THE READER'S CATALOG

SECOND EDITION

AN ANNOTATED SELECTION OF
MORE THAN 40,000 OF THE BEST BOOKS
IN PRINT IN OVER 300 CATEGORIES

Edited by Geoffrey O'Brien

STEPHANIE SMITH, EDITORIAL DIRECTOR/ASSOCIATE PUBLISHER

NEIL GORDON, EXECUTIVE AND ELECTRONIC EDITOR

REA S. HEDERMAN, PUBLISHER

JASON EPSTEIN, FOUNDING PUBLISHER

THE READER'S CATALOG
250 WEST 57TH STREET, NEW YORK, NEW YORK 10107

Library of Congress Cataloging-in-Publication Data

The reader's catalog: an annotated selection of more than 40,000 of
the best books in print in over 300 categories / edited by Geoffrey
O'Brien.—2nd ed.
p. cm.
Includes index.
ISBN 0-924322-01-2 (alk. paper)
1. Best books. I. O'Brien, Geoffrey, 1948-
Z1035.R263 1996 96-42428
011'.73--dc20 CIP

Grateful acknowledgement is made for permission to reprint from the following
copyrighted work: "(Pardon Me) I've Got Someone To Kill" by Aubrey Mayhew
and Johnny Paycheck © 1966 by Dream City Music—Renewed

Published simultaneously in the United States of America and Canada.
PRINTED IN THE UNITED STATES OF AMERICA

Editor
Geoffrey O'Brien

Editorial Director
Stephanie Smith

Executive and Electronic Editor
Neil Gordon

Senior Editors
Peter McCarthy
Don Hymans

Consulting Senior Editor
Edwin Frank

Associate Editor
Tracy A. Smith

Contributing Editors
Mark Caldwell
David Ebony
Claire Copley Eisenberg
Barbara Epstein
Jason Epstein
Jay A. Fernandez
Rea S. Hederman
Lawrence Klepp
Scott Malcomson
Albert Mobilio
Helen Morris
Cornelia Read
Marc Romano
Israel Rosenfeld
Tracy L. Shupp
Robert B. Silvers
Lee Smith
Evan Spring
Cynthia Stewart-Rinier
Tara Thomas
Samuel Truitt
Stephen Wasserstein
Doron Weber
Peter Zabelskis

Operations
Yongsun A. Bark, Director
Margarette Devlin
Alexander Sang
Yumiko Ishizuka
Richard Sang
Wena Khan
Diane Seltzer

Editorial Staff
Sara Kramer
Elaine Smith
Faith O'Han
Deborah Schneider

Book Design
Richard Saul Wurman

Assistant Designer
Tom Wood

Consulting Designers
Jenoa Brown
Tibor Kalman

Illustrator
David Levine

Cover Design
Angela Hederman

Publicity
Rose marie Morse

Production
William Stahl
Peter Sciabarra
&
Beverly Steiner at Inforonics, Inc.,
Erik Rieselbach
Janet Noble
Reed LeFevre
Judy Glasser

Contributors

Meena Alexander • Mindy Aloff • Hilary Ainger • Laurie Baum • Neil Belton • Paolo Berdini • Russell A. Berman • Paul Bernabeo • John Bierhorst • Stephen Bodio • James Boylan • Janet Byrne • Mary Cargill • Elizabeth Cavicchi • Andrew Cockburn • Andrew Cohen • Peter Cole • Joel Colton • Pablo Conrad • Lewis Coser • David Cronin • Mark D. Cummings • Diane Kender Dittrick • Mark Dittrick • Peggy Dye • Sue Elwyn • Tony Eprile • Helen Epstein • Jacob Epstein • Mary Anne Evans • James Fallows • Martin Filler • Ronald E. Findlay • Henry Flesh • Stephen William Foster • Edward Fox • Martin Gardner • Gary Giddins • Cyril Glasse • Joe Glickman • Arthur S. Goldwag • Marilyn Greco • David Guss • Ellen Handy • Peter Hay • David C. Hendrickson • David Herlihy • Rabbi Arthur Hertzberg • David Hinton • Jennifer Howard • Ewa Jankowska-Lategano • Kathrine Jason • Alison Karasz • Karyn Kay • Walter Kendrick • August Kleinzahler • Verlyn Klinkenborg • Heidi Knecht • Bernard Knox • Robert Lamberton • Paul Landau • Ira M. Lapidus • Sherman E. Lee • Jonathan Lieberson • Wendy Lochner • Pam Lord • Richard John Lynn • Joseph Masheck • Andrew McCord • Michael McGerr • Bruce McPherson • Louis Menand • David Mermelstein • John Miller • Stuart Miller • Richard Morris • Barbara Probst Morrow • Michael Moskowitz • Deborah Nadler • Maryann Napoli • Charlotte Nekola • Carly O'Brien • Craig Osbern • Elaine Pagels • Samuel M. Paley • Jerry E. Patterson • Tom Piazza • Darryl Pinckney • David Potenziani • George Preston • Missy Prowell • Diane Ravitch • Evie Righter • Diane Roback • Bruce Robbins • Patricia Romanowski • Edward Rothstein • Josh Rubins • William M. Sanders • Luc Sante • Hiroaki Sato • Robert Schirmer • John Schulian • Barry Schwabsky • Leonard Schwartz • Baird Searles • Mark Selden • Michael Sells • Vijay Seshadri • Michael Shae • Anna Shapiro • Myrna Smith • Nancy Spector • William R. Spiegelberger • Art Spiegelman • Gloria Steinem • Irwin Stern • Bhob Stewart • Brian Swann • Claudia Swan • Nathaniel Tarn • William Taylor • Diane Tong • Jessica Teich • David Tuller • Alice K. Turner • Stephen J. Vogel • Priscilla Wald • Carl Waldman • Mark Wasserman • Marjorie Welish • David Wheeler • Susan Wheeler • Arnold Wilson • Michael Wood • Elisabeth Wynhausen • Michael Zeilik

David Levine by David Levine

David Levine

David Levine is staff artist of *The New York Review of Books* and a frequent contributor of caricatures to other publications, including *The New Yorker*.

Following are comments made upon his induction into the Institute of Arts and Letters: His "caricatures are endowed with a brilliance of representation and a penetrative immediacy that bespeak a Victorian brutality and indeed their power, in part, is derived from earlier paradigms, but their relevant piercing to the heart of personality is Levine's alone, and a expression of his simple but profoundly evocative deployment of graphic means. David Levine's work is virtually unique in the US today and it is the graphic issue of a rare and incessantly original talent."

A Note to Our Readers

Culture: acquainting ourselves with the best that has been thought and said in the world, and thus with the history of the human spirit.
—Matthew Arnold

Established in 1989 by Jason Epstein, editorial director of Random House, and the poet, author, and editor Geoffrey O'Brien, The Reader's Catalog is an annotated listing of the 40,000 best books in print in America. As such, it aims to embody Matthew Arnold's famous ideal in a unique hybrid of the perfect bookstore, in which nothing ever goes out of stock, and the perfect reference book, in which an easy-to-use, thematic organization makes titles readily accessible.

Over 320 categories — often introduced with informative text — provide the book's basic organization, while many of the individual books listed have been supplied with concise, descriptive annotations. The Reader's Catalog provides basic knowledge in a wealth of different areas, making it not only an essential work of reference but a pleasure to read in its own right.

Three years ago, the First Edition of The Reader's Catalog sold out the last of its 150,000 copies. We have, however, continued to distill in biannual updates the enormous variety of books published each season, bringing discriminating selections of the best new books in every field of human knowledge to readers around the world, and offering them a simple way to order books from America, at American prices. And now we are delighted to present this Second Edition of The Reader's Catalog, incorporating all the erudition and organization of the first, and adding to it the accumulated experience of seven years.

Over half of the entries are new, and the book as a whole has been entirely recast in a distinctive, user-friendly format designed by Richard Saul Wurman, organizer of the TED Conference and prize-winning designer of information-intensive books. The book is organized around a simple tab system and includes extensive indexes as well as illustrations by the renowned caricaturist, David Levine. It also features new and updated annotations as well as over 35 original and imaginative timelines and maps that introduce subjects and historical eras in a bold and intriguing graphic format. Once again, The Reader's Catalog has found a new and unusual way to explore the world of books.

While the most exacting efforts have been made to ensure full accuracy at the time of publication, we cannot guarantee that all the books we have listed will continue to be in print and available. A printed catalog is subject to the inevitable limitations of the publishing industry: tens of thousands of books are published each year in America, and once published, they don't sit still. Prices increase, titles are delayed, stock sells out. Books fall out of print, others come back in paperback; publishers go out of business, others set up shop. Some titles are published by tiny presses without distributors; others by massive conglomerates with byzantine warehouses.

You can keep up with the latest releases, however, by receiving our **FREE** biannual updates. Simply mail or fax us the address portion of the order form at the back of the book, and we will enter your subscription. And for up-to-the-minute information about the newest books please visit our website at **WWW.NYBOOKS.COM**, where, over the coming half year, we will make available the entire Reader's Catalog. With cross-referencing, full Boolean searching, and simple ordering procedures, The Reader's Catalog Online offers the unique editorial qualities of the Second Edition and links them to the bibliographic resources of the World Wide Web.

Part 1

World History & Current Affairs

Edward Gibbon

1 Qin Shi Huangdi, Emperor of China (221–207 BC)
The first emperor of unified China was an intelligent and efficient administrator with a bad case of paranoia. Qin went everywhere under heavy guard and riddled the walls of his palace with secret passages to ensure a quick escape. He even commanded that a vast army of terracotta warriors be assembled to protect him in the tomb. In 213 Qin decided to obliterate history. He ordered every book in China burned, making exceptions, however, of medical and technical treatises and of his own family history.

138

2 Commodus, Emperor of Rome (180–192)
"The meanest of the populace were affected with indignation when they beheld their sovereign enter the lists as a gladiator. He chose the habit and arms of the secutor, whose combat with the retiarius formed one of the most lively scenes in the bloody sports of the amphitheater. The secutor was armed with a helmet, sword, and buckler; his naked opponent had only a large net and trident. The emperor fought in this character seven hundred and thirty-five times. It may easily be supposed that he was always successful."

—Edward Gibbon
The Decline and Fall of the Roman Empire

23

3 Justinian, Emperor of Byzantium (527–565)
"Some who were in the Emperor's company at night thought they saw a strange demonic form in his place. One man declared that he more than once rose suddenly and walked around and around the room, and his head would momentarily disappear, while the rest of his body continued making these long circuits. A second man said that he stood by the Emperor's side as he sat and saw his face suddenly transformed to a shapeless lump of flesh: neither eyebrows nor eyes were in their normal position, and it showed no other distinguishing feature at all."

— Procopius
The Secret History

25

4 Charles VI , King of France (1380–1422)
Known both as the Mad and the Well Beloved, Charles had "two pronounced aversions: for the *fleur-de-lys* entwined with his own name in the royal coat-of-arms, which he tried to deface in a rage whenever he saw it, and for his wife. If she approached him he would cry, 'Who is this woman the sight of whom torments me? Find out what she wants and free me from her demands, that she may follow me no more."

—Barbara Tuchman
A Distant Mirror

36

5 Ibrahim the Debauched, Ottoman Sultan (1640–1648)
The sole descendant of the race of Osman was encouraged in his fondness for women by his mother. Believing sensual delight to be directly proportional to physical size, he dispatched messengers to discover the world's biggest woman: a gigantic Armenian. Ibrahim's mother soon became jealous and had her strangled, after which she had her son declared mad for seeking to "ruin his empire through murder, shame, and corruption." Ibrahim was deposed, murdered, and succeeded, with his mother's blessing, by the 8-year-old son and heir his debauchery had conveniently provided.

118

6 Ali, Pasha of Yannina (c. 1787–1822)
Ali, a former highwayman, was notorious for his cruelty and for his refinement.
"In a marble-paved pavilion, where a spring
Of living water from the center rose,
Whose bubbling did a genial freshness fling,
And soft voluptuous couches breathed repose,
ALI reclined, a man of war and woes:
Yet in his lineaments ye cannot trace
While Gentleness her milder radiance throws
Along that aged venerable face,
The deeds that lurk beneath, and stain him with disgrace."

—Lord Byron
Childe Harold's Pilgrimage

119

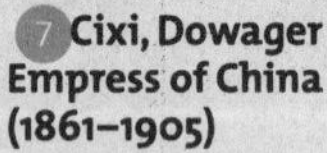

7 Cixi, Dowager Empress of China (1861–1905)
Cixi took funds meant for China's naval defense against its Japanese and European enemies and used them to build herself the Summer Palace. The crowning glory of its extensive grounds was a lifesize ship made of stone.

141

8 Paul I, Czar of Russia (1796–1801)
The son of Catherine the Great court-martialed and executed a rat for knocking over his toy soldiers. He himself was later murdered by his nobles and replaced by his son.

101

9 Queen Joe of Whale Cay (1900–1993)
In 1923, Marion Barbara Carstairs purchased her West Indian domain for $8,000 after a lifetime chasing speed records in powerboats named *Estelle.* Unauthorized visitors were greeted with blasts from a sawed-off shotgun, and the punishment for anyone who failed to live respectably was banishment. The queen was stern when it came to the dietary habits of her subjects, encouraging the consumption of vegetables and posting such signs as "If brown rice is good enough for me, it is good enough, or even too good, for the people." Carstairs abdicated abruptly in 1944 and went to Florida to build warships.

305

10 Jean Bedel Bokassa, Emperor, Central African Empire (1976–1979)
Bokassa took over leadership of the Central African Republic in a 1966 coup and proclaimed himself emperor ten years later. He spent some 25 million dollars on his coronation ceremony, two million of which went to pay for his crown alone. He was later deposed and charged with numerous crimes, including procuring bodies for consumption from the national morgue. Since his release from prison, he has become a vegetarian and renounced the world.

130

11 Kim Jong Il (1994–)
The current ruler of North Korea is known for his height-enhancing hairstyle and internationally unrivaled purchases of 50-year-old Hennessey Paradis Scotch (at $630 per bottle). A passionate film buff, he kidnapped one of his favorite actresses and a Japanese film director to make movies for him. The true extent of his power is unclear, but he has recently been elevated from Dear Leader to Great Leader Comrade, just a notch below his departed father's position of Great Leader President.

154

Trade in the Ancient World

1 Alexandria
This famous center of learning, founded by Alexander the Great in 332 BC, boasted such distinguished citizens as Euclid, Archimedes, Plotinus, and the astronomer-emperor Ptolemy. Alexandria was a vast entrepot for trade between the Red Sea and the Mediterranean. It was from here that the Egyptian wheat that fed the Roman Empire departed.
19

2 Ashok
The documented history of India begins with this Buddhist ruler. The system of well-shaded roads he built helped to promote trade and to draw the subcontinent together; it "acquired a political unity not matched in extent for over 2000 years. Ashok enjoined respect for the dignity of all men, and, above all, religious toleration."
—J.R. Roberts
A History of the World
134

3 The Chinese Empire
The Qin dynasty first unified China (hence the name) in 221 BC. In spite of shifting boundaries and changing dynasties, the empire remained intact until 1911.
138

4 Currency
Middle Eastern merchants had introduced silver bars or rings as currency by 2000 BC. About the same time, cowrie shells began to serve the same purpose in the Far East.
115

5 Hordes
The barren lands to the west and north of China were "peopled by pastoral tribes who were what they would remain until their decline in the mid-17th century: hordes of violent, cruel, pillaging horsemen full of daredevil courage" (Fernand Braudel). In the third century BC, their incursions led the Chinese to begin construction of the Great Wall, while many hundreds of years later their raids drove the Goths before them to the south—where they in turn destroyed the Roman Empire.
138

6 The Mandarins
Dynasties came and went in China, but the cadre of meticulously trained officials who actually ran the country always remained. The sage Mencius explained: "The pursuits of men of quality are not those of the poor. Those who work with their brains govern the others; those who work with physical strength are governed by them." In ancient China, as in the modern world, meritocracy masked the brute exercise of power.
139

7 Palmyra
Even in one of the ancient world's most flourishing entrepots, trade involved significant risks. Citizens who successfully planned or led a great caravan received the honor of having their statues erected along the city's major thoroughfares.
27

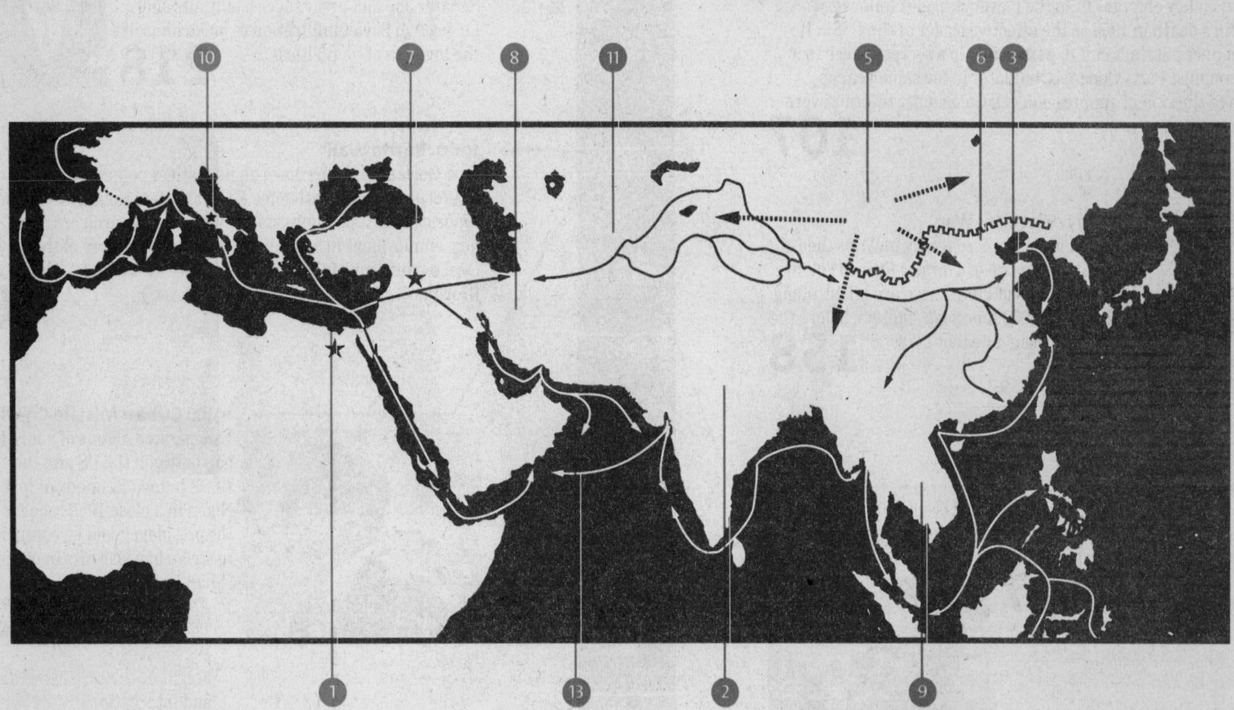

8 The Persian Empire
If the center of the ancient world was anywhere, it was Persia, which was first unified under Cyrus the Great in 515 BC. A bastion of religious tolerance and and an all-important conduit of goods and ideas between East and West, Persia remained a great empire until the advent of Islam nearly a thousand years later.
117

9 Rice
Wet rice, the staple food of the orient, was first cultivated in Southeast Asia, from where it spread to China and India. Oriental cultures, by contrast to those of the occident, have always been primarily vegetarian.
155

10 Rome
Rome exported glass, copper, tin, red coral, textiles, pottery—and above all, the currency in which traders throughout the world did business.
23

11 The Silk Route
By the second century BC, the Chinese had succeeded in securing the plains of Turkestan from the hordes, allowing the establishment of a regular silk route to the Middle East.
140

12 Slavery
Forced labor was the foundation of the Western economies. The vast plantations and seafaring galleys of the Roman Empire in particular depended upon slave labor. Slavery existed in India and China as well, but on a much smaller scale.
27

13 The Spice Route
The discovery of the monsoon by the Greek pilot Hippalus around 100 BC transformed sea trade between Europe, India, and the Far East. Ships sailed east with the winds of the summer monsoon and returned with the westward breezes of the winter.
28

Cold War Capsules

1940 · 1945 · 1950 · 1955 · 1960 · 1965 · 1970 · 1975 · 1980 · 1985 · 1990

May 1945: Fall of Germany
"The Second World War had, in terms of Europe's political geography, a very simple outcome: Germany lost and Russia won. Considering Russia's past sufferings and present strength, Stalin's territorial demands were mainly remarkable for their modesty."
—Colin McEvedy
The Penguin Atlas of Recent History

74

August 1945: Hiroshima and Nagasaki
Some 200,000 people are killed when the US drops the newly developed atom bomb on two Japanese cities. The Soviet Union acquires the bomb in 1949, and a nuclear arms race starts that continues for another 40 years.

150

1947: The Marshall Plan
The US Secretary of State's plan providing financial assistance to help rebuild war-torn Germany and Europe is approved by Congress as an anti-communist measure.

82

1948: Berlin Blockade
"The Russians' basic concern was to prevent the reemergence of a reunited, economically powerful Germany not under their influence" (J.M. Roberts, *A History of the World*). A Western airlift sustains the besieged city.

106

1949: James D. Forrestal
Truman's former Secretary of Defense kills himself when he sees Russians swarming through the bedroom window. The next year, Senator Joe McCarthy successfully airs similar fears of Soviet infiltration to make himself the big man of US politics.

218

1954–75: Vietnam War
Anti-communism increasingly involves the US in a war for control of a former French colony. Untold millions of Vietnamese are killed, along with some 50,000 American soldiers, before the US withdraws in defeat in 1973.

158

1956: Nikita Khrushchev
Khrushchev emerges from the power struggles following Stalin's death in 1953 as the effective leader of the USSR. He denounces Stalin's cult of personality in a secret speech to a Communist Party Congress, but later in the same year approves the violent suppression of a Communist reform government of Hungary.

107

1960: Berlin Wall
East Germany clamps down on its restless population, while California, blessed with huge Federal defense outlays, becomes America's most populous state. "Weapons research created new employment in a manner that left the memory of the New Deal experiments in public expenditure far behind." (Hugh Brogan, *The Penguin History of the U.S.A.*)

8

1962: Cuban Missile Crisis
Exaggerated claims of a missile gap between the US and the USSR helped Kennedy defeat Nixon in a close 1960 race for the presidency, and he continues to strike hawkish airs in office: "Shall I take Cuba out?"

192

1964: Leonid Brezhnev
Brezhnev helps to oust Khrushchev and eventually becomes president of the USSR. Under his leadership the country bankrupts itself trying to achieve military parity with the US.

107

1976: Détente
Race riots and massive anti-Vietnam war demonstrations in the US, and the Soviet Union's violent suppression in Czechoslovakia of another Communist reform government, are succeeded by a period of détente between the two superpowers in which they sign a number of significant arms limitations accords.

106

1984: The Evil Empire
With the US caught in a deep economic recession, Reagan attacks the Soviet Union as an "Evil Empire" in a speech to the British Parliament. "The Reaganite cold war was directed not only against the 'Evil Empire' abroad but against the memory of FDR. Its enemy was liberalism as much as communism." (Eric Hobsbawm, *The Age of Extremes*)

224

1985: Mikhail Gorbachev
Over the next six years, this energetic new leader of the USSR will astonish the world by promoting economic and political reform at home and disarmament abroad, though his efforts to restore the Soviet Union to health will only hasten its demise.

107

1990: Germany Reunited
The Berlin Wall falls and the Communist regimes of Soviet Union's Eastern European satellite states fall with it. Reunited, Germany stands for the first time as Europe's dominant and unchallenged economic and political power.

85

The Varieties of Civilization

"History is a discipline widely cultivated among nations and races. It is eagerly sought after. The men in the street, the ordinary people, aspire to know it. Kings and leaders vie for it.

Both the learned and the ignorant are able to understand it. For on the surface history is no more than information about political events, dynasties, and occurrences of the remote past, elegantly presented and spiced with proverbs. It serves to entertain large, crowded gatherings and brings to us an understanding of human affairs. It shows how changing conditions affect [human affairs], how certain dynasties came to occupy an ever wider space in the world, and how they settled the earth until they heard the call and their time was up.

The inner meaning of history, on the other hand, involves speculation and an attempt to get at the truth, and deep knowledge of the how and why of events. History, therefore, is firmly rooted in philosophy. It deserves to be accounted a branch of it."
—Ibn Khaldûhn, *The Muqaddimah: An Introduction to History* [late 14th century].

World Histories

Fernand **Braudel**

A History of Civilizations

First written in 1962 and denounced for its anti-ethnocentric approach, Braudel's study is now seen as a paradigm of modern scholarship. The first serious work to expand the scope of inquiry beyond events, dates, and personages to view the sweeping continuities and patterns of civilization since the eighth century

See also **FERNAND BRAUDEL** under **THE EXPANSION OF EUROPE: EMPIRE AND COMMERCE** under **EARLY MODERN EUROPE**

0-14-012489-6 PENGUIN PB $14.95

William H. **McNeill**

The Rise of the West: A History of the Human Community

Traces the fundamental interrelations among different cultures throughout history, challenging the idea that separate civilizations evolved on largely independent paths

0-226-56141-0 CHICAGO PB $22.95

R.R. **Palmer** & Joel **Colton**

A History of the Modern World

The seventh edition of a classic textbook whose focus is on Europe since the Renaissance

0-07-040830-0 MCGRAW HILL PB $39.75

J.M. **Roberts**

A Concise History of the World

A compact edition of Roberts's highly acclaimed *History of the World*, about which the London *Sunday Telegraph* declared, "There is nothing better of its kind"

0-19-521151-0 OXFORD $35.00

John **Romer** & Elizabeth **Romer**

The Seven Wonders of the World

The companion to the television series measures the Seven Wonders of the World as the yardsticks of human achievement over the past 5,000 years—a wondrously vivid visit, given that none other than the Egyptian pyramids can be seen today. Drawing on history and archaeology, the book traces the hunt for the Seven Wonders, and a remarkable set of photographs recreate the magnificent environments of the ancient marvels

0-8050-4122-2 HOLT $30.00

Hugh **Thomas**

World History: The Story of Mankind from Prehistory to the Present

Thomas has written no less than the entire history of man, beginning with our earliest ancestors. Thematically organized, this new edition includes, notably, a revision of the Cold War chapters, a new epilogue, and new maps. "A remarkable tour de force, at once informative, lively, and coherent... irresistible reading"—*The Baltimore Sun*

0-06-017477-3 HARPERCOLLINS $35.00

Readings in Western Civilization

John W. **Boyer** & Julius **Kirshner**, editors

University of Chicago Readings in Western Civilization

A widely used, authoritative collection of source materials

Volume 1
The Greek Polis

0-226-06934-6 CHICAGO $25.00
0-226-06935-4 CHICAGO PB $11.95

Volume 2
Late Republic and Principate

0-226-06936-2 CHICAGO $25.00
0-226-06937-0 CHICAGO PB $12.95

Volume 3
The Church in the Roman Empire

0-226-06938-9 CHICAGO $20.00
0-226-06939-7 CHICAGO PB $12.95

Volume 4
Medieval Europe

0-226-06942-7 CHICAGO $30.00
0-226-06943-5 CHICAGO PB $16.95

Volume 5
The Renaissance

0-226-06944-3 CHICAGO $30.00
0-226-06945-1 CHICAGO PB $14.95

Volume 6
Early Modern Europe: Crisis of Authority

0-226-06948-6 CHICAGO PB $17.95

Volume 7
The Old Regime and the French Revolution

0-226-06949-4 CHICAGO $33.00
0-226-06950-8 CHICAGO PB $13.95

Volume 8
Nineteenth-Century Europe

0-226-06951-6 CHICAGO $37.50
0-226-06952-4 CHICAGO PB $16.95

Volume 9
Twentieth-Century Europe

0-226-06953-2 CHICAGO $40.00
0-226-06954-0 CHICAGO PB $17.95

William H. **McNeill**

History of Western Civilization: A Handbook

0-226-56159-3 CHICAGO $48.00
0-226-56160-7 CHICAGO PB $22.00

Asia

Cyril E. **Black** & others

The Modernization of Inner Asia

A college text with a solid authorship team

0-87332-779-9 SHARPE PB $28.95

William T. **De Barry**

East Asian Civilizations: A Dialogue in Five Stages

0-674-22406-X HARVARD PB $13.50

John K. **Fairbank** & Edwin O. **Reischauer**

East Asia: Tradition and Transformation

This book remains the most widely used introduction to the history and culture of East Asia

See also **GENERAL HISTORIES** under **CHINA**
See also **EAST ASIA AS ECONOMIC AND POLITICAL REGION: GENERAL STUDIES** under **SOUTHEAST ASIA AND THE PHILIPPINES**

0-395-45023-3 HOUGHTON MIFFLIN $56.75

Christopher **Howe** & Brian **Hook**

China and Japan: History, Trends, Prospects

0-19-828932-4 CLARENDON PB $23.00

Eric **Jones** & others, editors

Coming Full Circle: An Economic History of the Pacific Rim

0-8133-1241-8 WESTVIEW PB $13.95

Jaroslav **Kreji**

Before the European Challenge: The Great Civilizations of Asia and the Middle East

0-7914-0169-3 NYU PB $21.95

David **Morgan**

The Mongols

The amazing military career of Genghis Khan and the impact of the Mongols on the peoples they conquered in Russia, China, Persia, and Europe

0-631-17563-6 BLACKWELL PB $22.95

Rhoads **Murphey**

A History of Asia

0-673-99407-4 HARPERCOLLINS PB $38.14

Conrad **Schirokauer**

A Brief History of Chinese and Japanese Civilizations

A sweeping bird's-eye view of the cultural and political history of the two great Asian powers

0-15-505569-0 H.B.J. PB $36.58

The 20th Century

Raymond **Aron**

The Century of Total War

0-313-22852-3 GREENWOOD $59.75

Norman **Davies**

Europe: A History

The latest by the distinguished historian, published in the fall of 1996

0-19-520912-5 OXFORD $29.95

Felix **Gilbert**

The End of the European Era: 1890 to the Present

The "present" is 1983

0-393-96059-5 NORTON PB $15.95

H. Stuart **Hughes** & James **Wilkinson**

Contemporary Europe: A History

An intelligent textbook on Europe since 1914; now in its 8th edition

0-13-169947-4 PRENTICE HALL $41.90

Paul **Johnson**

Modern Times: The World from the Twenties to the Eighties

A tour de force from the British neo-conservative, stressing the dangers of the consolidation of state power

0-06-092283-4 HARPERPERENNIAL PB $20.00

William R. **Keylor**

The Twentieth-Century World: An International History

Properly sets Europe in a global context

See also **THE 20TH-CENTURY WORLD** under **INTERNATIONAL RELATIONS AND STRATEGIC STUDIES** in **SOCIAL STUDIES**

0-19-506804-1 OXFORD PB $21.00

Gabriel **Kolko**

Century of War: Politics, Conflict, & Society Since 1914

Traces the social, political, and technological changes etched onto human society by 100 years of war

1-56584-192-1 NEW PRESS PB $15.95

Neil J. **Kressel**

Mass Hate: The Global Rise of Genocide and Terror

0-306-45271-5 PLENUM $25.95

Michael R. **Marrus**

The Unwanted: European Refugees in the Twentieth Century

Those displaced by the Nazis, the Spanish Civil War, the Cold War, and other 20th-century crises

0-19-503615-8 OXFORD $30.00

Robert O. **Paxton**

Europe in the Twentieth Century

0-15-52471-9 HARCOURT BRACE $42.56
0-15-524719-0 H.B.J. $53.87

Theodore H. **Von Laue**

The World Revolution of Westernization: The Twentieth Century in Global Perspective

How Westernization has caused the global violence and warfare of this century, accounting for world wars, the rise of communism and fascism, decolonization, and contemporary dictatorship

0-19-504907-1 OXFORD PB $16.95

Daniel **Yergin**

The Prize: The Epic Quest for Oil, Money, and Power

The 20th century depicted as a protracted fight over oil. "*The Prize* should be read by everyone who wants to know why nations struggle over the control of oil resources"
—John Chancellor, NBC News

0-671-50248-4 TOUCHSTONE PB $27.95

Cultural Politics and Nationalism

Benedict **Anderson**

Imaged Communities: Reflections on the Origin and Spread of Nationalism

The sense of *nationality* is the personal and cultural feeling of belonging to a nation. Anderson probes the impact of print during the Reformation, the independence movements of 18th-century America, the Meiji Restoration, and more

0-8052-7178-3 VERSO PB $16.95

Henry Louis **Gates** & Kwame Anthony **Appiah**, editors

The Dictionary of Global Culture

0-394-58581-X KNOPF $35.00

Jack **Goody**

The East and the West

Challenges several Eurocentric assumptions, including the notion of a special Western rationality. A wide-ranging and provocative study

0-521-55673-2 CAMBRIDGE PB $18.95

Eric **Hobsbawm**

Primitive Rebels

0-393-00328-0 NORTON PB $10.95

Michael **Ignatieff**

Blood and Belonging: Journeys into the New Nationalism

"Vivid and readable...provides unforgettable impressions of societies that are going in the wrong direction on the highway to brotherhood and unity"—David Fromkin, *Book World*

0-374-52448-3 NOONDAY PB $11.00

Anthony D. **Smith**

The Ethnic Origins of Nations

0-631-16169-4 BLACKWELL PB $22.95

D.A. **Low**

The Egalitarian Moment: Asia and Africa, 1950-1980

Surveys a major feature of twentieth-century world history, arguably affecting more people than the rise and fall of Soviet communism: the failure to create egalitarian rural societies—in Egypt, Iran, India, Vietman, and Ethiopia—despite landlord abolition

0-521-56765-3 CAMBRIDGE PB $14.95

Economic History

Alfred D. **Chandler**, Jr.

Scale and Scope: The Dynamics of Industrial Capitalism

Chandler studies the pattern of industrial competitiveness in the three leading industrial nations—the US, Germany, and Britain—from the 1880s to the 1940s. He shows how large firms developed by exploring economies of scale and scope which required investments in production facilities, marketing and distribution networks, and management organization. The first companies to make these investments dominated their industries for decades

0-674-78994-6 HARVARD $42.50

Philip D. **Curtin**

Cross-Cultural Trade in World History

Silk from China to Rome, African ivory, the Indian Ocean spice trade: the colorful world of exchange over two millennia

See also **GENERAL HISTORIES** under **AFRICA**

0-521-26931-8 CAMBRIDGE PB $16.95

Thomas L. **Haskell** & Richard F. **Teichgraeber**, editors

The Culture of the Market

Ranging over historical, geographical, and theoretical terrain. Includes "The Ruling Class in the Marketplace: Nobles and Money in Early Modern France" by Jonathan Dewald; "An Entrepreneur in Spite of Himself: Edgar Degas and the Market" by Marilyn R. Brown; and "New Cultural Heroes in the Early National Period" by Joyce Appleby

0-521-56478-6 CAMBRIDGE PB $19.95

Douglass C. **North** & Robert **Paul**

The Rise of the Western World: A New Economic History

Offers a unified explanation for the growth of Western Europe between 900 A.D. and 1700. North won the Nobel Prize for economics in 1993 for applying economic theory and quantitative methods to historical problems

0-521-29099-6 CAMBRIDGE PB $15.95

Karl **Polanyi**

The Great Transformation: The Political and Economic Origins of Our Time

0-8070-5679-0 BEACON PB $16.00

W.W. **Rostow**

The Stages of Economic Growth

0-521-40070-8 CAMBRIDGE $65.00
0-521-40928-4 CAMBRIDGE PB $20.95

H.W. **Spiegel**

The Growth of Economic Thought

A roughly 900-page synthesis that charts the main currents of economic thinking from ancient times to the contemporary period. A valuable survey of the ideas of the great economists; less useful in recent macroeconomic theory

0-8223-0973-4 DUKE PB $34.95

Intellectual History

Jacob **Bronowski** & Bruce **Mazlish**

The Western Intellectual Tradition: From Leonardo to Hegel

0-06-133001-9 HARPERCOLLINS PB $21.60

Douglas A. **Irwin**

Against the Tide: An Intellectual History of Free Trade

How the idea of free trade has withstood challenges since the age of the physiocrats; an accessible, nontechnical discussion

0-691-01138-9 PRINCETON $29.95

Dominick **LaCapra** & Steven L. **Kaplan**, editors

Modern European Intellectual History: Reappraisals and New Perspectives

0-8014-9881-3 CORNELL PB $17.95

Henri-Jean **Martin**

The History and Power of Writing

0-226-50835-8 CHICAGO $39.95
0-226-50836-6 CHICAGO PB $18.95

Robert **Nisbet**

History of the Idea of Progress

1-56000-713-3 TRANSACTION PB $21.95

Terence **Ranger** & Paul **Slack**, editors

Epidemics and Ideas: Essays on the Historical Perception of Ideas

Views of medicine and disease, and the ways in which people have defined the "health" of society in general terms

0-521-55831-X CAMBRIDGE PB $19.95

John Ralston **Saul**

Voltaire's Bastards: The Dictatorship of Reason in the West

0-679-74819-9 VINTAGE PB $16.00

Benjamin **Schwartz**

The World of Thought in Ancient China

This most important recent study investigates the thinkers—including Confucius—of the golden age of Chinese thought between the 6th and 3rd centuries BC

See also **CHINESE THOUGHT** under **TOPICS IN IMPERIAL CIVILIZATION** under **CHINA**

0-674-96190-0 HARVARD $37.00
0-674-96191-9 HARVARD PB $18.95

Roland N. **Stromberg**

European Intellectual History Since 1789

0-13-105990-4 PRENTICE HALL PB $30.92

Science and Technology

Science

Daniel **Boorstin**

The Discoverers: A History of Man's Search to Know His World and Himself

0-394-40229-4 RANDOM HOUSE $45.00
0-394-72625-1 RANDOM HOUSE PB $16.00

William **Brock**

The Norton History of Chemistry

0-393-03536-0 NORTON $35.00
0-393-31043-4 NORTON PB $15.95

Harold R. **Dorn**

The Geography of Science

How science developed in different parts of the world—and why

0-8018-4151-8 JOHNS HOPKINS $38.00

Toby **Huff**

The Rise of Early Modern Science: Islam, China, and the West

0-521-49833-3 CAMBRIDGE PB $18.95

David C. **Lindberg**

The Beginnings of Western Science: The European Scientific Tradition in Philosophical, Religious, and Institutional Context, 600 B.C. to A.D. 1450

"A triumph… Provides us for the first time with an authoritative account of Western science from its beginnings to the height of the medieval scientific achievement"—Richard C. Dales, *American Historical Review*

0-226-48231-6 CHICAGO PB $22.50

Anthony **Serafini**

The Epic History of Biology

0-306-44511-5 PLENUM $27.95

Andrew **Whitaker**

Einstein, Bohr, and the Quantum Dilemma

Includes nontechnical and nonmathematical accounts of the many current experimental and theoretical developments in quantum theory; "probably the most successful physical theory in the history of science"

0-521-48428-6 CAMBRIDGE PB $27.95

Trevor **Williams**

Science: A History of Discovery in the Twentieth Century

0-19-520843-9 OXFORD $40.00

Albert Einstein

Technology

Ahmad **Al-Hassan** & Donald **Hill**

Islamic Technology: An Illustrated History

0-521-42239-6 CAMBRIDGE PB $29.95

R.A. **Buchanan**

The Power of the Machine: The Impact of Technology from 1700 to the Present Day

0-14-017063-4 PENGUIN PB $13.95

Alexander **Hellemans** & Brian **Bunch**

The Timetables of Technology: A Chronology of the Most Important People and Events in the History of Technology

0-671-76918-9 SIMON & SCHUSTER $35.00

Patrice **Higonet** & others, editors

Favorites of Fortune: Technology, Growth, and Economic Development Since the Industrial Revolution

A galaxy of distinguished economists and historians pit economic history against the shaky assumptions of the classical economic theory of natural growth. Includes "The Conquest of High Mortality and Hunger in Europe and America: Timing and Mechanisms" by Robert W. Fogel; "Dear Labor, Cheap Labor, and the Industrial Revolution" by Joel Mokyr; "The Huguenots and the English Financial Revolution" by Francois Crouzet; and "Creating Competitive Capability: Innovation and Investment in the United States, Great Britian, and Germany from the 1870s to World War I" by Alfred D. Chandler, Jr.

0-674-29521-8 HARVARD PB $19.95

Richard L. **Hills**

Power from Wind: A History of Windmill Technology

From the inception of windpower around 1000 A.D. "An important contribution to the history of technology"—*Science*

0-521-56686-X CAMBRIDGE PB $29.95

Ian **McNeil** & Lance **Day**, editors

Biographical Dictionary of the History of Technology

0-415-06042-7 ROUTLEDGE $150.00

Arnold **Pacey**

Technology in World Civilization: A Thousand-Year History

A concise survey of the development of technology, from a global rather than Europe-centered viewpoint. Fascinating for its accounts of Islamic irrigation techniques, Chinese iron smelting, and the gunpowder empires of Asia. One of *Library Journal's* "Best Sci-Tech Books of 1990"

See also **HISTORY OF SCIENCE AND TECHNOLOGY** under **SCIENCE AND TECHNOLOGY** in **SCIENCE**

0-262-66072-5 MIT PB $13.50

Paper-making also came to Europe via Spain...The paper was made from the same vegetable fibers as linen cloth (and usually from linen rags), which first had to be pounded in water until a pulp was formed. The process had been invented in China long before, where it replaced an even older method of making paper-like material from mulberry bark. Knowledge of the technique entered the Islamic world in AD 751 after a battle in Central Asia between Chinese forces and an Arab-led army. Chinese prisoners-of-war skilled in paper-making set up a workshop in Samarqand, and from there other workmen went to Baghdad...The manufacture of paper meant that books became more widely available. By AD 900 there were over a hundred shops in Baghdad employing scribes and binders to produce books for sale, and soon there were even some public libraries.

TECHNOLOGY IN WORLD CIVILIZATION: A THOUSAND-YEAR HISTORY

John H. **Pryor**

Geography, Technology and War: Studies in the Maritime History of the Mediterranean, 649-1571

0-521-42892-0 CAMBRIDGE PB $19.95

Perspectives in History

William J. **Baker**

Sports in the Western World

"Every...sporting event from amateur Olympics to professional media hype [is] presented in this thorough, well-composed chronicle"
—*Best Sellers*

0-252-06042-3 ILLINOIS PB $12.95

Daniel J. **Boorstin**

Cleopatra's Nose: Essays on the Unexpected

Pulitzer Prize-winning Boorstin (*The Discoverers, The Creators, The Americans*) seems to go from strength to strength in his illuminating ventures into history. *Cleopatra's Nose* compiles a number of essays united by the theme of how discovery, often, only increases ignorance. What were the historical opportunities of the New World? How has the Industrial Age confused and contradicted Darwinian expectations?

0-679-43505-0 RANDOM HOUSE $23.00
0-679-75518-7 VINTAGE PB $12.00

Daniel J. **Boorstin**

The Creators: A History of Heroes of the Imagination

The ambitious national bestseller is now available in paperback. A mosaic of biographies—Homer, Joyce, Picasso, Stravinsky —which paints a panoramic view of human creativity over 3,000 years. "A remarkable achievement and a pleasure to read"—*NY Times Book Review*

0-679-74375-8 VINTAGE PB $17.00

Leo **Braudy**

The Frenzy of Renown: Fame and Its History

By the author of *The World in a Frame: What We See in Films*

0-19-504003-1 OXFORD $35.00

Jan **Bremmer**
& Herman **Roodenburg**, editors

A Cultural History of Gesture

An intriguing approach to history, this book documents the vocabulary of body movements through the ages. "Bringing acute personal insight as well as far-ranging scholarly research to bear, the contributors to this volume uncover the meanings behind body language"
—Marina Warner

0-8014-2744-4 CORNELL $49.00
0-8014-8023-X CORNELL PB $15.95

John **Carey**, editor

Eyewitness to History

An engaging collection of snapshots great and small: Rome burns, AD 64; dinner with Attila the Hun, c. AD 450; the murder of Thomas à Becket, December 29; 1170; Marie Antoinette at the opera, July 1792; the conquest of Everest, May 29, 1953; and more

0-674-28750-9 HARVARD $29.95
0-380-70895-7 AVON PB $13.00

Mark Nathan **Cohen**

Health and the Rise of Civilization

0-300-04006-7 YALE $37.00

Alain **Corbin**

The Foul and the Fragrant: Odor and the French Social Imagination

An offbeat look at the 18th and 19th centuries. "Reminds us that social history, too long sanitized and too often abstract, must make room for the senses"
—Michael Bums, *LA Times Book Review*

0-674-31176-0 HARVARD PB $15.95

The Lure of the Sea: The Discovery of the Seaside in the Western World, 1750-1840

The environment as a human construct and how "the desire for the shore swelled and spread between 1750 and 1840" in England, France, and Germany. A history of imagination and of social practices

0-14-024799-8 PENGUIN PB $14.95

Mark **Girouard**

Cities and People

An ideal survey; beautifully illustrated

0-300-03502-0 YALE $60.00
0-300-03968-9 YALE PB $27.50

Greil **Marcus**

Lipstick Traces: A Secret History of the Twentieth Century

The "counterhistory" of hidden cultural movements

0-674-53581-2 HARVARD PB $16.95

Walter A. **McDougall**

Let the Sea Make a Noise...: The Making of the North Pacific from Magellan to MacArthur

0-380-72467-7 AVON PB $17.50

William H. **McNeill**

Keeping Together in Time: Dance and Drill in Human History

See also **BODY SCIENCE, KINESICS, TECHNIQUE, AND PEDAGOGY** under **DANCE** in **PERFORMING ARTS AND MEDIA**

0-674-50229-9 HARVARD $22.00

Plagues and Peoples

An important essay whose focus is larger than the 14th century

See also **THE 14TH CENTURY: BLACK DEATH AND ECONOMIC DEPRESSION** under **MEDIEVAL AND RENAISSANCE EUROPE**

0-8446-6492-8 SMITH $21.75
0-385-12122-9 DOUBLEDAY PB $9.95

Henry **Petroski**

The Evolution of Useful Things: How Everyday Artifacts—from Forks and Pins to Paper Clips and Zippers—Came to Be as They Are

Petroski, author of *The Pencil*, is a virtuoso when writing about everyday objects. Dredging up great anecdotes and unforeseen connections in the history of the invention of small things, Petroski shows how crazy ideas finally become accepted (cf. the man behind the pop-top lid)

See also **SCIENTIFIC THOUGHT AND DISCOVERY** under **SCIENCE AND TECHNOLOGY** in **SCIENCE**

0-679-41226-3 KNOPF $24.00
5-679-64039-2 VINTAGE PB $13.00

Richard **Sennett**

Flesh and Stone: The Body and the City in Western Civilization

The original and innovative Sennett engages the life of cities, from ancient Athens to modern New York, over 2,500 years and, through the eyes of their inhabitants, finds a significant lesson about the quality of life. "By exposing the principles of individualism and personal comfort that form the most fundamental assumptions of 20th-century consumer culture, Sennett reminds modern readers that they trade a great deal for comfort—namely their engagement with one another. In so doing, he debunks the myth that the evolution of cities has been one of unfettered progress, or that progress is synonymous with improvement. Passionate, exhaustively researched, and original"
—*Kirkus Reviews*

See also **PERSONAL AND PSYCHIC DEVELOPMENT** under **SPIRITUALITY** under **SPIRITUALITY** in **RELIGION, SPIRITUALITY, AND PHILOSOPHY**

0-393-03684-7 NORTON $27.50

Gerrit L. **Verschuur**

Hidden Attraction: The Mystery and History of Magnetism

From alchemical experiments through the more tangible works of Faraday, Maxwell, Hertz, and other great pioneers, to state-of-the-art theories that see magnetism as a basic force in the universe

0-19-510655-5 OXFORD PB....$14.95

G.J. **Whitrow**

Time in History: Views of Time from Prehistory to the Present Day

0-19-285211-6 OXFORD PB....$11.95

John Noble **Wilford**

The Mapmakers: The Story of the Great Pioneers in Cartography from Antiquity to the Space Age

0-394-75303-8 RANDOM HOUSE PB....$19.00

Sexuality and Private Life

Philippe **Ariès** & Andre **Bejin**, editors

Western Sexuality: Practice and Precept in Past and Present Times

Essays from French, Italian, and English scholars on the Western models of marriage, love within and outside marriage, and changing sexual practices

TRANSLATED BY ANTHONY FORSTER

0-631-14989-9 BLACKWELL PB....$22.95

Philippe **Ariès** & Georges **Duby**, editors

A History of Private Life

Paul **Veyne**, editor

Volume 1
From Pagan Rome to Byzantium

Stimulating essays by historians and literary critics. "One of the most arresting, original and rewarding historical surveys to be published in many years"—Bernard Knox, *Atlantic Monthly*

See also **SOCIAL LIFE** under **TOPICS IN ROMAN HISTORY** under **ANCIENT ROME**

0-674-39975-7 HARVARD....$42.50
0-674-39974-9 HARVARD PB....$19.95

Georges **Duby**, editor

Volume 2
Revelations of the Medieval World

TRANSLATED BY ARTHUR GOLDHAMMER

0-674-39976-5 HARVARD....$39.95
0-674-40001-1 HARVARD PB....$19.95

The bath and steam room were places of relaxation, where people went not only to cleanse their bodies but also to talk, rest, and amuse themselves. What better place for amorous encounters of every kind? Some baths had such bad reputations that it was generally considered disreputable to work in a bathhouse or as a masseuse. The erotic connotations of water color the descriptions of furtive encounters at the baths of Bourbon-l'Archambault in *Flamenca*, an Occitanian poem of guilty love. The immodest and the innocent met in the baths; bathers were scrutinized, judged, desired, seduced. The exchanges of glances that must have taken place are not hard to imagine.

VOLUME 2: REVELATIONS OF THE MEDIEVAL WORLD

Roger **Chartier**, editor

Volume 3
Passions of the Renaissance

The third volume in this ambitious and highly acclaimed five-volume series. It continues the examination of the social forces that shaped private lives and historic events from the Renaissance to the Age of Enlightenment. "A feast for the eye; it is fascinating, often compelling in its exquisite details"
—*NY Times Book Review*

0-674-39977-3 HARVARD....$39.95
0-674-40002-X HARVARD PB....$18.95

Michelle **Perrot**, editor

Volume 4
From the Fires of Revolution to the Great War

The fourth volume in a highly acclaimed series, addressing such themes as "The Sweet Delights of Home," "The Family Triumphant," and "Private Spaces." With 406 halftone and 16 color illustrations

0-674-39978-1 HARVARD....$39.95
0-674-40003-8 HARVARD PB....$19.95

Antoine **Prost** & Gérard **Vincent**, editors

Volume 5
Riddles of Identity in Modern Times

The last volume in the acclaimed French series which opened new, intimate perspectives on history. The drastic changes in European and American family life in the 20th century provide the focal point here. 16 color and 230 black-and-white illustrations

0-674-39979-X HARVARD....$39.95
0-674-40004-6 HARVARD PB....$19.95

Terry **Castle**

Apparitional Lesbian: Female Homosexuality and Modern Culture

0-231-07652-5 COLUMBIA....$32.50

Michel **Feher**, editor

Fragments for a History of the Human Body

Essays by leading social historians; published by Zone books and distributed by MIT Press. "Michel Feher has assembled an all-star Euro-crit team, with MVPs like Julia Kristeva, Jean Starobinski, and Jean-Pierre Vernant, to perform an exhaustive physical exam: no body part is left unpoked"—Albert Mobilio, *VLS*

Volume 1
0-942299-23-X MIT PB....$34.95

Volume 2
0-942299-24-8 MIT PB....$34.95

Volume 3
0-942299-28-0 MIT PB....$34.95

Stephen **Kern**

The Culture of Love: Victorians to Moderns

Makes excursions into popular culture and into art, moving from the Brontës to Henry Miller, and from Victorian genre painting to Picasso to reveal the changing nature of intimate personal experience

0-674-17959-5 HARVARD PB....$16.95

Jeffrey **Merick** & Bryant T. **Ragan**, Jr., editors

Homosexuality in Modern France

The realities and representations of same-sex sexuality in the 18th, 19th, and 20th centuries

0-19-509304-6 OXFORD PB....$19.95

Ray **Porter** & Lesley **Hall**

The Facts of Life: The Creation of Sexual Knowledge in Britian, 1650-1950

How people arrived at sexual attitudes, how sexual information was culturally transmitted, and how printed books about sex shaped popular opinion. Argues that the modernization of sex made for increasing alienation between men and women as sexual roles became more polarized

0-300-06221-4 YALE....$35.00

Roy **Porter** & Mikulas **Teich**, editors

Sexual Science, Sexual Knowledge: The History of Sexuality

0-521-44891-3 CAMBRIDGE PB....$19.95

Paul **Robinson**

The Modernization of Sex: Havelock Ellis, Alfred Kinsey, William Masters and Virginia Johnson

0-8014-9539-3 CORNELL PB....$15.95

Colin **Spencer**

Homosexuality in History

A comprehensive and readable survey

0-15-100223-1 HARCOURT BRACE....$29.00

William Irwin **Thompson**

The Time Falling Bodies Take to Light: Mythology, Sexuality, and the Origins of Culture

0-312-16062-3 ST. MARTIN'S PB....$13.95

Theodore **Zeldin**

An Intimate History of Humanity

By the author of *France, 1848-1945: Intellect, Taste, and Anxiety*

0-06-092691-0 HARPERPERENNIAL PB....$15.00

The Family

Roderick **Phillips**

Putting Asunder: A History of Divorce in Western Society

0-521-32434-3 CAMBRIDGE....$69.95

Michael **Anderson**

Approaches to the History of the Western Family, 1500-1914

A short but comprehensive survey focusing on Western Europe and North America

0-521-55793-3 CAMBRIDGE PB $9.95

Philippe **Ariès**

Centuries of Childhood: A Social History of Family Life

TRANSLATED BY ROBERT BALDICK

0-394-70286-7 RANDOM HOUSE PB $16.00

André **Burguière** & others, editors

A History of the Family

Volume I Distant Worlds, Ancient Worlds

0-674-39675-8 HARVARD $39.95

Volume II The Impact of Modernity

0-674-39676-6 HARVARD $39.95

John **Harriss**, editor

The Family: A Social History of the Twentieth Century

An illustrated overview, written by a team of distinguished historians, of the remarkable evolution of family structures in modern times under the impact of technology and rapid cultural change. With 300 photographs and 50 full-color drawings

0-19-520844-7 OXFORD $40.00

Food and Pharmaceuticals

Sophie **Coe** and Michael **Coe**

The True History of Chocolate

From the sacred drink of the Aztecs to Hershey's Kisses

050-001693-3 THAMES & HUDSON $27.50

Henry **Hobhouse**

Seeds of Change: Five Plants that Transformed Mankind

How quinine, sugar cane, tea, cotton, and the potato changed the course of human history. "Infused with witty speculation and the courage to suggest new ways at looking at the cause and effect of world events"—*Smithsonian*

0-06-091440-8 HARPERCOLLINS PB $13.00
0-333-58263-2 MCCLELLAND & STEWART PB $22.99

Sidney W. **Mintz**

Sweetness and Power: The Place of Sugar in Modern History

How Europe and America transformed sugar from a rare foreign luxury to a staple of modern life

0-14-009233-1 VIKING PB $13.95

Richard **Rudgley**

Essential Substances: A Cultural History of Intoxicants in Society

1-56836-016-9 KODANSHA $22.00
1-56836-075-4 KODANSHA PB $12.00

Roy **Porter** & Mikulas **Teich**, editors

Drugs and Narcotics in History

0-521-43163-8 CAMBRIDGE $49.95

Redcliffe **Salaman**

The History and Social Influence of the Potato

0-521-31623-5 CAMBRIDGE PB $27.95

Wolfgang **Schivelbusch**

Tastes of Paradise: A Social History of Spices, Stimulants, and Intoxicants

Highly recommended study by the author of *Disenchanted Night: The Industrialization of Light in the Nineteenth Century*

0-679-74438-X VINTAGE PB $13.00

Women and Gender Studies

For related reading, see WOMEN'S STUDIES in SOCIAL STUDIES

Bonnie S. **Anderson** & Judith **Zinsser**

A History of Their Own: Women in Europe from Prehistory to the Present

Both volumes are organized according to women's societal roles. The first volume covers the history of women to the Renaissance, the second from the 17th century to the present

Volume 1

0-06-091452-1 HARPERCOLLINS PB $18.00

Volume 2

0-06-091563-3 HARPERCOLLINS PB $18.00

Renate **Bridenthal**, editor

Becoming Visible: Women in European History

See also **EUROPEAN HISTORY** under **WOMEN'S STUDIES** in **SOCIAL STUDIES**

0-395-41950-6 HOUGHTON MIFFLIN PB $33.96

Mark **Brietenberg**

Anxious Masculinity in Early Modern England

Explores jealousy, cuckoldry, heterosexual desire, and the perpetuation of "patriarchal ideologies in a gendered economy." Explores the works of writers such as Shakespeare, Montaigne, Bacon, and Jane Anger

0-521-48588-6 CAMBRIDGE PB $16.95

Margaret **Creighton** & Lisa **Norling**, editors

Iron Men, Wooden Women: Gender and Seafaring in the Atlantic World, 1700-1920

Among other topics, the careers of female pirates, such as Anne Bonny and Mary Read, as well as those of other women—"transvestite heroines"—who dressed as men to serve on the crews of sailing ships. Contributors include Marcus Rediker, Laura Tabili, and Lilian Nayder

0-8018-5160-2 JOHNS HOPKINS PB $16.95

Vern **Bullough** & Bonnie **Bullough**

Women and Prostitution: A Social History

0-87975-372-2 PROMETHEUS PB $22.95

Janice **Delaney**

The Curse: A Cultural History of Menstruation

"By providing a broad cultural reading... the authors make an important feminist and scholarly statement about women and the continuing impact of 'menstrual politics'" —Paula A. Treichler

0-252-01452-9 ILLINOIS PB $13.95

Geoff **Dench**

Transforming Men: Changing Patterns of Dependency and Dominance in Gender Relations

"A highly original, pithy and controversial book"—Asa Briggs

1-56000-232-8 TRANSACTION $29.95

Flapper

Antonia **Fraser**

The Warrior Queens

0-679-72816-3 VINTAGE PB $14.00

Olwen **Hufton**

The Prospect Before Her: A History of Women in Western Europe, 1500-1800

See also **WORLD HISTORY** under **WOMEN'S STUDIES** in **SOCIAL STUDIES**

0-679-45030-0 KNOPF $35.00

Gerda **Lerner**

The Creation of Feminist Consciousness: From the Middle Ages to Eighteen-Seventy

"A compelling argument constructed by a distinguished and well-respected historian of women"—Judith M. Bennett, University of North Carolina, Chapel Hill

See also **FEMINIST THEORY** under **WOMEN'S STUDIES** in **SOCIAL STUDIES**

0-19-506604-9 OXFORD $30.00
0-19-509060-8 OXFORD PB $11.95

Gerda **Lerner**

The Creation of Patriarchy

"Dramatically reopens a chapter of women's history that historians had thought was forever closed to them—the origins of the collective dominance of women by men"
—Katherine Kish Sklar, UCLA

0-19-505185-8 OXFORD PB $12.95

George L. **Mosse**

The Image of Man: The Creation of Modern Masculinity

The masculine stereotype as it evolved in modern Western culture

0-19-510101-4 OXFORD $25.00

David F. **Noble**

A World Without Women: The Christian Clerical Culture of Western Science

Suggests, among other things, a "defeminization" at the core of the modern scientific enterprise

See also **HISTORY OF SCIENCE AND TECHNOLOGY** under **SCIENCE AND TECHNOLOGY** in **SCIENCE**

0-19-508435-7 OXFORD PB $12.95

Joan **Scott**, editor

Feminism and History

A cross-disciplinary selection of articles on the future direction of women's history: from the experience of women in colonial Asia to the ideology of sexual difference in Nazi Germany

0-19-875169-9 OXFORD PB $19.95

Environmental Studies

For related reading, see THE ENVIRONMENT in SCIENCE

Anna **Branwell**

Fading of the Greens: The Decline of Environmental Politics in the West

0-300-06040-8 YALE $28.00

Lester R. **Brown**

Who Will Feed China? Wake Up Call for a Small Planet

The president of the Worldwatch Institute predicts that the potential for a grain deficit in China could trigger a world food shortage

0-393-31409-X NORTON PB $8.95

Richard H. **Grove**

Green Imperialism: Colonial Expansion, Tropical Island Edens and the Origins of Environmentalism, 1600-1860

The significance of Utopian, Physiocratic, and medical thinking in the history of environmentalist ideas and the role of the ocean island "Eden" as a vehicle for the new conceptions of nature

0-521-56513-8 CAMBRIDGE PB $18.95

Joel E. **Cohen**

How Many People Can the Earth Support?

By the head of the Laboratory of Populations at the Rockefeller University

0-393-03862-9 NORTON $30.00
0-393-31495-2 NORTON PB $14.95

Carolyn **Merchant**

The Death of Nature: Women, Ecology, and the Scientific Revolution

0-06-250595-5 HARPERCOLLINS PB $14.00

Earthcare: Women and the Environment

0-415-90888-4 ROUTLEDGE PB $16.95

Reference

For related reading, see HISTORICAL AND POLITICAL ATLASES under GEOGRAPHICAL INFORMATION under REFERENCE in BUSINESS AND REFERENCE

Alan **Axelrod** & Charles **Phillips**

What Everyone Should Know About the 20th Century

Summarizes the 200 most important events since 1900

1-55850-506-7 ADAMS $16.00

Geoffrey **Barraclough**, editor

The Times Concise Atlas of World History

0-8437-1145-0 HAMMOND PB $27.95

Paul F. **Boller**, Jr. & John **George**

They Never Said It: A Book of Fake Quotes, Misquotes, and Misleading Attributions

0-19-505541-1 OXFORD $22.00

Arthur **Cotterell**, editor

The Penguin Encyclopedia of Classical Civilizations

This absorbing book encourages a new approach to the classical world by offering a superb survey of the whole

0-14-051344-2 PENGUIN PB $19.95

Robert H. **Ferrell** & Richard **Natkiel**

Atlas of American History

Informed text, historical paintings, and color photos. The maps range from the Atlantic trade in 1770 to presidential elections from 1800 to 1980

See also **REFERENCE** under **TEXTBOOKS** under **SURVEYS OF US HISTORY** in **HISTORY OF THE AMERICAS**

0-8160-3441-9 FACTS ON FILE $29.95
0-8160-2884-2 FACTS ON FILE PB $19.95

Bernard **Grun**

The Timetables of History: A Horizontal Linkage of People and Events

Based on Werner Stein's *Kulturfahrplan*

0-671-74271-X TOUCHSTONE PB $20.00

Colin **McEvedy**, editor

The Penguin Atlas of Medieval History

0-14-051249-7 PENGUIN PB $12.95

The Penguin Atlas of Modern History: To 1815

0-14-051153-9 VIKING PB $10.95

The Penguin Atlas of North American History: To 1870

0-14-051128-8 PENGUIN PB $11.95

The Penguin Atlas of Recent History

See also **HISTORICAL AND POLITICAL ATLASES** under **GEOGRAPHICAL INFORMATION** under **REFERENCE** in **BUSINESS AND REFERENCE**

0-14-051154-7 PENGUIN PB $11.95

Archaeology

Archaeology is the systematic study of the material remains of human behavior in the past. Stuart Piggot called it "the science of rubbish," and it is by carefully examining bits of pottery, sword handles, and scraps of papyrus that an archaeologist is able to piece together the habits of a society that may have disappeared millennia before.

To make full use of their finds, archaeologists have developed a battery of techniques. Some, like thermoluminescence and cobalt dating, are extremely sophisticated; others are merely a matter of common sense. One useful technique resulted from the identification of certain types of pottery with certain eras. Now, any dig is carefully conducted so that the pottery at the various strata can date other objects on the same level.

Books on context and dating techniques have much of the same fascination as Sherlock Holmes's explanation of his "methods." Whether ancient societies were nomadic cattle-herders or were ruled in the name of god-kings by priestly bureaucracies, we have few written records. All we know must be deduced from their bronze implements, broken chariot wheels, or their circles of monumental stone. Although this does not yield history, it allows us to paint a haunting picture of the way of life of many strange, distant peoples now gone forever.

General Archaeology

Warwick **Bray** & David **Trump**

The Penguin Dictionary of Archaeology

References to all areas of archaeological interest—Baal, the Yang Shao culture of neolithic China, the nutcracker men of prehistoric Africa—as well as explanations of the specialized vocabulary

0-14-051116-4 VIKING PB $14.95

C.W. **Ceram**
Gods, Graves, and Scholars: The Story of Archaeology
Communicates the excitement of a science that requires the nerves of an adventurer and the mind of a first-rate detective
0-394-74319-9 VINTAGE PB........$12.00

Brian M. **Fagan**
Archaeology: A Brief Introduction
The goals of archaeology, problems of finding and excavating sites, of dating artifacts and reconstructing cultures from them
0-673-52525-2 HARPERCOLLINS PB........$25.00

Kevin **Greene**
Archaeology: The History, Principles, and Methods of Modern Archaeology
0-8122-1570-2 PENNSYLVANIA PB........$19.95

Sharman Apt **Russell**
When the Land Was Young: Reflections on American Archaeology
From an 8,000-year-old burial site in eastern Florida to the cutting edge of present-day archaeology, Russel skillfully weaves together the human emotions and technical expertise of archaeologists in an intense and exciting exploration of a fascinating scientific quest
0-201-40698-5 ADDISON-WESLEY........$23.00

Robert **Wenke**
Patterns in Prehistory: Humankind's First Three Million Years
See also **PALEOANTHROPOLOGY** under **PALEONTOLOGY AND EVOLUTION** under **LIFE SCIENCES** in **SCIENCE**
0-19-505522-5 OXFORD PB........$28.00

Archaeological Techniques and Philosophy

George **Bass**, editor
Ships and Shipwrecks of the Americas: A History Based on Underwater Archaeology
A richly illustrated picture book
0-500-05049-X THAMES & HUDSON........$40.00
0-500-27892-X THAMES & HUDSON PB........$24.95

Jacob **Bronowski**
The Ascent of Man
The charm and eloquence of Bronowski's writing are complemented by plentiful illustrations from the popular television series of the 1970s
0-316-10933-9 LITTLE, BROWN PB........$29.95

Roland **Etienne** & Francoise **Etienne**
The Search for Ancient Greece
0-8109-2804-3 ABRAMS PB........$12.95

Peter **James**
Centuries of Darkness
0-8135-1951-9 RUTGERS PB........$16.95

Ian **Hodder**
Reading the Past: Current Approaches to Interpretation in Archaeology
A controversial adaptation of new semiotic approaches to the archaeological recreation of cultures
0-521-40142-9 CAMBRIDGE........$40.00
0-521-40957-8 CAMBRIDGE PB........$14.95

Bruce **Koklick**
Puritans in Babylon: Ancient Near East and American Intellectual Life
1-880493-0 PRINCETON........$29.95

Paul **MacKendrick**
The Greek Stones Speak: The Story of Archaeology in Greek Lands
0-393-30111-7 NORTON PB........$14.95

Jane **McIntosh**
The Practical Archaeologist
Explains in clear and practical detail how we know about the past and how our knowledge is increasing
0-8160-1400-0 FACTS ON FILE........$24.95
0-8160-1814-6 FACTS ON FILE PB........$15.95

Ralph **Merrifield**
The Archaeology of Ritual and Magic
Examines the *longue durée* of ritual below cultural and ideological change, from pristine animism to rationalistic thought
0-941533-25-5 NEW AMSTERDAM........$25.00
0-941533-26-3 NEW AMSTERDAM PB........$15.95

Philip **Rahtz**
Invitation to Archaeology
"Today's garbage is tomorrow's archaeology." An introduction to the methods enlivened with the quirks of some of the methodologists
0-631-14106-5 BLACKWELL........$24.95
0-631-18067-2 BLACKWELL PB........$17.95

Bruce G. **Trigger**
Gordon Childe: Revolutions in Archaeology
0-231-05038-0 COLUMBIA........$47.00

A History of Archaeological Thought
A survey of archaeological theory from the middle ages to now
0-521-33818-2 CAMBRIDGE........$22.95

Language and Writing

Archaeology also builds up its pictures of lost peoples from fragments of writing, whether ritual inscriptions or palace inventories, on stone or papyrus, and from whatever traces it can find of the once-vast oral tradition.

The series Reading the Past is published jointly by University of California Press and the British Museum. Amply illustrated, these books serve as excellent introductions to the writing systems of the ancient world.

Y. John **Chadwick**
Linear B and Related Scripts
How the script of the Minoan bureaucracy was discovered, deciphered, and interpreted. The diagrams of hieroglyphics and their meanings are especially helpful
See also **EARLY GREEK AND MINOAN PERIODS** under **ANCIENT GREECE**
0-520-06019-9 CALIFORNIA PB........$11.00

B.F. **Cook**
Greek Inscriptions
0-520-06113-6 CALIFORNIA PB........$11.00

W.V. **Davies**
Egyptian Hieroglyphs
Explanation of their principles, origins, development, and use, as well as the history of their decipherment
See also **ANCIENT EGYPTIAN LITERATURE** in **LITERATURE OF EUROPE, AFRICA, AND ASIA**
0-520-06287-6 CALIFORNIA PB........$11.00

Umberto **Eco**
The Search for the Perfect Language
0-631-1746-5 BLACKWELL........$24.95

David **Diringer**
The Book Before Printing: Ancient, Medieval and Oriental
0-8446-5926-6 SMITH........$18.00
0-486-24243-9 DOVER PB........$12.95

Jack **Goody**
The Interface Between the Written and the Oral
Considers this complex interplay in three ways: as internal to certain societies; in relationship between oral and written societies; and in the linguistic life of the individual
0-521-33794-1 CAMBRIDGE PB........$19.95

John **Healey**
The Early Alphabet
0-520-07309-6 CALIFORNIA PB........$11.00

Joyce **Marcus**
Mesoamerican Writing Systems: Propaganda, Myth and History in Four Ancient Civilizations
Superb archeological study of the role of hieroglyphic writing in pre-Hispanic Aztec, Mixtec, Zapotec, and Maya states
See also **MEXICO AND CENTRAL AMERICA: GENERAL WORKS** under **NATIVE AMERICAN CULTURES: CENTRAL AND SOUTH AMERICA** in **HISTORY OF THE AMERICAS**
0-691-09474-8 PRINCETON........$60.00

R.I. **Page**

Runes

Runes were the alphabet of the ancient Celts

0-520-06114-4 CALIFORNIA PB $11.00

Colin **Renfrew**

Archaeology and Language: The Puzzle of Indo-European Origins

A remarkable synthesis of archaeology and linguistics. Renfrew pushes the earliest date of the Indo-European occupation of Europe back to 6000 BC and demonstrates its agricultural character. Highly recommended

0-521-38675-6 CAMBRIDGE PB $19.95

Denise **Schmandt-Besserat**

How Writing Came About

From the award-winning author of *Before Writing*, which is currently unavailable, a study on the origins of writing

0-292-77710-8 UTEXA $19.95

C.B. **Walker**

Cuneiform

The writing system of Mesopotamia, its origins and development, the scribes who used it and their libraries, and its modern decipherment

0-520-06115-2 CALIFORNIA PB $11.00

In most periods, with the exception of the Old Babylonian, it is the formal libraries from palace and temple that preserved the mass of literary texts…The literary libraries largely consisted of standard texts copied and recopied from one generation to the next. Occasional new texts were added from time to time, but they were few by comparison with the great mass of traditional material. Much of this was not what we today would regard as literature, even if Assyriologists continue to call it such. The largest group of texts consists of omens, collections of observations made over hundreds of years concerned with the stars, the appearance of the liver of a sacrificial sheep, the movements of birds, etc. Other categories of texts were the lexical lists, incantations, prayers, and the well-known epic literature. The late Leo Oppenheim, in a summary of traditional Mesopotamian literature, calculated that the whole of the standard corpus as represented in a library like Ashurbanipal's could have run to as many as fifteen hundred different tablets of between eighty and two hundred lines each; for many texts Ashurbanipal had several copies.

CUNEIFORM

The Archaeology of Civilizations

Julian **Burger**

The Gaia Atlas of First Peoples: The Future for the Indigenous World

The first volume in the new Gaia Futures series: a sourcebook on native people in the world today—from the Maori of New Zealand to the Sanema of Venezuela—and their struggle to survive the onslaughts of industrial development and environmental decay

0-385-26653-7 DOUBLEDAY PB $15.95

John A.J. **Cowlett**

Ascent to Civilization: The Archaeology of Early Man

Our primitive beginnings at the remote and dimmest edge of human existence in Africa. Elaborately mapped and illustrated

0-07-544312-0 MCGRAW HILL PB $29.50

Riane **Eisler**

The Chalice and the Blade

Posits the golden age as a lost "Goddess culture," and how its end, amid chaotic conditions, bifurcated human cultural evolution

0-06-250289-1 HARPERCOLLINS PB $16.00

Harvey **Rachlin**

Lucy's Bones, Sacred Stones, and Einstein's Brain: The Remarkable Stories Behind the Great Objects and Artifacts of History, from Antiquity to the Modern Era

By telling the stories behind some of the greatest artifacts of history, Rachlin has found a way to animate the past. The Bayeux Tapestry tells the story of William's conquest of England; the skeletal remains of "Lucy" introduce us to our earliest human ancestors; and the rifle that killed JFK serves as a vivid evocation of that terrible assassination. From antiquity to the modern era, this is a unique introduction to some of history's critical moments

0-8050-3964-3 HOLT $27.50

Asia

Edmund **Capon**

Art and Archaeology in China

0-262-53034-1 MIT PB $13.95

Peter **Hopkirk**

Foreign Devils on the Silk Road: The Search for the Lost Cities and Treasures of Chinese Central Asia

See also **CENTRAL ASIA** under **ASIA** under **TRAVEL LITERATURE** in **FOOD, TRAVEL, AND LEISURE**

0-87023-435-8 MASSACHUSETTS PB $17.95

David N. **Keightly**

Sources of Shang History: The Oracle-Bone Inscriptions of Bronze Age China

Inscriptions carved on cattle scapulas and turtle shells dating from the second millenium BC are used to delineate the ethos of the first dynasty

0-520-02969-0 CALIFORNIA $70.00

0-520-05455-5 CALIFORNIA PB $35.00

Mesopotamia

The Mesopotamian city-state of Sumer disappeared from the annals of history until quite recently. It is not even mentioned in the Bible. But since its discovery in the course of digs by Assyriologists, it has become one of the marvels of archaeology. A complete civilization based on a complex irrigation system, it also invented the potter's wheel, the wagon wheel, the sailboat, bronze-casting, and a system of writing on clay used all over the Near East for 2,000 years.

Seton **Lloyd**

Foundations in the Dust: The Story of Mesopotamian Exploration

Knits the lives and work of the great Assyriologists from Layard to Woolley into an exciting narrative

0-404-15364-X AMS $21.50

J.N. **Postgate**

Early Mesopotamia: Society and Economy at the Dawn of History

0-415-11032-7 ROUTLEDGE PB $25.00

H.W.F. **Saggs**

Babylonians

0-8061-2765-1 OKLAHOMA $28.95

Egypt

Howard **Carter** & A.C. **Mace**

The Discovery of the Tomb of Tutankhamen

The original story by the discoverer and excavator

0-8446-5562-7 SMITH $20.50

Graham **Hancock** & Robert **Bauval**

The Message of the Sphinx: A Quest for the Hidden Legacy of Mankind

0-517-70503-6 CROWN $27.50

T.G. **James**

Excavating in Egypt

Egyptian civilization and the explorations that uncovered it

0-226-39192-2 CHICAGO PB $14.95

Nancy **Thomas**

The American Discovery of Ancient Egypt

ESSAYS BY GERRY D. SCOTT III & BRUCE G. TRIGGER

0-8109-6312-4 L.A. COUNTY MUSEUM $49.50

Northern Europe

Rodney **Castleden**

The Stonehenge People: An Exploration of Life in Neolithic Britain, 4100-2000 B.C.

Investigates the purpose of the building, how the huge bluestones were hauled from the sacred mountains of the west to Salisbury Plain, and the customs of the builders

0-415-04065-5 ROUTLEDGE PB $14.95

Barry **Cunliffe**

Danebury: Anatomy of an Iron Age

Illustrated

0-906780-29-2 HUMANITIES PB $42.00

Barry **Cunliffe**, editor

The Oxford Illustrated Prehistory of Europe

Compresses the most recent archaeological discoveries into a coherent vision of life in Europe prior to classical Greece. Ranges from the Stone Age to the march of the barbarians, from northern Europe to the Mediterranean. Lavishly illustrated and far-reaching in scope

0-19-814385-0 OXFORD $49.95

Prudence **Jones** & Nigel **Pennick**

A History of Pagan Europe

See also **EUROPEAN MYTHOLOGY** under **MYTHOLOGY AND FOLKLORE** in **RELIGION, SPIRITUALITY, AND PHILOSOPHY**

0-415-09136-5 ROUTLEDGE $25.00

Roger **Joussaume**

Dolmens for the Dead: Megalith-Building Throughout the World

The ancient chamber-tombs constructed with huge untrimmed rocks provide information about burial rites, social organization, and religious customs of prehistoric Europe. Illustrated

TRANSLATED BY ANNE & CHRISTOPHER CHIPPINDALE

0-8014-2156-X CORNELL $39.95

Britain from Celts to Angles

For related reading, see GREAT BRITAIN AND IRELAND in this section

C.J. **Arnold**

An Archaeology of the Early Anglo-Saxon Kingdoms

0-415-00349-0 ROUTLEDGE $67.00

T.B. **Barry**

The Archaeology of Medieval Ireland

0-416-30370-6 ROUTLEDGE PB $14.95

Stuart **Piggott**

The Druids

A study of the ancient Celtic priests

0-500-27363-4 NORTON PB $15.95

John **Sharkey**

Celtic Mysteries

0-8446-6312-3 SMITH $25.00

0-500-81009-5 THAMES & HUDSON PB $15.95

Charles **Thomas**

Celtic Britain

0-500-02107-4 THAMES & HUDSON $22.50

American Southwest

For related reading, see NATIVE AMERICAN CULTURES: NORTH AMERICA in HISTORY OF THE AMERICAS

George J. **Gumerman**

A View from Black Mesa: The Changing Face of Archaeology

0-8165-0848-8 ARIZONA $24.95

0-8165-1340-6 ARIZONA PB $16.95

Robert H. **Lister** & Florence C. **Lister**

Those Who Came Before: Southwestern Archaeology in the National Park System

PHOTOGRAPHS BY DAVID MUENCH

0-911408-62-2 SW PARKS PB $12.95

John C. **McGregor**

Southwestern Archaeology

0-252-00989-4 ILLINOIS PB $19.95

Central and South America

For related reading, see NATIVE AMERICAN CULTURES: CENTRAL AND SOUTH AMERICA in HISTORY OF THE AMERICAS

Michael **Coe**

The Maya

An authoritative history

050-027716-8 THAMES & HUDSON PB $15.95

Nigel **Davies**

The Aztecs: A History

From their rude beginnings to their rise to domination over a large part of Mesoamerica and their defeat at the hands of the conquistadores

0-8061-1691-9 OKLAHOMA PB $19.95

Evan **Hadingham**

Lines to the Mountain Gods: Nazca and the Mysteries of Peru

0-8061-2130-0 OKLAHOMA PB $18.95

Norman **Hammond**

Ancient Maya Civilization

The discovery of the ancient Maya centers deep in the forests of central America and the rise and fall of classic Mayan civilization

0-8135-0906-8 RUTGERS PB $17.95

L. Bruce **Hunter**

A Guide to Ancient Mexican Ruins

Part fun guide, part cultural history of the ruins of the Toltec, Zapotec, Mixtec, and Aztec peoples

0-8061-1407-X OKLAHOMA PB $15.95

Tony **Morrison**

Pathways to the Gods: The Mystery of the Andes Lines

Who built the Nazca lines that extend for up to 20 miles on a desolate Peruvian plain, and why? This popular book by a BBC producer incorporates work by Gerald Hawkins of the Smithsonian and Maria Reiche, who has worked in Peru since the 1940s

0-89733-282-2 ACADEMY CHICAGO PB $9.95

Dennis **Tedlock**, translator

Popol Vuh

The newest translation of the Quiche Maya classic combines anthropological and literary values

See also **THE MAYA** under **NATIVE AMERICAN CULTURES: CENTRAL AND SOUTH AMERICA** in **HISTORY OF THE AMERICAS**

See also **MEXICO, CENTRAL AND SOUTH AMERICA** under **TRADITIONAL LITERATURE: POETRY, STORIES, ORATORY** under **NATIVE AMERICAN LITERATURES** in **LITERATURE OF THE AMERICAS**

0-684-81845-0 TOUCHSTONE PB $15.00

The Ancient Near East

Some of the most spectacular achievements of archaeology have been among the ruins of the great civilizations that flourished between the valley of the Tigris and the Euphrates and the Mediterranean coast. From this arid land sprang Sumer, Assyria, and Babylon, the first known civilizations, whose achievements in writing, technical invention, and religion gave an impetus to subsequent, more familiar cultures.

Robert **Drews**

The Coming of the Greeks: Indo-European Conquests in the Aegean and the Near East

0-691-03592-X PRINCETON $49.50

0-691-02951-2 PRINCETON PB $14.95

The End of the Bronze Age: Changes in Warfare and the Catastrophe ca. 1200 B.C.

The end of the Levantine, Hittite, Trojan, and Mycenaean kingdoms and the advent of a dark age that would last more than 400 years

0-691-02591-6 PRINCETON PB $14.95

Henri **Frankfort**

Kingship and the Gods: A Study of Ancient Near Eastern Religion as the Integration of Society and Nature

The differences between the social and religious forms developed in the natural fertility of the Nile valley and the more arid Mesopotamian plains

PREFACE BY SAMUEL N. KRAMER

0-226-26011-9 CHICAGO PB $23.95

O.R. **Gurney**

The Hittites

New, revised edition of the standard English introduction to the life, history, and culture of the Hittites of Central Anatolia (Turkey)

0-14-012601-5 PENGUIN PB $12.95

Henri **Frankfort**, editor

The Intellectual Adventure of Ancient Man: An Essay on Speculative Thought in the Ancient Near East

How abstract reasoning evolved from the primitive poetic mind that divined invisible agencies behind each natural phenomenon

0-226-26008-9 CHICAGO PB $14.95

William W. **Hallo** & William K. **Simpson**

The Ancient Near East: A History

A parallel history of ancient Egypt and the ancient Near East for general readers

0-15-502755-7 H.B.J. PB $28.60

Hans J. **Nissen**

The Early History of the Ancient Near East, 9000-2000 B.C.

0-226-58658-8 CHICAGO PB $21.95

Wolfram **von Soden**

The Ancient Orient: An Introduction to the Study of the Ancient Near East

TRANSLATED BY SONALD G. SCHLEY

0-8028-0142-0 EERDMANS PB $15.00

Mesopotamia

Jeremy **Black** & Anthony **Green**

Gods, Demons and Symbols of Ancient Mesopotamia: An Illustrated Dictionary

Well informed and up-to-date illustrated dictionary by two scholars who have made their career out of clarifying the confusing array of religious representations in pre-classical Mesopotamia

See also **MESOPOTAMIA** under **THE ANCIENT WORLD: EGYPT AND MESOPOTAMIA** under **MYTHOLOGY AND FOLKLORE** in **RELIGION, SPIRITUALITY, AND PHILOSOPHY**

0-292-70794-0 TEXAS PB $19.95

Jean **Bottero**

Mesopotamia: Writing, Reasoning, and the Gods

"A very readable guide to Bottero's view of Mesopotamian history, religion, and literature that can be described as thought-provoking, challenging and insightful"
—*Religious Studies Review*

0-226-06727-0 CHICAGO PB $16.95

Thorkild **Jacobsen**

The Treasures of Darkness: A History of Mesopotamian Religion

A study based on Sumerian mythological literature

0-300-02291-3 YALE PB $17.00

Samuel N. **Kramer**

The Sumerians: Their History, Culture and Character

The doyen of Sumerologists uses the ancient texts to demonstrate the common humanity of the forgotten civilization

0-226-45238-7 CHICAGO PB $15.95

A. Leo **Oppenheim**

Ancient Mesopotamia: Portrait of a Dead Civilization

City life, the scribes, kings, and "scientists" of ancient Mesopotamia

0-226-63187-7 CHICAGO PB $17.95

Georges **Roux**

Ancient Iraq

Covers with a light but exact touch the political, cultural, and economic history from the prehistoric to the Christian period

0-14-012523-X PENGUIN PB $14.95

Leonard **Woolley**

The Sumerians

The great British archaeologist describes the people whose achievements influenced the course of Western civilization for 2000 years before their very name faded from historical records

0-393-00292-6 NORTON PB $9.95

Egypt

Ancient Egypt's history has a longer span than Western Europe from the time of Julius Caesar to our own day. Yet the power of the priestly bureaucracy that upheld the god-king was such that in all that time very little change can be discerned. By its very strangeness, this religion fascinates us; and the excavators of the great tombs built to preserve the body for its other-worldly journey have revealed many of its mysteries. The excellent studies of Egyptian religion are matched by many works giving detailed accounts of the daily life of the people.

Alberto **Siliotti**

Egypt: Splendors of an Ancient Civilization

A photo journey up the Nile highlights national monuments and treasures

See also **AFRICA** under **TRAVEL PHOTOGRAPHY** in **FOOD, TRAVEL, AND LEISURE**

0-500-01647-X THAMES & HUDSON $50.00

Jean **Vercoutter**

The Search for Ancient Egypt

0-8109-2817-5 ABRAMS PB $12.95

History

Cyril **Aldred**

Akhenaten: King of Egypt

The king who tried to replace the entrenched religious bureaucracy with his own worship of the sun disk

0-500-27621-8 THAMES & HUDSON PB $24.95

Cyril **Aldred**

Egypt to the End of the Old Kingdom

Using a wealth of art objects, Aldred recreates Egypt under pharaonic rule, a refinement of the African worship of an omnipotent, rain-making god-king

0-500-29001-6 THAMES & HUDSON PB $12.95

Alan K. **Bowman**

Egypt After the Pharaohs: 332 B.C.-A.D. 642

Egypt under the Macedonian and Roman Empires, until the Muslim invasion. "A valuable history. It presents a picture of daily life in Egypt that was neither Greek nor Pharaonic but a fusion of interweaving cultures"
—*Christian Science Monitor*

0-520-20531-6 CALIFORNIA PB $15.95

Nicolas **Grimal**

A History of Ancient Egypt

TRANSLATED BY IAN SHAW

0-631-19396-0 BLACKWELL PB $22.95

Donald B. **Redford**

Akhenaten: The Heretic King

Eunuch king, disguised woman, mentor of Moses? These are only some of the speculations surrounding this potent but obscure monarch. Scholar and general reader alike will benefit from this fresh portrait

0-691-00217-7 PRINCETON PB $22.50

George **Steindorff** & Keith C. **Seele**

When Egypt Ruled the East: From the Eighteenth to the Twentieth Dynasty

The period of Egypt's greatest imperial expansion after the overthrow of the Hyksos, the invading Asiatic shepherd kings

0-226-77199-7 CHICAGO PB $13.95

L.A. **Waddell**

Egyptian Civilization: Its Sumerian Origin and Real Chronology

0-317-53201-4 NOONTIDE $12.00

Culture and Society

Cyril **Aldred**

The Egyptians

A popular and instructive introduction to their history and culture by the British art historian

0-500-27345-6 THAMES & HUDSON PB $15.95

T.G.H. **James**

Ancient Egypt: The Land and Its Legacy

0-292-72062-9 TEXAS $34.95

Jill **Kamil**

The Ancient Egyptians: A Popular Introduction to Life in the Pyramid Age

977-424-294-7 AMERICAN U. OF CAIRO $24.95

Jill **Kamil**

Coptic Egypt: A History and Guide

977-424-104-5 AMERICAN U. OF CAIRO PB.............$15.00

Pierre **Montet**

Everyday Life in Egypt in the Days of Rameses the Great

Life in Egypt during the reign of the pharaoh most likely to have tangled with Moses

0-8371-7446-5 GREENWOOD.............$65.00
0-8122-1113-8 PENNSYLVANIA PB.............$21.95

Gay **Robins**

Women in Ancient Egypt

0-674-95468-8 HARVARD PB.............$18.95

Mirian **Stead**

Egyptian Life

0-674-24151-7 HARVARD PB.............$12.50

John A. **Wilson**

The Culture of Ancient Egypt

0-226-90152-1 CHICAGO PB.............$11.95

Pyramids, Mummies, and Obelisks

Carol **Andrews**

Egyptian Mummies

0-674-24152-5 HARVARD PB.............$11.95

Sue **Daria**

Mummies and Magic: The Funerary Arts of Ancient Egypt

0-87846-303-8 DALLAS MUSEUM OF ART PB.............$29.95

I.E.S. **Edwards**

The Pyramids of Egypt

The rise and decline of the massive funerary monuments, from the step-pyramids and mastabas of the early dynasties to the attempt to foil grave robbers with the cliff-tombs of the Valley of the Kings

0-14-013634-7 PENGUIN PB.............$14.95

Christine **el Mahdy**

Mummies, Myth and Magic: In Ancient Egypt

See also **ART OF EGYPT AND THE ANCIENT NEAR EAST** in **ART**

0-500-05055-4 THAMES & HUDSON PB.............$19.95

John **Romer**

Ancient Lives: The Story of the Pharaoh's Tombmakers

The tombmakers lived outside Thebes in a tighttly-packed village filled with ritual experts and craftsmen who made the figures of the gods

0-8050-1244-3 HOLT PB.............$18.95

John H. **Taylor**

Unwrapping a Mummy

The unwrapping and scientific examination of Horemkenesi, an Egyptian priest and official who lived in Thebes in the eleventh century BC

0-292-78141-5 TEXAS PB.............$18.95

Peter **Tompkins**

Secrets of the Great Pyramid

Adventures and discoveries of the explorers and scientists who, for 200 years, have been probing the mysteries of the Great Pyramid of Cheops

0-88365-957-3 BUDGET BOOK.............$16.98

Beliefs and Knowledge

Bob **Brier**

Ancient Egyptian Magic

An up-to-date account of the role of the magician in every aspect of Egyptian life—from mummificaton to love potions

0-688-00796-1 MORROW PB.............$12.95

Geraldine **Pinch**

Magic in Ancient Egypt

"A thorough and thoughtful treatment of a world in which science, magic, and religion coexisted"—*Natural History*

0-292-76559-2 TEXAS PB.............$18.95

A.J. **Spencer**

Death in Ancient Egypt

The origin and development of burial practices

0-14-022294-4 PENGUIN PB.............$12.00

Language, Ciphers, and Hieroglyphics

Maria C. **Betro**

Hieroglyphics: The Writing of Ancient Egypt

0-7892-0232-8 ABBEVILLE.............$29.95

Edward **Chiera**

They Wrote on Clay: The Babylonian Tablets Speak Today

A friendly view of the Mesopotamian cultures through the written word of professional scribes

EDITED BY G.G. CAMERON

0-226-10425-7 CHICAGO PB.............$13.95

E.A. Wallis **Budge**

Egyptian Hieroglyphic Dictionary

Volume 1

0-486-23615-3 DOVER PB.............$18.95

Volume 2

0-486-23616-1 DOVER PB.............$18.95

Egyptian Language: Easy Lessons in Egyptian Hieroglyphics with Sign List

0-486-21394-3 DOVER PB.............$6.95

Reference

John **Baines** & Jaromir **Malek**

Atlas of Ancient Egypt

Comprehensive, easy-to-use compendium of major Egyptian archeological sites, well illustrated with photos, charts, reconstructions, graphs

0-87196-334-5 FACTS ON FILE.............$45.00

Michael **Grant**

Ancient History Atlas

Europe and the Mediterranean world, including Egypt and the Near East

See also **REFERENCE** under **TOPICS IN ROMAN HISTORY** under **ANCIENT ROME**

0-915262-73-8 DURST PB.............$12.00

George **Hart**

A Dictionary of Egyptian Gods and Goddesses

Gives full information in an attractive format with line drawings of the Egyptian symbols and images of their deities

0-7102-0167-2 ROUTLEDGE PB.............$12.95

Manfred **Lurker**

Gods and Symbols of Ancient Egypt: An Illustrated Dictionary

See also **EGYPT** under **THE ANCIENT WORLD: EGYPT AND MESOPOTAMIA** under **MYTHOLOGY AND FOLKLORE** in **RELIGION, SPIRITUALITY, AND PHILOSOPHY**

EDITED BY PETER A. CLAYTON

0-500-27253-0 NORTON PB.............$15.95

Palestine and the Bible

The archaeology of the Bible has a special interest, since for many people it is not merely a question of recreating a dead past but also of assisting in the exposition of living faiths. A number of works in this field employ archaeological discoveries to interpret the biblical text. This combination of text and artifact can yield rich results both in corroborating biblical accounts and adding to our understanding of the ancient societies. The evidence provided by the remains of devastated cities can bring to light information on both Solomon's monopoly of the Palestinian metal industry and the invasion of Canaan in Exodus.

John **Finegan**

Light from the Ancient East

The material world inhabited by the prophets and the apostles

Volume 1

0-691-00208-8 PRINCETON PB.............$24.95

Volume 2

0-686-76901-5 PRINCETON.............$90.00

Theodor H. **Gaster**, translator

The Dead Sea Scriptures

A selection of the Essene texts and other scriptures that were found in caves near the Dead Sea in 1947 and subsequent years, and that reveal much about sectarian religious life in ancient Judaea

See also **APOCRYPHA AND OTHER TEXTS** under **BIBLES AND COMMENTARY** under **CHRISTIANITY** in **RELIGION, SPIRITUALITY, AND PHILOSOPHY**

0-385-08859-0 DOUBLEDAY PB.............$13.95

Werner **Keller**

The Bible as History

The classic textbook in this genre

0-553-27943-2 BDD PB.............$6.99

Jerome **Murphy-O'Connor**

The Holy Land: An Archaeological Guide from Earliest Time to 1700

A popular, accurate introductory guide, easily used

0-19-285269-8 OXFORD PB $15.95

Geza **Vermes**

The Dead Sea Scrolls: Qumran in Perspective

Their discovery, authentication, and dating, and the evidence they provide of the beliefs and practices of the Essene community

0-8006-1435-6 FORTRESS PB $14.00

The Dead Sea Scrolls in English

A translation of the Hebrew and Aramaic documents discovered in the 1940s and dating from 200 BCE to the 1st century CE, offering unparalleled insights into post-biblical Jewish life; a revised and updated edition

See also THE DEAD SEA SCROLLS under LATER ANTIQUITY under JUDAISM in RELIGION, SPIRITUALITY, AND PHILOSOPHY

0-14-013544-8 PENGUIN PB $12.00

Cities and Sites

Louis **Frederic** & Jean Louis **Nou**

Borobudur

0-7892-0134-8 ABBEVILLE $125.00

Serge **Lancel**

Carthage: A History

TRANSLATED BY ANTONIA NEVILL

1-55786-468-3 BLACKWELL $34.95

Amihai **Mazar**

Archaeology of the Land of the Bible 10,000-586 B.C.E.

0-385-23970-X DOUBLEDAY $37.50

0-385-42590-2 ANCHOR PB $24.95

F.E. **Peters**

Jerusalem: The Holy City in the Eyes of Chroniclers, Visitors, Pilgrims, and Prophets from the Days of Abraham to the Beginnings of Modern Times

Reactions of visitors through the ages, in their own words

0-691-07300-7 PRINCETON $65.00

0-691-00641-5 PRINCETON PB $19.95

Ephraim **Stern** & Ayelet **Lewinson-Gilboa**

The New Encyclopedia of Archaeological Excavations in the Holy Land

The comprehensive four-volume encyclopedia with articles on all the major sites in southern Syria, many written by the archaeologists who participated in the findings

EDITED BY JOSEPH AVIRAM

0-13-276288-9 SIMON & SCHUSTER $375.00

Veronica **Tatton-Brown**

Ancient Cyprus

The unique and distinctive culture of Cyprus developed from its position at the crossroads of Mediterranean cultures. With color and black-and-white illustrations

0-674-03307-8 HARVARD PB $11.50

Caroline **Moorehead**

Lost and Found: The 9,000 Treasures of Troy: Heinrich Schliemann and the Gold that Got Away

In 1873 the pioneering archaeologist Heinrich Schliemann discovered the lost gold of Priam, king of ancient Troy, and smuggled it out to Berlin. In 1945 the treasure, which had been pillaged by the Nazis, disappeared from the German capital only to be found again recently in Moscow. Moorehead (*Bertrand Russell*, *Freya Stark*) tells the exciting story of this treasure, and along the way gives a thrilling account of her investigative adventure in search of it

0-670-85679-7 VIKING $24.95

David A. **Traill**

Schliemann of Troy: Treasure and Deceit

Schliemann, a phenomenal traveler as well as a linguist with a command of fifteen languages, was referred to by Traill as "…the emblematic archaeologist of all time"

0-312-14042-8 ST. MARTIN'S $24.95

Ancient Greece

The study of ancient Greek history has, for centuries, provided the West with political models. In addition to describing diplomacy and war, Greek historians speculated on the effect of the political structure on behavior, and their speculations gave subsequent generations a language with which to debate their own policies. This tradition is still alive. During the Cold War, Gore Vidal suggested that rulers on both sides of the Iron Curtain might benefit from study of Thucydides on the Peloponnesian War, in which a dashing, expansionist Athens broke itself against the stolid rock of militarist Sparta. The debate engendered by these opposed systems swayed to and fro for 2,400 years and continues to thread its way through modern history.

Although support is almost unanimous today for democratic Athens, questions persist about the nature of a democracy based on slavery. The following books are thus part of an ongoing argument about our own place in the larger world of political participation.

General Political History

J.K. **Davies**

Democracy and Classical Greece

The problem of sources for ancient history complements the investigation of what made Greece not so much a cultural continuum as a political patchwork

0-8047-1226-3 STANFORD PB $14.95

Socrates

John **Fine**

The Ancient Greeks: A Critical History

The most current one-volume overview of history and culture based on up-to-date findings and interpretations

0-674-03314-0 HARVARD PB $24.50

Peter **Green**

Ancient Greece: An Illustrated History

0-500-27161-5 NORTON PB $15.95

Donald **Kagan**

Pericles of Athens and the Birth of Democracy

Kagan, the leading contemporary historian of Periclean Athens, offers a compelling biography of its founding figure. His account of democracy's difficult birth could not be more relevant

0-02-916825-2 FREE PRESS $29.95

General Cultural History

Antony **Andrewes**

The Greeks

Greek society in archaic and classical times

0-393-00877-0 NORTON PB $10.95

John **Boardman** & others, editors

The Oxford History of the Classical World: Greece and the Hellenistic World

Thirty contributors whose essays range in subject from the Homeric hero to the twilight of the classical pantheon

0-19-282165-2 OXFORD PB $21.50

Kenneth **Dover**

The Greeks

"A resilient, satirical, cheeky people who wanted clear and sane answers to the questions Why? and Why not?"—from the Introduction

0-292-72724-0 TEXAS PB $12.95

James D. **Faubion**

Modern Greek Lessons: A Primer in Historical Constructivism

An innovative study of the Athenian cultural elite and a critical re-articulation of social theory

0-691-09473-X PRINCETON $45.00
0-691-00050-6 PRINCETON PB $18.95

M.I. **Finley**

Ancient Greeks

The Dark Ages following the destruction of Mycenae, the tyrants and lawgivers of archaic Greece, and the achievements and final decline of the city-state

0-14-013707-6 VIKING PB $10.95

Simon **Hornblower**

The Greek World, 479-323 B.C.

The great age of Greece begins with the defeat of Xerxes at Salamis and culminates with Alexander's incursion into Nepal

0-415-06557-7 ROUTLEDGE PB $17.95

Jean-Pierre **Vernant**, editor

The Greeks

0-226-85383-7 CHICAGO PB $15.95

Early Greek and Minoan Periods

Arthur Evans's discovery of the palace of Minos at Knossos on Crete revealed that a great maritime civilization had flourished in the Mediterranean from 2000 to 1400 BC.

W.R. **Biers**

Archaeology of Greece

The physical remains interpreted against the political and social background of the period between the age of the Homeric heroes and the era of the first colonies

0-8014-2082-2 CORNELL $52.50

Walter **Burkert**

Orientalizing Revolution: Near Eastern Influence on Greek Culture in the Early Archaic Age

An acclaimed study that focuses on the period 750-650 B.C., when Assyrian conquest, Phoenician commerce, and Greek exploration of both East and West mixed

TRANSLATED BY MARGARET E. PINDAR

0-674-64364-X HARVARD PB $14.95

Y. John **Chadwick**

Linear B and Related Scripts

How the script of the Minoan bureaucracy was discovered, deciphered, and interpreted. The diagrams of hieroglyphics and their meanings are especially helpful

See also LANGUAGE AND WRITING under ARCHAEOLOGY

0-520-06019-9 CALIFORNIA PB $11.00

Y. John **Chadwick**

The Mycenaean World

0-521-29037-6 CAMBRIDGE PB $21.95

Oliver **Dickinson**

The Aegean Bronze Age

The rise and fall of the Minoan and Mycenaean civilizations. Explores a network of themes including settlement, economy, foreign contact, religion, and burial customs

0-521-45664-9 CAMBRIDGE PB $28.95

M.I. **Finley**

Early Greece: The Bronze and Archaic Ages

Reconstructs the lost cultures of Crete and Troy from archaeological and mythological evidence

0-393-30051-X NORTON PB $9.95

The World of Odysseus

The revision of Finley's 1956 book locating the world of the *Odyssey* in the early Dark Age of Greece. A pioneering application of sociological and anthropological insights. "Finley's magnificent work has long been one of the treasures of my library"—Mary Renault

See also STUDIES OF INDIVIDUAL AUTHORS under CRITICAL STUDIES under ANCIENT GREEK LITERATURE in LITERATURE OF EUROPE, AFRICA, AND ASIA

0-14-013686-X PENGUIN PB $10.95

J. Lesley **Fitton**

The Discovery of the Greek Bronze Age

Fitton, a Greek and Roman antiquities curator at the British Museum, traces the coming of age of archaeological science. From the earliest travelers and Schliemann's excavation at Troy to contemporary archaeological digs, Fitton provides a concise summation of a compelling world of discovery

0-674-21188-X HARVARD $29.95

Michael **Grant**

The Ancient Mediterranean

0-452-01037-3 NEW AMERICAN LIBRARY PB $13.95

Reynold **Higgins**

Minoan and Mycenaean Art

0-500-18184-5 OXFORD $19.95

R.F. **Hoddinott**

The Thracians

0-500-02099-X THAMES & HUDSON $19.95

Aubrey **Snodgrass**

Archaic Greece

A portrait of a violent yet creative culture based on archaeological discoveries

0-520-04373-1 CALIFORNIA PB $15.00

Emily T. **Vermeule**

Greece in the Bronze Age

From the first inhabitants to the fall of the Mycenaean palace-towns in the 13th century BC, with special attention to the tragic encounter between the Minoan and Mycenaean empires

0-226-85354-3 CHICAGO PB $19.95

The Greek Wars

Peter **Green**

The Year of Salamis, 480-479 B.C.: The Greco-Persian Wars

This is a reissue with a new foreword of *Xerxes at Salamis*, originally published in 1970

0-520-20573-1 CALIFORNIA $24.95
0-520-20313-5 CALIFORNIA PB $15.00

Donald **Kagan**

The Outbreak of the Peloponnesian War

These four volumes, by a distinguished historian at Yale, re-examine Thucydides's *History of the Peloponnesian War*

0-8014-0501-7 CORNELL $47.50
0-8014-9556-3 CORNELL PB $16.95

The Archidamian War

0-8014-0889-X CORNELL $47.50
0-8014-9714-0 CORNELL PB $16.95

The Peace of Nicias and the Sicilian Expedition

0-8014-1367-2 CORNELL $47.50
0-8014-9940-2 CORNELL PB $16.95

The Fall of the Athenian Empire

0-8014-1935-2 CORNELL $47.50
0-8014-9984-4 CORNELL PB $16.95

Macedon and Alexander

A.B. **Bosworth**

Conquest and Empire: The Reign of Alexander the Great

0-521-34320-8 CAMBRIDGE $64.95
0-521-40679-X CAMBRIDGE PB $12.95

Robin Lane **Fox**

Alexander the Great

0-14-008878-4 PENGUIN PB $13.95

Peter **Green**

Alexander of Macedon, 356-323 B.C.: A Historical Biography

Green, a classicist who is also a novelist, presents the conqueror as a complex and contradictory personality. "The strength of Green's book…lies in his ability to create coherent and exciting narrative out of modern scholarly controversy: he has written a very fine biography"—Oswyn Murray, *Greece and Rome*

0-520-07166-2 CALIFORNIA PB $16.95

J.R. **Hamilton**

Alexander the Great

Emphasis on the Macedonian Alexander—his hard drinking and political cunning—and his limited influence on the spread of Hellenism

0-8229-6084-2 PITTSBURGH PB $15.95

Mary **Renault**

Renault uses her wide knowledge of the ancient world to depict daily life during the war with Sparta and the conquests of Alexander.

Mary **Renault**

The Nature of Alexander

A biography by the famous novelist. "The perfect companion to her Alexander novels" —*Wall Street Journal*

0-394-73825-X RANDOM HOUSE PB $11.00

Ulrich **Wilcken**

Alexander the Great

Alexander as the military missionary for the spread of Hellenism through the Persian and Egyptian monarchies

0-393-00381-7 NORTON PB $12.95

The Hellenistic World

An overlooked but important aspect of the ancient Greeks is their 200-year domination of Asia Minor, the Middle East, Egypt, and Persia. Though politically disunited, they achieved hegemony for the cultural products of Athenian democracy, which spread out from the great centers of Antioch and Alexandria.

Luciano **Canfora**

The Vanished Library: A Wonder of the Ancient World

An erudite investigation—sometimes adopting the tone of fiction—into the library of Alexandria and its ultimate fate

0-520-07255-3 CALIFORNIA PB $15.95

Peter M. **Fraser**

Cities of Alexander the Great

Suggests that Alexander founded far fewer cities than usually supposed

0-19-815006-7 OXFORD $72.00

Peter **Green**

Alexander to Actium: An Essay on the Historical Evolution of the Hellenistic Age

Spans an entire age—past the fall of the Roman republic and the emergence of Augustus as sole ruler of the Mediterranean

0-520-05611-6 CALIFORNIA $70.00
0-520-08349-0 CALIFORNIA PB $39.95

Amelie **Kuhrt** & Susan **Sherwin-White**, editors

Hellenism in the East: Greek and Non-Greek Civilizations from Syria to Central Asia After Alexander

The continuity of Mesopotamian civilizations under the Seleucid successors of Alexander

0-520-06054-7 CALIFORNIA $50.00

Arnaldo **Momigliano**

Alien Wisdom: The Limits of Hellenization

The dean of ancient historiographers considers the conflict between Greek culture and its Middle Eastern opponents

0-521-20876-9 CAMBRIDGE $50.00
0-521-38761-2 CAMBRIDGE PB $19.95

F.W. **Walbank**

The Hellenistic World

This excellent introduction to the post-conquest period includes the individual kingdoms of the Attalids, Ptolemies, and Seleucids, and the remarkable achievements of Alexandrian astronomy and literary scholarship

0-674-38726-0 HARVARD PB $14.50

Ancient Greek Classics

P.E. **Easterling** & Bernard **Knox**, editors

The Cambridge History of Classical Literature: Greek Literature

An ingeniously organized group effort, offering a coherent and highly credible survey. Tremendously valuable bibliography

See also **GENERAL STUDIES** under **CRITICAL STUDIES** under **ANCIENT GREEK LITERATURE** in **LITERATURE OF EUROPE, AFRICA, AND ASIA**

0-521-21042-9 CAMBRIDGE $125.00

Aeschylus

The Oresteia

Includes *Agamemnon, The Libation Bearers,* and *The Eumenides*. A verse translation in a more modern idiom than Lattimore's. Highly recommended

See also **AESCHYLUS** under **TRAGEDY** under **THE CLASSICAL PERIOD** under **ANCIENT GREEK LITERATURE** in **LITERATURE OF EUROPE, AFRICA, AND ASIA**

TRANSLATED BY ROBERT FAGLES

0-14-044333-9 PENGUIN PB $8.95

Aristophanes

Three Comedies

Includes *The Birds, The Clouds,* and *The Wasps*

See also **COMEDY** under **THE CLASSICAL PERIOD** under **ANCIENT GREEK LITERATURE** in **LITERATURE OF EUROPE, AFRICA, AND ASIA**

EDITED BY WILLIAM ARROWSMITH

0-472-06153-4 MICHIGAN PB $13.95

Aristotle

Introduction to Aristotle

Includes the *Nicomachean Ethics,* the *Politics,* the *Poetics,* and selections from other works

See also **ARISTOTLE** under **PHILOSOPHY** in **RELIGION, SPIRITUALITY, AND PHILOSOPHY**

EDITED BY RICHARD MCKEON

0-679-60027-2 MODERN LIBRARY $18.50

Arrian

The Campaigns of Alexander

Alexander as heroic leader, magnanimous and brilliant, by a Greek historian of the Age of the Antonines

TRANSLATED BY AUBREY DE SELINCOURT

0-14-044253-7 PENGUIN PB $12.95

Euripides

Three Tragedies

Includes *Electra, The Phoenician Women,* and *The Bacchae*

See also **EURIPIDES** under **TRAGEDY** under **THE CLASSICAL PERIOD** under **ANCIENT GREEK LITERATURE** in **LITERATURE OF EUROPE, AFRICA, AND ASIA**

TRANSLATED BY EMILY VERMEULE, ELIZABETH WYCKOFF & WILLIAM ARROWSMITH

EDITED BY DAVID GRENE & RICHMOND LATTIMORE

0-226-30784-0 CHICAGO PB $8.95

M.I. **Finley**, editor

Portable Greek Historians

Selections from Herodotus, Thucydides, Xenophon, and Polybius provide an introduction to the first historians

0-14-015065-X VIKING PB $13.95

Herodotus

The Histories

Father of history; father of lies—Herodotus has both reputations. The new translation upholds the reputation of this bestiary of ancient customs, which becomes a history of Greek resistance to the invasion of the Persian king Xerxes in 480 BC

See also **HISTORY** under **THE CLASSICAL PERIOD** under **ANCIENT GREEK LITERATURE** in **LITERATURE OF EUROPE, AFRICA, AND ASIA**

TRANSLATED BY DAVID GRENE

0-226-32770-1 CHICAGO $35.00
0-226-32772-8 CHICAGO PB $13.95

The Persian Wars

TRANSLATED BY GEORGE RAWLINSON

INTRODUCTION BY R.B. GODOLPHIN

0-394-30954-5 MCGRAW HILL PB $10.71

Hesiod

Theogony & Works and Days

A verse translation with very generous notes. Remarkable for its use of parallels from modern Greek folklore

See also **HESIOD** under **THE ARCHAIC PERIOD** under **ANCIENT GREEK LITERATURE** in **LITERATURE OF EUROPE, AFRICA, AND ASIA**

TRANSLATED BY APOSTOLOS N. ATHANASSAKIS

0-8018-2999-2 JOHNS HOPKINS PB $9.95

Homer

The Iliad of Homer

An "Iliad of woes" that does remarkable justice to the somber majesty of the original. Lattimore, an accomplished scholar and a fine poet in his own right, attempts to match the length of the Homeric line and, to some extent, the formulaic nature of the language, rendering the Greek with astonishing immediacy

See also **THE ILIAD** under **HOMER** under **THE ARCHAIC PERIOD** under **ANCIENT GREEK LITERATURE** in **LITERATURE OF EUROPE, AFRICA, AND ASIA**

TRANSLATED BY RICHMOND LATTIMORE

0-226-46940-9 CHICAGO PB $9.95

The Iliad of Homer

A long-awaited new version of *The Iliad* by a scholar whose earlier translations of Aeschylus and Sophocles have won wide acclaim

TRANSLATED BY ROBERT FAGLES

INTRODUCTION AND NOTES BY BERNARD KNOX

0-670-83510-2 VIKING $40.00

The Odyssey

Faithfulness to the repetitive use of formulaic phrases helps recapture the cadence of oral poetry

See also **THE ODYSSEY** under **HOMER** under **THE ARCHAIC PERIOD** under **ANCIENT GREEK LITERATURE** in **LITERATURE OF EUROPE, AFRICA, AND ASIA**

TRANSLATED BY RICHMOND LATTIMORE

0-06-090479-8 HARPERCOLLINS PB $13.00

The Odyssey

A new and highly acclaimed translation with a significant introduction by Bernard Knox

TRANSLATED BY ROBERT FAGLES

0-670-82162-4 VIKING $35.00

Peter **Jay**, editor

The Greek Anthology

A selection in modern verse translation

See also **THE GREEK ANTHOLOGY** under **THE ARCHAIC PERIOD** under **ANCIENT GREEK LITERATURE** in **LITERATURE OF EUROPE, AFRICA, AND ASIA**

0-14-044285-5 PENGUIN PB $10.95

Pausanias

Guide to Greece

A selection from the 2nd-century BC description by Pausanias, reorganized around a geographical pattern more useful to the tourist than that of the original

Volume 1

Northern Greece

See also **GREEK KNOWLEDGE** under **ANCIENT GREEK LITERATURE** in **LITERATURE OF EUROPE, AFRICA, AND ASIA**

0-14-044225-1 PENGUIN PB $13.95

Volume 2

Southern Greece

0-14-044226-X PENGUIN PB $13.95

Pindar

Pindar's Victory Songs

TRANSLATED BY FRANK NISETICH

0-8018-2350-1 JOHNS HOPKINS $45.00
0-8018-2356-0 JOHNS HOPKINS PB $16.95

Plato

The Portable Plato

Includes *The Republic*, the *Phaedo*, the *Symposium*, and the *Protagoras*

See also **PLATO** under **PHILOSOPHY** in **RELIGION, SPIRITUALITY, AND PHILOSOPHY**

EDITED BY SCOTT BUCHANAN

0-14-015040-4 VIKING PB $14.95

Plutarch

The Age of Alexander

The will to power of Alexander's generals and the courage of those who opposed them

TRANSLATED BY IAN SCOTT-KILVERT

0-14-044286-3 PENGUIN PB $11.95

Plutarch

Plutarch on Sparta

0-14-044463-7 PENGUIN PB $10.95

The Rise and Fall of Athens: Nine Greek Lives

The gritty personalities of the men who made Athens great and led her to defeat

TRANSLATED BY IAN SCOTT-KILVERT

0-14-044102-6 PENGUIN PB $9.95

Quintus Curtius **Rufus**

The History of Alexander

Alexander as the favorite of fortune corrupted by his heady successes, portrayed by a Roman aristocrat of the early empire

TRANSLATED BY JOHN YARDLEY

INTRODUCTION BY HECKEL WALDEMAR

0-14-044412-2 PENGUIN PB $10.95

A. N.W. **Saunders**, translator

Greek Political Oratory

A record of Athenian politics through the speeches of its greatest orators, from Pericles to Demosthenes

0-14-144223-5 PENGUIN PB $8.95

Sophocles

The Three Theban Plays

Includes *Antigone, Oedipus the King,* and *Oedipus at Colonus*. This highly readable translation has many advantages over the Grene/Fitzgerald/Wyckoff translations in the Chicago series: the plays are arranged in the order in which they were written, and Bernard Knox has contributed introductions and notes about the plays' relationship to the audience that first viewed them in the Theater of Dionysus

See also **SOPHOCLES** under **TRAGEDY** under **THE CLASSICAL PERIOD** under **ANCIENT GREEK LITERATURE** in **LITERATURE OF EUROPE, AFRICA, AND ASIA**

TRANSLATED BY ROBERT FAGLES

0-14-044425-4 PENGUIN PB $8.95

Robert B. **Strassler**

Thucydides: A Comprehensive Guide to the Peloponnesian War

A newly revised edition of the Richard Crawley, with maps, annotations, and appendices, and an encyclopedic index

INTRODUCTION BY VICTOR DAVIS HANSON

0-02-913395-5 FREE PRESS $15.00

Thucydides

The History of the Peloponnesian War

Seapower was the key to Greek victory in the Persian War, and the Athenians used the navy to dominate other Greek states until the tragic conflict with Sparta destroyed her empire. This unflinching record by an exiled Athenian general established a standard for accurate history writing

See also **HISTORY** under **THE CLASSICAL PERIOD** under **ANCIENT GREEK LITERATURE** in **LITERATURE OF EUROPE, AFRICA, AND ASIA**

TRANSLATED BY REX WARNER

0-14-044039-9 PENGUIN PB $10.95

The Peloponnesian War: The Complete Hobbes Translation

Thucydides' great history as translated by philosopher Thomas Hobbes and first published in 1629. "Thomas Hobbes' translation of Thucydides brings together the magisterial prose of one of the greatest writers of the English language and the depth of mind and experience of one of the greatest writers of history in any language"—David Grene

WITH NOTES AND INTRODUCTION BY DAVID GRENE

0-226-80106-3 CHICAGO PB $17.95

Xenophon

A History of My Times

Life in the defeated Athenian Empire, with personal reminiscences of Plato and Socrates

TRANSLATED BY REX WARNER

0-14-044175-1 PENGUIN PB $10.95

The March Up Country: A Modern Translation of the Anabasis

Stranded in the heart of the Persian Empire, a Greek contingent fights its way north from Babylon to the Black Sea

TRANSLATED BY W.H. ROUSE

0-472-06095-3 MICHIGAN PB $14.95

Topics in Ancient Greek History

Arts

John **Boardman**

Greek Sculpture: The Archaic Period

An informative handbook to works of the 8th-6th centuries BC, reviewing their public function and artistic development

See also **GREECE** under **ART OF THE CLASSICAL WORLD** in **ART**

0-500-18166-7 NORTON $19.95
0-500-20198-6 THAMES & HUDSON PB $14.95

Jacqueline **de Romilly**

A Short History of Greek Literature

0-226-14311-2 CHICAGO $32.50
0-226-14312-0 CHICAGO PB $12.00

Jeffrey M. **Hurwit**

Art and Culture of Early Greece, 1100-480 B.C.

Illustrated introduction to the cultural context of art from the Archaic period to the eve of the Persian War in its political and philosophical background

0-8014-1767-8 CORNELL $59.50
0-8014-9401-X CORNELL PB $18.95

Susan **Woodford**

An Introduction to Greek Art

"Imparts a radiant lustre to the Greeks and their artistic creations, drawn from her special sensitivity to their inner spirit"
—D.G. Mitter, Harvard University Art Museums

0-8014-1994-8 CORNELL $52.50
0-8014-9480-X CORNELL PB $22.95

The Parthenon
A lucid and scholarly introduction to the monument and its elaborate sculptural program
See also **GREEK AND ROMAN** under **EUROPEAN ARCHITECTURE TO 1900** in **ARCHITECTURE, DESIGN, AND HOMES**
0-521-22629-5 CAMBRIDGE PB $9.95

Religion and Philosophy

Walter **Burkert**
Ancient Mystery Cults
The most eminent contemporary historian of ancient Greek religion discusses the cults of Demeter, Dionysus, the Great Mother, Isis, and Mithras, and describes initiation rituals, priestly organization, and secret rites
See also **ANCIENT MEDITERRANEAN RELIGIONS** under **WORLD RELIGION** in **RELIGION, SPIRITUALITY, AND PHILOSOPHY**
0-674-03387-6 HARVARD PB $12.95

Marcel **Detienne**
The Masters of Truth in Archaic Greece
0-942299-85-X MIT $22.50

Marcel **Detienne** & Jean-Pierre **Vernant**
The Cuisine of Sacrifice Among the Greeks
0-226-14351-1 CHICAGO $39.95
0-226-14353-8 CHICAGO PB $15.95

E. R. **Dodds**
The Greeks and the Irrational
The sources of Greek rationalism are to be found in primitive modes of thought
See also **OTHER TOPICS IN ANCIENT PHILOSOPHY** under **PHILOSOPHY** in **RELIGION, SPIRITUALITY, AND PHILOSOPHY**
0-8446-6224-0 SMITH $24.05
0-520-00327-6 CALIFORNIA PB $15.00

Joseph **Fontenrose**
Python: A Study of Delphic Myth
0-520-04091-0 CALIFORNIA PB $13.00

Jon D. **Mikalson**
Athenian Popular Religion
Religious beliefs of Athens in the fifth and fourth centuries BC drawn from contemporary sources—state decrees, sacred laws, religious dedications, and epitaphs
0-8078-4194-3 NORTH CAROLINA PB $12.95

Robert **Parker**
Athenian Religion: A History
How did people actually worship the gods? Was Socrates's trial a crisis for religion or the state, or both? These and other questions are addressed in what may become the authoritative work on the subject. Published in 1996
0-19-814979-4 OXFORD $52.00

Miasma: Pollution and Purification in Early Greek Religion
First published in 1983, this is a penetrating analysis of Greek social values
0-19-814835-6 OXFORD $85.00

Paul **Veyne**
Did the Greeks Believe in Their Myths?: An Essay on the Constitutive Imagination
"Brilliant and exhilarating"—*TLS*
0-226-85434-5 CHICAGO PB $11.95

Women in Antiquity

Elizabeth Wayland **Barber**
Women's Work: The First 20,000 Years: Women, Cloth, and Society in Early Times
A general history of early weaving, although of particular interest to those interested in Minoan and Mycenaean societies
0-393-31348-4 NORTON PB $13.00

Eva **Cantarella**
Pandora's Daughters: The Role and Status of Women in Greek and Roman Antiquity
Draws upon the evidence of myth, ritual, and literature to question whether women were actually subjugated to the extent that the laws imply
TRANSLATED BY MAUREEN B. FANT
FOREWORD BY MARY R. LEFKOWITZ
0-8018-3385-X JOHNS HOPKINS PB $14.95

Paul **Friedrich**
The Meaning of Aphrodite
The goddess of love as a complex figure at the border of sexuality and abstinence
0-226-26483-1 CHICAGO PB $11.00

Mary R. **Lefkowitz** & Maureen B. **Fant**
Women's Life in Greece and Rome: A Source Book in Translation
"The texts are well and widely chosen, and newly translated...The modern reader can enter the ancient world through this text"
—Peter Parsons, *London Review of Books*
0-8018-4474-6 JOHNS HOPKINS $38.50
0-8018-4475-4 JOHNS HOPKINS PB $14.95

G.E.R. **Lloyd**
Science, Folklore and Ideology
Scientific views and ideals of the ruling elite as they supported their opinions of female social and biological inferiority
0-521-27307-2 CAMBRIDGE PB $27.95

Sarah B. **Pomeroy**
Goddesses, Whores, Wives, and Slaves: Women in Classical Antiquity
0-8052-0530-6 SCHOCKEN PB $16.00

Philip E. **Slater**
The Glory of Hera: Greek Mythology and the Greek Family
Matriarchal dominance in Greek society both encouraged and stymied the male child's urge to heroic behavior
0-691-00222-3 PRINCETON PB $18.95

Private Life, Sexuality, and Recreation

K.J. **Dover**
Greek Homosexuality
"A landmark study—with philosophical brilliance and scholarly objectivity, he presents facts that can no longer be ignored"
—Erich Segal
See also **HISTORY** under **GAY, LESBIAN, AND BISEXUAL STUDIES** in **SOCIAL STUDIES**
0-674-36270-5 HARVARD PB $15.00

David M. **Halperin**
One Hundred Years of Homosexuality & Other Essays on Greek Love
Suggests that we need a framework other than our own contemporary values to interpret Greek sexuality, and that such a new interpretation might well transform our own culture
0-415-90097-2 ROUTLEDGE PB $18.95

Michael B. **Poliakoff**
Combat Sports in the Ancient World: Competition, Violence and Culture
0-300-06312-1 YALE PB $15.00

Giulia **Sissa**
Greek Virginity
Drama, philosophy, myth, vase paintings, and religious practices are used to expose the classical conceptions of sexual purity and of the female body as vehicle and vessel
TRANSLATED BY ARTHUR GOLDHAMMER
0-674-36320-5 HARVARD $32.00

Waldo E. **Sweet**
Sport and Recreation in Ancient Greece
FOREWORD BY ERICH SEGAL
0-19-504127-5 OXFORD PB $16.95

John J. **Winkler**
The Constraints of Desire: The Anthropology of Sex and Gender in Ancient Greece
"Contains some sparkling treatments of particular texts. Particularly rewarding is a chapter on the comparatively unfamiliar subject of the Greek magical spells that claimed to induce a woman to fall helplessly in love with a man"—Jasper Griffin, *NY Review of Books*
0-415-90123-5 ROUTLEDGE PB $17.95

Fikret **Yegul**
Baths and Bathing in Classical Antiquity
10262-74018-4 MIT PB $35.00

Politics and Ideas

The Greek rationalist methodology that intuited the atom and measured the circumference of the earth remains an outstanding contribution to civilization. Though progress has overtaken most of their discoveries, the extent of the knowledge the Greeks acquired before the fall of the classical world can still amaze us.

A.H. **Jones**

Athenian Democracy

The merits and demerits of ancient Athens: cradle of democracy or slave society ruled by effete intellectuals?

0-8018-3380-9 JOHNS HOPKINS PB $13.95

Eva C. **Keuls**

The Reign of the Phallus: Sexual Politics in Ancient Athens

Everywhere the citizenry of ancient Athens turned, they were confronted by the phallus. Painted on vases, carved in stone, held aloft in gigantic form during processions, and depicted in theater. Kuels explains the effect this symbol had on art, myth, family life, law, politics, and even foreign policy. Includes 345 reproductions

0-520-07929-9 CALIFORNIA PB $18.00

G.E.R. **Lloyd**

Early Greek Science: Thales to Aristotle

0-393-00583-6 NORTON PB $7.95

Greek Science After Aristotle

The Greeks were the first to explain natural phenomena in naturalistic terms. Lloyd places their scientific achievement in its social setting and discusses the motives of individual thinkers

0-393-00780-4 NORTON PB $10.95

D.R. **Ricks**

Early Greek Astronomy to Aristotle

The astronomy of Homer and Hesiod, of the pre-Socratics, of Plato, Eudoxus, and Aristotle

0-8014-9310-2 CORNELL PB $16.95

S. **Sambursky**

Physics of the Stoics

The Stoic continuum theory is described and traced to earlier sources, and the more rigorous elaborations are discussed

0-691-08478-5 PRINCETON $37.50
0-691-02412-X PRINCETON PB $14.95

I. F. Stone

I.F. **Stone**

The Trial of Socrates

The most emphatic treatment of the trial of Socrates as a political event, with the twist that the philosopher had it coming

See also **SOCRATES** under **PHILOSOPHY** in **RELIGION, SPIRITUALITY, AND PHILOSOPHY**

0-385-26032-6 ANCHOR PB $12.95

Gregory **Vlastos**

Studies in Greek Philosophy

Volume 1 The Presocratics

See also **ENCYCLOPEDIAS AND HISTORIES OF PHILOSOPHY** under **PHILOSOPHY** in **RELIGION, SPIRITUALITY, AND PHILOSOPHY**

0-691-03310-2 PRINCETON $49.50

Volume 2 Socrates, Plato, and Their Tradition

0-691-03311-0 PRINCETON $49.50

Society and Economy

Yvon **Garlan**

Slavery in Ancient Greece

The best recent book on the complex interweaving of slave and freeborn members of ancient society, where both often worked side by side and joined the same craft clubs

0-8014-1841-0 CORNELL $41.50
0-8014-9504-0 CORNELL PB $16.95

Victor Davis **Hanson**

The Other Greeks: The Family Farm and the Agrarian Roots of the Western Civilization

0-02-913751-9 FREE PRESS $28.00

John **Morrison** & John **Coates**

The Athenian Trireme: The History and Reconstruction of an Ancient Greek Warship

0-521-31100-4 CAMBRIDGE PB $22.95

The Greek City

Numa **de Coulanges**

The Ancient City: A Classic Study of the Religious and Civil Institutions of Ancient Greece and Rome

FOREWORD BY ARNALDO MOMIGLIANO & S.C. HUMPHREYS

0-8018-2304-8 JOHNS HOPKINS PB $16.95

R.E. **Wycherly**

How the Greeks Built Cities

Urban architectural forms reflect the inner nature growing out of the needs, ways of life, traditions, and ideas of the citizens

0-393-00814-2 NORTON PB $9.95

Greek Influence

Martin **Bernal**

Black Athena, The Afro-Asiatic Roots of Classical Civilization, Volume 1: The Fabrication of Ancient Greece, 1785-1985

Argues that the Egyptian and Middle Eastern sources of Greek civilization were downplayed in the interests of the northern peoples who proclaimed themselves heirs to Greek scientific thought

0-8135-1277-8 RUTGERS PB $16.95

Black Athena, The Afro-Asiatic Roots of Classical Civilization, Volume 2: The Archaeological and Documentary Evidence

0-8135-1584-X RUTGERS PB $17.95

Mary **Lefkowitz**

Not Out of Africa: How Afrocentrism Became an Excuse to Teach Myth as History

The distinguished classicist shows why there is no reason to think the Greeks stole their civilization from Africa; a cogent argument against teaching "feel good history" in order to raise self-esteem

See also **NEW DIRECTIONS** under **HISTORIOGRAPHY**

0-465-09837-1 BASIC $24.00

Ian **Jenkins**

Greek and Roman Life

0-674-36307-8 HARVARD PB $12.00

Hugh **Lloyd-Jones**

Blood for the Ghosts: Classical Influences in the Nineteenth and Twentieth Centuries

0-8018-3017-6 JOHNS HOPKINS $36.00

Reference

Robert **Graves**

The Greek Myths

Volume 1

The scattered elements of these classical myths are organized into fluent narratives, with copious indexes, cross-references, and discussions of problems of historical and anthropological interpretation

See also **CLASSICAL MYTHOLOGY: ANCIENT GREECE AND ROME** under **MYTHOLOGY AND FOLKLORE** in **RELIGION, SPIRITUALITY, AND PHILOSOPHY**

0-14-001026-2 VIKING PB $7.00

Volume 2

0-14-001027-0 PENGUIN PB $8.95

Peter **Levi**

Atlas of the Greek World

0-87196-448-1 FACTS ON FILE $45.00

Betty **Radice**

Who's Who in the Ancient World

"One person's pointers to some of the classical names that have kept their vitality—as poetic symbols, themes in music, paintings or drama, or forces in the western unconscious"—from the introduction

See also **REFERENCE** under **TOPICS IN ROMAN HISTORY** under **ANCIENT ROME**

0-14-051055-9 VIKING PB $12.50

Richard J.A. **Talbert**

Atlas of Classical History

Maps, diagrams, and commentary, from the Bronze Age to Constantine

See also **REFERENCE** under **TOPICS IN ROMAN HISTORY** under **ANCIENT ROME**

0-415-03463-9 ROUTLEDGE PB $19.95

Ancient Rome

Imperial Rome's achievement was enormous. No empire has ever conquered so many peoples by force and established stable rule over them for so long. Modern national territories that fell under Rome's mandate run from Great Britain to Turkey and from Syria to Morocco. The edifice as a whole lasted for more than 400 years, and the Byzantine eastern portion survived the barbarian invasions and the power of Islam until 1453. Even in its death, Rome left as a legacy to Europe an ideal of unity that has influenced politicians and political theorists to the present.

But it had a dreadful cost. First, the republican government that presided over most of the conquests was insufficient to govern the immense territorial acquisitions and gave way after civil war to the despotic rule of a single man—the emperor. And second, the stable administration was imposed and maintained by military brutalities, the uprooting of whole populations, and genocide.

Its costs show up in a continuous dark commentary from the Roman historians themselves to current writers. Beginning with Tacitus and Suetonius, the value of the imperial settlement has been brought into doubt. Historians of this school look back to the republic, the period of Rome's greatest expansion, to study the source of its power and the reasons for its fall. And in our own age of destructive demagoguery, they find the character of Julius Caesar, the first to establish single rule on a populist base, particularly controversial.

Edward **Gibbon**

Edward Gibbon (1737-1794) devoted his life to what is still the only work on Rome that starts with Marcus Aurelius in AD 161 and continues to the fall of Constantinople in 1453, from the height of empire to the eve of Columbus's voyage, taking in the history of peoples from the Orkneys to Turkestan.

The Decline and Fall of the Roman Empire

Whet your appetite with this one-volume abridgment, but don't miss the main course

See also **PROSE** under **THE RESTORATION AND THE 18TH CENTURY** in **LITERATURE OF THE BRITISH ISLES**

EDITED BY DERO A. SAUNDERS & CHARLES A. ROBINSON, JR.

0-14-043189-6 PENGUIN PB $13.95

Edward **Gibbon**

The History of the Decline and Fall of the Roman Empire

Bury's scholarly edition is still unsurpassed; his footnotes and appendices are a compendium of classical knowledge in themselves. A seven-volume reprint

EDITED BY JOHN B. BURY

0-7139-9124-0 ALLEN LANE $150.00

The History of the Decline and Fall of the Roman Empire

This convenient edition contains the complete original work

Volume 1

See also **PROSE** under **THE RESTORATION AND THE 18TH CENTURY** in **LITERATURE OF THE BRITISH ISLES**

0-14-043393-7 PENGUIN PB $24.95

Volume 2

See also **PROSE** under **THE RESTORATION AND THE 18TH CENTURY** in **LITERATURE OF THE BRITISH ISLES**

0-14-043394-5 PENGUIN PB $24.95

Volume 3

See also **PROSE** under **THE RESTORATION AND THE 18TH CENTURY** in **LITERATURE OF THE BRITISH ISLES**

0-14-043395-3 PENGUIN PB $24.95

R.H. **Barrow**

The Romans

A brief but excellent introduction which proposes that the Roman genius is of vital importance for understanding ourselves

0-14-013502-2 PENGUIN PB $10.95

John **Boardman** & others

The Roman World

This collection of essays forms an agreeable and informative introduction to all aspects of life in ancient Rome

0-19-282166-0 OXFORD PB $21.50

Michael **Grant**

History of Rome

The rise and fall. Illustrated with useful maps, family trees, and lists of emperors

0-02-345610-8 PRENTICE HALL PB $50.00

Marcel **LeGlay** & others

A History of Rome

TRANSLATED BY ANTONIA NEVILL

0-631-19458-4 BLACKWELL PB $24.95

From Antiquity to Feudalism

The Etruscans and Early Rome

Axel **Boethius**

Etruscan and Early Roman Architecture

From 1400 BC to the Hellenized buildings of Pompeii and Herculaneum

See also **GREEK AND ROMAN** under **EUROPEAN ARCHITECTURE TO 1900** in **ARCHITECTURE, DESIGN, AND HOMES**

0-300-05290-1 PENGUIN PB $25.00

Otto J. **Brendel**

Etruscan Art

Centered in the life of the family and a continuing life in the tomb, Etruscan art is private, aristocratic, and luxurious. Brendel's book is the first important study of Etruscan sculpture, wall-painting, metalware, ceramics and jewelry, which, though influenced by Greek artforms, were profoundly original

See also **ART OF THE CLASSICAL WORLD** in **ART**

0-300-06446-2 YALE PB $27.50

Republic to Empire

Michael **Crawford**

The Roman Republic

Its history and constitution from its establishment after the fall of the kings in the 6th century BC to the triumph of Augustus

0-674-77927-4 HARVARD PB $14.50

Erich S. **Gruen**

Culture and National Identity in Republican Rome

What happened when the Roman ruling class confronted the glories of Greek civilization? The meeting of the Roman and Hellenic cultures and how Rome expropriated Hellenic culture to serve its national ends, to define the distinctive features of Roman values, and to enhance its civic and religious life

0-8014-8041-8 CORNELL PB $17.95

Studies in Greek Culture and Roman Policy

The impact of Greek learning, literature, and religion on central aspects of Roman life in the middle Republic

0-520-20483-2 CALIFORNIA PB $14.95

Kurt A. **Raaflaub** & **Mark Toher**, editors

Between Republic and Empire: Interpretations of Augustus and His Principate

0-520-08447-0 CALIFORNIA PB $27.50

Henry T. **Rowell**

Rome in the Augustan Age

0-8061-0956-4 OKLAHOMA PB $12.95

H.H. **Scullard**

From the Gracchi to Nero: A History of Rome from 133 B.C. to A.D. 68

Populist resistance to patrician power leads to the first imperial dynasty

0-415-02527-3 ROUTLEDGE PB $18.95

Ronald **Syme**

The Roman Revolution

A classic from the 1930s, still essential on the revolution that overturned the republic and established the empire after Antony and Cleopatra's defeat at Actium in 31 BC

0-19-881001-6 OXFORD PB $19.95

Colin **Wells**
The Roman Empire
Balances a description of central government against life in the provinces
0-8047-1237-9 STANFORD $45.00

Zvi **Yavetz**
Julius Caesar and His Public Image
Exposes the myth of Caesar as enlightened despot
0-8014-1440-7 CORNELL $39.95

Late Empire

"But the empire of the Romans filled the world, and, when that empire fell into the hands of a single person, the world became a safe and dreary prison for his enemies. The slave of imperial despotism, whether he was condemned to drag his gilded chain in Rome and the senate, or to wear out a life of exile on the barren rock of Seriphus or the frozen banks of the Danube, expected his fate in silent despair. To resist was fatal, and it was impossible to fly. On every side he was encompassed with a vast extent of sea and land, which he could never hope to traverse without being discovered, seized and restored to his irritated master. Beyond the frontiers, his anxious view could discover nothing, except the ocean, inhospitable deserts, hostile tribes of barbarians, of fierce manners and unknown language, or dependent kings, who would gladly purchase the emperor's protection by the sacrifice of an obnoxious fugitive. 'Wherever you are,' said Cicero to the exiled Marcellus, 'remember that you are equally within the power of the conqueror.'"—Edward Gibbon, *The Decline and Fall of the Roman Empire*.

Peter **Brown**
The Making of Late Antiquity
In an epoch-making shift, the civic culture of the Antonines gives way to the religious cultism of the late empire
0-674-54320-3 HARVARD PB $20.00

Jacob **Burckhardt**
The Age of Constantine the Great
TRANSLATED BY MOSES HADES
0-520-04680-3 CALIFORNIA PB $15.95

J.B. **Bury**
History of the Later Roman Empire: From the Death of Theodosius I to the Death of Justinian
The tragic history, from the struggle between the two barbarians, Alaric and Stilicho, for the fate of Rome, to its recovery by Belisarius under the Byzantine emperor Justinian

Volume 1
0-486-20398-0 DOVER PB $12.95

Volume 2
0-486-20399-9 DOVER PB $12.95

Averil **Cameron**
The Later Roman Empire
0-674-51194-8 HARVARD PB $14.00

Michael **Grant**
The Severans: The Changed Roman Empire
0-415-12772-6 ROUTLEDGE $24.95

A.H. **Jones**
The Later Roman Empire, 284-602: A Social, Economic, and Administrative Survey
The classic study, available for the first time in paperback. One of the most eminent ancient historians surveys social, economic, and administrative developments, from the restructuring of the empire by Diocletian to its collapse in the West in 476

Volume 1
0-8018-3348-5 JOHNS HOPKINS $49.95
0-8018-3353-1 JOHNS HOPKINS PB $27.50

Volume 2
0-8018-3349-3 JOHNS HOPKINS $49.50
0-8018-3354-X JOHNS HOPKINS PB $24.50

Stephen **Williams**
Diocletian and the Roman Recovery
After the disastrous invasions and civil wars of the third century, Diocletian restores stability through a drastic change in the system of government
0-415-91827-8 ROUTLEDGE PB $25.00

Late Antiquity: Classical Culture After the Fall

Perry **Anderson**
Passages from Antiquity to Feudalism
A British Marxist history of the empire and the barbarian invaders, by the author of *Lineages of the Absolutist State*
0-86091-709-6 VERSO PB $19.95

Peter **Brown**
The World of Late Antiquity
0-393-95803-5 NORTON PB $12.95

Garth **Fowden**
Empire to Commonwealth: Consequences of Monotheism in Late Antiquity
0-691-01545-7 PRINCETON PB $12.95

Ancient Roman Sources

"All over the field Roman soldiers lay dead in their thousands, horse and foot mingled, as the shifting phases of the battle, or the attempt to escape had brought them together. Here and there wounded men smeared with blood, recovering consciousness in the morning cold, were dispatched by a quick blow as they struggled to rise from amongst the corpses; others with the sinews in their thighs and behind the knees sliced through, bared their throats and necks and begged anyone to spill what little blood they had left. Some had their heads buried in the ground, having choked themselves to death by digging holes and smothering their faces in the earth. Strangest of all was a Numidian, with nose and ears horribly lacerated, still breathing, pinned beneath the body of a Roman who, when his sword-arm failed, had died tearing his foe in bestial fury with his teeth."—Livy, *Hannibal in Italy*

Anthony R. **Birley**, translator & editor
Lives of the Later Caesars
The unsolved mystery of their authorship does not detract from the fascination of these brief biographies of some of the greatest emperors—Trajan, Hadrian, and Marcus Aurelius
0-14-044308-8 PENGUIN PB $10.95

Julius **Caesar**
The Civil War
After conquering Gaul, Caesar turns his armies against the Senate
TRANSLATED BY JANE F. MITCHELL
0-14-044187-5 PENGUIN PB $8.95

Cassius **Dio**
The Roman History: The Reign of Augustus
Augustan politics by a professional politican in 2nd-century Rome
TRANSLATED BY IAN SCOTT-KILVERT
INTRODUCTION BY JOHN CARTER
0-14-044448-3 PENGUIN PB $12.95

Flavius **Josephus**
The Jewish War
The rebellion against Roman power whose failure initiated the Diaspora—by a leader of the Jews
See also **BIBLICAL AND ANCIENT HISTORY** under **JEWISH HISTORY**
TRANSLATED BY G.A. WILLIAMSON
EDITED BY E. MARY SMALLWOOD
0-14-044420-3 PENGUIN PB $10.95

The Works of Josephus
The tenacious struggle against total domination by one of the empire's victims
0-913573-86-8 HENDRICKSON $24.95

Titus **Livy**
The Early History of Rome
From the mythic times of Romulus to the hardships of recovery after the sack of Rome by the Gauls
TRANSLATED BY AUBREY DE SELINCOURT
0-14-044104-2 PENGUIN PB $10.95

Rome and Italy
Early Roman expansion into surrounding territory
0-14-044388-6 PENGUIN PB $9.95

Rome and the Mediterranean
Roman armies move east to confront the rulers of the remnants of Alexander's empire in Macedonia, Syria, and Egypt
TRANSLATED BY HENRY BETTENSON.
0-14-044318-5 PENGUIN PB $12.95

The War with Hannibal
Rome's most dangerous hour. How the early republic survived invasion by Carthage, her greatest rival, for control of the Mediterranean
TRANSLATED BY AUBREY DE SELINCOURT
0-14-044145-X PENGUIN PB $9.95

Ammianus **Marcellinus**

The Later Roman Empire (A.D. 353-378)

A pagan historian writes a florid and somber account of the early Christian empire. Gibbon praised him as "an accurate and faithful guide, who has composed the history of his own times without indulging the prejudices and passions which usually affect the mind of a contemporary"

See also **LATE WRITERS** under **LATIN LITERATURE** in **LITERATURE OF EUROPE, AFRICA, AND ASIA**

EDITED BY WALTER HAMILTON

INTRODUCTION BY ANDREW WALLACE-HADRILL

0-14-044406-8 PENGUIN PB........$14.95

Plutarch

Makers of Rome

Contains the lives of Coriolanus, Fabius Maximus, Marcellus, Cato the Elder, Tiberius Gracchus, Gaius Gracchus, Sertorius, Brutus, and Mark Antony

TRANSLATED BY IAN SCOTT-KILVERT

0-14-044158-1 PENGUIN PB........$12.95

Polybius

Polybius on Roman Imperialism

The noble Greek hostage whose history combines the excitement of the war against Hannibal with still-valid insights into the reasons for Roman dominance

TRANSLATED BY EVELYN S. SHUCKBURGH

EDITED BY ALVIN H. BERNSTEIN

0-89526-902-3 REGNERY PB........$10.95

The Rise of the Roman Empire

More engrossing reading about the growth of Roman power; an expert translation

TRANSLATED BY IAN SCOTT-KILVERT

0-14-044362-2 PENGUIN PB........$11.95

Procopius

The Secret History

The seamy underside of the Byzantine court—fascinating reading

TRANSLATED BY G.A. WILLIAMSON

0-14-044182-4 PENGUIN PB........$10.95

The Secret History

TRANSLATED BY RICHARD ATWATER

FOREWORD BY A.E. BOAK

0-472-08728-2 MICHIGAN PB........$9.95

Sallust

The Jugurthine War & the Conspiracy of Catiline

Perils at home and abroad. Marius becomes the first Roman to turn his armies against the Senate: Cicero defends the republic against the designs of yet another disgruntled young aristocrat

TRANSLATED BY S.A. HANDFORD

0-14-044132-8 PENGUIN PB........$9.95

Suetonius

The Twelve Caesars: An Illustrated Edition

Madness and perversity among the supremely powerful

See also **SILVER AGE** under **LATIN LITERATURE** in **LITERATURE OF EUROPE, AFRICA, AND ASIA**

TRANSLATED BY ROBERT GRAVES

0-14-044072-0 PENGUIN PB........$11.95

Julius Caesar

Tacitus

Agricola & Germania

A patrician soldier's exemplary career and wistful regret for Rome's lost primitivism in a study of the ancient Germans

TRANSLATED BY HUGH MATTINGLY

0-14-044241-3 PENGUIN PB........$10.95

Annals of Imperial Rome

This ironic depiction of the gradual loss of freedom among Romans under the first emperors includes memorable vignettes of Messalina's career and the failed plot against Nero. Tacitus's influence on later European writers is incalculable

See also **SILVER AGE** under **LATIN LITERATURE** in **LITERATURE OF EUROPE, AFRICA, AND ASIA**

TRANSLATED BY MICHAEL GRANT

0-14-044060-7 PENGUIN PB........$9.95

Complete Works

EDITED BY MOSES HADES

0-07-553639-0 MCGRAW HILL PB........$18.40

The Histories

AD 69: the year of the four emperors. Chaos following Nero's suicide allows Tacitus to deploy his narrative verve on the events of the civil war

TRANSLATED BY KENNETH WELLESLEY

0-14-044150-6 PENGUIN PB........$11.95

Roman Portraits

"Whenever Britannicus was seated at his meal, it was a settled rule that an attendant should taste his food and liquor. To preserve this custom, and prevent detection by the attendant's death, an innocent beverage, without any infusion that could hurt, was tried by the proper officer, and presented to the prince. He found it too hot, and returned it. Cold water, in which the poison had been mixed, was immediately poured into the cup. Britannicus drank freely; the effect was violent, and, in an instant, it seized the powers of life: his limbs were palsied, his breath was suppressed, and his utterance failed. The company were thrown into consternation. Some rushed out of the room, but others, who had more discernment, stayed, though in astonishment, with their eyes fixed on Nero, who lay stretched at ease on his couch, with an air of innocence, and without emotion."—Tacitus, *Annals of Imperial Rome*

Royston **Lambert**

Beloved and God

An investigation of the mysterious death of Hadrian's lover Antinous, in the Nile; the cult of his memory recreates the *fin de siècle* mood of Rome's Silver Age

0-8216-2003-7 LYLE STUART PB........$9.95

Christian **Meier**

Caesar: A Biography

0-465-00894-1 BASIC........$30.00

Zvi **Yavetz**

Julius Caesar and His Public Image

Exposes the myth of Caesar as enlightened despot

0-8014-1440-7 CORNELL........$39.95

Miriam T. **Griffin**

Nero: The End of a Dynasty

Nero was only the stepson of the emperor Claudius. Through the machinations of his mother, Agrippina, he was declared successor to the throne over the claim of Britannicus, the real heir. Matricide and this playboy's tragic flaws led to his own early suicide and the fall of the Julio-Claudian dynasty

0-300-03285-4 YALE........$17.00

Samuel N.C. **Lieu** & Dominic **Montserrat**, editors

From Constantine to Julian: Pagan and Byzantine Views

0-415-09336-8 ROUTLEDGE PB........$22.95

William L. **MacDonald** & John A. **Pinto**

Hadrian's Villa and Its Legacy

0-300-05381-9 YALE........$55.00

Joseph **Peebles**

Hannibal, the Ultimate Warrior: The Untold Story

0-9644758-1-2 PEEBCO........$19.95

D.C.A. **Shotter**

Nero

0-415-12931-1 ROUTLEDGE........$25.00

Topics in Roman History

"Constantine promoted the spread of Christianity beyond the frontiers, still more within them. He tried to reclaim heretics and schismatics. His motive, however, was not to save souls but, one almost might say, bodies. He aimed at the prosperity of his reign and realm through ensuring to God acceptable worship, and by prosperity he evidently had in mind quite material well-being: an end to civil war, security along the borders, plentiful crops for a plentiful population—in short, peace, and its products. Few of the essential elements of Christian belief interested Constantine very much—neither God's mercy nor man's sinfulness, neither damnation nor salvation, neither brotherly love, nor, needless to say, humility. Ardent in his convictions he remained nevertheless oblivious to their moral implications."—Ramsay MacMullen, *Christianizing the Roman Empire*

Religion

Stephen **Benko**

Pagan Rome and the Early Christians

0-253-34286-4 INDIANA $26.95
0-253-20385-6 INDIANA PB $10.95

Peter **Brown**

Augustine of Hippo: A Biography

A comprehensive biography of the fourth-century Christian convert whose theology formed a bridge between the ancient and medieval churches and defined such essential Christian doctrines as grace and original sin

See also **AUGUSTINE** under **PHILOSOPHY** in **RELIGION, SPIRITUALITY, AND PHILOSOPHY**

See also **SAINTS** under **BIOGRAPHIES** under **CHRISTIANITY** in **RELIGION, SPIRITUALITY, AND PHILOSOPHY**

0-520-01411-1 CALIFORNIA PB $16.00

The Rise of Western Christendom: Triumph and Diversity, 200–1000 A.D.

1-557-86136-6 BLACKWELL $24.95

The Body and Society: Men, Women and Sexual Renunciation in Early Christianity

Brown (*The World of Late Antiquity*) is one of the great living scholars of early Christianity, and *The Body and Society* is perhaps his most important work to date. *The New York Review of Books* called it "a profound sociological and intellectual study…a magesterial survey, a lasting work of scholarship"

0-231-06101-3 COLUMBIA PB $19.50

The Cult of the Saints: Its Rise and Function in Latin Christianity

The saints succeed the ancient heroes

See also **BEGINNINGS AND EARLY HISTORY** under **HISTORY** under **CHRISTIANITY** in **RELIGION, SPIRITUALITY, AND PHILOSOPHY**

0-226-07622-9 CHICAGO PB $9.95

St. Jerome

Peter **Brown**

Society and the Holy in Late Antiquity

0-520-04305-7 CALIFORNIA $50.00
0-520-06800-9 CALIFORNIA PB $14.00

Franz **Cumont**

The Mysteries of Mithra

A 1911 study about the Persian religion that gave us Sunday and Christmas and almost beat out Christianity for dominance in the Roman Empire

TRANSLATED BY THOMAS J. MCCORMACK

0-486-20323-9 DOVER PB $8.95

E.R. **Dodds**

Pagan and Christian in an Age of Anxiety: Some Aspects of Religious Experience from Marcus Aurelius to Constantine

See also **ELAINE PAGLES'S PICKS** under **COMPARATIVE RELIGION** under **WORLD RELIGION** in **RELIGION, SPIRITUALITY, AND PHILOSOPHY**

0-521-38599-7 CAMBRIDGE $18.95
0-393-00545-3 CAMBRIDGE PB $5.95

John **Ferguson**

The Religions of the Roman Empire

A variegated picture of religious life as its importance increased during the 2nd and 3rd centuries

0-8014-0567-X CORNELL $45.00
0-8014-9311-0 CORNELL PB $15.95

George **Luck**, editor

Arcana Mundi: Magic and the Occult in the Greek and Roman Worlds

A collection of ancient texts translated, annotated, and introduced by Luck. A first-rate comprehensive sourcebook and introduction to magic as practiced by witches and sorcerers, magicians and astrologers

0-8018-2548-2 JOHNS HOPKINS PB $15.95

Ramsay **MacMullen**

Christianizing the Roman Empire

The social forces involved in the spread of Christianity, from supernatural contests between rival wonder-workers to imperial coercion under Constantine

0-300-03216-1 YALE $27.00
0-300-03642-6 YALE PB $14.00

Paganism in the Roman Empire

The movement from rationalism to eastern occultism prepares the way for Christianity

0-300-02984-5 YALE PB $15.00

Arnaldo **Momigliano**

On Pagans, Jews and Christians

Roman religion, the historiography of Josephus, and the transformations of Judaism in the classical period are among the topics addressed

0-8195-6218-1 WESLEYAN PB $19.95

R.M. **Ogilvie**

Romans and Their Gods in the Age of Augustus

Religion in the early empire was tolerant but failed because the world changed from rationalist to mystic

0-393-00543-7 NORTON PB $10.95

Elaine **Pagels**

The Gnostic Gospels

The historical and theological implications of an ancient library of Gnostic texts, including Gospels attributing the esoteric, paradoxical teachings of the Gnostics to Jesus, found near Nag Hammadi in upper Egypt in 1945

See also **GNOSTICISM** under **HISTORY** under **CHRISTIANITY** in **RELIGION, SPIRITUALITY, AND PHILOSOPHY**

0-394-74043-2 VINTAGE PB $9.00

The Gnostic Paul: Gnostic Exegesis of the Pauline Letters

See also **COMPARATIVE RELIGION** under **WORLD RELIGION** in **RELIGION, SPIRITUALITY, AND PHILOSOPHY**

1-56338-039-0 TRINITY PB $14.95

Rodney **Stark**

The Rise of Christianity: A Sociologist Reconsiders History

"A marvelous exercise in sociological imagination"—Andrew M. Greeley

See also **BEGINNINGS AND EARLY HISTORY** under **HISTORY** under **CHRISTIANITY** in **RELIGION, SPIRITUALITY, AND PHILOSOPHY**

0-691-02749-8 PRINCETON $24.95

Robert L. **Wilken**

The Christians as the Romans Saw Them

The views of the most cogent pagan opponents of Christianity, from the philosopher Celsus to Julian the Apostate, in a mix of social and intellectual history

0-300-03066-5 YALE $27.00
0-300-03627-2 YALE PB $13.00

Women and the Family

J.P. **Balsdon**

Roman Women: Their History and Habits

From first ladies of the empire to the Roman housewife, with portraits of the powerful wives and mothers who made imperial policy

0-8371-8040-6 GREENWOOD $59.75

Kate **Cooper**

The Virgin and the Bride: Idealized Womanhood in Late Antiquity

Dramatically changing ideas about sexuality, family, and morality in an age of cultural revolution

0-674-93949-2 HARVARD $37.50

Beryl **Rawon**, editor

Marriage, Divorce and Children in Ancient Rome

The sentimental ideal versus everyday reality. Considers the impact of high mortality rates, status, and fostering on the family in ancient Rome

0-19-815045-8 OXFORD PB $24.00

Richard P. **Saller**

Patriarchy, Property and Death in the Roman Family

A book of genuine importance by one of the leading scholars in the field

0-521-32603-6 CAMBRIDGE $54.95

Arts

Richard **Brilliant**

Visual Narratives: Story-Telling in Etruscan and Roman Art

0-8014-1558-6 CORNELL..$47.50

J.B. **Ward-Perkins**

Roman Imperial Architecture

The Hellenistic tradition revolutionized by the Roman invention of concrete. Fully illustrated

0-300-05292-8 PENGUIN PB..$26.50

Mortimer **Wheeler**

Roman Art and Architecture

A survey of architecture, town planning, sculpture and painting, as well as silver, glass, pottery, and other achievements

See also **ROME** under **ART OF THE CLASSICAL WORLD** in **ART**

0-500-20021-1 THAMES & HUDSON PB..................$14.95

Social Life

Philippe **Ariès** & Georges **Duby**, editors

A History of Private Life

Paul **Veyne**, editor

Volume 1 From Pagan Rome to Byzantium

Stimulating essays by historians and literary critics. "One of the most arresting, original and rewarding historical surveys to be published in many years"—Bernard Knox, *Atlantic Monthly*. The first volume has to do specifically with Greece and Rome

See also **SEXUALITY AND PRIVATE LIFE** under **PERSPECTIVES IN HISTORY** under **THE VARIETIES OF CIVILIZATION**

0-674-39975-7 HARVARD..$42.50

0-674-39974-9 HARVARD PB..$19.95

Keith R. **Bradley**

Slaves and Masters in the Roman Empire: A Study in Social Control

0-19-520607-X OXFORD PB..$13.95

Jerome **Carcopino**

Daily Life in Ancient Rome: The People and the City at the Height of the Empire

Splendor and squalor, spectacle and daily routine, recreated from archaeological findings and ancient literature

TRANSLATED BY E.O. LORIMER

0-300-00031-6 YALE PB..$17.00

Thomas **Hope**

Costumes of the Greeks and Romans

Early 19th-century classic line renderings of authentic costumes of many classes and occupations, including armor and household objects

0-8446-2274-5 SMITH..$20.80

0-486-20021-3 DOVER PB..$8.95

Petronius

The Satyricon

A 1996 translation of the first-century novel. A chronology, introduction, and commentary provide background on Petronius's social milieu

See also **SILVER AGE** under **LATIN LITERATURE** in **LITERATURE OF EUROPE, AFRICA, AND ASIA**

TRANSLATED & EDITED BY R. BRACHT BRANHAM & DANIEL KINNEY

0-520-20599-5 CALIFORNIA..$28.00

Caligula

Thomas **Wiedemann**

Greek and Roman Slavery

New translations of 243 texts and inscriptions on slavery from fifth- and fourth-century Greece and Rome

0-415-02972-4 ROUTLEDGE PB..$24.95

Cities

Robert **Etienne**

Pompeii: The Day a City Died

0-8109-2855-8 ABRAMS PB..$12.95

Christopher **Hibbert**

Rome: The Biography of a City

This combination of portrait, history, and guidebook captures the seductive beauty of the Eternal City. Lavishly illustrated

See also **RENAISSANCE CITIES** under **RENAISSANCE ITALY AND THE COMING OF HUMANISM** under **MEDIEVAL AND RENAISSANCE EUROPE**

0-14-007078-8 PENGUIN PB..$24.95

Richard **Krautheimer**

Three Christian Capitals: Topography and Politics

Rome, Milan, and Constantinople. Architectural masterpieces illuminate the shaping of life by power politics and religious beliefs

0-520-04541-6 CALIFORNIA..$42.50

0-520-06034-2 CALIFORNIA PB..$17.00

John E. **Stambaugh**

The Ancient Roman City

The details and texture of daily existence—apartment houses and street vendors, taverns and graffiti, water deliverymen and dry cleaners

0-8018-3692-1 JOHNS HOPKINS PB..........................$14.95

0-8018-3574-7 JOHNS HOPKINS PB..........................$48.50

The Melting-Pot Empire

Peter **Blair**

Roman Britain and Early England, 55 B.C. to A.D. 871

The transition from Roman rule to Saxon England, using archaeological and written sources

0-393-00361-2 NORTON PB..$12.95

Walter **Goffart**

Barbarians and Romans, A.D. 418-584: The Techniques of Accommodation

How the Germans settled within the frontiers of the western empire

0-691-10231-7 PRINCETON PB..$19.95

Martin **Goodman**

The Ruling Class of Judaea: The Origins of the Jewish Revolt Against Rome, A.D. 66-70

0-521-33401-2 CAMBRIDGE..$69.95

0-521-44782-8 CAMBRIDGE PB..$21.95

Fergus **Millar**

The Roman Near East, 31 B.C.-A.D. 337

This beautifully produced book brings up to date and replaces some of the classic synthesizing works of ancient history by A.H.M. Jones, notably *The Greek City from Alexander to Justinian*. A major achievement

0-674-77885-5 HARVARD..$47.50

Justine **Randers-Pherson**

Barbarians and Romans: The Birth Struggle of Europe, A.D. 400-700

Province-by-province account of the transformation of late antiquity into the Middle Ages under the impact of the northern invaders

0-8061-1818-0 OKLAHOMA $37.95
0-8061-2511-X OKLAHOMA PB $15.95

Military

Arthur **Ferrill**

The Fall of the Roman Empire: The Military Explanation

See also **ANCIENT WARFARE** under **WARS THROUGH THE AGES** under **MILITARY AFFAIRS**

0-500-27495-9 NORTON PB $15.95

Edward **Lutwak**

The Grand Strategy of the Roman Empire: From the First Century A.D. to the Third

0-801-82158-4 UHPKN PB $14.95

Reference

For related reading, see THE EXPANSION OF EUROPE: EMPIRE AND COMMERCE under EARLY MODERN EUROPE

For related reading, see US HISTORY TO THE CIVIL WAR

Matthew **Bunson**

A Dictionary of the Roman Empire

Easy to read, interesting, and concise

0-19-510233-9 OXFORD PB $18.95

Tim **Cornell** & John **Matthews**

Atlas of the Roman World

Detailed maps, colorful illustrations, informative text: more than an atlas, a glimpse of a world

0-87196-652-2 FACTS ON FILE $45.00

Michael **Grant**

Ancient History Atlas

Europe and the Mediterranean world, including Egypt and the Near East

See also **REFERENCE** under **ARCHAEOLOGY**

0-915262-73-8 DURST PB $12.00

Claude **Moatti**

The Search for Ancient Rome

0-8109-2839-6 ABRAMS PB $12.95

Betty **Radice**

Who's Who in the Ancient World

"One person's pointers to some of the classical names that have kept their vitality—as poetic symbols, themes in music, paintings or drama, or forces in the Western unconscious" —from the introduction

See also **REFERENCE** under **ANCIENT GREECE**

0-14-051055-9 VIKING PB $12.50

Colin **McEvedy**

The Penguin Atlas of Ancient History

0-14-051151-2 PENGUIN PB $12.00

Richard J.A. **Talbert**

Atlas of Classical History

Maps, diagrams, and commentary: from the Bronze Age to Constantine

See also **REFERENCE** under **ANCIENT GREECE**

0-415-03463-9 ROUTLEDGE PB $19.95

K.D. **White**

Agricultural Implements and Farm Equipment in the Roman World

"Will be the standard work of reference on its subject for a long time"—*TLS*

0-8018-5423-7 JOHNS HOPKINS PB $25.95

Greek and Roman Technology

From farm implements to hydraulic engineering. Includes illustrations and helpful diagrams

0-8014-1439-3 CORNELL $52.50

Historical Fiction

Robert **Graves**

Graves combines stunning powers of characterization and storytelling with deep historical knowledge of such diverse areas as mythical Greece, classical Rome, Byzantium, and colonial America.

Robert Graves

Claudius the God and His Wife Messalina

The sequel to *I, Claudius,* in which the new emperor and his wife, the infamous Messalina, fall prey to the evils of power

See also **HISTORICAL AND ROMANTIC FICTION** in **POPULAR READING**

See also **THE EARLY 20TH CENTURY** under **20TH-CENTURY BRITISH AND IRISH FICTION** in **LITERATURE OF THE BRITISH ISLES**

0-679-72573-3 VINTAGE PB $14.00

I, Claudius

The pedantic ugly duckling of the imperial family survives mad rulers and political purges to inherit the Roman Empire

See also **THE EARLY 20TH CENTURY** under **20TH-CENTURY BRITISH AND IRISH FICTION** in **LITERATURE OF THE BRITISH ISLES**

0-394-60811-9 MODERN LIBRARY $15.00
0-679-72477-X VINTAGE PB $13.00

Gore **Vidal**

Julian

The 4th-century Roman emperor portrayed with sympathetic irony by the author of *Hollywood*

See also **SINCE 1945** under **20TH-CENTURY AMERICAN FICTION** in **LITERATURE OF THE AMERICAS**

0-345-32908-2 BALLANTINE PB $5.95

Gore Vidal

Thornton **Wilder**

The Ides of March

Intimate portrait of Caesar in the months before his assassination

See also **FROM THE TURN OF THE CENTURY TO WORLD WAR II** under **20TH-CENTURY AMERICAN FICTION** in **LITERATURE OF THE AMERICAS**

1-56849-445-9 BUCCANEER $24.95

Marguerite **Yourcenar**

Memoirs of Hadrian

Yourcenar's major work, which presents the fictitious memoirs of the Roman emperor, earned her a place among the great contemporary French writers

See also **FICTION** under **MODERN FRENCH LITERATURE** in **LITERATURE OF EUROPE, AFRICA, AND ASIA**

0-374-50348-6 FS&G PB $14.00

The slightest and most superficial of contacts are enough for us with most persons, or prove even too much. But when these contacts persist and multiply about one unique being, to the point of embracing him entirely, when each fraction of a body becomes laden for us with meaning as overpowering as that of the face itself, when this one creature haunts us like music and torments us like a problem (instead of inspiring in us, at most, mere irritation, amusement, or boredom), when he passes from the periphery of our universe to its center, and finally becomes for us more indispensable than ourselves, then the astonishing prodigy takes place where I see much more an invasion of the flesh by the spirit than a simple play of the body alone.
MEMOIRS OF HADRIAN

Medieval and Renaissance Europe

The term "Middle Ages," possibly first used as early as 1469, originally described that period of history between the decline of learning in late antiquity and the "Renaissance" of classical studies in 15th-century Italy. Since then, the period has acquired various reputations, good and bad: "medieval" may suggest "superstitious," "unenlightened," "backward," and "feudal," but equally "pious," "faithful," "chivalrous," "noble," and "romantic."

Few would now attempt to color these thousand years of history with a single brush. Instead, recent scholarship has stressed the changes within the medieval epoch. The most popular current chronology recognizes three major divisions of medieval history, each with its own principal themes. The early Middle Ages, extending roughly from the fall of the Roman Empire in the West to c. 1000, witnessed the formation of a new cultural community in the European West, comprised of Latins, Germans, Celts, Slavs, and others; each of these peoples retained its own cultural character but all of them came to share common values and attitudes. This was "the making of Europe."

In the central period of medieval history, from about 1000 to 1350, the European community was profoundly reorganized and took on many of the social and cultural traits it would retain through the Renaissance and Reformation, up until the economic and political revolutions of the 18th and 19th centuries. The central Middle Ages, in other words, created "traditional" Europe.

Finally, the late period, from c. 1350 to 1500, was a time of many spectacular disasters, brought on by plagues, famines, and incessant wars. Out of this age of crisis and readjustment, Europe declined in population but gained a more powerful technology (through printing, guns, sails, and other inventions), a richer culture (with a revival of things classical), and more effective political institutions (best embodied by the "new" national monarchies). By the late 15th century, Europe was equipped for its great worldwide expansion in the early modern period. The discovery of America in 1492 is only one of several dates used to mark the end of the Middle Ages, but it may be the best. The discovery opened Europe to a wider world and thereby changed it, and the world, forever.

General Histories

Philippe **Contamine**

War in the Middle Ages

A sophisticated study of war in all its aspects—technological, economic, political and cultural. Highly recommended

See also **THE MIDDLE AGES** under **WARS THROUGH THE AGES** under **MILITARY AFFAIRS**

0-631-13142-6 BLACKWELL $24.95

Georges **Duby**

France in the Middle Ages: 987-1460

From the co-author of the widely acclaimed *A History of Private Life* comes this lavishly illustrated history, a treasure trove for francophiles and historians alike. This unique volume traces France from fragmented Capetian nation in the 10th century to European power in the 15th

TRANSLATED BY JULIET VALE

0-631-18945-9 BLACKWELL PB $22.95

Hans-Werner **Goetz**

Life in the Middle Ages: From the Seventh to the Thirteenth Century

Historian Goetz takes readers back to the Middle Ages with this lively account of "everyday history." Of interest to historians and history buffs alike, the in-depth research presents a vivid picture of day-to-day life from peasantry to ruling class

0-268-01300-4 NOTRE DAME $52.00
0-268-01301-2 NOTRE DAME PB $23.00

James **Harpur** & Elizabeth **Hallam**

Revelations: The Medieval World

0-8050-4140-0 HOLT $35.00

C. Warren **Hollister**

Medieval Europe: A Short History

A well-written introduction

0-394-34186-4 RANDOM HOUSE $16.95
0-07-029637-5 MCGRAW HILL PB $32.30

George **Holmes**

The Oxford Illustrated History of Medieval Europe

Balanced treatment of Europe, north and south, with admirable use of illustrations

0-19-820073-0 OXFORD $49.95
0-19-285220-5 OXFORD PB $22.50

Nicholas **Hooper** & Matthew **Bennet**

The Cambridge Atlas of Medieval History: Warfare: 768-1487

A lively, illustrated volume aimed at the general reader. With 100 maps and battle plans

See also **REFERENCE** under **MILITARY AFFAIRS**

0-521-44049-1 CAMBRIDGE $39.95

Jacques **Le Goff**

Medieval Civilization, 400-1500

A survey by one of the great medievalists of our time

0-631-17566-0 BLACKWELL PB $24.95

H.R. **Loyn**, editor

The Middle Ages: A Concise Encyclopedia

A compact, profusely illustrated reference source to the culture and history of the Middle Ages, drawing on the wealth of recent scholarship that has opened up new areas of study within the period. "The coverage is impressive, giving due attention to all of Europe and the Middle East, to all phases of economic, social, political, intellectual, and spiritual life"—*Choice*

0-500-27645-5 THAMES & HUDSON PB $24.95

Henri **Pirenne**

Economic and Social History of Medieval Europe

A much-criticized classic by one of this century's major historians; still worth exploring

TRANSLATED BY I.E. CLEGG

0-15-627533-3 HARCOURT BRACE PB $10.00

Jean W. **Sedlar**

East Central Europe in the Middle Ages, 1000-1500

0-295-97290-4 WASHINGTON $50.00

Richard W. **Southern**

The Making of the Middle Ages

0-300-00230-0 YALE PB $13.00

Sources and Documents

David **Herlihy**, editor

Medieval Culture and Society

An overview from peasants to poets in the Documentary History of Western Civilization series

0-88133-747-1 WAVELAND PB $13.95

James B. **Ross** & Mary M. **McLaughlin**, editors

The Portable Medieval Reader

A well-edited collection drawing on many rare sources

See also **MEDIEVAL LITERATURE** in **LITERATURE OF EUROPE, AFRICA, AND ASIA**

0-14-015046-3 VIKING PB $14.95

Cultural and Intellectual History

J.H. **Burns**, editor

The Cambridge History of Medieval Political Thought, c. 350-c.1450

An invaluable work of reference, less successful as a synthesis

0-521-24324-6 CAMBRIDGE $110.00
0-521-42388-0 CAMBRIDGE PB $39.95

Norman F. **Cantor**

The Civilization of the Middle Ages

0-06-092553-1 HARPERPERENNIAL PB $16.00

Peter **Dronke**

History of 12th-Century Western Philosophy

0-521-25896-0 CAMBRIDGE $89.95
0-521-42907-2 CAMBRIDGE PB $31.95

Valerie I.J. **Flint**

The Rise of Magic in Early Medieval Europe

0-691-03165-7 PRINCETON $65.00
0-691-00110-3 PRINCETON PB $17.95

Geoffrey Chaucer

Aron **Gurevich**

Medieval Popular Culture: Problems of Belief and Perception

Probes the lives of saints, miracle stories, descriptions of fantastic travels, and catechisms to reconstruct the beliefs of the "silent majority" of medieval men and women

0-521-38658-6 CAMBRIDGE PB $19.95

Michael **Haren**

Medieval Thought: The Western Intellectual Tradition from Antiquity to the 13th Century

0-8020-2868-3 TORONTO $60.00
0-8020-7758-7 TORONTO PB $20.95

Charles H. **Haskins**

The Renaissance of the Twelfth Century

Argues that the Middle Ages had a "Renaissance," too

0-674-76075-1 HARVARD PB $15.95

Ernst H. **Kantorowicz**

The King's Two Bodies: A Study of Medieval Political Theology

A classic analysis of the overlap between medieval religious and political ideas

0-691-02018-3 PRINCETON PB $19.95

Paul Oskar **Kristeller**

Medieval Aspects of Renaissance Learning

0-231-07950-8 COLUMBIA $45.00
0-231-07951-6 COLUMBIA PB $16.00

Jacques **Le Goff**

The Birth of Purgatory

Suggests that purgatory was transformed from a state to a place in the 12th century, even as a new "spiritual accounting" entered the practice of penitence

TRANSLATED BY ARTHUR GOLDHAMMER

0-226-47083-0 CHICAGO PB $19.95

Intellectuals in the Middle Ages

With the creation of universities in the great cities of medieval Europe a new kind of person was born: neither monk nor knight, churchman nor courtier, these first professional academics effected an irrevocable shift in culture. "The richness, imaginativeness and sheer learning of Le Goff's work cannot be summarized and demands to be experienced"—M.T. Clanchy, *TLS*

0-631-17078-2 BLACKWELL $49.95
0-631-18519-4 BLACKWELL PB $17.95

The Medieval Imagination

TRANSLATED BY ARTHUR GOLDHAMMER

0-226-47084-9 CHICAGO $29.95

Time, Work, and Culture in the Middle Ages

Collected essays, illustrating the use of anthropological concepts and methods

TRANSLATED BY ARTHUR GOLDHAMMER

0-226-47081-4 CHICAGO PB $22.50

Robert I. **Moore**

The Formation of a Persecuting Society

0-631-17145-2 BLACKWELL PB $22.95

Social and Economic History

"One economic system replaces another only after it has passed through a long and varied obstacle course. History is people and the instigators of capitalism were usurers: merchants of the future, sellers of time...These men were Christians but it was not the *earthly* consequences of the Church's condemnation of usury that restrained them; it was the agonizing fear of Hell. In a society where all conscience was a religious conscience, obstacles were first of all—or finally—religious. The hope of escaping Hell, thanks to purgatory, permitted the usurer to propel the economy and society of the thirteenth century ahead toward capitalism."
—Jacques Le Goff, *Your Money or Your Life: Economy and Religion in the Middle Ages*.

John W. **Baldwin**

The Language of Sex: Five Voices from Northern France Around 1200

The theological doctrine of Augustine, the medical theories of Galen, the Ovidian literature of the schools, contemporary romances, and the emerging voices of the *fabliaux*—at a critical moment in the development of European ideas about sexual desire, morality, and gender

0-226-03614-6 CHICAGO PB $17.95

Marc **Bloch**

French Rural History: An Essay on Its Basic Characteristics

A master historian makes the seemingly dull countryside come alive

TRANSLATED BY JANET SONDHEIMER

0-520-01660-2 CALIFORNIA PB $17.00

Dyan **Elliott**

Spiritual Marriage: Sexual Abstinence in Medieval Wedlock

"I loved this book for its magnificent scholarship, clarity of expression, provocative ideas, and scholarly modesty"—Penelope D. Johnson, *American Historical Review*

0-691-08649-4 PRINCETON $49.50

John **Boswell**

Christianity, Social Tolerance, and Homosexuality: Gay People in Western Europe from the Beginning of the Christian Era to the 14th Century

An erudite examination of Christian attitudes toward homosexuality, arguing that tolerance changed into intolerance as the Middle Ages progressed

See also **HISTORY** under **GAY, LESBIAN, AND BISEXUAL STUDIES** in **SOCIAL STUDIES**

0-226-06711-4 CHICAGO PB $19.95

The Kindness of Strangers: The Abandonment of Children in Western Europe from Late Antiquity to the Renaissance

0-679-72499-0 VINTAGE PB $14.25

Georges **Duby**

The Knight, the Lady and the Priest: The Making of Modern Marriage in Medieval France

The dispute between the aristocracy of northern France and the Church in the 12th century over the rules of marriage. "An important book for anyone interested in the origins of contemporary sexual roles and mores"
—*LA Times Book Review*

TRANSLATED BY BARBARA BRAY

0-226-16768-2 CHICAGO PB $14.95

Love in the Middle Ages

The unequaled master of medieval social history examines courtly poetry and love, arguing that the structure of sexual relationship took its cue from feudalism—a bastion of masculinity. Beautifully written, *Love in the Middle Ages* universalizes the interest of questions once addressed only by students of history and women's studies

0-226-16773-9 CHICAGO $37.50

Rural Economy and Country Life in the Medieval West

A survey of European farming from c. 800 to 1400, with special attention to France

TRANSLATED BY CYNTHIA POSTAN

0-87249-347-4 SOUTH CAROLINA PB $21.95

Frances **Gies** & Joseph **Gies**

Life in a Medieval City

A well-written social history

0-06-090880-7 HARPERCOLLINS PB $13.00

Marriage and the Family in the Middle Ages

A readable summary of recent work

0-06-091468-8 HARPERCOLLINS PB $14.00

Jean **Gimpel**

The Medieval Machine: The Industrial Revolution of the Middle Ages

An enthusiastic account of medieval technological innovations

0-14-004514-7 PENGUIN PB $12.95

Jack **Goody**

The Development of the Family and Marriage in Europe

An anthropologist looks at medieval marriages, with debatable conclusions

0-521-28925-4 CAMBRIDGE PB $23.95

David **Herlihy**

Medieval Households

The making of modern households in medieval Europe

0-674-56376-X HARVARD PB $17.00

Emmanuel Le Roy **Ladurie**

Montaillou: The Promised Land of Error

A sometimes shocking picture of a community in the Pyrenees, and of the lives, beliefs, and behavior of its people

TRANSLATED BY BARBARA BRAY

0-394-72964-1 RANDOM HOUSE PB $13.50

Jacques **Le Goff**

Your Money or Your Life: Economy and Religion in the Middle Ages

A brief monograph by the co-director of the journal *Annales-sociétés-civilisations*

TRANSLATED BY PATRICIA RANUM

0-942299-14-0 MIT $24.95
0-942299-15-9 MIT PB $10.95

Michel **Mollat**

The Poor in the Middle Ages: An Essay in Social History

The ever-present poor, viewed under multiple aspects

TRANSLATED BY ARTHUR GOLDHAMMER

0-300-02789-3 YALE $45.00
0-300-04605-7 YALE PB $19.00

George J. **Ovitt**

The Restoration of Perfection: Labor and Technology in Medieval Culture

An original exploration of the relationship between speculations on the nature of the universe and technological innovation

0-8135-1235-2 RUTGERS $32.00

Henri **Pirenne**

Medieval Cities: Their Origins and the Revival of Trade

By an old master of economic history, to be admired more than believed

TRANSLATED BY F.D. HALSEY

0-691-00760-8 PRINCETON PB $13.95

M.M. **Postan**

Medieval Trade and Finance

Reprinted studies by the most prominent English economic historian of the past generation

0-521-08745-7 CAMBRIDGE $74.95

Eileen **Power**

Medieval People

A classic reconstruction of individual lives—nobles, merchants, monks, and others

0-06-463253-9 HARPERCOLLINS PB $6.95
0-06-092275-3 HARPERCOLLINS PB $12.00

Jaques **Rossiaud**

Medieval Prostitution

0-63119992-6 BLACKWELL PB $21.95

William H. **TeBrake**

A Plague of Insurrection: Popular Politics and Peasant Revolt in Flanders, 1323-1328

0-8122-3241-0 PENNSYLVANIA $29.95
0-8122-1526-5 PENNSYLVANIA PB $13.95

Lynn **White**, Jr.

Medieval Technology and Social Change

Beautiful essays on warfare, stirrups, plows, and cranks

0-19-500266-0 OXFORD PB $10.95

Women

Rudolph M. **Bell**

Holy Anorexia

Psychological portraits of more than 250 Italian women from the 13th century to the present. "According to Bell, the demon that spurs self-starvation in women is an ever-elusive ideal: in modern America, 'bodily health, thinness, and self-control'; in medieval Christendom, 'spiritual health, fasting, and self-denial.' In both cases, anorexia represents a woman's 'war against bodily urges' in a search for autonomy from a suffocating, male-dominated society"
—*Kirkus Reviews*

EPILOGUE BY WILLIAM N. DAVIS

0-226-04205-7 CHICAGO PB $12.95

Judith M. **Bennett**

Women in the Medieval English Countryside: Gender and Household in Brigstock Before the Plague

There was no "golden age" for women in early medieval society

0-19-504094-5 OXFORD $55.00
0-19-504561-0 OXFORD PB $17.95

Alcuin **Blamires**, editor

Woman Defamed and Woman Defended: An Anthology of Medieval Texts

See also **MEDIEVAL HISTORY** under **EUROPEAN HISTORY** under **WOMEN'S STUDIES** in **SOCIAL STUDIES**

0-19-811971-2 OXFORD $59.00
0-19-871039-9 OXFORD PB $17.95

Judith C. **Brown**

Immodest Acts: The Life of a Lesbian Nun in Renaissance Italy

Reconstructed from the archives of a church investigation, the story of an abbess who had an affair with a nun

See also **HISTORY** under **GAY, LESBIAN, AND BISEXUAL STUDIES** in **SOCIAL STUDIES**

0-19-503675-1 OXFORD $25.00
0-19-504225-5 OXFORD PB $11.95

Caroline W. **Bynum**

Holy Feast and Holy Fast: The Religious Significance of Food to Medieval Women

The subjects of this book were "extravagant in their bodily self-denial and self-immolation, and their craving for the Eucharist of the Holy Feast was the complement to their extreme fasting practice, their Holy Fast"—*NY Review of Books*

0-520-06329-5 CALIFORNIA PB $15.95

Penny Schine **Gold**

The Lady and the Virgin: Image, Attitude, and Experience in 12th Century France

Images of women that have endured into the modern era: the secular image of the *dame* of romance and the religious image of Notre Dame, the Virgin Mary

FOREWORD BY CATHARINE R. STIMPSON

0-226-30088-9 CHICAGO PB $11.95

Martha C. **Howell**

Women, Production and Patriarchy in Late Medieval Cities

Working women at Leiden and Cologne, viewed in Marxist perspective

0-226-35503-9 CHICAGO $25.00
0-226-35504-7 CHICAGO PB $18.95

Ruth Mazo **Karras**

Common Women: Prostitution and Sexuality in Medieval England

The daily lives of streetwalkers, brothel workers, and the medieval equivalent of call girls—and their customers

0-19-506242-6 OXFORD $35.00

Religious History

Paul J. **Archambault**, editor

A Monk's Confession: The Memoirs of Guibert of Nogent

TRANSLATED BY PAUL J. ARCHAMBAULT

0-271-01481-4 PENN STATE $35.00
0-271-01482-2 PENN STATE PB $14.95

Caroline Walker **Bynum**

The Resurrection of the Body in Western Christianity, 200-1336

0-231-08127-8 COLUMBIA PB $17.50

Norman **Cohn**

The Pursuit of the Millennium: Revolutionary Millenarians and the Mystical Anarchists of the Middle Ages

Popular religious and social movements from the 11th to the 16th century. "A work of the first order...of great originality and power"
—Isaiah Berlin

0-19-500456-6 OXFORD PB $15.95

Meister **Eckhart**

Meister Eckhart: A Modern Translation

See also **CHRISTIAN MYSTICISM** under **CHRISTIANITY** in **RELIGION, SPIRITUALITY, AND PHILOSOPHY**

TRANSLATED BY R.F. BLAKENEY

0-06-130008-X HARPERCOLLINS PB $14.00

There is the soul's day and God's day. A day, whether six or seven ago, or more than six thousand years ago, is just as near to the present as yesterday. Why? Because all time is contained in the present Now-moment. Time comes of the revolution of the heavens and day began with the first revolution. The soul's day falls within this time and consists of the natural light in which things are seen. God's day, however, is the complete day, comprising both day and night. It is the real Now-moment, which for the soul is eternity's day, on which the Father begets his only begotten Son and the soul is reborn in God. Whenever this birth occurs, it is the soul giving birth to the only begotten Son.

MEISTER ECKHART: A MODERN TRANSLATJON

Amos **Funkenstein**

Theology and the Scientific Imagination from the Middle Ages to the Seventeenth Century

See also **THE SCIENTIFIC REVOLUTION** under **HISTORY OF SCIENCE AND TECHNOLOGY** under **SCIENCE AND TECHNOLOGY** in **SCIENCE**

0-691-02425-1 PRINCETON PB $22.50

Malcolm **Lambert**

Medieval Heresy: Popular Movements from the Georgian Reform to the Reformation

A subtle, thorough account of late medieval heresies that does justice to both the theological and the historical background

See also **MIDDLE AGES AND RENAISSANCE** under **HISTORY** under **CHRISTIANITY** in **RELIGION, SPIRITUALITY, AND PHILOSOPHY**

0-631-17432-X BLACKWELL PB $23.95

Thomas **Noble**

Soldiers of Christ: Saints and Saints' Lives from Late Antiquity and the Early Middle Ages

EDITED BY THOMAS HEAD

0-271-01345-1 PENN STATE PB $18.95

Steven **Runciman**

The Medieval Manichee: A Study of the Christian Dualist Heresy

Messalians, Borborites, Paulicans, Bogomils, Patarenes, Cathars—the strange and often compelling heretical sects which believed that the world is the creation of a demon, in a succinct and learned account by a distinguished British historian

See also **MIDDLE AGES AND RENAISSANCE** under **HISTORY** under **CHRISTIANITY** in **RELIGION, SPIRITUALITY, AND PHILOSOPHY**

0-521-28926-2 CAMBRIDGE PB $19.95

W.L. **Wakefield** & A.P. **Evans**, editors

Heresies of the High Middle Ages

0-231-09632-1 COLUMBIA PB $18.00

Jewry

Jeremy **Cohen**

The Friars and the Jews: The Evolution of Medieval Anti-Judaism

Reasons for and results of the mendicant antagonism against the Jews

See also **THE MIDDLE AGES** under **JEWISH HISTORY**

0-8014-9266-1 CORNELL PB $14.95

Mark R. **Cohen**

Under Crescent and Cross

0-691-03378-1 PRINCETON $39.50

The Medieval Aesthetic

Henry **Adams**

Mont Saint-Michel and Chartres

A study of the medieval imagination through the religion, art, and architecture of the 12th century. "From beginning to end, it reads as from a man in the fresh morning of life, with a frolic power unusual to historic literature" —William James

See also **THE 19TH CENTURY: AFTER THE CIVIL WAR** under **AMERICAN LITERATURE TO 1900** in **LITERATURE OF THE AMERICAS**

INTRODUCTION BY RAYMOND CARNEY

0-14-039054-5 PENGUIN PB $11.95

Henry Adams

Wolfgang **Braunfelds**

Monasteries of Western Europe: The Architecture of the Orders

A major investigation of the relation of architectural style to liturgy and ritual

See also **GOTHIC AND ROMANESQUE** under **EUROPEAN ARCHITECTURE TO 1900** in **ARCHITECTURE, DESIGN, AND HOMES**

0-500-27201-8 THAMES & HUDSON PB $34.95

Georges **Duby**

The Age of the Cathedrals: Art and Society, 980-1240

A survey of medieval mentalities as reflected in the architecture of the monastery, the cathedral, and the palace

0-226-16770-4 CHICAGO PB $17.95

Umberto **Eco**

Art and Beauty in the Middle Ages

A brief introduction to the subject, much of it repeated from Eco's book on Aquinas' aesthetics

See also **OTHER MEDIEVAL PHILOSOPHERS** under **PHILOSOPHY** in **RELIGION, SPIRITUALITY, AND PHILOSOPHY**

0-300-04207-8 YALE PB $10.00

Johan **Huizinga**

The Autumn of the Middle Ages

A new translation of one of the twentieth century's great works in European history

TRANSLATED BY RODNEY J. PAYTON & ULRICH MAMMITZSCH

0-226-35992-1 CHICAGO $39.95

Erwin **Panofsky**

Gothic Architecture and Scholasticism: An Inquiry into the Analogy of the Arts, Philosophy, and Religion in the Middle Ages

How architectural style and structure replicated scholastic definitions of the order and form of thought

0-452-00995-2 NEW AMERICAN LIBRARY PB $12.95

Marilyn **Stokstad**

Medieval Art

A recent study notable for covering a broad geographical range of artistic production, placing works within their social and aesthetic context. With maps, chronological table, and a glossary

See also **MEDIEVAL ART: 600-1400** under **EUROPEAN ART: BYZANTINE AND MEDIEVAL** in **ART**

0-06-430132-X ICON PB $30.00

Europe and the Rest of the World

Janet **Abu-Lughod**

Before European Hegemony: The World System A.D. 1250-1350

A fascinating attempt to achieve an integrated picture of the interconnections between the commercial cities of Western Europe, the merchant mariners of Genoa and Venice, the Mongols, the Islamic world centered in Baghdad, and the civilizations of India and China. "A fine example of sociological imagination and historical generalization" —Ashraf Ghani, Johns Hopkins University

0-19-506774-6 OXFORD PB $18.95

Marco **Polo**

The Travels of Marco Polo

The Italian trader who followed the Silk Road opened by the Mongol invasion and became the advisor of Kublai Khan

Volume 1

See also **MEDIEVAL LITERATURE** in **LITERATURE OF EUROPE, AFRICA, AND ASIA**

See also **BIOGRAPHIES AND MEMOIRS** under **TOPICS IN IMPERIAL CIVILIZATION** under **CHINA**

0-486-27587-6 DOVER PB $17.95

Volume 2

0-486-27586-8 DOVER PB $17.95

The Early Middle Ages

For related reading, see ANCIENT ROME

Roger **Collins**

Early Medieval Europe: 300-1000

The distinguished author of *Early Medieval Spain* and *The Basques* has written a readable overview of one of the most fascinating historical periods, from the fall of the Roman Empire to the beginning of the Western revival under the Carolingians

0-312-06198-6 ST. MARTIN'S PB $16.95

The Barbarians and the Barbarian Kingdoms

Thomas S. **Burns**

A History of the Ostrogoths

A reconstruction of the culture and a tracking of the movements of a principal Germanic people

0-253-20600-6 INDIANA PB $18.95

Patrick J. **Geary**

Before France and Germany: The Creation and Transformation of the Merovingian World

An illuminated look at a dark epoch

0-19-504457-6 OXFORD $29.95

0-19-504458-4 OXFORD PB $16.95

Simon **Keynes** & Michael **Lapidge**, translators

Alfred the Great

Includes Asser's contemporaneous *Life of King Alfred* and other writings of the period

0-14-044409-2 PENGUIN PB $12.95

Alfred P. **Smyth**

King Alfred the Great

A new interpertation which rejects the image of a neurotic and invalid king. Instead we are shown a man of remarkable drive and intelligence, who had been a scholar all his life

0-19-822989-5 OXFORD $35.00

E.A. **Thompson**

The Huns

0-631-15899-5 BLACKWELL $29.95

J.M. **Wallace-Hadrill**

The Long-Haired Kings and Other Stories in Frankish History

The roots of royal authority in Frankland, now reprinted in a scholarly series from Toronto

0-8020-6500-7 TORONTO PB $15.95

Herwig **Wolfram**

History of the Goths

How the barbarian world of the Goths was both a creation of and a key element of the late Roman world. A 613-page history incorporates important findings since the last German edition of 1980

TRANSLATED BY THOMAS J. DUNLAP

0-520-06983-8 CALIFORNIA PB $18.95

Charlemagne and the Making of Europe

Einhard & Notker the Stammerer

Two Lives of Charlemagne

TRANSLATED BY LEWIS THORPE

0-14-044213-8 PENGUIN PB $9.95

Heinrich **Fichtenau**

The Carolingian Empire

A survey of Carolingian Europe, stressing oppression and depression; available in reprint edition

TRANSLATED BY PETER MUNZ

0-8020-6367-5 TORONTO PB $13.95

Robert **Harrison** & Glyn **Burgess**, translators

The Song of Roland

A lucid and energetic poetic translation of the great medieval epic, which tells of the death in battle of Charlemagne's commander in the Pyrenees

0-451-62822-5 NEW AMERICAN LIBRARY PB $4.99

0-14-044532-3 PENGUIN PB $8.95

The battle rages, spreads throughout the hosts: Count Roland pays no heed to his own safetybut plies his lance as long as its shaft holds—with fifteen blows it's splintered and is useless—and then unsheathes his good sword Durendal. He spurs his horse and goes against Chernuble: he breaks the helmet on which rubies gleam; he slices downward through the coif and hair and cuts between the eyes, down through his face the shiny hauberk made of fine-linked mail, entirely through the torso to the groin, and through the saddle trimmed with beaten gold. The body of the horse slows down the sword, which, seeking out no joint, divides the spine: both fall down dead upon the field's thick grass. He says then: "Coward, you have come in vain! Mohammed will not give you any help; no glutton such as you will win this fight."

THE SONG OF ROLAND

Richard **Hodges** & David **Whitehouse**

Mohammed, Charlemagne and the Origins of Europe: The Pirenne Thesis in the Light of Archaeology

A pioneering effort to apply archaeological evidence to historical problems. "Succeeds...not only in integrating archaeology with traditionally researched history but also interweaving European and Islamic history in the early medieval period"—*American Historical Review*

0-8014-9262-9 CORNELL PB $12.95

Pierre **Riche**

The Carolingians: A Family Who Forged Europe

TRANSLATED BY MICHAEL IDOMIR ALLEN

0-8122-1342-4 PENNSYLVANIA PB $20.95

Daily Life in the World of Charlemagne

The few sources of the Carolingian world expertly gathered, sifted, and interpreted

TRANSLATED BY JO ANN MCNAMARA

0-8122-1096-4 PENNSYLVANIA PB $20.95

Suzanne F. **Wemple**

Women in Frankish Society: Marriage and the Cloister, 500-900

Finds a deterioration of women's status as the early Middle Ages progressed

0-8122-1209-6 PENNSYLVANIA PB $24.95

Byzantium

Anna **Comnena**

The Alexiad of Anna Comnena

A biography of Alexius I (1081-1118) by his daughter, who demonstrates a gift for fast-moving narrative and shrewd character sketches

See also MEDIEVAL LITERATURE in LITERATURE OF EUROPE, AFRICA, AND ASIA

TRANSLATED BY E.R.A. SEWTER

0-14-044215-4 PENGUIN PB $10.95

Deno J. **Geanakopolos**, editor

Byzantine Church, Society, and Civilization Seen Through Contemporary Eyes

A gold mine of sources on the Byzantine church, society, and civilization, knit together with an analytical commentary

0-226-28460-3 CHICAGO $32.50

0-226-28461-1 CHICAGO PB $29.00

Donald M. **Nichol**

The Reluctant Emperor: A Biography of John Cantacuzene, Byzantine Emperor and Monk, c.1295-1383

One of the most unusual Byzantine emperors, who dealt in his reign (1347-1354) with the earliest leaders of the Ottoman Turks, the merchants of Venice and Genoa, and Stephen Dusan of Serbia, and who subsequently spent thirty years as a monk

0-521-55256-7 CAMBRIDGE $39.95

The End of the Byzantine Empire

0-8419-5826-2 HOLMES & MEIER PB $14.95

John Julius **Norwich**

Byzantium: The Early Centuries

The Byzantine Empire during the five centuries before the emergence of Charlemagne's Holy Roman Empire; with 32 pages of illustrations

0-679-41650-1 KNOPF $35.00

0-394-53778-5 KNOPF $45.00

Byzantium: The Decline and Fall

0-679-41650-1 KNOPF $35.00

Michael **Psellus**

Fourteen Byzantine Rulers

A translation of the *Chronographia*, tracing the decline of Byzantium, by an adviser, friend, and tutor to successive emperors

TRANSLATED BY E.R.A. SEWTER

0-14-044169-7 PENGUIN PB $10.95

Mark **Whittow**
The Making of Byzantium, A.D. 600-1025
The origins of Russia, relations with the nomad powers of the steppe world, the competitions between Bulgars, Romans, and Slavs in the Balkans, and the frequently ignored region of the Transcaucasus are all given extended treatment. "An excellent book"—Cyril Mango
0-520-20496-4 CALIFORNIA........$45.00
0-520-20497-2 CALIFORNIA PB........$17.95

Vikings and Normans

Robert **Bartlett**
The Making of Europe: Conquest, Colonization, and Cultural Change, 950-1350
0-691-03298-X PRINCETON........$49.50
0-691-03780-9 PRINCETON PB........$17.95

Yves **Cohat**
The Vikings: Lords of the Seas
0-8109-2865-5 ABRAMS PB........$12.95

Kathleen **Gormley** & others
The Norman Impact on the Medieval World
From about 900 to 1348. Charts the Norman conquest of England and expansion into Wales and Scotland, and the limits of their control in Ireland
0-521-46601-6 CAMBRIDGE PB........$10.95

James **Graham-Campbell**
Cultural Atlas of the Vikings
0-8160-3004-9 FACTS ON FILE........$45.00

Gwyn **Jones**
A History of the Vikings
The best recent survey
0-19-285139-X OXFORD PB........$15.95

Peter H. **Sawyer**
Kings and Vikings
A critical appraisal of the difficult sources that illuminate the Vikings
0-416-74190-8 ROUTLEDGE PB........$16.95

Culture

Thomas **Cahill**
How the Irish Saved Civilization: The Untold Story of Ireland's Heroic Role from the Fall of Rome to the Rise of Medieval Europe
See also **BEGINNINGS AND EARLY HISTORY** under **HISTORY** under **CHRISTIANITY** in **RELIGION, SPIRITUALITY, AND PHILOSOPHY**
0-385-41849-3 ANCHOR PB........$12.95

Richard C. **Dales**
The Intellectual Life of Western Europe in the Middle Ages
90-04-09622-1 E.J. BRILL PB........$50.50

G.R. **Evans**
The Thought of Gregory the Great
The thought of Gregory the Great was normative for medieval society
0-521-36826-X CAMBRIDGE PB........$16.95

Patrick J. **Geary**
Phantoms of Remembrance: Memory and Oblivion at the End of the First Millenium
"A strickingly original story of the ways in which men and women of the 11th century recorded, interpreted, and used their memories of the past"—Thomas Head, Washington University
0-691-02603-3 PRINCETON........$16.95

Frances **Gies** & Joseph **Gies**
Cathedral, Forge, and Waterwheel: Technology and Invention in the Middle Ages
0-06-092581-7 HARPERPERENNIAL PB........$14.00

Walter **Goffart**
The Narrators of Barbarian History (A.D. 550-800): Jordanes, Gregory of Tours, Bede, and Paul the Deacon
Critical appraisals of the four historians to whom we owe nearly all our knowledge of early medieval political history
0-691-05514-9 PRINCETON........$69.50

Jean **Leclercq**
Love of Learning and Desire for God: A Study of Monastic Culture
A modern monk admires early monastic culture
0-8232-0407-3 FORDHAM PB........$14.00

Rosamond **McKitterick**, editor
Carolingian Culture: Emulation and Innovation
0-521-40586-6 CAMBRIDGE PB........$24.95

Pierre **Riche**
Education and Culture in the Barbarian West: Sixth Through Eighth Centuries
Comprehensive survey of formal education under chiefly monastic auspices
TRANSLATED BY J.J. CONTRENI
0-87249-376-8 SOUTH CAROLINA PB........$14.95

The High Middle Ages: Empire and Papacy

Malcolm **Barber**
The Two Cities: Medieval Europe, 1050-1320
0-415-09682-0 ROUTLEDGE PB........$19.95

Geoffrey **Barraclough**
The Medieval Papacy
0-393-95100-6 NORTON PB........$9.95

The Origins of Modern Germany
In fact a history of medieval Germany stressing real rather than ideological motors in its development
0-393-30153-2 NORTON PB........$15.95

Arno **Borst**
Medieval Worlds: Barbarians, Heretics and Artists in the Middle Ages
How knights, witches and heretics, monks and kings, women poets and university professors existed in the medieval world."[A] brilliant study"—Christopher Brooke
0-226-06657-6 CHICAGO PB........$17.95

Horst **Fuhrmann**
Germany in the High Middle Ages
TRANSLATED BY TIMOTHY REUTER
0-521-26638-6 CAMBRIDGE........$44.95
0-521-31980-3 CAMBRIDGE PB........$15.95

Francis **Oakley**
The Western Church in the Later Middle Ages
0-8014-1208-0 CORNELL........$45.00
0-8014-9347-1 CORNELL PB........$13.95

Marie **Tanner**
The Last Descendant of Aeneas: The Hapsburgs and the Mythic Image of the Emperor from Antiquity to the Renaissance
0-300-05488-2 YALE........$52.50

Feudal Institutions

Marc **Bloch**
Feudal Society
Without question, one of the most influential works of history written in the 20th century
Volume 1
0-226-05978-2 CHICAGO PB........$9.95
Volume 2
0-226-05979-0 CHICAGO PB........$9.95

Georges **Duby**
The Chivalrous Society
Essays on feudal organization and culture in the central Middle Ages
TRANSLATED BY CYNTHIA POSTAN
0-520-04271-9 CALIFORNIA PB........$15.00

Love and Marriage in the Middle Ages
An ideal entree into Duby's ideas about love, spousal decorum, family structure, and their cultural context in bodily and spiritual values
0-226-16774-7 CHICAGO PB........$14.95

The Three Orders: Feudal Society Imagined
A lengthy examination of feudal ideas on social order, extending into the 17th century
TRANSLATED BY ARTHUR GOLDHAMMER
0-226-16772-0 CHICAGO PB........$19.95

Francois L. **Ganshof**

Feudalism

The best short introduction available

TRANSLATED BY PHILIP GRIERSON

0-8020-7158-9 TORONTO PB $13.95

Carl **Stephenson**

Medieval Feudalism

An easy introduction

TRANSLATED BY JULIA E. EDMONDSON

0-8014-9013-8 CORNELL PB $6.95

Chivalry

Georges **Duby**

William Marshal: The Flower of Chivalry

In large part a paraphrase of and comment on a contemporary *chanson de geste*

TRANSLATED BY RICHARD HOWARD

0-394-75154-X PANTHEON PB $12.00

Frances **Gies**

The Knight in History

A short, graceful introduction to medieval knighthood

0-06-091413-0 HARPERCOLLINS PB $13.50

Maurice **Keen**

Chivalry

An admiring account that finds in medieval chivalry the model for modern views of officers and gentlemen. "A rich book, making effective use of all sorts of documents. Mr. Keen moves easily across Europe in search of the international spirit of chivalry"
—David Herlihy, *NY Times Book Review*

0-300-03360-5 YALE PB $17.00

The Feudal Principalities of England and France

For related reading, see GREAT BRITAIN AND IRELAND

M.T. **Clanchy**

From Memory to Written Record: England 1066-1307

0-631-16857-5 BLACKWELL PB $22.95

Geoffrey of Monmouth

The History of the Kings of Britain

See also **MEDIEVAL LITERATURE** in **LITERATURE OF EUROPE, AFRICA, AND ASIA**

TRANSLATED BY LEWIS THORPE

0-14-044170-0 PENGUIN PB $11.95

Elizabeth **Hallam**, editor

The Plantagenet Chronicles

Brilliant combination of translated chronicles, informative essays, and beautiful illustrations

INTRODUCTION BY H.R. TREVOR-ROPER

0-517-14076-4 CRESCENT $19.99

Matthew **Strickland**

War and Chivalry: The Conduct and Perception of War in England and Normandy, 1066-1217

0-521-44392-X CAMBRIDGE $69.95

Hugh M. **Thomas**

Vassals, Heiresses, Crusaders, and Thugs: The Gentry of Angevin Yorkshire, 1154-1216

0-8122-3159-7 PENNSYLVANIA $34.95

Spain

Stephen P. **Bensch**

Barcelona and Its Rulers, 1096-1291

0-521-43511-0 CAMBRIDGE $65.00

Roger **Collins**

The Arab Conquest of Spain

0-631-19405-3 BLACKWELL PB $20.95

The Basques

Summarizes modern historical discoveries concerning the oldest surviving people of Europe

0-631-17565-2 BLACKWELL PB $22.95

Sylvia Remie **Constable**

Trade and Traders in Muslim Spain: The Commercial Realignment of the Iberian Peninsula, 900-1500

Drawn from hundreds of bits of data gleaned from Arabic, Judeo-Arabic, Latin, and vernacular Spanish sources, this study examines the ports, shipping, and routes that served Muslim Spain's vibrant commerce

0-521-43075-5 CAMBRIDGE $59.95

Richard **Fletcher**

The Quest For El Cid

A fascinating piece of historical detective work, looking for the real El Cid beneath the overlay of legend that has grown up around Spain's national hero. "A splendid achievement, a work of investigative scholarship presented with verve and style"—Raymond Carr, *Sunday Telegraph*

0-19-506955-2 OXFORD PB $10.95

Vivian **Mann**, editor

Convivencia: Jews, Muslims, and Christians in Medieval Spain

Published in concert with a major exhibition at the Jewish Museum in New York. "Splendidly illustrated…provocative essays…"
—Publishers Weekly

0-8076-1283-9 BRAZILLER $50.00

0-8076-1286-3 BRAZILLER PB $25.00

Bernard F. **Reilly**

The Contest of Christian and Muslim Spain: 1031-1157

0-631-19964-0 BLACKWELL PB $21.95

Benzion **Netanyahu**

The Origins of the Inquisition in Fifteenth Century Spain

Examines Spanish anti-Semitism from its origins and argues that the brutal anti-conversion movement that led to the Inquisition was also responsible for the massacre of the Jews in Spain in 1391 and their forced conversion to Christianity

0-679-41065-1 RANDOM HOUSE $60.00

Joseph F. **O'Callaghan**

A History of Medieval Spain

0-8014-9264-5 CORNELL PB $25.00

David **Wasserstein**

The Rise and Fall of the Party-Kings: Politics and Society in Islamic Spain, 1002-1086

0-691-05436-3 PRINCETON $42.50

The Crusades

"If an outsider were to strike any of your kin down, would you not avenge your blood-relative? How much more ought you to avenge your God…whom you see reproached, banished from his estates, crucified?"—Baldric of Bourgueil, late 11th century, cited in Jonathan Riley-Smith's *The Crusades: A Short History*

For related reading, see THE ISLAMIC WORLD TO WORLD WAR I

Malcolm **Barber**

The New Knighthood: A History of the Order of the Temple

How the Order of the Temple became one of the most powerful corporate entities of the Middle Ages, and how it precipitously fell

0-521-55872-7 CAMBRIDGE PB $11.95

The Trial of the Templars

0-521-21896-9 CAMBRIDGE $59.95

0-521-45727-0 CAMBRIDGE PB $11.95

Edward **Burman**

The Templars: Knights of God

The dramatic history of one of three great military religious orders founded during the crusades, to its violent suppression by Philip IV of France in 1307

0-89281-221-4 INNER TRADITIONS PB $12.95

0-85030-396-6 INNER TRADITIONS PB $9.95

John **France**

Victory in the East: A Military History of the First Crusade

How crusader armies, commanded by men of genuine military talent, evolved through experience in the field. Not just a work for military fans; places great emphasis on negotiations of the crusaders with Byzantium and Fatimid Egypt

0-521-41969-7 CAMBRIDGE $59.95

Archibald R. **Lewis**

Nomads and Crusaders: A.D. 1000-1368

How Central Asian nomads and European crusaders changed the balance of world power, leaving Europe in a position of dominance. "A fine, arresting book with a clear and novel thesis and a firm grasp of geography...Strongly recommended"—William H. McNeill

0-253-20652-9 INDIANA PB $11.95

Jonathan **Riley-Smith**

The Crusades: A Short History

An excellent and brief one-volume account

0-300-04700-2 YALE PB $16.00

Jonathan **Riley-Smith**, editor

The Oxford Illustrated History of the Crusades

0-198-20435-3 OXFORD PB $45.00

Steven **Runciman**

History of the Crusades

The standard work. "The best scholarly survey of the subject by a single author"
—English Historical Review

Volume 1
The First Crusade and the Foundation of the Kingdom of Jerusalem

See also **THE CRUSADES** under **THE ISLAMIC WORLD TO WORLD WAR I**

0-521-34770-X CAMBRIDGE PB $19.95

Volume 2
Kingdom of Jerusalem and the Frankish East, 1100-1187

0-521-34771-8 CAMBRIDGE PB $19.95

Volume 3
Kingdom of Acre and the Later Crusades

0-521-34772-6 CAMBRIDGE PB $19.95

The Sicilian Vespers: A History of the Mediterranean World in the Later Thirteenth Century

The career and vast ambitions of Charles of Anjou

0-521-43774-1 CAMBRIDGE PB $11.95

Joseph R. **Strayer**

The Albigensian Crusades

Compact account of how the Catholic north overran the heretical south in 13th-century France, with a new epilogue by Carol Lansing

0-472-06476-2 MICHIGAN PB $16.95

Geoffrey de **Villehardouin** &
Jean de **Joinville**

Chronicles of the Crusades

Firsthand accounts by two French noblemen who took part in the crusades

See also **MIDDLE AGES** under **FRENCH LITERATURE TO 1900** in **LITERATURE OF EUROPE, AFRICA, AND ASIA**

TRANSLATED BY MARGARET R.B. SHAW

0-14-044124-7 PENGUIN PB $12.95

Medieval Portraits

David **Abulafia**

Frederick II: A Medieval Emperor

0-19-508040-8 OXFORD PB $15.95

Amy **Kelly**

Eleanor of Aquitaine and the Four Kings

The strong-willed woman who married two kings and gave birth to two others

See also **MEDIEVAL PORTRAITS** under **HIGHLIGHTS OF MEDIEVAL ENGLAND AND IRELAND** under **GREAT BRITAIN AND IRELAND**

0-674-24254-8 HARVARD PB $14.95

J.R. **Maddicott**

Simon de Montfort

A central figure in the civil war of the 1260s has now been accorded a major modern study worthy of his importance

0-521-37636-X CAMBRIDGE PB $22.95

Donald M. **Nicol**

The Immortal Emperor: The Life and Legend of Constantine Palaiologos, Last Emperor of the Romans

0-521-41456-3 CAMBRIDGE $39.95
0-521-46717-9 CAMBRIDGE PB $9.95

Jean **Richard** & others

Saint Louis: Crusader King of France

TRANSLATED BY J. BIRRELL

0-521-38156-8 CAMBRIDGE $69.95

W.L. **Warren**

Henry II

The king best remembered for his struggles with Thomas Becket and Eleanor of Aquitaine. "A fine work by a professional historian who can write"—A.L. Rowse

See also **MEDIEVAL PORTRAITS** under **HIGHLIGHTS OF MEDIEVAL ENGLAND AND IRELAND** under **GREAT BRITAIN AND IRELAND**

0-520-03494-5 CALIFORNIA PB $16.95

The 14th Century: Black Death and Economic Depression

T.H. **Aston** & C.H. **Philpin**, editors

The Brenner Debate: Agrarian Class Structure and Economic Development in Pre-Industrial Europe

Spirited disputes over whether excess population or class oppression led to the great population collapse of the late Middle Ages

0-521-34933-8 CAMBRIDGE PB $22.95

Piero **Camporesi**

Bread of Dreams: Food and Fantasy in Early Modern Europe

TRANSLATED BY DAVID GENTILCORE

0-226-09258-5 CHICAGO PB $16.95

Ann G. **Carmichael**

Plague and the Poor in Renaissance Florence

A study not only of plague but of the common causes of death; part of the Cambridge History of Medicine Series

0-521-26833-8 CAMBRIDGE $52.95

Robert S. **Gottfried**

The Black Death: Natural and Human Disaster in Medieval Europe

"Marks a distinct intellectual advance...a powerful reminder of how drastically ecological balances can be upset"—William H. McNeil

0-02-912370-4 FREE PRESS PB $16.95

William C. **Jordan**

The Great Famine: Northern Europe in the Early Fourteenth Century

0-691-01134-6 PRINCETON $29.95

William H. **McNeill**

Plagues and Peoples

An important essay whose focus is larger than the 14th century

See also **PERSPECTIVES IN HISTORY** under **THE VARIETIES OF CIVILIZATION**

0-8446-6492-8 SMITH $21.75
0-385-12122-9 DOUBLEDAY PB $9.95

Colin **Platt**

King Death: The Black Death and Its Aftermath in Late-Medieval England

0-8020-7900-8 TORONTO PB $18.95

Barbara **Tuchman**

A Distant Mirror: The Calamitous 14th Century

"What Mrs. Tuchman does superbly is to tell *how* it was"—Lawrence Stone

0-394-40026-7 RANDOM HOUSE $50.00

Ann **Wroe**

A Fool and His Money: Life in a Partitioned Town in Fourteenth-Century France

0-8090-4595-8 HILL & WANG $22.00

Hans **Zinsser**

Rats, Lice and History

A bacteriologist on the struggle to conquer the scourge of typhus

See also **DISEASE AND RESEARCH** under **MEDICINE** in **SCIENCE**

0-316-98896-0 LITTLE, BROWN PB $13.95

Wars and Revolts

Christopher **Allmand**

The Hundred Years War: England and France at War, 1300-1450

0-521-31923-4 CAMBRIDGE PB.....$16.95

Anne **Curry**

The Hundred Years War

0-333-53176-0 ST. MARTIN'S PB.....$16.95

Jean **Froissart**

Chronicles

Froissart's book is a triumph both of literary art and reportorial skill. To read his firsthand accounts of the Hundred Years War, the Black Death, or the court of Richard II is to breathe the air of the 14th century

See also **MIDDLE AGES** under **FRENCH LITERATURE TO 1900** in **LITERATURE OF EUROPE, AFRICA, AND ASIA**

TRANSLATED BY GEOFFREY BRERETON

0-14-044200-6 PENGUIN PB.....$11.95

Charles **Ross**

The Wars of the Roses: A Concise History

Suggests that the gloom of 15th-century England has been too often exaggerated

See also **THE TUDORS: 1485-1603** under **GREAT BRITAIN AND IRELAND**

0-500-27407-X THAMES & HUDSON PB.....$15.95

Renaissance Italy and the Coming of Humanism

Hans **Baron**

Crisis of the Early Italian Renaissance: Civic Humanism and Republican Liberty in an Age of Classicism and Tyranny

0-691-00752-7 PRINCETON PB.....$24.95

Michael **Baxandall**

Giotto and the Orators: Humanist Observers of Painting in Italy and the Discovery of Pictorial Composition, 1350-1450

A detailed and fascinating examination of the literary and pictorial culture of the early Renaissance

0-19-817178-1 OXFORD.....$15.50

Painting and Experience in Fifteenth-Century Italy

Early Renaissance painting as a reflection of the society from which it evolved

See also **THE RISE OF ITALIAN PAINTING** under **MEDIEVAL ART: 600-1400** under **EUROPEAN ART: BYZANTINE AND MEDIEVAL** in **ART**

0-19-282144-X OXFORD PB.....$13.95

Peter **Burke**

The Italian Renaissance: Culture and Society in Italy

Unusual approaches to usual subjects

0-691-09431-4 PRINCETON.....$49.50

0-691-02838-9 PRINCETON PB.....$17.95

William J. **Bouwsma**

Venice and the Defense of Republican Liberty: Renaissance Values in the Age of the Counter Reformation

A new look at the Renaissance, focusing on the Venetian republic. "One of the most important contributions to Renaissance historiography in recent memory"—*Journal of Modern History*

0-520-05221-8 CALIFORNIA PB.....$16.00

Gene **Brucker**

Renaissance Florence

"There is no other book about Florence in this period which combines such a broad range of archival sources—family records, records of church and state—with standard literary sources in such an original and effective way" —*American Historical Review*

0-520-04919-5 CALIFORNIA.....$50.00

0-520-04695-1 CALIFORNIA PB.....$14.95

The Society of Renaissance Florence: A Documentary Study

Excerpts from original documents that reveal something about the emotions, passions, and temperaments of Renaissance Florentines, from family squabbles to prostitution to business fortunes

0-06-131607-5 HARPERCOLLINS PB.....$14.50

Giovanni and Lusanna

In 1455, Lusanna, a beautiful Florentine woman of the artisan class, brought suit against her wealthy, high-born lover Giovanni, who had contracted to marry a young aristocrat. "At its core, this splendid study is about stubborn love and the forms of law, and the impossibility of each to accommodate the ultimate claims of the other"—A. Bartlett Giamatti

0-520-05655-8 CALIFORNIA.....$28.00

0-520-06328-7 CALIFORNIA PB.....$12.95

A. Bartlett **Giamatti**

The Earthly Paradise and the Renaissance Epic

"An original approach to Spenser and Milton...This is comparative literature as it ought to be done"—*NY Review of Books*

0-393-30573-2 NORTON PB.....$8.95

Richard A. **Goldthwaite**

The Building of Renaissance Florence: An Economic and Social History

A splendid view of the city's 16th-century architectural transformation

0-8018-2977-1 SOFTSHELL PB.....$18.95

Wealth and the Demand for Art in Italy, 1300-1600

To Burckhardt's assertion that the Renaissance was the discovery of the world and man, Goldthwaite adds the dimension of the discovery of the world of things—and the modern material culture of conspicuous consumption

0-8018-5235-8 JOHNS HOPKINS PB.....$15.95

J.R. **Hale**

Renaissance Europe: The Individual and Society, 1480-1520

0-520-03471-6 CALIFORNIA PB.....$15.95

War and Society in Renaissance Europe, 1450-1620

0-8018-3196-2 JOHNS HOPKINS PB.....$14.95

J.R. **Hale**, editor

A Concise Encyclopedia of the Italian Renaissance

A sturdy and exhaustive illustrated reference book for the general reader

See also **ITALY** under **EUROPEAN ART: THE RENAISSANCE** in **ART**

0-500-23333-0 NORTON.....$19.95

0-500-20191-9 THAMES & HUDSON PB.....$14.95

Denys **Hay**

The Italian Renaissance in Its Historical Background

0-521-29104-6 CAMBRIDGE PB.....$19.95

David **Herlihy** & Christiane **Klapisch-Zuber**

Tuscans and Their Families: A Study of the Florentine Catasto of 1427

0-300-04611-1 YALE PB.....$18.00

George **Holmes**

Art and Politics in Renaissance Italy: British Academy Lectures

0-19-726159-0 OXFORD PB.....$19.95

The Florentine Enlightenment

0-19-820292-X OXFORD PB.....$24.95

Christiane **Klapisch-Zuber**

Women, Family, and Ritual in Renaissance Italy

A living picture of the Tuscan household—its size and composition, its values and priorities—drawn from the detailed records of tax collectors, as well as business and household accounts

TRANSLATED BY LYDIA G. COCHRANE

FOREWORD BY DAVID HERLIHY

0-226-43926-7 CHICAGO PB.....$14.95

Jill **Kraye**, editor

The Cambridge Companion to Renaissance Humanism

Fourteen essays on all aspects of the movement: from its origins in Italy to the works of More, Sidney, and Shakespeare

0-521-43624-9 CAMBRIDGE PB.....$18.95

Paul Oskar **Kristeller**

Renaissance Thought and Its Sources

Kristeller is one of the foremost authorities on Renaissance intellectual history

0-231-04513-1 COLUMBIA PB.....$22.00

Sebastian **de Grazia**
Machiavelli in Hell
Winner of the Pulitzer Prize in biography: a stunningly intimate approach to the great political philosopher. "Complex, brilliant, attractive, at times profound"
—*Christian Science Monitor*
See also **STUDIES OF INDIVIDUAL AUTHORS** under **CRITICAL STUDIES** under **ITALIAN LITERATURE** in **LITERATURE OF EUROPE, AFRICA, AND ASIA**
0-691-00861-2 VINTAGE PB $14.95

Ian **Maclean**
The Renaissance Notion of Woman: A Study in the Fortunes of Scholasticism and Medical Science in European Intellectual Life
See also **WORLD HISTORY** under **WOMEN'S STUDIES** in **SOCIAL STUDIES**
0-521-27436-2 CAMBRIDGE PB $15.95

Lauro **Martines**
Power and Imagination: City-States in Renaissance Italy
0-8018-3643-3 JOHNS HOPKINS PB $15.95

Christopher **Hibbert**
The House of Medici: Its Rise and Fall
0-688-05339-4 MORROW PB $13.00

James **Saslow**
The Medici Wedding of 1589: Florentine Festival as Theatrum Mundi
The marriage of Grand Duke Ferdinando de' Medici and the French princess Christine of Lorraine, a landmark event in Renaissance art, architecture, theatre, music, and political and ceremonial life
0-300-06447-0 YALE $45.00

Peter **Partner**
Renaissance Rome: A Portrait of a Society, 1500-1559
0-520-03945-9 CALIFORNIA PB $15.00

Armando **Petrucci**
Writers and Readers in Medieval Italy: Studies in the History of Written Culture
TRANSLATED BY CHARLES RADDING
0-300-06089-0 YALE $30.00

Mark **Phillips**
The Memoir of Marco Parenti: A Life in Medici Florence
The public and private life of a 15th-century silk merchant. "Combines very careful and sound scholarship with intellectual originality and a remarkable sense for literary presentation"
—Felix Gilbert
0-691-05502-5 PRINCETON $45.00
0-691-00833-7 PRINCETON PB $15.95

J.H. **Plumb**
The Italian Renaissance
0-8281-0485-9 AMERICAN HERITAGE PB $13.95

Michael **Rocke**
Forbidden Friendships: Homosexuality and Male Culture in Renaissance Florence
Suggests that nearly all Florentine males had some kind of same-sex experience as part of their normal sexual life
0-19-506975-7 OXFORD $30.00

James B. **Ross** & Mary M. **McLaughlin**, editors
The Portable Renaissance Reader
See also **GENERAL ANTHOLOGIES** under **WORLD LITERATURE: WORLD LITERATURE SURVEYS AND ANTHOLOGIES** in **LITERATURE OF EUROPE, AFRICA, AND ASIA**
0-14-015061-7 VIKING PB $14.95

Jonathan **Sawday**
The Body Emblazoned: Dissection and the Human Body in Renaissance Culture
A work of interdisciplinary scholarship
0-415-04444-8 ROUTLEDGE $45.00

Christine **Shaw**
Julius II: The Warrior Pope
0-631-16738-2 BLACKWELL $41.95

Renaissance Classics

Gene **Brucker**, editor
Two Memoirs of Renaissance Florence: The Diaries of Buonaccorso Pitti and Gregorio Dati
TRANSLATED BY JULIA MARTINES
0-88133-622-X WAVELAND PB $8.95

Francesco **Guicciardini**
The History of Italy
A well-translated abridgment of Guicciardini's four-volume masterpiece
TRANSLATED BY SIDNEY ALEXANDER
0-691-00800-0 PRINCETON PB $19.95

Niccolo **Machiavelli**
The radical innovation of Machiavelli was to base political theory on experience rather than edifying ideals; in his work he drew on history as well as on his own career as a Florentine diplomat. His ambiguous legacy includes both modern empirical political science and the realpolitik of the nation-state as a law unto itself.
Discourses on Livy
See also **CLASSICS** under **POLITICAL THOUGHT** in **SOCIAL STUDIES**
See also **HUMANISM** under **THE RENAISSANCE** under **ITALIAN LITERATURE** in **LITERATURE OF EUROPE, AFRICA, AND ASIA**
TRANSLATED BY HARVEY C. MANSFIELD
0-226-50035-7 CHICAGO $34.95

The Prince
TRANSLATED BY GEORGE BULL
0-14-044107-7 PENGUIN PB $5.95

Machiavelli

Giorgio **Vasari**
Lives of the Artists
First published in 1550, this book is a primary source on Renaissance art and artists
0-14-044460-2 PENGUIN PB $11.95

Renaissance Cities

Michael **Levey** & others
Florence: A Portrait
0-674-30657-0 HARVARD $35.00

Mary **McCarthy**
The Stones of Florence
A perceptive look into the spirit of one of Italy's greatest cities
See also **EUROPE SINCE 1945** under **EUROPE** under **TRAVEL LITERATURE** in **FOOD, TRAVEL, AND LEISURE**
0-15-185079-8 HARCOURT BRACE $49.95
0-15-685081-8 HARCOURT BRACE PB $19.95

Charles R. **Mack**
Pienza: The Creation of a Renaissance City
Rebuilt by Pius II as a Renaissance model, the small hill town embodied the theoretical propositions of Brunelleschi and Alberti
0-8014-1699-X CORNELL $49.95

David **Coffin**
The Villa in the Life of Renaissance Rome
The change in function of the country residence from a productive farm to a center of pleasurable relaxation
See also **ITALIAN RENAISSANCE CITIES** under **ITALIAN RENAISSANCE** under **EUROPEAN ARCHITECTURE TO 1900** in **ARCHITECTURE, DESIGN, AND HOMES**
0-691-00279-7 PRINCETON PB $26.95

Christopher **Hibbert**

Rome: The Biography of a City

This combination of portrait, history, and guidebook captures the seductive beauty of the Eternal City. Lavishly illustrated

See also **CITIES** under **TOPICS IN ROMAN HISTORY** under **ANCIENT ROME**

0-14-007078-8 PENGUIN PB $24.95

Daniel **Huguenin** & others

The Glory of Venice

2-87939-096-6 STEWART, TABORI PB $24.95

John **Ruskin**

The Stones of Venice

An original and illuminating commentary on the city's monuments

0-918825-13-X MOYER BELL $34.95
0-306-80244-9 DA CAPO PB $11.95

Erasmus and the Northern Renaissance

"Here a new watchword comes to the fore: back to the sources! It is not merely an intellectual, philological requirement; it is equally an ethical and aesthetic necessity of life. The original and pure, all that is not yet overgrown or has not passed through many hands, has such a potent charm. Erasmus compared it to an apple which we ourselves pick off the tree. To recall the world to the ancient simplicity of science, to lead it back from the now turbid pools to those living and most pure fountain-heads, those most limpid sources of gospel doctrine—thus he saw the task of divinity."
—Johan Huizinga, *Erasmus and the Age of Reformation*

Desiderius **Erasmus**

The Essential Erasmus

Includes *The Praise of Folly, The Complaint of Peace, An Inquiry Concerning Faith,* and other writings

EDITED BY JOHN P. DOLAN

0-452-00673-2 NEW AMERICAN LIBRARY PB $11.95

The Praise of Folly

The great satirical work by the renowned northern humanist

TRANSLATED BY BETTY RADICE

0-472-06023-6 MICHIGAN PB $12.95

Erasmus

M.A. **Screech**

Erasmus: Ecstasy and the Praise of Folly

"To the familiar portrait of Erasmus as critic and mischievous observer of his time, as humourist, as philological custodian of the Ancients and as international pacificist, Screech has added the dimension of Erasmus as a guide to the human soul"—Margaret Mann Phillips, *Colloque Erasmien de Liege*

0-14-055235-9 PENGUIN PB $7.95

Johan **Huizinga**

Erasmus of Rotterdam

An account by a great modern historian

0-7148-3366-5 PHAIDON PB $14.95

Introductions to Modern European History

T.C.W. **Blanning**, editor

The Oxford Illustrated History of Modern Europe

0-19-820374-8 OXFORD $45.00

Robert P. **Libbon**

Instant European History: From the French Revolution to the Cold War

A complete education without tuition. Humorous, fact-filled, and fun

0-449-90702-3 FAWCETT PB $10.00

John **Merriman**

A History of Modern Europe

Emphasizes the social basis of historical change, in politics, culture, the organization of work, and war. A 1200-page text by the Yale historian and author of *Red City: Limoges and the French Nineteenth Century*

0-393-96885-5 NORTON PB $39.95

The People of Europe

Luigi **Barzini**

The Italians

Their manners and morals. "Searching into every corner of Italian life and scrutinizing every cliche concerning it, from the charm of the people (an illusion, he maintains) to the consolations of *La Dolce Vita* (another one), Mr. Barzini has written an invaluable and astringent guidebook to his country"—*New Yorker*

0-8446-6146-5 SMITH $23.55
0-689-70540-9 ATHENEUM PB $13.00

Gordon A. **Craig**

The Germans

The paradoxes that have produced great music, art, literature—and Hitler

0-452-01085-3 MERIDIAN PB $13.95

David M. **Crowe**

A History of the Gypsies of Eastern Europe and Russia

See also **GYPSIES** under **REGIONAL AND NATIONAL HISTORIES**

0-312-12946-7 ST. MARTIN'S PB $14.95

Patrick **Galliou** & Michael **Jones**

The Bretons

An addition to the fascinating Peoples of Europe series, joining previous volumes on the Mongols, the Basques, and the Franks. The authors probe the archaeological and historical roots of the Armorican culture from the paleolithic era onward

0-631-16406-5 BLACKWELL $36.95
0-631-20105-X BLACKWELL PB $21.95

Hedrick **Smith**

The Russians

0-345-31746-7 BALLANTINE PB $6.99

Regional and National Histories

For related reading, see GREAT BRITAIN and IRELAND

For related reading, see RUSSIAN STUDIES

Eastern Europe and Poland

Neal **Ascherson**

The Struggles for Poland

An illustrated companion to the PBS documentary covering the broad sweep of Poland's tragic past

0-394-55997-5 RANDOM HOUSE $5.98

Norman **Davies**

God's Playground: A History of Poland

"The best introduction available to the incredible imbroglio of Polish history"
—Stanislaw Baranczak, *New Republic*

Volume 1
The Origins to 1795

0-231-05351-7 COLUMBIA PB $27.50

Volume 2
1795 to the Present

0-231-05353-3 COLUMBIA $22.50

Heart of Europe: A Short History of Poland

Starting with the Solidarity movement and working back to the 18th-century partitions, a view of Poland as the geographical and symbolic heart of Europe

0-19-285152-7 OXFORD PB $14.95

Francis **Dvornik**

The Slavs in European History and Civilization

0-8135-0799-5 RUTGERS PB $20.00

E. Garrison **Walters**
The Other Europe: Eastern Europe to 1945
0-8156-2440-9 SYRACUSE PB $17.50

France

Alfred **Cobban**
A History of Modern France
An excellent survey by the late British historian
Volume 1 1715-1799
0-14-013825-0 VIKING PB $12.95
Volume 2 1799-1870
0-14-013826-9 VIKING PB $12.95
Volume 3 1871-1962
0-14-013827-7 VIKING PB $13.95

Napoleon in Russia

Pierre **Goubert**
The Course of French History
A useful synthesis by the author of *Louis XIV and Twenty Million Frenchmen*
TRANSLATED BY MAARTEN ULTEE
0-415-06671-9 ROUTLEDGE PB $18.95

Colin **Jones**
The Cambridge Illustrated History of France
Excellent illustrations and lively writing make this an attractive introduction to the political and social history of France from the earliest times to the present
0-521-43294-4 CAMBRIDGE $39.95

Charles **Tilly**
The Contentious French
A social historian on urban and provincial uprisings throughout the modern period
See also **HISTORICAL SOCIOLOGY** under **TOPICS IN MODERN SOCIOLOGY** under **SOCIOLOGY** in **SOCIAL STUDIES**
0-674-16695-7 HARVARD $32.50
0-674-16696-5 HARVARD PB $16.00

Roger **Price**
A Concise History of France
One of the Cambridge Concise Histories
0-521-36809-X CAMBRIDGE PB $15.95

Herbert **Tint**
France Since 1918
0-312-30315-7 ST. MARTIN'S $29.95

Gordon **Wright**
France in Modern Times
0-393-96705-0 NORTON PB $22.95

Germany

V.R. **Berghahn**
Modern Germany: Society, Economy and Politics in the Twentieth Century
A crisp account beginning with the rapid industrialization of the pre-World War I era and focusing on social and economic developments
0-521-34748-3 CAMBRIDGE PB $18.95

Mary **Fulbrook**
A Concise History of Germany
A handy, brief synthesis
0-521-36836-7 CAMBRIDGE PB $14.95

Hajo **Holborn**
A History of Modern Germany
The standard survey of German history published in 1964. A "massive and unmatched reconstruction of the German past"—Fritz Stern
Volume 1 The Reformation
0-691-00795-0 PRINCETON PB $18.95
Volume 2 1648-1840
0-691-00796-9 PRINCETON PB $22.95
Volume 3 1840-1945
0-691-00797-7 PRINCETON PB $19.95

James J. **Sheehan**
German History: 1770-1866
0-19-822120-7 OXFORD $79.00
0-19-820432-9 OXFORD PB $29.95

Greece and the Balkans

R.J. **Crampton**
A Short History of Modern Bulgaria
From Bulgaria's liberation from the Ottoman Empire in 1878 to the present; a good introduction
0-521-25340-3 CAMBRIDGE $59.95
0-521-27323-4 CAMBRIDGE PB $22.95

John V.A. **Fine**
The Early Medieval Balkans
0-472-08149-7 MICHIGAN PB $24.95
The Late Medieval Balkans
0-472-08260-4 MICHIGAN PB $27.95

Barbara **Jelavich**
History of the Balkans
Volume 1 Eighteenth and Nineteenth Centuries
0-521-27458-3 CAMBRIDGE PB $24.95
Volume 2 Twentieth Century
0-521-27459-1 CAMBRIDGE PB $24.95

Charles **Jelavich** & Barbara **Jelavich**
The Establishment of the Balkan National States, 1804-1920
0-295-96413-8 WASHINGTON PB $25.00

Noel **Malcolm**
Bosnia: A Short History
A reliable historical guide to the roots of the Bosnian conflict
0-8147-5520-8 NYU $26.95
0-8147-5561-5 NYU PB $18.95

Fred **Singleton**
A Short History of the Yugoslav Peoples
0-521-27485-0 CAMBRIDGE PB $19.95

John **Wilkes**
The Illyrians
A history of Albania and the Albanians
0-631-14671-7 BLACKWELL $54.95

Italy

Spencer **Di Scala**
Italy: From Revolution to Republic
A good survey from 1700 to the 20th century
0-8133-1343-0 WESTVIEW PB $21.95

Christopher **Duggan**
A Concise History of Italy
0-521-40848-2 CAMBRIDGE PB $14.95

Scandinavia

Michael **Roberts**
The Swedish Imperial Experience, 1560-1718
Sweden's important role in European affairs in the 17th century
0-521-27889-9 CAMBRIDGE PB $19.95

Birgit **Sawyer** & Peter **Sawyer**
Medieval Scandinavia: From Conversion to Reformation, circa 800-1500
0-8166-1739-2 MINNESOTA PB $19.95

Fred **Singleton**

A Short History of Finland

0-521-32275-8 CAMBRIDGE....$49.95
0-521-31136-5 CAMBRIDGE PB....$18.95

The Netherlands and the Low Countries

Jonathan **Israel**

The Dutch Republic: Its Rise, Greatness, and Fall, 1477-1806

Illustrated
0-19-873072-1 OXFORD....$45.00

Dutch Primacy in World Trade, 1585-1740

0-19-821139-2 OXFORD PB....$35.00

E.H. **Kossman**

The Low Countries, 1750-1940

A comparative approach to why Belgium and the Netherlands, despite many similarities, embarked on different courses of development
0-19-822108-8 OXFORD....$89.00

Simon **Schama**

The Embarrassment of Riches: An Interpretation of Dutch Culture in the Golden Age

The Dutch and early capitalism in the 17th century
0-394-51075-5 KNOPF....$39.95

The Hapsburg Empire, Modern Austria and Hungary

Charles **Ingrao**

The Habsburg Monarchy, 1618-1815

Challenges the conventional notion of the empire's backwardness as it explores the progressive judicial and educational systems under the Habsburgs
0-521-38900-3 CAMBRIDGE PB....$15.95

Barbara **Jelavich**

Modern Austria: Empire and Republic, 1800-1986

Political history and foreign policy, from the Congress of Vienna to the 1986 elections
0-521-30320-6 CAMBRIDGE....$69.95
0-521-31625-1 CAMBRIDGE PB....$18.95

A.J.P. **Taylor**

The Habsburg Monarchy, 1809-1918: A History of the Austrian Empire and Austria-Hungary

First published in 1941 and still essential reading for all students of the period. "A very good book indeed, brilliant, acid and penetrating"—Alan Bullock
See also **19TH-CENTURY AUSTRIA AND THE HABSBURGS** under **19TH-CENTURY EUROPE**
0-226-79145-9 CHICAGO PB....$12.95

Robert A. **Kann**

A History of the Habsburg Empire, 1526-1918

An essential one-volume survey
0-520-04206-9 CALIFORNIA PB....$18.95

Spain and Portugal

David **Birmingham**

A Concise History of Portugal

0-521-43880-2 CAMBRIDGE PB....$14.95

Raymond **Carr**

Spain: 1808-1975

Economic, political, and social history to the death of Franco; with an extensive bibliographical essay
0-19-822128-2 OXFORD PB....$35.00

John **Crow**

Spain the Root and the Flower: An Interpretation of Spain and the Spanish People

An older, idiosyncratic study
0-520-05123-8 CALIFORNIA....$55.00
0-520-05133-5 CALIFORNIA PB....$15.95

David R. **Ringrose**

Spain, Europe, and the "Spanish Miracle," 1700-1900

A challenging study that promises to change our understanding of modern Spain
0-521-43486-6 CAMBRIDGE....$64.95

Gypsies

The word *Gypsy* derives from *Egypt*, where many people mistakenly thought Gypsies originated. In fact, the Gypsies (or *Rom* in their own language, *Romany*) started out in northern India. Beginning around the 10th century, many of them left in several waves, moving westward into Europe. No one knows exactly why they left India (though there are countless theories), but the routes as well as the times of their various migrations can be traced through linguistic evidence.

Being outsiders, Gypsies were persecuted everywhere they went, by enslavement, systematic deportation, and massacre. Officially freed in the mid-19th century, the Gypsies have endured programs of forced assimilation in many countries, as well as unofficial pressures to abandon their culture. As Jean-Pierre Liegeois has remarked, "the Gypsies, moving about in their nomadic groups, were seen as physically threatening and ideologically disruptive. Their very existence constituted dissidence." Violence against Gypsies reached a peak during the Second World War when the Nazis attempted to wipe out the entire Gypsy race in Europe. At least half a million Gypsies perished in the Holocaust.

The following list of books deal with both historical and contemporary issues.

Thomas **Acton**

Gypsies

A politically aware overview of the culture, history, and struggles of the many different groups of Gypsies. Written for young people
0-382-06645-6 SILVER, BURDETT....$16.96

David M. **Crowe**

A History of the Gypsies of Eastern Europe and Russia

See also **THE PEOPLE OF EUROPE**
0-312-12946-7 ST. MARTIN'S PB....$14.95

Isabel **Fonseca**

Bury Me Standing: The Gypsies and Their Journey

The mythic world of the Gypsies—a worldwide diaspora of 12 million people, little understood and much reviled—is brought to life by journalist Fonseca. Benefiting from the revolutions of 1989, Fonseca traveled to Bulgaria, Poland, Romania, Albania, and the former Yugoslavia to document the little-known Romany world
0-679-40678-6 KNOPF....$25.00

Ian **Hancock**

The Pariah Syndrome: An Account of Gypsy Slavery and Persecution

An illuminating account by a Gypsy of his people's oppression, including the murder of at least half a million Gypsies at the hands of the Nazis
See also **GENERAL SURVEYS** under **THE HOLOCAUST**
0-89720-079-9 KAROMA PB....$25.00

Josef **Koudelka** & Willy **Guy**

Gypsies

Sixty of Koudelka's intense black-and-white photographs, most of them taken among isolated Gypsy settlements in East Slovakia. Willy Guy's succinct essay provides historical and political background
0-89381-491-1 APERTURE....$49.95

Jean-Pierre **Liegeois**

Gypsies: An Illustrated History

An excellent and insightful history illustrated with black-and-white photographs
0-86356-025-3 ZED PB....$15.00

David **Mayall**

Gypsy-Travellers in Nineteenth-Century Society

Reconstructs the Gypsy lifestyles of the period and examines the negative stereotypes that arose as a result of conflict
0-521-32397-5 CAMBRIDGE....$79.95

Bertha B. **Quintana** & Lois G. **Floyd**

Que Gitano!: Gypsies of Southern Spain

Through observation and interviews, an anthropologist and a psychologist examine the nature of the Sacro Monte Gypsies and their critical views of American culture
0-88133-217-8 WAVELAND PB....$9.50

Anne **Sutherland**
Gypsies: The Hidden Americans
Describes a predominantly Kalderash community in California (here called Barvale). The book is brought to life by the major contribution of social worker Jan Tompkins
0-88133-235-6 WAVELAND PB....................$12.95

Marlene **Sway**
Familiar Strangers: Gypsy Life in America
0-252-01512-6 ILLINOIS....................$24.95
0-252-06116-0 ILLINOIS PB....................$8.95

Diane **Tong**
Gypsy Folktales
An international collection of 80 stories, many never before published; with an insert of 16 black-and-white photographs of Greek Gypsies
0-15-637989-9 HARCOURT BRACE PB....................$15.00

Jan **Yoors**
The Gypsies
A lyrical celebration of life on the road with a group of Lowara horse traders
0-88133-305-0 WAVELAND PB....................$10.95

Early Modern Europe

Jeremy **Black**
The Rise of the European Powers, 1679-1793
A survey that gives equal emphasis to both Western and Eastern Europe, including neglected topics such as the Baltics after the Great Northern War and the role of the Turks
0-7131-6537-5 ARNOLD PB....................$15.95

Leonard **Krieger**
Kings and Philosophers, 1689-1789
0-393-09905-9 NORTON PB....................$12.95

John F. **New**
The Renaissance and Reformation: A Short History
0-07-554681-7 MCGRAW HILL PB....................$31.90

Theodore K. **Rabb**
The Struggle for Stability in Early Modern Europe
0-19-501956-3 OXFORD PB....................$14.95

Eugene F. **Rice**, Jr.
The Foundations of Early Modern Europe, 1460-1559
From the development of movable metal type, perfected in Mainz about 1450, through the English Reformation
0-393-96304-7 NORTON PB....................$11.95

Geoffrey **Treasure**
The Making of Modern Europe, 1648-1780
0-416-72370-5 ROUTLEDGE PB....................$17.95

Hugh **Trevor-Roper**
From Counter-Reformation to Glorious Revolution
This selection of the best writings from one of the greatest living historians ranges over subjects from Matteo Ricci's 16th-century mission to China to the plunder of European artistic treasure to Hugo Grotius's plans to create a universal Anglican church. "[T]he most eloquent, sophisticated and assured historian of our age"—Noel Annan
0-226-81230-8 CHICAGO....................$29.95

Rosario **Villari**, editor
Baroque Personae
Informative essays on the nun, the courtier, the soldier, and others who populated the seventeenth century
TRANSLATED BY LYDIA G. COCHRANE
0-226-85637-2 CHICAGO PB....................$18.95

Reformation and Counter-Reformation

For related reading, see GREAT BRITAIN AND IRELAND

For related reading, see CHRISTIANITY

Robert **Bireley**
The Counter-Reformation Prince: Anti-Machiavellianism or Catholic Statecraft in Early Modern Europe
0-8078-1925-5 NORTH CAROLINA....................$49.95

Peter **Blickle**
Communal Reformation: The Quest for Salvation in Sixteenth-Century Germany
See also **REFORMATION** under **HISTORY** under **CHRISTIANITY** in **RELIGION, SPIRITUALITY, AND PHILOSOPHY**
TRANSLATED BY THOMAS DUNLAP
0-391-03730-7 HUMANITIES....................$49.95

The Revolution of 1525: The German Peasants' Revolution from a New Perspective
A seminal book from a non-Marxist historian; first published in 1981
TRANSLATED BY THOMAS A. BRADY
0-8018-3162-8 JOHNS HOPKINS PB....................$12.95

John **Bossy**
Christianity in the West, 1400-1700
A systematic exposition of pre-Reformation Christianity and the forces that undermined it
0-19-289162-6 OXFORD PB....................$16.95

Owen **Chadwick**
The Reformation
Part of the Pelican History of the Church series
See also **REFORMATION** under **HISTORY** under **CHRISTIANITY** in **RELIGION, SPIRITUALITY, AND PHILOSOPHY**
0-14-013757-2 VIKING PB....................$12.00

Oliver Cromwell

A.G. **Dickens**
The Counter-Reformation
How the Catholic Church sought to regain its spiritual dominion after the abuses of the Renaissance papacy
0-393-95086-7 NORTON PB....................$9.95

Richard S. **Dunn**
The Age of Religious Wars, 1559-1689
Chapters include "Calvinism Versus Catholicism in Western Europe" and "The Century of Genius," with discussions of Newton, Montaigne, Pascal, Hobbes, Rubens, Velazquez, Bernini, and Rembrandt
0-393-09021-3 NORTON PB....................$10.95

Mark **Greengrass**
The French Reformation
A good, brief introduction, first published in 1987
0-631-14516-8 BLACKWELL PB....................$11.95

Hans **Hillerbrand**, editor
The Protestant Reformation
Excerpts from Luther, Calvin, and Zwingli, plus additional documents tracing the Reformation through the Anabaptists and developments in England
0-06-131342-4 HARPERCOLLINS PB....................$14.50

R. Po-chia **Hsia**

The German People and the Reformation

Essays on how the religious schisms of 16th-century Europe affected the lives of ordinary Germans

0-8014-9485-0 CORNELL PB $14.95

Carter **Lindberg**

The European Reformations

1-55786-575-2 BLACKWELL PB $22.95

Heiko A. **Oberman**

The Reformation: Roots and Ramifications

0-8028-0825-5 EERDMANS PB $30.00

Steven **Ozment**

The Age of Reform, 1250-1550: An Intellectual and Religious History of Late Medieval and Reformation Europe

See also **REFORMATION** under **HISTORY** under **CHRISTIANITY** in **RELIGION, SPIRITUALITY, AND PHILOSOPHY**

0-300-02760-5 YALE PB $19.00

Protestants: The Birth of a Revolution

In a closely reasoned and convincing social history, Ozment, a distinguished scholar, shows that the Protestant Reformation, in attacking ritual and ceremony, supported individualism. In addition, through diaries and letters, Ozment offers insight into the emotional makeup of the first Protestants. "To read Steven Ozment is to believe that history is a living art"—Richard Marius, Harvard University

See also **PROTESTANT** under **HISTORY** under **CHRISTIANITY** in **RELIGION, SPIRITUALITY, AND PHILOSOPHY**

0-385-47101-7 DOUBLEDAY PB $12.95

Steven **Ozment**, editor

When Fathers Ruled: Family Life in Reformation Europe

0-674-95120-4 HARVARD $31.95

Jaroslav **Pelikan** & others

The Reformation of the Bible: The Bible of the Reformation

The book serves as the catalog for a major exhibition of early Bibles and Reformation texts

0-941881-18-0 YALE PB $10.00

Ernest G. **Schwiebert**

Luther and His Times: The Reformation from a New Perspective

0-570-03246-6 CONCORDIA $27.95

Bard **Thompson**

Humanists and Reformers: A History of the Renaissance and the Reformation

A solid survey with excellent color plates

0-8028-3691-7 EERDMANS $40.00

Andrew **Pettegree** & others, editors

Calvinism in Europe, 1540-1620

0-521-43269-3 CAMBRIDGE $59.95

J. Denny **Weaver**

Becoming Anabaptist: The Origin and Significance of Sixteenth-Century Anabaptism

A very readable yet scholarly introduction to Anabaptist origins

0-8361-3434-6 HERALD PB $14.95

Donald J. **Wilcox**

In Search of God and Self: Renaissance and Reformation Thought

See also **REFORMATION** under **HISTORY** under **CHRISTIANITY** in **RELIGION, SPIRITUALITY, AND PHILOSOPHY**

0-88133-276-3 WAVELAND PB $16.95

The Printing Revolution and Reading

Alain **Boureau**

The Culture of Print: Power and the Uses of Print in Early Modern Europe

This collection offers challenging scholarly assessments of the nature of reading and the use of posters, broadsheets, and flysheets in Western Europe. Contributions by Alain Boureau, Roger Chartier, Marie-Elisabeth Ducreux, and others. "Each essay…reveals surprising ways in which printed books and pamphlets entered into the world of seeing, talking, praying and ruling of early modern Europe…Fairy tales, saints' lives and emblem books existed not as disembodied genres but as printed objects in vital social exchange"—Natalie Zemon Davis

0-691-05580-7 PRINCETON $57.50

William **Eamon**

Science and the Secrets of Nature: Books of Secrets in Medieval and Early Modern Culture

How to sire mulitcolored horses, produce nuts without shells, and create an egg the size of a human head. "[A] lively account of authors and writings that were always unacademic, unscrupulous, unprofessional, turbulent, and unsettled: that is to say, an account of the popular or seamy side of medicine and natural knowledge in medieval and early modern times"—*Nature*

0-691-02602-5 PRINCETON PB $18.95

Elizabeth L. **Eisenstein**

The Printing Press as an Agent of Change

0-521-29955-1 CAMBRIDGE PB $44.95

The Printing Revolution in Early Modern Europe

A shorter statement of the same thesis, with pictures

0-521-44770-4 CAMBRIDGE PB $12.95

Lucien **Febvre** & Henri-Jean **Martin**

The Coming of the Book: The Impact of Printing, 1450-1800

In the 40 years between the Gutenberg Bible and the close of the 15th century, more than 20 million printed volumes were manufactured in Europe; between 1500 and 1600, between 150 and 200 million. Febvre and Martin's classic study conveys the revolutionary impact of printing on early modern Europe. "One of the most exciting scholarly books ever written on printing"—H.R. Trevor-Roper

TRANSLATED BY DAVID GERARD

EDITED BY GEOFFREY NOWELL-SMITH & DAVID WOOTTON

0-86091-797-5 VERSO PB $19.95

Francois **Furet** & Jacques **Ozouf**

Reading and Writing: Literacy in France from Calvin to Jules Ferry

From the Protestant Reformation to the New Imperialism

0-521-22389-X CAMBRIDGE $79.95

0-521-27402-8 CAMBRIDGE PB $21.95

Janet **Ing**

Johann Gutenberg and His Bible

Illustrated

0-945074-00-X DAWSONS $27.50

Henri-Jean **Martin**

The French Book: Religion, Absolutism, and Readership, 1585-1715

Intellectual history that treats the relationship between politics and ideas. Investigates such topics as the founding of royal and university libraries, Richelieu's cultural program, censorship, the first illustrated "coffee table" books, and the invention of the paragraph to facilitate reading

TRANSLATED BY PAUL SAENGER & NADINE SAENGER

0-8018-5419-9 JOHNS HOPKINS PB $13.95

James **Raven** & others, editors

The Practice and Representation of Reading in England

How did people read in the past? Where, when, and why? Tapping fields as diverse as medieval pedagogy, the history of science, and social and literary history, this text explores the history of readers and reading

0-521-48093-0 CAMBRIDGE $54.95

Religion and Capitalism

R.H. **Tawney**

Religion and the Rise of Capitalism

Tawney evaluates Weber's theory of the Protestant ethic and suggests a revision, providing an account of conscious and unconscious attitudes about business in the early modern period

0-8446-1446-7 SMITH $14.50

Max **Weber**

The Protestant Ethic and the Spirit of Capitalism

Weber's classic argument, first published in 1904, that the spread of Protestantism directly affected the rise of the capitalist ethic

See also CLASSICAL EUROPEAN SOCIOLOGY under SOCIOLOGY in SOCIAL STUDIES

0-02-424860-6 PRENTICE HALL PB $34.40

Reformers and Revolutionaries

William J. **Bouwsma**

John Calvin: A Sixteenth Century Portrait

"By intense reading in Calvin's work [Bouwsma] has come up with a 20th-century psychological scheme, giving a genuinely new insight into the man and into the 16th century as a whole" —*NY Times*

0-19-504394-4 OXFORD $35.00
0-19-505951-4 OXFORD PB $14.95

Martin **Luther**

Martin Luther: Selections from His Writings

A sampling of Luther's theological, exegetical, and polemical works

See also THEOLOGY under THEOLOGY AND DOCTRINE under CHRISTIANITY in RELIGION, SPIRITUALITY, AND PHILOSOPHY

EDITED BY JOHN DILLENBERGER

0-385-09876-6 DOUBLEDAY PB $11.95

Roland H. **Bainton**

Here I Stand: A Life of Martin Luther

A classic study

See also PROTESTANTS under BIOGRAPHIES under CHRISTIANITY in RELIGION, SPIRITUALITY, AND PHILOSOPHY

0-8446-6225-9 SMITH $19.00
0-687-16895-3 ABINGDON PB $5.95

Erik **Erikson**

Young Man Luther

The origins of Luther's rebelliousness and later authoritarianism; one of the most successful forays into psychobiography, by the author of *Childhood, Youth and Crisis*

See also ERIK H. ERIKSON under POST-FREUDIAN THEORISTS under PSYCHOLOGY in SOCIAL STUDIES

0-393-31036-1 NORTON PB $9.95

James M. **Kittelson**

Luther the Reformer

A reliable and up-to-date biography especially written for the nonspecialist; first published in 1986

0-8066-2315-2 AUGSBURG FORTRESS PB $14.99

Heiko A. **Oberman**

Luther: Man Between God and the Devil

A brilliant biography by a leading Luther authority

0-385-42278-4 IMAGE PB $16.00

W.P. **Stephens**

Zwingli: An Introduction to His Thought

Study of the Swiss reformer Ulrich Zwingli (1481-1531). Readers should also consult the best account of Zwingli's life and thought in English: G.R. Potter's *Zwingli* (1976), which is out of print

0-19-826363-5 OXFORD PB $19.95

Demons, Witchcraft, and Magic

Bengt **Ankarloo** & Gustav **Henningsen**

Early Modern European Witchcraft

0-19-820388-8 OXFORD PB $19.95

Jonathan **Barry** & others, editors

Witchcraft in Early Modern Europe: Studies in Culture and Belief

Building on the pioneer work of Keith Thomas's *Religion and the Decline of Magic,* these essays explore issues of power, gender, and language, with examples from England, France, Germany, and the Spanish New World

0-521-55224-9 CAMBRIDGE $59.95

Anne Llewellyn **Barstow**

Witchcraze: A New History of the European Witch-Hunts

0-06-251036-3 HARPERCOLLINS PB $13.00

Robin **Briggs**

Witches and Neighbors: A History of European Witchcraft

0-670-83589-7 VIKING $32.95

Joan P. **Couliano**

Eros and Magic in the Renaissance

Magic as a manipulative psychology of motives, especially erotic ones

See also ROMANIAN LITERATURE under EASTERN EUROPEAN LITERATURE in LITERATURE OF EUROPE, AFRICA, AND ASIA

TRANSLATED BY MARGARET COOK

FOREWORD BY MIRCEA ELIADE

0-226-12315-4 CHICAGO $34.95
0-226-12316-2 CHICAGO PB $14.95

Carlo **Ginzburg**

The Cheese and the Worms: The Cosmos of a Sixteenth-Century Miller

A miller in Italy burned as a heretic under the Inquisition. "By the end of the book, the reader who has followed Dr. Ginzburg in his wanderings through the labyrinthine mind of the miller of Friuli will take leave of this strange and quirky old man with genuine regret" —*NY Review of Books*

TRANSLATED BY JOHN & ANNE TEDESCHI

0-8018-4387-1 JOHNS HOPKINS PB $13.95

Carlo **Ginzburg**

Ecstasies: Deciphering the Witches' Sabbath

Ginzburg, author of such brilliant earlier studies as *The Cheese and the Worms* and *Night Battles*, challenges the received wisdom on European witchcraft by positing an actual body of hidden belief

TRANSLATED BY RAYMOND ROSENTHAL

0-394-58163-6 PANTHEON $25.00

Night Battles: Witchcraft and Agrarian Cults in the Sixteenth and Seventeenth Centuries

The Inquisition's persecution of a simple peasant society deeply rooted in fertility cults

TRANSLATED BY JOHN & ANNE TEDESCHI

0-8018-4386-3 PENGUIN PB $13.95

R. Po-chia **Hsia**

The Myth of Ritual Murder: Jews and Magic in Reformation Germany

Throughout the 16th century, German Jews were persecuted for the alleged ritual murders of Christian children, whose blood was erroneously believed to have played a role in Jewish magical rites

0-300-04120-9 YALE $40.00
0-300-04746-0 YALE PB $15.00

Richard **Kieckhefer**

Magic in the Middle Ages

This comprehensive history from c. 500 to 1500 shows how magic served as a point of contact between the popular and elite classes. The chapter on necromancy is the book's most original

0-521-31202-7 CAMBRIDGE PB $14.95

Jules **Michelet**

Witchcraft, Sorcery and Superstition

A 19th-century classic and the grandfather of all books about witchcraft and its history

0-806-51686-0 CITADEL PB $12.95

Jeffrey Burton **Russell**

A History of Witchcraft: Sorcerers, Heretics and Pagans

See also THE OCCULT, WITCHCRAFT, AND THE DEVIL under WORLD RELIGION in RELIGION, SPIRITUALITY, AND PHILOSOPHY

0-8446-6052-3 SMITH $23.30
0-500-27242-5 THAMES & HUDSON PB $14.95

Early Modern Popular Culture

Peter **Burke**

Popular Culture in Early Modern Europe

0-06-131928-7 HARPERCOLLINS PB $21.60

Piero **Camporesi**

Bread of Dreams: Food and Fantasy in Early Modern Europe

How many poor and ordinary people lived in a state of permanent hallucination, drugged by hunger or by bread adulterated with hallucinogenic herbs or fungi

0-226-09257-7 CHICAGO $27.50

Alexandra Parma **Cook** & Noble David **Cook**

Good Faith and Truthful Ignorance: A Case of Transatlantic Bigamy

In 1557, after 20 years in Peru, Francisco Noguerol de Ulloa returned home to Spain with his second wife. Upon his arrival, he was charged with bigamy, arrested and jailed. Through their account of this singular incident, two scholars vividly reveal the 16th century as it was lived by the underclasses. "A remarkably juicy tale that opens a window onto daily life at the height of the conquest of the Americas" —Mary Talbott

0-8223-1086-4 DUKE $23.95
0-8223-1222-0 DUKE PB $14.95

Natalie Zemon **Davis**

Fiction in the Archives: Pardon Tales and Their Tellers in Sixteenth-Century France

"Her original and detailed exploration of the stories French men and women told to save their lives challenges the conventional boundaries between fiction and truth" —Stephen Greenblatt

See also EARLY MODERN FRANCE

0-8047-1799-0 STANFORD PB $13.95

Steven **Ozment**

The Burgermeister's Daughter: Scandal in a Sixteenth-Century German Town

In the tradition of Natalie Zemon Davis and Emmanuel LeRoy Ladurie, Ozment explores the private life history of a woman from the town of Hall in Swabia, Anna Buschler. "As we read Anna's pleading, passionate, arrogant letters, she becomes a recognizable person in an impossible but imaginable situation. Those few outpourings provide a splendid and very unusual entry into the private life of the distant past" —*NY Times Book Review*

0-312-13939-X ST. MARTIN'S $23.95

Three Behaim Boys: Growing up in Early Modern Germany, A Chronicle of Their Lives

0-300-04670-7 YALE $32.00
0-300-05133-6 YALE PB $16.00

Steven **Ozment**, editor

Magdalena and Balthasar: An Intimate Portrait of Life in Sixteenth-Century Europe Revealed in the Letters of a Nuremberg Husband and Wife

0-300-04378-3 YALE PB $12.00

Pamela H. **Smith**

The Business of Alchemy: Science and Culture in the Holy Roman Empire

A portrait of intellectual life in the late 17th-century Habsburg territories, in the tradition of the pioneering work of Frances Yates. "This is a really smart historian with an excellent first book who should be urged to write the next installment, and to grapple with German science as it developed in the subsequent century, in the process taking on the larger questions that make the cultural meanings of Western science fascinating"—Margaret C. Jacob, New School for Social Research

0-691-05691-9 PRINCETON $45.00

The Expansion of Europe: Empire and Commerce

For related reading, see US HISTORY TO THE CIVIL WAR in HISTORY OF THE AMERICAS

Exploration

Felipe **Fernandez-Armesto**

Columbus

A meticulously researched biography of the explorer, showing him as a self-taught social climber often at odds with his society, and charting his voyages and subsequent career as colonial administrator. With eight pages of illustrations and a chronology

0-19-215898-8 OXFORD $30.00

Samuel Eliot **Morison**

Admiral of the Ocean Sea: A Life of Christopher Columbus

The achievements and tribulations of the explorer

ILLUSTRATED BY ERWIN RAISZ & BERTRAM GREENE

0-316-58478-9 LITTLE, BROWN $24.95

Christopher Columbus

• Alfred W. **Crosby**

Ecological Imperialism: The Biological Expansion of Europe, 900-1900

0-521-32009-7 CAMBRIDGE $44.95
0-521-45690-8 CAMBRIDGE PB $12.95

Luciano **Formisano**, editor

Letters from a New World: Amerigo Vespucci's Discovery of America

First complete English translation of the letters of the cartographer who gave his name to the new world

TRANSLATED BY DAVID JACOBSON

0-941419-62-2 MARSILIO $24.00

Donald S. **Johnson**

Charting the Sea of Darkness: The Four Voyages of Henry Hudson

1-56836-105-X KODANSHA PB $14.00

J.H. **Parry**

The Age of Reconnaissance: Discovery, Exploration, and Settlement, 1450-1650

0-520-04235-2 CALIFORNIA PB $15.00

Antonio **Pigafetta**

The First Voyage Around the World, 1519-1522

Diary of a crew member of Magellan's historic voyage

1-56886-005-6 MARSILIO PB $16.95

The Colonial Empires

For related reading, see LATIN AMERICA AND THE CARIBBEAN in HISTORY OF THE AMERICAS

Clinton **Black**

Pirates of the West Indies

The life and times of ten of the Caribbean's most famous pirates, including the "prince of pirates" Henry Morgan; Edward Teach, alias Blackbeard; and "Calico Jack" Rackman and his accomplices Ann Bonney and Mary Read

0-521-35818-3 CAMBRIDGE PB $15.50

C.R. **Boxer**

The Dutch Seaborne Empire

In the 17th century the Dutch dominated trade. Ships traveled as far as modern-day New York and Nagasaki, and settlements were founded in Indonesia and South Africa

0-14-013618-5 PENGUIN PB $12.95

James C. **Boyajian**

Portuguese Trade in Asia Under the Habsburgs, 1580-1640

"A superbly researched work, rich in provocative and revisionist interpretation, whose sources, ideas, and references will be mined by historians"—*Canadial Journal of History*

0-8018-4405-3 JOHNS HOPKINS $48.95

Lyle N. **McAlister**

Spain and Portugal in the New World, 1492-1700

See also THE COLONIAL PERIOD under LATIN AMERICA AND THE CARIBBEAN in HISTORY OF THE AMERICAS

0-8166-1218-8 MINNESOTA PB $19.95

Stephen J. **Greenblatt**

Marvelous Possessions: The Wonder of the New World

An imaginative scholar's reconstruction of the way Europeans represented non-Europeans and took possession of their lands. Studying travel narratives, legal documents, and official reports, Greenblatt shows how the sense of wonder was harnessed to the process of appropriation

0-226-30651-8 CHICAGO $28.95
0-226-30652-6 CHICAGO PB $12.95

Stephen **Greenblatt**, editor

New World Encounters

0-520-08021-1 CALIFORNIA PB $15.95

Gert **Oostindle**, editor

Fifty Years Later: Antislavery, Capitalism and Modernity in the Dutch Orbit

"No aspect of the global history of slavery and emancipation has been so neglected and misunderstood as the 'case of the Dutch.' Gert Oostindle's volume of essays on the Dutch abolition of slavery from the Caribbean to the Cape Colony and Southeast Asia fills an immense black hole"—David Brion Davis

0-8229-5587-3 PITTSBURGH PB $22.50

J.H. **Parry**

The Spanish Seaborne Empire

A distinguished scholar looks at the first of the great seaborne empires of Western Europe and its impact on America. "Likely to remain the standard volume on the society created by the development and decline of the Spanish empire"—*NY Times Book Review*

0-520-07140-9 CALIFORNIA PB $14.00

Sanjay **Subrahmanyam**

The Portugese Empire in Asia, 1500-1700: A Political and Economic History

0-582-05068-5 LONGMAN PB $34.50

James D. **Tracy**, editor

The Political Economy of Merchant Empires: State Power and World Trade, 1350-1750

0-521-41046-0 CAMBRIDGE $69.95
0-521-57464-1 CAMBRIDGE PB $19.95

The Triumph of Capitalism

Jean **Baechler**, editor

Europe and the Rise of Capitalism

Essays addressing one of the great historical questions: Why did massive social and economic development take place in Western Europe rather than in other comparably advanced civilizations in early modern times?

0-631-16942-3 BLACKWELL PB $22.95

J. **De Vries**

The Economy of Europe in an Age of Crisis: 1600-1750

0-521-29050-3 CAMBRIDGE PB $18.95

Rodney **Hilton** & Maurice **Dobb**

The Transition from Feudalism to Capitalism

Participants in the "transition debate" of the early 1950s include Maurice Dobb, Paul Sweezy, and Christopher Hill. Their contributions are reprinted here, along with essays by Pierre Vilar and Eric Hobsbawm

0-312-81454-2 ST. MARTIN'S $39.95
0-86091-701-0 VERSO PB $17.95

Albert O. **Hirschman**

The Passions and the Interests: Political Arguments for Capitalism Before Its Triumph

The debate over the justification of economic gain (and hence capitalism) in this era

See also **ECONOMIC DEVELOPMENT AND INTERNATIONAL TRADE** under **ECONOMICS** in **SOCIAL STUDIES**

0-691-00357-2 PRINCETON PB $12.95

Fernand Braudel

Braudel's *The Mediterranean World in The Age of Phillip II*, partly written while he was held as a prisoner of war by the Nazis, was published in 1949 and remains one of the century's seminal works of history. Braudel and the French *Annales* school with which he was associated, helped turn historians' attention from traditional political and military studies to the consideration of large scale structural determinants of change and social history. Braudel's *The Identity of France* is, unfortunately, currently out of print.

Fernand **Braudel**

The Mediterranean and the Mediterranean World in the Age of Philip II

A magisterial example of *Annales* history, stressing the importance of geography, climate, and population as influences on political and military events and culminating in the struggle for mastery in the Mediterranean between Turks and Spaniards

Volume 1

0-520-20308-9 CALIFORNIA PB $19.95

No region of the Mediterranean was free from the scourge. Catalonia, Calabria and Albania, all notorious regions in this respect, by no means had a monopoly of brigandage. It cropped up everywhere in various guises, political, social, economic, terrorist; at the gates of Alexandria in Egypt or of Damascus and Aleppo; in the countryside round Naples, where watch towers were built to warn of brigands and in the Roman Campagna, where brush fires were sometimes ordered to smoke out bands of robbers who found abundant cover there; even in a state so apparently well-policed as Venice. When the sultan's army marched along the Stambul road to Adrianople, Nis, Belgrade and on into Hungary, it left behind along the roadside seams of hanged brigands whom it had disturbed in their lairs.
THE MEDITERRANEAN AND THE MEDITERRANEAN WORLD IN THE AGE OF PHILIP II

Volume 2

0-520-20330-5 CALIFORNIA PB $19.95

Civilization and Capitalism, 15th-18th Century,

Volume 1: The Structures of Everyday Life

0-520-08114-5 CALIFORNIA PB $24.95

Volume 2: The Wheels of Commerce

0-520-08115-3 CALIFORNIA PB $24.95

A History of Civilizations

First written in 1962 and denounced for its anti-ethnocentric approach, Braudel's study is now seen as a paradigm of modern scholarship. The first serious work to expand the scope of inquiry beyond events, dates, and personages to view the sweeping continuities and patterns of civilization since the eighth century

See also **WORLD HISTORIES** under **THE VARIETIES OF CIVILIZATION**

0-14-012489-6 PENGUIN PB $14.95

On History

The most famous member of the *Annales* school discusses the method used in such works as *The Structures of Everyday Life*

See also **THE GREAT TRADITION** under **HISTORIOGRAPHY**

TRANSLATED BY SARAH MATTHEWS

0-226-07151-0 CHICAGO PB $11.95

The Perspective of the World

0-520-08116-1 CALIFORNIA PB $24.95

The Thirty Years' War, 1618-1648

A series of protracted wars, the Thirty Years' War was something of a European civil war between the Habsburg Empire and other powers. It consisted of four phases: the Bohemian (1618-1625), the Danish (1625-1629), the Swedish (1630-1635), and the Swedish-French (1635-1648). Is it an accident that it peaked—as did the English Civil War—at the same time as the fall of the Ming dynasty in China (1644)? From Bourbon France to Tokugawa Japan, Europe and Asia experienced a midcentury upheaval that some historians call "the crisis of the 17th century."

Geoffrey **Parker**, editor

The Thirty Years' War

A valuable collection of essays

0-415-02534-6 ROUTLEDGE PB $17.95

Geoffrey **Parker** & Lesley M. **Smith**, editors

The General Crisis of the Seventeenth Century

Essays in the debate over the existence and nature of a political and economic "general crisis" in Europe in the 17th century

0-7102-0545-7 ROUTLEDGE PB $22.00

J.V. **Polisensky**

War and Society in Europe, 1618-1648

0-521-21659-1 CAMBRIDGE $64.95

B.F. **Porshnev**
Muscovy and Sweden in the Thirty Years' War, 1630-1655
The first English translation of important writings on the other Thirty Years War by a major Soviet historian
TRANSLATED BY BRIAN PEARCE
EDITED BY PAUL DUKES
0-521-45139-6 CAMBRIDGE $54.95

Henrik **Tikkanen**
The Thirty Years' War
TRANSLATED BY GEORGE & L.T. BLECHER
0-8032-9407-7 NEBRASKA PB $8.95

Spain: Golden Age and Decline

James S. **Amelang**
Honored Citizens of Barcelona: Patrician Culture and Class Relations, 1490-1714
How the Catalan feudal aristocracy merged with the urban oligarchy to form a civil ruling class; published in 1986
0-691-05461-4 PRINCETON $39.50

James S. **Amelang**, translator & editor
A Journal of the Plague Year: The Diary of the Barcelona Tanner Miquel Parets, 1651
An engrossing eyewitness account of the devastating epidemic that killed at least 15,000 people in Barcelona in 1651. The journal offers an unusual glimpse of an ordinary citizen caught up in public disaster
0-19-506455-0 OXFORD $29.95

Just think about a person who, during other sickness, was taken care of by his or her spouse, and was able to see his relatives and friends, and was given everything he needed. And then you see the same person during the plague being nursed by a stranger with no love for him, or perhaps never seen or known by him before, and he had to receive everything from this person without being consoled by any other. And many times all this nurse did was to make the patient die more quickly, because the sooner he died the sooner the nurse got the 18 to 20 pounds or however much they had agreed on for the quarantine, and then the nurse would be free to go elsewhere.
A JOURNAL OF THE PLAGUE YEAR: THE DIARY OF THE BARCELONA TANNER MIQUEL PARETS, 1651

Marina S. **Brownlee** & Hans Ulrich **Gumbrecht**, editors
Cultural Authority in the Golden Age of Spain
0-8018-4937-3 JOHNS HOPKINS PB $16.95

Marcelin **Defourneaux**
Daily Life in Spain in the Golden Age
TRANSLATED BY NEWTON BRANCH
0-8047-1036-8 STANFORD $39.50
0-8047-1029-5 STANFORD PB $14.95

Cervantes

J. H. **Elliott**
The Count-Duke of Olivares: The Statesman in an Age of Decline
Don Gaspar de Gusman, count-duke of Olivares, right-hand adviser to Philip IV and archrival of Richelieu. "The finest biography ever written on a Spanish statesman"
—Raymond Carr, *NY Review of Books*
0-300-04499-2 YALE PB $22.00

Imperial Spain: 1469-1716
The essential work in English on this period by the leading authority
0-14-013517-0 PENGUIN PB $12.95

Carlos **Fuentes**
The Buried Mirror: Reflections on Spain and the New World
Turning his novelist's eye to history, Fuentes provides a fascinating view of Hispanic culture on both sides of the Atlantic. Rich in both metaphor and historical detail, this perceptively illustrated volume brings a remarkable heritage and present-day culture alive. "Fuentes has written what may be the freshest and most inspiring Quincentennial history"
—Washington Post
0-395-67281-3 HOUGHTON MIFFLIN PB $29.95

A.W. **Lovett**
Early Habsburg Spain, 1517-1598
A very useful study of the reigns of Charles V and Philip II, published in 1986
0-19-822138-X OXFORD PB $24.95

John **Lynch**
Bourbon Spain, 1700-1808
After a startling collapse in the second half of the 17th century, Spain made an economic and cultural comeback. "Takes its place as the best general book in any language on the Spanish eighteenth century"
—J.H. Elliott, *NY Review of Books*
0-631-14576-1 BLACKWELL $64.95

Cecil **Roth**
The Spanish Inquisition
0-393-00255-1 NORTON PB $11.95

Helen **Nader**
Liberty in Absolutist Spain: The Habsburg Sale of Towns, 1516-1700
Focuses on the significance of municipal government in Spain and the consequences of the practice of selling towns their independence as a fund-raising gimmick
0-8018-4731-1 JOHNS HOPKINS PB $19.95

Norman **Roth**
Conversos, Inquisition, and the Expulsion of the Jews from Spain
See also **THE MIDDLE AGES** under **JEWISH HISTORY**
0-299-14230-2 WISCONSIN $50.00

The Spanish Armada

Spain's abortive invasion of England in 1588 helped to spell an end to Spanish Imperial hegemony over Europe. It also proved a defining event in the nationalist mythology of England.

Felipe **Fernandez-Armesto**
The Spanish Armada: The Experience of War in 1588
0-19-285196-9 OXFORD $12.95

Colin **Martin** & Geoffrey **Parker**
The Spanish Armada
0-393-30926-6 NORTON PB $11.95

Peter **Padfield**
Armada: A Celebration of the Four Hundredth Anniversary of the Defeat of the Spanish Armada, 1588-1988
0-87021-006-8 NAVAL INSTITUTE $29.95

Peter **Pierson**
Commander of the Armada: The Seventh Duke of Medina Sidonia
0-300-04408-9 YALE $35.00

Early Modern France

William **Beik**
Absolutism and Society in Seventeenth-Century France: State Power and Provincial Aristocracy in Languedoc
0-521-36782-4 CAMBRIDGE PB $21.95

David **Buisseret**
Henry IV
Flippantly remarking that "Paris is worth a mass," Henry converted to Catholicism, bringing the Bourbons to the throne in 1589 and establishing a dynasty that would rule, not without interruption, until 1830
0-04-445635-2 UNWIN HYMAN PB $17.95

James B. **Collins**

The State in Early Modern France

Graduate-level analysis from an expert on fiscal policy in the age of Henry IV and Louis XIII; part of the New Approaches to European History Series

0-521-38724-8 CAMBRIDGE PB $15.95

Natalie Zemon **Davis**

Fiction in the Archives: Pardon Tales and Their Tellers in Sixteenth-Century France

"Her original and detailed exploration of the stories French men and women told to save their lives challenges the conventional boundaries between fiction and truth" —Stephen Greenblatt

See also EARLY MODERN POPULAR CULTURE

0-8047-1799-0 STANFORD PB $13.95

The Return of Martin Guerre

"One can only admire Natalie Davis for the major work of historical reconstruction she has performed without any kind of ideological bias...The movie was great but Natalie Davis' book is even better"—Emmanuel LeRoy Ladurie, *NY Review of Books*

0-674-76691-1 HARVARD PB $12.00

Society and Culture in Early Modern France

Eight essays from the social historian at Princeton

0-8047-0868-1 STANFORD $49.50
0-8047-0972-6 STANFORD PB $17.95

Barbara B. **Diefendorf**

Paris City Councillors in the Sixteenth Century: The Politics of Patrimony

The social and economic process that made houses and miniature castles fashionable

0-691-05362-6 PRINCETON $47.50

Lucien **Febvre**

Life in Renaissance France

A splendid account of life at the court of Francis I (1515-1547), and of the new aristocracy of parvenus by the great 20th-century French historian

TRANSLATED BY MARIAN ROTHSTEIN

0-674-53180-9 HARVARD PB $11.95

The Problem of Unbelief in the Sixteenth Century: The Religion of Rabelais

TRANSLATED BY BEATRICE GOTTLIEB

0-674-70826-1 HARVARD PB $23.50

Mack P. **Holt**

The French Wars of Religion, 1562-1629

A compact study that draws on the latest scholarship

0-521-35873-6 CAMBRIDGE PB $15.95

Emmanuel LeRoy **Ladurie**

The Ancien Regime: A History of France, 1610-1770

TRANSLATED BY MARK GREENGRASS

0-631-17028-6 BLACKWELL $52.95

Robert M. **Kingdon**

Myths About the St. Bartholomew's Day Massacres, 1572-1576

How the new medium of print was used by Protestants to perpetuate the myths and propaganda that helped shape reaction to the catastrophe

0-674-59831-8 HARVARD $37.00

Ruth **Kleinman**

Anne of Austria: Queen of France

Louis XIII's wife, Louis XIV's mother, Cardinal Mazarin's secret lover. "Traditionally scholars have dismissed Anne as almost a nonentity—lazy, fat, stupid, and of little influence in the government. Kleinman offers convincing revisions of each of these assumptions"—*Choice*

0-8142-0429-5 OHIO STATE PB $24.50

R.J. **Knecht**

Francis I

Contemporary of Henry VIII, Charles V, and Suleiman the Magnificent, this king presided over Renaissance France. "A model of what a dense historical biography should be" —*Times* (London)

0-521-27887-2 CAMBRIDGE PB $24.95

Renaissance Warrior and Patron: The Reign of Francis I

0-521-57885-X CAMBRIDGE PB $27.95

Robert **Mandrou**

Introduction to Modern France, 1500-1640: An Essay in Historical Psychology

More from the *Annales* school and its interpretation of the *mentalité,* or collective outlook, of different classes

TRANSLATED BY R.E. HALLMARK

0-8419-0245-3 HOLMES & MEIER $35.00

Louis **Marin**

Portrait of the King

The images and symbols of royalty, from a historian and semiotician

TRANSLATED BY MARTHA M. HOULE

0-8166-1603-5 MINNESOTA $39.95

A. Lloyd **Moote**

Louis XIII, The Just

The hapless monarch of Dumas' *The Three Musketeers* in a new biography. "A powerfully convincing portrait of one of the most inarticulate kings in European history" —Orest Ranum

0-520-06485-2 CALIFORNIA $55.00

Roland **Mousnier**

The Institutions of France Under the Absolute Monarchy, 1598-1789

Challenges both Marxist and *Annales* writers by arguing that the need for greater revenues, due to constant warfare, forced the monarchy to move from a system of administration in which offices were owned

Volume 1 Society and the State

0-226-54327-7 CHICAGO $55.00

Volume 2 The Organs of State and Society

0-226-54328-5 CHICAGO $66.00

Nancy Lyman **Roelker**

One King, One Faith

Argues that not only the body politic but the body social was defined by Gallic Catholicism. "Will be the definitive work on the Parlement in the Reformation and Wars of Religion"—Orest Ranum

0-520-08626-0 CALIFORNIA $65.00

Queen of Navarre, Jeanne D'albret, 1528-1572

0-674-74150-1 HARVARD $42.50

J.H. **Salmon**

Renaissance and Revolt: Essays in the Intellectual and Social History of Early France

0-521-32769-5 CAMBRIDGE $85.00

David **Thomson**

Renaissance Paris

An architectural history

0-520-05347-8 CALIFORNIA $47.50
0-520-05359-1 CALIFORNIA PB $18.95

Frances **Yates**

French Academies of the Sixteenth Century

0-7102-1373-5 ROUTLEDGE $45.00

Louis XIV and the Ancien Régime

Lenin wrote that the old regime has no beginning, only an end. And for Tocqueville, two generations before him, the roots of the great French Revolution were to be located in the centralizing power of Louis XIV's efficiently run state.

Maurice **Ashley**

Louis XIV and the Greatness of France

0-02-901080-2 FREE PRESS PB $14.95

Nancy Nichols **Barker**

Brother to the Sun King: Philippe, Duke of Orleans

0-8018-3791-X JOHNS HOPKINS $45.00

David A. **Bell**

Lawyers and Citizens: The Making of a Political Elite in Old Regime France

An important new study by a Yale historian

0-19-507670-2 OXFORD $45.00

Nancy **Milford**

The Sun King

A lively, popular account

0-140-23967-7 PENGUIN $10.95

Paul Freart **de Chantelou**

Diary of the Cavaliere: Bernini's Visit to France in 1665

The 66-year-old Bernini arrived in Paris commissioned to redesign the Louvre. Chantelou, assigned by the king to attend him, kept a diary of the visit

0-691-04028-1 PRINCETON $54.50

Daniel **Gordon**

Citizens Without Sovereignty: Equality and Sociability in French Thought, 1670-1789

Reveals some of the profound flaws of the *ancien régime* state

0-691-05699-4 PRINCETON $39.50

Pierre **Goubert**

The French Peasantry in the Seventeenth Century

TRANSLATED BY IAN PATTERSON

0-521-26007-8 CAMBRIDGE $59.95

0-521-31269-8 CAMBRIDGE PB $18.95

Louis XIV and Twenty Million Frenchmen

Rather than focusing on the glitter of Versailles, an *Annales* historian portrays the ordinary men and women of the age

0-394-71751-1 RANDOM HOUSE PB $10.00

John **Hardman**

French Politics, 1774-1789: From the Ascension of Louis XVI to the Bastille

By the author of *Louis XVI*

0-582-23649-5 LONGMAN PB $27.92

Julian **Swann**

Politics and the Parlement of Paris Under Louis XV, 1754-1774

0-521-48362-X CAMBRIDGE PB $29.95

Voltaire

Jonathan D. **Spence**

The Question of Hu

The story of one man who came from China to France in the 1720s

See also **CHINA AND THE WEST** under **CULTURE, SOCIETY, AND ECONOMY** under **TOPICS IN IMPERIAL CIVILIZATION** under **CHINA**

0-679-72580-6 VINTAGE PB $14.00

The Netherlands

Herbert H. **Rowen**

John De Witt: Statesman of the True Freedom

0-521-30391-5 CAMBRIDGE $59.95

The Princes of Orange: The Stadholders in the Dutch Republic

First published in 1988

0-521-39653-0 CAMBRIDGE PB $18.95

Austria and the German-Speaking States

Derek **Beales**

Joseph II: In the Shadow of Theresa, 1741-1780

The apprenticeship of "the most radical of the enlightened despots" traces the development of Joseph's strange personality; the first of two planned volumes, the second due out late 1997

0-521-24240-1 CAMBRIDGE $90.00

Gordon A. **Craig**

The Politics of the Prussian Army, 1640-1945

A pioneer study of 1955 arguing against the popular belief that "the Germans are by nature subservient to authority, militaristic, and aggressive." For Craig these qualities "are not inherent in the German character but are rather—as Franz Neumann has written—'products of a structure which vitiated the attempts to create a viable democracy' "

0-19-500257-1 OXFORD PB $19.95

Christopher **Duffy**

Frederick the Great: A Military Life

Solid military history with superb battle maps and tactical analysis

0-415-00276-1 ROUTLEDGE PB $19.95

Nancy **Milford**

Frederick the Great

A vivid re-creation of Frederick's life

0-140-03653-9 PENGUIN $10.95

Gerhard **Ritter**

Frederick the Great: A Historical Profile

Not a biography but a series of essays; this translation is based on the third edition of 1954

TRANSLATED WITH AN INTRODUCTION BY PETER PARET

0-520-02775-2 CALIFORNIA PB $13.00

Margaret **Shennan**

The Rise of Brandenburg-Prussia

How the energetic Hohenzollern rulers raised a small frontier state into a world-class power

0-415-12938-9 ROUTE PB $9.95

Frederick the Great

The Ottoman Empire

For related reading, see THE ISLAMIC WORLD TO WORLD WAR I

Norman **Itzkowitz**

Ottoman Empire and Islamic Tradition

See also **THE RISE AND FALL OF THE OTTOMANS** under **THE ISLAMIC WORLD TO WORLD WAR I**

0-226-38806-9 CHICAGO PB $8.95

Lord **Kinross**

The Ottoman Centuries: The Rise and Fall of the Turkish Empire

The best one-volume history by the man Arnold Toynbee calls "a master of character-drawing and a master of narrative"

See also **THE RISE AND FALL OF THE OTTOMANS** under **THE ISLAMIC WORLD TO WORLD WAR I**

0-688-08093-6 MORROW PB $14.95

Bernard **Lewis**

The Muslim Discovery of Europe

A great historian uses journals, letters, diaries, dispatches, and books to reveal a 700-year-old relationship

0-393-30233-4 NORTON PB $13.95

Brummett **Palmira**

Ottoman Seapower and Levantine Diplomacy in the Age of Discovery

0-7914-1702-6 SUNY PB $21.95

Peter F. **Sugar**
Southeastern Europe Under Ottoman Rule, 1354-1804
0-295-96033-7 WASHINGTON PB........................$25.00

The Scientific Revolution

The scientific revolution did more than dislodge the earth from the astronomic centrality it had held since antiquity. By Newton's death in 1725, the scientific method had become firmly established as a means of seeking truth. It was widely believed that the universe was governed by uniform laws that the human mind could ascertain. From there it was a short step to the Enlightenment and the discovery of similar laws for human society as well.

For related reading, see SCIENCE AND TECHNOLOGY in SCIENCE

Marie **Boas**
Scientific Renaissance, 1450-1630
Excellent on the relation of magic to science and in its treatment of Galileo's trial
See also **THE SCIENTIFIC REVOLUTION** under **HISTORY OF SCIENCE AND TECHNOLOGY** under **SCIENCE AND TECHNOLOGY** in **SCIENCE**
0-486-28115-9 DOVER PB........................$10.95

I. Bernard **Cohen**
The Birth of a New Physics
A terse survey of astronomy from Copernicus to Newton. Students with some math will profit from the extensive formulas and diagrams
0-393-01994-2 NORTON........................$19.95
0-393-30045-5 NORTON PB........................$10.95

Thomas **Goldstein**
The Dawn of Modern Science: From the Arabs to Leonardo Da Vinci
See also **ANCIENT AND MEDIEVAL SCIENCE** under **HISTORY OF SCIENCE AND TECHNOLOGY** under **SCIENCE AND TECHNOLOGY** in **SCIENCE**
0-306-80637-1 DA CAPO PB........................$14.95

Margaret **Jacob**
The Cultural Meaning of the Scientific Revolution
The road from the scientific to the industrial revolution
See also **THE SCIENTIFIC REVOLUTION** under **HISTORY OF SCIENCE AND TECHNOLOGY** under **SCIENCE AND TECHNOLOGY** in **SCIENCE**
0-07-554361-3 MCGRAW HILL PB........................$21.75

Alexandre **Koyre**
From the Closed World to the Infinite Universe
0-8018-0347-0 JOHNS HOPKINS PB........................$15.95

Thomas **Kuhn**
The Copernican Revolution
A outstanding account of the impact of the revolution in astronomy by the author of *The Structure of Scientific Revolutions*
See also **HISTORY OF ASTRONOMY** under **ASTRONOMY** in **SCIENCE**
0-674-17103-9 HARVARD PB........................$12.95

The Structure of Scientific Revolutions
0-295-96033-7 UCHTR........................$10.95

Galileo and Newton

Galileo **Galilei**
Dialogues Concerning Two New Chief World Systems, Ptolemaic and Copernican
See also **HISTORY OF PHYSICS** under **PHYSICS** in **SCIENCE**
0-520-00450-7 CALIFORNIA PB........................$17.95

Mario **Biagioli**
Galileo, Courtier: The Practice of Science in the Culture of Absolutism
Galileo as scheming baroque courtier. "An entirely plausible portrait, argued with vigor, swagger, and immense knowledge of Italian court culture. This fashionably 'self-fashioning' Galileo suits our academic times"
—Steven Shapin, UC, San Diego
0-226-04559-5 CHICAGO........................$32.95

Maurice A. **Finocchiaro**, translator
The Galileo Affair: A Documentary History
Galileo was tried and condemned as a heretic by the Inquisition in 1633, an episode in the history of science that remains a subject of controversy
See also **BIOGRAPHIES AND AUTOBIOGRAPHIES** under **PHYSICS** in **SCIENCE**
0-520-06662-6 CALIFORNIA PB........................$16.00

Pietro **Redondi**
Galileo: Heretic
"Redondi places before us not just Galileo but the entire milieu that surrounded the dispute of the 'new science' during a crucial twenty-year period of the 17th century"—Italo Calvino
See also **BIOGRAPHIES AND AUTOBIOGRAPHIES** under **PHYSICS** in **SCIENCE**
TRANSLATED BY RAYMOND ROSENTHAL
0-691-08451-3 PRINCETON........................$49.50
0-691-02426-X PRINCETON PB........................$17.95

Galileo

Michael **Sharratt**
Galileo: Decisive Innovator
An entertaining biography of the Inquisition's most dazzling victim
0-521-56671-1 CAMBRIDGE PB........................$18.95

Gale **Christianson**
In the Presence of the Creator: Isaac Newton and His Times
See also **BIOGRAPHIES AND AUTOBIOGRAPHIES** under **PHYSICS** in **SCIENCE**
0-02-905190-8 FREE PRESS........................$29.95

A. Rupert **Hall**
Isaac Newton: Adventurer in Thought
An absorbing biography of Isaac Newton (1642-1727), historian, theologian, chemist, civil servant, natural philosopher—and mathematician. Argues that Newton cannot simply be explained as a Platonist or mystic
0-521-56669-X CAMBRIDGE PB........................$19.95

Newton

Richard S. **Westfall**
Never at Rest: A Biography of Isaac Newton
A masterful rendering, from his absorption with Christian chronology to his tenure as master of the British Mint
See also **BIOGRAPHIES AND AUTOBIOGRAPHIES** under **PHYSICS** in **SCIENCE**
0-521-27435-4 CAMBRIDGE PB........................$36.95

The Age of Enlightenment

Though France was certainly its epicenter, the Enlightenment was a cosmopolitan movement, disrespectful of national boundaries. By the 1770s, to be "enlightened" meant to be in the forefront of intellectual thought throughout the Western world.

For related reading, see PHILOSOPHY in RELIGION, SPIRITUALITY, AND PHILOSOPHY

Harvey **Chisick**
The Limits of Reform in the Enlightenment
0-691-05305-7 PRINCETON........................$49.50

Gerald **Cragg**

The Church and the Age of Reason

0-14-013761-0 VIKING PB $12.95

Maurice William **Cranston**

The Solitary Self: Jean-Jacques Rousseau in Exile and Adversity

0-226-11865-7 CHICAGO $29.95

Robert **Darnton**

The Business of Enlightenment: A Publishing History of the Encyclopédie, 1775-1800

One of several important books from a historian whose intriguing approach has shed new light on 18th-century France

0-674-08785-2 HARVARD $42.50
0-674-08786-0 HARVARD PB $14.95

The Forbidden Best-Sellers of Pre-Revolutionary France

0-393-31442-1 NORTON PB $14.95

The Great Cat Massacre

A venture into popular culture in the Enlightenment age, which tells a good deal about the collective mentality of the working and other classes

0-394-72927-7 RANDOM HOUSE PB $13.00

The Kiss of Lamourette: Reflections in Cultural History

Essays ranging from the meaning of the French Revolution to the presence of the past in Poland's Solidarity movement. By the witty and entertaining Princeton historian and author of *The Great Cat Massacre*

0-393-02753-8 NORTON PB $19.95

The Literary Underground of the Old Regime

The underbelly of the Enlightenment: how Grub Street served as the ideological precursor of the radicalism of the Great Revolution

0-674-53656-8 HARVARD $27.00
0-674-53657-6 HARVARD PB $9.95

Perhaps the most outspoken *libelle*—a pamphlet so sensational and so widely read that it became virtually a prototype of the genre—was the work that especially horrified Voltaire: *Le Gazetier cuirassé* by Charles Theveneau de Morande. Morande mixed specific calumny and general declamation in brief, punchy paragraphs, which anticipated the style of gossip columnists in the modern yellow press. He promised to reveal "behind-the-scenes secrets" *(secrets des coulisses)* in the tradition of the *chronique scandaleuse*. But he provided more than scandal…

This sexual sensationalism conveyed a social message: the aristocracy had degenerated to the point of being unable to reproduce itself; the great nobles were either impotent or deviant; their wives were forced to seek satisfaction from their servants, representatives of the more virile lower classes; and everywhere among *les grands* incest and venereal disease had extinguished the last sparks of humanity.

THE LITERARY UNDERGROUND OF THE OLD REGIME

Mesmerism and the End of the Enlightenment in France

0-674-56950-4 HARVARD $20.00
0-674-56951-2 HARVARD PB $12.95

Arthur **Donovan**

Antoine Lavoisier: Science, Administration and Revolution

An accessible account that devotes equal attention to the development of Lavoisier's oxygen theory of combustion and to his efforts as a public administrator before and during the French Revolution

0-521-56672-X CAMBRIDGE PB $24.95

Peter **Gay**

The Enlightenment: An Interpretation

A massive compendium of the ideas of major and minor figures revolving around the theme of their devaluation of the culture of classical antiquity

Volume 1 The Rise of Modern Paganism

0-393-00870-3 NORTON PB $15.95

Volume 2 The Science of Freedom

0-393-00875-4 NORTON PB $16.95

Jean Marie **Goulemot**

Forbidden Texts: Erotic Literature and Its Readers in 18th Century France

0-8122-3319-0 PENNSYLVANIA $32.95

Norman **Hampson**

The Enlightenment: An Evaluation of Its Assumptions, Attitudes and Values

Argues that the Enlightenment set out to free mankind from superstition and pessimism and establish a reasonable world experiment and progress. Yet by 1760, in the works of Rousseau, Kant, and Goethe, there was a new awareness of self that had eluded their predecessors

0-14-013745-9 PENGUIN PB $12.00

Isaac **Kramnick**, editor

The Portable Enlightenment Reader

Includes writings by Kant, Diderot, Voltaire, Newton, Rousseau, Locke, Franklin, Jefferson, Madison, and Paine, among others

0-14-024566-9 PENGUIN PB $14.95

George **Rude**

Europe in the Eighteenth Century: Aristocracy and the Bourgeois Challenge

A succinct account of institutions, economies, war, and the circulation of ideas in terms of social pressures and needs. Rude pays particular attention to the role of popular protest as a factor of change

0-674-26921-7 HARVARD PB $15.95

Barbara Maria **Stafford**

Artful Science: Enlightenment Entertainment and the Eclipse of Visual Education

A learned reworking of the 18th century. Celebrates the role of visual play and sees "the multiple, multiform images of the new computer era not as the end of rational thought but rather as the revival of a tradition that was repressed by the nineteenth-century victory of print culture"

—David Vincent, *American Historical Review*

0-262-69181-7 MIT PB $20.00

Franco **Venturi**

The End of the Old Regime in Europe, 1768-1776

From the Greek uprising of 1770 and the Pugachev revolt in Russia to the crisis of reform in France and the outbreak of the American Revolution. "Venturi presents a panorama of Europe during the critical years when the Old Regime in many countries drifted toward its end. The skillful and fluent translation by Burr Litchfield makes the book a pleasure to read"

—R.R. Palmer

TRANSLATED BY R. BURR LITCHFIELD

0-691-05564-5 PRINCETON $60.00

Isser **Woloch**

Eighteenth Century Europe: Tradition and Progress, 1715-1789

0-393-95214-2 NORTON PB $12.95

Samia I. **Spencer**, editor

French Women and the Age of Enlightenment

See also **MODERN EUROPEAN HISTORY** under **EUROPEAN HISTORY** under **WOMEN'S STUDIES** in **SOCIAL STUDIES**

INTRODUCTION BY ELIZABETH FOX-GENOVESE

0-253-32481-5 INDIANA $45.00
0-253-20725-8 INDIANA PB $6.95

Lindsay **Wilson**

Women and Medicine in the French Enlightenment: The Debate over Maladies des Femmes

The discrepancy between the soaring aspirations of professional knowledge and its fractured achievements in practice

0-8018-4438-X JOHNS HOPKINS $39.95

The Thought of the Philosophes

Carl **Becker**

The Heavenly City of the Eighteenth-Century Philosophers

A provocative essay from the 1920s that portrays the 18th-century writers as utopians substituting their own cosmogony and dogma for the older Christian ones; faulted by many commentators for giving inadequate credit to the philosophers for their pragmatism, but still a pleasure to read

0-300-00017-0 YALE PB $13.00

A. Owen **Aldridge**

Voltaire and the Century of Light

0-691-06287-0 PRINCETON $67.50

Ernst **Cassirer**

The Philosophy of the Enlightenment

Powerful insights derived from considerations of specific figures from Bayle to Kant

TRANSLATED BY F. KOELIN & J. PETTEGROVE

0-691-01963-0 PRINCETON PB $16.95

The Enlightenment: A Sampler

Marie Jean **Condorcet**

Sketch For a Historical Picture of the Progress of the Human Mind

0-88355-838-6 HYPERION $25.00

Denis **Diderot**

Rameau's Nephew and D'Alembert's Dream

Two of Diderot's most famous works in one volume

TRANSLATED BY LEONARD TANCOCK

0-14-044173-5 PENGUIN PB $10.95

Thomas **Jefferson**

Writings

A comprehensive gathering of Jefferson's remarkably varied writings, including *Autobiography, A Summary View of the Rights of British America, Public Papers, Miscellany*, and a large selection of letters. The letters in particular create a three-dimensional and often surprising portrait. Jefferson envisioned a nation of prosperous farmers who he thought were far more likely than city-dwellers to cultivate the virtues of self-reliance, hard work, moderation, and common sense on which a free society depends

0-940450-16-X VIKING $35.00

Jean-Jacques **Rousseau**

The Essential Rousseau

Includes Rousseau's *Social Contract, Discourse on Inequality, Discourse on Arts and Sciences*, and *The Creed of a Savoyard Priest*

TRANSLATED BY LOWELL BAIR

ILLUSTRATED BY MATTHEW JOSEPHSON

0-452-01031-4

NEW AMERICAN LIBRARY PB $12.95

Voltaire

The Portable Voltaire

Including *Candide* (Part 1), *Zadig Micromegas, The Story of a Good Brahmin*, selections from the *Philosophical Dictionary, The English Letters, The Lisbon Earthquake, Essay on the Manners and Spirit of Nations*, and 35 selected letters

EDITED BY BEN R. REDMAN

0-14-015041-2 VIKING PB $14.95

Laurence **Dickey**

Hegel: Religion, Economics, and the Politics of Spirit, 1770-1807

Argues that Hegel's work is best understood in the context of the eighteenth-century liberalization of German Protestantism

0-521-38912-7 CAMBRIDGE PB $24.95

Peter **Gay**

Voltaire's Politics

0-300-04095-4 YALE PB $21.00

Knud **Haakonssen**, editor

Enlightenment and Religion: Rational Dissent in Eighteenth-Century Britian

Fresh, interdisciplinary essays on English Enlightenment culture; contributors include R.K. Webb, Alan Saunders, and Iain McCalman

0-521-56060-8 CAMBRIDGE $59.95

Jean **Le Rond d'Alembert**

Preliminary Discourse to the Encyclopedia of Diderot

0-226-13476-8 CHICAGO PB $10.95

Julien **Offray de La Mettrie**

La Mettrie: Machine Man & Other Writings

A new translation of *Machine Man* by La Mettrie (1709-1751), the most uncompromising of the 18th-century materialists, along with his most important other philosophical works, translated into English for the first time

EDITED BY ANN THOMSON

0-521-47849-9 CAMBRIDGE PB $18.95

Ira **Wade**

The Structure and Form of the French Enlightenment

Volume 1 Esprit Philosophique

0-691-05256-5 PRINCETON $85.00

Volume 2 Esprit Revolutionnaire

0-691-05257-3 PRINCETON $55.00

Style, Fashion, and Food

Anne **Hollander**

Sex and Suits

The art critic and author (*Moving Pictures*) brings her piercing eye to bear on the history of women's clothing from the late Middle Ages to the present. "This iconoclastic, continually stimulating essay argues that women's clothes, even after 1800, slavishly echoed ancient, traditional sartorial custom; modernizing women's clothing has meant copying men's garments, directly or indirectly"
—*Publishers Weekly*

See also **HISTORY OF FASHION** under **FASHION AND COSTUME** in **ARCHITECTURE, DESIGN, AND HOMES**

1-56836-101-7 KODANSHA PB $13.00

Leora **Auslander**

Taste and Power: Furnishing Modern France

Louis XIV, regency, rococo, neoclassical, empire, art nouveau: the changing meaning of furniture from the mid-17th century to World War I. A rich book about many things

See also **FRENCH FURNITURE** under **FURNITURE** under **EUROPEAN DECORATIVE ARTS** in **ARCHITECTURE, DESIGN, AND HOMES**

0-520-08894-8 CALIFORNIA $40.00

Jonathan **Brown**

Kings and Connoisseurs: Collecting Art in 17th-Century Europe

0-691-04497-X PRINCETON $49.50

Claire **Farago**, editor

Reframing the Renaissance: Visual Culture in Europe and Latin America, 1450-1650

See also **EUROPEAN ART: THE RENAISSANCE** in **ART**

0-300-06295-8 YALE $45.00

Philippe **Perrot**

Fashioning the Bourgeoisie: A History of Clothing in the Nineteenth Century

How the suit—dark, stiff, and austere—expressed the new self-image of the bourgeois male, who abandoned the "fashion game" of the old aristocracy to join "the inexorable tendency toward somberness and severity." Meanwhile, women continued to be adorned as ornamental objects

TRANSLATED BY RICHARD BIENVENU

0-691-03383-8 PRINCETON $35.00

T. Sarah **Peterson**

Acquired Taste: The French Origins of Modern Cooking

The Renaissance brought changes in what people ate and how they prepared food as much as it revolutionized the way we think

0-8014-3053-4 CORNELL $34.95

Aileen **Ribeiro**

The Art of Dress: Fashion in England and France, 1750-1820

0-300-06287-7 YALE $55.00

The French Revolution and Napoleon

"In 1789 France fell into revolution, and the world has never since been the same. The French Revolution was by far the most momentous upheaval of the whole revolutionary age. It replaced the 'old regime' with 'modern society,' and at its extreme phase it became very radical, so much so that all later revolutionary movements have looked back to it as a predecessor to themselves. At the time, in the age of the Democratic or Atlantic Revolution from the 1760s to 1848, the role of France was decisive…

The French Revolution, unlike the Russian or Chinese revolutions of the twentieth century, occurred in what was in many ways the most advanced country of the day. France was the center of the intellectual movement of the Enlightenment. French science then led the world. French books were read everywhere, and the newspapers and political journals which became very numerous after 1789 carried a message which hardly needed translation. French was a kind of international spoken language in the educated and aristocratic circles of many countries. France was also, potentially before 1789 and actually after 1793, the most powerful country in Europe."—R.R. Palmer & Joel Colton, *A History of the Modern World*

D.M.G. **Sutherland**

France 1789-1815: Revolution and Counter-Revolution

How counterrevolutionary movements affected the course of the Revolution and led to the failure of constitutional government; a good overview

0-19-520513-8 OXFORD PB........$18.95

Isser **Woloch**

The New Regime: Transformations of the French Civic Order, 1789-1820s

0-393-31397-2 NORTON PB........$16.95

The Revolution: 1789-1799

"His hands are tied, his head bare; the fatal moment is come. He advances to the edge of the Scaffold, his face is very red, and says: 'Frenchmen, I die innocent: it is from the Scaffold and near appearing before God that I tell you so. I pardon my enemies; I desire that France—' A General on horseback, Santerre or another, prances out, with uplifted hand: *'Tambours!'* The drums drown the voice. 'Executioners, do your duty!' The Executioners, desperate lest themselves be murdered (for Santerre and his Armed Ranks will strike, if they do not), seize the hapless Louis: six of them desperate, him singly desperate, struggling there; and bind him to their plank. Abbé Edgeworth, stopping, bespeaks him: 'Son of Saint Louis, ascend to Heaven.' The Axe clanks down; a King's Life is shorn away. It is Monday, the 21st of January 1793. He was aged Thirty-eight years four months and twenty-eight days."—Thomas Carlyle, *The French Revolution*

Jean-Paul **Bertaud**

The Army of the French Revolution

The foremost expert on the army of the Revolution, the first to be composed primarily of draftees in a war of national survival. Integrates military and social history to show how the army, as a "school for the republic," paved the way for Napoleon

TRANSLATED BY R.R. PALMER

0-691-05537-8 PRINCETON........$59.50

Marc **Bouloiseau**

The Jacobin Republic, 1792-1794

Despite the excesses of the Reign of Terror, the Jacobins initiated the modernization of French civil society

TRANSLATED BY JONATHAN MANDELBAUM

0-521-28918-1 CAMBRIDGE PB........$19.95

Thomas **Carlyle**

The French Revolution

A great work of literature and history

See also **19TH-CENTURY PROSE** under **THE 19TH CENTURY** in **LITERATURE OF THE BRITISH ISLES**

EDITED BY K.J. FIELDING & DAVID SORENSEN

0-19-281843-0 OXFORD PB........$14.95

Madame Lafarge

Richard **Cobb**

The People's Armies

"A kind of documentary film of what revolutionary France looked like, how different citizens behaved, what the attack on Catholicism meant in obscure villages, how food supplies were organized, and what revolutionary orthodoxy implied in the remoter provinces" —Norman Hampson, *NY Review of Books*

TRANSLATED BY MARIANNE ELLIOTT

0-300-02728-1 YALE........$63.00

William **Doyle**

The Oxford History of the French Revolution

A compact 480-page history. "A fair, and remarkably complete, account of both the Revolution itself and the years that preceded it…A significant contribution"—*Newsday*

0-19-285221-3 OXFORD PB........$14.95

P.M. **Jones**

The Peasantry in the French Revolution

This book fills a gap in the literature of the Revolution. Jones agrees with Georges Lefebvre's view that the peasantry held center stage during the early years of the Revolution; but he departs from Lefebvre's thesis that the peasantry's participation ran counter to the Revolution's capitalist thrust

0-521-33070-X CAMBRIDGE........$59.95

0-521-33716-X CAMBRIDGE PB........$22.95

David P. **Jordan**

The King's Trial: Louis XVI vs. the French Revolution

0-520-04399-5 CALIFORNIA PB........$14.95

Georges **Lefebvre**

The Coming of the French Revolution

A brief classic from the 1930s by the greatest authority on 18th-century French rural history. Lefebvre carries the events from the Aristocratic Reaction of 1787 to October 1789

TRANSLATED BY R.R. PALMER

0-691-00751-9 PRINCETON PB........$10.95

The French Revolution

A solid account that remains unmatched

Volume 1 From Its Origins to 1793

0-231-08598-2 COLUMBIA PB........$18.50

Volume 2 From 1793 to 1799

0-231-08599-0 COLUMBIA PB........$18.50

Darline Gay **Levy** & others, editors

Women in Revolutionary Paris, 1789-1795

0-252-00855-3 ILLINOIS PB........$15.95

R.R. **Palmer**

Twelve Who Ruled

The executive committee of the National Convention—the Committee of Public Safety—and the Reign of Terror, 1793-94

0-691-05119-4 PRINCETON........$58.00

0-691-00761-6 PRINCETON PB........$16.95

The Two Tocquevilles, Father and Son: Herve and Alexis de Tocqueville on the Coming of the French Revolution

0-691-05495-9 PRINCETON........$29.50

Alexis de Tocqueville

John **Paxton**

Companion to the French Revolution

A-to-Z coverage of names, dates, places, and definitions, from the storming of the Bastille to the Napoleonic era

0-8160-1937-1 FACTS ON FILE PB....$12.95

R.B. **Rose**

Gracchus Babeuf: The First Revolutionary Communist

Babeuf's "Conspiracy of Equals" was put down and Babeuf was tried and executed in 1797

0-8047-0949-1 STANFORD....$52.50

George **Rude**

The Crowd in the French Revolution

Riots and riot makers as a key component in the Revolution

0-19-500370-5 OXFORD PB....$14.95

Albert **Soboul**

The Sans-Culottes: The Popular Movement and Revolutionary Government, 1793-1794

The *sans-culottes* were primarily artisans, master craftsmen, shopkeepers, small merchants, and domestic servants, those who for the most part wore long trousers, not the breeches of the aristocracy

0-691-00782-9 PRINCETON PB....$16.95

J.M. **Thompson**

The French Revolution

A clear and factual account, over 40 years old. "The most precise and satisfying history of the French Revolution for many years to come" —A.J.P. Taylor

0-631-11921-3 BLACKWELL PB....$24.95

Michel **Vovelle**

The Fall of the French Monarchy, 1787-1792

A sophisticated chronology from the old regime to the fall of the monarchy on August 10, 1792; by a leading undoctrinaire Marxist

TRANSLATED BY SUSAN BURKE

0-521-24723-3 CAMBRIDGE....$54.50

0-521-28916-5 CAMBRIDGE PB....$22.95

Denis **Woronoff**

The Thermidorean Regime and the Directory, 1794-1799

TRANSLATED BY JULIAN JACKSON

0-521-24725-X CAMBRIDGE....$59.95

Interpreting the Revolution

"Though the Jacobins, as every history relentlessly points out, were great respecters of property, their war was a war against commercial capitalism. They may not have intended it that way at the beginning, but their incessant rhetoric against 'rich egoists' and the incrimination of the commercial and financial elites in federalism meant that, in practice, mercantile and industrial enterprise—unless it had been pulled into the service of the military—was itself attacked. Not surprisingly, then, it was the great growth areas of eighteenth-century France—the Atlantic and Mediterranean ports, the textile towns of the north and the east, the great metropolis of Lyon—which were the major casualties of the Revolution. The 'bourgeoisie' which Marxist history long believed to be the essential beneficiaries of the Revolution was, in fact, its principal victim."—Simon Schama, *Citizens: A Chronicle of the French Revolution*.

Alexis **de Tocqueville**

The Old Regime and the French Revolution

Still the greatest interpretive work on the subject and a masterpiece of historical thinking. "One of the very few 19th-century studies of the French Revolution that have not been rendered obsolete by the work of later historians" —John Gross, *NY Times*

TRANSLATED BY STUART GILBERT

EDITED BY J.P. MAYER & A.P. KERR

0-385-09260-1 DOUBLEDAY PB....$11.00

Keith **Baker**

Inventing the French Revolution: Essays on French Political Culture in the Eighteenth Century

0-521-38578-4 CAMBRIDGE PB....$24.95

Edmund **Burke**

Reflections on the Revolution in France

Burke, who had supported the American Revolution as a vindication of traditional English liberties, produced in *Reflections on the Revolution in France* (1790) the most influential arguments against the French Revolution and in the process invented conservatism as a distinct political philosophy. He favored gradual reform based on experience and local tradition, which distinguishes his conservatism from the more iron-handed and pessimistic variety developed on the Continent by De Maistre and others

See also **CLASSICS** under **POLITICAL THOUGHT** in **SOCIAL STUDIES**

0-14-043204-3 PENGUIN PB....$9.95

It is now sixteen or seventeen years since I saw the queen of France, then the dauphiness, at Versailles; and surely never lighted on this orb, which she hardly seemed to touch, a more delightful vision...Oh! What a revolution! and what an heart must I have, to contemplate without emotion that elevation and that fall!...I thought ten thousand swords must have leaped from their scabbards to avenge even a look that threatened her with insult.—But the age of chivalry is gone.—That of sophisters, economists, and calculators, has succeded; and the glory of Europe is extinguished for ever. Never, never more, shall we behold that generous loyalty to rank and sex, that proud submission, that dignified obedience, that subordination of the heart, which kept alive, even in servitude itself, the spirit of an exalted freedom.

REFLECTIONS ON THE REVOLUTION IN FRANCE

Thomas Paine

Alfred **Cobban**

The Social Interpretation of the French Revolution

A provocative, iconoclastic lecture of the early 1960s by the distinguished English historian. "Stimulating and challenging to all those who have so far accepted the orthodox 'bourgeois versus aristocrat' theory" —*Times Educational Supplement*

0-521-09548-4 CAMBRIDGE PB....$16.95

George C. **Comninel**

Rethinking the French Revolution: Marxism and the Revisionist Challenge

A sociologist suggests that Marxists have lapsed into abstractions on the question of the transition from feudalism to capitalism. He argues instead for a return to the principles of historical materialism that found their mature expression in *Capital*

FOREWORD BY GEORGE RUDE

0-86091-179-9 VERSO....$34.95

0-86091-890-4 VERSO PB....$18.95

William **Doyle**

Origins of the French Revolution

The second edition of this clear and thoughtful book originally released in 1981. "A synthesis worthwhile for any historian or educated reader" —*Journal of Modern History*

0-19-822284-X OXFORD PB....$19.95

Francois **Furet**

Interpreting the French Revolution

The Revolution in light of contemporary experience and the writings of Tocqueville and Cochin; a brilliant and challenging response to the grip of academic Marxism

TRANSLATED BY ELBORG FORSTER

0-521-28049-4 CAMBRIDGE PB....$19.95

Marx and the French Revolution

TRANSLATED BY DEBORAH KAN FURET

0-226-27338-5 CHICAGO....$34.95

Revolutionary France: 1770-1880

See also **FRANCE** under **19TH-CENTURY EUROPE**

0-631-17029-4 BLACKWELL....$59.95

0-631-19808-3 BLACKWELL PB....$21.95

Francois **Furet** & Mona **Ozouf**

A Critical Dictionary of the French Revolution

This exciting book is organized by key words and themes under five chief categories: events, actors, institutions and creations, ideas, and historians and commentators. "A stunning vindication of the centrality of politics and the lasting significance of the event. Some of the essays—Furet on Quinet, Higonnet on the Sans-Culottes, Ozouf on Revolutionary Religion—are miniature masterpieces" —Simon Schama

TRANSLATED BY ARTHUR GOLDHAMMER

0-674-17728-2 BELKNAP $100.00

Eric **Hobsawm**

Echoes of the Marseillaise: Two Centuries Look Back on the French Revoluton

See also **NEW DIRECTIONS** under **HISTORIOGRAPHY**

0-8135-1524-6 RUTGERS PB $9.95

Lynn **Hunt**

Politics, Culture and Class in the French Revolution

This scholarly analysis emphasizes the importance of rhetoric, ritual, and ceremony in the revolution

0-520-05740-6 CALIFORNIA PB $14.95

Emmet **Kennedy**

A Cultural History of French Revolution

A comprehensive cultural history of painting, music, fiction, theater, science, education, philosophy, and religion. Includes 95 illustrations

0-300-04426-7 YALE $50.00
0-300-05013-5 YALE PB $23.00

Ted W. **Margadant**

Urban Rivalries in the French Revolution

In a revolution we think of as primarily urban, the division of France into departments revealed a widespread oppositon to the dominance of provincial capitals, "a kind of championing of the towns against the cities." This richly detailed study is divided into three sections: "The Institutional Crisis of the Old Regime"; "The Rhetoric and Politics of Space"; and "The Fate of Small Towns"

0-691-00891-4 PRINCETON PB $26.95

Mona **Ozouf**

Festivals and the French Revolution

"With enormously rich original materials, she has fashioned a means of understanding revolutionary culture through its symbolic forms"—Lynn Hunt

TRANSLATED BY ALAN SHERIDAN

0-674-29883-7 HARVARD $48.00
0-674-29884-5 HARVARD PB $18.95

Jean **Starobinski**

1789: The Emblems of Reason

Sophisticated analysis of the painting and sculpture the revolutionaries used to purvey their new ideas

TRANSLATED BY BARBARA BRAY

0-8139-0915-5 VIRGINIA $35.00
0-262-69122-1 MIT PB $18.95

The Revolution and the World

Geoffrey **Best**, editor

The Permanent Revolution: The French Revolution and Its Legacy, 1789-1989

Essays on the Revolution's legacy, from the practice of nationalism to the pursuit of human rights, to the ways people make revolutions. Contributors include Conor Cruise O'Brien, George Steiner, Norman Hampson, and Eugene Weber

0-226-04428-9 CHICAGO PB $13.50

Charles **Breunig**

The Age of Revolution, 1789-1850

0-393-09143-0 NORTON PB $10.95

Crane **Brinton**

The Anatomy of Revolution

A provocative effort to compare the English, American, French, and Russian revolutions

0-8446-1740-7 SMITH $20.00
0-394-70044-9 RANDOM HOUSE PB $8.00

Norman **Hampson**

The First European Revolution, 1776-1815

0-393-95096-4 NORTON PB $9.95

R.R. **Palmer**

The Age of the Democratic Revolution: A Political History of Europe and America, 1760-1800 Volume I The Challenge

A masterful work of historical synthesis, which compares the constitutional history of Western civilization at the time of the French and American Revolutions. Winner of the Bancroft Prize. The second volume, *The Struggle* is currently out of print

See also **INTERPRETING THE REVOLUTION**

0-691-00569-9 PRINCETON PB $21.95

Simon **Schama**

Patriots and Liberators: Revolution in the Netherlands, 1780-1813

The definitive study of the Batavian republic and the kingdom of Holland, by the author of *Citizens: A Chronicle of the French Revolution*

0-679-72949-6 VINTAGE PB $15.00

The Age of Napoleon

For related reading, see MILITARY AFFAIRS

Enno E. **Kraehe**

Metternich's German Policy: The Congress of Vienna, 1814-1815

0-691-10133-7 PRINCETON PB $24.95

Louis **Bergeron**

France Under Napoleon

An important contribution of recent scholarship, this is a strong analysis of French society and the nature of the Napoleonic system; originally published in France as *L'Episode Napoleonien: Aspects Interieurs*, 1799-1815

TRANSLATED BY R.R. PALMER

0-691-00789-6 PRINCETON PB $18.95

David **Chandler**

The Military Maxims of Napoleon

Napoleon's thoughts on the art of war, tactics, strategies, and command

See also **THE NAPOLEONIC ERA** under **WARS THROUGH THE AGES** under **MILITARY AFFAIRS**

0-947898-64-6 GREENHILL $24.95

John R. **Elting**

Swords Around a Throne: Napoleon's Grande Armé

An American military historian's view of Napoleonic warfare

See also **THE NAPOLEONIC ERA** under **WARS THROUGH THE AGES** under **MILITARY AFFAIRS**

0-02-909501-8 FREE PRESS $50.00

David **Hamilton-Williams**

The Fall of Napoleon: The Final Betrayal

Charts military events and the clandestine diplomatic intrigues linking Britain, Austria, Russia, and Prussia in the quest for the emperor's demise

0-471-11862-1 WILEY $30.00
0-471-16077-6 WILEY PB $19.95

Waterloo: New Perspectives: The Great Battle Reappraised

0-471-14571-8 WILEY PB $19.95

J. Christopher **Herold**, editor

The Mind of Napoleon: A Selection of His Written and Spoken Words

0-231-08523-0 COLUMBIA PB $21.00

Proctor Paterson **Jones**

Napoleon: An Intimate Account of the Years of Supremacy

The finest collection of Napoleonic art and memorabilia ever assembled: paintings, sketches, engravings, objects d'art, maps, weapons, personal effects, and more. Juxtaposes two accounts, both long out of print—the reminiscences of Napoleon's secretary, the Baron de Meneval, and his valet, Constant Wairy

0-679-41458-4 RANDOM HOUSE $95.00

Norman **Mackenzie**

The Escape from Elba: The Fall and Flight of Napoleon, 1814-1815

The emperor's exile and triumphant return to the Tuileries—and his final defeat

0-19-215863-5 OXFORD $30.00

Felix **Markham**

Napoleon

An excellent short biography

0-451-62798-9 NEW AMERICAN LIBRARY PB $5.99

Rory **Muir**

Britain and the Defeat of Napoleon, 1807-1815

The national effort: how politics, the press, the crown, civilians, and soldiers together defeated Napoleon

0-300-06443-8 YALE $45.00

George F. **Nafziger**

Napoleon's Invasion of Russia

Assembling an army of nearly 600,000, the largest force under a single command seen in Europe until that time, Napoleon crossed the Russian frontier on June 23, 1812, in a campaign that culminated in the Battle of Borodino on September 7. Includes 16 maps and appendices with valuable documents

See also **THE NAPOLEONIC ERA** under **WARS THROUGH THE AGES** under **MILITARY AFFAIRS**

FOREWORD BY DAVID CHANDLER

0-89141-322-7 PRESIDIO $45.00

G.E. **Rothenberg**

The Art of Warfare in the Age of Napoleon

Insights into the character of warfare of the age and Napoleon's military style

See also **THE NAPOLEONIC ERA** under **WARS THROUGH THE AGES** under **MILITARY AFFAIRS**

0-253-20260-4 INDIANA PB $12.95

Biographical Studies

Marie-France **Boyer**

The Private Realm of Marie Antoinette

The visual legacy of the queen consort of France, protector and patron of the most gifted craftsmen of the day

PHOTOGRAPHS BY FRANCOIS HALARD

0-500-01690-9 THAMES & HUDSON $19.95

Evangeline **Bruce**

Napoleon and Josephine: An Improbable Marriage

0-02-517810-5 DREW $32.00
1-57566-056-3 KENSINGTON PB $16.00

Duff **Cooper**

Talleyrand

An old regime bishop whose political agility kept him on top—through the Revolution, the Empire, and the Restoration. First published in 1932

0-8047-0616-6 STANFORD $49.50

Jonathan **Dewald**

The European Nobility, 1400-1800

A leading historian of France offers the first comprehensive history of Europe's nobility between the Renaissance and the advent of Napoleon

0-521-42528-X CAMBRIDGE PB $15.95

John **Hardman**

Louis XVI

0-300-06077-7 YALE PB $18.00

Ernest J. **Knapton**

Empress Josephine

0-674-25201-2 HARVARD PB $9.95

David P. **Jordan**

The Revolutionary Career of Maximilien Robespierre

0-226-41037-4 CHICAGO PB $23.95

Lloyd **Kramer**

Lafayette in Two Worlds: Public Cultures and Personal Identities in an Age of Revolutions

An informal, if flawed, intellectual biography

0-8078-2258-2 UNC $39.95

Barbara **Luttrell**

Mirabeau

A 1991 study of one of the ablest leaders of the Revolution and a leading advocate of constitutional parliamentary monarchy, the Comte de Mirabeau (1749-1791)

0-8093-1705-2 SOUTHERN ILLINOIS $34.95

Douglas L. **Wilson** & others, editors

Thomas Jefferson Abroad

Letters and documents written during Jefferson's five years as minister to the court of Louis XVI

0-679-60186-4 MODERN LIBRARY $18.00

19th-Century Europe

Revolution and Napoleonic rule raised the political consciousness of much of Europe's lower middle class, which found itself actively seeking self-government, freedom, and an end to foreign domination. At the same time, another revolution as cataclysmic as the French Revolution began to take form. As the Industrial Revolution spread, so too did socialism and other movements for social reform.

Dudley **Baines**

Emigration From Europe, 1815-1930

Why sixty million people left Europe for overseas destinations in this period

0-521-55783-6 CAMBRIDGE PB $9.95

Robert **Gildea**

Barricades and Borders: Europe 1800-1914

Second edition of a comprehensive survey that incorporates the results of recent research on topics such as population, social mobility, and intellectual trends; a solid introduction

0-19-820625-9 OXFORD PB $24.95

Norman **Rich**

The Age of Nationalism and Reform, 1850-1890

Chapters include "The Intellectual and Cultural Climate" and "The Course of Reform: Great Britain and Russia"

0-393-09183-X NORTON PB $9.95

Theodore S. **Hamerow**

The Birth of a New Europe: State and Society in the Nineteenth Century

The rise of the working and middle classes, the growth of literacy and the extension of the ballot, and the profound transformation brought about by the Industrial Revolution

0-8078-1548-9 NORTH CAROLINA $45.00
0-8078-4239-7 NORTH CAROLINA PB $19.95

Paul W. **Schroeder**

The Transformation of European Politics, 1763-1848

An appealing and cogent reinterpretation; a welcome addition to the Oxford History of Modern Europe

0-19-822119-3 OXFORD $59.00

David **Thomson**

Europe Since Napoleon

0-394-30539-9 KNOPF $26.00

Revolution and Reaction: 1815-1848

Henry A. **Kissinger**

A World Restored: Metternich, Castlereagh and the Problems of Peace, 1812-1822

Shrewd insights into the reconstruction of Europe following the collapse of Napoleonic France

0-8446-2384-9 SMITH $18.05
0-395-17229-2 HOUGHTON MIFFLIN PB $14.95

Lewis **Namier**

1848: The Revolution of the Intellectuals

The great Polish-born historian of the politics of 18th-century England on the Revolution in Central Europe. First published in 1946

0-19-726111-6 OXFORD PB $15.95

Priscilla **Robertson**

The Revolutions of 1848: A Social History

0-691-05147-X PRINCETON PB $18.95

Peter N. **Stearns**

1848: The Revolutionary Tide in Europe

The 1815 settlement imposed on France lasted until revolutions broke out all over Europe; published in 1974

0-393-09311-5 NORTON PB $11.95

J.R. **Talmon**

Romanticism and Revolt

The idealism of the reformers and revolutionaries set in the context of Romanticism

0-393-95081-6 NORTON PB $9.95

The Industrial Revolution

For related reading, see THE 19TH CENTURY AND THE INDUSTRIAL REVOLUTION under GREAT BRITAIN AND IRELAND

David S. **Landes**

The Unbound Prometheus: Technological Change and Industrial Development in Western Europe from 1750 to the Present

Landes's study is widely regarded as a classic

0-521-09418-6 CAMBRIDGE PB $19.95

Sidney **Pollard**

Peaceful Conquest: The Industrialization of Europe, 1760-1970

The three stages of industrial development on the Continent

0-19-877095-2 OXFORD PB $19.95

Kirkpatrick **Sale**

Rebels Against the Future: The Luddites and Their War on the Industrial Revolution, Lessons for the Computer Age

In this illuminating study of the Luddite rebellion against industrialization, Sale finds not only a fascinating history but also a dramatically relevant lesson about intellectual and ethical concerns in the computer age. "If Sale's book serves no other purpose than getting us to ask ourselves whether technology serves us or we serve technology, it will be worth reading" —*Washington Post*

0-201-40718-3 ADDISON-WESLEY PB $13.00

France

"I have taken as models the political institutions that once before, at the turn of the century, in similar circumstances, gave new strength to a shaken society and raised France to the height of prosperity and grandeur. I have taken as models the institutions that, instead of vanishing at the first outbreak of popular disturbances, were toppled only by the coalition of all of Europe against us. In short, I asked myself: since France has been functioning for the past fifty years only thanks to the administrative, military, judiciary, religious and financial organizations of the Consulate and the Empire, why should we not also adopt the political institutions of that period? As the creation of the same mind, they must surely embody the same national character and the same practical usefulness."—Louis Bonaparte (later Napoleon III), 14 January 1852, quoted in *The Rise and Fall of the Second Empire, 152-1871*, by Alain Plessis.

Maurice **Agulhon**

The Republican Experiment, 1848-1852

TRANSLATED BY JANET LLOYD

0-521-28988-2 CAMBRIDGE PB $19.95

Metternich

John **Bierman**

Napoleon III and His Carnival Empire

The public and private life of the adventurer who presided over France in the age of Offenbach and impressionism

0-312-03900-X ST. MARTIN'S PB $14.95

Rupert **Christiansen**

Paris Babylon: The Story of the Paris Commune

The glittering capital of Europe was at the height of its decadence. But it was also about to be brought down by the Franco-Prussian War and handed into the conflagration of the Commune

0-670-83131-X VIKING $23.95

Alain **Corbin**

Women for Hire: Prostitution and Sexuality in France After 1850

The first systematic study of the commercial and political aspects of the sex trade, with a special focus on the role of brothel-based prostitution as an enterprise integral to capitalism. This innovative work is now a classic in its genre

TRANSLATED BY ALAN SHERIDAN

0-674-95543-9 HARVARD $46.00

Francois **Delaporte**

Disease and Civilization: The Cholera in Paris, 1832

0-262-54055-X MIT PB $9.95

Judith **Devlin**

The Superstitious Mind: French Peasants and the Supernatural in the Nineteenth Century

0-300-03710-4 YALE $40.00

Francois **Furet**

Revolutionary France: 1770-1880

See also **THE FRENCH REVOLUTION AND NAPOLEON**

0-631-17029-4 BLACKWELL $59.95

0-631-19808-3 BLACKWELL PB $21.95

Otto **Friedrich**

Olympia: Paris in the Age of Manet

From the author of the widely acclaimed *City of Nets* comes a portrait of 19th-century Paris in what *New York* magazine called "a francophile's feast." This masterful work brings a time and place to life by combining social history, culture, politics, and anecdote. "A vibrant… idiosyncratic book, enlarging the effect of many definitive histories of the time"—*LA Times*

0-671-86411-4 TOUCHSTONE PB $14.00

David P. **Jordan**

Transforming Paris: The Life and Labors of Baron Haussmann

Though neither architect nor engineer, Haussmann transformed the capital of France during his seventeen years as Prefect of the Seine under Napoleon III

0-226-41038-2 CHICAGO PB $17.95

Herbert **Lottman**

The French Rothschilds: The Great Banking Dynasty Through Two Turbulent Centuries

0-517-59229-0 CROWN $30.00

Roger **Magraw**

France 1815-1914: The Bourgeois Century

The consolidation of bourgeois strength after 1789

0-19-520510-3 OXFORD $39.95

0-19-520503-0 OXFORD PB $17.95

Michael **Marrinan**

Painting Politics for Louis Philippe: Art and Ideology in Orléanist France, 1830-1848

The depiction of revolutionary themes in the world of the *Comedie Humaine*, with special attention paid to Guizot's role in choosing revolutionary subjects for public buildings

0-300-03853-4 YALE $50.00

Karl **Marx**

The Eighteenth Brumaire of Louis Bonaparte

"History repeats itself, the first time as tragedy, the second time as farce": Marx's scathingly political analysis of Louis Bonaparte's conservative authoritarian state and his coup d'etat of 1852 is considered a masterpiece of politically engaged history writing

0-7178-0056-3 INTERNATIONAL PUB PB $4.95

John M. **Merriman**

The Red City: Limoges and the French Nineteenth Century

One hundred years in the life of Limoges, France's first socialist city: the story of urban transformation, political radicalism, and the making of a powerful working class. "A city could not hope to have a better biographer" —*Contemporary French Civilization*

0-19-503590-9 OXFORD $45.00

0-19-505682-5 OXFORD PB $19.95

Michael B. **Miller**
The Bon Marché: Bourgeois Culture and the Department Store, 1869-1920
0-691-03494-X PRINCETON PB $16.95

R.R. **Palmer**, editor
From Jacobin to Liberal: Marc-Antoine Jullien, 1775-1848
Portrays France's transition from revolutionary republicanism to the more placid liberalism of the nineteenth century
0-691-03299-8 PRINCETON $45.00

Alain **Plessis**
The Rise and Fall of the Second Empire, 1852-1871
A period of plentiful but dear money. An age that saw the creation of *Les Miserables*, *Olympia*, and the French protectorate over Cambodia. Plessis's study is a good attempt to reveal the period's rich complexity
TRANSLATED BY JONATHAN MANDELBAUM
0-521-35856-6 CAMBRIDGE PB $17.95

Charles **Rearick**
Pleasures of the Belle Epoque: Entertainment and Festivity in Turn-of-the-Century France
0-300-03230-7 YALE $40.00
0-300-04381-3 YALE PB $22.00

Joan Wallach **Scott**
Only Paradoxes to Offer: French Feminists and the Rights of Man
Focuses on four feminist activists: Olympe de Gouges, who wrote the *Declaration of the Rights of Woman and Citizen* during the Revolution; Jeanne Deroin, utopian socialist and candidate for legislative office in 1848; Hubertine Auclert, the leading suffragist of the Third Republic; and Medeleine Pelletier, a psychiatrist in the early 20th century who argued that women must "virilize" themselves in order to gain equality
0-674-63930-8 HARVARD $27.95

Debora **Silverman**
Art Nouveau in Fin-de-Siècle France
Republican politicians, museum curators, wealthy collectors, and luxury artisans in an allied quest for stylistic innovation based on the rediscovery of the 18th century-rococo arts
0-520-06322-8 CALIFORNIA $50.00
0-520-08088-2 CALIFORNIA PB $22.50

Andrea **Weiss**
Paris Was a Woman: Portraits from the Left Bank
Weiss, the award-winning filmmaker and historian (*Before Stonewall*), has collected a stunning scrapbook from the lesbian literati subculture that thrived in Paris at the turn of the century. This montage of letters, photos, journals, and drawings from the likes of Colette, Djuna Barnes, Gertrude and Alice, H.D., and Sylvia Beach recreates the radically new creative energy of this extraordinary moment in history
0-06-251313-3 HARPERCOLLINS PB $20.00

Colette

Eugen **Weber**
France, Fin-de-Siècle
"The epoch immortalized by Marcel Proust in *Remembrance of Things Past* has now found a historian equal to the task of capturing its tones and textures"
—Lynn Hunt, *LA Times Book Review*
0-674-31812-9 HARVARD $32.00
0-674-31813-7 HARVARD PB $14.95

Theodore **Zeldin**
France 1848-1945
Volume 1 Intellect and Pride
0-19-822177-0 OXFORD PB $29.95
Volume 5 Ambition and Love
0-19-822178-9 OXFORD PB $32.00

Emile **Zola**
The Dreyfus Affair: "J'Accuse" and Other Writings
Provides in English the full extent of Zola's writings on the Dreyfus affair
EDITED BY ALAIN PAGES
TRANSLATED BY ELEANOR LEVIEUX
0-300-06689-9 YALE $32.50

Jean-Denis **Bredin**
The Affair: The Case of Alfred Dreyfus
See also **ENLIGHTENMENT, REFORM, ASSIMILATION** under **MODERN EUROPE** under **JEWISH HISTORY**
TRANSLATED BY JEFFREY MEHLMAN
0-8076-1175-1 BRAZILLER PB $19.95

Germany

David **Barclay** & Eric **Weitz**, editors
Between Reform and Revolution: German Socialism and Communism from 1840 to 1990
1-57181-000-5 BERGHAHN $59.95

Otto **Friedrich**
Blood & Iron: From Bismarck to Hitler, the Von Moltke Family's Impact on German History
0-06-016866-8 HARPERCOLLINS $30.00

Theodore S. **Hamerow**
Restoration, Revolution, Reaction: Economics and Politics in Germany, 1815-1871
The German states during the years in which Austria and Prussia competed for leadership, and in which economic ties prepared the way for political unification
0-691-00755-1 PRINCETON PB $18.95

Friedrich **Meinecke**
The Age of German Liberation, 1795-1815
The perspective of a great German historian
TRANSLATED BY PETER PARET & HELMUT FISCHER
0-520-02792-2 CALIFORNIA $50.00

Thomas **Nipperdey**
Germany from Napoleon to Bismarck, 1800-1866
The seismic effect of Napoleon on the German *ancien régime*, the fate of the revolutions of 1848-49, and the rise of Bismarck; by one of Germany's leading historians, who died in 1992
TRANSLATED BY DANIEL NOLAN
0-691-02636-X PRINCETON $69.95

Peter **Paret**
The Berlin Secession: Modernism and Its Enemies in Imperial Germany
0-674-06774-6 HARVARD PB $15.95

German Cultural Studies

Russell A. **Berman**
Cultural Studies in Modern Germany: History, Representation and Nationhood
"Modern Germany" is Germany in the 20th century
0-299-14014-8 WISCONSIN PB $14.95

Helmut Kohl

David B. **Dennis**
Beethoven in German Politics, 1879-1989
0-300-06399-7 YALE $30.00

Peter **Friszsche**

Reading Berlin 1900

With cameo appearances by Georg Simmel, Walter Benjamin, and Alfred Doblin. "How the city was perceived and tamed and how it touched all aspects of life"—George Mosse

0-674-74881-6 HARVARD $39.95

George **Himmelheber**

Biedermeier, 1815-1835: Architecture, Painting, Sculpture, Decorative Art, Fashion

Named for the pseudonym of a group of German poets, Biedermeier was a movement which made high style comfortable and affordable

See also GENERAL under EUROPEAN DECORATIVE ARTS in ARCHITECTURE, DESIGN, AND HOMES

3-7913-1023-2 PRESTEL $75.00
3-7913-1620-6 PRESTEL PB $29.95

Klaus **Kreimeier**

The UFA Story: A History of Germany's Greatest Film Company, 1918-1945

The company that produced Fritz Lang's *Metropolis* and made stars of Emil Jannings and Marlene Dietrich

TRANSLATED BY ROBERT & RITA KIMBER

0-8090-9483-5 HILL & WANG $35.00

Ben **MacIntyre**

Forgotten Fatherland: The Search for Elisabeth Nietzsche

0-06-097561-X HARPERPERENNIAL PB $12.00

Frederic **Spotts**

Beyreuth: A History of the Wagner Festival

0-300-06665-1 YALE PB $18.00

Bismarck

Otto von Bismarck (1815-1898) was the chief architect of the German Empire created in 1871. Skillfully marshalling popular support, he conducted victorious wars against Austria (in 1866) and France (in 1870) and made Prussia the cornerstone of a Germany that would dominate Europe.

"Nietzsche was seventeen when Bismarck came to power and went insane a year before the Iron Chancellor was dismissed from office. Nietzsche's time is the Bismarck era. It was during Bismarck's rise to power and through the climactic events of the 1860s that Nietzsche and his generation came of age politically."
—Peter Bergmann, *Nietzsche: The Last Antipolitical German*

Erich **Eyck**

Bismarck and the German Empire

0-393-00235-7 NORTON PB $11.95

Theodore S. **Hamerow**

Otto von Bismarck: A Historical Assessment

0-669-82008-3 HEATH PB $14.00

Lothar **Gall**

Bismarck: The White Revolutionary

The name Bismarck stands for the political and social development of central Europe in the second half of the 19th century, and the internal shape that Germany assumed. Gall asks: How much of all this was Bismarck's personal achievement? Did one man put the German nation on the disastrously wrong course that culminated in 1933? Or were there deeper trends?

Volume 1 1815-1871

0-04-445778-2 UNWIN HYMAN PB $19.95

Volume 2 1871-1898

0-04-445779-0 UNWIN HYMAN PB $22.95

George O. **Kent**

Bismarck and His Times

A solid, up-to-date approach

0-8093-0859-2 SOUTHERN ILLINOIS PB $15.95

Fritz **Stern**

Gold and Iron: Bismarck, Bleishroder and the Building of the German Empire

Bismarck's modus operandi after unification; the story of a Jewish banker and the creator of the Second Reich. "A major contribution to our understanding of some of the great themes of modern European history—the relations between Jews and Germans, between economics and politics, between banking and diplomacy"
—James Joll, *NY Times Book Review*

0-394-74034-3 RANDOM HOUSE PB $19.56

Otto von Bismarck

A.J.P. **Taylor**

Bismarck: The Man and the Statesman

First published in 1955. Performs "the difficult task of compressing the most earth-shattering career between Napoleon and Hitler into fewer than 300 pages with conspicuous success"—*TLS*

0-394-70387-1 RANDOM HOUSE PB $10.00

Imperial Germany

Michael **Balfour**

The Kaiser and His Times

0-393-00661-1 NORTON PB $14.95

V.R. **Berghahn**

Germany and the Approach of War in 1914

By the modern German historian at Brown University

0-312-09993-2 ST. MARTIN'S $39.95
0-312-32480-4 ST. MARTIN'S PB $19.35

David **Blackbourn** & Geoffrey **Eley**

The Peculiarities of German History: Bourgeois Society and Politics in Nineteenth-Century Germany

Reevaluation of the assumptions thought to distinguish modern German history from that of other nations

0-19-873057-8 OXFORD PB $21.00

Geoffrey **Eley**

From Unification to Nazism: Reinterpreting the German Past

0-415-08488-1 UNWIN HYMAN PB $22.95

Peter **Hoffmann**

Stauffenberg: A Family History, 1905-1944

Count von Stauffenberg led the plot to assassinate Hitler

0-521-45307-0 CAMBRIDGE $39.95

Thomas **Kohut**

Wilhelm II and the Germans: A Study in Leadership

0-19-506172-1 OXFORD $45.00

Jules **Laforgue**

Berlin: The City and the Court

The French symbolist poet's record of his five years (1881-1886) in Berlin as reader to the Francophile Empress Augusta. "Laforgue is a sharp, thorough and often wickedly funny observer of Prussian manners, dress and mores"—*Publishers Weekly*

TRANSLATED BY WILLIAM JAY SMITH

1-88598-302-6 TURTLE POINT PB $13.95

Hannah **Pakula**

An Uncommon Woman: Empress Frederick, Daughter of Queen Victoria, Wife of the Crown Prince of Prussia, Mother of Kaiser Wilhelm

0-684-80818-8 SIMON & SCHUSTER $35.00

Hans-Ulrich **Wehler**

The German Empire, 1871-1918

TRANSLATED BY KIM TRAYNOR

0-907582-22-2 BERG $59.95

John C.G. **Rohl**

The Kaiser and his Court

Provocative essays on the absolutist culture of the court and of Berlin society, as well as the extent of the exiled Wilhelm II's anti-Semitism

TRANSLATED BY TERRENCE F. COLE

0-521-56504-9 CAMBRIDGE PB $18.95

Fritz **Stern**

Dreams and Delusions: The Drama of German History

"Stern writes with all the poignancy of one who loves German civilization deeply and is determined to fathom how it could have done such terrible violence to others, and to itself" —David P. Calleo, *Foreign Affairs*

See also WHY HITLER CAME TO POWER under THE THIRD REICH under 20TH-CENTURY EUROPE TO THE SECOND WORLD WAR

0-394-75772-6 VINTAGE PB $14.00

19th-Century Austria and the Habsburgs

Edward **Crankshaw**

The Fall of the House of Habsburg

Emperor Franz Josef and the last decades of the Austro-Hungarian Empire

0-14-006459-1 PENGUIN PB $14.95

Istvan **Deak**

Beyond Nationalism: A Social and Political History of the Habsburg Officer Corps

0-19-504505-X OXFORD $48.00

The Lawful Revolution: Louis Kossuth and the Hungarians, 1848-1849

0-231-04602-2 COLUMBIA $25.00

Alexander **Gerschenkron**, editor

An Economic Spurt that Failed: Four Lectures on Austrian Economic History

0-691-04216-0 PRINCETON $26.50

Alice **Hanson**

Musical Life in Biedermeier Vienna

With the fall of the old regime, the culture of the bourgeoisie begins to dominate in Europe

0-521-25799-9 CAMBRIDGE $49.50

William M. **Johnston**

The Austrian Mind: An Intellectual and Social History, 1848-1938

0-520-04955-1 CALIFORNIA PB $16.00

John **Lukacs**

Budapest 1900: A Historical Portrait of a City and Its Culture

0-8021-3250-2 GROVE PB $10.95

1900 was both a milestone and a turning point in the history of Budapest. It has a meaning that is more than chronological. It provides a contrast with Vienna 1900 and Paris 1900—two capital cities of capital importance for the culture of the Western world—about which so many books have been written. The *belle epoque* is a pleasant nostalgic phrase, but the crisis of an older France and the breaking away from the ideas, ideals and standards of the nineteenth century had begun in Paris fifteen or even twenty-five years before 1900. In Vienna, too, 1900 was the end of the Austrian *fin-de-siécle* with many of its interesting artistic and intellectual symptoms and alarming manifestations. In Budapest, *le mal* (if it was as *mal-de-siécle)* was only about to begin.

BUDAPEST 1900: A HISTORICAL PORTRAIT OF A CITY AND ITS CULTURE

Frederic **Morton**

A Nervous Splendor: Vienna, 1888-1889

0-14-005667-X VIKING PB $11.95

Geoffrey **Wawro**

The Austro-Prussian War: Austria's War with Prussia and Italy in 1866

Prussia's successful invasion of Habsburg Bohemia and the wretched collapse of the Austrian army in July 1866

0-521-56059-4 CAMBRIDGE $59.95

Andrew **Wheatcroft**

The Habsburgs: Embodying Empire

By the author of the *The Ottomans; Dissolving Images*

0-670-85490-5 VIKING $34.95

A.J.P. **Taylor**

The Habsburg Monarchy, 1809-1918: A History of the Austrian Empire and Austria-Hungary

First published in 1941 and still essential reading for all students of the period. "A very good book indeed, brilliant, acid and penetrating"—Alan Bullock

See also THE HAPSBURG EMPIRE, MODERN AUSTRIA AND HUNGARY under REGIONAL AND NATIONAL HISTORIES under INTRODUCTIONS TO MODERN EUROPEAN HISTORY

0-226-79145-9 CHICAGO PB $12.95

19th-Century Italy

Christopher **Duggan**

Fascism and the Mafia

Examines private papers, police files, and trial proceedings in the period from 1860 through the 1920s and concludes that the idea of the Mafia is a fiction, the result of political calculation and real misunderstanding of the behavior of Sicilians

0-300-04372-4 YALE $35.00

Gaetano **Salvemini**

Mazzini

A classic biography of Giuseppe Mazzini (1805-1872), republican and democrat, Romantic intellectual and publicist, and founder of the "Young Italy" society

0-8047-0496-1 STANFORD $32.50

Denis **Mack Smith**

Italy and Its Monarchy

With the monarchy as its focus, Mack Smith assesses Italy's political history from the Risorgimento to the foundation of the Italian Republic

0-300-04661-8 YALE $40.00

Mazzini

0-300-05884-5 YALE $35.00

0-300-06884-0 YALE PB $16.00

Guiseppe Mazzini

Stuart **Woolf**

A History of Italy, 1700-1860: The Social Constraints of Political Change

0-415-06607-7 ROUTLEDGE PB $22.95

The Rise of Marxism

For related reading, see POLITICAL THOUGHT in SOCIAL STUDIES

Eugene **Kamenka**, editor

The Portable Karl Marx

Includes *The Communist Manifesto, The German Ideology,* selections from *Capital*, letters, and other documents

See also LEFTISM AND MARXISM under POLITICAL THOUGHT in SOCIAL STUDIES

0-14-015096-X VIKING PB $14.95

George **Lichtheim**

Marxism: An History and Critical Study

Balanced study by a humanist Marxist reveals strengths and weaknesses of a major 19th-century mode of thought

0-231-05425-4 COLUMBIA PB $19.50

Frank E. **Manuel**

A Requiem for Karl Marx

"The materials—the Hegelian theory of history, Smith, Ricardo, Malthus, the Parliamentary Blue Books—were all waiting to be combined in a new science of society. Only Marx achieved this prodigious synthesis. Manuel's book leaves us with a sense of wonder at the achievement" —Michael Ignatieff, *New Republic*

0-674-76326-2 HARVARD $24.95

David **McLellan**

Marxism After Marx

An essential text by a leading figure in the field of Marxist studies

0-395-31541-7 HOUGHTON MIFFLIN PB $11.95

John **Torrance**

Karl Marx's Theory of Ideas

0-521-44066-1 CAMBRIDGE $59.95

Robert C. **Tucker**, editor

The Marx-Engels Reader

A comprehensive anthology including *The Communist Manifesto,* selections from *Capital, The Grundrisse,* and other writings

0-393-09040-X NORTON PB $15.95

Biographical Studies

Isaiah **Berlin**

Karl Marx: His Life and Environment

0-19-510326-2 OXFORD PB $12.95

J.D. **Hunley**

The Life and Thought of Friedrich Engels: A Reinterpretation

0-300-04923-4 YALE $25.00

Socialist and Labor Movements

Tony **Judt**

Marxism and the French Left: Studies on Labour and Politics in France, 1830-1981

Essays on labor, socialism, and communism in France

0-19-821578-9 OXFORD PB $19.95

V.R. **Lorwin**

The French Labor Movement

0-674-32200-2 HARVARD $22.50

Bernard H. **Moss**

The Origins of the French Labor Movement: Socialism of Skilled Workers, 1930-1940

0-520-04101-1 CALIFORNIA $37.50

Carl E. **Schorske**

German Social Democracy, 1905-1918: The Development of the Great Schism

0-674-35125-8 HARVARD PB $12.50

The Reader's Catalog
250 West 57th Street
New York, NY 10107

Ideas, Culture, and Society

Jacques **Barzun**

Classic, Romantic and Modern

The erudite pundit surveys the great style movements of modernity

0-226-03852-1 CHICAGO PB $12.95

Owen **Chadwick**

The Secularization of the European Mind in the Nineteenth Century

An account by an eminent historian of religion

0-521-39829-0 CAMBRIDGE PB $11.95

Louis **Dumont**

German Ideology: From France to Germany and Back

Looks at Goethe, Troeltsch, Thomas Mann, and others in an assessment of European culture and cultural interaction

0-226-16952-9 CHICAGO $32.50
0-226-16953-7 CHICAGO PB $14.95

Peter **Gay**

The Bourgeois Experience: Victoria To Freud

Volume 1 Education of the Senses

Sexuality in the bourgeois age

0-19-503352-3 OXFORD $35.00
0-19-503728-6 OXFORD PB $15.95

Volume 2 The Tender Passion

Bourgeois theories of love, homosexuality, and sublimation

0-19-505183-1 OXFORD PB $15.95

Volume 3 The Cultivation of Hatred

0-393-31224-0 NORTON PB $15.00

Volume 4 The Naked Heart

0-393-03813-0 NORTON $29.95
0-393-31515-0 NORTON PB $15.00

Thomas **Harrison**

1910: The Emancipation of Dissonance

The intellectual intricacies of Mitteleuropa on the eve of World War I. Explores the essential themes and concerns of E xpressionism in the work of Egon Schiele, George Trakl, Wassily Kandinsky, George Lukacs, Georg Simmel, Dino Campana, and Arnold Schoenberg

0-520-20043-8 CALIFORNIA $30.00

H. Stuart **Hughes**

Consciousness and Society: The Reorientation of European Social Thought, 1890-1930

For all its limitations, this remains the best introduction to the intellectual revolution of the period

0-394-70201-8 RANDOM HOUSE PB $9.75

Albert S. **Lindemann**

The Jew Accused: Three Anti-Semitic Affairs—Dreyfus, Beilis, Frank, 1894-1915

Three well-publicized affairs in France, Russia, and the United States

0-521-44761-5 CAMBRIDGE PB $15.95

Franco **Moretti**

The Way of the World: The Bildungsroman in European Culture

"Youth" as the new hero of 19th-century society and the symbol of modernity in works of Goethe, Austen, Balzac, Stendhal, Dickens, Flaubert, and George Eliot

TRANSLATED BY ALBERT SBRAGIA

0-86091-159-4 VERSO $60.00
0-86091-891-2 VERSO PB $20.00

Jeffrey S. **Weiss**

The Popular Culture of Modern Art: Picasso, Duchamp, and Avant-Gardism, 1909-1917

A cultural history of the deeply ambiguous relationship between modern art and popular culture, focusing on the work of Picasso and Duchamp in the first two decades of the century

See also **SPECIAL TOPICS** under **GENERAL** under **20TH-CENTURY ART** in **ART**

0-300-05895-0 YALE $47.50

Freud

For related reading, see FREUD under PSYCHOLOGY in SOCIAL STUDIES

Frederick **Crews** & others

The Memory Wars: Freud's Legacy in Dispute

A strongly argued and controversial polemic against both Freud and the contemporary recovered memory movement. "In the two essays that form the core of this book, Frederick Crews convincingly dismantles the entire Freudian enterprise from beginning to end" —John F. Kihlstrom

See also **THE REACTION AGAINST FREUD** under **FREUD** under **PSYCHOLOGY** in **SOCIAL STUDIES**

0-940322-04-8 NY REVIEW $22.95

Peter **Gay**, editor

The Freud Reader

Fifty-one texts in a single 800-page volume

See also **FREUD** under **PSYCHOLOGY** in **SOCIAL STUDIES**

0-393-31403-0 NORTON PB $18.95

Sander L. **Gilman**

The Case of Sigmund Freud: Medicine and Identity at the Fin-de-Siècle

0-8018-4974-8 JOHNS HOPKINS PB $15.95

Freud, Race, and Gender

0-691-02586-X PRINCETON PB $14.95

Philip **Rieff**

Freud: The Mind of a Moralist

Offers an excellent entry into Freud's thinking

See also **ABOUT FREUD** under **FREUD** under **PSYCHOLOGY** in **SOCIAL STUDIES**

0-226-71639-2 CHICAGO PB $25.00

Paul W. **Robinson**

Freud and His Critics

"Since we all speak Freud now, it is useful to know what we are talking about"
—Peter Gay, *American Historical Review*

See also **ABOUT FREUD** under **FREUD** under **PSYCHOLOGY** in **SOCIAL STUDIES**

0-520-08029-7 CALIFORNIA $30.00

The New Imperialism

"If France took the whole of Africa," an English colonial critic suggested in 1857, "I do not see what harm she would do us or anybody else save herself." Yet within 15 years, Benjamin Disraeli challenged Britain to "be a great country, an Imperial country, a country where your sons, when they rise, rise to paramount positions and obtain not merely the esteem of their countrymen, but command the respect of the world." By World War I about one-quarter of the world's land surface was carved up as colonies among a half-dozen states. This was the era of the "new imperialism."

The books that follow cover not only Europe's colonial expansion in the late 19th century, but newer forms of political and economic imperialism as they developed in the 20th century.

For related reading, see GREAT BRITAIN AND IRELAND

For related reading, see ECONOMICS in SOCIAL STUDIES

Raymond **Betts**

Uncertain Dimensions: Western Overseas Empires in the Twentieth Century

0-8166-1309-5 MINNESOTA PB $15.95

Eric J. **Hobsbawm**

The Age of Empire, 1875-1914

"Few, if any, present practitioners of the historian's craft can equal the astonishing and dazzling craft of Mr. Hobsbawm's scholarship"
—*NY Times Book Review*

See also **IMPERIALISM AND COLONIALISM** under **THE VICTORIAN ERA** under **GREAT BRITAIN AND IRELAND**

0-679-72175-4 VINTAGE PB $15.00

J.A. **Hobson**

Imperialism

The term "imperialism" exploded into general use in the 1890s. When the British liberal J.A. Hobson wrote his study in 1902 it was "on everybody's lips...and used to denote the most powerful movement in the current politics of the western world." Hobson stressed economic motivations and the need for outlets for "surplus capital" as the cause of expansion

See also **IMPERIALISM** under **ECONOMICS** in **SOCIAL STUDIES**

INTRODUCTION BY P. SIEGELMAN

0-472-06103-8 MICHIGAN PB $17.95

Ian **Copeland**

The Burden of Empire: Perspectives on Imperialism and Colonialism

0-19-553208-2 OXFORD PB $24.95

V.I. **Lenin**

Imperialism: The Highest Stage of Capitalism

A radical "student" of Hobson, Lenin argued a decade later that the new imperialism had economic roots in a new *phase* of capitalism, which resulted in "the territorial division of the world among the great capitalist powers"

See also **IMPERIALISM** under **ECONOMICS** in **SOCIAL STUDIES**

0-7178-0098-9 INTERNATIONAL PUB PB $2.95

John **Lowe**

The Great Powers, Imperialism and the German Problem, 1865-1925

0-415-10444-0 ROUTLEDGE PB $16.95

Bernard **Semmel**

The Liberal Ideal and the Demons of Empire: Theories of Imperialism from Adam Smith to Lenin

"Will be unquestionably useful to historians—particularly those outside the confines of European expansion"—R.K. Webb

0-8018-4540-8 JOHNS HOPKINS $36.00

The Colonial Empires

For related reading, see AFRICA

Paul H. **Clyde** & Burton F. **Beers**

The Far East: A History of Western Impacts and Eastern Responses, 1830-1975

Treats Japan and Southeast Asia as well as China

0-88133-612-2 WAVELAND PB $30.95

Philip D. **Curtin**

Death by Migration: Europe's Encounter with the Tropical World in the Nineteenth Century

0-521-38922-4 CAMBRIDGE PB $16.95

David Levering **Lewis**

The Race to Fashoda

Fast-paced story of the European scramble for Africa

0-8050-3556-7 HOLT PB $13.95

Roger **Owen**

The Middle East in the World Economy, 1800-1914

0-416-14270-2 METHUEN $45.00
1-85043-658-4 I.B. TAURIS PB $19.95

Thomas **Pakenham**

The Scramble For Africa: The White Man's Conquest of the Dark Continent from 1876-1910

A dramatic telling of the imperialist struggle over Africa, a quick and violent grab for territory in which Britain, France, Germany, Belgium, and Italy vied for power and markets. In a mere 34 years the European powers carved up an entire continent. Pakenham offers an engrossing—and appalling—narrative of panoramic scope

See also **AFRICA AND THE WEST** under **GENERAL HISTORIES** under **AFRICA**

0-380-71999-1 AVON PB $16.00

David Livingstone

Douglas **Porch**

The French Foreign Legion

Much romanticized but barely known in its reality, the French Foreign Legion has had a more morally dubious history than Ouida's popular novel, *Under Two Flags* might indicate. Porch has written a fascinating and revealing history of the unit. "Excellent...This book has been an education for me"
—Phillip Knightley, *NY Times Book Review*

0-06-016652-5 HARPERPERENNIAL PB $35.00

By 1932, the image of the Legion as a band of romantic outcasts was already well enough established to place Sidi-bel-Abbes on the tourist itinerary before World War II...As the Legion's place in the public imagination grew in the interwar years, the mysteries that shrouded its collective character deepened. And as it became increasingly the focus of popular attention, so the process of character definition became a very self-conscious one in the Legion. The Legion's myths, heretofore an informal and half-formed collection of regimental lore and vague public perception, were collected, expanded, ritualized and given official status, while its "traditions" were not only codified and standardized, but in some instances actually invented.

THE FRENCH FOREIGN LEGION

H.L. **Wesseling**

Divide and Rule: The Partition of Africa, 1880-1914

A lively, accessible synthesis of the carving up of Africa; by a professor of history at the University of Leiden, Holland

TRANSLATED BY ARNOLD J. POMERANS

0-275-95138-3 PRAEGER PB $29.95

Eric R. **Wolf**
Europe and the People Without History
A cross-disciplinary study of European colonialism looking outward from "native" societies
ILLUSTRATED BY NOEL L. DIAZ
0-520-04459-2 CALIFORNIA....$50.00
0-520-04898-9 CALIFORNIA PB....$18.00

Cecil Rhodes

20th-Century Europe to the Second World War

World War I

"No power had any overall, conscious designs for war in 1914. Nowhere, even in the summer of 1914, was a calculated, advance decision made for global war. Rather, the powers, as a result of Sarajevo, became involved in a series of moves and countermoves...that stage by stage, step by step, imperceptibly at times, and hardly ever with any true vision of the consequences, placed them in a position from which there was no way back to the negotiating table."
—Joachim Remak, *The Origins of World War I*

Diplomatic Background

George F. **Kennan**
The Decline of Bismarck's European Order: Franco-Russian Relations, 1875-1890
A search for the origins of Europe's "delicious euphoria" over the outbreak of war. Kennan is "at his best when revealing how human frailties played havoc with national interests"
—Theodore Zeldin
0-691-05282-4 PRINCETON....$60.00

Robert K. **Massie**
Dreadnought: Britain, Germany, and the Coming of the Great War
0-345-37556-4 BALAT PB....$17.50

Paul **Kennedy**
The Rise of the Anglo-German Antagonism: 1860-1914
Reaches beyond diplomatic history to compare the two societies and the changes that led to unbearable friction between them. "An imaginatively researched, innovative study of one of the most important historical questions of the pre-1914 period"—Fritz Stern
0-948660-06-6 HUMANITIES PB....$25.00

Joachim **Remak**
The Origins of World War I
0-03-082839-2
HOLT RINEHART & WINSTON PB....$19.62

A.J.P. **Taylor**
The Struggle for Mastery in Europe: 1848-1918
In the period between the fall of Metternich and the advent of Wilson and Lenin, nationalism, tempered by the balance of power, dominated European relations. "One of the glories of 20th-century writing"—*Observer*
0-19-822101-0 OXFORD....$65.00

Barbara **Tuchman**
The Proud Tower
Patricians and anarchists: Europe and America in the years before the Great War
0-345-40501-3 BALLANTINE PB....$14.00

The Great War

For related reading, see GREAT BRITAIN AND IRELAND

Robert B. **Asprey**
The German High Command at War: Hindenburg and Ludendorff Conduct World War I
0-688-12842-4 QUILL PB....$15.00

Hugh **Cecil**
The Flower of Battle: How Britain Wrote the Great War
1-88364-205-1 STEERFORTH....$32.00

Richard **Cork**
A Bitter Truth: The Avant-Garde, Art, and the Great War
The first world war had an immensely powerful effect on the artists who participated in it. This lavishly illustrated book is the first to bring together the full international array of images spawned by the great war. It shows how avant-garde painters, sculptors, and printmakers challenged the propaganda of recruitment by producing art that reflected the degradation of the trenches
See also **SPECIAL TOPICS** under **GENERAL** under **20TH-CENTURY ART** in **ART**
0-300-05704-0 YALE....$60.00

Byron **Farwell**
The Great War in Africa 1914-1918
0-393-30564-3 NORTON PB....$13.95

Martin **Gilbert**
The First World War: A Complete History
0-8050-4734-4 HOLT PB....$19.95

B.H. Liddell **Hart**
The Real War, 1914-1918
A largely military history, written in 1930 by the famous wartime strategist
See also **WORLD WAR I** under **WARS THROUGH THE AGES** under **MILITARY AFFAIRS**
0-316-52505-7 LITTLE, BROWN PB....$16.95

Anthony **Livesey**, editor
The Historical Atlas of World War I
Stunning battle maps, overlays, photos, paintings, and authoritative summaries are the highlights of this magnificent atlas. Published to coincide with the 75th anniversary of the Treaty of Versailles, it reminds us of how the contemporary concept of "global warfare" came to be born
0-8050-2651-7 HOLT....$45.00

Erich Maria **Remarque**
All Quiet on the Western Front
Incinerated by the Nazis in 1933, this famous war novel depicts the horror of the front "on a quiet day?" with deliberately brutal realism
See also **FICTION AND OTHER PROSE** under **MODERN GERMAN LITERATURE: TO 1945** under **GERMAN LITERATURE** in **LITERATURE OF EUROPE, AFRICA, AND ASIA**
TRANSLATED BY A.W. WHEEN
0-316-73992-8 LITTLE, BROWN....$21.95
0-449-21394-3 FAWCETT PB....$5.99

Keith **Robbins**
The First World War
The major battles against the backdrop of cultural, literary, and diplomatic developments
0-19-289149-9 OXFORD PB....$15.95

Tim **Travers**
The Killing Ground: The British Army, the Western Front and the Emergence of Modern Warfare, 1900-1918
0-04-445736-7 UNWIN HYMAN PB....$24.95

Barbara **Tuchman**
The Guns of August
The outbreak of W.W.I
0-345-38623-X BALAT PB....$14.00

Amos N. **Wilder**
Armageddon Revisited: A World War I Journal
As a volunteer ambulance driver, Wilder traveled from the Western Front to the mountains of Macedonia. What he saw and experienced was vividly captured in his journals and in letters to his parents (and to his brother, Thornton Wilder) back home. "Dramatic, enlightening, and gripping...a major contribution"
—Louis Martz, Yale University
0-300-05560-9 YALE....$26.00

Denis **Winter**

Death's Men: Soldiers of the Great War

The individual British soldier, in the trenches with five million of his countrymen

See also WORLD WAR I under WARS THROUGH THE AGES under MILITARY AFFAIRS

See also ARMAGGEDON: 1914-1918 under THE 20TH CENTURY under GREAT BRITAIN AND IRELAND

0-14-016822-2 PENGUIN PB $12.00

A Broken World: The Interwar Years

Despite the ravages of war, the Europe of 1919 seemed more "a broken world," in Raymond Sontag's phrase, than a Europe destroyed. Yet the hope that the Europeans could pick up where they had left off in 1914 and once again find prosperity was shattered by the Great Depression and the ascension of Hitler in 1933. The Depression cast its political shadow over the entire decade, passing the threat—and often the triumph—of dictatorship over much of the continent.

Modris **Eksteins**

Rites of Spring: The Great War and the Birth of the Modern Age

A cultural history of the influence of World War I on Western society, opening with the premiere performance of Stravinsky's *Le Sacre du Printemps* in Paris and ending with Hitler committing suicide in his Berlin bunker while his officers danced in the cafeteria

0-385-41202-9 ANCHOR PB $14.00

Gerald D. **Feldman**

The Great Disorder: Politics, Economics, and Society in the German Inflation, 1914-1924

"A sweeping history of Germany in the age of inflation"—*The Historian*

0-19-510114-6 OXFORD PB $39.95

Felix **Gilbert**

A European Past: Memoirs, 1905-1945

A historian's early years. By the editor of *The Norton History of Modern Europe*

0-393-02552-7 NORTON $19.95

David Clay **Large**

Between Two Fires: Europe's Path in the 1930s

A series of vivid portraits portrays the European drama in the decade before the war. Among other themes Large assesses the Stavisky Affair, the Night of the Long Knives, the Spanish Civil War and the destruction of Guernica, and the Munich Conference of 1938

0-393-02751-1 NORTON $22.50

Sally **Marks**

The Illusion of Peace: International Relations, 1918-1933

0-312-40635-5 ST. MARTIN'S PB $21.99

Marc **Trachtenberg**

Reparation in World Politics: France and European Economic Diplomacy, 1916-1923

A lucid examination of the complicated war debts-reparations question

0-231-04786-X COLUMBIA $59.50

Paris Was Yesterday: France Between the Wars

Joel **Colton**

Leon Blum: Humanist in Politics

France's first socialist prime minister; by the co-author, with R.R. Palmer, of A *History of the Modern World*

0-8223-0762-6 DUKE PB $23.95

John E. **Dreifort**

Myopic Grandeur: The Ambivalence of French Foreign Policy Toward the Far East, 1919-1945

0-87338-441-5 KENT STATE $35.00

Romy **Golan**

Modernity and Nostalgia: Art and Politics in France Between the Wars

0-300-06350-4 YALE $45.00

Julian **Jackson**

The Popular Front in France: Defending Democracy, 1934-1938

"Provides the first history of the French Popular Front in English, and fills that surprising gap with scholarly distinction" —*International Affairs*

0-521-31252-3 CAMBRIDGE PB $29.95

Michael B. **Miller**

Shanghai on the Metro: Spies, Intrigue, and the French Between the Wars

First published in 1994

0-520-08519-1 CALIFORNIA $35.00

Eugen **Weber**

The Hollow Years: France in the 1930s

0-393-31479-0 NORTON PB $14.95

Coco Chanel

The Rise of Italian Fascism

Alexander **De Grand**

Italian Fascism: Its Origins and Development

0-8032-6578-6 NEBRASKA PB $12.00

Victoria **De Grazia**

The Culture of Consent: Mass Organization of Leisure in Fascist Italy

What the regime meant in practice to the average Italian

0-521-23705-X CAMBRIDGE $65.00

How Fascism Ruled Women: Italy, 1922-1945

0-520-07456-4 CALIFORNIA $35.00
0-520-06027-X CALIFORNIA PB $14.00

Denis Mack **Smith**

Mussolini: A Biography

Authoritative and accessible, and rapidly becoming the standard English biography. "While his book may not be psychohistory in the strict sense of the term, there hovers in the background of his account the sort of informed professional understanding that has inspired the best work in that genre"—H. Stuart Hughes

0-394-71658-2 RANDOM HOUSE PB $18.00

Central and Eastern Europe Between the Wars

Ivo **Banac**

The National Question in Yugoslavia: Origins, History, Politics

"Succeeds in disentangling the astonishing complexities of the Yugoslav situation between 1918 and 1921, and points convincingly to the likely causes of the dramatic developments that followed the creation of Europe's last great multinational state" —Istvan Deak, *NY Review of Books*

0-8014-1675-2 CORNELL $55.00
0-8014-9493-1 CORNELL PB $17.95

Igor **Lukes**

Czechoslovakia Between Stalin and Hitler: The Diplomacy of Edvard Benes in the 1930s

The attempts to secure the existence of the Republic of Czechoslovakia in the treacherous space between the millstones of the East and West. "One of the most important and interesting studies of the events which led to World War II"—Adam B. Ulam

0-19-510267-3 OXFORD PB $29.95

Joseph **Rothschild**

East Central Europe Between the Two World Wars

0-295-95357-8 WASHINGTON PB $25.00

The Third Reich

Portraits of Weimar

Michael **Brenner**
The Renaissance of Jewish Culture in Weimar Germany
Offers fresh insight into modern questions of Jewish existence, identity, and integration into other cultures
0-300-06262-1 YALE $30.00

Wolf von **Eckhardt** & Sander L. **Gilman**
Bertold Brecht's Berlin: A Scrapbook of the Twenties
0-8032-9612-6 NEBRASKA PB $25.00

Peter **Gay**
Weimar Culture: The Outsider as Insider
A large-scale account of a vital and catastrophic era of modern times
0-313-22972-4 GREENWOOD $59.75
0-06-131482-X HARPERCOLLINS PB $18.90

Anton **Kaes** & others
Weimar Republic Source Book
Highly recommended anthology of texts, many appearing here in English for the first time. "An indispensable, enthralling, properly ambitious book"—Susan Sontag
0-520-06775-4 CALIFORNIA PB $24.95

John **Willett**
Art and Politics in the Weimar Period: The New Sobriety, 1917-1933
From the German typographic revolution to the Brecht-Weill partnership. "An original and challenging book, thoroughly researched and aptly illustrated"—*Times* (London)
See also **THEORY AND CRITICISM** under **ART HISTORY: GENERAL STUDIES** in **ART**
See also **EXPRESSIONISM AND THE BLUE RIDER** under **20TH-CENTURY ART** in **ART**
See also **CRITICAL STUDIES** under **GERMAN LITERATURE** in **LITERATURE OF EUROPE, AFRICA, AND ASIA**
0-306-80724-6 DA CAPO PB $17.95

Why Hitler Came to Power

Theodore **Abel**
Why Hitler Came into Power
FOREWORD BY THOMAS CHILDERS
0-674-95200-6 HARVARD PB $15.95

David **Abraham**
The Collapse of the Weimar Republic: Political Economy and Crisis
Reissued version of the controversial analysis of the fall of Weimar and rise of Hitler
0-8419-1083-9 HOLMES & MEIER $45.00
0-8419-1084-7 HOLMES & MEIER PB $18.95

Adolf Hitler

Thomas **Childers**
The Nazi Voter: The Social Foundations of Fascism in Germany, 1919-1933
Statistical analysis that illuminates upper and lower-middle-class electoral support for the Nazis
0-8078-4147-1 NORTH CAROLINA PB $16.95

Sebastian **Haffner**
The Ailing Empire: Germany from Bismarck to Hitler
By the author of *The Meaning of Hitler*
0-88064-127-4 FROMM PB $9.95

A.J. **Nicholls**
Weimar and the Rise of Hitler
A good introduction
0-312-05795-4 ST. MARTIN'S $45.00
0-312-86067-6 ST. MARTIN'S PB $16.00

Fritz **Stern**
Dreams and Delusions: The Drama of German History
"Stern writes with all the poignancy of one who loves German civilization deeply and is determined to fathom how it could have done such terrible violence to others, and to itself"
—David P. Calleo, *Foreign Affairs*
See also **GERMANY** under **19TH-CENTURY EUROPE**
0-394-75772-6 VINTAGE PB $14.00

Life, Death, and Politics in the Third Reich

Peter **Adam**
The Art of the Third Reich
0-8109-1912-5 ABRAMS $49.50
0-8109-2615-6 ABRAMS PB $19.95

Karl-Dietrich **Bracher**
The German Dictatorship: The Origins, Structure, and Effects of National Socialism
According to Fritz Stern, probably the most authoritative account
TRANSLATED BY JEAN STEINBERG
INTRODUCTION BY PETER GAY
0-275-83780-7
HOLT RINEHART & WINSTON PB $34.95

Alfred M. **de Zayas**
The Wehrmacht War Crimes Bureau, 1939-1945
FOREWORD BY HOWARD S. LEVIE
0-8032-9908-7 NEBRASKA PB $16.95

Bernt **Engelmann**
In Hitler's Germany: Everyday Life in the Third Reich
Interviews with the "silent" generation
TRANSLATED BY KRISHNA WINSTON
FOREWORD BY STUDS TERKEL
0-8052-0864-X SCHOCKEN PB $15.10

Klaus P. **Fischer**
Nazi Germany: A New History
0-8264-0797-8 CONTINUUM $37.50
0-8264-0906-7 CONTINUUM PB $24.95

Michael **Freeman**
Atlas of Nazi Germany: A Political, Economic and Social Anatomy of the Third Reich
Second edition published in 1996
0-02-910681-8 MACMILLAN $75.00

Henry **Grosshans**
Hitler and the Artists
How Hitler's perverse notions of cultural advancement led to clashes with many of Germany's major artists; illustrated
0-8419-0746-3 HOLMES & MEIER $34.50

Hilmar **Hoffmann**
The Triumph of Propaganda: Film and National Socialism, 1933-1945
TRANSLATED BY V.R. BERGHAHN & JOHN BROADWIN
1-57181-066-8 BERGHAHN $42.00

David **Irving**
Göring: A Biography
Reichsmarschal, drug addict, and onetime mental patient, Hermann Göring was Hitler's alter ego and chosen successor. This is the first full-length biography of him and the only one in print
0-380-70824-8 AVON PB $12.95

Claudia **Koonz**
Mothers in the Fatherland: Women, Family Life and Nazi Politics
Traces the role of women in the massive German war effort
See also **MODERN EUROPEAN HISTORY** under **EUROPEAN HISTORY** under **WOMEN'S STUDIES** in **SOCIAL STUDIES**
0-312-02256-5 ST. MARTIN'S PB $17.95

Robert Jay **Lifton**

The Nazi Doctors: Medical Killing and the Psychology of Genocide

"Breaks through the frontiers of historiography to provide a convincing psychological interpretation of the Third Reich and the crimes of National Socialism"
—Neal Ascherson, NY *Review of Books*

0-465-04905-2 BASIC PB $18.50

Richard **Mandell**

The Nazi Olympics

A look at the 1936 Munich Olympics, one of the most bizarre episodes in modern sports

0-252-01325-5 ILLINOIS PB $12.95

George L. **Mosse**

Nazi Culture

Choice selections from the newspapers, the literature, and the public pronouncements of the age

0-8052-0668-X SCHOCKEN PB $16.95

J. **Noakes** & Geoffrey **Pridham**, editors

Nazism 1919-1945

Volume I
The Rise to Power

0-85989-472-X EXETER PB $12.95

Volume II
State, Economy, and Society

0-85989-461-4 EXETER PB $15.95

Volume III
Foreign Policy, War, and Racial Extermination

0-85989-474-6 EXETER PB $18.95

Richard **Overy**

The Nazi Economic Recovery, 1932-1938

Argues that the war preparation that took place in the 1930s was incompatible with long-term economic recovery, and that the German economic miracle did not occur until *after* 1945. Fully revised and updated 1996 edition of the Macmillan title of 1982

0-521-55767-4 CAMBRIDGE PB $9.95

Alison **Owings**

Frauen: German Women Recall the Third Reich

"A remarkable work of history that stands out from the vast library of World War II studies for its sheer intimacy and its sometimes startling perspectives"—*LA Times Book Review*

0-8135-1992-6 RUTGERS $45.00
0-8135-2200-5 RUTGERS PB $16.95

Jack N. **Porter**

Sexual Politics in the Third Reich: The Persecution of Homosexuals During the Holocaust

0-932270-05-0 SPENCER PB $24.95

Robert N. **Proctor**

Racial Hygiene: Medicine Under the Nazis

0-674-74578-7 HARVARD PB $16.95

Joachim **Remak**, editor

The Nazi Years: A Documentary History

0-88133-527-4 WAVELAND PB $9.95

David **Schoenbaum**

Hitler's Social Revolution: Class and Status in Nazi Germany, 1933-1939

Argues that Hitler, by leveling classes, accomplished a social revolution

0-393-31554-1 NORTON PB $14.95

William L. **Shirer**

The Rise and Fall of the Third Reich

The popular journalistic account; readers should also consult Joachim Fest's *Hitler*

0-517-10294-3 CRESCENT $19.99
0-449-21977-1 FAWCETT PB $7.99

Ronald **Smelser**

Robert Ley: Hitler's Labor Front Leader

The architect of the German Labor Front. Corrupt and alcoholic, Ley typified the criminal mentality of the Nazi elite

0-85496-161-5 BERG $38.00

Albert **Speer**

Inside the Third Reich

An insider's account of Hitler's machine, to be read with caution

0-02-037500-X MACMILLAN PB $16.00

Marie **Vassiltchikov**

Berlin Diaries, 1940-1945

EDITED BY ANNE FREEDGOOD

0-394-75777-7 VINTAGE PB $14.00

John **Weiss**

Ideology of Death: Why the Holocaust Happened in Germany

1-56663-088-6 DEE $29.95

Hitler: Studies in Tyranny

Alan **Bullock**

Hitler: A Study in Tyranny

A solid biography; tells as much about the times as the man. "Remains the best biography of Adolf Hitler in English"
—Gordon A. Craig, *NY Review of Books*

See also **THE HIGH COMMAND** under **MEMOIRS AND BIOGRAPHIES** under **THE SECOND WORLD WAR**

0-06-092020-3 HARPERCOLLINS PB $17.00

William **Carr**

Hitler: A Study in Personality and Politics

0-7131-6462-X ARNOLD PB $18.95

Marlis **Steinert**

Hitler: A Biography

TRANSLATED BY STEVEN RENDALL

0-393-03867-X NORTON $27.50

Joachim C. **Fest**

Hitler

"An enormous mural of sorcery, conquest, war and destruction"—*Nation*

TRANSLATED BY RICHARD & CLARA WINSTON

0-15-640946-1 HARCOURT BRACE PB $18.95

Sebastian **Haffner**

The Meaning of Hitler

The psychological and historical forces that shaped the mind of Hitler and made his rise possible

TRANSLATED BY EWALD OSERS

0-674-55775-1 HARVARD PB $11.95

Adolf **Hitler**

Mein Kampf

Hitler's vituperative autobiography, written while he was in prison for his beer-hall *putsch*, gives his theories of Aryan superiority, Jewish conspiracy and democratic degeneracy, and provides a blueprint of his totalitarian regime and war aims

See also **FASCISM AND TOTALITARIANISM** under **POLITICAL THOUGHT** in **SOCIAL STUDIES**

TRANSLATED BY RALPH MANHEIM

0-395-07801-6 HOUGHTON MIFFLIN $24.95
0-395-08362-1 HOUGHTON MIFFLIN PB $16.95

J.P. **Stern**

Hitler: The Fuhrer and the People

0-520-02952-6 CALIFORNIA PB $13.95

John **Toland**

Adolf Hitler

"The first book that anyone who wants to learn about Hitler or the war in Europe must read!"
—*Newsweek*

0-385-42053-6 DOUBLEDAY PB $19.95

H.R. **Trevor-Roper**

The Last Days of Hitler

See also **EUROPE** under **THE END OF THE WAR** under **THE SECOND WORLD WAR**

0-226-81224-3 CHICAGO PB $14.95

Zbynek **Zeman**

Heckling Hitler: Caricatures of the Third Reich

A study of anti-Nazi cartoons, with profiles of the artists and numerous illustrations

See also **POLITICAL CARTOONISTS** under **COMICS** in **POPULAR READING**

0-87451-403-7 NEW ENGLAND PB $19.95

Fascism and Totalitarianism: General Studies

"Totalitarianism is the antithesis of liberalism and its most implacable enemy. It rejects the philosophical principles on which the liberal order rests. It denies the ultimate worth of the individual, valuing him only insofar as he is useful to the state or national community...It also denies the fundamental harmony of human interests, stressing instead the universality of conflict, whether social, national, or racial. From the point of view of these assumptions, totalitarianism is a conservative creed. It is a mass-oriented movement, harnessing the emotions and aspirations of the multitude not to satisfy them but, with their help, to destroy resistance to total power whether at home or abroad. It is conservative in its aims and radical in its means."—Richard Pipes, *Western Civilization: The Struggle for Empire to Europe in the Modern World*

Richard **Bessel**, editor
Fascist Italy and Nazi Germany: Comparisons and Contrasts
Ten essays on two regimes central to 20th-century history
0-521-47711-5 CAMBRIDGE PB $18.95

Mussolini

Martin **Blinkhorn**, editor
Fascists and Conservatives
Thirteen contributors explore the relationship between the radical right and the conservative right within Italy, Germany, Spain, Portugal, France, Britain, Austria, Romania, Greece, and the Nordic countries
0-04-940087-8 UNWIN HYMAN PB $24.95

Alan **Bullock**
Hitler and Stalin: Parallel Lives
A magisterial dual biography of the two great leaders of totalitarian societies
0-679-72994-1 VINTAGE PB $22.00

F.L. **Carsten**
The Rise of Fascism
0-520-04307-3 CALIFORNIA $40.00
0-520-04643-9 CALIFORNIA PB $15.95

Stanley G. **Payne**
Fascism: A Comparative Approach Toward a Definition
0-299-08060-9 WISCONSIN $25.00
0-299-08064-1 WISCONSIN PB $9.95

Fritz **Stern**
The Politics of Cultural Despair: A Study in the Rise of the Germanic Ideology
The development of Nazi ideology, as evidenced by the writings of three German cultural critics, Paul de Lagarde, Julius Langbehn, and Moeller van den Bruck
0-520-02626-8 CALIFORNIA PB $15.00

Zeev **Sternhell**
The Birth of Fascist Ideology: From Cultural Rebellion to Political Revolution
0-691-03289-0 PRINCETON $45.00

The Spanish Civil War

Gabriel **Jackson**
The Spanish Republic and the Civil War, 1931-1939
Polished, detailed account, sympathetic to the liberal Republican cause
0-691-00757-8 PRINCETON PB $24.95

Laurie **Lee**
A Moment of War
As a wartime volunteer from England, Lee walked across the Pyrenees to Spain,, and into the most terrible period of the Spanish Civil War. This is the memoir of Lee's participation in the war and a moving account of returning to and remembering the scenes he witnessed there. "Aches with unforgotten cold, and trembles with unforgotten terror"—*The Guardian.*
1-56584-173-5 NEW PRESS PB $9.95

Nancy **MacDonald**
Homage to the Spanish Exiles: Voices from the Spanish Civil War
INTRODUCTION BY MARY MCCARTHY
0-89885-325-7 HUMAN SCIENCES $28.95

Shirley **Mangini-Gonzalez**
Memories of Resistance: Women's Voices from the Spanish Civil War
0-300-05816-0 YALE $27.50

Cary **Nelson** & Jefferson **Hendricks**, editors
Madrid 1937: Letters of the Abraham Lincoln Brigade from the Spanish Civil War
0-415-91408-6 ROUTLEDGE $40.00

George **Orwell**
Homage to Catalonia
Memoirs of fighting for the Republicans
See also **20TH-CENTURY BRITISH ESSAYS AND OTHER PROSE** in **LITERATURE OF THE BRITISH ISLES**
INTRODUCTION BY LIONEL TRILLING
0-15-642117-8 HARCOURT BRACE PB $8.00

Stanley G. **Payne**
Falange: A History of Spanish Fascism
0-8047-0059-1 STANFORD PB $14.95

The Franco Regime, 1936-1975
0-299-11070-2 WISCONSIN $30.00

Spain's First Democracy: The Second Republic, 1931-1936
0-299-13674-4 WISCONSIN PB $19.95

Hugh **Thomas**
The Spanish Civil War
0-671-75876-4 TOUCHSTONE PB $20.00

The Second World War

General Histories

Peter **Calvocoressi**
Total War: Causes and Courses of the Second World War
If you're looking for only one book on the war, this is it. Revised and expanded since its original 1972 publication, this 1989 edition incorporates the latest research in governmental archives. Of special importance is the new information on Ultra intelligence, the decipherment of the German secret code. "As good a one-volume history of World War II as we are likely to get" —*Chicago Tribune Book World*
0-679-75843-7 PANTHEON $20.00

John **Charmley**
Churchill's Grand Alliance
0-15-127581-5 HARCOURT BRACE $26.00
0-15-600470-4 HARCOURT BRACE PB $18.00

Kati **David**
A Child's War: World War II Through the Eyes of Children
"A rare and poignant account of World War II as witnessed through the eyes of 15 children of different faiths and countries …a book that could well be read by young people to discover the sorrow's instead of the glories of war" —Herbert Mitgang, *NY Times*
0-941423-24-7 FOUR WALLS $17.95

Roy **Douglas**
The World War 1939-1945: The Cartoonist's Vision
Wartime cartoons from various combatant and neutral nations; features 247 cartoons
0-415-03049-8 ROUTLEDGE PB $29.95

Martin **Gilbert**
The Second World War: A Complete History
Virtually a day-by-day account, from the German invasion of Poland on September 1, 1939, to the postwar aftermath with its changing perceptions. Gilbert is particularly sensitive to the war's victims, both civilian and military. Over 102 expertly drawn maps and 130 black-and-white photographs help make this a valuable addition to any World War II library
0-8050-0534-X HOLT $29.95
0-8050-1788-7 HOLT PB $19.95

John **Keegan**
The Second World War
A thorough, 592-page history of World War II from the eminent military historian, with fascinating discussions of the tactics and strategies deployed in five crucial battles
0-670-77921-0 VIKING $24.95

Robert **Leckie**

Delivered from Evil: The Saga of World War II

A one-volume history that makes excellent use of first-person testimonies

0-06-091535-8 HARPERCOLLINS PB $20.00

J. Robert **Moskin**

Mr. Truman's War: The Final Victories of World War II and the Birth of the Postwar World

The first months of Truman's presidency included the defeat of the Nazis and Japan, the birth of the United Nations, the dropping of the atom bomb, and the beginning of the Cold War. As such Truman faced in his first months, as David McCullough wrote, "a greater surge of history, with larger, more difficult, more far-reaching decisions than any president before him." Moskin's dramatic chronicle and analysis captures this key period of the century in unprecedented vividness

0-679-40936-X RANDOM HOUSE $30.00

Richard **Overy**

Why the Allies Won

Why an Axis victory was very nearly attained in 1942, and how the allies regained military superiority at the war's critical turning point

0-393-03925-0 NORTON $29.95

R.A.C. **Parker**

Struggle for Survival: The History of the Second World War

"A magnificent achievement… As a one-volume survey, it is unlikely to be surpassed"—Kenneth O. Morgan. 24 photographs, 14 maps

0-19-219126-8 OXFORD $27.50

0-19-289112-X OXFORD PB $11.95

C.J. **Sulzberger**

World War II

"An objective and engrossing commentary"
—San Francisco Chronicle

0-8281-0331-3 AMERICAN HERITAGE PB $13.95

Gerhard L. **Weinberg**

Germany, Hitler, and World War II: Essays in Modern German and World History

Includes careful examinations of the Holocaust, the connection between the European and Pacific theaters of war, and comparative analysis of the leadership styles of Hitler, Stalin, Roosevelt, and Tojo

0-521-56626-6 CAMBRIDGE PB $15.95

A World at Arms: A Global History of World War II

The author's enormous theme is that, while the Axis partners in World War I fought mainly to maintain traditional balances of power, in World War II they sought a total reordering of resources and populations. The world was in dire shape, he suggests, and we're lucky to have gotten through it with so *little* destruction. "Rich in content and sharply interpretive, Weinberg's book is a stunning achievement"
—Publishers Weekly

0-521-44317-2 CAMBRIDGE $39.95

0-521-55879-4 CAMBRIDGE PB $19.95

Gordon **Wright**

The Ordeal of Total War, 1939-1945

Originally published in the late 1960s, this remains a good survey of the war's military, diplomatic, social, technological, and psychological ramifications

0-06-131408-0 HARPERCOLLINS PB $14.50

Winston S. **Churchill**

The Second World War

Volume 1
The Gathering Storm

The origins of, and entry into, the war and Churchill's appointment as prime minister at age 65

See also **WINSTON CHURCHILL** under **THE 20TH CENTURY** under **GREAT BRITAIN AND IRELAND**

0-395-41055-X HOUGHTON MIFFLIN PB.......$16.95

Volume 2
Their Finest Hour

The months from May to December 1940

0-395-07536-X HOUGHTON MIFFLIN $35.00

0-395-41056-8 HOUGHTON MIFFLIN PB.......$14.95

Volume 3
Grand Alliance

1941: the year of the sinking of the Bismarck, Hitler's invasion of Russia, Pearl Harbor, and the formation of the "Grand Alliance"

0-395-07538-6 HOUGHTON MIFFLIN $35.00

Volume 4
The Hinge of Fate

The turning of the tide in the Pacific and North Africa

0-395-07539-4 HOUGHTON MIFFLIN $35.00

0-395-41058-4 HOUGHTON MIFFLIN PB.......$14.95

Volume 5
Closing the Ring

Allied efforts up to the Normandy invasion. This volume is currently out of print

0-395-41059-2 HOUGHTON MIFFLIN $9.95

Volume 6
Triumph and Tragedy

0-395-41060-6 HOUGHTON MIFFLIN PB.......$14.95

Reference

Mark Mayo **Boatner**

Biographical Dictionary of World War II

See also **BIOGRAPHICAL DICTIONARIES** under **GENERAL INFORMATION** under **REFERENCE** in **BUSINESS AND REFERENCE**

0-89141-548-3 PRESIDIO PB $50.00

I.C.B. **Dear**

The Oxford Companion to World War II

Seventeen hundred entries cover World War II in its entirety

0-19-866225-4 OXFORD $60.00

John **Keegan**

The Times Atlas of the Second World War

A remarkable, truly outstanding and original production without an equivalent …it offers page after page of stunning and eye-catching images of the war, and employs a variety of techniques … A stunning work of reference and a great educational tool"
—Paul Kennedy, *NY Times*

0-517-12377-0 CRESCENT $29.99

The Road to War

Anthony **Adamthwaite**

The Making of the Second World War

0-415-90716-0 UNWIN HYMAN PB $19.95

FDR

Robert **Divine**

The Reluctant Belligerent: American Entry into World War II

0-07-554672-8 MCGRAW HILL PB $19.15

Waldo **Heinrichs**

Threshold of War: Franklin D. Roosevelt and American Entry into World War II

Roosevelt emerges as a cautious and deliberate leader in this narrative of the climactic months leading up to Pearl Harbor

0-19-506168-3 OXFORD PB $11.95

Eberhard **Jackel**

Hitler's World View: A Blueprint for Power

FOREWORD BY FRANKLIN L. FORD

0-674-40425-4 HARVARD PB $12.95

Gordon **Martel**, editor

The Origins of the Second World War Reconsidered: The A.J.P. Taylor Debate After Twenty-Five Years

0-415-08420-2 UNWIN HYMAN PB $24.95

Anthony **Read** & David **Fisher**
The Deadly Embrace: Hitler, Stalin, and the Nazi-Soviet Pact, 1939-1941
"The story of the 'monstrous chess game' the two dictators…proceeded to play, using whole countries as pieces while preparing for a battlefield confrontation that would exceed anything before or since in bloodshed" —*Publishers Weekly*
See also **WORLD WAR II** under **THE STALIN ERA** under **RUSSIAN STUDIES**
0-393-02528-4 NORTON $25.00
0-393-30651-8 NORTON PB $12.95

Norman **Rich**
Hitler's War Aims: Ideology, the Nazi State, and the Course of Expansion
A good overview by a shrewd historian of diplomacy
0-393-00802-9 NORTON PB $12.95

A.J.P. **Taylor**
The Origins of the Second World War
Taylor's influential work remains a controversial one, arguing that responsibility for the war and its devastation is too complex an issue to be blamed entirely on Hitler
0-684-82947-9 SCRIBNERS PB $14.00

The United States and World War II

Michael C.C. **Adams**
The Best War Ever: America and World War II
0-8018-4696-X JOHNS HOPKINS $38.95
0-8018-4697-8 JOHNS HOPKINS PB $13.95

David **Brinkley**
Washington Goes to War
0-345-40730-4 BALLANTINE PB $12.00

Robert **Dallek**
Franklin D. Roosevelt and American Foreign Policy, 1932-1945
The first full-scale history of American diplomacy during the Roosevelt presidency
See also **THE GREAT DEPRESSION AND THE NEW DEAL** under **US HISTORY, 1877-1945** in **HISTORY OF THE AMERICAS**
0-19-509732-7 OXFORD PB $18.95

Diane Burke **Fessler**
No Time for Fear: Voices of American Military Nurses in World War II
0-87013-416-7 MICHIGAN STATE $34.95

Robert **Heide** & John **Gilman**
Home Front America: Popular Culture of the World War II Era
0-8118-0927-7 CHRONICLE PB $17.95

Sherna Berger **Gluck**
Rosie the Riveter Revisited: Women, the War and Social Change
An oral history of the women who went to work to help with the war effort and the lives they led after the war ended
See also **AMERICA'S WORKING WOMEN** under **AMERICAN HISTORY** under **WOMEN'S STUDIES** in **SOCIAL STUDIES**
0-8057-9022-5 TWAYNE $22.95
0-452-01024-1 NEW AMERICAN LIBRARY PB $12.95

Samuel **Hynes**
Reporting World War II: American Journalism, 1938-1946
Volume I
See also **THE AGE OF THE REPORTER: SINCE 1880** under **HISTORY** under **JOURNALISM** in **PERFORMING ARTS AND MEDIA**
1-88301-104-3 LIBRARY OF AMERICA $35.00
Volume II
See also **THE AGE OF THE REPORTER: SINCE 1880** under **HISTORY** under **JOURNALISM** in **PERFORMING ARTS AND MEDIA**
1-88301-105-1 LIBRARY OF AMERICA $35.00

Allen W. **Koop**
Stark Decency: German Prisoners of War in a New England Village
0-87451-468-1 NEW ENGLAND PB $13.95

Judy Barrett **Littoff** & David C. **Smith**
Since You Went Away: World War II Letters from American Women on the Home Front
A collection of letters from women to their men fighting overseas. Worthwhile reading
0-19-506795-9 OXFORD $27.50
0-7006-0714-5 KANSAS PB $15.95

Alan S. **Milward**
War Economy and Society: 1939-1945
The war years with a focus on economic issues
0-520-03942-4 CALIFORNIA PB $15.95

William L. **O'Neill**
Democracy at War: America's Fight at Home and Abroad in World War II
"A grand and sensitive synthesis of what the war meant to an entire generation and of how unity, valor and victory came only after a period of unpreparedness, confusion and reluctance. O'Neill writes with vivid clarity—*Houston Chronicle*
0-02-923678-9 FREE PRESS $24.95
0-674-19737-2 HARVARD PB $16.95

Norman **Polmar** & Thomas B. **Allen**
World War II: America at War, 1941-1945
The war from an American perspective; offers a complete military history and a panorama of U.S. wartime life and events. Originally published in 1991
0-679-77039-9 RANDOM HOUSE PB $20.00

Geoffrey **Perret**
Days of Sadness, Years of Triumph: The American People, 1939-1945
0-299-10394-3 WISCONSIN PB $17.50

Stephen W. **Sears**, editor
Eyewitness to World War II: The Best of American Heritage
0-395-61903-3 HOUGHTON MIFFLIN PB $9.95

Studs **Terkel**
The Good War: An Oral History of World War II
Interviews with men and women, whites, blacks, and Asians, combat soldiers, officers, and those who stayed at home
0-345-32568-0 BALLANTINE PB $7.99

William M. **Tuttle**, Jr.
Daddy's Gone to War: The Second World War in the Lives of America's Children
While WWII changed the geography of Europe, it also transformed the landscape of the American family. An analysis of the war's impact on a generation of Americans who were permanently altered and who themselves thus altered America. "Artful and absorbing" —*Kirkus Reviews*
0-19-504905-5 OXFORD $30.00

Nancy Baker **Wise** & Christy **Wise**
A Mouthful of Rivets: Women in World War II
"Together, mother and daughter have written a delightful, absorbing book of real-life stories: what women's lives were really like on the home front—and the factory front—during World War II"—*LA Times*
1-55542-703-0 JOSSEY-BASS $25.00

America's Concentration Camps

In one of the ugliest episodes in wartime America, some 120,000 Japanese-Americans were evacuated from their homes and relocated to internment camps in the months following the attack on Pearl Harbor. Renewed attention to the subject—culminating in reparations payments offered to the remaining victims by the US government—has produced books that focus both on the politics and human consequences of the internment.

Deborah **Gesensway**
Beyond Words: Images from America's Concentration Camps
The authors "have collected from attics, basements, and college libraries prison paintings by internees, ranging from comic caricatures to desolate landscapes…The result is not only beyond words, it is even beyond newsreels, since the moving hand of art is always present"—*NY Times Book Review*
0-8014-1919-0 CORNELL $42.50
0-8014-9522-9 CORNELL PB $21.95

Peter **Irons**

Justice at War: The Inside Story of the Japanese American Internment

The role of the Justice Department and interviews with participants, including the three defendants in the cases that reached the Supreme Court

0-520-08312-1 CALIFORNIA PB $14.95

The War in Europe

General Military Accounts

Matthew **Cooper**

The German Army, 1933-1945—Its Political and Military Failure

0-8128-8519-8 SCARBOROUGH PB $17.95

Michael **Howard**

Strategic Deception in the Second World War

0-393-31293-3 NORTON PB $13.95

F.W. von **Mellenthin**

Panzer Battles

0-345-32158-8 BALLANTINE PB $6.95

Germany

For related reading, see 20TH-CENTURY EUROPE TO THE SECOND WORLD WAR

Wilhelm **Diest** & Manfred **Messerschmidt**

Germany and the Second World War: The Build-Up of German Aggression

0-19-822866-X OXFORD $145.00

Klaus A. **Maier** & Horst **Rohde**

Germany and the Second World War: Germany's Initial Conquests in Europe

0-19-822885-6 OXFORD $95.00

Thomas **Powers**

Heisenberg's War

The story of the German atom program and the Allied response; demonstrates why, despite all the Nazis' technological might, they failed to build an atomic bomb. The drama involves the century's leading physicists, including Niels Bohr and Robert Oppenheimer, and centers around Werner Heisenberg, whose unwillingness to give Hitler a weapon of such magnitude may have spared the world vast destruction. "A comprehensive and resonant overview, notable for its compassionate perspectives on the moral dilemmas faced by men of genius…in a global conflict"—*Kirkus Reviews*

0-394-51411-4 KNOPF $27.50

Bernd **Stegemann** & others

Germany and the Second World War: The Mediterranean, South-East Europe, and North Africa 1939-1941

0-19-822884-8 OXFORD $105.00

Britain

Paul **Fussell**

Wartime: Understanding and Behavior in the Second World War

Explores the psychological culture of Britons and Americans during World War II. Fussell frankly confronts the "euphemism and rationalization" needed to deal with the often unacceptable reality from 1939 to 1945. Chapters include "Chickenshit, An Anatomy," "Drinking Far Too Much, Copulating Too Little," "Reading in Wartime," and "The Real War Will Never Get in the Books"

See also **HISTORY, POLITICS, AND SOCIETY** under **20TH-CENTURY AMERICAN ESSAYS AND JOURNALISM** in **LITERATURE OF THE AMERICAS**

0-19-503797-9 OXFORD $27.50
0-19-506577-8 OXFORD PB $12.95

Italy

MacGregor **Knox**

Mussolini Unleashed, 1939-1941: Politics and Strategy in Fascist Italy's Last War

0-521-23917-6 CAMBRIDGE $69.95
0-521-33835-2 CAMBRIDGE PB $19.95

Iris **Origo**

War in Val D'orcia: An Italian War Diary 1943-1944

FOREWORD BY DENIS MACK SMITH

0-87923-476-8 GODINE PB $13.95

France

Marguerite **Duras**

The War: A Memoir

Paris during the Nazi occupation and the first month of liberation

See also **FICTION** under **MODERN FRENCH LITERATURE** in **LITERATURE OF EUROPE, AFRICA, AND ASIA**

TRANSLATED BY BARBARA BRAY

1-56584-221-9 NEW PRESS PB $10.00

Michael R. **Marrus** & Robert O. **Paxton**

Vichy France and the Jews

A landmark study, focusing on the long denial of French collaboration in Hitler's "Final Solution"

See also **HOLOCAUST EXPERIENCES: FROM PARIS TO WARSAW** under **THE HOLOCAUST**

0-8047-2499-7 STANFORD PB $17.95

Marshal Petain

Robert O. **Paxton**

Vichy France: Old Guard and New Order, 1940-1944

"With the publication of *Vichy France,* [the] conventional apologia for Vichy is revealed for what it has always been: an alibi that made it easier for a generation of Frenchmen to live with themselves. Paxton's study tells us as much of the truth about Vichy as we are likely to have for a long time"
—Nicholas Wahl, Princeton University

0-231-05426-2 COLUMBIA $59.50

William L. **Shirer**

The Collapse of the Third Republic: An Inquiry into the Fall of France in 1940

0-306-80562-6 DA CAPO PB $22.95

John F. **Sweets**

Choices in Vichy France: The French Under Nazi Occupation

Popular responses to, and rejections of, Nazism in Clermont-Ferrand, near the Occupation capital

0-19-509052-7 OXFORD PB $15.95

Tzvetan **Todorov**

A French Tragedy: Scenes of the Civil War, Summer 1944

TRANSLATED BY MARY BYRD KELLY

0-874-51747-8 UDART $19.95

Poland

Richard C. **Lukas**

The Forgotten Holocaust: The Poles Under German Occupation, 1939-1944

0-8131-1566-3 KENTUCKY $24.00
0-87052-632-4 HIPPOCRENE PB $9.95

Steven **Zaloga** & Victor **Madej**

The Polish Campaign of 1939

An account of the Polish invasion from the perspective of the Polish Army; challenges the idea that the German victory was an easy one

0-87052-013-X HIPPOCRENE PB $11.95

Russia

Otto Preston **Chaney**

Zhukov

A biography of Stalin's greatest general

0-806-12807-0 UOKLA $39.95

David M. **Glantz** & Johnathan M. **House**

When Titans Clashed: How the Red Army Stopped Hitler

A brilliant, thorough history of the war in the east, to which Nazi Germany commited three quarters of its military might

0-700-60717-X UKANS $29.95

Bruce **Myles**

Night Witches: The Untold Story of Soviet Women in Combat

As the Nazis swept into the Soviet Union in 1941, the Russian air force sought female volunteers in a desperate attempt to fill its diminishing ranks. Three regiments of young women were trained as combat pilots, partaking in some of the war's fiercest battles and receiving the Soviet Union's highest decorations for bravery. Called "night witches" by their German foes, these women helped to turn the tide of the war. An unusual perspective on recent history

0-89733-288-1 ACADEMY CHICAGO PB $7.95

Roger R. **Reese**

Stalin's Reluctant Soldiers: A Social History of the Red Army, 1925-1941

The make-up of the army that was to (eventually) defeat Hitler

0-700-60717-X UKANS $29.95

Alexander **Werth**

Russia at War, 1941-1945

The classic history of the Soviet Union at war; precise, literate, thought-provoking, and a must for the student of World War II

See also WORLD WAR II under THE STALIN ERA under RUSSIAN STUDIES

0-88184-084-X CARROLL & GRAF PB $17.95

This scene of filth and suffering in that yard of the Red Army House was my last glimpse of Stalingrad. I remembered the long anxious days of the summer of 1942, and the nights of the London blitz, and the photographs of Hitler, smirking as he stood on the steps of the Madeleine in Paris, and the weary days of '38 and '39 when a jittery Europe would tune in to Berlin and hear Hitler's yells accompanied by the cannibal roar of the German mob. And there seemed a rough but divine justice in those frozen cesspools with their diarrhoea, and those horses' bones, and those starved yellow corpses in the yard of the Red Army House at Stalingrad.

RUSSIA AT WAR, 1941-1945

The Resistance

Jorgen **Haestrup**

European Resistance Movements, 1939-1945: A Complete History

0-313-28131-9 MECKLER $79.50

Peter **Hoffmann**

German Resistance to Hitler

See also RESCUE AND RESISTANCE under THE HOLOCAUST

0-674-35085-5 HARVARD $34.50

0-674-35086-3 HARVARD PB $15.95

Margaret L. **Rossiter**

Women in the Resistance

0-275-90222-6 PRAEGER $59.95

Inge **Scholl**

White Rose: Munich, 1942-1943

The story of courageous Catholic teenagers who opposed Hitler, by the sister of Sophie Scholl, one of the executed leaders of the group

TRANSLATED BY ARTHUR R. SCHULTZ

0-8195-6086-3 WESLEYAN PB $13.95

Margaret C. **Wietz**

Sisters in the Resistance: How Women Fought to Free France, 1940-1945

0-471-12676-4 WILEY $30.00

Jan **Yoors**

Crossing: A Journal of Survival and Resistance in World War II

An impassioned account of the author's recruitment by the British into World War II Resistance work and his subsequent enlisting of Lowara and Churara Gypsies in anti-Nazi activities

0-88133-364-6 WAVELAND PB $10.95

The War in Europe: The Western Front

The Opening Campaign

Marc **Bloch**

Strange Defeat: A Statement of Evidence Written in 1940

A moving testimonial by a distinguished medievalist, shot for his Resistance activities

TRANSLATED BY GERARD M. HOPKINS

0-374-90665-3 HIPPOCRENE $20.00

0-393-00371-X NORTON PB $9.95

James S. **Corum**

The Roots of Blitzkrieg: Hans von Seeckt and German Military Reform

Explores the lessons learned by the German military from the course of World War I

0-7006-0628-9 KANSAS PB $14.95

Walter **Lord**

The Miracle of Dunkirk

Was Dunkirk a defeat, a moral victory, or a lost opportunity? Lord explores the series of crises that led to encirclement and escape at a small town on the Belgian seacoast

0-670-28630-3 VIKING $17.95

Patrick **Turnbull**

Dunkirk: Anatomy of Disaster

0-8419-0396-4 HOLMES & MEIER $35.00

The Battle of Britain

Richard **Hough** & Denis **Richards**

The Battle of Britain: The Greatest Air Battle of World War II

0-393-30734-4 NORTON PB $17.95

Philip **Kaplan** & Richard **Collier**, editors

Their Finest Hour: The Battle of Britain Remembered

1-55859-047-1 ARTABRAS $29.98

John **Lukacs**

The Duel: 10 May - 31 July 1940: The Eighty Day Struggle Between Churchill and Hitler

0-395-61863-0 HOUGHTON MIFFLIN PB $10.95

Peter **Townsend**

The Odds Against Us: Memoirs of Aerial Combat at Night During the Battle of Britain

0-8217-2495-9 ZEBRA PB $4.50

D-Day and the Normandy Campaign

Stephen E. **Ambrose**

"D-Day" June 6, 1944: The Climatic Battle of World War II

"Once in a while a book comes along to lift us into another time and the gripping drama of a great heroic event. This is such a book. Extraordinary"—David McCullough

0-684-80137-X SIMON & SCHUSTER PB $16.00

Pegasus Bridge: June 6, 1944

0-671-67156-1 TOUCHSTONE PB $10.00

Donald M. **Goldstein** & others

D-Day Normandy: The Story and Photographs

The bestselling co-authors of *At Dawn We Slept* and *Miracle at Midway* again combine their formidable talents and insight to provide text for this 50th anniversary commemorative volume of "the longest day." Contains rare Allied and Third Reich photographs never before published.

0-02-881057-0 BRASSEY'S DEFENSE $30.00

Gordon **Harrison**

United States Army in World War II: European Theater of Operations, Cross-Channel Attack

The army's official history of D-Day

0-318-22740-1

GOVERNMENT PRINTING OFFICE $36.25

John **Keegan**

Six Armies in Normandy: From D-Day to the Liberation of Paris

Highly recommended account

0-14-005293-3 PENGUIN PB $9.95

Henry **Maule**

Caen: The Brutal Battle and Breakout from Normandy

A look at a key operation of the campaign; part of the Battle Standards Series

0-8095-7502-7 BORGO $25.00

Cornelius **Ryan**

The Longest Day

The oral history of June 6, 1944

0-671-89091-3 TOUCHSTONE PB $11.00

Theodore A. **Wilson**, editor

D-Day 1944

"Readers may be astonished at how much scholarly digging and the release of once-secret information have transformed the history of this campaign. At times it seems like a whole new war"—*New York Time Book Review*

FOREWORD BY JOHN S.D. EISENHOWER

0-7006-0674-2 KANSAS PB $22.50

From D-Day to V-E Day

William B. **Breuer**

Operation Dragoon: The Allied Invasion of the South of France

Operation Dragoon involved 1000 ships, 3000 aircraft, and one million troops

0-89141-601-3 PRESIDIO PB $14.95

Ken **Hechler**

The Bridge at Remagen

The story of the first Allied bridgehead over the Rhine

0-929521-79-X

MOTORBOOKS INTERNATIONAL PB $12.95

Robert A. **Miller**

August 1944

A day-by-day account of a crucial turning point

0-89141-316-2 PRESIDIO $17.95

0-89141-594-7 PRESIDIO PB $14.95

Cornelius **Ryan**

A Bridge Too Far

A thorough history of the Anglo-American drive to the Rhine at Arnheim in September 1944, a lost gamble to end the war that year

0-684-80330-5 TOUBK PB $15.00

Russell F. **Weigley**

Eisenhower's Lieutenants: The Campaign of France and Germany 1944-1945

Inspired by Freeman's Civil War classic, *Lee's Lieutenants*, this is a magnificent, scholarly approach, from the daily activity on the front to the problems of setting and achieving objectives in an incompletely unified Allied camp

0-253-13333-5 INDIANA $42.00

0-253-20608-1 INDIANA PB $19.95

The War in Europe: The Eastern Front

Alan **Clark**

Barbarossa: The Russian-German Conflict, 1941-1945

0-688-04268-6 MORROW PB $13.00

Harrison E. **Salisbury**

The Nine Hundred Days: The Siege of Leningrad

0-306-80253-8 DA CAPO PB $16.95

The Mediterranean War

Ernle **Bradford**

Siege: Malta, 1940-1943

A tiny island only 60 miles from Italy, Malta endured attack and siege for three years, refusing to surrender to the combined efforts of Italy and Germany. Currently, this large-print edition is the only one available

0-7089-1755-0 ULVERSCROFT $15.95

S.W. **Pack**

Invasion North Africa, 1942

Brief illustrated account of America's first amphibious attack in the European theater

0-684-15921-X SCRIBNERS $12.95

The Pacific War

Overviews

John **Costello**

The Pacific War, 1941-1945: The First Comprehensive One-Volume Account of the Causes and Conduct of World War II in the Pacific

See also **IMPERIAL JAPAN AND THE PACIFIC WAR** under **FROM THE MEIJI RESTORATION TO THE END OF THE EMPIRE: 1868-1945** under **JAPAN**

0-688-01620-0 MORROW PB $17.95

Thomas R. **Havens**

Valley of Darkness: The Japanese People and World War II

0-8191-5495-4

UNIVERSITY PRESS OF AMERICA PB $24.50

John W. **Dower**

War Without Mercy: Race and Power in the Pacific War

A history of anti-Japanese attitudes in America and anti-Western attitudes in Japan. "A cautionary tale for all peoples, now and in the future"—*Foreign Affairs*

0-394-75172-8 PANTHEON PB $15.00

Saburo **Ienaga**

The Pacific War, 1931-1945

A harsh critique of Japanese aggression by a leading Japanese scholar

TRANSLATED BY FRANK BALDWIN

0-394-73496-3 RANDOM HOUSE PB $13.00

Akira **Iriye**

Power and Culture: The Japanese-American War, 1941-1945

0-674-69582-8 HARVARD PB $22.50

Ronald H. **Spector**

Eagle Against the Sun: The American War with Japan

0-02-930360-5 FREE PRESS $29.95

0-394-74101-3 RANDOM HOUSE PB $17.00

E. T. **Wooldridge**, editor

Carrier Warfare in the Pacific

An oral history that includes the experiences of pilots, seamen, officers, and enlisted men in the Pacific Theater. Compelling first-hand accounts make this a unique historical contribution. "These memoirs will forever chronicle the determination and the daring feats of courageous people"
—John B. Connally, from the Foreword

1-56098-264-0 SMITHSONIAN $24.95

Pearl Harbor

Gordon W. **Prange**

At Dawn We Slept: The Untold Story of Pearl Harbor

Perhaps the best book on the subject

0-14-015734-4 VIKING PB $19.95

John J. **Stephan**

Hawaii Under the Rising Sun: Japan's Plans for Conquest After Pearl Harbor

"Will give a fresh perspective on the place of the Hawaiian islands in Japanese strategy and war aims"—*History*

0-8248-0872-X HAWAII $14.95

John **Toland**

Infamy: Pearl Harbor and Its Aftermath

Argues that FDR and others had prior knowledge of the Japanese attack

0-425-09040-X BERKLEY PB $5.95

The Philippines

Donald **Knox**

Death March: The Survivors of Bataan

PREFACE BY STANLEY L. FALK

0-15-625224-4 HARCOURT BRACE PB $13.00

Midway

Mitsuo **Fuchida** & Masatke **Okumiya**

Midway: The Battle that Doomed Japan

At Midway, Japan lost air superiority over the Pacific, and effective naval superiority as well

1-55750-575-6 NAVAL INSTITUTE $32.95

0-345-34691-2 BALLANTINE PB $5.99

Gordon W. **Prange**

Miracle at Midway

0-14-006814-7 VIKING PB $16.95

The Island War

Eric **Bergerud**

Touched with Fire: Land Warfare in the South Pacific

A revelatory and heart-stopping account of the regular infantrymen who struggled to contain the Japanese advance—a terrifyingly real story that is often overshadowed by the dropping of the atomic bomb. Based on hundreds of hours of interviews and placed in context of military analysis, this is an authentic and authoritative account

0-670-86158-8 VIKING $34.95

Harry **Gailey**

Peleliu: 1944

0-933852-41-X NAUTICAL & AVIATION $26.95

Brig. Gen. Samuel B. **Griffith II**

The Battle for Guadalcanal

The capture of the island by American marine and naval forces

0-933852-04-5 NAUTICAL & AVIATION $25.95

Robert **Leckie**

Okinawa: The Last Battle of World War II

A fast-paced, thought-provoking, stirring re-creation of one of World War II's most desperate and bloody battles

0-14-017389-7 PENGUIN PB $13.95

Bill D. **Ross**

Iwo Jima: Legacy of Valor

0-394-74288-5 RANDOM HOUSE PB $14.00

Carl **Solberg**

Decision and Dissent: With Halsey at Leyte Gulf

1-55750-791-0 NAVAL INSTITUTE $26.95

The War in the Air

Capt. Eric **Brown**, RN (Ret.)

Duels in the Sky: World War II Naval Aircraft in Combat

0-87021-063-7 NAVAL INSTITUTE $29.95

Thomas **Childers**

Wings of Morning: The Story of the Last American Bomber Shot Down over Germany in World War II

"Childers has often made me laugh and think. *Wings of Morning* made me weep and wonder"—Walter A. McDougall

0-201-40722-1 ADDISON-WESLEY PB $12.00

Jean Hascall **Cole**

Women Pilots of World War II

See also **WORLD HISTORY** under **WOMEN'S STUDIES** in **SOCIAL STUDIES**

0-87480-493-0 UTAH PB $12.95

Gerard M. **Devlin**

Paratrooper: The Saga of the U.S. Army and Marine Parachute and Glider Combat Troops During World War II

FOREWORD BY WILLIAM P. YARBOROUGH

0-312-59652-9 ST. MARTIN'S PB $14.95

Williamson **Murray**

Luftwaffe

An account of its downfall

0-933852-45-2 NAUTICAL & AVIATION $32.95

Ronard **Schaffer**

Wings of Judgment: American Bombing in World War II

War's terrible choices ensured that Dresden, Berlin, and dozens of other cities would not survive, but that Rome and Florence would be preserved

0-19-505640-X OXFORD PB $15.95

Michael S. **Sherry**

The Rise of American Air Power: The Creation of Armageddon

An in-depth history of American strategic bombing

See also **AIR POWER** under **MILITARY AFFAIRS**

0-300-03600-0 YALE $20.00

0-300-04414-3 YALE PB $20.00

The War at Sea

Paul S. **Dull**

A Battle History of the Imperial Japanese Navy: 1941-1945

A well-researched general history

0-87021-097-1 NAVAL INSTITUTE $36.95

Russell **Grenfell**

The Bismarck Episode

The sinking of the 42,000-ton Bismarck in May 1941 was both a military and psychological victory

0-8446-4024-7 SMITH $14.50

Jeter A. **Isely** & Philip **Crowl**

U.S. Marines and Amphibious War

A first-rate account of all the marine actions in the Pacific

0-686-31000-4 MARINE CORPS ASSOCIATION $15.95

Samuel Eliot **Morison**

The Two-Ocean War: A Short History of the United States Navy in the Second World War

0-316-58366-9 LITTLE, BROWN $37.50

0-316-58352-9 LITTLE, BROWN PB $22.95

Timothy **Mulligan**

Lone Wolf: The Life and Death of U-Boat Ace Werner Henke

0-8061-2780-5 OKLAHOMA PB $15.95

R. Adm. Richard H. **O'Kane**, USN (Ret.)

Wahoo: The Patrols of America's Most Famous World War II Submarine

The successes of the USS *Wahoo* recreated by the man who was the sub's exec for many of its war patrols

0-89141-572-6 PRESIDIO PB $15.95

Edward **Stafford**

The Big E

0-87021-036-X NAVAL INSTITUTE $32.95

Burkhard **von Mullenheim-Rechberg**

Battleship Bismarck: A Survivor's Story

0-87021-027-0 NAVAL INSTITUTE $29.95

Spies and Code-Breakers

Anthony C. **Brown**

Bodyguard of Lies

0-688-10281-6 QUILL PB $17.95

Edwin T. **Layton** & others

And I Was There: Pearl Harbor and Midway—Breaking the Secrets

0-688-06968-1 MORROW PB $15.00

John **Prados**

Combined Fleet Decoded: The Secret History of American Intelligence and the Japanese Navy in World War II

A recent, fascinating history

0-679-43701-0 RANDO $37.50

Gordon W. **Prange** & D.M. **Goldstein**

Target Tokyo: The Story of the Sorge Spy Ring

A look at Soviet spy Richard Sorge, who was tried and hanged by the Japanese in 1941

See also **ESPIONAGE TALES** under **ESPIONAGE** in **POPULAR READING**

0-07-050677-9 MCGRAW HILL $24.95

Countess Aline **Romanones**

The Spy Wore Red: My Adventures as an Undercover Agent in World War II

Memoirs of an American model who, in 1943, infiltrated the upper levels of Spanish society in order to uncover high-society intelligence links to Hitler

0-515-10653-4 CHARTER PB $5.99

Bradley F. **Smith**

Sharing Secrets with Stalin: British-American Intelligence Cooperation with Soviet Russia, 1941-1945

From the respected Modern War Studies series

0-700-60800-1 UKANS $35.00

John H. **Waller**

The Unseen War in Europe: Espionage and Conspiracy in the Second World War

Beginning with the war's onset when Great Britian lost virtually all of its agents in Europe to a sting operation run by Nazi intelligence, this is a narrative of a war of wits

0-679-44826-8 RANDOM HOUSE $35.00

Wesley K. **Wark**

The Ultimate Enemy: British Intelligence and Nazi Germany, 1933-1939

0-8014-1821-6 CORNELL $39.95

The End of the War

Europe

Martin **Gilbert**

The Day the War Ended: May 8, 1945—Victory in Europe

Gilbert, celebrated for his histories of the two World Wars, the Holocaust, and his life of Churchill, addresses the final day of the war in Europe

0-8050-3926-0 HOLT $30.00

Robert **Leckie**

The Last Great Victory: The End of World War II

0-525-93687-4 DUTTON $35.00

Anthony **Read** & David **Fisher**

The Fall of Berlin

0-393-03472-0 NORTON $29.95

H.R. **Trevor-Roper**

The Last Days of Hitler

See also **HITLER: STUDIES IN TYRANNY** under **20TH-CENTURY EUROPE TO THE SECOND WORLD WAR**

0-226-81224-3 CHICAGO PB $14.95

The Pacific: Hiroshima and Nagasaki

John **Hersey**

Hiroshima

Hersey's masterpiece tells what happened on August 6, 1945, through the memories of survivors

0-679-72103-7 VINTAGE PB $5.50

Philip **Nobile**

Judgement at the Smithsonian: The Bombing of Hiroshima and Nagasaki

The uncensored script of the Smithsonian's 50th anniversary exhibit of the Enola Gay

1-56924-841-9 MARLOWE PB $12.95

Richard **Rhodes**

The Making of the Atomic Bomb

"The comprehensive history of the bomb and also a work of literature"—Tracy Kidder

0-671-65719-4 SIMON & SCHUSTER PB $14.95

Martin J. **Sherwin**

A World Destroyed: Hiroshima and the Origins of the Arms Race

The best analysis of the decision to drop the bomb

See also **THE ATOMIC BOMB** under **FROM THE MEIJI RESTORATION TO THE END OF THE EMPIRE: 1868-1945** under **JAPAN**

0-394-75204-X VINTAGE PB $15.00

Ronald **Takaki**

Hiroshima: Why America Dropped the Atomic Bomb

From the psychological makeup of Harry Truman to the prevalent anti-Asian prejudice in America, Takaki presents a definitive study of why we dropped the bomb. "A lively, complex, multi-dimensional, and wonderfully undogmatic and inconclusive account of the American decision to use the atomic bomb—exactly the sort of book that is needed to stimulate debate and reflection"—Michael Walzer

0-316-83122-0 LITTLE, BROWN $19.95
0-316-83124-7 LITTLE, BROWN PB $11.95

Memoirs and Biographies

Erica **Fischer**

Aimee & Jaguar: A Love Story, Berlin 1943

This is a unique and tragic account of a World War II love affair, set in the little-explored territory of the Nazi persecution of homosexuals. A young Jewish lesbian and a gentile wife and mother, in love during the war, try to maintain a haven of peace as Berlin goes mad. But the Nazis will not permit it, deporting the Jewish partner to a ghetto, then a concentration camp. Now 80, the gentile partner tells her tragic story to the feminist writer and journalist Erica Fischer, who presents the story against its historical background with great sympathy and authenticity

0-06-018350-0 HARPERCOLLINS $24.00

Jonathan **Kaufman**

A Hole in the Heart of the World: Being Jewish in Eastern Europe After World War II

0-670-86747-0 VIKING $42.00

Gitta **Sereny**

Albert Speer: His Battle with Truth

The Nazi war criminal, considered through a decade of research, years of conversation, and access to private papers and intimate friends. Sereny takes us from Speer's childhood to his conviction at Nuremberg and his life in Spandau prison, struggling with his guilt. An access of remarkable depth and intimacy to the Nazi mind

0-394-52915-4 KNOPF $35.00

The High Command

A.J.P. **Taylor**

The War Lords

The five great leaders of the war: Churchill, Hitler, Mussolini, Roosevelt, and Stalin

0-14-004638-0 VIKING PB $11.95

Robert **Blake** & others, editors

Churchill

29 essays by renowned historians and political leaders that assess different aspects of Churchill's almost mythic career. Robin Edmonds reveals Churchill's lifelong antipathy to Russia; David Cannadine tackles his family, and more. "Expert essays on a fascinating subject…solid reading for anyone interested in 20th-century history"—*Kirkus Reviews*

0-19-820317-9 OXFORD $39.00

Winston Churchill

Paul D. **Bunker**

Bunker's War: The World War II Diary of Col. Paul D. Bunker

A personal account of Corregidor and the Philippines

0-89141-538-6 PRESIDIO $27.95

John **Charmley**

Churchill: The End of Glory, a Political Biography

The result of 15 years of research, this widely acclaimed biography dispels the myths created by Churchill as well as by his official biographer. "Probably the most important revisionist text to be published since the war"—*The London Times*

0-15-117881-X HARCOURT BRACE $34.95

Norman **Gelb**

Ike and Monty: Generals at War

An account of the close but stormy relationship between Eisenhower and Montgomery

0-688-1436-6 QUILL PB $15.00

C.R. **Messenger**, editor

Hitler's Gladiator: The Life of SS-Obergruppenfuhrer and General der Waffen-SS Sepp Dietrich

"Sepp" Dietrich managed to combine a career as a fanatic Nazi with that of a successful panzer commander. He was executed in 1945 for atrocities carried out during the Battle of the Bulge

0-08-031207-1 BRASSEY'S DEFENSE $32.95

E.B. **Potter**

Bull Halsey: A Biography

0-87021-146-3 NAVAL INSTITUTE $34.95

Correlli **Barnett**, editor

Hitler's Generals

Includes Rommel, Model, Student, and Beck

0-688-10383-9 QUILL PB $14.95

Alan **Bullock**

Hitler: A Study in Tyranny

A solid biography; tells as much about the times as the man. "Remains the best biography of Adolf Hitler in English"
—Gordon A. Craig, *NY Review of Books*

See also **HITLER: STUDIES IN TYRANNY** under **20TH-CENTURY EUROPE TO THE SECOND WORLD WAR**

0-06-092020-3 HARPERCOLLINS PB $17.00

Hitler and Stalin: Parallel Lives

A magisterial dual biography of the two great leaders of totalitarian societies

See also **FASCISM AND TOTALITARIANISM** under **POLITICAL THOUGHT** in **SOCIAL STUDIES**

See also **FASCISM AND TOTALITARIANISM: GENERAL STUDIES** under **20TH-CENTURY EUROPE TO THE SECOND WORLD WAR**

0-679-72994-1 VINTAGE PB $22.00

William **Manchester**

American Caesar: Douglas MacArthur, 1880-1964

The US commander-in chief in the Pacific: enigmatic, charismatic, revered and despised, but never ignored

0-316-54498-1 LITTLE, BROWN $40.00
0-440-30424-5 LAUREL LEAF PB $7.99

Geoffrey **Perret**

Old Soldiers Never Die: The Life of Douglas MacArthur

This 1996 biography concludes that MacArthur "at his best" was perhaps second only to Ulysses S. Grant among American military commanders

0-679-42882-8 RANDOM HOUSE $32.50

Douglas MacArthur

E.B. **Potter**

Nimitz

Biography of the commander of the US Pacific Fleet

0-87021-492-6 NAVAL INSTITUTE $35.00

John **Baynes**

Forgotten Victor: The Life of General Sir Richard O'Connor

0-08-036269-9 BRASSEY'S DEFENSE $24.95

Martin **Blumenson**

Patton: The Man Behind the Legend, 1885-1945

Individual to the point of eccentricity, this cavalry-officer-turned-commander's outbursts and mannerisms won him fame, but almost destroyed his career. Though he showed an awesome ability to advance rapidly against the enemy, he has been accused of sacrificing his men for eye-catching victories

0-688-13795-4 QUILL PB $15.00

The Patton Papers 1: 1885-1940

0-395-12706-8 HOUGHTON MIFFLIN $45.00

The Patton Papers 2: 1940-1945

0-306-80717-3 DA CAPO PB $19.95

Carlo **D'Este**

Patton: A Genius for War

0-06-016455-7 HARPERCOLLINS $35.00

George S. **Patton**

War as I Knew It

The principles forged from the general's fighting experience in three wars

0-553-25991-1 BDD PB $6.99

Warren F. **Kimball**, editor

Churchill and Roosevelt: The Complete Correspondence

An encyclopedic collection covering every aspect of the war years. Together with Kimball's commentary, the three volumes of letters provide a major interpretive account of Anglo-American diplomacy

0-691-05649-8 PRINCETON $350.00
0-691-00817-5 PRINCETON PB $85.00

Francis **Lowenheim**, editor

Roosevelt and Churchill: Their Secret Wartime Correspondence

Six hundred of the most interesting letters from an extraordinarily candid correspondence

0-306-80390-9 DA CAPO PB $17.95

Eric **Larrabee**

Commander in Chief: Franklin Delano Roosevelt, His Lieutenants and Their War

0-671-66382-8 SIMON & SCHUSTER PB $18.00

Robert **Conquest**

Stalin: Breaker of Nations

0-14-016953-9 PENGUIN PB $13.95

Alonzo L. **Hamby**

Man of the People: The Life of Harry S. Truman

0-19-504546-7 OXFORD $35.00

Hiroyuki **Agawa**

The Reluctant Admiral: Yamamoto and the Imperial Navy

Convinced by several visits to the US that America's industrial strength was bound to prevail in a prolonged war, Yamamoto's strategy—typified by the attack on Pearl Harbor—emphasized knock-out blows against the US Navy, designed to force America to early negotiations

See also **IMPERIAL JAPAN AND THE PACIFIC WAR** under **FROM THE MEIJI RESTORATION TO THE END OF THE EMPIRE: 1868-1945** under **JAPAN**

TRANSLATED BY JOHN BESTER

0-87011-512-X KODANSHA PB $10.00

The Men in the Field

Tom **Blackburn** & Eric **Hamel**

The Jolly Rogers: The Story of Tom Blackburn and Navy Fighting Squadron Vf-17

0-671-69493-6 POCKET PB $5.99

Gregory **Boyington**

Baa Baa Black Sheep

0-553-26350-1 BDD PB $5.99

John **Campbell**, editor

The Experience of World War II

0-19-520792-0 OXFORD $40.00

Keith **Douglas**

Alamein to Zem Zem

A memoir of the North Africa campaign

EDITED BY DESMOND GRAHAM

0-571-16264-9 FABER PB $10.95

Edwin P. **Hoyt**

The GI's War: The Story of American Soldiers in Europe in World War II

0-306-80448-4 DA CAPO PB $16.95

Robert B. **Ellis**

See Naples and Die: A World War II Memoir of a United States Army Ski Trooper in the Mountains of Italy

0-7864-0199-0 MCFARLAND LIBRARY EDITION $29.50

James J. **Fahey**

Pacific War Diary, Illustrated

First published in 1963, Fahey's hugely popular World War II diary is again available, this time with 64 photographs drawn from US Navy and Army services. Since diaries were forbidden by military regulations, Fahey's portrait of an "ordinary seaman" during the war is unique. "Fahey conveys [what] thousands of his fellows have never managed to convey to wives or friends back home: this is what it was like"—*Time*

INTRODUCTION BY ROGER PINEAU

0-295-97304-8 WASHINGTON PB $29.95

D. F. **Loza** & James F. **Gebhardt**

Commanding the Red Army's Sherman Tanks: The World War II Memoirs of a Hero of the Soviet Union: Dmitry Loza

0-8032-2920-8 NEBRASKA....$25.00

Dan **McCullen**

Lest We Forget: A POW Memoir of World War II

1-56474-191-5 FITHIAN PRESS....$25.00

Mack **Morriss** & others

South Pacific Diary, 1942-1943

0-8131-1969-3 KENTUCKY....$24.95

Carl S. **Nordin**

We Were Next to Nothing: An American POW's Account of Japanese Prison Camps and Deliverance in World War

0-7864-0274-1 MCFARLAND LIBRARY EDITION.....$28.95

Hiroo **Onoda**

No Surrender: My Thirty-Year War

Onoda, a lieutenant in the Philippines, spent 29 years in the jungle before learning that the war was over

See also **IMPERIAL JAPAN AND THE PACIFIC WAR** under **FROM THE MEIJI RESTORATION TO THE END OF THE EMPIRE: 1868-1945** under **JAPAN**

TRANSLATED BY CHARLES TERRY

0-87011-240-6 FS&G....$2.98

Colonel R. Bruce **Porter** & Eric **Hammel**

Ace!: A Marine Night Fighter Pilot in World War II

0-935553-01-0 PACIFICA....$25.00

Mark **Scott** & Semoyn **Krasilshchik**

Yanks Meet Reds: Recollections of US and Soviet Vets from the Linkup in World War II

American and Soviet veterans offer eyewitness accounts from the Elbe River in 1945

0-8095-4055-X BORGO $24.95

Jack **Stenbuck**

Typewriter Battalion: Dramatic Frontline Dispatches from World War II

See also **THE AGE OF THE REPORTER: SINCE 1880** under **HISTORY** under **JOURNALISM** in **PERFORMING ARTS AND MEDIA**

0-688-14190-0 MORROW....$23.00

The Holocaust

The growing field of "Holocaust Studies" not only includes several first-rate general histories, but a wide range of memoirs, works of fiction, criticisms of Allied inaction, and philosophical ruminations as well. Among the best surveys are: Lucy Dawidowicz's *The War Against the Jews, 1933-1945* (1975) and Martin Gilbert's *The Holocaust* (1985).

Much of the work listed below transcends the strict boundaries of historical research. An increasing flow of survivors' memoirs translates cold numbers into deeply personal tales. Several volumes have collected the artwork of the victims themselves. Novelists (as well as filmmakers) have also taken on the difficult task of exploring the psychic and physical brutality of the Nazi era.

For related reading, see JUDAISM in RELIGION, SPIRITUALITY, AND PHILOSOPHY

For related reading, see YIDDISH LANGUAGE AND LITERATURE

Jeshajahu **Weinberg** & Rina **Elieli**

The Holocaust Museum in Washington: The Story of Its Creation

Since its opening in 1993, 5,000 visitors a day have waited in line to visit the challenging and remarkable United States Holocaust Memorial Museum. This is the story of its creation. It explains the philosophy behind the museum, its educational mission, its conception of historical truth and narrative presentation. An important statement on the museum's mission

FOREWORD BY CHAIM POTOK

0-8478-1906-X ST. MARTIN'S....$45.00
0-8478-1907-8 RIZZOLI PB....$29.95

General Surveys

Michael **Berenbaum**

The World Must Know: The History of the Holocaust as Told in the United States Holocaust Memorial Museum

0-316-09135-9 LITTLE, BROWN....$40.00
0-252-06027-X ILLINOIS PB....$12.95

Christopher R. **Browning**

The Path to Genocide: Essays on Launching the Final Solution

0-521-55878-6 CAMBRIDGE PB....$10.95

Richard **Breitman**

The Architect of Genocide: Himmler and the Final Solution

A carefully documented look at the crucial role of Himmler, the head of the SS, in organizing the Holocaust

0-87451-596-3 BRANDEIS PB....$19.95

Lucy S. **Dawidowicz**

The War Against the Jews, 1933-1945

A narrative account of the attempted extermination of the Jews, from the death squads to the ghettoes and death camps

0-553-34532-X BANTAM PB....$15.95

Deborah **Dwork** & Robert-Jan **Van Pelt**

Auschwitz: 1270-1995

Founded by Germans in 1270, Auschwitz (Oswiecim in Polish) became a pawn in diplomatic battles between Germany, Poland, Bohemia, and Hungary. The notorious concentration camp was established in 1940. "Using 224 photographs and architectural plans, as well as oral histories of survivors, this careful, detatched study traces the camp's evolution into a site where more than one million people were killed"—*Publishers Weekly*

0-393-03933-1 NORTON....$35.00

Martin **Gilbert**

Atlas of the Holocaust

This volume, from the author of *Churchill: A Life*, geographically traces the Nazis' attempt to annihilate the Jews of Europe. Beginning with isolated incidents of prewar violence and expanding in scope with the Third Reich's rise to power, it includes expulsions, forced marches, mass executions, and concentration camps. 316 fully annotated maps drawn by the author

0-688-12364-3 MORROW....$20.00

The Holocaust: The History of the Jews of Europe During the Second World War

A definitive narrative weaving historical research and survivors' testimony into one of the most gripping accounts of the Nazi genocide

0-8050-0348-7 HOLT PB....$18.95

As well as the six million Jews who were murdered, more than ten million other non-combatants were killed by the Nazis. Under the Nazi scheme, Poles, Czechs, Serbs and Russians were to become subject peoples: slaves, the workers of the New Order. The Jews were to disappear altogether. It was the Jews alone who were marked out to be destroyed in their entirety: every Jewish man woman and child, so that there would be no future Jewish life in Europe. Against the eight million Jews who lived in Europe in 1939, the Nazi bureaucracy assembled all the concerted skills and mechanics of a modern state: the police, the railways, the civil service, the industrial power of the Reich; poison gas, soldiers, mercenaries, criminals, machine guns, artillery; and over all, a massive apparatus of deception.

THE HOLOCAUST: THE HISTORY OF THE JEWS OF EUROPE DURING THE SECOND WORLD WAR

Daniel J. **Goldhagen**

Hitler's Willing Executioners: Ordinary Germans and the Holocaust

This study revisits a question often treated as settled: How could the Holocaust have happened? Goldhagen's controversial response explores German society and its tradition of anti-Semitism, marshalling shocking new primary evidence to argue that the perpetrators of the Final Solution were not monsters but ordinary Germans only too eager to participate in the attempted extermination of the Jews

0-679-44695-8 KNOPF $30.00
0-679-77268-5 VINTAGE $16.00

Ian **Hancock**

The Pariah Syndrome: An Account of Gypsy Slavery and Persecution

An illuminating account by a Gypsy of his people's oppression, including the murder of at least half a million Gypsies at the hands of the Nazis

See also **GYPSIES** under **REGIONAL AND NATIONAL HISTORIES** under **INTRODUCTIONS TO MODERN EUROPEAN HISTORY**

0-89720-079-9 KAROMA PB $25.00

Raul **Hilberg**

The Destruction of the European Jews

This massive account, first published in 1961, is filled with facts, figures, and a thorough dissection of how the genocide was carried out. In Hilberg's words, "it is not a book about the Jews. It is a book about people who destroyed the Jews." Hardcover version is a 3-volume set

0-8419-0832-X ERGO $159.50
0-8419-0910-5 HOLMES & MEIER PB $17.95

The Politics of Memory: The Path of a Holocaust Historian

1-56663-116-5 DEE $22.50

Steve T. **Katz**

The Holocaust in Historical Context, Volume I: The Holocaust and Mass Death Before the Modern Age

In the first, and currently only, volume of his comparative analysis of the unthinkable, the author offers a thoroughly documented and well reasoned claim that the Holocaust was an unparalleled, singular event in human history. "Promises to be one of the most important works in the area of Holocaust studies"—Elie Weisel

0-19-507220-0 OXFORD $49.95

Michael R. **Marrus**

The Holocaust in History

0-452-00953-7 PLUME PB $12.95

Richard **Plant**

The Pink Triangle: The Nazi War Against Homosexuals

History of discrimination against gays in World War II Europe

See also **HISTORY** under **GAY, LESBIAN, AND BISEXUAL STUDIES** in **SOCIAL STUDIES**

0-8050-0600-1 HOLT PB $13.00

Tzvetan **Todorov**

Facing the Extreme: Moral Life in the Concentration Camps

A masterful study

TRANSLATED BY ARTHUR DENNER & ABIGAIL POLLAK

0-805-04263-6 HOLT $27.50

Leni **Yahil**

The Holocaust: The Fate of European Jewry, 1932-1945

First published in Israel in 1987, Yahil's monumental 861-page work has been called the most authoritative history of the Holocaust ever written

0-19-504522-X OXFORD $39.95

Holocaust Experiences: From Paris to Warsaw

The Nazi domination of Europe meant a Holocaust not only of death factories but also of ghettoes, murderous roving bands, mass shootings, deportations, starvation, and hiding.

Alan **Adelson** & Robert **Lapides**, editors

Lodz Ghetto: Inside a Community Under Siege

Diaries, notebooks, stories, and journals written by prisoners of the Lodz Ghetto. "Any moment now, the search will begin. If they find our hiding place, I will leave these notebooks in the dungeon. They might be our last trace" —from the diary of Jakub Poznanski

0-04-003228-7 PENGUIN PB $17.95

Jacques **Adler**

The Jews of Paris and the Final Solution: Communal Response and Internal Conflict, 1940-1944

"As objective as it is horrifying, a work which historians of the occupation were lacking" —*Vingtiéme Siecle*

0-19-504305-7 OXFORD $45.00
0-19-504306-5 OXFORD PB $19.95

Haim **Avni**

Spain, the Jews, and Franco

Based on new materials detailing the Franco regime's aid to refugees from Nazism

TRANSLATED BY EMANUEL SHIMONI

0-8276-0188-3 JEWISH PUB SOCIETY $19.95

Yehuda **Bauer**

Jews for Sale?: Nazi-Jewish Negotiations, 1939-1945

0-300-05913-2 YALE $35.00
0-300-06852-2 YALE PB $15.00

Randolph L. **Braham**

The Politics of Genocide: The Holocaust in Hungary

A definitive study, in two volumes

0-88033-247-6
EAST EUROPEAN MONOGRAPHS $283.50

Lucy S. **Dawidowicz**

A Holocaust Reader

A collection of documents about the destruction and martyrdom of the European Jewish Community under German occupation during WWII.

0-874-41236-6 BEHRM $15.95

Terrence **Des Pres**

The Survivor: An Anatomy of Life in the Death Camps

0-19-502703-5 OXFORD PB $11.95

Lucjan **Dobroszycki**, editor

The Chronicle of the Lodz Ghetto, 1941-1944

The painstakingly detailed diary of life and administration in Europe's second largest ghetto, reduced from 163,177 people in 1941 to 877 in 1944. A chilling document

0-300-03924-7 YALE PB $28.50

Konnilyn **Feig**

Hitler's Death Camps: The Sanity of Madness

An "unsparing compilation of the collective camp experience … written with sensitivity, power, and emotion" —*American Historical Review*

0-8419-0675-0 HOLMES & MEIER $47.95

Rena Kornreich **Gelissen** & Heather Dune **Macadam**

Rena's Promise: A Story of Sisters in Auschwitz

This woman's account of survival in Auschwitz is more than a heartwrenching story of survival; it is also a testament to the power of an unusual relationship between sisters—how the love for a younger sister stengthened the elder's will to stay alive."A woman's account of survival—not sentimental, certainly not sweet or nostalgic, but guided through the abyss of evil and horror by both the smallest and greatest of human connections… A powerful work of witness and endurance"—Marcie Hershman

0-8070-7070-X BEACON $23.00

Yisrael **Gutman**

The Jews of Warsaw, 1939-1943: Ghetto, Underground, Revolt

The outstanding example of Jewish resistance dramatically reconstructed

TRANSLATED BY INA FRIEDMAN

0-253-33174-9 INDIANA $42.00
0-253-20511-5 INDIANA PB $18.95

Shimon **Huberband**

Kiddush Hashem: Jewish Religious and Cultural Life in Poland During the Holocaust

Told by a Warsaw rabbi

TRANSLATED BY DAVID E. FISHMAN
EDITED BY JEFFREY S. GUROCK & ROBERT S. HIRT

0-88125-118-6 KTAV $35.00
0-88125-121-6 KTAV PB $22.95

Hans **Jonas**

Mortality and Morality: A Search for Good after Auschwitz

See also **OTHER 20TH-CENTURY PHILOSOPHERS** under **PHILOSOPHY** in **RELIGION, SPIRITUALITY, AND PHILOSOPHY**

0-8101-1286-8 NORTHWESTERN PB $22.50

Michael R. **Marrus** & Robert O. **Paxton**

Vichy France and the Jews

A landmark study, focusing on the long denial of French collaboration in Hitler's "Final Solution"

See also **FRANCE** under **THE WAR IN EUROPE** under **THE SECOND WORLD WAR**

0-8047-2499-7 STANFORD PB $17.95

Donna F. **Ryan**

The Holocaust and the Jews of Marseille: The Enforcement of Anti-Semitic Policies in Vichy France

0-252-02227-0 ILLINOIS $36.95
0-252-06530-1 ILLINOIS PB $15.95

Paul **Webster**

Petain's Crime: The Complete Story of French Collaboration in the Holocaust

A detailed telling of the unpleasant story of how the French government enthusiastically assisted in the extermination of European Jews

0-929587-55-3 DEE $24.95

First-Person Accounts

First-person accounts—Anne Frank's diary of a hidden life in occupied Holland, Primo Levi's chronicle of humanity gone haywire at Auschwitz—do what most histories cannot: they distill the horror of mass murder into the story of a single tortured life.

Alan **Adelson**, editor

The Diary of Dawid Sierakowiak: Five Notebooks from the Lodz Ghetto

TRANSLATED BY KAMIL TUROWSKI

0-19-510450-1 OXFORD $25.00

Wladyslaw **Bartoszewski**

The Warsaw Ghetto: A Christian's Testimony

Memoir of a Polish Catholic who served as liaison between Jewish leaders in the ghetto and the Polish underground

FOREWORD BY STANISLAW LEM

0-8070-5602-2 BEACON $14.95

Bruno **Bettelheim**

The Informed Heart: Autonomy in a Mass Age

The noted psychologist and educator, a prisoner at Dachau and Buchenwald in 1938-39, offers psychological parallels between life in the camps and the loss of self in today's "mass society"

0-02-903200-8 FREE PRESS $29.95

Tadeusz **Borowski**

This Way for the Gas, Ladies and Gentlemen

A collection of concentration camp stories written by a non-Jewish prisoner of Auschwitz. "...the difference between executioners and victims is stripped of all greatness and pathos; it is brutally reduced to a second bowl of soup, an extra blanket, or the luxury of a silk shirt and shoes with thick soles..."—Jan Kott

TRANSLATED BY BARBARA VEDDER

0-04-008624-7 PENGUIN PB $11.95

Shlomo **Breznitz**

Memory Fields

Saved from transport to Auschwitz when his parents persuaded a Catholic orphanage in Czechoslovakia to accept him, Breznitz spent the war hiding his circumcised-penis, and memorizing the Catholic litany so well he was chosen to recite for the prelate. Today he is a psychology professor at the University of Haifa. "By authority of his excellent prose, discomfiting honesty, risky form, and shattering fidelity to the traps of remembering the nearly unbearable, Breznitz has produced a Holocaust memoir that stands with the best of them"—*Kirkus Reviews*

0-679-40403-1 KNOPF $21.00

Charles **Delbo**

Auschwitz and After

0-300-06208-7 YALE $25.00

Anne **Frank**

Anne Frank: The Diary of a Young Girl

0-385-04019-9 DOUBLEDAY $24.95
0-8359-0235-8 GLOBE FEARON PB $10.60

The Diary of a Young Girl, The Definitive Edition

This edition of Anne Frank's diary restores the 30 percent of material excised by her father

See also **YOUNG ADULT NONFICTION** in **BOOKS FOR YOUNG READERS**

0-385-47378-8 DOUBLEDAY $25.00

The Diary of Anne Frank: The Critical Edition

An exhaustively detailed version of the acclaimed diary, including material not found in the standard edition

TRANSLATED BY ARNOLD J. POMERANS
EDITED BY NETHERLANDS STATE INSTITUTE FOR WAR DOCUMENTATION

0-385-24023-6 DOUBLEDAY $49.95

Miep **Gies** & Alison L. **Gold**

Anne Frank Remembered: The Story of the Woman Who Helped to Hide the Frank Family

0-671-66234-1 SIMON & SCHUSTER PB $12.00

Rian **Verhoeven** & others

Anne Frank: Beyond the Diary: A Photographic Remembrance

Includes more than 100 photographs, many never before published eyewitness accounts by those who knew the family, and illustrations revealing the family's secret living-quarters. Excerpts from the diary further illuminate this young girl whose tragedy has inspired and educated millions

0-670-84932-4 VIKING $17.00

Janusz **Korczak**

Ghetto Diary

0-8052-5004-2 UNITES STATES HOLOCAUST $16.95

Primo **Levi**

Survival in Auschwitz

"Documentary evidence of the first order of the inhumanity of man to man in our time" —*American Journal of Sociology*

See also **ESSAYS, MEMOIRS, AND OTHER PROSE** under **THE 20TH CENTURY** under **ITALIAN LITERATURE** in **LITERATURE OF EUROPE, AFRICA, AND ASIA**

0-684-82680-1 COLLIER PB $11.00

Now everyone is busy scraping the bottom of his bowl with his spoon so as not to waste the last drops of the soup; a confused, metallic clatter, signifying the end of the day. Silence slowly prevails and then, from my bunk on the top row, I see and hear old Kuhn praying aloud, with his beret on his head swaying backwards and forwards violently. Kuhn is thanking God because he has not been chosen. Kuhn is out of his senses. Does he not see Beppo the Greek in the bunk next to him, Beppo who is twenty years old and is going to the gas chamber the day after tomorrow and knows it and lies there looking fixedly at the light without saying anything and without even thinking any more? Can Kuhn fail to realize that next time it will be his turn? Does Kuhn not understand that what has happened today is an abomination, which no propitiatory prayer, no pardon, no expiation by the guilty, which nothing at all in the power of man can ever clean again. If I was God, I would spit at Kuhn's prayer.

SURVIVAL IN AUSCHWITZ

Michel **Mazor**

The Vanished City: Everyday Life in the Warsaw Ghetto

Arrested in the Warsaw Ghetto, Mazor was transported to Treblinka. Though he managed to escape to freedom, he chose to return, and now brings to life in chilling detail the daily heroism and horrors of life in the Ghetto. Passionate and disturbing, Mazor's indictment extends beyond the Nazis to include the Jewish administrators and police who gave in to the corruption

TRANSLATED BY DAVID JACOBSON

0-941419-93-2 MARSILIO $24.00

Yehuda **Nir**

The Lost Childhood

0-425-15547-1 BERKLEY PB $5.99

Boris **Pahor**

Pilgrim Among the Shadows: A Memoir

An insightful memoir by a Slovak survivor and medic in Belsen, Harzungen, and Dachau, written on the occasion of his visit to a camp 50 years after

0-15-171958-6 HARVEST $20.00

Blanca **Rosenberg**

To Tell at Last: Survival Under False Identity, 1941-45

0-252-01998-9 ILLINOIS $19.95
0-252-06520-4 ILLINOIS PB $12.95

Calel **Perechodnik**

Am I A Murderer? Testament of a Jewish Ghetto Policeman

A young Polish Jew, who died in 1944, chronicles his life under the Nazis. "Stunning. [A] blistering record of the Final Solution by a witness, victim, and collaborator"
—*Publishers Weekly*

TRANSLATED & EDITED BY FRANK FOX

0-8133-2702-4 HARPERCOLLINS $26.50

Emmanuel **Ringelblum**

Polish-Jewish Relations During the Second World War

Accounts of interactions between Poles and Jews during World War II

EDITED BY JOSEPH KERMISH

0-810-00963-8 NORTHWESTERN PB $19.95

Pierre **Seel**

I, Pierre Seel, Deported Homosexual: A Memoir of Nazi Terror

The tragedy of the homosexual Holocaust is brought vividly to life by one who, at the age of 58, came out of the closet to tell his harrowing story. "His account of his suffering and his plea for justice are heartrending in their dignified restraint"—*Publishers Weekly*

See also **BIOGRAPHIES** under **GAY, LESBIAN, AND BISEXUAL STUDIES** in **SOCIAL STUDIES**

TRANSLATED BY JOACHIM NEUGROSCHEL

0-465-04501-4 BASIC PB $12.00

Erno **Szep**

The Smell of Humans: A Memoir of the Holocaust in Hungary

1-85866-011-4 OXFORD PB $17.95

Avraham **Tory**

Surviving the Holocaust: The Kovno Ghetto Diary

"I wrote the diary at all hours, in the early hours of the morning, in bed at night, between meetings of the Council... During meetings I sometimes wrote headings, quotes, summaries, dates, and names of places and people on scraps of paper or in notebooks, lest I forget and make mistakes." A chronicle of life and death in the Jewish ghetto of Kovno, Lithuania, from June 1941 to January 1944. Includes 70 illustrations and 9 maps, with textual and historical notes by Dina Porat

EDITED BY MARTIN GILBERT

TRANSLATED BY JERZY MICHALOWICZ

0-674-85810-7 HARVARD $45.00

Rescue and Resistance

Uplifting tales of those who risked their lives to resist persecution and murder range from the efforts of individuals, like Sweden's Raoul Wallenberg, who used his position to save thousands of Hungarian Jews, to Denmark's collective action to resist Hitler. They also tell of the Jewish partisans whose underground activities challenge the notion that the Jews marched to their graves like "sheep to the slaughter."

Robert **Abzug**

Inside the Vicious Heart: Americans and the Liberation of Nazi Concentration Camps

0-19-503597-6 OXFORD $30.00

0-19-504236-0 OXFORD PB $13.95

Philip **Hallie**

Lest Innocent Blood Be Shed

How a French village under the Occupation organized to save Jews

0-06-132051-X HARPERPERENNIAL PB $13.00

Ernest G. **Heppner**

Shanghai Refuge: A Memoir of the World War II Jewish Ghetto

Born into a middle-class Jewish-German family, Heppner's privileged life ended with "Crystal Night." Fleeing the Nazis, his family made their way to the unlikely haven of Shanghai, the only port which did not require a visa. Now he chronicles the hardships and triumphs of the voyage, life in the Shanghai ghetto, and eventual immigration to the United States

0-8032-2368-4 NEBRASKA $25.00

Every morning, before classes started, rain or shine, we assembled in the school yard. Standing at attention one morning I pretended that my right arm hurt and that I was unable to raise it and salute the Swastika flag while the Horst Wessel song, anthem of the Brown Shirts, was played.

SHANGHAI REFUGE: A MEMOIR OF THE WORLD WAR II JEWISH GHETTO

John **Bierman**

Righteous Gentile: The Story of Raoul Wallenberg, Missing Hero of the Holocaust

"I don't know of any other man whom I would rather nominate for the Nobel Peace Prize than Raoul Wallenberg"—Simon Wiesenthal

0-14-024664-9 PENGUIN PB $11.95

Raoul Wallenberg

Peter **Hoffmann**

German Resistance to Hitler

See also **THE RESISTANCE** under **THE WAR IN EUROPE** under **THE SECOND WORLD WAR**

0-674-35085-5 HARVARD $34.50

0-674-35086-3 HARVARD PB $15.95

Thomas **Keneally**

Schindler's List

The story of a Catholic director of a Nazi factory—and prison camp—who saved many Jewish lives, reconstructed from the testimony of those who came to be known as *Schindlerjuden*

See also **AUSTRALIAN LITERATURE** in **LITERATURE OF EUROPE, AFRICA, AND ASIA**

0-671-51688-4 SIMON & SCHUSTER $25.00

0-671-88031-4 TOUCHSTONE PB $12.00

Samuel P. **Oliner** & Pearl M. **Oliner**

The Altruistic Personality: Rescuers of Jews in Nazi Europe

Interviews with 700 people who did—and did not—save European Jews, aimed at discovering what led people to risk their lives to save others

0-02-923829-3 FREE PRESS PB $16.95

Hannah **Senesh**

Hannah Senesh: Her Life and Diary

A major hero in Israel, Senesh was a pioneer Zionist, killed by the Nazis at the age of 23 after a failed attempt to rescue Hungarian Jews

See also **BIOGRAPHY** under **JEWISH HISTORY**

TRANSLATED BY MARTA COHN

INTRODUCTION BY ABBA EBAN

0-8052-0410-5 SCHOCKEN PB $16.00

Hannah Senesh (photo courtesy of Schocken Books)

Nechama **Tec**

When Light Pierced the Darkness: Christian Rescue of Jews in Poland

Based on 500 case histories of people who risked death to open their doors to Jews; by a Polish Jew aided by Christians

0-19-503643-3 OXFORD $27.95

0-19-505194-7 OXFORD PB $11.95

While Six Million Died: The World and the Holocaust

The response of the world—particularly the United States and its allies—to the plight of Europe's Jews has become a major source of research and controversy. In 1966 Arthur Morse's *While Six Million Died* demonstrated that more than simple disbelief led to Allied inaction. Since then, led by the pioneering work of historian David Wyman, many factors have been blamed for the apathetic response to Hitler's ongoing murder of Jews: anti-Semitism, opposition to immigration, the silence of the Catholic church, insecurity and ineffective leadership among American Jews, Britain's troubles in Palestine, and even Franklin Roosevelt's own indifference.

Lucy S. **Dawidowicz**

The Holocaust and the Historians

Why many of the world's historians have paid little attention to Hitler's mass murder of the Jews

0-674-40567-6 HARVARD PB $12.95

Leonard **Dinnerstein**

America and the Survivors of the Holocaust

Chronicles the postwar mistreatment of refugees and their arrival in the United States. "The shocking story of antisemitism, neglect, and heroic effort is laid bare here" —*Publishers Weekly*

0-231-04177-2 COLUMBIA PB $19.50

Lucjan **Dobroszycki** & Jeffrey S. **Gurock**, editors

The Holocaust in the Soviet Union: Studies and Sources on the Destruction of the Jews in the Nazi-Occupied Territories of the USSR, 1941-1945

1-56324-173-0 SHARPE $68.95
1-56324-174-9 SHARPE PB $28.95

Seymour Maxwell **Finger**, editor

American Jewry During the Holocaust

A report sponsored by the American Jewish Commission on the Holocaust

0-8419-7506-X HOLMES & MEIER PB $35.00

Martin **Gilbert**

Auschwitz and the Allies

A disturbing chronicle of Allied inaction

0-8050-1462-4 HOLT PB $15.95

David S. **Wyman**

The Abandonment of the Jews

The definitive account of American apathy to the Jewish plight in the Holocaust. "We will not see a better book on this subject in our lifetime" —Leonard Dinnerstein, *Journal of American History*

INTRODUCTION BY ELIE WIESEL
0-394-74077-7 RANDOM HOUSE PB $16.00

Tom **Segev**

The Seventh Million: The Israelis and the Holocaust

See also **ISRAEL SINCE 1948** under **ISRAEL** under **THE CONTEMPORARY MIDDLE EAST**

TRANSLATED BY HAIM WATZMAN
0-8090-8563-1 HILL & WANG $27.50
0-8090-1570-6 HILL & WANG PB $15.00

Art and Literature

Judy **Chicago**

The Holocaust Project: From Darkness into Light

Combining paintings, photography, tapestries, and stained glass. Best known for her innovative exhibitions *The Dinner Party* and *The Birth Project*, Chicago chronicles the artistic, intellectual, and personal exploration of the Final Solution. 40 pages of full-color art; 150 black-and-white photographs

0-670-84212-5 VIKING $40.00
0-14-015991-6 PENGUIN PB $22.50

Judith E. **Doneson**

The Holocaust in American Film

Argues that the presentation of the Holocaust has been influenced by such American social issues as McCarthyism, civil rights, Vietnam, and black-Jewish tensions

0-8276-0284-7 JEWISH PUB SOCIETY $29.95

Yaffa **Eliach**

Hasidic Tales of the Holocaust

Over 85 stories of Hasidim, their destruction and survival, in the form of classic Hasidic tales

0-19-503199-7 OXFORD $30.00
0-679-72043-X VINTAGE PB $12.00

Erich **Hartmann**

In the Camps

On the 50th anniversary of the liberation of the last Nazi concentration camp, Hartmann (Magnum Photos) documents the camps as they exist today

0-393-03772-X NORTON $35.00

Annette **Insdorf**

Indelible Shadows: Film and the Holocaust

FOREWORD BY ELIE WIESEL
0-521-37810-9 CAMBRIDGE PB $20.95

Claude **Lanzmann**

Shoah: An Oral History of the Holocaust

Complete text of the landmark film

See also **INDIVIDUAL FILMS** under **SCREENPLAYS** under **FILM** in **PERFORMING ARTS AND MEDIA**

FOREWORD BY SIMONE DE BEAUVOIR
0-306-80665-7 DA CAPO PB $12.95

Teresa **Swiebocka**, editor

Auschwitz: A History in Photographs

0-253-35581-8 INDIANA $75.00

Hana **Volavkova**, editor

I Never Saw Another Butterfly: Children's Drawings and Poems from Terezin Concentration Camp, 1942-1944

TRANSLATED BY JEANNE NEMCOVA
0-8052-1015-6 SCHOCKEN PB $14.00

Holocaust Fiction

Saul **Bellow**

Mr. Sammler's Planet

An elderly but vivacious man casts a skeptical eye on Manhattan in the radical '60s

See also **SINCE 1945** under **20TH-CENTURY AMERICAN FICTION** in **LITERATURE OF THE AMERICAS**

0-14-007317-5 VIKING PB $11.00
0-14-018936-X PENGUIN PB $11.95

Leslie **Epstein**

King of the Jews

0-393-30959-2 NORTON PB $9.95

Lawrence **Graver**

An Obsession with Anne Frank: Meyer Levin and the Diary

A novelist's passionate involvement with Anne Frank's diary veers into paranoia

0-520-20124-8 CALIFORNIA $28.00

John **Hersey**

The Wall

The famous novel of life in the Warsaw ghetto during World War II

See also **THE '50S** under **THE GREAT FICTION BESTSELLERS 1930-1995** in **POPULAR READING**

0-394-75696-7 VINTAGE PB $14.00

Jerzy **Kosinski**

The Painted Bird

A nightmarish vision of Eastern Europe during World War II

0-8021-3422-X GROVE PB $10.00

Primo **Levi**

If Not Now, When?

A novel of Jewish resistance to the Nazis

See also **FICTION** under **THE 20TH CENTURY** under **ITALIAN LITERATURE** in **LITERATURE OF EUROPE, AFRICA, AND ASIA**

TRANSLATED BY WILLIAM WEAVER
0-14-008492-4 PENGUIN PB $11.00

Janos **Nyiri**

Battlefields and Playgrounds

Called "the best novel about the Holocaust ever written" by *The Observer* (London), Nyiri's spellbinding book depicts the survival of a Jewish boy in a world of adults gone mad—war-torn Budapest. "If this were simply a book of consuming interest to those concerned with Hungary, or the war, or the Jews, it would be worth reading. But it is much more. It is an adventure story full of suspense, a child study of outstanding merit, an enthralling family saga, a highly entertaining and enlightening novel" —*The Literary Review* [London]

TRANSLATED BY WILLIAM BRANDON AND THE AUTHOR
0-374-10918-4 FS&G $25.00

Cynthia **Ozick**

The Shawl

0-394-58199-7 KNOPF $12.95

Andre **Schwarz-Bart**

The Last of the Just

A novel of the Holocaust. "Transcends the definition of fiction. It's part history, part vision, forged into a single echoing, terrifying outcry" —*NY Times*

See also **FICTION** under **MODERN FRENCH LITERATURE** in **LITERATURE OF EUROPE, AFRICA, AND ASIA**

TRANSLATED BY STEPHEN BECKER

0-689-70365-1 MACMILLAN PB $15.95

Art **Spiegelman**

Maus: A Survivor's Tale

When Art Spiegelman undertook an epic account of the Holocaust and its impact on the American son of an Auschwitz survivor in the form of a comic book featuring mice, cats, and other emblematic animals, few could have foreseen the masterpiece that resulted. Available in separate volumes or as a set, in both paperback and hardcover. "The most affecting and successful narrative ever done about the Holocaust"—*Wall Street Journal*

Volume 1
My Father Bleeds History

See also **AMERICAN GRAPHIC NOVELS** under **COMICS** in **POPULAR READING**

0-394-54155-3 PANTHEON $22.00
0-394-74723-2 PANTHEON PB $14.00

Volume 2
And Here My Troubles Began

0-394-55655-0 PANTHEON $22.00
0-679-72977-1 PANTHEON PB $14.00

Boxed set of both volumes

0-679-41038-4 PANTHEON $44.00
0-679-74840-7 PANTHEON PB $28.00

Art Spiegelman (photo by Nancy Crampton)

William **Styron**

Sophie's Choice

The terrible secret of a 1940s immigrant to New York

0-679-73637-9 VINTAGE PB $13.00

Abraham **Sutzkever**

A. Sutzkever: Selected Poetry and Prose

EDITED AND TRANSLATED BY BARBARA HARSHAV AND BENJAMIN HARSHAV

0-520-06539-5 CALIFORNIA $40.00

Leon **Uris**

Mila 18

Leon Uris's fictional account of a family trapped in the horrors of the Warsaw Ghetto.

See also **THE '60S** under **THE GREAT FICTION BESTSELLERS 1930-1995** in **POPULAR READING**

0-553-24160-5 BDD PB $7.99

Elie Wiesel

Beginning with the publication of his first novel, *Night*, a loosely fictionalized account of his haunted memories of Auschwitz, Wiesel has recorded the tragedy both of death and of survival. His recent books have branched into the realms of Soviet Jews, Hasidism, and Biblical Studies; several of his nonfiction works can be found in the Judaism chapter. Wiesel won the 1986 Nobel Peace Prize.

Elie **Wiesel**

The Accident

0-374-52311-8 HILL & WANG PB $8.00

Night

0-553-27253-5 BDD PB $4.99

Dawn

An Auschwitz survivor faces his own life-and-death dilemma as a member of the Zionist underground

0-553-22536-7 BDD PB $4.99

Twilight

0-8052-1058-X RANDOM HOUSE PB $12.00

The Night Trilogy: Night, Dawn, the Accident

0-374-52140-9 HILL & WANG PB $11.00

All the Rivers Run to the Sea: Memoirs

These long-anticipated memoirs tell of Wiesel's childhood in Auschwitz and Buchenwald and his rebirth in a French orphanage. What followed was a life filled with despair, faith, and struggle amid the richness of Jewish scripture, French culture, and the birth of Israel

See also **STUDIES OF INDIVIDUAL AUTHORS** under **CRITICAL STUDIES** under **MODERN FRENCH LITERATURE** in **LITERATURE OF EUROPE, AFRICA, AND ASIA**

0-7862-0673-X GK HALL $30.95
0-679-43916-1 KNOPF $30.00

A Beggar in Jerusalem

0-8052-0897-6 SCHOCKEN PB $14.00

The Forgotten

0-8052-1019-9 SCHOCKEN PB $12.00

From the Kingdom of Memory

0-8052-1020-2 SCHOCKEN PB $12.00

The Gates of the Forest

A young survivor of the Nazis travels a strange, folkloric path through the underground forests of Europe

0-8052-0896-8 SCHOCKEN PB $13.00

Legends of Our Time

Wiesel recounts the deeds and visions of extraordinary people

0-8052-0714-7 SCHOCKEN PB $14.00

Elie Wiesel (photo by Philippe Halsman)

The Town Behind the Wall

0-8052-1045-8 SCHOCKEN PB $13.00

The Trial of God: A Play in Three Acts

In 1649 in Shamgorod, three actors and the three survivors of a pogrom attempt to stage a trial of God for what He allowed to happen to His people in this "tragic farce"

0-8052-0809-7 SCHOCKEN PB $12.00

Elie **Wiesel** & François **Mitterand**

Memoir in Two Voices

See also **RECENT HISTORY AND CURRENT AFFAIRS** under **FRANCE SINCE 1945** under **EUROPE SINCE 1945**

1-55970-338-5 ARCADE $21.95

The Postwar Trials and the Nazi Hunters

Hannah **Arendt**

Eichmann in Jerusalem: A Report of the Banality of Evil

Haunting reflections on Eichmann's role in the "Final Solution," written during his war-crimes trial in Jerusalem

0-14-004450-7 PENGUIN PB $17.00

Robert E. **Conot**

Justice At Nuremberg

A dramatic account of the trial

0-88184-032-7 CARROLL & GRAF PB $13.95

Joseph E. **Persico**

Nuremberg: Infamy on Trial

0-14-016622-X PENGUIN PB $14.95

Telford **Taylor**

The Anatomy of the Nuremberg Trials: A Personal Memoir

A thorough, impeccably accurate account of the trials at Nuremberg

0-316-83400-9 LITTLE, BROWN PB $18.95

Epilogue: Children of the Holocaust

John **Borneman** & Jeffrey M. **Peck**
Sojourners: The Return of German Jews and the Question of Identity
0-8032-1255-0 NEBRASKA........$40.00

Helen **Epstein**
Children of the Holocaust: Conversations with Sons and Daughters of Survivors
How the Holocaust has affected the children of survivors
0-14-011284-7 PENGUIN PB........$12.95

Barbara **Heimannsberg** & Cristoph J. **Schmidt**, editors
The Collective Silence: German Identity and the Legacy of Shame
A remarkable collection of interviews, conducted by a team of distinguished psychotherapists, with children, grandchildren, and families of Holocaust survivors, resisters, and Nazis. A fascinating revelation of a legacy of guilt, abuse, and shame
TR. GORDAN WHEELER & CYNTHIA OUDEJANS HARRIS
1-55542-556-9 JOSSEY-BASS........$30.95

Bjorn **Krondorfer**
Remembrance and Reconciliation: Encounters Between Young Jews and Germans
"An important and sensitive book that opens a new window into young and conscientious minds, Jewish or German, and characterizes their perplexity about one another honestly and vividly"—Geoffrey Hartman
0-300-05959-0 YALE........$27.50

Elena **Lapin**
Jewish Voices, German Words: Growing Up Jewish in Postwar Germany and Austria
The strange experience of growing up Jewish in postwar Germany teaches singular lessons about religion and identity, about Germany, about assimilation. This "wonderful selection of voices [shows] the reality and complexity of life for Jews in Germany today"—Ruth Gay
0-945774-23-0 CATBIRD........$23.95

Facing the Holocaust

Lawrence L. **Langer**
Admitting the Holocaust: Collected Essays
"Clear, persuasive, and compelling"
—*Detroit Free Press*
0-19-510648-2 OXFORD PB........$11.95

Pierre **Vidal-Naquet**
Assassins of Memory: Essays on the Denial of the Holocaust
0-231-07458-1 COLUMBIA........$29.50
0-231-07459-X COLUMBIA PB........$16.00

Charles S. **Maier**
The Unmasterable Past: History, Holocaust, and German National Identity
"For the very large segment of the American public that does not read German, the book is a discreet Baedecker to very unfamiliar—and often ugly—territory"
—Norman Bimbaum, *The Nation*
0-674-92976-4 HARVARD PB........$12.00

Robert **Melson**
Revolution and Genocide: On the Origins of the Armenian Genocide and the Holocaust
Focuses on the Jews in Imperial Germany and the Armenians in the Ottoman Empire, as well as mass killings in the Soviet Union and Cambodia, to create a framework for understanding the link between genocide and revolution
0-226-51991-0 CHICAGO PB........$16.95

Europe Since 1945

For related reading, see INTERNATIONAL RELATIONS AND STRATEGIC STUDIES in SOCIAL STUDIES

Tony **Judt**
A Grand Illusion: An Essay on Europe
A look at Europe's future by a frequent contributor to *The New York Review of Books*
0-8090-5093-5 HILL & WANG........$25.00

Cold War Europe

Warren **Cohen**, editor
The Cambridge History of American Foreign Relations Volume 4: America in the Age of Soviet Power, 1945-1991
0520483816 CAMBRIDGE PB........$15.95

Robert V. **Daniels**
Year of the Heroic Guerrilla: World Revolution and Counterrevolution in 1968
From Paris to Beijing, from Saigon to Washington. "One of the first works I would recommend to anyone who is freshly coming to this topic"—Paul Berman
0-674-96451-9 HARVARD PB........$15.95

Abbott **Gleason**
Totalitarianism: The Inner History of the Cold War
"A valuable document of the moral-political development of a generation"
—Ernest Gellner, *New Republic*
0-19-505017-7 OXFORD........$25.00

Charles **Gati**
Hungary and the Soviet Bloc
0-8223-0684-0 DUKE........$48.00

Michael J. **Hogan**
The Marshall Plan: America, Britain, and the Reconstruction of Western Europe, 1947-1952
0-521-25140-0 CAMBRIDGE........$65.00
0-521-37840-0 CAMBRIDGE PB........$19.95

H. Stuart **Hughes**
Sophisticated Rebels: The Political Culture of European Dissent, 1968-1987
What happened to the revolutionary spirit after 1968? Hughes suggests that dissenters learned their lesson and began to pursue their goals in patient, realistic, limited fashion
0-674-82130-0 HARVARD........$29.00
0-674-82131-9 HARVARD PB........$9.95

Jane **Kramer**
Europeans
An elegant and witty series of essays by a *New Yorker* contributor. Chapters include "Being German," "Danton and Robespierre," and "Mitterand's Monarchy"
See also **HISTORY, POLITICS, AND SOCIETY** under **20TH-CENTURY AMERICAN ESSAYS AND JOURNALISM** in **LITERATURE OF THE AMERICAS**
0-374-14939-9 FS&G........$22.95

Alan S. **Milward**
The Reconstruction of Western Europe, 1945-51
An economic history of the reconstruction and a search for the origins of the Great Boom of the 1950s and 1960s
0-520-05206-4 CALIFORNIA........$55.00
0-520-06035-0 CALIFORNIA PB........$18.95

Thomas **Parrish**
The Cold War Encyclopedia
0-8050-2778-5 HOLT........$60.00

Derek W. **Urwin**
A Dictionary of European History and Politics, 1945-1995
0-582-25874-X LONGMAN PB........$20.39

The Collapse of Communism and the New Nationalism

Richard **Caplan** & John **Feffer**, editors
Europe's New Nationalism: States and Minorities in Conflict
The rebirth of nationalism as a threat to stability since the Cold War. Essayists include Michael Ignatieff, Mary Kaldor, and Adam Michnik
0-19-509149-3 OXFORD PB........$16.95

Hans Magnus **Enzensberger**

Civil Wars: From LA to Bosnia

A leading European analyst confronts the post-Cold War world, torn by civil wars and ethnic strife. He traces the evolving ideas of nationhood, loyalty, and community in Central Europe and applies them elsewhere, such as to the riots in Los Angeles. A provocative and controversial essay on self-destruction and mass madness. "Magnificient…a tremendous blast to destroy illusion, and to restore a modest but permanent hope"—E.J. Hobsbawn

1-56584-208-1 NEW PRESS $18.00

Julia **Kristeva**

Nations Without Nationalism

Kristeva, the psychoanalyst and critic, makes a plea for tolerance and commonality. With the rise of neo-Nazi groups in Germany and the National Front in France, the author looks at the origins of nationalism to explain the pervasiveness of hate. From discussions on Montesquieu's notion of *esprit général,* to Harlem Desir, founder of the French antiracist SOS Racisme, Kristeva's commitment to social justice and reconciliation is a fresh reminder of what is our primary responsibility

0-231-08105-7 COLUMBIA $10.00

Jack F. **Matlock**, Jr.

Autopsy on An Empire: The American Ambassador's Account of the Collapse of the Soviet Union

"No other American had the opportunity to observe the Soviet government's collapse at such close range"—Richard Pipes

0-679-41376-6 RANDOM HOUSE $40.00

Daniel Patrick **Moynihan**

Pandaemonium: Ethnicity in International Politics

Moynihan predicted the Soviet Union's collapse before anyone else, as he understood the abiding power of nationalism and ethnic self-identity. This book takes a pan-global look at ethnicity, arguing that it has been and will be a controlling factor in international politics. Although we have seen an emergence of dozens of new countries in the last few decades, and certainly ethnic warring is a reality, we needn't descend into an age of "ethnic cleansing," Moynihan insists—the dynamics of such conflict can be moderated

0-19-827787-3 OXFORD $22.00

Samuel F. **Wells**, Jr. &
Paul Bailey **Smith**, editors

New European Orders, 1919 and 1991

Compares and contrasts 1991's creation of a new order in Europe with 1919's, in the belief that many of the issues dealt with after the Cold War had their origins in World War I and its peace settlement

0-943875-76-5 WOODROW WILSON CENTER $32.50

Eastern Europe

Wladyslaw T. **Bartoszewski**

The Convent at Auschwitz

0-8076-1267-7 BRAZILLER $17.95

Ivan T. **Berend**

Central and Eastern Europe 1944-1993: Detour from the Periphery to the Periphery

The fortunes of the postwar socialist regimes in Eastern Europe, distinguished here by a unique combination of time, region, and topic

0-521-55066-1 CAMBRIDGE $59.95

William M. **Brinton** & Alan **Rinzler**, editors

Without Force or Lies: Voices from the Revolution of Central Europe, 1989-1990

Vaclav Havel, Josef Skvorecky, and Günter Grass are among the contributors to this anthology of forceful statements on what is happening in Eastern Europe

0-916515-92-3 MERCURY HOUSE PB $10.95

Juris **Dreifelds**

Latvia in Transition

From Moscow-dominated Soviet republic to independent and interdependent state

0-521-55537-X CAMBRIDGE PB $19.95

Alexander **Dubcek** & Jiri **Hochman**

Hope Dies Last: The Autobiography of Alexander Dubcek

The humanist social reformer and hero of the Prague Spring of 1968 completed this memoir just prior to his death. Dubcek intimately describes his singular journey from a Nazi resister in World War II to the betrayals of communism that brutally "removed" him from power. "A vigorous, engrossing autobiography" —*Publishers Weekly*

1-56836-000-2 KODANSHA $27.50

Paul **Hockenos**

Free to Hate: The Rise of the Right in Post-Communist Eastern Europe

0-415-91058-7 ROUTLEDGE PB $17.95

Lloyd **Jones**

Biografi: A Traveler's Tale

"*Biografi* is travel writing as it should be: with an intellectual and emotional investment in the country which is its subject [Albania]" —*TLS* [London]

See also **THE COMMONWEALTH OF INDEPENDENT STATES** under **EUROPE** under **TRAVEL LITERATURE** in **FOOD, TRAVEL, AND LEISURE**

0-374-11318-1 FS&G $19.00
0-15-600128-4 HARVEST PB $10.95

Ivan **Klima**

The Spirit of Prague and Other Essays

This collection of essays from the Czech author of *Waiting for the Darkness, Waiting for the Light* charts five critical decades in the history of Czechoslovakia. From his early witnessing of Nazi occupation to his life in the Stalinist regimes of the '50s, from the celebrations of Prague Spring to the Velvet Revolution, Klima offers a keen and sensitive view of a life in his country's tumultuous history. "Ivan Klima is a writer of enormous power and originality. His work is a sort of alchemy; it makes gold out of the base metals of state repression and the spiritual constriction it spawns"—*NY Times*

See also **CZECH LITERATURE** under **EASTERN EUROPEAN LITERATURE** in **LITERATURE OF EUROPE, AFRICA, AND ASIA**

0-9645611-2-3 CONSORTIUM PB $10.95

Janos **Kornai**

The Road to a Free Economy: Shifting from a Socialist System—The Example of Hungary

A preeminent Hungarian economist tackles the problems of moving from central economic planning toward a free market. "A wise and masterful analysis… Bold and penetrating" —Jeffrey D. Sachs, Harvard University

0-393-02887-9 NORTON PB $16.95

Vaclav Havel

Eda **Kriseova**

Vaclav Havel: The Authorized Biography

Full of vivid anecdotes and first-hand accounts of dissidents and fellow artists (like director Milos Forman) who know Havel best. Written by his confidante and long-time assistant, this book gives an inside look at the man who was the most unusual—and heartening—chief of state in the world

0-312-10317-4 PHAROS $22.95

Taras **Kuzio** & Andrew **Wilson**

Ukraine: From Perestroika to Independence

0-312-08652-0 ST. MARTIN'S $35.00

Peter **Laufer**

Iron Curtain Rising: A Personal Journey Through the Changing Landscape of Eastern Europe

An international correspondent's exhilarating and personal account of his travels through Eastern Europe as he collects a great variety of anecdotes, conversations, and opinions on the matter of the region's new-found political freedom. "I could actually feel, see, hear, and smell the revolution as I read *Iron Curtain Rising*"—Jim Farley, ABC News

1-56279-015-3 MERCURY HOUSE $19.50

Anatol **Lieven**

The Baltic Revolution

Presents an in-depth portrait of the past and likely outcome for the future of the Baltic states of Latvia, Estonia, and Lithuania. From conquest by Christians to life under Soviet rule to more recent struggles of ethnic conflict

0-300-05552-8 YALE $35.00
0-300-06078-5 YALE PB $16.00

Adam **Michnik**

The Church and the Left

A vanguard dissident, who did most of his writing in jail, discusses the surreal alliance between the Vatican and the left that led to the collapse of Polish communist rule. "Michnik is one of those who bring honor to the last two decades of the 20th century"—Czeslaw Milosz

EDITED, TRANSLATED, AND WITH AN INTRODUCTION BY DAVID OST

0-226-52424-8 CHICAGO $27.50

Kazimierz Z. **Poznanski**

Poland's Protracted Transition: Institutional Change and Economic Growth, 1971-1993

A reevaluation of conventional views of communist economies and the post-communist transition. Argues that the political pressures that affected the communist system have continued to have a disastrous impact in recent "shock therapy" reforms

0-521-55639-2 CAMBRIDGE PB $19.95

Angelo Maria **Ripellino**

Magic Prague

0-520-07352-5 CALIFORNIA $35.00

Joseph **Rothschild**

Return to Diversity: A Political History of East Central Europe Since World War II

This short history must be ranked as an invaluable resource for anyone interested in the pathbreaking events in Eastern Europe. "The essential facts and trends, soberly and deftly interpreted"—*Foreign Affairs*

0-19-507381-9 OXFORD $39.95

Yugoslavia

Rabia **Ali** & Lawrence **Lifschultz**

Why Bosnia?: Writings on the Balkan War

Brilliant, horrifying, informative essays about and by Bosnians. One of the finest books of the decade

0-9630587-8-9 PAMPHLETEERS $35.00
0-9630587-9-7 PAMPHLETEERS PB $19.95

Beverly **Allen**

Rape Warfare: The Hidden Genocide in Bosnia-Herzegovina and Croatia

0-8166-2818-1 MINNESOTA $19.95

Melissa **Bokovy** & others

State-Society Relations in Yugoslavia, 1945-1992

0-312-12690-5 ST. MARTIN'S $45.00

Norman **Cigar**

Genocide in Bosnia: The Policy of "Ethnic Cleansing"

0-89096-638-9 TEXAS A & M $29.95

Bogdan **Denitch**

The Tragic Death of Yugoslavia

0-8166-2458-5 MINNESOTA $44.95
0-8166-2459-3 MINNESOTA PB $24.95

Zlatko **Dizdarevizc**

Portraits of Sarajevo

0-88064-167-3 FROMM $19.95

Alex N. **Dragnich**

Serbs and Croats: The Struggle in Yugoslavia

This book tells a painful ethnic history, of killings of Serbs and Jews by fascist Croatians during World War II and of killings of Croatians by Serbs. It explains how Tito's apparent triumph of independent statehood became the struggle that rages today. "Concise, lucid history...a floodlight on the tragic drama unfolding in Yugoslavia"—*Publishers Weekly*

0-15-181073-7 HARCOURT BRACE $22.95
0-15-680663-0 HARCOURT BRACE PB $10.95

Slavenka **Drakulic**

The Balkan Express: Fragments from the Other Side of War

Personal essays from the Croatian journalist and novelist that bear witness to the way in which the war, by forcing upon her an ethnic "identity," has stripped her of her individuality—"the most precious property I had accumulated in my forty years of life." "An admirable, deeply felt, mosaiclike portrait of one of the most appalling grotesqueries of modern history"
—*Kirkus Reviews*

0-393-03496-8 NORTON $19.95

How We Survived Communism and Even Laughed

Nineteen essays that describe the daily struggles of women under the Marxist regime in the former Yugoslavia. "Drakulic's voice belongs to the world. If the purpose of bringing down the walls of Eastern Europe had been only for us to hear it, that would have been reason enough"
—Gloria Steinem

0-06-097540-7 HARPERPERENNIAL PB $12.50

Misha **Glenny**

The Fall of Yugoslavia: The Third Balkan War

Glenny's books have been influential in Western debate over the former Yugoslavia. "Vigorous, passionate, humane and extremely readable... For an account of what has actually happened...Glenny's book so far stands unparalled"—*The New Republic*

See also AFTER THE COLD WAR: THE FORMER SOVIET UNION AND EASTERN BLOC under INTERNATIONAL RELATIONS AND STRATEGIC STUDIES in SOCIAL STUDIES

0-14-023586-8 PENGUIN PB $10.95

Brian **Hall**

The Impossible Country: A Journey Through the Last Days of Yugoslavia

"A tragic portrait and an excellent piece of writing...Hall presents with sympathy, and frequently with humor the inhabitants of a country that never was a country"
—*Atlantic Monthly*

0-14-024923-0 PENGUIN PB $11.95

Jill A. **Irvine**

The Croat Question: Partisan Politics in the Formation of the Yugoslav Socialist State

0-8133-8542-3 WESTVIEW $71.50

Robert D. **Kaplan**

Balkan Ghosts: A Journey Through History

"Combines up-to-the-minute political reporting and literary, travel writing...[Kaplan's prose] is vivid, controlled, and sensitive"—*New Yorker*

0-312-08701-2 ST. MARTIN'S $22.95
0-679-74981-0 VINTAGE PB $13.00

Robert Kaplan
(photo credit: Susan Muhlhauser)

Franklin **Lindsay**
Beacons in the Night: With the OSS and Tito's Partisans in Wartime Yugoslavia
0-8047-2123-8 STANFORD $45.00

Ratko Mladic

Peter **Maas**
Love Thy Neighbor: A Story of War
Maas, a staff writer for *The Washington Post*, takes us deep into the former Yugoslavia in a book that travels from the eerie and grotesque to the ironic and heartbreaking. A terrible picture of the chaos of war
0-679-44433-5 KNOPF $25.00

Scott **Malcomson**
Borderlands: Nation and Empire
0-571-19815-5 FABER $22.95

Scott Malcomson
(photo credit: Sylvia Plachy)

David **Owen**
Balkan Odyssey
Chief European Community negotiator in Bosnia, David Owen provides a shocking account of the international peace effort following the breakup of the former Yugoslavia. A personal chronicle and rare look inside the world of international diplomacy
0-15-100221-5 HARCOURT BRACE $25.00

David **Rieff**
Slaughterhouse: Bosnia and the Failure of the West
0-684-81903-1 TOUCHSTONE PB $12.00

James **Seroka** & Vukasin **Pavlovic**
The Tragedy in Yugoslavia: The Failure of Democratic Transformation
1-56324-392-X SHARPE PB $23.95

Laura **Silber** & Allan **Little**
Yugoslavia: Death of a Nation
1-57500-005-9 T.V. BOOKS $29.95

Muslim refugees run into the woods, crowd into trucks, some are shot dead while trying to escape a Serb onslaught. Serb refugees form endless convoys of tractors, fleeing a Croatian advance. Blackened skeletons of buildings shape Sarajevo's skyline.
YUGOSLAVIA: DEATH OF A NATION

Dubravka **Ugresic**
Have a Nice Day: From the Balkan War to the American Dream
A native of Zagreb transplanted to Connecticut writes of the mind-blowing contrast between two poles of the Western world—the war-torn former Yugoslavia and Middletown, Connecticut
0-670-86016-6 VIKING $21.95

Warren **Zimmermann**
Origins of a Catastrophe: Yugoslavia and Its Destroyers
0-8129-6399-7 TIME BOOKS $25.00

Germany Since 1945

Noel **Annan**
Changing Enemies: The Defeat and Regeneration of Germany
0-393-03988-9 NORTON $35.00

Timothy Garton **Ash**
In Europe's Name: Germany and the Divided Continent
0-679-75557-8 VINTAGE PB $15.00

Leslie **Colitt**
Spymaster: The Real-Life "Karla," His Moles, and the East German Police
See also **ESPIONAGE TALES** under **ESPIONAGE** in **POPULAR READING**
0-201-40738-8 ADDISON-WESLEY $23.00

Ralf **Dahrendorf**
Society and Democracy in Germany
A German sociologist attempts to describe the "whole" of his own society
0-393-00953-X NORTON PB $10.95

Robert **Darnton**
Berlin Journal: 1989-1990
0-393-31018-3 NORTON PB $10.95

Konrad **Jarausch**
The Rush to German Unity
Explores the issues and problems raised by unification; published in 1994
0-19-508577-9 OXFORD PB $15.95

Gregory W. **Sandford**
From Hitler to Ulbricht: The Communist Reconstruction of East Germany, 1945-46
0-691-05367-7 PRINCETON $37.50

Yaron **Svoray** & Nick **Taylor**
In Hitler's Shadow: An Israeli's Amazing Journey Inside Germany's Neo-Nazi Movement
A real-life thriller in a deadly, terrifying world. Yaron Svoray, backed by the Simon Wiesenthal Center, penetrated and documented the dangerous and pernicious underworld of neo-Nazi skinheads and far-right nationalists in Germany. He found a clear and present threat posed by far-flung groups with frighteningly "respectable" connections, not only in Germany but in the United States–a militant and organized minority unrepentant about Germany's past and determined to restore Nazism in its future
0-385-47284-6 DOUBLEDAY $24.95

Henry A. **Turner**, Jr.
The Two Germanies Since 1945: East and West
From the Nazi surrender to the Bundestag elections of 1987
0-300-03865-8 YALE $27.00

Ian **Buruma**
The Wages of Guilt: Memories of War in Germany and Japan
The conflicting moral response to defeat and atrocity is the subject of this illuminating work. Buruma (*Playing the Game*) contrasts East Germany's reaction to the Holocaust with that of the West and analyzes the dual symbol of Hiroshima, offering insight into essential questions of morality and nationalism
See also **DOMESTIC POLITICS** under **OVERVIEWS OF CONTEMPORARY JAPAN** under **JAPAN**
0-374-28595-0 FS&G $25.00

France Since 1945

Robert **Gildea**
France Since 1945
By the author of *Barricades and Borders: Europe 1800-1914*
0-19-219246-9 OXFORD $32.00

Hugh **Gough**
De Gaulle and Twentieth-Century France
EDITED BY JOHN HORNE
0-340-58826-8 ARNOLD PB $19.95

Jean **Lacouture**

De Gaulle: The Rebel, 1890-1944

The first volume of a definitive biography of De Gaulle, tracing his life from his early career in World War I to his triumphant leadership during the liberation of Paris in 1944

0-393-02699-X NORTON $29.95

Charles de Gaulle

De Gaulle: The Ruler 1945-1970

A distinguished French journalist and biographer traces De Gaulle's return to France in 1944 to his death in 1970. This second volume covers the enigmatic general's two terms as President of France, his sudden resignation in 1946, and his triumphant return to power after the collapse of the Fourth Republic in 1958

0-393-03084-9 NORTON $29.95

Maurice **Larkin**

France Since the Popular Front: Government and Politics, 1936-1986

The evolution of French political life from the short-lived ministries of the Third and Fourth Republics to the greater stability of the Fifth Republic. Close attention is given to key figures and the crises of 1940, 1958, and 1968

0-19-873035-7 OXFORD PB $24.95

Marcel **Ophuls**

Hotel Terminus: The Life and Times of Klaus Barbie

0-671-68703-4 POSEIDON $18.95

Jean-Pierre **Rioux**

The Fourth Republic, 1944-1958

TRANSLATED BY GODFREY ROGERS

0-521-38916-X CAMBRIDGE PB $19.95

Henry **Rousso**

The Vichy Syndrome: History and Memory in France Since 1944

A study not of the Vichy regime itself, but of how subsequent generations of French people have dealt with the troubling legacy of occupation and collaboration. "Unusual and original...The study enlarges our sense of what historical explanation can be and how history may intersect with popular memory"
—Robert O. Paxton

0-674-93538-1 HARVARD $42.50

Recent History and Current Affairs

John **Ardagh**

France Today

Among the many topics Ardagh treats are the position of women, the role of education, Club Mediterranée, *nouvelle cuisine,* and the cinema. This revised edition of *France in the 1980s* is by the author of *Germany and the Germans*

0-14-010098-9 PENGUIN PB $12.00

Raymonde **Carroll**

Cultural Misunderstandings: The French-American Experience

A native of Tunisia, educated in France and the US, probes the clash of cultures in such topics as party manners, child-rearing, privacy, and using the telephone

TRANSLATED BY CAROL VOLK

0-226-09498-7 CHICAGO PB $11.95

J.B. **Duroselle**

France and the United States: From the Beginnings to the Present Day

This edition originally published in 1978

TRANSLATED BY DEREK COLTMAN

0-8057-9205-8 TWAYNE PB $15.95

Douglas **Porch**

The French Secret Service: From the Dreyfus Affair to the Gulf War

See also ESPIONAGE TALES under ESPIONAGE in POPULAR READING

0-374-15853-3 FS&G $32.50

Daniel **Singer**

Is Socialism Doomed?: The Meaning of Mitterrand

The collapse of the Socialist party during Mitterrand's first term

0-19-504925-X OXFORD $30.00

Elie **Weisel** & François **Mitterand**

Memoir in Two Voices

See also ELIE WIESEL under ART AND LITERATURE under THE HOLOCAUST

1-55970-338-5 ARCADE $21.95

Netherlands Since 1945

Allison **Blakely**

Blacks in the Dutch World: The Evolution of Racial Imagery in a Modern Society

A truly impressive study that insists on ambiguity about racial attitudes. Topics include: African-influenced place names in the Netherlands; black bogeymen in Dutch culture; the images of blacks in Dutch songs, nursery rhymes, and commercial products; black dances in Curaçao; the image of blacks in Dutch cartoons and jokes; Africans as soldiers in the Dutch East Indian army; black servants in the Netherlands; and black sailors

0-253-31191-8 INDIANA $35.00

Italy Since 1945

Diego **Gambetta**

The Sicilian Mafia: The Business of Private Protection

"A dazzling combination of economic theory and sociological insight to make sense of a significant but mysterious social institution"
—Robert Snyder

0-674-80742-1 HARVARD PB $18.95

H. Stuart **Hughes**

Prisoners of Hope: The Silver Age of the Italian Jews, 1924-1974

0-674-70727-3 HARVARD $25.00

Joseph **La Palombara**

Democracy, Italian Style

The foremost authority on the subject looks at the apparent chaos and instability of Italian democracy. "Journalists and diplomats should read this book. So should the tourists who flock to Italy each summer"
—*London Review of Books*

0-300-04411-9 YALE PB $14.00

Patrick **McCarthy**

The Crisis of the Italian State: From the Origins of the Cold War to the Fall of Berlusconi

0-312-12667-0 ST. MARTIN'S $35.00

H.M. **Scobie**

The Italian Economy in the 1990s

0-415-13936-8 ROUTLEDGE $65.00

Frederic **Sports** & Theodor **Wieser**

Italy: A Difficult Democracy

An explanation of democracy in the least-understood major European state

0-521-30451-2 CAMBRIDGE $69.95
0-521-31511-5 CAMBRIDGE PB $18.95

Alexander **Stille**

Excellent Cadavers: The Mafia and the Death of the First Italian Republic

0-679-42579-9 PANTHEON $27.50
0-679-76863-7 VINTAGE PB $14.00

Spain and Portugal Since 1945

Raymond **Carr** & Juan P. **Fusi**

Spain: Dictatorship to Democracy

The end of Francoism and Spain's abrupt jump into modernity

0-04-946014-5 UNWIN HYMAN PB $21.95

Richard **Gillespie** & others

Democratic Spain: Reshaping External Relations in a Changing World

0-415-11326-1 ROUTLEDGE PB $19.95

Hugo G. **Ferreira** & Michael W. **Marshall**
Portugal's Revolution
0-521-32204-9 CAMBRIDGE........$65.00

Joseph **Harrison**
The Spanish Economy: From the Civil War to the European Community
A concise discussion, under 100 pages, on Spain—from backward agrarian economy to active member of the European Community. In the New Studies in Economic and Social History series
0-521-55772-0 CAMBRIDGE PB........$9.95

John **Hooper**
The Spaniards: A Portrait of the New Spain
Life in post-Franco Spain
0-14-009808-9 PENGUIN PB........$12.00

Charles **Powell**
Juan Carlos of Spain: Self-Made Monarch
0-312-12752-9 ST. MARTIN'S........$59.95

Greece and Turkey Since 1945

Richard **Clogg**
Parties and Elections in Greece: The Search For Legitimacy
The antecedents of the present party system and the structure of the parties currently in power
0-8223-0823-1 DUKE PB........$23.95

Nicholas **Gage**
Eleni
0-345-32494-3 BALLANTINE PB........$5.95

Dankwart A. **Rustow**
Turkey: America's Forgotten Ally
Turkey's crucial role in American global strategy and the dynamic changes taking place within Turkish society
0-87609-065-X
COUNCIL ON FOREIGN RELATIONS PB........$12.95

Other Developments

Amy **Janello** & Brennon **Jones**
A Global Affair: An Inside Look at the United Nations
Images and anecdotes of the UN's first fifty years
0-9646322-0-9 JONES & JANELLO........$35.00

Stanley **Meisler**
United Nations: The First Fifty Years
A recent and comprehensive study
0-8711361-6-3 GROVE........$24.00

Bernard **Wasserstein**
Vanishing Diaspora: The Jews in Europe Since 1945
In 1939 there were 10 million Jews in Europe; in 1945 four million; today there are under two million. On current projections the Jews will become virtually extinct as a significant element in European society over the course of the 21st century
0-674-93196-3 HARVARD........$27.95

Great Britain and Ireland

Introductory Works

England

Asa **Briggs**
A Social History of England: From the Romans to Mrs. Thatcher
0-297-83262-X WEIDENFELD & NICOLSON........$39.95

Trevor O. **Lloyd**
The British Empire, 1558-1983
0-19-873025-X OXFORD PB........$22.00

Kenneth O. **Morgan**, editor
The Oxford Illustrated History of Britain
This beautifully produced volume traces the British Isles and people from earliest times to the present and includes contributions by ten British historians
0-19-822684-5 OXFORD........$49.95
0-19-285202-7 OXFORD PB........$17.95

G.M. **Trevelyan**
A Shortened History of England
A somewhat dated but good old-fashioned Whig historical survey
0-14-010241-8 VIKING PB........$12.00

R.K. **Webb**
Modern England: From the Eighteenth Century to the Present
A comprehensive text designed for the American reader and probably the best introduction for this period
0-06-046974-9 HARPERCOLLINS PB........$37.46

Scotland and Wales

J.D. **Mackie**
A History of Scotland
A fine, brief synthesis
0-14-013649-5 VIKING PB........$13.95

Fitzroy **Maclean**
A Concise History of Scotland
Illustrated
0-500-27706-0 THAMES & HUDSON PB........$15.95

Kenneth O. **Morgan**
Rebirth of a Nation: Wales, 1880-1980
0-19-821760-9 OXFORD PB........$15.95

Ireland

Thomas **Bartlett**
Irish Studies: A General Introduction
0-389-20805-1 BARNES & NOBLE........$45.00

Thomas **Bartlett** & Keith **Jeffery**, editors
A Military History of Ireland
An illustrated history, beyond the traditional confines of battles and tactics, from the earliest times to the present
0-521-41599-3 CAMBRIDGE........$49.95

Karl **Bottingheimer**
Ireland and the Irish: A Short History
From the Celtic and Viking inheritance to the "Irish abroad," with a concluding chapter on Irish literature
0-231-04610-3 COLUMBIA........$49.50
0-231-04611-1 COLUMBIA PB........$18.00

Denis **Donoghue**
We Irish: Essays on Irish Literature and Society
See also GENERAL HISTORIES AND STUDIES under ANTHOLOGIES AND STUDIES in LITERATURE OF THE BRITISH ISLES
0-520-06425-9 CALIFORNIA PB........$14.00

R.F. **Foster**
Modern Ireland, 1600-1972
"Sure to become the standard against which similar books are judged for a long time to come"
—Andrew M. Greeley, *NY Times Book Review*
0-14-013250-3 PENGUIN PB........$16.95

R.F. **Foster**, editor
The Oxford Illustrated History of Ireland
This comprehensive history designed for the general reader offers a full account of Irish history from prehistoric times to the present. Over 200 illustrations including 24 in color make this a particularly attractive book
0-19-822970-4 OXFORD........$49.95
0-19-285245-0 OXFORD PB........$22.50

Peter **Fry** & Fiona Somerset **Fry**
A History of Ireland
Useful and balanced outline to the present day; illustrated
0-415-04888-5 ROUTLEDGE PB........$18.95

Henry **Glassie**

Passing the Time in Ballymenone

A remarkable study revealing the complexity of traditional culture in a small agricultural community. Glassie provides everything: political ballads, potato farming, parlor decorations, jokes, and much more

0-253-20987-0 INDIANA PB $27.95

Robert **Kee**

The Green Flag

Volume 1
The Most Distressful Country

0-14-014758-6 PENGUIN PB $12.95

Volume 2
The Bold Fenian Men

0-14-014760-8 PENGUIN PB $12.95

Volume 3
Ourselves Alone

0-14-014756-X PENGUIN PB $13.95

J.J. **Lee**

Ireland, 1912-1985: Politics and Society

0-521-37741-2 CAMBRIDGE PB $38.95

T.W. **Moody** & F.X. **Martin**, editors

The Course of Irish History

0-85342-710-0 ROBERTS RINEHART PB $27.95

Kathleen J. **Ryan** & Bernard **Share**, editors

Irish Traditions

INTRODUCTION BY JAMES PLUNKETT

0-8109-8096-7 ABRADALE $19.98

Roger **Stalley**

The Cistercian Monasteries of Ireland

0-300-03737-6 YALE $50.00
0-300-04546-8 YALE PB $29.95

Topics in British History

Cultural and Social Life

Kenneth **Baker**, editor

The Faber Book of English History in Verse

Works of Shakespeare, Milton, Swift, Blake, Eliot, Larkin, and others

0-571-15062-4 FABER PB $14.95

Ilana K. **Ben-Amos**

Adolescence and Youth in Early-Modern England

0-300-05597-8 YALE $35.00

Ronald **Blythe**

Akenfield: Portrait of an English Village

A classic focusing on one village on the Suffolk coast

0-394-73847-0 RANDOM HOUSE PB $10.65

David Hackett **Fischer**

Albion's Seed: Four British Folkways in America

"It is the first in a series of volumes that he hopes will eventually constitute a cultural history of the United States....This book starts with a bang...a big bang....Remarkable....A revisionist blockbuster"
—Gordon Wood, *The New Republic*

See also **CULTURAL AND SOCIAL HISTORY** under **TOPICS IN AMERICAN STUDIES** in **HISTORY OF THE AMERICAS**

0-19-503794-4 OXFORD $40.00
0-19-506905-6 OXFORD PB $24.95

Antonia **Fraser**

The Weaker Vessel: Woman's Lot in Seventeenth-Century England

"An almost encyclopedic chronicle of women in 17th-century England ... wives, warriors, heiresses, preachers ... alive with anecdote after anecdote"—*NY Times*

See also **MODERN EUROPEAN HISTORY** under **EUROPEAN HISTORY** under **WOMEN'S STUDIES** in **SOCIAL STUDIES**

0-394-73251-0 RANDOM HOUSE PB $18.00

Geoffrey **Hughes**

Words in Time: A Social History of the English Vocabulary

The fascinating origin of words: "blurb" comes from "Miss Linda Blurb" who appeared on an American book cover around 1900; and more

See also **ABOUT LANGUAGE** under **REFERENCE** in **BUSINESS AND REFERENCE**

0-631-17321-8 BLACKWELL PB $20.95

Peter **Laslett**

The World We Have Lost: England Before the Industrial Age

0-02-367860-7 SCRIBNERS PB $46.00

William Roger **Louis**, editor

Adventures with Britannia: Personalities, Politics, and Culture in Britain

Essays include "The Myth of T.E. Lawrence" by Albert Hourani; "Winston Churchill as Historian" by Robert Blake; "How Liberal was John Stuart Mill?" by Joseph Hamburger; and "Who Cares about Cyril Connolly?" by Jeremy Lewis. "Scholarship at its most humane, true scholarship worn lightly in its off-duty moments, relaxed, informative, sometimes humorous"
—Michael Holroyd

0-292-74689-X TEXAS PB $17.95

Mark **Overton**

Agricultural Revolution in England: The Transformation of the Agrarian Economy, 1500-1850

Designed for students, this valuble study combines new material with analysis of the existing literature

0-521-56859-5 CAMBRIDGE PB $19.95

Simon **Shepherd** & Peter **Womack**

English Drama: A Cultural History

0-631-16812-5 BLACKWELL $64.95
0-631-19938-1 BLACKWELL PB $22.95

Roy **Porter**

Disease, Medicine and Society in England, 1550-1860

An expert's brief and authoritative study, available in a second edition

0-521-55791-7 CAMBRIDGE PB $9.95

Lawrence **Stone**

Broken Lives: Separation and Divorce in England, 1660-1857

0-19-820254-7 OXFORD $35.00

The Family, Sex and Marriage in England, 1500-1800

0-06-131979-1 HARPERCOLLINS PB $21.60

Lawrence **Stone** & Jeanne C. **Stone**

An Open Elite?: England, 1540-1880

A test of the long-held notion that landed society was opened to infiltration by families newly made rich through trade, office, or the professions

0-19-285149-7 OXFORD PB $16.95

John K. **Walton** & James **Walvin**, editors

Leisure in Britain, 1780-1939

0-7190-1946-X ST. MARTIN'S PB $22.95

Town and Country

Mark **Girouard**

The English Town: A History of Urban Life

0-300-04635-9 YALE $50.00

Mark **Giroud**

Victorian Pubs

A photographic essay: interiors and exteriors of gin palaces, many still in existence today

0-300-03199-8 YALE $37.50
0-300-03201-3 YALE PB $22.50

London

Paul **Bailey**

The Oxford Book of London

The life and growth of the city from the Middle Ages to present day, chronicled through the works of such renowned authors as Charles Dickens, Ben Jonson, William Wordsworth, George Bernard Shaw, Daniel Defoe, John Evelyn, and Samuel Pepys

See also **GREAT BRITAIN AND IRELAND** under **TRAVEL LITERATURE** in **FOOD, TRAVEL, AND LEISURE**

0-19-214192-9 OXFORD $25.00
0-19-283244-1 OXFORD PB $13.95

Roy **Porter**

London: A Social History

The social historian of medicine looks at the great metropolis. Chapters include "Commercial City: 1650-1800," "Culture City: Life under the Georges," and "Swinging London, Dangling Economy: 1945-1975"

0-674-53838-2 HARVARD $29.95

John **Russell**

London

St. Paul's Cathedral to Regent's Park; Canaletto to Gainsborough; Pinter in the West End to momentous occasions in the House of Commons—all London is brought to life by one of its most literate lovers

0-8109-3570-8 ABRAMS $49.50
0-8109-2673-3 ABRAMS PB $24.95

Monarchy

John **Cannon** & Ralph **Griffiths**

The Oxford Illustrated History of the British Monarchy

The crown's full history since Anglo-Saxon times. Includes 130 color illustrations, 270 black-and-white pictures, six color maps, and ten genealogies

0-19-822786-8 OXFORD $55.00

Antonia **Fraser**

The Lives of the Kings and Queens of England

0-520-20409-3 CALIFORNIA PB $19.95

Sea Power

Paul M. **Kennedy**

The Rise and Fall of British Naval Mastery

The author of *The Rise and Fall of the Great Powers* surveys his subject from the Tudors to the present day. "A work of the first importance"—*International Historical Review*

0-948660-01-5 HUMANITIES PB $25.00

Reference

Christopher **Bayley**, editor

Atlas of the British Empire

0-8160-1995-9 FACTS ON FILE $40.00

Christopher **Haigh**

The Cambridge Historical Encyclopedia of Great Britain and Ireland

0-521-39552-6 CAMBRIDGE PB $29.95

Elizabeth **Hallam**, editor

The Plantagenet Encyclopedia

0-517-14081-0 CRESCENT $19.99

David **Hey**, editor

The Oxford Companion to Local and Family History

Entries range from minstrels and monasteries to E.P. Thompson and trade unions

0-19-211688-6 OXFORD $49.95

Alan **Palmer** & Victoria **Palmer**

Who's Who in Bloomsbury

0-312-01630-1 ST. MARTIN'S $35.00

David **Hume**

From the Invasion of Julius Caesar to the Revolution of 1688: The History of England

Volume 1

From Early Britain to King John

From the invasion of Julius Caesar to the Revolution in 1688

See also **THE 18TH CENTURY**

0-86597-021-1 LIBERTY FUND $20.00
0-86597-022-X LIBERTY FUND PB $7.50

Volume 2

From John to Henry VI

See also **THE 18TH CENTURY**

0-86597-026-2 LIBERTY FUND $20.00
0-86597-027-0 LIBERTY FUND PB $7.50

Volume 3

From Henry VII to Mary

See also **THE 18TH CENTURY**

0-86597-028-9 LIBERTY FUND $20.00
0-86597-029-7 LIBERTY FUND PB $7.50

Volume 4

Elizabeth I

See also **THE 18TH CENTURY**

0-86597-030-0 LIBERTY FUND $20.00
0-86597-031-9 LIBERTY FUND PB $7.50

Volume 5

From James I to Charles I

See also **THE 18TH CENTURY**

0-86597-032-7 LIBERTY FUND $20.00
0-86597-033-5 LIBERTY FUND PB $7.50

Volume 6

From the Commonwealth to the Glorious Revolution

See also **THE 18TH CENTURY**

0-86597-034-3 LIBERTY FUND $20.00
0-86597-035-1 LIBERTY FUND PB $7.50

Elizabeth **Longford**, editor

The Oxford Book of Royal Anecdotes

"Absolutely jam-packed with tempting tidbits" —*Library Journal*

0-19-282851-7 OXFORD PB $13.95

Alan **Palmer**

Who's Who in Shakespeare's England

Over 700 biographies of leading figures in the arts, politics, the church, the court, the secret service, as well as the theater and literary world

0-312-87096-5 ST. MARTIN'S $32.50

Early British History: From Prehistory to 1066

Kevin **Crossley-Holland**, editor

The Anglo-Saxon World: An Anthology

A compact collection of documents and poems, including a complete translation of *Beowulf*

See also **BRITISH AND CELTIC** under **EUROPEAN MYTHOLOGY** under **MYTHOLOGY AND FOLKLORE** in **RELIGION, SPIRITUALITY, AND PHILOSOPHY**

See also **THE ANGLO-SAXON PERIOD** in **LITERATURE OF THE BRITISH ISLES**

0-85115-169-8 ROCHESTER $45.00
0-19-281632-2 OXFORD PB $9.95

Dorothy **Whitelock**

The Beginnings of English Society

0-14-020245-5 VIKING PB $8.95

Highlights of Medieval England and Ireland

At the height of the Plantagenet (Norman) dynasty, the kings of England considered their holdings in France as valuable as anything they ruled in Britain. For the medieval period, therefore, the history of England cannot be separated from that of France.

For related reading, see ARCHAEOLOGY and MEDIEVAL AND RENAISSANCE EUROPE

Christopher **Daniell**

Death and Burial in Medieval England, 1066-1550

0-415-11629-5 ROUTLEDGE $42.00

Chris **Given-Wilson**

The Illustrated History of Late Medieval England

0-7190-4153-8 MANCHESTER $25.00
0-7190-4152-X MANCHESTER $40.00

Rosemary **Horrox**

Fifteenth-Century Attitudes: Perceptions of Society in Late Medieval England

0-521-58986-X CAMBRIDGE PB $18.95

A.R. **Myers**

England in the Late Middle Ages

0-14-013766-1 VIKING PB $7.00

Austin Lane **Poole**

From Domesday Book to Magna Carta, 1087-1216

Part of the Oxford History of England Series

0-19-821707-2 OXFORD $65.00
0-19-285287-6 OXFORD PB $18.95

Michael **Richter**

Medieval Ireland: The Enduring Tradition

TRANSLATED BY BRIAN STORE

0-312-15812-2 ST. MARTIN'S PB $17.95

Medieval Portraits

Frank **Barlow**

Thomas Becket

0-520-05920-4 CALIFORNIA $40.00
0-520-07175-1 CALIFORNIA PB $16.00

Edward the Confessor

0-520-05319-2 CALIFORNIA PB $15.95

Amy **Kelly**

Eleanor of Aquitaine and the Four Kings

The strong-willed woman who married two kings and gave birth to two others

See also **MEDIEVAL PORTRAITS** under **THE HIGH MIDDLE AGES: EMPIRE AND PAPACY** under **MEDIEVAL AND RENAISSANCE EUROPE**

0-674-24254-8 HARVARD PB $14.95

D.D.R. **Owen**

Eleanor of Aquitaine: Queen and Legend

"This biography succeeds where so many others have failed precisely because of its honesty and its refusal to compromise with the evidence" —*History*

0-631-20101-7 BLACKWELL PB $19.95

Chris **Given-Wilson** & Alice **Curteis**

The Royal Bastards of Medieval England

Despite ecclesiastical disapproval, noble bastardy was not a major barrier to success. Chapters include "Sex, Love and Illegitimacy" and "The Bastards of Richard I and King John"

0-415-02826-4 ROUTLEDGE PB $22.95

Sir Thomas More

W.L. **Warren**

Henry II

The king best remembered for his struggles with Thomas A. Becket and Eleanor of Aquitaine. "A fine work by a professional historian who can write"—A.L. Rowse

See also **MEDIEVAL PORTRAITS** under **THE HIGH MIDDLE AGES: EMPIRE AND PAPACY** under **MEDIEVAL AND RENAISSANCE EUROPE**

0-520-03494-5 CALIFORNIA PB $16.95

King John

0-520-03643-3 CALIFORNIA PB $18.95

Charles **Ross**

Richard III

Richard ruled for only 26 months, but remains one of the most controversial English monarchs. Ross argues that his resort to violent means and illegal actions to attain his ends was, in his day, by no means unique

0-520-05075-4 CALIFORNIA PB $14.00

J.F. **Webb** & others, editors

The Age of Bede

0-14-044437-8 PENGUIN PB $8.95

David C. **Douglas**

William the Conqueror: The Norman Impact upon England

0-520-00350-0 CALIFORNIA PB $16.00

The Tudors: 1485-1603

The years 1485 and 1603 are strictly the political anchors, demarcating control of the crown by a Welsh family over three generations. The underlying social and economic developments that carried England into the modern world are not easily confined to specific years.

Richard **Barber**, editor

The Pastons: A Family in the Wars of the Roses

A fascinating, uniquely detailed portrait of daily life in England during the 15th century

See also **PROSE** under **MEDIEVAL LITERATURE** in **LITERATURE OF THE BRITISH ISLES**

0-85115-338-0 BOYDELL & BREWER PB $23.00

Muriel **Byrne** & Bridget **Boland**, editors

The Lisle Letters: An Abridgment

A collection of early 16th-century letters written to and from Arthur Plantagenet, Viscount Lisle, offering a revealing mirror of life at the beginning of the Renaissance

See also **PROSE** under **THE 16TH CENTURY** in **LITERATURE OF THE BRITISH ISLES**

0-226-08810-3 CHICAGO PB $12.95

G.R. **Elton**

England Under the Tudors

0-415-06533-X ROUTLEDGE PB $19.95

John **Guy**

Tudor England

A 608-page study that assesses new debates on the course of the English Reformation and the strength and weaknesses of Tudor government at a local and national level. The "myth" of Elizabeth is debunked

0-19-285213-2 OXFORD PB $19.95

John **Morrill**, editor

The Oxford Illustrated History of Tudor and Stuart Britain

Contains 250 photographs and maps, many in color

0-19-820325-X OXFORD $45.00

Charles **Ross**

The Wars of the Roses: A Concise History

Suggests that the gloom of 15th-century England has been too often exaggerated

See also **WARS AND REVOLTS** under **THE 14TH CENTURY: BLACK DEATH AND ECONOMIC DEPRESSION** under **MEDIEVAL AND RENAISSANCE EUROPE**

0-500-27407-X THAMES & HUDSON PB $15.95

Conrad **Russell**

The Crisis of Parliaments: English History, 1509-1660

An excellent synthesis that departs from the traditional dynastic periodization

0-19-913034-5 OXFORD PB $19.95

Wars of the Roses

0-345-40433-5 BALLANTINE PB $12.95

Henry **Williams**

The Tudor Regime

0-19-822678-0 OXFORD PB $24.00

The Reformation Through the Reign of Elizabeth I

Though the major effect of the English Reformation was largely political, it could not have happened had England not felt the spiritual crisis of the century. The rise of Calvinism in the form of Puritanism was as much a part of the process as Henry VIII's theatrics.

For related reading, see EARLY MODERN EUROPE

Wallace T. **MacCaffrey**

Queen Elizabeth and the Making of Policy, 1572-1588

Includes the religious issues that continued to divide the country

0-691-10112-4 PRINCETON PB $19.95

A.L. **Rowse**

The England of Elizabeth

0-299-07724-1 WISCONSIN PB $16.50

Roy **Strong**

The Cult of Elizabeth: Elizabethan Portraiture and Pageantry

With 94 black-and-white photos and four color plates

See also **NORTHERN EUROPE** under **EUROPEAN ART: THE RENAISSANCE** in **ART**

0-520-05840-2 CALIFORNIA $55.00

0-520-05841-0 CALIFORNIA PB $18.95

R.B. **Wernham**

The Making of Elizabethan Foreign Policy, 1558-1603

0-520-03974-2 CALIFORNIA PB $15.00

Biography

Eric **Ives**

Anne Boleyn

"A lush took at Tudor court life, with its elegant official celebrations, its moves from castle to castle, its cut-throat games of one-upsmanship and faction"—*Washington Book Review*

0-631-16065-5 BLACKWELL PB $22.95

Retha M. **Warnicke**

The Rise and Fall of Anne Boleyn

A fresh investigation of the behind-the-scenes forces that led to Anne's execution

0-521-40677-3 CAMBRIDGE PB..........$12.95

Anne Boleyn

Diarmaid **MacCulloch**

Thomas Cranmer: A Life

Named archbishop of Canterbury by Henry VIII in 1533, Cranmer (1489-1556) was one of the principal figures of the English Reformation. He was burned at the stake by Mary I

0-300-06688-0 YALE..........$35.00

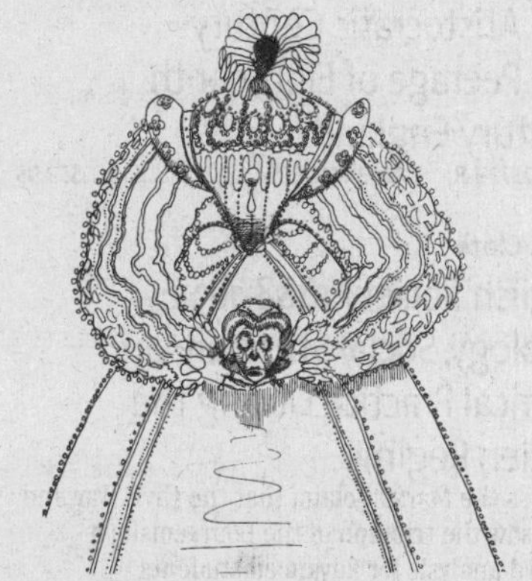

Mary, Queen of Scots

Antonia **Fraser**

The Wives of Henry VIII

Fraser pushes aside the stereotypes surrounding Henry's wives and makes them memorable for their own achievements, as well as their fateful link to Henry's Tudor court—Anne Boleyn, the champion of religious reform; the touchingly dignified Anne of Cleves; the reckless and naive Katherine Howard; and the quietly subversive Catherine Parr

0-679-73001-X VINTAGE PB..........$15.00

Karen **Lindsey**

Divorced, Beheaded, Survived: A Feminist Reinterpretation of the Wives of Henry VIII

"Lindsey is insightful and disarmingly funny in her musings on Henry and his sorry wives"
—*Arizona Republic*

0-201-40823-6 ADDISON-WESLEY PB..........$13.00

J.J. **Scarisbrick**

Henry VIII

The standard, solid biography

0-520-01130-9 CALIFORNIA PB..........$14.95

Antonia **Fraser**

Mary Queen of Scots

The tragic life of Elizabeth's Catholic rival, whom Elizabeth put to death in 1587

0-385-31129-X DELTA PB..........$17.95

Alison **Weir**

The Children of Henry VIII

0-345-39118-7 BALLANTINE..........$25.00

The Century of Revolution

"In order to close this part of British history, it is also necessary to relate the dissolution of the monarchy in England: That event soon followed upon the execution of the monarch. When the peers met, on the day appointed in their adjournment, they entered upon business, and sent down some votes to the commons, of which the latter deigned not to take the least notice. In a few days, the lower house passed a vote, that they would make no more addresses to the house of peers, nor receive any from them; and that that house was useless and dangerous, and was therefore to be abolished. A like vote passed with regard to the monarchy…The commons ordered a new great seal to be engraved, on which that assembly was represented, with this legend, ON THE FIRST YEAR OF FREEDOM, BY GOD'S BLESSING, RESTORED, 1648. The forms of all public business were changed from the king's name to that of the keepers of the liberties of England. And it was declared high treason to proclaim, or any otherwise acknowledge Charles Stuart, commonly called prince of Wales."
—David Hume, *A History of England*

Robert **Ashton**

Counter-Revolution: The Second Civil War and Its Origins, 1646-1648

0-300-06114-5 YALE..........$50.00

G.E. **Aylmer**

Rebellion or Revolution?: England, 1640-1660

Argues that the Revolution came from the middle class and the Puritans; rebellion from both aristocratic and popular elements

0-19-289212-6 OXFORD PB..........$16.95

Glenn **Burgess**

Absolute Monarchy and the Stuart Constitution

Holds that our common understanding of 17th-century English politics is oversimplified and inaccurate. The "constitutionalism" of common lawyers and parliamentarians was quite different from current notions of that term, and it was Charles I's inappropriate exploitation of agreed prerogatives that ruptured the "pacified politics" of which the early modern English were so proud

0-300-06532-9 YALE..........$30.00

Peter Beresford **Ellis**

Hell or Connaught: The Cromwellian Colonisation of Ireland

Following the execution of Charles I in 1649, Cromwell reduced the last bastions of royal support at Drogheda and Wexford, and redistributed confiscated estates among parliamentary supporters

0-85640-404-7 DUFOUR PB..........$13.95

Antonia **Fraser**

Cromwell: The Lord Protector

0-917657-90-X FINE PB..........$17.95

Peter **Gaunt**

Oliver Cromwell

0-631-18356-6 BLACKWELL..........$24.95

Christopher **Hill**

The Century of Revolution, 1603-1714

England on the path to Parliamentary rule, literary achievement, religious toleration, and scientific accomplishment. An ideal introduction

0-393-01573-4 NORTON..........$19.95
0-393-30016-1 NORTON PB..........$9.95

The English Bible and the Seventeenth Century Revolution

0-14-015990-8 PENGUIN PB..........$13.95

Some Intellectual Consequences of the English Revolution

0-299-08140-0 WISCONSIN..........$19.50
0-299-08144-3 WISCONSIN PB..........$9.95

A Tinker and a Poor Man: John Bunyan and His Church, 1628-1688

The first biography in many decades of the controversial literary genius of the English Revolution

0-393-30662-3 NORTON PB..........$10.95

The World Turned Upside Down: Radical Ideas During the English Revolution

Diggers, Ranters, Quakers, Levellers—and the social and theological impulses that gave rise to them. The "worm's eye view" of the Civil War

0-14-013732-7 VIKING PB..........$13.95

S.J. **Houston**

James I

0-582-35208-8 LONGMAN PB..........$22.25

Ronald **Hutton**

The Restoration: A Political and Religious History of England and Wales, 1659-1667

The transformation of Cromwell's commonwealth into the restoration monarchy

0-19-822698-5 OXFORD..........$45.00

Nigel **Smith**

Literature and Revolution in England, 1640-1660

0-300-05974-4 YALE..........$45.00

Kevin **Sharpe**

The Personal Rule of Charles I

How, in 1625, Charles I transformed the political landscape of Britain, dissolved parliament, and began a period of eleven years of personal rule. "A book written with verve, lucidity, and grace"—*Sunday Telegraph*

0-300-06596-5 YALE PB $25.00

Lawrence **Stone**

The Crisis of the Aristocracy, 1558-1641

Argues that the relative decline of the aristocracy—not the rise or fall of the gentry—was the fundamental social change in pre-Civil War England

0-19-821314-X OXFORD $75.00
0-19-500274-1 OXFORD PB $14.95

H.R. **Trevor-Roper**

Catholics, Anglicans and Puritans: Seventeenth Century Essays

New essays on Nicholas Hill, the Atomist; Laudianism and political power; James Ussher, Archbishop of Armagh; the Great Tew circle; Milton in politics

0-226-81228-6 CHICAGO $27.50

David **Underdown**

Fire from Heaven: Life in an English Town in the Seventeenth Century

By the author of *Pride's Purge: Politics in the Puritan Revolution*

0-300-05990-6 YALE PB $18.00

Revel, Riot and Rebellion: Popular Politics and Culture in England 1603-1660

A pioneering synthesis linking festive culture with political allegiance

0-19-285193-4 OXFORD PB $17.95

Sources

Samuel **Pepys**

The Shorter Pepys

"Pepys's diary is the cheerful self-report, not of the man eminent in naval history, nor of the historical witness, but of the unobjectionable hedonist"—Geoffrey Grigson

See also **PROSE** under **THE RESTORATION AND THE 18TH CENTURY** in **LITERATURE OF THE BRITISH ISLES**

EDITED BY ROBERT LATHAM

0-520-03426-0 CALIFORNIA $50.00

Samuel Pepys

David **Lagomarsino** & Charles T. **Woods**, editors

The Trial of Charles I: A Documentary History

0-87451-499-1 NEW ENGLAND PB $15.95

David **Wooton**, editor

Divine Right and Democracy: An Anthology of Political Writing in Stuart England

A collection of 33 speeches, essays, and polemical pamphlets by authors ranging from Charles I and James VI to Richard Hooker, Algernon Sidney, and John Locke

0-14-043250-7 PENGUIN PB $12.95

The Later Stuarts and the Glorious Revolution

G.N. **Clark**

The Later Stuarts, 1660-1714

A classic particularly good on old-fashioned politics

0-19-821702-1 OXFORD $75.00

Tim **Harris**

London Crowds in the Reign of Charles II: Propaganda and Politics from the Restoration Until the Exclusion Crisis

0-521-32623-0 CAMBRIDGE $59.95
0-521-39845-2 CAMBRIDGE PB $18.95

J.P. **Kenyon**

Stuart England

0-14-013768-8 PENGUIN PB $7.95

Thomas Babington **Macaulay**

The History of England

The classic Whig history of the 1850s celebrates the constitutional legacy of the Glorious Revolution and spans the period 1685-1702

EDITED, ABRIDGED & WITH AN INTRODUCTION BY H.R. TREVOR-ROPER

0-14-043133-0 PENGUIN PB $10.95

Sir Patrick **MacRory**

The Siege of Derry

The failure of King James II to capture Londonderry prepared to the Restoration final defeat of Stuart hopes at the Boyne in 1690

0-19-285182-9 OXFORD PB $13.95

W.A. **Speck**

The Reluctant Revolutionaries: Englishmen and the Revolution of 1688

The year that marked a decisive, though not inevitable, movement toward a mixed, constitutional monarchy

0-19-822768-X OXFORD $49.95

Stability and Strife: England 1714-1760

The best synthesis for the period, incorporating political, economic and social developments

0-674-83350-3 HARVARD PB $14.50

G.M. **Trevelyan**

The English Revolution, 1688-1689

Suggests that the Revolution strengthened conservatism but that its results made it a turning point in history. "The traditional Whig view at its best—the view of Locke, Burke, and Macaulay"—*Guardian*

0-19-500263-6 OXFORD PB $7.95

Henri **van der Zee** & Barbara **van der Zee**

1688: Revolution in the Family

How the Glorious Revolution was an intimate family affair

0-14-008354-5 PENGUIN PB $7.95

Stephen Saunders **Webb**

Lord Churchill's Coup: The Anglo-American Empire and the Glorious Revolution Reconsidered

0-394-54980-5 KNOPF $30.00

The 18th Century

Theo **Barker** & Dorian **Gerhold**

The Rise of Road Transport, 1700-1900

The significance of roads in an age of canals and, later, railways

0-521-55773-9 CAMBRIDGE PB $9.95

John **Cannon**

The Aristocratic Century: The Peerage of Eighteenth Century England

0-521-25729-8 CAMBRIDGE $59.95

J.C.D. **Clark**

English Society 1688-1832: Ideology, Social Structure and Political Practice During the Ancien Regime

Revises the Marxist claim that the Civil War and 1688 saw the triumph of the bourgeoisie; a shrewd analysis for advanced students

0-521-30922-0 CAMBRIDGE $79.95

Revolution and Rebellion: State and Society in England in the Seventeenth and Eighteenth Centuries

Reviews the polemics around the rise of capitalism and democracy in England

0-521-33063-7 CAMBRIDGE $49.95
0-521-33710-0 CAMBRIDGE PB $19.95

Linda **Colley**

Britons: Forging a Nation, 1701-1837

0-300-05925-6 YALE PB $15.00

Diana **Donald**

The Age of Caricature: Satirical Prints in the Age of George III

The great age of humorous and vital cartooning

0-300-06605-8 YALE $60.00

Daniel **Defoe**

A Tour Through the Whole Island of Great Britain

Businessman, journalist, soldier, and spy, Defoe toured Britain from 1724 to 1726. "Far the best authority for early 18th-century England" —Dorothy George

See also **PROSE** under **THE RESTORATION AND THE 18TH CENTURY** in **LITERATURE OF THE BRITISH ISLES**

0-14-043066-0 PENGUIN PB $13.95

David **Hume**

The History of England: From the Invasion of Julius Caesar to the Revolution of 1688 Volume 6 From the Commonwealth to the Glorious Revolution

See also **REFERENCE**

0-86597-034-3 LIBERTY FUND $20.00
0-86597-035-1 LIBERTY FUND PB $7.50

Derek **Jarrett**

England in the Age of Hogarth

0-300-03609-4 YALE PB $15.00

J.M. **Neeson**

Commoners: Common Right, Enclosure and Social Change in England, 1700-1820

Challenges the view that England had no peasantry or that it had disappeared before industrialization. A paperback editon of one of the most original contributions to English rural history in the past generation

0-521-56774-2 CAMBRIDGE PB $24.95

Richard **Pares**

King George III and the Politicians

"Full of wit and gaiety, enlivened with anecdote and a delight to read"—A.J.P. Taylor

0-19-821240-2 OXFORD $55.00

J.H. **Plumb**

The Growth of Political Stability in England, 1675-1725

"By providing this illuminating introduction to the political scene when Walpole first entered the Commons, he has done much to clear up the complexities of a very confusing period and lay the basis for a new interpretation" —Dorothy Marshall

0-391-01908-2 HUMANITIES PB $17.50

Roy **Porter**

Mind-Forg'd Manacles: A History of Madness in England from the Restoration to the Regency

Argues that before the advent of the public asylum all was not apathy, cruelty, and corruption. "A brilliant British answer to Foucault"—Elaine Showalter

0-674-57617-9 HARVARD $43.00

Biography

Conor Cruise **O'Brien**

The Great Melody: A Thematic Biography of Edmund Burke

0-226-61651-7 CHICAGO PB $24.95

Flora **Fraser**

The Unruly Queen: The Life of Queen Caroline

0-394-56146-5 KNOPF $35.00

John C. **Beaglehole**

The Life of Captain James Cook

A classic study and the first full-scale biography to do justice to the exploits and achievements of the intrepid navigator and explorer

See also **CAPTAIN COOK** under **POLYNESIA** under **AUSTRALIA, NEW ZEALAND, AND POLYNESIA**

0-8047-0848-7 STANFORD $65.00
0-8047-2009-6 STANFORD PB $24.95

James Cook

Richard **Hough**

Captain James Cook: A Biography

0-393-03680-4 NORTON $29.95
0-393-31519-3 NORTON PB $15.00

H. Larry **Ingle**

First Among Friends: George Fox and the Creation of Quakerism

"Valuable in reminding us of the most important dimension of the history of the seventeenth century, which was the searing intensity of its religious beliefs" —David Underdown, *New Republic*

0-19-510117-0 OXFORD PB $19.95

L.G. **Mitchell**

Charles James Fox

0-19-820104-4 OXFORD $49.95

Brian W. **Hill**

Robert Harley: Speaker, Secretary of State, and Prime Minister

A pioneer of parliamentary government, Harley turned the "country" Tories into an effective opposition in the reigns of William III and Anne

0-300-04284-1 YALE $40.00

Christopher **Hibbert**

Nelson: A Personal History

The victor of the battles of the Nile (1798), Copenhagen (1801), and Trafalgar (1805); by the author of *The Days of the French Revolution*

0-201-40800-7 ADDISON-WESLEY PB $16.00

Tom **Pocock**

Horatio Nelson

A popular biography, especially of interest to those intrigued by that Hamilton woman

0-7126-6123-9 TRAFALGAR SQUARE PB $15.95

Ian Simpsson **Ross**

The Life of Adam Smith

Student at Glasgow and Oxford, freelance lecturer in rhetoric, innovative university lecturer, tutor on the grand tour of the Continent with the young duke of Buccleuch, acclaimed political economist, and founder of the modern discipline of economics

0-19-828821-2 OXFORD $35.00

The 19th Century and the Industrial Revolution

"Were we to characterize this age of ours by any single epithet we should be tempted to call it, above all others, the Mechanical Age...The same habit regulates not our modes of action alone but our modes of thought and feeling. Men are grown mechanical in head and in heart as well as in hand."
—Thomas Carlyle, *Signs of the Times* [1829].

Anna **Clark**

The Struggle for the Breeches: Gender and the Making of the British Working Class

Spinners and weavers, radical politics and Chartism, the world of E.P. Thompson framed in terms of the gender conflict that characterized work and organizations within the working class. "A stunning achievement...promises to set the terms of debate over politics, class, and gender for many years to come"—Deborah Valenze, *American Historical Review*

0-520-08624-4 CALIFORNIA $35.00

E.J. **Hobsbawm**

Industry and Empire: The Making of Modern English Society

Britain's heady ride as the world's first industrial power, and the years that followed

0-14-013749-1 VIKING PB $14.95

Harold **Perkin**

The Origins of Modern English Society, 1780-1880

Bold and provocative; the birth of the new class society and its mid-Victorian maturity

0-415-05922-4 ROUTLEDGE PB $17.95

E.P. **Thompson**

The Making of the English Working Class

A pioneer study of working class culture in the Romantic Age

0-394-70322-7 RANDOM HOUSE PB $24.00

David **Thomson**

England in the Nineteenth Century

0-14-013770-X VIKING PB $9.95

Raymond **Williams**

Culture and Society: 1780-1950

From Edmund Burke and William Cobbett to F.R. Leavis and George Orwell. Written from an independent Left standpoint, this critical history is exactly to the point of contemporary discussions of value"—Harold Rosenberg

0-231-02287-5 COLUMBIA $91.00
0-231-05701-6 COLUMBIA PB $19.00

The Industrial Revolution

"The Industrial Revolution marks the most fundamental transformation of human life in the history of the world recorded in written documents. For a brief period it coincided with the history of a single country, Great Britain. An entire world economy was thus built on, or rather around, Britain, and this country therefore temporarily rose to a position of global influence and power unparalleled by any state of its relative size before or since, and unlikely to be paralleled by any state in the foreseeable future. There was a moment in the world's history when Britain can be described, if we are not too pedantic, as its only workshop, its only massive importer and exporter, its only carrier, its only imperialist..."
—E.J. Hobsbawm, *Industry and Empire*

Maxine **Berg**

The Age of Manufactures, 1700-1820: Industry, Innovation, and Work in Britain

0-19-520500-6 OXFORD PB $15.95

Phyllis **Deane**

The First Industrial Revolution

0-521-29609-9 CAMBRIDGE PB $19.95

Peter **Mathias**

The First Industrial Nation: An Economic History of Britain, 1700-1914

0-415-02756-X ROUTLEDGE PB $16.95

Henry **Mayhew**

London Labour and the London Poor

Portraits of Dickens's London, first published in 1861

0-486-21934-8 DOVER PB $9.95

Protest, Reform, and the New Economic Thought

John **Bowditch** & Clement **Ramsland**, editors

Voices of the Industrial Revolution: Selected Readings from the Liberal Economists and Their Critics

0-472-06053-8 MICHIGAN PB $14.95

Thomas Carlyle

Thomas **Carlyle**

Past and Present

"It is a moral, political, historical, and a most questionable red hot indignant thing," Carlyle wrote of this volume, "for my heart is sick to look at the things now going on in England." Carlyle's principal contemporary social criticism, first published in 1843

See also **19TH-CENTURY PROSE** under **THE 19TH CENTURY** in **LITERATURE OF THE BRITISH ISLES**

EDITED BY RICHARD D. ALTICK

0-8147-0562-6 NYU PB $16.00

Selected Writings

In the highly rhetorical prose of such works as *Chartism* and *The French Revolution*, Carlyle established himself as a kind of official moral opposition to his era. The excitement and power of his finest works exerted a profound influence on writers as diverse as Mill and Emerson, Dickens and George Eliot, Thackeray and Whitman

See also **19TH-CENTURY PROSE** under **THE 19TH CENTURY** in **LITERATURE OF THE BRITISH ISLES**

EDITED BY A. SHELSTON

0-14-043065-2 PENGUIN PB $12.95

Seamus **Deane**

The French Revolution and Enlightenment in England, 1789-1832

The revolution's impact on English thought

0-674-32240-1 HARVARD $34.50

Friedrich **Engels**

The Condition of the Working Class in England

Engels' finest hour: a masterpiece of committed reporting on the appalling living and working conditions in industrialized Manchester

EDITED WITH AN INTRODUCTION BY VICTOR KIERNAN

0-14-044486-6 PENGUIN PB $11.95

The Condition of the Working Class in England

0-19-282955-6 OXFORD PB $7.95

Robert L. **Heilbroner**

The Worldly Philosophers: The Lives, Times, and Ideas of the Great Economic Thinkers

History of economic thought which examines the theories of such major figures as Smith, Ricardo, and Marx. Well-written and accessible

See also **GENERAL WORKS AND HISTORIES OF ECONOMIC THOUGHT** under **ECONOMICS** in **SOCIAL STUDIES**

0-671-63318-X TOUCHSTONE PB $14.00

Steven **Marcus**

Engels, Manchester, and the Working Class

Applies critical literary techniques to Victorian responses to the Industrial Revolution

0-393-30237-7 NORTON PB $8.95

Henry **Mayhew**

London Labour and the London Poor

SELECTED AND INTRODUCED BY VICTOR NEUBURG

0-14-043241-8 PENGUIN PB $11.95

Robert **Owen**

A New View of Society and Other Writings

EDITED WITH AN INTRODUCTION BY GREGORY CLAEYS

0-14-043348-1 PENGUIN PB $11.95

The Victorian Era

Patricia **Anderson**

When Passion Reigned: Sex and the Victorians

0-465-08991-7 BASIC $23.00
0-465-08992-5 BASIC PB $15.00

Walter **Bagehot**

The English Constitution

Editor of *The Economist* from 1861 until his death in 1877, Walter Bagehot brought fresh insights into the psychological underpinnings of political action. Many regard *The English Constitution* (1867) as still the best introduction to English political culture

0-8014-9023-5 CORNELL PB $10.95

Virginia **Berridge** & Griffith **Edwards**

Opium and the People: Opiate Use in Nineteenth-Century England

0-335-15278-3 TAYLOR & FRANCIS $99.00
0-335-15129-9 TAYLOR & FRANCIS PB $29.95

Asa **Briggs**

The Collected Essays of Asa Briggs

"An unrivaled panorama of the range and riches of Victorian life"—David Cannadine

Volume 1
Words, Numbers, Places, People

0-252-01216-X ILLINOIS $32.50
0-252-06004-0 ILLINOIS PB $16.95

Volume 2
Images, Problems, Standpoints, Forecasts

0-252-01217-8 ILLINOIS $37.50
0-252-06005-9 ILLINOIS PB $16.95

Victorian People: A Reassessment of Persons and Themes, 1851-1867

This revised and illustrated edition includes Briggs's famous essays on the Crystal Palace Exposition and Disraeli's "Leap in the Dark"

0-226-07488-9 CHICAGO PB $16.95

Victorian Things

The meaning of objects in the Victorian Age: cameras and spectacles, matches, hats, postage stamps, telephones, and typewriters

0-226-07483-8 CHICAGO $35.95

David **Cannadine**

The Decline and Fall of the British Aristocracy

"As late as the 1870s, [British] patricians were still the most wealthy, the most powerful, and the most glamorous people in the country, corporately—and understandably—conscious of themselves as God's elect…This book seeks to recover and recreate, to evoke and explain, the decline and fall of this once-preeminent elite" —David Cannadine

0-300-04761-4 YALE $47.50

Robert **Ensor**

England, 1870-1914

First published in 1936 and still remarkable for its appeal to students and general readers alike

0-19-821705-6 OXFORD $75.00

David **Feldman**

Englishmen and Jews: Social Relations and Political Culture, 1840-1914

0-300-05501-3 YALE $50.00

H.J. **Hanham**, editor

The Nineteenth Century Constitution, 1815-1914

Includes original documents and criticism

0-521-09560-3 CAMBRIDGE PB $39.95

Gertrude **Himmelfarb**

The De-Moralization of Society: From Victorian Virtues to Modern Values

0-679-76490-9 VINTAGE PB $13.00

Poverty and Compassion: The Moral Imagination of the Late Victorians

The Victorian debates about poverty and the policies that society ought to adopt with regard to it have a keen relevance to contemporary American dilemmas, as the distinguished historian shows in this study

0-679-40119-9 KNOPF $30.00

Victorian Minds: A Study of Intellectuals in Crisis and Ideologies in Transition

"Precise and discriminating…an exemplary study of the 19th century and a superb introduction to the 20th"—Robert A. Nisbet

1-56663-077-0 DEE PB $16.95

Michael **Mason**

The Making of Victorian Sexual Attitudes

"Reveals a wealth of nineteenth-century thought and behavior"—*London Review of Books*

0-19-285319-8 OXFORD PB $14.95

James **Morris**

Farewell the Trumpets: An Imperial Retreat

0-15-630286-1 HARCOURT BRACE PB $16.00

Pax Brittanica: The Climax of an Empire

0-15-671466-3 HARCOURT BRACE PB $16.00

Jonathan **Parry**

The Rise and Fall of Liberal Government in Victorian Britain

British Liberalism from 1830 to 1886, and its leaders from Grey to Gladstone and Hartington. Argues that Liberalism was a more coherent force than has generally been recognized

0-300-06718-6 YALE PB $20.00

Bernard **Semmel**

George Eliot and the Politics of National Inheritance

0-19-508657-0 OXFORD PB $17.95

F.M.L. **Thompson**

The Rise of Respectable Society: A Social History of Victorian Britain, 1830-1900

0-674-77285-7 HARVARD $44.00
0-674-77286-5 HARVARD PB $15.95

Gaye **Tuchman** & Nina E. **Fortin**

Edging Women Out: Victorian Novelists, Publishers, and Social Change

"How male writers invaded and took over this white-collar occupation is the phenomenon investigated in this bombshell of a book" —*Publishers Weekly*

0-300-04316-3 YALE $35.00

Judith R. **Walkowitz**

City of Dreadful Delight: Narratives of Sexual Danger in Late-Victorian England

"Empirical historians attuned to studying social relations rather than gender constructions will miss the narratives of *class* danger or conflict….But those who prefer a London filled with menacing Minotaurs, misogynistic journalists, patriarchal intellectuals, and fearful as well as intrepid women will find much inspiration in this richly conceptualized study"—L. Perry Curtis, Jr., Brown University

0-226-87146-0 CHICAGO PB $17.95

Prostitution and Victorian Society: Women, Class, and the State

0-521-27064-2 CAMBRIDGE PB $18.95

E. Llewellyn **Woodward**

The Age of Reform, 1815-1870

From Waterloo to Gladstone's first ministry. Part of the Oxford History of England; second edition

0-19-285262-0 OXFORD PB $19.95

G.M. **Young**

Victorian England: Portrait of an Age

0-19-500259-8 OXFORD PB $9.95

Ireland Under the Union

Thomas **Gallagher**

Paddy's Lament: Ireland, 1846-1847 Prelude to Hatred

The potato famine and its place in Irish resentment of England

0-15-670700-4 HARCOURT BRACE PB $14.00

Tom **Garvin**

Nationalist Revolutionaries in Ireland, 1858-1928

Suggests that the elite who came to power after 1921 were heavily influenced not only by old agrarian grievances but also by contemporary Catholic abhorrence of the Protestant and secular world

0-19-820134-6 OXFORD $48.00

Cormac O. **Grada**

The Great Irish Famine

Despite a devastating food shortage, the huge death toll of one million was hardly inevitable

0-521-55787-9 CAMBRIDGE PB $9.95

Kerby A. **Miller**

Emigrants and Exiles: Ireland and the Irish Exodus to North America

0-19-505187-4 OXFORD PB $18.95

Austen **Morgan**

James Connolly: A Political Biography

0-7190-2958-9 MANCHESTER PB $19.95

Eunan **O'Halpin**

The Decline of the Union: British Government in Ireland, 1892-1920

0-8156-2425-5 SYRACUSE $33.00

Robert **Scally**

The End of Hidden Ireland: Rebellion, Famine, and Emigration

"Scally combines the labor of an archivist with the speculative verve of an historian of mentalities"—*Washington Post*

0-19-510659-8 OXFORD PB $14.95

Imperialism and Colonialism

Roger **Adelson**

London and the Middle East: Money, Power and War, 1902-1922

0-300-06094-7 YALE $35.00

Lance E. **Davis** & Robert A. **Huttenback**

Mammon and the Pursuit of Empire: The Political Economy of British Imperialism, 1860-1912

Abridged

0-521-23612-6 CAMBRIDGE $49.95

0-521-35723-3 CAMBRIDGE PB $18.95

Byron **Farwell**

Mr. Kipling's Army: All the Queen's Men

Victoria's upstairs-downstairs army—the smallest ever to hold an empire

0-393-30444-2 NORTON PB $9.95

Queen Victoria's Little Wars

Worldwide military expeditions protected Britons and British interests. In the process, the British Empire quadrupled

0-393-30235-0 NORTON PB $13.00

Aaron L. **Friedberg**

The Weary Titan: Britain and the Experience of Relative Decline, 1895-1905

Highly praised scholarship in theory and history

0-691-05532-7 PRINCETON $55.00

0-691-00844-2 PRINCETON PB $17.95

A.N. **Porter**

The Atlas of British Overseas Expansion

0-13-051988-X SIMON & SCHUSTER $60.00

Eric J. **Hobsbawm**

The Age of Empire, 1875-1914

"Few, if any, present practitioners of the historian's craft can equal the astonishing and dazzling craft of Mr. Hobsbawm's scholarship" —*NY Times Book Review*

See also **THE NEW IMPERIALISM** under **19TH-CENTURY EUROPE**

0-679-72175-4 VINTAGE PB $15.00

P.J. **Marshall**, editor

The Cambridge Illustrated History of the British Empire

From the end of the American Revolution to the present day. Contributors include David Fieldhouse, Ravinder Kumar, Andrew Porter, and Tapin Raychaudhuri

0-521-43211-1 CAMBRIDGE $39.95

Thomas **Pakenham**

The Boer War

The costliest, bloodiest, and most humiliating war that Britain fought between 1815 and 1914; Pakenham's study is as fast-moving as a novel

See also **SOUTH AFRICA: HISTORY** under **AFRICA**

0-679-43087-4 RANDOM HOUSE $40.00

Eminent Victorians: Biographical Studies

John D. **Rosenberg**

Carlyle and the Burden of History

Illustrates how the author of *The French Revolution* was a great epic poet whose natural medium was prose and for whom history was prophecy, biography, and social criticism

See also **BIOGRAPHIES AND CRITICAL STUDIES** under **HISTORIOGRAPHY**

0-674-09754-8 HARVARD $23.50

Peter J. **Bowler**

Charles Darwin: The Man and His Influence

Darwin's work explained to a general audience

0-521-56668-1 CAMBRIDGE PB $15.95

Janet **Browne**

Charles Darwin: Voyaging

"There is no better chronicle of Darwin as human being, friend, and indefatigable scientist, nor anywhere a richer description of his milieu, his family, his social circle, and his scientific connections"—*New York Newsday*

0-691-02606-8 PRINCETON PB $18.95

Jane **Ridley**

Young Disraeli: 1804-1846

0-517-58643-6 CROWN $35.00

Paul **Smith**

Disraeli: A Brief Life

0-521-38150-9 CAMBRIDGE $39.95

P.J. **Jagger**, editor

Gladstone, Politics and Religion

Essays with contributions by Michael Foot and Robert Blake

0-312-32763-3 ST. MARTIN'S $22.50

Peter **Stansky**

Gladstone: A Progress in Politics

Head of the Liberal Party and prime minister four times—viewed largely through his parliamentary speeches

0-393-00037-0 NORTON PB $8.95

Bentley B. **Gilbert**

David Lloyd George: A Political Life

Prime minister of a coalition government during World War I, Lloyd George later presided over the decline of the Liberal Party

0-8142-0597-6 OHIO STATE $68.50

John **Clive**

Macaulay: The Shaping of the Historian

A National Book Award winner

See also **HISTORIOGRAPHY**

0-674-54005-0 BELKNAP PB $18.50

Flora **Fraser**, editor

Maud: The Illustrated Diary of a Victorian Woman

0-87701-429-9 CHRONICLE $6.98

E.P. **Thompson**

William Morris: Romantic to Revolutionary

0-8047-1509-2 STANFORD PB $24.95

M **Tamarkin**

Cecil Rhodes and the Cape Afrikaners: The Imperial Colossus and the Colonial Parish Pump

0-714-64627-X CASS $47.50

Kitty **Muggeridge** & others

Beatrice Webb: A Life, 1858-1943

1-566-63001-0 DEE $30.00

Sidney & Beatrice Webb

Julia **Briggs**

A Woman of Passion: The Life of E. Nesbit, 1858-1924

Biography of a founding member of the Fabian Society

0-941533-03-4 NEW AMSTERDAM $27.95

Muriel **Chamberlain**

Lord Palmerston

Foreign minister in several Whig cabinets throughout the 1830s and '40s, Palmerston became prime minister of a Whig-Peelite administration during the Crimean War and remained in office until his death in 1865

0-8132-0663-4 CATHOLIC UNIVERSITY $22.95
0-8132-0664-2 CATHOLIC UNIVERSITY PB $9.95

E.V. **Quinn** & others, editors

Dear Miss Nightingale: A Selection of Benjamin Jowett's Letters to Florence Nightingale, 1860-1893

0-19-822953-4 OXFORD $69.00

M. **Tamarkin**

Cecil Rhodes and the Cape Afrikaners: The Imperial Colossus and the Colonial Parish Pump

0-714-64627-X CASS $47.50

Noel **Annan**

Leslie Stephen: The Godless Victorian

0-226-02106-8 CHICAGO PB $17.95

Lytton **Strachey**

Eminent Victorians

Quietly devastating thumbnail biographies of four quintessential high Victorians (Cardinal Manning, Dr. Arnold, Florence Nightingale, and General Gordon)

See also **20TH-CENTURY BRITISH ESSAYS AND OTHER PROSE** in **LITERATURE OF THE BRITISH ISLES**

INTRODUCTION BY MICHAEL HOLROYD

0-15-628697-1 HARCOURT BRACE PB $10.00

Christopher **Hibbert**

Queen Victoria in Her Letters

0-14-057027-6 VIKING PB $3.98

Queen Victoria

Lytton **Strachey**

Queen Victoria

First published in 1921. "A masterpiece" —*New Statesman*

0-15-175695-3 HARCOURT BRACE $15.95
0-15-675696-X HARCOURT BRACE PB $14.00

Adrienne **Munich**

Queen Victoria's Secrets

In an artful blend of feminist, anthropological, and postcolonial approaches, Munich—Director of the Women's Studies Program at SUNY-Stony Brook—reassesses Victoria and the lasting grip she has held on her nation's imagination. Following the predominating concepts governing a Victorian woman's life—fashion, marriage, menopause—she offers a study of general interest and central importance, elucidating a figure who has become synonymous with sexual repression

See also **EUROPEAN HISTORY** under **WOMEN'S STUDIES** in **SOCIAL STUDIES**

0-231-10480-4 COLUMBIA $27.95

Patrick **French**

Younghusband: The Last Great Imperial Adventurer

A great telling of masterful life

0-002-15733-0 HARPERCOLLINS $30.00

The 20th Century

Michael **Dockrill** & Brian **McKercher**, editors

Diplomacy and World Power: Studies in British Foreign Policy, 1890-1950

From Britain's preeminent position as a world power to her relative decline after World War II

0-521-46243-6 CAMBRIDGE $59.95

Alfred F. **Havighurst**

Britain in Transition: The Twentieth Century

0-226-31971-7 CHICAGO $46.00
0-226-31970-9 CHICAGO PB $24.95

Trevor O. **Lloyd**

Empire to Welfare State: English History, 1906-1985

0-19-873111-6 OXFORD PB $24.95

Harold **Perkin**

The Rise of Professional Society: England Since 1880

0-415-00890-5 ROUTLEDGE PB $49.95

A.J.P. **Taylor**

English History, 1914-1945

An account by a distinguished historian known for his acid style and maverick views

0-19-821715-3 OXFORD $69.00
0-19-285268-X OXFORD PB $17.95

David **Thomson**

England in the Twentieth Century

0-14-013771-8 VIKING PB $6.95

Philip **Williamson**

National Crisis and National Government: British Politics, the Economy and Empire, 1926-1932

0-521-36137-0 CAMBRIDGE $95.00

Armaggedon: 1914-1918

"'You say the news from home must seem trivial compared with my experience out here,' wrote Noakes. 'Please don't get that impression. Out here news of home is like food and drink to us, however trivial. Indeed, this life is like a dream and the old life is the only reality. We live on memories. Our constant thought is—what are they doing home.' The parcels would give more tangible backing. Contents might range from the over-ripe partridge and a bunch of violets, which Ellis once got, through to the home-made cakes, Oxo cubes, chocolate bars and cigarettes which were the more common staple. The contents of all parcels naturally were shared out equally among mates. The thought was the private and valuable part." —Denis Winter, *Death's Men: Soldiers of the Great War*

John **Bourne**

Britain and the Great War, 1914-1918

0-7131-6523-5 ARNOLD PB $16.95

Vera **Brittain**

Testament of Youth

A classic memoir of Britain's war years

0-14-018844-4 PENGUIN PB $14.95
0-14-012251-6 PENGUIN PB $14.00

Paul **Fussell**

The Great War and Modern Memory

On the shattering of innocence in 1914-18 and the end of our concept that any war can be heroic. "An original and brilliant piece of cultural history and one of the most deeply moving books I have read in a long time" —Lionel Trilling

See also **HISTORY, POLITICS, AND SOCIETY** under **20TH-CENTURY AMERICAN ESSAYS AND JOURNALISM** in **LITERATURE OF THE AMERICAS**

0-19-502171-1 OXFORD PB $12.95

Robert **Graves**

Goodbye to All That

Graves's "bitter leave-taking of England" at 33, in a classic autobiography (first published in 1929) about coming of age in the trenches of World War I

See also **20TH-CENTURY BRITISH ESSAYS AND OTHER PROSE** in **LITERATURE OF THE BRITISH ISLES**

0-385-09330-6 DOUBLEDAY PB $10.95

Siegfried **Sassoon**

Though published as fiction, Sassoon's Sherston series is in fact an undisguised autobiography of his experiences in the Great War.

Memoirs of a Fox Hunting Man

The first volume of Sherston's memoirs recounts with nostalgia the prewar world of the sportsman and cricketer

0-571-06454-X FABER PB $12.95

Memoirs of an Infantry Officer

The second volume describes a young subaltern who protests against the horror of the trenches

0-571-06410-8 FABER PB $10.95

Denis **Winter**

Death's Men: Soldiers of the Great War

The individual British soldier, in the trenches with five million of his countrymen

See also **WORLD WAR I** under **WARS THROUGH THE AGES** under **MILITARY AFFAIRS**

See also **THE GREAT WAR** under **WORLD WAR I** under **20TH-CENTURY EUROPE TO THE SECOND WORLD WAR**

0-14-016822-2 PENGUIN PB $12.00

Robert **Wohl**

The Generation of 1914

An attempt to regain the true story of a generation "lost" to myth

0-674-34466-9 HARVARD PB $14.95

WWI Infantryman

Britain Between the Wars

Jan **Marsh**

Bloomsbury Women: Distinct Figures in Life and Art

Attractively illustrated with fine color plates

0-8050-4550-3 HOLT $29.95

George **Orwell**

The Road to Wigan Pier

A powerful account of unemployment and proletarian life in the north of England

See also **20TH-CENTURY BRITISH ESSAYS AND OTHER PROSE** in **LITERATURE OF THE BRITISH ISLES**

FOREWORD BY VICTOR GOLLANCZ

0-15-676750-3 HARCOURT BRACE PB $9.00

In Wigan I stayed for a while with a miner who was suffering from nystagmus. He could see across the room but not much further. He had been drawing compensation of twenty-nine shilling a week for the past nine months, but the colliery company were now talking of putting him on "partial compensation" of fourteen shilling a week ... Watching this man go to the colliery to draw his compensation, I was struck by the profound differences that are made by status. Here was a man who had been half blinded in one of the most useful of all jobs and was drawing a pension to which he had a perfect right, if anybody has a right to anything. Yet he could not, so to speak, demand this pension—he could not, for instance, draw it when and how he wanted it. He had to go to the colliery once a week at a time named by the company, and when he got there he was kept waiting about for hours in the cold wind. For all I know he was also expected to touch his cap and show gratitude to whomever paid him; at any rate he had to waste an afternoon and spend sixpence in bus fares. It is very different for a member of the bourgeoisie, even such a down at-heel member as I am. Even when I am on the verge of starvation I have certain rights attaching to my bourgeois status. I do not earn much more than a miner earns, but I do at least get it paid into my bank in a gentlemanly manner and can draw it out when I choose. And even when my account is exhausted the bank people are still passably polite.

THE ROAD TO WIGAN PIER

Winston Churchill

There is, unfortunately, no convenient single biography. Churchill's life must be pieced together, perhaps in too much detail, by several volumes. His *The Second World War*, for which he won the Nobel Prize in 1953, remains a perennial favorite.

Winston S. **Churchill**

The Second World War

Volume 1
The Gathering Storm

The origins of, and entry into, the war and Churchill's a appointment as prime minister at age 65

See also **GENERAL HISTORIES** under **THE SECOND WORLD WAR**

0-395-41055-X HOUGHTON MIFFLIN PB $16.95

Volume 2
Their Finest Hour

The months from May to December 1940

See also **GENERAL HISTORIES** under **THE SECOND WORLD WAR**

0-395-07536-X HOUGHTON MIFFLIN $35.00

0-395-41056-8 HOUGHTON MIFFLIN PB $14.95

Volume 3
The Grand Alliance

1941: the year of the sinking of the *Bismarck*, Hitler's invasion of Russia, Pearl Harbor, and the formation of the "Grand Alliance"

See also **GENERAL HISTORIES** under **THE SECOND WORLD WAR**

0-395-07538-6 HOUGHTON MIFFLIN $35.00

Volume 4
The Hinge of Fate

The turning of the tide in the Pacific and North Africa

See also **GENERAL HISTORIES** under **THE SECOND WORLD WAR**

0-395-07539-4 HOUGHTON MIFFLIN $35.00

0-395-41058-4 HOUGHTON MIFFLIN PB $14.95

Volume 5
Closing the Ring

Allied efforts up to the Normandy invasion. This volume is currently out of print

See also **GENERAL HISTORIES** under **THE SECOND WORLD WAR**

0-395-41059-2 HOUGHTON MIFFLIN $9.95

Volume 6
Triumph and Tragedy

See also **GENERAL HISTORIES** under **THE SECOND WORLD WAR**

0-395-41060-6 HOUGHTON MIFFLIN PB $9.95

Martin **Gilbert**

Churchill: A Life

Gilbert's eight-volume biography of Churchill, the definitive account of the statesman's career, was called "a brilliant historical tour de force" by TLS. Now Gilbert has distilled his 25 years of research into a single 1,088-page volume combining broad scope and intimate detail

0-8050-0615-X HOLT $35.00

0-517-09297-2 OUTLET PB $12.99

William **Manchester**

The Last Lion: Winston Spencer Churchill

Volume 1
Visions of Glory, 1874-1932

0-316-54503-1 LITTLE, BROWN $40.00

Volume 2

0-385-31331-4 DELL PB $17.95

Ted **Morgan**

Churchill: Young Man in a Hurry, 1874-1915

A popular account by the biographer of FDR and Somerset Maugham

9-998-11728-3 OLYMPIC PB $4.98

Britain Since 1945

Virginia **Berridge**

AIDS and the UK: The Making of Policy, 1981-1994

0-19-820473-6 OXFORD PB $23.00

Christopher **Booker**

The Neophiliacs: The Revolution in English Life in the Fifties and Sixties

0-7126-5505-0 TRAFALGAR SQUARE PB $17.95

Tom **Bower**

The Perfect English Spy: The Unknown Man in Charge During the Most Tumultuous, Scandal-Ridden Era in Espionage History

See also **ESPIONAGE TALES** under **ESPIONAGE** in **POPULAR READING**

0-312-13584-X ST. MARTIN'S $26.95

Bill **Buford**

Among the Thugs

Granta editor Bill Buford provides a chilling report from the front lines of England's out-of-control soccer scene in what the *LA Times Book Review* called, "Remarkable…vividly, comically and horrifyingly reported" and John Gregory Dunne praised as "*A Clockwork Orange* come to life"

0-393-03381-3 NORTON $22.95

English Thugs

Peter **Hennessy**

Whitehall

0-02-914441-8 FREE PRESS $40.00

Dennis **Kavanagh**

Thatcherism and British Politics: The End of Consensus

The dissolution of the Labour/ Conservative postwar consensus

0-19-827755-5 OXFORD PB $17.95

William Roger **Louis** & Hedley **Bull**, editors

The "Special Relationship": Anglo-American Relations Since 1945

See also **SPECIAL TOPICS IN AMERICAN FOREIGN POLICY** under **AMERICAN POLITICS AND FOREIGN POLICY** in **HISTORY OF THE AMERICAS**

0-19-820183-4 OXFORD PB $27.00

Kenneth O. **Morgan**

Labour in Power: 1945-1951

The government that shaped the welfare state

0-19-285150-0 OXFORD PB $19.95

Labour People: Leaders and Lieutenants, Hardie to Kinnock

Illustrated

0-19-285270-1 OXFORD PB $15.00

The People's Peace: British History 1945-1989

The editor of *The Oxford Illustrated History of Britain* takes a detailed and comprehensive look at Britain's evolution in the years after World War II. "In 44 years," he writes, "the British had yet to recover from victory in the Second World War, even though the Germans and Japanese had so manifestly recovered from defeat"

0-19-822764-7 OXFORD $35.00

Anthony Cave **Brown**

Treason in the Blood: H. St. John Philby, Kim Philby, and the Spy Case of the Century

Uniquely effective, this dual biography of Kim Philby—considered by the CIA to be "the most remarkable spy of our generation" and by the KGB "one of the most important men of the century"—and his father provides unmatched insight into the anatomy of treachery. With sources from America, Britain, Switzerland, France, and Moscow, as well as new photographs and KGB memoranda, this is an enormously compelling view of one of the century's most fascinating figures

See also **ESPIONAGE TALES** under **ESPIONAGE** in **POPULAR READING**

0-395-63119-X HOUGHTON MIFFLIN $29.95

Sir Robin **Renwick**

Fighting with Allies: America and England at Peace and War

The former British ambassador to the United States on the forging of the "special relationship" which reached its zenith in the Reagan-Thatcher years. "A lively analysis of the diplomacy that brought, and kept, the two [nations] together"—*Publishers Weekly*

0-8129-2709-5 TIME BOOKS $35.00

Alan **Sked** & Chris **Cook**

Post-War Britain: A Political History

0-06-496322-5 BARNES & NOBLE $38.50

20th-Century Biography

Philip **Norman**

Shout!: The Beatles in Their Generation

An international bestseller

See also **GROUPS AND INDIVIDUAL ARTISTS** under **ROCK** in **PERFORMING ARTS AND MEDIA**

0-684-83067-1 FIRESIDE PB $13.00

Paul **Berry** & others

Vera Britain: A Life

0-7011-2679-5 CHATTO & WINDUS $35.00

John **Charmley**

Chamberlain and the Lost Peace

0929587332 DEE $27.95

Quentin **Crisp**

The Naked Civil Servant

The autobiography of the English civil servant who chose to flaunt his homosexuality in conventional 1930s London

See also **BIOGRAPHIES** under **GAY, LESBIAN, AND BISEXUAL STUDIES** in **SOCIAL STUDIES**

0-452-25413-2 NEW AMERICAN LIBRARY PB $6.95

David **Dutton**

Anthony Eden: A Life and Reputation

Due out at the end of 1996, a biography of a premier British statesman

0-340-56168-8 ARNOLD (ARNOE) NC $42.00

Robert **Skidelsky**

John Maynard Keynes: Volume I, Hope Betrayed, 1883-1920

The well-received first volume of Skidelsky's examination of one of the 20th century's most prominent and influential economists

See also **JOHN MAYNARD KEYNES** under **GREAT ECONOMISTS** under **ECONOMICS** in **SOCIAL STUDIES**

0-14-023554-X PENGUIN PB $15.95

John Maynard Keynes

John Maynard Keynes: Volume II, The Economist as Savior, 1920-1937

Skidelsky's second volume follows Keynes into his most productive period as an economist, when he "set out to save a capitalist system he did not admire." Includes clear, concise explanations of his central theories

See also **JOHN MAYNARD KEYNES** under **GREAT ECONOMISTS** under **ECONOMICS** in **SOCIAL STUDIES**

0-14-023806-9 PENGUIN PB $16.95

Michael **Holroyd**

Lytton Strachey: A Biography

Highly recommended

0-374-52465-3 FS&G PB $17.00

Margaret **Thatcher**

The Downing Street Years

0-06-092563-9 HARPERPERENNIAL PB $16.00

The Path to Power

Written with wit, intellect, and passion, this riveting memoir provides insight into the making of one of the most influential leaders of the 20th century

0-06-092732-1 HARPERCOLLINS PB $18.00

Martin **Stannard**

Evelyn Waugh: The Early Years, 1903-1939

A life of wit, bravado, and colorful escapades; but in Waugh's own phrase, a "sad story" of one who was melancholy at heart

See also **THE 20TH CENTURY** under **STUDIES OF INDIVIDUAL AUTHORS** under **ANTHOLOGIES AND STUDIES** in **LITERATURE OF THE BRITISH ISLES**

0-393-02450-4 NORTON $24.95

0-393-30605-4 NORTON PB $10.95

Evelyn Waugh

The House of Windsor

"The populace cannot understand the bureaucracy; it can only worship the national idols."—George Bernard Shaw, "Maxims for Revolutionists" in *Man and Superman*

Caroline **Blackwood**

The Last of the Duchess

The subject is Wallace Warfield, Duchess of Windsor (1896-1986)

0-679-43970-6 PANTHEON $23.00

Jonathan **Dimbleby**

The Prince of Wales: A Biography

0-688-14615-5 QUILL PB $12.00

Sarah **Bradford**

Elizabeth: A Biography of Britain's Queen

Bradford—Viscountess Bangor in private life—has previously chronicled the lives of Cesare Borgia, Disraeli, Princess Grace, and King George VI. Here, she brings her unparalleled experience of Buckingham Palace to a revealing, lucid, and entirely captivating portrait of a sitting queen struggling with a dynasty in flux

0-374-14749-3 FS&G $30.00

Donald **Spoto**

The Decline and Fall of the House of Windsor

0-684-81544-3 SIMON & SCHUSTER $27.50
0-671-00230-9 POCKET PB $6.99

Brian **Hoey**

Monarchy: Behind the Scenes with the Royal Family

0-563-20672-1 BBC PB $11.95

A. N. **Wilson**

The Rise and Fall of the House of Windsor

From the scandals of the *annus horribilis,* 1992, A. N. Wilson *(Tolstoy, Jesus)* addresses the ultimate question: Can the Windsor family dynasty survive? "A thinking person's irreverent, entertaining, and knowledgeable guide to the monarchy"—*Kirkus Reviews*

0-393-03607-3 NORTON $22.00

Ireland Divided

Backed by German aid during the First World War, Sinn Fein, the military arm of the Irish independence movement, rebelled against British rule in 1916. In 1923 a settlement was reached, and Ireland was divided. Southern Ireland broke political relations with Britain and in 1949 became an independent republic.

Antagonism characterized Irish politics in the 1960s, with one current urging the healing of the rebellion's wounds, and the other urging the procurement of Northern Ireland into the republic. After civil rights demonstrations erupted in Northern Ireland in 1969, the IRA began its direct attacks on security forces which, in 1972, led to the collapse of the Northern Ireland government. Throughout the 1970s, '80s, and '90s the Provisional IRA, or "Provos," have continued their campaign of terror on British targets in Northern Ireland, Britain, and elsewhere, with a brief cessation between September 1994 and February 1996. The recent peace efforts broke down after a long dispute over the British requirement that the IRA disarm its members, and the IRA bombing campaign has resumed in London.

Paul **Bew** & Henry **Patterson**

The British State and the Ulster Crisis

Challenges the belief that Britain has maintained a coherent imperialist strategy in Northern Ireland

0-8052-7258-5 VERSO $24.95

Terence **Brown**

Ireland: A Social and Cultural History, 1922 to the Present

"Gaelic, peasant Ireland may still inspire idealists and delight tourists. Terence Brown shows how its influence…no longer dominates the essential Ireland of the later 20th century"—*Times Educational Supplement*

0-8014-9349-8 CORNELL PB $14.95

Tim P. **Coogan**

The IRA: A History

1-87937-399-8 ROBERTS RINEHART PB $17.95

Michael Collins: The Man Who Made Ireland

1-57098-075-6 ROBERTS RINEHART PB $16.95

Kevin **Toolis**

Rebel Hearts: Journeys Within the IRA's Soul

0-312-14478-4 ST. MARTIN'S $25.95

John **Darby**, editor

Northern Ireland: The Background to the Conflict

A dispassionate collection of essays pointing to accommodation in the subtle relations between Catholics and Protestants

0-8156-2417-4 SYRACUSE PB $14.95

Jack **Holland**

The American Connection: U.S. Guns, Money, and Influence in Northern Ireland

"Compulsory reading for those who wish to understand the place and influence of Irish-American nationalism on Anglo-Irish affairs" —*Boston Globe*

0-670-80894-6 VIKING $19.95

Tony **Parker**

May the Lord in His Mercy Be Kind to Belfast

An intriguing oral history of Belfast that illustrates, like nothing else, why the achievement of true peace in Ireland is such a fragile, obstacle-ridden process. "By turns moving, inspirational, appalling, and illuminating…Parker [shows] you the inside of this divided community in a way no historian or documentary-maker could…a landmark achievement"—Sue Wilson, *The List.* "Utterly compassionate…the best that I have read about that blighted province" —Edna O'Brien, *Daily Mail*

0-8050-3806-X HOLT PB $13.95

Russian Studies

Overviews of Russian History

Paul **Dukes**

A History of Russia: Medieval, Modern, Contemporary

0-8223-1096-1 DUKE PB $26.95

Brian **Moynahan**

The Russian Century: Birth of a Nation, 1894-1994

Three hundred never-before published photographs chart Russia from before the Revolution to the present day with originality, incisiveness, and sympathy. Beyond the familiar official images, Moynahan has unearthed intimate photographs of the Romanovs, of the Eastern front of World War I, of the cruelties of Stalin's purges and the hard life after the fall of communism. A unique and startling compilation of insights into Soviet life

INTRODUCTION BY YEVGENY YEVTUSHENKO

0-679-42075-4 RANDOM HOUSE $45.00

The Russian Century: A History of the Last Hundred Years

0-679-76436-4 RANDOM HOUSE PB $15.00

Nicholas V. **Riasanovsky**

A History of Russia

Abundantly detailed history with the imprimatur of a leading academic press

0-19-507462-9 OXFORD $38.00

Hedrick **Smith**

The Russians

An authoritative account of Russia from Rurik through Communism

0-345-31746-7 BALANTINE (BALAN) PB $6.99

J.N. **Westwood**

Endurance and Endeavour: Russian History, 1812-1986

The defeat of Napoleon paradoxically created the forces of nationalism and radicalism that overthrew the Romanov dynasty and led to the Soviet state

0-19-873103-5 OXFORD PB $22.50

Cultural and Intellectual History

James H. **Billington**

The Icon and the Axe: An Interpretive History of Russian Culture

"Will do more to make Russia understandable to the West than 50 cultural exchange sorties" —Elizabeth Janeway, *Books Today*

0-394-70846-6 RANDOM HOUSE PB $22.00

Robert V. **Daniels**

Russia: The Roots of Confrontation

Examines the traditional love/hate relationship between the Russian national character and the influence of the West

0-674-77966-5 HARVARD PB $14.95

Joanna **Hubbs**

Mother Russia: The Feminine Myth in Russian Culture

0-253-33860-3 INDIANA $36.95
0-253-20842-4 INDIANA PB $13.95

W.J. **Leatherbarrow**, editor

A Documentary History of Russian Thought: From the Enlightenment to Marxism

The gentry revolutionaries, the liberal westernizers, and the revolutionary populists; over 20 writers, social and political critics included, among them Belinsky, Herzen, Chernyshevsky, Dostoevsky, Bakunin, and Plekhanov

W.J. LEATHERBARROW & D.C. OFFORD, TRANSLATORS AND EDITORS

0-87501-019-9 ARDIS PB $18.95

Nikolai **Tolstoy**

The Tolstoys: Twenty-Four Generations of Russian History

A heavily illustrated view of Russian history through the eyes of its most creative family

0-688-06674-7 MORROW PB $4.98

Adam B. **Ulam**

Ideologies and Illusions: Revolutionary Thought from Herzen to Solzhenitsyn

Russia's vibrant intellectual tradition: from the aristocratic friend of the people of the 19th century to the dissident arch-foe of communism

0-674-44310-1 HARVARD $20.00

James **von Geldern** & Richard **Stites**, editors

Mass Culture in Soviet Russia: Tales, Poems, Songs, Movies, Plays, and Folklore, 1917-1953

0-253-20969-2 INDIANA PB $24.95

Andrzej **Walicki**

A History of Russian Thought: From the Enlightenment to Marxism

"The value of Walicki's book resides…in his ability to see the development of individual thinkers against a complex background and to relate them to earlier and later aspects of the movement"—Philip Pomper, *Russian History*

0-8047-1026-0 STANFORD $57.50
0-8047-1132-1 STANFORD PB $19.95

Origins and Feudalism

After the destruction of the Byzantine-inspired culture of Kiev by the Mongols in the 13th century, the Russian national identity reasserted itself through the gradual expansion of Moscow, a small fort-settlement town in the central plain.

Basil **Dmytryshyn**, editor

Medieval Russia: A Source Book, 900-1700

Illuminating documents reveal the laws and manners of primitive Russia until the time of Peter the Great

0-03-086441-0
HOLT RINEHART & WINSTON PB $24.50

John Lister Illingworth **Fennell**

A History of the Russian Church to 1448

0-582-08067-3 ADDISON-WESLEY PB $23.50

Charles J. **Halperin**

Russia and the Golden Horde: The Mongol Impact on Medieval Russian History

Argues that the Russian-Tatar relationship was complex, multifaceted, and by no means always hostile

0-253-20445-3 INDIANA PB $10.95

Richard **Hellie**

Slavery in Russia, 1450-1725

Makes us aware of the importance of slavery in early modern Russia by presenting comparisons with other slave-owning societies

0-226-32648-9 CHICAGO PB $20.00

Vladimir **Volkoff**

Vladimir: The Russian Viking

The powerful prince of Kiev, descendant of northern warrior-traders, who adopted the religion and culture of Byzantium in the 10th century

0-87951-234-2 OVERLOOK PB $12.95

Russia of the Czars

An alliance with the powerful monasteries enabled Ivan III, the Grand Duke of Moscow, to free himself from Tatar overlordship in the 15th century and, by adopting the imperial rank of Czar, establish an extreme version of autocratic divine right.

The reign of Peter the Great (1682-1725) ushered in one of the most productive and influential transformations in modern European history. It was Peter who broke the independent armed bands of the Streltsy, defeated the Swedes at Poltava, expanded Russia to the Baltic, and moved the capital from Moscow to the new city of St. Petersburg.

Evgenii V. **Anisimov**

The Reforms of Peter the Great: Progress Through Coercion in Russia

How Peter's measures worked to inhibit the development of capitalism in Russia and to create a "totalitarian-military-bureaucratic, police state." Anisimov is a research scholar of the St. Petersburg branch of the Institute of History of the Russian Academy of Sciences and a leading authority on the Petrine era

1-56324-047-5 SHARPE $66.95

Neal **Ascherson**

Black Sea

A book about a great inland sea and a European history from the time of Herodotus to the fall of communism

0-8090-3043-8 HILL & WANG $23.00

Paul **Bushkovitch**

Religion and Society in Russia: The Sixteenth and Seventeenth Centuries

0-19-506946-3 OXFORD $39.95

John T. **Alexander**

Catherine the Great: Life and Legend

A well-researched biography that judiciously examines the myths, Catherine's sexual voracity among others, that sprang up around this great ruler

0-19-505236-6 OXFORD $35.00
0-19-506162-4 OXFORD PB $15.95

Peter **Kurth**

Tsar: The Lost World of Nicholas and Alexandra

INTRODUCTION BY EDWARD RADZINSKY AND PHOTOGRAPHS BY PETER CHRISTOPHER

0-316-50787-3 LITTLE, BROWN $60.00

Catherine the Great

Henri **Troyat**

Catherine the Great

Mother, lover, victorious expansionist, empress of all the Russias, presented in an entertaining narrative

TRANSLATED BY JOAN PINKHAM

0-452-01120-5 MERIDIAN PB........................$14.95

It was a dream-like ride in the unreal glow of the northern night. The men marched without knowing exactly where they were going, nor what they were going to do, but their enthusiasm was totally engaged in this mad adventure, mingling as it did light and shade, duty and revolution, truth and illusion. At the head of the slow procession, a woman, perhaps the goddess of war. Behind her, the Orlov brothers and many officers, all of whom seemed to be in love with her. The military band played stirring tunes. And when it stopped, the soldiers struck up old marching songs, broken by happy shouts and whistles. Always the same cry: "Long live our little mother Catherine!" Each time she heard her name yelled by these rough throats, she quivered with almost sexual joy. That was what she needed: a people which would be for her like a many-shaped lover, always ardent and always submissive.

CATHERINE THE GREAT

Nadezhda **Durova**

The Cavalry Maiden: Journals of a Russian Officer in the Napoleonic Wars

TRANSLATED WITH AN INTRODUCTION BY MARY FLEMING ZIRIN

0-253-20549-2 INDIANA PB........................$12.95

Benson **Bobrick**

Fearful Majesty: The Life and Reign of Ivan the Terrible

1-55778-226-1 PARAGON PB........................$12.95

W. Bruce **Lincoln**

The Romanovs: Autocrats of All the Russias

Dynastic struggles following the death of Ivan the Terrible ended in 1613 with the accession of the Romanov family, which held supreme power until 1917

0-385-27908-6 DOUBLEDAY PB........................$18.95

Vasili **Klyuchevsky**

Peter the Great

An influential view by a 19th-century liberal Russian historian

TRANSLATED BY LILIANA ARCHIBALD

0-8070-5647-2 BEACON PB........................$16.00

Robert **Massie**

Peter the Great

A vivid, popular account used as the basis of an NBC mini-series

0-345-29806-3 BALLANTINE PB........................$14.00

Carolyn Johnston **Pouncy**, editor & translator

The Domestroi: Rules for Russian Households in the Time of Ivan the Terrible

0-801-42410-0 CORNELL PB........................$35.00

Donald J. **Raleigh**, editor

The Emperors and Empresses of Russia: Rediscovering the Romanovs

A valuable collection of documents compiled by A.A. Iskenderov

1-56324-760-7 SHARPE PB........................$23.95

Richard S. **Wortman**

Scenarios of Power: Myth and Ceremony in Russian Monarchy

0-691-03484-2 PRINCETON........................$49.50

Marquis **de Custine**

Letters from Russia

Russia's de Tocqueville

0-140-44548-X PENGUIN........................$9.95

The Old Regime

Paul **Avrich**

Russian Rebels, 1600-1800

Bolotnikov, Stenka Razin, Bulavin, and Pugachev:the four great Cossack-led peasant rebellions that shook the throne of the Romanovs

0-393-00836-3 NORTON PB........................$11.95

Jeffrey **Brooks**

When Russia Learned to Read: Literacy and Popular Literature, 1861-1917

"The popular books that entertained and instructed, reflected, and helped shape the values of millions of newly literate Russians, particularly during the last three decades of the Romanov empire"—Maurice Friedberg, *Political Science Quarterly*

0-691-00821-3 PRINCETON PB........................$16.95

Victoria E. **Bonnell**, editor

The Russian Worker: Life and Labor Under the Tsarist Regime

Personal accounts by sales clerks and textile mill and factory workers

0-520-04837-7 CALIFORNIA........................$42.50

Tolstoy

Laura **Engelstein**

The Keys to Happiness: Sex and the Search for Happiness in Fin-de-Siècle Russia

Assesses attitudes of the emerging bourgeois middle class—public activists, jurists, physicians, journalists, writers—and argues for a liberal civic culture that was much the same as that in Western Europe and the United States. "It is Engelstein's achievement to have examined with subtlety and complexity some of the most critical cultural dilemmas of that time…through the prism of discussions about sex"—Mark D. Steinberg, Yale University

0-8014-9958-5 CORNELL PB........................$16.95

Michael F. **Hamm**

Kiev: A Portrait, 1800-1917

A splendid urban center in medieval times, Kiev became a major metropolis in late Imperial Russia: one of Europe's most diverse cities, with a distinctive mix of Ukrainians, Poles, Russians, and Jews

0-691-02585-1 PRINCETON PB........................$16.95

Alexander **Herzen**

Letters from France and Italy, 1847-1852

Exiled in Europe in 1847, Herzen experienced the 1848 revolutions first-hand before settling in England in 1852. "A pivotal text in the development of Russian Populism and the Russian Opposition movement" —Marshall Shatz, UMass, Boston

TRANSLATED AND EDITED BY JUDITH E. ZIMMERMAN

0-8229-3890-1 PITTSBURGH........................$59.95

Mikhail P. **Iroshnikov**
Before the Revolution: St. Petersburg in Photographs, 1890-1914
A lost world on the brink of irrevocable change: pictures of high and low, splendor and misery, with portraits of figures including Nicholas and Alexandra, Rasputin, Lenin, Pavlova, Rimsky-Korsakov, Blok, and Nabokov
0-8109-3813-8 ABRAMS $60.00

Steven G. **Marks**
Road to Power: The Trans-Siberian Railroad and the Colonization of Asian Russia, 1850-1917
0-8014-2533-6 CORNELL $35.00

Robert K. **Massie**
The Romanovs: The Final Chapter
Massie, the Pulitzer Prize-winning author of *Nicholas and Alexandra,* unravels the great murder mystery of what in fact happened to the last Russian tsar and his family in Ekaterinburg. This dramatic, endlessly suspenseful story of slaughter, cover-up, and the long search for the truth reads like a detective thriller, only the characters range from Lenin to James Baker, Boris Yeltsin, Prince Philip, a host of forensic experts, and DNA scientists
0-394-58048-6 RANDOM HOUSE $25.00
0-345-40640-0 BALLANTINE PB $12.95

Nicholas and Alexandra
A popular biography of the last Romanovs, an inward-looking family unable to cope with the forces that brought the Bolsheviks to power
0-440-36358-6 BDD PB $7.99

Thomas C. **Owen**
The Corporation Under Russian Law, 1800-1917: A Study in Tsarist Economic Policy
0-521-39126-1 CAMBRIDGE $65.00

Russian Corporate Capitalism from Peter the Great to Perestroika
0-19-509677-0 OXFORD $55.00

Edvard **Radzinsky**
The Life and Death of Nicholas II
0-385-46962-4 ANCHOR PB $14.95

Marc **Raeff**
Understanding Imperial Russia: State and Society in the Old Regime
The Russia of the czars, both in its own right and as a basis for the emergence of the Soviet Union
TRANSLATED BY ARTHUR GOLDHAMMER
0-231-05843-8 COLUMBIA PB $17.00

Priscilla **Roosevelt**
Life on the Russian Country Estate: A Social and Cultural History
0-300-05595-1 YALE $45.00

G.T. **Robinson**
Rural Russia Under the Old Regime: A History of the Landlord-Peasant World and a Prologue to the Peasant Revolution of 1917
0-520-01075-2 CALIFORNIA PB $15.00

Hugh **Seton-Watson**
The Russian Empire, 1801-1917
From Alexander I to the abdication of Nicholas II. As the Russian Empire expanded into Western Europe, India, and the dominions of Turkey, internal dissension reached critical proportions
0-19-822152-5 OXFORD PB $35.00

Roots of Revolution

"You are not alone, workers and peasants of Russia! If you succeed in overthrowing, crushing and destroying the tyrants of feudal, police-ridden landlord and tsarist Russia your victory will serve as a signal for a world struggle against the tyranny of capital."—V.I. Lenin, 1905, quoted in *The Age of Empire*, by Eric Hobsbawm

Abraham **Ascher**
The Revolution of 1905: Russia in Disarray
The army stayed loyal during the massive popular revolution following Russia's defeat by Japan, but the constitutional reforms only staved off 1917
0-8047-1436-3 STANFORD $65.00
0-8047-2328-1 STANFORD PB $18.95

Samuel H. **Baron**
Plekhanov in Russian History and Soviet Historiography
Study of the father of Russian Marxism, Georgy Valentinovich Plekhanov (1856-1918), who split with the Bolsheviks and died in exile
0-8229-3788-3 PITTSBURGH $59.95

Isaiah **Berlin**
Russian Thinkers
This collection of essays includes the famous "The Hedgehog and the Fox," as well as comparisons of Herzen and Bakunin
See also **GENERAL STUDIES** under **CRITICAL STUDIES** under **RUSSIAN LITERATURE** in **LITERATURE OF EUROPE, AFRICA, AND ASIA**
0-14-013625-8 VIKING PB $10.95

Victoria E. **Bonnell**
Roots of Rebellion: Workers' Politics and Organizations in St. Petersburg and Moscow, 1900-1914
0-520-04740-0 CALIFORNIA $52.50
0-520-05114-9 CALIFORNIA PB $16.00

Robert **Edelman**
Proletarian Peasants: The Revolution of 1905 in Russia's Southwest
A case study of a peasant revolt in the Ukraine
0-8014-2000-8 CORNELL $39.95
0-8014-9473-7 CORNELL PB $13.95

Anatole G. **Mazour**
The First Russian Revolution, 1825: The Decembrist Movement
The failed attempt at aristocratic reforms by officers returning from France is seen as the beginning of the movement that toppled czarism
0-8047-0081-8 STANFORD $45.00

Thomas S. **Pearson**
Russian Officialdom in Crisis: Autocracy and Local Self Government, 1861-1900
Why did the Russian government introduce counterreforms at the local level? The author assesses the government's "increasing futility at managing rural administrative development with its paternalistic bureaucracy and traditional corporate institutions…" Thus, the Russian Empire remained a top-heavy autocracy
0-521-36127-3 CAMBRIDGE $69.95

World War I

George F. **Kennan**
Russia Leaves the War: Soviet-American Relations, 1917-1920
From the Bolshevik revolution to the Russo-Polish War by one of America's leading diplomats and historians. Winner of the Pulitzer Prize and the National Book Award
0-691-00841-8 PRINCETON PB $18.95

W. Bruce **Lincoln**
In War's Dark Shadow: The Russians Before the Great War
The age of the Triple Entente, with a militarily unprepared Russia backing France against Germany despite the pressure of internal disorder
0-19-508953-7 OXFORD PB $16.95

Passage Through Armageddon: The Russians in War and Revolution, 1914-1918
"Events canter across the pages of *Passage Through Armageddon* faster than Cossack cavalrymen chasing a Bolshevik"
—*NY Times Book Review*
0-19-508954-5 OXFORD PB $18.95

The Revolution

An army demoralized by its failure against Germany and a czar absent from the capital paved the way for the first revolution in February, 1917. The subsequent leadership vacuum allowed the highly motivated Bolsheviks under Lenin's direction to take control of the government in October.

E.H. **Carr**
The Bolshevik Revolution Volume 1
An unrivaled account from a sympathetic and left-wing perspective. Carr analyzes the events from 1898 to 1917, the provisional constitution, and the Bolshevik takeover
0-393-30195-8 NORTON PB $12.95

E.H. **Carr**

Volume 2

1917-1919, From the Overthrow of the Tsar to the Assumption of Power by the Bolsheviks

The civil war, the revolt of the peasantry, and the decline of industrial output leads to greater repression and the New Economic Policy

0-393-30197-4 NORTON PB $13.95

Volume 3

1919-1921, From the Civil War to the Consolidation of Power

The foreign policy of the new communist state as it faces the stress of international confrontation

0-393-30199-0 NORTON PB $14.95

Paul **Dukes**

October and the World: Perspectives on the Russian Revolution

0-312-58096-7 ST. MARTIN'S $29.95

Sheila **Fitzpatrick**

The Russian Revolution

The entire revolutionary period, from 1905 to Stalin

0-19-289257-6 OXFORD PB $11.95

Daniel H. **Kaiser**

The Workers' Revolution in Russia, 1917: The View from Below

0-521-34971-0 CAMBRIDGE PB $12.95

Tim **McDaniel**

Autocracy, Capitalism, and Revolution in Russia

New synthesis of "class" and "mass" explanations for the revolution shows how the cross-purposes of capitalism and autocracy hindered reform

0-520-06071-7 CALIFORNIA PB $17.95

Richard **Pipes**

The Russian Revolution

Pipes follows up his *Russia Under the Old Regime* with this immense 976-page history of the revolution, from the rise of discontent in the 1890s to the abortive 1905 revolution and the decisive events of 1917. Illustrated with 100 photographs

0-394-50241-8 KNOPF $40.00

0-679-73660-3 MCKAY PB $22.00

A Concise History of the Russian Revolution

The Baird Professor of History at Harvard, Pipes recounts the "sequence of violent and disruptive acts" that led to the revolution. From Lenin's seizure of power, the murder of the Romanovs, and the birth of totalitarianism, this is sure to be a standard reference on the Russian Revolution for many years to come

0-679-42277-3 KNOPF $30.00

John **Reed**

Ten Days that Shook the World

The American radical journalist's eyewitness account of the Bolshevik seizure of power records the excitement of the October days and the beginnings of his own disillusionment

EDITED BY BERTRAM D. WOLFE

0-14-018293-4 VIKING PB $9.95

Harrison E. **Salisbury**

Black Night, White Snow: Russia's Revolutions, 1905-1917

A journalist's account of Russian politics and society as the reign of the Romanovs crumbled

0-306-80154-X DA CAPO PB $16.95

Harold **Shukman**, editor

The Blackwell Encyclopedia of the Russian Revolution

An illustrated volume offering a comprehensive chronology and biographies of key figures

0-631-19525-4 BLACKWELL PB $25.95

Mark D. **Steinberg**, and Vladimir M. **Khrustalev**

The Fall of the Romanovs: Political Dreams and Personal Struggles in a Time of Revolution

0-300-06557-4 YALE $27.50

The Fate of the Revolution

Paul **Avrich**

Kronstadt 1921

The brutal suppression of the sailors' revolt against the Bolshevik regime they had helped bring to power

0-691-00868-X PRINCETON PB $13.95

Fernando **Claudin**

The Communist Movement: From Comintern to Cominform

A Marxist looks at international communism under Lenin and Stalin; a 2-volume set

TRANSLATED BY BRIAN PEARCE

0-85345-366-7 MONTHLY REVIEW $27.00

0-85345-402-7 MONTHLY REVIEW PB $11.90

Stephen F. **Cohen**

Rethinking the Soviet Experience: Politics and History Since 1917

A survey that challenges the West's conventional wisdom on former Soviet affairs

0-19-506635-9 OXFORD $33.00

0-19-505714-7 OXFORD PB $8.95

Robert V. **Daniels**, editor

A Documentary History of Communism and the World: From Revolution to Collapse

0-87451-678-1 VERMONT PB $21.00

Peter **Hopkirk**

Setting the East Ablaze: Lenin's Dream of an Empire in Asia

1-56836-102-5 KODANSHA PB $14.00

Geoffrey **Hoskins**

The First Socialist Society: A History of the Soviet Union from Within

"For the general reader a very good introduction to the phantasmagoric history of the Communist state and for the specialist, a valuable aid" —*TLS*

0-674-30443-8 HARVARD PB $17.95

Jon **Jacobson**

When the Soviet Union Entered World Politics

A 1994 survey of Soviet foreign policy in the period 1917-1945

0-520-08976-6 CALIFORNIA PB $18.00

Olga **Narkiewicz**

Soviet Leaders: From the Cult of Personality to Collective Rule

0-312-74857-4 ST. MARTIN'S $45.00

Richard **Pipes**

The Formation of the Soviet Union: Communism and Nationalism, 1917-1923

0-674-30950-2 HARVARD $35.00

Russia Under the Bolshevik Regime

The second book in Pipes' monumental work on the Russian Revolution covers the years 1918 to the death of Lenin in 1924. Among the author's many insights is how deeply Hitler was influenced by the totalitarian Soviet model. A highly informative look at one of the 20th century's defining political phenomena

0-679-76184-5 VINTAGE PB $19.00

Richard **Stites**, editor

Revolutionary Dreams: Utopian and Experimental Life in the Russian Revolution

The emotional and expressive realm of the revolution in artistic artifacts, science fiction, invented rituals, and literary utopias

0-19-505536-5 OXFORD $45.00

Biography: The Revolutionary Era

Peter **Kurth**

Anastasia: The Riddle of Anna Anderson

Anna Anderson claimed that she was Anastasia—Nicholas II's youngest daughter—and that she had, in fact, survived the massacre at Ekaterinburg

0-316-50717-2 LITTLE, BROWN PB $15.95

Isaac **Babel**

1920 Diary

Tracks Babel's experiences riding with the Cossack cavalry during the Polish-Soviet war of 1919-1920

TRANSLATED BY H.T. WILLETTS

0-300-05966-3 YALE $22.00

Stephen F. **Cohen**

Bukharin and the Bolshevik Revolution: A Political Biography, 1888-1938

Bukharin's rise and fall, focusing on the period from Lenin's death in 1924 to Stalin's rise in 1929

0-19-502697-7 OXFORD PB $15.95

Richard **Abraham**

Alexander Kerensky: The First Love of the Revolution

A biography of the leading politician during the chaos between the czar's abdication in March and the Bolshevik takeover in October, 1917

0-231-06108-0 COLUMBIA $50.00
0-231-06109-9 COLUMBIA PB $19.50

N.K. **Krupskaya**

Reminiscences of Lenin

An intimate recollection of the Bolshevik leader by his wife

0-7178-0253-1 INTERNATIONAL PUB $7.50
0-7178-0254-X INTERNATIONAL PUB PB $4.95

Philip **Pomper**

Lenin, Trotsky, and Stalin: The Intelligentsia and Power

0-231-06906-5 COLUMBIA $50.00
0-231-06907-3 COLUMBIA PB $17.50

Vladimir Ilich **Lenin**

Unknown Lenin Archive

EDITED BY RICHARD PIPES

0-300-06919-7 YALE $27.50

Warren **Lerner**

Karl Radek: The Last Internationalist

Communism's brilliant publicist who fell victim to Stalin's purge of the Old Bolsheviks

0-8047-0722-7 STANFORD $37.50

Leon **Trotsky**

Despite his success as minister of war and creator of the Red Army, Trotsky was outmaneuvered by Stalin, exiled to the West, and eventually assassinated in Mexico.

The Revolution Betrayed

Despite the bitterness of recent exile, an objective view prevails in this critique of Stalin's revival of Russian absolutism

TRANSLATED BY MAX EASTMAN

0-87348-225-5 PATHFINDER $60.00
0-929087-48-8 LABOR PUBLICATIONS PB $18.95
0-87348-226-3 PATHFINDER PB $19.95

History of the Russian Revolution

0-913460-83-4 PATHFINDER PB $35.95

My Life

Considerable literary merit enhances the interest of this autobiography of a revolutionary written in 1930, the year after Trotsky's expulsion from the Soviet Union

0-87348-144-5 PATHFINDER PB $26.95

Dmitri **Volkogonov**

Trotsky: The Eternal Revolutionary

A monumental biography by a Kremlin insider

0-684-82293-8 FREE PRESS $32.50

The Stalin Era

Amy **Knight**

Beria: Stalin's First Lieutenant

In the 1920s Lavrenti Pavlovich Beria (1899-1953) mercilessly purged the Georgian, Armenian, and Azerbaijan Communist parties of "national deviationists." From 1938 to 1953 he headed the Soviet People's Commissariat for Internal Affairs, supervising internal security and intelligence. This portrait of Stalin's notorious police chief and powerful lieutenant first appeared in 1994

0-691-03257-2 PRINCETON $39.50

Robert **Conquest**

The Great Terror: A Reassessment

Conquest's study of Stalin's terror, first published in 1968 and out of print for many years, has now been reissued in a completely new edition. "The only scrupulous, non-partisan, and adequate book on the subject"
—George F. Kennan

0-19-505580-2 OXFORD $35.00

Harvest of Sorrow: Soviet Collectivization and the Terror-Famine

A graphic portrayal of the political ruthlessness with which Stalin stifled opposition and imposed his collectivization and industrialization programs

0-19-505180-7 OXFORD PB $12.95

Stalin and the Kirov Murder

Stalin's Reichstag fire: a political murder on his own orders gave Stalin the opportunity to inaugurate the treason trials that liquidated his old comrades-in-arms

0-19-506337-6 OXFORD PB $7.95

Sheila **Fitzpatrick**

Stalin's Peasants: Resistance and Survival in the Russian Village After Collectivization

Explores village culture, questions of authority and leadership, feuds, denunciations, rumors, and religious observance

0-19-510459-5 OXFORD PB $18.95

Joseph Stalin

Veronique **Garros** and others, editors

Intimacy and Terror: Soviet Diaries of the 1930's

1-565-84200-6 NEW PRESS $27.50

Eugenia Semyonovna **Ginzburg**

Journey into the Whirlwind

Memoir of years in prison and labor camps under Stalin

0-15-646509-4 HARCOURT BRACE PB $13.00

David **Holloway**

Stalin and the Bomb: The Soviet Union and Atomic Energy, 1939-1956

"A work on the largest scale, one that advances our understanding and is likely to remain definitive for years to come"—*NY Times Book Review*

0-300-06664-3 YALE PB $18.00

Stephen **Kotkin**

Magnetic Mountain: Stalinism as a Civilization

0-520-06908-0 CALIFORNIA $55.00

Moshe **Lewin**

The Making of the Soviet System: Essays in the Social History of Interwar Russia

1-56584-125-5 NEW PRESS PB $16.95

Russian Peasants and Soviet Power: A Study of Collectivization

0-393-00752-9 NORTON PB $18.95

Roy **Medvedev**

Let History Judge: The Origins and Consequences of Stalinism

A revised and enlarged edition

TRANSLATED & EDITED BY GEORGE SHRIVER

0-231-06350-4 COLUMBIA $75.00
0-231-06351-2 COLUMBIA PB $24.50

Louis **Rapoport**

Stalin's War Against the Jews: The Doctors' Plot and the "Soviet Solution"

The arrest in 1952 of nine Kremlin doctors, all Jewish, on charges of attempting to poison Soviet leaders triggered a wave of anti-Semitic hysteria. Rapoport describes how Stalin orchestrated the "plot," and how only his death prevented far worse consequences

0-02-925821-9 FREE PRESS $27.95

Suzanne **Rosenberg**

A Soviet Odyssey

A young Communist woman's tortuous encounter with Stalinist Siberia offers a rare glimpse of both Soviet life and the Stalinist era

0-14-012927-8 PENGUIN PB $8.95

Joseph **Stalin**

Stalin's Letters to Molotov, 1925-1936

TRANSLATED BY CATHERINE FITZPATRICK

0-300-06211-7 YALE $30.00

S.J. **Taylor**

Stalin's Apologist: Walter Duranty, The New York Times' Man in Moscow

Witty, engaging, and flamboyant, Duranty was the person most credited with helping to gain US recognition for the Soviet state. Yet Taylor argues that he played a crucial role in perpetrating some of the greatest lies of this century

0-19-505700-7 OXFORD..$30.00

Robert W. **Thurston**

Life and Terror in Stalin's Russia, 1934-1941

Revisionist argument that coercion was not the key factor in keeping the regime in power; more important was voluntary support. A highly controversial account

0-300-06401-2 YALE..$30.00

Arkady **Vaksberg**

Stalin Against the Jews

0-679-75959-X VINTAGE PB..$13.00

Hilda **Vitzthum**

Torn Out by the Roots: The Recollections of a Former Communist

Vitzthum and her husband were loyal communists. But as members of the educated class, they became victims of Stalin's paranoia. This harrowing account details her nearly ten years in a Soviet labor camp. She chronicles the daily horrors as well as infrequent acts of kindness and compassion she witnessed. "This moving, remarkably vivid memoir provides a woman's unflinching perspective on the Soviet Gulag"—*Publishers Weekly*

TRANSLATED WITH AN INTRODUCTION BY PAUL SCHACH

0-8032-4660-9 NEBRASKA..$27.50

Portraits of Stalin

"Stalin's head had 'a solid peasant look about it,' but his face was pock-marked and his teeth uneven. His eyes were dark brown with a tinge of hazel. He had a stiff left arm and shoulder, the result of an accident when he was about ten. His torso was short and narrow and his arms were too long. Like many ambition-driven men he was very short, only about five feet two inches. He raised himself an inch or so by specially built shoes, and at the May Day and 7 November parades stood on a wooden slab which gave him another inch or two."
—Robert Conquest, *The Great Terror*

Milovan **Djilas**

Conversations with Stalin

Memoir by one of Tito's top aides, ousted from the Communist Party in 1954

TRANSLATED BY MICHAEL B. PETROVICH

0-15-622591-3 HARCOURT BRACE PB..$8.95

Adam B. **Ulam**

Stalin: The Man and His Era

A mammoth portrait of Stalin and the development of the Soviet state

0-8070-7005-X BEACON PB..$21.00

Daniel **Rancour-Leferriere**

The Mind of Stalin: A Psychoanalytic Study

Psychoanalysis used to answer a host of questions: What did Stalin's paranoia and narcissism mean in the Soviet context? What were his attitudes toward women and homosexuals? Why did he trust Hitler? What were the psychological consequences of his bodily defects? A complex and original study

0-87501-053-9 ARDIS..$17.95

Edvard **Radzinsky**

Stalin: The First In-Depth Biography Based on Explosive New Documents from Russia's Secret Files

0-385-47397-4 DOUBLEDAY..$30.00

Dmitri **Volkogonov**

Stalin: Triumph and Tragedy

Portrait by the Soviet army official and Yeltsin adviser who died in 1995. "The more [Volkogonov] studied the historical sources, the more his disillusionment grew: his unfailing loyalty to the Communist cause utlimately turned into passionate hatred. In his last years he acted like a man awakened from a long hypnotic sleep"
—Richard Pipes, *NY Times Book Review*

TRANSLATED BY HAROLD SHUKMAN

1-55958-216-2 PRIMA PB..$22.00

Robert C. **Tucker**

Stalin in Power: The Revolution from Above, 1928-1941

A compelling political and psychological portrait of Stalin, analyzing how he came to power and how he maintained his reign of terror

0-393-02881-X NORTON..$29.95

World War II

Vladimir **Karpov**

Russia At War, 1941-45

Highlights every major campaign with stunning photographs from the military archives of the Soviet Union; includes 320 illustrations

EDITED BY CAROLINE SCHOFIELD
INTRODUCTION BY HARRISON E. SALISBURY

0-86565-077-2 BOOK SALES..$19.98

Anthony **Read** & David **Fisher**

The Deadly Embrace: Hitler, Stalin, and the Nazi-Soviet Pact, 1939-1941

"The story of the 'monstrous chess game' the two dictators…proceeded to play, using whole countries as pieces while preparing for a battlefield confrontation that would exceed anything before or since in bloodshed"
—*Publishers Weekly*

See also **THE ROAD TO WAR** under **THE SECOND WORLD WAR**

0-393-02528-4 NORTON..$25.00
0-393-30651-8 NORTON PB..$12.95

David **Reynolds** & others, editors

Allies at War: The Soviet, American, and British Experience, 1939-1945

A 1994 collaboration on wartime diplomacy among British, American, and Russian historians

0-312-10259-3 ST. MARTIN'S..$59.95

Richard **Stites**, editor

Culture and Entertainment in Wartime Russia

0-253-20949-8 INDIANA PB..$15.95

Nina **Tumarkin**

The Living and the Dead: The Rise and Fall of the Cult of World War II in Russia

0-465-04144-2 BASIC PB..$15.00

Alexander **Werth**

Russia At War, 1941-1945

The classic history of the Soviet Union at war; precise, literate, thought-provoking, and a must for the student of World War II

See also **RUSSIA** under **THE WAR IN EUROPE** under **THE SECOND WORLD WAR**

0-88184-084-X CARROLL & GRAF PB..$17.95

This scene of filth and suffering in that yard of the Red Army House was my last glimpse of Stalingrad. I remembered the long anxious days of the summer of 1942, and the nights of the London blitz, and the photographs of Hitler, smirking as he stood on the steps of the Madeleine in Paris, and the weary days of '38 and '39 when a jittery Europe would tune in to Berlin and hear Hitler's yells accompanied by the cannibal roar of the German mob. And there seemed a rough but divine justice in those frozen cesspools with their diarrhoea, and those horses' bones, and those starved yellow corpses in the yard of the Red Army House at Stalingrad.
RUSSIA AT WAR, 1941-1945

The Cold War

"With Communists we cannot say it with flowers…The cold war must be fought with as much energy and singlemindedness as the shooting war…"—Harold Macmillan, House of Commons, 23 March 1949

Anatoly **Dobrynin**

In Confidence: Moscow's Ambassador to America's Six Cold War Presidents

0-8129-2328-6 TIME BOOKS..$30.00
0-8129-2894-6 TIME BOOKS PB..$18.00

Michael **Parenti**

The Sword and the Dollar: Imperialism, Revolution and the Arms Race

Emphasizes the role of American-based corporations in determining US foreign policy

0-312-02295-6 ST. MARTIN'S..$16.95
0-312-01167-9 ST. MARTIN'S PB..$19.99

John Lewis **Gaddis**

The Long Peace: Inquiries into the History of the Cold War

A collection of essays notable for their mastery of historical sources and for an attempt to identify the elements of stability within the Soviet-American competition

See also **THE COLD WAR** under **INTERNATIONAL RELATIONS AND STRATEGIC STUDIES** in **SOCIAL STUDIES**

0-19-504336-7 OXFORD........$30.00
0-19-504335-9 OXFORD PB........$11.95

The United States and the Origins of the Cold War, 1941-1947

A post-revisionist analysis of American policy

0-231-03289-7 COLUMBIA........$59.50
0-231-08302-5 COLUMBIA PB........$17.50

Vladislav **Zubok** & Constantine **Pleshakov**

Inside the Kremlin's Cold War: From Stalin to Khruschev

The volatile period from 1945 to 1962

0-674-45531-2 HARVARD........$29.95

The Soviet Union: From Krushchev to Gorbachev

Stephen F. **Cohen**

Sovieticus: American Perceptions and Soviet Realities

Collected columns from *The Nation*

0-393-30338-1 NORTON PB........$7.95

Timothy **Colton**

Moscow: Governing the Socialist Metropolis

A roughly 900-page history of the "lynchpin of the Soviet system and exemplar of its ideology"

0-674-58741-3 HARVARD........$45.00

Mikhail S. **Gorbachev**

Memoirs

0-385-48019-9 DOUBLEDAY........$35.00

Perestroika: New Thinking for Our Country and the World

The glasnost czar's own blueprint for domestic and world reform

See also **INTERNATIONAL POLITICAL ECONOMY** under **INTERNATIONAL RELATIONS AND STRATEGIC STUDIES** in **SOCIAL STUDIES**

0-85124-501-3 DUFOUR........$40.00

The Search for a New Beginning: Developing a New Civilization

A thoughtful blueprint for the new world order eloquently evokes JFK, William Faulkner, and Native American wisdom in the service of a global civilization built on diversity, democracy, environmentalism, and peace. The architect of the Cold War's end turns his inspired eye toward the future

TRANSLATED BY PAVEL PALAZCHENKO

0-06-251338-9 HARPERCOLLINS........$12.00

Yegor **Ligachev**

Inside Gorbachev's Kremlin: The Memoirs of Yegor Ligachev

Originally Gorbachev's ally, Ligachev led the split in the Soviet leadership when it became clear the reforms would mean the end of communism. His memoir chronicles the breakup of the USSR in idiosyncratic but revealing terms. "At once self serving, instructive and tremendously thought-provoking"—*Publishers Weekly*

0-8133-2887-X WESTVIEW PB........$19.50

Political memoirs suffered the same fate as history writing, historians, and millions of other people in the Soviet Union: they were repressed, forbidden, and heavily censored.

INSIDE GORBACHEV'S KREMLIN: THE MEMOIRS OF YEGOR LIGACHEV

David **Remnick**

Lenin's Tomb: The Last Days of the Soviet Empire

A vivid, bestselling account of the end of the Soviet empire

0-679-75125-4 VINTAGE PB........$14.00

David K. **Shipler**

Russia: Broken Idols, Solemn Dreams

The impact of Gorbachev on the lives of ordinary Russians; revised and expanded

0-8129-1788-X TIME BOOKS........$6.98

Dissidents

For related reading, see JEWISH HISTORY

Stephen F. **Cohen**, editor

An End to Silence: Uncensored Opinion in the Soviet Union

Excerpts from Roy Medvedev's underground magazine, *Political Diary*, circulated between 1964 and 1971

0-393-30127-3 NORTON PB........$9.95

Natan **Sharansky**

Fear No Evil

Autobiographical account by the most famous Jewish refusenik of his voyage through Soviet prisons and ultimately to Israel

TRANSLATED BY STEFANI HOFFMAN

0-8027-2540-6 WALKER PB........$12.95

Aleksandr **Solzhenitsyn**

The Gulag Archipelago

A monumental exposé of the Stalinist period, based on the author's experience in forced labor camps and in exile

See also **CONTEMPORARY RUSSIAN WRITERS** under **RUSSIAN LITERATURE** in **LITERATURE OF EUROPE, AFRICA, AND ASIA**

TRANSLATED BY THOMAS WHITNEY & HARRY WILLETTS

0-06-092104-8 HARPERPERENNIAL PB........$17.50

Romnald **Spasowski**

The Liberation of One

Autobiography of the highest-ranking Soviet official to defect to the West

9-99-848427-8 HARCOURT BRACE........$5.98

Andrei **Sakharov**

Memoirs

The life of the most famous dissident of recent Soviet history. "Sakharov's sense of rightness, like that of scientist-moralists from Galileo to Oppenheimer, is rooted in his understanding of the scientific problems of light and time, his first-hand appreciation of both the laws of the universe and man's tragic ability to turn progress into catastrophe"—David Remnick, *NY Review of Books*

0-394-53740-8 KNOPF........$29.95

Andrei Sakharov

The Soviet Union Abroad: Twilight of the Cold War

Seweryn **Bialer**, editor

Dangerous Relations: The Soviet Union in World Politics, 1970-1982

0-19-503237-3 OXFORD........$29.95
0-19-503424-4 OXFORD PB........$9.95

Artyom **Borovik**

The Hidden War: A Russian Journalist's Account of the Soviet War in Afghanistan

"I have read no other account of the war in Afghanistan equal to this—an eyewitness account of the soldier's experiences, free from politics. In other words, this is literature, not journalism,"—Graham Greene

See also **AFGHANISTAN** under **THE INDIAN SUBCONTINENT**

0-87113-283-4 ATLANTIC MONTHLY PB........$18.95

Zbigniew K. **Brzezinski**

Soviet Bloc: Unity and Conflict

A 1967 analysis of the factions of world communism from the man who would become Jimmy Carter's National Security Adviser

0-674-82548-9 HARVARD PB........$16.95

Helene Carrere **d'Encausse**

Big Brother: The Soviet Union and Soviet Europe

From the postwar "Stalinization" of Eastern Europe to the continuing eruptions of nationalism to the age of Gorbachev; from a noted French political scientist

TRANSLATED BY GEORGE HOLOCH

0-8419-1042-1 HOLMES & MEIER........$39.50
0-8419-1043-X HOLMES & MEIER PB........$24.50

Helene Carrere **d'Encausse**

The End of the Soviet Empire: The Triumph of the Republics

An examination of the dissolution of the Soviet Union's Communist Party. D'Encausse—one of France's most exalted political professors and the third woman ever to be elected to the Académie Francaise—argues that the grassroots nationalist movements, as opposed to glasnost and perestroika, are the only means of rebuilding a healthy, pluralistic society to replace the former Soviet Union

0-465-09812-6 BASIC PB $24.00

Amin **Saikal** & William **Maley**, editors

The Soviet Withdrawal from Afghanistan

0-521-37577-0 CAMBRIDGE $49.95
0-521-37588-6 CAMBRIDGE PB $16.95

After the End of the Soviet Union

Walter **Adams** & James W. **Brock**

Adam Smith Goes to Moscow: A Dialogue on Radical Reform

A brief treatment, published in 1993

0-691-00053-0 PRINCETON PB $12.95

Ryszard **Kapuscinski**

Imperium

Kapuscinski brings stylistic originality, personal experience, and penetrating reportage to the many long-buried identities now emerging from the fall of the Soviet empire. "The author's prognosis is not reassuring: He quotes Nicholas driving his troika over the fields in Tolstoy's *War and Peace,* 'Heaven only knows where we are going, and heaven knows what is happening to us.' "Sensitive and searching"—*Kirkus Reviews*

See also **POLISH LITERATURE** under **EASTERN EUROPEAN LITERATURE** in **LITERATURE OF EUROPE, AFRICA, AND ASIA**

0-679-42619-1 KNOPF $24.00
0-679-74780-X VINTAGE PB $13.00

Vladimir **Kvint**

The Barefoot Shoemaker: Capitalizing on the New Russia

A Siberian who worked in mines and factories as well as in the corridors of power in Moscow, Kvint is today a professor of International Business at Fordham and an advisor to Fortune 500 companies considering joint ventures. "All business in Russia is personal," he observes, "so you need to know the personalities." Invaluable information and illuminating portraits of Russian characters across the business spectrum, from ministers to black marketeers

1-55970-182-X ARCADE $24.95

Michael **McFaul** & Sergei **Markov**

The Troubled Birth of Russian Democracy: Parties, Personalities and Programs

The state of Russian politics, published in 1993

0-8179-9232-4 HOOVER PB $24.95

Vladimir **Morozov**, editor

Who's Who in Russia and the CIS Republics

A roughly 325-page reference published in 1995

0-8050-2691-6 HOLT $60.00

Lev **Poliakov**

Russia: A Portrait

Pictures from the cutting edge of cataclysmic change, by an outstanding contemporary Soviet photographer

INTRODUCTION BY JOSEPH BRODSKY

0-374-25290-4 FS&G $14.98

David **Pryce-Jones**

The Strange Death of the Soviet Empire

0-8050-4154-0 HOLT $30.00

Peter **Shearman**, editor

Russian Foreign Policy Since 1990

0-8133-2633-8 WESTVIEW PB $19.95

Vladimir **Solvyov** & Elena **Klepikova**

Zhirinovsky: Russian Fascism and the Making of a Dictator

0-201-40948-8 ADDISON-WESLEY $25.00

Aleksandr **Solzhenitsyn**

The Russian Question Toward the End of the Twentieth Century

The Nobel laureate traces four centuries of Russian history and looks toward the future

0-374-25291-2 FS&G $15.00

Jonathan **Steele**

Eternal Russia: Yeltsin, Gorbachev, and the Mirage of Democracy

One of the most interesting of a slew of recent journalistic accounts, published in 1994

0-674-26838-5 HARVARD PB $15.95

Mikhail Gorbachev

Boris **Yeltsin**

The Struggle for Russia

"Extraordinary... Yeltsin shows that he can make a brave and hopeful case for himself—and for the Russia he may still create"—*Newsweek*

0-8129-2533-5 TIME BOOKS PB $14.00

Boris Yeltsin

The Post-Soviet Republics

Ali **Bantiazizi** & Myron **Wiener**, editors

New Geopolitics of Central Asia

A 1994 study of the new Islamic states

0-253-20918-8 INDIANA PB $15.95

Levon **Chorbajian** & others

The Caucasian Knot: The History and Geopolitics of Nagorno-Karabagh

1-85649-288-5 ZED PB $22.50

Karen **Dashiwa** & Bruce **Parrott**

Russia and the New States of Eurasia: The Politics of Upheaval

A 1994 assessment of recent changes and future directions

0-521-45895-1 CAMBRIDGE PB $21.95

Roger D. **Kangas**

Uzbekistan in the Twentieth Century: Political Development and the Evolution of Power

0-312-09679-8 ST. MARTIN'S $49.95

Bohdan **Nahaylo** & Victor **Swoboda**

Soviet Disunion: A History of the Nationalities Problem in the USSR

How the Soviet Union historically behaved as a conquering empire, crushing resistance from its subject peoples and imposing alien values. The authors probe the enormous difficulties the government faced as it tried to deal with an explosion of protest

0-02-922401-2 FREE PRESS $35.00

Martha Brill **Olcott**

The Kazakhs

0-8179-9352-5 HOOVER PB $20.95

Ronald Grigor **Suny**

The Making of the Georgian Nation

By the author of *Looking Toward Ararat: Armenia in Modern History*

0-253-20915-3 INDIANA PB $17.95

Crime

Stephen **Handelman**

Comrade Criminal: The Rise of the New Russian Mafia

0-300-06352-0 YALE $27.50

Jewish History

"Jewish history can be presented as a succession of climaxes and catastrophes. It can also be seen as an endless continuum of patient study, fruitful industry and communal routine, much of it unrecorded...Over 4,000 years the Jews proved themselves not only great survivors but extraordinarily skillful in adapting to the societies among which fate thrust them, and in gathering whatever human comforts they had to offer. No people has been more fertile in enriching poverty or humanizing wealth, or in turning misfortune to creative account. This capacity springs from a moral philosophy both solid and subtle, which has changed remarkably little over the millennia precisely because it has been seen to serve the purposes of those who share it. Countless Jews, in all ages, have groaned under the burden of Judaism. But they have continued to carry it because they have known, in their hearts, that it carried them. The Jews were survivors because they possessed the law of survival."

—Paul Johnson, *A History of the Jews*

General Histories

H.H. **Ben-Sasson**, editor

A History of the Jewish People

Six Hebrew University scholars trace the history of the Jews. "Breaks new ground for a one-volume history, both in its range and in its authority"—*Commentary*

See also **RESOURCES** under **HOW-TO: RITUAL AND PRACTICE** under **JUDAISM** in **RELIGION, SPIRITUALITY, AND PHILOSOPHY**

0-674-39731-2 HARVARD PB $26.50

Elena Romero **Castello** & Uriel Maclas **Kapon**, editors

The Jews and Europe: 2000 Years of History

This intelligently produced survey features attractive plates and perceptive text; not your run-of-the-mill coffee table book

0-8050-3526-5 HOLT $50.00

Chaim **Potok**

Wanderings: Chaim Potok's History of the Jews

0-449-21582-2 FAWCETT PB $6.99

Max I. **Dimont**

Jews, God and History

"By far the liveliest popular history of the Jewish people that I have ever read"
—Richard B. Morris

0-451-62866-7 MENTOR PB $6.99

Paul **Johnson**

A History of the Jews

This survey of 4000 years emphasizes the impact of Jewish genius and imagination on the world. Beautifully written

0-06-091533-1 HARPERCOLLINS PB $16.00

Paul **Mendes-Flohr** & Jehuda **Reinharz**

The Jew in the Modern World: A Documentary History

A collection of original source materials

0-19-502631-4 OXFORD $37.50
0-19-502632-2 OXFORD PB $24.95

Nitza **Rosovsky**, editor

City of the Great King: Jerusalem from David to the Present

A single magnificent volume brings to life the majestic story of the world's holiest city. From its natural scenic splendor to its architectural fascination, Rosovsky's portrait also tells the city's history and the history of its centrality to the three monotheisms. A splendid book for travelers and armchair travelers alike

See also **THE NEAR AND MIDDLE EAST** under **ASIA** under **TRAVEL LITERATURE** in **FOOD, TRAVEL, AND LEISURE**

0-674-13190-8 HARVARD $39.95

Leo W. **Schwarz**, editor

Great Ages and Ideas of the Jewish People

A collection of essays

0-394-60413-X MODERN LIBRARY $17.00

Pierre **Vidal-Naquet**

The Jews: History, Memory, and the Present

The preeminent French historian draws on his seemingly bottomless erudition to trace the history of the Jews from ancient Rome through modern Israel. Along the way he delves deeply into the shocking dishonesty of Holocaust denial; the Dreyfus affair; and his own childhood in Vichy, from where his family was deported and destroyed. "Mr. Vidal-Naquet's intellectual and moral power achieves, in the end, a deep appreciation of the absolute centrality of truth to the twin tasks of writing history and preserving memory"—*NY Times Book Review*

See also **MODERN THEOLOGY AND PHILOSOPHY** under **JUDAISM** in **RELIGION, SPIRITUALITY, AND PHILOSOPHY**

0-231-10208-9 COLUMBIA $29.50

Yosef Hayim **Yerushalmi**

Zakhor: Jewish History and Jewish Memory

Essays on Jewish collective memory; winner of the National Jewish Book Award for history (1982)

0-295-97519-9 WASHINGTON PB $12.95

Reference

Joseph **Alpher**, editor

Encyclopedia of Jewish History

Detailed and illustrated entries on the major figures, places, and events of Jewish history

0-8160-1220-2 FACTS ON FILE $40.00

Dan **Cohn-Sherbok**

Atlas of Jewish History

An exceptional, fascinating guide to the vicissitudes of Jewish history from ancient diasporic times to the present. A partial peek at the contents: "From Herod to Rebellion," "Judaism Under Islam in the Middle Ages," "Medieval Jewish Thought," "Eastern European Jewry in the Early Modern Period," "The Holocaust," "Israel." Illustrated with over 100 maps

See also **REFERENCE WORKS** under **WORLD RELIGION** in **RELIGION, SPIRITUALITY, AND PHILOSOPHY**

See also **RESOURCES** under **HOW-TO: RITUAL AND PRACTICE** under **JUDAISM** in **RELIGION, SPIRITUALITY, AND PHILOSOPHY**

0-415-08684-1 ROUTLEDGE $62.95
0-415-08800-3 ROUTLEDGE PB $24.95

Martin **Gilbert**

Atlas of Jewish History

Jewish history, migration and life through the ages, told through 121 maps

CARTOGRAPHY BY ARTHUR BANKS

0-688-12264-7 MORROW $20.00

Martin **Gilbert**, editor

The Illustrated Atlas of Jewish Civilization

A magnificent overview of Jewish history, with 200 illustrations and 100 full-color maps

0-02-543415-2 MACMILLAN $40.00

Judah **Gribetz**, & Eli **Barnavi**, editors

The Timetables of Jewish History

This book provides a chronology of important people and events in Jewish history. Its nearly 9,000 entries are listed by date, and horizontally linked so that readers can put events in Jewish history into a larger context. Includes 100 photos and engravings, maps, charts, and glossary

0-671-88577-4 TOUCHSTONE PB $20.00

A Historical Atlas of the Jewish People: From the Time of the Patriarchs to the Present

This important and beautiful volume presents the 4,000-year history of the Jewish people with a thousand maps, drawings, photos, paintings, chronologies, and commentaries by dozens of experts. A comprehensive reference and resource, it is certain to become a popular and treasured gift

0-679-40332-9 SCHOCKEN $50.00

Barry W. **Holtz**

The Schocken Guide to Jewish Books: Where to Start Reading About Jewish History, Literature, and Culture

0-8052-1005-9 SCHOCKEN PB $17.00

Biblical and Ancient History

Yohanan **Aharoni**

The Land of the Bible: A Historical Geography

TRANSLATED BY ANSON F. RAINEY

0-664-24266-9 KNOX PB $23.00

Meron **Benvenisti**

City of Stone: The Hidden History of Jerusalem

See also **LATE ARRIVALS**

0-520-20521-9 CALIFORNIA $24.95

Elias **Bickerman**

The Jews in the Greek Age

0-674-47490-2 HARVARD $39.95
0-674-47491-0 HARVARD PB $14.95

John **Bright**

A History of Israel

A sophisticated history of the ancient period

0-664-21381-2 KNOX $36.00

Steven **Fine**, editor

Sacred Realm: The Emergence of the Synagogue in the Ancient World

This book is an accompaniment to the *Sacred Realm* exhibition at the Yeshiva University Museum in New York

0-19-510225-8 OXFORD PB $25.00

Louis **Finkelstein**

Akiba: Scholar, Saint and Martyr

The definitive story of perhaps the most famous Jewish martyr of all time, Rabbi Akiba ben Joseph

0-87668-806-7 ARONSON $30.00

Flavius **Josephus**

The Jewish War

The rebellion against Roman power whose failure initiated the Diaspora—by a leader of the Jews

See also **ANCIENT ROMAN SOURCES** under **ANCIENT ROME**

TRANSLATED BY G.A. WILLIAMSON

EDITED BY E. MARY SMALLWOOD

0-14-044420-3 PENGUIN PB $10.95

Jacob **Neusner**

A History of the Jews in Babylonia: The Parthian Period

0-89130-738-9 SCHOLARS PB $22.00

The Pharisees: Rabbinic Perspectives

0-88125-067-8 KTAV PB $19.95

Max **Weber**

Ancient Judaism

"No one who has occupied himself with the study of Israelite culture can fail to admire the great sweep, the prevailing accuracy, and the true sensitivity of Weber's sociological analysis"—*Commentary*

TRANSLATED & EDITED BY DON MARTINDALE & HANS GARTH

0-02-934130-2 FREE PRESS PB $17.95

The Middle Ages

For related reading, see MEDIEVAL and RENAISSANCE EUROPE

Israel **Abrahams**

Jewish Life in the Middle Ages

0-8276-0542-0 JEWISH PUB SOCIETY $19.95
0-8276-0479-3 JEWISH PUB SOCIETY PB $9.95

Eliyahu **Ashtor**

The Jews of Moslem Spain

Three volumes in one

See also **ANTI-SEMITISM**

0-8276-0432-7 JEWISH PUB SOCIETY $38.95

Yitzhak F. **Baer**

Galut

See also **BIBLICAL COMMENTARY** under **THE BIBLE** under **JUDAISM** in **RELIGION, SPIRITUALITY, AND PHILOSOPHY**

INTRODUCTION BY JACOB NEUSNER

0-8191-5783-X UNIVERSITY PRESS OF AMERICA PB $15.50

History of the Jews in Christian Spain

0-8276-0431-9 JEWISH PUB SOCIETY PB $39.95

Robert **Chazan**

European Jewry and the First Crusade

One of the unanticipated results of the First Crusade in 1095 was a series of violent assaults on major Jewish communities in the Rhineland. "Takes us deep into the thoughts and feelings of Ashkenazic Judaism in its early, formative stages, and into its historical circumstances as an integral and highly significant part of Western Europe in the central Middle Ages" —*International History Review*

0-520-20506-5 CALIFORNIA PB $17.95

Jeremy **Cohen**

The Friars and the Jews: The Evolution of Medieval Anti-Judaism

Reasons for and results of the mendicant antagonism against the Jews

See also **JEWRY** under **RELIGIOUS HISTORY** under **MEDIEVAL AND RENAISSANCE EUROPE**

0-8014-9266-1 CORNELL PB $14.95

Paloma **Diaz-Maz**

Sephardim: The Jews from Spain

"An authoritative, well-organized, and very readable guide...[that] covers virtually every facet of Sephardic culture, from rites to language, from early history to the most recent developments worldwide" —Myron Lichtblau, Syracuse University

0-226-14483-6 CHICAGO $32.50

Nathan **Hanover**

The Abyss of Despair

Recounts the brutal 17th-century Chmielnicki massacres

TRANSLATED BY ABRAHAM J. MESCH

INTRODUCTION BY WILLIAM B. HELMREICH

0-87855-927-2 TRANSACTION PB $21.95

Bernard W. **Lewis**

The Jews of Islam

"Lewis refuses...simplistic approaches and tries to explain the complex and often contradictory history of Jewish-Muslim relations over fourteen hundred years" —Norman A. Stillman, *NY Review of Books*

0-691-00807-8 PRINCETON PB $13.95

Ivan G. **Marcus**

Rituals of Childhood: Jewish Acculturation in Medieval Europe

"This fascinating story of how young Jewish boys were introduced to formal Torah study in the Middle Ages presents a new perspective on many questions of medieval history"—William Chester Jordan, Princeton University

0-300-05998-1 YALE $25.00

Leon **Nemoy**, translator

Karaite Anthology: Excerpts from the Early Literature

A collection of writings covering the thought and beliefs of the influential sect, to about 1500

0-300-00792-2 YALE $45.00
0-300-03929-8 YALE PB $21.00

Cecil **Roth**

The Jews in the Renaissance

0-8276-0103-4 JEWISH PUB SOCIETY PB $8.95

Spinoza

Norman **Roth**

Conversos, Inquisition, and the Expulsion of the Jews from Spain

See also **SPAIN: GOLDEN AGE AND DECLINE** under **EARLY MODERN EUROPE**

0-299-14230-2 WISCONSIN $50.00

Howard M. **Sachar**

Farewell España: The World of the Sephardim Remembered

Sachar documents and analyzes the rich world of Sephardic Jewry following their expulsionfrom the golden age of medieval Spain to their varied lives throughout Western Europe, the Balkans, Turkey, and Israel. A personal and illuminating tour of the vein of Judaism that produced Maimonides, Spinoza, Disraeli, and Mendes-France

0-679-40960-2 KNOPF $30.00
0-679-73846-0 VINTAGE PB $15.00

Gershom **Scholem**

Sabbatai Sevi: The Mystical Messiah

A detailed and authoritative account of the messianic 17th-century Sabbatian movement from its inception to its founder's death

0-691-01809-X PRINCETON PB $29.95

Norman A. **Stillman**

The Jews of Arab Lands: A History and Source Book

"Clarifies two seemingly opposite interpretations of Muslim-Jewish relations—that Jewish life under Islam was the antithesis of medieval European persecution, and that the Jews were a persecuted minority in the Mideast"
—*Kirkus Reviews*

0-8276-0370-3 JEWISH PUB SOCIETY $39.95
0-8276-0198-0 JEWISH PUB SOCIETY PB $19.95

Kenneth R. **Stone**

Alienated Minority: The Jews of Medieval Latin Europe

0-674-01593-2 HARVARD PB $21.00

Modern Europe

Enlightenment, Reform, Assimilation

George E. **Berkley**

Vienna and Its Jews: The Tragedy of Success, 1880-1980s

FOREWORD BY HARRY ZOHN

0-8191-6816-5 MADISON $24.95

Jean-Denis **Bredin**

The Affair: The Case of Alfred Dreyfus

See also **FRANCE** under **19TH-CENTURY EUROPE**

TRANSLATED BY JEFFREY MEHLMAN

0-8076-1175-1 BRAZILLER PB $19.95

Arthur **Hertzberg**

The French Enlightenment and the Jews: The Origins of Modern Anti-Semitism

0-231-07385-2 COLUMBIA PB $19.50

Raphael **Mahler**

Hasidism and the Jewish Enlightenment: Their Confrontation in Galicia and Poland in the First Half of the Nineteenth Century

A major study of the bitter struggle between the Hasidim and the adherents of the *Haskalah*, or Jewish Enlightenment, during a watershed period

TRANSLATED BY EUGENE ORENSTEIN & AARON & JENNY MACHLOWITZ KLEIN

0-8276-0233-2 JEWISH PUB SOCIETY $29.95

Jacob **Katz**

Out of the Ghetto: The Social Background of Jewish Emancipation, 1770-1870

The effect of the transition into society-at-large on both Jews and Gentiles

0-674-64775-0 HARVARD $28.50
0-8052-0601-9 SCHOCKEN PB $15.00

David **Sorkin**

Moses Mendelssohn and the Religious Enlightenment

How Mendelssohn, like the Protestant and Catholic thinkers of the Enlightenment, attempted to use the science and philosophy of the 18th century to renew faith

0-520-20261-9 CALIFORNIA $40.00

Michael A. **Meyer**

Origins of the Modern Jew: Jewish Identity and Europe

"*Origins of the Modern Jew* is a scholarly analysis of Judaism's attempt to maintain itself within the framework of European culture in Germany from 1749 to 1824, a quest that has continued to be at the core of Jewish concern ever since"—*The Jewish Digest*

0-8143-1470-8 WAYNE STATE PB $14.95

Response to Modernity: A History of the Reform Movement in Judaism

0-8143-2555-6 WAYNE STATE PB $18.95

Leon **Modena**

The Autobiography of a 17th-Century Venetian Rabbi: Leon Modena's Life of Judah

A fascinating account of an intellectual figure in the early modern Italian Jewish community

EDITED AND TRANSLATED BY MARK R. COHEN

0-691-05529-7 PRINCETON $55.00
0-691-00824-8 PRINCETON PB $17.95

Michael **Ragussis**

Figures of Conversion: "The Jewish Question" and English National Identity

0-8223-1570-X DUKE PB $16.95

Rachel **Salamander**

The Jewish World of Yesterday: 1860-1938

A bestseller in its German-language edition, this survey of Jewish life before World War II offers a superbly detailed and deeply moving recreation of a vanished world. Its 425 sepia-tone illustrations are supplemented by a choice of texts by the leading writers and thinkers of the period, including Freud, Bloch, Wittgenstein, Buber, Schnitzler, and Arendt

0-8478-1415-7 RIZZOLI $70.00

Max **Wiener**

Abraham Geiger and Liberal Judaism: The Challenge of the Nineteenth Century

0-87820-800-3 BEHRMAN PB $9.95

Eastern Europe

Ruth Ellen **Gruber**

Upon the Doorposts of Thy House: Jewish Life in East-Central Europe, Yesterday and Today

From the opulence of modern Budapest to forlorn villages in southern Poland. The author visits shtetls, medieval ghettoes, synagogues, cemeteries, and death camps in order to compile an evocative account of what was lost and what remains

0-471-59568-3 WILEY $24.95

Celia **Heller**

On the Edge of Destruction: Jews of Poland Between the Two World Wars

An excellent account of the social trends in Europe's largest Jewish community before the Holocaust

0-8143-2494-0 WAYNE STATE PB $16.95

Abraham Joshua **Heschel**

The Earth Is the Lord's: The Inner World of the Jew in Eastern Europe

1-87904-542-7 JEWISH LIGHTS PB $12.95

Ezra **Mendelsohn**

The Jews of East-Central Europe Between the World Wars

A much-needed, first-rate study of interwar Jewish life and community

0-253-20418-6 INDIANA PB $15.95

Isaac Bashevis **Singer**

In My Father's Court

A beautiful, evocative memoir of growing up in Warsaw as the son of a famous rabbi

See also **ISAAC BASHEVIS SINGER** under **YIDDISH LANGUAGE AND LITERATURE** in **LITERATURE OF EUROPE, AFRICA, AND ASIA**

0-374-50592-6 NOONDAY PB $12.00

Isaac Bashevis Singer

Henry J. **Tobias**
The Jewish Bund in Russia from Its Origins to 1905
0-8047-0764-2 STANFORD $52.50

Mark **Zborowski** & Elizabeth **Herzog**
Life Is with People: The Culture of the Shtetl
A somewhat sentimentalized but detailed account of daily life in small Jewish towns
INTRODUCTION BY MARGARET MEAD
0-8052-1054-7 SCHOCKEN PB $16.00

Anti-Semitism

David **Berger**, editor
History and Hate: The Dimensions of Anti-Semitism
Essays by experts on different eras of Jewish history
0-8276-0267-7 JEWISH PUB SOCIETY $19.95

Werner **Bergmann** & Rainer **Erb**
Anti-Semitism in Germany
1-56000-270-0 RUTGERS $39.95

Frank **Felsenstein**
Anti-Semitic Stereotypes: A Paradigm of Otherness in English Popular Culture, 1660-1830
"All the familiar nightmares are here, along with a few inventive twists"
—Lawrence Lipking, *New Republic*
0-8018-4903-9 JOHNS HOPKINS $39.95

Jacob **Katz**
Exclusiveness and Tolerance: Studies in Jewish-Gentile Relations in Medieval and Modern Times
0-87441-365-6 BEHRMAN PB $12.95

From Prejudice to Destruction: Anti-Semitism, 1700-1933
Blends the history of ideas with social analysis, viewing modern anti-Semitism as a direct outgrowth of traditional Christian anti-Semitism
0-674-32507-9 HARVARD PB $18.50

Jean-Paul **Sartre**
Anti-Semite and Jew
A challenge to anti-Semitism from a non-Jewish point of view. "One of the most brilliant psychological analyses of the marginal Jew and the fanatical anti-Semite that has ever been published"—Sidney Hook
See also **SARTRE** under **PHILOSOPHY** in **RELIGION, SPIRITUALITY, AND PHILOSOPHY**
See also **ESSAYS: PERSONAL, LITERARY, PHILOSOPHICAL** under **MODERN FRENCH LITERATURE** in **LITERATURE OF EUROPE, AFRICA, AND ASIA**
0-8052-1047-4 SCHOCKEN PB $12.00

Jean-Paul Sartre

Benjamin W. **Segel**
A Lie and a Libel: The History of The Protocols of the Elders of Zion
TRANSLATED AND EDITED BY RICHARD S. LEVY
0-8032-4243-3 NEBRASKA $25.00
0-8032-9245-7 NEBRASKA PB $10.00

Joshua **Trachtenberg**
The Devil and the Jews: The Medieval Conception of the Jew and Its Relation to Modern Anti-Semitism
Traces anti-Semitism to the medieval view of the Jew as a devil; first published in 1943
FOREWORD BY MARC SAPERSTEIN
0-8276-0227-8 JEWISH PUB SOCIETY PB $12.95

Origins of Zionism

For related reading, see THE CONTEMPORARY MIDDLE EAST

Ian **Buruma**
Wages of Guilt: Memoirs of War in Germany and Japan
0-452-01156-6 PENGUIN PB $12.95

Benjamin **Halpern**
A Clash of Heroes: Brandeis, Weizmann and American Zionism
0-19-504062-7 OXFORD $45.00

Walter **Laqueur**
A History of Zionism
The classic historical analysis of Zionism
0-8052-0899-2 RANDOM HOUSE PB $16.00

Sergio I. **Minerbi**
The Vatican and Zionism: Conflict in the Holy Land, 1895-1925
A close look at the little-known and often antagonistic relations between the Catholic Church and the founders of Zionism
0-19-505892-5 OXFORD $30.00

David **Vital**
The Origins of Zionism
A two-part history of Zionist thought and politics; this volume ends with the First Zionist Congress (1897)
0-19-827439-4 OXFORD PB $31.00

Zionism: The Formative Years
0-19-827443-2 OXFORD $62.00
0-19-827715-6 OXFORD PB $29.95

Bernard **Avishai**
The Tragedy of Zionism: Revolution and Democracy in the Land of Israel
See also **ISRAEL SINCE 1948** under **ISRAEL** under **THE CONTEMPORARY MIDDLE EAST**
0-374-27863-6 FS&G $5.98

Russia and the Soviet Union

For related reading, see Russian Studies

Bella **Chagall** & Marc **Chagall**
Burning Lights: A Unique Double Portrait of the Warm World of Russian Jewry
A memoir with text by Bella Chagall and 36 drawings by Marc Chagall recalls their young lives in the Russian-Jewish market town of Vitebsk
0-930395-26-3 BIBLIO $42.00

Jacques **Kornberg**
Theodor Herzl: From Assimilation to Zionism
0-253-33203-6 INDIANA $25.95

John D. **Klier** & Shlomo **Lambroza**
Pogroms: Anti-Jewish Violence in Modern Russian History
0-521-40532-7 CAMBRIDGE $69.95

John Doyle **Klier**
Imperial Russia's Jewish Question, 1855-1881
0-521-46035-2 CAMBRIDGE $69.95

Jews in America

General Histories

Neil M. **Cowan** & Ruth Schwartz **Cowan**
Our Parents' Lives: The Americanization of Eastern European Jews
An oral history of the immigrant experience in the early 20th century
0-8135-2296-X RUTGERS PB $16.95

Harriet **Fred** & Rochlin **Fred**

Pioneer Jews: A New Life in the Far West

A picture book with text. "The stereotype of the urban Jew is vigorously, and even exuberantly, rejected in this colorful history"
—*Chicago Sun-Times*

0-395-42639-1 HOUGHTON MIFFLIN PB $18.95

Myrna Katz **Frommer** & Harvey **Frommer**

Growing Up in Jewish America: An Oral History

This oral history from the acclaimed authors of *It Happened in Brooklyn* and *It Happened in the Catskills* brings together the voices of 100 men and women, from 22 to 99 years old. Together, their childhood memories paint a unique portrait of growing up Jewish in America, not just in Brooklyn or Los Angeles, but in places as diverse as Maine, South Dakota, Texas, and South Carolina. The result is a witty and perceptive volume as much about being American as it is about being Jewish

0-15-100132-4 HARCOURT BRACE $25.00

Nathan **Glazer**

American Judaism

EDITED BY DANIEL J. BOORSTIN

0-226-29843-4 CHICAGO PB $18.95

Calvin **Goldscheider** & Alan S. **Zuckerman**

The Transformation of The Jews

0-226-30148-6 CHICAGO PB $10.95

Ben **Halpern**

The American Jew: A Zionistic Analysis

0-8052-0742-2 SCHOCKEN PB $6.95

Paula E. **Hyman**

Gender and Assimilation in Modern Jewish History : The Roles and Representation of Women

A history of Jewish assimilation in America as experienced by women. "Meticulously researched and eloquently written, Hyman's work will become the standard reference in Jewish women's history…"
—Marion Kaplan, Queens College

See also **AMERICA'S WORKING WOMEN** under **AMERICAN HISTORY** under **WOMEN'S STUDIES** in **SOCIAL STUDIES**

0-295-97425-7 WASHINGTON $30.00
0-295-97426-5 WASHINGTON PB $14.95

Jenna Weissman **Joselit**

The Wonders of America: Reinventing Jewish Culture, 1880-1950

"Felicitously written, filled with entertaining and often hilarious details"
—Phillip Lopate, *NY Times Book Review*

See also **JEWISH-AMERICANS** under **THE MELTING POT** under **AMERICAN PEOPLE AND PLACES** in **HISTORY OF THE AMERICAS**

0-8090-1586-2 HILL & WANG PB $14.00

David **Leviatin**

Followers of the Trail: Jewish Working-Class Radicals in America

0-300-04354-6 YALE $40.00

Kenneth **Libo** & Irving **Howe**

We Live There Too: Their Own Words, Pioneer Jews and the Westward Movement of America, 1630-1930

A large coffee-table picture book with text, documenting the westward journeys of American Jews

0-312-85867-1 ST. MARTIN'S PB $14.95

Deborah Dash **Moore**

To the Golden Cities: Pursuing the American Jewish Dream in Miami and L.A.

Attracted by palm trees, bungalows, and sunshine as much as by economic opportunity, Jews flocked to the South and West by the tens of thousands after World War II

0-674-89305-0 HARVARD PB $15.95

Dan A. **Oren**

Joining the Club: A History of Jews at Yale

0-300-03330-3 YALE $45.00
0-300-04384-8 YALE PB $19.00

Jonathan D. **Sarna**, editor

The American Jewish Experience

0-8419-0934-2 HOLMES & MEIER $37.95

The American Jewish Experience: A Reader

0-8419-1376-5 HOLMES & MEIER PB $19.95

Chaim I. **Waxman**

America's Jews in Transition

0-87722-329-7 TEMPLE PB $18.95

Jack **Wertheimer**, editor

The American Synagogue: A Sanctuary Transformed: A Centennial Publication of the Jewish Theological

0-87451-709-5 BRANDEIS PB $19.95

Orthodoxy

Lis **Harris**

Holy Days: The World of a Hasidic Family

"What is special about Lis Harris is her combination of openness and skepticism toward her subject. *Holy Days* is a deeply felt and informative introduction to an appealing sect of fundamentalist faith"—*NY Times*

0-684-81366-1 MACMILLAN PB $12.00

Assimilation and Intermarriage

Steven M. **Cohen**

American Assimilation or Jewish Revival?

As American Jews grow further from their European pasts, are they becoming more American or are they undergoing a great revival?

0-253-30608-6 INDIANA $11.95

Egon **Mayer**

Love and Tradition: Marriage Between Jews and Christians

Sociologist Mayer interviewed hundreds of intermarried couples and their children and assesses their motivations and religious identities

0-306-42043-0 PLENUM $19.95

Anti-Semitism in America

Jerome A. **Chanes**, editor

Antisemitism in America Today: Outspoken Experts Explode the Myths

Chanes includes incisive assessments written just for this volume by nineteen leading Jewish thinkers and authorities. These experts explore the history, psychology, expression, and dynamics of anti-Semitism in America. "No one who reads these up-to-the-minute essays will fail to be informed and perplexed. Describing the countertendencies of skinhead hatred, feminist and black antisemitism, and a general decline in prejudice, the work of the brilliant journalists and scholars in this book will spark debate for years to come"—Cynthia Fuchs Epstein, City University of New York Graduate Center

1-55972-290-8 BIRCH LANE $27.50

Leonard **Dinnerstein**

Antisemitism in America

History of prejudice against Jews in the United States from colonial times to the present. "The most comprehensive and up-to-date history of American antisemitism… Concise, highly readable… A major contribution"
—Philip Perlmuter, *Boston Globe*

0-09-503780-4 OXFORD $30.00
0-09-510012-X OXFORD PB $15.95

The Leo Frank Case

The infamous case of the southern Jewish man blamed and lynched for the murder of a factory girl

0-8203-0965-6 GEORGIA PB $14.95

Uneasy at Home: Antisemitism and the American Jewish Experience

0-231-06252-4 COLUMBIA $36.00

David A. **Gerber**, editor

Anti-Semitism in American History

0-252-01214-3 ILLINOIS $34.95
0-252-01477-4 ILLINOIS PB $13.95

Harold E. **Quinley** & Charles Y. **Glock**
Anti-Semitism in America
0-87855-940-X TRANSACTION PB............$21.95

The Lower East Side and the Jews of New York

Arthur A. **Goren**
New York Jews and the Quest For Community
Covers the attempts of early-20th-century New York Jews to form a central communal structure
0-231-03422-9 COLUMBIA............$37.50

Irving **Howe**
World of Our Fathers
The classic, beautifully written account of the Jewish migration from Europe to the United States, with detailed looks at everything from Yiddish theater to the Jewish labor movement
0-15-146353-0 HARCOURT BRACE............$34.95
0-8052-0928-X SCHOCKEN PB............$19.00

Ronald **Sanders**
The Downtown Jews: Portraits of an Immigrant Generation
0-486-25510-7 DOVER PB............$10.95

Anzia **Yezierska**
Hungry Hearts
Fictional tale of tenement life on the Lower East Side of New York City by author of *Red Ribbon on a White Horse*
0-451-52641-4 SIGNET PB............$4.95

Red Ribbon on a White Horse
Early autobiography of young immigrant woman who rises out of the tenements of New York's Lower East Side to become a successful writer, only to be thrust back into the world she tried to leave behind in the wake of the Great Depression
0-89255-124-0 PERSEA PB............$9.95

Other Jewish Experiences

Phyllis Cohen **Albert**
Contemporary French Jewry
0-8419-0933-4 HOLMES & MEIER PB............$14.50

Jonathan **Boyarin**
Polish Jews in Paris: The Ethnography of Memory
0-253-31252-3 INDIANA............$10.95

Thinking in Jewish
0-226-06927-3 CHICAGO PB............$14.95

Avigdor **Dagan**, editor
The Jews of Czechoslovakia
Volume 1
A trilogy, from the founding of the first republic in 1918 to the advent of communism in 1948
0-8276-0339-8 JEWISH PUB SOCIETY............$29.95
Volume 2
0-8276-0146-8 JEWISH PUB SOCIETY............$29.95
Volume 3
Covers the Holocaust and the rebuilding of the Jewish community after the war
0-8276-0230-8 JEWISH PUB SOCIETY............$29.95

Michael **Pollak**
Mandarins, Jews, and Missionaries: The Jewish Experience in the Chinese Empire
The Jews of Kaifeng China
0-8276-0229-4 JEWISH PUB SOCIETY PB............$14.95

Howard Morley **Sachar**
Diaspora: An Inquiry Into the Contemporary Jewish World
A survey of recent Jewish history outside the US and Israel
0-06-091347-9 OLYMPIC PB............$2.98

Sidney **Shapiro**, editor
Jews in Old China
Fascinating essays by Chinese scholars about the Jewish presence in China as early as the 8th century BC; translated and compiled by Shapiro
0-87052-553-0 HIPPOCRENE PB............$8.95

Biography

Eli N. **Evans**
Judah P. Benjamin: The Jewish Confederate
Born in St. Croix, raised in South Carolina, and educated at Yale, Benjamin was Attorney General, Secretary of War, and Secretary of State for the Confederacy in the American Civil War
0-02-909911-0 FREE PRESS PB............$14.95

Walter **Benjamin**
This incisive critic and cultural historian, who strove to balance the conflicting influences of Marxism and Jewish theology, committed suicide rather than fall into the hands of the Gestapo

Reflections: Essays, Aphorisms, Autobiographical Writings
See also **FICTION AND OTHER PROSE** under **MODERN GERMAN LITERATURE: TO 1945** under **GERMAN LITERATURE** in **LITERATURE OF EUROPE, AFRICA, AND ASIA**
TRANSLATED BY EDMUND JEPHCOTT
EDITED BY PETER DEMETZ
0-8052-0802-X SCHOCKEN PB............$15.00

Gershom **Scholem**
Walter Benjamin: The Story of a Friendship
Memoir of the friendship between two noted scholars
See also **STUDIES OF INDIVIDUAL AUTHORS** under **CRITICAL STUDIES** under **GERMAN LITERATURE** in **LITERATURE OF EUROPE, AFRICA, AND ASIA**
TRANSLATED BY HARRY ZOHN
0-8276-0197-2 JEWISH PUB SOCIETY............$17.95

Philippa **Strum**
Louis D. Brandeis: Justice For the People
0-674-53921-4 HARVARD............$39.95

Shlomo **Avineri**
Moses Hess: Prophet of Communism and Zionism
"A compact, lucid study of a notable thinker of the 19th century whose insight reached into the 20th"—*Journal of Jewish Studies*
0-8147-0584-7 NYU............$50.00

Franz **Kobler**, editor
Letters of Jews Through the Ages
The history of Jews, through their correspondence
Volume 1
0-85222-212-2 HEBREW PB............$7.95
Volume 2
0-85222-213-0 HEBREW PB............$7.95

Jonathan D. **Sarna**
Jacksonian Jew: The Two Worlds of Mordecai Noah
0-8419-0567-3 HOLMES & MEIER............$37.95

Dan V. **Segre**
Memoirs of a Fortunate Jew: An Italian Story
An odyssey through fascist Italy and the founding of Israel
1-56821-437-5 ARONSON............$20.00

Hannah **Senesh**
Hannah Senesh: Her Life and Diary
A major hero in Israel, Senesh was a pioneer Zionist, killed by the Nazis at the age of 23 after a failed attempt to rescue Hungarian Jews
See also **RESCUE AND RESISTANCE** under **THE HOLOCAUST**
TRANSLATED BY MARTA COHN
INTRODUCTION BY ABBA EBAN
0-8052-0410-5 SCHOCKEN PB............$16.00

Hannah Senesh (photo courtesy of Schocken Books)

Melvin I. **Urofsky** & others, editors
Half Brother, Half Son: The Letters of Louis D. Brandeis to Felix Frankfurter
0-8061-2303-6 OKLAHOMA............$55.00

Jewish Culture

For related reading, see YIDDISH LANGUAGE AND LITERATURE in LITERATURE OF EUROPE, AFRICA, AND ASIA

For related reading, see MODERN HEBREW LITERATURE in LITERATURE OF EUROPE, AFRICA, AND ASIA

For related reading, see JUDAISM in RELIGION, SPIRITUALITY, AND PHILOSOPHY

Nathan **Ausubel**, editor

A Treasury of Jewish Folklore

A compendium of stories, traditions, legends, humor, wisdom, and folk songs

See also **THE LANGUAGE** under **YIDDISH LANGUAGE AND LITERATURE** in **LITERATURE OF EUROPE, AFRICA, AND ASIA**

0-517-50293-3 CROWN $22.00

Joseph L. **Baron**, editor

A Treasury of Jewish Quotations

1-56821-948-2 ARONSON PB $40.00

Robert **Eisenberg**

Boychiks in the Hood: Travels in the Haisidic Underground

Takes us on a tour of "the Hasidic underground." With him we meet an ex-Deadhead Hasid in Antwerp, roller-blading kosher butchers in Minnesota, and a karate champion-turned-rabbi in Israel

0-06-251222-6 HARPERCOLLINS $20.00

Neal **Gabler**

An Empire of Their Own: How the Jews Invented Hollywood

An examination of the careers of Samuel Goldwyn, Louis B. Mayer, and other movie producers, showing how they successfully imposed their fantasies of American life onto the American screen

See also **FILM IN AMERICA** under **FILM** in **PERFORMING ARTS AND MEDIA**

0-385-26557-3 ANCHOR PB $14.00

Samuel Goldwyn

Joseph **Gutmann**

Hebrew Manuscript Painting

A vast range of illustrations of Jewish customs and holiday observances in manuscripts from Germany, Spain, Italy, and Islamic countries

0-8076-0891-2 BRAZILLER PB $12.95

A. Z. **Idelsohn**

Jewish Music

0-486-27147-1 DOVER PB $13.95

David G. **Roskies**

Against the Apocalypse: Responses to Catastrophe in Modern Jewish Culture

The Holocaust in the context of generations of Jewish response to persecutions. "Densely argued, richly allusive, exemplary in its far-ranging scholarship"—*TLS*

0-674-00915-0 HARVARD $32.00

The Literature of Destruction: Jewish Responses to Catastrophe

Anthology of literary responses to catastrophic events in the history of the Jewish people. Included are never-before-translated accounts from diaries and journals of Jewish prisoners of Nazi Germany

0-8276-0314-2 JEWISH PUB SOCIETY $47.50

0-8276-0414-9 JEWISH PUB SOCIETY PB $24.95

Jerome **Rothenberg**

Exiled in the Word: Poems & Other Visions of the Jews from Tribal Times to Present

The poetic anthologies of Jerome Rothenberg—*Technicians of the Sacred, Shaking the Pumpkin,* and many others—have been among the most influential of our time. In this new, more compact version of the long-out-of-print *A Big Jewish Book*, he and Harris Lenowitz create a highly personal collage of Jewish traditions both orthodox and heretical focusing, in Rothenberg's words, "on a poetic/visionary continuum & on the mystical & magical"

See also **ANTHOLOGIES** under **MODERN HEBREW LITERATURE** in **LITERATURE OF EUROPE, AFRICA, AND ASIA**

1-55659-026-1 COPPER CANYON PB $12.00

Pinhas **Sadeh**

Jewish Folktales

See also **FOLKLORE** under **MYTHOLOGY AND FOLKLORE** in **RELIGION, SPIRITUALITY, AND PHILOSOPHY**

0-385-19574-5 ANCHOR PB $16.00

Howard **Schwartz**, editor

Miriam's Tambourine: Jewish Folktales from Around the World

Fifty folktales, from the Jewish version of "Snow White" to the tales of the *Ba'al Shem Tov*

0-19-282136-9 OXFORD PB $13.95

The Islamic World to World War I

Islamic civilization began with Muhammad in the 7th century: new forms of polity, religion, and culture were established—first in the Middle East between 600 and 1200, then in much of the rest of Central and Southern Asia, North Africa, Sub-Saharan Africa, and Eastern Europe. Today, Islam is the religion of 900 million people and it is expanding rapidly in Asia, Africa, and the Americas.

Islam's success has inspired pride and faith among its numerous adherents, but it has also provoked suspicion, fear, and contempt from outsiders. Ever since the Middle Ages, Europeans have been trying to comprehend, and to contend with, this intimate, ambivalent adversary. As soldiers confronted Muslim warriors on the battlefields of Spain and Palestine, medieval scholars translated the Qur'an and Islamic philosophy into Latin. From the 15th to the 18th centuries, Europeans anguished over the threat of the Ottoman Empire, but delighted in Oriental fashion and taste.

In the 18th century, the tide was reversed: Europeans began to push back the Ottoman Empire and to conquer formerly Muslim lands. Even today, the legacy of colonialism, the struggle between Israel and the Arabs, and the Islamic revival make the confrontation between Islam and the West a passionate issue.

Akbar S. **Ahmed**

Discovering Islam: Making Sense of Muslim History and Society

0-415-03930-4 ROUTLEDGE PB $16.95

Frederick M. **Denny**

Islam and the Muslim Community

An interpretation of Muslim doctrines, devotional practices, and institutions which provides a ready understanding of current world events involving Muslims

0-06-061875-2 HARPERCOLLINS PB $12.00

Gerhard **Endress**

An Introduction to Islam

0-231-06581-7 COLUMBIA PB $17.50

Philip K. **Hitti**

A History of the Arabs

The best one-volume political and cultural history of Islam, from its origins in the 7th century until the end of Ottoman rule

0-312-37520-4 ST. MARTIN'S PB $45.32

Marshall G. **Hodgson**

The Venture of Islam: Conscience and History in World Civilization

Hodgson is particularly sensitive to cultural and literary issues and to the meaning of religious discourse. This work resounds with his idiosyncratic and brilliant voice; winner of the Ralph Waldo Emerson Award

Marshall G. **Hodgson**

The Venture of Islam: Conscience and History in World Civilization

Volume 1
The Classical Age of Islam
0-226-34683-8 CHICAGO PB $19.95

Volume 2
The Expansion of Islam in the Middle Periods
0-226-34684-6 CHICAGO PB $22.50

Volume 3
The Gunpowder Empire and Modern Times
0-226-34665-4 CHICAGO PB $15.95

P.M. **Holt**, editor

Cambridge History of Islam
This sturdy and reliable reference work by Western scholars is an excellent source; a 4-volume set

Volume 1A
Central Islamic Lands from Pre-Islamic Times to the First World War
0-521-29135-6 CAMBRIDGE PB $47.95

Volume 1B
Central Islamic Lands Since 1918
0-521-29136-4 CAMBRIDGE PB $47.95

Volume 2A
The Indian Subcontinent, Africa and the Muslim West
0-521-29137-2 CAMBRIDGE PB $47.95

Volume 2B
Islamic Society and Civilization
0-521-29138-0 CAMBRIDGE PB $47.95

Albert **Hourani**

A History of the Arab Peoples
A 576-page synthesis by a distinguished scholar. "Hourani covers twelve centuries of social, economic, political, and cultural life in a work already being hailed as both comprehensive and definitive"—*Newsweek*

See also **GENERAL STUDIES** under **ISLAM** in **RELIGION, SPIRITUALITY, AND PHILOSOPHY**

0-674-39565-4 HARVARD $27.50
0-446-39392-4 WARNER PB $15.99

Even if the ruler was unjust or impious, it was generally accepted that he should still be obeyed, for any kind of order was better than anarchy; as Ghazali said, "the tyranny of a sultan for a hundred years causes less damage than one year's tyranny exercised by the subjects against one another." Revolt was justified only against a ruler who clearly went against a command of God or His prophet. This did not mean, however, that 'ulama should look on an unjust ruler in the way in which they looked on a just one. A powerful tradition among the 'ulama (among Sunnis and Shi'is alike) was that they should keep their distance from the rulers of the world. Ghazali quoted a hadith: "in Hell there is a valley uniquely reserved for 'ulama who visit kings."
A HISTORY OF THE ARAB PEOPLES

Ira M. **Lapidus**

A History of Islamic Societies
An enormously useful 1,000-page survey. "Belongs to a rare breed of works which appear only once every two decades"
—*Third World Quarterly*

0-521-22552-3 CAMBRIDGE $85.00
0-521-29549-1 CAMBRIDGE PB $29.95

Bernard **Lewis**

Race and Slavery in the Middle East: An Historical Inquiry
The history of slavery in the region where it lasted longest; written with characteristic erudition and stylistic elegance by the author of *The Muslim Discovery of Europe* and *The Jew of Islam*

0-19-506283-3 OXFORD $30.00

The myth of Islamic racial innocence was a Western creation and served a Western purpose. Not for the first time, a mythologized and idealized Islam provided a stick with which to chastise Western failings. In the eighteenth century, the philosophers of the Enlightenment had praised Islam for its lack of dogmas and mysteries, its freedom from priests and Inquisitors and other persecutors—recognizing real qualities but exaggerating them as polemical weapon against the Christian churches and clergy...In the same way, the myth of total racial harmony in the Islamic world appears to have arisen as a reproach to the practices of white men in the Americas and in Southern Africa, beside which indeed even Islamic realities shone in contrast.
RACE AND SLAVERY IN THE MIDDLE EAST: AN HISTORICAL INQUIRY

King Faisal

Maxime **Rodinson**

The Arabs
A great scholar's study of the Arabs from their first eruption into history to their complex presence in the contemporary world
TRANSLATED BY ARTHUR GOLDHAMMER

0-226-72356-9 CHICAGO PB $13.00

Europe and the Mystique of Islam
TRANSLATED BY ROGER VEINUS

0-295-96485-5 WASHINGTON PB $12.95

Islamic Sources

Hilal **Al-Sabi**

Rusum Dar Al-Khila Fah (Rules and Regulations of the Abbasid Court)
EDITED BY ELIE A. SALEM

0-8156-6046-4 SYRACUSE $19.95

Al-Tabari

The History of Al-Tabari
This 10th-century compilation remains the indispensable source for Islam's early history, as well as for the declining years of the Persian Empire. Working in the traditional form of the "universal history," Al-Tabari recounts human history from an Islamic view, from Creation, Adam and Eve, the Flood, and the Prophets to the birth of Islam and the growth of the Islamic empire. The SUNY series is the first attempt to translate this enormous work—perhaps the greatest work of classical Arab historiography—into English. It is still incomplete; this list provides a sampling of the volumes now available

Volume 1
From Creation to the Flood
0-88706-562-7 SUNY $64.50

Volume 4
The Ancient Kingdoms
0-88706-181-8 SUNY $49.50
0-88706-182-6 SUNY PB $18.95

Volume 6
Muhammad at Mecca
0-88706-706-9 SUNY $44.50
0-88706-707-7 SUNY PB $16.95

Volume 7
The Foundation of the Community: Muhammad at Al-Madinah, A.D. 622-627
0-88706-344-6 SUNY $57.50
0-88706-345-4 SUNY PB $19.95

Volume 9
The Last Years of the Prophet, A.D. 630-632
0-88706-691-7 SUNY $49.50
0-88706-692-5 SUNY PB $19.95

Volume 25
The Later Marwanids
0-88706-569-4 SUNY $49.50
0-88706-570-8 SUNY PB $19.95

Volume 27
The Abbasid Revolution, A.D. 743-750
0-87395-884-5 SUNY $44.50
0-7914-0625-3 SUNY PB $18.95

Volume 30
The Abbasid Caliphate in Equilibrium: The Caliphates of Musa Al-Hadi and Harun Al-Rashid, A.D. 785-809
0-88706-564-3 SUNY $49.50
0-88706-566-X SUNY PB $24.95

Volume 35
The Crisis of the Abbasid Caliphate, A.D. 862-869
0-87395-883-7 SUNY........$44.50
0-7914-0627-X SUNY PB........$16.95

Volume 38
The Return of the Caliphate to Baghdad, A.D. 892-915
0-87395-876-4 SUNY........$44.50
0-7914-0626-1 SUNY PB........$18.95

Ibn **Khaldun**
The Muqaddimah: Abridged Edition
A single volume abridgment of the 14th-century masterpiece of Islamic historiography. "Should make the essential ideas of Ibn Khaldun accessible to a wide circle of readers"—*TLS*
See also **THE CLASSICS** under **HISTORIOGRAPHY**
TRANSLATED BY FRANZ ROSENTHAL
EDITED BY N.J. DAWOOD
0-691-01754-9 PRINCETON PB........$16.95

Usamah Ibn **Minqidh**
An Arab-Syrian Gentleman and Warrior in the Period of the Crusades: Memories of Usamah Ibn Munqidh
TRANSLATED BY PHILIP K. HITTI
0-691-02269-0 PRINCETON PB........$15.95

Lawrence I. Albrecht **Noth**
The Early Arabic Historical Tradition: A Source-Critical Study
0-87850-082-0 DARWIN........$27.50

Muhammad and the Qur'an

Karen **Armstrong**
Muhammad: A Biography of the Prophet
This highly readable, even-handed study examines Muhammad's life within the context of the emergence of Islam out of the cultural upheaval of seventh-century Arabia and its subsequent encounters with the West. "Portrays Muhammad as a passionate, complex, fallible human being"—*Publishers Weekly*
See also **THE LIFE AND CAREER OF MUHAMMAD** under **ISLAM** in **RELIGION, SPIRITUALITY, AND PHILOSOPHY**
0-06-250886-5 HARPERCOLLINS PB........$13.00

It has been difficult for Western people to understand the violent Muslim reaction to Salman Rushdie's fictional portrait of Muhammad in "The Satanic Verses." It seemed incredible that a novel could inspire such murderous hatred, a reaction which was regarded as proof of the incurable intolerance of Islam.
MUHAMMAD: A BIOGRAPHY OF THE PROPHET

F.E. **Peters**
Muhammad and the Origins of Islam
0-7914-1876-6 SUNY PB........$19.95

Michael **Cook**
Muhammad
A concise summary, from the Past Masters series
See also **THE LIFE AND CAREER OF MUHAMMAD** under **ISLAM** in **RELIGION, SPIRITUALITY, AND PHILOSOPHY**
0-19-287605-8 OXFORD PB........$8.95

Muhammad Marmaduke **Pickthall**, translator
The Meaning of the Glorious Koran
A literal translation in which each verse is followed by a brief explanation of its historical and religious meaning
See also **THE QU'RAN** under **ISLAM** in **RELIGION, SPIRITUALITY, AND PHILOSOPHY**
0-686-18531-5 KAZI PB........$5.95
0-451-62745-8 NEW AMERICAN LIBRARY PB........$6.99

W. Montgomery **Watt**
Muhammad: Prophet and Statesman
A concise biography by a leading scholar of Muhammad's career
See also **THE LIFE AND CAREER OF MUHAMMAD** under **ISLAM** in **RELIGION, SPIRITUALITY, AND PHILOSOPHY**
0-19-881078-4 OXFORD PB........$10.95

Early Islamic History

These books are good general surveys from the beginning of the Muslim era, AD 622 to 1258.

Bernard **Lewis**
The Arabs in History
0-19-285258-2 OXFORD PB........$12.95

The Assassins: A Radical Sect in Islam
A basic introduction to one of history's most intriguing sects, which threatened the Abbasid Empire with syllogism and dagger
0-19-520550-2 OXFORD PB........$10.95

Bernard **Lewis**, translator & editor
Islam: From the Prophet Muhammad to the Capture of Constantinople
Volume 1
Politics and War
0-19-505087-8 OXFORD PB........$15.95

Volume 2
Religion and Society
0-19-505088-6 OXFORD PB........$16.95

J.J. **Saunders**
A History of Medieval Islam
The rise and fall of the Caliphate and its relationship with the Christian world. The mission of Muhammad, the Arab conquests, the rise and decline of the empire of the caliphs, the coming of the Seljuk Turks, the Crusades, the Mongol invasions, and the character of the great Arabic civilization, which contributed directly to the European Renaissance
0-7100-0050-2 ROUTLEDGE PB........$17.95

Islam in Iran

Clifford E. **Bosworth**
The Cambridge History of Iran
An excellent history, of which the second and fourth volumes are currently out of print

Volume 1
The Land of Iran
0-521-06935-1 CAMBRIDGE........$130.00

Volume 2
The Median and Archaemenian Periods
0-521-20091-1 CAMBRIDGE........$145.00

Volume 3
The Seleucid, Parthian and Sasanid Periods
EDITED BY E. YARSHATER
0-521-24693-8 CAMBRIDGE........$140.00

Volume 4
From the Arab Invasion to the Saljuqs
0-521-20093-8 CAMBRIDGE........$130.00

Volume 5
The Saljuq and Mongol Periods
EDITED BY J.A. BOYLE
0-521-06936-X CAMBRIDGE........$125.00

Volume 6
The Timurid and Sefavid Periods
EDITED BY PETER JACKSON
0-521-20094-6 CAMBRIDGE........$150.00

Volume 7
From Nadir Shah to the Islamic Republic
EDITED BY PETER AVERY
0-521-20095-4 CAMBRIDGE........$150.00

The Crusades

Francesco **Gabrieli**, editor & translator
Arab Historians of the Crusades
The "other side" of the Holy War
TRANSLATED FROM THE ITALIAN BY E.J. COSTELLO
0-520-05224-2 CALIFORNIA PB........$15.95

Malcolm Cameron **Lyons** & D.E.P. **Jackson**
Saladin: The Politics of the Holy War
"The best book yet written about him in English"—*TLS*
0-521-31739-8 CAMBRIDGE PB........$26.95

Amin **Maalouf**
The Crusades Through Arab Eyes
0-8052-0898-4 SCHOCKEN PB........$16.00

Wearing no turban, his head shaved as a sign of mourning, the venerable qadi Abu Sa'ad al-Harawi burst with a loud cry into the spacious diwan of the caliph al-Mustanzir Billah, a throng of companions, young and old, trailing in his wake. Noisily assenting to his every word, they, like him, offered the chilling spectacle of long

beards and shaven skulls. A few of the court dignitaries tried to calm him, but al-Harawi swept them aside with brusque disdain, strode resolutely to the center of the hall, and then, with the searing eloquence of the seasoned preacher declaiming from his pulpit, proceeded to lecture all those present, without regard to rank. "How dare you slumber in the shade of complacent safety," he began, "leading lives as frivolous as garden flowers, while your brothers in Syria have no dwelling place save the saddles of camels and the bellies of vultures? Blood has been spilled! Beautiful young girls have been shamed, and must now hide their sweet faces in their hands! Shall the valorous Arabs resign themselves to insult, and the valiant Persians accept dishonor?"
THE CRUSADES THROUGH ARAB EYES

Steven **Runciman**
History of the Crusades
The standard work. "The best scholarly survey of the subject by a single author"
—*English Historical Review*

Volume 1
The First Crusade and the Foundation of the Kingdom of Jerusalem
0-521-34770-X CAMBRIDGE PB........$19.95

Volume 2
The Kingdom of Jerusalem and the Frankish East, 1100-1187
0-521-34771-8 CAMBRIDGE PB........$19.95

Volume 3
The Kingdom of Acre and the Later Crusades
See also THE CRUSADES under THE HIGH MIDDLE AGES: EMPIRE AND PAPACY under MEDIEVAL AND RENAISSANCE EUROPE
0-521-34772-6 CAMBRIDGE PB........$19.95

The Rise and Fall of the Ottomans

The Ottoman Empire emerged in the early 14th century under the legendary Osman I, reached its apogee in the 16th century under Suleiman the Magnificent, whose forces threatened the gates of Vienna, and gradually diminished thereafter until Mehmed VI, who was sent into exile by Mustafa Kemal (Atatürk) in the 20th century.

For related reading, see MEDIEVAL AND RENAISSANCE EUROPE

For related reading, see EARLY MODERN EUROPE

Franz **Babinger**
Mehmed the Conqueror and His Time
TRANSLATED BY RALPH MANNHEIM
EDITED BY WILLIAM HICKMAN
0-691-01078-1 PRINCETON PB........$19.95

Godfrey **Goodwin**
A History of Ottoman Architecture
0-500-27429-0 THAMES & HUDSON PB........$34.95

Norman **Itzkowitz**
Ottoman Empire and Islamic Tradition
See also THE OTTOMAN EMPIRE under EARLY MODERN EUROPE
0-226-38806-9 CHICAGO PB........$8.95

Lord **Kinross**
The Ottoman Centuries: The Rise and Fall of the Turkish Empire
The best one-volume history by the man Arnold Toynbee calls "a master of character-drawing and a master of narrative"
See also THE OTTOMAN EMPIRE under EARLY MODERN EUROPE
0-688-08093-6 MORROW PB........$14.95

Alan **Palmer**
The Decline and Fall of the Ottoman Empire
0-87131-754-0 EVANS........$22.50

Andrew **Wheatcroft**
The Ottomans
0-670-84412-8 VIKING........$29.95
0-14-016879-6 PENGUIN PB........$13.95

Islamic Dominions

Jamil M. **Abun Nasr**
A History of the Maghrib in the Islamic Period
0-521-33184-6 CAMBRIDGE........$65.00
0-521-33767-4 CAMBRIDGE PB........$36.95

Richard **Fletcher**
Moorish Spain
0-520-08496-9 CALIFORNIA PB........$13.95

A favourite wife of al-Mu'tamid was a Christian girl from the north. He found her weeping one day for the winter snows which she would never see again in Seville. To comfort her he assembled an army of gardeners who planted by night a forest of almond trees in blossom outside her apartments in the palace. In the morning he led her to the window: "See my love, there is your snow!" Sheer literary convention, of course: similar stories are told of other princesses in other times and places. But it is significant that in eleventh-century al-Andalus it was to the Abbasid court that the story became attached.
MOORISH SPAIN

L.P. **Harvey**
Islamic Spain: 1250 to 1500
Three centuries of Islamic civilization in Spain, viewed from a social, political, and cultural perspective
0-226-31960-1 CHICAGO PB........$47.00

Peter M. **Holt**
Egypt and the Fertile Crescent, 1516-1922: A Political History
The internal politics of the Ottoman Empire in Egypt, and the fate of its subsequent subsidiaries
0-8014-9079-0 CORNELL PB........$17.95

Robert **Irwin**
The Middle East in the Middle Ages: The Early Mamluk Sultanate, 1250-1382
0-8093-1286-7 SOUTHERN ILLINOIS........$29.95

W. Montgomery **Watt** & Pierre **Cachia**
A Short History of Islamic Spain
Recalls some of the most glorious political and cultural achievements in the history of the peninsula, which have been almost forgotten since the Christian recovery
0-85224-332-4 COLUMBIA PB........$13.50

The Medieval Middle Eastern World

Community and Society

Sheila S. **Blair** & Jonathan M. **Bloom**
The Art and Architecture of Islam
"A volume that will stand the test of time and that I, and anyone interested in Islamic art, will refer to again and again"—Hugh Kennedy, *American Historical Review*
See also ISLAMIC ART AND ARCHITECTURE in ART
0-300-05888-8 YALE........$70.00

Alev Lytle **Croutier**
Harem: The World Behind the Veil
A serious examination of a topic that has long been a subject of intense and often prurient Western curiosity. Lavishly illustrated with paintings, woodcuts, miniatures, and photographs
1-55859-159-1 ABBEVILLE PB........$17.95

Ross E. **Dunn**
The Adventures of Ibn Battuta: A Muslim Traveler of the Fourteenth Century
This entertaining account of the remarkable traveler provides a detailed picture of the 14th-century Islamic world
0-520-06743-6 CALIFORNIA PB........$15.95

Ralph S. **Hattox**
Coffee and Coffeehouses: The Origins of a Social Beverage in the Medieval Near East
The early history of coffee, from its use in Sufi rituals to its widespread consumption in medieval Muslim coffeehouses
0-295-96231-3 WASHINGTON PB........$12.95

Bernard **Lewis**

The Political Language of Islam

A brief and scintillating discussion by a great historian, based on direct examination of documents in Arabic, Persian, and Turkish. "Lewis's style, combining erudition with a simple elegance and subtle humor, continues to inspire"—*Middle East Review*

0-226-47693-6 CHICAGO PB........$11.95

Bernard **Lewis**, editor

The World of Islam

This splendidly illustrated anthology offers an introduction to the diversity of Islamic civilization, with full attention to its artistic legacy. Contains 495 illustrations, 160 in color

See also **GENERAL STUDIES** under **ISLAM** in **RELIGION, SPIRITUALITY, AND PHILOSOPHY**

0-500-27624-2 NORTON PB........$29.95

Reference

Ismail Al **Farugi**

The Cultural Atlas of Islam

0-02-910190-5 MACMILLAN........$125.00

H.A. **Gibb** & J.H. **Kramers**

Shorter Encyclopedia of Islam

Focuses on religious issues

90-04-00681-8 E.J. BRILL........$78.00

Francis **Robinson**

Atlas of the Islamic World Since 1500

0-87196-629-8 FACTS ON FILE........$45.00

Islam and the West

Robert J. **Allison**

The Crescent Obscured: The United States and the Muslim World, 1776-1815

0-19-508612-0 OXFORD........$35.00

Islam in European Thought

0-521-42120-9 CAMBRIDGE PB........$17.95

Robert **Kaplan**

The Arabists: The Romance of an American Elite

0-02-916785-X FREE PRESS........$24.95

Bernard **Lewis**

Islam and the West

An important and controversial study by a leading scholar of Islam

See also **GENERAL STUDIES** under **ISLAM** in **RELIGION, SPIRITUALITY, AND PHILOSOPHY**

0-19-507619-2 OXFORD........$27.50

0-19-509061-6 OXFORD PB........$13.95

The Contemporary Middle East

John **Bulloch** & others

No Friends but the Mountains: The Tragic History of the Kurds

The nationalistic aspirations of the Kurds—the world's largest group of stateless people—have been exploited from the days of the Ottoman Empire. Written by two veteran Middle East correspondents, *No Friends but the Mountains* is a comprehensive account of the origins and history of the Kurds—and one that explains the centrality of the Kurds to the complex politics of the region in the aftermath of the Gulf War

0-19-508075-0 OXFORD........$30.00

Edmund **Burke**, III & Ira M. **Lapidus**, editors

Islam, Politics, and Social Movements

The "new social" and "new cultural" history used to explore the social protest and political resistance movements in Islamic countries in the 19th and 20th centuries. Contributions from specialists on Islamic North Africa, Egypt, the Arab fertile crescent, Iran, and India

0-520-06868-8 CALIFORNIA PB........$13.95

Clifford **Geertz**

Islam Observed: Religious Development in Morocco and Indonesia

The anthropologist draws conclusions about the nature of religious belief from the development of a single creed, Islam, in two quite different civilizations

See also **ISLAM TODAY** under **ISLAM** in **RELIGION, SPIRITUALITY, AND PHILOSOPHY**

0-226-28511-1 CHICAGO PB........$7.95

Arthur **Goldschmidt**, Jr.

A Concise History of the Middle East

Conversational, direct, and trenchant history with incisive but sympathetic critiques of all the parties involved; revised

0-8133-1117-9 WESTVIEW........$61.00

0-8133-1118-7 WESTVIEW PB........$24.95

Albert **Hourani**

Arabic Thought in the Liberal Age, 1798-1939

Demonstrates how two streams of thought, one aiming to restore the social principles of Islam, the other justifying the separation of religion and politics, merge to create contemporary nationalisms

0-521-27423-0 CAMBRIDGE PB........$28.95

David **Lamb**

The Arabs: Journeys Beyond the Mirage

Inside the Arab world, in the journalistic tradition of John Gunther

0-394-75758-0 VINTAGE PB........$15.00

Barbara **Tuchman**

Bible and Sword: England and Palestine from the Bronze Age to Balfour

Traces a crucial relationship through the Crusades, the need to secure passage to India, and the impassioned tourism of the 19th century

0-345-31427-1 BALLANTINE PB........$15.00

Milton **Viorst**

Sandcastles: The Arabs in Search of the Modern World

New Yorker writer interviews Nobel Prize-winner Mahfouz on the secret splendors of Cairo and travels to Syria, Lebanon, Kuwait, Jordan, and to the Palestinian camps. The Arab state, he concludes, are "as fragile as sandcastles." A book that emphasizes, and clarifies, the cultural complexities of the region. "An informed, intelligent, and remarkably unbiased judgment to a timely subject"—*Kirkus Reviews*

0-679-40599-2 KNOPF........$25.00

Contemporary Politics and Society

Fouad **Ajami**

The Arab Predicament: Arab Political Thought and Practice Since 1967

"Ajami understands Arab politics; though angry and impatient with its shortcomings, he empathizes with it; though passionate, he writes with insight and clarity"—*Middle East Journal*

See also **ISLAM TODAY** under **ISLAM** in **RELIGION, SPIRITUALITY, AND PHILOSOPHY**

0-521-43243-X CAMBRIDGE........$49.95

0-521-43833-0 CAMBRIDGE PB........$11.95

Jimmy **Carter**

The Blood of Abraham: Insights into the Middle East

The former president's analysis of the area of his greatest success and greatest failure

1-55728-293-5 ARKANSAS PB........$18.00

Guilain **Denoeux**

Urban Unrest in the Middle East: A Comparative Study of Informal Networks in Egypt, Iran, and Lebanon

An original contribution to the debate over the political consequences of urbanization in what used to be called the Third World

0-7914-1524-4 SUNY PB........$17.95

Dale F. **Eickelman** & James **Piscatori**

Muslim Politics

How the politics of Islam play out in the daily lives of Muslims throughout the world; an attempt to demystify "Muslim politics" for a wide audience

0-691-00870-1 PRINCETON PB............$13.95

Michael **Field**

Inside the Arab World

Includes developments since the Gulf War and the pact between Israel and the PLO. "With a refreshing lack of stridency…charts a course from the decay of the Ottoman empire to the uncertainties of today"—*Economist*

0-674-45521-5 HARVARD PB............$15.95

Thomas **Friedman**

From Beirut to Jerusalem

A personal account of the conflicts between Arab and Israeli by the Pulitzer Prize-winning correspondent. "A sparkling intellectual guidebook…an engrossing journey not to be missed"—*The Wall Street Journal*

See also **HISTORY, POLITICS, AND SOCIETY** under **20TH-CENTURY AMERICAN ESSAYS AND JOURNALISM** in **LITERATURE OF THE AMERICAS**

0-374-15895-9 FS&G............$25.00
0-385-41372-6 ANCHOR PB............$14.00

David **Fromkin**

A Peace to End All Peace: Creating the Modern Middle East, 1914-1922

The best survey of the early-20th-century background of today's crises: how the collapse of the Ottoman Empire and the subsequent involvement of Great Britain and France laid the groundwork for contemporary problems in the Middle East. The international cast includes David Lloyd George, Lawrence of Arabia, Kitchener of Khartoum, V.I. Lenin, Chaim Weizmann, David Ben-Gurion, Ibn Saud, Kemal Ataturk, and Winston Churchill

0-380-71300-4 AVON PB............$14.95

Iraq: 1918

Unlike Arab nationalists, who were thinking in terms of political unity on a large scale, there were those who questioned whether even attempting to unite the Mesopotamian provinces might not be too ambitious to be practical. Gertrude Bell, working on her own plans for unified Iraq, was cautioned by an American missionary that she was ignoring rooted historical realities in doing so. "You are flying in the face of four millenniums of history if you try to draw a line around Iraq and call it a political entity! Assyria always looked to the west and east and north, and Babylonia to the south. They have never been an independent unit. You've got to get them integrated, but it must be done gradually. They have no conception of nationhood yet."

A PEACE TO END ALL PEACE: CREATING THE MODERN MIDDLE EAST, 1914-1922

Charles **Glass**

Tribes with Flags: A Dangerous Passage Through the Chaos of the Middle East

A journey from the southern Turkish coast around the bay of Alexandretta through Syria, Israel, Jordan, and Lebanon—the entire spectrum of Levantine life—by the veteran Middle East journalist

0-87113-457-8 ATLANTIC MONTHLY PB............$12.95

T.E. Lawrence

Albert **Hourani**

The Modern Middle East: A Reader

0-520-08241-9 CALIFORNIA PB............$20.00

Kanan **Makiya**

Cruelty and Silence: War, Tyranny, Uprising, and the Arab World

0-393-31141-4 NORTON PB............$10.95

Fatima **Mernissi**

Islam and Democracy: Fear of the Modern World

How can the Islamic world achieve democracy, asks the author of this provocative work, if those opposing fundamentalism have to use the same sacred texts as the violent fundamentalists? Essential reading on democracy and human rights in Islamic culture by a noted Moroccan professor of sociology

0-201-60883-9 ADDISON-WESLEY............$24.95

Judith **Miller**

God Has Ninety-Nine Names: A Reporter's Journey Through a Militant Middle East

This country-by-country account of today's Middle East is based on the author's unique access and experience as the Cairo bureau chief of *The New York Times* and special correspondent during the Gulf War. With her we visit the Hezbollah headquarters in Lebanon, the royal palace in Amman, the slums of Cairo, and an Israeli interrogation cell. And we come to understand that there is no unified Arab world and no single Islam, but rather a struggle for power and identity and a battle between secularism and militant fundamentalism

See also **ISLAM TODAY** under **ISLAM** in **RELIGION, SPIRITUALITY, AND PHILOSOPHY**

0-684-80973-7 SIMON & SCHUSTER............$30.00

Edward **Mortimer**

Farm and Power: The Politics of Islam

0-394-71173-4 RANDOM HOUSE PB............$13.32

Edward W. **Said**

Covering Islam: How the Media and the Experts Determine How We See the Rest of the World

0-394-74808-5 RANDOM HOUSE PB............$12.00

Joyce Shira **Starr**

Covenant over Middle Eastern Waters: Key to World Survival

0-8050-3019-0 HOLT............$25.00

Robin **Wright**

Sacred Rage: The Wrath of Militant Islam

A Middle East correspondent approaches Islamic fundamentalism through first-hand knowledge of Beirut, Damascus, and Teheran, combined with interviews of guerrillas and religious leaders

0-671-60113-X SIMON & SCHUSTER............$17.95

Women

Geraldine **Brooks**

Nine Parts of Desire: The Hidden World of Islamic Women

The prize-winning UN correspondent for *The Wall Street Journal* spent six years in the Middle East covering wars, insurrections, and the grim eruptions of fundamentalism. When her Egyptian translator gave up a Harvard scholarship to take the veil, Brooks's sharp analytic eye focused on the complex political, religious, and cultural forces defining the restricted life of women in Islam. From tea with Khomeini's widow to a Saudi Arabian bacchanal, Brooks explores the surprising world of Islamic women and finds a flowering of feminism behind the *chador*

0-385-47577-2 ANCHOR PB............$12.95

Elizabeth Warnock **Fernea**

Women and the Family in the Middle East: New Voices of Change

A progress report: essays, stories, life histories, poems, and documents

0-292-75529-5 TEXAS PB............$16.95

Sarah **Graham-Brown**

Images of Women: The Portrayal of Women in Photography of the Middle East, 1860-1950

0-231-06826-3 COLUMBIA............$49.50
0-231-06827-1 COLUMBIA PB............$23.50

Nadia **Hijab**

Womanpower: The Arab Debate on Women at Work

0-521-26992-X CAMBRIDGE PB............$18.95

Fatima **Mernissi**

Beyond the Veil: Male-Female Dynamics in Modern Muslim Society

An exploration of the suppression of female sexuality in the Muslim tradition, and the disorienting effect of modern life; revised edition

See also **WOMEN AND SEXUALITY** under **SPECIALIZED STUDIES** under **ANTHROPOLOGY** in **SOCIAL STUDIES**

0-253-20423-2 INDIANA PB....................$10.95

Freidoune **Sahebjam**

The Stoning of Soraya M.

The author of this unforgettable story had fled to Paris after he was condemned to death by the Khomeni regime for his writings. In 1987 he returned, incognito, to Iran, where he came upon the story of Soraya M., a quiet, faithful wife mired in drudgery and abuse. Eager to get rid of her, her husband accused her of adultery. Judged guilty by virtue of her stunned silence, she was buried up to her neck and stoned to death by her fellow villagers. Her father threw the first stone. "An indelible retelling—implacable, elegiac, simmering with moral outrage.... Brilliantly written and translated"—*Kirkus Reviews*

See also **THE ISLAMIC REPUBLIC** under **IRAN**

1-55970-270-2 ARCADE PB....................$9.95

"Remember that this woman was not the first woman to be stoned to death in our country since the law of the Almighty has been reinstated here. Dozens of others before her have met a like fate, and others will follow if, once again, God is desecrated or defiled...God willed that I save your village from evil and from sin."
—Sheik Hassanin in THE STONING OF SORAYA M.

Society

Akbar S. **Ahmad**

Towards an Islamic Anthropology

0-317-52455-0 NEW ERA PB....................$3.50

Allen **Douglas** & Fedwa **Malti-Douglas**

Arab Comic Strips

0-253-31814-9 INDIANA....................$39.95
0-253-20831-9 INDIANA PB....................$19.95

Dale F. **Eickelman**

The Middle East: An Anthropological Approach

0-13-582289-0 PRENTICE HALL PB....................$44.95

Elizabeth Warnock **Fernea** & Robert A. **Fernea**

The Arab World: Personal Encounters

Anecdotes of the anthropologists' experiences counteract the stereotypes

0-385-23973-4 ANCHOR PB....................$14.00

Brinkley **Messick**

The Calligraphic State: Textual Domination and History in a Muslim Society

0-520-07605-2 CALIFORNIA....................$42.50
0-520-20515-4 CALIFORNIA PB....................$18.95

Fundamentalism

Richard W. **Bulliet**

Islam: The View from the Edge

0-231-08218-5 COLUMBIA....................$34.50
0-231-08219-3 COLUMBIA PB....................$16.00

John L. **Esposito**

Voices of Resurgent Islam

Muslim and non-Muslim scholars of history, religion, and political science offer direct access to the nature and agenda of contemporary Islam

0-19-503339-6 OXFORD....................$38.00
0-19-503340-X OXFORD PB....................$17.95

Henry **Munson**, Jr.

Islam and Revolution in the Middle East

0-300-04127-6 YALE....................$22.50
0-300-04604-9 YALE PB....................$12.00

V.S. Naipaul

V.S. **Naipaul**

Among the Believers: An Islamic Journey

A foremost novelist, essayist, and frequently controversial sociopolitical critic, born of Indian parents in Trinidad but a British resident since the 1950s, provides commentary on Iran, Pakistan, Malaysia, and Indonesia, to the "Islamic Winter" of the final chapter

See also **TRINIDAD AND TOBAGO** under **CARIBBEAN LITERATURE** in **LITERATURE OF THE AMERICAS**

See also **THE NEAR AND MIDDLE EAST** under **ASIA** under **TRAVEL LITERATURE** in **FOOD, TRAVEL, AND LEISURE**

0-394-71195-5 RANDOM HOUSE PB....................$15.00

Yann **Richard**

Shi'ite Islam

"A primer and introduction to Shi'itism and...a brilliant account of revolutionary theory in Iran"—Ira M. Lapidus

TRANSLATED BY ANTONIA NEVILL

1-55786-470-5 BLACKWELL PB....................$21.95

Egypt

Selma **Botman**

Egypt from Independence to Revolution, 1919-1952

0-8156-2531-6 SYRACUSE PB....................$14.95

Amitav **Ghosh**

In an Antique Land

A vivid account of ancient and modern Egypt in which the author-historian uncovers the life of a slave who lived 800 years ago. Combining history with cultural investigation, travel writing with storytelling, Ghosh explains the strange and intense relationship that developed across centuries between his subject and himself

See also **NORTH AFRICA** under **AFRICA** under **TRAVEL LITERATURE** in **FOOD, TRAVEL, AND LEISURE**

0-679-72783-3 VINTAGE PB....................$13.00

By the time the trading nations of the Indian Ocean began to realize that their old understandings had been rendered defunct by the Europeans it was already too late. In 1509 AD the fate of that ancient trading culture was sealed in a naval engagement that was sadly, perhaps pathetically, evocative of its ethos: a transcontinental fleet, hastily put together by the Muslim potentate of Gujarat, the Hindu ruler of Calicut, and the Sultan of Egypt was attacked and defeated by a Portuguese force off the shores of Diu, in Gujarat. As always, the determination of a small, united band of soldiers triumphed easily over the rich confusions that accompany a culture of accommodation and compromise.
IN AN ANTIQUE LAND

Derek **Hopwood**

Egypt: Politics and Society, 1945-1984

0-415-09432-1 ROUTLEDGE PB....................$16.95

William Roger **Louis** & Roger **Owen**, editors

Suez 1956: The Crisis and Its Consequences

0-19-820141-9 OXFORD PB....................$45.00

Anwar Sadat

Ghali **Shoukri**

Egypt, Portrait of a President: Sadat's Road to Jerusalem

0-86232-072-0 HUMANITIES PB $12.50

P.J. **Vatikiotis**

History of Modern Egypt: From Muhammad Ali to Mubarak

0-8018-4215-8 JOHNS HOPKINS PB $18.95

John **Waterbury**

The Egypt of Nasser and Sadat: The Political Economy of Two Regimes

Probes the failure of the socialist transformation of Egypt under two presidents

0-691-07650-2 PRINCETON $68.00
0-691-10147-7 PRINCETON PB $21.95

Iran

Said Amir **Arjomand**

The Shadow of God and the Hidden Name: Religion, Political Order, and Societal Change in Shi'ite Iran from the Beginning to 1890

Influenced by Max Weber, this is both a history and sociology of the long relationship between Shi'ism and political organization

0-226-02782-1 CHICAGO $28.00
0-226-02784-8 CHICAGO PB $14.95

Cosroe **Chaqueri**

The Soviet Socialist Republic of Iran, 1920-1921: Birth of the Trauma

Original scholarship on a fascinating aspect of 20th century Iranian history

0-8229-3792-1 PITTSBURGH $75.00

Shusha **Guppy**

The Blindfold Horse: Memories of a Persian Childhood

"A gifted weaver of tales with an artist's eye for sketching characters in context. Guppy evokes the magic, cultural traditions and social fabric of her growing-up years, which were greatly affected by both Reza Shah's efforts to westernize Persia in the 1920s and the ensuing revolution led by bigoted Mullahs"
—*Publishers Weekly*

0-8070-7043-2 BEACON PB $12.95

From dawn till dusk the Bazaar seethed with a motley crowd of shoppers, peddlers, porters and errand-boys, brokers, layabouts and beggars, who bargained, pleaded, haggled and proclaimed their sincerity and honesty.
THE BLINDFOLD HORSE: MEMORIES OF A PERSIAN CHILDHOOD

Inge Demant **Mortensen**

Nomads of Luristan and Their Material Culture

0-500-01572-4 THAMES & HUDSON $50.00

Sayyed Mohammed Ali **Jamalzadeh**

Isfahan Is Half the World: Memories of a Persian Boyhood

Life in Iran at the turn of the century in the family of an enlightened Muslim clergyman

0-691-10186-8 PRINCETON PB $17.50

The Iranian Revolution

Ervand **Abrahamian**

The Iranian Mojahedin

Probes the social background of their leadership, the Marxist influence of their interpretation of Islam, and why they failed to gain political power in the early stages of the Revolution

0-300-05267-7 YALE PB $19.00

Said Amir **Arjomand**

The Turban for the Crown: The Islamic Revolution in Iran

0-19-504257-3 OXFORD $35.00
0-19-504258-1 OXFORD PB $11.95

Ryszard **Kapuscinski**

Shah of Shahs

Verbal snapshots capture the theater of the popular Islamic revolution that toppled the Shah

See also **POLISH LITERATURE** under **EASTERN EUROPEAN LITERATURE** in **LITERATURE OF EUROPE, AFRICA, AND ASIA**

TRANSLATED BY W.R. BRAND & K. MROCZKOWSKA-BRAND

0-679-73801-0 VINTAGE PB $11.00

Nikki R. **Keddie** & Yann **Richard**

Roots of Revolution: An Interpretive History of Modern Iran

"If one has a limited time to gain an appreciation of the revolutionary force of Islam in Iran, it should be spent here"
—Scott Armstrong, *Washington Post Book World*

0-300-02606-4 YALE $40.00
0-300-02611-0 YALE PB $17.00

The Islamic Republic

Cheryl **Benard** & Zatmay **Khalilzad**

The Government of God: Iran's Islamic Republic

0-231-05376-2 COLUMBIA $45.50
0-231-05377-0 COLUMBIA PB $16.50

Richard **Cottam**

Iran and the United States: A Cold War Case Study

A State Department veteran traces the flaws in the US relationship with Iran, culminating in the arms-for-hostages scandal

0-8229-3588-0 PITTSBURGH $49.95

Sandra **Mackey**

The Iranians: Persia, Islam and the Soul of a Nation

0-525-94005-7 DUTTON $26.95

Roy **Mottahedeh**

The Mantle of the Prophet: Religion and Politics in Contemporary Iran

0-394-74865-4 RANDOM HOUSE PB $17.00

Freidoune **Sahebjam**

The Stoning of Soraya M.

See also **WOMEN** under **CONTEMPORARY POLITICS AND SOCIETY**

1-55970-270-2 ARCADE PB $9.95

Iraq

Efraim **Karsh** & Inari **Rautsi**

Saddam Hussein: A Political Biography

The authors seek to explain Saddam Hussein's paranoia and ruthlessness by examining his background, motives, and the often brutal context of Iraqi politics

0-02-917063-X FREE PRESS $27.95

Kanan **Makiya**

Cruelty and Silence: War, Tyranny, and Uprising in the Arab World

0-393-03108-X NORTON $22.95

Christine **Moss-Helms**

Iraq: Eastern Flank of the Arab World

Analyzes the power of tradition, the rise of the Ba'ath Socialist party, and the war with Iran

0-8157-3556-1 BROOKINGS PB $28.95

Yitzhak **Nakash**

The Shi'is of Iraq

0-691-03431-1 PRINCETON $45.00

G.L. **Simons**

Iraq: From Sumer to Saddam

0-312-16052-6 ST. MARTIN'S PB $17.95

The Iran-Iraq War

M.S. **El Azhary**, editor

The Iran-Iraq War: An Historical, Economic and Political Analysis

0-312-43583-5 ST. MARTIN'S $29.95

Majid **Khadduri**

The Gulf War: The Origins and Implications of the Iraq-Iran Conflict

Hostilities over boundaries, religion, and ethnic groups, particularly since World War II, get close attention from a military expert and Arab scholar at Johns Hopkins

0-19-508384-9 OXFORD $25.00

Edgar **O'Ballance**

The Gulf War: 1980-1987

0-08-034747-9 BRASSEY'S DEFENSE $43.00

Saddam Hussein

Senator Simpson:…The last thing you talked about was democracy. Democracy is a very confusing issue. I believe that your problems lie with the Western media, and not with the U.S. government. As long as you are isolated from the media, the press—and it is a haughty and pampered press—they all consider themselves political geniuses. That is, the journalists do. They are very cynical. What I advise is that you invite them to come here and see for themselves.

President Hussein: They are welcome. We hope they will come to see Iraq, and after they do, write whatever they like, and say that they liked this and they didn't like that. No, we are not at all too sensitive toward the media. We hope they will come. I will grant your Ambassador my approval for all the media in the US. We welcome anyone who wants to come here: there is no veto against anyone…—*Conversation between Senator Alan Simpson and President Saddam Hussein, Baghdad, April 12, 1990*

THE MARCH TO WAR

The Gulf Conflict, 1990-1991

Lawrence **Freedman** & Efraim **Karsh**

The Gulf Conflict: 1990-1991, Diplomacy and War in the New World Order

Throughout their discussion of the events surrounding the war, Freedman and Karsh address not only American but European, Soviet, and Middle Eastern decisions. They show how President Bush found it necessary to buttress Gorbachev and to set aside Tiananmen Square in order to marshall the support he needed for his air war on Iraq. "It is unlikely that there will be a better balanced or more comprehensive chronicle"

—H.D.S. Greenaway, *NY Times Book Review*

0-691-08627-3 PRINCETON $45.00

Michael **Kelly**

Martyr's Day: Chronicle of a Small War

Kelly was an eyewitness to almost every major event of the Gulf War: the bombing of Baghdad, the attacks on Israel, the American assault into Kuwait, and the tragic events in Kurdestan. His dispatches won him a National Magazine Award and an Overseas Press Club Award. This narrative covers the war in human terms, capturing Kelly's own extraordinary experiences as well as the political and social consequences of the war

See also **REPORTING** under **20TH-CENTURY AMERICAN ESSAYS AND JOURNALISM** in **LITERATURE OF THE AMERICAS**

0-679-75014-2 VINTAGE PB $12.00

James **Ridgeway**, editor

The March to War

A casebook on the Gulf War, with a chronology of events and a well-chosen selection of relevant transcripts and press clippings. Ridgeway writes the "Moving Target" political column for the *Village Voice*

0-941423-61-1 FOUR WALLS PB $9.95

Elaine **Sciolino**

The Outlaw State: Saddam Hussein's Quest for Power and the Gulf Crisis

An authoritative analysis of Saddam Hussein's motives and background, and of the forces with which he collaborated and eventually collided. Sciolino is a diplomatic correspondent for the *New York Times*. "Riveting…A highly readable account of the events leading up to the Iraqi invasion of Kuwait and the conflict that followed…"—Gary Sick

0-471-54299-7 WILEY $22.95

Micah **Sifry**, editor

The Gulf War Reader: History, Documents, Opinions

A comprehensive anthology on the war, spanning the gamut of opinion on America's involvement. Contributors include: George Bush, Jimmy Carter, Walter Cronkite, Barbara Ehrenreich, David Halberstam, Christopher Hitchens, Saddam Hussein, Henry Kissinger, and William Safire. "A timely and indispensable guide to the underlying issues, interests, and passions that erupted in the world's first post-Cold War conflict"

—Eric Utne, editor-in-chief, *The Utne Reader*

0-8129-1947-5 TIME BOOKS PB $17.00

Hedrick **Smith**, editor

The Media and the Gulf War: The Press and Democracy in Wartime

The Gulf War established a new basis for media coverage, controlling the flow of information to an unprecedented degree. In this volume journalists, academics, and members of the military come together to discuss the issues raised by these new rules

0-932020-97-6 SEVEN LOCKS $9.95

Kenneth R. **Timmerman**

The Death Lobby: How the West Armed Iraq

Timmerman exposes the often-ignored story of how the US, England, Germany, and France helped create the Gulf crisis by their indiscriminate, enthusiastic sales of weaponry to Saddam Hussein. A riveting expose of the triumph of short-term profits over long-term self-interest

0-395-59305-0 HOUGHTON MIFFLIN $21.95

Israel

For related reading, see JEWISH HISTORY

Amos **Elon**

Jerusalem: City of Mirrors

The hub of three religions, Jerusalem is boldly heterogeneous. Powerful civilizations—Roman, Byzantine, Ottoman, and British—have fought to control it. Elon counts "twenty ruinous sieges, two intervals of total destruction, eighteen reconstructions, and at least eleven transitions from one religion to another." A native of the city, Elon writes perceptively yet informally. "A brilliantly illuminating book about the religion of nationalism no less than the religions of faith"—Philip Roth

1-56836-099-1 KODANSHA PB $13.00

Howard Morley **Sachar**

A History of Israel

Volume 1
From the Rise of Zionism to Our Time

An updated edition, due out in early 1997

0-679-44632-X KNOPF $25.00

Volume 2
From the Aftermath of the Yom Kippur War

0-19-504386-3 OXFORD $27.95

0-19-594623-4 OXFORD PB $12.95

Nadav **Safran**

Israel: The Embattled Ally

This in-depth story of Israel since its founding focuses on its relationship with the US and includes a brilliant analysis of Kissinger's Israel policy

See also **THE 20TH-CENTURY WORLD** under **INTERNATIONAL RELATIONS AND STRATEGIC STUDIES** in **SOCIAL STUDIES**

0-674-46881-3 HARVARD $42.50

0-674-46882-1 BELKNAP PB $19.95

Hershel **Shanks**

Jerusalem: An Archaeological Biography

The eminent archaeologist presents a beautifully illustrated, enormously readable archaeological history of Jerusalem. From the discovery of the crucified heel of a first-century Jewish rebel to the search for King David's tomb, Shanks enlivens history while simultaneously providing a fascinating account of the processes of archaeology

See also **COMPARATIVE RELIGION** under **WORLD RELIGION** in **RELIGION, SPIRITUALITY, AND PHILOSOPHY**

0-679-44526-9 RANDOM HOUSE $50.00

Andrew **Sinclair**

Jerusalem: The Endless Crusade

0-517-59476-5 CROWN $24.00

David **Vital**

The Future of the Jews

A challenging meditation on the increasing international isolation of Israel and the assimilation and lack of cohesion in Jewish communities in the Diaspora

0-674-33925-8 HARVARD $20.00

A.B. **Yehoshua** & Frederic **Brenner**

Israel

A beautiful coffee-table book commemorating Israel's history and 40th anniversary

0-06-015959-6 HARPER & ROW $30.00

Independence, 1948

Larry **Coffins** & Dominique **Lapierre**

O Jerusalem!

Bestselling account of the day-to-day story of the founding of the state of Israel in 1948

0-671-66241-4 TOUCHSTONE PB $16.00

Allon **Gal**

David Ben-Gurion and the American Alignment for a Jewish State

0-253-32534-X INDIANA $29.95

David Ben-Gurion

Jon **Kimche** & David **Kimche**

The Secret Roads: The Illegal Migration of a People

0-88355-329-5 HYPERION $23.00

Jehuda **Reinharz**

Chaim Weizmann: The Making of a Zionist

0-19-505069-X OXFORD PB $15.95

Shabtai **Teveth**

Ben-Gurion: The Burning Ground, 1886-1948

0-395-48358-1 HOUGHTON MIFFLIN PB $12.95

Israel Since 1948

Muki **Betser** & Robert **Rosenberg**

Secret Soldier

0-87113-637-6 ATLANTIC MONTHLY $23.00

Karen **Armstrong**

Jerusalem: One City, Three Faiths

The widely acclaimed author of *A History of God* continues her exploration of the varieties of religious experience with a riveting account of monotheism's epicenter. Tracing the city of Jerusalem from its beginnings three thousand years B.C.E., she shows it in its religious, mythic, and political aspects through to the present day. A *tour de force*

See also **COMPARATIVE RELIGION** under **WORLD RELIGION** in **RELIGION, SPIRITUALITY, AND PHILOSOPHY**

0-679-43596-4 KNOPF $30.00

Bernard **Avishai**

The Tragedy of Zionism: Revolution and Democracy in the Land of Israel

See also **ORIGINS OF ZIONISM** under **JEWISH HISTORY**

0-374-27863-6 FS&G $5.98

Amos **Elon**

Israelis: Founders and Sons

0-14-016969-5 PENGUIN PB $11.95

Moses **Hess**

The Revival of Israel: Rome and Jerusalem, the Last Nationalist Question

0-8032-7275-8 NEBRASKA PB $10.00

Shimon **Peres**

Battling For Peace: A Memoir

These candid memoirs go behind the scenes to tell of his quarrels with Golda Meir, the origins of Israel's nuclear program, the secret talks with King Hussein, and the path to Oslo

0-679-43617-0 RANDOM HOUSE $25.00

Golda Meir

Abraham **Rabinovich**

The Battle for Jerusalem: 20th Anniversary Edition

A *Jerusalem Post* reporter reconstructs the events of June 5-7, 1967

FOREWORD BY TEDDY KOLLEK

0-8276-0285-5 JEWISH PUB SOCIETY PB $17.95

Jerusalem on Earth: People, Passions, and Politics in the Holy City

0-02-925740-9 FREE PRESS $22.95

Tom **Segev**

The Seventh Million: The Israelis and the Holocaust

See also **THE HOLOCAUST**

TRANSLATED BY HAIM WATZMAN

0-8090-8563-1 HILL & WANG $27.50

0-8090-1570-6 HILL & WANG PB $15.00

Yitzhak **Shamir**

Summing Up: An Autobiography

Shamir's life is a fascinating journey from 1915 Poland, through his adventures in the shadowy Zionist underground, to the birth of Israel and the leadership of the country for which he spent his life fighting. It is also the inside story of a current of Israeli thought that opposed territorial compromise and was prepared to fight bitterly against any perceived threat to the Jewish state. A fascinating self-portrait of a kind of Zionism recent history has eclipsed

0-316-96825-0 LITTLE, BROWN $24.95

Robert **Wistrich**, editor

The Left Against Zion: Communism, Israel and the Middle East

0-85303-193-2 MITCHELL $25.00

Arabs, Israelis, and the Palestinian Question

American Friends Service Committee

A Compassionate Peace: A Future for Israel and the Palestinians

An updated version of the 1981 work by a Harvard educator

EDITED BY EVERETT MENDELSOHN

0-8090-1536-6 HILL & WANG PB $8.95

Meron **Bevenisti**

Intimate Enemies: Jews and Arabs in a Shared Land

The deputy mayor of Jerusalem from '71 to '78, largely responsible for administering Arab East Jerusalem, addresses the expectations for a "peaceful partition" in a brave and controversial book that argues that only a confederation of Israel and Palestine can bring a real and lasting peace. "Few Americans can appreciate the intensity, substance, and complexity of the struggles in Israel without reading this book" —Ian Lustick

FOREWORD BY THOMAS L. FRIEDMAN

0-520-08567-1 CALIFORNIA $24.95

Yitzhak Rabin

Arieh L. **Avneri**

The Claim of Dispossession: Jewish Land Settlement and the Arabs, 1878-1948

0-87855-964-7 TRANSACTION PB $16.95

Noam **Chomsky**

The Fateful Triangle: The United States, Israel and the Palestinians

A critical look at the situation in Israel that blames the US for what some perceive as the intransigence of Israeli government policies toward the Palestinians

0-89608-188-5 SOUTH END $40.00
0-89608-187-7 SOUTH END PB $18.00

Uri **Davis**

Israel: An Apartheid State

A prominent Israeli academic illustrates the legal provisions that institutionalize racial discrimination and considers the positions of various Israeli opposition movements

0-86232-317-7 ZED $39.95
0-86232-318-5 ZED PB $15.00

David **Grossman**

The Yellow Wind

A nonfictional account of relations between Arab and Jew in Israel's occupied territories

See also **FICTION** under **ISRAELI LITERATURE** under **MODERN HEBREW LITERATURE** in **LITERATURE OF EUROPE, AFRICA, AND ASIA**

TRANSLATED BY HAIM WATZMAN

0-374-29345-7 FS&G $17.95

Shulamith **Hareven**

The Vocabulary of Peace: Life, Culture, and Politics in the Middle East

Hareven proposes replacing the rhetoric of hate between Israelis and Palestinians with a "vocabulary of peace"

TRANSLATED BY MARCIA WEINSTEIN & OTHERS

1-56279-072-2 MERCURY HOUSE PB $14.95

Mark **Heller**

A Palestinian State: The Implications for Israel

A researcher at the Institute for Strategic Studies, Tel Aviv, argues that Israel's security may depend on the creation of a Palestinian state

0-674-65221-5 HARVARD $25.00
0-674-65222-3 HARVARD PB $8.95

Chaim **Herzog**

The Arab-Israel Wars: War and Peace in the Middle East

A largely military overview of more than three decades of Arab-Israeli warfare

0-394-71746-5 RANDOM HOUSE PB $16.00

Baruch **Kimmerling** & Joel S. **Migdal**

Palestinians: The Making of a People

Sensitively shows how this diffuse and tormented society has been forced to acquire a national identity through its interaction with the Israeli state

0-02-917321-3 FREE PRESS $32.95

Walter **Laqueur** & Barry **Rubin**, editors

The Israel-Arab Reader: A Documentary History of the Middle East Conflict

An illuminating collection of statements representing a wide range of views

0-14-024562-6 PENGUIN PB $15.95

David **McDowall**

Palestine and Israel: The Uprising and Beyond

"A masterpiece: by far the most penetrating and comprehensive analysis of the Palestine problem that I have read"
— Edward Mortimer, *The Financial Times*

0-520-06902-1 CALIFORNIA $32.50

Benny **Morris**

The Birth of the Palestinian Refugee Problem, 1947-1949

This 1988 book by an Israeli historian draws on previously unavailable sources to argue that neither the official Arab version—that Arabs were driven wholesale from their homes by Israeli terror—nor the official Israeli version—that Arab leaders broadcast orders for all Arabs to leave Palestine—is without serious omissions and historical distortions

0-521-33028-9 CAMBRIDGE $39.50
0-521-33889-1 CAMBRIDGE PB $22.95

Itamar **Rabinovich**

The Road Not Taken: Early Arab-Israeli Negotiations

Rabinovich, Rector of Tel Aviv University and author of *The War for Lebanon, 1970-1982*, takes a new look at the lost opportunities for negotiation between Israel and its Arab neighbors. He focuses on the talks that occurred between 1949 and 1952 in the wake of the 1948 war for independence, and shows how mistakes made then have precipitated deeper problems

0-19-506066-0 OXFORD $22.95

Rosemary Radford **Ruether** & Herman J. **Ruether**

The Wrath of Jonah: The Crisis of Religious Nationalism in the Israeli-Palestinian Conflict

0-06-066837-7 HARPERCOLLINS $19.95

Edward W. **Said**

Peace and Its Discontents: Essays on Palestine in the Middle East Peace Process

0-679-76725-8 VINTAGE PB $12.00

The Question of Palestine

In illumination of the tragic conflict from a Palestinian point of view

0-679-73988-2 VINTAGE PB $12.00

Gershon **Shafir**

Land, Labor and the Origins of the Israeli-Palestinian Conflict, 1882-1914

Challenges the "heroic myths" about the foundation of the state of Israel by investigating the struggle to control land and labor during the early Zionist enterprise. The author claims that it was not the imported Zionist ideas that were responsible for the character of the Israeli state, but the particular conditions of the local conflict between the European "settlers" and the Palestinian Arab population. "A groundbreaking analysis of the dynamics of Jewish-Arab relations"—Roger Owen

0-520-20401-8 CALIFORNIA PB $15.95

David **Shipler**

Arab and Jew: Wounded Spirits in a Promised Land

The origins of the prejudices currently intensified by war, terrorism, and religious fervor

0-14-010376-7 PENGUIN PB $11.95

Avi **Shlaim**

Collusion Across the Jordan: King Abdullah, the Zionist Movement, and the Partition of Palestine

Working from recently declassified documents, Shlaim tells of the clandestine diplomacy and collusion that left Palestinian Arabs without a homeland

0-231-06838-7 COLUMBIA $63.00

The PLO

Helena **Cobban**

The Palestinian Liberation Organisation: People, Power, and Politics

A Beirut correspondent shows the importance of Al-Fatah in the development of the PLO

0-521-27216-5 CAMBRIDGE PB $19.95

Alan **Hart**

Arafat: A Political Biography

The first American edition

0-253-32711-3 INDIANA $39.95
0-253-20516-6 INDIANA PB $7.50

Rashid **Khalidi**

Under Siege: P.L.O. Decisionmaking During the 1982 War

Inside view of the complex internal negotiations and military maneuvers behind the PLO evacuation of Beirut

0-231-06186-2 COLUMBIA $40.50
0-231-06187-0 COLUMBIA PB $14.50

Danny **Rubinstein**

The Mystery of Arafat

Rubinstein *(The People of Nowhere)* extracts the political history Arafat's years of deadly turmoil from lengthy interviews with Arafat

1-88364-210-8 STEERFORTH $18.00

Yitzhak Shamir & Yasir Arafat

Barbara **Victor**

A Voice of Reason: Hanan Ashrawi and Peace in the Middle East

Ashrawi is well known as the PLO's spokesperson during the Intifada and is single-handedly responsible for the change in the world's perception of the PLO from terrorists to diplomats. Victor shows that this consummate performance was all the more impressive, coming from a woman in a notoriously male-dominated world

0-15-103968-2 HARCOURT BRACE $24.95

Gaza and the West Bank

Paul **Cossali** & Clive **Robson**

Stateless in Gaza

0-86232-508-0 ZED $29.95
0-86232-509-9 ZED PB $9.95

Haim **Gordon**

Quicksand: Israel, the Intifada, and the Rise of Political Evil

The Israeli professor, long at the vanguard of his country's popular criticism of its govermnent's practices during the Intifada, writes movingly and honestly of his confusion at the cruelty of his country toward its Palestinian population. "Gordon...has acted with great courage and integrity, and sought to unearth the significance and import, and the social and psychological roots, of some of the most grim and shameful aspects of human life and practice. His reflections on these matters merit very careful attention"—Noam Chomsky

0-87013-364-0 MICHIGAN STATE $27.95

David **Grossman**

Sleeping on a Wire: Conversations with Palestinians in Israel

Almost onefifth of Israel's citizens are Arabs and they are in a painful position—Arabs in the eyes of Israel's Jewish population, Israelis to the Palestinians. As one man describes his current situation, "my people is at war with my country." This book provides a searching report on their plight by an Israeli Jew intent on understanding them. "A....writer of passionate self honesty, unafraid to ask terrible questions"
—Nadine Gordimer

TRANSLATED BY HAIM WATZMAN

0-374-17788-0 FS&G $22.00
0-374-52400-9 NOONDAY PB $10.00

The Peace Process Today

Hanan **Ashrawi**

This Side of Peace: A Personal Account

Ashrawi, Palestinian activist and negotiator, tells a moving story of life in the territories haunted by the promise of peace

0-684-80294-5 SIMON & SCHUSTER $25.00
0-684-82342-X TOUCHSTONE PB $13.00

Jane **Corbin**

The Norway Channel: The Secret Talks that Led to the Middle East Peace Accord

A BBC reporter tells the story behind the famous handshake in Washington between Yitzhak Rabin and Yasir Arafat in September, 1993. How did two Norwegians, a social scientist and a Foreign Ministry official, succeed in creating a common vision among top-ranking Israelis and Palestinians when even the superpowers had failed?

0-87113-576-0 GROVE $22.00

Mark A. **Heller** & Sari **Nusseibeh**

No Trumpets, No Drums: A Two-State Settlement of the Israeli-Palestinian Conflict

In an unusual collaboration, two writers from either side of the conflict share their own hard-won conviction that in the end reason will prevail in the Middle East. "An absorbing analytical narrative on how to dissolve petrified national differences...*No Trumpets, No Drums* could not have arrived at a better moment"
—J.C. Hurewitz, *NY Times*

0-8090-1562-5 HILL & WANG PB $10.00

Amos **Oz**

Israel, Palestine, and Peace: Essays

The "modern prophet of Israel" *(Sunday Telegraph)* brings his poetic vision and his voice of conscience to advocate a two-state solution

0-15-600192-6 HARVEST PB $11.00

Shimon **Peres**

The New Middle East

A compelling vision of social and economic revival in the Middle East by the former prime minister

0-8050-3811-6 HOLT PB $14.95

Jordan

Uriel **Dann**

King Hussein and the Challenge of Arab Radicalism: Jordan, 1955-1967

The unlikely story of the durability of Jordan and its Hashemite king in the growing years of Arab radicalism

0-19-507134-4 OXFORD PB $16.95

Shaul **Mishal**

West Bank-East Bank: The Palestinians in Jordan, 1949-1967

0-300-02191-7 YALE $20.00

Mahiha **Rashid al Madfai**

Jordan, the United States and the Middle East Peace Process, 1974-1991

0-521-41523-3 CAMBRIDGE $65.00

Lebanon

Fouad **Ajami**

The Vanished Imam: Musa Al Sadr and the Shia of Lebanon

The myth created by the disappearance of a modern-day imam leads to the revival of militant Shi'ism in Lebanon

0-8014-1910-7 CORNELL $29.95
0-8014-9416-8 CORNELL PB $15.95

Mahmoud **Darwish**

Memory for Forgetfulness: August, Beirut, 1982

0-520-08767-4 CALIFORNIA $35.00
0-520-08768-2 CALIFORNIA PB $12.00

Kamal **Salibi**

A House of Many Mansions: The History of Lebanon Reconsidered

0-520-06517-4 CALIFORNIA $35.00
0-520-07196-4 CALIFORNIA PB $15.00

North Africa and the Mediterranean

Algeria

Charles-Robert **Algeron**

Modern Algeria: A History from 1830 to the Present

0-86543-266-X AFRICA WORLD $45.00

Julia A. **Clancy-Smith**

Rebel and Saint: Muslim Notables, Populist Protest, Colonial Encounters: Algeria and Tunisia, 1800-1904

0-520-08242-7 CALIFORNIA....$45.00

Frantz **Fanon**

A Dying Colonialism

Tells how the native Algerians modified their colonized characteristics during the struggle to eject the French. Written by a member of the Algerian liberation movement (FLN)

See also **COLONIALISM** under **POLITICAL THOUGHT** in **SOCIAL STUDIES**

0-8021-5027-6 GROVE PB....$12.00

The Wretched of the Earth

On the need for national liberation movements to release themselves from European models and to develop programs that will apply to all of the world's oppressed. A widely influential book, first published in 1961—the classic and shattering anticolonial handbook from Algeria

See also **COLONIALISM** under **POLITICAL THOUGHT** in **SOCIAL STUDIES**

0-8021-5083-7 GROVE PB....$12.00

William **Spencer**

Algiers in the Age of the Corsairs

0-8061-1334-0 OKLAHOMA....$19.95

Libya

Ali Abdullatif **Ahmida**

The Making of Modern Libya: State Formation, Colonization, and Resistance, 1830-1932

0-7914-1762-X SUNY PB....$19.95

René **Lemarchand**, editor

The Green and the Black: Qadhafi's Policies in Africa

An effort to move beyond the "mad-dog" syndrome as an explanation of Qadhafi's foreign policy

0-253-32678-8 INDIANA....$32.50

Morocco and Tunisia

Douglas **Porch**

The Conquest of the Sahara

The dark side of France's "civilizing mission" and a rich tale of extravagant hopes, genius, and foolhardiness

0-88064-061-8 FROMM PB....$11.95

Michel **Vieuchange**

Smara: The Forbidden City

The diary of a young French adventurer who gave his life in the exploration of the ruins of this ancient Moroccan city

0-88001-146-7 ECCO PB....$9.50

Saudi Arabia

Joseph **Kostiner**

The Making of Saudi Arabia, 1916-1936: From Chieftaincy to Monarchical State

0-19-507440-8 OXFORD....$42.00

Robert **Lacey**

The Kingdom

The inside story of the family at the top of a feudal economy based on oil production, where computer printouts begin by praising the Lord and princesses are beheaded for adultery

0-380-61762-5 AVON PB....$5.95

Sandra **Mackey**

The Saudis: Inside the Desert Kingdom

An excellent overview of one of the world's most hermetic societies

0-452-01063-2 NEW AMERICAN LIBRARY PB....$10.95

Nadav **Safran**

Saudi Arabia: The Ceaseless Quest for Security

This demystification of Saudi policy is based upon the rulers' sense of domestic precariousness

0-8014-9484-2 CORNELL PB....$18.95

Syria

Philip S. **Khoury**

Syria and the French Mandate: The Politics of Arab Nation, 1920-1945

0-691-00843-4 PRINCETON PB....$26.95

Daniel **Pipes**

Greater Syria: The History of an Ambition

0-19-506021-0 OXFORD....$38.00

Patrick **Seale**

Asad: The Struggle for the Middle East

A pro-Syrian account of how Asad developed from a simple country boy into a politician of great subtlety. "A thriller, a textbook and an invaluable contemporary history"
—John le Carré

0-520-06667-7 CALIFORNIA....$40.00

The Struggle for Syria: A Study in Post-War Arab Politics

How the great powers' attempts to control the newly independent Arab states and the recent defeat in Palestine contributed to Syria as it is today

0-300-03944-1 YALE....$47.50

Turkey

Feroz **Ahmad**

The Making of Modern Turkey

The first modern secular state in a predominantly Islamic Middle East, Turkey has become a key, if reluctant, player in the geopolitical landscape. This excellent introduction combines history with in-depth analysis of the socioeconomic and political forces that continue to shape and transform this country

0-415-07835-0 ROUTLEDGE....$55.00
0-415-07836-9 ROUTLEDGE PB....$19.95

Marjorie Housepian **Dobkin**

Smyrna 1922: The Destruction of a City

The tragedy of the final expulsion of Greeks from Asia Minor

0-87338-359-1 KENT STATE PB....$14.00

Bernard **Lewis**

The Emergence of Modern Turkey

A brief and lucid interpretation by the well-known Middle East scholar

0-19-500344-6 OXFORD PB....$17.95

Armenia

Richard G. **Hovannisian**, editor

The Armenian Genocide in Perspective

0-88738-096-4 TRANSACTION....$32.95

Moses **Khorenats'i**

History of the Armenians

TRANSLATED BY R.W. THOMSON

0-674-39571-9 HARVARD....$30.00

Africa

General Histories

Donald **Crummey**, editor

Banditry, Rebellion and Social Protest in Africa

A look at decades of African protest in cultural phenomena such as work songs, stealing, and feigning illnesses

0-435-08011-3 HEINEMANN PB....$27.50

Philip D. **Curtin**

The Atlantic Slave Trade: A Census

This definitive summary vastly revised previous estimates of the traffic in people

0-299-05404-7 WISCONSIN PB....$16.95

Philip D. **Curtin**

Cross-Cultural Trade in World History

Silk from China to Rome, African ivory, the Indian Ocean spice trade: the colorful world of exchange over two millennia

See also ECONOMIC HISTORY under THE VARIETIES OF CIVILIZATION

0-521-26931-8 CAMBRIDGE PB $16.95

Basil **Davidson**

Africa in History

0-684-82667-4 SCRIBNERS PB $16.00

Africa in History—Themes & Outlines

0-02-042791-3 COLLIER PB $16.00

The African Genius: An Introduction to African Social and Cultural History

0-316-17432-7 LITTLE, BROWN PB $13.95

The African Slave Trade

Between the 15th and 19th centuries, perhaps 50 million men, women, and children were captured, bought, or kidnapped from Africa by European slave traders. This is an expanded edition of Davidson's classic account

0-316-17438-6 LITTLE, BROWN PB $12.95

The Lost Cities of Africa

Revised and reissued. "A book which must inspire all Africans to a pride in our past" —Kwame Nkrumah

0-316-17431-9 LITTLE, BROWN PB $14.95

Modern Africa

0-582-21288-X LONGMAN PB $30.75

The Search for Africa

0-8129-2527-0 TIME BOOKS PB $14.00

Cheikh Anta **Diop**

The African Origin of Civilization

African nationalist broadside against historians who sought to sever Egypt from Black Africa; bursting with energy and hyperbole

TRANSLATED & EDITED BY MERCER COOK

1-55652-072-7 INDEPENDENT PUBLISHERS GROUP PB $11.95

J.D. **Fage**

A History of Africa

An excellent introductory text

0-415-12721-1 ROUTLEDGE PB $24.95

Joseph E. **Harris**

Africans and Their History

A black American professor summarizes the literature

0-451-62556-0 MENTOR PB $4.99

John **Iliffe**

The African Poor: A History

That rare commodity in African history, an excellent synthesis. Includes sections on the urban poor, South African townships, and leprosy

0-521-34415-8 CAMBRIDGE $69.95

0-521-34877-3 CAMBRIDGE PB $28.95

John **Iliffe**

Africans: The History of a Continent

"Ranks with the best creative masters of the genre who defined the fields of African history"—Joseph C. Miller, University of Virginia

0-521-48235-6 CAMBRIDGE $64.95

0-521-48422-7 CAMBRIDGE PB $18.95

Robert **July**

An African Voice: The Role of the Humanities in Africa

Intellectual life, theater, and learning, all emphasizing African thinkers

0-8223-0769-3 DUKE PB $16.95

David **Lamb**

The Africans

A *Los Angeles Times* correspondent's impressions of 46 countries

0-394-75308-9 VINTAGE PB $13.00

Mark R. **Lipschutz** & R. Kent **Rasmussen**

Dictionary of African Historical Biography

An acclaimed reference work expanded and updated to include entries on over 800 people important in sub-Saharan history up to 1980

0-520-05179-3 CALIFORNIA $58.00

0-520-06611-1 CALIFORNIA PB $17.00

Phyllis M. **Martin** & Patrick **O'Meara**, editors

Africa

A compendium of essays on politics, culture, history

0-253-20392-9 INDIANA PB $17.95

Ali A. **Mazrui**

The Africans: A Triple Heritage

Companion to the controversial PBS series; an eclectic illustrated journey

0-275-92073-9 GREENWOOD PB $19.95

Roland **Oliver**

The African Experience: Major Themes in African History from Earliest Times to the Present

A grand chronicle of the history of Africa from the tribal settling of regions to the present-day nation-states. "An excellent introduction to African history, based on very wide scholarship, balanced in its approach to controversial issues, and written so that the lay reader has no difficulty in understanding it"—*TLS*

0-06-435850-X HARPERCOLLINS PB $23.00

Roland **Oliver** & Anthony **Atmore**

Africa Since 1800

The third edition of a standard text, focusing on the great civilizations and states of the 19th century

0-521-41946-8 CAMBRIDGE $55.00

Roland **Oliver** & J.D. **Fage**

A Short History of Africa

This excellent introduction has now reached its sixth edition

0-14-013601-0 PENGUIN PB $13.95

Patricia W. **Romero**, editor

Life Histories of African Women

Stories from seven regions, collected by noted specialists

0-948660-05-8 HUMANITIES PB $15.95

Ronald **Segal**

The Black Diaspora: Five Centuries of the Black Experience Outside Africa

"Deserves to be read by anyone who is troubled by the persistence of racism and devoted to the cause of human rights"—George M. Fredrickson

0-374-11396-3 FS&G $27.50

Jan **Vansina**

Oral Tradition as History

The pioneer of oral historiography speaks, drawing heavily from his knowledge of Africa

See also NEW DIRECTIONS under HISTORIOGRAPHY

0-299-10214-9 WISCONSIN PB $14.95

Africa and the West

W.E.B. **DuBois**

The World and Africa

The activist's personal and learned "Inquiry into the Part Which Africa has Played in Western History," which had a major impact on Afro-American thought

0-7178-0221-3 INTERNATIONAL PUB PB $7.95

Prosser **Gifford** & William Roger **Louis**, editors

Decolonization and African Independence: The Transfers of Power, 1960-1980

0-300-04070-9 YALE $60.00

0-300-04388-0 YALE PB $22.00

Sven **Lindqvist**

Exterminate All the Brutes: A Modern Odyssey into the Heart of Darkness

This unique study of Europe's troubling history in Africa, written in the form of a travel diary, constitutes a history of European racism over two centuries. "Everything that Lindqvist writes is hard-won fact based on sharp-eyed observation and diligent research. His books are informed by the analytical skills of a philosopher and constructed with the care and attention of a novelist"—Richard Gott

See also IMPORTANT RECENT WORK under POLITICAL THOUGHT in SOCIAL STUDIES

TRANSLATED BY JOAN TATE

1-56584-334-7 NEW PRESS $20.00

Thomas **Pakenham**

The Scramble For Africa: The White Man's Conquest of the Dark Continent from 1876-1910

A dramatic telling of the imperialist struggle over Africa, a quick and violent grab for territory in which Britain, France, Germany, Belgium, and Italy vied for power and markets. In a mere 34 years the European powers carved up an entire

continent. Pakenham offers an engrossing—and appalling—narrative of panoramic scope
See also **THE COLONIAL EMPIRES** under **THE NEW IMPERIALISM** under **19TH-CENTURY EUROPE**
0-380-71999-1 AVON PB $16.00

David Livingstone

Walter **Rodney**
How Europe Underdeveloped Africa
Sweeping Marxist history and indictment
0-88258-096-5 HOWARD PB $12.95

Religion and Culture

The extraordinary diversity of African civilization makes generalization difficult. The following books represent only a small sampling of the riches of African thought and culture.

Molefi Kete **Asante**
Afrocentricity
0-86543-067-5 AFRICA WORLD PB $9.95

William **Bascom**
African Art Cultural Perspective: An Introduction
See also **ARTS OF AFRICA** in **ART**
0-393-09375-1 NORTON PB $9.95

Francis **Bebey**
African Music: A People's Art
1-55652-128-6 LAWRENCE HILL PB $11.95

John M. **Chernoff**
African Rhythm and African Sensibility: Aesthetics and Social Action in African Musical Idioms
Travelogue and sociological investigation, based on travels in Ghana in the early 1970s
See also **ART** under **SPECIALIZED STUDIES** under **ANTHROPOLOGY** in **SOCIAL STUDIES**
See also **AFRICAN MUSIC** under **WORLD MUSIC: OTHER TRADITIONS** in **PERFORMING ARTS AND MEDIA**
0-226-10345-5 CHICAGO PB $13.95

Werner **Gillon**
A Short History of African Art
An excellent introduction, covering the major achievements of most African cultures
0-14-013611-8 PENGUIN PB $17.95

Ronnie **Graham**
The Da Capo Guide to Contemporary African Music
For both layman and expert, a reliable reference on modern African music, arranged by country, region, and artist, with a good index
See also **AFRICAN MUSIC** under **WORLD MUSIC: OTHER TRADITIONS** in **PERFORMING ARTS AND MEDIA**
0-306-80325-9 DA CAPO PB $13.95

Marcel **Griaule**
Conversations with Ogotemmeli: An Introduction to Dogon Religious Ideas
An illuminating presentation of the complex cosmology underlying the Dogon culture of West Africa
See also **RELIGION** under **SPECIALIZED STUDIES** under **ANTHROPOLOGY** in **SOCIAL STUDIES**
INTRODUCTION BY GERMAINE DIETERLEN
0-19-519821-2 OXFORD PB $14.95

Nancy **Hafkin** & Edna G. **Bay**, editors
Women in Africa: Studies in Social and Economic Change
0-8047-0906-8 STANFORD $45.00
0-8047-1011-2 STANFORD PB $15.95

Adrian **Hastings**
The Church in Africa, 1450-1950
An authoritative history of the Christian Church. "Strikingly original; and the framework is indubitably African"—*TLS*
0-19-826399-6 OXFORD PB $24.95

Robert Farris **Thompson**
Flash of the Spirit: African and Afro-American Art and Philosophy
One of the most provocative scholars on the continuity of African art and ritual in the New World
See also **ARTS OF AFRICA** in **ART**
0-394-72369-4 RANDOM HOUSE PB $13.00

Victor **Turner**
The Forest of Symbols: Aspects of Ndembu Ritual
The work of a great anthropologist
See also **ESSAYS IN ANTHROPOLOGY** under **ANTHROPOLOGY** in **SOCIAL STUDIES**
0-8014-9101-0 CORNELL PB $15.95

Revelation and Divination in Ndembu Ritual
Required reading for those interested in religious rituals, as well as rituals of everyday life which have no religious underpinnings
See also **RELIGION** under **SPECIALIZED STUDIES** under **ANTHROPOLOGY** in **SOCIAL STUDIES**
0-8014-9158-4 CORNELL PB $15.95

European Explorers in Africa

Anne **Hugon**
The Exploration of Africa: From Cairo to the Cape
0-8109-2810-8 ABRAMS PB $12.95

Frank **McLynn**
Hearts of Darkness: The European Exploration of Africa
Blood, sweat, tears, heroics, and death are the constants in this superb account of the opening of a dangerous continent. An amazing array of dedicated explorers, would-be rulers, visionary traders, earnest anthropologists, lunatic loners, and others get their moments in a narrative solidly based on well recounted history
0-7867-0084-X CARROLL & GRAF PB $14.95

Henry M. **Stanley**
Through the Dark Continent: Or the Sources of the Nile Around the Great Lakes of Equatorial Africa and Down the Livingstone River to the Atlantic Ocean
Volume 1
0-486-25667-7 DOVER PB $11.95
Volume 2
0-486-25668-5 DOVER PB $10.95

Regional Histories

West Africa

Lucy **Ecreevey**, editor
Women Farmers in Africa: Rural Development in Mali and the Sahel
Critical essays approach development in the driest of agricultural landscapes
0-8156-2358-5 SYRACUSE $29.95

Robert **Smith**
Kingdoms of the Yoruba
Now in its third edition, this is an outstanding synthesis for anthropologists and historians, and for students at all college levels
0-299-11600-X WISCONSIN $39.75

Central Africa

Karen **Fields**
Revival and Rebellion in Colonial Central Africa
Provocative account of religious violence. Was the colonial regime a theocracy?
0-691-09409-8 PRINCETON $50.00

Samuel H. **Nelson**

Colonialism in the Congo Basin, 1880-1940

0-89680-180-2 OHIO PB $23.00

John **Thornton**

The Kingdom of Kongo: Civil War and Transition, 1641-1718

0-299-09290-9 WISCONSIN $27.50

East Africa

Steven **Feierman**

The Shambaa Kingdom

The rise and fall of an inland dynasty in Tanzania, using a Lévi-Straussian analysis of myth

0-299-06360-7 WISCONSIN $32.50

Graham **Hancock**

African Ark: People and Ancient Cultures of Ethiopia and the Horn of Africa

The journalist Graham Hancock joins with photographers Carol Beckwith and Angela Fisher to offer a remarkable look at the peoples and cultures of the Horn of Africa, encompassing Ethiopia, Sudan, Somalia, and parts of Kenya

0-8109-1902-8 ABRAMS $65.00

John **Iliffe**

A Modern History of Tanganyika

0-521-29611-0 CAMBRIDGE PB $44.95

John **Middleton**

The World of the Swahili: An African Mercantile Civilization

0-300-06080-7 YALE PB $17.00

David **Robinson**

The Holy War of Umar Tal: The Western Sudan in the Mid-Nineteenth Century

Scholarly use of sources in tandem with an enthralling narrative of Islamic holy war in West Africa

0-19-822720-5 OXFORD $111.00

Thomas **Spear** & Richard **Waller**

Being Maasai: Ethnicity and Identity in East Africa

0-8214-1045-8 OHIO PB $19.95

Southern Africa

Gwendolyn **Carter**

International Politics in Southern Africa

0-253-34285-6 INDIANA $13.95
0-253-20281-7 INDIANA PB $3.95

Terence O. **Ranger**

Revolt in Southern Rhodesia, 1896-97

Insurrection in colonial Africa from the African side. Factually flawed yet tremendously influential, especially in Zimbabwe

0-435-94800-8 HEINEMANN PB $17.50

Elizabeth **Schmidt**

Peasants, Traders, and Wives: Shona Women in the History of Zimbabwe, 1870-1939

0-435-08066-0 HEINEMANN PB $22.95

Laurens **van der Post**

The Lost World of the Kalahari

"A journey in a great wasteland and a search for some pure remnant of the unique and almost vanished First People of my native land, the Bushmen of Africa," writes van der Post

See also **SUB-SAHARAN AFRICA** under **AFRICA** under **TRAVEL LITERATURE** in **FOOD, TRAVEL, AND LEISURE**

0-15-653706-0 HARCOURT BRACE PB $11.00

Current Affairs in Africa

Political scientists have traditionally structured their writing on Africa around a series of politico-economic theories. Today, more weight is given to the actions of Africans as participants in their own political and social fortunes—or misfortunes, as the case may be.

George B.N. **Ayittey**

Africa Betrayed

0-312-08058-1 ST. MARTIN'S $35.00
0-312-10400-6 ST. MARTIN'S PB $19.95

George C. **Bond** & others, editors

AIDS in Africa and the Caribbean

0-8133-2878-0 WESTVIEW $56.00
0-8133-2879-9 WESTVIEW PB $21.95

Raymond W. **Copson**

Africa's Wars and Prospects for Peace

1-56324-300-8 SHARPE $59.95
1-56324-301-6 SHARPE PB $23.95

Bill **Freund**

The Making of Contemporary Africa: The Development of African Society Since 1800

A materialist's sweeping view; focuses on the means of production and the relationship between capital and labor in development

0-253-28600-X INDIANA PB $13.95

Gaim **Kibreab**

Reflections on the African Refugee Problem

0-86543-006-3 AFRICA WORLD $25.00
0-86543-007-1 AFRICA WORLD PB $7.95

E. Wayne **Nafziger**

Inequality in Africa: Political Elites, Proletariat, Peasants and the Poor

0-521-26881-8 CAMBRIDGE $59.95
0-521-31703-7 CAMBRIDGE PB $16.95

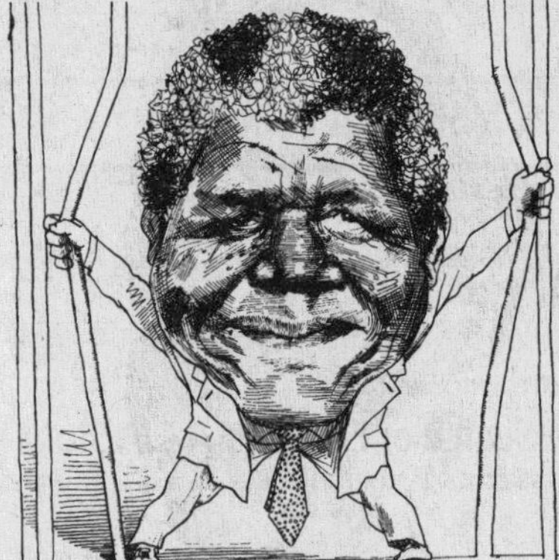

Nelson Mandela

Peter Anyang **Nyongo**

Popular Struggles for Democracy in Africa

0-86232-736-9 ZED $49.95
0-86232-737-7 ZED PB $17.50

Georges **Nzongola-Ntalaja**

Revolution and Counter Revolution in Africa: Essays in Contemporary Politics

Excellent survey of a thorny issue

0-86232-750-4 ZED $42.95

Richard **Sandbrook** & Judith **Barker**

The Politics of Africa's Economic Stagnation

Who profits and who loses

0-521-31961-7 CAMBRIDGE PB $17.95

Wole **Soyinka**

Winner of the Nobel Prize for Literature in 1986, Soyinka's work is complex and wide-ranging. His plays are a sophisticated blend of African dance rhythms, Yoruba mythology, and oral storytelling combined with Western imagery. Many of these plays have been performed by Soyinka's own company, Masks. Soyinka was jailed by the Nigerian government for 27 months for his criticism of their policies, and his experiences are chillingly narrated in The Man Died.

The Open Sore of a Continent

0-19-510557-5 OXFORD $19.95

Immanuel **Wallerstein**

Africa and the Modern World

A collection of articles. Wallerstein evolved his "world system" theory out of his Africanist background, later supplemented by his reading of Fernand Braudel

0-86543-021-7 AFRICA WORLD $32.00
0-86543-022-5 AFRICA WORLD PB $10.95

Crawford **Young**

Ideology and Development in Africa

Masterful synthesis by the premier political scientist working in Central Africa

0-300-02744-3 YALE....$40.00
0-300-03096-7 YALE PB....$20.00

A National Focus

Angola

John **Stockwell**

In Search of Enemies: A CIA Story

0-393-00926-2 NORTON PB....$10.95

Côte d'Ivoire

Barbara **Lewis**

The Ivory Coast

0-86531-023-8 WESTVIEW....$49.00

Carol **Spindel**

In the Shadow of the Sacred Grove

An account of a yearlong stay in a remote Ivory Coast village

0-679-72214-9 VINTAGE PB....$13.00

Eritrea

James **Firebrace** & Stuart **Holland**

Never Kneel Down: Drought, Development and Liberation in Eritrea

Results of a British fact-finding mission to Eritrea, land of brutal war, drought, and famine

PREFACE BY NEIL KINNOCK

0-932415-00-8 RED SEA....$29.95
0-932415-01-6 RED SEA PB....$9.95

Robert **Machida**

Eritrea: The Struggle for Independence

The roots of the costly 25-year civil war in the African Horn by an American who lived in Ethiopia in the 1970s

0-932415-24-5 RED SEA PB....$5.95

Ethiopia

Kurt **Jansson** & others

The Ethiopian Famine

The directors of the UN and Oxfam relief efforts offer their views on the natural and political causes of the famine

0-86232-835-7 ZED PB....$17.50

Ryszard **Kapuscinski**

The Emperor: Downfall of an Autocrat

The Polish journalist's depiction of the outrageous pomp and decadence at the Ethiopian court, through interviews with Haile Selassie's servants

See also **POLISH LITERATURE** under **EASTERN EUROPEAN LITERATURE** in **LITERATURE OF EUROPE, AFRICA, AND ASIA**

TRANSLATED BY WILLIAM R. BRAND & KATARZYNA MROCZKOWSKA-BRAND

0-679-72203-3 VINTAGE PB....$10.00

Edmond J. **Keller**

Revolutionary Ethiopia: From Empire to People's Republic

The historical roots, development, and results of the Ethiopian revolution of 1974. Essential for understanding the politics of Ethiopia's famine

0-253-35014-X INDIANA....$35.00
0-253-20646-4 INDIANA PB....$6.95

Kenya

David William **Cohen** & E.S. Atieno **Odhiambo**

Burying SM: The Politics of Knowledge and the Sociology of Power in Africa

Silvano Milea (SM) Otieno, a distinguished Kenyan barrister, died suddenly of a heart attack on December 20, 1986. For the next six months his embalmed corpse, stored at a Nairobi morturary, became the focus of a legal struggle that riveted the attention of a nation. In dispute was the proper site for SM's burial: his estate near Nairobi, close to his wife's Kikuyu people; or his birthplace in Nyalgunga in the Luo homeland in western Kenya

0-435-08063-6 HEINEMANN PB....$19.95

Jomo **Kenyatta**

Facing Mount Kenya

0-394-70210-7 RANDOM HOUSE PB....$7.09

David **Throup**

The Economic and Social Origins of Mau Mau

The great explosion of African violence in Kenya, 1954

0-8214-0883-6 OHIO....$29.95
0-8214-0884-4 OHIO PB....$15.95

Liberia

Augustine **Konneh**

Religion, Commerce, and the Intergration of the Madingo in Liberia

0-7618-0355-6 UNIVERSITY PRESS OF AMERICA...$16.50

Syrulwa L. **Somah**

Historical Settlement of Liberia and Its Environmental Impact

0-8191-9654-1
UNIVERSITY PRESS OF AMERICA PB....$29.50

Antonio **McDaniel**

Swing Low, Sweet Chariot: The Mortality Cost of Colonizing Liberia in the Nineteenth Century

0-226-55724-3 CHICAGO....$34.00

Mozambique

Mark **Chingono**

The State, Violence and Development: The Political Economy of War in Mozambique

1-85972-077-3 AVEBURY PB....$68.95

Joseph **Hanlon**

Mozambique: The Revolution Under Fire

Vignettes of daily life along with numerous photos and maps make sense of the complex story of droughts, policy blunders, and civil war with South Africa-backed troops; by a veteran BBC correspondent

0-86232-940-X ZED....$49.95
0-86232-941-8 ZED PB....$17.50

Jason **Laure** & Ettagale **Blauer**

Mozambique: Enchantment of the World

0-516-02636-4 CHILDRENS PRESS....$30.00

Malyn **Newitt**

A History of Mozambique

Published in 1995

0-253-34006-3 INDIANA....$59.95
0-253-34007-1 INDIANA PB....$27.50

Rachel **Waterhouse**

Mozambique: Rising from the Ashes

0-85598-341-8 HUMANITIES PB....$9.95

Nigeria

Thomas J. **Biersteker**

Multinationals, the State, and Control of the Nigerian Economy

Who wields corporate power in Africa's most populous and influential nation?

0-691-07728-2 PRINCETON....$57.00
0-691-02261-5 PRINCETON PB....$15.95

N. C. **McClintock**

Kingdoms in the Sand and Sun: An African Path to Independence

1-85043-522-7 I.B. TAURIS....$39.50

Sudan

David A. **Korn**

Assassination in Khartoum

0-253-33202-8 INDIANA....$24.95

Alexander **De Waal**

Famine that Kills: Darfur, Sudan, 1984-1985

0-19-827349-5 OXFORD $36.00
0-19-827749-0 OXFORD PB $12.95

Uganda

Holger Bernt **Hansen** & Michael **Twaddle**, editors

Uganda Now

A 1988 collection of essays. Christine Obbo's contribution traces the roots of Uganda's social and political violence to the colonial period

0-8214-0896-8 OHIO $29.95
0-8214-0897-6 OHIO PB $15.95

Phares **Mutibwa**

Uganda Since Independence: A Story of Unfulfilled Hopes

A 1992 survey

0-86543-357-7 AFRICA WORLD PB $16.95

Amii **Omara-Otunnu**

Politics and the Military in Uganda, 1890-1985

0-312-00046-4 ST. MARTIN'S $39.95

Christopher **Wrigley**

Kingship and State: The Buganda Dynasty

0-521-47370-5 CAMBRIDGE $64.95

Zaire

Paul **Hyland**

The Black Heart: A Voyage into Central Africa

A voyage up the Congo through the heart of Zaire

0-7089-8625-0 CHARNWOOD $24.95

Winsome J. **Leslie**

Zaire: Continuity and Political Change in an Oppressive State

0-86531-298-2 WESTVIEW $59.00

Michael G. **Schatzberg**

The Dialectics of Oppression in Zaire

Argues that scarcity and insecurity have become twin motors of a dialectic of oppression, resulting in coercion, corruption, exploitation, and fear

0-253-31703-7 INDIANA $25.00
0-253-20694-4 INDIANA PB $10.95

Mobutu or Chaos?: The United States and Zaire, 1960-1990

A 125-page white paper

0-8191-8131-5 FOREIGN POLICY PB $18.50

Nzongola-Ntalaja, editor

The Crisis in Zaire: Myths and Realities

0-86543-023-3 AFRICA WORLD $32.00
0-86543-024-1 AFRICA WORLD PB $11.95

Helen **Winternitz**

East Along the Equator: A Journey Up the Congo

Rendezvous with Zaire's secret police in a modern-day Conradian "journey upriver"

0-87113-162-5 ATLANTIC MONTHLY PB $9.95

Zimbabwe

Andre **Astrow**

Zimbabwe: A Revolution That Lost Its Way?

Yes, indeed, writes this socialist and critic

0-86232-140-9 ZED $35.00

Peter **Godwin**

Mukiwa: A White Boy in Africa

Godwin *(Rhodesians Never Die)* recreates his 1960s youth in white Rhodesia, his "racial enlightenment within a system of extreme conservatism," his departure for studies in England, and his return as a lawyer and journalist

0-87113-621-X GROVE $24.00

David **Martin** & Phyllis **Johnson**

The Struggle for Zimbabwe

INTRODUCTION BY ROBERT MUGABE

0-85345-599-6 MONTHLY REVIEW PB $10.00

Other

Alain **Destexhe** & Alison **Marschner**

Rwanda and Genocide in the Twentieth Century

0-8147-1873-6 NYU $19.95

Tony **Hodges**

Western Sahara: The Roots of a Desert War

The first full story of the politics, mineral riches, and foreign powers on the scene, and other stakes in Western Sahara's fight to reverse Morocco's annexation of 1975

0-88208-151-9 LAWRENCE HILL $19.95

Fergal **Keane**

Season of Blood: A Rwandan Journey

0-670-86205-3 VIKING $21.95

Robert **Klitgaard**

Tropical Gangsters

A remarkable first-hand account of a young economist's experiences in the small West African nation of Equatorial Guinea. "Klitgaard manages to be clear-headed about everything that is wrong with his beloved Equatorial Guinea … without losing his sense of warmth and respect for the people he dealt with there"—James Fallows

0-465-08758-2 BASIC PB $22.95

Gerard **Prunier**

The Rwanda Crisis: History of a Genocide

0-231-10408-1 COLUMBIA $29.95

Janet G. **Vaillant**

Black, French, and African: A Life of Leopold Sedar Senghor

A biography of the poet and intellectual who became the first president of Senegal

See also **ANTHOLOGIES AND CRITICAL STUDIES** under **AFRICAN LITERATURE** in **LITERATURE OF EUROPE, AFRICA, AND ASIA**

0-674-07623-0 HARVARD $32.50

South Africa: History

World interest, together with the long tradition of scholarship from within South Africa itself, has resulted in a rich historical tradition.

A new chapter in South African history began with the end of apartheid in 1991, when parliament voted to nullify first the apartheid laws regarding property ownership and then the Population Registration Act of 1950, which classified all South Africans by race at birth. The ANC approved a plan in 1993 to allow minority parties to participate in the government for five years after the end of white rule, and in February of that year, the first nonwhites entered the cabinet. The ANC was victorious in the 1994 election, and Nelson Mandela, promising to usher in a new era, was sworn in as the country's new president on May 10. Mandela, 78, recently announced, however, that he will not run again in the upcoming 1999 elections.

Keletso E. **Atkins**

The Moon Is Down! Give Us Our Money!: The Cultural Origins of an African Work Ethic, Natal, South Africa, 1843-1900

0-435-08078-4 HEINEMANN PB $22.95

William **Beinart** & Colin **Bundy**, editors

Hidden Struggles in Rural South Africa

An anthology of works on millenarianism and revolt

0-520-05779-1 CALIFORNIA $50.00
0-520-05780-5 CALIFORNIA PB $17.00

Colin **Bundy**

The Rise and Fall of the South African Peasantry

What happened to Africans—farmers all—as the Boers commanded the building of modern South Africa

0-520-03754-5 CALIFORNIA $55.00

Peter **Kallaway** & Patrick **Pearson**

Johannesburg: Images and Continuities—A History of Working-Class Life Through Pictures, 1885-1935

Fascinating archival photos with explanations

0-86975-303-7 OHIO PB $19.95

T.R.H. **Davenport**
South Africa: A Modern History
An excellent survey, now in its third edition
0-8020-5940-6 TORONTO $60.00
0-8020-6880-4 TORONTO PB $27.50

Stefan **Kanfer**
The Last Empire: South Africa, Diamonds, and De Beers from Cecil Rhodes to the Oppenheimers
0-374-15207-1 FS&G $25.00

J.D. **Omer-Cooper**
A History of Southern Africa
A solid history in an attractive format
0-435-08095-4 HEINEMANN PB $22.50

Charles van **Onselen**
The Small Matter of a Horse: The Life of "Nongoloza" Mathebula, 1867-1948
Published in 1984
0-86975-239-1 RAVAN PB $8.95

Thomas **Pakenham**
The Boer War
The costliest, bloodiest, and most humiliating war that Britain fought between 1815 and 1914; Pakenham's study is as fast-moving as a novel
See also **IMPERIALISM AND COLONIALISM** under **THE VICTORIAN ERA** under **GREAT BRITAIN AND IRELAND**
0679430874 RANDOM HOUSE $40.00

Robert I. **Rotberg** & Miles F. **Shore**
The Founder: Cecil Rhodes and the Pursuit of Power
The clergyman's son from Hertfordshire, who went to South Africa at the age of 20 because of poor health, and became one of the great diamond magnates of his day. "Without Rhodes's historical invervention, neither colonial Rhodesia nor modern South Africa would have been possible, but neither would Zimbabwe—or whatever emerges in South Africa when the present system goes"
—Geoffrey Wheatcroft, *NY Times Book Review*
0-19-504968-3 OXFORD $45.00

Leonard **Thompson**
A History of South Africa, Second Edition
Elegantly written, well-illustrated with contemporary engravings and photographs, a valuable contribution by a leading historian in the field. "Both accurate and authentic, written in a delightful literary style"
—Archbishop Desmond Tutu
0-300-06543-4 YALE PB $17.00

Monica **Wilson** &
Leonard M. **Thompson**, editors
A History of South Africa to 1870
Originally published as volume 1 of the *Oxford History of South Africa*, this ground-breaking work has been supplied with new illustrations. Highly recommended
0-86531-582-5 WESTVIEW PB $21.00

Charles **van Onselen**
Kas Maine, Son of Shield and Plow: The Life and Times of an African Sharecropper
The story of Kas Maine (pronounced MY-ee-neh), cobbler, saddle maker, cattle speculator, livestock breeder, who lived long enough to experience just about all the phases of modern South African history; related by a historian at the University of Witwatersrand. "An absorbing life story, one in the developing tradition of the study of ordinary lives that upon examination turn out not to be so ordinary after all"
—Richard Bernstein, *NY Times*
0-8090-9603-X HILL & WANG $35.00

Zulu

In the 1820s, a small polity controlled first by Dingiswayo and then by his protégé, Shaka, swept up southeastern Africa in a brilliant conquest. Modifying hunting techniques into a modern form of warfare completely unlike "ritualized" battle, Shaka forged a large military state. Known and feared throughout southern Africa, the Zulu kingdom persisted until 1879, when the English defeated a large contingent of troops and divided the domain.

Axel-Ivar **Berglund**
Zulu Thought: Patterns and Symbolism
0-253-21205-7 INDIANA PB $9.95

David **Clammer**
The Zulu War
The massacre of the British at Isandhlwana and the defense at Rorke's Drift; includes maps, photographs, and illustrations
See also **WARS OF IMPERIALISM** under **WARS THROUGH THE AGES** under **MILITARY AFFAIRS**
0-8095-7525-6 BORGO $25.00

E.A. **Ritter**
Shaka Zulu
A rendition based on the royal Zulu account
0-14-004826-X VIKING PB $11.95

South Africa Since 1948

Herbert **Adam** & Kogila **Moody**
South Africa Without Apartheid
Controversial liberal argument for a democratic "corporate federalism" compromise with Afrikaners; published in 1986
0-520-05769-4 CALIFORNIA $38.00
0-520-05770-8 CALIFORNIA PB $16.00

Mary **Benson**
Nelson Mandela: The Man and the Movement
A biography published while Mandela was still in prison
FOREWORD BY DESMOND TUTU
0-393-30322-5 NORTON PB $8.95

Donald **Woods**
Biko
The book that inspired the film *Cry Freedom*
0-8050-1899-9 HOLT PB $13.95

Belinda **Bozzoli**
Class, Community and Conflict: South African Perspectives
From a 1984 history symposium in South Africa
0-86975-281-2 RAVAN PB $22.95

John W. **Cell**
The Highest Stage of White Supremacy
The development of segregation in the US South compared with apartheid in South Africa
0-521-24096-4 CAMBRIDGE $75.00
0-521-27061-8 CAMBRIDGE PB $15.95

O. Tambo

Cedric **de Beer**
The South African Disease: Apartheid Health and Health Services
How South Africa stopped keeping track of black mortality when the statistics became embarrassing; published in 1986
0-86543-038-1 AFRICA WORLD $19.95
0-86543-039-X AFRICA WORLD PB $7.95

Don **Foster** & Dennis **Davis**
Detention and Torture in South Africa: Psychological, Legal and Historical Studies
Interviews with nearly 200 survivors form the basis of this meticulous and credible report
0-312-00785-X ST. MARTIN'S $39.95

George M. **Fredrickson**
Black Liberation: A Comparative History of Black Ideologies in the United States and South Africa
0-19-505749-X OXFORD $30.00
0-19-510978-3 OXFORD PB $14.95

Stanley **Greenberg**

Legitimating the Illegitimate: State, Markets and Resistance in South Africa

An academic but unmatched account of government policy, ideology, and struggles among the rulers of South Africa under apartheid; published in 1987

0-520-06010-5 CALIFORNIA $45.00
0-520-06011-3 CALIFORNIA PB $15.95

Joseph **Hanlon**

Beggar Your Neighbors: Apartheid Power in South Africa

South Africa's extrusion of its conflict onto foreign soil, including first-hand reports on terrorism in Mozambique; published in 1986

0-253-33131-5 INDIANA $39.95

Sheridan **Johns** & R. Hunt **Davis**, Jr., editors

Mandela, Tambo, and the African National Congress: The Struggle Against Apartheid, 1948-1990: A Documentary Survey

0-19-505784-8 OXFORD PB $15.95

Rian **Malan**

My Traitor's Heart: A South African Exile Returns to Face His Country

An Afrikaner exile returns to South Africa. "His stories are haunting the way bad dreams are. They fascinate us, and only in retrospect do we realize their horror"
—Vincent Crapanzano, *NY Times Book Review*

See also **CENTRAL AND SOUTHERN AFRICA** under **AFRICAN LITERATURE** in **LITERATURE OF EUROPE, AFRICA, AND ASIA**

0-679-73215-2 VINTAGE PB $14.00

Sebastian **Mallaby**

After Apartheid: The Future of South Africa

The social schisms of South Africa—racial, economic, and philosophical—have developed over centuries, but the country now faces the most crucial period in its bloody history. Mallaby offers an intelligent treatment of the risks and opportunities the nation confronts as apartheid is dismantled

0-8129-1938-6 TIME BOOKS $22.00
0-8129-2204-2 TIME BOOKS PB $14.00

Mark **Mathabane**

Kaffir Boy: The True Story of a Black Youth's Coming of Age in Apartheid South Africa

See also **CENTRAL AND SOUTHERN AFRICA** under **AFRICAN LITERATURE** in **LITERATURE OF EUROPE, AFRICA, AND ASIA**

0-02-034530-5 COLLIER PB $10.00

Leonard M. **Thompson**

The Political Mythology of Apartheid

How the Afrikaner people have interpreted history to sustain their notion of destiny

0-300-03368-0 YALE $30.00
0-300-03512-8 YALE PB $15.00

Desmond **Tutu**

The Rainbow People of God: The Making of a Peaceful Revolution

The Nobel Peace Prize-winner details the events leading up to the historic April 1994 open election in South Africa. From his letter as a young priest to Prime Minister Vorster to his sermon at the grave of Steve Biko, this collection documents a heroic freedom fighter's lifelong struggle against oppression

0-385-48374-0 IMAGE PB $12.95
0-385-47546-2 DOUBLEDAY $22.95

Nelson Mandela

Nelson **Mandela**

Long Walk to Freedom: The Autobiography of Nelson Mandela

The moral and practical leader of the anti-apartheid movement, winner of the 1993 Nobel Peace Prize, and an international symbol of human dignity and justice, has written the story of his life. His childhood as the foster son of a Tembu chief, his years of imprisonment, his setbacks and his ultimate triumph are powerfully and eloquently narrated

0-316-54585-6 LITTLE, BROWN $24.95
0-316-54818-9 LITTLE, BROWN PB $13.95

The Struggle Is My Life

Speeches and writings from before his imprisonment and an account of his life afterward

0-87348-594-7 PATHFINDER $50.00
0-87348-593-9 PATHFINDER PB $15.95

Winnie **Mandela**

Part of My Soul Went with Him

Her life, her cause, and moving reflections on her husband

0-393-30290-3 NORTON PB $6.95

The Indian Subcontinent

Following the standard practice of its time with respect to European history, the first edition of the *Oxford History of India* divided its subject into three categories: ancient (prehistoric, Vedic, Classical), medieval (Islamic), and modern (British). Although these categories are even more inappropriate for India than they are for Europe, they have been employed here to some extent because they reflect very well the relative availability of books on successive periods of Indian history. General-interest surveys of ancient and classical Indian cultures are extremely hard to come by; the situation is better for the Islamic period, and there is a relative abundance of material on the British and post-Independence era.

Given such uneven distribution, the reader interested in either the full sweep of Indian history or in a detailed understanding of particular events is forced to rely on texts that are not properly considered historical.

Ainslee **Embree** & Stephen **Hay**, editors

Sources of Indian Tradition

Ainslee **Embree**, editor

Volume 1

A new edition of an anthology that has become a classic. "A serious, careful, dependable book, broader and more varied even than the old *Sources*...This is *the* primary study of Indian civilizations"—Wendy D. O'Flaherty

See also **THE INDIAN TRADITIONS** under **ASIAN RELIGION AND PHILOSOPHY** in **RELIGION, SPIRITUALITY, AND PHILOSOPHY**

0-231-06651-1 COLUMBIA PB $19.50

Stephen **Hay**, editor

Volume 2

The second volume of the newly revised *Sources*, with much new material and short but illuminating introductions to each phase of the modern era

See also **THE INDIAN TRADITIONS** under **ASIAN RELIGION AND PHILOSOPHY** in **RELIGION, SPIRITUALITY, AND PHILOSOPHY**

0-231-06414-4 COLUMBIA $65.00
0-231-06415-2 COLUMBIA PB $19.50

A.L. **Basham**, editor

A Cultural History of India

Essays on the whole range of Indian cultural history, from noted contributors

0-19-561520-4 OXFORD $37.50

Cambridge University Press

The Cambridge Economic History of India

Tapan **Raychaudhuri** & Irfan **Habib**

Volume 1
1200-1750

Both volumes in this survey are first-rate and highly recommended. This volume has 9 maps

0-521-22692-9 CAMBRIDGE $125.00

Dharma **Kumar** & Meghnad **Desai**

Volume 2
1751-1970

With 12 maps and 20 diagrams

0-521-22802-6 CAMBRIDGE $155.00

Louis **Dumont**

Homo Hierarchicus: The Caste System and Its Implications

The most thorough and sophisticated analysis of the caste system ever written. A landmark in Indian studies and also an example of French rationalism

See also **POWER AND POLITICS** under **SPECIALIZED STUDIES** under **ANTHROPOLOGY** in **SOCIAL STUDIES**

TRANSLATED BY BASIA GULATI

0-226-16963-4 CHICAGO PB $18.95

Wilhelm **Halbfass**

India and Europe: An Essay in Understanding

The intellectual encounter of India and the West from pre-Alexandrian antiquity to the present. Examines India's role in European philosophical thought and the impact of the West on India

0-88706-794-8 SUNY $64.50
0-88706-795-6 SUNY PB $21.95

J.C. **Harle**

Art and Architecture of the Indian Subcontinent

A thoroughgoing and enormously erudite survey of Indian art, replete with information on intellectual, cultural, and social life

See also **INDIA** under **EAST ASIAN ART** in **ART**

0-300-05329-0 PENGUIN PB $26.50

Brigid **Keenan**

Travels in Kashmir: A Popular History of Its People, Places and Crafts

0-19-282791-X OXFORD PB $11.95

Francis **Robinson**, editor

The Cambridge Encyclopedia of India, Pakistan, Bangladesh, Sri Lanka, Nepal, Bhutan and the Maldives

0-521-33451-9 CAMBRIDGE $69.95

Vincent **Smith**

The Oxford History of India

The original text of the standard history, revised and edited in places, but left largely intact. An excellent survey now in its fourth edition

EDITED BY PERCIVAL SPEAR

0-19-561297-3 OXFORD PB $14.95

Romila **Thapar**, editor

A History of India

Romila **Thapar**

Volume 1

The first of a two-volume overview of Indian history, written by the foremost historian of ancient India

0-14-013835-8 VIKING PB $12.95

Percival **Spear**

Volume 2

The second volume covers the Islamic and modern periods and is a good place for the novice to begin exploring

0-14-013836-6 VIKING PB $13.95

Stanley **Wolpert**

A New History of India

A highly readable account that places modern Indian developments in their historical context. An excellent starting point for readers unfamiliar with India

0-19-507660-5 OXFORD PB $19.95

From Prehistoric India to the Classical Periods

Bridget **Allchin** & Raymond **Allchin**

The Rise of Civilization in India and Pakistan

The standard historical text on pre-Aryan India, incorporating all of the current archaeological evidence

0-521-28550-X CAMBRIDGE PB $36.95

A.K. **Coomaraswamy** & Nivedita **Coomaraswamy**

Myths of the Hindus and Buddhists

A very engaging retelling of Indian myths; co-authored by the renowned art historian A.K. Coomaraswamy

0-486-21759-0 DOVER PB $9.95

J.L. **Jaini**

Outlines of Jainism

A well-written, straightforward account of one of the major offshoots of the Vedantic tradition

See also **JAINISM** under **OTHER RELIGIONS OF INDIA** under **ASIAN RELIGION AND PHILOSOPHY** in **RELIGION, SPIRITUALITY, AND PHILOSOPHY**

0-88355-801-7 HYPERION $23.25

G.L. **Possehl**, editor

The Harapan Civilization

A beautifully produced book examining the first of India's urban cultures

1-88157-018-5 SCIENCE $92.50

Kumkum **Roy**

The Emergence of Monarchy in North India: Eighth to Fifth Centuries B.C.: As Reflected in the Brahmanical Tradition

0-19-563416-0 OXFORD $29.95

Romila **Thapar**

From Lineage to State: Social Formations of the Mid-First Millennium B.C. in the Ganges Valley

An ingenious discussion of the formation of classical Indian society, using a wide variety of sources

0-19-561394-5 OXFORD $28.00

Interpreting Early India

0-19-563342-3 OXFORD PB $7.95

Robert C. **Zaehner**

Hinduism

The best available single-volume treatment of the subject

0-19-88812-X OXFORD PB $10.95

The Islamic Period

S. **Arasaratnam**

Maritime India in the Seventeenth Century

0-19-563424-1 OXFORD $24.95

Richard **Eaton**

The Sufis of Bijapur, 1300-1700: The Social Roles of Sufis in Medieval India

A highly praised account of religious and political life in the pre-Mughal kingdoms of the Deccan

0-691-03110-X PRINCETON $55.00

Hamilton A. **Gibb**

Mohammedanism: An Historical Survey

An authority noted for his powers of synthesis and lucid, succinct exposition masterfully presents the subject

See also **GENERAL STUDIES** under **ISLAM** in **RELIGION, SPIRITUALITY, AND PHILOSOPHY**

0-19-500245-8 OXFORD PB $8.95

Stewart **Gordon**

Marathas, Marauders and State Formation in Eighteenth Century India

0-19-563386-5 OXFORD $23.00

Ifran **Habib**

An Atlas of the Mughal Empire

A prime source of statistics and geographical information about one of the most powerful empires the world has ever known

0-19-560379-6 OXFORD $85.00

John F. **Richards**

The Mughal Empire

One of the largest, most magnificent centralized states in the early modern period; from its creation in 1526 to its breakup in 1720. Winner of Choice Outstanding Academic Books 1995

0-521-56603-7 CAMBRIDGE PB $19.95

The British Period

The British period has an enormous literature associated with it. The following list provides representative samples of this writing; it is not meant to be exhaustive.

C.A. **Bayly**

Indian Society and the Making of the British Empire

One of the best contemporary historians of India examines the internal forces that made British rule possible

0-521-38650-0 CAMBRIDGE PB $18.95

Richard **Burton**

Goa, and the Blue Mountains: Or, Six Months of Sick Leave

An account of the famous traveler's journey through southwest India, from Bombay to Goa, while on sick leave from the British Indian army. A facsimile edition of the original 1851 text

INTRODUCTION BY DANE KENNEDY

0-520-07611-7 CALIFORNIA PB $16.00

Christopher **Ondaatje**

Sindh Revisited: A Journey in the Footsteps of Captain Sir Richard Francis Burton

An account of the author's years spent in India attempting to ferret out the secrets of the famous explorer's seven years in India. It additionally provides a fascinating contrast between contemporary India and that of the time of Burton's writings

See also **INDIA** under **ASIA** under **TRAVEL LITERATURE** in **FOOD, TRAVEL, AND LEISURE**

0-00-255436-4 HARPERCOLLINS $30.00

Henry **Dodwell**

Dupleix and Clive: Beginning of Empire

The genesis of the divide-and-rule policy of British expansion placed in the context of both Indian political environments and the worldwide rivalry between England and France

0-7146-1125-5 FRANK CASS $32.00

Michael **Fisher**

The Politics of the British Annexation of India, 1757-1857

From the *Oxford Indian History* series

0-19-562860-8 OXFORD $24.95

Ranajit **Guha**

Elementary Aspects of Peasant Insurgency in Colonial India

The work of a major historian on the subject

0-19-563157-9 OXFORD PB $8.95

David **Hardiman**

Peasant Resistance in India, 1858-1914

0-19-563390-3 OXFORD PB $7.95

Peter **Hopkirk**

The Great Game: The Struggle for Empire in Central Asia

The epic struggle for the riches of India and the East by the two central imperial powers of the 19th century: Victorian Britain and Czarist Russia. "Describes vividly the contested lands and cities whose very names conjure up mystery, romance, and high adventure..."
—*NY Times Book Review*

1-56836-022-3 KODANSHA PB $16.00

David **Lelyveld**

Aligarh's First Generation: Muslim Solidarity in British India

Focuses on the Mohammadan Anglo Oriental College and the challenges of colonialism and nationalism

0-19-563665-1 OXFORD PB $15.95

T.M. **Luhrmann**

The Good Parsi: The Fate of a Colonial Elite in a Postcolonial Society

How these Zoroastrian people adopted the manners, dress, and aspirations of their British colonizers—and were richly rewarded. And how Indian independence ushered in their decline

0-674-35676-4 HARVARD PB $22.95

James **Morris**

Heaven's Command: An Imperial Progress

The story of various military campaigns by a well-known journalist. The chapters on the Indian Rebellion of 1857 are quite enjoyable

0-15-640006-5 HARCOURT BRACE PB $14.95

Pratapaditya **Pal** & Vidya **Dehejia**

From Merchants to Emperors: British Artists and India, 1757-1930

0-8014-9386-2 CORNELL PB $32.50

Percival **Spear**

The Oxford History of Modern India: 1749-1975

An elegantly written but conventional account that tends to avoid the knottier problems of British rule

0-19-561076-8 OXFORD PB $13.95

Andrew **Ward**

Our Bones Are Scattered: The Cawnpore Massacres and the Indian Mutiny of 1857

The doomed world of the British East India Company's domain. "A grand and terrible epic of violence and retribution that is as harrowing as it is irresistibly readable"
—*American Heritage Magazine*

0-8050-2437-9 HOLT $30.00

Nationalism and Independence

General Histories

Paul R. **Brass**

The Politics of India Since Independence

India's major political, cultural, and economic changes and crises, and the drives of its national leadership to build a unified state and dynamic economy

0-521-45970-2 CAMBRIDGE PB $19.95

Judith M. **Brown**

Modern India: The Origins of a South Asian Democracy

A highly intelligent and valuable survey of the modern era

0-19-913124-4 OXFORD $55.00
0-19-873113-2 OXFORD PB $23.00

Sarvepalli **Gopal**

Jawaharlal Nehru: A Biography

The authorized biography of the nationalist leader and first prime minister of India

Volume 1

0-674-47310-8 HARVARD $41.50

Volume 2

0-674-47311-6 HARVARD $37.50

Volume 3

0-674-47312-4 HARVARD $35.00

Elias **Khoury**

The Journey of Little Gandhi

0-8166-1995-6 MINNESOTA $17.95

Stanley **Kochanek**

The Congress Party of India: The Dynamics of a One-Party Democracy

The political structure of independent India

0-691-03013-8 PRINCETON BOOK COMPANY $75.00

Ved **Mehta**

A Family Affair: India Under Three Prime Ministers

Mehta brings his characteristic insight to this examination of India's ruling dynasty

0-19-503118-0 OXFORD $25.00

Mahatma Gandhi and his Apostles

0-300-05539-0 YALE PB $16.00

Portrait of India

0-300-05538-2 YALE PB $20.00

Gandhi

Dennis **Dalton**

Mahatma Gandhi: Nonviolent Power in Action

A compelling and readable analysis of the Mahatma as an ethical theorist *and* a political activist. Dalton, a professor of political science at Barnard, traces the central connection between Gandhi's political philosophy and his social activism from its origins in South Africa to the historic Calcutta fast of 1947. Comparing Gandhi with Martin Luther King, Jr., and Malcolm X, Dalton shows the continuing relevance of Gandhi's experience today

0-231-08118-9 COLUMBIA $34.50
0-231-08119-7 COLUMBIA PB $15.50

Mohandas K. **Gandhi**

Autobiography: The Story of My Experiments with Truth

A 20th-century classic

See also **MODERN TRENDS** under **HINDUISM** under **ASIAN RELIGION AND PHILOSOPHY** in **RELIGION, SPIRITUALITY, AND PHILOSOPHY**
See also **NONVIOLENT POLITICS** under **POLITICAL THOUGHT** in **SOCIAL STUDIES**

0-486-24593-4 DOVER PB $8.95

The Essential Gandhi

A well-chosen selection of Gandhi's writings

See also **NONVIOLENT POLITICS** under **POLITICAL THOUGHT** in **SOCIAL STUDIES**

EDITED BY LOUIS FISCHER

0-394-71466-0 VINTAGE PB $11.00

B.R. **Nanda**

Mahatma Gandhi: A Biography

The authoritative account

81-224-0723-4 WILEY $56.00
0-19-563855-7 OXFORD PB $13.95

Gandhi

Current Affairs

Rolf **Caseen**

India: Population, Economy, Society

The country's population problem and its impact on the society

0-8419-0300-X HOLMES & MEIER $49.50
0-8419-0648-3 HOLMES & MEIER PB $19.50

Gita Mehta

Icarma Cola: The Marketing of the Mysic East

0-679-75433-4 VINTAGE PB $10.00

V.S. **Naipaul**

India: A Million Mutinies Now

Naipaul's impassioned account of India, his ancestral country. Shaped by his obsession with the subcontinent, to him at once a homeland and an alien nation, this landmark achievement follows up on the book he wrote on first venturing there 30 years ago. "Naipaul's book partakes of the excellence of every category and fulfills itself in one of the oldest and rarest forms—prophecy. It bears witness, in unforgettable language, to the best of hopes in the worst of times"—*Christian Science Monitor*

See also **CARIBBEAN LITERATURE** in **LITERATURE OF THE AMERICAS**

0-670-83702-4 VIKING $24.95
0-14-015680-1 PENGUIN PB $14.95

To awaken to history was to cease to live instinctively. It was to begin to see oneself and one's group the way the outside world saw one; and it was to know a kind of rage. India was now full of this rage. There had been a general awakening. But everyone awakened first to his own group or community; every group thought itself unique in its awakening; and every group sought to separate its rage from the rage of other groups.

INDIA: A MILLION MUTINIES NOW

Pakistan

Carved out of the northwestern provinces of the Indian subcontinent, the predominantly Muslim state of Pakistan came into existence in 1947. Since independence, political parties have functioned only intermittently and martial law has been periodically imposed, keeping Pakistan always one step away from an established democracy.

Closely tied with the United States, Pakistan was often perceived as a buffer against communism, and was effectively used to channel arms to the Afghan rebels against the Soviet-backed Kabul regime.

Stanley **Wolpert**

Zulfi Bhutto of Pakistan: His Life and Times

The wealthy lawyer who headed the government of Pakistan from 1971 to 1977 and the father of Benazir Bhutto

0-19-507661-3 OXFORD $35.00

David G. **Mandelbaum**

Women's Seclusion and Men's Honor: Sex Roles in North India, Bangladesh, and Pakistan

0-8165-1400-3 ARIZONA PB $15.50

Afghanistan

The mountainous terrain of the Himalayan foothills has helped to preserve the independence of the Islamic population (over 20 million at last count in 1993) for hundreds of years. For the British Empire it was the turbulent northwest frontier. The former Soviet Union was the most recent expansionist power to retreat before the hardiness and pugnacity of the inhabitants. By the time they completed their pullout in 1989, more than 15,000 Soviet soldiers had been killed.

Najibullah declared a state of emergency three days after the completion of the Soviet withdrawal, then replaced non-Communist members of the cabinet with Communist constituents. After a failed coup attempt in 1990, and the formation of the virtually powerless Homeland party in June of that year, the United States and the former Soviet Union agreed to end military aid to the Kabul government and the rebels. In 1992 rebels forced Najibullah out of power, leaving ethnic and political rivals vying for control.

Raja **Anwar**

The Tragedy of Afghanistan: A First-Hand Account

Conversations in an Afghan prison with leaders of both factions of Afghan communism provide the basis of this readable analysis

TRANSLATED BY KHALID HASAN

0-86091-979-X VERSO PB $19.95

Artyom **Borovik**

The Hidden War: A Russian Journalist's Account of the Soviet War in Afghanistan

"I have read no other account of the war in Afghanistan equal to this—an eyewitness account of the soldier's experiences, free from politics. In other words, this is literature, not journalism"—Graham Greene

See also **THE SOVIET UNION ABROAD: TWILIGHT OF THE COLD WAR** under **THE SOVIET UNION: FROM KRUSHCHEV TO GORBACHEV** under **RUSSIAN STUDIES**

0-87113-283-4 ATLANTIC MONTHLY PB $18.95

Henry S. **Bradsher**

Afghanistan and the Soviet Union

0-8223-0556-9 DUKE $39.95

Sandy **Gall**

Behind Russian Lines: An Afghan Journal

0-312-07260-0 ST. MARTIN'S $35.00

René **Grousset**

The Empire of the Steppes: A History of Central Asia

0-8135-1304-9 RUTGERS PB $20.00

Olivier **Roy**

Islam and Resistance in Afghanistan

0-521-32833-0 CAMBRIDGE $29.95
0-521-39700-6 CAMBRIDGE PB $19.95

Barnett R. **Rubin**

The Fragmentation of Afghanistan: State Formation and Collapse in the International System

0-300-05963-9 YALE $37.50

Sri Lanka

After nearly four and a half decades of foreign domination, beginning with the Portuguese and followed by the Dutch and the British, Sri Lanka (formerly Ceylon) became an independent state in 1948.

Located off the southern tip of India, the island enjoyed uninterrupted progress until recently. The minority (Hindu) Tamil population (20 percent) claims that its demands for equal opportunities in the (Buddhist) Sinhalese-dominated state have not been dealt with fairly. Since 1983, the country has been torn by civil war, with the body count up to 40,000 in 1995, despite a brief period of enforced peace between 1987 and 1990. With the resumption of the civil war in 1995, newly elected president Chandrika Kumartatunga offered the rebels administrative control of one of eight proposed new regions. Hopes for ending the civil war suffered a setback on January 31, 1996, with a Tamil rebel car bombing in Colombo's financial district.

Pranay **Gupte**

Sri Lanka: Unrest in Paradise

0-87131-529-7 EVANS $17.95

China

General Histories

John K. **Fairbank** & Edwin O. **Reischauer**

East Asia: Tradition and Transformation

This book remains the most widely used introduction to the history and culture of East Asia

See also **ASIA** under **WORLD HISTORIES** under **THE VARIETIES OF CIVILIZATION**

See also **EAST ASIA AS ECONOMIC AND POLITICAL REGION: GENERAL STUDIES** under **SOUTHEAST ASIA AND THE PHILIPPINES**

0-395-45023-3 HOUGHTON MIFFLIN $56.76

Jacques **Gernet**

A History of Chinese Civilization

An elegantly written one-volume history, which defines the political, social, and intellectual trends from China's past and present

0-521-24130-8 CAMBRIDGE $94.95
0-521-49781-7 CAMBRIDGE PB $24.95

Ray **Huang**

China: A Macro History

A compressed and very readable interpretation of the full sweep of Chinese history clarifying underlying patterns relevant to today's events

0-87332-728-4 SHARPE PB $19.95

W.J.F. **Jenner**

The Tyranny of History: The Roots of China's Crisis

0-14-014677-6 PENGUIN PB $12.95

S. Robert **Ramsey**

The Languages of China

This wonderfully informative book provides a regional, social, and demographic history along with its compelling study of the many languages of China

0-691-01468-X PRINCETON PB $18.95

Edward H. **Schaefer**

The Vermilion Bird: T'ang Images of the South

See also **T'ANG POETRY** under **CRITICAL STUDIES OF CLASSICAL CHINESE LITERATURE** under **CLASSICAL CHINESE LITERATURE** in **LITERATURE OF EUROPE, AFRICA, AND ASIA**

0-520-05463-6 CALIFORNIA PB $17.00

Jonathan D. **Spence**

Chinese Roundabout: Essays in History and Culture

0-393-03355-4 NORTON $24.95

0-393-30994-0 NORTON PB $12.95

Imperial China

Charles **Hucker**

China to 1850: A Short History

Brisk and reliable introduction to the pre-modern era

0-8047-0957-2 STANFORD $24.50

0-8047-0958-0 STANFORD PB $9.95

Charles O. **Hucker**

China's Imperial Past: An Introduction to Chinese History and Culture

"An eminently sound introduction to its subject," this volume offers a record of major events, a history of ideas, political institutions, socio-economics, literature, and art

0-8047-0887-8 STANFORD $57.50

Sechin **Jagchid** & Van Jay **Symons**

Peace, War, and Trade Along the Great Wall: Nomadic-Chinese Interaction Through Two Millennia

0-253-33187-0 INDIANA $15.95

Owen **Lattimore**

Inner Asian Frontiers of China

0-19-582781-3 OXFORD $35.00

Endymion **Wilkinson**

History of Imperial China

0-674-39680-4 HARVARD PB $16.00

Modern China

John K. **Fairbank**

The Great Chinese Revolution: 1800-1985

A brilliant summary

0-06-039076-X HARPERCOLLINS PB $14.00

Immanuel **Hsu**

The Rise of Modern China

0-19-505867-4 OXFORD $38.00

Mao Tse-Tung

Maurice **Meisner**

Mao's China and After

The most comprehensive of the new texts, and the strongest and most provocative in its treatment of politics and ideology

0-02-920870-X FREE PRESS $29.95

0-02-920880-7 FREE PRESS PB $18.95

Jonathan D. **Spence**

The Gate of Heavenly Peace: The Chinese and Their Revolution, 1895-1980

A century of change, through portraits of revolutionary leaders. "A magical symphony that tells us as no conventional history could of the agony of a nation in awesome labor" —Harrison E. Salisbury

0-14-006279-3 VIKING PB $13.95

The Search For Modern China

An immense, profusely illustrated history of China since the 17th century. "Will remain unrivaled for a generation to come…*The Search for Modern China* will give its readers a new appreciation of America's China problem and, more important, the Chinese people's problems" —John K. Fairbank, *NY Review of Books*

0-393-02708-2 NORTON $32.95

0-393-30780-8 NORTON PB $26.95

Reference

Caroline **Blunden** & Mark **Elvin**

A Cultural Atlas of China

A socio-anthropological compendium useful as background to the study of art

See also **CHINA** under **EAST ASIAN ART** in **ART**

0-87196-132-6 FACTS ON FILE $45.00

Hugh B. **O'Neill**

Companion to Chinese History

Handy reference combining a who's who, a gazetteer, a chronology, and a mini-atlas

0-87196-841-X FACTS ON FILE $27.50

0-8160-1825-1 FACTS ON FILE PB $14.95

Cambridge University Press

The Cambridge History of China

The Cambridge History of China spans the Course of Chinese history and provides a scholarly treatment with exhaustive references. New volumes will appear annually

Volume 1 The Ch'in and Han Empires, 221 B.C.-220 A.D.

0-521-24327-0 CAMBRIDGE $155.00

Volume 2

0-521-24328-9 CAMBRIDGE $85.00

Volume 3 Sui and T'ang China, 589-906, Part I

0-521-21446-7 CAMBRIDGE $155.00

Volume 4

0-521-24329-7 CAMBRIDGE $85.00

Volume 5

0-521-24330-0 CAMBRIDGE $85.00

Volume 6 Alien Regimes and Border States, 907-1368

See also **IMPERIAL CHINA**

0-521-24331-9 CAMBRIDGE $125.00

Volume 7 Ming China, 1368-1644, Part 2

0-521-24332-7 CAMBRIDGE $155.00

Volume 10 Late Ch'ing, 1800-1911, Part I

0-521-21447-5 CAMBRIDGE $155.00

Volume 11 Late Ch'ing, 1800-1911, Part 2

0-521-22029-7 CAMBRIDGE $155.00

Volume 12 Republican China, 1912-1949, Part 1

0-521-23541-3 CAMBRIDGE $165.00

Volume 13 Republican China, 1912-1949, Part 2

0-521-24338-6 CAMBRIDGE $155.00

Volume 14 The People's Republic of China, 1949-1976

0-521-24336-X CAMBRIDGE $135.00

Volume 15 The People's Republic, Part II: Revolutions within the Chinese Revolution

0-521-24337-8 CAMBRIDGE $140.00

Archaeology and Early Chinese Civilization

Burton Watson, translator

Courtier and Commoner in Ancient China: Selections from the History of Former Han by Pan Ku

An early Chinese history, demonstrating the richness of the written historical tradition

0-231-08354-8 COLUMBIA PB $18.00

Records of the Historian

Selections from Ssu-ma Ch'ien's *Shih Chi*, one of the great early Chinese histories on the founding of the Han dynasty

0-231-03321-4 COLUMBIA PB $24.50

Selections from the Tso Chuan: China's Oldest Narrative History

A literary and historical masterpiece of the 3rd century BC

0-231-06715-1 COLUMBIA PB $15.50

Topics in Imperial Civilization

Dynastic Politics

Beatrice **Bartlett**

Monarchs and Ministers: The Grand Councils in Mid-Ch'ing China, 1723-1820

0-520-08645-7 CALIFORNIA PB $19.00

John **Chaffee**

The Thorny Gates of Learning in Sung China

The stability and conservatism of Chinese government was achieved by the Confucian ideal of a highly developed bureaucracy. Chaffee focuses on its effectiveness in the Sung dynasty

0-7914-2423-5 SUNY $59.50

0-7914-2424-3 SUNY PB $19.95

Ray **Huang**

1587, a Year of No Significance: The Ming Dynasty in Decline

"Cleverly constructed and deliberately paradoxical. If 1587 is of no significance in the larger view, it is nevertheless full of incident, and each incident carries promise of future drama"—Jonathan D. Spence

0-300-02884-9 YALE PB $17.00

Robert **Marshall**

Storm from the East: From Ghengis Khan to Khubilai Khan

0-520-08300-8 CALIFORNIA $30.00

Shih-Shan **Tsai**

The Eunuchs in the Ming Dynasty

0-7914-2688-2 SUNY PB $18.95

Ichisadu **Miyazaki**

China's Examination Hell: The Civil Service Examination of Imperial China

For two millennia, the bureaucracy was the only outlet for rising talent. This book details types of questions from the ferocious exams, the psychological and financial burdens on the students, and such problems as nepotism and cheating

0-300-02639-0 YALE PB $11.00

Frederic **Wakeman**

The Great Enterprise: The Manchu Reconstruction of Imperial Order in 17th Century China

Winner of the Bancroft Prize; a 2-volume work

0-520-04804-0 CALIFORNIA $110.00

Biographies and Memoirs

Jonathan D. **Spence**

Emperor of China: Self-Portrait of K'ang-Hsi

Selections from the writings of one of the great emperors, a contemporary of Louis XIV and Peter the Great. His border treaty with Russia was the first ever between China and a Western power

0-679-72074-X VINTAGE PB $14.00

Morris **Rossabi**

Khubilai Khan: His Life and Times

The first and greatest of the Mongol rulers of China. He sent letters to the pope through Marco Polo, but burned the Taoist sacred books and installed ignorant Mongol soldiers over mandarin administrators

0-520-06740-1 CALIFORNIA PB $16.95

Marco **Polo**

The Travels of Marco Polo

The Italian trader who followed the Silk Road opened by the Mongol invasion and became the advisor of Khubilai Khan. He dictated his adventures in an Ottoman Turkish prison

Volume 1

See also **EUROPE AND THE REST OF THE WORLD** under **MEDIEVAL AND RENAISSANCE EUROPE**

See also **MEDIEVAL LITERATURE**

0-486-27587-6 DOVER PB $17.95

Volume 2

See also **EUROPE AND THE REST OF THE WORLD** under **MEDIEVAL AND RENAISSANCE EUROPE**

See also **MEDIEVAL LITERATURE**

0-486-27586-8 DOVER PB $17.95

The Travels of Marco Polo

See also **MEDIEVAL LITERATURE** in **LITERATURE OF EUROPE, AFRICA, AND ASIA**

TRANSLATED BY RONALD LATHAM

0-14-044057-7 PENGUIN PB $10.95

Richard **Strassberg**

The World of K'ung Shang-Jen: A Man of Letters in Early Ch'ing China

The world of a Confucian scholar/official

See also **DRAMA** under **CRITICAL STUDIES OF CLASSICAL CHINESE LITERATURE** under **CLASSICAL CHINESE LITERATURE** in **LITERATURE OF EUROPE, AFRICA, AND ASIA**

INTRODUCTION BY CYRIL BIRCH

0-231-05530-7 COLUMBIA $59.00

Chinese Thought

Jerry **Dennerline**

Qian Mu and the World of Seven Mansions

The life of one man provides the background for a penetrating analysis of Confucianism as a moral system during a time of great political and intellectual upheaval

0-300-04296-5 YALE $27.00

Joseph **Levenson**

Confucian China and Its Modern Fate: A Trilogy

Studies the continuity of the classical dilemmas of Chinese history—the intellectual and ethical tradition, and the tensions between the monarchy and the bureaucracy

0-520-00736-0 CALIFORNIA $55.00

0-520-00737-9 CALIFORNIA PB $22.50

Donald S. **Lopez**, Jr., editor

Religions of China in Practice

0-691-02144-9 PRINCETON $59.50

0-691-02143-0 PRINCETON PB $19.95

Daniel C. **Overmyer**

Religions of China

A concise and agreeable sketch of the interaction of the three vibrant ways of thought—Confucian, Taoist, and Buddhist

0-06-066401-0 HARPERCOLLINS PB $11.00

Benjamin **Schwartz**

The World of Thought in Ancient China

The most important recent study investigates the thinkers—including Confucius—of the golden age of Chinese thought between the 6th and 3rd centuries BC

See also **INTELLECTUAL HISTORY** under **THE VARIETIES OF CIVILIZATION**

0-674-96190-0 HARVARD $37.00

0-674-96191-9 HARVARD PB $18.95

Sun **Tzu**

The Art of War

Written in China more than 2000 years ago, this series of aphoristic essays is the first known study of the planning and conduct of military operations

See also **ANCIENT WARFARE** under **WARS THROUGH THE AGES** under **MILITARY AFFAIRS**

TRANSLATED WITH AN INTRODUCTION BY SAMUEL B. GRIFFITH

0-19-501540-1 OXFORD $19.95

0-19-501476-6 OXFORD PB $8.95

Meir **Shahar** & Robert P **Weller**, editors
Unruly Gods: Divinity and Society in China
0-8248-1724-9 HAWAII $32.00

Max **Weber**
The Religion of China: Confucianism and Taoism
In this famous work, Weber, the master sociologist of religion, argues that China's religious ethic impeded the development of a rational capitalist economy
See also **CLASSICAL EUROPEAN SOCIOLOGY** under **SOCIOLOGY** in **SOCIAL STUDIES**
See also **THE CHINESE TRADITIONS** under **ASIAN RELIGION AND PHILOSOPHY** in **RELIGION, SPIRITUALITY, AND PHILOSOPHY**
0-02-934450-6 FREE PRESS PB $19.95

Arthur **Wright**
Confucianism and Chinese Civilization
The system of moral order that restored Chinese society again and again to long periods of stability and creative achievement
0-8047-0891-6 STANFORD PB $17.95

Buddhism in Chinese History
A short, clearly written work for the general reader. "Throws light on the renewed process of borrowing and adaptation taking place in China today"—Derk Bodde
See also **GENERAL STUDIES** under **CHINESE BUDDHISM** under **ASIAN RELIGION AND PHILOSOPHY** in **RELIGION, SPIRITUALITY, AND PHILOSOPHY**
0-8047-0548-8 STANFORD PB $10.95

Culture, Society, and Economy

Mark **Elvin**
Pattern of the Chinese Past: A Social and Economic Interpretation
A controversial interpretation of China's longterm development trajectory
0-8047-0826-6 STANFORD $47.50
0-8047-0876-2 STANFORD PB $16.95

Jacques **Gernet**
Buddhism in Chinese Society: An Economic History from the Fifth to the Tenth Century
TRANSLATED BY FRANCISCUS VERELLEN
0-231-07380-1 COLUMBIA $42.50

Daily Life in China on the Eve of the Mongol Invasion, 1250-1276
A fascinating account of Chinese customs, beliefs, institutions, and the splendid lifestyle of Hangchow, the capital of the doomed Sung dynasty
0-8047-0720-0 STANFORD PB $12.95

Bret **Hinsch**
Passions of the Cut Sleeve: The Male Homosexual Tradition in China
0-520-06720-7 CALIFORNIA $35.00

Chao **Kang**
Man and Land in Chinese History: An Economic Analysis
Agriculture from ancient to modern times
0-8047-1271-9 STANFORD $42.50

Xinru **Liu**
Silk and Religion: An Exploration of Material Life and the Thought of People, A.D. 600-1200
More than a study of China, this is an exploration of the long-distance silk trade in Eurasia, which was established centuries before the emergence of the Tang dynasty. The author is at the Chinese Academy of Social Sciences, Beijing
0-19-563655-4 OXFORD $22.95

Susan **Mann**
Precious Records: Women in China's Long Eighteenth Century
0-8047-2743-0 STANFORD $42.00

Susan **Naquin** & Evelyn S. **Rawski**
Chinese Society in the Eighteenth Century
"[An] interesting and well-informed survey of China between about 1680 and 1820"
—W.J.F. Jenner, *Asian Affairs*
0-300-03848-8 YALE $32.00
0-300-04602-2 YALE PB $17.00

Edward **Schaefer**
The Golden Peaches of Samarkand
0-520-05462-8 CALIFORNIA PB $18.95

Edward Schafer is the Sinologists' Vladimir Nabokov. His feeling for Tang China, informed by an abiding interest in the natural world and an uncompromising attention to accuracy, recalls the sensibility of an emigre whose homeland has been irrevocably altered in his absence. When he describes the silk route, as he does here, his precision of detail renders material the source of so many Western dreams of the rich and exotic.
THE GOLDEN PEACHES OF SAMARKAND

Salley Hovey **Wriggins**
Xuanzang: A Buddhist Pilgrim on the Silk Road
The saga of the seventh-century Chinese monk Xuanzang, who completed a 16-year journey to discover the heart of Buddhism at its source in India; richly illustrated. "A significant introduction to an extraordinary traveler's extraordinary contribution to Buddhist history"—*Publishers Weekly*
0-8133-2801-2 WESTVIEW $32.50

Madeleine **Zelin**
The Magistrate's Tale: Rationalizing Fiscal Reform in Eighteenth Century Ch'ing China
A lucid explanation of Ch'ing economy and finance
0-520-04930-6 CALIFORNIA $55.00
0-520-07898-5 CALIFORNIA PB $16.95

China and the West

David S.G. **Goodman**, editor
China and the West: Ideas and Activists
0-7190-2941-4 MANCHESTER $59.95

Alain **Peyrefitte**
The Immobile Empire
A recounting of the first official British diplomatic mission to Imperial China in the 18th century. The Chinese view of the visit is supplied by Peyrefitte, providing a classic account of deliberate misunderstanding and genuine mystification on both sides, and a penetrating look at Chinese foreign policy in the mid-Qing Dynasty
0-394-58654-9 KNOPF $30.00

Jonathan D. **Spence**
The Memory Palace of Matteo Ricci
"Bodhisattva" Ricci was the first Jesuit to realize that the Chinese literati could be reached by introducing the arts and sciences of Europe
0-14-008098-8 VIKING PB $14.95

The Question of Hu
The story of one man who came from China to France in the 1720s
See also **LOUIS XIV AND THE ANCIEN REGIME** under **EARLY MODERN FRANCE** under **EARLY MODERN EUROPE**
0-679-72580-6 VINTAGE PB $14.00

The End of Imperial Power

So remote were Chinese perceptions of the West that in less than 50 years, between the embassy of Lord MacCartney in 1793 and the outbreak of the Opium War in 1839, Britain went from being "a small barbarian island where the women wear their hair loose" to being a dominant power in China. The Chinese were never to catch up. The consequences were futile popular rebellions against the encroachments of 19th-century imperialism and the eventual collapse of the Ch'ing dynasty in 1911. After the failure of the Republic to control the feuding warlords, whatever stability Chiang Kai-shek might have imposed was destroyed by the Japanese invasion of 1932.

Guy **Alitto**
The Last Confucian: Liang Shuming and the Chinese Dilemma of Modernity
Presents the conservative thinker as an opponent of the alienation of technological society
0-520-05318-4 CALIFORNIA PB $15.00

Jean **Chesneaux**, editor
Popular Movements and Secret Societies in China, 1840-1950
Runaway inflation, government corruption, and foreign invasion created huge popular uprisings with messianic overtones throughout the 19th century
0-8047-0790-1 STANFORD $47.50

Joseph W. **Esherick**

The Origins of the Boxer Uprising

The revolt against European imperialism was not inspired by antagonism to the dynasty but by resentment of alien influence. Winner of the John K. Fairbank Prize in East Asian History

0-520-06459-3 CALIFORNIA PB $17.00

Peter **Fleming**

The Siege at Peking

A sympathetic but basically Western account of the Boxer uprising that pinned Europeans in their embassies for almost two months in 1900

0-19-583735-5 OXFORD PB $11.95

Philip **Kuhn**

Rebellion and Its Enemies in Late Imperial China: Militarization and Social Structure, 1796-1864

The gradual erosion of central power led to the temporary success of the T'ai P'ing rebellion, whose motives ranged from mystical to social reformist. It prohibited drugs and alcohol, and asserted equality of the sexes

0-674-74954-5 HARVARD PB $14.95

Elizabeth **Perry**

Rebels and Revolutionaries in North China, 1845-1945

A study of three rebellions, in the area from which Mao marched on Peking, shows the importance of topography and peasant support for guerrilla movements

0-8047-1175-5 STANFORD PB $15.95

Douglas R. **Reynolds**

China, 1898-1912: The Xinzheng Revolution and Japan

0-674-11660-7 HARVARD $32.00

Jonathan D. **Spence**

God's Chinese Son: The Taiping Heavenly Kingdom of Hong Xiuquan

The Sterling Professor of History at Yale, Spence provides a brilliant narrative investigation of Hong Xiuquan, a religious visionary whose 19th-century dynasty cost at least 20 million Chinese their lives. Through Hong's 11-year reign, Spence tells a story of radical social reform, roving bandits, pirates, and a spectacular vision of clashing armies over a vast territory. History at its most compelling

0-393-03844-0 NORTON $27.50

0-393-31556-8 NORTON PB $15.95

Frederic **Wakeman**

The Fall of Imperial China

Combines a description of the cycle of the dynasties with a history of the decline and fall of the Ch'ing under European pressure

0-02-933680-5 FREE PRESS PB $17.95

Arthur **Waley**

The Opium War Through Chinese Eyes

These superbly translated diaries, autobiographies, and confessions of the Chinese participants are animated by brief connecting narratives

0-8047-0611-5 STANFORD PB $12.95

Mary **Wright**

The Last Stand of Chinese Conservatism: The Tung-Chih Restoration, 1862-1874

A useful starting point for exploring the tensions in Chinese politics and statecraft as the Ch'ing dynasty confronted the unfamiliar challenge of imperialism

0-8047-0475-9 STANFORD $57.50

0-8047-0476-7 STANFORD PB $17.95

Biography

John Maxwell **Hamilton**

Edgar Snow: A Biography

The life of the American midwesterner whose love for China and the oppressed gained him access to the inner circle around Mao both before and after his rise to power

0-253-31909-9 INDIANA $9.95

Edgar Snow

S. Bernard **Thomas**

Season of High Adventure: Edgar Snow in China

0-520-20276-7 CALIFORNIA $34.95

Jonathan D. **Spence**

The Death of Woman Wang

The plight of a Chinese peasant woman

0-14-005121-X PENGUIN PB $10.95

Sterling **Seagrave**

Dragon Lady: The Life and Legend of the Last Empress of China

"*Dragon Lady* not only details Dowager Empress Tzu Hsi's life in a fresh way…but is full of resonances with China's contemporary struggle"—*Washington Post Book World*

0-679-73369-8 VINTAGE PB $16.00

Caleb **Carr**

The Devil Soldier: The Story of Frederick Townsend Ward

Carr has rendered a gripping portrait of the mercenary and adventurer who was the first American ever to be made a mandarin in Imperial China. Ward, who by the age of 27 had fought with Garibaldi in South America and the French army in the Crimea, was the man who marshalled the famous native troop of "devil soldiers" to fight the Taiping army in Shanghai

0-679-76128-4 RANDOM HOUSE PB $15.00

Republican and Nationalist China

Sherman **Cochran**, editor

One Day in China: May 21, 1936

0-300-03400-8 YALE PB $16.00

Lloyd E. **Eastman**

Family, Field, and Ancestors: Constancy and Change in China's Social and Economic History, 1550-1949

Argues that modern China is the product less of sudden revolutionary change than forces at work since the 16th century

0-19-505270-6 OXFORD PB $16.95

Shinkichi **Eto** & Harold **Schiffrin**

1911 Revolution in China

The events leading up to the revolution that overthrew the Ch'ing dynasty and established the Republic under the leadership of Sun Yat-Sen

0-86008-349-7 TOKYO $37.50

Edward **Friedman**

Backward Toward Revolution: The Chinese Revolutionary Party

0-520-03279-9 CALIFORNIA PB $13.00

Tien Hung-Mao

Government and Politics in Kuomintang China, 1927-1937

0-8047-0812-6 STANFORD $37.50

Brian G. **Martin**

The Shanghai Green Gang: Politics and Organized Crime, 1919-1937

Argues that the Green Gang, the most powerful secret society in China during the first half of the 20th century, was a resilient social organization that adapted successfully to the complex environment of a modern urban society

0-520-20114-0 CALIFORNIA $40.00

Stirling **Seagrave**

The Soong Dynasty

The popular account of the influential merchant clan that set policy for nationalist China by marrying its daughters to Sun Yat-Sen, Chiang Kai-shek, and the finance czar H.H. Kung

0-06-091318-5 HARPERCOLLINS PB $17.00

Arthur N. **Waldron**

The Chinese Civil Wars, 1911-1949

0-340-58264-2 ARNOLD PB $16.95

James **Sheridan**

China in Disintegration: The Republican Era in Chinese History, 1912-1949

Stimulating narrative of the chaotic years of the warlords, the Japanese invasion, and the rise of Mao

0-02-928650-6 FREE PRESS PB $19.95

James **Sheridan**

Chinese Warlord: The Career of Feng Yu-Hsiang

"Tracing the career of the colorful 'Christian general,' it also analyzes the essence of warlordism"—John K. Fairbank

0-8047-0145-8 STANFORD $52.50

C. Martin **Wilbur**

Sun Yat-Sen: Frustrated Patriot

After losing control of the revolution to the forces of reaction, Sun founded the Kuomintang and formed an alliance with the communists in an attempt to provide stability for China

0-231-04036-9 COLUMBIA $62.00

The Communist Revolution

The corruption of the Kuomintang under Chiang Kai-shek and its failure to withstand the Japanese effectively undermined its support before and during the Second World War. Mao and the communists, however, had survived annihilation at the hands of the KMT by the Long March from Kiangsi province to Yenan, a distance of 6,000 miles. They flourished at their new base, where they initiated popular land reforms, and soon became strong enough to cause serious losses to the Japanese. After the war their disciplined and confident troops expelled Chiang and his followers to the island of Formosa (Taiwan) and began the reconstruction of mainland China along the lines of the Russian example.

For related reading, see THE SECOND WORLD WAR

Lucien **Bianco**

Origins of the Chinese Revolution: 1915-1949

Places China's modern revolution in the context of such movements since 1789, emphasizing its roots in the peasantry

0-8047-0827-4 STANFORD PB $12.95

John **Boyle**

China and Japan at War: 1937-1945

The politics of collaboration

0-8047-0800-2 STANFORD $55.00

Jean **Chesneaux**

The Chinese Labor Movement

The leading study of labor and the communist movement

0-8047-0644-1 STANFORD $67.50

Edwin **Hoyt**

The Rise of the Chinese Republic: From the Last Emperor to Deng Xiaoping

Fast-paced narrative covers all the bases from the 1911 revolution to the tentative capitalist ventures of the 1980s

0-306-80426-3 DA CAPO PB $13.95

Harold **Isaacs**

Tragedy of the Chinese Revolution

Valuable work by an excellent scholar

0-8047-0415-5 STANFORD $52.50
0-8047-0416-3 STANFORD PB $17.95

Chalmers **Johnson**

Peasant Nationalism and Communist Power: The Emergence of Revolutionary China, 1937-1945

0-8047-0073-7 STANFORD $37.50
0-8047-0074-5 STANFORD PB $14.95

Odd Arne **Westad**

Cold War and Revolution: Soviet-American Rivalry and the Origins of the Chinese Civil War, 1944-1946

0-231-07985-0 COLUMBIA PB $17.00

Mao

Stuart R. **Schram**

The Thought of Mao Tse-Tung

A pioneering collection, presenting both the original texts and their official, revised versions

0-521-32549-8 CAMBRIDGE $60.00
0-521-31062-8 CAMBRIDGE PB $21.95

Edgar **Snow**

Red Star over China

A journalistic classic on the early communist movement, including the autobiography of Mao as told to Snow in 1936

INTRODUCTION BY JOHN K. FAIRBANK

0-8021-5093-4 GROVE PB $15.95

Mao Zedong

The Writings of Mao

Volume 1: September 1949-December 1955

The first three of a projected five volumes in an authoritative collection

EDITED BY MICHAEL Y.M. KAU & JOHN LEUNG

0-87332-391-2 SHARPE $132.95

Volume 2: January 1956-December 1957

EDITED BY MICHAEL Y.M. KAU & JOHN LEUNG

0-87332-392-0 SHARPE $132.95

Volume 3: 1949-1976

EDITED BY MICHAEL Y.M. KAU & JOHN LEUNG

0-87332-393-9 SHARPE $95.00

Li **Zhisui** & Anne **Thurston**

The Private Life of Chairman Mao

"From now on, no one will be able to pretend to understand Chairman Mao's place in history without reference to this revealing account" —Professor Lucian Pye, MIT

0-679-76443-7 RANDOM HOUSE PB $20.00

The People's Republic

A. Doak **Barnett**

China's Far West: Four Decades of Change

0-8133-1774-6 WESTVIEW PB $24.95

B. Michael **Frolic**

Mao's People: Sixteen Portraits of Life in Revolutionary China

0-674-54846-9 HARVARD $25.00
0-674-54845-0 HARVARD PB $17.95

John **Gittings**

The Role of the Chinese Army

0-19-500160-5 OXFORD $19.95

Harry **Harding**

Organizing China: The Problem of Bureaucracy, 1949-1976

0-8047-1080-5 STANFORD $52.50

William A. **Joseph**

The Critique of Ultra-Leftism in China, 1958-1981

0-8047-1208-5 STANFORD $42.50

Witold **Rodzinski**

The People's Republic of China: A Concise Political History

Poland's ambassador to China separates fact from myth and propaganda

0-02-926872-9 FREE PRESS PB $14.95

Franz **Schurmann**

Ideology and Organization in Communist China

How the Chinese communists substituted their own ideas and methods for the traditional social system

0-520-01153-8 CALIFORNIA PB $16.00

Mark **Selden**, editor

The People's Republic of China: A Documentary History of Revolutionary Change

Traces the shifting contours of China's political economy

0-85345-532-5 MONTHLY REVIEW PB $18.00

Andrew G. **Walder**

Communist Neo-Traditionalism: Work and Authority in Chinese Industry

Traces the parallels between traditional and post-revolutionary work relations

0-520-06470-4 CALIFORNIA PB $15.00

The Cultural Revolution

In 1966 Mao instigated a new phase of the revolution with the intention of revivifying his political project. The Red Guard, an organization of fanatical teenagers who had grown up since

1949, were encouraged to overturn any person, idea, or institution smacking of fuedal imperialist influence. So nurse's aides became surgeons overnight, physicists became turnip farmers, most of China's statuary was defaced, and China's wealth of drama and operatic tradition was replaced with 8 facile operas commissioned by Mao's wife, Jiang Qing. The best and the brightest were silenced, many forever

Anita **Chan** & others

Chen Village: The Recent History of a Peasant Community in Mao's China

Based on refugee interviews, the political history of a south China rural community, from the Socialist Education Movement through the Cultural Revolution

0-520-08108-0 CALIFORNIA........$45.00

Lowell **Dittmer**

Liu Shao-Ch'i and the Chinese Cultural Revolution: The Politics of Mass Criticism

The most prominent of the old guard who suffered humiliation and disgrace during the Cultural Revolution

0-520-02574-1 CALIFORNIA........$52.00

Roderick **MacFarquar**

The Origins of the Cultural Revolution

Personality conflicts, the Sino-Soviet break, and the horrendous failure of the Great Leap Forward all contributed to the human tragedy

Volume 1
Contradictions Among the People, 1956-1957

0-231-08385-8 COLUMBIA PB........$19.00

Volume 2
The Great Leap Forward, 1958-1960

0-231-05716-4 COLUMBIA........$56.50

0-231-05717-2 COLUMBIA PB........$24.50

Anchee **Min**

Red Azalea

Min's life as a communist postulant and drone was forever altered when, from a pool of 20,000 applicants, she was chosen to play the lead in an opera by Madame Mao. Surviving a love affair with Madame's cultural advisor, the death of Mao, a bout with TB, and the ubiquitous political uncertainties of China, Min managed to emigrate to Chicago, where she now lives. "A haunting and quietly dramatic coming-of-age story with a cultural cataclysm as its backdrop"—*Kirkus Reviews*

See also **MEMOIRS**

0-425-14776-2 BERKLEY PB........$6.99

Tsou Tang

The Cultural Revolution and Post-Mao Reforms: A Historical Perspective

An informed overview locating China's tumultuous political transformations against the background both of the imperial state and contemporary Leninist states

0-226-81513-7 CHICAGO........$32.50

0-226-81514-5 CHICAGO PB........$18.00

Zhai Zhenhua

Red Flower of China

Born two years after the Communist Party seized power in China, Zhu Zhenhua grew up in the movement. When the Red Guards sprang to power at Mao's behest she was a young student, passionately loyal to the party. Now she recounts her days within the Red Guard, the violence of "home raids,"and the purging, during which time she was sent to a peasant labor camp

See also **COMMUNIST LITERATURE SINCE 1949** under **FROM 1949 TO THE PRESENT** under **MODERN CHINESE LITERATURE** in **LITERATURE OF EUROPE, AFRICA, AND ASIA**

0-939149-83-4 SOHO........$24.00

1-56947-009-X SOHO PB........$13.00

China After Mao

Following Mao's death and the arrest of the "Gang of Four," China embarked on the most profound socioeconomic transformation since the collectivization, nationalization, and commune formation of 1955-58. The emergence of a broadly based, student-led democracy movement in May, 1989, and the brutal suppression of it cast doubt on the economic reform program and on the communist regime itself.

President Clinton's renewal of China's most favored nation trading status has been hotly debated. Human rights groups have exerted pressure on the nation for its poor human rights record, and in 1994 President Jiang Zemin promised a visiting American delegation that he would make an effort to improve it.

Richard **Baum**

Burying Mao: Chinese Politics in the Age of Deng Xiaoping

"How factions, the bane of Chinese politics, align and realign"—*TLS*

0-691-03637-3 PRINCETON PB........$18.95

Michel **Chossudovsky**

Towards Capitalist Restoration?: Chinese Socialism After Mao

0-312-81134-9 ST. MARTIN'S........$39.95

0-312-81135-7 ST. MARTIN'S PB........$18.95

John K. **Fairbank**

China Watch

A collection of Fairbank's expert musings on the peculiar relationship between the US and China

0-674-11765-4 HARVARD........$27.50

John **Gardner**

Chinese Politics and the Succession to Mao

Inner sanctum power-plays for the party succession, from the ill-fated Lin Biao, shot down while fleeing to Russia, to the eventual emergence of Deng Xiaoping

0-8419-0809-5 HOLMES & MEIER PB........$19.50

Maurice **Meisner**

The Deng Xiaoping Era: An Inquiry into the Fate of Chinese Socialism, 1978-1994

0-8090-7815-5 HILL & WANG........$27.50

Ross Gregory **Garnaut** & others, editors

The Third Revolution in the Chinese Countryside

"The first revolution in the Chinese countryside was the land reform after 1949. The second was the shift to the household responsibility system as a basis for agricultural production. This set the scene for the third revolution." Contributions by experts on the Chinese economy

0-521-55409-8 CAMBRIDGE........$54.95

Immanuel C.Y. **Hsu**

China Without Mao: The Search for a New Order

Focuses on the passage from an ideology-based political and economic structure to market-based socialism

0-19-506055-5 OXFORD........$38.00

0-19-506056-3 OXFORD PB........$11.95

Ezra F. **Vogel**

One Step Ahead in China: Guangdong Under Reform

0-674-63911-1 HARVARD PB........$16.95

Democracy and Dissent

Geremie **Barme** & Linda **Javin**, editors

New Ghosts, Old Dreams: Chinese Rebel Voices

A compendium of Chinese dissent in the last decade, excerpting fiction, poetry, songs, speeches, satire, newspaper articles, and even a television miniseries. This is the first English publication of this material, much of which was not widely available in China. "One of the rare books that actually gets through the impervious skin of China. From literature to dissident politics and pop culture to underground poetry, it is all here in a fascinating potpourri" —Orville Schell

0-8129-1927-0 TIME BOOKS........$30.00

Gregor **Benton** & Alan **Hunter**, editors

Wild Lily, Prairie Fire: China's Road to Democracy, Yan'an to Tian'Anmen, 1942-1989

0-691-04359-0 PRINCETON........$49.50

0-691-04358-2 PRINCETON PB........$19.95

Liu Binyan

People or Monsters? & Other Stories and Reportage from China After Mao

INTRODUCTION BY LEO OU-FAN LEE

0-253-34329-1 INDIANA........$20.00

0-253-20313-9 INDIANA PB........$4.95

Craig **Calhoun**

Neither Gods nor Emperors: Students and the Struggle for Democracy in China

0-520-08826-3 CALIFORNIA........$37.50

Randle **Edwards** & Andrew **Nathan**

Human Rights in Contemporary China

0-231-06180-3 COLUMBIA $37.50
0-231-06181-1 COLUMBIA PB $16.00

Merle **Goldman**

China's Intellectuals: Advice and Dissent

A good introduction to the role of intellectuals in the People's Republic

0-674-11970-3 HARVARD $29.00
0-674-11971-1 HARVARD PB $13.50

Literary Dissent in Communist China

Profiles the major revolutionary writers and discusses their conflict with the Communist party

See also **CRITICAL STUDIES OF MODERN CHINESE LITERATURE** under **MODERN CHINESE LITERATURE** in **LITERATURE OF EUROPE, AFRICA, AND ASIA**

0-674-53625-8 HARVARD $25.50

Merle **Goldman** & others, editors

China's Intellectuals and the State: In Search of a New Relationship

0-674-11972-X HARVARD PB $18.00

Andrew **Nathan**

Chinese Democracy

The work of a top scholar

0-520-05933-6 CALIFORNIA PB $14.00

Hongda Harry **Wu**

Troublemaker: One Man's Crusade Against China's Cruelty

See also **CONTEMPORARY CHINESE SOCIETY**

0-8129-6374-1 TIME BOOKS $25.00

Contemporary Chinese Society

William P. **Alford**

To Steal a Book Is an Elegant Offense: Intellectual Property Law in Chinese Civilization (Studies in East Asian Law, Harvard University)

Alford is the Jonathan Spence of Chinese legal studies. His insight into the cultural psychology of intellectual property, Chinese and Western, is intriguing and acute. This small volume traces the history of intellectual property law in China, offering an informed view of the prospects for Chinese intellectual property law

0-8047-2270-6 STANFORD $39.50

Godwin C. **Chu** & Frances L.K. **Hsu**

China's New Social Fabric

Argues that the enormous conservatism of local communities in China is still the glue that holds the new state together

0-7103-0050-6 KEGAN & PAUL PB $35.00

Lester R. **Brown**

Who Will Feed China?: Wake-Up Call for a Small Planet

From the World Watch Institute, an informative if over-pessimistic assessment of food availability in China and its impact on the rest of the world

0-393-31409-X NORTON PB $8.95

Hsu-Tung **Chang** & **Zhang Xudong**

Chinese Modernism in the Era of Reforms: Cultural Fever, Avant-Garde Fiction and the New Chinese Cinema

0-8223-1846-6 DUKE PB $21.95

J.A. **Cohen** & R. **Edwards**

Essays on China's Legal Tradition

The authors' involvement in China's nascent legal system (as longterm consultants for Chinese lawmakers and for American firms involved in China today) and their historical erudition are apparent in this valuable resource for all who would have a better understanding of the background and application of law in China

0-691-09238-9 PRINCETON $63.00

Elisabeth **Croll**

The Family Rice Bowl: Food and Domestic Economy in China

A comprehensive and thoughtful critical introduction to the country's economic development since 1949

0-86232-125-5 ZED PB $17.50

William **Hinton**

Shenfan: The Continuing Revolution in a Chinese Village

0-436-19630-1 RANDOM HOUSE $12.98

Alan **Hunter** & Kim-Kwong **Chan**

Protestantism in Contemporary China

0-521-44161-7 CAMBRIDGE $69.95

Alastair Iain **Johnston**

Cultural Realism: Strategic Culture and Grand Strategy in Chinese History

Johnston is an expert on the Chinese military, both historical and current, and brings his erudition to this lucid and serious reflection on strategy

0-691-02996-2 PRINCETON $39.50

Kenneth G. **Lieberthal** & David M. **Lampton**, editor

Bureaucracy, Politics, and Decision Making in Post-Mao China

Chinese policy is frequently regarded as the product of a monolithic authority. Lieberthal and Lampton effectively dispel this notion, revealing the myriad spheres of influence brought to bear on decisions large and small. A very useful and readable study for people who do business in China, and for anyone seeking a clearer notion of how China works

0-520-07356-8 CALIFORNIA $48.00

Nicholas **Lardy**

Economic Growth and Distribution in China

0-521-21904-3 CAMBRIDGE $65.00

Victor **Lippit**

The Economic Development of China

Early-20th-century economics and the attempt at socialist development since 1949

0-87332-404-8 SHARPE PB $23.95

Alan P. L. **Liu**

Mass Politics in the People's Republic: State and Society in Contemporary China

0-8133-1335-X WESTVIEW PB $19.95

Steven **Mosher**

Broken Earth: The Rural Chinese

"For readers wishing to go beyond the tales of happy workers and barefoot doctors, this book is highly recommended"—*Boston Herald*

0-02-921720-2 FREE PRESS PB $17.95

Leo **Orleans**

Every Fifth Child: The Population of China

0-8047-0819-3 STANFORD $32.50

Lynn **Pan**

Tracing It Home: A Chinese Journey

Pan sets out on a search for her roots following the unexpected death of her mother. The journey leads her from the remote reaches of Canada to Shanghai in the '40s and '50s. There she discovers a world rich in triumph, tragedy, and scandal on the brink of communist takeover. "The finest sort of historical and social writing: living, unpretentious, and moving, but with no recriminations or garment rending"
—*Kirkus Reviews*

1-56836-009-6 KODANSHA $22.00

William L. **Parish** & Martin K. **Whyte**

Village and Family in Contemporary China

A good introduction to both city and countryside

0-226-64591-6 CHICAGO PB $16.00

Dwight H. **Perkins** & **Shahid Yusuf**

Rural Development in China

0-8018-3261-6 JOHNS HOPKINS $28.95
0-8018-3066-4 JOHNS HOPKINS PB $14.95

Vaclav **Smil**

China's Environmental Crisis: An Inquiry into the Limits of National Development

An informed and balanced account of China's current environmental status, with an analysis of domestic and international implications of current trends

1-56324-041-6 SHARPE PB $22.95

Thomas G. **Rawski**
Economic Growth and Employment in China
0-19-520151-5 OXFORD $22.00

Gordon **White** & others
In Search of Civil Society: Market Reform and Social Change in Contemporary China
0-19-828956-1 OXFORD $65.00

Hongda Harry **Wu**
Troublemaker: One Man's Crusade Against China's Cruelty
See also DEMOCRACY AND DISSENT under CHINA AFTER MAO
0-8129-6374-1 TIME BOOKS $25.00

Jianying **Zha**
China Pop: How Soap Operas, Tabloids, and Bestsellers Are Transforming China
See also CHINESE LITERATURE SINCE 1949 under CRITICAL STUDIES OF MODERN CHINESE LITERATURE under MODERN CHINESE LITERATURE in LITERATURE OF EUROPE, AFRICA, AND ASIA
1-56584-249-9 NEW PRESS $20.00
1-56584-250-2 NEW PRESS PB $12.00

Women and the Family

Several recent books provide overviews of the changing position of Chinese women in the 20th century who are engaged in the often conflicting issues of feminism and socialist revolution.

Julie **Checkoway**
Little Sister: In Search of the Shadow of Chinese Women
0-670-84878-6 VIKING $22.95

Christina Kelley **Gilmartin**
Engendering the Chinese Revolution: Radical Women, Communist Politics, and Mass Movements in the 1920s
0-520-20346-1 CALIFORNIA PB $15.00

Ono **Kazuko**
Chinese Women in a Century of Revolution, 1850-1950
The only comprehensive history of women in China, from the Taiping rebellion to the People's Republic
0-8047-1496-7 STANFORD $39.50
0-8047-1497-5 STANFORD PB $13.95

William **Kessen**, editor
Childhood in China
Detailed observations of children's behavior successfully convey the feeling of childhood in the Peoples' Republic
0-300-01910-6 YALE $30.00

Alice P. **Lin**
Grandmother Had No Name
A Chinese-born New York professional's confrontation with the inequities of gender and culture in her own heritage
0-8351-2034-1 CHINA BOOKS PB $9.95

Judith **Stacey**
Patriarchy and Socialist Revolution in China
The limits of women's liberation
0-520-04826-1 CALIFORNIA PB $14.95

Denyse **Verschuur-Basse**
Chinese Women Speak
TRANSLATED BY ELIZABETH RAUCH-NOLAN
0-275-95393-9 PRAEGER $49.95

Margery **Wolf** & Roxane **Witke**, editors
Women in Chinese Society
0-8047-0874-6 STANFORD $45.00

Foreign Relations

Harry **Harding**
China's Foreign Relations in the 1980s
0-300-03207-2 YALE $30.00
0-300-03628-0 YALE PB $14.00

George **Segal**
China Defending
0-19-827470-X OXFORD $49.95

John S. **Service**, editor
Golden Inches: The China Memoir of Grace Service
0-520-06656-1 CALIFORNIA PB $19.95

Jay **Taylor**
China and Southeast Asia: Peking's Relations with Revolutionary Movements
0-89206-213-4
CENTER FOR STRATEGIC & INT STUDIES PB $10.50

Allen S. **Whiting**
China Crosses the Yalu: The Decision to Enter the Korean War
0-8047-0627-1 STANFORD $37.50
0-8047-0629-8 STANFORD PB $12.95

Michael **Yahuda**
Towards the End of Isolationism: China's Foreign Policy After Mao
0-312-81142-X ST. MARTIN'S PB $11.95

The United States and China

Rosemary **Foot**
The Practice of Power: American Relations with China Since 1949
0-19-827878-0 OXFORD $35.00

John K. **Fairbank**
The United States and China
A popular work which offers both an overview of Chinese society and a history of Sino-American relations
0-674-92438-X HARVARD PB $18.95

Robert **Garson**
The United States and China Since 1949: A Troubled Affair
0-8386-3610-1 FAIRLEIGH DICKINSON $38.50

Michael **Hunt**
The Making of a Special Relationship: The United States and China to 1914
0-231-05517-X COLUMBIA PB $19.50

Ernest **May** & John K. **Fairbank**
America's China Trade in Historical Perspective
A reassessment of the Sino-American relationship from the perspective of investment and trade
0-674-03075-3 HARVARD $25.00

Michael **Schaller**
The United States and China in the Twentieth Century
A brief and incisive overview
0-19-505866-6 OXFORD PB $14.95

Memoirs

Ma **Bo**
Blood Red Sunset: A Memoir of the Chinese Cultural Revolution
This unflinching memoir by a former Red Guard was first banned in China and then became one of its biggest bestsellers ever
TRANSLATED BY HOWARD GOLDBLATT
0-14-015942-8 PENGUIN PB $12.95

Jung **Chang**
Wild Swans: Three Daughters of China
"Her family chronicle resembles a popular novel that stars strong, beautiful women and provides cameo roles for famous men. But *Wild Swans* is no romance. It's a story, at once grim and appealing, about the survival of a Chinese family through a century of disaster"—*The New Yorker*
0-385-42547-3 SIMON & SCHUSTER PB $14.95

Pang-Mei Natasha **Chang**
Bound Feet and Western Dress: A Memoir
0-385-47963-8 BDD $22.95

Nien **Cheng**
Life and Death in Shanghai
"The most powerful account yet of the Cultural Revolution…[it] echoes Kafka and Solzhenitsyn"—*Washington Post*
0-14-010870-X PENGUIN PB $13.95

Liang **Heng** & others

Son of the Revolution

Liang Heng recounts his participation in the Cultural Revolution as a youth from an intellectual family set adrift by the political upheavals since 1957

0-394-72274-4 RANDOM HOUSE PB $13.00

Reginald F. **Johnston**

Twilight in the Forbidden City

Recommended for any curious visitor to Beijing, this volume, written when the city was still an intact symbol of Imperial Manchu power, provides an anecdotal guide to the geography of old Peking. Travel books fail to note many of the sites described here, much less the details of everyday life, many of which still hold true

0-8488-1390-1 AMEREON $32.95

Owen **Lattimore**

The Desert Road to Turkestan

Lattimore's account of traveling in a camel caravan through inner Mongolia, published in 1929, reveals the lives and customs of "camel pullers" and Chinese traders

See also **CENTRAL ASIA** under **ASIA** under **TRAVEL LITERATURE** in **FOOD, TRAVEL, AND LEISURE**

1-56836-070-3 KODANSHA PB $16.00

Anchee **Min**

Red Azalea

"A haunting and quietly dramatic coming-of-age story with a cultural cataclysm as its backdrop"—*Kirkus Reviews*

See also **THE CULTURAL REVOLUTION** under **THE COMMUNIST REVOLUTION**

0-425-14776-2 BERKLEY PB $6.99

Tim **Severin**

The China Voyage: Across the Pacific by Bamboo Raft

The award-winning author of *The Brendan Voyage*, who specializes in recreating historic voyages, reconstructs a 60-foot bamboo raft believed to be a replica of the vessel used by ancient explorers and attempts to duplicate a crossing of the Pacific first accomplished in 218 BC. The result is a gripping narrative by a gifted writer and intrepid explorer

0-201-48394-7 ADDISON-WESLEY $25.00
0-201-44197-7 ADDISON-WESLEY PB $12.00

Pirates had not been very high on my list of concerns when I began to prepare the China Voyage expedition nearly three years before. Then my thoughts had been about more obvious matters such as the risk of typhoons, how to raise enough money to finance the project, or whether a raft of bamboos would stay afloat long enough to carry five or six people across the vastness of the Pacific Ocean from China to America. Above all, I had to be sure such a journey was justified.
THE CHINA VOYAGE: ACROSS THE PACIFIC BY BAMBOO RAFT

Betty Peh-Ti **Wei**

Old Shanghai (Images of Asia)

An ideal resource for the history minded traveler

0-19-585747-X OXFORD $16.95

Harry **Wu**

Bitter Winds: A Memoir of My Years in China's Gulag

0-471-55645-9 WILEY $22.95
0-471-11425-1 WILEY PB $14.95

Gao Yuan

Born Red: A Chronicle of the Cultural Revolution

The view from an elite school

0-8047-1368-5 STANFORD $47.50
0-8047-1369-3 STANFORD PB $12.95

Daiyun **Yue** & Carolyn **Wakeman**

To the Storm: The Odyssey of a Revolutionary Chinese Woman

A painstaking account of the torture and turmoil inflicted on intellectuals during the Cultural Revolution. The author has since been restored to the party and continues to teach at Beijing University

0-520-06029-6 CALIFORNIA PB $13.00

Tibet

The **Dalai Lama** & Glen **Rowell**

Freedom in Exile: The Autobiography of the Dalai Lama

The spiritual leader of the Tibetan people describes his childhood, the Chinese invasion, and his escape to India, followed by 100,000 other refugees

See also **EASTERN** under **20TH-CENTURY SPIRITUAL LEADERS** under **SPIRITUALITY** in **RELIGION, SPIRITUALITY, AND PHILOSOPHY**

0-06-098701-4 HARPERCOLLINS PB $13.00

The **Dalai Lama**

My Tibet

0-520-07109-3 CALIFORNIA $40.00
0-520-08948-0 CALIFORNIA PB $25.00

The Dalai Lama

Lee **Feigon**

Demystifying Tibet: Unlocking the Secrets of the Land of the Snows

A scholarly, unromantic look at this vast land and its people, featuring the author's well-researched argument against China's historical claim to sovereignty over Tibet. Also noteworthy is his stunning description of contemporary Lhasa

See also **CENTRAL ASIA** under **ASIA** under **TRAVEL LITERATURE** in **FOOD, TRAVEL, AND LEISURE**

1-56663-089-4 DEE $27.50

Melvyn C. **Goldstein**

A History of Modern Tibet, 1913-1951: The Demise of the Lamaist State

A 936-page history of the theocratic state of Tibet in modern times, and its eventual collapse in the face of Chinese invasion. "Goldstein's marvelous book, while compassionate, is also clearsighted…A magnificent study of modern Tibet"—Jonathan Mirsky, *NY Review of Books*

0-520-07590-0 CALIFORNIA PB $29.95

A.T. **Grunfeld**

The Making of Modern Tibet

An introduction to China's stormy relations with Tibet

0-86232-482-3 SHARPE PB $15.95

Roger **Hicks**

Hidden Tibet: The Land and Its People

A photographic record of life in Tibet as it has been lived for thousands of years

1-85230-030-2 ELEMENT PB $17.95

Peter **Hopkirk**

Trespassers on the Roof of the World

1-56836-050-9 KODANSHA PB $14.00

Chogyam **Trungpa**

Born in Tibet

This autobiography of a Tibetan lama includes the gripping tale of his escape from invading Chinese troops in 1959

See also **EASTERN** under **20TH-CENTURY SPIRITUAL LEADERS** under **SPIRITUALITY** in **RELIGION, SPIRITUALITY, AND PHILOSOPHY**

1-57062-116-0 SHAMBHALA PB $15.00

Shakabpa **Wang-Chug-Day-Den**

One Hundred Thousand Moons: A Political History of Tibet

This extraordinary history of Tibet covers the period from the 1840s to the 1960s, after the Chinese invasion, and is writtten by a high official in the Tibetan government prior to the Chinese takeover. "There is no doubt [this book] will be of immense value in presenting a true picture of Tibet, particularly today, when there is a great need for it"—The Dalai Lama

Volume I

0-06-017399-8 HARPERCOLLINS $40.00

Volume II

0-06-017416-1 HARPERCOLLINS $40.00

Japan

Kenneth B. **Pyle**

The Making of Modern Japan

Argues that modern Japan was a deliberate creation: the Meiji Restoration of 1866 was a pragmatic nationalist response to the challenges of Western imperial power. A narrative of Japan's development from the sixteenth century to contemporary times in 300 pages. Second edition

0-669-20020-4 HEATH PB $35.00

General Studies

Jon **Livingston**, editor

The Japan Reader

Volume I

See also **FROM THE MEIJI RESTORATION TO THE END OF THE EMPIRE: 1868–1945**

0-06-092409-8 HARPERPERENNIAL PB $17.00

Volume II

See also **FROM THE MEIJI RESTORATION TO THE END OF THE EMPIRE: 1868–1945**

0-06-092410-1 HARPERPERENNIAL PB $17.00

Ministry of Foreign Affairs, editor

Japan: Profile of a Nation

Over 200 articles organized into seven thematic sections (Geography, History, Government and Diplomacy, Economy, Society, Culture, and Life) make up this readable and detailed portrait of Japan

4-7700-1918-1 KODANSHA $25.00

Edwin O. **Reischauer**

Japan: The Story of a Nation

A sympathetic survey by a leading Japan specialist

0-07-557074-2 MCGRAW HILL PB $28.90

Conrad **Totman**

Japan Before Perry: A Short History

0-520-04134-8 CALIFORNIA PB $15.00

Burton **Watson**

The Rainbow World: Japan in Essays and Translations

Watson, a distinguished translator and interpreter of Chinese and Japanese literature, writes of his long experience in Japan, beginning with his first glimpses of it in 1945. "A fresh and insightful miscellany from the mature experience of a great and graceful scholar"—Gary Snyder

See also **CRITICAL STUDIES AND HISTORIES** under **JAPANESE LITERATURE** in **LITERATURE OF EUROPE, AFRICA, AND ASIA**

0-913089-06-0 BROKEN MOON PB $10.00

Languages like English or Chinese achieve a scurrilous effect by the addition of epithets or expletives that serve to suggest all sorts of awful things about the parentage or moral habits of the person addressed. Japanese, on the other hand, gets the same effect by purely formal means. Just as there is an elaborate set of honorific pronouns, verbs, and verb endings which are used to express varying degrees of respect...so there is a complementary set for expressing varying degrees of contempt. The sting of the latter comes not from any scurrility explicit in the words themselves, but from the insulting implication of inferior social status they carry.

THE RAINBOW WORLD: JAPAN IN ESSAYS AND TRANSLATIONS

Traditional Culture

Robert C. **Christopher**

The Japanese Mind

0-449-90120-3 FAWCETT PB $11.00

Ruth **Benedict**

The Chrysanthemum and the Sword: Patterns of Japanese Culture

A study dating from the 1940s, by a leading anthropologist

See also **CLASSICS** under **GENERAL ANTHROPOLOGICAL STUDIES** under **ANTHROPOLOGY** in **SOCIAL STUDIES**

0-395-50075-3 HOUGHTON MIFFLIN PB $12.95

Martin **Collcutt** & others

The Cultural Atlas of Japan

0-8160-1927-4 FACTS ON FILE $45.00

Marius **Jansen**, editor

Warrior Rule in Japan

How the struggle of competing leagues of fighting men, from the 12th to the 19th century, dominated Japanese political history

0-521-48404-9 CAMBRIDGE PB $17.95

Joseph M **Kitagawa**

On Understanding Japanese Religion

0-691-10229-5 PRINCETON PB $17.95

George **Sansom**

Japan: A Short Cultural History

0-8047-0954-8 STANFORD PB $19.95

Robert J. **Smith**

Japanese Society: Tradition, Self and the Social Order

0-521-31552-2 CAMBRIDGE PB $17.95

H. Paul **Varley**

Japanese Culture: A Short History

A summary of artistic, social, and political forces

ILLUSTRATED BY JOE SHULMAN

0-8248-0927-0 HAWAII PB $13.00

Martial Arts

Ivan **Morris**

The Nobility of Failure: Tragic Heroes in the History of Japan

A witty and poignant study of how defenders of lost causes have been the most enduring Japanese heroes

0-374-52120-4 NOONDAY PB $17.00

Yagyu **Munenori**

The Sword and the Mind

A translation of the classic treatise on swordsmanship

See also **MARTIAL ARTS** under **FITNESS** in **LIFESTYLES AND PRACTICAL ADVICE**

TRANSLATED BY HIROAKI SATO

0-87951-256-3 OVERLOOK PB $11.95

Hiroaki **Sato**

Legends of the Samurai

A rich documentary survey of the culture of bushido—the way of the warrior—as it evolved from the earliest historical period

0-87951-619-4 OVERLOOK $29.95

Yamamoto **Tsunetomo**

Hagakure: The Book of the Samurai

"The most influential of all samurai treatises" —Ivan Morris

TRANSLATED BY WILLIAM S. WILSON

0-87011-378-X KODANSHA $20.00

4-7700-1106-7 KODANSHA PB $8.00

The Japanese Way: Specialized Studies

Donald **Richie**

A Taste of Japan, Food Fact and Fable: What the People Eat, Customs and Etiquette

"In his very entertaining way, Mr. Richie makes you feel familiar with the basic vocabulary you need to really experience and enjoy Japanese food the way the Japanese do"—Alice Waters

4-7700-1707-3 KODANSHA PB $18.00

A.L. **Sadler**

Cha-No-Yu: The Japanese Tea Ceremony

A reprint of the 1933 classic, this is one of the most helpful publications on the subject—detailed, and by no means too susceptible to the mystique of tea

0-8048-1224-1 TUTTLE PB $14.95

Oliver **Statler**

Japanese Inn: A Reconstruction of the Past

The succeeding generations of a family of innkeepers, recounted in novelistic style; one of the best introductory books on Japanese tradition

0-8248-0818-5 HAWAII PB $9.95

Junichiro **Tanizaki**

In Praise of Shadows

A brief and indispensable essay on traditional aesthetics by one of Japan's greatest modern writers

0-918172-02-0 LEETE'S ISLAND PB $5.95

Reference

John W. **Dower**

Japanese History and Culture from Ancient to Modern Times: Seven Basic Bibliographies

1-55876-098-9 WIENER PB $34.95

Janet E. **Hunter**

A Concise Dictionary of Modern Japanese History

0-520-04557-2 CALIFORNIA PB $17.00

Japan to 1600

After achieving a high state of civilization by the middle of the first millennium, Japanese society remained at the mercy of warring feudal overlords until final unification under the Tokugawa shogunate in 1603.

George **Sansom**

Sansom's monumental work is still the most complete general history of Japan to the Meiji Restoration.

A History of Japan: To 1334
0-8047-0523-2 STANFORD PB $18.95

A History of Japan, 1334-1615
0-8047-0525-9 STANFORD PB $18.95

A History of Japan, 1615-1867
0-8047-0527-5 STANFORD PB $14.95

Heian Period: 794-1185

Ivan **Morris**

The World of the Shining Prince
A splendid recreation of the court society that created *The Tale of Genji* and other literary masterpieces

See also **DRAMA** under **CRITICAL STUDIES AND HISTORIES** under **JAPANESE LITERATURE** in **LITERATURE OF EUROPE, AFRICA, AND ASIA**

1-56836-029-0 KODANSHA PB $15.00

Kamakura, Muromachi, and Shokuhō Periods: 1185-1600

Mary E. **Berry**

Hideyoshi
Toyotomi Hideyoshi, who built Osaka Castle and invaded Korea, ruled supreme in Japan from 1590 until his death in 1598

0-674-39026-1 HARVARD PB $14.00

John Whitney **Hall** & others, editors

Japan Before Tokugawa: Political Consolidation in Economic Growth, 1500 to 1650
0-691-05308-1 PRINCETON $60.00
0-691-10216-3 PRINCETON PB $22.95

Jeffrey P. **Mass**

The Development of Kamakura Rule, 1180-1250: A History with Documents
0-8047-1003-1 STANFORD $45.00

Jeffrey P. **Mass** & William B. **Hauser**, editors

The Bakufu in Japanese History
The techniques through which military overlords from the Heian period to the Meiji Restoration turned the emperor into a puppet

0-8047-1278-6 STANFORD $45.00
0-8047-2210-2 STANFORD PB $16.95

The Tokugawa Period: 1600-1868

Chie **Nakane**, editor

Tokugawa Japan
0-86008-447-7 TOKYO PB $42.50

Thomas C. **Smith**

Tokugawa Ieyasu: Shogun
In 1603, the year James VI of Scotland became James I of England, Ieyasu took the title of Shogun and established the Tokugawa line

0-89346-210-1 HEIAN PB $12.95

Conrad **Totman**

Collapse of the Tokugawa Bakufu: 1862-1868
0-8248-0614-X HAWAII $25.00

Early Modern Japan
0-520-20356-9 CALIFORNIA PB $18.95

Stephan **Vlastos**

Protests and Uprisings in Tokugawa Japan
0-520-07203-0 CALIFORNIA PB $15.00

Anne **Walthall**

Social Protest and Popular Culture in 18th-Century Japan
0-8165-0961-1 ARIZONA $23.00

Society, Culture, and Ideas

Herbert P. **Bix**

Peasant Protest in Japan: 1590-1884
A superb reconstruction of rural class conflict

0-300-05251-0 YALE PB $19.00

Nakae **Chomin**

A Discourse by Three Drunkards on Government
An early Japanese view of the West

TRANSLATED BY NOBUKO TSUKUI

0-8348-0192-2 WEATHERHILL PB $12.50

Donald **Keene**

The Japanese Discovery of Europe, 1720-1830
A well-told history of Japan's sometimes contradictory approaches to the West

0-8047-0669-7 STANFORD PB $14.95

Gary **Leupp**

Male Colors: The Construction of Homosexuality in Tokugawa
0-520-08627-9 CALIFORNIA $35.00

James L. **McClain**

Kanazawa: A 17th-Century Japanese Castle Town
0-300-02736-2 YALE $32.00

Masao **Maruyama**

Studies in the Intellectual History of Tokugawa Japan
TRANSLATED BY MIKISO HANE

0-691-00832-9 PRINCETON PB $23.95

Masao **Miyoshi**

As We Saw Them: The First Japanese Embassy to the United States
A brilliant history, lavishly documented, of the beginnings of U.S.-Japanese relations in the 19th century

1-568-36028-2 YALE $32.00

Tetsuo **Najita**

Japan: The Intellectual Foundations of Modern Japanese Politics
Incisive and original

0-226-56803-2 CHICAGO PB $11.95

Visions of Virtue in Tokugawa Japan: The Kaitokudo Merchant Academy of Osaka
A study of the development of the merchant discourse on political economy during the 18th century

0-226-56804-0 CHICAGO $37.50
0-226-56805-9 CHICAGO PB $18.95

Peter **Nosco**, editor

Confucianism and Tokugawa Culture
0-691-00839-6 PRINCETON PB $18.95

Thomas C. **Smith**

Nakahara: Family Farming and Population in a Japanese Village, 1717-1830
With Smith's *Agrarian Origins* (listed in "Rural Society" below), this is a classic study of the early modern period

0-8047-0928-9 STANFORD $32.50

From the Meiji Restoration to the End of the Empire: 1868-1945

"What the Japanese wanted from the West was primarily science, technology, and organization. They were content enough with the innermost substance of their culture, their moral ideas, their family life, their arts and amusements, their religious conceptions, though even in these they showed an uncommon adaptability. Essentially it was to protect their internal substance, their Japanese culture, that they took over the external apparatus of Western civilization."—R.R. Palmer & Joel Colton, *A History of the Modern World*.

W.G. **Beasley**

The Meiji Restoration
The classic study

0-8047-0815-0 STANFORD $65.00

Mikiso **Hane**

Modern Japan: A Historical Survey

"Hane has a keen eye for vivid small events as well as for the great triumphs and tragedies in Japan's emergence as a great power" —John W. Dower

0-8133-1367-8 WESTVIEW.....$61.00
0-8133-1368-6 WESTVIEW PB.....$24.95

Peasants, Rebels and Outcasts: The Underside of Modern Japan

A spirited guide to the dark side of Japan's drive to empire and to the life of the lower classes, themes once largely ignored by Western historians

0-394-71040-1 RANDOM HOUSE PB.....$13.32

Thomas M. **Huber**

The Revolutionary Origins of Modern Japan

0-8047-1048-1 STANFORD.....$37.50
0-8047-1755-9 STANFORD PB.....$14.95

Marius B. **Jansen**

Sakamoto Ryoma and the Meiji Restoration

Highly educated, like many of his peers, Sakamoto Ryomo was a key player in ending Tokugawa rule

0-231-10173-2 COLUMBIA PB.....$17.50

Jon **Livingston**, editor

The Japan Reader

Volume I

See also **GENERAL STUDIES**

0-06-092409-8 HARPERPERENNIAL PB.....$17.00

Volume II

See also **GENERAL STUDIES**

0-06-092410-1 HARPERPERENNIAL PB.....$17.00

W.J. **Macpherson**

The Economic Development of Japan, 1868-1941

The rise of Japan from a position of relative international obscurity in the mid-19th century to that of industrial power

0-521-55792-5 CAMBRIDGE PB.....$9.95

Barrington **Moore**, Jr.

Social Origins of Dictatorship and Democracy

See also **HISTORICAL SOCIOLOGY** under **TOPICS IN MODERN SOCIOLOGY** under **SOCIOLOGY** in **SOCIAL STUDIES**

0-8070-5073-3 BEACON PB.....$20.00

Society and Culture

William **Beasley**

Japan Encounters the Barbarian: Japanese Travellers in America and Europe, 1860-1873

0-300-06324-5 YALE.....$30.00

Nakano **Makiko**

Makiko's Diary

EDITED AND TRANSLATED BY KAZUKO SMITH

0-8047-2441-5 STANFORD PB.....$14.95

Yukichi **Fukuzawa**

Autobiography

The story of the founder of Keio University and one of Meiji Japan's great Westernizers

TRANSLATED BY EIICHI KIYOOKA

0-231-08373-4 COLUMBIA PB.....$20.00

Carol **Gluck**

Japan's Modern Myths: Ideology in the Late Meiji Period

A study of the invention of Japanese "national" traits when the country decided to modernize in the last quarter of the 19th century

0-691-00812-4 PRINCETON PB.....$18.95

David G. **Goodman** & Masanoii **Miyazawa**

Jews in the Japanese Mind: The History and Uses of a Cultural Stereotype

Incisive study of Japanese anti-Semitism, historical and modern

0029124824 FREE PRESS.....$24.95

Mikiso **Hane**, translator & editor

Reflections on the Way to the Gallows: Rebel Women in Pre-War Japan

Translations of memoirs, diaries, and essays by women in protest movements

0-520-06259-0 CALIFORNIA.....$35.00
0-520-08421-7 CALIFORNIA PB.....$14.95

Yoichi **Harashima**

Meiji Japan Through Woodblock Prints

0-86008-450-7 TOKYO.....$250.00

Germaine **Hoston**

Marxism and the Crisis of Development in Pre-War Japan

Penetrating analysis of Marxist controversy in political thought and historiography during the 1920s and '30s

0-691-07722-3 PRINCETON.....$59.50
0-691-10206-6 PRINCETON PB.....$19.95

Donald **Keene**

Appreciations of Japanese Culture

4-7700-0956-9 KODANSHA PB.....$10.00

Robert A. **Rosenstone**

Mirror in the Shrine: American Encounters with Meiji Japan

Three very different Westerners: the missionary William Elliot Griffis, the scientist Edward S. Morse, and the writer Lafcadio Hearn

0-674-57641-1 HARVARD.....$34.50
0-674-57642-X HARVARD PB.....$15.00

Edward G. **Seidensticker**

Low City, High City: Tokyo from Edo to the Earthquake, 1867-1923

A history of Tokyo's refined and low-life quarters in the era before the Great Earthquake of 1923

0-674-53939-7 HARVARD PB.....$14.95

Sharon L. **Sievers**

Flowers in Salt: The Beginnings of Feminist Consciousness in Modern Japan

0-8047-1382-0 STANFORD PB.....$12.95

Robert J. **Smith** & Ella L. **Wiswell**

The Women of Suye Mura

Presents first-hand observations of the condition of rural women in the 1930s

0-226-76345-5 CHICAGO PB.....$14.95

Thomas C. **Smith**

The Agrarian Origins of Modern Japan

See also **RURAL SOCIETY** under **CONTEMPORARY SOCIETY AND CULTURE**

0-8047-0530-5 STANFORD.....$25.00
0-8047-0531-3 STANFORD PB.....$12.95

Imperial Japan and the Pacific War

For related reading, see THE SECOND WORLD WAR

Hiroyuki **Agawa**

The Reluctant Admiral: Yamamoto and the Imperial Navy

Convinced by several visits to the US that America's industrial strength was bound to prevail in a prolonged war, Yamamoto's strategy—typified by the attack on Pearl Harbor—emphasized knock-out blows against the US Navy, designed to force America to early negotiations

See also **THE HIGH COMMAND** under **MEMOIRS AND BIOGRAPHIES** under **THE SECOND WORLD WAR**

TRANSLATED BY JOHN BESTER

0-87011-512-X KODANSHA PB.....$10.00

Michael A. **Barnhart**

Japan Prepares for Total War: The Search For Economic Security, 1919-1941

Illuminates Japan's drive for a world empire in the first half of the 20th century

0-8014-9529-6 CORNELL PB.....$14.95

Haruko Taya **Cook** & Theodore F. **Cook**

Japan at War: An Oral History

1-56584-039-9 NEW PRESS PB.....$14.95

John **Costello**

The Pacific War, 1941-1945: The First Comprehensive One-Volume Account of the Causes and Conduct of World War II in the Pacific

See also **OVERVIEWS** under **THE PACIFIC WAR** under **THE SECOND WORLD WAR**

0-688-01620-0 MORROW PB.....$17.95

Hirohito

John W. **Dower**

War Without Mercy: Race and Power in the Pacific War

A history of anti-Japanese attitudes in America and anti-Western attitudes in Japan. "A cautionary tale for all peoples, now and in the future"—*Foreign Affairs*

See also **OVERVIEWS** under **THE PACIFIC WAR** under **THE SECOND WORLD WAR**

0-394-75172-8 PANTHEON PB $15.00

Peter **Duus** & others, editors

The Japanese Wartime Empire, 1931-1945

The empire at war. Essay subjects include the creation of an East Asian economic bloc centered in northeastern Asia, the mobilization of human and physical resources in the older established areas of Japanese colonial rule, and the penetration and occupation of Southeast Asia

0-691-04382-5 PRINCETON $49.50

Thomas R. **Havens**

Valley of Darkness: The Japanese People and World War II

See also **OVERVIEWS** under **THE PACIFIC WAR** under **THE SECOND WORLD WAR**

0-8191-5495-4
UNIVERSITY PRESS OF AMERICA PB $24.50

Saburo **Ienaga**

The Pacific War, 1931-1945

A harsh critique of Japanese aggression by a leading Japanese scholar

See also **OVERVIEWS** under **THE PACIFIC WAR** under **THE SECOND WORLD WAR**

TRANSLATED BY FRANK BALDWIN

0-394-73496-3 RANDOM HOUSE PB $13.00

Akira **Iriye**

Power and Culture: The Japanese-American War, 1941-1945

See also **OVERVIEWS** under **THE PACIFIC WAR** under **THE SECOND WORLD WAR**

0-674-69582-8 HARVARD PB $22.50

Sharon **Minichiello**

Retreat from Reform: Patterns of Political Behavior in Interwar Japan

0-8248-0778-2 HAWAII $18.00

Ramon **Myers** & Mark **Peattie**, editors

The Japanese Colonial Empire: 1895-1945

0-691-10222-8 PRINCETON PB $24.95

Ronald H. **Spector**

Eagle Against the Sun: The American War with Japan

See also **OVERVIEWS** under **THE PACIFIC WAR** under **THE SECOND WORLD WAR**

0-02-930360-5 FREE PRESS $29.95
0-394-74101-3 RANDOM HOUSE PB $17.00

John J. **Stephan**

Hawaii Under the Rising Sun: Japan's Plans for Conquest After Pearl Harbor

"Will give a fresh perspective on the place of the Hawaiian islands in Japanese strategy and war aims"—*History*

See also **PEARL HARBOR** under **THE PACIFIC WAR** under **THE SECOND WORLD WAR**

0-8248-0872-X HAWAII $14.95

Shunsuke **Tsurumi**

An Intellectual History of Wartime Japan, 1931-1945

A wide-ranging and provocative survey

0-7103-0072-7 ROUTLEDGE $76.50

The Atomic Bomb

Thomas B. **Allen** & Norman **Polmar**

Code-Name Downfall: The Secret Plan to Invade Japan—And Why Truman Dropped the Bomb

0-684-80406-9 SIMON & SCHUSTER $25.00

Gar **Alperovitz**

The Decision to use the Atomic Bomb

0-679-76285-X VINTAGE PB $16.00

Michael J. **Hogan**, editor

Hiroshima in History and Memory

Prominent historians survey the Hiroshima story, from the American decision to drop the first atomic bomb to the controversy over the Enola Gay exhibit in Washington, D.C.

0-521-56682-7 CAMBRIDGE PB $17.95

Robert James **Maddox**

Weapons for Victory: The Hiroshima Decision Fifty Years Later

0-8262-1037-6 MISSOURI $19.95

Jay Robert **Lifton**

Hiroshima in America: Fifty Years of Denial

0-399-14072-7 PUTNAM $27.50

Death in Life: Survivors of Hiroshima

A classic psychological study of the emotional scars left by the bomb

0-8078-4344-X NORTH CAROLINA PB $22.50

Ibuse **Masuji**

Black Rain

A devastating, detailed account of the day the bomb dropped on Hiroshima, told from the perspective of a minor local official

See also **FICTION AND OTHER PROSE** under **THE MODERN PERIOD: SINCE 1850** under **JAPANESE LITERATURE** in **LITERATURE OF EUROPE, AFRICA, AND ASIA**

TRANSLATED BY JOHN BESTER

0-87011-364-X KODANSHA PB $10.00

Keiji **Nakazawa**

Barefoot Gen: A Cartoon Story of Hiroshima

Nakazawa was a child in Hiroshima when the bomb fell, and in the dense and realistic *Barefoot Gen* he recounts his life up to and including that day

See also **JAPANESE COMICS** under **COMICS** in **POPULAR READING**

0-86571-095-3 NEW SOCIETY PB $12.95

Martin J. **Sherwin**

A World Destroyed: Hiroshima and the Origins of the Arms Race

The best analysis of the decision to drop the bomb

See also **THE PACIFIC: HIROSHIMA AND NAGASAKI** under **THE END OF THE WAR** under **THE SECOND WORLD WAR**

0-394-75204-X VINTAGE PB $15.00

Ronald **Takaki**

Hiroshima: Why America Dropped the Atomic Bomb

From the psychological makeup of Harry Truman to the prevalent anti-Asian prejudice in America, Takaki presents a definitive study of why we dropped the bomb. "A lively, complex, multi-dimensional, and wonderfully undogmatic and inconclusive account of the American decision to use the atomic bomb—exactly the sort of book that is needed to stimulate debate and reflection"—Michael Walzer

See also **THE PACIFIC: HIROSHIMA AND NAGASAKI** under **THE END OF THE WAR** under **THE SECOND WORLD WAR**

0-316-83122-0 LITTLE, BROWN $19.95
0-316-83124-7 LITTLE, BROWN PB $11.95

The American Occupation

Ian **Buruma**

The Wages of Guilt: Memories of War in Germany and Japan

The conflicting moral response to defeat and atrocity is the subject of this illuminating work. Buruma (*Playing the Game*) contrasts East Germany's reaction to the Holocaust with that of the West and analyzes the dual symbol of

Hiroshima, offering insight into essential questions of morality and nationalism
See also **DOMESTIC POLITICS** under **OVERVIEWS OF CONTEMPORARY JAPAN**
See also **GERMANY SINCE 1945**
0-374-28595-0 FS&G $25.00

Ian Buruma

John W. **Dower**
Empire and Aftermath: Yoshida Shigeru and the Japanese Experience, 1878-1994
Illuminates the period by focusing on Yoshida Shigeru, who played a major role in shaping Japan's response to the postwar years
0-674-25126-1 HARVARD PB $14.00

Japan in War and Peace: Selected Essays
1-56584-067-4 NEW PRESS $30.00
1-56584-279-0 NEW PRESS PB $14.95

Kazuo **Kawai**
Japan's American Interlude
0-226-42775-7 CHICAGO PB $18.00

Michael **Schaller**
The American Occupation of Japan: The Origins of the Cold War in Asia
Argues that the reconstruction of postwar Japan shaped not only that country's future but also US policy throughout postwar Asia, leading up to the interventions in China, Korea, and Vietnam
See also **THE COLD WAR** under **THE TRUMAN AND EISENHOWER YEARS** under **US HISTORY, 1945 TO THE PRESENT** in **HISTORY OF THE AMERICAS**
0-19-505190-4 OXFORD PB $13.95

Saburo **Shiroyama**
War Criminal: The Life and Death of Hirota Koki
Hirota was the only civilian among the convicted war criminals executed in 1948; Shiroyama suggests that he was denied full justice
TRANSLATED BY JOHN BESTER
0-87011-368-2 KODANSHA PB $6.95

Overviews of Contemporary Japan

Roger **Buckley**
Japan Today
0-521-38885-6 CAMBRIDGE PB $13.95

Andrew **Gordon**, editor
Postwar Japan as History
Sixteen essays first published in 1993
0-520-07475-0 CALIFORNIA PB $18.00

Edwin O. **Reischauer**
The Japanese Today: Change and Continuity
An updated and greatly expanded edition of *The Japanese*; one of the most popular overviews
0-674-47181-4 HARVARD $36.00
0-674-47182-2 HARVARD PB $11.95

Karel **van Wolferen**
The Enigma of Japanese Power: People and Politics in a Stateless Nation
A Dutch journalist who lives in Tokyo probes the "elusive state," "Japanese culture as ideology," and "the system as religion" in an intriguing look at one of the world's economic superpowers. "Forceful and important" —James Fallows, *Atlantic*
0-679-72802-3 VINTAGE PB $17.00

Ann **Waswo**
Modern Japanese Society
A brief, accessible introduction to Japanese society since the late 19th century
0-19-289228-2 OXFORD PB $14.95

International Relations

Sydney **Giffard**
Japan Among the Powers, 1890-1990
0-300-05847-0 YALE $32.50

Thomas R. **Havens**
Fire Across the Sea: The Vietnam War and Japan, 1965-1975
A chronicle of Japan's important anti-Vietnam War movement
0-691-05491-6 PRINCETON $50.00
0-691-00811-6 PRINCETON PB $19.95

Domestic Politics

David E. **Apter** & Nagayo **Sawa**
Against the State: Politics and Social Protest in Japan
0-674-00921-5 HARVARD PB $13.95

Ian **Buruma**
The Wages of Guilt: Memories of War in Germany and Japan
See also **GERMANY SINCE 1945** under **EUROPE SINCE 1945**
See also **THE AMERICAN OCCUPATION** under **FROM THE MEIJI RESTORATION TO THE END OF THE EMPIRE: 1868-1945**
0-374-28595-0 FS&G $25.00

Gerald L. **Curtis**
The Japanese Way of Politics
A comprehensive study of party politics in today's Japan
0-231-06680-5 COLUMBIA $55.00
0-231-06681-3 COLUMBIA PB $17.00

Joe **Moore**
Japanese Workers and the Struggle For Power, 1945-1947
Moore effectively demolishes the myth of the docile Japanese worker
0-299-09320-4 WISCONSIN $23.95

Tetsuo **Najita**, editor
Conflict in Modern Japanese History: The Neglected Tradition
Pathbreaking essays on an underinvestigated element of Japanese society
0-691-05364-2 PRINCETON $65.00
0-691-10137-X PRINCETON PB $25.00

T.J. **Pempel**
Policy and Politics in Japan: Creative Conservatism
Presents a useful selection of Japanese documents
0-87722-250-9 TEMPLE PB $19.95

Economics and Business

James **Abegglen** & George **Stalk**, Jr.
Kaisha, the Japanese Corporation: How Marketing, Money and Manpower Strategy, Not Management Style, Make the Japanese World Pacesetters
Abegglen, a longtime resident of Tokyo, is a leading authority on Japanese business
See also **THE JAPANESE CHALLENGE AND AMERICA'S ECONOMIC FUTURE** under **BUSINESS, INDUSTRY, AND FINANCE** in **BUSINESS AND REFERENCE**
0-465-03712-7 BASIC PB $17.00

Rodney **Clark**
The Japanese Company
0-300-02646-3 YALE PB $18.00

Ronald **Dore**
Flexible Rigidities: Industrial Policy and Structural Adjustment in the Japanese Economy, 1970-1980
0-8047-1328-6 STANFORD $42.50
0-8047-1465-7 STANFORD PB $14.95

James **Fallows**
Looking at the Sun
0-679-76162-4 VINTAGE PB $14.00

David **Halberstam**
The Reckoning
Halberstam charts the humbling of Ford Motor Company against the rise of Japan's Nissan
See also **THE JAPANESE CHALLENGE AND AMERICA'S ECONOMIC FUTURE** under **BUSINESS, INDUSTRY, AND FINANCE** in **BUSINESS AND REFERENCE**
0-380-70447-1 AVON PB $6.50

Shotaro **Ishinomori**
Japan, Inc.: Introduction to Japanese Economics
A full-scale comic book version of a textbook on the Japanese economy, with a melodramatic plot to speed things along
See also **JAPANESE COMICS** under **COMICS** in **POPULAR READING**
INTRODUCTION BY PETER DUUS
0-520-06289-2 CALIFORNIA PB $15.95

Chalmers **Johnson**
Japan: Who Governs?: The Rise of the Developmental State
Argues that Japan's successful economic system is one in which service is highly valued; where state bureaucracy attracts the best young minds; and where "guidance" by the state is both accepted and ubiquitous
0-393-31450-2 NORTON PB $13.95

Miti and the Japanese Miracle: The Group of Industrial Policy, 1925-1975
The classic study of Japanese economic planning; dense but worth the effort
See also **THE JAPANESE CHALLENGE AND AMERICA'S ECONOMIC FUTURE** under **BUSINESS, INDUSTRY, AND FINANCE** in **BUSINESS AND REFERENCE**
0-8047-1206-9 STANFORD PB $16.95

Michio **Morishima**
Why Has Japan Succeeded?: Western Technology and the Japanese Ethos
0-521-26903-2 CAMBRIDGE PB $15.95

Akio **Morita** & others
Made in Japan: Akio Morita and the Sony Corporation
One of Japan's most creative business leaders tells his company's story and reflects on technology, world trade, and differences between his country and the US
See also **CORPORATE LEADERSHIP AND CEO BIOGRAPHIES** under **BUSINESS, INDUSTRY, AND FINANCE** in **BUSINESS AND REFERENCE**
0-451-15171-2 NEW AMERICAN LIBRARY PB $6.99

Takafusa **Nakamura**
The Postwar Japanese Economy: Its Development and Structure
A valuable survey now in its second edition
0-86008-514-7 TOKYO PB $34.00

Nakasone

Kenichi **Ohmae**
Triad Power: The Coming Shape of Global Competition
Ohmae contends that companies, consumers, and cultures are becoming the same around the world, and that Japan, the US, and Europe must become more tightly integrated
0-02-923470-0 FREE PRESS $32.95

Terutomo **Ozawa**
Multinationalism, Japanese Style: The Political Economy of Outward Dependency
An introduction to the conglomerates now making their challenge on a global scale
0-691-00367-X PRINCETON PB $12.95

Clyde V. **Prestowitz**, Jr.
Trading Places: How We Allowed Japan to Take the Lead
A former high-ranking Commerce Department official makes a convincing case for get-tough trade policies with Japan
See also **THE JAPANESE CHALLENGE AND AMERICA'S ECONOMIC FUTURE** under **BUSINESS, INDUSTRY, AND FINANCE** in **BUSINESS AND REFERENCE**
0-465-08679-9 BASIC PB $18.00

Raymond **Vernon**
Two Hungry Giants: The United States and Japan in the Quest For Oil and Ores
0-674-91470-8 HARVARD $25.95

Management and Labor

Ronald **Dore**
British Factory-Japanese Factory: The Origins of National Diversity in Employment Relations
0-520-02495-8 CALIFORNIA PB $16.00

Kunio **Odaka**
Toward Industrial Democracy: Management and the Workers in Modern Japan
0-674-89816-8 HARVARD $18.50

Kenichi **Ohmae**
The Mind of the Strategist: The Art of Japanese Business
0-07-047595-4 MCGRAW HILL $29.95
0-07-047904-6 MCGRAW HILL PB $12.95

Lester C. **Thurow**, editor
The Management Challenge: Japanese Views
Of the many recent studies of Japanese management, this is one of the most insightful
0-262-20053-8 MIT $22.50
0-262-70033-6 MIT PB $11.95

Contemporary Society and Culture

Theodore C. **Bestor**
Neighborhood Tokyo
An anthropologist considers the uses of tradition in contemporary urban Japan
0-8047-1439-8 STANFORD $47.50
0-8047-1797-4 STANFORD PB $15.95

D.W. **Brackett**
Holy Terror: Armageddon in Tokyo
0-8348-0353-4 WEATHERHILL $24.95

Winston **Davis**
Dojo: Magic and Exorcism in Modern Japan
A lively study of one of Japan's new religions, Sukyo Mahikari
0-8047-1053-8 STANFORD $47.50
0-8047-1131-3 STANFORD PB $16.95

David **Desser**
Eros Plus Massacre: An Introduction to the Japanese New Wave Cinema
A thematic survey of Japan's New Wave, focusing on the work of such directors as Oshima, Shinoda, Imamura, and Yoshida
See also **JAPAN** under **NATIONAL CINEMAS** under **FILM** in **PERFORMING ARTS AND MEDIA**
0-253-20469-0 INDIANA PB $5.25

Takeo **Doi**
The Anatomy of Dependence
A book the Japanese themselves take very seriously as a key to their character, written by a leading psychologist
TRANSLATED BY JOHN BESTER
0-87011-494-8 KODANSHA PB $10.00

The Anatomy of Self
Doi's most recent work deals with the role of the individual in Japan
0-87011-902-8 KODANSHA PB $9.00

Ronald **Dore**

Taking Japan Seriously: A Confucian Perspective on Leading Economic Issues

Emphasizes the Confucian impetus for many of Japan's accomplishments

0-8047-1350-2 STANFORD $42.50
0-8047-1401-0 STANFORD PB $14.95

Matthews Masayuki **Hamabata**

Crested Kimono: Power and Love in the Japanese Business Family

Portrays very real people trying to make sense of their lives—trying to reconcile the roles and duties dictated by custom with changing expectations in the cosmopolitan milieu of today's Japan

0-8014-2333-3 CORNELL $29.95

Norie **Huddle** & others

Island of Dreams: Environmental Crisis in Japan

AFTERWORD BY RALPH NADER

0-87047-028-0 SCHENKMAN PB $19.95

Robert Jay **Lifton**

Six Lives, Six Deaths

0-300-02266-2 YALE $42.00
0-300-02600-5 YALE PB $17.00

Chie **Nakane**

Japanese Society

"Miss Nakane has distilled into 150 pages a gin-crisp, clear, and fresh primer on what is Japanese about modes of human relating in Japan .... If you have time for just one book on Japan, try this one"—*Asian Student*

0-520-02154-1 CALIFORNIA PB $13.95

Haru M. **Reischauer**

Samurai and Silk: A Japanese and American Heritage

Several generations of a Japanese aristocratic family, by the wife of Edwin O. Reischauer. "Beautifully written, with a sense of intimacy that only first-hand experience and family traditions could confer"—John Gross, *NY Times*

0-674-78801-X HARVARD PB $17.95

Frederik **Schodt**

Manga! Manga!: The World of Japanese Comics

A superbly researched and elegantly written history of Japanese comics, including 96 pages of complete translated stories. "Definitive…An unlikely fusion of scholarship, enthusiasm, and wit"—*Village Voice*

See also **JAPANESE COMICS** under **COMICS** in **POPULAR READING**

0-87011-752-1 KODANSHA PB $22.00

Frederik L. **Schodt**

Inside the Robot Kingdom: Japan, Mechatronics, and the Coming Robotopia

How Japanese popular culture has embraced robots as friendly heroes in films, toys, comic books, and the impact of the robotics industry on Japan's economy

0-87011-918-4 KODANSHA PB $12.95

Christopher **Seymour**

Yakuza Diary: Doing Time in the Japanese Underworld

From drug deals and gun-selling to political bribery, Seymour provides a telling account of a little-known world

0-87113-604-X GROVE $22.00

Shunsuke **Tsurumi**

A Cultural History of Postwar Japan, 1945-1980

Touches on everything from comic books to the war crimes trial

0-7103-0259-2 KEGAN & PAUL $76.50

Merry **White**

The Japanese Overseas: Can They Go Home Again?

Examines the cultural isolation faced by overseas Japanese workers when they return home

0-02-935091-3 FREE PRESS $27.95
0-691-00871-X PRINCETON PB $13.95

Education

Joy **Hendry**

Becoming Japanese: The World of the Pre-School Child

0-8248-1092-9 HAWAII $18.00
0-8248-1215-8 HAWAII PB $11.95

Thomas P. **Rohlen**

Japan's High Schools

A remarkably full and comprehensive account

0-520-04863-6 CALIFORNIA PB $16.00

Barbara **Rose**

Tsuda Umeko and Women's Education in Japan

Biography of the pioneer founder of Tsuda College

0-300-05177-8 YALE $27.00

Merry **White**

The Japanese Educational Challenge: A Commitment to Children

0-02-933801-8 MACMILLAN PB $14.95

Rural Society

Ronald **Dore**

Shinohata: Portrait of a Japanese Village

An acclaimed portrait of rural life

0-520-08628-7 CALIFORNIA PB $14.95

Thomas C. **Smith**

The Agrarian Origins of Modern Japan

See also **SOCIETY AND CULTURE** under **FROM THE MEIJI RESTORATION TO THE END OF THE EMPIRE: 1868-1945**

0-8047-0530-5 STANFORD $25.00
0-8047-0531-3 STANFORD PB $12.95

Women and the Family

Gail Lee **Bernstein**

Haruko's World: A Japanese Farm Woman and Her Community

0-8047-1174-7 STANFORD $37.50
0-8047-1287-5 STANFORD PB $12.95

Gail Lee **Bernstein**, editor

Recreating Japanese Women, 1600-1945

"A splendid collection of studies on the definition of women's roles" —Kenneth B. Pyle. Published in 1991

0-520-07017-8 CALIFORNIA PB $16.95

Kittredge **Cherry**

Womansword: What Japanese Words Say About Women

The role of women in Japanese culture, as exemplified in the meaning and usage of 80 words

4-7700-1655-7 KODANSHA PB $8.00

Anne E. **Imamura**, editor

Re-Imagining Japanese Women

Brings up to date the work of Gail Lee Bernstein's *Recreating Japanese Women, 1600-1945.* Published in 1996

0-520-20263-5 CALIFORNIA PB $18.00

Shidzue **Ishimoto**

Facing Two Ways: The Story of My Life

EDITED BY BARBARA MOLONY

0-8047-1239-5 STANFORD $52.50
0-8047-1240-9 STANFORD PB $17.95

Takie S. **Lebra**

Japanese Women: Constraint and Fulfillment

0-8248-1025-2 HAWAII PB $10.00

E. Patricia **Tsurumi**

Factory Girls: Women in the Thread Mills of Meiji Japan

The exploitation of women in the textiles factories

0-691-00035-2 PRINCETON PB $14.95

Korea

"Koreans call their country Choson…'The Land of the Morning Calm.' Despite the country's indigenous name, the history of Korea has been anything but calm, with successive invasions by the Chinese, the Mongols and the Japanese. Today's division of Korea has added a new dimension to this turbulent past…Following the destruction of the Korean War, the economy remained very weak for a decade…Following a military coup in 1961, South Korea enjoyed both political stability and economic growth which, within 20 years, turned the Republic of Korea into an advanced industrial country…From less than $40 million in 1961, exports rose to about

$455 million in 1968…to over $15 billion in 1979; per capita national income during the same period increased from $82 per annum to about $1500. The GNP jumped from $2 billion to $60 billion… The ROK had become in effect an advanced industrial country, second only to Japan in the Far East."
—David Rees, *A Short History of Modern Korea*

One Nation: To 1945

Peter **Duus**
The Abacus and the Sword
Military and economic factors in Japan's takeover of Korea in the late 19th century
0-520-08614-7 CALIFORNIA..$45.00

Jattyun Kim **Haboush**
A Heritage of Kings: One Man's Monarchy in the Confucian World
"Elegant biographical study of Yongjo, one of Korea's most illustrious and yet tragic kings"
—Laurel Kendall
0-231-06656-2 COLUMBIA..$52.50

Woo-Keun **Han**
The History of Korea
"A survey of Korean history which is clearly in a class by itself"—*Library Journal*
TRANSLATED BY KYUNG-SHIK LEE
EDITED BY GRAFTON K. MINTZ
0-8248-0334-5 HAWAII PB..$13.00

Ki-Baik **Lee**
A New History of Korea
A meticulously indexed book, strong on the development of Korean culture. "The best and most comprehensive general history of Korea published to date"—*History*
TRANSLATED BY EDWARD WAGNER & EDWARD SCHULTZ
0-674-61576-X HARVARD PB..$14.95

Stewart **Lone** & Gavan **McCormack**
Korea Since 1850
0-312-09686-0 ST. MARTIN'S PB..$16.95

The Korean War

Bevin **Alexander**
Korea: The First War We Lost
0-7818-0065-X HIPPOCRENE PB..$16.95

Bruce **Cumings**
The Origins of the Korean War: Liberation and the Emergence of Separate Regimes
An in-depth examination of the road into and out of war
0-691-10113-2 PRINCETON PB..$26.95

J.C. **Goulden**
Korea: The Untold Story of the War
A popular history
0-07-023580-5 MCGRAW HILL PB..$14.95

Max **Hastings**
The Korean War
A preeminent military historian draws from the accounts of more than 200 veterans to chart the first war the US could not win. "Must reading for any American who wants to understand some of the watershed events of the post World War II period"—Richard M. Nixon
0-671-66834-X TOUCHSTONE PB..$14.00

Burton **Kaufman**
The Korean War: The Challenges in Crisis, Credibility and Command
See also **THE KOREAN WAR** under **THE TRUMAN AND EISENHOWER YEARS** under **US HISTORY, 1945 TO THE PRESENT** in **HISTORY OF THE AMERICAS**
0-07-554665-5 KNOPF PB..$30.00

Donald **Knox**
The Korean War
A masterful oral history
Volume 1: Pusan to Chosin
0-15-647200-7 HARCOURT BRACE PB..$16.95
Volume 2: Uncertain Victory
0-15-647201-5 HARCOURT BRACE PB..$14.95

Callum A. **MacDonald**
Korea: The War Before Vietnam
0-02-919621-3 FREE PRESS..$32.95

Matthew B. **Ridgway**
The Korean War: How We Met the Challenge
The general who took over from MacArthur in 1951 "deals harshly with those who shout 'There is no substitute for victory' without really knowing what victory means"
—J.M. Allison, *Saturday Review*
0-306-80267-8 DA CAPO PB..$13.95

William **Stueck**
The Korean War: An International History
0-691-03767-1 PRINCETON..$39.50

Korea Divided

Recent student riots calling for the unification of North and South Korea have brought the world's attention to the largest standoff of opposing troops in the world. Although fighting ended in 1953 with an armistice, no peace treaty ever marked an official end to the war.

Nancy **Abelmann**
Echoes of the Past, Epics of Dissent: A South Korean Social Protest Movement
How farmers, students, and organizers joined to protest the corporate ownership of tenant plots never distributed in the 1949 Land Reform. By an anthropologist at the Universtiy of Illinois, Urbana-Champaign
0-520-20418-2 CALIFORNIA PB..$18.00

William J. **Barnds**, editor
The Two Koreas in East Asian Affairs
0-8147-0988-5 NYU..$50.00

Michel **Brun**
Incident at Sakhalin: The True Mission of KAL 007
The KAL 007 tragedy, in which 269 civilians died and the world came closer to nuclear war than at any time since the Cuban Missile Crisis, has remained unresolved. "The results of this… tenacious investigation show that we must not let governments continue to suppress the truth of how this wholly unnecessary tragedy came about"
—Nan Moore Oldham, mother of KAL 007 victim
1-56858-054-1 FOUR WALLS..$24.95

Mark **Clifford**
Troubled Tiger: The Businessmen, Bureaucrats, and Generals in South Korea
1-56324-386-5 SHARPE..$64.95
1-56324-387-3 SHARPE PB..$22.95

Barry K. **Gills**
Korea Versus Korea: Political Economy, Diplomacy, and Contested Legitimacy
Timely and authoritative
0-415-14231-8 ROUTLEDGE..$42.00

James **Hoare**
North Korea
A recent history that draws heavily on sociological studies
0-198-28022-X OXFORD PB..$16.95

Kim Dae **Jung**
Prison Writings
A trenchant view of the dictatorship and the tumultuous politics of South Korea by the long-incarcerated opposition leader
0-520-05482-2 CALIFORNIA..$40.00

Kim Dae Jung

K. Connie **Kang**

Home Was the Land of Morning Calm

0-201-62684-5 ADDISON-WESLEY $23.00

Teishintai—the "comfort-women brigade"—was a dreaded word, known to every Korean. To avoid being abducted by Japanese agents, some girls dressed like boys and wore farmer's straw hats when they went outdoors. Poor peasant girls from the countryside were favorite targets, but everyone else worried, too. "We were warned about the Teishintai all the time," said my mother. Her parents kept a close watch over her and her two younger sisters, because every girl was a potential sex slave for the Japanese military. Innocent girls were kidnapped from their homes while they picked wild vegetables for dinner or washed clothes by the stream. Poor country girls running errands in the marketplace were lured by tales of desirable factory jobs. All together, the Japanese recruited or abducted more than one hundred thousand Korean girls and young women, who were forced to follow Japanese soldiers to Manchuria and China, and later, throughout Southeast Asia.
HOME WAS THE LAND OF MORNING CALM

Byung C. **Koh**

The Foreign Policy Systems of North and South Korea

0-520-04805-9 CALIFORNIA $45.00

Chong-Sik **Lee**

Korean Workers' Party: A Short History

EDITED BY R.F. STEER

0-8179-6852-0 HOOVER PB $7.95

Donald **MacDonald**

The Koreans: Contemporary Politics and Society

0-8133-0966-2 WESTVIEW $62.50
0-8133-0967-0 WESTVIEW PB $19.95

Edward **Olsen**

U.S. Policy and the Two Koreas

The military, commercial, and political interests of the United States in North and South Korea

0-8133-0593-4 WESTVIEW PB $27.00

Hazel **Smith**, Chris **Rhodes**, and Diana **Pritchard**, editors

North Korea in the New World Order

Somewhat academic, but a comprehensive analysis of North Korea and the international community

0-312-16011-9 ST. MARTINS $65.00

David I. **Steinberg**

The Republic of Korea: Economic Transformation and Social Change

0-86531-720-8 WESTVIEW PB $59.50

Culture

Stanley H. **Barkan**, editor

South Korean Poets of Resistance

TRANSLATED BY KO WON

0-89304-606-X CROSS-CULTURAL $15.00
0-89304-607-8 CROSS-CULTURAL PB $5.00

Chongwha **Chung**, editor

Korean Classical Literature: An Anthology

See also KOREAN LITERATURE under OTHER ASIAN LITERATURES in LITERATURE OF EUROPE, AFRICA, AND ASIA

0-7103-0279-7 ROUTLEDGE $42.50

Lady **Hyegyong**

The Memoirs of Lady Heygyong: The Autobiographical Writings of a Crown Princess of Eighteenth-Century Korea

The drama of Korean court life, written from 1795 to 1805, available for the first time in English translation. Published in 1996

TRANSLATED AND EDITED BY JAHYAN KIM HABOUSH

0-520-20055-1 CALIFORNIA PB $17.95

Laurel **Kendall**

The Life and Hard Times of a Korean Shaman: Of Tales and the Telling of Tales

An innovative re-creation of the dramatic life story of a woman many times wronged by men, finally claimed by the spirits, and now a practicing yarn-spinning shaman and ritual specialist

0-8248-1145-3 HAWAII PB $11.00

Shamans, Housewives and Restless Spirits: Women in Korean Ritual Life

A reconsideration of Korean notions of family and kin through an analysis of women's beliefs and practices

0-8248-1142-9 HAWAII PB $11.00

Southeast Asia and the Philippines

John **Cady**

The History of Postwar Southeast Asia: Independence Problems

0-8214-0160-2 OHIO $30.00

The Southeast Asian World

0-88273-502-0 FORUM PB $6.95

J.M. **Gullick**, editor

Adventures and Encounters: Europeans in South-East Asia

An anthology of European writings: from Portuguese and Spanish spice traders to nineteenth-century naturalists

967-65-3090-5 OXFORD PB $29.95

Donald G. **McCloud**

System and Process in Southeast Asia: The Evolution of a Region

0-86531-587-6 WESTVIEW $51.50

Clark **Neher**

Politics in Southeast Asia

0-87047-011-6 SCHENKMAN PB $15.95

Milton **Osborne**

Southeast Asia: An Illustrated Introduction

0-04-442215-6 PAUL & CO PB $19.95

Lucian W. **Pye** & Mary W. **Pye**

Asian Power and Politics: The Cultural Dimensions of Authority

"Will be the subject of much scholarly debate"
—*Foreign Affairs*

0-674-04979-9 HARVARD PB $19.95

Anthony **Reid**

Southeast Asia in the Age of Commerce 1450-1680: The Lands Below the Winds, Volume 1

A total history encompassing a fascinating gamut of social and cultural structures from diet to law to sex to war

0-300-04750-9 YALE PB $17.00

Southeast Asia in the Age of Commerce 1450-1680: Expansion and Crisis, Volume 2

0-300-06516-7 YALE PB $17.00

Karl J. **Schmidt**

An Atlas and Survey of South Asian History

1-56324-334-2 SHARPE PB $24.95

David J. **Steinberg**, editor

In Search of Southeast Asia: A Modern History

Using an overall thematic structure, seven leading Asian historians explore how Southeast Asian people are adapting their cultures to a swiftly changing world

0-8248-1110-0 HAWAII PB $19.00

R.H. **Taylor**, editor

The Politics of Elections in Southeast Asia

Eleven separate studies focusing on countries that have conducted multi-party elections since the 1940s and '50s, notably Indonesia, Malaysia, the Philippines, Thailand, Cambodia, and Burma/Myanmar. Contributors include Benedict Anderson, Suchit Bunbongkarn, and Dan Lev

0-521-56443-3 CAMBRIDGE PB $17.95

Lea E. **Williams**

Southeast Asia: A History

Considers men and movements of influence in Southeast Asia: Sukarno, Ho Chi Minh, Ferdinand Marcos, and the Viet Minh

0-19-502000-6 OXFORD PB $16.95

Burma (Myanmar)

Independent in 1948 after more than a century of British rule, and with a more remote history of Chinese domination, this large Buddhist state has been a "nominally civilian" one-party Socialist Democratic Republic since 1974.

In July of 1988 U Ne Win resigned from the Burmese Socialist Party and in September the civilian government was overthrown by military junta leader Saw Maung. Although its leaders were in jail under house arrest, the National League for Democracy won by a landslide in the May 1990 election. Saw Maung resigned in 1992, and in April martial law was lifted. In 1993 the ruling junta extended the house arrest of Nobel Peace Prize winner Aung San Sun Kyi.

John **Cady**

The United States and Burma

0-674-92320-0 HARVARD $22.00

Aung San Sun **Kyi**

Freedom from Fear

A collection of writings from the detained Burmese opposition leader, who was awarded the 1991 Nobel Peace Prize. The volume, compiled by her husband, Michael Aris, is divided into two parts. The first is composed of writings undertaken in Oxford, Kyoto, and Simla, India, before she returned to Myanmar in 1988. The second contains interviews, speeches, and essays she authored after becoming involved in the democracy movement there. Mrs. Aung San Sun Kyi has been under house arrest since July 1989

0-14-025317-3 PENGUIN PB $13.95

George **Orwell**

Burmese Days

An early novel based on Orwell's experiences in the colonial service

See also **THE EARLY 20TH CENTURY** under **20TH-CENTURY BRITISH AND IRISH FICTION** in **LITERATURE OF THE BRITISH ISLES**

0-15-614850-1 HARCOURT BRACE PB $8.95

Robert H. **Taylor**

The State in Burma

An impressive array of source materials helps to unravel the history of Burma's political development since the early 1960s, when the military took power

0-8248-1141-0 HAWAII $32.00

Cambodia

Between the splendors of the Khmer Angkor empire (800–1220) and the infamies of the Pol Pot/Khmer Rouge regime (1975–1979) Cambodia also knew a century of French rule, until independence under King Sihanouk in 1953. Efforts to steer clear of the Vietnam War were thwarted by United States interventions in the early 1970s. War with one foe or another has remained a fact of life ever since, although the bloodshed appeared to peak under Pol Pot, who annihilated an estimated two to four million Cambodians. In the UN-backed free elections of 1993, the royalist party prevailed. By September of that year the constitution was changed to restore the monarchy, with Prince Sihanouk as ruler. In 1994 the Khmer Rouge sent 55,000 people fleeing their homes after stepping up attacks in western Cambodia.

David A. **Ablin** & Marlowe **Hood**, editors

The Cambodian Agony

Specialists in Indochinese politics address the major issues confronting the country in the aftermath of the Pol Pot regime, which provoked the most radical social upheaval in any country in recorded history

0-87332-754-3 SHARPE PB $25.95

Prince Sihanouk

David P. **Chandler** & Ben **Kiernan**, editors

Revolution and Its Aftermath in Kampuchea: Eight Essays

0-938692-05-4 YALE PB $14.00

Richard **Dudman**

Forty Days with the Enemy

The story of a journalist held captive by guerrillas in Cambodia

0-87140-259-9 NORTON PB $2.45

May M. **Ebihara** & others, editors

Cambodian Culture Since 1975: Homeland and Exile

0-8014-8173-2 CORNELL PB $13.95

Karl D. **Jackson**, editor

Cambodia, 1975-1978: Rendezvous with Death

0-691-07807-6 PRINCETON $60.00

Ian **Mabbet** & David **Chandler**

The Khemers

0-631-20298-6 BLACKWELL PB $19.95

Michael **Vickery**

Cambodia: 1975-1982

Fluent in all Khmer patois, Vickery based his study on discussions with hundreds of refugees

0-89608-190-7 SOUTH END $40.00
0-89608-189-3 SOUTH END PB .... $16.

Hong Kong

"Hong Kong seldom was a very characteristic British possession. In its affairs we see reflected not only the decline of a historical genre—it is the last great *European* colony, too—but the shifting aspirations of communism and capitalism, the resurgence of the new Asia, the rising power of technology. As it prepares to withdraw at last from the British imperium, it is like a mirror to the world, or perhaps a geomancer's compass."—Jan Morris, *Hong Kong*

Bruce Bueno **de Mesquita**

Forecasting Political Events: The Future of Hong Kong

0-300-04279-5 YALE PB $14.00

Norman J. **Miners**

The Government and Politics of Hong Kong

An authoritative reference on the administration of the Crown Colony; discusses the changes following the 1984 Sino-British agreement on Hong Kong's restoration to the mainland

0-19-585425-X OXFORD PB $21.00

Jan **Morris**

Hong Kong

A great travel writer's montage of imperial history and modern capitalism shows the precipitous contrasts between primitive poverty and outrageous wealth

See also **CHINA** under **ASIA** under **TRAVEL LITERATURE** in **FOOD, TRAVEL, AND LEISURE**

0-679-72486-9 VINTAGE PB $15.00

Lau **Siu-Kai**

Society and Politics in Hong Kong

0-312-73892-7 ST. MARTIN'S $25.00

Frank **Welsh**

A Borrowed Place: The History of Hong Kong

"A magnificent, much-needed, and compendious history"—*NY Review of Books*

1-56836-134-3 KODANSHA PB $16.00

Indonesia

Currently fifth in world population, with more than 200 million people scattered across some 13,000 islands, Indonesia is potentially the richest state in Southeast Asia. Moslem by the 15th century, it is now the world's largest Islamic republic. Dutch occupation culminated in membership in the Netherlands kingdom after World War I, until Sukarno proclaimed independence in 1945. His Sino-Soviet-oriented "guided (i.e., non-parliamentary) democracy" was ousted by General Suharto in 1967 after a series of virulent anti-communist purges claiming, it is said, over a quarter of a million victims. The Suharto regime boasts political—and economic—stability, with more open policies toward both China and the West. The 1,000-member People's Consultive Assembly reelected the unopposed Suharto in March 1993. Concerns about increasing unrest were raised when anti-Chinese riots broke out in 1994.

Karl D. **Jackson** & Lucian W. **Pye**, editors

Political Power and Communications in Indonesia

0-520-04205-0 CALIFORNIA PB........$16.00

M.C. **Ricklefs**

A History of Modern Indonesia

0-8047-2194-7 STANFORD........$49.50
0-8047-2195-5 STANFORD PB........$16.95

Laos

After enjoying a heyday in the late 17th century, the Lao kingdom declined, eventually suffering the ignominy of incorporation into French Indochina until 1953. A monarchic regime was finally overthrown in 1975 by Pathet-Lao communists. The educated elite fled while others ended up in "re-education centers," from which many never reemerged.

Timothy **Castle**

At War in the Shadow of Vietnam

U.S. covert activity in Laos, 1955-1975

See also **THE CAMBODIAN CONFLICT** under **THE VIETNAM WAR** in **HISTORY OF THE AMERICAS**

0-231-07977-X COLUMBIA PB........$15.00

Arthur **Dommen**

Laos: Keystone of Indochina

0-86531-771-2 WESTVIEW........$69.50

Malaysia, Singapore, and Brunei

The original Federation of Malaysia, created in 1963 after nearly 100 years of British rule, included Singapore as well as Sabah and Sarawak. Singapore withdrew in 1965. Since then the two countries have become industrial and financial powers with standards of living among the highest in Asia.

Barbara **Andaya** & Leonard **Andaya**

A History of Malaysia

0-312-38121-2 ST. MARTIN'S PB........$16.95

Leonard **Andaya**

The World of Maluku: Eastern Indonesia in the Early Modern Period

0-8248-1490-8 HAWAII........$38.00

S. **Baring-Gould** & C.A. **Bampfylde**

A History of Sarawak Under Its Two White Rajahs, 1839-1908

0-19-588926-6 OXFORD........$78.00

R.S. **Milne** & Diane **Mauzy**

Malaysia: Tradition, Modernity, and Islam

0-7146-2988-X FRANK CASS........$45.00

James **Minchin**

No Man Is an Island: A Study of Singapore's Lee Kuan Yew

A critical biography

0-04-400028-6 UNWIN HYMAN PB........$17.95

Janet **Salaff**

State and Family in Singapore: Structuring an Industrial Society

A detailed analysis of the dramatic shift in emphasis from labor-intensive to capital-intensive society, based on a methodology of interview and follow-up

0-8014-2140-3 CORNELL........$42.50

James C. **Scott**

Weapons of the Weak: Everyday Forms of Peasant Resistance

0-300-03641-8 YALE PB........$19.00

Florian **von Alten**

The Role of Government in the Singapore Economy

3-631-48325-2 LANG PB........$39.95

Ching-Hwang **Yen**

A Social History of the Chinese in Singapore and Malaya, 1800-1911

0-19-582666-3 OXFORD........$45.00

The Philippines

The sprawling archipelago was propelled into the limelight in early 1986 with the ouster of the Marcos regime by the popular rebellion led by Corazon Aquino, widow of the opposition leader Benigno Aquino assassinated in 1983. Following over three centuries of Spanish rule, the islands were ceded to the United States in 1898 and did not gain independence until after World War II. Sporadic leftist activism has plagued each corrupt presidency since, and leftist insurgency continues to threaten each succeeding administration.

In May 1992, General Fidel Ramos, backed by the outgoing Corazon Aquino, won the presidency in a seven-way race, while control of the Congress went to the opposition. The government signed a cease-fire pact in January 1994 in an important step toward ending the long-standing war with Muslim separatists, and in August 1996 President Ramos and rebel chief Nur Misuari declared an end to the war which has killed 120,000 Filipinos.

John **Bresnan**, editor

Crisis in the Philippines: The Marcos Era and Beyond

"The background behind the newspaper headlines and television segments"
—Stanley Karnow

0-691-05490-8 PRINCETON........$49.50
0-691-00810-8 PRINCETON PB........$16.95

Claude **Buss**

Cory Aquino and the People of the Philippines

"From his presence behind the scenes and his access to the movers and shakers of the period, he weaves a political tale with skill and understanding"—Philip Habib

0-317-61916-0 STANFORD........$16.95

E. San **Juan**

Crisis in the Philippines: The Making of a Revolution

An insider's scrutiny of the relentless avalanche of political events which culminated in the slaying of the opposition leader Aquino

FOREWORD BY GEORGE WALD

0-89789-085-X BERGIN & GARVEY........$55.00

Stanley **Karnow**

In Our Image: America's Empire in the Philippines

An excellent history of US involvement in the Philippines by the author of *Vietnam: A History*

See also **SPECIAL TOPICS IN AMERICAN FOREIGN POLICY** under **AMERICAN POLITICS AND FOREIGN POLICY** in **HISTORY OF THE AMERICAS**

0-87124-125-0 FOREIGN POLICY PB........$5.95

Benedict J. **Kerkvliet**

The Huk Rebellion: A Study of Peasant Revolt in the Philippines

0-520-04635-8 CALIFORNIA PB........$18.00

Richard J. **Kessler**

Rebellion and Repression in the Philippines

0-300-04406-2 YALE........$32.00
0-300-05130-1 YALE PB........$15.00

David J. **Steinberg**

The Philippines: A Singular and a Plural Place

0-8133-2038-0 WESTVIEW PB........$19.95

Taiwan

"Taiwan…is a modern nation, albeit without official independence. This has created a problem of identity which is quite different in kind from the divisions of many centuries ago: How can a modern Chinese state identify itself with Chinese civilization if it is not 'China'? The temporary answer is to hold up the illusion that it is."
—Ian Buruma, *God's Dust: A Modern Asian Journey*

Thomas **Gold**

State and Society in the Taiwan Miracle

0-87332-399-8 SHARPE PB........$23.95

Victor **Li**

The Future of Taiwan: A Difference of Opinion

0-87332-173-1 SHARPE........$45.00

Burton **Pasternak**

Kinship and Community in Two Chinese Villages

0-8047-0823-1 STANFORD $32.50

Murray A. **Rubinstein**, editor

The Other Taiwan: 1945 to the Present

1-56324-193-5 SHARPE PB $25.95

Yu-Shan **Wu**

Comparative Economic Transformations: Mainland China, Hungary, the Soviet Union, and Taiwan

0-8047-2388-5 STANFORD $45.00

Thailand

The populous Buddhist kingdom is the only Southeast Asian country never to have been occupied by a European colonial power. (In the later 19th century it served as a buffer between French Indochina and British Burma.)

Representative government was introduced in the 1930s, diminishing the absolute nature of the monarchy. The last two decades have been punctuated by coups large and small. The country's already serious domestic problems—inflation, crime, AIDS, child pornography, and widespread social unrest—were compounded by an influx of refugees from neighboring Cambodia.

In the 1992 Parliamentary elections more than half of the vacant seats went to pro-military parties. Violent street clashes broke out between pro-democracy civilians and the military after the top military commander was appointed prime minister in April. He was replaced in September 1992 by Chuan Leekpai.

David **Elliott**

Thailand: Origins of Military Rule

FOREWORD BY MALCOLM CALDWELL

0-905762-11-8 LAWRENCE HILL PB $12.50

Paul **Lewis** & Elaine **Lewis**

Peoples of the Golden Triangle: Six Tribes in Thailand

0-500-97314-8 THAMES & HUDSON $40.00

Ross **Prizzia**

Thailand in Transition: The Role of Oppositional Forces

0-8248-0977-7 HAWAII PB $9.00

David K. **Wyatt**

Thailand: A Short History

The history of the Thai people from the early centuries AD to 1982. The standard account

0-300-03582-9 YALE PB $18.00

Vietnam

Under Chinese suzerainty until the 15th century, Vietnam was unified by France in 1887. Divided after Ho Chi Minh's triumph at Dien Bien Phu in 1954, it was finally reunified in 1975 when communist forces occupied Saigon.

After the end of the war the Vietnamese government tried to lead the whole country into socialism. But economic difficulties and foreign policy problems created severe hardship, and Vietnamese leaders are now attempting to guide the country through the transition to a market economy, which it appears to relish.

For related reading, see THE VIETNAM WAR in HISTORY OF THE AMERICAS

John **Balaban**, editor

Vietnam: A Traveler's Literary Companion

See also **SOUTHEAST ASIAN LITERATURE** under **OTHER ASIAN LITERATURES** in **LITERATURE OF EUROPE, AFRICA, AND ASIA**

1-88351-302-2 WHEREABOUTS PRESS PB $12.95

Lou **Dematteis**

A Portrait of Vietnam

A beautiful and compelling portrait of Vietnam as it emerges from a long period of isolation. Focusing his camera on the daily lives of ordinary people, Dematteis documents a vibrant, rapidly changing country just opening its doors to the world

FOREWORD BY OLIVER STONE

0-393-31429-4 NORTON PB $22.50

William **Duiker**

Vietnam Since the Fall of Saigon

0-89680-162-4 OHIO PB $20.00

James P. **Harrison**

The Endless War: Vietnam's Struggle For Independence

A leading Sinologist covers all sides, including some of the fullest characterizations of the Vietnamese; with a new preface

See also **GENERAL HISTORIES** under **THE VIETNAM WAR** in **HISTORY OF THE AMERICAS**

0-231-06909-X COLUMBIA PB $17.00

Le Ly **Hayslip**

When Heaven and Earth Changed Places: A Vietnamese Woman's Journey from War to Peace

0-452-27168-1 PLUME PB $12.00

Murray **Hiebert**

Chasing the Tigers: A Portrait of the New Vietnam

1-56836-139-4 KODANSHA $25.00

Hue-Tam **Ho Tai**

Millenarianism and Peasant Politics in Vietnam

0-674-57555-5 HARVARD $40.00

Henry **Kamm**

Dragon Ascending: Vietnam and the Vietnamese

1-55970-306-7 ARCADE $24.95

1-55970-355-5 ARCADE PB $12.95

Stanley **Karnow**

Vietnam: A History

A first-rate survey of the American era in Vietnam

0-14-014533-8 PENGUIN PB $17.95

David **Marr**

Vietnam 1945

See also **GENERAL HISTORIES** under **THE VIETNAM WAR** in **HISTORY OF THE AMERICAS**

0-520-07833-0 CALIFORNIA $50.00

Hue-Tam Ho **Tai**

Radicalism and the Origins of the Vietnamese Revolution

"Sets out to challenge the assumption so prevalent in earlier works which compressed the history of the Vietnamese Revolution into the history of communism. In her quest she marshals an impressive range of material—much of it unknown in the West"—Al Richardson, *Analysis*

0-674-74613-9 HARVARD PB $17.95

Keith W. **Taylor**

The Birth of Vietnam

0-520-07417-3 CALIFORNIA PB $16.95

Ho Chi Minh

East Asia as an Economic and Political Region: General Studies

John K. **Fairbank** & Edwin O. **Reischauer**

East Asia: Tradition and Transformation

This book remains the most widely used introduction to the history and culture of East Asia

See also **ASIA** under **WORLD HISTORIES** under **THE VARIETIES OF CIVILIZATION**

See also **GENERAL HISTORIES** under **CHINA**

0-395-45023-3 HOUGHTON MIFFLIN $56.75

Peter **Hayes**

American Lake: Nuclear Peril in the Pacific

Why World War III is more likely to begin in the Pacific than in the Middle East or Europe

See also **NUCLEAR STRATEGY** under **NUCLEAR WEAPONS AND ARMS CONTROL** under **INTERNATIONAL RELATIONS AND STRATEGIC STUDIES** in **SOCIAL STUDIES**

0-14-009396-6 PENGUIN PB $6.95

Akira **Iriye**

The World of Asia

0-88273-500-4 FORUM PB $18.95

Staffan B. **Linder**

The Pacific Century: Economic and Political Consequences of Asian-Pacific Dynamism

See also **ECONOMIC DEVELOPMENT AND INTERNATIONAL TRADE** under **ECONOMICS** in **SOCIAL STUDIES**

0-8047-1294-8 STANFORD $27.50
0-8047-1305-7 STANFORD PB $11.95

Australia, New Zealand, and Polynesia

Australia

"I grew up with a skimpy sense of colonial Australia. Convict history was ignored in schools and little taught in universities—indeed, the idea that the convicts might *have* a history worth telling was foreign to Australians in the 1950s and 1960s. Even in the mid-1970s only one general history of the System (as transportation, assignment and secondary punishment in colonial Australia were loosely called) was in print: A.G.L. Shaw's pioneering study *Convicts and the Colonies*. An unstated bias rooted deep in Australian life seemed to wish that 'real' Australian history had begun with Australian respectability—with the flood of money from gold and wool, the opening of the continent, the creation of an Australian middle class. Behind the bright diorama of Australia Felix lurked the convicts, some 160,000 of them, clanking their fetters in the penumbral darkness. But on the feelings and experiences of these men and women, little was written. They were statistics, and finally embarrassments."
—Robert Hughes, *The Fatal Shore*

Jan **Bassett**, editor

The Oxford Dictionary of Australian History

0-19-553243-0 OXFORD $49.95

S.L. **Goldberg** & F.B. **Smith**, editors

Australian Cultural History

0-521-37758-7 CAMBRIDGE PB $18.95

Gregory **Melleuish**

Cultural Liberalism in Australia: A Study in Intellectual and Cultural History

Argues that cultural liberalism is central to the Australian experience of modernity

0-521-47969-X CAMBRIDGE $42.00

The Oxford History of Australia

Oxford

The Oxford History of Australia

Geoffrey **Balton**, editor

Volume I

0-19-554609-1 OXFORD $39.95

Jan **Kociumbas**, editor

Volume II 1770-1860, Possessions

0-19-553744-0 OXFORD PB $29.95

Beverley **Kingston**, editor

Volume III 1860-1900, Glad, Confident Morning

0-19-553519-7 OXFORD PB $19.95

Stuart F. **MacIntyre**, editor

Volume IV 1901-1942, The Succeeding Age

0-19-554612-1 OXFORD $45.00
0-19-553518-9 OXFORD PB $19.95

Geoffrey **Bolton**, editor

Volume V 1942-1988, Middle Way

0-19-554613-X OXFORD $39.95

Aboriginal History

"There have been two versions of Australian history since 1788. Most Australians and their governments have based their understanding on the school history books, in which Australia was 'founded' (not taken or conquered) in 1788; and Australian law assumes that there was no law before that date. But new techniques of research, and new ways of using old ones, are literally 'uncovering' what happened over an enormous range of time, probably at least 400 centuries of 'prehistory' before the 1.91 centuries of recorded history based on documents written by the whites."—*Handbook for Aboriginal and Islander History*

Geoffrey **Blainey**

Triumph of the Nomads: A History of Aboriginal Australia

A recent and necessary examination of the complex societies of the continent's earliest indigenous inhabitants, honored more by time than by their European co-habitants

0-87951-084-6 VIKING PB $13.95

H.C. **Coombs**

Aboriginal Autonomy: Issues and Strategies

Discusses issues of land tenure and relations with the Australian government

0-521-44637-6 CAMBRIDGE PB $10.00

Sally **Morgan**

My Place

An exploration of the author's Aboriginal roots. "Sally Morgan's extraordinary work is about a quest for the past of one person and one family, an individual past which turns out to be a communal past, which is, in turn, the history of a people"—Janette Turner Hospital, *NY Times*

See also **ANTHOLOGIES** under **AUSTRALIAN LITERATURE** in **LITERATURE OF EUROPE, AFRICA, AND ASIA**

0-316-58289-1 LITTLE, BROWN PB $13.95

Eric **Venbrux**

A Death in the Tiwi Islands: Conflict, Ritual and Social Life in an Australian Aboriginal Community

0-521-47351-9 CAMBRIDGE $49.95

W. Lloyd **Warner**

Black Civilization: A Social Study of an Australian Tribe

Fieldwork carried out in the 1920s by a cultural anthropologist among the Murngin in the farthest Australian north. "The first to deal with the amplitude of the structure and supernaturalism of a tropical Australian people"—from the foreword

0-8446-0954-4 SMITH $14.50

19th-Century Australia

Paul **Carter**

The Road to Botany Bay: An Exploration of Landscape and History

"An impressive exploration on the nature of emptiness, place-names, convict behaviour and history itself—a remapping of the European settlement of Australia"— Murray Bail

0-226-09516-9 CHICAGO PB $20.50

Alexander **Harris**

Settlers and Convicts

A 19th-century account by an "emigrant mechanic" of somewhat mysterious identity and one of the liveliest extant records of early colonial life as seen by an ordinary man

FOREWORD BY C.M. CLARK

0-522-83944-4 MELBOURNE PB $19.95

Robert **Hughes**

The Fatal Shore

"Hughes has a story to tell as vivid, large-scale and appalling as anything by Dickens or Solzhenitsyn, but one that's virtually unknown—until the writing of this splendid book"
—Susan Sontag

0-394-75366-6 VINTAGE PB $17.00

Deborah **Oxley**

Convict Maids: The Forced Migration of Women to Australia

Looks at the female convicts transported from Britain and Ireland to New South Wales between 1826 and 1840 and refutes the notion that these women were prostitutes and criminals. Rather they were skilled, literate, young, and healthy—and they helped put the colony on its feet

0-521-44131-5 CAMBRIDGE $54.95
0-521-44677-5 CAMBRIDGE PB $10.00

20th-Century Australia

Akin to Canada in its continental vastness, modern Australia, with roughly 17.8 million inhabitants, boasts a population slightly smaller than the greater New York area.

Tom **Griffiths**

Hunters and Collectors: The Antiquarian Imagination in Australia

Historical consciousness and environmental sensibilities in European Australia from the mid-19th century to the present

0-521-48281-X CAMBRIDGE $64.95
0-521-48349-2 CAMBRIDGE PB ....

Mark **Hearn** & Harry **Knowles**

One Big Union: A History of the Austalian Workers Union, 1886-1994

One of the most influential unions in Australia's political and industrial history—and the individuals who made it

0-521-55138-2 CAMBRIDGE $64.95
0-521-55897-2 CAMBRIDGE PB $42.00

William S. **Livingston** & W. Roger **Louis**, editors

Australia, New Zealand, and the Pacific Islands Since the First World War

A sharp analysis of transformations wrought by three principal factors: dwindling British power, rising United States influence, and various forms of nationalism

0-292-70344-9 TEXAS $20.00

New Zealand

Discovered by the Dutch in 1642 and formally annexed by Britain two centuries later, New Zealand has been a self-governing sliver of Britishness since 1852. It bears a similarity to the Scandinavian democracies in its pioneering championship of social welfare programs, some of which date back to the turn of the century. As an outspoken exponent of anti-nuclear environmentalism, it shamed the French government over the Greenpeace/*Rainbow Warrior* incident, and confronted the United States over nuclear-armed naval ships.

Faced with the global changes of the 1990s, New Zealand governments pursued domestic policies of deregulation and the cutting of social benefits.

James N. **Bade**, editor

The German Connection: New Zealand and German-Speaking Europe in the Nineteenth Century

0-19-558283-7 OXFORD PB $45.00

Jonathan **Boston** & Martin **Holland**, editors

The Fourth Labour Government

0-19-558213-6 OXFORD PB $32.50

Charles **Higham**

The Maoris

0-8225-1229-7 LERNER LIBRARY EDITION $13.50

Ian **McGibbon**

New Zealand and the Korean War

Volume I
Politics and Diplomacy

0-19-558253-5 OXFORD $59.00

Volume II
Combat Operations

0-19-558343-4 OXFORD $75.00

Richard **Mulgan**

Democracy and Power in New Zealand: A Study in New Zealand Polities

0-19-558106-7 OXFORD PB $19.95

Geoffrey **Palmer**

Unbridled Power: A Study of New Zealand's Constitution and Government

0-19-558170-9 OXFORD PB $26.00

K. **Sinclair**

History of New Zealand

0-14-020344-3 PENGUIN PB $7.95

Polynesia

The umbrella term describes the area of Oceania which contains the principal island nations of Samoa, Tonga, Fiji, and the Solomons, as well as the Hawaiian islands and French Polynesia, where Kanak autonomy claims have exposed the persistence of colonialism. The South Seas are studded with some 25,000 islands in all—and a total population of 1.5 million.

John C. **Beaglehole**

The Exploration of the Pacific

Delves into the driving ideas behind the exploration of the Pacific, and describes the epic voyages of Magellan, Drake, Mendana, Quiros, Tasman, and others

0-8047-0310-8 STANFORD $49.50
0-8047-0311-6 STANFORD PB $15.95

Thomas **Harding** & Ben **Wallace**

Cultures of the Pacific

0-02-913800-0 FREE PRESS PB $16.95

K. R. **Howe**

Where the Waves Fall: A New South Sea Islands History from First Settlement to Colonial Rule

0-8248-1186-0 HAWAII PB $20.00

Edward **Joesting**

Hawaii: An Uncommon History

0-393-00907-6 NORTON PB $10.95

Patrick V. **Kirch**

The Evolution of the Polynesian Chiefdoms

0-521-27316-1 CAMBRIDGE PB $31.95

Stephanie **Lawson**

Traditon Versus Democracy in the South Pacific: Fiji, Tonga and Western Samoa

How political elites use the idea of "tradition" to legitimize practices and institutions. A critical approach to the political implications of romanticizing non-Western cultural traditions, especially in terms of democratic development

0-521-49638-1 CAMBRIDGE $59.95

David **Lewis**

We, the Navigators: The Ancient Art of Landfinding in the Pacific

0-8248-1582-3 HAWAII PB $24.95
0-8248-0394-9 HAWAII PB $10.95

Herman **Melville**

Typee: A Peep at Polynesian Life

Melville's first book, based on his experiences among cannibals in the Marquesas, became a bestseller in 1846

See also **THE 19TH CENTURY: TO THE CIVIL WAR** under **AMERICAN LITERATURE TO 1900** in **LITERATURE OF THE AMERICAS**

EDITED BY GEORGE WOODCOCK

0-14-043070-9 PENGUIN PB $9.95

Alan **Moorehead**

The Fatal Impact: The Invasion of the South Pacific, 1767-1840

Focus on three distinct sites—lush Tahiti, the temperate east coast of Australia, and the bleak south polar regions

FOREWORD BY MANNING CLARK

0-935180-77-X MUTUAL PUBLICATIONS PB $4.95

Marshall **Sahlins**

Islands of History

"Deeply grounded in Polynesian ethnography, but also wide-ranging in its comparative references, in Pacific history and in broad statements of history/anthropological method"—*TLS*

See also **ESSAYS IN ANTHROPOLOGY** under **ANTHROPOLOGY** in **SOCIAL STUDIES**

0-226-73358-0 CHICAGO PB $11.95

Bernard **Smith**

European Vision and the South Pacific

An illustrated book surveying the work of artists attached to voyages of exploration

0-300-04479-8 YALE PB $35.00

Robert Louis **Stevenson**

In the South Seas

Firsthand impressions of the Marquesas and the Paumotus and Gilbert Islands

See also **AUSTRALIA, NEW ZEALAND, AND THE SOUTH PACIFIC** under **TRAVEL LITERATURE** in **FOOD, TRAVEL, AND LEISURE**

See also **19TH-CENTURY PROSE** under **THE 19TH CENTURY** in **LITERATURE OF THE BRITISH ISLES**

0-7103-0140-5 ROUTLEDGE PB $25.50

Captain Cook

Captain James **Cook**

Explorations of Captain James Cook in the Pacific, as Told by Selections of His Own Journals, 1768-1779

See also **AUSTRALIA, NEW ZEALAND, AND THE SOUTH PACIFIC** under **TRAVEL LITERATURE** in **FOOD, TRAVEL, AND LEISURE**

0-486-22766-9 DOVER PB $9.95

John C. **Beaglehole**

The Life of Captain James Cook

A classic study and the first full-scale biography to do justice to the exploits and achievements of the intrepid navigator and explorer

See also **BIOGRAPHY** under **THE 18TH CENTURY** under **GREAT BRITAIN AND IRELAND**

0-8047-0848-7 STANFORD $65.00

0-8047-2009-6 STANFORD PB $24.95

Gananath **Obeyesekere**

The Apotheosis of Captain Cook: European Mythmaking in the Pacific

A Sri Lankan anthropologist attacks his eminent colleague, Marshall Sahlins, for having misrepresented native Hawaiians as being unable to reason like Europeans—and as unable to realize that Captain Cook wasn't a god

See also **CRITICAL ANTHROPOLOGY** under **ANTHROPOLOGY** in **SOCIAL STUDIES**

0-691-03621-7 PRINCETON PB $13.95

Lynne **Withey**

Voyages of Discovery: Captain Cook and the Exploration of the Pacific

0-520-06564-6 CALIFORNIA PB $15.00

Military Affairs

For related reading, see INTERNATIONAL RELATIONS AND STRATEGIC STUDIES in SOCIAL STUDIES

Military History

Histories of specific wars can be found throughout the various history chapters, including the Second World War, the Civil War and Reconstruction, and the Vietnam War. The books below provide overviews of military history in the world and in the United States.

General Histories

Eliot A. **Cohen** & John **Gooch**

Military Misfortunes: The Anatomy of Failure in War

An analysis of such defeats as the British invasion of Gallipoli in 1915 and the Arab surprise attack against Israel in 1973

0-679-73296-9 VINTAGE PB $13.00

Hans **Delbruck**

History of the Art of War

A classic, monumental history of warfare first published during the early decades of the 20th century. Delbruck includes many detailed analyses of famous battles

Volume 1
Warfare in Antiquity

0-8032-9199-X NEBRASKA PB $20.00

Volume 2
The Barbarian Invasions

0-8032-9200-7 NEBRASKA PB $18.00

Volume 3
Medieval Warfare

0-8032-6585-9 NEBRASKA PB $25.00

Volume 4
The Dawn of Modern Warfare

0-8032-6586-7 NEBRASKA PB $17.00

Paul **Fussell**, editor

The Norton Book of Modern War

A 720-page anthology of writing prompted by the wars of the 20th century, from Rupert Brooke and Ernest Hemingway to ordinary people who recorded their experiences in letters, diaries, and oral histories

0-393-02909-3 NORTON $24.95

Richard **Holmes**

Acts of War: The Behavior of Men in Battle

0-02-914851-0 FREE PRESS PB $16.95

Michael **Howard**

War in European History

Short and authoritative study of warfare as it has developed from the Middle Ages to the present

See also **STRATEGIC STUDIES** under **INTERNATIONAL RELATIONS AND STRATEGIC STUDIES** in **SOCIAL STUDIES**

0-19-289095-6 OXFORD PB $15.95

John F. **Hutchinson**

Champions of Charity: War and the Rise of the Red Cross

Argues that the world's Red Cross organizations failed in their aim to make war more humane; rather, their principal achievement in the nineteenth and early twentieth centuries was to propagandize the values of militarism and wartime sacrifice and to encourage women to participate in the national war efforts

0-8133-2526-9 WESTVIEW $35.00

Archer **Jones**

The Art of War in the Western World

0-19-506241-8 OXFORD PB $22.95

John **Keegan**

A History of Warfare

One of the world's most respected military historians explores and illuminates mankind's seemingly infinite capacity for armed conflict, from primitive ritual to high-tech destruction. "Keegan concludes that global survival depends on our curbing humanity's vast capacity for destructive violence—and on this score, readers of his superb new survey will find, he's cautiously optimistic"—*Kirkus Reviews*

See also **STRATEGIC STUDIES** under **INTERNATIONAL RELATIONS AND STRATEGIC STUDIES** in **SOCIAL STUDIES**

0-394-58801-0 KNOPF $30.00

0-679-73082-6 VINTAGE PB $15.00

Paul **Kennedy**

The Rise and Fall of the Great Powers: Economic Change and Military Conflict, 1500-2000

A work of extraordinary breadth, this national bestseller examines cases of "imperial overstretch" in the past and concludes with a somber warning for the contemporary prospects of preserving the Pax Americana

0-679-72019-7 VINTAGE PB $16.00

Paul M. **Kennedy**, editor

Grand Strategies in War and Peace

Kennedy and other scholars pursue some of the themes he enunciated in *The Rise and Fall of the Great Powers:* the trade-offs that nations have had to make among their political, economic, and military goals, and how this applies to America's future

0-300-04944-7 YALE $30.00

William H. **McNeill**

The Pursuit of Power: Technology, Armed Force, and Society Since AD 1000

Society's conflicts and dilemmas from the cross-bow to the nuclear missile; the arms race as the motor of progress. "A grand synthesis … that tells us almost as much about the history of butter as the history of guns"
—*Washington Post Book World*

0-226-56158-5 CHICAGO PB $13.95

Robert L. **O'Connell**

Of Arms and Men: A History of War, Weapons and Aggression

From prehistoric times to the nuclear age, focusing on how social and economic conditions interact with weapons and the tactics employed in warfare

0-19-505359-1 OXFORD $29.95

0-19-505360-5 OXFORD PB $12.95

Geoffrey **Parker**

The Cambridge Illustrated History of Warfare

0-521-44073-4 CAMBRIDGE $39.95

Richard A. **Preston** & Sydney F. **Wise**

In Arms: A History of Warfare and Its Interrelationships with Western Society

0-03-033428-4 HOLT PB $27.93

Martin L. **van Creveld**

Supplying War: Logistics from Wallerstein to Patton

The "nuts and bolts" of war, from the Thirty Years War to World War II

0-521-29793-1 CAMBRIDGE PB $19.95

Technology and War: From 2000 B.C. to the Present

0-02-933153-6 FREE PRESS PB $17.95

American Military History

Jim **Crace**

Signals of Distress

See also **THE MIDDLE GENERATION** under **20TH-CENTURY BRITISH AND IRISH FICTION** in **LITERATURE OF THE BRITISH ISLES**

0-374-26379-5 FS&G $22.00
0-88001-486-5 ECCO PB $15.00

Charles E. **Heller** & William A. **Stofft**, editors

America's First Battles, 1776-1950

0-7006-0276-3 KANSAS $29.95
0-7006-0277-1 KANSAS PB $15.95

Maj. Gen. Jeanne **Holm**, USAF (Ret)

Women in the Military: An Unfinished Revolution

A historical account of women in the American military

0-89141-450-9 PRESIDIO $27.50
0-89141-513-0 PRESIDIO PB $16.95

Edwin P. **Hoyt**

America's Wars

By a leading American military historian

0-306-80338-0 DA CAPO PB $14.95

John **Keegan**

Fields of Battle: The Wars for North America

A tour of the major fields of battle on the North American continent, from the arrival of the first Europeans in the 16th century to the final defeat of the Native American population in the 19th. Throughout, Keegan emphasizes how the continent's unique geography has determined the strategy and outcome of our military history and the competition for our land's wealth and natural resources. An original and impassioned analysis

0-679-42413-X KNOPF $30.00

Allan R. **Millett** & Peter **Maslowski**

For the Common Defense: A Military History of the United States, 1607-1983

A good survey

0-02-921597-8 FREE PRESS PB $22.95

Colonel Michael Lee **Lanning**

Senseless Secrets: The Failures of U.S. Military Intelligence, From George Washington to the Present

Despite the enormous amount of national resources poured into its coffers, the American military intelligence community has provided the country with complete failures: Ticonderoga, Little Big Horn, Pearl Harbor, Tet, Grenada, Panama, to name just a few of its major debacles. Lanning, a decorated US Army veteran and public affairs officer to General Schwarzkopf, offers an insider's account of how and why this enormously expensive—28 billion dollars annually—item in the military budget has failed its country time after time after time

1-55972-322-X BIRCH LANE $24.95

Russell F. **Weigley**

The American Way of War: A History of U.S. Military Strategy and Policy

The best introduction to American military thought. Published in 1973

See also **STRATEGIC STUDIES** under **INTERNATIONAL RELATIONS AND STRATEGIC STUDIES** in **SOCIAL STUDIES**

0-253-28029-X INDIANA PB $16.95

T. Harry **Williams**

A History of American Wars: From Colonial Times to World War I

Americans at war, by the biographer of Huey Long

0-8071-1234-8 LOUSIANA STATE PB $14.95

Atlases

Arthur **Banks**

A World Atlas of Military History, 1860-1945

An emphasis on the American Civil War, World War I, and World War II

0-306-80332-1 DA CAPO PB $12.95

Jeremy **Black**

The Cambridge Illustrated Atlas of Warfare: Renaissance to Revolution, 1472-1792

With particular attention paid to the effects of European military expansion on the Americas, Africa, Asia, and the Mediterranean

0-521-47033-1 CAMBRIDGE $39.95

Martin **Gilbert**

Atlas of the First World War

Covers all aspects of the war in 159 maps

CARTOGRAPHY BY ARTHUR BANKS
INTRODUCTION BY VISCOUNT MONTGOMERY OF ALAMEIN

0-88029-020-X HIPPOCRENE $17.95

Tom **Hartman** & John **Mitchell**

A World Atlas of Military History, 1945-1984

A map and text history of conflicts in the Middle East, Africa, India, China, Korea, Southeast Asia, Central and South America, and Europe

0-306-80316-X DA CAPO PB $14.95

Theory and Strategy

Karl von **Clausewitz**

On War

0-679-42043-6 KNOPF $23.00
0-14-044427-0 PENGUIN PB $9.95

Trevor N. **Dupuy**

Understanding War: History and Theory of Combat

By the co-author of *The Encyclopedia of Military History*

0-913729-57-4 PARAGON $24.95

Alfred Thayer **Mahan**

The Influence of Sea Power upon History, 1660-1805

The book that inspired America's entry into the battleship era

0-486-25509-3 DOVER PB $12.95

Williamson **Murray** & others

The Making of Strategy: Rulers, States, and War

Seventeen case studies analyze how strategists have sought to implement a course of action against their adversaries

0-521-56627-4 CAMBRIDGE PB $19.95

Martin **van Creveld**

The Transformation of War

Van Creveld takes a position against Clausewitz's assumption that war is rational, arguing that modern technology and techniques of terrorism and guerilla warfare have created conditions that exceed rational analysis

0-02-933155-2 FREE PRESS $29.95

> Doubtless the process by which the state will lose its monopoly over armed violence…will be gradual, uneven, and spasmodic. Things will happen at a different pace in different parts of the world. Most likely, disintegration will be accompanied by violent upheavals similar to those which in Europe began during the Reformation and culminated in the Thirty Years' War.
>
> THE TRANSFORMATION OF WAR

Wars Through the Ages

For related reading, see THE SECOND WORLD WAR

For related reading, see THE CIVIL WAR AND RECONSTRUCTION

For related reading, see THE VIETNAM WAR

Ancient Warfare

Arthur **Ferrill**

The Fall of the Roman Empire: The Military Explanation

See also **MILITARY** under **TOPICS IN ROMAN HISTORY** under **ANCIENT ROME**

0-500-27495-9 NORTON PB $15.95

Donald W. **Engels**

Alexander the Great and the Logistics of the Macedonian Army

"Careful analyses of terrain, climate and supply … are combined in a masterly fashion to help account for Alexander's strategic decisions" —*NY Review of Books*

0-520-04272-7 CALIFORNIA PB $13.95

J. F.C. **Fuller**

The Generalship of Alexander the Great

0-306-80371-2 DA CAPO PB $14.95

Victor Davis **Hanson**

The Western Way of War: Infantry Battle in Classical Greece

What happened on the battlefields of ancient Greece, and how those battles have affected war to the present day

INTRODUCTION BY JOHN KEEGAN

0-19-506588-3 OXFORD PB $12.95

Chester G. **Starr**

The Influence of Sea Power in Ancient History

0-19-505667-1 OXFORD PB $12.95

Edward **Luttwak**

The Grand Strategy of the Roman Empire

"Brings detailed insights into the working of Roman military organization, in strategy and tactics"—E. Badian

See also **INTERNATIONAL SYSTEM TO 1900** under **INTERNATIONAL RELATIONS AND STRATEGIC STUDIES** in **SOCIAL STUDIES**

0-8018-2158-4 JOHNS HOPKINS PB $14.95

Sun **Tzu**

The Art of War

Written in China more than 2000 years ago, this series of aphoristic essays is the first known study of the planning and conduct of military operations

See also **CHINESE THOUGHT** under **TOPICS IN IMPERIAL CIVILIZATION** under **CHINA**

TRANSLATED WITH AN INTRODUCTION BY SAMUEL B. GRIFFITH

0-19-501540-1 OXFORD $19.95

0-19-501476-6 OXFORD PB $8.95

The Middle Ages

Michael **Bennett**

The Battle of Bosworth

The battle of 1485 that ended Richard III's short reign and established the Tudor dynasty

0-312-06972-3 ST. MARTIN'S $35.00

0-312-10320-4 ST. MARTIN'S PB $19.95

Malcolm **Billings**

The Cross and the Crescent: A History of the Crusades

The pageantry and clash of battle, the toll of disease; from the first crusade to Napoleon's taking of Malta. Over 200 illustrations

0-8069-6904-0 STERLING PB $19.95

Philippe **Contamine**

War in the Middle Ages

A sophisticated study of war in all its aspects—technological, economic, political and cultural. Highly recommended

See also **GENERAL HISTORIES** under **MEDIEVAL AND RENAISSANCE EUROPE**

0-631-13142-6 BLACKWELL $24.95

Tim **Newark**

Medieval Warlords

ILLUSTRATED BY ANGUS MCBRIDE

0-7137-2234-7 BLANDFORD PB $16.95

Michael **Prestwich**

Armies and Warfare in the Middle Ages: The English Experience

While military life in this era is sometimes pictured in terms of romantic knights in armor, the reality more often consisted of men struggling against cold and damp, and against elusive forces who refused to do battle. An appealing social history of war

0-300-06452-7 YALE $37.50

Early Modern Warfare

Jeremy **Black**

European Warfare, 1660-1815

0-300-06170-6 YALE $32.50

David B. **Ralston**

Importing the European Army: The Introduction of European Military Techniques and Institutions in the Extra-European World, 1600-1914

How five countries refashioned their armed forces along European lines. The examples are Russia, the Ottoman Empire, Egypt, China, and Japan

0-226-70319-3 CHICAGO PB $14.95

The Napoleonic Era

David **Chandler**

The Campaigns of Napoleon: The Mind and Method of History's Greatest Soldier

0-02-523660-1 MACMILLAN $75.00

The Military Maxims of Napoleon

Napoleon's thoughts on the art of war, tactics, strategies, and command

See also **THE AGE OF NAPOLEON** under **THE FRENCH REVOLUTION AND NAPOLEON**

0-947898-64-6 GREENHILL $24.95

John R. **Elting**

Swords Around a Throne: Napoleon's Grande Armée

An American military historian's view of Napoleonic warfare

See also **THE AGE OF NAPOLEON** under **THE FRENCH REVOLUTION AND NAPOLEON**

0-02-909501-8 FREE PRESS $50.00

Philip J. **Haythornthwaite**

Napoleon's Military Machine

How the ragged armies of the French Revolution were transformed into the era's best fighting force. This is a big, lavishly illustrated book

1-88511-918-6 SARPEDON $37.95

John **Lynn**

Bayonets of the Republic: Motivation and Tactics in the Army of Revolutionary France

0-8133-2945-0 WESTVIEW PB $24.95

George F. **Nafziger**

Napoleon's Invasion of Russia

Assembling an army of nearly 600,000, the largest force under a single command seen in Europe until that time, Napoleon crossed the Russian frontier on June 23, 1812, in a campaign that culminated in the Battle of Borodino on September 7. Includes 16 maps and appendices with valuable documents

See also **THE AGE OF NAPOLEON** under **THE FRENCH REVOLUTION AND NAPOLEON**

FOREWORD BY DAVID CHANDLER

0-89141-322-7 PRESIDIO $45.00

G.E. **Rothenberg**

The Art of Warfare in the Age of Napoleon

Insights into the character of warfare of the age and Napoleon's military style

See also **THE AGE OF NAPOLEON** under **THE FRENCH REVOLUTION AND NAPOLEON**

0-253-20260-4 INDIANA PB $12.95

Wars of Imperialism

Michael **Barthorp**

The Zulu War: A Pictorial History

0-7137-1469-7 STERLING PB $14.95

David **Clammer**

The Zulu War

The massacre of the British at Isandhlwana and the defense at Rorke's Drift; includes maps, photographs, and illustrations

See also **ZULU** under **SOUTH AFRICA: HISTORY** under **AFRICA**

0-8095-7525-6 BORGO $25.00

World War I

For related reading, see 20TH-CENTURY EUROPE TO THE SECOND WORLD WAR

For related reading, see GREAT BRITAIN AND IRELAND

For related reading, see US HISTORY, 1877-1945

For related reading, see RUSSIAN STUDIES

Robert A. **Doughty**

The Seeds of Disaster: The Development of French Army Doctrine

0-208-02096-9 SHOE STRING $32.50

John **Ellis**

Eye-Deep in Hell: Trench Warfare in World War I

0-8018-3947-5 JOHNS HOPKINS PB $14.95

Paddy **Griffith**

Battle Tactics of the Western Front

How the Allied army gradually improved its techniques and technology and eventually demonstrated a battlefield skill and mobility that would rarely be surpassed even during World War II

0-300-06663-5 YALE PB $17.00

B.H. Liddell **Hart**

The Real War, 1914-1918

A largely military history, written in 1930 by the famous wartime strategist

See also **THE GREAT WAR** under **WORLD WAR I** under **20TH-CENTURY EUROPE TO THE SECOND WORLD WAR**

0-316-52505-7 LITTLE, BROWN PB $16.95

Alan **Moorehead**

Gallipoli

The disastrous Allied campaign in Turkey

0-345-33088-9 BALLANTINE PB $5.95

Myron J. **Smith**, Jr.

World War I in the Air: A Bibliography and Chronology

0-8108-0990-7 SCARECROW $25.00

Tim **Travers**

The Killing Ground: The British Army, the Western Front and the Emergence of Modern Warfare, 1900-1918

See also **THE GREAT WAR** under **WORLD WAR I** under **20TH-CENTURY EUROPE TO THE SECOND WORLD WAR**

0-04-445736-7 UNWIN HYMAN PB $24.95

Denis **Winter**

Death's Men: Soldiers of the Great War

The individual British soldier, in the trenches with five million of his countrymen

See also **ARMAGGEDON: 1914-1918** under **THE 20TH CENTURY** under **GREAT BRITAIN AND IRELAND**

See also **THE GREAT WAR** under **WORLD WAR I** under **20TH-CENTURY EUROPE TO THE SECOND WORLD WAR**

0-14-016822-2 PENGUIN PB $12.00

Recent Wars

Manuel **De Landa**

War in the Age of Intelligent Machines

Throughout history, technological change has been linked to military thinking and military applications. From the Greek phalanx to the 19th-century invention of the conoidal bullet to today's computerized weapons systems, De Landa takes a close look at this connection

0-942299-75-2 ZONE PB $16.95

US Armed Forces

The US Army

Edward M. **Coffman**

The Old Army: A Portrait of the American Army in Peacetime, 1794-1898

The only comprehensive study of the people who made up the "garrison world" in the peacetime intervals between the war for Independence and the Spanish-American War, particularly the lonely men of Northern cities for whom enlistment was a "choice of evils"

0-19-503750-2 OXFORD $40.00
0-19-504555-6 OXFORD PB $22.00

Richard H. **Kohn**

Eagle and Sword: The Beginnings of the Military Establishment in America

0-02-918350-2 FREE PRESS PB $16.95

H. Norman **Schwarzkopf** & Peter **Petre**

It Doesn't Take a Hero

"Stormin' Norman" was always the right man for the job—as a cadet at West Point, on two tours of duty in Vietnam, in the 1983 operation against Grenada, and in the Gulf War. Sometimes shocking, sometimes funny, his stories of behind-the-scenes events in combat and at headquarters illuminate the changes in the military during the last two decades

0-553-56338-6 BDD PB $6.99

General H. Norman Schwarzkopf (credit: ©1992 Michael A. Gorenflo)

The US Navy

Robert G. **Albion**

The Makers of Naval Policy, 1798-1947

EDITED BY ROWENA REED

0-87021-360-1 NAVAL INSTITUTE $39.95

Paolo E. **Coletta**

The American Naval Heritage in Brief

0-8191-5596-9 UNIVERSITY PRESS $66.50
0-8191-5597-7 UNIVERSITY PRESS PB $38.50

Raimondo **Luraghi**

A History of the Confederate Navy

Argues that the gravest threat to the South was not, as commonly held, the Federal blockade, but the Union's amphibious and riverine operations. "One of the most prominent European scholars of the Civil War weighs in with a provocative revisionist study… [A] notable addition to Civil War maritime history" —*Publishers Weekly*

See also **THE WAR AT SEA** under **THE CIVIL WAR AND RECONSTRUCTION** in **HISTORY OF THE AMERICAS**

1-55750-527-6 NAVAL INSTITUTE $39.95

Robert L. **O'Connell**

Sacred Vessels: The Cult of the Battleship and the Rise of the U.S. Navy

An irreverent and cautionary history of the modern battleship and its overvalued place in US history

0-19-508006-8 OXFORD PB $15.95

Jack **Sweetman**, editor

American Naval History: An Illustrated Chronology of the U.S. Navy and Marine Corps, 1775 to the Present

1-55750-785-6 NAVAL INSTITUTE $45.00

The US Marines

Allan R. **Millett**

Semper Fidelis: The History of the U.S. Marine Corps

0-02-921596-X FREE PRESS PB $19.95

Robert J. **Moskin**

The U.S. Marine Corps Story

The second edition of a popular textbook

0-316-58558-0 LITTLE, BROWN PB $27.50

Agostino **von Hassell**

Warriors: The United States Marines

A photographic journal of the Marines, based on 60,000 miles of travel over eight years

0-943231-08-6 HOWELL $24.95

Other US Forces

Robert E. **Johnson**

Guardians of the Sea: A History of the U.S. Coast Guard, 1915 to the Present

0-87021-720-8 NAVAL INSTITUTE $35.00

US Military Leadership

Joseph G. **Dawson**, editor
Commanders in Chief: Presidential Leadership in Modern Wars
0-7006-0579-7 KANSAS PB $12.95

Edgar F. **Puryear**, Jr.
Stars in Flight: A Study in Air Force Character and Leadership
The careers of the first five chiefs of staff of the Air Force: Arnold, Spaatz, Twining, Vandenberg, and White
0-89141-127-5 PRESIDIO $14.95
0-89141-128-3 PRESIDIO PB $8.95

Air Power

Michael S. **Sherry**
The Rise of American Air Power: The Creation of Armageddon
An in-depth history of American strategic bombing
See also THE WAR IN THE AIR under THE SECOND WORLD WAR
0-300-04414-3 YALE PB $20.00

Aircraft

George **Hall**
Top Gun: The Navy's Fighter Weapons School
0-87938-520-0
MOTORBOOKS INTERNATIONAL PB $14.95

C.J. **Heatley III**
Forged in Steel: U.S. Marine Corps Aviation
Color photographs of the A-4 Skyhawk, "Whiskey" Cobra helicopter, F-18 fighter, and many others
INTRODUCTION BY JOHN GLENN
0-943231-00-0 HOWELL $24.95

Robert **Jackson**
NATO Air Power
A heavily illustrated guide
0-89141-294-8 PRESIDIO $17.98

Piet Hein **Meijering**
Signed with Their Honor: Air Chivalry During the Two World Wars
1-55778-116-8 PARAGON $18.95

Peter B. **Mersky**
U.S. Marine Corps Aviation: 1912 to the Present
From the Western Front through Vietnam and beyond
0-933852-39-8 NAUTICAL & AVIATION $26.95

Michael **O'Leary**
U.S. Sky Spies Since World War I
0-7137-1555-3 STERLING $24.95

Ben R. **Rich** & Leo **Janos**
Skunk Works
The true story of America's most successful and secret aerospace operation, Lockheed's Skunk Works and its aviation triumphs, from the U-2 spy plane to the Stealth bomber
0-316-74330-5 LITTLE, BROWN $24.95

David **Wragg**
Airlift: A History of Military Air Transport
A heavily illustrated history that includes the C-130 Hercules and helicopters in Vietnam and the British "air bridge" in the Falklands
0-89141-282-4 PRESIDIO $17.98

Space

Craig **Ryan**
The Pre-Astronauts: Manned Ballooning on the Threshhold of Space
The story of the early, daring space pioneers who explored the stratosphere in tiny capsules suspended beneath plastic balloons
1-55750-732-5 NAVAL INSTITUTE $29.95

Alan **Shepard** & Deke **Slayton**
Moon Shot: The Inside Story of America's Race to the Moon
"A first-hand, white-knuckle, behind-the-scenes account of the race to the moon by America's coolest astronaut and colleagues. It's rich in unfamiliar anecdotes, funny and surprisingly moving"—Carl Sagan
1-57036-167-3 TURNER PB $12.95

World War II Aircraft

Mark **Meyer**
Classics: U.S. Aircraft of World War II
Color photographs of the classic planes, by a *Time* magazine photographer
TEXT BY WALTER J. BOYNE
0-943231-41-8 HOWELL PB $24.95

Jerry **Scutts**
Spitfire in Action
0-89747-092-3 SQUADRON SIGNAL PB $7.95

Tanks and Armored Vehicles

R.P. **Hunnicutt**
Patton: A History of the American Battle Tank
FOREWORD BY DONN A STARRY
0-89141-230-1 PRESIDIO $60.00

Charles **Messenger**
Anti-Armour Warfare
An experienced tank commander shows how today's anti-armor battle might be fought
0-7110-1396-9 HIPPOCRENE $19.95

Ships and Sea Warfare

G. **Albrecht**, editor
Weyer's Warships of the World, 1988-89
More than 600 drawings and 900 photos of ships in all the world's navies; in English and German
FOREWORD BY NORMAN POLMAR
0-933852-75-4 NAUTICAL & AVIATION $78.95

James J. **Colledge**
Ships of the Royal Navy: An Historical Index
0-87021-652-X NAVAL INSTITUTE $37.95

Peter **Garrison**
CV: Carrier Aviation
The story of the aircraft carrier, which changed the face of war at sea; third edition
PHOTOGRAPHS BY GEORGE HALL
0-89141-299-9 PRESIDIO PB $9.98

Hans **Hansen**
Ships of the German Fleet, 1849-1945
0-87021-654-6 NAVAL INSTITUTE $41.95

Brian **Lavery**
The Arming and Fitting of English Ships of War, 1600-1815
0-87021-009-2 NAVAL INSTITUTE $59.95

Archibald R. **Lewis** & Timothy J. **Runyan**
European Naval and Maritime History
0-253-32082-8 INDIANA $24.95
0-253-20573-5 INDIANA PB $10.95

Emanuel Raymond **Lewis**
Seacoast Fortifications of the United States
A history of the Army's coast artillery from colonial times to the end of World War II
0-89141-257-3 NAVAL INSTITUTE PB $8.95

World War II Ships

Norman **Polmar** & Dorr B. **Carpenter**
Submarines of the Imperial Japanese Navy
0-87021-682-1 NAVAL INSTITUTE $37.95

Uniforms and Insignia

Anthony J. **Bryant**
Samurai: 1550-1600
ILLUSTRATED BY ANGUS MCBRIDE
1-85532-345-1 OSPREY PB $12.95

Brian L. **David**
German Army Uniforms and Insignia, 1933-1945
1-85409-158-1 ARMS & ARMOUR $29.95

Col. John R. **Elting**
Napoleonic Uniforms
ILLUSTRATED BY HERBERT KNOTEL
0-02-897115-9 MACMILLAN $250.00

Philip J. **Haythornthwaite**
Uniforms of the Civil War: In Color
0-8069-5846-4 STERLING PB $14.95

Philip **Katcher**
Civil War Uniforms: A Photo Guide: Confederate Forces
1-85409-333-9 ARMS & ARMOUR PB $12.95

Wade **Krawczyk**
German Army Uniforms of World War II: In Color Photographs
0-7603-0249-9
MOTORBOOKS INTERNATIONAL $39.95

Jon A. **Maguire**
Gear Up!: Flight Clothing & Equipment of USAAF Airmen in World War II
0-88740-744-7 SCHIFFER $45.00

John **Mollo**
Uniforms of the American Revolution
ILLUSTRATED BY MALCOLM MCGREGOR
0-8069-8240-3 STERLING PB $14.95

Anton **Shalito** & Ilya **Savchenkov**
Red Army Uniforms of World War II in Colour Photographs
1-87200-459-8 WINDROW & GREENE PB $15.95

Gordon **Williamson**
The Iron Cross: A History, 1813-1957
0-9624883-8-0 REDDICK ENTERPRISES $19.95

War Games

James F. **Dunnigan**
The Complete Wargames Handbook: How to Play, Design, and Find Them
0-688-10368-5 QUILL PB $12.00

Paul **Haque**
Naval Wargaming
1-85260-143-4
MOTORBOOKS INTERNATIONAL $24.95

Reference

Frank **Cox**
The NCO Guide
0-8117-2565-0 STACKPOLE PB $17.95

Lawrence P. **Crocker**
The Army Officer's Guide
0-8117-2510-3 STACKPOLE PB $19.95

R. Ernest **Dupuy** & Trevor N. **Dupuy**
The Harper Encyclopedia of Military History: From 3500 to the Present
The updated fourth edition includes treatments of the winding down of the Soviet-Afghan War, the Persian Gulf War, and the collapse of the Soviet and Eastern European governments. With clear-to-read and concise chronologies throughout
0-06-270056-1 HARPERCOLLINS $70.00

Trevor N. **Dupuy** & others
Dictionary of Military Terms
0-8242-0717-3 H.W. WILSON $42.00

Max **Hastings**, editor
The Oxford Book of Military Anecdotes
0-19-214107-4 OXFORD $25.00
0-19-520528-6 OXFORD PB $11.95

Nicholas **Hooper** & Matthew **Bennet**
The Cambridge Atlas of Medieval History: Warfare: 768-1487
A lively, illustrated volume aimed at the general reader. With 100 maps and battle plans
See also **GENERAL HISTORIES** under **MEDIEVAL AND RENAISSANCE EUROPE**
0-521-44049-1 CAMBRIDGE $39.95

John **MacDonald**
Great Battlefields of the World
INTRODUCTION BY LEN DEIGHTON
FOREWORD BY JOHN HACKETT
0-02-044464-8 MACMILLAN PB $25.95

Historiography

The Classics

Jacob **Burckhardt**
Reflections on History
A cultural historian for whom art and literature are as important as political institutions
INTRODUCTION BY GOTTFRIED DIETZE
0-913966-37-1 LIBERTY FUND $15.00

The Civilization of the Renaissance in Italy
0-679-60169-4 RANDOM HOUSE $15.50
0-14-044534-X PENGUIN PB $12.95

Wilhelm **Dilthey**
Introduction to the Human Sciences: An Attempt to Lay a Foundation for the Study of Society and History
The great 19th-century German theorist attempted to attain objectively valid interpretations of the inner life of past cultures
See also **PHILOSOPHY** in **RELIGION, SPIRITUALITY, AND PHILOSOPHY**
TRANSLATED & EDITED BY RAMON J. BETANZOS
0-691-07307-4 PRINCETON $65.00

Francesco **Guicciardini**
Maxims and Reflections
The Florentine historian was one of the first to make the distinction between history and romance
0-8122-1037-9 PENNSYLVANIA PB $17.95

G.W.F. **Hegel**
Lectures on the Philosophy of History
History as the rational process of the spirit of world freedom from the ancient Orient through classical Greece to 19th-century Europe
See also **HEGEL** under **PHILOSOPHY** in **RELIGION, SPIRITUALITY, AND PHILOSOPHY**
TRANSLATED BY J. SIBREE
INTRODUCTION BY C.J. FRIEDRICH
0-486-20112-0 DOVER PB $9.95

Philosophy of Right
Hegel's political philosophy was conservative, though liberal in the context of contemporary Prussia. He favored constitutional monarchy based on family and guild in which liberty was balanced with public order
See also **HEGEL** under **PHILOSOPHY** in **RELIGION, SPIRITUALITY, AND PHILOSOPHY**
See also **CLASSICS** under **POLITICAL THOUGHT** in **SOCIAL STUDIES**
TRANSLATED BY T.M. KNOX
0-19-500276-8 OXFORD PB $18.95

Niccolo **Machiavelli**

The radical innovation of Machiavelli was to base political theory on experience rather than edifying ideals, and he drew on history (in his Discourses*) as well as his own career as a Florentine diplomat. His ambiguous legacy includes both modern empirical political science and the Realpolitik of the nation-state as a law unto itself*

Machiavelli

The Discourses
A commentary on Livy's history of Rome
See also **CLASSICS** under **POLITICAL THOUGHT** in **SOCIAL STUDIES**
EDITED BY BERNARD CRICK
0-14-044428-9 PENGUIN PB $9.95

Florentine Histories

See also **CLASSICS** under **POLITICAL THOUGHT** in **SOCIAL STUDIES**

TRANSLATED BY LAURA BANFIELD & HARVEY MANSFIELD

0-691-05521-1 PRINCETON $65.00

0-691-00863-9 PRINCETON PB $17.95

History of Florence and of the Affairs of Italy

See also **CLASSICS** under **POLITICAL THOUGHT** in **SOCIAL STUDIES**

0-8446-2503-5 SMITH $18.25

The Portable Machiavelli

Contains *The Prince,* excerpts from *The Discourses* (Machiavelli's commentary on Roman history), and other writings

See also **HUMANISM** under **THE RENAISSANCE** under **ITALIAN LITERATURE** in **LITERATURE OF EUROPE, AFRICA, AND ASIA**

See also **CLASSICS** under **POLITICAL THOUGHT** in **SOCIAL STUDIES**

TRANSLATED BY MARK MUSA & PETER BONDANELLA

0-14-015092-7 VIKING PB $14.95

The Prince

See also **CLASSICS** under **POLITICAL THOUGHT** in **SOCIAL STUDIES**

See also **RENAISSANCE CLASSICS** under **RENAISSANCE ITALY AND THE COMING OF HUMANISM** under **MEDIEVAL AND RENAISSANCE EUROPE**

TRANSLATED BY GEORGE BULL

0-14-044107-7 PENGUIN PB $5.95

Ibn **Khaldun**

The Muqaddimah: Abridged Edition

A single-volume abridgement of the 14th-century masterpiece of Islamic historiography. "Should make the essential ideas of Ibn Khaldun accessible to a wide circle of readers"—*TLS*

See also **ISLAMIC SOURCES** under **THE ISLAMIC WORLD TO WORLD WAR I**

TRANSLATED BY FRANZ ROSENTHAL

EDITED BY N.J. DAWOOD

0-691-01754-9 PRINCETON PB $16.95

Charles de **Montesquieu**

The Spirit of the Laws

The first structuralist shows the variety of political constitutions by collecting and categorizing historical evidence from all times and place

0-02-849270-6 FREE PRESS PB $15.95

The Spirit of the Laws: A Compendium of the First English Edition Together with an English Translation of an Essay on Causes Affecting Mind and Characters

In his greatest work, published in 1748, Montesquieu argues that a separation of government functions will ensure individual liberty

EDITED BY DAVID W. CARRITHERS

0-520-02566-0 CALIFORNIA $55.00

0-520-03455-4 CALIFORNIA PB $16.95

The Persian Letters

A satire on French institutions, thinly disguised as the observations of two Persians visiting Paris

See also **THE AGE OF CLASSICISM** under **FRENCH LITERATURE TO 1900** in **LITERATURE OF EUROPE, AFRICA, AND ASIA**

TRANSLATED BY C.J. BETTS

0-14-044281-2 PENGUIN PB $10.95

Friedrich **Nietzsche**

Human, All Too Human: A Book for Free Spirits

See also **NIETZSCHE** under **PHILOSOPHY** in **RELIGION, SPIRITUALITY, AND PHILOSOPHY**

TRANSLATED BY MARION FABER AND STEPHEN LEHMANN

0-8032-8368-7 NEBRASKA PB $12.00

Untimely Meditations

Nietzsche's early critical assessment of his influences: Schopenhauer, Wagner, academic history and philology, and the rationalist biblical critic David Strauss

See also **NIETZSCHE** under **PHILOSOPHY** in **RELIGION, SPIRITUALITY, AND PHILOSOPHY**

TRANSLATED BY R.J. HOLLINGDALE

0-521-28927-0 CAMBRIDGE PB $17.95

The Use and Abuse of History

Deeply influenced by Emerson, the philosopher criticizes the 19th-century dependence on history at the expense of living in the present

TRANSLATED BY ADRIAN COLLINS

INTRODUCTION BY J. KRAFT

0-02-323730-9 PRENTICE HALL PB $11.00

Oswald **Spengler**

The Decline of the West

This World War I-inspired meditation on the doom of Western civilization is still interesting for its depiction of the centralization of control over the culture industry. Available as a complete set or in an abridged edition

EDITED BY HELMUT WERNER

0-394-42176-0 RANDOM HOUSE $40.00

Alexis de **Tocqueville**

Journeys to England and Ireland

INTRODUCTION BY J.P. MAYER

0-88738-716-0 TRANSACTION PB $19.95

Recollections of the French Revolution

EDITED WITH AN INTRODUCTION BY J.P. MAYER

PREFACE BY FERNAND BRAUDEL

9-990-08518-8 TRANSACTION PB $19.95

Selected Letters on Politics and Society

TRANSLATED BY JAMES TOUPIN

EDITED BY ROGER BOESCHE

0-520-05047-9 CALIFORNIA $37.50

0-520-05751-1 CALIFORNIA PB $15.00

Arnold **Toynbee**

A Study of History

An enormous sweep over nations and epochs firmly situates Western civilization in the last five minutes of the clock of history

Volume 1: An Abridgement of Volumes 1-6

0-19-505080-0 OXFORD PB $16.95

Volume 2 An Abridgement of Volumes 7-10

0-19-505081-9 OXFORD PB $16.95

Giambattista **Vico**

The New Science of Giambattista Vico

Vico's 1725 treatise was the first modern study of myth, foreshadowing later anthropological views: "The fables of the gods are true histories of customs." This groundbreaking work was the first to treat the internal dynamics of primitive cultures and offered a cyclical alternative to the Enlightenment's belief that history means progress

See also **VICO** under **PHILOSOPHY** in **RELIGION, SPIRITUALITY, AND PHILOSOPHY**

See also **GENERAL INTRODUCTIONS** under **MYTHOLOGY AND FOLKLORE** in **RELIGION, SPIRITUALITY, AND PHILOSOPHY**

TRANSLATED BY THOMAS G. BERGIN & MAX FISCH

0-8014-9265-3 CORNELL PB $15.95

The Great Tradition

Herbert **Butterfield**

The Whig Interpretation of History

One of the earliest books to question the 19th-century interpretation of Britain's constitutional development

0-393-00318-3 NORTON PB $8.95

John **Cannon**, editor

The Blackwell Dictionary of Historians

More than 200 contributors have created an authoritative work, including extensive entries on more than 500 historians from Herodotus to the present, and numerous historiographical essays on a wide range of topics

0-631-14708-X BLACKWELL $99.95

Norman F. **Cantor** & Richard I. **Schneider**

How to Study History

Excellent practical guide for the beginner

0-88295-709-0 HARLAN DAVIDSON PB $13.95

E.H. **Carr**

What Is History?

Classic by a great British historian of the Russian Revolution

0-394-70391-X RANDOM HOUSE PB $7.98

R.G. **Collingwood**

The Idea of History

Collingwood is the chief English exponent of historical idealism: that reality is essentially historical and a collaborative work of human imagination

See also **COLLINGWOOD** under **PHILOSOPHY** in **RELIGION, SPIRITUALITY, AND PHILOSOPHY**

EDITED BY T.M. KNOX

0-19-285306-6 OXFORD PB $14.95

Will **Durant** & Ariel **Durant**

The Lessons of History

Four decades of research, knowledge, and insights are distilled here in a single volume that illuminates the pivotal lessons of history. Presented in the same lively and highly readable style that has been enlightening readers of the 11-volume *The Story of Civilization* for more than 50 years

0-671-41333-3 SIMON & SCHUSTER $17.95

Robert W. **Fogel** & G.R. **Elton**

Which Road to the Past?: Views of History

Illuminating discussion between Fogel, a leading practitioner of quantitative methods, and Elton, the late Tudor historian and defender of traditional history

0-300-03011-8 YALE $27.00
0-300-03278-1 YALE PB $13.00

Gertrude **Himmelfarb**

The New History and the Old

A highly critical look at the trends of recent decades

0-674-61580-8 HARVARD $32.00
0-674-61581-6 HARVARD PB $13.95

Johan **Huizinga**

Men and Ideas: History, the Middle Ages, the Renaissance

Historiography from the author of *The Waning of the Middle Ages*

INTRODUCTION BY BERT F. HOSELITZ

0-691-00802-7 PRINCETON PB $18.95

Georg **Lukacs**

The Historical Novel

TRANSLATED BY HANNAH & STANLEY MITCHELL

0-8032-7910-8 NEBRASKA PB $13.00

Main Trends in History

0-8419-1287-4 HOLMES & MEIER $45.00
0-8419-1062-6 HOLMES & MEIER PB $19.95

Frank E. **Manuel**

Shapes of Philosophical History

Cultivated lectures on the patterns that man has tried to find in history from Daniel to Immanuel Kant

0-8047-0248-9 STANFORD $24.50

Arnaldo **Momigliano**

The Classical Foundations of Modern Historiography

"Vintage Momigliano, full of deep learning, new associations, sound judgments, mastery of a broad range of literature from several different cultures, and all bearing the inimitable stamp of one of this century's leading intellectual historians"—Ronald S. Stroud, University of California, Berkeley

0-520-07870-5 CALIFORNIA PB $13.00

Karl R. **Popper**

The Poverty of Historicism

The most famous attack on history-writing in which theories overwhelm facts

0-7448-0052-8 ROUTLEDGE PB $10.95

Fritz **Stern**, editor

The Varieties of History: From Voltaire to the Present

A canny selection of seminal texts in the history of historiography

0-394-71962-X RANDOM HOUSE PB $17.00

C. Vann **Woodward**

The Future of the Past: Historical Writings

0-195-05704-9 OXFORD $24.95

Robin W. **Winks**, editor

The Historian as Detective: Essays on Evidence

A variety of historians apply their deductive talents to the elucidation of mysteries from medieval murders to Edgar Allan Poe thrillers

0-06-131933-3 HARPERCOLLINS PB $16.00

The *Annales* School

The highly influential French school, named for its own periodical, *Annales—societés—civilisations,* has a methodological rather than a political orientation. Its early focus was on the *mentalité*, the cultural and religious particularity of past periods, derived from little-used documents such as heresy trial records and private letter caches. Later writers developed the idea of the *longue durée* as a supplement to the interpretation of political, military, and constitutional events. They analyzed the effect of geological, social, and technological changes spanning hundreds and even thousands of years.

Marc **Bloch**

Feudal Society

A great work of social history by the co-founder (with Lucien Fèbre) of the *Annales* school

Volume I
The Growth of Ties of Dependence

0-22605978-2 CHICAGO PB $9.95

Volume II
Social Classes and Political Organization

0-22605979-0 CHICAGO PB $9.95

Fernand **Braudel**

On History

The most famous member of the *Annales* school discusses the method used in such works as *The Structures of Everyday Life*

See also **FERNAND BRAUDEL** under **THE EXPANSION OF EUROPE: EMPIRE AND COMMERCE** under **EARLY MODERN EUROPE**

TRANSLATED BY SARAH MATTHEWS

0-226-07151-0 CHICAGO PB $11.95

Emmanuel Le Roy **Ladurie**

The Mind and Method of the Historian

The historian who used Inquisition records in his depiction of a 13th-century village discusses his working methods

TRANSLATED BY SIAN & BEN REYNOLDS

0-226-47326-0 CHICAGO $26.00

New Directions

Bernard **Bailyn**

On the Teaching and Writing of History

"[Full of] wisdom and charm…a book which deserves a much larger audience"—*TLS*

0-87451-720-6 NEW ENGLAND PB $9.95

Robert H. **Canary** & Henry **Kozicki**, editors

The Writing of History: Literary Form and Historical Understanding

Language is the new subjectivity: these essays show how rhetorical tropes distort the historian's desire to reproduce reality

0-299-07570-2 WISCONSIN $32.50

Norman F. **Cantor**

Inventing the Middle Ages: The Lives, Works, and Ideas of the Great Medievalists of the Twentieth Century

A tale of how nearly all of our ideas about the Middle Ages were actually created in this century by 20 scholars—including J.R.R. Tolkein and C.S. Lewis. It is both an artful description of a group of fascinating people and an intellectual history of our century. "A highly impassioned and personal book"
—*Washington Post Book World*

0-688-12302-3 QUILL PB $12.00

Philippe **Carrard**

Poetics of the New History: French Historical Discourse from Braudel to Chartier

A professor of French looks at the *Annales* tradition of historiography in the light of literary theory—specifically theory of narration, theory of enunciation, rhetoric, and stylistics

0-8018-5233-1 JOHNS HOPKINS PB $16.95

Roger **Chartier**

Cultural History: Between Practices and Representations

TRANSLATED BY LYDIA COCHRANE

0-8014-2223-X CORNELL $37.50

Michel **de Certeau**

The Writing of History

0-231-05575-7 COLUMBIA PB $17.00

Georges **Duby**

History Continues

The grand old man of medieval history reflects on his fascinating intellectual odyssey, casting light on his methods of research, on the meaning of history, and on the French milieu in which he has played a leading part for five decades. "Beautifully evokes the vocation, craft, and career of one of this century's outstanding medievalists"
—Julius Kirshner, University of Chicago

TRANSLATED BY ARTHUR GOLDHAMMER

0-226-16775-5 CHICAGO $24.95

David Hackett **Fischer**

Historian's Fallacies: Toward a Logic of Historical Thought

A classic of the early 1970s, by the author of *Paul Revere's Ride*

0-06-131545-1 HARPERCOLLINS PB $18.65

Peter **Gay**

Freud for Historians

0-19-503586-0 OXFORD $25.00
0-19-504228-X OXFORD PB $11.95

Francois **Furet**

In the Workshop of History

Essays on the Enlightenment, the French Revolution, and anti-Semitism in France

TRANSLATED BY JONATHAN MANDELBAUM

0-226-27336-9 CHICAGO $27.50

Robert **Gildea**

The Past in French History

Champions a renewal of political history and argues that in collective memory and commemoration—not in race, class, or even creed—political communities find their unity

0-300-05799-7 YALE $45.00

0-300-06711-9 YALE PB $20.00

Carlo **Ginzburg**

Clues, Myths, and the Historical Method

TRANSLATED BY JOHN TEDESCHI & ANNE C. TEDESCHI

0-8018-3458-9 JOHNS HOPKINS $35.00

Jürgen **Habermas**

The New Conservatism: Cultural Criticism and the Historians' Debate

0-262-08188-1 MIT $30.00

Francis **Haskell**

History and Its Images: Art and Interpretation of the Past

How history, one literary branch of the humanist tradition, regarded the visual arts between the fifteenth and early twentieth centuries

See also **THEORY AND CRITICISM** under **ART HISTORY: GENERAL STUDIES** in **ART**

0-300-05540-4 YALE $50.00

J.H. **Hexter**

On Historians: Reappraisals of Some of the Masters of Modern History

0-674-63427-6 HARVARD PB $12.95

Eric **Hobsbawm** & Terence **Ranger**, editors

The Invention of Tradition

Just how old are traditions? These essays will tell you precisely when the tartan was invented and describe the mixture of Ali Baba and Lohengrin that was cooked up for the great 1870 durbar at Delhi

0-521-43773-3 CAMBRIDGE PB $12.95

Eric **Hobsbawm**

Echoes of the Marseillaise: Two Centuries Look Back on the French Revolution

See also **INTERPRETING THE REVOLUTION** under **THE FRENCH REVOLUTION AND NAPOLEON**

0-8135-1524-6 RUTGERS PB $9.95

Lynn **Hunt**, editor

The New Cultural History

0-520-06428-3 CALIFORNIA $45.00

0-520-06429-1 CALIFORNIA PB $13.95

Patrick H. **Hutton**

History as an Art of Memory

0-87451-631-5 VERMONT $40.00

0-87451-637-4 VERMONT PB $17.95

Georg **Iggers**

The German Conception of History

0-8195-6080-4 WESLEYAN PB $21.00

New Directions in European Historiography

Excellent coverage of the current trend—*Annales*, Modern German, Marxist—with some historical background

0-8195-6071-5 WESLEYAN PB $19.95

Dominick **LaCapra**

History and Criticism

Attempts to locate ways of doing history that will incorporate new rhetorical criticism while retaining a sense of the difference of the past

0-8014-9324-2 CORNELL PB $11.95

History, Politics, and the Novel

0-8014-2033-4 CORNELL $36.50

0-8014-9577-6 CORNELL PB $13.95

Mary **Lefkowitz**

Not Out of Africa: How Afrocentrism Became an Excuse to Teach Myth as History

The distinguished classicist shows why there is no reason to think the Greeks stole their civilization from Africa; a cogent argument against teaching "feel-good history" in order to raise self-esteem

See also **GREEK INFLUENCE** under **TOPICS IN ANCIENT GREEK HISTORY** under **ANCIENT GREECE**

0-465-09837-1 BASIC $24.00

David **Lowenthal**

The Past Is a Foreign Country

An illustrated personal investigation into the persistence of the past in our daily lives through architecture, sculpture, and the sites of great events

0-521-22415-2 CAMBRIDGE $54.95

0-521-29480-0 CAMBRIDGE PB $24.95

Edward **Muir** & Guido **Ruggiero**, editors

Microhistory and the Lost Peoples of Europe

The notion of microhistory—the intense study of a particular individual, community, or event—evolved in the 1970s and '80s in the Italian journal *Quaderni Storici*, under the editorship of Carlo Ginzburg and Carlo Poni, from which the essays in this collection are taken. Reacting against the long-term, generalizing perspectives of most historians, the contributors try to focus as concretely as possible on otherwise obscure persons and events, restricting themselves to the local level on which most history actually occurs

0-8018-4183-6 JOHNS HOPKINS PB $14.95

Richard **Rorty** & others, editors

Philosophy in History: Essays in the Historiography of Philosophy

Sixteen essays on the nature of philosophy and its history

0-521-27330-7 CAMBRIDGE PB $19.95

Jacques **Ravel** & Lynn **Hunt**, editors

French Histories: French Constructions of the Past

Contributors include Ernst Labrousse, Pierre Vilar, Francois Furet, Bernard Bailyn, Immanuel Wallerstein, and J.H. Hexter, among many others

TRANSLATED BY ARTHUR GOLDHAMMER

1-56584-195-6 NEW PRESS $40.00

Paul **Ricoeur**

Time and Narrative

Volume 1

0-226-71332-6 CHICAGO PB $13.95

Volume 2

0-226-71334-2 CHICAGO PB $13.95

Volume 3

0-226-71336-9 CHICAGO PB $13.95

Simon **Schama**

Landscape and Memory

Schama argues that the landcape of the West is a treasury of myths, legends, identities and mysteries

0-679-40255-1 KNOPF $40.00

Lawrence **Stone**

The Past and the Present

0-7102-1193-7 ROUTLEDGE PB $17.95

Richard **Terdiman**

Present Past: Modernity and the Memory Crisis

A work primarily in literary studies of relevance to historians, with discussions of Musset, Baudelaire, Proust, Freud, Lukacs, and the Frankfurt school. "Suggests an important role for historians in dealing with the current perplexities in the realm of memory, history, and theory"—Herman Lebovics, SUNY, Stony Brook

0-8014-8132-5 CORNELL PB $18.95

Paul **Thompson**

The Voice of the Past: Oral History

Oral history records the lives of ordinary people through their own voices

0-19-289216-9 OXFORD PB $19.95

Hayden **White**

The Content of the Form: Narrative Discourse and Historical Representation

The foremost proponent of history as a rhetorical form rather than a representation of reality makes a series of powerful arguments in this and the following books

0-8018-2937-2 JOHNS HOPKINS $38.50

0-8018-4115-1 JOHNS HOPKINS PB $14.95

Metahistory: The Historical Imagination in Nineteenth-Century Europe

Hegel, Michelet, Ranke, Tocqueville, Burckhardt, Marx, Nietzsche, and Croce

0-8018-1761-7 JOHNS HOPKINS PB $16.95

Jan **Vansina**

Oral Tradition as History

The pioneer of oral historiography speaks, drawing heavily from his knowledge of Africa

See also **GENERAL HISTORIES** under **AFRICA**

0-299-10214-9 WISCONSIN PB $14.95

Biographies and Critical Studies

Hugh **Tulloch**

Acton

0-312-02726-5 ST. MARTIN'S $24.95

John D. **Rosenberg**

Carlyle and the Burden of History

Illustrates how the author of *The French Revolution* was a great epic poet whose natural medium was prose and for whom history was prophecy, biography, and social criticism

See also **EMINENT VICTORIANS: BIOGRAPHICAL STUDIES** under **GREAT BRITAIN AND IRELAND**

0-674-09754-8 HARVARD $23.50

Jacob **Owensby**

Dilthey and the Narrative of History

Renders the thought of German cultural philosopher Wilhelm Dilthey (1833-1911) plausible to a poststructuralist readership

0-8014-3011-9 CORNELL $29.95

Norma **Thompson**

Herodotus and the Origins of the Political Community: Arion's Leap

Explains historical tales, contending that the "father of history" recognized the importance of compelling stories: that stories bind together one polity as distinct from another

0-300-06260-5 YALE $25.00

G.R. **Elton**

F.W. Maitland

0-300-03528-4 YALE $22.00

Leonard **Krieger**

Ranke: The Meaning of History

0-226-45349-9 CHICAGO $37.50

Robert **Boesche**

The Strange Liberalism of Alexis de Tocqueville

"Uncommonly provocative and culturally annotated"
—George Armstrong Kelly, *New Republic*

0-8014-1964-6 CORNELL $37.50

Peter **Singer**

Marx

0-19-287510-8 OXFORD PB $7.95

William H. **McNeill**

Arnold J. Toynbee: A Life

"A rare treat...poignant and perceptive"
—*Library Journal*

0-19-505863-1 OXFORD $30.00
0-19-506335-X OXFORD PB $10.95

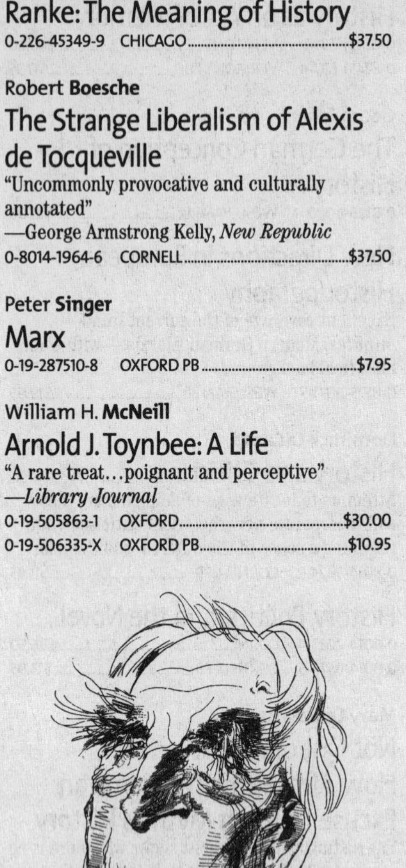

Arnold Toynbee

John **Clive**

Macaulay: The Shaping of the Historian

A National Book Award winner

See also **EMINENT VICTORIANS: BIOGRAPHICAL STUDIES** under **GREAT BRITAIN AND IRELAND**

0-674-54005-0 HARVARD PB $18.50

Late Arrivals

Samuel W. **Mitcham**

Why Hitler

0-275-95485-4 PRAEGER $25.00

Victor **Perera**

The Cross and the Pear Tree: A Sephardic Journey

0-520-20652-5 CALIFORNIA $14.95

Steven **Shapin**

The Scientific Revolution

0-226-75020-5 CHICAGO $19.95
0-226-75021-3 CHICAGO PB $42.01

H.J.A. **Sire**

The Knights of Malta

0-300-05502-1 YALE $50.00
0-300-06885-9 YALE PB $25.00

History of the Americas

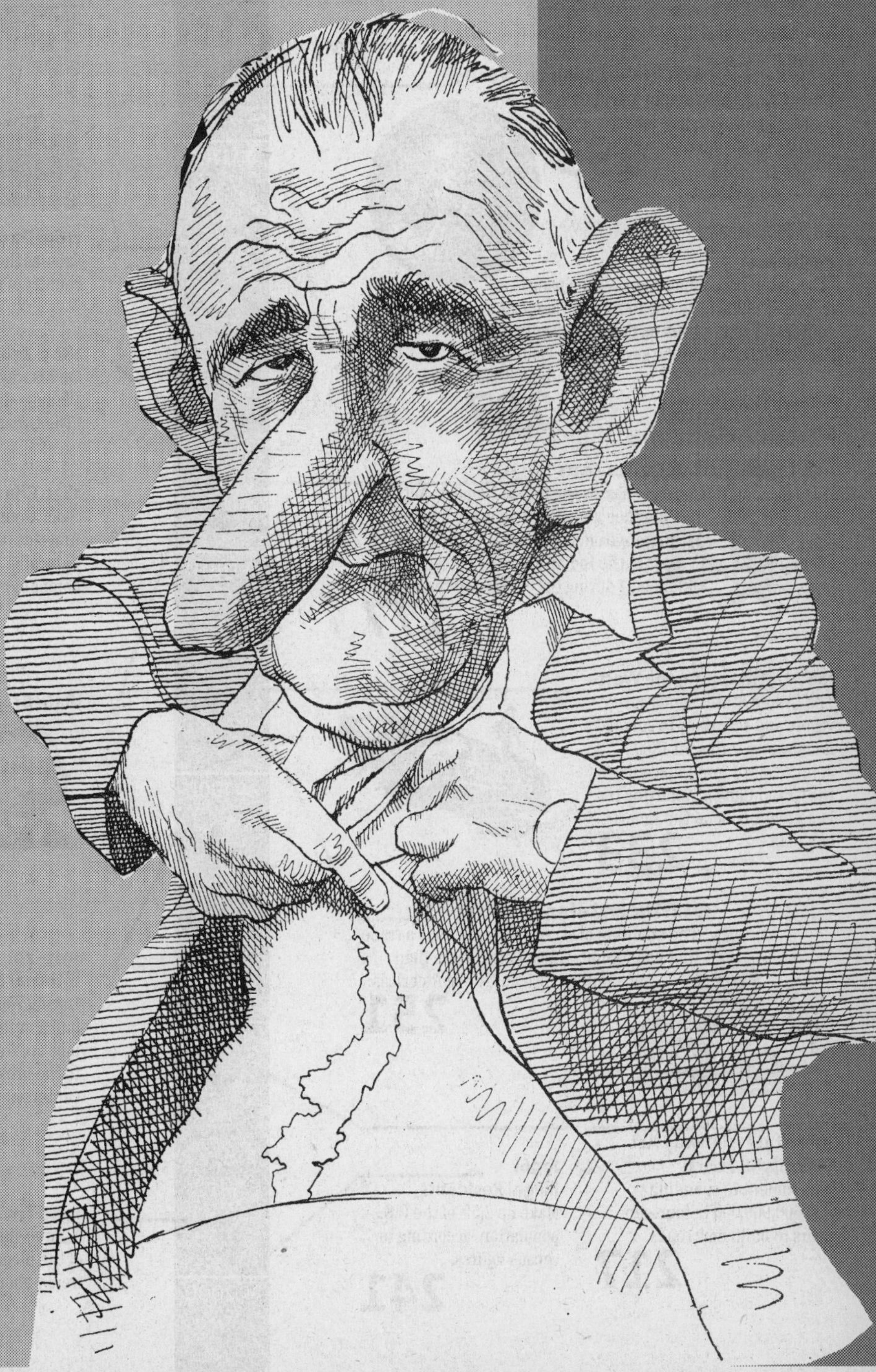

L.B.J.

Migration & Exploration

28,000 BC: Ice Age
As oceans shrink, mammoth-hunters follow a land bridge across the Bering Strait into North America.
175

1345: Aztecs
Migrating south, they see an island in the great lake of Mexico and an eagle perched on a cactus with a snake struggling in its beak. Here they found the city of Tenochtitlán.
187

1541: Francesco de Orallana
A Spanish explorer sails up a vast river, returning with tales of fierce female warriors. The river is named the Amazon.
298

1682: René-Robert Cavelier, Sieur de La Salle
Descends the Mississippi and claims it and all its watershed for France. He is killed by his men.
193

Pestilence:
"The indigenous population of the Spanish colonies, which at the beginning of European contact may have been as much as 50 million, fell to about 4 million in the seventeenth century."
—Richard Hofstedter
297

1831: Trail of Tears
Congress passes the Indian Removal Act. Cherokee and other tribes are forced to migrate from native lands in the Southeast to the Indian Territory (present-day Oklahoma) during the coldest winter in fifty years.
177

1867–79: Mapping the West
The United States sends surveyors and scientists to survey its new territories. In 1869 John Wesley Powell floats down the Grand Canyon, charting the last great blank on the American map.
233

1888: The End of an Industry
The abolition of slavery in Brazil ends a trade that had forcibly transplanted more than nine million Africans to the Americas.
251

1956: Interstate Highway Act
Commits US federal government to spending $33,500,000,000 in fourteen years to build new roads.
217

1996: Illegal Residents
Make up 2.5% of the U.S. population, according to census figures.
241

c. 1000 AD: Leif Erikson
Discovers Vinland, full of "grapes and self-sown wheat," somewhere along the northeast coast of the U.S. or Canada (neither later Vikings nor contemporary historians can figure out where).
193

1513: Balboa
Crosses the Panamanian isthmus to the Pacific Ocean, claiming all it touches for Spain. His rivals conspire to have him seized, condemned for treason, and beheaded.
297

1610: Henry Hudson
Finds Hudson Bay while searching for the Northwest Passage. Set adrift with his teenage son in an open boat by a mutinous crew, he is never seen again.
193

1769: Daniel Boone
Crosses the Cumberland Gap into the bluegrass country of Kentucky.
233

1805: Zebulon Pike
On his way to the Rio Grande, he traverses the Great Plains—dubbing the future breadbasket of America "The Great American Desert."
233

1831: Charles Darwin
Sails around the tip of South America to the Galapagos as naturalist (and captain's dinner companion) aboard the *Beagle*.
560

1846: Brigham Young
After the lynching of Joseph Smith, he leads the Latter Day Saints (Mormons) from Illinois to the promised land of Deseret, where they found the great Salt Lake City.
233

Immigrants
Over 20,000,000 Europeans emigrate to America between the Civil War and World War I.
241

1915–20: Internal Migration
During World War I, more than half a million American blacks migrate from Southern farms to the urban manufacturing centers of the North.
251

1993: The Golden Venture
A cargo ship runs aground in Long Island Sound, killing many of the illegal Chinese immigrants packed aboard it. A media frenzy about illegal immigration ensues.
243

AD 1000 · AD 1500 · AD 1600 · AD 1700 · AD 1800 · AD 1850 · AD 1900 · AD 1950 · AD 2000

Settlements in The Americas

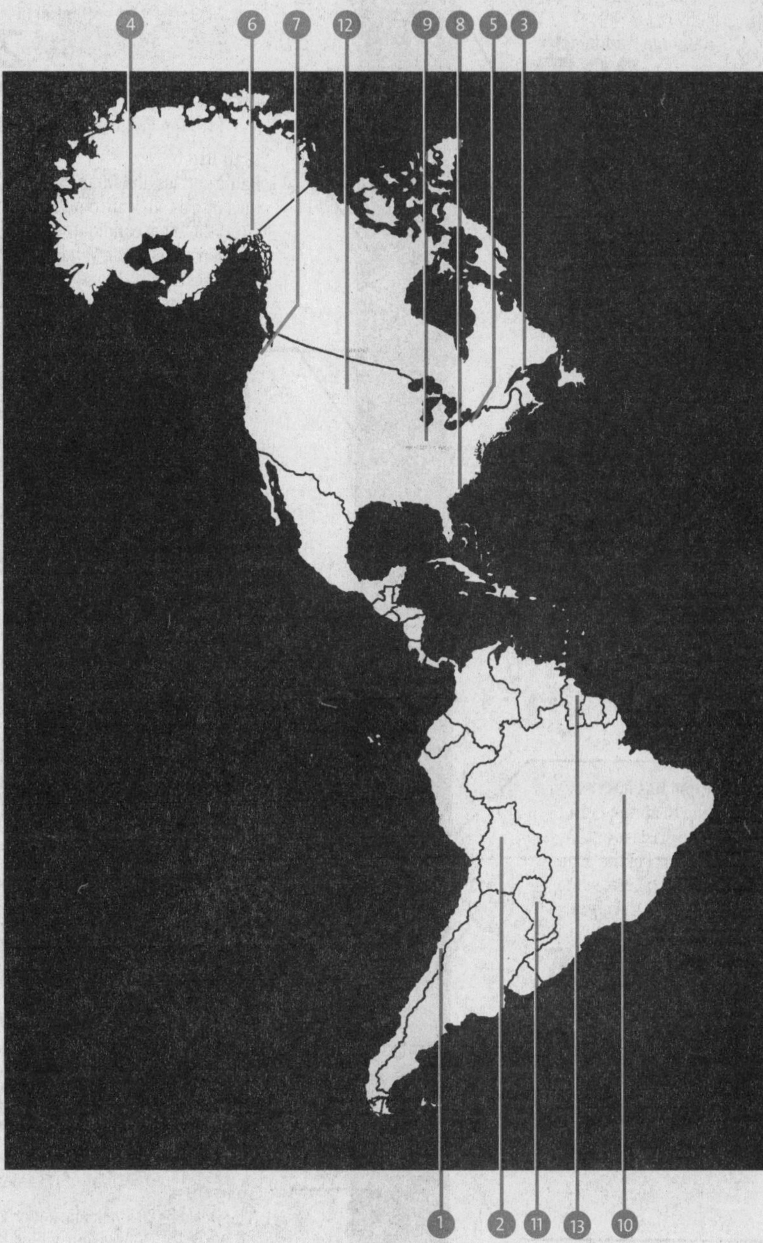

1 Monte Verde, Chile
The earliest known human habitations in the Americas dating from c.10,000 BC, are in evidence here.

13

2 Potosi, Bolivia
At 13,000+ feet, Potosi is one of the highest cities in the world. It is the site of vast silver mines that paid the expenses of the Spanish Empire for 50 years after their discovery in 1545.

304

3 Magdalen Islands
The first English Puritans in America settled here in the Gulf of St. Lawrence, north of Prince Edward Island.

194

4 Brobdingnag
The country of giants, discovered on the northwest coast of North America by Lemuel Gulliver in 1703.

—*Jonathan Swift*
Gulliver's Travels

800

5 The Ordinance of 1785
This measure ordered the Northwest Territory surveyed in one-mile-square sections. "Government surveyors laid out a baseline westward from the precise point where the Ohio River left the State of Pennsylvania. The grid was an infinitely reproducible pattern, the perfect machine for national expansion."

—*The Oxford History of the American West*

193

6 New Archangel
The capital of Russian Alaska was established in 1808. The Russians made serfs of the native Aleuts and demanded they hunt furs for a Russian-American company. The US purchased Alaska from Russia in 1867.

193

7 Ft. Astoria
John Jacob Astor established this fur-trading outpost at the mouth of the Columbia river in 1811: the first American settlement on the Pacific coast.

232

8 Sea Islands, South Carolina
Home to the first cotton plantations, the Sea Islands were part of the land distributed to freed slaves by the federal government after the Civil War. Largely cut off from the rest of America until well into the 20c, the islands are still inhabited primarily by African Americans, who speak a distinctive dialect called Gullah, a mixture of English and African languages.

250

9 New Harmony, Indiana
In 1824 Robert Owen, a utopian social planner, purchased Harmony, Indiana, from the religious leader George Rapp. New Harmony, the first American community to offer universal public education, failed after 10 years.

191

10 Manaus
Capital of the Brazilian state of Manaus. The 19c rubber boom led to a period of spectacular, though brief, prosperity.

301

11 Nueva Germania, Paraguay
Elizabeth Nietzsche (sister of the philosopher) and her husband, the racist theorist Bernard Förster, founded an Aryan settlement here in the late 19c. The colony failed after 3 years, but the descendents of several Nueva Germanian families remain.

305

12 Boys Town, Nebraska
Founded by Edward J. Flanagan in 1917 for homeless and abandoned boys.

291

13 Jonestown, Guyana
In 1979, almost a thousand followers of the religious leader Jim Jones killed themselves by drinking Kool-Aid laced with cyanide, while others were shot or injected with cyanide. Jones himself either committed suicide or was murdered.

322

Boom and Bust

1790 Boom
"Houses are rebuilt, fields enclosed, stocks of cattle which were destroyed are replaced, and many a desolated territory assumes again the cheerful appearance of cultivation. The arts of peace, such as clearing rivers, building bridges, and establishing conveniences for traveling are assiduously promoted. In short, the foundation of a great empire is laid."
—George Washington
200

1800

1815 Boom
Bad harvests in Europe prompt demand for US wheat and maize; the influx of hard cash leads to a frenzy of financial speculation.
280

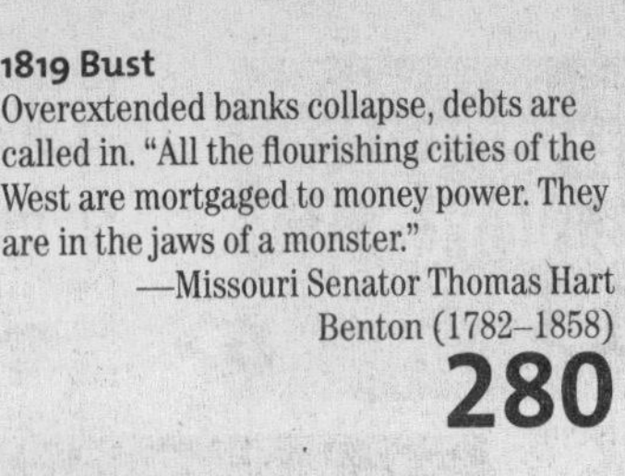

1819 Bust
Overextended banks collapse, debts are called in. "All the flourishing cities of the West are mortgaged to money power. They are in the jaws of a monster."
—Missouri Senator Thomas Hart Benton (1782–1858)
280

1825

1839 Bust
Bankruptcies and financial panic in 1837 turn into a full-scale depression two years later; the Whig candidate Harrison defeats Jackson's successor, Van Buren, in the 1840 presidential election.
200

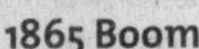

1850

1857 Bust
Repercussions of a collapsing world market hit the North hard, while the South continues to prosper. Planters build splendid mansions and expand their operations, comfortable in the certainty that the industrial North offers no challenge to the supremacy of cotton and slavery.
238

1865 Boom
To meet the demands of running the Civil War, the Republicans have to override the old Jacksonian policies limiting federal involvement in the economy. They establish a national currency and an extensive railway system—major factors in the vast postwar expansion of the Gilded Age.
213

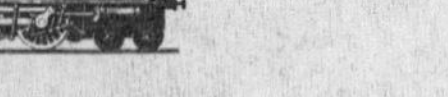

1875

1873 Bust
Though late-19c America enjoys unprececented levels of economic growth, it is also beset by recurrent—and increasingly cataclysmic—financial collapses. Speculation is uncontrolled, while the growth of industry means the economy has become ever more complexly intertwined. A single financial failure could have devastating consequences for the nation.
213

1893 Bust
The second great crisis of the Gilded Age: rapid business expansion exhausts financial resources, leading to abrupt contraction, and a ruinous panic ensues. With the crisis over, bankers like J.P. Morgan set out to assume control of the economy from the industrialists who had exercised it before, while the devasted farmers of the south and west launch the great Populist movement against the gold standard.
275

1900

1907 Bust
"For a week in October, a team of New York bankers, led by Pierpont Morgan, struggled heroically against a crisis which threatened to bring down the whole American financial and economic structure; they prevailed, but it had been a close-run thing."
—Hugh Brogan
The Penguin History of the U.S.A.
281

1920s Boom
"The business of America is business."
—Calvin Coolidge
215

1925

1929 Bust
The October 29 stock market crash brings on the Great Depression, which lasts until America enters World War II. Fearing revolution, business accepts the greater government involvement in its affairs entailed by FDR's New Deal.
216

1945–1974 Boom
Emerging undamaged out of WWII, the US enters a Golden Age in which economic growth is spurred by military spending and technological innovation. "The ideal to which the Golden Age aspired was production, or even service, without humans: automated robots assembling cars, silent voids filled with banks of computers, trains without drivers. Human beings were essential only as buyers."
—Eric Hobsbawm
The Age of Extremes
217

1950

1975

1974 Bust
The oil crisis is followed by the high inflation of the 1970s and a sharp reduction in productivity.
495

1989 Bust
In 1984 Ronald Reagan says "It's morning in America," but despite an economic boomlet and an upsurge in speculation that produces numerous millionaires, average wages and salaries drop and income differentials are wider than at any time since the late 19c. After the stock market collapse in October 1989 and the huge banking crisis that follows, the economy goes into a recession from which it only begins to recover in the mid-1990s.

224

Native American Cultures: North America

"Despite vast study by scientists and a voluminous literature of modern knowledge about Indians, still common are ignorance and misconceptions, many of them resulting from the white man's continuing inability to regard Indians save from his own European-based point of view. Today most Indians on both continents have been conquered and enfolded within the conquerors' own cultures; but the span of time since the various phases of the conquest ended has been short, and numerous Indians still cling to traits that are centuries, if not millennia, old and cannot be quickly shed." —Alvin M. Josephy, Jr., *The Indian Heritage of America*

General Works

William **Brandon**

Indians

A strong, compact narrative

0-8281-0301-1 AMERICAN HERITAGE PB $12.95

Angie **Debo**

A History of the Indians of the United States

0-8061-1888-1 OKLAHOMA PB $17.95

Harold E. **Driver**

Indians of North America

One of the most useful overviews. This revised edition incorporates recent archaeological findings and devotes much space to the 20th century

0-226-16467-5 CHICAGO PB $29.95

Brian M. **Fagan**

Ancient North America: The Archaeology of a Continent

Traces the entire course of native American history from the first appearance of humans in the New World 14,000 years ago to the cataclysmic aftermath of European settlement. "A heroic effort to synopsize the occupational history of the United States and Canada...An excellent introductory text" *—American Antiquity*

0-500-05075-9 THAMES & HUDSON $45.00
0-500-27606-4 THAMES & HUDSON PB $34.95

Kingdoms of Gold, Kingdoms of Jade: The Americas Before Columbus

The author of *The Journey from Eden* draws on history, archaeology, ethnography, mythology, and art history to create a stunning overview of the civilizations of the Americas before Columbus. The most recent research, such as tomb discoveries and new advances in the decipherment of Mayan hieroglyphs, is incorporated. Includes 140 illustrations, 20 in color

0-500-05062-7 THAMES & HUDSON $24.95

Peter **Farb**

Man's Rise to Civilization: Cultural Ascent of the Indians of North America

Revised edition of the landmark 1968 book that marked the first comprehensive examination of the culture and history of North American Indians and inspired a rebirth of popular interest

0-14-015323-3 PENGUIN PB $14.00

Arlene **Hirschfelder**, editor

Native Heritage: Personal Accounts by American Indians, 1790 to Present

0-02-860412-1 MACMILLAN PB $15.00

Alvin M. **Josephy**, Jr.

500 Nations: An Illustrated History of North American Indians

A big, handsome book

0-679-42930-1 KNOPF $50.00

America in 1492: The World of the Indian Peoples Before the Arrival of Columbus from Prehistoric Times Through the 15th Century

0-679-74337-5 VINTAGE PB $18.00

The Indian Heritage of America

An encyclopedic work by one of the best historians of Indian America, surveying tribal cultures region by region

0-395-57320-3 HOUGHTON MIFFLIN PB $13.95

Philip **Kopper**

The Smithsonian Book of North Americans Indians: Before the Coming of the Europeans

Features 293 full-color illustrations

0-8109-1510-3 ABRAMS $39.95

Min **Lee**, editor

Larousse Dictionary of North American History

Superficial but useful reference for beginners

0-7523-0005-9 LAROUSSE PB $8.95

William H. **MacLeish**

The Day Before America

0-395-74014-2 DORLING KINDERSLEY PB $11.95

Lee **Miller**, editor

From the Heart: Voices of the American Indian

0-679-43549-2 KNOPF $24.00
0-679-76891-2 VINTAGE PB $14.00

Russel **Thornton**

American Indian Holocaust and Survival: A Population History Since 1492

From the leading scholar in the field of American Indian demography

0-8061-2220-X OKLAHOMA PB $16.95

Ruth M. **Underhill**

Red Man's America: History of Indians in the United States

ILLUSTRATED BY MARIANNE STOLLER

0-226-84165-0 CHICAGO PB $18.95

Herman J. **Viola**

After Columbus: The Smithsonian Chronicle of the North American Indians

A profusely illustrated account of over 500 years of cultural change among the North American Indians. With 265 color and 77 black-and-white illustrations, and many maps

0-89599-031-8 SMITHSONIAN PB $24.95

Carl **Waldman**

Atlas of the North American Indian

Contains over 100 maps, with an extensive text treating prehistory, culture, wars, land cessions, and contemporary issues

ILLUSTRATED BY MOLLY BRAUN

0-87196-850-9 FACTS ON FILE $35.00
0-8160-2136-8 FACTS ON FILE PB $18.95

Encyclopedia of Native American Tribes

Appropriate for both adult and young readers

ILLUSTRATED BY MOLLY BRAUN

0-8160-1421-3 FACTS ON FILE $45.00

Jack **Weatherford**

Indian Givers: How the Indians of the Americas Transformed the World

Contributions in business, government, medicine, architecture, agriculture, and many other social and cultural affairs

0-449-90496-2 FAWCETT PB $10.00

Clark **Wissler**

Indians of the United States: Four Centuries of Their History and Culture

Unusual in that it traces the tribes by language family rather than by culture area

0-385-02019-8 DOUBLEDAY PB $11.95

Evelyn **Wolfson**

From Abenaki to Zuni: A Dictionary of Native American Tribes

0-8027-7445-8 WALKER PB $9.95

Prehistory

Michael **Coe** & others

Atlas of Ancient America

A guide to the Americas before Columbus

0-8160-1199-0 FACTS ON FILE $45.00

Frederick Hadleigh **West**, editor

American Beginnings: The Prehistory and Paleoecology of Beringia

0-226-89399-5 CHICAGO $75.00

Dean R. **Snow**

The Archaeology of North America

How archaeologists investigate the origins and prehistory of American Indians; part of the fine *Indians of North America* series for young adults

0-7910-0353-1 CHELSEA HOUSE PB $8.95

Early Paintings and Photographs

Edward S. **Curtis**

Visions of a Vanishing Race

TEXT BY FLORENCE CARTER GRAYBILL & VICTOR BOESIN

0-88394-089-2 PROMONTORY $24.98

George **Catlin**

Letters and Notes on the Manners, Customs and Conditions of the North American Indians

The classic early account of life among the Plains Indians

Volume 1

0-517-14744-0 GRAMERCY $22.99

Volume 2

0-486-22119-9 DOVER PB $9.95

North American Indians

The classic two-part account abridged in one volume

INTRODUCTION BY PETER MATTHIESSEN

0-14-017014-6 PENGUIN PB $12.95

Edward S. **Curtis**

The North American Indians

A new edition of Aperture's superb selection of photographs from Edward S. Curtis's legendary 20-volume work which appeared between 1896 and 1930. Curtis's commitment to recording Native American cultures is made movingly evident in these indelible images

PHOTOGRAPHS BY EDWARD S. CURTIS

0-89381-492-X FS&G PB $19.95

Christopher **Cardozo**, editor

Native Nations: First Americans as Seen by Edward S. Curtis

0-8212-2052-7 BULFINCH $60.00

Laurie **Lawlor**

Shadow Catcher: The Life and Work of Edward S. Curtis

Traces his life and work from boyhood in Wisconsin through completion of the North American Indian Collection in the 1930s to his death in 1952

0-8027-8288-4 WALKER $19.95

0-8027-8289-2 WALKER LIBRARY EDITION $20.85

Ulrich W. **Hiesinger**

Indian Lives

A photographic record from the Civil War to Wounded Knee

3-7913-1422-X PRESTEL $35.00

M.R. **Harrington**

The Indians of New Jersey: Dickon Among the Lenapes

The culture, crafts, and language of the Lenapes—with line drawings and a glossary—as seen through the eyes of a fictional shipwrecked English boy

0-8135-0425-2 RUTGERS PB $12.95

Sandy **Johnson**

The Book of Elders: The Life Stories and Wisdom of Great American Indians

"A stirring and wonderful book. The portraits are wonderful"—Peter Matthiessen

PHOTOS BY DAN BUDNICK

0-06-250837-7 HARPERCOLLINS PB $25.00

Paul **Kane**

Wanderings of an Artist Among the Indians of North America

0-486-29031-X DOVER PB $10.95

David **Penney**

Art of the American Indian Frontier: A Portfolio

Penney, curator of Native American Art at the Detroit Institute of Art, documents the extraordinary body of Native American art from the North American woodlands and plains

See also **NORTH AMERICA** under **NATIVE AMERICAN ARTS** in **ART**

0-295-97318-8 DETROIT INSTITUTE PB $39.95

1-56584-251-0 NEW PRESS PB $18.95

Reader's Digest

America's Fascinating Indian Heritage: The First Americans: Their Customs, Art, History and How They Lived

Readable one-volume synthesis with many photos

0-89577-372-4 READER'S DIGEST $30.00

David **Thomas** & others, editors

The Native Americans: An Illustrated History

Sumptuous photos; companion to the Turner Broadcasting presentation

1-87868-542-2 TURNER $50.00

1-57036-239-4 TURNER PB $29.95

Geoffrey **Turner**

Indians of North America

Popular, gracefully written picture book

0-8069-8616-6 STERLING PB $14.95

William **Webb** & Robert **Weinstein**

Dwellers at the Source: Southwestern Indian Photographs of A.C. Vroman, 1895-1904

0-8263-1009-5 NEW MEXICO PB $35.00

Regional and Tribal Studies

Northeast and Great Lakes

James **Axtell**, editor

The Indian Peoples of Eastern America: A Documentary History of the Sexes

Customs of the woodland Indians of the Northeast; consisting of 7 primary source materials arranged according to social rites of passage

0-19-502741-8 OXFORD PB $15.95

Kathleen J. **Bragdon**

Native People of Southern New England, 1500-1650

0-8061-2803-8 OKLAHOMA $28.95

Cadwallader **Colden**

The History of the Five Indian Nations

An 18th-century account of the Iroquois League

0-8014-9086-3 CORNELL PB $8.95

Edmund J. **Danziger**, Jr.

The Chippewas of Lake Superior

0-8061-2246-3 OKLAHOMA PB $15.95

Robert **Grumet**

The Lenapes

0-7910-0385-X CHELSEA HOUSE PB $8.95

George T. **Hunt**

Wars of the Iroquois: A Study in Intertribal Trade Relations

0-7812-5158-3 REPRINT SERVICES $79.00

Isabel T. **Kelsay**

Joseph Brant, 1743-1807: Man of Two Worlds

The Mohawk chief who sided with the British during the American Revolution

0-8156-0208-1 SYRACUSE PB $22.50

Lewis Henry **Morgan**

League of the Iroquois

A classic study, first published in 1851, of an American Indian tribe. With original illustrations

0-8065-0917-1 CITADEL PB $10.95

Arthur C. **Parker**

Seneca Myths and Folk Tales

0-8032-8723-2 NEBRASKA PB $15.00

Stephen R. **Potter**

Commoners, Tributes and Chiefs: The Development of Algonquin Culture

From 200 to 1650, using archaeology and ethnohistory

0-8139-1540-6 VIRGINIA PB $12.95

Dean R. **Snow**
The Iroquois
1-55786-938-3 BLACKWELL PB $19.95

Helen H. **Tanner**, editor
Atlas of Great Lakes Indian History
Contains 33 newly researched maps. "Far and away one of this century's landmark works on American Indian history—absolutely indispensable…A quantum leap forward in the study and understanding of the Indian past" —Alvin M. Joseph, Jr.
CARTOGRAPHY BY MIKLOS PINTHER
0-8061-1515-7 OKLAHOMA $85.00
0-8061-2056-8 OKLAHOMA PB $45.00

Bruce G. **Trigger**
The Children of Aataentsic: A History of the Huron People to 1660
A remarkably detailed work that attempts to avoid the Eurocentric bias of earlier writers
0-7735-0626-8 MCGILL $80.00
0-7735-0627-6 MCGILL PB $29.95

C. Keith **Wilbur**
Woodland Indians
1-56440-625-3 GLOBE PEQUOT PB $16.95

Southeastern

William L. **Anderson**, editor
Cherokee Removal: Before and After
Eight interdisciplinary essays by prominent scholars, including three of Cherokee descent, on the forced relocation of 1838
0-8203-1482-X GEORGIA PB $12.95

Lawrence A. **Clayton**
The De Soto Chronicles
0-8173-0593-9 ALABAMA $50.00

James W. **Covington**
The Seminoles of Florida
0-8130-1196-5 FLORIDA $49.95
0-8130-1204-X FLORIDA PB $18.95

Angie **Debo**
And Still the Waters Run: The Betrayal of the Five Civilized Tribes
Classic work, first published in 1940, which tells the tragic tale of the liquidation of the independent Indian republics of the Choctaws, Chickasaws, Cherokees, Creeks, and Seminoles in Oklahoma territory
0-691-00578-8 PRINCETON PB $16.95

The Rise and Fall of the Choctaw Republic
0-8061-1247-6 OKLAHOMA PB $15.95

John **Ehle**
Trail of Tears: The Rise and Fall of the Cherokee Nation
0-385-23953-X ANCHOR $30.00
0-385-23954-8 ANCHOR PB $12.95

Grant **Foreman**
Indian Removal: The Emigration of the Five Civilized Tribes of Indians
The forced removals to Indian Territory in the 1830s
See also **ANTEBELLUM AMERICA AND THE AGE OF JACKSON** under **US HISTORY TO THE CIVIL WAR**
0-8061-1172-0 OKLAHOMA PB $18.95

J.T. **Glisson**
The Creek
0-8130-1184-1 FLORIDA $29.95
0-8130-1185-X FLORIDA PB $16.95

Charles **Hudson**
The Southeastern Indians
0-87049-248-9 TENNESSEE PB $18.95

Duane H. **King**, editor
The Cherokee Indian Nation: A Troubled History
0-87049-227-6 TENNESSEE $22.95

Robert H. **Lowie**
The Crow Indians
This 1935 study resulted from many years of fieldwork under the auspices of the American Museum of Natural History
See also **CLASSIC ETHNOGRAPHIES** under **ANTHROPOLOGY** in **SOCIAL STUDIES**
0-8032-7909-4 NEBRASKA PB $12.00

Wilma **Mankiller** & Michael **Wallis**
Mankiller: A Chief and Her People
0-312-09868-5 ST. MARTIN'S $22.95

William G. **McLoughlin**
After the Trail of Tears: The Cherokees' Struggle for Sovereignty, 1839-1880
0-8078-2111-X NORTH CAROLINA $45.00
0-8078-4433-0 NORTH CAROLINA PB $18.95

Gerald T. **Milanich** & Charles **Hudson**
Hernando De Soto and the Indians of Florida
0-8130-1170-1 FLORIDA $39.95

Jerald T. **Milanich**
The Timucua
1-55786-488-8 BLACKWELL $29.95

Mallory McCane **O'Connor**
Lost Cities of the Ancient Southeast
0-8130-1350-X FLORIDA $49.95

Theda **Perdue**
Slavery and the Evolution of Cherokee Society, 1540-1866
0-87049-530-5 TENNESSEE PB $14.95

Russel **Thronton**
The Cherokees: A Population History
0-8032-9410-7 NEBRASKA PB $14.00

Time-Life, editors
Tribes of the Southern Woodlands
Part of the colorful Time-Life *American Indian* series
0-8094-9550-3 TIME BOOKS $19.95

Grace Steele **Woodward**
The Cherokees
How the fabled people reached a higher peak of civilization between 1540 and 1906 than any other North American tribe
0-8061-1815-6 OKLAHOMA PB $17.95

J. Leitch **Wright**, Jr.
Creeks and Seminoles: The Destruction and Regeneration of the Muscogulge People
The best one-volume work on the subject, showing that the sense of identity in these tribes was stronger than believed
0-8032-9728-9 NEBRASKA PB $15.00

Plains, Plateau, and Great Basin

Harvey **Arden**
Noble Red Man: Lakota Wisdomkeeper Mathew King
1-88522-301-3 BEYOND WORDS $16.95

Norman **Bancroft-Hunt**
Indians of the Great Plains
Photographic history includes the Cheyenne, Crow, Apache, Blackfoot, and Sioux
PHOTOS BY WERNER FORMAN
0-8061-2465-2 OKLAHOMA PB $22.95

Donald J. **Berthrong**
The Southern Cheyennes
Takes this tribe's history up to the present
0-8061-1199-2 OKLAHOMA PB $17.95

William **Black Elk** & William S. **Lyons**
Black Elk: The Sacred Ways of a Lakota
0-06-250074-0 HARPERCOLLINS PB $11.00

Edwin T. **Denig**
Five Indian Tribes of the Upper Missouri: Sioux, Arickaras, Assiniboines, Crees and Crows
A firsthand account by a fur trader who married an Assiniboine woman and lived among various tribes from 1833 to 1858
EDITED BY JOHN EWERS
0-8061-1308-1 OKLAHOMA PB $14.95

Vera Louise **Drysdale**
The Gift of the Sacred Pipe
0-8061-2311-7 OKLAHOMA PB $29.95

John **Ewers**
The Blackfeet: Raiders on the Northwestern Plains
An ethnic history to 1930, including all three divisions of the Blackfeet: Piegan, Blood, and Siksika
0-8061-1836-9 OKLAHOMA PB $16.95

Norman **Gelb**, editor

Jonathan Carver's Travels Through America, 1776-1778: An Explorer's Portrait of the American Wilderness

First popular American travel book—published in 1778—and international bestseller. Fascinating, detailed account of the lives of the Plains Indians

0-471-11876-1 WILEY PB $14.95

George B. **Grinnell**

The Fighting Cheyennes

Nineteenth-century wars with other tribes and subsequently with whites

INTRODUCTION BY STANLEY VESTAL

0-8061-1839-3 OKLAHOMA PB $19.95

George E. **Hyde**

Red Cloud's Folk: A History of the Oglala Sioux Indians

The migration of the Oglala Sioux from the upper Mississippi to the Powder River in Montana

FOREWORD BY ROYAL B. HASSRICK

0-8061-1520-3 OKLAHOMA PB $15.95

Spotted Tail's Folk: A History of the Brule Sioux

0-8061-1380-4 OKLAHOMA PB $15.95

Robert H. **Lowie**

Indians of the Plains

A concise survey, first published in 1954

FOREWORD BY HARRY L. SHAPIRO

0-8032-7907-8 NEBRASKA PB $8.95

Thomas E. **Mails**

The Mystic Warriors of the Plain

The culture, arts, crafts, and religion of the Plains Indians, profusely illustrated. Used by Kevin Costner as a resource for *Dances with Wolves*

1-57178-002-5 COUNCIL OAK $49.95

Mildred P. **Mayhall**

The Kiowas

0-8061-0987-4 OKLAHOMA PB $17.95

Walter **McClintock**

Old Indian Trails

Originally published in 1923, this is a classic long unavailable. McClintock was "adopted" as a member of the Blackfoot tribe and recorded its customs, legends, religious rites, and daily life

FOREWORD BY WILLIAM LEAST HEAT-MOON

0-395-61155-5 HOUGHTON MIFFLIN PB $12.95

Jacqueline **Peterson**

Sacred Encounters: Father De Smet and the Indians of the Rocky Mountains West

0-8061-2575-6 OKLAHOMA $49.95

0-8061-2576-4 OKLAHOMA PB $24.95

Pauk **Radin**

The Winnebago Tribe

A classic work first published in 1823 as the annual report of the Bureau of Ethnology and still considered the best authority

0-8032-5710-4 NEBRASKA PB $18.95

Maria **Sandoz**

Love Song to the Plains

A lyric salute to the Great Plains and its people from the noted regional historian

0-8032-5172-6 NEBRASKA PB $12.95

Mark **St. Pierre** & Tilda Long **Soldier**

Walking in the Sacred Manner: The Spiritual Power and Legacy of American Plains Indians

0-684-80200-7 TOUCHSTONE PB $12.00

William E. **Unrau**

The Kansa Indians: History of the Wind People, 1673-1873

From first contact with whites to migration and settlement in eastern Kansas

FOREWORD BY R. DAVID EDMUNDS

0-8061-1965-9 OKLAHOMA PB $14.95

James R. **Walker**

Lakota

0-8032-9706-8 NEBRASKA PB $15.00

Lakota Society

A physician on the Pine Ridge Reservation from 1896 to 1914, Walker recorded a wealth of information on the traditional lifeways of the Oglala Sioux

0-8032-9737-8 NEBRASKA PB $10.95

Gene **Wellfish**

The Lost Universe: Pawnee Life and Culture

Narrative of one typical year in a Pawnee village

0-8032-5871-2 NEBRASKA PB $16.95

Southwestern

Maximilien **Bruggmann** & Sylvio **Acatos**

Pueblos: Prehistoric Indian Cultures of the Southwest

Fourteen centuries of flourishing Native American culture

0-8160-2437-5 FACTS ON FILE $45.00

Carlos **Castaneda**

The Teachings of Don Juan: A Yaqui Way of Knowledge

Castaneda's accounts of his mystical experiences with Don Juan, a Yaqui Indian, became bestsellers

See also **WESTERN** under **20TH-CENTURY SPIRITUAL LEADERS** under **SPIRITUALITY** under **SPIRITUALITY** in **RELIGION, SPIRITUALITY, AND PHILOSOPHY**

0-520-00217-2 CALIFORNIA $35.00

0-671-72791-5 WASHINGTON SQUARE PB $14.00

Harold **Courlander**

The Fourth World of the Hopis

The epic story of the Hopi Indians as preserved in their legends and traditions. "Little short of spellbinding"—*Publishers Weekly*

0-8263-1011-7 NEW MEXICO PB $12.95

John **Cremony**

Life Among the Apaches

A basic source on Apache beliefs, tribal life, and fighting tactics, first published in 1868 and still informative despite its ethnocentrism

0-8032-6312-0 NEBRASKA PB $10.95

Frank Hamilton **Cushing**

Zuni: Selected Writings of Frank Hamilton Cushing

Cushing stayed with the Zuni from 1879 to 1884, the first professional anthropologist to live among his subjects. His writings are of far more than historical interest

EDITED BY JESSE GREEN

0-8032-2100-2 NEBRASKA $40.00

0-8032-7007-0 NEBRASKA PB $12.95

Bertha P. **Dutton**

American Indians of the Southwest

A history of the Apache, Navajo, and Pueblo peoples, updated with information on current issues

0-8263-0704-3 NEW MEXICO PB $16.95

T.R. **Fehrenbach**

Comanches: The Destruction of a People

Authoritative account of the most powerful Indian tribe that became the single greatest obstacle to Anglo-American expansion. "For a complete history of the Comanches this book probably has no equal"—Dee Brown

0-306-80586-3 DA CAPO PB $16.95

William M. **Ferguson**

Anasazi Ruins of the Southwest

Twenty-five hundred years of the Southwest tribes

0-8263-0874-0 NEW MEXICO PB $32.50

Edward T. **Hall**

West of the '30s: Discoveries Among the Navajo and Hopi

0-385-42422-1 ANCHOR PB $9.95

Peter **Iverson**

The Navajos

An overview of the largest Indian tribe in the U.S. today, part of the fine *Indians of North America* series

0-7910-0390-6 CHELSEA HOUSE PB $8.95

Clyde **Kluckhohn** & Dorothy **Leighton**

The Navajo

1974 republication of original 1946 edition. "This collaboration between an anthropologist and a medico-psychiatrist has been a fortunate one" —*NY Times*

0-674-60603-5 HARVARD PB $14.95

Frank C. **Lockwood**

The Apache Indians

"Undoubtedly the best account for the general reader"—*Christian Science Monitor*

0-8032-7925-6 NEBRASKA PB $15.00

Carroll L. **Riley**

Rio Del Norte: People of the Upper Rio Grande from Earliest Times to the Pueblo Revolt

Twelve thousand years of history

0-87480-466-3 UTAH $29.95
0-87480-496-5 UTAH PB $15.95

Willard H. **Rollings**

The Comanche

Part of the Smithsonian's *Indians of North America* series

0-7910-0359-0 CHELSEA HOUSE PB $8.95

Scott **Rushforth** & Steadman **Upham**

A Hopi Social History: Anthropological Perspectives on Sociocultural Persistence and Change

Case histories from the western Pueblo region from late prehistory through modernization in the 20th century

0-292-73067-5 TEXAS PB $18.95

Dan L. **Thrapp**

Victorio and the Mimbres Apaches

The Mimbres from their first American contacts in 1849 to the massacre of 1880, with a biography of their war leader, Victorio

0-8061-1645-5 OKLAHOMA PB $16.95

Ruth M. **Underhill**

The Navajos

0-8061-1816-4 OKLAHOMA PB $14.95

California

John **Fahey**

The Kalispel Indians: The History of a Hunting People

0-8061-2000-2 OKLAHOMA $26.95

Robert F. **Heizer** & Albert B. **Elsasser**

The Natural World of the California Indians

This highly detailed guide situates the Indians within the interlocked, self-sustaining ecosystem they inhabited and summarizes the destruction of their ways

0-520-03896-7 CALIFORNIA PB $14.95

Robert F. **Heizer** & Theodora **Kroeber**, editors

Ishi the Last Yahi: A Documentary History

0-520-04366-9 CALIFORNIA PB $15.95

Robert F. **Heizer** & M.A. **Whipple**, editors

The California Indians: A Source Book

0-520-02031-6 CALIFORNIA PB $24.95

Theodora **Kroeber**

Ishi in Two Worlds: Biography of the Last Wild Indian in North America

0-520-03152-0 CALIFORNIA $50.00
0-520-00675-5 CALIFORNIA PB $13.95

Keith A. **Murray**

The Modocs and Their War

Describes the beliefs that led the Modocs of northern California to war in 1872

0-8061-1331-6 OKLAHOMA PB $14.95

Stephen **Powers**

Tribes of California

INTRODUCTION BY ROBERT F. HEIZER

0-520-03023-0 CALIFORNIA $50.00
0-520-03172-5 CALIFORNIA PB $15.95

Time-Life editors

The Indians of California

Part of the colorful Time-Life *American Indian* series

0-8094-9587-2 TIME BOOKS $19.95

Northwest Coast

Peter R. **Gerber** & Maximilian **Bruggmann**

Indians of the Northwest Coast

0-8160-2028-0 FACTS ON FILE $45.00

Alvin M. **Josephy**, Jr.

The Nez Percé Indians and the Opening of the Northwest

0-8032-7551-X NEBRASKA PB $16.95

Peter Skeene **Ogden**

Traits of American Indian Life and Character

Day-to-day life among the original inhabitants of the Oregon Territory, from one of the first individuals to penetrate the vast wilderness of the American Far West. Originally published in 1853

0-486-28436-0 DOVER PB $6.95

Time-Life editors

Indians of the Western Range

Part of the colorful Time-Life *American Indian* series

0-8094-9725-5 TIME BOOKS $19.95

Northern Canadian and Arctic Peoples

Don E. **Dumond**

The Eskimos and Aleuts: Their Archaeology and Early History

"One of the most provocative holistic statements of Arctic prehistory"—*Alaska Journal*

0-500-27479-7 THAMES & HUDSON PB $11.95

Diamond **Jenness**

The Indians of Canada

0-8020-6326-8 TORONTO PB $23.95

Richard K. **Nelson**

Hunters of the Northern Ice

INTRODUCTION BY WILLIAM S. LAUGHLIN

0-226-57176-9 CHICAGO PB $15.95

Dorothy Jean **Ray**

A Legacy of Arctic Art

See also **NORTH AMERICA** under **NATIVE AMERICAN ARTS** in **ART**

0-295-97507-5 WASHINGTON $40.00
0-295-97518-0 WASHINGTON PB $24.95

Ulli **Steltzer**

Inuit: The North in Transition

0-226-77247-0 CHICAGO PB $22.50

Indian-White Relations: General Studies

"Every European 'discoverer' had Indian guides. Every European colonizer had Indian instruction and assistance. Ethnocentric semantics have hidden the chief role of Indians in the creation of American society by reserving exclusively for Europeans the honorable title of 'pioneer' and contrasting it to the lowly status of 'native,' but the European vanguard were pupils in the Indian school. Indians brought to their symbiotic partnership with Europeans the experience and knowledge of millennia of genuine pioneering. What American society owes to Indian society, as much as to any other source, is the mere fact of its existence."
—Francis Jennings, *The Invasion of America*

James **Axtell**

The European and the Indian: Essays in the Ethnohistory of Colonial North America

A blend of history and anthropology, drawing on archaeology, linguistics, literature, and art

See also **THE NEW COLONIES** under **US HISTORY TO THE CIVIL WAR**

0-19-502904-6 OXFORD PB $12.95

The Invasion Within: The Contest of Cultures in Colonial North America

Relations among root cultures in Canada—Indian, French, and English. "The best introduction now available to the problem of cultural conversion in the New World"
—William Cronon

See also **THE NEW COLONIES** under **US HISTORY TO THE CIVIL WAR**

0-19-504154-2 OXFORD PB $17.95

Robert F. **Berkhofer**, Jr.

The White Man's Indian: Images of the American Indian from Columbus to the Present

0-394-72794-0 RANDOM HOUSE PB $8.75

Stephen **Cornell**

The Return of the Native: American Indian Political Resurgence

The active response of American Indians to European power, in the context of political mobilization among subordinated groups

0-19-506575-1 OXFORD PB $16.95

Frederick **Dimmer**

Captured by the Indians: 15 Firsthand Accounts, 1750-1870

Vivid eyewitness narratives by those who survived the ordeal of captivity

0-486-24901-8 DOVER PB $8.95

Brian W. **Dippie**

The Vanishing American: White Attitudes and U.S. Indian Policy

Argues that the Native American is doomed to disappear from the face of the earth

0-7006-0507-X KANSAS PB $14.95

William T. **Hagan**

American Indians

Third edition of a concise, standard history of Indian-white relations, with a new chapter on the 1970s and 1980s

0-226-31237-2 CHICAGO PB $14.95

Helen Hunt **Jackson**

A Century of Dishonor: A Sketch of the United States Government's Dealings with Some of the Indian Tribes

First published in 1881

0-8061-2726-0 OKLAHOMA PB $14.95

Alvin M. **Josephy**, Jr.

The Patriot Chiefs: A Chronicle of American Indian Resistance

"Josephy places his Indian heroes in a broad historical setting and pictures them as fighters for freedom in the American tradition"
—*NY Times Book Review*

See also **INDIAN WARS**

0-14-023463-2 PENGUIN PB $11.95

Peter **Nabokov**, editor

Native American Testimony: An Anthology of Indian and White Relations

PREFACE BY VINE DELORIA, JR.

0-14-012986-3 PENGUIN PB $15.95

Edward H. **Spicer**

Cycles of Conquest: The Impact of Spain, Mexico and the United States on Indians of the Southwest, 1533-1960

0-8165-0021-5 ARIZONA PB $21.50

Richard **VanDerBeets**, editor

Held Captive by Indians: Selected Narratives, 1642-1886

0-87049-840-1 TENNESSEE PB $18.95

Francis P. **Prucha**

The Great Father: United States Government and the American Indians

An abridgment of Prucha's massive study. "The most important history ever published about the formulation of federal Indian policies in the United States"—*Minnesota History*

0-8032-8712-7 NEBRASKA PB $13.95

The Indians in American Society: From the Revolutionary War to the Present

The transformation from self-sufficiency into dependency

0-520-05503-9 CALIFORNIA $38.00
0-520-06344-9 CALIFORNIA PB $12.95

Documents of the US Indian Policy

A selection of the essential documents that marked significant formulations of policy in the conduct of Indian affairs by the U.S. government between 1783 and 1973

0-8032-8726-7 NEBRASKA PB $16.00

William W. **Savage**, editor

Indian Life: Transforming an American Myth

This look at the white man's perception of the Indian from 1877 to 1914 shows how the dominant whites varied their idea of the Indian to conform to political and economic utility

0-8061-2513-6 OKLAHOMA PB $14.95

Ronald **Wright**

Stolen Continents: The "New World" Through Indian Eyes

A historian and philosopher examines how five great American civilizations—Aztec, Mayan, Inca, Cherokee, Iroquois—were invaded, colonized, and suppressed by the Europeans, yet still managed to survive

0-395-65975-2 HOUGHTON MIFFLIN PB $14.95

Special Studies

"In ordinary conversation, Apaches address each other in low, softly modulated tones and at a pace they consider measured and deliberate. By comparison, they say, they are forcefully struck by the speech of Anglo-Americans, which is regularly described as being too fast, too loud, and too 'tense.'...Among themselves, Apaches associate these ...phenomena with the expression of criticism and indignant self-assertion—with the voice of a woman scolding a child, for example, or with that of a man responding to an insult. As a result, Anglo-Americans, even when speaking in a manner that they consider genial and relaxed, may easily give the impression of being vexed and irate. Most Apaches recognize this disjunction and on occasions find it amusing, as when they observe, 'Whitemen are angry even when they're friendly.'"—Keith H. Basso, *Portraits of The Whiteman*

Keith H. **Basso**

Portraits of "The Whiteman": Linguistic Play and Cultural Symbols Among the Western Apache

Investigates a complex form of joking in which Apaches stage carefully crafted imitations of Anglo-Americans

0-521-29593-9 CAMBRIDGE PB $15.95

Robert A. **Clark**, editor

The Killing of Chief Crazy Horse

Viewed from three eyewitnesses: an Indian, an Indian-white, and a white doctor

0-8032-6330-9 NEBRASKA PB $6.95

Denys **Delage**

Bitter Feasts: Amerindians and Europeans in Northeastern North America 1600-64

0-7748-0434-3 BRITISH COLUMBIA $60.00
0-7748-0451-3 BRITISH COLUMBIA PB $29.95

Gregory Evans **Dowd**

A Spirited Resistance: The North American Indian Struggle for Unity, 1745-1815

0-8018-4236-0 JOHNS HOPKINS $45.00
0-8018-4609-9 JOHNS HOPKINS PB $14.95

Charles **Eastman**

Indian Boyhood

An autobiography by a Santee Sioux who sought to bring Indians and whites together

0-486-22037-0 DOVER PB $5.95

Renee Samson **Flood**

Lost Bird of Wounded Knee: Spirit of the Lakota

Heart-rending history of the baby girl who survived the massacre of Wounded Knee and was adopted, then abused, by Brigadier General Leonard W. Colby

0-684-19512-7 SCRIBNERS $25.00

Tom **Hatley**

The Dividing Paths: Cherokees and South Carolinians Through the Revolutionary Era

Award-winning book traces the interactions between the Cherokee people and the settlers of South Carolina

0-19-509638-X OXFORD PB $19.95

Francis **Jennings**

The Ambiguous Iroquois Empire: The Covenant Chain Confederation of Indian Tribes with English Colonies

See also **THE NEW COLONIES** under **US HISTORY TO THE CIVIL WAR**

0-393-30302-0 NORTON PB $16.95

Empire of Fortune: Crowns, Colonies, and Tribes in the Seven Years War in America

0-393-02537-3 NORTON $27.50
0-393-30640-2 NORTON PB $16.95

Francis **Jennings**

The Invasion of America: Indians, Colonialism, and the Cant of Conquest

A startlingly revised and richly documented picture of Puritans and Indians in the 17th century. "Will surprise many readers with its revelations"—Dee Brown

0-393-00830-4 NORTON PB $11.95

Bruce E. **Johansen**

Forgotten Founders: How the American Indians Helped Shape Democracy

"Rarely has a book given me more information and a worse conscience. It tells what one should know of how the first Americans governed themselves and in many ways set an example for the Europeans"—John Kenneth Galbraith

0-916782-90-5 HARVARD COMMON PB $9.95

Fanny **Kelly**

My Captivity Among the Sioux Indians

"…this republication of the original 1871 edition with illustrations is one of the most distinguished examples of the last period of the captivity narrative"—Jules Zanger

0-8065-1434-5 CITADEL PB $10.95

William G. **McLoughlin**

Cherokee Renascence in the New Republic

The stresses of acculturation between 1794 and 1833, from clashes with the federal government to internal divisions

0-691-00627-X PRINCETON PB $19.95

James Willard **Schultz**

Blackfeet and Buffalo: Memories of Life Among the Indians

Unique reporting from a fur trader who became an adoptive Indian and married one

0-8061-1700-1 OKLAHOMA PB $14.95

Bernard W. **Sheehan**

Seeds of Extinction: Jeffersonian Philanthropy and the American Indian

0-393-00716-2 NORTON PB $9.95

Wiley **Sword**

President Washington's Indian War: The Struggle for the Old Northwest, 1790-1795

The little-known story of how the United States gained control in modern-day Ohio, Illinois, Indiana, Wisconsin, and Michigan

0-8061-2488-1 OKLAHOMA PB $16.95

Alan T. **Vaughan**

New England Frontier: Puritans and Indians, 1620-1675

Third edition of this standard authority on Puritan-Indian relations from the landing of the Mayflower through King Philip's War

0-8061-2718-X OKLAHOMA PB $16.95

Edmund Wilson

Edmund **Wilson** & Joseph **Mitchell**

Apologies to the Iroquois & A Study of The Mohawks in High Steel

On *Apologies to the Iroquois:* "Provocatively suggests that the great American ideal of liberty, followed by western Christian culture, forgot itself when it came to grips with the Indian and his differentness. It hasn't remembered itself yet"—*Christian Science Monitor*

0-8156-2564-2 SYRACUSE PB $15.95

Indian Wars

Gary Clayton **Anderson** & Alan R. **Woolworth**, editors

Through Dakota Eyes: Narrative Accounts of the Minnesota Indian War of 1862

Multiple eyewitness views of a devastating conflict

0-87351-216-2 MINNESOTA HISTORICAL PB $11.95

Merrill D. **Beal**

I Will Fight No More Forever: Chief Joseph and the Nez Perce War

0-295-74009-4 WASHINGTON PB $14.95

Jason **Betzinez** & Wilbur S. **Nye**

I Fought with Geronimo

The memoirs of Betzinez, Geronimo's cousin, who survived until 1959. "The Apache wars from the inside looking out"—Angie Debo, *NY Times*

ILLUSTRATED BY J. FRANKLIN WHITMAN. JR.

0-8032-6086-5 NEBRASKA PB $8.95

John G. **Bourke**

An Apache Campaign in Sierra Madre: An Account of the Expedition in Pursuit of the Hostile Chiricahua Apaches in the Spring of 1883

Crook's pursuit of Geronimo from Arizona to Mexico in 1883

FOREWORD BY JOSEPH C. PORTER

0-8032-6085-7 NEBRASKA PB $7.95

On the Border with Crook

"Capt. John G. Bourke understood the Apache people and the Apache country… as a soldier, as a scholar, and as a man with eager sympathies for nearly all things human"—J. Frank Dobie

0-8032-5741-4 NEBRASKA PB $14.00

Cyrus Townsend **Brady**

Indian Fights and Fighters

0-8032-5743-0 NEBRASKA PB $15.00

Dee **Brown**

Bury My Heart at Wounded Knee: An Indian History of the American West

0-8050-1730-5 HOLT PB $14.95

Art **Burton**

Black, Red and Deadly: Black and Indian Gunfighters of the Indian Territories, 1870-1907

The exploits of Cherokee Bill and other black and Indian outlaws and lawmen

0-89015-798-7 EAKINS $24.95

0-89015-994-7 EAKINS PB $16.95

Forest **Carter**

Watch for Me on the Mountain

A novel about Geronimo and the Indian Nation. "Can surely stand comparison with the best novels of Indian life we have"—Larry McMurtry

0-385-30082-4 DELACORTE PB $11.95

Will Levington **Comfort**

Apache

0-8032-6319-8 NEBRASKA PB $11.95

Britton **Davis**

The Truth About Geronimo

The first-hand 1929 account of the Geronimo campaign by an Indian Scout officer who knew many of the combatants personally

0-8032-5840-2 NEBRASKA PB $10.95

Angie **Debo**

Geronimo

A scholarly, prizewinning biography, readable and balanced

0-8061-1828-8 OKLAHOMA PB $18.95

Charles **Eastman**

Indian Heroes and Great Chieftains

0-8032-6720-7 NEBRASKA PB $9.95

R. David **Edmunds**

The Shawnee Prophet

"Previous historians have stressed the role of Tecumseh in the creation of an anti-American confederacy, in the years before 1812. Edmunds demonstrate that Tecumseh's brother Tenskwatawa, the Prophet, launched the movement and dominated it for several years" —*Montana*

0-8032-6711-8 NEBRASKA PB $9.95

Tecumseh and the Quest for Indian Leadership

0-673-39336-4 FORESMAN PB $16.20

Odie B. **Faulk**

The Geronimo Campaign

"The best account of this phase of Geronimo's life since *The Truth About Geronimo*"—*Choice*

0-19-508351-2 OXFORD PB $9.95

Alexander B. **Adams**

Geronimo

Well-researched biography of the great Indian warrrior and the removal of the Apaches from New Mexico lands

0-306-80394-1 DA CAPO PB $14.95

Jerome A. **Greene**

Slim Buttes, 1876: An Episode of the Great Sioux War

Military history of the campaign and the battle that ended it

0-8061-2261-7 OKLAHOMA PB $14.95

Jerome A. **Greene**, editor

Lakota and Cheyenne: Indian Views of the Great Sioux War, 1876-1877

The Indians' own story of the war forced on them by the U.S. Government

0-8061-2681-7 OKLAHOMA $24.95

Bruce **Hampton**

Children of Grace: The Nez Perce War of 1877

A powerful account of one of the most shameful chapters in frontier history

0-380-72487-1 AVON PB $12.50

Laurence **Hauptman**

Between Two Fires: American Indians in the Civil War

The important role of some 20,000 American Indians who served in the Civil War

0-02-914180-X FREE PRESS $25.00

0-684-82668-2 FREE PRESS PB $13.00

Stan **Hoig**

The Sand Creek Massacre

0-8061-1147-X OKLAHOMA PB $13.95

Richard E. **Jensen**, editor

Eyewitness at Wounded Knee

This climactic episode of the Indian Wars was documented by 143 photographs taken before and immediately after the massacre. Published for the first time in 1991

0-8032-1409-X NEBRASKA $45.00

Members of the Potomac Corral of the Westerners

Great Western Indian Fights

A vivid recreation of over 20 battles between 1832 and 1891 that were considered crucial in the opening of the American West to white settlement

0-8032-5186-6 NEBRASKA PB $10.95

Bill **Neeley**

The Last Comanche: The Life and Times of Quanah Parker

A major study of the great warrior

0-471-11722-6 WILEY $24.95

Alvin M. **Josephy**, Jr.

The Patriot Chiefs: A Chronicle of American Indian Resistance

"Josephy places his Indian heroes in a broad historical setting and pictures them as fighters for freedom in the American tradition"
—*NY Times Book Review*

See also **INDIAN-WHITE RELATIONS**

0-14-023463-2 PENGUIN PB $11.95

S.L.A **Marshall**

Crimsoned Prairie: The Indian Wars

The first study of the military tactics employed by the Plains Indians and the U.S. Army in their long war for the American frontier, by a renowned military historian

0-306-80226-0 DA CAPO PB $12.95

John G. **Neihardt**

The Twilight of the Sioux

The epic poem dealing with the tragic defeat of the Plains Indians

0-8032-5734-1 NEBRASKA PB $10.95

Stanely **Noyes**

Los Comanches: The Horse People, 1751-1845

Sweeping history of the tribe which dominated the southern plains for a hundred years

0-8263-1548-8 NEW MEXICO PB $19.95

David **Robert**

Once They Moved Like the Wind

Exciting, epic tale of Cochise, Geronimo, and the Apache Wars

0-671-88556-1 TOUCHSTONE PB $14.00

Duane **Schultz**

Month of Freezing Rain: The Sand Creek Massacre, November 1864

0-312-06417-9 ST. MARTIN'S PB $12.95

John **Sugden**

Tecumseh's Last Stand

How tribes of the Old Northwest joined with the British to resist American expansion during the War of 1812

0-8061-2242-0 OKLAHOMA PB $16.95

Time-Life editors

The War for the Plains

Part of the colorful Time-Life *American Indian* series

0-8094-9445-0 TIME BOOKS $19.95

Clifford E. **Trafzer**

The Kit Carson Campaign: The Last Great Navajo War

A detailed account of the notorious 1860s campaign, told from the Navajo point of view using oral histories and archival material

0-8061-2265-X OKLAHOMA PB $14.95

Robert M. **Utley** & Wilcomb E. **Washburn**

Indian Wars

A well-told, one-volume history

See also **WARS AND CONFLICTS** under **AMERICAN REGIONAL HISTORY: THE WEST AND THE SOUTH**

0-8281-0202-3 AMERICAN HERITAGE PB $13.95

Robert M. **Utley**

Frontier Regulars: The United States Army and the Indians, 1866-1891

The final, massive drive by the Army to subdue and control the Indians

See also **WARS AND CONFLICTS** under **AMERICAN REGIONAL HISTORY: THE WEST AND THE SOUTH**

0-8032-9551-0 NEBRASKA PB $17.95

Frontiersmen in Blue: The United States Army and the Indian, 1848-1865

0-8032-9550-2 NEBRASKA PB $16.95

The Indian Frontier of the American West, 1846-1890

The irreconcilable conflict between Indians and whites in the American West, told with admirable balance and skill

0-8263-0716-7 NEW MEXICO PB $15.95

Captain Eugene F. **Ware**

The Indian War of 1864

Vivid, first-hand account by the soldier charged with keeping overland routes free from Indian attack, originally published in 1911

0-8032-9749-1 NEBRASKA PB $14.95

Paul I. **Wellman**

Death on the Prairie: The Thirty Years' Struggle for the Western Plains

Beginning with the Minnesota Sioux uprising in 1862

0-8032-9721-1 NEBRASKA PB $12.95

General Custer

Stephen E. **Ambrose**

Crazy Horse and Custer

Parallel lives converging at the Little Bighorn

0-385-47966-2 ANCHOR PB $15.95

Evan S. **Connell**

Son of the Morning Star: Custer and the Little Bighorn

"An unconventional, highly evocative retelling of the celebrated military disaster ...One of the Ten Best of 1984"—*Time*

0-06-097161-4 HARPERCOLLINS PB $10.95

W.A. **Graham**

The Reno Court of Inquiry: Abstract of the Official Record of Proceedings

An abstract of the original 1300-page court proceedings from the inquiry investigating the battle

0-8117-1416-0 STACKPOLE $19.95

The Story of the Little Big Horn

The first book-length study of the Little Bighorn, published in 1926 by an Army colonel

0-8117-0346-0 STACKPOLE $19.95

0-8032-7026-7 NEBRASKA PB $9.95

John S. **Gray**

Centennial Campaign: The Sioux War of 1876

0-8061-2152-1 OKLAHOMA PB $18.95

Elizabeth **Custer**

Following the Guidon: Into the Indian Wars with General Custer and the Seventh Cavalry

Originally published in 1890, a personal account by Custer's wife, who spent the rest of her life (she lived 57 years after his death) trying to defend her husband's reputation

0-8032-6362-7 NEBRASKA PB $12.95

Tenting on the Plains: Or, General Custer in Kansas and Texas

The second in her trilogy of her life with the general focuses on the period immediately following the Civil War

0-8061-2668-XOKLAHOMA PB $12.95

George A. **Custer**

My Life on the Plains: Or, Personal Experiences with Indians

Covers the years 1867-69, including the Battle of the Washita

0-8061-1357-XOKLAHOMA PB $11.95

Marguerite **Merington**, editor

The Custer Story: The Life and Intimate Letters of General George A. Custer and His Wife Elizabeth

The letters provide a rare and unusual contribution to the basic data of America's social and military history—"a wife's eye view of war and soldiering"
—*Saturday Review of Literature*

0-8032-8138-2 NEBRASKA PB $11.95

David Humphreys **Miller**

Custer's Fall: The Indian Side of the Story

Starting in the 1930s, Miller collected first-hand accounts from 71 Indian survivors of the Battle of the Little Bighorn

0-452-01095-0 PENGUIN PB $11.95

Jay **Monaghan**

Custer: The Life of General George Armstrong Custer

0-8032-5732-5 NEBRASKA PB $15.95

E. Lisle **Reedstrom**

Custer's Seventh Cavalry: From Fort Riley to the Little Big Horn

Scores of period photographs, archival records, and documents about the famous 7th Cavalry

0-8069-8762-6 STERLING PB $16.95

Mary **Sandoz**

Crazy Horse: The Strange Man of the Oglalas

The classic 1942 biography, reissued. "Here is a glorious hero tale told with beauty and power…the story of a great American"
—*NY Times*

0-8032-9211-2 NEBRASKA PB $12.00

Edgar I. **Stewart**

Custer's Luck

"The most comprehensive single picture of all the causative forces that culminated on that brassy-hot and dusty day along the Little Big Horn"—*San Francisco Chronicle*

0-8061-1632-3 OKLAHOMA PB $18.95

William O. **Taylor**

With Custer on the Little Bighorn

This extraordinary book is no less than an eyewitness account of Little Bighorn by a soldier who recorded it in minute-to-minute detail. Taylor, who served in the Seventh US Cavalry from 1872 to 1877, spent 30 years writing this memoir, which is presented here with full annotations, explanatory sidebars, and fully illustrated with duotone photographs

EDITED BY GREG MARTIN

0-670-86803-5 VIKING $27.95

Robert M. **Utley**

Cavalier in Buckskin: George Armstrong Custer and the Western Military Frontier

0-8061-2292-7 OKLAHOMA PB $13.95

The Lance and the Shield: The Life and Times of Sitting Bull

A compelling portrait, chosen as a *New York Times* Notable Book of the Year

0-345-38938-7 BALLANTINE PB $14.00

Frederic F. **Van de Water**

Glory-Hunter: A Life of General Custer

"A complex and unsparing analysis"—William Rose Benet, *Saturday Review of Literature*

0-87266-034-6 ARGOSY ANTIQUARIAN $20.00

J.W. **Vaughan**

With Crook at the Rosebud

A major battle eight days before Little Bighorn when General Crook thought he had beaten Crazy Horse—when in fact it was a stalemate that put his troops out of commission and unable to help Custer

0-8117-1911-1 STACKPOLE $19.95

Stanley **Vestal**

Sitting Bull: Champion of the Sioux

An apologia for a true apostle of freedom

0-8061-2219-6 OKLAHOMA PB $15.95

Warpath: The True Story of the Fighting Sioux, Told in a Biography of Chief White Bull

In 1932, Chief White Bull, nephew of Sitting Bull, told his story to Vestal, who corroborated it

0-8032-9601-0 NEBRASKA PB $11.00

James **Welch** & Paul **Stekler**

Killing Custer: The Battle of the Little Big Horn and the Fate of the Plains Indians

Eloquent rethinking of the Little Bighorn for a multicultural society

0-393-03657-X NORTON $25.00
0-14-025176-6 PENGUIN PB $13.95

Frederick **Whittaker**

A Complete Life of General George A. Custer

"No Custer library is complete without Whittaker's work, which is essential to understanding the Custer legend"
—Robert M. Utley

Volume I Through the Civil War

0-8032-9742-4 NEBRASKA PB $12.95

Volume II From Appomattox to the Little Bighorn

0-8032-9743-2 NEBRASKA PB $12.95

Modern Indian Life: Contemporary Issues

Paula Gunn **Allen**

The Sacred Hoop: Recovering the Feminine in American Indian Traditions

0-8070-4601-9 BEACON PB $14.00

Russel L. **Barsh** & James Y. **Henderson**

The Road: Indian Tribes and Political Liberty

0-520-04636-6 CALIFORNIA PB $13.00

Gretchen M. **Bataille** & Kathleen Mullen **Sands**

American Indian Women: Telling Their Lives

"A unique and intimate record. All 21 autobiographies signal Native American women's diversity and unity"—*Library Journal*

0-8032-6082-2 NEBRASKA PB $9.95

Menno **Boldt**

The Quest for Justice: Aboriginal Peoples and Aboriginal Rights

0-8020-6589-9 TORONTO PB $22.95

Ruth McDonald **Boyer** & Narcissus Duffy **Gayton**

Apache Mothers and Daughters

See also **MOTHERHOOD** under **THE FEMALE EXPERIENCE** under **WOMEN'S STUDIES** in **SOCIAL STUDIES**

0-8061-2447-4 OKLAHOMA $24.95

Lloyd **Burton**

American Indian Water Rights and the Limits of Law

"As the governmental institution ostensibly least susceptible to shifting political currents and

most sensitive to the honoring of governmental obligations, the federal judiciary has emerged over the course of this century as the primary definer and defender of the Indian water right"
0-7006-0601-7 KANSAS PB....$12.95

Ward **Churchill**
Indians Я Us?
The outspoken activist for Indian rights argues against the commercialization in Native American classrooms and discusses the challenges of modern education
1-56751-020-5 COMMON COURAGE PB....$14.95

Vine **Deloria**, Jr.
Behind the Trail of Broken Treaties: An Indian Declaration of Independence
The events and issues surrounding the 1973 occupation of Wounded Knee
0-292-70754-1 TEXAS PB....$14.95

The Nations Within: The Past and Future of American Indian Sovereignty
0-394-72566-2 PANTHEON PB....$13.32

Vine **Deloria**, Jr., editor
American Indian Policy in the Twentieth Century
The present realities and future possibilities of American Indian policy, from a historical and legal point of view
0-8061-1897-0 OKLAHOMA....$24.95

Vine **Deloria**, Jr. & Clifford M. **Lytle**
American Indians, American Justice
0-292-73834-X TEXAS PB....$12.95

Mike **Fedullo**
Light of the Feather
In the tradition of *Strange Inequalities*, a teacher's journey into Native American classrooms and the challenges of modern education
0-385-47136-X ANCHOR PB....$14.00

Rayna **Green**
Women in American Indian Society
See also **ANTHROPOLOGY AND CROSS-CULTURE STUDIES** under **WOMEN'S STUDIES** in **SOCIAL STUDIES**
0-7910-0401-5 CHELSEA HOUSE PB....$8.95

Peter **Iverson**, editor
The Plains Indians of the Twentieth Century
A pioneering anthology that emphasizes the maintenance of tribal identity despite many changes and adaptations
0-8061-1959-4 OKLAHOMA PB....$14.95

Alvin M. **Josephy**, Jr.
Now that the Buffalo's Gone: A Study of Today's American Indian
The histories of seven Indian tribes serves to illustrate Indian-white relations, including racial stereotyping, self-determination, and control of tribal affairs and resources
0-8061-1915-2 OKLAHOMA PB....$17.95

Red Power: The American Indians' Fight for Freedom
A documentary history of the American Indian movement of the 1960s, exploring such areas as employment, education, health, and land rights
0-8032-7563-3 NEBRASKA PB....$9.95

Arnold **Krupat**
The Turn to the Native: Studies in Criticism and Culture
0-8032-2735-3 NEBRASKA....$30.00

L.G. **Moses** & Raymond **Wilson**, editors
Indian Lives: Essays on Nineteenth and Twentieth Century Native American Leaders
0-8263-0815-5 NEW MEXICO PB....$14.95

Patricia **Riley**, editor
Growing Up Native American: An Anthology
Mandatory boarding school, suburban alienation, and the recollection of a first buffalo hunt are among the surprising subjects of these sketches, novel excerpts, and stories. Contributors include Mary Tall Mountain, Black Elk, and Louise Erdrich
0-380-72417-0 AVON PB....$11.00

Paul Chaat **Smith** & Robert Allen **Warrior**
Like a Hurricane: The Indian Movement from Alcatraz to Wounded Knee
1-56584-316-9 NEW PRESS....$25.00

Barbara **Tedlock**
The Beautiful and the Dangerous: Encounters with the Zuni Indians
In this provocative work, an anthropologist recounts her experience among the Zunis in New Mexico, whom she often visited for over 20 years
0-14-017812-0 PENGUIN PB....$12.95

Charles F. **Wilkinson**
American Indians, Time and the Law
Highly informed analysis of the Supreme Court's work in Indian law since 1959
0-300-04136-5 YALE PB....$14.00

John R. **Wunder**
"Retained by the People": A History of American Indians and the Bill of Rights
The first in-depth look at the subject, part of the *Bicentennial Essays on the Bill of Rights*
0-19-505563-2 OXFORD PB....$16.95

Aspects of Traditional Culture

H. David **Brumble III**
American Indian Autobiography
Interdisciplinary study that discusses narratives in historical terms
0-520-07182-4 CALIFORNIA PB....$15.00

Elsie Claw **Parsons**, editor
American Indian Life
A classic collection of 27 stories about American Indians representing two dozen tribes from the Eskimos to the Mayans. Most of the authors are ethnologists or anthropologists
0-8032-8728-3 NEBRASKA PB....$12.95

Douglas **Preston**
Talking to the Ground: One Family's Journey on Horseback Across the Sacred Land of the Navajo
Popular and evocative
0-684-80391-7 SIMON & SCHUSTER....$24.00
0-8263-1740-5 NEW MEXICO PB....$18.95

Memoirs and Reminiscences

Mary **Brave Bird** & Richard **Erdoes**
Ohitika Woman
0-06-097583-0 HARPERPERENNIAL PB....$13.00

Joseph Iron Eye **Dudley**
Choteau Creek: A Sioux Reminiscence
Ordained minister and cultural lecturer Dudley contends that little has been written about the everyday comings and goings of reservation life. Born on a Sioux reservation in South Dakota, his memories of being raised by his grandparents makes for a compelling look at the forces that shape Native Americans
0-446-39519-6 WARNER PB....$12.99

Gabriel **Horn**
Native Heart: An American Indian Odyssey
1-88003-207-4 NEW WORLD PB....$13.95

Ecology and Economy

William **Cronon**
Changes in the Land: Indians, Colonists, and the Ecology of New England
"Combines ecological and cultural analysis into a cogent, sophisticated, and balanced study of Indian-White contact"
—Richard White, Michigan State University
See also **THE NEW COLONIES** under **US HISTORY TO THE CIVIL WAR**
0-8090-0158-6 FS&G PB....$9.95

Peter C. **Mancall**

Deadly Medicine: Indians and Alcohol in Early America

A well-researched study of how alcohol abuse was encouraged by whites both as an instrument of free market capitalism and colonial Indian policy

0-8014-2762-2 CORNELL $29.95

Calvin **Martin**

Keepers of the Game: Indian-Animal Relationship and the Fur Trade

A controversial study suggesting that Indian attitudes toward animals were disrupted by the fur trade with the whites

INTRODUCTION BY NANCY LURIE

0-520-03519-4 CALIFORNIA $38.00

0-520-04637-4 CALIFORNIA PB $15.95

Virgil J. **Vogel**

American Indian Medicine

Medicinal practices and theories of disease, with a listing of Indian contributions to pharmacology

0-8061-2293-5 OKLAHOMA PB $24.95

Religion and Mythology

Paula Gunn **Allen**

Grandmothers of the Light: A Medicine Woman's Sourcebook

A retelling of 21 traditional stories—from Cherokee and Navajo to Aztec and Maya—steeped in the female supernatural

See also **WOMEN AND RELIGION** under **WORLD RELIGION** in **RELIGION, SPIRITUALITY, AND PHILOSOPHY**

0-8070-8103-5 BEACON PB $14.00

Ooma-oo, long ago. The Spider was in the place where only she was. There was no light or dark, there was no warm wind, no rain or thunder. There was no cold, or ice or snow. There was only the Spider. She was a great wise woman, whose powers are beyond imagining. No medicine person, no conjurer or shaman, no witch or sorcerer, no scientist or inventor can imagine how great her power is. Her power is complete and total. It is pure, and cleaner than the void. It is the power of thought, we say, but not the kind of thought people do all the time. It's like the power of dream, but more pure. Like the spirit of vision, but more clear. It has no shape or movement, because it just is. It is the power that creates all that is, and it is the power of all that is.

GRANDMOTHERS OF THE LIGHT: A MEDICINE WOMAN'S SOURCEBOOK

0-8070-8102-7 BEACON PB $19.95

Donald **Bahr**, editor

The Short Swift Time of Gods on Earth

The Hokokam Chronicles of the Pima Indians told in narrative and song. The most complete version of the origin of the world according to the Pima of Arizona

0-520-08468-3 CALIFORNIA PB $16.95

Vine **Deloria**, Jr.

God Is Red

1-55591-904-9 NORTH AMERICAN PRESS $22.95

Garrick A. **Bailey**

The Osage and the Invisible World: From the Works of Francis La Flesche

0-8061-2743-0 OKLAHOMA $29.95

John **Bierhorst**

The Mythology of North America

A systematic survey of heroes, goddesses, and spirits, from the Arctic regions to the Southwest. Illustrated

0-688-06666-6 MORROW PB $12.50

Henry W. **Bowden**

American Indians and Christian Missions: Studies in Cultural Conflict

0-226-06812-9 CHICAGO PB $17.95

Doug **Boyd**

Rolling Thunder

American Indian culture and society viewed through a shaman's chronicles

0-385-28859-X DELTA PB $12.95

Dee **Brown**

Dee Brown's Folktales of the Native American

Thirty-six stories gathered from numerous tribes and retold by Dee Brown

0-8050-2607-X HOLT PB $9.95

Joseph E. **Brown**, editor

The Sacred Pipe: Black Elk's Account of the Seven Rites of the Oglala Sioux

0-8061-0272-1 OKLAHOMA $26.95

0-8061-2124-6 OKLAHOMA PB $10.95

Raymond J. **DeMallie**, editor

The Sixth Grandfather: Black Elk's Teachings Given to John Neihardt

0-8032-6564-6 NEBRASKA PB $12.95

George A. **Dorsey**

The Mythology of the Wichita

0-8061-2778-3 OKLAHOMA PB $13.95

Richard **Erdoes** & Alfonso **Ortiz**

American Indian Myths and Legends

"...probably the most comprehensive and diverse collection of American Indian legends ever compiled"—*Dee Brown*

See also **NATIVE AMERICAN** under **THE WESTERN HEMISPHERE** under **MYTHOLOGY AND FOLKLORE** in **RELIGION, SPIRITUALITY, AND PHILOSOPHY**

0-394-74018-1 PANTHEON PB $18.00

Sam D. **Gill**

Mother Earth

Tracing the evolution of female earth imagery in North America from the 16th century to the present, this study offers a radical rethinking of the Mother Earth concept

0-226-29371-8 CHICAGO PB $11.95

Jamake **Highwater**

The Primal Mind: Visions and Reality in Indian America

Contrasts the ideas and intellectual aims of Western culture with the life-styles and world views of North American tribal people

0-452-00966-9 NEW AMERICAN LIBRARY PB $11.95

Ake **Hultkrantz**

Native Religions of North America

An impressive synthesis from one of the leading authorities on American Indian religions

0-06-064061-8 HARPERCOLLINS PB $12.00

Weston **La Barre**

The Peyote Cult

0-8061-2214-5 OKLAHOMA PB $17.95

Frank B. **Linderman**

Pretty-Shield: Medicine Woman of the Crows

0-8032-5791-0 NEBRASKA PB $9.95

James **Mooney**

The Ghost-Dance Religion and the Sioux Outbreak of 1890

A classic anthropological study showing how the Ghost Dance, which raised white fears of an Indian outbreak that eventually led to Wounded Knee, was a legitimate religious movement

EDITED BY ANTHONY F. WALLACE

0-8032-3155-5 NEBRASKA $65.00

0-8032-8177-3 NEBRASKA PB $25.00

Barbara G. **Myerhoff**

Peyote Hunt: The Sacred Journey of the Huichol Indians

Description of the pilgrimage to collect peyote, with an overview of Huichol religion

0-8014-9137-1 CORNELL PB $11.95

John G. **Neihardt**

Black Elk Speaks: Being the Life Story of a Holy Man of the Oglala Sioux

See also **AUTOBIOGRAPHICAL ACCOUNTS** under **NATIVE AMERICAN LITERATURES** in **LITERATURE OF THE AMERICAS**

INTRODUCTION BY VINE DELORIA, JR.

0-8032-3301-9 NEBRASKA $25.00

0-8032-8359-8 NEBRASKA PB $9.95

William K. **Powers**

Oglala Religion

The durability of Oglala beliefs in the face of overwhelming obstacles

0-8032-8706-2 NEBRASKA PB $11.00

Lewis **Spence**

The Myths of the North American Indians

The major myths, with illustrations and maps, collected by the distinguished British anthropologist and folklorist and originally published in 1914

0-486-25967-6 DOVER PB $8.95

Michael F. **Steltenkamp**

Black Elk: Holy Man of the Oglala

0-8061-2541-1 OKLAHOMA $19.95

Barbara **Tedlock** & Dennis **Tedlock**, editors
Teachings from the American Earth: Indian Religion and Philosophy
0-87140-146-0 LIVERIGHT PB $10.95

Hamilton A. **Tyler**
Pueblo Gods and Myths
Composite picture of the Pueblo Indian gods and lesser supernaturals, using the Indians' own words to retell the myths
0-8061-1112-7 OKLAHOMA PB $14.95

Ruth M. **Undergill**
Red Man's Religion
Classic account of the religions of American Indians north of the Rio Grande
0-226-84167-7 CHICAGO PB $16.95

Frank **Walers**
Book of the Hopi
Thirty elders of the ancient Hopi tribe of northern Arizona reveal the Hopi worldview in written form for the first time
0-14-004527-9 VIKING PB $12.95

Ray A. **Williamson**
Living the Sky: The Cosmos of the American Indian
Astronomy and Native American beliefs
0-8061-2034-7 OKLAHOMA PB $19.95

Music, Dance, and Games

Stewart **Culin**
Games of the North American Indians
0-486-23125-9 DOVER PB $16.95

James **Mooney**
Native American Dance: Ceremonies and Social Traditions
A collection of essays on Indian dance, with photos. "Fascinating and beautifully put together"—Peter Matthiessen
1-56373-021-9 STARWOOD PB $29.95

Peter Matthiessen

Alice C. **Fletcher** & James R. **Murie**
The Hako: Song, Pipe, and Unity in a Pawnee Calumet Ceremony
See also **TRADITIONAL LITERATURE: POETRY, STORIES, ORATORY** under **NATIVE AMERICAN LITERATURES** in **LITERATURE OF THE AMERICAS**
0-8032-6889-0 NEBRASKA PB $16.95

Reginald **Laubin** & Gladys **Laubin**
Indian Dances of North America: Their Importance to Indian Life
Includes descriptions, costumes, and musical accompaniment; illustrated with paintings, drawings, and photographs
FOREWORD BY LOUIS R BRUCE
0-8061-2172-6 OKLAHOMA PB $22.95

Language

"It has not been possible so far to determine how many different languages and dialects have been spoken in the Americas. Many tongues have become extinct. But linguistic scholar Morris Swadesh believes that when the whites arrived in the New World, Indians were speaking some 2,200 different languages, many of them possessing regional variations. Other students have estimated that there were at least 200 mutually unintelligible languages among the native peoples north of Mexico, at least another 350 in Mexico and Central America, and considerably more than 1,000 in the Caribbean and South America."—Alvin M. Josephy, Jr., *The Indian Heritage of America*

W.P. **Clark**
The Indian Sign Language
Originally written in 1884 for the U.S. Army and based on first-hand observation of Plains Indian life. Corrects many stereotypes
0-8032-6309-0 NEBRASKA PB $12.95

Charles L. **Cutler**
O Brave New Words!: Native American Loanwords in Current English
"It should be enjoyed by enthusiasts of American history, of American Indian studies, and of word origins"—William O. Bright
0-8061-2655-8 OKLAHOMA $24.95

Gerard **Hausman**
Turtle Island Alphabet
A lexicon of Native American symbols and culture
FOREWARD BY N. SCOTT MOMADAY
0-312-07103-5 ST. MARTIN'S $19.95

John **Rydjord**
Indian Place Names: Their Origin, Evolution, and Meanings, Collected in Kansas from the Siouan, Algonquian, Shoshonean, Caddoan, Iroquoian, and Other Tongues
0-8061-0801-0 OKLAHOMA $32.95
0-8061-1763-X OKLAHOMA PB $18.95

Travel Guides

Arnold **Marquis**
A Guide to America's Indians: Ceremonials, Reservations, and Museums
Basic information for the traveler
0-8061-1148-8 OKLAHOMA PB $19.95

Ralph **Shanks** & Lisa W. **Shanks**
North American Indian Travel Guide
Now in its fifth edition
0-930268-12-1 COSTANO PB $17.95

Native American Cultures: Central and South America

Stuart J. **Fiedel**
Prehistory of the Americas
This textbook takes an evolutionary approach to the prehistories of North, Central, and South America, from 10,000 BC to 1530 AD
0-521-42544-1 CAMBRIDGE PB $22.95

Mexico and Central America: General Works

Anthony F. **Aveni**
Skywatchers of Ancient Mexico
Archaeoastronomy of Mesoamerica; illustrated
See also **HISTORY OF ASTRONOMY** under **ASTRONOMY** in **SCIENCE**
0-292-77578-4 TEXAS PB $24.95

Beatriz Pastor **Bodmer**
The Armature of Conquest: Spanish Accounts of the Discovery of America, 1492-1589
0-8047-1977-2 STANFORD $49.50
0-8047-2470-9 STANFORD PB $16.95

David **Carrasco**
Religions of Mesoamerica
0-06-061325-4 HARPERCOLLINS PB $12.00

Flora **Clancy** & Jeremy A. **Sabloff**, editors
Pyramids
0-89599-039-3 SMITHSONIAN $23.45

Michael D. **Coe**
Mexico
A brief introduction to the archaic cultures, the Olmecs, the classic civilizations of Teotihuacan and Monte Alban, and the postclassic Toltecs and Aztecs
0-500-27328-6 THAMES & HUDSON PB $14.95

Nigel **Davies**

The Ancient Kingdoms of Mexico

Spans four civilizations in ancient Mexico—Olmec, Toltec, Aztec, Teotihuacan—from 1500 BC to 1500 AD

See also **PRE-COLUMBIAN ERA** under **LATIN AMERICA AND THE CARIBBEAN**

0-14-013587-1 VIKING PB $12.95

Patricia **de Fuentes**, editor & translator

The Conquistadors: A First Person Account of the Conquest of Mexico

Distorted and Eurocentric but offers an invaluable eyewitness view of the Spanish conquest

0-8061-2562-4 OKLAHOMA PB $17.95

Bartoleme **de Las Casas**

The Devastation of the Indies: A Brief Account

In 1552, after 40 years of witnessing and opposing countless acts of brutality in the new Spanish colonies, this Spanish priest—an acquaintance of Cortes and Pisarro and a shipmate of Velasquez—published this eyewitness account of the first modern genocide and caused a storm of controversy that persists to this day. Casas argued that the early evangelizing vision of Christopher Columbus, whose discourses he preserved and edited, was corrupted by later conquistadores into a genocidal colonization

TRANSLATED BY HERMA BRIFFAULT

0-8018-4430-4 JOHNS HOPKINS PB $11.95

Roberta H. **Markman** & Peter T. **Markman**

Masks of the Spirit: Image and Metaphor in Mesoamerica

0-520-06418-6 CALIFORNIA $69.00

J.M.G. **Le Clezio**

The Mexican Dream

0-226-11002-8 CHICAGO $22.50

William **Madsen** & Claudia **Madsen**

A Guide to Mexican Witchcraft

Compact description for the general reader, with emphasis on modern Aztecs, or Nahuas, of central Mexico

0-912434-10-4 MEXICS PB $5.00

Joyce **Marcus**

Mesoamerican Writing Systems: Propaganda, Myth and History in Four Ancient Civilizations

Superb archaeological study of the role of hieroglyphic writing in pre-Hispanic Aztec, Mixtec, Zapotec, and Maya states

See also **LANGUAGE AND WRITING** under **ARCHAEOLOGY** in **WORLD HISTORY AND CURRENT AFFAIRS**

0-691-09474-8 PRINCETON $60.00

Hugh **Thomas**

The Cities of Ancient Mexico: Reconstructing a Lost World

Instead of focusing on individual societies, this leading scholar emphasizes the unity of Mexican civilization

0-500-27588-2 THAMES & HUDSON PB $14.95

John Lloyd **Stephens**

Incidents of Travel in Yucatan

Originally published in 1843, Stephens reveals Yucatan villages of 150 years ago, when cacao beans were used for money

See also **MEXICO** under **THE CARIBBEAN AND CENTRAL AMERICA** under **TRAVEL LITERATURE** in **FOOD, TRAVEL, AND LEISURE**

NEW EDITION BY KARL ACKERMAN

1-56098-652-2 SMITHSONIAN $36.50
1-56098-651-4 SMITHSONIAN PB $13.95

Conquest: Montezuma, Cortes, and the Fall of Old Mexico

See also **FROM THE CONQUEST TO THE 20TH CENTURY** under **MEXICO** under **LATIN AMERICA AND THE CARIBBEAN**

0-671-51104-1 TOUCHSTONE PB $16.00

The Olmec, Toltec, and Mixtec

Michael **Coe**, editor

The Olmec World: Ritual and Rulership

Essays by Michael D. Coe, Richard A. Diehl, and others

0-8109-6311-6 PRINCETON $75.00

Michael D. **Coe** & Richard A. **Diehl**

In the Land of the Olmec

Results of a large-scale expedition to explore the age and nature of the Olmec, in volumes respectively titled *The Archaeology of San Lorenzo Tenochtitlan* and *The People of the River*; illustrated

0-292-77549-0 TEXAS $100.00

Nigel **Davies**

The Toltec Heritage: From the Fall of Tula to the Rise of Tenochtitlan

0-8061-1505-X OKLAHOMA $37.95

Ronald **Spores**

The Mixtecs in Ancient and Colonial Times

0-8061-1884-9 OKLAHOMA $34.95

The Aztecs

Frances F. **Berdan**

The Aztecs

Part of the Smithsonian's fine *Indians of North America* series for young adults

1-55546-692-3 CHELSEA HOUSE $19.95

John **Bierhorst**

The Hungry Woman: Myths and Legends of the Aztecs

A wide-ranging selection of Aztec lore in new English versions

0-688-12301-5 QUILL PB $9.00

Warwick **Bray**

Everyday Life of the Aztecs

Using archaeological evidence and early documentary sources, tries to reconstruct life in Mexico on the eve of Cortes's conquest in 1519

0-87226-245-6 BEDRICK PB $7.95

Johanna **Broda**

The Great Temple of Tenochtitlan: Center and Periphery in the Aztec World

The nature and significance of the Templo Mayor, the great double pyramid excavated in Mexico City from 1978 to 1982. Includes black-and-white photographs

0-520-05602-7 CALIFORNIA $48.00
0-520-06597-2 CALIFORNIA PB $21.00

David **Carrasco**

Quetzalcoatl and the Irony of Empire: Myths and Prophecies in the Aztec Tradition

Mesoamerican cultural history through an exploration of the symbolism of this complex diety figure

0-226-09490-1 CHICAGO PB $16.95

Alfonso **Caso**

The Aztecs: People of the Sun

A popular introduction to Aztec religion, illustrated with full-color paintings by Miguel Covarrubias

0-8061-0414-7 OKLAHOMA PB $17.95

Bernard Ortiz **de Montellano**

Aztec Medicine, Health and Nutrition

A thorough work which argues that, contrary to popular belief, the Aztecs were a thriving, well-nourished, and healthy people at the time of the conquest

0-8135-1563-7 RUTGERS PB $16.00

Bernal **Diaz Del Castillo**

The Conquest of New Spain

Fifty years after Cortes defeated the Aztecs, Díaz, who served under Cortes, wrote this account of Montezuma's death, the massacre of the natives, and the eventual capture of the capital of Mexico

See also **THE CONQUEST** under **LATIN AMERICA AND THE CARIBBEAN**

TRANSLATED BY J.M. COHEN

0-14-044123-9 PENGUIN PB $10.95

Charles **Gibson**

The Aztecs Under Spanish Rule: A History of the Indians of the Valley of Mexico, 1519-1810

Strong on economic issues and political life. Detailed and scholarly, one of the great works of Latin American history

0-8047-0912-2 STANFORD PB $24.95

Fernando **Horcasitas**

The Aztecs Then and Now

Concise introduction to the Aztecs of ancient and modern times; illustrated

0-912434-22-8 MEXICS PB $9.00

Jacques **Soustelle**

Daily Life of the Aztecs on the Eve of the Spanish Conquest

Customs, manners, life cycle, and daily round

0-8047-0721-9 STANFORD PB $13.95

Benjamin **Keen**

The Aztec Image in Western Thought

Detailed study of Aztec influences in Western art, literature, and philosophy from the Renaissance to the present; illustrated

0-8135-0698-0 RUTGERS $65.00
0-8135-1572-6 RUTGERS PB $22.95

Miguel **Leon-Portilla**

The Broken Spears: The Aztec Account of the Conquest of Mexico

Compiled from Sahagun's Florentine Codex and other 16th-century sources

0-8070-5501-8 BEACON PB $14.00

Hernando **Ruiz de Alarcon**

Treatise on the Heathen Superstitions that Today Live Among the Indians Native to This New Spain, 1629

A more scholarly edition of Alarcon's treatise on Aztec sorcery

TRANSLATED BY J. RICHARD ANDREWS & ROSS HASSIG

0-8061-2031-2 OKLAHOMA PB $21.95

Bernardino **de Sahagun**

The Florentine Codex: General History of the Things of New Spain

The Florentine Codex is a primary source for Aztec studies. This complete English-Nahuatl edition is available in 12 books plus an introductory volume. The illustrations by native artists are reproduced in black and white. Of particular interest are volumes 3 and 12

0-87480-082-X UTAH $40.00

The Maya

Claude **Baudez** & Sydney **Picasso**

Lost Cities of the Maya

0-8109-2841-8 ABRAMS PB $12.95

Gary **Bevington**

The Maya

A serious guide to the language and culture of the Yucatan, including how to communicate with the Maya in their native language

0-292-70812-2 TEXAS PB $14.95

Inga **Clendinnen**

Ambivalent Conquests: Maya and Spaniard in Yucatan, 1517-1570

0-521-33397-0 CAMBRIDGE $59.95
0-521-37981-4 CAMBRIDGE PB $15.95

Michael D. **Coe**

Breaking the Maya Code

A lively, informative account of how Maya hieroglyphic writing was finally deciphered, by a distinguished Mayanist

See also **SYMBOLS AND SEMIOTICS** under **SPECIALIZED STUDIES** under **ANTHROPOLOGY** in **SOCIAL STUDIES**

0-500-27721-4 THAMES & HUDSON PB $14.95

The Maya

A general introduction, with emphasis on the ancient Maya

See also **MEXICO AND CENTRAL AMERICA** under **NATIVE AMERICAN ARTS** in **ART**

0-500-57745-5 THAMES & HUDSON PB $14.95

T. Patrick **Culbert**

Maya Civilization

0-89599-036-9 SMITHSONIAN $23.45

Friar Diego **De Landa** & William **Gates**, translator

Yucatan: Before and After the Conquest

Classic 16th-century account of Mayan civilization, with 120 illustrations, written by Landa to defend himself against charges of despotic mismanagement. "99 percent of what we know today of the Mayas we know as a result either of what Landa has told us in the pages that follow or have learned in the use and study of what he told"—William Gates

See also **THE CONQUEST** under **LATIN AMERICA AND THE CARIBBEAN**

0-486-23622-6 DOVER PB $5.95

Nancy M. **Farriss**

Maya Society Under Colonial Rule: The Collective Enterprise of Survival

0-691-10158-2 PRINCETON PB $26.95

David **Friedel** & others

Maya Cosmos: Three Thousand Years of the Shaman's Path

A synthesis of Maya religious thought, ancient and modern, with emphasis on the Classic Period, A.D. 200-900. Illustrated with photographs and line drawings

0-688-14069-6 QUILL PB $15.00

C. Bruce **Hunter**

A Guide to Ancient Maya Ruins

0-8061-1992-6 OKLAHOMA PB $17.95

Joyce **Kelly**

An Archeological Guide to Mexico's Yucatan Peninsula

Covers 91 sites and 18 museums

0-8061-2585-3 OKLAHOMA PB $19.95

Miguel **León-Protilla**

Time and Reality in the Thought of the Maya

A classic in anthropology, this work explores the peculiar Mayan obsession with time which sets them apart from all other people in history

0-8061-2308-7 OKLAHOMA PB $15.95

Sylvanus G. **Morley** & George W. **Brainerd**

The Ancient Maya

A comprehensive introduction, now in its fourth revision; illustrated

0-8047-1137-2 STANFORD $45.00
0-8047-1288-3 STANFORD PB $19.95

Sylvanus Griswold **Morley**

An Introduction to the Study of the Mayan Hieroglyphics

Modern republication of the original 1915 text. While some important new material has since been uncovered, this remains the only book to make elements of the Mayan system accessible to the beginner

0-486-23108-9 DOVER PB $8.95

Jeremy A. **Sabloff**

The New Archeology and the Ancient Maya

Using the Maya as a case study, shows how changes in the practice of archaeology have given birth to a new science that is changing our understanding of past civilizations. With large photographs and illustrations

0-7167-5054-6 FREEMAN $32.95

Linda **Schele** & David **Friedel**

A Forest of Kings: The Untold Story of the Ancient Maya

Using recent interpretations of Mayan hieroglyphics, this richly detailed work tells the story of Mayan kingship, from the first great pyramid builders 2,000 years ago to the decline of the Mayan civilization and its destruction by the Spanish. Illustrated with photographs and line drawings

0-688-11204-8 QUILL PB $17.95

Linda **Schele** & Mary **Miller**, editors

The Blood of Kings: Dynasty and Ritual in Maya Art

0-807-61278-2 BRAZILLER PB $29.95

James D. **Sexton**, editor & translator

Maya Folk Tales: Folklore from Lake Atitla, Guatemala

A broad selection of folkloric voices, the results of twenty years of research and travel by the eminent anthropologist

0-385-42253-9 ANCHOR PB $14.95

Robert J. **Sharer**

The Ancient Maya

0-8047-2310-9 STANFORD PB $27.50

Barbara **Tedlock**

Time and the Highland Maya

A revised edition of a landmark in ethnographic study of the Maya, this work focuses on rituals and cosmology among the contemporary Quiche Maya Indians of highland Guatemala

0-8263-1358-2 NEW MEXICO PB $15.95

Dennis **Tedlock**, translator

Popol Vuh: The Maya Book of the Dawn of Life

The newest translation of the Quiche Maya classic combines anthropological and literary values

See also **MEXICO, CENTRAL AND SOUTH AMERICA** under **TRADITIONAL LITERATURE: POETRY, STORIES, ORATORY** under **NATIVE AMERICAN LITERATURES** in **LITERATURE OF THE AMERICAS**

0-684-81845-0 TOUCHSTONE PB $15.00

J. Eric **Thompson**

A Catalog of Maya Heiroglyphics

Lists all known Mayan hieroglyphs, assigns them a number, and tries to list every occurrence of every glyph. "Everyone interested in Mayan writing will have to refer to it constantly" —*American Journal of Archeology*

0-8061-2260-9 OKLAHOMA PB $21.95

Maya Hieroglyphic Writing: An Introduction

Specialists find chapter twelve out of date, but Thompson's massive, well-illustrated treatment remains the best introduction to the subject

0-8061-0958-0 OKLAHOMA PB $38.95

Maya History and Religion

Collected scholarly articles on demography, cultural boundaries, tobacco use, trade relations, rituals, and creation myths

0-8061-2247-1 OKLAHOMA PB $17.95

Lawana Hooper **Trout**

The Maya

Concise overview, part of the Smithsonian's fine *Indians of North America* series for young adults

0-7910-0387-6 CHELSEA HOUSE PB $8.95

Mayan Culture in the Modern Period

Victoria Reifler **Bricker**

Ritual Humor in Highland Chiapas

Fiesta lore of the modern Tzotzil-speaking Indians of southern Mexico

0-292-77029-4 TEXAS PB $8.95

Robert M. **Carmack**, editor

Harvest of Violence: The Maya Indians and the Guatemalan Crisis

Articles by a dozen specialists documenting the effects of civil war on the Guatemalan Maya in the 1980s

0-8061-2459-8 OKLAHOMA PB $13.95

N. Ross **Crumrine**

The Maya Indians of Sonora: A People Who Refuse to Die

General history and ethnography, highlighting recent revitalization movements

0-88133-358-1 WAVELAND PB $9.50

Victor **Perera** & Robert D. **Bruce**

The Last Lords of Palenque: The Lacandon Mayas of the Mexican Rain Forest

0-520-05309-5 CALIFORNIA PB $13.00

Ricardo **Pozas**

Juan the Chamula: An Ethnological Recreation of the Life of a Mexican Indian

Composite life story of a typical Tzotzil Maya

0-520-01027-2 CALIFORNIA PB $13.95

Nelson **Reed**

The Caste War of Yucatan

The great Mayan revolt against Mexican authority in the middle of the 19th century

See also **FROM THE CONQUEST TO THE 20TH CENTURY** under **MEXICO** under **LATIN AMERICA AND THE CARIBBEAN**

0-8047-0165-2 STANFORD PB $14.95

Evan Z. **Vogt**

The Zinacantecos of Mexico: A Modern Maya Way of Life

Concise ethnography of the Tzotzil Maya of Zinacantan, Chiapas, by the director of the Harvard Chiapas Project

0-03-084016-3 HOLT RINEHART & WINSTON PB $13.30

South America

Threatened more than ever by technological change and rampant land development, the native cultures of South America remain little known. The wide-ranging titles below (history, anthropology, travel literature, ecology, and even fiction) present many aspects of a complex situation.

Ellen B. **Basso**

In Favor of Deceit: A Study of Tricksters in an Amazonian Society

Based on years of research with the Kalapalo Indians of Brazil, this work is the first study of a trickster tradition in a native South American culture

0-8165-1022-9 ARIZONA $52.00

Karen Olsen **Bruhns**

Ancient South America

Ten millenia of history before the Incas

0-521-27761-2 CAMBRIDGE PB $23.95

Richard L. **Burger**

Chavin and the Origins of Andean Civilization

Outsize book with drawings, maps, and photos that offers an excellent introduction to early Andean prehistory for the general reader

0-500-27816-4 THAMES & HUDSON PB $29.95

Catherine **Caufield**

In the Rainforest: Report from a Strange, Beautiful, Imperiled World

One of the best discussions of the destruction of rainforests

0-226-09786-2 CHICAGO PB $14.95

Napoleon A. **Chagnon**

Yanomamo: The Fierce People

The controversial study of South America's largest remaining group of hunters and gatherers

0-03-032819-5 HARCOURT BRACE $15.96

Pierre **Clastres**

Society Against the State: Essays in Political Anthropology

A classic work now back in print

0-942299-00-0 ZONE $24.95

Jon Christopher **Crocker**

Vital Souls: Bororo Cosmology, Natural Symbolism and Shamanism

One of several ethnographies emerging from Harvard's Central Brazil Project of the 1960s

0-8165-0877-1 ARIZONA $45.95

Marlene Dobkin **de Rios**

Visionary Vine: Hallucinogenic Healing in the Peruvian Amazon

0-88133-093-0 WAVELAND PB $9.95

Philippe **Descola**

The Spears of Twilight: Three Years Among the Jivaro Indians of South America

Under the tutelage of Claude Lévi-Strauss, the author spent three years with the Jivaro Indians in the jungle of the Upper Amazon. In this fascinating tour of the Jivaros' daily life, Descola has also told the story of his own evolving sympathy for and understanding of an utterly alien culture. "An admirable book…it proves that subjectivity and objectivity can go hand in hand when they are served by a true literary gift"—Claude Lévi-Strauss

See also **GENERAL ANTHROPOLOGICAL STUDIES** under **ANTHROPOLOGY** in **SOCIAL STUDIES**

TRANSLATED FROM BY JANET LLOYD

1-56584-228-6 NEW PRESS $25.00

Edward G. **Goodman**

The Explorers of South America

A 400-year narrative that recounts the gradually increasing knowledge of South America—a knowedge acquired through the efforts of explorers who ventured forth with varying purposes

0-8061-2420-2 OKLAHOMA PB $15.95

Thomas **Gregor**

Mehinaku: The Drama of Daily Life in a Brazilian Indian Village

0-226-30746-8 CHICAGO PB $14.95

David M. **Guss**

To Weave and Sing: Art, Symbol, and Narrative in the South American Rainforest

0-520-07185-9 CALIFORNIA PB $17.00

Michael **Harriet**

The Jivaro: People of the Sacred Waterfalls

The standard ethnography of Ecuador's Shuar people, famous for their custom of shrinking heads

0-520-05065-7 CALIFORNIA PB $14.95

John **Hemming**

Red Gold: The Conquest of the Brazilian Indians, 1500-1760

0-299-09600-9 WISCONSIN $32.50

Richard W. **Keatinge**, editor

Peruvian Prehistory

Survey of the cultural evolution of Peru from 10,000 BC to the arrival of the Spanish in 1534

0-521-27555-5 CAMBRIDGE PB $23.95

Joe **Kane**

Savages

New Yorker readers have long been familiar with Kane's brave and literate environmental reporting from the Amazon—indeed, his *Running the Amazon* was a *New York Times* bestseller. This first-hand account of a small band of Amazonian warriors and their battle to preserve their traditional life against the encroachment of oil companies, missionaries, bureaucrats, and environmentalists is at once hilarious and heartbreaking, a tragic and fascinating story of the tenacious and delicate survival of a determinedly primitive people

See also **REGIONAL GUIDES AND STUDIES** under **NATURE STUDY** in **SCIENCE**

0-679-41191-7 KNOPF $25.00

Jacques **Lizot**

Tales of Yanomami: Daily Life in the Venezuela Forest

Written as a rebuttal of Chagnon's *Yanomamo:* a compelling story

0-521-40672-2 CAMBRIDGE PB $11.95

Yolanda **Murphy** & Robert F. **Murphy**

Women of the Forest

An analysis of the Mundurucu of Brazil with particular attention to the role of women

0-231-06089-0 COLUMBIA PB $15.50

June **Nash**

We Eat the Mines and the Mines Eat Us: Dependency and Exploitation in Bolivian Tin Mines

See also **NEW ETHNOGRAPHIES** under **CRITICAL ANTHROPOLOGY** under **ANTHROPOLOGY** in **SOCIAL STUDIES**

0-231-04710-X COLUMBIA $34.00
0-231-08051-4 COLUMBIA PB $19.00

Redmond **O'Hanlon**

In Trouble Again: A Journey Between the Orinoco and the Amazon

The story of "O'Hanlon hacking his way up an unmapped tributary of the Amazon, fearful of ending his days in someone's cooking pot" —Jonathan Raban

See also **SOUTH AMERICA** under **TRAVEL LITERATURE** in **FOOD, TRAVEL, AND LEISURE**

0-679-72714-0 VINTAGE PB $12.00

Michel **Perrin**

The Way of the Dead Indians: Guajiro Myths and Symbols

A passionate interpretation of Guajiro life as seen through its myths

TRANSLATED BY MICHAEL FINEBERG

0-292-79039-2 TEXAS PB $14.95

Michael **Sallnow**

Pilgrims of the Andes: Regional Cults in Cusco

An extremely readable history of several of Peru's most popular religious cults

0-87474-826-7 SMITHSONIAN $39.00

Tobias **Schneebaum**

Keep the River on Your Right

Fascinating account of an artist's exploration in the Peruvian Amazon

0-8021-3133-6 GROVE PB $10.95

Gary **Urton**, editor

Animal Myths and Metaphors in South America

A good introduction by eight of South America's most interesting anthropologists

0-87480-205-9 UTAH PB $20.00

Norman E. **Whitten**, Jr.

Sicuanga Runa: The Other Side of Development in Amazonian Ecuador

A sophisticated account of cultural resilience and adaptation

0-252-01117-1 ILLINOIS $29.95

Incas

Burr Cartwright **Brundage**

Empire of the Inca

"A book for the public and especially for those who prefer to get their education through a beautifully written piece of literature" —*American Antiquity*

FOREWORD BY ARNOLD TOYNBEE

0-8061-1924-1 OKLAHOMA PB $17.95

Bernabe **Cobo**

History of the Inca Empire

Based on Father Bernabe Cobo's early-17th-century text, *Historia del Nuevo Mundo*

TRANSLATED BY ROLAND HAMILTON
FOREWORD BY JOHN H. ROWE

0-292-73025-X TEXAS PB $14.95

Inca Religion and Customs

0-292-73861-7 TEXAS PB $14.95

Geoffrey W. **Conrad** & Arthur A. **Demarest**

Religion and Empire: The Dynamics of Aztec and Inca Expansionism

An analysis of the two largest states of pre-Columbian America that argues for the role of ideology in cultural development

0-521-31896-3 CAMBRIDGE PB $24.95

John **Hemming**

The Conquest of the Incas

The first of Hemming's impressive volumes on the European occupation of South America

ILLUSTRATED BY K.C. JORDAN

0-15-622300-7 HARCOURT BRACE PB $21.00

Sydney D. **Kirkpatrick**

Lords of Sipan: A True History of Pre-Inca Tombs, Archeology and Crime

Adventure tale of grave robbers who stumbled onto the treasure of the Moche empire, a major pre-Inca civilization

0-8050-2817-X OWLET PB $14.95

Nigel **Davis**

The Incas

0-87081-360-9 COLORADO $29.95

Frank **Salomon**

Native Lords of Quito in the Age of the Incas: The Political Economy of North-Andean Chiefdoms

How Ecuador was affected by Inca expansion in pre-conquest times

0-521-30299-4 CAMBRIDGE $75.00

Irene **Silverblatt**

Moon, Sun, and Witches: Gender Ideologies and Class in Inca and Colonial Peru

The women's world in the Peruvian Andes before and after the Spanish conquest and Inquisition

0-691-02258-5 PRINCETON PB $15.95

Gary **Urton**

The History of a Myth: Pacariqtambo and the Origin of the Incas

Examines the social-historical context of this myth between 1532 and 1572

0-292-73057-8 TEXAS PB $10.95

Surveys of US History

General Histories

Bruce **Ackerman**

We the People: Foundations

Part one of a projected three-volume reinterpretation of constitutional history by a renowned legal scholar. "This book is one of the most important contributions to American constitutional thought in the last half-century"—*The New Republic*

0-674-94841-6 HARVARD PB $10.95

Hugh **Brogan**

The Longman/Pelican History of the United States of America

One of the best surveys happens to be by a British historian

0-14-013460-3 VIKING PB $16.95

James MacGregor **Burns**

The American Experiment

Volume 1
The Vineyard of Liberty

0-394-71629-9 VINTAGE PB $25.00

Volume 2
The Workshop of Democracy

0-394-74320-2 VINTAGE PB $25.00

Volume 3
The Crosswinds of Freedom from Roosevelt to Reagan
0-679-72819-8 VINTAGE PB $25.00

Peter N. **Carroll** & David W. **Noble**
The Free and the Unfree: A New History of the United States
The story of Native Americans, blacks, immigrants, religious minorities, and women
0-14-022827-6 VIKING PB $8.95

Carl N. **Degler**
Out of Our Past: The Forces that Shaped Modern America
A good introduction
0-06-131985-6 HARPERCOLLINS PB $17.00

Larry **Gonick**
The Cartoon Guide to U.S. History
Volume 1
A History of the United States to 1877
See also **OTHER COMICS** under **COMICS** in **POPULAR READING**
See also **CONTEMPORARY COMIC STRIP ARTISTS AND CARTOONISTS** under **COMICS** in **POPULAR READING**
0-15-500730-0 HARCOURT BRACE $47.55

Volume 2
A History of the United States since 1865
0-15-500731-9 HARCOURT BRACE $47.55

Maldwyn A. **Jones**
The Limits of Liberty: American History, 1607-1980
0-19-913130-9 OXFORD PB $22.50

Roger G. **Kennedy**
Rediscovering America: Journeys Through Our Forgotten Past
Offbeat history from the director of the Smithsonian Institution's Museum of American History. "The aim of these lively essays is to startle (and perhaps shame) the reader into a new curiosity about American history, both ancient and modern"—*TLS*
0-395-62895-4 HOUGHTON MIFFLIN PB $14.95

Donald **Meinig**
The Shaping of America
In two volumes
0-300-05658-3 YALE $50.00
0-300-03882-8 YALE PB $22.00

Samuel Eliot **Morison** & others
The Growth of the American Republic
Volume 1
To 1877
0-19-502593-8 OXFORD $36.00
0-19-503181-4 OXFORD PB $24.95

Volume 2
Since 1865
0-19-502594-6 OXFORD $36.00
0-19-503182-2 OXFORD PB $24.95

Francis **Parkman**
France and England in North America
Two great empires maneuver for dominance on hostile and unfamiliar terrain; a classic of 19th-century historical writing, despite its obvious biases

Volume 1
See also **LIBRARY OF AMERICA** in **LITERATURE OF THE AMERICAS**
0-940450-10-0 LIBRARY OF AMERICA $40.00

Volume 2
0-940450-11-9 LIBRARY OF AMERICA $40.00

Richard **Shenkman** & Kurt **Reiger**
One-Night Stands with American History: Odd, Amusing, and Little-Known Incidents
J. Edgar Hoover refused to allow people to walk on his shadow; in 1721, women were in such short supply that the government of France shipped 25 prostitutes to the colonies
0-688-01399-6 MORROW PB $9.00

Carl **Sifakis**
American Eccentrics: 140 of the Greatest Human Interest Stories Ever Told
0-88365-864-X GALAHAD $9.98

Peter **Stevens**
The Mayflower Murderer and Other Forgotten Firsts in American History
All kinds of little-known but compelling "firsts" surface in this book, from the story of the *Mayflower's* one bad apple, loud-mouthed Peter Billington, who shot and killed one of his Plymouth neighbors and was hanged for it, to the first woman who demanded a vote in 1648
0-688-13515-3 QUILL PB $10.00

William **Strauss** & Neil **Howe**
Generations: The History of America's Future, 1584-2069
The history of America as a succession of generational biographies—broken down into four types, which repeat sequentially in a fixed pattern. "A provocative, erudite and engaging analysis of the rhythms of American life"—*Newsweek*
0-688-11912-3 MORROW PB $12.00

Richard **Hofstadter**, editor
Volume II
From the Revolution to the Civil War, 1765-1865
Significant documents from one hundred years of fervent debate, with commentary and notes by the Pulitzer Prize-winning historian
0-394-70541-6 RANDOM HOUSE PB $10.00

Richard **Hofstadter** & Beatrice **Hofstadter**
Volume III
From Reconstruction to the Present Day
Through the 1960s
0-394-70842-3 VINTAGE PB $12.00

Clarence L. **VerSteeg** & Richard **Hofstadter**, editors
Great Issues in American History
Volume I
From Settlement to Revolution, 1584-1776
A wide sampling of selections from the major political controversies in the colonial period, with useful introductions and explanatory notes
0-394-70540-8 RANDOM HOUSE PB $12.00

Textbooks

Paul **Boyer**
Enduring Vision: A History of the American People
A hugely successful collaborative text aimed squarely at the "middle of the market" and first published in 1990; now in its fourth edition
0-669-42651-2 HEATH $62.36

Frances **FitzGerald**
America Revised
A biting critique of how textbooks portray the American past
0-394-74439-X VINTAGE PB $8.87

John A. **Garraty**
A Short History of the American Nation
A well-written text by a noted Columbia historian
0-06-042415-X HARPERCOLLINS PB $27.00

Joan R. **Gundersen** & Marshall **Smelser**
American History at a Glance: From the Exploration of the New World to the Present
Basic summary of significant events and trends
0-06-273292-7 HARPERPERENNIAL PB $13.00

Samuel Eliot **Morison**
A Concise History of the American Republic
An abbreviated version of *The Growth of the American Republic,* revised to include the Carter and Reagan administrations; available in a 1 or 2-volume edition
0-19-503180-6 OXFORD PB $32.00

Mary B. **Norton** & others
A People and a Nation: The United States
A social emphasis
0-395-74568-3 HOUGH PB $37.50

George Brown **Tindall** &
David E. **Shi**, editors

Everyday Life in America

David F. **Hawke**

Volume I
Everyday Life in Early America

By the author of *Nuts and Bolts of the Past: A History of American Technology, 1777-1860*

0-809-59165-0 OBORGO $33.00
0-06-091251-0 OHARPERCOLLINS PB $13.00

Stephanie Grauman **Wolf**

Volume II
As Various as Their Land: The Everyday Lives of 18th-Century Americans

"Wolf's splendid account of eighteenth-century life reflects the newest scholarship and introduces us to a colonial American society that was complex, lively, and rapidly changing"—Linda K. Kerber

0-06-0092537-X HARPERPERENNIAL PB $13.50

Jack **Larkin**

Volume III
The Reshaping of Everyday Life, 1790-1840

By the chief historian at Old Sturbridge Village in Sturbridge, Massachusetts. "Virtually all human activity in the late 18th and early 19th centuries comes in for scrutiny in this compact and insightful work"
—*NY Times Book Review*

0-06-091606-0 OHARPERCOLLINS PB $14.00

Daniel E. **Sutherland**

Volume IV
The Expansion of Everyday Life, 1860-1876

0-06-091639-7 OHARPERCOLLINS PB $14.00

Thomas J. **Schlereth**

Volume V
Victorian America: Transformations in Everyday Life, 1876-1915

How, in this period of rapid social change, the country's population doubled and the foundations of a consumer society were laid. Chapters include "Moving," "Working," "Housing," "Consuming," "Playing," "Striving," and "Living and Dying"

0-06-092160-9 OHARPERPERENNIAL PB $14.00

Harvey **Green**

Volume VI
The Uncertainty of Everyday Life, 1915-1945

0-06-092414-4 OHARPERPERENNIAL PB......$12.00

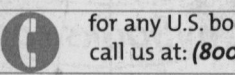

Popular Reading

Alan **Axlerod** & Charles **Phillips**

What Every American Should Know About American History: 200 Events that Shaped the Nation

The crash course, palm-sized. "Cogently written, concisely thorough and admirably informative"—*Library Journal*

See also **ONE-VOLUME ENCYCLOPEDIAS** under **REFERENCE** in **BUSINESS AND REFERENCE**

1-55850-309-9 ADAMS PB $10.95

Kenneth C. **Davis**

Don't Know Much About History: Everything You Need to Know About American History but Never Learned

A bestseller, written in a breezy question-and-answer format

0-380-71252-0 AVON PB $12.50

John **Whitcomb** & Claire **Whitcomb**

O Say Can You See: Unexpected Anecdotes About American History

Amusing anecdotes, arranged in list format

0-688-08664-0 MORROW PB $10.95

Reference

Vincent J. **Esposito**

The West Point Atlas of American Wars
Volume I
1689-1900

Subsequent volumes have yet to appear

0-8050-3391-2 HOLT $75.00

William J. **Federer**

America's God and Country Encyclopedia of Quotations

Useful reference for speeches, papers, debates, and essays as well as solid source of general knowledge

1-88056-305-3 SPRING ARBOR PB $19.99

Robert H. **Ferrell** & Richard **Natkiel**

Atlas of American History

Informed text, historical paintings, and color photos. The maps range from the Atlantic trade in 1770 to presidential elections from 1800 to 1980

See also **REFERENCE** under **THE VARIETIES OF CIVILIZATION** in **WORLD HISTORY AND CURRENT AFFAIRS**

0-8160-2883-3 FACTS $29.95
0-8160-2544-4 FACTS PB $19.95

John Anthony **Scott**

The Story of America: A National Geographic Picture Atlas

Lavishly illustrated. Oversized

0-87044-887-0 NATIONAL GEOGRAPHIC $25.00

Eric **Foner** & John A. **Garraty**, editors

The Reader's Encyclopedia of American History

A scholarly reference book for the general reader, this 1,000-page volume incorporates the work of nearly 400 specialists to present a thematically arranged guide to American history. Readable and comprehensive

0-395-51372-3 HOUGHTON MIFFLIN $35.00

John A. **Garraty**

1001 Things Everyone Should Know About American History

A zippy, entertaining cram course in the people, the places, and the politics that make up America's colorful past, by a distinguished historian. With 400 illustrations

0-385-42577-5 MAIN STREET PB $12.00

Richard B. **Morris**, editor

Encyclopedia of American History

0-06-181605-1 HARPERCOLLINS $39.95

US History to the Civil War

This chapter and the two that follow are devoted to a basic outline of social and political history, from America's exploration and settlement to the present. Subsequent chapters deal with aspects of the national experience and current scene whose inclusion here might hamper the general flow of events.

Essays and Reflections

Henry **Adams**

The U.S. in 1800

The essays on social history which constitute the first six chapters of his book on Thomas Jefferson

0-8014-9014-6 CORNELL PB $8.95

Thomas Jefferson

James **Axtell**

Beyond 1492: Encounters in Colonial North America

Collection of essays by a leading ethnohistorian on the 500th anniversary of Columbus. Focuses on the key role of the imagination in our perception of strangers and in the writing of history

0-19-508033-5 OXFORD PB $17.95

Daniel J. **Boorstin**

Hidden History: Exploring Our Secret Past

Essays from the Pulitzer Prize-winning historian

0-679-72223-8 VINTAGE PB $14.00

Richard **Hofstadter**

The American Political Tradition and the Men Who Made It

Insightful essays on outstanding political leaders by one of the great postwar historians

See also **POLITICAL HISTORY** under **AMERICAN POLITICS AND FOREIGN POLICY**

FOREWORD BY CHRISTOPHER LASCH

0-394-48880-6 RANDOM HOUSE $26.00
0-679-72315-3 VINTAGE PB $13.00

Thomas **Jefferson**

The Portable Thomas Jefferson

See also **THE EARLY COLONIAL PERIOD** under **AMERICAN LITERATURE TO 1900** in **LITERATURE OF THE AMERICAS**

EDITED BY MERRILL D. PETERSON

0-14-015080-3 VIKING PB $14.95

Michael **Kammen**

People of Paradox: An Inquiry Concerning the Origins of American Civilization

How the 17th- and 18th-century colonies helped form a style and temper that foreshadows our own

0-8014-9755-8 CORNELL PB $16.95

David M. **Potter**

People of Plenty: Economic Abundance and the American Character

0-226-67633-1 CHICAGO PB $11.95

Arthur M. **Schlesinger**

The Birth of the Nation

The distinguished historian and father of Arthur M. Schlesinger, Jr. offers a rich portrait of American life in the mid to late eighteenth century

0-395-31675-8 HOUGHTON MIFFLIN PB $14.95

Arthur M. **Schlesinger**, Jr.

The Cycles of American History

0-395-45400-X HOUGHTON MIFFLIN PB $14.95

The European Discovery of America

John **Bakeless**

America as Seen by Its First Explorers: The Eyes of Discovery

0-486-26031-3 DOVER PB $9.95

Emerson W. **Baker** & others

American Beginnings: Exploration, Culture, and Cartography in the Land of Norumbega

0-8032-4554-8 NEBRASKA $35.00

Christopher Columbus

Christopher **Columbus**

The Diario of Christopher Columbus's First Voyage to America, 1492-1493

"The single most important piece of Columbus scholarship to appear in a long, long time" —Robert Fuson, University of South Florida

TRANSLATED & EDITED BY OLIVER DUNN & JAMES E. KELLEY, JR.

0-8061-2101-7 OKLAHOMA $70.00

Alvar Nunez Cabeza **de Vaca**

Adventures in the Unknown Interior of America

The story of the ill-fated Nervaez expedition to Florida; one of the most astonishing narratives of early American exploration

TRANSLATED WITH NOTES BY CYCLONE COVEY

0-8263-0656-X NEW MEXICO PB $9.95

George Francis **Dow** & John Henry **Edmonds**

The Pirates of the New England Coast, 1630-1730

0-486-29064-6 DOVER PB $11.95

Anthony **Grafton**

New Worlds, Ancient Texts: The Power of Tradition and the Shock of Discovery

How the evidence of the New World shook the foundations of the old, upsetting the authority of the ancient texts that had guided Europeans so far afield

0-674-61875-0 HARVARD $29.95

Gianni **Granzotto**

Christopher Columbus

A tale of royal intrigue and great sea adventure

TRANSLATED BY STEPHEN SARTARELLI

0-8061-2100-9 OKLAHOMA PB $14.95

Ted **Morgan**

Wilderness at Dawn: Settling of the North American Continent

A sweeping, well-researched panorama, from the Pulitzer Prize-winning journalist and historian

0-671-88237-6 TOUCHSTONE PB $15.00

Samuel Eliot **Morison**

The European Discovery of America: The Northern Voyages

A gripping account of every voyage to the New World before 1600, by the historian who dominates the field

Volume 1: A.D. 500-1600

0-19-501823-0 OXFORD $39.95
0-19-501371-0 OXFORD PB $19.95

Volume 2: A.D. 1492-1616

0-19-501823-0 OXFORD $39.95
0-19-508272-9 OXFORD PB $19.95

The Great Explorers: The European Discovery of America

A popular condensation of Morison's two longer volumes

0-19-504222-0 OXFORD PB $21.95

Ivan van **Sertima**

They Came Before Columbus: The African Presence in Ancient America

A provocative and detailed account of African explorers

See also **HISTORY** under **AFRICAN-AMERICAN STUDIES**

0-394-40245-6 RANDOM HOUSE $23.00
0-679-72530-X VINTAGE PB $14.95

David E. **Stannard**

American Holocaust: Columbus and the Conquest of the New World

The true significance of the "discovery" of America, argues the author, was to provide Europe with a new place in which to wage its Holy Christian war

0-19-507581-1 OXFORD $35.00

Tzvetan **Todorov**

The Conquest of America

"An original argument…The extraordinary story of the first encounter of Europeans and Americans"—*NY Review of Books*

0-06-091214-6 HARPERPERENNIAL PB $12.00

Richard C. **Trexler**

Sex and Conquest: Gendered Violence, Political Order, and the European Conquest of the Americas

0-8014-3224-3 CORNELL $29.95

Frederick **Turner**

Beyond Geography: The Western Spirit Against the Wilderness

A dazzling exploration—historical, philosophical, literary—of the European experience in the New World

0-8135-1909-8 RUTGERS PB $15.00

The New Colonies

Early American settlements are a natural subject for historians interested in social, particularly family, life. Increased sensitivity about race has not only led to outstanding studies of the first confrontation of Native Americans, whites, and blacks, but has also increased our perception of the social and ideological origins of the Revolutionary War.

William L. **Andrews**, editor

Journeys in New Worlds: Early American Women's Narratives

Four remarkable memoirs by American women of the 17th and 18th centuries: accounts of captivity, indentured servitude, travel, and spiritual awakening by Mary Rowlandson, Sarah Kemble Knight, Elizabeth Ashbridge, and Elizabeth House Trist

0-299-12584-X WISCONSIN PB..........$10.95

It was a solemn Sight to see so many Christians lying in their blood, some here and some there, like a company of Sheep torn by Wolves; all of them stript naked by a company of hell-hounds, roaring, singing, ranting, and insulting as if they would have torn our very hearts out; yet the Lord, by his Almighty power, preserved a number of us from death, for there were twenty-four of us taken alive; and carried Captive.—From "The Captivity and Restoration of Mrs. Mary Rowlandson"

JOURNEYS IN NEW WORLDS: EARLY AMERICAN WOMEN'S NARRATIVES

James **Axtell**

The European and the Indian: Essays in the Ethnohistory of Colonial North America

A blend of history and anthropology, drawing on archaeology, linguistics, literature, and art

See also **INDIAN-WHITE RELATIONS** under **NATIVE AMERICAN CULTURES: NORTH AMERICA**

0-19-502904-6 OXFORD PB..........$12.95

The Invasion Within: The Contest of Cultures in Colonial North America

Relations among root cultures in Canada—Indian, French, and English. "The best introduction now available to the problem of cultural conversion in the New World"
—William Cronon

0-19-504154-2 OXFORD PB..........$17.95

Carol **Berkin** & Eric **Foner**

First Generations: Women in Colonial America

A feminist perspective with an emphasis on gender and class. "[Berkin's] analysis of Native American and African-American women, as well as of how the American Revolution affected female roles, is enlightening"
—*Publishers Weekly*

See also **COLONIAL AMERICA** under **AMERICAN HISTORY** under **WOMEN'S STUDIES** in **SOCIAL STUDIES**

0-8090-4561-3 HILL & WANG..........$23.00

Bernard Bailyn

The Origins of American Politics

"...these well-argued essays represent the first sustained and systematic attempt to provide a comprehensive and integrated analysis of all elements of American political life during the late colonial period"—*The New-York Historical Society Quarterly*

0-394-70865-2 RANDOM HOUSE PB..........$6.20

The Peopling of British North America: An Introduction

Three fine essays exploring the migration of Europeans to North America

0-394-75779-3 VINTAGE PB..........$9.00

Voyagers to the West: A Passage in the Peopling of America on the Eve of the Revolution

Using such research techniques as computerized demographic analysis, Bailyn explores the lives and attitudes of colonial Americans in this Pulitzer Prize-winning book

0-394-51569-2 KNOPF..........$35.00
0-394-75778-5 VINTAGE PB..........$19.00

T.H. **Breen**

Puritans and Adventurers: Change and Persistence in Early America

Essays on how the local origins of English colonists influenced their attitudes, and on contrasts between the settlements in Massachusetts and Virginia

0-19-503207-1 OXFORD PB..........$15.95

William **Cronon**

Changes in the Land: Indians, Colonists, and the Ecology of New England

"Combines ecological and cultural analysis into a cogent, sophisticated, and balanced study of Indian-White contact"
—Richard White, Michigan State University

See also **ECOLOGY AND ECONOMY** under **ASPECTS OF TRADITIONAL CULTURE** under **NATIVE AMERICAN CULTURES: NORTH AMERICA**

0-8090-0158-6 FS&G PB..........$9.95

James **Deetz**

In Small Things Forgotten: The Archaeology of Early American Life

Traces the development of the Anglo-American tradition in the 17th century and the culture of black Americans through artifacts

0-385-08031-X DOUBLEDAY PB..........$11.00

David Hackett **Fischer**

Albion's Seed: Four British Folkways in America

"It is the first in a series of volumes that he hopes will eventually constitute a cultural history of the United States....This book starts with a bang...a big bang....Remarkable....A revisionist blockbuster"
—Gordon Wood, *The New Republic*

See also **CULTURAL AND SOCIAL LIFE** under **TOPICS IN BRITISH HISTORY** under **GREAT BRITAIN AND IRELAND** in **WORLD HISTORY AND CURRENT AFFAIRS**

0-19-503794-4 OXFORD..........$40.00
0-19-506905-6 OXFORD PB..........$24.95

Philip **Greven**

The Protestant Temperament: Patterns of Child-Rearing, Religious Experience, and the Self in Early America

"Interdisciplinary historical effort, in which children and women are deemed significant, in which the rituals of the home are understood to be intimately connected with the tactics of church and state"
—Ann Douglas, *NY Times Book Review*

0-226-30830-8 CHICAGO PB..........$15.95

David Freeman **Hawke**

Everyday Life in Early America

People seen in the vividness and hardship of their daily lives: living in cramped houses, drinking too much, governed by superstition, subject to epidemics, and coping with the guerrilla tactics of the Indians

0-8095-9165-0 BORGO..........$33.00
0-06-091251-0 HARPO PB..........$13.00

Francis **Jennings**

The Ambiguous Iroquois Empire: The Covenant Chain Confederation of Indian Tribes with English Colonies

0-393-30302-0 NORTON PB..........$16.95

Empire of Fortune: Crowns, Colonies, and Tribes in the Seven Years' War in America

0-393-02537-3 NORTON..........$27.50
0-393-30640-2 NORTON PB..........$16.95

The Invasion of America: Indians, Colonialism, and the Cant of Conquest

A startlingly revisionist and richly documented picture of Puritans and Indians in the 17th century. "Will surprise many readers with its revelations"—Dee Brown

0-393-00830-4 NORTON PB..........$11.95

Benjamin Woods **Labaree**

America's Nation-Time: 1607-1789

0-393-00821-5 NORTON PB..........$10.95

Wendy **Martin**, editor

Colonial American Travel Narratives

A collection of four tales that shed light on the physical and psychological challenges of colonial life

0-14-039088-X PENGUIN PB..........$12.95

John J. **McCusker** & Russell R. **Menard**

The Economy of British America, 1607-1789

0-8078-4351-2 NORTH CAROLINA PB..........$22.50

Gary B. **Nash**

Red, White, and Black: The Peoples of Early America

0-13-769878-X PRENTICE HALL PB $27.13

Mary Beth **Norton**

Founding Mothers & Fathers: Gendered Power and the Forming of American Society

This insightful study from the Mary Dolon Alger Professor of American History at Cornell focuses on the years from 1620 to 1670 to isolate the origin of "gendered power" in America. Demonstrating that early America drew little distinction between family and society, Norton shows that women wielding power within the family therefore were able to achieve great influence in society at large. She goes on to discuss the moment of change, when "public" and "private" were made separate, showing how the distinction gave women no role outside the home and set the stage for a sexual basis of discrimination that remains unresolved today

0-679-42965-4 KNOPF $35.00

Howard **Peckham**

Colonial Wars, 1689-1762

0-226-65314-5 CHICAGO PB $13.95

Richard C. **Simmons**

The American Colonies from Settlement to Independence

0-393-00999-8 NORTON PB $14.95

John **Smith**

Captain John Smith: A Select Edition of His Writings

A rich collection of writings, arranged thematically, focusing on the founding of Jamestown and on Smith's relations with the Indians

See also **THE EARLY COLONIAL PERIOD** under **AMERICAN LITERATURE TO 1900** in **LITERATURE OF THE AMERICAS**

EDITED BY KAREN ORDAHL KUPPERMAN

0-8078-1778-3 NORTH CAROLINA $45.00

0-8078-4208-7 NORTH CAROLINA PB $16.95

Clarence L. **Ver Steeg**

The Formative Years: 1607-1763

"Ver Steeg's central concern is with the forces that converted 'transplanted Englishmen' into 'provincial Americans.' [He] shows how cultural conditioning, not mere geography, caused the pattern of New England settlement to differ from that in Virginia. At the same time, in analyzing how abundant land, expanding trade, and immigration modified the European heritage, he persuasively argues that Frederick Jackson Turner's frontier hypothesis...is valid when applied to the settlement of the Old West"—from the Foreword

FOREWORD BY DAVID HERBERT DONALD

0-8090-0137-3 FS&G PB $10.95

David C. **Woodman**

Unraveling the Franklin Mystery: Inuit Testimony

This new examination of Sir John Franklin's ill-fated Arctic expedition reconstructs events surrounding the mysterious loss of both ships and all hands by giving new credence to the testimony of Inuit witnesses

0-7735-0833-3 MCGILL $42.95

Puritan Lives

Though Puritanism was fundamentally a religious movement, books about the Puritan experience are listed here because of its adherents' extraordinary influence on all of American society.

Andrew **Delbanco**

The Puritan Ordeal

Emphasizes that they left England to escape the acquisitive life and because, as immigrants, they believed their lives could be renewed. Winner of Columbia University's Lionel Trilling Award

0-674-74056-4 HARVARD PB $16.95

John **Demos**

The Unredeemed Captive: A Family Story from Early America

A prominent Puritan family struggles to rescue their young daughter from a Native American tribe, only to discover she is not being held against her will

0-679-75961-1 VINTAGE PB $13.00

George Francis **Dow**

Everyday Life in the Massachusetts Bay Colony

Furniture, clothing, sports, trade, medicine, crime and punishment, and manners, with detailed lists of such things as inventories of shops and homes

0-486-25565-4 DOVER PB $9.95

Richard **Godbeer**

The Devil's Dominion: Magic and Religion in Early New England

"Godbeer shows us that popular belief in magic underlay most accusations of witchcraft, even in the Salem epidemic, and he also shows that popular belief did not necessarily ascribe the efficacy of magic and by consequence of witchcraft to the devil"—*NY Review of Books*

0-521-40329-4 CAMBRIDGE $33.95

0-521-46670-9 CAMBRIDGE PB $14.95

Michael G. **Hall**

The Last American Puritan: The Life of Increase Mather

0-8195-6238-6 WESLEYAN PB $24.00

Perry **Miller**

The New England Mind

One of the great books of American history written in this century. "The historical process whereby Puritan became Yankee—as part of that larger process whereby the Reformation became the Enlightenment" —*Christian Science Monitor*

See also **GENERAL STUDIES TO 1900** under **AMERICAN LITERATURE: ANTHOLOGIES AND CRITICAL STUDIES** in **LITERATURE OF THE AMERICAS**

Volume 1 From Colony to Province

0-674-61301-5 HARVARD PB $16.95

Volume 2 The Seventeenth Century

0-674-61306-6 HARVARD PB $16.95

Karen Ordahl **Kupperman**

Providence Island, 1630-1641: The Other Puritan Colony

0-521-55835-2 CAMBRIDGE PB $18.95

Edmund S. **Morgan**

The Puritan Family: Religion and Domestic Relations in Seventeenth Century New England

0-06-131227-4 HARPERCOLLINS PB $13.00

Visible Saints: The History of a Puritan Idea

0-8014-9041-3 CORNELL PB $9.95

James G. **Mosely**

John Winthrop's World: History as a Story: The Story as History

"...promises to be a lasting contribution to New England Puritan studies as well as a book of great importance to a more general audience of people interested in religion's role in shaping American consciousness and character" —Amanda Porterfield

0-299-13534-9 WISCONSIN PB $14.95

David E. **Stannard**

The Puritan Way of Death: A Study in Religion, Culture, and Social Change

Probes the idea of death and the problem of mortality in Puritan midmodern America

0-19-502521-0 OXFORD PB $10.95

Harry S. **Stout**

The New England Soul: Preaching and Religious Culture in Colonial New England

The first comprehensive analysis of preaching in colonial New England examines more than 2000 sermons spanning five generations of ministers

0-19-505645-0 OXFORD PB $19.95

The Witches of New England

Paul **Boyer** & Stephen **Nissenbaum**

By Salem Possessed: The Social Origins of Witchcraft

"An illuminating and imaginative interpretation of the social and moral state of Salem Village in 1692"—*NY Review of Books*

0-674-78526-6 HARVARD PB $13.50

Paul **Boyer** & Stephen **Nissenbaum**, editors

Salem-Village Witchcraft: A Documentary Record of Local Conflict in Colonial New England

Includes transcripts of the preliminary proceedings and much of the testimony against five accused witches, two contemporary narratives of the 1692 witchcraft outbreak, and several sermons delivered in response to the trials

1-55553-165-2 NORTHEASTERN PB $15.95

John Putnam **Demos**

Entertaining Satan: Witchcraft and the Culture of Early New England

An outstanding work on the social and psychological roots of witchcraft, including case histories of various episodes

0-19-503378-7 OXFORD PB $16.95

David D. **Hall**

Witch Hunting in Seventeenth-Century New England: A Documentary History 1638-1692

Excellent collection that illuminates the social history of New England

1-55553-085-0 NORTHEASTERN PB $15.95

Chadwick **Hansen**

Witchcraft at Salem

Argues that witchcraft actually was practiced in 17th-century New England. "A story that departs significantly from the traditional version…undermines the work of generations of American historians who could make sense of the witchcraft trials only by seeing evidence of fraud, malice, and the harsh moral politics that marked Puritanism"—*NY Times Book Review*

0-8076-1137-9 BRAZILLER PB $8.95

Peter Charles **Hoffer**

The Devil's Disciples: Makers of the Salem Witchcraft Trials

0-8018-5200-5 JOHNS HOPKINS $29.95

0-8018-5201-3 JOHNS HOPKINS PB $10.00

Carol F. **Karlsen**

The Devil in the Shape of a Woman: Witchcraft in Colonial New England

"The assumptions, explicit and implicit, that governed the everyday relationships of men and women in early New England"
—Edmund S. Morgan

0-679-72184-3 VINTAGE PB $13.00

Marion L. **Starkey**

The Devil in Massachusetts: A Modern Enquiry into the Salem Witch Trials

Modern psychiatry takes on the notorious trials of 1692; first published in 1949

0-385-03509-8 DOUBLEDAY PB $11.00

Southern Colonies

T.H. **Breen**

Tobacco Culture: The Mentality of the Great Tidewater Planters on the Eve of Revolution

"Breen's major contribution is to delineate the 'mentality' of the great planters of the period when private and public distress converged"
—Peter S. Onuf, *William & Mary Quarterly*

0-691-00596-6 PRINCETON PB $12.95

T.H. **Breen** & Stephen **Innes**

Myne Owne Ground: Race and Freedom on Virginia's Eastern Shore, 1640-1676

The story of several blacks who amassed property, established plantations, and lived for several generations as free members of Virginia society

0-19-503206-3 OXFORD PB $14.95

Rhys **Isaac**

The Transformation of Virginia, 1740-1790

Pulitzer Prize-winning social history on the effect of religious revival and political revolution

0-8078-1489-X NORTH CAROLINA $45.00

0-8078-4116-1 NORTH CAROLINA PB $12.95

Thomas **Jefferson**

Notes on the State of Virginia

A new edition of Jefferson's 1781 survey, originally written as a response to the questions of a French diplomat

See also **THE 18TH CENTURY** under **AMERICAN LITERATURE TO 1900** in **LITERATURE OF THE AMERICAS**

EDITED BY WILLIAM PEDEN

0-8078-4588-4 NORTH CAROLINA PB $14.95

Allan **Kulikoff**

Tobacco and Slaves: The Development of Southern Cultures in the Chesapeake, 1680-1800

The changing social relations, among both blacks and whites, explored in a "true synthesis dealing with the entire Chesapeake region"
—*Register of the Kentucky Historical Society*

0-8078-1671-X NORTH CAROLINA $39.95

0-8078-4224-9 NORTH CAROLINA PB $16.95

Kenneth A. **Lockridge**

The Diary and Life of William Byrd II of Virginia, 1674-1744

0-8078-1736-8 NORTH CAROLINA $29.95

Edmund S. **Morgan**

American Slavery, American Freedom: The Ordeal of Colonial Virginia

0-393-09156-2 NORTON PB $10.95

Gerald W. **Mullin**

Flight and Rebellion: Slave Resistance in Eighteenth Century Virginia

0-19-501788-9 OXFORD PB $9.95

Darrett B. **Rutman** & Anita H. **Rutman**

A Place in Time: Middlesex County, Virginia, 1650-1750

0-393-30318-7 NORTON PB $11.95

Peter H. **Wood**

Black Majority: Negroes in Colonial South Carolina from 1670 Through the Stono Rebellion

0-393-00777-4 NORTON PB $9.95

The American Revolution

John R. **Alden**

A History of the American Revolution

0-306-80366-6 DA CAPO PB $16.95

Fred **Anderson**

A People's Army: Massachusetts Soldiers and Society in the Seven Years' War

This fine example of the "new military history" gauges the impact of the French and Indian War on a generation of colonists

0-393-95520-6 NORTON PB $8.95

Bernard **Bailyn**

The Ideological Origins of the American Revolution

A landmark study that examines pamphlet literature and stresses the role of Whig thought in the emergence of revolutionary consciousness. "One cannot claim to understand the Revolution without having read this book"
—*NY Times Book Review*

0-674-44301-2 HARVARD PB $12.95

The Ordeal of Thomas Hutchinson

A fine biography of the unpopular governor of Massachusetts, 1771-1774

0-674-64161-2 HARVARD PB $15.50

Jack P. **Greene**

Peripheries and Center: Constitutional Development in the Extended Polities of the British Empire and the United States, 1607-1788

0-393-30661-5 NORTON PB $10.95

Jack P. **Greene** & J.R. **Role**, editor

The Blackwell Encyclopedia of the American Revolution

A terrific sourcebook edited by two top historians

1-55786-547-7 BLACKWELL PB $24.95

Linda K. **Kerber**

Women of the Republic: Intellect and Ideology in Revolutionary America

0-393-30345-4 NORTON PB $12.95

Benjamin Woods **Labaree**

The Boston Tea Party

The dumping of tea into Boston Harbor on the night of December 16, 1773, as a protest against the trade monopoly of the British East India Company, was a major turning point in the road to revolution. "A brilliant and scholarly demonstration of the way a single act of violence can affect the course of history"—Julian P. Boyd, editor, *The Papers of Thomas Jefferson*

0-930350-05-7 NORTHEASTERN PB $16.95

Pauline **Maier**

From Resistance to Revolution: Colonial Radicals and the Development of American Opposition to Britain, 1765-1776

0-394-71937-9 NORTON PB....................$11.95

John C. **Miller**

The Origins of the American Revolution

"The full story of the decade before the Revolution is here recounted with uniformly crisp phrasing, incisive comment, and apt quotation"—*Yale Review*

0-8047-0594-1 STANFORD PB....................$18.95

Edmund S. **Morgan**

The Birth of the Republic, 1763-89

Covering the Revolutionary War and the Confederation periods. Now in its third edition

0226-537579-9 CHICAGO PB....................$9.95

The Challenge of the American Revolution

Essays on events and ideas that formed the background to revolution, with a controversial interpretation of slavery and class conflict

0-393-00876-2 NORTON PB....................$8.95

Inventing the People: The Rise of Popular Sovereignty in England and America

0-393-30623-2 NORTON PB....................$10.95

Gary B. **Nash**

The Urban Crucible: Social Change, Political Consciousness and the Origins of the American Revolution

An attempt to tie the Revolution in part to social conflict among the colonists themselves

0-674-93059-2 HARVARD PB....................$15.95

Clinton **Rossiter**

The First American Revolution: The American Colonies on the Eve of Independence

0-15-631121-6 HARCOURT BRACE PB....................$9.95

Garry **Wills**

Inventing America: Jefferson's Declaration of Independence

An adept and controversial analysis compares Jefferson's original draft with the final accepted version–thereby challenging many long-cherished assumptions about both the man and the document

1-56849-536-6 BUCCANEER....................$29.95

The Revolutionary War

"But what do we mean by the American Revolution? Do we mean the American war? The Revolution was effected before the war commenced. The Revolution was in the minds and hearts of the people; a change in their religious sentiments, of their duties and obligations...This radical change in the principles, opinions, sentiments, and affections of the people was the real American Revolution."—John Adams to Hezekiah Niles, 1818, quoted in Bernard Bailyn, *The Ideological Origins of the American Revolution*

John R. **Alden**

The American Revolution, 1775-1783

0-06-133011-6 HARPERCOLLINS PB....................$14.50

The South in the Revolution, 1763-1789

0-8071-0003-X LOUSIANA STATE....................$37.50

0-8071-0013-7 LOUSIANA STATE PB....................$16.95

Henry Steele **Commager** & Richard B. **Morris**

The Spirit of 1776: The Story of the American Revolution as Told by the Participants

"For readers who like their history straight from the sources, *The Spirit of 1776* is the best they can find on the Revolution. Anyone with an interest in the roots of American history and national character has much to learn from it" —C. Vann Woodward. Over 1,300 pages

0-306-80620-7 DA CAPO PB....................$27.95

Don **Cook**

The Long Fuse: How England Lost the American Colonies, 1760-1785

"This book by one of our best foreign correspondents brings new immediacy, color and insight to a forgotten dimension of the American Revolution. It is time for Americans to learn how the War for Independence struck the British" —Arthur Schlesinger, Jr.

0-87113-588-4 GROVE....................$24.00

0-87113-661-9 ATLANTIC MONTHLY PB....................$14.00

Edward **Countryman**

The American Revolution

"A balanced view of how the Revolution was made by a variety of social groups… and how, in turn, these groups were transformed by the Revolutionary experience"—Gary B. Nash, UCLA

EDITED BY ERIC FONER

0-8090-0162-4 FS&G PB....................$9.95

Theodore **Draper**

A Struggle for Power: The American Revolution

The great American historian delivers an extraordinary account of the origins and nature of the American Revolution. Rejecting the dominant view that ideology motivated the colonists to rebel, he shows that the struggle for power was an inevitable result of colonialism's economic constraints. "Fresh, detailed and crisp writing, and ideas are handled as skillfully as are men and mobs"—Esmond Wright

0-8129-2575-0 TIME BOOKS....................$35.00

Jack P. **Greene**, editor

Colonies to Nation, 1763-1789: A Documentary History of the American Revolution

0-393-09229-1 NORTON PB....................$18.95

Benjamin Franklin

Jonathan R. **Dull**

A Diplomatic History of the American Revolution

A good introduction. Interested readers should also look at R.R. Palmer's *The Age of the Democractic Revolution* for the European context of the war

0-300-03886-0 YALE PB....................$17.00

David Hackett **Fischer**

Paul Revere's Ride

When Paul Revere and his alarm riders set out on April 18, 1775, they did not call out that "the British are coming." In fact, most still considered themselves British. In the first serious look at a great mythical episode in the making of our republic, Fischer explores the complex figure of Paul Revere and the events leading up to that famous night

0-19-508847-6 OXFORD....................$30.00

0-19-509831-5 OXFORD PB....................$15.95

John J. **Gallagher**

The Battle of Brooklyn, 1776

The largest and bloodiest clash of the American Revolution, seen, despite its defeat for the colonists, as containing the kind of American courage and resolve that would result in independence

1-88511-902-X SARPEDON....................$24.95

Merrill **Jensen**

The Articles of Confederation: An Interpretation of the Social-Constitutional History of the American Revolution, 1774-1781

"…an admirable analysis. It presents, in succinct form, the results of a generation of study in this chapter of our history and summarizes fairly the conclusions of that study"—Henry Steele Commager

0-299-00204-7 WISCONSIN PB....................$15.50

Robert **Middlekauff**

The Glorious Cause: The American Revolution, 1763-1789

Proves that traditional narrative on a grand scale is still one of the most rewarding offerings of history

0-19-503575-5 OXFORD PB....................$18.95

Jack N. **Rakove**

The Beginnings of National Politics: An Interpretive History of the Continental Congress

0-8018-2864-3 JOHNS HOPKINS PB $15.95

John Philip **Reid**

Constitutional History of the American Revolution

An abridged edition of his four-volume work, which shows the significant role played by constitutional disputes in precipitating the American Revolution

0-299-14664-2 WISCONSIN PB $14.95

Barbara W. **Tuchman**

The First Salute

The author of *The Guns of August* and *A Distant Mirror* brings her talents to an episode of the Revolutionary War, showing how not only England and America were affected by the Revolution, but the rest of Europe as well

0-345-33667-4 BALLANTINE PB $14.00

Harry M. **Ward**

The American Revolution: Nationhood Achieved, 1763-1788

A scholarly, detailed, and measured overview of the Revolutionary experience

0-312-07162-0 ST. MARTIN'S PB $26.66

Gordon S. **Wood**

The Creation of the American Republic, 1776-1787

An important study emphasizing the role of ideas and their influence on founding the new nation

0-393-31040-X NORTON PB $14.95

The Radicalism of the American Revolution

0-679-73688-3 RANDOM HOUSE PB $15.00

Revolutionary Lives

Bernard **Bailyn**

Faces of Revolution: Personalities and Themes in the Struggle for American Independence

Collection of essays from the foremost historian of the American Revolution, winner of two Pulitzer Prizes: "explores revolutionary action as a study in character"—*Newsday*

0-394-49895-X KNOPF $29.95
0-679-73623-9 VINTAGE PB $16.00

Michelle A. **Bellesiles**

Revolutionary Outlaws: Ethan Allen and the Struggle for Independence on the Early American Frontier

Politics, biography, and social history in this analysis of Vermont and its formative role in frontier experience and revolution

0-8139-1603-8 VIRGINIA PB $17.50

Linda Grant **De Pauw**

Founding Mothers: Women of America in the Revolutionary Era

"A notable contribution toward dusting off women's history for young people"—*Booklist*

0-395-70109-0 SANDPIPER PB $5.95

A.J. **Langguth**

Patriots: The Men Who Started the American Revolution

0-671-67562-1 TOUCHSTONE PB $16.00

Benjamin **Quarles**

The Negro in the American Revolution

See also **HISTORY** under **AFRICAN-AMERICAN STUDIES**

08087808334 NORTH CAROLINA $27.50

George F. **Scheer** & Hugh F. **Rankin**

Rebels and Redcoats: The American Revolution Through the Eyes of Those Who Fought and Lived It

"I know of no other book where either the professional student or the general reader can attain, in one vivid apprehension, a more stimulating sense of what it truly was to have been there, of what it meant for humanity, patriot or redcoat, to have fought there"—Perry Miller

0-306-80307-0 DA CAPO PB $15.95

The Making of the Constitution

Long preoccupied by the motives of the members of the Philadelphia Convention, historians now seem uncertain about the precise mix of economic interests, democratic values, and conservative intentions that spurred the framers.

Bernard **Bailyn**, editor

The Debate on the Constitution

Employing newspaper articles, pamphlets, and letters, this collection captures the energy and the eloquence of Franklin, Madison, Jefferson, Washington, Patrick Henry, and other less recognized voices as they took part in the "bloodless revolution" that formed the government of the United States. Each volume includes the full texts of the Declaration of Independence, the Articles of Confederation, and the Constitution. "For Americans this is Shakespeare, and more. Not only is it wonderful writing, it is wonderful thinking"—Nina Totenberg

Volume 1 September 17, 1787 to January 12, 1788

See also **THE CONSTITUTION** under **LAW** in **SOCIAL STUDIES**

See also **LIBRARY OF AMERICA** in **LITERATURE OF THE AMERICAS**

0-940450-42-9 LIBRARY OF AMERICA $35.00

Volume 2 January 14, 1788 to August 9, 1788

0-940450-64-X LIBRARY OF AMERICA $35.00
0-940450-81-X BOXED SET $70.00

Charles A. **Beard**

An Economic Interpretation of the Constitution of the United States

With a new introduction by Forrest McDonald. The famous thesis, first published in 1913, that the document was shaped by men whose commercial interests were served by its provisions

0-02-902480-3 FREE PRESS PB $14.95

Richard **Beeman**, editor

Beyond Confederation: Origin of the Constitution and American National Identity

Essays that probe the ideological background of the Constitution, the rigors of its writing and ratification, and the problems it provoked and faced immediately afterward

0-8078-1719-8 NORTH CAROLINA $34.95
0-8078-4172-2 NORTH CAROLINA PB $13.95

Catherine Drinker **Bowen**

Miracle at Philadelphia: The Story of the Constitutional Convention, May to September 1787

FOREWORD BY WARREN E. BURGER

0-316-10398-5 LITTLE, BROWN PB $14.95

James MacGregor **Burns** & Stewart **Burns**

A People's Charter: The Pursuit of Rights in America

A history of the ideas that gave birth to the Bill of Rights—and the often ferocious struggles that have erupted around it in the last 200 years. "A majestic chronicle that covers history, political science and the philosophy behind the social contract…a bold and pathbreaking book"—*NY Times*

0-679-74172-0 VINTAGE PB $16.00

Carl Van **Doren**

The Great Rehearsal: The Story of the Making and Ratifying of the Constitution of the United States

A very readable day-to-day account

0-313-23492-2 GREENWOOD $65.00

Max **Farrand**

The Framing of the Constitution of the United States

A classic in American constitutional history, Farrand's famous account of the Federal Convention presents a vivid analysis of the conditions, the convictions, and the men who framed the Constitution of the United States

0-300-00079-0 YALE PB $15.00

Jerry **Fresia**

Toward an American Revolution: Exposing the Constitution and Other Illusions

Argues that the true intent of the Founding Fathers was to protect property and ensure that the poorer majority would have no real voice in political affairs

0-89608-297-0 SOUTH END PB $12.00

John A. **Garraty**, editor

Quarrels that Have Shaped the Constitution

Twenty leading historians describe landmark cases that have altered the Constitution

0-06-132084-6 HARPERCOLLINS PB....$19.58

Alexander Hamilton

Alexander **Hamilton** & others

The Federalist Papers

The original 18th-century text of the series of controversial essays advocating the popular ratification of the Constitution as a new charter of government. With Madison's marginal notations and useful, expert commentary by Wills

EDITED BY GARY WILLS

0-553-21340-7 BDD PB....$5.95

Angela Roddey **Holder**

The Meaning of the Constitution

The Constitution explained, phrase by phrase

FOREWORD BY HENRY STEELE COMMAGER

0-8120-3847-9 BARRONS PB....$11.95

Michael **Kammen**, editor

The Origins of the American Constitution: A Documentary History

The fundamental documents needed to understand the genesis and evolution of the US Constitution, edited by the Pulitzer Prize-winning historian

0-14-008744-4 PENGUIN PB....$12.95

Ralph **Ketcham**

The Anti-Federalist Papers and the Constitutional Convention Debates

The dissenting opinions of such statesmen as Patrick Henry and John DeWitt

0-451-62525-0 MENTOR PB....$7.99

Christopher **Lincoln Collier** & James **Lincoln Collier**

Decision in Philadelphia: The Constitutional Convention of 1787

A popular retelling

0-345-34652-1 BALLANTINE PB....$5.99

Jackson Turner **Main**

The Anti-Federalists: Critics of the Constitution, 1781-1788

0-393-00760-X NORTON PB....$11.95

Forrest **McDonald**

Novus Ordo Seclorum: The Intellectual Origin of the Constitution

"A realistic, tough-minded book about the role of ideas among practical men of affairs at a pivotal and difficult moment in human history"
—Michael Kammen

0-7006-0311-5 KANSAS PB....$9.95

Jack N. **Rakove**

Original Meanings: Politics and Ideas in the Making of the Constitution

An original examination of a key concept in constitutional interpretation: the framers' intentions. Setting the Constitution in its original context, and examining the debates surrounding its framing and ratification, Rakove allows us access into essential nuances that are vital to understanding the original intentions of both the framers and ratifiers, as well as the citizens they represented

0-394-57858-9 KNOPF....$35.00

Clinton **Rossiter**

1787: The Grand Convention

"No one has so successfully captured the human elements of the gathering at Philadelphia"
—from the Foreword by Richard B. Morris

0-393-30404-3 NORTON PB....$13.95

Herbert J. **Storing**

What the Anti-Federalists Were For: The Political Thought of the Opponents of the Constitution

Superb introduction to the thoughts and principles of the anti-Federalists, whose contibutions include the Bill of Rights and discussion of such modern concepts as big government and infringement of personal liberty

0-226-77574-7 CHICAGO PB....$6.95

Herbert J. **Storing**, editor

The Anti-Federalist: Writings by Opponents of the Constitution

"This abridgment provides us with the best of anti-Federalist thought, presented in sufficient detail so that we can more fully appreciate the dialogue that took place between the Federalists and the anti-Federalists and which, in fact, continues in contemporary American society"
—Ralph A. Rossum

0-226-77565-8 CHICAGO PB....$15.95

David B. **Szatmary**

Shays' Rebellion: The Making of an Agrarian Insurrection

A brief account of the 1786 rebellion that played a key role in strengthening the public desire for a strong, constitutional Federal government

0-87023-419-6 MASSACHUSETTS PB....$15.95

The New Nation

Henry **Adams**

History of the United States During the Administrations of Jefferson and Madison, Volume 1

"All things considered, I suspect that it is the greatest historical work in English, with the probable exception of *The Decline and Fall of the Roman Empire*...The history is penetrated with precise intelligence in all its parts: it is in this quality, I think, that it surpasses any historical masterpiece with which I am acquainted"—Yvor Winters

See also LIBRARY OF AMERICA in LITERATURE OF THE AMERICAS

0-940450-34-8 LIBRARY OF AMERICA....$35.00

History of the United States During the Administrations of Jefferson and Madison, Volume 2

See also LIBRARY OF AMERICA in LITERATURE OF THE AMERICAS

0-940450-35-6 VIKING....$40.00

The United States were supposed to have stabbed England in the back at the moment when her hands were tied, when her existence was in the most deadly peril and her anxieties were most heavy. England never could forgive treason so base and cowardice so vile. That Madison had been from the first a tool and accomplice of Bonaparte was thenceforward so fixed an idea in British history that time could not shake it. Indeed, so complicated and so historical had the causes of war become that no one even in America could explain or understand them, while Englishmen could see only that America required England as the price of peace to destroy herself by abandoning her naval power, and that England preferred to die fighting rather than to die by her own hand. The American party in England was extinguished; no further protest was heard against the war; and the British people thought moodily of revenge.

HISTORY OF THE UNITED STATES DURING THE ADMINISTRATIONS OF JEFFERSON AND MADISON

Henry Adams

Joyce **Appleby**
Capitalism and a New Social Order: The Republican Vision of the 1790s
Examines the fusion of ideas and circumstances that made possible the triumph of Jeffersonian Republicans, America's first popular political movement
0-8147-0583-9 NYU PB $15.00

Daniel J. **Boorstin**
The Lost World of Thomas Jefferson
The concepts of the Jeffersonian Circle: God, nature, equality, toleration, education, and government, and the worldview that underlies them
See also **INTELLECTUAL HISTORY** under **TOPICS IN AMERICAN STUDIES**
0-226-06497-2 CHICAGO PB $14.95

Roger H. **Brown**
The Republic in Peril, 1812
0-393-00578-X NORTON PB $9.95

Harry L. **Coles**
The War of 1812
A compact history
0-226-11350-7 CHICAGO PB $16.95

Marcus **Cunliffe**
The Nation Takes Shape, 1789-1837
Provides excellent background and analysis of the period
0-226-12667-6 CHICAGO PB $14.95

Stanley **Elkins** & Eric **McKitrick**
The Age of Federalism: The Early American Republic, 1788-1800
A comprehensive synthesis of the problems faced by the new nation and the individuals—Washington, Hamilton, Adams, Madison, Jefferson—who tried to solve them
See also **THE MAKING OF THE CONSTITUTION**
0195068905 OXFORD $39.95
0-19-509381-X OXFORD PB $19.95

Donald R. **Hickey**
The War of 1812: A Forgotten Conflict
0-252-01613-0 ILLINOIS PB $32.50

Ralph **Ketcham**
Presidents Above Party: The First American Presidency, 1789-1829
0-8078-4179-X NORTH CAROLINA PB $14.95

Lloyd S. **Kramer**, editor
Paine and Jefferson on Liberty
The major texts from the two most significant thinkers on liberty in America, part of the *Milestones of Thought* series
0-8044-6382-4 UNGAR PB $9.95

Ernest R. **May**
The Making of the Monroe Doctrine
The doctrine was as much the work of England's Canning as America's John Quincy Adams
0-674-54341-6 HARVARD PB $14.95

Richard K. **Mathews**
The Radical Politics of Thomas Jefferson: A Revisionist View
"Liberals and the Jefferson cult will hate it. Conservatives and Hamiltonians will love it...because Mathews has demonstrated, with Jefferson's own words, that the man was precisely the kind of wild-eyed political quack that the 'high Federalists' understood him to be"—Forrest McDonald
0-7006-0293-3 KANSAS PB $7.95

John Quincy Adams

Forrest **McDonald**
The Presidency of Thomas Jefferson
"An elegant and revelatory analysis"
—Gore Vidal
0-7006-0330-1 KANSAS PB $9.95

David R. **Palmer**
1794: America, Its Army, and the Birth of a Nation
"Palmer takes a 'history as story' approach in describing how the nation's army took shape"
—*Publishers Weekly*
0-89141-561-0 BERKELEY PB $14.95

George Green **Shackleford**
Thomas Jefferson's Travels in Europe, 1784-1789
"To understand how Jefferson completed his metamorphosis from a talented provincial (into America's most sophisticated national leader) it is necessary to reconstitute what he saw on his European journeys, to describe where he lived in Europe and to speak of how his European friends influenced him"
—from *Thomas Jefferson's Travels in Europe*
0-8018-4843-1 JOHNS HOPKINS $34.95

James Roger **Sharp**
American Politics in the Early Republic: The New Nation in Crisis
"The liveliest exposition yet of the roots of our present political power struggles"
—William Safire
0-300-05530-7 YALE $35.00
0-300-06519-1 YALE PB $15.00

Thomas P. **Slaughter**
The Whiskey Rebellion: Frontier Epilogue to the American Revolution
It took 13,000 soldiers in 1794 to crush the first large-scale resistance to federal law under the Constitution
0-19-505191-2 OXFORD PB $11.95

Marshall **Smelser**
The Democratic Republic, 1801-1815
An introduction to the era of Jefferson, Madison, Randolph, Burr, and Pickering; part of the *New American Nation* series
INTRODUCTION BY HENRY STEELE COMMAGER & RICHARD B. MORRIS
0-88133-668-8 WAVELAND PB $14.95

Daniel E. **Williams**
Pillars of Salt: An Anthology of Early American Criminal Narratives
0-945612-31-1 MADISON $34.95
0-945612-37-0 MADISON PB $19.95

James S. **Young**
The Washington Community: 1800-1828
Fascinating study of the difficulties of establishing a truly representative national government
0-231-08381-5 COLUMBIA PB $19.50

Antebellum America and the Age of Jackson

Historians have had a special affinity for the Jacksonian era because it seemed to parallel the politics of the mid-20th century: Andrew Jackson and Franklin Roosevelt both represented the forces of democracy in the battle against special privilege. Historians now see that a more complex pattern of social conflict spurred the vigorous public life of the 1830s. They've begun to wonder, too, just how democratic the vaunted "Jacksonian democracy" really was.

Tyler **Anbinder**
Nativism & Slavery: The Northern Know Nothings and the Politics of the 1850s
First book-length study of the northern party whose phenomenal success in the pre-Civil War era was linked to its anti-immigrant and anti-Catholic political agenda as well as to the firm stance its northern members took against the extension of slavery. A 1992 *New York Times* Notable Book of the Year
0-19-508922-7 OXFORD PB $16.95

George **Dangerfield**
The Era of Good Feelings
The years of transition from Jefferson to Jackson, from a benign to a strong central government. By the Pulitzer Prize-winning historian
0-929587-14-6 DEE PB $14.95

Donald B. **Cole**

The Presidency of Andrew Jackson

"This is the best account I have read of the presidency of Andrew Jackson. [It] is distinguished for its erudition, lucidity, fairness, and balance, while finding the essentials of such issues as … Indian removal, nullification, the bank war, the emergence of the two-party system, and the surprisingly complex character of the Old Hero himself"—Robert McColley, *American Historical Review*

0-7006-0600-9 KANSAS $29.95

Henry Steele **Commager**

Commager on Tocqueville

0-8262-0897-5 MISSOURI $24.95
0-8262-0941-6 MISSOURI PB $14.95

Alexis de Tocqueville

Richard E. **Ellis**

The Union at Risk: Jacksonian Democracy, States' Rights and the Nullification Crisis

"Shows how the states-rights bulwark of Jefferson's yeoman republic became the bulwark of slavery"—Charles Sellers

0-19-506187-X OXFORD PB $17.95

Grant **Foreman**

Indian Removal: The Emigration of the Five Civilized Tribes of Indians

The forced removals to Indian Territory in the 1830s

See also **SOUTHEASTERN** under **REGIONAL AND TRIBAL STUDIES** under **NATIVE AMERICAN CULTURES: NORTH AMERICA**

0-8061-1172-0 OKLAHOMA PB $18.95

William W. **Freehling**

The Road to Disunion: Secessionists at Bay, 1776-1854

Sweeping political and social history of the antebellum South. "A brilliant synthesis" —*The Washington Times*

0-19-507259-6 OXFORD PB $18.95

Marvin **Meyers**

Jacksonian Persuasion: Politics and Belief

0-8047-0506-2 STANFORD PB $12.95

Edward **Pessen**

Jacksonian America: Society, Personality, and Politics

In Pessen's own words, "The time has come for a comprehensive reexamination of the Jacksonian era." A strong statement of newer research on "the inegalitarian society"

0-252-01237-2 ILLINOIS PB $14.95

Robert **Remini**

Andrew Jackson and the Bank War

Remini is the leading authority on the Jacksonian era. His prize-winning biography of Jackson is listed in the biography section of "American History to the Civil War"

0-393-09757-9 NORTON PB $7.95

The Revolutionary Age of Andrew Jackson

Superb narrative history, from one of the foremost historians of the Jacksonian era

0-06-132074-9 HARPERCOLLINS PB $13.50

Anne C. **Rose**

Voices of the Marketplace: American Thought and Culture, 1830-1860

A reinterpretation of antebellum culture, focusing on Christianity, democracy, and capitalism

0-8057-9075-6 TWAYNE PB $15.95

Arthur M. **Schlesinger**, Jr.

The Age of Jackson

The classic analogy between the New Deal and the Jacksonian era

0-316-77343-3 LITTLE, BROWN PB $17.95

Andrew Jackson

Alexis **de Tocqueville**

Democracy in America

"America," Tocqueville wrote to John Stuart Mill, "was only my framework; democracy was my subject." A 1960s translation of Tocqueville's masterpiece

TRANSLATED BY GEORGE LAWRENCE

0-394-42186-8 KNOPF $50.00
0-06-091522-6 HARPERCOLLINS PB $20.00

Paul A. **Varg**

U.S. Foreign Relations, 1820-1860

0-87013-212-1 MICHIGAN STATE $15.00

Anthony F.C. **Wallace**

The Long, Bitter Trail: Andrew Jackson and the Indians

"This informative, insightful and sobering study deserves the attention of all who would understand American Indian policy, not just in Jackson's period but in our own" —Howard Lamar, Yale

0-8090-1552-8 HILL & WANG PB $7.95

The Mexican War

John S.D. **Eisenhower**

So Far from God: The U.S. War with Mexico, 1846-48

"A brilliant match of painstaking scholarship and engrossing interpretation"—James A. Michener

0-385-41214-2 ANCHOR PB $14.95

Robert W. **Johannsen**

To the Halls of Montezuma: The Mexican War in the American Imagination

0-19-503518-6 OXFORD $35.00
0-19-504981-0 OXFORD PB $17.95

Otis A. **Singletary**

The Mexican War

0-226-76061-8 CHICAGO PB $12.95

Slavery and Black Lives

Roger D. **Abrahams**

Singing the Master: The Emergence of African-American Culture in the Plantation South

"Impressive…A scrupulously researched work enlarging our understanding of an integral aspect of slave culture" —*Washington Post Book World*

0-14-017919-4 PENGUIN PB $12.95

Terry **Alford**

Prince Among Slaves

0-19-504223-9 OXFORD PB $11.95

Ira **Berlin**

Slaves Without Masters: The Free Negro in the Antebellum South

How the thousands of Southern blacks who enjoyed freedom before the Civil War tried to maintain their liberty within the grip of the slave system

1-56584-028-3 NEW PRESS PB $14.95

Ira **Berlin** & others

Slaves No More: Three Essays on Emancipation and the Civil War

Three essays on the destruction of slavery and the redefinition of freedom. Drawn from *Freedom: A Documentary History of Emancipation, 1861-1867.* "This generation's most significant encounter with the American past"—*NY Times*

0-521-43692-3 CAMBRIDGE PB $13.95

John W. **Blassingame**

The Slave Community: Plantation Life in the Antebellum South

See also SLAVERY under HISTORY under AFRICAN-AMERICAN STUDIES

0-19-502563-6 OXFORD PB $16.95

Madeline **Burnside** & Rosemarie **Robotham**, editors

Spirits of the Passage: The Transatlantic Slave Trade in the Seventeenth Century

0-684-81819-1 SIMON & SCHUSTER $35.00

Leonard P. **Curry**

The Free Black in Urban America, 1800-1850: The Shadow of the Dream

0-226-13125-4 CHICAGO PB $17.95

David Brion **Davis**

The Problem of Slavery in Western Culture

0-19-505639-6 OXFORD PB $16.95

Slavery and Human Progress

A complete survey covering slavery from the early expansion of Europe to the present

0-19-503439-2 OXFORD $40.00

0-19-503733-2 OXFORD PB $13.95

Stanley M. **Elkins**

Slavery: A Problem in American Institutional and Intellectual Life

0-226-20477-4 CHICAGO PB $14.95

Robert W. **Fogel**

Without Consent or Contract: The Rise and Fall of American Slavery

0-393-30753-0 NORTON PB $14.95

Elizabeth **Fox-Genovese**

Within the Plantation Household: Black and White Women of the South

Argues that class and race did affect women's experiences and that slaves and slaveholders were never linked in sisterhood

See also SLAVERY under HISTORY under AFRICAN-AMERICAN STUDIES

0-8078-1808-9 NORTH CAROLINA $39.95

0-8078-4232-X NORTH CAROLINA PB $16.95

Eugene D. **Genovese**

Roll, Jordan, Roll: The World the Slaves Made

An enduring classic. "Genovese's great gift is his ability to penetrate the minds of both slaves and masters, revealing not only how they viewed themselves and each other, but also how their contradictory perceptions interacted"
—David Brion Davis, *NY Times Book Review*

See also SLAVERY under HISTORY under AFRICAN-AMERICAN STUDIES

0-394-71652-3 RANDOM HOUSE PB $18.00

The Slaveholders' Dilemma: Freedom and Progress in Southern Conservative Thought, 1820-1860

0-87249-995-2 SOUTH CAROLINA PB $12.95

The World the Slaveholders Made: Two Essays in Interpretation

A comparative history of slavery and the Virginia pro-slavery ideologue George Fitzhugh

See also THE ANTEBELLUM SOUTH under AMERICAN REGIONAL HISTORY: THE WEST AND THE SOUTH

0-8195-6204-1 WESLEYAN PB $19.95

Stanley **Harold**

The Abolitionists and the South, 1831-1861

Argues for greater involvement in abolitionism by the border slave states. "This is a pathbreaking work that will significantly alter interpretations of abolitionism"
—James L. Huston

0-8131-1906-5 KENTUCKY $29.95

Michael P. **Johnson** & James L. **Roark**

Black Masters: A Free Family of Color in the Old South

0-393-30314-4 NORTON PB $14.95

Leon F. **Litwack**

Been in the Storm So Long: The Aftermath of Slavery

Explores the lives of ex-slaves and their masters to uncover the mutual dependency of blacks and whites during and after the Civil War

0-394-74398-9 RANDOM HOUSE PB $17.78

Leslie H. **Owens**

This Species of Property: Slave Life and Culture in the Old South

0-19-502245-9 OXFORD PB $10.95

Albert J. **Raboteau**

Slave Religion: The Invisible Institution in the Antebellum South

Slave religion from its African roots through its reinterpretation under Christianity

0-19-502705-1 OXFORD PB $14.95

Mechal **Sobel**

Trabelin' On: The Slave Journey to an Afro-Baptist Faith

A religious history of the slaves and free blacks of antebellum America. "Takes seriously the religion of black people and shows its creative power to construct a sacred cosmos"—Andrew E. Murray, *Journal of American History*

See also RELIGION under CULTURE under AFRICAN-AMERICAN STUDIES

0-8371-9887-9 GREENWOOD $79.50

0-691-00603-2 PRINCETON PB $16.95

Kenneth M. **Stampp**

The Peculiar Institution

0-679-72307-2 VINTAGE PB $13.00

Hugh **Thomas**

The Slave Trade

0-684-81063-8 SIMON & SCHUSTER $35.00

Reformers and Abolitionists

Merton L. **Dillon**

Abolitionists: The Growth of a Dissenting Minority

0-393-00957-2 NORTON PB $8.95

Ann **Douglas**

The Feminization of American Culture

Traces today's culture back to its Victorian roots

See also SUFFRAGE, LIBERATION, AND BEYOND under AMERICAN HISTORY under WOMEN'S STUDIES in SOCIAL STUDIES

0-385-24241-7 ANCHOR PB $14.00

Barbara L. **Epstein**

The Politics of Domesticity: Women, Evangelism, and Temperance in Nineteenth-Century America

0-8195-6184-3 WESLEYAN PB $13.95

Paul E. **Johnson**

A Shopkeeper's Millennium: Society and Revivals in Rochester, New York, 1815-1837

0-8090-0136-5 FS&G PB $9.95

Stephen B. **Oates**

To Purge this Land with Blood: A Biography of John Brown

Hanged for leading an armed insurrection in 1859, Brown had planned to found an abolitionist republic and wage guerrilla war on slavery

0-87023-458-7 MASSACHUSETTS PB $20.95

John Brown

Steven **Mintz**

Moralists and Modernizers: America's Pre-Civil War Reformers

Fascinating analysis of the America's first age of reform and its roots not only in fears of social disorder, family fragmentation, and widening class divisions but in a millennialist sense of possibility

0-8018-5081-9 JOHNS HOPKINS PB $13.95

James B. **Stewart**

Holy Warriors: The Abolitionists and American Slavery

0-8090-0123-3 FS&G PB $8.95

Ronald G. **Walters**

The Antislavery Appeal: American Abolitionism After 1830

0-393-95444-7 NORTON PB $6.95

The Romantic Age and the American Renaissance

Carl J. **Guarneri**

The Utopian Alternative: Fourierism in Nineteenth Century America

Traces the American Fourierist movement from its roots in religious, social, and economic upheaval of the 1830s through its bold communal efforts of the 1840s to its lingering twilight after the Civil War. "This work should stand as a scholarly landmark for another half-century"—*American Historical Review*

0-8014-8197-X CORNELL PB $17.95

Ralph Waldo Emerson

David S. **Reynolds**

Beneath the American Renaissance: The Subversive Imagination in the Age of Emerson and Melville

See also **THE 19TH CENTURY** under **GENERAL STUDIES TO 1900** under **AMERICAN LITERATURE: ANTHOLOGIES AND CRITICAL STUDIES** in **LITERATURE OF THE AMERICAS**

0-674-06565-4 HARVARD PB $19.50

Biography

Lester J. **Cappon**

The Adams-Jefferson Letters: The Complete Correspondence Between Thomas Jefferson and Abigail and John Adams

Begins in 1777, ceases in 1801 after Jefferson's defeat of Adams for the presidency, resumes in 1812, and continues until the death of both on July 4, 1826

0-8078-4230-3 NORTH CAROLINA PB $19.95

Peter **Shaw**

The Character of John Adams

0-393-00856-8 NORTON PB $7.95

Edith B. **Gelles**

Portia: The World of Abigail Adams

0-253-32553-6 INDIANA $25.95

Paul C. **Nagel**

The Adams Women: Abigail and Louisa Adams, Their Sisters and Daughters

0-19-503874-6 OXFORD $30.00

Thomas P. **Slaughter**

The Natures of John and William Bartram

See also **NATURE STUDY** in **SCIENCE**

0-679-43045-8 KNOPF $27.50

John Mack **Faragher**

Daniel Boone: The Life and Legend of an American Pioneer

"A brilliant biography"—*NY Times Book Review*

0-8050-3007-7 OWLET PB $14.95

Nat **Brandt**

The Congressman Who Got Away with Murder

0-8156-0277-4 SYRACUSE PB $14.95

Stephen **Burroughs**

Memoirs of Stephen Burroughs

The shady colonial character whose alleged indiscretions included impersonating a minister on the eve of Shays' Rebellion, counterfeiting, and committing robbery and rape

1-55553-035-4 NORTHEASTERN PB $16.95

William S. **McFeely**

Frederick Douglass

Orator, writer, and abolitionist leader, Douglass was one of the most influential voices in the struggle against slavery. McFeely gives us not a hagiography but a rounded portrait of a complex figure

0-393-02823-2 NORTON $24.95

Francis **Jennings**

Benjamin Franklin, Politician

0-393-03983-8 NORTON $27.50

John **Niven**

John C. Calhoun and the Price of the Union

0-8071-1858-3 LOUSIANA STATE PB $12.95

John C. Calhoun

Esmond **Wright**

Franklin of Philadelphia

0-674-31810-2 HARVARD PB $14.95

Forrest **McDonald**

Alexander Hamilton

A serious biography focusing on Hamilton's abilities and accomplishments as the first Secretary of the Treasury

0-393-30048-X NORTON PB $15.95

David S. **Lifton**

The Raven: A Biography of Sam Houston

A Pulitzer Prize-winning biography of the rebel elected president of the Republic of Texas in 1836

INTRODUCTION BY HENRY STEELE COMMAGER

0-292-77040-5 TEXAS PB $14.95

Robert V. **Remini**

The Life of Andrew Jackson

A new one-volume version of Remini's prizewinning 3-volume biography of Jackson, portrayed here as heroic and larger than life

0-14-013267-8 PENGUIN PB $13.95

John William **Ward**

Andrew Jackson: Symbol for an Age

How Jackson's image as a victorious general, rough-hewn frontiersman, and man of iron will made him the legendary figure of his age

0-19-500699-2 OXFORD PB $10.95

Fawn M. **Brodie**

Thomas Jefferson: An Intimate History

Highly controversial biography that makes much of Jefferson's relationship with his slave mistress, Sally Hemmings

0-553-27335-3 BDD PB $7.99

Noble E. **Cunningham**, Jr.

In Pursuit of Reason: The Life of Thomas Jefferson

0-8071-1375-1 LOUSIANA STATE $24.95
0-345-35380-3 BALLANTINE PB $14.00

Dumas **Malone**

Jefferson and His Time

Volume 1: Jefferson the Virginian

0-316-54474-4 LITTLE, BROWN $29.95
0-316-54472-8 LITTLE, BROWN PB $15.95

Volume 2: Jefferson and the Rights of Man

0-316-54472-8 LITTLE, BROWN PB $15.95

Volume 3: Jefferson and the Ordeal of liberty

0-316-54475-2 LITTLE, BROWN $29.95
0-316-54469-8 LITTLE, BROWN PB $15.95

Volume 4: Jefferson the President: First term, 1801-1805

0-316-54467-1 LITTLE, BROWN $29.95
0-316-54466-3 LITTLE, BROWN PB $15.95

Volume 5: Jefferson the President: Second term

0-316-54465-5 LITTLE, BROWN $29.95
0-316-54464-7 LITTLE, BROWN PB $15.95

Volume 6: The Sage of Monticello

0-316-54463-9 LITTLE, BROWN $29.95
0-316-54478-7 LITTLE, BROWN PB $15.95

Jack **McLaughlin**

Jefferson and Monticello: The Biography of a Builder

National Book Award nominee (1988)

See also **INDIVIDUAL ARCHITECTS** under **AMERICAN ARCHITECTURE TO 1900** in **ARCHITECTURE, DESIGN, AND HOMES**

0-8050-1463-2 HOLT PB $14.95

Merrill D. **Peterson**

Thomas Jefferson and the New Nation

0-19-501909-1 OXFORD PB $24.95

James Morton **Smith**

The Republic of Letters: The Correspondence Between Thomas Jefferson and James Madison

The complete correspondence, in three volumes, between the two greatest philosopher-statesmen of the American Enlightenment

0-393-03691-X NORTON $150.00

Claude-Anne **Lopez** & others

The Private Franklin: The Man and His Family

"Seen not as a scientist, philosopher, and a statesman, but as a son, brother, husband, uncle, father, and grandfather"—*Library Journal*

0-393-30227-X NORTON PB $9.95

Susan R. **Stein**

The World of Thomas Jefferson at Monticello

A comprehensive presentation of the wonderful objects and furniture with which Jefferson filled his home

See also **INDIVIDUAL ARCHITECTS** under **AMERICAN ARCHITECTURE TO 1900** in **ARCHITECTURE, DESIGN, AND HOMES**

0-8109-3967-3 ABRAMS $65.00

Stella **Tillyard**

Aristocrats: Caroline, Emily, Louisa, and Sarah Lennox, 1740-1832

"*Aristocrats* has extraordinary density and breadth... This is an absolutely splendid book and a work of art as well. History is the category, but history of a relatively rare sort: popular history, devoid of ideological bias or careerism, written at a level that elevates it to high history"—Jonathan Yardley, *Washington Post*

0-374-52447-5 NOONDAY PB $16.00

Charles F. **Hobson**

The Great Chief Justice: John Marshall and the Rule of Law

Hobson, the editor of Marshall's papers, on the life of Marshall's mind. Impressively researched and clearly written

0-7006-0788-9 KANSAS $35.00

Esther **Forbes**

Paul Revere and the World He Lived In

A Pulitzer Prize-winning biography (1943); part of the American Heritage Library

0-8446-6526-6 SMITH $21.05
0-395-08370-2 HOUGHTON MIFFLIN PB $14.95

John D. **Alden**

George Washington: A Biography

0-8071-1153-8 LOUSIANA STATE PB $14.95

James T. **Flexner**

George Washington

Volume 1 The Forge of Experience, 1732-1775

0-316-28597-8 LITTLE, BROWN $40.00

Volume 2 In the American Revolution, 1775-1783

0-316-28595-1 LITTLE, BROWN $40.00

Volume 3 And the New Nation, 1783-1793

0-316-28600-1 LITTLE, BROWN $40.00

Volume 4 Anguish and Farewell, 1793-1799

0-316-28602-8 LITTLE, BROWN $35.00

Barry **Schwartz**

George Washington: The Making of an American Symbol

0-02-928141-5 FREE PRESS $35.00
0-8014-9747-7 CORNELL PB $14.95

George Washington

Mason Locke **Weems**

The Life of Washington

INTRODUCTION BY PETER S. ONUF

1-56324-699-6 SHARPE PB $15.95

Richard Norton **Smith**

Patriarch: George Washington and the New American Nation

Smith offers up a George Washington more interesting and human than any previously seen—vain, but a hero nonetheless

0-395-52442-3 HOUGHTON MIFFLIN $24.95

Merrill D. **Peterson**

The Great Triumvirate: Webster, Clay, and Calhoun

A sweeping biography of the foremost statesmen who personified their respective regions in antebellum America. "[Peterson's] details enable us to recognize how little the practices of parliamentary democracy have changed" —*New Yorker*

0-19-503877-0 OXFORD $35.00

The Civil War and Reconstruction

The literature of the Civil War—the "American Iliad," as Gore Vidal calls it—is enormous. Much of it is popular military history for the enthusiast. The titles here are only a sample of a much larger field, which is best surveyed in a good library. Many of these books, while exploring the larger context of the war, focus on specific events and highlight their cataclysmic effects on the young nation. *Battle Cry of Freedom* relates how George Ticknor, a retired Harvard professor, wrote in 1869 that the Civil War created a "great gulf between what happened before in our century and what has happened since, or what is likely to happen hereafter. It does not seem to me as if I were living in the country in which I was born."

Surveys of the Civil War Era: 1845-1877

Curt **Anders**

Hearts in Conflict: A One-Volume History of the Civil War

More than just recounting battles, noted author Anders portrays the social history, political atmosphere, and personalities that led America into its most bloody, perilous, and tragic war. Fully illustrated

1-55972-184-7 BIRCH LANE $29.95

James M. **McPherson**

Battle Cry of Freedom: The Eve of the Civil War

Starting with the war with Mexico, McPherson traces the contradictions and confusions that separated North and South to the point of war—and carries the story to Appomattox. A national bestseller and winner of the Pulitzer Prize

0-19-503863-0 OXFORD $45.00
0-345-35942-9 BALLANTINE PB $18.00

Richard H. **Sewell**

A House Divided: Sectionalism and Civil War, 1848-1865

"The North and South may not have been distinct cultures, but by mid-century each section *thought* of itself as possessing a distinct and superior way of life, one shaped most profoundly by the absence or presence of human bondage"—Richard H. Sewell

0-8018-3532-1 JOHNS HOPKINS PB $11.95

Irwin **Unger**

Instant American History: Through the Civil War and Reconstruction

Amusing bite-size summaries with cartoons, illustrations, and lists from a Puliter Prize-winning historian

0-449-90695-7 FAWCETT PB $10.00

General Histories of the War: 1861-1865

Bruce **Catton**

The American Heritage New History of the Civil War

EDITED BY JAMES MCPHERSON

0-670-86804-3 VIKING $50.00

Martin **Crawford**

William Howard Russell's Civil War

Russell's *My Diary, North and South,* written in the 1860's while he was the *Times* of London's war correspondent, formed contemporary British opinion of the Civil War. These are the notes on which he based the work: his impressions of living in 19th-century America—its food, fashions, politicians, and soldiers—his meetings with Seward, Lincoln, and McClellan, his tours of prisons and cotton fields. Includes illustrations and an excellent biography of Russell by the editor

0-8203-1369-6 GEORGIA $40.00

William C. **Davies** & Bell I. **Wiley**, editors

Photographic History of the Civil War

Over 4,000 photographs exhaustively document the leaders, heroes, campaigns, and battles of the Civil War; accompanied by informative, comprehensive, and scholarly texts

Volume I
Fort Sumter to Gettysburg

1-88482-208-8 BLACK DOG $39.98

Volume II
Vicksburg to Appomattox

1-88482-209-6 BLACK DOG $39.98

Shelby **Foote**

The Civil War: A Narrative

A panoramic military study, slightly biased toward the Confederate viewpoint

Volume 1
Fort Sumter to Perryville

0-394-74623-6 VINTAGE PB $24.00

Volume 2
Fredericksburg to Meridian

0-394-74621-X VINTAGE PB $24.00

Volume 3
Red River to Appomattox

0-394-74622-8 VINTAGE PB $24.00

Margaret **Leech**

Reveille in Washington, 1860-1865

A Pulitzer Prize-winning (1942) history of Washington, D.C., during the war

0-88184-732-1 CARROLL & GRAF PB $12.95

John **MacDonald**

Great Battles of the Civil War

A glorious picture book that uses computer graphics to recreate the great battles

0-02-034554-2 MACMILLAN PB $22.95

James **McPherson**

Drawn with the Sword: Reflections on the American Civil War

0-19-509679-7 OXFORD $25.00

James M. **McPherson**

What They Fought For, 1861-1865

An eye-opening study of Civil War ideology by a Pulitzer Prize-winning historian

0-8071-1904-0 LOUSIANA STATE $16.95
0-385-47634-5 ANCHOR PB $10.00

Phillip Shaw **Paludan**

A People's Contest: The Union and the Civil War, 1861-1865

Chapters include "Congress and the 'Capitalists" and "Frankenstein and Everyman: Sherman, Grant, and Modern War"

0-06-015903-0 HARPERCOLLINS PB $27.95

Brian C. **Pohanka** & Constance **Sullivan**, editors

Landscapes of the Civil War

0-679-44178-6 KNOPF $40.00

Stephen W. **Sears**, editor

Civil War: The Best of American Heritage

0-395-61905-X AMERICAN HERITAGE $19.95

Geoffrey C. **Ward** & others

The Civil War: An Illustrated History

The famous illustrated account of the most important event in U.S. history, based on the award-winning PBS series now in paperback. National Book Critics Circle Award winner Ward wrote the text with the Burnses, the series producers; five historians, including Shelby Foote and C. Vann Woodward, contribute essays. Includes a frameable map

0-394-56285-2 KNOPF $60.00
0-679-74277-8 KNOPF PB $35.00

Reference

Mark M. **Boatner III**

The Civil War Dictionary

Over 4000 entries including 2000 biographical sketches, major battles, lesser engagements and skirmishes, weapons, military terms and definitions; 86 specially prepared maps and diagrams; all carefully cross-referenced

0-8129-1689-1 MCKAY $30.00

Patricia L. **Faust**, editor

Historical Times Illustrated Encyclopedia of the Civil War

0-06-181261-7 HARPER & ROW $39.95
0-06-273116-5 HARPERPERENNIAL PB $27.50

E.B. **Long** & Barbara **Long**

The Civil War Day by Day: An Almanac, 1861-1865

0-306-80255-4 DA CAPO PB $22.50

The Gathering Storm

"As to the policy I 'seem to be pursuing,' as you say, I have not meant to leave any one in doubt. I would save the Union. I would save it the shortest way under the Constitution. The sooner the national authority can be restored, the nearer the Union will be 'the Union as it was.' If there be those who would not save the Union unless they could at the same time save slavery, I do not agree with them. If there be those who would not save the Union unless they could at the same time destroy slavery, I do not agree with them. My paramount objective in this struggle is to save the Union, and is not either to save or to destroy slavery. If I could save the Union without freeing any slave, I would do it; and if I could save it by freeing some and leaving others alone, I would also do that. What I do about slavery, and the colored race, I do because I believe it helps to save the Union; and what I forbear, I forbear because I do not believe it would help to save the Union."
—Abraham Lincoln in a letter to Horace Greeley, editor of the New York *Tribune*, published August 22, 1862

Paul M. **Angle**, editor

Created Equal?: The Complete Lincoln-Douglas Debates of 1858

0-226-02084-3 CHICAGO PB $18.95

David Herbert **Donald**

Lincoln Reconsidered: Essays on the Civil War Era

0-394-70190-9 VINTAGE PB $11.00

Paul **Finkelman**, editor

His Soul Goes Marching On: Responses to John Brown and the Harper's Ferry Raid

Ten essays on Brown's legacy. "By illuminating the complex meanings of John Brown's raid as well as the American and European reactions to his martyrdom, the authors move well beyond the specific event. They enrich our understanding of the Civil War"—David Brion Davis

0-8139-1537-6 VIRGINIA PB $19.95

Eric **Foner**

Free Soil, Free Labor, Free Men: The Ideology of the Republican Party Before the Civil War

A significant reevaluation of the causes of the war

0-19-501352-2 OXFORD PB $10.95

Oscar **Handlin** & Lillian **Handlin**

Abraham Lincoln and the Union

0-673-39340-2 FORESMAN PB $16.20

Michael F. **Holt**

The Political Crisis of the 1850s

0-393-95370-X NORTON PB $9.95

Robert W. **Johannsen**, editor

The Lincoln-Douglas Debates of 1858

0-19-500921-5 OXFORD PB $15.95

David M. **Potter**

Lincoln and His Party in the Secession Crisis

0-8071-2027-8 LOUSIANA STATE PB $16.95

David M. **Potter** & Don **Fehrenbacher**

The Impending Crisis, 1848-1861

An often brilliant political history of the collision of North and South over slavery

0-06-131929-5 HARPERCOLLINS PB $21.60

Edward J. **Renehan**, Jr.

The Secret Six: The True Tale of the Men Who Conspired with John Brown

"In vivid prose, *The Secret Six* unravels the mystery of the six prominent abolitionists who supported John Brown but abandoned him to his fate after the ill-starred raid at Harper's Ferry. Edward Renehan has made an important contribution to our understanding of the Civil War and its causes"—James M. McPherson

0-517-59028-X CROWN $25.00

Kenneth M. **Stampp**

America in 1857: A Nation on the Brink

A fine portrait of a decisive—and disastrous—year, from the dean of Civil War historians

0-19-503902-5 OXFORD $35.00
0-19-507481-5 OXFORD PB $16.95

The Causes of the Civil War

Blends the conclusions of historians with the writings of contemporaries. Excerpts from the Lincoln-Douglas debates and vivid commentaries by Horace Greeley, John C. Calhoun, and Jefferson Davis are included in this revised edition

0-8446-2993-6 SMITH $18.30
0-671-62237-4 TOUCHSTONE PB $10.00

The Imperiled Union: Essays on the Background of the Civil War

The long-standing controversy about the cause and inevitability of the sectional crisis as well as other key questions

0-19-502991-7 OXFORD PB $12.95

The Confederacy

Burke **Davis**

The Long Surrender: The Collapse of the Confederacy and the Flight of Jefferson Davis

0-679-72409-5 VINTAGE PB $14.00

Jefferson Davis

Jefferson **Davis**

The Rise and Fall of the Confederate Government

Davis was in his late '60s when he began this long, carefully researched account of the secessionist government over which he presided. With a foreword by James M. McPherson

Volume 1

0-306-80418-2 DA CAPO PB $17.95

Volume 2

0-306-80419-0 DA CAPO PB $17.95

William C. **Davis**

"A Government of Our Own": The Making of the Confederacy

A definitive account of the formation of the Southern Confederacy and its leading personalities

0-02-907735-4 FREE PRESS $27.95

Clement **Eaton**

History of the Southern Confederacy

0-02-908710-4 FREE PRESS PB $15.95

Lacy K. **Ford**, Jr.

Origins of Southern Radicalism: The South Carolina Upcountry, 1800-1860

This new study analyzes the circumstances and values of white society in a hotbed of proslavery Southern radicalism

0-19-506961-7 OXFORD PB $18.95

Rod **Gragg**, editor

The Illustrated Confederate Reader

A collection of personal experiences and eyewitness accounts by Southern soldiers and civilians

0-06-092074-2 HARPERCOLLINS PB $18.00

David S. **Heidler**

Pulling the Temple Down: The Fire-Eaters and the Destruction of the Union

The first comprehensive study of the political mavericks who led the fight for secession

0-8117-0634-6 STACKPOLE $22.95

Robert Selph **Henry**

The Story of the Confederacy

0-306-80370-4 DA CAPO PB $14.95

Mark E. **Neely**, Jr.

The Confederate Image: Prints of the Lost Cause

The popular lithographs and engravings cherished by Southerners after the Civil War

0-8078-1742-2 NORTH CAROLINA $45.00

George **Rable**

The Confederate Republic: A Revolution Against Politics

0-8078-2144-6 NORTH CAROLINA $34.95

William Robert **Taylor**

Cavalier and Yankee: The Old South and American National Character

A highly recommended study

0-19-508284-2 OXFORD PB $18.95

Frank E. **Vandiver**

Their Tattered Flags: The Epic of the Confederacy

0-89096-355-X TEXAS A & M PB $15.95

Emory M. **Thomas**

The Confederacy as a Revolutionary Experience

Points to the far-reaching governmental changes introduced by the Confederacy as a major source of dissatisfaction within the wartime South. "The Confederate government, albeit unwittingly, transformed the South from a states rights confederation into a centralized, national state"

0-87249-780-1 SOUTH CAROLINA PB $9.95

The Confederate Nation, 1861 to 1865

"A serious, scholarly, readable work…that rounds up modern scholarship and offers a fresh and detached view of the whole subject"
—C. Vann Woodward, *New Republic*

0-06-131965-1 HARPERCOLLINS PB $18.90

The Leaders

Lincoln

"Earlier in the summer I occasionally saw the President and his wife, toward the latter part of the afternoon, out in a barouche, on a pleasure ride through the city...They pass'd me once very close, and I saw the President in the face fully, as if they were moving slowly, and his look, though abstracted happen'd to be directed steadily in my eye. He bow'd and smiled, but far beneath his smile I noticed well the expression I have alluded to. None of the artists or pictures has caught the deep, though subtle and indirect expression of this man's face. There is something else there. One of the great painters of two or three centuries ago is needed."
—Walt Whitman, from "Specimen Days" in *Complete Poetry and Collected Prose*

Gabor **Boritt** & others, editors

The Historian's Lincoln: Pseudohistory, Psychohistory and History

Different views of Lincoln and his place in American history

0-252-01527-4 ILLINOIS $29.95
0-252-06544-1 ILLINOIS PB $16.95

William **Hanchett**

The Lincoln Murder Conspiracies

Debunks the many conspiracy theories that have flourished since Lincoln's assassination

0-252-01361-1 ILLINOIS PB $11.95

Jim **Bishop**

The Day Lincoln Was Shot

A well-documented minute-by-minute chronicle of one momentous presidential assassination

0-06-080005-4 HARPERCOLLINS PB $6.50

Gabor S. **Boritt**

Lincoln's Generals

Edited by a seminal Lincoln historian, this fascinating collection of essays looks beyond the packaged version of Lincoln's Civil War triumph to the turbulent relationship the President had with his generals

0-19-508505-1 OXFORD $22.00
0-19-510110-3 OXFORD PB $11.95

LaWanda **Cox**

Lincoln and Black Freedom: A Study in Presidential Leadership

An award-winning analysis of Lincoln's objectives and priorities for Reconstruction with special focus on Louisiana, which became a showcase of wartime reconstruction efforts

0-87249-997-9 SOUTH CAROLINA PB $14.95

Robert V. **Bruce**

Lincoln and the Tools of War

0-252-06090-3 ILLINOIS PB $11.95

David Herbert **Donald**

Lincoln

Perhaps *the* Lincoln biography of its generation draws on Lincoln's personal papers and the vast, unexplored records of his legal practice to recreate his world with immediacy and rich detail

See also **LATE ARRIVALS**

0-684-80846-3 SIMON & SCHUSTER $35.00
0-684-82535-X TOUCHSTONE PB $17.00

Don **Fehrenbacher**

Prelude to Greatness: Lincoln in the 1850s

0-8047-0120-2 STANFORD PB $11.95

Russell **Freedman**

Lincoln: A Photobiography

An ambitious book with far more information than usual in juvenile biographies. The illustrations are from contemporary sources. For attentive readers eleven and up. Newbery Medal 1988

See also **YOUNG ADULT NONFICTION** in **BOOKS FOR YOUNG READERS**
See also **YOUNG ADULT FICTION** in **BOOKS FOR YOUNG READERS**

0-395-51848-2 CLARION PB $7.95

Abraham Lincoln

Timothy S. **Good**

We Saw Lincoln Shot: One Hundred Eyewitness Accounts

0-87805-778-1 MISSISSIPPI $42.50
0-87805-779-X MISSISSIPPI PB $17.95

J. David **Greenstone**

The Lincoln Persuasion: Remaking American Liberalism

"…a brilliant reexamination of the Lincoln myth. Its argument, to oversimplify, is that, perhaps better than any other leader in our country's history, Lincoln was able to combine a passionate commitment to changing the country with the political realism required to change the country without tearing it apart"
—*The Chicago Sun Times*

0-691-03764-7 PRINCETON PB $13.95

William Henry **Herndon**

Life of Lincoln

First published in 1889. "William H. Herndon had a closer acquaintance with his law partner, Abraham Lincoln, and a better understanding of his complex personality than any other student ever had. For this reason, for all its limitations, Herndon's *Lincoln* remains a classic—the essential book that any serious student of Abraham Lincoln must read"
—David Herbert Donald, Harvard University

0-306-80195-7 DA CAPO PB $14.95

John Paul **Jones**, editor

Dr. Mudd and the Lincoln Assassination: The Case Reopened

The proceedings of a Moot Court of Military Appeal to hear the case of Dr. Samuel A. Mudd, who was convicted of conspiring with John Wilkes Booth to kill President Lincoln. "Here is history at its best, relived with all its controversies, passions, and struggles for justice"—Senator Paul Simon

0-938289-50-0 STACKPOLE $24.95

Philip B. **Kunhardt**

Lincoln

An affordable paperback edition of the best-selling companion volume to the acclaimed television documentary. With over 700 images and the first use of the exhaustive Meserve Lincoln Archive, this is a thorough picture of the great American president

0-679-40862-2 KNOPF $50.00

Abraham **Lincoln**

The Portable Abraham Lincoln

EDITED BY ANDREW DELBANCO

0-14-017031-6 VIKING PB $12.00

Speeches and Writings, 1832-1858

For the first time, a compact, comprehensive presentation of Lincoln's writings. Each volume includes a useful and well-documented chronology of the president's life. "The greatest mystery of our most mysterious president is how, with almost no formal education and with no vast reading, he made himself a master of American prose, unique among our statesmen, no great thing, but unique among our writers, a very great thing indeed, as this volume demonstrates"—Gore Vidal. Includes *Speeches, Letters, and Miscellaneous Writings* and the complete text of *The Lincoln-Douglas Debates*

See also **LIBRARY OF AMERICA** in **LITERATURE OF THE AMERICAS**

0-940450-43-7 LIBRARY OF AMERICA $35.00

Speeches and Writings, 1859-1865

Includes *Speeches, Letters, and Miscellaneous Writings* and *Presidential Messages and Proclamations*

See also **LIBRARY OF AMERICA** in **LITERATURE OF THE AMERICAS**

0-940450-63-1 LIBRARY OF AMERICA $35.00
0-940450-68-2
LIBRARY OF AMERICA BOXED SET $70.00

Stephen B. **Oates**

Abraham Lincoln: The Man Behind the Myths

0-06-092472-1 HARPERPERENNIAL PB $12.50

James M. **McPherson**

Abraham Lincoln and the Second American Revolution

The author of *Battle Cry of Freedom* seeks to determine how much of a radical Lincoln was: "Abraham Lincoln was not Maximilien de Robespierre. No Confederate leaders went to the guillotine. Yet the Civil War changed the United States as thoroughly as the French Revolution changed that country"

0-19-505542-X OXFORD $20.00

Lincoln grew up close to the rhythms of nature, of wild beasts and farm animals, of forest and running water, of seasons and crops and of people who got their meager living from the land. These things, more than books, furnished his earliest education. They infused his speech with the images of nature. And when he turned to books, what were his favorites? They were the King James Bible, *Aesop's Fables, Pilgrim's Progress,* and Shakespeare's plays. What do these four have in common? They are rich in figurative language—in allegory, parable, fable, metaphor—in words and stories that seem to say one thing but mean another, in images that illustrate something more profound than their surface appearance.

ABRAHAM LINCOLN AND THE SECOND AMERICAN REVOLUTION

Marc E. **Neely**, Jr.

The Fate of Liberty: Abraham Lincoln and Civil Liberties

A Pulitzer Prize-winning exploration of Lincoln's constitutional policies, including his controversial restriction of civil liberties and the abuses of power that arose under martial law

0-19-508032-7 OXFORD PB..........$14.95

With Malice Toward None: The Life of Abraham Lincoln

"An admirable job in portraying Lincoln's life and character, the conquest of his deficiencies and the out-maneuvering of political jackals" —*Publishers Weekly*

0-06-013283-3 HARPERPERENNIAL PB..........$15.00

Merrill D. **Peterson**

Lincoln in American Memory

By the author of *The Great Triumvirate*

0-19-506570-0 OXFORD..........$35.00
0-19-509645-2 OXFORD PB..........$15.95

William A. **Tidwell**

Come Retribution: The Confederate Secret Service and the Assassination of Lincoln

New evidence that Lincoln's death emerged from a Confederate plot

0-87805-347-6 MISSISSIPPI..........$24.95

T. Harry **Williams**

Lincoln and the Radicals

Distinguished, dramatic history. "It brings within easy compass all the struggle which went on ceaselessly between the so-called radicals in Congress and the Republican Party, who sought to make the war an instrument for social revolution in the South, and Lincoln, whose aim at the start, in common with most Northern conservatives, was simply to preserve the union"—*Christian Century*

0-299-00274-8 WISCONSIN PB..........$15.95

Garry **Wills**

Lincoln at Gettysburg

A subtle and brilliant study of the Gettysburg Address as well as an account of the literary genius of Lincoln. The author explores the undiscovered message in this great document. "In precision and economy of language it emulates Lincoln's masterpiece…a stunning tour de force"—*NY Review of Books*

0-671-76956-1 TOUCHSTONE PB..........$23.00

Lincoln at Gettysburg: The Words that Remade America

0-671-86742-3 TOUCHSTONE PB..........$12.00

Carl **Sandburg**

Mary Lincoln: Wife and Widow

A classic portrait by the distinguished poet, originally published in 1932 and long out of print

1-55709-248-6 APPLEWOOD PB..........$12.95

Abraham Lincoln: The Prairie Years and the War Years

0-88365-832-1 GALAHAD..........$16.98

Carl Sandburg

John G. **Nicolay** &
Michael **Burlingame**, editors

An Oral History of Abraham Lincoln

0-8093-2054-1 SOUTHERN ILLINOIS..........$29.95

Confederates and Yankees

Clement **Eaton**

Jefferson Davis: The Sphinx of the Confederacy

A graduate of West Point, Davis was respected for his humane treatment of his slaves. Unfortunately for the South, he neither excelled as a military thinker nor delegated authority effectively

0-02-908700-7 FREE PRESS PB..........$15.95

Joseph T. **Glatthaar**

Partners in Command: The Relationships Between Leaders in the Civil War

Spotlights six relationships: Robert E. Lee and Thomas J. Jackson; Abraham Lincoln and George B. McClellan; Jefferson Davis and Joseph E. Johnston; Ulysses S. Grant and William T. Sherman; Grant, Sherman, and David D. Porter; and Lincoln and Grant

0-02-911817-4 FREE PRESS..........$24.95

Ulysses S. Grant

Ulysses S. **Grant**

Memoirs and Selected Letters

Grant's eloquently understated memoirs are an insufficiently recognized American literary classic. "Perhaps the most revelatory autobiography of high command to exist in any language"—John Keegan

See also LIBRARY OF AMERICA in LITERATURE OF THE AMERICAS

0-940450-58-5 LIBRARY OF AMERICA..........$35.00

Personal Memoirs of U.S. Grant

Written as he was dying, Grant's autobiography is a powerful account of his failings and triumphs. Mark Twain called Grant's memoirs "the best of any general's since Caesar"

INTRODUCTION BY WILLIAM S. MCFEELY

0-306-80172-8 DA CAPO PB..........$15.95

William S. **McFeely**

Grant: A Biography

Winner of the Pulitzer Prize for biography (1982)

0-393-30046-3 NORTON PB..........$16.95

James I. **Robertson**, Jr.

General A.P. Hill: The Story of a Confederate Warrior

One of "Lee's Lieutenants," Hill was an excellent subordinate who saw action in every major conflict in the Eastern theater

0-679-73888-6 VINTAGE PB..........$14.00

Frank E. **Vandiver**

Mighty Stonewall

A recent biography of General "Stonewall" Jackson

0-89096-384-3 TEXAS A & M..........$27.50
0-89096-391-6 TEXAS A & M PB..........$16.95

Byron **Farwell**

Stonewall: A Biography of General Thomas J. Jackson

0-393-31086-8 NORTON PB..........$15.95

Thomas Lee **Connelly**

The Marble Man: Robert E. Lee and His Image in American Society

0-8071-0474-4 LOUSIANA STATE PB $11.95

Charles Bracelen **Flood**

Lee: The Last Years

The story of Lee's efforts to heal the wounds of war

0-395-34637-1 HOUGHTON MIFFLIN PB $15.95

Douglas S. **Freeman**

Lee's Lieutenants: A Study in Command

A history of the war in the East and the Army of North Virginia, including biographies of dozens of high-ranking officers. Its complex appreciation of tactics and strategies makes it a classic study of battle and the issues of command

Volume 1 Manassas to Malvern Hill

0-684-18748-5 MACMILLAN PB $23.00

Volume 2 Cedar Mountain to Chancellorsville

0-684-18749-3 MACMILLAN PB $23.00

Volume 3 Gettysburg to Appomattox

0-684-18750-7 MACMILLAN PB $23.00

Douglas S. **Freeman**

Lee

0-684-17427-8 COLLIER PB $21.00

William **Piston**

Lee's Tarnished Lieutenant: James Longstreet and His Place in Southern History

Despite errors at Seven Pines and Second Manassas, Longstreet justified Lee's confidence in him at Antietam and Fredericksburg, but showed little aptitude for independent command

0-8203-0907-9 GEORGIA $24.95
0-8203-1229-0 GEORGIA PB $11.95

Stephen W. **Sears**

George B. McClellan: The Young Napoleon

At 35, he commanded all the Northern armies; at 37, he was nominated for the presidency by the Democratic party. McClellan's importance in shaping the cause of the Union during the Civil War was—Sears argues—matched only by Lincoln, Grant, and Sherman

0-89919-264-5 TICKNOR & FIELDS $24.95

Allan **Pinkerton**

The Spy of the Rebellion: A True History of the Spy System of the United States Army During the Late Rebellion, Revealing Many Secrets of the War

1-55613-441-X HERITAGE PB $35.00

Gary W. **Gallagher**

Stephen Dodson Ramseur: Lee's Gallant General

Based largely on the letters of a young Confederate officer at war, this is a study of one of the South's most talented commanders

0-8078-1627-2 NORTH CAROLINA $29.95
0-8078-4522-1 NORTH CAROLINA PB $14.95

George Green **Shackelford**

George Wythe Randolph and the Confederate Elite

The grandson of Thomas Jefferson, Randolph became secretary of war in 1862. This study reveals his role in recruiting a technocracy to run the war economy

0-8203-0998-2 GEORGIA $25.00

Paul A. **Hutton**

Phil Sheridan and His Army

Though his career got off to a slow start, "Little Phil" proved an audacious and effective commander, breaking the Confederate line at Chattanooga and conducting a devastating campaign along the Shenandoah in '64-'65

0-8032-7227-8 NEBRASKA PB $19.95

Michael **Fellman**

Citizen Sherman: A Life of William Tecumseh Sherman

Fellman (professor, Simon Fraser University; *Inside War*) masters the contradictions and implications of Sherman's complex and controversial place in American history

0-679-42966-2 RANDOM HOUSE $30.00

John F. **Marszalek**

Sherman: A Soldier's Passion for Order

0-02-920135-7 FREE PRESS $35.00
0-679-74989-6 VINTAGE PB $17.00

William T. **Sherman**

Memoirs of General W.T. Sherman

"Sherman's story of his march on the South must be one of the most articulate and engrossing ever written by an important general. It creates the appalled suspense of a kind of Grand Guignol horror, as we follow this intrepid and disciplined man, in many ways so sympathetic, going further and further in destructiveness, and recounting the process with the utmost exactitude and without the slightest compunction"
—Edmund Wilson

See also **LIBRARY OF AMERICA** in **LITERATURE OF THE AMERICAS**

0-940450-65-8 LIBRARY OF AMERICA $35.00
0-6-80213-9DA CAPO PB $17.95

The Soldiers

"E.H. Hampton of the 58th North Carolina wrote the widow of a comrade that her husband had only been wounded in the hand, and that the real cause of his death was the doctor's neglect; 'the doctor was very mean to him and did not treat him right.' A federal cavalryman told his wife, 'When a person is sick in camp they might as well dig a hole and put him in as to take him to one of thee (sic) infernal hells called hospitals.' One man in his regiment had died neglected, while nearby hospital attendants played euchre. After the war another soldier vividly remembered a one-eyed man in the ambulance corps who neglected the wounded to rob the dead."—Reid Mitchell, *Civil War Soldiers: Their Expectations and Their Experiences*

Nat **Brandt**

The Man Who Tried to Burn New York

Focuses on the trial of Robert Cobb Kennedy, the last Confederate hanged for spying

0-8156-0227-8 SYRACUSE PB $10.95

Dudley Taylor **Cornish**

The Sable Arm: Black Troops in the Union Army, 1861-1865

Black soldiers fought in every theater of the war, and by its end they made up one-tenth of the Union army

FOREWORD BY HERMAN HATTAWAY

0-7006-0328-X KANSAS PB $9.95

Henry Kyd **Douglas**

I Rode with Stonewall

Evokes the day-by-day sense of Confederate army life

0-8078-0337-5 NORTH CAROLINA $29.95

Edwin C. **Fishel**

The Secret War for the Union: The Untold Story of Military Intelligence in the Civil War

Fishel, an intelligence officer with the NSA for 30 years, a reporter, and a World War II intelligence agent, turns his practiced attention to an area of the Civil War that has long been misunderstood. Although central to the war's progress, records of intelligence activity has been hidden for nearly a century, only now uncovered by the author during the 40 years of research that has resulted in this book. What these records reveal radically alters our understanding of the war that divided America. "A groundbreaking study of military intelligence in the Civil War. A very important book"
—Stephen Spears

0-395-74281-1 HOUGHTON MIFFLIN $35.00

B.P. **Gallaway**

The Ragged Rebel: A Common Soldier in W.H. Parsons' Texas Cavalry, 1861-1865

A young Texas farmer in the Confederate cavalry

0-292-77047-2 TEXAS PB $12.95

Thomas Wentworth **Higginson**

Army Life in a Black Regiment

A classic by the preacher-soldier who commanded the First South Carolina, composed of runaway slaves

See also **SOLDIERS** under **BLACK VOICES, BLACK LIVES** under **AFRICAN-AMERICAN STUDIES**

0-87928-022-0 CORNER HOUSE $23.95
0-393-30157-5 NORTON PB $9.95

Gerald F. **Linderman**
Embattled Courage: The Experience of Battle in the American Civil War
0-02-919761-9 FREE PRESS PB $14.95

Kevin H. **Siepel**
Rebel: The Life and Times of John Singleton Mosby
A guerrilla fighter of the Confederacy. "Decent, solid, popular biography"—*Village Voice*
0-312-01507-0 ST. MARTIN'S PB $9.95

Thomas W. **Osborn**
The Fiery Trail: A Union Officer's Account of Sherman's Last Campaigns
FOREWORD BY WILLIAM S. MCFEELY
0-87049-500-3 TENNESSEE $31.95

John **Ransom**
John Ransom's Andersonville Diary
INTRODUCTION BY BRUCE CATTON
0-425-10554-7 BERKELEY PB $4.95

Edwin S. **Redkey**, editor
A Grand Army of Black Men: Letters from African-American Soldiers in the Union Army, 1861-1865
0-521-43998-1 CAMBRIDGE PB $19.95

James **Robertson**, Jr.
Soldiers Blue and Gray
An in-depth treatment of Civil War soldier life
0-87249-572-8 SOUTH CAROLINA $24.95

Stephen Z. **Starr**
The Union Cavalry in the Civil War
Volume 1 From Fort Sumter to Gettysburg
0-8071-0484-1 LOUISIANA STATE $39.95
Volume 2 The War in the East, from Gettysburg to Appomattox, 1863-1865
0-8071-0859-6 LOUISIANA STATE $39.95
Volume 3 The War in the West, 1861-1865
0-8071-1209-7 LOUISIANA STATE $39.95

Annette **Tapert**
The Brothers' War: Civil War Letters to Their Loved Ones from the Blue and Gray
0-679-72211-4 VINTAGE PB $13.00

Bell Irvin **Wiley**
The Life of Billy Yank: The Common Soldier of the Union
These two classic studies are valuable for their discussion of volunteerism
0-8071-0476-0 LOUISIANA STATE PB $11.95

The Life of Johnny Reb: The Common Soldier of the Confederacy
0-8071-0475-2 LOUISIANA STATE PB $11.95

The Civilians

Iver **Bernstein**
The New York City Draft Riots: Their Significance for American Society and Politics in the Age of the Civil War
"An original work in the historiography of Civil War America and labor history"—*NY Times Book Review*
0-19-505006-1 OXFORD $35.00
0-19-507130-1 OXFORD PB $19.95

John R. **Brumgardt**, editor
Civil War Nurse: The Diary and Letters of Hannah Ropes
The chief nurse of the Union Hospital in Washington, DC, describes her experiences and comments on notable political personalities
0-87049-790-1 TENNESSEE PB $11.95

Mary **Chesnut**
Mary Chesnut's Civil War
A spirited diary by the wife of a leading South Carolina Confederate
EDITED BY C. VANN WOODWARD
0-300-02979-9 YALE PB $19.95

Stanton **Garner**
The Civil War World of Herman Melville
An exemplary exercise in literary history, especially for the way it connects each of the poems in Melville's *Battle-Pieces* (1866) to its historical background
0-7006-0602-5 KANSAS $29.95

James M. **Greiner** & Janet L. **Coryell**
A Surgeon's Civil War: The Letters and Diary of Daniel M. Holt, M.D.
Civil War hospitals were all too often battlefields of a different kind, with appalling death tolls resulting from primitive care. Camp life, army politics, and omnipresent medical challenges are presented in high relief from the unique vantage point of an enlightened volunteer surgeon
EDITED BY JAMES R. SMITHER
0-87338-538-1 KENT STATE PB $18.00

John Vance **Lauderdale**
The Wounded River: The Civil War Letters of John Vance Lauderdale, M.D
From the Battle of Shiloh through the assassination of Lincoln, we share the experience and views of an enlightened surgeon faced with the horrors of war as his hospital ship plies the Mississippi, Ohio, and Tennessee rivers
EDITED BY PETER JOSYPH
0-87013-328-4 MICHIGAN STATE $29.95

Elizabeth D. **Leonard**
Yankee Women: Gender Battles in the Civil War
A frontline nurse, a community organizer, and a licensed doctor in the American Civil War
0-393-31372-7 NORTON PB $12.95

Robert Manson **Myers**
The Children of Pride: A True Story of Georgia and the Civil War
Abridged edition of the award-winning collection of letters of a Georgia plantation family; tells of the Old South and its destruction
0-300-04053-9 YALE PB $22.00

Elizabeth Brown **Pryor**
Clara Barton: Professional Angel
Barton organized an agency for getting medical supplies and care to the soldiers. In 1869 she went to Switzerland as a member of the Red Cross and succeeded in 1882 in having the US sign the Geneva agreement
0-8122-1273-8 PENNSYLVANIA PB $25.95

Anne C. **Rose**
Victorian America and the Civil War
"Through a study of seventy-five white middle-class Victorians, Anne C.Rose has created a compelling portrait of Civil War era American culture.... [A]n ingenious inquiry into middle-class culture and how the Civil War changed or amplified trends that had begun a decade or two earlier"—*Journal of the Early Republic*
0-521-47883-9 CAMBRIDGE PB $15.95

John **Rozier**, editor
The Granite Farm Letters: The Civil War Correspondence of Edgeworth and Sallie Bird
The letters of a Georgia plantation family span the entire Civil War era. From Sallie Bird in Gordonsville, Virginia, to her daughter Saida: "I believe if I were a man I would never lay down my arms in this glorious struggle, till the fiendish invader was driven back step-by-step from our soil"
FOREWORD BY THEODORE ROSENGARTEN
0-8203-1042-5 GEORGIA $29.95

Louis M. **Starr**
Bohemian Brigade
How the Civil War, and the reporters who covered it, created a 19th-century news revolution
0-299-11340-X WISCONSIN $35.00

Battles and Campaigns: The War in the East

Bull Run and the Peninsular Campaign

Joseph P. **Cullen**
The Peninsula Campaign, 1862: McClellan and Lee Struggle for Richmond
"In ten days I shall be in Richmond," McClellan boasted in 1862. But Lee emerged as the South's military genius while McClellan, "the Little

Napoleon," earned his reputation for procrastination and politicking
0-8117-1220-6 OUTLET $2.98

William C. **Davis**
Battle at Bull Run: A History of the First Major Campaign of the Civil War
The first—and what many thought would be the last—conflict of the war shattered the innocence of both victor and vanquished
0-8071-0867-7 LOUISIANA STATE PB $11.95

Robert E. Lee

John J. **Hennessy**
Return to Bull Run: The Campaign and Battle of Second Manassas
Culminates in the battle of August 29-30, 1862, which marked a highpoint in Robert E. Lee's campaign against George B. McClellan and John Pope
0-671-88989-3 TOUCHSTONE PB $17.00

Antietam and Chancellorsville

Stephen W. **Sears**
Chancellorsville
Robert E. Lee's decisive defeat at Gettysburg was preceded, ironically, by his greatest triumph, at Chancellorsville, in which he sent Stonewall Jackson on his famous 12-mile march and destroyed half the Union army. Stephen Sears examines this victory in vivid detail, drawing on a wealth of new sources, to write the definitive history of a central moment in the Civil War. "The finest and most provocative Civil War historian writing today"—*Chicago Tribune*
0-395-63417-2 HOUGHTON MIFFLIN $29.95

Landscape Turned Red: The Battle of Antietam
0-395-65668-0 TICKNOR & FIELDS PB $14.95

Gettysburg

Edwin B. **Coddington**
The Gettysburg Campaign: A Study in Command
0-684-18152-5 MACMILLAN PB $23.95

Harry W. **Pfanz**
Gettysburg: The Second Day
An exhaustive—almost 600-page—inquiry into the critical engagement of the most brutal, decisive battle of the war, by a former military historian at Gettysburg National Park. With 60 illustrations and 13 maps
0-8078-1749-X NORTH CAROLINA $37.50

Sherman's March

John G. **Barrett**
Sherman's March Through the Carolinas
"A scholarly and temperate account of a part of the Civil War which even yet can hardly be viewed without emotion"
—*NY Times Book Review*
0-8078-0701-X NORTH CAROLINA $27.50

Burke **Davis**
Sherman's March: The First Full-Length Narration of General William T. Sherman's Devastating March Through Georgia and the Carolinas
Taking off from their victories in Tennessee, the Union forces moved southeast to Atlanta, then north through the Carolinas, to menace Richmond from the south
0-394-75763-7 VINTAGE PB $12.00

William T. Sherman

Lee **Kennett**
Marching Through Georgia: The Story of Soldiers and Civilians During Sherman's Campaign
Kennett casts a new light on America's most colorful, talked-about, and bitterly remembered campaign
0-06-092745-3 HARPERCOLLINS PB $15.00

The Road to Appomattox

Bruce **Catton**
Grant Takes Command
Along with *Grant Moves South* (see below), the best military biography of the war
0-316-13240-3 LITTLE, BROWN PB $15.95

A Stillness at Appomattox
0-385-04451-8 ANCHOR PB $12.95

Gordon C. **Rhea**
The Battle of the Wilderness: May 5-6, 1864
The Wilderness as a classic study of the chaos that accompanies battle, and of two gamblers—Grant and Lee—who sought to exploit the chaos. "Rhea untangles as well as anyone the complex detail [of the battle]"
—Edward Hagerman, York University
0-8071-1873-7 LOUISIANA STATE $34.95

William G. **Robertson**
Back Door to Richmond: The Bermuda Hundred Campaign, April-June 1864
0-87413-303-3 DELAWARE $42.50
0-8071-1672-6 LOUSIANA STATE PB $9.95

Battles and Campaigns: The War in the West

Bruce **Catton**
Grant Moves South
Particularly good on Grant at Vicksburg
0-316-13244-6 LITTLE, BROWN PB $16.95

Ray C. **Colton**
The Civil War in the Western Territories: Arizona, Colorado, New Mexico, and Utah
The story of a little-known arena
0-8061-1902-0 OKLAHOMA PB $14.95

William C. **Davis**
The Orphan Brigade: The Kentucky Confederates Who Couldn't Go Home
0-8071-1077-9 LOUSIANA STATE PB $11.95

Thomas Goodrich **March**
Black Flag: Guerrilla Warfare on the Western Border, 1861-1865
0-253-32599-4 INDIANA $24.95

Jay **Monaghan**
Civil War on the Western Border, 1854-1865
The bloody first phase of the war began at least six years before the First Bull Run with the conflict between the proslavery elements from Missouri and the New England abolitionists who migrated to Kansas
0-8032-8126-9 NEBRASKA PB $13.95

Shiloh

More Americans fell at Shiloh in two days than in all the battles of the Revolution, the War of 1812, and the Mexican War combined.

James L. **McDonough**
Shiloh: In Hell Before Night
"The best book devoted entirely to Shiloh yet to be published"—Thomas Connelly, *Journal of American History*
0-87049-199-7 TENNESSEE $31.95
0-87049-232-2 TENNESSEE PB $16.95

David **Miller**
The Road to Shiloh
0-8094-4712-6 TIME BOOKS $18.95

The Battle for Tennessee

Next to Virginia, Tennessee saw more military action than any state during the Civil War.

Thomas Lee **Connelly**
Army of the Heartland: The Army of Tennessee, 1861-1862
0-8071-0404-3 LOUSIANA STATE $24.95

Autumn of Glory: The Army of Tennessee, 1862-1865
0-8071-0445-0 LOUSIANA STATE $34.95

Civil War Tennessee
Short, historically accurate, and easy to read
0-87049-284-5 TENNESSEE $9.95
0-87049-261-6 TENNESSEE PB $5.50

Larry J. **Daniels**
Cannoneers in Gray: The Field Artillery of the Army of Tennessee, 1861-1865
The difficulties of artillery warfare in the western theater
0-8173-0481-9 ALABAMA PB $22.50

Stanley F. **Horn**
The Decisive Battle of Nashville
The battle that ended the Confederacy's last offensive action and removed the Confederate Army of Tennessee from the field as an effective fighting force
0-8071-1709-9 LOUISIANA STATE PB $11.95

James Lee **McDonough**
Stones River: Bloody Winter in Tennessee
"Attractive to any Civil War buff"
—Timothy D. Johnson, *Alabama Historian*
0-87049-301-9 TENNESSEE $31.95
0-87049-373-6 TENNESSEE PB $16.95

James Lee **McDonough** & Thomas Lee **Connelly**
Five Tragic Hours: The Battle of Franklin
In a single day in November 1864, nearly 2000 Confederates lost their lives in a senseless attack against a well-fortified Union position
0-87049-396-5 TENNESSEE $31.95
0-87049-397-3 TENNESSEE PB $16.95

Vicksburg

With the garrison reduced to eating rats, Vicksburg fell on July 4, 1863, a day after the end of Gettysburg. Its loss gave Union gunboats control of the Mississippi, and isolated Texas and Arkansas from the Confederacy.

Shelby **Foote**
The Beleaguered City: The Vicksburg Campaign, Dec. 1862-July 1863
0-679-60170-8 MODERN LIBRARY $14.50

A.A. **Hoehling**
Vicksburg: 47 Days of Siege
0-8117-2980-X STACKPOLE PB $16.95

Earl S. **Miers**
The Web of Victory: Grant at Vicksburg
0-8071-1199-6 LOUISIANA STATE PB $14.95

The War at Sea

Bern **Anderson**
By Sea and by River: A Naval History of the Civil War
0-306-80367-4 DA CAPO PB $13.95

William C. **Davis**
Duel Between the First Ironclads
0-8071-0868-5 LOUISIANA STATE PB $9.95

Raimondo **Luraghi**
A History of the Confederate Navy
Argues that the gravest threat to the South was not, as commonly held, the Federal blockade but the Union's amphibious and riverine operations. "One of the most prominent European scholars of the Civil War weighs in with a provocative revisionist study... [A] notable addition to Civil War maritime history"—*Publishers Weekly*
See also **THE US NAVY** under **ARMIES OF THE WORLD** under **MILITARY AFFAIRS** in **WORLD HISTORY AND CURRENT AFFAIRS**
1-55750-527-6 NAVAL INSTITUTE $39.95

Charles G. **Summersell**
CSS Alabama: Builder, Captain, and Plans
Built at Liverpool despite Britain's official neutrality, this Confederate raider took 69 Union ships in two years, traveling from Indochina to Cherbourg, before she was sunk by the *USS Kearsarge*
0-8173-0209-3 ALABAMA $39.50

The Outcome

Richard E. **Beringer** & Herman **Hattaway**
Why the South Lost the Civil War
Argues that the erosion of nationalism and morale, more than defeat in battle, led to the South's collapse. "The wholesale desertion that took away 40 percent of the Confederate armies east of the Mississippi in the fall and early winter of 1864-65 showed that, before a full-scale resort to guerrilla warfare loomed as the alternative, a critical number of Confederates had given to the cause all that their commitment warranted"—from the Epilogue
0-8203-0815-3 GEORGIA $34.95
0-8203-1396-3 GEORGIA PB $19.95

David Herbert **Donald**, editor
Why the North Won the Civil War
FOREWORD BY U.S. GRANT III
0-02-031660-7 MACMILLAN PB $5.95
1-87789-112-6 PAPERBOOK PB $2.50

Edward **Hagerman**
The American Civil War and the Origins of Modern Warfare
The Civil War's commanders had to abandon the Napoleonic tradition and create new forms of tactical organization. Hagerman argues that their armies were the first to confront the full impact of mid-19th-century industrial technology on weapons, trench warfare, and logistics
0-253-30546-2 INDIANA $37.50

Stetson **Kennedy**
After Appomatox: How the South Won the War
Controversial work, based on newly discovered evidence, arguing that the verdict of Appomatox was reversed during Reconstruction
0-8130-1341-0 FLORIDA $49.95

Reconstruction

Edward L. **Ayers**
The Promise of the New South: Life After Reconstruction
"An ambitious and challenging reassessment of the years after Reconstruction"
—*NY Times Book Review*
0-19-508548-5 OXFORD PB $16.95

Dan T. **Carter**
When the War Was Over: The Failure of Self-Reconstruction in the South, 1865-1867
0-8071-1204-6 LOUISIANA STATE PB $11.95

Richard Nelson **Current**

Those Terrible Carpetbaggers: A Reinterpretation

A revision of the traditional image of the carpetbaggers as evil moneygrubbers, demonstrating that many were highly educated, had served well in the Union army, and, in some cases, brought their own money to help refurbish the war-torn South

0-19-504872-5 OXFORD $35.00
0-19-504873-3 OXFORD PB $12.95

Eric **Foner**

Reconstruction: America's Unfinished Revolution, 1863-1877

"With this book, Mr. Foner becomes the pre-eminent historian of Reconstruction"—William S. McFeely. Winner of the *LA Times* Book Award

0-06-091453-X HARPERCOLLINS PB $20.00

A Short History of Reconstruction, 1863-1877

An abridged version of *Reconstruction*

0-06-096431-6 HARPERCOLLINS PB $13.00

Eric **Foner** & Olivia **Mahoney**

America's Reconstruction: People and Politics After the Civil War

The companion volume to the Valentine Museum's exhibit on Reconstruction in Richmond, Va., with a wealth of documentation

0-06-096989-X HARPERPERENNIAL PB $17.50

Gaines M. **Foster**

Ghosts of the Confederacy: Defeat, the Lost Cause, and the Emergence of the New South

Argues that, contrary to folklore, Southerners accepted their loss, embraced reunification, and helped to foster sectional reconciliation

0-19-505420-2 OXFORD PB $19.95

Michael L. **Benedict**

The Impeachment and Trial of Andrew Johnson

The Republicans failed by a single vote to impeach Lincoln's successor

0-393-09418-9 NORTON PB $8.95

Eric L. **McKitrick**

Andrew Johnson and Reconstruction

Challenges the long-standing idea of Johnson as a misunderstood statesman, arguing that he was a small-minded, vindictive, stubborn man whose rigid determination to defy Northern majority opinion thwarted the postwar reunion of North and South

0-19-505707-4 OXFORD PB $18.95

Nell Irvin **Painter**

Exodusters: Black Migration to Kansas After Reconstruction

By the author of *Standing at Armageddon*

0-393-00951-3 NORTON PB $10.95

C. Vann **Woodward**

Origins of the New South, 1877-1913

A Brancroft Prize winner

0-8071-0019-6 LOUISIANA STATE PB $17.95

Michael **Perman**

Emancipation and Reconstruction, 1862-1879

The attempt to establish a two-party political system in the South. Suggests that the key to Reconstruction politics can be found in the factions that developed within the two parties

0-88295-836-4 HARLAN DAVIDSON PB $11.95

The Road to Redemption: Southern Politics, 1869-1879

0-8078-1526-8 NORTH CAROLINA $45.00
0-8078-4141-2 NORTH CAROLINA PB $14.95

Kenneth M. **Stampp**

The Era of Reconstruction: 1865-1877

Discards many popular notions, arguing that the radical governments—despite their shortcomings—were more democratic than any the South had known; that their record included a substantial list of achievements, and that "scalawag" and "carpetbagger" are not altogether justified terms

0-394-70388-X RANDOM HOUSE PB $10.65

US History, 1877-1945

For World War II, please see World History

Alan **Brinkley**

The Unfinished Nation

0-07-008219-7 MCGRAW HILL $42.00

Samuel P. **Hays**

The Response to Industrialism 1885-1914

0-226-32164-9 CHICAGO PB $13.95

Morton **Keller**

Regulating a New Society: Public Policy and Social Change in America, 1900-1933

"No historian has attempted such a comprehensive review of the policy response to early twentieth-century economic change. His accomplishment is stunning"
—*Journal of Policy History*

0-674-75366-6 HARVARD $49.95

Walter **LaFeber**

The American Century: A History of the United States Since the 1890s

0-07-035772-2 MCGRAW HILL PB $41.25

Gail **Buckland** & **Kevin Baker,** editors

The American Century

America since 1900, lavishly illustrated

0-679-41070-8 KNOPF $42.00

The Gilded Age and the Progressive Era

Once, historians neatly divided the period from the end of Reconstruction to World War I: a corrupt "Gilded Age" in the late 19th century, replete with greedy robber-baron industrialists and corrupt politicians, was followed around 1900 by a generation-long "Progressive Era," marked by crusading reformism and good government. In recent years, the dividing line has been blurred. The Gilded Age no longer seems so simplistic; reform clearly began before the turn of the century. And something called "Progressivism" may never have existed at all.

Ernest **Samuels**, editor

Henry Adams: Selected Letters

"These brilliant letters are an incomparable commentary on politics, literature, science and the world at large in the last half of the ninteenth century"—Alfred Kazin

0-674-38757-0 HARVARD $32.50

Jane **Addams**

Twenty Years at Hull House

The most famous settlement house, founded in Chicago in 1889

0-451-51955-8 NEW AMERICAN LIBRARY PB $4.95

Frederick Lewis **Allen**

The Big Change: America Transforms Itself, 1900-1950

"A mellow and thoroughly charming volume which tells the story of the changing American scene with humor and affection"—Peter Gay, *The Nation*

0-06-132082-X HARPERCOLLINS PB $14.50

Eliot **Asinof**

Eight Men Out: The Black Sox and the 1919 World Series

The Black Sox scandal of 1919 tarnished one of America's most cherished institutions

0-8050-0346-0 HOLT PB $12.95

Gerald **Berk**

Alternative Tracks: The Constitution of American Industrial Order, 1865-1917

Questions whether technology or the laws of economics made bigness inevitable. The author examines railroad consolidation, republican values, and public policy, and in the process illuminates the path to 20th-century statism and monopoly

0-8018-4656-0 JOHNS HOPKINS $40.00

Sean Dennis **Cashman**

America in the Age of the Titans

An interdisciplinary journey through the Progressive Era

0-8147-1411-0 NYU PB $18.50

America in the Gilded Age: From the Death of Lincoln to the Rise of Theodore Roosevelt

Personalities and events in the age of industry, immigration, urbanization, and the politics of Reconstruction and Populism

0-8147-1494-3 NYU $50.00

George **Cooper**

Lost Love: A True Story of Passion, Murder and Justice in Old New York

Sensational murder trial in New York after the Civil War. "History at its best—dramatic, riveting and heart-rending"—Doris Kearns Goodwin

See also **CRIME AND PUNISHMENT** under **TOPICS IN AMERICAN STUDIES**

0-679-75699-X VINTAGE PB $12.00

George Cooper (photo by Lawrence Blume)

John Milton **Cooper**, Jr.

Pivotal Decades: The United States, 1900-1920

A panoramic view of the period when Roosevelt and Wilson reigned

0-393-95655-5 NORTON PB $15.95

Mario R. **DiNunzio**, editor

Theodore Roosevelt: An American Mind: Selected Writings

"Controversial, but consistently provoking and entertaining"—*Publishers Weekly*

See also **HISTORY, POLITICS, AND SOCIETY** under **20TH-CENTURY AMERICAN ESSAYS AND JOURNALISM** in **LITERATURE OF THE AMERICAS**

0-14-024520-0 PENGUIN PB $13.95

Lawrence **Goodwyn**

The Populist Moment: A Short History of the Agrarian Revolt in America

An abridged version of Goodwyn's massive *Democratic Promise;* a major reinterpretation of the most important reform movement of the late 19th century

0-19-502417-6 OXFORD PB $12.95

Richard **Hofstadter**

The Age of Reform: From Bryan to FDR

A classic, Pulitzer Prize-winning (1956) work

0-394-41442-X RANDOM HOUSE $16.95

0-394-70095-3 RANDOM HOUSE PB $10.00

Social Darwinism in American Thought

A major analysis of the social philosophies of the intellectual movements of the Gilded Age and Progressive Era

0-8070-5461-5 BEACON PB $15.00

Michael T. **Isenberg**

John L. Sullivan and His America

How an outlaw in an outlawed sport became one of America's first national celebrities; as much a history of national culture in the Gilded Age as a story of a boxing hero

0-252-01381-6 ILLINOIS $29.95

Gabriel **Kolko**

The Triumph of Conservatism: A Reinterpretation of American History, 1900-1916

Argues that Progressivism was a profoundly conservative effort to maintain existing political and social relations in a new economic context

0-02-916650-0 FREE PRESS PB $16.95

David J. **Langum**

Crossing over the Line: Legislating Morality and the Mann Act

"It will be the definitive study of the rise and fall this ignoble experiment in behavior control" —Lawrence M. Friedman

0-226-46880-1 CHICAGO $24.95

O. Winston **Link**, photographer

Steam, Steel, & Stars: America's Last Steam Railroad

"Visions as captivating to gaze upon as they are invaluable as social documentation. A photographic masterpiece"—*Booklist*

0-8109-2587-7 ABRAMS PB $19.95

David **Lowe**, editor

The Great Chicago Fire in Eyewitness Accounts and Sixty-Three Contemporary Photographs and Illustrations

0-486-23771-0 DOVER PB $7.95

Tom **Lutz**

American Nervousness, 1903: An Anecdotal History

"Tom Lutz brings back into modern awareness one of the least understood but most fascinating illnesses of the Victorian period… A marvelous book"—*The Wall Street Journal*

0-8014-9878-3 CORNELL PB $14.95

David **McCullough**

McCullough's epic style brings to life the dramatic stories often shunned by academic historians. The following volumes cover the tremendous engineering feats of the Panama Canal and Brooklyn Bridge, a disastrous flood, and the boyhood of one of the century's most colorful presidents

The Great Bridge: The Epic Story of the Building of the Brooklyn Bridge

A classic account of one of the greatest engineering feats of all time

0-671-45711-X SIMON & SCHUSTER PB $16.00

The Johnstown Flood

More than 2000 people were killed on May 31, 1889, when a dam built to create a lake for an exclusive summer resort collapsed

0-671-20714-8 TOUCHSTONE PB $11.00

Teddy Roosevelt

Mornings on Horseback

A biography of the young Teddy Roosevelt

0-671-44754-8 SIMON & SCHUSTER PB $15.00

The Path Between the Seas: The Creation of the Panama Canal, 1870-1914

A gripping narrative of the extraordinary construction job between the Atlantic and Pacific oceans, by the Pulitzer Prize-winning author

See also **PANAMA** *under* **LATIN AMERICA AND THE CARIBBEAN**

0-671-24409-4 SIMON & SCHUSTER PB $14.95

Nell Irvin **Painter**

Standing At Armageddon: The United States, 1877-1919

A history of politics and labor that pays due attention to the dispossessed, including the working class, women, and blacks

0-393-30588-0 NORTON PB $14.95

Henry **Petroski**

Engineers of Dreams: Great Bridge Builders and the Spanning of America

0-679-43939-0 KNOPF $30.00

Jacob **Riis**

How the Other Half Lives

The tenements of turn-of-the-century New York

0-87928-033-6 CORNER HOUSE $26.95

Theodore **Roosevelt**

The Rough Riders

Roosevelt's gripping account of the colorful regiment he led into battle—and fame—in the Spanish-American War, thus beginning his march to the Presidency

0-306-80405-0 DA CAPO PB $13.95

Lewis L. **Gould**

The Presidency of Theodore Roosevelt

"This book deserves to be read by a large general audience trying to understand not only Roosevelt but also the development of the modern presidency. It will become the standard work on the subject"—Robert Dallek

0-7006-0565-7 KANSAS PB $14.95

Charles E. **Rosenberg**

The Trial of the Assassin Guiteau: Psychiatry and the Law in the Gilded Age

0-226-72717-3 CHICAGO PB $14.95

Carroll **Smith-Rosenberg**

Disorderly Conduct: Visions of Gender in Victorian America

How and why male-female relations, families, sex, and social custom changed as the US embarked on industrialization

0-19-504039-2 OXFORD PB $13.95

Lincoln **Steffens**

The Shame of the Cities

0-374-52373-8 HILL & WANG PB $9.00

Richard Samuel **West**

Satire on Stone: The Political Cartoons of Joseph Keppler

America's leading political cartoonist of the 1880s; includes reproductions of 170 cartoons, many republished for the first time

FOREWORD BY JIM BORGMAN

0-252-01497-9 ILLINOIS $39.95

Robert H. **Wiebe**

The Search for Order: 1877-1920

A provocative argument about the transformation of America from a collection of isolated "island communities" at the end of Reconstruction into a centralized, bureaucratized organizational society by World War I

0-8090-0104-7 FS&G PB $10.95

The Road to World Power

Robert L. **Beisner**

Twelve Against Empire: The Anti-Imperialists, 1898-1900

The leaders of the protest against the Spanish-American War, including William James, Charles Eliot Norton, Andrew Carnegie, and Benjamin Harrison

1-87917-610-6 IMPRINT PB $15.95

Walter **LaFeber**

The New Empire: An Interpretation of American Expansion, 1860-1898

0-8014-9048-0 CORNELL PB $14.95

The Panama Canal: The Crisis in Historical Perspective

See also SPECIAL TOPICS IN AMERICAN FOREIGN POLICY under AMERICAN POLITICS AND FOREIGN POLICY

0-19-505930-1 OXFORD PB $13.75

H. Wayne **Morgan**

America's Road to Empire: The War with Spain and Overseas Expansion

0-394-34198-8 MCGRAW HILL PB $8.95

G.J.A. **O'Toole**

The Spanish War: An American Epic, 1898

Narrative history of the turning point that ended an era of isolation and inaugurated a system of alliances and spheres of influence whose legacy is still felt

0-393-30304-7 NORTON PB $15.95

World War I

America's brief involvement in World War I resulted in considerably fewer casualties than those suffered by Europe, but the war had a powerful impact. The books below describe both the horrors of combat and the social changes that swept the nation.

Edward M. **Coffman**

The War to End All Wars: The American Military Experience in World War I

Vividly recounts the short but often horrifying experience of US soldiers

0-299-10964-X WISCONSIN PB $16.95

Maurine Wiener **Greenwald**

Women, War and Work: The Impact of World War I on Women Workers in the United States

Case studies in a national context. "...One of the most valuable contibutions to date to our understanding of women's role as workers in the American economy"
—*American Historical Review*

0-8014-9733-7 CORNELL PB $14.95

Ross **Gregory**

The Origins of American Intervention in the First World War

0-393-09980-6 NORTON PB $6.95

David M. **Kennedy**

Over Here: The First World War and American Society

A wide-ranging social history covering such topics as the repression of dissent; the special implications of the war for intellectuals, blacks, and workers; and the quality of Wilson's presidential leadership

0-19-503209-8 OXFORD PB $13.95

Thomas **Knock**

To End All Wars: Woodrow Wilson and the Quest for a New World Order

"This superbly researched study of Woodrow Wilson and the League of Nations...challenges virtually every recent historian who has tackled the subject. Knock demands that we see Wilson in a genuinely new framework and succeeds admirably"—*The American Historical Review*

0-691-00150-2 PRINCETON PB $16.95

Woodrow Wilson

N. Gordon **Levin**

Woodrow Wilson and World Politics: America's Response to War and Revolution

0-19-500803-0 OXFORD PB $16.95

Elton E. **Mackin**

Suddenly We Didn't Want to Die: Memoirs of a World War I Marine

Published 20 years after the author's death, this World War I diary brings to life the horror and heroes of the "war to end all wars" from the timeless point of view of a young soldier

0-89141-498-3 PRESIDIO $19.95
0-89141-593-9 PRESIDIO PB $14.95

Paul L. **Murphy**

World War I and the Origin of Civil Liberties in the United States

How the prosecution of more than 2,000 cases under the Espionage and Sedition Acts led to a new and widespread movement to protect civil liberties

0-393-95012-3 NORTON PB $9.95

Neil A. **Wynn**

From Progressivism to Prosperity: World War I and American Society

A British historian's analysis of how World War I pushed America into the 20th century

0-8419-1107-X HOLMES & MEIER PB $19.95

The Roaring '20s

Although the decade still appears flashy and excessive, it is now more commonly seen as a bridge between the Progressive Era and the New Deal—perhaps because of the ongoing rehabilitation of Herbert Hoover, a more compelling figure than he appeared in traditional views.

Edward **Behr**

Prohibition: The Thirteen Years that Changed America

1-55970-356-3 ARCADE $24.95

Paul A. **Carter**
The '20s in America
0-88295-717-1 HARLAN DAVIDSON PB $11.95

Norman **Clark**
Deliver Us from Evil: An Interpretation of American Prohibition
0-393-09170-8 NORTON PB $9.95

The Dry Years
0-295-96466-9 WASHINGTON PB $14.95

Ann **Douglas**
Terrible Honesty: Mongrel Manhattan in the 1920s
0-374-52462-9 NOONDAY PB $15.00

Lynn **Dumenil**
Modern Temper: American Culture and Society in the 1920s
Intelligent recreation and rethinking of the decade
0-8090-1566-8 HILL & WANG PB $10.95

Paula S. **Fass**
The Damned and the Beautiful: American Youth in the 1920s
The explosive changes that took place as the Roaring '20s broke with Victorian traditions
0-19-502492-3 OXFORD PB $14.95

Ray **Ginger**
Six Days or Forever?: Tennessee vs. John Thomas Scopes
The full story of the "Monkey Trial" of 1925
0-19-519784-4 OXFORD PB $10.95

Colin **Gordon**
New Deals: Business, Labor, and Politics in America, 1920-1935
0-521-45755-6 CAMBRIDGE PB $18.95

Frederick **Lewis Allen**
Only Yesterday: An Informal History of the 1920s
A classic, first published in 1931
0-06-080004-6 HARPERCOLLINS PB $7.50

Robert **Sobel**
The Great Bull Market: Wall Street in the 1920s
0-393-09817-6 NORTON PB $6.95

Doris **Stevens**
Jailed for Freedom: American Women Win the Vote
First published in 1920, this reissue of Stevens's dramatic reportage commemorates the 75th anniversary of the 19th Amendment. "A vivid partisan account that clearly conveys the excitement of both battle and victory"
—Publishers Weekly

See also **SUFFRAGE, LIBERATION, AND BEYOND** under **AMERICAN HISTORY** under **WOMEN'S STUDIES** *in* **SOCIAL STUDIES**

EDITED BY CAROL O'HARE
0-939165-25-2 NEWSAGE PB $12.95

Ellen **Williamson**
When We Went First Class: A Recollection of Good Times
An unabashedly nostalgic voyage through the high life of the '20s, '30s, and '40s, part of the Iowa Heritage series
0-813-81083-0 IOWA PB $10.95

William **Young** & David E. **Kaiser**
Postmortem: New Evidence in the Case of Sacco and Vanzetti
0-87023-479-X MASSACHUSETTS PB $15.95

The Great Depression and the New Deal

Anthony **Badger**
The New Deal: The Depression Years, 1933-1940
0-374-52174-3 FS&G PB $10.95

Ann **Banks**, editor
First Person America
Many of the nation's finest young writers interviewed ordinary Americans for the Federal Writers' Project; this sampling offers a rewarding glimpse of America during the Depression and the era of World War II
0-394-74796-8 NORTON PB $10.00

Alan **Brinkley**
Voices of Protest: Huey Long, Father Coughlin and the Great Depression
Two major demagogues and their genius for voicing—and manipulating—the needs and hopes of ordinary people ruined by the Depression
0-394-71628-0 RANDOM HOUSE PB $13.00

FDR

Terry A. **Cooney**
Balancing Acts: American Thought and Culture in the 1930s
The contradictions and tensions of a society battling to preserve and escape tradition
0-8057-9069-1 TWAYNE PB $15.95

Hope Hale **Davis**
Great Day Coming: A Memoir of the 1930s
The lure of love and Communism, affectingly told
1-88364-217-5 STEERFORTH $24.00

Steve **Fraser** & Gary **Gerstle**, editors
The Rise and Fall of the New Deal Order, 1930-1980
Essays that "demonstrate afresh how the New Deal continues to influence twentieth-century American politics and political economy"
—Jordan A. Schwarz
0-691-00607-5 PRINCETON PB $16.95

Irwin F. **Gellman**
Secret Affairs: Franklin Roosevelt, Cordell Hull, and Sumner Welles
0-8018-5083-5 JOHNS HOPKINS $35.00

Ellis W. **Hawley**
The New Deal and the Problem of Monopoly: A Study in Economic Ambivalence
Argues that FDR's seeming inconsistency on monopoly policy was a result of political pressures, not muddy thinking. A "major contribution to the history of economic thought"—*The Journal of American History*
0-8232-1609-8 FORDHAM PB $20.00

Frederick **Lewis Allen**
Since Yesterday—The 1930s in America: September 3, 1929, to September 3, 1939
Another classic, from 1939. "Conveys the impression of the American people telling their own story in autobiographical form"—*NY Times*
0-06-091322-3 HARPERCOLLINS PB $14.00

Robert S. **McElvaine**
The Great Depression: America, 1929-1941
A comprehensive narrative account of all aspects of the Depression
0-8129-2327-8 TIME BOOKS PB $15.00

Robert S. **McElvaine**, editor
Down and Out in the Great Depression: Letters from the Forgotten Man
0-8078-4099-8 NORTH CAROLINA PB $12.95

Russell D. **Buhite** & others
FDR's Fireside Chats
Complete texts of the 31 fireside chats FDR delivered over the radio during his 13 years as president
0-14-017905-4 PENGUIN PB $12.50

Kenneth S. **Davis**
FDR: The New Deal Years, 1933-1937
An excellent synthesis
0-679-41541-6 RANDOM HOUSE $35.00

Robert **Dallek**

Franklin D. Roosevelt and American Foreign Policy, 1932-1945

The first full-scale history of American diplomacy during the Roosevelt presidency

See also **THE UNITED STATES AND WORLD WAR II** under **THE SECOND WORLD WAR** in **WORLD HISTORY AND CURRENT AFFAIRS**

0-19-509732-7 OXFORD PB $18.95

Robert E. **Herzstein**

Roosevelt & Hitler: Prelude to War

"Mr Herzstein's picture of Roosevelt as a consistent anti-Nazi who aimed to defeat fascism at home and abroad is indisputable" —*The Historian*

0-471-03341-3 WILEY PB $16.95

William E. **Leuchtenburg**

Franklin D. Roosevelt and the New Deal, 1932-1940

This was, for over two decades, the best one-volume account of the period

0-06-133025-6 HARPERCOLLINS PB $19.58

In the Shadow of FDR: From Harry Truman to Ronald Reagan

"Shrewdly sets forth the special cruelty of the dilemma Roosevelt's successors have all faced: 'If he did not walk in FDR's footsteps, he ran the risk of having it said that he was not a Roosevelt but a Hoover. Yet to the extent that he did copy FDR, he lost any chance of marking out his own claim to recognition' "—*NY Times Book Review*

0-8014-9303-X CORNELL PB $14.95

The Perils of Prosperity

Entertaining and highly recommended account of the transformation of America from a decentralized, agrarian nation into the urban, industrialized capital of the world

0-226-47369-4 CHICAGO PB $10.95

Robert **Shogan**

Hard Bargain: How FDR Twisted Churchill's Arm, Evaded the Law and Changed the Role of the American Presidency

"Robert Shogan leads us through one of the most intricate, important and precedent-setting deals of the twentieth century in an absorbing account of FDR at his best and worst" —Stephen Ambrose

0-689-12160-1 SCRIBNERS $24.00

Arthur M. **Schlesinger**, Jr.

The Coming of the New Deal

0-395-48905-9 AMERICAN HERITAGE PB $15.95

The Crisis of the Old Order

0-395-48903-2 AMERICAN HERITAGE PB $11.95

The Politics of Upheaval

0-395-48904-0 HOUGHTON MIFFLIN PB $11.95

Harvard **Sitkoff**, editor

Fifty Years Later: The New Deal Evaluated

0-07-554460-1 RANDOM HOUSE PB $24.40

Joseph E. **Stevens**

Hoover Dam: An American Adventure

Nearly 5000 workers toiled around the clock through the worst years of the Depression to build the dam that would harness the Colorado River and transform the West

0-8061-2283-8 OKLAHOMA PB $14.95

Studs **Terkel**

Hard Times: An Oral History of the Great Depression

0-394-74691-0 PANTHEON PB $13.00

Donald **Warren**

Radio Priest: Charles Coughlin, the Father of Hate Radio

0-684-82403-5 FREE PRESS $27.50

T.H. **Watkins**

The Great Depression: America in the 1930s

0-316-92453-9 LITTLE, BROWN $24.95
0-316-92454-7 LITTLE, BROWN PB $12.95

US 1945 to the Present

Paul **Boyer**

Promises to Keep: The United States Since World War II

A useful, 550-page college survey published in 1995. Chapters include "Crucible of Change: World War II and the Forging of Modern America"; "From *Sputnik* to the Nuclear Brink to Vietnam: The Cold War Heats Up"; and "Prime-Time Politics: The Reagan Years"

0-669-20350-5 HEATH PB $29.33

Lois **Gordon** & Alan **Gordon**

The Columbia Chronicles of American Life, 1910-1992

0-231-08100-6 COLUMBIA $39.95

1945 to the Present: "The American Century"

In 1941 Henry Luce, the founder of *Time*, called on a powerful United States to become "the Good Samaritan of the entire world," and proclaimed this the "American Century."

Stephen **Ambrose**

Rise to Globalism: American Foreign Policy Since 1938

The fifth edition includes analyses of the Iran-Contra Affair, the Nicaraguan revolution, international terrorism, superpower summits, and other recent developments

See also **20TH-CENTURY DIPLOMACY** under **FOREIGN POLICY AND DIPLOMATIC HISTORY** under **AMERICAN POLITICS AND FOREIGN POLICY**

0-14-017536-9 PENGUIN PB $13.95

William **Chafe**

The Paradox of Change: American Women in the 20th Century

A valuable survey, first published in 1991

0-19-504419-3 OXFORD PB $11.95

The Unfinished Journey: America Since World War II

Highlights the paradoxes of postwar reform and reaction, and shows how things might have been different

0-19-506626-X OXFORD $45.00
0-19-506627-8 OXFORD PB $18.95

William H. **Chafe** & Harvard **Sitkoff**

A History of Our Time: Readings on Postwar America

Anthology of articles and essays with lively intros and first-person accounts by participants

0-19-506616-2 OXFORD PB $17.95

Dwight D. Eisenhower

David **Fromkin**

In the Time of the Americans: FDR, Truman, Eisenhower, Marshall, MacArthur— The Generation that Changed America's Role in the World

0-394-58901-7 KNOPF $30.00
0-679-76728-2 VINTAGE PB $16.00

Douglas MacArthur

Otis L. **Graham**, Jr.

Toward a Planned Society: From Roosevelt to Nixon

The beginnings and development of national growth policies and machinery

0-19-501985-7 OXFORD $25.00

Stanley **Hochman** & Eleanor **Hochman**

A Dictionary of Contemporary American History: 1945 to the Present

Seven hundred entries through the 1990s. "An excellent, quick-reference source on recent U.S. political and cultural history"—*Library Journal*

0-451-17807-6 SIGNET PB $7.99

William **Manchester**

The Glory and the Dream: A Narrative History of America, 1932-1972

"This fluent, likable, can't-put-it-down narrative history of America from the Bonus Army to Watergate is popular history in our special tradition" —Alfred Kazin, *NY Times Book Review*

0-553-34589-3 BANTAM PB $27.95

James **Reston**

Deadline: Our Times and the *New York Times*

One of the great American journalists of the century tells of his long career at the *New York Times*, from 1939 to 1989, a period during which he won two Pulitzers

0-394-58558-5 TIMES BOOKS PB $25.00

The Truman and Eisenhower Years

Bruce **Cook**

The Beat Generation: The Tumultuous '50s Decade and Its Impact on Today

Solid literary journalism

0-688-13452-1 QUILL PB $12.00

John Patrick **Diggins**

The Proud Decades: America in War and Peace, 1941-1960

This portrait of a triumphant America gives "the overview we have needed of that mid-century shift that changed the course of American life—even before it entered the '60s"—Walter LaFeber

0-393-95656-3 NORTON PB $14.95

Stephen E. **Ambrose**

Eisenhower: Soldier and President

0-671-74758-4 TOUCHSTONE PB $16.00

Kenneth S. **Davis**

Dwight D. Eisenhower: Soldier of Democracy

0-8317-5714-0 SMITHMARK $12.98

Susan **Eisenhower**

Mrs. Ike: Memoirs and Reflections on the Life of Mamie Eisenhower

0-374-21514-6 FS&G $25.00

Fred I. **Greenstein**

The Hidden-Hand Presidency: Eisenhower as Leader

0-465-02951-5 JOHNS HOPKINS PB $14.95

Audrey **Kahin** & George **Kahin**

Subversion as Foreign Policy: The Secret Eisenhower and Dulles Debacle in Indonesia

"A wholly original study of United States foreign policy and the destruction of a fragile democracy in Southeast Asia's largest nation" —Gabriel Kolko

1-56584-244-8 NEW PRESS $25.00

Chester J. **Pach**, Jr. & others

The Presidency of Dwight D. Eisenhower: Revised Edition

This revision is essentially a completely new book which draws on all the Eisenhower scholarship of the past decade (the bibliography is a tour de force, by itself worth the price of the book). Pach has incorporated the work of the revisionists, hardly under way when Richardson wrote the first edition, and added the insights and criticisms of the post-revisionists. "The best single volume now available on the Eisenhower presidency"—Stephen E. Ambrose

0-7006-0437-5 KANSAS PB $12.95

Eric F. **Goldman**

The Crucial Decade and After: America, 1945-1960

0-394-70183-6 RANDOM HOUSE PB $10.00

David **Halberstam**

The '50s

Pulitzer Prize-winning Halberstam presents a sweeping cultural, political, and scientific portrait of America's pivotal decade. "Compulsively readable, with familiar events and people grown fresh in the telling" —*Kirkus Reviews*

0-679-74725-7 RANDOM HOUSE PB $29.95

William L. **O'Neill**

American High: The Years of Confidence, 1945-1960

0-02-923679-7 FREE PRESS PB $14.95

Harry S Truman

Frank **Kofsky**

Harry S. Truman and the War Scare of 1948: A Successful Campaign to Deceive the Nation

How Truman, along with Marshall and Forrestal, systematically deceived Congress and the public into thinking the USSR was about to launch World War III by attacking Western Europe

0-312-12329-9 ST. MARTIN'S PB $16.95

David **McCullough**

Truman

A biography that received much attention when it was first published in 1992

0-671-45654-7 SIMON & SCHUSTER $30.00
0-671-86920-5 TOUCHSTONE PB $16.00

The Cold War

H.W. **Brands**

The Devil We Knew: Americans and the Cold War

This engaging volume offers readers a full assessment of the policies, politics, paranoia, and price Americans paid for the Cold War

0-19-507499-8 OXFORD $35.00
0-19-509377-1 OXFORD PB $11.95

Warren I. **Cohen**

The Cambridge History of American Foreign Relations: America in the Age of Soviet Power, 1945-1991

The first post-Cold War analysis of the origins of Soviet-American confrontation and its extension from Europe to the Third World

0-521-48381-6 CAMBRIDGE PB $15.95

Robert A. **Divine**

Eisenhower and the Cold War

How Ike shaped the nation's foreign policy during eight critical years

0-19-502824-4 OXFORD PB $8.95

Tom **Engelhart**

The End of Victory Culture: Cold War America and the Disillusioning of a Generation

0-465-01984-6 BASIC $25.00

John Lewis **Gaddis**

The United States and the End of the Cold War: Implications, Reconsiderations, Provocations

One of the first explanations of how and why the Cold War ended so abruptly. "A thought-provoking 40-year look backwards" —*The Economist*

0-19-508551-5 OXFORD PB $13.95

Fraser J. **Harbutt**

The Iron Curtain: Churchill, America and the Origins of the Cold War

0-19-505422-9 OXFORD PB $17.95

George F. Kennan: Cold War Iconoclast

0-231-06894-8 COLUMBIA $46.50
0-231-06895-6 COLUMBIA PB $17.00

George F. Kennan

Melvyn P. **Leffler**

A Preponderance of Power: National Security, the Truman Administration, and the Cold War

An excellent reassessment, first published in 1992

0-8047-2218-8 STANFORD PB $24.95

Melvyn P. **Leffler** & David S. **Painter**

Origins of the Cold War: An International History

Collection of 15 papers providing the latest research and interpretation. Part of the *Rewriting Histories* series

0-415-09694-4 ROUTLEDGE PB $16.95

Thomas J. **McCormick**

America's Half-Century: United States Foreign Policy in the Cold War and After

In this new (1993) edition of his acclaimed study, McCormick investigates the gradual decline of U.S. hegemony during the Cold War period

0-8018-5011-8 JOHNS HOPKINS PB $13.95

Guy **Oakes**

The Imaginary War: Civil Defense and the American Cold War Culture

A convincing analysis of the civil defense program as an exercise in propaganda that was part of the official mythmaking of the Cold War

0-19-509027-6 OXFORD $29.95

Thomas G. **Paterson**

On Every Front: The Making of the Cold War

0-393-03060-1 NORTON $24.95
0-393-96435-3 NORTON PB $11.95

Richard **Rhodes**

Dark Sun: The Making of the Hydrogen Bomb

Rhodes reveals the secret details not only of how, but of *why* we built the ultimate machine of destruction

0-684-80400-X SIMON & SCHUSTER $32.50

Michael **Schaller**

The American Occupation of Japan: The Origins of the Cold War in Asia

Argues that the reconstruction of postwar Japan shaped not only that country's future but also US policy throughout postwar Asia, leading up to the interventions in China, Korea, and Vietnam

See also **THE AMERICAN OCCUPATION** under **FROM THE MEIJI RESTORATION TO THE END OF THE EMPIRE: 1868-1945** under **JAPAN** in **WORLD HISTORY AND CURRENT AFFAIRS**

0-19-505190-4 OXFORD PB $13.95

Martin **Walker**

The Cold War: A History

"The first major study for the general reader of the Cold War as history"—Ronald Steel

See also **THE COLD WAR** under **INTERNATIONAL RELATIONS AND STRATEGIC STUDIES** in **SOCIAL STUDIES**

0-8050-3454-5 HOLT $30.00
0-8050-3454-4 HOLT PB $14.00

Randall B. **Woods** & Howard **Jones**

Dawning of the Cold War: The United States Quest for Order

"The most satisfactory narrative history we now have of how the Cold War came about" —*American Historical Review*

0-8203-1265-7 GEORGIA $35.00
1-5663-0479-9 DEE PB $12.95

The Korean War

Historians have recently shown a revival of interest in the Korean War. Several detailed accounts chronicle the first major conflict of the Cold War, which took more than three million Korean and 30,000 American lives.

Burton **Kaufman**

The Korean War: The Challenges in Crisis, Credibility and Command

See also **THE KOREAN WAR** under **KOREA** in **WORLD HISTORY AND CURRENT AFFAIRS**

0-07-034150-8 MCGRAW HILL $25.00

Donald **Knox**

The Korean War: Pusan to Chosin, an Oral History

The first six months, told almost entirely in the words of American participants

0-15-647200-7 HARCOURT BRACE PB $16.95

The Korean War: Uncertain Victory

The second volume of Knox's oral history

See also **THE KOREAN WAR** under **KOREA** in **WORLD HISTORY AND CURRENT AFFAIRS**

ADDITIONAL TEXT BY ALFRED COPPEL

0-15-147289-0 HARCOURT BRACE $29.95
0-15-647201-5 HARCOURT BRACE PB $14.95

James L. **Stokesbury**

A Short History of the Korean War

A brief introduction for the layman. "Enough battle detail to produce a flesh-and-blood book, not just a diplomatic and strategic overview" —Harry Levins, *St. Louis Post-Dispatch*

0-688-09513-5 QUILL PB $8.95

John B. **Toland**

In Mortal Combat: Korea 1950-1953

A gripping narrative of America's first limited war, drawing on interviews with over 200 members of the American military and scrupulous research in both Chinese and North Korean archives, to which Toland was the first Westerner allowed access

0-688-10079-1 QUILL PB $25.00

The McCarthy Era

More than 30 years after his death, McCarthy has few admirers, but the abiding questions of his era—the morality of informing, the threat of native radicalism, the persecution of Communist sympathizers, the question of ultimate guilt—remain at the heart of political debate.

Sally **Belfrage**

UnAmerican Activities: A Memoir of the '50s

"A memoir of extraordinary grace and wit, Belfrage's child's-eye view of a shameful period in American politics is among the most human and compulsively readable documents to have emerged from the Red-baiting era" —*Harper's Bazaar*

0-06-092626-0 HARPERPERENNIAL PB $13.00

Walter **Bernstein**

Inside Out: A Memoir of the Blacklist

See also **FILM IN AMERICA** under **FILM** in **PERFORMING ARTS AND MEDIA**

0-394-58341-8 KNOPF $24.00

Whittaker **Chambers**

Witness

The autobiographical account of one of the most controversial episodes of the McCarthy era

PREFACE BY ROBERT NOVAK

0-89526-789-6 REGNERY PB $14.95

Joe McCarthy

Richard M. **Fried**

Nightmare in Red: The McCarthy Era in Perspective

0-19-504360-X OXFORD PB $22.95

Griffin **Fariello**

Red Scare: Memories of the American Inquisition—An Oral History

"A vital chapter in American history in the actual words of the up-against-the-wall heroes and heroines who experienced the witch hunts of McCarthy & Co. This is must reading" —Studs Terkel

0-393-03732-0 NORTON $29.95
0-380-72711-0 AVON PB $15.00

Robert **Griffith**

The Politics of Fear: Joseph R. McCarthy and the Senate

0-87023-555-9 MASSACHUSETTS PB $19.95

John E. **Haynes**

Red Scare or Red Menace?: American Communism and Anticommunism in the Cold War Era

1-56663-090-8 DEE $24.95

Stanley I. **Kutler**

The American Inquisition: Justice and Injustice in the Cold War

0-8090-0157-8 FS&G PB $10.95

Victor **Navasky**

Naming Names

The definitive liberal account of the HUAC hearings, focusing on the morality of informing

0-14-005942-3 PENGUIN PB $12.00

David M. **Oshinsky**

A Conspiracy So Immense: The World of Joe McCarthy

A detailed account recreating (often with actual dialogue) many of the Wisconsin senator's probes into government agencies

0-02-923760-2 FREE PRESS PB $18.95

Camelot: The Kennedy Years

Noam **Chomsky**

Rethinking Camelot: JFK, the Vietnam War, and US Political Culture

Dismisses the Camelot legend and the belief that JFK would have withdrawn from Vietnam. Chomsky contends that US institutions and political culture, not individual presidents, are the key to understanding US behavior during the war

0-89608-458-2 SOUTH END PB $14.00

Carl **Anthony**

As We Remember Her: The Impact of Jacqueline Kennedy Onassis in Her Own Words and in the Recollections of Others

0-06-017690-3 HARPERCOLLINS $25.00

Peter **Collier** & David **Horowitz**

The Kennedys: An American Drama

0-446-32702-6 WARNER PB $6.99

Leo **Damore**

The Cape Cod Years of John Fitzgerald Kennedy

Damore brings to life the compound in Hyannisport and shows that it is ineluctably bound to the Kennedy family history and myth, putting both in clear focus to arrive at an original understanding of America's first family. "A book to buy and keep…an important new chapter in the story of J.F.K." —*Boston Sunday Globe*

1-88836-312-6 SEVEN STORIES PB $12.95

Senatorial Privilege: The Chappaquiddick Coverup

0-89526-564-8 REGNERY $21.95

John H. **Davis**

The Bouviers: From Waterloo to the Kennedys and Beyond

Updated with "intimate details" of the final days of Jacqueline Bouvier Kennedy Onassis. "Davis does a magnificent job of narrating his family chronicle"—*LA Times*

1-88260-519-5 NATIONAL PRESS PB $14.95

Barbara **Gibson** & Ted **Schwartz**

Rose Kennedy and Her Family: The Best and Worst of Their Times and Lives

Tidbits from her personal secretary within a broader biography

1-55972-299-1 BIRCH LANE $22.50

Ronald **Goldfarb**

Perfect Villains, Imperfect Heroes: Robert F. Kennedy's War Against Organized Crime

0-679-43565-4 RANDOM HOUSE $26.00

Robert Kennedy

Doris Kearns **Goodwin**

The Fitzgeralds and the Kennedys: An American Saga

Bestselling account of the famous immigrant families and the political power they wielded

0-312-90933-0 ST. MARTIN'S PB $5.95

Jim F. **Heath**

Decade of Disillusionment: The Kennedy-Johnson Years

0-253-20201-9 INDIANA $9.95

Trumbull **Higgins**

The Perfect Failure: Kennedy, Eisenhower, and the CIA at the Bay of Pigs

0-393-30563-5 NORTON PB $7.95

Nigel **Hamilton**

JFK: Reckless Youth

"Hamilton refuses to turn away from the sheer paradox and ambiguity of the man—the narcissism and self-deprecation, charm and coldness, loyalty and cruelty…It is a book not only about a remarkable young John F. Kennedy, but also about American democracy's own still reckless age"—*NY Times Book Review*

0-679-41216-6 RANDOM HOUSE $30.00

Robert F. **Kennedy**

The Enemy Within: The McClellan Committee's Crusade Against Jimmy Hoffa and Corrupt Labor Unions

"Well before he became Attorney General in 1961, Robert Kennedy had developed a deep concern about the pervasive threat of organized crime in our society. In this book, he laid out the facts, and it is one of his lasting contibutions to the nation"—Senator Edward M. Kennedy

0-306-80590-1 DA CAPO PB $14.95

Thirteen Days: A Memoir of the Cuban Missile Crisis

0-393-09896-6 NORTON PB $6.95

Wayne **Koestenbaum**

Jackie Under My Skin: Interpreting an Icon

Traces Jackie through the metaphoric females in literature, film, and the popular imagination

0-374-28446-6 FS&G $21.00
0-452-27649-7 PLUME PB $12.95

Dan E. **Moldea**

The Killing of Robert F. Kennedy: An Investigation of Motive, Means and Opportunity

"Moldea's book is a must-read for all those concerned about the official version of the assassination of RFK"—G. Robert Blakey

0-393-03791-6 NORTON $27.50
0-393-31534-7 NORTON PB $14.00

Arthur M. **Schlesinger**, Jr.

Robert Kennedy and His Times

0-345-32547-8 BALLANTINE PB $6.95

A Thousand Days: John F. Kennedy in the White House

One of America's best-known historians, Schlesinger embodies the liberal tradition of historical writing. Known for his interpretations of the Jacksonian and New Deal eras—and for linking their democratic traditions—Schlesinger is also a chief defender of the Kennedy legacy

0-449-30021-8 FAWCETT PB $6.95

John Fitzgerald Kennedy

The Kennedy Assassination

The Dallas Morning News

November 22: The Day Remembered

A minute-by-minute account, with more than 100 photographs, from coverage of the JFK assassination by Dallas's largest newspaper

0-87833-711-3 TAYLOR PB $11.95

Edward J. **Epstein**

The Assassination Chronicles: Inquest, Counterplot and Legend

Includes the complete text of *Inquest* (the study of the Warren Commission Report), *Counterplot* (the report of Jim Garrison's prosecution of Clay Shaw), and *Legend* (the investigation of Oswald's possible links to the KGB and the CIA)

0-88184-909-X CARROLL & GRAF PB $14.95

Robert J. **Groden**

The Killing of a President: The Complete Photographic Record of the JFK Assassinaton, the Conspiracy and the Cover-Up

The author was the Staff Photographic Consultant to the House Select Committee on Assassinations for three years and a consultant on Oliver Stone's film *JFK*

INTRODUCTION BY OLIVER STONE

0-14-024003-9 STUDIO PB $21.95

Henry **Hurt**

Reasonable Doubt: An Investigation into the Assassination of John F. Kennedy

"A powerful case for conspiracy with… methodical, meticulous re-examination of the evidence"—*San Francisco Chronicle*

0-8050-0360-6 HOLT PB $16.95

Michael L. **Kurtz**

Crime of the Century: The Kennedy Assassination from a Historian's Perspective

Analyzes investigations into the assassination, outlines major areas of controversy, argues that the most popular conspiracy theories fail to fit the facts, and offers a new theory of the assassination

0-87049-479-1 TENNESSEE PB $14.95

Mark **Lane**

Rush to Judgement

A bestseller. "…Will live as a classic. Lane's book proves once and forever that the assassination of President Kennedy is more of a mystery today than when it occurred"—Norman Mailer

1-56025-043-7 THUNDER'S MOUTH PB $13.95

David S. **Lifton**

Best Evidence: Disguise and Deception in the Assassination of John F. Kennedy

A meticulously detailed, bestselling argument for a conspiracy to murder JFK

0-451-17573-5 SIGNET PB $6.99

Harrison Edward **Livingston**

High Treason 2: The Great Cover-Up: The Assassination of President John F. Kennedy

Also a bestseller

0-7867-0017-3 CARROLL & GRAF PB $16.95

Carl **Oglesby**

The JFK Assassination: The Facts and the Theories

From the co-director of the Assassination Information Bureau

0-451-17476-3 SIGNET PB $4.99

Norman **Mailer**

Oswald's Tale: An American Mystery

This monumental portrait combines a novelist's breadth with a reporter's research to bring a president's assassin to life

0-679-42535-7 RANDOM HOUSE $30.00
0-345-40437-8 BALLANTINE PB $18.00

Gerald L. **Posner**

Case Closed: Lee Harvey Oswald and the Assassination of JFK

"By far the most lucid and compelling account of what probably happened in Dallas—and what almost certainly did not. No serious historian who writes about the assassination in the future will be able to ignore it"—*NY Times*

0-385-47446-6 ANCHOR PB $14.95

David **Scheim**

Contract on America: The Mafia Murder of President John F. Kennedy

0-8217-3833-X ZEBRA PB $5.99

The Warren Commission

The Warren Commission Report: Report of the President's Commission on the Assassination of President John F. Kennedy

Over 800 pages comprising the official, complete, and unabridged report, itself an object of as much controversy as its purported subject

0-312-08257-6 ST. MARTIN'S PB $12.95

Gary **Wills** & others

Jack Ruby

0-306-80564-2 DA CAPO PB $13.95

Civil Rights

Liva **Baker**

The Second Battle of New Orleans: The Hundred-Year Battle to Integrate the Schools

Following *Brown v. Board of Education,* the landmark ruling declaring racial segregation in public schools unconstitutional, the city of New Orleans began a seven-year struggle toward integration. This follows the tumultuous events and introduces a cast of historic characters: Ruby Bridges, a six-year-old black girl who endured appalling threats; Skelly Wright, a white federal judge who risked career and life to enforce the law; the young Thurgood Marshall, then working at the NAACP; and many others who took part in a key moment of American history

See also **THE CIVIL RIGHTS MOVEMENT AND BEYOND** under **AFRICAN-AMERICAN STUDIES**

0-06-016808-0 HARPERCOLLINS $32.00

Rhoda Lois **Blumberg**

Civil Rights: The 1960s' Freedom Struggle

This 1991 overview of the civil-rights revolution provides a good introduction to a subject whose literature is now immense

0-8057-9734-3 TWAYNE PB $15.95

Taylor **Branch**

Parting the Waters: America in the King Years, 1954-1963

A powerful, scrupulously detailed account of the early civil rights years

See also **THE CIVIL RIGHTS MOVEMENT AND BEYOND** under **AFRICAN-AMERICAN STUDIES**

0-671-68742-5 TOUCHSTONE PB $16.00

Hugh Davis **Graham**

Civil Rights and the Presidency: Race and Gender in American Politics, 1960-1972

0-19-507322-3 OXFORD PB $15.95

E. Culpepper **Clark**

The Schoolhouse Door: Segregation's Last Stand at the University of Alabama

The antecedents and repercussions of George Wallace's 1963 defiance of court-ordered desegregation and his backing down before Kennedy, who went on TV to call civil rights a "moral issue"

0-19-509658-4 OXFORD PB $15.95

Michael D. **Davis** & Hunter R. **Clark**

Thurgood Marshall: Warrior at the Bar, Rebel on the Bench

A landmark biography of the first African-American to serve on the United States Supreme Court. The authors trace Marshall's career as a pioneering civil rights lawyer and one of this country's great liberal justices, offering insights into some of the most sensitive social issues of our time

1-55972-133-2 BIRCH LANE $24.95

John **Egerton**

Speak Now Against the Day: The Generation Before the Civil Rights Movement in the South

"Throws much-needed light on a biracial Gideon's army of heroic Southerners who fought the good fight years before the civil rights movement flourished"—Studs Turkel

0-679-40808-8 KNOPF $35.00

James Max **Fendrich**

Ideal Citizens: The Legacy of the Civil Rights Movement

Traces the social and political careers of black and white civil rights activists and their nonactivist counterparts over a quarter of a century

See also **THE CIVIL RIGHTS MOVEMENT AND BEYOND** under **AFRICAN-AMERICAN STUDIES**

0-7914-1324-1 SUNY PB $16,95

Melissa Fay **Greene**

The Temple Bombing

0-201-62206-8 ADDISON-WESLEY $25.00

Henry **Hampton** & Steve **Fayer**

Voices of Freedom: An Oral History of the Civil Rights Movement from the 1950s Through the 1980s

Companion volume to *Eyes on the Prize*, drawing on nearly one thousand interviews. "A vast choral pageant that recounts the momentous work of the civil rights struggle" —*NY Times Book Review*

See also **THE CIVIL RIGHTS MOVEMENT AND BEYOND** under **AFRICAN-AMERICAN STUDIES**

0-553-35232-6 BANTAM PB $18.95

Doug **McAdam**

Freedom Summer

In 1964, over 1000 mostly white college students arrived in Mississippi as part of a campaign to register black voters. By summer's end, four had died and hundreds had endured bombings, hearings, and arrests

0-19-506472-0 OXFORD PB $13.95

Anne **Moody**

Coming of Age in Mississippi

A memoir of lynchings, economic hardship, and the brutal times of a black female civil rights activist of the '60s

See also **THE CIVIL RIGHTS MOVEMENT AND BEYOND** under **AFRICAN-AMERICAN STUDIES**

0-440-31488-7 LAUREL LEAF PB $6.50

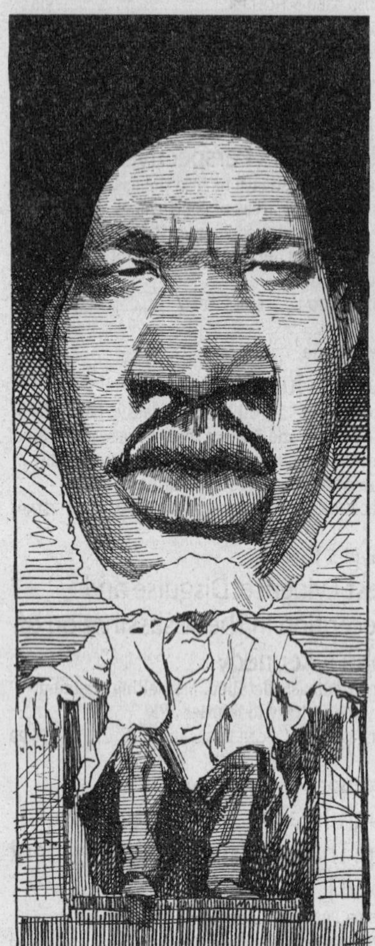

Martin Luther King, Jr.

Stephen B. **Oates**

Let the Trumpet Sound: The Life of Martin Luther King, Jr.

See also **20TH-CENTURY** under **BIOGRAPHIES** under **CHRISTIANITY** in **RELIGION, SPIRITUALITY, AND PHILOSOPHY**

0-06-092473-X HARPERPERENNIAL PB $16.00

William **Pepper**

Orders to Kill: The Truth About the Murder of Martin Luther King

0-7867-0253-2 CARROLL & GRAF $28.00

Maryanne **Vollers**

Ghosts of Mississippi

National Book Award finalist—a brilliant examination of the 1963 murder of civil rights leader Medgar Evers and the three-decade crusade to convict his murderer. "...Prizewinning journalism, a compelling tale that speaks volumes about the transformation of the Deep South—and of America"—David Lamb

0-316-91485-1 LITTLE, BROWN $24.95
0-316-91471-1 LITTLE, BROWN PB $13.95

Juan **Williams**

Eyes on the Prize: America's Civil Rights Years, 1954-1965

Illustrated accompaniment to the PBS television series

See also **THE CIVIL RIGHTS MOVEMENT AND BEYOND** under **AFRICAN-AMERICAN STUDIES**

INTRODUCTION BY JULIAN BOND

0-14-009653-1 PENGUIN PB $14.95

The '60s

"By the time the decade reached its end with episodes like the Weatherman rampage in Chicago, 'the '60s' represented not just a span of time but an impetuous, extreme spirit—youthful and reckless, searching and headstrong, foolhardy, romantic, willing to try almost anything...The spirit of ecstatic freedom proved impossible to sustain. The Movement collapsed, leaving behind a congeries of smaller single-issue movements, demanding peace in Vietnam, dignity for blacks, liberation for women, respect for homosexuality, reverence for the balance of nature. Frustrated revolutionists built bombs, turning reveries of freedom into cruel, ineffectual outbursts of terrorism. And one by one, the political pilgrims who had created 'the '60s' fell back to earth."—James Miller, *"Democracy Is in the Streets": From Port Huron to the Siege of Chicago*

Terry **Anderson**

The Movement and the '60s

0-19-510457-9 OXFORD PB $16.95

Paul **Berman**

A Tale of Two Utopias: The Political Journey of the Generation of 1968

Berman, a staff writer for *The New Yorker* and a MacArthur Fellow, captures a 30-year journey through the American left, following the growth of the '68 generation from the flowering of liberal passions to the philosophical confusion of Communism's downfall and "the end of history"

0-393-03927-7 NORTON $24.00

Scott L. **Bills**

Kent State/May 4: Echoes Through a Decade

The killing of four students—three of them bystanders—at a college protest was the climactic event of a tumultuous decade; this anthology offers essays and interviews with those touched by the violence

0-87338-360-5 KENT STATE PB $14.00

John H. **Bunzel**, editor

Political Passages: Journeys of Chance Through Two Decades

Essays reflecting on the legacy of the '60s, by such writers as Carol Iannone, Michael Novak, Ronald Radosh, and Richard Rodriguez

0-02-904921-0 FREE PRESS $27.95

David Mark **Chalmers**

And the Crooked Places Made Straight: The Struggle for Social Change in the 1960's

0-8018-4174-7 JOHNS HOPKINS PB $12.95

Peter **Clecak**

America's Quest for the Ideal Self: Dissent and Fulfillment in the '60s and 70s

Argues for one extended period, marked by a quest for individual self-fulfillment

0-19-503544-5 OXFORD PB $18.95

Peter **Collier** & David **Horowitz**

Destructive Generation: Second Thoughts About the '60s

The authors of *The Kennedys* argue that the leftist ideology of the 1960s damaged the nation

0-684-82641-0 FREE PRESS PB $14.00

David **Farber**

The Age of Great Dreams: America in the 1960s

Beyond the clichéd images of psychedelic rock posters shines the decade that changed the world in the context of the New Deal, America's postwar rise to a superpower global position, and the coming of age of a mass media marketplace

0-8090-2401-2 HILL & WANG $25.00
0-8090-1567-6 FS&G PB $11.95

Chicago '68

The full story of the epochal event told from three perspectives: Yippies, antiwar protesters, and Mayor Daley and his police

0-226-23800-8 CHICAGO $29.95
0-226-23801-6 CHICAGO PB $14.95

David **Farber**, editor

The '60s: From Memory to History

Eleven essays by young scholars. "A unique and necessary contribution to our understanding of the '60s, one that should help wrench discussions away from the nostalgic realm where even among academics they have remained for far too long"—Robert A. Rosenstone, CIT

0-8078-4462-4 NORTH CAROLINA PB $15.95

Todd **Gitlin**

The '60s: Years of Hope, Days of Rage

"Brilliant in its understanding of the New Left as a genuinely American insurgency, rooted in the mass culture of the '50s; and brave for its revealingly self-critical analysis of why that movement faded all too soon"
—Barbara Ehrenreich

0-553-34601-6 BANTAM PB $15.95

Kenneth J. **Heineman**

Campus Wars: The Peace Movement at American State Universities in the Vietnam Era

0-8147-3512-6 NYU PB $18.95

Abbie **Hoffman**

The Best of Abbie Hoffman: Selections from *Revolution for the Hell of It, Woodstock Nation,* and *Steal This Book*

0-941423-27-1 FOUR WALLS $21.95
0-941423-42-5 FOUR WALLS PB $14.95

Steal This Book

"*[Steal This Book]* reads as if Hoffman decided it was time to sit down and advise his children on what to avoid and what was worth having in America. He says that if you want to be free, then America might kill you. You must know certain things if you are to survive…"
—Dotson Rader, *NY Times Book Review*

1-56858-053-3 FOUR WALLS PB $9.95

Abbie Hoffman

Gerald **Howard**, editor

The '60s: The Art, Attitudes, Politics, and Media of our Most Explosive Decade

A wide selection of essays about the '60s and from the '60s

1-56924-824-9 MARLOWE PB $14.95

Andrew **Jamison** & Ron **Eyerman**

Seeds of the '60s

An intimate portrait of the intellectual legacy that the '60s inherited

0-520-08516-7 CALIFORNIA $25.00
0-520-20341-0 CALIFORNIA PB $12.95

Myron **Magnet**

The Dream and the Nightmare: The '60s Legacy to the Underclass

"To read Magnet is to realize that the conservative critique of contemporary America is the more—indeed, the only—radical critique just now"—George F. Will

0-688-13512-9 QUILL PB $12.00

Allen J. **Matusow**

The Unraveling of America: A History of Liberalism in the 1960s

"May well be the definitive analysis"
—Bill Youngblood, *Fort Worth Star Telegram*

0-06-132058-7 HARPERCOLLINS PB $17.00

Joan K. **Morrison** & Robert K. **Morrison**

From Camelot to Kent State: The '60s Experience in the Words of Those Who Lived It

0-8129-1715-4 TIMES BOOKS PB $17.00

William L. **O'Neill**

Coming Apart: An Informal History of America in the 1960s

0-8129-6223-0 TIMES BOOKS PB $14.00

W.J. **Rorabaugh**

Berkeley at War: The 1960s

The best account of People's Park and its repercussions; published in 1989

0-19-506667-7 OXFORD PB $13.95

Nora **Sayre**

'60s Going on '70s

"The best reportage on the '60s"
—*NY Times Book Review*

0-8135-2193-9 RUTGERS PB $18.95

Jay **Stevens**

Storming Heaven: LSD and the American Dream

Charts LSD's brief but convulsive reign in America, from CIA projects of chemical warfare to Timothy Leary's turning on

0-06-097172-X HARPERCOLLINS PB $14.00

Barbara L **Tischler**, editor

Sights on the '60s

Offers useful information on the New Left and counterculture

0-8135-1793-1 RUTGERS PB $15.00

"Hippies"

Peter O. **Whitmer** & Bruce van **Wyngarden**

Aquarius Revisited: Seven Who Created the '60s Counterculture that Changed America

The decade dissected through the lives and ideas of William Burroughs, Allen Ginsberg, Ken Kesey, Timothy Leary, Norman Mailer, Tom Robbins, and Hunter S. Thompson

0-8065-1222-9 CITADEL PB $10.95

Harris **Wofford**

Of Kennedys and Kings: Making Sense of the '60s

An illuminating, anecdotal account of the '60s by the US Senator from Pennsylvania who was a special assistant to JFK, adviser to Martin Luther King, and cofounder of the Peace Corps

0-8229-5808-2 PITTSBURGH PB $16.95

The Nixon Years

Richard M. **Nixon**
No More Vietnams
0-380-70119-7 AVON PB $4.99

The Real War
0-671-70617-9 TOUCHSTONE PB $12.95

Monica **Crowley**
Nixon Off the Record
0-679-45681-3 RANDOM HOUSE $23.00

J. Anthony **Lukas**
Common Ground: A Turbulent Decade in the Lives of Three American Families
0-394-74616-3 VINTAGE PB $17.00

Stephen E. **Ambrose**
Nixon: Ruin and Recovery, 1973-1990
The Watergate debacle and after: Ambrose traces Richard Nixon's self-destruction and then examines the equally remarkable process by which he resurrected himself as "elder statesman"
0-671-69188-0 TOUCHSTONE PB $27.50

Fawn M. **Brodie**
Richard Nixon: The Shaping of His Character
0-393-01467-3 NORTON $18.95

W.D. **Ehrhart**
Busted: A Vietman Veteran in Nixon's America
Part of a fine autobiographical trilogy exploring the legacy of Vietnam
See also **MEMOIRS** under **THE VIETNAM WAR**
0-87023-955-4 MASSACHUSETTS $21.95

H.R. **Haldeman**
The Haldeman Diaries: Inside the Nixon White House
From the controversial chief of staff who meticulously recorded everything. "A record of the way the Oval Office works that may never again be matched"—*The Washington Times*
0-425-14827-0 BERKLEY PB $7.99

Gerald Ford

Joe **McGinniss**
The Selling of the President, 1968
How Nixon was successfully repackaged by advertising advisers during the 1968 presidential campaign
0-14-011240-5 PENGUIN PB $13.95

Roger **Morris**
Richard Milhous Nixon: The Rise of an American Politician
"A massive, powerful biographical portrait of the 37th President as a full, if flawed, human being and not merely a symbol to be accepted or rejected on partisan grounds"
—Kevin Starr, *NY Times*
0-8050-1121-8 HOLT $29.95

Jonathan **Schell**
The Time of Illusion
Beautifully analyzes Nixon's administration
0-394-72217-5 RANDOM HOUSE PB $9.75

Terry **Terriff**
The Nixon Administration and the Making of US Nuclear Strategy
A scholarly critique of the Nixon administration's doctrine of "limited nuclear options"
0-8014-3082-8 CORNELL $35.00

Tom **Wicker**
One of Us: Richard Nixon and the American Dream
"Mr. Wicker's knowledge, insight and fairness have enabled him…to see [Nixon]…as a more representative and a more tragically interesting figure than either the implausible heir of Metternich or the dark creation of liberal paranoia"
—Godfrey Hodgson, *NY Times Book Review*
0-394-55066-8 RANDOM HOUSE PB $24.95

Garry **Wills**
Nixon Agonistes: The Crisis of the Self-Made Man
A first-rate analysis of a troubled presidency, perhaps the finest of Wills's commentaries on recent commanders-in-chief
0-87797-198-6 CHEROKEE $34.95

Bob **Woodward**
The Final Days
Nixon's last days in the White House and his struggle against resignation
0-671-69087-6 TOUCHSTONE PB $8.95

Bob **Woodward** & Carl **Bernstein**
All the President's Men
How two green *Washington Post* reporters toppled a presidency
0-671-89441-2 TOUCHSTONE PB $12.00

Carter and the '70s

Douglas **Brinkley**
Jimmy Carter: The Post-Presidential Years
0-679-44742-3 RANDOM HOUSE PB $25.00

Peter N. **Carroll**
It Seemed Like Nothing Happened: America in the 1970s
Argues that, in fact, the decade was filled with dramatic events and changes
0-8135-1538-6 RUTGERS PB $15.00

Jimmy **Carter**
Keeping Faith: Memoirs of a President
0-553-05023-0 BANTAM DOUBLEDAY DELL $22.50

Turning Point: A Candidate, a State and a Nation Come of Age
See also **THE PRESIDENCY** under **AMERICAN POLITICS AND FOREIGN POLICY**
0-8129-2299-9 TIMES BOOKS PB $13.00

Jimmy Carter (credit: ©Rick Diamond Photography, Inc.)

Gaddis **Smith**
Morality, Reason and Power: American Diplomacy in the Carter Years
A Yale historian's analysis of Carter's foreign policy
0-8090-0168-3 HILL & WANG PB $11.95

The Reagan Years

Tom **Blanton**, editor
White House E-Mail: The Top-Secret Messages the Reagan/Bush White House Thought They Had Destroyed
North, Poindexter, Hall, Powell, and others gossip and joke electronically
1-56584-276-6 NEW PRESS PB $14.95

Paul **Boyer**, editor
Reagan as President: Contemporary Views of the Man, His Politics and His Policies
Close to 100 articles ranging from the intensely admiring to the deeply critical
0-929587-28-6 DEE PB $8.95

Donald T. **Regan**
For the Record: From Wall Street to Washington
0-312-91518-7 ST. MARTIN'S PB $4.95

Ronald Reagan

Peter **Irons**

Brennan vs. Rehnquist: The Battle For the Constitution

The 20-year fight for control of the Supreme Court between Eisenhower appointee Brennan and Nixon's Rehnquist is a story that illuminates and dramatizes the central issues of democracy in our time

0-679-42436-9 KNOPF $27.50

Claus **Jensen**

No Downlink: A Dramatic Narrative about the Challenger Incident and Our Time

See also **SPACE EXPLORATION** under **ASTRONOMY** in **SCIENCE**

0-374-12036-6 FS&G $25.00

Kevin **Phillips**

The Politics of Rich and Poor: The American Electorate in the Reagan Aftermath

A probe of the consequences of Reaganism and the widening gap between rich and poor. The incisive conservative political analyst, who named the Sunbelt and blueprinted Nixon's emerging Republican majority, predicts a swing toward a new populism

0-06-097396-X HARPERCOLLINS PB $11.00

George P. **Schultz**

Turmoil and Triumph: Diplomacy, Power and the Victory of the American Ideal

The former secretary of state's bestselling chronicle of the Reagan years. "The most detailed, vivid, outspoken, and reliable record we probably shall have of the 1980s"
—*American Historical Review*

0-684-80332-1 TOUCHSTONE PB $20.00

Robert **Timberg**

The Nightingale's Song

Five US Naval Academy graduates who served in Vietnam and rose to prominence, then became embroiled in controversy under Ronald Reagan

0-684-82673-9 TOUCHSTONE PB $14.00

Gary **Sick**

October Surprise: America's Hostages and the Election of Ronald Reagan

A disturbing, meticulously documented account of the secret hostage deals that ensured the election of Reagan in 1980, written by the National Security Council staff member who first broke the story. Peopled by greedy spies, unscrupulous mullahs, arms dealers looking to make a quick million, and the ubiquitous, conveniently deceased William Casey

0-8129-1989-0 TIMES BOOKS PB $23.00

A U.S. brigadier general was summoned to the office of General David Jones, the chairman of the Joint Chiefs of Staff, and was told that the President [Carter] had approved the planning and development of a new operation to rescue the U.S hostages…His name was Richard V. Secord

OCTOBER SURPRISE: AMERICA'S HOSTAGES AND THE ELECTION OF RONALD REAGAN

Stephen **Vaughn**

Ronald Reagan in Hollywood: Movies and Politics

Reveals the performing craft of Ronald Reagan in radio and in films such as *Kings Row* (1942), *Voice of the Turtle* (1947), *John Loves Mary* (1949), and *The Girl from Jones Beach* (1949). "This book is not about 'The Films of Ronald Reagan,' but instead about the films set against the background of the studio, the country, and the star, whose transition from liberal to conservative has already been noted, but not in this way"—Bernard F. Dick

0-521-44080-7 CAMBRIDGE $27.95

George F. **Will**

Will, one of our best-known political commentators, has built a reputation based as much on his eloquence as his conservative outlook

The Morning After: American Successes and Excesses, 1981-1986

See also **CURRENT POLITICAL THOUGHT AND ISSUES** under **AMERICAN POLITICS AND FOREIGN POLICY**
See also **HISTORY, POLITICS, AND SOCIETY** under **20TH-CENTURY AMERICAN ESSAYS AND JOURNALISM**

0-02-934430-1 FREE PRESS $24.95

Realignments: Bush, Clinton, and the Republican Resurgence

Charles F. **Allen** & others

The Comeback Kid: The Life and Career of Bill Clinton

Includes extensive interviews with both the candidate and his wife, Hillary, and with friends, former teachers, and others. It traces Clinton's career and inquires how he has dealt with everything from charges of an illicit 12-year affair to his alleged avoidance of the draft

1-55972-154-5 BIRCH LANE $18.95

David **Brock**

The Seduction of Hillary Rodham

A new biography by the conservative writer

0-684-83451-0 SIMON & SCHUSTER $26.00

Elizabeth **Drew**

Showdown: The Struggle Between the Gingrich Congress and the Clinton White House

0-684-81518-4 SIMON & SCHUSTER $25.00

James William **Gibson**

Warrior Dreams: Paramilitary Culture in Post-Vietnam America

Combat magazines, films, novels: a vast fantasy of violence thrives in America and has spawned the militaristic realities of the Aryan Nation, contract killers, and mercenaries in Central America. Gibson maps the new American war zone as a theorist and gonzo journalist, providing a fascinating tour of paintball games, shooting ranges, and soldier of fortune conventions

0-8090-9666-8 HILL & WANG $23.00
0-8090-1578-1 HILL & WANG $12.00

Bill Clinton

David **Maraniss**

First in His Class: The Biography of Bill Clinton

0-684-81890-6 TOUCHSTONE PB $14.00

Jim **Moore**

Clinton: Young Man in a Hurry

The key to understanding Clinton the presidential candidate, Moore says, is knowing Clinton the governor. *Young Man in a Hurry* paints a detailed portrait of Clinton's record in Arkansas, on education, the state's economy, and on both his successes and failures. It also examines Clinton's presidential platform

1-56530-006-8 SUMMIT $22.95

Roger **Morris**

Partners in Power: The Clintons and Their America

A senior staff member of the National Security Council under Johnson and Nixon, Morris offers an insider's analysis of the Washington maze that Clinton inherited—lobbyists, key committee staffers, the military, and the Capitol Hill bureaucracy—and delivers an incisive status report on how the Clinton administration is negotiating this obstacle course to deliver on its promises of change

0-8050-2804-8 HOLT $27.50

Martin **Walker**

The President We Deserve: Bill Clinton and the New American

0-517-59871-X CROWN $27.50

Peggy **Noonan**

Life, Liberty, and the Pursuit of Happiness

Noonan's bestseller *What I Saw at the Revolution* provided a revealing look into the Reagan White House. Here, she gives us her view from another perch: as a single mother in New York who returns as the Republican prodigal daughter in an attempt to resuscitate the dying Bush regime

0-679-40160-1 RANDOM HOUSE $23.00
1-55850-509-1 ADAMS PB $10.95

David G. **Savage**

Turning Right

A controversial and well-documented critical guide to the Rehnquist court

0-471-53660-1 WILEY $22.95

Biographies

Howard B. **Schaffer**

Chester Bowles: New Dealer in the Cold War

Chester Bowles (1901-1986) headed his own successful advertising firm (1929-1941) before beginning a long career in public service. Elected Democratic governor of Connecticut in 1948, he was the first to set up a State Commission on Civil Rights. As a highly visible ambassador to India during the Truman administration, Bowles developed a sympathetic understanding of India's economic problems and its policy of nonalignment. He returned to New Delhi during the Kennedy and Johnson administrations. "[A] carefully crafted and thoughtful portrait"
—Gary R. Hess, author of *Vietnam and the United States: Origins and Legacy of War*

0-674-11390-X HARVARD $29.95

Lawrence **Levine**

Defender of the Faith: William Jennings Bryan—the Last Decade, 1915-1925

0-674-19542-6 HARVARD PB $15.95

Donald R. **McCoy**

Calvin Coolidge: The Quiet President

"McCoy [shows] that Coolidge was a fairminded, sincere, assiduous, and idealistic president"
—*American Historical Review*

0-7006-0351-4 KANSAS PB $14.95

Mike **Royko**

Boss: Richard J. Daley of Chicago

A sardonic portrait by the Chicago columnist which presents Chicago's mayor from 1955 to 1976 as the quintessential big-city boss

0-452-26167-8 NEW AMERICAN LIBRARY PB $10.95

Hollinger **Barnard**, editor

Outside the Magic Circle: The Autobiography of Virginia Foster Durr

The metamorphosis of a Southern belle into a New Deal liberal and champion of civil rights

FOREWORD BY STUDS TERKEL

0-8173-0517-3 ALABAMA PB $17.95

Randall Bennett **Woods**

Fulbright: A Biography

Authoritative study of the Arkansas senator. Fulbright (1905-1995) served as chairman of the Senate Committee on Foreign Relations from 1959 to 1974, from whose vantage he challenged the use of executive power in determining foreign policy

0-521-48262-3 CAMBRIDGE $29.95

Robert Alan **Goldberg**

Barry Goldwater

0-300-06261-3 YALE $27.50

Barry Goldwater

Barry M. **Goldwater**

Goldwater

Autobiography of the man who lost to LBJ in a landslide but inaugurated the "new conservatism" that led to the electoral triumph of Ronald Reagan

0-312-92000-8 ST. MARTIN'S PB $5.95

David **Gollaher**

Voice for the Mad: The Life of Dorothea Dix

0-02-912399-2 FREE PRESS $28.00

Woody **Guthrie**

Bound For Glory

0-8446-6178-3 SMITH $22.25
0-452-26445-6 NEW AMERICAN LIBRARY PB $13.95

Edward Jay **Epstein**

The Three Lives of Armand Hammer

See also **CORPORATE LEADERSHIP AND CEO BIOGRAPHIES** under **BUSINESS, INDUSTRY, AND FINANCE** in **BUSINESS AND REFERENCE**

0-679-44802-0 RANDOM HOUSE $30.00

George H. **Nash**

The Life of Herbert Hoover

Volume 1
The Engineer, 1874-1914

0-393-01634-X NORTON $25.00

Volume 2
The Humanitarian, 1914-1917

0-393-02550-5 NORTON $25.00

Volume 3
Master of Emergencies, 1917-1918

0-393-03841-6 NORTON $45.00

Curt **Gentry**

J. Edgar Hoover: The Man and the Secrets

The most revealing book ever written about the FBI chief sets forth in shocking detail the undue influence he wielded over American governments and his agency's long record of distortion and corruption. With new information from hidden FBI files

0-393-02404-0 NORTON $29.95
0-452-26904-0 PLUME PB $15.00

Richard G. **Powers**

Secrecy and Power: The Life of J. Edgar Hoover

See also **THE CIA, FBI, AND ESPIONAGE** under **AMERICAN POLITICS AND FOREIGN POLICY**

0-02-925061-7 FREE PRESS PB $18.95

Robert **Caro**

The Path to Power: The Years of Lyndon Johnson

0-394-49973-5 KNOPF $29.95
0-394-71654-X VINTAGE PB $9.95

Means of Ascent: The Years of Lyndon Johnson

The highly admired but controversial biography continues. During Johnson's middle years the focus is on the Texas senatorial election of 1948, Coke Stevenson, and Johnson's aggressive personality

0-394-52835-2 KNOPF $24.95

Huey Long

Robert **Dallek**

Lone Star Rising: Lyndon B. Johnson and His Times, 1908-1960

An impressively researched account of LBJ's rise to power, the first of a projected two-volume biography

0-19-505435-0 OXFORD $35.00
0-19-507904-3 OXFORD PB $16.95

As Hubert Humphrey recalled: "Lyndon kept saying that we had to wait until McCarthy began attacking the more conservative, the respected, the senators of what you might call the old school." Johnson had also warned Humphrey to keep away from McCarthy. "He just eats fellows like you. You're nourishment for him…The only way we'll ever get Joe McCarthy is when he starts attacking some conservatives around here, and then we'll put an end to it." Johnson had told Maury Maverick that he deplored the "hysteria around the country and in the Government," but "you have got to realize that atmosphere can be dispelled only by letting it run its course so that people can see for themselves what is really behind all the noise." McCarthy is "the sorriest senator up here," Johnson had told Bobby Baker. "Can't tie his goddamn shoes. But he's riding high now, he's got people scared to death some Communist will strangle 'em in their sleep, and anybody who takes him on before the fevers cool—well, you don't get in a pissin' contest with a polecat."
LONE STAR RISING: LYNDON B. JOHNSON AND HIS TIMES, 1908-1960

Christopher **Matthews**

Kennedy and Nixon: The Rivalry that Shaped Postwar America

The rivalry between Richard Nixon and JFK is not only of biographical interest, but also had lasting impact on contemporary American history. Provides new insight into two towering American presidencies

0-684-81030-1 SIMON & SCHUSTER $25.00

Walter **Isaacson**

Kissinger: A Biography

An examination of the life of the master diplomat and Nixon's secretary of state

See also **MEMOIRS AND BIOGRAPHIES** under **AMERICAN POLITICS AND FOREIGN POLICY**

0-671-87236-2 TOUCHSTONE PB $16.00

Henry Kissinger

T. Harry **Williams**

Huey Long

Full-scale biography of Louisiana's "Kingfish"; the nonfiction version of *All the King's Men*

0-394-42954-0 RANDOM HOUSE $40.00
0-394-74790-9 RANDOM HOUSE PB $21.00

Michael **Schaller**

Douglas MacArthur: The Far Eastern General

0-19-506332-5 OXFORD PB $12.95

Frank E. **Vandiver**

Black Jack: The Life and Times of John J. Pershing

A 2-volume set

0-89096-024-0 TEXAS A & M $49.95

John J. Pershing

William **Manchester**

Disturber of the Peace: The Life of H.L. Mencken

The best biography of the exuberant iconoclast who did much to establish the cultural tone of the '20s

0-87023-544-3 MASSACHUSETTS PB $19.95

Robert **Caro**

The Power Broker: Robert Moses and the Fall of New York

Combines good reporting and good writing, and reminds that no interesting public figure is a stick figure

0-394-48076-7 KNOPF $45.00
0-394-72024-5 RANDOM HOUSE PB $24.00

Joann **Robinson**

Abraham Went Out: A Biography of A.J. Muste

Biography of the noted peace, labor, and civil rights activist

0-87722-231-2 TEMPLE $27.95
0-87722-560-5 TEMPLE PB $14.95

Tip **O'Neill**

Man of the House: The Life and Political Memoirs of Speaker Tip O'Neill

0-312-91191-2 ST. MARTIN'S PB $4.95

Roger A. **Bruns**

The Damndest Radical: The Life and World of Ben Reitman, Chicago's Celebrated Social Reformer, Hobo King, and Whorehouse Physician

0-252-00984-3 ILLINOIS $29.95

Blanche Wiesen **Cook**

Eleanor Roosevelt Volume I, 1884-1933

This vivid and controversial biography describes the emergence of an insecure and repressed voting woman from a constricted background to a political force in her own right. "Blanche Cook has resurrected the Eleanor Roosevelt who was not only a woman of power and influence, a woman who changed the lives of millions, but, moreover, a thoroughly interesting human being….The freshness and centeredness of Blanche Cook's view of Eleanor make her book fascinating reading in this political season"—Abigail McCarthy, *Washington Post Book World*

See also **FIRST FAMILIES** under **THE PRESIDENCY** under **AMERICAN POLITICS AND FOREIGN POLICY**

0-14-009460-1 PENGUIN PB $14.95

However much her political vigor, new friends and public prominence might disturb the older members of her family, she herself greeted every new controversy with verve. Eleanor Roosevelt had become a feminist. She fought for women's rights steadfastly and with determination; she championed equality in public and private matters; and she herself used the word "feminist." But during the 1920s, the bitterly divisive Equal Rights Amendment ripped the women's movement apart, obscuring for decades the full dimensions of historical feminism—and ER's leadership role within it.
ELEANOR ROOSEVELT: VOLUME I, 1884-1933

Volume II: 1934-1962

0-670-84498-5 PENGUIN $24.95

Edmund **Morris**

The Rise of Theodore Roosevelt

The popular biography by Reagan's official biographer; excellent on Roosevelt's personality, but weaker on his politics

0-345-33902-9 BALLANTINE PB $16.00

Joan **Paterson Kerr**

A Bully Father: Theodore Roosevelt's Letters to His Children with a Biographical Essay and Notes

Long out of print, the witty and warm letters of Roosevelt to his six children reveal a portrait of the president unattainable by any other means. From their home in Long Island's Oyster Bay to the White House, the Roosevelts' family life revolved around the father as a loving, guiding, attentive man—one whom his wife once called "the oldest and rather worst child." "These letters…lift Roosevelt to a higher level of purely literary attainment than any of his other published writings. They are of tremendously absorbing interest from any angle of view"
—The Evening Sun, 1919

INTRODUCTION BY DAVID MCCULLOUGH

0-679-43948-X RANDOM HOUSE $25.00

Kenneth S. **Davis**

FDR: The New York Years 1928-1933

0-679-75301-X RANDOM HOUSE PB $15.00

William **Lanouette** & others

Genius in the Shadows: A Biography of Leo Szilard, the Man Behind the Bomb

Szilard's copious brainstorms made possible information theory, the atomic bomb, and Enrico Fermi's patent for CP-1. But General Groves, head of the Manhattan Project, considered him a "pushy Jew" and tried to get him interned during the war. "*Genius in the Shadows* leaves no doubt that this bizarre Hungarian was one of the great minds of our time, of any time...Mind-blowing Szilardian anecdotes make this one of the most entertaining stories in recent years"
—Dick Teresi, *NY Times Book Review*

See also **BIOGRAPHIES AND AUTOBIOGRAPHIES** under **PHYSICS** in **SCIENCE**

0-226-46888-7 CHICAGO PB $18.95

Oscar **Handlin**

Al Smith and His America

A sympathetic portrait of the four-term New York governor, the first Roman Catholic to run for president

1-55553-021-4 NORTHEASTERN PB $14.95

Jean H. **Baker**

The Stevensons: A Biography of An American Family

0-393-03874-2 NORTON $30.00

Margaret **Truman**

Bess W. Truman

0-02-529470-9 MACMILLAN $19.95

Harry S Truman

Best-selling biography by the late president's daughter

0-380-72112-0 AVON PB $12.50

Stockton **Axson**

"Brother Woodrow": A Memoir of Woodrow Wilson

0-691-03255-6 PRINCETON $29.95

John M. **Cooper**, Jr.

The Warrior and the Priest: Woodrow Wilson and Theodore Roosevelt

A comparative biography of the two dominant figures whose sophistication and character—and struggles with each other—set the tone for political debate for much of the century

0-674-94751-7 HARVARD PB $16.95

Alexander L. **George** & others

Woodrow Wilson and Colonel House: A Personality Study

The complex interrelationship of Wilson and his closest adviser, blending historical research and psychoanalytic theory

0-486-21144-4 DOVER PB $11.95

Lois Beachy **Underhill**

The Woman Who Ran for President: The Many Lives of Victoria Woodhull

"An utterly fascinating, overdue tribute to an extraordinary feminist maverick, as well as a significant contribution to the history of feminism and the suffrage movement"
—*Booklist*

See also **BIOGRAPHIES, AUTOBIOGRAPHIES, AND LETTERS** under **ANTHOLOGIES OF WOMEN'S WRITING** under **WOMEN'S STUDIES** in **SOCIAL STUDIES**

INTRODUCTION BY GLORIA STEINEM

0-14-025638-5 PENGUIN PB $13.95

The Vietnam War

"In human terms at least, the war in Vietnam was a war that nobody won—a struggle between victims. Its origins were complex, its lessons disputed, its legacy still to be assessed by future generations. But whether a valid venture or a misguided endeavor, it was a tragedy of epic dimensions."
—Stanley Karnow, *Vietnam: A History*

General Histories

Marvin E. **Gettleman**, editor

Vietnam and America: A Documented History

Documents from World War II to America's defeat in 1975

0-8021-3362-2 GROVE PB $16.95

James P. **Harrison**

The Endless War: Vietnam's Struggle for Independence

A leading Sinologist covers all sides, including some of the fullest characterizations of the Vietnamese; with a new preface

See also **VIETNAM** under **SOUTHEAST ASIA AND THE PHILIPPINES** in **WORLD HISTORY AND CURRENT AFFAIRS**

0-231-06909-X COLUMBIA PB $17.00

George C. **Herring**

America's Longest War: The United States and Vietnam, 1950-1975

Focuses on the geopolitical and cultural effects; a favorite on university campuses

0-07-554795-3 MCGRAW HILL PB $19.15

Martha **Hess**

Then the Americans Came

Twenty years after the last American helicopter lifted off from Vietnamese soil comes the first book detailing the war as lived and recounted by the Vietnamese people

0-941423-92-1 FOUR WALLS $22.95
0-8135-2145-9 RUTGERS PB $14.95

Maurice **Isserman**

Witness to War: Vietnam

0-399-52162-3 PERIGEE PB $12.00

Stanley **Karnow**

Vietnam: A History

A first-rate survey of the American era in Vietnam

See also **VIETNAM** under **SOUTHEAST ASIA AND THE PHILIPPINES** in **WORLD HISTORY AND CURRENT AFFAIRS**

0-14-014533-8 PENGUIN PB $17.95

Guenter **Lewy**

America in Vietnam

0-19-502732-9 OXFORD PB $13.95

David **Marr**

Vietnam 1945

0-520-07833-0 CALIFORNIA $50.00

Gareth **Porter**, editor

Vietnam: A History in Documents

INTRODUCTION BY GLORIA EMERSON

0-8014-2168-3 CORNELL $29.95

Grace **Sevy**

The American Experience in Vietnam: A Reader

0-8061-2390-7 OKLAHOMA PB $14.95

The Politics

Christian G. **Appy**

Working-Class War: American Combat Soldiers and Vietnam

Appy shows that social class was the most important factor determining which Americans fought and died in Vietnam: a full *80 percent* of enlisted men came from poor or working-class families

0-8078-2057-1 NORTH CAROLINA $45.00
0-8078-4391-1 NORTH CAROLINA PB $15.95

Larry **Berman**

Lyndon Johnson's War

0-393-30778-6 NORTON PB $9.95

Planning a Tragedy: The Americanization of the War in Vietnam

0-393-95326-2 NORTON PB $8.95

Robert **Buzzanco**

Masters of War: Military Dissent and Politics in the Vietnam Era

Die-hard defenders of the US role in Vietnam have long argued that America's defeat was the fault of President Johnson and his staff, who forced willing and able troops to "fight with one hand tied behind their backs." In fact, Buzzanco shows, the political will for war was fully in place, and the troops were undercut rather by civil-military acrimony, interservice rivalries, military dissent, and ever-present politics

0-521-48046-9 CAMBRIDGE $29.95

Bernard B. **Fall**

Street Without Joy

A military and political history of the pre-American conflict; first published in 1961

0-8117-1700-3 STACKPOLE $22.95

Frances **FitzGerald**

Fire in the Lake: The Vietnamese and the Americans in Vietnam

A prizewinning 1973 classic (Pulitzer, National Book Award, and Bancroft) looks at US intervention from the vantage point of Vietnamese culture and society

0-679-72394-3 VINTAGE PB $15.00

Lloyd C. **Gardner**

Approaching Vietnam: From World War II Through Dienbienphu

Analyzes events from 1941 to 1954. "Illuminates not only the origins of the Vietnam War, but the creation of the postwar world"—Ronald Steel

0-393-30578-3 NORTON PB $9.95

Pay Any Price: Lyndon Johnson and the Wars for Vietnam

Blending political biography and diplomatic history and using the newly declassified documents of the Johnson Library, Gardner brings the tragedy of Vietnam into an original political, historical, and ideological focus. Here are the behind-the-scenes decision-making, the miscalculations, the moral obtuseness, the blind optimism that created the fatal combination of fulfilling the Kennedy anticommunist pledge in Southeast Asia while also attempting to create the Great Society at home

1-56663-087-8 DEE $35.00

Leslie **Gelb** & Richard K. **Betts**

The Irony of Vietnam: The System Worked

One of the best scholarly reviews of American political decision-making on the war through 1968

0-8157-3071-3 BROOKINGS PB $18.95

David **Halberstam**

The Best and the Brightest

The founding of Kennedy's "Camelot" and how America's "best and brightest" designed a disastrous war

0-449-90870-4 FAWCETT PB $15.00

The Making of a Quagmire

A personal account of Vietnam in 1961-62 with an inside look at the press in conflict with officialdom

0-07-555092-X MCGRAW HILL PB $16.15

George C. **Herring**, editor

The Pentagon Papers

An abridged version of the shattering government report leaked to *The New York Times* by Daniel Ellsberg

0-070-28380-X MCGRAW HILL PB $14.25

Townsend **Hoopes**

The Limits of Intervention

0-393-30427-2 NORTON PB $7.95

Michael H. **Hunt**

Lyndon Johnson's War: America's Cold War Crusade in Vietnam, 1945-1965

Drawing on new sources in Washington, Hanoi, and the LBJ Library in Austin, Texas, this leading scholar of US-Asian relations explores the values, choices, and miscalculations that shaped the Cold War crusade in Vietnam from Truman to Johnson and brought tragic consequences to all its participants

0-8090-5023-4 HILL & WANG $18.00

Gabriel **Kolko**

Anatomy of War: Vietnam, the United States, and the Modern Historical Experience

"A book that goes far beyond the ambitions of earlier writers by synthesizing the difficult story of United States intervention with the yet more complicated internal dynamic of the Vietnamese Revolution. Stylish, passionate, stimulating and provocative"—*Manchester Guardian*

1-56584-218-9 NEW PRESS PB $17.95

Robert S. **McNamara** & Brian **VanDemark**

In Retrospect: The Tragedy and Lessons of Vietnam

Twenty years after the fall of Saigon, the defense secretary for Kennedy and Johnson breaks his silence and casts a revealing new light on why we went to Vietnam and what happened there

0-8129-2523-8 TIMES BOOKS $27.50

0-679-76749-5 VINTAGE PB $15.00

Myra **McPherson**

Long Time Passing: Vietnam and the Haunted Generation

"Myra MacPherson's book belongs with the best of works on Vietnam and there has been no better body of war literature that I know of" —Joseph Heller

0-385-47016-9 ANCHOR PB $15.95

William **Prochnau**

Once Upon a Distant War: Young War Correspondents and the Early Vietnam Battles

The former national correspondent for the *Washington Post* vividly renders the world of David Halberstam, Neil Sheehan, and Mal Browne, the brash young reporters who arrived in Saigon in the early '60s and became harsh and outraged critics of America's secret war. Their energy and skepticism would define how Americans at home came to see our military's activities in Vietnam and thereby change the nature of the war. Serialized in *Vanity Fair* and appeared as an HBO feature

0-8129-2633-1 TIMES BOOKS $27.50

Daniel Ellsberg

David **Rudenstine**

The Day the Presses Stopped: A History of the Pentagon Papers Case

0-520-08672-4 CALIFORNIA $34.95

Neil **Sheehan**

A Bright Shining Lie: John Paul Vann and America in Vietnam

A magisterial view of the war, told through the life of John Paul Vann, the colonel who was "the closest thing the US had to Lawrence of Arabia"

0-679-72414-1 VINTAGE PB $16.00

Kathleen J. **Turner**

Lyndon Johnson's Dual War: Vietnam and the Press

Johnson's ultimately unsuccessful struggle to gain the support of the press for the war in Vietnam

See also **THE PRESS AND GOVERNMENT** under **JOURNALISM TODAY** under **JOURNALISM** in **PERFORMING ARTS AND MEDIA**

0-226-81731-8 CHICAGO $25.00

0-226-81732-6 CHICAGO PB $14.95

Tom **Wells**

The War Within: America's Battle Over Vietnam

Interviewing virtually every important figure from the era—Dean Rusk to Daniel Ellsberg—Wells shows how the rift over Vietnam has shaped the America of today

FOREWORD BY TODD GITLIN

0-520-08367-9 CALIFORNIA $30.00

William Appleman **Williams**, editor

America in Vietnam

Public attitudes, government deceptions, and the media's impact on public support for the war; based on documents from the CIA, the media, Congress, and the government

0-393-30555-4 NORTON PB $12.95

Antiwar Movement

Many general histories include accounts of the antiwar movement and the drift of public opinion against escalating the conflict. Readers should also consult the many recent books on the 1960s, listed in "US History, 1945 to the Present," for broader views of the protests and politics.

Melvin **Small**

Covering Dissent: The Media and the Anti-Vietnam War Movement

"Melvin Small's invaluable book persuasively analyzes media coverage of the antiwar movement and in doing so shatters the persistent and mischievous notion that the media lionized the antiwar movement and undermined support for the war" —George C. Herring

0-8135-2107-6 RUTGERS PB $16.00

Johnson, Nixon, and the Doves

A history of the antiwar movement

0-8135-1287-5 RUTGERS $35.00

0-8135-1288-3 RUTGERS PB $12.00

The Battlefield

Phillip B. **Davidson**

Vietnam at War: The History, 1946-1975

A new overview of the fighting, from training and management to the battlefield, with special attention to the strategies of senior North Vietnamese general Vo Nguyen Giap

0-19-506792-4 OXFORD PB $19.95

Van Tien **Dung**

Our Great Spring Victory: An Account of the Liberation of the South

The war from the side of the senior North Vietnamese general

0-85345-409-4 MONTHLY REVIEW $15.00

Ellen **Frey-Wouters** & Robert S. **Laufer**

Legacy of a War: The American Soldier in Vietnam

0-87332-354-8 SHARPE $66.95

0-87332-562-1 SHARPE PB $23.95

Michael **Herr**

Dispatches

The ground war through the eyes of a first-time war correspondent; highly recommended

See also **REPORTING** under **20TH-CENTURY AMERICAN ESSAYS AND JOURNALISM** in **LITERATURE OF THE AMERICAS**

0-679-73525-9 VINTAGE PB $11.00

Andrew F. **Krepinevich**, Jr.

The Army and Vietnam

A US Army major analyzes the American military's flawed reliance on the conventional warfare tactics of World War II

0-8018-3657-3 JOHNS HOPKINS PB $15.95

Harry G. **Summers**, Jr.

Vietnam War Almanac

Over 440 articles on battles, weapons, military units, and key concepts, with maps and photos

0-8160-1017-X FACTS ON FILE $27.95

Strategy

James W. **Gibson**

The Perfect War: The War We Couldn't Lose and How We Did

How American planners slipped into the never-never land of technology and lost touch with reality on the battlefield

0-394-75704-1 VINTAGE PB $14.21

Bruce **Palmer**, Jr.

The 25-Year War: America's Military Role in Vietnam

A four-star general and deputy to Westmoreland reviews key wins and losses

0-8131-1513-2 KENTUCKY $27.00

John **Prados**

The Hidden History of the Vietnam War

Concentrating on crucial battles and actions, Prados determines the real circumstances leading to the astounding American military defeat

1-56663-079-7 DEE $27.50

Campaigns and Controversies

Mark **Clodfelter**

The Limits of Air Power: The American Bombing of Vietnam

0-02-905990-9 FREE PRESS $32.95

Don **Oberdorfer**

Tet: Turning Point in the Vietnam War

Retraces the surprise attacks that ripped across South Vietnam during the Vietnamese New Year in 1968

0-306-80210-4 DA CAPO PB $11.95

Ronald H. **Spector**

After Tet: The Bloodiest Year in Vietnam

0-02-930380-X FREE PRESS $29.95

0-679-75046-0 VINTAGE PB $14.00

Personal Battle Accounts

Mark **Baker**

Nam: The Vietnam War in the Words of the Men and Women Who Fought There

0-425-10144-4 BERKLEY PB $5.99

We took the gooks' weapons off them and stacked the bodies next to each other. You ever see them safari pictures when they go to Africa and they kill an elephant? The hunter steps on the head and he puts his rifle on it, like a picture of Teddy Roosevelt with a water buffalo. This is what it was like in Nam. They shot up the bodies, then they would pile the bodies up. Then they would call over the news people, like NBC news or CBS. They wasn't out there when we was shooting, but they was out there when it was over for the body count. They took pictures of the bodies strewed out there and the Americans standing around. It was like a trophy. Hey, this is trophy day. What is the hunter's kill?

NAM: THE VIETNAM WAR IN THE WORDS OF THE MEN AND WOMEN WHO FOUGHT THERE

Matthew **Brennan**

Brennan's War

A member of Blue Platoon of First Squadron, 9th Calvary—nicknamed the "headhunters" because of their high kill rate—relives the action of 1965-69

0-671-70595-4 POCKET PB $5.99

R.D. **Camp** & Eric **Hammel**

Lima-6: A Marine Company Commander in Vietnam

0-671-70436-2 POCKET PB $4.99

Philip D. **Chinnery**

Life on the Line: Stories of Vietnam Air Combat

Includes many photos

0-312-02599-8 ST. MARTIN'S $17.95

Frederick **Downs**

The Killing Zone: My Life in the Vietnam War

Detailed characterizations of men under combat

0-393-07531-1 NORTON $13.95

0-393-31089-2 NORTON PB $9.95

Bernard **Edelman**, editor

Dear America: Letters Home from Vietnam

Companion to the HBO TV special

0-671-66112-4 POCKET PB $14.00

Ron **Kovic**

Born on the Fourth of July

Paralyzed from the waist down in combat, Kovic relates his conversion from warrior and victim to antiwar activist. Book on which Oliver Stone's movie of the same name was based

0-671-73914-X POCKET PB $5.50

Robert **Mason**

Chickenhawk: A Shattering Personal Account of the Helicopter War in Vietnam

By a veteran of a thousand combat flights

0-14-007218-7 VIKING PB $10.95

Harold G. **Moore** & Joseph **Galloway**

We Were Soldiers Once...and Young: Ia Drang—The Battle that Changed the War in Vietnam

By the American officer who led the fight and the journalist who accompanied him, a blow-by-blow reenactment of the battle that marked the beginning of the massive ground war in Vietnam

0-06-097576-8 HARPERPERENNIAL PB $14.00

Al **Santoli**

Everything We Had: An Oral History of the Vietnam War by 33 American Soldiers Who Fought It

0-345-32279-7 BALLANTINE PB $5.95

John **Trotti**

Phantom Over Vietnam

A fighter pilot tells how it felt

0-89141-599-8 PRESIDIO $14.95

Keith **Walker**

A Piece of My Heart: The Stories of Twenty-Six American Women Who Served in Vietnam

0-345-33997-5 BALLANTINE PB $5.99

The Cambodian Conflict

Timothy **Castle**

At War in the Shadow of Vietnam

U.S. covert activity in Laos, 1955-1975

See also **LAOS** under **SOUTHEAST ASIA AND THE PHILIPPINES** in **WORLD HISTORY AND CURRENT AFFAIRS**

0-231-07977-X COLUMBIA PB $15.00

Martin **Goldstein**

American Policy Toward Laos

0-8386-1131-1 ASSOCIATED UNIVERSITIES $30.00

Kregg P.J. **Jorgenson**

MIA Rescue: LRRP Manhunt in the Jungle

0-87364-822-6 PALADIN $29.95

Jacques **Leslie**

The Mark: A War Correspondent's Memoir of Vietnam and Cambodia

1-56858-024-X FOUR WALLS $22.00

Marie Alexandrine **Martin** & Mark W. **McLeod**

Cambodia: A Shattered Society

0-520-07052-6 CALIFORNIA $40.00

The Aftermath

Thomas A. **Bass**

Vietnamerica: The War Comes Home

Bui Doi, "the dust of life." So were the half-Asian children of American servicemen in Vietnam called, and indeed, with the US unwilling to recognize them and the Asians only too ready to ostracize them, the appellation was apt. By the time America opened its doors to them in 1989, their average age was 19

1-56947-050-2 SOHO $25.00

Mitch **Epstein**

Vietnam: A Book of Changes

0-393-04027-5 NORTON $35.00

H. Bruce **Franklin**

M.I.A. or Mythmaking in America: How and Why Belief in Live POWs Has Possessed a Nation

"It uncovers the political sources and historical development of a national cult of grievance, whose persistence distorts our understanding of the Vietnam War and our responses to current issues in foreign affairs…A major contribution"—Richard Slotkin

0-8135-2001-0 RUTGERS PB $9.95

Bill **McCloud**

What Should We Tell Our Children About Vietnam?

0-8061-2229-3 OKLAHOMA $18.95

Jeremy **Hein**

From Vietnam, Laos and Cambodia: A Refugee Experience in the United States

The story of southeast Asian refugee settlement in the US during the past two decades, combining scholarship, demographic studies, and personal experience

0-8057-8433-0 TWAYNE PB $14.95

Laura **Palmer**

Shrapnel in the Heart: Letters and Remembrances from the Vietnam Veterans Memorial

"Helps restore humanity to a generation of young Americans who were depersonalized and dehumanized by the political passions of an unpopular war"—Ted Koppel

0-394-75988-5 VINTAGE PB $11.00

Jan **Scruggs** & Joel **Swerdlow**

To Heal a Nation: The Vietnam Veterans Memorial

The inside story of building the memorial in Washington, by a leading participant. An oversized book with many photos and a list of the Americans killed in Vietnam

0-06-092344-X HARPERPERENNIAL PB $20.00

Usha **Welaratna**

Beyond the Killing Fields: The Voice of Nine Cambodian Survivors in America

Extensive interviews and historical background depict the lives of Cambodians before the Khmer Rouge, during the ensuing holocaust, and to their ultimate journey to America

0-8047-2139-4 STANFORD $39.50
0-8047-2372-9 STANFORD PB $15.95

Literature: Fiction and Poetry

Donald **Anderson**, editor

Aftermath: An Anthology of Post-Vietnam Fiction

FORWARD BY GEORGE C. HERRING

0-8050-3656-3 HOLT PB $12.95

H. Bruce **Franklin**, editor

The Vietnam War in Songs, Poems and Stories

0-312-11552-0 ST. MARTIN'S PB $9.99

Graham **Greene**

The Quiet American

A prescient novel of Vietnam, published in 1955: cynical British opium addict's resentment of American inheritors of French colonialism leads to betrayal and murder

See also **THE EARLY 20TH CENTURY** under **20TH-CENTURY BRITISH AND IRISH FICTION** in **LITERATURE OF THE BRITISH ISLES**

0-679-60014-0 MODERN LIBRARY $13.50
0-14-018500-3 PENGUIN PB $10.95

Jon **Hasford**

The Short Timers

The inspiration for Stanley Kubrick's ***Full Metal Jacket***

0-553-26739-6 BDD PB $3.50

Larry **Heinemann**

Paco's Story

The lone survivor of an attack that killed his 90-man company returns to civilian life as a Valium-popping dishwasher in a small town cafe. Winner of the National Book Award (1987)

0-14-012761-5 VIKING PB $11.95

Tim **O'Brien**

"[O'Brien's] landscapes have the breadth and scope of Tolstoy's and the essential American wonder and innocence of his vision deserves to stand beside that of Stephen Crane"
—National Book Award Committee

Going After Cacciato

A soldier dreams he and his platoon pursue a deserter on a fantastic voyage to Paris

See also **SINCE 1945** under **20TH-CENTURY AMERICAN FICTION** in **LITERATURE OF THE AMERICAS**

0-385-28349-0 DELACORTE PB $11.95
0-440-21439-4 DELL PB $6.99

In the Lake of the Woods

From the National Book Award winner, a powerful revisiting of the legacy of the war in Southeast Asia and the return of a buried memory of the infamous Thuan Yen massacre

0-395-48889-3 HOUGHTON MIFFLIN $21.95
0-14-025094-8 PENGUIN PB $10.95

The Things They Carried

0-14-014773-X PENGUIN PB $10.95

James **Webb**, Jr.

Fields of Fire

0-671-73138-6 POCKET PB $6.50

Stephen **Wright**

Meditations in Green

The corruption and decay of Spec. 4 Griffin, who had planned to glide through the war untouched

0-385-31521-X DELTA PB $11.95

Memoirs

Philip **Caputo**

A Rumor of War

A powerful account of the author's experience in the war

See also **MEMOIRS AND JOURNALS** under **20TH-CENTURY AMERICAN ESSAYS AND JOURNALISM** in **LITERATURE OF THE AMERICAS**

0-345-38656-6 BALLANTINE PB $12.00

W.D. **Ehrhart**

Busted: A Vietnam Veteran in Nixon's America

Part of a fine autobiographical trilogy exploring the legacy of Vietnam

See also **THE NIXON YEARS** under **US HISTORY, 1945 TO THE PRESENT**

0-87023-955-4 MASSACHUSETTS $21.95

Tobias **Wolff**

In Pharoah's Army: Memoirs of the Lost War

In this sequel to his celebrated *This Boy's Life* Wolff gives us an honest and unsparing tour of duty in Vietnam. A paratrooper and Green Beret who survived service in the Mekong Delta, Wolff documents, with biographical exactitude and literary grace, the price of survival

See also **MEMOIRS AND JOURNALS** under **20TH-CENTURY AMERICAN ESSAYS AND JOURNALISM** in **LITERATURE OF THE AMERICAS**

0-679-40217-9 KNOPF $23.00

American Regional History: The West and the South

The Western Frontier: Overviews

"Americans had a safety valve for social danger, a bank account on which they might continually draw to meet losses. This was the vast unoccupied domain that stretched from the borders of the settled area to the Pacific Ocean...No grave social problem could exist while the wilderness at the edge of civilizations opened wide its portals to all who were oppressed, to all who with strong arms and stout heart desired to hew out a home and a career for themselves. Here was an opportunity for social development continually to begin over again, wherever society gave signs of breaking into classes. Here was a magic fountain of youth in which America continually bathed and was rejuvenated."—Frederick Jackson Turner, quoted in Henry Nash Smith's *Virgin Land: The American West as Symbol and Myth*

Susan **Armitage** & Elizabeth **Jameson**

The Women's West

Collection of 21 articles creates a multidimensional picture of Western women and challenges the traditional emphasis on a frontier settled by Anglo men

0-8061-2067-3 OKLAHOMA PB $16.95

Richard A. **Bartlett**

The New Country: A Social History of the American Frontier, 1776-1890

A spirited account focusing on settlement of the country, the settlers' racial and ethnic composition, agriculture, transportation, and the nature of frontier society

0-19-502021-9 OXFORD PB $24.95

Dee **Brown**

Hear that Lonesome Whistle Blow: Railroads in the West

A readable, popular account of the transcontinental railroads

0-671-89939-2 TOUCHSTONE PB $12.00

Ray Allen **Billington**

Land of Savagery, Land of Promise: The European Image of the American Frontier in the Nineteenth Century

What a typical European would have read about America during the period, from the premier frontier historian

0-8061-1929-2 OKLAHOMA PB $15.95

Wondrous Times on the Frontier

"An entertaining social history and a useful reminder of the merriment and amusement that existed, at least in small part, alongside the better-known frontier facts of loneliness, disease and fear"—*Milwaukee Journal*

0-06-097492-3 HARPERPERENNIAL PB $12.00

Robert **Clark**

River of the West: Stories from the Columbia

A revisionist history of that great river of the American West and of the American imagination

0-06-258516-9 HARPERCOLLINS $22.00

David **Dary**

Seeking Pleasure in the Old West

After a hard day's work winning the West, what did the early Americans on the frontier do to relax? Drawing on journals, memoirs, and first-hand accounts, David Dary—prize-winning author of *Cowboy Culture*—details the pleasures of the pioneers: from Indian foot races, mountain men at rendezvous, and gambling to spelling bees, church socials, and Fourth of July picnics. A vivid portrait of a rarely documented dimension of life in the West

0-394-56178-3 KNOPF $30.00

Bernard **DeVoto**

Across the Wide Missouri

Bancroft Prize-winning chronicle of the Rocky Mountain fur trade during its climax and decline; part of the American Heritage Library

0-395-08374-5 HOUGHTON MIFFLIN PB $13.95

The Course of Empire

DeVoto's trilogy tells the story of the emigrants, soldiers, refugees, heroes, villains, and bystanders of the antebellum West.

0-88411-292-6 AMEREON $31.95
0-395-51014-7 HOUGHTON MIFFLIN PB $12.95

Leroy R. **Hafen**, editor

Mountain Men and Fur Traders of the Far West

Brief biographies of 18 representative Mountain Men—the fur traders and trappers who explored the Far West in the first half of the 19th century—culled from the massive 10-volume original

0-8032-7210-3 NEBRASKA PB $12.95

Howard R. **Lamar**, editor

Reader's Encyclopedia of the American West

Over 2400 entries on its people, places, institutions, and ideas; a magnificent, endlessly entertaining reference work

0-06-270048-0 HARPERCOLLINS $50.00

Allan W. **Eckert**

The Conquerors: A Narrative

Eckert's six-part series traces the full story of the westward expansion.

0-553-25820-6 BDD PB $7.50

The Frontiersmen: A Narrative

0-553-25799-4 BDD PB $7.50

Gateway to Empire

0-553-26010-3 BDD PB $6.99

Wilderness Empire

0-553-26488-5 BDD PB $6.99

Clyde A. **Milner**

The Oxford History of the American West

The ultimate sourcebook of the West—from the Navajo settlement of the Southwest over 700 years ago to the neon of Las Vegas today. Over 200 illustrations, with text written by 28 leading historians of the West

0-19-505968-9 OXFORD $49.95

Martin **Ridge**

Rand McNally Atlas of American Frontiers

The development of the West, as seen through superb historical maps and photographs, with a scholarly text (outsize)

0-528-83493-2 RAND MCNALLY $49.95

Theodore **Roosevelt**

The Winning of the West: From the Alleghenies to the Mississippi, 1769-1776

The president-to-be's ambitious 4-volume epic about the conquest of the American West, begun in 1888. "[R]emains one of the greatest works of western history......It reflects the character of its author. It is sometimes quirky and full of prejudices and blind spots but it is cultivated and sweeping in its learning and encompassing in its judgements"—John Milton Cooper, Jr.

Volume I

0-8032-8954-5 NEBRASKA PB $15.00

Volume II

0-8032-8955-3 NEBRASKA PB $15.00

Volume III

0-8032-8956-1 NEBRASKA PB $15.00

Volume IV

0-8032-8957-X NEBRASKA PB $15.00

Henry Nash **Smith**

Virgin Land: The American West as Symbol and Myth

"The rise and decline of the conception of the West as an agrarian utopia—the myth of the 'garden of the world' "—*The Nation*

0-674-93955-7 HARVARD PB $13.95

Frederick Jackson **Turner**

The Frontier in American History

In 1893, Turner was the first to theorize that the frontier, with its endless possibilities for social regeneration, gave America its uniquely individualistic and democratic society

0-88275-347-9 KRIEGER $35.70
0-8165-0946-8 ARIZONA PB $19.50

Geoffrey C. **Ward**

The West: An Illustrated History

"Following the format of *The Civil War* and *Baseball*, two earlier book companions to Ken Burns's television series, this [is a] beautifully designed, handsomely illustrated and stylishly written social history"—*Publishers Weekly*

See also LATE ARRIVALS

0-316-92236-6 LITTLE, BROWN $60.00

Walter P. **Webb**

The Great Frontier

The frontier of America as only part of a vast movement to colonize all of the world's unexploited, habitable regions

INTRODUCTION BY ARNOLD J. TOYNBEE

0-8032-9711-4 NEBRASKA PB $9.95

David J. **Weber**

The Spanish Frontier in North America

"Splendid...Weber surveys the history of the so-called 'Spanish' borderlands of America in a grand sweep which seems to combine the narrative approach...with the cultural and ethnohistorical insights of a new generation of historians"—J.H. Elliott

0-300-05198-0 YALE $40.00

0-300-05917-5 YALE PB $18.00

Richard **White**

"It's Your Misfortune and None of My Own": A New History of the American West

0-8061-2567-5 OKLAHOMA PB $21.95

Richard **White** & Patricia Nelson **Limerick**

The Frontier in American Culture

"In this beautifully illustrated volume, two of the nation's leading western historians offer brilliant and provocative insight into why the frontier has had such a longstanding and problematic hold on American national thought"—William Cronon

EDITED BY JAMES R. GROSSMAN

0-520-08844-1 CALIFORNIA PB $15.00

Art of the West

Leonard **Engel**, editor

The Big Empty: Essays on Western Landscapes as Narrative

0-8263-1473-2 NEW MEXICO $35.00

William H. **Goetzmann** & William N. **Goetzmann**

The West of the Imagination

0-393-02370-2 NORTON PB $34.95

Helene Wickham **Koon**

Gold Rush Performers: A Biographical Dictionary of Actors, Singers, Dancers, Musicians, Circus Performers and Minstrel Players of America's Far West

0-89950-923-1 MCFARLAND $49.95

Kay Aiken **Reeve**

Santa Fe and Taos, 1898-1942: An American Cultural Center

0-87404-126-0 TEXAS WESTERN PB $10.00

Western Explorations

Stephen E. **Ambrose**

Undaunted Courage: Meriwether Lewis, Thomas Jefferson, and the Opening of the American West

0-684-81107-3 SIMON & SCHUSTER $27.50

William H. **Goetzmann**

Exploration and Empire: The Explorer and the Scientist in the American West

0-87611-135-5

TEXAS STATE HISTORICAL SOCIETY $21.95

New Lands, New Men: America and the Second Great Age of Discovery

Explorations from the 17th to the 19th centuries of the Pacific Northwest, as well as the oceans, Japan, and the polar religions. "Ultimately a tale of high adventure—both in the physical and intellectual sense"—*Texas Monthly*

0-670-81068-1 VIKING $6.98

Leroy R. **Hafen** & Ann W. **Hafen**

Old Spanish Trail, Santa Fe to Los Angeles: With Extracts from Contemporary Records

0-8032-7261-8 NEBRASKA PB $12.95

David Freeman **Hawke**

Those Tremendous Mountains: The Story of the Lewis and Clark Expedition

"Makes clear the scientific value of the expedition without in any way dulling its impact as high and heroic adventure"—*New Yorker*

0-393-30289-X NORTON PB $8.95

David **Lavender**

The Way to the Western Sea: Lewis and Clark Across the Continent

"A valuable new history of the expedition" —*Washington Post*

0-385-41155-3 ANCHOR PB $14.00

Meriwether **Lewis** & William **Clark**

The Journals of Lewis and Clark

A one-volume abridgment of the account by the explorers who saw the American West before white settlement

EDITED BY BERNARD DEVOTO

0-395-08380-X HOUGHTON MIFFLIN PB $14.95

John Wesley **Powell**

The Exploration of the Colorado River and Its Canyons

The classic first-hand account

0-486-20094-9 DOVER PB $8.95

Zebulon M. **Pike**

The Expeditions of Zebulon Montgomery

From the diaries of the daring young army officer who commanded two major exploratory expeditions in the newly acquired Louisiana Territory. Two volumes

Volume I

0-486-25255-8 DOVER PB $12.95

Volume II

0-486-25254-X DOVER PB $12.95

Wallace **Stegner**

Beyond the Hundredth Meridian: John Wesley Powell and the Second Opening of the West

"The one-armed Civil War hero who explored the great canyons of the Colorado River and then launched a political struggle for a sensible water policy for the West was certainly larger than life"—*Accent*

INTRODUCTION BY BERNARD DEVOTO

0-14-015994-0 PENGUIN PB $13.95

James Josiah **Webb**

Adventures in the Santa Fe Trade, 1844-1847

The journals of a Santa Fe trader provide a wealth of information on trappers, Mexicans, and Indian tribes of the old Southwest

EDITED BY RALPH P. BIEBER

0-8032-9772-6 NEBRASKA PB $12.00

America Moves West

Leonard J. **Arrington**

Great Basin Kingdom: An Economic History of the Latter-Day Saints, 1830-1900

0-87480-420-5 UTAH PB $14.95

Juanita **Brooks**

The Mountain Meadows Massacre

"This book remains the definitve study of that dark day in the history of Utah when an emigrant wagon crossing southern Utah was attacked by Indians and Mormons and all of the emigrants, with the exception of a few children, were slaughtered"—*Library Journal*

0-8061-2318-4 OKLAHOMA PB $17.95

Hiram Martin **Chittenden**

The American Fur Trade of the Far West

A classic history, nearly a century old

Volume 1

0-8032-6320-1 NEBRASKA PB $17.95

Volume 2

0-8032-6321-X NEBRASKA PB $11.95

Michael **Conforti**

Art and Life on the Upper Mississippi, 1880-1915

0-87413-560-5 DELAWARE $65.00

William C. **Davis**

A Way Through the Wilderness: The Natchez Trace and Civilization of the Southern Frontier

Thoroughly researched and evocative

0-06-016921-4 HARPERCOLLINS $30.00

James R. **Dickinson**

Home on the Range: A Century on the High Plains

"This is not history from the bottom up but from the inside out—life on the High Plains experienced viscerally, then reflected on shrewdly; a rare combination of emotion and analysis"—Gary Wills

0-689-12194-6 SCRIBNERS $24.00

John **Hildebrand**

Mapping the Farm: The Chronicle of a Family

0-679-43009-1 VILLARD $23.00

Julie Roy **Jeffrey**

Frontier Women: The Trans-Mississippi West, 1840-1880

How women took on roles normally reserved for men, yet clung to the Victorian values that defined their era

0-8090-0141-1 FS&G PB $10.00

David **Lavender**

The Great West

0-8281-0303-8 AMERICAN HERITAGE PB $13.95

Westward Vision: The Story of the Oregon Trail

The efforts of emigration societies, missionaries, and early pioneers and the routes they took to the "Promised Land"

ILLUSTRATED BY MARIAN EBERT

0-8032-7915-9 NEBRASKA PB $15.00

Michael **Lesy**

Wisconsin Death Trip

"Michael Lesy's grim collection of American Gothic uses old glass-plate negatives to clobber an old myth: the idyll of 'pioneers' escaping the city's evils to reap happiness on the open prairies....Lesy's reading of rural decay is history with a wrench"—*Newsweek*

0-385-41215-0 ANCHOR PB $19.95

Randolph B. **Marcy**

The Prairie Traveler: A Hand-Book for Overland Expeditions

Originally published in 1859, this bestselling guide became the principal manual for westward-bound pioneers. Today it provides a vivid sense of the dangers involved in making the trek

0-918222-89-3 APPLEWOOD PB $10.95

Gerald **McFarland**

A Scattered People: An American Family Moves West

A vivid personal history of one family's migration over almost two centuries

0-87023-765-9 MASSACHUSETTS PB $16.95

Sandra L. **Myres**

Westering Women and the Frontier Experience, 1800-1915

0-8263-0626-8 NEW MEXICO PB $16.95

John G. **Neihardt**

The Mountain Men

The first volume in the two-volume *Cycle of the West*, which "celebrates the great mood of courage that was developed west of the Missouri River in the nineteenth century." Considered by many to be Neihardt's masterwork

0-8032-5733-3 NEBRASKA PB $12.95

Francis **Parkman**

The Oregon Trail

A vivid account of Parkman's journey to Wyoming, published in 1849

See also **THE 19TH CENTURY: TO THE CIVIL WAR** under **AMERICAN LITERATURE TO 1900** in **LITERATURE OF THE AMERICAS**

EDITED BY DAVID LEVIN

0-451-52513-2 NEW AMERICAN LIBRARY PB $4.95

0-14-039042-1 VIKING PB $11.95

The Oregon Trail, The Conspiracy of Pontiac

See also **LIBRARY OF AMERICA** in **LITERATURE OF THE AMERICAS**

0-940450-54-2 LIBRARY OF AMERICA $35.00

0-517-14765-3 LIBRARY OF AMERICA PB $11.99

E.N. **Feltskog**, editor

Francis Parkman: The Oregon Trail

The definitive edition. "The most authoritative text, based on scholarly collection of all editions published in Parkman's lifetime and containing excellent critical and analytical introduction, textual and factual notes, Frederic Remington's illustrations and map. This splendid edition is essential to an understanding of the Oregon Trail"—Robert L. Gale

0-8032-8739-9 NEBRASKA PB $22.50

Francis Parkman

Fred **Reinfeld**

Pony Express

0-8032-5786-4 NEBRASKA PB $6.00

Lillian **Schlissel**

Far from Home: Families of the Westward Journey

Letters and diaries tell the stories of three families who ventured West

PREFACE BY ROBERT COLES

0-8052-0977-8 SCHOCKEN PB $14.00

Women's Diaries of the Westward Journey

A newly expanded edition of personal writings by American frontier women, which includes a new introduction by the author. "Important for anyone who wants a clearer understanding of the people, and particularly the women, who shaped a good part of the nation"—*NY Times*. "A major revelation in the recording of American history"—*San Francisco Chronicle*

INTRODUCTION BY CARL DEGLER

0-8052-1004-0 SCHOCKEN PB $14.00

It rains and snows. We start this morning around the falls with our wagons...I carry my babe and lead, or rather carry, another through snow, mud and water, almost to my knees. It is the worst road...I went ahead with my children and I was afraid to look behind me for fear of seeing the wagons turn over into the mud...My children gave out with cold and fatigue and could not travel, and the boys had to unhitch the oxen and bring them and carry the children on to camp. I was so cold and numb I could not tell by feeling that I had any feet at all...there was not one dry thread on one of us—not even my babe....

WOMEN'S DIARIES OF THE WESTWARD JOURNEY

Raymond W. **Settle** & Mary L. **Settle**

Saddles and Spurs: The Pony Express Saga

0-8032-5765-1 NEBRASKA PB $9.95

Elinore Pruit **Stewart**

Letters of a Woman Homesteader

Basis of the movie *Heartland*, a first-person account of life on the American frontier by a young widowed mother who took up homesteading in Wyoming in 1909 to prove that a woman could ranch

0-395-32137-9 HOUGHTON MIFFLIN PB $7.95

George R. **Stewart**

Ordeal by Hunger: The Story of the Donner Party

The true story of the group that set out for California in 1846, and, trapped by winter in the High Sierras, turned cannibal

0-395-61159-8 HOUGHTON MIFFLIN PB $13.95

Irving **Stone**

Men to Match My Mountains

The great popularizer's saga of the winning of the West

0-425-10544-X BERKELEY PB $16.95

Joanna **Stratton**

Pioneer Women: Voices from the Kansas Frontier

"A striking testimonial to the too often overlooked feminine half of the pioneer experience"—*Cleveland Plain Dealer*

0-671-44748-3 SIMON & SCHUSTER PB $12.95

R.B. **Stratton**
The Captivity of the Oatman Girls
A bestseller when it first appeared in 1857, this recounts the massacre of the Oatman family on the Santa Fe Trail and the captivity of two of their daughters
0-8032-9139-6 NEBRASKA PB $11.95

John D. **Unruh**, Jr.
The Plains Across: The Overland Emigrants and the Trans-Mississippi West, 1840-60
0-252-00698-4 ILLINOIS $49.95
0-252-06360-0 ILLINOIS PB $19.95

Walter P. **Webb**
The Great Plains
0-8032-9702-5 NEBRASKA PB $14.95

Legendary Figures and Places

Richard **Aquila**, editor
Wanted Dead or Alive: The American West in Popular Culture
0-252-02224-6 ILLINOIS $29.95

Don **Russell**
The Lives and Legends of Buffalo Bill
0-8061-1537-8 OKLAHOMA PB $21.95

Duncan **Aikman**
Calamity Jane and the Lady Wildcats
First published in 1927, this account also tells of Belle Starr, Madame Moustache, Poker Alice Tubbs, and Carrie Nation
INTRODUCTION BY WATSON PARKER
0-8032-5911-5 NEBRASKA PB $12.95

M. Morgan **Estergreen**
Kit Carson: A Portrait in Courage
0-8061-1601-3 OKLAHOMA PB $16.95

David **Crockett**
A Narrative of the Life of David Crockett of the State of Tennessee
Readers "should find this carefully researched and authoritative edition, which extricates the man from the myth, a valuable addition to the frontier history, biography, and literature of Tennessee and America"—Robert E. Dalton, *Tennessee History Quarterly*
0-87049-533-X TENNESSEE PB $14.95

Michael A. **Lofaro**, editor
Davy Crockett: The Man, the Legacy
0-87049-507-0 TENNESSEE PB $16.00

Stuart N. **Lake**
Wyatt Earp: Frontier Marshall
The authorized, action-packed biography
0-671-88537-5 POCKET PB $6.50

Thelma S. **Guild** & others
Kit Carson: A Pattern for Heroes
"The authors show how Carson gradually evolved from antagonist to friend of the Indian"
—*American West*
0-8032-7027-5 NEBRASKA PB $12.95

Joseph G. **Rosa**
The West of Wild Bill Hickock
"This is Wild Bill and the Wild West made easy. It is a skillful blend of photographs with useful, brief and well-organized information"
—*The Historian*
0806126899 OKLAHOMA PB $15.95

Tom **Horn**
Life of Tom Horn, Government Scout and Interpreter, Written by Himself, Together with His Letters and Statements by His Friends: A Vindication
INTRODUCTION BY DEAN KRAKEL
0-8061-1044-9 OKLAHOMA PB $10.95
0-87380-154-7 RIO GRANDE PB $12.00

Joseph C. **Rosa** & others
Buffalo Bill and His Wild West: A Pictorial Biography
0-7006-0399-9 KANSAS PB $14.95

Dan L. **Thrapp**
Encyclopedia of Frontier Biography, 3 Volumes
Profiles of 4500 frontier figures, from the famous—Billy the Kidd, Daniel Boone, Calamity Jane—to the lesser-known
0-8032-4425-8 NEBRASKA $150.00
Volume 1: A-F
0-8032-9418-2 NEBRASKA PB $20.00
Volume 2: G-O
0-8032-9419-0 NEBRASKA PB $20.00
Volume 3: P-Z
0-8032-9420-4 NEBRASKA PB $20.00

Outlaws and Vigilantes

Pearl **Baker**
The Wild Bunch at Robbers Roost
A history of the famous Utah desert hideout that often sheltered the notorious Wild Bunch in the 1890s
0-8032-6089-X BROMPTON PB $8.95

Pat **Garrett**
The Authentic Life of Billy the Kid
The original biography of one of the Old West's most famous outlaws, by the man who shot him
0-8061-1195-X OKLAHOMA PB $9.95

Jon **Tuska**
Billy the Kid: A Handbook
"This is an excellent book—the best to date on the Kid and the making of the legend"
—*Western Historical Quarterly*
0-8032-9406-9 NEBRASKA PB $9.95

Robert M. **Utley**
Billy the Kid: A Short and Violent Life
Utley, a distinguished historian of the American West, synthesizes all that we know of the obscure and troubled career of Henry McCarty, aka Billy Bonney, from his birth in New York's Irish slums to his death, aged 21, at the hands of Pat Garrett. A fascinating glimpse of the often sordid reality behind an enduring folk legend
0-8032-4553-X NEBRASKA PB $22.95

High Noon in Lincoln: Violence on the Western Frontier
Story of the 1878 Lincoln County War of New Mexico
0-8263-1201-2 NEW MEXICO PB $14.95

John **Boessenecker**
Badge and Buckshot: Lawlessness in Old California
The true stories of the once-famous peace officers and outlaws of old California, including Ben Thorn, the iron-willed but scandal-plagued sheriff of Calaveras County; the Coates-Frost feud, which left 14 men dead; and Captain Ingram's Rangers, who raided stagecoaches during the Civil War
0-8061-2097-5 OKLAHOMA $26.95
0-8061-2510-1 OKLAHOMA PB $12.95

John **Toland**
The Dillinger Days
A hard-headed, meticulously researched account of the brief but significant career of Dillinger, Public Enemy Number One, and the outlaw era
0-306-80626-6 DA CAPO PB $14.95

Thomas J. **Dimsdale**
The Vigilantes of Montana
A 19th-century account of the coming of law & order
0-8061-1379-0 OKLAHOMA PB $10.95

John Wesley **Hardin**
The Life of John Wesley Hardin as Written by Himself
INTRODUCTION BY ROBERT G. MCCUBBIN
0-8061-1051-1 OKLAHOMA PB $10.95

Larry C. **Bradley**
Jesse James: The Making of a Legend: An Account of the Much-Mythicized Missouri Bandit
0-9604370-0-2 LARREN PB $8.95

Phillip W. **Steele**
Jesse and Frank James: The Family History
0-88289-653-9 PELICAN PB $7.95

Robert **Love**
The Rise and Fall of Jesse James
The real story of a much-romanticized killer
0-8032-7932-9 BROMPTON PB $15.00

Paula Mitchell **Marks**
And Die in the West: The Story of the O.K. Corral Gunfight
A detailed narrative account of the celebrated gunfight of 1881
0-8061-2888-7 OKLAHOMA $25.00

Roger D. **McGrath**

Gunfighters, Highwaymen and Vigilantes: Violence on the Frontier

McGrath's "comparisons between crime rates in the east and on the frontier, in the present and the past, are both unique and convincing, and...[his] criticisms of other writers on frontier violence are telling"
—Ralph Mann, *New Mexico History Review*

0-520-06026-1 CALIFORNIA PB $15.00

A.S. **Mercer**

The Banditti of the Plains

FOREWORD BY WILLIAM H. KITTRELL

0-8061-1315-4 OKLAHOMA PB $10.95

John Rollin **Ridge (Yellow Bird)**

The Life and Adventures of Joaquin Murieta, the Celebrated California Bandit

INTRODUCTION BY HENRY JACKSON

0-8061-1429-0 OKLAHOMA PB $11.95

Bill **O'Neal**

Encyclopedia of Western Gunfighters

0-8061-1508-4 OKLAHOMA $37.95
0-8061-2335-4 OKLAHOMA PB $19.95

Frank Richard **Prassel**

The Great American Outlaw: A Legacy of Fact and Fiction

A comprehensive account that tries to separate fact from fiction while freely admitting the futility of such a task

0-8061-2534-9 OKLAHOMA $29.95

Joseph G. **Rosa**

Age of the Gunfighter: Men and Weapons on the Frontier, 1840-1900

0-8061-2761-9 OKLAHOMA PB $19.95

Glenn **Shirley**

Belle Starr and Her Times: The Literature, the Facts and the Legends

0-8061-2276-5 OKLAHOMA PB $14.95

Paul I. **Wellman**

A Dynasty of Western Outlaws

"...less morbid, better documented, and more interpretively written than the earlier galleries of western outlaws... a book of historical value in a field that too long has been left to legend and folklore"—*NY Times Book Review*

0-8032-9709-2 NEBRASKA PB $11.95

Cattlemen and Miners

Lewis **Atherton**

The Cattle Kings

0-8032-5759-7 NEBRASKA PB $9.95

Andy **Adams**

The Log of a Cowboy: A Narrative of the Old Trail Days

0-87928-067-0 CORNER HOUSE $26.95
0-8032-5000-2 NEBRASKA PB $9.95

Nannie T. **Alderson** & Helena H. **Smith**

A Bride Goes West

Memoir of ranching life in Montana

ILLUSTRATED BY J. COSGROVE, JR.

0-8032-5001-0 NEBRASKA PB $9.95

Robert R. **Dykstra**

The Cattle Towns

Social and political diversions in the early days of Dodge City and Abilene

0-8032-6561-1 NEBRASKA PB $15.00

Anne **Ellis**

The Life of an Ordinary Woman

Adventures and hardships of pioneer life in the mining camps and communities of the central Rocky Mountains. "Anne Ellis has added something to the story of the West as well as told an appealing and thrilling tale of how one woman faced the adventure of living"
—*NY Times*

See also **AMERICA MOVES WEST**

0-395-54412-2 HOUGHTON MIFFLIN PB $12.95

Teresa **Jordan**

Cowgirls: Women of the American West

An oral history of 28 contemporary women

0-8032-7575-7 NEBRASKA PB $14.00

Thomas J. **Noel**

The City and the Saloon: Denver, 1858-1916

0-8032-3306-X NEBRASKA PB $19.95

Malcolm J. **Rohrbough**

Aspen: The History of a Silver-Mining Town, 1879-1893

"How the mining frontier of the Colorado Rockies 'worked,' from its shaky first days, to its boom years, to ghost town"
—Walter Nugent, University of Notre Dame

0-19-504064-3 OXFORD PB $25.00

John **Seelye**, editor

Stories of the Old West: Tales of the Mining Camp & Cattle Ranch

0-14-014550-8 PENGUIN PB $13.95

Charles A. **Siringo**

A Texas Cowboy: Or, Fifteen Years On the Hurricane Deck of a Spanish Pony

0-8032-9111-6 NEBRASKA PB $10.00

Duane A. **Smith**

Rocky Mountain Mining Camps: The Urban Frontier

The overnight change from mining camps to towns and the urban problems that came with it

0-87081-266-1 COLORADO PB $17.50

Wars and Conflicts

Rebecca **Solnit**

Savage Dreams: A Journey Into the Hidden Wars of the American West

"It is an innovative combination of naturalism, history, autobiography, and social commentary, replete with the smells, touches, sights, and moods of desert and country"—Lucy R. Lippard

0-87156-526-9 SIERRA CLUB $22.00
0-679-76660-X VINTAGE PB $13.00

Robert M. **Utley**

Frontier Regulars: The United States Army and the Indian, 1866-1891

The final, massive drive by the Regular Army to subdue and control the Indians

See also **INDIAN WARS** under **NATIVE AMERICAN CULTURES: NORTH AMERICA**

0-8032-9551-0 NEBRASKA PB $17.95

Frontiersmen in Blue: The United States Army and the Indian, 1848-1865

0-8032-9550-2 NEBRASKA PB $16.95

Robert M. **Utley** & Wilcomb E. **Washburn**

Indian Wars

A well-told one-volume history

0-8281-0202-3 AMERICAN HERITAGE PB $13.95

The Making of Western States

Texas

Donald E. **Chipman**

Spanish Texas, 1519-1821

Chipman's excellent scholarship relates the ebbs and flows of Spanish Texas over three centuries. "From the founding of the first mission in 1682," the author writes, "to the last in 1793, there were close to forty different sites in Texas. Individual religious outposts lasted for less than a year to more than a hundred, but rarely were even a dozen in operation at the same time." Neatly complements David J. Weber's *Spanish Frontier in North America*

0-292-77656-X TEXAS $30.00
0-292-77659-4 TEXAS PB $14.95

Jose Enrique **de La Pena**

With Santa Anna in Texas: A Personal Narrative of the Revolution

Based on the diary of a captain in the Mexican Army, perhaps the best eyewitness account of the siege of the Alamo

TRANSLATED BY CARMEN PERRY
INTRODUCTION BY LLERENA FRIEND

0-89096-527-7 TEXAS A & M PB $14.95

David G. **McComb**

Texas: An Illustrated History

Photographs and illustrations with an entertaining and informative text

See also **SOUTHERN PLACES** under **THE NEW SOUTH**

0-19-509246-5 OXFORD $22.95
0-292-74665-2 TEXAS PB $12.95

David **Montejano**

Anglos and Mexicans in the Making of Texas, 1836-1986

0-292-77596-2 TEXAS PB $14.95

John M. **Myers**

The Alamo

0-8032-5779-1 NEBRASKA PB $8.95

John D. **Weaver**

The Brownsville Raid

This gripping 1970 expose of the 1906 injustice visited upon African-American troops in the town of Brownsville, Texas, led to Congressional action and posthumous rectification

0-89096-528-5 TEXAS A & M PB $12.95

John Hoyt **Williams**

Sam Houston: A Biography of the Father of Texas

As a teenager Houston ignored his family and rode among the Cherokee. As a man he routed the Mexican army in an unprovoked land grab, then fought tooth and nail to prevent Texas from seceding from the Union. His passion for alcohol was legendary, and he died with hardly a penny to his name

0-671-74641-3 TOUCHSTONE PB $25.00

California

William **Bronson**

The Earth Shook, the Sky Burned: A Moving Record of America's Great Earthquake and Fire, San Francisco, April 18, 1906

0-87701-389-6 CROWN PB $16.95

Chauncey L. **Canfield**, editor

The Diary of a Forty-Niner

"A remarkable drama"—*NY Times*, 1921

0-9627987-3-8 TURTLE POINT PB $12.95

James N. **Gregory**

American Exodus: The Dust Bowl Migration and Okie Culture in California

0-19-504423-1 OXFORD PB $24.95

Richard E. **Lingenfelter**

Death Valley and the Amargosa: A Land of Illusion

"Death Valley is a wilderness of extremes—the lowest, the driest, the hottest—and not surprisingly, its human history represents one more extreme, a bumptious, sleazy, hilarious Wild West Show"—Mark Munro, *Boston Globe*

0-520-06356-2 CALIFORNIA PB $18.95

David **Reid**, editor

Sex, Death, and God in L.A.

0-520-08640-6 CALIFORNIA PB $13.00

Kevin **Starr**

Americans and the California Dream, 1850-1915

"Demonstrates how idea, myth, misconception and hope shaped and often distorted a developing society"—*LA Times*

0-19-501644-0 OXFORD $35.00

Inventing the Dream: California Through the Progressive Era

Part two of Starr's cultural history focuses on the emergence of Southern California as a regional culture in its own right

0-19-503489-9 OXFORD $35.00

Other States

Odie **Faulk**

Arizona: A Short History

0-8061-1222-0 OKLAHOMA PB $14.95

Claus M. **Naske** & others

Alaska: A History of the 49th State

0-8061-2573-X OKLAHOMA PB $17.95

Kenneth Ross **Toole**

Montana: An Uncommon Land

0-8061-1890-3 OKLAHOMA PB $14.95

Edwin C. **McReynolds**

Oklahoma: The Story of Its Past and Present

0-8061-0509-7 OKLAHOMA $22.95

The 20th-Century West

Carl **Abbott**

The Metropolitan Frontier: Cities in the Modern American West

Stresses the unfairness of holding up Western cities against the idealized models of New York and Paris. "Elbow room has provided the opportunity to create entirely new communities," Abbott writes, "and to realize extreme patterns of dispersal and decentralization." For good or bad, Western cities remain pacesetters

0-8165-1129-2 ARIZONA $39.95
0-8165-1570-0 ARIZONA PB $19.95

Robert G. **Athearn**

The Mythic West in Twentieth-Century America

0-7006-0304-2 KANSAS $29.95
0-7006-0377-8 KANSAS PB $12.95

Philip L. **Fradkin**

Sagebrush Country: Land and the American West

A history of the Uinta National Forest that stretches through Utah, Wyoming, and Colorado, linking the past with such current issues as water rights, tensions between government and developers, and conflicts between conservationists and local residents

0-8165-1236-1 ARIZONA PB $19.95

Margot **Liberty** & Ray **Head**

Working Cowboy: Recollections of Ray Holmes

Born in Hulett, Wyoming, in 1911, Holmes spent his life on horseback and working with livestock. A cowboy through and through, he tells us of calving, working cattle, branding, herd management, and all that makes up the day-to-day adventure of a cowboy's life. "A good book, a fresh narrative, vivid and interesting"
—Larry McMurtry

0-8061-2692-2 OKLAHOMA $28.95

Fay E. **Ward**

The Cowboy at Work: All About His Job and How He Does It

A detailed account by an experienced practitioner

FOREWORD BY JOHN R. ERICKSON

0-8061-2051-7 OKLAHOMA PB $18.95

Patricia Nelson **Limerick**

Unbroken Past of the American West

A new interpretation, demonstrating strong continuities between the trappers, traders, Indians, farmers, oilmen, cowboys, and sheriffs of the Old West and the economic realities of today's West

0-393-30497-3 NORTON PB $12.95

Patricia Nelson **Limerick** & others, editors

Trails: Toward a New Western History

A collection of essays seeking a new, wider view of the West, in terms of race, ethnicity, gender, and the environment

0-7006-0501-0 KANSAS PB $12.95

Ann M. **Low**

Dust Bowl Diary

An autobiography of a girl growing up on a stock farm in North Dakota during the late 1920s and 1930s. "A lovingly detailed, sometimes humorous and often painful account"
—*LA Times Book Review*

0-8032-7913-2 NEBRASKA PB $8.95

Richard **Lowitt**

The New Deal and the West

How the New Deal combatted droughts, dust storms, locusts, and the Depression

FOREWORD BY MARTIN RIDGE

0-8061-2557-8 OKLAHOMA PB $14.95

Michael P. **Malone** & Richard W. **Etulain**

The American West: A Twentieth-Century History

0-8032-8167-6 NEBRASKA PB $14.95

Marc **Reisner**

Cadillac Desert: The American West and Its Disappearing Water

"A savagely witty history of America's reckless depletion of its water resources"—*Newsday*

0-14-017824-4 PENGUIN PB $14.99

Dan **Morgan**
Rising in The West: The True Story of an "Okie" Family from the Great Depression Through the Reagan Years
0-679-74593-9 VINTAGE PB $15.00

Earl **Pomeroy**
In Search of the Golden West: The Tourist in Western America
"Pomeroy has given us an acute, engaging and provocative book: a lively look at ourselves as both dudes and dude-wranglers over a century in which both time and tide were westward running"—*Saturday Review*
0-8032-8725-9 NEBRASKA PB $9.95

William G. **Robbins**
Colony and Empire: The Capitalist Transformation of the American West
A historian argues that global capitalism had a more profound impact on the modern West than individual initiative
0-7006-0645-9 KANSAS $29.95

David **Spanier**
Welcome to the Pleasuredome: Inside Las Vegas
0-87417-213-6 NEVADA PB $17.95

Mike **Tronnes**, editor
Literary Las Vegas
0-8050-3669-5 HOLT $30.00
0-8050-3670-9 HOLT PB $12.95

Peter **Wiley** & Robert **Gottlieb**
Empires in the Sun: The Rise of the New American West
"A good old fashioned muckraking journey through the slimy greed-and-growth politics of the American Southwest"—Edward Abbey
0-8165-0911-5 ARIZONA PB $18.95

Donald **Worster**
Rivers of Empire: Water, Aridity, and the Growth of the American West
0-19-507806-3 OXFORD PB $16.95

Under Western Skies: Nature and History in the American West
Eleven essays on subjects as varied as the decline of the cowboy, the ecology of livestock ranching, and the Dakotas' struggle to regain the Black Hills. Achieves a philosophical balance and a poetic clarity
0-19-505820-8 OXFORD $30.00

The South: Overviews

The South remains the strongest regional specialty in American historiography. The literature of Southern history is not only vast but also includes some of the most important historical writing we have.

Wilbur Joseph **Cash**
The Mind of the South
0-8446-6632-7 SMITH $22.75
0-679-73647-6 VINTAGE PB $13.00

Larry J. **Griffin** & Don Harrison **Doyle**, editors
The South as an American Problem
Twelve essayists on the modern South's persistent image as a people and place at odds with mainstream America's ideals and values
0-8203-1729-2 GEORGIA $29.95
0-8203-1752-7 GEORGIA PB $18.95

Charles Reagan **Wilson**
Judgment and Grace in Dixie: Southern Faiths from Faulkner to Elvis
By the co-editor of *The Encyclopedia of Southern Culture*
0-8203-1753-5 GEORGIA $29.95

Charles Reagan **Wilson** & William **Ferris**, editors
The Encyclopedia of Southern Culture
A monumental effort compiling the work of more than 800 scholars and writers. "Mirrors the very best of what has lately come to be called 'the new South' "—Alex Haley
0-8078-1823-2 NORTH CAROLINA $69.95

C. Vann **Woodward**
The Burden of Southern History, Third Editon
The third edition of this landmark historical text, with a new essay, "Look Away, Look Away" and previously uncollected appreciations of Robert Penn Warren and William Faulkner
0-8071-1891-5 LOUSIANA STATE PB $11.95

The Future of the Past
A collection of essays, addresses, and major book reviews spanning the past two decades, from the Pulitzer Prize-winning historian
0-19-505744-9 OXFORD $30.00

The Antebellum South

Edward L. **Ayers**
Vengeance and Justice: Crime and Punishment in the 19th-Century American South
0-19-503988-2 OXFORD PB $17.95

William **Bartram**
Travels of William Bartram
Illustrated edition of 18th-century classic of natural science and observation of southern North America. The book was a source for Coleridge's *Kubla Khan* and *The Rime of The Ancient Mariner* and highly regarded by Wordsworth and Emerson
EDITED BY MARK VAN DOREN
0-486-20013-2 DOVER PB $8.95

Carol **Bleser**
The Hammonds of Redcliffe
0-19-504984-5 OXFORD PB $19.95

Carol **Bleser**, editor
Secret and Sacred: The Diaries of James Henry Hammond, a Southern Slaveholder
0-19-505308-7 OXFORD $29.95

Steven A. **Charming**
Crisis of Fear: Secession in South Carolina
0-393-00730-8 NORTON PB $10.95

Avery O. **Craven**
Edmund Ruffin, Southerner: A Study in Secession
The ardent Southern nationalist who fired the first shot at Fort Sumter and killed himself after Appomattox
0-8071-0104-4 LSU PB $12.95

Christie Anne **Farnham**
The Education of the Southern Belle: Higher Education and Student Socialization in the Antebellum South
How higher education, posing no serious challenge to the dominant ideology of womanhood and "gentleness," was more accepted for white women in the slave-owning South than in the North before 1860
0-8147-2615-1 NYU $45.00
0-8147-2634-8 NYU PB $16.95

Drew G. **Faust**
James Henry Hammond and the Old South: A Design For Mastery
0-8071-1048-5 LOUSIANA STATE $37.50
0-8071-1248-8 LOUSIANA STATE PB $14.95

Eugene D. **Genovese**
The World the Slaveholders Made: Two Essays in Interpretation
A comparative history of slavery and the Virginia pro-slavery ideologue George Fitzhugh
See also SLAVERY AND BLACK LIVES under US HISTORY TO THE CIVIL WAR
0-8195-6204-1 WESLEYAN PB $19.95

David King **Gleason**
Virginia Plantation Homes
0-8071-1570-3 LOUISIANA STATE $45.00

Kenneth S. **Greenberg**
Masters and Statesmen: The Political Culture of American Slavery
0-8018-3744-8 JOHNS HOPKINS PB $13.95

Martha **McCulloch-Williams**
Dishes and Beverages of the Old South
A facsimile of the original (1913). " 'Must' reading for anyone who wants to understand the history and culture of the real South" —Stephen A. Smith
INTRODUCTION BY JOHN EGERTON
0-87049-580-1 TENNESSEE $16.95

Frank L. **Owsley**
Plain Folk of the Old South
FOREWORD BY GRADY MCWHINEY
0-8071-1062-0 LOUISIANA STATE $25.00
0-8071-1063-9 LOUISIANA STATE PB $9.95

Steven M. **Stowe**
Intimacy and Power in the Old South: Ritual in the Lives of the Planters
0-8018-3388-4 JOHNS HOPKINS $45.00
0-8018-4113-5 JOHNS HOPKINS PB $16.95

Bertram **Wyatt-Brown**
Honor and Violence in the Old South
0-19-504242-5 OXFORD PB $10.95

After Slavery: Origins of the New South

David **Carlton**
Mill and Town in South Carolina, 1880-1920
0-8071-1042-6 LOUISIANA STATE $35.00
0-8071-1059-0 LOUISIANA STATE PB $14.95

Pete **Daniel**
Deep'n as It Come: The 1927 Mississippi River Flood
1-55728-401-6 ARKANSAS PB $20.00

The Shadow of Slavery: Peonage in the South, 1901-1969
0-252-06146-2 ILLINOIS PB $11.95

Steven **Hahn**
The Roots of Southern Populism: Yeoman Farmers and the Transformation of the Georgia Upcountry, 1850-1890
0-19-503508-9 OXFORD PB $18.95

Howard N. **Rabinowitz**
Race Relations in the Urban South, 1865-1890
A classic work, first published in 1978, on post-emancipation black life and culture during the painful transition from slavery to freedom. Focusing on such cities as Richmond, Raleigh, Atlanta, Montgomery, and Nashville, Rabinowitz argues that segregation emerged in Southern cities after 1865 in part because blacks expected equal conditions in the provision of services and because they viewed segregation as an improvement over exclusion. "The most thorough and important study we have had on any period or sample of race relations in the South"—C. Vann Woodward
FOREWORD BY GEORGE W. FREDRICKSON
0-8203-1880-9 GEORGIA PB $24.95

Louis D. **Rubin**, editor
I'll Take My Stand: The South and the Agrarian Tradition
0-8446-1245-6 SMITH $19.25
0-8071-0357-8 LOUISIANA STATE PB $11.95

Barton C. **Shaw**
The Wool-Hat Boys: Georgia's Populist Party
0-8071-1148-1 LOUISIANA STATE $32.50

Stewart E. **Tolnay** & E.M. **Beck**
A Festival of Violence: An Analysis of Southern Lynchings, 1882-1930
A detailed statistical study of lynching in ten Southern states; shows that economic factors (such as the price of cotton) and status were at the heart of this violent practice
0-252-06413-5 ILLINOIS PB $19.95

Alan W. **Trelease**
White Terror: The Ku Klux Klan Conspiracy and Southern Reconstruction
"The fullest narrative history of the subject we are likely to have"—C. Vann Woodward
0-8071-1953-9 LOUISIANA STATE PB $17.95

Christopher **Waldrep**
Night Riders: Defending Community in the Black Patch, 1890-1915
The making of a unique society along the Tennessee-Kentucky border
0-8223-1359-6 DUKE $47.95
0-8223-1393-6 DUKE PB $17.95

Altina L. **Waller**
Feud: Hatfields, McCoys, and Social Change in Appalachia, 1860-1900
The legendary struggle as a symbol of economic and social struggle between local interests and outside industrialists
0-8078-1770-8 NORTH CAROLINA $45.00
0-8078-4216-8 NORTH CAROLINA PB $16.95

Joel **Williamson**
William Faulkner and Southern History
Probes the world that created William Faulkner, the rough, racist Mississippi of the late 19th century. In the author's words, it discusses "the universe of race, class, sex, and violence, of family, clan, and community that affected him so profoundly and about which he wrote with such telling effect"
0-19-507404-1 OXFORD $35.00
0-19-510129-4 OXFORD PB $17.95

C. Vann **Woodward**
Origins of the New South, 1877-1913
Still overshadows its entire field more than 30 years after publication. A landmark of American historical writing
0-8071-0009-9 LOUISIANA STATE $37.50

Gavin **Wright**, editor
The Political Economy of the Cotton South
0-393-09038-8 NORTON PB $8.95

The New South

Colin **Crawford**
Uproar at Dancing Rabbit Creek: The Battle Over Race, Class, and the Environment in the New South
See also **ETHNICITY AND RACE RELATIONS** under **TOPICS IN MODERN SOCIOLOGY** under **SOCIOLOGY** in **SOCIAL STUDIES**
0-201-62723-X ADDISON-WESLEY $24.00

Dewey W. **Grantham**
The South in Modern America: A Region at Odds
"...a superb study. Readers seeking a compact, up-to-date history of the New South need look no farther than this book"—*NY Times Book Review*
0-06-092208-7 HARPERPERENNIAL PB $16.00

Jack T. **Kirby**
Rural Worlds Lost: The American South, 1920-1960
0-8071-1360-3 LOUISIANA STATE PB $14.95

A.J. **Liebling**
Earl of Louisiana
FOREWORD BY T. HARRY WILLIAMS
0-8071-0203-2 LOUISIANA STATE PB $11.95

Anne C. **Loveland**
Lillian Smith: A Southerner Confronting the South
0-8071-1343-3 LOUISIANA STATE $32.50

William A. **Percy**
Lanterns on the Levee: Recollections of a Planter's Son
INTRODUCTION BY WALKER PERCY
0-8071-1184-8 LOUISIANA STATE $24.95
0-8071-0072-2 LOUISIANA STATE PB $11.95

John S. **Reed**
The Enduring South: Subcultural Persistence in Mass Society
FOREWORD BY EDWIN M. YODER, JR.
0-8078-4162-5 NORTH CAROLINA PB $11.95

Daniel J. **Singal**
The War Within: From Victorian to Modernist Thought in the South, 1919-1945
0-8078-1505-5 NORTH CAROLINA $39.95
0-8078-4087-4 NORTH CAROLINA PB $19.95

George B. **Tindall**
The Emergence of the New South, 1913-1945
0-8071-0020-X LSV PB $14.95

Southern Places

Harley E. **Jolley**

The Blue Ridge Parkway

An illustrated history and guide

0-87049-100-8 TENNESSEE PB $14.00

Harry M. **Caudill**

Night Comes to the Cumberlands: A Biography of a Depressed Area

The impoverished people and land in a region of Appalachia where coal mining is king. "The story of how this rich and beautiful land was changed into an ugly, poverty-ridden place of desolation"—*NY Times*

0-316-13212-8 LITTLE, BROWN PB $14.95

William S. **Ward**

A Literary History of Kentucky

0-87049-577-1 TENNESSEE $40.00

0-87049-578-X TENNESSEE PB $21.95

Reid **Mitchell**

All on a Mardi Gras Day: Episodes in the History of New Orleans Carnival

"The author is from New Orleans and places himself within the narrative. This is an excellent illustration of the new type of social history as narrative that fuses sociological and historical motifs"—Joseph Boskin

0-674-01622-X HARVARD $29.95

Robert **Tallant**

Mardi Gras...As It Was

A tour of Mardi Gras traditions, first published in 1947

0-88289-722-5 PELICAN PB $8.95

William S. **Powell**

North Carolina Through Four Centuries

A single volume on the events and people that have shaped the history of the Tarheel state

0-8078-1846-1 NORTH CAROLINA $34.95

Dan T. **Carter**

Scottsboro: A Tragedy of the American South

0-8071-0498-1 LOUISIANA STATE PB $14.95

Robert E. **Corlew**

Tennessee: A Short History

The second edition of this work traces the state from its beginnings to 1978, offering a searching appraisal of its development and future

0-87049-647-6 TENNESSEE PB $18.95

David G. **McComb**

Texas: An Illustrated History

Photographs and illustrations with an entertaining and informative text

See also **TEXAS** under **THE MAKING OF WESTERN STATES**

0-19-509246-5 OXFORD $22.95

0-292-74665-2 TEXAS PB $12.95

Lawrence H. **Larsen**

The Urban South: A History

0-8131-0309-6 KENTUCKY $25.00

0-292-74665-2 TEXAS PB $12.95

Other Regions

Wayne **Bernhardson** & Marisa **Gierlich**

Rocky Mountain States

0-86442-241-5 LONELY PLANET PB $21.95

John R. **Borchert**

America's Northern Heartland

0-8166-1499-7 MINNESOTA PB $24.95

Howard **Mansfield**

In the Memory House

Explores the culture of modern memory by revisiting the cultural history of New England

1-55591-162-5 FULCRUM $19.95

1-55591-247-8 FULCRUM PB $12.95

James C. **Nylander**

Our Own Snug Fireside: Images of the New England Home, 1760-1860

"This imaginatively illustrated book is dedicated to the notion that the details of everyday life form the core of human experience"—*NY Times*

0-300-05953-1 YALE PB $18.00

Robert E. **Pike**

Tall Trees, Tough Men: An Anecdotal and Pictorial History of Logging and Log-Driving in New England

"The author's lively prose matches the temper of his subject...This is basic history, geography, psychology, economics and folklore all rolled into one top-quality volume" —*NY Times Book Review*

0-393-30185-0 NORTON PB $11.95

John **Stilgoe**

Common Landscape of America, 1580-1845

A sweeping view of how Americans have mastered and been mastered by the lands they settled

0-300-03046-0 YALE PB $20.00

American People and Places

Wesley **Brown** & Amy **Ling**, editors

Imagining America: Stories from the Promised Land

Thirty-six short stories by Bernard Malamud, Louise Erdrich, Oscar Hijuelos, Grace Paley, Alice Walker, and others attempt to capture the American experience. "A marvelous anthology"—*Washington Post Book World*

0-89255-167-4 PERSEA PB $11.95

Visions of America: Personal Narratives from the Promised Land

Thirty American writers of varied ethnic and cultural backgrounds offer their personal stories of the American experience. Diverse and insightful, includes contributions by James Baldwin, Joan Didion, Maxine Hong Kingston, Anton Shammas, and Bharati Mukherjee

0-89255-173-9 PERSEA $29.95

0-89255-174-7 PERSEA PB $11.95

On a peaceful Sunday morning December 7, 1941, Henry, Sumi, and I were at choir rehearsal singing ourselves hoarse in preparation for the annual Christmas recital of Handel's "Messiah." Suddenly Chuck Mizuno...burst into the chapel, gasping as if he had sprinted all the way up the stairs.

"Listen, everybody!" he shouted. "Japan just bombed Pearl Harbor—in Hawaii! It's war!"

With that, Chuck swept out of the room, a swirl of young men following in his wake. Henry was one of them. The rest of us stayed, rooted to our places like a row of marionettes. I felt as if a fist had smashed my pleasant little existence, breaking it into jigsaw puzzle pieces. An old wound opened up again, and I found myself shrinking inwardly from my Japanese blood, the blood of an enemy. I knew instinctively that the fact that I was an American by birthright was not going to help me escape the consequences of this unhappy war.—*Monic Sone*

VISIONS OF AMERICA: PERSONAL NARRATIVES FROM THE PROMISED LAND

Joel **Garreau**

The Nine Nations of North America

Divides America into nine nations, including MexAmerica, Dixie, and the Breadbasket, and analyzes each region's prospects for the future

0-380-57885-9 AVON PB $12.50

John F. **Sears**

Sacred Places: American Tourist Attractions in the Nineteenth Century

Sears has discovered unexpected fascinations in the relations between 19th-century Americans and their native scenery. A new national identity took shape against the background of "sacred places" like Niagara Falls, the Hudson Valley, the White Mountains, Yosemite, and Yellowstone—while a profitable tourist industry also flourished. The book is enriched by profuse illustrations and unusual source materials

See also **THE UNITED STATES** under **TRAVEL GUIDES** in **FOOD, TRAVEL, AND LEISURE**

0-19-505350-8 OXFORD $27.95

Michael **Zuckerman**

Almost Chosen People: Oblique Biographies in the American Grain

One of America's most controversial and iconoclastic social historians takes on America's most beloved personalities in this thought-provoking volume of essays. Among his subjects are the Puritans, Benjamin Franklin, P.T. Barnum, Ronald Reagan, and Dr. Benjamin Spock

0-520-06651-0 CALIFORNIA $30.00

Immigration

"So we come finally to a paradox in assessing the impact of immigration. Clearly, it has enhanced the variety of American culture. Its diversifying influence is imprinted in the American ideal of nationality, in the American religious pattern, and in the sheer presence of so many different human types. On the other hand, the diversities have given way time and again to pressures for uniformity, which have come not just from older Americans but which immigrants and their children have also shaped and inspired. Through the systems of mass production and mass communications, America and its immigrants assimilated one another within an urban, technological culture that overrode distinctions of place, class, and ethnic type.

Yet the distinctions were never obliterated, the assimilation never wholly satisfying or complete. Today many Americans are rebuilding ethnic identities, and are discovering that America no longer looks as monolithic as it did a few years ago. Other societies have had a simpler experience with immigrant groups, either absorbing them or acquiescing in their separateness. In American life these contrary impulses mingle, their tensions unresolved, their implications still unfolding."—John Higham, *Send These to Me: Immigrants in Urban America*

John **Bodnar**
The Transplanted: A History of Immigrants in Urban America
Summarizes the newer view that immigrants maintained a separate identity in their national traditions
0-253-20416-X INDIANA PB $13.95

Lewis A. **Coser**
Refugee Scholars in America: Their Impact and Their Experiences
0-300-03193-9 YALE $38.00

Roger **Daniels**
Coming to America: A History of Immigration and Ethnicity in American Life
Readable one-volume synthesis tracing the migration of refugees nationality by nationality
0-06-092100-5 HARPERPERENNIAL PB $16.00

Leonard **Dinnerstein**
Natives and Strangers: Ethnic Groups and the Building of America
The role of blacks, Indians, and immigrant minorities in transforming colonial society into a nation
0-19-505722-8 OXFORD PB $16.95

Goergie Ann **Geyer**
Americans No More
The conservative columnist looks at immigration and citizenship in the U.S. today
0-871-13650-3 ATLANTIC MONTHLY $23.00

Nathan **Glazer** & Daniel P. **Moynihan**
Beyond the Melting Pot: The Negroes, Puerto Ricans, Jews, Italians, and Irish of New York City
See also **ETHNICITY AND RACE RELATIONS** under **TOPICS IN MODERN SOCIOLOGY** under **SOCIOLOGY** in **SOCIAL STUDIES**
0-262-57022-X MIT PB $17.50

Daniel Patrick Moynihan

Oscar **Handlin**
Boston's Immigrants: A Study in Acculturation
An early landmark study (1941) of ethnic acculturation. "The first historical case study of the impact of immigrants upon a particular society and of the adjustment of the immigrants to that society"
—*American Journal of Sociology*
0-674-07986-8 HARVARD PB $15.95

The Uprooted: The Story of the Great Migrations that Made the American People
The Pulitzer Prize-winning story (1952) of immigrant lives, cut off from their heritage by distance and American culture
0-316-34313-7 LITTLE, BROWN PB $12.95

John **Higham**
Send These to Me: Immigrants in Urban America
Essays on Jewish immigration, anti-Semitism, and other topics
0-8018-2438-9 JOHNS HOPKINS PB $14.95

Dirk **Hoerder**, editor
Struggle a Hard Battle: Essays on Working-Class Immigrants
0-87580-112-9 NORTHERN ILLINOIS $25.00
0-87580-533-7 NORTHERN ILLINOIS PB $9.50

Maldwyn Allen **Jones**
American Immigration
A survey from 1607 to 1959, analyzing the forces that uprooted Europeans and their roles in America's sectional conflicts, labor movements, westward expansion, and foreign policy
0-226-40633-4 CHICAGO PB $18.95

Thomas **Kessner**
The Golden Door: Italian and Jewish Immigrant Mobility in New York City, 1880-1915
How two immigrant groups, with differing results, used New York not only as an entry port but also as a stepping-stone to Americanization
0-19-502161-4 OXFORD PB $14.95

Thomas **Kessner** & Betty Boyd **Caroli**
Today's Immigrants, Their Stories: A New Look at the Newest Americans
0-19-503270-5 OXFORD PB $9.95

Stanley **Lieberson**
A Piece of the Pie: Black and White Immigrants Since 1880
See also **RACE RELATIONS** under **AFRICAN-AMERICAN STUDIES**
0-520-04362-6 CALIFORNIA PB $17.00

Joan **Morrison** & Charlotte **Fox**
American Mosaic: The Immigrant Experience in the Words of Those Who Lived It
From the turn of the century to present day, 140 immigrants from six continents and 50 countries recount their personal tragedies and triumphs in their adopted country
0-8229-3753-0 PITTSBURGH $49.95
0-8229-5488-5 PITTSBURGH PB $10.95

David M. **Reimers**
Still the Golden Door: The Third World Comes to America
Charts the shift in immigration that has brought an influx of newcomers from the Third World
0-231-07680-0 COLUMBIA $52.50
0-231-07681-9 COLUMBIA PB $17.00

Ronald **Takaki**, editor
Takaki writes with unusual clarity and erudition about race in America, whether in the past or today. His work also introduces Asian Americans into a debate normally dominated by blacks and whites.

From Different Shores: Perspectives on Race and Ethnicity in America
0-19-508368-7 OXFORD PB $18.95

Stephan **Thernstrom** & others, editors
Harvard Encyclopedia of American Ethnic Groups
A splendid resource on American immigration and ethnicity
0-674-37512-2 HARVARD $115.00

Thomas **Wheeler**, editor

Immigrant Experience: The Anguish of Becoming American

Personal narratives on the immigrant experience

0-14-015446-9 VIKING PB $10.95

Virginia **Yans-McLaughlin**, editor

Immigration Reconsidered: History, Sociology and Politics

Interdisciplinary collection of essays from leading scholars; provides a global perspective on immigration to the United States and challenges many previously accepted concepts

0-19-505511-X OXFORD PB $18.95

Ethnic and Race Relations

Derrick **Bell**

Confronting Authority: Reflections of an Ardent Protester

In 1992 Bell resigned from a tenured position at Harvard Law School to protest the lack of tenuring for any women of color. Here, he sagely examines not only his own, but also many other examples of dissent, and provides a convincing argument for individual action against unjustly used authority. "As a writer and teacher [Bell] conveys profound insights...from a life devoted to a higher and better vision for humankind"
—Jesse Jackson

See also **RACE RELATIONS** under **AFRICAN-AMERICAN STUDIES**

0-8070-0926-1 BEACON $20.00
0-8070-0927-X BEACON PB $12.00

Oliver C. **Cox**

Caste, Class, and Race

A cross-cultural view that tackles such times and places as India, the Middle Ages, and contemporary America

0-85345-116-8 MONTHLY REVIEW PB $22.00

Kimberle **Crenshaw**

Critical Race Theory: The Key Writings that Formed the Movement

Kendall Thomas, Cornel West, Derrick Bell, Cheryl Harris, Lani Guinier...the contributors to this volume make up a virtual Who's Who of the progressive intellectuals who have redefined the grounds on which race, law, and power are discussed in America

See also **LEGAL THEORY** under **LAW** in **SOCIAL STUDIES**

1-56584-270-7 NEW PRESS $60.00
1-56584-271-5 NEW PRESS PB $30.00

Alexander **Deconde**

Ethnicity, Race and American Foreign Policy: A History

Systematically examines the role of "ethnoracial" influences in the history of US foreign policy from the founding of Jamestown in 1607 to the Persian Gulf War in 1991

1-55553-215-2 NORTHEASTERN PB $15.95

Nathan **Glazer**

Affirmative Discrimination: Ethnic Inequality and Public Policy

0-674-00730-1 HARVARD PB $14.50

Leonard **Dinnerstein**

Antisemitism in America

Taking the Crown Heights riot as his point of entry and working his way back to the earliest Jews in the US, Dinnerstein provides a comprehensive and disturbing account of the persistence of anti-Jewish prejudice in the land of opportunity

0-19-503780-4 OXFORD $30.00

bell **hooks**

Killing Rage: Ending Racism

Recently named by the *Utne Reader* as one of the "100 Visionaries Who Could Change Your Life," bell hooks has been among our country's premier cultural and social critics for years. The 23 essays here address the fight against racism and sexism, and how those two battles are intimately interrelated in the American scene. From internalized racism in movies and media to black anti-Semitism, hooks draws from her enormous spectrum of reference an enduring lesson about the possibility of change

See also **AMERICAN POLITICS** under **POLITICAL THOUGHT**

0-8050-3782-9 HOLT $20.00

[These essays] bear witness to the passion for racial justice that remains a powerful legacy handed down to this generation from the freedom fighters of all races who dared to create an anti-racist discourse, who dared to create and sustain an anti-racist social movement...I testify in this writing—bear witness to the reality that our many cultures can be remade, that this nation can be transformed, that we can resist racism and in the act of resistance recover ourselves and be renewed.

KILLING RAGE: ENDING RACISM

bell hooks

Mickey **Kaus**

The End of Equality

"Provocative...bold...moving....A valuable contribution to the continuing debate on race and class in America"
—J. Anthony Lukas, *NY Times Book Review*

See also **CLASS IN AMERICA**

0-465-09816-9 BASIC PB $12.00

Thomas F. **Pettigrew**

The Sociology of Race Relations: Reflection and Reform

0-02-925110-9 FREE PRESS PB $19.95

C. Eric **Lincoln**

Coming Through the Fire: Surviving Race and Place in America

Lincoln was born in a rural town in northern Alabama, and is today professor emeritus of religion and culture at Duke University, the founding president of the Black Academy of Arts and Letters, and a fellow of the American Academy of Arts and Sciences. Lincoln explores such issues as biracial relationships, black-on-black violence, and the relationship between blacks and Jews

See also **RACE RELATIONS** under **AFRICAN-AMERICAN STUDIES**

WITH A FOREWORD BY HENRY LOUIS GATES, JR.

0-8223-1736-2 DUKE $17.95

Richard **Polenberg**

One Nation Divisible: Class, Race and Ethnicity in the United States Since 1938

"Deftly manipulates a wide variety of materials, from the perplexing statistical profiles provided by government surveys to the work of social scientists Gunnar Myrdal, Ashley Montagu, and David Riesman, to the poetry of Nikki Giovanni and the fiction of Joseph Heller"
—Alan M. Kraut, *Washington Star*

See also **ETHNICITY AND RACE RELATIONS** under **TOPICS IN MODERN SOCIOLOGY** under **SOCIOLOGY** in **SOCIAL STUDIES**

0-14-015999-1 VIKING PB $9.95

Carl T. **Rowan**

The Coming Race War in America: A Wake-Up Call

0-316-75980-5 LITTLE, BROWN $22.95

Thomas **Sowell**

Ethnic America: A History

0-465-02075-5 BASIC PB $16.00

Marcelo M. **Suarez-Orozco**

Central American Refugees and U.S. High Schools: A Psychosocial Study of Motivation and Achievement

Looks at students from El Salvador, Guatemala, and Nicaragua in major American cities to explain why so many Central American immigrant youths stay in school and succeed, and why their success rate is greater than other ethnic groups

0-8047-1498-3 STANFORD $35.00

Studs **Terkel**

Race: How Blacks and Whites Think and Feel About the American Obsession

"If we submit to the truth and wisdom of [Terkel's] witnesses who refuse to succumb to cynicism and disbelief, we will understand...that our once stated goal of a racially integrated society can be achieved"
—Henry Hampton, *NY Times Book Review*

0-385-46889-X ANCHOR PB $14.00

David T. **Wellman**

Portraits of White Racism

This disquieting study includes five chapters of interviews to bolster its central premise that racism is not an individual expression of hatred, but rather a culturally acceptable set of beliefs designed to maintain a white-based power structure

0-521-45051-9 CAMBRIDGE........$49.95
0-521-45668-1 CAMBRIDGE PB........$14.95

Cornel **West** & Michael **Lerner**

Jews and Blacks: The Hard Hunt for Common Ground

See also **RACE RELATIONS** under **AFRICAN-AMERICAN STUDIES**

0-399-14046-8 PUTNAM........$24.95

Nativism, Bigotry, and the Extreme Right

James **Coates**

Armed and Dangerous: The Rise of the Survivalist Right

"Introduces us to the world of those who live by the gun, and who plan to succeed the rest of us by surviving the coming Apocalypse and rebuilding a pure Aryan race"
—Christopher Hitchens, *Newsday*

0-8090-0174-8 FS&G PB........$11.00

Morris **Dees** & Steve **Fiffer**

Hate on Trial: The Case Against America's Most Dangerous Neo-Nazi

In one of his greatest victories, Dees, the leading civil rights attorney, won a case holding the Klan responsible for a crime of some of its members. When an Ethiopian college student was killed in Portland, Oregon, by skinheads in 1988, Dees went after Tom Metzger—overlord of the White Aryan Resistance—who, he was convinced, had incited the kids to this act of violence. "Scary stuff…with a gripping courtroom confrontation between hatred and righteousness"
—*Kirkus Reviews*

067040614X VILLARD........$21.00

Raphael S. **Ezekiel**

The Racist Mind: Portraits of American Neo-Nazis and Klansmen

"A profoundly disturbing vision of the malaise rumbling around in the belly of America… uncomfortable but necessary reading"
—Rosellen Brown

0-670-83958-2 VIKING........$24.95
0-14-023449-7 PENGUIN PB........$12.95

John **Higham**

Strangers in the Land: Patterns of American Nativism, 1860-1920s

A scholarly study of restrictive immigration

0-8135-1317-0 RUTGERS........$40.00
0-8135-1308-1 RUTGERS PB........$16.00

Nancy **MacLean**

Behind the Mask of Chivalry: The Making of the Ku Klux Klan

An award-winning, well-researched study of the inner workings of the Ku Klux Klan in the '20s; illuminated by a modern understanding of race, gender, and class

0-19-509836-6 OXFORD PB........$13.95

Kenneth S. **Stern**

A Force Upon the Plain: The American Militia Movement and the Politics of Hate

Showing the continuity between the Klan, the Order, Christian Identity, and other right-wing movements and today's domestic terrorists, the former director of the National Organization Against Terrorism explains the sense of siege among the movements' adherents and their feeling that national leaders cannot be trusted

0-684-81916-3 SIMON & SCHUSTER........$24.00

Elisabeth **Young-Bruehl**

The Anatomy of Prejudices

The well-known biographer of Hannah Arendt and Anna Freud asks a central question: what is prejudice and how does prejudice manifest itself in our behavior? From the offhand slight to the full-scale war, Young-Bruehl draws a subtle and precise portrait of the different types of prejudice, and brings its troubling effects into view

0-674-03190-3 HARVARD........$35.00

The Melting Pot

Sanford J. **Ungar**

Fresh Blood: The New American Immigrants

Ungar, a former host of NPR's *All Things Considered*, addresses the most inflammatory issue in America today. Who are today's immigrants? Are they a drain on our resources or an enrichment to our culture? From Koreans in Los Angeles to Poles in Chicago, from Cubans in Miami to Irish in Boston, Ungar shows that far from being a national threat, the "salad bowl" of immigration is a vital force of renewal in our culture

0-684-80860-9 SIMON & SCHUSTER........$25.00

African-Americans

K. Anthony **Appiah** & Amy **Gutmann**

Color Conscious: The Political Morality of Race

0-691-02661-0 PRINCETON........$21.95

Stanley **Crouch**

The All-American Skin Game, Or, The Decoy of Race: The Long and the Short of It, 1990-1994

A maverick writer and editor, Crouch has long been undermining our accepted wisdom, liberal and conservative alike, about race in America. Here again, he takes on the full spectrum of views about race in America: the myth of the rebel, Afro-American literature, the tribalism of minority politics. "[Stanley Crouch] is the black writer whose unorthodox views and attacks on liberals, feminists, and Black Power leaders often send ethnic militants into paroxysms of anger"—*NY Times*. "Behind his dissenter's rhetoric and hangman's mask, Stanley Crouch is actually a benign and eloquent provocateur"
—Ralph Ellison

0-679-44202-2 PANTHEON........$24.00
0-679-77660-5 VINTAGE PB........$13.00

Henry Louis **Gates**, Jr. & Cornel **West**

The Future of the Race

Two of our foremost African-American intellectuals take W.E.B. DuBois's "The Talented Tenth" as their point of departure for a consideration of the future of the black community in America

See also **POLITICAL THEORY AND MOVEMENTS** under **AFRICAN-AMERICAN STUDIES**

0-679-44405-X KNOPF........$21.00

Henry Louis Gates, Jr.

Douglas S. **Massey** & Nancy A. **Denton**

American Apartheid: Segregation and the Making of the Underclass

Persistent poverty of American blacks, Massey and Denton argue convincingly, can be linked to the unparalleled degree of segregation they experience, segregation that cuts them off from the opportunities other Americans enjoy, and in turn further reinforces their segregation

0-674-01820-6 HARVARD........$37.00

Asian-Americans

R. David **Arkush** & Leo O. **Lee**, editors

Land Without Ghosts: Chinese Impressions of America from the Mid-Nineteenth Century to the Present

0-520-08424-1 CALIFORNIA PB........$15.95

James M. **Freeman**

Hearts of Sorrow: Vietnamese-American Lives

First-person accounts by 14 Vietnamese who made new lives in the United States: a winner of the American Book Award of the Before Columbus Foundation

0-8047-1890-3 STANFORD PB $18.95

Yuji **Ichioka**

The Issei: The World of the First Generation Japanese Immigrants, 1885-1924

0-02-932435-1 FREE PRESS PB $16.95

Nazli **Kibria**

Family Tightrope: The Changing Lives of Vietnamese Americans

Twelve working-class households in Philadelphia. A well-researched "participant-observer" study in 200 pages

0-691-03260-2 PRINCETON $35.00
0-691-02115-5 PRINCETON PB $14.95

Peter **Kwong**

The New Chinatown

0-374-52121-2 NOONDAY PB $9.95

Valerie J. **Matsumoto**

Farming the Home Place: A Japanese American Community in California, 1919-1982

Founded in 1919 by a handful of families, the Cortez Colony was a community of Japanese American immigrants in California's San Joaquin Valley, a colony that still exists

0-8014-8115-5 CORNELL PB $15.95

Victor De Bary **Nee** & Brett De Bary **Nee**

Longtime Californ': A Documentary Study of an American Chinatown

A fascinating portrait of San Francisco's Chinatown

0-8047-1335-9 STANFORD $49.50
0-8047-1336-7 STANFORD PB $16.95

German-Americans

Jay P. **Dolan**

The Immigrant Church: New York's Irish and German-Catholics, 1815-1865

FOREWORD BY MARTIN E. MARTY

0-268-01151-6 NOTRE DAME PB $7.95

Frederick C. **Luebke**

Bonds of Loyalty: German-Americans and World War I

German immigrants found that latent tensions erupted into manifest hostilities at the outbreak of war, even though most German-Americans remained loyal to their adopted country

0-87580-514-0 NORTHERN ILLINOIS PB $10.50

Walter D. **Kamphoefner** & others, editors

News from the Land of Freedom: German Immigrants Write Home

German-American cultural identity has been sublimated since the outset of World War I, when national feeling against "the krauts" first ran high. The editors have recreated a lost view of the New World. "Most of what comes through... is the sense of immediacy one often gets from good novels and so seldom finds in conventional history"
—Martin E. Marty, *NY Times Book Review*

TRANSLATED BY SUSAN CARTER VOGEL

0-8014-2523-9 CORNELL $39.95

Hispanic-Americans

Rodolfo **Acuna**

Occupied America: A History of Chicanos

0-06-040163-X HARPERCOLLINS PB $36.11

Ted **Conover**

Coyotes

Disguised as a Mexican alien, the author followed the harrowing path through today's underground railroad, over the American border, and into the world of illegal aliens

0-394-75518-9 VINTAGE PB $13.00

Miriam **Davidson**

Convictions of the Heart: Jim Corbett and the Sanctuary Movement

0-8165-1034-2 ARIZONA $29.95
0-8165-1107-1 ARIZONA PB $10.95

Matt S. **Meier** & Feliciano **Rivera**

Mexican Americans, American Mexicans: From Conquistadors to Chicanos

0-8090-1559-5 HILL & WANG PB $10.95

Genaro M. **Padilla**

My History, Not Yours: The Formation of Mexican American Autobiography

The editor of *The Short Stories of Fray Angelico Chavez* looks at how men and women of Mexican descent resisted cultural destruction by using autobiography as a weapon of struggle. "A major entry in the rewriting of nineteenth-century U.S. and Chicano history"
—*American Historical Review*

0-299-13970-0 WISCONSIN $40.00
0-299-13974-3 WISCONSIN PB $17.95

David **Rieff**

The Exile: Cuba in the Heart of Miami

The acclaimed author of *Going to Miami* delivers a report on what may be the most culturally and economically significant immigrant group since the Jews of the 19th century: Miami's Cubans

0-671-77604-5 TOUCHSTONE PB $21.00

Ricardo **Romo**

East Los Angeles: History of a Barrio

0-292-72041-6 TEXAS PB $12.95

Irish-Americans

Dennis **Clark**

The Irish in Philadelphia: Ten Generations of Urban Experience

0-87722-227-4 TEMPLE PB $16.95

Andrew M. **Greeley**

The Irish-Americans: The Rise to Money and Power

Argues that "Irish-Catholic Americans have become the most successful educational, occupational, and economic gentile ethnic group in America"—*NY Times Book Review*

0-446-38558-1 WARNER PB $12.99

William D. **Griffin**

The Book of Irish Americans

"A slightly proud compendium of facts and figures, outrages and delights, history, lore and legend about the greater glories of the Irish in the new land"—From the jacket copy

0-8129-1264-0 TIMES BOOKS PB $16.95

Thomas **O'Connor**

The Boston Irish: A Political History

1-55553-220-9 NORTHEASTERN $24.95
0-316-62661-9 LITTLE, BROWN PB $14.95

Italian-Americans

John W. **Briggs**

An Italian Passage: Immigrants to Three American Cities, 1890-1930

0-300-02095-3 YALE $45.00

Donna R. **Gabaccia**

From Sicily to Elizabeth Street: Housing and Social Change Among Italian Immigrants, 1880-1930

0-87395-768-7 SUNY $64.50
0-87395-769-5 SUNY PB $19.95

Jerre **Mangione** & Ben **Morreale**

La Storia: Five Centuries of the Italian-American Experience

Combines historical research with oral history to describe the contribution of Italian immigrants to our culture, from the forgotten Fillipo Mazzei, alive during the American Revolution, to little-known Italian-American enclaves in the West. "A magnificent saga that illuminates a century of accomplishments and struggle"
—*Publishers Weekly*

0-06-092441-1 HARPERPERENNIAL PB $17.00

Pasquale **Spagnuolo**

One Barber's Story: From Sicily to America

Charming personal vignette of an immigrant barber who captivated New York's cultural and literary elite

0-312-11872-4 ST. MARTIN'S $18.95

Gay **Talese**

Unto the Sons

Bestseller about the journey of Talese's family from Italy to America, which takes on an emblematic quality about the Italian immigrant experience

0-8041-1033-6 IVY PB $5.99

Virginia **Yans-McLaughlin**

Family and Community: Italian Immigrants in Buffalo, 1880-1930

0-8014-1036-3 CORNELL $45.00
0-252-00916-9 ILLINOIS PB $11.95

Jewish-Americans

Joyce **Antler**

The Journey Home: A Celebration of Jewish Women in the American Century

See also **HISTORICAL BIOGRAPHIES** under **AMERICAN HISTORY** under **WOMEN'S STUDIES** in **SOCIAL STUDIES**

0-684-83444-8 FREE PRESS $27.50

Jenna Weissman **Joselit**

The Wonders of America: Reinventing Jewish Culture, 1880-1950

"Felicitously written, filled with entertaining and often hilarious details"
—Phillip Lopate, *NY Times Book Review*

See also **GENERAL HISTORIES** under **JEWS IN AMERICA** under **JEWISH HISTORY** in **WORLD HISTORY AND CURRENT AFFAIRS**

0-8090-1586-2 HILL & WANG PB $14.00

Stefan **Kanfer**

A Summer World: The Attempt to Build a Jewish Eden in the Catskills, from the Days of the Ghetto to the Rise and Decline of the Borscht Belt

The Catskill Mountains, New York, as haven for Yiddishkeit

0-374-27180-1 FS&G $22.95

Kenneth I. **Kann**

Comerades and Chicken Ranchers: The Story of a California Jewish Community

In the most unlikely setting, Kann brings a vibrant Jewish community back to life in an oral history that covers three generations and more than 200 interviews

0-8014-2807-6 CORNELL $38.95
0-8014-8075-2 CORNELL PB $17.95

Seymour Martin **Lipset** & Earl **Raab**

Jews and the New American Scene

"Powerful new insights into how the three prongs of my own identity as woman, American, and Jew have meshed together"—Betty Friedan

0-674-47493-7 HARVARD $22.95

Howard M. **Sachar**

A History of the Jews in America

From science to crime, movies to politics, this sprawling history presents 500 years of Jewish influence, contributions, and culture in America

0-679-74530-0 VINTAGE PB $20.00

Other Groups

Robert **Mirak**

Torn Between Two Lands: Armenians in America, 1890-World War I

0-674-89541-X HARVARD PB $12.95

Gregory **Orfalea**

Before the Flames: A Quest for the History of Arab-Americans

Orfalea's search for identity took him on a ten-year odyssey from Los Angeles to his family's ancestral village in Syria

0-292-70748-7 TEXAS $24.95

James S. **Pula**

Polish Americans: An Ethnic Community

"The best survey of Polish America to date"
—William Galush

0-8057-8438-1 TWAYNE PB $17.95

Class in America

"Class distinctions in America are so complicated and subtle that foreign visitors often miss the nuances and sometimes even the existence of a class structure. So powerful is 'the fable of equality,' as Frances Trollope called it when she toured America in 1832, so embarrassed is the government to confront the subject—in the thousands of measurements pouring from its bureaus, social class is not officially recognized—that it's easy for visitors not to notice the way the class system works. A case in point is the experience of Walter Allen, the British novelist and literary critic. Before he came over here to teach at a college in the 1950s, he imagined that 'class scarcely existed in America, except, perhaps, as divisions between ethnic groups or successive waves of immigrants.' But living a while in Grand Rapids opened his eyes: there he learned of the snob power of New England and the pliability of the locals to the long-wielded moral and cultural authority of old families."—Paul Fussell, *Class*

Paul **Fussell**

Class: A Guide Through the American Status System

"Fussell identifies the class significance of not only clothes and houses but cars, food, language, vacations, reading habits and much more... Frighteningly acute"—Alison Lurie

See also **HISTORY, POLITICS, AND SOCIETY** under **20TH-CENTURY AMERICAN ESSAYS AND JOURNALISM** in **LITERATURE OF THE AMERICAS**

0-671-79225-3 TOUCHSTONE PB $10.00

Christopher **Hitchens**

Blood, Class, and Nostalgia: Anglo-American Ironies

How Britain's "special relationship" with the US has influenced American foreign policy and the domestic scene as well, with profound English influences on scholarship, manners, ethnicity, and taste

0-374-11443-9 FS&G $22.95

In the United States, it is considered extremely insulting to say of somebody that he or she is "history." To be told "You're history" is to be condemned as a has-been. I know of no other country that has this everyday dismissal in its idiom. But then, I know of no other country that has such a a great weakness for things that originated in England—the has-been country par excellence. (A British person, seeking to be extremely self-deprecating about something in his or her own past, might say modestly and dismissively, "But that's all ancient history." I trust the distinction is plain.)

BLOOD, CLASS, AND NOSTALGIA: ANGLO-AMERICAN IRONIES

Mickey **Kaus**

The End of Equality

"Provocative...bold...moving....A valuable contribution to the continuing debate on race and class in America"
—J. Anthony Lukas, *NY Times Book Review*

See also **ETHNIC AND RACE RELATIONS**

0-465-09816-9 BASIC PB $12.00

Social Mobility

Matthew **Edel** & others

Shaky Palaces: Home Ownership and Social Mobility in Boston, 1870-1970

0-231-05626-5 COLUMBIA $47.50
0-231-05627-3 COLUMBIA PB $20.00

Frank **Levy**

Dollars and Dreams: The Changing American Income Distribution

Argues that a family's chances of attaining the middle-class dream have declined significantly since 1973

0-87154-523-3 RUSSELL SAGE PB $14.95

Katherine S. **Newman**

Declining Fortunes: The Withering of the American Dream

The author of *Falling from Grace* spent years conducting interviews with postwar suburban

parents and their babyboom children to provide this probing look at the damage that economic decline has done to the people of America
0-465-01593-X BASIC PB $23.00

Kevin **Phillips**
Boiling Point: Republicans, Democrats, and the Decline of Middle-Class Prosperity
Examines the middle class's declining influence. "In the political business, very few people deserve the appellation 'genius.' Kevin Phillips is decidedly one of them"—James Carville
See also **THE AMERICAN ECONOMY TODAY** under **ECONOMICS** in **SOCIAL STUDIES**
0-06-097582-2 HARPERCOLLINS PB $13.50

Stephan **Thernstrom**
Poverty and Progress: Social Mobility in a Nineteenth-Century City
An exciting social history that uses census records and other previously neglected sources to recover the lives of ordinary people
0-674-69501-1 HARVARD PB $13.95

The Upper Class

Nelson W. **Aldrich**, Jr.
Old Money: The Mythology of America's Upper Class
"A revealing document not just about one social class in America but about class itself"
—Richard Sennett
1-88055-964-1 ALLWORTH PB $16.95

E. Digby **Baltzell**
Philadelphia Gentlemen: The Making of a National Upper Class
A first-rate study of the rise of the Eastern urban aristocracy
0-88738-789-6 TRANSACTION PB $21.95

The Protestant Establishment
An interesting study of the role of upper-class anti-Semitism
0-300-03917-4 YALE $50.00
0-300-03818-6 YALE PB $18.00

Puritan Boston and Quaker Philadelphia
The leading families of two leading cities—and how they have differed throughout their history
0-02-901320-8 FREE PRESS $45.00
1-56000-830-X TRANSACTION PB $24.95

Frederic C. **Jaher**
The Urban Establishment: Upper Strata in Boston, New York, Charleston, Chicago and Los Angeles
An encyclopedic study full of fascinating data
0-252-00827-8 ILLINOIS $49.95
0-252-00932-0 ILLINOIS PB $19.95

Jerry E. **Patterson**
The Vanderbilts
0-8109-1748-3 ABRAMS $49.50

Bernice **Kert**
Abby Aldrich Rockefeller: The Woman in the Family
A complete portrait of the strong-willed and independent woman who provided the philanthropic vision of the Rockefeller fortune, from the Museum of Modern Art to the continued charitable work of her children and grandchildren
0-394-56975-X RANDOM HOUSE $35.00

The Middle Class

John S. **Gilkeson**, Jr.
Middle-Class Providence, 1820-1940
Focuses on middle-class voluntary associations of the period
0-691-04734-0 PRINCETON $60.00

Karen **Halttunen**
Confident Men and Painted Women: A Study of Middle-Class Culture in America, 1830-1870
0-300-03788-0 YALE PB $17.00

Colleen **McDannell**
The Christian Home in Victorian America, 1840-1900
See also **EARLY AMERICA** under **RELIGION IN AMERICA** under **TOPICS IN AMERICAN STUDIES**
0-253-31376-7 INDIANA $25.00

Katherine S. **Newman**
Falling from Grace: The Experience of Downward Mobility in the American Middle Class
Until recently America's middle class believed it could only move up the social ladder
0-02-923121-3 FREE PRESS $29.95
0-679-72397-8 VINTAGE PB $13.00

The Poor

"If we strip away the rhetoric of the right and the left, a surprising consensus emerges. There is broad agreement that America has developed an underclass, although some would prefer another term. There is sharp disagreement about the causes of this underclass, but rarely about its effects. Those on the right tend to use words like 'pathology,' 'passivity,' and 'hostility'; those on the left tend to speak of 'despair,' 'hopelessness,' and 'alienation'—different words that often mean the same thing. As Jacob Riis warned more than a century ago, a 'few generations' of slum life might produce monsters. For the first time in America's relatively young history, the ghetto has become a permanent home for too many broken families. For some, upward mobility is a lie, and organized society is the enemy; for others, the temporary crutch of welfare has turned into a straitjacket of permanent dependency. Whether you are compassionate or scared, the underclass should command your attention."
—Ken Auletta, *The Underclass*

R.H. **Bremner**
The Discovery of Poverty in the U.S.
1-56000-582-3 TRANSACTION PB $21.95

Children's Defense Fund
Wasting America's Future
An urgent look at the meaning of a frightening statistic: one in every five American children is living below the government-defined poverty line of $12,000. This book studies the terrible effects of poverty on infant mortality, children's injuries, abuse, neglect, and health
INTRODUCTION BY MARIAN WRIGHT EDELMAN
0-8070-4106-8 BEACON $35.00
0-8070-4107-6 BEACON PB $18.00

Michael **Harrington**
The Other America: Poverty in the United States
This classic portrait caused a sensation when it first appeared in 1962, and deeply influenced New Left politics; revised edition
0-02-020763-8 COLLIER PB $9.00

Christopher **Jencks**
Rethinking Social Policy: Race, Poverty and the Underclass
0-06-097534-2 HARPERPERENNIAL PB $13.00

Jacqueline **Jones**
The Dispossessed: America's Underclasses from the Civil War to the Present
"...one of the few scholars who has succeeded in clarifying, in specific historical discussions, the extremely complex relationship between race and class"
—David Brion Davis, *NY Review of Books*
0-465-01674-X BASIC PB $16.00

Jonathan **Kozol**
Amazing Grace: The Lives of Children and the Conscience of a Nation
See also **URBAN SOCIOLOGY** under **TOPICS IN MODERN SOCIOLOGY** under **SOCIOLOGY** in **SOCIAL STUDIES**
0-517-79999-5 CROWN $23.00
0-06-097697-7 HARPERPERENNIAL PB $13.50

Susan **Sheehan**
Life for Me Ain't Been No Crystal Stair
A terrifying legacy of institutional abuse and neglect charted through the prism of Crystal Taylor, a 14-year-old mother whose newborn baby is immediately put into foster care while Crystal moves among a myriad of group homes and halfway houses, trying to acquire the necessary skills for a normal life. Serialized to great acclaim in *The New Yorker*. "A relentless and dispassionate chronicle of shattered lives and inadequate institutions"—*Kirkus Reviews*
0-679-75450-4 VINTAGE PB $11.00

Ruth **Sidel**
Women and Children Last: The Plight of Poor Women in Affluent America
A fine study of the "feminization of poverty"
0-14-016766-8 PENGUIN PB $11.95

The Homeless

Rick **Beard**, editor
On Being Homeless: Historical Perspectives
0-8135-1508-4 RUTGERS PB $16.95

Michael **Elliott**
Why the Homeless Don't Have Homes and What to Do About It
After 14 years of working with the homeless, Elliott has constructed a compassionate and pragmatic solution: accountability of the homeless and cooperation from the government, churches, and community organizations in a unified approach to solving one of our most persistent and tragic problems
0-8298-0965-1 PILGRIM PB $9.95

Christopher **Jencks**
The Homeless
0-674-40596-X HARVARD PB $10.00

Jonathan **Kozol**
Rachel and Her Children: Homeless Families in America
A harrowing portrait by the author of *Death at an Early Age*
0-449-90339-7 FAWCETT PB $10.00

Charles A. **Kroloff**
54 Ways You Can Help the Homeless
Practical suggestions on how to give effective personal aid to the most neglected segment of our society. From the founder of the Interfaith Council for the Homeless. All publisher's profits will be donated to homeless relief organizations
0-88363-888-6 LEVIN PB $1.95

Elliot **Liebow**
Tell Them Who I Am: The Lives of Homeless Women
The renowned anthropologist and author of the classic *Tally's Corner* gives us another book written in the participant-observer mode. This one documents the patterns and routines of homeless women: how they meet their needs for shelter, food, religious solace, and companionship
0-02-919095-9 FREE PRESS $27.95

Richard H. **Ropers**
The Invisible Homeless: A New Urban Ecology
This new study shows that at least 250,000 people nationwide are homeless on any given night
0-89885-406-7 INSIGHT $32.95

Welfare and Social Policy

Nathan **Glazer**
The Limits of Social Policy
0-674-53443-3 HARVARD $32.00
0-674-53444-1 HARVARD PB $13.95

Forrest **Chisman** & Alan **Pifer**
Government for the People: The Federal Social Role—What It Is, What It Should Be
Challenges widely held assumptions about social security, social spending, welfare, and other aspects of social policy
0-393-30526-0 NORTON PB $9.95

Sheldon H. **Danziger** & Daniel H. **Weinberg**, editors
Fighting Poverty: What Works and What Doesn't
Economists, sociologists and political scientists assess the antipoverty policies of the last 20 years
0-674-30085-8 HARVARD $40.00

James Dale **Davidson** & Lord William **Rees-Mogg**
The Sovereign Individual: How to Survive and Thrive During the Collapse of the Welfare State
0-684-81007-7 SIMON & SCHUSTER $25.00

David T. **Ellwood**
Poor Support: Poverty in the American Family
0-465-05995-3 BASIC PB $13.00

Michael **Kammen**
Sphere of Liberty: Changing Perceptions of Liberty in American Culture
Divided into three insightful essays: the colonial and Revolutionary periods, the 19th century, and the 20th century
0-8014-9682-9 CORNELL PB $12.95

Michael B. **Katz**
In the Shadow of the Poor-House: A Social History of Welfare in America
Suggests that America has the resources and competence to eliminate poverty, hunger, and inadequate housing through creative public policy
0-465-03226-5 BASIC BOOKS PB $16.00

Edward **Luttwak**
The Endangered American Dream: How to Stop the United States from Becoming a Third World Country and How to Win the Geo-Economic Struggle for Industrial Supremacy
The author, director of Geo-Economics at Georgetown University's Center for Strategic and International Studies, prescribes some dire medicine for our diseased economy: a heavy value-added tax and strict, uniform educational standards. If not, he warns, by the year 2020 the U.S. will look woefully like Mexico or Argentina. "A powerful, tough-minded, alarming report" —*Publishers Weekly*
See also **THE AMERICAN ECONOMY TODAY** under **ECONOMICS** in **SOCIAL STUDIES**
0-671-89667-9 TOUCHSTONE PB $14.00

Charles **Murray**
Losing Ground: American Social Policy, 1950-1980
Argues that the ambitious programs of the Great Society not only didn't work but actually made things worse
0-465-04233-3 BASIC PB $16.00

Frances Fox **Piven**
Regulating the Poor: The Functions of Public Welfare
"The central thesis is crucial for understanding the dramatic rise in welfare rolls that has been taking place in recent years"—Herbert Gans
0-679-74516-5 VINTAGE PB $13.00

Frances Fox **Piven** & Richard A. **Cloward**
The New Class War: Reagan's Attack on the Welfare State and Its Consequences
0-394-70647-1 RANDOM HOUSE PB $9.75

Lisbeth B. **Schorr** & Daniel **Schorr**
Within Our Reach: Breaking the Cycle of Disadvantage
FOREWORD BY JUDITH VIORST
0-385-24244-1 ANCHOR PB $12.95

Walter I. **Trattner**, editor
Social Welfare or Social Control?: Some Historical Reflections on "Regulating the Poor"
A historical critique that takes issue with the social control thesis offered by Piven and Cloward, who offer a spirited rebuttal
0-87049-374-4 TENNESSEE $25.00
0-87049-375-2 TENNESSEE PB $15.00

Urban America

Alexander B. **Callow**, Jr., editor
American Urban History: An Interpretive Reader with Commentaries
Thirty-two essays examine the development of cities from colonial times to the present, addressing the question of whether American urban history reflected our national history or whether it developed on a divergent path
0-19-502981-X OXFORD PB $21.00

Jane **Jacobs**
The Death and Life of Great American Cities
An attack on the principles and aims that have shaped modern orthodox city planning and rebuilding. "This is one of the most remarkable books ever written about the city"—William Whyte
See also **CITIES AND CITY PLANNING** under **CRITICISM** under **20TH-CENTURY ARCHITECTURE** in **ARCHITECTURE, DESIGN, AND HOMES**
0-679-60047-7 MODERN LIBRARY $17.50
0-679-74195-X VINTAGE PB $13.00

Edge of Empire: Post Colonialism and the City
0-415-12007-1 ROUTLEDGE PB $19.95

David R. **Goldfield** & Blaine A. **Brownell**
Urban America: A History
0-395-46501-X HOUGHTON MIFFLIN PB $41.16

Jon C. **Teaford**
The Twentieth-Century American City
A slim, scholarly volume contrasting the promise and reality of urban life
0-8018-4551-3 JOHNS HOPKINS PB $13.95

Special Studies

Gunther **Barth**
City People: The Rise of Modern City Culture in 19th-Century America
0-19-503194-6 OXFORD PB $10.95

Thomas **Bender**
Toward an Urban Vision: Ideas and Institutions in Nineteenth-Century America
Explores the distinctive "urban vision" that sought to reconcile America's rural heritage with its new industrial life
0-8018-2925-9 JOHNS HOPKINS PB $14.95

Richard M. **Bernard** & Bradley R. **Rice**, editors
Sunbelt Cities: Politics and Growth Since World War II
0-292-77580-6 TEXAS PB $14.95

Children's Express
Voices from the Future: Children Speak About Violence in America
Children's Express, a Peabody and Emmy Award-winning news organization run by young editors and reporters, interviews teenagers from all racial and economic groups—gang members, skinheads, and homeless kids—about violence and its impact on American society
EDITED BY SUSAN GOODWILLIE
0-517-59494-3 CROWN $20.00

Herbert **Croly**
The Promise of American Life
FOREWORD BY MICHAEL E. MCGERR
1-55553-062-1 NORTHEASTERN PB $16.95

Kenneth **Fox**
Metropolitan America: Urban Life and Urban Policy in the United States, 1940-1980
This comprehensive history emphasizes the interaction between government policy and metropolitan development
0-87805-283-6 MISSISSIPPI $37.50
0-8135-1506-8 RUTGERS PB $15.00

Zane L. **Miller**
The Urbanization of Modern America: A Brief History
0-15-593657-3 HARCOURT BRACE PB $25.94

Roberta Brandes **Gratz**
The Living City
The rejuvenation of urban areas demonstrates the successes that come from "thinking small in a big way"
0-89133-246-4 PRESERVATION PB $16.95

Ira **Katznelson**
City Trenches: Urban Politics and the Patterning of Class in the United States
"The most persuasive analysis I have ever encountered of...the sources and nature of political turmoil in American cities during the 1960s, and how political order was restored at the end of that turbulent decade"
—Martin Shefter, Cornell University
See also **20TH-CENTURY HISTORIES AND STUDIES** under **AMERICAN LABOR AND RADICAL MOVEMENTS**
0-226-42673-4 CHICAGO PB $17.95

Jonathan **Kozol**
Death at an Early Age: The Destruction of the Hearts and Minds of Negro Children in the Boston Public Schools
An indictment of public education, from the front lines of 1964 Boston. "A very disturbing book. He is writing of the Boston Public School system, but he could be writing of the system in almost any city in the country"—*Christian Science Monitor*
See also **THE STATE OF THE SCHOOLS** under **EDUCATION** in **SOCIAL STUDIES**
0-452-26292-5 NEW AMERICAN LIBRARY PB $11.95

Savage Inequalities: Children in America's Schools
See also **THE STATE OF THE SCHOOLS** under **EDUCATION** in **SOCIAL STUDIES**
0-06-097499-0 HARPERPERENNIAL PB $13.50

Bradford **Luckingham**
Minorities in Phoenix: A Profile of Mexican American, Chinese American, and African American Communities, 1862-1992
0-8165-1457-7 ARIZONA $39.50

William H. **Pease** & Jane H. **Pease**
The Web of Progress: Private Values and Public Styles in Boston and Charleston, 1828-1843
"Enriches our understanding of both cities and highlights the distinctive influences that shaped each of them"
—Richard P. McCormick, Rutgers University
0-19-503467-8 OXFORD $36.00
0-8203-1390-4 GEORGIA PB $18.00

Marc H. **Rose**
Cities of Heat and Light: Domesticating Gas and Electricity in Urban America
The importance of culture, politics, and urban growth in shaping technological change in the cities of North America, taking Denver and Kansas City as test cases
0-271-01349-4 PENN STATE $34.50

Luis J. **Rodriguez**
Always Running: La Vida Loca—Gang Days in L.A.
0-671-88231-7 TOUCHSTONE PB $10.00

David **Schuyler**
The New Urban Landscape: The Redefinition of City Form in 19th-Century America
The failed effort to use public space and recreation to reform cramped urban life
0-8018-3748-0 JOHNS HOPKINS PB $12.95

Carl **Smith**
Urban Disorder and the Shape of Belief: The Great Chicago Fire, the Haymarket Bomb and the Model Town of Pullman
How responses to disaster have deeply affected cities in the United States, in this case 19th-century Chicago
0-226-76416-8 CHICAGO $35.00
0-226-76417-6 CHICAGO PB $18.95

Richard C. **Wade**
Urban Frontier: The Rise of Western Cities, 1790-1830
0-674-93075-4 HARVARD $25.00
0-252-06422-4 ILLINOIS PB $18.95

Sam Bass **Warner**, Jr.
The Private City: Philadelphia in Three Periods of Its Growth
0-8122-8061-X PENNSYLVANIA $37.95

William Julius **Wilson**
The Truly Disadvantaged: The Inner City, the Underclass and Public Policy
See also **RACE RELATIONS** under **AFRICAN-AMERICAN STUDIES**
0-226-90131-9 CHICAGO PB $13.95

William Julius **Wilson**, editor
The Ghetto Underclass
See also **URBAN SOCIOLOGY** under **TOPICS IN MODERN SOCIOLOGY** under **SOCIOLOGY** in **SOCIAL STUDIES**
0-8039-5272-4 SAGE PB $19.95

Suburbia

Henry C. **Binford**
The First Suburbs: Residential Communities on the Boston Periphery, 1815-1860
Argues that peripheral communities began to modernize before mass transportation linked the city to the outskirts
0-226-05159-5 CHICAGO PB $13.95

John R. **Stilgoe**
Borderland: Origins of the American Suburb, 1820-1939
A highly praised new study
0-300-04866-1 YALE PB $20.00

Robert A. **Fishman**

Bourgeois Utopias: The Rise and Fall of Suburbia

From its origins in 18th-century London to its fall in the sprawl of Los Angeles

0-465-00747-3 BASIC BOOKS PB $13.00

Kenneth T. **Jackson**

Crabgrass Frontier: The Suburbanization of America

A Bancroft Prize-winning study. "Among the many interpretations, attacks, sociological reviews and other accounts of surburbia's spread since 1945, Mr. Jackson's stands out as the most comprehensive"
—Grady Clay, *NY Times Book Review*

0-19-504983-7 OXFORD PB $14.95

Zane L. **Miller**

Suburb: Neighborhood and Community in Forest Park, Ohio, 1935-1976

0-87049-289-6 TENNESSEE $32.50

Sam Bass **Warner**, Jr.

Streetcar Suburbs: The Process of Growth in Boston, 1870-1900

0-674-84213-8 HARVARD $21.00
0-674-84211-1 HARVARD PB $11.95

Housing

The following books on domestic architecture imaginatively use houses to explore family life and broader social conflicts, particularly in the late 19th and early 20th centuries.

Richard L. **Bushman**

The Refinement of America: Persons, Houses, Cities

0-679-74414-2 VINTAGE PB $18.00

Clifford E. **Clark**, Jr.

The American Family Home, 1800-1960

0-8078-1675-2 NORTH CAROLINA $39.95
0-8078-4151-X NORTH CAROLINA PB $19.95

Dolores **Hayden**

The Grand Domestic Revolution: A History of Feminist Designs for American Homes, Neighborhood, and Cities

0-262-58055-1 MIT PB $18.95

Gwendolyn **Wright**

Building the Dream: A Social History of Housing in America

An original, lucid exploration of the relationship between the way we build our homes and our images of ourselves

0-262-73064-2 MIT PB $16.95

American Cities

Webb **Garrison**

The Legacy of Atlanta: A Short History

0-934601-14-3 PEACHTREE PB $8.95

Sam Bass **Warner**, Jr.

To Dwell Is to Garden: A History of Boston's Community Gardens

1-55553-007-9 NORTHEASTERN $24.95

William **Cronon**

Nature's Metropolis: Chicago and the West, 1848-1893

The author of the brilliant *Changes in the Land* writes about the rise of Chicago and its interactions with the frontier from which it emerged

0-393-02921-2 NORTON $27.50

Michael H. **Ebner**

Creating Chicago's North Shore: A Suburban History

0-226-18205-3 CHICAGO $39.95

Harold M. **Mayer** & others

Chicago: Growth of a Metropolis

0-226-51274-6 CHICAGO PB $28.95

Frank B. **Woodford** & others

All Our Yesterdays: A Brief History of Detroit

0-8143-1381-7 WAYNE STATE PB $14.95

Michael J. **McDonald** & others

Knoxville, Tennessee: Continuity and Change in an Appalachian City

0-87049-393-0 TENNESSEE $35.00
0-87049-648-4 TENNESSEE PB $16.00

Scott L. **Bottles**

Los Angeles and the Automobile: The Making of the Modern City

0-520-05795-3 CALIFORNIA $45.00
0-520-07395-9 CALIFORNIA PB $15.00

John Walton **Caughey** & others

Los Angeles: Biography of a City

A collection of historical and literary essays

0-520-03410-4 CALIFORNIA PB $15.00

Russell F. **Weigley**, editor

Philadelphia: Three Hundred Year History

0-393-01610-2 NORTON $17.95

Constance M. **Green**

Washington: A History of the Capital

0-691-00585-0 PRINCETON PB $24.95

David L. **Lewis** & others

District of Columbia: A Bicentennial History

0-393-05601-5 NORTON $14.95

Robert **Reed**

Old Washington, D.C., in Early Photographs

0-8446-5804-9 SMITH $19.00
0-486-23869-5 DOVER PB $12.95

New York

George G. **Foster**

New York by Gas-Light and Other Urban Sketches

A scandalous bestseller when first published in 1850, Foster's book is a journalistic guide to New York's dark side: "the festivities of prostitution, the orgies of pauperism, the haunts of theft and murder, the scenes of drunkenness and beastly debauch"

EDITED WITH AN INTRODUCTION BY STUART M. BLUMIN

0-520-06722-3 CALIFORNIA PB $13.95

Paul A. **Gilje**

The Road to Mobocracy: Popular Disorder in New York City, 1763-1834

0-8078-1743-0 NORTH CAROLINA $39.95

Helen **Hanff**

Letter from New York

Writings on life in New York from the author of *84, Charing Cross Road.* Tree-lighting at Christmas, life in a high-rise, dog stories, and block parties—Hanff's dexterous touch has enthralled BBC listeners for six years. A charming collection

1-55921-064-8 MOYER BELL $16.95

Eric **Homberger** & Alice **Hudson**, editors

The Historical Atlas of New York City

Even if you are not a New Yorker, this will intrigue you

See also **HISTORICAL AND POLITICAL ATLASES** under **GEOGRAPHICAL INFORMATION** under **REFERENCE** in **BUSINESS AND REFERENCE**

0-8050-2649-5 HOLT $45.00

Clifton **Hood**

722 Miles: The Building of the Subways and How They Transformed New York

The intimidating job of building beneath Manhattan's irregular terrain; how, when the Interborough Rapid Transit subway opened in 1904, New Yorkers went "subway mad"; and more. This is a first-rate history

0-8018-5244-7 JOHNS HOPKINS PB $15.95

Kenneth T. **Jackson**

The Encyclopedia of New York City

0-300-05536-6 YALE $60.00

Roy **Rosenzweig** & Elizabeth **Blackmar**

The Park and the People: A History of Central Park

When Olmsted and Vaux designed the park in the 1850s in an effort to create a public space similar to Europe's grand examples, they could never have foreseen all the ways it would alter city history and become an arena for so many dramatic gatherings. "A deeply felt celebration of the role of public space in fostering a truly democratic polity"
—Robert Fishman, *NY Times Book Review*

0-8014-2516-6 CORNELL $39.95

Luc **Sante**

Low Life: Lures and Snares of Old New York

Manhattan from 1840 to 1919, with all its dens of vice and low entertainment: a richly anecdotal tour of an alluring and dangerous city

0-374-19414-9 FS&G $27.50

Concert saloons were actually a specific and distinct phenomenon… The sucker would be strongly encouraged to buy numerous drinks for himself and for a minimum of one female companion, whose drinks would be heavily watered or consist simply of colored water, and which would cost twice as much as the man's, which were themselves expensive for the time, from fifteen to twenty-five cents. The women did not receive wages but worked on a percentage basis. Sex did not occur on the premises, and in fact usually did not occur at all; obstreperous customers were treated to knockout drops.

LOW LIFE: LURES AND SNARES OF OLD NEW YORK

Martin **Shefter**

Political Crisis—Fiscal Crisis: The Collapse and Revival of New York City

The definitive study of the 1975 fiscal crisis that drove New York City to the brink of bankruptcy, by a Cornell political scientist

0-231-07942-7 COLUMBIA $45.00
0-231-07943-5 COLUMBIA PB $13.50

William R. **Taylor**, editor

Inventing Times Square: Commerce and Culture at the Crossroads of the World

0-8018-5337-0 JOHNS HOPKINS PB $19.95

Caroline F. **Ware**

Greenwich Village, 1920-1930

0-520-08566-3 CALIFORNIA PB $16.00

Elliot **Willensky**

When Brooklyn Was the World: 1920-1957

A well-illustrated backward glance

0-517-55858-0 HARMONY $24.00

African-American Studies

"The history of the American Negro is the history of this strife, —this longing to attain self-conscious manhood, to merge his double self into a better and truer self. In this merging he wishes neither of the other selves to be lost. He would not Africanize America, for America has too much to teach the world and Africa. He would not bleach his Negro soul in a flood of white Americanism, for he knows that Negro blood has a message for the world. He simply wishes to make it possible for a man to be both a Negro and an American, without being cursed and spit upon by his fellows, without having the doors of Opportunity closed roughly in his face."—W.E.B. DuBois, "The Souls of Black Folk," from *Writings*

History

Mary Frances **Berry** & John W. **Blassingame**

Long Memory: The Black Experience in America

0-19-502910-0 OXFORD PB $19.95

W.E.B. **DuBois**

Writings

This volume contains DuBois's most important historical and autobiographical writings, including *The Suppression of the African Slave-Trade, The Souls of Black Folk,* and *Dusk of Dawn*

See also **LIBRARY OF AMERICA** in **LITERATURE OF THE AMERICAS**

0-940450-33-X LIBRARY OF AMERICA $35.00

John Hope **Franklin** & Alfred **Moss**, Jr.

From Slavery to Freedom: A History of Negro Americans

0-07-021907-9 MCGRAW HILL PB $37.50

Vincent **Harding**

There Is a River: The Black Struggle for Freedom in America

0-15-689089-5 HARCOURT BRACE PB $14.00

William Loren **Katz**

Black Indians: A Hidden Heritage

Crispus Attucks, Cherokee Bill, and the "Dusky Demon" are among the figures in this chronicle of the little-known history of the African-American/Native American alliance

0-689-31196-6 ATHENEUM $17.00

Gerda **Lerner**, editor

Black Woman in White America: A Documentary History

"A stunning collection of documents by black women about themselves"—*Washington Post*

See also **AFRICAN-AMERICAN HISTORY** under **AMERICAN HISTORY** under **WOMEN'S STUDIES** in **SOCIAL STUDIES**

0-679-74314-6 VINTAGE PB $15.00

Darlene Clark **Hine**

The State of Afro-American History: Past, Present, and Future

0-8071-1581-9 LSU PB $11.95

Wilson J. **Moses**

The Golden Age of Black Nationalism, 1850-1925

0-19-520639-8 OXFORD PB $11.95

Hortense **Powdermaker**

After Freedom: A Cultural Study in the Deep South

A classic, first published in 1939, which offers the first complete ethnography of an African-American community in the U.S.

0-299-13784-8 WISCONSIN PB $17.95

Benjamin **Quarles**

The Negro in the American Revolution

See also **REVOLUTIONARY LIVES** under **THE REVOLUTIONARY WAR** under **US HISTORY TO THE CIVIL WAR**

08087808334 NORTH CAROLINA $27.50

Sandi **Russell**

Render Me My Song: African-American Women Writers from Slavery to the Present

Beginning with Phyllis Wheatley, who survived the slave ships to become the most renowned woman poet in 18th-century America, Russell chronicles the lives and work of such giants as Sojourner Truth, Zora Neale Hurston, and also this generation's Toni Morrison, Gloria Naylor, Alice Walker, and Ntozake Shange

0-312-07074-8 ST. MARTIN'S PB $9.95

Ivan Van **Sertima**

They Came Before Columbus: The African Presence in Ancient America

A provocative and detailed account of African explorers

See also **THE EUROPEAN DISCOVERY OF AMERICA** under **US HISTORY TO THE CIVIL WAR**

0-394-40245-6 RANDOM HOUSE $23.00
0-679-72530-X RANDOM HOUSE PB $14.95

Encyclopedias and Picture Books

Nancy **Cunard**, editor

Negro: An Anthology

A broad examination of black life in the Americas, Europe, and Africa; first published in 1934

ABRIDGED WITH AN INTRODUCTION BY HUGH FORD

0-8264-0862-1 CHIRON PB $39.50

W. Augustus **Low** & Virgil A. **Clift**

Encyclopedia of Black America

Offers a variety of special sections, including slavery, folklore, religion, education, the NAACP, and the Black Panther Party

0-306-80221-X DA CAPO PB $35.00

J.A. **Rogers**

World's Great Men of Color

An encyclopedia of notable figures since the 18th century. Entries include Pushkin, Alexandre Dumas, and Marcus Garvey

Volume 1

0-684-81581-8 TOUCHSTONE PB $15.00

Volume 2

0-684-81582-6 TOUCHSTONE PB $15.00

Columbus **Salley**

The Black 100: A Ranking of the Most Influential African-Americans, Past and Present

A compendium of significant African-Americans, past and present, which identifies "the collective giants on whose shoulders African-Americans stand in their unending quest for full economic, political and social quality." With 120 photographs and drawings. "A useful mini-collection of profiles of black American leaders"—*Publishers Weekly*

0-8065-1299-7 CITADEL $21.95

Richard **Wright**, editor

Twelve Million Black Voices: A Folk History of the Negro in the U.S.

A Wright essay accompanies stunning photographs of blacks in the '30s, depicting sharecroppers and city-dwellers alike

PHOTOGRAPHS BY EDWIN ROSSKAM

0-938410-44-X THUNDER'S MOUTH PB $15.95

Slavery

Ira **Berlin**, editor

The Destruction of Slavery

0-521-22979-0 CAMBRIDGE $69.95

Free at Last: A Documentary History of Slavery, Freedom, and the Civil War

1-56584-015-1 NEW PRODUCTS DEVELOPMENT $27.50

1-56584-120-4 NEW PRESS PB $15.95

Elizabeth **Fox-Genovese**

Within the Plantation Household: Black and White Women of the South

Argues that class and race affected women's experiences and that slaves and slaveholders were never linked in sisterhood

See also **SLAVERY AND BLACK LIVES** under **US HISTORY TO THE CIVIL WAR**

0-8078-1808-9 NORTH CAROLINA $39.95

0-8078-4232-X NORTH CAROLINA PB $16.95

Eugene D. **Genovese**

Roll, Jordan, Roll: The World the Slaves Made

An enduring classic. "Genovese's great gift is his ability to penetrate the minds of both slaves and masters, revealing not only how they viewed themselves and each other, but also how their contradictory perceptions interacted" —David Brion Davis, *NY Times Book Review*

See also **SLAVERY AND BLACK LIVES** under **US HISTORY TO THE CIVIL WAR**

0-394-71652-3 RANDOM HOUSE PB $18.00

John W. **Blassingame**

The Slave Community: Plantation Life in the Ante-Bellum South

See also **SLAVERY AND BLACK LIVES** under **US HISTORY TO THE CIVIL WAR**

0-19-502563-6 OXFORD PB $16.95

Kent Anderson **Leslie**

Woman of Color, Daughter of Privilege: Amanda America Dickson, 1849-1893

This well-researched narrative documents the life of an illegitimate mulatto woman who inherited a large amount of land from her plantation-owner father. The court battle contesting her right to inherit serves to expose 19th-century racial ambiguities

0-8203-1688-1 GEORGIA $29.95

0-8203-1871-X GEORGIA PB $14.95

Melton A. **McLaurin**

Celia, a Slave

The historical narrative of the slave girl who, having been adopted at fourteen, endured years of sexual abuse by her master, Robert Newsome, and finally killed him. Despite much sympathy from whites concerning her predicament, she was ultimately executed

See also **AFRICAN-AMERICAN HISTORY** under **AMERICAN HISTORY** under **WOMEN'S STUDIES** in **SOCIAL STUDIES**

0-8203-1352-1 GEORGIA $19.95

Sterling **Stuckey**

Slave Culture: Nationalist Theory and the Foundations of Black America

0-19-504265-4 OXFORD $32.50

Deborah Gray **White**

Ar'n't I a Woman?: Female Slaves in the Plantation South

An important study of the women who faced the double burdens of sexism and racism

0-393-30406-X NORTON PB $8.95

The North

America's northern industrial cities have long seemed to glisten with opportunity for southern blacks and West Indians; their northward migration and the subsequent rise of the urban ghetto marked a turning point in the nation's political and social history. From the cultural mecca of 1920s Harlem to the controversial gentrification of 1980s slums, black neighborhoods have played a leading role in the shape and economy of American cities.

Houston A. **Baker**, Jr.

Modernism and the Harlem Renaissance

See also **GENERAL STUDIES: THE 20TH CENTURY** under **AMERICAN LITERATURE: ANTHOLOGIES AND CRITICAL STUDIES** in **LITERATURE OF THE AMERICAS**

0-226-03525-5 CHICAGO PB $10.95

Kenneth B. **Clark**

Dark Ghetto: Dilemmas of Social Power

A sweeping overview of housing, schools, psychology, and the politics of the Harlem ghetto, by a leading sociologist of race

FOREWORD BY GUNNAR MYRDAL

0-8195-6226-2 WESLEYAN PB $17.95

Dennis C. **Dickerson**

Out of the Crucible: Black Steelworkers in Western Pennsylvania, 1875-1980

0-88706-305-5 SUNY $74.50

0-88706-306-3 SUNY PB $19.95

Arnold R. **Hirsch**

Making the Second Ghetto: Race and Housing in Chicago, 1940-1960

0-521-24569-9 CAMBRIDGE $47.95

Nathan I. **Huggins**

Harlem Renaissance

The first full-scale story of 1920s Harlem in the context of American history, including artistic, cultural, political, and social developments

0-19-501665-3 OXFORD PB $16.95

Nicholas **Lemann**

The Promised Land: The Great Black Migration and How It Changed America

"Richly informative...When [Lemann] reminds us that there has been only one nonfiction book entirely on the post-1940 black migration and we think of the continuing flood of books on the civil rights movement, our respect for his decision grows. He has fulfilled an important and neglected need"—C. Vann Woodward

0-394-56004-3 KNOPF $24.95

0-679-73347-7 VINTAGE PB $14.00

Elliot **Liebow**

Tally's Corner

The classic sociological study of black street life

0-316-52514-6 LITTLE, BROWN PB $10.95

James M. **McPherson**

The Abolitionist Legacy: From Reconstruction to the NAACP

0-691-10039-X PRINCETON PB $14.95

Mark **Naison**

Communists in Harlem During the Depression

Blunders and heady adventures; winner of the American Political Science Association Ralph Bunche Award (1984)

0-252-00644-5 ILLINOIS $34.95

0-8021-5183-3 GROVE PB $9.95

Allan H. **Spear**

Black Chicago: The Making of a Negro Ghetto, 1890-1920

0-226-76857-0 CHICAGO PB $13.95

Joe W. **Trotter**, Jr.

Black Milwaukee: The Making of an Industrial Proletariat, 1915-45

How factory jobs were a step up from sharecropping and house service

0-252-01124-4 ILLINOIS $29.95
0-252-06035-0 ILLINOIS PB $11.95

The Civil Rights Movement and Beyond

Often regarded as a time of unprecedented alliance between blacks and whites, the civil rights decade marked a full-scale war on racial inequality that had been long in preparation. The Rev. Martin Luther King, Jr.'s 1963 March on Washington, with 200,000 in attendance, was among the highlights of an inspirational movement that placed intense pressure on the federal government, whose most significant response to the growing unrest of those years was the Civil Rights Act of 1964.

Harry S. **Ashmore**

Hearts and Minds: A Personal Chronicle of Race in America

The civil rights movement as seen by the former editor of the *Arkansas Gazette,* whose editorials advocating integration won him a Pulitzer Prize

INTRODUCTION BY HAROLD FLEMING

0-932020-58-5 SEVEN LOCKS PB $14.95

Liva **Baker**

The Second Battle of New Orleans: The Hundred-Year Battle to Integrate the Schools

Following *Brown v. Board of Education,* the landmark ruling declaring racial segregation in public schools unconstitutional, the city of New Orleans began a seven-year struggle toward integration. This follows the tumultuous events and introduces a cast of historic characters: Ruby Bridges, a six-year-old black girl who endured appalling threats; Skelly Wright, a white federal judge who risked career and life to enforce the law; the young Thurgood Marshall, then working at the NAACP; and many others who took part in a key moment of American history

See also **CIVIL RIGHTS** under **US HISTORY, 1945 TO THE PRESENT**

0-06-016808-0 HARPERCOLLINS $32.00

Taylor **Branch**

Parting the Waters: America in the King Years, 1954-1963

A powerful, scrupulously detailed account of the early civil rights years

See also **CIVIL RIGHTS** under **US HISTORY, 1945 TO THE PRESENT**

0-671-68742-5 TOUCHSTONE PB $16.00

John Langston **Gwaltney**

Drylongso: A Self-Portrait of Black America

These eloquent and, at times, disturbing testimonies, conducted in the early '70s with "drylongso," or ordinary people, are among the most illuminating of core black culture

1-56584-080-1 NEW PRESS PB $12.95

Stokely **Carmichael** & Charles V. **Hamilton**

Black Power: The Politics of Liberation in America

0-679-74313-8 VINTAGE PB $11.00

Clayborne **Carson**

In Struggle: SNCC and the Black Awakening of the 1960s

0-674-44727-1 HARVARD PB $15.95

William Henry **Chafe**

Civilities and Civil Rights: Greensboro, North Carolina, and the Black Struggle For Freedom

0-19-502625-X OXFORD $24.95
0-19-502919-4 OXFORD PB $10.95

Ward **Churchill** & Jim Vander **Wall**

Agents of Repression: The FBI's Secret Wars Against the Black Panther Party and the American Indian Movement

See also **THE CIA, FBI, AND ESPIONAGE** under **AMERICAN POLITICS AND FOREIGN POLICY**

0-89608-293-8 SOUTH END PB $16.00

Thomas C. **Dent** & Tom **Dent**

Southern Journey: A Return to the Civil Rights Movement

0-688-14099-8 MORROW $25.00

James Max **Fendrich**

Ideal Citizens: The Legacy of the Civil Rights Movement

Traces the social and political careers of black and white civil rights activists and their nonactivist counterparts over a quarter of a century

See also **CIVIL RIGHTS** under **US HISTORY, 1945 TO THE PRESENT**

0-7914-1324-1 SUNY PB $16.95

Robin **Gooding-Williams**, editor

Reading Rodney King—Reading Urban Uprising

0-415-90734-9 ROUTLEDGE $55.00
0-415-90735-7 ROUTLEDGE PB $16.95

Melissa Faye **Greene**

Praying for Sheetrock

A small southern town's awakening to civil rights in the '70s and a black man who leads the call. "An inspiring and absorbing account of the struggle for human dignity and racial equality in McIntosh County, Georgia"
—Coretta Scott King

0-449-90753-8 FAWCETT PB $11.00

Martin Luther **King**, Jr.

I Have a Dream

A 30th-anniversary gift edition of the inspiring speech that seared the imperative of racial justice into our national psyche

See also **NONVIOLENT POLITICS** under **POLITICAL THOUGHT** in **SOCIAL STUDIES**

0-06-250947-0 HARPERCOLLINS $12.00
0-590-20516-1 SCHOLASTIC $25.00

Henry **Hampton** & Steve **Fayer**

Voices of Freedom: An Oral History of the Civil Rights Movement from the 1950s through the 1980s

Companion volume to *Eyes on the Prize*, drawing on nearly one thousand interviews. "A vast choral pageant that recounts the momentous work of the civil rights struggle"
—*NY Times Book Review*

See also **CIVIL RIGHTS** under **US HISTORY, 1945 TO THE PRESENT**

0-553-35232-6 BANTAM PB $18.95

Anne **Moody**

Coming of Age in Mississippi

A memoir of lynchings, economic hardship, and the brutal times of a black female civil rights activist of the '60s

See also **CIVIL RIGHTS** under **US HISTORY, 1945 TO THE PRESENT**

0-440-31488-7 LAUREL LEAF PB $6.50

Aldon D. **Morris**

The Origins of the Civil Rights Movement: Black Communities Organizing for Change

See also **ETHNICITY AND RACE RELATIONS** under **TOPICS IN MODERN SOCIOLOGY** under **SOCIOLOGY** in **SOCIAL STUDIES**

0-02-922130-7 FREE PRESS PB $16.95

Adam **Nossiter**

Of Long Memory: Mississippi and the Murder of Medgar Evers

Covers the 1963 murder of Evers through the 1994 conviction of his murderer, and along the way shows how Mississippi has painfully confronted its past. A *New York Times* Notable Book of the Year

0-201-48339-4 ADDISON-WESLEY PB $12.00

Kenneth **O'Reilly**

"Racial Matters": The FBI's Secret File on Black America, 1960-1972

How J. Edgar Hoover and his bureau did their best to undermine Martin Luther King and the civil rights movement

0-02-923681-9 FREE PRESS $24.95
0-02-923682-7 FREE PRESS PB $16.95

Charles M. **Payne**

I've Got the Light of Freedom: The Organizing Tradition and the Mississippi Freedom Struggle

In this history of the early civil rights movement in the South, Payne demonstrates that working-class rural blacks—and especially women—led the movement in the most dangerous parts of the South

0-520-08515-9 CALIFORNIA $28.00

Pete **Seeger** & Robert S. **Reiser**

Everybody Says Freedom: The Civil Rights Movement in Words, Pictures, and Song

0-393-30604-6 NORTON PB $18.95

Howell **Raines**
My Soul Is Rested: Movement Days in the Deep South Remembered
Resisters and civil rights leaders tell of their lives; with testimonies from Bull Connor, Martin Luther King, Jr., George Wallace, and Rosa Parks
0-14-006753-1 VIKING PB $12.95

Jo Ann Gibson **Robinson**
The Montgomery Bus Boycott and the Women Who Started It: The Memoir of Jo Ann Gibson Robinson
An autobiographical account of one of the most successful tactics of the civil rights era
EDITED BY DAVID J. GARROW
0-87049-524-0 TENNESSEE $36.00
0-87049-527-5 TENNESSEE PB $15.95

Howard **Smead**
Blood Justice: The Lynching of Mack Charles Parker
A chilling reconstruction of a Mississippi lynching and the subsequent FBI investigation
0-19-505429-6 OXFORD PB $10.95

Thomas **Sowell**
Civil Rights: Rhetoric or Reality?
A critical look at the movement by the author of *The Economics and Politics of Race*
0-688-06269-5 MORROW PB $6.95

Maryanne **Vollers**
Ghosts of Mississippi
National Book Award finalist—a brilliant examination of the 1963 murder of civil rights leader Medgar Evers and the three-decade crusade to convict his murderer. "Prizewinning journalism, a compelling tale that speaks volumes about the transformation of the Deep South—and of America"—David Lamb
See also **CIVIL RIGHTS** under **US HISTORY, 1945 TO THE PRESENT**
0-316-91485-1 LITTLE, BROWN $24.95
0-316-91471-1 LITTLE, BROWN PB $13.95

Stephen J. **Whitfield**
A Death in the Delta: The Story of Emmett Till
In August 1955, 14-year-old Emmett Till was lynched for allegedly making a pass at a white woman, but an all-white jury acquitted the white defendants who went on trial for the lynching
0-8018-4326-X JOHNS HOPKINS PB $13.95

Juan **Williams**
Eyes on the Prize: America's Civil Rights Years, 1954-1965
Illustrated accompaniment to the PBS television series
See also **CIVIL RIGHTS** under **US HISTORY, 1945 TO THE PRESENT**
INTRODUCTION BY JULIAN BOND
0-14-009653-1 PENGUIN PB $14.95

Andrew **Young**
An Easy Burden: The Civil Rights Movement and the Transformation of America
0-06-017362-9 HARPERCOLLINS $26.00

Race Relations

Robert Sam **Anson**
Best Intentions: The Education and Killing of Edmund Perry
The story of an Exeter student from Harlem killed by a white policeman in an alleged holdup attempt
0-394-75707-6 VINTAGE PB $12.00

James **Baldwin**
The Evidence of Things Not Seen
The Atlanta serial murders of the '80s moved Baldwin to write about collective responsibility in the trial of the black man accused
INTRODUCTION BY WILLIAM STYRON
0-8050-3939-2 HOLT PB $9.95

James Baldwin

Derrick **Bell**
And We Are Not Saved: The Elusive Quest for Racial Justice
Freedom and full rights are still not realities for African-Americans, according to a Harvard law professor
0-465-00329-X BASIC PB $14.00

Confronting Authority: Reflections of an Ardent Protester
In 1992 Bell resigned from a tenured position at Harvard Law School to protest the lack of tenuring for any women of color. Here, he sagely examines not only his own, but many other examples of dissent, and provides a convincing argument for individual action against unjustly used authority. "As a writer and teacher [Bell] conveys profound insights…from a life devoted to a higher and better vision for humankind" —Jesse Jackson
See also **ETHNIC AND RACE RELATIONS** under **AMERICAN PEOPLE AND PLACES**
0-8070-0926-1 BEACON $20.00
0-8070-0927-X BEACON PB $12.00

Gospel Choirs: Psalms of Survival in an Alien Land Called Home
Bell uses allegorical stories and encounters with fictional characters to confront the most vexing issues of the day: the *Bell Curve* controversies, the Contract with America, the media's depiction of black men, and more
0-465-02412-2 BASIC $23.00

Faces at the Bottom of the Well: The Permanence of Racism
This civil rights activist has a sobering thesis: "racism is an integral, permanent and destructive component of this society." "A starkly existentialist vision…effective…chilling ….The stories challenge old assumptions and linger in the mind"—*NY Times Book Review*
0-465-06814-6 BASIC PB $12.00

We must see this country's history of slavery, not as an insuperable racial barrier to blacks, but as a legacy of enlightenment from our enslaved forebears reminding us that if they survived the ultimate form of racism, we and those whites who stand with us can at least view racial oppression in its many contemporary forms without underestimating its critical importance and likely permanent status in this country.

To initiate the reconsideration, I want to set forth this proposition, which will be easier to reject than refute: *Black people will never gain full equality in this country. Even those herculean efforts we hail as successful will produce no more than temporary "peaks of progress," short-lived victories that slide into irrelevance as racial patterns adapt in ways that maintain white dominance. This is a hard-to-accept fact that all history verifies. We must acknowledge it, not as a sign of submission, but as an act of ultimate defiance.*
FACES AT THE BOTTOM OF THE WELL: THE PERMANENCE OF RACISM

Derrick Bell (©Ken Shung)

Paul **Berman**
Blacks and Jews: Alliances and Arguments
0-385-31473-6 DELTA PB $12.95

Joseph **Boskin**
Sambo: The Rise and Demise of an American Jester
"A major contribution to the study of stereotypes, the history of theatrical and other entertainments in America, and the analysis of material culture in the United States" —*Philadelphia Inquirer*
0-19-505658-2 OXFORD PB $10.95

Kevin **Flynn** & Gary **Gerhardt**
The Silent Brotherhood: Inside America's Racist Underground
0-451-16786-4 NEW AMERICAN LIBRARY PB $6.99

John Hope **Franklin**

Racial Equity in America

The expensive volume is a limited slipcase edition that also includes *The Color Line: Legacy for the Twenty-First century*

0-8262-0913-0 MISSOURI $159.00
0-8262-0912-2 MISSOURI PB $12.95

George M. **Frederickson**

The Black Image in the White Mind: The Debate on Afro-American Character and Destiny, 1817-1914

0-685-93763-1 IRVINGTON $30.50
0-8195-6188-6 WESLEYAN PB $19.95

White Supremacy: A Comparative Study in American and South African History

0-19-502759-0 OXFORD $45.00
0-19-503042-7 OXFORD PB $12.95

Nikki **Giovanni**

Racism 101

Provocative essays from the outspoken and popular poet, on figures ranging from Spike Lee ("self-serving and devoid of historical perspective") to *Star Trek's* Uhura ("the voice of the entire Federation") and from W.E.B. DuBois to Toni Morrison. "The general rage may be mellower with age, but Giovanni's ability to provoke with barbed comment remains much in evidence"—*Kirkus Reviews.* "A performing voice capable of dizzying displays of virtuosity" —Virginia Fowler

See also **AFROCENTRISM AND OTHER TRENDS** under **CULTURE**

0-688-14234-6 QUILL PB $11.00

Walt **Harrington**

Crossings: A White Man's Journey into Black America

Harrington, married to a black woman with whom he has two children, one day at the dentist overheard a racist joke. "This idiot's talking about my children!" the author realized. The experience sent him on a journey into black neighborhoods across the U.S., determined to understand race and to know what black experience is really like

0-06-092462-4 HARPERPERENNIAL PB $13.00

A. Leon **Higginbotham**

In the Matter of Color

0-19-502387-0 OXFORD $40.00
0-19-502745-0 OXFORD PB $15.95

Anita **Hill** & Emma Coleman **Jordan**, editors

Race, Gender and Power in America

Essays that explore the volatile American politics of race and gender in the wake of the Clarence Thomas confirmation hearings. Includes Hill's first published piece on the hearings and contributions by Anna Deveare Smith, Harvard's Charles J. Ogletree, Professor Emma Coleman Jordan, and Chief Judge Emeritus A. Leon Higgenbotham

0-19-508774-7 OXFORD $25.00

bell **hooks**

Killing Rage: Ending Racism

Recently named by the *Utne Reader* as one of the "100 Visionaries Who Could Change Your Life," bell hooks has been among our country's premier cultural and social critics for years. The 23 essays here address the fight against racism and sexism, and how those two battles are intimately interrelated in the American scene. From internalized racism in movies and media to African-American anti-Semitism, hooks draws from her enormous spectrum of reference an enduring lesson about the possibility of change

See also **AMERICAN POLITICS** under **POLITICAL THOUGHT** in **SOCIAL STUDIES**

0-8050-3782-9 HOLT $20.00

Michael **Lerner** & Cornel **West**

Jews & Blacks: A Dialogue on Race, Religion, and Culture in America

0-452-27591-1 PLUME PB $12.95

Stanley **Lieberson**

A Piece of the Pie: Black and White Immigrants Since 1880

See also **IMMIGRATION** under **AMERICAN PEOPLE AND PLACES**

0-520-04362-6 CALIFORNIA PB $17.00

C. Eric **Lincoln**

Coming Through the Fire: Surviving Race and Place in America

Lincoln was born in a rural town in northern Alabama and today, is professor emeritus of religion and culture at Duke University, the founding president of the Black Academy of Arts and Letters, and a fellow of the American Academy of Arts and Sciences. Here he explores such issues as biracial relationships, violence among African-Americans, and the relationship between African-Americans and Jews

See also **ETHNIC AND RACE RELATIONS** under **AMERICAN PEOPLE AND PLACES**

WITH A FOREWORD BY HENRY LOUIS GATES, JR.

0-8223-1736-2 DUKE $17.95

Bernard **Magubane**

The Ties that Bind: African-American Consciousness of Africa

A startling analysis of African-American self-prejudice

0-86543-036-5 AFRICA WORLD $35.00
0-86543-037-3 AFRICA WORLD PB $12.95

Toni **Morrison**, editor

Race-ing Justice, En-Gendering Power: Essays on Anita Hill, Clarence Thomas, and the Construction of Social Reality

Published to coincide with the first anniversary of the political scandal that shook the country, this book brings together 17 essays by prominent scholars—black, white, male, and female—on the historical, political, and sexual consequences of the Thomas/Hill affair

See also **CURRENT POLITICAL THOUGHT AND ISSUES** under **AMERICAN POLITICS AND FOREIGN POLICY**

0-679-74145-3 PANTHEON PB $15.00

Thomas F. **Pettigrew**

The Sociology of Race Relations: Reflection and Reform

0-02-925110-9 FREE PRESS PB $19.95

Alphonso **Pinkney**

The Myth of Black Progress

A statistically rich refutation of the argument that African-Americans have progressed greatly since the 1964 Civil Rights Act in income, employment, educational access, and growth of a middle class

0-521-31047-4 CAMBRIDGE PB $15.95

Patricia **Raybon**

My First White Friend: Confessions on Race, Love, & Forgiveness

0-670-85956-7 VIKING $22.95

Howard **Schuman** & others

Racial Attitudes in America: Trends and Interpretations

0-674-74574-4 HARVARD $33.00
0-674-74573-6 HARVARD PB $14.95

Thomas **Sowell**

The Economics and Politics of Race: An International Perspective

Provocative analysis of the relative significance of race in society, both in the US and elsewhere. Sowell is America's leading black conservative thinker

See also **DISCRIMINATION, EDUCATION, AND INCOME** under **SPECIAL TOPICS** under **ECONOMICS** in **SOCIAL STUDIES**

0-688-04832-3 MORROW PB $9.95

C. Vann **Woodward**

American Counterpoint: Slavery and Racism in the North-South Dialogue

0-19-503269-1 OXFORD PB $9.95

The Strange Career of Jim Crow

A brief but outstanding account of segregation

0-19-501805-2 OXFORD PB $10.95

Cornel **West**

Race Matters

0-8070-0918-0 BEACON $15.00
0-679-74986-1 VINTAGE PB $10.00

Cornel **West** & Michael **Lerner**

Jews and Blacks: The Hard Hunt for Common Ground

0-399-14046-8 PUTNAM $24.95

Joel **Williamson**

A Rage for Order: Black-White Relations in the American South Since Emancipation

0-19-504025-2 OXFORD PB $12.95

Bruce M. **Wright**

Black Robes, White Justice

A black New York City judge and poet investigates racism in the American legal system

0-8184-0573-2 LYLE STUART PB $12.95

William Julius **Wilson**

The Declining Significance of Race: Blacks and Changing American Institutions

0-226-90129-7 CHICAGO PB $10.95

The Truly Disadvantaged: The Inner City, the Underclass and Public Policy

See also **URBAN SOCIOLOGY** under **TOPICS IN MODERN SOCIOLOGY** under **SOCIOLOGY**

0-226-90131-9 CHICAGO PB $13.95

Forrest G. **Wood**

The Arrogance of Faith: Christianity and Race in America from the Colonial Era to the Twentieth Century

A controversial and groundbreaking study of the ways in which Christian churches in America have been guilty of complicity with racism

0-394-57993-3 NORTHEASTERN PB $29.95

Facing Black Violence

Geoffrey **Canada**

Fist Stick Knife Gun: A Personal History of Violence in America

See also **CRIME AND PUNISHMENT** under **TOPICS IN AMERICAN STUDIES**

0-8070-0423-5 BEACON PB $12.00

Richard **Majors** & Janet Mancini **Billson**

Cool Pose: The Dilemma of Black Manhood in America

The demeanor of African-American ghetto males is one of irony and superiority. But what are its consequences? Based on six years of research that included intensive personal interviews, this study theorizes an assortment of surprising and sometimes tragic conclusions. "A creative and dynamic contribution to the growing literature on the unique position of black males in American society"—Jewelle Taylor Gibbs

0-671-86572-2 TOUCHSTONE PB $10.00

Nathan **McCall**

Makes Me Wanna Holler: A Young Black Man in America

McCall's journey from teenage rapist and stickup artist to prison inmate, and, finally, after much struggle, to a coveted job at *The Washington Post* is told with wit, intelligence, and frank emotion. "So powerful that it will leave you shaken and educated. The book belongs in every prison library and affluent country club. No one will come away unrewarded"—*USA Today*

0-679-74070-8 VINTAGE PB $12.00

Jerome G. **Miller**

Search and Destroy: African-American Males in the Criminal Justice System

Among other facts, this 1996 study shows that around the country, 90 percent of those arrested on drug charges are black, even though African-Americans make up only 12 percent of the population. "One of the most important and clear eyed challenges to date to the linking of crime and race and to the entire conservative anti-welfare, hard-on-crime agenda" —*Publishers Weekly*

See also **CRIME AND PUNISHMENT** under **TOPICS IN AMERICAN STUDIES**

0-521-46021-2 CAMBRIDGE $24.95

Political Theory and Movements

Barbara **Bergmann**

In Defense of Affirmative Action

This polemic argues in favor of the necessity and effectiveness of affirmative action programs. Bergman, who served on the staff of President Kennedy's Council of Economic Advisors, acknowledges the problems with quotas and considers the unfairness to white males inherent in the programs, but concludes that the implications of allowing sexual and racial discrimination to continue are far worse

See also **CURRENT POLITICAL THOUGHT AND ISSUES** under **AMERICAN POLITICS AND FOREIGN POLICY**

0-465-09833-9 BASIC $23.00

Harold **Cruse**

Crisis of the Negro Intellectual: A Historical Analysis of the Failure of Black Leadership

A forceful and disturbing book that has sacrificed none of its relevance since its first printing in 1967

0-688-03886-7 MORROW PB $14.95

Christopher **Edley**

Not All Black and White: Affirmative Action and American Values

0-8090-2955-3 HILL & WANG $15.00

Henry Louis **Gates**, Jr. & Cornel **West**

The Future of the Race

Two foremost African-American intellectuals take W.E.B. DuBois's "The Talented Tenth" as their point of departure for a consideration of the future of the black community in America

See also **AFRICAN-AMERICANS** under **THE MELTING POT** under **AMERICAN PEOPLE AND PLACES**

0-679-44405-X KNOPF $21.00

0-679-76378-3 VINTAGE $12.00

Gerald D. **Jaynes**

Branches Without Roots: The Genesis of the Black Working Class, 1862-1882

0-19-505575-6 OXFORD PB $17.95

William K. **Tabb**

The Political Economy of the Black Ghetto

Argues that a colonial relationship exists between ghettoes and the larger society

0-393-09930-X NORTON PB $6.95

Culture

Allison **Blakely**

Russia and the Negro: Blacks in Russian History and Thought

"Opens the field of Soviet scholarship to further investigations, fresh insights, and interpretations by those scholars who see the Negro's role in world affairs as a theme of unheralded significance"—Albert Parry

0-88258-175-9 HOWARD PB $14.95

Eugene D. **Genovese**

The Southern Front: History and Politics in the Cultural War

A collection of essays, addresses, and reviews from the mid-eighties to 1994, from one of the nation's preeminent scholars of Southern and African-American history

0-8262-1001-5 MISSOURI $29.95

Kathy **Russell** & others

The Color Complex: The Politics of Skin Color Among African-Americans

Argues that color—the varying hues of black—determines one's standing in the political, social, and professional hierarchies within the African-American community. The authors—a white woman, a black woman, and a black man—discuss the history of black-on-black prejudice and the tensions it has caused; they seek to heighten awareness about a subject long considered taboo

0-15-119164-6 HARCOURT BRACE $21.95

Patricia A. **Turner**

Heard It Through the Grapevine: Rumor in African-American Culture

0-520-08185-4 CALIFORNIA $25.00

0-520-08936-7 CALIFORNIA PB $12.95

Family

E. Franklin **Frazier**

Black Bourgeoisie: The Rise of a New Middle Class in the United States

This 1957 analysis of America's black middle class made "black bourgeoisie" as loaded a term as "yuppie" is today

WITH AN INTRODUCTION BY WILLIAM JULIUS WILSON

0-684-83241-0 FREE PRESS PB $12.00

Herbert G. **Gutman**

The Black Family in Slavery and Freedom, 1750-1925

"Gutman has successfully challenged the traditional view that slavery virtually destroyed the Afro-American family"—John Hope Franklin

0-394-72451-8 RANDOM HOUSE PB $22.00

Shirley Taylor **Haizlip**

The Sweeter the Juice: A Family Memoir in Black and White

0-671-89933-3 TOUCHSTONE PB....$11.00

Carole **Ione**

Pride of Family: Four Generations of American Women of Color

The author investigates the fascinating past of her family, going as far back as her great-grandmother Frances Anne Rollin, whose 1868 diary is a landmark. An eloquent and absorbing memoir

0-380-71934-7 AVON PB....$10.00

Carole Ione (credit: ©Gisela Gamper)

Women

Patricia **Bell-Scott**, editor

Double Stitch

Forty-seven black feminists explore their relationships with their mothers in this collection of stories, poems, and essays. Introduced by Maya Angelou, and including contributions by Alice Walker, bell hooks, Audre Lorde, Sonia Sanchez, and others, *Double Stitch* uses quilt-making as its central metaphor to construct a fine blend of writing and scholarship that chronicles poverty, sexism, racism, and triumph in spite of hardship. "A truly powerful collection, long overdue"—*Booklist*

0-8070-0910-5 BEACON....$19.95
0-06-097503-2 HARPERPERENNIAL PB....$13.00

Angela **Davis**

Women, Race and Class

0-394-71351-6 RANDOM HOUSE PB....$10.00

Gwendolyn **Etter-Lewis**

My Soul Is My Own: Oral Narratives of African-American Women in the Professions

A multidisciplinary approach to understanding the complex lives of those who crossed the threshold of white male-dominated professions in the early part of our century. A colonel, a physician, and a union organizer are among the extraordinary women who are visited in this volume

0-415-90559-1 ROUTLEDGE....$55.00
0-415-90560-5 ROUTLEDGE PB....$17.95

Paula **Giddings**

In Search of Sisterhood: Delta Sigma Theta and the Challenge of the Black Sorority Movement

A history of black women in American political, social, and economic affairs

0-688-05775-6 MORROW....$23.00
0-688-13509-9 QUILL PB....$14.00

Jacqueline **Jones**

Labor of Love, Labor of Sorrow: Black Women, Work and the Family from Slavery to the Present

Winner of the Bancroft Prize

See also **AFRICAN-AMERICAN HISTORY** under **AMERICAN HISTORY** under **WOMEN'S STUDIES** in **SOCIAL STUDIES**

0-394-74536-1 VINTAGE PB....$14.00

Religion

Maya **Angelou**

Heart of a Woman

See also **CLASSIC AUTOBIOGRAPHIES** under **BLACK VOICES, BLACK LIVES**

0-394-51273-1 RANDOM HOUSE....$24.95
0-553-24689-5 BDD PB....$5.50

Albert B. **Cleage**, Jr.

Black Christian Nationalism: New Directions for the Black Church

By the famous Detroit minister who shared platforms with Malcolm X

0-941205-00-2 LUXOR....$14.95
0-941205-01-0 LUXOR PB....$10.00

E. Franklin **Frazier** & C. Eric **Lincoln**

The Negro Church in America & the Black Church Since Frazier

Two important works

0-8052-0387-7 SCHOCKEN PB....$12.00

Mechal **Sobel**

Trabelin' On: The Slave Journey to an Afro-Baptist Faith

A religious history of the slaves and free blacks of antebellum America. "Takes seriously the religion of black people and shows its creative power to construct a sacred cosmos"—Andrew E. Murray, *Journal of American History*

See also **SLAVERY AND BLACK LIVES** under **US HISTORY TO THE CIVIL WAR**

0-8371-9887-9 GREENWOOD....$79.50
0-691-00603-2 PRINCETON PB....$16.95

Gayraud S. **Wilmore**

Black Religion and Black Radicalism: An Interpretation of the Religious History of Afro-American People

0-88344-032-6 ORBIS PB....$17.00

The Black Aesthetic

Donald **Bogle**

Toms, Coons, Mulattoes, Mammies and Bucks: An Interpretive History of Blacks in American Film

A historical overview of how Hollywood has portrayed blacks

See also **GENRES AND THEMES** under **FILM** in **PERFORMING ARTS AND MEDIA**

0-8264-0416-2 CONTINUUM PB....$15.95

J. L. **Dillard**

Black English: Its History and Usage in the United States

0-394-71872-0 RANDOM HOUSE PB....$11.00

Nelson **George**

Buppies, B-Boys, Baps, and Bohos: Notes on Post-Soul Black Culture

Journalist and award-winning author George surveys black culture's entry into the popular mainstream, from Superfly to Muhammed Ali to Michael Jordan. "Scholarly depth, and [a] gift for stylish, finger-on-the-pulse reporting" —*Publishers Weekly*

0-06-092201-X HARPERPERENNIAL PB....$11.00

Ira **Gitler**

Swing to Bop: An Oral History of the Transition in Jazz in the 1940s

"An era when black musicians tried innovatively to wrest control of their music from white big-band leaders"—Mel Watkins, *American Visions*

See also **BEBOP AND POST-BOP** under **SURVEYS OF JAZZ HISTORY** under **JAZZ** in **PERFORMING ARTS AND MEDIA**

0-19-505070-3 OXFORD PB....$13.95

Jim **Haskins**

Cotton Club

A history of Harlem's famous nightclub and its gangster-owners, white-only patrons, and black entertainers

0-7818-0248-2 HIPPOCRENE PB....$14.95

Charles **Johnson**

Being and Race: Black Writing Since 1970

See also **GENERAL STUDIES: THE 20TH CENTURY** under **AMERICAN LITERATURE: ANTHOLOGIES AND CRITICAL STUDIES** in **LITERATURE OF THE AMERICAS**

0-253-31165-9 INDIANA....$20.00
0-253-20537-9 INDIANA PB....$8.95

John Oliver **Killens** & Jerry W. **Ward**, Jr., editors

An important figure in the Black Arts movement of the '60s, Killens was a close friend of Martin Luther King, Jr. and other civil rights activists

Black Southern Voices: An Anthology of Fiction, Poetry, Drama, Nonfiction, and Critical Essays

This book represents the last project of Killens, who founded the Harlem Writers Guild, and who influenced a generation of black writers. Its 56

entries, in a wide variety of genres, demonstrate the existence of a black Southern literary tradition, one distinct from American writing in general and from black literature as a whole. It includes the work of Frederick Douglass, Zora Neale Hurston, Angela Davis, and Maya Angelou. "A magnificent homage to the memory of John Oliver Killens, and to the African-American literary tradition"—Henry Louis Gates, Jr.
0-452-01096-9 MERIDIAN PB $15.00

Lawrence W. **Levine**
Black Culture and Black Consciousness: Afro-American Folk Thought from Slavery to Freedom
0-19-502374-9 OXFORD PB $14.95

Alan **Pomerance**
Repeal of the Blues: How the Black Entertainers Influenced Civil Rights
0-8065-1105-2 CITADEL $17.95
0-8065-1244-X CITADEL PB $10.95

Folklore

Nearly every American black writer has touched on some aspect of folk culture. Zora Neale Hurston, a pioneering feminist and cultural anthropologist, incorporated a great deal of folk material into her writing, as did Langston Hughes. Its impression can be seen in the work of such early writers as Paul Laurence Dunbar and Jean Toomer, as well as in the contemporary contributions of Ishmael Reed, Alice Walker, and Toni Morrison.

Harold **Courlander**
A Treasury of Afro-American Folklore: The Oral Literature, Traditions, Recollections, Legends, Tales, Songs, Religious Beliefs, Customs and Sayings
See also **AFRICAN-AMERICAN** under **THE WESTERN HEMISPHERE** under **MYTHOLOGY AND FOLKLORE** in **RELIGION, SPIRITUALITY, AND PHILOSOPHY**
1-56924-811-7 MARLOWE PB $14.95

Daryl C. **Dance**
Long Gone: The Mecklenberg Six and the Theme of Escape in Black Folklore
0-87049-512-7 TENNESSEE $28.00
9-99397-369-6 TENNESSEE PB $14.95

Shuckin' and Jivin'?: Folklore from Contemporary Black Americans
0-253-20265-5 INDIANA PB $15.95

Linda **Goss** & Marian E. **Barnes**, editors
Talk that Talk: An Anthology of African-American Storytelling
0-671-67167-7 SIMON & SCHUSTER $22.95
0-671-67168-5 TOUCHSTONE PB $13.00

J. Frank **Dobie**, editor
Coffee in the Gourd
0-87074-039-3 SMU $11.95

Zora Neale **Hurston**
Mules and Men
This classic was the first substantial collection of folktales by a black writer
ILLUSTRATED BY MIGUEL COVARRUBIAS
0-8095-9018-2 BORGO $33.00
0-06-091648-6 HARPERCOLLINS PB $13.50

Bessie **Jones** & Bess L. **Hawes**
Step It Down: Games, Plays, Songs, and Stories from the Afro-American Heritage
0-8203-0960-5 GEORGIA PB $12.95

Jane **Livingston** & John **Beardsley**
Black Folk Art in America, 1930-1980
FOREWORD BY PETER C. MARZIO
0-87805-158-9 MISSISSIPPI PB $29.95

Jakie L. **Pruett** & Everett B. **Cole**
As We Lived: Stories Told by Black Story Tellers
0-89015-309-4 EAKINS $9.95

Michael P. **Smith**
Spirit World: Pattern in the Expressive Folk Culture of Afro-American New Orleans
INTRODUCTION BY NICHOLAS R. SPITZER
0-88289-895-7 PELICAN PB $21.95

Geneval **Smitherman**
Talkin' and Testifying: The Language of Black America
0-8143-1805-3 WAYNE STATE PB $16.95

Afrocentrism and Other Trends

Nikki **Giovanni**
Racism 101
Provocative essays from the outspoken and popular poet, on figures ranging from Spike Lee ("self-serving and devoid of historical perspective") to *Star Trek's* Uhura ("the voice of the entire Federation") and from W.E.B. DuBois to Toni Morrison. "The general rage may be mellower with age, but Giovanni's ability to provoke with barbed comment remains much in evidence"—*Kirkus Reviews.* "A performing voice capable of dizzying displays of virtuosity" —Virginia Fowler
See also **RACE RELATIONS**
0-688-14234-6 QUILL PB $11.00

The Black Middle Class

Ellis **Cose**
The Rage of a Privileged Class
0-06-092594-9 HARPERPERENNIAL PB $12.00

Bart **Landry**
The New Black Middle Class
0-520-05942-5 CALIFORNIA $38.00
0-520-06465-8 CALIFORNIA PB $13.95

Leanita **McClain** & Clarence **Page**
What Killed Leanita McClain: Essays on Living in Both Black and White Worlds
The enigma of the African-American journalist Leanita McClain—the *Newsweek* and *Washington Post* essayist who, months after being named by *Glamour* one of the ten most outstanding career women in America, took her own life
1-87936-038-1 NOBLE $21.95

Richard **Sennett** & Jonathan **Cobb**
The Hidden Injuries of Class
A classic work on the conflicts of blue-collar America
0-393-31085-X NORTON PB $9.95

Black Voices, Black Lives

Anna Julia **Cooper**
A Voice from the South
Considered one of the original texts foretelling the black feminist movement, these essays offer unparalleled insight into the thought of black women writers in the 19th century. Originally published in 1892
INTRODUCTION BY MARY HELEN WASHINGTON
0-19-506323-6 OXFORD PB $12.95

Gerald **Early**, editor
Lure and Loathing
"…An illuminating book, filled with frank and revealing insights on the decisions and dilemmas that come with being black" —*NY Review of Books*
0-14-015937-1 PENGUIN PB $11.95

Gloria **Naylor**, editor
Children of the Night: The Best Short Stories by Black Writers, 1967 to the Present
The author of the National Book Award-winning *The Women of Brewster Place* collects a powerful group of stories by African-American writers: Maya Angelou, Ralph Ellison, Jamaica Kincaid, Terry McMillan, Rita Dove, James Baldwin, John Edgar Wideman, and many others. A collective and compelling portrait of the black experience in post-civil rights America
0-316-59926-3 LITTLE, BROWN $24.95
0-316-59923-9 LITTLE, BROWN PB $14.95

Classic Autobiographies

Claude **Brown**
Manchild in the Promised Land
Painfully honest autobiography of growing up in Harlem in the '40s and '50s
0-451-16827-5 NEW AMERICAN LIBRARY PB $6.99

William L. **Andrews**, editor

Sisters of the Spirit: Three Black Women's Autobiographies of the 19th Century

Three preachers of Christian Gospel who helped to launch a feminist revolution in American religious life

0-253-28704-9 INDIANA PB $11.95

To Tell a Free Story: The First Century of Afro-American Autobiography, 1760-1864

"Imaginatively combines literary criticism, anthropological theory, and history to provide a detailed, nuanced, and persuasive reading of Afro-American autobiography from its origins in the 18th century through emancipation"
—Julius S. Scott, *Journal of Southern History*

0-252-01222-4 ILLINOIS $29.95
0-252-06033-4 ILLINOIS PB $12.95

Maya **Angelou**

And Still I Rise

0-394-50252-3 RANDOM HOUSE $14.50

A Brave and Startling Truth

0-679-44904-3 RANDOM HOUSE $10.00

Gather Together in My Name

0-394-48692-7 RANDOM HOUSE $23.00
0-553-26066-9 BDD PB $5.50

Heart of a Woman

See also **RELIGION** under **CULTURE**

0-394-51273-1 RANDOM HOUSE $24.95
0-553-24689-5 BDD PB $5.50

I Know Why the Caged Bird Sings

Angelou's classic tale of her black girlhood in Arkansas, Chicago, and California, one of the finest coming-of-age novels ever written

See also **SINCE 1945** under **20TH-CENTURY AMERICAN FICTION** in **LITERATURE OF THE AMERICAS**

0-394-42986-9 RANDOM HOUSE $20.00
0-553-27937-8 BDD PB $5.50

Phenomenal Woman: Four Poems Celebrating Women

0-679-43924-2 RANDOM HOUSE $10.00

Frederick **Douglass**

Narrative of the Life of Frederick Douglass, an American Slave

First published in 1845, this became the most famous of all slave narratives

See also **THE 19TH CENTURY: TO THE CIVIL WAR** under **AMERICAN LITERATURE TO 1900** in **LITERATURE OF THE AMERICAS**

EDITED BY HOUSTON A. BAKER, JR.

0-14-039012-X PENGUIN PB $7.95

W.E.B. **DuBois**

Autobiography of W.E.B. DuBois: A Soliloquy of Viewing My Life from the Last Decade of Its First Century

0-7178-0235-3 INTERNATIONAL PUB $21.00
0-7178-0234-5 INTERNATIONAL PUB PB $10.95

John Hope **Franklin**, editor

Three Negro Classics

Includes Booker T. Washington's *Up from Slavery*, W.E.B. DuBois's *The Souls of Black Folk*, and James Weldon Johnson's *The Autobiography of an Ex-Coloured Man*

0-380-01581-1 AVON PB $5.99

Marita **Golden**

Migrations of the Heart

0-345-34669-6 BALLANTINE PB $5.99

Dick **Gregory** & Robert **Lipsyte**

Nigger

From poverty to celebrity status as a comedian and civil rights activist

0-671-73560-8 POCKET PB $5.99

John Howard **Griffin**

Black Like Me

A white writer chemically darkened his skin and traveled through the mid-1950s South; his journal, a longtime bestseller, offers chilling revelations

0-451-16317-6 NEW AMERICAN LIBRARY PB $4.99

Alex **Haley**

Roots

See also **YOUNG ADULT FICTION** in **BOOKS FOR YOUNG READERS**

See also **THE '70S** under **THE GREAT FICTION BESTSELLERS 1930-1995** in **POPULAR READING**

0-385-03787-2 DOUBLEDAY $25.00
0-440-17464-3 DELL PB $6.99

Langston **Hughes**

Hughes was the most important poet to come out of the Harlem Renaissance. He invented his own stanza forms or used blank verse to transcribe urban folk life and the mood of jazz and blues; he is probably the most widely read of all black poets, and by the time of his death in 1967 was known even by the man on the street as the poet laureate of the African-American people

I Wonder as I Wander

Hughes's autobiography covers his travels to Cuba, Haiti, Russia, Japan, and civil-war Spain during the '30s

0-8090-1550-1 HILL & WANG PB $14.00

Zora Neale **Hurston**

Zora Neale Hurston was a leading light of African-American writing in the '30s, but she died in obscurity and poverty in 1960, her books long out of print. Today Hurston's novels and folkloric studies are undergoing an extraordinary revival, making her more widely read than ever in her lifetime.

Dust Tracks on a Road: An Autobiography

"Warm, witty, imaginative, and down-to-earth by turns, *Dust Tracks on a Road* is a rich and winning book by one of our few, genuine Grade A folk writers"—*New Yorker*

See also **MEMOIRS AND JOURNALS** under **20TH-CENTURY AMERICAN ESSAYS AND JOURNALISM** in **LITERATURE OF THE AMERICAS**

0-06-092168-4 HARPERCOLLINS PB $13.00

Audre **Lorde**

Zami: A New Spelling of My Name

The late Poet Laureate of New York's stark tale of her own sexual and literary awakening

See also **POETRY SINCE 1945** under **20TH-CENTURY AMERICAN POETRY** in **LITERATURE OF THE AMERICAS**

0-89594-123-6 CROSSING $23.95
0-89594-122-8 CROSSING PB $12.95

Malcolm X

By Any Means Necessary

EDITED BY GEORGE BREITMAN

0-87348-754-0 PATHFINDER PB $15.95

Selected Speeches and Statements

EDITED BY GEORGE BREITMAN

0-8021-3051-8 GROVE PB $9.95

Malcolm X & Alex Haley

The Autobiography of Malcolm X

A compelling view of life as a man of color in America, from a childhood of poverty to the jitterbug days of Boston and Harlem. Malcolm X educated himself in prison, where he joined the Nation of Islam. His ultimate rejection of the movement's separatist ideology, after seeing people of all races worship together at Mecca, resulted in his assassination

See also **YOUNG ADULT FICTION** in **BOOKS FOR YOUNG READERS**

0-345-37671-4 BALLANTINE PB $12.00
0-345-35068-5 BALLANTINE PB $5.99

Paul **Robeson**

Here I Stand

Robeson's major autobiographical and political statement, from 1958

INTRODUCTION BY STERLING STUCKEY

0-8070-6445-9 BEACON PB $11.00

Philip S. **Foner**, editor

Paul Robeson Speaks

A collection of Robeson's writings, from his graduation oration at Rutgers in 1919 to pieces on the color bar, South Africa, and black history

0-8065-0815-9 CITADEL PB $12.00

Theodore **Rosengarten**

All God's Dangers: The Life of Nate Shaw

An award-winning oral history of a sharecropper in the post-Civil War South

0-394-72245-0 VINTAGE PB $12.95

Booker T. **Washington**

Up from Slavery

0-679-72761-2 VINTAGE PB $16.00

Voices from Slavery

"To the slave mother, New Year's day comes laden with peculiar sorrows. She sits on her cold cabin floor, watching the children who may all be torn from her the next morning; and often does she wish that she and they might die before the day dawns. She may be an ignorant creature, degraded by the system that has brutalized her from childhood; but she has a mother's instincts, and is capable of feeling a mother's agonies."—From *Linda: Incidents in the Life of a Slave Girl*, cited in Marion Wilson Starling, *The Slave Narrative: Its Place in American History*

T. Lindsay **Baker** & Julie P. **Baker**, editors

The WPA Oklahoma Slave Narratives

0-8061-2859-3 OKLAHOMA PB $24.95

John W. **Blassingame**, editor

Slave Testimony: Two Centuries of Letters, Speeches, Interviews, and Autobiographies

The largest annotated and authenticated account of slaves ever published in one volume

0-8071-0273-3 LSU PB $18.99

Linda **Brent**

Incidents in the Life of a Slave Girl

A stunning narrative of a slave girl who, after much struggle, escapes to the North

See also **AFRICAN-AMERICAN HISTORY** under **AMERICAN HISTORY** under **WOMEN'S STUDIES** in **SOCIAL STUDIES**

EDITED BY L. MARIA CHILD

PREFACE BY WALTER TELLER

0-15-644350-3 HARCOURT BRACE PB $7.95

Charlotte L. **Forten**

The Journal of Charlotte L. Forten: A Free Negro in a Slave Era

EDITED BY RAY A. BILLINGTON

0-393-00046-X NORTON PB $9.95

Henry Louis **Gates**, Jr., editor

Classic Slave Narratives

0-451-62726-1 NEW AMERICAN LIBRARY PB $5.99

James **Mellon**, editor

Bullwhip Days: The Slaves Remember

The Federal Writers' Project of the mid-thirties dispatched interviewers to collect the memories of the dwindling number of former slaves; 29 of these narrative oral histories plus other writings make up this new collection

0-380-70884-1 AVON PB $14.00

Moira **Ferguson**, editor

The History of Mary Prince, a West Indian Slave, Related by Herself

0-472-08246-9 MICHIGAN PB $10.95

Marion Wilson **Starling**

The Slave Narrative: Its Place in American History

The testimonies of 6000 blacks, before, during, and after slavery

0-88258-165-1 HOWARD PB $14.95

Leaders and Activists

Elaine **Brown**

A Taste of Power

An illustrated autobiography of the woman who took charge of the Black Panthers in 1974, as Huey Newton headed for refuge in Cuba

0-385-47107-6 ANCHOR PB $14.95

Eldredge **Cleaver**

Soul on Ice

Long out of print, Cleaver's prison memoir of what it means to be black in America is available again

0-440-21128-X DELL PB $6.50

Thulani **Davis**

Malcolm X: The Great Photographs

1-55670-312-0 STEWART, TABORI $40.00

1-55670-317-1 STEWART, TABORI PB $24.95

Waldo E. **Martin**

The Mind of Frederick Douglass

0-8078-1616-7 NORTH CAROLINA $39.95

0-8078-4148-X NORTH CAROLINA PB $15.95

W.E.B. **DuBois**

The Selected Speeches of W.E.B. DuBois

0-679-77199-9 MODERN LIBRARY PB $1.99

The Souls of Black Folk

First published in 1903, DuBois's witty, impassioned treatment of what it feels like to be a "problem" for white America remains popular today

See also **ETHNICITY AND RACE RELATIONS** under **TOPICS IN MODERN SOCIOLOGY** under **SOCIOLOGY** in **SOCIAL STUDIES**

0-679-60187-2 MODERN LIBRARY $14.50

0-679-72519-9 VINTAGE PB $11.50

W.E.B. DuBois

David **Levering**

W.E.B. Dubois: 1868-1919, Biography of a Race

0-8050-3568-0 HOLT PB $17.95

Manning **Marable**

W.E.B. Dubois: Black Radical Democrat

0-8057-7750-4 TWAYNE $28.95

Arthur J. **Magida**

Prophet of Rage: A Life of Louis Farrakhan and His Nation

Describes Louis Gene Walcott's youth in Boston's Roxbury and his drifting into black nationalism and the Nation of Islam, an analysis of the mythologies behind Farrakhan's religion, his prominence on American college campuses, and his headline-grabbing rhetoric

FORWARD BY JULIAN BOND

0-465-06436-1 HARPERCOLLINS $25.00

Louis Farrakhan

David J. **Garrow** & Martin Luther **King**, Jr.

Bearing the Cross: Martin Luther King, Jr., and the Southern Christian Leadership Conference, 1955-1968

0-394-75623-1 VINTAGE PB $18.00

Judith **Stein**

The World of Marcus Garvey: Race and Class in Modern Society

0-8071-1670-X LSU PB $12.95

Paul Carter **Harrison**

Black Light

This photo-essay celebrates the black heroes of the struggle against social oppression. It includes profiles and photographs of Maya Angelou, Ice Cube, Malcolm X, Jackie Joyner-Kersey, Arthur Ashe, Lorraine Hansberry, Colin Powell, Martin Luther King, Jr., Bill Cosby, Katherine Dunham, Muhammed Ali, and many others

INTRODUCTION DANNY GLOVER

PREFACE BY BILL DUKE

1-56025-060-7 THUNDER'S MOUTH PB $14.95

Robert **Hill** & others, editors

Marcus Garvey: Life and Lessons

0-520-06214-0 CALIFORNIA $40.00

Nell Irvin **Painter**

The Narrative of Hosea Hudson: His Life as a Negro Communist in the South

0-393-31015-9 NORTON PB $12.95

Charlayne **Hunter-Gault**

In My Place

The coming-of-age story of the MacNeil/Lehrer News Hour national correspondent during the time that marked the demise of the Jim Crow laws. "*In My Place* makes a whole, pure sound like a musical note rising from that old, segregated world"—*NY Times Book Review*

0-679-74818-0 VINTAGE PB $11.00

Adolph L. **Reed**

The Jesse Jackson Phenomenon: The Crisis of Purpose in Afro-American Politics

0-300-03543-8 YALE $22.50

Jesse Jackson

David J. **Garrow**

The FBI and Martin Luther King, Jr.

0-14-006486-9 VIKING PB $11.95

Martin Luther **King**, Jr.

Strength to Love

INTRODUCTION BY CORETTA SCOTT KING

0-8006-1441-0 FORTRESS PB $10.00

Mark **Lane** & Dick **Gregory**

Murder in Memphis: The FBI and the Martin Luther King Assassination

Lane, the campaign manager of JFK's 1960 presidential race, and Gregory, comic, writer, and activist, reach grim conclusions about King's death

1-56025-056-9 THUNDER'S MOUTH PB $13.95

Steven **Barboza**

American Jihad: Islam After Malcom X

See also **ISLAM TODAY** under **ISLAM** in **RELIGION, SPIRITUALITY, AND PHILOSOPHY**

0-385-47011-8 DOUBLEDAY $25.00

0-385-47694-9 IMAGE PB $14.00

Karl **Evanzz**

The Judas Factor: The Plot to Kill Malcolm X

Analysts of American politics have long speculated about the complex machinations that may have gone into Malcolm X's murder. Here, journalist Evanzz's thorough research suggests that the FBI and CIA were working in tandem with the Nation of Islam, and that there may have been enough fear and hatred of Malcolm within the NOI to plot his assassination. "Vastly convincing"—*Kirkus Reviews*

1-56025-049-6 THUNDER'S MOUTH $22.95

David **Gallen**

Malcolm X: As They Knew Him

The controversial civil rights leader remembered. Commentary by Maya Angelou, William Kunstler, Mike Wallace, Robert Penn Warren, James Baldwin, and Alex Haley. A poignant and true remembrance

0-88184-850-6 CARROLL & GRAF PB $11.95

Bruce **Perry**

Malcolm

Eighteen years after beginning research on Malcolm X, Perry places "the man beside the myth and thus give[s] a fuller portrait of a figure who is probably the most compelling presence in black American political life today"
—*NY Times Book Review*

0-88268-103-6 STATION HILL $24.95

William **Strickland**

Malcolm X: Make It Plain

Based on the PBS series by the producers of *Eyes on the Prize*, this extraordinary volume features rare photos as well as personal remembrances, providing a detailed and dramatic portrait of one of America's most provocative and influential figures

0-670-84893-X VIKING $29.95

Joe **Wood**, editor

Malcolm X: In Our Own Image

0-312-06609-0 ST. MARTIN'S $18.95

Nelson **Peery**

Black Fire: The Making of an American Revolutionary

An elegantly told story of an African-American's political awakening. From rural Minnesota to a tour of duty in the all-black 93rd Infantry, "Peery writes with intelligence, grace, and humor. His autobiography provides not only a portrait of a fascinating life but a history of 20th-century black radicalism"—*Kirkus Reviews*. "A well-told, scathing story and it resounds with a sense of justice"—*New Yorker*

1-56584-159-X NEW PRESS PB $11.95

Wil **Haygood**

King of the Cats: The Life and Times of Adam Clayton Powell, Jr.

The brilliant and seductive Powell, the grandson of a slave, replaced his father as pastor of the Abyssinian Church in Harlem, went on to marry a showgirl, started his own newspaper, and ran for New York City Council. In 1945 he became Harlem's first black congressman and helped lead the war against poverty and racial discrimination

0-395-70068-X HOUGHTON MIFFLIN PB $14.95

Jervis A. **Anderson**

A. Philip Randolph: A Biographical Portrait

The rise of a young radical street orator in Harlem to national labor leader of sleeping-car porters

0-520-05505-5 CALIFORNIA PB $15.95

Paul **Robeson**, Jr.

Paul Robeson, Jr. Speaks to America

Robeson attacks mainstream American culture in a series of essays on his father (Paul Robeson), Clarence Thomas, liberals and conservatives, and gender and minorities. "I have seldom read a book…with as much prophetic good sense as this one"
—David Levering Lewis

0-8135-1985-3 RUTGERS $17.95

0-8135-2322-2 RUTGERS PB $15.95

Assata **Shakur**

Assata: An Autobiography

As a leader of the Black Panther party in 1973, Assata Shakur was charged with murder in a shoot-out with state troopers; she later escaped from prison, went underground, and, living in Cuba, wrote this memoir of prison and the life that led her to join the Panthers

0-88208-221-3 LAWRENCE HILL $18.95

Maria W. **Stewart**

Maria W. Stewart, America's First Black Woman Political Writer: Essays and Speeches

EDITED BY MARILYN RICHARDSON

0-253-20446-1 INDIANA PB $9.95

Booker T. **Washington**

The Negro in the South

0-8216-0183-0 LYLE STUART PB $7.95

Roger **Wilkins**

A Man's Life: An Autobiography

The life of the former US assistant attorney general and Pulitzer Prize-winning journalist

0-918024-83-8 OX BOW PB $15.95

Roy **Wilkins** & others

Standing Fast: The Autobiography of Roy Wilkins

The civil rights leader and a major force in the NAACP

0-306-80566-9 DA CAPO PB $14.95

John Hope **Franklin**

George Washington Williams: A Biography

The self-made intellectual, long overlooked, who wrote the first history of blacks in America

0-226-26084-4 CHICAGO PB $16.00

Scientists and Educators

Daisy **Bates**

The Long Shadow of Little Rock

Memoir of a key figure in the fight to integrate Central High in Little Rock

0-938626-75-2 ARKANSAS PB $12.00

Linda O. **McMurry**

George Washington Carver: Scientist and Symbol

0-19-503205-5 OXFORD PB $12.95

Septima **Clark**

Ready from Within: Septima Clark and the Civil Rights Movements

A South Carolina teacher fired for joining the NAACP in 1965 went on to organize "freedom" schools and register voters

EDITED BY CYNTHIA S. BROWN

0-86543-174-4 AFRICA WORLD PB $9.95

Henry Louis **Gates**, Jr.

Colored People: A Memoir

A rich and touching memoir of growing up in a West Virginia hill town by the chairman of the Afro-American Studies department at Harvard. Gates recalls a vanishing America—one marked by the presence of town heroes and rogues, where a family's most guarded secret was a potato salad recipe and the annual mill picnic was the social event of the year

0-679-42179-3 KNOPF $25.00

Kenneth R. **Manning**

Black Apollo of Science: The Life of Ernest Everett Just

The zoologist at Woods Hole, Massachusetts

0-19-503498-8 OXFORD PB $13.95

Benjamin E. **Mays**

Born to Rebel: An Autobiography by Benjamin E. Mays

Born the son of a sharecropper in 1894, Mays rose to become president of Morehouse College in Atlanta

INTRODUCTION BY ORVILLE V. BURTON

0-8203-0881-1 GEORGIA PB $14.95

Louis R. **Harlan**

Booker T. Washington: The Making of a Black Leader, 1856-1901

The man, his era, and the problem of living in the face of racial injustice; a Pulitzer Prize-winning study (1984)

0-19-504229-8 OXFORD PB $16.95

Artists and Literary Figures

Maya **Angelou**

Wouldn't Take Nothing for My Journey Now

Angelou relates the sexual abuse she endured as a child, the poverty, the challenge of being black in America while also pondering her own sense of faith

See also **MEMOIRS AND JOURNALS** under **20TH-CENTURY AMERICAN ESSAYS AND JOURNALISM** in **LITERATURE OF THE AMERICAS**

0-679-42743-0 RANDOM HOUSE $17.00

0-553-56907-4 BDD PB $5.50

Houston A. **Baker**, Jr.

Black Studies, Rap, and the Academy

See also **RAP, R&B, MOTOWN, AND SOUL** under **ROCK** in **PERFORMING ARTS AND MEDIA**

0-226-03520-4 CHICAGO $16.95

Joanne M. **Braxton** &
Andreé Nicola **McLaughlin**, editors

Wild Women in the Whirlwind: Afro-American Culture and the Contemporary Literary Renaissance

Includes essays on feminist theory and women artists

0-8135-1442-8 RUTGERS PB $16.95

Margaret **Busby**, editor

Daughters of Africa

Two hundred writers, from the ancient Egyptian Queen Hatshepsut to Terry MacMillan, contribute to 2,000 years of black women's writing: memoirs, fiction, poetry, journalism, drama, and more. "Magnificent…A stunning wealth of writing….Contains all the great, enduring themes of literature"
—*Washington Post Book World*

0-345-38268-4 BALLANTINE PB $19.95

Frank Marshall **Davis**

Livin' the Blues: Memoirs of a Black Journalist and Poet

Davis was a renowned poet and journalist of the '30s and '40s who published four volumes of poetry, edited four newspapers, and wrote jazz criticism. But he renounced his writing career in 1948 and moved to Hawaii, forgotten until the '60s, when the Black Arts movement rediscovered him. "Adds a fearless new voice to the black Renaissance"—*Kirkus Reviews*

EDITED, WITH AN INTRODUCTION BY JOHN EDGAR TIDWELL

0-299-13500-4 WISCONSIN $16.95

The blues? We were formally introduced when I was eight; even then I had the feeling we weren't really strangers. So when the blues grabbed me and held on, it was like meeting a long lost brother

LIVIN' THE BLUES: MEMOIRS OF A BLACK JOURNALIST AND POET

Katherine **Dunham**

A Touch of Innocence: Memoirs of Childhood

See also **MODERN DANCERS, CHOREOGRAPHERS, AND SCHOOLS** under **THE 20TH CENTURY** under **DANCE** in **PERFORMING ARTS AND MEDIA**

0-226-17112-4 CHICAGO PB $12.95

Robert E. **Hemenway**

Zora Neale Hurston: A Literary Biography

See also **THE 20TH CENTURY** under **STUDIES OF INDIVIDUAL AUTHORS** under **AMERICAN LITERATURE: ANTHOLOGIES AND CRITICAL STUDIES** in **LITERATURE OF THE AMERICAS**

FOREWORD BY ALICE WALKER

0-252-00807-3 ILLINOIS PB $12.50

Fenton **Johnson**

Geography of the Heart: A Memoir

0-684-81417-X SCRIBNERS $22.00

Richard **Marshall**

Jean-Michel Basquiat

The exhibition catalog of a major Basquiat retrospective that toured the country in 1996. An unprecedented survey of Basquiat's short and brilliant career, from his graffiti-inspired beginnings in the company of Keith Haring and Kenny Scharf to his death at 28 in 1988. Written under the direction of the curator at the Whitney, the text discusses Basquiat's influences and the position of the African-American artist today

See also **AMERICAN ART OF THE '60S AND '70S** under **ART SINCE 1945** in **ART**

0-8109-6814-2 ABRAMS PB $35.00

Arnold **Rampersad** & Langston **Hughes**

The Life of Langston Hughes

Volume 1, 1902-1941: I Too, Sing America

See also **THE 20TH CENTURY** under **STUDIES OF INDIVIDUAL AUTHORS (ALPHABETICAL BY SUBJECT)** under **AMERICAN LITERATURE: ANTHOLOGIES AND CRITICAL STUDIES** in **LITERATURE OF THE AMERICAS**

0-19-504011-2 OXFORD $39.95

0-19-505426-1 OXFORD PB $15.95

Volume 2, 1941-1967: I Dream a World

See also **THE 20TH CENTURY** under **STUDIES OF INDIVIDUAL AUTHORS (ALPHABETICAL BY SUBJECT)** under **AMERICAN LITERATURE: ANTHOLOGIES AND CRITICAL STUDIES** in **LITERATURE OF THE AMERICAS**

0-19-506169-1 OXFORD PB $17.95

Alice **Walker**

The Same River Twice: Honoring the Difficult

The autobiography of one of this century's most important African-American woman writers

See also **MEMOIRS AND JOURNALS** under **20TH-CENTURY AMERICAN ESSAYS AND JOURNALISM** in **LITERATURE OF THE AMERICAS**

0-684-81419-6 SCRIBNERS $24.00

John Edgar **Wideman**

Fatheralong: A Meditation on Fathers and Sons, Race and Society

A meditation on "fathers, color, roots, time, and language" that is also a summing up of a man's escape from the prison of racial ideology. "Our most powerful and accomplished artist of the urban black world"—*LA Times Book Review*

See also **MEMOIRS AND JOURNALS** under **20TH-CENTURY AMERICAN ESSAYS AND JOURNALISM** in **LITERATURE OF THE AMERICAS**

0-679-40720-0 PANTHEON $21.00

Athletes and Entertainers

Hank **Aaron** & Lonnie **Wheeler**

I Had a Hammer: The Hank Aaron Story

The autobiography of the greatest home run hitter in baseball history

See also **BASEBALL** under **SPORTS** in **FOOD, TRAVEL, AND LEISURE**

0-06-016321-6 HARPERCOLLINS PB $21.95

Arthur R. **Ashe**, Jr.

Hard Road to Glory: A History of the African-American Athlete

A sport-by-sport narrative account, with an extensive reference section on the successes of black athletes

Volume 1
1619-1918
1-56743-006-6 AMISTAD $29.95

Volume 2
1919-1945
1-56743-007-4 AMISTAD $39.95

Volume 3
Since 1946
1-56743-008-2 AMISTAD $39.95

Jean-Claude **Baker** & others

Josephine: The Josephine Baker Story

"Bravo! Her exotic beauty, flaming ambition, flashing eyes, rolling hips, and large peculiarities seduce the reader"—Maya Angelou

1-55850-472-9 ADAMS PB $12.95

Josephine **Baker** & others

Josephine

The dramatic story of the American dancer who became the toast of Paris in the '20s and a spy for the Allies in World War II

TRANSLATED BY MARIANA FITZPATRICK

1-56924-978-4 MARLOWE PB $12.00

Donald **Bogle** & others

Louis Armstrong: A Cultural Legacy

See also **STUDIES AND INDIVIDUAL ARTISTS** under **JAZZ** in **PERFORMING ARTS AND MEDIA**

0-295-97383-8 WASHINGTON PB $29.95

Miles **Davis**

Miles: The Autobiography

A tough, rapid-fire narration of Davis' musical career, from his collaboration with Charlie Parker in the '40s through the famous fities quartet and the later fusion experiments. A frank and sometimes harsh representation of the rarely shown realities of the jazz scene

See also **STUDIES AND INDIVIDUAL ARTISTS** under **JAZZ** in **PERFORMING ARTS AND MEDIA**

0-671-72582-3 TOUCHSTONE PB $14.00

Mark **Tucker**, editor

The Duke Ellington Reader

A trove, with more surprises than all the conventional Ellington biographies put together. This would make any jazz lover's top ten

See also **STUDIES AND INDIVIDUAL ARTISTS** under **JAZZ** in **PERFORMING ARTS AND MEDIA**

0-19-505410-5 OXFORD $30.00

Thomas **Hauser** & Muhammad **Ali**

Muhammad Ali: In Perspective

See also **BOXING AND WRESTLING** under **SPORTS** in **FOOD, TRAVEL, AND LEISURE**

0-00-649124-3 COLLINS SAN FRANCISCO PB $25.00

Robert **Waldron**

Oprah!

The national bestseller about TV star Oprah Winfrey

0-312-92529-8 ST. MARTIN'S PB $3.95

Gil **Noble**

Black Is the Color of My TV Tube

The autobiographical odyssey of a star black reporter, one of first in the industry during the '60s

0-8184-0538-4 CAROL PB $9.95

William J. **Baker**

Jesse Owens: An American Life

"The story of the ultimate black American sports hero and how he was used and abused"
—Marty Glickman

0-02-901760-2 FREE PRESS PB $14.95

Susan **Robeson**

The Whole World in His Hands: A Pictorial Biography of Paul Robeson

A beautifully illustrated book by his grandchild

0-8065-0977-5 LYLE STUART PB $14.95

Jackie **Robinson** & Jules **Tygiel**

The Jackie Robinson Reader: Writings By and About Jackie Robinson

See also **BASEBALL BIOGRAPHIES** under **BASEBALL** under **SPORTS** in **FOOD, TRAVEL, AND LEISURE**

0-525-94096-0 DUTTON $25.00

Rachel **Robinson** & Lee **Daniels**

Jackie Robinson: An Intimate Portrait

Available fall 1997

See also **BASEBALL BIOGRAPHIES** under **BASEBALL** under **SPORTS** in **FOOD, TRAVEL, AND LEISURE**

0-8109-3792-1 ABRAMS $29.95

Lewis **Porter**, editor

A Lester Young Reader

See also **STUDIES AND INDIVIDUAL ARTISTS** under **JAZZ** in **PERFORMING ARTS AND MEDIA**

1-56098-065-6 SMITHSONIAN PB $19.95

Soldiers

Thomas Wentworth **Higginson**

Army Life in a Black Regiment

A classic by the preacher-soldier who commanded the First South Carolina, composed of runaway slaves

See also **THE SOLDIERS** under **THE CIVIL WAR AND RECONSTRUCTION**

0-87928-022-0 CORNER HOUSE $23.95
0-393-30157-5 NORTON PB $9.95

Bernard C. **Nalty**

Strength for the Fight: A History of Black Americans in the Military

The story of blacks in the armed forces from the 17th century to the 1980s. "Institutional history at its best... will become the standard work in its field"—*Journal of American History*

0-02-922411-X FREE PRESS PB $16.95

Virginia Matzke **Adams**, editor

On the Altar of Freedom: A Black Soldier's Civil War Letters from the Front

James Henry Gooding of the 54th Massachusetts Regiment describes the soldiers' progress from training through the long siege of Charleston. One of a handful of primary documents on the black militia during the Civil War

0-87023-745-4 MASSACHUSETTS $27.50

At the first charge the 54th rushed to within twenty yards of the ditches, and, as might be expected of raw recruits, wavered—but at the second advance they gained the parapet. The color bearer of the State colors was killed on the parapet. Col. Shaw seized the staff when the standard bearer fell, and in less than a minute after, the Colonel fell himself. When the men saw their gallant leader fall, they made a desperate effort to get him out, but they were either shot down, or reeled in the ditch below. One man succeeded in getting hold of the State color staff, but the color was completely torn in pieces.

ON THE ALTAR OF FREEDOM: A BLACK SOLDIER'S CIVIL WAR LETTERS FROM THE FRONT

American Politics and Foreign Policy

Political History

Samuel H. **Beer**

To Make a Nation: The Rediscovery of American Federalism

Theories of nationalism and federalism from 17th-century British republicans to today. "This is Beer's magnum opus, the work which draws together his incomparable knowledge, gained over 60 years of study, of American and British political theory and historical practice"
—Patrick Riley, University of Wisconsin

0-674-89318-2 HARVARD PB $17.95

David H. **Bennett**

The Party of Fear: From Nativist Movements to the New Right in American History

Asks important questions about how Americans define themselves and about the need of some segments of society to lash out against people and ideas considered alien, from the anti-Catholic hysteria of the 19th century to present-day New Right and Neo-Nazi groups. "A superbly well-informed narrative history of nativist and post-nativist political movements from the 1790s to the 1980s"—*Journal of American History*

0-8078-1772-4 NORTH CAROLINA $37.50
0-679-72861-9 VINTAGE PB $16.95

Richard F. **Bensel**

Sectionalism and American Political Development, 1880-1980

0-299-09834-6 WISCONSIN PB $14.95

Barry M. **Bleichman**

The Politics of National Security: Congress and U.S. Defense Policy

Reviews interactions between the executive and legislative branches over the last two decades and concludes that Congress is an equal partner in making national security policy

0-19-507705-9 OXFORD PB $18.95

John **Bodnar**

Remaking America: Public Memory, Commemoration and Patriotism in the Twentieth Century

On the social meaning of public ceremonials; especially good on public memory within ethnic groups

0-691-03495-8 PRINCETON PB $15.95

Daniel J. **Boorstin**

The Genius of American Politics

0-226-06491-3 CHICAGO PB $9.95

James W. **Clarke**

American Assassins: The Darker Side of Politics

0-691-02221-6 PRINCETON PB $16.95

Kenneth **Cmiel**

Democratic Eloquence: The Fight over Popular Speech in Nineteenth Century America

"A penetrating account of the long debate about the kind of public language appropriate for a democratic society"—Christopher Lasch

0-520-07485-8 CALIFORNIA PB $15.95

Felix **Gilbert**

To the Farewell Address: Ideas of Early American Policy

A study of European influences on those who developed American foreign policy, as expressed in Washington's Farewell Address. "While this study is primarily addressed to professional historians and other students of history, it is of the greatest practical importance to all who desire to take a more intelligent interest in the nature of the aspirations and motives, the hopes and fears, that characterize the complex society of which America consists"—*The Personalist*. Winner of the Bancroft Prize

0-691-00574-5 PRINCETON PB $10.95

Alonzo L. **Hamby**

Liberalism and Its Challengers: FDR to Reagan

0-19-503419-8 OXFORD PB $16.95

Louis **Hartz**

The Liberal Tradition in America: An Interpretation of American Political Thought Since the Revolution

0-15-651269-6 HARCOURT BRACE PB $10.95

Samuel P. **Hays**

American Political History as Social Analysis

Pathbreaking essays on the social base of political behavior and the structure of modern society

0-87049-276-4 TENNESSEE $45.00

Richard **Hofstadter**

The American Political Tradition and the Men Who Made It

Insightful essays on outstanding political leaders by one of the great postwar historians

See also **ESSAYS AND REFLECTIONS** under **US HISTORY TO THE CIVIL WAR**

FOREWORD BY CHRISTOPHER LASCH

0-394-48880-6 RANDOM HOUSE $26.00
0-679-72315-3 VINTAGE PB $13.00

Morris **Janowitz**

The Last Half-Century: Societal Change and Politics in America

0-226-39306-2 CHICAGO $35.00
0-226-39307-0 CHICAGO PB $19.50

Robert **Kelley**

The Cultural Pattern in American Politics: The First Century

The ethnic and religious roots of political behavior

0-8191-1825-7 UNIVERSITY PRESS OF AMERICA PB $23.00

V.O. **Key**, Jr.

Southern Politics in State and Nation

A new edition of a massive work originally published in 1949

0-87049-435-X TENNESSEE PB $18.00

Susan **Kismaric**

American Politicians: Photographs from 1843 to 1993

A superb collection showing how photography has pictured and helped to transform American politics, published in conjunction with a Museum of Modern Art exhibit

See also **PHOTOJOURNALISM AND HISTORICAL DOCUMENTARY** under **PHOTOGRAPHY** in **ART**

0-8109-6135-0 MOMA $39.95

Alpheus Thomas **Mason** & Gordon E. **Baker**, editors

Free Government in the Making: Readings in American Political Thought

A comprehensive collection of documents updated to include the role of women and minorities

0-19-503524-0 OXFORD $36.00

Richard L. **McCormick**

The Party Period and Public Policy: American Politics from the Age of Jackson to the Progressive Era

An important recent work

0-19-504784-2 OXFORD PB $18.95

Thomas K. **McCraw**

Prophets of Regulation: Charles Francis Adams, Louis D. Brandeis, James M. Landis, Alfred E. Kahn

A Pulitzer Prize-winning study (1984) using biography to probe the development of government economic regulation

0-674-71607-8 HARVARD $32.00
0-674-71608-6 HARVARD PB $14.95

Daniel Patrick **Moynihan**

On the Law of Nations

"An impassioned and well-reasoned plea for a return to the rule of international law. Sure to raise hackles—and hopes—in D.C. and beyond"—*Kirkus Reviews*

0-674-63576-0 HARVARD PB $10.95

Richard Gid **Powers**

Not Without Honor: The History of American Anticommunism

0-684-82427-2 FREE PRESS $30.00

Shelley **Ross**

Fall from Grace: Sex, Scandal and Corruption in American Politics from 1702 to the Present

Strange but true tales: New York's governor Lord Cornbury, who wore hooped skirts and women's accessories as a tribute to Queen Anne; Grover Cleveland's illegitimate child; and many others

0-345-35381-1 BALLANTINE PB $10.00

Stephen **Skowronek**

The Politics Presidents Make: Leadership from John Adams to George Bush

"…a book that kicks aside all the conventional ways of thinking about presidential leadership and erects a daring, powerful analytic machine that compels attention"—Hugo Heclo

0-674-68936-4 HARVARD PB $15.95

John Adams

Page **Smith**

Democracy on Trial

0-684-80354-2 SIMON & SCHUSTER $27.50

William **Steigerwald**

Wilsonian Idealism in America

The legacy of Wilsonianism from its origins in the internationalist movement to its resurgence in Desert Storm

0-8014-2936-6 CORNELL $37.50

Democrats and Republicans

John Calvin **Batchelor**

Ain't You Glad You Joined the Republicans?: A Short History of the G.O.P.

0-8050-3267-3 HOLT $25.00

Bob Dole

Ralph M. **Goldman**

Search for Consensus: The Story of the Democratic Party

0-87722-152-9 TEMPLE $34.95

David R. **Mayhew**

Placing Parties in American Politics: Organization, Electoral Settings, and Government Activity in the Twentieth Century

A serious academic study by a Yale scholar

0-691-02249-6 PRINCETON PB $11.50

Ronald **Radosh**

Divided They Fell: The Demise of the Democratic Party, 1964-1996

0-684-82810-3 FREE PRESS $25.00

Robert Allen **Rutland**

The Democrats: From Jefferson to Clinton

The noted American historian's readable, balanced account of the Democratic Party, from its founding to its current triumphs and failures under William Jefferson Clinton. "A perceptive and engaging survey that can be thoroughly enjoyed by the professional historian and layman alike"—*Journal of Southern History*

WITH A FOREWORD BY JIMMY CARTER

0-8262-1034-1 MISSOURI PB $19.95

James L. **Sundquist**

Dynamics of the Party System: Alignment and Realignment of Political Parties in the United States

0-8157-8225-X BROOKINGS PB $18.95

Voting

Angus **Campbell**

The American Voter

0-226-09254-2 CHICAGO PB $34.00

League of Women Voters

Choosing the President: A Citizen's Guide to the Electoral Process

The most comprehensive guide to the election process available; the essential information for making every vote count. "No voter should be without the basic information and explanations contained in this handbook"
—Theodore Sorenson

See also **THE PRESIDENCY**

1-55821-171-3 LYONS & BURFORD PB $15.95

Abigail M. **Thernstrom**

Whose Votes Count?: Affirmative Action and Minority Voting Rights

0-674-95196-4 HARVARD PB $13.95

Marjorie Spruill **Wheeler**, editor

One Woman, One Vote

This fascinating and revealing anthology by noted suffrage historians exposes the sexism, as well as the shocking racism and classism, entrenched in the long struggle for the 19th Amendment. "The ideal guide…and as such, an important step into our future"—Susan Faludi, *Backlash: The Undeclared War Against American Women*

See also **SUFFRAGE, LIBERATION, AND BEYOND** under **AMERICAN HISTORY** under **WOMEN'S STUDIES** in **SOCIAL STUDIES**

0-939165-26-0 NEWSAGE PB $18.95

The Congress

"The principle of the independence of the states triumphed in the formation of the Senate, and that of the sovereignty of the nation in the composition of the House of Representatives. Each state was to send two senators to Congress, and a number of representatives proportional to its population. It results from this arrangement that the state of New York has at the present day thirty-three representatives, and only two senators; the state of Delaware has two senators, and only one representative; the state of Delaware is therefore equal to the state of New York in the Senate, while the latter has thirty-three times the influence of the former in the House of Representatives. Thus the minority of the nation in the Senate may paralyze the decisions of the majority represented in the other house, which is contrary to the spirit of constitutional government."
—Alexis de Tocqueville, *Democracy in America*

Paul **Boller**

Congressional Anecdotes

Ten chapters by subject with essays and amusing stories (e.g., the congressman who asked why the Israelis and Arabs can't settle their differences like "good Christians") from the bestselling author of *Presidential Anecdotes*

0-19-506092-X OXFORD $22.95

Morris P. **Fiorina**

Congress: Keystone of the Washington Establishment

0-300-04640-5 YALE PB $11.00

Robert **Goehlert** & John **Sayre**

The United States Congress

0-87187-810-0
CONGRESSIONAL QUARTERLY $195.00

Loch K. **Johnson**

A Season of Inquiry: Congress and Intelligence

"Especially useful in underlining the complexities in major oversight efforts"
—Morris Ogul, University of Pittsburgh

0-534-10597-1 HARCOURT BRACE PB $19.95

David R. **Mayhew**

Congress: The Electoral Connection

0-300-01809-6 YALE PB $12.00

Walter **Oleszek**

Congressional Procedures and the Policy Process

0-87187-477-6
CONGRESSIONAL QUARTERLY PB $24.95

Timothy J. **Penny** & Major **Garrett**

Common Cents

An insider's view of what is wrong with Congress

0-316-69912-8 LITTLE, BROWN $21.95
0-380-72719-6 AVON PB $12.00

George E. **Reedy**

The U.S. Senate: Paralysis or Search for Consensus?

0-313-26614-X GREENWOOD $55.00

Senator Warren **Rudman**

In Combat: Twelve Years in the U.S. Senate

0-679-44135-2 RANDOM HOUSE $27.50

James L. **Sundquist**

The Decline and Resurgence of Congress

0-8157-8224-1 BROOKINGS $44.95
0-8157-8223-3 BROOKINGS PB $19.95

The Presidency

Paul F. **Boller**, Jr.

Presidential Campaigns

Entertaining history of the showdowns for the nation's highest office

0-19-503722-7 OXFORD PB $10.95

James David **Barber**

The Pulse of Politics: The Rhythm of Presidential Elections in the Twentieth Century

A 1974 study by a leading student of the presidency

1-56000-589-0 TRANSACTION PB $21.95

Presidential Anecdotes

0-19-510715-2 OXFORD $30.00
0-19-509731-9 OXFORD PB $13.95

Carl M. **Brauer**

Presidential Transitions: Eisenhower Through Reagan

How five newly elected presidents created their administrations

0-19-505655-8 OXFORD PB $9.95

Jimmy **Carter**

Turning Point: A Candidate, a State and a Nation Come of Age

See also CARTER AND THE 70'S under US HISTORY, 1945 TO THE PRESENT

0-8129-2299-9 TIME BOOKS PB $13.00

Hedley **Donovan**

Roosevelt to Reagan: A Reporter's Encounters with Nine Presidents

0-06-039042-5 HARPERCOLLINS $19.95

Fred I. **Greenstein**, editor

Leadership in the Modern Presidency

0-674-51855-1 HARVARD PB $17.95

Gregg **Herken**

Cardinal Choices

Herken documents the dwindling involvement of the scientific community in US nuclear arms policy since before WWII. From Truman's decision, against scientific advice, to use the bomb at Hiroshima without previously demonstrating it on an uninhabited area, through Reagan's inability to fill the post of science advisor, Herken tells a tale of governmental mismanagement of the science community. "Herken's clear, well-documented writing and his close attention to the human element make for a fascinating and wisely cautionary study"— *Kirkus Reviews*

0-19-507210-3 OXFORD $24.95

Kathleen Hall **Jamieson**

Eloquence in an Electronic Age: The Transformation of Political Speechmaking

The impact of TV and radio on political oratory

0-19-503826-6 OXFORD $27.95
0-19-506317-1 OXFORD PB $12.95

Packaging the Presidency

Chronicles the strategies for winning voters' hearts and ballots, focusing on the elections from Eisenhower to Reagan

0-19-507299-5 OXFORD PB $15.95

Kathleen Hall **Jamieson** & David S. **Birdsell**

Presidential Debates: Their Power, Problems and Promise

Includes numerous suggestions for improving debates

0-19-506660-X OXFORD PB $16.95

Barbara **Kellerman**

The Political Presidency: The Practice of Leadership from Kennedy Through Reagan

How six presidents handled the most important domestic policy issues

0-19-504037-6 OXFORD PB $16.95

Stephen F. **Knott**

Secret and Sanctioned: Covert Operations and the American Presidency

The doctrine of plausible deniability and the innovative presidential maneuver of hiding covert actions from Congress were brought to the public's attention during the Iran-Contra scandal. But long before even the early Cold War—since, in fact, the Founding Fathers themselves—presidents have relied upon the clandestine and the unscrupulous. George Washington used invisible ink and created cutout businesses; Jefferson plotted to overthrow the Pasha of Tripoli; Lincoln used disinformation to influence foreign opinion during the Civil War

0-19-510098-0 OXFORD $27.50

Harold J. **Laski**

The American Presidency: An Interpretation

First published in 1940 and still essential. "One of the best books ever written about the institutions of another country by a foreign observer"
—Kingsley Martin, *New Statesman and Nation*

0-87855-821-7 TRANSACTION PB $18.95

League of Women Voters

Choosing the President: A Citizen's Guide to the Electoral Process

The most comprehensive guide to the election process available, the essential information for making every vote count. "No voter should be without the basic information and explanations contained in this handbook"
—Theodore Sorenson

1-55821-171-3 LYONS & BURFORD PB $15.95

Davis Newton **Lott**

The Presidents Speak: The Inaugural Addresses of the American Presidents, from Washington to Clinton

With paragraph-by-paragraph annotations and useful introductions. "A marvelous and valuable collection...a must for any student of American history"—Robert V. Remini

0-8050-3305-X HOLT $35.00

Richard P. **McCormick**

The Presidential Game: The Origins of American Presidential Politics

The origins of presidential politics and why the selection process has become something quite different from that intended by the framers of the Constitution

0-19-503455-4 OXFORD PB $16.95

Forrest **McDonald**

The American Presidency: An Intellectual History

"At last a grand and sweeping history of the presidency. It has just enough partisan bite to keep from being aloof but it is magisterial nevertheless. And it crackles. Will be required reading"—Leonard W. Levy

0-7006-0652-1 KANSAS $29.95

W. Dale **Nelson**

The President Is at Camp David

"A delightful book depicting the role of the presidential retreat in the lives of modern American presidents"—*Boston Globe*

0-8156-0318-5 SYRACUSE $24.95

Richard E. **Neustadt**

Presidential Power and the Modern Presidents: The Politics of Leadership from Roosevelt to Reagan

Neustadt offers compelling appraisals of presidential style and skill. We see Eisenhower keeping the US out of active combat in Vietnam, Kennedy during the Bay of Pigs, Carter handling the Burt Lance affair

0-02-922795-X FREE PRESS PB $22.95

Edward **Pessen**

The Log Cabin Myth: The Social Backgrounds of the Presidents

0-8446-1404-1 SMITH $12.75

William H. **Rehnquist**

Grand Inquests: The Historic Impeachments of Justice Samuel Chase and President Andrew Johnson

In a rare contribution to scholarship outside the Court, Chief Justice Rehnquist turns a historian's eye to two cases that shaped American political and legal history

0-688-12839-4 QUILL PB $15.00

Eileen **Shields-West**

The World Almanac of Presidential Campaigns

Despite the furor over mudslinging in recent Presidential races, few recall that in the contest's history, epithets such as "carbuncle-faced old drunkard," "howling atheist," "pickpocket," "gorilla," "syphilitic," or even "murderer" have been traditionally hurled among our candidates

0-88687-609-5 PHAROS PB $10.95

Michael P. **Riccards**

The Ferocious Engine of Democracy: A History of the American Presidency

"…a broad sweeping history of the Republic through the actions of its presidents, from Washington to Bush. It's an important, even controversial view of how some presidents exercised leadership, or failed to, and how the country survived its glories and failures in the White House"
—Herbert Mitgang, from the Foreword

Volume 1

1-56833-041-3 MADISON $34.95

Volume 2

1-56833-042-1 MADISON $34.95

Clinton **Rossiter**

The American Presidency

A widely consulted introduction to its history and political culture, by the late Cornell professor
INTRODUCTION BY MICHAEL NELSON
0-8018-3545-3 JOHNS HOPKINS PB $14.95

Franklin **Steiner**

The Religious Beliefs of Our Presidents: From Washington to FDR

The first 32 presidents organized by religious affiliation, including such categories as "Presidents Whose Religious Beliefs Are Doubtful"
0-87975-975-5 PROMETHEUS PB $16.95

Steve **Tally**

Bland Ambition: From Adams to Quayle—The Cranks, Criminals, Tax Cheats and Golfers Who Made It to Vice President

Breezy, irreverent, and funny
0-15-613140-4 HARCOURT BRACE PB $10.95

Kenneth T. **Walsh**

Feeding the Beast: The White House versus the Press

See also **THE IMPACT OF THE MEDIA** under **TOPICS** in **AMERICAN STUDIES**
0-679-44290-1 RANDOM HOUSE $25.00

Bob **Woodward**

The Choice

The inimitable Woodward—author of seven *New York Times* bestsellers—takes us behind the scenes of the 1996 race, with the incumbent and all his challengers. From fundamental questions to detailed assessments of their strategies, skills, and compromises as they try to capitalize on the changing political climate, *The Choice* offers unprecedented insight into how we elect an American president
0-684-81308-4 SIMON & SCHUSTER $26.00

The Reader's Catalog
250 West 57th Street
New York, NY 10107

First Families

Paul F. **Boller, Jr.**

Presidential Wives

Includes a biographical essay on each First Lady, followed by a selection of revealing anecdotes. "Just before Inauguration Day, Mrs. Eisenhower received a beautiful embossed invitation to the inaugural ball. 'What should we do about this,' she asked Ike. 'Turn it down,' he said with a straight face. 'Tell them we've got another engagement'"
0-19-503763-4 OXFORD $27.50
0-19-505976-X OXFORD PB $11.95

Betty Boyd **Caroli**

First Ladies

Wives from Martha to Nancy come alive through their backgrounds, successes, and failures; including Jane Pierce, who prayed her husband would lose the election, Edith Wilson, who virtually became president herself after her husband's stroke, and Pat Nixon, who perfected what some have called "the robot image"
0-19-505654-X OXFORD PB $13.95

Blanche Wiesen **Cook**

Eleanor Roosevelt

Volume I, 1884-1933

This vivid and controversial biography describes the emergence of an insecure and repressed voting woman from a constricted background to a political force in her own right. "Blanche Cook has resurrected the Eleanor Roosevelt who was not only a woman of power and influence, a woman who changed the lives of millions, but, moreover, a thoroughly interesting human being.…The freshness and centeredness of Blanche Cook's view of Eleanor make her book fascinating reading in this political season"
—Abigail McCarthy, *Washington Post Book World*
See also **BIOGRAPHIES** under **US HISTORY, 1945 TO THE PRESENT**
0-14-009460-1 PENGUIN PB $14.95

However much her political vigor, new friends and public prominence might disturb the older members of her family, she herself greeted every new controversy with verve. Eleanor Roosevelt had become a feminist. She fought for women's rights steadfastly and with determination; she championed equality in public and private matters; and she herself used the word "feminist." But during the 1920s, the bitterly divisive Equal Rights Amendment ripped the women's movement apart, obscuring for decades the full dimensions of historical feminism—and ER's leadership role within it.
ELEANOR ROOSEVELT: VOLUME I, 1884-1933

Volume 2, 11934-1962

0-670-84498-5 PENGUIN $24.95

Wendell **Garrett**

Our Changing White House

"…Now, in the pages of this wonderful book, the White House doors open wide, offering readers a chance to share in two hundred years' worth of stories and history that are uniquely American"—Barbara Bush
1-55553-222-5 NORTHEASTERN $40.00

Eleanor Roosevelt

Margaret **Truman**

First Ladies

Daughter of President Truman and bestselling author, Margaret Truman offers a well-informed, intimate look at 29 women who served as First Lady. Interviews with those who have recently held the post—Lady Bird Johnson, Hillary Clinton, Nancy Reagan—complement recollections of First Ladies past, from Jacqueline Kennedy to Mary Lincoln, and together combine to draw an extraordinary portrait of marriage in the White House
0-449-22323-X FAWCETT PB $12.95

Eleanor peppered her letters to friends with references to her attempts to influence both legislation and appointments, and she discussed powerful Washington figures as colleagues rather than superiors. After meeting with Postmaster General James Farley and his aides to "start them off on patronage for women," she judged both Harry Hopkins and Secretary of Interior Harold Ickes "good to work with;" and when Hopkins came through with improvements in school lunches, she upgraded her estimate of him to "swell."
FIRST LADIES

Recent Presidential Elections

Jimmy **Carter**

Electing Jimmy Carter: The Campaign of 1976

"A fascinating portrait"—Tom Wicker
0-8071-1916-4 LSU $24.95

Mary **Matalin** & James **Carville**

All's Fair: Love, War, and Running for President

Matalin ran the Bush campaign; Carville, Clinton's—they tell a strangely romantic story, as outspoken about relationships as they are about how presidents are elected
0-679-43103-9 RANDOM HOUSE $24.00

Hunter S. **Thompson**

Better than Sex: Fear and Loathing on the Campaign Trail, 1992

"Memorable, …Packed with egocentric anecdotes, musings and reprints of memos, faxes and scrawled handwritten notes"—*Philadelphia Inquirer*
0-679-42447-4 RANDOM HOUSE $23.00
0-345-39635-9 BALLANTINE PB $12.95

Current Political Thought and Issues

Tom **Athanasiou**

Divided Planet: The Ecology of Rich and Poor

Examining today's major threats to the environment, *Divided Planet* shows that the real issues of pollution, ozone depletion, deforestation, and the like can only be addressed with money, incentives, and the will to change an economic system

See also **INDUSTRIAL HAZARDS AND SOLID WASTES** under **NATURAL RESOURCES AT RISK** under **THE ENVIRONMENT** in **SCIENCE**

0-316-05635-9 LITTLE, BROWN $24.95

James **Atlas**

Battle of the Books: The Curriculum Debate in America

Students are what they read, Atlas argues; choosing our children's books is an incredibly important task. As ethnic groups assert themselves and reject assimilation, our need for common ground grows ever greater. The author suggests that unless there are common beliefs on which to build consensus, there may soon be no common heritage, no shared vision of the future

See also **KULTURKAMPF: THE WAR OVER THE CANON** under **THE STATE OF THE SCHOOLS** under **EDUCATION** in **SOCIAL STUDIES**

0-393-31070-1 NORTON PB $8.95

James David **Barber** & Barbara **Kellerman**

Women Leaders in American Politics

0-13-962267-5 PRENTICE HALL PB $36.40

Barbara **Bergmann**

In Defense of Affirmative Action

This polemic argues in favor of the necessity and effectiveness of affirmative action programs. Bergmann, who served on the staff of President Kennedy's Council of Economic Advisors, acknowledges the problems with quotas and considers the unfairness to white males inherent in the programs, but concludes that the implications of allowing sexual and racial discrimination to continue are far worse

See also **POLITICAL THEORY AND MOVEMENTS** under **AFRICAN-AMERICAN STUDIES**

0-465-09833-9 BASIC $23.00

Fred **Block**

The Vampire State: And Other Myths and Fallacies About the U.S. Economy

INTRODUCTION BY ROBERT HEILBRONER

1-56584-193-X NEW PRESS $23.00

Walter Dean **Burnham**

The Current Crisis in American Politics

0-19-503219-5 OXFORD $35.00

Patrick H. **Caddell**

The Fire this Time: The Failure of Two-Party Politics and the Rise of the American People

0-87113-639-2 GROVE $22.00

Stephen **Carter**

Reflections of an Affirmative Action Baby

Argues for conservatism as a dissent against civil rights orthodoxy

See also **ETHNICITY AND RACE RELATIONS** under **TOPICS IN MODERN SOCIOLOGY** under **SOCIOLOGY** in **SOCIAL STUDIES**

0-465-06869-3 BASIC PB $14.50

Integrity

0-465-03466-7 BASIC $24.00

0-465-03468-3 BASIC PB $10.00

Mario **Cuomo**

Common Sense

"We should have all the government we need—but only the government we need, and that need must be defined one issue at a time." The voice of Mario Cuomo offers a path for dignity instead of despair to the underprivileged and suggests ways to recapture our dominance in the global economy. Whether one wishes to embrace an open-minded liberalism or an intelligent conservatism, Cuomo provides support against "Gingrichism," trumped-up rhetoric, and the political exploitation of fears and dissatisfactions. An important call to action for those who, conservative or liberal, believe in American constitutional democracy

0-684-81517-6 SIMON & SCHUSTER $21.00

Robert A. **Dahl**

Who Governs?: Democracy and Power in an American City

A classic study of how local American government really works, first published in 1961 and based on a study of New Haven politics

0-300-00051-0 YALE PB $18.00

John Patrick **Diggins**

The Lost Soul of American Politics: Virtue, Self-Interest, and the Foundations of Liberalism

0-226-14877-7 CHICAGO PB $24.95

Frederick M. **Dolan**

Allegories of America: Narratives, Metaphysics, Politics

Examines what it means to be an American in terms of political theory

0-8014-8200-3 CORNELL PB $15.95

Thomas Byrne **Edsall**

The New Politics of Inequality

A *Washington Post* reporter examines how control of the nation's tax and spending policies is increasingly falling into the hands of the affluent

0-393-30250-4 NORTON PB $8.95

James F. **Dunnigan** & Albert A. **Nofi**

Dirty Little Secrets: Military Information You're Not Supposed to Know

The myths, mysteries, and boondoggles for which our military has become famous: the official 18-page-long Defense Department recipe for fruitcake, the tanks that use just as much fuel standing still as they do in motion, and the annual cost of military aircraft collisions with birds ($100 million, 20 dead or injured pilots)

0-688-11270-6 QUILL PB $13.00

Richard J. **Ellis**

American Political Cultures

Published in 1993; by the author of *Presidential Lightning Rods: The Politics of Blame Avoidance*. "For those who see everywhere the one-dimensionality of American life, Ellis's book should provide fifteen minutes of relief" —John Patrick Diggins

0-19-507900-0 OXFORD $49.95

0-19-511138-9 C.A.B. INTERNATIONAL PB $18.95

John Kenneth **Galbraith**

The Culture of Contentment

Considers the growth of an affluent class content with its own prospects and unconcerned with the penury surrounding it—and the possible consequences for society at large

See also **THE AMERICAN ECONOMY TODAY** under **ECONOMICS** in **SOCIAL STUDIES**

0-395-66919-7 HOUGHTON MIFFLIN PB $10.95

John Kenneth Galbraith

The Good Society

A blueprint for a better America, written for a general audience

See also **THE AMERICAN ECONOMY TODAY** under **ECONOMICS** in **SOCIAL STUDIES**

0-395-71328-5 HOUGHTON MIFFLIN $21.95

Myron Peretz **Glazer** & Penina Migdal **Glazer**

The Whistle-Blowers: Exposing Corruption in Government and Industry

A full-scale study of the people who have put their careers and lives on the line to expose dangerous or illegal situations

0-465-09174-1 BASIC PB $9.95

Joel M. **Gora**

The Right to Protest: The Basic ACLU Guide to Free Expression

Provides detailed guidance on what does and does not constitute an illegitimate restraint on free expression. Packs a remarkable quantity of detailed information on recent court decisions and the legal nuances of current debates on "fighting words," bigoted speech, obscenity, government-funded art, and surveillance techniques

0-8093-1699-4 SOUTHERN ILLINOIS PB $7.95

David **Green**

The Language of Politics in America

"This survey is studded with insights and underscores key patterns in the evolution of our national discourse: the pervasive superficiality and self-contradictions; the invariable domination of expediency over principle, ambiguity over precision, partisanship over critical perspective"—*NY Times Book Review*

0-8014-8054-X CORNELL PB $14.95

William **Greider**

Who Will Tell the People?: The Betrayal of American Democracy

"At the very moment when Western democracies and capitalism have triumphed over the Communist alternative, their own systems of self-government are being gradually unravelled by the market system," writes the author. His book pinpoints how special interest groups, money, and influence have completely taken over the American political system

See also **AMERICAN POLITICS** under **POLITICAL THOUGHT** in **SOCIAL STUDIES**

0-671-86740-7 TOUCHSTONE PB $13.00

Allen D. **Hertzke**

Representing God in Washington: The Role of Religious Lobbies in the American Polity

0-87049-553-4 TENNESSEE $35.00
0-87049-570-4 TENNESSEE PB $16.00

Samuel P. **Huntington**

American Politics: The Promise of Disharmony

Examines the gap between American political ideals and actual performance

0-674-03021-4 HARVARD PB $15.50

Jane **Jacobs**

Systems of Survival: A Dialogue on the Moral Foundations of Commerce and Politics

There are "takers" (hunters, foragers) and there are "traders" (outward-looking exchangers of goods), and from these two types, says the author, spring the contradictory ethical codes that govern human behavior

0-679-74816-4 VINTAGE PB $13.00

Haynes **Johnson** & David S. **Broder**

The System: The American Way of Politics Stretched to the Breaking Point

0-316-46969-6 LITTLE, BROWN $25.95

Richard D. **Kahlenberg**

The Remedy: Class, Race, and Affirmative Action

Kahlenberg—professor of law and contributor to *The Washington Post, New Republic,* and elsewhere—argues for a return to the roots of affirmative action. His damning analysis shows that affirmative action programs have become a means to achieve racial diversity, even if that entails preferring wealthy blacks over poor whites, rather than a means to help the disadvantaged regardless of their race

0-465-09823-1 BASIC $25.00

Steven **Kelman**

Making Public Policy: A Hopeful View of American Government

Why the system works better than most Americans believe; by a professor at the John F. Kennedy School of Government

0-465-04335-6 BASIC BOOKS PB $14.00

James S. **Kunen**

Reckless Disregard: Corporate Greed, Government Indifference, and the Kentucky School Bus Crash

The author of *The Strawberry Statement* assigned to report for *People* magazine on the deadliest drunk-driving incident in history

0-671-70533-4 SIMON & SCHUSTER $23.00

Michael **Lerner**

The Politics of Meaning: Affirming Hope and Possibility in an Age of Cynicism

Lerner, a rabbi, psychotherapist, and editor of *Tikkun* magazine, offers a spiritual and ethical program for reconstituting liberalism as a mainstream American force, all the while sharpening its challenge to the right's usurpation of family and religious values

0-201-47966-4 ADDISON-WESLEY $24.00

Theodore J. **Lowi**

The End of Liberalism: The Second Republic of the United States

0-393-09000-0 NORTON PB $14.95

Dave **Marsh**

Fifty Ways to Fight Censorship

Rock critic Marsh takes on Jesse Helms, Tipper Gore, the American Family Association, the Eagle Forum, the National Organization for Women, the networks, the newspapers, the movie industry, and all the other forces he sees as conspiring to restrict free expression in America

1-56025-011-9 THUNDER'S MOUTH PB $5.95

Patricia G. **Miller**

The Worst of Times: Illegal Abortion—Survivors, Practitioners, Coroners, Cops, and Children of Women Who Died Talk about Its Horrors

This work of oral history, published on the 20th anniversary of *Roe v. Wade,* demonstrates that, no matter what, American women will have abortions, whether legal or not, whether by doctors or by back-alley abortionists

See also **THE ABORTION DEBATE** under **THE FEMALE EXPERIENCE** under **WOMEN'S STUDIES** in **SOCIAL STUDIES**

0-06-099512-2 HARPERPERENNIAL PB $12.00

I was so terrified I couldn't move or speak or even think. I just huddled there in the front seat. I didn't know where I was going or what was going to be done to me. I had no idea. Was someone going to cut my head off or cut my belly open?

THE WORST OF TIMES: ILLEGAL ABORTION—SURVIVORS, PRACTITIONERS, CORONERS, COPS, AND CHILDREN OF WOMEN WHO DIED TALK ABOUT ITS HORRORS

Jack **Mitchell**

Executive Privilege: Two Centuries of Scandals

Mitchell makes clear that presidential abuses of power began with George Washington, but distinguishes between the first president's minor graft and Hoover's giveaway of natural resources, or the Reagan administration's arms-profiteering and subversion of constitutional process

0-7818-0063-3 HIPPOCRENE $24.95

Richard D. **Mohr**

A More Perfect Union: Why Straight America Must Stand Up for Gay Rights

"A powerful book whose timing is just perfect. Send this book to your family, friends, and political allies"—David Mixner

See also **POLITICS AND LAW** under **GAY LIFE AND CULTURE** under **GAY, LESBIAN, AND BISEXUAL STUDIES** in **SOCIAL STUDIES**

0-8070-7933-2 BEACON PB $9.00

Toni **Morrison**, editor

Race-ing Justice, En-gendering Power: Essays on Anita Hill, Clarence Thomas, and the Construction of Social Reality

Published to coincide with the first anniversary of the political scandal that shook the country, this book brings together 17 essays by prominent scholars—black, white, male, and female—on the historical, political, and sexual consequences of the Thomas/Hill affair

See also **RACE RELATIONS** under **AFRICAN-AMERICAN STUDIES**

0-679-74145-3 PANTHEON PB $15.00

Ralph **Nader** & Wesley J. **Smith**

No Contest: How the Power Lawyers Are Perverting Justice in America

Far from being crippled by frivolous lawsuits brought by individuals, the authors reveal a shockingly corrupt world in which corporate lawyers are using superior resources and secrecy to restrict, maybe even eliminate, our access to justice

See also **LEGAL THEORY** under **LAW** in **SOCIAL STUDIES**

0-679-42972-7 RANDOM HOUSE $25.00

H.G. **Nicholas**

The Nature of American Politics

Traces the evolution of the American political process, including an assessment of its current participation and manipulation

0-19-827483-1 OXFORD $28.00

Thomas E. **Patterson**

Out of Order

A pointed examination of how the news media have replaced political parties in the election of public officials, and how this chaotic, image-obsessed, sensation-crazed, and often destructive process has weakened America

0-679-41929-2 KNOPF $23.00

Gerald **Posner**

Ross Perot and Third Party Politics

0-679-44731-8 RANDOM HOUSE $25.00

Jonathan **Rauch**

Demosclerosis: The Silent Killer of American Government

0-8129-2632-3 TIME BOOKS PB $14.00

Eric **Redman**

The Dance of Legislation

A case study of the complexity of American legislative politics, tracing the drafting and passing of a single piece of legislation, the National Health Service Bill; by a former Senate aide

0-671-21746-1 SIMON & SCHUSTER PB $11.00

Charles A. **Reich**

Opposing the System

0-517-59777-2 CROWN $23.00

Leo P. **Ribuffo**

Right Center Left: Essays in American History

0-8135-1775-3 RUTGERS $45.00
0-8135-1776-1 RUTGERS PB $16.95

Elliot **Richardson**

Reflections of a Radical Moderate

While best known for his refusal to follow Nixon's order to fire the Watergate special prosecutor, Richardson held other important positions: secretary of defense, attorney general, under secretary of state. His essays address the vast majority of voters who have lost faith in American government, reflecting on what it means to be American today

0-679-42820-8 PANTHEON $24.00

Michael **Rogin**

Ronald Reagan, the Movie: And Other Episodes in Political Demonology

"A dazzling, heady…exploration of 'the countersubversive tradition and political demonology' in America since colonial times" —Phillip French, *Observer*

0-520-06469-0 CALIFORNIA PB $16.95

Lyman Tower **Sargent**, editor

Extremism in America: A Reader

This collection of left- and right-wing extremist texts, from the Students for a Democratic Society to the racist Aryan Nation, paints a vivid portrait of life on the political fringes

0-8147-8011-3 NYU PB $17.95

Arthur M. **Schlesinger**, Jr.

The Vital Center: The Politics of Freedom

Schlesinger's treatise on maintaining the balance between extremes in American politics, first published in 1949

0-306-80323-2 DA CAPO PB $10.95

Arthur M. Schlesinger, Jr.

Jonathan E. **Schwarz**

America's Hidden Success: A Reassessment of Public Policy from Kennedy to Reagan

"Shows that America's political and economic institutions have performed much better than commonly thought"— Aaron Wildavsky, University of California at Berkeley

0-393-30447-7 NORTON PB $8.95

Harold **Seidman** & Robert S. **Gilmour**

Politics, Position and Power: From the Positive to the Regulatory State

An inside view of the federal administration as it effects and is affected by competing forces for power, position, and political advantage; revised edition

0-19-503991-2 OXFORD PB $13.95

Hedrick **Smith**

The Power Game: How Washington Works

Jargon is a vital element of the Washington game. Washington jargon is impenetrable and often deliberately so, to exclude all but the initiated

0-345-36015-X BALLANTINE PB $6.95

For starters: unless you're President Reagan, you can't be a major player in budget politics unless you know the difference between constant dollars and current dollars, between outlays and obligations, between the baseline and the out-years; you can't enter the arena of arms control without some grasp of launchers, throwweight, and RVs.… You will also know that bogeys are the spending targets the secretary of defense gives the armed services and that beam-splitters are the nearly invisible TelePromTers that flash the text of a speech to the president as he turns his head from side to side.

THE POWER GAME: HOW WASHINGTON WORKS

Susan J. **Tolchin** & Martin **Tolchin**

Dismantling America: The Rush to Deregulate

0-19-503577-1 OXFORD PB $9.95

Donald **Wallace**

The American Century: The Rise and Decline of the United States as a World Power

0-300-05721-0 YALE $35.00

Jim **Wallis**

The Soul of Politics: A Practical and Prophetic Vision for Change

Behind the doomsday media view of societal breakdown and political intransigence Wallis documents a world of hope: LA gang members working against violence, South African youths working for democracy, and grassroots groups rebuilding local communities

FOREWORD BY GARRY WILLS
PREFACE BY CORNEL WEST

1-56584-204-9 NEW PRESS $19.95

Michael **Walzer**

What It Means to Be an American: Essays on the American Identity

Our political system works both for and in favor of differences and achieves cohesion through ideals of citizenship rather than cultural or ethnic identity, the author says

0-941419-66-5 MARSILIO $18.00

Cornel **West**

Keeping Faith: Philosophy and Race in America

Essays on race, social theory, American pragmatism, and the limitations of liberation, from the insightful author of *Race Matters*

0-415-90486-2 ROUTLEDGE $29.95
0-415-91028-5 ROUTLEDGE PB $17.95

George F. **Will**

Will, one of our best-known political commentators, has built a reputation based as much on his eloquence as his conservative outlook.

The Morning After: American Successes and Excesses, 1981–1986

See also **THE REAGAN YEARS** under **US HISTORY, 1945 TO THE PRESENT**
See also **HISTORY, POLITICS, AND SOCIETY** under **20TH-CENTURY AMERICAN ESSAYS AND JOURNALISM**

0-02-934430-1 FREE PRESS $24.95

Restoration: Congress, Term Limits and the Recovery of Deliberative Democracy

"*Restoration* is a biting, humorous and perceptive sifting of much of the sand that fouls the national political machinery. Mr. Will has accurately charted the fault lines in the national political terrain"—*NY Times Book Review*

0-02-934713-0 FREE PRESS PB $12.95

James Q. **Wilson**

American Government: Institutions and Policies

A bestselling textbook now in its fourth edition

0-669-15430-X HEATH $52.65

Conservatism and the New Right

Ronald Reagan's stunning victory in 1980 paved the way for the cult of the right-wing personality. The books listed below represent the most recent of them in print.

Patrick **Allitt**

Catholic Intellectuals and Conservative Politics in America, 1950-1985

The fullest account to date of Catholic social theorists, scholars, and polemicists (such as William F. Buckley) and their place in the wider context of post-World War II America. "[Shows] the diversity, tensions, and (sometimes ironic) shifts within the Catholic Right"
—Leo P. Ribuffo, George Washington University

0-8014-8300-X CORNELL PB $15.95

William J. **Bennett**

The Moral Compass

0-684-80313-5 SIMON & SCHUSTER $30.00
0-684-83578-9 TOUCHSTONE PB $16.00

William F. **Buckley**, Jr.

Happy Days Were Here Again: Reflections of a Libertarian Journalist

In his latest collection, the undisputed king of the conservative movement targets Idi Amin, the Sandinistas, fundamentalists, Bush ("his supreme preppiness"), Charles and Diana, and nearly every other icon of the era. "A bravura performance"—*Kirkus Reviews*

1-55850-471-0 ADAMS PB $12.95

William F. Buckley, Jr.

Dan T. **Carter**

The Politics of Rage

The first study of George Wallace in 20 years, and, although unauthorized, the most authoritative. Carter, an eminent Southern historian, gives a vivid account of a central figure in right-wing American politics: the four-time Alabama governor, who spearheaded the anti-integrationist movement in the '60s, was central to the rise of Reaganism in the '80s, and remained a pivotal figure in the Republican revolution of the '90s. A relevant study of the growing influence of white backlash, blue-collar resentment, and the religious right in contemporary American politics

0-684-80916-8 SIMON & SCHUSTER $30.00

Alexander **Cockburn** & Ken **Silverstein**

Washington Babylon

Cockburn and Silverstein cast a jaundiced eye across the Washington landscape, from the liberal elite to the cult of Gingrich. Along the way they direct a keen glance toward Congress, the overwhelming power of the big bureaucracies, and the lawyer-lobbyists who manage the traffic of money and favors. Blistering stuff from two informed, committed, and skeptical observers of the scene inside the Beltway

1-85984-092-2 VERSO PB $17.00

Michael **D'Antonio**

Fall from Grace: The Failed Crusade of the Christian Right

D'Antonio, a *Newsday* correspondent, examines the new Christian right through its leaders (Jerry Falwell, Pat Robertson) and followers, concluding that the recent scandals (Jim and Tammy Bakker, Jimmy Swaggart) are leading to the inevitable collapse of the movement. "An intelligent survey of modern evangelicals' activities"—Garry Wills, *NY Review of Books*

See also **REVIVALS AND EVANGELICALISM** under **RELIGION IN AMERICA** under **TOPICS IN AMERICAN STUDIES**

0-8135-1896-2 RUTGERS PB $14.95

Louis **Filler**, editor

A Dictionary of American Conservatism

Entries on politicians, parties, programs, triumphs, and setbacks

0-8065-1087-0 CITADEL PB $12.95

Gary **Franks**

Searching for the Promised Land: The Odyssey of an African-American Conservative

The first black conservative "on the Hill," Representative Gary Franks writes here of his own experiences fighting the predominantly liberal Congressional Black Caucus and NAACP, while developing his informed opinions on welfare, the American family, the Supreme Court, and other relevant and hotly debated topics in today's political scene

0-06-039156-1 HARPERCOLLINS $24.00

Mark **Gerson**

The Neo-Conservative Vision: From the Cold War to the Culture Wars

The definitive new study of this important movement in American political thought

1-56833-054-5 MADISON $27.95

Mark **Gerson**, editor

The Essential Neo-Conservative Reader

0-201-47968-0 ADDISON-WESLEY $27.50

Michael **Lind**

Up from Conservatism: Why the Right Is Wrong for America

A disaffected protegé of William F. Buckley analyzes what is wrong with the American right

0-684-82761-1 FREE PRESS $23.00

Gertrude **Himmelfarb**

On Looking into the Abyss: Untimely Thoughts on Culture and Society

From a major neo-conservative intellectual; a collection of essays that considers the cultural dilemmas of modern America from a conservative viewpoint

See also **CULTURAL AND SOCIAL HISTORY**

0-679-42826-7 KNOPF $23.00
0-679-75923-9 VINTAGE PB $12.00

Michael W. **Miles**

The Odyssey of the American Right

0-19-502774-4 OXFORD $30.00

Gillian **Peele**

Revival and Reaction: The Right in Contemporary America

0-19-821132-5 OXFORD PB $22.00

Ralph **Reed**

Active Faith: How Christians Are Changing the Face of American Politics

0-684-82758-1 FREE PRESS $25.00

Jim **Wallis**

The Soul of Politics

FOREWORD BY GARRY WILLS AND PREFACE BY CORNEL WEST

0-15-600328-7 HARVEST PB $12.00

George F. **Will**

Suddenly: The American Ideal Abroad and at Home, 1986–1990

"For barbed, moral, conservative political commentary Will has few peers—as this excellent roundup attests"—*Kirkus Reviews*

0-02-934436-0 FREE PRESS PB $14.95

Liberals and the Left

Allida M. **Black**

Casting Her Own Shadow: Eleanor Roosevelt and the Shaping of Postwar Liberalism

Assistant professor of American studies and history at Pennsylvania State University reconstructs Eleanor Roosevelt's role as an underestimated but major force from 1945 until she died in 1962. "Her principled stand for low-cost and public housing, affirmative action, regulation of the corporations, U.S. support for the United Nations—key planks in the liberal agenda under siege today—makes this a timely reassessment"—*Publishers Weekly*

See also **HISTORICAL BIOGRAPHIES** under **AMERICAN HISTORY** under **WOMEN'S STUDIES** in **SOCIAL STUDIES**

0-231-10404-9 COLUMBIA $29.95

Helen C. **Camp**

Iron in Her Soul: Elizabeth Gurley Flynn and the American Left

First full-length biography of America's foremost woman communist

0-87422-106-4 WASHINGTON PB $28.00

James **Carville**

We're Right, They're Not: A Handbook for Spirited Progressives

Chief strategist for the campaign that brought Clinton to the White House, Carville responds to the Contract with America. With trademark acuity of argument and common-sensical wit, he staunchly defends a strong government and offers a politically realistic and feasible program for a Democratic platform that builds upon the nation's best liberal traditions

0-679-76978-1 RANDOM HOUSE PB........................$10.00

William H. **Chafe**

Never Stop Running: Allard Lowenstein and the Struggle to Save American Liberalism

A Jew who feared he looked too Jewish, a homosexual who was deeply ashamed of his longings, Lowenstein was one of the most influential and successful organizers of the civil rights and antiwar movements of the '60s and '70s, until his assassination in 1980. "A biography...written by a wise and thoughtful historian who uses one life to tell us much about a nation's experience in the 1960's and 1970's"—Robert Coles

0-465-00103-3 BASIC........................$28.00

Noam **Chomsky**

Chronicles of Dissent

A wonderful introduction to the controversial Chomskian political perspective, these interviews range across history from Columbus to the recent Gulf War. The Israeli and US dependent relationship, the decline of language because of propaganda, and American imperialist designs are themes to which he continually returns. "Chomsky at his most accessible..."—Howard Zinn

See also **LEFTISM AND MARXISM** under **POLITICAL THOUGHT** in **SOCIAL STUDIES**

INTRODUCTION BY ALEXANDER COCKBURN

0-9628838-9-1 COMMON COURAGE........................$29.95
0-9628838-8-3 COMMON COURAGE PB........................$16.95

Robert **Cohen**

When the Old Left Was Young: Student Radicals and America's First Mass Student Movement, 1929–1941

0-19-506099-7 OXFORD........................$55.00

Mike **Davis** & Michael **Sprinker**

Reshaping the U.S. Left: Popular Struggles in the 1980s

Essays on the successes and current activities of leftist groups, including the Central American solidarity campaigns, the sanctuary movement, the women's peace movement, and labor struggles

0-86091-909-9 VERSO PB........................$19.95

John Patrick **Diggins**

The Rise and Fall of the American Left

"A balanced history of leftist American politics in the 20th century...Admirably nonpartisan" —*Washington Post*

0-393-30917-7 NORTON PB........................$13.95

Elizabeth **Holtzman**

Leading with My Left: One Woman's Life in the Political Arena

WITH CYNTHIA L. COOPER

1-55970-302-4 ARCADE........................$24.95

Michael **Moore**

Downsize This!: Random Threats from an Unarmed American

Seriously funny musings. "Michael Moore is a hybrid of two Ralphs—Kramden and Nader—and he is blessed with brilliant comic timing" —*Time*

See also **HUMOR WRITERS** under **HUMOR** in **POPULAR READING**

0-517-70739-X CROWN........................$21.00

Robert B. **Reich**

Tales of a New America: The Anxious Liberal's Guide to the Future

"The reigning myths of the Reagan era lie in shambles after his searching probe" — *Commonwealth*

0-394-75706-8 VINTAGE PB........................$13.00

Allida M. Carl T. **Rowan**

Dream Makers, Dream Breakers: The World of Justice Thurgood Marshall

Marshall changed America. As a lawyer, he argued 31 cases before the Supreme Court and lost just three. As a justice himself, he influenced fellow justices in cases involving abortion rights, voting rights, and constitutional protection for the accused

See also **LAWYERS AND JUDGES** under **LEGAL HISTORY** under **LAW** in **SOCIAL STUDIES**

0-316-75979-1 LITTLE, BROWN PB........................$12.95

Patricia Cayo **Sexton**

The War on Labor and the Left: Understanding America's Unique Conservatism

"Patricia Sexton has written a very readable survey of the American Labor-Left, showing how it has met with fiery repressive measures from government and business and how it has nonetheless won sizable victories for American workers and others"—Irving Howe

See also **20TH-CENTURY HISTORIES AND STUDIES** under **AMERICAN LABOR AND RADICAL MOVEMENTS**

0-8133-1063-6 WESTVIEW PB........................$17.95

Charles **Shipman**

It Had to Be Revolution: Memoirs of an American Radical

Draft resister, political refugee, founding member of the Mexican Communist Party, railroad executive, and an investment columnist for *Wall Street Journal*—Shipman was all of these. His unusual memoir chronicles the early years of the American left, as well as the author's friendship with Lenin, Trotsky, John Reed, and Bertolt Brecht. "Both an autobiographical cliffhanger and an important historical document"—*Kirkus Reviews*

0-8014-2180-2 CORNELL........................$31.50

Foreign Policy and Diplomatic History

Cambridge University Press

The Cambridge History of American Foreign Relations

On the series: "Happily, the new four-volume *Cambridge History of American Foreign Relations* provides an opportunity to scan the past two centuries for indications of the shape of foreign policy in the post–Cold War world. Each of the four books stands on its own"—*World Policy Journal*

Volume I
The Creation of a Republican Empire, 1776-1865

"...a skilled and absorbing diplomatic history by a scholar who masterfully combines expertise with readability" —Arthur Schlesinger, Jr.

0-521-38209-2 CAMBRIDGE........................$29.95

Volume II
The Search for Opportunity, 1865-1913

0-521-38185-1 CAMBRIDGE........................$29.95

Volume III
The Globalizing of America, 1913-1945

0-521-38206-8 CAMBRIDGE........................$29.95

Volume IV
America in the Age of Soviet Power, 1945-1991

0-521-38193-24 CAMBRIDGE........................$29.95

G.J.A. **O'Toole**

Honorable Treachery: A History of U.S. Intelligence, Espionage, and Covert Action from the American Revolution to the CIA

The first comprehensive history of American intelligence. Historian and former intelligence officer O'Toole recounts every important intelligence operation since the country began, placing each in historical context, and demonstrating that such activities have played a critical role during our history

0-87113-492-6 ATLANTIC MONTHLY PB........................$15.00

Overviews

Howard **Jones**

The Course of American Diplomacy: From the Revolution to the Present

Volume 1

0-534-10603-X DORSEY PB........................$20.95

Volume 2

0-534-10606-4 DORSEY PB........................$20.95

Thomas A. **Bailey**

A Diplomatic History of the American People

Surveys social, political, economic, and diplomatic developments from colonial times to post–World War II, in a lively prose style

0-13-214726-2 PRENTICE HALL $66.00

William H. **Becker** & Samuel F. **Wells**

Economics and World Power: An Assessment of American Diplomacy Since 1789

0-231-04370-8 COLUMBIA $71.00
0-231-04371-6 COLUMBIA PB $17.00

Jerald A. **Combs**

American Diplomatic History: Two Centuries of Changing Interpretations

0-520-04590-4 CALIFORNIA $47.50
0-520-05893-3 CALIFORNIA PB $15.00

Robert H. **Ferrell**

American Diplomacy

0-393-09309-3 NORTON $28.95

Walter **LaFeber**

The American Age: United States Foreign Policy at Home and Abroad since 1750

0-393-96474-4 NORTON PB $25.95

20th-Century Diplomacy

Stephen **Ambrose**

Rise to Globalism: American Foreign Policy Since 1938

The fifth edition includes analyses of the Iran-Contra affair, the Nicaraguan revolution, international terrorism, superpower summits, and other recent developments

See also **1945 TO THE PRESENT: "THE AMERICAN CENTURY"** under **US HISTORY, 1945 TO THE PRESENT**

0-14-017536-9 PENGUIN PB $13.95

C.J. **Bartlett**

The Rise and Fall of the Pax Americana: U.S. Foreign Policy in the Twentieth Century

0-312-68355-3 ST. MARTIN'S $29.95

John **Ehrman**

The Rise of Neoconservatism: Intellectuals and Foreign Affairs, 1945-1994

0-300-06025-4 YALE $35.00
0-300-06870-0 YALE PB $14.00

Lloyd C. **Garner**

A Covenant with Power: America and World Order from Wilson to Reagan

0-19-504009-0 OXFORD PB $14.95

George **Bush** & Brent **Scowcroft**

American Foreign Policy

The collapse of the Soviet Union, the unification of Germany, and the Gulf War against Saddam Hussein were high points of the Bush presidency. Using his diary, Bush, along with his national security advisor Brent Scowcroft, analyzes these issues

0-679-43248-5 KNOPF $30.00

John **Harper**, editor

American Visions of Europe: Franklin D. Roosevelt, George F. Kennan, and Dean G. Acheson

A readable, engaging, and thoughtful examination of the three prime movers of 20th-century American diplomacy. "Harper creatively melds biography with cultural and diplomatic history in this triptych of portraits of important architects of US policy toward Europe during the American Century"—*Kirkus Reviews*

0-521-45483-2 CAMBRIDGE $29.95
0-521-56628-2 CAMBRIDGE PB $16.95

Richard **Nixon**

Beyond Peace

Refuting isolationists of both the Right and the Left, Nixon says that our foreign policy is inextricably tied to the spiritual and economic development of our life at home. The current policy crises—should America intervene in Bosnia? in Somalia? in Haiti?—may be symptomatic of a troubling ailment in the national heart

0-679-43323-6 RANDOM HOUSE $23.00

Richard Nixon

Robert A. **Pastor**

Condemned to Repetition: The United States and Nicaragua

Was "the first extensive insider's account of U.S. policy-making toward Nicaragua during the crucial four-year period that began in 1977" —*Washington Post Book World*

0-691-07752-5 PRINCETON $59.50
0-691-02291-7 PRINCETON PB $15.95

Robert D. **Schulzinger**

American Diplomacy in the 20th Century

A comprehensive survey blending historical narrative with analysis of how and why policy is made

0-19-508061-0 OXFORD PB $17.95

Ronald **Steel**

Temptations of a Superpower: America's Foreign Policy after the Cold War

"Steel makes what should be, but seldom is, an obvious point: that American foreign policy continues to operate within a framework designed for a world that no longer exists....scathing and effective"—Alan Brinkley

See also **INTERNATIONAL RELATIONS AND STRATEGIC STUDIES** in **SOCIAL STUDIES**

0-674-87340-8 HARVARD $18.95
0-674-87341-6 HARVARD PB $10.95

Special Topics in American Foreign Policy

James A. **Bill**

The Eagle and the Lion: The Tragedy of American-Iranian Relations

0-300-04412-7 YALE PB $18.00

Central Intelligence Agency

The Secret Cuban Missile Crisis Documents

Comprised of recently declassified documents, including formerly top secret cables, memos, briefing papers, and maps, this volume provides insight into not only one of the most harrowing events of the 20th century, but into the CIA itself

0-02-881083-X BRASSEY'S DEFENSE PB $21.00

Lawrence **Chang** & Peter **Kornbluh**, editors

The Cuban Missile Crisis, 1962: A National Security Archive Documents Reader

Newly declassified primary documents that include correspondence between Kennedy, Krushchev, and Castro reveal how close to nuclear holocaust we actually were 35 years ago

1-56584-019-4 NEW PRESS $25.00

Andrew **Cockburn** & Leslie **Cockburn**

Dangerous Liaison: The Inside Story of the U.S.-Israeli Covert Relationship

A controversial, highly critical look at the often secretive relationship between American and Israeli intelligence and military agencies, and the ramifications of this relationship on international politics

0-06-016444-1 HARPERPERENNIAL PB $25.00

Richard E. **Feinberg**

The Intemperate Zone: The Third World Challenge to U.S. Foreign Policy

0-393-30143-5 NORTON PB $8.95

John S.D. **Eisenhower**

Intervention!: The United States and the Mexican Revolution, 1913-1917

"This terrific story, superbly told by John Eisenhower, could not be more timely. Reagan's, Bush's and Clinton's interventions in third world countries run parallel to Wilson's in Mexico, including the same mistakes and unhappy consequences"—Stephen Ambrose

0-393-31318-2 NORTON PB $14.00

Stanley **Karnow**

In Our Image: America's Empire in the Philippines

An excellent history of U.S. involvement in the Philippines by the author of *Vietnam: A History*

See also THE PHILIPPINES under SOUTHEAST ASIA AND THE PHILIPPINES in WORLD HISTORY AND CURRENT AFFAIRS

0-87124-125-0 FOREIGN POLICY PB $5.95

Walter **LaFeber**

Inevitable Revolutions: The United States in Central America

With one third of its contents new, this revised edition of the former bestseller by the noted historian is still timely and includes a scathing analysis of the Reagan-Bush policy in Central America

0-393-30964-9 NORTON PB $13.95

The Panama Canal: The Crisis in Historical Perspective

See also THE ROAD TO WORLD POWER under US HISTORY, 1877-1945

0-19-505930-1 OXFORD PB $13.75

Anthony **Lake**

Somoza Falling: A Case Study in the Making of U.S. Foreign Policy

Based on the 1978 Nicaraguan crisis

See also NICARAGUA under LATIN AMERICA AND THE CARIBBEAN

0-87023-733-0 MASSACHUSETTS PB $17.95

William Roger **Louis** & Hedley **Bull**, editors

The "Special Relationship": Anglo-American Relations Since 1945

See also BRITAIN SINCE 1945 under GREAT BRITAIN AND IRELAND in WORLD HISTORY AND CURRENT AFFAIRS

0-19-820183-4 OXFORD PB $27.00

Robert J. **McMahon**

The Cold War on the Periphery: The United States, India, and Pakistan

0-231-08226-6 COLUMBIA $34.50
0-231-08227-4 COLUMBIA PB $17.50

Yossi **Melman** & Dan **Raviv**

Friends in Deed: Inside the U.S.-Israeli Alliance

"For detailed research, readable analysis, and endlessly interesting anecdotes, it would be hard to top this splendid book"
—*Washington Times*

0-7868-8090-2 HYPERION PB $14.95

Bernard S. **Morris**

Communism, Revolution, and American Policy

A revised edition of the author's influential 1966 study *International Communism and American Policy*

0-8223-0706-5 DUKE $35.00
0-8223-0760-X DUKE PB $14.95

Chester D. **Pach**

Arming the Free World

Documents the United States government's practice of providing arms to a variety of countries—a great many of them dangerous—throughout the world. Pach also traces the huge role that military aid plays in foreign policy

0-8078-1943-3 NORTH CAROLINA $16.95

Thomas G. **Paterson**

Contesting Castro: The United States and the Triumph of the Cuban Revolution

0-19-508630-9 OXFORD $30.00
0-19-510120-0 OXFORD PB $14.95

Meeting the Communist Threat: Truman to Reagan

A distinguished diplomatic historian traces why and how Americans have perceived and exaggerated the Communist threat, with devastating critiques of Kennedy's foreign policy, Reagan's rewriting of the Vietnam War, and Congress's inability to oversee the CIA's covert activities

0-19-504533-5 OXFORD $29.95
0-19-504532-7 OXFORD PB $10.95

Jimmy M. **Skaggs**

The Great Guano Rush: Entrepreneurs and American Overseas Expansion

How 19th-century America acquired islands around the world, from Haiti to the central Pacific

0-312-12339-6 ST. MARTIN'S PB $16.95

Holly **Sklar**

Washington's War on Nicaragua

0-89608-296-2 SOUTH END $35.00
0-89608-295-4 SOUTH END PB $15.00

The Iran-Contra Scandal

Neil C. **Livingstone** & Terrell E. **Arnold**

Beyond the Iran-Contra Crisis: The Shape of U.S. Anti-Terrorism Policy in the Post-Reagan Era

0-669-16467-4 LEXINGTON PB $19.95

Malcolm **Byrne** & Peter **Kornbluh**, editors

The Iran-Contra Affair: A National Security Archive Documents Reader

A casebook of documents crucial to a thorough understanding of "Irangate," the most puzzling and disturbing government scam since Watergate. Includes Oliver North's diaries, a chronology of key events, and a systematic glossary of the major players

FOREWORD BY THEODORE DRAPER

1-56584-024-0 NEW PRESS $40.00
1-56584-047-X NEW PRESS PB $24.95

Jonathan **Marshall**

The Iran-Contra Connection: Secret Teams and Covert Operations in the Reagan Era

Views the Iran-Contra affair as a function of ongoing CIA and extra-CIA operations including drug-trafficking, gun-running, government-toppling, and assassination

0-921689-14-4 BLACK ROSE PB $19.99

Bill **Moyers**

The Secret Government: The Constitution in Crisis

Both a history of events culminating in the Iran-Contra affair and an analysis of the threat posed by the growth of the secret government; based on the PBS documentary

INTRODUCTION BY HENRY STEELE COMMAGER

0-932020-85-2 SEVEN LOCKS $16.95
0-932020-84-4 SEVEN LOCKS PB $9.95

Samuel **Segev**

The Iranian Triangle: The Untold Story of Israel's Role in the Iran-Contra Affair

0-02-928341-8 FREE PRESS $29.95

The CIA, FBI, and Espionage

James **Adams**

Sellout: Aldrich Ames and the Corruption of the CIA

See also ESPIONAGE TALES under ESPIONAGE in POPULAR READING

0-670-86236-3 VIKING $23.95

Peter **Maas**

Killer Spy: The Inside Story of the FBI's Pursuit and Capture of Aldrich Ames, America's Deadliest Spy

0-446-51973-1 WARNER $21.95
0-446-60279-5 WARNER PB $6.50

William **Burroughs**

Deep Black: Space Espionage and National Security

High technology and intelligence collection. "More remarkable than exploits of human spies"
—*NY Times*

0-425-10879-1 BERKLEY PB $6.99

William B. **Beuer**

J. Edgar Hoover and His G-Men

Chronicles the early years, when Hoover and his crimebusters achieved legendary success and status

0-275-94990-7 BERGIN & GARVEY $24.95

J. Edgar Hoover

Ward **Churchill** & Jim Vander **Wall**

Agents of Repression: The FBI's Secret Wars against the Black Panther Party and the American Indian Movement

See also THE CIVIL RIGHTS MOVEMENT AND BEYOND under AFRICAN-AMERICAN STUDIES

0-89608-293-8 SOUTH END PB $16.00

Cartha D. "Deke" **DeLoach**

Hoover's FBI: The Inside Story by Hoover's Trusted Lieutenant

A 28-year veteran and number three at the FBI gives us the scoop

0-89526-479-X REGNERY $27.50

William **Hood**

Mole: The True Story of the First Russian Spy to Become an American Counterspy

"William Hood, an old OSS and CIA hand, has written a real-life spy thriller"—*The Economist*

0-02-881079-1 BRASSEY'S DEFENSE PB $14.95

Ronald **Kessler**

Spy vs. Spy: The Shocking True Inside Story of the FBI's Secret War Against Soviet Agents in America

"A notable coup"—*Chicago Tribune*

0-671-67967-8 POCKET PB $5.99

Edward Lee **Howard**

Safe House: The Compelling Memoir of the Only CIA Spy to Seek Asylum in Russia

Howard recounts the history of his defection to the KGB from his rising-star position in the CIA. A thrilling political and personal story from a recently bygone time. "Since he jumped from a car on a darkened Santa Fe street…Howard has led a life of intrigue worthy of a Tom Clancy novel"—*Albuquerque Journal*

1-88260-515-2 NATIONAL PRESS $23.95

Rhodri **Jeffreys-Jones**

The CIA and American Democracy

0-300-05017-8 YALE PB $18.00

Marita **Lorenz**

Marita: One Woman's Extraordinary Tale of Love and Espionage

Castro's lover and the mother of his child, Marita was kidnapped by the CIA and recruited as Fidel's most promising would-be assassin. The snaky road of espionage led her to Dallas with Lee Harvey Oswald, to the boudoir of Venezuelan strongman Marcos Perez Jimenez, and, finally, to Queens, New York, where she lives today under the constant harassment of the CIA

1-56025-055-0 THUNDER'S MOUTH $22.95

John **Marks**

The Search for the "Manchurian Candidate": The CIA and Mind Control

Working from thousands of pages of newly released documents, Marks has investigated CIA experiments in mind control and programmed assassins, producing what *New York* Magazine called "the CIA exposé to end all CIA exposés."

0-393-30794-8 NORTON PB $10.95

Richard G. **Powers**

Secrecy and Power: The Life of J. Edgar Hoover

0-02-925061-7 FREE PRESS PB $18.95

Natalie **Robins**

Alien Ink: The FBI's War on Freedom of Expression

"The book's superb documentation draws on secret files, obtained by the author, on hundreds of subjects….Contributes greatly to an understanding of the dark underside of American culture and offers a prescription for altered priorities in the agendas of intelligence agencies"—*NY Times*

0-8135-1954-3 RUTGERS PB $14.95

Jeffrey D. **Simon**

The Terrorist Trap: America's Experience with Terrorism

"Simon's book is tremendous in making us understand the history, the reality and the ongoing danger of terrorism"—Pierre Salinger

0-253-35249-5 INDIANA $29.95

Athan **Theoharis**

J. Edgar Hoover, Sex and Crime: An Historical Antidote

Theoharis refutes claims that Hoover was secretly homosexual, and emphasizes Hoover's Cold War activities against American citizens and the culture of lawlessness within the FBI

1-56663-071-1 DEE $19.95

Evan **Thomas**

The Very Best Men: The Early Years of the CIA

Four central figures in the CIA bureaucracy serve as the optic nerve through which Thomas (assistant managing editor, *Newsweek*) analyzes the great days of the CIA, from World War II to Vietnam. The covert overthrow of foreign governments, bribing heads of state, and plotting assassinations in the global secret war against communism—such were the jobs of the "best and the brightest." Exclusive access and extensive interviews serve as the basis for an original account of the president's personal action arm: four men who were volunteered to accomplish covertly what our government was not allowed to do constitutionally

0-684-81025-5 SIMON & SCHUSTER $27.50

0-684-82538-4 TOUCHSTONE PB $15.00

William W. **Turner**

Hoover's FBI

By a ten-year FBI agent. "A powerful case against Hoover and the Agency"—*The Nation*

1-56025-063-1 THUNDER'S MOUTH PB $12.95

H. Bradford **Westerfield**, editor

Inside the CIA's Private World: Declassified Articles from the Agency's Internal Journal, 1955-1992

"A brilliant selection from the CIA's secret Cold War archive—gripping, haunting, intellectually challenging and as tantalizing as Le Carré" —Bob Woodward

0-300-06026-2 YALE $35.00

Bob **Woodward**

Veil: The Secret Wars of the CIA, 1981-1987

The bestselling account of William Casey's CIA

0-671-66159-0 POCKET PB $5.99

Memoirs and Biographies

Zbigniew **Brzezinski**

Power and Principle: Memoirs of the National Security Adviser, 1977-1981

"Fascinating as an insight into how a crucial part of government works, intimidating as a reflection of what it takes to go forth in bureaucratic wars, and appealing in its candor"—Flora Lewis, *NY Times*

0-374-23665-8 FS&G $100.00

0-374-51877-7 FS&G PB $11.95

Robert D. **Schulzinger**

Henry Kissinger: Doctor of Diplomacy

0-231-06952-9 COLUMBIA $44.50

Douglas **Frantz** & others

Friends in High Places: The Rise and Fall of Clark Clifford

The first biography of Clifford, who, in his long career, served as Kennedy's personal lawyer and Johnson's secretary of defense before becoming involved with the "outlaw bank," the Bank of Commerce and Credit International, and so ending his public life

0-316-29162-5 LITTLE, BROWN.................$24.95

Waldo H. **Heinrichs**, Jr.

American Ambassador: Joseph C. Grew and the Development of the United States Diplomatic Tradition

0-19-504159-3 OXFORD PB.................$22.00

Walter **Isaacson**

Kissinger: A Biography

An examination of the life of the master diplomat and Nixon's secretary of state

See also **BIOGRAPHIES** under **US HISTORY, 1945 TO THE PRESENT**

0-671-87236-2 TOUCHSTONE PB.................$16.00

Walter **Isaacson**

The Wise Men: Six Friends and the World They Made

How Robert Lowell, John McCloy, Averell Harriman, Charles Bohlen, George Kennan, and Dean Acheson shaped American policy in the postwar world

0-671-65712-7 TOUCHSTONE PB.................$15.95

Colin L. **Powell** & Joseph **Persico**

My American Journey

And what a journey it was. From the South Bronx through combat in Vietnam to chairman of the Joint Chiefs of Staff, strategist of Desert Storm, and advisor to presidents Democratic and Republican alike, Powell writes with candor and vision of his passage to the highest point in America's political landscape. A revealing self-portrait

0-679-76511-5 RANDOM HOUSE PB.................$25.95

0-345-40728-8 BALLANTINE PB.................$6.99

Colin Powell

Richard **Secord**

Honored and Betrayed

From organizing the secret war over Laos through his days working with presidents Bush and Reagan in the covert arms deals, Secord has played a central role in American politics. This memoir frankly assigns praise and blame to many of his powerful colleagues, including LBJ, Carter, Reagan, Bush, and Ollie North. "Only in Washington did I discover the bureaucratic art of 'forgetting,' and I have to admit I never developed a taste or aptitude for it"
—from *Honored and Betrayed*

0-471-57328-0 WILEY.................$24.95

About two hours later, after Tom Green had returned, President Reagan called Ollie. Despite all that had happened, North actually came to attention when he picked up the phone—a completely spontaneous, touching, and, I think, telling gesture on Ollie's part. Colonel Chauvin, say goodbye to the Gipper.

The President told North he was "a national hero."

"Well, Mr. President," Ollie answered, "I'm just sorry that my attempts to serve you have turned out as they have."

"Let me talk to him," I asked. Ollie glanced at me but continued listening to the President.

"Let me talk to him!" I said loudly, hoping to be heard on the other end. It was not a request.

Ollie hung up looking proud and drained.

Jesus, I thought. I was so mad I could hardly speak. All the President had to do was make one ceremonial, hypocritical phone call and Ollie was floating on cloud nine.

HONORED AND BETRAYED

American Labor and Radical Movements

Heavily influenced by European scholarship, a "new labor history" emerged in the 1960s, shifting attention from unions and organized labor to working-class life and culture itself.

General Histories

American Social History Project, CUNY

Who Built America?: Working People and the Nation's Economy, Politics, Culture and Society

"An extremely insightful and thoughtful compendium of social and labor history skillfully interwoven with a far more critical than usual political history of the nation

Volume I
Through the Civil War, Reconstruction and the Railroad Strike of 1877

0-679-73022-2 PANTHEON PB.................$22.50

Volume II
From the Gilded Age to the Present

0-679-73022-3 PANTHEON PB.................$22.50

Paul **Buhle** & Alan **Dawley**, editors

Working for Democracy: American Workers from the Revolution to the Present

ESSAYS BY ERIC FONER, NELL IRVIN PAINTER, DAVID MONTGOMERY, BARBARA MEYER WERTHEIMER, MANNING MARABLE

0-252-01220-8 ILLINOIS.................$24.95

0-252-01221-6 ILLINOIS PB.................$9.95

Philip S. **Foner**, editor

History of the Labor Movement in the United States

A Marxist-oriented narrative

Volume 1
From Colonial Times to the Foundation of the American Federation of Labor

0-7178-0091-1 INTERNATIONAL PUB.................$19.00

0-7178-0376-7 INTERNATIONAL PUB PB.................$6.95

Volume 2
From the Foundation of the American Federation of Labor to the Emergence of American Imperialism

0-7178-0092-X INTERNATIONAL PUB.................$19.00

0-7178-0388-0 INTERNATIONAL PUB PB.................$4.95

Volume 3
The Policies and Practices of the American Federation of Labor, 1900-1909

0-7178-0389-9 INTERNATIONAL PUB PB.................$4.95

Volume 4
The Industrial Workers of the World, 1905-1917

0-7178-0396-1 INTERNATIONAL PUB PB.................$12.95

Volume 5
The AFL in the Progressive Era, 1910-1915

0-7178-0562-X INTERNATIONAL PUB PB.................$4.95

Volume 6
On the Eve of America's Entrance into World War I, 1915-1916

0-686-97775-0 INTERNATIONAL PUB PB.................$5.75

Volume 7
Labor and World War I, 1914-1918

0-7178-0638-3 INTERNATIONAL PUB.................$21.00

0-7178-0627-8 INTERNATIONAL PUB PB.................$9.95

Volume 8
Postwar Struggles, 1918-1920

0-7178-0653-7 INTERNATIONAL PUB.................$19.00

0-7178-0652-9 INTERNATIONAL PUB PB.................$8.95

Volume 9
The T.U.E.L., 1925-1929

0-7178-0690-1 INTERNATIONAL PUB.................$19.00

Volume 10
The T.U.E.L. to the End of the Gompers Era

0-7178-0674-X INTERNATIONAL PUB.................$12.50

Karen **Orren**
Belated Feudalism: Labor, the Law and Liberal Development in the United States
"Orren's forcefully written book brings an entirely new perspective to the place of labor in the United States and goes beyond that to fresh insights on corporate capitalism itself"
—Theodore J. Lowi
0-521-42254-X CAMBRIDGE PB $18.95

Joseph G. **Rayback**
A History of American Labor
First published in 1959
0-02-925850-2 FREE PRESS PB $19.95

Samuel **Yellen**
American Labor Struggles, 1877-1934
Ten decisive confrontations between owners and workers; first published in 1936
0-913460-33-8 PATHFINDER PB $21.95

Essays

Paul S. **Adler**, editor
Technology and the Future of Work
0-19-507171-9 OXFORD $42.00

Eileen **Boris** & Elisabeth **Prugl**, editors
Homeworkers in Global Perspective: Invisible No More
0-415-91007-2 ROUTLEDGE PB $19.95

David **Brody**
Workers in Industrial America: Essays on the 20th-Century Struggle
0-19-504504-1 OXFORD PB $14.95

Leon **Fink**
In Search of the Working Class: Essays in American Labor History and Political Culture
0-252-06368-6 ILLINOIS PB $17.95

Michael H. **Frisch** & Daniel J. **Walkowitz**
Working Class-America: Essays on Labor, Community and American Society
Ten original essays in the "new" labor history
0-252-00954-1 ILLINOIS PB $12.95

Herbert G. **Gutman**
Power and Culture: Essays in the American Working Class
A final collection from the late historian
EDITED BY IRA BERLIN
1-56584-010-0 NEW PRESS PB $14.95

Work, Culture, and Society in Industrializing America
0-394-72251-5 RANDOM HOUSE PB $10.56

Herbert G. **Gutman** & Donald H. **Bell**, editors
The New England Working Class and the New Labor History
0-252-01300-X ILLINOIS $37.50

Heidi I. **Hartmann** & others, editors
Computer Chips and Paper Clips: Technology and Women's Employment
0-309-03688-7 NATIONAL ACADEMY PB $19.95

Daniel J. **Leab**, editor
The Labor History Reader
An anthology from the journal *Labor History*
INTRODUCTION BY DAVID BRODY & HERBERT G. GUTMAN
0-252-01198-8 ILLINOIS PB $17.95

David **Montgomery**
Workers' Control in America: Studies in the History of Work, Technology, and Labor Struggles
0-521-28006-0 CAMBRIDGE PB $16.95

Charles **Stephenson** & Robert **Asher**, editors
Life and Labor: Dimensions of Working-Class History
0-88706-173-7 SUNY $59.50
0-88706-172-9 SUNY PB $21.95

The Early Years: From Crafts to Industry

Stephen **Innes**
Work and Labor in Early America
"Especially strong in detailing the process of work and the consciousness of workers in rural America"
—Allan Kulikoff, University of Northern Illinois
0-8078-1798-8 NORTH CAROLINA $37.50

Marcus **Rediker**
Between the Devil and the Deep Blue Sea: Merchant Seamen, Pirates and the Anglo-American Maritime World, 1700-1750
0-521-30342-7 CAMBRIDGE $44.95
0-521-45720-3 CAMBRIDGE PB $11.95

W.J. **Rorabaugh**
The Craft Apprentice: From Franklin to the Machine Age in America
0-19-503647-6 OXFORD $34.00
0-19-505189-0 OXFORD PB $17.95

Steven J. **Ross**
Workers on the Edge: Work, Leisure and Politics in Industrializing Cincinnati, 1788-1890
0-231-05520-X COLUMBIA $53.50

Charles G. **Steffen**
Mechanics of Baltimore: Workers and Politics in the Age of Revolution, 1763-1812
Urban craftsmen in early American political life
0-252-01088-4 ILLINOIS $29.95

Laurel Thatcher **Ulrich**
A Midwife's Tale: The Life of Martha Ballard, Based on Her Diary, 1785-1812
Maine in the Federalist era
0-679-73376-0 VINTAGE PB $13.00

Sean **Wilentz**
Chants Democratic: New York City and the Rise of the American Working Class, 1788-1850
An important and beautifully written work by a Princeton historian
0-19-504012-0 OXFORD PB $13.95

Industrial America: To 1920

The Industrial Workers of the World—or Wobblies, as they came to be known—was the first labor organization committed to the idea that a giant union of all workers could crush the capitalist system. Though it lasted less than two decades, the IWW has long since remained a preeminent symbol of radical American unionism.

Paul **Avrich**
The Haymarket Tragedy
On May 4, 1886, in Chicago, center for the campaign for the eight-hour workday, seven people were killed when a bomb was hurled into the ranks of an anarchist protest meeting
0-691-00600-8 PRINCETON PB $19.95

Jeremy **Brecher**
Strike!
A sympathetic history
0-8467-0364-5 SOUTH END PB $15.00

David **Brody**
Labor in Crisis: The Steel Strike of 1919
0-313-23499-X GREENWOOD $55.00
0-252-01373-5 ILLINOIS PB $10.95

Stanley **Buder**
Pullman: An Experiment in Industrial Order and Community Planning, 1880-1930
The fate of the company town rocked by the great strike of 1894
0-19-500838-3 OXFORD PB $14.95

Dan **Clawson**
Bureaucracy and the Labor Process: The Transformation of U.S. Industry, 1860-1920
0-85345-543-0 MONTHLY REVIEW PB $15.00

Alan **Dawley**

Class and Community: The Industrial Revolution in Lynn

"The author brilliantly examines the structure and culture of Lynn shoemakers, their relations with the owners, changes in their work situation due to the displacement of craft skills by factory machines, local and vocational distribution of property and income, social and geographical mobility"—*Historian*

0-674-13395-1 HARVARD PB $15.95

Thomas **Dublin**

Women at Work: The Transformation of Work and Community in Lowell, Massachusetts, 1826-1860

Winner of the Bancroft Prize; deals with the first generation of American women to face the demands of industrial capitalism

0-231-04167-5 COLUMBIA PB $18.00

Melvyn **Dubofsky**

Industrialism and the American Worker, 1865-1920

EDITED BY JOHN HOPE FRANKLIN & ABRAHAM EISENSTADT

0-88295-831-3 HARLAN DAVIDSON PB $11.95

Leon **Fink**

Workingmen's Democracy: The Knights of Labor and American Politics

Uses community studies to raise broader critical issues about the Knights

0-252-01256-9 ILLINOIS PB $11.95

Philip S. **Foner**, editor

The Great Labor Uprising of 1877

Argues that what began as a railroad workers' strike became the first "general strike" in American history

0-913460-56-7 PATHFINDER $50.00

0-913460-57-5 PATHFINDER PB $18.95

Jacquelyn Dowd **Hall** & others

Like a Family: The Making of a Southern Cotton Mill World

Life in the early mills and the technological changes that transformed them

0-8078-1754-6 NORTH CAROLINA $45.00

0-393-30619-4 NORTON PB $12.95

Dirk **Hoerder**, editor

American Labor and Immigrant History, 1877-1920s: Recent European Research

0-252-00963-0 ILLINOIS $29.95

Ira **Katznelson** & Aristide R. **Zolberg**, editors

Working-Class Formation: 19th-Century Patterns in Western Europe and the United States

How and when the idea of class became central to the ideologies and actions of working people, and the political consequences of that consciousness

0-691-10207-4 PRINCETON PB $21.95

Joyce **Kornbluh**, editor

Rebel Voices: An IWW Anthology

0-88286-145-X KERR $42.50

0-88286-120-4 KERR PB $30.00

Milton **Meltzer**

Bread and Roses: The Struggle of American Labor, 1865-1915

See also **THE EARLY YEARS: FROM CRAFTS TO INDUSTRY**

0-8160-2371-9 FACTS ON FILE $17.95

In a little room in this big, black shed—a little room not twenty feet square—forty boys are picking their lives away. The floor of the room is an inclined plane, and a stream of coal pours constantly in. They work here, in this little black hole, all and every day, trying to keep cool in summer, trying to keep warm in winter, picking away among the black coals, bending over 'til their little spines are curved, never saying a word all the live-long day. These little fellows go to work in this cold dreary room at seven o'clock in the morning and work'til it is too dark to see any longer. For this they get $1 to $3 a week. Not three boys in this roomful could read or write. Shut in from everything that is pleasant, with no chance to learn, with nothing to do but work, grinding their little lives away in this dusty room they are no more than the wire screens that separate the great lumps of coal from the small. They had no games; when their day's work is done they are too tired for that. They know nothing but the difference between slate and coal. *The breaker room in the Hickory Colliery near St. Clair, Pennsylvania, described by a contemporary (1877)*

BREAD AND ROSES: THE STRUGGLE OF AMERICAN LABOR, 1865-1915

Gwendolyn **Mink**

Old Labor and New Immigrants in American Political Development: Union, Party and State, 1875-1920

Traces the political implications of union leaders' attitudes toward immigrants

0-8014-1863-1 CORNELL $37.95

0-8014-9680-2 CORNELL PB $15.95

David **Montgomery**

Beyond Equality: Labor and the Radical Republicans, 1862-1872

A landmark study

0-252-00869-3 ILLINOIS PB $15.95

Citizen Worker: The Experience of Workers in the United States with Democracy and the Free Market during the Nineteenth Century

"To understand the ideological and social transformations at work in this era one could have no better guide than David Montgomery, the nation's foremost labor historian—his book is short but rich, full of explosive insights and subtle distinctions"—*The Nation*

0-521-48380-8 CAMBRIDGE PB $13.95

The Fall of the House of Labor: The Workplace, the State, and American Labor Activism, 1865-1925

0-521-22579-5 CAMBRIDGE $47.95

0-521-37982-2 CAMBRIDGE PB $18.95

Lon **Savage**

Thunder in the Mountains: The West Virginia Mine War, 1920-21

A history of the bloody civil insurrection that pitted the coal companies against the Appalachian miners. Forms the backdrop to John Sayles film *Matewan*

0-8229-5426-5 PITTSBURGH PB $14.95

Daniel J. **Walkowitz**

Worker City, Company Town: Iron and Cotton-Worker Protest in Troy and Cohoes, New York, 1855-1884

Why labor was assertive in one place and quiescent in another

0-252-00667-4 ILLINOIS $29.95

0-252-00915-0 ILLINOIS PB $11.95

Anthony F.C. **Wallace**

Rockdale: The Growth of an American Village in the Early Industrial Revolution

0-393-00991-2 NORTON PB $14.95

St. Clair: A Nineteenth-Century Coal Town's Experience with a Disaster-Prone Industry

The anthracite colliery and the workingman's town that was totally dependent on it

0-8014-9900-3 CORNELL PB $15.95

Ulla **Wikander** & others, editors

Protecting Women: Labor Legislation in Europe, the United States, and Australia, 1880-1920

0-252-06464-X ILLINOIS PB $19.95

20th-Century Histories and Studies

Stanley **Aronowitz**

False Promises: The Shaping of American Working-Class Consciousness

First published in 1973

0-8223-1181-X DUKE $34.95

0-8223-1198-4 DUKE PB $18.95

David **Bensman** & Roberta **Lynch**

Rusted Dreams: Hard Times in a Steel Community

"Traces the history of Chicago's Southeast Side, the growth and demise of its neighborhoods, and the steel industry in relation to global competition"—Phyllis Janik, *Chicago Tribune*

0-520-06302-3 CALIFORNIA PB $13.95

Farrell **Dobbes**

Teamster Rebellion: The 1930s Strike and Organizing Drive that Transformed the Labor Movement in the Midwest

From a leader of the strike and a socialist

0-913460-03-6 PATHFINDER PB $16.95

Ronald W. **Edsforth**
Class Conflict and Cultural Consensus: The Making of a Mass Consumer Society in Flint, Michigan
0-8135-1105-4 RUTGERS PB $15.00

Richard **Feldman** & Michael **Betzold**, editors
End of the Line: Autoworkers and the American Dream: An Illustrated Oral History
0-252-06148-9 ILLINOIS PB $11.95

David **Gartman**
Auto Slavery: The Labor Process in the American Automobile Industry, 1897-1950
0-8135-1181-X RUTGERS $45.00
0-8135-1104-6 RUTGERS PB $20.00

William B. **Gould**, IV
A Primer on American Labor Law
An overview of its background, historical development, basic principles, and current status
0-262-07149-5 MIT $37.50
0-262-57099-8 MIT PB $18.50

Charles C. **Heckscher**
The New Unionism: Employee Involvement in the Changing Corporation
A call for a new system of "associational" unionism
0-8014-8357-3 I.L.R. PB $16.95

Ira **Katznelson**
City Trenches: Urban Politics and the Patterning of Class in the United States
"The most persuasive analysis I have ever encountered of...the sources and nature of political turmoil in American cities during the 1960s, and how political order was restored at the end of that turbulent decade"
—Martin Shefter, Cornell University
See also **SPECIAL STUDIES** under **URBAN AMERICA** under **AMERICAN PEOPLE AND PLACES**
0-226-42673-4 CHICAGO PB $17.95

Nelson **Lichtenstein**
Labor's War at Home: The CIO in World War II
"A brilliant peek into the origins of the postwar welfare-warfare state"—Melvyn Dubofsky
0-521-33573-6 CAMBRIDGE PB $18.95

The Most Dangerous Man in Detroit: Walter Reuther and the Fate of American Labor
0-465-09080-X BASIC $35.00

Seymour Martin **Lipset**, editor
Unions in Transition: Entering the Second Century
0-917616-74-X I.C.S. $29.95
0-917616-73-1 I.C.S. PB $12.95

Alice **Lynd** & Staughton **Lynd**, editors
Rank and File: Personal Histories of Working-Class Organizers
Organizers from World War I to the present
0-85345-752-2 MONTHLY REVIEW PB $12.00

Mark H. **Maier**
City Unions: Managing Discontent in New York City
A history of New York's municipal unions and the rise of collective bargaining from 1896 to the present
0-8135-1228-X RUTGERS $28.00
0-8135-1229-8 RUTGERS PB $12.00

August **Meier** & Elliott **Rudwick**
Black Detroit and the Rise of the UAW
"By ignoring the conventional lines between labor and black history, Meier and Rudwick have found an unexplored middle ground—the net of relations between the black community and the white economic institutions"—David Brody, University of California at Davis
0-19-502895-3 OXFORD PB $9.95

Ronald W. **Schatz**
The Electrical Workers: A History of Labor at General Electric and Westinghouse, 1923-60
The rise and decline of unionism at two technologically advanced corporations
0-252-01438-3 ILLINOIS PB $11.95

Patricia Cayo **Sexton**
The War on Labor and the Left: Understanding America's Unique Conservatism
"Patricia Sexton has written a very readable survey of the American Labor-Left, showing how it has met with fiery repressive measures from government and business and how it has nonetheless won sizable victories for American workers and others"—Irving Howe
See also **LIBERALS AND THE LEFT** under **CURRENT POLITICAL THOUGHT AND ISSUES** under **AMERICAN POLITICS AND FOREIGN POLICY**
0-8133-1063-6 WESTVIEW PB $17.95

Harvey **Swados**
On the Line
0-252-06055-5 ILLINOIS PB $9.95

Christopher L. **Tomlins**
The State and the Unions: Labor Relations, Law, and the Organized Labor Movement in America, 1880-1960
"Combines a sure knowledge of the labor movement with a profound understanding of the origins of modern labor law"
— Stanley N. Katz, Princeton University
0-521-31452-6 CAMBRIDGE PB $17.95

Robert **Zieger**
American Workers, American Unions, 1920-1985
0-8018-4943-8 JOHNS HOPKINS $35.00
0-8018-4944-6 JOHNS HOPKINS PB $13.95

Sociological Studies

Michael **Burawoy**
Manufacturing Consent: Changes in the Labor Process under Monopoly Capitalism
An unorthodox Marxist theory of the capitalist labor process, based in part on the author's experiences as a machine operator in a Chicago factory
0-226-08038-2 CHICAGO PB $12.95

William **Form**
Divided We Stand: Working-Class Stratification in America
0-252-01168-6 ILLINOIS $29.95

David **Halle**
America's Working Man: Work, Home and Politics Among Blue-Collar Property Owners
Based on interviews at an automated chemical plant in New Jersey
0-226-31365-4 CHICAGO $29.95
0-226-31366-2 CHICAGO PB $18.95

Rosabeth M. **Kanter**
The Change Masters: Innovation for Productivity in the American Corporation
0-671-52800-9 SIMON & SCHUSTER PB $12.00

William **Kornblum**
Blue Collar Community
The complex social organization of the South Chicago steel-mill community
FOREWORD BY MORRIS JANOWITZ
0-226-45037-6 CHICAGO $14.95

Lillian **Rubin**
Worlds of Pain: Life in the Working-Class Family
0-465-09248-9 BASIC PB $16.00

Socialists, Communists, and Radicals

Paul **Avrich**
Anarchist Portraits
A collection of portraits of anarchists in America, Russia, and Europe; American topics include "Proudhon and America," "Sacco and Vanzetti: The Italian Anarchist Background," and "Mollie Steimer: An Anarchist Life"
0-691-04753-7 PRINCETON $55.00

Daniel **Bell**
Marxian Socialism in the United States
0-8014-8309-3 CORNELL PB $16.95

Theodore **Draper**
The Roots of American Communism
0-929587-00-6 DEE PB $11.95

Mari Jo **Buhle**

Women and American Socialism, 1870-1920

"Throws new light not only on the history of socialism in this period but on temperance, populism, labor, social purity, and even on progressivism"
—Eli Zaretsky, *Reviews in American History*

0-252-00873-1 ILLINOIS $34.95
0-252-01045-0 ILLINOIS PB $12.95

David **Caute**

The Fellow-Travellers: Intellectual Friends of Communism

The revised edition of Caute's highly praised work

0-300-04195-0 YALE $45.00
0-300-03875-5 YALE PB $20.00

Richard H. **Crossman**, editor

The God that Failed

The classic statement of disillusionment with communism

FOREWORD BY NORMAN PODHORETZ

0-89526-867-1 REGNERY PB $12.95

Peter **Drucker**

Max Shachtman and His Left: A Socialist's Odyssey through the "American Century"

The Trotskyist Max Shachtman died in 1972 in obscurity. He played an honorable role in denouncing Stalin's Moscow trials, led various Trotskyist sects in the '30s, '40s, and '50s, and moved among interesting circles, knowing or influencing (at various times) Dwight MacDonald, Irving Howe, Irving Kristol, Seymour Martin Lipset, C.L.R. James, and Michael Harrington. "[Charts] the dynamics of the political sect, with its patriarchal hierarchies, punitive rituals of self-discipline and self-abasement, and internal rivalries"
—Maurice Isserman, author of *Which Side Were You On?: The American Communist Party during the Second World War*

0-391-03815-X HUMANITIES $49.95
0-391-03816-8 HUMANITIES PB $18.50

Richard **Flacks**

Marketing History: The Radical Tradition in American Life

0-231-04832-7 COLUMBIA $50.00

Philip S. **Foner**, editor

Mother Jones Speaks: Collected Writings and Speeches

0-913460-88-5 PATHFINDER $70.00
0-913460-89-3 PATHFINDER PB $28.95

John **Chalberg**

Emma Goldman: American Individualist

An emigrée from Russia, Goldman was a proponent of free love and violent revolution who was eventually deported from the United States for her radical politics

1-88674-636-2 HARPERCOLLINS PB $15.95

Candace **Falk**

Love, Anarchy and Emma Goldman: A Biography

"With marvelous clarity and depth, Candace Falk illuminates for us an Emma Goldman shaped by her time yet presaging in her life the situation and conflicts of women in our time"
—Tillie Olsen

0-8135-1513-0 RUTGERS PB $14.95

Emma **Goldman**

Living My Life

Volume 1

0-486-22543-7 DOVER PB $8.95

Volume 2

0-486-22544-5 DOVER PB $10.95

James R. **Green**

Grass-Roots Socialism: Radical Movements in the Southwest, 1895-1943

0-8071-0773-5 LSU PB $14.95

Irving **Howe**

Socialism and America

Six essays from a leading American intellectual

0-15-683520-7 HARCOURT BRACE PB $5.95

Maurice **Isserman**

If I Had a Hammer...: The Death of the Old Left and the Birth of the New Left

0-252-06338-4 ILLINOIS PB $12.95

Mark E. **Kann**

Middle-Class Radicalism in Santa Monica

"Though superficially a narrow study of 'radicalism in one city,' it actually says more about the nature of, and prospects for, the American Left today than any book I can remember"—Philip Green, Smith College

0-87722-526-5 TEMPLE PB $16.95

Roger **Keeran**

The Communist Party and the Auto Workers' Unions

"The first...to separate the genuine achievement of the communists in the labor movement during the New Deal both from the hagiography of...admirers...and from the knee-jerk anticommunism of the right"—John H.M. Laslett

0-253-15754-4 INDIANA $25.00
0-7178-0639-1 INTERNATIONAL PUB PB $8.75

Harvey **Klehr**

Far Left of Center: The American Radical Left Today

0-88738-217-7 TRANSACTION $32.95
0-88738-875-2 TRANSACTION PB $18.95

Harvey **Klehr** & others

The Secret World of American Communism

"This book contains the first new revelation about American communism in a generation. It is superbly edited and admirably presented" —Theodore Draper

0-300-06183-8 YALE $30.00

John H.M. **Laslett** & Seymour Martin **Lipset**, editors

Failure of a Dream?: Essays in the History of American Socialism

Revised edition

0-520-04452-5 CALIFORNIA PB $16.00

Stephen **Meyer**

"Stalin over Wisconsin": The Making and Unmaking of Militant Unionism, 1900-1950

0-8135-1798-2 RUTGERS $45.00

Bruce **Nelson**

Workers on the Waterfront: Seamen, Longshoremen, and Unionism in the 1930s

0-252-06144-6 ILLINOIS PB $11.95

Bruce C. **Nelson**

Beyond the Martyrs: A Social History of Chicago's Anarchists

Focuses on the rank-and-file workers whose lives exploded in the Haymarket tragedy

0-8135-1345-6 RUTGERS PB $15.00

Eileen **Philipson**

Ethel Rosenberg: Behind the Myths

"Contributes to women's history and biography and to radical history, particularly to our understastanding of family and gender relations"—Nancy Chodorow

0-8135-1917-9 RUTGERS PB $14.95

Bud **Schultz** & Ruth **Schultz**

Recollections of Political Repression in America

Oral histories of the victims. "For all the outrages described in this book, it is not defeat that resounds but a steadfast defiance and the knowledge that the fight for civil liberties is a continuous one"—*NY Times Book Review*

0-520-07197-2 CALIFORNIA PB $15.95

Alan M. **Wald**

The New York Intellectuals: The Rise and Decline of the Anti-Stalinist Left from the 1930s to the 1980s

"Wald's grasp of the ideological twists and turns of his protagonists is first-rate. ...His story has an epic sweep"—*Village Voice*

0-8078-4169-2 NORTH CAROLINA PB $17.95

James **Weinstein**

The Decline of Socialism in America: 1912-1925

A recently reissued history

0-8135-1068-6 RUTGERS $40.00

The Decline of Organized Labor

Michael **Goldfield**

The Decline of Organized Labor in the United States

0-226-30103-6 CHICAGO PB $13.95

Juliet B. **Schor**

The Overworked American: The Unexpected Decline of Leisure

"Deserves to be widely read, and to rekindle a debate about working hours that was prematurely extinguished decades ago" —Robert Kuttner, *NY Times Book Review*

0-465-05434-X BASIC PB $13.00

Biography

Mary V. **Dearborn**

Queen of Bohemia: The Life of Louise Bryant

Known as the wife of radical journalist John Reed, Louise Bryant was a pioneering reporter in her own right, as well as a social activist, a committed feminist, and a champion of sexual freedom. The first comprehensive account of her life introduces us to a central presence on the stage of our century, traveling from Greenwich Village to the Russian Front and through friendships with Eugene O'Neill, Sylvia Beach, and Janet Flanner

0-395-68396-3 HOUGHTON MIFFLIN $24.95

Richard Griswold **del Castillo** & others

Cesar Chavez: A Triumph of the Spirit

0-8061-2758-9 OKLAHOMA $19.95

Paul **Avrich**

An American Anarchist: The Life of Voltairine De Cleyre

"Avrich has greatly enriched our knowledge and understanding of life as it was for hundreds of ordinary men and women who dared to stand for a new order"—*Choice*

0-691-04657-3 PRINCETON $49.50

Melvyn **Dubofsky** & Warren **Van Tine**, editors

Labor Leaders in America

Profiles include Samuel Gompers, Eugene V. Debs, Sidney Hillman, A. Philip Randolph, Jimmy Hoffa, and Cesar Chavez

0-252-01327-1 ILLINOIS $39.95
0-252-01343-3 ILLINOIS PB $14.95

Rosalyn **Baxandall**

Words on Fire: The Life and Writing of Elizabeth Gurley Flynn

The heroine of left-wing causes (1890-1964)

0-8135-1240-9 RUTGERS $40.00
0-8135-1241-7 RUTGERS PB $15.00

Elizabeth Gurley **Flynn**

Rebel Girl: An Autobiography, My First Life

0-7178-0368-6 INTERNATIONAL PUB PB $9.95

Alix Kates **Shulman**, editor

Red Emma Speaks: An Emma Goldman Reader

0-391-03952-0 HUMANITIES $19.95

Harold **Livesay**

Samuel Gompers and Organized Labor in America

0-88133-751-X WAVELAND PB $10.50

Steven **Fraser**

Labor Will Rule: Sidney Hillman and the Rise of American Labor

Hillman forced labor issues onto a national consciousness obsessed with consumerism and social climbing. A Lithuanian immigrant and founder of the CIO, his amazing life serves as a microcosm of the American labor movement

0-8014-8126-0 CORNELL PB $16.95

Craig **Phelan**

Divided Loyalties: The Public and Private Life of Labor Leader John Mitchell

The first comprehensive biography of the United Mine Workers leader by a historian

0-7914-2088-4 SUNY PB $21.75

Steve **Nelson**

Steve Nelson, American Radical

0-8229-3441-8 PITTSBURGH $49.95
0-8229-5471-0 PITTSBURGH PB $19.95

Nick **Salvatore**

Eugene V. Debs: Citizen and Socialist

Winner of the Dunning and Bancroft prizes. "This book's distinction is its exploration of Debs's social milieu, its analysis of his tortured passage from right-wing craft unionism to left-wing socialism, and its penetrating insights into the failure of socialism in America" —William N. Harbaugh, *New Republic*

0-252-01148-1 ILLINOIS PB $13.95

Eugene V. Debs

John **Barnard**

Walter Reuther and the Rise of the Autoworkers

0-673-39320-8 FORESMAN PB $15.53

Dorothy **Gallagher**

All the Right Enemies: The Life and Murder of Carlo Tresca

The 1943 murder of the noted socialist-turned-anarchist has never been solved

0-8135-1310-3 RUTGERS $24.95
0-14-012400-4 PENGUIN PB $8.95

Topics in American Studies

General Histories

Eric **Foner**, editor

The New American History

Essays by leading historians, part of the *Critical Perspectives of the Past* series

0-87722-698-9 TEMPLE $39.95

David W. **Noble**

The End of American History: Democracy, Capitalism, and the Metaphor of Two Worlds in Anglo-American Historical Writing

0-8166-1416-4 MINNESOTA PB $14.95

Economic History

Michael A. **Bernstein**

The Great Depression: Delayed Recovery and Economic Change in America, 1929-1939

A serious economic analysis of the Depression years

0-521-37985-7 CAMBRIDGE PB $16.95

Thomas C. **Cochran**

Frontiers of Change: Early Industrialism in America

0-19-503284-5 OXFORD PB $14.95

Milton **Friedman** & Anna Jacobson **Schwartz**

A Monetary History of the United States, 1867-1960

"The numerical account is dexterously and gracefully interwoven with a history of monetary institutions, legislation, policies, personalities, and politics"—James Tobin, *American Economic Review*

0-691-00354-8 PRINCETON PB $39.50

Douglass C. **North**

Economic Growth of the United States, 1790-1860

A classic study by the Nobel Prize winner

0-393-00346-9 NORTON PB $11.95

Martin J. **Sklar**

The Corporate Reconstruction of American Capitalism, 1890-1916: The Market, the Law and Politics

0-521-31382-1 CAMBRIDGE PB $20.95

Herbert **Stein**

Presidential Economics: The Making of Economic Policy from Roosevelt to Reagan and Beyond

0-8447-3851-4 AEI PB $19.75

Farming in America

Craig **Canine**

Dream Reaper: The Story of an Old-Fashioned Inventor in the High-Tech, High Stakes World of Modern Technology

A lively account of the invention of a new reaper combine in the '90s, as well as a general history of American large-scale agriculture

0-679-41272-7 KNOPF $25.00

Pete **Daniel**

Breaking the Land: The Transformation of Cotton, Tobacco, and Rice Cultures since 1880

0-252-01391-3 ILLINOIS PB $14.95

Steven **Hahn** & Jonathan **Prude**, editors

The Countryside in the Age of Capitalist Transformation

0-8078-1666-3 NORTH CAROLINA $49.95
0-8078-4139-0 NORTH CAROLINA PB $16.95

Victor Davis **Hanson**

Fields Without Dreams: Defending the Agrarian Idea

A Beautifully written essay, by a classics professor, of the decline of the family farm in America

0-684-82299-7 FREE PRESS $23.00
0-684-835570-3 FREE PRESS PB $12.00

David Mas **Masumoto**

Epitaph for a Peach: Four Seasons on My Family Farm

See also **HISTORIES AND PERSONAL ACCOUNTS** under **FARMING AND AGRICULTURE** in **SCIENCE**

0-06-251025-8 HARPERCOLLINS PB $12.00

Howard S. **Russell**

Long, Deep Furrow: Three Centuries of Farming in New England

EDITED AND ABRIDGED BY MARK LAPPING

0-87451-214-X NEW ENGLAND PB $24.95

Patrick H. **Mooney** & Theo J. **Majka**

Farmers' and Farm Workers' Movements: Social Protest in American Agriculture

"Not since Carl Taylor's *The Farmers' Movement* was published forty years ago have American sociologists taken on the ambitious agenda of examining the history and current prospects of farmers' and farm workers' movements and struggles in a single book. Mooney and Majka's study is an essential source for understanding the history of these movements, their contemporary significance, and the dilemma of strategy they now face"—Frederik H. Buttel

0-8057-3870-3 TWAYNE PB $15.95

John L. **Shover**

First Majority, Last Minority: The Transforming of Rural Life in America

0-87580-056-4 NORTHERN ILLINOIS $22.00
0-87580-522-1 NORTHERN ILLINOIS PB $14.00

M. Suzanne **Sontag** & Margaret M. **Bubolz**

Families on Small Farms: Case Studies in Human Ecology

0-87013-409-4 MICHIGAN STATE $45.00

Business History

Alfred D. **Chandler**, Jr.

Strategy and Structure: Chapters in the History of the American Industrial Enterprise

An influential study of corporate reorganization

0-262-53009-0 MIT PB $17.50

The Visible Hand: The Managerial Revolution in American Business

A Pulitzer Prize-winning study of the emergence of large-scale organizations

0-674-94051-2 HARVARD $48.00
0-674-94052-0 HARVARD PB $16.95

Alfred D. **Chandler**, Jr. &
Herman **Daems**, editors

Managerial Hierarchies: Comparative Perspectives on the Rise of the Modern Industrial Enterprise

The beginnings of a more comparative economic history

0-674-54740-3 HARVARD $24.95
0-674-54741-1 HARVARD PB $9.95

Jonathan **Hughes**

The Vital Few: The Entrepreneur and American Economic Progress

0-19-504038-4 OXFORD PB $15.95

Glenn **Porter**

The Rise of Big Business

0-88295-882-8 HARLAN DAVIDSON PB $8.95

The Business Barons

Harold C. **Livesay**

American Made: Men Who Shaped the American Economy

An interesting set of biographical vignettes

0-673-39346-1 FORESMAN PB $26.33

Andrew Carnegie and the Rise of Big Business

The short version of Carnegie's life

0-673-39344-5 FORESMAN PB $16.20

Joseph F. **Wall**

Andrew Carnegie

The long version of Carnegie's life

0-8229-3828-6 PITTSBURGH $49.95
0-8229-5904-6 PITTSBURGH PB $22.50

Robert **Lenzner**

The Great Getty

Popular biography of the man long known as the world's richest magnate

0-517-56222-7 CROWN $18.95

Maury **Klein**

The Life and Legend of Jay Gould

Gould portrayed as far more complex and sympathetic than the amoral, daring investor and railroad czar of popular image

0-8018-2880-5 JOHNS HOPKINS $39.95

Ron **Chernow**

The House of Morgan

Winner of the National Book Award for Non-Fiction. "Utterly absorbing…Not merely the chronicle of an institution, but indeed of American finance and society"
—*New York Observer*

0-671-73400-8 TOUCHSTONE PB $16.00

Matthew **Josephson**

The Robber Barons: The Great American Capitalists, 1861-1901

0-8488-0091-5 AMEREON $28.95
0-15-676790-2 HARCOURT BRACE PB $12.95

Wall Street Culture of the '80s and '90s

Connie **Bruck**

The Predators' Ball: The Junk Bond Raiders and the Man Who Staked Them

A glimpse inside Michael Milken's securities empire and the giant deals he engineered. Intelligent analysis and entertaining stories, including feared raider Carl Icahn's Monopoly game with real money

See also **WALL STREET AND CORPORATE FINANCE** under **BUSINESS, INDUSTRY, AND FINANCE** in **BUSINESS AND REFERENCE**

0-14-012090-4 PENGUIN PB $12.95

Bryan **Burrough** & John **Helyar**

Barbarians at the Gate: The Fall of RJR Nabisco

The largest corporate takeover in American history covered in detail by two business reporters; the gripping story of buyout kings, Wall Street institutions, and gigantic corporations caught in a struggle for power

0-06-016172-8 HARPERCOLLINS PB $22.50

Michael **Lewis**

The Money Culture

The author of the outstanding *Liar's Poker,* Lewis relates more tales from his days as a trainee at Salomon Brothers, investment banker, and financial journalist in London and later Japan. "A wry, wicked account…falls somewhere between *Wealth of Nations* and *Animal House*"—*Newsweek*

0-393-03037-7 PENGUIN PB $19.95

Liar's Poker: Rising Through the Wreckage on Wall Street

0-14-014345-9 PENGUIN PB $11.95

James B. **Stewart**

Den of Thieves

"Stewart takes the reader through the maze of arcane Wall Street dealings as if he were writing a detective story"—*Philadelphia Inquirer*

0-671-63802-5 TOUCHSTONE PB $12.00

History of Consumerism

Though it is difficult to avoid clichés about the spread of conformity and the stimulation of unnecessary demands, several historians have written works that provide fresh insights into American culture.

Susan **Porter Benson**

Counter Cultures: Saleswomen, Managers, and Customers in American Department Stores, 1890-1940

0-252-01252-6 ILLINOIS $27.50
0-252-06013-X ILLINOIS PB $12.95

Daniel **Horowitz**

The Morality of Spending: Attitudes toward the Consumer Society in America, 1875-1940

0-929587-77-4 DEE PB $12.95

William **Leach**

Land of Desire: Merchants, Power, and the Rise of a New American Culture

"With its extraordinarily rich panorama of persons, things, and events, and its continual flow of pertinent commentary and provocative speculation, this volume deepens our understanding of the cultural effects of consumer society, how they came about, and what degradations they imply for civil life" —Alan Trachtenberg

0-679-75411-3 VINTAGE PB $16.00

David E. **Shi**

The Simple Life: Plain Living and High Thinking in American Culture

0-19-504013-9 OXFORD PB $12.95

History of Advertising

Stuart **Ewen**

Captains of Consciousness

0-07-019846-2 MCGRAW HILL PB $6.95

Roland **Marchand**

Advertising the American Dream: Making Way for Modernity, 1920-1940

How advertising manipulated modern art and photography to promote an enduring consumption ethic

0-520-05253-6 CALIFORNIA $50.00
0-520-05885-2 CALIFORNIA PB $21.95

James B. **Twitchell**

Adcult USA: The Triumph of Advertising in American Culture

0-231-10324-7 COLUMBIA $24.95

The lingo of Adcult is not tied to folk traditions or wisdom. It is tied to a product. Without a second thought, we immediately recognize such phrases as the "Teflon president," "McPaper," "Velveeta-voiced," "Mr. Clean politician," "doc in the box," "Maalox moment," "Pepto Bismol pink," and even "the Edsel of…" because the codes of communication have been resettled on advertising claims. Think only of the hundreds of times you've heard turns on "I can't believe I ate the whole thing," "You deserve a break today," "When E.F. Hutton talks," and "Where the rubber meets the road," and you will realize that, like jazz riffs, we play with the language of Adcult because we know that the tune is already familiar.
ADCULT USA: THE TRIUMPH OF ADVERTISING IN AMERICAN CULTURE

History of Science and Technology

I. Bernard **Cohen**

Science and the Founding Fathers: Science in the Political Thought of Thomas Jefferson, Benjamin Franklin, John Adams, and James Madison

0-393-03501-8 NORTON $25.00
0-393-31510-X NORTON PB $15.95

David F. **Noble**

Forces of Production: A Social History of Industrial Automation

"Approaches technology from a leftist perspective, a viewpoint that is largely lacking in the existing historical literature" —Philip M. Boffey, *NY Times Book Review*

0-19-504046-5 OXFORD PB $17.95

James Madison

Industrial Revolutions

Roger **Bilstein**

Flight in America: From the Wrights to the Astronauts

"From technological trends and research and development to the effect of air travel on the expansion of major league baseball in the 1950s and 1960s…A superior work"—William F. Trimble, *Journal of American History*

0-8018-4828-8 JOHNS HOPKINS PB $16.95

James J. **Flink**

The Automobile Age

A sweeping social history of the car and its impact on American society

See also **CARS** under **BOATS, CARS, PLANES, AND TRAINS** in **FOOD, TRAVEL, AND LEISURE**

0-262-56055-0 MIT PB $19.00

Brooke **Hindle** & Steven **Lubar**

Engines of Change: The American Industrial Revolution, 1790-1860

0-87474-539-X SMITHSONIAN PB $16.95

David A. **Hounshell**

From the American System to Mass Production, 1800-1932: The Development of Manufacturing Technology in the United States

0-8018-3158-X JOHNS HOPKINS PB $18.95

David A. **Hounshell** & John Kenly **Smith**, Jr.

Science and Corporate Strategy: DuPont R&D, 1902-1980

A corporate history of the role of research in the development of DuPont products

0-521-32767-9 CAMBRIDGE $44.95

Thomas P. **Hughes**

American Genesis: A Century of Technological Enthusiasm, 1870-1970

0-14-009741-4 PENGUIN PB $17.95

Linda **Leuzzi**
Life in America 100 Years Ago: Transportation
Slender, profusely illustrated series of books. This one shows how the steam and gasoline engines revolutionized American transportation at the turn of the century and made Americans the constant travelers they are today
0-7910-2841-0 CHELSEA HOUSE EDITION $18.95

Albro **Martin**
Railroads Triumphant: The Growth, Rejection, and Rebirth of a Vital American Force
An intriguing examination of the history and future of railroads in America
0-19-503853-3 OXFORD $35.00

Otto **Mayr** & Robert C. **Post**, editors
Yankee Enterprise: The Rise of the American System of Manufactures
0-87474-631-0 SMITHSONIAN PB $14.95

David F. **Noble**
America by Design: Science, Technology, and the Rise of Corporate Capitalism
0-19-502618-7 OXFORD PB $12.95

Richard **Preston**
American Steel
A revealing portrait of the steel industry in America, and a detailed account of the building of a billion-dollar business
0-380-71822-7 AVON PB $11.00

Inventions

Hugh G. **Aitken**
Syntony and Spark: The Origins of Radio
0-691-02392-1 PRINCETON PB $17.95

Tom **Crouch**
The Bishop's Boys: A Life of Wilbur and Orville Wright
Focuses on the brothers' early family life and their technological innovation in the context of its time
0-393-30695-X NORTON PB $18.95

A Dream of Wings: Americans and the Airplane, 1875-1905
0-87474-325-7 SMITHSONIAN PB $19.95

John **Ellis**
The Social History of the Machine Gun
"It's hard to imagine a more stimulating way to study human destructiveness"
— Christopher Lehmann-Haupt, *NY Times*
FOREWORD BY EDWARD C. EZELL
0-405-14209-9 AYER $19.95
0-8018-3358-2 JOHNS HOPKINS PB $13.95

Rachel **Fermi** & Esther **Samra**
Picturing the Bomb: Photographs from the Secret World of the Manhattan Project
INTRODUCTION BY RICHARD RHODES
0-8109-3735-2 ABRAMS $39.95

James G. **Hershberg**
James B. Conant: Harvard to Hiroshima and the Making of the Nuclear Age
See also **HISTORY OF SCIENCE** in **AMERICA** under **HISTORY OF SCIENCE AND TECHNOLOGY** under **SCIENCE AND TECHNOLOGY** in **SCIENCE**
0-8047-2619-1 STANFORD PB $29.95

James B. Conant

Reese V. **Jenkins**
Images and Enterprise: Technology and the American Photographic Industry, 1839-1925
Technological changes that culminated in George Eastman's creation of the Kodak system of amateur photography in the 1880s
0-8018-3549-6 JOHNS HOPKINS PB $24.95

The Space Age

Andrew **Chaikin**
A Man on the Moon: The Voyage of the Apollo Astronauts
"The authoritative masterpiece"—*LA Times*. A *New York Times* Notable Book of the Year
0-14-009706-6 PENGUIN PB $15.95

Tom **Wolfe**
The Right Stuff
The full, irreverent story of the first Americans in space
See also **REPORTING** under **20TH-CENTURY AMERICAN ESSAYS AND JOURNALISM** in **LITERATURE OF THE AMERICAS**
0-374-25033-2 FS&G $30.00
0-553-27556-9 BDD PB $6.99

Michael **Collins**
Liftoff: The Story of America's Adventure in Space
The American space program, by an astronaut
0-8021-3188-3 GROVE PB $12.95

Donald K. **Slayton** & Michael **Cassut**
Deke!: U.S. Manned Space from Mercury to the Shuttle
By the first chief of America's Astronaut Corps and a key figure in the space program
0-312-85918-X FORGE PB $14.95

Paul B. **Stares**
The Militarization of Space: U.S. Policy, 1945-1994
The change from relatively peaceful exploration of space to the beginnings of a new militarization in the late 1970s
0-8014-1810-0 CORNELL $38.50
0-8014-9471-0 CORNELL PB $15.95

Technology and Culture

Claude S. **Fischer**
America Calling: A Social History of the Telephone to 1940
0-520-08647-3 CALIFORNIA PB $16.00

Michael **O'Malley**
Keeping Watch: A History of American Time
1-56098-672-7 SMITHSONIAN PB $16.95

Carroll W. **Pursell**, Jr.
The Machine in America: A Social History of Technology
From the medieval farm implements brought by the first colonists to the invisible links of the Internet, how technology has affected our lives
See also **HISTORY OF SCIENCE** in **AMERICA** under **HISTORY OF SCIENCE AND TECHNOLOGY** under **SCIENCE AND TECHNOLOGY** in **SCIENCE**
0-8018-4817-2 JOHNS HOPKINS $45.00
0-8018-4818-0 JOHNS HOPKINS PB $15.95

Cecelia **Tichi**
Shifting Gears: Technology, Literature, Culture in Modernist America
0-8078-1715-5 NORTH CAROLINA $45.00
0-8078-4167-6 NORTH CAROLINA PB $17.95

Science and Machines

Daniel J. **Kevles**
In the Name of Eugenics: Genetics and the Uses of Human Heredity
"It stands as a powerful warning against anyone today who would use the fruits of legitimate science to bolster arguments and policies that echo the social and racial prejudice of the past"—*Washington Post*
See also **GENETIC ENGINEERING AND BIOTECHNOLOGY** under **GENETICS** under **LIFE SCIENCES** in **SCIENCE**
0-674-44557-0 HARVARD PB $16.95

John S. **Haller**, Jr.

American Medicine in Transition, 1840-1910

0-252-00806-5 ILLINOIS.......$39.95

Regina **Morantz-Sanchez**

Sympathy and Science: Women Physicians in American Medicine

See also **THE MEDICAL PROFESSION** under **MEDICINE** in **SCIENCE**

0-19-503627-1 OXFORD.......$24.95
0-19-504985-3 OXFORD PB.......$12.95

James **Patterson**

The Dread Disease: Cancer and Modern American Culture

0-674-21625-3 HARVARD.......$36.00
0-674-21626-1 HARVARD PB.......$17.95

Nathan **Reingold**, editor

Science in Nineteenth-Century America: A Documentary History

0-226-70947-7 CHICAGO PB.......$15.00

Charles E. **Rosenberg**

The Cholera Years: The United States in 1832, 1849, and 1866

"A masterful analysis of the moral and social interest attached to epidemic disease, providing generally applicable insights into how the connections between social change, changes in knowledge, and changes in technical practice may be conceived"—Steven Shapin, *TLS*

0-226-72677-0 CHICAGO PB.......$11.95

Randy **Shilts**

And the Band Played On: Politics, People, and the AIDS Epidemic

The groundbreaking masterpiece of investigative reporting reveals, in the mishandling of the AIDS epidemic, the inadequacies of a government obsessed with budget considerations, health authorities more interested in politics than public health, and scientists overly concerned with international prestige. "A heroic work of journalism on what must rank as one of the foremost catastrophes of modern history" —*NY Times*

See also **AIDS AND HEALTH** under **GAY, LESBIAN, AND BISEXUAL STUDIES** in **SOCIAL STUDIES**

0-14-023221-4 VIKING PB.......$15.00

Randy Shilts

Paul **Starr**

The Social Transformation of American Medicine

See also **HISTORY OF MEDICINE** under **MEDICINE** in **SCIENCE**

0-465-07935-0 BASIC BOOKS PB.......$20.00

Intellectual History

Guided by Christopher Lasch's extraordinary set of essays *The New Radicalism in America, 1889-1963*, now more than 25 years old, many of the newer works focus more on a history of intellectuals than on particular ideas. Some of the studies of slavery and racism (particularly by David Brion Davis) suggest the rich possibilities for intellectual history. The list below represents a mix of both newer works and some employing an older approach that should not be ignored.

Leslie Cohen **Berlowitz**, editor

America in Theory

Sixteen prominent thinkers examine the myths and theories that make up the idea of modern America

0-19-505396-6 OXFORD.......$29.95

Daniel J. **Boorstin**

The Lost World of Thomas Jefferson

The concepts of the Jeffersonian circle: God, nature, equality, toleration, education, and government, and the worldview that underlies them

See also **THE NEW NATION** under **US HISTORY TO THE CIVIL WAR**

0-226-06497-2 CHICAGO PB.......$14.95

Lawrence **Buell**

New England Literary Culture: From Revolution through Renaissance

0-521-37801-X CAMBRIDGE PB.......$23.95

Henry Steele **Commager**

The American Mind: An Interpretation of American Thought and Character since the 1880s

0-300-00046-4 YALE PB.......$20.00

Robert **Dawidoff**

The Genteel Tradition and the Sacred Rage: High Culture Versus Democracy in Adams, James, and Santayana

0-8078-2017-2 NORTH CAROLINA.......$34.95

Richard Wightman **Fox** & James T. **Kloppenberg**, editors

A Companion to American Thought

"Edited by two of America's most distinguished intellectual and cultural historians, *A Companion to American Thought* reflects the best contemporary scholarship across the humanities and social sciences. Its wide-ranging entries will make this an indispensable reference work for anyone interested in American culture"—Alan Brinkley

See also **EASTERN** under **20TH-CENTURY SPIRITUAL LEADERS** under **SPIRITUALITY** in **RELIGION, SPIRITUALITY, AND PHILOSOPHY**

1-55786-268-0 BLACKWELL.......$39.95

James B. **Gilbert**

Work without Salvation: America's Intellectual and Industrial Alienation, 1880-1910

0-8018-1954-7 JOHNS HOPKINS.......$30.00

Jack P. **Greene**

The Intellectual Construction of America: Exceptionalism and Identity from 1492 to 1800

An expansion of the Phelps lectures at New York University from 1990

0-8078-2097-0 NORTH CAROLINA.......$34.95
0-8139-1622-4 VIRGINIA.......$75.00

Carol **Highsmith** & Ted **Landphair**

The Library of Congress: America's Memory

Photographs with accompanying text provide an insider's look at the world's largest library

1-55591-188-9 FULCRUM PB.......$24.95

Richard **Hofstadter**

Anti-Intellectualism in American Life

1964 Pulitzer Prize winner. "A rich, complex, shifting picture of the life of the mind in a society dominated by the ideal of practical success" —Robert Peel, *Christian Science Monitor*

See also **RECENT PHILOSOPHY** under **THEORY AND PHILOSOPHY** under **EDUCATION** in **SOCIAL STUDIES**

0-394-70317-0 RANDOM HOUSE PB.......$16.00

David A. **Hollinger**

In the American Province: Studies in the History and Historiography of Ideas

0-8018-3826-6 JOHNS HOPKINS PB.......$13.95

Robert **Hughes**

The Culture of Complaint: The Fraying of America

0-19-507676-1 OXFORD.......$22.00
0-446-67034-0 WARNER PB.......$11.99

David **Isay** & Harvey **Wang**

Holding On: Dreamers, Visionaries, Eccentrics and Other American Heroes

A longtime Woolworth's lunch-counter waitress. A moonshiner. Snake handlers in Jolo, West Virginia. The caretaker of America's only coon-dog graveyard in Vina, Alabama. Based on David Isay's award-winning NPR radio series of profiles, *The American Folklife Radio Project*, illustrated by Harvey Wang's incisive portraits, and introduced by none other than Henry Roth, this book documents a rare kind of American

FOREWORD BY HENRY ROTH

0-393-03754-1 NORTON.......$25.00

Russell **Jacoby**

The Last Intellectuals: American Culture in the Age of Academe

Analyzes the disappearance of the nonacademic intellectual—people like Dwight Macdonald, Lewis Mumford, and Edmund Wilson—in an age dominated by suburbanization and gentrification

0-374-52175-1 FS&G PB $14.00

Dwight Macdonald

Michael **Kammen**

Mystic Chords of Memory: The Transformation of Tradition in American Culture

A panoramic cultural history that asks how "the land of the future" acquired a past and to what extent our collective memory of that past—as embodied in our traditions—has been distorted or even manufactured. "Brilliant, idiosyncratic…presented with superlative style laced with wit"—*NY Times Book Review*

0-394-57769-8 KNOPF $40.00
0-679-74177-1 VINTAGE PB $23.00

James T. **Kloppenberg**

Uncertain Victory: Social Democracy and Progressivism in European and American Thought, 1870-1920

Pivotal intellectual figures—William James, John Dewey, Dilthey, Green, Sidgwick, Fouillee—and their influence on the next generation—Lippmann, Bernstein, Weber, and others

0-19-505304-4 OXFORD PB $19.95

Christopher **Lasch**

The Culture of Narcissism

Trenchant critique of "the dotage of bourgeois society"

0-393-30738-7 NORTON PB $11.95

The New Radicalism in America, 1889-1963: The Intellectual as a Social Type

0-393-30319-5 NORTON PB $8.95

Henry F. **May**

The End of American Innocence: A Study of the First Years of Our Own Time, 1912-1917

Traces the intellectual and cultural transformations associated with the 1920s to their origins

0-231-09652-6 COLUMBIA $49.50
0-231-09653-4 COLUMBIA PB $18.50

The Enlightenment in America

0-19-502367-6 OXFORD PB $17.95

Roderick **Nash**

Wilderness and the American Mind

See also **ESSAYS** under **THE OUTDOORS** in **FOOD, TRAVEL, AND LEISURE**

0-300-02910-1 YALE PB $16.00

Vernon Louis **Parrington**

Main Currents in American Thought

Volume 1
The Colonial Mind, 1620-1800

0-8061-2080-0 OKLAHOMA PB $18.95

Volume 2
The Romantic Revolution in America, 1800-1860

0-8061-2081-9 OKLAHOMA PB $19.95

Lewis **Perry**

Intellectual Life in America: A History

The background and roles of intellectuals in different eras of American history

0-226-66101-6 CHICAGO PB $18.95

James B. **Twitchell**

Carnival Culture: The Trashing of Taste in America

A provocative examination of the forces that have sullied popular taste in the United States. "An amusing insightful…revelation of why the castle of cards that was academic and cultural canonicity in America tumbled"—Ray Brown, founder, Popular Culture Association

0-231-07830-7 COLUMBIA $34.50

Katharine **Washburn** & John **Thornton**, editors

Dumbing Down: Essays on the Strip-Mining of American Culture

0-393-03829-7 NORTON $25.00

R. Jackson **Wilson**

Figures of Speech: American Writers and the Literary Marketplace, from Benjamin Franklin to Emily Dickinson

Was publication, as Emily Dickinson wrote, "the auction of the mind?" Wilson suggests that the writers he studies were never free from the tensions that the new capitalism evoked

0-8018-4003-1 JOHNS HOPKINS PB $15.95

New York Intellectuals

Alexander **Bloom**

Prodigal Sons: The New York Intellectuals and Their World

In America the fusing of Marxism and modernism was attempted by the so-called New York intellectuals, chief among whom were Irving Howe and Lionel Trilling

0-19-505177-7 OXFORD PB $11.95

Alan M. **Wald**

The New York Intellectuals: The Rise and Decline of the Anti-Stalinist Left from the 1930s to the 1980s

0-8078-1716-3 NORTH CAROLINA $39.95

Cultural and Social History

Elizabeth **Aldrich**

From the Ballroom to Hell: Grace and Folly in Nineteenth-Century Dance

Evoking a mostly forgotten social milieu, Aldrich describes with wit and insight the ballroom dance, etiquette, music, and fashion

See also **THE 19TH CENTURY** under **DANCE** in **PERFORMING ARTS AND MEDIA**

0-8101-0913-1 NORTHWESTERN PB $19.95

Erik **Barnouw**

Tube of Plenty: The Evolution of American Television

See also **TELEVISION** in **PERFORMING ARTS AND MEDIA**

0-19-506484-4 OXFORD PB $16.95

Rick **Beard** & Leslie **Cohen Berlowitz**, editors

Greenwich Village: Culture and Counterculture

Twenty-two essays explore the historical and cultural dimensions of that tiny, labyrinthine section of Manhattan known as Greenwich Village, refuge for free blacks, avant-garde artists, and sexual and political nonconformists throughout its history. Includes 140 photographs and visual images from the Museum of the City of New York

0-8135-1946-2 RUTGERS $29.95

William J. **Bennett**

The Index of Leading Cultural Indicators: Facts and Figures on the State of American Society

0-671-88326-7 TOUCHSTONE PB $8.95

Daniel **Boorstin**

Americans: The National Experience

Volume 1
The Colonial Experience

0-394-41506-X RANDOM HOUSE $40.00
0-394-70513-0 RANDOM HOUSE PB $13.00

Daniel **Boorstin**

Volume 2
The National Experience

0-394-70358-8 RANDOM HOUSE PB $14.00

Ask the *bartender* (1855) to *set 'em up* (1851)! Do you want only a *snifter* (1848), or do you prefer a drink precisely measured by a *jigger* (1836)...? Ask for a *long drink* (1828), unless you prefer your whiskey *straight* (1862; the English word was *neat*). Would you like an *eggnog* (1775), a *mint-julep* (1809), or some kind of *cobbler* (1840), for example, a *sherry cobbler* (1841)?...The world-famous *cocktail*—destined to become one of the most prolific American inventions, linguistic or otherwise—came not from a later effete era, but from that same Gothic Age. Its first recorded use, in the Hudson, New York *Balance (and Columbian Repository)* on May 13, 1806, explained: "*Cock tail*, then, is a stimulating liquor, composed of spirits of any kind, *sugar, water,* and *bitters*—it is vulgarly called *bittered sling*...it is said, also, to be of great use to a democratic candidate: because, a person having swallowed a glass of it, is ready to swallow anything else."
VOLUME 2: THE NATIONAL EXPERIENCE

Volume 3
The Democratic Experience

0-394-41453-5 RANDOM HOUSE $35.00
0-394-71011-8 RANDOM HOUSE PB $16.00

Paul **Boyer**

By the Bomb's Early Light: American Thought and Culture at the Dawn of the Atomic Age

Documents "how the bomb figured in the nation's public discourse and popular mythology between 1945 and 1950...an era brought vividly back to life in this rich and disturbing chronicle"—*Newsweek*

0-8078-4480-2 NORTH CAROLINA PB $16.95

When Time Shall Be No More: Prophecy Belief in Modern American Culture

0-674-95128-X HARVARD $35.00

Douglas **Brinkley**

The Magic Bus: An American Odyssey

"The ultimate road trip, a rollicking tour of American history seen through the eyes of a remarkable professor and his students"
—*New Orleans Times-Picayune*

0-385-47419-9 ANCHOR PB $14.95

John C. **Burnham**

Bad Habits: Drinking, Smoking, Taking Drugs, Gambling, Sexual Misbehavior and Swearing in American History

In an historical investigation into why so many people engage in what are considered "bad" behaviors, Burnham has discovered how a coalition of economic interests has exploited the quest for self-gratification: making the Marlboro Man a hero, turning sexual experience to commodity

0-8147-1187-1 NYU $50.00
0-8147-1224-X NYU PB $18.95

James M. **Cassedy**

Medicine in America: A Short History

From colonial times to present, linking medicine, health, and disease to larger events in US social history

0-8018-4208-5 JOHNS HOPKINS PB $13.95

Howard P. **Chudacoff**

How Old Are You?: Age Consciousness in American Culture

0-691-04768-5 PRINCETON $45.00

James **Conaway**

The Smithsonian: 150 Years of Adventure, Discovery, and Delight

Giant pandas, the Hope Diamond, the *Spirit of St. Louis:* since 1846, the Smithsonian Institution has housed a staggering variety of national treasures. On the occasion of its sesquicentennial, this entertaining and authoritative account of the great American institution brings its century and a half of history to life with hundreds of photographs, paintings, anecdotes, and profiles

See also **MUSEUMS AND COLLECTIONS** under **ART HISTORY: GENERAL STUDIES** in **ART**

0-679-44175-1 KNOPF $60.00

Michael **Davidson**

The San Francisco Renaissance: Poetics and Community at Mid-Century

The best cultural history of the Beats

See also **POETRY** under **GENERAL STUDIES: THE 20TH CENTURY** under **AMERICAN LITERATURE: ANTHOLOGIES AND CRITICAL STUDIES** in **LITERATURE OF THE AMERICAS**

0-521-25880-4 CAMBRIDGE $59.95
0-521-42304-X CAMBRIDGE PB $18.95

David Brion **Davis**

From Homicide to Slavery: Studies in American Culture

A leading historian of slavery probes such subjects as capital punishment, the cowboy as American hero, violence in American literature, and the rise of antislavery movements

0-19-505418-0 OXFORD PB $18.95

Andrew **Delbanco**

The Death of Satan: How Americans Have Lost the Sense of Evil

0-374-13566-5 FS&G $23.00

Lynn **Gamwell** & Nancy **Tomes**

Madness in America: Cultural and Medical Perceptions of Mental Illness before 1914

0-8014-3161-1 CORNELL $39.50

Todd **Gitlin**

The Twilight of Common Dreams: Why America Is Wracked by Culture Wars

0-8050-4090-0 HOLT $25.00

Robert Justin **Goldstein**

Saving "Old Glory": The History of the American Flag Desecration Controversy

From the Civil War to today. "It is the most complete treatment of this subject I have seen"—Ira Glasser

0-8133-2325-8 WESTVIEW $35.00

Neil **Harris**

The Artist in American Society: The Formative Years, 1790-1860

0-226-31754-4 CHICAGO PB $24.00

Suellen **Hoy**

Chasing Dirt: The American Pursuit of Cleanliness

How cleanliness became an essential ingredient of middle-class identity

0-19-509420-4 OXFORD $25.00

John F. **Kasson**

Rudeness and Civility: Manners in Nineteenth-Century Urban America

"Kasson adds an important and delightful dimension to our previously narrow understanding of everyday life in the United States"
—Michael Kammen

0-374-52299-5 NOONDAY PB $14.00

Bill **Kauffman**

America First!

FOREWORD BY GORE VIDAL

0-87975-956-9 PROMETHEUS $25.95

Pagan **Kennedy**

Platforms: A Microwaved Cultural Chronicle of the 1970s

The members of Generation X are a special breed, born in the '70s to parents who wore earth shoes and who tried, rather unsuccessfully, to reconcile the contradictory enticements of hedonism and social activism. X'er Pagan Kennedy, a widely published pop culture critic and novelist, is well equipped to reveal the complex gestalt of these wry, knowing, alienated, post-hippie romantics, just as they are getting ready to inherit the earth

0-312-10525-8 ST. MARTIN'S PB $13.95

W.T. **Lhamon**

Deliberate Speed: The Origins of a Cultural Style in the American 1950s

Offers a useful treatment of the growing dissent in the later '50s; first published in 1990

1-56098-316-7 SMITHSONIAN PB $15.95

Vincent de Paul **Lupiano** & Ken W. **Sayers**

It Was a Very Good Year: A Cultural History of the United States from 1776 to the Present

A year-by-year compilation, with the emphasis on popular culture

1-55850-419-2 ADAMS PB $15.00

John **Margolies**

Pump and Circumstance: Glory Days of the Gas Station

0-8212-2284-8 BULFINCH PB $17.95

Karal Ann **Marling**

George Washington Slept Here: Colonial Revivals and American Culture

0-674-34951-2 HARVARD $47.50

Alice Goldfarb **Marquis**

Art Lessons: Learning from the Rise and Fall of Public Arts Funding

"A revolutionary blueprint for democratizing public support for the arts"—*Publishers Weekly*

See also **THE ART WORLD** under **ART SINCE 1945** in **ART**

0-465-00438-5 BASIC PB $16.00

Lary **May**

Screening Out the Past: The Birth of Mass Culture and the Motion Picture Industry

0-226-51173-1 CHICAGO PB $14.95

Lary **May**, editor

Recasting America: Culture and Politics in the Age of Cold War

Essays by leading scholars on the convergence of politics and cultural change in postwar America

0-226-51175-8 CHICAGO $49.95

0-226-51176-6 CHICAGO PB $15.95

Neal R. **Peirce** & Jerry **Hagstrom**

The Book of America: Inside 50 States Today

A thick state-by-state guide

0-393-01639-0 NORTON $27.50

Richard **Shenkman**

"I Love Paul Revere Whether He Rode or Not"

A humorous collection of historical facts exposing many of our self-serving myths and illusions, from the bestselling author

0-06-092330-X HARPERCOLLINS PB $12.00

Paul Revere

Arthur M. **Schlesinger**, Jr.

The Disuniting of America

0-393-03380-5 NORTON $15.95

Debora **Silverman**

Selling Culture: Bloomingdale's, Diana Vreeland and the Aristocracy of Taste in Reagan's America

"Illuminates the mixture of fantasy and corruption that is the distinctive mark of both the aristocratic revival in fashion and the Reagan presidency"—Michael Rogin

0-679-75549-7 VINTAGE PB $20.00

Robert Blair **St. George**, editor

Material Life in America, 1600-1860

Essays by leading scholars on folklore, anthropology, decorative arts, and related subjects provide a multifaceted portrait of early American life

1-55553-019-2 NORTHEASTERN $55.00

1-55553-020-6 NORTHEASTERN PB $27.50

Ronald **Sukenick**

Down and In: Life in the Underground

The world of American underground culture

0-9626530-2-0 IN PRESS $17.95

Alan **Trachtenberg**

Reading American Photographs: Images as History from Mathew Brady to Walker Evans

The role of photographers in shaping the American perception of the past

See also **SPECIAL TOPICS** under **PHOTOGRAPHY** in **ART**

0-374-52249-9 HILL & WANG PB $16.00

Richard **Weiss**

The American Myth of Success: From Horatio Alger to Norman Vincent Peale

0-252-06043-1 ILLINOIS PB $10.95

Public Figures and Issues

Mary S. **Lovell**

The Sound of Wings: The Biography of Amelia Earhart

Examines Earhart's life from her tomboy childhood in Kansas and her obsession with airplanes to her relationship with G.P. Putnam, the publisher and PR genius, and their quest to keep Amelia's image an innovative one in the 1930s. In her new book, Mary S. Lovell, the author of the international bestseller *Straight on Till Morning: The Biography of Beryl Markham*, captures the reckless spirit of the "Golden Age of Flight"

0-312-03431-8 ST. MARTIN'S PB $22.95

Randall **Brink**

Lost Star: The Search for Amelia Earhart

Painstaking reconstruction argues that Earhart survived and was held as a POW by the Japanese with FDR's collusion

0-393-31311-5 NORTON PB $12.95

Amelia Earhart

Joyce **Milton**

Loss of Eden: A Biography of Charles and Anne Morrow Lindbergh

An extraordinary dual biography of one of the most celebrated couples in American history. Revealingly examines their respective childhoods, and their 45-year marriage. "Milton's authoritative and engrossing volume reshapes popular notions about its legendary subjects"—*Publishers Weekly*

0-06-092482-9 HARPERPERENNIAL PB $17.50

Lee **Hall**

Olmstead's America: An "Unpractical" Man and His Vision of Civilization

Examines the controversial life and work of the father of American landscape architecture, with particular attention to his ideas for integrating everyday life with nature

0-8212-1998-7 BULFINCH $40.00

Neil **Skolnick**

On the Ledge: A Doctor's Stories from the Inner City

Skolnick was an idealistic young doctor when he took his first job at a clinic in a Philadelphia project. The result is not only a riveting account of medical practice among the impoverished, but a compassionate cry to lawmakers and voters to consider the effect of legislative cuts on the nation's underprivileged and needy. An important work

0-571-19883-X FABER $19.95

Patients come into the office after drinking whiskey or shooting dope all weekend long, and I act as though I make a difference in their lives. If I were honest I could admit to them, and to myself, that the pills I prescribe for their high blood pressure have little chance of helping their true health problems. Their blood pressure alone is not going to kill them; their environment will.

ON THE LEDGE: A DOCTOR'S STORIES FROM THE INNER CITY

Leisure

Robert **Bogdan**

Freak Show: Presenting Human Oddities for Amusement and Profit

Social history of the freak show, for 100 years one of the most popular forms of entertainment in the US. "A fine example of what has emerged as a major genre in the field of social history: the study of phenomena on the margins of society in order to illuminate developments at the core"—*Atlantic*

0-226-06312-7 CHICAGO PB $16.95

Donna **Braden**

Leisure and Entertainment in America

Includes hundreds of black-and-white and color illustrations

0-8143-2153-4 WAYNE STATE $45.00
0-8143-2154-2 WAYNE STATE PB $24.95

Lewis A. **Erenberg**

Steppin' Out: New York Nightlife and the Transformation of American Culture, 1890-1930

From the Gay '90s through the Jazz Age, New York nightlife was both a symbol and catalyst of America's liberation from the Victorian period

0-313-21342-9 GREENWOOD $49.95
0-226-21515-6 CHICAGO PB $16.95

George W. **Hilton**

Eastland: Legacy of the *Titanic*

A landmark study of the *Eastland,* the Great Lakes steamer that capsized on the Chicago River in 1915, drowning more than 800 passengers. Hilton traces the tragedy, showing the drama of technical, maritime and, above all, political forces that led the ship to turn turtle. One hundred photographs, maps, and diagrams.

0-8047-2291-9 STANFORD $45.00

John F. **Kasson**

Amusing the Millions: Coney Island at the Turn of the Century

An excellent short illustrated history of the meaning of the amusement park

0-8090-0133-0 FS&G PB $9.95

David **Nasaw**

Children of the City: at Work and at Play

See also YOUTH under RITES OF PASSAGE

0-19-504015-5 OXFORD PB $11.95

Going Out: The Rise and Fall of Public Amusements

Focusing on the 1800s through the First World War, Nasaw looks at the institutions of vaudeville, baseball, amusement parks, dance halls, and motion pictures, whose rise marked an alternative to home-based entertainments and male-only saloons

0-465-02654-0 BASIC PB $14.00

Kathy **Peiss**

Cheap Amusements: Working Women and Leisure in Turn-of-the-Century New York

With colorful details about dance styles, silent-movie plots, and amusement parks, this book shows how working women spent their free time and money

0-87722-500-1 TEMPLE PB $16.95

W.J. **Rorabaugh**

The Alcoholic Republic: An American Tradition

The changes in drinking patterns between 1790 and 1840 and the psychological factors that helped produce the temperance movement

0-19-502990-9 OXFORD PB $12.95

Roy **Rosenzweig**

Eight Hours for What We Will: Workers and Leisure in an Industrial City, 1870-1920

A superb study with implications far beyond its subject of Worcester, Massachusetts

0-521-31397-X CAMBRIDGE PB $15.95

A.H. **Saxon**

P.T. Barnum: The Legend and the Man

0-231-05686-9 COLUMBIA $35.00
0-231-05687-7 COLUMBIA PB $16.50

Sports in America

Elliott J. **Gorn**

The Manly Art: Bare-Knuckle Prize Fighting in America

"First-rate social history rendered in felicitous prose....Gorn masterfully blends boiling prose and social history"—*Chicago Sun-Times*

0-8014-1920-4 CORNELL $39.95
0-8014-9582-2 CORNELL PB $15.95

Harvey **Green**

Fit for America: Health, Fitness, Sport and American Society

0-8018-3642-5 JOHNS HOPKINS PB $13.95

Allen **Guttmann**

From Ritual to Record: The Nature of Modern Sports

0-231-08369-6 COLUMBIA PB $16.50

Thomas **Mallon**

Rockets and Rodeos: And Other American Spectacles

Depicting the idiosyncracies of those themes American: The launching of the space shuttle *Discovery,* a commemoration of the bombing of Pearl Harbor, the trial of a murderer in New York, and Robert Redford's Sundance Festival, this is a cross-country trip to relish

0-89919-939-9 TICKNOR & FIELDS $19.95

Richard D. **Mandell**

Sport: A Cultural History

0-231-05470-X COLUMBIA $52.50
0-231-05471-8 COLUMBIA PB $18.50

Donald J. **Mrozek**

Sport and American Mentality, 1880-1910

"A fine example of the social history of sport" —Allen Guttmann, *American Historical Review*

0-87049-394-9 TENNESSEE $36.00
0-87049-395-7 TENNESSEE PB $18.00

Steven A. **Riess**, editor

The American Sporting Experience: A Historical Anthology of Sport in America

0-88011-210-7 HUMAN KINETICS PB $25.00

Jeffrey T. **Sammons**

Beyond the Ring: The Role of Boxing in American Society

An ambitious work tracing the history of heavyweight boxing from an illegal activity to a vaunted big business, and how it reflects social change

0-252-01473-1 ILLINOIS $34.95
0-252-06145-4 ILLINOIS PB $14.95

Paul D. **Staudohar**, editor

Baseball's Best Short Stories

A common ground for many of America's best writers, the baseball story is a literary form in its own right. This collection includes stories by T. Coraghessan Boyle, Michael Chabon, Zane Grey, Ring Lardner, James Thurber, P.G. Wodehouse, Garrison Keillor, Robert Penn Warren, and other fans of the American pastime

1-55652-247-9 CHICAGO REVIEW $20.00

Religion in America

S.E. **Ahlstrom**

A Religious History of the American People

0-300-01762-6 YALE PB $27.00

Stephen L. **Carter**

The Culture of Disbelief: How American Law and Politics Trivialize Religious Devotion

0-385-47498-9 ANCHOR PB $14.95

William A. **Clebsch**

From Sacred to Profane America: The Role of Religion in American History

0-89130-517-3 SCHOLARS $15.95

Winthrop **Hudson**

Religion in America: An Historical Account of the Development of American Religious Life

0-02-357830-0 MACMILLAN PB $39.20

Jay P. **Dolan**

The American Catholic Experience: A History from Colonial Times to the Present

How Catholicism spread across the New World and how it deals with pressing social issues of today

See also **ROMAN CATHOLIC** under **HISTORY** under **CHRISTIANITY** in **RELIGION, SPIRITUALITY, AND PHILOSOPHY**

0-268-00639-3 NOTRE DAME PB $18.50

Catherine L. **Albanese**

Nature Religion in America: From the Algonkian Indians to the New Age

A preliminary guide to a vast and previously uncharted religious world. Albanese argues for a classic American double vision of nature, notably articulated by Emerson and Thoreau

0-226-01145-3 CHICAGO PB $24.95

Henry Thoreau

Roger **Finke** & Rodney **Stark**

The Churching of America, 1776-1990: Winners and Losers in Our Religious Economy

"A brilliant and revolutionary analysis of the social history of American religion, one which will become required reading….The conclusion, that organized religion has been enormously successful in American society, challenges all conventional wisdom"—Andrew M. Greeley

0-8135-1837-7 RUTGERS $30.00
0-8135-1838-5 RUTGERS PB $15.95

Nathan O. **Hatch**

The Democratization of American Christianity

0-300-04470-4 YALE PB $25.00

Martin E. **Marty**

Modern American Religion Volume I The Irony of It All, 1893-1919

0-226-50893-5 CHICAGO $29.95

Volume II The Noise of Conflict, 1919-1941

0-226-50895-1 CHICAGO $29.95

Volume III Under God Indivisible, 1941-1960

022650986 CHICAGO $34.95

Pilgrims in Their Own Land

0-14-008268-9 PENGUIN PB $13.95

Henry F. **May**

Ideas, Faiths, and Feelings: Essays on American Intellectual and Religious History, 1952-1982

0-19-503236-5 OXFORD PB $9.95

William G. **McLoughlin**

Revivals, Awakenings, and Reform: An Essay on Religion and Social Change in America, 1607-1977

0-226-56092-9 CHICAGO PB $10.95

R. Laurence **Moore**

Religious Outsiders and the Making of Americans

0-19-505188-2 OXFORD PB $17.95

Mark **Silk**

Spiritual Politics: Religion and America since World War II

"Demonstrates at once the pervasiveness of evangelical religion and politics in American life and the paradoxes that have resulted since 1945 from the nation's alleged commitment to the 'Judeo-Christian' tradition"—Daniel Aaron

0-345-36983-1 BALLANTINE PB $12.95

Early America

Paul K. **Conkin**

The Uneasy Center: Reformed Christianity in Antebellum America

Conkin (Distinguished Professor of History, Vanderbilt University) offers a comprehensive account of mainline American Protestantism from the colonial era to the Civil War

0-8078-2180-2 NORTH CAROLINA $39.95
0-8078-4492-6 NORTH CAROLINA PB $16.95

Thomas J. **Curry**

The First Freedoms: Church and State in America to the Passage of the First Amendment

0-19-505181-5 OXFORD PB $19.95

Paul E. **Johnson** & Sean **Wilentz**

The Kingdom of Mathias: A Story of Sex and Salvation in 19th-Century America

The riveting, true-life tale of a corrupt self-proclaimed prophet during the religious revival of the Second Great Awakening, with nods to Waco and Jonestown

0-19-503827-4 OXFORD $25.00
0-19-509835-8 OXFORD PB $11.95

Jama **Lazerow**

Religion and the Working Class in Antebellum America

1-56098-544-5 SMITHSONIAN $39.50

Leonard W. **Levy**

The Establishment Clause: Religion and the First Amendment

0-8078-2156-X NORTH CAROLINA $37.50

David S. **Lovejoy**

Religious Enthusiasm in the New World: Heresy to Revolution

0-674-75864-1 HARVARD $37.00

Colleen **McDannell**

The Christian Home in Victorian America, 1840-1900

See also **THE MIDDLE CLASS** under **AMERICAN PEOPLE AND PLACES**

0-253-31376-7 INDIANA $25.00

Ronald L. **Numbers** & Jonathan M. **Butler**, editors

The Disappointed: Millerism and Millenarianism in the 19th Century

0-87049-793-6 TENNESSEE PB $14.95

James **Turner**

Without God, without Creed: The Origins of Unbelief in America

0-8018-3407-4 JOHNS HOPKINS PB $15.95

Special Studies

Priscilla J. **Brewer**

Shaker Communities, Shaker Lives

"Draws from sociology, statistics, social history, and cultural history to provide a well-reasoned, thoroughly researched analysis of the dynamics of Shaker development and decline"—*Choice*

0-87451-400-2 NEW ENGLAND PB $18.95

James J. **Hennesey**

American Catholics: A History of the Roman Catholic Community in the United States

0-19-503268-3 OXFORD PB $15.95

John A. **Hostetler**

Amish Society

The third edition of a noted work on Amish culture, religious beliefs, community and family life, and interactions with outsiders

0-8018-4441-X JOHNS HOPKINS $45.00
0-8018-4442-8 JOHNS HOPKINS PB $14.95

Winthrop S. **Hudson**

American Protestantism

0-226-35803-8 CHICAGO PB $8.00

William R. **Hutchinson**
The Modernist Impulse in American Protestantism
One of the most authoritative writers on American religion traces liberal thought in American Protestantism from the 1870s to the 1930s
0-8223-1248-4 DUKE PB $15.95

Donald R. **Kraybill**
The Riddle of Amish Culture
0-8018-3681-6 JOHNS HOPKINS $45.00
0-8018-3682-4 JOHNS HOPKINS PB $12.95

Joseph M. **Murphy**
Santeria: An African Religion in America
"His engaging picture of Santeria, the Yoruba religion now practiced in the US by way of Cuba, is fresh, startling, then strangely attractive and even inspiring"—Harvey Cox, Harvard Divinity School
0-942272-22-6 ORIGINAL PB $10.95

Jon H. **Roberts**
Darwinism and the Divine in America: Protestant Intellectuals and Organic Evolution, 1859-1900
Scholarly analysis of the changing stategies that American Protestant thinkers employed in grappling with the revolutionary implications of Darwin's theory of organic evolution
0-299-11590-9 WISCONSIN $26.75

Bruce A. **Rosenberg**
Can These Bones Live?: The Art of the American Folk Preacher
"One can see the folk artist in action, feel his imagery, his language unfold in a dynamic process of interaction between his audience and himself, one aiding and stimulating the other in a mutual ritual"— David C. Fowler
0-252-01415-4 ILLINOIS $39.95
0-252-01416-2 ILLINOIS PB $14.95

Jan **Shipps**
Mormonism: The Story of a New Religious Tradition
0-252-01417-0 ILLINOIS PB $11.95

Robert **Wuthnow**
The Restructuring of American Religion: Society and Faith since World War II
"No one book could possibly do service as a sociological map of the current state of American religion, but if readers were confined to only one, this could, arguably, be it"—John A. Coleman
0-691-02057-4 PRINCETON PB $15.95

Susan M. **Yohn**
A Contest of Faiths: Missionary Women and Pluralism in the American Southwest
"…makes an important contribution to the literature on women missionaries by connecting the history of evangelical women to the transformation of liberalism in 19th- and 20th-century American reform circles"—Peggy Pascoe
0-8014-8273-9 CORNELL PB $16.95

Revivals and Evangelicalism

Michael **D'Antonio**
Fall from Grace: The Failed Crusade of the Christian Right
D'Antonio, a *Newsday* correspondent, examines the new Christian right through its leaders (Jerry Falwell, Pat Robertson) and followers, concluding that the recent scandals (Jim and Tammy Bakker, Jimmy Swaggart) are leading to the inevitable collapse of the movement. "An intelligent survey of modern evangelicals' activities"—Garry Wills, *NY Review of Books*
See also **CONSERVATISM AND THE NEW RIGHT** under **CURRENT POLITICAL THOUGHT AND ISSUES** under **AMERICAN POLITICS AND FOREIGN POLICY**
0-8135-1896-2 RUTGERS PB $14.95

David E. **Harrell**, Jr.
All Things Are Possible: The Healing and Charismatic Revivals in Modern America
0-253-20221-3 INDIANA PB $15.95

James D. **Hunter**
American Evangelicalism: Conservative Religion and the Quandary of Modernity
0-933951-27-2 LOCUST HILL $45.00
0-8135-0985-8 RUTGERS PB $14.00

Evangelicalism: The Coming Generation
0-226-36083-0 CHICAGO PB $14.95

George M. **Marsden**
Fundamentalism and American Culture: The Shaping of Twentieth-Century Evangelicalism, 1870-1925
0-19-503083-4 OXFORD PB $12.95

Religion in America Today

Michael **Barkun**
Religion and the Racist Right: The Origins of the Christian Identity Movement
0-8078-4451-9 NORTH CAROLINA PB $15.95

Dallas A. **Blanchard** & Terry J. **Prewitt**
Religious Violence and Abortion: The Gideon Project
The authors explore the phenomenon of violence by the religious right while focusing on the specific case of a Pensacola, Florida bombing of an abortion clinic. They warn that fundamentalists will continue to use violence in reaction not only to legalized abortion, but also to such issues as pornography, homosexuality, equality for women, and prayer in public schools
See also **THE ABORTION DEBATE** under **THE FEMALE EXPERIENCE** under **WOMEN'S STUDIES** in **SOCIAL STUDIES**
0-8130-1193-0 FLORIDA $39.95
0-8130-1194-9 FLORIDA PB $17.95

Dennis **Covington**
Salvation on Sand Mountain: Snake Handling and Redemption in Southern Appalachia
A reporter's investigation of a case of attempted murder (by snake) among fundamentalist Protestants whose services include the handling of poisonous snakes leads to a spiritual reassessment of his life and to his own participation in the snake-handling rites
See also **MEMOIRS AND JOURNALS** under **20TH-CENTURY AMERICAN ESSAYS AND JOURNALISM** in **LITERATURE OF THE AMERICAS**
0-14-025458-7 PENGUIN PB $11.95

Samuel G. **Freedman**
Upon this Rock: The Miracles of a Black Church
Johnny Ray Youngblood—the enigmatic pastor of the St. Paul Community Baptist Church in East New York—is a controversial miracle worker building hope in a desperate place. "This stunning book has much to say about religion and race, cities and change, community and faith"—*Publishers Weekly*
0-06-016610-X HARPERCOLLINS PB $22.50

Biographies

Anne **Taylor**
Annie Besant: A Biography
0-19-211796-3 OXFORD $65.00

Thomas **Sugrue**
There Is a River: The Story of Edgar Cayce
A biography of Cayce
0-87604-151-9 ARE PRESS PB $6.95

Robert **Coles**
Dorothy Day: A Radical Devotion
The author writes as a close friend of Day, the radical Catholic who fed, clothed, and befriended the destitute for over 50 years
0-201-07974-7 ADDISON-WESLEY PB $14.00

Robert David **Thomas**
"With Bleeding Footsteps": Mary Baker Eddy's Path to Religious Leadership
Brilliantly combines history and psychoanalysis to reveal the singular circumstances that led a New England farm girl to found the Christian Science Church, one of the most wide-reaching American religious organizations of her time. As the story of a middle-class Protestant who possessed a rare lucidity and conviction about suffering and renewal, the book is fascinating in its spiritual, social, and feminist implications
0-679-41495-9 KNOPF $27.50

Robert M. **Miller**
Harry Emerson Fosdick: Preacher, Pastor, Prophet
0-19-503512-7 OXFORD $49.95

William **Martin**

A Prophet with Honor: The Billy Graham Story

"Thoroughly researched, lucidly written…it is sure to become a classic in the field of American religion"—Harry S. Stout. "A thoughtful and probing book that preserves Billy Graham's glory while revealing a complex and flawed man" —*LA Times Book Review*

0-688-11906-9 MORROW PB $13.00

Edith L. **Blumhofer**

Aimée Semple McPherson: Everybody's Sister

A detailed and scholarly biography of the Los Angeles-based Aimée McPherson (1890-1944), who in offering a beguiling blend of religious fundamentalism, faith healing, and show-biz glitz anticipated the television evangelists of a later day

0-8028-3752-2 EERDMANS $24.99
0-8028-0155-2 EERDMANS PB $15.00

Daniel Mark **Epstein**

Sister Aimée: Life of Aimée Semple McPherson

The stormy, scandal-disrupted career of the Canadian-born woman who became a flamboyant and very popular radio evangelist in Los Angeles in the 1920s and '30s

See also **20TH-CENTURY** under **BIOGRAPHIES** under **CHRISTIANITY** in **RELIGION, SPIRITUALITY, AND PHILOSOPHY**

0-15-182688-9 HARCOURT BRACE $27.95
0-15-600093-8 HARVEST PB $14.95

Michael **Mott**

The Seven Mountains of Thomas Merton

Biography of the scholar and Trappist monk

0-15-680681-9 HARVEST PB $17.95

Thomas Merton

David E. **Harrell**, Jr.

Oral Roberts: An American Life

Scrupulously objective, this biography vividly conveys the changes in American Pentecostal culture over the past 50 years

0-253-15844-3 INDIANA $12.95

Leonard J. **Arrington**

Brigham Young: American Moses

0-252-01296-8 ILLINOIS PB $15.95

History of Family Life

Rosalind **Barnett** & Caryl **Rivers**

He Works/She Works: How the New American Family Is Making It Work

A study sponsored by the National Institutes of Health investigated two-income households. Although the study is of white and heterosexual couples, there is valuable insight into the dynamic of all contemporary working couples

See also **MARRIAGE** under **COURTSHIP, LOVE, SEX, AND MARRIAGE** in **LIFESTYLES AND PRACTICAL ADVICE**

0-06-251080-0 HARPERCOLLINS $24.00

Mary Frances **Berry**

The Politics of Parenthood: Child Care, Women's Rights, and the Myth of the Good Mother

Berry argues that the lessons of the past, including the experiences of African Americans and Native Americans, teach that what matters is not who cares for children, but how they are cared for. "An important and comprehensive reference for those involved in both gender battles and the fight for comprehensive child-care"—*Kirkus Reviews*

See also **MOTHERS** under **BEING A PARENT** under **PARENTING** in **LIFESTYLES AND PRACTICAL ADVICE**

0-14-023360-1 PENGUIN PB $11.95

John Putnam **Demos**

Little Commonwealth: Family Life in Plymouth Colony

Roles and relationships within the family in the early Pilgrim communities

0-8446-6308-5 SMITH $20.80
0-19-501355-7 OXFORD PB $8.95

Past, Present, and Personal: The Family and the Life Course in American History

The changing nature of fatherhood, the experience of middle age in colonial times and the present, and the historian's role in discussions of present-day policymaking

0-19-503777-4 OXFORD $30.00
0-19-504766-4 OXFORD PB $10.95

Marian Wright **Edelman**

Families in Peril: An Agenda for Social Change

The president of the Children's Defense Fund charts such growing problems for both whites and blacks as teen pregnancy, joblessness, and single-parent households and offers suggestions for widespread change

0-674-29229-4 HARVARD PB $8.95

Ian **Frazier**

Family

Searching for "a meaning that would defeat death," *New Yorker* contributor Frazier retraces the history of his family from early colonial times to the present

0-374-15319-1 FS&G $23.00

Linda **Gordon**

Heroes of Their Own Lives: The Politics and History of Family Violence, Boston, 1880-1960

0-14-010468-2 PENGUIN PB $13.95

Robert L. **Griswold**

Family and Divorce in California, 1850-1890: Victorian Illusions and Everyday Realities

A study of 400 divorce cases, with insights into family values, sexuality, parenthood, and domestic violence

0-87395-633-8 SUNY $64.50

Michael **Grossberg**

Governing the Health: Law and the Family in Nineteenth-Century America

0-8078-4225-7 NORTH CAROLINA PB $22.50

Shere **Hite**

The Hite Report on the Family: Growing Up under Patriarchy

A statement signed by Stephen Jay Gould, Gloria Steinem, Susan Faludi, and others said: "The latest book by ground-breaking researcher Shere Hite could be a major contribution to the US's ongoing debate over…'family values'"

See also **CRITICAL COMMENTARY ON AMERICAN CULTURE** under **TOPICS IN MODERN SOCIOLOGY** under **SOCIOLOGY** in **SOCIAL STUDIES**

0-8021-1570-5 GROVE $22.00

Christopher **Lasch**

Haven in a Heartless World: The Family Besieged

The more the family is needed as a refuge, the less it serves as one

See also **NON-MARXIST SOCIALISM** under **POLITICAL THOUGHT** in **SOCIAL STUDIES**

0-393-31303-4 NORTON PB $12.95

Christopher Lasch

Steven **Mintz** & Susan **Kellogg**

Domestic Revolutions: A Social History of Domestic Family Life

An overview of changes in the family in the last 300 years, including a look at today's family

0-02-921291-X FREE PRESS PB $13.95

Barry **Levy**

Quakers and the American Family: British Settlement in the Delaware Valley

Argues that the Quakers played a pivotal role in the development of American family ideology and the belief that morally self-sufficient nuclear households must serve as the foundation of a republican society

0-19-504976-4 OXFORD PB $18.95

Mary Ann **Mason**

From Fathers' Property to Children's Rights: The History of Child Custody in the United States

"A first rate book. Mason combines a lively style with sound scholarship as she traces the historic roots of contemporary child custody issues from colonial times to illuminate the crosscurrents of community values and the bitter legal controversies of the present"—Judith L. Wallerstein

0-231-08046-8 COLUMBIA $40.00

Elaine Tyler **May**

Barren in the Promised Land: Childless Americans and the Pursuit of Happiness

"An admirable job of charting the history of childbearing, why we do it, or don't, and how we as a society feel about it"—*LA Times*

0-465-00608-6 BASIC PB $15.00

Great Expectations: Marriage and Divorce in Post-Victorian America

Why did the divorce rate rise by 2000 percent between 1867 and 1929? May analyzed over 1000 divorce cases across the country to provide quantitative and personal accounts

0-226-51170-7 CHICAGO PB $11.95

Homeward Bound: American Families in the Cold War Era

0-465-03055-6 BASIC BOOKS PB $17.50

Steven **Mintz**

A Prison of Expectations: The Family in Victorian Culture

Investigates the private lives of five famous and influential novelists—Robert Louis Stevenson, George Eliot, Harriet Beecher Stowe, Catharine Sedgwick, and Samuel Butler—to show the intersection between family dynamics and the larger culture during the 19th century

0-8147-5391-4 NYU PB $17.50

Mary P. **Ryan**

Cradle of the Middle Class: The Family in Oneida County, New York, 1790-1865

0-521-27403-6 CAMBRIDGE PB $17.95

Richard **Sennett**

Families against the City: Middle-Class Homes of Industrial Chicago, 1872-1890

0-674-29226-X HARVARD PB $12.95

Charlotte **Nekola**

Dream House: A Memoir

Nekola came of age in the '50s, in a squeaky-clean suburban home with a new car in the garage, cocktails in the evening, mom in the kitchen, and a hard-working dad arriving home in the evenings. Only dad was an alcoholic, and mom died of cancer, and sister drifted slowly into homelessness

0-393-03433-X NORTON $18.95

Daniel Blake **Smith**

Inside the Great House: Planter Family Life in 18th-Century Chesapeake Society

A key period that saw a change from a patriarchal, authoritarian, and emotionally restrained family into a more intimate, child-centered family life marked by close emotional bonds and growing autonomy

0-8014-9380-3 CORNELL PB $14.95

Richard W. **Wertz** & Dorothy C. **Wertz**

Lying-In: A History of Childbirth in America

See also **CHILDBIRTH** under **PARENTING** in **LIFESTYLES AND PRACTICAL ADVICE**

0-300-04088-1 YALE $35.00
0-300-04087-3 YALE PB $18.00

Rites of Passage

Courtship

Beth L. **Bailey**

From Front Porch to Back Seat: Courtship in 20th-Century America

0-8018-3609-3 JOHNS HOPKINS $35.00
0-8018-3935-1 JOHNS HOPKINS PB $13.95

Helen **Lefkowitz-Horowitz** & Kathy **Peiss**, editors

Love Across the Color Line: The Letters of Alice Hanley to Channing Lewis

The letters exchanged between a white working-class woman and her African-American lover in turn-of-the-century Massachusetts

1-55849-024-8 MASSACHUSETTS PB $12.95

Youth

James B. **Gilbert**

A Cycle of Outrage: America's Reaction to the Juvenile Delinquent in the 1950s

Includes, along with much else related to the rise of American youth culture, a detailed account of Frederic Wertham's notorious crusade against comic books

0-19-503721-9 OXFORD $30.00

N. Ray **Hiner** & Joseph M. **Hawes**

Growing Up in America: Children in Historical Perspective

0-252-01218-6 ILLINOIS PB $13.95

David **Nasaw**

Children of the City: At Work and at Play

See also **LEISURE**

0-19-504015-5 OXFORD PB $11.95

Grace **Palladino**

Teenagers: An American History

0-465-00767-8 BASIC $25.00

Aging

Daniel **Callahan**

Setting Limits: Medical Goals in an Aging Society

Argues that society must limit the money spent on care that is merely life-extending and concentrate on relief for the suffering

See also **MEDICAL CARE AND HEALTH POLICY** under **MEDICINE** in **SCIENCE**

0-87840-572-0 GEORGETOWN PB $15.95

Carole **Haber** & Brian **Gratton**

Old Age and the Search for Security: An American Social History

An intelligent synthesis of existing old-age history that offers new interpretations and insights

0-253-20836-X INDIANA PB $15.95

Beth H. **Hess** & Elizabeth W. **Marbum**, editors

Growing Old in America: New Perspectives on Old Age

Essays on public policy, history, and the sociology of aging

0-88738-846-9 TRANSACTION PB $24.95

Alan **Pifer** & Lydia **Bronte**, editors

Our Aging Society: Paradox and Promise

How the aging population can be turned into a public asset instead of a problem

0-393-30334-9 NORTON PB $15.95

History of Sexuality

Allan M. **Brandt**

No Magic Bullet: A Social History of Venereal Disease in the United States since 1880

Includes a section on AIDS

0-19-503469-4 OXFORD $32.00
0-19-504237-9 OXFORD PB $12.95

Richard **Dooling**

Blue Streak: Swearing, Free Speech, and Sexual Harassment

0-679-44471-8 RANDOM HOUSE $23.00

George **Chauncey**

Gay New York: Gender, Urban Culture, and the Making of the Gay Male World, 1890-1940

Gay life before the Second World War

0-465-02621-4 BASIC PB $15.00

John **Costello**

Virtue under Fire: How World War II Changed Our Social and Sexual Attitudes

How the brutality of war and women's economic emancipation in wartime America set the stage for postwar social change

0-88064-070-7 FROMM PB $9.95

John **D'Emilio** & Estelle B. **Freedman**

Intimate Matters: A History of Sexuality in America

A serious and provocative scholarly study

See also **SEX** under **COURTSHIP, LOVE, SEX, AND MARRIAGE** in **LIFESTYLES AND PRACTICAL ADVICE**

0-06-091550-1 HARPERCOLLINS PB $14.00

John S. **Haller** & Robin M. **Haller**

The Physician and Sexuality in Victorian America

0-8093-2009-6 SOUTHERN ILLINOIS PB $18.95

Elizabeth Lapovsky **Kennedy** & Madeline D. **Davis**

Boots of Leather, Slippers of Gold: The History of a Lesbian Community

This very first community study of lesbians, researched over 13 years, includes such topics as sex, relationships, coming out, motherhood, work, oppression and pride. *"Boots of Leather, Slippers of Gold* honors all of us....[It] opens up the heart and mind....[It] breaks new ground in women's history, lesbian history, and the history of desire as a lived force in a community under siege"—Joan Nestle, co-founder of the Lesbian Herstory Archives

See also **HISTORY** under **GAY, LESBIAN, AND BISEXUAL STUDIES** in **SOCIAL STUDIES**

0-415-90293-2 ROUTLEDGE $39.95

0-14-023550-7 PENGUIN PB $13.95

Peter **Laufer**

A Question of Consent: Innocence and Complicity in the Glen Ridge Rape Case

The true story behind the famous 1993 rape case in Glen Ridge, New Jersey, and the courtroom drama in which a mentally retarded girl was portrayed as a seductress, while her rapists—although convicted—were excused as all-American boys. Laufer concludes that the case is representative of much greater problems within our society: racism, sexism, and deeply ingrained faults in the judicial system

See also **RAPE, INCEST, AND BATTERED WOMEN** under **THE FEMALE EXPERIENCE** under **WOMEN'S STUDIES** in **SOCIAL STUDIES**

1-56279-059-5 MERCURY HOUSE $19.95

Ellen **Messer** & Kathryn E. **May**

Back Rooms: Voices from the Illegal Abortion Era

Frontline tales from women who had backroom abortions before *Roe v. Wade*

See also **THE ABORTION DEBATE** under **THE FEMALE EXPERIENCE** under **WOMEN'S STUDIES** in **SOCIAL STUDIES**

FOREWORD BY MARGE PIERCY

0-87975-876-7 PROMETHEUS PB $17.95

James C. **Mohr**

Abortion in America: The Origins and Evolution of National Policy, 1800-1900

See also **THE ABORTION DEBATE** under **THE FEMALE EXPERIENCE** under **WOMEN'S STUDIES** in **SOCIAL STUDIES**

0-19-502616-0 OXFORD PB $11.95

Sylvia **Plachy** & James **Ridgeway**

Red Light: Inside the Sex Industry

1-57687-000-6 D.A.P. $39.95

Katie **Roiphe**

Last Night in Paradise: Sex and Morals at the Century's End

See also **LATE ARRIVALS** in **SOCIAL STUDIES**

0-316-75439-0 LITTLE, BROWN $21.95

Steven **Seidman**

Romantic Longings: Love in America, 1830-1980

Drawing on sex surveys, advice literature, autobiographies, and novels, Seidman charts the birth of the culture of eroticism in the post–World War II years, when sex was transformed from a Victorian spiritual ideal to a modern expression of intimacy and pleasure

0-415-90828-0 ROUTLEDGE PB $17.95

Prostitution

Anne M. **Butler**

Daughters of Joy, Sisters of Misery: Prostitutes in the American West, 1865-90

"Butler has portrayed the stark realities of prostitution in the American West with sensitivity and insight"—*Southwest Review*

0-252-01466-9 ILLINOIS PB $12.95

Timothy J. **Gilfoyle**

City of Eros: New York City, Prostitution, and the Commercialization of Sex, 1790-1920

Gilfoyle's pioneering work makes it clear that the business of sex played an integral part in forming New York's neighborhoods, social roles, and politics. "A revealing peek at a Gotham that exceeded our own anything-goes sexual license and urban misery"—*Kirkus Reviews*

See also **CRIME, DELINQUENCY, AND DEVIANCE** under **TOPICS IN MODERN SOCIOLOGY** under **SOCIOLOGY** in **SOCIAL STUDIES**

0-393-31108-2 NORTON PB $13.95

Marion S. **Goldman**

Gold Diggers and Silver Miners: Prostitution and Social Life on the Comstock Lode

0-472-06332-4 MICHIGAN PB $17.95

Barbara Meil **Hobson**

Uneasy Virtue: The Politics of Prostitution and the American Reform Tradition

"How and why we regulate prostitution, who America's prostitutes were, and how our practice and attitudes contrast with those of Europe"—Caroll Smith-Rosenberg, University of Pennsylvania

0-226-34557-2 CHICAGO PB $17.95

Gail **Pheterson**, editor

A Vindication of the Rights of Whores

Members of "the world's oldest profession" are given voice in this remarkable volume. A collection that defines and illuminates the differences and similarities of prostitutes and their lives from around the world. "Genuinely radical, courageous and strong" —Catherine Stimpson, Rutgers University

0-931188-73-3 SEAL PB $16.95

I enter a plea of innocence for all those incarcerated for prostitution and cheer on all those who have the courage to speak out on their own behalf. Hopefully this book will generate the kind of thinking and awareness and activism necessary to right the wrongs committed against whores for centuries.— *Margo St. James*

A VINDICATION OF THE RIGHTS OF WHORES

Ruth **Rosen**

The Lost Sisterhood: Prostitution in America, 1900-1918

A vivid study of an era in which prostitution became a widespread concern of the American public

0-8018-2664-0 JOHNS HOPKINS $32.50

0-8018-2665-9 JOHNS HOPKINS PB $13.95

Drug Abuse

William M. **Adler**

Land of Opportunity: One Family's Quest for the American Dream in the Age of Crack

The American Dream—only the product was cocaine. Combining investigative journalism with a larger social analysis of the post-agricultural South and post-industrial North, Adler tells a dramatic tale of the widest-reaching social implications

0-87113-593-0 GROVE $22.00

Dan **Baum**

Wasted: How America Got Addicted to Its War on Drugs

0-316-08412-3 LITTLE, BROWN $24.95

Eva **Bertram** & others
Drug War Politics: The Price of Denial
0-520-20598-7 CALIFORNIA PB $17.95

David T. **Courtwright**
Addicts Who Survived: An Oral History of Narcotic Use in America, 1923-1965
Life in the drug subculture during the era of strict narcotic control
FOREWORD BY CLAUDE BROWN
0-87049-587-9 TENNESSEE $32.00

Stanton A. **Glantz** & others
Cigarette Papers
FOREWORD BY C. EVERETT KOOP
0-520-20572-3 CALIFORNIA $29.95

Philip J. **Hilts**
Smokescreen: The Truth Behind the Tobacco Industry Cover-Up
A *New York Times* reporter offers a fast-paced tour through the revelations that have Big Tobacco on the defensive
0-201-48836-1 ADDISON-WESLEY $22.00

Abbie **Hoffman** & Jonathan **Silvers**
Steal this Urine Test: Fighting Drug Hysteria in America
The late author of *Steal this Book* argues that the current wave of drug testing is an unconstitutional and dangerous assault, comparable to the loyalty oaths of the 1950s
0-14-010400-3 PENGUIN PB $11.95

Richard **Klein**
Cigarettes Are Sublime
0-8223-1401-0 DUKE $24.95

David F. **Musto**
The American Disease: Origins of Narcotic Control
A history of the relationship between public outcry against drugs and prohibitive drug laws, including today's anti-drug campaigns
0-19-505211-0 OXFORD PB $14.95

Crime and Punishment

Geoffrey **Canada**
Fist Stick Knife Gun: A Personal History of Violence in America
See also FACING BLACK VIOLENCE under RACE RELATIONS under AFRICAN-AMERICAN STUDIES
0-8070-0423-5 BEACON PB $12.00

Alice Morse **Earle**
Curious Punishments of Bygone Days
A catalog of early American crimes and their punishments—including the pillories, the stocks, and the scarlet letter—originally published in 1896 by a noted social historian on everyday life in colonial America
1-55709-249-4 APPLEWOOD PB $10.95

Paul **Chevigny**
Edge of the Knife: Police Violence and Accountability in Six Cities of the Americas
1-56584-183-2 NEW PRESS $25.00

George **Cooper**
Lost Love: A True Story of Passion, Murder and Justice in Old New York
Sensational murder trial in New York after the Civil War. "History at its best—dramatic, riveting and heartrending"—Doris Kearns Goodwin
See also THE GILDED AGE AND THE PROGRESSIVE ERA under US HISTORY, 1877-1945
0-679-75699-X VINTAGE PB $12.00

George Cooper (photo by Lawrence Blume)

John **DeSantis**
The New Untouchables
DeSantis reveals a pattern of police brutality and cover-up throughout the country
1-87936-031-4 NOBLE $22.95

Ronald A. **Farrell** & Carole **Case**
The Black Book and the Mob: The Untold Story of the Control of Nevada's Casinos
0-299-14750-9 WISCONSIN $44.00
0-299-14754-1 WISCONSIN PB $17.95

Lawrence M. **Friedman**
Crime and Punishment in American History
Urges the value of historical understanding, "tinged with the viewpoint of the social sciences." By the author of *Legal Culture and the Legal Profession*
0-465-01487-9 BASIC PB $17.00

William **Kleinknecht**
The New Ethnic Mob: The Changing Face of Organized Crime in America
0-684-82294-6 FREE PRESS $25.00

Robert **Lacey**
Little Man: Meyer Lansky and the Gangster Life
A look at the legendary—and much-mythologized—gangster and associate of Arnold Rothstein, Lucky Luciano, and Bugsy Siegel
0-316-51168-4 LITTLE, BROWN $24.95

Wendy **Lesser**
Pictures at an Execution: An Inquiry into the Subject of Murder
0-674-66735-2 HARVARD $24.95

Coramae Richey **Mann**
Unequal Justice: A Question of Color
A synthesis of present research on race and crime with cross-cultural analyses of four US minority groups. The results make clear that people of color do not in any way receive equal treatment under America's judicial system. While that finding alone only affirms what many have long known, the book also describes how and why such injustice occurs. "Mann has produced an illuminating, thoroughly researched, and comprehensive treatment of the experiences of minorities in the criminal justice system"—Mary Frances Berry, US Commission on Civil Rights
0-253-33676-7 INDIANA $35.00
0-253-20783-5 INDIANA PB $15.95

Peter **McWilliams**
Ain't Nobody's Business If You Do
Why does the government jail people for offering "unapproved" therapies to the terminally ill whom the establishment has already "given up for dead?" This is one of many consensual crimes—the others are sex, unconventional worship, and recreational drug taking—that the author questions in his infuriated, often funny reclamation of our Bill of Rights. "One of the most important books to be published in 1993. One of the greatest collections of funny, hilarious, unusual and trenchant remarks ever"—Liz Smith
0-931580-53-6 PRELUDE $22.95

Jerome G. **Miller**
Search and Destroy: African-American Males in the Criminal Justice System
Among other facts, this 1996 study shows that, around the country, 90 percent of those arrested on drug charges are black, even though African Americans make up only 12 percent of the population. "One of the most important and clear-eyed challenges to date to the linking of crime and race and to the entire conservative anti-welfare, hard-on-crime agenda" —*Publishers Weekly*
See also FACING BLACK VIOLENCE under RACE RELATIONS under AFRICAN-AMERICAN STUDIES
0-521-46021-2 CAMBRIDGE $24.95

Daniel **Monti**
Wannabe: Gangs in Suburbs and Schools
A vivid portrayal of gang life based on over 100 interviews in which the author illustrates how boys and girls become involved with gang violence and discusses the nature of their strong allegiances. He concludes that gangs provide a means of entry into the conventionality and adulthood that their members profess to disdain
1-55786-615-5 BLACKWELL PB $17.95

Thomas **Puccio** & Dan **Collins**
In the Name of the Law
The defense attorney who freed Claus von Bulow writes of his experience as a federal prosecutor
0-393-03728-2 NORTON $25.00

Helen **Prejean**

Dead Man Walking: An Eyewitness Account of the Death Penalty in the United States

A unique perspective on one of the greatest moral dilemmas in America, from a nun who works closely with both death-row inmates and the families of victims. Without denying the inmates' brutality, she nonetheless comes down squarely against institutionalized killing of criminals. "Sister Prejean…is an excellent writer, direct and honest and unsentimental; her accounts of crime and punishment are gripping, and her argument is persuasive"—*NY Times Book Review*

See also **CRIMINAL LAW AND THE DEATH PENALTY** under **CURRENT LEGAL AFFAIRS** under **LAW** in **SOCIAL STUDIES**

0-679-64131-9 UNKNOWN PB $12.00

Piri **Thomas**

Seven Long Times

1-55885-105-4 ARTE PUBLICO PB $9.95

The Impact of the Media

Helen **Benedict**

Virgin or Vamp: How the Press Covers Sex Crimes

Most cases of sexual violence are painted alike, the author argues: the alleged victim is either sexually suspect or absolutely virginal; the man is either a reluctant participant or a monster. Benedict examines four crimes—including the famous "preppy murder" and Central Park jogger cases—to show how traditional views of women still prevail in the media

0-19-506680-4 OXFORD $30.00

Susan J. **Douglas**

Where the Girls Are: Growing Up Female with the Mass Media

Deconstructs pop culture's mind-bending messages to women over the past four decades

See also **ADOLESCENCE** under **THE FEMALE EXPERIENCE** under **WOMEN'S STUDIES** in **SOCIAL STUDIES**

0-8129-2530-0 TIME BOOKS PB $15.00

Norman M. **Klein**

Seven Minutes: The Life and Death of the American Animated Cartoon

The late, lamented cartoon short, which had ceased to exist by the '60s, was an art form as tightly controlled as a minuet—and one fraught with complex pressures. Cartoons reflected changing styles of design, fashion, and economics while evoking the harried nature of daily life. "No one has a view of animation as broad and yet as detailed as Norman Klein's. From the nuances of the art clear out to its richest social implications, he's consistently lucid and stimulating"—Hugh Kenner

See also **FILM IN AMERICA** under **FILM** in **PERFORMING ARTS AND MEDIA**

0-86091-396-1 VERSO $29.95

1-85984-150-3 VERSO PB $19.95

Karal Ann **Marling**

As Seen on TV: The Visual Culture of Everyday Life in the 1950s

The 1950s seen as a decade of design dominated by the new impact of television

0-674-04882-2 HARVARD $24.95

Karl **Meyer**

Pundits, Poets and Wits: An Omnibus of American Newspaper Columns

An anthology of 72 of America's finest columnists. "An irresistibly oddball history of American life"—*Washington Post Book World*

See also **REPORTING** under **20TH-CENTURY AMERICAN ESSAYS AND JOURNALISM** in **LITERATURE OF THE AMERICAS**

0-19-507137-9 OXFORD PB $13.95

Tom **Shachtman**

The Inarticulate Society: Eloquence and Culture in America

How Americans have become increasingly inarticulate and how this linguistic crisis may presage a larger breakdown in democratic governance

0-02-928375-2 FREE PRESS $25.00

Kenneth T. **Walsh**

Feeding the Beast: The White House versus the Press

See also **THE PRESIDENCY** under **AMERICAN POLITICS AND FOREIGN POLICY**

0-679-44290-1 RANDOM HOUSE $25.00

Tom **Wicker**

A Time to Die: The Attica Prison Revolt

The former *New York Times* columnist's gripping account of the 1971 prison revolt and the massacre that followed

0-8032-9756-4 NEBRASKA PB $12.95

Canada

The world's second-largest nation (in area) has a population smaller than California's; 90 percent of the 25 million Canadians occupy just 10 percent of the land. The theory "fewer people, less bother" may help explain Canada's relatively smooth political ride over the past two centuries. A slight tremor was registered in 1967 when De Gaulle uttered his *"Vive le Quebec libre!"* exhortation, after which separatist sentiment occasionally developed into urban terrorist episodes. Fifteen years later, the Constitution Act formalized the already existing state of independence from Britain.

In more recent times, there have been problems related to a significant influx of immigrants, more than five million in all since World War II. A certain amount of regional push-and-pull has brought an acceleration of domestic redistribution policies. Internationally, Canada has matured from a somewhat subservient posture into a role of more self-assertive nationhood—particularly in relation to the United States.

General Histories

Goeffrey **Matthews** & R. Cole **Harris**, editors

Historical Atlas of Canada

R. Cole **Harris**, editor

Volume 1 From the Beginning to 1800

Seventy full-color double-page plates illuminate the impact of the Europeans on Canada, paying close attention to individual frontier settlements. Volumes on the 19th and 20th centuries are forthcoming

0-8020-2495-5 TORONTO $95.00

R. Louis **Gentilcore** & others, editors

Volume 2 The Land Transformed, 1800-1891

0-8020-3447-0 TORONTO $95.00

Donald **Kerr**, editor

Volume 3 Addressing the Twentieth Century, 1891-1961

0-8020-3448-9 TORONTO $95.00

Kenneth **MacNaught**

The Penguin History of Canada

The British dominion from Champlain, the first French explorer, to Trudeau, the last French prime minister

0-14-014998-8 PENGUIN PB $13.95

William L. **Morton**

The Canadian Identity

An interpretation of the history and distinctive national character of Canadians and their attitudes toward Britain and America

0-8020-6139-7 TORONTO PB $13.95

R.T. **Naylor**

Canada in the European Age, 1453-1919

0-919573-70-3 NEWSTAR $39.95

0-919573-69-X NEWSTAR PB $19.95

Doug **Owram**

Promise of Eden: The Canadian Expansionist Movement and the Idea of the West

How 19th-century opinions about the Northwest changed from despising it as an inhospitable region to seeing it as a land of opportunity

0-8020-7390-5 TORONTO PB $22.95

John **Porter**

Vertical Mosaic: An Analysis of Social Class and Power in Canada

0-8020-6055-2 TORONTO PB $19.95

George **Woodcock**

The Century that Made Us: Canada, 1814-1914

0-19-540703-2 OXFORD PB $21.00

Colonial Times

Pierre **Berton**

The Invasion of Canada: 1812-1813

A popular history of the War of 1812 and what led up to it

0-7710-1235-7 MCCLELLAND & STEWART $29.95

Flames across the Border: 1813-1814

A continuation of *The Invasion of Canada*

0-7710-1244-6 MCCLELLAND & STEWART $29.95

Peter C. **Newman**

Caesars of the Wilderness: The Company of Adventurers

The eventful tale of the trading posts that systematically conquered the vast territory that is modern Canada

0-14-011456-4 PENGUIN PB $10.95

Company of Adventurers: The Story of the Hudson's Bay Company

The expansion of the world's largest trading company into the North American wilderness

0-14-006720-5 VIKING PB $9.95

Francis **Parkman**

France and England in North America

Two great empires maneuver for dominance on hostile and unfamiliar terrain; a classic of 19th-century historical writing, despite its obvious biases

Volume 1

0-940450-10-0 LIBRARY OF AMERICA $32.50

Volume 2

See also **LIBRARY OF AMERICA** in **LITERATURE OF THE AMERICAS**

See also **GENERAL HISTORIES** under **SURVEYS OF US HISTORY**

0940-45011 LIBRARY OF AMERICA $37.50

Bruce **Trigger**

Natives and Newcomers: Canada's Heroic Age Reconsidered

A major Canadian anthropologist reinterprets the history of New France. "A landmark, a milestone, epochal in its field"—*Toronto Star*

0-7735-0595-4 TORONTO PB $22.95

Immigrants

"In 1869 the Northwest Territories reverted to the Crown...In the whole of this western empire there was a settled population of about 7,000. Fort Garry, on the present site of Winnipeg, was the hub of settlement. Its population of slightly more than 5,000 was composed of Métis (mixed Indian and white), scattered English speaking farmers, a handful of Americans...and a small group of very active Canadians."— Kenneth McNaught, *The Penguin History of Canada*

Kay J. **Anderson**

Vancouver's Chinatown: Racial Discourse in Canada, 1875-1980

0-7735-1329-9 MCGILL PB $19.95

Tara Singh **Bains** & Hugh **Johnson**

The Four Quarters of the Night: The Life Journey of an Emigrant Sikh

0-7735-1265-9 MCGILL $44.95

0-7735-1266-7 MCGILL PB $19.95

Patrick **Dunae**

Gentlemen Emigrants: From the British Public Schools to the Canadian Frontier

0-88894-324-5 MADRONA $16.95

Bruce S. **Elliott**

Irish Migrants in the Canadas: A New Approach

A focus on a single social group illuminates the migration process from the Atlantic coast to the Ottawa Valley and the Huron Tract

0-7735-0703-5 MCGILL PB $22.95

Canada at War

World War II claimed 42,000 Canadian lives, a figure slightly smaller than in World War 1. Canada's thriving war economy enabled her to offer valuable aid to Britain.

Ken **Bell**

The Way We Were

The combat photographer presents side-by-side photographs of Canadian battle sites from Normandy to the Rhine as they were then and as they are now

0-8020-3990-1 TORONTO $45.00

A.M.J. **Hyatt**

General Sir Arthur Currie: A Military Biography

Currie, the "amateur" soldier of the First World War, had all the instincts of a professional, and he used them to minimize the destruction of the young troops under his command

0-8020-2603-6 TORONTO $30.00

Desmond **Morton** & Glenn **Wright**

Winning the Second Battle: Canadian Veterans and the Civilian Life, 1915-1930

"Readers may be astonished," the authors argue, "to find veterans as the focus and the origin of many of the institutions of our modern industrial society. The re-establishment of veterans became a justification for a National Employment Service. If veterans were entitled to income maintenance and medical care, how could legitimate boundaries be set without, at some point, including the entire citizenry?"

0-8020-5705-5 TORONTO $45.00

0-8020-6634-8 TORONTO PB $18.95

Thomas P. **Socknat**

Witness against War: Pacificism in Canada, 1900-1945

Study of a small but forceful minority in Canadian society, radicalized by the First World War and the peace movement of the interwar years

0-8020-5704-7 TORONTO $40.00

0-8020-6632-1 TORONTO PB $17.95

French Canada and Quebec

Quebec's push for secession, which emerged in the 1960s with militant agitation to separate from Canada and establish a French-speaking nation, has persisted into the '90s. Several constitutional amendment proposals have been drafted, approved, then rejected when they went to the vote.

William D. **Coleman**

The Independence Movement in Quebec, 1945-1980

The coalition that united the francophone business class, middle class, and organized labor in the aftermath of the "Quiet Revolution"

0-8020-6542-2 TORONTO PB $18.95

John **Fitzmaurice**

Quebec and Canada: Past, Present and Future

0-312-65921-0 ST. MARTIN'S $45.00

Richard **Handler**

Nationalism and the Politics of Culture in Quebec

Experimental ethnography through rhetorical analysis brings history, sociology, and philosophy to bear on this vexing problem

0-299-11510-0 WISCONSIN $39.50

0-299-11514-3 WISCONSIN PB $15.75

Canada Today

Robert **Bothwell** & others

Canada, 1900-45

How the everyday lives of Canadians were shaped by the state and by concrete developments in the economy. The authors examine the political currents running through Canada during two wars and assess their impact on social and cultural institutions

0-8020-6801-4 TORONTO PB $21.95

Canada since 1945: Politics, Power and Provincialism

A general history of the postwar years

0-8020-2647-8 TORONTO $45.00

William R. **Duggan**

Our Neighbours Upstairs: The Canadians

A personal view by an old "Canadian hand" in the foreign office

0-88229-530-6 NELSON-HALL $28.95

Dawn **Fuller**

The Heart of Joshua

A personal account of a mother's struggle against her infant's heart problems and a look into the relative merits of Canadian and US health systems

0-8020-5764-0 TORONTO $30.00

0-8020-6675-5 TORONTO PB $12.95

Hugh **Johnston**

The Voyage of the Komagata Maru: The Sikh Challenge to Canada's Colour Bar

0-19-561164-0 OXFORD $22.00
0-7748-0340-1 BRITISH COLUMBIA PB $15.95

Angela **Miles** & Geraldine **Finn**, editors

Feminism in Canada: From Pressure to Politics

0-919619-02-9 BLACK ROSE $39.95

Denis **Smith**

Diplomacy of Fear: Canada and the Cold War, 1941-1948

Canada carves its own pathway through the shifting alliances of Allied and postwar politics

0-8020-6684-4 TORONTO PB $17.95

Charles **Taylor**

Snow Job: Canada, the United States and Vietnam, 1954-1973

0-88784-619-X HOUSE OF ANANSI PB $7.95

Biographies and Memoirs

L. Ian **MacDonald**

Mulroney: The Making of the Prime Minister

0-7710-5469-6 MCCLELLAND & STEWART $22.95

Laura Goodman **Salverson**

Confessions of an Immigrant's Daughter

0-8020-2424-6 TORONTO $30.00
0-8020-6434-5 TORONTO PB $17.95

Pierre Elliott **Trudeau**

Memoirs

0-7710-0036-7 MCCLELLAND & STEWART $29.95

The Constitution

The last legislative link with Britain was severed in 1982, when Queen Elizabeth signed the Constitution Act. Until then (since the British North America Act of 1867), approval from Parliament in London had been required for any constitutional amendment.

Paul C. **Bartholomew** & Joseph F. **Menez**

Summaries of the Leading Cases on the Constitution

0-8226-3008-7 ROWMAN & LITTLEFIELD PB $21.95

Robert **Bothwell**

Canada and Quebec: One Country, Two Histories

0-7748-0524-2 BRITISH COLUMBIA $34.95
0-7748-0542-0 BRITISH COLUMBIA PB $24.95

C.E.S. **Franks**

The Parliament of Canada

A recent Gallup poll found that a majority of Canadians had little or no interest in Parliament, considering it neither important nor effective. Franks examines the theories of parliamentary government and the proposed reforms to the Senate and the electoral system

0-8020-6651-8 TORONTO PB $18.95

Culture and Society

Alan **Filewood**

Collective Encounters: Documentary Theatre in English Canada

0-8020-6669-0 TORONTO PB $16.95

Northrop **Frye**

Divisions on the Ground: Essays on Canadian Culture

The old maestro draws universal applications from Canadian topics

0-88784-093-0 HOUSE OF ANANSI $12.95

Richard **Gruneau** & David **Whitson**

Hockey Night in Canada: Sports, Identities, and Cultural Politics

0-920059-05-8 GARAMOND PB $21.95

Louis A. **Knafla** & Susan **Binnie**, editors

Law, Society, and the State

0-8020-6971-1 TORONTO PB $24.95

A.B. **McKillop**

Contours of Canadian Thought

Explores the thought of a number of English-Canadian thinkers from the 1860s to the 1920s. Chapters include "Evolution, Ethnology, and the Poetic Fancy" and "Science, Authority, and the American Empire"

0-8020-6652-6 TORONTO PB $13.95

Janet **Noel**

Canada Dry: Temperance Crusades Before Confederation

0-8020-6976-2 TORONTO PB $19.95

Jeremy **Webber**

Reimagining Canada: Language, Culture, Community and the Canadian Constitution

0-7735-1146-6 MCGILL $49.95
0-7735-1152-0 MCGILL PB $19.95

Suzanne **Zeller**

Inventing Canada: Early Victorian Science and the Idea of a Transcontinental Nation

The role of science in the expansion of a local into a transcontinental state

0-8020-2644-3 TORONTO $40.00
0-8020-6606-2 TORONTO PB $18.95

Latin America and the Caribbean

General Histories

Leslie **Bethell**, editor

The Cambridge History of Latin America

Volume I
Colonial Latin America, Part I
0-521-23223-6 CAMBRIDGE $119.95

Volume II
Colonial Latin America, Part II
0-521-24516-8 CAMBRIDGE $135.00

Volume III
From Independence to c. 1870
0-521-23224-4 CAMBRIDGE $125.00

Volume IV
c. 1870-1930, Part I
0-521-23225-2 CAMBRIDGE $125.00

Volume V
c. 1870-1930, Part II
0-521-24517-6 CAMBRIDGE $135.00

Volume VI
Latin America since 1930: Economy, Society, and Politics, Part 1
0-521-23226-0 CAMBRIDGE $85.00

Volume VII
Latin America since 1930: Economy, Society, and Politics, Part 2
0-521-46556-7 CAMBRIDGE $85.00

Volume VIII
Latin America since 1930s: Mexico, Central America, and the Caribbean
0-521-24518-4 CAMBRIDGE $125.00

Volume IX
0-521-39524-0 CAMBRIDGE $25.00

Volume X
Latin America since 1930: Ideas, Culture, and Society
0-521-49594-6 CAMBRIDGE $110.00

Volume XI
Bibliographical Essays
0-521-39525-9 CAMBRIDGE $89.95

E. Bradford **Burns**

Latin America: A Concise Interpretive History

A lively examination that focuses on the post-independence era

0-13-501321-6 PRENTICE HALL $35.30

John **Crow**

The Epic of Latin America

Dated, but offers solid information and is still fun to read

0-520-03776-6 CALIFORNIA PB $19.95

Tulio Halperin **Donghi**

The Contemporary History of Latin America

A translation with some new chapters of the classic work which for 25 years has been the most influential and widely read general history of Latin America in the Spanish-speaking world

0-8223-1374-X DUKE PB $23.95

Eduardo **Galeano**

Open Veins of Latin America: Five Centuries of the Pillage of a Continent

"Eminent Latin American author Galeano is both an impassioned and hard-nosed scholar in this well-documented, Marxist-oriented history of Latin America as an exploited continent from Columbus to the present"—*Publishers Weekly*

0-85345-308-X MONTHLY REVIEW PB $15.00

Alan **Gilbert**

Latin America

Concise, scholarly text with maps, photos, and case studies focusing on the social and economic development from the 16th century to the present. Part of a Routledge series on Third World development

0-415-04199-6 ROUTLEDGE PB $14.95

Himilce **Novas**

Everything You Wanted to Know About Latino History

A very light, popular overview for the general US reader in a question-and-answer format. Example: "If Columbus was Italian, why do Hispanics celebrate Columbus Day?"

0-452-27100-2 PLUME PB $12.95

George **Pendle**

The Penguin History of Latin America

"A beginner's guide to the continent…lively and full of anecdotes"—*Financial Times*

0-14-020620-5 PENGUIN PB $15.95

Alain **Rouquie**

The Military and the State in Latin America

0-520-06664-2 CALIFORNIA PB $15.00

Thomas E. **Skidmore** & Peter H. **Smith**

Modern Latin America

Two professors provide a succinct, informed introduction to Latin American history using a case-studies approach to guide students. This revised third edition contains chapters on the end of the Cold War and international drug trafficking

0-19-507649-4 OXFORD PB $22.00

Howard J. **Wiarda** & Harvey F. **Kline**, editors

Latin American Politics and Development

This useful introduction to the complexities of Latin American politics brings together experts on 20 countries who present an updated analysis based on the trend toward democratization

0-8133-0821-6 WESTVIEW PB $26.95

Pre-Columbian Era

Nigel **Davies**

The Ancient Kingdoms of Mexico

Spans four civilizations in ancient Mexico—Olmec, Toltec, Aztec, Teotihuacan—from 1500 BC to 1500 AD

See also MEXICO AND CENTRAL AMERICA: GENERAL WORKS under NATIVE AMERICAN CULTURES: CENTRAL AND SOUTH AMERICA

0-14-013587-1 VIKING PB $12.95

The Inca **Garcilaso de la Vega**

Royal Commentaries of the Incas and General History of Peru

Born in 1539, Garcilaso de la Vega was the illegitimate son of a Spanish cavalier and an Inca princess. His work is an account of the origin, growth, and destruction of the Inca empire, from its legendary birth until the death in 1572 of its last independent ruler

TRANSLATED BY HAROLD V. LIVERMORE
FOREWORD BY ARNOLD J. TOYNBEE

0-292-77038-3 TEXAS PB $17.95

R.C. **Padden**

The Hummingbird and the Hawk: Conquest and Sovereignty in the Valley of Mexico, 1503-1541

A graphic, controversial interpretation of Aztec history and society. "A book in the tradition of the great 19th-century histories: impressive in its form and style, it moves inexorably to its tragic conclusion"—*New Yorker*

0-06-131898-1 HARPERCOLLINS PB $19.58

Well before daybreak of the opening day, legionnaires prepared the victims, who were put in close single file down the steps of the great pyramid, through the city, out over the causeways, and as far as the eye could see. For the average person viewing the spectacle from his rooftop, it would appear that the victims stretched in lines to the ends of the earth. The bulk of the unfortunates were from hostile provinces and the swollen ranks of slavery. On the pyramid's summit four slabs had been set up, one at the head of each staircase, for Tlacaellel and the three kings of the Triple Alliance, all of whom were to begin the affair as sacrificial priests. All was in readiness; the lines of victims were strung out for miles, with great reservoirs at their ends, thousands of trapped humans milling about like cattle, awaiting their turn in the line that was about to move. Suddenly, the brilliantly arrayed kings appeared on the platform and silence fell over the city…great snakeskin drums began to throb, announcing that the lines could now begin to move. The lambs were slaughtered with machine-like precision; as the knife wielders fell exhausted, they were replaced by fresh priests who lifted the heavy blade and let it fall in precise and measured strokes until their arms grew weary; others stepped in without losing a beat. A refinement of mass sacrificial technique was apparent; it took but seconds to dispatch each victim.

THE HUMMINGBIRD AND THE HAWK: CONQUEST AND SOVEREIGNTY IN THE VALLEY OF MEXICO, 1503-1541

Jacques **Soustelle**

Daily Life of the Aztecs on the Eve of the Spanish Conquest

08047 07219 STANFORD PB $12.95

Eric **Wolf**

Sons of the Shaking Earth

A brilliant account of the history and society of Mesoamerica

0-226-90500-4 CHICAGO PB $13.95

The Conquest

Alvar Nuñez **Cabeza de Vaca**

Castaways

0-520-07062-3 CALIFORNIA $30.00
0-520-07063-1 CALIFORNIA PB $13.00

Hernando **Cortes**

Letters from Mexico

Written to Charles V between 1519 and 1526, *Cartas de Relación* is a unique rendition of the conquest by the conqueror himself

TRANSLATED BY ANTHONY R. PAGDEN
INTRODUCTION BY J.H. ELLIOTT

0-300-03799-6 YALE PB $23.00

The Inca **Garcilaso de la Vega**

The Florida of the Inca

Garcilaso de la Vega recounts de Soto's march through the jungles, swampland, and forests between Florida and the Mississippi Valley; the first complete English translation since its publication in Spanish nearly four centuries ago

TRANSLATED BY JOHN & JEANNETTE VARNER

0-292-72434-9 TEXAS PB $24.95

Friar Diego **de Landa**

Yucatan: Before and after the Conquest

Classic 16th-century account of Mayan civilization with 120 illustrations, written by Landa to defend himself against charges of despotic mismanagement. "99 percent of what we know today of the Mayas we know as a result either of what Landa has told us in the pages that follow or have learned in the use and study of what he told"—William Gates

See also THE MAYA under NATIVE AMERICAN CULTURES: CENTRAL AND SOUTH AMERICA

TRANSLATED BY WILLIAM GATES

0-486-23622-6 DOVER PB $5.95

Bartolome **de Las Casas**

In Defense of the Indians

0-87580-042-4 NORTHERN ILLINOIS $30.00
0-87580-556-6 NORTHERN ILLINOIS PB $18.00

William H. **Prescott**

History of the Conquest of Mexico & The Conquest of Peru

Two classics in one volume, dating from the 1840s

0-394-60729-5 RANDOM HOUSE $22.00

Bernal **Díaz Del Castillo**

The Conquest of New Spain

Fifty years after Cortes defeated the Aztecs, Díaz, who served under Cortes, wrote this account of Montezuma's death, the massacre by the Spaniards, and the eventual capture of the capital of Mexico

See also **THE AZTECS** under **NATIVE AMERICAN CULTURES: CENTRAL AND SOUTH AMERICA**

TRANSLATED BY J.M. COHEN

0-14-044123-9 PENGUIN PB $10.95

Eduardo **Galeano**

Memory of Fire

Volume 1

for Volume 2, see "Independence" below

Genesis

0-394-74730-5 PANTHEON PB $16.00

He was old, or felt he was. There wouldn't be enough time, nor would the weary heart hold out. Juan Ponce de Leon wanted to discover and win the unconquered world that the Florida islands had announced. He wanted to dwarf the memory of Christopher Columbus by the grandeur of his feats. Here he landed, following the magic river that crosses the garden of delights. Instead of the fountain of youth, he has met this arrow that penetrates his breast. He will never bathe in the waters that restore energy to the muscles and shine to the eyes without erasing the experience of the mature spirit. The soldiers carry him in their arms toward the ship. The conquered captain murmurs complaints like a newborn baby, but his years remain many and he is still aging. The men carrying him confirm without astonishment that here a new defeat has occurred in the continuous struggle between the alwayses and the nevers.

VOLUME 1: GENESIS

Miguel **Leon-Portilla**

The Broken Spears: The Aztec Account of the Conquest of Mexico

Compiled from Sahagun's Florentine Codex and other 16th-century sources

See also **THE AZTECS** under **NATIVE AMERICAN CULTURES: CENTRAL AND SOUTH AMERICA**

0-8070-5501-8 BEACON PB $14.00

Walter D. **Mignolo**

The Darker Side of the Renaissance: Literacy, Territoriality and Colonization

Breaks down traditional barriers in looking at the colonization of the New World

0-472-10327-X MICHIGAN $42.50

The Colonial Period

C.H. **Haring**

The Spanish Empire in America

A one-volume synthesis of the Spanish colonies in America from 1492 to the wars of independence in the early 19th century. "A completely successful book"—*NY Times*

0-15-684701-9 HARCOURT BRACE PB $7.95

James **Lockhart** & Stuart **Schwartz**

Early Latin America: A History of Colonial Spanish America and Brazil

0-521-29929-2 CAMBRIDGE PB $19.95

Lyle N. **McAlister**

Spain and Portugal in the New World, 1492-1700

See also **THE COLONIAL EMPIRES** under **THE EXPANSION OF EUROPE: EMPIRE AND COMMERCE** under **EARLY MODERN EUROPE** in **WORLD HISTORY AND CURRENT AFFAIRS**

0-8166-1218-8 MINNESOTA PB $19.95

Stanley J. **Stein** & Barbara H. **Stein**

Colonial Heritage of Latin America: Essays on Economic Dependence in Perspective

Six essays on colonial institutions and social attitudes. "The value of this book lies in the demonstration that the peculiar form of direct colonial dependence of Latin America…was almost inevitably succeeded by the neocolonialism of the nineteenth and twentieth centuries"
—E.J. Hobsbawm, *NY Review of Books*

0-19-501292-5 OXFORD PB $14.95

William B. **Taylor**

Drinking, Homicide, and Rebellion in Colonial Mexican Villages

How Indians adjusted to Spanish rule

0-8047-1112-7 STANFORD PB $12.95

Slavery and Piracy

Hilary **Beckles** & Varence **Shepherd**, editor

Caribbean Slave Society and Economy

A scholarly collection of essays on Caribbean slave systems; reflects recent research for students

1-56584-086-0 NEW PRESS PB $20.00

B.R. **Burg**

Sodomy and the Pirate Tradition: English Sea Rovers in the Seventeenth-Century Caribbean

The sexual mores and practices of English buccaneers in the 17th century

See also **HISTORY** under **GAY, LESBIAN, AND BISEXUAL STUDIES** in **SOCIAL STUDIES**

0-8147-1236-3 NYU PB $14.95

Barbara **Bush**

Slave Women in Caribbean Society, 1650-1838

The first study of slave women in the British Caribbean focuses on how their experience differed from that of black men

0-253-31284-1 INDIANA $31.50
0-253-21251-0 INDIANA PB $13.95

Katia M. **de Queiros Mattoso**

To Be a Slave in Brazil, 1500-1888

"A stunning tale of social and economic relations"—Shepard Foreman, *NY Times*

TRANSLATED BY ARTHUR GOLDHAMMER

0-8135-1154-2 RUTGERS $40.00
0-8135-1155-0 RUTGERS PB $16.00

Richard S. **Dunn**

Sugar and Slaves: The Rise of the Planter Class in the English West Indies, 1624-1713

The settlers of St. Christopher, Barbados, Nevis, Montserrat, Antigua, and Jamaica in the early colonial era

0-393-00692-1 NORTON PB $13.95

David **Eltis**

Economic Growth and the Ending of the Transatlantic Slave Trade

"No other scholar…rivals Eltis in tracing the connections between industrialization in Europe and coerced labor in the Americas;…in deciphering the covert activities of large multinational slaving firms; in mastering the details of slave ship tonnage, mortality, and voyage time; or in moving on a global scale from the plantations of Cuba and Brazil back to the sophisticated African slave-trading networks extending from Upper Guinea to Mozambique"
—David Brion Davis, *NY Review of Books*

0-19-504563-7 OXFORD PB $19.95

Peter **Gerhard**

Pirates of the Pacific: 1575-1742

"Peter Gerhard's sparkling account of swashbuckling pirates on the West Coast of Mexico illuminates a vital but often forgotten chapter in the history of international rivalry in the New World"
—John Jay TePaske, Duke University

0-8032-7030-5 NEBRASKA PB $9.95

Robert C. **Ritchie**

Captain Kidd and the War against the Pirates

0-674-09502-2 HARVARD PB $14.95

Captain Kidd

Herbert S. **Klein**

African Slavery in Latin America and the Caribbean

The evolution of slavery in Europe, Africa, and America, and the life and culture of some twelve million African slaves over five centuries

0-19-503838-X OXFORD PB.......$18.95

Richard **Price**

Maroon Societies: Rebel Slave Communities in the Americas

0-8018-2247-5 JOHNS HOPKINS PB.......$15.95

Rebecca J. **Scott**

Slave Emancipation in Cuba: The Transition to Free Labor, 1860-1899

The underlying social process that led to the end of a very profitable institution

0-691-10157-4 PRINCETON PB.......$19.95

Independence

"Whereas out of the North American struggle against the English, thirteen colonies became one United States, the Spanish American insurrections and wars prepared the way not for unity but for the emergence of seventeen separate republics. It has been argued that if Spanish American emancipation had been delayed for just fifty years, until railways could be built, such national fragmentation might have been avoided."—George Pendle, *The Penguin History of Latin America*

David **Bushnell** & Neill **Macaulay**

The Emergence of Latin America in the Nineteenth Century

A clear summary of, and guide to, the politics of the continent

0-19-508401-2 OXFORD.......$45.00

0-19-508402-0 OXFORD PB.......$17.95

Eduardo **Galeano**

Memory of Fire

For Volume 1, see "The Conquest" above

Volume 2 Faces and Masks

See also **MEXICO**

0-394-75167-1 PANTHEON PB.......$15.00

He came on the scene two years ago. In Paris they call him the *Black Spartacus.* Toussaint l'Ouverture has the body of a tadpole and lips that occupy almost all of his face. He was a coachman on a plantation. An old black man taught him to read and write, to cure sick horses, and to talk to men; but he learned on his own how to look not only with his eyes, and he knows how to see flight in every bird that sleeps.

VOLUME 2: FACES AND MASKS

John **Lynch**

The Spanish-American Revolutions, 1808-1826

0-393-95537-0 NORTON PB.......$13.95

Florence E. **Mallon**

Peasant and Nation: The Making of Postcolonial Mexico and Peru

0-520-08505-1 CALIFORNIA PB.......$19.00

Martin **Ros**

Night of Fire: The Black Napoleon and the Battle for Haiti

Dramatic tale of ex-slave Toussaint l'Ouverture's daring military campaign against the world's three largest colonial powers

0-9627613-7-0 SARPEDON PB.......$14.95

Argentina

Four times the size of Texas, Argentina is Latin America's second-largest nation, and one of the most prosperous. In the 20th century, however, Argentina has been beset by serious problems. Conservative administrations alternating with military rule produced a sequence of fierce dictatorships spanning much of the century. This pattern was broken by the victory of the moderate, civilian left in 1983, but, plagued by inflation and an energy crisis, 1989 elections returned the Perónist party to power when Carlos Saul Menem was elected the new president. His administration set in motion plans for a reversal of state control of business in favor of a free-market economy, which featured lowering tariffs and privatizing state-owned businesses.

David **Bushnell**

Reform and Reaction in the Platine Provinces, 1810-1852

Post-independence era Argentina

0-8130-0757-7 FLORIDA PB.......$24.95

D.C. **Platt** & Guido **Di Tella**, editors

Argentina, Australia and Canada: Studies in Comparative Development, 1870-1965

0-312-04868-8 ST. MARTIN'S.......$29.95

Robert A. **Potash**

The Army and Politics in Argentina, 1928-1945: Yrigoyen to Perón

With its companion volume below, a study of one of the most important institutions in modern Argentina—the military

0-8047-0683-2 STANFORD.......$45.00

The Army and Politics in Argentina, 1945-1962: Perón to Frondizi

0-8047-1056-2 STANFORD.......$52.50

David **Rock**

Argentina, 1560-1987: From Spanish Colonization to Alfonsin

Supplemented by a glossary of Spanish terms and a comprehensive bibliography. "Without question this is the best general history of Argentina in the English language"
—Thomas L. Whigham, *Latin America in Books*

0-520-06178-0 CALIFORNIA PB.......$18.00

Authoritarian Argentina: The Nationalist Movement, Its History and Its Impact

The first comprehensive history of the Nationalist movement in Argentina, which came to a head with the notorious "disappearances" of the 1970s. "More than a superb piece of scholarship, it is a warning and a diagnostic tool"
—*American Historical Review*

0-520-20352-6 CALIFORNIA PB.......$14.95

Kristin Hoffman **Ruggiero**

And Here the World Ends: The Life of an Argentine Village

A vivid narrative of contemporary rural life, revealing on a small scale the larger values of people living on the periphery of the modern world

0-8047-1379-0 STANFORD.......$39.50

Domingo F. **Sarmiento**

Life in the Argentine Republic in the Days of the Tyrants: Or, Civilization and Barbarism

A classic polemic against gaucho rule in the 19th century

TRANSLATED BY MARY T. MANN

0-02-851650-8 FREE PRESS PB.......$13.95

Nicolas **Shumway**

The Invention of Argentina

"An engaging account of the writing and debates of that remarkable group of ideologues who shaped Argentina's destiny, several of whom rose to become president of the republic"—*NY Times*

0-520-08284-2 CALIFORNIA PB.......$15.95

Horacio **Verbitsky**

The Flight: Confessions of an Argentine Dirty Warrior

INTRODUCTION BY JUAN MENDEZ, GENERAL COUNSEL, HUMAN RIGHTS WATCH

1-56584-009-7 NEW PRESS.......$22.00

Los Desaparecidos

In 1976 the military deposed Juan Perón's widow, Isabel, from power and proceeded to wage war against so-called subversives. Over 30,000 people "disappeared." Another 10,000 were executed. After enduring a seven-year reign of terror and a brief, disastrous war with Britain over the Falkland Islands, the Argentine people established a democratic government under Raúl Alfonsían. It was short-lived, however. Six years later, a Perónist party member was voted into office, and pardoned those involved in the 1970s war atrocities.

Argentine National Commission on the Disappeared

Nunca Más: The Report of the Argentine National Commission on the Disappeared

INTRODUCTION BY RONALD DWORKIN

0-374-22350-5 OLYMPIC.......$3.98

Andrew **Graham-Yooll**

A Matter of Fear: Portrait of an Argentinian Exile

0-88208-145-4 LAWRENCE HILL PB $7.95

Jacobo **Timerman**

Prisoner without a Name, Cell without a Number

"Ranks with Hannah Arendt's *Eichmann in Jerusalem* in its examination of the totalitarian mind, the role of anti-Semitism, and the silence"—Eliot Fremont-Smith, *Village Voice*

TRANSLATED BY TOBY TALBOT

0-679-72048-0 VINTAGE PB $10.00

Juan and Eva Perón

Robert **Crassweller**

Perón and the Enigmas of Argentina

0-393-30543-0 NORTON PB $14.95

Nicholas **Fraser** & Marysa **Navarro**

Eva Perón

"A fascinating, frightening, straightforward look at the ways a private mythology integrated a public personality"—*Cleveland Plain Dealer*

0-393-30238-5 NORTON PB $11.00

Juan Perón

Las Malvinas: The Falklands

Max **Hastings** & Simon **Jenkins**

The Battle for the Falklands

A diplomatic, military, and naval history of the events of May through July 1982

0-393-30198-2 NORTON PB $13.95

Martin **Middlebrook**

The Fight for the "Malvinas": The Argentine Forces in the Falklands War

0-670-82106-3 VIKING $6.98

Signals of War: The Falklands Conflict of 1982

0-691-02344-1 PRINCETON PB $17.95

Brazil

Occupying almost half the South American continent, Brazil, with its population of over 150 million, is custodian of the mighty Amazon, whose continued maintenance is a matter of worldwide concern. For these and other reasons, Brazil is rightly perceived as a world power to be reckoned with in the 21st century. However, it has not only vast, untapped resources but also one of the world's highest external debts and a similarly alarming rate of inflation. Vibrant and youthful, the nation is seen as a symbol of the future, yet half the population lives in poverty, a condition associated with decades of military and dictatorial rule. A civilian government was voted in by a democratic election in 1985, but the 75-year-old president-elect died before being sworn in, and his vice presidential running mate assumed office. Corruption characterized the succeeding administration, while the nation's inflation rate continued to soar at about 400 percent.

Roderick V. **Barman**

Brazil: The Forging of a Nation, 1798-1952

A new study, published in 1988, that challenges prevailing interpretations by suggesting a more traumatic birth for the Brazilian state

0-8047-1437-1 STANFORD $55.00

Bertha K. **Becker** & Claudio A.G. **Engler**

Brazil: A New Regional Power in the World Economy

Explores Brazil's entry into the capitalist world economy from its origins as a Portuguese colony to its status as a regional power in Latin America and the world's eighth largest economy

0-521-37905-9 CAMBRIDGE PB $18.95

José Maria **Bello**

A History of Modern Brazil, 1889-1964

Based on the 1959 fourth edition, the last to appear in the author's lifetime

TRANSLATED BY JAMES L. TAYLOR

CONCLUDING CHAPTER BY ROLLIE E. POPPINO

0-8047-0240-3 STANFORD PB $17.95

C.R. **Boxer**

The Golden Age of Brazil, 1659-1750: Growing Pains of a Colonial Society

0-312-12639-5 ST. MARTIN'S $49.95

E. Bradford **Burns**

A History of Brazil

Lively and authoritative; the best single-volume history

0-231-07955-9 COLUMBIA PB $22.50

Michael L. **Conniff** & Frank D. **McCann**, editors

Modern Brazil: Elites and Masses in Historical Perspective

Essays on the rural folk, urban workers, immigrants, and the mass media. "The clearest impression I have found in a single work of the origins, evolution, and present status of class and cultural distinctions within Brazilian society"—Rollie E. Poppino, University of California at Davis

0-8032-3131-8 NEBRASKA $40.00

0-8032-6348-1 NEBRASKA PB $17.50

Carolina Maria **De Jesus**

Child of the Dark: The Diary of Carolina Maria De Jesus

A raw, primitive journal of a street scavenger who fought daily for survival for herself and her three illegitimate children in the squalid Brazilian slums. "One of the most astonishing documents of the lower depths ever printed" —*Newsweek*

0-451-62731-8 NEW AMERICAN LIBRARY PB $5.99

Jean **de Lery**

History of a Voyage to the Land of Brazil Otherwise Called America

0-520-08274-5 CALIFORNIA PB $15.95

Peter **Evans**

Dependent Development: The Alliance of Multinational, State, and Local Capital in Brazil

The most important examination of economic development in the past two decades

See also **MODERNIZATION AND DEVELOPING NATIONS** under **TOPICS IN MODERN SOCIOLOGY** under **SOCIOLOGY** in **SOCIAL STUDIES**

0-691-02185-6 PRINCETON PB $14.95

Gilberto **Freyre**

The Mansions and the Shanties: The Making of Modern Brazil

TRANSLATED BY HARRIET DE ONIS

0-520-05681-7 CALIFORNIA PB $18.00

The Masters and the Slaves: A Study in the Development of Brazilian Civilization

TRANSLATED BY SAMUEL PUTNAM

0-520-05665-5 CALIFORNIA PB $18.95

Order and Progress: Brazil from Monarchy to Republic

The rise and fall of patriarchal society, by an acclaimed anthropologist of Brazil

TRANSLATED BY ROD W. HORTON

0-520-05682-5 CALIFORNIA PB $16.95

Orpheus and Power: The Movimento Negro of Rio de Janeiro and São Paulo, Brazil

0-691-03292-0 PRINCETON $29.95

David **Hess**

Samba in the Night: Spiritism in Brazil

See also **NATIVE AMERICAN** under **THE WESTERN HEMISPHERE** under **MYTHOLOGY AND FOLKLORE** in **RELIGION, SPIRITUALITY, AND PHILOSOPHY**

0-231-08432-3 COLUMBIA $29.50

David J. **Hess** & Roberto **DeMatta**, editor

The Brazilian Puzzle

0-231-10115-5 COLUMBIA PB $17.50

Javier **Martinez-Lara**

Building Democracy in Brazil: The Politics of Constitutional Change, 1985-95

0-312-16102-6 ST. MARTIN'S $25.00

Phyllis R. **Parker**

Brazil and the Quiet Intervention, 1964

"A convincing criticism of US–Latin American policy"—*Latin America in Books*

0-292-78507-0 TEXAS $14.50

Andrew **Revkin**

The Burning Season: The Murder of Chico Mendes and the Fight for the Amazon Rain Forest

"A lively narrative that reads like a murder story…rich with natural history and a broad view of the politics of Brazil that put the story in its full context"—*Miami Herald*

0-452-27405-2 PLUME PB $10.95

Alex **Shoumatoff**

The Rivers Amazon

0-87156-771-7 SIERRA CLUB PB $9.00

Thomas L. **Skidmore**

The Politics of Military Rule in Brazil, 1964-85

A bestseller in Brazil

0-19-506316-3 OXFORD PB $18.95

Alfred **Stepan**, editor

Democratizing Brazil: Problems of Transition and Consolidation

0-19-505152-1 OXFORD PB $16.95

Charles **Wagley**

Introduction to Brazil

Dated but still an excellent entry into the continent's largest country

0-231-03543-8 COLUMBIA PB $20.00

Chile

Under the thumb of General Pinochet since the 1973 overthrow of the Marxist Allende government, dissenting Chileans finally merged in 1988 to form a coalition concerted enough to reject Pinochet's quest for an extended mandate. The center-left coalition's candidate, Eduardo Frei, won the 1993 presidential election.

Marjorie **Agosin**

Tapestries of Hope, Threads of Love: The Arpillera Movement in Chile, 1974-1994

A testament to the women who translated the sorrow and pain of oppression into *apilleras*, patchwork tapestries which were memorials to the disappeared as well as quiet forms of rebellion

FORWARD BY ISABEL ALLENDE

0-8263-1692-1 NEW MEXICO PB $45.00

Leslie **Bethell**

Chile Since Independence

Relevant chapters from the *Cambridge History of Latin America*

0-521-43987-6 CAMBRIDGE PB $22.95

Simon **Collier** & William F. **Sater**

A History of Chile, 1880-1994

0-521-56075-6 CAMBRIDGE $54.95

0-521-56827-7 CAMBRIDGE PB $16.95

Pamela **Constable** & Arturo **Valenzuela**

A Nation of Enemies: Chile under Pinochet

0-393-30985-1 NORTON PB $12.95

Nathaniel **Davis**

The Last Two Years of Salvador Allende

0-8014-1791-0 CORNELL $39.95

Julio **Faundez**

Marxism and Democracy in Chile: From 1932 to the Fall of Allende

0-300-04024-5 YALE $35.00

Brian **Loveman**

Chile: The Legacy of Hispanic Capitalism

Tension between the Hispanic tradition in Chile and later outside factors—European capitalism, liberalism, Marxism, and the influence of the United States. "The best single volume on Chilean history"—Charles Bergquist

0-19-505219-6 OXFORD PB $19.95

Timothy R. **Scully**

Rethinking the Center: Party Politics in Nineteenth- and Twentieth-Century Chile

0-8047-1913-6 STANFORD $45.00

Peter **Winn**

Weavers of Revolution: The Yarur Workers and Chile's Road to Socialism

A reinterpretation of the Allende era through analysis of the dramatic seizure of the Yarur cotton mill in Santiago and its widely felt repercussions for Allende's revolution

0-19-504558-0 OXFORD PB $16.95

Mexico

T.R. **Fehrenbach**

Fire and Blood: A History of Mexico

A popular, well-researched history, packed with information

0-306-80628-2 DA CAPO PB $18.95

Eduardo **Galeano**

Memory of Fire

for Volumes 1 & 2, see "The Conquest" and "Independence" above

Volume 3 Century of the Wind

See also **THE REVOLUTIONARY PERIOD**

0-394-75726-2 PANTHEON PB $16.00

The hogs, the cows, the chickens, are they Zapatistas? And the jugs, the pans, the stewpots, what of them? Government troops have exterminated half the population of Morelos in these years of stubborn peasant war, and taken away everything. Only stones and charred stalks remain in the fields; the wreckage of a house, a woman heaving a plow. Of the men, any not dead or exiled have become outlaws. But the war continues. The war will continue as long as corn sprouts in secret mountain crannies, as long as Zapata's eyes flash.

VOLUME 3: CENTURY OF THE WIND

Michael C. **Meyer** & William L. **Sherman**

The Course of Mexican History

Revised 1995 fifth edition; a lavishly illustrated textbook distinguished by coverage of the pre-Columbian period and emphasis on social and cultural development

0-19-504201-8 OXFORD PB $24.95

Henry Bamford **Parkes**

History of Mexico

Originally published in 1938 and most recently revised in 1969. "…remarkably well-balanced and sound interpretation"— *New Republic*

0-395-08410-5 HOUGHTON MIFFLIN PB $13.95

Ramon Eduardo **Ruiz**

Triumphs and Tragedy: A History of the Mexican People

From the Olmec, Maya, and Aztec heritage to today, a sweeping, magisterial general history

0-393-31066-3 NORTON PB $15.95

From the Conquest to the 20th Century

J. **Bazant**

A Concise History of Mexico from Hidalgo to Cardenas, 1805-1940

From the era of independence through the administration of Lazaro Cardenas, the president who affirmed Mexico's control of its own natural resources, nationalized its oil industry, and distributed millions of acres to the peasants

0-521-29173-9 CAMBRIDGE PB $18.95

Howard **Campbell**

Zapotec Struggles

Fascinating account of Zapotec cultural revival (since 1930) in Oaxaca, Mexico

1-56098-268-3 SMITHSONIAN $45.00
1-56098-293-4 SMITHSONIAN PB $19.95

Jonathan **Kandell**

La Capitál: The Biography of Mexico City

An anecdotal rather than analytical narrative, focusing on personalities—Cortes, Archduke Maximilian, Porfirio Diaz, Diego Rivera—rather than on economic or political issues

0-8050-1267-2 HOLT PB $22.50

Jacques **Lafaye**

Quetzalcoatl and Guadalupe: The Formation of the Mexican National Consciousness, 1531-1813

The importance of religious beliefs in the formation of the Mexican nation: "a classic of Mexican history"—*NY Review of Books*

FOREWORD BY OCTAVIO PAZ

0-226-46788-0 CHICAGO PB $16.95

Colin M. **MacLachlan** & Jaime E. **Rodriguez**

The Forging of the Cosmic Race: A Reinterpretation of Colonial Mexico

0-520-04280-8 CALIFORNIA PB $15.95

Laurens B. **Perry**

Juarez and Díaz: Machine Politics in Mexico

Two of Mexico's greatest 19th-century leaders placed against a political backdrop

0-87580-058-0 NORTHERN ILLINOIS $29.00

Nelson **Reed**

The Caste War of Yucatan

The great Mayan revolt against Mexican authority in the middle of the 19th century

See also **MAYAN CULTURE IN THE MODERN PERIOD** under **THE MAYA** under **NATIVE AMERICAN CULTURES: CENTRAL AND SOUTH AMERICA**

0-8047-0165-2 STANFORD PB $14.95

Patricia **Seed**

To Love, Honor, and Obey in Colonial Mexico: Conflicts over Marriage Choice, 1574-1821

Focuses on nearly the entire colonial period in Mexico City

0-8047-1457-6 STANFORD $47.50
0-8047-2159-9 STANFORD PB $16.95

Hugh **Thomas**

Conquest: Montezuma, Cortes, and the Fall of Old Mexico

See also **MEXICO AND CENTRAL AMERICA: GENERAL WORKS** under **NATIVE AMERICAN CULTURES: CENTRAL AND SOUTH AMERICA**

0-671-51104-1 TOUCHSTONE PB $16.00

The Revolutionary Period

Eduardo **Galeano**

Memory of Fire Volume 3 Century of the Wind

0-394-75726-2 PANTHEON PB $16.00

The hogs, the cows, the chickens, are they Zapatistas? And the jugs, the pans, the stewpots, what of them? Government troops have exterminated half the population of Morelos in these years of stubborn peasant war, and taken away everything. Only stones and charred stalks remain in the fields; the wreckage of a house, a woman heaving a plow. Of the men, any not dead or exiled have become outlaws. But the war continues. The war will continue as long as corn sprouts in secret mountain crannies, as long as Zapata's eyes flash.

VOLUME 3: CENTURY OF THE WIND

John Mason **Hart**

Revolutionary Mexico: The Coming and Process of the Mexican Revolution

For Hart the revolution broke out during a global crisis and a wave of nationalistic revolution: in Iran (1905), Russia (1905), and China (1911)

0-520-05995-6 CALIFORNIA $50.00
0-520-06744-4 CALIFORNIA PB $15.95

Friedrich **Katz**

The Secret War in Mexico: Europe, the United States, and the Mexican Revolution

A tour de force exposition of diplomacy and domestic events. "The interplay among the revolutionary factions, the powers, and foreign investors in Mexico is analyzed in all its complexity"—Helen Delpar, *The Americas*

0-226-42589-4 CHICAGO PB $27.50

Alan **Knight**

The Mexican Revolution

A prize-winning study

Volume 1 Porfirians, Liberals and Peasants

0-8032-7770-9 NEBRASKA PB $22.50

Volume 2 Counter-Revolution and Reconstruction

0-8032-7771-7 NEBRASKA PB $22.50

John **Reed**

Insurgent Mexico

By the author of *Ten Days that Shook the World*

0-7178-0099-7 INTERNATIONAL PUB PB $7.95

Ramon E. **Ruiz**

The Great Rebellion: Mexico, 1905-1924

Entertaining mini-biographies

0-393-95129-4 NORTON PB $13.95

Shirlene **Sotto**

Emergence of the Modern Mexican Woman: Her Participation in Revolution and Struggle for Equality

0-912869-12-7 ARDEN PB $16.95

John **Womack**, Jr.

Zapata and the Mexican Revolution

Displays great sympathy for the peasants who made the revolution and their hero who embodied it

0-394-70853-9 RANDOM HOUSE PB $15.00

Contemporary Mexico

Frank **Cancian**

The Decline of Community in Zincantan: Economy, Public Life and Social Stratification

Ethnography of a Mexican community which was transformed by prosperity and government expansion

0-8047-2362-1 STANFORD PB $15.95

George **Collier**

Basta!: Land and the Zapatista Rebellion in Chiapas

Analysis of the forces that produced the Indian agrarian revolution on New Year's Day 1994

0-935028-65-X SUBTERRANEAN PB $12.95

Nora **Hamilton**

The Limits of State Autonomy: Post-Revolutionary Mexico

0-691-02211-9 PRINCETON PB $19.95

Judith Adler **Hellman**

Mexican Lives

"An important book composed of 15 timely focused snapshots of fascinating individuals who, collectively, tell a story about a nation in historic transition"—*Christian Science Monitor*

1-56584-178-6 NEW PRESS PB $11.95

Subcomandante **Marcos**

Shadows of Tender Fury: The Letters and Communiqués of Subcomandante Marcos and the Zapatista Army

TRANSLATED BY LESLIE LOPEZ

0-85345-918-5 MONTHLY REVIEW PB $15.00

Daniel **Nugent**

Spent Cartridges of Revolution: An Anthropological History of Namiquipas Chihuahua

Analysis of a town that seems to have been passed up by the revolution of 1910-1920

0-226-60742-9 CHICAGO PB $15.95

Andres **Oppenheimer**

Bordering on Chaos: Guerrillas, Stockbrokers, Politicians, and Mexico's Quest for Prosperity

0-316-65095-1 LITTLE, BROWN $25.95

Patrick **Oster**

The Mexicans: A Personal Portrait of a People

A journey into the United States's number three trading partner and number one source of illegal drugs; published in 1989

See also **ASPECTS OF MEXICAN CULTURE**

0-06-097310-2 HARPERCOLLINS PB $13.00

Robert A. **Pastor** & Jorge G. **Castaneda**

Limits to Friendship: The United States and Mexico

Explores the mutual mistrust and misconceptions that have characterized international relations. "Valuable, timely and fascinating"—*NY Times*

0-679-72543-1 VINTAGE PB $15.00

Alan **Riding**

Distant Neighbors: Portrait of the Mexicans

An excellent study by a former *New York Times* resident correspondent

0-679-72441-9 VINTAGE PB $13.00

David R. Davila **Villers**, editor

NAFTA, the First Year: A View from Mexico

0-7618-0391-2 UNIVERSITY PRESS OF AMERICA . $42.00

Sidney **Weintraub**

A Marriage of Convenience: Relations between Mexico and the United States—A Twentieth-Century Fund Report

0-19-506125-X OXFORD $29.95

Aspects of Mexican Culture

Roderic Ai **Camp**

Crossing Swords: Politics and Religion in Mexico

0-19-510784-5 OXFORD $42.00

Erich **Fromm** & Michael **MacCoby**

Social Character in a Mexican Village

1-56000-876-8 TRANSACTION PB $24.95

Oscar **Lewis**

The Children of Sanchez

"The stories were taken down by tape recorder, over a period of years, and under various circumstances. The result is a moving, strange tragedy, not an interview, a questionnaire, or a sociological study"—Elizabeth Hardwick

0-394-70280-8 RANDOM HOUSE PB $16.00

Five Families: Mexican Case Studies in the Culture of Poverty

"He was the first anthropologist to insist that there was a culture of poverty which deserved careful ethnographic study, and he invented the method of seeing individuals as they presented themselves within families"
—from the Introduction by Margaret Mead

0-465-09705-7 BASIC BOOKS PB $18.00

Carl J. **Mora**

Mexican Cinema: Reflections of a Society

See also **OTHER COUNTRIES** under **NATIONAL CINEMAS** under **FILM** in **PERFORMING ARTS AND MEDIA**

0-520-04304-9 CALIFORNIA PB $14.95

Patrick **Oster**

The Mexicans: A Personal Portrait of a People

A journey into the United States's number three trading partner and number one source of illegal drugs; published in 1989

See also **CONTEMPORARY MEXICO**

0-06-097310-2 HARPERCOLLINS PB $13.00

Octavio **Paz**

Alternating Current

See also **MEXICO** under **CRITICISM, MEMOIRS, AND OTHER PROSE** under **LATIN AMERICAN LITERATURE** in **LITERATURE OF THE AMERICAS**

1-55970-136-6 ARCADE PB $9.95

The Labyrinth of Solitude: Life and Thought in Mexico

Paz's famous essay on the Mexican character

See also **MEXICO** under **CRITICISM, MEMOIRS, AND OTHER PROSE** under **LATIN AMERICAN LITERATURE** in **LITERATURE OF THE AMERICAS**

TRANSLATED BY LYSANDER KEMP

0-8021-5042-X GROVE PB $13.95

Nations of South America

Bolivia

Oscar **Cornblit**

Power and Violence in the Colonial City: Oruro from the Mining Renaissance to the Rebellion of Tupac Amawu (1740-1782)

0-521-44148-X CAMBRIDGE $59.95

Bruce **Farcau**

The Chaco War: Bolivia and Paraguay, 1932-1935

0-275-95218-5 PRAEGER $59.95

Herbert S. **Klein**

Bolivia: The Evolution of a Multi-Ethnic Society

The preeminent American historian of Bolivia discusses one of the most colorful and dramatic nations in South America

0-19-505735-X OXFORD PB $16.95

Haciendas and Ayllus: Rural Society in the Bolivian Andes in the Eighteenth and Nineteenth Centuries

0-8047-2057-6 STANFORD $39.50

Eric **Lawlor**

In Bolivia

In the tradition of Paul Theroux, a dark and funny journey. Lawlor views Bolivia as a grand opera—with a tragic plot

0-394-75836-6 VINTAGE PB $12.00

Colombia

Colombia is now dominated by the nationwide violence caused by the thriving drug industry—the homicide rate is more than five times that of the United States. So it is all the more noteworthy that the country is one of the few in Latin America to function as a democracy.

Elizabeth E. **Brusco**

The Reformation of Machismo: Evangelical Conversion & Gender in Colombia

Shows how the asceticism required of evangelicals—no drinking, smoking, or extramarital relations—redirects male income back into the household

0-292-70821-1 TEXAS PB $14.95

Ana **Carrigan**

The Palace of Justice: A Colombian Tragedy

When the M-19 guerilla insurgency took the Palace of Justice hostage in Colombia, it defined a tragic moment in that nation's history. The elected president ceded control to the military and a bloodbath ensued, claiming the lives of insurgents, Supreme Court justices, and army personnel. This detailed study provides an unflinching look at the 27-hour turning point in Latin American politics. "Unsparing and convincingly documented"—*Kirkus Reviews*

0-941423-82-4 FOUR WALLS $22.95

Patrick **Clawson**

Colombia before Independence: Economy, Society, and Politics under Bouibon Rule

0-521-41641-8 CAMBRIDGE $65.00

Patrick **Clawson** & Lee **Rensselaer**

The Andean Cocaine Industry

0-312-12400-7 ST. MARTIN'S $35.00

Robert **Davis**, editor

A Historical Dictionary of Colombia

0-8108-2636-4 SCARECROW $62.50

Wendy **Ewald**

Magic Eyes: Scenes from an Andean Girlhood

True-life novel about magic, violence, and the power of seeing, told through native voices and photographs of a Colombian village

0-941920-21-6 BAY PB $18.95

Rakesh **Mohan**
Understanding the Developing Metropolis: Lessons from the City Study of Bogota and Cali, Colombia
0-19-520882-X OXFORD $32.95

Eduardo **Posada-Carbo**
The Colombian Caribbean: A Regional History, 1870-1950
0-19-820628-3 OXFORD $72.00

Ecuador

Blanca **Muratorio**
The Life and Times of Grandfather Alonso: Culture and History in the Upper Amazon
0-8135-1685-4 RUTGERS PB $15.00

Linda A. **Newson**
Life and Death in Early Colonial Ecuador
0-8061-2697-3 OKLAHOMA $45.00

Ronn F. **Pineo**
Social and Economic Reform in Ecuador: Life and Work in Guayaquil
0-8130-1437-9 FLORIDA $49.95

Douglas **Southgate** & Morris **Whitaker**
Economic Progress and the Environment: One Developing Country's Policy Crisis
0-19-508786-0 OXFORD $39.95

Mark J. **Van Aken**
King of the Night: Juan José Flores and Ecuador, 1824-1864
General Juan José Flores rose from humble origins in Venezuela to attain eminence in the wars of independence and the first presidency of Ecuador
0-520-06277-9 CALIFORNIA $50.00

Paraguay

R.B. **Cunninghame Graham**
A Vanished Arcadia: Being Some Account of the Jesuits in Paraguay in 1607-1767
From their arrival in South America in 1550 until their expulsion in 1767, the Jesuits sought to defend the Guarani Indian against enslavement by European settlers. Threats of relocation led to an uprising, and the Indian army was destroyed in 1756. This tragic story provides the background to Roland Joffe's film *The Mission*
0-8383-0949-6 HASKELL $75.00

Paul **Lewis**
Socialism, Liberalism and Dictatorship in Paraguay
0-275-90847-X PRAEGER $49.95

Paul H. **Lewis**
Political Parties and Generations in Paraguay's Liberal Era, 1869-1940
0-8078-2078-4 NORTH CAROLINA $39.95

R. Andrew **Nickson**
Historical Dictionary of Paraguay
0-8108-2643-7 SCARECROW $69.50

Peru

Abraham F. **Lowenthal**
The Peruvian Experiment: Continuity and Change under Military Rule
Evaluates the Peruvian military coup of 1968
0-691-10035-7 PRINCETON PB $19.95

Philip **Mauceri**
State under Siege: Ideology and Policy in Peru since 1973
0-8133-2753-9 WESTVIEW $49.00

Cynthia **McClintock** & Abraham F. **Lowenthal**, editors
The Peruvian Experiment Reconsidered
Essays on Peru, 1968-1980
0-691-07648-0 PRINCETON $70.00

Edmundo **Morales**
Cocaine: White Gold Rush in Peru
A look inside the underground industry
0-8165-1159-4 ARIZONA PB $14.95

Susan E. **Ramirez**
The World Upside Down: Cross-Cultural Contact and Conflict in Sixteenth-Century Peru
0-8047-2416-4 STANFORD $45.00

Veronica **Salles-Reese**
From Viracocha to the Virgin of Copacabana: Representation of the Sacred at Lake Titicaca
0-292-77713-2 TEXAS PB $15.00

Mark **Thurner**
From Two Republics to One Divided: Contradictions of Postcolonial Nation-Making in Andean Peru
0-8223-1812-1 DUKE PB $25.00

Karl S. **Zimmerer**
Changing Fortunes: Biodiversity and Peasant Livelihood in the Peruvian Andes
0-520-20303-8 CALIFORNIA $45.00

Uruguay

John Charles **Chasteen**
Heroes on Horseback: A Life and Times of the Last Gaucho Caudillos
0-8263-1598-4 NEW MEXICO PB $19.95

Simon G. **Hanson**
Utopia in Uruguay: Chapters in the Economic History of Uruguay
0-88355-885-8 HYPERION PB $23.00

Venezuela

Michael **Coppedge**
Strong Parties and Lame Ducks: Presidential Patriarchy and Factionalism in Venezuela
0-8047-2278-1 STANFORD $45.00

Brian Stuart **McBeth**
Juan Vincente Gomez and the Oil Companies in Venezuela, 1908-1935
0-521-24717-9 CAMBRIDGE $74.95

P. Michael **McKinley**
Pre-Revolutionary Caracas: Politics, Economy, and Society, 1777-1811
0-521-30450-4 CAMBRIDGE $69.95

Winthrop R. **Wright**
Cafe con Leche: Race, Class, and National Image in Venezuela
0-292-79080-5 TEXAS PB $12.95

The Caribbean

Ronald **Fernandez**
Cruising the Caribbean: U.S. Influence and Intervention in the 20th Century
A century of disastrous US policy in the region
1-56751-036-1 COMMON COURAGE PB $16.95

Franklin W. **Knight**
The Caribbean: The Genesis of a Fragmented Nationalism
Five centuries of economic and social development, emphasizing such areas as the slave-run plantation economy, US influence, and the effect of Castro's revolution
0-19-505441-5 OXFORD PB $18.95

Franklin W. **Knight** & Colin A. **Palmer**, editors
The Modern Caribbean
Thirteen original essays by experts
0-8078-4240-0 NORTH CAROLINA PB $16.95

Mindie **Lazarus-Black**
Legitimate Acts and Illegal Encounters: Law and Society in Antigua and Barbados
1-56098-327-2 SMITHSONIAN $49.00
1-56098-326-4 SMITHSONIAN PB $24.95

Gordon K. **Lewis**
The Growth of the Modern West Indies
The British and former British West Indian territories from the First World War through the 1960s
0-85345-130-3 MONTHLY REVIEW PB $15.00

Main Currents in Caribbean Thought: The Historical Evolution of Caribbean Society in Its Ideological Aspects, 1492-1900
How European, African, and Asian ideas became Creolized and Americanized, creating an entirely new ideology. "Written with verve, imagination and passion"—*TLS*
0-8018-3492-9 JOHNS HOPKINS PB $15.95

Clive Y. **Thomas**
The Poor and the Powerless: Economic Policy and Change in the Caribbean
A historical overview and contemporary analysis of development strategies in five English-speaking Caribbean countries
0-85345-744-1 MONTHLY REVIEW PB $17.00

Eric **Williams**
From Columbus to Castro: The History of the Caribbean
0-394-71502-0 VINTAGE PB $16.00

Cuba

Leslie **Bethel**, editor
Cuba: A Short History
This first-rate work brings together chapters from the *Cambridge History of Latin America*
0-521-43682-6 CAMBRIDGE PB ....

James A. **Michener** & John **King**
Six Days in Havana
A coffee-table book by the popular author that provides an entertaining behind-the-scenes view
0292776242 TEXAS $24.95

Louis A **Perez**, Jr.
Slaves, Sugar and Colonial Society: Travel Accounts of Cuba
"Perez's superb use of the accounts of travelers in Cuba during the 19th century substantially broadens our understanding of that first century of Spanish control of the island"
—*Christian Science Monitor*
0-8420-2415-8 SCHOLARLY RESOURCES PB $14.95

Sidney **Mintz**
Caribbean Transformations
0-231-07115-9 COLUMBIA PB $17.00

José **Martí**
The writings of the late 19th-century political journalist and activist José Martí had a profound influence on 20th-century Cuban politics. From 1881 to 1895 Martí lived most of the time in New York, where his initial sympathy for American democracy was transformed into an ardent hostility toward capitalism and most of its cultural implications.

On Art and Literature: Critical Writings
Includes essays on Goya, Emerson, Whitman, Pushkin, and Wilde
EDITED WITH AN INTRODUCTION BY PHILIP S. FONER
0-85345-590-2 MONTHLY REVIEW PB $15.00

Our America: Writings on Latin America and the Struggle for Cuban Independence
0-85345-495-7 MONTHLY REVIEW PB $10.00

G. L. **Simons** & Geoff **Simons**
Cuba: From Conquistador to Castro
0-312-12822-3 ST. MARTIN'S $29.95

Cuba under Communism

Gianni **Mina**
An Encounter with Fidel
Rare view of Castro based on a marathon interview prepared for Italian television. "This is the Fidel I believe I know: a man of austere ways and insatiable illusions, of cautious words and simple manner and incapable of conceiving of any idea which is not out of the ordinary"
—Gabriel Garcia Marquez
1-87528-422-2 OCEAN $34.95

Robert E. **Quirk**
Fidel Castro
From privileged childhood to "Maximum Leader," award-winning historian Quirk provides the most accurate picture yet of Castro, whose career has survived the fall of the Soviet Union and eight American presidents. "A balanced, well-written and definitive examination of the long, turbulent, and often unheroic career of the architect of Cuba's revolution"—*Kirkus Reviews*
0-393-03485-2 NORTON $35.00
0-393-31327-1 NORTON PB $16.00

Tad **Szulc**
Fidel: A Critical Portrait
The most thorough biography of the dictator to date; a critical assessment filled with good gossip and insights
0-380-69956-7 AVON PB $5.95

Yvonne **Daniel**
Rumba: Dance and Social Change in Contemporary Cuba
An ethnographic report on the rumba and its development from once a lower-class recreational dance to a symbol of egalitarianism in post-revolutionary Cuba
See also **DANCE AND ANTHROPOLOGY** under **SPECIAL TOPICS** under **DANCE** in **PERFORMING ARTS AND MEDIA**
0-253-31605-7 INDIANA $29.95
0-253-20948-X INDIANA PB $12.95

Lynn **Geldof**
Cubans: Voices of Change
32 conversations with Cubans who fled, those who stayed, and leading experts on Cuban policy
0-312-07689-4 ST. MARTIN'S PB $13.95

Che **Guevara**
Guerrilla Warfare
Guevara's works and the application of his theories to guerrilla campaigns in Central and South America; with useful maps and chronologies
INTRODUCTION & CASE STUDIES BY BRIAN LOVEMAN & THOMAS M. DAVIES, JR.
0-8032-7010-0 NEBRASKA PB $14.00

Che Guevara

Guillermo Cabrera **Infante**
Mea Cuba
"An enduringly original literary presence, unquestionably Cuba's most important living writer...His view of Cuba is as clear as it is relentless, and he has Cuba at heart"
—Alastair Reid, *NY Review of Books*
See also **CUBA** under **FICTION** under **LATIN AMERICAN LITERATURE** in **LITERATURE OF THE AMERICAS**
See also **CUBA** under **CRITICISM, MEMOIRS, AND OTHER PROSE** under **LATIN AMERICAN LITERATURE** in **LITERATURE OF THE AMERICAS**
TRANSLATED BY KENNETH HALL
0-374-20497-7 FS&G $23.00
0-374-52446-7 NOONDAY PB $15.00

Oscar **Lewis**
Four Women Living the Revolution: An Oral History of Contemporary Cuba
With its companion volume below, examines everyday life in Cuba
0-252-00639-9 ILLINOIS $39.95

Carlos **Lechuga**
In the Eye of the Storm: Castro, Krushchev, Kennedy and the Missile Crisis
An inside account by Cuba's former UN ambassador
1-87528-487-7 OCEAN PB $15.95

Kennedy & Krushchev

Oscar **Lewis** & others
Four Men Living the Revolution: An Oral History of Contemporary Cuba
0-252-00628-3 ILLINOIS $44.95

Louis A. **Perez**
Cuba: Between Reform and Revolution
0-19-509481-6 OXFORD $55.00
0-19-509482-4 OXFORD PB $19.95

Ramón E. **Ruiz**
Cuba: The Making of a Revolution
Argues that the revolution did not represent a sharp break with the past but grew out of events that had been developing for well over half a century
0-393-00513-5 NORTON PB $8.95

Lois M. **Smith** & Alfred **Padula**
Sex and Revolution: Women in Socialist Cuba
0-19-509490-5 OXFORD $39.95
0-19-509491-3 OXFORD PB $16.95

Haiti

Jean-Bertrand **Aristide**
Dignity
Published in 1996 by the president of Haiti
0-8139-1674-7 VIRGINIA $27.95

Joan **Dayan**
Haiti, History, and the Gods
0-520-08900-6 CALIFORNIA $35.00

Katherine **Dunham**
Island Possessed
This pioneering dancer, choreographer, and anthropologist who first visited Haiti as a graduate student offers vivid personal sketches of the island and its people
See also **MODERN DANCERS, CHOREOGRAPHERS, AND SCHOOLS** under **THE 20TH CENTURY** under **DANCE** in **PERFORMING ARTS AND MEDIA**
0-226-17113-2 CHICAGO PB $11.95

Paul **Farmer**
The Uses of Haiti
A physician with over a decade of experience in rural Haiti brings into relief the myriad forces that have long kept Haitians poor, sick, and silenced
1-56751-034-5 COMMON COURAGE PB $14.95

Carolyn E. **Frick**
The Making of Haiti: The Saint Domingue Revolution from Below
Revisionist analysis of the revolt of the slave underclass in 1791—"the only successful slave rebellion in history"—which argues that the slaves were the primary architects of their freedom and the colony's move to independence as the black republic of Haiti
0-87049-667-0 TENNESSEE PB $21.50

C.L.R. **James**
The Black Jacobins: Toussaint l'Ouverture and the San Domingo Revolution
James's most famous book, an influential interpretation of the Haitian revolution of the 1790s
See also **CARIBBEAN LITERATURE** in **LITERATURE OF THE AMERICAS**
0-679-72467-2 VINTAGE PB $14.00

Jean-Bertrand Aristide

NACLA, editor
Haiti: Dangerous Crossroads
Series of essays, from the Left, that were the first to analyze Haiti after US intervention in 1994
0-89608-505-8 SOUTH END PB $15.00

David **Nicholls**
From Dessalines to Duvalier: Race, Colour and National Independence in Haiti
0-8135-2239-0 RUTGERS $50.00
0-8135-2240-4 RUTGERS PB $18.95

Hans **Schmidt**
The U.S. Occupation of Haiti, 1915-1934
"A good history of a sordid intervention that submitted a people to autocratic rule and did little for economic development"—*NY Times*
0-8135-2203-X RUTGERS PB $15.95

Jamaica

Leonard E. **Barrett**, Sr.
The Rastafarians: Sounds of Cultural Dissonance
The best study of this controversial social and religious force. This updated edition includes new information on the impact of the deaths of Haile Selassie and Bob Marley
0-8070-1027-8 BEACON PB $15.00

Morris **Cargill**
Jamaica Farewell
Personal memoir of leave-taking from a widely respected Jamaican newspaper columnist whose family has lived on the island for three centuries
1-56980-031-6 BARRICADE PB $7.95

Barry **Chavannes**
Rastafari: Roots and Ideology
Historical-ethnographic work on the origins and practices of Rastafarianism
0-8156-0296-0 SYRACUSE PB $17.95

Daryl C. **Dance**
Folklore from Contemporary Jamaica
With brief critical introductions to each chapter, photographs, and original drawings
0-87049-566-6 TENNESSEE PB $16.00

Michael **Manley**
The Politics of Change: A Jamaican Testament
0-88258-049-3 HOWARD PB $15.95

Up the Down Escalator: Development and the International Economy—a Jamaican Case Study
0-88258-112-0 HOWARD $27.50

Puerto Rico

Raymond **Carr**
Puerto Rico: A Colonial Experiment
A dispassionate and disturbing analysis of Puerto Rico's relations with its imperial rulers from the time it was a Spanish colony to the present
0-8147-1389-0 NYU $45.00

Arturo Morales **Carrion**
Puerto Rico: A Political and Cultural History
The Puerto Rican search for identity
0-393-30193-1 NORTON PB $13.95

Edward **Rivera**
Family Installments: Memories of Growing Up Hispanic
A family's journey from a small Puerto Rican village to New York City. "An intense, living drama of the Puerto Rican diaspora"
—Geraldo Rivera
0-14-006726-4 VIKING PB $12.95

Cesar Andreu **Iglesias**, editor
Memoirs of Bernardo Vega: A Contribution to the History of the Puerto Rican Community in New York
Oral history of a Puerto Rican laborer in the early 1900s
TRANSLATED BY JUAN FLORES
0-85345-656-9 MONTHLY REVIEW PB $16.00

Sidney **Mintz**
Worker in the Cane: A Puerto Rican Life History
0-393-00731-6 NORTON PB $12.95

Central America

John A. **Booth** & Thomas W. **Walker**
Understanding Central America
"The most useful single volume on contemporary Central America"
—*Journal of Third World Studies*
0813382190 WESTVIEW PB $16.95

Victor **Bulmer-Thomas**
The Political Economy of Central America since 1920
A scholarly study of the five Central American republics by the co-editor of the *Journal of Latin American Studies*
0-521-34839-0 CAMBRIDGE PB $22.95

Noam **Chomsky**
Turning the Tide: U.S. Intervention in Central America: The Struggle for Peace
One of the region's fiercest left-wing critics looks at the aim and impact of US policy, especially in Nicaragua and El Salvador, and argues that US academics and the media distort the truth
0-89608-266-0 SOUTH END PB $16.00

Martha **Honey**
Hostile Acts: U.S. Policy in Costa Rica in the 1980s
How Reagan, Bush, and Iran-Contra operatives undermined Latin America's oldest democracy
0-8130-1250-3 FLORIDA PB $24.95

Lester D. **Langley** & Thomas **Schoonover**
The Banana Men: American Mercenaries and Entrepreneurs in Central America, 1880-1930
A saga of colorful characters and modernization, American-style
0-8131-1891-3 KENTUCKY $29.95

Thomas M. **Leonard**
The United States and Central America, 1944-1949: Perceptions of Political Dynamics
0-8173-0190-9 ALABAMA $26.50

Stephen G. **Rabe**
Eisenhower and Latin America: The Foreign Policy of Anticommunism
In portraying Eisenhower as a virulent cold warrior, the author challenges the revisionists who consider him a model of diplomatic restraint. "Should become the standard account"—Walter LaFeber
0-8078-4204-4 NORTH CAROLINA PB $14.95

Ralph L. **Woodward**, Jr.
Central America: A Nation Divided
This revised edition covers events since 1976, including US withdrawal of control from the Panama Canal, the Nicaraguan revolution, and civil war in El Salvador
0-19-503593-3 OXFORD PB $17.95

El Salvador

Robert **Armstrong** & Janet **Shenk**
El Salvador: The Face of Revolution
0-89608-137-0 SOUTH END PB $12.00

Roque **Dalton**
El Salvador at War: A Collage Epic
0-930656-54-7 MEP PB $10.95

Miguel Marmol
Testimony of a revolutionary, documenting historical and political events of El Salvador during the first decades of the 20th century
0-915306-68-9 CURBSTONE $19.95
0-915306-67-0 CURBSTONE PB $12.95

Joan Didion

Joan **Didion**
Salvador
"Didion has that rare gift, the ability to take in the essence of a country through her pores"
—Robert E. White, former US ambassador to El Salvador
See also REPORTING under 20TH-CENTURY AMERICAN ESSAYS AND JOURNALISM in LITERATURE OF THE AMERICAS
0-679-75183-1 VINTAGE PB $10.00

Teresa **Witfield**
Paying the Price: Ignacio Ellacuria and the Murdered Jesuits of El Salvador
1-56639-253-5 TEMPLE PB $19.95

Guatemala

George **Black** & others
Garrison Guatemala
From the democratic revolution of 1944 to the present
0-85345-665-8 MONTHLY REVIEW $25.00

Elizabeth **Burgos-Debray**, editor
I...Rigoberta Menchu: An Indian Woman in Guatemala
The stuff of everyday life in a Guatemalan Indian community. "A fascinating and moving description of the culture of an entire people"
—*Times* (London)
0-86091-788-6 VERSO PB $17.00

Piero **Gleijeses**
Shattered Hopes: The Guatemalan Revolution and the U.S., 1944-1954
The first revolution that saw true agrarian reform in Central America and its downfall by a CIA-orchestrated coup
0-691-02556-8 PRINCETON PB $17.95

Jill **Harbury**
Bridge of Courage: Life Stories of the Guatemalan Compañeros and Compañeras
Personal testimonies from a leftist perspective. "If we are to understand our neighbors below the border, their vision and hopes, this is the book to read"—Studs Terkel
1-56751-068-X COMMON COURAGE PB $14.95

Richard H. **Immerman**
The CIA in Guatemala: The Foreign Policy of Intervention
The US role in the overthrow of the democratic government of Guatemala in 1954; a tension-packed account
0-292-71083-6 TEXAS PB $15.95

Stephen **Schlesinger** & Stephen **Kinzer**
Bitter Fruit: The Untold Story of the American Coup in Guatemala
"Schlesinger and Kinzer have done the greatest service to truth and justice by presenting the untold story of the CIA coup"—Carlos Fuentes
0-385-18354-2 ANCHOR PB $12.95

Nicaragua

Claribel **Alegria** & Darwin **Flakoll**
Death of Somoza
1-88068-426-8 CURBSTONE PB $12.95

Violeta **Chamorro**
Dreams of the Heart: The Autobiography of Violeta Barrios de Chamorro, President of Nicaragua
0-684-81055-7 SIMON & SCHUSTER $25.00

Tomas **Borge**
The Patient Impatience: From Boyhood to Guerilla: A Personal Narrative of Nicaragua's Struggle for Liberation
The former Minister of the Interior and the sole surviving member of the founding Sandinistas provides a personal view of the Nicaraguan revolution
0-915306-97-2 CURBSTONE $24.95

Shirley **Christian**
Nicaragua: Revolution in the Family
"If you decided to read just one blow-by-blow account of recent Nicaraguan events, this should be it"—*Philadelphia Inquirer*
84-320-4762-7 PLANETA EDITORIAL PB $19.50

Forrest D. **Colburn**
Post-Revolutionary Nicaragua: State, Class, and the Dilemmas of Agrarian Policy
0-520-05524-1 CALIFORNIA $40.00
0-520-06166-7 CALIFORNIA PB $11.95

Richard L. **Harris** & Carlos M. **Vilas**, editors
Nicaragua: A Revolution Under Siege
0-86232-484-X ZED PB $15.00

Donald C. **Hodges**
Intellectual Foundations of the Nicaraguan Revolution
Argues that the leaders of the Nicaraguan Revolution were neither doctrinaire Marxist-Leninists nor reform-minded social democrats but, rather, represented the Latin American New Left that incorporated features of both; by the author of *Argentina, 1943-1987: The National Revolution and Resistance*
0-292-73838-2 TEXAS $27.50
0-292-73843-9 TEXAS PB $12.95

Anthony **Lake**
Somoza Falling: A Case Study in the Making of U.S. Foreign Policy
Based on the 1978 Nicaraguan crisis
See also SPECIAL TOPICS IN AMERICAN FOREIGN POLICY under AMERICAN POLITICS AND FOREIGN POLICY
0-87023-733-0 MASSACHUSETTS PB $17.95

Neill **Macaulay**
The Sandino Affair
Augusto Sandino, the rebel leader, anarcho-syndicalist, and opponent of US intervention, was murdered in 1934 by the National Guard, on the order of its leader, Anastasio Somoza Garcia
0-8223-0696-4 DUKE PB $18.95

Panama

Ulrich **Keller**, editor
The Building of the Panama Canal in Historic Photographs
0-486-24408-3 DOVER PB $10.95

Stephanie C. **Kane**
The Phantom Gringo Boat: Shamanic Discourse and Development in Panama
1-56098-360-4 SMITHSONIAN PB $19.95

David **McCullough**
The Path between the Seas: The Creation of the Panama Canal, 1870-1914
A gripping narrative of the extraordinary construction job between the Atlantic and Pacific oceans, by the Pulitzer Prize-winning author
See also THE GILDED AGE AND THE PROGRESSIVE ERA under US HISTORY, 1877-1945
0-671-24409-4 SIMON & SCHUSTER PB $14.95

Christopher **Ward**
Imperial Panama: Commerce and Conflict in Isthmian America, 1550-1800
0-8263-1434-1 NEW MEXICO $29.95

Almon R. **Wright**
Panama: Tension's Child, 1502-1989
0-533-08626-4 VANTAGE $16.95

Aspects of Latin America

Alma **Guillermoprieto**
The Heart That Bleeds: Latin America Now
0-679-75795-3 VINTAGE PB $13.00

Economic Development

There is an enormous controversy over the origins of Latin American underdevelopment.

Maria Ines **Bastos** & Charles **Cooper**
Politics of Technology in Latin America
0-415-12690-8 ROUTLEDGE $75.00

Victor **Bulmner-Thomas**, editor
The Economic History of Latin America since Independence
0-521-36872-3 CAMBRIDGE PB $17.95

Fernando H. **Cardoso** & Enzo **Faletto**
Dependency and Development in Latin America
The most persuasive elucidation of the "dependency" approach. Suggests that the dependency of Latin America stems not merely from the domination of the world market over national and "enclave" economies, but also from the more complex interaction of economic drives, political structures, social movements, and historically conditioned alliances. An essential book
TRANSLATED BY MARJORY MATTINGLY URQUIDI
0-520-03527-5 CALIFORNIA PB $14.95

David **Collier**
The New Authoritarianism in Latin America
Essays by leading economists, political scientists, and sociologists explain the rise of authoritarian regimes and their relationship to the problems of economic development
0-691-02194-5 PRINCETON PB $19.95

Frederick **Cooper** & others
Confronting Historical Paradigms: Peasants, Labor, and the Capitalist World System in Africa and Latin America
0-299-13684-1 WISCONSIN PB $15.95

Hernando **de Soto**
The Other Path: The Invisible Revolution in the Third World
Using Lima, Peru as a case study, shows how the world of the black marketeers and the underground economy holds great promise —*New York Times*
0-06-091640-0 HARPERCOLLINS PB $15.00

Jeffrey A. **Frieden**
Debt, Development and Democracy: Modern Political Economy and Latin America
The interplay between politics and economics—especially lobbying by powerful interest groups—in the region's five largest debtor states: Argentina, Brazil, Chile, Mexico, and Venezuela
0-691-00399-8 PRINCETON PB $18.95

Celso **Furtado**
Economic Development of Latin America
A highy recommended book
0-521-29070-8 CAMBRIDGE PB $22.95

Religion

Phillip **Berryman**
Liberation Theology
A sympathetic exposition by an American Catholic antiwar activist and former priest
0-394-74652-X PANTHEON PB $11.00

Penny **Lernoux**
Cry of the People: The Struggle for Human Rights in Latin America—the Catholic Church in Conflict with U.S. Policy
Argues that the metamorphosis of the Catholic Church is the most significant development in Latin America since the Cuban revolution. "Powerful and important…Lernoux writes with intelligence and passion"—*Nation*
0-14-006047-2 PENGUIN PB $9.95

Michael **Lowy**
The War of the Gods: Religion and Politics in Latin America
1-85984-907-5 VERSO $42.00

Daniel H. **Levine**

Religion and Politics in Latin America: The Catholic Church in Venezuela and Colombia

0-691-02200-3 PRINCETON PB $15.95

Politics

Robert J. **Alexander**

The ABC Presidents: Conversations and Correspondence with the Presidents of Argentina, Brazil and Chile

0-275-94110-8 PRAEGER $47.95

Charles **Bergquist**

Labor in Latin America

Comparative essays on Chile, Argentina, Venezuela, and Colombia

0-8047-1253-0 STANFORD $57.50

John A. **Booth** & Mitchell A. **Seligson**, editors

Political Participation in Latin America

Volume 1 is out of print

Volume 2 Politics and the Poor

0-8419-0406-5 HOLMES & MEIER PB $14.00

Ruth Berins **Collier** & David **Collier**

Shaping the Political Arena: Critical Junctures, the Labor Movement and Regime Dynamics in Latin America

0-691-02313-1 PRINCETON PB $24.95

Juan E. **Corradi** & others

Fear at the Edge: State Terror and Resistance in Latin America

0-520-07705-9 CALIFORNIA PB $14.00

John J. **Johnson**

Political Change in Latin America: The Emergence of the Huddle Sectors

A classic that looked to the middle class as the key to Latin American democracy. Discredited in the 1960s and 1970s, it is now making a comeback

0-8047-0528-3 STANFORD $42.50

Bruce **Marcus** & Michael **Taber**, editors

Maurice Bishop Speaks: The Grenada Revolution, 1979-83

A collection of speeches by the late prime minister

0-87348-612-9 PATHFINDER PB $20.95

Guillermo **O'Donnell**, editor

Transitions from Authoritarian Rule: Tentative Conclusions about Uncertain Democracies

0-8018-2682-9 JOHNS HOPKINS PB $8.95

Guillermo **O'Donnell** & Philippe C. **Schmitter**, editors

Transitions from Authoritarian Rule: Comparative Perspectives

0-8018-3192-X JOHNS HOPKINS PB $12.50

John A. **Peeler**

Latin American Democracies

0-8078-4153-6 NORTH CAROLINA PB $13.95

Sarah A. **Radcliffe** & Sallie **Westwood**

Remaking the Nation: Identity and Politics in Latin America

0-415-12337-2 ROUTLEDGE PB $25.00

Alfred **Stepan**

Rethinking Military Politics: Brazil and the Southern Cone

0-691-07750-9 PRINCETON $29.00

0-691-02274-7 PRINCETON PB $11.95

Gary W. **Wynia**

The Politics of Latin American Development

One of the best overviews

0-521-27842-2 CAMBRIDGE PB $16.95

International Relations and Finance

Pedro-Pablo **Kuczynski**

Latin American Debt

The debt crisis from the high inflation and cheap credit of the 1970s through 1987, when the total amount owed by all Latin American countries was five times their combined earnings from exports. By a former Peruvian cabinet member and investment banker

0-8018-3660-3 JOHNS HOPKINS PB $13.95

John D. **Martz**

United States Policy in Latin America: A Quarter Century of Crisis and Challenge, 1961-1986

Topics include Johnson's invasion of the Dominican Republic, Nixon's actions against the Marxist regime in Chile, and Carter's negotiation of the Panama Canal treaties

0-8032-8189-7 NEBRASKA PB $25.00

Lars **Schoultz**

Human Rights and United States Policy toward Latin America

From the early 1960s through 1980

0-691-02204-6 PRINCETON PB $18.95

Barbara **Stallings**

Banker to the World: U.S. Portfolio Investment in Latin America, 1900-1986

"Stands out for its historical perspective, useful collection of data, sound economic analysis, and cool understanding. It is at the same time scholarly and accessible"—Charles P. Kindleberger

0-520-06164-0 CALIFORNIA PB $15.00

Social Thought, Culture, and Aesthetics

Julianne **Burton**, editor

Cinema and Social Change in Latin America

Twenty interviews with key figures of Latin American cinema, covering three decades and ranging from Argentina to Mexico

See also **OTHER COUNTRIES** under **NATIONAL CINEMAS** under **FILM** in **PERFORMING ARTS AND MEDIA**

0-292-72453-5 TEXAS $25.00

0-292-72454-3 TEXAS PB $16.95

Jan **Carew**

Fulcrums of Change: Origins of Racism in the Americas and Other Essays

The Guyanese poet and novelist on racism, exile, and imperialism

0-86543-033-0 AFRICA WORLD PB $9.95

Asunción **Lavrin**

Women, Feminism, and Social Change in Argentina, Chile, and Uruguay, 1890-1940

0-8032-2897-X NEBRASKA $60.00

Francesca **Miller**

Latin American Women and the Search for Social Justice

The first comprehensive history of women in Latin America, showing their role in the politics of reform, national liberation, democracy, and international feminism

0-87451-558-0 NEW ENGLAND PB $19.95

Sally **Price** & Richard **Price**

Equatoria

Experimental, post-modernist travelogue and critique of the rainforest of French Guiana, focusing on the major concerns of anthropology and how it should represent different cultures

0-415-90895-7 ROUTLEDGE PB $17.95

Margaret **Randall**

Sandino's Daughters Revisited: Feminism in Nicaragua

In 1989, Randall revisited a group of Nicaraguan women she first interviewed 10 years earlier during their struggle against Somoza. The result is a moving account of the relationship between feminism and revolution as it is expressed in the daily lives of Nicaraguan women—how the revolution made them strong and how it also held them back

0-8135-2025-8 RUTGERS PB $16.95

José Enrique **Rodo**

Ariel

First published in 1900 in Uruguay, *Ariel* is Latin America's most famous essay on aesthetic and philosophical sensibility, as well as its most discussed treatise on hemispheric relations

TRANSLATED BY MARGARET SAYERS PEDEN

PROLOGUE BY CARLOS FUENTES

0-292-70396-1 TEXAS PB $9.95

Helen I. **Safa**

The Myth of the Male Breadwinner: Women and Industrialization in the Caribbean

Based on studies of industrial workers, argues that women have been more successful in challenging their subordination in the home than in the workplace or political parties

0-8133-1212-4 WESTVIEW PB $18.95

Pedro Perez **Sarduy** & Jean **Stubbs**, editors

Afrocuba: An Anthology of Cuban Writing on Race, Politics, and Culture

Looks at black experience in Cuba through the island's writers, scholars, and artists

1-87528-441-9 OCEAN PB $17.95

Judith A. **Weiss**

Latin American Popular Theater

Interdisciplinary study on evolution of the theater, especially the New Popular Theater

0-8263-1401-5 NEW MEXICO $42.50

Late Arrivals

Noam **Chomsky** & R.C. **Lewontin**

The Cold War and the University: Toward an Intellectual History of the Postwar Years

1-56584-005-4 NEW PRESS $25.00

Noam Chomsky

Tom **Clancy**

Marine: A Guided Tour of a Marine Expeditionary Unit

0-425-15454-8 BERKELEY PB $16.00

Mary B. **Davis**, editor

Native America in the Twentieth Century: An Encyclopedia

0-8153-2583-5 GARLAND PB $24.95

Albert **French**

Patches of Fire: A Story of War and Redemption

The experience of black soldiers in Vietnam

0-385-48363-5 ANCHOR $22.95

Stephen B. **Goddard**

Getting There: The Epic Struggle between Road and Rail in the American Century

0-465-02639-7 BASIC $28.00
0-226-30043-9 CHICAGO PB $15.95

Lewis L. **Gould**, editor

American First Ladies: Their Lives and Their Legacy

0-8153-2585-1 GARLAND PB $22.95

Paul **Hendrickson**

The Living and the Dead: Robert McNamara and Five Lost Lives of a Lost War

0-679-42761-9 KNOPF $27.50

Oliver Wendell **Holmes** & Felix **Frankfurter**

Holmes and Frankfurter: Their Correspondence, 1912-34

EDITED BY ROBERT M. MENNEL

0-87451-758-3 NEW HAMPSHIRE $45.00

Frederick E. **Hoxie**, editor

Encyclopedia of North American Indians

0-395-66921-9 HOUGHTON MIFFLIN $39.95

Marybeth **Lorbiecki**

Aldo Leopold: A Fierce Green Fire

1-56044-478-9 FALCN $19.95

David Herbert **Donald**

Lincoln

Perhaps *the* Lincoln biography of its generation draws on Lincoln's personal papers and the vast, unexplored records of his legal practice to recreate his world with immediacy and rich detail

See also **LINCOLN** under **THE LEADERS** under **THE CIVIL WAR AND RECONSTRUCTION**

0-684-80846-3 SIMON & SCHUSTER $35.00
0-684-82535-X TOUCHSTONE PB $17.00

John H. **Moore**

The Cheyenne

1-55786-484-5 BLACKWELL $27.95

Joseph A. **Page**

The Brazilians

A study of contemporary Brazilian culture and society

0-201-40913-5 ADDISON-WESLEY $27.50
0-201-44191-8 ADDISON-WESLEY PB $17.00

Eva **Perón**

In My Own Words: Evita

1-56584-353-3 NEW PRESS PB $9.95

Cedric J. **Robinson**

Black Movements in America

0-415-91222-9 ROUTLEDGE $59.95
0-415-91223-7 ROUTLEDGE PB $16.95

Jonathan **Schell**

World Enough and Time: A Political Chronicle

1-55921-177-6 MOYER BELL $24.95

Michael Ernest **Smith**

The Aztecs

1-55786-496-9 BLACKWELL $25.95

Geoffrey C. **Ward**

The West: An Illustrated History

"Following the format of *The Civil War* and *Baseball*, two earlier book companions to Ken Burns's television series, this [is a] beautifully designed, handsomely illustrated and stylishly written social history"—*Publishers Weekly*

See also **THE WESTERN FRONTIER: OVERVIEWS** under **AMERICAN REGIONAL HISTORY: THE WEST AND THE SOUTH**

0-316-92236-6 LITTLE, BROWN $60.00

Roger **Warner**

Shooting at the Moon: The CIA's War in Laos

1-88364-236-1 STEERFORTH PB $18.00

Part 3

Religion & Philosophy

Friedrich Nietzsche

Negations

Socrates (469–399 BC)
The unexamined life is not worth living.
387

Plato (c. 428–347 BC)
There will be no end to the trouble of states, or indeed of humanity itself, till philosophers become kings in this world, or till those we call kings and rulers really and truly become philosophers.
387

Aristotle (384–399 BC)
It is evident that the city-state is a creation by nature, and that man is by nature a political animal, and it is clear that, just as some are by nature free, others are by nature slaves, and for the latter the condition of slavery is both beneficial and just.
388

Francis Bacon (1561–1626)
Knowledge itself is power.
392

Thomas Hobbes (1588–1679)
Words are wise men's counters, they but reckon with them; but they are the money of fools, that value them by the authority of an Aristotle, a Cicero, or a Thomas, or any other doctor whatsoever, if but a man.
392

René Descartes (1596–1650)
I will suppose therefore that not God, but some malicious demon of the utmost power and cunning has employed all his energies in order to deceive me. I shall think that the sky, the air, the earth, colors, shapes, sounds and all external things are merely the delusions of dreams which he has devised to ensnare my judgment.
392

Blaise Pascal (1623–1662)
Let us say "Either God is or he is not." To which view shall we be inclined? Reason cannot decide this question. Infinite chaos separates us. At the far end of this infinite distance a coin is being spun which will come down either heads or tails. How will you wager? Reason cannot make you choose either, reason cannot prove either wrong.
350

Benedict Spinoza (1632–1677)
Except God, no substance can be or be conceived.
393

David Hume (1711–1776)
The question is, how far we ought to yield to these illusions.
394

Immanuel Kant (1724–1804)
It is precisely in knowing its limits that philosophy consists.
396

G.W.F. Hegel (1770–1831)
What is rational is actual and what is actual is rational. On this conviction the plain man like the philosopher takes his stand, and from it philosophy starts in its study of the universe of mind as well as the universe of nature.
396

Karl Marx (1818–1883)
To be radical is to grasp the root of the matter. But for the human being the root is the human being himself. The criticism of religion ends with the teaching that *the human being is the highest being for the human being,* hence with the *categorical imperative to overthrow all relations* in which the human being is a degraded, enslaved, forsaken, despicable being.
399

Søren Kierkegaard (1813–1855)
Most people are subjective toward themselves and objective toward all others—frightfully objective sometimes—but the task is precisely to be objective toward oneself and subjective toward all others.
398

Friedrich Nietzsche (1844–1900)
What are man's truths ultimately? Merely his *irrefutable* errors.
400

Martin Heidegger (1889–1976)
The Nothing nothings.
405

Theodor Adorno (1903–1969)
There is nothing innocuous left. Even the blossoming tree lies the moment it is seen without the shadow of terror; even the innocent "How lovely!" becomes an excuse for an existence outrageously unlovely, and there is no longer beauty or consolation except in the gaze falling on horror, withstanding it, and in unalleviated consciousness of negativity holding fast to the possibility of what is better.
408

Willard V.O. Quine (1908–)
To be is to be the value of a variable.
413

500BC
AD0
AD1500
AD1600
AD1700
AD1800
AD1900

St. Paul (c. AD 10–65/7)
A devout Pharisee who had been a student of the great rabbi Gemaliel, Paul was a determined and violent opponent of the followers of Jesus until a blinding vision on the road to Damascus led him to join them: "For the good that I would, I do not; but the evil which I would not, that I do."
—Romans 7:15
353

Simon Magus (c.100)
Prophet, miracle worker, and magician—this contemporary of the apostles preached a Gnostic doctrine of fallen creation and is said to have died while attempting to fly. For the Church Fathers, he stood as the father of all heresy but "his influence has been still more extensive: Simon employed the Latin cognomen Faustus and traveled with a certain Helena who claimed to be Helen of Troy reborn; few admirers of Marlowe and Goethe have an inkling that their hero is the descendant of a Gnostic sectarian." —Hans Jonas
The Gnostic Religion
353

Marcion (c. 85–160)
Marcion took the Pauline doctrine of the antagonisms of flesh and spirit and of Jewish law and Christian grace to a Gnostic limit, insisting that the Hebrew scriptures were nothing but a devilish fiction. In his *Antitheses* he explains why the ancient patriarchs did not heed Christ's call when He came to lead them out of hell: "The sinners listened to His words and were all saved; but the saints, believing as usual that they were being tested, rejected His words and were all damned.
360

Tertullian (c. 160–225)
Tertullian first articulated the doctrine of the Trinity, and his assertion that the simple authority of the Church was the only necessary basis for accepting its extraordinary claims and promises—"I believe because it is absurd"—was fundamental in the espousal of orthodoxy as a virtue in its own right. Nonetheless, Tertullian died a heretic: an adherent of the Montanists, who believed that the Holy Spirit was still active on earth.
353

The Brotherhood of the Free Spirit (14c)
The spiritual disposition of the mystical and antinomian Brotherhood emerges clearly in Henry Suso's account of meeting with a spirit. "Where have you come from?" Suso asked. "From nowhere." "What are you?" "I am not." "What do you wish for?" "Nothing." "This is a miracle!" Suso exclaimed, "what is your name?" "I am called Nameless Wildness and my insight leads to that untrammeled freedom when a man lives according to all his caprices without distinguishing between God and himself."
354

William Erbery (d.1654)
The intertwined theological and political disputes that provoked the English revolution and continued throughout the short life of the Commonwealth led some believers—John Milton among them—to withdraw from any form of organized worship. Such men were called Seekers, and William Erbery, who denounced the Commonwealth's control of worship as much as he had previously denounced that of the Crown, was prominent among them. "To be solitary and walk alone is a wilderness condition, which with God is the most comfortable state."
354

Sabbatai Zevi (1626–1676)
A rabbi with a manic streak, Sabbatai declared himself the Messiah in 1665. The news spread throughout the Diaspora, and he gained numerous followers, who however were bitterly disappointed the next year when, under pressure from the Turks, Sabbatai converted to Islam. Nathan of Gaza, his most devoted disciple, argued that precisely this apostasy proved Sabbatai's legitimacy—only Messiah could number himself among the unbelievers without sin.
343

William Blake (1757–1827)
"A MEMORABLE FANCY: As I was walking among the fires of hell, delighted with the enjoyments of Genius, which to the angels look like torment and insanity, I collected some of their proverbs.

"When I came home, on the abyss of the five senses, I saw a mighty devil folded in black clouds, hovering on the sides of the rock. With corroding fires he wrote the following sentence now perceived by the minds of men, and read by them on earth:

How do you know but ev'ry bird that cuts the airy sphere
Is an immense world of delight, closed to your senses five?"

—*The Marriage of Heaven and Hell*
802

A.N. Kirilov (19c)
"I don't understand how up to now an atheist could know there was no God, and still not kill himself immediately. To realize there is no God, but at the same time not to realize that one is become God oneself is absurd, or one would certainly kill oneself. If you realize it—you're sovereign and won't kill yourself; you'll live in great glory. But one person, he who comes first, must certainly kill himself, or who'll make a start and prove it? So I must certainly kill myself."
—Fyodor Dostoevsky
Demons
976

William James (1842–1910)
James argued against the religious skepticism of modern science even as he affirmed a constitutive role for human will in the realization of the divine—which makes him a heretic by anybody's books. "One who should shut himself up in snarling logicality and try to make the gods extort his recognition willy-nilly might cut himself off forever from his only opportunity of making the gods' acquaintance. The feeling, forced on us we know not whence, that by obstinately believing there are gods (although not to do so would be so easy both for our logic and our life) we are doing the universe the deepest service we can, seems part of the living essence of the religious hypothesis."
—*"The Will to Believe"*
400

Hazel Motes (20c)
"Sweet Jesus Christ Crucified, I want to tell you people something. Maybe you think you're not clean because you don't believe. Well you are clean, let me tell you that. Every one of you people are clean and let me tell you why if you think it is because of Jesus Christ Crucified you're wrong. I don't say he wasn't crucified but I say it wasn't for you. Listen here, I'm a preacher myself and I preach the truth… I'm a member and a preacher to that church where the blind don't see and the lame don't walk and what is dead stays that way."
—Flannery O'Connor
Wise Blood
667

Salman Rushdie (1947–)
The Muslim-born Rushdie was denounced as a heretic and sentenced to death by the Ayatollah Khomeini for the content of his novel *The Satanic Verses*: "How unconfident of Itself this Deity was, Who didn't want Its finest creations to know right from wrong; and Who reigned by terror, insisting upon the unqualified submission of even Its closest associates, packing off all dissidents to its blazing Siberias, the gulag-infernos of Hell… he checked himself. These were satanic thoughts, put into his head by Iblis-Beelzebub-Shaitan."
839

World Religion

"Let us consider the deepest and most fundamental element in all strong and sincerely felt religious emotion…Let us follow it up with every effort of sympathy and imaginative intuition wherever it is to be found, in the lives of those around us, in sudden, strong ebullitions of personal piety…in the fixed and ordered solemnities of rites and liturgies, and again in the atmosphere that clings to old religious monuments and buildings, to temples and to churches. If we do so we shall find we are dealing with something for which there is only one appropriate expression, *'mysterium tremendum.'* The feeling of it may at times come sweeping like a gentle tide, pervading the mind with a tranquil mood of deepest worship…It may burst in sudden eruption up from the depths of the soul with spasms and convulsions, and lead to the strangest excitements, to intoxicated frenzy, to transport, and to ecstasy…It may become the hushed, trembling, and speechless humility of the creature in the presence of—whom or what? In the presence of that which is a *mystery* inexpressible and above all creatures."—Rudolf Otto in *The Idea of the Holy*

Under this heading we have grouped general and comparative studies of religion, and books that focus on such special topics as mysticism, religious skepticism, and the occult. Books dealing specifically with the major world faiths will be found under a series of separate headings immediately following this introductory section.

Classics of Western Religious Thought

Saint Thomas **Aquinas**

Selected Philosophical Writings

A recommended selection

See also **ST. THOMAS AQUINAS** under **PHILOSOPHY**

0-19-282946-7 OXFORD PB $13.95

Saint **Augustine**

The City of God

The first Christian philosophy of history. A monumental response to pagan interpretations of the decline of Rome

See also **CLASSICS** under **CHRISTIANITY**

See also **LATE WRITERS** under **LATIN LITERATURE** in **LITERATURE OF EUROPE, AFRICA, AND ASIA**

TRANSLATED BY HENRY BETTENSON

0-14-044426-2 PENGUIN PB $15.95

The City of God

TRANSLATED BY MARCUS DODS

0-679-60087-6 MODERN LIBRARY $20.00

The Confessions of St. Augustine

The first systematic philosopher of the Church describes his own conversion and seeks to reconcile Biblical faith with the Platonic tradition

0-385-02955-1 DOUBLEDAY PB $7.95

The Confessions

"The *Confessions* is more than a narrative of conversion. It is a work of rare sophistication and intricacy, in which even the apparently simple autobiographical narrative often carries harmonics of deeper meaning" —from the translator's introduction

TRANSLATED BY HENRY CHADWICK

0-19-281779-5 OXFORD $30.00

0-19-281774-4 OXFORD PB $6.95

And so step by step I ascended from bodies to the soul which perceives through the body, and from there to its inward force, to which bodily senses report external sensations, this being as high as the beasts go. From there again I ascended to the power of reasoning to which is to be attributed the power of judging the deliverances of the bodily senses. This power, which in myself I found to be mutable, raised itself to the level of its own intelligence, and led my thinking out of the ruts of habit. It withdrew itself from the contradictory swarms of imaginative fantasies, so as to discover the light by which it was flooded.

THE CONFESSIONS

Boethius

The Consolation of Philosophy

The Roman adviser to the Gothic king Theodoric wrote this amalgamation of Roman and Christian wisdom while awaiting execution

See also **BOETHIUS** under **OTHER MEDIEVAL PHILOSOPHERS** under **PHILOSOPHY**

See also **EARLY CHRISTIAN WRITINGS** under **CLASSICS** under **CHRISTIANITY**

TRANSLATED BY V.E. WATTS

0-14-044208-1 PENGUIN PB $10.95

Martin **Buber**

I and Thou

A classic of religious existentialism.

See also **HASIDIM** under **JUDAISM**

See also **MODERN THEOLOGY AND PHILOSOPHY** under **JUDAISM**

TRANSLATED BY WALTER KAUFFMAN & S.G. SMITH

0-684-71725-5 MACMILLAN PB $10.00

0-684-18254-8 SCRIBNERS PB $5.95

Martin Buber

William **James**

The Varieties of Religious Experience

A wide-ranging masterpiece that highlights the personal, subjective, and mystical aspects of religion—an approach that coincides with contemporary tastes

See also **WILLIAM JAMES** under **PHILOSOPHY**

0-14-039034-0 PENGUIN PB $10.95

Our normal waking consciousness, rational consciousness as we call it, is but one special type of consciousness, whilst all about it, parted from it by the filmiest of screens, there lie potential forms of consciousness entirely different. We may go through life without suspecting their existence; but apply the requisite stimulus, and at a touch they are there in all their completeness, definite types of mentality which probably somewhere have their field of application and adaptation. No account of the universe in its totality can be final which leaves these other forms of consciousness quite disregarded. How to regard them is the question—for they are so discontinuous with ordinary consciousness. Yet they may determine attitudes though they cannot furnish formulas, and open a region though they fail to give a map. At any rate they forbid a premature closing of our accounts with reality.

THE VARIETIES OF RELIGIOUS EXPERIENCE

William James

Søren **Kierkegaard**

Fear and Trembling

A meditation on the biblical sacrifice of Isaac and on the difficult Christianity of the "Knight of Faith"

See also **KIERKEGAARD** under **PHILOSOPHY**

TRANSLATED BY ALASTAIR HANNAY

0-14-044449-1 PENGUIN PB $9.95

Moses **Maimonides**

The Guide of the Perplexed

A reconciliation of the Old Testament and Aristotle by the great 12th-century Jewish philosopher

Volume 1

See also **EARLY PHILOSOPHICAL TEXTS** under **JUDAISM**

0-226-50230-9 CHICAGO PB $25.00

Volume 2

0-226-50231-7 CHICAGO PB $25.00

John Henry **Newman**

Apologia Pro Vita Sua

A humane and intellectually incisive testament to Newman's fervent yet independent-minded Catholic faith

See also **19TH-CENTURY PROSE** under **THE 19TH CENTURY** in **LITERATURE OF THE BRITISH ISLES**

See also **CLASSICS** under **CHRISTIANITY**

EDITED BY DAVID DELAURA

0-393-09766-8 NORTON PB $14.95

Rudolf **Otto**

The Idea of the Holy

First published in Germany in 1917, this influential work set the agenda for much of 20th-century theology by attempting to isolate an irreducible, nonrational sense of mystery in religious experience

See also **CHRISTIAN MYSTICISM** under **CHRISTIANITY**

TRANSLATED BY JOHN W. HARVEY

0-19-500210-5 OXFORD PB $10.95

Blaise **Pascal**

Pensées

See also **THE AGE OF CLASSICISM** under **FRENCH LITERATURE TO 1900** in **LITERATURE OF EUROPE, AFRICA, AND ASIA**

TRANSLATED BY A.J. KRAILSHEIMER

0-14-044645-1 PENGUIN PB $9.95

Pensées and Other Writings

TRANSLATED BY HONOR LEVI

0-19-282990-4 OXFORD PB $8.95

Simone **Weil**

Waiting for God

Searching spiritual autobiography by a brilliant and austere writer of Jewish origins who was drawn to an existentialist Christianity influenced by Pascal, Kierkegaard, and her own mystical experience

See also **ESSAYS: PERSONAL, LITERARY, PHILOSOPHICAL** under **MODERN FRENCH LITERATURE** in **LITERATURE OF EUROPE, AFRICA, AND ASIA**

TRANSLATED BY EMMA CRAUFURD

0-06-090295-7 HARPERPERENNIAL PB $12.00

General Surveys and Studies

Archie J. **Bahm**

The World's Living Religions

An authoritative, detailed study not only of the five major religions, but of the lesser-known ones such as Jainism, Taoism, Shintoism, and even Humanism. By revealing the essential similarities among the religions, Bahm suggests the existence of a universal spiritual doctrine. Ideal for the student and the general reader alike. "This compact, introductory treatment is impartial, insightful and shows the author to be well informed"
—*Journal for the Scientific Study of Religion*

0-87573-000-0 ASIAN HUMANITIES PB $12.95

Robert O. **Ballou**, editor

The Portable World Bible

Selections from the scriptures of major world religions

0-14-015005-6 VIKING PB $14.95

Steve **Bruce**

Religions in the Modern World: From Cathedrals to Cults

0-19-878151-2 OXFORD PB $14.95

Michael **Carrithers**

Founders of Faith: The Buddha, Confucius, Jesus, and Mohammed

Four self-contained studies on the inspirers of the world's most widespread religious traditions exploring how, and why, these four traditions continue to influence the way people think and live. Lucidly written, authoritative, rooted in history and theology, it is "a handy introduction to the founders of the world's major religious traditions"—Jon R. Stone

0-19-283066-X OXFORD PB $12.95

Mircea **Eliade**

A History of Religious Ideas

A monumental work, one of the crowning achievements of the great Romanian scholar who died in 1986. In these three volumes Eliade traces religious development from prehistory to the Reformation

Volume 1
From the Stone Age to the Eleusinian Mysteries

TRANSLATED BY WILLARD R. TRASK

0-226-20400-6 CHICAGO $33.00

0-226-20401-4 CHICAGO PB $21.95

Volume 2
From Gautama Buddha to the Triumph of Christianity

TRANSLATED BY WILLARD R. TRASK

0-226-20403-0 CAMBRIDGE PB $21.95

Volume 3
From Muhammad to the Age of Reforms

TRANSLATED BY ALF HILTEBEITEL AND DIANE APOSTLOS-CAPPADONA

0-226-20404-9 CHICAGO PB $21.95

Daniel L. **Pals**

Seven Theories of Religion

Religious scholar Pals turns to the fundamental questions of religion: the origins of religious thought and the power of religious ideas. He examines seven classic theories of religion—E.B.Tylor's animism, James Frazer's *The Golden Bough*, "reductionist" explanations of Freud, Durkheim, and Marx, and finally Mircea Eliade, E.E. Evans-Pritchard, and Clifford Geertz. In the end, this accessible book succeeds in constructing an appreciation of religion's human dimension and the purposes that inspire it

0-19-508724-0 OXFORD $19.95

Geoffrey **Parrinder**, editor

World Religions: From Ancient History to the Present

Clear, historically comprehensive accounts by leading scholars, profusely illustrated

0-87196-129-6 FACTS ON FILE $40.00

0-8160-1289-X FACTS ON FILE PB $17.95

Arvind **Sharma**, editor

Our Religions: The Seven World Religions

Published to coincide with the 1993 Parliament of World Religions, this book is a first of its kind. It gathers seven renowned theologians and scholars and asks each to present a contemporary and historical perspective on his or her own tradition. Contributors are: Sharma on Hinduism, Masao Abe on Buddhism, Tu Wei-Ming on Confucianism, Liu Xiaogan on Taoism, Jacob Neusner on Judaism, Harvey Cox on Christianity, and Seyyed Hossein Nasr on Islam

0-06-067700-7 HARPERCOLLINS PB $20.00

Ninian **Smart**

Dimensions of the Sacred: An Anatomy of the World's Beliefs

From one of the great historians of religion, a thorough look at how humans worldwide endeavor to put meaning on existence. "A kind of anatomy of spirituality, designed to advance understanding of the practical and theoretical aspects of a variety of world religions, Smart's book is important reading..."—*Publishers Weekly*

See also **GENERAL BOOKS** under **SPIRITUALITY**

0-520-20777-7 CALIFORNIA $29.95

The Religious Experience

0-02-412141-X PRENTICE HALL PB $37.25

The Religious Experience of Mankind

This illustrated historical survey by the eminent comparative religion scholar is widely used as a college text

0-02-412130-4 MACMILLAN PB $37.00

Huston **Smith**

The Illustrated World's Religions: A Guide to Our Wisdom Traditions

Detailed, absorbing, richly illustrated: this is a thoroughly researched, informative, and fascinating presentation of the differences and similarities among the world's religions. Smith has "passionate intellect and immense heart...He is the world's ambassador to religions everywhere."—Thomas Moore. "If one buys only one of the number of recent introductions to world religions, this should be it"—*Publishers Weekly*

0-06-067440-7 HARPERCOLLINS PB $22.00

The Religions of Man

A good introductory account of the beliefs of the major world religions

0-06-080972-8 HARPERCOLLINS PB $7.00

Samantha **Trenoweth**

The Future of God: Personal Adventures in Spirituality with Thirteen of Today's Eminent Thinkers

Interviews with a few of the most renowned spiritual thinkers of this century, including Paul Davies, Ina May Gaskin, Bishop Desmond Tutu, Matthew Fox, Rabbi Harold Kushner, the Dalai Lama, and Floyd Red Crow Westerman

1-86429-023-4 MILLENNIUM BOOKS PB $14.95

Comparative Religion

Karen **Armstrong**

A History of God: The 4000-Year Quest of Judaism, Christianity, and Islam

Using historical, philosophical, and intellectual evidence, Armstrong discusses the experience of God in the three monotheistic traditions. She shows how, throughout the centuries, each one subtly adapted its conception of God to changing times, while retaining a fundamental and passionate belief in God's existence. "This is the most fascinating and learned survey of the biggest wild goose chase in history—the quest for God. Karen Armstrong is a genius"
—A.N. Wilson, author of *Jesus: A Life*

0-679-42600-0 KNOPF $27.50

Karen **Armstrong**

Jerusalem: One City, Three Faiths

The widely acclaimed author of *A History of God* continues her exploration of the varieties of religious experience with a riveting account of monotheism's epicenter. Tracing the city of Jerusalem from its beginnings three thousand years B.C.E., she shows it in its religious, mythic, and political aspects through to the present day. A tour de force

See also **ISRAEL SINCE 1948** under **ISRAEL** under **THE CONTEMPORARY MIDDLE EAST** in **WORLD HISTORY AND CURRENT AFFAIRS**

0-679-43596-4 KNOPF $30.00

Stephen **Batchelor**

The Awakening of the West: The Encounter of Buddhism and Western Culture

A history of the West's encounters with Buddhism, from ancient Greece to the 20th century

0-938077-68-6 PARALLAX $30.00
0-938077-69-4 PARALLAX BP $18.00

Harold **Bloom**

Omens of Millennium: The Gnosis of Angels, Dreams and Resurrection

"A dazzling account of the Gnostic, Jewish, and Islamic roots of American spirituality by our most prominent literary and religious critic. *Omens of the Millennium* is one of those magnificent works of religious interpretation and synthesis that appear only once in a generation"—Bentley Layton, Professor of Religious Studies, Yale

1-57322-045-0 PUTNAM $24.95

Harold Bloom

Mary **Douglas**

Natural Symbols: Explorations in Cosmology

A British anthropologist's comments on religion and social order

0-415-13825-6 ROUTLEDGE $42.00
0-415-13826-4 ROUTLEDGE PB $16.95

Purity and Danger: An Analysis of the Concepts of Pollution and Taboo

See also **SYMBOLS AND SEMIOTICS** under **SPECIALIZED STUDIES** under **ANTHROPOLOGY** in **SOCIAL STUDIES**

0-415-06608-5 ROUTLEDGE PB $14.95

Mircea **Eliade**

The Sacred and the Profane: The Nature of Religion

Eliade's incomparably fluent exploration of recurrent themes in world religions —an excellent introduction

TRANSLATED BY WILLARD R. TRASK

0-15-679201-X HARCOURT BRACE PB $9.00

Roberta **Harris**

The World of the Bible

This illustrated book covers the full range of Biblical life by tracing the development of Islam, Judaism, and Christianity

0-500-05073-2 THAMES & HUDSON $29.95

Stephen **Hayward** & Sara **Lefanu**, editors

God: An Anthology of Fiction

Each author sounds the theme of his or her religious background, be it Zoroastrian or Jewish, Roman Catholic or Muslim. Contributors include David Plante, Joyce Carol Oates, Gabriel Josipovici, Bapsi Sidhwa, and Michele Roberts

1-85242-259-9 SERPENT'S TAIL PB $13.99

Leonard W. **Levy**

Blasphemy: Verbal Offense Against the Sacred from Moses to Salman Rushdie

How religious and political authorities have defined religious, philosophical, and literary ideas as blasphemous since ancient Israel and Greece

0-679-40236-5 KNOPF $35.00
0-8078-4515-9 NORTH CAROLINA PB $18.95

Jacob **Neusner**

Children of the Flesh, Children of the Promise: A Rabbi Talks with Paul

A modern Jewish thinker in fictional dialogue with the first Christian theologian, Paul

0-8298-1026-9 PILGRIM PB $14.95

Philip **Novak**

The World's Wisdom: Sacred Texts of the World's Religions

FOREWORD BY HUSTON SMITH

0-06-066342-1 HARPERCOLLINS PB $14.00

Elaine **Pagels**

Adam, Eve, and the Serpent

The evolution of Christian thought—from an early emphasis on freedom to the asceticism and determinism that prevailed through the writings of Augustine—as reflected in orthodox and Gnostic interpretations of the story of Adam and Eve

0-679-72232-7 RANDOM HOUSE PB $10.00

The Gnostic Gospels

The historical and theological implications of an ancient library of Gnostic texts, including Gospels attributing the esoteric, paradoxical teachings of the Gnostics to Jesus, found near Nag Hammadi in upper Egypt in 1945

See also **GNOSTICISM** under **HISTORY** under **CHRISTIANITY**

0-394-74043-2 VINTAGE PB $9.00

The Gnostic Paul: Gnostic Exegesis of the Pauline Letters

See also **RELIGION** under **TOPICS IN ROMAN HISTORY** under **ANCIENT ROME**

1-56338-039-0 TRINITY PB $14.95

The Origin of Satan

Tracing the Devil from the Old to the New Testament, Pagels confronts an issue long ignored by modern theologians—the Church's demonization of Jews, pagans, and dissenting Christians (heretics)—and identifies this as one of the most disturbing and enduring aspects of Western civilization

See also **THE OCCULT, WITCHCRAFT, AND THE DEVIL**

0-679-40140-7 RANDOM HOUSE $23.00
0-679-73118-0 VINTAGE PB $12.00

Geoffrey **Parrinder**

Sex in the World's Religions

A concise survey of sexual attitudes, taboos, and practices

0-19-520202-3 OXFORD PB $15.95

F.E. **Peters**

The Children of Abraham: Judaism, Christianity, Islam

A study of the development of three interdependent and often mutually intolerant faiths, with discussions of scripture, mysticism, asceticism, and theology

0-691-02030-2 PRINCETON PB $13.95

Hershel **Shanks**

Jerusalem: An Archaeological Biography

The eminent archaeologist presents a beautifully illustrated, enormously readable archaeological history of Jerusalem. From the discovery of the crucified heel of a first-century Jewish rebel to the search for King David's tomb, Shanks enlivens history while simultaneously providing a fascinating account of the processes of archaeology

0-679-44526-9 RANDOM HOUSE $50.00

Ninian **Smart**

Worldviews: Crosscultural Explorations in Human Beliefs

Smart, an eminent 20th-century scholar of comparative religion, discusses six dimensions of religion—experiential, mythic, doctrinal, ethical, ritual, and social—in cultures throughout the world, and speculates on the future of religion and ideology

0-02-412010-3 PRENTICE HALL PB $22.00

Andrew **Wilson**, editor

World Scripture: A Comparative Anthology of Sacred Texts

1-55778-723-9 CONTINUUM PB $19.95

Elaine Pagels' Picks

Lucius **Apuleius**

The Golden Ass

A humorous, first-person account of one man's "conversion" to the worship of the goddess Isis and his initiation into her mysteries in the second-century Roman empire

See also **ANCIENT MEDITERRANEAN RELIGIONS**

TRANSLATED BY ROBERT GRAVES

0-374-50532-2 FS&G PB $11.00

Saint **Augustine**

The Confessions

Augustine's classic spiritual autobiography, tracing his passage from boyhood sin through Manichaeanism to Christian conversion

See also **AUGUSTINE** under **PHILOSOPHY**

TRANSLATED BY R.S. PINE-COFFIN

0-14-044114-X PENGUIN PB $8.95

Marcus **Aurelius**

Meditations

Marcus Aurelius, philosopher-emperor of Rome (c. 160), wrote these reflections on human character, power, and mortality at night, mostly while camped with his soldiers on campaign

See also **STOICS AND EPICUREANS** under **PHILOSOPHY**

TRANSLATED BY MAXWELL STANIFORTH

0-14-044140-9 PENGUIN PB $9.95

Peter **Brown**

Augustine of Hippo: A Biography

A comprehensive biography of the fourth-century Christian convert whose theology formed a bridge between the ancient and medieval churches and defined such essential Christian doctrines as grace and original sin

See also **SAINTS** under **BIOGRAPHIES** under **CHRISTIANITY**

0-520-01411-1 CALIFORNIA PB $16.00

Elaine Pagels

E.R. **Dodds**

Pagan and Christian in an Age of Anxiety: Some Aspects of Religious Experience from Marcus Aurelius to Constantine

0-521-38599-7 CAMBRIDGE PB $18.95

Elisabeth **Fiorenza**, editor

In Memory of Her: A Feminist Theological Reconstruction of Christian Origins

A highly provocative and influential work that is transforming feminist thinking about the Bible

See also **WOMEN AND RELIGION**

0-8245-1357-6 CROSSROAD PB $17.95

Hans **Jonas**

The Gnostic Religion

The classic early study of the Gnostic religion written from an existentialist viewpoint before the discovery of a major library of Gnostic sources at Nag Hammadi in upper Egypt in 1945

0-8446-2339-3 SMITH $27.75

0-8070-5799-1 BEACON PB $17.00

Howard Clark **Kee**

Jesus in History: An Approach to the Study of the Gospels

A lucid presentation of sources for study of the gospels, and of ways that scholarly views of the New Testament have changed in the past hundred years

0-15-501125-1 HARCOURT BRACE PB $24.50

Bentley **Layton**

The Gnostic Scriptures

A recent translation of many major Gnostic sources, well-annotated with good historical commentary

0-385-17447-0 DOUBLEDAY $35.00

0-385-47843-7 BANTAM PB $22.00

Thomas **Merton**

The Wisdom of the Desert

See also **EARLY CHRISTIAN WRITINGS** under **CLASSICS** under **CHRISTIANITY**

0-8112-0102-3 NEW DIRECTIONS PB $6.95

Helen **Waddell**

The Desert Fathers

Translation of an ancient collection of anecdotes about the radical desert hermits of Egypt

0-472-06008-2 MICHIGAN PB $16.95

Ancient Mediterranean Religions

Lucius **Apuleius**

The Golden Ass

TRANSLATED BY ROBERT GRAVES

0-374-50532-2 FS&G PB $11.00

Walter **Burkert**

Ancient Mystery Cults

The most eminent contemporary historian of ancient Greek religion discusses the cults of Demeter, Dionysus, the Great Mother, Isis, and Mithras, and describes initiation rituals, priestly organization, and secret rites

See also **RELIGION AND PHILOSOPHY** under **TOPICS IN ANCIENT GREEK HISTORY** under **ANCIENT GREECE** in **WORLD HISTORY AND CURRENT AFFAIRS**

0-674-03387-6 HARVARD PB $12.95

Greek Religion

"A masterpiece, packed with learning but also rich in ideas and connections of every sort…Nobody else could have produced an account of the subject of comparable range and power"—*NY Review of Books*

See also **RELIGION** under **SPECIALIZED STUDIES** under **ANTHROPOLOGY** in **SOCIAL STUDIES**

0-674-36281-0 HARVARD PB $17.95

Homo Necans: The Anthropology of Ancient Greek Sacrificial Ritual and Myth

TRANSLATED BY PETER BING

0-520-05875-5 CALIFORNIA PB $16.00

E.R. **Dodds**

Pagan and Christian in an Age of Anxiety: Some Aspects of Religious Experience from Marcus Aurelius to Constantine

See also **RELIGION** under **TOPICS IN ROMAN HISTORY**

0-521-38599-7 CAMBRIDGE PB $18.95

Georges **Dumézil**

Archaic Roman Religion

0-8018-5483-0 JOHNS HOPKINS $25.00

Jane Ellen **Harrison**

Prolegomena to the Study of Greek Religion

See also **OTHER TOPICS IN ANCIENT PHILOSOPHY** under **PHILOSOPHY**

0-691-01514-7 PRINCETON PB $19.95

Byron E. **Shafer**, editor

Religion in Ancient Egypt: Gods, Myths, and Personal Practice

The newest findings of Egyptology are brought to bear in these studies of Egyptian religion, with a special emphasis on the experience of the individual believer

See also **EGYPT** under **THE ANCIENT WORLD: EGYPT AND MESOPOTAMIA** under **MYTHOLOGY AND FOLKLORE**

0-8014-9786-8 CORNELL PB $13.95

Mysticism

Samuel **Angus**

The Mystery Religions: A Study in the Religious Background of Early Christianity

A classic history of religion examining cryptic rites and beliefs such as the Dionysian and Orphic mysteries and the cults of Isis and Mithras

See also **RELIGION** under **SPECIALIZED STUDIES** under **ANTHROPOLOGY** in **SOCIAL STUDIES**

0-486-23124-0 DOVER PB $8.95

Karen **Armstrong**

Visions of God: Four Medieval Mystics and Their Writings

A selection from four English mystics—Richard Rolle, Walter Hilton, Dame Julian of Norwich, and the author of *The Cloud of Unknowing*—with an introduction by Armstrong, author of *A History of God*

0-553-35199-0 BANTAM PB $10.95

Arthur C. **Danto**

Mysticism and Morality: Oriental Thought and Moral Philosophy

A closely argued account of Buddhism, Taoism, and Hinduism and their divergence from Western moral teachings

0-231-06639-2 COLUMBIA PB $16.50

Felicitas D. **Goodman**

Where the Spirits Ride the Wind: Trance Journeys and Other Ecstatic Experiences

Goodman looks at shamanistic practices in a fresh light, examining the means by which trance states were actually induced

0-253-32764-4 INDIANA $35.00

Frank C. **Happold**

Mysticism

A good entry to the subject combining general remarks with an anthology of crucial texts

0-14-013746-7 VIKING PB $12.95

Holger **Kalweit**

Dreamtime and Inner Space: The World of the Shaman

A survey of shamanism in Africa, Australia, Asia, Siberia, and the Americas, and a comparison with modern scientific studies of altered consciousness

FOREWORD BY ELISABETH KUBLER-ROSS

0-87773-406-2 SHAMBHALA PB $22.50

Marvin W. **Meyer**, editor

The Ancient Mysteries: A Sourcebook

Sacred texts of the ancient mystery religions, including the cults of the Great Mother, Isis and Osiris, Dionysus, Mithras, and Jewish and Christian mysteries

0-06-065576-3 HARPERCOLLINS PB $18.00

Philosophy and Religion

Martin **Buber**

On Intersubjectivity and Cultural Creativity

One of the foremost religious philosophers of the century examines the dialogues between individuals on the one hand and God on the other

EDITED WITH AN INTRODUCTION BY S.N. EISENSTADT

0-226-07805-1 CHICAGO $44.00

0-226-07807-8 CHICAGO PB $15.95

Charles **Hartshorne**

Omnipotence and Other Theological Mistakes

A critique of mainstream theology by a leading exponent of "process philosophy"

0-87395-771-7 SUNY PB $16.95

Abraham Joshua **Heschel**

Moral Grandeur and Spiritual Audacity: Essays

The five parts of this splendid collection cover the full range of Heschel's thought, moving from "Existence and Celebration" to "Toward a Just Society" and "The Holy Dimension." "One of the truly great men of our day and age, a truly great prophet"—Martin Luther King, Jr.

See also **MODERN THEOLOGY AND PHILOSOPHY** under **JUDAISM**

EDITED BY SUSANNAH HESCHEL

0-374-19980-9 FS&G $27.50

John **Macquarrie**

Existentialism

An introduction to an important influence on 20th-century religious thought

0-14-013616-9 PENGUIN PB $12.95

Wayne **Proudfoot**

Religious Experience

An argument against the theological tendency to detach religion from its contexts in history, society, and individual psychology

0-520-06128-4 CALIFORNIA PB $14.95

Science and Religion

George **Johnson**

Fire in the Mind: Science, Faith, and the Search for Order

After visiting scientific think tanks, the science writer considers the boundaries between chaos and order, belief and fact

See also **SCIENCE IN TODAY'S SOCIETY** under **HISTORY OF SCIENCE AND TECHNOLOGY** under **SCIENCE AND TECHNOLOGY** in **SCIENCE**

0-679-41192-5 KNOPF $30.00

0-679-74021-X VINTAGE PB $14.00

Ian **Stewart** & Martin **Golubitsky**

Fearful Symmetry: Is God a Geometer?

From the authors of *Does God Play Dice?* mathematical and philosophical musings on the apparently ordered nature of the world

See also **PHILOSOPHY OF MATHEMATICS** under **MATHEMATICS** in **SCIENCE**

0-631-18251-9 BLACKWELL $25.95

0-14-013047-0 PENGUIN PB $12.50

Richard **Swinburne**

Is There a God?

An Oxford professor of Christian religion asks the fundamental question, presenting a powerful case for the existence of God, rigorously argued with the methods of scientific reasoning. From black holes to quarks, Swinburne argues, science again and again brings us closer to understanding how the universe works, and in so doing leads us to a greater appreciation of the great question of *why* it is there at all. The unifying answer, according to Swineburne's readable and compelling argument, is a theistic one

0-19-823544-5 OXFORD $19.95

0-19-823545-3 OXFORD PB $9.95

Frank **Tipler**

The Physics of Immortality: Modern Cosmology, God and the Resurrection of the Dead

A big book that addresses the often-remarked, little-understood nexus of quantum physics and theology. Rigorously drawing on quantum mechanics information theory and advanced mathematics, in the context of Jewish messianism, deism, and diverse theological concepts of immortality, Tipler articulates his "Omega Point" proof of God's existence

See also **THE NEW PHYSICS** under **METAPHYSICS** under **SPIRITUALITY**

0-385-46799-0 ANCHOR PB $14.95

Skepticism and Atheism

Paul **Blanshard**, editor

Classics of Free Thought

An introduction to the tradition of skeptical humanism

0-87975-421-4 PROMETHEUS PB $18.95

David **Hume**

Dialogues Concerning Natural Religion and the Natural History of Religion

See also **HUME** under **PHILOSOPHY**

EDITED BY J.C.A. GASKIN

0-19-282932-7 OXFORD PB $7.95

Paul **Kurtz**

In Defense of Secular Humanism

Kurtz is a leading philosophical champion of scientific skepticism

0-87975-221-1 PROMETHEUS $28.95

0-87975-228-9 PROMETHEUS PB $19.95

H.L. **Mencken**

Prejudices: A Selection

These essays by the great American journalist include some of his sardonic writings on religion

See also **HISTORY, POLITICS, AND SOCIETY** under **20TH-CENTURY AMERICAN ESSAYS AND JOURNALISM** in **LITERATURE OF THE AMERICAS**

EDITED BY JAMES T. FARRELL

0-8018-5341-9 JOHNS HOPKINS PB $15.95

Friedrich **Nietzsche**

The Twilight of the Idols & the Anti-Christ

Two polemical and incandescent late works: one a succinct summary of major themes; the other a serious attempt at a cultural psychology of Buddhism and Christianity

See also **NIETZSCHE** under **PHILOSOPHY**

TRANSLATED BY R.J. HOLLINGDALE

0-14-044514-5 PENGUIN PB $10.95

Bertrand **Russell**

Why I Am Not a Christian & Other Essays on Religion and Related Subjects

Essays 1899-1954, all centering on one deeply held belief: "I am as firmly convinced that religions do harm as I am that they are untrue"—Bertrand Russell

See also **20TH-CENTURY BRITISH ESSAYS AND OTHER PROSE**

0-671-20323-1 SIMON & SCHUSTER PB $12.00

Percy Bysshe **Shelley**

The Necessity of Atheism: And Other Essays

Shelley was expelled from Oxford for the title essay, which argues that neither reason nor religious testimony can establish the existence of a god. This essay and the book's other two works—*A Logical Objection to Christianity* and *A Refutation of Deism*—confirm the Romantic poet's importance as a humanist essayist

0-87975-774-4 PROMETHEUS $24.95

Roger E. **Greeley**, editor

The Best of Robert Ingersoll

Selections from the iconoclastic work of the eloquent 19th-century American agnostic

0-87975-209-2 PROMETHEUS PB $19.95

Psychology and Religion

Joseph F. **Byrnes**

The Psychology of Religion

The best overview of 20th-century theories of religion and of psychological research on religious experience

0-02-903580-5 FREE PRESS $32.95

Sigmund **Freud**

The Future of an Illusion

Psychoanalysis as the most powerful argument against the consolations of religion

See also **FREUD** under **PSYCHOLOGY** in **SOCIAL STUDIES**

EDITED BY JAMES STRACHEY

0-393-00831-2 NORTON PB $7.95

Moses and Monotheism

Freud speculates that modern science developed out of the asceticism fostered by monotheism

See also **CLASSICAL EUROPEAN SOCIOLOGY** under **SOCIOLOGY** in **SOCIAL STUDIES**

0-394-70014-7 RANDOM HOUSE PB $8.00

Erich **Fromm**

Psychoanalysis and Religion

0-300-00089-8 YALE PB $9.00

Erich Fromm

Karen **Horney**

Final Lectures

See also **KAREN HORNEY** under **POST-FREUDIAN THEORISTS** under **PSYCHOLOGY** in **SOCIAL STUDIES**

0-393-30755-7 NORTON PB $6.95

Carl **Jung**

Modern Man in Search of a Soul

A diagnosis of the spiritual restlessness and emptiness of modern civilization which also serves as a basic introduction to Jung's thought on dream analysis, the collective unconscious, and the relation between psychology and religion. It includes "Freud and Jung: Contrast"

See also **JUNG** under **PSYCHOLOGY** in **SOCIAL STUDIES**

0-15-661206-2 HARCOURT BRACE PB $9.00

Abraham H. **Maslow**

Religions, Values, and Peak Experiences

The most influential advocate of a psychology of self-realization, Maslow finds religious experience at the heart of the "peak experience" achieved by healthy, fully functioning individuals

See also **HUMAN POTENTIAL PSYCHOLOGY** under **PSYCHOLOGY** in **SOCIAL STUDIES**

0-14-004262-8 VIKING PB $6.00

Donald **Meyer**

The Positives:Religion as Pop Psychology from Mary Baker Eddy to Oral Roberts

An engaging survey of the irrepressible, optimistic, positive-thinking strain in American culture and religion

0-8195-6166-5 WESLEYAN PB $19.95

Oral Roberts

Ann **Ulanov** & Barry **Ulanov**

Religion and the Unconscious

A scholarly exposition of religious psychology, from a Jungian perspective

0-664-24657-5 KNOX PB $16.00

Religion and Society

Peter L. **Berger**

The Sacred Canopy: Elements of a Sociological Theory of Religion

A controversial book by a contemporary sociologist of knowledge

0-385-07305-4 ANCHOR PB $9.95

Harold J. **Berman**

Law and Revolution: The Formation of the Western Legal Tradition

Berman's history of the development of Western law is a mind-altering account of the formative institutions of the Western moral, political, and intellectual outlook

See also **LEGAL HISTORY** under **LAW** in **SOCIAL STUDIES**

0-674-51776-8 HARVARD PB $19.95

Robert **Coles**

The Spiritual Life of Children

Coles' continuing series on the mental life of children focuses here on such topics as God, salvation, and the meaning of life

See also **CHILD PSYCHOLOGY** under **PSYCHOLOGY** in **SOCIAL STUDIES**

0-395-55999-5 HOUGHTON MIFFLIN $22.95

0-395-59923-7 HOUGHTON MIFFLIN PB $10.95

Emile **Durkheim**

The Elementary Forms of the Religious Life

A classic study that explains the function of the totem and introduces a distinction between the sacred and profane

See also **CLASSICAL EUROPEAN SOCIOLOGY** under **SOCIOLOGY** in **SOCIAL STUDIES**

TRANSLATED BY JOSEPH W. SWAIN

0-02-908010-X FREE PRESS PB $16.95

Pope John Paul II

Crossing the Threshold of Hope

The Pope's reflections on God, prophecy, salvation, Judaism, and the fall of Communism

See also **CONTEMPORARY ISSUES** under **THEOLOGY AND DOCTRINE** under **CHRISTIANITY**

0-679-76561-1 RANDOM HOUSE PB $11.00

Max **Weber**

The Sociology of Religion

0-8070-4205-6 BEACON PB $16.00

Women and Religion

Paula Gunn **Allen**

Grandmothers of the Light: A Medicine Woman's Sourcebook

A retelling of 21 traditional stories—from Cherokee and Navajo to Aztec and Maya—steeped in the female supernatural

See also **RELIGION AND MYTHOLOGY** under **ASPECTS OF TRADITIONAL CULTURE** under **NATIVE AMERICAN CULTURES: NORTH AMERICA** in **HISTORY OF THE AMERICAS**

0-8070-8103-5 BEACON PB $14.00

0-8070-8102-7 BEACON PB $19.95

Ooma-oo, long ago. The Spider was in the place where only she was. There was no light or dark, there was no warm wind, no rain or thunder. There was no cold, or ice or snow. There was only the Spider. She was a great wise woman, whose powers are beyond imagining. No medicine person, no conjurer or shaman, no witch or sorcerer, no scientist or inventor can imagine how great her power is. Her power is complete and total. It is pure, and cleaner than the void. It is the power of thought, we say, but not the kind of thought people do all the time. It's like the power of dream, but more pure. Like the spirit of vision, but more clear. It has no shape or movement, because it just is. It is the power that creates all that is, and it is the power of all that is.
GRANDMOTHERS OF THE LIGHT: A MEDICINE WOMAN'S SOURCEBOOK

Carol P. **Christ** & Judith **Plaskow**

Womanspirit Rising: A Feminist Reader in Religion

An anthology of feminist religious scholarship

See also **THEOLOGY** under **FEMINIST THEORY** under **WOMEN'S STUDIES** in **SOCIAL STUDIES**

0-06-061385-8 HARPERCOLLINS PB $12.00

Christine **Downing**

The Goddess: Mythological Images of the Feminine

Female figures in Greek myth

0-8245-0091-1 CROSSROAD $14.95

0-8245-0624-3 CROSSROAD PB $11.95

Elisabeth **Fiorenza**, editor

In Memory of Her: A Feminist Theological Reconstruction of Christian Origins

A highly provocative and influential work that is transforming feminist thinking about the Bible

See also **ELAINE PAGLES'S PICKS** under **COMPARATIVE RELIGION**

0-8245-1357-6 CROSSROAD PB $17.95

Susan **Haskins**

Mary Magdalen: Myth and Metaphor

"A bold revisionist study…Whether writing about medieval relics, renaissance painting, or Victorian pornography, [Haskins] succeeds in demonstrating how her subject served as a canvas onto which each era projected its fears and fantasies about women's sexuality" —*Washington Post Book World*

See also **BEGINNINGS AND EARLY HISTORY** under **HISTORY** under **CHRISTIANITY**

1-57322-509-6 RIVERHEAD PB $16.00

Margaret R. **Miles**

Carnal Knowing: Female Nakedness and Religious Meaning in the Christian West

Miles examines the emotional and spiritual significance of the idea and the image of unclothed women throughout the history of Christianity in the West. "An absorbing illustrated history of how women's nakedness has figured in Christian thought and iconography"—*Harvard Magazine*

0-679-73401-5 VINTAGE PB $15.00

Barbara H. **Rigney**

Lilith's Daughters: Women and Religion in Contemporary Fiction

A short but wide-ranging and influential study of religious themes in women's fiction

0-299-08960-6 WISCONSIN $17.50

Susan Starr **Sered**

Priestess, Mother, Sacred Sister: Religions Dominated by Women

The first comparative study of the feminine in the world's religions delves into Korean shamanism, Christian Science, the ancestral cults among black Caribs, Shakerism, and contemporary feminist spirituality, finding links in the handling of death, birth, the winds of fortune, and the ultimate questions of deities unknown. A pioneering study by the author of *Women as Ritual Experts*

0-19-508395-4 OXFORD $27.50

Fulvio **Tomizza**

Heavenly Supper: The Story of Maria Janis

Maria Janis, a poor and devout peasant woman, claimed to have subsisted for five years solely on a diet of the bread and wine of Holy Communion. This is a fictionalized account of her life by a skilled novelist, reconstructed from her trial as a heretic before the Venetian Holy Office of the Inquisition in 1662

TRANSLATED BY ANNE JACOBSON SCHURRE

0-226-80789-4 CHICAGO $24.95

Some time after she had vowed to subject herself completely to the will of God, the idea "passed one day through her heart" of taking no nourishment other than the bread of heaven. Then just after she had taken communion, she felt herself fall into "an ocean of infinitive love." She began by fasting for a week, then skipped communion and began to eat again. But that day she was so ill that she felt constrained, and at the same time encouraged, to extend her fast to fifteen and then twenty days…Hence she decided to renounce forever all food and all drink and to take communion every day.

HEAVENLY SUPPER: THE STORY OF MARIA JANIS

Marina **Warner**

Alone of All Her Sex: The Myth and the Cult of the Virgin Mary

The relationship between images of Mary in church iconography and doctrine and the subordinate role of women endorsed by the church. "Explores the cult in all its ramifications, peeling aside each successive accretion of doctrine and devotion in order to examine its moral, social, and emotional implications" —Keith Thomas, *NY Review of Books*

0-394-71155-6 RANDOM HOUSE PB $18.00

In medieval miracle stories, statues and paintings, in accordance with iconodule belief, are constantly coming to life. In many the Virgin weeps, as she did in 1953 in Syracuse and elsewhere more recently; in one, a Saracen is converted when her breasts become flesh and flow with oil; in a very popular tale, a woman begs the Virgin to spare her dying child, and to make sure, seizes the Christ child from her arms as a hostage and only returns him to his mother on the recovery of her own child. In yet another miracle, the Virgin breaks out in a sweat as she tries to restrain her son's almighty and vengeful arm from striking a sinner down.

ALONE OF ALL HER SEX: THE MYTH AND THE CULT OF THE VIRGIN MARY

Emilie **Zum Brunn** & Georgette **Epiney-Burgard**

Women Mystics in Medieval Europe

Long overlooked by scholars, female mystics are now a topic of research and debate. Hildegard of Bingen, Hadewijch of Antwerp, Beatrice of Nazareth, Mechthild of Magdeburg, and Marguerite Porete are presented here in rich detail

TRANSLATED BY SHEILA HUGHES

1-55778-196-6 PARAGON PB $12.95

Religion in the Modern World

Robert N. **Bellah**

Beyond Belief: Essays on Religion in a Post-Traditional World

By a leading American sociologist of religion

0-520-07394-0 CALIFORNIA PB $15.00

Ronald **Cole-Turner** & Brent **Waters**

Pastoral Genetics: Theology and Care at the Beginning of Life

As human genetics transforms conception and childbirth, and more and more prenatal tests for genetic conditions are conducted, today's clergy are forced to confront unprecedented ethical and theological questions. Here, two experienced theologians describe the range of religious and ethical responses available, basing their thought on a vision of divine creation functioning through evolutionary and genetic processes. "Eminently useful…the theological boldness, based upon Christology, is to be welcomed"—J. Robert Nelson

0-8298-1077-3 PILGRIM PB $15.95

Victor **Frankel**

Man's Search For Meaning

"A moving, compressed account of a psychiatrist's reflections on his experiences in Auschwitz and their implications"—Elaine Pagels

0-671-24422-1 SIMON & SCHUSTER PB $10.00

Cults

Robert S. **Ellwood** & Harry **Partin**

Religious and Spiritual Groups in Modern America

An excellent survey of recent eccentric groups, including spiritualists, theosophists, Zen, neopagans, Scientologists, and others

0-13-773045-4 PRENTICE HALL PB $42.00

J. Gordon **Melton**

The Encyclopedic Handbook of Cults in America

A comprehensive guide to beliefs, organization, and origins by the author of major reference works on American religion

See also **REFERENCE WORKS**

0-8153-0502-8 GARLAND $65.00

James D. **Tabor** & Eugene V. **Gallagher**

Why Waco?: Cults and the Battle for Religious Freedom in America

0-520-20186-8 CALIFORNIA $24.95

The Occult, Witchcraft, and the Devil

Carlo **Ginzburg**

Ecstasies: Deciphering the Witches' Sabbath

TRANSLATED BY RAYMOND ROSENTHAL

0-140-15858-8 PENGUIN PB $16.00

Joan P. **Couliano**

Eros and Magic in the Renaissance

Magic as a manipulative psychology of motives, especially erotic ones

See also **ROMANIAN LITERATURE** under **EASTERN EUROPEAN LITERATURE** in **LITERATURE OF EUROPE, AFRICA, AND ASIA**

TRANSLATED BY MARGARET COOK

FOREWORD BY MIRCEA ELIADE

0-226-12315-4 CHICAGO $34.95

0-226-12316-2 CHICAGO PB $14.95

Nevill **Drury**

Dictionary of Mysticism and the Occult

A sympathetic guide to occult and mystical concepts, rites, and practitioners

See also **REFERENCE** under **CHRISTIANITY**

0-87436-699-2 ABC CLIO $55.00

1-85327-075-X PRISM PB $14.95

Mircea **Eliade**

Occultism, Witchcraft, and Cultural Fashion: Essays in Comparative Religions

Discourses on the occult, Gnosticism, Tantric Buddhism, and contemporary culture

See also **MIRCEA ELIADE**

0-226-20392-1 CHICAGO PB $11.95

Gerald **Messadié**

A History of the Devil

A sweeping revisionist history of Satan— whom the author claims, was first invented in the fifth century B.C. by Iranian priests

TRANSLATED BY MARC ROM

1-568-36081-9 KODANSHA $27.00

Bernard **McGinn**

Antichrist: Two Thousand Years of the Human Fascination with Evil

The Antichrist as an essential figure of Christian faith, from the early Christian communities to the apocalyptic visions of contemporary fundamentalists. A richly detailed illustrated history of "Christ's alter ego"

See also **BEGINNINGS AND EARLY HISTORY** under **HISTORY** under **CHRISTIANITY**

0-06-065543-7 HARPERCOLLINS $32.50

0-06-065282-9 HARPERCOLLINS PB $15.00

Elaine **Pagels**

The Origin of Satan

Tracing the Devil from the Old to the New Testament, Pagels confronts an issue long ignored by modern theologians—the Church's demonization of Jews, pagans, and dissenting Christians (heretics)—and identifies this as one of the most disturbing and enduring aspects of Western civilization

0-679-40140-7 RANDOM HOUSE $23.00

0-679-73118-0 VINTAGE PB $12.00

Kurt **Seligmann**

The History of Magic and the Occult

Magic, astrology, and alchemy in Western culture

0-517-15032-8 GRAMERCY $25.00

Jeffrey Burton **Russell**

The Devil: Perceptions of Evil from Antiquity to Primitive Christianity

This and its successors constitute a thorough history of the personification of evil in the Western world. Russell's scholarly and engrosing books also provide an excellent intellectual history to the Church, tracking the devil through Western literature and philosphy: Milleu's Satan, Goethe's Mephistopheles, Martin Luther's home remedies for disposing of Satan

0-8014-0938-1 CORNELL $37.50

0-8014-9409-5 CORNELL PB $14.95

Satan: The Early Christian Tradition

0-8014-1267-6 CORNELL $37.50

0-8014-9413-3 CORNELL PB $13.95

Lucifer: The Devil in the Middle Ages

0-8014-1503-9 CORNELL $37.50

0-8014-9429-X CORNELL PB $15.95

Mephistopheles: The Devil in the Modern World

0-8014-1808-9 CORNELL $37.50

0-8014-9718-3 CORNELL PB $14.95

A History of Witchcraft: Sorcerers, Heretics and Pagans

See also **DEMONS, WITCHCRAFT, AND MAGIC** under **EARLY MODERN EUROPE** in **WORLD HISTORY AND CURRENT AFFAIRS**

0-500-27242-5 THAMES & HUDSON PB $14.95

Reference Works

Donald **Attwater** & Catherine Rachel **John**

The Penguin Dictionary of Saints

An invaluable work of reference, this dictionary explores the major saints, many of whom played important roles in history, as well as those who are less well known

See also **SAINTS** under **BIOGRAPHIES** under **CHRISTIANITY**

0-14-051312-4 PENGUIN PB $13.95

Robert E. **Bell**

Women of Classical Mythology: A Biographical Dictionary

The first comprehensive dictionary of mythological women, most of whom have gotten little recognition in standard works on mythology. Includes information on many little-known figures and takes a contemporary look at better-known ones like Medusa and Aphrodite. Each character entry includes a list of works and stories in which the figure appears

See also **REFERENCE** under **WOMEN'S STUDIES** in **SOCIAL STUDIES**

0-87436-581-3 ABC CLIO $60.00

0-19-507977-9 OXFORD PB $14.95

Dan **Cohn-Sherbok**

Atlas of Jewish History

An exceptional, fascinating guide to the vicissitudes of Jewish history from ancient diasporic times to the present. A partial peek at the contents: "From Herod to Rebellion," "Judaism Under Islam in the Middle Ages," "Medieval Jewish Thought," "Eastern European Jewry in the Early Modern Period," "The Holocaust, Israel." Illustrated with over 100 maps

See also **REFERENCE** under **GENERAL HISTORIES** under **JEWISH HISTORY**

0-415-08684-1 ROUTLEDGE $62.95

0-415-08800-3 ROUTLEDGE PB $24.95

Joan **Comay**

Who's Who in the Old Testament

Placing the huge cast of characters populating the Old Testament in their geographic and historical contexts, this definitive, accessibly written, 3,000-entry volume is an essential source for both readers of the Bible and readers of the great works of Western literature that rely on biblical allusions

See also **THE BIBLE** under **REFERENCE** under **CHRISTIANITY**

0-19-521029-8 OXFORD PB $16.95

Mircea **Eliade**, editor

The Encyclopedia of Religion

The most comprehensive and culturally sympathetic reference work on religion in English; a 16-volume set

0-02-897135-3 MACMILLAN $650.00

Pierre **Grimal**

The Penguin Dictionary of Classical Mythology

See also **CLASSICAL MYTHOLOGY: ANCIENT GREECE AND ROME** under **MYTHOLOGY AND FOLKLORE**

0-14-051235-7 PENGUIN PB $14.95

James **Harpur**

The Atlas of Sacred Places: Meeting Points of Heaven and Earth

An atlas of more than 30 sites, from Mexico to Norway to China, where communities located the numinous. Illustrated

0-8050-2775-0 HOLT $45.00

John R. **Hinnells**, editor

A Handbook of Living Religions

0-14-022342-8 PENGUIN PB $8.95

0-14-013599-5 VIKING PB $14.95

The Penguin Dictionary of Religions

A compact and extremely useful reference source on religious history, doctrine, and terminology

0-14-051106-7 PENGUIN PB $12.95

David Adams **Leeming** & Margaret Adams **Leeming**

A Dictionary of Creation Myths

See also **GENERAL INTRODUCTIONS** under **MYTHOLOGY AND FOLKLORE**

0-19-510275-4 OXFORD PB $15.95

William L. **Reese**

Dictionary of Philosophy and Religion

0-391-03865-6 HUMANITIES PB $25.00

J. Gordon **Melton**

The Encyclopedic Handbook of Cults in America

A comprehensive guide to beliefs, organization, and origins by the author of major reference works on American religion

See also **CULTS** under **RELIGION IN THE MODERN WORLD**

0-8153-0502-8 GARLAND $65.00

J. Gordon **Melton**, editor

Encyclopedia of American Religions

The most thorough guide, taking in everything from mainstream denominations to obscure flying saucer cults, and often as entertaining as it is authoritative

0-8103-5491-8 GALE $145.00

Iona **Opie** & Moira **Tatem**, editors

A Dictionary of Superstition

From the albatross to the yawn, the dangers of sleeping in the moonlight and the curative properties of horsehairs, thousands of folk beliefs, largely drawn from the British Isles

0-19-211597-9 OXFORD $39.95

Shambhala Editors

The Encyclopedia of Eastern Philosophy and Religion: Buddhism, Hinduism, Taoism, Zen

A complete survey of the teachers, traditions, and terminology of Eastern wisdom. Over 4,000 entries, including short essays on important philosophers and different schools of Asian religious belief, make this an indispensable reference for students, scholars, and those with a personal interest in Eastern mystical thought

See also **INTRODUCTIONS AND SURVEYS** under **ASIAN RELIGION AND PHILOSOPHY**

0-87773-980-3 SHAMBHALA PB $25.00

Jonathan Z. **Smith**, editor

The HarperCollins Dictionary of Religion

More than 3,100 articles, 11 in-depth essays on the major religions, time lines, maps and drawings, color-photo inserts and graphs. This unbiased, accessible resource assembled by a distinguished editorial board offers a complex overview of the people, places, practices, and writings of the entire religious world

0-06-067515-2 HARPERCOLLINS $45.00

Geoffrey **Wigoder**, editor

The Encyclopedia of Judaism

See also **RESOURCES** under **HOW-TO: RITUAL AND PRACTICE** under **JUDAISM**

0-02-628410-3 MACMILLAN $75.00

Mircea Eliade

Mircea Eliade (1907-1986) has been one of the most influential writers on comparative religion and mythology in this century. For the convenience of readers who wish to explore his entire work, as an author and as an editor, we present a fuller listing of those titles currently available, including memoirs and works of fiction.

Mircea **Eliade**

The Sacred and the Profane: The Nature of Religion

Eliade's incomparably fluent exploration of recurrent themes in world religions—an excellent introduction

See also **COMPARATIVE RELIGION**

TRANSLATED BY WILLARD R. TRASK

0-15-679201-X HARCOURT BRACE PB $9.00

Autobiography

Volume 1

1907-1937, Journey East, Journey West

0-226-20411-1 CHICAGO $23.95

Volume 2

1937-1960, Exile's Odyssey

0-226-20411-1 CHICAGO $23.95

The Forge and the Crucible: The Origins and Structures of Alchemy

TRANSLATED BY STEPHEN CORRIN

0-226-20390-5 CHICAGO PB $12.95

A History of Religious Ideas

A monumental work, one of the crowning achievements of the great Romanian scholar. In these three volumes Eliade traces religious development from prehistory to the Reformation

Volume 1

From the Stone Age to the Eleusinian Mysteries

See also **GENERAL SURVEYS AND STUDIES**

TRANSLATED BY WILLARD R. TRASK

0-226-20400-6 CHICAGO $33.00

0-226-20401-4 CHICAGO PB $21.95

Volume 2

From Gautama Buddha to the Triumph of Christianity

TRANSLATED BY WILLARD R. TRASK

0-226-20403-0 CAMBRIDGE PB $21.95

Volume 3

From Muhammad to the Age of Reforms

TRANSLATED BY ALF HILTEBEITEL AND DIANE APOSTLOS-CAPPADONA

0-226-20404-9 CHICAGO PB $21.95

Myth and Reality

Although resolutely empirical in his approach to history and anthropology, Eliade suggests that particular historical patterns all point to a universal and ahistorical experience of the sacred

See also **GENERAL INTRODUCTIONS** under **MYTHOLOGY AND FOLKLORE**

0-06-131369-6 HARPERCOLLINS PB $13.50

The Myth of the Eternal Return

An influential study of history and mythical time. Using Eastern European folk materials, Eliade traces the transmutation of historical events into myths

See also **ROMANIAN LITERATURE** under **EASTERN EUROPEAN LITERATURE** in **LITERATURE OF EUROPE, AFRICA, AND ASIA**

TRANSLATED BY WILLARD R. TRASK

0-691-09798-4 PRINCETON $37.50

0-691-01777-8 PRINCETON PB $9.95

Myths, Dreams, and Mysteries: The Encounter Between Contemporary Faiths and Archaic Realities

See also **GENERAL INTRODUCTIONS** under **MYTHOLOGY AND FOLKLORE**

0-06-131943-0 HARPERCOLLINS PB $13.00

Occultism, Witchcraft, and Cultural Fashion: Essays in Comparative Religions

Discourses on the occult, Gnosticism, Tantric Buddhism, and contemporary culture

See also **THE OCCULT, WITCHCRAFT, AND THE DEVIL**

0-226-20392-1 CHICAGO PB $11.95

The Old Man and the Bureaucrats

A short novel set in the author's native Romania

TRANSLATED BY MARY STEVENSON

0-268-01497-3 NOTRE DAME $15.00

The Quest: History and Meaning in Religion

0-226-20386-7 CHICAGO PB $14.95

Rites and Symbols of Initiation

0-88214-358-1 SPRING PB $16.00

Shamanism: Archaic Techniques of Ecstasy

Eliade's study of shamanism is one of his greatest and most influential works. He takes a global approach to the subject but focuses particularly on the traditions of North and Central Asia

See also **INNER ASIAN TRADITIONS** under **ASIAN RELIGION AND PHILOSOPHY**

TRANSLATED BY WILLARD R. TRASK

0-691-01779-4 PRINCETON PB $17.95

Healer and psychopomp, the shaman is these because he commands the techniques of ecstasy—that is, because his soul can safely abandon his body and roam at vast distances, can penetrate the underworld and rise to the sky. Through his own ecstatic experience he knows the roads of the extraterrestrial regions. He can go below and above because he has already been there. The danger of losing his way in these forbidden regions is still great; but sanctified by his initiation and furnished with his guardian spirits, the shaman is the only human being able to challenge the danger and venture into a mystical geography.

SHAMANISM: ARCHAIC TECHNIQUES OF ECSTASY

Symbolism, the Sacred and the Arts

EDITED BY DIANE APOSTOLOS-CAPPADONA

0-8245-0723-1 CROSSROAD $18.95

Yoga: Immortality and Freedom

See also **GENERAL STUDIES** under **HINDUISM** under **ASIAN RELIGION AND PHILOSOPHY**

TRANSLATED BY WILLARD R. TRASK

0-691-01764-6 PRINCETON PB $15.95

From the time of the Upanishads India rejects the world as it is and devalues life as it reveals itself to the eyes of the sage—ephemeral, painful, illusory. Such a conception leads neither to nihilism nor pessimism. *This* world is rejected, *this* life depreciated because it is known that *something else* exists, beyond becoming, beyond temporality, beyond suffering. In religious terms,

it could almost be said that India rejects the *profane* cosmos and *profane* life, because it thirsts for a *sacred* world and a *sacred* mode of being.
YOGA: IMMORTALITY AND FREEDOM

Mircea **Eliade** & others

The Eliade Guide to World Religions: The Authoritative Compendium of the 33 Major Religious Traditions

Based on Mircea Eliade's three-volume *History of Religious Ideas,* this volume offers an encyclopedic A-to-Z digest of the world's great religions as interpreted by an inspiring scholar

0-06-062145-1 HARPERCOLLINS........$24.00

Mythology and Folklore

General Introductions

Yves **Bonnefoy**, editor

American, African, and Old European Mythologies

TRANSLATED UNDER THE DIRECTION OF WENDY DONIGER

0-226-06457-3 CHICAGO PB........$27.50

Asian Mythologies

TRANSLATED UNDER THE DIRECTION OF WENDY DONIGER

0-226-06456-5 CHICAGO PB........$28.95

Greek and Egyptian Mythologies

TRANSLATED UNDER THE DIRECTION OF WENDY DONIGER

0-226-06454-9 CHICAGO PB........$26.95

Roman and European Mythologies

TRANSLATED UNDER THE DIRECTION OF WENDY DONIGER

0-226-06455-7 CHICAGO PB........$26.95

Thomas **Bulfinch**

The Age of Fable: Myths of Greece and Rome

The first and best-known volume of Bulfinch's famous work, focusing on Greek and Roman mythology; illustrated

INTRODUCTION BY JOSEPH CAMPBELL

0-14-005643-2 VIKING PB........$24.95

The clouds begin to smoke, and the mountain tops take fire; the fields are parched with heat, the plants wither, the trees with their leafy branches burn, the harvest is ablaze! But these are small things. Great cities perished, with their walls and towers; whole nations with their people were consumed to ashes! The forest-clad mountains burned, Athos and Taurus and Tmolus and Oete; Ida, once celebrated for fountains, but now all dry; the Muses' mountain Helicon, and Haemus; Aetna, with fires within and without, and Parnassus, with his two peaks, and Rhodope, forced at last to part with his snowy crown.
THE AGE OF FABLE: MYTHS OF GREECE AND ROME

Bulfinch's Mythology: The Age of Chivalry and Legends of Charlemagne or Romance in the Middle Ages

The enduring popular 19th-century retelling of Greek, Roman, and medieval myths and legends

0-394-60437-7 MODERN LIBRARY........$20.00
0-452-01153-1 PENGUIN PB........$14.95

Joseph **Campbell**

Campbell's work combines scholarship, Jungian depth psychology, and inspirational writing, and remains an immensely popular introduction. His approach reflects the continuing relevance of mythological symbols even—or especially—in our secular, mythless age.

The Flight of the Wild Gander

Fairy tales and myths interpreted in relation to science, psychology, religion, and modern life

0-06-096981-4 HARPERPERENNIAL PB........$13.00

The Hero with a Thousand Faces

This best-seller attempts to discover an archetypal "monomyth" within the myths of various cultures

0-691-09743-7 PRINCETON........$65.00
0-691-01784-0 PRINCETON PB........$12.95

Joseph Campbell

The Inner Reaches of Outer Space: Metaphor as Myth and as Religion

A distillation of the author's lifework

0-06-096353-0 HARPERPERENNIAL PB........$12.00

The Masks of God

Campbell's major work of comparative mythology

Volume 1 Primitive Mythology

0-14-019443-6 ARKANA PB........$14.95

Volume 2 Oriental Mythology

0-14-019442-8 ARKANA PB........$15.95

Volume 3 Occidental Mythology

0-14-019441-X ARKANA PB........$15.95

Volume 4 Creative Mythology

0-14-019440-1 ARKANA PB........$15.95

Joseph **Campbell** & M.J. **Abadie**

The Mythic Image

Mythological art from all cultures and periods, with commentary

0-691-01839-1 PRINCETON PB........$29.95

Joseph **Campbell** & Bill **Moyers**

The Power of Myth

A transcript of the popular television series

0-385-24774-5 DOUBLEDAY........$24.95
0-385-41886-8 ANCHOR PB........$12.00

Diane **Osbon**

A Joseph Campbell Companion: Reflections on the Art of Living

Highlights of Campbell's 1984 seminar at Big Sur's Esalen Institute. During the 30-day session, Campbell shared with 10 students the fruits of his life-long study of spiritual awakening and the art of living in the sacred

0-06-016718-1 HARPERCOLLINS........$25.00

Giorgio **de Santillana** & Hertha **von Dechend**

Hamlet's Mill: An Essay on Myth and the Frame of Time

A highly original examination of the origins of human knowledge and the relation of myth to science

0-87923-215-3 GODINE PB........$18.95

Mircea **Eliade**

Myth and Reality

0-06-131369-6 HARPERCOLLINS PB........$13.50

The Myth of the Eternal Return

TRANSLATED BY WILLARD R. TRASK

0-691-09798-4 PRINCETON........$37.50
0-691-01777-8 PRINCETON PB........$9.95

Myths, Dreams, and Mysteries: The Encounter Between Contemporary Faiths and Archaic Realities

0-06-131943-0 HARPERCOLLINS PB........$13.00

Ernst **Cassirer**

Language and Myth

An important study of the relation of myth, language, and thought, by a German neo-Kantian philosopher

TRANSLATED BY SUSANNE K. LANGER

0-486-20051-5 DOVER PB........$4.95

James G. **Frazer**

The Golden Bough

The ideas in Frazer's bold and pioneering study of ancient European myths, published in 1890 and subsequently revised and expanded, have been thoroughly absorbed into our culture, most visibly in the work of Sigmund Freud and the poetry of T.S. Eliot

See also **CLASSICS** under **GENERAL ANTHROPOLOGICAL STUDIES** under **ANTHROPOLOGY** in **SOCIAL STUDIES**

EDITED AND ABRIDGED BY THEODORE GASTER

0-517-33633-2 GRAMERCY........$12.99
0-19-282934-3 OXFORD PB........$17.95

James G. **Frazer**

The Golden Bough

Frazer's complete classic in a 13-volume set. Includes *The Magic Art and the Evolution of Kings, Taboo and the Perils of the Soul; The Dying God; Adonis, Attis, Osiris, Spirits of the Corn and of the Wild; The Scapegoat; Balder the Beautiful; The Fire Festivals of Europe and the Doctrines of the Eternal Soul; Bibliograpby and General Index*; and *Aftermath: A Supplement*

0-312-33215-7 ST. MARTIN'S $450.00

Robert **Graves**

The White Goddess: A Historical Grammar of Poetic Myth

An eccentric and engaging study of poetry and its relation to muses and myths, mainly Celtic and Greek; in the author's words, "a very difficult book, as well as a very queer one"

See also **20TH-CENTURY BRITISH ESSAYS AND OTHER PROSE** in **LITERATURE OF THE BRITISH ISLES**

0-374-50493-8 FS&G PB $15.00

Carl **Jung** & Karl **Kerenyi**

Essays on a Science of Mythology

An approach based on Jung's theory of a collective unconcious

See also **JUNG** under **PSYCHOLOGY** in **SOCIAL STUDIES**

0-691-01756-5 PRINCETON PB $11.95

C. G. Jung
(photo courtesy of Wide World)

G.S. **Kirk**

Myth: Its Meaning and Functions in Ancient and Other Cultures

The relation of myth to the unconscious and to folklore and ritual, the theory of structuralism, and the influence of Near Eastern mythology on Greek thought

0-520-02389-7 CALIFORNIA PB $16.95

David Adams **Leeming** &
Margaret Adams **Leeming**

A Dictionary of Creation Myths

See also **REFERENCE WORKS** under **WORLD RELIGION**

0-19-510275-4 OXFORD PB $15.95

Anthony S. **Mercatante**

The Facts on File Encyclopedia of World Mythology and Legend

0-8160-1049-8 FACTS ON FILE $95.00

Carl **Olson**, editor

The Book of the Goddess

A sourcebook of essays on the female deities of Eastern and Western cultures, including the Sophia of the Gnostics, the Virgin Mary, and the Hindu goddesses

0-8245-0689-8 CROSSROAD PB $15.95

Barbara C. **Sproul**

Primal Myths: Creating the World

"A representative, well-chosen collection, from good sources, well presented for use either as an introduction to the study of mythology or as a convenient reference work and refresher of memory"—Joseph Campbell

0-06-067501-2 HARPERCOLLINS PB $17.00

The All-Lord said, after he had come into being: "I am he who came into being as Khepri. When I had come into being, being (itself) came into being, and all beings came into being after I came into being. Many were the beings which came forth from my mouth, before heaven came into being, before earth came into being, before the ground and creeping things had been created in this place. I put together (some) of them in Nun as weary ones, before I could find a place in which I might stand. It (seemed) advantageous to me in my heart; I planned with my face; and I made (in concept) every form when I was alone, before I had spat out what was Shu, before I had Sputtered out what was Tefnut, and before (any) other had come into being who could act with me."—From the ancient Egyptian text *The Repulsing of the Dragon and the Creation*
PRIMAL MYTHS: CREATING THE WORLD

Giambattista **Vico**

The New Science of Giambattista Vico

Vico's 1725 treatise was the first modern study of myth, foreshadowing later anthropological views: "The fables of the gods are true histories of customs." This groundbreaking work was the first to treat the internal dynamics of primitive cultures and offered a cyclical alternative to the Enlightenment's belief that history means progress

See also **VICO** under **PHILOSOPHY**

TRANSLATED BY THOMAS G. BERGIN & MAX FISCH

0-8014-9265-3 CORNELL PB $15.95

Roy **Willis**, editor

World Mythology

The myths of birth, loss, death, famine, abundance, longing, greed, love, and power comprise a portrait of the emotional and imaginative landscape of humankind. Common mythological themes from diverse corners of the world are linked and explored, both as aspects of a single unified psyche and as rich regional expressions of their own. 500 photographs, charts, and maps

See also **ONE-VOLUME ENCYCLOPEDIAS** under **REFERENCE** in **BUSINESS AND REFERENCE**

0-8050-2701-7 HOLT $45.00

The Ancient World: Egypt and Mesopotamia

Egypt

E.A. Wallis **Budge**

The Gods of the Egyptians: Studies in Egyptian Mythology

A major study, covering the myths of Thoth and Isis, the Book of the Dead, the cult of Osiris, and the mythological associations of animals and birds. Many illustrations

Volume 1

0-486-22055-9 DOVER PB $12.95

Volume 2

0-486-22056-7 DOVER PB $12.95

Osiris and the Egyptian Resurrection

Volume 1

0-486-22780-4 DOVER PB $10.95

Volume 2

0-486-22781-2 DOVER PB $9.95

Hasan M. **El-Shamy**, editor

Folktales of Egypt

FOREWORD BY RICHARD M. DORSON

0-226-20625-4 CHICAGO PB $19.00

Manfred **Lurker**

Gods and Symbols of Ancient Egypt: An Illustrated Dictionary

See also **REFERENCE** under **ARCHAEOLOGY** in **WORLD HISTORY AND CURRENT AFFAIRS**

EDITED BY PETER A. CLAYTON

0-500-27253-0 NORTON PB $15.95

R.A. **Schwaller de Lubicz**

The Temple of Man

TRANSLATED BY DEBORAH LAWLOR AND ROBERT LAWLOR

0-89281-570-1 INNER TRADITIONS $100.00

Byron E. **Shafer**, editor

Religion in Ancient Egypt: Gods, Myths, and Personal Practice

The newest findings of Egyptology are brought to bear in these studies of Egyptian religion, with a special emphasis on the experience of the individual believer

See also **ANCIENT MEDITERRANEAN RELIGIONS** under **WORLD RELIGION**

0-8014-9786-8 CORNELL PB $13.95

Mesopotamia

Jeremy **Black** & Anthony **Green**

Gods, Demons and Symbols of Ancient Mesopotamia: An Illustrated Dictionary

Well informed and up-to-date illustrated dictionary by two scholars who have made their career out

of clarifying the confusing array of religious representations in pre-classical Mesopotamia
See also **MESOPOTAMIA** under **THE ANCIENT NEAR EAST** under **ARCHAEOLOGY** in **WORLD HISTORY AND CURRENT AFFAIRS**
0-292-70794-0 TEXAS PB $19.95

S. H. **Hooke**
Middle Eastern Mythology
A compact summary of the mythology of the Egyptians, Babylonians, Assyrians, Hittites, Canaanites, and Hebrews, in the light of 20th-century archaeological discoveries. Hooke also discusses influences on early Christianity
0-14-013687-8 VIKING PB $9.00

Classical Mythology: Ancient Greece and Rome

Walter **Burkert**
Structure and History in Greek Mythology
A rare combination of fine scholarship with imagination and humor
0-520-04770-2 CALIFORNIA PB $16.00

Roberto **Calasso**
The Marriage of Cadmus and Harmony
A beautifully written recounting of and meditation on Greek myths
0-394-58154-7 KNOPF $25.00
0-679-73348-5 VINTAGE PB $13.00

Dionysus's phallus is more hallucinogenic than coercive. It is close to a fungus, or a parasite in nature, or to the toxic grass stuffed in the cavity of the thyrsus. It has none of the faithfulness of the farmer's crop, it won't stretch out in the plowed furrow where Iasion made love to Demeter, nor does it push its way up amid flourishing harvest fields, but rather in the most intractable woodland. It is a metallic tip concealed beneath innocuous green leaves. It doesn't intoxicate to promote growth; yet, growth sustains intoxication, as the stem of a goblet holds up the wine. Dionysus is not a useful god who helps weave or knot things together, but a god who loosens and unties.
THE MARRIAGE OF CADMUS AND HARMONY

F.M. **Cornford**
From Religion to Philosophy: A Study in the Origins of Western Speculation
A classic study of early Greek thought, applying anthropological insights and scholarship to the "very first utterance of philosophers," the Presocratic thinkers of the sixth century BC
0-691-02076-0 PRINCETON PB $13.95

Fritz **Graf**
Greek Mythology: An Introduction
See also **GENERAL STUDIES** under **CRITICAL STUDIES** under **ANCIENT GREEK LITERATURE** in **LITERATURE OF EUROPE, AFRICA, AND ASIA**
0-8018-4657-9 JOHNS HOPKINS $35.95

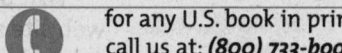

Robert **Graves**
Graves combines stunning powers of characterization and storytelling with deep historical knowledge of such diverse areas as mythical Greece, classical Rome, Byzantium, and colonial America.

Greek Myths
Drawn from the definitive classic, this condensed edition cites the legends of birth and the lives of the great Olympians, from Andromeda and Aphrodite to Narcissus and Zeus. Illustrated by the artists of ancient Greece
See also **ANTHOLOGIES** under **ANCIENT GREEK LITERATURE** in **LITERATURE OF EUROPE, AFRICA, AND ASIA**
0-918825-80-6 MOYER BELL $27.95
0-14-007602-6 PENGUIN PB $17.95

The Greek Myths
The scattered elements of these classical myths are organized into fluent narratives, with copious indexes, cross-references, and discussions of problems of historical and anthropological interpretation
Volume 1
0-14-001026-2 VIKING PB $7.00
Volume 2
0-14-001027-0 PENGUIN PB $8.95

Robert Graves

Pierre **Grimal**
The Dictionary of Classical Mythology
The complete story of every mythic figure and type—gods and mortals, centaurs, satyrs, nymphs, and dryads—with illustrations from classical art, maps, and genealogical charts. "It will indeed be a learned reader who does not find something he did not previously know on almost every page"—*TLS*
0-631-20102-5 BLACKWELL PB $24.95

The Penguin Dictionary of Classical Mythology
0-14-051235-7 PENGUIN PB $14.95

Rhoda A. **Hendricks**, translator
Classical Gods and Heroes: Myths as Retold by the Ancient Authors
Selections from Hesiod, Ovid, Sophocles, Catullus, and others, with glossary and maps
0-688-05279-7 MORROW PB $12.95

Carl **Kerenyi**
The Gods of the Greeks
The Greek myths, humanistically reinterpreted in terms of their continued relevance to contemporary life
0-500-27048-1 NORTON PB $14.95

G.S. **Kirk**
The Nature of Greek Myths
A systematic examination, including an overview of the leading theories and speculation on the transition from mythology to philosophy
0-14-013536-7 VIKING PB $11.95

Jane Davidson **Reid** & Chris **Rohmann**
The Oxford Guide to Classical Mythology in the Arts, 1300-1900s
0-19-504998-5 OXFORD $225.00

Gustav **Schwab**
Gods and Heroes
A 19th-century German compendium of myths and legends drawn from Greek and Roman literature
0-394-73402-5 PANTHEON PB $20.00

European Mythology

Georges **Dumézil**
The Stakes of the Warrior
The tragic warrior-hero as a crucial figure in Indo-European mythology
TRANSLATED BY DAVID WEEKS
0-520-04834-2 CALIFORNIA $35.00

Marija **Gimbutas**
Goddesses and Gods of Old Europe, 7000 to 3500 B.C.: Myths, Legends, and Cult Images
0-520-04655-2 CALIFORNIA PB $17.95

Prudence **Jones** & Nigel **Pennick**
A History of Pagan Europe
See also **NORTHERN EUROPE** under **THE ARCHAEOLOGY OF CIVILIZATIONS** under **ARCHAEOLOGY** in **WORLD HISTORY AND CURRENT AFFAIRS**
0-415-09136-5 ROUTLEDGE $25.00

Jessie L. **Weston**
From Ritual to Romance
This classic study of European mythology, with the notable inclusion of the Grail legend, was a major source for T.S. Eliots' *The Waste Land*
0-691-02107-4 PRINCETON PB $10.95

British and Celtic

Norma Lorre **Goodrich**
King Arthur
A medieval scholar searches archaeology, history, and romance for the truth of the Arthurian legend
0-06-097182-7 HARPERCOLLINS PB $16.00

Norris J. **Lacy**, editor
The Arthurian Encyclopedia
See also **HISTORIES AND CRITICAL STUDIES** under **MEDIEVAL LITERATURE** in **LITERATURE OF EUROPE, AFRICA, AND ASIA**
0-87226-164-6 BEDRICK PB $16.95

Sir Thomas **Malory**

Le Morte D'Arthur

See also **PROSE** under **MEDIEVAL LITERATURE** in **LITERATURE OF THE BRITISH ISLES**

0-679-60099-X MODERN LIBRARY $21.00

John **Steinbeck**

The Acts of King Arthur and His Noble Knights

Steinbeck's modernization of the *Morte d'Arthur*—which he considered among the greatest challenges of his career—"embellishes Malory's spare legend with a richness of detail that transfers the vision, makes it no one but Steinbeck's"
—John Gardner, *NY Times Book Review*

0-374-52378-9 NOONDAY PB $17.00

John Steinbeck

T.H. **White**

The Once and Future King

This retelling of King Arthur was the basis for *Camelot,* and contains fascinating information about living in the Dark Age

See also **THE EARLY 20TH CENTURY** under **20TH-CENTURY BRITISH AND IRISH FICTION** in **LITERATURE OF THE BRITISH ISLES**

0-441-62740-4 ACE PB $6.99

Kevin **Crossley-Holland**, editor

The Anglo-Saxon World: An Anthology

A compact collection of documents and poems, including a complete translation of *Beowulf*

See also **THE ANGLO-SAXON PERIOD** in **LITERATURE OF THE BRITISH ISLES**

0-85115-169-8 ROCHESTER $45.00
0-19-281632-2 OXFORD PB $9.95

Patrick K. **Ford**, editor

The Mabinogi & Other Medieval Welsh Tales

Celtic literature unadulterated by the French Arthurian romances, constituting the core of the ancient Welsh mythological cycle

0-520-03414-7 CALIFORNIA PB $15.95

Jeffrey **Gantz**, translator

Early Irish Myths and Sagas

See also **CELTIC LITERATURE** in **LITERATURE OF THE BRITISH ISLES**

0-14-044397-5 PENGUIN PB $9.95

Norma Lorre **Goodrich**

The Holy Grail

Stripping away layers of myth and fiction surrounding the Grail, Goodrich explores 2,000 years of Christian, Hebraic, Celtic, and academic lore. An unusual, rich, and immensely readable study

See also **BEGINNINGS AND EARLY HISTORY** under **HISTORY** under **CHRISTIANITY**

0-06-092204-4 HARPERPERENNIAL PB $14.00

Merlin

Passages from ancient sources brought together in a fascinating narrative recreate the magical thinking of the early Middle Ages

0-06-097183-5 HARPERCOLLINS PB $16.00

Kenneth Hartstone **Jackson**, editor

A Celtic Miscellany

Prose and verse from six Celtic languages, including bardic elegies, heroic tales, and the literature of love

See also **CELTIC LITERATURE** in **LITERATURE OF THE BRITISH ISLES**

0-14-044247-2 PENGUIN PB $12.95

Roger Sherman **Loomis**

Grail: From Celtic Myth to Christian Symbol

0-691-02075-2 PRINCETON PB $12.95

G. Ronald **Murphy**

The Heliand: The Saxon Gospel

0-19-507375-9 OXFORD $35.00

Ward **Rutherford**

Celtic Mythology: The Nature and Influence of Celtic Mythology from Druidism to Arthurian Legend

0-85030-551-9 AQUARIAN PB $10.95

William Butler **Yeats**, editor

Irish Fairy and Folktales

0-679-60094-9 MODERN LIBRARY $14.50

Norse

Padraic **Colum**

Nordic Gods and Heroes

0-486-28912-5 DOVER PB $8.95

Kevin **Crossley-Holland**, editor

The Norse Myths

A vivid new rendering

0-394-74846-8 RANDOM HOUSE PB $16.00

H.R. Ellis **Davidson**

Gods and Myths of Northern Europe

A renowned scholar explores Viking mythology, relating cultic practices to daily life and speculating on the eclipse of pagan beliefs by Christianity

0-14-013627-4 VIKING PB $10.95

Carolyne **Larrington**, translator

The Poetic Edda

Compiled in Iceland in the 12th or 13th century, *The Poetic Edda* is the principal compendium of Norse mythology

0-19-282383-3 OXFORD PB $10.95

Elias **Lonnrot**

The Kalevala

See also **FINNISH LITERATURE** under **SCANDINAVIAN LITERATURE** in **LITERATURE OF EUROPE, AFRICA, AND ASIA**

TRANSLATED BY KEITH BOSLEY

0-19-281700-0 OXFORD PB $13.95

Snorri **Sturluson**

The Prose Edda of Snorri Sturluson: Tales from Norse Mythology

Originally penned as a manual in skaldic (courtly) poetry

See also **OLD NORSE AND ICELANDIC LITERATURE** under **SCANDINAVIAN LITERATURE** in **LITERATURE OF EUROPE, AFRICA, AND ASIA**

TRANSLATED BY JEAN YOUNG

0-520-01232-1 CALIFORNIA PB $12.00

Russian and Slavic

Elizabeth **Warner**

Heroes, Monsters and Other Worlds from Russian Mythology

0-87226-925-6 BEDRICK LIBRARY EDITION $24.95

The Non-Western World

African

Harold **Coulander** & Ousmane **Sako**

The Heart of the Ngoni: Heroes of the African Kingdom

0-87023-929-5 MASSACHUSETTS PB $13.95

Bernard B. **Dadie**

The Black Cloth: A Collection of African Folk Tales

Stories rich in humor and inventiveness, retold by the distinguished Ivory Coast poet, novelist, and statesman

See also **ANTHOLOGIES AND CRITICAL STUDIES** under **AFRICAN LITERATURE** in **LITERATURE OF EUROPE, AFRICA, AND ASIA**

TRANSLATED BY KAREN C. HATCH
FOREWORD BY E'-KIA MPHAHLELE

0-87023-557-5 MASSACHUSETTS PB $13.95

Paul **Radin**, editor

African Folktales

Stories from sub-Saharan Africa including those of the Hausa, the Bantu, the Bushmen, and the Zulu, compiled by a distinguished American anthropologist

0-8052-0732-5 SCHOCKEN PB $14.95

Arab

Iner **Bushnaq**, editor

Arab Folktales

"Beautifully edited, translated, and annotated" —Edward W. Said

0-394-75179-5 PANTHEON PB $18.00

There is in the Koran a whole *sura*, or chapter, named for the Djinn. Indeed, just as God created man from potter's clay, so he formed the Djinn from a smokeless fire. He sent the prophet to enlighten both worlds of sentient beings, that of the Ins, or humans, and that of the Djinn, or spirits. Much of the excitement in the tales of magic lies in the removal of the boundary between the two worlds. Whether they are potential helpers to be wooed or dangerous enemies to be overcome, the spirits are as much a part of the landscape as the heroes. When a merchant watering his camels pulls a handsome youth up from the bottom of the well with his rope, or when a prince hunting in the wilderness comes upon a girl whose hair shines like threads of gold, the question "Are You Ins or are you Djinn?" is asked as a matter of course.

ARAB FOLKTALES

Husain **Haddawy**, translator

The Arabian Nights

The most authentic translation of the classic of Oriental storytelling. "Haddawy's *Arabian Nights* is ... indispensable. He has given us not a new version of an old favorite, but a work we've never known"— *Village Voice*

See also **CLASSICAL LITERATURE** under **ARABIC LITERATURE** in **LITERATURE OF EUROPE, AFRICA, AND ASIA**

0-679-41338-3 KNOPF $20.00

0-393-02707-4 NORTON $27.95

0-393-31367-0 NORTON PB $14.95

The Arabian Nights II: Sinbad and Other Popular Stories

0-393-31517-7 NORTON PB $14.95

Robert **Irwin**

The Arabian Nights: A Companion

0-7139-9105-4 ALLEN LANE $24.95

Chinese

Anne M. **Birrell**

Chinese Mythology: An Introduction

0-8018-4595-5 JOHNS HOPKINS $34.95

Yin-Lien **Chin**

Traditional Chinese Folktales

A collection of 12 tales from different provinces of China

1-56324-800-X SHARPE PB $12.50

Moss **Roberts**, editor

Chinese Fairy Tales and Fantasies

See also **SHORT STORIES** under **FICTION** under **CLASSICAL CHINESE LITERATURE** in **LITERATURE OF EUROPE, AFRICA, AND ASIA**

0-394-73994-9 RANDOM HOUSE PB $14.00

Indian

Brenda E.F. **Beck**, editor

Folktales of India

Nearly 100 tales from 14 languages, arranged by theme

FOREWORD BY A.K. RAMANUJAN

0-226-04082-8 CHICAGO PB $19.95

R.K. **Narayan**, translator

The Ramayana: The Indian Epic

A fluent retelling of the story by India's foremost contemporary writer

See also **THE VEDAS AND THE GREAT EPICS** under **SANSKRIT LITERATURE** under **LITERATURES OF INDIA**

0-14-018700-6 PENGUIN PB $9.95

Wendy Doniger **O'Flaherty**

Dreams, Illusion and Other Realities

The role of dreams and dreaming in Indian religion, philosophy, literature, and art

0-226-61855-2 CHICAGO PB $22.95

Women, Androgynes, and Other Mythical Beasts

Sexual symbolism and themes in Indian myth and ritual. "An important, provocative and original work...splendid translations, and exegesis of so many, and so different, Sanskrit texts"—Mircea Eliade

0-226-61849-8 CHICAGO $33.00

0-226-61850-1 CHICAGO PB $17.95

Wendy Doniger **O'Flaherty**, translator

Hindu Myths

A kaleidoscopic survey with selections from the Vedas, the medieval pantheon, and the mythology of Krishna and the minor gods

0-14-044306-1 PENGUIN PB $9.95

A. K. **Ramanujan**, editor

Folktales of India: A Selection of Oral Tales from Twenty Languages

An exquisite compilation of tales and legends from a variety of Indian traditions, edited by a scholar renowned for his many volumes of poetic translations.

0-394-55479-5 PANTHEON PB $23.00

Heinrich **Zimmer**

Myths and Symbols in Indian Art and Civilization

0-691-01778-6 PRINCETON PB $10.95

Japanese

David F. **Hadland**

Myths and Legends of Japan

0-486-27045-9 DOVER PB $9.95

Juliet **Piggott**

Japanese Mythology

Mythological art with historical background and a selection of myths, legends, and tales

0-911745-09-2 BEDRICK LIBRARY EDITION $24.95

Royall **Tyler**

Japanese Tales

The most extensive Japanese folk tale collection available

See also **TALES, DIARIES, AND ESSAYS** under **THE HEIAN PERIOD (794–1185)** under **JAPANESE LITERATURE** in **LITERATURE OF EUROPE, AFRICA, AND ASIA**

0-394-75656-8 PANTHEON PB $17.00

Oceanian

Rosemary **Crumlin** & Anthony **Knight**

Aboriginal Art and Spirituality

The sacred art of the Australian aborigines—representing a heritage that goes back 40,000 years—has in recent years attracted increasing attention for both its aesthetic and religious aspects. The 82 contemporary examples reproduced here in full color and with detailed commentary show the continuing vitality of this most ancient of traditions

0-85924-998-0 HARPERCOLLINS PB $29.95

Tibetan

Sylvia **Gretchen**

Hero of the Land of Snow

Traditional Tibetan myth for children

0-89800-202-8 DHARMA PB $7.95

Laurence Austine **Waddell**

Tibetan Buddhism

Covers mystic cults, symbolism, mythology, and the relation to Indian Buddhism

0-486-20130-9 DOVER PB $13.95

The Western Hemisphere

African-American

Harold **Courlander**

A Treasury of Afro-American Folklore: The Oral Literature, Traditions, Recollections, Legends, Tales, Songs, Religious Beliefs, Customs and Sayings

See also **FOLKLORE** under **CULTURE** under **AFRICAN-AMERICAN STUDIES** in **HISTORY OF THE AMERICAS**

1-56924-811-7 MARLOWE PB $14.95

Virginia **Hamilton**

Her Stories: African American Folktales, Fairy Tales and True Tales

A collection for children

See also **FICTION** under **BOOKS FOR EIGHTS, NINES, AND UP** in **BOOKS FOR YOUNG READERS**

0-590-47370-0 SCHOLASTIC $19.95

Robert D. **San Souci**

John and Mr. Bear: An African-American Folktale

0-8037-1766-0 PENGUIN $25.00

American

Walter **Blair**

Tall Tale America: A Legendary History of Our Humorous Heroes

0-226-05596-5 CHICAGO PB $17.95

Jan H. **Brunvand**

The Choking Doberman & Other "New" Urban Legends

Brunvand's journeys into the byways of urban folklore to explore apocryphal—and often horrific things—usually described as having happened to "a friend of a friend"

0-393-30321-7 NORTON PB $9.95

The Mexican Pet: More "New" Urban Legends and Some Old Favorites

0-393-30542-2 NORTON PB $10.95

The Vanishing Hitchhiker: American Urban Legends and Their Meanings

0-393-95169-3 NORTON PB $9.95

Alan **Dundes** & Carl R. **Pagter**

Work Hard and You Shall Be Rewarded: Urban Folklore from the Paperwork Empire

A serious but entertaining survey of contemporary materials that proliferate through photocopying rather than oral tradition

0-8143-1866-5 WAYNE STATE $34.95

Alan **Dundes**

When You're Up to Your Ass in Alligators: More Urban Folklore from the Paperwork Empire

A follow-up to *Work Hard and You Shall Be Rewarded*

0-8143-1867-3 WAYNE STATE PB $15.95

Mary **Knapp** & Herbert **Knapp**

One Potato, Two Potato: The Folklore of American Children

0-393-09039-6 NORTON PB $7.95

Vance **Randolph**

Ozark Magic and Folklore

A noted study first published in 1947

0-486-21181-9 DOVER PB $7.95

Caribbean

Maya **Deren**

Divine Horsemen: The Living Gods of Haiti

A study of voodoo owing much to the experiences of the author, a leading experimental filmmaker of the 1940s

See also **RELIGIONS OF AFRICA AND THE AFRICAN DIASPORA**

FOREWORD BY JOSEPH CAMPBELL

0-914232-63-0 MCPHERSON PB $15.00

Wade **Davis**

Passage of Darkness: The Ethnobiology of the Haitian Zombie

A controversial account of Davis' attempt to explain the zombie phenomenon. "Davis broke into that amazing world for the first time and what he found has, I think, possible transoceanic resonance…He has written of one of the most fascinating and most misunderstood phenomena of all the Black Americas"—Robert Farris Thompson

0-8078-1776-7 NORTH CAROLINA $39.95
0-8078-4210-9 NORTH CAROLINA PB $15.95

Native American

John **Bierhorst**

The Mythology of Mexico and Central America

The region's basic myths shed light on the writing of history, the rise of nationalism, and the nature of mythology itself

0-688-06721-2 MORROW $17.00

The Mythology of North America

A systematic survey of heroes, goddesses, and spirits, from the Arctic regions to the Southwest. Illustrated

See also **RELIGION AND MYTHOLOGY** under **ASPECTS OF TRADITIONAL CULTURE** under **NATIVE AMERICAN CULTURES: NORTH AMERICA** in **HISTORY OF THE AMERICAS**

0-688-06666-6 MORROW PB $12.50

Frank H. **Cushing**

Zuni Folk Tales

0-404-11836-4 AMS $68.75
0-8165-0986-7 ARIZONA PB $17.95

Richard **Erdoes** & Alfonso **Ortiz**

American Indian Myths and Legends

"…probably the most comprehensive and diverse collection of American Indian legends ever compiled"—Dee Brown

0-394-74018-1 PANTHEON PB $18.00

Sam D. **Gill** & Irene F. **Sullivan**

Dictionary of Native American Mythology

0-87436-621-6 ABC CLIO $69.50
0-19-508602-3 OXFORD PB $17.95

Emilio Abreu **Gomez**

Canek: History and Legend of a Maya Hero

TRANSLATED BY MARIO L. DAVILA & CARTER WILSON

0-520-03148-2 CALIFORNIA $38.00

Edwin S. **Hall**, Jr.

The Eskimo Storyteller: Folktales from Noatak, Alaska

0-87049-603-4 TENNESSEE PB $16.95

David **Hess**

Samba in the Night: Spiritism in Brazil

See also **BRAZIL** under **LATIN AMERICA AND THE CARIBBEAN** in **HISTORY OF THE AMERICAS**

0-231-08432-3 COLUMBIA $29.50

Basil **Johnston**

The Manitous: The Spiritual World of the Ojibway

"An extraordinary glimpse into a rich and meaningful mythology"—*Kirkus Reviews*

0-06-092735-6 HARPERCOLLINS PB $12.00

Jeff **King**

Where the Two Came to Their Father: A Navaho War Ceremonial

The ethnologist Maud Oakes was "given" this version of the Navaho creation myth in the 1940s by the medicine man Jeff King, along with eighteen ceremonial paintings; the original publication was the first title in the famous Bollingen Series

TEXT AND PAINTINGS RECORDED BY MAUD OAKES
COMMENTARY BY JOSEPH CAMPBELL

0-691-02069-8 PRINCETON PB $14.95

Archie Fire **Lame Deer** & Richard **Erdoes**

Gift of Power: The Life and Teaching of a Lakota Medicine Man

0-671-88802-1 WASHINGTON SQUARE PB $5.50

Lawrence **Millman**

A Kayak Full of Ghosts: Eskimo Tales

0-88496-267-9 CAPRA PB $9.95

Stith **Thompson**

Folktales of the North American Indians: Selected and Annotated

1-572-15196-X WORLD PUB $12.99

Marion **Wood**

Spirits, Heroes and Hunters from North American Indian Mythology

ILLUSTRATED BY JOHN SIBBICK

0-87226-903-5 BEDRICK LIBRARY EDITION $24.95

Folklore

Peter C. **Asbjornsen** & Jorgen **Moe**

Norwegian Folk Tales

0-394-71054-1 PANTHEON PB $14.00

Bruno **Bettelheim**

The Uses of Enchantment: The Meaning and Importance of Fairy Tales

A classic study by this distinguished psychologist and interpreter of childhood who links folk tales to children's most pressing emotional needs

See also **CHILD PSYCHOLOGY** under **PSYCHOLOGY** in **SOCIAL STUDIES**

0-679-72393-5 VINTAGE PB $13.00

Bruno Bettelheim

Italo **Calvino**

"Calvino does what very few writers can do: he describes imaginary worlds with the most extraordinary precision and beauty" —Gore Vidal

Italian Folktales

Lovers, saints, rogues, kings, peasants, and animals, in tales from every region of Italy, retold by the distinguished novelist

TRANSLATED BY GEORGE MARTIN

0-15-145770-0 HARCOURT BRACE....$27.95

0-394-74909-X HARCOURT BRACE PB....$11.95

Italo Calvino

Joanna **Cole**

Best Loved Folktales of the World

Over 200 stories, arranged geographically, including *Snow White, The Indian Cinderella,* and *The Magic Orange Tree*

0-385-18949-4 ANCHOR PB....$14.95

Richard M. **Dorson**, editor

Folktales Told Around the World

Brings together the work of field workers, folklorists, and storytellers, with an emphasis on contemporary folk narrative

0-226-15874-8 CHICAGO PB....$26.50

Handbook of American Folklore

0-253-20373-2 INDIANA PB....$18.95

Henry **Glassie**, editor

Irish Folktales

0-394-74637-6 PANTHEON PB....$17.00

Shahrukh **Husain**, editor

Daughters of the Moon: Witch Tales from Around the World

Folklorist, writer, and psychotherapist Husain has collected over 50 stories of witchcraft from over 30 different cultures: *femmes fatales* who doom men; child-eating hags; witches who can become animals; and mysterious wise women

0-571-19856-2 FABER....$22.95

Max **Luthi**

The European Folktale: Form and Nature

A classic attempt to define the essential laws of the genre

0-253-20393-7 INDIANA PB....$11.95

Once Upon a Time: On the Nature of Fairy Tales

Essays on such celebrated stories as *Hansel and Gretel, Sleeping Beauty*, and *Rapunzel*

0-253-20203-5 INDIANA PB....$10.95

Raphael **Patai**

On Jewish Folklore

0-8143-2437-1 WAYNE STATE PB....$18.95

Pinhas **Sadeh**

Jewish Folktales

See also **JEWISH CULTURE** under **JEWISH HISTORY** in **WORLD HISTORY AND CURRENT AFFAIRS**

0-385-19574-5 ANCHOR PB....$16.00

Howard **Schwartz**

Lilith's Cave: Jewish Tales of the Supernatural

Wonderful translations and retellings of 50 stories from the long Jewish tradition of the fantastic. Dybbuks, dangerous mirrors, werewolves, and wandering spirits are among the uncanny presences that haunt these pages

0-19-506726-6 OXFORD PB....$12.95

Stith **Thompson**

Motif-Index of Folk Literature: A Classification of Narrative Elements in Folktales, Ballads, Myths, Fables, Medieval Romanas, Exempla, Fabliaux

An important study

0-253-33884-0 INDIANA....$65.00

Jacob **Grimm** & Wilhelm K. **Grimm**

The Complete Fairy Tales of the Brothers Grimm

Vivid, striking, raucous, violent, filled with the rhythms of folklore and song. "Clearly the text of choice for any reader. With its outstanding introduction and notes…Zipes's edition deserves to become the standard translation" —Donald Haase, *The German Quarterly*

TRANSLATED BY JACK ZIPES

0-553-37101-0 BANTAM PB....$15.95

Grimm's Tales for Young and Old: The Complete Stories

A fine new translation of the powerful and haunting European folk tales collected by the Grimm brothers in the early 19th century

TRANSLATED BY RALPH MANHEIM

0-385-18950-8 DOUBLEDAY PB....$16.95

Grimm Brothers

W.B. **Yeats**, editor

Fairy and Folk Tales of Ireland

Fairies, leprechauns, ghosts, witches, princesses, devils, and others, compiled by Yeats in the 1880s

See also **CELTIC LITERATURE** in **LITERATURE OF THE BRITISH ISLES**

FOREWORD BY BENEDICT KIELY

0-02-055640-3 MACMILLAN PB....$11.00

Heinrich **Zimmer**

The King and the Corpse: Tales of the Soul's Conquest of Evil

Tales of the soul's conquest of evil, culled from Eastern and Western folk literature and retold by the renowned Indologist and Jungian

See also **TALES** under **SANSKRIT LITERATURE** under **LITERATURES OF INDIA** in **LITERATURE OF EUROPE, AFRICA, AND ASIA**

EDITED BY JOSEPH CAMPBELL

0-691-01776-X PRINCETON PB....$12.95

Jack **Zipes**

Breaking the Magic Spell: Radical Theories of Folk and Fairy Tales

0-416-01001-6 ROUTLEDGE PB....$10.95

Asian Religion and Philosophy

Western interest in the religions of Asia has a long history; Greek ambassadors reported on Indian religious observances in the 3rd century BC, and references to Buddhism can be found in early Christian writings. European colonial and missionary efforts after the 16th century led to increased contact, and the intellectual sympathy for Chinese culture and the climate of tolerance that came out of the Enlightenment fostered a desire to understand Eastern traditions on their own terms. In the 19th century, the study of Asian languages and the progress of historical and philological disciplines prepared the way for the immense increase in the knowledge of Asian religions in our own time.

Introductions and Surveys

Joseph **Campbell**

Baksheesh and Brahman: The Indian Journal, 1954-1955

A set of journals kept by Joseph Campbell during his travels through India, Sri Lanka, Thailand, and Japan offer an opportunity to see those Asian cultures through the eyes of the renowned scholar and mythologist. They also present an intimate glimpse of a private man

0-06-016889-7 HARPERCOLLINS....$25.00

Journey to the Sun's Door: The Asian Journals, 1954-1955

0-06-092477-2 HARPERCOLLINS PB....$12.00

Joseph M. **Kitagawa**

Religions of the East

An excellent comparative study

1-55612-140-7 SHEED & WARD PB....$7.95

Yong C. **Kim**

Oriental Thought: An Introduction to the Philosophical and Religious Thought of Asia

0-8226-0365-9 ROWMAN & LITTLEFIELD PB............$14.25

Hajime **Nakamura**

Ways of Thinking of Eastern Peoples: India, China, Tibet, Japan

An introduction by an eminent Japanese scholar

EDITED BY PHILIP P. WIENER

0-8248-0078-8 HAWAII PB............$17.00

Shambhala Editors

The Encyclopedia of Eastern Philosophy and Religion: Buddhism, Hinduism, Taoism, Zen

A complete survey of the teachers, traditions, and terminology of Eastern wisdom. Over 4,000 entries, including short essays on important philosophers and different schools of Asian religious belief, make this an indispensable reference for students, scholars, and those with a personal interest in Eastern mystical thought

See also **REFERENCE WORKS** under **WORLD RELIGION**

0-87773-980-3 SHAMBHALA PB............$25.00

The Indian Traditions

Embree **Ainslee** & Stephen **Hay**, editors

Sources of Indian Tradition

Embree **Ainslee**, editor

Volume 1

A new edition of an anthology that has become a classic. "A serious, careful, dependable book, broader and more varied even than the old *Sources*...This is *the* primary study of Indian civilizations"—Wendy D. O'Flaherty

See also **THE INDIAN SUBCONTINENT** in **WORLD HISTORY AND CURRENT AFFAIRS**

0-231-06651-1 COLUMBIA PB............$19.50

Stephen **Hay**, editor

Volume 2

The second volume of the newly revised *Sources*, with much new material and short but illuminating introductions on each phase of the modern era

0-231-06414-4 COLUMBIA............$65.00

0-231-06415-2 COLUMBIA PB............$19.50

Sarvepalli **Radhakrishnan** & Charles A. **Moore**, editors

A Source Book in Indian Philosophy

"This long-awaited book gives a splendid coverage of indispensable source material in Indian philosophy"—Dale Riepe

0-691-01958-4 PRINCETON PB............$19.95

Heinrich **Zimmer**

Philosophies of India

Wide-ranging and profound, Zimmer's famous study remains a modern classic in Asian studies

EDITED BY JOSEPH CAMPBELL

0-691-01758-1 PRINCETON PB............$19.95

Hinduism

Classic Texts

Cornelia **Dimmitt**, editor

Classical Hindu Mythology: A Reader in the Sanskrit Puranas

Extracts from the Puranas—encyclopedic repositories of Hindu myths, legends, and customs—with excellent introductory material

TRANSLATED BY J.A. VAN BUITENEN

0-87722-122-7 TEMPLE PB............$22.95

Romesh C. **Dutt**

The Mahabharata: Epic of the Bharatas

81-242-0057-2 SOUTH ASIA PB............$7.00

Sachindra K. **Majumbar**, translator

The Bhagavad Gita: A Scriptive for the Future

A good translation of the most sacred Hindu text, with commentary designed to demonstrate the applicability of the Gita's teaching to everyone, regardless of their religion or philosphy

0-89581-885-X ASIAN HUMANITIES............$45.00

0-89581-896-5 ASIAN HUMANITIES PB............$14.95

Barbara Stoler **Miller**, translator

Bhagavad-Gita: Krishna's Counsel in Time of War

A very precise translation. Unlike Zaehner's work, which reflects the subtle influence of its translator's Roman Catholicism, this version maintains a rigorous neutrality with respect to interpretation

0-231-06468-3 COLUMBIA............$29.50

0-553-21365-2 BDD PB............$4.95

S. **Radhakrishnan**, translator

The Bhagavadgita

81-7223-087-7 HARPERCOLLINS PB............$7.00

J.A. **Van Buitenen**, editor & translator

The Bhagavadgita in the Mahabharata: A Bilingual Edition

This sacred poem, part of the epic *Mahabharata*, is a dialogue between Krishna and the warrior Arjuna on the conflict between action and contemplation. Van Buitenen's superb translation is presented with facing Sanskrit text

0-226-84662-8 CHICAGO PB............$11.95

Robert C. **Zaehner**, translator & editor

The Bhagavad-Gita

India's most sacred text, translated by a distinguished student of comparative religion

See also **THE VEDAS AND THE GREAT EPICS** under **SANSKRIT LITERATURE** under **LITERATURES OF INDIA** in **LITERATURE OF EUROPE, AFRICA, AND ASIA**

0-19-501666-1 OXFORD PB............$15.95

Ishikawa **Jun**

The Bodhisattva

0-231-06962-6 COLUMBIA............$45.00

Juan **Mascaro**, translator

The Upanishads

A fine translation of the most important and original text of Indian religious thought

0-8488-0339-6 AMEREON............$16.95

0-14-044163-8 PENGUIN PB............$7.95

OM. In the center of the castle of Brahman, our own body, there is a small shrine in the form of a lotus-flower, and within can be found a small space. We should find who dwells there, and we should want to know him.

And if anyone ask, "Who is he who dwells in a small shrine in the form of a lotus-flower in the centre of the castle of Brahman? Whom should we want to find and to know?" we can answer:

"The little space within the heart is as great as this vast universe. The heavens and the earth are there, and the sun, and the moon, and the stars; fire and lightning and winds are there; and all that now is and all that is not: for the whole universe is in Him and He dwells within our heart."

THE UPANISHADS

R.K. **Narayan**, translator

The Ramayana: The Indian Epic

A fluent retelling of the story by India's foremost contemporary writer

See also **INDIAN** under **THE NON-WESTERN WORLD** under **MYTHOLOGY AND FOLKLORE**

0-14-018700-6 PENGUIN PB............$9.95

0-14-004428-0 PENGUIN PB............$7.00

Wendy Doniger **O'Flaherty**, editor

The Rig Veda

The standard contemporary English version of one of the world's oldest religious texts, containing a beautiful version of the Vedic hymn to creation, the earliest extant lyric poem

0-14-044402-5 PENGUIN PB............$11.95

General Studies

Eliot **Deutsch**

Advaita Vedanta: A Philosophical Reconstruction

An interpretation of the religious and philosophical system of Sankara, perhaps India's greatest religious figure

0-8248-0271-3 HAWAII PB............$7.00

Mircea **Eliade**

Yoga: Immortality and Freedom

See also **MIRCEA ELIADE** under **WORLD RELIGION**

TRANSLATED BY WILLARD R. TRASK

0-691-01764-6 PRINCETON PB............$15.95

From the time of the Upanishads India rejects the world as it is and devalues life as it reveals itself to the eyes of the sage—ephemeral, painful, illusory. Such a conception leads neither to nihilism nor pessimism. *This* world is rejected, *this* life depreciated because it is known that *something else* exists, beyond becoming, beyond temporality, beyond suffering. In religious terms, it could almost be said that India rejects the *profane* cosmos and *profane* life, because it thirsts for a *sacred* world and a *sacred* mode of being.

YOGA: IMMORTALITY AND FREEDOM

Ainslie T. **Embree**, editor
The Hindu Tradition
Selected readings from the tradition, modestly annotated
0-394-71702-3 RANDOM HOUSE PB $7.98

John S. **Hawley** & Donna M. **Wulff**, editors
The Divine Consort: Radha and the Goddesses of India
An anthology examining feminine aspects of divinity in the Indian tradition. "A shower of insights on the male/female polarity itself, in all its subtlety, tensions and potential glory" —Huston Smith
81-208-0940-8 SOUTH ASIA $28.50

Devi: Goddesses of India
0-520-20058-6 CALIFORNIA PB $17.95

David **Kinsley**
Hindu Goddesses: Visions of the Divine Feminine in the Hindu Religious Tradition
0-520-06339-2 CALIFORNIA PB $14.95

Wendy Doniger **O'Flaherty**
The Origins of Evil in Hindu Mythology
Enriched, like all this author's works, by remarkable insight and erudition. "The range and number of myths handled is dazzling… A major contribution to the study of religion in general and Hinduism in particular"—*TLS*
0-520-04098-8 CALIFORNIA PB $17.00

Siva: The Erotic Ascetic
A detailed survey of the major mythic themes, centered on the paradox of the god's dual role as ascetic and heroic lover
0-19-520250-3 OXFORD PB $14.95

R.C. **Zaehner**
Hinduism
A lucid, topical presentation of major themes in the tradition
0-19-888012-X OXFORD PB $12.95

Modern Trends

Margaret **Chatterjee**
Gandhi's Religious Thought
A short book that makes clear the range and flexibility of Gandhi's religious thought and its fusion with his commitment to social justice
0-268-01011-0 NOTRE DAME PB $11.95

Mohandas K. **Gandhi**
Autobiography: The Story of My Experiments with Truth
A 20th-century classic
See also **NONVIOLENT POLITICS** under **POLITICAL THOUGHT** in **SOCIAL STUDIES**
0-486-24593-4 DOVER PB $8.95

J. **Krishnamurti**
On Conflict
0-06-251016-9 HARPERCOLLINS PB $10.00

On Fear
0-06-251014-2 HARPERCOLLINS PB $11.00

On Knowledge and Learning
"A master of reality"—Henry Miller
0-06-251011-8 HARPERCOLLINS PB $12.00

On Truth
"To read big thoughts is to face oneself and the world with an astonishing morning freshness" —Anne Morrow Lindbergh
0-06-251012-6 HARPERCOLLINS PB $12.00

Christopher **Isherwood**
Ramakrishna and His Disciples
A good introduction to the thought of the 19th-century visionary and exponent of religious unity, by the author of *Goodbye to Berlin* and *My Guru and His Disciple*
0-87481-037-X VEDANTA PB $12.9

Christopher Isherwood

Evelyne **Blau**
Krishnamurti: 100 Years
This biography turns to a group of "witnesses" to explore the vast spiritual dimensions of Krishnamurti's life of teaching to an ever-growing following of disciples. Including the recollections of Aldous Huxley, Joseph Campbell, Henry Miller, and Van Morrison
1-55670-407-0 STEWART, TABORI $29.95

Buddhism in India

Classic Texts

Edward **Conze**, translator
Buddhist Scriptures
The selections are arranged by topic and are taken almost entirely from Sanskrit Buddhist texts
0-14-044088-7 PENGUIN PB $9.95

E.B. **Cowell**, editor
Buddhist Mahayana Texts
Recommended for its translation of the three chief scriptures of Pure Land Buddhism
0-486-25552-2 DOVER PB $9.95

Juan **Mascaro**, translator
The Dhammapada
One of the loveliest texts of Buddhist literature, treasured for its aphoristic moral instructions, in a translation sensitive to its literary quality
0-14-044284-7 PENGUIN PB $7.95

D.T. **Suzuki**, translator
The Lankavatara Sutra: A Mahayana Text
Contains material central to the Yogacara wing of Buddhist thought
9-5763-8031-6 ORIENTAL BOOK STORE $30.00

Alex **Wayman** & Hideko **Wayman**, translators
The Lion's Roar of Queen Srimala: A Buddhist Scripture on the Tathagatagarbha Theory
81-208-0731-6 MOTILAL BANARSIDASS $20.00

General Studies

Archie J. **Bahm**
Philosophy of the Buddha
An illuminating introduction and guide to Buddhism, explaining the philosophy of Gotama through a careful examination of the original sources. "…the most fundamentally intelligent and illuminating book about Pali Buddhism which I have read" —Alan Watts, author of *The Way of Zen*
0-87573-025-6 ASIAN HUMANITIES PB $12.95

Edward **Conze**
Buddhism:Its Essence and Development
An overview of the main themes of the tradition and its historical development
8-1215-0631-Y SOUTH ASIA $19.50

Walpola **Rahula**
What the Buddha Taught
An excellent overview of basic Buddhist thought from the perspective of the Theravada school
FOREWORD BY PAUL DEMIEVILLE
0-8021-3031-3 GROVE PB $11.00

Richard H. **Robinson** & Willard L. **Johnson**
The Buddhist Religion: A Historical Introduction
An excellent survey, with an extensive bibliography
0-534-01027-X WADSWORTH PB $25.00

Nyanaponika **Thera**
The Heart of Buddhist Meditation
Outlines the Theravada program of "meditation" and the practice of "mindfulness" *(satipatthana)*
0-87728-073-8 WEISER PB $11.00

Other Religions of India

Jainism

J.L. **Jaini**

Outlines of Jainism

A well-written, straightforward account of one of the major offshoots of the Vedantic tradition

See also **FROM PREHISTORIC INDIA TO THE CLASSICAL PERIODS** under **THE INDIAN SUBCONTINENT** in **WORLD HISTORY AND CURRENT AFFAIRS**

0-88355-801-7 HYPERION $23.25

Michael **Tobias**

Life Force: The World of Jainism

Although it is one of the world's oldest religions, little is known about Jainism outside of India. Its precepts of ecological awareness and nonviolence resonate in modern environmental and political issues, rendering it particularily relevant to the modern world. Currently out of print

0-89581-899-X ASIAN HUMANITIES PB $12.95

Sikhism

W.H. **McLeod**

Historical Dictionary of Sikhism

0-8108-3035-3 SCARECROW $55.00

The Sikhs:History, Religion and Society

A lucid introduction, surveying the 16th-century beginnings of the sect, as well as doctrine, literature, history, and cultural identity

0-231-06814-X COLUMBIA $49.50
0-231-06815-8 COLUMBIA PB $14.50

J.P.S. **Vberoi**

Religion, Civil Society and the State: A Study of Sikhism

0-19-563691-0 OXFORD $18.95

Zoroastrianism

The Persian Zoroastrians who settled in India in the latter half of the first millennium became known as Parsis. The following are a few general works on the Zoroastrian tradition and its Indian vicissitudes.

Mary **Boyce**, editor

Zoroastrianism

A highly recommended history aimed at the more advanced student

0-939214-89-X MAZDA $25.00
9-991112-99-5 MAZDA PB $16.95

S.A. **Nigosian**

The Zoroastrian Faith:Tradition and Modern Research

0-7735-1144-X MCGILL PB $17.95

The Chinese Traditions

Wing-tsit **Chan**

Chu Hsi: New Studies

An extensive account of the ideas of the twelfth-century neo-Confucian philosopher

0-8248-1201-8 HAWAII $40.00
0-312-13470-3 ST. MARTIN'S $39.95

Wing-tsit **Chan**, editor

A Source Book in Chinese Philosophy

An accessible and fascinating historical anthology, with introductory discussions of each period or school."Heroically [the editor] translates his philosophers himself, with the result that for the first time the entire map is seen through a consistent eye"—Robert Payne

0-691-01964-9 PRINCETON PB $19.95

Herrlee G. **Creel**

Chinese Thought from Confucius to Mao Tse-Tung

0-226-12030-9 CHICAGO PB $13.95

William T. **De Bary**, editor

Sources of Chinese Tradition

Volume 1

This invaluable survey of Chinese intellectual history is a collection of translated sources with introductions

0-231-08602-4 COLUMBIA PB $19.50

Volume 2

0-231-08603-2 COLUMBIA PB $17.00

Arthur **Waley**

Three Ways of Thought in Ancient China

For generations this has been the classic introduction to Confucianism, Taoism, and "Realism" (Legalism). "The book is full of memorable phrases and amusing aphorisms. It reveals a world at once close to us and very far away"—Peter Quennell, *New Statesman*

0-8047-1169-0 STANFORD PB $10.95

Max **Weber**

The Religion of China: Confucianism and Taoism

In this most famous work, Weber, the master sociologist of religion, argues that China's religious ethic impeded the development of a rational capitalist economy

See also **CHINESE THOUGHT** under **TOPICS IN IMPERIAL CIVILIZATION** under **CHINA** in **WORLD HISTORY AND CURRENT AFFAIRS**

0-02-934450-6 FREE PRESS PB $19.95

Fung **Yu-Lan**

A History of Chinese Philosophy

The classic history

Volume 1

0-691-02021-3 PRINCETON PB $27.50

Volume 2

0-691-02022-1 PRINCETON PB $37.50

Cheng

Nagarjuna's Twelve Gate Treatise

A concise summary of Nagarjuna's thoughts from early Chinese sources

90-277-1380-4 REIDL $72.50

Confucianism

"The Master said, Be of unwavering good faith, love learning, if attacked be ready to die for the good Way. Do not enter a State that pursues dangerous courses, nor stay in one where the people have rebelled. When the Way prevails under Heaven, then show yourself; when it does not prevail, then hide. When the Way prevails in your own land, count it a disgrace to be needy and obscure; when the Way does not prevail in your land, then count it a disgrace to be rich and honoured."—Confucius, *The Analects*, Translated by Arthur Waley

Classic Texts

Tsai Chih **Chung**

Confucius Speaks: Words to Live By

TRANSLATED BY BRIAN BRUYA

0-385-48034-2 ANCHOR PB $10.95

Confucius

The Analects

The best of the modern translations of the aphorisms of Confucius, superbly illustrated

TRANSLATED BY D.C. LAU

0-14-044348-7 PENGUIN PB $9.95

The Analects of Confucius

An excellent translation published in 1939, with a good introduction and biography of Confucius

TRANSLATED BY ARTHUR WALEY

0-679-72296-3 VINTAGE PB $10.00

The Confucian Analects, the Great Learning & the Doctrine of the Mean

Three of the so-called Four Books (the fourth being the *Mencius*) that formed the core of the official Confucian curriculum

EDITED BY JAMES LEGGE

0-486-22746-4 DOVER PB $12.95

Chu **Hsi** & Lu **Tsu-Ch'ien**

Reflections on Things at Hand: The Neo-Confucian Anthology

A collection assembled in the 12th century by Chu Hsi, the neo-Confucian movement's foremost figure. His thought defined the official state orthodoxy until the creation of the Republic of China in 1912

TRANSLATED BY WING-TSIT CHAN

0-231-06037-8 COLUMBIA $18.50

Mencius

Mencius

The best modern translation of the second most influential thinker in the Confucian tradition

TRANSLATED BY D.C. LAU

0-14-044228-6 PENGUIN PB $10.95

Richard **Wilhelm** & C.F. **Baynes**, translators

I Ching, or the Book of Changes

Confucius' attention to this divination text (he allegedly wrote its most important commentary) ensured its central role in Chinese thought

0-691-09750-X PRINCETON $19.95

Richard **Lynn**

The Classic of Changes: A New Translation of the I Ching

The ancient Chinese book of divination

0-231-08294-0 COLUMBIA $19.95

Ling **Ch'**

I Ching: A Classic Chinese Oracle

EDITED BY RALPH SAWYER

TRANSLATED BY MEI-CHUN LEE

0-570-62083-0 SHAMBALA $16.00

Burton **Watson**, translator & editor

Basic Writings of Mo Tzu, Hsun Tzu, & Han Fei Tzu

A fine translation of the classical neo-Confucian thinker Mo Tzu, the Confucian reformist Hsun Tzu, and the legalist Han Fei Tzu

0-231-02515-7 COLUMBIA $21.50

General Studies

Wing-tsit **Chan**, editor

Chu Hsi and Neo-Confucianism

0-8248-0961-0 HAWAII $30.00

William T. **de Bary**

Neo-Confucian Orthodoxy and the Learning of the Heart-Mind

0-231-05229-4 COLUMBIA PB $18.00

Herbert **Fingarette**

Confucius: The Secular as Sacred

A penetrating and highly original interpretation of Confucian thought, particularly concerned with the centrality of ritual in everyday life

0-06-131682-2 HARPERCOLLINS PB $13.00

Taoism

"But to wear out your brain trying to make things into one without realizing that they are all the same—this is called 'three in the morning.' What do I mean by 'three in the morning'? When the monkey trainer was handing out acorns, he said, 'You get three in the morning and four at night.' This made all the monkeys furious. 'Well, then,' he said, 'you get four in the morning and three at night.' The monkeys were all delighted. There was no change in the reality behind the words, and yet the monkeys responded with joy and anger. Let them, if they want to. So the sage harmonizes with both right and wrong and rests in Heaven the Equalizer. This is called walking two roads."—Chuang Tzu, *The Complete Works*, translated by Burton Watson.

Classic Texts

Tsai Chih **Chung**

The Tao Speaks

Through a series of enchanting cartoon panels, Chung introduces us to the classic work of the great Chinese philosopher Lao Tzu

0-385-47259-5 ANCHOR PB $10.95

Thomas **Cleary**

The Essential Tao

By freeing Taoist philosophy and religion from the "mist of mystical allure and vague sentiment, Cleary is finally making them authentically available"—Jacob Needleman, author of *The Heart of Philosophy*

0-06-250162-3 HARPERCOLLINS PB $18.00

Thomas **Cleary**, translator

The Book of Balance and Harmony

A famous anthology of writings by a 13th-century Taoist master. "This collection, compiled by one of the master's disciples and still current in Taoist circles of East Asia, provides a most unusual compendium of the teachings of Complete Reality Taoism, including its theoretical and practical basis in classical Taoism"—from the translator's introduction

0-86547-363-3 NORTH POINT PB $12.00

A.C. **Graham**, translator

The Book of Lieh-Tzu: A Classic of the Tao

"The *Lieh-Tzu* ranks with the *Lao Tzu* and *Chuang Tzu* as one of the most eloquent and influential expositions of Taoist philosophy. This definitive translation by Professor Graham does full justice to the subtlety of thought and literary effectiveness of the text"—Burton Watson

0-231-07237-6 MORNINGSIDE PB $15.50

Victor **Mair**, translator

Wandering on the Way: Early Taoist Tales and Parables of Chuang Tzu

0-553-37406-0 BANTAM PB $11.95

Chuang **Tzu**

The Book of Chuang Tzu

A new, complete translation of the classic Taoist text

TRANSLATED BY MARTIN PALMER WITH ELIZABETH BREUILLY, CHANG WAI MING, AND JAY RAMSAY

0-14-019488-6 ARKANA PB $13.95

The Complete Works of Chuang Tzu

A delightful translation of this classic Taoist text, preserving all the humor, paradox, and deliberate ambiguity of the original

TRANSLATED BY BURTON WATSON

FOREWORD BY WILLIAM T. DE BARY

0-231-03147-5 COLUMBIA $50.00

Brian **Walker**

Hua Hu Ching: The Unknown Teachings of Lao Tzu

0-06-069245-6 HARPERCOLLINS PB $10.00

Lao **Tzu**

Tao Te Ching

The classical text of Taoism in a gracefully poetic new translation by a writer whose other translations range from the Gospels to Rilke. "Beautiful and accessible; the English, as 'fluid as melting ice,' is a joy to read throughout" —*The New Republic*

TRANSLATED BY STEPHEN MITCHELL

0-06-091608-7 HARPERCOLLINS PB $11.00

Tao Te Ching

The first volume in Ballantine's new Classics of Ancient China series is a new translation of the fundamental text of Taoism. This edition is based on newly discovered copies of the text which are five centuries earlier than any previously known. "No one can understand Chinese philosophy, religion, art or social ethics without reading the *Te-Tao Ching.* We welcome, therefore, the translation of the recently discovered, the earliest, the most authentic texts"—Wing-tsit Chan

TRANSLATED BY ROBERT G. HENRICKS

0-345-34790-0 BALLANTINE PB $19.95

The Tao Te Ching: The Book of Meaning and Life

The Taoist classic, probably the work of a number of writers over a long period, but attributed to a contemporary of Confucius called Lao Tzu ("the Old Man")

TRANSLATED BY RICHARD WILHELM

0-14-019060-0 VIKING PB $10.95

The Way and Its Power: A Study of the Tao Te Ching and Its Place in Chinese Thought

A highly recommended translation of the *Tao Te Ching* with an excellent introduction

TRANSLATED BY ARTHUR WALEY

0-8021-5085-3 GROVE PB $10.95

Hua **Ching**, elucidator

Hua Hu Ching: The Later Teachings of Lao Tzu

A Taoist master's accessible translation of a companion text to the Tao Te Ching

1-57062-079-2 SHAMBHALA PB $10.00

General Studies

Herrlee G. **Creel**

What Is Taoism?: & Other Studies in Chinese Cultural History

0-226-12047-3 CHICAGO PB $18.00

Benjamin **Hoff**

The Tao of Pooh and the Te of Piglet: Box Set

"Te" is a Chinese word meaning virtue, and *The Te of Piglet* is the virtue of the small. The author conducts a sagacious dialogue between Piglet, Eeyore, Tigger, and the rest of the Pooh gang, interspersed with traditional Taoist stories. A boxed gift set of the two volumes that have sold over a million copies

0-525-48609-7 DUTTON $34.95

0-14-095144-X PENGUIN PB $21.90

Max **Kaltenmark**
Lao-Tzu and Taoism
A brief survey by an eminent French scholar
0-8047-0689-1 STANFORD PB........$10.95

Thomas **Merton**
The Way of Chuang Tzu
A sympathetic account by the Catholic scholar and poet
0-8112-0103-1 NEW DIRECTIONS PB........$7.95
0-87773-676-6 SHAMBHALA PB........$6.00

Holmes **Welch**
Taoism: The Parting of the Way
A wonderful brief introduction, containing much material on religious Taoism not easily found elsewhere and emphasizing the gulf between Taoist mysticism and Taoist practice
0-8070-5973-0 BEACON PB........$13.00

Chinese Buddhism

Classic Texts

Thomas **Cleary**, translator
The Flower Ornament Scripture: A Translation of the Avatamsaka Sutra
0-87773-940-4 SHAMBHALA........$78.60

Leon **Hurvitz**, editor
Scripture of the Lotus Blossom of the Fine Dharma: The Lotus Sutra
A faithful elegant translation of one of the most popular scriptures in East Asian Buddhism
0-231-03920-4 COLUMBIA PB........$20.00

Shambhala Editors
The Zen Teachings of Huang Po
One of the most crucial and sublime manuals of Zen training, by the great ninth-century master who served as mentor to the famous Lin-chi. John Blofeld brings a knowledge and understanding to his translation that makes it thoroughly accessible to Western readers. An exceptional opportunity to enter the stratosphere of the rare spiritual mind of Huang Po
See also **ZEN AND CH'AN**
0-87773-969-2 SHAMBHALA PB........$6.00

General Studies

Kenneth **Ch'en**
Buddhism in China: A Historical Survey
The standard account, unsurpassed for its panoramic scope
0-691-00015-8 PRINCETON PB........$22.95

Kogen **Mizuno**
The Buddhist Sutras: Origin, Development, Transmission
Development of the codified and edited discourses of the Buddha with particular attention to the Chinese Buddhist canon
4-333-01028-4 ORIENT BOOK PB........$10.95

Arthur F. **Wright**
Buddhism in Chinese History
A short, clearly written work for the general reader. "Throws light on the renewed process of borrowing and adaptation taking place in China today"—Derk Bodde
See also **CHINESE THOUGHT** under **TOPICS IN IMPERIAL CIVILIZATION** under **CHINA** in **WORLD HISTORY AND CURRENT AFFAIRS**
0-8047-0548-8 STANFORD PB........$10.95

The Japanese Traditions

Robert N. **Bellah**
Tokugawa Religion
A classic study by the leading American sociologist of religion. In the manner of Max Weber, Bellah traces the origins of Japanese modernization to the religious ethos of the Tokugawa period (1600-1868). "Remains a landmark reference in Japanese studies…[by a] sensitive and critical interpreter of modernization"
—Tetsuo Najita, University of Chicago
0-02-902460-9 FREE PRESS PB........$14.95

William T. **De Bary**
Sources of Japanese Tradition
An essential collection of annotated religious and philosophical writings
Volume 1
0-231-08605-9 COLUMBIA PB........$18.00
Volume 2
0-231-08604-0 COLUMBIA PB........$19.00

Byron H. **Earhart**
The Religions of Japan: Many Traditions Within One Sacred Day
A brief analysis taking both historical and thematic approaches
0-06-062112-5 HARPERCOLLINS PB........$12.00

Joseph M. **Kitagawa**
Religion in Japanese History
The standard account by one of the most perceptive modern interpreters
0-231-02834-2 COLUMBIA........$55.50
0-231-02838-5 COLUMBIA PB........$19.50

Sokyo **Ono**
Shinto: The Kami Way
A brief exposition of Japan's earliest religious traditions
0-8048-0525-3 TUTTLE PB........$12.95

Royall **Tyler**
The Miracles of the Kasuga Deity
0-231-06958-8 COLUMBIA........$50.00

Japanese Buddhism

Dennis **Hirota**, editor
Wind in the Pines: Classic Writings of the Way of Tea as a Buddhist Path
0-87573-073-6 JAIN........$60.00

Yoshita S. **Hakeda**, translator
Kukai: Major Works, Translated with an Account of His Life and a Study of His Thought
An introduction to the 8th-century scholar and saint, one of the most influential figures in Japanese Buddhism. "Hakeda's achievement in arriving at these lively and intelligible translations is of the highest order"—*Choice*
0-231-05933-7 COLUMBIA PB........$19.50

Zen and Ch'an

Western interest in Zen Buddhism (and its Chinese precursor Ch'an) is reflected in the immense English-language literature on the subject. Listed below are some reliable introductory works, as well as many others that reflect America's ongoing fascination with Zen.

Heinrich **Dumoulin**
Zen Buddhism: A History
Volume 1
India and China
A rich and detailed account of the roots of the Zen tradition and its ramifications throughout Asia. The first volume covers India and China
0-02-908260-9 MACMILLAN........$17.95
Volume 2
Japan
0-02-908240-4 MACMILLAN PB........$23.00

Robert **Aitken**
Encouraging Words: Zen Teachings by a Western Buddhist
Aitken is one of the few American Zen Buddhist masters. His teachings over two decades are collected in this book, which brings Zen precepts to bear on contemporary questions of family life and sexual relationships. It includes a collection of important *sutras* and an annotated guide for further reading
0-679-41701-X PANTHEON PB........$20.00

The Mind of Clover: In Zen Buddhist Ethics
Applications of Zen to the modern world. "Clear, down to earth, and excellently crafted while full of depth, Zen spirit, and humanity"
—*Religious Studies Review*
0-86547-158-4 NORTH POINT PB........$12.00

Original Dwelling Place: Zen Buddhist Essays
An American Zen roshi provides a chronicle of his journey to Zen Buddhism
See also **WESTERN** under **20TH-CENTURY SPIRITUAL LEADERS** under **SPIRITUALITY**
1-88717-816-3 COUNTERPOINT........$22.00

Taking the Path of Zen
0-86547-080-4 NORTH POINT PB........$10.00

Chang **Chung-Yuan**, translator
Original Teachings of Ch'an Buddhism: Selected from the Transmission of the Lamp
0-679-75824-0 PANTHEON PB........$14.00

Urs **App**

Master Yunmen: From the Record of the Chan Teacher "Gate-of-the-Clouds"

The first thorough account of the life and teachings of Zen Master Yunmen, who eschewed traditionalist sermons in favor of straight talk, sarcasm, yelps, and whacks. Based on ten years of research by App, an associate director of the International Research Institute for Zen Buddhism in Kyoto

1-56836-004-5 KODANSHA $27.50
1-56836-005-3 KODANSHA PB $13.00

Bodhidharma

The Zen Teaching of Bodhidharma

Bodhidharma was the legendary Indian monk who brought Zen Buddhism to China. Red Pine, the translator of these four texts traditionally attributed to Bodhidharma, writes in his introduction: "Bodhidharma's approach to zen was unique. As he says in these sermons, 'Seeing your nature is zen…Not thinking about anything is zen…Everything you do is zen.'…Instead of telling his disciples to purify their minds, he pointed them to rock walls, to the movements of tigers and cranes, to a hollow reed floating across the Yangtze, to a single sandal"

TRANSLATED WITH INTRODUCTION BY RED PINE

0-86547-399-4 NORTH POINT PB $11.00

Thomas **Cleary**

Zen Antics: One Hundred Stories of Enlightenment

The author has been described by *New Age Journal* as "history's single most prolific translator of primary East Asian sacred texts." Now he introduces us to a classic collection of over 100 inspirational and simple Zen stories from some of the most influential Chinese and Japanese Zen masters, many appearing in English for the first time

0-87773-944-7 SHAMBHALA PB $10.00

Thomas **Cleary**, translator

Rational Zen: The Mind of Dogen Zenji

0-87773-689-8 SHAMBHALA $20.00
0-87773-973-0 SHAMBHALA PB $14.00

Shobogenzo: Zen Essays by Dogen

0-8248-1401-0 HAWAII PB $13.00

Heinrich **Dumoulin**

Zen Buddhism in the 20th Century

0-8348-0247-3 WEATHERHILL PB $14.95

Ch'an Master **Foyen**

Instant Zen: Waking Up in the Present

TRANSLATED BY THOMAS CLEARY

1-55643-193-7 NORTH ATLANTIC PB $12.95

Joseph **Goldstein**

Insight Meditation

"A delightful, compelling, and down-to-earth look at a wide range of key issues…"
—Jon Kabat-Zinn

1-57062-025-3 SHAMBHALA PB $12.00

Thich Naht **Hanh**

Zen Keys: A Guide to Zen Practice

0-385-47561-6 BANTAM PB $11.00

Peter **Haskel**, translator

Bankei Zen: Translations from the Record of Bankei

0-8021-3184-0 GROVE PB $11.95

Eugen **Herrigel**

Zen in the Art of Archery

This remarkable book discusses how the practice of archery helps toward an understanding of Zen. Eugen Herrigel spent a five-year apprenticeship in Japanese archery that resulted in his deep understanding of Zen and this wonderful book, written long before martial arts became a fad. Although not specially about martial arts, it captures the philosophy of training that distinguishes Asian martial arts from Western fencing or boxing

See also **MARTIAL ARTS** under **FITNESS** in **LIFESTYLES AND PRACTICAL ADVICE**

0-679-72297-1 VINTAGE PB $10.00

Zen Master **Hongzhi**

Cultivating the Empty Field: The Silent Illumination of Zen Master Hongzhi

TRANSLATED BY TAIGEN DANIEL LEIGHTON

0-86547-474-5 NORTH POINT $24.95
0-86547-475-3 NORTH POINT PB $11.95

Dainin **Katagiri**

Returning to Silence: Zen Practice in Daily Life

0-87773-431-3 SHAMBHALA PB $15.00

Zen Master **Keizan**

Transmission of Light: Zen in the Art of Enlightenment

0-86547-433-8 NORTH POINT PB $14.95

Kenneth **Kraft**, editor

Zen: Tradition and Transition

An anthology dealing with the whole range of modern developments in Zen. The contributors include Burton Watson, Philip Yampolsky, Chang Shen-yen, and Albert Low

0-8021-3162-X GROVE PB $10.95

Isshu **Miura** & Ruth F. **Sasaki**

The Zen Koan

A well-documented study of the form's history

0-15-699981-1 HARCOURT BRACE PB $10.00

Takpo Tashi **Namgyal**

Mahamudra: The Quintessence of Mind and Meditation

A major meditation text of the Kagyu sect

TRANSLATED BY LOBSANG P. LHALUNGPA

0-87773-360-0 RANDOM HOUSE PB $30.00

Huang **Po**

The Zen Teaching of Huang Po on the Transmission of the Mind

A classic of Ch'an Buddhism, dating from the T'ang dynasty

TRANSLATED BY JOHN BLOFELD

0-3943-1721-5 GROVE PB $10.95

William **Powell**, translator

The Record of Tung-Shan

0-8248-1070-8 HAWAII PB $9.00

A.F. **Price** & Wong **Mou-Lam**, translators

The Diamond Sutra & the Sutra of Hui Neng

A new edition of two important documents of Buddhist and Zen thought

0-87773-005-9 SHAMBHALA PB $14.00

Paul **Reps**, editor

Zen Flesh, Zen Bones: A Collection of Zen and Pre-Zen Writings

A lively anthology of koans that has entertained and stimulated generations of students

0-385-08130-8 DOUBLEDAY PB $8.95

David **Schiller**

The Little Zen Companion

A collection of quotes, phrases, koans, haiku poetry, and other works whose maverick Zen spirit offers another way of looking at the world. Includes short biographies of Zen followers, a glossary of interesting terms, enlightenment experiences, and more

1-56305-467-1 WORKMAN PB $6.95

Katsuki **Sekida**

Zen Training: Methods and Philosophy

0-8348-0114-0 WEATHERHILL PB $15.00

Lawrence **Shainberg**

Ambivalent Zen: A Memoir

An American's revelations and disappointments in the lifelong study of Zen

0-679-44116-6 PANTHEON $24.00

Shambhala Editors

The Zen Teachings of Huang Po

One of the most crucial and sublime manuals of Zen training, by the great ninth-century master who served as mentor to the famous Lin-chi. John Blofeld brings a knowledge and understanding to his translation that makes it thoroughly accessible to Western readers. An exceptional opportunity to enter the stratosphere of the rare spiritual mind of Huang Po

See also **CLASSIC TEXTS** under **CHINESE BUDDHISM**

0-87773-969-2 SHAMBHALA PB $6.00

Lucien **Stryk**

The Awakened Self: Encounters with Zen

"No one has done more than Stryk to introduce Americans to the work of Zen masters, past and present…"
—Dennis Lynch, *American Poetry Review*

1-56836-046-0 KODANSHA PB $15.00

Lucien **Stryk** & Takashi **Ikemoto**, editors

Zen Poems of China and Japan: The Crane's Bill

One hundred fifty poems ranging from the 9th to the 19th century. "A fine chronological anthology of Buddhist writings"—*Choice*

0-8021-3019-4 GROVE PB $7.95

Soiku **Shigematsu**

A Zen Forest: Sayings of the Masters

Over 1200 Chinese and Japanese aphorisms from the *Zenrin Kushu* (Zen Forest Sayings Anthology)

FOREWORD BY GARY SNYDER

0-8348-0259-7 WEATHERHILL PB $7.95

A Zen Harvest: Japanese Folk Zen Sayings

Short poems related to the Zen tradition of *jakugo* (capping-phrase exercises): "Ears / Hear and Eyes / See, / Then what does / Mind do?"

0-86547-328-5 NORTH POINT PB $12.95

Soiku Shigematsu
(photo courtesy of Soiku Shigematsu)

D.T. **Suzuki**

An Introduction to Zen Buddhism

A widely consulted guide by the leading expositor of Zen to the West

FOREWORD BY C.G. JUNG

0-8021-3055-0 GROVE PB $7.95

Manual of Zen Buddhism

Prayers, sutras, and sayings that have long been part of the Zen tradition

See also **EASTERN TRADITIONS** under **SPIRITUALITY**

0-8021-3065-8 GROVE PB $11.00

Zen and Japanese Culture

0-691-01770-0 PRINCETON PB $16.95

Shunryu **Suzuki**

Zen Mind

"A primer on what Zen is and how a person can begin to practice it"—*Publishers Weekly*

0-8348-0079-9 WEATHERHILL PB $7.95

Helen **Tworkov**

Zen in America: Five Teachers and the Search for an American Buddhism

"Entertaining…A lively introduction to the earthy, human side of an austere faith"
—*Kirkus Reviews*

1-56836-030-4 KODANSHA PB $15.00

Norman **Waddell**, translator

Unborn: The Life and Teaching of Zen Master Bankei 1622-1693

0-86547-153-3 NORTH POINT PB $11.95

Burton **Watson**, translator

The Zen Teachings of Master Lin-Chi

One of the foremost texts of Zen literature, this has been made popular in the West through the writings of D.T. Suzuki and is now available in an original translation for the first time. Innovative teaching methods and colorful language characterize the insights and exploits of this great 9th-century master

0-87773-891-2 SHAMBHALA PB $10.00

Alan **Watts**

The Way of Zen

0-679-72301-3 VINTAGE PB $9.00

Philip B. **Yampolsky**, translator

The Platform Sutra of the Sixth Patriarch

"Without sacrificing scholarly accuracy, Yampolsky has produced a lucid and idiomatic translation which even the layman can enjoy"
—*Literature East and West*

0-231-08361-0 COLUMBIA PB $17.50

The Zen Master Hakuin: Selected Writing

0-231-06041-6 COLUMBIA PB $18.50

Yuan-Wu & others

Zen Letters: Teachings of Yuanwu

0-87773-931-5 SHAMBHALA PB $10.00

Southeast Asian Religion

Clifford **Geertz**

The Religion of Java

An authoritative work on modern Javanese religion by a powerful and original thinker

0-226-28510-3 CHICAGO PB $15.95

Raphael **Israeli**, editor

The Crescent in the East

Essays on Islam in Malaysia, Indonesia, and the Philippines

0-391-02099-4 HUMANITIES $25.00

Robert C. **Lester**

Theravada Buddhism in Southeast Asia

A good, clearly written survey of Theravada Buddhist doctrine and the function of religion in the societies of mainland Southeast Asia

0-472-06184-4 MICHIGAN PB $16.95

Tibetan Religion

Stephan **Beyer**

The Cult of Tara: Magic and Ritual in Tibet

A lucid and sophisticated analysis of the cult of the great savioress, demonstrating the way in which religious and magical elements complement each other in religious ritual

INTRODUCTION BY KEES BOLLE

0-520-03635-2 CALIFORNIA PB $18.00

The **Dalai Lama**

The Way to Freedom: Core Teachings of Tibetan Buddhism

A new series—Library of Tibet—is inaugurated by his Holiness the Dalai Lama and will serve to explore the culture, history, politics, and spirituality of Tibetan Buddhism. This volume, translated for the first time into English, is considered to be the essence of 1,000 years of Buddhist teaching and the heart of Tibetan practice. Presented in an easy to understand manner perfect for those already practicing as well as for the beginner

See also **EASTERN TRADITIONS** under **SPIRITUALITY**

0-06-061722-5 HARPERCOLLINS $16.00

Dalai Lama, the Meaning of Life: From a Buddhist Perspective

The Dalai Lama explains the Buddhist Wheel of Life, the nature of suffering and how to transcend it, while answering personal and philosophical questions from his listeners. Edited from a series of talks in London

See also **EASTERN** under **20TH-CENTURY SPIRITUAL LEADERS** under **SPIRITUALITY**

EDITED BY TENZIN GYATSO

TRANSLATED BY JEFFREY HOPKINS

0-86171-096-7 WISDOM PB $12.50

Essential Teachings

1-55643-192-9 NORTH ATLANTIC PB $12.95

The World of Tibetan Buddhism

With a foreword by Richard Gere, this book by His Holiness the Dalai Lama provides an overview of the philosophy and practice of Tibetan Buddhism. Lucid and detailed, this is an invaluable tool for both the curious and the practiced

0-86171-100-9 WISDOM $25.00

A Flash of Lightning in the Dark of the Night: A Guide to the Bodhisattva's Way of Life

The Dalai Lama engages in a dialogue with the well-known sutra of Mahayana Buddhism. The bodhisattva's enemies, he explains, are the ego, the passions, and hatred; his allies are generosity and patience. His ultimate goal: complete and liberating compassion. Written with the wisdom and integrity that have made this enduring holy leader an inspiration to millions

0-87773-971-4 SHAMBHALA PB $10.00

The **Dalai Lama** & Donald S. **Lopez**, editors

Awakening the Mind, Lightening the Heart: Core Teachings of Tibetan Buddhism

Wisdom and compassion are the two most important elements in the Buddhist path to enlightenment. Here, in lucid, simple, and elegant prose, His Holiness the Dalai Lama offers practical steps for developing compassion in our daily lives. "The Dalai Lama writes with charisma and authority"
—*San Francisco Chronicle*

See also **WESTERN** under **20TH-CENTURY SPIRITUAL LEADERS** under **SPIRITUALITY**

0-06-061688-1 HARPERCOLLINS $20.00

W.Y. **Evans-Wentz**, editor & translator

Tibetan Yoga and Secret Doctrines

The best work by a popular but not always reliable interpreter of Tibetan religion

0-19-500278-4 OXFORD PB $14.95

Francesca **Fremantle** & Chogyam **Trungpa**, translators

The Tibetan Book of the Dead: The Great Liberation Through Hearing in the Bardo

Although it is by no means the central work of the Tibetan Buddhist tradition (whatever its estimation in the West), this work remains a fascinating account of Tibetan beliefs about the state immediately following death and preceding the next rebirth

0-87773-074-1 RANDOM HOUSE PB $10.00
0-87773-675-8 SHAMBHALA PB $7.00

Geshe K. **Gyatso**

The Clear Light of Bliss

An exposition of one of the central meditative practices of the advanced Anuttarayoga Tantras

TRANSLATED BY TENZIN NORBU
EDITED BY CHRIS COLB & JONATHAN LANDOW

0-948006-21-8 THARPA PB $19.95

Lobsang P. **Lhalunga**, translator

The Life of Milarepa

A rendering of a popular Tibetan biography of perhaps the best-known and most venerated of all Buddhists in Tibet

0-14-019350-2 ARKANA PB $13.95

Namkhai **Norbu**

Crystal and the Way of Light: Sutra, Tantra, and Dzogchen

One of the very finest introductions to Dzogchen tradition by a living master, teaching in U.S. and Europe

0-14-019314-6 VIKING PB $13.95

Orient Foundation & Graham **Coleman**, editors

A Handbook of Tibetan Culture: A Guide to Tibetan Centers and Resources Throughout the World

Since 1959, when the Chinese annexed Tibet and drove its culture and religion into exile, a huge and vibrant network has sprung up worldwide to keep Tibetan Buddhism and national identity alive. With the database of the Orient Foundation at his disposal, Coleman was able to compile this invaluable guide to the far-flung organizations and centers of the unsurrendering Tibetan diaspora

1-57062-002-4 SHAMBHALA PB $18.00

John M. **Reynolds**, editor

Self-Liberation Through Seeing With Naked Awareness

One of the half dozen major Dzogchen texts

0-88268-050-1 STATION HILL PB $14.95

Miranda **Shaw**

Passionate Enlightenment: Women in Tantric Buddhism

"A groundbreaking book"—Robert Thurman

0-691-01090-0 PRINCETON PB $13.95

Sogyal **Rinpoche**

The Tibetan Book of Living and Dying

"A magnificent achievement. In its power to touch the heart, to awaken consciousness, it is an inestimable gift"
—*San Francisco Chronicle Book Review*

FOREWORD BY THE DALAI LAMA

0-06-250793-1 HARPERCOLLINS $26.00
0-06-250834-2 HARPERCOLLINS PB $16.00

R.A. **Stein**

Tibetan Civilization

An authoritative study with a useful table of key terms

TRANSLATED BY J.E. DRIVER

0-8047-0806-1 STANFORD $47.50
0-8047-0901-7 STANFORD PB $15.95

Tulku **Thondup**

Enlightened Journey: The Practice of Buddhism as Daily Life

A guide to active Buddhism by an exponent of Tibetan Buddhism

1-57062-021-0 SHAMBHALA PB $16.00

Robert A.F. **Thurman**

Essential Tibetan Buddhism

Despite the growing popularity of Tibetan Buddhism, many of its core beliefs remain little understood in America. Here, the foremost Tibetan Buddhist scholar, a professor at Columbia University and practicing Buddhist monk, offers a much-needed, comprehensive guide to the essential riches of Tibetan Buddhism. Complemented by glossaries, notes, and bibliographies for further reading

0-06-251048-7 HARPERCOLLINS $20.00

Inside Tibetan Buddhism: Rituals and Symbols Revealed

Color photographs of Tibetan Buddhist art, ritual, and meditation—some with the Dalai Lama or Western as well as Tibetan followers—accompanied by a clear explanatory text by an eminent American scholar

0-00-638299-1 COLLINS SAN FRANCISCO PB $20.00

Tenzin **Wangyal**

Wonders of the Natural Mind: The Essence of Dzogchen in the Native Bon Tradition of Tibet

The most important work on Tibetan Bon since Snellgrove's "Nine Ways of Bon"

0-88268-117-6 STATION HILL PB $15.95

Buddhism as a Pan-Asian Religion

Heinz **Bechert** & Richard **Gombrich**, editors

The World of Buddhism

The 2,500-year history of the oldest world religion surveyed by leading experts in the field. The 297 illustrations, 82 in color, provide an introduction to a cluster of great artistic traditions

0-500-27628-5 THAMES & HUDSON PB $29.95

W. Theodore **De Bary**, editor

The Buddhist Tradition: In India, China and Japan

Readings from the various literatures of Buddhism with brief introductions and annotations

0-394-71696-5 MODERN LIBRARY PB $9.75

Louis **Frederic**

Buddhism: Flammarion Iconographic Guides

Authoritative, easy to use, this is an abundantly illustrated introduction to the iconic figures of Buddhism from India, Nepal, and Tibet, to Southeast Asia, China, and Japan. Copious notes, bibliographies, and indices make this an invaluable guide to iconography as well as a splendid introduction to Buddhism as a whole

2-08-013582-1 ABBEVILLE $45.00
2-08-013558-9 ABBEVILLE PB $24.95

Thich Nhat **Hanh**

The Miracle of Mindfulness: A Manual on Meditation

"One of the best available introductions to the wisdom and beauty of meditation practice"—*New Age Journal*

See also **EASTERN** under **20TH-CENTURY SPIRITUAL LEADERS** under **SPIRITUALITY**

0-8070-1232-7 BEACON $16.00
0-8070-1201-7 BEACON PB $11.00

Thundering Silence: Sutra on Knowing the Better Way to Catch a Snake

Rich comments on this ancient sutra explain the subtle difference between indulgence and attachment on the one hand, and appreciating life's pleasures on the other. Thich Nhat Hanh suggests that this sutra opens the door to Mahayana Buddhist thought and practice

0-938077-64-3 PARALLAX PB $7.00

Donald S. **Lopez**

Buddhism in Practice

This volume contains 48 difficult-to-find texts from India, China, Japan, Nepal, and elsewhere to illustrate, in unusually revealing ways, the vast scope of Buddhist practice in Asia. An ideal introduction to Buddhism and a delightful sourcebook for scholars. "These selections consistently reveal new vistas on the Buddhist landscape or illuminate old views from new angles"—John S. Strong

0-691-04442-2 PRINCETON $59.50
0-691-04441-4 PRINCETON PB $19.95

Tom **Lowenstein**

The Vision of the Buddha

The Living Wisdom Series presents key issues of body, mind, and spirit in a format that combines plentiful color illustration and authoritative texts. "The books in this intriguing series are tantalizing glimpses of their subjects for the lay reader"—*Dallas Morning News*

0-316-53431-5 LITTLE, BROWN PB $14.95

Hans W. **Schumann**
Buddhism
An outstanding primer of Buddhist thought that includes a sympathetic treatment of the main schools of Mahayana Buddhism
0-8356-0452-7 THEOSOPHICAL PB $8.95

John **Snelling**
The Buddhist Handbook: A Complete Guide to Buddhist Schools, Teaching, Practice, and History
A survey of the complex traditions of Buddhism from early history and meditation practices to the international influence of Buddhism in the modern world, including its contribution to psychotherapy
0-89281-319-9 INNER TRADITIONS PB $16.95

Inner Asian Traditions

Mircea **Eliade**
Shamanism: Archaic Techniques of Ecstasy
Eliade's study of shamanism is one of his greatest and most influential works. He takes a global approach to the subject but focuses particularly on the traditions of North and Central Asia
See also **MIRCEA ELIADE** under **WORLD RELIGION**
See also **NEW PAGANISM** under **METAPHYSICS** under **SPIRITUALITY**
TRANSLATED BY WILLARD R. TRASK
0-691-01779-4 PRINCETON PB $17.95

Walther **Heissig**
The Religions of Mongolia
An authoritative study that focuses on the non-Buddhist component of Mongol religion
0-520-03857-6 CALIFORNIA $45.00

Religions of Africa and the African Diaspora

Jason **Berry**
The Spirit of Black Hawk: A Mystery of Africans and Indians
The complex story of how an African-American sect in New Orleans came to honor the Illinois chief Black Hawk as its guiding spirit
0-87805-806-0 MISSISSIPPI $20.00

Serge **Bramly**
Macumba: The Teachings of Maria-Jose Mother of the Gods
0-87286-286-0 CITY LIGHTS PB $12.95

Laennec **Húrbon**
Voodoo: Search for the Spirit
TRANSLATED BY LORY FRANKEL
0-8109-2857-4 ABRAMS PB $12.95

Maya **Deren**
Divine Horsemen: The Living Gods of Haiti
A study of voodoo owing much to the experiences of the author, a leading experimental filmmaker of the 1940s
See also **CARIBBEAN** under **THE WESTERN HEMISPHERE** under **MYTHOLOGY AND FOLKLORE**
FOREWORD BY JOSEPH CAMPBELL
0-914232-63-0 MCPHERSON PB $15.00

Miguel **Gonzalez-Wippler**
Legends of Santeria
1-56718-328-X LLEWELLYN PB $9.95

Alfred **Metraux**
Voodoo in Haiti
An Anthropologist discusses the history and origin of voodoo as well as the rituals of *mambos* and adepts
08052=08941 SCHOCKEN PB $17.00

Malidoma Patrice **Some**
Of Water and the Spirit: Ritual, Magic, and Initiation in the Life of an African Shaman
0-14-019496-7 PENGUIN PB $12.95

Judaism

The following books focus primarily on Judaism as both a religion and a way of life. Books that explore the various other aspects of Jewish existence can be found in the chapters on Jewish History, Hebrew Literature, Yiddish Literature, the Holocaust, and the Contemporary Middle East.

The Bible

The volumes of biblical translation and commentary listed below reflect a continuing discussion over biblical interpretation. The Five Scrolls were edited by scholars who are identified with Reform Judaism; the commentaries contained in the Soncino Books of the Bible are an anthology of Orthodox interpretation. The authors in the section of commentaries represent their own individual views; none of them speaks for a party.

Martin **Buber** & Franz **Rosenzweig**
Scripture and Translation
0-253-31272-8 INDIANA $26.50

Everett **Fox**
The Five Books of Moses: The Schocken Bible
The books of Moses—Genesis, Exodus, Leviticus, Numbers, and Deuteronomy—newly translated to render the full force of the Bible's original rhetoric and poetry into modern, believable English. "A real breakthrough in the English translation of the Bible... It opens up the biblical text... in new and refreshing ways"—Peter Machinist, Harvard University. "A feast of satisfaction for those of us who always wanted to know what the Hebrew words really said! Anyone who has ever loved the Bible as revelation or poetry, as history or myth, will treasure this book"—Anne Rice
See also **BIBLES AND COMMENTARY** under **CHRISTIANITY**
0-8052-4061-6 SCHOCKEN $50.00

J.H. **Hertz**
The Pentateuch & Haftorahs
Torah readings grouped with their Haftorah readings, in Hebrew and English
0-900689-21-8 SONCINO $30.00

Jewish Publication Society
The Prophets: Nevi'im
0-8276-0096-8 JEWISH PUB SOCIETY $19.95

Tanakh: A New Translation of the Holy Scriptures According to the Traditional Hebrew Text
All three volumes collected in a new English translation prepared by scholars from the three main branches of American Judaism; also available as individual volumes
0-8276-0252-9 JEWISH PUB SOCIETY $26.95

The Torah: The 5 Books of Moses
0-8276-0015-1 JEWISH PUB SOCIETY $15.95

The Writings: Ketubim
0-8276-0202-2 JEWISH PUB SOCIETY $19.95

Stephen **Mitchell**, translator
The Book of Job
An acclaimed translation that highlights *Job*'s literary qualities. "Stephen Mitchell's version of *Job* succeeds in conveying a rush, a momentum, that are insistent, at times awesome, and often the bearers of a new insight into the meaning and power of the unique original"—W.S. Merwin
0-06-096959-8 HARPERPERENNIAL PB $11.00

Genesis: A New Translation and Interpretation
The companion volume to the PBS series by Bill Moyers, this translation and interpretation of the Book of Genesis comes from the celebrated translator of the *Tao Te Ching* and *The Book of Job*. Placing the great biblical stories in a modern context, this is a rare opportunity to understand both the original intent of this seminal text as well as its modern relevance
See also **BIBLES AND COMMENTARY** under **CHRISTIANITY**
0-06-017249-5 HARPERCOLLINS $20.00

W. Gunther **Plaut** & Bernard J. **Bamberger**
The Torah: A Modern Commentary
A Reform-movement edition of the 5 Books of Moses
0-8074-0055-6 U.A.H.C. $40.0

Jack **Miles**
God: A Biography
In this slightly mischievous book, Miles reads the Old Testament, book by book, as if they formed a novel with God as the main character
0-679-41833-4 KNOPF $27.50
0-679-74368-5 VINTAGE PB $15.00

Biblical Commentary

S. Y. **Agnon**, editor

Present at Sinai: The Giving of the Law

Nobel Laureate Agnon centers his study of the focal point of Jewish consciousness on the verses of the Torah, augmenting them with ancient and medieval commentaries and his own trenchant observations

0-8276-0503-X JEWISH PUB SOCIETY $40.00

Robert **Alter**

The Art of Biblical Narrative

A commentary on the Bible as a literary work. "Alter's book may open up the Bible to those who usually avoid it, and offer new insights to those who know it well"
—Elaine Pagels, *New Republic*

See also **THE BIBLE** under **LITERARY CRITICISM** in **LITERATURE OF EUROPE, AFRICA, AND ASIA**

0-465-00427-X BASIC BOOKS PB $13.00

Robert **Alter**, translator

Genesis

New contemporary translation and commentary on the founding book of the Bible. "Here is the *Genesis* for our generation and beyond. An occasion for praise..."
—Robert Fagles, Princeton University

0-393-03981-1 NORTON $25.00

Robert **Alter** & Frank **Kermode**

The Literary Guide to the Bible

"A veritable thesaurus of literary and human evaluation of the Scriptures, both absorbing and authoritative"
—Amos N. Wilder, Harvard University

0-674-87530-3 HARVARD $46.95
0-674-87531-1 HARVARD PB $16.95

Yitzhak F. **Baer**

Galut

See also **THE MIDDLE AGES** under **JEWISH HISTORY** in **WORLD HISTORY AND CURRENT AFFAIRS**

INTRODUCTION BY JACOB NEUSNER

0-8191-5783-X UNIVERSITY PRESS OF AMERICA PB $15.50

Harold **Bloom** & David **Rosenberg**

The Book of J

Harold Bloom's idiosyncratic and controversial interpretation of the earliest stratum of the Hebrew Bible, or Old Testament, accompanied by David Rosenberg's new translation. Bloom speculates that the author of the earliest Jewish scriptures was a woman

0-679-73624-7 VINTAGE PB $13.00

Louis **Ginzberg**

Legends of the Bible

"An unusual treat"—*Jewish Ledger*

0-8276-0404-1 JEWISH PUB SOCIETY PB $19.95

Legends of the Jews

A classic collection of biblical stories and legends

Volume 1

0-8276-0340-1 JEWISH PUB SOCIETY $29.95

Volume 2

0-8276-0341-X JEWISH PUB SOCIETY $29.95

Volume 3

0-8276-0342-8 JEWISH PUB SOCIETY $29.95

Volume 4

0-8276-0343-6 JEWISH PUB SOCIETY $29.95

Volume 5 Notes to Volumes 1 & 2

0-8276-0344-4 JEWISH PUB SOCIETY $29.95

Volume 6

0-8276-0345-2 JEWISH PUB SOCIETY $29.95

Volume 7

9-9954-0682-9 JEWISH PUB SOCIETY $29.95

Robert **Gordis**

Koheleth: The Man and His World—A Study of Ecclesiastes

A thorough analysis of the book of Ecclesiastes in the context of both the literature of its time and its relevance to moderm thought

1-56821-601-7 ARONSON PB $25.00

Abraham Joshua **Heschel**

The Prophets

"Heschel seeks not so much to expound the message of the prophets against the background of their times and to fix their place in the history of Israel's religion, as to explore the phenomenon of prophecy as such, to analyze its fundamental presuppositions and the nature of prophetic inspiration"—John Bright

Volume 1 An Introduction

0-06-131421-8 HARPERCOLLINS PB $14.00

Volume 2

0-06-131557-5 HARPERCOLLINS PB $14.00

James L. **Kugel**

In Potiphar's House: The Interpretive Life of Biblical Texts

0-674-44563-5 HARVARD PB $15.95

Robert **Alter**

The Art of Biblical Poetry

0-465-00431-8 BASIC PAPER $14.50

Dale J. **Pritchard**

The Bible in a Nutshell

0-87573-029-9 JAIN $6.95

David **Rosenberg**, editor

Congregation: Contemporary Writers Read the Jewish Bible

The continuing relevance of the Bible to the life and work of contemporary writers, including Isaac Bashevis Singer, Mordecai Richler, and Cynthia Ozick

0-15-146350-6 HARCOURT BRACE PB $29.95

Samuel **Sandmel**

The Hebrew Scriptures: An Introduction to Their Literature and Religious Ideas

0-19-502369-2 OXFORD PB $22.00

William **Safire**

The First Dissident: What We Can Learn About Protest and Politics from the Book of Job

Safire, Pulitzer Prize-winning political columnist and writer on language, sees Job as a dissenter against authority and explores ways the biblical book can inspire and instruct. He cites the need for dissent in the shaping of power, and applies the lessons of Job's struggle to our own times

0-679-74858-X RANDOM HOUSE PB $12.00

William Safire

Nahum M. **Sarna**

Exploring Exodus: The Heritage of Biblical Israel

Sarna demonstrates the significance of Israel's revolutionary monotheism by analyzing how and why the biblical text represents an original departure in religious imagination

0-8052-0830-5 SCHOCKEN PB $14.00

Understanding Genesis: The Heritage of Biblical Israel

"The most comprehensive and careful interpretation of the Bible's initial book in light of the extrabiblical sources"
—*Journal of Biblical Literature*

0-8052-0253-6 SCHOCKEN PB $14.00

Shalom **Spiegel**

The Last Trial: On the Legend and Lore of the Command to Abraham to Offer Isaac as a Sacrifice—The Akedah

A learned book on a key episode in the demonstration of Jewish faith that figured strongly in the Hebrew liturgy of the 12th and 13th centuries

1-87904-529-X JEWISH LIGHTS PB $17.95

Elie **Wiesel**

Five Biblical Portraits

Portraits of Saul, Jonah, Jeremiah, Elijah, and Joshua

0-268-00962-7 NOTRE DAME PB $7.95

Messengers of God: Biblical Portraits and Legends

Original thoughts on the stories of Adam, Cain and Abel, the sacrifice of Isaac, Jacob and the angel, Joseph, Moses, Job, and others

0-671-54134-X SUMMIT PB $11.00

Later Antiquity

Edgar **Goodspeed**

The Apocrypha: An American Translation

Includes such key works as Maccabees I and II, The Wisdom of Solomon, and the Book of Judith

INTRODUCTION BY MOSES HADAS

0-394-70163-1 VINTAGE PB $14.00

Martin S. **Jaffee**

Early Judaism: Religious Worlds of the First Judaic Millenium

0-13-519323-0 PRENTICE HALL PB $29.33

Jacob **Neuser** & William Scott **Green**, editors

Dictionary of Judaism in the Biblical Period: 450 B.C.E. to 600 C.E.

0-02-897288-0 MACMILLAN $25.00

The Dead Sea Scrolls

The most epochal find of recent times: the texts of the Jewish monastic community that flourished in the age of Augustus whose tenets have been suggested as the source of Christian thought. But the scrolls are also valuable in their own right. The story of their discovery is no less fabulous than the texts themselves with their protagonists, the Righteous Teacher and the Wicked Priest, and the millenial "War of the Children of Darkness Against the Children of Light"

Robert **Eisenman** & Michael **Wise**

The Dead Sea Scrolls Uncovered

1-85230-368-9 ELEMENT $24.95

0-14-023250-8 PENGUIN PB $12.95

Florentino Garcia **Martinez**

The Dead Sea Scrolls Translated: The Qumram Texts in English

0-8028-4193-7 EERDMANS PB $30.00

Laurence H. **Schiffman**

Reclaiming The Dead Sea Scrolls: Their True Meaning for Judaism and Christianity

"The most thorough and authoritative of the new books occasioned by the full release of the Dead Sea Scrolls"—*Kirkus Reviews*

0-385-48121-7 DOUBLEDAY PB $24.95

Geza **Vermes**

The Dead Sea Scrolls in English

A translation of the Hebrew and Aramaic documents discovered in the 1940s and dating from 200 BCE to the 1st century CE, offering unparalleled insights into post-biblical Jewish life; a revised and updated edition

See also **PALESTINE AND THE BIBLE** under **ARCHAEOLOGY** in **WORLD HISTORY AND CURRENT AFFAIRS**

0-14-013544-8 PENGUIN PB $12.00

Michael **Wise** & others

The Dead Sea Scrolls: A New Translation

0-06-069200-6 HARPERCOLLINS $35.00

The Talmud

"Historically speaking, the Talmud is the central pillar of Jewish culture. This culture is many faceted, but each of its numerous aspects is connected in some way with the Talmud. This is true not only of the literature that deals directly with the interpretation or continuation of the Talmud, but also of all other types of Jewish creativity. Halakhic literature is, of course, based entirely on the Talmud, but most original Jewish philosophy has also drawn inspiration from it in one way or another. It is impossible to approach biblical exegesis or Jewish or esoteric philosophy without knowledge of the Talmud. Even works that have no ostensible connection with talmudic literature—like poetry or prayers—are inspired by it in various ways. The student who claims to understand the significance and intention of material will realize, after close perusal of this literature, how barren are the attempts to absorb Jewish knowledge while ignoring its basic sources."
—Adin Steinsaltz, *The Essential Talmud*

Adin **Steinsaltz**

The Essential Talmud

A clear and intelligent guide to the history, structure and content, and method of the Talmud

0-465-02063-1 BASIC PB $16.00

Adin **Steinsaltz**

The Talmud: The Steinsaltz Edition

Volume 1
Tractate Bava Metzia, Part 1

0-394-57666-7 RANDOM HOUSE $50.00

Volume 2
Tractate Bava Metzia, Part 2

0-394-58233-0 RANDOM HOUSE $45.00

Volume 3
Tractate Bava Metzia, Part 3

0-394-58234-9 RANDOM HOUSE $45.00

Volume 4
Tractate Bava Metzia, Part 4

0-394-58853-3 RANDOM HOUSE $45.00

Volume 5
Tractate Bava Metzia, Part 5

0-679-41379-0 RANDOM HOUSE $45.00

Volume 6
Tractate Bava Metzia, Part 6

0-679-41378-2 RANDOM HOUSE $50.00

Volume 7
Tractate Ketubot, Part 1

0-679-40769-3 RANDOM HOUSE $45.00

Volume 8
Tractate Ketubot, Part 2

0-679-41632-3 RANDOM HOUSE $45.00

Volume 9
Tractate Ketubot, Part 3

0-679-42694-9 RANDOM HOUSE $50.00

Volume 10
Tractate Ketubot, Part 4

0-679-42899-2 RANDOM HOUSE $45.00

Volume 11
Tractate Ketubot, Part 5

0-679-44397-5 RANDOM HOUSE $50.00

Volume 12
Tractate Ketubot, Part 5

0-679-42962-X RANDOM HOUSE $50.00

Volume 13
Tractate Ta'Anit, Part 1

0-679-42961-1 RANDOM HOUSE $45.00

Volume 14
Tractate Ta'Anit, Part 2

0-679-44398-3 RANDOM HOUSE $50.00

Volume 15
Tractate Sanhedrin

0-679-45222-2 RANDOM HOUSE $50.00

Adin **Steinsaltz**

The Talmud: The Steinsaltz Edition, A Reference Guide

This indispensable accompaniment to the Steinsaltz Talmud offers a guide to the nature and historical background of the Talmud, guidelines for study, and detailed glossaries of Mishnaic methodology, Talmudic terminology and hermeneutics, and Halakhic concepts and terms

0-394-57665-9 RANDOM HOUSE $50.00

Hayim Nahman **Bialik** & Yehoshua Hana **Ravnitzky**, editors

The Book of Legends: Legends from the Talmud and Midrash

0-8052-4113-2 SCHOCKEN $75.00

Abraham **Cohen**

Everyman's Talmud

A classic, straightforward introduction to the fundamental concepts of the Talmud

0-8052-0497-0 SCHOCKEN PB $17.00

Emmanuel **Levinas**

Nine Talmudic Readings

See also **OTHER 20TH-CENTURY PHILOSOPHERS** under **PHILOSOPHY**

TRANSLATED BY ANNETTE ARONOWICZ

0-253-20876-9 INDIANA PB $11.95

Herbert **Danby**, translator & editor

The Mishnah

The standard reference work, a one-volume translation of the entire Mishnah by a noted Christian scholar

0-19-815402-X OXFORD $69.00

Philip **Blackman**, translator

The Mishnah

The entire, fully indexed work, in Hebrew and English; a 7-volume set

0-910818-00-2 JUDAICA $100.00

Jacob **Neusner**

The Mishnah: A New Translation

A formal-analytical rendering of the entire Mishnah, keeping as close to a literal translation as possible, by a leading scholar

0-300-03065-7 YALE $75.00

1-56338-021-8 TRINITY PB $16.95

Marc-Alain **Ouaknin**

The Burnt Book: Reading the Talmud

0-691-03729-9 PRINCETON $35.00

Esra **Shereshevsky**

Rashi

A biography of Rabbi Solomon Ben Isaac (1040-1105), the foremost Jewish Talmud commentator of all time

0-87203-101-2 SEPHER-HERMON $17.50

Ephraim E. **Urbach**

The Sages: The World and Wisdom of the Rabbis of the Talmud

A landmark examination of the ancient texts that form the basis for the rabbinic code of ethics and the conduct of daily life

TRANSLATED BY ISRAEL ABRAHAMS

0-674-78523-1 HARVARD PB $27.50

Early Philosophical Texts

J. David **Bleich**

With Perfect Faith: The Foundations of Jewish Belief

A collection of medieval philosophical writings

0-87068-452-3 KTAV PB $20.00

Marvin **Fox**

Interpreting Maimonides: Studies in Methodology, Metaphysics, and Moral Philosophy

0-226-25942-0 CHICAGO PB $15.95

Moses **Maimonides**

The Guide of the Perplexed

A reconciliation of the Old Testament and Aristotle by the great 12th-century Jewish philosopher

Volume 1

See also **CLASSICS OF WESTERN RELIGIOUS THOUGHT** under **WORLD RELIGION**

0-226-50230-9 CHICAGO PB $25.00

Volume 2

0-226-50231-7 CHICAGO PB $25.00

Isadore **Twersky**, editor

A Maimonides Reader

Excerpts from the great medieval philosopher, including pieces from his two greatest works: *Guide of the Perplexed* and *Mishneh Torah*

0-87441-206-4 BEHRMAN PB $15.95

Mysticism and Hasidism

Mysticism and Kabbalah

Johann **Reuchlin**

On the Art of the Kabbalah

0-8032-8946-4 NEBRASKA PB $15.00

Raphael **Patai**

The Jewish Alchemists: A History and Source Book

A history of medieval Jewish alchemy and its relation to Kabbalist mysticism

0-691-03290-4 PRINCETON $65.00

Gershom **Scholem**

Kabbalah

The history and basic ideas of the Kabbalah, plus detailed entries on a wide range of concepts and personalities in the mystical literature; by the leading authority on Jewish mysticism

0-452-01007-1 NEW AMERICAN LIBRARY PB $14.95

Major Trends in Jewish Mysticism

A collection of lectures on the features of the movement that began in antiquity and continues in Hasidism today

0-8052-1042-3 SCHOCKEN PB $16.00

The Messianic Idea in Judaism & Other Essays on Jewish Spirituality

Scholem explores the complex relationship between mysticism and Messianism in Jewish thought

0-8052-0362-1 SCHOCKEN PB $15.00

Origins of the Kabbalah

Now in paperback: a crucial work by the great scholar of Jewish mysticism. "[Scholem's] work… constitutes one of the major achievements of the historical imagination in our time"
—Robert Alter, *Commentary*

0-691-02047-7 PRINCETON PB $18.95

Gershom Scholem

Aryeh **Wineman**

Mystic Tales from the Zohar

0-8276-0515-3 JEWISH PUB SOCIETY $34.95

Hasidism

Martin **Buber**

The Legend of the Baal-Shem

The greatest Jewish philosopher of the 20th century reflects on the 18th century mystic and healer who founded Hasidism and sought holiness in ordinary life instead of asceticism

0-691-04389-2 PRINCETON PB $12.95

The Origin and Meaning of Hasidism

Compares Hasidism with Biblical prophecy, Spinoza, Freud, Christianity, Zen Buddhism, and more

0-391-03549-5 HUMANITIES PB $19.95

Tales of the Hasidim

This edition contains both Volume 1: The Early Masters, and Volume 2: The Later Masters

0-8052-0995-6 SCHOCKEN PB $20.00

Samuel H. **Dresner**

Zaddik: The Doctrine of the Zaddik According to the Writings of Rabbi Yaakov Yosef of Polnoy

PREFACE BY ABRAHAM JOSHUA HESCHEL

1-56821-312-3 ARONSON PB $25.00

Louis I. **Newman**, editor

The Hasidic Anthology: Tales and Teachings of the Hasidim

Translations of writings and documents covering the history and practice of Hasidic life

See also **BIBLICAL COMMENTARY** under **THE BIBLE**

0-87668-968-3 ARONSON $40.00

Elie **Wiesel**

Souls on Fire: Portraits and Legends of Hasidic Masters

Writings about the Hasidic sects. "These tales, although they are the kernel of a highly developed form of Jewish mysticism, have a basic human interest that transcends the dividing lines of religion"
—Alan Pryce-Jones, *Washington Post*

0-671-44171-X SIMON & SCHUSTER PB $13.00

Anthologies of Basic Texts

David **Curzon**, editor

Modern Poems on the Bible: An Anthology

0-8276-0449-1 JEWISH PUB SOCIETY $35.00

Solomon **Ganzfried**

Code of Jewish Law

A one-volume English edition of the 16th-century guide to orthodox Jewish law (the Kitzur Shulhan Arukh)

TRANSLATED BY HYMAN E. GOLDIN

0-88482-423-3 HEBREW $23.50

0-88482-779-8 HEBREW PB $16.95

Nahum **Glatzer**, editor

The Judaic Tradition: Jewish Writing from Antiquity to the Modern Age

A comprehensive collection including selections from ancient, medieval, and modern Judaism on topics ranging from the nature of God to the politics of modern Zionism. "An outstanding anthology of Jewish thought, full of substance and yet highly readable and well organized"
—Emil L. Fackenheim

0-87668-984-5 ARONSON $35.00

0-87441-344-3 BEHRMAN PB $15.95

Barry **Holtz**, editor
Back to the Sources: Reading the Classic Jewish Texts
"The best and most comprehensive introduction available"—Harold Bloom
0-671-60596-8 SUMMIT PB $13.00

Modern Theology and Philosophy

David S. **Ariel**
What Do Jews Believe?: The Spiritual Foundations of Judaism
"A remarkably rich and useful one-volume introduction to millennia of Jewish beliefs" —*Kirkus Reviews*
0-8052-1059-8 SCHOCKEN PB $13.00

Eugene B. **Borowitz**
Liberal Judaism
A study of Reform Judaism
0-8074-0264-8 U.A.H.C. PB $9.95

Daniel **Boyarin**
Carnal Israel: Reading Sex in Talmudic Culture
The bearing of Talmudic interpretation on sex, women, and the body
0-520-08012-2 CALIFORNIA $40.00

Martin **Buber**
I and Thou
A classic of religious existentialism. Please see Hasidim under Judaism for Buber's other works
See also **CLASSICS OF WESTERN RELIGIOUS THOUGHT** under **WORLD RELIGION**
TRANSLATED BY WALTER KAUFFMAN & S.G. SMITH
0-684-71725-5 MACMILLAN PB $10.00
0-684-18254-8 SCRIBNERS PB $5.95

On Judaism
"These twelve essays bring together, for the first time in English, Buber's most important articulations of thought on the value and role of Judaism"—*Kirkus Reviews*
0-8052-1050-4 SCHOCKEN PB $13.00

Maurice **Friedman**
Encounter on the Narrow Ridge: A Life of Martin Buber
"Friedman analyzes succinctly, but with great care, Buber's responses to the important events of the 20th century: the two World Wars, the Holocaust, post war Germany from 1945-1961, and the establishment of Israel and the Jewish-Arab problem...Highly recommended to all libraries"—*Library Journal*
1-55778-596-1 PARAGON PB $18.95

Arthur A. **Cohen** & Paul **Mendes-Flohr**, editors
Contemporary Jewish Religious Thought
An ample collection: 140 essays from such major figures as Emil Fackenheim, Jacob Neusner, Gerson Cohen, and others
0-02-906040-0 FREE PRESS PB $27.95

Emil L. **Fackenheim**
To Mend the World
A major work on post-Holocaust spiritual survival by a German-born rabbi and Jewish philosopher
0-253-32114-X INDIANA PB $17.50

Andrew M. **Greeley** & Jacob **Neusner**
Common Ground: A Priest and a Rabbi Read the Scripture Together
See also **CONTEMPORARY ISSUES** under **THEOLOGY AND DOCTRINE** under **CHRISTIANITY**
FOREWORD BY MARTIN E. MARTY
0-8298-1120-6 PILGRIM PB $16.95

Hafetz **Hayyim**
Ahavath Chesed: The Love of Kindness as Required by God
A very important work on the fundamental Jewish concept of kindness by one of the greatest religious leaders of Eastern Europe's Jews, Rabbi Israel Meir ha-Kohen, better known as the Hafetz Hayyim
TRANSLATED BY LEONARD OSCHRY
0-87306-110-1 PHILIPP FELDHEIM $14.95

Abraham Joshua **Heschel**
Between God and Man: An Interpretation of Judaism
An anthology of key writings by a leading modern Jewish philosopher
EDITED BY FRITZ A. ROTHSCHILD
0-02-914510-4 FREE PRESS PB $14.95

God in Search of Man: A Philosophy of Judaism
0-374-51331-7 FS&G PB $16.00

Man Is Not Alone: A Philosopy of Religion
0-374-51328-7 FS&G PB $14.00

Moral Grandeur and Spiritual Audacity: Essays
The five parts of this splendid collection cover the full range of Heschel's thought, moving from "Existence and Celebration" to "Toward a Just Society" and "The Holy Dimension." "One of the truly great men of our day and age, a truly great prophet"—Martin Luther King, Jr.
See also **PHILOSOPHY AND RELIGION** under **WORLD RELIGION**
EDITED BY SUSANNAH HESCHEL
0-374-19980-9 FS&G $27.50

Louis **Jacobs**
The Book of Jewish Belief
0-87441-379-6 BEHRMAN PB $11.50

Mordecai M. **Kaplan**
Dynamic Judaism: The Essential Writings of Mordecai M. Kaplan
An anthology of works by the founder of the Reconstructionist movement that offers clear insight into Kaplan's thought and the philosophy of the fourth major branch of American Judaism
EDITED BY EMANUEL S. GOLDSMITH & MEL SCULT
0-8232-1310-2 FORDHAM PB $16.95

Judaism as a Civilization
Kaplan's major work on the principles of Reconstructionist Judaism
0-8276-0529-3 JEWISH PUB SOCIETY PB $29.95

David **Landau**
Piety and Power: The World of Jewish Fundamentalism
This disturbing book, by a senior political correspondent for the Israeli newspaper *Maariv*, provides the reader with a rare view of the self-contained world of the *haredim* communities—the sect whose dramatic post-Holocaust revival has deepened the bitter conflict over the soul of Israel
0-8090-7605-5 HILL & WANG $27.50

Michael **Lerner**
Jewish Renewal: A Path of Healing and Transformation
"Michael Lerner constructs an impassioned yet pragmatic approach to a spiritual revitalization that is at once proud of a group identity while also being outward-focused in its deep concern with the world"—John Brown Child
0-06-097675-6 HARPERPERENNIAL PB $15.00

Moses **Luzzatto**
Moses Luzzatto (known in Hebrew as Moshe Chaim) was an 18th-century Italian-born Hebrew poet and mystic. He is often called the "father of modern Hebrew literature."
The Path of the Just
Moral guidelines from the Hebrew poet, kabbalist, and ethical thinker
See also **THE 18TH AND 19TH CENTURIES** under **MODERN HEBREW LITERATURE** in **LITERATURE OF EUROPE, AFRICA, AND ASIA**
1-56821-596-7 ARONSON $30.00
0-87306-114-4 FELDHEIM $16.95

Arnaldo **Momigliano**
Essays on Ancient and Modern Judaism
During the final 20 years of his life, the eminent classicist Momigliano wrote essays on a variety of Jewish individuals and themes, relating them to the breadth of Hellenic and European thought. "Perhaps [Momigliano's] most solid achievement in the study of Jews was to help to locate them properly in relation to Greek and Roman society and ideas...But most lasting of all are the acute evaluations of Jewish scholars like himself whose sometimes precarious position in the modern world sharpened their understanding of the ancient"—*TLS*
0-226-53381-6 CHICAGO $24.95

Franz **Rosenzweig**
The Star of Redemption
Significant contribution to modern Jewish theology and existential philosophy of the twentieth century
TRANSLATED BY WILLIAM W. HALLO
FOREWORD BY NAHUM N. GLATZER
0-268-01718-2 NOTRE DAME PB $19.50

Michael **Shevack** & Jack **Bemporad**
Stupid Ways, Smart Ways to Think About God
As the title suggests, some interesting ways to include God in one's daily life
0-89243-821-5 TRIUMPH PB $8.95

Abba Hillel **Silver**

Where Judaism Differs: An Inquiry into the Distinctiveness of Judaism

A key work by a noted American rabbi and Zionist leader (1893-1963)

0-87668-957-8 ARONSON $25.00

Joseph B. **Soloveitchik**

Halakhic Man

A basic theological statement on the importance of halakhah, or law, in Jewish life

TRANSLATED BY LAWRENCE KAPLAN

0-8276-0222-7 JEWISH PUB SOCIETY PB $12.95

Pierre **Vidal-Naquet**

The Jews: History, Memory, and the Present

The pre-eminent French historian draws on his seemingly bottomless erudition to trace the history of the Jews from ancient Rome through modern Israel. Along the way he delves deeply into the shocking dishonesty of Holocaust denial; the Dreyfus affair; and his own childhood in Vichy, from where his family was deported and destroyed. "Mr. Vidal-Naquet's intellectual and moral power achieves, in the end, a deep appreciation of the absolute centrality of truth to the twin tasks of writing history and preserving memory"—*NY Times Book Review*

See also **GENERAL HISTORIES** under **JEWISH HISTORY** in **WORLD HISTORY AND CURRENT AFFAIRS**

0-231-10208-9 COLUMBIA $29.50

Arthur **Waskow**

Down-to-Earth Judaism: Modern Theology and Philosophy

"Waskow shows us artfully and unpretentiously how Judaism lives in us and how we live in Judaism"—Rabbi Nina Beth Cardin

0-688-11840-2 MORROW $25.00

Herman **Wouk**

This Is My God: The Jewish Way of Life

Includes "Israel at Forty: The Land and the Faith"

0-316-95507-8 LITTLE, BROWN $17.95

How-To: Ritual and Practice

The Basics of Judaism

Marc D. **Angel**

The Rhythms of Jewish Living: The Sephardic Approach

0-87203-126-8 SEPHER-HERMON $14.95

Hayim Halevy **Donin**

To Be a Jew

A comprehensive guide to Jewish law and life from a modern Orthodox perspective, covering everything from prayer to birth control

0-465-08632-2 BASIC PB $16.00

To Pray as a Jew: A Guide to the Prayer Book and the Synagogue Service

Includes texts of prayers and songs

0-465-08628-4 BASIC $25.00

0-465-08633-0 BASIC PB $16.50

Wayne **Dosick**

Living in Judaism: The Complete Guide to Jewish Belief, Tradition and Practice

This wide-ranging resource allows easy access to the essentials of Jewish belief and tradition. Dosick, a rabbi and professor, has assembled a perfect introduction for people new to Jewish observance

0-06-062119-2 HARPERCOLLINS $27.50

Marcia **Falk**

The Book of Blessings: A Re-Creation of Jewish Prayer

"When a new movement arises in Judaism," writes Rachel Adler, "invariably it publishes a prayer book as its manifesto." Here, Falk presents a collection of blessings, poems, meditations, and rituals for contemporary Jewish life that includes women in its rituals. Unusually relevant to our times

0-06-062340-3 HARPERCOLLINS $50.00

Blu **Greenberg**

How to Run a Traditional Jewish Household

0-671-60270-5 SIMON & SCHUSTER PB $14.95

David C. **Gross**

1,201 Questions and Answers About Judaism

"Ideal for busy people seeking ready answers on the basic questions of Judaism and the Jewish people"—Rabbi Alexander Schindler, President, Union of American Hebrew Congregations

0-7818-0050-1 HIPPOCRENE PB $14.95

Aryeh **Kaplan**

Jewish Meditation: A Practical Guide

"A guide to Jewish prayer and meditation that is both grounded in the tradition and genuinely mind-expanding"—William Novak

0-8052-0781-3 SCHOCKEN PB $12.00

Morris N. **Kertzer**

What Is a Jew?

Questions and answers on Jewish life, religion, and culture ranging from birth control to Jewish attitudes toward the New Testament

0-02-086350-0 COLLIER PB $8.00

Alfred J. **Kolatch**

The Jewish Book of Why

A question-and-answer approach to the fundamental tenets and practices of Judaism

0-8246-0256-0 JONATHAN DAVID $18.95

The Second Jewish Book of Why

A sequel, addressing more complex and controversial issues of modern Jewish life

0-8246-0305-2 JONATHAN DAVID $18.95

Harold **Meek**

The Synagogue

A glorious photographic tour through the world's—and history's—synagogues: Venice, the Renaissance, Jewish communities worldwide. This book presents a history of Jewish life and worship through the eyes of a renowned architectural historian

0-7148-2932-3 PHAIDON $59.95

Dennis **Prager** & Joseph **Telushkin**

The Nine Questions People Ask About Judaism

"The intelligent skeptic's guide to Judaism" —Herman Wouk

0-671-62261-7 SIMON & SCHUSTER PB $10.00

Michael **Strassfeld** & others

The First Jewish Catalog: A Do-It-Yourself Kit

A best selling volume offering practical guidelines on everything from keeping kosher to crocheting *kippot*

0-8276-0042-9 JEWISH PUB SOCIETY PB $17.95

David J. **Wolpe**

In Speech and in Silence: The Jewish Quest for God

A collection of moving meditations, *In Speech and in Silence* explores the spiritual uses of silences and prayers—based on the idea that if words are the avenue of spirituality, silence is the destination. "In the search for spiritual renewal, Rabbi Wolpe is proving to be one of our most eloquent voices"
—David Ellenson, Hebrew Union College

0-8050-2816-1 OWLET PB $9.95

Why Be Jewish?

"A deeply inspirational guide to Jewish spiritual seekers. It is an ideal book for someone returning to Judaism or looking to understand the mystery of Jewish survival"
—Dr. David S. Ariel

0-8050-3927-9 HOLT PB $9.95

Sabbath and Holidays

Theodor H. **Gaster**

Festivals of the Jewish Year: A Modern Interpretation and Guide

0-8446-2113-7 SMITH $21.00

Irvin **Greenberg**

The Jewish Way: Living the Holidays

An easy-to-understand guide for enriching the spiritual aspect of all the Jewish holidays by a fuller comprehension of their historic origins, ceremonial rituals, and religious significance. Also covered are Yom Hashoah (Holocaust Remembrance Day) and Yom Ha'Atzmaut (Israel Independence Day). "Perceptive, enriching, profoundly moving—this volume by Irving Greenberg will further inspire his many followers who wish to understand and receive the joy and anguish of the Jewish tradition"
—Elie Wiesel

0-671-87303-2 TOUCHSTONE PB $13.00

S.Y. **Agnon**

The first and only Hebrew writer to win the Nobel Prize for literature, Agnon used the resources of midrashic, Hasidic, and folk literature to create a unique prose style. Edmund Wilson called him "a man of unquestionable genius."

Days of Awe: A Treasury of Tradition, Legends and Learned Commentaries Concerning Rosh Ha-Shanah, Yom Kippur and the Days Between

See also THE PIONEER PERIOD under MODERN HEBREW LITERATURE in LITERATURE OF EUROPE, AFRICA, AND ASIA

INTRODUCTION BY JUDAH GOLDIN

0-8052-1048-2 SCHOCKEN PB $15.00
0-8052-0100-9 SCHOCKEN PB $15.00

S.Y. Agnon

Abraham Joshua **Heschel**

The Sabbath

Heschel, internationally known scholar, author, activist, theologian, and professor of ethics and mysticism at the Jewish Theological Seminary in New York, wrote this classic of spiritual literature in 1951. Reissued here with Ilya Schor's original woodcuts, Heschel's meditation on the meaning of the sabbath offers a profound insight into Judaism and the meaning of the seventh day. "Heschel writes prose that sings and soars in the warm, intuitive tradition of the great 18th-century Hasidic masters from whom he is descended"—*Time*

WOODCUTS BY ILYA SCHOR

0-374-25321-8 FS&G $15.00

Peter S. **Knobel**, editor

The Gates of the Seasons: A Guide to the Jewish Year

Holidays, festivals, the Sabbath, and other special days, from the perspective of the Reform movement

0-916694-92-5
CENTRAL CONFERENCE OF AMERICAN RABBIS $12.95

Joan **Nathan**

The Children's Jewish Holiday Kitchen: 70 Ways to Have Fun with Your Kids and Make Your Family's Celebrations Special

ILLUSTRATIONS BY BROOKE SCUDDER

0-8052-4130-2 RANDOM HOUSE $18.00

Hayyim **Schauss**

The Jewish Festivals: History and Observance

The background and meaning of the major Jewish holidays, including a calendar of dates for the next two decades

0-8052-0413-X SCHOCKEN PB $16.00

Isaac Bashevis **Singer**

The Power of Light: Eight Stories of Hanukkah

The late Nobel Prize-winning author presents eight autobiographically inspired tales, one for each night of Hanukkah. His simple yet powerful tales of the triumph of love are further enhanced by Irene Lieblich's full-color illustrations, culled from memories of her childhood village near Singer's own in Poland. All ages

See also FICTION under BOOKS FOR EIGHTS, NINES, AND UP in BOOKS FOR YOUNG READERS
See also ISAAC BASHEVIS SINGER under YIDDISH LANGUAGE AND LITERATURE in LITERATURE OF EUROPE, AFRICA, AND ASIA

ILLUSTRATED BY IRENE LIEBLICH

0-374-36099-5 SUNBURST $15.00
0-374-45984-3 FS&G PB $8.95

Isaac Bashevis Singer

Michael **Strassfeld**

Jewish Holidays

An informative guide from the coauthor of the popular Jewish Catalog series

ILLUSTRATED BY BETSY P. TEUTSCH
COMMENTARIES BY ARNOLD EISEN

0-06-272008-2 HARPERCOLLINS PB $22.00

Arthur **Waskow**

Seasons of Our Joy: A Celebration of Modern Jewish Renewal

A "New Age" guide to Jewish holidays

0-8070-3611-0 BEACON PB $15.00

Passover

Nahum **Glatzer**, editor

The Passover Haggadah

Illustrated with woodcuts from the first illuminated Haggadah, Prague, 1526

0-8052-0624-8 SCHOCKEN PB $6.95

Herbert **Bronstein**, editor

A Passover Haggadah: The New Union Haggadah

Prepared by the Central Conference of American Rabbis

0-916694-05-4
CENTRAL CONFERENCE OF AMERICAN RABBIS PB ... $13.95

The Schocken Passover Haggadah

0-8052-1067-9 SCHOCKEN PB $11.00

David **Goldstein**, editor

The Ashkenazi Haggadah

The Passover Haggadah has been, for centuries, the inspiration for some of the most beautiful Hebrew illuminated manuscripts, including this splendid one

0-8109-1819-6 ABRAMS $75.00

Raphael **Loewe**, editor

The Rylands Haggadah: Medieval Sephardi Masterpiece in Facsimile

A replication of a 14th-century edition of an original Sephardic Haggadah housed in Manchester, England

0-8109-1568-5 ABRAMS $75.00

Elie **Wiesel**

A Passover Haggadah

Nobel laureate Wiesel and artist Mark Podwal celebrate Israel's liberation from Egypt with these striking new interpretations of the traditional Jewish Passover text, the *Haggadah.* Wiesel's poetic commentaries accompany the original Hebrew text, along with a complete new translation and 40 two-color drawings by Podwal

0-671-73541-1 SIMON & SCHUSTER $30.00
0-671-79996-7 SIMON & SCHUSTER PB $15.00

Women

Susannah **Heschel**, editor

On Being a Jewish Feminist: A Reader

"Superb collection…on the feminist side of Judaism and the woman as outsider"
—Jack Nusan Porter

0-8052-0745-7 SCHOCKEN PB $15.00

Judith **Plaskow**

Standing Again at Sinai: Judaism from a Feminist Perspective

0-06-066684-6 HARPERCOLLINS PB $16.00

Letty Cottin **Pogrebin**

Deborah, Golda, and Me: Being Female and Jewish in America

"Ms. Pogrebin grapples heroically with a difficult and problematic subject: to reconcile feminism and Judaism, and to create a meaningful life that integrates both"—*NY Times Book Review*

0-385-42512-0 ANCHOR PB $14.95

Norman **Tamor**

A Book of Jewish Women's Prayers

1-56821-298-4 ARONSON $30.00

Ellen M. **Umansky** & Diane **Ashton**, editors
Four Centuries of Jewish Women's Spirituality: A Sourcebook
"From 1560 to today, the voices of Jewish women are reflected in never-before-published diary entries, letters, prayers, sermons, and speeches"—Pamela Griner Leavy
0-8070-3613-7 BEACON PB $19.00

Children

Hayim Halevy **Donin**
To Raise a Jewish Child: A Guide for Parents
"The 'Jewish Dr. Spock' offers parents warm, contemporary but traditional advice" —*Baltimore Jewish Times*
0-465-08626-8 BASIC $19.95
0-465-08635-7 BASIC PB $13.00

Rabbi E.B. **Freedman** & others
What Does Being Jewish Mean?: Read-Aloud Responses to Questions Children Ask About History, Culture, and Religion
0-671-76574-4 SIMON & SCHUSTER PB $10.00

Harold S. **Kushner**
When Children Ask About God
By the best selling author of *When Bad Things Happen to Good People*
0-8052-0879-8 SCHOCKEN PB $10.00

David **Wolpe**
Teaching Your Children About God: A Modern Jewish Approach
0-06-097647-0 HARPERPERENNIAL PB $12.00

Marriage and Weddings

Anita **Diamant**
The New Jewish Wedding
An overview of traditional practice and its variations for those who want to fashion their own ceremony
0-671-62882-8 SUMMIT PB $11.00

Self-Help

Harold S. **Kushner**
When Bad Things Happen to Good People
A best-selling guide to crisis management, from a noted rabbi
See also **GENERAL** under **SELF-HELP** in **LIFESTYLES AND PRACTICAL ADVICE**
0-380-60392-6 AVON PB $5.50

Maurice **Lamm**
The Jewish Way in Death and Mourning
Practical and spiritual guidelines
0-8246-0126-2 JONATHAN DAVID PB $14.00

Travel

Noah **Benshea**, editor
The Word: Jewish Wisdom Through Time: A Spiritual Sourcebook
0-679-42584-5 VILLARD $25.00

Ben G. **Frank**
A Travel Guide to Jewish Europe
1-56554-037-9 PELICAN PB $18.95

Stephen W. **Massil**, editor
Jewish Travel Guide 1996
0-85303-318-8 SEPHER-HERMON PB $13.95

Alan M. **Tigay**, editor
The Jewish Traveler: Hadassah Magazine's Guide to the World's Jewish Communities and Sights
A wealth of information on kosher restaurants, places of worship, Jewish community centers, historical sights, and Jewish life
1-56821-078-7 ARONSON PB $30.00

Resources

H.H. **Ben-Sasson**, editor
A History of the Jewish People
Six Hebrew University scholars trace the history of the Jews. "Breaks new ground for a one-volume history, both in its range and in its authority"—*Commentary*
See also **GENERAL HISTORIES** under **JEWISH HISTORY** in **WORLD HISTORY AND CURRENT AFFAIRS**
0-674-39731-2 HARVARD PB $26.50

Dan **Cohn-Sherbok**
Atlas of Jewish History
An exceptional, fascinating guide to the vicissitudes of Jewish history from ancient diasporic times to the present. A partial peek at the contents: "From Herod to Rebellion," "Judaism under Islam in the Middle Ages," "Medieval Jewish Thought," "Eastern European Jewry in the Early Modern Period," "The Holocaust, Israel." Illustrated with over 100 maps
See also **REFERENCE** under **GENERAL HISTORIES** under **JEWISH HISTORY**
0-415-08684-1 ROUTLEDGE $62.95
0-415-08800-3 ROUTLEDGE PB $24.95

Benzion **Netanyahu**
The Origins of the Inquisition in Fifteenth Century Spain
Examines Spanish anti-Semitism from its origins and argues that the brutal anti-converso movement that led to the Inquisition was also responsible for the massacre of the Jews in Spain in 1391 and for their forced conversion to Christianity
See also **SPAIN** under **THE HIGH MIDDLE AGES: EMPIRE AND PAPACY** under **MEDIEVAL AND RENAISSANCE EUROPE** in **WORLD HISTORY AND CURRENT AFFAIRS**
0-679-41065-1 RANDOM HOUSE $60.00

Michael **Strassfeld**
The First Jewish Catalog: A Do-It-Yourself Kit
0-827-60042-9 JEWISH PUB SOCIETY PB $17.95

The Second Jewish Catalog: Sources and Resources
0-8276-0084-4 JEWISH PUB SOCIETY PB $17.95

The Third Jewish Catalog: Creating Community: With a Cumulative Index to All 3 Catalogs
0-827-60083-2 JEWISH PUB SOCIETY PB $17.95

Joseph **Telushkin**
Jewish Literacy: The Most Important Things to Know About the Jewish Religion, Its People and Its History
Concise encyclopedia-formatted reference guide to Jewish history, ritual, and culture. "What a powerful difference it would make if we possessed a source for acquiring the common knowledge which every literate Jew should have. Well, Joseph Telushkin has provided this very thing with his new book, *Jewish Literacy*. It is a dream come true"—Dr. Jack Schechter, Jewish Theological Seminary of America
0-688-08506-7 MORROW $24.95

Jewish Wisdom: Ethical, Spiritual, and Historical Lessons from the Great Works and Thinkers
"No single book can summarize the collective statement of the Jewish people, but Rabbi Telushkin's anthology goes a long way toward collecting the wisest thoughts of a civilization that transcends thousands of years" —Alan M. Dershowitz, Felix Frankfurter Professor of Law, Harvard University
0-688-12958-7 MORROW $25.00

Geoffrey **Wigoder**, editor
The Encyclopedia of Judaism
See also **REFERENCE WORKS** under **WORLD RELIGION**
0-02-628410-3 MACMILLAN $75.00

Christianity

Bibles and Commentary

George **Aichele**, editor
The Postmodern Bible
0-300-06090-4 YALE $35.00

Ward **Allen**, editor
Translating for King James: Notes Made by a Translator of King James's Bible
0-8265-1246-1 VANDERBILT PB $19.95

Ernest Sutherland **Bates**, editor

The Bible

When first published almost half a century ago, this version of the Old and New Testaments caused a sensation. Bates had deleted repetitions, genealogies, legal codes, and reformatted the familiar King James text into a single column. The result was wholly readable and enjoyable. Now, newly updated and compiled according to modern biblical scholarship, this timeless edition is even better

0-671-87959-6 POSEIDON $25.00

Thomas **Brodie**

The Gospel According to John: A Literary and Theological Commentary

0-19-505800-3 OXFORD $59.00

Cambridge University Press

The Holy Bible: King James Version

With presentation page, concordance, eight maps in color, and gazetteer; bound in black imitation leather

0-521-16110-X CAMBRIDGE $46.99

Everett **Fox**, translator

The Five Books of Moses: The Schocken Bible

The books of Moses—Genesis, Exodus, Leviticus, Numbers, and Deuteronomy—newly translated to render the full force of the Bible's original rhetoric and poetry into modern, believable English. "A real breakthrough in the English translation of the Bible...It opens up the biblical text...in new and refreshing ways"—Peter Machinist, Harvard University. "A feast of satisfaction for those of us who always wanted to know what the Hebrew words really said! Anyone who has ever loved the Bible as revelation or poetry, as history or myth, will treasure this book"—Anne Rice

See also **THE BIBLE** under **JUDAISM**

0-8052-4061-6 SCHOCKEN $50.00

George M. **Lamsa**, translator

The Holy Bible: From the Ancient Eastern Text

A translation from the ancient Aramaic text

0-06-064923-2 HARPERCOLLINS PB $32.00

Bruce **Metzger** & Roland E. **Murphy**, editors

The New Oxford Annotated Bible: With the Apocrypha—an Ecumenical Study Bible

The full text of the New Revised Standard Version of the Bible, accompanied by introductions to each book, essays on the forms of biblical literature, detailed annotations and elucidations, supplementary articles on relevant areas such as geography, modern textual scholarship, Hebrew poetry, and 14 full color maps

0-19-528356-2 OXFORD $39.95

Paul R. **Raabe**

Obadiah: A New Translation with Introduction and Commentary

0-385-41268-1 BDD $35.00

Stephen **Mitchell**, translator

Genesis: A New Translation and Interpretation

The companion volume to the PBS series by Bill Moyers, this translation and interpretation of the Book of Genesis comes from the celebrated translator of the *Tao Te Ching* and the *Book of Job*. Placing the great biblical stories in a modern context, this is a rare opportunity to understand both the original intent of this seminal text as well as its modern relevance

0-06-017249-5 HARPERCOLLINS $20.00

Stephen D. **Moore**

Literary Criticism and the Gospels

A comprehensive survey of the new theories of literary criticism as applied to the study of the Gospels. Gives an overview of all the work in the field

0-300-04525-5 YALE $32.50
0-300-04525-5 YALE PB $13.00

The Old Testament: The King James Version

INTRODUCTION BY GEORGE STEINER

0-679-45102-1 KNOPF $35.00

J.B. **Phillips**, translator

The New Testament in Modern English

Effective precisely because of its almost matter-of-fact tone

0-02-596970-6 MACMILLAN $14.95
0-02-088490-7 MACMILLAN PB $10.00

William **Tyndale**, translator

The New Testament

Tyndale completed his translation in 1525. The first vernacular English version of any part of the Bible to be published, it seems the basis for the King James version

See also **PROSE** under **THE 16TH CENTURY** in **LITERATURE OF THE BRITISH ISLES**

EDITED AND INTRODUCED BY DAVID DANIELL

0-300-04419-4 YALE $32.00
0-300-06580-9 YALE PB $15.00

Henry **Wansbrough**, editor

The New Jerusalem Bible

This version is a tribute to the monumental advances made in biblical scholarship since the previous edition in 1966. Translated directly from the original Hebrew, Aramaic, and Greek texts, this Bible represents "The best of the modern translations"—*The Living Church*

0-385-14264-1 DOUBLEDAY $37.50
0-385-24833-4 DOUBLEDAY PB $24.95

The New Testament of the New Jerusalem Bible

A contemporary Catholic translation

0-385-23706-5 IMAGE PB $12.00

Apocrypha and Other Texts

Willis **Barnstone**, editor

The Other Bible

Jewish Pseudepigrapha, Christian Apocrypha, Gnostic scriptures, the Kabbalah, and the Dead Sea Scrolls

0-06-250030-9 HARPERCOLLINS PB $28.00

James H. **Charlesworth**, editor

Old Testament Pseudepigrapha

Jewish and Hellenistic texts that served as sources for or are otherwise related to the canonical Old Testament scriptures

0-385-09630-5 DOUBLEDAY $49.95

Theodor H. **Gaster**, translator

The Dead Sea Scriptures

A selection of the Essene texts and other scriptures that were found in caves near the Dead Sea in 1947 and subsequent years, and that reveal much about sectarian religious life in ancient Judaea

See also **PALESTINE AND THE BIBLE** under **ARCHAEOLOGY** in **WORLD HISTORY AND CURRENT AFFAIRS**

0-385-08859-0 DOUBLEDAY PB $13.95

Marvin **Meyer** & Harold **Bloom**

The Gospel of Thomas: The Hidden Sayings of Jesus

Discovered in 1945, the Thomas gospel is thought by many scholars to contain authentic sayings of Jesus not found in the four canonical gospels, as well as somewhat different versions of established sayings. Devoid of narrative framework and clearly influenced by Gnosticism, the proverbs and aphorisms have a paradoxical, Zen-like quality. Bloom, America's preeminent literary critic, adds commentary to Meyer's masterly rendering. "Tells us more about the historical Jesus than all the Dead Sea Scrolls put together"—John Dominic Crossan

0-06-065581-X HARPERCOLLINS $17.00

David **Rosenberg**

The Lost Book of Paradise: Adam and Eve in the Garden of Eden

The co-author of the controversial *Book of J* employs his formidable scholarship to "reimagine" a lost epic poem in which Adam was seduced not by Eve but by a female snake named Lilith. The result is a story of equality between the sexes and sensitivity to and connection with the Earth and humanity. An exciting challenge to our assumptions about the book of creation. "Breathtaking...This is a major work"—Grace Schulman, *The Nation*

0-7868-8073-2 HYPERION PB $12.95

David Rosenberg (photo by Layle Silbert)

Classics

The following are of historical interest as founding texts that have influenced several generations of anthropologists.

George **Appleton**, editor
The Oxford Book of Prayer
See also **PRAYER AND CONTEMPLATION** under **PRACTISE OF FAITH**
0-19-213222-9 OXFORD $29.95

Saint Thomas Aquinas
Summa Theologiae: A Concise Translation
EDITED BY TIMOTHY MCDERMOTT
0-87061-210-7 CHRISTIAN CLASSICS PB $29.95

Saint Francis De Sales
Introduction to the Devout Life
"One of the great religious and devotional masterpieces of all time"
—*The Journal of Religious Thought*
See also **PRAYER AND CONTEMPLATION** under **PRACTISE OF FAITH**
TRANSLATED BY JOHN K. RYAN
0-385-03009-6 DOUBLEDAY PB $11.95

The greatness of this work is shown in what may be called the symmetry of the Saint's thought. Throughout the work delicate balance and just proportions are preserved. Saint Francis avoids the extremes that lead to danger or are themselves dangerous. —From the translator's preface, **INTRODUCTION TO THE DEVOUT LIFE**

Saint Augustine
The City of God
See also **LATE WRITERS** under **LATIN LITERATURE** in **LITERATURE OF EUROPE, AFRICA, AND ASIA**
TRANSLATED BY HENRY BETTENSON
0-14-044426-2 PENGUIN PB $15.95

The City of God
The first Christian philosophy of history. A monumental response to pagan interpretations of the decline of Rome
TRANSLATED BY MARCUS DODS
0-679-60087-6 MODERN LIBRARY $20.00

The Confessions
Augustine's classic spiritual autobiography, tracing his passage from boyhood sin through Manichaeanism to Christian conversion
See also **ELAINE PAGLES'S PICKS** under **COMPARATIVE RELIGION** under **WORLD RELIGION**
TRANSLATED BY R.S. PINE-COFFIN
0-14-044114-X PENGUIN PB $8.95

The Trinity
See also **AUGUSTINE** under **PHILOSOPHY**
0-911782-96-6 NEWCI PB $24.95

Saint Francis of Assisi
The Little Flowers of St. Francis
A compilation of anecdotes (some apocryphal) that convey the joyful faith of the medieval saint
TRANSLATED BY RAPHAEL BROWN
0-385-07544-8 DOUBLEDAY PB $7.95

John **Bunyan**
The Pilgrim's Progress
After the Bible the most-read book in the history of English literature
See also **PROSE** under **THE EARLY 17TH CENTURY** in **LITERATURE OF THE BRITISH ISLES**
EDITED BY ROGER SHATTUCK
0-14-043004-0 PENGUIN PB $7.95

Century **Hutchinson**, editor
The Book of Common Prayer
The essential prayer book for millions of Christians, *The Book of Common Prayer* contains morning and evening prayers, litanies, Thanksgivings, the Eucharist, Collects, Baptisms, and various special prayers. Includes 185 color medieval illuminated manuscript reproductions from museums and libraries worldwide. Full-cloth binding with colored endpapers, head and tail bands, and silk ribbon marker
0-8050-2284-8 HOLT $27.95

Oxford University Press
The Book of Common Prayer & Administration of the Sacraments: According to the Use of the Church of England
The liturgy of the Anglican communion, originally adopted in 1549
See also **PROTESTANT** under **HISTORY**
0-19-130601-0 OXFORD $19.95

Thomas à **Kempis**
The Imitation of Christ
After the Bible, this 15th-century devotional work, distinguished by its simplicity and spiritual purity, is probably the most influential Christian book ever written
TRANSLATED BY LEO SHERLEY-PRICE
0-14-044027-5 PENGUIN PB $9.95

Søren **Kierkegaard**
Attack Upon "Christendom"
Kiekegaard's polemic against the conventional, repectable Christianity of the churches
TRANSLATED BY WALTER LOWRIE
INTRODUCTION BY H.A. JOHNSON
0-691-01950-9 PRINCETON PB $13.95

Fear and Trembling
A meditation on the biblical sacrifice of Isaac and on the difficult Christianity of the "Knight of Faith"
See also **CLASSICS OF WESTERN RELIGIOUS THOUGHT** under **WORLD RELIGION**
TRANSLATED BY ALASTAIR HANNAY
0-14-044449-1 PENGUIN PB $9.95

A Kierkegaard Anthology
These writings by the founder of existentialist religious thought emphasize the risk and irrationality of faith.
EDITED BY ROBERT BRETALL
0-691-01978-9 PRINCETON PB $16.95

The Sickness Unto Death
Kierkegaard's most famous work is subtitled "A Christian Psychological Exposition for Upbuilding and Awakening"
See also **KIERKEGAARD** under **PHILOSOPHY**
TRANSLATED BY HOWARD V. HONG & EDNA H. HONG
0-691-02028-0 PRINCETON PB $13.95

C. S. **Lewis**
The Essential C. S. Lewis
EDITED BY LYLE W. DORSETT
0-684-82374-8 TOUCHSTONE PB $14.00

C.S. Lewis

Mere Christianity: Comprising the Case for Christianity, Christian Behaviour, and Beyond
One of Lewis' most popular books, originally broadcast as informal radio "talks" and later published as three separate books
See also **WESTERN** under **20TH-CENTURY SPIRITUAL LEADERS** under **SPIRITUALITY**
0-684-82378-0 TOUCHSTONE PB $6.00

The Problem of Pain
"A theologian for everyman"—Anthony Burgess
0-02-086850-2 MACMILLAN PB $4.95

The Screwtape Letters
A classic satiric work consisting of a series of letters from Screwtape, an elderly devil, advising his nephew Wormwood, an apprentice devil, how to corrupt his earthly "patient"
INTRODUCTION BY RICHARD GILMAN
0-451-62821-7 MENTOR PB $4.99

Surprised by Joy: The Shape of My Early Life
Lewis' spiritual journey from Christianity to atheism and back again to Christianity. "Anyone approaching this book as a study in the psychology of conversion will find the greatest interest in the dual paths—intellectual and intuitive—which converged at last"
—*Saturday Review*
0-15-100185-5 HARCOURT BRACE $16.00
0-15-687011-8 HARCOURT BRACE PB $9.00

Thomas **Merton**
The Seven Storey Mountain
The autobiography of the influential American Catholic poet, scholar, and monk
0-15-680679-7 HARCOURT BRACE PB $12.00

John Henry **Newman**
Apologia Pro Vita Sua
A humane and intellectually incisive testament to Newman's fervent yet independent-minded Catholic faith
See also **19TH-CENTURY PROSE** under **THE 19TH CENTURY** in **LITERATURE OF THE BRITISH ISLES**
EDITED BY DAVID DELAURA
0-393-09766-8 NORTON PB $14.95

John Henry **Newman**

Apologia Pro Vita Sua

0-460-87232-X EVERYMAN'S PB $10.95
0-14-043374-0 PENGUIN PB $12.95

An Essay in Aid of a Grammar of Assent

A theological classic on the nature of faith and knowledge
INTRODUCTION BY NICHOLAS LASH
0-268-01000-5 NOTRE DAME PB $16.50

An Essay on the Development of Christian Doctrine

0-268-00921-X NOTRE DAME PB $14.95

Parochial and Plain Sermons

0-89870-136-8 IGNATIUS $49.00

Bertrand **Russell**

Why I Am Not a Christian & Other Essays on Religion and Related Subjects

Essays 1899-1954, all centering on one deeply held belief: "I am as firmly convinced that religions do harm as I am that they are untrue"—Bertrand Russell
See also **SKEPTICISM AND ATHEISM** under **WORLD RELIGION**
0-671-20323-1 SIMON & SCHUSTER PB $12.00

Blaise **Pascal**

Pensées and Other Writings

See also **THE AGE OF CLASSICISM** under **FRENCH LITERATURE TO 1900**
TRANSLATED BY HONOR LEVI
0-19-282990-4 OXFORD PB $8.95

Blaise Pascal

Friedrich **Schleiermacher**

On Religion: Speeches to Its Cultured Despisers

One of the most important works of Protestant theology; an attempt to reconcile Christianity and Romanticism by finding the essence of religion in the suggestions of infinity that permeate everyday existence
INTRODUCTION BY RUDOLPH OTTO
0-521-35789-6 CAMBRIDGE PB $20.95

On Religion: Speeches to Its Cultured Despisers

0-521-47975-4 CAMBRIDGE PB $18.95

Leo **Tolstoy**

The Kingdom of God Is Within You

Tolstoy's plea for Christian anarchism, and a scathing attack on the state and militarism
TRANSLATED BY CONSTANCE GARNETT
FOREWORD BY MARTIN GREEN
0-8032-9404-2 NEBRASKA PB $12.00

Simone **Weil**

Waiting For God

Searching spiritual autobiography by a brilliant and austere writer of Jewish origins who was drawn to an existentialist Christianity influenced by Pascal, Kierkegaard, and her own mystical experience
See also **CLASSICS OF WESTERN RELIGIOUS THOUGHT** under **WORLD RELIGION**
TRANSLATED BY EMMA CRAUFURD
0-06-090295-7 HARPERPERENNIAL PB $12.00

Simon Weil

Early Christian Writings

Henry **Bettenson**, translator

The Early Christian Fathers: A Selection from the Writings of the Fathers from St. Clement of Rome to St. Athanasius

0-19-283009-0 OXFORD PB $16.95

Boethius

The Consolation of Philosophy

The Roman adviser to the Gothic king Theodoric wrote this amalgamation of Roman and Christian wisdom while awaiting execution
See also **BOETHIUS** under **OTHER MEDIEVAL PHILOSOPHERS** under **PHILOSOPHY**
TRANSLATED BY V.E. WATTS
0-14-044208-1 PENGUIN PB $10.95

Wayne A. **Meeks**, editor

Writings of St. Paul

0-393-09979-2 NORTON PB $12.95

Maxwell **Staniforth**, translator

Early Christian Writings: The Apostolic Fathers

A selection of doctrinal and controversial works by the earliest Christian theologians
0-14-044475-0 PENGUIN PB $9.95

Saint John of the Cross

The Collected Works of St. John of the Cross

Explores the sensuality of the soul. These are love songs to God
EDITED BY KICRAN KAVANAUGH
TRANSLATED BY OTILIO RODRIQUEZ
0-935216-15-4 ICSPB PB $17.95

The Dark Night of the Soul and the Living Flame of Love: St. John of the Cross

One of the greatest works of mystical literature, by the 16th-century Spanish monk and poet
EDITED BY ROBERT VAN DE WEYER
0-00-627934-1 HARPERCOLLINS PB $11.00

Thomas **Merton**

The Wisdom of the Desert

See also **ELAINE PAGLES'S PICKS** under **COMPARATIVE RELIGION** under **WORLD RELIGION**
0-8112-0102-3 NEW DIRECTIONS PB $6.95

Helen **Waddell**

The Desert Fathers

Translation of an ancient collection of anecdotes about the radical desert hermits of Egypt
See also **ELAINE PAGLES'S PICKS** under **COMPARATIVE RELIGION** under **WORLD RELIGION**
0-472-06008-2 MICHIGAN PB $16.95

Christian Mysticism

Meister **Eckhart**

Meister Eckhart: A Modern Translation

See also **RELIGIOUS HISTORY** under **MEDIEVAL AND RENAISSANCE EUROPE** in **WORLD HISTORY AND CURRENT AFFAIRS**
TRANSLATED BY R.F. BLAKENEY
0-06-130008-X HARPERCOLLINS PB $14.00

There is the soul's day and God's day. A day, whether six or seven ago, or more than six thousand years ago, is just as near to the present as yesterday. Why? Because all time is contained in the present Now-moment. Time comes of the revolution of the heavens and day began with the first revolution. The soul's day falls within this time and consists of the natural light in which things are seen. God's day, however, is the complete day, comprising both day and night. It is the real Now-moment, which for the soul is eternity's day, on which the Father begets his only begotten Son and the soul is reborn in God. Whenever this birth occurs, it is the soul giving birth to the only begotten Son.
MEISTER ECKHART: A MODERN TRANSLATION

Meister Eckhart from Whom God Hid Nothing: Sermons, Writings, and Sayings

EDITED BY DAVID O'NEIL
1-57062-139-X SHAMBHALA PB $11.00

Carol Lee **Flinders**

Enduring Grace: Living Portraits of Seven Women Mystics

See also **WOMEN** under **GENERAL TOPICS**
0-06-062645-3 HARPERCOLLINS PB $15.00

Monica **Furlong**, editor

Visions & Longings: Medieval Women Mystics

1-57062-125-X SHAMBHALA $20.00

David **Hazard**

You Set My Spirit Free: A 40-Day Journey in the Company of John of the Cross

1-55661-481-0 BETHANY PB $8.99

Hildegard of Bingen

Book of Divine Works with Letters and Sayings

In the last volume of her trilogy, *Liber divinorum operum,* written between 1163 and 1173, Hildegard addresses the concept of creation and the Creator God

EDITED BY MATTHEW FOX

0-939680-35-1 BEAR PB $16.00

Hildegard of Bingen: Scivias

0-8091-3130-7 PAULIST PB $22.95

The Illuminations

At the age of 42, Hildegard of Bingen began to experience her famous visions, which she recorded in the form of paintings known as "illuminations." Twenty-four of these works are recorded here, with commentary by Matthew Fox. Hildegard's own text describing the visions appears in her book *Scivias*

0-939680-21-1 BEAR PB $18.95

Symphonia

The *Symphonia celestium revelationum* (or Symphony of the Harmony of the Celestial Revelations) is a collection of words to accompany Hildegard's 77 musical compositions. One of the few female composers on record, she viewed music as the truest metaphor for the human relationship with God, explaining, "The word stands for the body, but the symphony stands for the spirit"

INTRODUCTION, TRANSLATION, AND COMMENTARY BY BARBARA NEWMAN

0-8014-9514-8 CORNELL PB $13.95

Sabina **Flanagan**

Hildegard of Bingen, 1098-1179: A Visionary Life

The first full-scale biography of a remarkable medieval visionary, healer, and poet

0-415-05793-0 ROUTLEDGE PB $15.95

Barbara **Lachman**

The Journal of Hildegard of Bingen

The imagined diary is drawn from the prolific scientific, autobiographical, and visionary writings of this remarkable médieval abbess and mystic. It is both a vivid evocation of the medieval mind and a literary tour de force. "A delightful fictional memoir" —*Publishers Weekly*

0-517-59169-3 CROWN $20.00

Andrew **Louth**

The Origins of the Christian Mystical Tradition

0-19-826668-5 OXFORD PB $21.00

Thomas **Merton**

Ways of the Christian Mystics

Part of the Shambhala Pocket Classics series

See also **WESTERN** under **20TH-CENTURY SPIRITUAL LEADERS** under **SPIRITUALITY**

1-57062-030-X SHAMBHALA PB $6.00

Walter **Hilton**

The Ladder of Perfection

Hilton remains the most accessible of the 14th-century mystics; this book of advice to a female hermit is his best-known work

See also **PROSE** under **MEDIEVAL LITERATURE** in **LITERATURE OF THE BRITISH ISLES**

0-14-044511-0 PENGUIN PB $6.95

Julian of Norwich

Revelations of Divine Love

Perhaps the best-known of medieval mystical meditations. It includes the phrase made famous by T.S. Eliot's *Four Quartets:* "All shall be well and all shall be well and all manner of thing shall be well"

TRANSLATED BY CLIFTON WOLTERS

0-14-044177-8 PENGUIN PB $9.95

Rudolf **Otto**

The Idea of the Holy

First published in Germany in 1917, this influential work set the agenda for much of 20th-century theology by attempting to isolate an irreducible, nonrational sense of mystery in religious experience

See also **CLASSICS OF WESTERN RELIGIOUS THOUGHT** under **WORLD RELIGION**

TRANSLATED BY JOHN W. HARVEY

0-19-500210-5 OXFORD PB $10.95

Elizabeth Alvida **Petroff**

Body and Soul: Essays on Medieval Women and Mysticism

0-19-508454-3 OXFORD $38.00

0-19-508455-1 OXFORD PB $14.95

Teresa of Avila

The Life of Teresa of Jesus: The Autobiography of Teresa of Avila

The life story of the 16th-century mystic. Beloved for the last 400 years for her spiritually infused literary works, hers is one of the rare female voices to have survived from the pre-modern era

See also **SAINTS** under **BIOGRAPHIES**

TRANSLATED AND EDITED BY E. ALLISON PEERS

INTRODUCTION BY BENEDICTA WARD

0-385-01109-1 DOUBLEDAY PB $12.95

Robert Van De **Weyer**, editor

The Interior Castle: Teresa of Avila

0-00-627935-X HARPERCOLLINS PB $10.00

Clifton **Wolters**, editor

The Cloud of Unknowing & Other Works

A classic mystical work, written anonymously in England in the 14th century

0-14-044385-1 PENGUIN PB $10.95

History

Surveys

Paul **Carus**

The History of the Devil and the Idea of Evil

0-517-15064-6 GRAMERCY $12.99

David **Christie-Murray**

A History of Heresy

0-19-285210-8 OXFORD PB $12.95

W.H. **Frend**

The Rise of Christianity

A monumental, richly detailed history of the first 600 years or Christianity, from its Jewish origins to the formation of the medieval church, with special attention to heresy, schisms, theology, and social and political background. Illustrated

0-8006-1931-5 FORTRESS PB $30.00

Paul **Johnson**

A History of Christianity

A clear, vigorous survey by an English Catholic journalist and scholar. "The best one-volume history of Christianity ever done" —*Christian Century*

0-689-70591-3 ATHENEUM PB $17.95

Kenneth S. **Latourette**

A History of Christianity

A superb scholarly work that pays ampleattention to the Eastern church

Volume 1 Beginning to 1500

0-06-064952-6 HARPERCOLLINS PB $23.00

Volume 2 Reformation to the Present

0-06-064953-4 HARPERCOLLINS PB $28.35

John **McManus**, editor

The Oxford History of Christianity

An excellent one-volume history, also available as *The Oxford Illustrated History of Christianity*

0-19-285291-4 OXFORD PB $16.95

Gerald **Messadié**

A History of the Devil

1-56836-081-9 KODANSHA $27.00

Alice K. **Turner**

The History of Hell

Hell has always inspired artists more than its pastoral, conflict-free counterpart upstairs. Turner guides us through the doctrines and depictions, from *Gilgamesh* to Beckett, Homer to Freud. With 32 pages of full-color reproductions, and 30 black-and-white illustrations

0-15-140934-X HARCOURT BRACE $29.95

Williston **Walker**

A History of the Christian Church

A classic textbook, recently revised, with a clear, concise presentation of historical and theological developments

0-02-423870-8 SCRIBNERS $74.00

Orthodox

Sebastian **Brock**

Syriac Father on Prayer and the Spritual Life

0-87907-901-1 CISTERCIAN PUBNS..........$19.95

G.K. **Chesterton** & Fred **Williams**

Orthodoxy

Written in 1908

0-89870-552-5 IGNATIUS PB..........$9.95

People have fallen into a foolish habit of speaking of orthodoxy as something heavy, humdrum and safe. There was never anything so perilous or so exciting ... It was sanity: and to be sane is more dramatic than to be mad.

ORTHODOXY

J.M. **Hussey**

The Orthodox Church in the Byzantine Empire

0-19826-456-9 CLARENDON PRESS..........$22.95

Andrew **Louth**

Maximus The Confessor (Early Church Fathers)

0-41511-846-8 ROUTLEDGE..........$16.95

John **Meyendorff**

Imperial Unity and Christian Divisions: The Church, 450-680AD

0-88141-055-1 ST. VLADIMIRS SEMINARY PRESS..$16.95

Jaroslav **Pelikan**

Imago Dei: The Byzantine Apologia for Icons

The renowned historian of theology recounts one of the most striking episodes in the history of Christianity: the Byzantine Iconoclast rejection of sacred images, and their eventual restoration

0-691-09970-7 PRINCETON..........$49.50

Timothy **Ware**

The Orthodox Church

A history covering the last 2000 years, and a survey of the doctrines and rituals of contemporary Orthodoxy

0-14-014656-3 PENGUIN PB..........$12.95

Roman Catholic

Thomas **Bokenkotter**

A Concise History of the Catholic Church

A lucid, balanced account by a Catholic scholar of the institutional and doctrinal evolution of the Church and the controversies that accompanied it. Especially good in clarifying the divisions over such issues as conciliar reform, Jansenism, liberalism and modernism

0-385-13015-5 IMAGE PB..........$11.00

Essential Catholicism: Dynamics of Faith and Belief

0-385-23243-8 IMAGE PB..........$14.00

Jay P. **Dolan**

The American Catholic Experience: A History from Colonial Times to the Present

How Catholicism spread across the New World and how it deals with pressing social issues of today

0-268-00639-3 NOTRE DAME PB..........$18.50

Dinesh **D'Souza**

Catholic Classics

0-87973-545-7 OURSN PB..........$6.95

The Catholic Classics II

0-87973-423-X OURSN PB..........$6.95

Jean **Lacouture**

Jesuits: A Multibiography

TRANSLATED BY JEREMY LEGGATT

1-88717-805-8 COUNTERPOINT..........$29.50

John W. **O'Malley**

The First Jesuits

Follows the society from 1540 to 1565 as it takes shape according to Loyola's vision and in response to the church heirarchy, the needs of the lay community, and the strong personalities of its founders

0-674-30312-1 HARVARD..........$37.50

0-674-30313-X HARVARD PB..........$16.95

Liguori Editorial Staff, editor

Catechism of the Catholic Church

0-89243-565-8 LIGUO..........$19.95

0-89243-566-6 LIGUO PB..........$9.95

Richard P. **McBrien**

Catholicism: New Study

0-06-065405-8 HARPERCOLLINS PB..........$36.00

John **McQuiston II**

Always We Begin Again: The Benedictine Way of Living

0-8192-1648-8 MOREHOUSE PB..........$7.95

Timothy E. **O'Connell**

Principles for a Catholic Morality

0-06-254865-4 HARPERCOLLINS PB..........$22.95

Paul **Wilkes**

The Good Enough Catholic: A Guide for the Perplexed

0-345-39543-3 BALLANTINE..........$25.00

Kenneth L. **Woodward**

Making Saints: How the Catholic Church Determines Who Becomes a Saint, Who Doesn't and Why

0-684-81530-3 TOUCHSTONE PB..........$14.00

Protestant

John **Dillenberger** & Claude **Welch**

Protestant Christianity

A history with an emphasis on doctrine

0-02-329601-1 MACMILLAN PB..........$37.00

Stephen **Neill**

Anglicanism

0-19-520033-0 OXFORD PB..........$24.95

Oxford University Press

The Book of Common Prayer & Administration of the Sacraments: According to the Use of the Church of England

The liturgy of the Anglican communion, originally adopted in 1549

See also **CLASSICS**

0-19-130601-0 OXFORD..........$19.95

Steven **Ozment**

Protestants: The Birth of a Revolution

In a closely reasoned and convincing social history, Ozment, a distinguished scholar, shows that the Protestant Reformation, in attacking ritual and ceremony, supported individualism. In addition, through diaries and letters, Ozment offers insight into the emotional makeup of the first Protestants. "To read Steven Ozment is to believe that history is a living art"
—Richard Marius, Harvard University

See also **REFORMATION AND COUNTER-REFORMATION** under **EARLY MODERN EUROPE** in **WORLD HISTORY AND CURRENT AFFAIRS**

0-385-47101-7 DOUBLEDAY PB..........$12.95

Histories of the Bible

F.F. **Bruce**

The History of the Bible in English

0-19-520088-8 OXFORD PB..........$12.95

Cambridge University Press

The Cambridge History of the Bible

A three-volume set of which the third is out of print

Volume 1
From the Beginnings to Jerome

0-521-09973-0 CAMBRIDGE PB..........$54.95

Volume 2
The West from the Fathers to the Reformation

0-521-29017-1 CAMBRIDGE PB..........$49.95

Beginnings and Early History

Thomas **Cahill**

How the Irish Saved Civilization: The Untold Story of Ireland's Heroic Role from the Fall of Rome to the Rise of Medieval Europe

See also **CULTURE** under **THE EARLY MIDDLE AGES** under **MEDIEVAL AND RENAISSANCE EUROPE** in **WORLD HISTORY AND CURRENT AFFAIRS**

0-385-41849-3 ANCHOR PB..........$12.95

Peter **Brown**

The Cult of the Saints: Its Rise and Function in Latin Christianity

The saints succeed the ancient heroes

0-226-07622-9 CHICAGO PB $9.95

Saint Jerome

E.R. **Dodds**

Pagan and Christian in an Age of Anxiety: Some Aspects of Religious Experience from Marcus Aurelius to Constantine

See also **RELIGION** under **TOPICS IN ROMAN HISTORY** under **ANCIENT ROME**

0-521-38599-7 CAMBRIDGE $18.95
0-393-00545-3 CAMBRIDGE PB $5.95

Eusebius

The History of the Church from Christ to Constantine

The first chronicle of the Christian church, written in the early 4th century by the bishop of Palestine, and concentrating on the Eastern church and the defeat of heresy

TRANSLATED BY G.A. WILLIAMSON

0-14-044138-7 PENGUIN PB $10.95

Elisabeth **Fiorenza**, editor

In Memory of Her: A Feminist Theological Reconstruction of Christian Origins

A highly provocative and influential work that is transforming feminist thinking about the Bible

See also **WOMEN AND RELIGION** under **WORLD RELIGION**

0-8245-1357-6 CROSSROAD PB $17.95

Susan **Haskins**

Mary Magdalen: Myth and Metaphor

"A bold revisionist study…Whether writing about medeival relics, renaissance painting, or Victorian pornography, [Haskins] succeeds in demonstrating how her subject served as a canvas onto which each era projected its fears and fantasies about women's sexuality" —*Washington Post Book World*

1-57322-509-6 RIVERHEAD PB $16.00

Gerhart B. **Ladner**

God, Cosmos, and Humankind: The World of Early Christian Symbolism

0-520-08549-3 CALIFORNIA $45.00

Hyam **Maccoby**

The Mythmaker: Paul and the Invention of Christianity

A provocative work arguing that Jesus remained a faithful Jew and that Christianity was created by Paul, who synthesized it out of Gnosticism and Hellenistic mystery cults, in the process giving it an anti-Semitic taint

0-06-250585-8 HARPERCOLLINS PB $12.00

Burton L. **Mack**

The Lost Gospel: The Book of Q and Christian Origins

"A powerful and persuasive analysis emphasizing this lost gospel's role in both the church politics of the first century and the scholarly politics of the twentieth"—John Dominic Crossan

0-06-065375-2 HARPERCOLLINS PB $14.00

Who Wrote the New Testament? The Making of the Christian Myth

"A powerful, compact, yet detailed introduction to the New Testament and the origins of Christianity. Mack has sketched the panorama of early Christian literature and social development …a lucid, convincing and magisterial performance"—Robert W. Funk

0-06-065517-8 HARPERCOLLINS $24.00
0-06-065518-6 HARPERCOLLINS PB $15.00

Bernard **McGinn**

Antichrist: Two Thousand Years of the Human Fascination with Evil

The Antichrist as an essential figure of Christian faith from the early Christian communities to the apocalyptic visions of contemporary fundamentalists. A richly detailed illustrated history of "Christ's alter ego"

See also **THE OCCULT, WITCHCRAFT, AND THE DEVIL** under **WORLD RELIGION**

0-06-065543-7 HARPERCOLLINS $32.50
0-06-065282-9 HARPERCOLLINS PB $15.00

Wayne A. **Meeks**

The First Urban Christians: The Social World of the Apostle Paul

Who were the Christians to whom Paul preached? What were their class, ethnic, and family backgrounds, their neighborhoods, daily life, and view of the world? Meeks offers answers to these questions

0-300-03244-7 YALE PB $16.00

Elaine **Pagels**

Adam, Eve, and the Serpent

The evolution of Christian thought—from an early emphasis on freedom to the asceticism and determinism that prevailed through the writings of Augustine—as reflected in orthodox and Gnostic interpretations of the story of Adam and Eve

See also **AUGUSTINE** under **PHILOSOPHY**

0-679-72232-7 RANDOM HOUSE PB $10.00

In a world in which Christians not only were free to follow their faith but were officially encouraged to do so, Augustine came to read the story of Adam and Eve very differently than had the majority of his Jewish and Christian predecessors. What they had read for centuries as a story of human freedom became, in his hands, a story of human bondage. Most Jews and Christians had agreed that God gave humankind in creation the gift of moral freedom, and that Adam's misuse of it brought death upon his progeny. But Augustine went further: Adam's sin not only caused our mortality but cost us our moral freedom, irreversibly corrupted our experience of sexuality (which Augustine tended to identify with original sin), and made us incapable of genuine political freedom.

ADAM, EVE, AND THE SERPENT

The Origin of Satan

Tracing the Devil from the Old to the New Testament, Pagels confronts an issue long ignored by modern theologians—the Church's demonization of Jews, pagans, and dissenting Christians (heretics)—and identifies this as one of the most disturbing and enduring aspects of Western civilization

See also **COMPARATIVE RELIGION** under **WORLD RELIGION**

0-679-40140-7 RANDOM HOUSE $23.00
0-679-73118-0 VINTAGE PB $12.00

E.P. **Sanders**

Paul and Palestinian Judaism: A Comparison of Patterns of Religion

Paul's ideas in the context of the contemporary Judaism he renounced

0-8006-1899-8 FORTRESS PB $28.00

Rodney **Stark**

The Rise of Christianity: A Sociologist Reconsiders History

"A marvelous exercise in sociological imagination"—Andrew M. Greeley

See also **RELIGION** under **TOPICS IN ROMAN HISTORY** under **ANCIENT ROME** in **WORLD HISTORY AND CURRENT AFFAIRS**

0-691-02749-8 PRINCETON $24.95

Gnosticism

Gnosticism, which teaches the cosmic redemption of the spirit through knowledge, and posits a radical separation between spirit and matter, has received much attention since the discovery of the Nag Hammadi scrolls in Egypt in 1945.

Charles W. **Hedrick**, Sr. & Robert **Hodgson**, Jr.

Nag Hammadi, Gnosticism, and Early Christianity

Emphasizes the significance of these texts

0-913573-16-7 HENDRICKSON PB $14.95

Hans **Jonas**

The Gnostic Religion

The classic early study of the Gnostic religion written from an existentialist viewpoint before the discovery of a major library of Gnostic sources at Nag Hammadi

0-8446-2339-3 SMITH $27.75
0-8070-5799-1 BEACON PB $17.00

Bentley **Layton**

The Gnostic Scriptures

A recent translation of many major Gnostic sources, well-annotated with good historical commentary

0-385-17447-0 DOUBLEDAY $35.00
0-385-47843-7 BANTAM PB $22.00

Elaine **Pagels**

The Gnostic Gospels

The historical and theological implications of an ancient library of Gnostic texts, including Gospels attributing the esoteric, paradoxical teachings of the Gnostics to Jesus

0-394-74043-2 VINTAGE PB $9.00

The Gnostic Paul: Gnostic Exegesis of the Pauline Letters

1-56338-039-0 TRINITY PB $14.95

Kurt **Rudolph**

Gnosis: The Nature and History of Gnosticism

An authoritative study of the doctrines and rites of Gnostic sects and their enduring influence on Christianity

0-06-067018-5 HARPERCOLLINS PB $22.00

Middle Ages and Renaissance

John **Boswell**

Same-Sex Unions in Premodern Europe

This scholarly work examines homosexual relations in the Eastern Orthodox and Catholic churches during the Middle Ages

See also **HISTORY** under **GAY, LESBIAN, AND BISEXUAL STUDIES** in **SOCIAL STUDIES**

0-679-75164-5 VINTAGE PB $13.00

Malcolm **Lambert**

Medieval Heresy: Popular Movements from the Georgian Reform to the Reformation

A subtle, thorough account of late medieval heresies that does justice to both the theological and the historical background

See also **RELIGIOUS HISTORY** under **MEDIEVAL AND RENAISSANCE EUROPE** in **WORLD HISTORY AND CURRENT AFFAIRS**

0-631-17432-X BLACKWELL PB $23.95

Steven **Runciman**

The Medieval Manichee: A Study of the Christian Dualist Heresy

Messalians, Borborites, Paulicans, Bogomils, Patarenes, Cathars—the strange and often compelling heretical sects which believed that the world is the creation of a demon, in a succinct and learned account by a distinguished British historian

0-521-28926-2 CAMBRIDGE PB $19.95

Leo **Steinberg**

The Sexuality of Christ in Renaissance Art and in Modern Oblivion

Steinberg argues that there was a theological significance to Renaissance depictions of Jesus' phallus, erect and otherwise, that modern scholarship has repressed

See also **THE RISE OF ITALIAN PAINTING** under **MEDIEVAL ART: 600-1400** under **EUROPEAN ART: BYZANTINE AND MEDIEVAL** in **ART**

0-226-77186-5 CHICAGO $85.00
0-226-77187-3 CHICAGO PB $29.95

Reformation

Roland H. **Bainton**

The Reformation of the Sixteenth Century

A lucid account of the various Protestant Reformers and their churches, with an emphasis on doctrine and ideas

INTRODUCTION BY JAROSLAV PELIKAN

0-8070-1301-3 FS&G PB $15.95

Peter **Blickle**

Communal Reformation: The Quest for Salvation in Sixteenth-Century Germany

TRANSLATED BY THOMAS DUNLAP

0-391-03730-7 HUMANITIES $49.95

Owen **Chadwick**

The Reformation

Part of the Pelican History of the Church series

See also **REFORMATION AND COUNTER-REFORMATION** under **EARLY MODERN EUROPE** in **WORLD HISTORY AND CURRENT AFFAIRS**

0-14-013757-2 VIKING PB $12.00

C. Scott **Dixon**

The Reformation and Rural Society: The Parishes of Brandenburg-Ansbach-Kulmbach, 1528-1603

0-521-48311-5 CAMBRIDGE $49.95

Hans **Hillerbrand**, editor

The Protestant Reformation

Excerpts from Luther, Calvin, and Zwingli, plus additional documents tracing the Reformation through the Anabaptists and developments in England

0-06-131342-4 HARPERCOLLINS PB $14.50

The Oxford Encyclopedia of the Reformation

0-19-506493-3 OXFORD $450.00

Steven **Ozment**

The Age of Reform, 1250-1550: An Intellectual and Religious History of Late Medieval and Reformation Europe

0-300-02760-5 YALE PB $19.00

Jaroslav **Pelikan** & others

The Reformation of the Bible: The Bible of the Reformation

The book serves as the catalog for a major exhibition of early Bibles and Reformation texts

0-941881-18-0 YALE PB $10.00

Donald J. **Wilcox**

In Search of God and Self: Renaissance and Reformation Thought

0-88133-276-3 WAVELAND PB $16.95

George H. **Williams**

The Radical Reformation

A detailed history of the Anabaptists andother radical sects that emerged from the Reformation

0-940474-15-8 16TH CENTURY JOURNAL $125.00

Third World

Stephen **Neill**

A History of Christian Missions

The best general account of Christian missionary efforts

0-14-022736-9 PENGUIN PB $7.95

North America

Laurence **Moore**

Selling God: American Religion in the Marketplace of Culture

A wide-ranging history of the marketing of religion in American life, from early use of advertising techniques to Scientology, evangelical publishing, and millennial merchandise

0-19-509838-2 OXFORD PB $12.95

Reynolds **Price**

Three Gospels

A leading American novelist's version of Jesus' life, based on Mark, John, and his own imaginative reconstruction

0-7838-1854-8 GK HALL $22.95

Biographies

Jack **Miles**

God: A Biography

In this slightly mischievous book, Miles reads the Old Testament, book by book, as if they formed a novel with God as the main character

See also **THE BIBLE** under **JUDAISM**

0-679-41833-4 KNOPF $27.50
0-679-74368-5 VINTAGE PB $15.00

The Life of Jesus

John Dominic **Crossan**

The Essential Jesus: Original Sayings and Earliest Images

Crossan, professor of biblical studies and an authority on Jesus, paints a concise and controversial picture of Jesus as he was before the Gospels and before 2000 years of Church history. This fresh translation of Jesus' earliest sayings shows not a god, but a revolutionary healer and leader

0-06-251045-2 HARPERCOLLINS PB $12.00

The Historical Jesus: The Life of a Mediterranean Jewish Peasant

A seminal work—Crossan examines Jesus the man, carefully reconstructing the social and spiritual milieu that he represented. In the

author's view, Jesus was a sophisticated and courageous peasant, both a compassionate healer and a revolutionary radical. "The most important scholarly book about Jesus in many decades"—Marcus Borg
0-06-061629-6 HARPERCOLLINS PB $18.00
0-06-061607-5 HARPERCOLLINS PB $30.00

Who Killed Jesus?: Exposing the Roots of Anti-Semitism in the Gospel Story of the Death of Jesus
An examination of the influence of anti-Semitism in the Gospel accounts of Jesus' death. "Intellectually convincing and brilliantly written"—Arthur Hertzberg
0-06-061480-3 HARPERCOLLINS PB $14.00

Robert **Eisenman**
James the Brother of Jesus: The Key to Unlocking the History of Early Christianity and the Dead Sea Scrolls
Eisenman, the scholar who introduced the Dead Sea Scrolls to the public, compellingly argues that it is James, not Peter, who was the true spiritual heir to Jesus. To find the historical James, he says, is to find new and startling insight into the historical Jesus. Drawing on early Church texts and the Scrolls, Eisenman rescues James from oblivion and resurrects him as a fascinating and central figure in early Christianity
0-670-86932-5 VIKING $39.95

Robert W. **Funk** & Roy W. **Hoover**, editors
The Five Gospels: The Search For the Authentic Words of Jesus
Did Jesus really give the Sermon on the Mount? Is the Lord's Prayer his own words? A distinguished group of biblical scholars gives us new insight into the authenticity of more than 1,500 sayings attributed to Jesus. Color-coded by degree of probablility to which the scholars deemed each saying to be the actual words of Jesus, this is a controversial and compelling addition to biblical scholarship and the quest for the historical Jesus
0-02-541949-8 MACMILLAN $35.00

Michael **Grant**
Jesus: A Historian's Review of the Gospels
A distinguished British historian's attempt to put the composition of the gospels into a historical context that includes the apocalyptic hopes of the Jews, the development of the early Christian church, and the Jewish War of A.D. 66-70
0-02-085251-7 MACMILLAN PB $12.00

Elmer R. **Gruber** & Holger **Kersten**
The Original Jesus: The Buddhist Sources of Christianity
A provocative account of Jesus' life and teachings, speculating that Jesus was brought up by Asian missionaries of Theravada Buddhism and stressing the parallels between the earliest sayings attributed to Jesus (known as the "Q" material) and Buddhist texts
1-85230-835-4 ELEMENT PB $14.95

John P. **Meier**
A Marginal Jew
A comprehensive, meticulous study of the elusive "historical" or "authentic" Jesus, taking into account varying interpretations of the evidence and assessing the significance of the quest. "His thorough chapters... [are] gently skeptical, always admirably clear... [and] are tackled with an enthusiasm and honest effort that will make this book accessible to a wide circle of readers"—*NY Times Book Review*
Volume 1
0-385-26425-9 DOUBLEDAY $35.00
Volume2
0-385-46992-6 DOUBLEDAY $35.00

Christen Peter **Thiede** & Matthew **d'Ancona**
Eyewitness to Jesus: Amazing New Manuscript Evidence About the Origins of One Gospel
Three small fragments of the Gospel of St. Matthew, kept for nearly a century in a display case at an Oxford College, were, the authors argue, written as early as A.D. 60, making the gospel stories earlier and perhaps more reliable than had been thought by most New Testament scholars
0-385-48051-2 DOUBLEDAY $23.95

Benjamin **Urrutia** & Guy **Davenport**, translators
The Logia of Yeshua: The Sayings of Jesus
"Faith can move mountains." "Be as watchful as snakes and as innocent as doves." More than 100 aphoristic, metaphoric, self-contained, and memorable sayings guide us through the paradoxical, ironic, and timeless messages which were the essence of Jesus' teaching
WITH AN INTRODUCTION BY THE TRANSLATORS
1-88717-818-X COUNTERPOINT $14.00

A.N. **Wilson**
Jesus: A Life
Wilson's seeks to separate fact, or at least probability, from myth and theological distortion. What is provable about the death and resurrection? When did the radical Judaism Jesus preached transform itself into Christianity? To what extent was Jesus connected with the Zealots and other Jews who called for rebellion against Roman rule? "A biography worthy of its subject"—*LA Times*
0-393-03087-3 NORTON $22.95

Ian **Wilson**
Jesus: The Evidence
An illustrated survey of recent scholarship, with the prolific British author's own conclusions about Jesus' life and teachings
0-06-250973-X HARPERCOLLINS PB $17.00

Saints

Donald **Attwater** & Catherine Rachel **John**
The Penguin Dictionary of Saints
An invaluable work of reference, this dictionary explores the major saints, many of whom played important roles in history, as well as those who are less well known
0-14-051312-4 PENGUIN PB $13.95

Peter **Brown**
Augustine of Hippo: A Biography
A comprehensive biography of the fourth-century Christian convert whose theology formed a bridge between the ancient and medieval churches and defined such essential Christian doctrines as grace and original sin
0-520-01411-1 CALIFORNIA PB $16.00

The Cult of the Saints: Its Rise and Function in Latin Christianity
The saints succeed the ancient heroes
See also **BEGINNINGS AND EARLY HISTORY** under **HISTORY**
0-226-07622-9 CHICAGO PB $9.95

Alban **Butler**
Butler's Lives of the Saints
A revised and abridged version of the 18th-century classic
EDITED BY MICHAEL WALSH
0-06-069299-5 HARPERCOLLINS PB $20.00

Saint Caterina da Siena
Catherine of Siena: The Dialogue
EDITED BY SUZANNE NOFFKE
0-8091-2233-2 PAULIST PB $18.95

G.K. **Chesterton**
Saint Thomas Aquinas
A short, vigorous, informal biography
0-385-09002-1 IMAGE PB $10.00

Gaston **Duchet-Suchaux** & Michel **Pastoureau**
The Bible and the Saints: A Flammarion Iconographic Guide
2-08-013575-9 ABBEVILLE $45.00

Michael S. **Durham**
Miracles of Mary: Apparitions, Legends and Miraculous Works of the Blessed Virgin Mary
0-06-062131-1 HARPERCOLLINS $25.00

Paul **Elie**, editor
A Tremor of Bliss: Contemporary Writers on the Saints
Contributors include Kathryn Harrison on Saint Catherine of Siena, Bruce Bawer on Saint Francis of Assisi, Francine Prose on Saint Teresa of Avila, and Enrique Fernandez on Saint Lazarus
0-15-100101-4 HARCOURT BRACE $22.00

Julien **Green**
God's Fool: The Life and Times of Francis of Assisi
A biography by an outstanding French novelist
0-06-063464-2 HARPERCOLLINS PB $13.00

Saint Ignatius of Loyola
The Spiritual Exercises of St. Ignatius
TRANSLATED BY ANTHONY MOTTOLA
0-385-02436-3 DOUBLEDAY PB $8.95

Anthony **Kenny**

Thomas More

A biography of the humanist and Catholic martyr by a prolific and wide-ranging British philosopher

See also **MEDIEVAL AND RENAISSANCE** under **STUDIES OF INDIVIDUAL AUTHORS** under **ANTHOLOGIES AND STUDIES** in **LITERATURE OF THE BRITISH ISLES**

0-19-287573-6 OXFORD PB $7.95

Tom **Morgan**

Saints:A Visual Almanac of the Virtuous, Pure, Praiseworthy, and Good

Medieval, Renaissance, Baroque, and contemporary imagery of saints accompany concise, accessible retellings of over 120 of their lives, from the household names to the obscure. A list of their attributes and feast days round off this appealing compendium

0-8118-0549-2 CHRONICLE $16.95

Saint Ignatius Loyola

The Autobiography of St. Ignatius Loyola

EDITED BY JOHN C. OLIN

0-8232-1480-X FORDHAM PB $15.00

Vita **Sackville-West**

Saint Joan of Arc: Born January 6, 1412, Burned as a Heretic May 20, 1431, Canonized as a Saint May 16, 1920

0-385-42109-5 IMAGE PB $13.95

Saint Teresa of Avila

Way of Perfection

First published in 1583, this simple and practical guide to the practice of prayer stresses the importance of active love, detachment, and humility

See also **PRAYER AND CONTEMPLATION** under **PRACTISE OF FAITH**

0-385-06539-6 IMAGE PB $9.95

The Life of Teresa of Jesus: The Autobiography of Teresa of Avila

The life story of the 16th-century mystic. Beloved for the last 400 years for her spiritually infused literary works, hers is one of the rare female voices to have survived from the pre-modern era

See also **CHRISTIAN MYSTICISM**

TRANSLATED AND EDITED BY E. ALLISON PEERS

INTRODUCTION BY BENEDICTA WARD

0-385-01109-1 DOUBLEDAY PB $12.95

Saint Thérésé of Lisieux

The Autobiography of Saint Thérése of Lisieux: The Story of a Soul

Saint Thérése's life dramatizes Christ's teaching "become as little children." Indeed, she was living proof that, as her autobiography attests, "great love, not great deeds, is the essence of sanctity."

TRANSLATED BY JOHN BEEVERS

0-385-02903-9 DOUBLEDAY PB $8.95

Protestants

Roland H. **Bainton**

Here I Stand: A Life of Martin Luther

A classic study

See also **REFORMERS AND REVOLUTIONARIES** under **REFORMATION AND COUNTER-REFORMATION** under **EARLY MODERN EUROPE** in **WORLD HISTORY AND CURRENT AFFAIRS**

0-8446-6225-9 SMITH $19.00

0-687-16895-3 ABINGDON PB $5.95

Fawn M. **Brodie**

No Man Knows My History: The Life of Joseph Smith

The best biography of Mormonism's founder

0-394-46967-4 KNOPF $35.00

Francois **Wendel**

Calvin: Origins and Development of His Religious Thought

A biographical outline and a systematic exposition of his ideas on faith, predestination, the sacraments, and other theological and institutional questions

TRANSLATED BY PHILIP MAIRET

0-939464-44-6 LABYRINTH PB $16.95

Willa **Cather** & others

The Life of Mary Baker G. Eddy and the History of Christian Science

This controversial biography of the founder of the Christian Science Church was serialized in *McClure's Magazine* in 1907-8, and later published as a book. It disappeared almost overnight and has been difficult to find ever since. "Contains some of the finest portrait sketches and reflections on human nature that [Willa Cather] would ever write"
—David Stouck

0-8032-1453-7 NEBRASKA $45.00

0-8032-6349-X NEBRASKA PB $14.95

Mary Baker Eddy

V.H. **Green**

John Wesley

An excellent account of the founder of Methodism

0-8191-6461-5 PRESS OF AMERICA PB $18.00

20th Century

Richard **Fox**

Reinhold Niebuhr

A biography of the most important modern American Protestant thinker

0-8014-8369-7 CORNELL PB $16.95

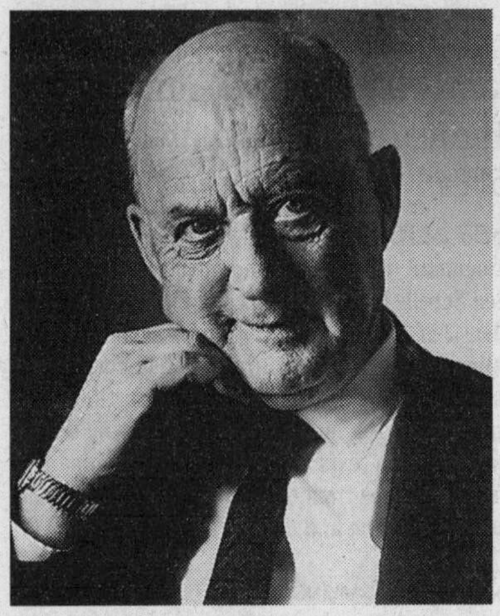

Reinhold Niebuhr (photo courtesy of Associated Press)

Daniel Mark **Epstein**

Sister Aimée: Life of Aimée Semple McPherson

The stormy, scandal-disrupted career of the Canadian-born woman who became a flamboyant and very popular radio evangelist in Los Angeles in the 1920s and '30s

See also **PUBLIC FIGURES AND ISSUES** under **TOPICS IN AMERICAN STUDIES** in **HISTORY OF THE AMERICAS**

0-15-182688-9 HARCOURT BRACE $27.95

0-15-600093-8 HARVEST PB $14.95

C.L. **Franklin**

Give Me this Mountain: Life History and Selected Sermons

FOREWORD BY JESSE L. JACKSON

0-252-06087-3 ILLINOIS PB $12.95

Thomas **Merton**

The Journals of Thomas Merton

Patrick **Hart**, editor

Volume 1 Run to the Mountain: The Story of a Vocation: 1939-1941

Merton, the Trappist monk and writer, specified that his journals not be published until 25 years after his death. This volume, the first of seven (all to be published by 1998), offers a glimpse of the young, pre-monastic Merton as a graduate student in Greenwich Village, grappling with rejection by *New Yorker* and other magazine editors and struggling with probing theological and ethical questions that would lead him to discover his true vocation. "This is just the right time to renew our appreciation for the eternal in the world by reading the gutsy, thoughtful, passionate journals of Thomas Merton" —Thomas Moore

0-06-065475-9 HARPERCOLLINS PB $15.00

Jonathan **Montado**, editor

Volume 2

Entering the Silence: Becoming a Monk & Writer: 1941-1952

0-06-065477-5 HARPERCOLLINS PB $14.00

Lawrence **Cunningham**, editor

Volume 3

A Search for Solitude: Pursuing the Monk's True Life: 1952-1960

The third volume of Merton's journals offers "unique insight into the mind and heart of the most important spiritual writer of the twentieth century" (Henri Nouwen). Ranging from his monastic routine to his exploration of Zen, existentialism, Latin American culture, and Marxism, this fascinating volume completes Merton's record of his spiritual odyssey

0-06-065479-1 HARPERCOLLINS PB $14.00

Victor A. **Kramer**, editor

Volume 4

Turning Toward the World: The Pivotal Years: 1960-1963

0-06-065481-3 HARPERCOLLINS PB $10.00

Thomas **Merton**

The Seven Storey Mountain

The autobiography of the influential American Catholic poet, scholar, and monk

See also **WESTERN** under **20TH-CENTURY SPIRITUAL LEADERS** under **SPIRITUALITY**

0-15-680679-7 HARCOURT BRACE PB $12.00

Mother Teresa

A Simple Path

An autobiography

0-345-39745-2 BALLANTINE $20.00

There is something else to remember—that this kind of love begins at home. We cannot give to the outside world what we don't have on the inside. This is very important. If I can't see God's love in my brother and sister then how can I see that love in somebody else? How can I give it to somebody else? Everybody has got some good. Some hide it, some neglect it, but it is there.
A SIMPLE PATH

Mother Teresa & Jose Luis **Gonzalez-Balado**

Mother Teresa: In My Own Words

0-89243-858-4 LIGUORI $11.95

Christopher **Hitchens**

The Missionary Position: Mother Teresa in Theory and Practice

A short, iconoclastic analysis of the Albanian missionary, Nobel Peace Prize winner, and future saint, questioning the efficacy of her devotion to the Third World poor and criticizing her ties with authoritarian regimes

1-85984-929-6 VERSO $14.95

Michael **Mott**

The Seven Mountains of Thomas Merton

"A stunning portrait of a complex and holy man"—*Boston Globe*

0-395-40451-7 HARVEST PB $17.95

Thomas **Merton** & William J. **Shannon**, editor

Witness to Freedom: The Letters of Thomas Merton in Times of Crisis

"In these impassioned, searching letters… Merton reflects his commitment to nuclear disarmament, his immersion in Gandhi's philosophy of nonviolence, his growing ecological awareness, and his quest for a political philosophy of freedom grounded in his Catholic faith"—*Publishers Weekly*

0-15-600274-4 HARVEST PB $16.00

Thomas Merton

Stephen B. **Oates**

Let the Trumpet Sound: The Life of Martin Luther King, Jr.

See also **CIVIL RIGHTS** under **US HISTORY, 1945 TO THE PRESENT** in **HISTORY OF THE AMERICAS**

0-06-092473-X HARPERPERENNIAL PB $16.00

Tad **Szulc**

Pope John Paul II: The Biography

A political and diplomatic as well as religious story, stressing John Paul's role in the collapse of communism in eastern Europe

0-671-00047-0 POCKET PB $6.99

Dan **Wakefield**

Returning: A Spiritual Journey

An autobiographical account of how a middle-aged novelist and screenwriter recovered his faith after years of drifting, drinking, and personal crisis

See also **WESTERN** under **20TH-CENTURY SPIRITUAL LEADERS** under **SPIRITUALITY**

0-14-025493-5 PENGUIN PB $10.00

Theology and Doctrine

The following titles will provide the reader with introductions to and summaries of the major Christian thinkers, although clearly no attempt can be made to represent all views.

For related reading, see PHILOSOPHY

History of Doctrine

Rudolf **Bultmann**

Jesus and the Word

A 1926 work by one of the most influential of modern Protestant theologians

0-684-17596-7 MACMILLAN $40.00

J.N. **Kelly**

Early Christian Doctrines

The development of Christian belief and dogma from the early Fathers to the 5th century

0-06-064334-X HARPERCOLLINS PB $20.25

John **Macquarrie**

Principles of Christian Theology

A clear, incisive discussion of the major themes of Christian thought as applied to problems of contemporary life

0-02-374510-X SCRIBNERS PB $48.00

Colleen **McDannell** & Bernhard **Lang**

Heaven: A History

The evolution of the doctrines and concepts of Heaven in Christian thought

0-300-04858-0 YALE PB $17.00

Jaroslav **Pelikan**

The Christian Tradition: A History of the Development of Doctrine

A comprehensive treatment, written by a master

Volume 1

Emergence of the Catholic Tradition, 100-600

0-226-65370-6 CHICAGO $36.00
0-226-65371-4 CHICAGO PB $14.95

Volume 2

The Spirit of Eastern Christendom, 600-1700

0-226-65372-2 CHICAGO $36.00
0-226-65373-0 CHICAGO PB $13.95

Volume 3

The Growth of Medieval Theology, 600-1300

0-226-65374-9 CHICAGO $40.50
0-226-65375-7 CHICAGO PB $14.95

Volume 4

Reformation of Church and Dogma, 1300-1700

0-226-65376-5 CHICAGO $34.95
0-226-65377-3 CHICAGO PB $16.95

Volume 5

Christian Doctrine and Modern Culture, 1700-Present

0-226-65378-1 CHICAGO $34.95
0-226-65380-3 CHICAGO PB $14.95

John **Meyendorff**
Byzantine Theology: Historical Trends and Doctrinal Themes
The best guide to the development of Orthodoxy
0-8232-0967-9 FORDHAM PB $16.00

Theology

Hans Urs von **Balthasar**
Dare We Hope "That All Men Be Saved"?: With a Short Discourse on Hell
0-89870-207-0 IGNATIUS PB $11.95

Karl **Barth**
Dogmatics in Outline
A summary of *Church Dogmatics,* Barth's systematic, multivolume exposition of neo-orthodoxy, one of the great theological works of the 20th century
0-06-130056-X HARPERCOLLINS PB $12.00

Dietrich **Bonhoeffer**
The Cost of Discipleship
Based on the Sermon on the Mount, this work by the German Lutheran theologian martyred by the Nazis challenges the notion of "cheap grace"
0-8446-5960-6 SMITH $20.75
0-02-083850-6 MACMILLAN PB $6.95

John **Calvin**
The Institutes of Christian Religion
Calvin's central presentation of his Reformation theology
EDITED BY TONY LANE & HILARY OSBORNE
0-8010-2524-9 BAKER PB $11.99

Richard Elliott **Friedman**
The Disappearance of God: A Divine Mystery
0-316-29434-9 LITTLE, BROWN $24.95

The Disappearance of God: Searching for the Hidden Face of God
0-06-062258-X HARPERCOLLINS PB $14.00

B. A. **Gerrish**
Continuing the Reformation: Essays on Modern Religious Thought
One of the most distinguished theologians of our time examines, in 12 essays, how faith itself has become a primary object of inquiry, both in the new philosophy of religion and in the new style of church theology. Includes essays on Martin Luther and the Reformation, religious belief and the Age of Reason, and Friedrich Schleiermacher and the renewal of Protestant theology
0-226-28870-6 CHICAGO $54.00
0-226-28871-4 CHICAGO PB $19.95

Richard M. **Gula**
Reason Informed by Faith: Foundations of Catholic Morality
0-8091-3066-1 PAULIST PB $12.95

Gustavo **Gutierrez**
A Theology of Liberation: History, Politics and Salvation
0-88344-542-5 ORBIS PB $18.50

Hans **Kung**
Does God Exist?: An Answer for Today
TRANSLATED BY EDWARD QUINN
0-8245-1119-0 CROSSROAD PB $29.50

On Being a Christian
What it means to be a Christian today in a world of science, technology, political and personal crisis; a challenging statement of faith by a controversial German theologian
0-385-19286-X DOUBLEDAY PB $19.95

Martin **Luther**
Martin Luther: Selections from His Writings
A sampling of Luther's theological, exegetical, and polemical works
See also **REFORMERS AND REVOLUTIONARIES** under **REFORMATION AND COUNTER-REFORMATION** under **EARLY MODERN EUROPE** in **WORLD HISTORY AND CURRENT AFFAIRS**
EDITED BY JOHN DILLENBERGER
0-385-09876-6 DOUBLEDAY PB $11.95

Martin Luther

J.A. **Lyons**
Cosmic Christ in Origen and Teilhard de Chardin
0-19-826721-5 OXFORD $59.00

Bernard L. **Marthaler**
Creed
0-89622-537-2 TWETH PB $19.95

Reinhold **Niebuhr**
The Essential Reinhold Niebuhr: Selected Essays and Addresses
Taken from the writings of the most influential 20th-century American Protestant thinker. Niebuhr was particularly concerned with the relation between religion and the sociopolitical social order
EDITED BY ROBERT M. BROWN
0-300-04001-6 YALE PB $15.00

Karl **Rahner**
The Content of Faith: The Best of Karl Rahner's Theological Writings
EDITED BY KARL LEHMANN AND ALBERT RAFFELT
0-8245-1221-9 CROSSROAD $42.50

The Great Church Year: The Best of Karl Rahner's Homilies, Sermons, and Meditations
0-8245-1430-0 CROSSROAD PB $19.95

Joseph **Ratzinger**
Introduction to Christianity
TRANSLATED BY J.R. FOSTER
0-89870-316-6 IGNATIUS PB $14.95

Lynda **Sexson**
Ordinarily Sacred
0-8139-1416-7 VIRGINIA PB $12.50

George **Steiner**
No Passion Spent: Essays 1978-1995
See also **LITERARY ESSAYISTS** under **LITERARY CRITICISM** in **LITERATURE OF EUROPE, AFRICA, AND ASIA**
0-300-06630-9 YALE $30.00

Pierre **Teilhard de Chardin**
The Heart of Matter
This spiritual autobiography sums up Chardin's vision, which he arrives at by separate but converging roads of science and religion
0-15-640004-9 HARCOURT BRACE PB $9.00

The Phenomenon of Man
The principal exposition of his evolutionary theology
0-06-090495-X HARPERCOLLINS PB $13.50

Paul **Tillich**
Dynamics of Faith
The best introduction to Tillich's existentialist theology
0-06-130042-X HARPERCOLLINS PB $13.00

Systematic Theology
0-226-80336-8 CHICAGO $75.00

Contemporary Issues

Jack **Bemporad** & Michael **Sheback**
Our Age: The Historic New Era of Christian-Jewish Understanding
FOREWORD BY CARDINAL JOHN O'CONNOR
1-56548-081-3 NEW CITY PB $6.95

Leonardo **Boff**
Liberating Grace
An exposition of liberation theology by a Brazilian theologian who has been embroiled in controversy with the Vatican
TRANSLATED BY JOHN DRURY
0-88344-282-5 ORBIS PB $16.95

G.K. **Chesterton** & Alvaro **De Silva**
Brave New Family
0-89870-314-X IGNATIUS PB $12.95

Dietrich **Bonhoeffer**

Letters and Papers from Prison

Writings from a Nazi prison by the martyred German theologian

0-02-083920-0 MACMILLAN PB $12.00

Matthew **Fox**

The Coming of the Cosmic Christ: The Healing of Mother Earth and the Birth of a Global Renaissance

See also **WESTERN** under **20TH-CENTURY SPIRITUAL LEADERS** under **SPIRITUALITY**

0-06-062915-0 HARPERCOLLINS PB $16.00

Creation Spirituality: Liberating Gifts for the Peoples of the Earth

Fox's attempt to find an early Christian tradition compatible with contemporary social, environmental, and feminist concerns

0-06-062917-7 HARPERCOLLINS PB $15.00

Thomas C. **Fox**

Sexuality and Catholicism

An excellent survey of Catholic teachings and practice concerning women, birth control, abortion, celibacy, and homosexuality, with discussions of such institutional problems as clerical abuse of children

See also **SEX** under **COURTSHIP, LOVE, SEX, AND MARRIAGE** in **LIFESTYLES AND PRACTICAL ADVICE**

0-8076-1396-7 BRAZILLER $27.50

Andrew **Greeley**

Andrew Greeley's World: An Anthology of Critical Essays, 1986-88

0-446-38989-7 WARNER PB $14.95

How to Save the Catholic Church

0-670-38475-5 VIKING $16.95

Andrew M. **Greeley** & Jacob **Neusner**

Common Ground: A Priest and a Rabbi Read the Scripture Together

See also **MODERN THEOLOGY AND PHILOSOPHY** under **JUDAISM**

FOREWORD BY MARTIN E. MARTY

0-8298-1120-6 PILGRIM PB $16.95

Paul G. **Hiebert** & Eloise Hiebert **Meneses**

Incarnational Ministry: Planting Churches in Band, Tribal, Peasant, and Urban Societies

0-8010-2009-3 BAKER PB $19.99

Paul F. **Knitter**

Jesus and the Other Names: Christian Mission and Global Responsibility

1-57075-053-X ORBIS PB $17.00

Mark A. **Noll**

The Scandal of the Evangelical Mind

0-8028-3715-8 EERDMANS $20.00
0-8028-4180-5 EERDMANS PB $16.00

Malachi **Martin**

The Jesuits: The Society of Jesus and the Betrayal of the Roman Catholic Church

The author, a conservative American Catholic, argues that the Jesuits, after a long history of serving the papacy, have been transformed in the last 20 years into a radical conspiracy against the traditional church and the West

0-671-65716-X TOUCHSTONE PB $12.00

Ronald L. **Numbers**

The Creationists

A study of religious opposition to the theory of evolution and attempts to reconcile the Genesis account of creation with science, from the time of Darwin to the present

0-520-08393-8 CALIFORNIA PB $15.95

Pope John Paul II

Crossing the Threshold of Hope

The Pope's reflections on God, prophecy, salvation, Judaism, and the fall of communism

See also **RELIGION AND SOCIETY** under **WORLD RELIGION**

0-679-76561-1 RANDOM HOUSE PB $11.00

Love and Responsibility

TRANSLATED BY H.T. WILLETTS

0-374-19247-2 FS&G $15.00

Uta **Ränke-Heineman**

Eunuchs for the Kingdom of Heaven: Women, Sexuality, and the Catholic Church

A Catholic theologian maintains that the Church has manipulated biblical doctrine in order to denigrate women and their sexuality through deification of the Virgin, and that clerical celibacy and the prohibition of birth control flout common sense

0-14-016500-2 PENGUIN PB $11.95

David **Rosenberg**, editor

Communion: Contemporary Writers Reveal the Bible in their Lives

Contributors include Robert Coles, Jayne Anne Phillips, Elizabeth Hardwick, Bharati Mukherjee, and Bill McKibben

0-385-47483-0 ANCHOR $30.00

Albert **Schweitzer**

The Spiritual Life: Selected Writings of Albert Schweitzer

WITH INTRODUCTIONS BY ROBERT COLES AND SENATOR BOB KERRY

0-88001-466-0 ECCO PB $14.00

Nolan **Sidney** & Mary **Sidney**

Christian Pilgrimage in Modern Western Europe

A commanding exploration of religious shrines in modern Roman Catholicism, ranging from a discussion of obscure chapels to the world-famous shrines at Rome, Lourdes, and Fatima

0-8078-4389-X NORTH CAROLINA PB $18.95

General Topics

G. K. **Chesterton**

Brave New Family: Men and Women, Children, Sex, Divorce, Marriage, and the Family

0-89870-318-2 IGNATIUS $19.95

Women

Karen **Armstrong**

Through the Narrow Gate

0-312-11903-8 ST. MARTIN'S PB $10.95

Caroline Walker **Bynum**

Fragmentation and Redemption: Essays on Gender and the Human Body in Medieval Religion

0-942299-62-0 ZONE PB $16.95

Jesus as Mother: Studies in the Spirituality of the High Middle Ages

0-520-05222-6 CALIFORNIA PB $15.95

Nancy **Fierro**

Hildegard of Bingen and Her Vision of the Feminine

1-55612-753-7 SHEED & WARD PB $7.95

Carol Lee **Flinders**

Enduring Grace: Living Portraits of Seven Women Mystics

See also **CHRISTIAN MYSTICISM**

0-06-062645-3 HARPERCOLLINS PB $15.00

Nicole **Gausseron**

The Little Notebook: A Contemporary Woman's Encounters with Jesus

FOREWORD BY JOSEPH F. GIRZONE

0-06-063097-3 HARPERCOLLINS PB $12.00

Margery **Kempe**

The Book of Margery Kempe

A religious work with a fascinating autobiographical dimension, including an unforgettable account of Kempe's trial for heresy

See also **MEDIEVAL LITERATURE** in **LITERATURE OF EUROPE, AFRICA, AND ASIA**

TRANSLATED BY BARRY WINDEATT

0-14-043251-5 PENGUIN PB $10.95

Pope John Paul II

On the Dignity and Vocation of Women: Mulieris Dignitatem

1-55586-244-6 UNSHD PB $4.95

Barbara G. **Walker**

Woman's Dictionary of Symbols and Sacred Objects

0-06-250923-3 HARPERCOLLINS PB $25.00

Ewa **Kuryluk**

Veronica and Her Cloth: History, Symbolism, and Structure of a "True" Image

The author has chosen a popular theme of art and story—that the portrait of Jesus was imprinted on Saint Veronica's veil when she wiped his bleeding face as he was on his way to Golgotha. "[Kuryluk] has the gift of bold intellectual imagination, and [it] makes exhilirating reading"—Marina Warner

0-631-17813-9 BLACKWELL $31.95

Rosemary Radford **Ruether**

Womanguides: Readings Toward a Feminist Theology

"This integrative work…helps uncover a female modeling of wisdom that has been buried under centuries of male-interpreted doctrine. The foremothers are all here, and their stories are allowed to shine"—*Utne Reader*

See also **THEOLOGY** under **FEMINIST THEORY** under **WOMEN'S STUDIES** in **SOCIAL STUDIES**

0-8070-1235-1 BEACON PB $15.00

Practice of Faith

Prayer and Contemplation

George **Appleton**, editor

The Oxford Book of Prayer

See also **CLASSICS**

0-19-213222-9 OXFORD $29.95

Oscar **Cullmann**

Prayer in the New Testament

Answers modern questions about prayer. Simple, and clear

0-8006-2944-2 FORTRESS PB $19.00

Saint Francis de Sales

Introduction to the Devout Life

"One of the great religious and devotional masterpieces of all time"
—*The Journal of Religious Thought*

See also **CLASSICS**

TRANSLATED BY JOHN K. RYAN

0-385-03009-6 DOUBLEDAY PB $11.95

William **Johnston**, editor

The Cloud of Unknowing and the Book of Privy Counseling

0-385-03097-5 IMAGE PB $8.00

Thomas **Keating**

Open Mind, Open Heart: The Contemplative Dimension of the Gospel

The history of contemplative prayer and step-by-step guidance in the method of centering prayer by "the leader within the Catholic world in the task of recovering our Christian contemplative heritage"—Ewert Cousins

0-8264-0696-3 ELEMENT PB $11.95

Thomas à **Kempis**

The Imitation of Christ

0-385-02861-X DOUBLEDAY PB $8.95

Madeleine **L'Engle** & Carole F. **Chase**

Glimpses of Grace: Daily Thoughts and Reflections

0-06-065281-0 HARPERCOLLINS $25.00

0-06-065280-2 HARPERCOLLINS PB $18.00

Thomas **Merton**

Contemplative Prayer

Brings in texts from Scripture and from writers in the long tradition of Western contemplative spirituality. "Every page shows the rough texture of lived experience"—*America*

INTRODUCTION BY THICH NHAT HANH

0-385-09219-9 IMAGE PB $7.95

> Meditation has no point and no reality unless it is rooted in life.
> CONTEMPLATIVE PRAYER

Thoughts in Solitude

The vital importance of solitude and silence in everyday life is the theme of this collection of reflections and meditations by the influential Trappist monk. Chapters cover such topics as the true meaning of poverty, the liberating effect of humility, the relationship between spiritual and mental life, and the positive experience of knowing one's nothingness

See also **WESTERN** under **20TH-CENTURY SPIRITUAL LEADERS** under **SPIRITUALITY**

0-374-51325-2 FS&G PB $7.00

0-87773-920-X SHAMBHALA PB $6.00

Karl **Rahner**

On Prayer

Written for a talk Rahner gave at a German cathedral in the immediate aftermath of WWII, *On Prayer* is a stern call to truer prayer and a wise elucidation of what prayer is and how it works

0-8146-2171-6 LITUR PB $6.95

Saint Teresa of Avila

Way of Perfection

First published in 1583, this simple and practical guide to the practice of prayer stresses the importance of active love, detachment and humility

See also **SAINTS** under **BIOGRAPHIES**

0-385-06539-6 IMAGE PB $9.95

Hans Urs **von Balthasar**

Prayer

Balthasar is one of the great theologians of the twentieth century

0-89870-074-4 IGNATIUS PB $12.95

Holidays and Rituals

Leigh **Grant**

The Twelve Days of Christmas: A Celebration and History

In charming paintings and a delightful text, artist Leigh Grant takes us to the origins of the standard holiday songs, presenting us not only with an interpretation of each day of Christmas, but an explanation of the many Christmas traditions and references that lie behind each verse. Fresh and engaging, this is a lovely way to re-experience the "Twelve Days of Christmas"

0-8109-3881-2 ABRAMS $14.95

Reference

Donald **Attwater** & Catherine Rachel **John**

The Penguin Dictionary of Saints

An invaluable work of reference, this dictionary explores the major saints, many of whom played important roles in history, as well as those who are less well known

See also **SAINTS** under **BIOGRAPHIES**

0-14-051312-4 PENGUIN PB $13.95

David **Barrett**, editor

World Christian Encyclopedia: A Comparative Survey of Churches and Religions in the Modern World, A.D. 1900 to 2000

A monumental guide to contemporary Christianity, with information and statistics on all churches and sects for every country

0-19-507963-9 OXFORD $300.00

Chas S. **Clifton**, editor

Encyclopedia of Heresies and Heretics

The tradition of heretics in Christianity is a long one that includes not only madmen and witches, but also Augustine, Joan of Arc, and early followers of St. Francis of Assisi—the history of heresy is ultimately and fascinatingly intertwined with history of the Church of Rome

See also **ONE-VOLUME ENCYCLOPEDIAS** under **REFERENCE** in **BUSINESS AND REFERENCE**

0-87436-600-3 ABC CLIO $50.00

F.L. **Cross** & Elizabeth A. **Livingstone**

The Oxford Dictionary of the Christian Church

A standard work, concise, scholarly, and thorough, with more than 6,000 articles on important figures, events, movements, and ideas in Eastern and Western Christianity

0-19-211545-6 OXFORD $65.00

Nevill **Drury**

Dictionary of Mysticism and the Occult

A sympathetic guide to occult and mystical concepts, rites, and practitioners

See also **THE OCCULT, WITCHCRAFT, AND THE DEVIL** under **WORLD RELIGION**

0-87436-699-2 ABC CLIO $55.00

1-85327-075-X PRISM PB $14.95

Gaston **Duchet-Suchaux** & Michel **Pastoureau**

The Bible and the Saints

Clearly and simply, this invaluable resource covers over 300 Christian saints and other characters from the Old and New Testaments with lucid definitions of the attributes by which they are known in Western and Byzantine art. Also, the Apocrypha, significant religious scenes, and a complete bestiary of both real and imaginary beasts make this a handy guide for art lovers

See also **REFERENCE** under **ART HISTORY: GENERAL STUDIES** in **ART**

2-08-013564-3 ABBEVILLE PB $24.95

David Hugh **Farmer**, editor

The Oxford Dictionary of Saints

0-19-283069-4 OXFORD PB $15.95

Van A. **Harvey**

A Handbook of Theological Terms

Three hundred short essays, mainly Protestant in approach, that help penetrate the language of contemporary theology

0-02-085430-7 MACMILLAN PB $7.00

Elizabeth A. **Livingstone**, editor

The Concise Oxford Dictionary of the Christian Church

0-19-283014-7 OXFORD PB $12.95

The Bible

Mathew **Black** & H.H. **Rowley**

Peake's Commentary on the Bible

0-415-05147-9 ROUTLEDGE PB $20.00

W.R.F **Browning**

A Dictionary of the Bible

0-19-211691-6 OXFORD $25.00

Ronald **Brownrigg**

Who's Who in the New Testament

0-19-521031-X OXFORD PB $15.95

Keith R. **Crim** & George A. **Buttrick**

The Interpreter's Dictionary of the Bible

The standard dictionary: defines every proper name, place, and episode in the Bible; explains concepts, doctrines, and rituals; includes maps, pronunciation guides, and bibliographies. Contributions, generally Protestant in approach, from 253 scholars

0-687-19268-4 ABINGDON $199.95

Keith R. **Crim**, editor

The Interpreter's Dictionary of the Bible: Supplementary Volume

An updated, cross-referenced supplement to the above

0-687-19269-2 ABINGDON $44.95

Peter **Calvocoressi**, editor

Who's Who in the Bible

0-14-051212-8 PENGUIN PB $13.95

Joan **Comay**

Who's Who in the Old Testament

Placing the huge cast of characters populating the Old Testament in their geographic and historical contexts, this definitive, accessibly written, 3,000-entry volume is an essential source for both readers of the Bible and readers of the great works of Western literature that rely on biblical allusions

See also **REFERENCE WORKS** under **WORLD RELIGION**

0-19-521029-8 OXFORD PB $16.95

Mark **Levine** & Eugene **Rachlis**, editors

The Complete Book of Bible Quotations

0-671-70551-2 POCKET PB $18.00

Charles M. **Laymon**, editor

The Interpreter's One-Volume Commentary on the Bible

A succinct exposition with clearly written contributions from 70 Protestant scholars on geography, historical background and chronology, biblical languages, units of measurement and money, with many maps and charts

0-687-19299-4 ABINGDON $39.95

Bruce M. **Metzger** & Michael D. **Coogan**, editors

The Oxford Companion to the Bible

Far more comprehensive than "standard Bible dictionaries," this guide features not only traditional definitions, references, and maps, but more than 700 articles by 250 scholars relating to everything from homosexuality in the Bible and the Bible's influence on literature to women's issues and extended entries on concepts such as immortality, sin, and the Holy Spirit

0-19-504645-5 OXFORD $55.00

The **Reader's Digest**

Who's Who in the Bible

An illustrated A-to-Z format provides concise and in-depth portraits of over 500 biblical characters, from prophets to beggars. With color maps, genealogies, and ample documentation

See also **BIOGRAPHICAL DICTIONARIES** under **GENERAL INFORMATION** under **REFERENCE** in **BUSINESS AND REFERENCE**

0-89577-618-9 READER'S DIGEST $32.00

William **Smith**

Smith's Bible Dictionary

0-8407-5542-2 NELSON $12.95

0-8407-3085-3 NELSON PB $9.99

Robert **Young**

Young's Analytical Concordance to the Bible

The classic concordance, originally published in 1879, with 311,000 references, and with the original Hebrew and Greek words listed under each English entry; includes a guide to the pronunciation of proper names

0-917006-29-1 HENDRICKSON $29.95

Islam

In this section will be found titles relating directly to the history, doctrines, and practice of Islam as a religion. In view of the difficulty of separating the religious from the social and cultural, the following headings should also be consulted for a fuller picture: the Islamic World, The Contemporary Middle East, Arabic Literature, Persian Literature, and Islamic Art and Architecture.

General Studies

Arthur J. **Arberry**

Aspects of Islamic Civilization as Depicted in the Original Texts

A very useful anthology by a great translator

0-472-06130-5 MICHIGAN PB $18.95

John L. **Esposito**

Islam: The Straight Path

An overall guide to Islam in its religious, cultural, and political aspects. "Explains in a very cogent manner the religious ramifications of contemporary Islamic society"—*Booklist*

0-19-506225-6 OXFORD $27.50

0-19-504399-5 OXFORD PB $15.95

Hamilton A. **Gibb**

Mohammedanism: An Historical Survey

An authority noted for his powers of synthesis and lucid, succinct exposition masterfully presents the subject

See also **THE ISLAMIC PERIOD** under **THE INDIAN SUBCONTINENT** in **WORLD HISTORY AND CURRENT AFFAIRS**

0-19-500245-8 OXFORD PB $8.95

Albert **Hourani**

A History of the Arab Peoples

A 576-page synthesis by a distinguished scholar. "Hourani covers twelve centuries of social, economic, political, and cultural life in a work already being hailed as both comprehensive and definitive"—*Newsweek*

See also **THE ISLAMIC WORLD TO WORLD WAR I** in **WORLD HISTORY AND CURRENT AFFAIRS**

0-674-39565-4 HARVARD $27.50

0-446-39392-4 WARNER PB $15.99

Even if the ruler was unjust or impious, it was generally accepted that he should still be obeyed, for any kind of order was better than anarchy; as Ghazali said, "the tyranny of a sultan for a hundred years causes less damage than one year's tyranny exercised by the subjects against one another." Revolt was justified only against a ruler who clearly went against a command of God or His prophet. This did not mean, however, that 'ulama should look on an unjust ruler in the way in which they looked on a just one. A powerful tradition among the 'ulama (among Sunnis and Shi'is alike) was that they should keep their distance from the rulers of the world. Ghazali quoted a hadith: "in Hell there is a valley uniquely reserved for 'ulama who visit kings."

A HISTORY OF THE ARAB PEOPLES

Charles **Le Gai Eaton**

Islam and the Destiny of Man

0-88706-163-X SUNY PB $18.95

Bernard **Lewis**

Islam and the West

An important and controversial study by a leading scholar of Islam

See also **ISLAM AND THE WEST** under **THE ISLAMIC WORLD TO WORLD WAR I** in **WORLD HISTORY AND CURRENT AFFAIRS**

0-19-507619-2 OXFORD $27.50

0-19-509061-6 OXFORD PB $13.95

Bernard **Lewis**, editor

The World of Islam

This splendidly illustrated anthology offers an introduction to the diversity of Islamic civilization, with full attention to its artistic legacy. Contains 495 illustrations, 160 in color

0-500-27624-2 NORTON PB $29.95

F.E. **Peters**

The Hajj: The Muslim Pilgrimage to Mecca and the Holy Places

The central ritual of Islam presented in rich detail

0-691-02120-1 PRINCETON $49.50
0-691-02619-X PRINCETON PB $18.95

A Reader on Classical Islam

Selections from the Qur'an and the major philosophers, theologians, and commentators of the Islamic Golden Age covering all aspects of faith, law, practice, and mysticism

0-691-03394-3 PRINCETON $60.00
0-691-00040-9 PRINCETON PB $19.95

Fazlur **Rahman**

Islam

A highly respected Muslim scholar explains his religion

0-226-70281-2 CHICAGO PB $11.95

E. **Van Donzel**, editor

Islamic Desk Reference

Concise, factual, and all-inclusive, this compilation from *The Encyclopedia of Islam* opens the massive and varied Muslim world to our examination. Maps, genealogies, diagrams, and illustrations bring one of the world's vibrant religions and cultures home

90-04-09738-4 E.J. BRILL $87.50

David **Waines**

An Introduction to Islam

A fascinating and complex introduction to one of the world's great monotheistic traditions

0-521-41880-1 CAMBRIDGE $49.95
0-521-42929-3 CAMBRIDGE PB $15.95

Peter Lamborn **Wilson**

Scandal: Essays in Islamic Heresy

Freewheeling explorations of the unorthodox in Islam, on such subjects as "Secrets of the Assassins," "Imaginal Yoga and Sacred Pedophilia in Persian Sufism," and "A Note on the Use of Wine, Hemp & Opium"

0-936756-14-4 AUTONOMEDIA PB $10.00

The Qur'an

Muslims believe the Qur'an (or Koran) to be God's very words revealed to Muhammad. It is the basis and immutable reference point of Islamic civilization. Many Muslims turn to it daily to guide their actions.

Ahmad **Ali**, translator

Al-Qur'an: A Contemporary Translation

A new scholarly version

0-691-02046-9 PRINCETON PB $16.95

Arthur J. **Arberry**

The Koran Interpreted

A brilliant, not always literal rendition of the original

0-02-083260-5 MACMILLAN PB $17.00

N. R. **Dawood**, translator

The Koran

An accessible prose version, with the traditional order of chapters changed

0-14-044052-6 PENGUIN PB $6.95

N.J. **Dawood**, translator

The Koran: With Parallel Arabic Text

0-14-044542-0 PENGUIN PB $21.95

Abdel Muhammad **Haleem**

Understanding the Qur'an: Themes and Style

1-86064-009-5 ST. MARTIN'S $23.95

Muhammad Marmaduke **Pickthall**, translator

The Meaning of the Glorious Koran

A literal translation in which each verse is followed by a brief explanation of its historical and religious meaning

See also **MUHAMMAD AND THE QUR'AN** under **THE ISLAMIC WORLD TO WORLD WAR I** in **WORLD HISTORY AND CURRENT AFFAIRS**

9-995-71217-2 NEW AMERICAN LIBRARY PB $6.99

Fazlur **Rahman**

Major Themes in the Qur'an

A clear explanation of the Qur'an's view of man and the world, by a respected Muslim scholar who taught in the West

0-88297-027-5 BIBLIO PB $16.00

The Life and Career of Muhammad

Karen **Armstrong**

Muhammad: A Biography of the Prophet

This highly readable, even-handed study examines Muhammad's life within the context of the emergence of Islam out of the cultural upheaval of seventh-century Arabia and its subsequent encounters with the West. "Portrays Muhammad as a passionate, complex, fallible human being"—*Publishers Weekly*

See also **MUHAMMAD AND THE QUR'AN** under **THE ISLAMIC WORLD TO WORLD WAR I** in **WORLD HISTORY AND CURRENT AFFAIRS**

0-06-250886-5 HARPERCOLLINS PB $13.00

It has been difficult for Western people to understand the violent Muslim reaction to Salman Rushdie's fictional portrait of Muhammad in "The Satanic Verses." It seemed incredible that a novel could inspire such murderous hatred, a reaction which was regarded as proof of the incurable intolerance of Islam.

MUHAMMAD: A BIOGRAPHY OF THE PROPHET

Michael **Cook**

Muhammad

A concise summary, from the Past Masters series

0-19-287605-8 OXFORD PB $8.95

Martin **Lings**

Muhammad

A fresh and direct life of the Prophet based upon the most authoritative early biography and traditions. The story comes to life for the modern reader

0-89281-170-6 INNER TRADITIONS PB $16.95

W. Montgomery **Watt**

Muhammad: Prophet and Statesman

A concise biography by a leading scholar of Muhammad's career

See also **MUHAMMAD AND THE QUR'AN** under **THE ISLAMIC WORLD TO WORLD WAR I** in **WORLD HISTORY AND CURRENT AFFAIRS**

0-19-881078-4 OXFORD PB $10.95

Islamic Theology and Law

Al-Ghazali

On the Duties of Brotherhood

0-686-83895-5 NEW ERA PB $4.95

Avicenna

Avicenna on Theology

Selections from the theological work of an eleventh-century Persian physician and philosopher strongly influenced by Aristotle and Neoplatonism

TRANSLATED BY ARTHUR J. ARBERRY

0-88355-676-6 HYPERION $18.00

Shems **Friedlander** &
Al-Hajj Shaikh **Muzaffereddin**

Ninety-Nine Names of Allah: The Beautiful Names

0-06-063034-5 HARPERCOLLINS PB $10.00

Ignaz **Goldziher**

Introduction to Islamic Theology and Law

Important scholarly essays by a distinguished Islamicist

0-691-10099-3 PRINCETON PB $17.95

Islamic Philosophy

Henry **Corbin**

Cyclical Time and Ismaili Gnosis

Studies in a form of Gnosticism that developed within the medieval Islamic world

0-7103-0048-4 RUTLEDGE PB $34.00

Majid **Fakhry**

A History of Islamic Philosophy

A widely used study of the subject

0-231-05533-1 COLUMBIA PB $21.00

Oliver **Leaman**

An Introduction to Medieval Islamic Philosophy

A succinct account of the major ideas of Ghazali, Averroes, Avicenna, and others

0-521-28911-4 CAMBRIDGE PB $21.95

W. Montgomery **Watt**

Islamic Philosophy and Theology

0-7486-0749-8 EDINBURGH PB $23.00

The Shi'a

The Shi'a, a sect constituting roughly 10 percent of the Islamic world, is itself divided into several groups. Recent events have brought the Shi'a, or Shi'ites, to prominence on the world scene.

Henry **Corbin**

Spiritual Body and Celestial Earth: From Mazdean Iran to Shi'ite Iran

How the mystical and cosmological ideas of Shi'ite Islam were influenced by the traditional religion of Persia

TRANSLATED BY NANCY PEARSON

0-691-01883-9 PRINCETON PB $18.95

Reinhold **Loeffler**

Islam in Practice: Religious Beliefs in a Persian Village

Interviews about religious beliefs with a diverse selection of individuals in an Iranian Shi'ite village, forming a vivid picture of the faith of ordinary Muslims

0-88706-679-8 SUNY PB $21.95

Matti **Moosa**

Extremist Shi'ites: The Ghulat Sects

An illuminating study of the beliefs and practices of the Ahl'i Haqq and the Nusayris. The latter, although a small minority, are the dominant group in the Syrian government today

0-8156-2411-5 SYRACUSE $39.95

Abdulaziz A. **Sachedina**

Islamic Messianism: The Ideal of the Mahdi in Twelver Shi'ism

A survey of the conflicting beliefs about Al-Mahdi, the Shi'ite Islamic messiah

0-87395-458-0 SUNY PB $24.95

Sufism

Sufism is the mysticism of Islam. Rich in poetry, music, and intellectual ideas, the Sufis have walked (as al-Ghazati wrote) "in the light of prophecy" and have continuously inspired Islamic civilization. They are much studied today in the West.

Ahmad **Ghazzali**

Sawanih: Inspiration from the World of Pure Spirits—The Oldest Persian Sufi Treatise on Love

0-7103-0091-3 ROUTLEDGE $42.50

Arthur J. **Arberry**

The Doctrine of the Sufis

A translation of the writings of a medieval Sufi, al-Kalabadhi

0-521-29218-2 CAMBRIDGE PB $19.95

Mojdeh **Bayat** & Mohammad Ali **Jamnia**

Tales from the Land of the Sufis

Stories have always been central to the teachings of Sufism, and in this collection by two initiates of the order some of the most famous and resonant tales from Persia are retold. In one, a fool's eccentric behavior veils his deep wisdom; in another, stern-faced Moses learns a lesson in worship from a simple shepherd

0-87773-955-2 SHAMBHALA PB $16.00

Henry **Corbin**

Creative Imagination in the Sufism of Ibn Arabi

TRANSLATED BY RALPH MANHEIM

0-691-01828-6 PRINCETON PB $19.95

Ibn Abbad of Ronda

Letters on the Sufi Path

A Muslim mystic's advice and instruction to disciples on the spiritual path. Ranks with the Philokalia in depth and inspiration

TRANSLATED BY JOHN RENARD, S.J.

PREFACE BY ANNEMARIE SCHIMMEL

0-8091-2730-X PAULIST PB $9.95

Louis **Massignon**

Essay on the Origins of the Technical Language of Islamic Mystics

See also **BACKGROUND STUDIES** under **ARABIC LITERATURE** in **LITERATURE OF EUROPE, AFRICA, AND ASIA**

0-268-00928-7 NOTRE DAME $34.95

The Passion of Al-Hallaj: Mystic and Martyr of Islam

This fascinating study of a mysterious figure opens the door onto the brilliant intellectual richness of 10th-century Baghdad. Scholarly, demanding, and immensely instructive

0-691-09910-3 PRINCETON $210.00

Sayyed H. **Nasr**

Sufi Essays

Discusses the centrality of Sufi mysticism to Islam, and Sufi teachings on how a turning inward toward the Divine Presence brings together the divine essence of the human soul. Nasr also discusses the relation of Sufism to the universal mystical impulse, to other religions, and to the modern world

0-7914-1052-8 SUNY PB $16.95

Jalal ad-Din **Rumi**

Open Secret: Versions of Rumi

New translations of a Sufi poet, by a poet and a Persian scholar in collaboration

TRANSLATED BY JOHN MOYNE & COLEMAN BARKS

0-939660-06-7 THRESHOLD PB $10.00

In Rumi's poetry there is always the mystery of the pronouns. Who is this you he addresses?… Pronouns dissolve within the pressure of Rumi's recognition of his true identity. The essential power of Rumi's poetry is ecstasy, an ecstasy melting the confinement of the ego into a larger, elastic, cross-pollinating dance of Selves.

OPEN SECRET: VERSIONS OF RUMI

The Sufi Path of Love

TRANSLATED BY WILLIAM C. CHITTICK

0-87395-724-5 SUNY PB $16.95

Unseen Rain: Quatrains of Rumi

About 200 quatrains, in fresh versions by the translators of *Open Secret*

TRANSLATED BY JOHN MOYNE & COLEMAN BARKS

0-939660-16-4 THRESHOLD PB $10.00

Annemarie **Schimmel**

Mystical Dimensions of Islam

A sensitive and scholarly account of the history, doctrines, and practices of Sufism. "Beautifully written. The best and most comprehensive study on Islamic mysticism in the English language" —*Religious Studies Review*

0-8078-1271-4 NORTH CAROLINA PB $18.95

Behind all created beauty the mystic sees a witness to the source of eternal beauty—the ruby is the heart of the stone, which has been transformed into a priceless jewel through patience and shedding its blood; the emerald is powerful like the mystical leader, blinding the eyes of the serpents or the enemies of faith. The millstone turns in its restless journey like the Sufi, and the waterwheel sighs like the lover who is separated from his home and his friend. Rain is God's mercy, which revives the heart that has become lowly as dust; sun is His glory, to be contemplated through the multicolored prisms of created things. The breeze of His loving-kindness makes the growing boughs and buds dance, and the storm of His wrath uproots the dried-up bushes and trees that lack the sap of love.

MYSTICAL DIMENSIONS OF ISLAM

Idries **Shah**

Learning How to Learn: Psychology and Spirituality in the Sufi Way

The Sufi expert offers a series of questions and answers that illustrate how traditional Sufi concepts can resolve our social, psychological, and spiritual problems. Drawing on classic Sufi writings, Eastern parables of Jesus, and encounters with contemporaries, Shah offers a simple and beautiful introduction to Sufi wisdom

0-14-019513-0 PENGUIN PB $11.95

Islam Today

Fouad **Ajami**

The Arab Predicament: Arab Political Thought and Practice Since 1967

"Ajami understands Arab politics; though angry and impatient with its shortcomings, he empathizes with it; though passionate, he writes with insight and clarity"—*Middle East Journal*

See also **CONTEMPORARY POLITICS AND SOCIETY** under **THE CONTEMPORARY MIDDLE EAST** in **WORLD HISTORY AND CURRENT AFFAIRS**

0-521-43243-X CAMBRIDGE $49.95

0-521-43833-0 CAMBRIDGE PB $11.95

Steven **Barboza**

American Jihad: Islam After Malcom X

See also **LEADERS AND ACTIVISTS** under **BLACK VOICES, BLACK LIVES** under **AFRICAN-AMERICAN STUDIES** in **HISTORY OF THE AMERICAS**

0-385-47011-8 DOUBLEDAY $25.00

0-385-47694-9 IMAGE PB $14.00

John L. **Esposito**

The Islamic Threat: Myth or Reality?

"A useful antidote to the barrage of exaggerated views on Islam"—*NY Times*

0-19-508666-X OXFORD PB $9.95

Clifford **Geertz**

Islam Observed: Religious Development in Morocco and Indonesia

The anthropologist draws conclusions about the nature of religious belief from the development of a single creed, Islam, in two quite different civilizations

0-226-28511-1 CHICAGO PB $7.95

Judith **Miller**

God Has Ninety-Nine Names: A Reporter's Journey Through a Militant Middle East

This country-by-country account of today's Middle East is based on the author's unique access and experience as the Cairo bureau chief of *The New York Times* and special correspondent during the Gulf War. With her we visit the Hezbollah headquarters in Lebanon, the royal palace in Amman, the slums of Cairo, and an Israeli interrogation cell. And we come to understand that there is no unified Arab world and no single Islam, but rather a struggle for power and identity and a battle between secularism and militant fundamentalism

0-684-80973-7 SIMON & SCHUSTER $30.00

Spirituality

Metaphysics

General Books

Elaine **Edgar**

A Journey Between the Souls: The Story of a Soldier and a Pharaoh

The fascinating account of the man who slept for seven years guarding King Tutankhamen's tomb

1-88858-000-3 WHITE BOUCKE PB $16.95

Jess **Hollenback**

Mysticism: Experience, Response, and Empowerment

An impressive volume on extraordinary experience

0-271-01552-7 PENN STATE PB $25.00

Prince **Michael of Greece** & Anthony **Roberts**, translator

Living with Ghosts: Eleven Extraordinary Tales

Eleven first-person accounts of European palace and castle hauntings, with photographs

0-393-03952-8 NORTON $25.00

for any U.S. book
in print *fax* us at:
(212) 307-1973

New Paganism

Jose **Arguelles**

The Mayan Factor: Path Beyond Technology

The Maya mysteries and their relevance for the New Age

0-939680-38-6 BEAR PB $16.00

Raymond **Buckland**

Buckland's Complete Book of Witchcraft

An essential step-by-step how-to

0-87542-050-8 LLEWELLYN PB $14.95

Witchcraft from the Inside: Origins of the Fastest Growing Religious Movement in America

The history of wicca in America

EDITED BY RICHARD PIPES

1-56718-101-5 LLEWELLYN PB $12.95

Zsuzsanna E. **Budapest**

Grandmother Moon: Lunar Magic in Our Lives: Spells, Rituals, Goddesses, Legends, & Emotions Under the Moon

Feminist witch discusses how to tap the moon's power

See also **WOMEN'S SPIRITUALITY** under **SPIRITUALITY**

0-06-250114-3 HARPERCOLLINS PB $18.00

The Grandmother of Time: A Woman's Book of Celebrations, Spells, and Sacred Objects for Every Month of the Year

How to integrate wiccan practice into daily life; new approaches to ritual

0-06-250109-7 HARPERCOLLINS PB $17.00

The Holy Book of Women's Mysteries: Feminist Witchcraft, Goddess Rituals, Spellcasting, & Other Womanly Arts

A feminist survival guide of witchcraft, health, and nutrition. "*The Holy Book* is original, gentle, wonderful, magical, large in scope, hugely imaginative, a guide…wholesome food for the womansoul"

—Phyllis Chesler, *Women and Madness*

0-914728-67-9 BOOK PEOPLE PB $17.50

Pauline **Campanelli**

Ancient Ways: Reclaiming Pagan Traditions

Covers Imbolc, Vernal Equinox, and other seasonal rituals

0-87542-090-7 LLEWELLYN PB $14.95

Chas S. **Clifton**, editor

Witchcraft Today

Neo-pagans discuss their religion in modern times

Book 1: The Modern Craft Movement

0-87542-377-9 LLEWELLYN PB $9.95

Book 2: Modern Rites of Passage

0-87542-378-7 LLEWELLYN PB $9.95

Book 3: Shamanism and Witchcraft

1-567-18150-3 LLEWELLYN PB $9.95

Book 4: Challenges of the Modern Witch

1-567-18151-1 LLEWELLYN PB $12.95

Gerina **Dunwich**

Wicca Craft

Dunwich, a historian and practitioner of witchcraft, gives an entertaining and informative look at the symbolism and ideology of wicca culture. Includes recipes and instructions for concocting the perfect spell

0-8065-1238-5 CITADEL PB $8.95

Mircea **Eliade**

Shamanism: Archaic Techniques of Ecstasy

Eliade's study of shamanism is one of his greatest and most influential works. He takes a global approach to the subject but focuses particularly on the traditions of North and Central Asia

See also **MIRCEA ELIADE** under **WORLD RELIGION**

TRANSLATED BY WILLARD R. TRASK

0-691-01779-4 PRINCETON PB $17.95

Ellen Evert **Hopman** & Lawrence **Bond**

People of the Earth: The New Pagans Speak Out

Interviews with those who are practicing ancient worship, such as Margot Adler, Starhawk, Susun Weed, and Z. Budapest

0-89281-559-0 INNER TRADITIONS PB $19.95

Caitlin **Libera**

Creating Circles of Power & Magic: A Woman's Guide to Sacred Community

An exploration of group dynamics from those unhappy with the modern religious experience

0-89594-712-9 CROSSING PB $12.95

Victoria **Ransom** & Henrietta **Bernstein**

The Crone Oracles: Initiate's Guide to the Ancient Mysteries

Initiation cycles, sexual enlightenment from the Ancient Mother Goddess of the Temple of Mysteries in Eleusis that Greece worshipped over 3,000 years ago

0-87728-800-3 WEISER PB $12.95

Luisah **Teish**

Carnival of the Spirit: Seasonal Celebrations and Rites of Passage

A personal blend of ritual, traditional tales, and advice for those who follow the seasons, from an Oshun priestess

0-06-250868-7 HARPERCOLLINS PB $12.00

Divination

Tarot is most often associated with divination; however, many choose to use it as a means for meditation or as a focus for self-understanding. The I Ching is an ancient Chinese tradition using geometric diagrams—please see Confucianism under Asian Religions for these books; runes are ancient characters and letters used for prognostication; and astrology is the study of planets and their effect on the world.

Nathaniel **Altman**

The Palmistry Workbook

0-85030-352-4 STERLING PB $14.95

Ted **Andrews**

Crystal Balls & Crystal Bowls: Tools for Ancient Scrying & Modern Seership

Healing, divination, astral projection, and clairvoyance through the aid of the crystal ball and bowl

1-56718-026-4 LLEWELLYN PB $12.95

How to See and Read the Aura

Provides exercises to build aura reading and interpretation skills as well as advice on how to balance your own aura

0-87542-013-3 LLEWELLYN PB $3.95

Barbara **Bishop**

Numerology: Universal Vibrations of Numbers

A workbook for calculating and interpreting numerical vibrations and using them in everyday life

0-87542-056-7 LLEWELLYN PB $12.95

Ruth **Gardner**

Instant Handwriting Analysis: A Key to Personal Success

How to use graphology for self-understanding, with illustrations that help illuminate the meaning of various types of handwriting. Includes resources for continuing study

0-87542-251-9 LLEWELLYN PB $15.95

William **Hewitt**

Tea Leaf Reading

Step-by-step instructions for preparing a cup of tea to reading and interpreting tea-leaf symbols. With comprehensive glossary of hundreds of tea-leaf images

0-87542-308-6 LLEWELLYN PB $3.95

Patricia **Telesco**

The Victorian Flower Oracle: The Language of Nature

Learn to create your own magically charged oracle and discover the divinatory interpretations of 79 flowers, herbs, and trees

0-87542-786-3 LLEWELLYN PB $12.95

Brandon **Toropov**

I-Ching for Beginners

A layman's guide to the ancient Chinese system of divination

0-86316-230-4 HARLEM RIVER PRESS PB $11.00

Edred **Thorsson**

The Book of Ogham: The Celtic Tree Oracle

The Celtic Ogham alphabet is the basis of this system of divination. Druid lore and Celtic spirituality are also provided to augment the practitioner's understanding of the system's symbols and meaning

0-87542-783-9 LLEWELLYN PB $12.95

Tarot

The origins of tarot—the deck of cards widely used for fortune-telling and other divination purposes—are hotly disputed. Many believe that the method was created in ancient Egypt, reaching Europe by Gypsy migrations; indeed, Gypsies around the world today remain among the foremost practitioners of the art of reading tarot cards.

There is still great variety in methods of interpretation and in the decks used by the different tarot traditions, although they may have some of the same symbolic cards, such as the juggler, high priestess, and hanged man. Among the more famous decks is that designed by 20th-century magician Aleister Crowley.

Sylvia **Abraham**

How to Read the Tarot

How to read any tarot deck of both the Major and Minor Arcana

1-56718-001-9 LLEWELLYN PB $4.99

Eileen **Connolly**

The Tarot: A New Handbook for the Apprentice

0-87877-162-X UNITED STATES GAMES SYSTEMS PB .. $15.00

Aleister **Crowley**

The Book of Thoth

0-87728-268-4 WEISER PB $12.95

Aleister Crowley

Alfred **Douglas**

Tarot: The Origins, Meaning and Uses of the Cards

The historical, mystical, and psychological significance of tarot cards; with instructions on how to read them

0-14-019239-5 VIKING PB $10.00

Jean **Freer**

The New Feminist Tarot

0-8095-7057-2 BORGO $27.00

David **Godwin**

How to Choose Your Own Tarot

This guidebook explains how to shop for apersonal tarot deck for divination, magic, or meditation

1-56718-323-9 LLEWELLYN PB $4.99

P. Scott **Hollander**

Tarot for Beginners

How to use the cards for meditation and self-enlightenment as well as for divination

1-56718-363-8 LLEWELLYN PB $12.95

Runes

Ralph **Blum**, editor

The New Book of Runes: A Handbook for the Use of an Ancient Oracle—The Viking Runes

0-312-09758-1 ST. MARTIN'S $29.95

Lisa **Peschel**

A Practical Guide to the Runes: Their Uses in Divination and Magic

How to use runes on a daily basis to improve quality of life

0-87542-593-3 LLEWELLYN PB $4.99

Richard **Webster**

Omens, Oghams and Oracles: Divination in the Druidic Tradition

How to use the 25 Ogham fews and the druid sticks as well as sky stones, touchstones, and bodhran drums through illustration and geomantic figures

1-56718-800-1 LLEWELLYN PB $12.95

Astrology

Astrology—the interpretation of how the movements of stars and planets affect events on earth—originated in ancient Mesopotamia, and flourished during the Hellenistic period, when the zodiac was established. Hundreds of books explain how to create and read astrological charts, but the following are among the clearest and most interesting.

Linda **Goodman**

Linda Goodman's Love Signs: A New Approach to the Human Heart

From the late, popular astrologer

0-06-096896-6 HARPERPERENNIAL PB $18.00

Rose **Lineman** & Jan **Popelka**

Compendium of Astrology

0-914918-43-5 SCHIFFER PB $24.95

William **Hewitt**

Astrology for Beginners: An Easy Guide to Understanding & Interpreting Your Chart

How to make a chart the easy way. References for advanced study also included

0-87542-307-8 LLEWELLYN PB........$9.95

Chris **Marshall**

The Complete Book of Chinese Horoscopes

With a punch-out wheel for your own use

1-55670-490-9 STEWART, TABORI........$22.50

Joan **McEvers**, editor

Intimate Relationships: The Astrology of Attraction

Nine astrology experts discuss sex, love, and marriage

0-87542-386-8 LLEWELLYN PB........$14.95

Dennis **Oakland**

Your Planetary Personality: Everything You Need to Make Sense of Your Horoscope

In-depth planetary positions discussed for use in analyzing fears, emotional blocks, relationships, and more

0-87542-594-1 LLEWELLYN PB........$24.95

Dane **Rudhyar**

The Astrological Houses: The Spectrum of Individual Experience

0-916360-24-5 C.R.C.S. PB........$12.95

Frances **Sakoian** & Louis **Acker**

The Astrologer's Handbook

A popular guide to interpreting and creating natal charts

0-06-272004-X HARPERCOLLINS PB........$13.00

Gloria **Star**

Optimum Child: Developing Your Child's Fullest Potential Through Astrology

An in-depth astrological analysis of childhood

0-87542-740-5 LLEWELLYN PB........$9.95

Suzanne **White**

The New Astrology

Ancient craft updated for the '90s

0-312-01797-9 ST. MARTIN'S PB........$15.95

David **Williams**

Astro-Economics: The Study of Astrology and the Business Cycle

How astrology can be used to forecast stock market and business trends

0-87542-882-7 LLEWELLYN PB........$3.00

Sandra Harrisson **Young** & Edna **Rowland**

Destined for Murder: Profiles of Six Serial Killers with Astrological Commentary

An analysis of six murderers' birth charts

1-56718-832-X LLEWELLYN PB........$12.95

Near-Death and Out-of-Body Experiences

Dannion **Brinkley** & Paul **Perry**

At Peace in the Light: The Further Adventures of a Reluctant Psychic Who Reveals the Secret of Your Spiritual Powers

The Southern good ol' boy who had his life transformed by two near-death experiences updates us on his "grief centers" and his compassionate hospice work

FOREWORD BY JAMES REDFIELD

0-06-017674-1 HARPERCOLLINS........$20.00

0-06-109446-3 HARPERCOLLINS PB........$5.99

Saved by the Light: The True Story of a Man Who Died Twice and the Profound Revelations He Received

A well-written description of Brinkley's two near-death experiences

0-679-43176-4 VILLARD PB........$5.99

William **Buhlman**

Adventures Beyond the Body: Proving Your Immortality Through Out-of-Body Travel

Buhlman finds startling evidence that astral travel can help verify the existence of the soul, expand consciousness, teach us about past lives, and enhance our present lives

0-06-251371-0 HARPERCOLLINS PB........$14.00

Mally **Cox-Chapman**

The Case for Heaven: Near Death Experiences as Evidence of the Afterlife

Based on interviews with over 50 people who experienced near death, Cox-Chapman explores the commonalities and what they suggest about the evidence of an afterlife

0-399-14024-7 PUTNAM........$19.95

0-425-15401-7 BERKELEY PB........$12.00

Betty J. **Eadie**

Embraced by the Light

A woman's recounting of her near-death experience; over five million copies sold

0-533-5659-15 BANTAM PB........$5.99

The Awakening Heart: My Continuing Journey to Love

Eadie's update on how her experiences in the light have further transformed her life

0-671-55868-4 POCKET........$20.00

Melita

The Llewellyn Practical Guide to Astral Projection: The Out-of-Body Experience

A how-to for moving consciousness through space, time, and other dimensions, with exercises that develop new skills

0-87542-181-4 LLEWELLYN PB........$9.95

Raymond A. **Moody**, Jr.

Life After Life

Near-death experiences related by the doctor who was the first to explore this compelling phenomenon

0-89176-037-7 MOCKINGBIRD........$14.95

0-553-27484-8 BDD PB........$5.99

Dianne **Morrissey**

Anyone Can See the Light: The 7 Keys to a Guided Out-of-Body Experience

Explains the difference between out-of-body and near-death experiences and gives tips on how to achieve an out-of-body experience

1-88347-813-8 STILLPOINT........$18.95

Melvin **Morse** & Paul **Perry**

Transformed by the Light: The Powerful Effect of Near-Death Experiences on People's Lives

Seattle pediatrician interviewed dozens of people who have undergone a near-death experience and recorded how these people have been changed for the better

0-8041-1183-9 IVY PB........$5.99

David **Seltzer**

Raising the Dead: A Doctor's Encounter with His Own Mortality

"One of the most bizarre near-death experiences ever recorded. A fascinating tale"
—*NY Times Book Review*

0-14-023489-6 PENGUIN PB........$9.95

Reincarnation

Reincarnation—also called "transmigration of the soul"—is the belief that after the death of the body, the soul passes into another body, whether animal or human. Although many ancient societies believed in some form of reincarnation, the doctrine reached its most developed form in India. An individual was reborn lower or higher up on the scale of possible rebirths depending upon "karma"—the sum total of a person's good and bad deeds.

Experiments in hypnotic regression have enhanced its popularity in recent decades; one particularly famous example, in the 1950s, was the account of a Colorado housewife who was purportedly an Irish girl—Bridey Murphy—in a prior life.

Ted **Andrews**

How to Uncover Your Past Lives

How to safely regress from nine different techniques to access past lives

0-87542-022-2 LLEWELLYN PB........$4.99

Gina **Cerminara**

Many Mansions: The Edgar Cayce Story of Reincarnation

0-451-16817-8 NEW AMERICAN LIBRARY PB........$5.99

Jonathan **Cott**

The Search For Omm Sety: A Story of Eternal Love

Reliving an affair with an Egyptian pharaoh

0-446-39040-2 WARNER PB $9.95

David **Darling**

Zen Physics: The Logic of Death, the Science of Reincarnation

The tenets of Buddhism are elegantly combined with hard scientific data in a proof of reincarnation. Culminating years of research in astrophyics, anthropology, Eastern religions, philosophy, and psychology, Darling takes us on an adventure whose outcome is the inevitability of afterlife

0-06-017352-1 HARPERCOLLINS $23.00

Joseph **Head**, editor

Reincarnation: The Phoenix Fire Mystery

How renowned historical figures have viewed reincarnation

1-55700-026-3 THEOSOPHICAL PB $19.00

Shirley **MacLaine**

It's All in the Playing

0-553-05267-5 BDD $18.95

Out on a Limb

0-553-05035-4 BDD $15.95

0-553-27370-1 BDD PB $6.50

Roger **Woolger**

Other Lives, Other Selves: A Jungian Psychotherapist Discovers Past Lives

0-553-34595-8 BANTAM PB $12.95

Between Lives

Michael **Newton**

Journey of Souls: Case Studies of Life Between Lives

The testimony of 29 subjects attempts to confirm the veracity of the immortal soul with abundant detail on the death experience and the spirit world. Tips on recognizing soulmates and much more

1-56718-485-5 LLEWELLYN PB $12.95

Afterlife

M. Scott **Peck**

In Heaven as on Earth: A Vision of the Afterlife

Peck turns from the enormously popular form of his spiritual guides to undertake an exploration of the afterlife in the form of a novel. When the book's narrator, a psychiatrist much like Peck, awakens into the afterlife, he begins an adventure that leads him to the fundamental moral principles that transcend mortality

See also **WESTERN** under **20TH-CENTURY SPIRITUAL LEADERS** under **SPIRITUALITY**

0-7868-6204-1 HYPERION $19.95

T. Lobsang **Rampa**

Feeding the Flame

Mystical revelations on life after death, suicide, astral body travel

0-938294-89-X INNER LIGHT PB $12.95

Darryl **Reanney**

After Death: A New Future for Human Consciousness

The late New Zealand molecular biologist discusses fear of death and our notion of time

0-688-14420-9 MORROW $23.00

Soul Travel

D.J. **Conway**

Astral Love: Romance, Ecstasy & Higher Consciousness

In a world full of frightening sexual realities—both physical and emotional—astral sex magick offers the safest sex around. This is a guide to finding astral ecstasy and, when desire for more fleshy involvement surfaces, guidance from your astral partner to find the right earthly lover

1-56718-161-9 LLEWELLYN PB $12.95

Past-Life Regression

Florence Wagner **McLain**

A Practical Guide to Past Life Regression

This guide provides help for retrieving past life memories and learning how to use them

0-87542-510-0 LLEWELLYN PB $7.95

Psychic Phenomena

Spiritual or paranormal phenomena are dismissed by many critics as nonsense or fraud. Yet some writers and scientists, including those below, have sought to explore the relationship between such experiences and the rigorous demands of the natural sciences.

Ted **Andrews**

How to Develop and Use Psychometry

Psychometry is the ability to read the psychic imprints on objects, people, and places. Includes over 25 exercises to help in the step-by-step process of elevating psychic abilities

1-56718-025-6 LLEWELLYN PB $4.99

How to Meet & Work with Spirit Guides

How to access guardian angels, nature spirits, familiars, dead friends, and family members

0-87542-008-7 LLEWELLYN PB $4.99

Ruth **Montgomery** & Joanne **Garland**

Ruth Montgomery: Herald of the New Age

Spiritual autobiography of the psychic

0-449-21252-1 CREST PB $5.99

Loyd **Auerbach**

Psychic Dreaming: A Parapsychologist's Handbook

Astral travel in the dream state, and tips on how to identify and use psychic dreaming elements to achieve a variety of personal goals

0-446-36056-2 WARNER PB $5.50

Reincarnation, Channeling, and Possession

This book attempts to answer scientifically the long-asked questions associated with transmigration

0-446-36333-2 WARNER PB $5.99

Patricia **Collins**

Psychic New York: A Guide to Astrologers, Tarot Readers, Psychics, Palmists, & Numerologists

The complete guide to where to go for psychic healing. Includes brief introductions to all the occult arts

1-88549-228-6 CITY & CO. PB $13.00

FATE magazine

Psychic Pets & Spirit Animals: True Stories from the Files of FATE

Psychic pets, ghost animals, animal omens, and near-death pet experiences are among the many paranormal animal experiences explored here

1-56718-299-2 LLEWELLYN PB $4.99

Linda **Georgian**

Communicating with the Dead: Reaching Friends and Loved Ones Who Have Passed On to Another Dimension

The TV psychic explains this surprisingly common event

0-684-810880-3 SIMON & SCHUSTER PB $11.00

Creating Your Own Future: A Practical Guide to Developing Your Psychic and Spiritual Powers

How to tap into your psychic self, from the founder and host of the Psychic Friend's Network

0-684-81089-1 FIRESIDE PB $12.00

Hans **Hozer**

The Directory of Psychics: How to Find, Evaluate, and Communicate with Professional Psychics and Mediums

A paranormal expert presents a useful guide to finding and working with psychics, how to consult one, evaluate services, and how to avoid charlatans

0-8092-3561-7 CONTEMPORARY PB $12.95

Jean-Charles **de Fontbrune**

Nostradamus: Countdown to Apocalypse

0-8050-1048-3 HOLT PB $14.95

Erika **Cheetham**, editor

The Prophecies of Nostradamus: The Man Who Saw Tomorrow

Nostradamus was renowned in the 16th century for his predictions. Though they can be hard to decipher, since they are expressed in complex symbolism and anagrams, some are remarkably accurate, with uncanny descriptions of, for example, the French Revolution; some can be interpreted as predicting World War II and, around the year 2000, the end of the world

0-425-08757-3 BERKLEY PB $5.50
0-399-50345-5 PERIGEE PB $10.95

John **Hogue**

Nostradamus: The New Revelations

All 34,000 words of Nostradamus's original writings computer-analyzed. The results presented in unique and attractive layout with four-color illustrations and archival photographs

1-85230-683-1 ELEMENT PB $19.95

Peter **Lorie**

Nostradamus: The Millennium and Beyond—The Prophecies to 2016

Even for confirmed skeptics, the predictions of Nostradamus make intriguing reading. Lorie and astrologer Liz Greene unravel the puzzle of the ancient verses to formulate prediction for the coming millennium and beyond. Includes photographs, original drawings, and "special effects"

0-671-89656-3 SIMON & SCHUSTER $22.50

Judith **Orloff**

Second Sight: The Personal Story of a Psychiatrist Clairvoyant

A unique autobiography by a physician who learns to accept her psychic gifts and incorporates them into her practice

0-446-51842-5 WARN $22.95

J.B. **Rhine**

Extra-Sensory Perception

Rhine coined the term ESP; when his book received a positive review in the *NY Times*, it fostered widespread interest among the public that has continued to the present

0-8283-1464-0 BRANDEN PB $14.95

Channeling

Judy **Boss**

In Silence They Return

The author's spiritual awakening through her discovery of automatic writing after the death of her husband

087542081X LLEWELLYN PB $5.95

Edain **McCoy**

How to Do Automatic Writing

Learn how to receive and interpret written messages channeled through you from other intelligences

1-56718-662-9 LLEWELLYN PB $3.99

Suzane **Northrup** & Kate **McLoughlin**

The Seance: Healing Messages from Beyond

Testimonials and instruction on communication with the spirit world

0-440-22176-5 DELL PB $5.99

UFOs

Unidentified Flying Objects have been hotly debated for much of this century. Thousands of sightings over the years have convinced many people that UFOs have, indeed, come from outer space; some individuals actually claim to have not only seen UFOs but to have been abducted by aliens.

George **Andrews**

Extra-Terrestrials Among Us

Evidence that alien beings are living on earth

0-87542-010-9 LLEWELLYN PB $4.95

Norman **Briazack** & Simon **Mennick**

The UFO Guidebook

Encyclopedia of UFO-related topics

0-8065-0763-2 LYLE STUART PB $4.95

Michael **Craft**

Alien Impact: A Comprehensive Look at the Evidence of Human/Alien Contact

Explains the entire range of human contact with aliens, from angels to beings from other planets. Also makes the point that as humans become more technologically advanced, so do aliens

0-312-14438-5 ST. MARTIN'S $23.95

Lawrence **Fawcett** & Barry J. **Greenwood**

The UFO Cover-Up: What the Government Won't Say

From two authors who have investigated UFOs for decades

0-671-76555-8 FIRESIDE PB $10.00

Budd **Hopkins**

Witnessed: The True Story of the Brooklyn Bridge UFO Abductions

This account features a 16-page black-and-white insert

0-671-56915-5 POCKET $23.00

Patrick **Huyghe**

The Field Guide to Extraterrestrials

Where to find sighting locations

0-380-78128-X AVON PB $16.50

John E. **Mack**

Abduction: Human Encounters with Aliens

The book that started it all

0-345-39300-7 DEL REY PB $6.99

Robert **Temple**

The Sirius Mystery

Evidence of visits by beings from Sirius

0-89281-163-3 INNER TRADITIONS PB $16.95

The New Physics

Jack **Cohen** & Ian **Stewart**

The Collapse of Chaos: Discovering Simplicity in a Complex World

The authors combine chaos and complexity into a theory that derives simplicity from the interaction of the two

0-14-017874-0 PENGUIN PB $13.95

Allan **Combs** & Mark **Holland**

Synchronicity: Science, Myth and the Trickster

A discussion of the phenomenon of synchronicity, picking up threads from psychology, spirituality, and physics

1-56924-845-1 MARLOWE PB $10.95

Francis **Crick**

The Astonishing Hypothesis: The Scientific Search for the Soul

"…a fascinating argument that consciousness and what has long been called the soul are now accessible to scientific investigation"
—Carl Sagan, *Cosmos*

0-684-80158-2 TOUCHSTONE PB $14.00

Michael **Heim**

The Metaphysics of Virtual Reality

An exploration of the question of how our sense of reality changes with the advent of virtual reality technologies

0-19-509258-9 OXFORD PB $9.95

Nick **Herbert**

Elemental Mind: Human Consciousness and the New Physics

"…Herbert scrutinizes recent brain research, reviews highly conjectural quantum models of mind, and outlines his own theory…which, if true, might help explain paranormal phenomena"—*Publishers Weekly*

See also **THE NEUROSCIENCES AND THE BRAIN** under **BIOLOGY** under **LIFE SCIENCES** in **SCIENCE**

0-452-27245-9 PLUME PB $11.95

Martha **Heyneman**

The Breathing Cathedral: Feeling Our Way into a Living Cosmos

A sweeping survey from Dante to Stephen Hawking in the quest for discovering our place in the universe

0-87156-687-7 SIERRA CLUB $25.00

J. Allan **Hobson**

The Chemistry of Conscious States: How the Brain Changes Its Mind

Hobson, a world-renowned neuroscientist, has the rare gift of rendering the complexity of the brain clear and accessible to the general reader. With lively anecdotes and familiar examples, he explains how the chemistry of the brain creates the bewildering range of conscious experience

See also **NONCOGNITIVE PERSPECTIVES OF THE MIND** under **SPECIAL TOPICS IN PSYCHOLOGY** under **PSYCHOLOGY** in **SOCIAL STUDIES**

0-316-36754-0 LITTLE, BROWN $24.95

Daniel C. **Matt**

God & the Big Bang: Discovering Harmony Between Science & Spirituality

An unraveling of one of humankind's tightest knots

1-87904-548-6 JEWISH LIGHTS $22.95

Chet **Raymo**

The Soul of the Night: An Astronomical Pilgrimage

An astronomer's essays on the night sky and his ruminations on reason and faith

1-88691-311-0 HUNGRY MIND PB $15.00

Michael S. **Schneider**

A Beginner's Guide to Constructing the Universe: The Mathematical Archetypes of Nature, Art, and Science, A Voyage from 1 to 10

An elegantly illustrated meditation on both the uses and the beauties of numbers and geometrical shapes; subtle and original, Schneider lucidly explores arcane territory without demanding advanced mathematical training of his reader

See also **GENERAL INTRODUCTIONS** under **INTRODUCTIONS TO MATHEMATICS** under **MATHEMATICS** in **SCIENCE**

0-06-016939-7 HARPERCOLLINS $30.00
0-06-092671-6 HARPERPERENNIAL PB $17.50

Brian **Swimme**

The Hidden Heart of the Cosmos: Humanity and the New Story

From a cosmologist (*The Universe Is a Green Dragon*) who now considers the spiritual implications of science's theories and discoveries about the birth of the universe

1-57075-058-0 ORBIS $15.00

Michael **Talbot**

The Holographic Universe

Fascinating and elegantly written, tackles the new theory of reality to explain the mind's paranormal abilities, the new physics, and the riddles of the brain and body

0-06-092258-3 HARPERPERENNIAL PB $13.50

Frank **Tipler**

The Physics of Immortality: Modern Cosmology, God and the Resurrection of the Dead

A big book that addresses the often-remarked, little-understood nexus of quantum physics and theology. Rigorously drawing on quantum mechanics, information theory, and advanced mathematics, in the context of Jewish messianism, deism, and diverse theological concepts of immortality, Tipler articulates his "Omega Point" proof of God's existence

See also **SCIENCE AND RELIGION** under **WORLD RELIGION**

0-385-46799-0 ANCHOR PB $14.95

19th-Century Spiritualist Revival

Helena **Blavatsky**

The Secret Doctrine

Madame Blavatsky, co-founder with Henry Steel Olcott of the Theosophical Society, claimed that she had been chosen by superhuman mahatmas to reveal ancient knowledge to the world and perform miracles. This is a two-volume abridged version of her masterpiece

0-911500-00-6 THEOSOPHICAL $21.00

K. Paul **Johnson**

The Masters Revealed: Madame Blavatsky and the Myth of the Great White Lodge

0-7914-2064-7 SUNY PB $18.95

Robert **McDermott**, editor

The Essential Rudolf Steiner

Steiner believed that man's attachment to material possessions had crippled his innate ability to participate in spiritual processes, and that only extensive training of the consciousness could help recapture that ability. His philosophy was the basis for the Waldorf School movement

See also **CLASSICS** under **THEORY AND PHILOSOPHY** under **EDUCATION** in **SOCIAL STUDIES**

0-06-065345-0 HARPERCOLLINS PB $20.00

Rudolf **Steiner**

Theosophy: An Introduction to Supersensible Knowledge of the World and the Destination of Man

0-88010-179-2 ANTHROPOSOPHIC $18.95
0-910142-39-4 ANTHROPOSOPHIC PB $6.95

Emanuel **Swedenborg**

Divine Love and Wisdom

The 18th-century scientist, inventor, philosopher, and visionary helped point the way for man to be reunited with God. His descriptions of the spiritual world influenced William Blake, the most mystical of the Romantic poets, as well as the spiritualists of the 19th-century revival

0-87785-129-8 SWEDENBORG FOUNDATION PB ... $6.95

Heaven and Hell

0-87785-167-0 SWEDENBORG FOUNDATION PB $7.95

The Occult

Philip S. **Berg**

Kabbalah for the Layman

Vol. 1

Rabbi Berg traces Kabbalah thought from its early beginnings to the 20th century, and explores the concept of reincarnation

0-943688-01-9 KABBALAH CENTRE PB $11.95

Vol. 2

0-943688-83-3 KABBALAH CENTRE PB $10.95

Vol. 3

0-943688-70-1 KABBALAH CENTRE PB $10.95

Grillot **de Givry**

Witchcraft, Magic, and Alchemy

0-486-22493-7 DOVER PB $12.95

Charles **Fielding**

The Practical Quabalah

Combines Jungian psychology and Western mystery tradition with the esoteric symbolism of the Tree of Life, and looks specifically at personality, karma, reincarnation, and the importance of ritual

0-87728-654-X WEISER PB $11.00

Anton Szandor **LaVey**

The Satanic Bible

The "Black Pope" of the Church of Satan presents the devil's scriptures and the keys in Enochian

0-380-01539-0 AVON PB $10.00

Debbie **Nathan** & Michael **Snedeker**

Satan's Silence: Ritual Abuse and the Making of a Modern American Witch-Hunt

Accusations of ritual sexual abuse of children are rampant in America today, and yet, when such accusations are closely examined, it's clear that they often are leveled without a shred of evidence. Journalist Nathan and criminal defense lawyer Snedeker examine this phenomenon—a true witch hunt—in America today and show how a conspiracy of values among the federal government, feminists, and fundamentalists has promoted it

0-465-07180-5 BASIC $25.00

James **Randi**

An Encyclopedia of Lies, Frauds, and Hoaxes of the Occult and Supernatural

A fascinating compendium of all kinds of shenanigans from "The Amazing" Randi

0-312-13066-X ST. MARTIN'S $24.95

Magic

Abramelin the Mage

The Book of the Sacred Magic

This edition is a republication of the 1900 edition, which is based on the 15th-century manuscript. Abramelin was an Egyptian magician and this is a system based on a mix of Hellenism and the Cabala for both black and white magic

0-486-23211-5 DOVER PB $8.95

Tara **Buckland**

How to Make an Easy Charm to Attract Love in Your Life

From the Egyptians, harmless charms for catching that elusive love

0-87542-087-7 LLEWELLYN PB $3.95

D.J. **Conway**

Moon Magick: Myth & Magic, Crafts & Recipes, Rituals & Spells

Understanding the moon's cycles and how they affect mood

1-56718-167-8 LLEWELLYN PB $16.95

Aleister **Crowley**

The Book of Lies

A collection of paradoxes

0-87728-516-0 WEISER PB $8.95

Liber Aleph: The Book of Wisdom or Folly

Written in New York City at the end of World War I, this work set down many concepts still of interest today

0-87728-729-5 WEISER PB $16.00

Barrie **Dolnick**

Simple Spells for Success: Ancient Practices for Creating Abundance and Prosperity

Attracting money, continuted growth, personal power, and other spells for financial success

0-517-70338-0 CROWN $18.00

Dion **Fortune**

Applied Magic and Aspects of Occultism

From the founder of the Society of Inner Light, a selection of Fortune's writings on all manner of concerns for those interested in the occult

0-85030-665-5 AQUARIAN PB $15.95

David Allen **Hulse**

The Key of It All: An Encyclopedic Guide to the Sacred Languages and Magickal Systems of the World—The Eastern Mysteries

0-87542-318-3 LLEWELLYN PB $24.95

Konstantinos

Summoning Spirits: The Art of Magical Evocation

A complete manual for evoking spirits to effect life changes, with descriptions of over 50 entities to evoke

1-56718-381-6 LLEWELLYN PB $14.95

James R. **Lewis**, editor

Magical Religion and Modern Witchcraft

A professor of religion has compiled an anthology of writing from contemporary neo-pagans

0-7914-2890-7 SUNY PB $19.95

S. L. MacGregor **Mathers**

Astral Projection, Ritual Magic, and Alchemy

Edited by Francis King, this book presents the Flying Rolls work of Golden Dawn members

See also **ALCHEMY**

0-89281-164-1 DESTINY PB $10.95

W. Somerset **Maugham**

The Magician

A melodramatic tale based on the career of the sinister magus Aleister Crowley

See also **THE EARLY 20TH CENTURY** under **20TH-CENTURY BRITISH AND IRISH FICTION** in **LITERATURE OF THE BRITISH ISLES**

0-14-018595-X VIKING PB $11.95

Phoenix **McFarland**

The Complete Book of Magical Names

The only compilation of nonbiblical monikers is gleaned from modern and ancient sources

1-56718-251-8 LLEWELLYN PB $19.95

Marina **Medici**

Good Magic

Incantations, herbs, flowers, and natural elements to channel energy

0-671-76316-4 PRENTICE HALL PB $18.00

Love Magic

4-color photos and illustrations enhance discussion of spells, incantations, and romantic potions

0-671-79684-4 FIRESIDE PB $16.00

Nema

Maat Magick: A Guide to Self-Initiation

The Egyptian goddess of truth and justice revealed by a practicing wiccan

0-87728-827-5 WEISER PB $14.95

Nigel **Pennick**

Magical Alphabets

The secrets and significance of ancient scripts, including Greek, Hebrew, Oghan, runic, and alchemical alphabets

0-87728-747-3 WEISER PB $12.95

Elizabeth **Pepper** & John **Wilcock**

The Witches' Almanac: Spring 1996 to Spring 1997

A complete guide to lunar harmony, notes on planetary aspects and their influence on each sun sign, herbal and animal secrets, incantations

0-88496-407-8 WITCHES' ALMANAC PB $6.95

Steve **Richards**

Invisibility: Mastering the Art of Vanishing

A unique how-to

1-85538-168-0 AQUARIAN PB $9.00

Tetragrammation: The Secret to Evoking Angelic Powers and the Key to the Apocalypse

The four Hebrew letters IHVH is the occult key that unlocks the secret of tarot, astrology, the Old Testament, the Book of Revelations, the Kabbalah, and modern ritual magic

1-56718-744-7 LLEWELLYN PB $24.95

Donald **Tyson**

How to Make and Use a Magic Mirror

The ancient art of scrying into the black mirror

0-919345-31-X PHOENIX PROJECTS PB $8.95

Bill **Whitcomb**

The Magician's Companion: A Practical Encyclopedic Guide to Magical and Religious Symbolism

Eastern and Western magical systems. Rituals, exercises, organizations, periodicals also are listed

0-87542-868-1 LLEWELLYN PB $24.95

Alchemy

The effort to transform base metals into silver or gold had its roots in ancient China, India, and Greece. When interest in the art was revived in the Middle Ages, it was given the Arabic name "alchemy." By the Renaissance, leading scientists were starting to doubt the possibility of transmuting one metal into another. That possibility was not irrefutably disproved until the 19th century. Nonetheless, the ancient and medieval alchemists, in the process of developing their theories, offered valuable contributions to the world of science: the techniques and equipment they used helped lay the foundation for modern-day chemistry.

Frater **Albertus**

Alchemist's Handbook

A working manual

0-87728-655-8 WEISER PB $12.50

Stanislas Klossowski **de Rola**

Alchemy: The Secret Art

0-500-81003-6 THAMES & HUDSON PB $14.95

S. L. MacGregor **Mathers**

Astral Projection, Ritual Magic, and Alchemy

Edited by Francis King, this book presents the Flying Rolls work of Golden Dawn members

See also **MAGIC**

0-89281-164-1 DESTINY PB $10.95

H. Stanley **Redgrove**

Alchemy, Ancient and Modern

1-56459-143-3 KESSINGER PB $17.95

Amber **Wolfe**

Personal Alchemy

The secrets to using color and light rays for healing

0-87542-890-8 LLEWELLYN PB $17.95

Spirituality

General Books

David **Abram**

The Spell of the Sensuous: Perception and Language in a More-than-Human World

How language forms and informs perception. "This book of David Abram lights up the landscape of language, mind, history" —Gary Snyder

0-679-43819-X PANTHEON $25.00

Cass **Adams**

The Soul Unearthed: Celebrating Wildness & Personal Renewal Through Nature

An anthology of 60 stories, essays, poems, and interviews that explore how wildness affects us spiritually

0-87477-838-7 PUTNAM PB $14.95

Robert **Aitken** & David **Steindl-Rast**

The Ground We Share: Everyday Practice, Buddhist and Christian

In a series of dialogues, Zen master Aitken and Benedictine monk Steindl-Rast find common ground

1-57062-219-1 SHAMBHALA PB $15.00

Richard **Bach**

Stranger to the Ground

See also **WESTERN** under **20TH-CENTURY SPIRITUAL LEADERS**

0-440-20658-8 DELL PB $5.99

Sister Wendy **Beckett**

The Gaze of Love: Meditations on Art and Spiritual Transformation

0-06-060828-5 HARPERCOLLINS PB $16.00

Thomas **Berry**

Creative Energy: Bearing Witness for the Earth

Eco-theology adapted from *The Dream of the Earth*

0-87156-854-3 SIERRA CLUB PB $9.00

Jeffrey **Boyd**

Reclaiming the Soul: The Search for Meaning in a Self-Centered Culture

A psychiatrist of 25 years' experience and an Episcopal minister, Boyd argues against the thrust of the mental health movement, positing instead that the modern search for meaning is best understood as a search for the soul. Examining the biblical understanding of the soul and tracing the development of its definition to modern days, Boyd's revolutionary argument is an effort to restore the centrality of a conception of God rather than a conviction of self

0-8298-1080-3 PILGRIM PB $15.95

Alan **Briskin**

The Stirring of the Soul in the Workplace

"Criticizing the sterility of much contemporary business practice and much modern spirituality, Briskin provides suggestions for soulfully reinvigorating the workplace"
—*Publishers Weekly*

0-7879-0281-0 JOSSEY-BASS $27.95

Richard **Bucke**

Cosmic Consciousness

A classic text examining man's mystical nature

0-8065-0211-8 CITADEL PB $12.95

Ken **Carey**

The Third Millennium: Living in the Posthistoric World

Carey explores our social structures, relationship to the environment, work, economy, and more in his determination to open "access [to] higher-frequency thought"

0-06-251408-3 HARPERCOLLINS PB $12.00

Tilden **Edwards**

Living in the Presence: Spiritual Exercises to Open Our Lives to the Awareness of God

0-06-062127-3 HARPERCOLLINS PB $12.00

The **Dalai Lama**

Beyond Dogma: Dialogues and Discourses

A discussion of current issues such as AIDS and human rights from the exiled leader of Tibet

See also **EASTERN** under **20TH-CENTURY SPIRITUAL LEADERS**

1-55643-218-6 NORTH ATLANTIC PB $14.95

Morgan Simone **Daleo**

Curriculum of Love: Cultivating the Spiritual Nature of Children

Based on Christian values but flavored with Eastern philosophy, each of the 10 chapters provides art, storytelling, and music activities to illustrate history, compassion, beauty, balance, joy, harmony, mindfulness, service, self-reliance, and community

See also **INNER AND OUTER DISCIPLINE** under **BEING A PARENT** under **PARENTING** in **LIFESTYLES AND PRACTICAL ADVICE**

0-9648799-4-8 GRACE PB $17.95

Diana L. **Eck**

Encountering God: A Spiritual Journey from Bozeman to Banaras

In the spirit of the ecumenical movement, Eck, a lifelong Methodist and a professor of comparative religion at Harvard, reveals how her encounters with the great religions of the East—Hinduism, Buddhism, and Islam—challenged, and eventually enriched, her Christian beliefs

0-8070-7303-2 BEACON PB $14.00

Our experience with people of other faiths may be difficult or rewarding, or both. In any case our "interfaith dialogue" does not usually begin with philosophy or theory, but with experience and relationships. Individually and collectively, our experience has now begun to challenge traditional religious thinking and to contribute decisively to the reformulation of our theologies.
ENCOUNTERING GOD: A SPIRITUAL JOURNEY FROM BOZEMAN TO BANARAS

George R. **Elder**

An Encyclopedia of Archetypal Symbolism—Volume 2: The Body

Developed from the resources in the Archive for Research in Archetypal Symbolism, this second volume concentrates on the human body as the center of insight and the sacred. "This is an astonishing book, an important publishing event and a significant sourcebook of body wisdom" —*Publishers Weekly*. The first volume is currently out of print

1-57062-096-2 SHAMBHALA $124.50

William **Elliott**

Tying Rocks to Clouds: Meetings and Conversations with Wise and Spiritual People

By a mental health worker who traveled the globe to ask fundamental questions of existence from Ram Dass, Mother Theresa, and psychologist B.F. Skinner, among others

0-385-48191-8 IMAGE PB $12.95

Foundation for Inner Peace

A Course in Miracles: Combined Volume

Presents a non-dualistic philosophical system with an emphasis on forgiveness. Contains Text, the Workbook for Students, and the Manual for Teachers

0-670-86975-9 VIKING $29.95

Judith **Handelsman**

Growing Myself: A Spiritual Journey Through Gardening

Former gardening columnist for *New Age Journal* learns to listen to plants

0-525-94057-X DUTTON $21.95

Linda **Hogan**

Dwellings: Reflections on the Natural World

The award-winning Chickasaw poet writes about the nature of nature

See also **ESSAYS, MEDITATIONS, AND CLASSICS** under **NATURE STUDY** in **SCIENCE**

0-393-03784-3 NORTON $21.00
0-684-83033-7 TOUCHSTONE PB $11.00

Paul **Johnson**

The Quest for God

The author of the bestselling *Modern Times*, *Intellectuals*, and *A History of the Jews* offers a study of the central and enigmatic relationship between mankind and God, and how this relationship has evolved in modern times. Who is God? Is there any progress in our comprehension of Him? Can He be reached through prayer?

0-06-017344-0 HARPERCOLLINS $24.00

Blackwolf **Jones** & Gina **Jones**

Earth Dance Drum: A Celebration of Life

Personal insights relate to the dance at a Pow Wow, with a spiritual explanation of the dances themselves by a licensed psychotherapist

1-88139-448-4 COMMUNE-A-KEY PB $16.95

Stephen **Levine** & Ondrea **Levine**

Embracing the Beloved: Relationship as a Path of Awakening

Free-form poetry and practical meditation techniques on the healing potential of love and the family. "If you aspire to transform an intimate relationship towards a realization, *Embracing the Beloved* is the most subtly articulated 'how-to' book available"—Ram Dass

See also **WESTERN** under **20TH-CENTURY SPIRITUAL LEADERS**

See also **MEDITATIONS**

0-385-42526-0 DOUBLEDAY $21.95
0-385-42527-9 ANCHOR PB $11.00

Susan Chernak **McElroy**

Animals as Teachers and Healers: True Stories and Reflections

"The ultimate importance of this book is to elevate the status and significance of animals in society, which is long overdue for the good of animals, and for humanity"—Michael W. Fox

0-939165-27-9 NEWSAGE PB $12.95

Sogyal **Rinpoche**

Living and Dying Every Day: A Daily Meditation Book

"...Rinpoche is without peer"
—*NY Times Book Review*

0-06-251126-2 HARPERCOLLINS PB $12.00

Victor **Sanchez**

Toltecs of the New Millennium

An anthropologist reexamines academic parameters during a trip to Mexico to study the social customs of the Wirrarika tribe. Included here is his examination of the ways that psychoactives such as LSD and peyote generate states of religious consciousness. He also explores the traditions of the Aztecs and the Toltecs. "This is an interesting read and a revealing examination of a sacred terrain"
—*Publishers Weekly*

1-87918-135-5 BEAR PB $14.00

Scott Russell **Sanders**

Staying Put: Making a Home in a Restless World

"In the tradition of Wendell Berry, Sanders champions fidelity to place, informed by ecological awareness, arguing that intimacy with one's home region is the grounding for global knowledge...A wise and beautifully written book"—*Publishers Weekly*

0-8070-6341-X BEACON PB $12.95

Loyalty to place arises from sources deeper than narcissism. It arises from our need to be at home on the earth. We marry ourselves to the creation by knowing and cherishing a particular place, just as we join ourselves to the human family by marrying a particular man or woman. If the marriage is deep, divorce is painful.
STAYING PUT: MAKING A HOME IN A RESTLESS WORLD

His Holiness Shantanand **Saraswati**

The Man Who Wanted to Meet God: Myths and Stories that Explain the Inexplicable

0-517-88520-4 BELL TOWER PB $16.00

Morrie **Schwartz**

Letting Go: Morrie's Reflections on Living While Dying

The story of a confrontation with terminal illness and death which came out of interviews with Schwartz—a retired university professor facing Lou Gehrig's Disease—on ABC's "Nightline" and NPR's "Talk of the Nation"

See also **DEATH AND MOURNING** under **SELF-HELP** in **LIFESTYLES AND PRACTICAL ADVICE**

0-8027-1315-7 WALKER $18.00

Carolyn R. **Shaffer** & Kristin **Anundsen**

Creating Community Anywhere: Finding Support and Connection in a Fragmented World

The authors provide step-by-step instructions for establishing everything from intellectual salons and spiritual communities to computer networks and study groups. "The most comprehensive book about the community movement in all its variety"—M. Scott Peck

0-87477-746-1 PERIGEE PB $15.95

Charles **Simpkinson** &
Anne **Simpkinson**, editors

Sacred Stories: A Celebration of the Power of Stories to Transform and Heal

The editors of *Common Boundary* magazine bring together stories whose universality tap into the purgative yearnings of the human soul. Jungians, spiritualists, political figures, and writers of wisdom interpret and celebrate the primal, regenerative powers of fiction. Contributors include Maya Angelou, Robert Bly, Sam Keen, Mary Catherine Bateson, and Al Gore

0-06-250852-0 HARPERCOLLINS PB $14.00

Ninian **Smart**

Dimensions of the Sacred: An Anatomy of the World's Beliefs

From one of the great historians of religion, a thorough look at how humans worldwide endeavor to put meaning into existence. "A kind of anatomy of spirituality, designed to advance understanding of the practical and theoretical aspects of a variety of world religions, Smart's book is important reading..."
—*Publishers Weekly*

See also **GENERAL SURVEYS AND STUDIES** under **WORLD RELIGION**

0-520-20777-7 CALIFORNIA $29.95

Elaine **St. James**

Living the Simple Life: 100 Steps to Scaling Down and Enjoying More

The simplicity movement has gained enormous popularity in America, where thousands have turned away from the fast track toward a simpler, less expensive life centered on peace, spirituality, and health. Bestselling author St. James follows her canonical *Simplify Your Life* and *Inner Simplicity* with this practical 100-step guide to scaling down

See also **LIVING SIMPLY**

0-7868-6219-X HYPERION $14.95

Anthony **Storr**

Feet of Clay—Saints, Sinners, and Madmen: A Study of Gurus

Psychotherapist and author of *Solitude* Storr paints some vivid portraits of spiritual leaders such as David Koresh, Jung, Freud, and Jesus

0-684-82818-9 FREE PRESS $24.00

Charles T. **Tart**

Living the Mindful Life: A Workbook for Living in the Present Moment

1-57062-003-2 SHAMBHALA PB $14.00

William Irwin **Thompson**

Coming into Being: Artifacts and Texts in the Evolution of Consciousness

Evidence of the pending change of consciousness is found in ancient religious texts and artifacts

0-312-15834-3 ST. MARTIN'S $24.95

Lucinda **Vardey**, editor

God in All Worlds: An Anthology of Contemporary Spiritual Writing

Thomas Merton and Krishnamurti, Albert Einstein and Mother Theresa—this splendid anthology manages to sample virtually every spiritual tradition in the world. Taoism, Gaia, and New Age beliefs; Hans Kung, Martin Buber, the Dalai Lama; Allen Ginsberg, Graham Greene, Aldous Huxley; Martin Luther King, Jr., Vaclav Havel; Carl Jung, M. Scott Peck; and more...A cornucopia of spiritual thought and voices

0-679-44214-6 PANTHEON $35.00

Neal Donald **Walsch**

Conversations with God: Uncommon Dialogue Book 1

This quiet and elegant volume reflects on the ways of the heart in reference, and sometimes in opposition, to Biblical dogma

1-57174-048-1 HAMPTON ROADS PB $10.95

Kenneth **Wapnick**

A Course in Miracles: What It Says

Audio cassette from the most prominent practictioner of A Course in Miracles

0-14-086354-0 HIGHBRIDGE AUDIO $9.95

Ken **Wilber**

Sex, Ecology, Spirituality: The Spirit of Evolution

The evolution of humankind is Wilber's passion—which way that evolution turns is his imperative concern in this original and innovative book

See also **EVOLUTION AND THE ORIGINS OF LIFE** under **PALEONTOLOGY AND EVOLUTION** under **LIFE SCIENCES** in **SCIENCE**

1-57062-072-5 SHAMBHALA $39.50

Robert L. **Wise**

Quest for the Soul: Our Search for Deeper Meaning

Discusses why we are spiritual beings, from a Christian point of view

0-7852-7554-1 NELSON PB $14.99

Eastern Traditions

A fascination with all things Eastern has spurred many writers and thinkers to find ways of adapting ancient teachings to make them accessible to modern audiences. The result, as these titles indicate, is often a curious blend of classic Eastern mysticism and Western pragmatism and materialism.

Hadrat **'Ali**

Living and Dying with Grace

Thomas Cleary brings the aphoristic spiritual insight of Sufism to the affairs of daily life. 400 teachings of the great Sufi master 'Ali concerning the virtues of generosity, intelligence, perseverance, integrity, and calm reflection

TRANSLATED BY THOMAS CLEARY

1-57062-065-2 SHAMBHALA $16.00

Charlotte Joko **Beck**

Nothing Special: Living Zen

The challenge of incorporating Zen principles into the practice of everyday living is not impossible. So says author Beck in this intriguing new book on living a life free from illusion, projection, and desire. Rooted in ancient practices and written for those who seek a more fulfilling life path of harmony and joy. With Steve Smith, author of *Everyday Zen*

0-06-250256-5 HARPERCOLLINS PB........................$16.00

Sylvia **Boorstein**

It's Easier than You Think: The Buddhist Way to Happiness

The "Jewish grandmother boddhisattva" exemplifies her renowned honesty and wisdom in this simple guide to the Buddhist practice of everyday life. "Sylvia Boorstein finds in the very fabric of daily life the essence of a great wisdom tradition. In her inimitable way, she reminds us that the opportunities for spiritual practice are everywhere"—Ram Dass

0-06-251293-5 HARPERCOLLINS $18.00

Pema **Chodron**

Start Where You Are: A Guide to Compassionate Living

This how-to uses a framework of 59 Tibetan Buddhist maxims that help the individual let go of fear and, starting with the self, to live with compassion as a driving value

See also **VALUES** under **QUALITY OF LIFE** under **SELF-HELP** in **LIFESTYLES AND PRACTICAL ADVICE**

0-87773-880-7 SHAMBHALA PB..............................$12.00

Huang **Chung-lian**

Embrace Tiger, Return to Mountain: The Essence of Tai Ji

0-89087-504-9 CELESTIAL ARTS PB............................$14.95

The **Dalai Lama**

The Way to Freedom: Core Teachings of Tibetan Buddhism

A new series—Library of Tibet—is inaugurated by his Holiness the Dalai Lama and will serve to explore the culture, history, politics, and spirituality of Tibetan Buddhism. This volume, translated for the first time into English, is considered to be the essence of 1,000 years of Buddhist teaching and the heart of Tibetan practice. Presented in an easy-to-understand manner perfect for those already practicing as well as for the beginner

See also **TIBETAN RELIGION** under **ASIAN RELIGION AND PHILOSOPHY**

0-06-061722-5 HARPERCOLLINS $16.00

The **Dalai Lama** & others

The Good Heart: A Buddhist Perspective on the Teachings of Jesus

The record of the 1994 John Main Seminar sponsored by the World Community for Christian Meditation led by the Dalai Lama. These are his thoughts on New Testament selections, many of which he had never read before. As a consequence, "familar passages are renewed and opened to unexpected insights…This is a fascinating book which deserves a great deal of attention in these times of multicultural exchange"—*Publishers Weekly*

See also **EASTERN** under **20TH-CENTURY SPIRITUAL LEADERS**

0-86171-114-9 WISDOM..$25.00

Neil **Douglas-Klotz**, translator

Desert Wisdom: Sacred Middle Eastern Writings from the Goddess Through the Sufis

The Aramaic words of Jesus, Zoroastrian texts, ancient Judaic writings, Gnosticism, and Sufi mysticism are included in this volume

0-06-061996-1 HARPERCOLLINS..............................$20.00

Sandy **Eastoak**, editor

Dharma Family Treasures: Sharing Mindfulness with Children

A collection of writings about sharing Buddhist practice with children. Contributors, including Thich Nhat Hanh and Sahel Estoak-Siletz (age 5), present insights and stories about living as a Buddhist family

1-55643-172-4 NORTH ATLANTIC PB $14.95

Mark **Epstein**

Thoughts Without a Thinker: Psychotherapy from a Buddhist Perceptive

"No facile synthesis of the two systems here, but rather a thoughtful account that allows their paths to converge and diverge without losing sight of the distinctive contributions of each to deeper self-understanding"—*Kirkus Reviews*

0-465-03931-6 BASIC $22.00

Thich Nhat **Hanh**

Thich Nhat Hanh, a renowned Buddhist who was nominated for the Nobel Peace Prize, is a prolific and multifaceted writer whose works examine topics such as nonviolent social change, meditation, and Eastern philosophy

Being Peace

"A jewel of love and wisdom"—*Small Press*

See also **EASTERN** under **20TH-CENTURY SPIRITUAL LEADERS**

0-938077-00-7 PARALLAX PB $10.00

John **Heider**

The Tao of Leadership: Lao Tzu's Tao Te Ching Adapted for a New Age

Adaptation of a Chinese classic

0-89334-079-0 HUMANICS PB $16.95

Eva Rudy **Jansen**

The Book of Buddhas: Ritual Symbolism Used on Buddhist Statuary and Ritual Objects

Explains for Western students the symbolism of ritual objects through text and detailed illustrations

90-74597-02-5 WEISER PB.......................................$10.95

The Book of Hindu Imagery: The Gods and Their Symbols

Over 100 illustrations portray the important deities and their divine manifestations

90-74597-07-6 WEISER PB.......................................$12.95

Singing Bowls: A Practical Handbook of Instruction and Use

The Himalyan bowls that produce meditative and special sounds, "sound massage". How to use them and how to find the right bowl for you

90-800594-7-1 WEISER PB.......................................$10.95

Greg **Johanson** & Ron **Kurtz**

Grace Unfolding: Psychotherapy in the Spirit of the Tao-Te Ching

"A fascinating blend of Eastern spirituality, Western psychotherapy, feminist consciousness, and real caring"—Riane Eisler

0-517-88130-6 HARMONY PB $10.00

Deng **Ming-Dao**

Everyday Tao: Living with Balance and Harmony

The companion volume to *365 Tao*; the author discusses Taoism in application to everyday life. He also presents Chinese ideograms and their translations, which offer reflections for following the Tao

0-06-251395-8 HARPERCOLLINS PB..........................$14.00

365 Tao: Daily Meditations

0-06-250223-9 HARPERCOLLINS PB..........................$15.00

Lati **Rinbochay** & Jeffrey **Hopkins**

Death, Intermediate State, and Rebirth in Tibetan Buddhism

Tibetan-Buddhist philosophy of death and dying

0-937938-00-9 SNOW LION PB..................................$9.95

Sharon **Salzberg**

Lovingkindness: The Revolutionary Art of Happiness

Lovingkindness, described by the Buddha as "the liberation of the heart which is love," teaches us to combat our fear of intimacy and find a greater sense of connection with others—and with ourselves

1-57062-037-7 SHAMBHALA......................................$18.00

David **Schneider**

Street Zen: The Life and Work of Issan Dorsey

"A fascinating book. I think Issan's story contributes significantly to the history of the gay community and its response to AIDS, as well as to the history of Buddhism in America"
—Randy Shilts, author of *And the Band Played On*

0-87773-914-5 SHAMBHALA PB..............................$13.00

Idries **Shah**

The Way of the Sufi

Sufi traditions and stories

0-14-019252-2 ARKANA PB.......................................$12.95

D.T. **Suzuki**

Manual of Zen Buddhism

Prayers, sutras, and sayings that have long been part of the Zen tradition

See also **ZEN AND CH'AN** under **ASIAN RELIGION AND PHILOSOPHY**

0-8021-3065-8 GROVE PB $11.00

Kazuaki **Tanahashi** &
Tensho David **Schneider**

Essential Zen

Koans, stories, quotes, and examples, with texts from diverse Zen teachers—both Eastern and Western—comprise this concise and essential introduction to the practice, as Jim Harrison put it elsewhere, of "inviting your devils in and offering them tea"

0-06-251046-0 HARPERCOLLINS PB $12.00

Meditation

Meditation is a practice in which intense concentration upon an object or sound leads to a higher state of consciousness, understanding, or awareness. Recent scientific studies have indicated that meditative techniques actually have an effect on brain waves, pulse, and respiratory rates, and can help alleviate stress-related conditions.

Jalaja **Bonheim**

The Serpent and the Wave: A Guide to Movement Meditation

"...an important work...that adds fascinating and subtle dimensions to meditation..."—Diana Saltoon, *The Common Book of Consciousness*

0-89087-657-6 CELESTIAL ARTS PB $14.95

Thomas **Cleary**, translator

Buddhist Yoga: A Comprehensive Course

A major text in "The Doctrine of Consciousness" and "The Practice of Yoga," this is an essential preparation for the practice of yoga and meditation

1-57062-018-0 SHAMBHALA PB $10.00

Ram **Dass**

Journey of Awakening: A Meditator's Guidebook

The book's many illustrations and clear text are perfect for the beginner

See also **WESTERN** under **20TH-CENTURY SPIRITUAL LEADERS**

0-553-28572-6 BDD PB $5.99

George **Fowler**

Learning to Dance Inside: Getting to the Heart of Meditation

Fowler (*Dance of a Fallen Monk*) left his Trappist order after adhering to a 17-year vow of silence to conduct his spiritual quest on his own terms. Here, unlike other meditation books, he focuses not on the techniques of meditative practice but on understanding the contemplative state of meditation, demonstrating the delight and "dance" that are the aim of the discipline

0-201-41039-7 ADDISON-WESLEY $18.00

Henepola **Gunaratana**

Mindfulness in Plain English

A step-by-step guide to Insight Meditation through everyday examples of the basic Vipassana teachings

0-86171-064-9 WISDOM PB $12.95

Thich Nhat **Hanh**

The Miracle of Mindfulness: A Manual on Meditation

"One of the best available introductions to the wisdom and beauty of meditation practice" —*New Age Journal*

See also **EASTERN** under **20TH-CENTURY SPIRITUAL LEADERS**

0-8070-1232-7 BEACON $16.00
0-8070-1201-7 BEACON PB $11.00

Willard **Johnson**

Riding the Ox Home: A History of Meditation from Shamanism to Science

0-8070-1305-6 BEACON PB $12.00

Yogi Mahesh **Marharishi**

Science of Being and Art of Living: Transcendental Meditation

0-451-15386-3 MERIDIAN PB $5.99

Pandit **Rajmani Tigunait**

The Power of Mantra & the Mystery of Initiation

Mantra, "the word that protects by being repeated", is discussed as a means to peace and well-being

1-88764-508-X YOGA PB $14.95

Tulku **Thondup**

The Healing Power of the Mind: Simple Meditation Exercises for Health, Well-Being, and Enlightenment

A survey of healing practices of Nyingma Buddhism, the oldest school of Buddhism in Tibet. "In simple language, Thondup presents an ancient transformative approach to the true nature of the mind and the sources of suffering. The uncomplicated exercises and insights he presents provide an important link between body and mind that strengthens the immmune system and reinforces the health of the student"—*Publishers Weekly*

1-57062-239-6 SHAMBHALA $22.00

Mark **Verman**

The History and Varieties of Jewish Meditation

Uniquely combines the history and practice of meditation. "Verman beautifully grounds the contemporary practice of Jewish meditation in the history of Judaism itself" —*Publishers Weekly*

1-56821-522-3 ARONSON $30.00

Donald J. **Walters**

Superconsciousness: A Guide to Meditation

How to tap the power of conciousness for self-enlightenment, by one who has practiced meditation for over 50 years

0-446-67173-8 WARNER PB $10.99

Women's Spirituality

Lynn **Andrews**

Crystal Woman: The Sisters of the Dreamtime

True story of the author's spiritual search in the Australian outback

0-446-38572-7 WARNER PB $12.99

Star Woman

Continuation of the saga

0-446-38566-2 WARNER PB $12.99

Nicky **Arden**

The Spirits Speak: One Woman's Journey into the African Spirit World

A white, middle-aged expatriate from South Africa returns to her homeland to live among the Zulu. This is the story of how she apprentices herself to a mystical practitioner of the healing arts and learns how to heal body and soul

0-8050-4207-5 HOLT $22.50

Martine **Batchelor**

Walking on Lotus Flowers: Buddhist Women Working, Loving and Meditating

0-7225-3231-8 HARPERCOLLINS PB $18.00

Sue **Bender**

Everyday Sacred: A Woman's Journey Home

Over 200,000 people bought Bender's *Plain and Simple*, a chronicle of the spiritual journey that led her to live with the Amish. Now she tells the story of her return home to the pressured and time-starved world, a place she finds transformed by her new and simple conception of the sacred

0-06-251289-7 HARPERCOLLINS $20.00
0-06-251290-0 HARPERCOLLINS PB $13.00

Plain and Simple: A Woman's Journey to the Amish

0-06-250186-0 HARPERCOLLINS PB $14.00

Sandy **Boucher**

Turning the Wheel: American Women Creating the New Buddhism

An intimate look at the lives of women who are the teachers, scholars, nuns, and followers of a newly evolving Buddhist practice in this country. "The issues are substantial, the women gutsy and insightful, and Ms. Boucher's analysis refreshingly balanced and sane" —Katy Butler, *NY Times Book Review*

0-8070-7305-9 BEACON PB $16.00

Doris **Grumbach**

Fifty Days of Solitude

Novelist and essayist Grumbach reports on 50 days of self-imposed solitude in the Maine countryside. She finds "the universal solitude in which we have all lived, try as we might to escape it"

0-8070-7060-2 BEACON $15.00
0-8070-7061-0 BEACON PB $10.00

Zsuzsanna E. **Budapest**

Grandmother Moon: Lunar Magic in Our Lives: Spells, Rituals, Goddesses, Legends, & Emotions Under the Moon

Feminist witch discusses how to tap the moon's power

See also **NEW PAGANISM** under **METAPHYSICS**

0-06-250114-3 HARPERCOLLINS PB....................$18.00

The Grandmother of Time: A Woman's Book of Celebrations, Spells, and Sacred Objects for Every Month of the Year

How to integrate wiccan practice into daily life; new approaches to ritual

See also **NEW PAGANISM** under **METAPHYSICS**

0-06-250109-7 HARPERCOLLINS PB....................$17.00

The Holy Book of Women's Mysteries: Feminist Witchcraft, Goddess Rituals, Spellcasting, & Other Womanly Arts

A feminist survival guide to witchcraft, health, and nutrition. "*The Holy Book* is original, gentle, wonderful, magical, large in scope, hugely imaginative, ...wholesome food for the womansoul"
—Phyllis Chesler, *Women and Madness*

See also **NEW PAGANISM** under **METAPHYSICS**

0-914728-67-9 BOOK PEOPLE PB....................$17.50

Susan **Cahill**, editor

Wise Women: An Anthology of Spirituality

From Ishtar of Babylonia to Hildegard of Bingen and on to the contemporary Buddhist shaman Joan Hilfax, this anthology unites 2,000 years of women's voices in their expression of spiritual identity. Poetry, essays, prayers, memoirs, and theology draw these diverse women together across time as they explore the conflicts of love, loss, and aging, as well as the opportunities for freedom, artistic expression, and political action

0-393-03946-3 NORTON....................$27.50

Kim **Chernin**

In My Father's Garden: The Roots of My Spiritual Journey

Chernin (*In My Mother's House*, *A Different Kind of Listening*), a liberal Californian psychoanalyst and writer, describes the central influence of her father—particularly the image of him working quietly in his garden—upon her feminism and spirituality. Through three personal stories, she reflects on her realization that her model for action remains her radical mother, but that her sense of underlying order in the world comes from the quiet and retiring spirit of her father

1-56512-100-7 ALGONQUIN....................$17.95

Elizabeth **Davis** & Carol **Leonard**

The Women's Wheel of Life: Thirteen Archetypes of Woman at Her Fullest Power

The Matriarch, or the Queen of the Harvest: a model for women in their 40s, finished with raising children but not yet old, at the height of their sexual and professional powers. This archetype is just one of 13 offered here as a new vision of a woman's middle years, a vision based on women's health, spirituality, and psychology, and drawn from over 100 interviews with women who are following a revolutionary path to more powerful living

See also **AGING** under **THE FEMALE EXPERIENCE** under **WOMEN'S STUDIES** in **SOCIAL STUDIES**

0-670-86227-4 VIKING....................$22.95

Kathy **Keay**

Dancing on Mountains: An Anthology of Women's Spiritual Writings

0-551-02922-6 HARPERCOLLINS PB....................$25.00

Sue Monk **Kidd**

The Dance of the Dissident Daughter: A Woman's Journey from Christian Tradition to the Sacred Feminine

0-06-064588-1 HARPERCOLLINS....................$20.00
0-06-064589-X HARPERCOLLINS PB....................$10.00

Caitlin **Libera**

Creating Circles of Power & Magic: A Woman's Guide to Sacred Community

An exploration of group dynamics from those unhappy with modern religious experience

See also **NEW PAGANISM** under **METAPHYSICS**

0-89594-712-9 CROSSING PB....................$12.95

Ann **Linnea**

Deep Water Passage: A Midlife Journey

Ann Linnea, on her 43rd birthday, reflected to herself that although her life was full with children, marriage, and work, she still longed for something more. She found it by leaving the next morning to circumnavigate Lake Superior's 1,200-mile perimeter in 65 days, through storm, cold, and exhaustion. It was a trip that, in the end, exposed the spiritual poverty of her comfortable middle-class existence and allowed her to embark on a new, richer life

0-316-52683-5 LITTLE, BROWN....................$22.95

Jennifer **Louden**

The Woman's Comfort Book: A Self-Nuturing Guide for Restoring Balance in Your Life

0-06-250531-9 HARPERCOLLINS PB....................$16.00

Sara **Maitland**

A Big Enough God

As a Christian and a feminist, Maitland defines faith as a radical act, theology as the art of telling—and listening to—stories about the divine, and God as someone beyond image and gender

See also **THEOLOGY** under **FEMINIST THEORY** under **WOMEN'S STUDIES** in **SOCIAL STUDIES**

0-8050-4183-4 HOLT....................$22.50

Diane **Stein**

The Woman's Spirituality Book

A "herstory" of civilization

0-87542-761-8 LLEWELLYN PB....................$12.95

Maura **O'Halloran**

Pure Heart, Enlightened Mind: The Zen Journal and Letters of Maura "Soshin" O'Halloran

"A fascinating portrait of an apprentice sage... The book unfolds as a grand adventure"
—*NY Times Book Review*

1-57322-503-7 RIVERHEAD PB....................$13.00

Victoria **Ransom** & Henrietta **Bernstein**

The Crone Oracles: Initiate's Guide to the Ancient Mysteries

Initiation cycles, sexual enlightenment from the Ancient Mother Goddess of the Temple of Mysteries in Eleusis that Greece worshipped over 3,000 years ago

See also **NEW PAGANISM** under **METAPHYSICS**

0-87728-800-3 WEISER PB....................$12.95

Lizelle **Reymond**

To Live Within: A Woman's Spiritual Pilgrimage in a Himalayan Hermitage

FOREWORD BY JACOB NEEDLEMAN

0-915801-54-X RUDRA PB....................$14.95

Terry Tempest **Williams**

An Unspoken Hunger: Stories from the Field

"Intensely experienced, smartly delivered vignettes on the power of place, and in particular the special connections among women, spirituality, and the earth. With an observant eye and a breathtaking frame of reference, Williams fluently explores the meeting ground of place, spirit, and emotion"
—*Kirkus Reviews*

0-679-75256-0 VINTAGE PB....................$10.00

Men's Spirituality

Marvin **Allen** & Jo **Robinson**

In the Company of Men: A New Approach to Healing for Husbands, Fathers, and Friends

0-679-42287-0 RANDOM HOUSE....................$12.00

Stephen Blake **Boyd**

The Men We Long to Be: Beyond Domination to a New Christian Understanding of Manhood

Observations about male expectations, including the growing refusal among men to be "pc," are discussed

0-06-061038-7 HARPERCOLLINS....................$19.00
0-06-061039-5 HARPERCOLLINS PB....................$10.00

John **Carmody**

Toward a Male Spirituality

In a departure from the Muscular Christianity genre so prevalent among the Promise Keepers, Carmody opens the way to a more personal and thoughtful male spirituality

0-89622-410-4 TWETH PB....................$7.95

Mark G. **Boyer**
Biblical Reflections on Male Spirituality
0-8146-2323-9 LITUR PB $9.95

Philip **Culbertson**
New Adam: The Future of Male Spirituality
0-8006-2512-9 FORT PB $13.00

Joseph **Jastrab** & Ron **Schaumburg**
Sacred Manhood, Sacred Earth: A Vision Quest into the Wilderness of a Man's Heart
0-06-016945-1 HARPERCOLLINS $22.00

Kenneth **Johnson** & Marguerite **Elsbeth**
The Grail Castle: Male Myths & Mysteries in the Celtic Tradition
Explains how to integrate the four archetypes: the Father, the Warrior, the Lover, and the Wise Man
1-56718-369-7 LLEWELLYN PB $12.00

Glen A. **Mazis**
The Trickster, Magician & Grieving Man: Reconnecting Men with Earth
1-87918-111-8 BEAR PB $12.95

Bill **McCartney**
What Makes a Man: Twelve Promises that Will Change Your Life
Written by the University of Colorado football coach who started the national, patriarchal Christian revivalist-style movement, the Promise Keepers
0-89109-730-9 NAV PRESS PB $6.00

James B. **Nelson**
The Intimate Connection: Male Sexuality, Masculine Spirituality
0-664-24065-8 KNOX PB $13.00

Alan **Richardson**
Earth God Rising: The Return of the Male Mysteries
How to tap into the psychological and spiritutal heritage of the ancients
0-87542-672-7 LLEWELLYN PB $9.95

Richard **Rohr**
The Wild Man's Journey: Reflections on Male Spirituality
0-86716-128-0 STANT $17.95

John **Rowan**
Healing the Male Psyche: Therapy as Initiation
0-415-10049-6 ROUTLEDGE PB $19.95

Personal and Psychic Development

Hal **Bennett**
The Lens of Perception
Self-empowerment through guided imagery
0-89087-492-1 CELESTIAL ARTS PB $6.95

Robert **Benson**
Between the Dreaming and the Coming True
Elegant bundles of wisdom illuminate one man's struggle with depression. "Benson has given us that rare gift, a thought-provoking record of his own spiritual quest for God through the dark night of depression"—*Publishers Weekly*
See also **DEPRESSION** under **SELF-HELP** in **LIFESTYLES AND PRACTICAL ADVICE**
0-06-060973-7 HARPERCOLLINS $18.00
0-06-060900-1 HARPERCOLLINS PB $10.00

Lynne **Bundesen**
One Prayer at a Time: A Day-to-Day Path to Spiritual Growth
0-684-81114-6 SIMON & SCHUSTER $20.00

Leo **Buscaglia**
Living, Loving and Learning
0-449-90181-5 FAWCETT PB $10.00

Personhood
0-449-90199-8 FAWCETT PB $10.00

Richard **Carlson** & Benjamin **Shield**, editors
Handbook for the Soul
More than 30 original essays by some of the most celebrated spiritual writers of our time—Jack Kornfield, Bernie Siegel, John Gray, Robert Fulghum, Thomas Moore, and others—are gathered together here, each speaking directly to the question of how best to understand and nurture our soul in today's fast-paced world
FOREWORD BY MARIANNE WILLIAMSON
0-316-12812-0 LITTLE, BROWN $22.95
0-316-12822-8 LITTLE, BROWN PB $12.95

James P. **Carse**
Breakfast at the Victory: The Mysticism of Ordinary Experience
Destined to become a classic of spiritual writing from the director of religious studies at New York University and inspired by the words of the Sufi poet Jala al-Din Rumi: "A mystic is one who finds joy in the heart when grief comes." The one-legged owner of a luncheonette; a sailing error stranding the author on Lake Michigan; the death of his wife—Carse fills the painful void of damaged ego with the wisdom of soul
0-06-251171-8 HARPERCOLLINS PB $11.00

As ego, my wealth, intelligence, moral goodness, social class are what they are only in contrast to the person next to me. Whether or not we are believers, we oppose the natural and the supernatural; we are here and wordly, God is there and otherwordly.
BREAKFAST AT THE VICTORY: THE MYSTICISM OF ORDINARY EXPERIENCE

Phil **Cousineau**, editor
Soul: An Archeology
Thoughtful meditations on the idea of the soul—from Socrates to current bestseller Thomas Moore, and including Ralph Waldo Emerson, Milan Kundera, Ray Charles, Hildegard of Bingen, Tracy Kidder, and Jack Kerouac. Rich reflections, poems, and cross-cultural observations make this "a wonderful volume…a treasure house of wisdom and hope" —Joan Halifax, author of *The Fruitful Darkness*
0-06-250243-3 HARPERCOLLINS PB $13.00

The grove faced west and formed a kind of kiva or womblike container. This enclosure had all the power of an ancient shrine; as the sun left the sky awash in crimson flames, I learned a way of being in the world and in transition. Something in my soul changed as the earth underwent its own transfiguration and the day's activity gave way to the long slow respiratory of the night.—*Valerie Andrews*
SOUL: AN ARCHEOLOGY

Mihaly **Csikszentmihalyi**
The Evolving Self: A Psychology for the Third Millennium
The bestselling author of *Flow* presents a compelling thesis for a science-based approach to morality in the coming years.
"Csikszentmihalyi is a man obsessed by happiness"—*NY Times Magazine*
"A book...with momentous implications for the future"—Howard Gardner
0-06-092192-7 HARPERCOLLINS PB $13.00

Flow: The Psychology of Optimal Experience
See also **RATIONAL AND REALITY THERAPY** under **DISORDERS AND TREATMENT** under **PSYCHOLOGY** in **SOCIAL STUDIES**
0-06-092043-2 HARPERCOLLINS PB $13.50

Denning & Phillips
The Development of Psychic Powers
A step-by-step aid for exercising the entire range of psychic powers, from ESP and divination to spirit communication and psychokinesis
0-87542-191-1 LLEWELLYN PB $9.95

Shakti **Gawain**
Creative Visualization
1-880-03262-7 NEW WORLD PB $9.95

Mark **Gerzon**
Listening to Midlife: Turning Your Crisis into a Quest
Making the most out of getting older
1-57062-168-3 SHAMBHALA PB $15.00

Eileen R. **Hannegan**
Know Your Truth, Speak Your Truth, Live Your Truth
Stories, exercises, and affirmations to guide the individual to live from the authentic self
1-88522-334-X BEYOND WORDS PB $12.95

Roger **Housden**

Retreat: Time Apart for Silence and Solitude

Spanning the world's traditions of solitude and contemplation, retreat leader Housden provides a breathtaking, illustrated guide to the wide range of approaches in the practice of retreat, from a walk in the woods to a three-year silent stint in the mountains of Tibet. Since he explains the four directions a retreat can take—the Way of the Heart, Knowledge, Body, Art—seekers can choose the path most suited to them

0-06-063905-9 HARPERCOLLINS PB........................$18.00

James W. **Jones**

In the Middle of this Road We Call Our Life: The Courage to Search for Something More

"This book rests on a simple but profound truth: Spiritual meaning is vital to human life... Will help restore meaning and purpose to anyone who reads it"—Larry Dossey

0-06-250960-8 HARPERCOLLINS........................$20.00
0-06-250961-6 HARPERCOLLINS PB........................$12.00

H. Spencer **Lewis**

Mental Poisoning

How to resist negative mental energies

0-912057-49-1 AMORC PB........................$9.95

Angela **Mattey**

The Key to Spiritual and Psychic Development: Table Tipping

How to connect with spirit guides

1-882-33600-6 TAM ENTERPRISES PB........................$13.95

Dan **Menkin**

Transformation Through Bodywork: Using Touch Therapies for Inner Peace

An exploration of several types of bodywork as tools for healing, self-discovery, finding and creating a sense of ease

See also **HEALING HANDS** under **ALTERNATIVE THERAPIES** under **HOLISTIC MEDICINE** under **HEALTH** in **LIFESTYLES AND PRACTICAL ADVICE**

1-87918-134-7 BEAR PB........................$16.00

D. Patrick **Miller**

The Book of Practical Faith: A Path to Useful Spirituality

0-8050-4179-6 HOLT........................$14.95

Kent **Nerburn**

Simple Truths: Clear and Gentle Guidance on the Big Issues in Life

Brief, non-sentimental observations on work, love, death, and other topics

1-88003-292-9 NEW WORLD........................$10.50

Michael P. **Nichols**

The Lost Art of Listening

"This book is an antidote to the sense of diminishment experienced by so many as our culture short-circuits our need for interchange with others"—Marion F. Solomon

0-89862-267-0 GUILFORD........................$26.95
1-57230-131-7 GUILFORD PB........................$14.95

Pat **Rodegast** & Judith **Stanton**, editors

Emmanuel's Book: A Manual for Living Comfortably in the Cosmos

Advice from a spirit named Emmanuel. A provocative and popular book

0-553-34387-4 BANTAM PB........................$12.95

Geneen **Roth**

Appetites: On the Search for True Nourishment

"The gift of this book is its soul-baring honesty in touching our longing. Geneen grapples with the demons of appetite, and wins us over with her humanity, her laughter, and a wise, knowing heart"—Jack Kornfield

0-525-94076-6 PENGUIN........................$20.95

Richard **Sennett**

Flesh and Stone: The Body and the City in Western Civilization

The original and innovative Sennett engages the life of cities, from ancient Athens to modern New York, over 2,500 years and, through the eyes of their inhabitants, finds a significant lesson about the quality of life. "By exposing the principles of individualism and personal comfort that form the most fundamental assumptions of 20th-century consumer culture, Sennett reminds modern readers that they trade a great deal for comfort—namely their engagement with one another. In so doing, he debunks the myth that the evolution of cities has been one of unfettered progress, or that progress is synonymous with improvement. Passionate, exhaustively researched, and original"—*Kirkus Reviews*

See also **PERSPECTIVES IN HISTORY** under **THE VARIETIES OF CIVILIZATION** in **WORLD HISTORY AND CURRENT AFFAIRS**

0-393-03684-7 NORTON........................$27.50

Chogyam **Trungpa**

Cutting Through Spiritual Materialism

0-87773-050-4 SHAMBHALA PB........................$14.00

The Path Is the Goal

Teachings that provide an essential foundation to the practice of meditation

See also **EASTERN** under **20TH-CENTURY SPIRITUAL LEADERS**

0-87773-970-6 SHAMBHALA PB........................$10.00

Enneagrams

Renee **Baron** & Elizabeth **Wagele**

Are You My Type, Am I Yours: Relationships Made Easy Through the Enneagram

"The enneagram can be invaluable in love! [It] can help you figure out whether you'll click—or clash"—*Mademoisselle*

0-06-251248-X HARPER & ROW PB........................$14.00

Alan **Fensin**

Spiritual Truth: Using the Enneagram

How to use the knowledge of enneagrams for enhancing spiritual life

0-9622183-3-2 WAY ENTERPRISES PB........................$11.95

Joel **Friedlander**

Body Types: The Enneagram of Essence Types

Uses a mix of ancient mythology and planetary types to understand personality types

0-936385-25-1 INNER JOURNEY PB........................$14.95

Kathleen **Henley** & Theodore **Dobson**

My Best Self: Using the Enneagram to Free the Soul

Finding the hidden way to integrate one's personality for a fuller life

0-06-250332-4 HARPERCOLLINS PB........................$13.00

Margaret Frings **Keyes**

Emotions and the Enneagram

How to use enneagrams to overcome anger, anxiety, and depression

1-88204-209-3 MOLYSDATUR PB........................$14.95

Helen **Palmer**

The Enneagram in Love and Work: Understanding Your Intimate and Business Relationships

An introduction to the nine body types, with an explanation of the strengths, weaknesses, and potentials of each

0-06-250721-4 HARPERCOLLINS PB........................$14.00

Inspirational

Jimmy **Carter**

Living Faith

0-8129-2736-2 TIME BOOKS........................$23.00

Larry **Dossey**

Prayer Is Good Medicine: How to Reap the Healing Benefits of Prayer

"Dossey shows us how we can create a lasting partnership between faith and medicine" —Deepak Chopra. His latest

See also **GENERAL** under **HOLISTIC MEDICINE** under **HEALTH** in **LIFESTYLES AND PRACTICAL ADVICE**

0-06-251423-7 HARPERCOLLINS........................$20.00

Marian Wright **Edelman**

Guide My Feet: Meditations and Prayers on Loving and Working for Children

Edelman is founder and president of the Children's Defense fund, author of *New York Times* bestseller *The Measure of Our Success*, and a nationally prominent voice in children's issues. Here she returns to her South Carolina childhood to mine the spiritual bedrock of her own family and bring it to us in a book of heartfelt and tough-minded meditations and prayers. Sure to be of inspiration to many who struggle to live with and work for children

0-8070-2308-6 BEACON........................$17.95

Desmond **Tutu**

An African Prayer Book

0-8027-2701-8 WALKER PB........................$10.95

Thomas **Moore**

Meditations: On the Monk Who Dwells in Daily Life

Drawing on his 12 years living as a monk and expanding the themes of his two monumental bestsellers, *Care of the Soul* and *Soul Mates*, Moore offers a series of one-page meditations to suggest ways of finding spirituality and nourishment for the soul in daily life. "[Moore] is a literate, informed, and careful participant observer, and his mediations are full of practical insights for life…. The collection is as much about the poetry and music of our lives together as about overly religious discipline"—*Booklist*

0-06-092700-3 HARPERPERENNIAL PB $10.00

Elizabeth **Roberts** & Elias **Amidon**, editors

Life Prayers from Around the World

Poetry, political wisdom, and commemorations from Hildegard of Bingen, Gary Snyder, Nelson Mandela, and sources including Native American chants and classical Chinese verse

See also **MEDITATIONS** under **ADDICTION AND RECOVERY** under **SELF-HELP** in **LIFESTYLES AND PRACTICAL ADVICE**

0-06-251377-X HARPERCOLLINS PB $15.00

Living Simply

Robert A. **Alper**

Life Doesn't Get Any Better than This: The Holiness of Little Daily Dramas

Rabbi, stand-up comic, and parent offers insights into the humorous and poignant experiences of daily life

0-89243-932-7 TRIUMPH PB $12.00

Joe **Dominguez** & Vicki **Robin**

Your Money or Your Life: Transforming Your Relationship with Money and Achieving Financial Independence

The authors, who now live on $12,000 a year, speak to a growing American trend: the simplification of life and therefore control over finances. Based on the idea that we do not need all that money can buy, this book teaches us how to get out of debt in order to live more fulfilling lives. Frugality, the authors say, teaches us how to respect our life values, time, and energy

0-14-016715-3 PENGUIN PB $11.95

Duane **Elgin**

Voluntary Simplicity: Toward a Way of Life that Is Outwardly Simple, Inwardly Rich

Not about poverty, but about balance, updated for the '90s

0-688-12119-5 QUILL PB $10.00

Carla **Emery**

The Encyclopedia of Country Living

0-912365-95-1 SASQUATCH PB $27.95

Ann Wall **Frank**

Bless this House

"We make our homes sacred," says the author, "by loving them." Anecdotes include those about her grandmother's home, where she says she learned about sacred space

0-8092-3197-2 CONTEMPORARY PB $12.95

Richard J. **Leider** & David A. **Shapiro**

Repacking Your Bags: Lighten Your Load for the Rest of Your Life

Bite-size advice from a career development counselor on how to live a life of purpose

1-88105-267-2 BERRETT-KOEHLER $21.95

Timothy **Miller**

How to Want What You Have: Discovering the Magic and Grandeur of Everyday Existence

The psychotherapist presents three principles to achieve happiness with what you have: compassion, attention, and gratitude. *Publishers Weekly* writes, "Realistic solace for the discontented"

0-8050-3317-3 HOLT $19.95

Jan **Mitchell**

Home Sweeter Home

Based on the premise that happiness and inner peace are not found externally, but from right where you live, Mitchell gives tips on a variety of ways to create a home that is enjoyable, healthy, and spiritually rich

1-88522-333-1 BEYOND WORDS PB $12.95

Thomas **Moore**

The Reenchantment of Everyday Life

Illustrious and widely read, Moore (*Care of the Soul*, *Soul Mates*) furthers his reflection on the centrality of soul by focusing on daily life, from food to politics, showing the meaning and fulfillment that can be found in a genuine engagement with the quotidian, an engagement that implies and reflects the needs of the heart

See also **WESTERN** under **20TH-CENTURY SPIRITUAL LEADERS**

0-06-017209-6 HARPERCOLLINS $25.00

Beverly **Potter**

Finding a Path with a Heart: How to Go from Burnout to Bliss

How to get to the blissful state, from an organizational psychologist

0-914171-74-7 RONIN PB $14.95

Witold **Rybczynski**

Waiting for the Weekend

"Witty and racy…What *Home* and *The Most Beautiful House in the World* did for personal space, *Waiting for the Weekend* does for personal time"—*San Francisco Chronicle*

0-14-012663-5 PENGUIN PB $10.00

Joseph **Sharp**

Living Our Dying: A Way to the Sacred in Everyday Life

From a long-term survivor of AIDS who believes that in order to appreciate life's preciousness, we must stay aware of our transience

0-7868-6230-0 HYPERION $19.95

Elaine **St. James**

Living the Simple Life: 100 Steps to Scaling Down and Enjoying More

The simplicity movement has gained enormous popularity in America, where thousands have turned away from the fast track toward a simpler, less expensive life centered on peace, spirituality, and health. Bestselling author St. James follows her canonical *Simplify Your Life* and *Inner Simplicity* with this practical 100-step guide to scaling down

0-7868-6219-X HYPERION $14.95

Mary **Swander**

Out of this World: A Journey of Healing

A woman's inspiring memoir of healing from a devastating environmental illness—and of creating a simpler life for herself—by living in rural Iowa

See also **MEMOIRS AND JOURNALS** under **20TH-CENTURY AMERICAN ESSAYS AND JOURNALISM** in **LITERATURE OF THE AMERICAS**

0-14-024170-1 PENGUIN PB $11.95

Aliske **Webb**

Twelve Golden Threads

Lessons about serene living the author learned as a girl while quilting with her grandmother

0-06-017463-3 HARPERCOLLINS PB $18.00

Claude **Whitmyer**, editor

Mindfulness and Meaningful Work: Explorations in Right Livelihood

A wholly relevant volume from the distinguished Buddhist publisher Parallax offers a collection of essays on the integration of mindfulness and ethics in the workplace. Thich Nhat Hanh, Shunyru Suzuki, Gary Snyder, Robert Aitken, and Ellen Langer are some of the contributors who encourage all of us to find work that is meaningful, life-affirming and non-exploitive—and to point the way for others as well

0-938077-54-6 PARALLAX PB $16.00

Mindfulness puts us in a constant present, releasing us from the clatter of distracting thoughts so that our energy, creativity, and productivity are undiluted. You become your most effective. Attention is power, and those who work in a state of mindful awareness bring an almost supernatural power to what they do.—*Marsha Sinetar*

MINDFULNESS AND MEANINGFUL WORK: EXPLORATIONS IN RIGHT LIVELIHOOD

20th-Century Spiritual Leaders

Throughout this century, a number of individuals have attracted significant followings through their teachings, writings, and activities.

Eastern

Gautama **Chopra**

Child of the Dawn: A Magical Journey of Awakening

1-87842-424-6 AMBER-ALLEN $16.00

H. **Murphet**

Sai Baba, Man of Miracles

Satya Sai Baba is one of the most influential and important gurus in India today. His performance of miracles is well-documented and his following is currently growing into the millions—in both the East and the West

0-87728-335-4 WEISER PB $9.95

The **Dalai Lama**

The Way to Freedom: Core Teachings of Tibetan Buddhism

A new series—Library of Tibet—is inaugurated by his Holiness the Dalai Lama and will serve to explore the culture, history, politics, and spirituality of Tibetan Buddhism. This volume, translated for the first time into English, is considered to be the essence of 1,000 years of Buddhist teaching and the heart of Tibetan practice. Presented in an easy-to-understand manner perfect for those already practicing as well as for the beginner

See also **TIBETAN RELIGION** under **ASIAN RELIGION AND PHILOSOPHY**

0-06-061722-5 HARPERCOLLINS $16.00

Beyond Dogma: Dialogues and Discourses

A discussion of current issues such as AIDS and human rights from the exiled leader of Tibet

See also **GENERAL BOOKS**

1-55643-218-6 NORTH ATLANTIC PB $14.95

A Flash of Lightning in the Dark of the Night: A Guide to the Bodhisattva's Way of Life

The Dalai Lama engages in a dialogue with the well-known sutra of Mahayana Buddhism. The bodhisattva's enemies, he explains, are the ego, the passions, and hatred; his allies are generosity and patience. His ultimate goal: complete and liberating compassion. Written with the wisdom and integrity that have made this enduring holy leader an inspiration to millions

0-87773-971-4 SHAMBHALA PB $10.00

Freedom in Exile: The Autobiography of the Dalai Lama

The spiritual leader of the Tibetan people describes his childhood, the Chinese invasion, and his escape to India, followed by 100,000 other refugees

0-06-039116-2 HARPERCOLLINS $22.95
0-06-098701-4 HARPERCOLLINS PB $13.00

The Meaning of Life from a Buddhist Perspective

The Dalai Lama explains the Buddhist Wheel of Life, the nature of suffering and how to transcend it, while answering personal and philosophical questions from his listeners. Edited from a series of talks in London

See also **TIBETAN RELIGION** under **ASIAN RELIGION AND PHILOSOPHY**

EDITED BY TENZIN GYATSO
TRANSLATED BY JEFFREY HOPKINS

0-86171-096-7 WISDOM PB $12.50

The Path to Enlightenment

EDITED BY GLENN MULLIN

1-55939-032-8 SNOW LION PB $14.95

The **Dalai Lama** & Jean-Claude **Carriere**

Violence and Compassion: Dialogues on the World Today

0-385-47960-3 DOUBLEDAY $20.00

The **Dalai Lama** & Alexander **Norman**

Ethics for the Next Millennium

1-57322-025-6 PUTNAM $23.95

The **Dalai Lama** & Others

The Good Heart: A Buddhist Perspective on the Teachings of Jesus

The record of the 1994 John Main Seminar sponsored by the World Community for Christian Meditation led by The Dalai Lama. These are his thoughts on New Testament selections, many of which he had never read before. As a consequence, "familar passages are renewed and opened to unexpected insights…This is a fascinating book which deserves a great deal of attention in these times of multicultural exchange"—*Publishers Weekly*

0-86171-114-9 WISDOM $25.00

The **Dalai Lama** & Glen **Rowell**

My Tibet

See also **TIBET** under **CHINA** in **WORLD HISTORY AND CURRENT AFFAIRS**

0-520-07109-3 CALIFORNIA $40.00
0-520-08948-0 CALIFORNIA PB $25.00

Dalai Lama

Thich Nhat **Hahn**

Peace Is Every Step: The Path of Mindfulness in Everyday Life

0-553-35139-7 BANTAM PB $10.95

The Sutra on the Eight Realizations of the Great Beings

0-938077-07-4 PARALLAX PB $3.00

Thich Nhat **Hahn**

Thich Nhat Hanh, a renowned Buddhist who was nominated for the Nobel Peace Prize, is a prolific and multifaceted writer whose works examine topics such as nonviolent social change, meditation, and Eastern philosophy

Being Peace

"A jewel of love and wisdom"—*Small Press*

See also **EASTERN TRADITIONS**

0-938077-00-7 PARALLAX PB $10.00

The Blooming of a Lotus: Guided Meditation Exercises for Healing and Transformation

Makes available to readers his highly respected method of entering the realm of peace during meditation

0-8070-1222-X BEACON $14.00

A Joyful Path: Community, Transformation and Peace

A collection of stories from residents of and visitors to Thich Nhat Hanh's Buddhist retreat

0-938077-76-7 PARALLAX PB $25.00

Love in Action: Writings on Nonviolent Social Change

A collection of Thich Nhat Hanh's reflections on the devastation of war, on its roots within us, and on the need for spiritual motivation in political action. This book shows how to cultivate altruistic love as a means for achieving nonviolent social transformation. It also contains a beautifully rendered portrait of Vietnam's indigenous Montagnard hill tribe, whose way of life suggests a path to peace. "This meditation of Nhat Hanh [is] peaceful and serious, theologically profound, hopeful, light…a passage by water from time to timelessness" —Daniel Berrigan, from the foreword

0-938077-63-5 PARALLAX PB $13.50

The Miracle of Mindfulness: A Manual on Meditation

"One of the best available introductions to the wisdom and beauty of meditation practice" —*New Age Journal*

See also **BUDDHISM AS A PAN-ASIAN RELIGION** under **ASIAN RELIGION AND PHILOSOPHY**
See also **MEDITATION**

0-8070-1232-7 BEACON $16.00
0-8070-1201-7 BEACON PB $11.00

Touching Peace: Practicing the Art of Mindful Living

This sequel to *Being Peace* develops teachings on how the practice of peace and mindfulness in everyday life provides insights into the roots of war, addiction, and alienation

0-938077-57-0 PARALLAX PB $10.00

Sandy **Johnson**

The Book of Tibetan Elders: The Life Stories and Wisdom of the Great Spiritual Masters of Tibet

"Johnson's spiritual travelogue not only reveals the timeless wisdom of these great teachers as they live patiently the lessons of Buddhism in a homeland occupied by China, but also reveals the ways in which she is enlightened by her encounter with these men"—*Publishers Weekly*

1-57322-023-X RIVERHEAD $24.95

Jiddu **Krishnamurti**

The First and Last Freedom

An Indian philosopher and spiritual guide

INTRODUCTION BY ALDOUS HUXLEY

0-06-064831-7 HARPERCOLLINS PB $14.00

Osho **Rajneesh**
Gold Nuggets
3-89338-107-4 OSHOA $12.95

The Language of Existence
3-89338-054-X OSHOA $11.95

Meditation: The First and Last Freedom: A Practical Guide to Meditation
3-89338-128-7 ST. MARTIN'S $16.95

Zen: The Mystery and the Poetry of the Beyond
3-89338-082-5 OSHOA $14.95

Swami **Rama**
The Art of Joyful Living: Meditation and Daily Life
0-89389-117-7 OSHOA PB $12.95

Love and Family Life
0-89389-133-9 OSHOA PB $9.95

Meditation and Its Practice
0-89389-130-4 OSHOA PB $10.95

Nitnem: Spiritual Practices of Sikhism
9-991-63309-X HIMALAYAN PB $9.95

Wisdom of the Ancient Sages: Mundaka Upanishad
0-89389-120-7 OSHOA PB $10.95

Carole **Tonkinson**, editor
Big Sky Mind: Buddhism and the Beat Generation
1-57322-501-0 RIVERHEAD PB $15.00

Chogyam **Trungpa**
Born in Tibet
This autobiography of a Tibetan lama includes the gripping tale of his escape from invading Chinese troops in 1959

See also **TIBET** under **CHINA** in **WORLD HISTORY AND CURRENT AFFAIRS**

1-57062-116-0 SHAMBHALA PB $15.00

Cutting Through Spiritual Materialism
See also **PERSONAL AND PSYCHIC DEVELOPMENT**

0-87773-050-4 SHAMBHALA PB $14.00

The Path Is the Goal
Teachings that provide an essential foundation to the practice of meditation

0-87773-970-6 SHAMBHALA PB $10.00

Shambhald: Sacred Path of the Warrior
0-87773-264-7 SHAMBHALA PB $13.00

Paramahansa **Yogananda**
Autobiography of a Yogi
Yogananda was the first great master of India to live in the West for a long period. In this book he explains the subtle but definite laws by which yogis perform miracles and gain self-mastery

0-87612-083-4 OSHOA PB $11.50

The Divine Romance
0-87612-241-1 SELF PB $11.50

How You Can Talk With God
0-87612-160-1 SELF PB $.95

The Science of Religion
0-937134-16-3 AMRITA PB $8.95

Western

Robert **Aitken**
Original Dwelling Place: Zen Buddhist Essays
An American Zen roshi provides a chronicle of his journey to Zen Buddhism

See also **ZEN AND CH'AN** under **ASIAN RELIGION AND PHILOSOPHY**

1-88717-816-3 COUNTERPOINT $22.00

Richard **Bach**
Illusions: The Adventure of a Reluctant Messiah
0-385-28501-9 DOUBLEDAY $18.95
0-440-20488-7 DELL PB $5.99

Nothing by Chance
0-440-20656-1 DELL PB $5.99

Running from Safety: An Adventure of the Spirit
0-385-31528-7 DELTA PB $11.95

Stranger to the Ground
See also **GENERAL BOOKS**

0-440-20658-8 DELL PB $5.99

There's No Such Place as Far Away
See also **THE '70S** under **THE GREAT FICTION BESTSELLERS 1930-1995** in **POPULAR READING**

ILLUSTRATED BY RON WEGEN

0-385-30211-8 DELACORTE $18.95

Robert **Bly**
Iron John: A Book About Men
The quintessential men's movement manual

See also **MEN'S STUDIES** in **SOCIAL STUDIES**

0201417205 ADDISON WESLEY $19.95
0-679-73119-9 VINTAGE PB $11.00

The Sibling Society
Moving his mythic perspective beyond the individual, Bly looks to the psychic problems of our public life for an insight into why our culture is adrift. Using the psychological lessons of ancient folktales, Bly issues a condemnation of television, consumerism, and spiritual impoverishment

See also **HISTORY, POLITICS, AND SOCIETY** under **20TH-CENTURY AMERICAN ESSAYS AND JOURNALISM** in **LITERATURE OF THE AMERICAS**

0-201-40646-2 ADDISON-WESLEY $25.00

Jack **Canfield**
A 3rd Serving of Chicken Soup for the Soul: 101 More Stories to Open the Heart and Rekindle the Spirit
EDITED BY MARK VICTOR HANSEN

1-55874-379-0 HEALTH COMM PB $12.95

Chicken Soup for the Surviving Soul: 101 Stories to Comfort Cancer Patients and Their Loved Ones
1-55874-402-9 HEALTH COMM PB $12.95

Jack **Canfield** & Mark Victor **Hansen**
A 2nd Helping of Chicken Soup for the Soul: 101 More Stories to Open the Heart and Rekindle the Spirit
1-55874-331-6 HEALTH COMM PB $12.95

The Aladdin Factor
0-425-15075-5 BERKELEY PB $13.00

Chicken Soup for the Soul: 101 Stories to Open the Heart & Rekindle the Spirit
1-55874-262-X HEALTH COMMUN PB $12.95

Jack **Canfield** & Jacqueline **Miller**
Heart at Work: Stories and Strategies for Building Self-Esteem and Reawakening the Soul at Work
Inspiring personal testimonies from Nelson Mandela, Mother Theresa, and others

See also **SELF-ESTEEM** under **QUALITY OF LIFE** under **SELF-HELP** in **LIFESTYLES AND PRACTICAL ADVICE**

0-07-011643-1 MCGRAW HILL PB $14.95

Carlos **Castaneda**
The Teachings of Don Juan: A Yaqui Way of Knowledge
Castaneda's accounts of his mystical experiences with Don Juan, a Yaqui Indian, became bestsellers

See also **OTHER GROUPS AND TOPICS** under **NATIVE AMERICAN CULTURES: CENTRAL AND SOUTH AMERICA** in **HISTORY OF THE AMERICAS**

0-520-00217-2 CALIFORNIA $35.00
0-671-72791-5 WASHINGTON SQUARE PB $14.00

A Separate Reality: Further Conversations with Don Juan
0-671-73249-8 WASHINGTON SQUARE PB $12.00

Journey to Ixlan: The Lessons of Don Juan
0-671-73246-3 WASHINGTON SQUARE PB $14.00

Tales of Power
0-671-73252-8 WASHINGTON SQUARE PB $14.00

Hilda **Charlton**
Hell-Bent for Heaven: The Autobiography of Hilda
0-927383-15-2 GOLDEN QUEST PB $9.95

The New Sun
0-927383-01-2 GOLDEN QUEST PB $8.95

Pioneers of the Soul
0-927383-12-8 GOLDEN QUEST PB $11.95

Saints Alive
0-927383-00-4 GOLDEN QUEST PB $12.95

Eileen **Caddy**

God Spoke to Me

0-905249-81-X DEVORSS PB $14.95

Deepak **Chopra**

Ageless Body, Timeless Mind: The Quantum Alternative to Growing Old

Combining ancient wisdom with the latest scientific data, he shows how many of the effects of the aging process are avoidable and suggests ways to prevent physical vitality, creativity, memory, and self-esteem from waning with the passing years

See also **AGING** under **HEALTH** in **LIFESTYLES AND PRACTICAL ADVICE**

0-517-59257-6 HARMONY $23.00
0-517-88212-4 CROWN PB $14.00
0-517-59818-3 RANDOM HOUSE PB $12.50

Creating Health: How to Wake Up the Body's Intelligence

This revised edition of Chopra's classic work introduces the reader to the basics of Ayurveda, the 6,000-year-old tradition of health care from India, which Dr. Chopra, the former chief of staff for the New England Memorial Hospital, has brought to national attention. "Chopra communicates excitement on the cutting edge of today's mind/body medicine with the sophistication of a medical insider"
—*Harvard Magazine*

See also **AYURVEDIC** under **ALTERNATIVE THERAPIES** under **HOLISTIC MEDICINE** under **HEALTH** in **LIFESTYLES AND PRACTICAL ADVICE**

0-395-75515-8 HOUGHTON MIFFLIN PB $11.95

The Path to Love: Creating a Passionate Life

0-679-45827-1 RANDOM HOUSE $19.95

The Spirit of Love: 11 Spiritual Lessons for Creating the Love You Want

0-517-70622-9 HARMONY $16.95

The Way of the Wizard: 20 Lessons for Living a Magical Life

Deepak Chopra's *The Seven Spiritual Laws of Success* and *Ageless Body, Timeless Mind* were both *New York Times* bestsellers and, more important, vastly enhanced the quality of life for millions. Here, Chopra elucidates 20 principles of spiritual alchemy for discovering and mastering the full—indeed, the boundless—possibilities of the world around us

See also **GENERAL** under **SELF-HELP** in **LIFESTYLES AND PRACTICAL ADVICE**

0-517-70434-X HARMONY $15.95

Alan **Cohen**

A Deep Breath of Life: Daily Inspiration for Heart-Centered Living

1-56170-337-0 HAY HOUSE PB $12.00

The Dragon Doesn't Live Here Anymore: Loving Fully, Living Freely

1-56170-281-1 HAY HOUSE $16.95

I Had It All the Time: When Self-Improvement Gives Way tp Ecstasy

1-56170-286-2 HAY HOUSE PB $16.95

Joy Is My Compass

1-56170-341-9 HAY HOUSE PB $11.95

Lifestyles of the Rich in Spirit: Living in a Win-Win World

1-56170-339-7 HAY HOUSE PB $12.95

Rising in Love: Opening Your Heart in All Your Relationships

1-56170-340-0 HAY HOUSE PB $10.95

Andrew **Cohen**

Autobiography of an Awakening

0-9622678-4-8 MOKSHA PB $10.95

The Challenge of Enlightenment: A Voyage into the Multidimensional Integrity of Nonduality

1-88392-914-8 MOKSHA PB $6.00

Enlightenment is a Secret: Teachings of Liberations

1-88392-908-3 MOKSHA PB $14.95

My Master Is My Self: The Birth of a Spiritual Teacher

1-88392-907-5 MOKSHA PB $10.95

No Relationship to Thought

1-88392-910-5 MOKSHA PB $16.00

An Unconditional Relationship to Life: The Odyssey of a Young American Spiritual Teacher

1-88392-904-0 MOKSHA PB $10.95

Who Has the Courage to Stand Alone in Truth?

0-9622678-6-4 MOKSHA PB $4.00

Ram **Dass**

Journey of Awakening: A Meditator's Guidebook

The book's many illustrations and clear text are perfect for the beginner

See also **MEDITATION**

0-553-28572-6 BDD PB $5.99

Ram **Dass** & Mirabai **Bush**

Compassion in Action: Setting Out on the Path of Service

0-517-88500-X CROWN PB $12.00

Ram **Dass** & Paul **Gorman**

How Can I Help: Stories and Reflections on Service

0-394-72947-1 KNOPF PB $9.95

Ram **Dass** & Stephen **Levine**

Grist for the Mill

0-89087-499-9 CELESTIAL ARTS PB $9.95

Benjamin B. **Ferencz** & Ken **Keyes**, Jr.

Planethood: The Key to Your Future

0-915972-21-2 LOVE LINE PB

Emmet **Fox**

Alter Your Life

0-06-250897-0 HARPERCOLLINS PB $12.00

The Emmet Fox Treasury: Five Spiritual Classics

0-06-062860-X HARPERCOLLINS PB $25.00

Find and Use Your Inner Power

0-06-250407-X HARPERCOLLINS PB $12.00

Make Your Life Worthwhile

0-06-062913-4 HARPERCOLLINS PB $12.00

The Sermon on the Mount: The Key to Success in Life and the Lord's Prayer: An Interpretation

0-06-062862-6 HARPERCOLLINS PB $10.00

Matthew **Fox**

The Coming of the Cosmic Christ: The Healing of Mother Earth and the Birth of a Global Renaissance

See also **CONTEMPORARY ISSUES** under **THEOLOGY AND DOCTRINE** under **CHRISTIANITY**

0-06-062915-0 HARPERCOLLINS PB $16.00

Confessions: The Making of a Post-Denominational Priest

0-06-062965-7 HARPERCOLLINS PB $14.00

Creation Spirituality: Liberating Gifts for the Peoples of the Earth

Fox's attempt to find an early Christian tradition compatible with contemporary social, environmental, and feminist concerns

See also **CONTEMPORARY ISSUES** under **THEOLOGY AND DOCTRINE** under **CHRISTIANITY**

0-06-062917-7 HARPERCOLLINS PB $15.00

In the Beginning There Was Joy

ILLUSTRATED BY JANE TATTERSFIELD

0-8245-1505-6 CROSSROAD $14.95

The Reinvention of Work: A New Vision of Livelihood

0-06-063062-0 HARPERCOLLINS PB $14.00

Matthew **Fox** & Rupert **Sheldrake**

Natural Grace: Dialogues on Creation, Darkness, and the Soul in Spirituality and Science

0-385-48356-2 DOUBLEDAY $22.00

The Physics of Angels: Exploring the Realm Where Science and Spirit Meet

0-06-062864-2 HARPERCOLLINS PB $16.00

Shakti **Gawain**

Awakening: A Daily Guide to Conscious Living

1-88259-105-4 NATARAJ PB $12.95

Shakti **Gawain**

Creative Visualization: Use the Power of Your Imagination to Create What You Want in Your Life

1-88003-262-7 NEW WORLD PB $9.95

Living in the Light: A Guide to Personal and Planetary Transformation

0-553-56104-9 BDD PB $5.50

The Path of Transformation: How Healing Ourselves Can Change the World

1-88259-115-1 NATARAJ PB $11.95

Joel S. **Goldsmith**

The Art of Meditation

0-06-250379-0 HARPERCOLLINS PB $10.00

Man Was Not Born to Cry

0-8065-0915-5 CITADEL PB $7.95

The Mystical I

EDITED BY LORRAINE SINKLER

0-06-250818-0 HARPERCOLLINS PB $10.00

Practicing the Presence: The Inspirational Guide to Regaining Meaning and Sense of Purpose in Your Life

0-06-250399-5 HARPERCOLLINS PB $11.00

Daniel **Goleman** & Stephen **Levine**

Worlds in Harmony: Dialogues on Compassionate Action: His Holiness the Dalai Lama

0-938077-77-5 PARALLAX PB $12.50

G.I. **Gurdjieff**

The writings of an Armenian mystic

Beelzebub's Tales to His Grandson: An Objectively Impartial Criticism of the Life of Man

0-67-0841-250 ARKANSAS $50.00

Meetings with Remarkable Men

0-14-019037-6 DUTTON PB $11.95

G.I. Gurdjieff

Louise **Hay**

You Can Heal Your Life

See also **MIND-BODY HEALING** under **HOLISTIC MEDICINE** under **HEALTH** in **LIFESTYLES AND PRACTICAL ADVICE**

1-56170-094-0 HAY HOUSE PB $16.95

Heal Your Body: The Mental Causes for Physical Illness and the Metaphysical Way to Overcome Them

0-937611-35-2 HAY HOUSE PB $6.95

Heart Thoughts: A Treasury of Inner Wisdom

EDITED BY LINDA CARWIN TOMCHIN

1-56170-045-2 HAY HOUSE PB $10.00

Life!: Reflections on Your Journey

1-56170-312-5 HAY HOUSE PB $12.00

Love Yourself, Heal Your Life Workbook

EDITED BY GLENN KOLB

0-937611-69-7 HAY HOUSE PB $12.00

Meditations to Heal Your Life

1-56170-106-8 HAY HOUSE $12.95

Louise L. **Hay** & Linda Carwin **Tomchin**

The Power Is Within You

1-56170-023-1 HAY HOUSE PB $12.00

Ken **Keyes**, Jr.

The Power of Unconditional Love: 21 Guidelines for Beginning, Improving, and Changing Your Most Meaningful Relationships

0-915972-19-0 LOVE LINE PB $10.95

Your Road Map to Lifelong Happiness: A Guide to the Life You Want

0-915972-22-0 LOVE LINE PB $19.95

Ken **Keyes**, Jr. & Penny **Keyes**

Handbook to Higher Consciousness, The Workbook: A Daily Practice Book to Help You Increase Your Heart-to-Heart Loving and Happiness

0-915972-16-6 LOVE LINE PB $7.95

Stephen **Levine**

A Gradual Awakening

0-385-26218-3 ANCHOR PB $8.95

Guided Meditations, Explorations and Healings

0-385-41737-3 ANCHOR PB $11.95

Meetings at the Edge: Dialogues with the Grieving and the Dying, the Healing and the Healed

0-385-26220-5 DOUBLEDAY PB $10.95

Who Dies?: An Investigation of Conscious Living and Conscious Dying

0-385-26221-3 DOUBLEDAY PB $10.95

Stephen **Levine** & Ondrea **Levine**

Embracing the Beloved: Relationship as a Path of Awakening

Free-form poetry and practical meditation techniques on the healing potential of love and the family. "If you aspire to transform an intimate relationship towards a realization, *Embracing the Beloved* is the most subtly articulated 'how-to' book available"—Ram Dass

See also **GENERAL BOOKS**

See also **MEDITATIONS**

0-385-42526-0 DOUBLEDAY $21.95

0-385-42527-9 ANCHOR PB $11.00

C.S. **Lewis**

All My Road Before Me: The Diary of C.S. Lewis, 1922-1927

EDITED BY WALTER HOOPER

0-15-604643-1 HARCOURT BRACE PB $15.00

The Four Loves

0-15-132916-8 HARCOURT BRACE $18.00

God in the Dock: Essays on Theology and Ethics

EDITED BY WALTER HOOPER

0-8028-0868-9 EERDMANS PB $15.00

A Grief Observed

Lewis's effort to console himself after the death of his wife—and to defend against his loss of belief in God. "The author has done something I believed impossible—assuaged his own grief by conveying it"—Anne Freemantle

See also **DEATH OF A SPOUSE** under **DEATH AND MOURNING** under **SELF-HELP** in **LIFESTYLES AND PRACTICAL ADVICE**

0-553-27486-4 BDD PB $5.50

0-06-065284-5 HARPERCOLLINS PB $10.00

Mere Christianity: Comprising the Case for Christianity, Christian Behaviour, and Beyond

One of Lewis's most popular books, originally broadcast as informal radio "talks" and later published as three separate books

See also **CLASSICS** under **CHRISTIANITY**

0-684-82378-0 TOUCHSTONE PB $6.00

The Screwtape Letters

A classic satiric work consisting of a series of letters from Screwtape, an elderly devil, advising his nephew Wormwood, an apprentice devil, how to corrupt his earthly "patient"

INTRODUCTION BY RICHARD GILMAN

0-553-26369-2 BDD PB $4.50

0-451-62821-7 MENTOR PB $4.99

Surprised by Joy: The Shape of My Early Life

Lewis's spiritual journey from Christianity to atheism and back again to Christianity. "Anyone approaching this book as a study in the psychology of conversion will find the greatest interest in the dual paths—intellectual and

intuitive—which converged at last"
—*Saturday Review*
See also **20TH-CENTURY BRITISH ESSAYS AND OTHER PROSE** in **LITERATURE OF THE BRITISH ISLES**
See also **CLASSICS** under **CHRISTIANITY**
0-15-100185-5 HARCOURT BRACE $16.00
0-15-687011-8 HARCOURT BRACE PB $9.00

Thomas **Merton**

Conjectures of a Guilty Bystander
INTRODUCTION BY THOMAS MOORE
0-385-01018-4 IMAGE PB $12.00

Contemplative Prayer
Brings in texts from Scripture and from writers in the long tradition of Western contemplative spirituality. "Every page shows the rough texture of lived experience" —*America*
See also **PRAYER AND CONTEMPLATION** under **PRACTISE OF FAITH** under **CHRISTIANITY**
INTRODUCTION BY THICH NHAT HANH
0-385-09219-9 IMAGE PB $7.95

Meditation has no point and no reality unless it is rooted in life.
CONTEMPLATIVE PRAYER

The Courage for Truth: The Letters of Thomas Merton to Writers
EDITED BY CHRISTINE M. BOCHEN
0-15-600004-0 HARVEST PB $15.95

The Journals of Thomas Merton
Patrick **Hart**, editor

Volume 1
Run to the Mountain: The Story of a Vocation: 1939-1941
Merton, the Trappist monk and writer, specified that his journals not be published until 25 years after his death. This volume, the first of seven (all to be published by 1998), offers a glimpse of the young, pre-monastic Merton as a graduate student in Greenwich Village, grappling with rejection by *New Yorker* and other magazine editors and struggling with probing theological and ethical questions that would lead him to discover his true vocation. "This is just the right time to renew our appreciation for the eternal in the world by reading the gutsy, thoughtful, passionate journals of Thomas Merton"
—Thomas Moore
See also **20TH-CENTURY** under **BIOGRAPHIES** under **CHRISTIANITY**
0-06-065475-9 HARPERCOLLINS PB $15.00

Jonathan **Montado**, editor

Volume 2
Entering the Silence: Becoming a Monk & Writer: 1941-1952
See also **20TH-CENTURY** under **BIOGRAPHIES** under **CHRISTIANITY**
0-06-065477-5 HARPERCOLLINS PB $14.00

Lawrence **Cunningham**, editor

Volume 3
A Search for Solitude: Pursuing the Monk's True Life: 1952-1960
The third volume of Merton's "gutsy, thoughtful, passionate journals" (Thomas Moore) offers "unique insight into the mind and heart of the most important spiritual writer of the twentieth century" (Henri Nouwen). Ranging from his monastic routine to his exploration of Zen, existentialism, Latin American culture, and Marxism, this fascinating volume completes Merton's record of his spiritual odyssey
See also **20TH-CENTURY** under **BIOGRAPHIES** under **CHRISTIANITY**
0-06-065479-1 HARPERCOLLINS PB $14.00

Victor A. **Kramer**, editor

Volume 4
Turning Toward the World: The Pivotal Years: 1960-1963
0-06-065481-3 HARPERCOLLINS PB $10.01

Life and Holiness
0-385-48048-2 DOUBLEDAY PB $6.00

Love and Living
0-15-653895-4 HARCOURT BRACE PB $8.95

No Man Is an Island
0-15-665962-X HARCOURT BRACE PB $9.00

The Seven Storey Mountain
The autobiography of the influential American Catholic poet, scholar, and monk
See also **20TH-CENTURY** under **BIOGRAPHIES** under **CHRISTIANITY**
0-15-680679-7 HARCOURT BRACE PB $12.00

A Thomas Merton Reader
INTRODUCTION BY M. SCOTT PECK
0-385-03292-7 IMAGE PB $12.95

Thoughts in Solitude
The vital importance of solitude and silence in everyday life is the theme of this collection of reflections and meditations by the influential Trappist monk. Chapters cover such topics as the true meaning of poverty, the liberating effect of humility, the relationship between spiritual and mental life, and the positive experience of knowing one's nothingness
0-374-51325-2 FS&G PB $7.00
0-87773-920-X SHAMBHALA PB $6.00

Thoughts on the East
"Merton's works on Eastern thought provide the ordinary American, not necessarily religious, an excellent means for enlarging his appreciation of spiritual potentiality and his understanding of man's experiential nexus with reality"
—Hayden Carruth
0-8112-1293-9 NEW DIRECTIONS PB $6.00

Ways of the Christian Mystics
Part of the Shambhala Pocket Classics series
See also **CHRISTIAN MYSTICISM** under **CHRISTIANITY**
1-57062-030-X SHAMBHALA PB $6.00

Zen and the Birds of Appetite
0-8112-0104-X NORTON PB $7.95

Thomas **Merton** & Czeslaw **Milosz**

Striving Towards Being: The Letters of Thomas Merton and Czeslaw Milosz
EDITED BY ROBERT FAGEN
0-374-27100-3 FS&G $42.01

Thomas **Moore**

The Art of Soulwork: Living the Life of the Soul
0-7813-0004-5 NEW DIMENSION $15.95

Thomas **Merton** &
William J. **Shannon**, editor

Witness to Freedom: The Letters of Thomas Merton in Times of Crisis
"In these impassioned, searching letters…Merton reflects his commitment to nuclear disarmament, his immersion in Gandhi's philosophy of nonviolence, his growing ecological awareness, and his quest for a political philosophy of freedom grounded in his Catholic faith"—*Publishers Weekly*
See also **20TH-CENTURY** under **BIOGRAPHIES** under **CHRISTIANITY**
0-15-600274-4 HARVEST PB $16.00

Dan **Millman**

The Life You Were Born to Live: A Guide to Finding Your Purpose in Life
0-915811-60-X KRAMER PB $14.95

The Way of the Peaceful Warrior
0-915811-00-6 KRAMER PB $11.95

Care of the Soul: A Guide for Cultivating Depth and Sacredness in Everyday Life
"There is a depth and originality to Mr. Moore's observations"—*NY Times Book Review*
0-06-092224-9 HARPERPERENNIAL PB $13.50

Care of the Soul and Soul Mates: Boxed Gift Edition
The bestselling philosophical guides to spirituality, meaning, relationships, and soul work, published together in an elegant slipcase. "I devoured *Soul Mates* like some comfort food for the spirit…. Moore moves love off the fast track and into the realm of mystery and imagination where it belongs"
—Erica Abeel, *New Woman*
0-06-017173-1 HARPERCOLLINS $39.95

The Education of the Heart
0-06-017410-2 HARPERCOLLINS $25.00

A Magical Life
1-87932-348-6 SOUND HORIZONS $18.95

The Reenchantment of Everyday Life
Illustrious and widely read, Moore (*Care of the Soul*, *Soul Mates*) furthers his reflection on the centrality of soul by focusing on daily life, from food to politics, showing the meaning and fulfillment that can be found in a genuine engagement with the quotidian, an engagement that implies and reflects the needs of the heart
See also **LIVING SIMPLY**
0-06-017209-6 HARPERCOLLINS $25.00

Soul Mates: Honoring the Mysteries of Love and Relationship
Expands on Moore's hugely popular *Care of the Soul*, with special emphasis on the unexpected ways that we connect and enrich one another, and are able to cultivate our souls. His topics range from sexuality and jealousy to boredom and endings, and his references include Emily

Dickinson, Black Elk, and the Sufi poets, who all recognized the deepest and most transforming aspects of intimacy. Sure to speak to Moore's many fans

0-06-092575-2 HARPERPERENNIAL PB........$13.50

Like the resurrection of Jesus or the mission of Moses, the angelic visitation to Mohammed or the enlightenment of the Buddha, the heart has its own mysteries every bit as profound as the mysteries we encounter in the religions of the world. Everything associated with the heart—relationship, emotion, passion—can only be grasped and appreciated with the tools of religion and poetry.

SOUL MATES: HONORING THE MYSTERIES OF LOVE AND RELATIONSHIP

M. Scott **Peck**

Different Drum

0-671-66833-1 TOUCHSTONE PB........$12.00

Further Along the Road Less Traveled: The Unending Journey Toward Spiritual Growth

For the millions of devotees of the unmatched bestseller, *The Road Less Traveled*, here is Peck's eagerly awaited sequel. Having pondered the most frequent and essential questions asked at his nationwide lectures, Peck addresses such subjects as self-love versus self-esteem, sexuality and spirituality, addiction, mythology, and human nature. "It will hit the fast track fast, and keep on running and running and running" —*Kirkus Reviews*

0-671-78159-6 SIMON & SCHUSTER........$21.00
0-671-89288-6 TOUCHSTONE PB........$12.00

In Heaven as on Earth: A Vision of the Afterlife

Peck turns from the enormously popular form of his spiritual guides to undertake an exploration of the afterlife in the form of a novel. When the book's narrator, a psychiatrist much like Peck, awakens into the afterlife, he begins an adventure that leads him to the fundamental moral principles that transcend mortality

See also **AFTERLIFE** under **REINCARNATION** under **METAPHYSICS**

0-7868-6204-1 HYPERION........$19.95

In Search of Stones: A Pilgrimage of Faith, Reason, and Discovery

"Peck's soaring meditations on faith, art, despair and self-integration make this a rewarding spiritual odyssey"—*Publishers Weekly*

0-7868-6021-9 HYPERION........$22.95
0-7868-8164-X HYPERION PB........$13.95

The Road Less Traveled

0-671-67300-9 TOUCHSTONE PB........$14.00

The Road Less Traveled and Beyond: Spiritual Growth in an Age of Anxiety

0-684-81314-9 SIMON & SCHUSTER........$23.00

A World Waiting to Be Born: Rediscovering Civility

Peck, the acclaimed author of the eight-year bestseller *The Road Less Traveled*, convincingly argues that we have lost our civility, that subtle forms of offensive behavior have become acceptable in the US. He examines the consequences of our failure to care for one another, and uses examples from his practice to show a way back to social health

0-553-37317-X BANTAM PB........$12.95

Hugh **Prather**

Notes on How to Live in the World

0-385-18261-9 MAIN STREET PB........$9.95

Notes to Myself

0-553-27382-5 BDD PB........$5.50

Hugh **Prather** & Gayle **Prather**

I Will Never Leave You: How Couples Can Achieve the Power of Lasting Love

Human-potential workshop leaders and married couples present the eight stages of relationships

See also **MAINTAINING A RELATIONSHIP** under **COURTSHIP, LOVE, SEX, AND MARRIAGE** in **LIFESTYLES AND PRACTICAL ADVICE**

0533095331 BDD PB........$19.95

Spiritual Parenting: A Guide to Understanding and Nuturing the Heart of Your Child

Instilling virtues in your children

See also **INNER AND OUTER DISCIPLINE** under **BEING A PARENT** under **PARENTING** in **LIFESTYLES AND PRACTICAL ADVICE**

0-517-70385-8 HARMONY........$23.00

John Randolph **Price**

The Abundance Book

1-56170-347-8 HAY HOUSE PB........$7.00

Angel Energy: How to Harness the Power of Angels in Your Everyday Life

0-449-90983-2 FAWCETT PB........$12.00

The Angels Within Us

0-449-90784-8 FAWCETT PB........$12.00

The Superbeings

0-449-21543-1 FAWCETT PB........$5.99

John Randolph **Price** & John R. **Price**

Empowerment: You Can Do, Be, and Have All Things

1-56170-350-8 HAY HOUSE PB........$10.95

James **Redfield**

The Celestine Prophesy

The bestselling spiritual adventure of the '90s

0-446-51862-X WARNER........$19.95

The Tenth Insight: Holding the Vision: Futher Adventures of the Celestine Prophecy

0-446-51908-1 WARNER........$19.95

James **Redfield** & Carol **Adrienne**

The Tenth Insight: Holding the Vision: An Experimental Guide

0-446-67299-8 WARNER........$25.01

Sale Merrill **Redfield**

The Joy of Meditating: A Beginner's Guide to the Art of Meditation

INTRODUCTION BY JAMES REDFIELD

0-446-67234-3 WARNER PB........$8.99

Harold **Schulweis**

For Those Who Can't Believe: Overcoming the Obstacles to Faith

Rabbi Schulweis offers a Judaism as alive today as it was at its revolutionary inception. "All readers—believer and unbeliever alike—will appreciate [Schulweis's] forthrightness of thought and clarity of style"—Chaim Potok. "Simply the best book of its kind available: it speaks to the mind and to the heart"—Rabbi Harold S. Kushner. "I don't know of a better case for Judaism that is addressed to the contemporary Jew"—Ted Solotaroff

0-06-092651-1 HARPERPERENNIAL PB........$12.50

Tony **Schwartz**

What Really Matters: Searching for Wisdom in America

0-553-37492-3 BANTAM PB........$12.95

Marsha **Sinetar**

Do What You Love, the Money Will Follow: Discovering Your Right Livelihood

0-440-50160-1 DELL PB........$11.95

Elegant Choices, Healing Choices

0-8091-3010-6 PAULIST PB........$8.95

Ordinary People as Monks and Mystics: Lifestyles for Self-Discovery

0-8091-2773-3 PAULIST PB........$9.95

To Build the Life You Want, Create the Work You Love: The Spiritual Dimension of Entrepreneuring

0-312-14141-6 ST. MARTIN'S PB........$10.95

Lorraine **Sinkler**

The Alchemy of Awareness

0-9629119-3-3 DVORSS PB........$12.95

Dan **Wakefield**

Creating from the Spirit: Living Each Day as a Creative Act

The author of *Expect a Miracle* provides a way to enhance our basic creative nature

0-345-37430-4 BALLANTINE........$24.00

Expect a Miracle: The Miraculous Things that Happen to Ordinary People

0-8027-2702-6 WALKER PB........$18.95

Returning: A Spiritual Journey

An autobiographical account of how a middle-aged novelist and screenwriter recovered his

faith after years of drifting, drinking, and personal crisis
See also **20TH-CENTURY** under **BIOGRAPHIES** under **CHRISTIANITY**
0-14-025493-5 PENGUIN PB $10.00

Arthur I. **Waskow**
Godwrestling Round 2: Ancient Wisdom, Future Paths
A sequel to the classic but out of print 1978 volume from the pioneer of the Jewish renewal movement
1-87904-545-1 JEWISH LIGHTS $23.95

Marianne **Williamson**
Illuminata: Prayers for Everyday Life
Williamson distills the spiritual themes of *A Return to Love*—of which there are over one million copies sold—into a series of common prayers. Speaking directly to the new American spirituality, *Illuminata* offers particular insight to readers in twelve-step programs
0-679-43550-6 RANDOM HOUSE $20.00

A Return to Love
This bestseller offers us the way to return to the innocence and spontaneity of childhood, to reconnect with our natural tendencies for love. "Her honest accounts of different periods in her life will motivate readers for a long time to come. A *Return to Love* makes for very powerful reading"—Louise L. Hay
0-06-016374-7 HARPERCOLLINS PB $22.50

Philosophy

Philosophy begins, according to Aristotle, in wonder. From this auspicious beginning, it has arrived at some odd places—at the position, for instance, that the book you are holding in your hand has no physical existence (and neither does your hand). Even odder is that the history of philosophy consists of a long series of unsuccessful efforts to put an end to philosophy. Most philosophers have begun by trying to solve all major philosophical problems, and many of them have ended by announcing that they have done so. But few people—and no other philosophers—have agreed with them.

When we get beyond everyday routines, we are all likely to run up against mysteries that evoke perplexity and wonder. We are all capable of pondering the nature of knowledge, choice, mind, language; what it means to call an act good or evil or a painting beautiful; whether the soul is immortal or God exists. What philosophers have always attempted to do is to think clearly, precisely, and thoroughly about questions that most of us think about sporadically and vaguely.

Thus philosophy can be read as a way of thinking that offers a sense of clarification and cautious consolidation, a means of examining, testing, and ordering our values and beliefs. Conceived in this way, philosophy may live up to its original meaning: love of wisdom.

Introductions to Philosophy

Monroe C. **Beardsley**, editor
The European Philosophers from Descartes to Nietzsche
See also **READINGS IN PHILOSOPHY: ANTHOLOGIES ON SPECIAL TOPICS**
0-679-60024-8 MODERN LIBRARY $20.00

Malcolm **Budd**
Values of Art: Pictures, Poetry, and Music
Addresses fundamental problems in aesthetics
0-7139-9026-0 ALLEN LANE $24.95

Morris R. **Cohen** & Ernest **Nagel**
An Introduction to Logic
A naturalistic account of logic
0-87220-144-9 HACKETT PB $12.95

Frederick **Copleston**, S.J.
A History of Philosophy
Volume 1
TRANSLATED BY BEN FOWKES
0-14-044568-4 PENGUIN PB $16.95
Volume 1
Greece and Rome
0-385-46843-1 IMAGE PB $15.95
Volume 2
Medieval Philosophy
0-385-46844-X IMAGE PB $15.95
Volume 3
Late Medieval and Renaissance Philosophy
0-385-46845-8 IMAGE PB $15.95
Volume 4
From Descartes to Leibniz
0-385-47041-X DOUBLEDAY PB $15.95
Volume 5
The British Philosophers from Hobbes to Hume
0-385-47042-8 DOUBLEDAY PB $15.95
Volume 6
From the French Enlightenment to Kant
0-385-47043-6 DOUBLEDAY PB $15.95
Volume 7
From the Post-Kantian Idealists to Marx, Kierkegaard, and Nietzsche
0-385-47044-4 IMAGE PB $15.95
Volume 8
Empiricism, Idealism, and Pragmatism in Britain and America
0-385-47045-2 IMAGE PB $15.95
Volume 9
From the French Revolution to Sartre, Camus, and Lévi-Strauss
0-385-47046-0 IMAGE PB $16.95

Claude Lévi-Strauss

Gilles **Deleuze** & Felix **Guattari**
What is Philosophy?
See also **OTHER 20TH-CENTURY PHILOSOPHERS**
0-231-07988-5 COLUMBIA $29.95
0-231-07989-3 COLUMBIA PB $17.00

William K. **Frankena**
Ethics
A highly regarded introduction to the subject
0-13-290478-0 PRENTICE HALL PB $16.95

Jostein **Gaardner**
Sophie's World: A Novel About the History of Philosophy
A beguiling beginner's guide to Western philosophy in the form of a novel about a young Norwegian girl. "Remarkable…a whimsical and ingenious mystery novel that also happens to be a history of philosophy"
—*Washington Post Book World*
0-425-15225-1 BOULEVARD PB $6.99

Ian **Hacking**
Why Does Language Matter to Philosophy?
A historically informed reflection on the "linguistic turn" of modern philosophy
0-521-09998-6 CAMBRIDGE PB $18.95

John **Hospers**
An Introduction to Philosophical Analysis
The approach of the analytic school of philosophy that has dominated Anglo-American philosophy since World War II, explained by a leading practitioner
0-13-266305-8 PRENTICE HALL $45.00

C.E.M. **Joad**
Guide to Philosophy
A classic introduction to the subject from the first half of the century
0-486-20297-6 DOVER PB $12.95

Robert **Klee**
Introduction to the Philosophy of Science: Cutting Nature at Its Seams
0-19-510610-5 OXFORD $42.00

Thomas **Nagel**

What Does It All Mean?: A Very Short Introduction to Philosophy

A succinct survey of major problems—including "Other Minds," "Free Will," "Justice," and "The Meaning of Life"—by the American philosopher who wrote the famous essay "What Is It like to be a Bat?"

See also OTHER 20TH-CENTURY PHILOSOPHERS

0-19-505292-7 OXFORD $16.95
0-19-505216-1 OXFORD PB $10.95

Jacob **Needleman** &
David **Applebaum**, editors

Real Philosophy: An Anthology of the Universal Search for Meaning

Quotations from philosophers in all world traditions on such topics as "Who am I?" "Why am I here?" "Does God exist?" and "The spectrum of love"

0-14-019256-5 ARKANA PB $12.95

W. V. **Quine**

Methods of Logic

0-674-57176-2 HARVARD PB $16.95

Robert C. **Solomon**

Introducing Philosophy: A Text with Readings

0-15-541560-3 HARCOURT BRACE PB $22.95

Karsten J. **Struhl** & Paula R. **Struhl**, editors

Philosophy Now: An Introductory Reader

0-394-31852-8 RANDOM HOUSE PB $29.50

Encyclopedias and Histories of Philosophy

Robert **Audi**, editor

The Cambridge Dictionary of Philosophy

0-521-48328-X CAMBRIDGE PB $27.95

A.J. **Ayer** & Jane **O'Grady**, editors

A Dictionary of Philosophical Quotations

From Thales to Rawls and Derrida, with an emphasis on recent philosophy. "[A] history of Western philosophy, like Bertrand Russell's, but arranged alphabetically rather than chronologically, and by direct quotation rather than by precis…Everybody should have a copy"—Auberon Waugh

0-631-19478-9 BLACKWELL PB $22.95

Monroe C. **Beardsley**

Aesthetics from Classical Greece to the Present: A Short History

0-8173-6623-7 ALABAMA PB $16.50

Vincent **Descombes**

Modern French Philosophy

An interesting overview of the key figures in postwar French philosophy

0-521-29672-2 CAMBRIDGE PB $20.95

Isaiah **Berlin**, editor

The Age of Enlightenment: The Eighteenth Century Philosophers

0-452-00904-9 NEW AMERICAN LIBRARY PB $10.95

Isaiah Berlin

W.K. **Guthrie**

A History of Greek Philosophy

Volume 1
The Earlier Presocratics and the Pythagoreans

0-521-29420-7 CAMBRIDGE PB $38.95

Volume 2
The Presocratic Tradition from Parmenides to Democritus

0-521-29421-5 CAMBRIDGE PB $38.95

Volume 3
The Fifth-Century Enlightenment, Part 1: Socrates

0-521-09667-7 CAMBRIDGE PB $23.95

Volume 3
The Fifth-Century Enlightenment, Part 2: The Sophists

0-521-09666-9 CAMBRIDGE PB $29.95

Volume 4
Plato, The Man and His Dialogues: Earlier Period

0-521-31101-2 CAMBRIDGE PB $38.95

Volume 5
The Later Plato and the Academy

0-521-31102-0 CAMBRIDGE PB $38.95

Volume 6
Aristotle, An Encounter

0-521-23573-1 CAMBRIDGE $100.00
0-521-38760-4 CAMBRIDGE PB $34.95

D.W. **Hamlyn**

History of Western Philosophy

"Well-crafted and readable…neither laden with footnotes nor weighed down with technical language…a general guide to three millennia of philosophizing in the West"—*TLS*

0-14-022540-4 PENGUIN PB $6.95

Stuart **Hampshire**, editor

The Age of Reason: The Seventeenth Century Philosophers

An anthology of the founders of modern rationalist and empiricist philosophy, including Descartes, Malebranches, Bacon, Hobbes, and Leibniz

0-452-00989-8 NEW AMERICAN LIBRARY PB $9.95

Karl **Jaspers**

The Great Philosophers: Descartes, Pascal, Lessing, Kierkegaard, Nietzsche, Marx, Weber, Einstein

Jaspers engages in an intensely personal and skeptical dialogue with his "eternal contemporaries," of whom several were also his real contemporaries. "An expository, biographical, and critical study of great thinkers, written by one of the most eminent of contemporary existentialist philosophers" —*New Yorker*

TRANSLATED BY EDITH & LEONARD EHRLICH
FOREWORD BY MICHAEL ERMARTH

0-15-136943-7 HARCOURT BRACE $29.95

Anthony **Kenny**, editor

The Oxford History of Western Philosophy

Plato through Sartre, a dazzling tour in a beautifully illustrated Oxford edition. Kenny assembles a brilliant international team to bring into lively relief the story of our philosophical ideas. With a field of reference that ranges widely through human experience and includes subjects from medieval manuscripts to Gauguin and Magritte

0-19-824278-6 OXFORD $45.00

Arthur **Lovejoy**

The Great Chain of Being: A Study of the History of an Idea

This celebrated and highly influential study in the history of ideas considers one of the master metaphors of the western world

0-674-36153-9 HARVARD PB $15.95

Bertrand **Russell**

A History of Western Philosophy

A characteristically lucid, though highly opinionated, account stressing the historical context and the social and political implications of philosophical ideas

0-671-20158-1 SIMON & SCHUSTER PB $22.00

Richard **Tarnas**

The Passion of the Western Mind: Understanding the Ideas that Have Shaped our World View

"The most lucid and concise presentation I have read of the grand lines of what every student should know about the history of Western thought. The writing is elegant and carries the reader with the momentum of a novel" —Joseph Campbell

0-345-36809-6 BALLANTINE PB $14.00

Roger **Scruton**

A Short History of Modern Philosophy: From Descartes to Wittgenstein

A brisk, incisive, often iconoclastic history by a British philosopher who sees Wittgenstein's work as bringing to an end the isolated philosophical mind's quest for certainty that began with Descartes

0-415-13327-0 ROUTLEDGE $45.00
0-415-13035-2 ROUTLEDGE PB $10.95

Roger Scruton

Morton **White**, editor

The Age of Analysis: The Twentieth Century Philosophers

0-452-00830-1 NEW AMERICAN LIBRARY PB $11.95

The Presocratics

The chief pre-Socratic philosophers, whose work survives only in fragments, were concerned with the basic stuff, the underlying unity, of the universe. Thales thought it was water, Anaximander "the boundless." This culminated in the drastic monism of the Eleatic school, and Parmenides's contention that only unchanging being exists and that all motion and plurality are illusory—a point his follower Zeno tried to prove with his famous paradoxes. Heraclitus, on the other hand, claimed that all is ceaseless change and that everything contains and becomes its opposite.

Jonathan **Barnes**, editor

Early Greek Philosophy

Collects the extant writings of the Presocratics

See also **PHILOSOPHY** under **THE CLASSICAL PERIOD** under **ANCIENT GREEK LITERATURE** in **LITERATURE OF EUROPE, AFRICA, AND ASIA**

0-14-044461-0 PENGUIN PB $10.95

Martin **Heidegger**

Early Greek Thinking

According to Heidegger, Western philosophy not only begins with the Presocratics but culminates in ideas that are close to theirs

See also **HEIDEGGER**

TRANSLATED BY DAVID KRELL & FRANK CAPUZZI

0-06-063842-7 HARPERCOLLINS PB $16.20

Charles H. **Kahn**, editor

The Art and Thought of Heraclitus: An Edition of the Fragments with Translation and Commentary

0-521-28645-X CAMBRIDGE PB $34.95

Jonathan **Barnes**

The Presocratic Philosophers

A rigorous and precise study of the intriguing and sometimes baffling ideas of Greek pre-Socratic philosophy. "Lovers of the Presocratics will welcome this highly personal, vigorous and stimulating survey of the field"
— Charles H. Kahn, *Journal of Philosophy*

0-415-05079-0 ROUTLEDGE PB $27.95

Socrates

Socrates (469-399 B.C.) apparently wrote nothing; however, it is generally believed that the sly and relentless questioner of received opinions depicted in Plato's early dialogues faithfully represents him. The ethical intensity of Plato's Socrates—the injunction "know thyself" and the conviction that virtue is a form of knowledge—also rings true. Whatever his precise teachings, Socrates stands as a supreme example of the committed philosophical spirit.

I.F. **Stone**

The Trial of Socrates

The most emphatic treatment of the trial of Socrates as a political event, with the twist that the philosopher had it coming

See also **POLITICS AND IDEAS** under **TOPICS IN ANCIENT GREEK HISTORY** under **ANCIENT GREECE** in **WORLD HISTORY AND CURRENT AFFAIRS**

0-385-26032-6 ANCHOR PB $12.95

Gregory **Vlastos**, editor

The Philosophy of Socrates: A Collection of Critical Essays

An attempt to distinguish the authentic Socratic teaching from the dialogues of Plato and other sources

0-268-01537-6 NOTRE DAME PB $15.00

Socrates

Xenophon

Conversations of Socrates

See also **PHILOSOPHY** under **THE CLASSICAL PERIOD** under **ANCIENT GREEK LITERATURE** in **LITERATURE OF EUROPE, AFRICA, AND ASIA**

0-14-044517-X PENGUIN PB $11.95

Plato

Plato (427-347 B.C.) was a rationalist among poets and a poet among rationalists, who presented some of his most rigorous thought in such beautifully written dialogues as the *Phaedrus*, *Phaedo*, *Symposium*, and *Republic*. This severe moralist, who would have banned most forms of poetry, art, and music from his ideal city, has always appealed to poets, aesthetes, and visionaries, as well as to philosophers.

Plato

The Collected Dialogues of Plato

Edited by Edith Hamilton & Huntington Cairns

See also **PHILOSOPHY** under **THE CLASSICAL PERIOD** under **ANCIENT GREEK LITERATURE** in **LITERATURE OF EUROPE, AFRICA, AND ASIA**

0-691-09718-6 PRINCETON $37.50

Early Socratic Dialogues

The moral teachings of Socrates

EDITED WITH AN INTRODUCTION BY TREVOR J. SAUNDERS

0-14-044447-5 PENGUIN PB $9.95

Five Dialogues

TRANSLATED BY G.M. GRUBS

0-915145-23-5 HACKETT $27.95
0-915145-22-7 HACKETT PB $5.95

Gorgias

On the moral shortcomings of rhetoric, and a defense of justice against the idea that might makes right

TRANSLATED BY WALTER HAMILTON

0-14-044094-1 PENGUIN PB $7.95

The Last Days of Socrates

Includes *Euthyphro, Apology, Crito,* and the *Phaedo.* The speeches and teachings of Socrates at the time of his trial, and the doctrine of the immortality of the soul

TRANSLATED BY HUGH TREDENNICK

0-14-044037-2 PENGUIN PB $8.95

But I suggest, gentlemen, that the difficulty is not so much to escape death; the real difficulty is to escape from doing wrong, which is much fleeter of foot. In this present instance I, the slow old man, have been overtaken by the slower of the two, but my accusers, who are clever and quick, have been overtaken by the faster: by iniquity. When I leave this court I shall go away condemned by you to death, but they will go away convicted by Truth herself of depravity and wickedness... No doubt it was bound to be so, and I think the result is fair enough.—Socrates, *The Apology*

THE LAST DAYS OF SOCRATES

The Laws

A late work offering detailed practical legislation for a real, not ideal, state. Subjects range from education and elections to games and diet

TRANSLATED BY T.J. SAUNDERS

0-14-044222-7 PENGUIN PB $8.95

Phaedrus & Letters VII & VIII

The psychology of love

TRANSLATED BY WALTER HAMILTON

0-14-044275-8 PENGUIN PB $9.95

Philebus
The good in relation to pleasure and intelligence
TRANSLATED BY ROBIN A. WATERFIELD
0-14-044395-9 PENGUIN PB $7.95

The Portable Plato
Includes *The Republic*, the *Phaedo*, the *Symposium*, and the *Protagoras*
See also **ANCIENT GREEK CLASSICS** under **ANCIENT GREECE** in **WORLD HISTORY AND CURRENT AFFAIRS**
EDITED BY SCOTT BUCHANAN
0-14-015040-4 VIKING PB $14.95

Protagoras & Meno
In the *Protagoras* Socrates argues about goodness and pleasure with a Sophist famous for saying, "Man is the measure of all things." And in the *Meno* he offers a conception of knowledge as a recollection of something known before birth
TRANSLATED BY W.K. GUTHRIE
0-14-044068-2 PENGUIN PB $9.95

The Republic
TRANSLATED BY FRANCIS CORNFORD
0-19-500364-0 OXFORD PB $7.95

The Republic
Plato's most famous work presents the famous Allegory of the Cave, a version of his Theory of Forms, and a blueprint for an ideal state ruled by philosophers
TRANSLATED BY H.D. LEE
0-14-044048-8 PENGUIN PB $7.95

The Republic
This great 19th-century translation is distinguished for its literary style
TRANSLATED BY BENJAMIN JOWETT
0-394-70128-3 VINTAGE PB $9.00

The Republic
A careful translation with tendentious commentary by the neoconservative philosopher known for the *Closing of the American Mind*
TRANSLATED BY ALLAN BLOOM
0-465-06936-3 BASIC PB $15.00

The Republic
See also **PHILOSOPHY** under **THE CLASSICAL PERIOD** under **ANCIENT GREEK LITERATURE** in **LITERATURE OF EUROPE, AFRICA, AND ASIA**
TRANSLATED BY ROBIN WATERFIELD
0-19-212604-0 OXFORD $30.00
0-19-282909-2 OXFORD PB $5.95

Plato

The Symposium
A discussion of various forms of love, culminating with Socrates's exposition of "higher love"
TRANSLATED BY WALTER HAMILTON
0-14-044024-0 PENGUIN PB $7.95

Symposium
0-679-60197-X MODERN LIBRARY $13.50
0-02-360760-2 PRENTICE HALL PB $6.00

The Symposium of Plato
A new translation of Plato's famous dinner-party conversation about beauty and love, Platonic and otherwise
TRANSLATED BY TOM GRIFFITH
0-520-06694-4 CALIFORNIA PB $25.00

Theaetetus
A brilliant and rigorous inquiry into the nature of thought and knowledge, rejecting the view that sense perception is knowledge
EDITED WITH AN INTRODUCTION BY ROBIN A. WATERFIELD
0-14-044450-5 PENGUIN PB $8.95

Timaeus & Critias
Plato's cosmology and natural science; the *Timaeus* contains the earliest known form of the Atlantis legend
TRANSLATED BY H.D. LEE
0-14-044261-8 PENGUIN PB $9.95

The Works of Plato
0-679-60164-3 MODERN LIBRARY $19.00

Julia **Annas**
An Introduction to Plato's Republic
A remarkable achievement. Presents Plato as a philosophical educator rather than a dogmatist and discusses various problems raised by this difficult text
See also **STUDIES OF INDIVIDUAL AUTHORS** under **CRITICAL STUDIES** under **ANCIENT GREEK LITERATURE** in **LITERATURE OF EUROPE, AFRICA, AND ASIA**
0-19-827429-7 OXFORD PB $18.95

Hans-Georg **Gadamer**
Plato's Dialectical Ethics: Phenomenological Interpretations Relating to the Philebus
TRANSLATED BY ROBERT M. WALLACE
0-300-04807-6 YALE $32.50

R.M. **Hare**
Plato
A brief, elegant summary of the major arguments, from the Past Masters series
0-19-287585-X OXFORD PB $7.95

Eric **Havelock**
Preface to Plato
Perhaps the most influential discussion of the oral nature of early Greek literature
See also **GENERAL STUDIES** under **CRITICAL STUDIES** under **ANCIENT GREEK LITERATURE** in **LITERATURE OF EUROPE, AFRICA, AND ASIA**
0-674-69906-8 HARVARDP PB $16.95

Terence **Irwin**
Plato's Ethics
0-19-508645-7 OXFORD PB $22.00

Martha C. **Nussbaum**
The Fragility of Goodness: Luck and Ethics in Greek Tragedy and Philosophy
An important study of Greek culture encompassing literature as well as philosophical ethics
0-521-27702-7 CAMBRIDGE PB $31.95

Stanley **Rosen**
Plato's Statesman: The Web of Politics
0-300-06264-8 YALE $25.00

Leo **Strauss**
Studies in Platonic Political Philosophy
The influential German-born conservative philosopher discusses the political philosophy that was the key to his own ideas
EDITED BY THOMAS L. PANGLE
FOREWORD BY JOSEPH CROPSEY
0-226-77700-6 CHICAGO PB $16.95

Leo Strauss

Gregory **Vlastos**
Platonic Studies
0-691-10021-7 PRINCETON PB $24.95

Aristotle

Aristotle's (384-322 B.C.) monumental presence in Western philosophy means that he is almost as difficult to approach as he is to get around. He was the chief influence not only on medieval scholastic philosophy but also on all philosophy of a realist or empiricist tendency right up through 20th-century "ordinary language" philosophy. A great systematizer and classifier, he was called "the master of those who know" by Dante. Yet his surviving works consist solely of lecture notes, arranged in arbitrary order by editors. His dialogues, Platonic in tone, are lost. Aristotle's philosophy should be approached in the inquisitive, investigative spirit in which it was written.

Aristotle

Aristotle's Poetics

Aristotles's theory of tragedy as catharsis has been of crucial importance to subsequent literary theory

TRANSLATED BY S.H. BUTCHER

INTRODUCTION BY FRANCES FERGUSSON

0-8090-0527-1 FS&G PB $5.95

The Art of Rhetoric

0-14-044510-2 PENGUIN PB $11.95

The Athenian Constitution

TRANSLATED BY P.J. RHODES & MARTIN HURLIMANN

0-14-044431-9 PENGUIN PB $9.95

The Complete Works of Aristotle

The revised Oxford translation in a 2-volume set

See also **PHILOSOPHY** under **THE CLASSICAL PERIOD** under **ANCIENT GREEK LITERATURE** in **LITERATURE OF EUROPE, AFRICA, AND ASIA**

EDITED BY JONATHAN BARNES

0-691-09950-2 PRINCETON $79.00

De Anima: On the Soul

The relation of the soul to God and to intellectual and imaginative capacity

TRANSLATED BY HUGH LAWSON-TANCRED

0-14-044471-8 PENGUIN PB $10.95

Eudemian Ethics: Books I, II, and VIII

TRANSLATED BY MICHAEL WOODS

0-19-824020-1 OXFORD PB $29.95

Introduction to Aristotle

Includes the *Nicomachean Ethics,* the *Politics,* the *Poetics,* and selections from other works

See also **ANCIENT GREEK CLASSICS** under **ANCIENT GREECE** in **WORLD HISTORY AND CURRENT AFFAIRS**

EDITED BY RICHARD MCKEON

0-679-60027-2 MODERN LIBRARY $18.50

Metaphysics: Books Gamma, Delta, and Epsilon

TRANSLATED BY CHRISTOPHER KIRWAN

0-19-824087-2 OXFORD PB $24.95

Metaphysics Books Z and H

TRANSLATED BY DAVID BOSTOCK

0-19-823947-5 OXFORD PB $22.00

A New Aristotle Reader

EDITED BY J.L. ACKRILL

0-691-02043-4 PRINCETON PB $17.95

The Nicomachean Ethics

Ethics as an imprecise practical science; virtue as the mean between extremes

TRANSLATED BY SIR DAVID ROSS

REVISED TRANSLATION BY J.L. ACKRILL & J.O. URMSON

0-19-281518-0 OXFORD PB $6.95

Physics

0-19-282310-8 OXFORD PB $8.95

The Pocket Aristotle

EDITED BY JUSTIN KAPLAN

0-671-46377-2 POCKET PB $5.99

Politics

Treats man the political animal, and surveys the various kinds of states and their advantages and disadvantages

0-14-044421-1 PENGUIN PB $11.95

Jonathan **Barnes**

Aristotle

Barnes places Aristotle in historical context, as a controversial political figure and a member of Plato's philosophical school

0-19-287581-7 OXFORD PB $7.95

Jonathan **Lear**

Aristotle: The Desire to Understand

A lucid introduction and guide to Aristotle's central doctrines

0-521-34762-9 CAMBRIDGE PB $19.95

J.L. **Ackrill**, editor

Aristotle the Philosopher

Reveals why contemporary philosophers still draw from and return to Aristotle

0-19-289118-9 OXFORD PB $15.95

Sir David **Ross**

Aristotle

An excellent introduction

0-415-12068-3 ROUTLEDGE PB $18.95

Stoics and Epicureans

Marcus **Aurelius**

Meditations

Marcus Aurelius, philosopher-emperor of Rome (c. 160), wrote these reflections on human character, power, and mortality at night mostly while camped with his soldiers on campaign

See also **ELAINE PAGLES'S PICKS** under **COMPARATIVE RELIGION** under **WORLD RELIGION**

TRANSLATED BY MAXWELL STANIFORTH

0-14-044140-9 PENGUIN PB $9.95

Epictetus

The Discourses

0-460-87312-1 EVERYMAN'S PB $8.50

Epicurus

Epicurus: The Extant Remains, with a Short Critical Apparatus

Far from epicurean in the modern sense, Epicurus lived on bread and cheese and taught moderation and tranquility as the path to happiness

TRANSLATED BY CYRIL BAILEY

0-88355-789-4 HYPERION $37.00

Lucretius

The Nature of Things

An eloquent poetic exposition of materialism and atheism

TRANSLATED BY F.O. COPLEY

0-393-09094-9 NORTON PB $8.95

The Way Things Are: The De Rerum Natura of Titus Lucretius Carus

An excellent verse translation of the philosophical poem which exults in the freedom from tyrannical gods conferred by Epicurean materialism

See also **GOLDEN AGE** under **LATIN LITERATURE** in **LITERATURE OF EUROPE, AFRICA, AND ASIA**

TRANSLATED BY ROLFE HUMPHRIES

0-253-20125-X INDIANA PB $8.95

Seneca

Letter from a Stoic

The austere ideal of passionless virtue developed by the Stoics was never more eloquently urged than by the Roman essayist and dramatist Seneca

See also **SILVER AGE** under **LATIN LITERATURE** in **LITERATURE OF EUROPE, AFRICA, AND ASIA**

EDITED BY ROBIN CAMPBELL

0-14-044210-3 PENGUIN PB $9.95

The Stoic Philosophy of Seneca: Essays and Letters

See also **SILVER AGE** under **LATIN LITERATURE** in **LITERATURE OF EUROPE, AFRICA, AND ASIA**

EDITED BY MOSES HADAS

0-393-00459-7 NORTON PB $9.95

R. W. **Sharples**

Stoics, Epicureans and Sceptics

0-415-11034-3 ROUTLEDGE $42.00

Other Topics in Ancient Philosophy

E. R. **Dodds**

The Greeks and the Irrational

The sources of Greek rationalism are to be found in primitive modes of thought

See also **RELIGION AND PHILOSOPHY** under **TOPICS IN ANCIENT GREEK HISTORY** under **ANCIENT GREECE** in **WORLD HISTORY AND CURRENT AFFAIRS**

0-8446-6224-0 SMITH $24.05

0-520-00327-6 CALIFORNIA PB $15.00

Michel **Foucault**

The History of Sexuality, Volume 2: The Use of Pleasure

Foucault's last major project changed direction in the writing. Volume two alone addresses the sexual mores of the Ancients. "Required reading for those who cling to stereotyped ideas about our difference from the Greeks in terms of pagan license versus Christian austerity or their hedonism versus our anxiety"
—*LA Times Book Review*

See also **HISTORICAL SOCIOLOGY** under **TOPICS IN MODERN SOCIOLOGY** under **SOCIOLOGY** in **SOCIAL STUDIES**

0-394-75122-1 VINTAGE PB $13.00

David **Furley**

The Greek Cosmologists

A scholarly study of the philosophical materialism that began with Democritus

Volume 1

0-521-33328-8 CAMBRIDGE $59.95

Volume 2

0-521-33329-6 CAMBRIDGE $42.50

Jane Ellen **Harrison**

Prolegomena to the Study of Greek Religion

See also **ANCIENT MEDITERRANEAN RELIGIONS** under **WORLD RELIGION**

0-691-01514-7 PRINCETON PB $19.95

Werner W. **Jaeger**

Paideia: The Ideals of Greek Culture

Volume 1
Archaic Greece and the Mind of Athens
0-19-500425-6 OXFORD PB........$19.95

Volume 2
In Search of the Divine Centre
0-19-504047-3 OXFORD PB........$19.95

Volume 3
The Conflict of Ideals in the Age of Plato
0-19-504048-1 OXFORD PB........$19.95

Martha C. **Nussbaum**

The Therapy of Desire: Theory and Practice in Hellenistic Ethics
The convergence of ethics and therapeutic approaches to desire and happiness in Aristotle, Stoicism and Epicureanism

See also **OTHER 20TH-CENTURY PHILOSOPHERS**

0-691-03342-0 PRINCETON........$45.00
0-691-00052-2 PRINCETON PB........$16.95

Richard Broxton **Onians**

The Origins of European Thought About the Body, the Mind, the Soul, the World, Time, and Fate
0-521-34794-7 CAMBRIDGE PB........$31.95

Bruno **Snell**

The Discovery of the Mind in Greek Philosophy and Literature
0-486-24264-1 DOVER PB........$8.95

Gregory **Vlastos**

Studies in Greek Philosophy
The collected papers of the preeminent modern scholar of classical philosophy

Volume 1
The Presocratics
See also **POLITICS AND IDEAS** under **TOPICS IN ANCIENT GREEK HISTORY** under **ANCIENT GREECE** in **WORLD HISTORY AND CURRENT AFFAIRS**

0-691-03310-2 PRINCETON........$49.50

Volume 2
Socrates, Plato, and Their Tradition
See also **POLITICS AND IDEAS** under **TOPICS IN ANCIENT GREEK HISTORY** under **ANCIENT GREECE** in **WORLD HISTORY AND CURRENT AFFAIRS**

0-691-03311-0 PRINCETON........$49.50

Bernard **Williams**

Shame and Necessity
A discussion of ethical problems as reflected in classical Greek literature

See also **OTHER 20TH-CENTURY PHILOSOPHERS**

0-520-08046-7 CALIFORNIA........$30.00
0-520-08830-1 CALIFORNIA PB........$15.00

Plotinus

Some 600 years after Plato's death, Plotinus (205-270) turned Platonic philosophy into something more mystical, rarefied, and elaborate. His hierarchical chain of being continues to influence Christian thought and literature.

Plotinus

The Enneads
The famous MacKenna translation of the great mystical philosopher, now available in an inexpensive edition. The neo-Platonic thought of Plotinus is of incomparable importance in the development of Western philosophy; he also wrote with great beauty and concision. MacKenna's version has been described by George Steiner as "one of the masterpieces of modern English prose and formal sensibility"

TRANSLATED BY STEPHEN MACKENNA
0-14-044520-X PENGUIN PB........$13.95

> Many times it has happened: lifted out of the body into myself; becoming external to all other things and self-centered; beholding a marvelous beauty; then, more than ever, assured of community with the loftiest order; enacting the noblest life, acquiring identity with the divine, stationing within it by having attained that activity; poised above whatsoever within the intellectual is less than the supreme; yet, there comes the moment of descent from intellection to reasoning, and after that sojourn in the divine, I ask myself how it happens that I can now be descending, and how did the soul ever enter into my body, the soul which, even within the body, is the high thing it has shown itself to be.
>
> THE ENNEADS

The Essential Plotinus
TRANSLATED BY ELMER O'BRIEN
0-915144-09-3 HACKETT PB........$6.95

Augustine

Augustine (354-430) was the last great philosopher of classical antiquity and the first great philosopher of the Middle Ages. A Manichaean in his youth, he assimilated the neoPlatonism of Plotinus before formulating a Christian philosophy based on original sin and predestination.

Saint Augustine

The Confessions
Augustine's classic spiritual autobiography, tracing his passage from boyhood sin through Manichaeanism to Christian conversion

TRANSLATED BY R.S. PINE-COFFIN
0-14-044114-X PENGUIN PB........$8.95

The Trinity
See also **CLASSICS** under **CHRISTIANITY**

0-911782-96-6 NEWCI PB........$24.95

Henry **Chadwick**

Augustine
"Deep learning and lucidity make this a finely balanced and authoritative introduction to Augustine's thought"— *TLS*

0-19-287534-5 OXFORD PB........$7.95

Peter **Brown**

Augustine of Hippo: A Biography
A comprehensive biography of the fourth-century Christian convert whose theology formed a bridge between the ancient and medieval churches and defined such essential Christian doctrines as grace and original sin

See also **RELIGION** under **TOPICS IN ROMAN HISTORY** under **ANCIENT ROME**

0-520-01411-1 CALIFORNIA PB........$16.00

Elaine **Pagels**

Adam, Eve, and the Serpent
The evolution of Christian thought—from an early emphasis on freedom to the asceticism and determinism that prevailed through the writings of Augustine—as reflected in orthodox and Gnostic interpretations of the story of Adam and Eve

See also **COMPARATIVE RELIGION** under **WORLD RELIGION**

0-679-72232-7 RANDOM HOUSE PB........$10.00

> In a world in which Christians not only were free to follow their faith but were officially encouraged to do so, Augustine came to read the story of Adam and Eve very differently than had the majority of his Jewish and Christian predecessors. What they had read for centuries as a story of human freedom became, in his hands, a story of human bondage. Most Jews and Christians had agreed that God gave humankind in creation the gift of moral freedom, and that Adam's misuse of it brought death upon his progeny. But Augustine went further: Adam's sin not only caused our mortality but cost us our moral freedom, irreversibly corrupted our experience of sexuality (which Augustine tended to identify with original sin), and made us incapable of genuine political freedom.
>
> ADAM, EVE, AND THE SERPENT

Saint Thomas Aquinas

The Scholastics sought to synthesize Christian theology with philosophical rationalism, and Aquinas (1225-1274), whose thought fully assimilated that of Aristotle, achieved the most imposing and influential of such syntheses. Indeed, throughout his comprehensive, systematic philosophy he continually sought to reconcile opposing arguments. In the 19th century Aquinas's work was accepted by the Catholic church as the main philosophical basis of its doctrines.

Saint Thomas Aquinas

The Pocket Aquinas
EDITED BY V. BOURKE
0-671-73991-3 POCKET PB........$5.99

Selected Philosophical Writings
A recommended selection

See also **CLASSICS OF WESTERN RELIGIOUS THOUGHT** under **WORLD RELIGION**

0-19-282946-7 OXFORD PB........$13.95

Selected Writings of St. Thomas Aquinas
Includes *The Principles of Nature, On Being and Essence, On the Virtues in General,* and *On Free Choice*

TRANSLATED BY ROBERT P. GOODWIN
0-02-345050-9 PRENTICE HALL PB........$12.00

Frederick C. **Copleston**

Aquinas

A sympathetic account, stressing modern implications

0-14-020349-4 VIKING PB $12.00

Umberto **Eco**

The Aesthetics of Thomas Aquinas

Aquinas's criteria of beauty—integrity, proportion, and clarity—turn up in the work of the young James Joyce. Eco shows how Aquinas's ideas about music and poetry were integrated with his ideas about God and human nature

0-674-00676-3 HARVARD PB $14.00

Anthony **Kenny**

Aquinas

A short study comprising an account of Aquinas's life and works and his significance for philosophy; a summary of major metaphysical concepts; and an account of his philosophy of mind

0-19-287500-0 OXFORD PB $7.95

Paul E. **Sigmund**, editor

St. Thomas Aquinas on Politics and Ethics

Contains new translations of central selections from *The Summa Against the Gentiles*, *On Kingship or The Governance of Rulers*, and *The Summa of Theology.* Selected critical interpretations trace Aquinas's influence on Roman Catholicism during the Renaissance, on 19th-and 20th-century papal social thought, and on contemporary Christian Democratic political parties in Europe and Latin America

0-393-95243-6 NORTON PB $9.95

Other Medieval Philosophers

Meister **Eckhart**

Selected Writings

Eckhart's radical synthesis of neoPlatonism and Christian doctrine remains complex, challenging, and controversial

TRANSLATED BY OLIVER DAVIES

0-14-043343-0 PENGUIN PB $11.95

Umberto **Eco**

Art and Beauty in the Middle Ages

A brief introduction to the subject, much of it repeated from Eco's book on Aquinas's aesthetics

See also **THE MEDIEVAL AESTHETIC** under **MEDIEVAL AND RENAISSANCE EUROPE** in **WORLD HISTORY AND CURRENT AFFAIRS**

0-300-04207-8 YALE PB $10.00

Christopher **Martin**

An Introduction to Medieval Philosophy

0-7486-0790-0 EDINBURGH PB $25.00

Andrew B. **Schoedinger**

Readings in Medieval Philosophy

0-19-509293-7 OXFORD PB $29.95

Boethius

Boethius (c.475-525); a Christian Platonist who also drew on Aristotle, was the archetypal philosopher for the Middle Ages. Accused of treason, he wrote his *Consolation of Philosophy* while in prison awaiting execution.

Boethius

Boethius

Includes *Theological Tractate,* and *The Consolation of Philosophy*

See also **LATIN LITERATURE** under **THE LOEB CLASSICS** in **LITERATURE OF EUROPE, AFRICA, AND ASIA**

0-674-99083-8 HARVARD $18.95

The Consolation of Philosophy

The Roman adviser to the Gothic king Theodoric wrote this amalgamation of Roman and Christian wisdom while awaiting execution

See also **LATE WRITERS** under **LATIN LITERATURE** in **LITERATURE OF EUROPE, AFRICA, AND ASIA**

TRANSLATED BY V.E. WATTS

0-14-044208-1 PENGUIN PB $10.95

Saint Anselm

An originator of Scholastic philosophy, Anselm (c. 1033-1109) is best known as the inventor of the ontological proof for the existence of God, which holds that it is an essential part of God's perfection that he exist.

Saint Anselm

Basic Writings

EDITED BY SIDNEY N. DEANE

INTRODUCTION BY CHARLES HARTSHORNE

0-87548-109-4 OPEN COURT PB $9.00

Duns Scotus

The American philosopher C.S. Pierce, influenced by his theory of universals, called the 13th-century Franciscan Scholastic (1266-1308) one of the most profound metaphysicians who ever lived.

Duns **Scotus**

Philosophical Writings: A Selection

TRANSLATED BY ALLAN WOLTER & MARILYN M. ADAMS

0-87220-019-1 HACKETT $37.95

0-87220-018-3 HACKETT PB $14.95

Martha **Kneale** & William **Kneale**

The Development of Logic

A history of logic particularly useful for its treatment of Duns Scotus

0-19-824773-7 OXFORD PB $35.00

William of Ockham

The greatest Scholastic logician, Ockham (1285-1349) is best known for Ockham's razor, the too-often neglected principle that philosophical explanations should not multiply logical entities: "What can be done with fewer assumptions is done in vain with more."

William of **Ockham**

Philosophical Writings: A Selection

0-87220-078-7 HACKETT PB $14.95

Predestination, God's Foreknowledge, and Future Contingents

0-915144-14-X HACKETT $27.95

Renaissance Philosophers

Marsilio Ficino

The radiant and serene Platonism that pervades much of European Renaissance literature is largely due to Ficino (1433-1499), founder of the Platonic Academy in Florence. By making the first complete translation of Plato's dialogues and assimilating ancient neoPlatonism into his own thought, Ficino conveyed Platonic philosophy to modern Europe, especially the idea of love as presented in the *Symposium*.

Marsilio **Ficino**

The Book of Life

TRANSLATED BY CHARLES BOER

0-88214-212-7 SPRING PB $18.00

Meditations on the Soul: Selected Letters of Marsilio Ficino

EDITED BY CLEMENT SALAMAN

0-89281-567-1 INNER TRADITIONS $24.95

Giordano Bruno

The most famous and iconoclastic figure in Renaissance philosophy, Bruno (1548-1600) was its only martyr. Arrested by the Inquisition, he languished in prison for eight years and then was burned alive for heresy. A caustic critic of the static cosmos presented in Scholastic philosophy, Bruno evoked a universe containing an infinite number of worlds, a divine unity in which all opposites are reconciled. This pantheism edged into the occult: Bruno was an ardent champion of magic, hermetic philosophy, and astrology.

Giordano Bruno

Giordano **Bruno**

The Ash Wednesday Supper

Dialogues on the Copernican heliocentric theory, on magic, and on Bruno's concept of an animated cosmos

See also **HUMANISM** under **THE RENAISSANCE** under **ITALIAN LITERATURE** in **LITERATURE OF EUROPE, AFRICA, AND ASIA**

EDITED AND TRANSLATED BY EDWARD A. GOSSELIN & LAWRENCE S. LERNER

0-8020-7469-3 TORONTO PB $20.9

Giovanni Pico della Mirandola

Believing that a measure of truth could be found in all philosophies, Pico (1463-1494) not only drew on Aristotle, the Scholastics, and Plato, but also on Jewish Kabbalists and Renaissance Hermetic philosophers. His most famous and influential work, *The Oration on the Dignity of Man*, strikes a modern note through its uncompromising insistence on human freedom, by which man can sink to the lowest levels of existence or rise to the divine.

Giovanni Pico **della Mirandola**

Oration on the Dignity of Man

TRANSLATED BY A. ROBERT CAPONIGRI

0-89526-925-2 REGNERY PB $8.95

Frances **Yates**

Giordano Bruno and the Hermetic Tradition

The belief that magical and occult approaches to nature could be traced back to ancient Egypt—the legendary Hermes Trismegistus—pervaded Renaissance thought, especially neoPlatonism, and it was the inspiration for Bruno's attempt to retrieve a true religion of nature out of the Hermetic tradition

0-226-95003-4 CHICAGO PB $16.95

Bacon

The first great English essayist, Bacon (1561-1626) was also the first philosophical advocate of the scientific experimental method, which he said could give mankind mastery over nature.

Francis Bacon

Francis **Bacon**

The Advancement of Learning

See also **PROSE** under **THE EARLY 17TH CENTURY** in **LITERATURE OF THE BRITISH ISLES**

EDITED BY G.W. PITCHER

INTRODUCTION BY ARTHUR JOHNSTON

1-56459-436-X KESSINGER PB $16.95

The Essays

A few years after Montaigne invented the essay in French, Bacon composed his terse, epigrammatic, and shrewdly perceptive meditations, introducing the form into English

See also **PROSE** under **THE EARLY 17TH CENTURY** in **LITERATURE OF THE BRITISH ISLES**

EDITED BY JOHN PITCHER

0-14-043216-7 PENGUIN PB $10.95

The New Organon & Related Writings

Bacon's revolutionary philosophy of science

See also **PROSE** under **THE EARLY 17TH CENTURY** in **LITERATURE OF THE BRITISH ISLES**

EDITED BY FULTON H. ANDERSON

0-02-303380-0 BOBBS-MERRILL PB $17.40

Hobbes

Impressed by the results of Galileo's experiments, Thomas Hobbes (1588-1679) sought to apply mechanical principles to the study of human psychology. He was a pioneer materialist who became notorious, however, for his bold political theories. Hobbes lived through the English civil war, which gave him ample reason to believe that, in the absence of civil order, the life of man would be, as he famously put it, "solitary, poor, nasty, brutal, and short." He argued that the only escape from such a fate lay in accepting the absolute authority of the state.

Thomas **Hobbes**

The Elements of Law Natural and Politic: Part I, Human Nature; & Part II, De Corpore Politico

EDITED BY J.C.A. GASKIN

0-19-283121-6 OXFORD PB $8.95

Leviathan

This great work, published in 1651 and subjected to a parliamentary investigation for atheism, heavily influenced much subsequent British political theory

See also **CLASSICS** under **POLITICAL THOUGHT** in **SOCIAL STUDIES**

EDITED BY C.B. MACPHERSON

0-14-043195-0 PENGUIN PB $8.95

Whatsoever therefore is consequent to a time of Warre, where every man is Enemy to every man; the same is consequent to the time, wherein men live without other security, than what their own strength, and their own invention shall furnish them withall. In such condition, there is no place for Industry; because the fruit thereof is uncertain: and consequently no Culture of the Earth; no Navigation, nor use of the commodities that may be imported by Sea; no commodious Building; no Instruments of moving, and removing such things as require much force; no Knowledge of the face of the Earth; no account of Time; no Arts; no Letters; no Society; and which is worst of all, continuall feare, and danger of violent death; And the life of man, solitary, poore, nasty, brutish, and short.

LEVIATHAN

Man and Citizen: De Homine and De Cive

0-87220-111-2 HACKETT PB $9.95

Thomas Hobbes

Norberto **Bobbio**

Thomas Hobbes and the Natural Law Tradition

TRANSLATED BY DANIELA GOBETTI

0-226-06248-1 CHICAGO PB $15.95

Leo **Strauss**

The Political Philosophy of Hobbes: Its Basis and Its Genesis

0-226-77705-7 CHICAGO PB $13.95

Richard **Tuck**

Hobbes

A short introduction to Hobbes's thought

0-19-287668-6 OXFORD PB $8.95

Descartes

Descartes (1589-1660) thought that philosophy had lost ground to science as a description of the world. He rejected the subtle logical structures of the Scholastics and replaced them with the epistemological question of how it is we know what we know. For better or for worse, that has been the main preoccupation of philosophers ever since.

René **Descartes**

Discourse on Method & the Meditations

TRANSLATED BY F.E. SUTCLIFFE

0-14-044206-5 PENGUIN PB $6.95

I became aware that, while I decided thus to think that everything was false, it followed necessarily that I who thought thus must be something; and observing that this truth: *I think, therefore I am*, was so certain and so evident that all the most extravagant suppositions of the sceptics were not capable of shaking it, I judged that I could accept it without scruple as the first principle of the philosophy I was seeking.

DISCOURSE ON METHOD & THE MEDITATIONS

Discourse on the Method and Meditations on First Philosophy

EDITED BY DAVID WEISSMAN

0-300-06772-0 YALE $35.00
0-300-06773-9 YALE PB $15.00

Meditations on First Philosophy: With Selections from the Objections and Replies

TRANSLATED BY JOHN COTTINGHAM

0-521-55252-4 CAMBRIDGE $34.95
0-521-55818-2 CAMBRIDGE PB $12.95

The Philosophical Writings Volume 1

This volume contains Descartes' major philosophical works. Volume 2, containing his correspondence, is currently out of print

0-521-28807-X CAMBRIDGE PB $22.95

Antonio R. **Damasio**

Descartes' Error: Emotion, Reason, and the Human Brain

"Damasio's astonishing book takes us on a scientific journey into the brain that helps us see the source of our feelings, thoughts and desires, as well as our idiosyncratic creative and destructive behavior"—Jonas Salk. Damasio, a much-honored doctor and professor of neurology, draws on his treatment of brain-damaged patients to show, in direct contradiction to the durable Cartesian "mind-body duality," the interdependence of rationality and emotion

0-399-13894-3 PUTNAM $24.95
0-380-72647-5 AVON PB $12.50

Spinoza

The enigmatic Dutch philosopher Spinoza (1632-1677) was a controversial figure in his lifetime and an inspiration to such diverse later thinkers as Coleridge and Marx. He was a monist, arguing that all reality shares a single essence, but his work has received both materialist and idealist interpretations, and even been accused of pantheism. It is universally admired, however, for its beautiful and deeply considered design.

Baruch Spinoza

The Collected Works of Spinoza

EDITED BY EDWIN CURLEY

0-691-07222-1 PRINCETON $80.00

Baruch **Spinoza**

Ethics

TRANSLATED BY GEORGE ELIOT
EDITED BY JAMES HOGG

0-934710-05-8 SIMON $40.00

On the Improvement of the Understanding, Ethics, and Correspondence

An inexpensive edition of Spinoza's major works

0-486-20250-X DOVER PB $8.95

A Spinoza Reader: The Ethics and Other Works

0-691-03363-3 PRINCETON $55.00
0-691-00067-0 PRINCETON PB $14.95

Theologico-Political Treatise: Political Treatise

TRANSLATED BY R.H. ELWES

0-486-20249-6 DOVER PB $8.95

Richard H. **Popkin**

The History of Scepticism from Erasmus to Spinoza

"Demonstrates conclusively and in fascinating detail how the transmission of ancient scepticism was a vital factor in the formation of modern thought"—M.F. Burnyeat

0-520-03876-2 CALIFORNIA PB $16.00

Leo **Strauss**

Spinoza's Critique of Religion

0-226-77688-3 CHICAGO PB $15.95

Harry A. **Wolfson**

The Philosophy of Spinoza: Unfolding the Latent Processes of His Reasoning

"Wolfson has tracked Spinoza to his lair in a work of scholarship and erudition hard to duplicate...He argues his thesis with persuasion and wit...and writes in a style that is a model of clarity"—*New Republic*

0-674-66595-3 HARVARD PB $25.95

Yirmiahu **Yovel**

Spinoza and Other Heretics

Volume 1
The Marrano of Reason

0-691-02078-7 PRINCETON PB $14.95

Volume 2
The Adventures of Immanence

0-691-02079-5 PRINCETON PB $14.95

Locke

John Locke (1632-1704) is equally important as the founder of British empiricism and the champion of political liberalism. The philosopher who best embodies the clarity and rationality of the Enlightenment, he is very much present in contemporary philosophical and political debates.

John **Locke**

An Essay Concerning Human Understanding

This important work was greatly influenced by Locke's reading of travel accounts, which for him and many of his contemporaries made up a "scientific" body of evidence from which to speculate on the nature of humanity

See also **PRECURSORS** under **GENERAL ANTHROPOLOGICAL STUDIES** under **ANTHROPOLOGY** in **SOCIAL STUDIES**

0-460-87355-5 EVERYMAN'S PB $8.95

John Locke

George **Berkeley** & others

The Empiricists

Includes Locke's *Essay Concerning Human Understanding*, Berkeley's *Principles of Human Knowledge* and *Three Dialogues*, and Hume's *Enquiry Concerning Human Understanding*

See also **BERKELEY**
See also **HUME**

0-385-09622-4 ANCHOR PB $11.00

John **Dunn**

Locke

An excellent introduction by an outstanding scholar

0-19-287560-4 OXFORD PB $7.95

Two Treatises of Government

0-460-87356-3 EVERYMAN'S PB $6.95

J.L. **Mackie**

Problems from Locke

Locke posed questions about knowledge and perception that philosophers are still trying to resolve

0-19-875036-6 OXFORD PB $19.95

Blackwell's Dictionaries

Blackwell presents a comprehensive series to the great philosophers Descartes, Locke, Rousseau, and Hegel. Arranged alphabetically for easy reference, each volume defines fundamental concepts and places each into historical and intellectual perspective. Written to be accessible to scholar and general reader alike, the listings are based on both the published and unpublished work of the philosophers. Includes a complete biographical outline of their lives, a complete bibliography of their work, as well as recommendations for further reading.

John **Cottingham**

A Descartes Dictionary

0-631-18538-0 BLACKWELL PB $20.95

N.J.H. **Dent**

A Rousseau Dictionary

0-631-17569-5 BLACKWELL PB $20.95

Michael **Inwood**

A Hegel Dictionary

0-631-17533-4 BLACKWELL PB $20.95

John **Yolton**

A Locke Dictionary

0-631-17547-4 BLACKWELL PB $39.95

Leibniz

Leibniz (1646-1710) was a daunting intellectual polymath, not only a philosopher but a diplomat, natural scientist, and mathematician who is credited with having invented calculus at the same time as, but independently of, Newton. His work in philosophy greatly influenced Kant, while his optimistic view that "this is the best of all possible worlds" was satirized in Voltaire's *Candide*.

Gottfried Wilhelm **Leibniz**

Discourse on Metaphysics and the Monadology

TRANSLATED BY GEORGE R. MONTGOMERY

0-87975-775-2 PROMETHEUS PB $6.95

Monadology & Other Philosophical Essays

In Liebniz's view in these essays, the world is composed of autonomous "monads" which do not interact but exist in preestablished harmony

0-02-406970-1 PRENTICE HALL PB $11.60

New Essays on Human Understanding

Reflections and arguments inspired by the philosophy of John Locke

EDITED BY PETER REMNANT & JONATHAN BENNETT

0-521-28539-9 CAMBRIDGE PB $25.95

The Political Writings of Leibniz

EDITED BY PATRICK RILEY

0-521-35380-7 CAMBRIDGE $54.95

Theodicy: Essays on the Goodness of God, the Freedom of Man, and the Origin of Evil

0-87548-437-9 OPEN COURT PB $13.00

Writings on China

0-8126-9251-9 OPEN COURT PB $17.95

Nicholas **Rescher**, editor

Leibniz: An Introduction to His Philosophy

0-7512-0275-4 ASHGATE $49.95

Vico

Vico (1688-1744) replaced Descarte's mathematical model of knowledge with a historical one: it is not nature but history that has constituted humanity as it is, and so it is through the historical study of such characteristic human attainments as language, mythology, and social institutions that we can understand ourselves best. Ignored in his own day, Vico had a strong influence on such writers as Michelet, Marx, and James Joyce.

Giambattista Vico

Giambattista **Vico**

The Autobiography of Giambattista Vico

A Venetian nobleman asked Vico to set down an account of his studies and intellectual development up to *The New Science*, and the result is one of the great European autobiographies

TRANSLATED BY MAX H. FISCH & THOMAS G. BERGIN

0-8014-9088-X CORNELL PB $14.95

The New Science of Giambattista Vico

Vico's 1725 treatise was the first modern study of myth, foreshadowing later anthropological views: "The fables of the gods are true histories of customs." This groundbreaking work was the first to treat the internal dynamics of primitive cultures and offered a cyclical alternative to the Enlightenment's belief that history means progress

See also **GENERAL INTRODUCTIONS** under **MYTHOLOGY AND FOLKLORE**

See also **THE CLASSICS** under **HISTORIOGRAPHY**

TRANSLATED BY THOMAS G. BERGIN & MAX FISCH

0-8014-9265-3 CORNELL PB $15.95

On Humanistic Education

0-8014-2838-6 CORNELL $29.95

0-8014-8087-6 CORNELL PB $11.95

Leon **Pompa**

Vico: A Study of the New Science

0-521-38217-3 CAMBRIDGE $49.95

0-521-38871-6 CAMBRIDGE PB $16.95

Berkeley

To be is to be perceived, Berkeley (1685-1753) taught; inanimate things exist only as they are perceived by animate beings. He developed this radical idealism partly to defend commonsense notions of knowledge against both science and skepticism, and partly to justify the existence of God, who, observing everything, becomes the ultimate guarantor of all sense perceptions. Berkeley is English empiricism stood on its head.

George **Berkeley**

Principles of Human Knowledge and Three Dialogues

Published in 1710, when Berkley was only 25, these works sum up his paradoxical contribution to philosophy—a radical antimaterialist metaphysics that presents itself as a defense of common sense

EDITED BY ROGER WOOLHOUSE

0-14-043293-0 PENGUIN PB $8.95

George **Berkeley** & others

The Empiricists

Includes Locke's *Essay Concerning Human Understanding*, Berkeley's *Principles of Human Knowledge* and *Three Dialogues*, and Hume's *Enquiry Concerning Human Understanding*

See also **LOCKE**

See also **HUME**

0-385-09622-4 ANCHOR PB $11.00

Hume

Empiricism gave way to scepticism in the work of Hume (1711-1776), a cheerful, engaging Scot who argued that there is no basis for believing in causation, the self, or a benevolent God, and that morality is at most a matter of psychology. Hume himself claimed that there was nothing about such disturbing conclusions that friendly conversation or a game of backgammon could not set right, but they shook his slightly younger German contemporary Kant out of a "dogmatic slumber" and roused him to a radical new defense of the eternal verities. An Anglo-German dialogue that has continued for two centuries resulted.

David **Hume**

Dialogues Concerning Natural Religion

Published posthumously, this is a brilliantly ironic and scandalous work of skepticism

0-317-30530-1 FREE PRESS PB $11.95

Dialogues Concerning Natural Religion and the Natural History of Religion

See also **SKEPTICISM AND ATHEISM** under **WORLD RELIGION**

EDITED BY J.C.A. GASKIN

0-19-282932-7 OXFORD PB $7.95

Enquiries Concerning Human Understanding and Concerning the Principles of Morals

EDITED BY P.H. NIDDITCH

0-19-824536-X OXFORD PB $15.95

Moral and Political Philosophy

0-317-30537-9 FREE PRESS PB $12.95

Political Essays

EDITED BY KNUD HAAKONSSEN

0-521-46093-X CAMBRIDGE $44.95

Selected Essays

EDITED BY STEPHEN COPLEY AND ANDREW EDGAR

0-19-283072-4 OXFORD PB $11.95

A Treatise of Human Nature

Hume's first book and central work, the outcome of eight years of intensive intellectual labor

EDITED BY ERNEST G. MOSSNER

0-14-043244-2 PENGUIN PB $9.95

Where am I, or what? From what causes do I derive my existence, and to what condition shall I return? Whose favour shall I court and whose anger must I dread? What beings surround me? and in whom have I any influence, or who have any influence on me? I am confounded with all these questions, and begin to fancy myself in the most deplorable condition imaginable, inviron'd with the deepest darkness, and utterly depriv'd of the use of every member and faculty. Most fortunately it happens, that since reason is incapable of dispelling these clouds, nature herself suffices to that purpose, and cures me of that philosophical melancholy and delirium, either by relaxing this bent of mind, or by some avocation… I dine, I play a game of back-gammon, I converse and am merry with my friends, and when after three or four hour's amusement, I wou'd return to these speculations, they appear so cold, and strain'd, and ridiculous, that I cannot find it in my heart to enter into them any farther.

A TREATISE OF HUMAN NATURE

George **Berkeley** & others

The Empiricists

Includes Locke's *Essay Concerning Human Understanding*, Berkeley's *Principles of Human Knowledge* and *Three Dialogues*, and Hume's *Enquiry Concerning Human Understanding*

See also BERKELEY

See also LOCKE

0-385-09622-4 ANCHOR PB $11.00

Barry **Stroud**

Hume

A superb, accessible study that emphasizes Hume's relevance to contemporary philosophy

0-415-03687-9 ROUTLEDGE PB $17.95

Rousseau

"Man is born free but is everywhere in chains." Rousseau (1712-1788) made an eloquent case for the goodness of human nature and natural moral sentiment and for replacing a corrupt social order with one based on liberty and equality. His ideas played a major role in the French Revolution, the Romantic movement, and every subsequent radical and utopian European movement through 1968.

Jean-Jacques **Rousseau**

Emile

Rousseau used a novel to expound his views on education

EDITED BY P.D. JIMACK

0-460-87380-6 EVERYMAN'S PB $6.95

The Confessions

This *philosophe* shared with his colleagues a loathing of the Old Regime, yet he also opposed certain of the Enlightenment's principal tenets. The keystone of Rousseau's writings: a self-portrait preserving the author's contradictions and self-doubts

See also THE ENLIGHTENMENT under FRENCH LITERATURE TO 1900 in LITERATURE OF EUROPE, AFRICA, AND ASIA

TRANSLATED BY J.M. COHEN

0-14-044033-X PENGUIN PB $8.95

A Discourse on Inequality

The book that first made Rousseau famous, on the happiness of a state of nature and the miseries of civilized sophistication

See also THE ENLIGHTENMENT under FRENCH LITERATURE TO 1900 in LITERATURE OF EUROPE, AFRICA, AND ASIA

TRANSLATED BY MAURICE CRANSTON

0-14-044439-4 PENGUIN PB $8.95

Jean-Jacques Rousseau

Discourse on Political Economy and the Social Contract & The Social Contract

See also THE ENLIGHTENMENT under FRENCH LITERATURE TO 1900 in LITERATURE OF EUROPE, AFRICA, AND ASIA

TRANSLATED BY CHRISTOPHER BETTS

0-19-282750-2 OXFORD PB $5.95

Discourse on the Origin of Inequality

See also THE ENLIGHTENMENT under FRENCH LITERATURE TO 1900 in LITERATURE OF EUROPE, AFRICA, AND ASIA

TRANSLATED BY FRANKLIN PHILIP

0-19-282947-5 OXFORD PB $7.95

Discourse on the Origins of Inequality

See also THE ENLIGHTENMENT under FRENCH LITERATURE TO 1900 in LITERATURE OF EUROPE, AFRICA, AND ASIA

EDITED BY ROGER D. MASTERS AND C. KELLY

0-87451-603-X NEW ENGLAND $40.00

Discourse on the Sciences and Arts

See also THE ENLIGHTENMENT under FRENCH LITERATURE TO 1900 in LITERATURE OF EUROPE, AFRICA, AND ASIA

EDITED BY ROGER D. MASTERS AND C. KELLY

0-87451-580-7 NEW ENGLAND $40.00

The Essential Rousseau

Includes Rousseau's *Social Contract, Discourse on Inequality, Discourse on Arts and Sciences*, and *The Creed of a Savoyard Priest*

See also THE ENLIGHTENMENT: A SAMPLER under THE AGE OF ENLIGHTENMENT under EARLY MODERN EUROPE in WORLD HISTORY AND CURRENT AFFAIRS

See also THE ENLIGHTENMENT under FRENCH LITERATURE TO 1900 in LITERATURE OF EUROPE, AFRICA, AND ASIA

TRANSLATED BY LOWELL BAIR

ILLUSTRATED BY MATTHEW JOSEPHSON

0-452-01031-4 NEW AMERICAN LIBRARY PB $12.95

La Nouvelle Héloise: Julie, Or the New Eloise

A portrayal of idealized conjugal fidelity set against a joyous rustic backdrop

See also THE ENLIGHTENMENT under FRENCH LITERATURE TO 1900 in LITERATURE OF EUROPE, AFRICA, AND ASIA

TRANSLATED BY JUDITH MCDOWELL

0-271-00602-1 PENN STATE PB $15.00

On the Origin of Language

See also THE ENLIGHTENMENT under FRENCH LITERATURE TO 1900 in LITERATURE OF EUROPE, AFRICA, AND ASIA

0-226-73012-3 CHICAGO PB $9.95

Reveries of the Solitary Walker

Evocations of wild natural beauty and the moral implications of solitude and independence

See also THE ENLIGHTENMENT under FRENCH LITERATURE TO 1900 in LITERATURE OF EUROPE, AFRICA, AND ASIA

TRANSLATED BY PETER FRANCE

0-14-044363-0 PENGUIN PB $7.95

Rousseau Selections

See also THE ENLIGHTENMENT under FRENCH LITERATURE TO 1900 in LITERATURE OF EUROPE, AFRICA, AND ASIA

EDITED BY PAUL EDWARDS

0-02-325521-8 MACMILLAN PB $18.00

The Social Contract

The chief work of Rousseau's political philosophy, in which the individual attains true freedom by submitting to the "general will"

See also CLASSICS under POLITICAL THOUGHT in SOCIAL STUDIES

See also THE ENLIGHTENMENT under FRENCH LITERATURE TO 1900 in LITERATURE OF EUROPE, AFRICA, AND ASIA

TRANSLATED BY MAURICE CRANSTON

0-14-044201-4 PENGUIN PB $7.95

The Social Contract and Discourses

See also THE ENLIGHTENMENT under FRENCH LITERATURE TO 1900 in LITERATURE OF EUROPE, AFRICA, AND ASIA

TRANSLATED BY G.D.H. COLE

0-460-87357-1 EVERYMAN'S PB $6.95

The Social Contract and the Discourses

See also THE ENLIGHTENMENT under FRENCH LITERATURE TO 1900 in LITERATURE OF EUROPE, AFRICA, AND ASIA

TRANSLATED BY G.D.H. COLE

0-679-42302-8 KNOPF $17.00

Jean **Starobinski**

Jean-Jacques Rousseau: Transparency and Obstruction

"The greatness of *Transparency and Obstruction* consists in its ability to draw the disconnected threads of Rousseau's life and works into one supremely coherent interpretation and to show how his personal drama opened a route into the major concerns of the 19th and 20th centuries"
—Robert Darnton, *NY Review of Books*.

TRANSLATED BY ARTHUR GOLDHAMMER

0-226-77126-1 CHICAGO $72.00

Kant

Kant (1724-1804) is perhaps the most universally respected of modern philosophers. The centerpiece of his "critical philosophy," *The Critique of Reason*, is a radical renovation of systematic metaphysics born of a profound confrontation with the skepticism of Hume. Kant's work in ethics and aesthetics has been hardly less influential.

Immanuel **Kant**

Anthropology from a Pragmatic Point of View

See also **PRECURSORS** under **GENERAL ANTHROPOLOGICAL STUDIES** under **ANTHROPOLOGY** in **SOCIAL STUDIES**

0-8093-2060-6 SOUTHERN ILLINOIS PB $16.95

Critique of Judgement

Kant's major work in aesthetics relates the beautiful and sublime to our capacities for understanding, and offers an analysis of teleological arguments applied to nature and theology

TRANSLATED BY J.C. MEREDITH

0-19-824589-0 OXFORD PB $21.00

Critique of Practical Reason

In Kant's full treatment of ethics, morality is seen as unconditional, constituting acts done for their own sake, not for some ulterior end

TRANSLATED BY LEWIS W. BECK

0-02-307753-0 MACMILLAN PB $13.00

Critique of Pure Reason

The major work of Kant's "critical philosophy," an intricate, profound, perennially challenging system of thought

EDITED BY NORMAN K. SMITH

0-312-45010-9 ST. MARTIN'S PB $17.35

Groundwork of the Metaphysics of Morals

The short but monumental treatise in which Kant presents his famous "categorical imperative": act so that you can accept the principle of your action as a universal law

TRANSLATED BY H.J. PATON

0-06-131159-6 HARPERCOLLINS PB $16.88

Kant's Political Writings

Kant as champion of liberalism

EDITED BY H. REISS

0-521-39185-7 CAMBRIDGE $49.95

On History

EDITED & TRANSLATED BY LEWIS W. BECK

0-02-307860-X PRENTICE HALL PB $7.00

Observations on the Feeling of the Beautiful and Sublime

An early treatise on the favorite distinction of 18th-century aesthetics

EDITED BY JOHN T. GOLDTHWAITE

0-520-04421-5 CALIFORNIA $28.00
0-520-07404-1 CALIFORNIA PB $13.95

Perpetual Peace and Other Essays on Politics, History, and Morals

0-915145-47-2 HACKETT PB $6.95

Religion Within Limits of Reason Alone

0-06-130067-5 HARPERCOLLINS PB $15.00

Hannah **Arendt**

Lectures on Kant's Political Philosophy

INTRODUCTION BY RONALD BEINER

0-226-02595-0 CHICAGO PB $10.95

Ernst **Cassirer**

Kant's Life and Thought

A lucid intellectual biography by a neo-Kantian philosopher

TRANSLATED BY STEPHAN KORNER

0-300-02982-9 YALE PB $18.00

P.F. **Strawson**

Bounds of Sense: An Essay on Kant's Critique of Pure Reason

A clear, scrupulous interpretation by a major British analytical philosopher

0-416-83560-0 ROUTLEDGE PB $18.95

Paul **Guyer**

Kant and the Experience of Freedom: Essays on Aesthetics and Morality

0-521-56833-1 CAMBRIDGE PB $18.95

Norman Kemp **Smith**

Commentary to Kant's Critique of Pure Reason

0-391-00457-3 HUMANITIES $65.00

Fichte

Fichte's (1762-1814) philosophy, with its emphasis on the absolute moral freedom of the transcendental ego, provides the bridge between Kant and the German Idealists. He is perhaps better known today for his avid German nationalism.

Johann Gottlieb **Fichte**

Fichte: Early Philosophical Writings

EDITED BY DANIEL BREAZEALE

0-8014-1779-1 CORNELL $55.00

The Vocation of Man

PETER PREUSS

0-87220-038-8 HACKETT $27.95
0-87220-037-X HACKETT PB $7.95

Bentham

Based on "the greatest happiness of the greatest number," Jeremy Bentham's (1748-1832) utilitarianism had, as he wished, a major impact on English social, political, and legal reform. Although his moral psychology seems crude in light of the discoveries of modern psychology, his ideas still influence modern economic and political thought.

Jeremy **Bentham**

A Fragment on Government

Bentham, an active reformer and a proponent of the doctrine of utilitarianism, argued that the greatest good for the greatest number should guide political judgments

See also **CLASSICS** under **POLITICAL THOUGHT** in **SOCIAL STUDIES**

0-313-22323-8 CAMBRIDGE PB $21.95

An Introduction to the Principles of Morals and Legislation

0-02-841200-1 FREE PRESS PB $14.95

The Panopticon and Other Prison Writings

EDITED BY MIRAN BOZOVIC

1-85984-083-3 VERSO PB $16.95

John Stuart **Mill** & Jeremy **Bentham**

Utilitarianism and Other Essays

See also **MILL**

0-14-043272-8 PENGUIN PB $9.95

Hegel

Hegel (1770-1831) viewed history as a sort of ongoing cosmic argument by which the Absolute Spirit becomes conscious of itself. His combination of rationalism, idealism, and history proved formidable, influencing Marxists, theologians, historians, and sociologists as well as modern philosophers, who have either had to assimilate Hegel or argue with him.

G.W.F. **Hegel**

The Essential Writings

Selections from *Phenomenology, Science of Logic, Philosophy of Nature,* and *Philosophy of Right*

EDITED BY FREDERICK G. WEISS

0-06-131831-0 HARPERCOLLINS PB $16.00

Hegel's Logic: Being Part One of the Encyclopedia of Philosophical Sciences (1830)

The fundamentals of the dialectic

FOREWORD BY JOHN N. FINDLAY

0-19-824512-2 THAMES & HUDSON PB $19.95

Hegel's Philosophy of Mind

0-19-875014-5 OXFORD PB $19.95

Introductory Lectures on Aesthetics

Hegel's lectures on aesthetics exercised a tremendous influence on later philosophers and helped to shape the field of art history

0-14-043335-X PENGUIN PB $11.95

Lectures on the History of Philosophy

Volume I
0-8032-7271-5 NEBRASKA PB $15.00

Volume II
0-8032-7272-3 NEBRASKA PB $15.00

Volume III
0-8032-7273-1 NEBRASKA PB $15.00

Lectures on the Philosophy of History
History as the rational process of the spirit of world freedom from the ancient Orient through classical Greece to 19th-century Europe

See also **THE CLASSICS** under **HISTORIOGRAPHY** in **WORLD HISTORY AND CURRENT AFFAIRS**

TRANSLATED BY J. SIBREE
INTRODUCTION BY C.J. FRIEDRICH
0-486-20112-0 DOVER PB $9.95

Philosophy of Right
Hegel's political philosophy was conservative, though liberal in the context of contemporary Prussia. He favored constitutional monarchy based on family and guild in which liberty was balanced with public order

See also **THE CLASSICS** under **HISTORIOGRAPHY** in **WORLD HISTORY AND CURRENT AFFAIRS**
See also **CLASSICS** under **POLITICAL THOUGHT** in **SOCIAL STUDIES**

TRANSLATED BY T.M. KNOX
0-19-500276-8 OXFORD PB $18.95

Theodor **Adorno**
Hegel: Three Studies
TRANSLATED BY SHIERRY WEBER NICHOLSEN
0-262-51080-4 MIT PB $12.50

J.N. **Findlay**
Hegel: A Re-Examination
0-7512-0180-4 ASHGATE $69.95

Jean **Hyppolite**
Genesis and Structure of Hegel's Phenomenology of Spirit
First published in France just after World War II, Hyppolite's interpretation reflects the tensions between existentialist and Marxist approaches to Hegel that were current in postwar French intellectural life. His students included Foucault, Derrida, and Deleuze
TRANSLATED BY SAMUEL CHERNIAK & JOHN HECKMAN
0-8101-0447-4 NORTHWESTERN $45.95

Alexandre **Kojéve**
Introduction to the Reading of Hegel: Lecture on the "Phenomenology of Spirit"
Sartre, Camus, and Merleau-Ponty studied with Kojeve
EDITED BY ALLAN BLOOM
0-8014-9203-3 CORNELL PB $15.95

Peter **Singer**
Hegel
A very good short introduction by a philosopher best known for his book *Animal Liberation*
0-19-287564-7 OXFORD PB $7.95

Jon **Stewart**, editor
The Hegel Myths and Legends
A defense of the "Continental" Hegel against distortions prevalent in Anglo-American interpretations including "The Myth that Hegel Glorified War" and "The Myth of the End of History"
0-8101-1301-5 NORTHWESTERN PB $29.95

Charles **Taylor**
Hegel
The distinguished Canadian philosopher, known for his work on modernity and authenticity, examines the thought of the philosopher who originated these themes
0-521-29199-2 CAMBRIDGE PB $34.95

Schelling

A philosophical wunderkind whose later career was overshadowed by that of his sometime friend Hegel, Schelling (1775-1854) took idealism to its limits: His philosophy is an elaborate demonstration of the oneness of absolutely everything, with special attention paid to nature and art. Coleridge was so fascinated by Schelling's work that he plagiarized it.

Friedrich **Schelling**
Ideas for a Philosophy of Nature
0-521-35733-0 CAMBRIDGE PB $28.95

On the History of Modern Philosophy
EDITED ANDREW BOWIE
0-521-40861-X CAMBRIDGE PB $18.95

The Philosophy of Art
0-8166-1684-1 MINNESOTA PB $21.95

System of Transcendental Idealism
0-8139-1458-2 VIRGINIA PB $16.50

Andrew **Bowie**
Schelling and Modern European Philosophy: An Introduction
0-415-10347-9 ROUTLEDGE PB $16.95

Schopenhauer

Defying the prevailing progressive rationalism of Hegel, Schopenhauer's (1788-1860) pessimistic philosophy described the world in terms of pure, irrational will, a ceaseless blind striving. Schopenhauer was the first major Western philosopher to be influenced by Buddhism, and despite his pessimism, he was one of the most popular 19th-century thinkers with the larger reading public.

Arthur **Schopenhauer**
Essays and Aphorisms
Schopenhauer's essays (on fame, style, genius, education) and incisive aphorisms demonstrate his mordant, sardonic genius
TRANSLATED BY R.J. HOLLINGDALE
0-14-044227-8 PENGUIN PB $9.95

The World as Will and Representation
His major philosophical work

Volume 1
0-486-21761-2 DOVER PB $11.95

Georg **Simmel**
Schopenhauer and Nietzsche
A study by the great German social and economic philosopher of two philosophers who rejected the progressive, optimistic assumptions of 19th-century civilization
0-252-06228-0 ILLINOIS PB $15.95

Feuerbach

Ludwig Feuerbach (1804-1872) is the overshadowed link between Hegel and Marx. He rejected Hegel for concealing theology in his rationalism and the empiricists for excluding consciousness from their materialism. His own rational humanism places human thought in the material world and resolves philosophy into the study of human society.

Ludwig **Feuerbach**
The Essence of Christianity
In his most famous work, Feuerbach sees religion as alienating humanity from itself
INTRODUCTION BY KARL BARTH
FOREWORD BY REINHOLD H. NIEBUHR
0-8446-2055-6 SMITH $25.50
0-87975-559-8 PROMETHEUS PB $8.95

Thoughts on Death and Immortality: From the Pages of a Thinker, Along with an Appendix of Theological Satirical Epigrams, Edited by One of His Friends
A caustic critic of theology, Feuerbach was an influence on the great 20th-century theologian Karl Barth, as well as on existentialists like Heidegger and Sartre
TRANSLATED BY JAMES A. MASSEY
0-520-04062-7 CALIFORNIA PB $12.00

Max **Wartofsky**
Feuerbach
0-521-28929-7 CAMBRIDGE PB $28.95

Mill

John Stuart Mill (1806-1873) took the harsh utilitarianism he inherited from his father and Bentham and reworked it until it assumed the richer, more flexible character of modern liberalism.

John Stuart **Mill**
Autobiography
EDITED BY JOHN ROBSON
0-14-043316-3 PENGUIN PB $9.95

Mill: Texts, Commentaries
A Norton Critical Edition
EDITED BY ALAN RYAN
0-393-97009-4 NORTON PB $10.00

John Stuart Mill

On Liberty

On Liberty (1859) is the most famous argument ever made for the liberal, tolerant, pluralistic, democratic point of view. After a nervous breakdown in his early twenties, Mill opened himself to Coleridge and the Romantics and tried to base his political philosophy on a broader view of human nature

See also **CLASSICS** under **POLITICAL THOUGHT** in **SOCIAL STUDIES**

EDITED BY GERTRUDE HIMMELFARB

0-14-043207-8 PENGUIN PB $8.95

But, indeed, the dictum that truth always triumphs over persecution is one of those pleasant falsehoods which men repeat after one another till they pass into commonplaces, but which all experience refutes. History teems with instances of truth put down by persecution. If not suppressed forever, it may be thrown back for centuries. To speak only of religious opinions: the Reformation broke out at least twenty times before Luther, and was put down. Arnold of Brescia was put down. Fra Dolcino was put down. Savonarola was put down. The Albigeois were put down. The Vaudois were put down. The Lollards were put down. The Hussites were put down…It is a piece of idle sentimentality that truth, merely as truth, has any inherent power denied to error of prevailing against the dungeon and the stake.

ON LIBERTY

On Liberty: With The Subjection of Women and Chapters on Socialism

On the Subjection of Women is an early and influential polemic in support of women's rights. In this foundational text of modern liberalism Mill argues that a good society must recognize human individuality as a basic value

See also **CLASSICS** under **POLITICAL THOUGHT** in **SOCIAL STUDIES**

EDITED BY STEFAN COLLINI

0-521-37917-2 CAMBRIDGE PB $8.95

On Liberty and Utilitarianism

0-679-41329-4 KNOPF $15.00

Principles of Political Economy and Chapters on Socialism

Two works

EDITED BY JONATHAN RILEY

0-19-283081-3 OXFORD PB $9.95

Utilitarianism

EDITED BY MARY WARNOCK

0-915144-41-7 HACKETT PB $3.95

John Stuart **Mill** & Jeremy **Bentham**

Utilitarianism and Other Essays

See also **BENTHAM**

0-14-043272-8 PENGUIN PB $9.95

Bernard **Semmel**

John Stuart Mill and the Pursuit of Virtue

0-300-03006-1 YALE $30.00

Kierkegaard

Choice is at the center of Kierkegaard's (1813-1855) philosophy. He hated any system that imposed a predetermined role on the individual, advocating risk and the confrontation of anxiety and dread. His own "leap of faith" led him to an austere Christianity, but the existentialist impulse in philosophy, which he was the first to formulate, has carried later thinkers to many different destinations.

Søren **Kierkegaard**

The Concept of Anxiety

Subtitled "A Simple Psychologically Orienting Deliberation on the Dogmatic Issue of Hereditary Sin"

TRANSLATED BY REIDER THOMTE

EDITED BY HOWARD V. & EDNA H. HONG

0-691-07244-2 PRINCETON $45.00

0-691-02011-6 PRINCETON PB $13.95

Concluding Unscientific Postscript

A typically offhand title masks what many consider Kierkegaard's greatest work

TRANSLATED BY D.F. SWENSON & WALTER LOWRIE

0-691-02083-3 PRINCETON PB $32.50

Concluding Unscientific Postscripts to Philosophical Fragments

EDITED BY HOWARD V. HONG AND EDNA H. HONG

0-691-07402-X PRINCETON $49.50

0-691-02081-7 PRINCETON PB $19.95

Eighteen Upbuilding Discourses

EDITED BY HOWARD V. HONG AND EDNA H. HONG

0-691-02087-6 PRINCETON PB $22.50

Either/Or

The choice between the aesthetic and the ethical ways of life, presented in a series of ironic essays including the famous "Diary of a Seducer" and a long commentary on Mozart's *Don Giovanni*

Volume 1

0-691-07315-5 PRINCETON $85.00

0-691-02041-8 PRINCETON PB $19.95

Volume 2

0-691-07316-3 PRINCETON $70.00

0-691-02042-6 PRINCETON PB $16.95

Either/Or: A Fragment of Life

Abridged

EDITED BY VICTOR EREMITA

0-14-044577-3 PENGUIN PB $14.95

Fear and Trembling

A meditation on the biblical sacrifice of Isaac and on the difficult Christianity of the "Knight of Faith"

See also **CLASSICS** under **CHRISTIANITY**

See also **CLASSICS OF WESTERN RELIGIOUS THOUGHT** under **WORLD RELIGION**

TRANSLATED BY ALASTAIR HANNAY

0-14-044449-1 PENGUIN PB $9.95

Fear and Trembling & Repetition

TRANSLATED AND EDITED BY HOWARD V. & EDNA H. HONG

0-691-02026-4 PRINCETON PB $16.95

Papers and Journals: A Selection

TRANSLATED BY ALASTAIR HANNAY

0-14-044589-7 PENGUIN PB $13.95

Parables of Kierkegaard

EDITED BY THOMAS C. ODEN

0-691-02053-1 PRINCETON PB $9.95

Philosophical Fragments: Or, a Fragment of Philosophy

TRANSLATED BY HOWARD V. & EDNA H. HONG

0-691-02036-1 PRINCETON PB $16.95

Practice in Christianity

EDITED BY HOWARD V. HONG AND EDNA H. HONG

0-691-02063-9 PRINCETON PB $16.95

The Sickness Unto Death

Kierkegaard's most famous work is subtitled "A Christian Psychological Exposition for Upbuilding and Awakening"

See also **CLASSICS** under **CHRISTIANITY**

TRANSLATED BY HOWARD V. HONG & EDNA H. HONG

0-691-02028-0 PRINCETON PB $13.95

Works of Love

EDITED BY HOWARD V. HONG AND EDNA H. HONG

0-691-03792-2 PRINCETON $65.00

Søren Kierkegaard

Walter **Lowrie**

A Short Life of Kierkegaard

An intellectual biography

0-691-01957-6 PRINCETON PB $15.95

Theodor W. **Adorno**

Kierkegaard: Construction of the Aesthetic

0-8166-1187-4 MINNESOTA PB $15.95

Marx

Marx (1818-1883) began as a philosopher before growing into an economist, sociologist, historian, and revolutionary. "The philosophers have only interpreted the world in various ways," he famously remarked, "the point however is to change it"—the repercussions to this philosophical point continue to be felt to this day.

Karl **Marx**

Capital: A Critique of Political Economy

Volume 1

See also **KARL MARX** under **GREAT ECONOMISTS** under **ECONOMICS** in **SOCIAL STUDIES**

0-14-044586-4 PENGUIN PB $14.95

Volume 2

0-14-044569-2 PENGUIN PB $14.95

Volume 3

0-14-044570-6 PENGUIN PB $14.95

Early Writings

Marx's mature economic doctrines were built upon his earlier philosophical preoccupations. This excellent selection includes the major writings of his youth

See also **LEFTISM AND MARXISM** under **POLITICAL THOUGHT** in **SOCIAL STUDIES**

TRANSLATED BY RODNEY LIVINGSTON & GREGOR BENTON

EDITED BY QUINTIN HOARE

0-394-72005-9 RANDOM HOUSE PB $16.00

Grundrisse: Foundations of the Critique of Political Economy

See also **LEFTISM AND MARXISM** under **POLITICAL THOUGHT** in **SOCIAL STUDIES**

TRANSLATED BY MARTIN NICOLAUS

0-14-044575-7 PENGUIN PB $17.95

Karl **Marx** & Frederich **Engels**

Collected Works

See also **KARL MARX** under **GREAT ECONOMISTS** under **ECONOMICS** in **SOCIAL STUDIES**

See also **GREAT ECONOMISTS** under **ECONOMICS** in **SOCIAL STUDIES**

0-7178-0537-9 INTERNATIONAL PUB $24.95

The Economic and Philosophic Manuscripts of 1844: Karl Marx and the Communist Manifesto

0-87975-446-X PROMETHEUS PB $6.95

The German Ideology

This attack on German philosophy after Hegel also includes a philosophical discussion of the good society. Includes Part 1 and selections from Parts 2 & 3

See also **LEFTISM AND MARXISM** under **POLITICAL THOUGHT** in **SOCIAL STUDIES**

EDITED BY C.J. ARTHUR

0-7178-0302-3 INTERNATIONAL PUB PB $6.95

Gerald Allan **Cohen**

History, Labour, and Freedom: Themes from Marx

0-19-824816-4 OXFORD PB $27.00

Marshall **Cohen** & others

Marx, Justice and History

0-691-07252-3 PRINCETON $25.50

Jon **Elster**

An Introduction to Karl Marx

0-521-33831-X CAMBRIDGE PB $16.95

Sidney **Hook**

From Hegel to Marx

0-231-09665-8 COLUMBIA PB $18.00

Marx and the Marxists: The Ambiguous Legacy

0-89874-443-1 KRIEGER PB $12.08

Marxism and Beyond

0-8476-7159-3 ROWMAN & LITTLEFIELD $35.00

Steven **Lukes**

Marxism and Morality

According to Lukes, the inability of Marxism to give an adequate account of human rights, justice, and the relation of ends and means has left it no resources with which to resist the crimes committed in its name; a cogent, closely argued case for a new Marxist moral theory that examines the moral and philosophical arguments of Trotsky, Sartre, Camus, Merleau-Ponty, Brecht, Koestler, and others

0-19-876101-5 OXFORD $32.50

0-19-282074-5 OXFORD PB $16.95

Istvan **Meszaros**

Beyond Capital: Toward a Theory of Transition

0-85345-881-2 MONTHLY REVIEW PB $25.00

Philosophy, Ideology, and Social Science: Essays in Negation and Affirmation

0-312-00231-9 ST. MARTIN'S PB $12.95

Bertell **Ollman**

Alienation: Marx's Conception of Man in Capitalist Society

Marx's theory of internal relations as the conceptual foundation of his views of alienation and ideology

0-521-29083-X CAMBRIDGE PB $23.95

Social and Sexual Revolution: Essays on Marx and Reich

0-89608-080-3 SOUTH END PB $7.50

Dilthey

Dilthey's (1833-1911) "philosophy of life" reflected his belief that philosophy must do justice to the fullness of human cultural and historical experience. A seminal figure in philosophical historicism, he argued that human subjects must be understood differently from natural objects and reinterpreted Kantian categories as historical "world views."

Wilhelm **Dilthey**

Hermeneutics and the Study of History

EDITED BY RUDOLF A. MAKKREEL & FRITHJOF RODI

0-691-00649-0 PRINCETON $59.50

Introduction to the Human Sciences: An Attempt to Lay a Foundation for the Study of Society and History

The great 19th-century German theorist attempted to attain objectively valid interpretations of the inner life of past cultures

TRANSLATED & EDITED BY RAMON J. BETANZOS

0-691-07307-4 PRINCETON $65.00

0-8143-1897-5 WAYNE STATE $49.95

Poetry and Experience

EDITED BY RUDOLF A. MAKKREEL & FRITHJOF RODI

0-691-07297-3 PRINCETON $47.00

0-691-02928-8 PRINCETON PB $21.95

Rudolf A. **Makkreel**

Dilthey: Philosopher of the Human Studies

0-691-02097-3 PRINCETON PB $19.95

Peirce

Peirce (1838-1914) was a secretive New England genius who did important work in logic and developed a peculiarly American philosophical approach: pragmatism. His ideas were not generally appreciated until after his death.

Charles S. **Peirce**

Philosophical Writings of Peirce

EDITED BY JUSTUS BUCHLER

0-486-20217-8 DOVER PB $9.95

Selected Writings

EDITED BY PHILIP P. WIENER

0-486-21634-9 DOVER PB $11.95

Writings of Charles S. Peirce: A Chronological Edition, 1879-1884

EDITED BY CHRISTIAN J.W. KLOESSEL

0-253-37204-6 INDIANA $67.50

Joseph **Brent**

Charles Sanders Peirce: A Life

A full, illustrated account of a brilliantly original and strangely self-sabotaging thinker

0-253-31267-1 INDIANA $35.00

Umberto **Eco** & Thomas A. **Sebeok**, editors

The Sign of Three: Dupin, Holmes, Peirce

A semiotic analysis of the relation of Peirce's philosophy to some aspects of detective fiction

0-253-20487-9 INDIANA PB $13.95

John K. **Sheriff**

Charles Peirce's Guess at the Riddle

Peirce as a philosopher of human and cosmic meaning and as an alternative to contemporary relativism and pessimism

0-253-20880-7 INDIANA PB $9.95

Nathan **Hauser** & Christian **Kloesel**, editors

The Essential Peirce: 1867-1893
0-253-20721-5 INDIANA PB $19.95

William James

James (1842-1910) was a robust and open-minded thinker whose range recalled that of the 17th-century philosopher-polymaths. James became the foremost champion of pragmatism, the theory that truth is determined by what works in practice. He made a pioneering contribution to scientific psychology, coining the term "stream of consciousness," and revolutionized the study of religion. His work, related to that of Bergson and Whitehead, has also exercised an influence on postwar analytic philosophy.

William James

William **James**

Essays in Pragmatism
Including "The Will to Believe," "The Sentiment of Rationality," "The Dilemma of Determinism," and "What Pragmatism Means"

See also **THE 19TH CENTURY: AFTER THE CIVIL WAR** under **AMERICAN LITERATURE TO 1900** in **LITERATURE OF THE AMERICAS**

0-02-847140-7 FREE PRESS PB $12.95

Pragmatism & the Meaning of Truth
INTRODUCTION BY A.J. AYER

0-674-69737-5 HARVARD PB $15.50

Some Problems of Philosophy: A Beginning of an Introduction to Philosophy
0-8032-7587-0 NEBRASKA PB $12.00

The Varieties of Religious Experience
A wide-ranging masterpiece that highlights the personal, subjective, and mystical aspects of religion—an approach that coincides with contemporary tastes

See also **CLASSICS OF WESTERN RELIGIOUS THOUGHT** under **WORLD RELIGION**

0-14-039034-0 PENGUIN PB $10.95

Our normal waking consciousness, rational consciousness as we call it, is but one special type of consciousness, whilst all about it, parted from it by the filmiest of screens, there lie potential forms of consciousness entirely different. We may go through life without suspecting their existence; but apply the requisite stimulus, and at a touch they are there in all their completeness, definite types of mentality which probably somewhere have their field of application and adaptation. No account of the universe in its totality can be final which leaves these other forms of consciousness quite disregarded. How to regard them is the question—for they are so discontinuous with ordinary consciousness. Yet they may determine attitudes though they cannot furnish formulas, and open a region though they fail to give a map. At any rate they forbid a premature closing of our accounts with reality.

THE VARIETIES OF RELIGIOUS EXPERIENCE

Writings 1878-1899
Includes *The Will To Believe and Other Essays in Popular Philosophy*, *Psychology: Briefer Course*, and excerpts from the monumental *Principles of Psychology*

See also **THE 19TH CENTURY: AFTER THE CIVIL WAR** under **AMERICAN LITERATURE TO 1900** in **LITERATURE OF THE AMERICAS**

See also **LIBRARY OF AMERICA** in **LITERATURE OF THE AMERICAS**

0-940450-72-0 LIBRARY OF AMERICA $35.00

Writings 1902-1910
Includes *The Varieties of Religious Experience*, *Pragmatism*, *A Pluralistic Universe*, *The Meaning of Truth*, *Some Problems of Philosophy*, and *Essays*

See also **LIBRARY OF AMERICA** in **LITERATURE OF THE AMERICAS**

0-940450-38-0 LIBRARY OF AMERICA $37.50

One need only shut oneself in a closet and begin to think of the fact of one's being there, of one's queer bodily shape in the darkness (a thing to make children scream at, as Stevenson says), of one's fantastic character and all, to have the wonder steal over the detail as much as over the general fact of being, and to see that it is only familiarity that blunts it. Not only that *anything* should be, but that *this* very thing should be, is mysterious! Philosophy stares, but brings no reasoned solution for from nothing to being there is no logical bridge. From *Some Problems of Philosophy*

WRITINGS 1902-1910

Linda **Simon**, editor

William James Remembered
0-8032-4248-4 NEBRASKA $30.0

Nietzsche

Nietzsche (1844-1900) regarded philosophical systems as instruments with which a philosopher deceives himself and others. His own philosophy was conveyed in swift, incisive, and deliberately provocative aphorisms, and many of his major ideas remain elusive. But the central problem he wished to diagnose is clear: nihilism. As the "death of God" penetrates modern culture, all ultimate values and truths must evaporate, and all that remains is an infinity of perspectives on a meaningless flux. To find values that can confront this nihilism, he examined the underlying motives of past and present cultures and moralities, calling for a "revaluation of values" that could say yes to life at its most terrible.

Friedrich **Nietzsche**

Basic Writings
TRANSLATED AND EDITED BY WALTER KAUFMANN

0-679-60000-0 MODERN LIBRARY $20.00

Beyond Good and Evil: Prelude to a Philosophy of the Future
Nietzsche's most complete presentation of his moral philosophy

TRANSLATED BY WALTER KAUFMANN

0-679-72465-6 VINTAGE PB $11.00

The Birth of Tragedy
Tragedy considered as a synthesis of the turbulent Dionysian and serene Apollonian elements in Greek culture, and Socrates as the embodiment of a perverse rationalism that killed it off

See also **DRAMATIC THEORY AND CRITICISM** under **THEATER** in **PERFORMING ARTS AND MEDIA**

TRANSLATED BY WALTER KAUFMANN

0-394-70369-3 RANDOM HOUSE PB $9.00

Daybreak: Thoughts on the Prejudices of Morality
The aphoristic books of Nietzsche's skeptical, rationalistic middle period owe much of their spirit and tone to the classical maxims of La Rochefoucauld and Chamfort. Many readers prefer them to his more polemical and rhapsodic later works

TRANSLATED BY R.J. HOLLINGDALE

0-521-28662-X CAMBRIDGE PB $17.95

Ecce Homo
A high-spirited, sometimes strident, often witty intellectual autobiography

TRANSLATED BY R.J. HOLLINGDALE

0-14-044515-3 PENGUIN PB $9.95

The Gay Science
Brilliant aphorisms that introduce themes prominent in Nietzsche's later work, including the death of God and the eternal recurrence

TRANSLATED BY WALTER KAUFMANN

0-394-71985-9 VINTAGE PB $10.00

Human, All Too Human
TRANSLATED BY GARY HANDWERK

0-8047-2665-5 STANFORD $29.95

Human, All Too Human: A Book for Free Spirits
See also **THE CLASSICS** under **HISTORIOGRAPHY** in **WORLD HISTORY AND CURRENT AFFAIRS**

TRANSLATED BY MARION FABER AND STEPHEN LEHMANN

0-8032-8368-7 NEBRASKA PB $12.00

Human, All Too Human: Including Assorted Opinions and Maxims & the Wanderer and His Shadow
The first work of Nietzsche's skeptical, antiromantic middle period, full of shrewd and lucid aphorisms
TRANSLATED BY R.J. HOLLINGDALE
INTRODUCTION BY ERICH HELLER
0-521-26543-6 CAMBRIDGE $75.00
0-521-31945-5 CAMBRIDGE PB $18.95

The New Nietzsche: Contemporary Styles of Interpretation
EDITED BY DAVID B. ALLISON
0-262-51034-0 MIT PB $17.00

On the Genealogy of Morality & Other Writings
EDITED BY KEITH ANSELL-PEARSON & CAROL DIETHE
0-521-40610-2 CAMBRIDGE PB $11.95

On the Genealogy of Morals
A speculative history of the conflict between a self-affirming "master" morality and a vengeful, guilt-mongering "slave" morality
TRANSLATED BY WALTER KAUFMANN
0-679-72462-1 VINTAGE PB $11.00

Philosophy and Truth: Selections from Nietzsche's Notebooks of the Early 1870s
EDITED BY DANIEL BREAZEALE
0-391-03671-8 HUMANITIES PB $15.95

The Portable Nietzsche
Includes selections from *Twilight of the Idols, The Anti-Christ,* and *Nietzsche Contra Wagner*
EDITED BY WALTER KAUFMANN
B01150625 PENGUIN PB $12.50

The Portable Nietzsche
A selection from the whole range of Nietzsche's work, including *Zarathustra, Twilight of the Idols, The Anti-Christ,* and *Nietzsche Contra Wagner*
EDITED BY WALTER KAUFMANN
0-14-015062-5 VIKING PB $14.95

Thus Soke Zarathustra: A Book for All and None
Nietzche's most famous and enduring work
0-679-60175-9 MODERN LIBRARY $14.50

The Twilight of the Idols & The Anti-Christ
Two polemical and incandescent late works, one a succinct summary of major themes, the other a serious attempt at a cultural psychology of Buddhism and Christianity
See also **SKEPTICISM AND ATHEISM** under **WORLD RELIGION**
TRANSLATED BY R.J. HOLLINGDALE
0-14-044514-5 PENGUIN PB $10.95

The Will to Power
Nietzsche's sister gathered passages from his notebooks and imposed an order and a title on them after he went mad. They are nevertheless illuminating fragments of his mature philosophy
TRANSLATED BY WALTER KAUFMANN
0-394-70437-1 RANDOM HOUSE PB $15.00

Unfashionable Observations
TRANSLATED BY RICHARD T. GRAY
0-8047-2382-6 STANFORD $29.95

Untimely Meditations
Nietzsche's early critical assessment of his influences: Schopenhauer, Wagner, academic history and philology, and the rationalist biblical critic David Strauss
See also **THE CLASSICS** under **HISTORIOGRAPHY** in **WORLD HISTORY AND CURRENT AFFAIRS**
TRANSLATED BY R.J. HOLLINGDALE
0-521-28927-0 CAMBRIDGE PB $17.95

Peter **Bergmann**
Nietzsche: The Last Antipolitical German
0-253-34061-6 INDIANA $31.95

Arthur C. **Danto**
Nietzsche as Philosopher
Concentrates on aspects of Nietzsche's work that anticipate the epistemological and linguistic concerns of 20th-century analytical philosophy
0-231-05053-4 COLUMBIA PB $16.50

Martin **Heidegger**
Nietzsche
Volumes 1 & 2
The Will to Power as Art & The Eternal Recurrence of the Same
See also **HEIDEGGER**
0-06-063841-9 HARPERCOLLINS PB $22.00

Volumes 3 & 4
The Will to Power as Knowledge and as Metaphysics & Nihilism
See also **HEIDEGGER**
0-06-063794-3 HARPERCOLLINS PB $22.00

Walter **Kaufmann**
Nietzsche: Philosopher, Psychologist, Antichrist
Kaufmann offers Nietzsche as a champion of free thought and a tough-minded, individualistic humanism
0-691-01983-5 PRINCETON PB $16.95

Alexander **Nehamas**
Nietzsche: Life as Literature
Argues that Nietzsche regarded life as a text to be both created and interpreted
0-674-62426-2 HARVARD PB $15.95

Fredrich Nietzsche

Graham **Parkes**
Composing the Soul: Reaches of Nietzsche's Psychology
Elaborating on Nietzsche's "polyphonic" idea of the psyche–its multiplicity of drives or personalities–Parkes consolidates Nietzsche's reputation as an original psychologist
0-226-64687-4 CHICAGO PB $19.95

Graham **Parkes**, editor
Nietzsche and Asian Thought
Parallels between Nietzsche's philosophy and Hinduism, Taoism, and other Asian philosophies, and the reception of his work in India, China, and Japan
0-226-64685-8 CHICAGO PB $14.95

Stanley **Rosen**
The Mask of Enlightenment: Nietzsche's Zarathustra
0-521-49889-9 CAMBRIDGE PB $18.95

Richard **Schacht**
Nietzsche
"Schacht's *Nietzsche*...is much more constructive and positive than Danto's and much more of an academic philosopher than Kaufman's"—Alexander Nehamas
0-415-09071-7 ROUTLEDGE PB $22.95

Peter R. **Sedgwick**, editor
Nietzsche: A Critical Reader
Nietzsche and postmodernism, sex, ethics, and aesthetics. Among the contributors are Heidegger and Derrida
0-631-19045-7 BLACKWELL PB $21.95

Peter **Sloterdijk**
Thinker on Stage: Nietzsche's Materialism
For Sloterdijk, Nietzsche is not "an exacting philologist behind a lectern but rather a thinker on stage, acting out a defiant psychodrama on universal suffering"
TRANSLATED BY JAMIE OWEN DANIEL
0-8166-1764-3 MINNESOTA $29.95
0-8166-1765-1 MINNESOTA PB $12.95

Joan **Stambaugh**
The Other Nietzsche
Stambaugh stresses Nietzsche's aesthetics and the lyrical, playful side of his philosophy and his style
0-7914-1700-X SUNY PB $16.95

J. P. **Stern**
A Study of Nietzsche
A study by a distinguished German-literature specialist
0-521-28380-9 CAMBRIDGE PB $18.9

Cambridge Companions

Jonathan **Barnes**, editor
The Cambridge Companion to Aristotle
0-521-41133-5 CAMBRIDGE $59.95

Frederick C. **Beiser**, editor
The Cambridge Companion to Hegel
0-521-38274-2 CAMBRIDGE $69.95
0-521-38711-6 CAMBRIDGE PB $20.95

Vere **Chappell**, editor
The Cambridge Companion to Locke
0-521-38371-4 CAMBRIDGE $65.00

John **Cottingham**, editor
The Cambridge Companion to Descartes
0-521-36623-2 CAMBRIDGE $65.00
0-521-36696-8 CAMBRIDGE PB $19.95

Don **Garrett**, editor
The Cambridge Companion to Spinoza
0-521-39235-7 CAMBRIDGE $59.95
0-521-39865-7 CAMBRIDGE PB $17.95

Lloyd P. **Gerson**, editor
The Cambridge Companion to Plotinus
0-521-47093-5 CAMBRIDGE $59.95
0-521-47676-3 CAMBRIDGE PB $18.95

Charles B. **Guignon**, editor
The Cambridge Companion to Heidegger
0-521-38597-0 CAMBRIDGE PB $19.95

Gary **Gutting**, editor
The Cambridge Companion to Foucault
0-521-40332-4 CAMBRIDGE $65.00
0-521-40887-3 CAMBRIDGE PB $18.95

Richard **Kraut**, editor
The Cambridge Companion to Plato
0-521-43018-6 CAMBRIDGE $65.00
0-521-43610-9 CAMBRIDGE PB $20.95

Bernd **Magnus** &
Kathleen Marie **Higgins**, editors
The Cambridge Companion to Nietzsche
0-521-36586-4 CAMBRIDGE $59.95
0-521-36767-0 CAMBRIDGE PB $17.95

David Fate **Norton**, editor
The Cambridge Companion to Hume
0-521-38273-4 CAMBRIDGE $69.95
0-521-38710-8 CAMBRIDGE PB $19.95

Markku **Peltonen**, editor
The Cambridge Companion to Bacon
0-521-43498-X CAMBRIDGE $54.95
0-521-43534-X CAMBRIDGE PB $18.95

Hans **Sluga** & David G. **Stern**, editors
The Cambridge Companion to Wittgenstein
0-521-46025-5 CAMBRIDGE $59.95
0-521-46591-5 CAMBRIDGE PB $25.00

Barry **Smith** &
David Woodruff **Smith**, editor
The Cambridge Companion to Husserl
0-521-43616-8 CAMBRIDGE PB $18.95

Tom **Sorell**, editor
The Cambridge Companion to Hobbes
0-521-41019-3 CAMBRIDGE $59.95
0-521-42244-2 CAMBRIDGE PB $17.95

Stephen K. **White**, editor
The Cambridge Companion to Habermas
Essays on Jurgen Habermas's relation to the Frankfurt school, to Marxism, and to postmodernism, and on his defense of modernity and his theory of communicative rationality
0-521-44666-X CAMBRIDGE PB $17.95

Bradley

Bradley (1844-1924) is the most important English-speaking philosopher to advance an idealist philosophy based on the work of Hegel.

F.H. **Bradley**
Ethical Studies
0-19-881039-3 OXFORD PB $26.00

Frege

Frege (1848-1925), a modest and retiring man who did little to make his revolutionary work in symbolic logic known in his day, has come to be considered a founder of modern analytic philosophy.

'Gottlob **Frege**
The Foundations of Arithmetic: A Logico-Mathematical Enquiry into the Concept of Number
0-8101-0605-1 NORTHWESTERN PB $15.95

Michael **Dummett**
Frege: Philosophy of Language
0-674-31931-1 HARVARD PB $25.95

The Interpretation of Frege's Philosophy
A study by a leading American analytic philosopher
0-674-45975-X HARVARD $50.00
0-674-45976-8 HARVARD PB $25.50

Dewey

Dewey (1859-1952) applied his theories of pragmatism to educational reform and liberal politics. For Dewey ideas have meaning, truth, and value insofar as they are effective in solving the problems encountered in immediate human experience.

John **Dewey**
Art as Experience
An influential modern study of aesthetics
0-399-50025-1 PERIGEE PB $9.00

Experience and Nature
0-486-20471-5 DOVER PB $9.95

Human Nature and Conduct
0-8093-1437-1 SOUTHERN ILLINOIS PB $14.95

The Philosophy of John Dewey
EDITED BY JOHN J. MCDERMOTT
0-226-14401-1 CHICAGO PB $24.95

The Political Writings
EDITED BY DEBRA MORRIS AND IAN SHAPIRO
0-87220-190-2 HACKETT PB $9.95

Reconstruction in Philosophy and Essays, 1920
EDITED BY JO ANN BOYDSTON
0-8093-1435-5 SOUTHERN ILLINOIS PB $14.95

John Dewey

Alan **Ryan**
John Dewey And The High Tide Of American Liberalism
See also **LIBERALISM** under **POLITICAL THOUGHT** in **SOCIAL STUDIES**
03933155AH NORTON PB $17.00

Sidney **Morgenbesser**, editor
Dewey and His Critics
0-931206-01-4 HACKETT PB $19.95

Robert B. **Westbrook**
John Dewey and American Democracy
0-8014-8111-2 CORNELL PB $16.95

Alan **Ryan**

John Dewey and the Tide of American Liberalism

Dewey's pragmatist philosophy was intended to have a close connection to social and political life, and in the era of the New Deal it became a major force in the development of liberalism

See also **LIBERALISM** under **POLITICAL THOUGHT** in **SOCIAL STUDIES**

0-393-03773-8 NORTON $30.00
0-393-31550-9 NORTON PB $17.00

Husserl

The aim of Husserl's (1859-1938) phenomenology is to examine the data of immediate experience with as few presuppositions as possible. Husserl advanced a theory of human consciousness as essentially intentional by way of bridging the mind-matter dualism that had troubled philosophers since Descartes.

Edmund **Husserl**

Crisis of European Sciences and Transcendental Phenomenology

0-8101-0458-X NORTHWESTERN PB $18.95

Experience and Judgement

0-8101-0595-0 NORTHWESTERN PB $22.95

Phenomenology and the Crisis of Philosophy

In this late (1935) work, Husserl places a new emphasis on the intersubjective community of individuals, as opposed to the transcendent ego, and on the *Lebenswelt*, the lived world that is the subject of phenomenology, as opposed to the world known to science

TRANSLATED BY QUENTIN LAUER

0-06-131170-7 HARPERCOLLINS PB $13.00

Jacques **Derrida**

Speech and Phenomena & Other Essays on Hussserl's Theory of Signs

The fashionable Derrida acknowledges his debt to the monkish professor

TRANSLATED BY DAVID B. ALLISON

0-8101-0397-4 NORTHWESTERN $24.95
0-8101-0590-X NORTHWESTERN PB $16.95

Emmanuel **Levinas**

The Theory of Intuition in Husserl's Phenomenology

See also **OTHER 20TH-CENTURY PHILOSOPHERS**

0-8101-1281-7 NORTHWESTERN PB $18.95

Paul **Ricoeur**

Husserl: An Analysis of His Phenomenology

TRANSLATED BY EDWARD G. BALLARD & LESTER EMBREE

0-8101-0209-9 NORTHWESTERN $26.95
0-8101-0530-6 NORTHWESTERN PB $22.50

Bergson

Bergson's (1859-1941) vitalism might be described as life for life's sake. Reacting against the drab scientific materialism and determinism of the late 19th century, he made the *élan vital* (life force) a metaphysical principle that lifts humanity above the mechanical repetitions of matter and serves as the creative secret of evolution. His intuitive, antirational philosophy was admired by Proust, William James, and T.S. Eliot, among others.

Henri **Bergson**

Creative Evolution

Bergson argues that the *élan vital* gives the process of evolution a creative freedom which distinguishes it from mechanistic or predetermined process

TRANSLATED BY ARTHUR MITCHELL

0-8191-3553-4 UNIVERSITY PRESS OF AMERICA PB $29.00

An Introduction to Metaphysics

TRANSLATED BY T.E. HULME

0-02-358470-X BOBBS-MERRILL PB $9.20

Matter and Memory

0-942299-05-1 ZONE PB $14.95

The Two Sources of Morality and Religion

0-268-01835-9 NOTRE DAME PB $13.95

Gilles **Deleuze**

Bergsonism

The French postmodernist philosopher finds in Bergson a philosopher— like Lucretius, Spinoza, Hume, and Nietzsche—"who seemed to be part of the history of philosophy, but who escaped from it in one respect altogether"

TRANSLATED BY HUGH TOMLINSON & BARBARA HABBERJAM

0-942299-06-X ZONE $24.95
0-942299-07-8 ZONE PB $12.95

Whitehead

Whitehead's (1861-1947) philosophical course diverged sharply from Russell's after their epochal collaboration on *Principia Mathematica*. While Russell tried to weld philosophy to physics, Whitehead warned against using physics to account for all reality. He developed a metaphysics "of process" by turns enthralling and abstruse, in which the universe consists of aggregates of becomings and God is identified as the source of creative possibility.

Alfred North **Whitehead**

Adventures of Ideas

A late and accessible presentation of his philosophy

0-02-935170-7 FREE PRESS PB $12.95

The Concept of Nature

An analysis of nature in terms of "events" and "objects" (which are recurrent patterns of events)

See also **ESSAYS, MEDITATIONS, AND CLASSICS** under **NATURE STUDY** in **SCIENCE**

0-521-09245-0 CAMBRIDGE PB $23.95

Alfred North Whitehead

Process and Reality

Whitehead's most systematic and difficult work of metaphysics

0-02-934570-7 FREE PRESS PB $16.95

Religion in the Making

EDITED BY RANDALL AUXIER

0-8232-1645-4 FORDHAM $29.95

Science and the Modern World

Whitehead's approach, at once philosophical and scientific, yields many unique insights; physics, for example, was originally an anti-intellectual activity

See also **SCIENCE AND TECHNOLOGY** in **SCIENCE**

0-02-935190-1 FREE PRESS PB $16.95

Alfred North **Whitehead** & Bertrand **Russell**

Principia Mathematica

A three-volume set

See also **RUSSELL**

0-521-06791-X CAMBRIDGE $525.00

Principia Mathematica

0-521-09187-X CAMBRIDGE PB $49.95

Victor **Lowe**

Alfred North Whitehead: The Man and His Work Volume 1 1861-1910

The most balanced and comprehensive account of Whitehead's character and philosophy

0-8018-2488-5 JOHNS HOPKINS $39.95

Santayana

Poet, novelist, essayist, and critic, Santayana (1863-1952) in his philosophy combined a firm naturalism with a serene sensibility informed by his Spanish Catholic background. In imperturbably lucid prose, Santayana set forth the realm of matter, established by our "animal faith," and the more compelling realm of essences, wherein our ideals, values, art, and ultimate interests lie.

Interpretations of Poetry and Religion: Critical Edition

0-262-19286-1 MIT $40.00

George Santayana

George **Santayana**

The Last Puritan

See also **FROM THE TURN OF THE CENTURY TO WORLD WAR II** under **20TH-CENTURY AMERICAN FICTION** in **LITERATURE OF THE AMERICAS**

0-262-19328-0 MIT $52.50
0-262-69178-7 MIT PB $19.95

Persons and Places: The Autobiography of George Santayana

EDITED BY WILLIAM HOLZBERGER & HERMAN SAATKAMP, JR.

0-262-69114-0 MIT PB $14.95

The Sense of Beauty: Being the Outline of Aesthetic Theory

0-262-19271-3 MIT $37.50

Timothy **Sprigge**

Santayana: An Examination of His Philosophy

0-415-11751-8 ROUTLEDGE PB $24.95

Unamuno

The greatest modern Spanish philosopher and a passionate student of *Don Quixote*, Unamuno (1864-1936) advocated discarding all illusions and resigning oneself to "the tragic sense of life."

Miguel de **Unamuno**

The Tragic Sense of Life in Men and Nations

Unamuno argues that the only common ground for humanity is the abyss of tragic despair that threatens each individual life

See also **THE GENERATION OF 1898** under **SPANISH LITERATURE** in **LITERATURE OF EUROPE, AFRICA, AND ASIA**

EDITED BY ANTHONY KERRIGAN

0-691-01820-0 PRINCETON PB $19.95

Victor **Ouimette**

Reason Aflame: Unamuno and the Heroic Will

0-300-01666-2 YALE $35.00

Croce

Croce (1866-1952) is the most important Italian philosopher after Vico, and learned from him and Hegel to place history at the center of philosophy. He is best known for his *Aesthetic*, in which he conceives of art as both expression and a form of intuitive knowledge.

Benedetto **Croce**

Aesthetic

Croce's most famous and influential work

See also **ESSAYS, MEMOIRS, AND OTHER PROSE** under **THE 20TH CENTURY** under **ITALIAN LITERATURE** in **LITERATURE OF EUROPE, AFRICA, AND ASIA**

TRANSLATED BY DOUGLAS AINSLIE

1-56000-818-0 TRANSACTION PB $29.95

Russell

Russell (1872-1970) is the principal figure in the evolution of English-language philosophy from speculation to analysis. He began as an idealist, but rejected his origins to pursue what he saw as a leaner and more precise kind of philosophy modeled on logic and mathematics.

Bertrand **Russell**

The Conquest of Happiness

0-87140-162-2 NORTON PB $11.00

My Philosophical Development

0-415-13601-6 UNWIN HYMAN PB $14.95

Our Knowledge of the External World

The search for the nature of our inner and outer worlds has long eluded the great philosophers. Now, Russell turns his extraordinary powers to the claims and achievements of the philosophers to explain why they regularly fall short of their aims."...a brilliant, lucid, and amusing book which...everyone can understand" —*New Statesman*

0-415-09605-7 ROUTLEDGE PB $14.95

Philosophical Essays

See also **20TH-CENTURY BRITISH ESSAYS AND OTHER PROSE** in **LITERATURE OF THE BRITISH ISLES**

0-415-10579-X ROUTLEDGE PB $10.95

The Principles of Mathematics

See also **GENERAL INTRODUCTIONS** under **INTRODUCTIONS TO MATHEMATICS** under **MATHEMATICS** in **SCIENCE**

0-393-31404-9 NORTON PB $17.95

The Problems of Philosophy

An early (1912) work summing up Russell's revolutionary work in epistemology and logic

0-19-500212-1 OXFORD PB $7.95

Ray **Monk**

Bertrand Russell: The Spirit of Solitude

The first volume of a new biographical study

0-684-82802-2 FREE PRESS $35.00

A.J. **Ayer**

Bertrand Russell as a Philosopher

"The confrontation or conjunction of Ayer and Russell is a notable event and has produced a remarkable book"—*Nation*

0-226-03343-0 CHICAGO PB $12.95

Alan **Ryan**

Bertrand Russell: A Political Life

0-19-508634-1 OXFORD PB $12.95

Alfred North **Whitehead** & Bertrand **Russell**

Principia Mathematica

A three-volume set

See also **WHITEHEAD**

0-521-06791-X CAMBRIDGE $525.00

Bertrand Russell

Moore

Moore (1873-1958) fired the first shot at the Hegelian idealism that dominated British philosophy at the turn of the century and then, with Russell, developed the analytical approach that replaced it. But Moore was less interested than Russell in mathematics, logic, and a logically purified philosophical language than in clarifying and defending a commonsense view of the world.

G.E. **Moore**

Principia Ethica

The book that became a kind of ethical handbook for the Bloomsbury Group is also one of the most important works of modern moral theory, stressing friendship, aesthetic pleasure, and other intrinsic goods

0-521-44378-4 CAMBRIDGE $54.95
0-521-44848-4 CAMBRIDGE PB $19.95

Paul A. **Schilpp**, editor

The Philosophy of G.E. Moore

A 2-volume set

0-87548-136-1 OPEN COURT $56.95
0-87548-285-6 OPEN COURT PB $28.95

Collingwood

Unsympathetic to the analytical trend of 20th-century British philosophy, Collingwood (1889-1943), an archaeologist as well as philosopher, is best known, like his mentor Croce, for his philosophy of history and art. His *Principles of Art* has been as much acclaimed by artists as by philosophers.

R.G. **Collingwood**

The Idea of History

Collingwood is the chief English exponent of historical idealism: that reality is essentially historical and a collaborative work of human imagination

See also **THE GREAT TRADITION** under **HISTORIOGRAPHY** in **WORLD HISTORY AND CURRENT AFFAIRS**

EDITED BY T.M. KNOX

0-19-285306-6 OXFORD PB $14.95

The Principles of Art

Colligwood defends the originality and autonomy of art by making a sharp distinction between art and craft

0-19-500209-1 OXFORD PB $11.95

Wittgenstein

Ludwig Wittgenstein (1889-1951) produced two landmarks in 20th-century philosophy, the second repudiating the first. The *Tractatus Logico- Philosophicus* is the consummation of logical atomism, the attempt to reduce language and knowledge to its fundamental logical forms. *Philosophical Investigations* presents a philosophy that "leaves everything as it is," contending that most philosophical problems are confusions resulting from inattention to ordinary language. The elliptical and penetrating aphorisms of *Philosophical Investigations*, in which such influential concepts as "language games," "family resemblances," and "forms of life" are developed, have had a revolutionary effect on postwar analytical philosophy.

Ludwig **Wittgenstein**

The Blue and Brown Books: Preliminary Studies for the Philosophical Investigations

Notebooks from Wittgenstein's later period. "There could be no better introduction to Wittgensteins' thought than the *Blue Book*, whose simplicity and forthrightness must make an instant appeal. The progressive complications of the *Brown Book* make a natural bridge to the still more subtle, but often confusing, exposition of the *Investigations*"—Max Black

0-06-131211-8 HARPERCOLLINS PB $14.00

Culture and Value

Wittgensteins' notes on art and ethics

0-226-90435-0 CHICAGO PB $9.95

Last Writings on the Philosophy of Psychology

EDITED BY G.H. VON WRIGHT & HEIKKI NYMAN

0-226-90425-3 CHICAGO PB $17.95

Notebooks, 1914-1916

0-226-90447-4 CHICAGO PB $14.95

On Certainty

0-06-131686-5 HARPERCOLLINS PB $13.00

Philosophical Grammar

0-520-03725-1 CALIFORNIA PB $13.95

Philosophical Investigations

Currently all American editions are out of print

0-02-428810-1 PRENTICE HALL $19.95

Philosophy may in no way interfere with the actual use of language; it can in the end only describe it. For it cannot give it any foundation either. It leaves everything as it is.
PHILOSOPHICAL INVESTIGATIONS

Philosophical Occasions: 1912-1951

0-87220-155-4 HACKETT $49.95
0-87220-154-6 HACKETT PB $24.95

Philosophical Remarks

0-226-90431-8 CHICAGO PB $16.95

Remarks on Colour

0-520-03727-8 CALIFORNIA PB $12.95

Remarks on the Foundations of Mathematics

0-262-73067-7 MIT PB $19.00

Remarks on the Philosophy of Psychology

0-226-90437-7 CHICAGO PB $17.95

Tractatus Logico-Philosophicus

Written mainly while Wittgenstein was serving in the Austrian army during World War I, this series of terse aphorisms became the chief influence on logical positivism

TRANSLATED BY C.K. OGDEN

0-415-02825-6 ROUTLEDGE PB $15.95

Tractatus Logico-Philosophicus

TRANSLATED BY D.F. PEARS & B.F. MCGUINNESS
INTRODUCTION BY BERTRAND RUSSELL

0-686-77038-2 HUMANITIES PB $15.95

Zettel

A notebook from the 1930s

TRANSLATED BY G.E.M. ANSCOMBE

0-520-01635-1 CALIFORNIA PB $12.95

Ludwig Wittgenstein

G.E.M. **Anscombe**

Introduction to Wittgenstein's Tractatus

FOREWORD BY H.J. PATON

0-8122-1019-0 PENNSYLVANIA PB $21.95

A.J. **Ayer**

Wittgenstein

A careful, fair-minded, and frank critical assessment by a major analytical philosopher. Addressing Wittgenstein's views on religion and psychology as well as on language and knowledge, Ayer concedes much to him while arguing that certain positions were "mistakes"

0-226-03337-6 CHICAGO PB $13.95

Robert J. **Fogelin**

Wittgenstein

A thorough study of Wittgenstein's *Tractatus* and later work emphasizing the radical originality of his point of view. "This is the best general introduction to Wittgenstein's work that I have read"— John R. Searle

0-7870-0007-8 NATIONAL ASSOCIATION OF COLLEGE STORES PB $21.58

Saul A. **Kripke**

Wittgenstein on Rules and Private Language

Kripke makes public the influence of Wittgenstein on his own thought

0-674-95401-7 HARVARD PB $13.00

Ray **Monk**

Ludwig Wittgenstein: The Duty of Genius

The most intimate account to date of the life of the 20th century's most influential philosopher. "Ray Monk succeeds both with the life and with the doctrines and he is the first person to make entirely clear the substantial interaction between them"
—Stuart Hampshire, *NY Review of Books*

0-14-015995-9 PENGUIN PB $15.95

Heidegger

Heidegger's (1889-1976) work is perhaps best understood as the consummate philosophical expression of the German romantic tradition. The search for an authentic way of being; the brooding contemplation of the solitary path that ends in death; the critique of society dominated by technology and out of touch with being; the conception of the poet as the guide back to being—all these are familiar elements of that tradition, as are the unsavory nationalistic and irrationalist overtones of the philosophy. Yet Heidegger no less than Nietzsche succeeded in transforming this tradition into something philosophically creative and provocative.

Martin **Heidegger**

The Basic Problems of Phenomenology

0-253-20478-X INDIANA PB $19.95

Basic Writings

EDITED BY DAVID F. KRELL

0-06-063845-1 HARPERCOLLINS PB $16.00

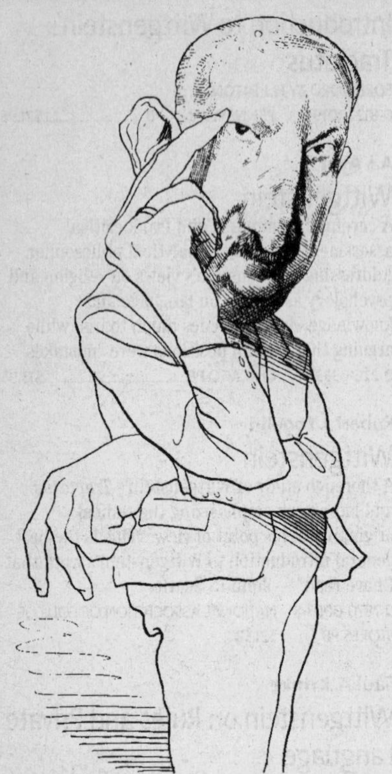

Martin Heidegger

Being and Time

Heidegger's magnum opus on the profound dimensions of ordinary, concrete aspects of the human condition

0-06-063850-8 HARPERCOLLINS $27.00
0-7914-2677-7 SUNY $57.50
0-7914-2678-5 SUNY PB $18.95

Early Greek Thinking

According to Heidegger, Western philosophy not only begins with the Presocratics but culminates in ideas that are close to theirs

See also THE PRESOCRATICS

TRANSLATED BY DAVID KRELL & FRANK CAPUZZI

0-06-063842-7 HARPERCOLLINS PB $16.20

History of the Concept of Time

0-253-20717-7 INDIANA PB $17.95

An Introduction to Metaphysics

0-300-01740-5 YALE PB $13.00

Nietzsche

Volumes 1 & 2
The Will to Power as Art & The Eternal Recurrence of the Same

See also NIETZSCHE

0-06-063841-9 HARPERCOLLINS PB $22.00

Volumes 3 & 4
The Will to Power as Knowledge and as Metaphysics & Nihilism

See also NIETZSCHE

0-06-063794-3 HARPERCOLLINS PB $22.00

On the Way to Language

0-06-063859-1 HARPERCOLLINS PB $13.00

Poetry, Language, Thought

Includes such essays as "The Origin of the Work of Art," "What Are Poets For?" and "The Thing" "As a whole this very valuable collection deals with the later Heidegger's highly aesthetic, highly poetic, view of Being and of Dasein's relationship to Being" -*Review of Metaphysics*

TRANSLATED BY ALBERT HOFSTADTER

0-06-090430-5 HARPERCOLLINS PB $13.00

The Question Concerning Technology, and Other Essays

See also CONSERVATISM under POLITICAL THOUGHT in SOCIAL STUDIES

0-06-131969-4 HARPERCOLLINS PB $13.50

Elzbieta **Ettinger**

Hannah Arendt - Martin Heidegger

The love affair between Heidegger and Arendt took place in the 1920s, when he was her teacher and she was his student. Valuable for the biographical light it sheds on the development of Arendt's thought

0-300-06407-1 YALE $16.00

Hannah Arendt

What Is Called Thinking?

TRANSLATED BY J. GLENN GRAY & FRED D. WIECK

0-06-090528-X HARPERCOLLINS PB $13.50

Hugo **Ott**

Martin Heidegger: An Intellectual and Political Portrait

A sensation when it was published in Germany, this book fully documents for the first time how one of this century's leading philosophers came to embrace and promote Nazism. "Excellent...In this indispensable book, Hugo Ott demonstrates that Heidegger's commitment to National Socialism was neither accidental nor unrelated...but was profound and enduring because he himself believed his philosophy was the spiritual core of that movement"—*TLS*

0-465-02898-5 BASIC $30.00

George **Steiner**

Martin Heidegger

"It would be hard to imagine a better introduction to the work of Martin Heidegger" —*New Republic*

0-8446-6384-0 SMITH $21.00
0-226-77232-2 CHICAGO PB $11.95

Theodor W. **Adorno**

The Jargon of Authenticity

An attack on Heideggerian existentialism

0-8101-0657-4 NORTHWESTERN PB $14.95

Logical Positivism

Logical positivism limited meaningful sentences to propositions that can be verified scientifically, and dismissed most traditional philosophy—notably metaphysics, ethics, and aesthetics—as nonsense. Its most prominent exponents were Rudolf Carnap, Moritz Schlick, and Otto Neurath.

A.J. **Ayer**

Language, Truth and Logic

Ayer's best-known work, making a classic case for scientific philosophy

0-8446-1571-4 SMITH $18.55

Logical Positivism

0-02-901130-2 FREE PRESS PB $17.95

More of My Life

Part of My Life is currently out of print. This is the second installment of Ayer's memoirs

0-19-281878-3 OXFORD $9.95

The Problem of Knowledge

0-14-020377-X VIKING PB $10.00

Rudolf **Carnap**

Introduction to Symbolic Logic and Its Applications

0-486-60453-5 DOVER PB $6.95

Meaning and Necessity: A Study in Semantics and Modal Logic

0-226-09347-6 CHICAGO PB $22.00

Onora **O'Neill**

Towards Justice and Virtue: A Constructive Account of Practical Reasoning

0-521-48095-7 CAMBRIDGE $54.95
0-521-48559-2 CAMBRIDGE PB $18.95

Hans **Reichenbach**

The Rise of Scientific Philosophy

A pungent critique of the Western metaphysical tradition, e.g. Hegel, from the point of view of logical positivism

0-520-01055-8 CALIFORNIA PB $13.00

Paul A. **Schilpp**, editor

The Philosophy of Rudolph Carnap

Twenty-six essays on the work of the most important member of the logical positivist school of philosophy and Carnap's reply to them, along with an autobiographical essay

0-8126-9153-9 OPEN COURT PB $28.95

Moritz **Schlick**

General Theory of Knowledge

0-87548-442-5 OPEN COURT PB $16.64

Sartre

The most famous and influential French philosopher of the century, Sartre (1905-1980) began with a Heideggerian existentialism that combined an affirmation of human freedom with an unflinching metaphysical pessimism. Stressing choice, commitment, and responsibility, he declared that man makes himself—but he also asserted that life is ultimately meaningless. He later attempted to reconcile his existentialist faith in freedom with a commitment to Marxist historical determinism and to revolutionary violence.

Jean-Paul Sartre

Jean-Paul **Sartre**
Hope Now: The 1980 Interviews
0-226-47630-8 CHICAGO $19.95

Jean-Paul **Sartre**
Anti-Semite and Jew
A challenge to anti-Semitism from a non-Jewish point of view. "One of the most brilliant psychological analyses of the marginal Jew and the fanatical anti-Semite that has ever been published"—Sidney Hook

See also **ANTI-SEMITISM** under **JEWISH HISTORY** in **WORLD HISTORY AND CURRENT AFFAIRS**
See also **ESSAYS: PERSONAL, LITERARY, PHILOSOPHICAL** under **MODERN FRENCH LITERATURE** in **LITERATURE OF EUROPE, AFRICA, AND ASIA**

0-8052-1047-4 SCHOCKEN PB $12.00
0-8052-0102-5 SCHOCKEN PB $12.00

Being and Nothingness
The major statement of Sartre's atheistic existentialism
TRANSLATED BY HAZEL E. BARNES
0-517-10185-8 GRAMERCY $12.99

Essays in Existentialism
INTRODUCTION BY S. WAHL
0-8065-0162-6 CITADEL PB $12.95

Existentialism and Humanism
0-8383-2148-8 HASKELL $49.95

Search for a Method
A work from Sartre's later Marxist phase
TRANSLATED BY HAZEL E. BARNES
0-394-70464-9 KNOPF PB $8.87

Paul A. **Schilpp**, editor
The Philosophy of Jean-Paul Sartre
Interpretive and critical essays with Sartre's replies
0-87548-354-2 OPEN COURT $56.95
0-8126-9150-4 OPEN COURT PB $29.95

Mary **Warnock**
Existentialism
A good introduction not only to Sartre but to the whole existentialist phenomenological tradition, with discussions of Husserl, Heidegger, Merleau-Ponty, Kierkegaard, and Nietzsche
0-19-888052-9 OXFORD PB $14.95

Merleau-Ponty

Often regarded as a disciple of Sartre, Merleau-Ponty (1908-1961) was a more rigorous and persistent exponent of phenomenology, paying close attention to problems of perception. Like Sartre, he attempted to fuse his early thought with orthodox Marxism, and like Sartre, he ended up quarreling with orthodox Marxists.

Maurice **Merleau-Ponty**
Adventures of the Dialectic
TRANSLATED BY JOSEPH J. BIEN
0-8101-0404-0 NORTHWESTERN $39.95
0-8101-0596-9 NORTHWESTERN PB $24.95

In Praise of Philosophy and Other Essays
0-8101-0796-1 NORTHWESTERN PB $15.95

Primacy of Perception
0-8101-0164-5 NORTHWESTERN PB $15.95

The Visible and the Invisible: Followed by Working Notes
0-8101-0457-1 NORTHWESTERN PB $22.50

Maurice Merleau-Ponty

Other 20th-Century Philosophers

Mortimer J. **Adler**
Art, the Arts, and the Great Ideas
Adler devotes his 57th book to an exploration of such words and concepts as "art," "idea," and "significance," using them to illuminate the relation between the root ideas of our culture and the great imaginative creations
0-02-500243-0 MACMILLAN $15.00

Giorgio Agamben
The Coming Community
TRANSLATED BY MICHAEL HARDT
0-8166-2235-3 MINNESOTA PB $16.95

Infancy and History: The Destruction of Experience
TRANSLATED BY LIZ HERON
0-86091-470-4 VERSO $59.95
0-86091-645-6 VERSO PB $18.95

Language and Death: The Place of Negativity
0-8166-1936-0 MINNESOTA $34.95
0-8166-1937-9 MINNESOTA PB $15.95

D.M. **Armstrong**
Universals and Scientific Realism
Volume 1
0-521-28033-8 CAMBRIDGE PB $20.95
Volume 2
0-521-28032-X CAMBRIDGE PB $17.95

Hannah **Arendt** & Karl **Jaspers**
Hannah Arendt—Karl Jaspers: Correspondence, 1926-1969
EDITED BY LOTTE KOHLER AND HANS SANER
0-156-22599-9 HARCOURT BRACE PB $19.95

Kenneth J. **Arrow**
Social Choice and Individual Values
A classic by the American Nobel laureate
See also **SOCIAL CHOICE AND GAME THEORY** under **SPECIAL TOPICS** under **ECONOMICS** in **SOCIAL STUDIES**
0-300-01364-7 YALE PB $12.00

J.L. **Austin**
How to Do Things with Words
The short but extremely influential work by the founder of speech act theory
See also **PIONEERS IN LINGUISTICS** under **LINGUISTICS** in **SOCIAL STUDIES**
EDITED BY J.O. URMSON AND MARINA SBISA
0-674-41152-8 HARVARD PB $10.50

Sense and Sensibilia
EDITED BY GEOFFREY J. WARNOCK
0-19-500307-1 OXFORD PB $11.95

Jean **Baudrillard**
This unclassifiable French theorist had a great influence in the Reagan years. His subject is usually a certain idea of America as a place where ideas have no purchase on the human imagination in any recognizable way—rather, America, and by extension global culture, is a

"site" where notions and images run against and over each other without any particular sensible pattern, where nothing is real and everything is a simulation:

Simulacra and Simulation

0-472-09521-8 MICHIGAN $34.50
0-472-06521-1 MICHIGAN PB $13.95

Brand **Blanshard**

A tenacious critic of analytical philosophy, existentialism, and other 20th-century tendencies, Blanshard is the most eminent champion of rational idealism in recent philosophy, giving it a less religious, more rigorous form than hsi 19th-century predecessors. He has forcefully upheld the rational basis of ethics against the prevalent emotive and relativistic theories.

Reason and Analysis

Consists largely of a spirited attack on twentieth-century analytic philosophy

0-87548-112-4 OPEN COURT PB $18.95

Hans **Blumenberg**

Work on Myth

0-262-52133-4 MIT PB $22.00

James M. **Buchanan**

The Limits of Liberty: Between Anarchy and Leviathan

A leading economist's examination of questions of freedom and authority within the framework of rights and rules established by a social contract theory of democracy

0-226-07820-5 CHICAGO PB $13.95

Malcolm **Budd**

Music and the Emotions: The Philosophical Theories

0-415-08779-1 ROUTLEDGE PB $16.95

Wittgenstein's Philosophy of Psychology

0-415-06452-X ROUTLEDGE PB $16.95

Stanley **Cavell**

The Claim of Reason

Clavell's magnum opus

0-195-03195-4 OXFORD PB $15.95

Conditions Handsome and Unhandsome: The Constitution of Emersonian Perfectionism

0-226-09821-4 CHICAGO PB $11.95

In Quest of the Ordinary: Lines of Skepticism and Romanticism

0-226-09818-4 CHICAGO PB $12.95

Must We Mean What We Say?

Early papers, including Cavell's reflections on his earlier career as a musician

0-521-29048-1 CAMBRIDGE PB $31.95

Philosophical Passages: Wittgenstein, Emerson, Austin, Derrida

0-631-19269-7 BLACKWELL $41.95
0-631-19271-9 BLACKWELL PB $20.95

Theodor **Adorno**

The leading figure of the postwar German Frankfurt school of philosophy and social theory, Adorno combined Marzxism and Freudianism in an attemt to vindicate an ideal of enlightened human freedom. A gifted musicologist and composer, he made several notable contributions to aesthetics.

Aesthetic Theory

Adorno's last work, newly translated

0-816-617996-6 MINNESOTA $39.95

Minima Moralia: Reflections from Damaged Life

These fragmentary reflections and essays on contemporary society were composed in America during and just after World War II. Adorno's most characteristic book and a brilliant stylistic achievement

See also **MARXISM AND THE FRANKFURT SCHOOL** under **SOCIOLOGY AFTER WEBER** under **SOCIOLOGY** in **SOCIAL STUDIES**

See also **THE FRANKFURT SCHOOL** under **CULTURAL CRITICISM** under **LITERARY THEORY** in **LITERATURE OF EUROPE, AFRICA, AND ASIA**

0-86091-704-5 VERSO PB $19.00

Negative Dialectics

Detailed critiques of Heidegger's *Being and Time*, Kant's *Critique of Practical Reason*, and Hegel's *Philosophy of Right*

0-8264-0132-5 CONTINUUM PB $19.95

Notes to Literature

A two-volume set. Includes Adorno's wonderful and revealing essay on writing essays

EDITED BY ROLF TIEDMAN

0-231-06333-4 COLUMBIA PB $16.00

Prisms

Essays on sundry subjects

See also **THE FRANKFURT SCHOOL** under **CULTURAL CRITICISM** under **LITERARY THEORY** in **LITERATURE OF EUROPE, AFRICA, AND ASIA**

TRANSLATED BY SAMUEL & SHERRY WEBER

0-262-51025-1 MIT PB $13.95

Quasi una Fantasia: Essays on Modern Music

Adorno composed as a young man and devoted much of his philosophical energy to a critical aesthetic of music

See also **CRITICAL ESSAYS** under **WESTERN CLASSICAL MUSIC** in **PERFORMING ARTS AND MEDIA**

TRANSLATED BY RODNEY LIVINGSTONE

0-86091-613-8 NORTON PB $19.95

Lambert **Zuidervaart**

Adorno's Aesthetic Theory: The Redemption of Illusion

0-262-74016-8 MIT $20.00

A Pitch of Philosophy: Autobiographical Exercises

0-674-66980-0 HARVARD $26.00
0-674-66981-9 HARVARD PB $14.95

Stanley **Cavell** & Stephen **Mulhall**

The Cavell Reader

0-631-19742-7 BLACKWELL $54.95
0-631-19743-5 BLACKWELL PB $21.95

David J. **Chalmers**

The Conscious Mind: In Search of a Fundamental Theory

A provocative new dualist approach to the problem of consciousness

0-19-510553-2 OXFORD $29.95

Paul M. **Churchland**

The Engine of Reason, the Seat of the Soul: A Philosophical Journey into the Brain

An important materialist contribution to the current debate about consciousness

0-262-03224-4 MIT $32.50
0-262-53142-9 MIT PB $17.50

Matter and Consciousness: A Contemporary Introduction to the Philosophy of Mind

0-262-53074-0 MIT PB $13.95

Arthur C. **Danto**

After the End of Art: Contemporary Art and the Pale of History

To be published February 1997

See also **THEORY AND CRITICISM** under **ART HISTORY: GENERAL STUDIES** in **ART**

0-691-01173-7 PRINCETON $24.95

Beyond the Brillo Box: The Visual Arts in Post-Historical Perspective

0-374-52391-6 NOONDAY PB $12.00

Embodied Meanings: Critical Essays & Aesthetic Meditations

0-374-52458-0 NOONDAY PB $14.00

The Philosophical Disenfranchisement of Art

See also **PHILOSOPHY AND ART** under **ART SINCE 1945** in **ART**

0-231-06364-4 COLUMBIA $39.50
0-231-06365-2 COLUMBIA PB $16.00

Narration and Knowledge

An analytical approach to the philosophy of history

0-231-06116-1 COLUMBIA $42.50
0-231-06117-X COLUMBIA PB $18.00

Encounters & Reflections: Art in the Historical Present

To be published February 1997

0-520-20846-3 CALIFORNIA $42.00

The Transfiguration of the Commonplace: A Philosophy of Art

A philosopher's mind at grips with a fascinating aesthetic situation, the identity of found things and artifacts mimicking them

See also **PHILOSOPHY AND ART** under **ART SINCE 1945** in **ART**

0-674-90346-3 HARVARD PB $12.95

Donald **Davidson**

The most important American analytic philosopher since Quine, Davidson has brought a fresh, subtle, and uncommonly rigorous approach to the questions of meaning and truth. He rejects not only pluralistic theories of interpretation but also atomistic theories of meaning in favor of a holistic theory of truth based on the coherence of entire sentences with one another.

Essays on Actions and Events
0-19-824637-4 OXFORD PB $24.00

Inquiries into Truth and Interpretation
0-19-875046-3 OXFORD PB $24.00

Donald Davidson

Gilles **Deleuze**

Empiricism and Subjectivity: An Essay on Hume's Theory of Human Nature
TRANSLATED BY CONSTANTIN BOUNDAS

0-231-06812-3 COLUMBIA $34.50

Expressionism in Philosophy: Spinoza
0-942299-50-7 ZONE $28.95

0-942299-51-5 ZONE PB $16.95

Negotiations: 1972-1990
TRANSLATED BY MARTIN JOUGHIN

0-231-07580-4 COLUMBIA $37.50

Gilles **Deleuze** & Felix **Guattari**

What Is Philosophy?
See also **INTRODUCTIONS TO PHILOSOPHY**

0-231-07988-5 COLUMBIA $29.95

0-231-07989-3 COLUMBIA PB $17.00

Gilles **Deleuze** & others

The Logic of Sense
0-231-05982-5 COLUMBIA $49.50

Daniel C. **Dennett**

Dennett makes a strong case for abandoning traditional humanistic and anthropocentric theories of consciousness, arguing in favor of an unapologetically hard-nosed scientific approach to the problem.

Consciousness Explained
"An extraordinarily rich perspective so often brilliant, so witty, and so informed by contemporary culture as to make pleasurable the reading of what is truly a complex and demanding text" —*Kirkus Reviews*

See also **HISTORIES AND INTRODUCTIONS** under **PSYCHOLOGY** in **SOCIAL STUDIES**

See also **THE NEUROSCIENCES AND THE BRAIN** under **BIOLOGY** under **LIFE SCIENCES** in **SCIENCE**

0-316-18065-3 LITTLE, BROWN $27.95

0-316-18066-1 LITTLE, BROWN PB $15.95

Content and Consciousness
0-415-10431-9 ROUTLEDGE PB $17.95

Darwin's Dangerous Idea: Evolution and the Meanings of Life
0-684-80290-2 SIMON & SCHUSTER $30.00

The Intentional Stance
0-262-04093-X BRADFORD $35.00

0-262-54053-3 MIT PB $19.00

Kinds of Minds: Toward an Understanding of Consciousness
0-465-07350-6 HARPERCOLLINS $20.00

Daniel Dennett

Jacques **Derrida**

Derrida's philosophy has brought the influence of Nietzsche and Heidegger to bear on questions of semiotics and literary language. He has been the chief philosophical exponent of deconstrutionism, which has had a pervasive influence on contemporary literary theory and confines itself to unmasking hidden assumptions and the prejudices of language.

Aporias
On death as limit and the limits of truth, with reflections on Seneca and Heidegger, among others

0-8047-2233-1 STANFORD $32.50

0-8047-2252-8 STANFORD PB $12.95

Dissemination
TRANSLATED BY BARBARA JOHNSON

0-226-14334-1 CHICAGO PB $17.95

Jaques Derrida

Limited Inc
Derrida's reply to American philosopher John Searles's criticisms

See also **POSTSTRUCTURALISM** under **LITERARY THEORY** in **LITERATURE OF EUROPE, AFRICA, AND ASIA**

TRANSLATED BY SAMUEL WEBER & JEFFREY MEHLMAN

0-8101-0788-0 NORTHWESTERN PB $13.95

Margins of Philosophy
Dismantles the philosophic tradition of Plato, Kant, Hegel, and Nietzsche, among others

See also **POSTSTRUCTURALISM** under **LITERARY THEORY** in **LITERATURE OF EUROPE, AFRICA, AND ASIA**

TRANSLATED BY ALAN BASS

0-226-14326-0 CHICAGO PB $15.95

Of Grammatology
See also **POSTSTRUCTURALISM** under **LITERARY THEORY** in **LITERATURE OF EUROPE, AFRICA, AND ASIA**

TRANSLATED BY GAYATRI C. SPIVAK

0-8018-1879-6 JOHNS HOPKINS PB $16.95

The Truth of Painting
"Calling into question every certain conclusion, Derrida exposes the impossibility of all final solutions"—*NY Times*

See also **THEORY AND CRITICISM** under **ART HISTORY: GENERAL STUDIES** in **ART**

See also **POSTSTRUCTURALISM** under **LITERARY THEORY** in **LITERATURE OF EUROPE, AFRICA, AND ASIA**

0-226-14324-4 CHICAGO PB $23.95

0-226-14323-6 CHICAGO PB $49.95

Writing and Difference
His most influential work on language and literature, bringing Hegel, Heidegger, Husserl, and Foucault to bear on the project of deconstructing the Western philosophical tradition and disclosing what that tradition has supressed

See also **POSTSTRUCTURALISM** under **LITERARY THEORY** in **LITERATURE OF EUROPE, AFRICA, AND ASIA**

TRANSLATED BY ALAN BASS

0-226-14329-5 CHICAGO PB $14.95

Vincent **Descombes**

The Barometer of Modern Reason: On the Philosophies of Current Events

A clearly written critique of current movements in continental philosophy

0-19-507990-6 OXFORD PB $19.95

Michael **Dummett**

Origins of Analytical Philosophy

0-674-64473-5 HARVARD PB $16.95

The Seas of Language

0-19-823621-2 OXFORD PB $19.95

Ronald **Dworkin**

Law's Empire

Dworkin is among the most eminent of contemporary legal philosophers, notable for finding a theoretical basis for liberal social policy.

See also **LIBERALISM** under **POLITICAL THOUGHT** in **SOCIAL STUDIES**

0-674-51836-5 HARVARD PB $16.95

A Matter of Principle

See also **LIBERALISM** under **POLITICAL THOUGHT** in **SOCIAL STUDIES**

0-674-55461-2 HARVARD PB $17.50

Taking Rights Seriously

"The most significant book on the philosophy of law in this decade"—*Ethics*

See also **LIBERALISM** under **POLITICAL THOUGHT** in **SOCIAL STUDIES**

0-674-86710-6 HARVARD $34.50

0-674-86711-4 HARVARD PB $15.95

Luc **Ferry**

Ferry's work reasserts a liberal ideal in opposition to the standard anti-humanist radicalism of postwar French philosophy.

Rights—The New Quarrel Between the Ancients and the Moderns

0-226-24471-7 CHICAGO $25.50

The System of Philosophies of History

TRANSLATED BY FRANKLIN PHILIP

0-226-24472-5 CHICAGO $29.95

Luc **Ferry** & Alain **Renaut**

French Philosophy of the Sixties: An Essay on Antihumanism

TRANSLATED BY MARY H.S. CATTANI

0-87023-694-6 MASSACHUSETTS $35.00

0-87023-695-4 MASSACHUSETTS PB $17.95

From the Rights of Man to the Republican Idea

0-226-24473-3 CHICAGO $27.95

Heidegger and Modernity

TRANSLATED BY FRANKLIN PHILIP

0-226-24462-8 CHICAGO $16.95

Paul **Feyerabend**

Killing Time

The maverick philosopher's autobiography

0-226-24531-4 CHICAGO $22.95

0-226-24532-2 CHICAGO PB $13.95

Against Method

Feyerabend, an Austrian-born American philosopher, remained the *enfant terrible* of the philosophy of science throughout his life, an iconoclast who relentlessly attacked the premises of modern science on behalf of a pluralist view of knowledge. This is his best-known book

0-86091-481-X VERSO $64.95

0-86091-646-4 VERSO PB $19.00

Philosophical Papers

Volume 1
Realism, Rationalism, and Scientific Method

0-521-22897-2 CAMBRIDGE $85.00

Volume 2
Problems of Empiricism

0-521-23964-8 CAMBRIDGE $75.00

0-521-31641-3 CAMBRIDGE PB $31.95

Alain **Finkielkraut**

The Defeat of the Mind

TRANSLATED BY JUDTIH FRIEDLANDER

0-231-08022-0 COLUMBIA $22.95

Jerry A. **Fodor**

The Elm and the Expert: Mentalese and Its Semantics

0-262-06170-8 MIT $22.00

0-262-56093-3 BRADFORDS DIRECTORY PB $10.00

A Theory of Content and Other Essays

0-262-06130-9 MIT $32.50

Michel **Foucault**

The Archaeology of Knowledge

See also **POSTWAR FRENCH AND BRITISH THOUGHT** under **SOCIOLOGY AFTER WEBER** under **SOCIOLOGY** in **SOCIAL STUDIES**

0-394-71106-8 PANTHEON PB $10.65

Ethics, Subjectivity, and Truth: Michel Foucault on Truth, Beauty and Power, 1954-1984

EDITED BY PAUL RABINOW

TRANSLATED BY ROBERT HURLEY

1-56584-352-5 NEW PRESS $25.00

The Foucault Reader

Presents many aspects of Foucault's investigation of the nature of power in society

See also **MICHEL FOUCAULT** under **POSTSTRUCTURALISM** under **LITERARY THEORY** in **LITERATURE OF EUROPE, AFRICA, AND ASIA**

See also **ESSAYS: PERSONAL, LITERARY, PHILOSOPHICAL** under **MODERN FRENCH LITERATURE** in **LITERATURE OF EUROPE, AFRICA, AND ASIA**

EDITED BY PAUL RABINOW

0-394-71340-0 RANDOM HOUSE PB $15.00

The Order of Things: An Archaeology of the Human Sciences

See also **POSTWAR FRENCH AND BRITISH THOUGHT** under **SOCIOLOGY AFTER WEBER** under **SOCIOLOGY** in **SOCIAL STUDIES**

0-679-75335-4 VINTAGE PB $13.00

Hans Georg **Gadamer**

The Enigma of Health: The Art of Healing in a Scientific Age

TRANSLATED BY JASON GEIGER & NICK WALKER

0-8047-2692-2 STANFORD PB $14.95

Truth and Method

Gadamer's magnum opus is a major treatise on hermeneutics

0-8264-0585-1 CONTINUUM PB $22.95

René **Girard**

Things Hidden Since the Foundation of the World

"Girard's thesis on mimetic desire and the spiral that leads to conflict, violence, and the eventual restoration of social order by means of sacrifice is known to readers of *Violence and the Sacred* and *The Scapegoat*. What the present work adds is a remarkable disclosure of the way in which Girard comes to his thesis…and shares his views on the 20th century"—*Religious Studies Review*

0-8047-2215-3 STANFORD PB $18.95

Nelson **Goodman**

Goodman is noted for his stress on the frames of reference through which we approach and construct the world.

Fact, Fiction and Forecast

0-674-29071-2 HARVARD PB $12.00

The Languages of Art

An acclaimed analytic philosophy of art in which the author argues (among other things) that perspective construction is conventional rather than real

See also **PHILOSOPHY AND ART** under **ART SINCE 1945** in **ART**

0-915144-34-4 HACKETT PB $12.95

Of Mind and Other Matters

0-674-63126-9 HARVARD PB $13.50

Ways of Worldmaking

A rigorously nominalist approach to epistemology

0-915144-52-2 HACKETT $29.95

0-915144-51-4 HACKETT PB $8.95

Susan **Haack**

Evidence and Inquiry: Towards Reconstruction in Epistemology

0-631-19679-X BLACKWELL PB $22.95

Ian **Hacking**

Rewriting the Soul: Multiple Personality and the Sciences of Memory

Hacking's studies provide a fresh and insightful view on this American phenomenon

See also **OTHER PROBLEMS** under **DISORDERS AND TREATMENT** under **PSYCHOLOGY** in **SOCIAL STUDIES**

0-691-03642-X PRINCETON $24.95

Stuart **Hampshire**

Innocence and Experience

A lucid defense of moral reasoning, confronting skeptics like Hume, Nietzsche, and Macchiavelli, and drawing on history and personal experience, by the British political and ethical philosopher

0-674-45448-0 HARVARD $29.95

Jurgen **Habermas**

Theory and Practice

TRANSLATED BY JOHN VIERTEL

0-8070-1527-X FS&G PB $17.00

The Theory of Communicative Action

Generally regarded as Habermas' chief work, arguing that the "life-world" of concrete social life and communication has been dislocated by bureaucratic and economic forms of power

Volume 1 Reason and the Rationalization of Society

0-8070-1507-5 FS&G PB $21.00

Volume 2 Lifeworld and System: Critique of Functionalist Reason

0-8070-1401-X BEACON $21.00

Jurgen Habermas

Karl **Jaspers**

Philosophy

Volumes one and two of Jaspers' comprehensive exposition of his philosophy are currently out of print

Volume 3

0-226-39494-8 CHICAGO $14.00

Hans **Jonas**

Mortality and Morality: A Search for Good after Auschwitz

See also **HOLOCAUST EXPERIENCES: FROM PARIS TO WARSAW** under **THE HOLOCAUST** in **WORLD HISTORY AND CURRENT AFFAIRS**

0-8101-1286-8 NORTHWESTERN PB $22.50

Saul A. **Kripke**

Naming and Necessity

Kripke's work runs against the tide of recent analytic philosophy by championing a rigorous theory of meaning and truth reminiscent of Russell and Frege

0-674-59846-6 HARVARD PB $12.95

Thomas S. **Kuhn**

The Structure of Scientific Revolutions

The classic study of the development and displacement of scientific "paradigms"

See also **SCIENTIFIC THOUGHT AND DISCOVERY** under **SCIENCE AND TECHNOLOGY** in **SCIENCE**

See also **HISTORICAL SOCIOLOGY** under **TOPICS IN MODERN SOCIOLOGY** under **SOCIOLOGY** in **SOCIAL STUDIES**

0-226-45803-2 CHICAGO $25.00

0-226-45804-0 CHICAGO PB $10.95

Philippe **Lacoue-Labarthe**

Musica Ficta (Figures of Wagner)

TRANSLATED BY FELICIA MCCARREN

0-8047-2376-1 STANFORD $35.00

0-8047-2385-0 STANFORD PB $13.95

The Subject of Philosophy

0-8166-1697-3 MINNESOTA $49.95

Philippe **Lacoue-Labarthe** & Jean-Luc **Nancy**

The Literary Absolute

A consideration of the philosophical character of German romanticism

0-88706-660-7 SUNY $59.50

0-88706-661-5 SUNY PB $19.95

The Title of the Letter: A Reading of Lacan

0-7914-0961-9 SUNY $49.50

0-7914-0962-7 SUNY PB $16.95

Lawrence **Lampert**

Leo Strauss and Nietzsche

"[Strauss] restores Platonic and Nietzschean teaching to their proper place, revives the enduring questions and oppositions set out in those teachings, and by implication calls decisively into account prevailing views in the contemporary philosophical world"—Alan Udoff

0-226-46825-9 CHICAGO $22.50

Berel **Lang**

Act and Idea in the Nazi Genocide

0-226-46868-2 CHICAGO $49.95

0-226-46869-0 CHICAGO PB $17.95

The Anatomy of Philosophical Style: Literary Philosophy and the Philosophy of Literature

0-631-17546-6 BLACKWELL PB $22.95

Heidegger's Silence

0-8014-3310-X CORNELL $19.95

Mind's Bodies: Thought in the Act

0-7914-2553-3 SUNY $39.50

0-7914-2554-1 SUNY PB $12.95

Writing and the Moral Self

0-415-90295-9 ROUTLEDGE $45.00

0-415-90296-7 ROUTLEDGE PB $16.95

Berel **Lang**, editor

Writing and the Holocaust

0-8419-1184-3 HOLMES & MEIER $45.00

0-8419-1185-1 HOLMES & MEIER PB $19.95

John **Lechte**

Fifty Key Contemporary Thinkers: From Structuralism to Postmodernity

Lechte leads us into the labyrinthine present tense of philosophical thought, with essays on Kafka, Freud, Chomsky, Derrida, Irigaray: 50 key thinkers who have taken us along the road from '60s Structuralism to the '90s "postmodernism"—a word bandied at cocktail parties but rarely understood

0-415-07408-8 ROUTLEDGE PB $15.95

Henri **Lefebvre**

Introduction to Modernity: Twelve Preludes September 1959-May 1961

TRANSLATED BY JOHN MOORE

1-85984-056-6 VERSO PB $23.00

Writing on Cities

A collection of major essays by the great Marxist theorist of cities and urban life

See also **AMERICAN CITIES** under **REGIONAL ARCHITECTURE** under **AMERICAN ARCHITECTURE TO 1900** in **ARCHITECTURE, DESIGN, AND HOMES**

EDITED AND TRANSLATED BY ELEONORE KOFMAN AND ELIZABETH LEBAS

0-631-19187-9 BLACKWELL $55.95

0-631-19188-7 BLACKWELL PB $19.95

Emmanuel **Levinas**

Basic Philosophical Writings

0-253-33078-5 INDIANA $35.00

The Levinas Reader

An accessible introduction to one of the most influential of contemporary European thinkers

EDITED BY SEAN HAND

0-631-16447-2 BLACKWELL PB $22.95

Outside the Subject

A series of essays by the eminent French phenomenologist, dealing with other philosophers such as Martin Buber and Jean Wahl and questions such as meaning, communication, and rights

0-8047-2197-1 STANFORD $35.00

0-8047-2199-8 STANFORD PB $17.95

Proper Names

TRANSLATED BY MICHAEL B. SMITH

0-8047-2352-4 STANFORD PB $14.95

The Theory of Intuition in Husserl's Phenomenology

See also **HUSSERL**

0-8101-1281-7 NORTHWESTERN PB $18.95

Time and the Other

TRANSLATED BY RICHARD A. COHEN

0-8207-0233-1 DUQUESNE PB $17.95

Jean-Francois **Lyotard**

The Inhuman: Reflections on Time

0-8047-2006-1 STANFORD $39.50

0-8047-2008-8 STANFORD PB $11.95

Lessons on the Analytic of the Sublime

0-8047-2241-2 STANFORD $39.50

0-8047-2242-0 STANFORD PB $14.95

Jean-Francois **Lyotard**

The Postmodern Explained : Correspondence, 1982-1985

0-8166-2211-6 MINNESOTA PB $12.95

Jean-Francois **Lyotard** & Robert **Harvey**

Toward the Postmodern

0-391-03890-7 HUMANITIES PB $17.50

Alasdair **MacIntyre**

After Virtue: A Study in Moral Theory

An important and controversial critique of Kantian and utilitarian versions of morality

0-268-00611-3 NOTRE DAME PB $15.00

Three Rival Versions of Moral Enquiry: Encyclopaedia, Genealogy, and Tradition

0-268-01877-4 NOTRE DAME PB $12.95

Whose Justice? Which Rationality?

Continues reflections begun in *After Virtue*

0-268-01944-4 NOTRE DAME PB $17.50

Gabriel **Marcel**

The Philosophy of Existentialism

Marcel was the foremost Catholic proponent of existentialism

0-8065-0901-5 LYLE STUART PB $8.95

Herbert **Marcuse**

Marcuse, another member of the Frankfurt school, became a chief intellectual sponsor of the New Left and the 1960s counterculture through his insistence that erotic liberation must accompany radical political and economic change.

Herbert Marcuse

One Dimensional Man

A scathing criticism of modern capitalism

See also **LEFTISM AND MARXISM** under **POLITICAL THOUGHT** in **SOCIAL STUDIES**

See also **MARXISM AND THE FRANKFURT SCHOOL** under **SOCIOLOGY AFTER WEBER** under **SOCIOLOGY** in **SOCIAL STUDIES**

0-8070-1417-6 BEACON PB $15.00

Eros and Civilization: A Philosophical Inquiry into Freud

Rejecting Freud's theory that civilization demands instinctual repression, Marcuse calls for a society in which sexual liberation will accompany political and economic liberation

See also **THE REACTION AGAINST FREUD** under **FREUD** under **PSYCHOLOGY** in **SOCIAL STUDIES**

See also **SOCIAL PSYCHOLOGY** under **PSYCHOLOGY** in **SOCIAL STUDIES**

See also **MARXISM AND THE FRANKFURT SCHOOL** under **SOCIOLOGY AFTER WEBER** under **SOCIOLOGY** in **SOCIAL STUDIES**

0-8070-1555-5 FS&G PB $15.00

Avishai **Margalit**

The Decent Society

TRANSLATED BY NAOMI GOLDBLUM

0-674-19436-5 HARVARD $35.00

Thomas **McCarthy**

The Critical Theory of Jurgen Habermas

A meticulous and illuminating exposition of Habermas's ideas by an American philosopher

0-262-63073-7 MIT PB $20.00

Mary **Midgley**

The Ethical Primate: Humans, Freedom and Morality

0-415-09530-1 ROUTLEDGE $29.95

Utopias, Dolphins and Computers: Some Problems in Philosophical Plumbing

0-415-13377-7 ROUTLEDGE $22.95

Mary **Mothersill**

Beauty Restored

A neo-Kantian aesthetic

0-937431-04-4 ADAMN PB $19.95

Ernest **Nagel**

The Structure of Science

0-915144-72-7 HACKETT $39.95

0-915144-71-9 HACKETT PB $19.95

Thomas **Nagel**

Mortal Questions

Includes the famous essay "What Is It Like To Be A Bat?"

0-52-140676-5 CAMBRIDGE PB $10.95

Other Minds: Critical Essays 1969-1994

0-19-509008-X OXFORD $24.95

The View from Nowhere

0-19-505644-2 OXFORD PB $16.95

What Does It All Mean?: A Very Short Introduction to Philosophy

A succinct survey of major problems—including "Other Minds," "Free Will," "Justice," and "The Meaning of Life"—by the American philosopher who wrote the famous essay "What is it like to Be a Bat?"

See also **INTRODUCTIONS TO PHILOSOPHY**

0-19-505292-7 OXFORD $16.95

0-19-505216-1 OXFORD PB $10.95

Iris **Murdoch**

Metaphysics as a Guide to Morals

Murdoch taught philosophy for many years as well as writing novels. This work offers a synthesis of her views on art and the moral life

0-14-017232-7 PENGUIN PB $15.96

Iris Murdoch

Jean-Luc **Nancy**

The Birth to Presence

A collection of intricate and subtle meditations, essays, and dialogues

0-8047-2060-6 STANFORD $49.50

0-8047-2189-0 STANFORD PB $16.95

The Experience of Freedom

A philosophy of freedom that owes much to Heidegger and resists the permutations of "necessity" found in both traditional metaphysics and Sartrean existentialism

0-8047-2175-0 STANFORD $39.50

0-8047-2190-4 STANFORD PB $13.95

Robert **Nozick**

Anarchy, State and Utopia

A brilliant and provocative work that offers a libertarian alternative to John Rawls's *Theory of Justice*

0-465-09720-0 BASIC BOOKS PB $18.50

The Nature of Rationality

The celebrated Harvard philosopher Nozick continues his search for the connections between philosophy and ordinary experience. In a lively, highly readable style, he shows how philosophic principles actually function in our day to-day thinking and in our efforts to live productively and peacefully with each other

0-691-07424-0 PRINCETON $35.00

Philosophical Explanations

"His arguments link his explanations to what he is rightly confident of … his vision of a persistent role for philosophy in common life" —*New Republic*

0-674-66448-5 HARVARD $42.50

0-674-66479-5 HARVARD PB $19.95

Martha C. **Nussbaum**

Love's Knowledge

0-1907485-8 OXFORD $19.95

The Therapy of Desire: Theory and Practice in Hellenistic Ethics

The convergence of ethics and therapeutic approaches to desire and happiness in Aristotle, Stoicism, and Epicureanism

See also **OTHER TOPICS IN ANCIENT PHILOSOPHY**

0-691-03342-0 PRINCETON $45.00
0-691-00052-2 PRINCETON PB $16.95

Michael **Oakeshott**

Rationalism in Politics and Other Essays

Essays by an influential British political philosopher calling into question the prevalence of ideology and systematic rationalism in modern politics and defending a less intrusive, tradition-respecting style of governance as essential to individualism and freedom

See also **CONSERVATISM** under **POLITICAL THOUGHT** in **SOCIAL STUDIES**

0-86597-094-7 LIBERTY FUND $21.00
0-86597-095-5 LIBERTY FUND PB $7.50

Anthony **O'Hear**

Karl Popper

Illustrates the nature of Popper's thought and examines his views on knowledge, science, probability, society, evolution, and the self

0-415-08480-6 ROUTLEDGE PB $18.95

Dereck **Parfit**

Reasons and Persons

"Parfit's book, besides contributing, as it certainly does, intellectual illumination and delight, may possibly do more: it may point the way to the emergence of a satisfactory theory of rational beneficence, and this might, in the long run, be capable of influencing political behavior"—P.F. Strawson, *NY Review of Books*

0-19-824908-X OXFORD PB $28.00

Robert M. **Pirsig**

Lila: An Inquiry Into Morals

The idiosyncratic philosopher, whose *Zen and the Art of Motorcycle Maintenance* became one of the most popular and influential books of the 1970s, has written a long-awaited continuation of his inquiry into what he calls the Metaphysics of Quality. "A marvelous improvisation on a most improbable quarter: sailing, philosophy, sex and madness"—*NY Times Book Review*

0-553-07737-6 BDD $22.50

Karl R. **Popper**

The Logic of Scientific Discovery

A classic work on the philosophy of science

See also **SCIENTIFIC THOUGHT AND DISCOVERY** under **SCIENCE AND TECHNOLOGY** in **SCIENCE**

0-415-07892-X ROUTLEDGE PB $22.95
0415007892X ROUTLEDGE PB $19.95

Objective Knowledge: An Evolutionary Approach

0-19-875024-2 OXFORD PB $19.95

Karl Popper

The Open Society and Its Enemies

Popper argues that the systematic philosophies of Plato, Hegel, and Marx laid the intellectual foundations for 20th-century totalitarianism; he advocates a democratic, "piecemeal" approach to politics

Volume 1

The Spell of Plato

See also **FASCISM AND TOTALITARIANISM** under **POLITICAL THOUGHT** in **SOCIAL STUDIES**

0-691-01968-1 PRINCETON PB $19.95

Volume 2

The High Tide of Prophecy

See also **FASCISM AND TOTALITARIANISM** under **POLITICAL THOUGHT** in **SOCIAL STUDIES**

0-691-01972-X PRINCETON PB $18.95

Popper Selections

Thirty excerpts from Popper's non-technical writings on the theory of knowledge, the philosophy of science, metaphysics, and social science

EDITED BY DAVID MILLER

0-691-07287-6 PRINCETON $65.00
0-691-02031-0 PRINCETON PB $17.95

Hilary **Putnam**

The Many Faces of Realism

0-8126-9043-5 OPEN COURT PB $10.95

Pragmatism: An Open Question

0-631-19343-X BLACKWELL PB $16.95

Reason, Truth, and History

A defense of rationality against both absolutist, ahistorical standards of rationality and radical subjectivism or relativism

0-521-23035-7 CAMBRIDGE $59.95
0-521-29776-1 CAMBRIDGE PB $18.95

Renewing Philosophy

0-674-76094-8 HARVARD PB $14.95

Words and Life

0-674-95607-9 HARVARD PB $19.95

W.V. **Quine**

Quine, an acute and original logician, is the most important American philosopher to work in the analytic tradition. Through his influence the center of philosophical activity has shifted to the United States.

From Stimulus to Science

0-674-32635-0 HARVARD $22.95

The Logic of Sequences: A Generalization of Principia Mathematica

0-8240-3210-1 GARLAND $25.00

Quiddities: An Intermittently Philosophical Dictionary

Plainspoken and beguiling short essays on a wide range of topics, including "Paradoxes," "Space -Time," "Creation," "Free Will," "Tolerance," and "Gambling"

0-674-74352-0 HARVARD PB $10.95

Selected Logic Papers

0-674-79837-6 HARVARD PB $16.95

The Roots of Reference

0-8126-9101-6 OPEN COURT PB $17.95

The Ways of Paradox and Other Essays

0-674-94837-8 HARVARD PB $14.95

Word and Object

0-262-67001-1 MIT PB $16.00

John **Rawls**

Rawl's Theory of Justice *is the most important book in ethical philosophy to appear in English since G.E. Moore's* Principia Ethica *of 1903.*

Political Liberalism

See also **LIBERALISM** under **POLITICAL THOUGHT** in **SOCIAL STUDIES**

0-231-05248-0 COLUMBIA $40.00
0-231-05249-9 COLUMBIA PB $15.00

A Theory of Justice

A broad and important work of philosophy elaborating the idea of "justice as fairness"

See also **LEGAL THEORY** under **LAW** in **SOCIAL STUDIES**

0-674-88014-5 HARVARD PB $18.95

John Rawls

Paul **Ricoeur**

The Philosophy of Paul Ricoeur

EDITED BY LEWIS EDWIN HAHN

0-8126-9259-4 OPEN COURT $56.95

Nicholas **Rescher**

Luck: The Brilliant Randomness of Everyday Life

Lively and provocative, this is a meditation on luck, fate, fortune, and chance that gives a philosopher's explication of the shape, operation, and management of luck in our chaotic world. Ranging from antiquity to the present, from lotteries to war, Rescher explains how we can reduce our reliance on luck alone to improve the odds in our everyday lives

0-374-19428-9 FS&G $19.00

Richard **Rorty**

Contingency, Irony, and Solidarity

Liberalism plus literary irony, or how to reinvent yourself in private while working for democratic reform in public. Rorty's neopragmatism synthesizes Continental philosphy and postmodernist atmospherics with the open-minded commitment to experience and experiment of James and Dewey

0-521-36781-6 CAMBRIDGE PB $16.95

Philosophy and the Mirror of Nature

Argues from a pragmatist perspective against philosophy's post-Cartesian epistemological obsession. One of the most significant and controversial works of modern philosophy

0-691-02016-7 PRINCETON PB $16.95

Gilbert **Ryle**

The Concept of Mind

Ryles's chief work argues against the dogma of the "ghost in the machine," the idea of an autonomous mind or soul inhabiting the body—an idea he regards as a linguistic illusion or "category mistake"

0-226-73295-9 CHICAGO PB $12.95

John R. **Searle**

The Construction of Social Reality

0-02-928045-1 FREE PRESS $25.00
0-684-83179-1 FREE PRESS PB $15.95

Intentionality: An Essay in the Philosophy of Mind

0-521-22895-6 CAMBRIDGE $74.95
0-521-27302-1 CAMBRIDGE PB $19.95

John Searle

Rediscovery of the Mind

Searle offers a philosophical perspective on the scientific debate about the relation between physical processes in the brain and subjective experience

See also **SCIENCE AND TECHNOLOGY** in **SCIENCE**

0-262-19321-3 MIT $30.00
0-262-69154-X BRADFORD PB $14.00

Amartya **Sen**

Inequality Reexamined

In democracies, "equality" is a notion most often taken for granted and usually misinterpreted. Harvard professor Sen argues that our differences should be celebrated, and our individual capabilities reappraised. "All people are created equal" may be a platitude that keeps us from gaining victory over poverty, racism, and other serious social problems

See also **POLITICS AND THE INTERNATIONAL ECONOMY** under **ECONOMICS** in **SOCIAL STUDIES**

0-674-45256-9 HARVARD PB $15.95

Gary H. **Stahl**

Human Transactions: The Emergence of Meaning in Time

1-56639-287-X TEMPLE $39.95

Leo **Strauss**

Liberalism Ancient and Modern

"Strauss is…indeed a friend of democracy when he summons true liberals to counteract the perverted liberalism that forgets quality, excellence, or virtue…Strauss shows that the deepest seriousness, with no bow to popularity, is the one thing most needful"
—from the Foreword by Allan Bloom

0-226-77689-1 CHICAGO PB $15.95

The Rebirth of Classical Political Rationalism

Essays and lectures by a philosopher who took Plato and Aristotle as his political guides

0-226-77715-4 CHICAGO PB $17.95

Thoughts on Machiavelli

Strauss's meditation on a philosopher whose subtlety and integrity he admired without admiring his philosophy

0-226-77702-2 CHICAGO PB $16.95

P.F. **Strawson**

Beginning as an exponent of ordinary-language analytical philosophy, Strawson developed a related position he called "descriptive metaphysics," the attempt to uncover and describe the actual, unchanging structures of human thought.

Individuals: An Essay in Descriptive Metaphysics

Strawson's most famous book, approaching metaphysical questions like the mind-body distinction through a careful examination of our concepts of "person"and "object"

0-416-68310-X ROUTLEDGE PB $16.95

Skepticism and Naturalism: Some Varieties

0-231-05916-7 COLUMBIA $30.00
0-231-05917-5 COLUMBIA PB $13.50

Charles **Taylor**

Ethics of Authenticity

A short exposition of taylor's recent thuoghts about society and identity

0-674-26873-6 HARVARD $18.95

Human Agency and Language

0-521-31750-9 CAMBRIDGE PB $24.95

Philosophical Arguments

0-674-66476-0 HARVARD $35.00

Philosophy and the Human Sciences

0-521-31749-5 CAMBRIDGE PB $23.95

Sources of the Self: The Making of the Modern Identity

This erudite and accessible book is a historical and critical consideration of what it means to have a self

0-674-82426-1 HARVARD PB $19.95

Charles **Taylor** & James **Tully**, editors

Philosophy in an Age of Pluralism: The Philosophy of Charles Taylor in Question

0-521-43742-3 CAMBRIDGE PB $18.95

Roberto **Unger**

Law in Modern Society: Toward a Criticism of Social Theory

The development of law and legal theory in the West and the increasing irrelevance of traditional concepts of legality due to social and cultural changes that demand a new integration of law with social theory

0-02-932880-2 FREE PRESS PB $18.95

Bruce **Vermazen** & Merrill B. **Hintikka**, editors

Essays on Davidson: Actions and Events

0-19-824749-4 OXFORD $39.95
0-19-824963-2 OXFORD PB $24.95

Michael **Walzer**

Spheres of Justice: A Defense of Pluralism and Equality

An ambitious, comprehensive study of the relation of social institutions to equality and justice, taking in such questions as citizenship, group membership, work, money, leisure, education, marriage and family, welfare, and religion, comparing a wide range of societies and historical periods

0-465-08189-4 BASIC BOOKS PB $18.50

Rolf **Wiggerhaus**

The Frankfurt School: Its History, Theories, and Political Significance

See also **MARXISM AND THE FRANKFURT SCHOOL** under **SOCIOLOGY AFTER WEBER** under **SOCIOLOGY** in **SOCIAL STUDIES**

TRANSLATED BY MICHAEL ROBERTSON

0-262-73113-4 MIT PB $29.95

Bernard **Williams**

Ethics and the Limits of Philosophy

"To read this book is to be taken through one of the most sophisticated discussions available of such questions by an engaging, skeptical, often wryly witty and extraordinarily subtle professional"—*NY Times Book Review*

0-674-26857-1 HARVARD $32.00
0-674-26858-X HARVARD PB $12.95

Making Sense of Humanity and Other Philosophical Papers 1982-1993

0-521-47279-2 CAMBRIDGE $49.95
0-521-47868-5 CAMBRIDGE PB $17.95

Morality: An Introduction to Ethics

Williams's agile and often witty prose rescues the subject from abstraction and aridity

0-521-45729-7 CAMBRIDGE PB $7.95

Shame and Necessity

A discussion of ethical problems as reflected in classical Greek literature

See also **OTHER TOPICS IN ANCIENT PHILOSOPHY**

0-520-08046-7 CALIFORNIA $30.00
0-520-08830-1 CALIFORNIA PB $15.00

Richard **Wollheim**

Art and Its Objects

An acclaimed work examining the representational properties of art from the point of view of aesthetics

See also **PHILOSOPHY AND ART** under **ART SINCE 1945** in **ART**
See also **THEORY AND CRITICISM** under **ART HISTORY: GENERAL STUDIES** in **ART**

0-521-43778-4 CAMBRIDGE PB $11.95

The Mind and Its Depths

0-674-57612-8 HARVARD PB $14.95

Painting as an Art

An important contribution to our understanding of how pictures are made; well illustrated

See also **THEORY AND CRITICISM** under **ART HISTORY: GENERAL STUDIES** in **ART**

0-691-09964-2 PRINCETON $85.00
0-691-01892-8 PRINCETON PB $35.00

Readings in Philosophy: Anthologies on Special Topics

Giovanna **Borradori**

The American Philosopher: Conversations with Quine, Davidson, Putnam, Nozick, Danto, Rorty, Cavell, MacIntyre, and Kuhn

Borradori is especially interested in the way American philosophy has diverged from, and in some cases found its way back to, Continental European concerns. Her incisive, well-informed questioning vividly evokes the differing approaches and personalities of these philosophers

0-226-06648-7 CHICAGO PB $13.95

Monroe C. **Beardsley**, editor

The European Philosophers from Descartes to Nietzsche

See also **INTRODUCTIONS TO PHILOSOPHY**

0-679-60024-8 MODERN LIBRARY $20.00

Edwin A. **Burtt**, editor

The English Philosophers from Bacon to Mill

0-394-60411-3 RANDOM HOUSE $21.00

George **Dickie** & others

Aesthetics: A Critical Anthology

0-312-00309-9 ST. MARTIN'S $55.98

Philippa **Foot**, editor

Theories of Ethics

0-19-875005-6 OXFORD PB $18.95

J.C. **Glover**, editor

The Philosophy of Mind

0-19-875038-2 OXFORD PB $15.95

Ian **Hacking**

Scientific Revolutions

0-19-875051-X OXFORD PB $15.95

Rom **Harre**

The Philosophies of Science: An Introductory Survey

0-19-289201-0 OXFORD PB $18.95

Albert **Hofstadter** & Richard **Kuhns**, editors

Philosophies of Art and Beauty: Selected Readings in Aesthetics from Plato to Heidegger

0-226-34812-1 CHICAGO PB $19.95

Kenneth G. **Lucey**, editor

On Knowing and the Known: Introductory Readings in Epistemology

1-57392-050-9 PROMETHEUS PB $22.95

Eric **Matthews**

Twentieth-Century French Philosophy

An assessment of key figures such as Bergson, Sartre, Marcel, Merleau-Ponty, Foucault, Derrida, and recent French feminists

0-19-289248-7 OXFORD PB $13.95

Martha C. **Nussbaum**

For Love of Country: Debating the Limits of Patriotism

An argument against patriotism as a parochial ideal, and for a view of ourselves as "citizens of the world." An astonishing range of writers from Robert Pinsky to Gertrude Himmelfarb, Elaine Scarry, Amartya Sen, and Cornel West respond in a series of brilliant essays

See also **IMPORTANT RECENT WORK** under **POLITICAL THOUGHT** in **SOCIAL STUDIES**

EDITED BY JOSHUA COHEN

0-8070-4313-3 BEACON PB $15.00

Hilary **Putnam**

Philosophy of Mathematics: Selected Readings

An anthology of papers

See also **PHILOSOPHY OF MATHEMATICS** under **MATHEMATICS** in **SCIENCE**

0-521-29648-X CAMBRIDGE PB $34.95

Anthony **Quinton**, editor

Political Philosophy

0-19-875002-1 OXFORD PB $14.95

Walter **Sinnott-Armstrong** & Mark **Timmons**

Moral Knowledge?: New Readings in Moral Epistemology

0-19-508989-8 OXFORD PB $24.00

Gary **Watson**

Free Will

0-19-875054-4 OXFORD PB $16.95

Part 4

Social Studies

Carl Jung

Sigmund Freud

Women: Body & Soul

1792: The Sceptre
"Taught from infancy that beauty is woman's sceptre, the mind shapes itself to the body, and roaming around its gilt cage, seeks only to adorn its prison."
—Mary Wollstonecraft
A Vindication of the Rights of Woman
423

1920: What We Miss
"To cast out and incorporate in a person of the opposite sex all that we miss in ourselves and desire in the universe and detest in humanity is a deep and universal instinct on the part of both men and women."
—Virginia Woolf
Essays
871

1939: Electrification of Texas Hill Country
At the start of F.D.R.'s first term, nine out of ten American farms lacked electricity. Every day, the typical farmer's wife had to haul two buckets of well-water, weighing over 30 pounds each, an average of 258 feet to her house.
434

JOHNSON CITY
HOME OF WORLDS LARGEST
RURAL ELECTRIFICATION
SYSTEM

1962: The Feminine Mystique
"It is time to stop exhorting mothers to 'love' their children more, and face the paradox between the mystique's demand that women devote themselves completely to their homes and their children, and the fact that most of the problems now being treated in child-guidance clinics are solved only when the mothers are helped to develop autonomous interests of their own and no longer need to fill their emotional needs through their children."
—Betty Friedan
422

1973: Roe v. Wade
Establishes that abortion should be a decision between a woman and her physician.
429

1990: The Workplace
Senate hearings on the nomination of Clarence Thomas to the Supreme Court popularize issue of sexual harassment in the workplace.
425

AD 1900

AD 1925

AD 1950

AD 1975

AD 1990

1893: Emma Goldman
"True emancipation begins neither at the polls nor in the courts. It begins in woman's soul. It is necessary that woman realize that her freedom will reach as far as her power to achieve her freedom reaches."
422

1914: The First Brassiere
For centuries female torsos have been laced into rigid whalebone corsets that restrict breathing, digestion, and movement. Now Mary Phelps Jacob (better known as Caresse Crosby) designs the brassiere, which lacks bones and leaves the midriff free.
431

1924: Divorce Eased
Courts begin to allow divorce based on want of affection in a marriage.
425

1942: Rosie the Riveter
Becomes a national symbol as nearly half of all US women work outside the home during the war.
435

1961: Oral Contraception Commercially Available
"I'm closing down your
brooder roost
'Cause now I've got the Pill."
—Loretta Lynn
"Nursery Hill"
435

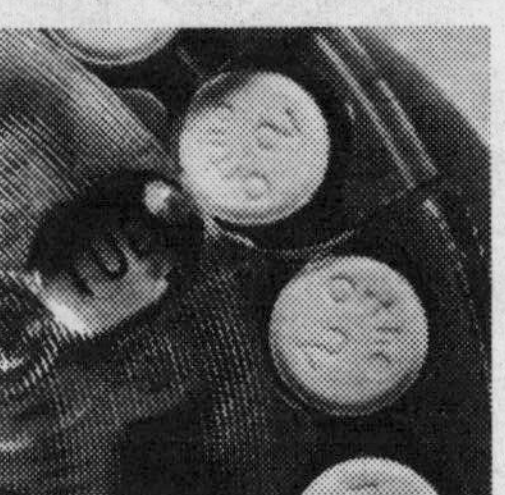

1965: Griswold v. Connecticut
Establishes that prohibiting the sale of birth control is unconstitutional, stating that "a zone of personal privacy exists in which state and governments may not interfere."
435

1987: Equality

"Equality means physical wholeness, virginity—for the woman, equality requires not ever having been reduced to that object of sensuality in order to be used as a tool of men's desire and satiation in sex."
—Andrea Dworkin
Intercourse
421

1994: Enlightenment
"An enlightened feminism of the 21st Century will embrace all sexuality and will turn away from delusionalism, sanctimony, prudery, and male-bashing."
—Camille Paglia
Vamps and Tramps
744

1 Aleutian Islands
When an Aleut dies, he is gutted, stuffed with dry grass, bundled up, and hung over his bed to dry in the smoky air of the communal longhouse for as long as a month (or longer if the bereaved survivors are particularly reluctant to see him go). The body is removed when it is completely dried out and taken, along with ritual objects and the deceased's favorite possessions, to a dry cave where it is left in the company of other "dry ones."

179

2 Bougainvillea, South Pacific
To become a Mumi, or "big man," among the Siuai you must:
1. Cut down on meat and coconuts
2. Work very hard
3. Build a longhouse
4. Give bigger and bigger parties in which ever greater quantities of coconut pies and sago almond puddings are served while you alone eat stale cakes and gristle
5. Line the longhouse with the skulls of your enemies
6. Gain renown as a killer of men and pigs.

455

3 Eleusis
"Tell those who assert the truth and certainty of sense objects to return to the most elementary school of wisdom, the Eleusinian mysteries of Ceres and of Bacchus, for they have still to learn the secret meaning of eating bread and drinking wine. Even the animals are not shut out from this wisdom. On the contrary, they show themselves to be most profoundly initiated into it; for they do not just stand idly in front of sensuous things as if these possessed intrinsic being, but, despairing of their reality, and completely assured of their nothingness, fall to without ceremony and eat them up. And all Nature, like the animals, celebrates these open Mysteries which teach the truth about sensuous things." —G.W.F. Hegel
The Phenomenology of Mind

396

4 Urban America
Young men in the big cities throw their tennis shoes over a telephone wire when they have lost their virginity.

292

5 Guatemala
A string is drawn through the tongue of a crouching woman, piercing the membrane that divides heaven from earth. The woman stares into the mouth of the Vision Serpent, while her blood drips onto a sheet of paper spread before her; the pattern it describes is taken to be the "voice of the gods." Bloodletting has been called the mortar of Mayan life, a ritual by which they maintain their connection to the fundamental forces of creation.

457

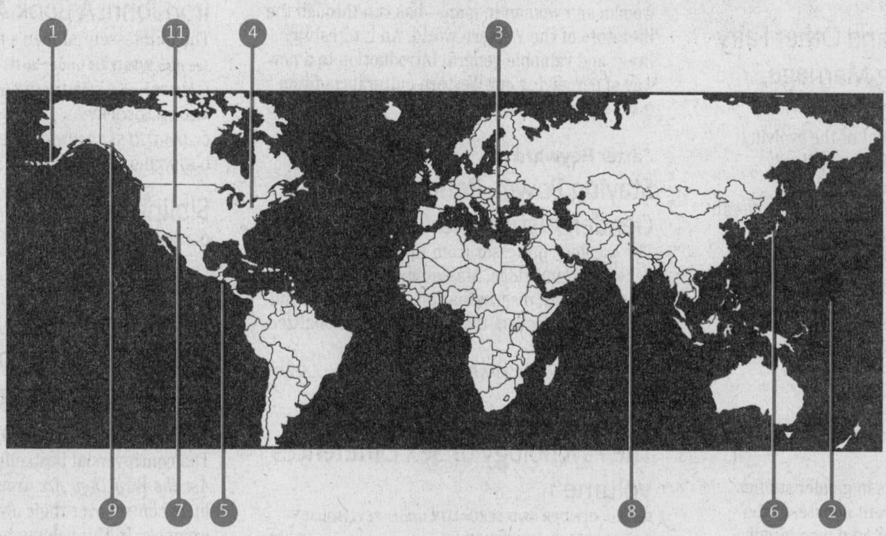

6 Heian (AD 950–1050) Japan
"On the last night of the year officials from the Ministry of Central Affairs join the Masters of Yin-Yang in a Service of Expulsion, during which special spells are recited. A Devil Chaser, who is selected from among the Imperial Attendants, dons a golden mask and a red skirt. Accompanied by twenty assistants, he makes his way through the Palace buildings and courtyards, twanging his bowstring, shooting arrows into the air, and striking his shield with a spear in order to expel all the devils and evil spirits before the beginning of the New Year's celebrations."
—Ivan Morris
World of the Shining Prince

336

7 New Mexico
Hopi childen carry their placentas in a bag around their necks until they are nine, at which age they eat them. Thus, symbolically, each consumes his own birth, assuming responsibility for it, and so is considered of age.

178

8 Tibet
When a lama dies, his soul immediately migrates to the body of a new child, whose location is gradually disclosed to the high priest through clues received in dreams: a glimpse of blue paint on a roof, or a shrub by a door, but never a sight of the child himself. Eventually, a team of monks is dispatched to search out the new lama in the dream place, which in some recent cases has proved as far afield as Spain and Seattle.

338

9 Tlingit
A Shaman's first dream: "Komwidapokuwia (Old Woman Medicine Power) took my soul to a house which looked like a white cloud in the west over the ocean. Then she took me to a domed house in the northeast of the morning star where she lives now. It was the rainbow. Inside there were four crescent moons, horns up. Rays like those of the sun came out of the house. In a little while it rained. Komwidapokuwia's hair hung to her knees and shone like stars. She gave me a song to cure all illness: 'The world has turned different, has turned white. The world has turned white and is moving around.'"
—Geza Roheim
The Gates of the Dream

469

10 Total Institutions
"The process of entrance brings loss and mortification. Staff employ what are called admission procedures, such as taking a life history, photographing, weighing, fingerprinting, assigning numbers, searching, listing personal possessions for storage, undressing, bathing, disinfecting, haircutting, issuing institutional clothing, instructing as to rules, and assigning to quarters.

"Admission procedures might better be called 'programming': in thus being squared away the new arrival allows himself to be shaped into an object that can be fed into the administrative machinery of the establishment, to be worked on smoothly by routine operations."
— Erving Goffman
Asylums

485

11 Colorado
On initiation night, the pledges of the University of Colorado's Chi Psi fraternity are blindfolded, spun around to organ music, and commanded to stiffen. They are then lifted into the air and lowered into a coffin, where their thumbs and forefingers are inserted into the eye-sockets of a skull. The coffin is nailed shut and covered with dirt. When the pledges are exhumed, they are reborn as brothers.

486

Gender Studies

Anne **Allison**

Nightwork: Sexuality, Pleasure, and Corporate Masculinity in a Tokyo Hostess Club

0-226-01485-1 CHICAGO $37.00
0-226-01487-8 CHICAGO PB $14.95

Asa **Baber**

Naked at Gender Gap

A guide to correct male behavior toward women in the '90s. "The picture Baber paints is funny, enraging and/or accurate, depending on where one stands"—*Publishers Weekly*

1-55972-114-6 BIRCH LANE $18.95

Regina **Barreca**

Perfect Husbands and Other Fairy Tales: Demystifying Marriage, Men, and Romance

A witty and engaging account of the evolving roles of husbands and wives in a radically changed world. As provocative as Colette Dowling's *The Cinderella Complex* and Deborah Tannen's *You Just Don't Understand*

See also **MARRIAGE** under **COURTSHIP, LOVE, SEX, AND MARRIAGE** in **LIFESTYLES AND PRACTICAL ADVICE**

0-517-59538-9 HARMONY $20.00

Sandra Lipsitz **Bem**

The Lenses of Gender: Transforming the Debate on Sexual Inequality

One of the leading scholars in gender studies brilliantly argues that current debate on the differences between women and men largely misses the point, and being indeed does so to the disadvantage of women. "Ultimately we need a psychological revolution that would have us all begin to view the biological fact of being male or female in much the same way as we now view the biological fact of being human, safely tucked away in the backs of our minds and left to its own devices"—Sandra Bem

0-300-05676-1 YALE $32.50
0-300-06163-3 YALE PB $15.00

Phyllis **Burke**

Gender Shock: Exploding the Myths of Male and Female

Burke believes that gender is a social construct, not a natural characteristic. She convincingly argues that the diagnostic category of Gender Identity Disorder (GID) should be abolished as well as the debilitating treatment for the "disorder"

0-385-47717-1 ANCHOR $23.95

Leslie **Feinberg**

Transgender Warriors: A History of Resistance from Joan of Arc to RuPaul

One of our most prominent gender-rights activists—winner of the ALA Gay and Lesbian Literature Award and the Lambda Literature Award—offers her personal journey through history, showing persuasively that crossing the cultural boundaries of gender is not new, but has a rich history stretching from Joan of Arc to Stonewall. Illustrated with historical images and contemporary photographs, *Transgender Warriors* is an eye-opening testament to a rebellious tradition

0-8070-7940-5 BEACON $27.50

Peter G. **Filene**

Him-Her-Self: Sex Roles in Modern America

0-8018-2893-7 JOHNS HOPKINS $38.00
0-8018-2895-3 JOHNS HOPKINS PB $13.95

Carolyn **Heilbrun**

Toward a Recognition of Androgyny

An eye-opening study of the ways in which the concept of androgyny—the realization of man in woman and woman in man—has run through the literature of the Western world. An interesting, lively, and valuable general introduction to a new way of perceiving our Western cultural tradition

0-393-31062-0 NORTON PB $9.95

Carter **Heyward**

Staying Power: Reflections on Gender, Justice and Compassion

The theology professor from Episcopal Divinity School in Cambridge, Massachusetts reflects on the patriarchy, discrimination, homophobia, and cultural imperialism that haunt institutionalized faith

0-8298-1027-7 PILGRIM PB $12.95

Eleanor E. **Maccoby** & Carol N. **Jacklin**

The Psychology of Sex Differences

Volume 1

See also **GENDER AND SEXUALITY** under **PSYCHOLOGY**

0-8047-0974-2 STANFORD PB $17.95

Volume 2

0-8147-4186-X NYU $150.00

Volume 3

0-8147-4187-8 NYU $143.75

Volume 4

0-8147-4188-6 NYU $143.75

Anne W. **Schaef**

Women's Reality: An Emerging Female System in the White Male Society

Explores the psychosocial differences between men and women

See also **FEMINIST THEORY** under **WOMEN'S STUDIES**

0-06-250770-2 HARPERCOLLINS PB $12.00

Eve Kosofsky **Sedgwick**

Tendencies

0-8223-1408-8 DUKE $44.95
0-8223-1421-5 DUKE PB $16.95

Deborah **Tannen**, editor

Gender and Conversational Interaction

The bestselling author's academic work

0-19-508194-3 OXFORD PB $18.95

Deborah **Tannen**

Talking from 9 to 5: How Women's and Men's Conversational Styles Affect Who Gets Heard, Who Gets Credit, and What Gets Done at Work

A fascinating look at the subtleties of speech and how they may affect your job as well as your relationships

See also **JOB SUCCESS** under **CAREERS** in **BUSINESS AND REFERENCE**

0-380-71783-2 AVON PB $12.50

Men's Studies

Robert **Bly**

Iron John: A Book About Men

The quintessential men's movement manual

See also **WESTERN** under **20TH-CENTURY SPIRITUAL LEADERS** under **SPIRITUALITY** in **RELIGION, SPIRITUALITY, AND PHILOSOPHY**

0-2014-1720-5 ADDISON WESLEY $19.95
0-679-73119-9 VINTAGE PB $11.00

Sibling Society

0-2014-0646-2 ADDISON WESLEY $25.00

Warren **Farrell**

The Myth of Male Power: Why Men Are the Disposable Sex—Fated for War, Programmed for Work, Divorced from Emotion

The controversial bestselling author of *Why Men Are the Way They Are* argues that men have little control over their own lives, much less women's. In this volume he takes on everything from sexual harassment, date rape, fathers' rights, and law. "I have never read a book that has stimulated me as much. Startling, original, powerful"—Nathaniel Branden, *The Psychology of Self-Esteem*

0-425-15523-4 BERKLEY $6.99

Ray **Gonzales**, editor

Muy Macho: Latino Men Confront Their Manhood

Male American writers of Latino descent such as Dagoberto Gilb, Rudolfo Anaya, Luis Rodriquez contribute essays to combat the stereotypes that plague Latino males

0-385-47861-5 ANCHOR $14.95

Christopher **Harding**, editor

Wingspan: Inside the Men's Movement

0-312-07886-2 LITUR PB $9.95

Sam **Keen**

Fire in the Belly: On Being a Man

"Brings to the men's movements a new kind of practical wisdom that should help both men and women"—John Bradshaw, *Homecoming*

0-553-35137-0 BANTAM PB $13.95

Arthur **Kroker** & Marilouise **Kroker**

The Hysterical Male: New Feminist Theory

Feminism in the '90s cannot exclude the male psyche, which is analyzed through the lens of psychoanalysis, art, theory, and culture

0-920393-69-1 ST. MARTIN'S PB $14.95

Michael **Schwalbe**

Unlocking the Iron Cage: The Men's Movement, Gender Politics, and American Culture

Associate professor of sociology analyzes those who participate in the men's movement and why. He theorizes on its good aspects as well as its failings

0-19-509229-5 OXFORD $27.50

John **Stoltenberg**

The End of Manhood: A Book for Men of Conscience

Radical pro-feminist and author of *Refusing to Be a Man,* Stoltenberg presents a new option for men who wish to become better than they are. Discussed in depth are such issues as male anxiety, peer pressure, and personal identity, while the myths of the new trend toward the cult of masculinity are dispelled by reason and logic. More than an examination of ideas, Stoltenberg provides a blueprint for putting conscience, passion, and a new integrated selfhood into everyday practice

0-452-27304-8 PLUME PB $10.95

Women's Studies

What are the sources and consequences of the differences between men and women? What are the implications of viewing gender as a social construct rather than as a biological mandate? How has the history of women differed from that of men? How are differences among women determined by race, class, and ethnicity? How do women view God and dogma? How have women contributed to the arts? Below is a compilation that reflects a diverse and rapidly growing body of literature addressing the central questions of women's studies.

Feminist Theory

Carol **Adams**

The Sexual Politics of Meat: A Feminist-Vegetarian Critical Theory

Understanding the reasons why people choose to be vegetarians will aid in understanding feminist critical theory. From a political and animal-rights activist

0-8264-0513-4 CONTINUUM PB $15.95

Judith **Butler**

Gender Trouble: Feminism and the Subversion of Identity

0-415-90043-3 ROUTLEDGE PB $16.95

Carol J. **Adams** & Josephine **Donovan**, editors

Animals & Women: Feminist Theoretical Explorations

Multidisciplinary essays explore the connections between animal defense and feminism. Discusses pornography, lab animals, wife beating, hunting, and factory farming. The premise is how we comprehend abuse of other species is directly linked to women's rights

0-8223-1667-6 DUKE PB $17.95

Alison **Blunt** & Gillian **Rose**, editors

Writing Women and Space: Colonial and Postcolonial Geographies

The question of domain is the focus in this collection of essays in which the authors explore the concept of physical space, its relationship to definition—both self and other—and how it has changed through history

0-89862-498-3 GUILFORD PB $17.95

Susan **Brownmiller**

Femininity

A historical and personal look at the accoutrements of femininity from 16th-century corsets to 20th-century cosmetics

0-449-90142-4 FAWCETT PB $11.00

Jill Ker **Conway** & Susan C. **Bourque**, editors

The Politics of Women's Education: Perspectives from Asia, Africa, and Latin America

In this fascinating volume, Third World women and men discuss the changing role of women's education, seen in many cases as a key to better lives of a struggle that has been waged for more than 25 years, the participants speak now about their triumphs and failures, and the work ahead. These genuine voices of the Third World are compelling reading that will challenge assumptions and raise new questions about the future

0-472-08328-7 MICHIGAN PB $16.95

Andrea **Dworkin**

Intercourse

A controversial work on how intercourse enslaves women

0-02-907970-5 FREE PRESS $27.95
0-02-907971-3 FREE PRESS PB $13.95

Scilla **Elworthy**

Power and Sex: A Book About Women

Male domination of society, says Elworthy, a UNESCO consultant and NATO researcher, has made the world a place where violence is endemic and the environment is in danger. Her provocative book looks at this abuse of power throughout the century, and offers a corrective: the Eastern archetype wherein self-knowledge, sexuality, and spiritual development lead to power without bullying, and to enhancing communication, defusing conflicts, and furthering justice

1-85230-788-9 ELEMENT $24.95

Simone **de Beauvoir**

The Second Sex

One of the most significant minds of the 20th century, de Beauvoir began this book to find out who and what she was as a woman, and ended up producing a seminal masterpiece of feminist thought.

See also **ESSAYS: PERSONAL, LITERARY, PHILOSOPHICAL** under **MODERN FRENCH LITERATURE** in **LITERATURE OF EUROPE, AFRICA, AND ASIA**

0-679-42016-9 KNOPF $20.00
0-679-72451-6 VINTAGE PB $14.00

Simone de Beauvoir

Barbara **Findlen**

Listen Up: Voices from the Next Feminist Generation

Findlen, the executive editor of *Ms.* magazine, collects 28 explorations by "third wave" feminists

1-87806-761-3 SEAL PB $12.95

Elizabeth **Fox-Genovese**

Feminism Without Illusions: A Critique of Individualism

A critical view of contemporary feminism from a distinguished historian and neo-conservative

0-8078-4372-5 NORTH CAROLINA PB $15.95

Marilyn **French**

Beyond Power: On Women, Men and Morals

"French does believe that, by and large, men and women live by different moralities, and that a woman's morality is better. Her book is…a plea for the world to adopt a feminine morality"—*Newsday*

0-345-33405-1 BALLANTINE PB $14.00

Nancy **Friday**

The Power of Beauty

Friday, bestselling author of *My Secret Garden* and *My Mother/My Self*, looks at the uses and abuses of beauty and appearance in the past and into the future. From the diaphragm to the WonderBra, she examines the history of women's views of themselves and looks ahead to a future in which we—men and women—might be freed from the twin traps of beauty and power

0-06-017140-5 HARPERCOLLINS $27.50

Betty **Friedan**
The Feminine Mystique
This 1963 book had a wide impact and continues to be read and relished
0-440-32497-1 DELL PB $6.99

Emma **Goldman**
The Traffic in Women & Other Essays on Feminism
Three key 1917 essays from the great anarchist
EDITED BY ALIX KATES SHULMAN
0-87810-001-6 TIMES CHANGE PB $4.25

Judy **Grahn**
Blood, Bread, and Roses: How Menstruation Created the World
"Using the lens of scholarship and the wit of personal experience, she restores the destroyed mythos of women's blood life…"
—Clarissa Pinkola Estes
0-8070-7505-1 BEACON PB $14.00

Susan **Griffin**
The Eros of Everyday Life: Essays on Ecology, Gender, and Society
Griffin, nominated both for a Pulitzer Prize and a National Book Critics Circle award, offers a collection of essays on the nature of women and their role in Western culture
0-385-47390-7 DOUBLEDAY $24.95
0-385-47399-0 ANCHOR PB $14.00

Sara **Halprin**
"Look at My Ugly Face!": Myths and Musings on Beauty and Other Perilous Obsessions with Women's Appearance
Halprin shows how women can enter a complex and creative interplay between roles of beauty and ugliness, each imbued with its own magical powers
0-14-023492-6 PENGUIN PB $12.95

Carolyn G. **Heilbrun**
Reinventing Womanhood
"Ranks with de Beauvoir's *The Second Sex* as a landmark work"—Claudia Dreifus
See also **FEMINIST CRITICISM** under **LITERARY THEORY** in **LITERATURE OF EUROPE, AFRICA, AND ASIA**
0-393-31076-0 NORTON PB $9.95

In the past those women who have made their way successfully into the male-dominated worlds of business, the arts, or the professions have done so as honorary men, neither admiring nor bonding with other women, offering no encouragement to those who might come after them, preserving the socially required "feminity," but sacrificing their womanhood.
REINVENTING WOMANHOOD
0-393-00997-1 NORTON PB $8.95

Patricia **Ireland**
What Women Want
This book, in which the president of NOW discusses her evolution from shy stewardess to national leader, is an "eminently readable autobiography [that will] inspire and enlighten activists of all stripes"—*Publishers Weekly*
0-525-93857-5 DUTTON $23.95

Maggie **Humm**, editor
Modern Feminisms: Literary, Political, Cultural
A comprehensive interdisciplinary historical feminist reader, with more than 70 selections from the works of Virginia Woolf, Simone de Beauvoir, Kate Millet, Adrienne Rich, and others. Includes a chronology of 20th-century women's politics and writing, entries on individual writers, a list for further reading, and a glossary of terms. "This book of classic essays will itself become a classic"
—Cheris Kramarae, *The Feminist Dictionary*
0-231-08072-7 COLUMBIA $45.00
0-231-08073-5 COLUMBIA PB $17.00

Luce **Irigaray**
Speculum of the Other Woman
Posits that masculine ideology is implicit in psychoanalytic theory and in Western discourse in general
See also **FEMINIST CRITICISM** under **LITERARY THEORY** in **LITERATURE OF EUROPE, AFRICA, AND ASIA**
TRANSLATED BY GILLIAN C. GILL
0-8014-9330-7 CORNELL PB $16.95

This Sex Which Is Not One
Reconsiders the question of female sexuality in a variety of contexts
TRANSLATED BY CATHERINE PORTER & CAROLYN BURKE
0-8014-1546-2 CORNELL $39.95
0-8014-9331-5 CORNELL PB $14.95

Ellen Zetzel **Lambert**
The Face of Love: Feminism and the Beauty Question
Through classics and personal experience the author tries to understand the "beauty myth." "In a book at once scholarly and deeply personal, Lambert aims to make beauty safe for feminists"—*Publishers Weekly*
0-8070-6500-5 BEACON $24.00

Eleanor B. **Leacock**
Myths of Male Dominance: Collected Articles
0-85345-538-4 MONTHLY REVIEW $13.00

Gerda **Lerner**
The Creation of Feminist Consciousness: From the Middle Ages to Eighteen-Seventy
"A compelling argument constructed by a distinguished and well-respected historian of women"—Judith M. Bennett, University of North Carolina, Chapel Hill
See also **WOMEN AND GENDER STUDIES** under **PERSPECTIVES IN HISTORY** under **THE VARIETIES OF CIVILIZATION** in **WORLD HISTORY AND CURRENT AFFAIRS**
0-19-506604-9 OXFORD $30.00
0-19-509060-8 OXFORD PB $11.95

Nan Bauer **Maglin**
"Bad Girls"/"Good Girls": Women, Sex, and Power in the Nineties
Twenty-four essays on feminism and the media that "boldly challenge the faux-fem superstars"—*Ms.*
0-8135-2250-1 RUTGERS $50.00
0-8135-2251-X RUTGERS PB $17.95

Audre **Lorde**
Sister Outsider
Collection of her essays on women, racism, and self-acceptance
0-89594-141-4 CROSSING PB $12.95

Elaine **Marks** & Isabelle **De Courtivron**, editors
New French Feminism: An Anthology
0-8052-0681-7 SCHOCKEN PB $14.00

John Stuart **Mill**
The Subjection of Women
First published in 1869, Mill's tract attacks the inequality manifested in marriage contracts, property rights, and women's responsibilities for family and marriage
0-87975-335-8 PROMETHEUS PB $4.95

Toril **Moi**
French Feminist Thought: A Reader
Writings by Julia Kristeva, Simone de Beauvoir, Anne Tristan, and others
0-631-14973-2 BLACKWELL PB $22.95

Robin **Morgan**
The Word of a Woman: Feminist Dispatches, 1968-1992
A collection from the editor of *Ms.* features her now-classic essays of feminist theory written in the late '60s and brought up to date by new introductory notes. Includes Morgan's more recent interviews with women of the Palestinian Intifada and women in the Philippines
0-393-03427-5 NORTON $19.95

Mariah Burton **Nelson**
The Stronger Women Get, the More Men Love Football: Sexism and the American Culture of Sports
A former player on the Women's Pro Basketball League argues that male hegemony in sports makes men fear strong women, which in turn causes prejudice and violence against them
0-15-181393-0 HARCOURT BRACE $22.95
0-380-72527-4 AVON PB $11.00

Barbara **Omolade**
The Rising Song of African American Women
Issues, both past and present, that have affected the black American female such as rape of slaves, single motherhood, academia, and other rarely discussed topics
0-415-90761-6 ROUTLEDGE PB $17.95

Daphne **Patai** & Noretta **Koertge**
Professing Feminism: Cautionary Tales from Inside the Strange World of Women's Studies
Doctrinaire politics and "ideological policing" in the classroom often preclude alterniative points of view, a dangerous situation, the authors conclude. "This unsparing account of the troubles that beset women's studies programs should incite vociferous debate"—*Publishers Weekly*
0-465-09821-5 BASIC $24.00

Janice G. **Raymond**

A Passion for Friends: Toward a Philosophy of Female Affection

0-8070-6739-3 FS&G PB $15.00

Evelyn **Reed**

Woman's Evolution: From Matriarchal Clan to Patriarchal Family

Reed hypothesizes that women played the leading role in prehistoric societies

0-87348-422-3 PATHFINDER PB $22.95

Anne W. **Schaef**

Women's Reality: An Emerging Female System in the White Male Society

Explores the psychosocial differences between men and women

See also **GENDER STUDIES**

0-06-250770-2 HARPERCOLLINS PB $12.00

Dale **Spender**

Nattering on the Net: Women, Power, and Cyberspace

An "examination of the state of literature, reading, and writers in the cyberage is spiked with a rallying cry for virtual sisterhood"—*Ms.*

1-87555-909-4 SPINIFEX PB $19.95

Gloria **Steinem**

Moving Beyond Words

One of our most influential feminists gives us an update of the movement and a synthesis of her most profound thoughts. Includes such classic essays as "Sex, Lies, and Advertising" and "The Trouble with Rich Women," as well as new writings never before published. An essential follow-up to Steinem's recent bestseller *Revolution from Within*

0-671-64972-8 SIMON & SCHUSTER $23.00

Outrageous Acts and Everyday Rebellions

A collection of writings, from notes on being a Playboy Bunny to profiles of women to satires like "If Men Could Menstruate"

0-8050-4202-4 HOLT PB $12.95

Susan **Ware**

Still Missing: Amelia Earhart and the Search for Modern Feminism

Explains the enduring fascination of Amelia Earhart in the context of the booming, optimistic '20s that spawned her. One of our first great feminist media stars fascinatingly revealed

0-393-03551-4 NORTON $22.00

Naomi **Wolf**

The Beauty Myth: How Images of Beauty Are Used Against Women

"A smart, angry, insightful book, and a clarion call to freedom. Every woman should read it" —Gloria Steinem

0-385-42397-7 ANCHOR PB $12.95

Georgia **Witkin**

The Truth About Women: Exposing the Devastating Myths that Hold Women Back

0-670-85060-8 VIKING $21.95

Mary **Wollstonecraft**

A Vindication of the Rights of Woman

A founding statement of feminism, first published in 1792, applying the egalitarian principles of the times to women

See also **CLASSICS** under **POLITICAL THOUGHT**

EDITED BY MIRIAM KRAMNICK

0-14-043382-1 PENGUIN PB $9.95

0-87975-525-3 PROMETHEUS PB $6.95

Theology

Carol P. **Christ** & Judith **Plaskow**

Womanspirit Rising: A Feminist Reader in Religion

An anthology of feminist religious scholarship

See also **WOMEN AND RELIGION** under **WORLD RELIGION** in **RELIGION, SPIRITUALITY, AND PHILOSOPHY**

0-06-061385-8 HARPERCOLLINS PB $12.00

Mary **Daly**

Beyond God the Father: Toward a Philosophy of Women's Liberation

"What other feminists have revealed by analyzing patriarchal society's political, economic, social and sexual institutions, Daly does for the spiritual institution…Not for the timid, this brilliant book calls for nothing short of the overthrow of patriarchy"—*Village Voice*

0-8070-1503-2 FS&G PB $15.00

Elisabeth Schussler **Fiorenza**

But She Said: Feminist Practices of Biblical Interpretation

Fiorenza, professor of Divinity at Harvard and author of the acclaimed *Bread Not Stone,* argues for a critical reinterpretation of biblical texts in order to establish a feminist basis for their reading. An important contribution to biblical studies

0-8070-1214-9 BEACON PB $24.00

Susan **Juster**

Disorderly Women: Sexual Politics and Evangelicalism in Revolutionary New England

See also **COLONIAL AMERICA** under **AMERICAN HISTORY**

0-8014-2732-0 CORNELL $32.95

0-8014-8388-3 CORNELL PB $14.95

Susan Hill **Lindley**

"You Have Stept Out of Your Place": A History of Women and Religion in America

0-664-22081-9 KNOX $35.00

Sara **Maitland**

A Big Enough God

As a Christian and a feminist, Maitland defines faith as a radical act, theology as the art of telling —and listening to —stories about the divine, and God as someone beyond image and gender

See also **WOMEN'S SPIRITUALITY** under **SPIRITUALITY** in **RELIGION, SPIRITUALITY, AND PHILOSOPHY**

0-8050-4183-4 HOLT $22.50

Carmel **McEnroy**

Guests in Their Own House: The Women of Vatican II

McEnroy is a sister of Mercy and theology professor who was fired from St. Meinrad Seminary in Indiana for her views on female ordination

0-8245-1547-1 CROSSROAD PB $15.95

Rosemary Radford **Ruether**

Sexism and God-Talk: Toward a Feminist Theology

This groundbreaking work of feminist theology is now reissued with a new introduction in a tenth-anniversary edition. "By the time Ruether finishes, systematic theology has undergone a radical critique from which it emerges transformed"—*NY Times Book Review.* "An impassioned plea for humane life on this planet"—*Philadelphia Inquirer*

0-8070-1205-X BEACON PB $15.00

Womanguides: Readings Toward a Feminist Theology

"This integrative work…helps uncover a female modeling of wisdom that has been buried under centuries of male-interpreted doctrine. The foremothers are all here, and their stories are allowed to shine"—*Utne Reader*

See also **WOMEN** under **GENERAL TOPICS** under **CHRISTIANITY** in **RELIGION, SPIRITUALITY, AND PHILOSOPHY**

0-8070-1235-1 BEACON PB $15.00

Letty M. **Russell** & Shannon **Clarkson**, editors

Dictionary of Feminist Theologies

Considered a major publishing event, this dictionary is the result of a four-year effort in which 180 authors and advisers participated. Although scholarly and in-depth, it will appeal to a wide audience of laypeople. It is a "volume not only destined to be the standard scholarly reference work in its area but also likely to become a touchstone text for students of religion, women's studies and American culture"—*Publishers Weekly*

0-664-22058-4 KNOX $39.00

Margaret **Starbird**

The Woman with the Alabaster Jar: Mary Magdalen and the Holy Grail

Though she set out to refute the suggestion that Jesus was actually married to Mary Magdalen, the author's research led her to new and compelling evidence not only for the existence of such a matrimony, but for a hidden body of believers who for centuries were forced underground. "An exciting narrative probing regions of thought long neglected. Magdalen, the Great Mary, emerges with new power" —John Shelby Spong, *Born of a Woman*

1-87918-103-7 BEAR PB $16.95

Elizabeth Cady **Stanton**

The Woman's Bible

Written in 1895, it is a series of feminist commentaries on the Scriptures by one of America's most thought-provoking radicals

1-55553-162-8 NORTHEASTERN PB $15.95

Nancy **Wilson**

Our Tribe: Queer Folks, God, Jesus, and the Bible

This ribald and funny manifesto from the radical ministry of the Reverend Nancy Wilson is, no matter how irreverent, a dead-serious mission to reclaim the Bible for lesbians and gay men. Framing a "queer theology," Rev. Wilson—senior pastor of the Metropolitan Community Church of Los Angeles—offers a path for all Christians, gay, lesbian and straight, into the next century

0-06-069396-7 HARPERCOLLINS PB $15.00

Economics

Barbara R. **Bergmann**

The Economic Emergence of Women

The transformation of women from homemakers to wage earners

See also **DISCRIMINATION, EDUCATION, AND INCOME** under **SPECIAL TOPICS** under **ECONOMICS**

0-465-01797-5 BASIC BOOKS PB $16.00

Margaret **Randall**

The Price We Pay: The Hidden Cost of Women's Relationship to Money

The history of women's economics is woven with personal stories of women and money

0-415-91203-2 ROUTLEDGE $59.95

Ruth **Sidel**

Keeping Women and Children Last: America's War on the Poor

A renowned sociologist revisits the explosive issue of women, children, and poverty ten years after the publication of her landmark work *Women and Children Last*

See also **CRITICAL COMMENTARY ON AMERICAN CULTURE** under **TOPICS IN MODERN SOCIOLOGY** under **SOCIOLOGY**

0-14-024663-0 PENGUIN PB $11.95

Careers and Money

Susan Witting **Albert**

Work of Her Own: How Women Create Success and Fulfillment Off the Traditional Career Track

No longer committed to the exclusive pursuit of success in the male-dominated workplace, and willing to sacrifice prestige, power, and money, the author and 80 other women whom she interviewed have created deeper senses of themselves through careers off the beaten path. An indispensable guide to other disillusioned women

0-87477-709-7 TARCHER PB $19.95

Nancy H. **Bancroft**

The Feminine Quest for Success: How to Prosper in Business and Be True to Yourself

Details five "Success Strategies" for professional and personal success

1-88105-262-1 BERRETT-KOEHLER $22.95

Judith **Briles**

Gender Traps: Confronting Confrontophobia, Toxic Bosses, & Other Landmines at Work

A guide for working women focuses on ten gender traps, or workplace problems that range from prejudice to sabotage

See also **JOB SUCCESS** under **CAREERS** in **BUSINESS AND REFERENCE**

0-07-007895-5 MCGRAW HILL $19.95

Joline **Godfrey**

Our Wildest Dream: Women Entrepreneurs Making Money, Having Fun, Doing Good

In this enlightening book, women (who own over 50 percent of new businesses) from across the country talk about their business successes and strategies. Filled with triumph and hope, they discuss the qualities—often ignored or not appreciated in a large corporation—that assured their success. "I felt affirmed and challenged as I reflect on these stories of business revolutionaries"—Kit Durgin, The Women's Foundation, San Francisco

0-88730-633-0 HARPERCOLLINS PB $12.00

Neal H. **Olshan**

Golden Handcuffs: How Women Can Break Free of Financial Dependence in Their Intimate Relationships

Olshan shows how to break the pattern of behavior and crippling state of mind that financial dependence often engenders. He provides a blueprint for equality in dependent relationships, including setting goals, honestly communicating needs, overcoming depression, and becoming more assertive

See also **MAINTAINING A RELATIONSHIP** under **COURTSHIP, LOVE, SEX, AND MARRIAGE** in **LIFESTYLES AND PRACTICAL ADVICE**

1-55972-202-9 BIRCH LANE $17.95

Karen **Salmansohn**

How to Succeed in Business Without a Penis

0-517-70668-7 HARMONY $21.00

Brett **Silverstein** & Deborah **Perlick**

The Cost of Competence: Gender Ambivalence, Eating Disorders and Depression in Women

Two psychologists study the connection among talent, depression, and eating disorders in women. Their conclusion: cultural prejudices and our ways of raising children lead women to equate thinness with success and femininity with failure

See also **EATING DISORDERS: ANOREXIA AND BULIMIA** under **SPECIFIC HEALTH PROBLEMS** under **HEALTH** in **LIFESTYLES AND PRACTICAL ADVICE**

0-19-506986-2 OXFORD $25.00

Elsa **Walsh**

Divided Lives: The Public and Private Lives of Three Accomplished Women

Walsh studies the lives of TV journalist Meredith Viera, First Lady of West Virginia Rachel Worby, and breast surgeon Alison Estabrook

0-684-80401-8 SIMON & SCHUSTER $23.50

0-385-48447-X ANCHOR PB $14.00

Science/Gender

Science has traditionally viewed itself as "objective," and therefore exempt from questions of gender. Feminist inquiry since the 1980s has challenged this assumption and refuted the idea of a biological basis for women's "inferiority."

Sandra **Harding**

Whose Science? Whose Technology?: Thinking from Women's Lives

"…an exciting contribution to the work on gender, race, and science"—Anne Faustino-Sterling, *Myths of Gender: Biological Theories*

0-8014-9746-9 CORNELL PB $14.95

Sarah Blaffer **Hardy**

The Woman that Never Evolved

New hypotheses on the evolution of women. "Provides the layperson with a fascinating account of the selective pressures that have shaped the behavior of males and females" —*Science*

0-674-95541-2 HARVARD PB $10.95

Evelyn Fox **Keller**

Reflections on Gender and Science

A widely read work that ponders why objectivity has been cast as "male" and subjectivity as "female"

See also **GENDER AND SEXUALITY** under **PSYCHOLOGY**

0-300-03636-1 YALE PB $12.00

Evelyn Fox **Keller** & Helen E. **Longine**

Feminism & Science

Seventeen outstanding articles argue for a feminist perspective on science

0-19-875146-X OXFORD PB $17.95

Margaret W. **Rossiter**

Women Scientists in America: Struggles and Strategies to 1940

"A record of hopes squelched, strategies thwarted, and uncomfortable compromises easily made"—Ruth Schwartz Cowan, *Journal of American History*

0-8018-2509-1 JOHNS HOPKINS PB $15.95

Politics, Law, and Equality

Mary Frances **Berry**

Why ERA Failed: Politics, Women's Rights, and the Amending Process of the Constitution

The noted historian and lawyer examines the systemic problems of politics and the amending process as they relate to the Equal Rights Amendment. "Berry has placed the rise and fall of the ERA into constitutional, political, and ideological contexts"—Blanche Wiesen Cook

0-253-20459-3 INDIANA PB $7.95

Ellen **Brava** & Ellen **Cassedy**

The 9 to 5 Guide to Combating Sexual Harassment

From the National Association of Working Women, this comprehensive volume provides all the information needed to combat sexual harassment

0-471-57576-3 WILEY PB $12.95

Jennifer **Coburn**

Take Back Your Power: A Working Woman's Response to Sexual Harassment

0-910383-13-8 ATRIUM $10.00

Zillah R. **Eisenstein**

The Female Body and the Law

The basis of sexual inequalities with an examination of issues including affirmative action, AIDS, surrogate motherhood, pornography, and abortion

0-520-06956-0 CALIFORNIA PB $15.00

Susan **Faludi**

Backlash: The Undeclared War Against American Women

"Fiery, scintillating…deserves the largest possible readership"—*Booklist.* "Enraging, enlightening, and invigorating, *Backlash* is, most of all, true"—*New York Newsday*

0-385-42507-4 ANCHOR PB $14.00

Joan **Hoff**

Law, Gender and Injustice: A Legal History of U.S. Women

0-8147-3509-6 NYU PB $22.50

Alison M. **Jaggar**

Feminist Politics and Human Nature

Analysis of liberal feminism, traditional Marxism, radical feminism, and socialist feminism

0-8476-7181-X ROWMAN & LITTLEFIELD $52.50
0-8476-7254-9 ROWMAN & LITTLEFIELD PB $18.95

Laura **Liswood**

Women World Leaders: Fifteen Great Politicians Tell Their Stories

Current and former prime ministers and presidents interviewed, including Benazir Bhutto of Pakistan, Margaret Thatcher of Great Britain, and Tansu Ciller of Turkey. Their family backgrounds, youthful political activism, leadership styles, and advice for those who wish to enter politics

0-04-440904-4 HARPERCOLLINS $26.00

Catherine A. **MacKinnon**

Feminism Unmodified: Discourses on Life and Law

Rape, abortion, athletics, sexual harassment, pornography, and other topics, developed from speeches by a noted feminist and legal scholar. "Fundamental to [MacKinnon's] radical feminism is the claim that gender is a system of dominance rather than of difference"
—Alison M. Jaggar, *NY Times*

0-674-29874-8 HARVARD PB $12.95

Sexual Harassment of Working Women: A Case of Sex Discrimination

0-300-02299-9 YALE PB $17.00

Pamela **McCorduck** & Nancy **Ramsey**

The Futures of Women: Scenarios for the Twenty-First Century

Using "scenario planning," the powerful new tool for understanding trends, the authors identify four alternatives for the social future of women: worldwide backlash against their gains; a golden age of equality; the status quo; and across-the-board sexual separatism—professional, political, and social. A fascinating report from two members of the Global Business Network, one the author of *The Fifth Generation*, the other a former senatorial legislative director and coauthor of *Nuclear Decision-Making*

0-201-48978-3 ADDISON-WESLEY $24.00

Robin **Morgan**

The Demon Lover: On the Sexuality of Terrorism

"By taking us to the sexual place where violence begins, *The Demon Lover* gives us a new belief that it can never be justified and is never inevitable"—Gloria Steinem

0-393-02642-6 NORTON $18.95

Pornography

Laura **Kipnis**

Bound and Gagged: Pornography and the Politics of Fantasy in America

Five essays by a "lively and engaging writer who argues, often convincingly, that we would be better off simply thinking of pornography as just another form of science fiction"
—*Publishers Weekly*

See also **THE DEBATE ON PORNOGRAPHY** under **LITERARY THEORY** in **LITERATURE OF EUROPE, AFRICA, AND ASIA**

0-8021-1584-5 GROVE $22.00

Catherine A. **MacKinnon**

Only Words

Pornography, MacKinnon contends, like hate speech and racial harassment, is an act of terror and should be legally treated as such. In the bold, compelling style that has made her one of our most provocative legal critics, she questions the enforcement of the First Amendment when it protects the very inequalities that the 14th Amendment is supposed to end

0-674-63933-2 HARVARD $14.95

Jose **Pierre**, editor

Investigating Sex: Surrealist Discussions, 1928-1932

This bestselling book destroyed forever the idea that Surrealism was a high-water mark in the effort to escape social constraints on sexuality. Leading surrealists are revealed here, in their own words, to have been juvenile, silly, and afraid of women

See also **ESSAYS: PERSONAL, LITERARY, PHILOSOPHICAL** under **MODERN FRENCH LITERATURE** in **LITERATURE OF EUROPE, AFRICA, AND ASIA**

TRANSLATED BY MALCOM IMRIE

0-86091-378-3 NORTON $24.95
0-86091-603-0 NORTON PB $16.95

Lynne **Segal** & Mary **McIntosh**, editors

Sex Exposed: Sexuality and the Pornography Debate

In this intriguing collection, feminists from America and Europe look at pornography as an exploitative medium and at its role in free society. Discussed are such topics as the dangerous alliance between anti-pornography feminists and the fanatical right; the new lesbian and bisexual pornography; censorship in relation to AIDS work; and the female nude in art. Contributors include Elizabeth Cowie, Harriett Gilbert, Robin Gorna, Jane Mills, Lynda Nead, Carol Smart, and others

0-8135-1937-3 RUTGERS $45.00
0-8135-1938-1 RUTGERS PB $14.95

Sallie **Tisdale**

Talk Dirty to Me

A defense of pornography by a pornography user

See also **THE DEBATE ON PORNOGRAPHY** under **LITERARY THEORY** in **LITERATURE OF EUROPE, AFRICA, AND ASIA**

0-385-46854-7 DOUBLEDAY $22.95

Crime

Ann **Jones**

Women Who Kill

Histories and punishments of battered and abused women who kill in self-defense

0-7710-7153-1 MCCLELLAND & STEWART PB $5.99

Renate **Siebert**

Secrets of Life and Death: Women and the Mafia

1-85984-903-2 VERSO $65.00
1-85984-023-X VERSO PB $20.00

The Female Experience

Adolescence

Susan J. **Douglas**

Where the Girls Are: Growing Up Female with the Mass Media

Deconstructs pop culture's mind-bending messages to women over the past four decades

See also **THE IMPACT OF THE MEDIA** under **TOPICS IN AMERICAN STUDIES** in **HISTORY OF THE AMERICAS**

0-8129-2530-0 TIME BOOKS PB $15.00

Madeleine **Blais**

In These Girls, Hope is a Muscle

"A warm, moving and optimistic book…a delight to read"—*Philadelphia Inquirer*

0-446-67210-6 WARNER PB $11.99

Lyn Mikel **Brown** & Carol **Gilligan**

Meeting at the Crossroads: Women's Psychology and Girls' Development

After talking with and listening to 100 adolescent girls, the authors, two noted psychologists, conclude that the passage to womanhood is too often a journey to silence. This book, destined to become a classic of women's studies, offers new insight into women's development, provides women ways to meet younger women at the crossroads, and helps them toward a more rewarding future

See also **CHILD PSYCHOLOGY** under **PSYCHOLOGY**

0-674-56464-2 HARVARD $19.95

0-345-38295-1 BALLANTINE PB $12.50

Our studies of women's psychological development began with listening to women's voices and hearing differences between the voices of women and men. Privileged men often spoke as if they were not living in relation with others—as if they were autonomous or self-governing, free to speak and move as they pleased. Women, in contrast, tended to speak of themselves as living in connection with others and yet described a relational crisis which was inherently paradoxical: a giving up of voice, an abandonment of self, for the sake of becoming a good woman and having relationships.

MEETING AT THE CROSSROADS: WOMEN'S PSYCHOLOGY AND GIRLS' DEVELOPMENT

Elizabeth **Debold** & others

Mother Daughter Revolution: From Betrayal to Power

This remarkable book identifies the roots of the crisis most girls experience in adolescence—that of a loss of self-confidence and a virtual silencing of self— a crisis that often effectively damages girls for life. Tying this in with the self-protective but ultimately self-defeating behavior many mothers unwittingly pass on to their teenage girls, the authors identify ways mothers subvert their daughters' strengths and show how the cycle can be broken. "A vital contribution to the discussion of girls and self-esteem" —Naomi Wolf, *The Beauty Myth*

0-201-63277-2 ADDISON-WESLEY $22.95

Roberta **Israeloff**

Lost & Found: A Woman Revisits Eighth Grade

A contributing editor of *Parents* magazine, the author explores a crucial year of her life that "serves a dual purpose here: it traces the twisting path by which she ultimately found a career as a writer, and it puts a human face on troubling statistics regarding girls' achievement in school"—*Publishers Weekly*

0-684-80081-0 SIMON & SCHUSTER $23.00

Mary **Pipher**

Reviviving Ophelia: Saving the Selves of Adolescent Girls

0-345-39282-5 BALLANTINE PB $12.50

Sue **Lees**

Sugar and Spice: Sexuality and Adolescent Girls

Examines the effects of such defining and limiting concepts as "slut" and "bitch" on girls in adolescence, when masculine and feminine identities are formed

See also **SEXUALITY**

0-14-016874-5 PENGUIN PB $12.95

Kristin **Luker**

Dubious Conceptions: The Politics of Teenage Pregnancy

A fresh analysis of society's prejudice against, in particular, the black teen mom, with the young mothers themselves speaking on their situation

See also **TEENAGE PREGNANCY** under **STAGES OF DEVELOPMENT** under **PARENTING** in **LIFESTYLES AND PRACTICAL ADVICE**

0-674-21702-0 HARVARD $24.95

Peggy **Orenstein**

Schoolgirls: Young Women, Self-Esteem, and the Confidence Gap

An increasing consciousness of how girls are short-changed by our educational system and our media characterizes contemporary child psychology. Girls' self-esteem drops horribly in adolescence; they learn to associate masculinity with opportunity, to concentrate self-image on sexual attractiveness, and to accept diminished expectations in their math and science performance. "Ardent and significant exploration of the adolescent roots of key women's issues"—*Kirkus Reviews*

0-385-42576-7 ANCHOR PB $12.95

Myra **Sadker** & David **Sadker**

Failing at Fairness: How Our Schools Cheat Girls

Gender inequality in the classroom and how to remedy it

0-684-80073-X TOUCHSTONE PB $12.00

Rickie **Solinger**

Wake Up Little Susie

Shocking documentation of the American double standard in the treatment and perception of pregnant teenagers. Solinger shows how white teenagers are allowed a second chance at respectability owing to the high demand for white adopted children, whereas young black women, with unmarketable children, continue to be villified. "[A] revelatory work with repercussions for today"—*Kirkus Reviews*

0-415-90448-X ROUTLEDGE $35.00

0-415-90894-9 ROUTLEDGE PB $16.95

Jill McLean **Taylor** & others

Between Voice and Silence: Women and Girls, Race and Relationships

A report on how and why girls at adolescence undergo such a profound and debilitating change in self-esteem. Here 26 girls from grades eight and nine of varying classes and races are considered

0-674-06879-3 HARVARD $22.00

Aging

See also AGING in HEALTH

Terri **Apter**

Secret Paths: Women in the New Midlife

Apter's study contrasts midlife for men—often a last effort at retaining a prolonged youth—to that of women

0-393-03766-5 NORTON $25.00

0-393-31500-2 NORTON PB $15.00

Caroline **Bird**

Lives of Our Own: Secrets of Salty Old Women

Bird's study of women 55 and older finds a surprising, and welcome, commonality: they enjoy life

0-395-65234-0 HOUGHTON MIFFLIN $22.95

Elizabeth **Davis** & Carol **Leonard**

The Women's Wheel of Life: Thirteen Archetypes of Woman at Her Fullest Power

The Matriarch, or the Queen of the Harvest: a model for women in their 40s, finished with raising children but not yet old, at the height of their sexual and professional powers. This archetype is just one of 13 offered here as a new vision of a woman's middle years, a vision based on women's health, spirituality, and psychology, and drawn from over 100 interviews with women who are following a revolutionary path to more powerful living

See also **WOMEN'S SPIRITUALITY** under **SPIRITUALITY** in **RELIGION, SPIRITUALITY, AND PHILOSOPHY**

0-670-86227-4 VIKING $22.95

Betty **Friedan**

The Fountain of Age

"A book that explodes the myths of aging—just as, 30 years ago, Friedan exploded the myth of the contented housewife"—*Kirkus Reviews*

See also **AGING** under **HEALTH** in **LIFESTYLES AND PRACTICAL ADVICE**

0-671-40027-4 SIMON & SCHUSTER $25.00

0-671-89853-1 TOUCHSTONE PB $15.00

Letty Cottin **Pogrebin**

Getting Over Getting Older: An Intimate Memoir

A founding editor at *Ms.* magazine and 55-year-old reflects on the inevitable

0-316-71263-9 LITTLE, BROWN $23.95

Sexuality

Lucy **Bland**

Banishing the Beast: Sexuality and the Early Feminists

A study of feminism in England between 1880 and 1914, "rich and engrossing" —*Publishers Weekly*

1-56584-307-X NEW PRESS $25.00

Jan **Bremmer**, editor

From Sappho to de Sade: Moments in the History of Sexuality

Pederasty and lesbian love in antiquity, incest in the Middle Ages, voyeurism in the rococo, prostitution in *fin-de-siècle* Vienna: the history of sexuality is anything but a confirmation of contemporary norms. An assortment of scholarly essays charting the shifting of sexual mores over the centuries

0-415-06300-0 ROUTLEDGE PB $18.95

Marquis de Sade

Andrea **Dworkin**

Intercourse

A controversial work on how intercourse enslaves women

See also **FEMINIST THEORY**

0-02-907970-5 FREE PRESS $27.95
0-02-907971-3 FREE PRESS PB $13.95

Barbara **Ehrenreich**

The Hearts of Men

Why men flee intimacy

0-385-17615-5 DOUBLEDAY PB $11.00

Re-Making Love: The Feminization of Sex

"It destroys the myth that only men had a sexual revolution and reclaims the power and pleasure inherent in sex for all of us"—Shere Hite

0-385-18499-9 ANCHOR PB $10.00

Riane **Eisler**

Sacred Pleasure: Sex, Myth, and the Politics of the Body—New Paths to Power and Love

Eisler studies sex and spirituality to point the way to the possibility of a revolutionary, fulfilling equality

See also **LOVE AND ROMANCE** under **COURTSHIP, LOVE, SEX, AND MARRIAGE** in **LIFESTYLES AND PRACTICAL ADVICE**

0-06-250293-X HARPERCOLLINS $25.00
0-06-250283-2 HARPERCOLLINS PB $15.00

Kate **Fillion**

Lip Service: Challenging the Sexual Script of the Modern Woman

0-06-017290-8 HARPERCOLLINS $23.00

Linda **Grant**

Sexing the Millennium: Women and the Sexual Revolution

An incisive examination of that brief period when sex seemed like the solution. In this lively and learned overview, Grant charts the historical origins of the sexual revolution, the puritanical backlash that followed, and our present condition as voyeurs. "Perhaps sex is just the ghost of freedom," writes Grant, "but until we have Utopia it can speak eloquently of what the heart desires." From the 17th-century Ranters' concept of sex as liberator to postmodern voyeurism, Grant charts it all in this exploration of the sexual revolution and its many implications. A heartfelt call for an integrated erotic existence

0-8021-3349-5 GROVE PB $12.00

Shere **Hite**

Women as Revolutionary Agents of Change: The Hite Reports & Beyond

A collection of essays outlining the methodology behind Hite's popular and widely publicized studies

PREFACE BY DALE SPENDER

0-299-14294-9 WISCONSIN PB $22.95

Women and Love: A Cultural Revolution in Progress

Hite's much-contested work is an analysis of the stages of falling in love, having a relationship, and getting married

0-312-91378-8 ST. MARTIN'S PB $5.95

Rape, Incest, and Battered Women

Louise **Armstrong**

Rocking the Cradle of Sexual Politics: What Happened When Women Said Incest

Posits that incest is fundamentally a political issue, not a personal, familial one as it is usually considered. Traces the history of incest over the past 15 years and how victims are stonewalled by the courts. "Her harrowing accounts of how incest has been dealt with in the courtroom will enrage readers"—*Publishers Weekly*

0-201-62471-0 ADDISON-WESLEY $23.00

Susan **Brownmiller**

Against Our Will: Men, Women, and Rape

"A history of rape in all its overt and subtle manifestations. It's a consciousness-raising session that should force both men and women to agonize over their assumptions"—*NY Times*

0-449-90820-8 FAWCETT PB $12.50

Donald Alexander **Downs**

More than Victims: Battered Women, the Syndrome Society, and the Law

0-226-16159-5 CHICAGO $27.50

Cynthia **Carosella**, editor

Who's Afraid of the Dark?: A Forum of Truth, Support, and Assurance for Those Affected by Rape

A rape survivor offers advice on rape and its aftermath through a collection of writings from women and men who have been raped

See also **RAPE** under **SELF-HELP** in **LIFESTYLES AND PRACTICAL ADVICE**

0-06-095072-2 HARPERPERENNIAL PB $12.00

Susan **Estrich**

Real Rape

An important book by the Harvard law professor

0-674-74944-8 HARVARD PB $12.00

Linda A. **Fairstein**

Sexual Violence: Our War Against Rape

"This book will stop your heart with its graphic tales of terror and sexual violence—all true. It's also a brilliant diary of hours of gritty, sleepless detective work, courtroom duels, and the passion of a great prosecutor"—Diane Sawyer

0-688-06715-8 MORROW $23.00
0-425-14780-0 BERKELEY PB $14.00

Linda Fairstein
(Photo credit: Sara Krulwich)

Leslie **Francis**, editor

Date Rape: Feminism, Philosophy, and the Law

The current thinking on the subject; focuses on communication before and during sex

0-271-01429-6 PENN STATE PB $13.95

Judith **Herman**

Father-Daughter Incest

An academic study of women as victims within families

See also **SEXUAL ABUSE** under **SELF-HELP** in **LIFESTYLES AND PRACTICAL ADVICE**

0-674-29506-4 HARVARD PB $12.95

Ann **Jones**

Next Time, She'll Be Dead: Battering and How to Stop It

In this impeccably researched critique, Jones (*Women Who Kill*) questions the very basis with which we view "domestic violence." "Male violence," she says, is a more apt term. One solution would be to shift the legal inquiry and focus from the "battered woman" to the "battering man." The scope of the problem? Four million US women are assaulted by their lovers or husbands each year. "A powerful, frightening report that drives home the fact that doing violence to another is tolerated in this society—especially if the victim is a female sex partner"—*Kirkus Reviews*

0-8070-6771-7 BEACON PB $12.00

Susan **Koppelman**, editor

Women in the Trees: Stories of Battering and Resistance by U.S. Women, 1839-1994

0-8070-6777-6 BEACON PB $16.00

Peter **Laufer**

A Question of Consent: Innocence and Complicity in the Glen Ridge Rape Case

The true story behind the famous 1993 rape case in Glen Ridge, New Jersey, and the courtroom drama in which a mentally retarded girl was portrayed as a seductress, while her rapists—although convicted—were excused as all-American boys. Laufer concludes that the case is representative of much greater problems within our society: racism, sexism, and deeply ingrained faults in the judicial system

1-56279-059-5 MERCURY HOUSE $19.95

Mary **Marecek**

Breaking Free from Partner Abuse

A simply written, helpful book filled with sound advice from women who have been there. Includes sections on legal rights, getting a perspective on and measuring violence, and how to get out of an abusive situation

0-930934-74-1 MORNING GLORY PB $7.95

Martha **Ramsey**

Where I Stopped: Remembering Rape at Thirteen

Raped at the age of 13, Ramsey discusses the effect of this traumatic event on her life and her sexuality. "...her prose itself—elegant, clear and sharply insightful—makes this memoir well worth reading for fans of personal narrative" —*Publishers Weekly*

0-399-14107-3 PUTNAM $24.95

Katie **Roiphe**

The Morning After: Fear, Sex, and Feminism on Campus

Roiphe looks at today's sexual politics on campus, and offers a scathing critique of the willingness she sees among women to embrace the role of the victim. A brave, outspoken book

0-316-75431-5 LITTLE, BROWN $19.95
0-316-75432-3 LITTLE, BROWN PB $8.95

Leora N. **Rosen**

The Hostage Child: Sex Abuse Allegations in Custody Disputes

Operation Z, a child advocacy group, gathered 206 cases and focused on five representative ones to illustrate an increasing antimother bias in the courts, where children are often remanded to the abusing father even though evidence of abuse is present

0-253-33045-9 INDIANA $29.95

Lenore E. **Walker**

The Battered Woman

"In addition to carefully written but inevitably disturbing case studies, Professor Walker's book includes sections on preventative remedies, including safehouses, and a careful discussion of psychotherapy"—*NY Times*

See also **BATTERED WOMEN** under **SELF-HELP** in **LIFESTYLES AND PRACTICAL ADVICE**

0-06-090742-8 HARPERCOLLINS PB $12.50

Robin **Warshaw**

I Never Called It Rape

The *Ms.* magazine report on recognizing, fighting, and surviving date and acquaintance rape

0-06-096276-3 HARPERPERENNIAL PB $11.00

Rosalind **Wiseman**

Defending Ourselves: A Guide to Prevention, Self-Defense, and Recovery from Rape

The founder and director of Woman's Way, a self-defense program, discusses in full all aspects of rape, how to protect yourself, and what to do if assaulted

0-374-52415-7 NOONDAY PB $10.00

The Abortion Debate

Dallas A. **Blanchard** & Terry J. **Prewitt**

Religious Violence and Abortion: The Gideon Project

The authors explore the phenomenon of violence by the religious right while focusing on the specific case of a Pensacola, Florida bombing of an abortion clinic. They warn that fundamentalists will continue to use violence in reaction not only to legalized abortion, but also to such issues as pornography, homosexuality, equality for females, and prayer in public schools

See also **RELIGION IN AMERICA TODAY** under **RELIGION IN AMERICA** under **TOPICS IN AMERICAN STUDIES** in **HISTORY OF THE AMERICAS**

0-8130-1193-0 FLORIDA $39.95
0-8130-1194-9 FLORIDA PB $17.95

Paige C. **Cunningham**, editor

Abortion and the Constitution: Reversing Roe v. Wade Through the Courts

This collection of essays points to the legal errors of the *Roe v. Wade* decision and suggests a course of litigation for its reversal

0-87840-447-3 GEORGETOWN PB $12.95

Cynthia R. **Daniels**

At Women's Expense: State Power and the Politics of Fetal Rights

Women's bodies have become battlegrounds in the struggle between fetal rights and women's rights. Examining benchmark legal cases concerned with forced medical treatment, fetal protectionism in the workplace, and drug and alcohol use and abuse, Daniels raises key questions about how a woman's reproductive capability affects her relationship to state power

0-674-05043-6 HARVARD $19.95

Ronald **Dworkin**

Life's Dominion: An Argument About Abortion, Euthanasia, and Individual Freedom

Dworkin, Professor of Jurisprudence at Oxford and of Law at NYU, offers an eloquent clarification of two of the most difficult issues of our time. The real question, he says, is not whether a fetus is a person, but how best to respect the universally shared philosophical/religious conviction that all human life is sacred. "Dworkin's landmark philosophical essay brings a new dimension to future debate about abortion and euthanasia" —*Publishers Weekly*

See also **CURRENT LEGAL AFFAIRS** under **LAW**

0-679-73319-1 VINTAGE PB $13.00

Ronald Dworkin

Marian **Faux**

Roe v. Wade: The Untold Story of the Landmark Decision That Made Abortion Legal

0-451-62719-9 MENTOR PB $5.50

Faye **Ginsburg**

Contested Lives: The Abortion Debate in an American Community

"Ginsburg demonstrates a fine sympathy for all of the protagonists and a profound historical understanding of the structural forces and the cultural traditions at work in the abortion controversy"—Judith Walkowitz

0-520-06492-5 CALIFORNIA $35.00

Thomas **Hilgers**, editor

New Perspectives on Human Abortion

Medical, legal, and social issues from a pro-life perspective

0-89093-379-0 UNIVERSITY PUBLICATIONS........$49.95

Carole **Joffe**

Doctors of Conscience: The Struggle to Provide Abortion Before and After Roe v. Wade

Despite the constitutionally mandated legality of abortion in America, access to safe medical abortions is rapidly narrowing. For this, Joffe argues in a novel and convincing thesis, the medical community is partly to blame. Even after *Roe v. Wade*, she demonstrates, mainstream medicine has failed to provide needed services and training and has stigmatized doctors who perform abortions. Doctors today who ensure safe abortions are subject to real threats to their professional standing and personal safety. "A book of major importance that looks at the abortion issue from a thoroughly fresh and critical perspective" —Rosalind Petchesky

See also **MEDICAL ETHICS** under **MEDICINE** in **SCIENCE**

0-8070-2100-8 BEACON........$24.00

William R. **LaFleur**

Liquid Life: Abortion and Buddhism in Japan

0-691-02965-2 PRINCETON PB........$14.95

Kristin **Luker**

Abortion and the Politics of Motherhood

A balanced analysis of the abortion debate. "Like all good science, her book tries to enlighten rather than to persuade" —*Boston Globe*

0-520-05597-7 CALIFORNIA PB........$15.95

Ellen **Messer** & Kathryn E. **May**

Back Rooms: Voices from the Illegal Abortion Era

Frontline tales from women who had backroom abortions before *Roe v. Wade*

See also **HISTORY OF SEXUALITY** under **TOPICS IN AMERICAN STUDIES** in **HISTORY OF THE AMERICAS**

FOREWORD BY MARGE PIERCY

0-87975-876-7 PROMETHEUS PB........$17.95

Patricia G. **Miller**

The Worst of Times: Illegal Abortion—Survivors, Practitioners, Coroners, Cops, and Children of Women Who Died Talk About Its Horrors

This work of oral history, published on the 20th anniversay of *Roe v. Wade*, demonstrates that, no matter what, American women will have abortions, whether legal or not, whether by doctors or by back-alley abortionists

See also **CURRENT POLITICAL THOUGHT AND ISSUES** under **AMERICAN POLITICS AND FOREIGN POLICY** in **HISTORY OF THE AMERICAS**

0-06-099512-2 HARPERPERENNIAL PB........$12.00

0-06-019034-5 HARPERPERENNIAL PB........$22.00

James C. **Mohr**

Abortion in America: The Origins and Evolution of National Policy, 1800-1900

0-19-502616-0 OXFORD PB........$11.95

Roger **Rosenblatt**

Life Itself: Abortion in the American Mind

The thesis of *Life Itself* challenges the agendas of both the pro-choice and pro-life factions in the American abortion debate—arguably the most divisive since slavery. Rosenblatt examines why this issue has been held hostage by the most vociferous advocates on both sides, though most Americans have profoundly mixed feelings on the subject, and details the history of the procedure

0-394-58244-6 VINTAGE PB........$20.00

Kathy **Rudy**

Beyond Pro-Life and Pro-Choice: Moral Diversity in the Abortion Debate

A professor of ethics and women's studies, Rudy argues that most individuals sustain not one simple opinion but complex, even contradictory beliefs about abortion, beliefs that exceed the limits of pro-life or pro-choice. Exploring the moral worlds of Catholicism, evangelical Christianity, feminism, and classical liberalism, Rudy brings to life the philosophical and religious underpinnings of our divergent beliefs, of which abortion is only a small, if troublesome, part. Rudy has "written a scholarly, opinionated critique of the abortion controversy" —*Publishers Weekly*

0-8070-0426-X BEACON........$23.00

Lloyd **Steffen**, editor

Abortion: A Reader

0-8298-1117-6 PILGRIM PB........$19.95

Motherhood

Nina **Barrett**

The Playgroup: Three Women Contend with the Myths of Motherhood

Barrett (*I Wish Someone Had Told Me*) turns her unique powers of observation to three mothers—one of them herself—who form a playgroup for their newborns in Chicago. One is depressed by her husband's sudden lack of interest in her; another is intent upon maintaining her career; while the third is content to surrender everything to the well-being of her child. "A penetrating, witty, moving exploration...that unfolds with the immediacy and suspense of a novel"—*Kirkus Reviews*

0-671-74710-X SIMON & SCHUSTER........$21.00

Evelyn **Bassoff**

Mothers and Daughters

From the mother's perspective; by a psychiatrist

See also **MOTHERS** under **BEING A PARENT** under **PARENTING** in **LIFESTYLES AND PRACTICAL ADVICE**

0-452-26319-0 PLUME PB........$12.95

Ruth McDonald **Boyer** & Narcissus Duffy **Gayton**

Apache Mothers and Daughters

See also **MODERN INDIAN LIFE: CONTEMPORARY ISSUES** under **NATIVE AMERICAN CULTURES: NORTH AMERICA** in **HISTORY OF THE AMERICAS**

0-8061-2447-4 OKLAHOMA........$24.95

Nancy **Chodorow**

The Reproduction of Mothering: Psychoanalysis and the Sociology of Gender

Why women in almost all societies are responsible for parenting. "Provides careful psychoanalytic grounding for the radical position that both sexes can and should parent equally, and—an additional boon—its style is not too academic"—*Ms.*

See also **GENDER AND SEXUALITY** under **PSYCHOLOGY**

0-520-03892-4 CALIFORNIA PB........$16.00

Diane **Eyer**

Motherguilt: How Our Culture Blames Mothers for What's Wrong with Society

0-8129-2416-9 TIME BOOKS........$25.00

Wendy **Kaminer**

A Fearful Freedom: Women's Flight from Equality

An argument against the "protectionist feminists" who believe that, though women are autonomous and self-reliant, they are mothers first. Kaminer advocates employer-sponsored childcare, parental leave programs, and greater male participation in the family

0-201-09234-4 ADDISON-WESLEY PB........$18.95

Katrina **Kenison** & Kathleen **Hirsch**, editors

Mothers: Twenty Stories of Contemporary Motherhood

See also **ANTHOLOGIES OF WOMEN'S WRITING**

0-86547-498-2 NORTH POINT........$22.00

Laurie **Lisle**

Without Child: Challenging the Stigma of Childlessness

The author weaves her own decision not to be a parent with cultural stereotypes regarding non-mothers and "...she points to the many ways a woman's childlessness, often perceived as selfish, can promote and nurture life-enhancing relationships"—*Publishers Weekly*

0-345-37327-8 BALLANTINE........$23.00

Melinda M. **Marshall**

Good Enough Mothers: Changing Expectations for Ourselves

With incisive commentary from experts, and inspiring examples of women who have figured out how to cope

1-56079-253-1 PETERSON'S........$18.95

1-56079-433-X PETERSON'S PB........$10.95

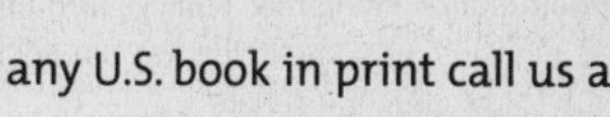

Tillie **Olsen** & others

Mothers & Daughters: That Special Quality, An Exploration in Photographs

The work of some 75 contemporary photographers is brought together with an insightful text by Estelle Jussim and a poetic essay by Tillie Olsen to create this "moving tribute to the emotional, cultural, and intellectual resources of women"—*USA Today*. Includes work by Bruce Davidson, Eudora Welty, Danny Lyon, and Nan Goldin

See also **SPECIAL TOPICS** under **PHOTOGRAPHY** in **ART**

0-89381-379-6 APERTURE PB $24.95

Shelley **Phillips**

Beyond the Myths: Mother-Daughter Relationships in Psychology, History, Literature and Everyday Life

Challenges the prejudices and myths that paralyze and gives new understanding to the complicated roles of fathers

0-14-025186-3 PENGUIN PB $14.95

Sandra **Pollack** & Jeanne **Vaughn**, editors

Politics of the Heart: A Lesbian Parenting Anthology

First-person accounts by lesbians with children

See also **GAY AND LESBIAN PARENTS** under **LOVERS, FAMILIES, AND FRIENDS** under **GAY, LESBIAN, AND BISEXUAL STUDIES**

0-932379-36-2 FIREBRAND $26.95
0-932379-35-4 FIREBRAND PB $12.95

Adrienne **Rich**

Of Woman Born: Motherhood as Experience and Institution

From one of the country's premier poets and essayists

0-393-02379-6 NORTON $17.95
0-393-30386-1 NORTON PB $10.95

Adrienne Rich (photo by Myriam Diaz-Diocaretz)

Jeanne **Safer**

Beyond Motherhood: Choosing a Life Without Children

The author presents her own story of her choice to be childless along with that of other women and couples. "Safer raises intelligent, stirring questions about how these women's childhoods, temperaments and career choices influenced their decision, and about the way our society treats these nonconformists"
—*Publishers Weekly*

0-671-79344-6 POCKET PB $12.00

Psychology

Mary Field **Belenky**

Women's Ways of Knowing: The Development of Self, Voice, and Mind

Interviews with 135 women of differing backgrounds, probing the question of why so many women are reluctant to speak out

0-465-09213-6 BASIC PB $16.00

Jessica **Benjamin**

The Bonds of Love: Psychoanalysis, Feminism, and the Problem of Domination

Analysis of the acceptance and perpetuation of relationships of domination and submission, from a leading theorist and psychoanalyst

See also **GENDER AND SEXUALITY** under **PSYCHOLOGY**

0-394-75730-0 PANTHEON PB $16.00

Carol **Gilligan**

In a Different Voice: Psychological Theory and Women's Development

Gilligan, a Harvard professor, argues that psychological development theories have been based on the experiences of men and suggests we reshape our understanding of human development to include women's voices

See also **GENDER AND SEXUALITY** under **PSYCHOLOGY**

0-674-44544-9 HARVARD PB $10.95

Karen **Horney**

Feminine Psychology

Horney rejects the feminine stereotypes embedded in orthodox Freudian psychology

EDITED BY HAROLD KELMAN

0-393-31080-9 NORTON PB $8.95

Doris **Howard**

A Guide to the Dynamics of Feminist Therapy

Essays on the practice of feminist psychotherapy

0-918393-37-X HARRINGTON PARK PB $24.95

Ellyn **Kaschak**

Engendered Lives: A New Psychology of Women's Experience

Kaschak demonstrates how gender bias is embedded in virtually all of our systems of self-understanding, from orthodox analysis to family therapy. She shows how psychological illnesses such as anxiety and eating disorders grow out of the ways women are made to conform

0-465-01349-X BASIC PB $15.00

Jean B. **Miller**

Toward a New Psychology of Women

An attempt to develop a new psychology out of the actual life experience of women, with many anecdotal case histories

0-8070-2909-2 BEACON PB $12.95

Harriet Goldhor **Lerner**

The Dance of Deception: Pretending and Truth-Telling

The bestselling author of *The Dance of Anger* and *The Dance of Intimacy* now follows up with an examination of feminine deceptions and their impact on self-esteem, intimacy, happiness, self-fulfillment, and society in general. Lerner's provocative and disturbing thesis is certain to sound familiar to generations of women

0-06-016816-1 HARPERCOLLINS PB $22.00

Juliet **Mitchell**

Psychoanalysis and Feminism

"Mitchell's attack on Reich, Laing, and the neofeminists is inspired by unflinching loyalty to the original psychoanalytic concepts, difficult, uncompromising and seemingly unflattering to women as these concepts are"
—Christopher Lasch, *NY Review of Books*

0-394-71442-3 RANDOM HOUSE PB $10.65

Susan **Swedo** & Henrietta **Leonard**

It's Not All in Your Head: The New Psychiatry for Women

0-06-251286-2 HARPERCOLLINS $25.00
0-06-251287-0 HARPERCOLLINS PB $14.00

Mary R. **Walsh**

The Psychology of Women: Ongoing Debates

A collection of essays on such questions as women's alleged proneness to masochism, the relevance of psychoanalytic theory to the psychology of women, androgyny, lesbianism, abortion, and pornography

0-300-03966-2 YALE PB $18.00

DeMaris S. **Wehr**

Jung and Feminism: Liberating Archetypes

Wehr suggests that Jung's theories and therapeutic ideas may be beneficial for women

0-8070-6735-0 BEACON PB $12.00

Anthropology and Cross-Culture Studies

Lila **Abu-Lughod**

Writing Women's Worlds: Bedouin Stories

Abu-Lughod, a professor of anthropology at New York University, tells the stories of Egyptian Bedouin women with whom she spent considerable time over the last decade. A portrayal of the family life and social customs of the Bedouin people, while also a critical discussion on the nature of anthropology, feminist theory and Third World women, and on current popular and scholarly preconceptions of the Muslim world

0-520-08304-0 CALIFORNIA PB $14.95

Rayna **Green**

Women in American Indian Society

See also **MODERN INDIAN LIFE: CONTEMPORARY ISSUES** under **NATIVE AMERICAN CULTURES: NORTH AMERICA** in **HISTORY OF THE AMERICAS**

0-7910-0401-5 CHELSEA HOUSE PB $8.95

Esther **Hicks**

Infibulation: Female Mutilation in Islamic Northeastern Africa

A scholarly and exhaustive look at the history of female circumcision and the social consequences for those in the faith as well as not

1-56000-841-5 TRANSACTION PB.....$21.95

Rosemary **Mahoney**

Whoredom in Kimmage: Irish Women Coming of Age

0-395-60201-7 HOUGHTON MIFFLIN.....$21.95
0-385-47450-4 ANCHOR PB.....$12.95

Margaret **Mead**

Male + Female

The classic study of the sexes by the anthropologist who started it all. This examination of seven Pacific Island cultures remains as relevant today as it did when it was first published in 1949

0-688-04676-7 MORROW PB.....$12.00

Margaret Mead

Sherry **Ortner** & Harriet **Whitehead**, editors

Sexual Meanings: The Cultural Construction of Gender and Sexuality

Detailed ethnographic studies

See also **WOMEN AND SEXUALITY** under **SPECIALIZED STUDIES** under **ANTHROPOLOGY**

0-521-28375-2 CAMBRIDGE PB.....$23.95

Michelle Z. **Rosaldo** & Louise **Lamphere**, editors

Woman, Culture, and Society

A well-chosen collection

See also **WOMEN AND SEXUALITY** under **SPECIALIZED STUDIES** under **ANTHROPOLOGY**

0-8047-0851-7 STANFORD PB.....$15.95

Judith E. **Tucker**, editor

Arab Women: Old Boundaries, New Frontiers

A discussion of the changing lives and roles of women in the Arab world during a time of radical change and fantastic opportunities by a distinguished group of feminist scholars. Among the more than dozen contributors are Sondra Hale, Margot Bedran, Souad Dajani, and Julie Peteet

0-253-36096-X INDIANA.....$39.95
0-253-20776-2 INDIANA PB.....$15.95

World History

History is one of the most richly developed fields in women's studies. New historical works document the role of women and correct the distortions of traditional accounts.

Ruth **Ashby** & Deborah Gore **Ohrn**

Herstory: Women Who Changed the World

From Sappho to Toni Morrison, this biographic encyclopedia is perfect for young adults and grownups who wish to learn of famous as well as unsung but important females

See also **REFERENCE**

INTRODUCTION BY GLORIA STEINEM

0-670-85434-4 VIKING.....$19.95

Marilyn J. **Boxer** & Jean H. **Quataert**, editors

Connecting Spheres: Women in the Western World, 1500 to the Present

Overviews of major periods along with writings on specific aspects of women's lives

FOREWORD BY JOAN W. SCOTT

0-19-504133-X OXFORD PB.....$16.95

Jean Hascall **Cole**

Women Pilots of World War II

See also **THE WAR IN THE AIR** under **THE SECOND WORLD WAR** in **WORLD HISTORY AND CURRENT AFFAIRS**

0-87480-493-0 UTAH PB.....$12.95

Irene M. **Franck** & David M. **Brownstone**

Women's World: A Time Line of Women in History

Women who have changed history, from Nefertiti to Janet Reno, chronologically arranged, illustrated with 105 photos, clearly presented with sidebars and annotations

0-06-273336-2 HARPERCOLLINS PB.....$22.50

Susan **Griffin**

A Chorus of Stones: The Private Life of War

"Part autobiographical memoir, part social history, Griffin's book ties scores of individuals to the wars they lived through or died in…"
—*NY Newsday*

0-385-41885-X ANCHOR PB.....$12.95

Olwen **Hufton**

The Prospect Before Her: A History of Women in Western Europe, 1500-1800

See also **WOMEN AND GENDER STUDIES** under **PERSPECTIVES IN HISTORY** under **THE VARIETIES OF CIVILIZATION** in **WORLD HISTORY AND CURRENT AFFAIRS**

0-679-45030-0 KNOPF.....$35.00

Gerda **Lerner**

The Creation of Patriarchy

"Dramatically reopens a chapter of women's history that historians had thought was forever closed to them—the origins of the collective dominance of women by men"
—Katherine Kish Sklar, UCLA

0-19-505185-8 OXFORD PB.....$12.95

Gerda **Lerner**

The Majority Finds Its Past: Placing Women in History

Twelve essays dealing with a range of feminist issues, focusing on women's role in history

0-19-502899-6 OXFORD PB.....$9.95

David E. **Jones**

Women Warriors: A History

Challenges the notion that only men are capable of fighting or leading in war

1-57488-106-X BRASSEYS.....$24.95

Ian **Maclean**

The Renaissance Notion of Woman: A Study in the Fortunes of Scholasticism and Medical Science in European Intellectual Life

See also **RENAISSANCE ITALY AND THE COMING OF HUMANISM** under **MEDIEVAL AND RENAISSANCE EUROPE** in **WORLD HISTORY AND CURRENT AFFAIRS**

0-521-27436-2 CAMBRIDGE PB.....$15.95

Margaret **MacMillan**

Women of the Raj

0-500-27898-9 THAMES & HUDSON PB.....$18.95

Rosalind **Miles**

Women's History of the World

Women's contributions on every level—domestic, emotional, social, sexual—as goddesses, war queens, scientists, artists, saints, and sinners. "An exuberant book written in a jazzy, colorful style sizzling with puns and startling images"—*Washington Post Book World*

See also **REFERENCE**

0-06-097317-X HARPERCOLLINS PB.....$13.00

Naomi **Shepherd**

A Price Below Rubies: Jewish Women as Rebels and Radicals

Examining the middle-class families in Czarist Russia that produced Populists and terrorists, Marxist teachers and theorists, American union organizers, European anarchists, and in many cases exiles and martyrs, Shepherd details the remarkable contribution of Jewish women to radical history (1870-1930). A fascinating biography of a distinct historical group of women in rebellion

0-674-70410-X HARVARD.....$27.95

Richard **Stites**

The Woman's Liberation Movement in Russia: Feminism, Nihilism, and Bolshevism, 1860-1930

An engrossing account that crosses over traditional chronological boundaries

0-691-10058-6 PRINCETON PB.....$21.95

Françoise **Thebaud** & others, editors

A History of Women in the West Volume I From Ancient Goddesses to Christian Saints

0-674-40370-3 HARVARD.....$29.95
0-674-40369-X HARVARD PB.....$15.95

Françoise **Thebaud** & others, editors

A History of Women in the West

Volume II

Silences of the Middle Ages

0-674-40368-1 HARVARD PB $16.95

Volume III

Renaissance and Enlightenment Paradoxes

0-674-40367-3 HARVARD PB $16.95

Volume IV

Emerging Feminism from Revolution to the World War

The fourth volume in this world-acclaimed series covers the 150 years after the French Revolution, when the subordination of women was recodified in new laws and rules, and the simultaneous emergence of feminism in the public arena as the pressures of industrialization drew women out of the home

0-674-40366-5 HARVARD PB $16.95

Volume V

Toward a Cultural Identity in the Twentieth Century

The fifth and final volume of this monumental work weighs our century's grand promises of liberation against such harsh realities as genocide, totalitarianism, and the democratization of "glamour." A brilliant and thoughtful history by renowned French scholars

0-674-40374-6 HARVARD $29.95
0-674-40365-7 HARVARD PB $16.95

American History

African-American History

Zita **Allen**

Black Women Leaders of the Civil Rights Movement

0-531-11271-3 FRANKLIN WATTS $22.70

Linda **Brent**

Incidents in the Life of a Slave Girl

A stunning narrative of a slave girl who, after much struggle, escapes to the North

See also **VOICES FROM SLAVERY** under **BLACK VOICES, BLACK LIVES** under **AFRICAN-AMERICAN STUDIES** in **HISTORY OF THE AMERICAS**

EDITED BY L. MARIA CHILD
PREFACE BY WALTER TELLER

0-15-644350-3 HARCOURT BRACE PB $7.95

Elizabeth **Clark-Lewis**

Living In, Living Out: African American Domestics and the Great Migration

A compilation of 81 oral histories from women who migrated as young girls from the rural South to find employment as live-in maids and childcare workers, and who eventually found independence "living out"

1-56836-124-6 KODANSHA PB $15.00

Paula **Giddings**

When and Where I Enter: The Impact of Black Women on Race and Sex

"History at its best—clear, intelligent, moving. Paula Giddings has written a book as priceless as its subject"—Toni Morrison

0-688-14650-3 QUILL PB $14.00

Glenda Elizabeth **Gilmore**

Gender and Jim Crow: Women and the Politics of White Supremacy in North Carolina, 1896-1920

0-8078-2287-6 NORTH CAROLINA $49.95
0-8078-4596-5 NORTH CAROLINA PB $17.95

Darlene Clark **Hine**

Black Women in America: An Historic Encyclopedia

These two volumes represent a long overdue, comprehensive assemblage of successful black women, deceased and living. Most entries are accompanied by a picture and a description of the woman's family to provide historical perspective and placement. Astronauts, orchestra conductors, mayors, welders, psychiatrists, bankers, maids, and lawyers—all great and inspiring and thoroughly, beautifully recorded on these pages. Alongside all the encyclopedias of great men, these volumes are sure to stand out

See also **REFERENCE**

0-926019-61-9 CARLSON $195.00
0-253-32774-1 INDIANA PB $49.95

Jacqueline **Jones**

Labor of Love, Labor of Sorrow: Black Women, Work and the Family from Slavery to the Present

Bancroft Prize winner

See also **WOMEN** under **CULTURE** under **AFRICAN-AMERICAN STUDIES** in **HISTORY OF THE AMERICAS**

0-394-74536-1 VINTAGE PB $14.00

Joyce A. **Ladner**

Tomorrow's Tomorrow: The Black Woman

A searching sociological study of black girls growing up in urban America. The author explores to what extent they represent the misconceptions of the black community

0-8032-7956-6 NEBRASKA PB $12.00

Gretchen **Lemke-Santangelo**

Abiding Courage: African American Migrant Women in the East Bay Community

A study of the movement of African-American women to Northern California's Bay Area between 1940 and 1945 to work in the wartime defense industry. Archival and oral records document their experiences at this historical nexus of social change

0-8078-4563-9 NORTH CAROLINA PB $14.95

Gerda **Lerner**, editor

Black Woman in White America: A Documentary History

"A stunning collection of documents by black women about themselves"—*Washington Post*

See also **HISTORY** under **AFRICAN-AMERICAN STUDIES** in **HISTORY OF THE AMERICAS**

0-679-74314-6 VINTAGE PB $15.00

Melton A. **McLaurin**

Celia, a Slave

The historical narrative of the slave girl who kills her master after being adopted at 14 and enduring years of sexual abuse. Despite much sympathy from whites concerning her predicament, she was ultimately executed

See also **SLAVERY** under **HISTORY** under **AFRICAN-AMERICAN STUDIES** in **HISTORY OF THE AMERICAS**

0-8203-1352-1 GEORGIA $19.95

Patricia **Morton**, editor

Discovering the Women in Slavery: Emancipating Perspectives on the American Past

Fourteen original essays on womens' experiences of American slavery, from perspectives that range from the slave woman herself to the slaveholding mistress to the free woman of color. Raises questions outside the conventional scope of the history of American slavery

0-8203-1757-8 GEORGIA PB $20.00

Leith **Mullings**

On Our Own Terms: Race, Class, and Gender in the Lives of African-American Women

0-415-91286-5 ROUTLEDGE PB $25.00

Overviews

William Henry **Chafe**

Women and Equality: Changing Patterns in American Culture

A provocative analysis of how sex roles have changed and how serious the remaining obstacles are to equality

0-19-502365-X OXFORD PB $10.95

Sara M. **Evans**

Born for Liberty: A History of Women in America

0-02-903090-0 FREE PRESS PB $18.95

Linda K. **Kerber**, editor

U.S. History as Women's History: New Feminist Essays

"Every scholar and activist concerned about public life and social change, feminist consciousness and empowerment, civil rights, human rights, and dignity for all people, will want to read and ponder this book"
—Blanch Wiesur Cook, *Eleanor Roosevelt*

0-8078-4495-0 NORTH CAROLINA PB $15.95

Linda K. **Kerber** &
Jane **De Hart Mathews**, editors
Women's America: Refocusing the Past
A collection of articles and documents tracing women's history from colonial times to the present, covering a wide range of subjects from obstetric practices in the 17th century to an analysis of contemporary feminism
0-19-506261-2 OXFORD $45.00
0-19-506262-0 OXFORD PB $19.95

Rosemary **Radford Ruether** &
Rosemary **Skinner Keller**, editors
In Our Own Voices: Four Centuries of American Women's Religious Writing
Brings to life the women in US religious history such as Sister Blandina Segale, who "kept the Billy the Kid gang from scalping doctors in Colorado," and Ida B. Wells-Barnett, who exposed the lynching of black men to the entire country and as a consequence had her life threatened
0-06-066843-1 HARPERCOLLINS $30.00
0-06-066840-7 HARPERCOLLINS PB $18.00

Colonial America

Carol **Berkin** & Eric **Foner**
First Generations: Women in Colonial America
A feminist perspective with an emphasis on gender and class. "[Berkin's] analysis of Native American and African American women, as well as of how the American Revolution affected female roles, is enlightening"—*Publishers Weekly*
See also **THE NEW COLONIES** under **US HISTORY TO THE CIVIL WAR** in **HISTORY OF THE AMERICAS**
0-8090-4561-3 HILL & WANG $23.00

Susan **Juster**
Disorderly Women: Sexual Politics and Evangelicalism in Revolutionary New England
See also **THEOLOGY** under **FEMINIST THEORY**
0-8014-2732-0 CORNELL $32.95
0-8014-8388-3 CORNELL PB $14.95

Laurel Thatcher **Ulrich**
Good Wives: Image and Reality in the Lives of Women in Northern New England, 1650 to 1750
The women of the period participated more vitally in the community and led more complex lives than has generally been supposed
0-679-73257-8 VINTAGE PB $12.00

The 19th Century and the Industrial Revolution

Lucy **Larcom**
A New England Girlhood
An 1889 account of life in the Lowell factories
0-87928-078-6 CORNER HOUSE $23.95
0-8446-2431-4 SMITH PB $12.00

Louisa May **Alcott**
The Feminist Alcott: Stories of a Woman's Power
Four fictional tales that reveal Alcott's rebellion against inequality
1-55553-266-7 NORTHEASTERN PB $14.95

Louisa May Alcott

Nancy F. **Cott**
The Bonds of Womanhood: "Woman's Sphere" in New England, 1780-1935
Emphasizes the virtues of women's activities that are usually denigrated
0-300-02289-1 YALE PB $14.00

Margaret **Fuller**
Woman in the Nineteenth Century
Fuller stresses in this 1845 work that men and women have a duty to fulfill their potential for the spiritual good of both sexes
See also **THE 19TH CENTURY: TO THE CIVIL WAR** under **AMERICAN LITERATURE TO 1900** in **LITERATURE OF THE AMERICAS**
0-393-00615-8 NORTON PB $9.95

Alice Ilgenfritz **Jones** & Ella **Merchant**
Unveiling a Parallel
An 1893 feminist utopian novel that has been out of print for decades, and an intriguing precursor to such titles as *Herland.* The book details two very different countries, discovered on the surface of Mars
EDITED AND WITH AN INTRODUCTION BY CAROL KOLMERTEN
0-8156-2538-3 SYRACUSE $34.50
0-8156-0259-6 SYRACUSE PB $12.95

Suzanne **Lebsock**
The Free Women of Petersburg: Status and Culture in a Southern Town, 1784-1860
Using Petersburg, Virginia as an example, Lebsock attempts to show that women were able to form an alternative value system in a society committed to slavery, dominance, and materialism
0-393-95264-9 NORTON PB $12.95

Cathy **Luchetti** & Carol **Olwell**
Women of the West
This book presents history not as it has been romanticized, but lived. It introduces us to 11 frontier women, including a Native American, an African American, and a doctor, and lets them tell their stories—through diaries, memoirs, letters, journals, and photos. "A human appeal barely touched in most history books of the westward expansion"—*The Kansas City Star*
0-517-59162-6 ORION PB $24.00

Janet **Robertson**
The Magnificent Mountain Women: Adventures in the Colorado Rockies
The stories of women from the 1850s to the 1980s who ventured into the mountains
0-8032-8933-2 NEBRASKA PB $10.95

Christine **Stansell**
City of Women: Sex and Class in New York, 1789-1860
A first-rate work of history focusing on economic and personal aspects of working-class women
0-252-01481-2 ILLINOIS PB $13.95

Walter **Sullivan**, editor
The War the Women Lived: Female Voices from the Confederate South
Diary excerpts from 23 white Southern women during the Civil War record the hardships endured and suffering witnessed as well as the risks assumed. Includes "many harrowing descriptions of the damage inflicted by Sherman's march through Georgia"
—*Publishers Weekly*
1-87994-130-9 J.S. SANDERS $24.95

Suffrage, Liberation, and Beyond

D'Ann **Campbell**
Women at War with America: Private Lives in a Patriotic Era
0-674-95475-0 HARVARD $32.00

Marcia **Cohen**
The Sisterhood: The True Story of the Women Who Changed the World
An intimate history of the women's movement, focusing on Betty Friedan, Gloria Steinem, Germaine Greer, and Kate Miller
0-7871-0468-X DOVE PB $15.95

Ann **Douglas**
The Feminization of American Culture
Traces today's culture back to its Victorian roots
See also **REFORMERS AND ABOLITIONISTS** under **US HISTORY TO THE CIVIL WAR** in **HISTORY OF THE AMERICAS**
0-385-24241-7 ANCHOR PB $14.00

Sara **Evans**

Personal Politics: The Roots of Women's Liberation in the Civil Rights Movement and the New Left

0-394-74228-1 RANDOM HOUSE PB $9.75

Eleanor **Flexner**

Century of Struggle: The Women's Rights Movement in the United States

0-674-10652-0 HARVARD PB $19.95

Aileen S. **Kraditor**

The Ideas of the Woman Suffrage Movement, 1880-1920

0-393-00039-7 NORTON PB $10.95

Nancy M. **Newman**, editor

A Voice of Our Own: Leading American Women Celebrate the Right to Vote

This collection of 28 essays by prominent American women to commemorate the 75th anniversary of the 19th Amendment was commissioned by the League of Women Voters. "Various contributors' retellings of the history of the women's suffrage movement provide an inspiring account of successful grassroots political activism"—*Publishers Weekly*

0-7879-0231-4 JOSSEY-BASS $24.00

Doris **Stevens**

Jailed for Freedom: American Women Win the Vote

First published in 1920, this reissue of Stevens's dramatic reportage commemorates the 75th anniversary of the 19th Amendment. "A vivid partisan account that clearly conveys the excitement of both battle and victory" —*Publishers Weekly*

See also **THE ROARING TWENTIES** under **US HISTORY, 1877-1945** in **HISTORY OF THE AMERICAS**

EDITED BY CAROL O'HARE

0-939165-25-2 NEWSAGE PB $12.95

Susan **Ware**

Beyond Suffrage: Women in the New Deal

The impact and attitudes of women in positions of national leadership in the 1930s

0-674-06921-8 HARVARD $30.00

Marjorie Spruill **Wheeler**, editor

One Woman, One Vote

This fascinating and revealing anthology companion to the PBS special by noted suffrage historians exposes the sexism, as well as the shocking racism and classism, entrenched in the long struggle for the 19th Amendment. "The ideal guide…and as such, an important step into our future"—Susan Faludi, *Backlash: The Undeclared War Against American Women*

See also **VOTING** under **DEMOCRATS AND REPUBLICANS** under **AMERICAN POLITICS AND FOREIGN POLICY** in **HISTORY OF THE AMERICAS**

0-939165-26-0 NEWSAGE PB $18.95

Marcia **Tucker**, editor

Bad Girls

0-262-70053-0 MIT PB $19.95

Linda **Witt** & others

Running as a Woman: Gender and Power in American Politics

Drawing on in-depth, candid interviews with Geraldine Ferraro, Pat Schroeder, Barbara Mikulski, and other major political figures, the authors explore the significant issues for women in public life: their marital status, the threat of sexual innuendo, what's involved in becoming a credible candidate, and raising enough money to run

See also **POLITICAL HISTORY** under **AMERICAN POLITICS AND FOREIGN POLICY** in **HISTORY OF THE AMERICAS**

0-02-920315-5 FREE PRESS $24.95

America's Working Women

See also ECONOMICS and CAREERS AND MONEY

Terri **Apter**

Working Women Don't Have Wives: Professional Success in the 1990s

A highly thoughtful and observant analysis of the plight of working women by the acclaimed author of *Altered Loves*. Based on ten years of interviews with professional women, the book finds that our failure to achieve equality rests not on some nefarious male conspiracy of dominance, but rather on a fundamental female conflict between work and family life. "Of appeal to anyone interested in understanding the feminist revolution"—*Kirkus Reviews*

0-312-09675-5 ST. MARTIN'S $19.95

What more and more people were pointing out was that women had been coerced into a series of choices which limited their lives far more that they had hitherto recognized. The rationale of the traditional division of labour was to men's advantage, and the consequenses for women of this traditional division of labour were disastrous: they became less than fully human. They lost self-respect, they lost power, they lost control over their lives.

WORKING WOMEN DON'T HAVE WIVES: PROFESSIONAL SUCCESS IN THE 1990S

Cynthia **Costello** & Barbara Kivimae **Krimgold**, editor

The American Woman 1996-1997: Women and Work

Up-to-date report on women's status in the work-place

1-55553-259-4 NORTHEASTERN $47.50

Margery W. **Davies**

Woman's Place Is at the Typewriter: Office Work and Office Workers, 1870-1930

0-87722-368-8 TEMPLE PB $16.95

Connie **Fletcher**

Breaking and Entering: Women Cops Talk About Life in the Ultimate Men's Club

Interviews of 106 female cops nationwide reveal the same sad story: every police department is a men's club where women are still not wanted

0-06-017311-4 HARPERCOLLINS $23.00

Sara **Friedman**

Work Matters: Women Talk About Their Work

"At work I pretend I don't have kids; at home I pretend I don't have a job"—A corporate executive. "If only I had a wife to wash my dirty overalls and fill my lunchpail every day, this job would be perfect"—A woman steelworker. In the tradition of *The Second Shift* and *Working*, this collection of 75 stories from working women goes behind the public debate to uncover the real changes in real lives that are revolutionizing the workplace

0-670-84203-6 VIKING $24.95

Carol A. B. **Giesen**

Coal Miners' Wives: Portraits of Endurance

Eighteen coal miners' wives aged 17 to 80 were interviewed to find out their coping mechanism for the stresses of having a beloved involved in one of the most dangerous and unsteady of jobs. "…provides an absorbing portrait of the hard impact of one industry on real women's lives" —*Publishers Weekly*

0-8131-0845-4 KENTUCKY PB $14.95

Penina **Glazer** & Miriam **Slater**

Unequal Colleagues: The Entrance of Women into the Professions, 1890-1940

0-8135-1187-9 RUTGERS PB $12.00

Paula E. **Hyman**

Gender and Assimilation in Modern Jewish History : The Roles and Representation of Women

A history of Jewish assimilation in America as experienced by women. "Meticulously researched and eloquently written, Hyman's work will become the standard reference in Jewish women's history…" —Marion Kaplan, Queens College

See also **GENERAL HISTORIES** under **JEWS IN AMERICA** under **JEWISH HISTORY** in **WORLD HISTORY AND CURRENT AFFAIRS**

0-295-97425-7 WASHINGTON $30.00

0-295-97426-5 WASHINGTON PB $14.95

David M. **Katzman**

Seven Days a Week: Women and Domestic Service in Industrializing America

The lives of domestics examined through their writings and interviews

0-252-00882-0 ILLINOIS PB $13.95

Sherna Berger **Gluck**
Rosie the Riveter Revisited: Women, the War and Social Change
An oral history of the women who went to work to help with the war effort and the lives they led after the war ended
See also **THE UNITED STATES AND WORLD WAR II** under **THE SECOND WORLD WAR** in **WORLD HISTORY AND CURRENT AFFAIRS**
0-8057-9022-5 TWAYNE.....$22.95
0-452-01024-1 NEW AMERICAN LIBRARY PB...$12.95

Nancy Baker **Wise** & Christy **Wise**
A Mouthful of Rivets: Women in World War II
"Together, mother and daughter have written a delightful, absorbing book of real-life stories: what women's lives were really like on the home front—and the factory front—during World War II"—*LA Times*
1-55542-703-0 JOSSEY-BASS.....$25.00

Christopher **Keane** & with Dottie **Thorson**
The Huntress: The True Saga of Dottie and Brandi Thorson, Modern Day Bounty Hunters
In 1994, Ralph Thorson, a famous bounty hunter, was killed by a car bomb by Q.D. Reese. Q.D. Reese set out to kill Thorson's wife, Dottie, and daughter, Brandi. This is their exciting and suspenseful story
1-55611-490-7 FINE.....$23.95

Ruth **Milkman**, editor
Women, Work and Protest: A Century of U.S. Women's Labor History
0-7100-9940-1 ROUTLEDGE PB.....$16.95

Judith **Rollins**
Between Women: Domestics and Their Employees
This history of domestic work brings up the issue of women using other women to enhance their status
0-87722-383-1 TEMPLE.....$32.95
0-87722-491-9 TEMPLE PB.....$17.95

Susan **Strasser**
Never Done: A History of American Housework
0-394-70841-5 RANDOM HOUSE PB.....$15.10

Leslie Woodcock **Tentler**
Wage-Earning Women: Industrial Work and Family Life in the United States, 1900-1930
The author reconstructs day-to-day realities of working women—on the job, in the home, and in the industrial neighborhoods of major cities
0-19-503211-X OXFORD PB.....$9.95

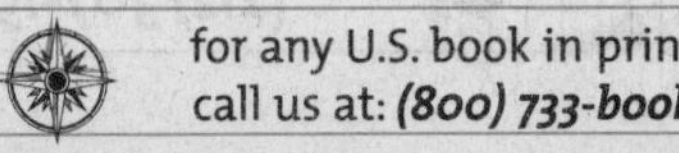

Historical Biographies

Joyce **Antler**
The Journey Home: A Celebration of Jewish Women in the American Century
See also **JEWISH-AMERICANS** under **THE MELTING POT** under **AMERICAN PEOPLE AND PLACES** in **HISTORY OF THE AMERICAS**
0-684-83444-8 FREE PRESS.....$27.50

Kathryn Kish **Sklar**
Catharine Beecher: A Study in American Domesticity
0-393-00812-6 NORTON PB.....$11.95

Jeanne **Boydston**
The Limits of Sisterhood: The Beecher Sisters on Women's Rights and Women's Sphere
Catherine, a writer and educator, Harriet, an author of novels, and Isabella, a political activist, were all committed to women's rights, but with different opinions on how this should be achieved
0-8078-4207-9 NORTH CAROLINA PB.....$16.95

Sharon McGrayne **Bertsch**
Nobel Prize Women in Science: Their Lives, Struggles and Momentous Discoveries
Over 400 men but only nine women have won the Nobel Prize in science. This is the first book-length examination of the work of female Nobel Prize winners and other deserving women denied recognition. An important and timely exposé
1-55972-146-4 BIRCH LANE.....$26.95

Ellen **Chesler**
Woman of Valor: Margaret Sanger and the Birth Control Movement in America
0-385-46980-2 ANCHOR.....$14.95

Sarah **Delany** & Elizabeth **Delany**
The Delany Sisters' Book of Wisdom
The observations (feisty) and advice (sage) of the bestselling sisters
1-56836-042-8 KODANSHA.....$15.00

Having Our Say: The Delany Sisters' First 100 Years
A century old each, the sisters from North Carolina were the first African-American professionals in the Harlem Renaissance to have lived to tell us of a lifetime of courage. A surprise bestseller
1-56836-010-X KODANSHA.....$20.00
0-385-31252-0 DELTA PB.....$9.95

Bell G. **Chevigny**, editor
The Woman and the Myth: Margaret Fuller's Life and Writings
Fuller (1810-1850) was a member of Emerson's circle, editor of *The Dial*, and a reporter for the *New York Tribune*
1-55553-181-4 NORTHEASTERN PB.....$16.95

Constance **Chen**
The Sex Side of Life: Mary Ware Dennett's Pioneering Battle for Birth Control and Sex Education
Mary Ware Dennett's credentials were impeccable: executive secretary of the American Woman Suffrage Association; founding organizer of the National Birth Control League; key member of the American Union Against Militarism (later the ACLU); and a founder of the first arts and crafts societies in America. Yet until now she has remained a little-known figure in American history. This engrossing biography resuscitates a key heroine in the progressive movement that radically changed sexual mores in our century
1-56584-132-8 NEW PRESS.....$25.00

The society she inherited was carefully circumscribed. Victorian mores were being codified into law. Men and women inhabited separate spheres, their very sexuality keeping them apart. Discomfort surrounding the human body was so extreme that even piano "limbs" had to be properly covered.
THE SEX SIDE OF LIFE: MARY WARE DENNETT'S PIONEERING BATTLE FOR BIRTH CONTROL AND SEX EDUCATION

Carolyn G. **Heilbrun**
Writing a Woman's Life
"Asserts that patriarchal culture has not only defined the limits of women's lives, it has determined what stories about women will be told"—*San Francisco Chronicle*
0-345-36256-X BALLANTINE PB.....$10.00

Joyce **Antler**
Lucy Sprague Mitchell
0-300-04176-4 YALE PB.....$22.00

Allida M. **Black**
Casting Her Own Shadow: Eleanor Roosevelt and the Shaping of Postwar Liberalism
Assistant professor of American studies and history at Pennsylvania State University reconstructs Eleanor Roosevelt's role as an underestimated but major force from 1945 until she died in 1962. "Her principled stand for low-cost and public housing, affirmative action, regulation of the corporations, U.S. support for the United Nations—key planks in the liberal agenda under siege today—makes this a timely reassessment"—*Publishers Weekly*
0-231-10404-9 COLUMBIA.....$29.95

Phyllis **Rose**, editor
The Norton Book of Women's Lives
Autobiographies, journals, and memoirs by Virginia Woolf, Joan Didion, and many more produce a fascinating portrait of the feminine sensibility in our century
0-393-03532-8 NORTON.....$30.00
0-393-31290-9 NORTON PB.....$17.95

Elisabeth **Griffith**
In Her Own Right: The Life of Elizabeth Cady Stanton
The definitive biography of a pioneer feminist
0-19-503729-4 OXFORD PB.....$14.95

Ruth **Bordin**

Frances Willard: A Biography

Believing that women could gain political power through the temperance crusade, Willard helped found the Prohibition Party. She served as the president of the Women's Christian Temperance Union and also stumped for women's suffrage

0-8078-1697-3 NORTH CAROLINA........................$34.95

European History

Bonnie S. **Anderson** & Judith **Zinsser**

A History of Their Own: Women in Europe from Prehistory to the Present

Both volumes are organized according to women's societal roles. The first volume covers the history of women to the Renaissance, the second from the 17th century to the present

Volume 1

See also **WOMEN AND GENDER STUDIES** under **PERSPECTIVES IN HISTORY** under **THE VARIETIES OF CIVILIZATION** in **WORLD HISTORY AND CURRENT AFFAIRS**

0-06-091452-1 HARPERCOLLINS PB........................$18.00

Volume 2

0-06-091563-3 HARPERCOLLINS PB........................$18.00

Elizabeth Wayland **Barber**

Women's Work: Women, Cloth, and Society in Early Times

A general history of early weaving, although of particular interest to those who wish to know more about Minoan and Mycenean societies

See also **WOMEN IN ANTIQUITY** under **TOPICS IN ANCIENT GREEK HISTORY** under **ANCIENT GREECE** in **WORLD HISTORY AND CURRENT AFFAIRS**

0-393-03506-9 NORTON........................$23.00
0-393-31348-4 NORTON PB........................$13.00

Susan G. **Bell**, editor

Women: From the Greeks to the French Revolution

0-8047-1082-1 STANFORD PB........................$16.95

Renate **Bridenthal**, editor

Becoming Visible: Women in European History

0-395-41950-6 HOUGHTON MIFFLIN PB..............$33.95

Queen Victoria

Adrienne **Munich**

Queen Victoria's Secrets

In an artful blend of feminist, anthropological, and postcolonial approaches, Munich—Director of the Women's Studies Program at SUNY Stony Brook—reassesses Victoria and the lasting grip she has held on her nation's imagination. Following the predominating concepts governing a Victorian woman's life—fashion, marriage, menopause—she offers a study of general interest and central importance, elucidating a figure who has become synonymous with sexual repression

0-231-10480-4 COLUMBIA........................$27.95

Medieval History

Alcuin **Blamires**, editor

Woman Defamed and Woman Defended: An Anthology of Medieval Texts

See also **WOMEN** under **SOCIAL AND ECONOMIC HISTORY** under **MEDIEVAL AND RENAISSANCE EUROPE** in **WORLD HISTORY AND CURRENT AFFAIRS**

0-19-811971-2 OXFORD........................$59.00
0-19-871039-9 OXFORD PB........................$17.95

Caroline Walker **Bynum**

Fragmentation and Redemption: Essays on Gender and the Human Body in Medieval Religion

Bynum (*Holy Feast and Holy Fast*) received a MacArthur fellowship for her exploratory work on medieval conceptions of the body. Here she examines ideas about the body of Christ, physical resurrection, eucharistic devotion, and the female body in relation to religious practice. "Caroline Bynum takes dark and sometimes fantastic topics and teases from them a marvelously vivid and compelling depiction of medieval religious life and especially of the differences between men's and women's religious practices"—Lynn Hunt

0-942299-63-9 ZONE........................$29.95

Trances, levitations, catatonic seizures or other forms of bodily rigidity, miraculous elongation or enlargement of parts of the body, swellings of sweet mucus in the throat (sometimes known as the "globus hystericus") and ecstatic nosebleeds are seldom if at all reported of male saints, but are quite common in the *vitae* of thirteenth and fourteenth-century women. The inability to eat anything except the eucharistic host (which Rudolph Bell calls "holy anorexia") is reported only of women for most of the Middle Ages. Although a few stories of fasting girls are told from Carolingian Europe, reports that see self-starvation as a manifestation of sanctity begin to proliferate about 1200.

FRAGMENTATION AND REDEMPTION: ESSAYS ON GENDER AND THE HUMAN BODY IN MEDIEVAL RELIGION

Monica **Furlong**, editor

Visions & Longings: Medieval Women Mystics

See also **CHRISTIAN MYSTICISM** under **CHRISTIANITY** in **RELIGION, SPIRITUALITY, AND PHILOSOPHY**

1-57062-125-X SHAMBHALA........................$20.00

Frances **Gies** & Joseph **Gies**

Women in the Middle Ages

An overview plus an in-depth study of the lives of seven women from different classes, countries, and centuries

0-06-092304-0 BARNES & NOBLE PB........................$12.50

Margaret W. **Labarge**

A Small Sound of the Trumpet: Women in Medieval Life

From queens to prostitutes, the daily lives and character sketches of various women

0-8070-5627-8 BEACON PB........................$18.00

Christine de **Pisan**

The Book of the City of Ladies

The author, often called the first French woman of letters, responded in prose and poetry to the prevailing misogyny of her time

See also **MIDDLE AGES** under **FRENCH LITERATURE TO 1900** in **LITERATURE OF EUROPE, AFRICA, AND ASIA**

TRANSLATED BY EARL RICHARDS

0-89255-066-X PERSEA PB........................$11.95

Jacques **Rossiaud**

Medieval Prostitution

A thorough and scholarly work that theorizes that because rape was common and considered a minor crime in 15th-century France, the ruling elite condoned and even encouraged prostitution and brothels as a means of social control

0-631-19992-6 BLACKWELL PB........................$21.95

Modern European History

Antonia **Fraser**

The Weaker Vessel: Woman's Lot in Seventeenth-Century England

"An almost encyclopedic chronicle of women in 17th-century England … wives, warriors, heiresses, preachers … alive with anecdote after anecdote"—*NY Times*

See also **CULTURAL AND SOCIAL LIFE** under **TOPICS IN BRITISH HISTORY** under **GREAT BRITAIN AND IRELAND** in **WORLD HISTORY AND CURRENT AFFAIRS**

0-394-73251-0 RANDOM HOUSE PB........................$18.00

Erna Olafson **Hellerstein**, editor

Victorian Women: A Documentary Account of Women's Lives in Nineteenth-Century England, France, and the United States

Diaries, letters, poems, wills, autobiographies, and other documents from women of all classes

0-8047-1096-1 STANFORD PB........................$22.50

Bridget **Hill**

Eighteenth Century Women: An Anthology

0-04-909014-3 UNWIN HYMAN PB........................$19.95

Claudia **Koonz**

Mothers in the Fatherland: Women, Family Life and Nazi Politics

Traces the role of women in the massive German war effort

0-312-02256-5 ST. MARTIN'S PB $17.95

James F. **McMillan**

Housewife or Harlot: The Place of Women in French Society, 1870-1940

0-312-39347-4 ST. MARTIN'S $29.95

Bruce **Seymour**

Lola Montez: A Life

Born in Ireland in 1820, Eliza Gilbert (Lola Montez's real name) was nomimally the child of an ensign in the British Army but in fact the illegitimate daughter of a country squire. The mistress of King Ludwig of Bavaria, she died in New York at the age of 56

0-300-06347-4 YALE $30.00

Martha **Vicinus**, editor

Suffer and Be Still: Women in the Victorian Age

0-253-35572-9 INDIANA $31.50
0-253-20168-3 INDIANA PB $13.95

Samia I. **Spencer**, editor

French Women and the Age of Enlightenment

See also **THE AGE OF ENLIGHTENMENT** under **EARLY MODERN EUROPE** in **WORLD HISTORY AND CURRENT AFFAIRS**

INTRODUCTION BY ELIZABETH FOX-GENOVESE

0-253-32481-5 INDIANA $45.00
0-253-20725-8 INDIANA PB $6.95

Arts and Letters

Art and Photography

Anna **Banti**

Artemisia

A fictional portrayal, first published in 1947, of the intriguing 17th-century Neapolitan portraitist Artemisia Gentileschi, by a woman writer who earned her success well before the feminist era

See also **FICTION** under **THE 20TH CENTURY** under **ITALIAN LITERATURE** in **LITERATURE OF EUROPE, AFRICA, AND ASIA**

TRANSLATED BY SHIRLEY D'ARDIA

0-8032-6119-5 NEBRASKA PB $10.00

Judy **Chicago**

Beyond the Flower: The Autobiography of a Feminist

0-670-85295-3 VIKING $27.95

The Dinner Party

Judy Chicago's multimedia exhibit, "The Dinner Party," a symbolically rich and complex visual chronicle of more than 1,000 women in Western civilization, was to the art world of the '70s what the first Impressionist exhibit had been to the Parisian art scene a century before. This new edition of the companion volume updates the history of the work with new illustrations and new material on the exhibits, themes, interpretation, and history

See also **THE CONTEMPORARY SCENE** under **ART SINCE 1945** in **ART**

0-670-85957-5 VIKING $45.00
0-14-024437-9 VIKING PB $24.95

Mary **Garrard**

Artemisia Gentileschi: The Female Hero in Italian Baroque Art

Perhaps the most important woman artist before the modern period, discussed in the first full-length study. Much is made of her unique representations of the female hero—Susanna, Judith, Lucretia, Cleopatra

See also **THE BAROQUE IN ITALY** under **EUROPEAN ART: BAROQUE AND ROCOCO** in **ART**

0-691-04050-8 PRINCETON $110.00
0-691-00285-1 PRINCETON PB $37.50

Guerrilla **Girls**

Confessions of the Guerrilla Girls: By the Guerrilla Girls Themselves, Whoever They Are

Combines the famous display—by the anonymous group who wear gorilla masks—of their ads, posters, and letter-writing campaigns that focus on the exclusion of women artists in museums and galleries

INTRODUCTION BY WHITNEY CHADWICK

0-06-095088-9 HARPERPERENNIAL PB $18.00

Lucy **Lippard**

The Pink Glass Swan: Feminist Essays on Art

Art critic since the '70s, Lippard includes here a collection of her work from various magazines as well as her previous books and offers what *Publishers Weekly* wrote is "a much broader reading of alternative culture, its politics and practices" than just of contemporary art and women

1-56584-213-8 NEW PRESS PB $20.00

Jeanne **Moutoussamy-Ashe**

Viewfinders: Black Women Photographers, 1839-1985

0-86316-159-6 WRITERS & READERS $39.95
0-86316-158-8 WRITERS & READERS PB $19.95

Eleanor **Munro**

Originals: American Women Artists

In addition to analyses of the women and their work, Munro offers a look into the mind of the artist: what it takes to be an artist and how it feels. Includes black-and-white and color reprints of artists' works

0-671-42812-8 SIMON & SCHUSTER PB $19.00

Linda **Nochlin**

Women, Art, and Power: and Other Essays

0-06-430183-4 ICON PB $14.00

Griselda **Pollock**

Vision and Difference: Femininity, Feminism, and the Histories of Art

0-415-00722-4 METHUEN PB $16.95

Raquel **Tibol**

Frida Kahlo: An Open Life

The author, one of Mexico's most respected art historians, was a close friend of Kahlo and Rivera, and as such is able to combine personal recollection with scholarship in this eclectic biography of one of the most idolized female artists of our time

See also **MEXICO AND CENTRAL AMERICA** under **NATIVE AMERICAN ARTS** in **ART**

TRANSLATED BY ELINOR RANDALL

0-8263-1418-X NEW MEXICO $19.95

Film

Molly **Haskell**

From Reverence to Rape: The Treatment of Women in the Movies

An excellent study of how film has reflected and reshaped images of women

See also **GENRES AND THEMES** under **FILM** in **PERFORMING ARTS AND MEDIA**

0-226-31885-0 CHICAGO PB $16.95

Humor

Regina **Barreca**, editor

The Penguin Book of Women's Humor

Called by *Ms.* magazine the "feminist humor maven," the author of the celebrated *They Used to Call Me Snow White…But I Drifted* has compiled the ultimate anthology of women's humor. From the 1700s to the 1900s, to politics, fate, and frustrations, selections include Anita Loos, Mae West, Lily Tomlin, Ntozake Shange, Jane Austen, Emily Dickinson, Dorothy Parker, and Cynthia Heimel

See also **HUMOR** in **POPULAR READING**

0-14-017294-7 PENGUIN PB $15.95

They Used to Call Me Snow White...But I Drifted

A sharply written exploration of women's humor that is tremendously funny in its own right. Here are women humorists from Jane Austen and Dorothy Parker to Lily Tomlin and Nicole Hollander, and their male detractors, from Oscar Wilde to Andrew Dice Clay and the late Sam Kinison. "Funny, painful, electric…a book not just about gender, but about life, fit to invigorate the learned and reeducate the blasé"
—Fay Weldon

0-14-016835-4 PENGUIN PB $11.95

When Elayne Boosler talks about the right-to-lifers' attitudes, she is challenging the entire conservative movement: "You ever notice that the same people who are against abortion are for capital punishment? Typical fisherman's attitude, throw 'em back when they're small and kill 'em when they're bigger."…She went on to illuminate the conservatives' approach to sex education: "Reagan was against sex education in the schools because he thought there was a connection between promiscuity and sex education—that kids did it because they learned about it. No way. I had four years of

algebra and I never do math. These guys say they're against abortion because birth is a miracle. Popcorn is a miracle, too, if you don't know how it's done."
THEY USED TO CALL ME SNOW WHITE...BUT I DRIFTED

Cynthia **Heimel**
If You Leave Me Can I Come Too?
Heimel is at the peak of her form in this collection of essays
See also HUMOR WRITERS under HUMOR in POPULAR READING
0-87113-603-1 GROVE $20.00

Sex Tips For Girls
A New York City humor columnist gives advice on "The Great Boyfriend Crunch," "Lingerie Dos and Don'ts," and "How to Cure a Broken Heart"
See also COURTSHIP AND DATING under COURTSHIP, LOVE, SEX, AND MARRIAGE in LIFESTYLES AND PRACTICAL ADVICE
0-671-47725-0 SIMON & SCHUSTER PB $9.00

When the Phone Doesn't Ring, It'll Be Me!
Caustic, wicked, and true, Heimel offers new and ever more bitterly hilarious observations on the war between the sexes. From nature and dogs to shopping and living, "Heimel gets funnier, meaner, and possibly even smarter, every time around"—*NY Times Book Review*
0-87113-634-1 GROVE PB $11.00

Vicki **Lon**
Uppity Women of Ancient Times
Humorous profiles of 200 women from the ages that includes Thais ("a brand-name courtesan from Athens"), Nefertiti ("the Jackie Kennedy of her day"), and Gorgo ("the Spartan Shirley Temple")
1-57324-010-9 CONARI PB $12.95

Katherine Ann **Samon**
Dates from Hell
A hilarious compendium of "horrible date" tales collected from the syndicated column, *Tales from the Front*
0-452-26778-1 PLUME PB $8.95

Claudia **Shear**
Blown Sideways Through Life: A Hilarious Tour de Resume
The actress/writer presents her job history while struggling through life. The play was a huge success
See also PERFORMANCE under 20TH-CENTURY AMERICAN DRAMA in LITERATURE OF THE AMERICAS
0-385-31315-2 DELTA PB $8.95

Music and Theater

Jane **Bowers** & Judith **Tick**, editors
Women Making Music: The Western Art Tradition, 1150-1950
Biographies of performers and composers with musical examples, from medieval chants to 20th-century compositions
0-252-01470-7 ILLINOIS PB $16.95

Mary A. **Bufwack** & Robert K. **Oermann**
Finding Her Voice: The Illustrated Guide to Women in Country Music
From Patsy Cline to Emmy Lou Harris. With black and white photographs throughout
See also GENERAL SURVEYS under COUNTRY AND FOLK MUSIC in PERFORMING ARTS AND MEDIA
0-8050-4265-2 HOLT PB $18.95

Sophie **Drinker**
Music and Women: The Story of Women in Their Relation to Music
Originally published in 1948, this reprint is a unique and radical criticism of the history of Western music and the ways women's contribution to music has been ignored or slighted
1-55861-120-7 FEMINIST PRESS $45.00
1-55861-116-9 FEMINIST PRESS PB $16.95

Karen **Malpede**
Martha Graham: The Evolution of Her Dance Theory and Drawing, 1926-1991
1-55652-141-3 INDEPENDENT PUB GROUP PB $14.95

Martha Graham

Carol **Neuls-Bates**, editor
Women in Music: An Anthology of Source Reading from the Middle Ages to the Present
1-55553-240-3 NORTHEASTERN PB $15.95

Amy **Raphael**
GRRRLS: Women Rewrite Back
British journalist interviews 14 contemporary female rockers including American groovettes Courtney Love, Liz Phair, Kim Gordon, and Tanya Donnelly
0-312-14109-2 ST. MARTIN'S PB $12.95

Anthologies of Women's Writing

Helen **Barolini**, editor
The Dream Book: An Anthology of Writings by Italian-American Women
Fiction, poetry, drama, essays, and memoirs
0-685-29570-2 AYER $19.95

Shari **Benstock**
Women of the Left Bank: Paris, 1900-1940
The lives and work of American, English, and French women in Paris, 1900-1940, including Gertrude Stein, Edith Wharton, and Jean Rhys
0-292-79029-5 TEXAS $29.95
0-292-79040-6 TEXAS PB $14.95

Pat **Califa**, editor
Forbidden Passages: Writings Banned in Canada
This free-speech anthology features writings detained by Canadian customs as they were on their way to Little Sister's, a Vancouver, BC, gay and lesbian bookstore
1-57344-019-1 CLEIS PB $14.95

Rebecca **Carroll**, editor
I Know What the Red Clay Looks Like: The Voice and Vision of Black Women Writers
Short biographies and interviews with African-American female writers where the object is to find out why, what, and for whom they write as well as who were their major inspirations. Includes Gloria Naylor, Lorene Cary, June Jordan, and others
0-517-88261-2 RANDOM HOUSE PB $12.00

Moira **Ferguson**, editor
First Feminists: British Women Writers, 1578-1799
0-253-28120-2 FEMINIST PRESS PB $18.95

Judith **Fetterley**, editor
Provisions: A Reader from Nineteenth-Century American Women
0-253-17040-0 INDIANA $35.00

Sandra **Gilbert** & Susan **Gubar**, editors
The Norton Anthology of Literature by Women: The Tradition in English
A well-edited and comprehensive collection of the writings of English-speaking women from the 14th century to the present, including Elizabeth I, Mary Wollstonecraft, George Eliot, Isak Dinesen, and Maxine Hong Kingston
0-393-95391-2 NORTON PB $39.95

Ayesha **Kagal** & Natasha **Perova**
Present Imperfect: Stories by Russian Women
0-8133-2676-1 WESTVIEW PB $17.00

Katherine **Govier**, editor

Without a Guide: Contemporary Women's Travel Adventures

A collection of travel essays from Alice Walker, E. Annie Proulx, and others

See also **ANTHOLOGIES** under **TRAVEL LITERATURE** in **FOOD, TRAVEL, AND LEISURE**

1-88691-304-8 CONSORTIUM PB.....$16.00

Beverly **Guy-Sheftall**, editor

Words of Fire: An Anthology of African-American Feminist Thought

"The indefatigable Beverly Guy-Sheftall has put together a breathtaking sweep of African-American feminist thought in one indispensable volume"—Elizabeth Spelman, Professor of Philosophy, Smith College

1-56584-256-1 NEW PRESS PB.....$21.95

Liz **Heron**, editor

City Women

In short stories and novel excerpts, some of the 20th century's most celebrated women writers lend their perspectives to life in New York, Buenos Aires, Leningrad, Shanghai, and other great cities where women have negotiated new freedoms and crossed cultural frontiers. An international anthology whose contributors include Jean Rhys, Christa Wolf, Flora Nwapa (of Nigeria), Toni Morrison, and Virginia Woolf

0-8070-8330-5 BEACON.....$30.00

Nancy **Hoffman** & Florence **Howe**, editors

Women Working: An Anthology of Stories and Poems

Thirty-four selections by such writers as Willa Cather, Zora Neale Hurston, Tillie Olsen, Alice Walker, and Sarah Orne Jewett

ILLUSTRATED BY ANN TOULMIN-ROTH

0-912670-57-6 FEMINIST PRESS PB.....$13.95

Teresa **Jordan** & James R. **Hepworth**

The Stories that Shape Us: Contemporary Women Write About the West

A collection of 25 essays about the West that are "fervently expressed feelings about family, gender and search for identity"
—*Publishers Weekly*

0-393-03723-1 NORTON.....$23.00
0-393-31451-0 NORTON PB.....$14.00

Katrina **Kenison** & Kathleen **Hirsch**, editors

Mothers: Twenty Stories of Contemporary Motherhood

See also **MOTHERHOOD** under **THE FEMALE EXPERIENCE**

0-86547-498-2 NORTH POINT.....$22.00

Alberto **Manguel**, editor

Other Fires: Short Fiction by Latin American Women

Stories by Brazilian, Argentinian, Colombian, Mexican, Cuban, and Uruguayan writers

See also **ANTHOLOGIES** under **LATIN AMERICAN LITERATURE** in **LITERATURE OF THE AMERICAS**

0-517-55870-X CLARKSON POTTER PB.....$12.00

Marlene Adler **Marks**

Nice Jewish Girls: Growing Up in America

Publishers Weekly wrote "This mixed but mostly marvelous collection of essays, fiction and poetry touches on the issues of being female and Jewish in America"

0-452-27397-8 PLUME PB.....$12.95

Wendy **Martin**, editor

The Beacon Book of Essays by Contemporary American Women

Publishers Weekly called this an "engrossing and lively collection," that features essays by women of differing ethnic backgrounds, religion, class, age, and sexual orientation. Included are Mary McCarthy, Adrienne Rich, Alice Walker, Margaret Mead, Mary Gordon, Carolyn Coma, Susan Faludi, Betty Friedan, and others

0-8070-6346-0 BEACON.....$26.00

We Are the Stories We Tell: The Best Short Stories by North American Women Since 1945

Selections include Alice Walker, Eudora Welty, Louise Erdrich, Joyce Carol Oates, Susan Minot, Anne Tyler, Maxine Hong Kingston, Ursula K. Le Guin, Mary McCarthy, and Tama Janowitz, as well as many others

0-679-72881-3 PANTHEON PB.....$15.00

Cris **Mazza** & Jeffrey **DeShell**, editors

Chick-Lit: On the Edge—New Women's Fiction Anthology

"...[E]ach one at least tries to make the leap through inventive form, style and content"
—*Publishers Weekly*

1-57366-005-1 BLACK ICE PB.....$11.95

Mandy **Merck**

Perversions: Deviant Readings

Sex, politics, and cultural criticism meet in this one-of-a-kind collection of provocative essays. Among the subjects are the feminist ethics of lesbian s/m; Simone de Beauvoir's obscure study of Brigitte Bardot; and the link between Andrea Dworkin's *Intercourse* and the glossy Hollywood product *Fatal Attraction*. Frequently suprising, sometimes shocking, this unique collection is ideal for the intellectually adventurous

0-415-90792-6 ROUTLEDGE PB.....$16.95

Robin **Morgan**, editor

Sisterhood Is Powerful: An Anthology of Writings from the Women's Liberation Movement

Articles, poems, photographs, manifestos, and personal accounts

0-394-70539-4 RANDOM HOUSE PB.....$16.00

Sara **Paretsky**, editor

Women on the Case: 26 Original Stories by the Best Women Crime Writers of Our Time

Includes writers Nancy Pickard, Frances Fyfield, Helga Anderle, Ruth Rendell, P.M. Carlson

0-385-31401-9 ANCHOR.....$21.95

Holly **Morris**, editor

A Different Angle: Fly Fishing Stories by Women

This anthology includes fresh prose by E. Annie Proulx, Pam Houston, Lorian Hemingway, Joan Wulff, Margot Page, and others; spans fishing from New York's Battenkill to Outer Mongolia

See also **TROUT, FLY-FISHING, AND FLY-TYING** under **FISHING** under **THE OUTDOORS** in **FOOD, TRAVEL, AND LEISURE**

1-87806-763-X SEAL.....$22.95
0-425-15134-4 BERKELEY PB.....$12.00

Holly Morris (photo by Harley Soltes)

Cherrie **Moraga** & Gloria **Anzaldua**, editors

This Bridge Called My Back: Writings by Radical Women of Color

Poetry, prose, and narrative by African-American, Asian-American, Latin American, and Native American women

ILLUSTRATED BY JOHNETTA TINKER

FOREWORD BY TONI CADE BAMBARA

0-913175-03-X KITCHEN TABLE PB.....$11.95

Gloria **Norris**, editor

The Seasons of Women: An Anthology

See also **ANTHOLOGIES** under **20TH-CENTURY AMERICAN ESSAYS AND JOURNALISM** in **LITERATURE OF THE AMERICAS**

0-393-03860-2 NORTON.....$27.50

Hillary **Pearlman**, editor

A Place Called Home: Twenty Writing Women Remember

Maxine Hong Kingston, Julie Smith, and 18 other women write about what home means

0-312-12793-6 ST. MARTIN'S.....$21.95

Brenda **Peterson**

Nature and Other Mothers: Personal Stories of Women and the Body of Earth

"Potent and poignant...Lively essays that mix politics, religion, nature, myth and memoir"
—*San Francisco Chronicle*

See also **ESSAYS, MEDITATIONS, AND CLASSICS** under **NATURE STUDY** in **SCIENCE**

0-449-90967-0 FAWCETT PB.....$12.00

Vicki **Piekarski**, editor

Westward the Women: An Anthology of Western Stories by Women

0-8263-1063-X NEW MEXICO PB $10.95

Jean Reith **Schroedel**

Alone in a Crowd: Women in the Trades Tell Their Stories

Twenty-five women with nontraditional blue-collar jobs talk about their experiences

0-87722-378-5 TEMPLE $32.95

Elaine **Showalter**, editor

Daughters of Decadence: Women Writers from the Fin-de-Siècle

A splendid collection of the best innovative fiction about, and often by, the "New Women" from turn-of-the-century America and Britain. Included are short stories by Charlotte Perkins Gilman, Edith Wharton, Kate Chopin, and Charlotte Mew, women whose works led to their being reviled as "literary degenerates" and "erotomaniacs." An important contribution to the study of women's fiction

0-8135-2015-0 RUTGERS $30.00
0-8135-2018-5 RUTGERS PB $14.95

Barbara **Smith**, editor

Home Girls: A Black Feminist Anthology

Writings by Audre Lorde, Alice Walker, Gloria T. Hull, and others

0-913175-02-1 NAIAD PB $15.95

Victoria **Sullivan** & James **Hatch**, editors

Plays by and about Women

0-394-71896-8 RANDOM HOUSE PB $10.00

Betty **Travitsky**, editor

The Paradise of Women: Writing by Englishwomen of the Renaissance

See also **PROSE** under **THE 16TH CENTURY** in **LITERATURE OF THE BRITISH ISLES**

0-231-06885-9 COLUMBIA PB $17.50

Joanne **Vickers** & Barbara I. **Thomas**

No More Frogs, No More Princes: Women Making Creative Choices at Midlife

Presenting 20 compelling autobiographical stories of typical American women boldly meeting the challenges of aging, this inspiring volume offers a clarion call to the possibilities of midlife creativity

0-89594-626-2 CROSSING $25.00
0-89594-625-4 CROSSING PB $10.95

Linda **Wagner-Martin** & Cathy N. **Davidson**, editors

The Oxford Book of Women's Writing in the United States

This anthology includes short stories, poems, essays, plays, speeches, erotica, letters, and even some recipes to provide a comprehensive view of the best women's writing in America

See also **SPECIALIZED ANTHOLOGIES** under **ANTHOLOGIES** under **AMERICAN LITERATURE: ANTHOLOGIES AND CRITICAL STUDIES** in **LITERATURE OF THE AMERICAS**

0-19-508706-2 OXFORD $30.00

Mary Helen **Washington**, editor

Black-Eyed Susans: Classic Stories By and About Black Women

Includes "If You're Light and Have Long Hair" by Gwendolyn Brooks and "A Sudden Trip Home in the Spring" by Alice Walker

0-385-26015-6 ANCHOR PB $14.00

Kathryn **Wilder**

Walking the Twilight II: Women Writers in the Southwest

Over 20 writers are featured

0-87358-648-4 NORTHLAND PB $14.95

Irene **Zahava**

Feminism 3: The Third Generation in Fiction

Stories from young American feminists

0-8133-2551-X WESTVIEW PB $18.00

Poetry Anthologies

Fleur **Adcock**, editor

The Faber Book of Twentieth Century Women's Poetry

Includes Stevie Smith, Edna St. Vincent Millay, Gwendolyn Brooks, and Denise Levertov

See also **POETRY ANTHOLOGIES** under **WORLD LITERATURE: WORLD LITERATURE SURVEYS AND ANTHOLOGIES** in **LITERATURE OF EUROPE, AFRICA, AND ASIA**

0-571-13693-1 FABER PB $13.95

Aliki **Barnstone** & Willis **Barnstone**

A Book of Women Poets: From Antiquity to Now

Among the 300 poets included are Anne Bradstreet, Anne Sexton, and Margaret Atwood

0-8052-0997-2 SCHOCKEN PB $20.00

Laura **Chester**, editor

Cradle and All: Women Writers on Pregnancy and Birth

An anthology of prose and poetry from 50 contemporary writers including Joyce Carol Oates, Adrienne Rich, and Erica Jong, capturing the pleasure and pain of motherhood

See also **PREGNANCY** under **PARENTING** in **LIFESTYLES AND PRACTICAL ADVICE**

0-571-12989-7 FABER PB $12.95

Roger **Lonsdale**, editor

Eighteenth-Century Women Poets

More than a hundred poets are featured in this groundbreaking collection, ranging in social status from the Countess of Winchilsea to the washerwoman Mary Collier, and including both well-known figures such as Lady Mary Wortley Montagu and Ann Radcliffe and hitherto obscure writers like Elizabeth Thomas, Mary Leapor, and Hannah More. The detailed biographical notes and scholarly introduction open up new perspectives on 18th-century literature

See also **ANTHOLOGIES** under **POETRY** under **THE RESTORATION AND THE 18TH CENTURY** in **LITERATURE OF THE BRITISH ISLES**

0-19-811769-8 OXFORD PB $35.00

Germaine **Greer**, editor

Kissing the Rod: An Anthology of 17th-Century Women's Verse

See also **ANTHOLOGIES** under **POETRY** under **THE EARLY 17TH CENTURY** in **LITERATURE OF THE BRITISH ISLES**

0-374-52164-6 FS&G PB $15.00

Germaine **Greer**

Slip-Shod Sybils: Recognition, Rejection, and the Woman Poet

0-670-84914-6 VIKING $20.00

Biographies, Autobiographies, and Letters

Lynn **Sherr**

Failure Is Impossible: Susan B. Anthony in Her Own Words

Anthony, the legendary suffragist, brought to life with her own words juxtaposed with contemporary reports and biographical essays. "Anyone who has thought of...Anthony as a dour profile on the $1 coin or a solemn sister of suffrage has a treat in store. In this wonderful book, we can practically hear the original Susan B. Anthony in all her richness and wisdom. She still speaks to us"—Ellen Goodman

0-8129-2718-4 TIME BOOKS PB $15.00

Jill Ker **Conway**, editor

Written by Herself: Autobiographies of American Women

An anthology of autobiographical writing by 25 American women, from fugitive slave Harriet Jacobs and Southern novelist Ellen Glasgow to feminist reformer Margaret Sanger and Zora Neale Hurston, as chosen by the bestselling author of *The Road From Coorain*

0-679-73633-6 VINTAGE PB $15.00

Janet **Flanner**

Darlinghissima: Letters to a Friend

Janet Flanner wrote about France for the *New Yorker* for 50 years under the pen name Genet. This collection includes her correspondence with her close friend Natalia D. Murray, written in a style far different from that of her magazine writing

EDITED BY NATALIA D. MURRAY

0-15-623937-X HARCOURT BRACE PB $10.95

Janet Flanner

Dorothy **Day**

The Long Loneliness: An Autobiography

The radical Catholic leader noted for her social programs

INTRODUCTION BY DANIEL BARRIGAN

0-06-061751-9 HARPERCOLLINS PB $14.00

Dorothy Day

Andrea **Gabor**

Einstein's Wife: Work and Marriage in the Lives of Five Great Twentieth-Century Women

Intimate portraits of five women: Milveva Maric, Einstein's wife and a talented scientist in her own right; Maria Goeppert Mayer, Nobel laureate and mother of two; Denise Scott, architect and wife of Robert Venturi; Lee Krasner, artist and wife of Jackson Pollock; and Sandra Day O'Connor

0-670-84210-9 VIKING $24.95

Patricia **Bell-Scott**

Life Notes: Personal Writings by Contemporary Black Women

Anthologized excerpts from journals and notebooks from such prominent writers as Jamaica Kincaid, bell hooks, and Audre Lorde

0093312062 NORTON PB $12.00

James **Lord**

Six Exceptional Women

The author of *Picasso and Dora* extends his memoir to other fascinating personalities of the Parisian scene, including Alice B. Toklas and the great French actress Arletty

0-374-26553-4 FS&G $27.50

Katha **Pollitt**

Reasonable Creatures: Essays on Women and Feminism

A collection of pieces from the prize-winning poet and essayist for *The Nation, New Yorker*, and *New York Times.* "[Pollitt] brings a lively wit and considerable erudition to analyzing topics ranging from date rape to media-bashing of Hillary Clinton, and she consistently sees past the ephemeral quality of specific newsmaking events to locate issues of enduring importance"—*Publishers Weekly*

See also **HISTORY, POLITICS, AND SOCIETY** under **20TH-CENTURY AMERICAN ESSAYS AND JOURNALISM** in **LITERATURE OF THE AMERICAS**

0-394-57060-X KNOPF $25.00

0-679-76278-7 VINTAGE PB $11.00

Carolyn G. **Heilbrun**

The Education of a Woman: The Life and Times of Gloria Steinem

An intimate portrait of the American feminist, editor, author, and icon, as well as an insightful study of four decades of feminism

0-385-31371-3 DIAL BOOKS $24.95

0-345-40621-4 BALLANTINE PB $12.95

Rinchen Dolma **Taring**

Daughter of Tibet

Born in 1910 to one of the oldest families in Tibet, Taring was the first Tibetan girl to speak and write English. Her moving personal story covers the crucial 50 years up to 1959, and her subsequent exile from Tibet and work among the refugees in India

0-86171-044-4 WISDOM PB $18.95

Alice **Walker**

In Search of Our Mother's Gardens

0-15-644544-1 HARCOURT BRACE PB $10.95

Living by the Word: Collected Writings

"One of the most important, grieving, graceful, and honest writers ever to come into print…She can teach you to care and she can make you laugh, if you got any soul left…Alice seems calm and gentle and small. But this is a powerful, big, even a wild book"—June Jordan

0-15-152900-0 HARCOURT BRACE $15.95

0-15-652865-7 HARCOURT BRACE PB $9.00

Lois Beachy **Underhill**

The Woman Who Ran for President: The Many Lives of Victoria Woodhull

"An utterly fascinating, overdue tribute to an extraordinary feminist maverick, as well as a significant contribution to the history of feminism and the suffrage movement"—*Booklist*

See also **BIOGRAPHIES** under **US HISTORY, 1945 TO THE PRESENT** in **HISTORY OF THE AMERICAS**

INTRODUCTION BY GLORIA STEINEM

0-14-025638-5 PENGUIN PB $13.95

Joan **Hardwick**

The Yeats Sisters: A Biography of Susan and Elizabeth Yeats

Moving and scholarly, Hardwick's portrait of Yeats's two sisters is both a contribution to women's history and to the history of English literature. She shows Susan and Elizabeth Yeats both in their roles supporting and publishing their Nobel Prize-winning brother and as artists and businesswomen in their own right, struggling to accomplish their visions in the decidedly ambivalent Irish society at the beginning of the century

0-04-440924-9 HARPERCOLLINS PB $15.00

Language

See also GENDER STUDIES

Jennifer **Coates**

Women, Men and Language

0-582-07492-4 LONGMAN PB $26.25

Alette Olin **Hill**

Mother Tongue, Father Time: A Decade of Linguistic Revolt

See also **LANGUAGE AND SOCIETY** under **LINGUISTICS**

0-253-20389-9 INDIANA PB $10.95

Reference

Ruth **Ashby** & Deborah Gore **Ohrn**

Herstory: Women Who Changed the World

From Sappho to Toni Morrison, this biographic encyclopedia is perfect for young adults and grownups who wish to learn of famous as well as unsung but important females

INTRODUCTION BY GLORIA STEINEM

0-670-85434-4 VIKING $19.95

Robert E. **Bell**

Women of Classical Mythology: A Biographical Dictionary

The first comprehensive dictionary of mythological women, most of whom have gotten little recognition in standard works on mythology. Includes information on many little-known figures and takes a contemporary look at better-known ones like Medusa and Aphrodite. Each character entry includes a list of works and stories in which the figure appears

See also **REFERENCE WORKS** under **WORLD RELIGION** in **RELIGION, SPIRITUALITY, AND PHILOSOPHY**

0-87436-581-3 ABC CLIO $60.00

0-19-507977-9 OXFORD PB $14.95

Deborah G. **Felder**

The 100 Most Influential Women of All Time: A Ranking Past and Present

From social reformers to scientists, educators, labor leaders, artists, performers, and sports figures, Felder has ranked the 100 most influential women of history in a detailed and insightful biographical compendium. Lucille Ball clocks in at 100, Sandra Day O'Connor at 86, Coco Chanel at 50, Simone de Beauvoir at 15, and Eleanor Roosevelt tops the field that also includes the Virgin Mary (10) and Marie Curie (2)

See also **BIOGRAPHICAL DICTIONARIES** under **GENERAL INFORMATION** under **REFERENCE** in **BUSINESS AND REFERENCE**

0-8065-1726-3 CITADEL $24.95

Barbara R. **Hauser**, editor

Women's Legal Guide

This essential guide to the law, by 29 female lawyers, provides up-to-date legal information on health care, marriage, divorce, adoption, the rights of lesbians, sexual discrimination, estate planning, and much more. "This is every woman's handy guide to charting one's way through a legal system filled with overt or covert bias against her sex. The authors can even make the summary statement of a pension plan sound interesting"—Jill Ker Conway

See also **REFERENCE AND PRACTICAL GUIDES** under **LAW**

FOREWORD BY ROBERTA COOPER RAMO, PRESIDENT OF THE AMERICAN BAR ASSOCIATION

1-55591-913-8 FULCRUM $39.95

1-55591-303-2 FULCRUM PB $22.95

Doris **Cole**

From Tipi to Skyscraper: A History of Women in Architecture

0-262-53033-3 MIT PB........$7.50

Sue **Heineman**

Timelines of American Women's History

An exploration of the significant achievements of women in US history through profiles and accounts

0-399-51986-6 PERIGEE PB........$15.00

Darlene Clark **Hine**

Black Women in America: An Historic Encyclopedia

These two volumes represent a long overdue, comprehensive assemblage of successful black women, deceased and living. Most entries are accompanied by a picture and a description of the woman's family to provide historical perspective and placement. Astronauts, orchestra conductors, mayors, welders, psychiatrists, bankers, maids, and lawyers—all great and inspiring and thoroughly, beautifully recorded on these pages. Alongside all the encyclopedias of great men, these volumes are sure to stand out

See also **AFRICAN-AMERICAN HISTORY** under **AMERICAN HISTORY**

0-926019-61-9 CARLSON........$195.00

0-253-32774-1 INDIANA PB........$49.95

Rosalind **Miles**

Women's History of the World

Women's contributions on every level—domestic, emotional, social, sexual—as goddesses, war queens, scientists, artists, saints, and sinners. "An exhuberant book written in a jazzy, colorful style sizzling with puns and startling images"—*Washington Post Book World*

0-06-097317-X HARPERCOLLINS PB........$13.00

Elaine **Partnow**, editor

The New Quotable Woman: The Definitive Treasury of Notable Words by Women from Eve to the Present

Over 15,000 quotes from more than 2,500 women on every subject imaginable

See also **QUOTATIONS** under **QUOTATIONS AND PROVERBS** under **REFERENCE** in **BUSINESS AND REFERENCE**

0-452-01099-3 PLUME PB........$15.00

Merlin **Stone**

Ancient Mirrors of Womanhood: A Treasury of Goddess and Heroine Lore from Around the World

ILLUSTRATED BY CYNTHIA STONE

0-8070-6751-2 BEACON PB........$16.00

Doris **Weatherford**

American Women's History: An A-to-Z of People, Organizations, Issues and Events

An inspirational volume that emphasizes the human by profiling such exemplary American women as Grace Abbott, the first advocate of prenatal care; Susan B. Anthony, who was arrested when she cast a presidential vote in 1872; and such pioneer artists in their fields as singer Marian Anderson and novelist Willa Cather

0-671-85028-8 MACMILLAN PB........$18.00

Gay, Lesbian, and Bisexual Studies

Just over twenty years ago the field of "gay studies" did not exist. Books on the subject of homosexuality were mostly sociological or academic, starting from the premise that homosexuality was an illness or a depravity, and justifying that premise with scientific arguments or psychological observations. The modern gay rights movement began in 1969, when a police raid on the Stonewall Inn in New York's Greenwich Village caused irate patrons to resist and riot. The ensuing gay movement has ignited an explosion in publishing, with major publishers regularly adding gay titles to their lists, while small gay-oriented presses thrive. Added to the existing literature of gay life and culture is the new category of gay and lesbian parents.

History

Until recently, many gay men and lesbian women shared no sense of a common history, for their past was hidden in shame and secrecy. Even if historians had wanted to tackle the subject, few publishers would have accepted a work focusing on gay history. Today, however, books on all aspects of that history—traditions in classical Greece, the persecution of homosexuals by the Nazis, the recent outing movement—are readily available.

Alan **Berube**

Coming Out Under Fire: The History of Gay Men and Women in World War Two

The stories include combat in the jungles of the Pacific, lesbians serving in the WAC, draftees coming out to their parents, gay nightlife in the wartime boom cities, and incarceration in the military's "queer stockades"

0-452-26598-3 PLUME PB........$12.95

When Lester Ellis, a Hollywood actor, completed and passed his physical examination, he recalled, "I was sent upstairs to see the psychiatrist. He said 'We have heard about men like you.' I said, 'We have heard about men like *you*, so don't start.' He said 'Do you want to be in the Armed Forces?' I said, 'As far as I am concerned, I am already in.' So he signed the paper and let me go."

COMING OUT UNDER FIRE: THE HISTORY OF GAY MEN AND WOMEN IN WORLD WAR TWO

John **Boswell**

Same-Sex Unions in Premodern Europe

This scholarly work examines homosexual relations in the Eastern Orthodox and Catholic churches during the Middle Ages

See also **MIDDLE AGES AND RENAISSANCE** under **HISTORY** under **CHRISTIANITY** in **RELIGION, SPIRITUALITY, AND PHILOSOPHY**

0-679-75164-5 VINTAGE PB........$13.00

Alan **Bray**

Homosexuality in Renaissance England

This classic work, first published in 1982, set the standard for the history of sexuality. "Its clarity and objectivity make it a pleasure to read" —*Times Literary Supplement*

0-231-10289-5 COLUMBIA PB........$12.00

Bernadette J. **Brooten**

Love Between Women: Early Christian Responses to Female Homoeroticism

Since men could not easily conceive of lesbianism, it was often not a concern. Brooten digs deep to analyze the ancients' response to women and homosexuality

0-226-07591-5 CHICAGO........$34.95

Judith C. **Brown**

Immodest Acts: The Life of a Lesbian Nun in Renaissance Italy

Reconstructed from the archives of a church investigation, the story that reads like a novel of an abbess who had an affair with a nun

See also **WOMEN** under **SOCIAL AND ECONOMIC HISTORY** under **MEDIEVAL AND RENAISSANCE EUROPE** in **WORLD HISTORY AND CURRENT AFFAIRS**

0-19-503675-1 OXFORD........$25.00

0-19-504225-5 OXFORD PB........$11.95

B.R. **Burg**

Sodomy and the Pirate Tradition: English Sea Rovers in the Seventeenth-Century Caribbean

The sexual mores and practices of English buccaneers in the 17th century

See also **SLAVERY AND PIRACY** under **LATIN AMERICA AND THE CARIBBEAN** in **HISTORY OF THE AMERICAS**

0-8147-1236-3 NYU PB........$14.95

John **D'Emilio**

Sexual Politics, Sexual Communities: The Making of a Homosexual Minority in the United States, 1940-1970

The rise of gay consciousness, from a historical perspective. "An intelligent, trustworthy, and welcome addition to our understanding of minority history"
—Peter G. Filene, *Journal of American History*

0-226-14266-3 CHICAGO PB........$11.95

K.J. **Dover**

Greek Homosexuality

"A landmark study—with philosophical brilliance and scholarly objectivity, he presents facts that can no longer be ignored"—Erich Segal

See also **PRIVATE LIFE, SEXUALITY, AND RECREATION** under **TOPICS IN ANCIENT GREEK HISTORY** under **ANCIENT GREECE** in **WORLD HISTORY AND CURRENT AFFAIRS**

0-674-36270-5 HARVARD PB........$15.00

Martin **Duberman**

About Time: Exploring the Gay Past

At times resembling a gay *Ripley's Believe It or Not*, a historical examination of gay life

0-452-01081-0 MERIDIAN PB........$15.95

Stonewall

"Illuminating…a vivid and stirring recreation of the Stonewall riot, probing beneath its symbolism to discover the social forces it unleashed"—*LA Times Book Review*

0-452-27206-8 PLUME PB $12.95

Martin **Duberman**, editor

Hidden from History

A comprehensive anthology covering many aspects of gay and lesbian history

0-452-01067-5 MERIDIAN PB $15.95

Lillian **Faderman**

Odd Girls and Twilight Lovers

An eclectic view of the history of lesbianism by the renowned author of *Surpassing the Love of Men*. "Faderman grasps the phenomenon of twentieth-century history—that its shaping histories are the issues of so-called minorities—and brings lesbian life out of the archives and onto the streets. A scholarly and fascinating study of the women whose sexuality and politics have profoundly affected mainstream America"—Jeanette Winterson

0-231-07488-3 COLUMBIA $35.00

0-14-017122-3 PENGUIN PB $13.95

Scotch Verdict

The award-winning author of *Odd Girls and Twilight Lovers* examines the famous case of two 19th-century schoolmistresses who were ruined by accusations of homosexuality (the basis for Lillian Hellman's *The Children's Hour)*. Using the trial, the accusations, and the public response, Faderman discusses women in the 19th century, and, more broadly, the sociosexual mores of the time. A piercing work of lesbian-feminist scholarship

0-231-08443-9 COLUMBIA PB $16.00

Surpassing the Love of Men: Romantic Friendship and Love Between Women from the Renaissance to the Present

"…a superb study that all who are interested in women, in sexuality, and in the family must read"—Carroll Smith-Rosenberg, University of Pennsylvania

0-688-13330-4 QUILL PB $15.00

Heinz **Heger**

The Men with the Pink Triangle

A first-hand account of gay men in Nazi concentration camps

TRANSLATED BY DAVID FERNBACH

0-932870-06-6 ALYSON PB $5.95

Jonathan N. **Katz**

The Invention of Heterosexuality

How language affects perception

See also **GENDER AND SEXUALITY** under **PSYCHOLOGY**

FOREWORD BY GORE VIDAL

0-525-93845-1 DUTTON $22.95

0-452-27542-3 DUTTON PB $13.95

Gerard **Kent** & Gert **Helema**, editors

The Pursuit of Sodomy: Male Homosexuality in Renaissance and Enlightenment Europe

0-86656-491-8 HAWORTH $59.95

0-918393-49-3 HAWORTH PB $19.95

Elizabeth Lapovsky **Kennedy** & Madeline D. **Davis**

Boots of Leather, Slippers of Gold: The History of a Lesbian Community

This very first community study of lesbians, researched over 13 years, includes such topics as sex, relationships, coming out, motherhood, work, oppression, and pride. *"Boots of Leather, Slippers of Gold* honors all of us ….[It] opens up the heart and mind…. [It] breaks new ground in women's history, lesbian history, and the history of desire as a lived force in a community under siege"—Joan Nestle, co-founder of the Lesbian Herstory Archives

See also **HISTORY OF SEXUALITY** under **TOPICS IN AMERICAN STUDIES** in **HISTORY OF THE AMERICAS**

0-415-90293-2 ROUTLEDGE $39.95

0-14-023550-7 PENGUIN PB $13.95

Salvatore **Licata** & Robert **Peterson**, editors

The Gay Past: A Collection of Historical Essays

Prominent academics' descriptions of attitudes toward homosexuality in earlier times

0-918393-11-6 HARRINGTON PARK PB $14.95

Eric **Marcus**

Making History: The Struggle for Gay and Lesbian Equal Rights 1945-1990

From the small, underground organizations to the national movement, Marcus depicts the individuals who, by constantly challenging the status quo, put their reputations on the line for the cause

0-06-016708-4 HARPERPERENNIAL PB $25.00

Esther **Newton**

Cherry Grove, Fire Island: Sixty Years in America's First Gay and Lesbian Town

How did this tiny resort community off the coast of New York become a crucible of gay identity and culture? Lively interviews with Grove residents aged 18 to 85 vividly evoke land development battles, legendary parties, and discrimination in the building of this important haven

0-8070-7927-8 BEACON PB $14.95

Don **Paulson** & Roger **Simpson**

An Evening at the Garden of Allah: A Gay Cabaret in Seattle

Over 20 patrons and performers remember the gay-owned cabaret that opened in Seattle in 1946 and recollect what it meant to be gay three decades before Stonewall. 70 black-and-white photos

0-231-09698-4 COLUMBIA $34.95

Richard **Plant**

The Pink Triangle: The Nazi War Against Homosexuals

History of discrimination against gays in World War II Europe

See also **GENERAL SURVEYS** under **THE HOLOCAUST** in **WORLD HISTORY AND CURRENT AFFAIRS**

0-8050-0600-1 HOLT PB $13.00

D. Michael **Quinn**

Same-Sex Dynamics Among Nineteenth-Century Americans: A Mormon Example

Until the mid-20th century the Mormon Church was surprisingly accepting of homosexual relationships. "Quinn's book is a model of critical religious history"—*Publishers Weekly*

0-252-02205-X ILLINOIS $29.95

Douglas **Sadownick**

Sex Between Men: An Intimate History of the Sex Lives of Gay Men Postwar to Present

From personal testimony, thoughtful commentary, and social history, this wide-ranging volume provides a full-scale psychosocial analysis of the sexual behavior of the modern gay man. The most complete description yet of the sexual consciousness now emerging from five decades of wildly divergent experience

0-06-251268-4 HARPERCOLLINS $25.00

Sarah **Schulman**

My American History: Lesbian and Gay Life During the Reagan/Bush Years

The prolific young novelist (*Empathy, People In Trouble*), activist (co-founder of Lesbian Avengers), and journalist (for *Village Voice, The Nation, NY Times*) has written an intensely personal political memoir of the '80s that accurately chronicles the sometimes lonely progressive struggles of those bleak Reagan-Bush years. "I admit that I am not typical," writes Schulman. "My view is not a typical view. I am thirty-four years old. This is, I suppose, volume one"

0-415-90852-3 ROUTLEDGE $49.95

0-415-90853-1 ROUTLEDGE PB $18.95

Rodger **Streitmatter**

Unspeakable: The Rise of the Gay and Lesbian Press in America

The author has "put together the definitive history of homosexual magazines, newspapers and even samizdat newsletters in the U.S. between 1947 and the present—[and] has done a masterful job of telling the complex story" —*Publishers Weekly*

0-571-19873-2 FABER $27.95

Andrea **Weiss** & Greta **Schiller**

Before Stonewall: The Making of a Gay and Lesbian Community

An illustrated guide to the Emmy-winning documentary

0-941483-20-7 NAIAD PB $7.95

Homophobia

Una **Fahy**

How to Make the World a Better Place for Gays and Lesbians

A practical handbook to counter and combat homophobia

0-446-67041-3 WARNER PB $9.99

Warren J. **Blumenfield**, editor

Homophobia: How We All Pay the Price

Essays, both personal and analytical, describe the cost of homophobia to our relationships, institutions, and other areas of national life. Includes an appendix on how to run an anti-homophobia workshop. "[M]akes forcefully clear that homophobia stunts the hater even as it oppresses the hated"—Martin B. Duberman. "It can help open our eyes…and prevent needless and tragic suffering"—Beth Winship

0-8070-7919-7 BEACON PB $18.00

Kevin **Jennings**, editor

One Teacher in 10: Gay and Lesbian Educators Tell Their Stories

Compilation of stories detailing the many ways teachers are fighting homophobia in the classroom

1-55583-263-6 ALYSON PB $9.95

Rita M. **Kissen**

The Last Closet: The Real Lives of Gay and Lesbian Teachers

The author interviewed 105 gay, lesbian, and bisexual teachers and other school staff. "A unique resource for teachers, parents and administrators who want to challenge homophobic stereotypes and improve the lives of gay and lesbian educators"—*Publishers Weekly*

0-435-07005-3 HEINEMANN $23.95

Richard D. **Mohr**

Gay Ideas: Outing and Other Controversies

Mohr seeks to determine how gays can assert themselves in a climate of repression, insisting that society can gain more from gay people than gay people can gain from society

0-8070-7921-9 BEACON PB $15.00

Michelangelo **Signorile**

Outing Yourself: How to Come Out as Lesbian or Gay to Your Family, Your Friends, and Your Coworkers

Out magazine columnist offers a 14-step program designed for self-acceptance and simple exercises to prepare for the process of coming out to family and colleagues

See also LOVERS, FAMILIES, AND FRIENDS

0-679-43838-6 RANDOM HOUSE $20.00
0-684-82617-8 FIRESIDE PB $11.00

Queer in America: Sex, the Media and the Closets of Power

From the man who "outed" Malcolm Forbes, who accused *The New York Times* of homophobia, and whom *Newsweek* named as one of the 100 members of the cultural elite, comes a no-holds-barred look at the "closets" of Washington, D.C., Hollywood, and the media. Praising gay-positive corporations in Silicon Valley, discussing growing up gay in Brooklyn, and accusing a person of national prominence of same-sex sexual harassment, Signorile gives voice to hundreds of homosexuals whose lives have been severely challenged by institutionalized homophobia

0-385-47377-X ANCHOR PB $14.00

Gay Life and Culture

Bruce **Bawer**, editor

Beyond Queer: Challenging Gay Left Orthodoxy

0-684-82766-2 FREE PRESS $25.00

A Place at the Table: The Gay Individual in American Society

Bawer (*Diminishing Fictions, The Screenplay's the Thing*) delivers a fresh, insightful, and provocative discussion on the role of homosexuals in society. Stripping away the misconceptions that underlie homophobia, he also criticizes the extremists in the gay movement who have been instrumental in promoting public misinformation about gay lifestyles. "Smashes the common stereotypes of gay people to smithereens" —Christopher Lehmann-Haupt

0-671-79533-3 POSEIDON $21.00
0-671-89439-0 TOUCHSTONE PB $12.00

Robin **Bernstein**, editor & Seth Clark **Silberman**

Generation Q

1-55583-356-X ALYSON PB $11.95

Leo **Bersani**

Homos

The widely respected literary and cultural critic looks at homosexuality in America

0-674-40619-2 HARVARD $22.95

Warren J. **Blumenfeld** & Diane **Raymond**

Looking at Gay and Lesbian Life

A well-documented and up-to-date look at issues central to the gay and lesbian experience, written by two leading activist scholars

0-8070-7923-5 BEACON PB $19.00

Keith **Boykin**

One More River to Cross: Black and Gay in America

As a former special media assistant to President Clinton, Boykin was the liaison to the gay and African-American communities. His book is the fascinating account of what he learned—not only how the straight world views gays and minorities, but how the gay world views itself

0-385-47982-4 READER'S CATALOG $23.95

Howard **Brown**

Familiar Faces, Hidden Lives: The Story of Homosexual Men in America Today

Accounts of contemporary gay men, written by a former New York City official

0-15-630120-2 HARCOURT BRACE PB $8.95

Kate **Chedgzoy**

Shakespeare's Queer Children: Sexual Politics and Contemporary Culture

How Shakespeare has been appropriated by culture illuminated through the works of Oscar Wilde, Angela Carter, and filmmaker Derek Jarman

0-7190-4658-0 MANCHESTER PB $19.95

Catherine **Chermayeff** & others, editors

Drag Diaries

The fastest-growing profession captured in interviews with those at the top: RuPaul, Lypsinka, Lady Bunny, and others with illustrations, bibliography, drag calendar, drag shopping guide, and filmography

0-8118-0895-5 CHRONICLE $17.95

Meryl **Cohn**

Do What I Say: Ms. Behavior's Guide to Gay and Lesbian Etiquette

0-395-74538-1 DORLING KINDERSLEY PB $11.95

Margaret L. **Cruikshank**, editor

The Lesbian Path

Collection of accounts of lesbian experiences

0-912516-96-8 SUBTERRANEAN PB $10.95

Alexander **Doty**

Keeping Things Perfectly Queer: Interpreting Mass Culture

Insightfully explores the uncategorizable space that "queerness"—be it heterosexual or gay—occupies in our culture. Jack Benny, Laverne & Shirley, and Pee-Wee Herman are among the spotlighted icons. "Alexander Doty has produced the most lucid expression so far of the value of queerness to cultural criticism. Each chapter is an innovation in its own right" —Andrew Ross, Princeton University

0-8166-2244-2 MINNESOTA $39.95
0-8166-2245-0 MINNESOTA PB $15.95

Lars **Eighner**

Gay Cosmos

The author of *Travels with Lizbeth* presents a collection of essays on the naturalness of all sexualities and "…provides a much needed cultural and historical context for homosexuality"—*Publishers Weekly*

1-56333-236-1 MASQUERADE PB $6.95

Lesley **Ferris**, editor

Crossing the Stage: Controversies on Cross-Dressing

0-415-06268-3 ROUTLEDGE $49.95
0-415-06269-1 ROUTLEDGE PB $15.95

David F. **Greenberg**

The Construction of Homosexuality

An exhaustive cross-cultural and historical account of homosexuality in its societal organization

0-226-30627-5 CHICAGO $42.00

Gilbert **Herdt**

Gay Culture in America: Essays from the Field

This collection of essays bears witness to the evolving institutions and wealth of gay culture. "Probes into life in gay society, delving well beyond the stereotypes…Highly recommended"—*Library Journal*

0-8070-7915-4 BEACON PB $15.00

Guy **Hocquenghem** &
Daniella **Dangoor**, translator

Homosexual Desire

INTRODUCTION BY MICHAEL MOON
PREFACE BY JEFFREY WEEKS
0-8223-1425-8 DUKE $34.95

Karla **Jay**, editor

Dyke Life: From Growing Up to Growing Old, a Celebration of the Lesbian Experience

English professor and longtime lesbian and gay-rights activist, Jay mixes the highly serious with the utterly irreverent in this wide-ranging book on growing up female and gay. From coming out to raising children, this is a collection of reflections that, addressing the specificity of the lesbian experience, is sure to be an authoritative classic
0-465-03907-3 BASIC $23.00
0-465-03908-1 BASIC PB $14.00

Seymour **Kleinberg**

Alienated Affections: Being Gay in America

Kleinberg investigates his own life in order to understand what it means to be gay in America, and discusses the "gay sensibility," passing as straight, the new masculinity of gay men, and aging
0-312-02158-5 ST. MARTIN'S PB $8.95

JoAnn **Loulan**

Lesbian Passion

A ground-breaking work on lesbian life, incorporating research from a study of 1,600 women
0-933216-29-7 SPINSTERS INK PB $12.95

Neil **Miller**

Out in the World: Gay and Lesbian Life from Buenos Aires to Bangkok

The author of *In Search of Gay America* (which is out of print) extends his exploration of gay cultures to the rest of the world. He examines persecution of gays in South America, their acceptance among native Australian peoples, their legal assimilation in Denmark, and their near-invisibility in Egypt. "A fascinating tour of the ways minorities of any sort...adapt to and influence their cultures"—*Kirkus Reviews*
See also **ANTHROPOLOGY**
0-679-74551-3 VINTAGE PB $13.00

Donald **Morton**, editor

The Material Queer: A LesBiGay Cultural Studies Reader

A Western Civ course on homosexuality in one volume. Includes among others: Freud, Barthes, Derrida, Foucault
0-8133-1927-7 WESTVIEW PB $25.00

Eve Kosofsky **Sedgwick**

Epistemology of the Closet

"Sedgwick's brilliant *Epistemology of the Closet* will have many lives: as a work of literary criticism, a cultural study, a political analysis; as a text for gay and straight, academic and nonacademic readers, and potentially as a landmark in the development of lesbian and gay studies...An extraordinary book"
—Julie Abraham, *Women's Review of Books*
0-520-07874-8 CALIFORNIA PB $14.95

Erica **Rand**

Barbie's Queer Accessories

The history of the doll and how she's been appropriated in art and popular culture, from an ACT UP member and assistant professor of art
0-8223-1604-8 DUKE $45.95
0-8223-1620-X DUKE PB $15.95

Arlene **Stein**, editor

Sisters, Sexperts, Queers: Beyond the Lesbian Nation

Essays that focus on the differences within the lesbian community—on class difference, on the politics of butch-fem identity, on lesbian pop stars, and on the rich diversity possible in lesbian culture. Contributions from Alisa Solomon, Jackie Goldsby, Maria Maggenti, and others show that shared sexual preference does not necessarily mean identical identity
0-452-26887-7 PLUME PB $12.95

Andrew **Sullivan**

Virtually Normal: An Argument About Homosexuality

The former editor of *The New Republic* offers an exploration, cogent and convincing, of the principal arguments about homosexuality from the Catholic Church to Michel Foucault. Dividing the debate into four competing politics—Prohibitionist, Liberationist, Conservative, and Liberal—Sullivan patiently explicates the weaknesses of each and proposes a new politic, reasoned and passionate, based on full societal equality for homosexuals
0-679-42382-6 KNOPF $22.00

Lindsy **Van Gelder** & Pamela Robin **Brandt**

The Girls in the Band: Into the Heart of Lesbian America

Birkenstocks to Doc Martens, this ground-breaking book draws on more than 100 interviews with gay women around the country to draw an unparalleled portrait of the lesbian today. An entertaining, enlightening, and appreciative tour of a burgeoning subculture
0-684-81118-9 SIMON & SCHUSTER $23.00

Martin S. **Weinberg**

Dual Attraction: Understanding Bisexuality

"Ground breaking...Offers us a new way to think about sexuality"—Virginia Johnson Masters
0-19-509841-2 OXFORD PB $15.95

Edmund **White**

States of Desire: Travels in Gay America

A study of contemporary gay American life, written by the prominent novelist
See also **REPORTING** under **20TH-CENTURY AMERICAN ESSAYS AND JOURNALISM** in **LITERATURE OF THE AMERICAS**
0-452-26689-0 PLUME PB $11.95

Lynn **Witt** & others, editors

Out in all Directions: The Almanac of Gay and Lesbian America

Ten chapters, dozens of photographs, and contributions from every corner of the United States constitute this essential guide to gay living in America. From gay and lesbian movie and television personalities, gay politicians, and the history of the struggle against AIDS, this is a vibrant and essential collection of articles, trivia, tidbits, and information about being gay and lesbian in America today
See also **TRAVEL** under **ANTHOLOGIES AND REFERENCE**
0-446-51822-0 WARNER $24.95

Careers

Gregory M. **Herek** & others, editors

Out in Force: Sexual Orientation and the Military

See also **MILITARY REFORM AND CIVIL-MILITARY RELATIONS** under **AMERICAN DEFENSE POLICY** under **INTERNATIONAL RELATIONS AND STRATEGIC STUDIES**
0-226-40048-4 CHICAGO PB $17.95

Richard A. **Rusi** &
Lourdes **Rodriguez-Nordes**

Out in the Workplace: The Pleasures and Perils of Coming Out on the Job

First-hand accounts from all professions with up-to-date information on the law pertinent to employment discrimination
1-55583-251-2 ALYSON PB $12.95

Randy **Shilts**

Conduct Unbecoming: Gays and Lesbians in the U.S. Military

The author of the hugely successful and influential *And the Band Played On* interviewed 1,000 gay service people, uncovering incredible stories of heroism and of persecution
0-312-09261-X ST. MARTIN'S $27.95

Randy Shilts

Politics and Law

Denis **Clifford** & Hayden **Curry**

A Legal Guide for Lesbian and Gay Couples

Practical book covering all legal aspects of couples living together
0-87337-269-7 NOLO PB $24.95

William **Eskridge** Jr.

The Case for Same-Sex Marriage: From Sexual Liberty to Civilized Commitment

"If all Americans could set aside their visceral responses to the words 'gay marriage' and read this book, the issue would be settled. Period" —Bruce Bawer, *Beyond Queer* and *A Place at the Table*

0-684-82404-3 FREE PRESS $25.00

Gary **Kinsman**

The Regulation of Desire: Sexuality in Canada

A sociologist studies the relationships among government regulation, social mores, and gay life in Canada

0-920057-79-9 BLACK ROSE $36.95
0-920057-81-0 TORONTO PB $16.95

Richard D. **Mohr**

A More Perfect Union: Why Straight America Must Stand Up for Gay Rights

"A powerful book whose timing is just perfect. Send this book to your family, friends, and political allies"—David Mixner

See also **CURRENT POLITICAL THOUGHT AND ISSUES** under **AMERICAN POLITICS AND FOREIGN POLICY** in **HISTORY OF THE AMERICAS**

0-8070-7933-2 BEACON PB $9.00

David E. **Newton**

Gay and Lesbian Rights

Newton provides a balanced study of gay and lesbian rights in America, including up-to-date information about relevant legislation

0-87436-745-X ABC CLIO $39.50

Richard A. **Posner** & Katharine B. **Silbaugh**, editors

A Guide to America's Sex Laws

A must for every activist, gay or straight

See also **REFERENCE AND PRACTICAL GUIDES** under **LAW**

0-226-67564-5 CHICAGO $26.95

Ruthann **Robson**

Lesbian (out)law: Survival Under the Rule of Law

An attorney on the faculty of CUNY Law School answers the question: How can lesbians use the law without being used by it?

See also **LEGAL THEORY** under **LAW**

1-56341-013-3 FIREBRAND $20.95
1-56341-012-5 FIREBRAND PB $9.95

William B. **Rubenstein**, editor

Lesbians, Gay Men, and the Law: A Reader

Rubenstein, Director of the Lesbian and Gay Rights Project for the ACLU, designed Harvard's first courses on homosexuality and the law. This anthology—which comes from those courses—places major gay-rights cases and other documents of the struggle in historical and political context

1-56584-027-5 NEW PRESS $45.00
1-56584-037-2 NEW PRESS PB $30.00

Sex and Sexuality

Gregory W. **Bredbeck**

Sodomy and Interpretation: Milton to Marlowe

An intriguing reexamination of Renaissance texts using the language and doctrine of such contemporary theorists as Foucault and Derrida

0-8014-2644-8 CORNELL $38.95
0-8014-9945-3 CORNELL PB $14.95

Susie **Bright**

Susie Bright's Sexual Reality: A Virtual Sex World Reader

With this new pop primer on sex, Bright continues her erotic travelogue. Whether it's sex talk with Camille Paglia or life on the less-traveled road, her frank and candid voice on the human sexual condition is always illuminating and entertaining. "A fascinating mix of the Madonna and Whore, Susie rides the gash between good girl and bad girl with great glee…Bright is irreverent, witty and wicked"—Wendy Chapkis, *Metro*

0-939416-58-1 CLEIS $24.95
0-939416-59-X CLEIS PB $9.95

Frank **Browning**

A Queer Geography: Journeys Toward a Sexual Self

National Public Radio reporter and author of *The Culture of Desire* discusses the quasi-religious quality that American gay political activism has and compares to it the ritualized gay sex among tribesmen of New Guinea, Brazil, and the Philippines

See also **ANTHROPOLOGY**

0-517-59857-4 CROWN $24.00

Chandler **Burr**

A Separate Creation: The Search for the Biological Origins of Sexual Orientation

"Burr's detailed, elegantly written report takes us to the front lines of research into a possible biological or genetic basis for homosexuality" —*Publishers Weekly*

See also **GENETICS** under **LIFE SCIENCES** in **SCIENCE**

0-7868-6081-2 HYPERION $24.95

John **De Cecco** & John **Elia**, editors

If You Seduce a Straight Person, Can You Make Them Gay?

In a coherent and rational discussion of the debate on whether or not people are born homosexual or become so at some point in their lives, the editors suggest an alternative view. That is, sexual orientation is determined by a mix of biological, personal, and cultural influences

1-56024-386-4 HAWORTH $49.95
1-56023-034-7 HARRINGTON PARK PB $14.95

Lindsey **Elder**

Early Embraces

Lesbian erotica

1-55583-354-3 ALYSON PB $11.95

Jonathan **Dollimore**

Sexual Dissidence: Augustine to Wilde, Freud to Foucault

The author draws on writers as varied as André Gide and Frantz Fanon, Sigmund Freud and St. Augustine to study the origins of Western attitudes toward homosexuality, and explains the paradox of a society obsessed with what it marginalizes

0-19-811269-6 OXFORD PB $18.95

Marjorie **Garber**

Vice Versa: Bisexuality and the Eroticism of Everyday Life

Harvard English professor (*Vested Interests: Cross-Dressing and Cultural Anxiety*) posits that sexuality is a continuum, not a "third" category or a period of confusion. She analyzes the lives of dozens of celebrities as well as bisexual themes in books and movies

0-684-80308-9 SIMON & SCHUSTER $30.00
0-684-82412-4 SIMON & SCHUSTER PB $16.00

Richard **Green**

The Sissy Boy Syndrome and the Development of Homosexuality

A study of the early life development of male homosexual behavior

0-300-03696-5 YALE $18.00

Dean **Hamer** & Peter **Copeland**

The Science of Desire: The Search for the Gay Gene and the Biology of Behavior

Hamer, a researcher at the National Cancer Institute, chronicles the scientific investigation that gave him the controversial hypothesis that he found the "gay gene"

0-671-88724-6 SIMON & SCHUSTER $23.00
0-684-80446-8 TOUCHSTONE PB $13.00

Karla **Jay**, editor

Lesbian Erotics

"Karla Jay is one of the authentic pioneers of lesbian studies. Here she brings together 16 essays on the once-taboo, now gloriously 'speakable' subject of lesbian sexuality" —Terry Castle, *The Apparitional Lesbian*

0-8147-4225-4 NYU PB $17.95

John **Preston** & Michael **Lowenthal**, editors

Flesh and the Word 3: An Anthology of Gay Erotic Writing

"The imagery here is often visceral, the language sophisticated and the humor on an even keel with eros"—*Publishers Weekly*

See also **EROTICA** under **COURTSHIP, LOVE, SEX, AND MARRIAGE** in **LIFESTYLES AND PRACTICAL ADVICE**

0-452-27252-1 PENGUIN PB $13.95

Esther D. **Rothblum** & Kathleen A. **Brehony**

Boston Marriages: Romantic But Asexual Relationships Among Contemporary Lesbians

"Boston marriages"—female partners who live together without having sexual relations—are here reexamined as a key to understanding lesbianism and the social construction of sexual identity. Are such partners lesbians? Should they even define themselves in sexual terms? These

essays examine both heterosexual and gay preconceptions about union
0-87023-876-0 MASSACHUSETTS PB $15.95

Charles **Silverstein** & Felice **Picano**
The New Joy of Gay Sex
Silverstein, co-author of the best selling *The Joy of Gay Sex,* and award-winning novelist Felice Picano have updated the original with all-new illustrations and a completely revised text to reflect the changing times and concerns of the gay community. Invaluable as an information resource, as a helpful aide for building self-esteem, and as a coming-out guide
0-06-092438-1 HARPERPERENNIAL PB $20.00

AIDS and Health

AIDS is the biggest crisis faced by the gay community since the beginning of the gay liberation movement. The many AIDS-related books include histories and politics of the disease, healthy life style how-tos, and spiritual or meditative essays on coping with the tragedy.

John G. **Bartlett** & Ann K. **Finkbeiner**
The Guide to Living with HIV Infection: Developed at the Johns Hopkins AIDS Clinic, Third Edition
How to negotiate the formidable challenges—medical, legal, psychological, and financial—presented by HIV. It includes updated information on new drugs, transmission of HIV, HIV and women, and much more. "An excellent resource for people with HIV infection, as well as those who live with or love them"
—Jane E. Brody, *NY Times*
See also **AIDS** under **SPECIFIC HEALTH PROBLEMS** under **HEALTH** in **LIFESTYLES AND PRACTICAL ADVICE**
0-8018-5358-3 JOHNS HOPKINS $40.00
0-8018-5359-1 JOHNS HOPKINS PB $15.95

Martin **Delaney** & Peter **Goldblum**
Strategies for Survival: A Gay Men's Health Manual for the Age of AIDS
A comprehensive guide covering gay health
See also **AIDS** under **SPECIFIC HEALTH PROBLEMS** under **HEALTH** in **LIFESTYLES AND PRACTICAL ADVICE**
0-312-00558-X ST. MARTIN'S PB $10.95

John Nguyet **Erni**
Unstable Frontiers: Technomedicine and the Cultural Politics of "Curing" AIDS
See also **MEDICAL AND RESEARCH ASPECTS** under **AIDS** under **MEDICINE** in **SCIENCE**
0-8166-2380-5 MINNESOTA $39.95
0-8166-2381-3 MINNESOTA PB $15.95

David B. **Feinberg**
Queer and Loathing: Rants and Raves of a Raging AIDS Clone
From the 1988 ACT UP seizure of FDA headquarters to the top ten creative solutions for Jesse Helms, Feinberg—who died of AIDS-related complications in 1994—was the ultimate chronicler, satirist, and black humorist of the tragedy of his own illness. "This is AIDS literature for a new generation—funny, impertinent, sexy, and enlightening."—*The Advocate*. "The ultimate gadfly of the epidemic…here's one book that deserves a place in a time capsule"—Armistead Maupin
WITH A NEW PREFACE BY TONY KUSHNER
0-14-024080-2 PENGUIN PB $11.95

Larry **Kramer**
Reports from the Holocaust: The Making of an AIDS Activist
A collection of essays on AIDS from 1978 to the present written by a leading gay activist and playwright, author of *The Normal Heart*
See also **AIDS** under **MEDICINE** in **SCIENCE**
0-312-11419-2 ST. MARTIN'S PB $13.95

Margaret R. **Rodway** & Brian L. **Wingrove**
The Healthy Homosexual
A psychological and sociological study
0-87212-180-1 LIBRA $9.95

Randy **Shilts**
And the Band Played On: Politics, People, and the AIDS Epidemic
The groundbreaking masterpiece of investigative reporting reveals, in the mishandling of the AIDS epidemic, the inadequacies of a government obsessed with budget considerations, health authorities more interested in politics than public health, and scientists overly concerned with international prestige. "A heroic work of journalism on what must rank as one of the foremost catastrophes of modern history"—*NY Times*
See also **AIDS** under **MEDICINE** in **SCIENCE**
0-14-023221-4 VIKING PB $15.00

Lovers, Families, and Friends

Fearing rejection, many gay men and lesbians find it difficult to tell their families and friends about their sexual orientation. A growing number of books have been written to help these loved ones understand and accept the situation. At the same time, gay men and women are addressing the issue of being parents themselves.

Betty **Berzon**
The Intimacy Dance: A Guide to Long-Term Success in Gay and Lesbian Relationships
A psychotherapist and author (*Permanent Partners*) emphasizes that positive attitude is a major factor to relationship success
0-525-94234-3 DUTTON $23.95

Permanent Partners: Building Gay and Lesbian Relationships that Last
A manual for gay and lesbian couples, written by a lesbian psychotherapist specializing in the counseling of same-sex couples
0-525-24698-3 PLUME PB $18.95

John D. **Cecco**, editor
Gay Relationships
A series of essays addressing gay relationships from a variety of perspectives
0-918393-33-7 HARRINGTON PARK PB $14.95

Don **Clark**
The New Loving Someone Gay
Updated version of a sympathetic guide for families and friends of gay men and women
0-89087-505-7 CELESTIAL ARTS PB $9.95

David P. **McWhirter** & Andrew M. **Mattison**
The Male Couple: How Relationships Develop
Sociological study of gay relationships
0-13-547563-5 PRENTICE HALL PB $14.95

Bob **Powers** & Alan **Ellis**
A Family and Friend's Guide to Sexual Orientation
How to be supportive to someone who is gay
0-415-91276-8 ROUTLEDGE PB $17.95

Michelangelo **Signorile**
Outing Yourself: How to Come Out as Lesbian or Gay to Your Family, Your Friends, and Your Coworkers
Out magazine columnist offers a 14-step program designed for self-acceptance and simple exercises to prepare for the process of coming out to family and colleagues
See also **HOMOPHOBIA**
0-679-43838-6 RANDOM HOUSE $20.00
0-684-82617-8 FIRESIDE PB $11.00

Suzanne **Slater**
The Lesbian Family Life Cycle
A psychotherapist who specializes in counseling lesbians presents a study for cohabiting lesbians in five stages. From being a couple through to retirement, she discusses how couples can cope with each stage of life
0-02-920895-5 FREE PRESS $25.00

Parents of Gays and Lesbians

Bev **Arthur** & Martin **Arthur**
Mama's Boy
A mother and her gay son discuss their relationship
0-89407-054-1 STRAWBERRY HILL PB $9.95

Robert **Bernstein**
Straight Parents, Gay Children: Keeping Families Together
1-56025-085-2 THUNDER'S MOUTH $24.95
1-56025-086-0 THUNDER'S MOUTH PB $12.95

Mary V. **Borhek**
Coming Out to Parents: A Two-Way Survival Guide for Lesbians and Gay Men and Their Parents
Revised and updated for the '90s with chapters on HIV/AIDS and theological issues
0-8298-0957-0 PILGRIM PB $14.95

Betty **Fairchild** & Nancy **Hayward**
Now that You Know: What Every Parent Should Know About Homosexuality
Advice for the parents of gays, written by two mothers with gay children
0-15-667702-4 HARCOURT BRACE PB $6.95

Gay and Lesbian Parents

Katherine **Arnup**, editor

Lesbian Parenting: Living with Pride & Prejudice

A complete and up-to-date anthology that covers the issues of insemination, adoption, rearing kids, and the law

0-921881-33-9 GYNERGY BOOKS PB $16.95

Frederick W. **Bozett**, editor

Gay and Lesbian Parents

Psychological, sociological, and legal aspects of gay parenting

0-275-92370-3 PRAEGER $55.00
0-275-92541-2 PRAEGER PB $19.95

Anndee **Hochman**

Everyday Acts & Small Subversions: Women Reinventing Family, Community and Home

"A compelling book about the options both straight and lesbian women have—and the complications and freedoms those options offer"—*The Oregonian*

See also **MOTHERS** under **BEING A PARENT** under **PARENTING** in **LIFESTYLES AND PRACTICAL ADVICE**

0-933377-25-8 EIGHTH MOUNTAIN PB $12.95

Ellen **Lewin**

Lesbian Mothers: Accounts of Gender in American Culture

Over 100 lesbian mothers tell their stories of how they came to motherhood, how they see children, relatives, and lovers, how they manage child custody and finances, and how they deal with threats to their rights as gay mothers

0-8014-2857-2 CORNELL $37.50
0-8014-8099-X CORNELL PB $14.95

April **Martin**

The Lesbian and Gay Parenting Handbook: Creating and Raising Our Families

A psychotherapist and a lesbian parent, the author sensitively addresses the many questions that confront gay parents. "What a gift April Martin has given us. Destined to become the primary guidebook to parenthood for lesbian and gay people"—Eric Marcus, *The Male Couple's Guide* and *Making History*

0-06-096929-6 HARPERPERENNIAL PB $16.00

Sandra **Pollack** & Jeanne **Vaughn**, editors

Politics of the Heart: A Lesbian Parenting Anthology

First-person accounts by lesbians with children

See also **MOTHERHOOD** under **THE FEMALE EXPERIENCE** under **WOMEN'S STUDIES**

0-932379-36-2 FIREBRAND $26.95
0-932379-35-4 FIREBRAND PB $12.95

John **Preston** & Michael **Lowenthal**, editors

Friends and Lovers: Gay Men Write About the Families They Create

"Any gay reader is bound to find in this collection a glimmer of his own experience…a way to think about the accidental arrangements of our lives that have created our families"—*Genre*

0-452-27254-8 PLUME PB $12.95

Gay and Lesbian Teenagers

Ellen **Bass** & Kate **Kaufman**

Free Your Mind: The Book for Gay, Lesbian, and Bisexual Youth and Their Allies

An invaluable step-by-step guide empowering gay youth to understand, accept, and celebrate their sexual orientation, come out to themselves, their families, and friends

0-06-095104-4 HARPERCOLLINS PB $14.00

Kurt **Chandler**

Passages of Pride: Lesbian and Gay Youth Come of Age

Zooms in on the lives of six gay and lesbian teenagers. The discussion on the origins of homosexuality, suicide, and family pressure makes the "book useful for parents and teachers"—*Publishers Weekly*

0-8129-2380-4 TIME BOOKS $23.00

Linnea **Due**

Joining the Tribe: Growing Up Gay & Lesbian in the 1990s

Interviews with gay, lesbian, and bisexual teenagers from a variety of backgrounds and cultures; the result, according to *Publishers Weekly*, is a "moving, vital pastiche"

038547004 ANCHOR PB $12.95

Gilbert **Herdt** & Andrew **Boxer**

Children of Horizons: How Gay and Lesbian Teens Are Leading a New Way Out of the Closet

And ethnographic study of the youth group at Horizons, Chicago's famous center for the gay and lesbian community. The study concludes that gay youth are as well socialized as their heterosexual counterparts when permitted to "come out" of their secretive, "homosexual" cocoons

0-8070-7928-6 BEACON $25.00

Rachel **Pollack** & Cheryl **Schwartz**

The Journey Out: A Guide for and About Lesbian, Gay, and Bisexual Teens

From sympathetic advice on coming out to explicit information on AIDS and other sexually transmitted diseases this is, *Publishers Weekly* wrote, a "candid, accessible resource" for ages 12 and up

0-670-85845-5 VIKING $14.99
0-14-037254-7 PUFFIN PB $6.99

Bennett **Singer**, editor

Growing Up Gay: An Anthology for Young People

In this remarkable and comprehensive first anthology for teenagers, there is fiction by James Baldwin and Rita Mae Brown; diary accounts of coming of age gay in the '80s and '90s; and essays on sexual identification, relationships, and finding safe places in a hostile world. Included are lists of gay and lesbian organizations and hotlines. Sober and funny

1-56584-102-6 NEW PRESS $21.95

Biographies

Victoria **Brownworth**

Too Queer: Essays from a Radical Life

The syndicated columnist "provides an urgent, sustaining, and very personal voice of dissent and resistance"—*Ms.*

1-56341-075-3 FIREBRAND $26.95
1-56341-074-5 FIREBRAND PB $13.95

Margarethe **Cammermeyer**

Serving in Silence

Notwithstanding her Bronze Star for duty in Vietnam, her award as Nurse of the Year by the VA, and her role as Chief Nurse of the Washington National Guard, Cammermeyer's distinguished medical career was cut short by her abrupt dismissal in 1992. The basis of her firing from lifelong military service? Sexual orientation. This important book provides a fresh view of the military, and of the overarching injustice of the Pentagon's stand on gay and lesbian personnel

0-670-85167-1 VIKING $22.95

Gerald **Clarke**

Capote: A Biography

See also **THE 20TH CENTURY** under **STUDIES OF INDIVIDUAL AUTHORS (ALPHABETICAL BY SUBJECT)** under **AMERICAN LITERATURE: ANTHOLOGIES AND CRITICAL STUDIES** in **LITERATURE OF THE AMERICAS**

0-345-36078-8 BALLANTINE PB $12.95

Jayne **County** & others

Man Enough to Be a Woman

"The saga of a true rock & roll eccentric, by turns mindlessly rambling and hilariously brash, this autobiography offers a raw and raunchy tour of the transsexual side of the underground music scene of the last 25 years" —*Publishers Weekly*

1-85242-338-2 SERPENT'S TAIL $17.99

Quentin **Crisp**

How to Become a Virgin

More reflections from Quentin Crisp

0-312-39543-4 ST. MARTIN'S $9.95

The Naked Civil Servant

The autobiography of the English civil servant who chose to flaunt his homosexuality in conventional 1930s London

See also **20TH-CENTURY BIOGRAPHY** under **GREAT BRITAIN AND IRELAND** in **WORLD HISTORY AND CURRENT AFFAIRS**

0-452-25413-2 NEW AMERICAN LIBRARY PB $6.95

Frank **DeCaro**

A Boy Named Phyllis: A Suburban Memoir

An antidote to the angst-ridden gay memoir. DeCaro, a contributing editor to *Martha Stewart Living* and author of the only gay humor column in a major newspaper, traces the development of his gay identity in the aluminum-sided wilds of New Jersey among working-class Italian folk. "Very touching and extremely funny. I loved it and wished I'd written it"—Quentin Crisp

0-670-86718-7 VIKING $22.95

Barbara **Haskell**

Charles Demuth

The life and work of the pioneering modernist, with more than 100 color illustrations

0-8109-1135-3 ABRAMS $49.50

Martin **Duberman**

Midlife Queer: Autobiography of a Decade

0-684-81836-1 SCRIBNERS $23.00

Aaron **Fricke**

Reflections of a Rock Lobster: A Story About Growing Up Gay

The story of the teenager whose right to take a same-sex date to his high school prom was upheld in a court case

0-932870-09-0 CONSORTIUM PB $5.95

Boze **Hadleigh**

Conversations with My Elders

Six famous gays (Sal Mineo, Luchino Visconti, Cecil Beaton, Rainier Werner Fassbinder, George Cukor, and Rock Hudson) talk frankly about their lives

INTRODUCTION BY QUENTIN CRISP

0-312-01404-X ST. MARTIN'S PB $7.95

Hall Carpenter Archives Lesbian Oral History Project

Inventing Ourselves: Lesbian Life Stories

0-415-02959-7 ROUTLEDGE PB $15.95

Alan **Helms**

Young Man from the Provinces: A Gay Life Before Stonewall

A story of one man's fast life with the famous as well as the notorious and his eventual self-destruction

0-571-19880-5 FABER $22.95

Christopher **Isherwood**

Christopher and His Kind

A partial autobiography covering the years from his first visit to Germany in 1929 to his move to the United States ten years later includes vignettes of Auden and Forster

See also **20TH-CENTURY BRITISH ESSAYS AND OTHER PROSE** in **LITERATURE OF THE BRITISH ISLES**

0-374-52036-4 FS&G PB $13.00

David **Kopay** & others

The David Kopay Story

The autobiography of the football running back, the first professional athlete publicly to reveal his homosexuality. "A dazzling and wonderful book"—Merle Miller

See also **BIOGRAPHIES** under **FOOTBALL** under **SPORTS** in **FOOD, TRAVEL, AND LEISURE**

FOREWORD BY DICK SCHAAP

1-55611-080-4 FINE PB $9.95

Charlotte **von Mahlsdorf**

I Am My Own Woman: The Outlaw Life of Charlotte von Mahlsdorf, Berlin's Most Distinguished Transvestite

A huge bestseller in Germany, this is the story of a remarkable life that "reads like a traditional action-adventure story—with a cross-dressing furniture buff as the hero"—*Publishers Weekly*

1-57344-010-8 CLEIS PB $12.95

Randy **Shilts**

The Mayor of Castro Street: The Life and Times of Harvey Milk

A biography of San Francisco's first openly gay elected official, who was assassinated in 1978

0-312-01900-9 ST. MARTIN'S PB $13.95

Paul **Morrissey**

Let Someone Hold You: The Journey of a Hospice Priest

0-8245-1408-4 CROSSROAD PB $16.95

Martina **Navratilova** & others

Martina

Even with eight Wimbledon titles under her belt, she remains one of the most misunderstood figures in sports. Here she writes candidly of her youth in Czechoslovakia, her emigration to the West, her bisexuality, and her well-known entourage of friends

See also **TENNIS BIOGRAPHIES** under **TENNIS** under **SPORTS** in **FOOD, TRAVEL, AND LEISURE**

0-449-20982-2 FAWCETT PB $5.99

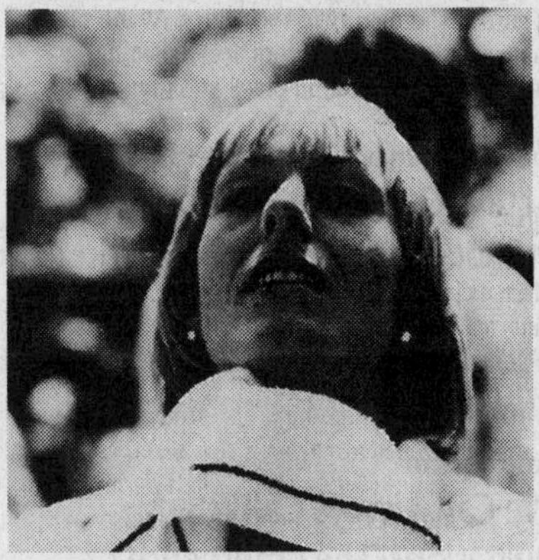

Martina Navartilova
(credit: © Carol L. Newsom)

Otis **Stuart**

Perpetual Motion: The Public and Private Lives of Rudolf Nureyev

The first American biography of the ballet legend who died in 1993 of AIDS

See also **BALLET DANCERS AND CHOREOGRAPHERS** under **THE 20TH CENTURY** under **DANCE** in **PERFORMING ARTS AND MEDIA**

0-671-87539-6 SIMON & SCHUSTER $24.00
0-452-27579-2 PLUME PB $13.95

Mark **Doty**

Heaven's Coast: A Memoir

National Book Critics Circle Award-winning poet Doty's story about the death of his lover from AIDS

0-06-017210-X HARPERCOLLINS $24.00

Ina **Russell**

Jeb and Dash: A Diary of Gay Life, 1918-1945

0-571-19847-3 FABER PB $14.95

Paul **Russell**

The Gay 100: A Ranking of the Most Influential Gay Men and Lesbians, Past and Present

From Sappho to Foucault, those women and men who have influenced gay and lesbian culture as well as culture in general are profiled with what *Publishers Weekly* calls "incisive essays"

See also **ANTHOLOGIES AND REFERENCE**

0-8065-1591-0 BIRCH LANE $24.95
0-8065-1783-2 CITADEL PB $19.95

Michael **Ryan**

Secret Life: An Autobiography

0-679-76776-2 VINTAGE PB $14.00

May **Sarton**

At 82: A Journal

"Memory is full of riches, grief, and joy" reads one entry of Sarton's newest diary, the rich record of the rhythms, recollections, and routines of the celebrated poet and journalist in her 82nd year. "It has been one of Sarton's gifts never to pretend that a woman's life is easier or simpler than it is, but to record its austerity and richness"—Marge Piercy

See also **MEMOIRS AND JOURNALS** under **20TH-CENTURY AMERICAN ESSAYS AND JOURNALISM** in **LITERATURE OF THE AMERICAS**

0-393-03889-0 NORTON $23.00

At Seventy: A Journal

Memoirs of the poet and novelist

0-393-30434-5 NORTON PB $7.95

Sarah **Schulman**

My American History: Lesbian and Gay Life During the Reagan/Bush Years

The prolific young novelist (*Empathy, People In Trouble*), activist (co-founder of Lesbian Avengers), and journalist (for *Village Voice, The Nation, NY Times*) has written an intensely personal political memoir of the '80s that accurately chronicles the sometimes lonely progressive struggles of those bleak Reagan-Bush years. "I admit that I am not typical," writes Schulman. "My view is not a typical view. I am thirty-four years old. This is, I suppose, volume one"

See also **HISTORY, POLITICS, AND SOCIETY** under **20TH-CENTURY AMERICAN ESSAYS AND JOURNALISM** in **LITERATURE OF THE AMERICAS**

0-415-90852-3 ROUTLEDGE $49.95
0-415-90853-1 ROUTLEDGE PB $18.95

Pierre **Seel**

I, Pierre Seel, Deported Homosexual: A Memoir of Nazi Terror

The tragedy of the homosexual Holocaust is brought vividly to life by one who, at the age of 58, came out of the closet to tell his harrowing story. "His account of his suffering and his plea for justice are heartrending in their dignified restraint"—*Publishers Weekly*

See also **FIRST-PERSON ACCOUNTS** under **THE HOLOCAUST** in **WORLD HISTORY AND CURRENT AFFAIRS**

TRANSLATED BY JOACHIM NEUGROSCHEL

0-465-04501-4 BASIC PB $12.00

Tom **Smith**

Half Straight: My Secret Bisexual Life

The autobiography of a man who leads a double life: the public life of father, grandfather, a businessman, and the secret, private life of a promiscuous homosexual. Tom Smith (a pseudonym) risked discovery by his family, friends, and colleagues to tell his candid story in hopes of reaching out to others like him. "This is as much their story as it is mine"—Tom Smith

0-87975-734-5 PROMETHEUS........$26.95

Arts and Letters

For Gay and Lesbian Fiction and Poetry please see the appropriate categories in the Literature sections

Roger **Baker**

Drag: A History of Female Impersonation in the Performing Arts

Publishers Weekly called *Drag* "a quiet, funny and superbly documented study that should appeal to a variety of readers"

0-8147-1254-1 NYU PB........$15.95

Emmanuel **Cooper**

The Sexual Perspective: Homosexuality and Art in the Last 100 Years in the West

A critical and sociological study of prominent gays in the arts

0-7102-0902-9 ROUTLEDGE PB........$18.95

Keith **Haring**

Keith Haring: Journals

Haring's journals not only tell the story of his friendships with Warhol, Leary, and Burroughs, but also illuminate the development of his work from early subway chalk sketches to international exhibitions, showing his deliberate, self-conscious, and extraordinarily successful effort to expand the boundaries of art

See also **AMERICAN ART OF THE 1960S AND '70S** under **ART SINCE 1945** in **ART**

INTRODUCTION BY DAVID HOCKNEY

0-670-84774-7 VIKING........$27.95

F. Valentine **Hooven**

Beefcake: The Muscle Magazines of America, 1950-1970

A compilation of photos in both color and black and white of America's hottest hunks

3-8228-8939-3 TASCHEN PB........$24.99

Sally **Munt**

New Lesbian Criticism: Literary and Cultural Readings

American and British contributors to *New Lesbian Criticism* examine recent literary texts by and about lesbians. Close readings of contemporary literature by Jeanette Winterson, Audre Lourde, Joanna Russ, Jane Rule, and others, as well as a look at lesbian pornography and other phenomena of popular culture

0-231-08018-2 COLUMBIA........$49.50
0-231-08019-0 COLUMBIA PB........$15.50

Rodger **Streitmatter**

Unspeakable: The Rise of the Gay and Lesbian Press in America

The author has "put together the definitive history of homosexual magazines, newspapers and even samizdat newsletters in the U.S. between 1947 and the present—[and] has done a masterful job of telling the complex story" —*Publishers Weekly*

See also **HISTORY**

0-571-19873-2 FABER........$27.95

Colin **Wilson**

The Misfits: A Study of Sexual Outsiders

An examination of prominent literary figures for whom unorthodox sexuality was an expression of creativity

0-88184-420-9 CARROLL & GRAF........$19.95

Theater and Film

Although those working in theater and film have always been aware of the contributions of gay men and lesbians, these contributions were usually invisible to members of the audience. Gay writers are now illuminating the prominence of gays in the history of these arts. At the same time, openly gay characters are becoming increasingly common in plays and films.

John M. **Clum**

Acting Gay: Male Homosexuality in Modern Drama

Clum examines the history of homosexuality in American and English theater from Noel Coward to John Guare

0-231-07510-3 COLUMBIA........$39.50

Kaier **Curtin**

We Can Always Call Them Bulgarians: The Emergence of Lesbians and Gay Men on the American Stage

A fascinating historical study

0-932870-36-8 ALYSON........$18.95

Martha **Gever**

Queer Looks: Perspectives on Lesbian and Gay Film and Video

A wide-ranging compilation of artists' statements and critical theory that explores the thin line between mainstream curiosity about queer films and the virulent censorship of the right. A plurality of aesthetics that includes work by John DiStefano, Alison Butler, B. Ruby Rich, and many more

0-415-90742-X ROUTLEDGE PB........$19.95

Boze **Hadleigh**

Hollywood Lesbians

Subjects include: Patsy Kelly, Judith Anderson, Marjorie Main, Barbara Stanwyck, Agnes Moorehead, Sandy Dennis, and Edith Head. *Publishers Weekly* reports, "...an enlightening picture emerges of Tinseltown, different from that presented in the fanzines"

1-56980-014-6 BARRICADE........$21.95
1-56980-067-7 BARRICADE PB........$14.95

Raymond **Murray**

Images in the Dark: An Encyclopedia of Gay and Lesbian Film and Video

Over 3,000 reviews and 200 biographies, some well known, some deeply buried. Hundreds of photos and detailed indices

See also **REFERENCE** under **FILM** in **PERFORMING ARTS AND MEDIA**

0-452-27627-6 PLUME PB........$19.95

Jenni **Olson**, editor

The Ultimate Guide to Lesbian & Gay Film & Video

1-85242-339-0 SERPENT'S TAIL PB........$25.00

Robert **Reinhardt**

Telling Moments: 16 Gay Monologues

A priest sliding toward heresy and an enraged abandoned lover are among the cast of monologuists in Reinhardt's revealing gallery of gay men. A striking and original work by the author of *History of Shadows,* which Randy Shilts called "the most profound book on gay life in America to be released in some time"

1-55783-163-7 APPLAUSE THEATRE PB........$8.95

Vito **Russo**

The Celluloid Closet: Homosexuality in the Movies

A groundbreaking, provocative study

See also **GENRES AND THEMES** under **FILM** in **PERFORMING ARTS AND MEDIA**

0-8095-9107-3 BORGO........$35.00
0-06-096132-5 HARPERCOLLINS PB........$14.00

Parker **Tyler**

Screening the Sexes: Homosexuality in the Movies

One of the premier film critics of our time observes the psychology of sex roles on the silver screen. "Verbally and intellectually limber, Parker Tyler puts on a strutting, joking, camping whale of a show: with a little gossip and lots of spice, he meets his subject with unfailing high spirits and passionate engagement" —Foster Hirsch, *Film Quarterly*

0-306-80543-X DA CAPO PB........$15.95

Andrea **Weiss**

Vampires and Violets: Lesbians in Film

With wit and political acumen, Weiss reclaims the secret history of gay women in film. From crossdressing stars like Garbo and Dietrich to movies such as *Rebecca, Silkwood,* and *The Color Purple,* this is a long-awaited and valuable resource

0-14-023100-5 PENGUIN PB........$12.50

Religion and Spirituality

Most established religions express disapproval or condemnation of homosexuality. In recent years, however, gay clergymen, laymen, and historians of religion have been challenging such teachings. By reexamining and refuting the assumptions underlying this prejudice, they have sought to establish a foundation for acceptance of gay men and women within various religious traditions, and to affirm the validity of their spiritual aspirations.

Brian **Bouldrey**, editor

Wrestling with the Angel: Faith and Religion in the lives of Gay Men

"A profound and absorbing new anthology…Brian Bouldrey has assembled 21 provocative essays by gay authors from a variety of faiths"—*Minneapolis Star Tribune*

1-57322-545-2 RIVERHEAD PB $14.00

Malcolm **Boyd**

Gay Priest: An Inner Journey

An Episcopalian minister comes out and challenges some teachings of the church

INTRODUCTION BY REV. PAUL MOORE, JR.

0-312-01031-1 ST. MARTIN'S PB $7.95

Bernadette J. **Brooten**

Love Between Women: Early Christian Responses to Female Homoeroticism

Since men could not easily conceive of lesbianism, it was often not a concern. Brooten digs deep to analyze the ancients' response to women and homosexuality

See also **HISTORY**

0-226-07591-5 CHICAGO $34.95

Rosemary **Curb** & Nancy **Manahan**, editors

Lesbian Nuns: Breaking Silence

A much-discussed study of a hidden aspect of Catholic life

0-930044-62-2 NAIAD PB $9.95

0-446-32659-3 WARNER PB $5.95

Keith **Hartman**

Congregations in Conflict: The Battle Over Homosexuality

Analysis of nine congregations in North Carolina and how they have dealt with the issue of homosexuality. "…an invaluable beginning to the healing of misunderstanding on all sides" —*Publishers Weekly*

0-8135-2229-3 RUTGERS $24.95

Tom **Horner**

Jonathan Loved David: Homosexuality in Biblical Times

A discussion of homosexuality in the Bible

0-664-24185-9 KNOX PB $13.00

John J. **McNeill**

The Church and the Homosexual

A sensitive discussion of the relationship between the Catholic church and gay men and women by a Jesuit priest and vocal church critic

0-8070-7931-6 BEACON PB $14.00

Freedom, Glorious Freedom: The Spiritual Journey to the Fullness of Life for Gays, Lesbians, and Everybody Else

The path toward full spiritual maturity and self-acceptance through the spirit of God. "A wonderful exploration of the spiritual journey we all can make…to come fully into ourselves as human beings…. It speaks to the best part of the Christian teachings and reminds us that Rome does not have the corner on truth" —*Bay Windows*

0-8070-7937-5 BEACON PB $14.00

Taking a Chance on God: Liberating Theology for Gays, Lesbians, and their Lovers, Families, and Friends

The foundation of a positive gay identity within the context of Christian faith. "McNeill draws on the insights of the gay and lesbian liberation movement, his counseling experience with lesbian and gay people, and a variety of faith traditions…to produce a unique, comprehensive, life-giving ethic"—*Equal Time*

0-8070-7945-6 BEACON PB $14.00

Will **Roscoe**, editor

Queer Spirits: A Gay Men's Myth Book

A leader in the US gay men's spirituality movement, the editor has compiled a collection of stories, myths, and poems that evoke a gay archetype, from Hans Christian Andersen's "The Ugly Duckling" to Zuni legends

0-8070-7938-3 BEACON $24.00

0-8070-7939-1 BEACON PB $15.00

Robin **Scroggs**

The New Testament and Homosexuality

Examines the cultural context of anti-gay attitudes in the New Testament

0-8006-1854-8 FORTRESS PB $14.00

Mark **Thompson**

Gay Spirit: Myth and Meaning

A collection of essays exploring the unique possibilities for gay people in human culture

0-312-01765-0 ST. MARTIN'S PB $11.95

Anthropology

Along with gay liberation has come a realization that different societies vary widely in their attitudes toward homosexuality.

Evelyn **Blackwood**, editor

The Many Faces of Homosexuality: Anthropological Approaches to Homosexual Behavior

Homosexuality in different historical periods and cultures

PREFACE BY JOHN DE CECCO

FOREWORD BY JOSEPH CARRIER

0-918393-20-5 HARRINGTON PARK PB $12.95

Frank **Browning**

A Queer Geography: Journeys Toward a Sexual Self

National Public Radio reporter and author of *The Culture of Desire* discusses the quasi-religious quality that American gay political activism has and compares it to the ritualized gay sex among tribesmen of New Guinea, Brazil, and the Philippines

See also **SEX AND SEXUALITY**

0-517-59857-4 CROWN $24.00

Russell **Leong**

Asian American Sexualities: Dimensions of the Gay and Lesbian Experience

A unique collection on the relationship of race and sexuality

0-415-91437-X ROUTLEDGE PB $16.95

Gary **Leupp**

Male Colors: The Construction of Homosexuality in Tokugawa Japan

A scholarly look at homoeroticism in early Modern Japan

See also **SOCIETY, CULTURE, AND IDEAS** under **THE TOKUGAWA PERIOD: 1600–1868** under **JAPAN** in **WORLD HISTORY AND CURRENT AFFAIRS**

0-520-08627-9 CALIFORNIA $35.00

Neil **Miller**

Out in the World: Gay and Lesbian Life from Buenos Aires to Bangkok

The author of *In Search of Gay America* extends his exploration of gay cultures to the rest of the world. He examines persecution of gays in South America, their acceptance among native Australian peoples, their legal assimilation in Denmark, and their near-invisibility in Egypt. "A fascinating tour of the ways minorities of any sort…adapt to, and influence their cultures"—*Kirkus Reviews*

See also **GAY LIFE AND CULTURE**

0-679-74551-3 VINTAGE PB $13.00

Frederick L. **Whitman** & Robin M. **Mathy**

Male Homosexuality in Four Societies: Brazil, Guatemala, the Philippines, and the United States

Results of a ten-year research study

0-275-90037-1 PRAEGER $42.95

Walter L. **Williams**

The Spirit and the Flesh: Sexual Diversity in American Indian Culture

"A valuable sourcebook, bringing together a wealth of information on the status of gender-variant men in a wide variety of Native American societies"—*San Francisco Chronicle*

See also **WOMEN AND SEXUALITY** under **SPECIALIZED STUDIES** under **ANTHROPOLOGY**

0-8070-4615-9 BEACON PB $16.00

Humor

Alison **Bechdel**

Unnatural Dykes to Watch Out For

The sixth collection of Bechdel's cartoons revisits Ginger, Mo, Lois, and Toni's early lives. Sordid, indecent, and absolutely hilarious are Bechdel's lampoons of lesbian life

1-56341-067-2 FIREBRAND PB $10.95

Jaffe **Cohen** & others
Growing Up Gay: From Left Out to Coming Out
Presented by the comedy team, Funny Gay Males, about coming of age
0-7868-8056-2 HYPERION PB $9.95

Joseph **Cohen**
You Know You're Gay When...: Those Unforgettable Moments that Make Us Who We Are
A humorous litmus test with drawings
0-8092-3320-7 CONTEMPORARY $9.95

Howard **Cruse**
Dancin' Nekkid with the Angels
Comic strips from the creator of Wendel
See also **CONTEMPORARY COMIC STRIP ARTISTS AND CARTOONISTS** under **COMICS** in **POPULAR READING**
0-312-01104-0 ST. MARTIN'S PB $9.95

Mary **Dugger**
The History of Lesbian Hair: And Other Tales of Bent Life in a Straight World
Advice on building your own lesbian and the "Downside to Lesbian Chic"
0-385-48037-7 DOUBLEDAY PB $10.95

Helen **Eisenbach**
Lesbianism Made Easy
This book is for those who are "lesbian impaired"
0-517-70475-7 CROWN $20.00

Charles **Flowers**
Out, Loud, & Laughing: A Collection of Gay and Lesbian Humor
A collection of monologues, sketches, and stories by 15 of today's leading gay and lesbian humorists
0-385-47618-3 ANCHOR PB $12.95

Karen **Rauch**
Why Gay Guys Are a Girls's Best Friend
Pays homage to the unique bond in cartoon format
0-684-80053-5 FIRESIDE PB $7.95

Shelly **Roberts**
Roberts' Rules of Lesbian Living
Humor columnist and business consultant Roberts writes, "The average lesbian date lasts approximately three years"
1-88352-309-5 SPINSTERS INK PB $5.95

Liz **Tracey** & Sydney **Pokorny**
So You Want to Be a Lesbian?
Chapters discuss "The Great Lesbian Bad Haircut Conspiracy" and "Lesbian Cuisine—Beyond Granola and Back Again"
0-312-14423-7 ST. MARTIN'S PB $12.95

Anthologies and Reference

Gerry **Kroll**, editor
The Alyson Almanac: 1997 Edition
1-55583-390-X ALYSON PB $11.95

Henry **Abelove**, editor
The Lesbian and Gay Studies Reader
Forty-two groundbreaking essays that explore a multitude of sexual, racial, ethnic, and socioeconomic experiences. Contributors include Kibena Mercer, Adrienne Rich, and Judith Butler. The most comprehensive multidisciplinary anthology of critical work in lesbian/gay studies
0-415-90518-4 ROUTLEDGE $65.00
0-415-90519-2 ROUTLEDGE PB $24.95

Mary Beth **Caschetta**
Lucy on the West Coast and Other Lesbian Short Fiction
1-55583-374-8 ALYSON $18.95

Stephen **Coote**, editor
The Penguin Book of Homosexual Verse
0-14-058551-6 PENGUIN PB $12.95

Wayne R. **Dynes**
Homosexuality: A Research Guide
Exhaustive reference book with 5,000 listings on gay history, health, legal issues, and other topics
0-8240-8692-9 GARLAND $60.00

Lillian **Faderman**
Chloe Plus Olivia: An Anthology of Lesbian Literature from the Seventeenth Century to the Present
"Illuminating...Her intelligence and acumen shine brightly...This massive book will be used all over the English-speaking world"
—*Lambda Book Report*
0-14-017248-3 PENGUIN PB $16.95

Jonathan **Goldberg**, editor
Queering the Renaissance
0-8223-1381-2 DUKE $54.95
0-8223-1385-5 DUKE PB $18.95

Judy **Grahn**
Another Mother Tongue: Gay Words, Gay Worlds
The derivations of gay and lesbian words, by an outstanding contemporary poet
0-8070-6717-2 BEACON PB $10.95

Marny **Hall**
The Lavender Couch: A Consumer's Guide to Psychotherapy for Lesbians and Gay Men
0-932870-41-4 ALYSON PB $7.95

Mark **Mitchell**, editor
The Penguin Book of Gay Short Stories
See also **SHORT STORY COLLECTIONS** under **20TH-CENTURY AMERICAN FICTION** in **LITERATURE OF THE AMERICAS**
0-670-85468-9 VIKING $27.50

Bruce **Morrow** & Charles **Rowell**, editors
Shade: An Anthology of Fiction by Gay Men of African Descent
Twenty-two stories by famous and unknown black gay writers
0-380-78305-3 AVON PB $7.50

The National Museum and Archive of Lesbian and Gay History
The Gay Almanac
The most complete reference book available on gay culture and history. Includes a directory of gay and lesbian community centers, timelines, dictionaries, quotes by and about gay men, statistics, a complete primer on AIDS, and much more
0-425-15300-2 BERKELEY PB $16.95

The Lesbian Almanac
Everything in the lesbian community's purview: directories, timelines, quotes, reading lists, and much more
0-425-15301-0 BERKELEY PB $16.95

Carol **Queen** & Lawrence **Schimel**, editors
Switch Hitters
Lesbians write gay male erotica, and gay men write lesbian erotica
1-57344-021-3 CLEIS PB $12.95

Margaret **Reynolds**, editor
The Penguin Book of Lesbian Short Stories
"...an adventurous anthology..."
—*Publishers Weekly*
0-14-024018-7 PENGUIN PB $13.95

Sean Stewart **Ruff**, editor
Go the Way Your Blood Beats: An Anthology of Lesbian and Gay Fiction by African-American Writers
Thirty-two stories from the well known, such as James Baldwin, to some unknown and previously unpublished writers
0-8050-4437-X OWL PB $16.95

Paul **Russell**
The Gay 100: A Ranking of the Most Influential Gay Men and Lesbians, Past and Present
From Sappho to Foucault, those women and men who have influenced gay and lesbian culture as well as culture in general are profiled with what *Publishers Weekly* calls "incisive essays"
See also **BIOGRAPHIES**
0-8065-1591-0 BIRCH LANE $24.95
0-8065-1783-2 CITADEL PB $19.95

George **Stambolian**, editor
Men on Men 4: Best New Gay Fiction
Fourth in the widely praised *Men on Men* series—anthologies of gay literature reflecting many cultures, backgrounds, and gay styles. Eighteen stories, with an introduction by Felice Picano that sets these important anthologies in the context of new gay writing
0-525-93504-5 PLUME PB $25.00

Leigh W. **Rutledge**

The Gay Book of Lists

Gay trivia and minutiae

1-55583-120-6 ALYSON PB $8.95

Claude J. **Summers**, editor

The Gay and Lesbian Literary Heritage: A Reader's Companion to the Writers and Their Work, from Antiquity to the Present

A bibliographic guide to gay and lesbian literature, transcultural and transhistorical

0-8050-2716-5 HOLT $45.00

Edmund **White**

The Faber Book of Gay Short Fiction

James Baldwin, E.M Forster, Henry James, Gore Vidal, Edmund White, and Tennessee Williams are just a few of the writers included in Faber & Faber's mammoth collection of gay short stories

0-571-14472-1 FABER $24.95

0-571-12908-0 FABER PB $16.95

Edmund White
(photo courtesy of Faber and Faber, Inc.)

James J. **Wilhelm**, editor

Gay and Lesbian Poetry: An Anthology from Sappho to Michelangelo

0-8153-1886-3 GARLAND PB $19.95

Terry **Wolverton** & Robert **Drake**, editors

Hers: Brilliant New Fiction by Lesbian Writers

Carole Maso, Sarah Schulman, Michelle T. Clingon, and Rebecca Brown are among the finest lesbian literary voices in America today, edited by Lambda Literary Award nominees Wolverton and Drake

See also **SHORT STORY COLLECTIONS** under **20TH-CENTURY AMERICAN FICTION** in **LITERATURE OF THE AMERICAS**

0-571-19866-X FABER PB $14.95

Travel

Specifically written for the gay traveler, guidebooks provide information about guesthouses, bars, restaurants, and other establishments around the country and the world.

David **Andrusia**

Gay Europe

"Practical and entertaining, this excellent travel guide should satisfy the wanderlust of every gay man who plans to go abroad"—Quentin Crisp

0-399-51910-6 PERIGEE PB $14.00

David **Appell** & Paul **Balido**, editors

Hot! International Gay: Love and Sex in Seven Languages

A pocket-size gay phrasebook with pickup lines, sex vocabulary, dating and health phrases in German, Spanish, French, Italian, Portugese, and Czech

1-88594-818-2 BABELCOM PB $12.95

Bent

The Bent Guide to Gay/Lesbian Canada: 1995-1996

Over 650 listings of bars, accommodations, shops, and tours for the gay traveler. Also includes maps to Canada's hottest gay and lesbian centers

1-55022-253-8 E.C.W. PB $9.95

Andrew **Collins**

Fodor's Gay Guide to the USA: The Only Comprehensive Guide for Gay and Lesbian Travelers

Forty destinations are covered with maps and listings of hotels, restaurants, and "scenes"

0-679-02909-5 FODOR'S PB $19.50

Damron

Damron Accommodations: United States and Canada

0-929435-18-4 DAMRON PB $18.95

The Damron Address Book: '96

0-929435-19-2 DAMRON PB $14.95

Lynn **Witt** & others, editors

Out in All Directions: The Almanac of Gay and Lesbian America

Ten chapters, dozens of photographs, and contributions from every corner of the United States constitute this essential guide to gay living in America. From gay and lesbian movie and television personalities, gay politicians, and the history of the struggle against AIDS, this is a vibrant and essential collection of articles, trivia, tidbits, and information about being gay and lesbian in America today

See also **GAY LIFE AND CULTURE**

0-446-51822-0 WARNER $24.95

Jeff **Yarbrough**, editor

Odysseus '96: The International Gay Travel Planner

Information on accommodations in the United States and around the world

1-88153-602-5 PUB. DISTRIBUTING CO. PB $25.00

Anthropology

The earliest "anthropology" available to us would probably be Herodotus's *History*, written in the 5th century BC, an odd, entertaining story which treats of many peoples, real and imagined, beyond the Greek world. Apart from Tacitus's anthropological book on Germans (98 AD), this is pretty much where anthropology remained until the Enlightenment.

From Michel de Montaigne, in his famous essay "On Cannibals" (1580), through John Locke and Thomas Hobbes in the 17th century and Jean-Jacques Rousseau and Montesquieu in the 18th, Europe's greatest thinkers raked through proto-anthropological texts, usually with hopes of discovering some universal pattern to human life.

By the end of the last century, anthropology had become a study in its own right, divided into physical anthropology, which concerned itself with man's evolving physical nature and is most active today in its study of genetics, and cultural anthropology, a less specialized inquiry into the nature of cultures. The classical form of cultural anthropology is ethnography, a treatment of a single society usually based on the fieldwork of an anthropologist who has spent time with the people under study.

After the second World War, and more vividly during and after the 1960s, anthropologists began to question seriously the morality of their profession, given its roots in European conquest. More fundamentally, some began to doubt the very possibility of someone from one culture ever understanding another culture. These debates have sometimes led to crippling self-doubt; at other times, they have inspired a new subtlety and humility in anthropological practice. As to whether an anthropologist can truly understand another culture, one might also ask whether one can ever understand oneself: both questions have been asked for millennia, and the answers, however overconfident at times, are usually worth hearing.

General Anthropological Studies

Franz **Boas**

Anthropology and Modern Life

First published in 1928

0-486-25245-0 DOVER PB $8.95

Michael **Carrithers**, editor

The Category of the Person

The concept "person" considered cross-culturally

0-521-27757-4 CAMBRIDGE PB $19.95

Philippe **Descola**

The Spears of Twilight: Three Years Among the Jivaro Indians of South America

Under the tutelage of Claude Lévi-Strauss, the author spent three years with the Jivaro Indians in the jungle of the Upper Amazon. In this fascinating tour of the Jivaros' daily life, Descola has also told the story of his own evolving sympathy for and understanding of an utterly alien culture. "An admirable book…it proves that subjectivity and objectivity can go hand in hand when they are served by a true literary gift"—Claude Lévi-Strauss

See also **OTHER GROUPS AND TOPICS** under **NATIVE AMERICAN CULTURES: CENTRAL AND SOUTH AMERICA** in **HISTORY OF THE AMERICAS**

TRANSLATED FROM FRENCH BY JANET LLOYD

1-56584-228-6 NEW PRESS $25.00

Marvin **Harris**

Our Kind: Who We Are, Where We Came From, Where We Are Going

0-06-015776-3 HARPERCOLLINS PB $22.95

Dan **Sperber**

On Anthropological Knowledge

Critical questions about what anthropologists know and how they come to know it

0-521-26748-X CAMBRIDGE $42.95

Eric R. **Wolf**

Anthropology

A brief, comprehensive overview

0-393-09290-9 NORTON PB $2.95

Precursors

Michel **de Montaigne**

The Complete Essays

Montaigne's essay "On Cannibals" may be the first modern anthropological essay—and it is still among the most elegant

See also **THE RENAISSANCE** under **FRENCH LITERATURE TO 1900** in **LITERATURE OF EUROPE, AFRICA, AND ASIA**

TRANSLATED BY M.A. SCREECH

0-14-044604-4 PENGUIN PB $22.50

Michel de Montaigne

Charles-Louis **de Montesquieu**

The Spirit of the Laws

The most complete examination of different systems of political organization by an Enlightenment thinker

See also **CLASSICS** under **POLITICAL THOUGHT**

0-521-36974-6 CAMBRIDGE PB $18.95

0-317-30542-5 FREE PRESS PB $13.95

Immanuel **Kant**

Anthropology from a Pragmatic Point of View

See also **KANT** under **PHILOSOPHY** in **RELIGION, SPIRITUALITY, AND PHILOSOPHY**

0-8093-2060-6 SOUTHERN ILLINOIS PB $16.95

John **Locke**

An Essay Concerning Human Understanding

This important work was greatly influenced by Locke's reading of travel accounts, which for him and many of his contemporaries made up a "scientific" body of evidence from which to speculate on the nature of humanity

See also **LOCKE** under **PHILOSOPHY** in **RELIGION, SPIRITUALITY, AND PHILOSOPHY**

0-460-87355-5 EVERYMAN'S PB $8.95

Jean-Jacques **Rousseau**

First and Second Discourse, Together with Replies to the Critics, & Essay on the Origin of Languages

The philosopher of the state of nature draws on travelers' tales to ponder "savage man." Includes *On the Origin and Foundations of Inequality Among Men*

See also **THE ENLIGHTENMENT** under **FRENCH LITERATURE TO 1900** in **LITERATURE OF EUROPE, AFRICA, AND ASIA**

TRANSLATED BY VICTOR GOUREVITCH

0-8095-9091-3 BORGO $37.00

0-06-132083-8 HARPERCOLLINS PB $16.00

Classics

Ruth **Benedict**

The Chrysanthemum and the Sword: Patterns of Japanese Culture

A study dating from the 1940s, by a leading anthropologist

See also **TRADITIONAL CULTURE** under **JAPAN** in **WORLD HISTORY AND CURRENT AFFAIRS**

0-395-50075-3 HOUGHTON MIFFLIN PB $12.95

Patterns of Culture

0-395-50088-5 HOUGHTON MIFFLIN PB $12.95

Franz **Boas**

Race, Language and Culture

This extremely influential early-20th-century anthropologist gives the clearest statement of the position that different cultures reflect underlying human characteristics

0-226-06241-4 CHICAGO PB $18.00

Emile **Durkheim** & Marcel **Mauss**

Primitive Classification

TRANSLATED BY RODNEY NEEDHAM

0-226-17334-8 CHICAGO PB $11.95

James G. **Frazer**

The Golden Bough

The ideas in Frazer's bold and pioneering study of ancient myths, published in 1890 and subsequently revised and expanded, have been thoroughly absorbed into our culture, most visibly in the work of Sigmund Freud and the poetry of T.S. Eliot

See also **GENERAL INTRODUCTIONS** under **MYTHOLOGY AND FOLKLORE** in **RELIGION, SPIRITUALITY, AND PHILOSOPHY**

EDITED AND ABRIDGED BY THEODORE GASTER

0-517-33633-2 GRAMERCY $12.99

0-19-282934-3 OXFORD PB $17.95

Clifford **Geertz**

The Interpretation of Cultures

Geertz's accessible 1973 book popularized the idea of reading cultures as "texts," thus bringing anthropology into closer touch with literary theory and helping to promote a new humility among postcolonial Western anthropologists

0-465-09719-7 BASIC BOOKS PB $20.00

Michel **Leiris**

Manhood: A Journey from Childhood into the Fierce Order of Virility

Leiris's work, based on field experience in colonial Africa, is peculiarly French in its autobiographical intensity. *Manhood* is a troubling study of the anthropologist's psychology

TRANSLATED BY LYDIA DAVIS

0-226-47141-1 CHICAGO PB $13.95

Claude **Lévi-Strauss**

Tristes Tropiques

Lévi-Strauss is the anthropologist most associated with "structuralism," the belief that societies are highly structured systems that share fundamental characteristics. Here, in an account of traveling and doing fieldwork in Brazil, he writes autobiographically as well as scientifically. Lévi-Strauss's most popular book is an unclassifiable work of genius

See also **CLAUDE LEVI-STRAUSS**

0-14-016562-2 PENGUIN PB $16.95

Bronislaw **Malinowski**

Argonauts of the Western Pacific

0-88133-084-1 WAVELAND PB $14.95

Marcel **Mauss**

The Gift: Forms and Functions of Exchange in Archaic Societies

Mauss's work provided the basis for subsequent work on reciprocity and exchange

0-393-30698-4 NORTON PB $9.95

Margaret **Mead**

Coming of Age in Samoa

A controversial account of female adolescence, published in 1928

See also **CLASSIC ETHNOGRAPHIES**

0-688-30974-7 MORROW PB $12.50

Edward L. **Schieffelin** & Robert **Crittenden**

Like People You See in a Dream: First Contact in Six Papuan Societies

The amazing story of how a team of ethnographers discovered six unknown Papuan tribes in the mid-30s, and how their journey nearly ended in disaster

0-8047-1899-7 STANFORD PB $16.95

Arnold **Van Gennep**
Rites of Passage
A classic French study of the ceremonies marking life transitions
TRANSLATED BY MONIKA VIZEDON & GABRIELLE CAFFEE
0-226-84849-3 CHICAGO PB $9.95

Research and Methodology

The following works address various aspects of "doing anthropology", from methodological theory to memoirs of experience in the field.

Jean-Paul **Dumont**
The Headman and I: Ambiguity and Ambivalence in the Fieldworking Experience
An examination of the assumptions and methods of fieldwork
0-88133-627-0 WAVELAND PB $9.95

Hussein M. **Fahim**, editor
Indigenous Anthropology in Non-Western Countries
0-89089-197-4 CAROLINA ACADEMIC $29.75

Peter **Matthiessen**
Under the Mountain Wall
Two seasons experienced by the Stone Age tribesmen of New Guinea
See also KOREA AND SOUTHEAST ASIA under ASIA under TRAVEL LITERATURE in FOOD, TRAVEL, AND LEISURE
See also ESSAYS, MEDITATIONS, AND CLASSICS under NATURE STUDY in SCIENCE
0-14-025270-3 PENGUIN PB $12.95

Paul **Rabinow**
Reflections on Fieldwork in Morocco
A work that takes anthropological field research itself as a subject of study
0-520-03529-1 CALIFORNIA PB $13.95

George W. **Stocking,** Jr.
Observers Observed: Essays on Ethnographic Fieldwork
0-299-09454-5 WISCONSIN PB $14.95

Edith **Turner**
The Spirit and the Drum: A Memoir of Africa
0-8165-1009-1 ARIZONA $11.95

Victor **Turner**
On the Edge of the Bush: Anthropology as Experience
Conveys the complexity of encountering "foreigness" and depicts "anthropology as experience" rather than merely as an academic exercise
EDITED BY EDITH TURNER
0-8165-0949-2 ARIZONA $40.95

History

The recent appearance of outstanding histories of anthropology is a welcome and exciting development.

Marvin **Harris**
The Rise of Anthropological Theory: A History of Theories of Culture
0-690-70322-8 CROWELL $66.49

Margaret **Hodgen**
Anthropology, History, and Cultural Change
0-8165-0451-2 ARIZONA PB $4.50

Classic Ethnographies

Different anthropologists would no doubt come up with vastly different lists of the five or ten most important descriptive classics in the field. But anyone with a serious interest in anthropology would be familiar with, for instance, the Nuer of Evans-Pritchard and with Firth's *Tikopia*. Some peoples made famous by anthropologists are known less for their culture *per se* than for the way the ethnographer wrote about them.

Gregory **Bateson**
Naven
An influential 1936 study of the rituals and culture of a New Guinea people
0-8047-0520-8 STANFORD PB $16.95

E.E. **Evans-Pritchard**
The Nuer: A Description of the Modes of Livelihood and Political Institutions of a Nilotic People
Published in 1940, this was the first in a celebrated series of ethnographies of a people apparently without government
0-19-500322-5 OXFORD PB $17.95

Raymond **Firth**
We, the Tikopia: A Sociological Study of Kinship in Primitive Polynesia
Firth's study of a Solomon Islands people first appeared in 1936
PREFACE BY BRONISLAW MALINOWSKI
0-8047-1202-6 STANFORD PB $19.95

R.F. **Fortune**
Sorcerers of Dobu: The Social Anthropology of the Dobu Islanders of the Western Pacific
0-88133-452-9 WAVELAND PB $12.95

Clifford **Geertz** & others
Meaning and Order in Moroccan Society
0-521-22175-7 CAMBRIDGE $65.00

Pierre-Jakez **Helias**
The Horse of Pride: Life in a Breton Village
TRANSLATED BY JUNE GUICHARNAUD
0-300-02599-8 YALE PB $16.00

Edmund R. **Leach**
Political Systems of Highlands Burma: A Study of Kachin Social Structure
Leach became the foremost English exponent of structuralist anthropology
0-485-19644-1 ATHLONE PB $25.00

Robert H. **Lowie**
The Crow Indians
This 1935 study resulted from many years of fieldwork under the auspices of the American Museum of Natural History
See also SOUTHEASTERN under REGIONAL AND TRIBAL STUDIES under NATIVE AMERICAN CULTURES: NORTH AMERICA in HISTORY OF THE AMERICAS
0-8032-7909-4 NEBRASKA PB $12.00

Margaret **Mead**
Coming of Age in Samoa
A controversial account of female adolescence, published in 1928
See also CLASSICS under GENERAL ANTHROPOLOGICAL STUDIES
0-688-30974-7 MORROW PB $12.50

Growing Up in New Guinea
0-688-07989-X MORROW PB $12.95

Alfonso **Ortiz**
The Tewa World: Space, Time, Being and Becoming in a Pueblo Society
0-226-63307-1 CHICAGO PB $10.95

Roy A. **Rappaport**
Pigs for the Ancestors: Ritual in the Ecology of a New Guinea People
0-300-03204-8 YALE $40.00

Kenneth E. **Read**
The High Valley
A narrative of fieldwork in New Guinea
0-231-05035-6 COLUMBIA PB $17.00

Colin M. **Turnbull**
The Forest People
A study of an exceptionally peace-loving tribe of pygmies. A great read
0-671-64099-2 TOUCHSTONE PB $11.00

The Mountain People
0-671-64098-4 TOUCHSTONE PB $12.00

Essays in Anthropology

Johannes **Fabian**
Time and the Other
0-231-05591-9 COLUMBIA PB $19.50

Charles O. **Frake**

Language and Cultural Description: Essays by Charles O. Frake

EDITED BY ANWAR S. DIL

0-8047-1074-0 STANFORD $47.50

Clifford **Geertz**

After the Fact

Both a memoir of fieldwork and further thoughts on the state of anthropology

0-674-00871-5 HARVARD $22.95

Local Knowledge: Further Essays in Interpretive Anthropology

Very readable and thought-provoking. "By displaying the tools with which an interpretive anthropologist works, he excites us over what is happening"—*NY Times*

0-465-04162-0 BASIC BOOKS PB $16.00

The concept of person is…an excellent vehicle by means of which to examine this whole question of how to go about poking into another people's turn of mind. In the first place, some sort of concept of this kind, one feels reasonably safe in saying, exists in recognizable form among all social groups. The notion of what persons are may be, from our point of view, sometimes more than a little odd. They may be conceived to dart about nervously at night shaped like fireflies. Essential elements of their psyches, like hatred, may be thought to be lodged in granular black bodies within their livers, discoverable upon autopsy. They may share their fates with *doppelganger* beasts, so that when the beast sickens or dies they sicken or die too. But at least some conception of what a human individual is, as opposed to a rock, an animal, a rainstorm, or a god, is, so far as I can see, universal.

LOCAL KNOWLEDGE: FURTHER ESSAYS IN INTERPRETIVE ANTHROPOLOGY

Works and Lives: The Anthropologist as Author

0-8047-1428-2 STANFORD $32.50

Edward T. **Hall**

Beyond Culture

0-385-12474-0 ANCHOR PB $12.00

The Dance of Life: The Other Dimension of Time

0-385-19248-7 ANCHOR PB $10.95

The Hidden Dimension

0-385-08476-5 ANCHOR PB $9.95

The Silent Language

0-385-05549-8 ANCHOR PB $9.95

Marvin **Harris**

Cannibals and Kings: The Origins of Cultures

0-679-72849-X VINTAGE PB $12.00

Cows, Pigs, Wars, and Witches: The Riddles of Culture

0-679-72468-0 VINTAGE PB $11.00

Marvin **Harris**

Cultural Materialism: The Struggle for a Science of Culture

0-394-74426-8 RANDOM HOUSE PB $18.00

Why Nothing Works: The Anthropology of Daily Life

0-671-63577-8 TOUCHSTONE PB $11.00

Michael **Jackson**

At Home in the World

A touching, often autobiographical account of the mind and work of the contemporary anthropologist

0-8223-1561-0 DUKE $21.95

Edmund R. **Leach**

Rethinking Anthropology

This collection of incisive essays includes Leach's famous work on the symbolic representation of time

0-485-19622-0 HUMANITIES PB $18.50

Rodney **Needham**

Circumstantial Deliveries

0-520-04389-8 CALIFORNIA $35.00

Structure and Sentiment: A Test Case in Social Anthropology

0-226-56989-6 CHICAGO PB $11.95

A.R. **Radcliffe-Brown**

Structure and Function in Primitive Society

Essays, mostly on kinship and social organization in Africa, making a strong case for social anthropology

0-02-925620-8 FREE PRESS PB $17.95

Roy A. **Rappaport**

Ecology, Meaning, and Religion

0-913028-65-7 NORTH ATLANTIC $25.00

0-938190-27-X NORTH ATLANTIC PB $14.95

Marshall **Sahlins**

Islands of History

"Deeply grounded in Polynesian ethnography, but also wide-ranging in its comparative references, in Pacific history and in broad statements of history/anthropological method"—*TLS*

See also **POLYNESIA** under **AUSTRALIA, NEW ZEALAND, AND POLYNESIA** in **WORLD HISTORY AND CURRENT AFFAIRS**

0-226-73358-0 CHICAGO PB $11.95

Victor **Turner**

The Forest of Symbols: Aspects of Ndembu Ritual

The work of a great anthropologist

See also **RELIGION AND CULTURE** under **AFRICA** in **WORLD HISTORY AND CURRENT AFFAIRS**

0-8014-9101-0 CORNELL PB $15.95

Claude Lévi-Strauss

While the structuralism of Lévi-Strauss appears to be passing out of fashion, his work remains a monument to anthropological expertise and sophistication.

Claude **Lévi-Strauss**

Elementary Structures of Kinship

See also **KINSHIP** under **SPECIALIZED STUDIES**

0-8070-4669-8 FS&G PB $22.00

Claude Lévi-Strauss

Introduction to a Science of Mythology Volume 1 The Raw and the Cooked

An astounding structural analysis, in which hundreds of myths of the peoples of the Americas are shown to be so many variations on a single theme. Unfortunately Volume 2 of this series is out of print

0-226-47487-9 CHICAGO PB $24.95

The Jealous Potter

TRANSLATED BY BENEDICTE CHORIER

0-226-47480-1 CHICAGO $23.95

0-226-47482-8 CHICAGO PB $15.95

Look, Listen, Read

The intellectual giant turns his attention to the interconnected ways in which we appreciate great works of painting, music, and literature. Reflecting on artists from Poussin to Ingres, relating their work to the music of Rameau and the poetry of Rimbaud, Lévi-Strauss shows the universal root of aesthetic judgments and the role of art in the human mind

See also **ART** under **SPECIALIZED STUDIES**

0-465-06880-4 BASIC $25.00

The Savage Mind

A bestseller in the 1960s, important for its analyses of myth, ritual, and social organization as well as for a controversial attack on Jean-Paul Sartre

See also **MAJOR TEXTS** under **SEMIOTICS AND STRUCTURALISM** under **LITERARY THEORY** in **LITERATURE OF EUROPE, AFRICA, AND ASIA**

0-226-47484-4 CHICAGO PB $16.95

The View from Afar

This engaging collection is closer in spirit to *Tristes Tropiques* than to Lévi-Strauss's more scholarly works

TRANSLATED BY JOACHIM NEUGROSCHEL & PHOEBE HOSS

0-226-47474-7 CHICAGO PB $16.50

Tristes Tropiques
Lévi-Strauss is the anthropologist most associated with "structuralism," the belief that societies are highly structured systems that share fundamental characteristics. Here, in an account of traveling and doing fieldwork in Brazil, he writes autobiographically as well as scientifically. Lévi-Strauss's most popular book is an unclassifiable work of genius

See also **CLASSICS** under **GENERAL ANTHROPOLOGICAL STUDIES**

0-14-016562-2 PENGUIN PB $16.95

Introduction to the Work of Marcel Mauss
Mauss, a major figure in the development of anthropology, taught at the University of Paris and founded the Institute of Ethnology there in 1925

0-7100-9066-8 ROUTLEDGE PB $14.95

Specialized Studies

Art

Franz **Boas**
Primitive Art
Examines art of the native population of the Pacific Northwest and uncovers an artistic "language"

0-8446-1695-8 SMITH $20.80
0-486-20025-6 DOVER PB $8.95

John M. **Chernoff**
African Rhythm and African Sensibility: Aesthetics and Social Action in African Musical Idioms
Travelogue and sociological investigation, based on travels in Ghana in the early 1970s

See also **RELIGION AND CULTURE** under **AFRICA** in **WORLD HISTORY AND CURRENT AFFAIRS**
See also **AFRICAN MUSIC** under **WORLD MUSIC: OTHER TRADITIONS** in **PERFORMING ARTS AND MEDIA**

0-226-10345-5 CHICAGO PB $13.95

Bennetta **Jules-Rosette**
The Messages of Tourist Art: An African Semiotic System in Comparative Perspective
0-306-41598-4 PLENUM $49.50

Jacques **Maquet**
The Aesthetic Experience: An Anthropologist Looks at the Visual Arts
0-300-04134-9 YALE PB $23.00

Gary **Witherspoon**
Language and Art in the Navajo Universe
Contains excellent ethnographic material

FOREWORD BY CLIFFORD GEERTZ

0-472-08966-8 MICHIGAN PB $21.95

Kinship

It used to be said that if an anthropologist did not publish work on kinship, his professional credentials would never be fully accepted. Although this is no longer assumed to be the case, the study of kinship is still viewed by many anthropologists as one of the few exclusive domains of their discipline.

E.E. **Evans-Pritchard**
Kinship and Marriage Among the Nuer
0-19-827847-0 CLARENDON PB $19.95

Clifford **Geertz** & Hildred **Geertz**
Kinship in Bali
0-226-28516-2 CHICAGO PB $13.95

Claude **Lévi-Strauss**
Elementary Structures of Kinship
See also **CLAUDE LÉVI-STRAUSS**

0-8070-4669-8 FS&G PB $22.00

Lewis Henry **Morgan**
Ancient Society
This work by the pioneering American ethnologist was first published in 1877

0-8165-0924-7 ARIZONA PB $22.95

David M. **Schneider**
American Kinship: A Cultural Account
Offers a powerful model of the culture of kinship in America and imparts much wisdom regarding cultural analysis

0-226-73930-9 CHICAGO PB $9.95

Life Histories

Ettore **Biocca**
Yanoama: The Narrative of a Young Girl Kidnapped by Amazonian Indians
"A unique document with no parallel in the history of American ethnology"
—*Kirkus Reviews*

TRANSLATED BY DENNIS RHODES

1-56836-108-4 KODANSHA PB $15.00

Vincent **Crapanzano**
Tuhami: Portrait of a Moroccan
A disturbing and puzzling story of the author's encounter with a far-from-typical Moroccan man

0-226-11871-1 CHICAGO PB $10.95

James D. **Sexton**
Campesino: The Diary of a Guatemalan Indian
0-8165-0814-3 ARIZONA $16.95

Marjorie **Shostak**
Nisa: The Life and Words of a !Kung Woman
0-394-71126-2 VINTAGE PB $10.65

Leo W. **Simmons**, editor
Sun Chief: The Autobiography of a Hopi Indian
FOREWORD BY ROBERT V. HINE

0-300-00227-0 YALE PB $16.00

Medicine

Medical anthropology explores the cross-cultural variations in the forms of medical knowledge and practice.

John M. **Janzen**
The Quest for Therapy in Lower Zaire
0-520-03295-0 CALIFORNIA $55.00
0-520-04633-1 CALIFORNIA PB $17.95

Arthur **Kleinman**
Patients and Healers in the Context of Culture: An Exploration of the Borderland Between Anthropology, Medicine, and Psychiatry
Kleinman is a psychiatrist whose work is particularly concerned with the various ways different cultures define and treat mental illness

0-520-04511-4 CALIFORNIA PB $16.00

Social Origins of Distress and Disease: Depression, Neurasthenia, and Pain in Modern China
0-300-04133-0 YALE PB $16.00

Psychology

Psychological anthropology investigates the relationship of personality to culture through a cross-cultural understanding of socialization, identity and identity formation, personal cultures, cultural creativity, life histories, psychopathology, and psychoanalysis.

Vincent **Crapanzano**
The Hamadsha: A Study in Moroccan Ethnopsychiatry
A striking interpretation of a "ritual" system for coping with stress and illness in Morocco which has religious overtones but which also carries on a Mediterranean tradition of ecstatic cults going back to Dionysus

0-520-04510-6 CALIFORNIA PB $16.95

Sue E. **Estroff**
Making It Crazy: An Ethnography of Psychiatric Clients in an American Community
FOREWORD BY H. RICHARD LAMB

0-520-05451-2 CALIFORNIA PB $14.00

George **Devereux**
Basic Problems of Ethnopsychiatry
TRANSLATED BY BASIA M. GULATI
0-226-14355-4 CHICAGO $37.50

Ted **Kerasote**
Bloodties: Nature, Culture and the Hunt
A provocative and compelling exploration of the most natural of all human urges. "Sad and strange, haunting and beautiful, *Bloodties* contains…all the honesty and strength we can stand"—Rick Bass
1-56836-027-4 KODANSHA PB $13.00

Gananath **Obeyesekere**
Medusa's Hair: An Essay on Personal Symbols and Religious Experience
0-226-61601-0 CHICAGO PB $10.95

Peggy R. **Sanday**
Divine Hunger: Cannibalism as a Cultural System
0-521-31114-4 CAMBRIDGE PB $19.95

Nancy **Scheper-Hughes**
Saints, Scholars and Schizophrenics: Mental Illness in Rural Ireland
A study of Ireland that makes an important contribution to the understanding of mental illness
0-520-04786-9 CALIFORNIA PB $15.95

Melford **Spiro**
Oedipus in the Trobriands
1-56000-627-7 TRANSACTION PB $19.95

Melford **Spiro** & Audrey G. **Spiro**
Children of the Kibbutz: A Study in Child Training and Personality
A reconsideration of Freudian concepts in a cross-cultural context
0-674-11606-2 HARVARD PB $17.95

Geoffrey M. **White** & John **Kirkpatrick**
Person, Self and Experience: Exploring Pacific Ethnopsychologies
0-520-06038-5 CALIFORNIA PB $15.95

Women and Sexuality

The literature on these topics has expanded dramatically over the last two decades. Topics of primary interest have included cultural variations in male and female roles and male-female dynamics, women's power, homosexuality in society, and the role of women in relation to social and cultural change.

Pat **Caplan**, editor
The Cultural Construction of Sexuality
0-415-04013-2 ROUTLEDGE PB $18.95

Susan **Dorsky**
Women of Amran: A Middle Eastern Ethnographic Study
0-87480-250-4 UTAH $22.50

Barbara **Ehrenreich** & Deirdre **English**
For Her Own Good: 150 Years of Experts' Advice to Women
The history of American women's dealings with the medical and psychological professions
0-385-12651-4 ANCHOR PB $11.00

Thomas **Gregor**
Anxious Pleasures: The Sexual Lives of an Amazonian People
0-226-30743-3 CHICAGO PB $15.95

Gilbert H. **Herdt**, editor
Ritualized Homosexuality in Melanesia
0-520-05037-1 CALIFORNIA $47.50
0-520-08096-3 CALIFORNIA PB $16.95

Bronislaw **Malinowski**
The Sexual Life of Savages
An early classic based on Malinowski's long sojourn among the Trobriand Islanders
PREFACE BY HAVELOCK ELLIS
0-8070-4607-8 BEACON PB $20.00

Fatima **Mernissi**
Beyond the Veil: Male-Female Dynamics in Modern Muslim Society
An exploration of the suppression of female sexuality in the Muslim tradition, and the disorienting effect of modern life; revised edition
See also **WOMEN** under **CONTEMPORARY POLITICS AND SOCIETY** under **THE CONTEMPORARY MIDDLE EAST** in **WORLD HISTORY AND CURRENT AFFAIRS**
0-253-20423-2 INDIANA PB $10.95

Sherry **Ortner** & Harriet **Whitehead**, editors
Sexual Meanings: The Cultural Construction of Gender and Sexuality
Detailed ethnographic studies
See also **ANTHROPOLOGY AND CROSS-CULTURE STUDIES** under **WOMEN'S STUDIES**
0-521-28375-2 CAMBRIDGE PB $23.95

Michelle Z. **Rosaldo** & Louise **Lamphere**, editors
Woman, Culture, and Society
A well-chosen collection
See also **ANTHROPOLOGY AND CROSS-CULTURE STUDIES** under **WOMEN'S STUDIES**
0-8047-0851-7 STANFORD PB $15.95

Walter L. **Williams**
The Spirit and the Flesh: Sexual Diversity in American Indian Culture
"A valuable sourcebook, bringing together a wealth of information on the status of gender-variant men in a wide variety of Native American societies"—*San Francisco Chronicle*
See also **ANTHROPOLOGY** under **GAY, LESBIAN, AND BISEXUAL STUDIES**
0-8070-4615-9 BEACON PB $16.00

Power and Politics

Louis **Dumont**
Homo Hierarchicus: The Caste System and Its Implications
The most thorough and sophisticated analysis of the caste system ever written. A landmark in Indian studies and also an example of French rationalism
See also **THE INDIAN SUBCONTINENT** in **WORLD HISTORY AND CURRENT AFFAIRS**
TRANSLATED BY BASIA GULATI
0-226-16963-4 CHICAGO PB $18.95

Clifford **Geertz**
Negara: The Theatre-State in 19th-Century Bali
0-691-05316-2 PRINCETON $55.00
0-691-00778-0 PRINCETON PB $16.95

Sidney W. **Mintz**
Sweetness and Power: The Place of Sugar in Modern History
How Europe and America transformed sugar from a rare foreign luxury to a staple of modern life
See also **FOOD AND PHARMACEUTICALS** under **PERSPECTIVES IN HISTORY** under **THE VARIETIES OF CIVILIZATION** in **WORLD HISTORY AND CURRENT AFFAIRS**
0-14-009233-1 VIKING PB $13.95

Fernando **Ortiz**
Cuban Counterpoint: Tobacco and Sugar
A brilliant analysis of the interplay between commodity production (tobacco and sugar) and Caribbean identity
TRANSLATED BY HARRIET DE ONIS
0-8223-1616-1 DUKE PB $18.95

Colonialism

Anthropology has been called a child of European colonialism, since so much ethnography was done under the umbrella of colonial administration. It would be an oversimplification, however, to regard all previous anthropology as a manifestation of "colonial discourse"; anthropologists have questioned both colonialism and its influence upon ethnographic practice.

Kwame Anthony **Appiah**
In My Father's House: Africa in the Philosophy of Culture
An extraordinarily rich collection of essays by an incisive Anglo-Asante philosopher on Africa, race, and the representation of both in Western and African traditions. Includes a penetrating discussion of genetic theories
0-19-506851-3 OXFORD $42.00
0-19-506852-1 OXFORD PB $11.95

Talal **Asad**, editor
Anthropology and the Colonial Encounter
0-391-00391-7 HUMANITIES PB $17.50

T.O. **Beidelman**

Colonial Evangelism: A Socio-Historical Study of an East African Mission at the Grassroots

0-253-31386-4 INDIANA $35.00

V.Y. **Mudimbe**

The Idea of Africa

A history of the idea of Africa that covers the ground from the ancient Greeks to today's Afrocentrism debates, Mudimbe's urbane book also discusses the history of African anthropology

0-253-20872-6 INDIANA PB $12.95

Edward W. **Said**

Orientalism

While not strictly speaking anthropology, Said's discussion of how "the Orient" was constructed by Westerners as an explanation of the nature of the West has had enormous influence on how people write about non-Western cultures

0-394-74067-X RANDOM HOUSE PB $14.00

Edward Said

Sara **Suleri**

Meatless Days

An odd, sensual, unsettling memoir of living in the shadow of British colonialism

0-226-77980-7 CHICAGO $21.95

0-226-77981-5 CHICAGO PB $11.95

Gauri **Viswanathan**

Masks of Conquest: Literary Studies and British Rule in India

An influential ethnography of the British educational system in colonial India

0-231-07084-5 COLUMBIA $36.50

Robert J.C. **Young**

Colonial Desire: Hybridity in Theory, Culture, and Race

An incisive, critical genealogy of culture as articulated through British colonial practices and imperial interventions

0-415-05373-0 ROUTLEDGE $59.95

0-415-05374-9 ROUTLEDGE PB $16.95

Language

Anthropologists regard language in its broadest sense: not just as vocabulary and syntax, but as a cultural phenomenon.

Joseph H. **Greenberg**

Language, Culture, and Communication: Essays by Joseph H. Greenberg

EDITED BY ANWAR S. DIL

0-8047-0781-2 STANFORD $49.50

Dell H. **Hymes**

Essays in the History of Linguistic Anthropology

90-272-4507-X BENJAMINS $87.00

Religion

Anthropologists are not concerned with the truth or falsity of religious systems, rituals, theologies, and symbolic representations. Their objective is to place religion in a social and cultural context that makes the behavior of believers intelligible.

Samuel **Angus**

The Mystery Religions: A Study in the Religious Background of Early Christianity

A classic history of religion examining cryptic rites and beliefs such as the Dionysian and Orphic mysteries and the cults of Isis and Mithras

See also **MYSTICISM** under **WORLD RELIGION** in **RELIGION, SPIRITUALITY, AND PHILOSOPHY**

0-486-23124-0 DOVER PB $8.95

Walter **Burkert**

Greek Religion

"A masterpiece, packed with learning but also rich in ideas and connections of every sort…Nobody else could have produced an account of the subject of comparable range and power"—*NY Review of Books*

See also **ANCIENT MEDITERRANEAN RELIGIONS** under **WORLD RELIGION** in **RELIGION, SPIRITUALITY, AND PHILOSOPHY**

0-674-36281-0 HARVARD PB $17.95

Homo Necans: The Anthropology of Ancient Greek Sacrificial Ritual and Myth

TRANSLATED BY PETER BING

0-520-05875-5 CALIFORNIA PB $16.00

Alan **Dundes**

The Study of Folklore

0-13-858944-5 PRENTICE HALL $65.84

E.E. **Evans-Pritchard**

Rituals of Primitive Religion

A lucid survey of the social anthropology of religious phenomena

0-19-823131-8 OXFORD PB $17.95

James W. **Fernandez**

Bwiti: An Ethnography of the Religious Imagination

An ethnographic study rich in texture and detail

0-691-10122-1 PRINCETON PB $39.50

Marcel **Griaule**

Conversations with Ogotemmeli: An Introduction to Dogon Religious Ideas

An illuminating presentation of the complex cosmology underlying the Dogon culture of West Africa

See also **RELIGION AND CULTURE** under **AFRICA** in **WORLD HISTORY AND CURRENT AFFAIRS**

INTRODUCTION BY GERMAINE DIETERLEN

0-19-519821-2 OXFORD PB $14.95

Gananath **Obeyesekere**

The Cult of the Goddess Pattini

A vividly detailed study of religion in Sri Lanka

0-226-61602-9 CHICAGO $42.50

Victor **Turner**

Revelation and Divination in Ndembu Ritual

Required reading for those interested in religious rituals, as well as rituals of everyday life which have no religious underpinnings

0-8014-9158-4 CORNELL PB $15.95

Symbols and Semiotics

The current generation of "symbolic anthropologists" has taken much of its inspiration from the work of David Schneider and Clifford Geertz; many have also profited from reading Roland Barthes and Claude Lévi-Strauss. The move toward applying symbolic interpretation to the secular and to the political arenas of modern life as well as to small-scale societies has broadened the scope of anthropology.

Arjun **Appadurai**

Social Life of Things: Symbol, Function, History

0-521-35726-8 CAMBRIDGE PB $20.95

Mary **Douglas**

Natural Symbols: Explorations in Cosmology

A British anthropologist's comments on religion and social order

See also **COMPARATIVE RELIGION** under **WORLD RELIGION** in **RELIGION, SPIRITUALITY, AND PHILOSOPHY**

0-415-13825-6 ROUTLEDGE $42.00

0-415-13826-4 ROUTLEDGE PB $16.95

Purity and Danger: An Analysis of the Concepts of Pollution and Taboo

0-415-06608-5 ROUTLEDGE PB $14.95

Roland **Barthes**

The Empire of Signs

The semiotics of Japan, from simple food to sumptuous gift wrapping

TRANSLATED BY RICHARD HOWARD

0-374-52207-3 FS&G PB $8.95

Roland Barthes

Mythologies

Barthes brings a highly literary anthropological technique to bear in these meditations on stripping and other Parisian activities

TRANSLATED BY ANNETTE LAVERS

0-374-52150-6 FS&G PB $9.95

Michael D. **Coe**

Breaking the Maya Code

A lively, informative account of how Maya hieroglyphic writing was finally decipered, by a distinguished Mayanist

See also **MEXICO AND CENTRAL AMERICA** under **NATIVE AMERICAN ARTS** in **ART**

0-500-27721-4 THAMES & HUDSON PB $14.95

James W. **Fernandez**

Persuasions and Performances: The Play of Tropes in Culture

Essays in symbolic anthropology with a traditional functional orientation

0-253-20374-0 INDIANA PB $15.95

James L. **Peacock**

Rites of Modernization: Symbolic and Social Aspects of Proletarian Drama

FOREWORD BY DELL HYMES

0-226-65131-2 CHICAGO PB $19.50

Dan **Sperber**

Rethinking Symbolism

Critical reflections

TRANSLATED BY A.L. MORTON

0-521-09967-6 CAMBRIDGE PB $16.95

Victor **Turner**

Dramas, Fields and Metaphors: Symbolic Action in Human Society

A collection of essays

0-8014-9151-7 CORNELL PB $15.95

Roy W. **Wagner**

Lethal Speech: Daribi Myth as Symbolic Obviation

Myth in New Guinea

0-8014-1193-9 CORNELL $29.95

Critical Anthropology

Since the 1960s and the end, more or less, of colonialism, anthropologists have engaged in a stern self-criticism that reached its peak in the late 1980s but continues today. Influenced by politics, anthropologists have critiqued their discipline's basis in European colonialism; influenced by literary theory, they have replaced an earlier generation's relative confidence in its ability to understand other cultures with what Clifford Geertz called a "pervasive nervousness," even a "hypochondria." The result has been a discipline afflicted by self-doubt—but also a discipline seeking new ways of writing about and understanding other cultures, ways that will do more than hold up distant peoples to a Western standard of coherence.

James A. **Boon**

Tribes, Other Scribes: Symbolic Anthropology in the Comparative Study of Cultures, Histories, Religions, and Texts

0-521-27197-5 CAMBRIDGE PB $22.95

Phyllis P. **Chock** & June R. **Wyman**

Discourse and the Social Life of Meaning

0-87474-308-7 SMITHSONIAN $29.95

James **Clifford** & George E. **Marcus**, editors

Writing Culture: The Poetics and Politics of Ethnography

This sometimes difficult, always thought-provoking collection brings together dissident voices questioning the very nature of anthropological practice

0-520-05729-5 CALIFORNIA PB $16.95

Stanley **Diamond**

In Search of the Primitive: A Critique of Civilization

Discusses the constraints imposed on anthropology by the Western domination of other cultures

FOREWORD BY ERIC R. WOLF

0-87855-582-X TRANSACTION PB $21.95

Bronislaw **Malinowski**

A Diary in the Strict Sense of the Term

When first published, this relentlessly self-revealing diary, kept while doing fieldwork in the Trobriand Islands, created storms of controversy and helped to demolish the notion of the anthropologist as neutral, objective observer

0-8047-1707-9 STANFORD PB $18.95

George E. **Marcus** & Michael M. **Fischer**

Anthropology as Cultural Critique: An Experimental Moment in the Human Sciences

Provides an overview of the social and cultural grounds of anthropology and offers speculation about its future

0-226-50449-2 CHICAGO PB $11.95

Gananath **Obeyesekere**

The Apotheosis of Captain Cook: European Mythmaking in the Pacific

A Sri Lankan anthropologist attacks his eminent colleague, Marshall Sahlins, for having misrepresented native Hawaiians as being unable to reason like Europeans—and as unable to realize that Captain Cook wasn't a god

See also **CAPTAIN COOK** under **POLYNESIA** under **AUSTRALIA, NEW ZEALAND, AND POLYNESIA** in **WORLD HISTORY AND CURRENT AFFAIRS**

0-691-03621-7 PRINCETON PB $13.95

Renato **Rosaldo**

Culture and Truth: The Remaking of Social Analysis

A well-written assessment of disciplinary self-doubt by a thoughtful anthropologist

0-8070-4623-X BEACON PB $14.00

Marshall **Sahlins**

Culture and Practical Reason

0-226-73361-0 CHICAGO PB $11.95

How "Natives" Think: About Captain Cook, For Example

Sahlins's scorching book-length reply to the attack on him by Obeyesekere. This seemingly minor battle revolves around most of the major issues in recent anthropological thinking

0-226-73368-8 CHICAGO $24.95
0-226-73369-6 CHICAGO PB $14.95

Michael **Taussig**

Shamanism, Colonialism, and the Wild Man: A Study in Terror and Healing

A rare and stimulating combination of in-depth fieldwork experience and current ideas in literary criticism, performance theory, and self-reflexive anthropology

0-226-79012-6 CHICAGO $35.95
0-226-79013-4 CHICAGO PB $19.95

Devil and Commodity Fetishism in South America

0-8078-4106-4 NORTH CAROLINA PB $12.95

Marianna **Torgovnick**

Gone Primitive: Savage Intellects, Modern Lives

A rough-and-tumble, ungenerous, but insightful critique of anthropology as, among other things, the sport of a particular type of white man. Includes an entertaining chapter on Tarzan and a bitter one on Malinowski

0-226-80832-7 CHICAGO PB $16.95

Anna Lowenhaupt **Tsing**

In the Realm of the Diamond Queen: Marginality in an Out-of-the-Way Place

An innovative ethnographic study of marginality, gender, and cultural reinvention in Indonesia

0-691-03335-8 PRINCETON $55.00
0-691-00051-4 PRINCETON PB $15.95

Rethinking Anthropology

The books grouped here are recent works that have been instrumental in furthering a reassessment from within of the history and practice of anthropology.

James **Clifford**

The Predicament of Culture: Twentieth-Century Ethnography, Literature, and Art

A lucid and stimulating recent collection that boldly crosses disciplinary lines

0-674-69843-6 HARVARD PB $18.95

George E. **Marcus**, editor

Rereading Cultural Anthropology

An up-to-date reader which provides an insightful glimpse into changing anthropologcial issues and approaches

0-8223-1279-4 DUKE $49.95
0-8223-1297-2 DUKE PB $16.95

Roy W. **Wagner**

The Invention of Culture

A "poetics of culture." Wagner argues that culture is not an object, but instead a process of constant modification, creativity, and innovation

0-226-86934-2 CHICAGO PB $12.95

New Ethnographies

Catherine J. **Allen**

The Hold Life Has: Coca and Cultural Identity in an Andean Community

A moving study of drug use and social structure in the Andes

0-87474-255-2 SMITHSONIAN PB $16.95

M.E. **Coombs-Schilling**

Sacred Performances: Islam, Sexuality, and Sacrifice

A strange, sometimes delirious study of the intersection of religion, politics, and everyday social life in Morocco, it embodies the best, and some of the worst, of contemporary ethnography

0-231-06975-8 COLUMBIA PB $17.00

Alan **Dundes**, editor

The Cockfight: A Case Book

0-299-14050-4 WISCONSIN $58.00
0-299-14054-7 WISCONSIN PB $19.95

Kevin **Dwyer**

Moroccan Dialogues: Anthropology in Question

0-8018-2759-0 JOHNS HOPKINS $47.50
0-88133-293-3 WAVELAND PB $11.95

Stephen William **Foster**

The Past Is Another Country: Representation, Historical Consciousness, and Resistance in the Blue Ridge

0-520-06251-5 CALIFORNIA $37.50

Abdellah **Hammoudi**

The Victim and Its Masks: An Essay on Sacrifice and Masquerade in the Maghreb

A study of structuralism in rural, post-colonial Morocco where tradition and change are both in question

TRANSLATED BY PAULA WISSING

0-226-31525-8 CHICAGO $39.95
0-226-31526-6 CHICAGO PB $16.95

Timothy J. **Knab**

A War of Witches: A Journey into the Underworld of the Contemporary Aztecs

0-06-251264-1 HARPERCOLLINS $22.00
0-06-251265-X HARPERCOLLINS PB $12.00

Smadar **Lavie**

The Poetics of Military Occupation: Mzeina Allegories of Bedouin Identity Under Israeli and Egyptian Rule

A lively ethnographic study that exposes the raw edge of the process of cultural fascination and illustrates the power of reflexive writing and ethnographic practice

0-520-06880-7 CALIFORNIA $35.00
0-520-07552-8 CALIFORNIA PB $16.00

Lamont **Lindstrom**

Cargo Cult: Strange Stories of Desire from Melanesia and Beyond

A model of reasoned ethnography, smoothly written and even entertaining without ever condescending to its subjects

0-8248-1526-2 HAWAII $36.00
0-8248-1563-7 HAWAII PB $14.95

Peter **Menzel**

Material World: A Global Family Portrait

TEXT BY CHARLES C. MANN AND INTRODUCTION BY PAUL KENNEDY

9995160765 SIERRA CLUB PB $20.00

Michael Z. **Rosaldo**

Knowledge and Passion

0-521-29562-9 CAMBRIDGE PB $20.95

June **Nash**

We Eat the Mines and the Mines Eat Us: Dependency and Exploitation in Bolivian Tin Mines

See also **SOUTH AMERICA** under **NATIVE AMERICAN CULTURES: CENTRAL AND SOUTH AMERICA** in **HISTORY OF THE AMERICAS**

0-231-04710-X COLUMBIA $34.00
0-231-08051-4 COLUMBIA PB $19.00

Renato **Rosaldo**

Ilongot Hunting, 1883-1974: A Study in Society and History

0-8047-1046-5 STANFORD $47.50
0-8047-1284-0 STANFORD PB $14.95

Alan R. **Sandstrom**

Corn Is Our Blood: Culture and Ethnic Identity in a Contemporary Aztec Indian Village

0-8061-2399-0 OKLAHOMA $42.50
0-8061-2403-2 OKLAHOMA PB $21.95

Nancy **Scheper-Hughes**

Death Without Weeping: The Violence of Everyday Life in Brazil

A chilling discription of Brazilian culture and motherhood in crisis written with grace and passion

0-520-07536-6 CALIFORNIA $39.95
0-520-07537-4 CALIFORNIA PB $18.95

Lesley A. **Sharp**

The Possessed and the Dispossessed: Spirits, Identity, and Power in a Madagascar Migrant Town

A carefully researched and innovative study of the complex relation of possession to society-wide issues of power, powerlessness, and change

0-520-08001-7 CALIFORNIA $45.00

Paul **Stoller**

Fusion of the Worlds: An Ethnography of Possession Among the Songhay of Niger

A penetrating study of African religious life that attempts to go beyond the limits of standard ethnographies

0-226-77544-5 CHICAGO $29.95

Sabra J. **Webber**

Romancing the Real: Folklore and Ethnographic Representation in North Africa

0-8122-8236-1 PENNSYLVANIA $31.95

Critical and Biographical Studies

Luigi **Cavalli-Sforza** &
Francesco **Cavalli-Sforza**
The Great Human Diasporas: A History of Diversity and Evolution
A compelling, comprehensible book on the history of evolution by one of the world's leading geneticists and his son, a documentary filmmaker
0-201-40755-8 ADDISON-WESLEY $27.50
0-201-44231-0 ADDISON-WESLEY PB $14.00

Luigi **Cavalli-Sforza**, & others
The History and Geography of Human Genes
A massive study of the diffusion of genetic characteristics across the globe
0-691-08750-4 PRINCETON $150.00

James L. **Newman**
The Peopling of Africa: A Geographic Interpretation
A reconsideration of the patterns of human origins in Africa and the diffusion of African peoples over time
0-300-06003-3 YALE $30.00

Alan **Walker** & Pat **Shipman**
The Wisdom of the Bones: In Search of Human Origins
A riveting account of the discovery of the Nariokotome Boy, a complete teenage skeleton believed by some to be the long-sought missing link between ape and modern man. Walker and Shipman, two of the word's foremost paleo-anthropologists, tell the fascinating story of the find and its sophisticated analysis, and show how from this singular discovery a world of information is revealed by the intricate detective work of their profession
0-679-42624-8 KNOPF $26.00

Biographies of Anthropologists

Mary Catherine **Bateson**
With a Daughter's Eye: A Memoir of Gregory Bateson and Margaret Mead
A personal, and at times, shocking account of two of our century's most brilliant citizens and how they used their ideas in their parenting methods
0-06-097573-3 HARPERPERENNIAL PB $13.00

Margaret **Caffrey**
Ruth Benedict: Stranger in This Land
A new biography of the author of *Patterns of Culture*
0-292-74655-5 TEXAS $19.95

Robert **Ackerman**
J.G. Frazer: Life and Work
0-521-34093-4 CAMBRIDGE PB $64.95

Margaret **Mead**
Blackberry Winter
A memoir rich in anecdotes and instructive details about Mead's work
0-317-60065-6 SMITH $25.05

Martin **Orans**
Not Even Wrong: Margaret Mead, Derek Freeman, and the Samoans
Sorts out the Mead-Freeman controversy over fieldwork methods
0-88316-564-3 CHANDLER & SHARP PB $14.95

Psychology

Histories and Introductions

Jerome **Bruner**
Acts of Meaning
A distinguished psychologist's critique of the current trend toward regarding the mind as an "information processor." Bruner feels that psychology must stop limiting itself to a computational model of mind in order to progress toward a "cultural psychology"
0-674-00361-6 HARVARD PB $12.00

Robert **Coles**
The Mind's Fate: A Psychiatrist Looks at His Profession
The Pulitzer Prize-winning psychiatrist's classic 1975 work is now available in a new edition, including 16 new essays. Illuminating essays explore an enormous range of psychiatric and psychological issues, including racism, psychoanalysis, the making of a moral life, and key theories of child development. "To read [Coles's] books is to make him a lasting friend"—*NY Times Book Review*.
"A colossal literary and scientific achievement"—*The Boston Globe*
0-316-15164-5 LITTLE, BROWN $25.95
0-316-15139-4 LITTLE, BROWN PB $14.95

Henri F. **Ellenberger**
The Discovery of the Unconscious: The History and Evolution of Dynamic Psychiatry
An excellent history of the exploration of the unconscious mind, from exorcists and hypnotists to Freud, Jung, and Adler
0-465-01673-1 BASIC BOOKS PB $40.00

Michel **Foucault**
Madness and Civilization: A History of Insanity in the Age of Reason
This 1961 study of madness—from the medieval "ship of fools" to 19th- century efforts to correct insanity through moral instruction—was Foucault's first major work
See also **HISTORICAL SOCIOLOGY** under **TOPICS IN MODERN SOCIOLOGY** under **SOCIOLOGY**
0-679-72110-X VINTAGE PB $12.00

Michel Foucault

Jan **Goldstein**
Console and Classify: The French Psychiatric Profession in the Nineteenth Century
0-521-39555-0 CAMBRIDGE PB $24.95

David **Hothersall**
History of Psychology
0-07-030512-9 MCGRAW HILL PB $52.15

William **James**
The Principles of Psychology
A classic that remains unsurpassed for its range of allusion to philosophy, the arts, and actual experience; although published in 1896, it is still a valuable introduction to such topics as the stream of consciousness, self-consciousness, perception, memory, emotion, instinct, and will

Volume 1
0-486-20381-6 DOVER PB $12.95

Volume 2
0-486-20382-4 DOVER PB $12.95

Psychology: The Briefer Course
EDITED BY GORDON ALLPORT
0-268-01557-0 NOTRE DAME PB $15.00

Jerome **Kagan** & Julius **Segal**
Psychology: An Introduction, Eighth Edition
The latest edition of a standard textbook, covering human psychology through all the stages of life
0-15-501476-5 HARCOURT BRACE PB $25.95

Stephen A. **Mitchell** & Margaret J. **Black**
Freud and Beyond: A History of Modern Psychoanalytic Thought
0-465-01404-6 BASIC $27.50

Janet **Sayers**
Mothers of Psychoanalysis: Helene Deutsch, Karen Horney, Anna Freud, & Melanie Klein
Females, Sayers intriguingly argues, gain a unique perspective and unique power as psychoanalysts and as theorists because of their experiences as mothers
0-393-30942-8 NORTON PB $12.95

Edward **Shorter**

From the Mind into the Body: The Cultural Origins of Psychosomatic Symptoms

According to the author, culture, class, ethnicity, and age all play a part in specific symptoms surrounding psychosomatic illness—women have more abdominal problems than men, Eastern European Jews have more nervous disorders than other ethnic groups

0-02-928666-2 FREE PRESS........$24.95

Herbert **Spiegelberg**

Phenomenology in Psychology & Psychiatry

0-8101-0624-8 NORTHWESTERN PB........$22.95

Robert I. **Watson**, editor

Basic Writings in the History of Psychology

Excerpts from Bacon, Hume, Kant, Helmholtz, Darwin, James, Freud, Jung, Skinner, and many others. Illustrated

0-19-502444-3 OXFORD PB........$19.95

Freud

Freud's theories can no longer be considered the rigorous scientific explanations he hoped he had achieved. Yet there is no doubt about their revolutionary impact, not only on psychology, but on almost every field of modern culture—anthropology, social and political theory, art, literature, criticism, philosophy, religion. His works have been called the "third blow" to Western anthropocentrism, after Copernicus and Darwin.

Sigmund **Freud**

The Basic Writings of Sigmund Freud

The anthology that introduced Freud to a wide American readership

0-679-60166-X MODERN LIBRARY........$20.00

Beyond the Pleasure Principle

An essay on the notion of a death instinct

0-393-00769-3 NORTON PB........$6.95

Civilization and Its Discontents

A pessimistic assessment of the instinctual cost of civilization

See also **CLASSICAL EUROPEAN SOCIOLOGY** under **SOCIOLOGY**

0-393-30158-3 NORTON PB........$7.95

The Diary of Sigmund Freud: 1929-1939

The first English-language publication of the daily chronicle that Freud maintained during the last ten years of his life in Vienna and London. Illustrated with 100 photographs from the Freud Museum. Translated and annotated by Michael Molnar

0-684-19329-9 SCRIBNERS........$50.00

The Ego and the Id

The book Freud himself identified as his last major contribution to psychoanalytic theory

0-393-00142-3 NORTON PB........$7.95

Dora: An Analysis of a Case of Hysteria

Perhaps Freud's best-known case study, and among his most fascinating demonstrations of psychoanalytic method

0-02-050987-1 COLLIER PB........$10.00

The Future of an Illusion

Psychoanalysis as the most powerful argument against the consolations of religion

See also **PSYCHOLOGY AND RELIGION** under **WORLD RELIGION** in **RELIGION, SPIRITUALITY, AND PHILOSOPHY**

EDITED BY JAMES STRACHEY

0-393-00831-2 NORTON PB........$7.95

General Psychological Theory

0-02-076350-6 MACMILLAN PB........$6.95

Inhibitions, Symptoms and Anxiety

0-393-00874-6 NORTON PB........$4.95

The Interpretation of Dreams

First published in 1900, this pioneering work introduced Freud's concept of the "Oedipus complex" and laid the foundation for many of his subsequent discoveries

0-380-01000-3 AVON PB........$4.95

Introductory Lectures on Psychoanalysis: A General Introduction to Psychoanalysis

Includes one section on "Parapraxes," a second on "Dreams," and a third on the "General Theory of the Neuroses"

0-87140-118-5 LIVERIGHT PB........$9.95

Jokes and Their Relation to the Unconscious

Written in response to Fliess's comment that *The Interpretation of Dreams* was too full of jokes

0-393-00145-8 NORTON PB........$7.95

Leonardo Da Vinci and a Memory of His Childhood

Freud applies his theories to the famously elusive Renaissance polymath

0-393-00149-0 NORTON PB........$5.95

New Introductory Lectures on Psychoanalysis

A supplement to the original, published in 1933

0-393-00743-X NORTON PB........$7.95

On Dreams

0-393-00144-X NORTON PB........$6.95

Sigmund Freud

An Outline of Psychoanalysis

Among Freud's last contributions, published posthumously in 1940

0-393-00151-2 NORTON PB........$6.95

The Psychopathology of Everyday Life

Includes "Forgetting," "Slips of the Tongue," "Bungled Actions," and "Superstitions and Errors"

0-393-00611-5 NORTON PB........$7.95

The Question of Lay Analysis

On the still-controversial question of whether or not the practice of psychoanalysis should be restricted to the medical profession

0-393-00503-8 NORTON PB........$4.95

Sexual Enlightenment in Children

The sexual awareness and preoccupation of children, and how the frustration of such feelings results in adult neuroses

0-02-076500-2 MACMILLAN PB........$7.00

Three Essays on the Theory of Sexuality

0-465-08606-3 BASIC BOOKS PB........$14.00

Totem and Taboo

Four essays first published as "Some Points of Agreement Between the Mental Lives of Savages and Neurotics," one of his original efforts to extend analysis of the individual psyche to culture and society

0-394-70124-0 RANDOM HOUSE PB........$8.00

Sigmund **Freud** & Josef **Breuer**

Studies on Hysteria

The pioneering 1895 collaboration that launched modern psychoanalysis, establishing a link between the bodily symptoms of hysteria and psychological trauma in early childhood

0-465-08276-9 BASIC BOOKS PB........$19.00

Peter **Gay**, editor

The Freud Reader

Fifty-one texts in a single 800-page volume

See also **FREUD** under **IDEAS, CULTURE, AND SOCIETY** under **19TH-CENTURY EUROPE** in **WORLD HISTORY AND CURRENT AFFAIRS**

0-393-31403-0 NORTON PB........$19.95

Andre **Haynal** & others, editors

The Correspondence of Sigmund Freud & Sandor Ferenczi

A 25-year-long correspondence between Freud and his younger Hungarian colleague

0-674-17418-6 HARVARD........$42.50

Philippe **Julien**

Jacques Lacan's Return to Freud: The Real, the Symbolic, & the Imaginary

An explanation—and defense—of Lacan's theories by one of his leading students

TRANSLATED BY DEVRA B. SIMIU

0-8147-4198-3 NYU........$45.00

0-8147-4226-2 NYU PB........$17.95

William **McGuire**, editor
The Freud/Jung Letters: The Correspondence Between Sigmund Freud and C.G. Jung
0-691-09890-5 PRINCETON $99.50

Jeffrey Moussaieff **Masson**, editor
The Complete Letters of Sigmund Freud to Wilhelm Fliess, 1887-1904
The highly interesting correspondence of Freud with his earliest (and perhaps his most eccentric) major colleague
0-674-15421-5 HARVARD PB $18.95

R. Andrew **Paskauskas**, editor
The Complete Correspondence of Sigmund Freud and Ernest Jones
A compendium of 671 letters between Freud and his loyal disciple and first biographer. Offers a first-hand account of the early years of psychoanalysis and revealing glimpses of its professional disputes and rivalries
0-674-15423-1 HARVARD $42.50

About Freud

Hannah S. **Decker**
Freud, Dora, and Vienna 1900
The case of the 18-year-old girl he called "Dora" was crucial for Freud. "By placing Dora into her environment, her family, her city, her religion, and her country, Decker has managed to recreate this complex person"—Peter Gay
0-02-907830-X FREE PRESS $27.95
0-02-907212-3 FREE PRESS PB $14.95

Seymour **Fisher** & Roger P. **Greenberg**
The Scientific Credibility of Freud's Theories and Theraphy
A survey of attempts to verify Freud's theories in empirical research
0-231-06215-X COLUMBIA PB $22.00

Lucy **Freeman**
Story of Anna O: The Woman Who Led Freud to Psychoanalysis
The story of one of the early patients who strongly influenced Freud's developing ideas about hysteria and the "talking cure"
1-56821-226-7 ARONSON PB $30.00

Peter **Gay**
Freud: A Life for Our Time
Scholarly, balanced, and deftly written, Gay's volume discusses the controversies currently swirling around Freud's reputation without losing sight of his importance
0-385-26256-6 ANCHOR PB $14.95

Adolf **Grunbaum**
The Foundations of Psychoanalysis: A Philosophical Critique
A thoroughgoing attack on Freud's scientific pretensions
0-520-05017-7 CALIFORNIA PB $15.95

Nathan G. **Hale**, Jr.
Freud & the Americans: The Origin & Foundation of the Psychoanalytic Movement in America, 1876-1918
An authoritative account of the scientific and cultural forces in late Victorian America that made the country receptive to Freud's ideas
0-19-501427-8 OXFORD $35.00

John **Kerr**
A Most Dangerous Method: The Story of Jung, Freud, and Sabina Spielrein
Sabina Spielrein was Jung's patient, lover, and colleague, as well as a confidante of Freud. She was the conduit through which each man learned of the private life of the other, and as such had a profound influence on the shaping of psychoanalysis. A fascinating work based on recently discovered diaries and journals
0-679-40412-0 KNOPF $30.00

Jonathan **Lear**
Love and Its Place in Nature: A Philosophical Analysis of Freudian Psychoanalysis
A lucid and accessible essay on the place of Freud's thought in Western traditions regarding the role of the individual. Lear focuses particularly on Freud's assertion that psychoanalysis is "a cure through love"
0-374-52320-7 NOONDAY PB $10.00

Philip **Rieff**
Freud: The Mind of a Moralist
Offers an excellent entry into Freud's thinking
See also **FREUD** under **IDEAS, CULTURE, AND SOCIETY** under **19TH-CENTURY EUROPE** in **WORLD HISTORY AND CURRENT AFFAIRS**
0-226-71639-2 CHICAGO PB $25.00

Paul W. **Robinson**
Freud and His Critics
"Since we all speak Freud now, it is useful to know what we are talking about"
—Peter Gay, *American Historical Review*
0-520-08029-7 CALIFORNIA $30.00

Frank **Sulloway**
Freud, Biologist of the Mind: Beyond the Psychoanalytic Legend
0-674-32335-1 HARVARD PB $21.50

Richard **Webster**
Why Freud Was Wrong
0-465-09128-8 BASIC PB $22.50

Richard **Wollheim**
Sigmund Freud
0-521-28385-X CAMBRIDGE PB $21.95

The Reaction Against Freud

Frederick **Crews** & others
The Memory Wars: Freud's Legacy in Dispute
A strongly argued and controversial polemic against both Freud and the contemporary recovered memory movement. "In the two essays that form the core of this book, Frederick Crews convincingly dismantles the entire Freudian enterprise from beginning to end"
—John F. Kihlstrom
See also **FREUD** under **IDEAS, CULTURE, AND SOCIETY** under **19TH-CENTURY EUROPE** in **WORLD HISTORY AND CURRENT AFFAIRS**
0-940322-04-8 NY REVIEW $22.95

Later Freudianism

Elizabeth Y. **Bruehl**
Anna Freud: A Biography
The authorized life of Freud's daughter. "A notable contribution to the burgeoning literature of psychoanalytic history and a convincing portrait of a remarkable woman"—*NY Times*
0-393-31157-0 NORTON PB $14.95

Morris N. **Eagle**
Recent Developments in Psychoanalysis
"The best survey of the current status of psychoanalytical theory that I have seen—clearly reasoned, incisive, balanced and fair in its judgments"
—Robert R. Holt, New York University
0-674-75080-2 HARVARD PB $15.95

Otto **Fenichel**
The Psychoanalytic Theory of Neurosis
The latest edition of a standard text
0-393-01019-8 NORTON $35.00

Anna **Freud**
The Ego and the Mechanisms of Defense
A survey of the neurotic symptoms—such as obsessive-compulsive traits—that are used by the ego to ward off threatening thoughts and impulses
0-8236-6871-1 INT'L UNIVERSITIES $30.00
0-8236-8035-5 INT'L UNIVERSITIES PB $24.95

Otto F. **Kernberg**
Borderline Conditions and Pathological Narcissism
Kernberg's work assimilates into Freudianism the study of conditions formerly thought to be beyond psychoanalytic treatment
0-87668-177-1 ARONSON PB $35.00

Object-Relations Theory & Clinical Psychoanalysis
1-56821-612-2 ARONSON PB $40.00

Severe Personality Disorders: Psychotherapeutic Strategies
0-300-05349-5 YALE PB $20.00

Janet **Malcolm**

Psychoanalysis: The Impossible Profession

A candid and controversial portrait of a practicing psychoanalyst in Manhattan

0-394-71034-7 RANDOM HOUSE PB........................$11.00

Janet Malcolm

Joyce **McDougall**

Theaters of the Mind: Illusion and Truth on the Psychoanalytic Stage

0-87630-648-2 BRUNNER & MAZEL PB..................$28.95

David **Shapiro**

Autonomy and Rigid Character

A study of rigidity of character and loss of autonomy as revealed in sado-masochistic, obsessive-compulsive, and paranoid conditions

0-465-00568-3 BASIC BOOKS PB..............................$15.00

Neurotic Styles

An acclaimed work of character analysis focusing on paranoid, hysterical, impulsive, and obsessive-compulsive neurotic styles

0-465-09502-X BASIC BOOKS PB..............................$15.00

Donald P. **Spence**

The Freudian Metaphor: Toward Paradigm Change in Psychoanalysis

0-393-70042-9 NORTON..$22.95

Narrative Truth and Historical Truth: Meaning and Interpretation in Psychoanalysis

0-393-30207-5 NORTON PB.....................................$10.95

Jung

Jung's ideas have had a more gradual impact than those of Freud. His psychological theories, with their somewhat esoteric overtones of idealist philosophy and mystical religion, their flirtation with Gnosticism, Alchemy, Tantric Buddhism, and the Occult, for a long time influenced mainly those who had come into contact with Jung himself or who had mastered his finely written but unsystematic works. More recently, however, the work of Joseph Campbell, Mircea Eliade, and others inspired by his synoptic view of mythology has awakened a much broader interest in his theories. His reputation has been enhanced by a general revival, during the last 25 years, of concern with spiritual values, Eastern and unorthodox forms of religious expression, and mythology.

Carl **Jung**

The Collected Works of C.G. Jung

Volume 1

Psychiatric Studies

Today such Jungian notions as *archetype* and *collective unconscious* are nearly as familiar as *introvert, extrovert,* and other aspects of Jung's influential theory of character types. Jung's own writings, less rigorous but more suggestive than Freud's, present the reader with a remarkable range of ideas and a fund of religious and historical allusions

0-691-09768-2 PRINCETON.....................................$55.00
0-691-01855-3 PRINCETON PB..............................$17.95

Volume 2

Experimental Researches

Includes nine studies on word association with two lectures on the association method

0-691-09764-X PRINCETON.....................................$65.00

Volume 3

Psychogenesis of Mental Disease

0-691-09769-0 PRINCETON.....................................$47.50
0-691-01859-6 PRINCETON PB..............................$16.95

Volume 4

Freud and Psychoanalysis

0-691-01864-2 PRINCETON PB..............................$17.95

Volume 5

Symbols of Transformation

Jung's groundbreaking early work on symbolism and myth

0-691-09775-5 PRINCETON.....................................$65.00
0-691-01815-4 PRINCETON PB..............................$19.95

Volume 6

Psychological Types

Jung's single most influential work, introducing opposed pairs of character types (introvert/extravert, intuitive/sensing, thinking/feeling, and judging/perceiving) and relating them to masculine and feminine psychology

0-691-09770-4 PRINCETON.....................................$75.00
0-691-01813-8 PRINCETON PB..............................$19.95

Volume 7

Two Essays on Analytical Psychology

Includes "The Relationship Between the Ego and the Unconscious" and "On the Psychology of the Unconscious"

0-691-09776-3 PRINCETON.....................................$49.50
0-691-01782-4 PRINCETON PB..............................$15.95

Volume 8

Structure and the Dynamics of the Psyche

0-691-09774-7 PRINCETON.....................................$75.00

Volume 9 (Part 1)

Archetypes and the Collective Unconscious

"His idea of archetypes involves profound attitudes towards man's existence and intimates values through which many people have found a new significance"—*Virginia Quarterly*

0-691-09761-5 PRINCETON.....................................$69.50
0-691-01833-2 PRINCETON PB..............................$19.95

Volume 9 (Part 2)

Aion

0-691-09759-3 PRINCETON.....................................$49.50
0-691-01826-X PRINCETON PB..............................$15.95

Volume 10

Civilization in Transition

0-691-09762-3 PRINCETON.....................................$69.50

Volume 11

Psychology and Religion

Includes "A Psychological Approach to the Dogma of the Trinity" and "Transformation Symbolism in the Mass," among many others

0-691-09772-0 PRINCETON.....................................$69.50

Volume 12

Psychology and Alchemy

Jung's major application of alchemical symbolism to depth psychology; profusely illustrated

0-691-09771-2 PRINCETON.....................................$75.00
0-691-01831-6 PRINCETON PB..............................$18.95

Volume 13

Alchemical Studies

0-691-09760-7 PRINCETON.....................................$49.50
0-691-01849-9 PRINCETON PB..............................$19.95

Volume 14

Mysterium Coniunctionis

A detailed study of the alchemical symbol of the "sacred wedding"

0-691-09766-6 PRINCETON.....................................$65.00
0-691-01816-2 PRINCETON PB..............................$22.50

Volume 15

The Spirit in Man, Art, and Literature

Essays on Paracelsus, Freud, Picasso, and James Joyce's *Ulysses* examining the qualities of personality that enable the creative spirit to introduce radical innovations

0-691-09773-9 PRINCETON.....................................$27.50
0-691-01775-1 PRINCETON PB..............................$11.95

Volume 16

Practice of Psychotherapy

Essays on the "Psychology of the Transference" and other subjects

0-691-09767-4 PRINCETON.....................................$49.50
0-691-01870-7 PRINCETON PB..............................$17.95

Volume 17

Development of Personality

Papers on child psychology, education, and related subjects

0-691-09763-1 PRINCETON.....................................$39.50
0-691-01838-3 PRINCETON PB..............................$14.95

Volume 18

The Symbolic Life

0-691-09892-1 PRINCETON.....................................$90.00

Carl **Jung**

The Collected Works of C.G. Jung

Volume 19

General Bibliography

0-691-09893-X PRINCETON $39.50

Volume 20

General Index

0-691-09867-0 PRINCETON $85.00

Analytical Psychology: Its Theory and Practice

Five lectures on psychological types, the personal and collective unconscious, archetypes, and dream analysis. "This, surely, is the most lucid, simple and orderly introduction to the basic principles and methods of the Jungian science of the psyche that has yet been offered to the public"—Joseph Campbell

0-394-70862-8 RANDOM HOUSE PB $10.00

Analytical Psychology: Notes of the Seminar Given in 1925

EDITED BY WILLIAM MCGUIRE

0-691-01918-5 PRINCETON PB $13.95

Answer to Job

A consideration of evil which reflects on its interdependence with good

0-691-01785-9 PRINCETON PB $8.95

Aspects of the Feminine

On marriage, Eros, the mother, the maiden, and the anima/animus concept

0-691-01845-6 PRINCETON PB $10.95

The Basic Writings of C.G. Jung

EDITED BY VIOLET S. DE LASZLO

0-394-60419-9 MODERN LIBRARY $14.95

C.G. Jung Speaking: Interviews and Encounters

0-691-01871-5 PRINCETON PB $18.95

Dreams

0-691-01792-1 PRINCETON PB $13.95

The Essential Jung

Includes an introduction summarizing Jung's thought and extracts prefaced by brief explanatory remarks. "The best introductory book for a serious reader"—*Virginia Quarterly Review*

EDITED BY ANTHONY STORR

0-691-02455-3 PRINCETON PB $14.95

Four Archetypes: Mother/Rebirth/ Spirit/Trickster

0-691-01766-2 PRINCETON PB $10.95

Memories, Dreams, Reflections

An autobiography with emphasis on his religious ideas, recorded and edited by Aniela Jaffe

0-679-72395-1 VINTAGE PB $13.00

Modern Man in Search of a Soul

A diagnosis of the spiritual restlessness and emptiness of modern civilization which also serves as a basic introduction to Jung's thought on dream analysis, the collective unconscious, and the relation between psychology and religion. It includes "Freud and Jung: Contrast"

See also **PSYCHOLOGY AND RELIGION** under **WORLD RELIGION** in **RELIGION, SPIRITUALITY, AND PHILOSOPHY**

0-15-661206-2 HARCOURT BRACE PB $9.00

On the Nature of the Psyche

0-691-01751-4 PRINCETON PB $10.95

Psyche and Symbol

Selections from Jung's writings on the archetypal origins and integrating function of symbols

EDITED BY VIOLET S. DE LASZLO

0-691-01903-7 PRINCETON PB $14.95

Psychological Reflections: A New Anthology of His Writings

Aphoristic selections from Jung's works

0-691-01786-7 PRINCETON PB $16.95

Psychology and Religion

Drawing on ancient and medieval Gnostic, alchemical, and occult literature, Jung discusses the religious symbolism and continuity of the unconscious processes

0-300-00137-1 YALE PB $10.00

Psychology and the East

0-691-01806-5 PRINCETON PB $12.95

Psychology and the Occult

0-691-01791-3 PRINCETON PB $10.95

Psychology and Western Religion

0-691-01862-6 PRINCETON PB $12.95

Psychology of Kundalini Yoga

0-691-02127-9 PRINCETON $24.95

The Psychology of Transference

0-691-01752-2 PRINCETON PB $12.95

Synchronicity

The psychological significance of meaningful coincidences

0-691-01794-8 PRINCETON PB $9.95

The Undiscovered Self

How the bureaucratic character of modern society stands in the way of full self-realization

0-451-62650-8 NEW AMERICAN LIBRARY PB $5.99

Carl **Jung** & Karl **Kerenyi**

Essays on a Science of Mythology

An approach based on Jung's theory of a collective unconscious

See also **GENERAL INTRODUCTIONS** under **MYTHOLOGY AND FOLKLORE** in **RELIGION, SPIRITUALITY, AND PHILOSOPHY**

0-691-01756-5 PRINCETON PB $11.95

Introductions to Jung

Stephenson **Bond**

Living Myth: Personal Meaning as a Way of Life

Bond, a Jungian psychotherapist, discusses the power of and need for mythic imagination in modern culture. Recognizing the decline of traditional myths in contemporary life, the author suggests that we look to such icons as baseball and the works of J.R.R. Tolkien, C.G. Jung, and Black Elk for cultural renewal

0-87773-861-0 SHAMBHALA PB $14.00

Edward F. **Edinger**

Ego and Archetype

A lucid synthesis of Jung's major ideas, taking in art, mythology, and religion, and emphasizing the human need for super-personal meaning that expresses itself in the convergence of ego and archetype

0-87773-576-X SHAMBHALA PB $20.00

Robert **Hopcke**

A Guided Tour of the Collected Works of C.G. Jung

0-87773-582-4 SHAMBHALA PB $16.00

Carl Jung

Andrew **Samuels**

Jung and the Post-Jungians

0-415-05904-6 ROUTLEDGE PB $14.95

June **Singer**

Boundaries of the Soul: The Practice of Jung's Psychology

"Certainly the very best introduction to Jung around...a beautifully conceived and constructed book with a personal quality that is warm and lovely and rich"— Joseph Campbell

0-385-06900-6 ANCHOR PB $11.95

Anthony **Stevens**

Jung

A concise introductory biography by a widely recognized authority on Jung; a volume in Oxford's "Past Masters" series

0-19-287686-4 OXFORD PB $7.95

Jungian Studies

M. Esther **Harding**

The "I" and the "Not-I": A Study in the Development of Consciousness

0-691-01796-4 PRINCETON PB $13.95

Psychic Energy: Its Source and Transformation

0-691-01790-5 PRINCETON PB $18.95

James **Hillman**

Anima: The Anatomy of a Personified Notion

0-88214-316-6 SPRING PB $16.00

Healing Fiction

0-88214-363-8 SPRING PB $15.00

Insearch: Psychology and Religion

0-88214-501-0 SPRING PB $15.00

Revisioning Psychology

An allusive philosophical and historical meditation on psychology and myth

0-06-090563-8 HARPERPERENNIAL PB $14.50

The Soul's Code

0-679-44522-6 RANDOM HOUSE $23.00

Erich **Neumann**

Amor and Psyche: The Psychic Development of the Feminine

0-691-01772-7 PRINCETON PB $9.95

Art and the Creative Unconscious

The best application of Jungian ideas to aesthetics

0-691-01773-5 PRINCETON PB $14.95

The Great Mother: An Analysis of an Archetype

0-691-01780-8 PRINCETON PB $18.95

The Origins and History of Consciousness

A study arguing that the individual and the human race as a whole pass through the same stages of archetypal development

0-691-01761-1 PRINCETON PB $16.95

Richard **Noll**

The Jung Cult

Views Jung as the founder of a new religion, and a rebel against the scientific tradition of psychoanalysis. "Disturbing and often illuminating"—*London Review of Books*

0-691-03724-8 PRINCETON $27.95

Carol **Pearson**

The Hero Within: Six Archetypes We Live By

0-86683-527-X HARPERCOLLINS PB $12.00

Marie-Louise **von Franz**

Puer Aeternus

A brilliant study of the psychology of the "eternal boy" and his fear of making commitments in love and work

0-938434-01-2 SIGO PB $16.95

Post-Freudian Theorists

Alfred Adler

Alfred **Adler**

Individual Psychology of Alfred Adler: A Systematic Presentation in Selections from His Writings

EDITED BY HEINZ L. ANSBACHER AND ROWENA R. ANSBACHER

0-06-131154-5 HARPERCOLLINS PB $16.00

Understanding Human Nature

TRANSLATED BY COLIN BRETT

1-85168-021-7 ONEWORLD PB $13.95

Edward **Hoffman**

The Drive for Self: Alfred Adler & the Founding of Individual Psychology

A thorough account of a figure who—though overshadowed by Freud and Jung in the history of psychoanalysis—pioneered influential psychological concepts like the inferiority complex and sibling rivalry

0-201-63280-2 ADDISON-WESLEY $27.00

0-201-44194-2 ADDISON-WESLEY PB $14.00

Erik H. Erikson

Erik H. **Erikson**

Adulthood: Essays

0-393-09086-8 NORTON PB $11.95

Childhood and Society

A reissue of the classic about the social significance of childhood by the Pulitzer Prize-winning writer. Brilliantly analyzes the relationship between childhood training and cultural accomplishment, as well as the elements of human motivation. "A rare and living combination of European and American thought in the human sciences"
—Margaret Mead, *American Scholar*

0-393-31068-X NORTON PB $9.95

Gandhi's Truth: On the Origins of Militant Nonviolence

The famous psychoanalytic approach to Gandhi's career

0-393-31034-5 NORTON PB $11.95

Identity: Youth and Crisis

0-393-31144-9 NORTON PB $9.95

Identity and the Life Cycle

Erikson's theory of eight stages in the human lifecycle had a revolutionary impact on developmental psychology; his conception of an "identity crisis" in adolescence is perhaps the best-known aspect of this approach

0-393-31132-5 NORTON PB $8.95

Insight and Responsibility

0-393-09451-0 NORTON PB $8.95

Life Cycle Completed

0-393-31215-1 NORTON PB $8.00

A Way of Looking at Things: Selected Papers of Erik H. Erikson, 1930-1980

EDITED BY STEPHEN P. SCHLEIN

0-393-02267-6 NORTON $29.95

Young Man Luther

The origins of Luther's rebelliousness and later authoritarianism; one of the most successful forays into psychobiography, by the author of *Childhood, Youth and Crisis*

See also **REFORMERS AND REVOLUTIONARIES** under **REFORMATION AND COUNTER-REFORMATION** under **EARLY MODERN EUROPE** in **WORLD HISTORY AND CURRENT AFFAIRS**

0-393-31036-1 NORTON PB $9.95

Erich Fromm

Erich **Fromm**

The Anatomy of Human Destructiveness

0-8050-1604-X HOLT PB $17.95

The Art of Loving

A famous work in which Fromm argues that the root of neurosis is an inability to love either oneself or others

0-06-091594-3 HARPERCOLLINS PB $11.00

The Essential Fromm

0-8264-0844-3 CONTINUUM $18.95

0-09-474450-5 TRANS-ATLANTIC PB $19.95

The Sane Society

The alienation of modern man in a society dominated by purely economic imperatives

0-8050-1402-0 HOLT PB $12.95

Erich **Fromm** & Rainer **Funk**, compiler

The Erich Fromm Reader

INTRODUCTION BY JOEL KOVEL

0-391-03856-7 HUMANITIES $39.95

0-391-03851-6 HUMANITIES PB $15.00

Erich **Fromm** & Rainer **Funk**, editor

On Being Human

INTRODUCTION BY RAINER FUNK

0-8264-0576-2 CONTINUUM $17.95

Karen Horney

Karen **Horney**

Final Lectures

0-393-30755-7 NORTON PB $6.95

Neurosis and Human Growth

A brilliant study of aggressive, compliant, and withdrawing forms of neurotic alienation

0-393-30775-1 NORTON PB $12.95

The Neurotic Personality of Our Time

Under Adler's influence, Horney abandoned her earlier Freudianism and developed her theory of neurotic pride that protects the fantasy-bound ideal self from reality

0-393-31097-3 NORTON PB $7.95

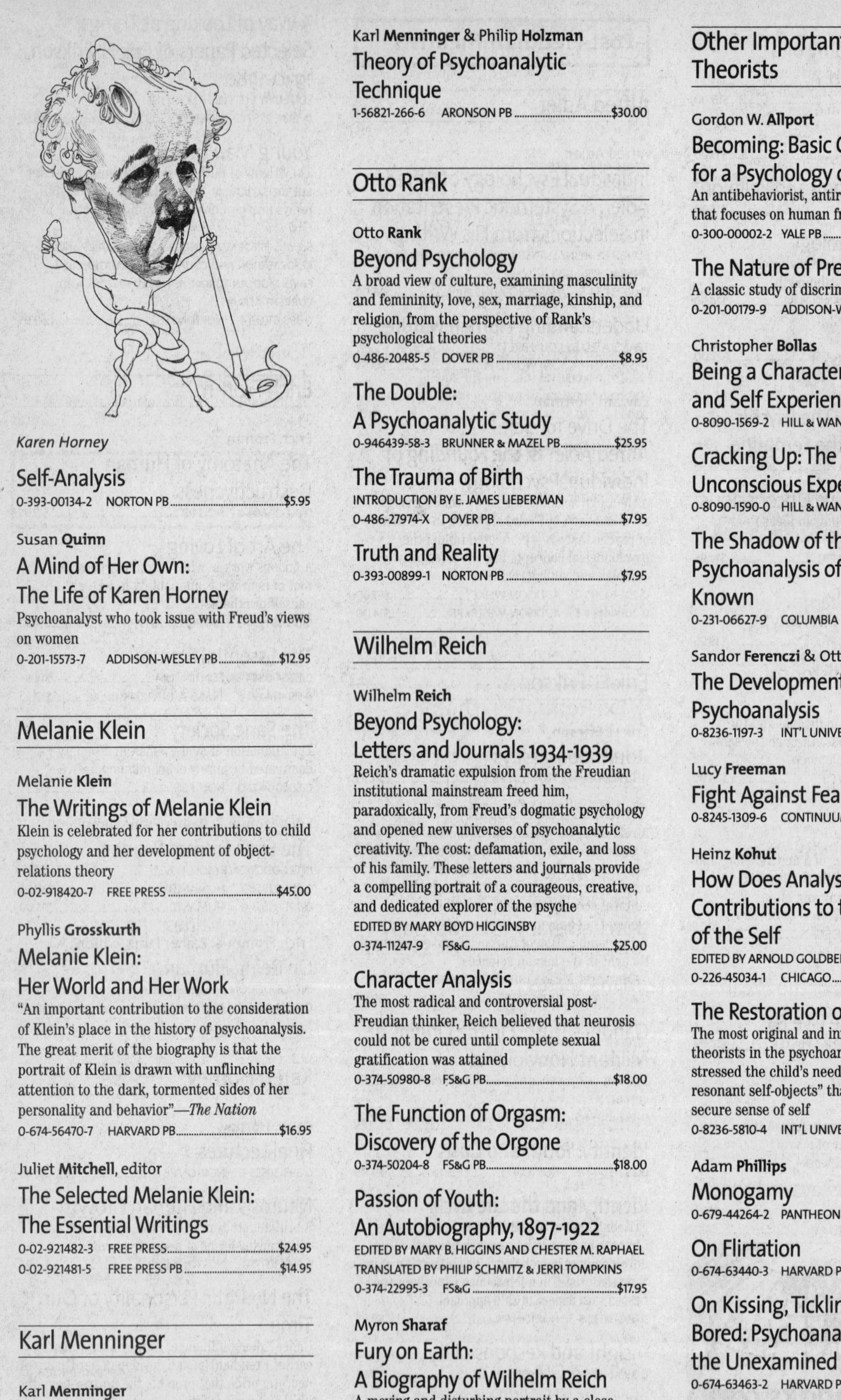

Karen Horney

Self-Analysis
0-393-00134-2 NORTON PB $5.95

Susan **Quinn**
A Mind of Her Own: The Life of Karen Horney
Psychoanalyst who took issue with Freud's views on women
0-201-15573-7 ADDISON-WESLEY PB $12.95

Melanie Klein

Melanie **Klein**
The Writings of Melanie Klein
Klein is celebrated for her contributions to child psychology and her development of object-relations theory
0-02-918420-7 FREE PRESS $45.00

Phyllis **Grosskurth**
Melanie Klein: Her World and Her Work
"An important contribution to the consideration of Klein's place in the history of psychoanalysis. The great merit of the biography is that the portrait of Klein is drawn with unflinching attention to the dark, tormented sides of her personality and behavior"—*The Nation*
0-674-56470-7 HARVARD PB $16.95

Juliet **Mitchell**, editor
The Selected Melanie Klein: The Essential Writings
0-02-921482-3 FREE PRESS $24.95
0-02-921481-5 FREE PRESS PB $14.95

Karl Menninger

Karl **Menninger**
Love Against Hate
0-15-653892-X HARCOURT BRACE PB $10.95

Karl **Menninger** & Philip **Holzman**
Theory of Psychoanalytic Technique
1-56821-266-6 ARONSON PB $30.00

Otto Rank

Otto **Rank**
Beyond Psychology
A broad view of culture, examining masculinity and femininity, love, sex, marriage, kinship, and religion, from the perspective of Rank's psychological theories
0-486-20485-5 DOVER PB $8.95

The Double: A Psychoanalytic Study
0-946439-58-3 BRUNNER & MAZEL PB $25.95

The Trauma of Birth
INTRODUCTION BY E. JAMES LIEBERMAN
0-486-27974-X DOVER PB $7.95

Truth and Reality
0-393-00899-1 NORTON PB $7.95

Wilhelm Reich

Wilhelm **Reich**
Beyond Psychology: Letters and Journals 1934-1939
Reich's dramatic expulsion from the Freudian institutional mainstream freed him, paradoxically, from Freud's dogmatic psychology and opened new universes of psychoanalytic creativity. The cost: defamation, exile, and loss of his family. These letters and journals provide a compelling portrait of a courageous, creative, and dedicated explorer of the psyche
EDITED BY MARY BOYD HIGGINSBY
0-374-11247-9 FS&G $25.00

Character Analysis
The most radical and controversial post-Freudian thinker, Reich believed that neurosis could not be cured until complete sexual gratification was attained
0-374-50980-8 FS&G PB $18.00

The Function of Orgasm: Discovery of the Orgone
0-374-50204-8 FS&G PB $18.00

Passion of Youth: An Autobiography, 1897-1922
EDITED BY MARY B. HIGGINS AND CHESTER M. RAPHAEL
TRANSLATED BY PHILIP SCHMITZ & JERRI TOMPKINS
0-374-22995-3 FS&G $17.95

Myron **Sharaf**
Fury on Earth: A Biography of Wilhelm Reich
A moving and disturbing portrait by a close associate
0-306-80575-8 DA CAPO PB $17.95

Other Important Post-Freudian Theorists

Gordon W. **Allport**
Becoming: Basic Considerations for a Psychology of Personality
An antibehaviorist, antireductionist psychology that focuses on human freedom
0-300-00002-2 YALE PB $10.00

The Nature of Prejudice
A classic study of discrimination
0-201-00179-9 ADDISON-WESLEY PB $16.00

Christopher **Bollas**
Being a Character: Psychoanalysis and Self Experience
0-8090-1569-2 HILL & WANG PB $11.00

Cracking Up: The Work of Unconscious Experience
0-8090-1590-0 HILL & WANG PB $13.00

The Shadow of the Object: Psychoanalysis of the Unthought Known
0-231-06627-9 COLUMBIA PB $16.50

Sandor **Ferenczi** & Otto **Rank**
The Development of Psychoanalysis
0-8236-1197-3 INT'L UNIVERSITIES $27.50

Lucy **Freeman**
Fight Against Fears
0-8245-1309-6 CONTINUUM PB $10.95

Heinz **Kohut**
How Does Analysis Cure?: Contributions to the Psychology of the Self
EDITED BY ARNOLD GOLDBERG & PAUL STEPANSKY
0-226-45034-1 CHICAGO $29.95

The Restoration of the Self
The most original and influential of recent theorists in the psychoanalytic tradition, Kohut stressed the child's need for "empathetically resonant self-objects" that reinforce the child's secure sense of self
0-8236-5810-4 INT'L UNIVERSITIES $55.00

Adam **Phillips**
Monogamy
0-679-44264-2 PANTHEON $18.00

On Flirtation
0-674-63440-3 HARVARD PB $14.00

On Kissing, Tickling, and Being Bored: Psychoanalytic Essays on the Unexamined Life
0-674-63463-2 HARVARD PB $12.00

Terrors and Experts
0-674-87479-X HARVARD $19.95

Jacques **Lacan**
Ecrits: A Selection
A useful compilation of Lacan's central writings—elliptical, sometimes obscure, but often strikingly original and always suggestive
TRANSLATED BY ALAN SHERIDAN
0-393-30047-1 NORTON PB $15.95

Jacques Lacan

The Four Fundamental Concepts of Psychoanalysis
The structure of psychoanalysis and language, and their relation to religion
0-393-00079-6 NORTON PB $14.95

Anika **Lemaire**
Jacques Lacan
A clear introduction to Lacan's thought
0-415-07844-X ROUTLEDGE PB $17.95

Theodor **Reik**
Listening with the Third Ear: The Inner Experience of a Psychoanalyst
0-374-51800-9 FS&G PB $16.95

Geza **Roheim**
The Eternal Ones of the Dream: Myth and Ritual, Dreams and Fantasies—Their Role in the Lives of Primitive Man
An application of Freudian theory to Australian aboriginal culture
0-8236-8044-4 INT'L UNIVERSITIES PB $24.95

Fire in the Dragon & Other Psychoanalytic Essays on Folklore
0-691-09471-3 PRINCETON $45.00
0-691-02868-0 PRINCETON PB $12.95

Gates of the Dream
0-8236-8060-6 INT'L UNIVERSITIES PB $24.95

Stuart **Schneiderman**
Jacques Lacan: The Death of an Intellectual Hero
A history of Lacan's work and of Freudianism in France by Lacan's leading American disciple
0-674-47116-4 HARVARD PB $12.95

Stuart **Schneiderman**, editor
Returning to Freud
An interview with a patient conducted by Lacan, and 15 case studies by his followers
0-300-02476-2 YALE $35.00
0-300-03932-8 YALE PB $13.00

Herbert S. **Strean**
Behind the Couch: Revelations of a Psychoanalyst
0-8245-1290-1 CONTINUUM PB $11.95

Harry Stack **Sullivan**
Clinical Studies in Psychiatry
0-393-00688-3 NORTON PB $14.95

Conceptions of Modern Psychiatry
Sullivan's central ideas on the role of interpersonal relations in personality formation
0-393-00740-5 NORTON PB $10.95

The Interpersonal Theory of Psychiatry
A systematic presentation of Sullivan's theories, which shifted the emphasis from personal, internal factors to social factors in explaining mental health and illness
0-393-00138-5 NORTON PB $5.95

Paul **Tolpin** & Marion **Tolpin**, editors
Lectures of Heinz Kohut
0-88163-116-7 ANALYTIC PRESS $49.95

Existential Psychology

Michel **Foucault** & Ludwig **Binswanger**
Dream & Existence
An important document in the history of existential psychology. EDITED BY KEITH HOELLER
0-391-03783-8 HUMANITIES PB $12.50

Viktor E. **Frankl**
The Doctor & the Soul: From Psychotherapy to Logotherapy
0-394-74317-2 RANDOM HOUSE PB $12.00

Man's Search for Meaning
The central statement of the theory of a human need for meaning in life that Frankl developed from his experience in a Nazi concentration camp
0-671-66736-X POCKET PB $5.99

The Will to Meaning: Foundations and Applications of Logotheraphy
0-452-01034-9 NEW AMERICAN LIBRARY PB $11.95

R.D. **Laing**
The Politics of the Family
The family as a system of complicated, interlocking, and interdependent relationships. "The basis of Laing's argument is that the concept of 'family' itself lies in the mutual collusion of those who believe themselves to be its members"
—*London Times Educational Supplement*
0-394-71809-7 RANDOM HOUSE PB $11.00

Self and Others
Laing sees schizophrenia as rooted in "ontological insecurity"
0-14-013467-0 VIKING PB $9.95

Rollo **May**
The Courage to Create
See also CREATIVITY under SPECIAL TOPICS IN PSYCHOLOGY
0-8446-6854-0 PEREGRINE SMITH $20.50
0-393-31106-6 NORTON PB $9.95

The Discovery of Being: Writings in Existential Psychology
A good short introduction to the major tenets of May's existential-humanist psychology
0-393-30315-2 NORTON PB $7.95

Love and Will
0-385-28590-6 DELACORTE PB $13.95

Jean-Paul **Sartre**
Existential Psychoanalysis
A spirited attack on Freudian determinism
0-89526-940-6 REGNERY PB $8.95

Human Potential Psychology

Roberto **Assagioli**
The Act of Will
The role of will in self-fulfillment, with exercises for strengthening it
0-14-019463-0 VIKING PB $12.95

Psychosynthesis
Argues that psychoanalysis is incomplete and that psychology must embrace the soul as well as the complexes
0-14-019460-6 PENGUIN PB $12.95

Abraham H. **Maslow**
The Farther Reaches of Human Nature
0-8446-6069-8 SMITH $22.50
0-14-019470-3 ARKANA PB $13.95

Religions, Values, and Peak Experiences
The most influential advocate of a psychology of self-realization, Maslow finds religious experience at the heart of the "peak experience" achieved by healthy, fully functioning individuals
See also PSYCHOLOGY AND RELIGION under WORLD RELIGION in RELIGION, SPIRITUALITY, AND PHILOSOPHY
0-14-004262-8 VIKING PB $6.00

Carl R. **Rogers**
A Carl Rogers Reader
EDITED BY HOWARD KIRSCHENBAUM & VALERIE L. HENDERSON
0-395-48357-3 HOUGHTON MIFFLIN PB $15.95

On Becoming a Person
A popular classic of the human potential movement
0-395-75531-X DORLING KINDERSLEY PB $12.95

A Way of Being
Rogers presents a humanistic psychotherapy based on self-acceptance and the full assimilation of the individual's experience
0-395-75530-1 DORLING KINDERSLEY PB $11.95

Behaviorism

M. **Baum**

Understanding Behaviorism

A clear and authoritative college-level text

0-06-500286-5 HARPERCOLLINS PB $23.95

Carl **Goldberg**

Speaking with the Devil: A Dialogue with Evil

How is evil distinguished from disturbed? What is malevolent behavior, and how does it differ from criminality? Using a perspective that mixes philosophy, theology, mythology, law, psychology, and literature, Goldberg establishes a cultural and historical overview of "evil." In dialogue with such books as Arendt's *Eichmann in Jerusalem* and Fromm's *The Heart of Man*, Goldberg—a psychoanalyst at New York University—offers a lucid discussion of the deepest human mystery

0-670-85557-X VIKING $27.95

Jerome **Kagan**

Galen's Prophecy: Temperament in Human Nature

Includes a history of the idea of temperament, an account of Kagan's career-long (and increasingly influential) study of the behavior of toddlers, and a balanced statement of his conclusion that character is strongly influenced by biology

See also **MISCELLANEOUS** under **SPECIAL TOPICS IN PSYCHOLOGY**

0-465-02612-5 BASIC PB $14.00

Howard **Rachlin**

Behavior & Mind: The Roots of Modern Psychology

0-19-507979-5 OXFORD $38.00

B.F. **Skinner**

About Behaviorism

Skinner assesses his life's work

0-394-71618-3 RANDOM HOUSE PB $9.00

Science and Human Behavior

The main statement of Skinner's behaviorist theory

0-02-929040-6 FREE PRESS PB $12.95

B.F. Skinner (photo by Nancy Crampton)

John B. **Watson**

Behaviorism

A clear exposition of the behaviorist approach to psychology written in 1925 by the American psychologist who first developed it

0-393-00524-0 NORTON PB $9.95

David **Weeks** & Jamie **James**

Eccentrics: A Study of Sanity and Strangeness

The emperor of the United States; the British security expert who wears green tights and carries a bow and arrow to the office; two Brooklyn artists who live as if it were 1895— all of these eccentrics, Dr. Weeks finds, are happier, healthier, and more creative than most conformists and have much to teach us about how to live "normal" lives. "A highly entertaining guide…Weeks has gathered together some remarkable examples of human oddity"
—*The Times* [London]

0-394-56565-7 VILLARD $23.00

1-56836-156-4 KODANSHA PB $10.00

The Cognitive Revolution

Peter **Baumgartner** & Sabine **Payr**, editors

Speaking Minds: Interviews with Twenty Eminent Cognitive Scientists

See also **THE NEUROSCIENCES AND THE BRAIN** under **BIOLOGY** under **LIFE SCIENCES** in **SCIENCE**

0-691-03678-0 PRINCETON $29.95

Jerome S. **Bruner**

Actual Minds, Possible Worlds

A cognitive approach to imaginative experience. "A splendid book, one which should contribute to the important reorientation that is taking place between psychology and the literary arts"—Howard Gardner

0-674-00366-7 HARVARD PB $12.00

Beyond the Information Given: Studies in the Psychology of Knowing

A classic which initiated the "cognitive revolution" against behaviorist-dominated psychology by stressing the mediation of cognitive processes in perception and behavior

EDITED BY JEREMY M. ANGLER

0-393-09363-8 NORTON PB $10.95

Michael C. **Corballis**

The Lopsided Ape: The Evolution of the Generative Mind

Corballis argues that the human intellect evolved through a development—unique to the species—of the left hemisphere of the brain, which allowed Homo sapiens to handle language and symbolic representation differently from other closely related primates

0-19-506675-8 OXFORD $35.00

0-19-508352-0 OXFORD PB $15.95

Merlin **Donald**

Origins of the Modern Mind: Three Stages in the Evolution of Culture & Cognition

"Whereas countless philosophers since Aristotle have attempted to define what is quintessentially human, Donald brings new knowledge of neuropsychology, ethology, and archaeology to propose a tripartite theory of the transition from ape to man. Using the fossil evidence of braincase size and tool-kit remains, Donald concludes that the australopithecines were limited to concrete/episodic minds: bipedal creatures able to benefit from pair-bonding, cooperative hunting, etc., but essentially of a seize-the-moment mentality. The first transition was to a "mimetic" culture: the era of Homo erectus in which mankind absorbed and refashioned events to create rituals, crafts, rhythms, dance, and other prelinguistic traditions. This was followed by the evolution to mythic cultures: the result of the acquisition of speech and the invention of symbols. The third transition carried oral speech to reading, writing, and an extended external memory store seen today in computer technology"
—*Kirkus Reviews*

0-674-64483-2 HARVARD $29.95

0-674-64484-0 HARVARD PB $16.95

Diane **Gillespie**

The Mind's We: Contextualism in Cognitive Psychology

Gillespie rejects a reductive analysis of human cognition, arguing instead for the importance of the total context within which perception and mental activity take place

0-8093-1675-7 SOUTHERN ILLINOIS $24.95

P.N. **Johnson-Laird**

The Computer and the Mind: An Introduction to Cognitive Science

0-674-15616-1 HARVARD PB $17.95

Jerome **Kagan**

Unstable Ideas: Temperament, Cognition, & Self

"The title refers to the problem of imprecise meaning in the use of scientific language for such terms as temperament, cognition, and self. Kagan makes a plea for more rigorous and innovative methods and a more powerful vocabulary in child development research"
—*NY Times*

0-674-93038-X HARVARD $32.00

0-674-93039-8 HARVARD PB $15.95

Joseph E. **LeDoux** & William **Hirst**, editors

Mind & Brain: Dialogues Between Cognitive Psychology & Neuroscience

A collection of essays and discussions by a number of well-known authorities in the field, covering problems of perception, attention, emotion, and memory

0-521-26756-0 CAMBRIDGE $85.00

0-521-31853-X CAMBRIDGE PB $33.95

Arnold **Trehub**

The Cognitive Brain

Trehub offers a complete paradigm for mental activity based on biology and physics, and accounting for all the daily tasks the brain performs. Intended for the non-specialist reader

0-262-70049-2 BRADFORD PB $18.00

The Human Mind and Artificial Intelligence

Margaret **Boden**

Computer Models of the Mind

A history and survey of how computers have helped us to understand the workings of the human mind

0-521-27033-2 CAMBRIDGE PB $22.95

Maureen **Caudill**

In Our Own Image: Building an Artificial Person

Surveys the current state of research on androids

0-19-507338-X OXFORD $27.50

0-19-508672-4 OXFORD PB $13.95

Daniel **Crevier**

AI: The Tumultuous History of the Search for Artificial Intelligence

0-465-00104-1 BASIC PB $14.00

David **Freedman**

Brainmakers: How Scientists Are Moving Beyond Computers to Create a Rival to the Human Brain

A chronicle of recent developments in Artificial Intelligence, based on interviews with leading researchers in the field

0-671-76079-3 SIMON & SCHUSTER $22.00

Douglas **Hofstadter**

Fluid Concepts & Creative Analogies: Computer Models of Mental Fluidity & Creativity

0-465-05154-5 BASIC $30.00

0-465-02475-0 BASIC PB $18.00

Godel, Escher, Bach: An Eternal Golden Braid

A consistently engaging and challenging meditation on puzzles and paradoxes of logic, mathematics, physics, art, and philosophy, presented in a series of essays and dialogues. "A wondrous book that unites and explains, in a very entertaining way, many of the important ideas of recent intellectual history"
—*Commonwealth*

See also **ARTIFICIAL INTELLIGENCE** under **THE COMPUTER REVOLUTION AND ARTIFICIAL INTELLIGENCE** in **SCIENCE**

0-394-75682-7 VINTAGE PB $18.00

Ray **Kurzweil**

Age of Intelligent Machines

Including essays by a number of experts on Artificial Intelligence, as well as Kurzweil's own wide-ranging survey

0-262-61079-5 MIT PB $27.50

Marvin **Minsky**

The Society of Mind

"Minsky explores means of explaining the world to a computer, translating it into language that you and I can understand. An ingenious and stimulating book"—*NY Times*

0-671-65713-5 SIMON & SCHUSTER PB $14.95

Theodore **Roszak**

The Cult of Information: The Folklore of Computers and the True Art of Thinking

A recent critique of computer enthusiasm

See also **THE CYBERNETIC SOCIETY** under **THE COMPUTER REVOLUTION AND ARTIFICIAL INTELLIGENCE** in **SCIENCE**

0-520-08584-1 CALIFORNIA PB $12.00

Roger **Schank** & Robert **Abelson**

Scripts, Plans, Goals, and Understanding: An Inquiry Into Human Knowledge Structures

0-89859-138-4 HALSTED PB $27.50

John **Searle**

Minds, Brains, and Science

A leading philosopher gives us a restrained attack on Artificial Intelligence

0-674-57633-0 HARVARD PB $8.95

John Searle

Norbert **Wiener**

Cybernetics: Control and Communication in the Animal and the Machine

Wiener invented the term "cybernetics" and suggested the possibility that the mathematical principles of communication and control that apply to machines also have broad implications in fields such as biology

0-262-73009-X MIT PB $13.95

The Human Use of Human Beings: Cybernetics & Society

0-306-80320-8 DA CAPO PB $11.95

Neurophysiological Approaches

Nancy C. **Andreasen**

The Broken Brain: The Biological Revolution in Psychology

A clear account of the biological basis of schizophrenia, depression, and other conditions

0-06-091272-3 HARPERCOLLINS PB $13.50

Gordon **Claridge**

Origins of Mental Illness

Argues that even severe mental disorders have their origins in common psychological and biological qualities

1-88353-601-4 HUMAN KNOWLEDGE PB $12.95

A.R. **Luria**

The Working Brain: An Introduction to Neuropsychology

Somewhat technical but filled with fascinating observations

See also **THE NEUROSCIENCES AND THE BRAIN** under **BIOLOGY** under **LIFE SCIENCES** in **SCIENCE**

0-465-09208-X BASIC BOOKS PB $17.00

Gestalt Psychology

Wofgang **Kohler**

Gestalt Psychology

0-87140-218-1 LIVERIGHT PB $11.95

The Mentality of Apes

0-87140-108-8 NORTON PB $3.95

Selected Papers of Wolfgang Kohler

EDITED BY SOLOMON E. ASCH & MARY HENLE

0-87140-505-9 NORTON $15.95

Max **Wertheimer**

Productive Thinking

One of the founders (with Kohler and Koffka) of Gestalt psychology, Wertheimer ranges beyond Gestalt theories of psychology to ethical and political questions

0-226-89376-6 CHICAGO PB $11.00

Social Psychology

Howard **Becker**

Outsiders: Studies in the Sociology of Deviance

"The most instructive and most interesting introduction to the subject of deviant behavior available"—Albert K. Cohen

See also **CRIME, DELINQUENCY, AND DEVIANCE** under **TOPICS IN MODERN SOCIOLOGY** under **SOCIOLOGY**

0-02-902140-5 FREE PRESS PB $14.95

Eric **Berne**

Games People Play: The Basic Handbook of Transactional Analysis

The popular account of role-playing in everyday life

0-345-32719-5 BALLANTINE PB $5.99

Norman O. **Brown**

Life Against Death: The Psychoanalytical Meaning of History

A book that had a major impact in the 1960s, calling for a liberated, nonhierarchical, playful sexuality, or "polymorphous perversity," that would free humanity from the reality principle

0-8195-6144-4 WESLEYAN PB $21.00

Love's Body

Originally published in 1966, Brown's sequel to his earlier *Life Against Death* was one of the most influential works of that decade

0-520-07106-9 CALIFORNIA PB $13.95

Roger **Brown**

Social Psychology

A collection of essays on recent research

0-02-908300-1 FREE PRESS $35.00

Herbert **Marcuse**

Marcuse, another member of the Frankfurt School, became a chief intellectual sponsor of the New Left and the 1960s counterculture through his insistence that erotic liberation must accompany radical political and economic change.

Eros and Civilization: A Philosophical Inquiry into Freud

Rejecting Freud's theory that civilization demands instinctual repression, Marcuse calls for a society in which sexual liberation will accompany political and economic liberation

See also MARXISM AND THE FRANKFURT SCHOOL under SOCIOLOGY AFTER WEBER under SOCIOLOGY

0-8070-1555-5 FS&G PB $15.00

Herbert Marcuse

Philip **Rieff**

Triumph of the Therapeutic: Uses of Faith After Freud

The cultural implications of the therapeutic model of human behavior

0-226-71646-5 CHICAGO PB $13.95

Reg **Theriault**

How to Tell When You're Tired: A Brief Examination of Work

0-393-03878-5 NORTON $18.00

0-393-31557-6 NORTON PB $13.00

Child Psychology

Bruno **Bettelheim**

A Good Enough Parent: A Book on Child Rearing

A guide to becoming a good enough—not a perfect—parent. "Bound to provide every reader with some nuggets of good sense and wisdom and young parents in particular with a challenge and an inspiration"—*Washington Post*

0-394-47148-2 VINTAGE PB $18.95

One ten-year old said when Santa Claus was discussed: "I know there is no Santa, and no Tooth Fairy who puts a dime under my pillow." And then she broke down, sobbing, "I hate reality." Her hatred of reality was the consequence of being forced too early to give up her wish-fulfilling fantasies....Belief in magic and the use of magical thinking to bind anxiety and also to rekindle and sustain hope for good things to come are needed by the young child to help him master the rest of reality.

A GOOD ENOUGH PARENT: A BOOK ON CHILD REARING

Bruno Bettelheim

Love Is Not Enough

Bettelheim's account of his observations and methods at the Sonia Shankman School and the implications for child psychology in general

0-02-903280-6 FREE PRESS $27.95

Truants from Life: The Rehabilitation of Emotionally Disturbed Children

Four case histories of severely disturbed children and the therapeutic teaching methods that Bettelheim used to guide them to normal lives; a widely influential work

0-02-903450-7 FREE PRESS PB $16.95

The Uses of Enchantment: The Meaning and Importance of Fairy Tales

A classic study by this distinguished psychologist and interpreter of childhood who links folk tales to children's most pressing emotional needs

See also FOLKLORE under MYTHOLOGY AND FOLKLORE in RELIGION, SPIRITUALITY, AND PHILOSOPHY

0-679-72393-5 VINTAGE PB $13.00

Nina **Sutton** & others

Bettelheim: A Life and a Legacy

Arrested by the Nazis for being a Jew, Bruno Bettelheim endured Buchenwald concentration camp for nearly a year. In the United States after the war, he achieved international acclaim as an innovator in the field of psychoanalysis. "Opens a closet of personal skeletons that will intrigue more than just professional psychologists"—*Publishers Weekly*

0-465-00635-3 BASIC $35.00

John **Bowlby**

Long neglected as a theorist of early childhood development, Bowlby has recently stimulated new attention, particularly for his ideas about the nature of the mother-child bond.

Attachment

0-465-00543-8 BASIC BOOKS PB $22.00

Separation: Anxiety & Anger

0-465-09716-2 BASIC BOOKS PB $20.00

Lyn Mikel **Brown** & Carol **Gilligan**

Meeting at the Crossroads: Women's Psychology and Girls' Development

After talking with and listening to 100 adolescent girls, the authors, two noted psychologists, conclude that the passage to womanhood is too often a journey to silence. This book, destined to become a classic of women's studies, offers new insight into women's development, provides women ways to meet younger women at the crossroads, and helps them toward a more rewarding future

See also ADOLESCENCE under THE FEMALE EXPERIENCE under WOMEN'S STUDIES

0-674-56464-2 HARVARD $19.95

0-345-38295-1 BALLANTINE PB $12.50

Robert **Coles**

The Moral Life of Children

How children struggle with moral choice in the US and elsewhere. "There is no one who is more interested in what children say, sing, don't say or don't sing—and why—than Robert Coles. He is to the stories that children have to tell what Homer was to the tale of the Trojan War" —Neil Postman, *NY Times Book Review*

0-395-59921-0 HOUGHTON MIFFLIN PB $10.95

The Political Life of Children

How children all over the world discover their political loyalties through language, nationalities, race, religion, exile, martyrdom, class, and revolution. "A major contribution to our understanding of how children become socialized"—*NY Times Book Review*

0-395-59922-9 HOUGHTON MIFFLIN PB $10.95

The Spiritual Life of Children

Coles's continuing series on the mental life of children focuses here on such topics as God, salvation, and the meaning of life

See also RELIGION AND SOCIETY under WORLD RELIGION in RELIGION, SPIRITUALITY, AND PHILOSOPHY

0-395-55999-5 HOUGHTON MIFFLIN $22.95

0-395-59923-7 HOUGHTON MIFFLIN PB $10.95

Margaret **Donaldson**

Children's Minds

"One of the most powerful, most wisely balanced and best informed books on the development of

the child's mind to have appeared in twenty years. Its implications for education are enormous"—Jerome S. Bruner
0-393-95101-4 NORTON PB $8.95

Judy **Dunn** & Carol **Kendrick**
Siblings: Love, Envy, and Understanding
0-674-80735-9 HARVARD $32.00

Katharine Davis **Fishman**
Behind the One-Way Mirror: Psychotherapy and Children
This study provides a practical basis for evaluating problems children may have, and gives an overview of how best to treat them
0-553-07886-0 BANTAM DOUBLEDAY DELL $27.50

Jean E. **Gombert**
Metalinguistic Development
TRANSLATED BY TIM POWNALL
0-226-30208-3 CHICAGO $60.00
0-226-30209-1 CHICAGO PB $27.50

Stanley I. **Greenspan**
Playground Politics: Understanding the Emotional Life of Your School-Age Child
A leading child psychologist shows the playground as the arena where foundations are laid for adult relationships, personal and professional, and offers a map for how to negotiate it. "Should be on the reading list of every parent with a child this age"—*The Boston Globe.* "Not only gives parents a great understanding of children in the middle years but gives excellent advice on how to support them better"—*Washington Post*
0-201-40830-9 ADDISON-WESLEY PB $12.00

Philip **Greven**
Spare the Child: The Religious Roots of Punishment and the Psychological Impact of Physical Abuse
Tracing the punishment of children from its historical roots to such contemporary manifestations as the fundamentalist child-rearing manual *Dare to Discipline,* Greven exposes the long-term psychological consequences of such abuse. "When you hurt a child," the author has said, "you teach him to hurt others and himself…I hope we can learn to rear children without inflicting pain and calling it discipline"
0-394-57860-0 VINTAGE PB $22.95

Jerome **Kagan**
Kagan's judicious, balanced, painstakingly designed and carefully accumulated research has won recognition as among the major 20th-century contributions to the study of character and development in the young child.

The Growth of the Child: Reflections on Human Development
0-393-95084-0 NORTON PB $5.95

The Nature of the Child
0-465-04852-8 BASIC PB $16.00

The Second Year: The Emergence of Self-Awareness
0-674-79662-4 HARVARD $19.50
0-674-79663-2 HARVARD PB $10.95

Kurt **Koffka**
Growth of the Mind
INTRODUCTION BY JAMES A. SCHELLENBERG
0-87855-360-6 TRANSACTION $34.95
0-87855-784-9 TRANSACTION PB $21.95

E. **Maccoby**
Social Development
A good introduction, stressing the parent-child relationship
0-15-581422-2 HARCOURT BRACE PB $28.60

Abraham H. **Maslow**, editor
Motivation and Personality
0-06-041987-3 HARPERCOLLINS PB $44.21

Alice **Miller**
The Drama of the Gifted Child
A theoretical book written by the Swiss psychoanalyst. She is a non-sectarian whose work strikes every creative person to the core, and who, in mid-life, became, through psychoanalytical insight, a very good painter
See also **ART SINCE 1945** in **ART**
0-465-01693-6 BASIC PB $12.00

For Your Own Good: Hidden Cruelty in Child-Rearing and the Roots of Violence
With a riveting chapter on Adolf Hitler's upbringing
TRANSLATED BY HILDEGARDE & HUNTER HANNUM
0-374-52269-3 NOONDAY PB $12.00

Thou Shalt Not Be Aware!: Society's Betrayal of the Child
"Long before child molestation became an appalling staple of the nightly news, Dr. Alice Miller formulated revolutionary psychological theories that might have prepared us for the grim actuality"—*LA Times Book Review*
0-452-00929-4 MERIDIAN PB $11.00

Patricia H. **Miller**
Theories of Developmental Psychology
0-7167-2309-3 FREEMAN PB $27.95

Paul H. **Mussen**
Child Development and Personality
0-06-044694-3 HARPERCOLLINS $37.50
0-06-045148-3 HARPERCOLLINS PB $9.50

Robert S. **Siegler**
Children's Thinking
0-13-131210-3 PRENTICE HALL PB $33.92

Valerie P. **Suransky**
The Erosion of Childhood
FOREWORD BY PAULO FREIRE
0-226-78007-4 CHICAGO PB $13.95

Richard **Weissbourd**
The Vulnerable Child: The Hidden Epidemic of Neglected and Troubled Children Even Within the Middle Class
A Harvard professor and special advisor on family issues to Al Gore, Weissbourd presents a surprising account of a middle-class epidemic of disadvantaged children. More than half of high school dropouts, he shows, have never been poor. Same for the children in unsafe homes. And as for the stereotypes of the inner-city disadvantaged, Weissbourd documents that 90 percent of America's poor do not live in urban environments. Fresh analysis and solid advice point out a new direction for protecting our children and our future
0-201-48395-5 ADDISON-WESLEY $22.00

Jean Piaget

Jean **Piaget**
The Child's Conception of the World
0-8226-0213-X LITTLEFIELD ADAMS PB $14.95

The Moral Judgment of the Child
Focusing on a game of marbles, Piaget and his associates analyze children's attitudes toward lying, cheating, adult authority, punishments, and responsibilities. "In a sense, child morality throws light on adult morality. If we want to form men and women, nothing will fit so well for the task as to study the laws that govern formation"—Jean Piaget
0-02-925240-7 FREE PRESS PB $17.95

The Origins of Intelligence in Children
An early and influential work on the relation of infantile sensory-motor experiences to cognitive development
0-8236-8207-2 INT'L UNIVERSITIES PB $24.95

Play, Dreams and Imitation in Childhood
Piaget's theories of the role of play in children's cognitive development have been borne out in studies throughout the world
0-393-00171-7 NORTON PB $11.95

Jean **Piaget** & Barbel **Inhelder**
Psychology of the Child
TRANSLATED BY HELEN WEAVER
0-465-09500-3 BASIC BOOKS PB $16.00

Dorothy **Singer** & Tracey A. **Revenson**, editors
A Piaget Primer
0-452-26346-8 NEW AMERICAN LIBRARY PB $9.95

Object-Relations Theory

Melanie **Klein** & Joan **Riviere**, editors
Love, Hate and Reparation
0-393-00260-8 NORTON PB $7.95

John **Bowlby**

Loss: Sadness and Depression

Bowlby demonstrated that attachment of the infant to the mother is of overwhelming importance in determining the individual's later security and success in forming relations with others, and that separation from or loss of the mother can have a devastating effect

0-465-04238-4 BASIC BOOKS PB $20.00

Melanie **Klein**

Narrative of a Child Analysis

Through her work in child psychology, Klein developed the original hypothesis of object-relations theory

0-02-918450-9 FREE PRESS $45.00

The Psychoanalysis of Children

Klein's influential work on child psychology stresses play and the child's relation to its mother

0-02-918430-4 FREE PRESS $45.00

D.W. **Winnicott**

Playing and Reality

0-422-78310-2 ROUTLEDGE PB $15.95

Thinking About Children

See also **BEING A PARENT** under **PARENTING** in **LIFESTYLES AND PRACTICAL ADVICE**

0-201-40700-0 ADDISON-WESLEY $25.00

Through Paediatrics to Psychoanalysis: Collected Papers

INTRODUCTION BY MASUD KHAN

0-87630-703-9 BRUNNER & MAZEL PB $37.95

Gender and Sexuality

Jessica **Benjamin**

The Bonds of Love: Psychoanalysis, Feminism, and the Problem of Domination

Analysis of the acceptance and perpetuation of relationships of domination and submission, from a leading theorist and psychoanalyst

See also **PSYCHOLOGY** under **WOMEN'S STUDIES**

0-394-75730-0 PANTHEON PB $16.00

David M. **Buss**

The Evolution of Desire: Strategies of Human Mating

See also **SEX** under **COURTSHIP, LOVE, SEX, AND MARRIAGE** in **LIFESTYLES AND PRACTICAL ADVICE**

0-465-02143-3 BASIC PB $13.00

Nancy **Chodorow**

The Reproduction of Mothering: Psychoanalysis and the Sociology of Gender

Why women in almost all societies are responsible for parenting. "Provides careful psychoanalytic grounding for the radical position that both sexes can and should parent equally, and—an additional boon—its style is not too academic"—*Ms.*

See also **MOTHERHOOD** under **THE FEMALE EXPERIENCE** under **WOMEN'S STUDIES**

0-520-03892-4 CALIFORNIA PB $16.00

Helene **Deutsch**

Psychoanalysis of the Sexual Functions of Women

0-946439-95-8 BRUNNER & MAZEL PB $28.95

Richard **Friedman**

Male Homosexuality: A Contemporary Psychoanalytic Perspective

A scholarly and judicious amassing of evidence against the traditional psychoanalytic definition of male homosexuality as a pathological condition

0-300-03963-8 YALE $50.00
0-300-04745-2 YALE PB $18.00

Linda D. **Garnets** & Douglas C. **Kimmel**, editors

Psychological Perspectives on Lesbian & Gay Male Experiences

0-231-07884-6 COLUMBIA $50.00
0-231-07885-4 COLUMBIA PB $27.50

Carol **Gilligan**

In a Different Voice: Psychological Theory and Women's Development

Gilligan, a Harvard professor, argues that psychological development theories have been based on the experiences of men and suggests we reshape our understanding of human development to include women's voices

0-674-44544-9 HARVARD PB $10.95

Maxine **Harris**

Sisters of the Shadow

A Jungian approach to the psychology of homeless women—and to the forces underlying their rejection by society

0-8061-2324-9 OKLAHOMA $19.95
0-8061-2502-0 OKLAHOMA PB $12.95

Karen **Horney**

Feminine Psychology

Horney rejects the feminine stereotypes embedded in orthodox Freudian psychology

EDITED BY HAROLD KELMAN

0-393-31080-9 NORTON PB $8.95

Ellyn **Kaschak**

Engendered Lives: A New Psychology of Women's Experience

Kaschak demonstrates how gender bias is embedded in virtually all of our systems of self-understanding, from orthodox analysis to family therapy. She shows how psychological illnesses such as anxiety and eating disorders grow out of the ways women are made to conform

0-465-01349-X BASIC PB $15.00

Jonathan N. **Katz**

The Invention of Heterosexuality

How language affects perception

See also **HISTORY** under **GAY, LESBIAN, AND BISEXUAL STUDIES**

FOREWORD BY GORE VIDAL

0-525-93845-1 DUTTON $22.95
0-452-27542-3 DUTTON PB $13.95

Evelyn Fox **Keller**

Reflections on Gender and Science

A widely read work that ponders why objectivity has been cast as "male" and subjectivity as "female"

See also **SCIENCE/GENDER** under **FEMINIST THEORY** under **WOMEN'S STUDIES**

0-300-03636-1 YALE PB $12.00

Simon **Le Vay**

The Sexual Brain

The author, mostly known for his theory on the difference between hypothalamic structure in homosexual and heterosexual men, suggests that sexual behavior can be understood by exploring how the brain develops. A fascinating tour though the territory of evolutionary theory, molecular genetics, and developmental psychology

See also **THE NEUROSCIENCES AND THE BRAIN** under **BIOLOGY** under **LIFE SCIENCES** in **SCIENCE**

0-262-12178-6 MIT $25.00
0-262-0936 MIT PB $10.95

Judith **Lorber**

Paradoxes of Gender

An authoritative formulation of the idea that gender is not simply a biological fact, but rather a cultural and social construct

0-300-05807-1 YALE $37.50

Eleanor E. **Maccoby** & Carol N. **Jacklin**

The Psychology of Sex Differences

Volume 1

See also **GENDER STUDIES**

0-8047-0974-2 STANFORD PB $17.95

Volume 2

0-8147-4186-X NYU $150.00

Volume 3

0-8147-4187-8 NYU $143.75

Volume 4

0-8147-4188-6 NYU $143.75

Jean B. **Miller**

Toward a New Psychology of Women

An attempt to develop a new psychology out of the actual life experience of women, with many anecdotal case histories

0-8070-2909-2 BEACON PB $12.95

Joseph H. **Smith** & Afaf M. **Mahfouz**, editors

Psychoanalysis, Feminism, & the Future of Gender

0-8018-4711-7 JOHNS HOPKINS $40.00
0-8018-4786-9 JOHNS HOPKINS PB $13.95

Mary R. **Walsh**

The Psychology of Women: Ongoing Debates

A collection of essays on such questions as women's alleged proneness to masochism, the relevance of psychoanalytic theory to the psychology of women, androgyny, lesbianism, abortion, and pornography

See also **PSYCHOLOGY** under **WOMEN'S STUDIES**

0-300-03966-2 YALE PB $18.00

Disorders and Treatment

Roy **Porter**, editor

The Anatomy of Madness

Essays on Samuel Johnson's melancholy, Darwin's view of madness, the idea of holy madness in Christianity, 18th-century and Victorian approaches to madness, and other topics. The second volume is out of print

Volume 1
People and Ideas

0-422-79430-9 ROUTLEDGE $67.00

Volume 3
The Asylum and Its Psychiatry

0-415-00859-X ROUTLEDGE $64.50

Depression

Peter R. **Breggin**

Talking Back to Prozac

A cautionary contrarian reaction to the recent tidal wave of publicity and comment in favor of drug therapy for depression

0-312-95606-1 ST. MARTIN'S PB $5.99

Robert **Burton**

The Anatomy of Melancholy

A classic of English literature, this eccentric, allusive, beautifully written 17th-century compendium of legend and lore on melancholy is also a psychologically acute account of depression, as caused by everything from love to religion

EDITED BY JOAN R. PETERS

1-56459-003-8 KESSINGER PB $50.00

Paul **Gilbert**

Depression: From Psychology to Brain State

0-89862-884-9 GUILFORD $45.00

Kay Redfield **Jamison**

An Unquiet Mind

Professor of psychiatry at Johns Hopkins and foremost authority on manic-depressive illness, Jamison offers a remarkable personal testimony about her own lifelong struggle with manic-depression. Vivid, direct, and witty, Dr. Jamison's memoir traces the growth and effect of her illness—an illness that finally led to a suicide attempt—and the slow and courageous process of mastering that illness through knowledge, medication, and self-discipline. An exhilarating and readable memoir

See also **DEPRESSION** under **SELF-HELP** in **LIFESTYLES AND PRACTICAL ADVICE**

0-679-44374-6 KNOPF $22.00
0-679-76330-9 RANDOM HOUSE PB $12.00

Donald F. **Klein** & Paul H. **Wender**

Understanding Depression: A Complete Guide to Its Diagnosis & Treatment

0-19-508669-4 OXFORD PB $7.95

Gerald **Klerman**

Interpersonal Psychotherapy of Depression

0-465-03396-2 BASIC BOOKS $37.50

Peter D. **Kramer**

Listening to Prozac: A Psychiatrist Explores Mood-Altering Drugs and the New Meaning of the Self

An expert in the field of drug therapy explores the implications of the drug that is currently prescribed to over 4,000,000 people. "[Kramer is] a warm-spirited, open-minded physician who has a thoughtful, wide-ranging mind…and a voice of earnest, unashamed speculation and reflection—subtle, suggestive, clarifying" —Robert Coles, *The Spiritual Life of Children*

See also **DRUG GUIDES** under **HEALTH** in **LIFESTYLES AND PRACTICAL ADVICE**

0-14-015940-1 PENGUIN PB $12.95

Peter **Lewisohn**

Control Your Depression

0-671-76242-7 SIMON & SCHUSTER PB $11.00

Alexander **Lowen**

Depression & the Body

0-14-019465-7 VIKING PB $12.95

William **Styron**

Darkness Visible: A Memoir of Madness

The novelist writes of his descent into depression, and how he recovered

See also **MEMOIRS AND JOURNALS** under **20TH-CENTURY AMERICAN ESSAYS AND JOURNALISM** in **LITERATURE OF THE AMERICAS**

0-394-58888-6 RANDOM HOUSE $15.95

Schizophrenia

Silvano **Arieti**

Understanding and Helping the Schizophrenic: A Guide for Family and Friends

A clear, practical guide, including advice on how to recognize the first signs of the illness which afflicts over three million Americans

1-56821-269-0 ARONSON PB $28.50

Peter **Barham**

Schizophrenia & Human Value

1-85343-196-6 FREE ASSOCIATION PB $21.00

Kayla F. **Bernheim** & Richard R.J. **Lewine**

Schizophrenia: Symptoms, Causes, Treatments

0-393-09017-5 NORTON PB $11.95

Mary **Boyle**

Schizophrenia: A Scientific Delusion

0-415-09700-2 ROUTLEDGE PB $22.50

R.D. **Laing**

The Divided Self

A famous and controversial existential analysis of schizophrenia

0-14-013537-5 VIKING PB $10.95

R.D. Laing

Susan **Sheehan**

Is There No Place on Earth for Me?

Winner of the Pulitzer Prize for nonfiction, Sheehan's intense, close-up chronicle of a young woman's struggle with schizophrenia is also a penetrating study of mental health care

See also **HISTORY, POLITICS, AND SOCIETY** under **20TH-CENTURY AMERICAN ESSAYS AND JOURNALISM** in **LITERATURE OF THE AMERICAS**

FOREWORD BY ROBERT M. COLES

0-394-71378-8 RANDOM HOUSE PB $13.00

Edward **Shorter**

From Paralysis to Fatigue: A History of Psychosomatic Illness in the Modern Era

A study of the manner in which symptoms of disease have changed to meet the expectations of doctors—from 19th-century "spinal irritation" to present-day "chronic fatigue syndrome." "Building on his vast and learned research in three languages, [Shorter] has created a compelling and sometimes poignant picture of our unending struggle against illness in a medicocentric world"—*NY Times Book Review*

See also **CHRONIC FATIGUE SYNDROME** under **SPECIFIC HEALTH PROBLEMS** under **HEALTH** in **LIFESTYLES AND PRACTICAL ADVICE**

0-02-928667-0 FREE PRESS PB $14.95

Thomas **Szasz**

Schizophrenia: The Sacred Symbol of Psychiatry

Argues that schizophrenia is not a genuine disease, but has been invented by psychiatrists as a way of locking up the nonconforming against their will

0-8156-0224-3 SYRACUSE PB $13.95

E. Fuller **Torrey**

Surviving Schizophrenia: A Family Manual

A guide to the nature, causes, symptoms, pathology, and treatment of the illness, from both the patient's and the family's perspective

0-19-096249-6 HARPER & ROW PB $13.00

Maryellen **Walsh**
Schizophrenia: Straight Talk for Family and Friends
0-688-12580-8 QUILL PB $10.00

John Kenneth **Wing**
Schizophrenia: Towards a New Synthesis
0-12-759450-7 ACADEMIC PRESS $36.50

Other Problems

Richard **Berendzen** & Laura **Palmer**
Come Here: A Man Overcomes the Tragic Aftermath of Childhood Sexual Abuse
President of American University, a brilliant astronomer, family man, Berendzen was at the height of his success when memories of his sexual abuse as a child provoked him into bizarre behavior. After a number of strange telephone calls were traced to his office, Berendzen resigned and entered John Hopkins Hospital. This is the courageous account of his slow and painful recovery. "Told with honesty, eloquence and humility. An inspiring and compelling work"—*Kirkus Reviews*
0-679-41777-X VILLARD $21.00

Donald W. **Goodman**
Anxiety
Theories, literary accounts, and case studies of phobias
0-19-503665-4 OXFORD $30.00

Temple **Grandin**
Thinking in Pictures: And Other Reports from My Life with Autism
0-679-77289-8 VINTAGE PB $12.00

Ián **Hacking**
Rewriting the Soul: Multiple Personality and the Sciences of Memory
Hacking's studies provide a fresh and insightful view on this American phenomenon
See also OTHER 20TH-CENTURY PHILOSOPHERS under PHILOSOPHY in RELIGION, SPIRITUALITY, AND PHILOSOPHY
0-691-03642-X PRINCETON $24.95

Diana Friel **McGowin**
Living in the Labyrinth: A Personal Journey Through the Maze of Alzheimer's
McGowin was a middle-aged legal assistant when she was diagnosed with early-onset Alzheimer's disease. Her heart-wrenching story is the first to describe its terrifying symptoms from a patient's point of view. An excellent resource for those affected, directly or indirectly, by this terminal illness
0-943873-18-5 ELDER PB $10.95

Alexander **Lowen**
Bioenergetics
Depression, fatigue, apathy, and their treatment through body training
0-14-019471-1 PENGUIN PB $12.95

Narcissism: Denial of the True Self
An analysis of narcissism as emotional numbness and how it can be treated by restoring the ability to feel
0-02-077290-4 MACMILLAN PB $8.00

Autism

Uta **Frith**
Autism: Explaining the Enigma
0-631-15833-2 BLACKWELL PB $19.95

Temple **Grandin**
Thinking in Pictures: And Other Reports from My Life with Autism
0-679-77289-8 VINTAGE PB $12.00

Catherine **Maurice**
Let Me Hear Your Voice: A Family's Triumph Over Autism
Written by a mother of two fully recovered autistic children, this is the best book available on the resources and varieties of therapies. "A lifeline to families in similar circumstances"—*Library Journal*
0-4499-0664-7 FAWCETT PB $12.00

Donna **Williams**
Like Color to the Blind: Soul Searching and Soul Finding
Williams (*Nobody Nowhere*, *Somebody Somewhere*) has previously chronicled her autistic childhood and her growth out of the sheltered bubble of autism into the real world. Here she tells the powerful sequel to the story, the emotional transformation of love and marriage that followed her emergence. "Donna Williams isn't just teaching us what it is like to be autistic. She is teaching us what it is like to be human"—*NY Times Book Review*
See also AUSTRALIAN LITERATURE in LITERATURE OF EUROPE, AFRICA, AND ASIA
0-8129-2640-4 TIME BOOKS $24.00

Nobody Nowhere: The Extraordinary Autobiography of an Autistic
A challenging, wrenching, and disturbing memoir. Williams is attached to the outside world firmly enough to evoke for the reader the disjointed, phantasmagoric, yet intensely vivid nature of her experiences as an autistic
0-8129-2042-2 TIME BOOKS $21.00
0-380-72217-8 AVON PB $10.00

Somebody Somewhere: Breaking Free from the World of Autism
"Williams continues to build a bridge between 'my' world and 'the' world"—*Publishers Weekly*
0-8129-2287-5 TIME BOOKS $23.00
0-8129-2524-6 TIME BOOKS PB $14.00

Jane **Phillips**
The Magic Daughter: A Memoir of Living with Multiple Personality Disorder
0-14-024455-7 PENGUIN PB $11.95

Judith L. **Rapoport**
The Boy Who Couldn't Stop Washing: The Experience and Treatment of Obsessive-Compulsive Disorder
"Using the case histories of more than a dozen doubters, checkers and innocent sinners obsessed with their imaginary crimes, Rapoport weaves a fascinating account of the symptoms, possible causes and, in some cases, cures" —*Psychology Today*
0-452-26365-4 PLUME PB $11.95

Case Histories

A.R. **Luria**
The Man with a Shattered World: The History of a Brain Wound
See also THE NEUROSCIENCES AND THE BRAIN under BIOLOGY under LIFE SCIENCES in SCIENCE
FOREWORD BY JEROME S. BRUNER
0-674-54625-3 HARVARD PB $11.95

The Mind of a Mnemonist: A Little Book About a Vast Memory
See also THE NEUROSCIENCES AND THE BRAIN under BIOLOGY under LIFE SCIENCES in SCIENCE
0-674-57622-5 HARVARD PB $12.95

Fayek **Nakhla** & Grace **Jackson**
Picking Up the Pieces: Two Accounts of a Psychoanalytic Journey
The first book about the psychoanalytic process ever to combine the views of both patient and doctor. An anguished woman and her doctor's dangerous decision to let her fully experience the often violent symptoms of her psychic disturbance so she could finally achieve the rebirth of her self
0-300-05653-2 YALE $20.00

Russ **Rymer**
Genie: An Abused Child's Flight from Silence
"A totally absorbing, unstoppable read…" —David Crystal, *The English Language*
0-06-092465-9 HARPERPERENNIAL PB $11.00

Oliver **Sacks**
An Anthropologist on Mars
Seven narratives of neurological disorder allow Dr. Sacks to continue his humane, poetic, and wonder-filled exploration of what it is to be human
See also THE NEUROSCIENCES AND THE BRAIN under BIOLOGY under LIFE SCIENCES in SCIENCE
0-679-43785-1 KNOPF $24.00
0-679-75697-3 VINTAGE PB $13.00

Oliver Sacks

Awakenings
A classic study
See also **MEMORY** under **SPECIAL TOPICS IN PSYCHOLOGY**
0-8095-9035-2 BORGO $29.00
0-8446-6277-1 SMITH $21.30
0-06-097368-4 HARPERPERENNIAL PB $13.00

A Leg to Stand On
A superbly written, often gripping account of Sacks's experiences after breaking a leg while climbing a mountain in Norway
0-06-097082-0 HARPER & ROW PB $13.00
0-06-092544-2 HARPERPERENNIAL PB $12.50

The Man Who Mistook His Wife for a Hat & Other Clinical Tales
"Dr. Sacks's most absorbing book...His tales are so compelling that many of them serve as eerie metaphors not only for the condition of modern medicine but of modern man"—*New York*
0-06-097079-0 HARPERCOLLINS PB $13.00

I tried one final test. It was still a cold day, in early spring, and I had thrown my coat and gloves on the sofa.

"What is this?" I asked, holding up a glove.

"May I examine it?" he asked, and, taking it from me, he proceeded to examine it as he had examined the geometrical shapes.

"A continuous surface," he announced at last, "infolded on itself. It appears to have"—he hesitated—"five outpouchings, if this is the word."

"Yes," I said cautiously. "You have given me a description. Now tell me what it is."

"A container of some sort?"

"Yes," I said, "and what would it contain?"

"It would contain its contents!" said Dr. P., with a laugh. "There are many possibilities. It could be a change purse, for example, for coins of five sizes. It could..."

I interrupted the barmy flow. "Does it not look familiar? Do you think it might contain, might fit, a part of your body?"

No light of recognition dawned on his face.

THE MAN WHO MISTOOK HIS WIFE FOR A HAT & OTHER CLINICAL TALES

Cognitive Therapy

Aaron T. **Beck**

Cognitive Therapy and the Emotional Disorders
An introduction to cognitive therapy, demonstrating the role of irrational and unrealistic "automatic thoughts" in depression and phobias and describing techniques for overcoming them
9993875376 NEW AMERICAN LIBRARY PB $12.00

Depression: Causes and Treatment
0-8122-1032-8 PENNSYLVANIA PB $20.95

David D. **Burns**

Feeling Good: The New Mood Therapy
See especially the chapters "Depression and Inventory Scale" and "Dysfunctional Attitudes Scale"
See also **HEALTH, EXERCISE, AND THERAPY** under **PEOPLE WITH DISABILITIES** in **LIFESTYLES AND PRACTICAL ADVICE**
0-688-03633-3 MORROW $25.00
0-451-15887-3 NEW AMERICAN LIBRARY PB $4.95

Rational and Reality Therapy

Albert **Ellis**

Anger: How to Live with and Without It
0-8065-0937-6 LYLE STUART PB $12.95

William **Glasser**

Control Therapy: A New Explanation of How We Control Our Lives
The connection between mental images and problems such as addiction
0-06-091292-8 HARPERCOLLINS PB $12.50

Positive Addiction
The importance of positive-reinforcing activities
0-06-091249-9 HARPERCOLLINS PB $12.00

Reality Therapy
Rejecting Freud and the concept of "mental illness," Glasser contends that the "mentally ill" are those who are unable to satisfy their needs realistically because they deny the reality of the world around them
0-06-090414-3 HARPERCOLLINS PB $11.00

Thomas S. **Szasz**

The Ethics of Psychoanalysis
0-8156-0229-4 SYRACUSE PB $14.95

The Myth of Mental Illness: Foundations of a Theory of Personal Conduct
This famous and provocative attack on the psychiatric profession rejects the medical pretenses of psychotherapy and advocates an approach that grants the individual full autonomy
0-06-091151-4 HARPERCOLLINS PB $13.50

Thomas S. **Szasz**

The Myth of Psychotherapy: Mental Healing as Religion, Rhetoric and Repression
0-8156-0223-5 SYRACUSE PB $13.95

Gestalt Therapy

Frederick S. **Perls**

Ego, Hunger and Aggression: A Revision of Freud's Theory and Method
An introduction by the founder of Gestalt as a form of psychotherapy
0-939266-18-0 GESTALT JOURNAL PB $20.00

Irving **Polster** & Miriam **Polster**

Gestalt Therapy Integrated: Contours of Theory and Practice
0-394-71006-1 RANDOM HOUSE PB $10.00

Joseph **Zinker**

Creative Process in Gestalt Therapy
0-394-72567-0 RANDOM HOUSE PB $13.00

Family Therapy

Augustus Y. **Napier** & Carl **Whitaker**

The Family Crucible: The Intense Experience of Family Therapy
0-06-091489-0 HARPERCOLLINS PB $13.00

Kathy **Weingarten**

The Mother's Voice
A therapist and parent's experience of breast cancer leads her to reflect on how best to introduce to her children this encounter with mortality. Both professionally rigorous and personally felt, the account charts her answer to that question. "[A] courageous, honest, and above all, useful book"—Sarah Ruddick
0-15-162680-4 HARCOURT BRACE $22.95

Child Therapy

Virginia M. **Axline**

Play Therapy
0-345-30335-0 BALLANTINE PB $5.95

D.W. **Winnicott**

Babies and Their Mothers
From the object-relations perspective
INTRODUCTION BY BENJAMIN SPOCK
0-201-63269-1 ADDISON-WESLEY PB $10.95

The Piggle
A detailed description of a single child therapy case
0-8236-4137-6 INT'L UNIVERSITIES $27.50

Special Topics in Psychology

Frans **De Waal**

Good Natured: The Origins of Right and Wrong in Humans and Other Animals

Do animals know right from wrong? Are only humans humane? The Dutch-born zoologist shows here that not only competition but cooperation and mutual assistance are key to the survival of species, and that morality, which is grounded in biology, is central to human and animals alike. In so doing, Dr. De Waal offers an entirely revolutionary view of what it means to be human

0-674-35660-8 HARVARD $24.95

Adriana **Rocha** & Kristi **Jorde**

A Child of Eternity: An Extraordinary Young Girl's Message from the World Beyond

FOREWORD BY JOAN BORYSENKO

0-345-38945-X BALLANTINE $23.00

Sleep and Dreams

Alexander **Borbely**

Secrets of Sleep

The latest word on sleep, dreams, and sleep disorders by one of the world's leading sleep researchers

See also SLEEP DISORDERS under SPECIFIC HEALTH PROBLEMS under HEALTH in LIFESTYLES AND PRACTICAL ADVICE

0-465-07593-2 BASIC BOOKS PB $16.00

Robert **Bosnak**

A Little Course in Dreams

This "basic handbook in Jungian dreamwork" offers a short, lucid introduction to remembering and recording dreams, analyzing a written dream text, and studying a series of dreams for underlying themes

FOREWORD BY DENISE LEVERTOV

0-87773-451-8 SHAMBHALA PB $10.00

Gayle **Delaney**, editor

New Directions in Dream Interpretation

Aimed at the professional but accessible to the general reader, this volume offers a practical guide to seven differing approaches to dream analysis

0-7914-1605-4 SUNY $59.50
0-7914-1606-2 SUNY PB $19.95

Lucy **Goodison**

The Dreams of Women: Exploring and Interpreting Women's Dreams

Goodison draws on a variety of techniques to offer this invitation to interpretation, for women, of women's dreams. An analysis and a tool kit, this volume allows women to understand the uniqueness of their dream imagery, and to use it for self-healing and self-understanding

0-393-03917-X NORTON $23.00

Jacob **Empson**

Sleep & Dreaming

0-13-302118-1 HARVESTER WHEATSHEAF PB $39.95

Bert O. **States**

Dreaming and Storytelling

In this fascinating exploration of the private and public imagination, the author draws on such diverse fields as neurobiology, psychology, literary theory, and dream theory to explore the meaning of dreams and their often subtle relationship to shared storytelling of literature and the cinema

0-8014-2896-3 CORNELL $27.50

Creativity

"The creative person is constantly seeking to discover himself, to remodel his own identity, and to find meaning in the universe by means of what he creates. He finds this to be a valuable integrating process which, like meditation or prayer, has little to do with other people, but which has its own separate validity. His most significant moments are those in which he attains some new insight, or makes some new discovery; and these moments are chiefly, if not invariably, those in which he is alone."
—Anthony Storr, *Solitude: A Return to the Self*.

Laurie S. **Adams**

Art & Psychoanalysis

A balanced evaluation of the often-controversial practice of interpreting works of art from psychoanalytical perspectives, informed by Adams's double competence as an art historian and practicing psychoanalyst

0-06-430206-7 ICON PB $20.00

Silvano **Arieti**

Creativity: The Magic Synthesis

"The most important work on creativity and its 'magic synthesis' that the world has yet had"
—Leon Edel

0-465-01442-9 BASIC BOOKS PB $28.35

Mihaly **Csikszentmihalyi**

Creativity: The Work and Lives of 91 Eminent People

Csikszentmihalyi's previous exploration of the creative process, *Flow*, was a phenomenal bestseller, rethinking human motivation and prescribing new paths to happiness. Here he offers a new understanding of creativity, drawing on hundreds of interviews with biologists, physicists, politicians, poets, artists, and business leaders, to show not only how understanding creativity can enrich our own lives, but how necessary it is for the future of our country to cultivate it

0-06-017133-2 HARPERCOLLINS $27.50

Flow: The Psychology of Optimal Experience

0-06-092043-2 HARPERCOLLINS PB $13.50

Betty **Edwards**

Drawing on the Right Side of the Brain: A Course in Enhancing Creativity and Artistic Confidence

0-87477-513-2 TARCHER PB $14.95

Howard **Gardner**

Art, Mind and Brain: A Cognitive Approach to Creativity

An impressive synthesis, drawing on Piaget, Chomsky, and Gombrich; contains discussions of Mozart and children's art, the effects of television on children, and the separate functions of the two halves of the brain

0-465-00445-8 BASIC PB $21.00

Creating Minds: An Anatomy of Creativity Seen Through the Lives of Freud, Einstein, Picasso, Stravinsky, Eliot, Graham, and Gandhi

Great minds of the 20th century who broke traditional modes of thought in their respective fields and accomplished the hitherto impossible. By studying patterns of behavior (abhorrence of the establishment, self-absorption) Gardner reveals certain common elements that he defines as essential for creativity. "Gardner is at his best: insightful, civilized, and precise. I can't think of a more stimulating book about creativity"—Mihaly Csikszentmihalyi

0-465-01455-0 BASIC $30.00

Igor Stravinsky (photo courtesy of Columbia Records)

Howard **Gardner** & Emma **Laskin**

Leading Minds: An Anatomy of Leadership

0-465-08280-7 BASIC PB $16.50

Willis **Harman** & Howard **Rheingold**

Higher Creativity: Liberating the Unconscious for Breakthrough Insight

0-87477-335-0 TARCHER PB $11.95

Rollo **May**

The Courage to Create

See also EXISTENTIAL PSYCHOLOGY

0-8446-6854-0 PEREGRINE SMITH $20.50
0-393-31106-6 NORTON PB $9.95

Alice **Miller**

The Untouched Key: Unnoticed Childhood Traumas in Creative People

How the trauma of childhood affected the creativity of such figures as Picasso, Dostoevsky, and Stalin

0-385-26764-9 ANCHOR PB $10.95

Anthony **Storr**

The Dynamics of Creation

A consistently intelligent and sensible discussion of the psychology of creativity; examples discussed range from Einstein and Newton to Chopin and Kafka

0-345-37673-0 BALLANTINE PB $10.00

Solitude: A Return to the Self

How psychologists underestimate the creative potential of solitude and the possibilities it offers for self-fulfillment

0-345-35847-3 BALLANTINE PB $11.00

Art and Perception

Rudolf **Arnheim**

Art and Visual Perception: A Psychology of the Creative Eye

Influenced by Gestalt psychology, Arnheim finds the relation of artistic form and perception in the operation of an ordering intelligence

0-520-02613-6 CALIFORNIA PB $17.95

Visual Thinking

To see is to think; why the act of perception is as complex and cognitive as any other mental act

0-520-01871-0 CALIFORNIA PB $15.95

E.H. **Gombrich**

Art & Illusion: A Study in the Psychology of Pictorial Presentation

A classic, groundbreaking examination of the ideal of representation in Western art and the means used to achieve it; profusely and brilliantly illustrated

0-691-09785-2 PRINCETON $80.00
0-691-01750-6 PRINCETON PB $29.95

The Sense of Order: A Study in the Psychology of Decorative Arts

See also **THEORY AND CRITICISM** under **ART HISTORY: GENERAL STUDIES** in **ART**

0-7148-2259-0 PHAIDON $24.95

Herman L. **Helmholtz**

On the Sensations of Tone

0-486-60753-4 DOVER PB $15.95

Stephen M. **Kosslyn**

Image & Brain: The Resolution of the Imagery Debate

A Harvard psychologist's theory of how the human brain processes complex images

0-262-11184-5 MIT $50.00

D. **Marr**

Vision

Marr's work on perception is among the most important contributions to the field in the last 50 years

0-7167-1567-8 FREEMAN PB $34.95

Robert L. **Solso**

Cognition & the Visual Arts

An illustrated exploration of the complex interplay between the visual arts and the mental processes of cognition and perception

0-262-19346-9 MIT $42.50

Language

Roger **Brown**

A First Language: The Early Stages

0-674-30325-3 HARVARD $33.00
0-674-30326-1 HARVARD PB $16.95

Jerome S. **Bruner**

Child's Talk: Learning to Use Language

"The cumulative effect of Bruner's writings has been to release a whole generation of researchers from the straitjacket of linguistic theory and laboratory experiments into studying social activities in their natural contexts...He offers wisdom and insights freely for any who wish to share in his search for a rich conception of the human mind"—*TLS*

0-393-95345-9 NORTON PB $7.95

Steven **Pinker**

The Language Instinct: How the Mind Creates Language

The co-director of the Center for Cognitive Science at MIT explains how we learn to talk, how the study of language can provide insight into how our genes interact with our experience to create behavior and thought, and how the arbitrary sounds we call language evoke emotion and meaning. "An extremely valuable book, very informative, and very well written"—Noam Chomsky

See also **LANGUAGE THEORY** under **LINGUISTICS**

0-688-12141-1 HARPERPERENNIAL PB $17.95

Andrew **Robinson**

The Story of Writing: Alphabets, Hieroglyphs, and Pictographs

0-500-01665-8 THAMES & HUDSON $29.95

Lev S. **Vygotsky**

Mind in Society: The Development of Higher Psychological Processes

EDITED BY MICHAEL COLE

0-674-57629-2 HARVARD PB $14.00

Thought and Language

EDITED BY ALEXEY KOZULIN

0-262-72010-8 MIT PB $16.00

Memory

Daniel **Goleman**

Vital Lies, Simple Truths: The Psychology of Self-Deception

How our lives are affected by our denial of painful insights and memories

0-684-83107-4 TOUCHSTONE PB $12.00

Elizabeth **Loftus** & Katherine **Ketchum**

The Myth of Repressed Memory

0-312-11454-0 ST. MARTIN'S $22.95
0-312-14123-8 ST. MARTIN'S PB $13.95

Steven **Rose**

The Making of Memory: From Molecules to Mind

0-385-47121-1 ANCHOR PB $14.00

Oliver **Sacks**

Awakenings

A classic study

See also **THE NEUROSCIENCES AND THE BRAIN** under **BIOLOGY**

0-8095-9035-2 BORGO $29.00
0-8446-6277-1 SMITH $21.30
0-06-097368-4 HARPERPERENNIAL PB $13.00

Noncognitive Perspectives of the Mind

Michael S. **Gazzaniga**

Nature's Mind: The Impact of Darwinian Selection on Thinking, Emotions, Sexuality, Language, & Intelligence

0-465-04863-3 BASIC PB $15.00

J. Allan **Hobson**

The Chemistry of Conscious States: How the Brain Changes Its Mind

Hobson, a world-renowned neuroscientist, has the rare gift of rendering the complexity of the brain clear and accessible to the general reader. With lively anecdotes and familiar examples, he explains how the chemistry of the brain creates the bewildering range of conscious experience

See also **THE NEW PHYSICS** under **METAPHYSICS** under **SPIRITUALITY** in **RELIGION, SPIRITUALITY, AND PHILOSOPHY**

0-316-36754-0 LITTLE, BROWN $24.95

Julian **Jaynes**

The Origin of Consciousness in the Breakdown of the Bicameral Mind

"When Julian Jaynes...speculates that until late in the second millennium BC men had no consciousness but were automatically obeying the voices of the gods, we are astounded but compelled to follow this remarkable thesis through all the corroborative evidence" —John Updike

0-395-56352-6 HOUGHTON MIFFLIN PB $16.95

Robert **Wright**

The Moral Animal: Evolutionary Psychology and Everyday Life

Evolutionary psychology is a potent new analytic tool for understanding human behavior, drawing on anthropology, biology, and psychology. "Many readers will feel uneasy reading Wright's dark and cynical portrayal of human nature ... [he] points to a growing body of evidence that says this is the way we are whether we like it or not, and he argues we're better off if we accept this fact"—*Kirkus Reviews*

0-679-76399-6 VINTAGE PB $14.00

Miscellaneous

Ernest **Becker**

The Denial of Death

Pulitzer Prize-winning book which argues that the repression of the knowledge of our own mortality is the source of much of our behavior and the root of anxiety and mental illness

0-02-902380-7 FREE PRESS PB $14.95

Escape from Evil

Becker's last work argues that man seeks victims and scapegoats to bolster his own fragile sense of mortality. "A profoundly nourishing book which is absolutely essential to the understanding of our troubled times"—Anaïs Nin

0-02-902450-1 FREE PRESS PB $14.95

Christopher **Bolla** & David **Sundelson**

The New Informants: The Betrayal of Confidentiality in Psychoanalysis and Psychotherapy

1-56821-595-9 ARONSON $22.00

Winifred **Gallagher**

I.D.: How Temperament and Experience Make You Who You Are

Drawing on behavioral science, genetics, psychoanalysis, neuroscience, and primatology, Gallagher provides here an up-to-the-minute account of the status of identity. Dividing human types into three distinct groups —sensitive, cool, and forceful—she concludes that genes and learning make us what we are: wonderful, mysterious, and complex

0-679-43018-0 RANDOM HOUSE $23.00

Daniel **Goleman**

Emotional Intelligence: Why It Can Matter More than IQ

The bestselling explanation of IQ

0-553-09503-X BDD $23.95

0-553-84007-X BANTAM PB $7.50

Susan **Griffin**

A Chorus of Stones: The Private Life of War

"Part autobiographical memoir, part social history, Griffin's book ties scores of individuals to the wars they lived through or died in..." —*NY Newsday*

See also **WORLD HISTORY** under **WOMEN'S STUDIES**

0-385-41885-X ANCHOR PB $12.95

Sue **Halpern**

Migrations to Solitude

Halpern examines the paradoxes of privacy: at what price we earn our distance, comfort, dignity, and seclusion, and the manner in which we try to breach the privacy of celebrities. "Offers much perspective on contemporary, secular America and a good deal of wisdom about life"—Robert Coles

0-679-40777-4 VINTAGE PB $20.00

Stanley **Milgram**

Obedience to Authority

An important study summing up recent research on why people submit to authority

0-06-131983-X HARPERCOLLINS PB $18.23

Jerome **Kagan**

Galen's Prophecy: Temperament in Human Nature

Includes a history of the idea of temperament, an account of Kagan's career-long (and increasingly influential) study of the behavior of toddlers, and a balanced statement of his conclusion that character is strongly influenced by biology

See also **BEHAVIORISM**

0-465-02612-5 BASIC PB $14.00

Robert **Ornstein**

The Psychology of Consciousness

A classic study of intuition, reason, and the improvement of mental functioning

0-14-017090-1 PENGUIN PB $11.95

The Roots of the Self: Unravelling the Mystery of Who We Are

Why do some people approach a roomful of strangers with enthusiasm while others feel dread? How much do the races and sexes differ? Using genetics, environment, and psychology, Ornstein (*The Psychology of Consciousness*) treats us to his intriguing musings on why we are the way we are. "[Ornstein] has always been on the frontier of new, speculative thinking about the workings of the mind"—Doris Lessing

0-06-250789-3 HARPERCOLLINS PB $12.00

Robert J. **Sternberg** &
Michael L. **Barnes**, editors

The Psychology of Love

A suprisingly revealing anthology of scientific approaches to the most unruly of subjects. "This impressive collection is informationally rich yet highly readable"—*Choice*

0-300-04589-1 YALE PB $20.00

Thomas S. **Szasz**

Psychiatric Justice

How psychiatric encroachments into the legal process violate the constitutional right to a fair and speedy trial

0-8156-0231-6 SYRACUSE PB $14.95

Carol **Tavris**

Anger: The Misunderstood Emotion

"Beautifully clarifies the difference between moral, useful anger and mere incivility or self-gratifying bad temper"—Morton Hunt

0-671-67523-0 TOUCHSTONE PB $11.00

Michael D. **Yapko**

Suggestions of Abuse: True and False Memories of Childhood Sexual Trauma

0-671-87431-4 SIMON & SCHUSTER $22.00

Reference

American Psychiatric Association Staff

Diagnostic & Statistical Manual of Mental Disorders: DSM-IV

The standard reference resource for mental health professionals (but also useful and informative for the general reader), offering an exhaustive catalogue of mental and emotional disorders and their symptoms

0-89042-061-0 AMERICAN PSYCHIATRIC $59.95

0-89042-062-9 AMERICAN PSYCHIATRIC PB $45.00

J.P. **Chaplin**

Dictionary of Psychology

0-440-31925-0 DELL PB $6.99

Stan **Gonilisco**

The McGraw-Hill Illustrated Encyclopedia of Robotics & Artificial Intelligence

0-07-023613-5 MCGRAW HILL $40.00

0-07-023614-3 MCGRAW HILL PB $24.95

R.L. **Gregory**, editor

The Oxford Companion to the Mind

Fascinating reference work encompassing philosophical and psychological approaches to everything concerning the human, from perception to art to religion

See also **THE NEUROSCIENCES AND THE BRAIN** under **BIOLOGY** under **LIFE SCIENCES** in **SCIENCE**

0-19-866124-X OXFORD $60.00

Rom **Harre** & Roger **Lamb**

The Encyclopedic Dictionary of Psychology

Scholarly articles on major concepts, approaches, and figures in all areas of psychology, with a particular stress on cognitive psychology, psycholinguistics, and neuropsychology

0-87967-885-2 DUSHKIN PB $12.45

Roy **Porter**, editor

The Faber Book of Madness

Includes excerpts from some of the world's greatest, and/or "mad" writers such as Auden, Brontë, Nietzsche, Pope, Plath, Rhys, Sexton, and Voltaire. "Salutary in what it reveals not so much about the mad, but about the way the sane think of them, treat them and usually fail to love them"—Jeanette Winterson

See also **GENERAL ANTHOLOGIES** under **WORLD LITERATURE: WORLD LITERATURE SURVEYS AND ANTHOLOGIES** in **LITERATURE OF EUROPE, AFRICA, AND ASIA**

0-571-14388-1 FABER PB $14.95

Benjamin B. **Wolman**

Dictionary of Behavioral Science

A guide to concepts and major figures in all areas of psychology and related fields such as psychiatry, biochemistry, psychopharmacology, and neurology

0-12-762455-4 ACADEMIC PRESS $39.95

Sociology

Classical European Sociology

While different historians trace the roots of sociological thought to the classical tradition, the French Enlightenment, or the Scottish moralists of the 18th century, most see the early 19th century as the birthdate of modern sociology. The discipline arose at a time when industrialism, urbanization, and modern capitalism required novel explanations. Its first major figures were Auguste Comte, the French thinker who gave the field its name, and the widely influential English writer Herbert Spencer. Founders of modern European sociology include the French scholar Emile Durkheim and the German social scientists Max Weber and Georg Simmel. Karl Marx did not see himself as a sociologist, since his works were not merely studies but contained a call to socialist action; however, his legacy has proved inspirational to generations of later scholars.

Auguste **Comte**

Introduction to Positive Philosophy

0-8722-0050-7 HACKETT PB $5.95

Emile **Durkheim**

One of the founders of modern sociology, Durkheim pioneered the use of empirical and statistical evidence. He is known for his analysis of religion and morality as "collective representations."

The Division of Labor in Society

TRANSLATED BY W. D. HALL

0-02-907960-8 FREE PRESS PB $16.95

The Elementary Forms of the Religious Life

A classic study that explains the function of the totem and introduces a distinction between the sacred and profane

See also **RELIGION AND SOCIETY** under **WORLD RELIGION** in **RELIGION, SPIRITUALITY, AND PHILOSOPHY**

TRANSLATED BY JOSEPH W. SWAIN

0-02-908010-X FREE PRESS PB $16.95

The Rules of Sociological Method & Selected Texts on Sociology and Its Method

TRANSLATED BY W.D. HALLS

EDITED BY STEVEN LUKAS

0-02-907940-3 FREE PRESS PB $16.95

Selected Writings

Although Comte set the theoretical foundation for the discipline of sociology, it was Durkheim who carried out the first systematic studies on a wide range of social phenomena, notably religion and class

EDITED BY ANTHONY GIDDENS

0-521-09712-6 CAMBRIDGE PB $18.95

Suicide: A Study in Sociology

The first systematic study of the subject is still indispensable

0-02-908660-4 FREE PRESS PB $16.95

Sigmund **Freud**

Although best known as the founder of psychoanalysis, Freud wrote in his later years on the relationship between sexuality and social organization, arguing that the two are in constant conflict. The three books below remain highly influential among sociologists and others seeking to understand how society controls sexual behavior.

Civilization and Its Discontents

A pessimistic assessment of the instinctual cost of civilization

See also **FREUD** under **PSYCHOLOGY**

0-393-30158-3 NORTON PB $7.95

Moses and Monotheism

Freud speculates that modern science developed out of the asceticism fostered by monotheism

See also **PSYCHOLOGY AND RELIGION** under **WORLD RELIGION** in **RELIGION, SPIRITUALITY, AND PHILOSOPHY**

0-394-70014-7 RANDOM HOUSE PB $8.00

Totem and Taboo

0-394-70124-0 RANDOM HOUSE PB $8.00

Charles **MacKay**

Extraordinary Popular Delusions and the Madness of Crowds

A perennial favorite that recounts Tulipmania and other misguided enthusiasms over the past few centuries. An exuberant survey of massive social delusions, it conveys the comic underside of sociology

0-517-53919-5 CROWN PB $11.00

Georg **Simmel**

Georg Simmel initiated the study of microsociology through his fascinating analyses of the differences between dyads and triads, and between small and large groups. As he himself put it, he was attempting to develop a geometry of social life. Although Simmel had few disciples in his native Germany, American sociologists have taken up his challenge.

Conflict and the Web of Group Affiliations

Simmel's highly original work on money and on social groups, which influenced Weber and other German contemporaries, has been considered up in recent years by American social and economic theorists

0-02-928840-1 FREE PRESS PB $13.95

Georg Simmel on Individuality and Social Forms

EDITED BY DONALD N. LEVINE

0-226-75776-5 CHICAGO PB $18.95

The Philosophy of Money

EDITED BY DAVID FRISBY

0-415-04641-6 ROUTLEDGE PB $22.95

The Sociology of Georg Simmel

EDITED BY KURT H. WOLFF

0-02-928920-3 FREE PRESS PB $15.95

Max **Weber**

Basic Concepts in Sociology

TRANSLATED BY H.P. SECHER

0-8065-0304-1 CITADEL PB $7.95

Ferdinand **Tonnies**

Ferdinand Tonnies on Sociology: Pure, Applied and Empirical Selected Writings

Tonnies's classic *Community and Society* appeared in 1887, and he remained at the forefront of German sociology until the Nazis dismissed him from his teaching post in 1933

0-226-80607-3 CHICAGO $30.00

Economy and Society

A two-volume set. Weber's most complete exposition of his sociological views and method

EDITED BY GUENTHER ROTH & CLAUS WITTICH

0-520-03500-3 CALIFORNIA PB $44.95

From Max Weber: Essay in Sociology

Weber saw culture and cultural values as determining forces in history. His studies of the development of such modern social institutions as bureaucracy and capitalism were groundbreaking works of historical interpretation as well as of social theory

TRANSLATED & EDITED BY H.H. GARTH & C. WRIGHT MILLS

0-19-500462-0 OXFORD PB $16.95

The Protestant Ethic and the Spirit of Capitalism

Weber's classic argument, first published in 1904, that the spread of Protestantism directly affected the rise of the capitalist ethic

See also **RELIGION AND CAPITALISM** under **REFORMATION AND COUNTER-REFORMATION** under **EARLY MODERN EUROPE** in **WORLD HISTORY AND CURRENT AFFAIRS**

0-02-424860-6 PRENTICE HALL PB $34.40

The Religion of China: Confucianism and Taoism

In this most famous work, Weber, the master sociologist of religion, argues that China's religious ethic impeded the development of a rational capitalist economy

See also **THE CHINESE TRADITIONS** under **ASIAN RELIGION AND PHILOSOPHY** in **RELIGION, SPIRITUALITY, AND PHILOSOPHY**

0-02-934440-9 FREE PRESS PB $19.95

The Sociology of Religion

See also **RELIGION AND SOCIETY** under **WORLD RELIGION** in **RELIGION, SPIRITUALITY, AND PHILOSOPHY**

0-8070-4205-6 BEACON PB $16.00

The Theory of Social and Economic Organization

TRANSLATED BY TALCOTT PARSONS

0-02-934930-3 FREE PRESS PB $19.95

Histories, Commentaries, and Biographies

Jeffrey C. **Alexander**

Durkheimian Sociology: Cultural Studies

0-521-39647-6 CAMBRIDGE PB $17.95

Neofunctionalism

1-55786-289-3 BLACKWELL PB $10.00

Jeffrey C. **Alexander**

Theoretical Logic in Sociology

Volume one is currently out of print

Volume 2
The Antinomies of Classical Thought—Marx and Durkheim

0-520-04481-9 CALIFORNIA $57.00
0-520-05613-2 CALIFORNIA PB $16.00

Volume 3
The Classical Attempt at Theoretical Synthesis—Max Weber

0-520-04482-7 CALIFORNIA $57.00
0-520-05614-0 CALIFORNIA PB $16.00

Steven **Lukes**

Emile Durkheim: His Life and Work—A Historical and Critical Study

0-8047-1282-4 STANFORD $67.50

Arthur **Mitzman**

Sociology and Estrangement: Three Sociologists of Imperial Germany

Analysis of Robert Michels, Werner Sombart, and Ferdinand Tonnies

0-88738-605-9 TRANSACTION PB $21.95

John Patrick **Diggins**

Max Weber: The Life and Work, A Passionate Reappraisal

One of the greatest social and political thinkers of the modern era is brought into precise new focus in this major biography

0-465-01750-9 BASIC $35.00

Max Weber

Dirk **Kasler**

Max Weber: An Introduction to His Life and Work

TRANSLATED BY PHILIPPA HURT

0-226-42560-6 CHICAGO PB $17.95

Arthur **Mitzman**

The Iron Cage: A Historical Interpretation of Max Weber

0-87855-984-1 TRANSACTION PB $19.95

Robert **Wuthnow**

Communities of Discourse: Ideology and Social Structure in the Reformation, the Enlightenment, and European Socialism

0-674-15164-X HARVARD $56.00
0-674-15165-8 HARVARD PB $32.00

Sociology After Weber

A product of Weimar Germany, the Frankfurt School attempted to develop a flexible Marxist theory of the role of ideas and culture in modern societies. Influenced by Freud, Simmel, and other "bourgeois" thinkers, it gradually lost faith in the redeeming role of the working class and assumed a more despairing stance toward the modern world. Alluding to their grand bourgeois life-style, Georg Lukacs once remarked of the school's adherents that they were rather comfortably installed in the "Hotel Abyss." The members of the Frankfurt School produced their major works in exile in America and in postwar Germany.

Marxism and the Frankfurt School

Theodor **Adorno**

Minima Moralia: Reflections from a Damaged Life

These fragmentary reflections and essays on contemporary society were composed in America during and just after World War II. Adorno's most characteristic book and a brilliant stylistic achievement

See also **OTHER 20TH-CENTURY PHILOSOPHERS** under **PHILOSOPHY** in **RELIGION, SPIRITUALITY, AND PHILOSOPHY**

0-86091-704-5 VERSO PB $19.00

Theodor **Adorno** & Else **Frenkel-Brunswik**

The Authoritarian Personality

Freudian psychoanalytic categories applied to the explanation of political authoritarianism

0-393-31112-0 NORTON PB $14.95

Jurgen **Habermas**

Knowledge and Human Interests

Habermas's special interest is a theory of social communication built upon the work of his teachers at the Frankfurt School. He is now recognized as a major figure in normative and analytical theory

TRANSLATED BY JEREMY J. SHAPIRO

0-8070-1541-5 BEACON $17.00

Legitimation Crisis

TRANSLATED BY THOMAS MCCARTHY

0-8070-1521-0 HARPERCOLLINS PB $14.00

The Philosophical Discourse of Modernity

Twelve unusually readable lectures in which Habermas makes his argument for "communicative rationality" against a host of thinkers from Hegel to Derrida

TRANSLATED BY FREDERICK G. LAWRENCE

0-262-58102-7 MIT PB $19.00

Max **Horkheimer**

Between Philosophy and Social Science: Early Writings

Includes Horkheimer's address from the 1930s on the purpose of the Institute of Social Research, as well as essays on the relationship between philosophy and social science that anticipate much later Continental thought

0-262-58142-6 BRADFORDS DIRECTORY PB $20.00

Critical Theory: Selected Essays

TRANSLATED BY MATTHEW J. O'CONNELL

0-8264-0083-3 CONTINUUM PB $16.95

The Eclipse of Reason

0-8264-0009-4 CONTINUUM PB $14.95

Martin **Jay**

Adorno

Clear writing makes the sometimes obstruse Adorno accessible

0-674-00515-5 HARVARD PB $12.95

The Dialectical Imagination: A History of the Frankfurt School and the Institute of Social Research, 1923-1950

Jay is the leading American historian and analyst of the Frankfurt School, and this book is the school's leading history. "A fascinating and indispensable contribution to the understanding of modern European thought"
—Raymond Williams

See also **OTHER 20TH-CENTURY PHILOSOPHERS** under **PHILOSOPHY** in **RELIGION, SPIRITUALITY, AND PHILOSOPHY**

See also **THE FRANKFURT SCHOOL** under **CULTURAL CRITICISM** under **LITERARY THEORY** in **LITERATURE OF EUROPE, AFRICA, AND ASIA**

0-520-20423-9 CALIFORNIA PB $13.95

Leo **Lowenthal**

Literature, Popular Culture, and Society

0-87015-166-5 PACIFIC PB $8.95

Herbert **Marcuse**

Marcuse, another member of the Frankfurt School, became a chief intellectual sponsor of the New Left and the 1960s counterculture through his insistence that erotic liberation must accompany radical political and economic change.

One Dimensional Man

A scathing criticism of modern capitalism

See also **LEFTISM AND MARXISM** under **POLITICAL THOUGHT**

0-8070-1417-6 BEACON PB $15.00

Herbert **Marcuse**

Eros and Civilization: A Philosophical Inquiry into Freud

Rejecting Freud's theory that civilization demands instinctual repression, Marcuse calls for a society in which sexual liberation will accompany political and economic liberation

See also **OTHER 20TH-CENTURY PHILOSOPHERS** under **PHILOSOPHY**

0-8070-1555-5 FS&G PB $15.00

Reason and Revolution: Hegel and the Rise of Theory

0-391-02999-1 HUMANITIES PB $18.50

Herbert Marcuse

Rolf **Wiggerhaus**

The Frankfurt School: Its History, Theories, and Political Significance

The latest and most comprehensive history of this group of influential intellectuals

See also **OTHER 20TH-CENTURY PHILOSOPHERS** under **PHILOSOPHY** in **RELIGION, SPIRITUALITY, AND PHILOSOPHY**

TRANSLATED BY MICHAEL ROBERTSON

0-262-73113-4 MIT PB $29.95

German Social Thought

After the Weimar period German thought laid particular stress on the sociology of knowledge. Following the lead of such predecessors as Karl Marx and Max Scheler, Karl Mannheim developed his distinctive approach to the study of ideas and intellectuals. Mannheim's work has been a focal point for scholars concerned with the relations between knowledge and society.

Peter L. **Berger**

The Sacred Canopy: Elements of a Sociological Theory of Religion

A controversial book by a contemporary sociologist of knowledge

See also **RELIGION AND SOCIETY** under **WORLD RELIGION** in **RELIGION, SPIRITUALITY, AND PHILOSOPHY**

0-385-07305-4 ANCHOR PB $9.95

Karl **Mannheim**

Ideology and Utopia: An Introduction to the Sociology of Knowledge

Mannheim's major work

0-15-643955-7 HARCOURT BRACE PB $14.00

Ralf **Dahrendorf**

Class and Conflict in Industrial Society

Dahrendorf is an outstanding conflict theorist and a past director of the London School of Economics

0-8047-0560-7 STANFORD $47.50

Essays in the Theory of Society

0-8047-0286-1 STANFORD $42.50
0-8047-0288-8 STANFORD PB $14.95

Postwar French and British Thought

Pierre **Bourdieu**

Distinction: A Social Critique of the Judgment of Taste

TRANSLATED BY RICHARD NICE

0-674-21277-0 HARVARD PB $21.00

Homo Academicus

A brilliant, bestselling self-analysis of the French academic world by its leading sociologist

See also **HIGHER EDUCATION** under **EDUCATION**

TRANSLATED BY PETER COLLIER

0-8047-1466-5 STANFORD $47.50
0-8047-1798-2 STANFORD PB $17.95

In Other Words: Essays Towards a Reflexive Sociology

0-8047-1557-2 STANFORD $37.50

The State Nobility 'Grandes Ecoles' and Esprit de Corps

0-8047-1778-8 STANFORD $55.00

Ernest **Gellner**

Plough, Sword and Book: The Structure of Human History

A synoptic view of human history by a distinguished British sociologist, emphasizing the power of new knowledge to transform social organization

0-226-28702-5 CHICAGO PB $17.95

Anthony **Giddens**

Central Problems in Social Theory: Action, Structure, and Contraction in Social Analysis

0-520-03975-0 CALIFORNIA PB $15.95

The Constitution of Society: Outline of the Theory of Structuration

0-520-05292-7 CALIFORNIA $50.00
0-520-05728-7 CALIFORNIA PB $16.95

The Nation-State and Violence: A Contemporary Critique of Historical Materialism

0-520-06039-3 CALIFORNIA PB $17.95

Sociology: A Brief but Critical Introduction

0-15-582001-X HARCOURT BRACE PB $22.61

Jack **Goody**

The Logic of Writing and the Organization of Society

A vivid treatment of how literacy and the production of knowledge determine social structures. Goody takes his examples mainly from the Near East and West Africa

0-521-33962-6 CAMBRIDGE PB $16.95

Stuart **Hall**

Resistance Through Rituals: Youth Subculture in Britain

Hall is a leading figure in cultural studies

0-00-302072-X UNWIN HYMAN PB $19.95

A.H. **Halsey** & Jerome **Karabel**, editors

Power and Ideology in Education

0-19-502139-8 OXFORD PB $27.00

Geoffrey **Hawthorn**

Enlightenment and Despair: A History of Social Theory

0-521-33721-6 CAMBRIDGE PB $19.95

Richard **Hoggart**

The Uses of Literacy

This famous and eloquent book about the reading habits of the English lower classes was a founding document in the sociological examination of popular culture now known as cultural studies

0-88738-892-2 TRANSACTION PB $21.95

The Way We Live Now

0-7011-6501-4 CHATTO & WINDUS $35.00

Charles **Lemert**, editor

French Sociology: Rupture and Renewal Since 1968

0-231-04698-7 COLUMBIA $66.50

Steven **Lukes**

Essays in Social Theory

0-231-04450-X COLUMBIA $43.00

Michael **Mann**

The Sources of Social Power Volume 1: A History of Power from the Beginning to A.D. 1760

A recent, original account of the origins of the modern European state, with particular emphasis on war making and the Christian church

0-521-31349-X CAMBRIDGE PB $31.95

Volume 2: The Rise of Classes and Nation-States

0-521-44585-X CAMBRIDGE PB $29.95

W.G. **Runciman**

A Treatise on Social Theory Volume 1: The Methodology of Social Theory

A brave attempt at sociology in the grand manner, but with an emphasis on the details of real life: "The distinctive problems of the social sciences," Runciman writes, "are problems of description and not of explanation"

0-521-27251-3 CAMBRIDGE PB $22.95

W.G. **Runciman**

Volume 2:
Substantive Social Theory
0-521-36983-5 CAMBRIDGE PB $24.95

Raymond **Williams**

The Sociology of Culture
An influential Marxist literary theorist and Cambridge professor who developed a sociological approach to this subject
0-226-89921-7 CHICAGO PB $14.95

Television
0-8195-6259-9 WESLEYAN PB $14.95

Writing in Society
0-86091-772-X VERSO PB $18.95

American Sociological Theory

Before 1900, American sociological theory remained largely dependent on European trends. But around the turn of the century more independent theorizing began to appear. Particularly noteworthy was the interactionist social psychology developed by the pragmatist philosopher and social psychologist George Herbert Mead and his close companion Charles Horton Cooley. The hallmark of their theory was a rejection of the Cartesian split between the ego and the surrounding world. Self and society, Cooley and Mead argued, are interdependent and develop simultaneously.

Early Founders

Charles Horton **Cooley**

Human Nature and the Social Order
0-87855-918-3 TRANSACTION PB $21.95

Social Organization: A Study of the Larger Mind
0-87855-824-1 TRANSACTION PB $24.95

Thorstein **Veblen**

Veblen gave a psychological spin to his analysis of American economic and social institutions.

Absentee Ownership
0-678-00048-4 AUGUSTUS KELLY $45.00
1-56000-922-5 TRANSACTION PB $24.95

Imperial Germany and the Industrial Revolution
INTRODUCTION BY J. DORFMAN
0-678-00050-6 AUGUSTUS KELLY $39.50

An Inquiry into the Nature of Peace
0-678-00052-2 AUGUSTUS KELLY $39.50

The Instinct of Workmanship
INTRODUCTION BY J. DORFMAN
0-678-00051-4 AUGUSTUS KELLY $37.50

The Theory of the Leisure Class
Veblen's classic social critique was first published in 1899
0-14-018795-2 PENGUIN PB $10.95

Alexis **de Tocqueville**

Democracy in America
Although not a sociologist, de Tocqueville wrote perhaps the most influential description of the peculiarities of American society—a 19th-century work that is still widely read and discussed today
0-8095-9076-X BORGO $47.00
0-679-43134-9 KNOPF $23.00

Alexis de Tocqueville

Democracy in America
Volume 1
0-679-72825-2 VINTAGE PB $12.00

Volume 2
0-679-72826-0 VINTAGE PB $12.00

George Herbert **Mead**

Mind, Self, and Society
EDITED BY CHARLES W. MORRIS
0-226-51668-7 CHICAGO PB $14.95

Postwar American Theory

Well into the 1960s, American sociological theory was dominated by what is known as structural functionalism, or functional theory. First developed by Durkheim and elaborated by the anthropologists Malinowski and Radcliffe-Brown, its chief American proponent was Talcott Parsons. The theory stresses analogies of the biological body with the social body. More recent theories take a variety of approaches, from the phenomenology of Alfred Schutz to the independent stances of Peter Blau, Edward Shils, and Arthur Stinchcombe.

William J. **Goode**

The Celebration of Heroes: Prestige as a Social Control System
0-520-03602-6 CALIFORNIA $49.95
0-520-03811-8 CALIFORNIA PB $14.95

Irving **Horowitz**

The Decomposition of Sociology
0-19-507316-9 OXFORD $35.00
0-19-509256-2 OXFORD PB $14.95

Robert K. **Merton**

Social Theory and Social Structure
0-02-921130-1 FREE PRESS $35.00

The Sociology of Science: Theoretical and Empirical Investigations
EDITED BY NORMAN STORER
0-226-52092-7 CHICAGO PB $19.95

C. Wright **Mills**

The Sociological Imagination
A classic, highly influential critique of sociological thought

See also **CRITICAL COMMENTARY ON AMERICAN CULTURE** under **TOPICS IN MODERN SOCIOLOGY**

0-19-500751-4 OXFORD PB $9.95

Talcott **Parsons**

Essays on Sociological Theory Pure and Applied
0-02-924030-1 FREE PRESS PB $18.95

The Social System
0-02-924190-1 FREE PRESS PB $22.95

The Structure of Social Action
The book that introduced the great European sociologists—Durkheim, Weber, Pareto—to American readers. The first volume is out of print

Volume 2
0-02-924250-9 FREE PRESS PB $21.95

Talcott Parsons on Institutions and Social Evolution: Selected Writings
EDITED BY LEON H. MAYHEW
0-226-64749-8 CHICAGO PB $14.95

Alfred **Schutz**

Alfred Schutz on Phenomenology and Social Relations: Selected Writings
EDITED BY HELMUT R. WAGNER
0-226-74153-2 CHICAGO PB $17.00

Phenomenology of the Social World
TRANSLATED BY GEORGE WALSH & FREDERICK LEHNERT
0-8101-0390-7 NORTHWESTERN PB $19.95

Edward **Shils**

The Calling of Sociology & Other Essays on the Pursuit of Learning
0-226-75323-9 CHICAGO $27.50

Arthur L. **Stinchcombe**

Economic Sociology
0-12-671382-0 ACADEMIC PRESS PB $36.00

Stratification and Organization: Selected Papers
0-521-32588-9 CAMBRIDGE $79.95

Topics in Modern Sociology

Microsociology

Georg Simmel initiated the study of microsociology through his fascinating analyses of the differences between dyads and triads, and between small and large groups. As he himself put it, he was attempting to develop a geometry of social life. Although Simmel had few disciples in his native Germany, American sociologists have taken up his challenge.

The late Erving Goffman was one of the rare authentic geniuses of American sociology. Although often impressionistic and loosely structured, his work has illuminated many aspects of interactive life: the dramatic nature of social interaction, role-playing in everyday life, and the management of the social self.

Peter M. **Blau**

Exchange and Power in Social Life

0-88738-628-8 TRANSACTION PB $21.95

Erving **Goffman**

The late Erving Goffman was one of the rare authentic geniuses of American sociology. Although often impressionistic and loosely structured, his work has illuminated many aspects of interactive life: the dramatic nature of social interaction, role-playing in everyday life, and the management of the social self.

Asylums: Essays on the Social Situation of Mental Patients and Other Inmates

0-385-00016-2 DOUBLEDAY PB $10.95

Frame Analysis: An Essay on the Organization of Experience

0-930350-91-X NORTHEASTERN PB $18.00

Interaction Ritual: Essays in Face-to-Face Behavior

0-394-70631-5 PANTHEON PB $9.98

The Presentation of Self in Everyday Life

0-385-09402-7 DOUBLEDAY PB $9.95

Historical Sociology

Reinhard **Bendix**

Kings or People: Power and the Mandate to Rule

0-520-04090-2 CALIFORNIA PB $17.95

Michel **Foucault**

The Archaeology of Knowledge

0-394-71106-8 PANTHEON PB $10.65

Discipline and Punish

A dizzying treatment of modern methods of social regulation, focused on criminology and penology

0-679-75255-2 VINTAGE PB $12.00

The Birth of the Clinic: An Archaeology of Medical Perception

A fascinating study critiquing the "rationality" of psychological treatments

0-394-71097-5 VINTAGE PB $9.00

The History of Sexuality

Volume 1
An Introduction

An examination of how rationalist social systems attempt to control the human body

0-679-72469-9 VINTAGE PB $10.00

Volume 2
The Use of Pleasure

Foucault's last major project changed direction in the writing. Volume Two alone addresses the sexual mores of the Ancients. "Required reading for those who cling to stereotyped ideas about our difference from the Greeks in terms of pagan license versus Christian austerity or their hedonism versus our anxiety"
—*LA Times Book Review*

0-394-75122-1 VINTAGE PB $13.00

Volume 3
The Care of the Self

0-394-74155-2 RANDOM HOUSE PB $12.00

Madness and Civilization: A History of Insanity in the Age of Reason

This 1961 study of madness—from the medieval "ship of fools" to 19th- century efforts to correct insanity through moral instruction—was Foucault's first major work

See also **HISTORIES AND INTRODUCTIONS** under **PSYCHOLOGY**

0-679-72110-X VINTAGE PB $12.00

The Order of Things: An Archaeology of the Human Sciences

See also **OTHER 20TH-CENTURY PHILOSOPHERS** under **PHILOSOPHY** in **RELIGION, SPIRITUALITY, AND PHILOSOPHY**

0-679-75335-4 VINTAGE PB $13.00

Beatrice **Gottlieb**

The Family in the Western World: From the Black Death to the Industrial Age

This history arrives just in time to show how "family values" isn't the age-old concept many take it for. Before the Industrial Revolution, Gottlieb found, most women were single up until their mid 20s; most households were not large; and inheritance was a decisive factor in respectability

0-19-507344-4 OXFORD $30.00

Hans **Haferkamp** & Neil J. **Smelser**, editors

Social Change and Modernity

0-520-06828-9 CALIFORNIA PB $18.00

Orlando **Patterson**

Slavery and Social Death: A Comparative Study

0-674-81083-X HARVARD PB $22.50

Thomas **Kuhn**

Social Theory: The Multicultural and Classic Readings

This invaluable collection brings together writings on social theory and its relation to the evident multiplicity of human cultures. The section introductions also act as a quick history of sociology, covering everything from Weber and Durkheim to Jacques Derrida and Václav Havel. Easily the best one-volume introduction to social theory

EDITED BY CHARLES LEMERT

0-8133-1584-0 WESTVIEW PB $23.95

Thomas S. **Kuhn**

The Structure of Scientific Revolutions

The classic study of the development and displacement of scientific "paradigms"

See also **SCIENTIFIC THOUGHT AND DISCOVERY** under **SCIENCE AND TECHNOLOGY** in **SCIENCE**

0-226-45803-2 CHICAGO $25.00
0-226-45808-3 CHICAGO PB $10.95

Barrington **Moore**, Jr.

Injustice: The Social Basis of Obedience and Revolt

0-87332-114-6 SHARPE $84.95
0-87332-145-6 SHARPE PB $29.95

Social Origins of Dictatorship and Democracy

See also **FROM THE MEIJI RESTORATION TO THE END OF THE EMPIRE: 1868-1945** under **JAPAN** in **WORLD HISTORY AND CURRENT AFFAIRS**

0-8070-5073-3 BEACON PB $20.00

Theda **Skocpol**

Social Policy in the United States: Future Possibilities in Historical Perspective

0-691-03786-8 PRINCETON $39.50

States and Social Revolutions

0-521-29499-1 CAMBRIDGE PB $20.95

Vision and Method in Historical Sociology

0-521-29724-9 CAMBRIDGE PB $19.95

Charles **Tilly**

The Contentious French

A social historian on urban and provincial uprisings throughout the modern period

See also **FRANCE** under **REGIONAL AND NATIONAL HISTORIES** under **INTRODUCTIONS TO MODERN EUROPEAN HISTORY** in **WORLD HISTORY AND CURRENT AFFAIRS**

0-674-16695-7 HARVARD $32.50
0-674-16696-5 HARVARD PB $16.00

From Mobilization to Revolution

0-07-554851-8 MCGRAW HILL PB $45.75

David **Zaret**

The Heavenly Contract: Ideology and Organization in Pre-Revolutionary Puritanism

0-226-97882-6 CHICAGO $22.50

Class Structure

Class and class structure remained taboo subjects in American sociology until the 1930s. Since then, however, they have attracted many of the best sociologists in the country. Because Marxist and neo-Marxist students of class are listed elsewhere, only non-Marxist work is listed here.

Peter **Blau** & Otis D. **Duncan**
The American Occupational Structure
0-02-903670-4 FREE PRESS PB $15.95

Richard F. **Hamilton** & James **Wright**
The State of the Masses
0-202-30324-1 DE GRUYTER $49.95
0-202-30325-X DE GRUYTER PB $26.95

Melvin **Kohn**
Class and Conformity: A Study in Values
0-226-45026-0 CHICAGO PB $19.95

Gerhard **Lenski**
Power and Privilege: A Theory of Social Stratification
0-8078-4119-6 NORTH CAROLINA PB $17.95

Robert King **Merton**
On Social Structure and Science
EDITED BY PIOTR SZTOMPKA
0-226-52070-6 CHICAGO $55.00
0-226-52071-4 CHICAGO PB $19.95

Critical Commentary on American Culture

In the immediate postwar years America bathed in warm feelings of self-satisfaction; but from the 1950s on, critical voices, radical, liberal, and conservative were increasingly audible.

Carol J. **Adams**
Neither Man or Beast: Feminism and the Defense of Animals
0-8264-0670-X CONTINUUM $24.95

Robert N. **Bellah**
Habits of the Heart: Individualism and Commitment in American Life
Bellah argues that Americans' increasing passion for self-therapy has undermined their commitment to the larger community
0-520-05388-5 CALIFORNIA $39.95
0-06-097027-8 HARPERCOLLINS PB $13.00

Fox **Butterfield**
All God's Children: The Bosket Family and the American Tradition of Violence
See also **MODERN CRIMINAL CASES** under **TRUE CRIME** in **POPULAR READING**
0-394-58286-1 KNOPF $27.50

Jean **Baudrillard**
America
A delirious travelogue in which the wandering Frenchman tries to make sense of the U.S.
0-86091-978-1 VERSO PB $18.00

Jean Baudrillard

Cool Memories
TRANSLATED BY CHRIS TURNER
0-86091-500-X VERSO PB $19.00

Cool Memories II 1987-1990
TRANSLATED BY CHRIS TURNER
0-8223-1793-1 DUKE PB $15.95

Daniel **Bell**
The Coming of Post-Industrial Society: A Venture in Social Forecasting
0-465-09713-8 BASIC BOOKS PB $18.00

The Cultural Contradictions of Capitalism
This edition marks the 20th anniversary of Bell's influential text
0-465-01499-2 BASIC PB $16.95

The End of Ideology
This influential book appeared in 1960
0-674-25229-2 HARVARD $36.00

Sara **Diamond**
Roads to Dominion: Right-Wing Movements and Political Power in the United States
0-89862-864-4 GUILFORD PB $19.95

David B. **Feinberg**
Queer and Loathing: Rants and Raves of a Raging AIDS Clone
See also **AIDS** under **MEDICINE** in **SCIENCE**
0-670-85766-1 VIKING $22.95

Herbert J. **Gans**
The War Against the Poor: The Underclass and Anti-Poverty Policy
The eminent Columbia professor and contributor to the *New York Times Magazine* and *The Nation* addresses the ubiquitous marginalization in America today of the "underclass," a term that has come to include welfare recipients, the working poor, teenage mothers, drug addicts, the homeless, and other members of the wide and disparate spectrum of disadvantaged citizens. We will continue, Gans's powerful argument shows, to relegate so many people to this underclass only at an enormous societal cost. "Gans lays bare America's obsession with the poor…[This] may be a painful book to read, but we avoid it at our peril"—Andrew Hacker. "For anyone wishing to understand the roots of today's political revolution in Washington, [this book]…is the place to start"—Anthony Lukas
0-465-01990-0 BASIC $22.00
0-465-01991-9 BASIC PB $14.00

Marjorie **Garber**
Dog Love
A look at America's obsession with canines
0-684-81871-X SIMON & SCHUSTER $24.00

Shere **Hite**
The Hite Report on the Family: Growing Up Under Patriarchy
A statement signed by Stephen Jay Gould, Gloria Steinem, Susan Faludi, and others said: "The latest book by ground-breaking researcher Shere Hite could be a major contribution to the US's ongoing debate over…'family values'"
See also **HISTORY OF FAMILY LIFE** under **TOPICS IN AMERICAN STUDIES** in **HISTORY OF THE AMERICAS**
0-8021-1570-5 GROVE $22.00

Richard **Hofstadter**
The Paranoid Style in American Politics
A much-quoted study of the sociology of American politics, emphasizing the creation of enemies—foreign and domestic—in order to give structure to political life
0-674-65461-7 HARVARD PB $15.95

Laura **Lederer** & Richard **Delgado**, editors
The Price We Pay: The Case Against Racist Speech, Hate Propaganda, and Pornography
0-8090-7883-X HILL & WANG $30.00
0-8090-1577-3 HILL & WANG PB $15.00

Lawrence W **Levine**
Highbrow/Lowbrow: The Emergence of Cultural Hierarchy in America
0-674-39077-6 HARVARD PB $15.00

Marshall **McLuhan**
Understanding Media: The Extensions of Man
The classic on information theory
0-262-63159-8 MIT PB $14.95

Marianne **Macy**

Working Sex: An Odyssey into Our Cultural Underworld

Transsexuals, prostitutes, exotic dancers, porn producers, sexual surrogates. From inside the sex industry, journalist Macy reports on the forbidden world of sex for sale, and using this rare vantage addresses debates on controversial social issues. What is pornography? How does it affect society's treatment of women? What role does the government have in legislating morality? With a frame of reference that runs from Foucault to Lou Reed, Macy brings a fresh perspective to the thorny and fascinating issues of sexual politics

0-7867-0249-4 CARROLL & GRAF $23.00

C. Wright **Mills**

Mills was a preeminent voice of radical dissent in the 1950s.

The Power Elite

0-19-500680-1 OXFORD PB $15.95

The Sociological Imagination

A classic, highly influential critique of sociological thought

See also **POSTWAR AMERICAN THEORY** under **AMERICAN SOCIOLOGICAL THEORY**

0-19-500751-4 OXFORD PB $9.95

White Collar: The American Middle Classes

0-19-500677-1 OXFORD PB $12.95

Michael **Parenti**

Against Empire

A leading voice in progressive political commentary, Parenti eloquently addresses the secret policies and hidden costs of the US empire, such as the lingering need for a huge military, the enormous cost of the CIA, and subsidies to corporations and banks at the expense of dwindling social services. "Parenti writes clear, smooth, often provocative prose, has a way of cutting to the heart of complex issues and knows how to tell a story"
—Allan Johnson

0-87286-298-4 CITY LIGHTS PB $12.95

David **Riesman**

The Lonely Crowd: A Study of the Changing American Character

Published in 1950, this famous book became a bestseller, popularizing the phrases "inner-directed" and "other-directed"

0-300-00193-2 YALE PB $17.00

Andrew **Ross**

The Chicago Gangster Theory of Life

An argument against the idea of scarcity; includes an excellent chapter on the Pacific Islands

0-86091-429-1 VERSO $24.95
0-86091-654-5 VERSO PB $17.95

Douglas **Rushkoff**

Playing the Future: How Kids' Culture Can Teach Us to Thrive in an Uncertain Future

0-06-017310-6 HARPERCOLLINS $25.00

Peggy Reeves **Sanday**

Fraternity Gang Rape: Sex, Brotherhood and Privilege on Campus

Sanday, examining the sociological roots of a prevalent although until recently rarely discussed phenomenon, tells us why the perpetrators view gang rape as a rite of passage, how university administrations justify their "boys will be boys" view, and the manner in which the victim is ultimately held responsible

0-8147-7902-6 NYU $37.50
0-8147-7961-1 NYU PB $15.95

Ruth **Sidel**

Keeping Women and Children Last: America's War on the Poor

A renowned sociologist revisits the explosive issue of women, children, and poverty ten years after the publication of her landmark work *Women and Children Last*

See also **ECONOMICS** under **FEMINIST THEORY** under **WOMEN'S STUDIES**

0-14-024663-0 PENGUIN PB $11.95

Nathaniel **Wice** & Steven **Daly**

Alt.Culture: From Acid Jazz to Zippies: The Underground Bible

This unique guide introduces nearly 1,000 items of alternative culture. Monty Python to gangsta rap; Bob Marley to Courtney Love; Prozac to Ecstacy; date-rape to eco-terrorism; phreaks; on-line music—a guide for the perplexed to the world beyond the mainstream

0-06-273383-4 HARPERCOLLINS PB $17.00

Modernization and Developing Nations

In the first two decades after World War II, studies of modernization and the Third World tended to be written in an optimistic spirit, generally assuming that the newly independent countries would overcome their difficulties, catch up with the West, and participate in a worldwide tendency toward progress and development.

Since the mid-1960s, however, this approach has come under increasing attack. Neo-Marxists and other theorists hold that the Third World's progress is compromised by its post-colonial dependence. Such critics also stress that conservative forces in Third World nations are likely to remain major obstacles to future development.

Arturo **Escobar**

Encountering Development: The Making and Unmaking of the Third World

A thorough and engaging critique of the Western belief in "development" as a natural process by which non-Western societies catch up to the West. Escobar treats development economists as a sociological group subject to social pressure and with distinct limitations

0-691-00102-2 PRINCETON PB $15.95

Reinhard **Bendix**

Work and Authority in Industry: Ideologies of Management in the Course of Industrialization

0-520-02628-4 CALIFORNIA PB $15.00

Peter **Evans**

Dependent Development: The Alliance of Multinational, State, and Local Capital in Brazil

The most important examination of economic development in the past two decades

See also **BRAZIL** under **LATIN AMERICA AND THE CARIBBEAN** in **HISTORY OF THE AMERICAS**

0-691-02185-6 PRINCETON PB $14.95

Alex **Inkeles**

Exploring Individual Modernity

0-231-05442-4 COLUMBIA $49.50
0-231-05443-2 COLUMBIA PB $17.00

Lloyd **Rudolph** & Susanne **Rudolph**

The Modernity of Tradition: Political Development in India

0-226-73137-5 CHICAGO PB $19.50

Ethnicity and Race Relations

The 1980s and 1990s saw an explosion of writing about race relations as the poverty of nonwhites deepened and both political parties questioned the validity of the Civil Rights era strategies for improving the status of nonwhites, particularly blacks, in American society.

Theodore **Allen**

The Invention of the White Race: Racial Oppression and Social Control

Mainly examines the "prehistory" of white racism by exploring the development of racist ideas in English relations with the Irish

0-86091-660-X VERSO PB $19.95

Molefi K. **Asante**

The Afrocentric Idea

A clear statement of Afrocentrist thinking, arguing that black Americans need to center their identity on Africa, and that much of Western religious and secular thought has its origins in Africa

0-87722-573-7 TEMPLE PB $14.95

Lerone **Bennett**, Jr.

Before the Mayflower: A History of Black America

Several decades old, but still the most fascinating one-volume history of black America, widely used by later writers

0-87485-029-0 JOHNSON $25.00
0-14-017822-8 PENGUIN PB $15.95

Charles M. **Christian**

Black Saga: The African American Experience

A useful year-by-year reference

0-395-68717-9 DORLING KINDERSLEY $35.00

Stephen **Carter**

Reflections of an Affirmative Action Baby

Argues for conservatism as a dissent against civil-rights orthodoxy

See also **CURRENT POLITICAL THOUGHT AND ISSUES** under **AMERICAN POLITICS AND FOREIGN POLICY** in **HISTORY OF THE AMERICAS**

0-465-06869-3 BASIC PB $14.50

Colin **Crawford**

Uproar at Dancing Rabbit Creek: The Battle over Race, Class, and the Environment in the New South

See also **THE NEW SOUTH** under **AMERICAN REGIONAL HISTORY: THE WEST AND THE SOUTH** in **HISTORY OF THE AMERICAS**

0-201-62723-X ADDISON-WESLEY $24.00

W.E.B. **DuBois**

The Souls of Black Folk

First published in 1903, DuBois's witty, impassioned treatment of what it feels like to be a "problem" for white America remains popular today

See also **LEADERS AND ACTIVISTS** under **BLACK VOICES, BLACK LIVES** under **AFRICAN-AMERICAN STUDIES** in **HISTORY OF THE AMERICAS**

0-679-60187-2 MODERN LIBRARY $14.50
0-679-72519-9 VINTAGE PB $11.50

W.E.B. DuBois

Nathan **Glazer** & Daniel P. **Moynihan**

Beyond the Melting Pot: The Negroes, Puerto Ricans, Jews, Italians, and Irish of New York City

See also **IMMIGRATION** under **AMERICAN PEOPLE AND PLACES** in **HISTORY OF THE AMERICAS**

0-262-57022-X MIT PB $17.50

Raphael S. **Ezekiel**

The Racist Mind: Portraits of American Neo-Nazis and Klansmen

"A profoundly disturbing vision of the malaise rumbling around in the belly of America...uncomfortable but necessary reading"—Rosellen Brown

See also **NATIVISM, BIGOTRY, AND THE EXTREME RIGHT** under **ETHNIC AND RACE RELATIONS** under **AMERICAN PEOPLE AND PLACES** in **HISTORY OF THE AMERICAS**

0-670-83958-2 VIKING $24.95
0-14-023449-7 PENGUIN PB $12.95

Kevin K. **Gaines**

Uplifting the Race: Black Leadership, Politics, and Culture in the Twentieth Century

0-8078-4543-4 NORTH CAROLINA PB $17.95

Jennifer L. **Hochschild**

Facing up to the American Dream: Race, Class, and the Soul of the Nation

A study of the "American dream" among blacks. "The most substantial and informative of the new books on race"—*NY Review of Books*

0-691-02957-1 PRINCETON $29.95

Reginald **Horsman**

Race and Manifest Destiny: The Origins of American Racial Anglo-Saxonism

0-674-94805-X HARVARD PB $16.95

Winthrop D. **Jordan**

The White Man's Burden: The Historical Origins of Racism in the United States

In this book and the one following, Jordan laid the groundwork for 20th-century thinking about the origins of American racism

0-19-501743-9 OXFORD PB $10.95

White over Black: American Attitudes Toward the Negro, 1550-1812

0-8078-1055-X NORTH CAROLINA $50.00
0-8078-4550-7 EARLY AM HISTORY PB $16.95

Paul Gordon **Lauren**

Power and Prejudice: The Politics and Diplomacy of Racial Discrimination

0-8133-2143-3 WESTVIEW PB $22.95

Michael **Lind**

The Next American Nation: The Origins and Future of Our National Identity

Lind traces the centrality of whiteness in defining Americans, then urges a Fourth American Revolution to create a truly color-blind nation

0-02-919103-3 FREE PRESS $25.00

Glenn C. **Loury**

One by One from the Inside Out: Race and Responsibility in America

Advocates self-improvement for black Americans rather than demands on white society and government for equality

0-02-919441-5 FREE PRESS $25.00

Aldon D. **Morris**

The Origins of the Civil Rights Movement: Black Communities Organizing for Change

See also **THE CIVIL RIGHTS MOVEMENT AND BEYOND** under **AFRICAN-AMERICAN STUDIES** in **HISTORY OF THE AMERICAS**

0-02-922130-7 FREE PRESS PB $16.95

Charles **Murray** & Richard J. **Hernstein**

The Bell Curve: The Reshaping of American Life by Differences in Intelligence

This fantastically controversial book was much debated if rarely read. Building on highly dubious research, the authors argued that there may be a genetic difference in intelligence between blacks and whites

0-02-914673-9 FREE PRESS $30.00

Charles Murray

Richard **Polenberg**

One Nation Divisible: Class, Race and Ethnicity in the United States Since 1938

"Deftly manipulates a wide variety of materials, from the perplexing statistical profiles provided by government surveys to the work of social scientists Gunnar Myrdal, Ashley Montagu, and David Riesman, to the poetry of Nikki Giovanni and the fiction of Joseph Heller"
—Alan M. Kraut, *Washington Star*

See also **ETHNIC AND RACE RELATIONS** under **AMERICAN PEOPLE AND PLACES** in **HISTORY OF THE AMERICAS**

0-14-015999-1 VIKING PB $13.95

Jonathan **Rieder**

Canarsie: The Jews and Italians of Brooklyn Against Liberalism

PHOTOGRAPHS BY LAURENCE LEVIN

0-674-09361-5 HARVARD PB $12.95

David **Roediger**

The Wages of Whiteness: Race and the Making of the American Working Class

A study of racial identity and the American worker

0-86091-550-6 VERSO PB $18.00

Alexander **Saxton**

The Rise and Fall of the White Republic: Class Politics and Mass Culture in Nineteenth-Century America

Considers the centrality of white identity to the construction of the American nation

0-86091-986-2 VERSO PB $22.95

Ilan **Stavans**

The Hispanic Condition: Reflections on Culture and Identity in America

A moving meditation on the "hyphenated" nature of being Hispanic in America

0-06-092693-7 HARPERPERENNIAL PB $13.00

Shelby **Steele**

The Content of Our Character: A New Vision of Race in America

Steele maintains that America is essentially a post-racist society, a key argument in black conservatism intended to show that blacks should drop an illusory "victim" status

0-06-097415-X HARPERCOLLINS PB $12.00

Alders **Stephanson**

Manifest Destiny: American Expansion and the Empire of Right

An engaging study of several centuries of American expansionism and its relation to white identity

0-8090-6721-8 HILL & WANG $17.95
0-8090-1584-6 HILL & WANG PB $7.95

Ronald **Takaki**

Takaki writes with unusual clarity and erudition about race in America, whether in the past or today. His work also introduces Asian Americans into a debate normally dominated by blacks and whites.

A Different Mirror: The Making of Multicultural America

0-316-83112-3 LITTLE, BROWN $29.95
0-316-83111-5 LITTLE, BROWN PB $13.95

Strangers from a Different Shore: A History of Asian-Americans

0-14-013885-4 PENGUIN PB $13.95

Urban Sociology

This popular field of inquiry was largely developed at the University of Chicago in the first half of this century. The major impetus came from Robert Park (1864-1944), who wrote many articles and introductions to his students' work but no full-scale book. Louis Wirth's *The Ghetto* (1928), an exemplary study of the Jewish ghetto, was largely inspired by Park's principles. The study of urban phenomena, somewhat neglected in the postwar years, has recently undergone a vigorous revival.

Elijah **Anderson**

Streetwise: Race, Class, and Change in an Urban Community

0-226-01816-4 CHICAGO PB $12.95

Mike **Davis**

City of Quartz: Excavating the Future of Los Angeles

A landmark study of the social politics of Los Angeles

0-679-73806-1 VINTAGE PB $14.00

W.E.B. **DuBois**

The Philadelphia Negro: A Social Study

First published in 1899 and surprisingly relevant today, DuBois's work was among the first to combine urban ethnography, statistics, and social history

0-8122-1573-7 PENNSYLVANIA PB $16.95

Claude S. **Fischer**

To Dwell Among Friends: Personal Networks in Town and City

0-226-25138-1 CHICAGO PB $22.00

The Urban Experience

0-15-593498-8 HARCOURT BRACE PB $19.95

Donna **Gaines**

Teenage Wasteland: America's Dead End Kids

0-06-097477-X HARPERPERENNIAL PB $12.50

Herbert J. **Gans**

The Levittowners: Ways of Life and Politics in a New Suburban Community

0-231-05570-6 COLUMBIA $59.00
0-231-05571-4 COLUMBIA PB $19.95

The Urban Villagers

0-02-911240-0 FREE PRESS PB $15.95

Jane **Jacobs**

The Economy of Cities

"This book is radiant with ideas about what makes cities rich or poor, how cities grow, and how city growth affects national economies"
—*New Yorker*

See also **CITIES AND CITY PLANNING** under **CRITICISM** under **20TH-CENTURY ARCHITECTURE** in **ARCHITECTURE, DESIGN, AND HOMES**

0-394-70584-X RANDOM HOUSE PB $10.00

Martin Sanchez **Jankowski**

Islands in the Streets: Gangs and American Urban Society

0-520-07434-3 CALIFORNIA PB $14.95

Alex **Kotlowitz**

There Are No Children Here: The Story of Two Boys Growing Up in America

A moving recent profile of two African-American boys in a Chicago housing project

0-385-26556-5 ANCHOR PB $12.95

Jonathan **Kozol**

Amazing Grace: The Lives of Children and the Conscience of a Nation

See also **THE POOR** under **AMERICAN PEOPLE AND PLACES** in **HISTORY OF THE AMERICAS**

0-517-79999-5 CROWN $23.00
0-06-097697-7 HARPERPERENNIAL PB $13.50

Robert S. **Lynd** & Helen M. **Lynd**

Middletown

0-15-659550-8 HARCOURT BRACE PB $13.95

Lewis **Mumford**

The Culture of Cities

0-15-623301-0 HARCOURT BRACE PB $22.00

Lewis Mumford

Robert E. **Park**

The City

0-226-64611-4 CHICAGO PB $15.95

Jeanne **Schinto**

Huddle Fever: Living in the Immigrant City

0-679-42121-1 KNOPF $24.00

Arthur J. **Vidich** & Joseph **Bensman**

Town in Mass Society: Class, Power and Religion in a Rural Community

0-691-02807-9 PRINCETON PB $19.95

Gerald **Suttles**
The Social Order of the Slum
0-226-78192-5 CHICAGO PB $12.95

William F. **Whyte**
Street Corner Society: The Social Structure of an Italian Slum
0-226-89545-9 CHICAGO PB $14.95

William Julius **Wilson**
The Truly Disadvantaged: The Inner City, the Underclass and Public Policy
See also **RACE RELATIONS** under **AFRICAN-AMERICAN STUDIES** in **HISTORY OF THE AMERICAS**
See also **SPECIAL STUDIES** under **URBAN AMERICA** under **AMERICAN PEOPLE AND PLACES** in **HISTORY OF THE AMERICAS**
0-226-90131-9 CHICAGO PB $13.95

William Julius **Wilson**, editor
The Ghetto Underclass
See also **SPECIAL STUDIES** under **URBAN AMERICA** under **AMERICAN PEOPLE AND PLACES** in **HISTORY OF THE AMERICAS**
0-8039-5272-4 SAGE PB $19.95

When Work Disappears: The World of the New Urban Poor
0-394-57935-6 KNOPF $26.00

Harvey **Zorbaugh**
The Gold Coast and the Slum: A Sociological Study of Chicago's Near Northside
0-226-98945-3 CHICAGO PB $22.00

Crime, Delinquency, and Deviance

Howard **Becker**
Outsiders: Studies in the Sociology of Deviance
"The most instructive and most interesting introduction to the subject of deviant behavior available"—Albert K. Cohen
See also **SOCIAL PSYCHOLOGY** under **PSYCHOLOGY**
0-02-902140-5 FREE PRESS PB $14.95

Donald **Black**
The Behavior of Law
0-12-102652-3 ACADEMIC PRESS PB $33.00

Phillipe **Bourgois**
In Search of Respect: Selling Crack in El Barrio
0-521-43518-8 CAMBRIDGE $25.00
0-521-57460-9 CAMBRIDGE PB $15.95

Albert K. **Cohen**
Delinquent Boys: The Culture of the Gang
0-02-905770-1 FREE PRESS PB $13.95

Steven R. **Donziger**, editor
The Real War on Crime: The Report of the National Criminal Justice Commission, First Edition
0-06-095165-6 HARPERPERENNIAL PB $15.00

Kai T. **Erikson**
Wayward Puritans: A Study in the Sociology of Deviance
0-02-332200-4 MACMILLAN PB $26.67

David O. **Friedrichs**
Trusted Criminals: White Collar Crime in Contemporary Society
0-534-50517-1 WADSWORTH PB $33.25

Timothy J. **Gilfoyle**
City of Eros: New York City, Prostitution, and the Commercialization of Sex, 1790-1920
Gilfoyle's pioneering work makes it clear that the business of sex played an integral part in forming New York's neighborhoods, social roles, and politics. "A revealing peek at a Gotham that exceeded our own anything-goes sexual license and urban misery"—*Kirkus Reviews*
See also **PROSTITUTION** under **HISTORY OF SEXUALITY** under **TOPICS IN AMERICAN STUDIES** in **HISTORY OF THE AMERICAS**
0-393-02800-3 NORTON $24.95
0-393-31108-2 NORTON PB $13.95

Wendy **Kaminer**
It's All the Rage: Crime and Culture
"No one concerned about crime policy should miss Kaminer's trenchant analysis"—*Booklist*
0-201-48833-7 ADDISON-WESLEY PB $13.00

Robert K. **Merton** & Robert **Nisbet**, editors
Contemporary Social Problems
0-15-513793-X HARCOURT BRACE $40.23

Sanyika **Shakur**
Monster: The Autobiography of an L.A. Gang Member
A fearless, terrifying memoir of growing up in the 1980s
0-14-023225-7 PENGUIN PB $10.95

Charles **Silberman**
Criminal Violence-Criminal Justice: Criminals, Police, Courts and Prisons in America
0-394-74147-1 RANDOM HOUSE PB $11.54

Edwin **Sutherland**
White Collar Crime: The Uncut Version
EDITED WITH AN INTRODUCTION BY GILBERT GEIS & COLIN GOFF
0-300-02921-7 YALE $42.00
0-300-03318-4 YALE PB $19.00

Gresham **Sykes**
Criminology, 2nd Edition
0-15-516118-0 HARCOURT BRACE $63.18

Terry **Williams**
Crack House: Notes from the End of the Line
Williams, a sociologist, virtually lived in a crackhouse with a "family" of crack users in New York to write this close, detailed, moving, and revealing study. An original ethnographic study of a people outside the mainstream, by a brilliant sociologist who writes without a word of jargon
0-201-56759-8 ADDISON-WESLEY $17.95

James Q. **Wilson**
Thinking About Crime
A leading conservative voice in the debate about crime
0-394-72917-X RANDOM HOUSE PB $13.00

James Q. **Wilson** & Richard J. **Hernstein**
Crime and Human Nature
0-671-62810-0 SIMON & SCHUSTER PB $17.00

James Q. Wilson

Texts and Reference

Lewis A. **Coser**
Introduction to Sociology
0-15-545919-8 HARCOURT BRACE PB $47.88

Dushkin Publishing Group
Encyclopedic Dictionary of Sociology
0-87967-886-0 DUSHKIN PB $12.45

Robert A. **Nisbet**
The Sociological Tradition
1-56000-667-6 TRANSACTION PB $21.95

Bryan **Turner**, editor
The Blackwell Companion to Social Theory
0-631-18399-X BLACKWELL $59.95
0-631-18401-5 BLACKWELL PB $24.95

Economics

Economics is the only social science comparable to the natural sciences in rigor and explanatory method. Like the phenomena treated by physics or chemistry, the data of economic life are pervasive and seemingly explainable by common-sense procedures. But the explanations of economic data, like those of physical states, go deeper than the connecting of observable events and may involve sophisticated mathematics. Economists explain the magnitude of prices and incomes by seeking out forces that exceed the wills, and even the comprehension, of most retailers and employers.

Economists must be sensitive to the historical nature of their discipline. The laws of economics may be true everywhere at present, but they have not always been true. Economic analysis has emerged under the particular conditions of capitalism, and its history is mainly a record of corrections imposed on pure theory by changes in economic life. Economists are thus forced to make an assumption that no physicist would accept: they assume that the laws of their science are subject to change by human action and can be useful in guiding that action.

General Works and Histories of Economic Thought

Christine **Ammer** & Dean S. **Ammer**

Dictionary of Business and Economics

Valuable for its emphasis on the application of economic ideas

0-02-900790-9 MACMILLAN........$40.00
0-02-901480-8 MACMILLAN PB........$29.95

Mark **Blaug**

Economic Theory in Retrospect

Excellent history by a neoclassical economist, for advanced students. Illustrated

0-521-31644-8 CAMBRIDGE PB........$29.95

Ronald H. **Coase**

Essays on Economics and Economists

Accessible recent essays by a distinguished economist

0-226-11103-2 CHICAGO PB........$12.95

Phyllis **Deane**

The Evolution of Economic Ideas

A streamlined history of difficult concepts by an authority on the industrial revolution in Britain

0-521-29315-4 CAMBRIDGE PB........$19.95

Maurice **Dobb**

Theories of Value and Distribution Since Adam Smith

Theories of value and price determination by a leading English Marxist

0-521-09936-6 CAMBRIDGE PB........$24.95

John **Eatwell** & others, editors

The New Palgrave: A Dictionary of Economics

The finest dictionary of economics and probably the best of all social-science reference works; available in a four-volume set

1-561-59041X-8 STOCKTON........$595.00

New Palgrave: Time Series & Statistics

0-393-95862-0 NORTON PB........$18.95

Capital Theory

0-393-95855-8 NORTON PB........$15.95

Finance

0-393-95857-4 NORTON PB........$14.95

Game Theory

0-393-95858-2 NORTON PB........$14.95

Amitai **Etzioni**

The Moral Dimension: Toward a New Economics

0-02-909901-3 FREE PRESS PB........$17.95

John Kenneth **Galbraith**

Economics in Perspective: A Critical History

The author is characteristically opinionated and irreverent in this survey of economic doctrines

0-395-48346-8 HOUGHTON MIFFLIN PB........$14.95

A Journey Through Economic Time: A Firsthand View

Galbraith's 30th book sums up his remarkable vision of 20th-century economic history, from the Russian Revolution and the "superbly insane decade of the twenties" to Reaganomics and the implications of communism's fall. The professor emeritus from Harvard treats us to his hindsight both as historian and participant in the shaping of the economic policies of the world

0-395-63751-1 HOUGHTON MIFFLIN........$24.95
0-395-74175-0 DORLING KINDERSLEY PB........$11.95

Short History of Financial Euphoria

0-14-023856-5 PENGUIN PB........$8.95

Robert L. **Heilbroner**

Behind the Veil of Economics: Essays in the Worldly Philosophy

0-393-30577-5 NORTON PB........$7.95

Teachings from the Worldly Philosophy

Heilbroner takes us on a tour through the history of economic thought from Aquinas to Adam Smith, Malthus, and John Maynard Keynes. The reader discovers the sturdiest principles of economic thought in a clearly written, thought-provoking guide

0-393-03919-6 NORTON........$27.50

The Worldly Philosophers: The Lives, Times, and Ideas of the Great Economic Thinkers

History of economic thought that examines the theories of such major figures as Smith, Ricardo, and Marx. Well-written and accessible

See also **PROTEST, REFORM, AND THE NEW ECONOMIC THOUGHT** under **THE 19TH CENTURY AND THE INDUSTRIAL REVOLUTION** under **GREAT BRITAIN AND IRELAND** in **WORLD HISTORY AND CURRENT AFFAIRS**

0-671-63318-X TOUCHSTONE PB........$14.00

Robert **Lekachman**

Capitalism for Beginners

Accessible, informative, and well illustrated

0-04-320195-4 WRITERS & READERS PB........$6.95

Joel **Mokyr**

The Lever of Riches: Technological Creativity and Economic Progress

A survey of creativity through history examining how Western countries can maintain, and developing nations can tap, their creative potential

0-19-507477-7 OXFORD PB........$14.95

Jurg **Niehans**

A History of Economic Theory: Classic Contributions, 1720-1980

0-8018-4976-4 JOHNS HOPKINS PB........$25.95

John **O'Shaughnessy**

Why People Buy

0-19-504087-2 OXFORD PB........$15.95

Michael **Parkin**

Economics

The third edition of a successful college textbook

0-201-53762-1 ADDISON-WESLEY........$61.28

David W. **Pearce**, editor

The MIT Dictionary of Modern Economics

0-262-66078-4 MIT PB........$18.50

Sidney **Pollard**, editor

Wealth and Poverty: An Economic History of the 20th Century

A lively survey of this century's economic history, designed for general readers usually intimidated by economics. Special features include debates on questions of particular importance: urban unemployment, the destruction of rainforests, Japanese management techniques

0-19-520821-8 OXFORD........$40.00

Paul **Samuelson** & William **Nordhaus**

Economics

The standard college text, written from the neoclassical standpoint but open to other approaches

0-07-054879-X MCGRAW HILL........$60.95

Charles E. **Staley**

A History of Economic Thought from Aristotle to Arrow

1-55786-031-9 BLACKWELL PB........$32.50

Herbert **Stein** & Murray **Foss**

An Illustrated Guide to the American Economy: A Hundred Key Issues

"A surprising little book by clear thinking authors"—*The Wall Street Journal*

0-8447-3801-8 AEI PB........$14.95

Pierre **Vilar**
A History of Gold and Money, 1450-1920
With almost obsessive attention, Vilar traces the history of gold and money as symbols of value that often drive men mad—solid economics, with a keen, sometimes comic grasp of social relations
TRANSLATED BY JUDITH WHITE
0-86091-798-3 VERSO PB..............................$19.95

Great Economists

Adam Smith

Adam **Smith**
Adam Smith (1723-1790) was the father of economics. He originated the idea that the unrestricted operations of a free market have the status of natural law; he was the first to note the importance of the division of labor and to hypothesize that the value of a commodity corresponds to its labor input.

The Wealth of Nations
First published in 1776
EDITED BY ANDREW SKINNER
0-14-043208-6 PENGUIN PB..............................$9.95

The Wealth of Nations
0-679-40564-X EVERYMAN'S..............................$20.00
0-679-42473-3 MODERN LIBRARY..............................$21.00

Thomas Malthus

Thomas **Malthus**
Thomas Malthus (1766-1834) was an economic pessimist who argued that increases in population would nullify gains in productivity and lead to widespread impoverishment.

An Essay on the Principle of Population
EDITED BY PHILIP APPLEMAN
0-393-09202-X NORTON PB..............................$10.95

David Ricardo

David **Ricardo**
David Ricardo (1772-1823) deepened Smith's economic vision by emphasizing conditions of production, thus clearing the way for Marx.

Works and Correspondence of David Ricardo: Principles of Political Economy
EDITED BY PIERO SRAFFA
0-521-28505-4 CAMBRIDGE PB..............................$29.95

John Stuart Mill

John Stuart **Mill**
Mill (1806-1873) offered a great synthesis of the major doctrines of classical political economy. He also introduced a supply-and-demand explanation of prices and an account of industrial growth that accommodated trade unionism.

Principles of Political Economy
See also **CLASSICS** under **POLITICAL THOUGHT**
EDITED BY DONALD WINCH
0-14-043260-4 PENGUIN PB..............................$11.95

Karl Marx

Karl **Marx**
Capital: A Critique of Political Economy
Volume 1
See also **MARX** under **PHILOSOPHY** in **RELIGION, SPIRITUALITY, AND PHILOSOPHY**
0-14-044568-4 PENGUIN PB..............................$15.95

Volume 2
0-14-044569-2 PENGUIN PB..............................$14.95

Volume 3
0-14-044570-6 PENGUIN PB..............................$14.95

Contribution to the Critique of Political Economy
0-7178-0041-5 INTERNATIONAL PUB PB..............................$5.95

Value, Price and Profit
TRANSLATED BY EDWARD AVELING
EDITED BY ELEANOR M. AVELING
0-88286-030-5 KERR PB..............................$5.00

Karl **Marx** & Frederich **Engels**
Collected Works
0-7178-0537-9 INTERNATIONAL PUB..............................$24.95

Paul A. **Baran** & Paul M. **Sweezy**
Monopoly Capital: An Essay on the American Economic and Social Order
An influential updating and reapplication of Marxist theory
0-85345-073-0 MONTHLY REVIEW PB..............................$18.00

Isaiah **Berlin**
Karl Marx: Life and Environment
The classic study, newly revised
0-19-520052-7 OXFORD PB..............................$9.95

G.A. **Cohen**
Karl Marx's Theory of History: A Defence
Arguably the most important work on Marxian social philosophy published in English in the last 50 years
See also **MARX** under **PHILOSOPHY** in **RELIGION, SPIRITUALITY, AND PHILOSOPHY**
See also **LEFTISM AND MARXISM** under **POLITICAL THOUGHT**
0-691-02008-6 PRINCETON PB..............................$17.95

Duncan K. **Foley**
Understanding *Capital*
A helpful guide to a forbidding work
0-674-92087-2 HARVARD..............................$24.00
0-674-92088-0 HARVARD PB..............................$15.95

Robert L. **Heilbroner**
Marxism: For and Against
A balanced appraisal of the economics of Marx and of his various disciples
0-393-95166-9 NORTON PB..............................$7.95

Ernest **Mandel**
The Marxist Theory of Alienation
0-87348-229-8 PATHFINDER..............................$30.00

Ronald L. **Meek**
Studies in the Labor Theory of Value
Valuable for its historical discussion of the sources of Marx's theories
0-85345-428-0 MONTHLY REVIEW PB..............................$10.00

I.I. **Rubin**
Essays on Marx's Theory of Value
An outstanding explication of the labor theory of value, by an early Soviet economist
TRANSLATED BY MILOS SAMARDZIJA & FREDY PERLMAN
0-919618-18-9 TORONTO PB..............................$18.99

Paul M. **Sweezy**
The Theory of Capitalist Development
A setting forth of Marxian concepts by the leading American Marxist economist of his time
0-85345-079-X MONTHLY REVIEW PB..............................$18.00

Alfred Marshall

Alfred **Marshall**
Alfred Marshall (1842-1924) was the principal architect of neoclassical economics and the developer of the modern theory of marginal utility

Principles of Economics
0-87991-051-8 PORCUPINE PB..............................$28.95

Friedrich von Hayek

Friedrich von **Hayek**
Friedrich von Hayek (1899-1992) offers the strongest modern argument for the political benefits of unregulated economic activity

Individualism and Economic Order
See also **CONSERVATISM** under **POLITICAL THOUGHT**
0-226-32093-6 CHICAGO PB..............................$16.95

Hayek on Hayek
An excellent introductory volume, unusually clear and concise
EDITED BY STEPHEN KRESGE AND LEIF WENAR
0-226-32062-6 CHICAGO..............................$27.50

Andrew **Gamble**
Hayek: The Iron Cage of Liberty
Gamble traces Hayek's development from his roots in Austrian economics and English liberalism to his critiques of socialism and conservatism, and argues that Hayek the social scientist must be separated from Hayek the ideologue before his insights can be fully appreciated
0-8133-3125-0 WESTVIEW..............................$51.00
0-8133-3126-9 WESTVIEW PB..............................$19.95

Steve **Fleetwood**

Hayek's Political Economy: The Socio-Economics of Order

0-415-12909-5 ROUTLEDGE $69.95

John Maynard Keynes

John Maynard **Keynes**

John Maynard Keynes (1883-1946) was the greatest economist of the 20th century. He not only revolutionized his discipline but also brought about changes in the economic policies of governments throughout the world.

The Economic Consequences of the Peace

A masterpiece of applied economics. Keynes foresaw the dire consequences of leaving Germany insolvent after World War I

INTRODUCTION BY ROBERT LEKACHMAN

0-14-011380-0 PENGUIN PB $12.00

General Theory of Employment, Interest and Money

Keynes's most complete elaboration of his theory that government investment will stimulate employment and reinvigorate depressed economies. First published in 1936

0-15-634711-3 HARCOURT BRACE PB....................$10.95

G.L. **Shackle**

The Years of High Theory: Invention and Tradition in Economic Thought, 1926-1939

A lively intellectual history of a rich period in economics that began with the first serious assaults on Marshall's theory of competition and ended with the deification of Keynes

0-521-27478-8 CAMBRIDGE PB....................$19.95

Robert **Skidelsky**

John Maynard Keynes, Volume I: Hope Betrayed, 1883-1920

The well-received first volume of Skidelsky's examination of one of the 20th century's most prominent and influential economists

See also **20TH-CENTURY BIOGRAPHY** under **GREAT BRITAIN AND IRELAND** in **WORLD HISTORY AND CURRENT AFFAIRS**

0-14-023554-X PENGUIN PB $15.95

John Maynard Keynes, Volume II: The Economist as Savior, 1920-1937

Skidelsky's second volume follows Keynes into his most productive period as an economist, when he "set out to save a capitalist system he did not admire." Includes clear, concise explanations of his central theories

See also **20TH-CENTURY BIOGRAPHY** under **GREAT BRITAIN AND IRELAND** in **WORLD HISTORY AND CURRENT AFFAIRS**

0-14-023806-9 PENGUIN PB....................$16.95

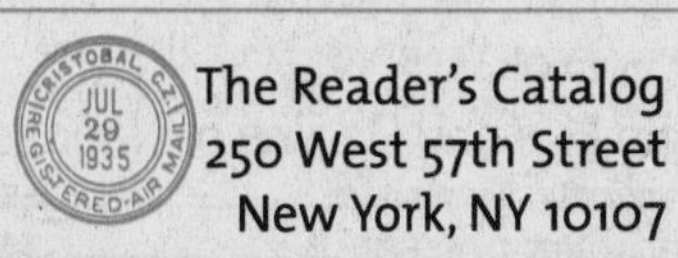

The Reader's Catalog
250 West 57th Street
New York, NY 10107

John Maynard Keynes

Contemporary Economists

Kenneth J. **Arrow**

Collected Papers of Kenneth J. Arrow

Volume 1 Choice and Justice

0-674-13760-4 HARVARD $32.00

Volume 2 General Equilibrium

0-674-13761-2 HARVARD $37.50

Volume 3 Individual Choice Under Certainty and Uncertainty

0-674-13762-0 HARVARD....................$36.00

Volume 4 The Economics of Information

0-674-13763-9 HARVARD....................$36.00

Volume 5 Production and Capital

0-674-13777-9 HARVARD $45.00

Volume 6 Applied Economics

0-674-13778-7 HARVARD $37.50

Gerard **Debreu**

Theory of Value: An Axiomatic Analysis of Economic Equilibrium

Debreu has developed, in partnership with Kenneth Arrow, the theory of general equilibrium; heavily mathematical

0-300-01559-3 YALE PB....................$12.00

Robert L. **Heilbroner**

Vision of the Future

"This is an exceedingly long short book," writes Heilbroner, economist, author and essayist, "stretching at least fifty thousand years into the past and who knows how many into the future"

0-19-509074-8 OXFORD....................$19.95

Paul **Samuelson**

Economics from the Heart: A Samuelson Sampler

EDITED BY MARYANN O. KEATING

0-913878-30-8 THOMAS HORTON & DAUGHTERS PB $5.95

Foundations of Economic Analysis

An important book, but highly mathematical

0-674-31301-1 HARVARD....................$34.95
0674313038 HARVARD PB $12.95

Robert M. **Solow**

Growth Theory: An Exposition

0-19-505609-4 OXFORD PB....................$14.95

Piero **Sraffa**

Production of Commodities by Means of Commodities

One of the most important works in economic theory after Keynes's *General Theory*. Sraffa resurrects Ricardo's theory of value, adjusts it to meet current requirements for explanations of value and price, and reaches conclusions that are similar to the tenets of general equilibrium developed by Arrow and Debreu from a completely different tradition; moderately advanced mathematics

0-521-09969-2 CAMBRIDGE PB....................$18.95

James **Tobin**

Asset Accumulation and Economic Activity

0-226-80502-6 CHICAGO PB....................$5.95

Essays in Economics

Volume 1 Macroeconomics

0-262-20062-7 MIT....................$67.50

Volume 2 Consumption and Economics

0-262-20064-3 MIT....................$65.00

Policies for Prosperity: Essays in a Keynesian Mode

EDITED BY PETER JACKSON

0-262-20066-X MIT....................$50.00

Milton Friedman and Monetarism

Milton **Friedman**

Capitalism and Freedom

Friedman is the principal exponent of monetarism, the view that the quantity of money is the determining factor in economic life

0-226-26401-7 CHICAGO PB....................$10.95

Milton **Friedman**
Essays in Positive Economics
0-226-26403-3 CHICAGO PB $19.95

Milton **Friedman** & Rose **Friedman**
Free to Choose: A Personal Statement
The bestselling polemic for a free-market society, from the conservative economist and his wife
0-15-133481-1 HARCOURT BRACE $16.95

N. Gregory **Mankiw**, editor
Monetary Policy
From a neo-Keynesian at Harvard
0-226-50308-9 CHICAGO $50.00

N. Gregory **Mankiw** & David **Romer**
The New Keynesian Economics
Volume 1
Imperfect Competition and Stickey Prices
0-262-63133-4 MIT PB $23.00
Volume 2
Coordination Failures and Real Rigidities
0-262-63134-2 MIT PB $23.00

Thomas **Mayer**
The Structure of Monetarism
0-393-09045-0 NORTON $11.95

Alan E.H. **Speight**
Consumption, Rational Expectations, and Liquidity: Theory and Evidence
0-312-04244-2 ST. MARTIN'S $39.95

Socialism

Joseph S. **Berliner**
Soviet Industry from Stalin to Gorbachev: Studies in Management and Innovation
Essays written over 35 years analyzing the structural problems that hampered Soviet economic performance since the Stalin Revolution
0-8014-2170-5 CORNELL $42.50

Maurice **Dobb**
Welfare Economics and the Elements of Socialism
0-521-07462-2 CAMBRIDGE $59.95
0-521-09937-4 CAMBRIDGE PB $24.95

David **Lane**
The End of Social Inequality: Class, Status and Power Under State Socialism
0-04-323025-3 UNWIN HYMAN PB $12.95

Alec **Nove**
The Economics of Feasible Socialism
0-04-446015-5 ROUTLEDGE PB $19.95

The Soviet Economic System
An introduction to the Soviet economy, updated to include an analysis of Gorbachev's reforms
0-04-335035-6 UNWIN HYMAN $29.50

Joseph A. **Schumpeter**
Capitalism, Socialism and Democracy
In this famous book, first published in 1942, Schumpeter predicts that capitalism will be crippled by its own achievements and will naturally evolve into socialism
0-8446-6027-2 SMITH $27.50

Paul M. **Sweezy**
Post-Revolutionary Society: Essays
0-85345-550-3 MONTHLY REVIEW $12.50
0-85345-551-1 MONTHLY REVIEW PB $10.00

Imperialism

Kenneth E. **Boulding** &
Tapan **Mukerjee**, editors
Economic Imperialism: A Book of Readings
0-472-08170-5 MICHIGAN PB $14.95

J.A. **Hobson**
Imperialism
The term "imperialism" exploded into general use in the 1890s. When the British liberal J.A. Hobson wrote his study in 1902 it was "on everybody's lips…and used to denote the most powerful movement in the current politics of the western world." Hobson stressed economic motivations and the need for outlets for "surplus capital" as the cause of expansion
See also **THE NEW IMPERIALISM** under **19TH-CENTURY EUROPE** in **WORLD HISTORY AND CURRENT AFFAIRS**
INTRODUCTION BY P. SIEGELMAN
0-472-06103-8 MICHIGAN PB $17.95

V.I. **Lenin**
Imperialism: The Highest Stage of Capitalism
A radical "student" of Hobson, Lenin argued a decade later that the new imperialism had economic roots in a new *phase* of capitalism, which resulted in "the territorial division of the world among the great capitalist powers"
See also **THE NEW IMPERIALISM** under **19TH-CENTURY EUROPE** in **WORLD HISTORY AND CURRENT AFFAIRS**
0-7178-0098-9 INTERNATIONAL PUB PB $2.95

Wolfgang J. **Mommsen**
Theories of Imperialism
TRANSLATED BY P.S. FALLA
0-226-53396-4 CHICAGO PB $13.00

Joseph A. **Schumpeter**
Imperialism and Social Classes
TRANSLATED BY HEINZ NORDEN
EDITED WITH AN INTRODUCTION BY PAUL M. SWEEZY
0-678-00020-4 AUGUSTUS KELLY $27.50

Economic Development and International Trade

Jagdish **Bhagwati**
Protectionism
0-262-02282-6 MIT $20.00

Richard E. **Caves**
Multinational Enterprise and Economic Growth
0-521-27115-0 CAMBRIDGE PB $23.95

W.M. **Corden**
Inflation, Exchange Rates, and the World Economy: Lectures on International Monetary Economics
0-226-11582-8 CHICAGO PB $12.95

Nigel **Harris**
The End of the Third World: Newly Industrializing Countries and the Decline of an Ideology
0-941533-14-X NEW AMSTERDAM $24.95

Albert O. **Hirschman**
The Passions and the Interests: Political Arguments for Capitalism Before Its Triumph
The debate over the justification of economic gain (and hence capitalism) in this era
See also **THE TRIUMPH OF CAPITALISM** under **THE EXPANSION OF EUROPE: EMPIRE AND COMMERCE** under **EARLY MODERN EUROPE** in **WORLD HISTORY AND CURRENT AFFAIRS**
0-691-00357-2 PRINCETON PB $12.95

Simon **Kuznets**
Growth, Population and Income Distribution
0-393-95061-1 NORTON $19.95

Staffan B. **Linder**
The Pacific Century: Economic and Political Consequences of Asian-Pacific Dynamism
See also **EAST ASIA AS ECONOMIC AND POLITICAL REGION: GENERAL STUDIES** under **SOUTHEAST ASIA AND THE PHILIPPINES** in **WORLD HISTORY AND CURRENT AFFAIRS**
0-8047-1294-8 STANFORD $27.50
0-8047-1305-7 STANFORD PB $11.95

Gerald M. **Meier** & Dudley **Seers**, editors
Pioneers in Development
0-19-520479-4 OXFORD PB $14.95

Mancur **Olson**
The Rise and Decline of Nations
0-300-02307-3 YALE $37.00
0-300-03079-7 YALE PB $15.00

Amartya **Sen**

Collective Choice and Social Welfare

0-444-85127-5 ELSEVIER $102.50

Resources, Values, and Development

0-674-76525-7 HARVARD $44.50

The Standard of Living

0-521-32101-8 CAMBRIDGE $47.95
0-521-36840-5 CAMBRIDGE PB $11.95

L.S. **Stavrianos**

Global Rift: The Third World Comes of Age

0-688-00657-4 MORROW PB $17.95

Politics and the International Economy

Michael **Albert**

Capitalism Versus Capitalism

Given the crippling deficit with which supply-side economics left America, did capitalism really triumph over communism with the fall of the Soviet Union? Albert, a leading European businessman, proposes an alternative to the economics of Reaganism: the Rhine Model, practiced in Europe and Japan, emphasizes collective achievement, public consensus, and a balanced society. A lucid, nontechnical account of a possible future global economy

1-56858-004-5 FOUR WALLS $25.95
1-56858-005-3 FOUR WALLS PB $12.95

Richard **Barnet** & John **Cavanaugh**

Global Dreams: Imperial Corporations and the New World Order

0-684-80027-6 TOUCHSTONE PB $15.00

Benjamin J. **Cohen**

In Whose Interest?: International Banking and American Foreign Policy

0-300-03614-0 YALE $40.00

Charles **Kindleberger**

Economic Response: Comparative Studies in Trade, Finance, and Growth

0-674-23025-6 HARVARD $31.00

Manias, Panics, and Crashes: A History of Financial Crises

The author, a professor emeritus at MIT, shows how financial institutions disintegrate and recommends seeking out a "lender of the last resort." Originally published in 1980

See also INTERNATIONAL POLITICAL ECONOMY under INTERNATIONAL RELATIONS AND STRATEGIC STUDIES

0-465-04404-2 BASIC BOOKS PB $17.50

Cheryl **Payer**

Lent and Lost: Foreign Credit and Third World Development

A well-reasoned attack on the World Bank, the IMF, and other international lending institutions

0-86232-953-1 ZED PB $15.00

Robert J.S. **Ross** & Kent C. **Trachte**

Global Capitalism: The New Leviathan

Attempts to describe how mobility of capital has led to a new kind of capitalism

0-7914-0340-8 SUNY PB $21.95

Anthony **Sampson**

The Money Lenders: The People and Politics of International Banking

0-844-66302-6 SMITH $20.80

Herman **Van der Wee**

Prosperity and Upheaval: The World Economy, 1945-1980

0-520-05709-0 CALIFORNIA $49.95

The American Economy Today

Gary S. **Becker**

Accounting for Tastes

By the 1992 winner of the Nobel prize in economics

0-674-54356-4 HARVARD $35.00

Treatise on the Family

0-674-90699-3 HARVARD PB $21.95

Barry **Bluestone** & Bennett **Harrison**

The Deindustrialization of America

0-465-01592-1 BASIC BOOKS PB $16.00

Samuel **Bowles** & others

After the Waste Land: A Democratic Economics for the Year 2000

0-87332-645-8 SHARPE PB $23.95

David **Card** & Alan B. **Krueger**

Myth and Measurement: The New Economics of the Minimum Wage

A seminal attack on the idea that minimum wages lead to economic decline

0-691-04390-6 PRINCETON $29.95

Sheldon **Danziger** & Peter **Gottschalk**

America Unequal

A clear analysis of inequality in the American economy and the perilous state of the middle and lower classes

0-87154-227-7 RUSSELL SAGE PB $16.95

Lloyd Jeffry **Dumas**

The Overburdened Economy

"Lloyd Dumas has challenged one of the implicit assumptions of the Keynesian Revolution and the national income statistics that embodied it: the assumption that all activity which is paid for must be productive"—Kenneth Boulding, former president of the American Economics Association

0-520-06169-1 CALIFORNIA PB $14.00

Thomas Byrne **Edsall** & Mary D. **Edsall**

Chain Reaction: The Impact of Race, Rights, and Taxes on American Politics

See also AMERICAN POLITICS under POLITICAL THOUGHT

0-393-30903-7 NORTON PB $10.95

Robert **Eisner**

How Real Is the Federal Deficit?

Eisner argues that fear of the deficit is exaggerated

0-02-909430-5 FREE PRESS $35.00

Martin **Feldstein**, editor

The American Economy in Transition

Twenty-nine contributors interpret the era of inflation and low productivity that followed the postwar boom; contributors include Richard Freeman, John T. Dunlop, Alan S. Blinder, Irving Kristol, James R. Schlesinger, and Paul Samuelson

0-226-24082-7 CHICAGO PB $22.00

Nancy **Folbre**

The New Field Guide to the U.S. Economy: A Compact and Irreverent Guide to Economic Life in America

1-56584-153-0 NEW PRESS PB $12.95

Nancy **Folbre** & Randy **Albelda**

The War on the Poor: A Defense Manual

Folbre specializes in marrying economics and social policy in clear prose

AND THE CENTER FOR POPULAR ECONOMICS

1-56584-262-6 NEW PRESS PB $11.95

Victor R. **Fuchs**

How We Live: An Economic Perspective on Americans from Birth to Death

Explores the intersection of economic conditions with stages in the life cycle

0-674-41226-5 HARVARD PB $13.50

David M. **Gordon**

Fat and Mean: The Corporate Squeeze of Working Americans and the Myth of Managerial "Downsizing"

0-684-82288-1 FREE PRESS $25.00

John Kenneth **Galbraith**

The Culture of Contentment

Considers the growth of an affluent class content with its own prospects and unconcerned with the penury surrounding it—and the possible consequences for society at large

See also **CURRENT POLITICAL THOUGHT AND ISSUES** under **AMERICAN POLITICS AND FOREIGN POLICY** in **HISTORY OF THE AMERICAS**

0-395-66919-7 HOUGHTON MIFFLIN PB $10.95

John Kenneth Galbraith

The Good Society

A blueprint for a better America, written for a general audience

0-395-71328-5 HOUGHTON MIFFLIN $21.95

Paul L. **Knox** & John A. **Agnew**

The Geography of the World Economy

0-7131-6517-0 ARNOLD PB $21.95

Paul R. **Krugman**

Pop Internationalism

From the author of *The Age of Diminished Expectations*, this compilation of his essays argues against the popular assertion that government and business need to forge a partnership in order to effectively compete in a global economy, pointing instead to the domestic problems which are the true cause of the slowed growth in Americans' real income

See also **THE INTERNATIONAL MARKETPLACE** under **BUSINESS, INDUSTRY, AND FINANCE** in **BUSINESS AND REFERENCE**

0-262-11210-8 MIT $22.50

Robert **Kuttner**

The End of Laissez Faire: National Purpose and the Global Economy After the Cold War

Kuttner examines the reemergence of the unrestricted market as an ideal in recent decades and how it flies in the face of economic realities: "The intriguing question is why the utopian vision of a pure market economy proved so potent—why it came back to life, after being so thoroughly discredited by events half a century ago"

0-394-57995-X KNOPF $27.50

Robert Z. **Lawrence**

Can America Compete?

0-8157-5175-3 BROOKINGS PB $9.95

Edward **Luttwak**

The Endangered American Dream: How to Stop the United States from Becoming a Third World Country and How to Win the Geo-Economic Struggle for Industrial Supremacy

The author, director of Geo-Economics at Georgetown University's Center for Strategic and International Studies, prescribes some dire medicine for our diseased economy: a heavy value-added tax and strict, uniform educational standards. If not, he warns, by the year 2020 the US will look woefully like Mexico or Argentina. "A powerful, tough-minded, alarming report" —*Publishers Weekly*

See also **WELFARE AND SOCIAL POLICY** under **AMERICAN PEOPLE AND PLACES** in **HISTORY OF THE AMERICAS**

0-671-89667-9 TOUCHSTONE PB $14.00

Alfred L. **Malabre**, Jr.

Understanding the New Economy

1-55623-117-2 IRWIN $30.00

Philip **Mattera**

Prosperity Lost: How a Decade of Greed Has Eroded Our Standard of Living and Endangered Our Children's Future

"A fine examination of how the U.S. economy fails to serve our most basic needs" —Doug Henwood

0-201-19897-5 ADDISON-WESLEY $19.95

Hyman P. **Minsky**

Stabilizing an Unstable Economy

0-300-04000-8 YALE $17.00

William A. **Niskanen**

Reaganomics: An Insider's Account of the Policies and the People

By a former member of the Council of Economic Advisers

0-19-505394-X OXFORD $30.00

Peter G. **Peterson**

Will America Grow Up Before It Grows Old?: How the Coming Social Security Crisis Threatens You, Your Family, and Your Country

By the director of the Federal Reserve Bank of New York. "[Peterson's] proposals for a graying America to return to an earlier generation's collective restraint are worthy advisories to which attention should be paid" —*Publishers Weekly*

See also **AMERICAN POLITICS** under **POLITICAL THOUGHT**

0-679-45256-7 MCKAY $21.00

Robert B. **Reich**

The Work of Nations: Preparing Ourselves for 21st Century Capitalism

Secretary of Labor Reich contends that in order to compete in the new world economy the US will have to ensure an educated workforce with marketable skills

0-394-58352-3 KNOPF $27.50

0-679-73615-8 VINTAGE PB $13.00

Lester C. **Thurow**

The Zero-Sum Society: Distribution and the Possibilities for Economic Change

Examines the effect of economic stagnation on the distribution of shares

0-14-005807-9 VIKING PB $12.95

Howard M. **Watchel**

The Money Mandarins: The Making of a New Supranational Economic Order

0-87332-704-7 SHARPE PB $28.95

Edward N. **Wolff**

Top Heavy: The Increasing Inequality of Wealth in America and What Can Be Done About It

By the New York University professor who is, perhaps, the leading American economist in the field of income inequality

0-87078-360-2 BROOKINGS PB $9.95

1-56584-347-9 NEW PRESS PB $7.95

Military Spending

Gregory A. **Bischak**, editor

Towards a Peace Economy in the United States: Essays on Military Industry, Disarmament and Economics

0-312-04731-2 ST. MARTIN'S $45.00

Ann **Markusen** & others

The Rise of the Gunbelt: The Military Remapping of Industrial America

0-19-506648-0 OXFORD $45.00

Seymour **Melman**

Profits Without Production

0-8122-1258-4 PENNSYLVANIA PB $19.95

Wayne **Sandholtz** & others

The Highest Stakes: The Economic Foundations of the Next Security System

0-19-508667-8 OXFORD PB $11.95

Todd **Sandler** & Keith **Hartley**

The Economics of Defence

0-521-44728-3 CAMBRIDGE PB $22.95

Special Topics

Microeconomics

William J. **Baumol** & Alan S. **Blinder**
Microeconomics
0-15-518865-8 HARCOURT BRACE PB $40.57

Laurence J. **Kotlikoff**
Generational Accounting: Knowing Who Pays, and When, for What We Spend
0-02-917585-2 FREE PRESS PB $14.95

W. Kip **Viscusi**
Fatal Tradeoffs: Public and Private Responsibilities for Risk
0-19-510293-2 OXFORD PB $18.95

W. Kip **Viscusi** & others
Economics of Regulation and Antitrust
0-262-22049-0 MIT $60.00

Discrimination, Education, and Income

Gary S. **Becker**
The Economics of Discrimination
0-226-04116-6 CHICAGO PB $11.95

Barbara R. **Bergmann**
The Economic Emergence of Women
The transformation of women from homemakers to wage earners
See also **ECONOMICS** under **FEMINIST THEORY** under **WOMEN'S STUDIES**
0-465-01797-5 BASIC BOOKS PB $16.00

Alan S. **Blinder**
Hard Heads, Soft Hearts: Tough-Minded Economics for a Just Society
0-201-14519-7 ADDISON-WESLEY PB $15.00

Melvin L. **Oliver** & Thomas M. **Shapiro**
Black Wealth/White Wealth: A New Perspective on Racial Inequality
"Documents how institutionalized racism has perpetuated deep inequalities in wealth and kept hard-working, thrifty black people from rising into the middle class"—Robin D.G. Kelley
0-415-91375-6 ROUTLEDGE $22.95

Theodore W. **Schultz**
Investing in People: The Economics of Population Quality
FOREWORD BY JOHN M. LETICHE
0-520-04437-1 CALIFORNIA $27.50
0-520-04787-7 CALIFORNIA PB $14.00

Michael **Reich**
Racial Inequality: A Political-Economic Analysis
0-691-04227-6 PRINCETON $45.00

Thomas **Sowell**
The Economics and Politics of Race: An International Perspective
Provocative analysis of the relative significance of race in society, both in the US and elsewhere. Sowell is America's leading black conservative thinker
See also **RACE RELATIONS** under **AFRICAN-AMERICAN STUDIES** in **HISTORY OF THE AMERICAS**
0-688-04832-3 MORROW PB $9.95

Urban Economics

James **Heilbrun**
Urban Economics and Public Policy
0-312-83442-X ST. MARTIN'S $50.65

Jane **Jacobs**
Cities and the Wealth of Nations: Principles of Economic Life
Jacobs's fullest and most recent statement of her view that cities are the engine of economic development
0-394-72911-0 RANDOM HOUSE PB $12.50

The Death and Life of Great American Cities
An attack on the principles and aims that have shaped modern orthodox city planning and rebuilding. "This is one of the most remarkable books ever written about the city"—William Whyte
See also **AMERICAN PEOPLE AND PLACES** in **HISTORY OF THE AMERICAS**
0-679-60047-7 MODERN LIBRARY $17.50
0-679-74195-X VINTAGE PB $13.00

The Economy of Cities
"This book is radiant with ideas about what makes cities rich or poor, how cities grow, and how city growth affects national economies" —*New Yorker*
See also **HISTORY, POLITICS, AND SOCIETY** under **20TH-CENTURY AMERICAN ESSAYS AND JOURNALISM** in **LITERATURE OF THE AMERICAS**
0-394-70584-X RANDOM HOUSE PB $10.00

William K. **Tabb**
The Long Default: New York City and the Urban Fiscal Crisis
0-85345-571-6 MONTHLY REVIEW $16.00
0-85345-572-4 MONTHLY REVIEW PB $10.00

The Economics of Energy and Environment

Edwin S. **Mills** & Philip F. **Graves**
The Economics of Environmental Quality
0-393-95270-3 NORTON $19.95

Cyrus **Bina**
The Economics of Oil Crisis: Theories of Oil Crisis, Oil Rent and Internationalization of Capital in the Oil Industry
0-312-23661-1 ST. MARTIN'S $35.00

Herman E. **Daly**
Beyond Growth: The Economics of Sustainable Development
Updating his iconoclastic work and providing a major new consideration of environmentalist economics, Daly draws on his experience at the World Bank to cast light on the key concept of "sustainable development." "Daly is turning economics inside out by putting the earth and its diminishing natural resources at the center of the field...a kind of reverse Copernican revolution in economics"—*Utne Reader*
0-8070-4708-2 BEACON $27.50

Bruce **Rich**
Mortgaging the Earth: The World Bank, Environmental Impoverishment, and the Crisis of Development
This explosive critique of the World Bank draws on back-corridor reports. Why is the bank—which lends $25 billion each year for huge agricultural and resettlement projects—so powerful? And why is it always unaccountable for the world's problems as it lends financial support to repressive military governments?
See also **INTERNATIONAL POLITICAL ECONOMY** under **INTERNATIONAL RELATIONS AND STRATEGIC STUDIES**
0-8070-4707-4 BEACON PB $16.00

E. F. **Schumacher**
Small Is Beautiful: Economics as if People Mattered
0-06-091630-3 HARPERCOLLINS PB $13.00

Social Choice and Game Theory

Kenneth J. **Arrow**
Social Choice and Individual Values
A classic by the American Nobel laureate
See also **OTHER 20TH-CENTURY PHILOSOPHERS** under **PHILOSOPHY** in **RELIGION, SPIRITUALITY, AND PHILOSOPHY**
0-300-01364-7 YALE PB $12.00

Robert **Axelrod**
The Evolution of Cooperation
0-465-02121-2 HARPERCOLLINS PB $17.00

Ken **Binmore**
Game Theory and the Social Contract: Playing Fair
0-262-02363-6 MIT $42.00

Ken **Binmore** & others
Frontiers of Game Theory
0-262-02356-3 MIT $47.50

James **Buchanan** & Gordon **Tullock**

The Calculus of Consent

0-472-06100-3 MICHIGAN PB $19.95

Oscar **Morgenstern** & John **von Neumann**

Theories of Games and Economic Behavior

Heavily mathematical

0-691-00362-9 PRINCETON PB $29.95

Thomas C. **Schelling**

Strategy of Conflict

0-674-84031-3 HARVARD PB $15.95

Political Thought

"Man is by nature a political animal," Aristotle wrote in his *Politics*. Western political thought has its origins in Ancient Greece, where the main issues were how to organize the state (democracy, or oligarchy?) and how to defend it. These issues haven't changed much since. The eternal negotiations between rulers and ruled, and among states, are the mainstays of political thought. In recent years, liberal democracy seems to have triumphed over its main modern rival, socialism. But competing systems—religious, nationalist, tribal, and communitarian—have shown remarkable vitality both in life and in political literature.

Classics

Aristotle

The Politics

The philosopher's attempt to make government "the subject of a single science," *The Politics* gives a clear, readable description of various types of government. Includes a defense of slavery, a central institution of Greek society at the time

EDITED BY STEPHEN EVERSON

0-521-35731-4 CAMBRIDGE PB $8.95

Walter **Bagehot**

Editor of The Economist *from 1861 until his death in 1877, Walter Bagehot brought fresh insights into the psychological underpinnings of political action. Many regard* The English Constitution *(1867) as still the best introduction to English political culture.*

The English Constitution

0-801-49023-5 CORNELL PB $10.95

Jeremy **Bentham**

A Fragment on Government

Bentham, an active reformer and a proponent of the doctrine of utilitarianism, argued that the greatest good for the greatest number should guide political judgments

See also **BENTHAM** under **PHILOSOPHY** in **RELIGION, SPIRITUALITY, AND PHILOSOPHY**

INTRODUCTION BY ROSS HARRISON

0-521-35054-9 CAMBRIDGE $21.95

Edmund **Burke**

Reflections on the Revolution in France

Burke, who had supported the American Revolution as a vindication of traditional English liberties, produced in *Reflections on the Revolution in France* (1790) the most influential arguments against the French Revolution and in the process invented conservatism as a distinct political philosophy. He favored gradual reform based on experience and local tradition, which distinguishes his conservatism from the more iron-handed and pessimistic variety developed on the Continent by De Maistre and others

See also **INTERPRETING THE REVOLUTION** under **THE FRENCH REVOLUTION AND NAPOLEON** in **WORLD HISTORY AND CURRENT AFFAIRS**

0-14-043204-3 PENGUIN PB $9.95

Thomas Paine

Marcus Tullius **Cicero**

On Government

The only Roman statesman to have left behind a full explanation of his theories, Cicero favored a constitution blending monarchy, oligarchy, and democracy

TRANSLATED BY MICHAEL GRANT

0-14-044595-1 PENGUIN PB $11.95

Benjamin **Constant**

Political Writings

A French-Swiss political writer, novelist, and statesman, Constant was an early and influential theorist of liberalism

TRANSLATED AND EDITED BY BIANCAMARIA FONTANA

0-521-31632-4 CAMBRIDGE PB $18.95

Charles-Louis **de Montesquieu**

The Spirit of the Laws

The most complete examination of different systems of political organization by an Enlightenment thinker

See also **PRECURSORS** under **GENERAL ANTHROPOLOGICAL STUDIES** under **ANTHROPOLOGY**

0-521-36974-6 CAMBRIDGE PB $18.95

0-317-30542-5 FREE PRESS PB $13.95

Charles **Fourier**

The Utopian Vision of Charles Fourier: Selected Texts on Work, Love and Passionate Attraction

The utopia of Fourier, conceived as a cooperative, egalitarian agricultural community, inspired Brook Farm, the transcendentalist experiment in Massachusetts, and other American cooperative settlements

TRANSLATED AND EDITED BY JONATHAN BEECHER & RICHARD BIENVENU

0-8262-0426-0 MISSOURI $42.00

0-8262-0413-9 MISSOURI PB $17.50

Sigmund **Freud**

Civilization and Its Discontents

0-393-30158-3 NORTON PB $7.95

William **Godwin**

An Enquiry Concerning Political Justice

Godwin was the most extreme of early English radicals. More anarchist than socialist, he believed that humanity could achieve perfection through political reform and saw the future in terms of small independent communities in which the individual would be allowed a maximum of personal freedom. His *Enquiry* appeared in 1793

EDITED BY ISAAC KRAMNICK

0-14-040030-3 PENGUIN PB $11.95

G.W.F. **Hegel**

Philosophy of Right

Hegel's political philosophy was conservative, though liberal in the context of contemporary Prussia. He favored constitutional monarchy based on family and guild in which liberty was balanced with public order

See also **HEGEL** under **PHILOSOPHY** in **RELIGION, SPIRITUALITY, AND PHILOSOPHY**

TRANSLATED BY T.M. KNOX

0-19-500276-8 OXFORD PB $18.95

Thomas **Hobbes**

Perhaps influenced by the unsettled times in which he lived, Hobbes took a dim view of human nature: in a state of nature the life of man was "solitary, poore, nasty, brutish, and short." Thus the main motive of political life is security, to be achieved by establishing a commonwealth through a social contract and setting up over it an absolute, undivided authority who will prevent it from dissolving into factionalism and civil war.

Leviathan

This great work, published in 1651 and subjected to a parliamentary investigation for atheism, heavily influenced much subsequent British political theory

See also **HOBBES** under **PHILOSOPHY** in **RELIGION, SPIRITUALITY, AND PHILOSOPHY**

EDITED BY C.B. MACPHERSON

0-14-043195-0 PENGUIN PB $8.95

Whatsoever therefore is consequent to a time of Warre, where every man is Enemy to every man; the same is consequent to the time, wherein men live without other security, than what their own strength, and their own invention shall furnish them withall. In such condition, there is no place for Industry; because the fruit thereof is uncertain: and consequently no Culture of the Earth; no Navigation, nor use of the commodities that may be imported by Sea; no commodious Building; no Instruments of moving, and removing such things as require much force; no Knowledge of the face of the Earth; no account of Time; no Arts; no Letters; no Society; and which is worst of all, continuall feare, and danger of violent death; And the life of man, solitary, poore, nasty, brutish, and short.

LEVIATHAN

of Time; no Arts; no Letters; no Society; and which is worst of all, continuall feare, and danger of violent death; And the life of man, solitary, poore, nasty, brutish, and short.
LEVIATHAN

Thomas **Jefferson**

Writings

A comprehensive gathering of Jefferson's remarkably varied writings, including *Autobiography, A Summary View of the Rights of British America, Public Papers, Miscellany*, and a large selection of letters. The letters in particular create a three-dimensional and often surprising portrait. Jefferson envisioned a nation of prosperous farmers who he thought were far more likely than city-dwellers to cultivate the virtues of self-reliance, hard work, moderation, and common sense on which a free society depends

See also **THE 18TH CENTURY** under **AMERICAN LITERATURE TO 1900** in **LITERATURE OF THE AMERICAS**

EDITED BY MERRIL D. PETERSON

0-940450-16-X LIBRARY OF AMERICA $35.00

Immanuel **Kant**

Political Writings

Includes the German philosopher's influential essays *Perpetual Peace* and *Idea for a Universal History with a Cosmopolitan Purpose*. Kant writes, "We can scarcely help feeling a certain distaste on observing [human] activities as enacted in the great world-drama," but he attempts "to discover a purpose in nature behind this senseless course of human events"

0-521-39837-1 CAMBRIDGE PB....................$16.95

Gottfried W. **Leibniz**

Political Writings

"Next to the honor of God the welfare of the Fatherland should properly be on the mind of every virtuous person"

0-521-35899-X CAMBRIDGE PB....................$18.95

John **Locke**

Two Treatises on Civil Government

Locke's theories on the "social contract" provided the theoretical basis for modern democratic government. He also proposed the "checks and balances" system which was later put into use by the US Constitution

EDITED BY PETER LASLETT

0-521-35730-6 CAMBRIDGE PB....................$10.95

Niccolo **Machiavelli**

The radical innovation of Machiavelli was to base political theory on experience rather than edifying ideals, and he drew on history (in his Discourses*) as well as his own career as a Florentine diplomat. His ambiguous legacy includes both modern empirical political science and the Realpolitik of the nation-state as a law unto itself.*

Discourses on Livy

See also **HUMANISM** under **THE RENAISSANCE** under **ITALIAN LITERATURE** in **LITERATURE OF EUROPE, AFRICA, AND ASIA**

TRANSLATED BY HARVEY C. MANSFIELD

0-226-50035-7 CHICAGO....................$34.95

The Discourses

A commentary on Livy's history of Rome

See also **THE CLASSICS** under **HISTORIOGRAPHY** in **WORLD HISTORY AND CURRENT AFFAIRS**

EDITED BY BERNARD CRICK

0-14-044428-9 PENGUIN PB....................$9.95

Florentine Histories

See also **THE CLASSICS** under **HISTORIOGRAPHY** in **WORLD HISTORY AND CURRENT AFFAIRS**

TRANSLATED BY LAURA BANFIELD & HARVEY MANSFIELD

0-691-05521-1 PRINCETON....................$65.00

0-691-00863-9 PRINCETON PB....................$17.95

History of Florence and of the Affairs of Italy

0-8446-2503-5 SMITH....................$18.25

The Portable Machiavelli

Contains *The Prince,* excerpts from *The Discourses* (Machiavelli's commentary on Roman history), and other writings

TRANSLATED BY MARK MUSA & PETER BONDANELLA

0-14-015092-7 VIKING PB....................$14.95

The Prince

See also **RENAISSANCE CLASSICS** under **RENAISSANCE ITALY AND THE COMING OF HUMANISM** under **MEDIEVAL AND RENAISSANCE EUROPE** in **WORLD HISTORY AND CURRENT AFFAIRS**

TRANSLATED BY GEORGE BULL

0-14-044107-7 PENGUIN PB....................$5.95

Niccolo Machiavelli

The Prince

EDITED BY QUENTIN SKINNER & RUSSELL PRICE

0-521-34240-6 CAMBRIDGE....................$21.95

0-521-34993-1 CAMBRIDGE PB....................$7.95

James **Madison** & others

The Federalist Papers

A defense of the US Constitution by several of America's most thoughtful Founders

EDITED BY ISAAC KRAMNICK

0-14-044495-5 PENGUIN PB....................$12.95

Karl **Marx** & Friedrich **Engels**

The Communist Manifesto

Marx and Engels's vivid call to arms, urging workers to unite and to overthrow capitalism

0-553-21406-3 BDD PB....................$3.95

John Stuart **Mill**

On Liberty

On Liberty (1859) is the most famous argument ever made for the liberal, tolerant, pluralistic, democratic point of view. After a nervous breakdown in his early twenties, Mill opened himself to Coleridge and the Romantics and tried to base his political philosophy on a broader view of human nature

EDITED BY GERTRUDE HIMMELFARB

0-14-043207-8 PENGUIN PB....................$8.95

But, indeed, the dictum that truth always triumphs over persecution is one of those pleasant falsehoods which men repeat after one another till they pass into commonplaces, but which all experience refutes. History teems with instances of truth put down by persecution. If not suppressed forever, it may be thrown back for centuries. To speak only of religious opinions: the Reformation broke out at least twenty times before Luther, and was put down. Arnold of Brescia was put down. Fra Dolcino was put down. Savonarola was put down. The Albigeois were put down. The Vaudois were put down. The Lollards were put down. The Hussites were put down…It is a piece of idle sentimentality that truth, merely as truth, has any inherent power denied to error of prevailing against the dungeon and the stake.
ON LIBERTY

On Liberty, The Subjection of Women, & Chapters on Socialism

In *On Liberty*, a foundational text of modern liberalism, Mill argues that a good society must recognize human individuality as a basic value. *On the Subjection of Women* is an early and influential polemic in support of women's rights

See also **MILL** under **PHILOSOPHY** in **RELIGION, SPIRITUALITY, AND PHILOSOPHY**

EDITED BY STEFAN COLLINI

0-521-37917-2 CAMBRIDGE PB....................$8.95

Principles of Political Economy

Mill (1806-1873) offered a great synthesis of the major doctrines of classical political economy. He also introduced a supply-and-demand explanation of prices and an account of industrial growth that accommodated trade unionism

See also **JOHN STUART MILL** under **GREAT ECONOMISTS** under **ECONOMICS**

EDITED BY DONALD WINCH

0-14-043260-4 PENGUIN PB....................$11.95

Thomas **More**

Utopia

More invented the word utopia (a pun in Greek on "good place"), and described a rational and tolerant communistic society that reflected his humanist sympathies and was very remote from the 16th-century England of Henry VIII in which he was eventually beheaded

See also **PROSE** under **THE 16TH CENTURY** in **LITERATURE OF THE BRITISH ISLES**

TRANSLATED BY PAUL TUMOR

0-14-044165-4 PENGUIN PB....................$6.95

William **Morris**

News from Nowhere

Morris was a Victorian Renaissance man, a fine poet, a major innovator in visual design, and a timeless socialist-activist. This 1891 novel describes an ideal rural socialist community

See also **19TH-CENTURY FICTION** under **THE 19TH CENTURY** in **LITERATURE OF THE BRITISH ISLES**

0-7100-6756-9 ROUTLEDGE PB....................$14.95

George **Orwell**

1984

Orwell's bleak 1948 vision of a totalitarian England under Big Brother

See also **THE EARLY 20TH CENTURY** under **20TH-CENTURY BRITISH AND IRISH FICTION** in **LITERATURE OF THE BRITISH ISLES**

84-233-0983-5 DESTINO PB $15.50
0-452-26293-3 NEW AMERICAN LIBRARY PB $11.95

Animal Farm

The famous satire on Soviet communism, depicted as a revolutionized barnyard in which "some animals are more equal than others"

0-452-26490-1 NEW AMERICAN LIBRARY PB $9.95

Thomas **Paine**

Common Sense

Paine's call to revolution sold over 100,000 copies in a three-month period in 1776

See also **THE 18TH CENTURY** under **AMERICAN LITERATURE TO 1900** in **LITERATURE OF THE AMERICAS**

0-14-039016-2 PENGUIN PB $6.95

Political Writings

EDITED BY BRUCE KUKLICK

0-521-36678-X CAMBRIDGE PB $8.95

The Rights of Man

A defense of the French Revolution against the attacks of Edmund Burke

0-14-039015-4 PENGUIN PB $8.95

Thomas Paine: Collected Writings

1-88301-103-5 LIBRARY OF AMERICA $35.00

The Thomas Paine Reader

Includes *Common Sense* and excerpts from *The Rights of Man*, *The American Crisis*, and *The Age of Reason*

See also **THE 18TH CENTURY** under **AMERICAN LITERATURE TO 1900** in **LITERATURE OF THE AMERICAS**

EDITED BY MICHAEL FOOT & ISAAC KRAMNICK

0-14-044496-3 PENGUIN PB $12.95

Plato

Dialogues of Plato

Plato's greatest dialogue, *The Republic*, tries to align justice with happiness and proposes that the ideal state would be ruled by philosophers schooled in the nature of virtue. His later work, *The Laws*, is a detailed blueprint for government

EDITED BY JUSTIN E. KAPLAN

0-671-52524-7 POCKET PB $5.99

Jean-Jacques **Rousseau**

Some of the profound contradictions in Rousseau's life found their way into his political philosophy, which is meant to show the way to freedom and equality but finds true freedom in the submission of the individual to the "general will." Rousseau has been seen as both the champion of revolution and individual liberty and the harbinger of 20th-century totalitarianism.

Political Writings

Contains the widely praised translation of *The Social Contract* (1762), the late and important *Considerations on the Government of Poland*, and the only published English translation of the fragment *Constitutional Project for Corsica*

EDITED BY FREDERICK WATKINS

0-299-111094-X UWISC PB $16.50

The Social Contract

The chief work of Rousseau's political philosophy, in which the individual attains true freedom by submitting to the "general will"

See also **ROUSSEAU** under **PHILOSOPHY** in **RELIGION, SPIRITUALITY, AND PHILOSOPHY**

TRANSLATED BY MAURICE CRANSTON

0-14-044201-4 PENGUIN PB $7.95

George H. **Sabine** & Thomas L. **Thorson**

A History of Political Theory

A broadly inclusive, excellent history of political thinking

0-03-080305-5 HOLT RINEHART & WINSTON $57.50

Edmund **Wilson**

To the Finland Station

The roots of modern radicalism, from Fourier and Saint-Simon to Marx and Lenin. "A work of the historical imagination at its most creative…puts us in touch with the revolutionary dreams and visions of our past" —*NY Times*

See also **LITERARY ESSAYISTS** under **LITERARY CRITICISM** in **LITERATURE OF EUROPE, AFRICA, AND ASIA**

0-374-51045-8 FS&G PB $16.00

Mary **Wollstonecraft**

A Vindication of the Rights of Woman

A founding statement of feminism, first published in 1792, applying the egalitarian principles of the times to women

See also **FEMINIST THEORY** under **WOMEN'S STUDIES**

EDITED BY MIRIAM KRAMNICK

0-14-043382-1 PENGUIN PB $9.95
0-87975-525-3 PROMETHEUS PB $6.95

Liberalism

Hannah **Arendt**

Essays in Understanding: 1930-1954

Arendt's insights on the nature of totalitarianism are central to contemporary political thought. These essays, including some that appear here in complete form for the first time, are seminal to her gestation as a philosopher. Edited and annotated by her longtime assistant, Jerome Kohn

0-15-172817-8 HARCOURT BRACE $39.95

The Human Condition

0-8446-6183-X SMITH $24.50
0-226-02593-4 CHICAGO PB $14.95

On Revolution

0-14-021681-2 VIKING PB $10.95

On Violence

0-15-669500-6 HARCOURT BRACE PB $7.00

Isaiah **Berlin**

Four Essays on Liberty

An exploration of the meaning of liberty in the context of modern ideologies, defending it as an ideal against theories of historical inevitability and monistic conceptions of political truth

0-19-281034-0 OXFORD PB $12.95

Norberto **Bobbio**

Liberalism and Democracy

A concise, elegant investigation of the uneasy relationship between liberal "negative liberty" and democratic "positive liberty" by a leading Italian political theorist

TRANSLATED BY MARTIN RYLE AND KATE SOPER

0-86091-985-4 VERSO PB $16.95

John **Dewey** & Jo A. **Boydston**, editor

John Dewey: The Later Works, 1925-1953

0-8093-1677-3 SOUTHERN ILLINOIS PB $14.95

Ronald **Dworkin**

A Matter of Principle

See also **OTHER 20TH-CENTURY PHILOSOPHERS** under **PHILOSOPHY** in **RELIGION, SPIRITUALITY, AND PHILOSOPHY**

0-674-55461-2 HARVARD PB $17.50

Taking Rights Seriously

"The most significant book on the philosophy of law in this decade"—*Ethics*

See also **OTHER 20TH-CENTURY PHILOSOPHERS** under **PHILOSOPHY** in **RELIGION, SPIRITUALITY, AND PHILOSOPHY**

0-674-86710-6 HARVARD $34.50
0-674-86711-4 HARVARD PB $15.95

Stephen **Holmes**

The Anatomy of Antiliberalism

0-674-03180-6 HARVARD $29.95
0-674-03185-7 HARVARD PB $15.95

Passions and Constraint: On the Theory of Liberal Democracy

0-226-34968-3 CHICAGO $29.95

C.B. **MacPherson**

The Rise and Fall of Economic Justice and Other Essays: The Role of State, Class, and Property in Twentieth-Century Democracy

Incisive essays by a clear-headed liberal

0-19-285186-1 OXFORD PB $14.95

Reinhold **Niebuhr**

Moral Man and Immoral Society: A Study in Ethics and Politics

Published in 1932, Niebuhr's most famous book is a classic of political realism that appeared when many people were looking for utopia. It stressed the inevitable selfishness of political entities and the perilous path of progress through inherent human limitations

0-684-71857-X MACMILLAN PB $13.00

John **Rawls**

Rawl's Theory of Justice *is the most important book in ethical philosophy to appear in English since G.E. Moore's* Principia Ethica *of 1903.*

Political Liberalism

See also **OTHER 20TH-CENTURY PHILOSOPHERS** under **PHILOSOPHY** in **RELIGION, SPIRITUALITY, AND PHILOSOPHY**

0-231-05248-0 COLUMBIA $40.00
0-231-05249-9 COLUMBIA PB $15.00

John Rawls

A Theory of Justice

A broad and important work of philosophy elaborating the idea of "justice as fairness"

See also **OTHER 20TH-CENTURY PHILOSOPHERS** under **PHILOSOPHY** in **RELIGION, SPIRITUALITY, AND PHILOSOPHY**

0-674-88014-5 HARVARD PB $18.95

Alan **Ryan**

John Dewey and the High Tide of American Liberalism

Dewey's pragmatist philosophy was intended to have a close connection to social and political life, and in the era of the New Deal it became a major force in the development of liberalism

See also **DEWEY** under **PHILOSOPHY** in **RELIGION, SPIRITUALITY, AND PHILOSOPHY**

0-393-03773-8 NORTON $30.00
0-393-31550-9 NORTON PB $17.00

Leftism and Marxism

Louis **Althusser**

For Marx

1-85984-146-5 VERSO PB $15.00

Lenin and Philosophy & Other Essays

0-85345-213-X MONTHLY REVIEW PB $16.00

Jonathan **Beecher**

Charles Fourier: The Visionary and His World

The most comprehensive biography to date of the French utopian socialist thinker of the early 19th century, whose radical ideas have continued to fascinate the 20th century

0-520-07179-4 CALIFORNIA PB $18.00

Ernst **Bloch**

Aesthetics and Politics

0-902308-38-6 VERSO $34.95
0-86091-722-3 VERSO PB $17.95

Cornelius **Castoriadis**

The Castoriadis Reader

1-55786-704-6 BLACKWELL PB $24.95

Nikolai **Chernyshevsky**

What Is to Be Done?

This novel of love and sacrifice by one of the Old Regime's most famous radical critics is a primary text of Russian feminism and socialism

See also **BEFORE THE 20TH CENTURY** under **RUSSIAN LITERATURE** in **LITERATURE OF EUROPE, AFRICA, AND ASIA**

TRANSLATED BY MICHAEL R. KATZ

0-8014-1744-9 CORNELL $46.50
0-8014-9547-4 CORNELL PB $14.95

Noam **Chomsky**

Chronicles of Dissent

A wonderful introduction to the controversial Chomskian political perspective, these interviews range across history from Columbus to the recent Gulf War. The Israeli and US dependent relationship, the decline of language because of propaganda, and American imperialist designs are themes to which he continually returns. "Chomsky at his most accessible…"—Howard Zinn

See also **LIBERALS AND THE LEFT** under **CURRENT POLITICAL THOUGHT AND ISSUES** under **AMERICAN POLITICS AND FOREIGN POLICY** in **HISTORY OF THE AMERICAS**

INTRODUCTION BY ALEXANDER COCKBURN

0-9628838-9-1 COMMON COURAGE $29.95
0-9628838-8-3 COMMON COURAGE PB $16.95

G.A. **Cohen**

Karl Marx's Theory of History: A Defence

Arguably the most important work on Marxian social philosophy published in English in the last 50 years

See also **KARL MARX** under **GREAT ECONOMISTS** under **ECONOMICS**

See also **MARX** under **PHILOSOPHY**

0-691-02008-6 PRINCETON PB $17.95

Guy **Debord**

Society of the Spectacle

In this influential work, the house philosopher of the elusive Situationist International, which came to public attention with the French student rebellion of 1968, analyzes modern capitalist society as a hypnotic show

See also **OTHER FRENCH THEORISTS** under **POSTSTRUCTURALISM** under **LITERARY THEORY** in **LITERATURE OF EUROPE, AFRICA, AND ASIA**

TRANSLATED BY DONALD NICHOLSON-SMITH

0-942299-80-9 ZONE $21.95
0-942299-79-5 ZONE PB $10.95

Jon **Elster**

Making Sense of Marx

A philosophical exponent of rational choice theory attempts to clarify Marx's strong arguments and dismiss his weak ones

0-521-29705-2 CAMBRIDGE PB $31.95

Antonio **Gramsci**

Further Selections from the Prison Notebooks

0-8166-2658-8 MINNESOTA $34.95

Letters from Prison

0-231-07554-5 COLUMBIA $42.50

Antonio **Gramsci**

Prison Notebooks: Selections

TRANSLATED BY QUINTIN HOARE & GEOFFREY N. SMITH

0-7178-0397-X INTERNATIONAL PUB PB $12.95

Che **Guevara**

The Motorcycle Diaries

A very entertaining account of a trip through Latin America by a young man who would become one of the 20th century's leading revolutionaries

1-85984-971-7 VERSO $50.00

Alexander **Herzen**

From the Other Shore & The Russian People and Socialism

From the Other Shore replaces Hegel's belief in an ineluctable logic of history with a stress on accident, chance, and the free improvisation of the individual

TRANSLATED BY MOURA BUDBERG

INTRODUCTION BY ISAIAH BERLIN

0-8305-0074-X HYPERION $26.00

My Past and Thoughts

This brilliant synthesis of personal memoir and social criticism by a great 19th-century Russian agitator and man of letters is an essential text

See also **BEFORE THE 20TH CENTURY** under **RUSSIAN LITERATURE** in **LITERATURE OF EUROPE, AFRICA, AND ASIA**

TRANSLATED BY J. D. DUFF

INTRODUCTION BY ISAIAH BERLIN

0-520-04191-7 CALIFORNIA $52.50
0-520-04210-7 CALIFORNIA PB $13.95

Alexander Herzen

Eric **Hobsbawm**

Politics for a Rational Left: Political Writing, 1977-1988

The distinguished historian and jazz critic is also an active and influential figure in the British left

0-86091-958-7 VERSO PB $17.95

Eugene **Kamenka**, editor

The Portable Karl Marx

Includes *The Communist Manifesto, The German Ideology,* selections from *Capital*, letters, and other documents

See also **THE RISE OF MARXISM** under **19TH-CENTURY EUROPE** in **WORLD HISTORY AND CURRENT AFFAIRS**

0-14-015096-X VIKING PB $14.95

Leszek **Kolakowski**

Main Currents of Marxism: Its Rise, Growth, and Dissolution Volume 1 The Founders

A classic, and highly critical, history by a Polish philosopher who fled the communist regime for England. Volumes 2 and 3 are out of print

See also **POLISH LITERATURE** under **EASTERN EUROPEAN LITERATURE** in **LITERATURE OF EUROPE, AFRICA, AND ASIA**

0-19-285107-1 OXFORD PB $16.95

Volume 2 The Golden Age

0-19-24569-6 OXFORD $42.00

Volume 3 The Breakdown

0-285109-8 OXFORD PB $16.95

V.I. **Lenin**

The Lenin Anthology

Lenin's revolutionary writings present what Lukacs called a "revolutionary Realpolitik" sharply distinct from classical Marxist theory and totalitarian Stalinist practice

EDITED BY ROBERT C. TUCKER

0-393-09236-4 NORTON PB $14.95

What Is to Be Done?

Lenin's main contribution to Marxist theory is his insistence on the role of a tightly disciplined revolutionary vanguard organization in bringing the working class into a revolutionary consciousness

0-14-018126-1 PENGUIN PB $9.95

Georg **Lukacs**

History and Class Consciousness

Written between 1919 and 1922, these essays focus on the concept of alienation in Marx's criticism of capitalist society and anticipate the 1960s revival of interest in the young, humanist Marx. Lukacs himself later disowned them

See also **MARX** under **PHILOSOPHY** in **RELIGION, SPIRITUALITY, AND PHILOSOPHY**

TRANSLATED BY RODNEY LIVINGSTONE

0-262-62020-0 MIT PB $16.00

Rosa **Luxemburg**

The National Question: Selected Writings by Rosa Luxemburg

Includes Luxemburg's argument for international worker solidarity in opposition to nationalism. Luxemburg was both the most uncompromising advocate of revolution in the German Social Democratic Party and a critic of Lenin's authoritarianism. She was killed by paramilitary forces during a 1919 uprising in Berlin

EDITED BY HORACE B. DAVIS

0-85345-355-1 MONTHLY REVIEW $16.50

Reform or Revolution

An attack on reformism

0-87348-303-0 PATHFINDER PB $9.95

Herbert **Marcuse**

Essays on Liberation

Marcuse makes the paradoxical claim that capitalism controls dissent by means of "repressive tolerance"

0-8070-0595-9 BEACON PB $12.00

Herbert **Marcuse**

One Dimensional Man

A scathing criticism of modern capitalism

See also **OTHER 20TH-CENTURY PHILOSOPHERS** under **PHILOSOPHY**

0-8070-1417-6 BEACON PB $15.00

Karl **Marx**

Early Writings

Marx's mature economic doctrines were built upon his earlier philosophical preoccupations. This excellent selection includes the major writings of his youth

See also **MARX** under **PHILOSOPHY** in **RELIGION, SPIRITUALITY, AND PHILOSOPHY**

TRANSLATED BY RODNEY LIVINGSTON & GREGOR BENTON

EDITED BY QUINTIN HOARE

0-394-72005-9 RANDOM HOUSE PB $16.00

Grundrisse: Foundations of the Critique of Political Economy

Marx's first large-scale consideration of the themes he addressed in *Capital* is an important work in its own right

See also **MARX** under **PHILOSOPHY** in **RELIGION, SPIRITUALITY, AND PHILOSOPHY**

TRANSLATED BY MARTIN NICOLAUS

0-14-044575-7 PENGUIN PB $17.95

Marx: Early Political Writings

EDITED BY JOSEPH O'MALLEY AND RICHARD A. DAVIS

0-521-34241-4 CAMBRIDGE $32.50

Marx: Later Political Writings

EDITED AND TRANSLATED BY TERRELL CARVER

0-521-36504-X CAMBRIDGE $34.95

Karl **Marx** & Friedrich **Engels**

The Communist Manifesto

0-19-282954-8 OXFORD PB $5.95

The German Ideology

This attack on German philosophy after Hegel also includes a philosophical discussion of the good society. Includes Part 1 and selections from Parts 2 & 3

EDITED BY C.J. ARTHUR

0-7178-0302-3 INTERNATIONAL PUB PB $6.95

David **McLellan, editor**

The Essential Left: Five Classic Texts on the Principles of Socialism

0-04-335056-9 UNWIN HYMAN PB $19.95

Ronald **Aronson**

Sartre's Second Critique

An analysis of Sartre's major late work of Marxist philosophy. *The Critique of Dialectical Reason* itself is currently out of print

0-226-02805-4 CHICAGO PB $13.95

Jerrold **Seigel**

Marx's Fate: The Shape of a Life

0-691-05259-X PRINCETON $65.00

0-271-00935-7 PENN STATE PB $18.95

Gary P. **Steenson**

Karl Kautsky, 1854-1938: Marxism in the Classical Years

0-8229-5443-5 PITTSBURGH PB $19.95

Thomas **Sowell**

Marxism: Philosophy and Economics

A critical analysis by the leading American black conservative thinker

0-688-06426-4 MORROW PB $12.00

Oscar **Wilde**

Soul of Man Under Socialism

0-88286-056-9 KERR PB $6.00

George **Woodcock**

Anarchism and Anarchists

1-55082-018-4 QUARRY PB $18.95

Non-Marxist Socialism

Mikhail **Bakunin**

God and the State

As an opponent of socialist authoritarianism and dogma, Bakunin became the chief alternative to Marx on the revolutionary left

INTRODUCTION BY PAUL AVRICH

0-486-22483-X DOVER PB $5.95

Murray **Bookchin**

From Urbanization to Cities: Toward a New Politics of Citizenship

0-304-32842-1 CASSELL PB $17.95

The Philosophy of Social Ecology: Essays on Dialectical Naturalism

1-55164-019-8 BLACK ROSE $48.99

1-55164-018-X BLACK ROSE PB $19.99

Re-Enchanting Humanity: A Defense of the Human Spirit

0-304-32839-1 CASSELL PB $17.95

Social Anarchism or Lifestyle Anarchism: An Unbridgeable Chasm

1-87317-683-X A.K. PRESS DISTRIBUTION PB $7.95

To Remember Spain: The Anarchist and Syndicalist Revolution of 1936

1-87317-687-2 A.K. PRESS DISTRIBUTION PB $6.00

Which Way for the Ecology Movement?

1-87317-626-0 A.K. PRESS DISTRIBUTION PB $6.00

Murray **Bookchin** & Dave **Foreman**

Defending the Earth: A Dialogue Between Murray Bookchin and Dave Foreman

EDITED BY STEVE CHASE

0-89608-382-9 SOUTH END PB $10.00

Robert A. **Dahl**

Dilemmas of Pluralist Democracy

On the possibility of a decentralized, worker-controlled socialist economy

0-300-03076-2 YALE PB $15.00

Robert A. **Dahl**

A Preface to Democratic Theory

The case for a new theoretical model of democracy to replace the traditional alternatives, Madisonian and populist, which, Dahl argues, no longer apply

0-226-13426-1 CHICAGO PB $7.95

Andre **Gorz**

Capitalism, Socialism, Ecology

TRANSLATED BY CHRIS TURNER

0-86091-477-1 VERSO $59.95
0-86091-647-2 VERSO PB $18.95

Paths to Paradise

0-86104-762-1 WESTVIEW PB $14.95

Peter **Kropotkin**

Memoirs of a Revolutionist

0-486-25745-2 DOVER PB $11.95

George **Orwell**

A Collection of Essays

Includes such classics as "Such, Such Were the Joys," "Shooting an Elephant," "Politics and the English Language," and "Why I Write"

See also **20TH-CENTURY BRITISH ESSAYS AND OTHER PROSE** in **LITERATURE OF THE BRITISH ISLES**

0-15-618600-4 HARCOURT BRACE PB $11.00

In Front of Your Nose

0-15-618623-3 HARCOURT BRACE PB $17.95

Georges **Sorel**

Reflections on Violence

Sorel's irrationalism and belief in revolutionary spontaneity and direct action were derived more from Nietzsche and Bergson than from Marx—he became a major influence on both anarcho-syndicalism and Italian fascism, and eventually on the New Left of the 1960s

0-8446-1416-5 SMITH $23.00

Nonviolent Politics

Mohandas K. **Gandhi**

Autobiography: The Story of My Experiments with Truth

A 20th-century classic

See also **GHANDI** under **NATIONALISM AND INDEPENDENCE** under **THE INDIAN SUBCONTINENT** in **WORLD HISTORY AND CURRENT AFFAIRS**

0-486-24593-4 DOVER PB $8.95

The Essential Gandhi

A well-chosen selection of Gandhi's writings

EDITED BY LOUIS FISCHER

0-394-71466-0 VINTAGE PB $11.00

Gandhi on Non-Violence: Selected Text from Gandhi's Non-Violence in Peace and War

EDITED BY THOMAS MERTON

1-57062-243-4 SHAMBHALA PB $6.00

Leo **Tolstoy**

The Law of Violence and the Law of Love

Tolstoy's Christian pacifism exercised a significant influence on Gandhi's thought

0-88695-016-3 CONCORD GROVE PB $10.95

Martin Luther **King**, Jr.

I Have a Dream

A 30th-anniversary gift edition of the inspiring speech that seared the imperative of racial justice into our national psyche

See also **THE CIVIL RIGHTS MOVEMENT AND BEYOND** under **AFRICAN-AMERICAN STUDIES** in **HISTORY OF THE AMERICAS**

0-590-20516-1 SCHOLASTIC $25.00
0-06-250552-1 HARPERCOLLINS PB $13.00

Martin Luther King, Jr.

Conservatism

Andrew **Dobson**

An Introduction to the Political Philosophy of José Ortega y Gasset

0-521-36068-4 CAMBRIDGE $59.95

Friedrich von **Hayek**

The laissez-faire theory that the Austrian-British economist Hayek introduced into Anglo-American political discourse was different from the traditional British versions; he saw economic development as a process of experiment and evolution too complex to be fully understood or managed. State intervention and planning could only impede the process. Hayek's influence on British prime minister Margaret Thatcher and on American conservatives made him a formative influence on policy in the 1980s.

The Constitution of Liberty

0-226-32084-7 CHICAGO PB $19.95

Individualism and Economic Order

See also **FRIEDRICH VON HAYEK** under **GREAT ECONOMISTS** under **ECONOMICS**

0-226-32093-6 CHICAGO PB $16.95

Martin **Heidegger**

The Question Concerning Technology, and Other Essays

See also **HEIDEGGER** under **PHILOSOPHY** in **RELIGION, SPIRITUALITY, AND PHILOSOPHY**

0-06-131969-4 HARPERCOLLINS PB $13.50

James D. **Hornfischer**, editor

Right Thinking: Conservative Common Sense Through the Ages

A slim compendium that brings the story up through Newt Gingrich

0-671-53559-5 POCKET PB $12.00

Russell **Kirk**, editor

The Portable Conservative Reader

A highly diverse collection of readings including Burke, John Adams, Hamilton, Calhoun, Tocqueville, Henry Adams, Santayana, T.S. Eliot, C.S. Lewis, Michael Oakeshott, and fiction by Conrad and Kipling

0-14-015095-1 VIKING PB $14.95

Irving **Kristol**

Neoconservatism: The Autobiography of an Idea/Selected Essays 1949-1995

0-02-874021-1 FREE PRESS $25.00

Michael **Oakeshott**

Morality and Politics in Modern Europe: The Harvard Lectures

EDITED BY SHIRLEY ROBIN LEWIN

0-300-05644-3 YALE $25.00

The Politics of Faith and the Politics of Scepticism: Selected Writings of Michael Oakeshott

EDITED BY TIMOTHY FULLER

0-300-06625-2 YALE $25.00

Rationalism in Politics and Other Essays

Essays by an influential British political philosopher calling into question the prevalence of ideology and systematic rationalism in modern politics and defending a less intrusive, tradition-respecting style of governance as essential to individualism and freedom

See also **OTHER 20TH-CENTURY PHILOSOPHERS** under **PHILOSOPHY** in **RELIGION, SPIRITUALITY, AND PHILOSOPHY**

0-86597-094-7 LIBERTY FUND $21.00
0-86597-095-5 LIBERTY FUND PB $7.50

Michael **Oakeshott**

Religion, Politics and the Moral Life

EDITED BY TIMOTHY FULLER

0-300-05643-5 YALE $25.00

The Voice of Liberal Learning: Michael Oakeshott on Education

0-300-04344-9 YALE $30.00

José **Ortega y Gasset**

The Revolt of the Masses

A famous and incisive study of the effects of bureaucracy, specialization, mass production, and cultural mediocrity on the European spirit

0-393-31095-7 NORTON PB $7.95

Carl **Schmitt**

The Concept of the Political

0-226-73886-8 CHICAGO PB $10.95

The Crisis of Parliamentary Democracy

0-262-69126-4 MIT PB $13.95

Political Theology: Four Chapters on the Concept of Sovereignty

0-262-69124-8 MIT PB $9.95

Thomas **Sowell**

A Conflict of Visions

How two radically opposed visions of human nature have manifested themselves in the political controversies of the past two centuries, including such contemporary issues as welfare reform, social justice, and crime

0-688-07951-2 MORROW PB $9.95

Leo **Strauss**

The City and Man

Strauss, a refugee from Hitler, saw as the chief threat to democracy the mass culture fostered by democracy itself

0-226-77701-4 CHICAGO PB $13.95

Natural Right and History

0-226-77694-8 CHICAGO PB $14.95

What Is Political Philosophy?

Essays on political philosophy, reason, history, Plato, Hobbes, and Locke by the influential German-born philosopher who produced two generations of disciples at the University of Chicago

0-226-77713-8 CHICAGO PB $15.95

Eric **Voegelin**

From Enlightenment to Revolution

The spiritual crisis of modern times seen in the attempts to create a new humanity in Marxism, Nietzscheanism, and Nazism

EDITED BY JOHN HALLOWELL

0-8223-0478-3 DUKE PB $18.95

Science, Politics and Gnosticism

A short study linking the alienated pessimism of the ancient Gnostic heresy with modern theories of alienation and revolutionary deliverance in Hegel, Marx, Nietzsche, and Nazism

0-89526-964-3 REGNERY PB $7.95

Richard **Weaver**

Ideas Have Consequences

A Platonic-Christian perspective on the modern fragmentation of humanity as revealed in philosophy, literature, psychology, and politics

0-226-87680-2 CHICAGO PB $9.95

Simone **Weil**

The Need for Roots: Prelude to a Declaration of Duties Toward Mankind

0-415-11959-6 ROUTLEDGE PB $15.95

Fascism and Totalitarianism

T.W. **Adorno**

The Authoritarian Personality

A psychoanalytic attempt to isolate personality traits that would predispose an individual to fascism

0-393-30042-0 NORTON PB $14.95

Hannah **Arendt**

The Origins of Totalitarianism

The classic study of totalitarianism, it connects the Fascist period to the rise of Stalinism and the nature of imperialism

0-15-670153-7 HARCOURT BRACE PB $15.00

Alan **Bullock**

Hitler and Stalin: Parallel Lives

A magisterial dual biography of the two great leaders of totalitarian societies

See also **FASCISM AND TOTALITARIANISM: GENERAL STUDIES** under **20TH-CENTURY EUROPE TO THE SECOND WORLD WAR** in **WORLD HISTORY AND CURRENT AFFAIRS**

0-679-72994-1 VINTAGE PB $22.00

Milovan **Djilas**

Djilas played leading roles in the prewar Yugoslav Communist Party and the resistance and held several high positions in Tito's government, making his scathing study of the new privileged ruling class that had developed in communist societies all the more devastating (it earned him years of confinement in Tito's prisons).

The New Class: An Analysis of the Communist System

0-15-665489-X HARCOURT BRACE PB $8.95

Roger **Griffin**, editor

Fascism

A very well edited selection of fascist texts from Europe and Asia

0-19-289249-5 OXFORD PB $16.95

Adolf **Hitler**

Mein Kampf

Hitler's vituperative autobiography, written while he was in prison for his beer-hall *putsch*, gives his theories of Aryan superiority, Jewish conspiracy and democratic degeneracy, and provides a blueprint of his totalitarian regime and war aims

See also **HITLER: STUDIES IN TYRANNY** under **20TH-CENTURY EUROPE TO THE SECOND WORLD WAR** in **WORLD HISTORY AND CURRENT AFFAIRS**

TRANSLATED BY RALPH MANHEIM

0-395-07801-6 HOUGHTON MIFFLIN $24.95

0-395-08362-1 HOUGHTON MIFFLIN PB $16.95

Walter **Laqueur**

Fascism: Past, Present, and Future

0-19-509245-7 OXFORD $25.00

Czeslaw **Milosz**

The Captive Mind

An analysis of the influence of Stalinist dogma on creativity by a onetime diplomat for the Polish Communist state who went into exile and became a Nobel Prize-winning poet

See also **POLISH LITERATURE** under **EASTERN EUROPEAN LITERATURE** in **LITERATURE OF EUROPE, AFRICA, AND ASIA**

0-8446-6615-7 SMITH $21.30

0-679-72856-2 VINTAGE PB $12.00

Stanley G. **Payne**

A History of Fascism, 1914-1945

See also **LATE ARRIVALS** in **WORLD HISTORY AND CURRENT AFFAIRS**

0-299-14870-X WISCONSIN $39.95

0-299-14874-2 WISCONSIN PB $19.95

Karl R. **Popper**

The Open Society and Its Enemies

Volume 1

The Spell of Plato

Popper argues that the systematic philosophies of Plato, Hegel, and Marx laid the intellectual foundations for 20th-century totalitarianism; he advocates a democratic "piecemeal" approach to politics

See also **OTHER 20TH-CENTURY PHILOSOPHERS** under **PHILOSOPHY** in **RELIGION, SPIRITUALITY, AND PHILOSOPHY**

0-691-01968-1 PRINCETON PB $19.95

Volume 2

The High Tide of Prophecy

See also **OTHER 20TH-CENTURY PHILOSOPHERS** under **PHILOSOPHY** in **RELIGION, SPIRITUALITY, AND PHILOSOPHY**

0-691-01972-X PRINCETON PB $18.95

Fritz **Stern**

Politics of Cultural Despair

Examines the thought of three German intellectuals who contributed to the development of Nazism

0-4200-2626-8 CALIFORNIA PB $15.00

Colonialism

Ali **Behdad**

Belated Travelers: Orientalism in the Age of Colonial Dissolution

A nuanced study of post-colonial orientation and desire which suggests that the cultural politics of the colonial era are revisited again and again in the present

0-8223-1454-1 DUKE $44.95

0-8223-1471-1 DUKE PB $15.95

Aime **Cesaire**

Discourse on Colonialism

A classic short essay by a great poet and a leader of the *Négritude* movement: "Colonialist Europe has grafted modern abuse onto ancient injustice, hateful racism onto old inequality"

TRANSLATED BY JOAN PINKLAM

0-85345-226-1 MONTHLY REVIEW PB $10.00

Frantz **Fanon**

Black Skin, White Masks

Fanon's first book analyzes the psychological costs, for both blacks and whites, of racism and colonialism

TRANSLATED BY CHARLES L. MAMANN

0-8021-5084-5 GROVE PB $12.00

A Dying Colonialism

Tells how the native Algerians modified their colonized characteristics during the struggle to eject the French

See also **ALGERIA** under **NORTH AFRICA AND THE MEDITERRANEAN** under **THE CONTEMPORARY MIDDLE EAST** in **WORLD HISTORY AND CURRENT AFFAIRS**

0-8021-5027-6 GROVE PB $12.00

Toward the African Revolution

A collection of essays on the prospects for a successful revolutionary liberation of Africa

TRANSLATED BY HAAKON CHEVALIER

0-8021-3090-9 GROVE PB $8.95

The Wretched of the Earth

On the need for national liberation movements to release themselves from European models and to develop programs that will apply to all of the world's oppressed. A widely influential book, first published in 1961—the classic and shattering anticolonial handbook from Algeria

See also **ALGERIA** under **NORTH AFRICA AND THE MEDITERRANEAN** under **THE CONTEMPORARY MIDDLE EAST** in **WORLD HISTORY AND CURRENT AFFAIRS**

0-8021-5083-7 GROVE PB $12.00

Nationalism

With the end of the Cold War, nationalism has been an increasingly compelling political form across the globe as has a certain tribalism. Both have inspired a considerable amount of writing from political theorists and historians attempting to describe a political belief that many had written off as archaic only a few years ago.

Benedict **Anderson**

Imagined Communities: Reflections on the Origin and Spread of Nationalism

Anderson's hugely influential 1983 book argued that national identity and national institutions are highly specific historical products. He emphasized the importance of print technologies in the process of nation-making

0-86091-546-8 VERSO PB $18.00

Homi K. **Bhabha**, editor

Nation and Narration

Collects essays, mainly by literary theorists, on the idea of the nation and how cultures create "nationness." Includes Ernest Renan's classic 1882 lecture, *What Is a Nation?*

0-415-01483-2 ROUTLEDGE PB $17.95

Partha **Chatterjee**

Nationalist Thought and the Colonial World: A Derivative Discourse

A blistering, eloquent attack on Western nationalism and its unhappy fate in the Third World by a noted Indian political philosopher

0-8166-2311-2 MINNESOTA PB $16.95

Walker **Connor**

Ethnonationalism: The Quest for Understanding

A collection of essays by an American political scientist who predicted decades ago that nationalism was unlikely to fade away

0-691-02563-0 PRINCETON PB $14.95

Francis **Fukuyama**

The End of History and the Last Man

0-02-910975-2 FREE PRESS $29.95

0-380-72002-7 AVON PB $13.00

People in the West themselves came to question whether liberal democracy was in fact a general aspiration of all mankind, and whether their earlier confidence that it was did not reflect a narrow ethnocentrism on their part…The suicidal self-destructiveness of the European state system in two world wars gave lie to the notion of superior Western rationality, while the distinction between civilized and barbarian that was instinctive to Europeans in the 19th century was much harder to make after the Nazi death camps.

THE END OF HISTORY AND THE LAST MAN

Liah **Greenfeld**

Nationalism: Five Roads to Modernity

An erudite and careful consideration of the evolution of nationalism in England, France, Russia, Germany, and the United States

0-674-60319-2 HARVARD PB $21.95

Eric **Hobsbawm**

Nations and Nationalism Since 1780: Programme, Myth, Reality

An elegant study by a British historian of the "invented" nature of nationalisms, which ends with the hope that nationalism is on the wane

0-521-43961-2 CAMBRIDGE PB $11.95

Joel **Kotkin**

Tribes: How Race, Religion and Identity Determine Success in the New Global Economy

The first post-Cold War book to argue that "tribal" characteristics determine how different groups prosper

0-679-75299-4 RANDOM HOUSE PB $13.00

Louis L. **Snyder**

Encyclopedia of Nationalism

A useful guide to the bewildering range of historical and current nationalisms

1-55778-167-2 PARAGON $35.00

J.L. **Talmon**

The Myth of the Nation and the Vision of Revolution: The Origins of Ideological Polarization in the Twentieth Century

0-8873-8844-2 TRANSACTION PB $24.95

American Politics

K. Anthony **Appiah** & Amy **Gutmann**

Color Conscious: The Political Morality of Race

See also **AFRICAN-AMERICANS** under **THE MELTING POT** under **AMERICAN PEOPLE AND PLACES** in **HISTORY OF THE AMERICAS**

0-691-02661-0 PRINCETON $21.95

Richard **Darman**

Who's in Control: The Polarization of American Politics and the Revival of the Sensible Center

0-684-81123-5 SIMON & SCHUSTER $25.00

E.J. **Dionne**

They Only Look Dead: Why Progressives Will Dominate the Next Political Era

0-684-80768-8 SIMON & SCHUSTER $24.00

Why Americans Hate Politics

0-671-77877-3 TOUCHSTONE PB $12.00

Thomas Byrne **Edsall**

Power and Money: Writings on Politics, 1971-1987

0-393-30615-1 NORTON PB $9.95

Thomas Byrne **Edsall** & Mary D. **Edsall**

Chain Reaction: The Impact of Race, Rights, and Taxes on American Politics

See also **THE AMERICAN ECONOMY TODAY** under **ECONOMICS**

0-393-30903-7 NORTON PB $10.95

Barbara **Ehrenreich**

Fear of Falling: The Inner Life of the Middle Class

Argues that the American middle class is characterized by a fear of losing its social position

0-06-097333-1 HARPERCOLLINS PB $13.00

Frank **Gatell** & others, editors

Growth of American Politics: A Modern Reader Since the Civil War

0-19-501547-9 OXFORD $9.95

Newt **Gingrich**

To Renew America

A statement of vision from the Speaker of the House who led the Republican revolution of 1994-95

0-06-109539-7 HARPERCOLLINS PB $6.99

Stanley B. **Greenberg**

Middle Class Dreams: The Political Power of the New American Majority

Careful analysis of what really makes up America's majority

0-8129-2345-6 TIME BOOKS $25.00

0-300-06712-7 YALE PB $15.00

William **Greider**

Who Will Tell the People?: The Betrayal of American Democracy

"At the very moment when Western democracies and capitalism have triumphed over the Communist alternative, their own systems of self-government are being gradually unravelled by the market system," writes the author. His book pinpoints how special interest groups, money, and influence have completely taken over the American political system

See also **CURRENT POLITICAL THOUGHT AND ISSUES** under **AMERICAN POLITICS AND FOREIGN POLICY** in **HISTORY OF THE AMERICAS**

0-671-86740-7 TOUCHSTONE PB $13.00

David A. **Hollinger**

Postethnic America: Beyond Multiculturalism

An agile account of American debates on cultural pluralism throughout the 20th century. Hollinger urges a "postethnic" definition of Americanness

0-465-05991-0 BASIC $22.00

bell **hooks**

Killing Rage: Ending Racism

Recently named by the *Utne Reader* as one of the "100 Visionaries Who Could Change Your Life," bell hooks has been among our country's premier cultural and social critics for years. The 23 essays here address the fight against racism and sexism, and how those two battles are intimately interrelated in the American scene. From internalized racism in movies and media to black anti-Semitism, hooks draws from her enormous spectrum of reference an enduring lesson about the possibility of change

See also **RACE RELATIONS** under **AFRICAN-AMERICAN STUDIES** in **HISTORY OF THE AMERICAS**

0-8050-3782-9 HOLT $20.00

bell hooks

Christopher **Lasch**

The Revolt of the Elites and the Betrayal of Democracy

0-393-03699-5 NORTON $22.00
0-393-31371-9 NORTON PB $12.95

Manning **Marable**

Beyond Black and White: Transforming African-American Politics

Essays toward renewed black activism and an end to racial inequality

1-85984-049-3 VERSO PB $17.00

Walter Benn **Michaels**

Our America: Nativism, Modernism, and Pluralism

Discusses, through literature and history, the different ways in which race has been used to understand Americanness

0-8223-1700-1 DUKE $24.95

Daniel P. **Moynihan**

Miles to Go: Attempts at Social Policy

0-674-57440-0 HARVARD $22.95

Kenneth **O'Reilly**

Nixon's Piano: Presidents and Racial Politics from Washington to Clinton

A careful historical study of the uses to which the "race card" has been put by American presidents

0-02-923685-1 FREE PRESS $27.50

Peter G. **Peterson**

Will America Grow Up Before It Grows Old?: How the Coming Social Security Crisis Threatens You, Your Family, and Your Country

By the director of the Federal Reserve Bank of New York. "[Peterson's] proposals for a graying America to return to an earlier generation's collective restraint are worthy advisories to which attention should be paid"
—*Publishers Weekly*

See also **THE AMERICAN ECONOMY TODAY** under **ECONOMICS**

0-679-45256-7 MCKAY $21.00

Kevin **Phillips**

Boiling Point: Republicans, Democrats, and the Decline of Middle-Class Prosperity

Examines the middle class's declining influence. "In the political business, very few people deserve the appellation 'genius.' Kevin Phillips is decidedly one of them"—James Carville, Clinton campaign strategist

See also **SOCIAL MOBILITY** under **AMERICAN PEOPLE AND PLACES** in **HISTORY OF THE AMERICAS**

0-06-097582-2 HARPERCOLLINS PB $13.50

Michael **Tomasky**

Left for Dead: The Life, Death, and Possible Resurrection of Progressive Politics in America

An argument for reviving the American left

0-684-82750-6 FREE PRESS $23.00

Jacob **Weisberg**

In Defense of Government: The Fall and Rise of Public Trust

A vigorous, well-researched argument for the importance of government's role in American society

0-684-81604-0 SCRIBNERS $22.00

Stephen R. **Weissman**

A Culture of Deference: Congress's Failure of Leadership in Foreign Policy

0-465-00761-9 BASIC $26.00
0-465-00732-5 BASIC PB $15.00

Cornel **West**

Race Matters

The theologist and philosopher discusses race in relation to America's social and spiritual predicaments

See also **RACE RELATIONS** under **AFRICAN-AMERICAN STUDIES** in **HISTORY OF THE AMERICAS**

0-8070-0918-0 BEACON $15.00
0-679-74986-1 VINTAGE PB $10.00

Robert H. **Wiebe**

Self Rule: A Cultural History of American Democracy

A fascinating history of the varying ways American democracy has defined "the people"

0-226-89562-9 CHICAGO $25.95

George F. **Will**

The Leveling Wind: Politics, the Culture and Other News

The fifth collection of columns, speeches, and reviews from the preeminent conservative commentator on the national scene

0-14-024702-5 PENGUIN PB $13.95

George F. Will

Daniel **Yergin** & Joseph **Stanislaw**

The Commanding Heights: The Battle Between Government and the Marketplace

0-684-82975-4 SIMON & SCHUSTER $22.00

Important Recent Work

Perry **Anderson**

The Ends of History

Is it truly Marxism that is collapsing as the century ends? Or is it capitalism?

1-85984-041-8 VERSO PB....$16.95

Homi **Bhabha**

The Location of Culture

A key collection of essays by a major cultural critic, this contains essential and challenging readings for anyone interested in the politics of culture

0-415-01635-5 ROUTLEDGE....$59.95
0-415-05406-0 ROUTLEDGE PB....$17.95

Derek Curtis **Bok**

The State of the Nation: Government and the Quest for a Better Society, 1960-1995

0-674-29210-3 HARVARD....$35.00

John **Dunn**

Western Political Theory in the Face of the Future

A deft assessment of Western political thought. "He has begun to show cogently in a quite new way why conventional political theory is now a subject of great political relevance. He does so in a short book of immense learning"—*London Review of Books*

0-521-43755-5 CAMBRIDGE PB....$10.95

Amitai **Etzioni**

Rights and the Common Good: The Communitarian Perspective

0-312-08968-6 ST. MARTIN'S PB....$21.32

The Spirit of Community: The Reinvention of American Society

0-671-88524-3 TOUCHSTONE PB....$12.00

Amitai **Etzioni**, editor

New Communitarian Thinking: Persons, Virtues, Institutions, and Communities

0-8139-1564-3 VIRGINIA....$55.00
0-8139-1569-4 VIRGINIA PB....$18.50

Francis **Fukuyama**

Trust: The New Foundations of Global Prosperity

See also **AFTER THE COLD WAR: THE FORMER SOVIET UNION AND EASTERN BLOC** under **INTERNATIONAL RELATIONS AND STRATEGIC STUDIES**

0-02-910976-0 FREE PRESS....$25.00
0-684-82525-2 FREE PRESS PB....$15.00

John **Gray**

Beyond the New Right: Markets, Government and the Common Environment

0-415-10706-7 ROUTLEDGE PB....$16.95

Post-Liberalism: Studies in Political Thought

0-415-08873-9 ROUTLEDGE....$49.95

Stephan **Haggard** & Robert R. **Kaufman**

The Political Economy of Democratic Transitions

Considers the political and economic difficulties of newly democratic states

0-691-02775-7 PRINCETON PB....$19.95

Ira **Katznelson**

Liberalism's Crooked Circle: Letters to Adam Michnik

0-691-03438-9 PRINCETON....$19.95

George **Lakoff**

Moral Politics: What Conservatives Know that Liberals Don't

0-226-46796-1 CHICAGO....$24.95

Michael **Lerner**

The Socialism of Fools: Anti-Semitism on the Left

0-935933-05-0 PUBLISHERS GROUP WEST PB....$10.00

Sven **Lindqvist**

Exterminate All the Brutes: A Modern Odyssey into the Heart of Darkness

This unique study of Europe's troubling history in Africa, written in the form of a travel diary, constitutes a history of European racism over two centuries. "Everything that Lindqvist writes is hard-won fact based on sharp-eyed observation and diligent research. His books are informed by the analytical skills of a philosopher and constructed with the care and attention of a novelist"—Richard Gott

See also **AFRICA AND THE WEST** under **GENERAL HISTORIES** under **AFRICA** in **WORLD HISTORY AND CURRENT AFFAIRS**

TRANSLATED BY JOAN TATE

1-56584-334-7 NEW PRESS....$20.00

Seymour Martin **Lipset**

Consensus and Conflict: Essays in Political Sociology

0-88738-051-4 TRANSACTION....$34.95
0-88738-608-3 TRANSACTION PB....$21.95

Political Man: The Social Bases of Politics

0-8018-2522-9 JOHNS HOPKINS PB....$15.95

Union Democracy: The Internal Politics of the International Typographical Union

0-02-919210-2 FREE PRESS PB....$18.95

Steven **Lukes**, editor

Power

0-8147-5030-3 NYU....$45.00
0-8147-5031-1 NYU PB....$17.50

Kenneth **Minogue**

Politics: A Very Short Introduction

A brisk tour of the varieties of Western political thought

0-19-285309-0 OXFORD PB....$7.95

Martha C. **Nussbaum**

For Love of Country: Debating the Limits of Patriotism

An argument against patriotism as a parochial ideal, and for a view of ourselves as "citizens of the world." An astonishing range of writers from Robert Pinsky to Gertrude Himmelfarb, Elaine Scarry, Amartya Sen, and Cornel West respond in a series of brilliant essays

See also **READINGS IN PHILOSOPHY: ANTHOLOGIES ON SPECIAL TOPICS** under **PHILOSOPHY** in **RELIGION, SPIRITUALITY, AND PHILOSOPHY**

EDITED BY JOSHUA COHEN

0-8070-4313-3 BEACON PB....$15.00

Karl Raimund **Popper** & Giancarlo **Bosetti**

The Lesson of This Century: With Two Talks on Freedom and the Democratic State

0-415-12958-3 ROUTLEDGE....$42.00

Michael J. **Sandel**

Democracy's Discontent: America in Search of a Public Philosophy

0-674-19744-5 HARVARD....$24.95

Liberalism and the Limits of Justice

0-521-56298-8 CAMBRIDGE....$49.95
0-521-56741-6 CAMBRIDGE PB....$15.95

Michael **Sandel**, editor

Liberalism and Its Critics

0-8147-7841-0 NYU PB....$17.50

John Ralston **Saul**

The Unconscious Civilization

0-684-83257-7 FREE PRESS....$22.00

Roberto **Unger**

Social Theory: Its Situation and Its Task: A Critical Introduction to Politics

0-521-32974-4 CAMBRIDGE....$54.95
0-521-33862-X CAMBRIDGE PB....$16.95

International Relations and Strategic Studies

The study of relations and conflicts among states has few obvious parameters. Theorists of the international system must have a solid grounding in the history of war, diplomacy, economics, law, and philosophy, all of which have their own canons of discourse. Most scholars also take a keen interest in contemporary political affairs; whether explicitly or implicitly, the truths inherent in past events have relevance to the concerns of the present day. In a world that lives daily with the specter of nuclear armageddon and financial catastrophe, questions about the nature of war are as urgent as ever.

Theories of International Relations

Historians explain particular events; political scientists classify, synthesize, and generalize. The following works include samples of both approaches, with emphasis on the latter. The causes of war, the nature of international change, the operation of the balance of power, and the institutions of international society are among the topics examined in these works, many of which are classics in the field of political writing.

Bernard **Brodie**

War and Politics

The distilled wisdom of the dean of American strategic studies, who died in 1978

0-02-315020-3 MACMILLAN PB........$46.00

Seyom **Brown**

Causes and Prevention of War

An examination of "the central survival question facing our species: How can we reduce the role of large-scale violence in world society?"

0-312-10269-0 ST. MARTIN'S........$45.00
0-312-12532-1 ST. MARTIN'S PB........$18.65

Hedley **Bull**

The Anarchical Society: A Study of Order in World Politics

Argues that the state system is not an obstacle to world order but its essential foundation

0-231-04133-0 COLUMBIA PB........$18.00

Robert **Gilpin**

War and Change in World Politics

An ambitious attempt to formulate a theory of international political change. "An intelligent and intellectually stimulating, if speculative, study of major issues in world politics"
—*Times Higher Education Supplement*

0-521-27376-5 CAMBRIDGE PB........$19.95

David **Kaiser**

Politics and War: European Conflict from Philip II to Hitler

Kaiser examines in revealing detail how political needs have led to war

0-674-68815-5 HARVARD........$38.00

Hans J. **Morgenthau**

Politics Among Nations

Morgenthau's 1948 work was a point of departure for a generation of scholars who took a "realistic" approach to international affairs. Now in its sixth edition, it remains worthy of serious study

EDITED BY KENNETH W. THOMPSON
0-07-554469-5 MCGRAW HILL........$71.65

Richard E. **Neustadt** & Ernest R. **May**

Thinking in Time: The Uses of History for Decision Makers

A Harvard political scientist and a Harvard historian offer rules that decisionmakers can follow to use history more widely and effectively

0-02-922791-7 FREE PRESS PB........$14.95

Stephen M. **Walt**

The Origins of Alliances

The author tests a variety of theories regarding the formation of alliances and concludes that states are more likely to "balance" rather than "bandwagon" when faced with would-be hegemons

0-8014-9418-4 CORNELL PB........$14.95

Kenneth N. **Waltz**

Man, the State and War: A Theoretical Analysis

Presents war as the result of three conflicting forms of interstate rivalry: as an expression of human nature, as a reflection of the internal character of the state, and as a consequence of the anarchical character of the state system

0-231-08564-8 COLUMBIA PB........$16.50

Theory of International Politics

A major treatise on international politics. This work is of great value for advanced students, but not recommended for beginners

0-07-554852-6 MCGRAW HILL PB........$48.40

Martin **Wight**

Power Politics

A neglected masterpiece, this book deserves a wide readership among students of international relations

EDITED BY HADLEY BULL
0-7185-1002-X PINTER PB........$21.95

International System to 1900

Michel W. **Doyle**

Empires

A wide-ranging account of the birth, life, and death of empires

0-8014-1756-2 CORNELL........$49.95
0-8014-9334-X CORNELL PB........$16.95

Murray G. **Forsyth**

Unions of States: Theory and Practice of Confederation

0-8419-0691-2 HOLMES & MEIER........$42.50
0-8419-0729-3 HOLMES & MEIER PB........$19.50

Edward V. **Gulick**

Europe's Classical Balance of Power

Gulick's case history is the Congress of Vienna. The first part of the work identifies the assumptions, aims, and applications of balance of power theory in the 18th century

0-393-00413-9 NORTON PB........$11.95

Edward **Luttwak**

The Grand Strategy of the Roman Empire

"Brings detailed insights into the working of Roman military organization, in strategy and tactics"—E. Badian

See also **MILITARY** under **TOPICS IN ROMAN HISTORY** under **ANCIENT ROME** in **WORLD HISTORY AND CURRENT AFFAIRS**

0-8018-2158-4 JOHNS HOPKINS PB........$14.95

Garrett **Mattingly**

Renaissance Diplomacy

The classic study of the age of Machiavelli

0-486-25570-0 DOVER PB........$8.95

The 20th-Century World

Geoffrey **Barraclough**

An Introduction to Contemporary History

First published in the early 1960s, this work remains a valuable introduction to the transformation of the international system in the 20th century

0-14-013513-8 VIKING PB........$9.95

David **Calleo**

The German Problem Reconsidered

An original essay on the central diplomatic question of the century from 1849 to 1948

0-521-29966-7 CAMBRIDGE PB........$18.95

Gordon A. **Craig**

Germany, 1866-1945

A superbly written book that traces the rise and fall of German power from Bismarck's victory over Austria in 1866 to Hitler's last days in the bunker

0-19-502724-8 OXFORD PB........$22.00

Gordon A. **Craig** &
Francis L. **Lowenheim**, editors

The Diplomats 1919-1939

0-691-03660-8 PRINCETON PB........$24.95

The Diplomats 1939-1979

0-691-03613-6 PRINCETON........$39.50

Graham **Hancock**

Lords of Poverty: The Power, Prestige, and Corruption of the International Aid Business

An unflattering portrait of the business and politics of foreign aid

0-87113-469-1 ATLANTIC MONTHLY PB........$10.95

William R. **Keylor**

The Twentieth-Century World: An International History

Properly sets Europe in a global context

See also **THE 20TH CENTURY** under **WORLD HISTORIES** under **THE VARIETIES OF CIVILIZATION** in **WORLD HISTORY AND CURRENT AFFAIRS**

0-19-506804-1 OXFORD PB........$21.00

George **Lenczowski**

The Middle East in World Affairs

A comprehensive work on the history, government, and politics of the Middle East to 1980

0-8014-1273-0 CORNELL........$49.95
0-8014-9872-4 CORNELL PB........$26.95

Stanley **Meisler**

United Nations: The First Fifty Years

See also **OTHER DEVELOPMENTS** under **EUROPE SINCE 1945** in **WORLD HISTORY AND CURRENT AFFAIRS**

0-87113-616-3 GROVE........$24.00

Frank **Ninkovich**

Modernity and Power: A History of the Domino Theory in the Twentieth Century

Artfully examines the shift in American policy from geopolitical realism to a struggle between "world opinion" and the forces of chaos

0-226-58651-0 CHICAGO PB $19.95

R.K. **Ramazani**

Revolutionary Iran: Challenge and Response in the Middle East

Published in 1987

0-8018-3377-9 JOHNS HOPKINS $49.50
0-8018-3610-7 JOHNS HOPKINS PB $14.95

Nadav **Safran**

Israel: The Embattled Ally

This in-depth story of Israel since its founding focuses on its relationship with the US and includes a brilliant analysis of Kissinger's Israel policy

See also **ISRAEL** under **THE CONTEMPORARY MIDDLE EAST** in **WORLD HISTORY AND CURRENT AFFAIRS**

0-674-46881-3 HARVARD $42.50
0-674-46882-1 HARVARD PB $19.95

Robert W. **Tucker** & Linda **Wrigley**, editors

The Atlantic Alliance and Its Critics

Excellent essays from Pierre Hassner, A.W. DePorte, Theodore Draper, Pierre Lelouche, Simon Serfaty, and Robert W. Tucker

0-275-91094-6 PRAEGER $49.95
0-275-91592-1 PRAEGER PB $14.95

D.C. **Watt**

Succeeding John Bull: America in Britain's Place, 1900-1975

An Englishman reviews the transition with a begrudging but always intelligent eye

0-521-25022-6 CAMBRIDGE $54.95

The Cold War

Seweryn **Bialer** & Michael **Mandelbaum**

The Global Rivals

The companion to the PBS series

0-679-72649-7 VINTAGE PB $9.95

Paul M. **Buhle** & Edward **Rice-Maximin**

William Appleman Williams: The Tragedy of Empire

A biography of a leading historian of the Cold War and critic of American empire-building

0-415-91131-1 ROUTLEDGE PB $18.95

Anton W. **DePorte**

Europe Between the Superpowers: The Enduring Balance

A clear-headed account of the origins of the Cold War, seeing it as a solution to the German problem

0-300-04081-4 YALE $35.00
0-300-03758-9 YALE PB $14.00

Tom **Engelhardt**

The End of Victory Culture: Cold War America and the Disillusioning of a Generation

0-465-01985-4 BASIC PB $14.00

John Lewis **Gaddis**

The Long Peace: Inquiries into the History of the Cold War

A collection of essays notable for their mastery of historical sources and for an attempt to identify the elements of stability within the Soviet-American competition

See also **THE COLD WAR** under **THE STALIN ERA** under **RUSSIAN STUDIES** in **WORLD HISTORY AND CURRENT AFFAIRS**

0-19-504336-7 OXFORD $30.00
0-19-504335-9 OXFORD PB $11.95

Lawrence S. **Kaplan**

NATO and the United States: The Enduring Alliance

The founding of NATO and the impact of such major events as the Korean War, the launching of Sputnik, and De Gaulle's decision to pull France out in 1966

0-8057-9221-X TWAYNE PB $15.95

Joseph S. **Nye**, Jr., editor

The Making of America's Soviet Policy

Contributors include Nye, Richard K. Betts, Ernest R. May, Stanley Hoffmann, and others

0-300-03140-8 YALE $40.00

Martin **Walker**

The Cold War: A History

"The first major study for the general reader of the Cold War as history"—Ronald Steel

See also **THE COLD WAR** under **THE TRUMAN AND EISENHOWER YEARS** under **US HISTORY, 1945 TO THE PRESENT** in **HISTORY OF THE AMERICAS**

0805034545 HOLT $30.00
0-8050-3454-4 HOLT PB $14.00

William Appleman **Williams**

"An American original...He stole time to create the most substantial one-man body of literature in our history. When he died at 79, he had no peer as the total American writer."
—Webster Scott, Life

The Tragedy of American Diplomacy

A classic examination of the profound contradictions between America's ideals and its actual uses of power, from the Open Door Notes of 1898 to the Bay of Pigs of 1961

See also **INTERPRETATIONS** under **FOREIGN POLICY AND DIPLOMATIC HISTORY** under **AMERICAN POLITICS AND FOREIGN POLICY** in **HISTORY OF THE AMERICAS**

0-393-30493-0 NORTON PB $11.95

After the Cold War: The Former Soviet Union and Eastern Bloc

Zbigniew **Brzezinski**

Out of Control: Global Turmoil on the Eve of the Twenty-First Century

President Carter's National Security Advisor serves up some dire, hardball warnings about the post-Cold War world. Brzezinski points out that in the 20th century, 167 million people have already been "extinguished" for political reasons, and it's difficult to argue with his fear that there will be more. "Brilliant, lucid and gripping"—*NY Times Book Review*

0-684-82636-4 COLLIER PB $11.00

Zbigniew Brzezinski

Nadia **Diuk** & Adrian **Karatnycky**

New Nations Rising: The Fall of the Soviets and the Challenge of Independence

A timely survey of the "new nations" that have emerged from the former Soviet bloc

0-471-58263-8 WILEY PB $14.95

Robert J. **Donia** & John V.A. **Fine**

Bosnia and Herzegovina: A Tradition Betrayed

Emphasizes the deep roots of Bosnia's multiethnic tradition

0-231-10160-0 COLUMBIA $32.50

Francis **Fukuyama**

Trust: The New Foundations of Global Prosperity

See also **IMPORTANT RECENT WORK** under **POLITICAL THOUGHT**

0-02-910976-0 FREE PRESS $25.00
0-684-82525-2 FREE PRESS PB $15.00

Misha **Glenny**

Glenny's books have been influential in Western debate over the former Yugoslavia.

The Fall of Yugoslavia: The Third Balkan War

"Vigorous, passionate, humane and extremely readable... For an account of what has actually happened...Glenny's book so far stands unparalled"—*The New Republic*

See also **THE BALKANS** under **EUROPE SINCE 1945** in **WORLD HISTORY AND CURRENT AFFAIRS**

0-14-023586-8 PENGUIN PB........$10.95

The Rebirth of History: Eastern Europe in the Age of Democracy

0-14-017286-6 PENGUIN PB........$11.95

Robert **Kaplan**

The Ends of the Earth: A Journey at the Dawn of the Twentieth Century

"In a controversial *Atlantic Monthly* article in 1994, Robert Kaplan predicted anarchy: extreme poverty and famine made worse by a widening gap between the ever more desperate underprivileged and the overprivileged who ignore them. Mr. Kaplan's dark prognosis...is eloquently illustrated and documented in *The Ends of the Earth*"—Peter Matthiessen

See also **EUROPE SINCE 1945** under **EUROPE** under **TRAVEL LITERATURE** in **FOOD, TRAVEL, AND LEISURE**

0-679-43148-9 RANDOM HOUSE........$27.50
0-679-75123-8 VINTAGE........$14.00

Paul **Kennedy**

Preparing for the Twenty-First Century

A grim preview of some of the threats facing humanity in the near future. "Penetrating...the book's impact is crushing"—*NY Times*

0-679-74705-2 VINTAGE PB........$14.00

Anatoly M. **Khazanov**

After the USSR: Ethnicity, Nationalism, and Politics in the Commonwealth of Independent States

0-299-14894-7 WISCONSIN PB........$13.95

Terrorism and Counter-Terrorism

Benjamin **Netanyahu**

Fighting Terrorism: How Democracies Can Defeat Domestic and International Terrorism

The current prime minister of Israel addresses the rise of terrorism in the world today, from the Oklahoma bombing to the sarin gas attack in Japan. From his wealth of experience, Netanyahu argues that domestic terror can be fought without any significant curtailment of civil liberties, but that international terrorism poses the greatest threat to democracy. How democracies can defend themselves against this new threat is the compelling and urgent center of this timely work

0-374-15492-9 FS&G........$17.00

International Political Economy

David A. **Baldwin**

Economic Statecraft

Examines not only the utility of economic statecraft but also its morality and legality and its role in the history of international thought

0-691-10175-2 PRINCETON PB........$19.95

David P. **Calleo**

The Imperious Economy

Closely examines the relationship between America's political ambitions and its monetary policy

0-674-44522-8 HARVARD........$28.00
0-674-44521-X HARVARD PB........$7.95

Robert **Gilpin**

The Political Economy of International Relations

Excellent study of the political and economic forces affecting money, trade, development, finance, and the multinational corporation; likely to become the standard text on the subject

0-691-07732-0 PRINCETON........$65.00
0-691-02262-3 PRINCETON PB........$16.95

Mikhail **Gorbachev**

Perestroika: New Thinking for Our Country and the World

A glimpse into the past

See also **THE SOVIET UNION: FROM KRUSHCHEV TO GORBACHEV** under **RUSSIAN STUDIES** in **WORLD HISTORY AND CURRENT AFFAIRS**

0-85124-501-3 DUFOUR........$40.00

Roger D. **Hansen**

Beyond the North-South Stalemate

0-07-026049-4 OVERSEAS DEVELOPMENT PB........$6.95

Ethan B. **Kapstein**

Governing the Global Economy: International Finance and the State

Banker and economist Kapstein analyzes the relationship between states and international banks in a period of increased globalization

0-674-35757-4 HARVARD........$29.95

Robert O. **Keohane**

After Hegemony: Cooperation and Discord in the World Political Economy

Keohane disputes the argument that the decline of American hegemony makes cooperation among the advanced capitalist nations impossible

0-691-07676-6 PRINCETON........$49.50
0-691-02228-3 PRINCETON PB........$15.95

Nicholas N. **Kittrie**

The War Against Authority: From the Crisis of Legitimacy to a New Social Contract

0-8018-5050-9 JOHNS HOPKINS........$29.95

Charles **Kindleberger**

Manias, Panics, and Crashes: A History of Financial Crises

The author, a professor emeritus at MIT, shows how financial institutions disintegrate and recommends seeking out a "lender of the last resort." Originally published in 1980

See also **POLITICS AND THE INTERNATIONAL ECONOMY** under **ECONOMICS**

0-465-04404-2 BASIC BOOKS PB........$17.50

Stephen D. **Krasner**

Structural Conflict: The Third World Against Global Liberalism

0-520-05478-4 CALIFORNIA PB........$15.95

Charles **Lipson**

Standing Guard: Protecting Foreign Capital in the Nineteenth and Twentieth Centuries

0-520-03468-6 CALIFORNIA........$47.50
0-520-05327-3 CALIFORNIA PB........$16.00

Gerald M. **Meier**

Emerging from Poverty: The Economics that Really Matters

An overview of the state of the economics of development; published in 1984

0-19-503714-6 OXFORD PB........$15.95

Bruce **Rich**

Mortgaging the Earth: The World Bank, Environmental Impoverishment, and the Crisis of Development

This explosive critique of the World Bank draws on back-corridor reports. Why is the bank—which lends $25 billion each year for huge agricultural and resettlement projects—so powerful? And why is it always unaccountable for the world's problems as it lends financial support to repressive military governments?

See also **THE ECONOMICS OF ENERGY AND ENVIRONMENT** under **SPECIAL TOPICS** under **ECONOMICS**

0-8070-4707-4 BEACON PB........$16.00

Richard **Rosecrance**

The Rise of the Trading State: Commerce and Conquest in the Modern World

Argues that a new "trading world" in international relations offers the possibility of escaping the "vicious cycle" of endemic warfare and of finding new patterns of cooperation among nation-states

0-465-07037-X BASIC BOOKS PB........$17.00

Law, Morality, and Justice

Charles R. **Beitz**

Political Theory and International Relations

Sets forth a case for a global redistribution of resources. Published in 1979

0-691-07614-6 PRINCETON........$37.50
0-691-02192-9 PRINCETON PB........$12.95

Thomas M. **Franck**

Nation Against Nation: What Happened to the U.N. Dream and What the U.S. Can Do About It

An examination of the United Nations by a law professor and former employee of the organization

0-19-503587-9 OXFORD $29.95

James **Muldoon**

The Americas in the Spanish World Order: The Justification for Conquest in the Seventeenth Century

An unusual study of the legal arguments for the Spanish takeover of the Americas. Muldoon probes the roots of modern international law and the moral justifications for international expansion

0-8122-3245-3 PENNSYLVANIA $32.95

Michael **Walzer**

Just and Unjust Wars

An excellent work notable not only for its conclusions but for its historical and logical method of discourse. Recommended for beginning and advanced students alike

0-465-03701-1 BASIC PB $17.00

Strategic Studies

Strategy, as Sir Basil Liddell-Hart once put it, is "the art of distributing and applying military means to fulfill the ends of policy." The following books take up a range of historical and contemporary problems in strategic studies, largely from an American perspective.

Carl von **Clausewitz**

On War

Clausewitz's study of war, first published in 1832, is generally acknowledged to be the great theoretical treatment of the subject. This edition contains valuable introductory essays by Paret, Howard, and Bernard Brodie that explain the influence and continuing relevance of *On War*, as well as an entertaining and instructive commentary on the text by Brodie

EDITED BY PETER PARET & MICHAEL HOWARD

0-691-05657-9 PRINCETON $70.00

Martin van **Creveld**

Command in War

The development of the nature of command from the Stone Age to Vietnam

0-674-14441-4 HARVARD PB $16.95

James T. **Johnson**

Can Modern War Be Just?

A distinguished historian of the "just war" examines a range of issues

0-300-03165-3 YALE $32.00

0-300-03626-4 YALE PB $14.00

John **Keegan**

The Face of Battle

A brilliant work on the predicament of individual soldiers in battle

0-14-004897-9 PENGUIN PB $12.95

Michael **Howard**

Clausewitz

An excellent short essay on the master of strategic thought. Highly recommended

0-19-287607-4 OXFORD PB $7.95

Carl von Clausewitz

War in European History

Short and authoritative study of warfare as it has developed from the Middle Ages to the present

See also **GENERAL HISTORIES** under **MILITARY HISTORY** under **MILITARY AFFAIRS** in **WORLD HISTORY AND CURRENT AFFAIRS**

0-19-289095-6 OXFORD PB $15.95

A History of Warfare

One of the world's most respected military historians explores and illuminates mankind's seemingly infinite capacity for armed conflict, from primitive ritual to high-tech destruction. "Keegan concludes that global survival depends on our curbing humanity's vast capacity for destructive violence—and on this score, readers of his superb new survey will find, he's cautiously optimistic"—*Kirkus Reviews*

See also **GENERAL HISTORIES** under **MILITARY HISTORY** under **MILITARY AFFAIRS** in **WORLD HISTORY AND CURRENT AFFAIRS**

0-394-58801-0 KNOPF $30.00

0-679-73082-6 VINTAGE PB $15.00

The Mask of Command

A comprehensive analysis of generalship

0-14-011406-8 PENGUIN PB $12.95

John J. **Mearsheimer**

Conventional Deterrence

How nations faced with the prospect of large-scale conventional war choose offensive or defensive strategies

0-8014-1569-1 CORNELL $39.95

0-8014-9346-3 CORNELL PB $14.95

Steven **Miller**, editor

Origins of the First World War: An International Security Reader

Essays on the relationship between military doctrine and the outbreak of the First World War

0-691-02349-2 PRINCETON PB $16.95

John **Mueller**

Retreat from Doomsday: The Obsolescence of Major War

Why a major war among the developed nations of the world has become increasingly unlikely

0-465-06939-8 BASIC $20.95

Peter **Paret** & others, editors

Of Modern Strategy: From Machiavelli to the Nuclear Age

An excellent compendium of essays from many of the leading historians of strategic thought

0-691-09235-4 PRINCETON $85.00

0-691-02764-1 PRINCETON PB $21.95

Theodore **Ropp**

War in the Modern World

A good introduction to the history of war since 1415

0-02-036390-7 MACMILLAN PB $11.00

Alvin **Toffler** & Heidi **Toffler**

War & Anti-War in the 21st Century

Two of the world's leading futurists and social thinkers *(Future Shock, The Third Wave)* offer a provocative vision of warfare in the past and intriguing insights into today's military conflicts by analyzing the horrifying reality of possible future war. The Tofflers hope to influence strategies for a war-free future

0-316-85024-1 LITTLE, BROWN $22.95

Russell F. **Weigley**

The American Way of War: A History of U.S. Military Strategy and Policy

The best introduction to American military thought. Published in 1973

See also **AMERICAN MILITARY HISTORY** under **MILITARY HISTORY** under **MILITARY AFFAIRS** in **WORLD HISTORY AND CURRENT AFFAIRS**

0-253-28029-X INDIANA PB $16.95

Nuclear Weapons and Arms Control

Howard **Ball**

Justice Downwind: America's Atomic Testing Program in the 1950s

The astonishing story of how the US exploded atomic weapons on its own soil between 1951 and 1963 as part of a postwar military nuclear testing program. "A praiseworthy job of exploring one of the great scandals of the atomic age"—*Chicago Sun-Times*

0-19-503672-7 OXFORD $30.00

0-19-505357-5 OXFORD PB $8.95

Glenn T. **Seaborg** & Benjamin S. **Loeb**
Kennedy, Khrushchev, and the Test Ban
0-520-04332-4 CALIFORNIA $32.50
0-520-04961-6 CALIFORNIA PB $13.00

Nuclear Strategy

Bruce G. **Blair**
Strategic Command and Control: Redefining the Nuclear Threat
An original study of the command and control of strategic weapons; published in 1985
0-8157-0982-X BROOKINGS $42.95
0-8157-0981-1 BROOKINGS PB $18.95

David **DeWitt**, editor
Nuclear Non-Proliferation and Global Security
Published in 1987
0-312-00367-6 ST. MARTIN'S $37.50

James F. **Dunnigan**
How to Make War: A Comprehensive Guide to Modern Warfare
"Why the most modern weapons will not work as expected and there's not much anyone can do about it"
0-688-12157-8 QUILL PB $15.00

Lawrence **Freedman**
The Evolution of Nuclear Strategy
Published in 1983
0-312-02843-1 ST. MARTIN'S PB $16.95

Peter **Hayes**
American Lake: Nuclear Peril in the Pacific
Why World War III is more likely to begin in the Pacific than in the Middle East or Europe
See also **EAST ASIA AS ECONOMIC AND POLITICAL REGION: GENERAL STUDIES** under **SOUTHEAST ASIA AND THE PHILIPPINES** in **WORLD HISTORY AND CURRENT AFFAIRS**
0-14-009396-6 PENGUIN PB $6.95

Charles W. **Kegley**, Jr. & Eugene R. **Wittkopf**, editors
The Nuclear Reader: Strategy, Weapons, War
Published in 1985
0-312-00498-2 ST. MARTIN'S PB $16.00

Henry A. **Kissinger**
Nuclear Weapons and Foreign Policy
0-86531-745-3 WESTVIEW PB $55.50

Robert W. **Tucker**
The Nuclear Debate: Deterrence and the Lapse of Faith
A 1985 study
0-8419-1038-3 HOLMES & MEIER $24.50
0-8419-1039-1 HOLMES & MEIER PB $9.95

Leonard C. **Lewin**
Report from Iron Mountain: On the Possibility and Desirability of Peace
A famous hoax from the '60s, *Report* presented a straightlaced argument for the economic and political necessity of permanent war written in Defense Department bureaucratese. All too believable, the book is still considered a genuine document by members of today's right-wing militias
0-684-82390-X FREE PRESS $20.00

Michael **Mandelbaum**
The Nuclear Future
A clear introduction published in 1983
0-8014-9254-8 CORNELL PB $10.95

The Nuclear Revolution: International Politics Before and After Hiroshima
0-521-23819-6 CAMBRIDGE $21.95

Nuclear Ethics

John **Finnis**
Nuclear Deterrence, Morality and Realism
A call for unilateral disarmament
0-19-824791-5 OXFORD PB $19.95

Lester **Grinspoon**, editor
The Long Darkness: Psychological and Moral Perspectives on Nuclear Winter
0-300-03664-7 YALE PB $13.00

Mark A. **Harwell**
Nuclear Winter
0-387-96093-7 SPRINGER-VERLAG $48.00

Joseph S. **Nye**, Jr.
Nuclear Ethics
A Harvard political scientist examines the ethical dilemmas raised by nuclear weapons
0-02-922460-8 FREE PRESS $22.95
0-02-923091-8 FREE PRESS PB $12.95

Fredric **Solomon** & Robert Q. **Marston**, editors
The Medical Implications of Nuclear War
FOREWORD BY LEWIS THOMAS
0-309-03636-4 NATIONAL ACADEMY PB $33.50

Spencer R. **Weart**
Nuclear Fear: A History of Images
See also **THE NUCLEAR AGE** under **TECHNOLOGY AND EDUCATION** under **EDUCATION**
0-674-62836-5 HARVARD PB $14.95

War in Space

Angelo **Coderilla**
While Others Build: A Commonsense Approach to the Strategic Defense Initiative
Published in 1988
0-02-905671-3 FREE PRESS $32.95

H. Bruce **Franklin**
War Stars: The Superweapon and the American Imagination
A history of the American belief that miraculous new weapons will somehow end war and ensure global triumph of American ideals
0-19-505295-1 OXFORD $30.00
0-19-506692-8 OXFORD PB $10.95

American Defense Policy

John L. **Gaddis**
Strategies of Containment: A Critical Appraisal of Postwar American National Security Policy
This reassessment, based on declassified documents, compares and evaluates the assumptions that shaped policy; published in 1982
0-19-503097-4 OXFORD PB $14.95

Norman A. **Graebner**, editor
The National Security: Its Theory and Practice in the United States, 1945-1960
Essays exploring policies of the Truman and Eisenhower administrations
0-19-503986-6 OXFORD $38.00
0-19-503987-4 OXFORD PB $8.95

David C. **Hendrickson**
The Future of American Strategy
Argues for the introduction of a new defense strategy in the 1990s, one that responds to budgetary pressures and that is more sensitive than the Reagan programs to foreign politics
0-8419-1104-5 HOLMES & MEIER $34.95
0-8419-1105-3 HOLMES & MEIER PB $16.95

George F. **Kennan**
American Diplomacy
A clearly written appraisal of 20th-century American diplomacy by one of its chief architects
0-226-43147-9 CHICAGO PB $8.95

Carnes **Lord**
The Presidency and the Management of National Security
A history of the National Security Council by a former member. Traces the NSC's transformation from an organization conceived as a constraint on presidential power into an instrument allowing the president greater control of the policymaking process
0-02-919341-9 FREE PRESS $32.95

Steven E. **Miller**, editor

Conventional Forces and American Defense Policy: An International Security Reader

Published in 1986

0-691-02246-1 PRINCETON PB $9.95

Naval Strategy and National Security: An International Security Reader

Published in 1988

0-691-02272-0 PRINCETON PB $14.95

Jeffrey **Record**

Revising U.S. Military Strategy: Tailoring Means to Ends

Combines a historical overview of postwar American strategy with recommendations for the future; published in 1984

0-08-031618-2 BRASSEY'S DEFENSE $12.00

Ronald **Steel**

Temptations of a Superpower: America's Foreign Policy After the Cold War

"Steel makes what should be, but seldom is, an obvious point: that American foreign policy continues to operate within a framework designed for a world that no longer exists....scathing and effective"—Alan Brinkley

See also **20TH-CENTURY DIPLOMACY** under **FOREIGN POLICY AND DIPLOMATIC HISTORY** under **AMERICAN POLITICS AND FOREIGN POLICY** in **HISTORY OF THE AMERICAS**

0-674-26837-7 HARVARD $27.95

0-674-87341-6 HARVARD PB $10.95

Military Reform and Civil-Military Relations

Asa A. **Clark** & Peter W. **Chiarelli**, editors

The Defense Reform Debate: Issues and Analysis

0-8018-3205-5 JOHNS HOPKINS $55.00

0-8018-3206-3 JOHNS HOPKINS PB $14.95

James **Coates** & Michael **Kilian**

Heavy Losses: The Dangerous Decline of American Defense

Two Washington journalists demonstrate how America's huge defense budget is mismanaged. Published in 1986

0-670-80484-3 VIKING $22.95

Eliot A. **Cohen**

Citizens and Soldiers: The Dilemmas of Military Service

0-8014-1581-0 CORNELL $42.50

Samuel P. **Huntington**

The Soldier and the State: The Theory and Politics of Civil-Military Relations

The classic study of American civil-military relations

0-674-81736-2 HARVARD PB $17.95

A. Ernest **Fitzgerald**

The Pentagonists: An Insider's View of Waste, Mismanagement, and Fraud in Defense Spending

The original "Defense Department whistle blower" tells of his fight for honest procurement practices, better equipment, and a defense of the taxpayers' interest

0-945999-26-7 LIBERTY TREE NETWORK $22.95

David C. **Hendrickson**

Reforming Defense: An Inquiry into the State of American Civil-Military Relations

The military reform movements of the 1980s, studied in the light of the dilemmas of civil-military relations

0-8018-3550-X JOHNS HOPKINS $24.50

Gregory M. **Herek** & others, editors

Out in Force: Sexual Orientation and the Military

See also **CAREERS** under **GAY LIFE AND CULTURE** under **GAY, LESBIAN, AND BISEXUAL STUDIES**

0-226-40048-4 CHICAGO PB $17.95

Randy **Shilts**

Conduct Unbecoming: Gays and Lesbians in the U.S. Military

0-449-90917-4 FAWCETT PB $16.00

Marc **Wolinsky**

Gays and the Military: Joseph Steffan Versus the United States

0-691-03307-2 PRINCETON $39.50

Law

Legal Theory

Barbara A. **Babcock**

Sex Discrimination and the Law: Causes and Remedies

Materials for a history of women's legal status

0-316-07420-9 LITTLE, BROWN $38.00

Benjamin N. **Cardozo**

The Nature of the Judicial Process

The classic 1921 work describing the process by which a judge decides a case

0-300-00033-2 YALE PB $12.00

Richard **Delgado**

Critical Race Theory: The Cutting Edge

1-56639-348-5 TEMPLE PB $24.95

Kimberle **Crenshaw**

Critical Race Theory: The Key Writings that Formed the Movement

Kendall Thomas, Cornel West, Derrick Bell, Cheryl Harris, Lani Guinier...the contributors to this volume make up a virtual Who's Who of the progressive intellectuals who have redefined the grounds on which race, law, and power are discussed in America

See also **ETHNIC AND RACE RELATIONS** under **AMERICAN PEOPLE AND PLACES** in **HISTORY OF THE AMERICAS**

1-56584-270-7 NEW PRESS $60.00

1-56584-271-5 NEW PRESS PB $30.00

Ronald **Dworkin**

Law's Empire

Dworkin is among the most eminent of contemporary legal philosophers, notable for finding a theoretical basis for liberal social policy.

See also **OTHER 20TH-CENTURY PHILOSOPHERS** under **PHILOSOPHY** in **RELIGION, SPIRITUALITY, AND PHILOSOPHY**

0-674-51836-5 HARVARD PB $16.95

George **Fletcher**

Rethinking Criminal Law

A reexamination of the theory underlying criminal law doctrine from the standpoint of moral philosophy

0-316-28592-7 LITTLE, BROWN $42.00

Lon L. **Fuller**

The Morality of Law

0-300-01070-2 YALE PB $13.00

Grant **Gilmore**

The Death of Contract

0-8142-0267-5 OHIO STATE PB $9.50

Amy **Gutmann**, editor

A Matter of Interpretation: Federal Courts and the Law

0-691-02630-0 PRINCETON $19.95

Herbert L. **Hart**

The Concept of Law

0-19-876072-8 OXFORD PB $19.95

Oliver Wendell **Holmes**

The Common Law

EDITED BY MARK DEWOLFE HOWE

0-316-37131-9 LITTLE, BROWN $45.00

0-316-37132-7 LITTLE, BROWN PB $16.95

Oliver Wendell **Holmes** & Richard A. **Posner**, editor

The Essential Holmes: Selections from the Letters, Speeches, Judicial Opinions and Other Writings

0-226-67552-1 CHICAGO $24.95

0-226-67554-8 CHICAGO PB $15.95

Ruthann **Robson**

Gay Men, Lesbians, and the Law

Legal theory from the foremost lesbian legal scholar

0-7910-2963-8 CHELSEA HOUSE PB $12.95

David **Kairys**, editor

The Politics of Law: A Progressive Critique

Essays emphasizing the highly contingent nature of legal principles

0-679-73161-X PANTHEON PB $21.00

Leo **Katz**

Bad Acts and Guilty Minds: Conundrums of the Criminal Law

The paradoxes of criminal law theory; aimed at the lay reader

0-226-42592-4 CHICAGO PB $15.95

Law and Literature: A Misunderstood Relation

"An outstanding work, as stimulating as it is intellectually distinguished"
—John Gross, *NY Times*

0-674-51468-8 HARVARD $38.00

Mari **Matsuda**

Words that Wound: Critical Race Theory, Assaultive Speech, and the First Amendment

0-8133-8428-1 WESTVIEW PB $16.95

Martha Craven **Nussbaum**

Poetic Justice: The Literary Imagination and Public Life

Reflections on justice that emerged from a law school seminar's reading of literary classics

0-8070-4108-4 BEACON $20.00

Richard A. **Posner**

The Economics of Justice

Justice and government intervention discussed by a leader of the "law and economics" school

0-674-23525-8 HARVARD $36.00
0-674-23526-6 HARVARD PB $17.95

Roscoe **Pound**

An Introduction to the Philosophy of Law

"The recognized American classic"
—*American Bar Association Journal*

0-300-00188-6 YALE PB $12.00

Lesbian (out)law: Survival Under the Rule of Law

An attorney on the faculty of CUNY Law School answers the question: How can lesbians use the law without being used by it?

See also **POLITICS AND LAW** under **GAY LIFE AND CULTURE** under **GAY, LESBIAN, AND BISEXUAL STUDIES**

1-56341-013-3 FIREBRAND $20.95
1-56341-012-5 FIREBRAND PB $9.95

Kim Lane **Scheppele**

Legal Secrets: Equality and Efficiency in the Common Law

Explores the broad issues of legal secrecy to challenge the economic theory of law and develop a new view of legal interpretation and legal morality. "Powerful and original"
—James S. Coleman, University of Chicago

0-226-73778-0 CHICAGO $54.00

Roberto **Unger**

The Critical Legal Studies Movement

0-674-17735-5 HARVARD $24.00
0-674-17736-3 HARVARD PB $12.95

What Should Legal Analysis Become

1-85984-969-5 VERSO $54.95
1-85984-100-7 VERSO PB $16.95

Legal History

Harold J. **Berman**

Law and Revolution: The Formation of the Western Legal Tradition

Berman's history of the development of Western law is a mind-altering account of the formative institutions of the Western moral, political, and intellectual outlook

See also **RELIGION AND SOCIETY** under **WORLD RELIGION** in **RELIGION, SPIRITUALITY, AND PHILOSOPHY**

0-674-51776-8 HARVARD PB $19.95

Anne Hobson **Freeman**

The Style of a Law Firm: Eight Gentlemen from Virginia

0-945575-25-4 ALGONQUIN $24.95

Lawrence M. **Friedman**

A History of American Law

"The best single, coherent history of American law that now exists…a stupendous achievement"—*NY Times Book Review*

0-671-52807-6 SIMON & SCHUSTER PB $22.00

Joan **Hoff**

Law, Gender and Injustice: A Legal History of U.S. Women

0-8147-3509-6 NYU PB $22.50

Leonard W. **Levy**

Origins of the Fifth Amendment

A 1969 Pulitzer Prize winner

0-02-919570-5 MACMILLAN $24.95
0-02-919580-2 FREE PRESS PB $14.95

H.L. **Pohlman**, editor

Political Thought and the American Judiciary

Gathers and analyzes key judicial decisions on such issues as equality and religious liberty

0-87023-830-2 MASSACHUSETTS PB $18.95

Richard A. **Posner**

The Federal Courts: Challenge and Reform

0-674-29626-5 HARVARD $37.50

Mark **Rose**

Authors and Owners: The Invention of Copyright

0-674-05308-7 HARVARD $29.00

Yves R. **Simon**

The Traditions of Natural Law: A Philosopher's Reflections

Both a history of natural law and a reflection on its uses

0-8232-0641-6 FORDHAM PB $19.95

The Supreme Court

Henry J. **Abraham**

Justices and Presidents: A Political History of Appointments to the Supreme Court

0-19-506557-3 OXFORD $45.00

Robert S. **Alley**

The Supreme Court on Church and State

0-19-505029-0 OXFORD PB $22.00

Archibald **Cox**

The Court and the Constitution

A history of the Supreme Court by the first Watergate Special Prosecutor and current head of Common Cause

0-395-48071-X HOUGHTON MIFFLIN PB $14.95

Kermit L. **Hall**

The Oxford Companion to the Supreme Court of the United States

Includes more than 1,000 entries, essays on major issues that have confronted the Court, plus biographies of all the justices

0-19-505835-6 OXFORD $55.00

Peter **Irons** & Stephanie **Guitton**

May It Please the Court: The Most Significant Oral Arguments Made Before the Supreme Court Since 1955

The Supreme Court's "greatest hits." Taped at the time of the proceedings, key arguments before the Supreme Court and justices' queries are now available in this unique book/cassette offering. Abortion rights, interracial marriage, school desegregation, sexual orientation, and Miranda rights are among the topics argued with passion. Justices and attorneys included are Thurgood Marshall, Abe Fortas, Robert Bork, Archibald Cox, Warren Burger, William Rehnquist, and Sandra Day O'Connor

1-56584-052-6 NEW PRESS PB $16.00

Joel D. **Joseph**

Black Mondays: Worst Decisions of the Supreme Court

FOREWORD BY THURGOOD MARSHALL

0-915765-65-9 NATIONAL PRESS PB $9.95

Anthony **Lewis**

Gideon's Trumpet

Bestselling account of the prisoner who took his case to the Supreme Court and forever changed the American criminal justice system

0-679-72312-9 VINTAGE PB $11.00

David **Kairys**

With Liberty and Justice for Some: A Critique of the Conservative Supreme Court

Kairys, a leading constitutional scholar and litigator, presents a fascinating—and devastating—look at changes wrought by the Reagan and Bush Supreme Courts. Exposing contradictions in conservative political thinking, he describes the erosion of the legal principles that embody American freedoms, and the retrenchments of our rights over the last decade. "A wonderful book, combining comprehensive knowledge, great historical insight, decent human values, and…storytelling skill"—Sylvia A. Law, New York University

1-56584-071-2 NEW PRESS $25.00
1-56584-059-3 NEW PRESS PB $12.95

Robert C. **McCloskey**

The American Supreme Court

0-226-55675-1 CHICAGO PB $10.95

William H. **Rehnquist**

The Supreme Court: How It Was, How It Is

The Chief Justice offers personal and general insights into the history and operation of the Court

0-688-08668-3 MORROW PB $15.00

Bernard **Schwartz**

The History of the Supreme Court

A very well written and illuminating history of the court

See also **LEGAL AND CONSTITUTIONAL HISTORY** under **TOPICS IN AMERICAN STUDIES** in **HISTORY OF THE AMERICAS**

0-19-508099-8 OXFORD $39.95
0-19-509387-9 OXFORD PB $16.95

Unpublished Opinions of the Burger Court

0-19-505317-6 OXFORD $49.95

Bob **Woodward**

The Brethren

A portrait of the Supreme Court at work

0-380-52183-0 AVON PB $6.99

Lawyers and Judges

Richard A. **Brisbin**

Justice Antonin Scalia and the Conservative Revival

0-801-85432-6 UHPKN $42.00

Hunter R. **Clark**

Justice Brennan: The Great Conciliator

1-55972-261-4 BIRCH LANE $24.95

Hella **Pick**

The Hidden Holmes: His Theory of Torts in History

0-674-39002-4 HARVARD $45.00

Peter **Irons**

Brennan vs. Rehnquist: The Battle for the Constitution

The 20-year fight for control of the Supreme Court between Eisenhower appointee Brennan and Nixon's Rehnquist is a story that illuminates and dramatizes the central issues of democracy in our time

See also **THE REAGAN YEARS** under **US HISTORY, 1945 TO THE PRESENT** in **HISTORY OF THE AMERICAS**

0-679-42436-9 KNOPF $27.50

Arthur **Weinberg**, editor

Justice Oliver Wendell Holmes: Law and the Inner Self

0-19-508182-X OXFORD $39.95
0-19-510128-6 OXFORD PB $18.95

Roy **Cohn** & Sidney **Zion**

The Autobiography of Roy Cohn

The notorious conservative lawyer and onetime aide to Joe McCarthy tells his story with the help of a liberal journalist

0-8184-0471-X LYLE STUART $18.95

Clare **Cushman**, editor

The Supreme Court Justices: Illustrated Biographies, 1789-1995

The lives of the 105 men and two women who have served as United States Supreme Court Justices. From farmers to soldiers, ministers, and musicians, their lives demonstrate a rich legacy of American law and show an enormous spectrum of legal philosophies and backgrounds. A fascinating collection, well written and concise

FOREWORD BY CHIEF JUSTICE WILLIAM H. REHNQUIST

1-56802-126-7 CONGRESSIONAL QUARTERLY PB. $33.95

Sue **Davis**

Justice Rehnquist and the Constitution

"Represents a remarkably comprehensive survey of Justice Rehnquist's constitutional positions and correctly identifies the major patterns in those positions"—Rogers M. Smith, Yale University

0-691-07800-9 PRINCETON $32.50

Jeffrey D. **Hockett**

New Deal Justice: The Constitutional Jurisprudence of Hugo L. Black, Felix Frankfurter, and Robert H. Jackson

0-8476-8210-2 ROWMAN & LITTLEFIELD $67.50
0-8476-8211-0 ROWMAN & LITTLEFIELD PB $24.95

Oliver Wendell **Holmes** & Felix **Frankfurter**

Holmes and Frankfurter: Their Correspondence, 1912-34

See also **LATE ARRIVALS** in **HISTORY OF THE AMERICAS**

EDITED BY ROBERT M. MENNEL

0-87451-758-3 NEW ENGLAND $45.00

Herbert Alan **Johnson**

The Chief Justiceship of John Marshall

1-57003-121-5 SOUTH CAROLINA $42.00

Charles F. **Hobson**

The Great Chief Justice: John Marshall and the Rule of Law

Hobson, the editor of Marshall's papers, on the life of Marshall's mind. Impressively researched and clearly written

See also **BIOGRAPHY** under **US HISTORY TO THE CIVIL WAR** in **HISTORY OF THE AMERICAS**

0-7006-0788-9 KANSAS $35.00

Jean Edward **Smith**

John Marshall: Defender of a Nation

0-8050-1389-X HOLT $35.00

Michael D. **Davis** & Hunter R. **Clark**

Thurgood Marshall: Warrior at the Bar, Rebel on the Bench

A landmark biography of the first African American to serve on the United States Supreme Court. The authors trace Marshall's career as a pioneering civil rights lawyer and one of this country's great liberal justices, offering insights into some of the most sensitive social issues of our time

See also **CIVIL RIGHTS** under **US HISTORY, 1945 TO THE PRESENT** in **HISTORY OF THE AMERICAS**

1-55972-133-2 BIRCH LANE $24.95

Carl T. **Rowan**

Dream Makers, Dream Breakers: The World of Justice Thurgood Marshall

Marshall changed America. As a lawyer, he argued 31 cases before the Supreme Court and lost just three. As a justice himself, he influenced fellow justices in cases involving abortion rights, voting rights, and constitutional protection for the accused

See also **LIBERALS AND THE LEFT** under **CURRENT POLITICAL THOUGHT AND ISSUES** under **AMERICAN POLITICS AND FOREIGN POLICY** in **HISTORY OF THE AMERICAS**

0-316-75979-1 LITTLE, BROWN PB $12.95

Hella **Pick**

Simon Wiesenthal: A Life in Search of Justice

1-55553-273-X NORTHEASTERN $29.95

Harold J. **Rothwax**

Guilty: The Collapse of Criminal Justice

The New York trial judge's reflections on the justice system in America today

0-446-67304-8 WARNER PB $12.99

Arthur **Weinberg**, editor

Attorney for the Damned: Clarence Darrow in the Courtroom

Darrow's work presented through a collection of his court summations and lectures. "Nothing gives quite the full flavor of the man as do these addresses"—William O. Douglas

FOREWORD BY WILLIAM O. DOUGLAS

0-226-13649-3 CHICAGO PB $18.95

Judge Judy **Sheindlin** & Josh **Getlin**

Don't Pee on My Leg and Tell Me It's Raining: America's Toughest Court Judge Speaks Out

Now a star on TV

0-06-017321-1 HARPERCOLLINS....$23.00

G. Edward **White**

The American Judicial Tradition: Profiles of Leading American Judges

The most famous appellate judges in American history, from John Marshall to Warren Burger; updated edition includes two new chapters, on William O. Douglas and the Burger Court

0-19-505685-X OXFORD PB....$15.95

The genesis of the American judicial tradition was the transformation of the office of appellate judge under John Marshall. This tradition has, since its origins, contained certain core elements: a measure of true independence and autonomy for the appellate judiciary from the other two branches of government; the extension, within limits, of judicial authority to questions of politics in addition to technical questions of law; and the presence of a set of internalized constraints upon the office of judge that circumscribe judicial freedom of choice and give the office an identity discrete from the personalities of the individuals who occupy it at any specific time. Since Marshall the appellate judiciary in America has been consciously aloof from direct participation in politics and an active and weighty political force that is at once the least regulated and the most constrained branch of American government. Marshall was the primary creator of this unique institutional role.
THE AMERICAN JUDICIAL TRADITION: PROFILES OF LEADING AMERICAN JUDGES

Earl Warren: A Public Life

0-19-503121-0 OXFORD....$35.00
0-19-504936-5 OXFORD PB....$13.95

Ed **Cray**

Chief Justice: A Biography of Earl Warren

0-684-80852-8 SIMON & SCHUSTER....$30.00

The Constitution

Bernard **Bailyn**, editor

The Debate on the Constitution

Employing newspaper articles, pamphlets, and letters, this collection captures the energy and the eloquence of Franklin, Madison, Jefferson, Washington, Patrick Henry, and other less recognized voices as they took part in the "bloodless revolution" that formed the government of the United States. Each volume includes the full texts of the Declaration of Independence, the Articles of Confederation, and the Constitution. "For Americans this is Shakespeare, and more. Not only is it wonderful writing, it is wonderful thinking"—Nina Totenberg

Volume 1 September 17, 1787 to January 12, 1788

See also **THE MAKING OF THE CONSTITUTION** under **US HISTORY TO THE CIVIL WAR** in **HISTORY OF THE AMERICAS**

0-940450-42-9 LIBRARY OF AMERICA....$35.00

Volume 2 January 14, 1788 to August 9, 1788

0-940450-64-X LIBRARY OF AMERICA....$35.00
0-940450-81-X LIBRARY OF AM BOXED SET....$70.00

Floyd G. **Cullop**

The Constitution of the United States: An Introduction

A very short, basic self-study book for beginners by a high school teacher

0-451-62724-5 NEW AMERICAN LIBRARY PB....$4.99

Ronald **Dworkin**

Freedom's Law: The Moral Reading of the American Constitution

0-674-31927-3 HARVARD....$35.00

John Hart **Ely**

On Constitutional Ground

0-691-08644-3 PRINCETON....$69.50
0-691-02553-3 PRINCETON PB....$24.95

Current Legal Affairs

Ellen **Alderman** & Caroline **Kennedy**

The Right to Privacy

The authors of the bestselling *In our Defense: The Bill of Rights in Action*—both practicing attorneys, one the daughter of JFK—deliver a knowing and intelligent account of our most basic and most contested civil right. Moving fluently among anecdotes, landmark trial decisions, and little-known cases, the authors consider questions such as the right to e-mail privacy on company computers, the right to a court-ordered cesarean to save an endangered fetus, and the defense against strip-searching: the broadest questions of privacy in the media, workplace, and in the world of information

0-679-41986-1 KNOPF....$26.95
0-679-74434-7 VINTAGE....$14.00

Jerold S. **Auerbach**

Justice Without Law?: Resolving Disputes Without Lawyers

Examines why Americans are the most litigious people in the world and looks through American history for alternatives to litigation in dispute settlement

0-19-503447-3 OXFORD PB....$9.95

Unequal Justice: Lawyers and Social Change in Modern America

"Stands as a powerful and well-documented indictment of the elite bar's failure to live up to the trust that has been bestowed upon it by our system of justice"—*NY Times*

0-19-502170-3 OXFORD PB....$13.95

Lee C. **Bollinger**

The Tolerant Society

Free speech in American society

0-19-504000-7 OXFORD....$30.00
0-19-505430-X OXFORD PB....$17.95

Alan M. **Dershowitz**

The Abuse Excuse: And Other Cop-Outs, Sob Stories, and Evasions of Responsibility

"Provocative...cogently reasoned...Dershowitz's writing is animated by a fierce sense of logic and a large measure of common sense...Lively and useful reading"—*NY Times*

0-316-18102-1 LITTLE, BROWN PB....$12.95

I.H.Ph. **Diederiks-Verschoor**

An Introduction to Space Law

90-6544-692-3 KLUWER LAW PB....$75.00

Ronald **Dworkin**

Life's Dominion: An Argument About Abortion, Euthanasia, and Individual Freedom

Dworkin, Professor of Jurisprudence at Oxford and of Law at NYU, offers an eloquent clarification of two of the most difficult issues of our time. The real question, he says, is not whether a fetus is a person, but how best to respect the universally shared philosophical/religious conviction that all human life is sacred. "Dworkin's landmark philosophical essay brings a new dimension to future debate about abortion and euthanasia" —*Publishers Weekly*

See also **THE ABORTION DEBATE** under **THE FEMALE EXPERIENCE** under **WOMEN'S STUDIES**

0-679-73319-1 VINTAGE PB....$13.00

Billie Wright **Dziech** &
Judge Charles B. **Schudson**

On Trial: America's Courts and Their Treatment of Sexually Abused Children

0-8070-0415-4 BEACON PB....$17.00

Mary Ann **Glendon**

Abortion and Divorce in Western Law

0-674-00161-3 HARVARD PB....$17.95

Kent **Greenwalt**

Fighting Words: Individuals, Communities, and Liberties of Speech

0-691-03638-1 PRINCETON....$29.95

Nat **Hentoff**

Free Speech for Me—But Not for Thee: How the American Left and Right Relentlessly Censor Each Other

0-06-099510-6 HARPERPERENNIAL PB....$13.00

Philip K. **Howard**

The Death of Common Sense: How Law is Suffocating America

0-679-42994-8 RANDOM HOUSE $18.00
0-446-67228-9 WARNER PB $10.99

Herbert **Jacob**

Silent Revolution: The Transformation of Divorce Law in the United States

"Well written, carefully researched, and persuasively argued"—Barbara J. Nelson, University of Minnesota
0-226-38951-0 CHICAGO $22.50

James B. **Jacobs**

Drunk Driving: An American Dilemma

An interdisciplinary study both of the social problem of drunk driving and of government policies and jurisprudence
FOREWORD BY FRANKLIN E. ZIMRING
0-226-38979-0 CHICAGO PB $15.95

Elizabeth **Mensch** & Alan **Freeman**

The Politics of Virtue: Is Abortion Debatable?

Originally published as a special issue of *The Georgia Law Review*, this revised and expanded edition takes the abortion debate to a new level. This fascinating volume is more than a one-sided critique; it seeks to untangle the strands of legal rights and theoretical concerns to get to the core of the issue
0-8223-1349-9 DUKE PB $15.95

Ralph **Nader** & Wesley J. **Smith**

No Contest: How the Power Lawyers Are Perverting Justice in America

Far from being crippled by frivolous lawsuits brought by individuals, the authors reveal a shockingly corrupt world in which corporate lawyers are using superior resources and secrecy to restrict, maybe even eliminate, our access to justice
See also CURRENT POLITICAL THOUGHT AND ISSUES under AMERICAN POLITICS AND FOREIGN POLICY in HISTORY OF THE AMERICAS
0-679-42972-7 RANDOM HOUSE $25.00

Eric **Neisser**

Recapturing the Spirit: Essays on the Bill of Rights at 200

Brisk essays from a leading civil libertarian
0-945612-23-0 MADISON PB $12.95

Laurence H. **Tribe**

Abortion: The Clash of Absolutes

A clear discussion by a constitutional scholar; includes comparative studies of abortion in other legal systems
0-393-02845-3 NORTON PB $19.95

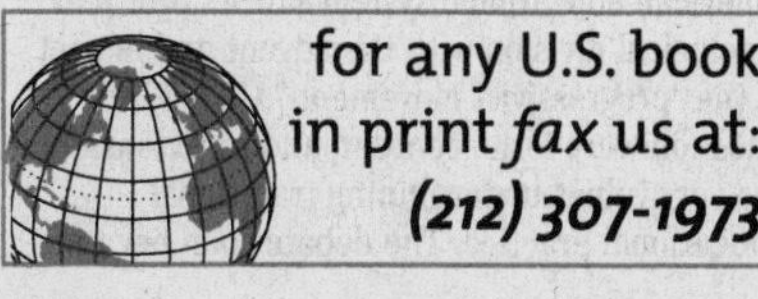
for any U.S. book
in print *fax* us at:
(212) 307-1973

Scott **Turow**

One L: An Inside Account of Life in the First Year of Harvard Law School

From the author of the bestselling *Presumed Innocent,* memoirs of an initiation by fire. "It should be read by anyone who has ever contemplated going to law school. Or anyone who has ever worried about being human" —Christopher Lehmann-Haupt, *NY Times*
0-446-35170-9 WARNER PB $5.99

Scott Turow

Patricia **Williams**

The Alchemy of Race and Rights

0-674-01471-5 HARVARD PB $12.95

Criminal Law and the Death Penalty

Hugo Adam **Bedau**, editor

The Death Penalty in America

0-19-502986-0 OXFORD $30.00
0-19-502987-9 OXFORD PB $13.95

Elizabeth F. **Loftus**

Eyewitness Testimony

Examines the fallibility of the eyewitness
9994814648 MICHIE BUTTERWORTH PB $25.00

Helen **Prejean**

Dead Man Walking: An Eyewitness Account of the Death Penalty in the United States

A unique perspective on one of the greatest moral dilemmas in America, from a nun who works closely both with death-row inmates and the families of victims. Without denying the inmates' brutality, she nonetheless comes down squarely against institutionalized killing of criminals. "Sister Prejean…is an excellent writer, direct and honest and unsentimental; her accounts of crime and punishment are gripping, and her argument is persuasive" —*NY Times Book Review*
See also CRIME AND PUNISHMENT under TOPICS IN AMERICAN STUDIES in HISTORY OF THE AMERICAS
0-679-64131-9 VINTAGE PB $12.00

Seymour **Wishman**

Anatomy of a Jury: The Inside Story of How Twelve Ordinary People Decide the Fate of an Accused Murderer

0-14-009851-8 VIKING PB $10.95

On Trial: Case Histories

Peter **Brooks** & Paul **Gewirtz**

Law's Stories: Narrative and Rhetoric in the Law

0-300-06675-9 YALE $30.00

Sara C. **Charles** & Eugene **Kennedy**

Defendant: A Psychiatrist on Trial for Medical Malpractice

A psychiatrist sued for malpractice by her suicidal patient describes her trial and reflects on the effects of the malpractice epidemic. "Absolutely hair-raising"—John Gregory Dunne
0-02-905910-0 FREE PRESS $29.95

Alan M. **Dershowitz**

The Best Defense

Courtroom adventures of Claus von Bulow's lawyer. "Has the feel of a vintage Coney Island roller coaster ride"—*Village Voice*
0-394-71380-X RANDOM HOUSE PB $14.00

Martin **Garbus**

Ready for the Defense

The lawyer discusses five of his cases, including his defenses of Lenny Bruce and Timothy Leary
0-88184-373-3 CARROLL & GRAF PB $4.95

Rodney R. **Jones**, editor

Disorderly Conduct: Verbatim

Intentionally and unintentionally humorous dialogue from actual court cases
0-393-30597-X NORTON PB $7.95

Jonathan **Harr**

A Civil Action

A *New York Times* and *New Yorker* writer delivers a terrifying and compelling insider's view of the law in America, centered on a group of leukemia victims in a small town north of Boston where the water supply has been poisoned by industrial chemicals. "A simply terrific book about the practice of law in America…Harr has captured more of the sham and nobility and greed of this troubled profession than anything I have read in years…By turns wildly funny and unspeakably sad"—J. Anthony Lukas. "Gripping and filled with tension…A compelling, fascinating read" —Tracy Kidder

0-394-56349-2 RANDOM HOUSE $25.00

Arthur **Kinoy**

Rights on Trial: The Odyssey of a People's Lawyer

The stories of Watergate, the Rosenbergs, the Montgomery bus boycott, and the Chicago Seven, all told by a lawyer who was there

0-674-77013-7 HARVARD $34.95
0-9641887-0-8 BERNEL PB $17.95

Steven **Phillips**

No Heroes, No Villains: The Story of a Murder Trial

First-hand account of a 1972 murder trial

0-394-72531-X RANDOM HOUSE PB $9.00

Charles **Rembar**

The End of Obscenity: The Trials of Lady Chatterley, Tropic of Cancer and Fanny Hill by the Lawyer Who Defended Them

0-06-097061-8 OLYMPIC PB $2.98

Peter H. **Schuck**

Agent Orange on Trial: Mass Toxic Disasters in the Courts

"A Dickensian drama of personality clashes, misguided idealism, power struggle, greed, immeasurable suffering and bitter disillusionment"—*USA Today*

0-674-01026-4 HARVARD PB $18.50

Richard B. **Sobol**

Bending the Law: The Story of the Dalkon Shield Bankruptcy

An account of the final days of the A.H. Robins Company, manufacturer of the defective Dalkon Shield IUD, which injured hundreds of thousands of women. Attorney Sobol paints a devastating portrait of the American litigation system

0-226-76753-1 CHICAGO PB $14.95

Gerald M. **Stern**

The Buffalo Creek Disaster: How the Survivors of One of the Worst Disasters in Coal-Mining History Brought Suit Against the Coal Company—and Won

0-394-72343-0 RANDOM HOUSE PB $7.00

Christopher **Darden**

In Contempt

The O.J. trial, by one of the prosecutors

0-694-51724-0 HARPC $18.00

Alan M. **Dershowitz**

Reasonable Doubts: The Criminal Justice System and the O.J. Simpson Case

0-684-83264-X TOUBK PB $12.00

Jeffrey **Toobin**

The Run of His Life: The People vs. O.J. Simpson

0-679-44170-0 RANDOM HOUSE $25.00

Reference and Practical Guides

Michael **Akehurst**

A Modern Introduction to International Law

An examination of the state of international law. Published in 1987

0-415-09081-4 ROUTLEDGE PB $24.95

Carl W. **Battle**

Legal-Wise

Providing detailed explanations and all the paperwork necessary to carry out everything from buying a house to composing a will, *Legal-Wise* obviates the need to hire a lawyer for many routine procedures

0-9607118-4-8 ALLWORTH PB $16.95

Senior Counsel: Legal and Financial Strategies for Age 50 and Beyond

"In this solid compendium of legal information, attorney Carl Battle covers not only the essential areas of health care and financial planning, but also has wise advice about travel, crime, employment, self-fulfillment, and much more"—William A. Bolger

1-88055-906-4 ALLWORTH PB $16.95

Henry C. **Black**

Black's Law Dictionary

0-314-76271-X WEST $36.95
0-314-88536-6 WEST PB $22.95

David John **Doukas** & William **Reichel**

Planning for Uncertainty: A Guide to Living Wills and Other Advance Directives for Health Care

This book will help prepare us all for the possibility that someday we may be unable to communicate our health-care decisions. As family doctors who have seen the devastating effects of prolonged and useless suffering, the authors are able to give us a clear and reliable guide on how to direct the final details of our lives, and what to take into account—medical choices, legal issues, and family concerns—when we do so

See also **HOSPITAL AND MEDICAL CARE** under **HEALTH** in **LIFESTYLES AND PRACTICAL ADVICE**

0-8018-4671-4 JOHNS HOPKINS PB $13.95

Michael **Gilbert**, editor

The Oxford Book of Legal Anecdotes

0-19-214112-0 OXFORD $24.95
0-19-282112-1 OXFORD PB $13.95

Barbara R. **Hauser**, editor

Women's Legal Guide

This essential guide to the law, by 29 female lawyers, provides up-to-date legal information on health care, marriage, divorce, adoption, the rights of lesbians, sexual discrimination, estate planning, and much more. "This is every woman's handy guide to charting one's way through a legal system filled with overt or covert bias against her sex. The authors can even make the summary statement of a pension plan sound interesting"—Jill Ker Conway

See also **REFERENCE** under **WOMEN'S STUDIES**

FOREWORD BY ROBERTA COOPER RAMO, PRESIDENT OF THE AMERICAN BAR ASSOCIATION

1-55591-913-8 FULCRUM $39.95
1-55591-303-2 FULCRUM PB $22.95

Thomas **Hauser**

The Family Legal Companion

Careful advice about all the legal problems one may encounter—consumer rights, employment, divorce, child custody, landlords, and more—in a simple question-and-answer format. "Hauser's straightforward presentation makes complicated lessons relatively easy to learn" —*Publishers Weekly*

1-88055-904-8 ALLWORTH PB $16.95

Richard A. **Posner** & Katharine B. **Silbaugh**, editors

A Guide to America's Sex Laws

A must for every activist, gay or straight

See also **POLITICS AND LAW** under **GAY LIFE AND CULTURE** under **GAY, LESBIAN, AND BISEXUAL STUDIES**

0-226-67564-5 CHICAGO $26.95

Daniel **Sitarz**

Divorce Yourself: The National No-Fault Divorce Kit

This bestselling, critically acclaimed legal reference on divorce offers detailed instructions, checklists, worksheets, and explanations for every step of a divorce in all 50 states and Washington, DC

See also **DIVORCE** under **SELF-HELP** in **LIFESTYLES AND PRACTICAL ADVICE**

0-935755-13-6 NOVA PB $24.95

Education

Every few years Americans seem to discover that their schools are in crisis. And each crisis produces a new set of critics, polemicists, and antagonists. In recent years, the subject has once again aroused controversy and concern, emerging from academic circles into the spotlight, and in the process generating best-sellers, television documentaries, front-page news, and campaign slogans. Yet for all its urgency, the fundamental issue of the debate remains the same: What should be the purpose of education in a democracy? Whatever those goals are, is our educational system living up to them?

The State of the Schools

During the late 1920s and early '30s the American educational system saw its first real ideological division with the advent and impact of the "progressivist movement." Called into question were form, content, and by extension, the very values underpinning traditional educational practice. The debate soon became charged with, then acquisitioned by partisan politics, which has served to keep the American educational system at the mercy of its wide political swings.

In the past half-century, traditionalists and progressives have waged verbal war with regularity. Their debate has ranged from practical disagreements over the most successful methods of conveying skills and knowledge, to deep divisions over the very essence of public education. Do children learn better in a tightly structured environment, or in a free system in which they learn to make decisions for themselves? Is a liberal education the birthright of all children in a democracy, or are some better served by technical and vocational training? The reform literature of the 1980s was in some ways a reaction against the progressivism of the 1960s. It was characterized by concern for academic standards, for reducing non-academic electives, and for bringing nearly all students into an academic curriculum.

The '90s have brought new pressures to bear on the already beleaguered system as schools across the nation face funding crises, an immigration backlash to dismantle bilingual education programs, and a push toward the privatization of education that continues to gain support among conservatives.

Mortimer J. **Adler**

The Paideia Proposal: An Educational Manifesto

A committee of leading educators proposes a democratic restructuring of basic schooling to overcome inherent elitism

0-02-064100-1 MACMILLAN PB $7.00

Mortimer Adler

Arthur **Bestor**

Educational Wastelands: The Retreat from Learning in Our Public Schools

A critique of progressivism in the 1950s with contributions by Clarence J. Karier & Foster McMurray

0-252-01226-7 ILLINOIS $29.95

John H. **Bunzel**, editor

Challenge to American Schools: The Case for Standards and Eleven Essays on the Current State of the Classroom

0-19-503556-9 OXFORD PB $28.00

Lisa **Delpit**

Other People's Children: Cultural Conflict in the Classroom

1-56584-180-8 NEW PRESS PB $11.95

Thomas **French**

South of Heaven: Welcome to High School at the End of the Twentieth Century

This sobering, intimate exploration of high school as it is today reveals the lives, loves, and fears of five students. "An exceptionally revealing—and sympathetic—journey into the isolated, high-pressure world of our teenagers"—*Kirkus Reviews*

0-671-89801-9 POCKET PB $12.00

J.I. **Goodlad**

A Place Called School

A statistically rich landmark study, with proposals for reform of secondary education

0-07-023627-5 MCGRAW HILL PB $16.95

Gerald **Grant**

The World We Created at Hamilton High

An in-depth look at a real (but disguised) American high school. "Gerald Grant moves the discourse of the debate on school renewal far beyond the slogans. He forces the reader to consider the school in larger context"
—Ernest L. Boyer

0-674-96201-X HARVARD PB $12.95

E. D. **Hirsch**

The Schools We Need: And Why We Don't Have Them

0-385-48457-7 DOUBLEDAY $24.95

Jonathan **Kozol**

Blueprint for a Democratic Education

By the author of the ground-breaking *Savage Inequalities,* this book proposes an overhaul of schools, calls for a countrywide commitment to equitable and adequately funded education, and outlines plans to make the goal attainable

0-517-59161-8 RANDOM HOUSE $17.00

Death at an Early Age: The Destruction of the Hearts and Minds of Negro Children in the Boston Public Schools

An indictment of public education, from the front lines in 1964 Boston. "A very disturbing book. He is writing of the Boston Public School system, but he could be writing of the system in almost any city in the country"
—*Christian Science Monitor*

0-452-26292-5 NEW AMERICAN LIBRARY PB $11.95

Savage Inequalities: Children in America's Schools

See also **SPECIAL STUDIES** under **URBAN AMERICA** under **AMERICAN PEOPLE AND PLACES** in **HISTORY OF THE AMERICAS**

0-06-097499-0 HARPERPERENNIAL PB $13.50

David **Levine** & others

Rethinking Schools: An Agenda for Change

1-56584-215-4 NEW PRESS PB $16.00

Sara L. **Lightfoot**

The Good High School: Portraits of Character and Culture

Six high schools in different types of communities, all with a reputation for excellence. "An antidote to despair and a road map to better education"
—Fred M. Hechinger, *NY Times*

0-465-02696-6 BASIC BOOKS PB $17.50

Paul Rogat **Loeb**

Generation at the Crossroads: Apathy and Action on the American Campus

0-8135-2256-0 RUTGERS PB $16.95

Mary Susan **Miller**

Save Our Schools: 66 Things You Can Do to Improve Your School Without Spending an Extra Penny

This call to grassroots activism in the classroom and beyond provides a wealth of tips for administrators, teachers, and parents. Ranging from the everyday to the inspired, it features dozens of success stories and step-by-step strategies for innovative change

0-06-250733-8 HARPERCOLLINS PB $8.00

Eleanor W. **Orr**

Twice as Less: Black English and the Performance of Black Students in Mathematics and Science

0-393-02392-3 NORTON $15.95
0-393-30585-6 NORTON PB $8.95

Jaroslav **Pelikan**

The Idea of the University: A Reexamination

Pelikan, a professor of history at Yale, compares the current state of the university with that in Cardinal Newman's classic of the last century

0-300-05725-3 YALE $35.00

Neil **Postman**

The End of Education: Redefining the Value of Schools

The New York University professor and chair of the Department of Culture and Communication turns his vast experience in social criticism to the imperative question of schooling in America. Postman analyzes the effect of modern technocracy on education and suggests a model in which schools can restore a sense of purpose and a respect for learning in their students.

Brilliant and affirmative, Postman has provided the response to *The Closing of the American Mind* and *Cultural Literacy*
0-679-43006-7 KNOPF $23.00

Arthur G. **Powell**
The Shopping Mall High School: Winners and Losers in the Educational Marketplace
0-395-42638-3 HOUGHTON MIFFLIN PB $12.95

Diane **Ravitch**
The Schools We Deserve: Reflections on the Educational Crisis of Our Time
Essays offering a reevaluation of contemporary educational issues, from a historical perspective
0-465-07234-8 BASIC BOOKS PB $16.00

Reforming Education: The Opening of the American Mind
0-02-030175-8 COLLIER PB $8.95

Mike **Rose**
Possible Lives: The Promise of Public Education
0-395-74546-2 HOUGHTON MIFFLIN $24.95
0-14-023617-1 PENGUIN PB $13.95

Michael **Rutter**
Fifteen Thousand Hours: Secondary Schools and Their Children
0-674-30026-2 HARVARD PB $12.00

Gilbert T. **Sewall**
Necessary Lessons: Decline and Renewal in American Schools
0-02-929030-9 FREE PRESS $27.95

Theodore **Sizer**
Horace's Hope: The Future of the American High School
0-395-73983-7 DORLING KINDERSLEY $21.95

Theodore R. **Sizer**
Horace's Compromise: The Dilemma of the American High School
An unflattering portrait, with proposals for reform
0-395-61158-X HOUGHTON MIFFLIN PB $10.95

Radical Critics on Left and Right

Since the 1960s, radical critics have subjected education to a searching examination, arguing that the flaws in the system are so deep and pervasive that the educational system itself is corrupt and beyond the help of reform.

Another source of radical criticism, however, comes from conservatives who assail John Dewey and progressive education as the philosophical source of irremediable error.

Michael W. **Apple**
Ideology and Curriculum
0-415-90266-5 ROUTLEDGE PB $15.95

Allan **Bloom**
The Closing of the American Mind: Education and the Crisis of Reason
The controversial book that helped set off the latest rounds in the culture wars
See also HIGHER EDUCATION
INTRODUCTION BY SAUL BELLOW
0-671-65715-1 TOUCHSTONE PB $12.00

Samuel **Bowles** & Herbert **Gintis**
Schooling in Capitalist America: Educational Reform and the Contradictions of Economic Life
A neo-Marxist critique of American education, from its historical origins. "A genuinely creative attempt to develop a Marxist point of view about the interaction between schooling and the labor market"—Mark Blaug, *Challenge*
0-465-09718-9 BASIC BOOKS PB $16.00

David **Bromwich**
Politics by Other Means: Higher Education and Group Thinking
He believes that genuine education must primarily be concerned with critical thinking and independence of mind, and that to impose a cultural and/or political slant is to detrimentally indoctrinate students. "A profoundly serious work, far better than any recent book on modern higher education"
—George Kateb, Princeton University
0-300-05702-4 YALE $35.00

I am concerned in these pages with two environments, a conservative political culture outside the academy and a radical political culture inside. Both, in the past decade, have isolated themselves from criticism, and both to an unprecedented degree have disciplined and stereotyped their products beyond the hope of self-criticism. Whatever good or useful about either of them is now far on the way to ruin. Both cultures have grown provincial rather than cosmopolitan: their members talk to the same people, receive the same narrow and defensive advice, from one occasion of judgment to the next.
POLITICS BY OTHER MEANS: HIGHER EDUCATION AND GROUP THINKING

Paulo **Freire**
Pedagogy of the Oppressed
On the ties between education and liberation, particularly in the Third World
TRANSLATED BY MYRA S. RAMOS
FOREWORD BY RICHARD SHAULL
0-8264-0611-4 CONTINUUM PB $12.95

Paul R. **Gross** & Norman **Levitt**
Higher Superstition: The Academic Left and Its Quarrels with Science
Attacks on the application of deconstruction to science
0-8018-4766-4 JOHNS HOPKINS $25.95

John **Holt**
How Children Fail
"What a wonderful world it would be if all children could have teachers like John Holt"
—*Library Journal*
0-201-48402-1 ADDISON-WESLEY PB $11.00

How Children Learn
Revised edition of a classic
0-201-48404-8 ADDISON-WESLEY PB $11.00

Kulturkampf: The War over the Canon

James **Atlas**
Battle of the Books: The Curriculum Debate in America
Students are what they read, Atlas argues; choosing our children's books is an incredibly important task. As ethnic groups assert themselves and reject assimilation, our need for common ground grows ever greater. The author suggests that unless there are common beliefs on which to build consensus, there may soon be no common heritage, no shared vision of the future
See also CURRENT POLITICAL THOUGHT AND ISSUES under AMERICAN POLITICS AND FOREIGN POLICY in HISTORY OF THE AMERICAS
0-393-03413-5 NORTON $17.95
0-393-31070-1 NORTON PB $8.95

Paul **Berman**, editor
Debating P.C.: The Controversy over Political Correctness on College Campuses
0-385-31533-3 LAUREL LEAF PB $11.95

Harold **Bloom**
The Western Canon: The Books and School of the Ages
The outstanding contemporary literary critic speaks up for the canon and names his candidates for inclusion
See also HAROLD BLOOM under SEMIOTICS AND STRUCTURALISM under LITERARY THEORY in LITERATURE OF EUROPE, AFRICA, AND ASIA
0-15-195747-9 HARCOURT BRACE $29.95
1-573-22514-2 RIVERHEAD PB $10.95

W.B. **Carnochan**
The Battleground of the Curriculum: Liberal Education and American Experience
0-8047-2147-5 STANFORD $35.00
0-8047-2364-8 STANFORD PB $13.95

J. North **Conway**
American Literacy: Fifty Books that Define Our Culture and Ourselves
0-688-14076-9 QUILL PB $12.00

Stanley **Fish**
There's No Such Thing as Free Speech: And It's a Good Thing Too
0-19-508018-1 OXFORD $27.50
0-19-508350-4 OXFORD PB $10.95

Henry Louis **Gates**, Jr.

Loose Canons: Notes on the Culture Wars

0-19-507519-6 OXFORD $25.00
0-19-509383-6 OXFORD PB $12.95

Gerald **Graff**

Beyond the Culture Wars: How Teaching the Conflicts Can Revitalize American Education

0-393-03424-0 NORTON $19.95
0-393-31113-9 NORTON PB $9.95

Bernard **Knox**

Backing into the Future: The Classical Tradition and Its Renewal

The renowned classicist and author of *The Oldest Dead White European Males* and *Essays Ancient and Modern* opens his new collection with a group of essays on heroes and poets, including one on Achilles and another on Ovid in exile

See also **GENERAL STUDIES** under **CRITICAL STUDIES** under **ANCIENT GREEK LITERATURE** in **LITERATURE OF EUROPE, AFRICA, AND ASIA**

0-393-03595-6 NORTON $25.00

The Oldest Dead White European Males

0-393-03492-5 NORTON $15.95
0-393-31233-X NORTON PB $9.95

Louis **Menand**, editor

The Future of Academic Freedom

0-226-52004-8 CHICAGO $24.95

Athanasios **Moulakis**

Liberal Education for a Technological Age

In this ground-breaking study by the noted educator and author, Moulakis reexamines and redefines the role of humanities in an educational system that is increasingly more focused on the specialized training of technocrats. Included among the topics are multiculturalism and "the canon," as well as global economic, ecological, and political issues

See also **TECHNOLOGY AND EDUCATION**

0-8262-0929-7 MISSOURI $24.95

Christopher **Newfield** & Ronald **Strickland**, editors

After Political Correctness: The Humanities and Society in the 1990s

0-8133-2337-1 WESTVIEW PB $24.95

Reading and Literacy

Sven **Birkets**

The Gutenberg Elegies: The Fate of Reading in the Electronic Age

0-571-19849-X FABER $22.95

Rudolf **Flesch**

Why Johnny Can't Read: And What You Can Do About It

Promotes the use of phonics, instead of the popular "look-and-say" method, to teach reading

0-06-091340-1 HARPERCOLLINS PB $12.00

Why Johnny Still Can't Read: A New Look at the Scandal of Our Schools

"I hope this book reaches a wide audience, because Flesch is right about phonics. Children want to learn to read; English is, for the most part, a phonetic language; once children learn the alphabetic code, they become readers. It is as simple as that"—John Merrow, *New Republic*

0-06-091031-3 HARPERCOLLINS PB $11.00

E. D. **Hirsch**, Jr. & others, editors

The Dictionary of Cultural Literacy

Revised and updated, this new edition provides a wealth of essential facts in fields that include politics, technology, medicine, history, and literature. Also includes new subjects based on readers' suggestions from the first edition, such as multiculturalism and African-American history. The only reference book to appear on the bestseller list

See also **ONE-VOLUME ENCYCLOPEDIAS** under **REFERENCE** in **BUSINESS AND REFERENCE**

0-395-65597-8 HOUGHTON MIFFLIN $24.95

E.D. **Hirsch**, Jr.

Cultural Literacy: What Every American Needs to Know

A call for a new emphasis on information—as opposed to skills—in education, including an exhaustive, 63-page appendix of names, dates, and terms that educated people should know. "Because it so powerfully demonstrates that reading—like thinking—is not a skill that can be separated from substance and content, I can think of no other book of recent years more important for the formulation of curriculum policy than this one"—Albert Shanker

0-394-75843-9 VINTAGE PB $10.00

E. D. **Hirsh Jr.** ,editor

What Your First Grader Needs to Know: Fundamentals of a Good First-Grade Education

0-385-41115-4 DOUBLEDAY $22.50
0-385-31026-9 DELTA PB $10.95

Ivan **Illich** & Barry **Sanders**

ABC: The Alphabetization of the Popular Mind

"A highly literate challenge to many fundamental assumptions about literacy" —Les Adler, *San Francisco Chronicle*

0-679-72192-4 VINTAGE PB $9.75

Mary V. **Jackson**

Engines of Instruction, Mischief, and Magic: Children's Literature in England from Its Beginnings to 1839

0-8032-7570-6 NEBRASKA PB $16.50

Jonathan **Kozol**

Illiterate America

Kozol's argument that one-third of all Americans are functionally illiterate sparked a national debate and helped bring the topic into the media limelight. "A stunning sequel to *Death at an Early Age*. Kozol, with passion and eloquence, reveals a devastating truth: Domestic illiteracy, en masse, is a graver threat than foreign weaponry"—Studs Terkel

0-452-26203-8 NEW AMERICAN LIBRARY PB $12.95

Teaching

Jacques **Barzun**

Teachers in America

A critical look at what's wrong with the way America's teachers are trained

0-913966-79-7 LIBERTY FUND PB $6.00

Marva **Collins** & Civia **Tamarkin**

Marva Collins' Way

The Chicago teacher who fought the status quo and founded her own school

0-87477-572-8 TARCHER PB $10.95

Howard **Gardner**

The Unschooled Mind: How Children Think and How Schools Should Teach

"An invaluable book for teachers, school administrators, parents, and policy makers" —*NY Times Book Review*

0-465-08895-3 BASIC PB $23.00

Gilbert **Higher**

The Art of Teaching

A classic on the principles of teaching

0-679-72314-5 VINTAGE PB $10.00

E. D. **Hirsch** & John **Holdren**

What Your Kindergartener Needs to Know: Preparing Your Child for a Lifetime of Learning

See also **EDUCATION** under **PARENTING** in **LIFESTYLES AND PRACTICAL ADVICE**

0-385-48117-9 BDD $24.95

William **James**

Talks to Teachers on Psychology and to Students on Some of Life's Ideals

INTRODUCTION BY P. WOODRING

0-393-00165-2 NORTON PB $10.95

Sharon L. **Kagan** & Edward F. **Zigler**, editors

Early Schooling: The National Debate

0-300-03995-6 YALE PB $17.00

Tracy **Kidder**

Among Schoolchildren

A year in the life of an American urban schoolteacher. Kidder's portrait of Mrs. Zajac restores the human element to the ongoing national debate on education, giving us not abstractions but the real human contact between teacher and students

0-395-47591-0 HOUGHTON MIFFLIN $21.95
0-380-71089-7 AVON PB $11.00

Kenneth **Koch**

Rose, Where Do You Get that Red: Teaching Great Poetry to Children

A poet and veteran teacher's iconoclastic method. "A handbook, anthology, and instructor's guide combined, Koch's work will instantly endear itself to writers and teachers of every age and competence"—*Library Journal*

0-679-72471-0 VINTAGE PB $12.00

Kenneth Koch

Herbert **Kohl**

"I Won't Learn from You": And Other Inquiries into the Control and Liberation of Learning

In the vanguard of educational theory, Kohl has forged new paths to the heart of the urban school crisis. Now available in book form, his acclaimed essay links the refusal to learn to students' sense that their dignity and self-worth are compromised by their teachers, schools, and society. Also included are three new essays: "The Tattooed Man: Against Stigma," "Beyond Not Learning: An Essay on Creative Maladjustment" and "Provocations: On Powerful Learning Experiences"

See also **EDUCATION** under **PARENTING** in **LIFESTYLES AND PRACTICAL ADVICE**

0-915943-64-6 MILKWEED PB $5.95

Not-learning tends to take place when someone has to deal with unavoidable challenges to her or his personal and family loyalties, integrity, and identity...To agree to learn from a stranger who does not respect your integrity causes a major loss of self. The only alternative is to not-learn and reject the stranger's world.

"I WON'T LEARN FROM YOU": AND OTHER INQUIRIES INTO THE CONTROL AND LIBERATION OF LEARNING

Dan C. **Lortie**

Schoolteacher: A Sociological Study

Classic study on the state of the profession, using interviews and surveys

0-226-49354-7 CHICAGO PB $12.95

Jay **Mathews**

Escalante: The Best Teacher in America

The story of the barrio high school teacher in East Los Angeles whose life was the basis for the film *Stand and Deliver*

0-8050-1195-1 HOLT PB $12.95

Vivian G. **Paley**

Boys and Girls: Superheroes in the Doll Corner

See also **BEING A PARENT** under **PARENTING** in **LIFESTYLES AND PRACTICAL ADVICE**

0-226-64492-8 CHICAGO PB $8.95

You Can't Say You Can't Play

This MacArthur Prize-winning kindergarten teacher attacked the roots of exclusion, rejection, and loneliness in the life of children and obtained a surprising glimpse into a child's view of the world

0-674-96590-6 HARVARD PB $10.00

Donald A. **Schon**

The Reflective Practitioner: How Professionals Think in Action

0-465-06878-2 BASIC PB $18.00

Kenneth A. **Strike** & Jonas **Soltis**

The Ethics of Teaching

0-8077-3141-2 TEACHER'S COLLEGE PB $11.95

Patrick **Welsh**

Tales out of School: A Teacher's Candid Account from the Front Lines of the American High School Today

0-670-80073-2 VIKING $15.95

Segregation, Integration, and Equal Opportunity

John **Devine**

Maximum Security: The Culture of Violence in Inner-City Schools

0-226-14386-4 CHICAGO $40.00
0-226-14387-2 CHICAGO PB $15.95

Paul R. **Dimond**

Beyond Busing: Inside the Challenge to Urban Segregation

0-472-10062-9 MICHIGAN $42.50

Paula S. **Fass**

Outside In: Minorities and the Transformation of American Education

0-19-503790-1 OXFORD $30.00

Thomas **James** & Henry M. **Levin**, editors

Public Dollars for Private Schools: The Case of Tuition Tax Credits

0-87722-386-6 TEMPLE PB $14.95

Richard **Kluger**

Simple Justice: The History of Brown v. Board of Education and Black America's Struggle for Equality

A marvelous journalistic account of the events leading up to the landmark Supreme Court decision

0-394-72255-8 RANDOM HOUSE PB $25.00

L. Scott **Miller**

An American Imperative: Accelerating Minority Educational Advancement

0-300-05793-8 YALE $37.50

Richard **Rodriguez**

Hunger of Memory: The Education of Richard Rodriguez, an Autobiography

An eloquent memoir from a Mexican-American intellectual. "Shows more insight and understanding into the familiar problems of contemporary American education than a roomful of studies and reports by social scientists"—Diane Ravitch

0-553-27293-4 BDD PB $5.99

J. Harvie **Wilkinson**

From Brown to Bakke: The Supreme Court and School Integration, 1954-1978

0-19-502897-X OXFORD PB $12.95

Raymond **Wolters**

The Burden of Brown: Thirty Years of School Desegregation

"A thoroughly researched and well-written description of the history of race relations since 1954 in the five school districts involved in the famous Brown decision"—L.E. Noble, Jr., *Choice*

0-87049-750-2 TENNESSEE PB $16.95

Edward **Zigler** & Susan **Muenchow**

Head Start: The Inside Story of America's Most Successful Educational Experiment

One of the few widely recognized successful education programs in America, Head Start has been fraught with political red tape and impeded by lack of support. Zigler and Muenchow recount its history and make recommendations for the program's future. "[This] informative, enjoyable and moving history provides a look at the politics of policymaking..."—*Publishers Weekly*

0-465-02885-3 BASIC PB $13.00

Theory and Philosophy

From Rousseau to Dewey and beyond, a handful of thinkers have had a major influence on the development of educational thinking. For much of the past century, philosophy of education in the United States may be seen as an extended commentary on—or debate with—the ideas of John Dewey (1859-1952). Even today, admirers invoke his name and words and critics assail his influence; his presence is inescapable.

Classics

Howard M. **Jones**, editor

Emerson on Education: Selections

0-8077-1584-0 TEACHER'S COLLEGE PB $8.00

John **Dewey**

Experience and Education

Dewey's concise statement on education, written more than two decades after *Democracy and Education*, and taking into account critics and his own experiences with progressive schools

0-02-013660-9 MACMILLAN PB $5.50

The School and Society & The Child and the Curriculum

0-226-14396-1 CHICAGO PB $9.95

Maria **Montessori**

The Discovery of the Child

From the first woman to receive a medical degree in Italy and originator of the Montessori method of educating small children that stresses self-motivation

0-345-33656-9 BALLANTINE PB $5.95

Robert **McDermott**, editor

The Essential Rudolf Steiner

Steiner believed that man's attachment to material possessions had crippled his innate ability to participate in spiritual processes, and that only extensive training of the consciousness could help recapture that ability. His philosophy was the basis for the Waldorf School movement

See also **19TH-CENTURY SPIRITUALIST REVIVAL** under **METAPHYSICS** under **SPIRITUALITY** in **RELIGION, SPIRITUALITY, AND PHILOSOPHY**

0-06-065345-0 HARPERCOLLINS PB $20.00

John Henry **Newman** & Frank M. **Turner**, editors

The Idea of a University

0-300-06404-7 YALE $35.00

Jean-Jacques **Rousseau**

Emile

Rousseau's treatise on education, advocating a return to nature and rural values

See also **THE ENLIGHTENMENT** under **FRENCH LITERATURE TO 1900** in **LITERATURE OF EUROPE, AFRICA, AND ASIA**

TRANSLATED BY ALLAN BLOOM

0-465-01931-5 BASIC BOOKS PB $20.00

Alfred North **Whitehead**

The Aims of Education

0-02-935180-4 FREE PRESS PB $16.95

Recent Philosophy

Stephen **Arons**

Compelling Belief: The Culture of American Schooling

A critique of the ideology of public education

0-87023-524-9 MASSACHUSETTS PB $16.95

Eva T.H. **Brann**

Paradoxes of Education in a Republic

0-226-07136-7 CHICAGO PB $13.50

Elizabeth **Hamstock**, editor

The Essential Montessori

0-452-26484-7 NEW AMERICAN LIBRARY PB $10.95

Jerome **Bruner**

The Culture of Education

In 1987 Bruner (*Acts of Meaning, On Knowing*) was awarded the International Balzac Prize for his "lifelong contribution to the understanding of the human mind." Here he applies the newly emerging "cultural psychology" to examine education's possibilities and failures as a tool for bringing the mind to its full potential through participation in culture. A challenging criticism of how we teach and how these methods can be reformed and enriched

0-674-17952-8 HARVARD $24.95

The Process of Education

The classic argument for the "spiral curriculum," in which basic concepts of science and the humanities are taught at an early age

0-674-71001-0 HARVARD PB $9.95

John W. **Gardner**

Excellence

Reflections on the importance of excellence in an egalitarian society. "A balanced, informed, and positive statement of democratic belief by a man who in temperament, experience and performance has shown himself to be a gifted educator"—Harold Taylor, *Saturday Review*

0-393-01848-2 NORTON $12.95

0-393-30377-2 NORTON PB $7.95

Henry A. **Giroux**

Schooling and the Struggle for Public Life: Critical Pedagogy in the Modern Age

The author urges a theory and practice that link schooling to the quest for a concrete form of democracy

0-8166-1705-8 MINNESOTA PB $14.95

Maxine **Greene**

Landscapes of Learning

Essays from a noted theorist on such topics as emancipatory education, social issues, and predicaments of women in American education

0-8077-2534-X TEACHER'S COLLEGE PB $18.95

Amy **Gutmann**

Democratic Education

"The book is free from technical jargon and other academic quirks, and nonprofessionals should find it both interesting and accessible" — William H. Nelson, University of Houston

0-691-07736-3 PRINCETON $49.50

Jacques **Maritain**

Education at the Crossroads

The Catholic philosopher's notes on Christian values and education

0-300-00163-0 YALE PB $11.00

Jane R. **Martin**

Reclaiming a Conversation: The Ideal of the Educated Woman

"Conversations" with Plato, Rousseau, Wollstonecraft, Beecher, and Gilman on how women should be educated in an ideal society

0-300-03999-9 YALE PB $13.00

Israel **Scheffler**

The Language of Education

0-398-01656-9 THOMAS $24.95

Jonas F. **Soltis**

Philosophy of Education Since Mid-Century

0-8077-2651-6 TEACHER'S COLLEGE PB $11.95

History of Education

Overviews

David B. **Tyack**

The One Best System: A History of American Urban Education

0-674-63782-8 HARVARD PB $16.50

R.R. **Palmer**

The Improvement of Humanity: Education and the French Revolution

By the co-author of *A History of the Modern World*

0-691-05434-7 PRINCETON $49.50

Diane **Ravitch**

The Troubled Crusade: American Education, 1945-1980

0-465-08757-4 BASIC BOOKS PB $18.00

History of American Education

Bernard **Bailyn**

Education in the Forming of American Society: Needs and Opportunities for Study

0-393-00643-3 NORTON PB $8.95

Benjamin R. **Barber**

An Aristocracy for Everyone: The Politics of Education and the Future of America

0-345-37040-6 BALLANTINE $20.00

0-19-509154-X OXFORD PB $11.95

Joan N. **Burstyn**

Victorian Education and the Ideal of Womanhood

0-389-20103-0 BARNES & NOBLE $44.00

Hugh D. **Graham**

The Uncertain Triumph: Federal Education Policy in the Kennedy and Johnson Years

0-8078-1599-3 NORTH CAROLINA $34.95

Robert L. **Hampel**

The Last Little Citadel: American High Schools Since 1940

FOREWORD BY THEODORE R. SIZER

0-395-36451-5 HOUGHTON MIFFLIN $15.95

Carl F. **Kaestle**
Pillars of the Republic: Common Schools and American Society, 1780-1960
EDITED BY ERIC FONER
0-8090-0154-3 FS&G PB $9.95

Ellen C. **Lagemann**
A Generation of Women: Education in the Lives of Progressive Reformers
0-674-34471-5 HARVARD $25.00

Henry J. **Perkinson**
Imperfect Panacea: American Faith in Education, 1865-1969
0-07-049348-0 MCGRAW HILL PB $23.25

Edward J. **Larson**
Trial and Error: The American Controversy over Creation and Evolution
0-19-506143-8 OXFORD PB $10.95

Lawrence A. **Cremin**, editor
The Republic and the School: Horace Mann on the Education of Free Men
0-8077-1206-X TEACHER'S COLLEGE PB $7.00

George M. **Marsden**
The Soul of the American University: From Protestant Establishment to Established Nonbelief
0-19-507046-1 OXFORD $35.00
0-19-510650-4 OXFORD PB $17.95

Paul E. **Peterson**
The Politics of School Reform, 1870-1940
0-226-66295-0 CHICAGO PB $14.50

David **Tyack**
Public Schools in Hard Times: The Great Depression and Recent Years
0-674-73800-4 HARVARD $30.00

David **Tyack** & Elisabeth **Hansot**
Managers of Virtue: Public School Leadership in America, 1820-1980
0-465-04374-7 BASIC BOOKS PB $15.00

International Education

Theodore Hsi-en **Chen**
Chinese Education Since 1949
0-08-023861-0 PERGAMON $44.00

John **Simmons**
The Education Dilemma
0-08-024303-7 PERGAMON PB $37.00

Benjamin **Duke**
The Japanese School: Lessons for Industrial America
FOREWORD BY CLARK KERR & JAMES M. HESTOR
0-275-92003-8 PRAEGER PB $19.95

Torstein **Husen**
The School in Question: A Comparative Study of the School and Its Future in Western Societies
0-19-874086-7 OXFORD PB $14.95

Higher Education

Alexander W. **Astin**
Four Critical Years: Effects of College on Beliefs, Attitudes, and Knowledge
0-87589-346-5 JOSSEY-BASS $29.95

Allan **Bloom**
The Closing of the American Mind: Education and the Crisis of Reason
The controversial book that helped set off the latest rounds in the culture wars

See also **RADICAL CRITICS ON LEFT AND RIGHT** under **THE STATE OF THE SCHOOLS**

INTRODUCTION BY SAUL BELLOW
0-671-65715-1 TOUCHSTONE PB $12.00

Derek C. **Bok**
Beyond the Ivory Tower: Social Responsibilities of the Modern University
0-674-06898-X HARVARD PB $10.95

Higher Learning
Wide-ranging thoughts on the purposes and practices of American higher education today, from a former president of Harvard
0-674-39175-6 HARVARD $24.95
0-674-39176-4 HARVARD PB $13.50

Pierre **Bourdieu**
Homo Academicus
A brilliant, bestselling self-analysis of the French academic world by its leading sociologist

See also **POSTWAR FRENCH AND BRITISH THOUGHT** under **SOCIOLOGY AFTER WEBER** under **SOCIOLOGY**

TRANSLATED BY PETER COLLIER
0-8047-1466-5 STANFORD $47.50
0-8047-1798-2 STANFORD PB $17.95

Steven M. **Cahn**
Saints and Scamps: Ethics in Academia
0-8476-7518-1 LITTLEFIELD ADAMS PB $9.95

Michael D. **Cohen** & James G. **March**
Leadership and Ambiguity
0-07-103224-X MCGRAW HILL PB $12.95

Clark **Kerr**
The Uses of the University
0-674-93171-8 HARVARD PB $13.95

A. Bartlett **Giamatti**
A Free and Ordered Space: The Real World of the University
0-393-30671-2 NORTON PB $9.95

Gerald **Grant** & David **Riesman**
The Perpetual Dream: Reform and Experiment in the American College
0-226-30606-2 CHICAGO PB $6.95

Helen Lefkowitz **Horowitz**
Campus Life: Undergraduate Cultures from the End of the 18th Century to the Present
0-226-35373-7 CHICAGO PB $17.95

Christopher **Jencks** & David **Riesman**
The Academic Revolution
The rise of faculty domination in the college and university world
0-226-39628-2 CHICAGO PB $10.95

Walter P. **Metzger**
Academic Freedom in the Age of the University
0-231-08512-5 COLUMBIA PB $17.00

Samuel Eliot **Morison**
Three Centuries of Harvard
0-674-88891-X BELKNAP PB $14.95

Conrad **Russell**
Academic Freedom
0-415-03714-X ROUTLEDGE $55.00
0-415-03715-8 ROUTLEDGE PB $15.95

Barbara M. **Solomon**
In the Company of Educated Women: History of Women and Education in America
0-300-03639-6 YALE PB $18.00

Technology and Education

President James A. Garfield is said to have remarked that the ideal college was Mark Hopkins on one end of a log and a student on the other. For years, that saying was reiterated, usually to reaffirm the importance of the relationship between the teacher and the student.

Since at least mid-century, however, technology has loomed large as the answer to those who have longed for a "teacher-proof" method of education. With each scientific advance, the promise of technology has seemed brighter. But amid the euphoria there are also warnings that the electronic cure for education's ills may be more dangerous than the disease itself.

Whether the computer, the videodisc, or some other version of the big screen will take Mark Hopkins' place remains to be seen.

Robert **Taylor**, editor
The Computer in the School: Tutor, Tutee, Tool
0-8077-2611-7 TEACHER'S COLLEGE PB $18.95

Larry **Cuban**

Teachers and Machines: The Classroom Use of Technology Since 1920

0-8077-2792-X TEACHER'S COLLEGE PB $13.95

Athanasios **Moulakis**

Liberal Education For a Technological Age

In this groundbreaking study by the noted educator and author, Moulakis reexamines and redefines the role of humanities in an educational system that is increasingly more focused on the specialized training of technocrats. Included among the topics are multiculturalism and "the canon," as well as global economic, ecological, and political issues

See also **KULTURKAMPF: THE WAR OVER THE CANON** under **THE STATE OF THE SCHOOLS**

0-8262-0929-7 MISSOURI $24.95

Neil **Postman**

Amusing Ourselves to Death: Public Discourse in the Age of Show Business

0-14-009438-5 VIKING PB $11.95

Theodore **Roszak**

The Cult of Information: The Folklore of Computers and the True Art of Thinking

A recent critique of computer enthusiasm

See also **THE CYBERNETIC SOCIETY** under **THE COMPUTER REVOLUTION AND ARTIFICIAL INTELLIGENCE** in **SCIENCE**

See also **THE HUMAN MIND AND ARTIFICIAL INTELLIGENCE** under **THE COGNITIVE REVOLUTION** under **PSYCHOLOGY**

0-520-08584-1 CALIFORNIA PB $12.00
0520085840 CALIFORNIA PB $1.00

Tom **Snyder** & Jane **Palmer**

In Search of the Most Amazing Thing: Children, Education and Computers

0-201-16437-X ADDISON WESLEY PB $12.95

Marie **Winn**

The Plug-In Drug: Television, Children and the Family

See also **TELEVISION AND SOCIETY** under **TELEVISION** in **PERFORMING ARTS AND MEDIA**

0-14-007698-0 VIKING PB $10.95

The Nuclear Age

David S. **Greenwald** & Steven J. **Zeitlin**

No Reason to Talk About It: Families Confront the Nuclear Taboo

0-393-70021-6 NORTON $22.95

Spencer R. **Weart**

Nuclear Fear: A History of Images

See also **NUCLEAR ETHICS** under **NUCLEAR WEAPONS AND ARMS CONTROL** under **INTERNATIONAL RELATIONS AND STRATEGIC STUDIES**

0-674-62836-5 HARVARD PB $14.95

Linguistics

Introductions to Language

Jean **Aitchison**

Teach Yourself Linguistics

This is an excellent, clearly presented introduction to the field, with many helpful diagrams

0-8442-3929-1 N.T.C. PB $12.95

Victoria **Fromkins** & Robert **Rodman**

An Introduction to Language

0-03-054983-3 HOLT RINEHART & WINSTON PB .$40.90

Kenneth **Katzner**

Languages of the World

0-7102-0861-8 ROUTLEDGE PB $14.95

Winfred P. **Lehmann**

Language: An Introduction

See also **ABOUT LANGUAGE** under **REFERENCE** in **BUSINESS AND REFERENCE**

0-07-554251-X RANDOM HOUSE PB $34.15

John **Lyons**

Language and Linguistics

Lyons has moved from a syntactic orientation to a romantic one

0-521-29775-3 CAMBRIDGE PB $19.95

Steven **Pinker**

The Language Instinct: How the Mind Creates Language

The co-director of the Center for Cognitive Science at MIT explains how we learn to talk, how the study of language can provide insight into how our genes interact with our experience to create behavior and thought, and how the arbitrary sounds we call language evoke emotion and meaning. "An extremely valuable book, very informative, and very well written"—Noam Chomsky

See also **LANGUAGE** under **SPECIAL TOPICS IN PSYCHOLOGY** under **PSYCHOLOGY**

0-688-12141-1 HARPERPERENNIAL PB $17.95

Geoffrey **Sampson**

Schools of Linguistics

"A fresh, funny, clear, literate and scholarly survey of the prelude and cacophonous themes of recent linguistic theory in the English-speaking world"—*Choice*

0-8047-1125-9 STANFORD PB $14.95

Ronald **Wardhaugh**

Introduction to Linguistics

0-07-068152-X MCGRAW HILL PB $67.15

Language Theory

Roger **Brown**

Words and Things

See also **ABOUT LANGUAGE** under **REFERENCE** in **BUSINESS AND REFERENCE**

0-02-904810-9 FREE PRESS PB $13.95

Philip S. **Dale**

Language Development: Structure and Function

0-03-089705-X HOLT RINEHART & WINSTON PB $35.91

Alison J. **Elliot**

Child Language

A clear and concise survey of the field of language acquisition

0-521-29556-4 CAMBRIDGE PB $19.95

Randy Allen **Harris**

The Linguistics Wars

0-19-509834-X OXFORD PB $16.95

Pioneers in Linguistics

J.L. **Austin**

How to Do Things with Words

The short but extremely influential work by the founder of speech-act theory

See also **OTHER 20TH-CENTURY PHILOSOPHERS** under **PHILOSOPHY** in **RELIGION, SPIRITUALITY, AND PHILOSOPHY**

EDITED BY J.O. URMSON AND MARINA SBISA

0-674-41152-8 HARVARD PB $10.50

Leonard **Bloomfield**

Language

The early American behaviorist cleared the ground for later scientific methods of language study; this summation of his views was published in 1933

FOREWORD BY CHARLES HOCKETT

0-226-06067-5 CHICAGO PB $26.00

A Leonard Bloomfield Anthology

EDITED BY CHARLES HOCKETT

0-226-06071-3 CHICAGO PB $14.95

Jonathan **Culler**

Ferdinand de Saussure

A brief introduction to the founder of semiotics and modern linguistics, aimed at the general reader

0-8014-9389-7 CORNELL PB $9.95

Ferdinand **de Saussure**

Course in General Linguistics

Published in 1916, this was the greatest single influence in detaching language study from the historical method of the 19th century and approaching it as a system

EDITED BY ROY HARRIS TRANSLATED BY WADE BASKIN

0-07-016524-6 MCGRAW HILL PB $11.25

Wilhelm **von Humboldt**

On Language: The Diversity of Human Language-Structure and Its Influence on the Mental Development of Mankind

A new translation of the milestone work by the early 19th-century philologist acknowledged by Chomsky as an early "transformationalist"

TRANSLATED BY PETER HEATH

INTRODUCTION BY HANS AARSLEFF

0-521-31513-1 CAMBRIDGE PB $31.95

Roman **Jakobson**

Language in Literature

Highly influential literary theory based on linguistics, by the cofounder of the Prague School

See also **FICTION AND OTHER PROSE** under **EARLY 20TH CENTURY** under **RUSSIAN LITERATURE** in **LITERATURE OF EUROPE, AFRICA, AND ASIA**

EDITED BY KRYSTYNA POMORSKA & STEPHEN RUDY

0-674-51027-5 BELKNAP $40.00

On Language

"An accessible collection of theoretical works by one of the most important and versatile linguists of the century"—*Russian Review*

See also **FICTION AND OTHER PROSE** under **EARLY 20TH CENTURY** under **RUSSIAN LITERATURE** in **LITERATURE OF EUROPE, AFRICA, AND ASIA**

See also **RUSSIAN FORMALISTS AND THE PRAGUE SCHOOL** under **SEMIOTICS AND STRUCTURALISM AND AFTER** under **LITERARY THEORY** in **LITERATURE OF EUROPE, AFRICA, AND ASIA**

EDITED BY LINDA R. WAUGH & MONIQUE MONVILLE-BURSTON

0-674-63536-1 BELKNAP PB $22.95

Roman **Jakobson** & Morris **Halle**

Fundamentals of Language

90-279-3074-0 WALTER DE GRUYTER PB $11.55

Roman **Jakobson** & Krystyna **Pomorska**

Dialogues

Intimate and casual interviews between the linguist and his wife give their thought a charming accessibility

See also **FICTION AND OTHER PROSE** under **EARLY 20TH CENTURY** under **RUSSIAN LITERATURE** in **LITERATURE OF EUROPE, AFRICA, AND ASIA**

0-262-60016-1 MIT PB $9.95

Edward **Sapir**

Language: An Introduction to the Study of Speech

With Whorf, Sapir was one of the originators of the idea that "the real world is unconsciously built up on the language habits of the group"; this classic study appeared in 1921

0-15-648233-9 HARCOURT BRACE PB $7.95

Selected Writings of Edward Sapir in Language, Culture, and Personality

EDITED BY DAVID G. MANDELBAUM

0-520-05594-2 CALIFORNIA PB $13.95

Benjamin Lee **Whorf**

Language, Thought and Reality: Selected Writings

A classic statement of the influence of language on perception, based on the study of Hopi and native Mexican languages

0-262-73006-5 MIT PB $18.00

Noam Chomsky

Chomsky is the founder of the major revolution in linguistics at mid-century that used the idea of "deep structure" to explain how a language user can generate an infinite variety of sentences without learning their individual forms.

Noam **Chomsky**

Knowledge of Language: Its Nature, Origin, and Use

0-275-90025-8 PRAEGER $55.00

Noam Chomsky

Language and Mind

0-15-549257-8 H.B.J. PB $23.61

Language and Thought

A printed lecture in which the famous linguistic theorist argues the study of language is central to cognitive psychology and the philosophy of mind

1-55921-076-1 MOYER BELL PB $9.95

Rules and Representations

0-231-04827-0 COLUMBIA PB $18.00

Gilbert **Harman**, editor

On Noam Chomsky: Critical Essays

0-87023-355-6 MASSACHUSETTS PB $18.95

Language and Society

John **DeFrancis**

Visible Speech: The Diverse Oneness of Writing Systems

0-8248-1207-7 HAWAII $28.00

Brock Haussamen

Revising the Rules: Traditional Grammar and Modern Linguistics

A discussion of the history of and the linguistic concepts behind the conventional rules of grammar. With suggested new formulations of the old rules

0-8403-9032-7 KENDALL/HUNT PB $219.95

C.A. **Ferguson** & Shirley Brice **Heath**, editors

Language in the United States of America

FOREWORD BY DELL H. HYMES

0-521-29834-2 CAMBRIDGE PB $33.95

Shirley Brice **Heath**

Ways with Words: Language, Life and Work in Communities and Classrooms

Two neighboring blue-collar communities, white Roadville and black Trackton, provide a comparison of language use based on education, upbringing, and working conditions

0-521-27319-6 CAMBRIDGE PB $26.95

Alette Olin **Hill**

Mother Tongue, Father Time: A Decade of Linguistic Revolt

See also **LANGUAGE** under **WOMEN'S STUDIES**

0-253-20389-9 INDIANA PB $10.95

Gunther **Kress** & Robert **Hodge**

Social Semiotics

Analyzes communication processes in literary texts, television, advertising billboards, and daily social interactions

0-8014-9515-6 CORNELL PB $16.95

William **Lutz**

The New Doublespeak: Why No One Knows What Anyone's Saying Anymore

0-06-017134-0 HARPERCOLLINS $23.00

Robert **McCrum**

The Story of English

A companion volume to the public television series. "The study of the language will never be the same again after the publication of this book. It travels at the speed of a bullet train to every corner of the globe where English is spoken. It also authentically describes the mysterious power of older dazzling forms of the language"—Robert Burchfield, Editor in Chief, *The Oxford Dictionaries*

See also **ABOUT LANGUAGE** under **REFERENCE** in **BUSINESS AND REFERENCE**

0-14-015405-1 PENGUIN PB $22.95

H.L. **Mencken**

The American Language

The classic work on the development of a specifically American vernacular that is also a history of the growth of the professions and the effect of immigration

0-394-73315-0 KNOPF PB $25.00

Frederick J. **Newmayer**

The Politics of Linguistics

Deals with 200 years of debate over whether language should be studied as an autonomous entity or as part of the cultural and social fabric

0-226-57722-8 CHICAGO PB $12.00

Wayne M. **Senner**, editor

The Origins of Writing

0-8032-4202-6 NEBRASKA PB $35.00

David **Simpson**

The Politics of American English, 1776-1850

The story of the fierce debate on both sides of the Atlantic over what American English was, what it might become, and what it ought to be

0-19-505643-4 OXFORD PB $18.95

Language and Literature

Roger **Fowler**

Linguistic Criticism

A leading British theorist looks at literature through the linguistic lens

0-19-289111-1 OXFORD PB $14.95

Umberto **Eco**

The Search for the Perfect Language

See also **ESSAYS, MEMOIRS, AND OTHER PROSE** under **THE 20TH CENTURY** under **ITALIAN LITERATURE** in **LITERATURE OF EUROPE, AFRICA, AND ASIA**

See also **LANGUAGE AND WRITING** under **ARCHAEOLOGY** in **WORLD HISTORY AND CURRENT AFFAIRS**

0-631-17465-6 BLACKWELL........................$24.95

Marshall **Edelson**

Language and Interpretation in Psychoanalysis

Attempts to link Chomsky and Freud, and offers interpretations of a Bach prelude and Wallace Stevens' "Snow Man"

0-226-18433-1 CHICAGO PB........................$9.00

John **Searle**

Expression and Meaning: Studies in the Theory of Speech Arts

One of the most influential theories applied by one of its leading exponents to metaphor and fiction

0-521-31393-7 CAMBRIDGE PB........................$20.95

Elizabeth C. **Traugott** & Mary L. **Pratt**

Linguistics for Students of Literature

0-15-551030-4 HARCOURT BRACE PB........................$31.92

Reference

Oswald **Ducrot** & Tzvetan **Todorov**

Encyclopedic Dictionary of the Sciences of Language

Excellent up-to-date collection of short articles that cover the major movements from transformational grammar to grammatology

TRANSLATED BY CATHERINE PORTER

0-8018-2857-0 JOHNS HOPKINS PB........................$18.95

Anatole V. **Lyovin**

An Introduction to the Languages of the World

0-19-508115-3 OXFORD........................$49.95

0-19-508116-1 OXFORD PB........................$24.95

Part 5

Science

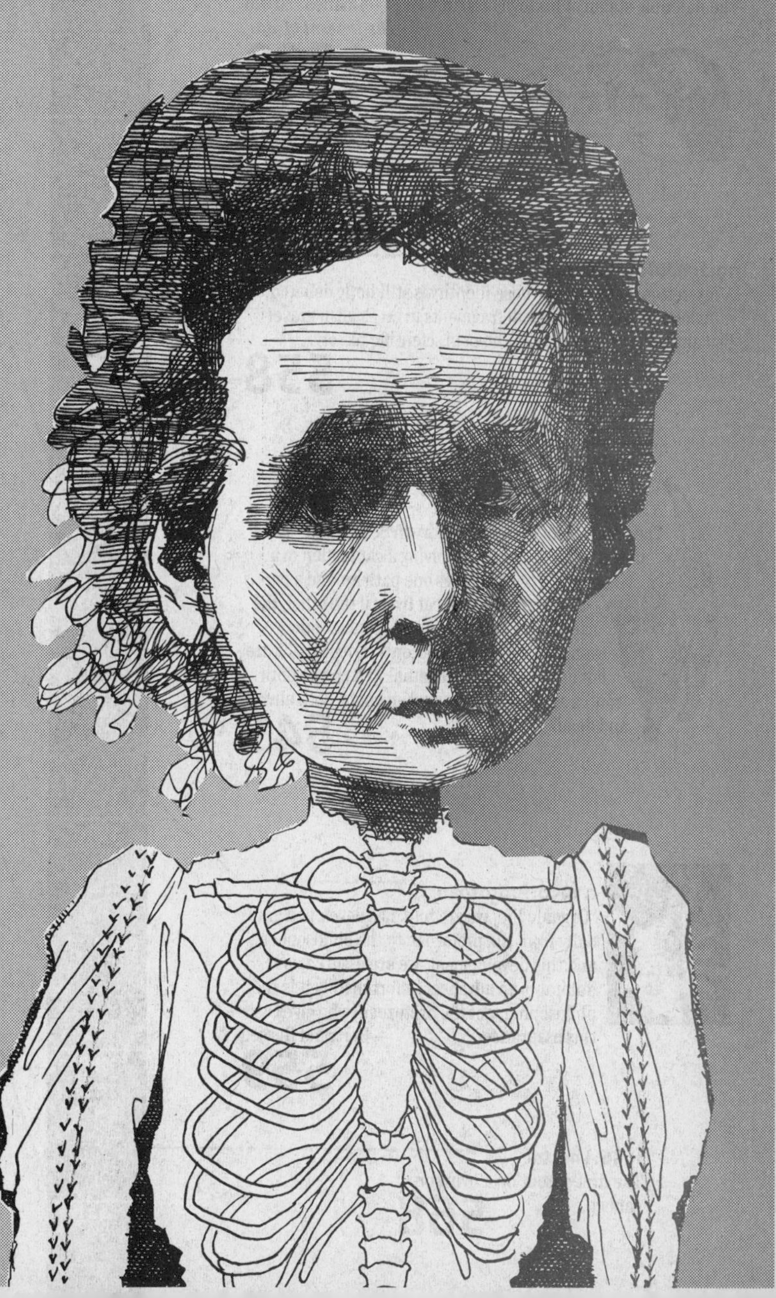

Marie Curie

Science: A Bestiary

1650 · 1700 · 1850 · 1875 · 1900 · 1925 · 1950 · 1975 · 1990

Half a Billion Years Ago: Hallucigenia
Peg-legging across the seafloor, Hallucigenia exemplified the bewildering anatomical diversity of Paleozoic life.

557

70 AD: Elephant
"It is a most surprising thing that the elephant is able not only to walk up the tightrope backwards, but to come down it as well with the head foremost." —Pliny the Elder

540

1856: Neanderthals
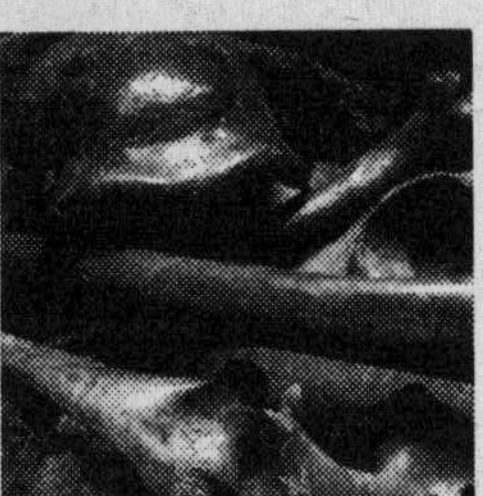
Were they our direct ancestors or an evolutionary dead end? The discovery of these bones, in the valley of the Neander near Düsseldorf, launched a stream of arguments, novels, and cartoons that tells us as much about our changing prejudices as about our much mocked kin.
558

1677: Spermatozoa
"The animalcules moved forward with a snake-like motion of the tail, as eels do when swimming in water."
—Antonie van Leeuwenhoek, pioneer of the microscope
567

1871: Homo Sapiens
"Man, with all his exalted powers, still bears in his bodily frame the indelible stamp of his lowly origin." —Charles Darwin *The Descent of Man*
560
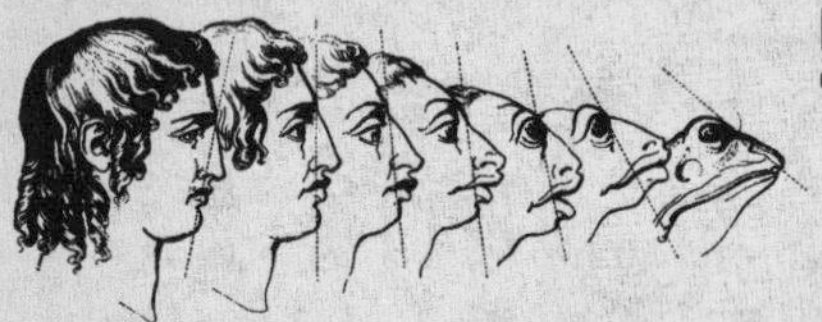

1871: Maxwell's Demon
Is invented by the great English physicist James Clerk Maxwell to break the second law of thermodynamics: that heat cannot pass from one body to a hotter body without work. The tiny demon selectively opens and shuts a gate between the two volumes of gas to let the more active molecules from the cooler gas into the hotter gas, making it hotter still, when in reality entropy would bring them both to the same temperature. Maxwell's whimsical metaphor has become a symbol of all attempts to escape the laws of thermodynamics.
547

1912: Piltdown Man
A mysterious scoundrel, whose identity is still hotly debated, mingles ape and human skull fragments in an English gravel bed and pulls off the greatest hoax in scientific history.
558

1914: Martha
With the death of the Cincinnati Zoo's last specimen, the passenger pigeon—once the world's most abundant bird—vanishes forever.
594

c. 1930: Schrödinger's Cat
The great quantum physicist Erwin Schrödinger imagined a "hellish device" involving a cat hidden in a box. If a photon takes one path around a particular crystal, the cat lives; if the other, the cat dies. In the "fuzziness" of subatomic events, however, the photon's various paths are not only potential but actual. If it can go both routes at once, can the unseen cat be both alive and dead?
545

c. 1945: Astronomer

"Whenever I see a frog's eye low in the water warily ogling the shoreward landscape, I always think inconsequentially of those twiddling mechanical eyes that mankind manipulates nightly from a thousand observatories."
—Loren Eiseley
549

c. 1950: Protozoan
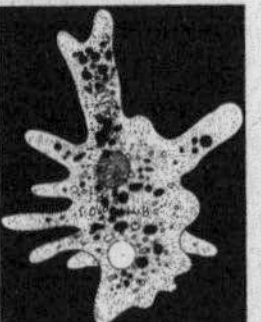
"Organic life, we are told, has developed gradually from the protozoan to the philosopher, and this development, we are assured, is indubitably an advance. Unfortunately it is the philosopher, not the protozoan, who gives us this assurance." —Bertrand Russell
559

1973: O Brave New World That Has Such People in It...
The first test-tube baby.
568

1986: Life, Inc.
The first patent on a living organism.
568

1989: The World Wide Web
Timothy Berners-Lee dreams up HTML (Hyper Text Markup Language) to help his fellow researchers' computers talk to each other, thereby spawning an electronic anaconda that is this moment wrapping our planet in its cybernetic coils.
596

At the Round Earth's Imagined Corners

1 c. 3000 BC: The Nile Valley
The world is a platter with a mountainous rim, floating upon primordial waters personified as the goddess Nun. Nun gives birth to the Nile, which bisects the earth's flat plain. Overhead the goddess Nut, crouching with only her fingers and toes touching the earth, forms the inverted bowl of the sky.

15

2 c. 400 BC: Athens
Aristotle proposes that the curved shape cutting across the face of the moon during a lunar eclipse is actually the shadow of a round earth. The fact that some stars seen above the horizon in Egypt sink below the horizon as one travels north shows the Earth to be round in three dimensions as well. His conclusion is widely accepted by educated people of classical and medieval Europe, although they also believe that the southern hemisphere is forever cut off by an impassably hot equator.

540

3 200 BC: Alexandria
Eratosthenes, librarian of Alexandria, calculates the circumference of the Earth. He observes that at noon on the summer solstice the angle of the sun's rays is 7.5 degrees from the vertical in Alexandria, but 0 degrees in the city of Syrene, about 500 miles due south. Using his fellow Alexandrian Euclid's geometry, he arrives at a fairly accurate figure: about 24,000 miles.

540

4 11C: Arabia
Al-Biruni founds the science of geodesy by calculating geographical longitude with spherical trigonometry.

539

5 India
Krishna's mother scolded her baby for eating dirt, but then saw "in his gaping mouth the whole universe in all its variety, with all the forms of life and time and nature and action and hopes, and her own village, and herself. Then she became afraid and confused."
—Wendy Doniger O'Flaherty
Hindu Myths

332

6 c. 1300: Mt. Purgatory
When Dante emerges from Hell's back door, he knows just where he is: on the opposite side of the globe, south of the impassable torrid zone. He describes constellations invisible from the inhabited part of the sphere: "I set my mind on the other pole, and I saw four stars never seen before but by the first people; the sky seemed to rejoice in their flames. Oh widowed region of the north, since thou art denied that sight!"

943

7 1420: Cape St. Vincent
At Portugal's southwest tip, Prince Henry the Navigator, seeking a sea route to India, founds a center of applied science, a combination think-tank and academy, to break down the medieval wall between scholarly astronomers and practical seafarers. Through the 1400s this is the only place in the world to learn the skills of deep-sea navigation. It is also where a shipwrecked young sailor, Christopher Columbus, washes ashore clinging to an oar.

45

14 Pangea
Dublin
London
Prague
Cape St. Vincent
Athens
Florence
Alexandria
Arabia
Nile
India
Antarctica
Mt. Purgatory

LATITUDE NORTH EQUATOR
TORRID ZONE
MERIDIAN
WEST
NORTH POLE
NADIR
SOUTH POLE
EQUINOX
EAST
ZENITH
LONGITUDE
Scale of Miles.
OCEAN-CHART.
11

8 c. 1620: Florence
"The Sun, with all the planets revolving around it and depending on it, can still ripen a bunch of grapes as though it had nothing else in the universe to do."
—Galileo Galilei

548

9 1610: Prague
"Provide ship or sails adapted to the heavenly breezes, and there will be some who will not fear even that void… So, for those who will come shortly to attempt this journey, let us establish the astronomy: Galileo, you of Jupiter, I of the Moon."
—Johannes Kepler

549

10 1759: London
For centuries mariners wandered the oceans unsure of their east-west position and untold numbers of ship wrecks resulted. John Harrison solves the most urgent scientific problem of his generation when he unveils "H-4"—"the most important timepiece ever made"—a spring-driven marine chronometer that allows the calculation of longitude at sea, and incidentally gives rise to the clocks and watches of our era.

540

11 1876: At Sea
"He had bought a large map representing the sea,
Without the least vestige of land:
And the crew were much pleased when they found it to be
A map they could all understand.
'What's the good of Mercator's North Poles and Equators,
Tropics, Zones, and Meridian Lines?'
So the Bellman would cry: and the crew would reply
'They are merely conventional signs!'"
—Lewis Carroll
"The Hunting of the Snark"

805

12 Antarctica
Geographers proposed a southern continent to counterbalance the weight of the known world almost two millennia before it was reached or even glimpsed by explorers. Antarctica's harsh climate, the abstract nature of the South Pole itself, and the unique absence of natives to provide directions or food made the mapping of Antarctica the last and purest epic of European exploration.

576

13 Black Hole
"You can't get there from here."
—Stephen Hawking

544

14 Pangea
The supercontinent, 220 million years ago. "Doesn't the east coast of S. America fit exactly against the west coast of Africa? The fit is even better if you look at a map of the floor of the Atlantic and compare the edges of the drop-off into the ocean basin… This is an idea I'll have to pursue…"
—Alfred Wegener, writing to his wife

576

15 Big Bang
"It may be that the Universe is just one of those things that happen from time to time."
—E. Tryon

550

16 1904: Dublin
"Meditations of evolution increasingly vaster: of the moon invisible in incipient lunation, approaching perigee of the infinite latiginous scintillating uncondensed Milky Way… of the parallax or parallactic drift of the so-called fixed stars, in reality evermoving wanderers from immeasurable remote eons to infinitely remote futures in comparison with which the years, threescore and ten, of allotted human life formed a parenthesis of infinitesimal brevity."
—James Joyce
Ulysses

823

Mathematics

The exponential growth of science and technology during the past 300 years could not have occurred without a corresponding increase in mathematical knowledge. Higher math today is fundamental not only in relativity theory and quantum mechanics, but also in the biological and medical fields where a firm grasp of probability and statistics is essential. Businessmen can perhaps get along without advanced math, but not economists. Not long ago Europeans who considered themselves educated were able to read and write Latin, a language replaced by mathematics, the new universal language of science and technology. Without some knowledge of its lower levels, a layman can no more comprehend modern science than he can understand the *Iliad* without knowing Homeric Greek.

Even though there are translations of Homer, "translations" by science writers presuppose some insight into mathematics. This is surely one reason for the growing demand for popularly written books about math. In surveying these works, keep in mind that no sharp line separates technical from non-technical. At one end of the spectrum are those books which only the professional mathematician can read. At the other are books written for children. Occasionally, a book published for the general reader will be harder to understand than a college textbook.

Introductions to Mathematics

General Introductions

John D. **Barrow**

Pi in the Sky: Counting, Thinking, and Being

"From the quest for artificial intelligence to physicists' search for a theory of Everything, Barrow shows how the crisis in mathematics touches the real world, too"—*Newsweek*

0-316-08259-7 LITTLE, BROWN PB $14.95

Eric Temple **Bell**

Mathematics: Queen and Servant of Science

0-317-70124-X MATHEMATICAL ASSOC PB $15.95

Bela **Bollobas**

Littlewood's Miscellany

0-521-33702-X CAMBRIDGE PB $19.95

Richard **Courant** & Herbert **Robbins**

What is Mathematics?: An Elementary Approach to Ideas and Methods

Going far beyond the rote memorization that passes for numbers literacy, this graceful and readable volume seeks to put the meaning back into mathematics. From natural numbers to the Continuum Hypothesis, *What is Mathematics?* opens up a world of understanding that can be read by beginners seeking an introduction to the subject and experts seeking to enhance their knowledge. "Without doubt, the work will have great influence. It should be in the hands of everyone, professional or otherwise, who is interested in scientific thinking"—*NY Times*

REVISED BY IAN STEWART

0-19-510519-2 OXFORD PB $18.95

Ivar **Ekeland**

The Broken Dice: And Other Mathematical Tales of Chance

Examining probability theory, particle physics, myths, and literature, the author, president of the Université Paris-Dauphine, explores the roles chance, fate, and chaos play in nature, society, and our daily lives. "Not just a literate work but a literary one"—*New Scientist*

0-226-19991-6 CHICAGO $19.95

Jan **Gullberg**

Mathematics: From the Birth of Numbers

0-393-04002-X NORTON $39.95

Lancelot **Hogben**

Mathematics For the Millions

Probably the most successful book ever intended as an introduction to elementary mathematics. "It makes alive the contents of the elements of mathematics"—Albert Einstein

0-393-31071-X NORTON PB $15.95

The relevance of no branch of mathematics to one or other aspect of the contemporary world's work is more wide open to dispute than is the theory of so-called probability. On the other hand, its unsavoury origin is on record. The first impetus came from a situation in which the dissolute nobility of France were competing in a race to ruin at the gaming tables. An algebraic calculus of probability takes its origin from a correspondence between Pascal and Fermat (about 1654) over the fortunes and misfortunes of the Chevalier de Mere, a great gambler and by that token "très bon esprit," but alas (wrote Pascal) "il n'est pas géomètre." Alas indeed. The Chevalier had made his pile by always betting small favorable odds on getting at least one six in 4 tosses of a die, and had then lost it by always betting small odds on getting at least one double six in 24 double tosses...The problem out of which the calculus took shape was...how to adjust the stakes in a game of chance in accordance with a rule which ensures success if applied consistently regardless of the fortunes of the session.

MATHEMATICS FOR THE MILLIONS

Morris **Kline**

Mathematics and the Physical World

The growth of mathematics, from arithmetic to calculus and the non-Euclidian geometries

0-486-24104-1 DOVER PB $10.95

Dan **Pedoe**

The Gentle Art of Mathematics

0-486-22949-1 DOVER PB $6.95

George **Polya**

How to Solve It

0-691-02356-5 PRINCETON PB $10.95

Rudy **Rucker**

Infinity and the Mind: The Science and Philosophy of the Infinite

0-553-25531-2 BDD PB $6.50

Mind Tools: The Five Levels of Mathematical Reality

"An original and fascinating look at various aspects of mathematics that is sure to fascinate the non-mathematician"—Isaac Asimov

0-395-46810-8 HOUGHTON MIFFLIN PB $12.95

Bertrand **Russell**

The Principles of Mathematics

See also RUSSELL under PHILOSOPHY in RELIGION, SPIRITUALITY, AND PHILOSOPHY

0-393-31404-9 NORTON PB $17.95
0-393-00249-7 NORTON PB $14.95

W.W. **Sawyer**

Prelude to Mathematics

A noted mathematician's account, with emphasis on novel aspects

0-486-24401-6 DOVER PB $5.95

Michael S. **Schneider**

A Beginner's Guide to Constructing the Universe: The Mathematical Archetypes of Nature, Art, and Science, A Voyage from 1 to 10

An elegantly illustrated meditation on both the uses and the beauties of numbers and geometrical shapes; subtle and original, Schneider lucidly explores arcane territory without demanding advanced mathematical training of his reader

See also THE NEW PHYSICS under METAPHYSICS under SPIRITUALITY in RELIGION, SPIRITUALITY, AND PHILOSOPHY

0-06-016939-7 HARPERCOLLINS $30.00
0-06-092671-6 HARPERPERENNIAL PB $17.50

Jagjit **Singh**

Great Ideas of Modern Mathematics

0-486-20587-8 DOVER PB $8.95

Ian **Stewart**

Nature's Numbers: The Unreal Reality of Mathematical Imagination

The author of *Does God Play Dice?* (see page 3) addresses essential new terms in our technological age: chaos, complexity, and virtual reality. Treating mathematics as the essential tool in understanding the increasingly complex world around us, Stewart offers a grasp of that tool's basic terms

0-465-07273-9 BASIC $20.00
0-465-07273-0 BASIC $20.00

Sheila **Tobias**

Overcoming Math Anxiety

Strategies for changing one's approach to math

0-393-03577-8 NORTON $23.00

Leo **Zippin**

Uses of Infinity

0-394-01563-0 MATHEMATICAL ASSOC PB $12.00

Claudia **Zaslavsky**

Fear of Math: How to Get Over It & Get on with Your Life

0-8135-2099-1 RUTGERS PB $14.95

Advanced Mathematical Studies

Philip **Davis** & Reuben **Hersh**

The Mathematical Experience

An exciting view of the development of mathematics for the general reader. Winner of an American Book Award

3-7643-3018-X BIRKHAUSER $29.95
0-395-32131-X HOUGHTON MIFFLIN PB $15.95

Heinrich **Dorrie**

One Hundred Great Problems of Elementary Mathematics: Their History and Solution

Problems that beset the great mathematicians

0-486-61348-8 DOVER PB $9.95

Paul **Hoffman**

Archimedes' Revenge: The Challenge of the Unknown

An engaging, anecdotal history of the problems that continue to puzzle mathematicians

0-449-21750-7 CREST PB $5.99

George **Polya**

Mathematics and Plausible Reasoning

Volumes are *Induction and Analogy in Mathematics* and *Patterns of Plausible Inference*

0-685-23091-0 PRINCETON $54.00

Reference

W. **Gellert**, editor

VNR Concise Encyclopedia of Mathematics

Advanced level

0-412-98421-0 CHAPMAN & HALL PB $24.95

Kiyoshi **Ito**, editor

Encyclopedic Dictionary of Mathematics

The highest level of difficulty

0-262-09026-0 MIT $385.00

N.J. **Sloane**

A Handbook of Integer Sequences

A marvelous reference that includes lists of more than 2000 integers and rules for generating them

0-12-648550-X ACADEMIC PRESS $80.00

History and Biography

Carl B. **Boyer**

A History of Mathematics

Especially recommended

0-471-54397-7 WILEY PB $32.95

Donald J. **Albers**, editor

More Mathematical People: Contemporary Conversations

A follow-up to the popular *Mathematical People*, showing a human aspect of mathematics that is too rarely seen. The subjects include Lipman Bets, Irving Kaplansky, Hans Lewy, Julia Robinson, and Mary Ellen Rudin. "The sheer pleasure mathematicians get from solving problems and making discoveries comes through in every interview"—Martin Gardner

0-12-048251-7 ACADEMIC PRESS PB $39.95

W.W. **Ball**

A Short Account of the History of Mathematics

Although written before 1900, still an excellent elementary account

0-486-20630-0 DOVER PB $11.95

E.T. **Bell**

Men of Mathematics

An outstanding early work. "Any [one] engaged in learning mathematics will profit by reading him"—Bertrand Russell

0-671-62818-6 TOUCHSTONE PB $14.95

Archimedes, Newton, and Gauss, these three, are in a class by themselves among the great mathematicians, and it is not for ordinary mortals to attempt to range them in order of merit. All three started tidal waves in both pure and applied mathematics: Archimedes esteemed his pure mathematics more highly than its applications; Newton appears to have found the chief justification for his mathematical inventions in the scientific uses to which he put them, while Gauss declared that it was all one to him whether he worked on the pure or the applied side
MEN OF MATHEMATICS

W.K. **Buehler**

Gauss: A Biographical Study

A fine biography of the great German mathematician

0-387-10662-6 SPRINGER-VERLAG $53.95

Florian **Cajori**

A History of Mathematics

A pre-1950 classic

0-8284-2303-2 CHELSEA $29.50

C. C. **Clawson**

The Mathematical Traveller: Exploring the Grand History of Numbers

An entertaining tour, ranging from the simple number systems devised by early and primitive cultures to the more challenging concepts of contemporary math (like irrational and transfinite numbers). Engaging and accessible

0-306-44645-6 PLENUM $25.95

William W. **Dunham**

Journey Through Genius: The Great Theorems of Mathematics

Explores 17 great watershed breakthroughs by 10 mathematicians, explaining their theorems and placing them in both biographical and historical contexts

0-471-50030-5 WILEY $29.95
0-14-014739-X PENGUIN PB $12.95

O.A. **Dilke**

Mathematics and Measurement

Classical and preclassical techniques of mapping, surveying, measurement, and mathematics in trade and astrology

0-520-06072-5 CALIFORNIA PB $11.00

Jesse **Dilson**

The Abacus: A Brief History of the World's First Computing System & How to Use It

0-312-10409-X ST. MARTIN'S PB $12.95

Howard **Eves**

Great Moments in Mathematics

A survey concluding in 1650

0-88385-310-8 MATHEMATICAL ASSOC PB $25.00

John **Fauvel** & others, editors

Mobius & His Band: Mathematics & Astronomy in Nineteenth-Century Germany

Essays by a gathering of distinguished scientific historians, placing the legendary German mathematician in context

0-19-853969-X OXFORD $35.00

K.O. **Friedrichs**

From Pythagoras to Einstein

0-88385-616-6 MATHEMATICAL ASSOC PB $8.00

Richard **Gillings**

Mathematics in the Time of the Pharaohs

A fascinating, notable work

0-486-24315-X DOVER PB $8.95

P.R. **Halmos**

I Want to Be a Mathematician

Crammed with anecdotes about famous friends, and pervaded with the subtle humor for which Halmos is known

0-387-96078-3 SPRINGER-VERLAG $64.95
0-88385-445-7 MATHEMATICAL ASSOC PB $25.00

Thomas **Heath**

A History of Greek Mathematics

Outstanding for its authoritative coverage

Volume 1

0-486-24073-8 DOVER PB $12.95

Volume 2

0-486-24074-6 DOVER PB $12.95

Robert **Kanigel**

The Man Who Knew Infinity: A Life of the Genius Ramanujan

A highly entertaining biography of a great scientist who rose out of obscurity in India to prominence within the English mathematical elite. Its description of life among the scientists includes insightful and moving portraits of great scientists, including his mentor, Godfrey Hardy. "Even a complete innumerate can enjoy Mr. Kanigel's richly detailed book"
—*NY Times Book Review*

0-671-75061-5 WASHINGTON SQUARE PB $12.00

Morris **Kline**

Mathematical Thought from Ancient to Modern Times

The most comprehensive history in English

0-19-501496-0 OXFORD $75.00

Mathematical Thought from Ancient to Modern Times

Volume 1

0-19-506135-7 OXFORD PB $16.95

Volume 2

0-19-506136-5 OXFORD PB $16.95

Volume 3

0-19-506137-3 OXFORD PB $16.95

Mathematics in Western Culture

Stresses the influence of math on science and the humanities

0-19-500714-X OXFORD PB $16.95

Ann **Koblitz**

A Convergence of Lives

A splendid biography of Sofia Kovalevskaia, "the greatest woman mathematician prior to the 20th century"
—*Dictionary of Scientific Biography*

0-8135-1962-4 RUTGERS $40.00

Lloyd **Motz** & Jefferson H. **Weaver**

The Story of Mathematics

A highly readable and admirably clear history of math from Euclid to the present (including treatments of chaos and symmetry theory), rooted in biographical sketches of mathematicians whose work broke new ground

0-306-44508-5 PLENUM $25.95
0-380-72458-8 AVON PB $14.00

Lynn M. **Osen**

Women in Mathematics

From Hypatia of 5th-century Alexandria, murdered by a fanatic mob, down to modern times

0-262-65009-6 MIT PB $13.95

C. **Reid**

Hilbert-Courant

Outstanding biographies of David Hilbert and Richard Courant

0-387-96256-5 SPRINGER-VERLAG PB $29.00

David E. **Smith**

A History of Mathematics

Volume 1

General Survey of the History of Elementary Mathematics

A reliable early work distinguished by hundreds of illustrations. Volume 1 is a chronological survey, Volume 2 is organized by topic

0-486-20429-4 DOVER PB $12.95

Volume 2

Special Topics of Elementary Math

0-486-20430-8 DOVER PB $13.95

Dirk **Struik**

A Concise History of Mathematics

A good brief history

0-486-60255-9 DOVER PB $8.95

S.M. **Ulam**

Adventures of a Mathematician

Entertaining account of the Polish mathematician who, with Edward Teller, invented the hydrogen bomb

0-520-07154-9 CALIFORNIA PB $18.95

Willard **van Orman Quine**

The Time of My Life: An Autobiography

Best known as a philosopher, Willard van Orman Quine made enormous contributions to set theory and logic

0-262-17003-5 MIT $35.00

Alistair M. **Wilson**

The Infinite in the Finite

0-19-853950-9 OXFORD $45.00

Philosophy of Mathematics

Philosophers are more interested in the philosophical foundations of mathematics than working mathematicians, but many books on the topic can be understood by outsiders.

Jacques **Hadamard**

Psychology of Invention in the Mathematical Field

Emphasizes mathematical creativity and offers insight into Einstein's thought processes

0-486-20107-4 DOVER PB $5.95

Godfrey **Hardy**

A Mathematician's Apology

Hardy's famous essay, with an introduction by C.P. Snow, is must reading

0-521-42706-1 CAMBRIDGE PB $8.95

Stephan **Korner**

The Philosophy of Mathematics: An Introduction Essay

An excellent introduction

0-486-25048-2 DOVER PB $8.95

Henri **Poincaré**

Science and Hypothesis

0-486-60221-4 DOVER PB $7.95

Science and Method

1-85506-431-6 THOEM PB $24.95

Hilary **Putnam**

Philosophy of Mathematics: Selected Readings

An anthology of papers

See also **READINGS IN PHILOSOPHY: ANTHOLOGIES ON SPECIAL TOPICS** under **PHILOSOPHY** in **RELIGION, SPIRITUALITY, AND PHILOSOPHY**

0-521-29648-X CAMBRIDGE PB $34.95

Paul **Watzlawick**, editor

The Invented Reality: How Do We Know What We Believe We Know?

0-393-01731-1 NORTON $23.95

Brian **Rotman**

Ad Infinitum – the Ghost in Turing's Machine: Taking God Out of Mathematics & Putting the Body Back In: An Essay in Corporeal Semiotics

0-8047-2127-0 STANFORD $39.50
0-8047-2128-9 STANFORD PB $14.95

Bertrand **Russell**

Introduction to Mathematical Philosophy

A classic

0-415-09604-9 ROUTLEDGE PB $15.95

Bertrand Russell

Ian **Stewart** & Martin **Golubitsky**

Fearful Symmetry: Is God a Geometer?

Mathematical and philosophical musings on the apparently ordered nature of the world from the authors of *Does God Play Dice?*

See also **SCIENCE AND RELIGION** under **WORLD RELIGION** in **RELIGION, SPIRITUALITY, AND PHILOSOPHY**

0-631-18251-9 BLACKWELL $25.95
0-14-013047-0 PENGUIN PB $12.50

Cultural Interpretations

Most mathematicians believe that mathematical structure is "out there," independent of the human mind, and that theorems are discovered, not created. However, some hold more subjective views, stressing mathematics as a cultural construct—like art, music, ethics, and even traffic regulations.

Morris **Kline**

Mathematics: The Loss of Certainty

0-19-502754-X OXFORD $27.95
0-19-503085-0 OXFORD PB $13.95

Mathematics and the Search For Knowledge

0-19-503533-X OXFORD $24.95
0-19-504230-1 OXFORD PB $10.95

Karl **Menninger**

Number Words & Number Symbols: A Cultural History of Numbers

A reprint of a now-classic exploration of how different cultures have treated numbers

TRANSLATED BY PAUL BRONEER

0-486-27096-3 DOVER PB $14.95

John Allen **Paulos**

Beyond Numeracy: Ruminations of a Numbers Man

An entertaining glance at a variety of mathematical concepts, from chaos and fractals to recursion and complexity

0-679-73807-X VINTAGE PB $13.00

Edward **Rothstein**

Emblems of Mind: The Inner Life of Music & Mathematics

0-8129-2298-0 TIME BOOKS $25.00
0-380-72747-1 AVON PB $13.00

Annemarie **Schimmel**

The Mystery of Numbers

Schimmel takes us on a tour of the powers attributed to numbers through the centuries, from Pythagorean and Platonist philosophy to the kabala and the Islamic Brethren. She examines individual numbers from one to 10,000, and discusses the meanings they hold in different traditions, from Semitic and Christian cultures to those of India, China, and the Americas

0-19-506303-1 OXFORD $25.00
0-19-508919-7 OXFORD PB $12.95

Number Theory

Tobias **Dantzig**

Number: The Language of Science

0-02-906990-4 FREE PRESS PB $16.95

Philip **Davis**

The Lore of Large Numbers

0-88385-606-9 MATHEMATICAL ASSOC PB $14.00

Ivan **Niven**

Irrational Numbers

0-88385-011-7 MATHEMATICAL ASSOC $28.00

Ivan **Niven** & Herbert **Zuckerman**

An Introduction to the Theory of Numbers

0-471-02851-7 WILEY $67.67

Oystein **Ore**

Invitation to Number Theory

0-88385-620-4 MATHEMATICAL ASSOC PB $17.00

Number Theory and Its History

0-486-65620-9 DOVER PB $9.95

Algebra and Combinatrics

There is a dearth of popularly written books on algebra (there are, of course, hundreds of textbooks).

Combinatrics

Combinatrics is one of the fastest-growing areas of mathematics.

Chung **Liu**

Introduction to Applied Combinatorial Mathematics

0-07-038124-0 MCGRAW HILL $84.80

Ivan **Niven**

The Mathematics of Choice

0-88385-615-8 MATHEMATICAL ASSOC PB $16.00

John **Riordan**

An Introduction to Combinatorial Analysis

One of the best and most widely used books on combinatrics; advanced level

0-691-08262-6 PRINCETON $37.50
0-691-02365-4 PRINCETON PB $16.95

Herbert **Ryser**

Combinatorial Mathematics

A good introduction and clear presentation of a difficult subject

0-88385-014-1 MATHEMATICAL ASSOC $25.00

Probability and Statistics

Richard **Brook**

The Fascination of Statistics

0-8247-7329-2 MARCEL DEKKER $49.75

Stephen **Campbell**

Flaws and Fallacies in Statistical Thinking

0-13-322214-4 PRENTICE HALL PB $43.00

Larry **Gonick** & Woollcott **Smith**

The Cartoon Guide to Statistics

Merging humor, concept, and cartoon, the authors (*The Cartoon History of the Universe*) cover the history of statistics, its applications in a wide variety of fields—from science to the humanities—then jump into such topics as probability theory, data analysis, and math-computer statistics

0-06-273102-5 HARPERCOLLINS PB $14.00

Robert **Hooke**

How to Tell the Liars from the Statisticians

0-8247-1817-8 MARCEL DEKKER $49.75

Darrel **Huff**

How to Lie with Statistics

0-393-09426-X NORTON PB $4.95

Frederick **Mosteller**

Fifty Challenging Problems in Probability

0-486-65355-2 DOVER PB $4.95

E.W. **Packel**

The Mathematics of Games and Gambling

A good survey of how mathematics can be used to analyze games of chance and skill

0-88385-628-X MATHEMATICAL ASSOC PB $17.50

Theodore **Porter**

The Rise of Statistical Thinking, 1820-1900

A nontechnical history that stresses the role of statistics in the natural and social sciences

0-691-02409-X PRINCETON PB $17.95

Stephen **Stigler**

The History of Statistics

Recommended history, up to 1900

0-674-40340-1 BELKNAP $40.00

Edward **Thorp**

Beat the Dealer: A Winning Strategy For the Game of Twenty-One

Edward Thorp startled the gambling world by writing the first general trade book on how to win the game of Black Jack. This created a wave of "counters" who still are able to win until the casino asks them to leave

0-394-70310-3 RANDOM HOUSE PB $10.00

Warren **Weaver**

Lady Luck: The Theory of Probability

The best popularly written introduction to probability theory

0-486-24342-7 DOVER PB $8.95

Game and Decision Theory

Introductory

Morton **Davis**

The Art of Decision-Making

Emphasizes the paradoxical aspects

0-387-96228-X SPRINGER-VERLAG $39.00

J.D. **Williams**

The Compleat Strategyst: Being a Primer on the Theory of Games of Strategy

Another fine elementary introduction

0-486-25101-2 DOVER PB $7.95

Higher-Level

Steven **Brams**

The Presidential Election Game

0-300-02254-9 YALE $37.00
0-300-02296-4 YALE PB $14.00

Superior Beings: If They Exist How Would We Know?
0-387-91223-1 SPRINGER-VERLAG $49.95
0-387-90877-3 SPRINGER-VERLAG PB $30.00

Richard **Jeffrey**
The Logic of Decision
0-226-39582-0 CHICAGO PB $17.95

Howard **Raiffa**
Decision Analysis: Introductory Lectures on Choices Under Uncertainty
0-07-554866-6 MCGRAW HILL PB $48.00

Catastrophy Theory, Chaos Theory, and Fractals

James **Gleick**
Chaos: Making a New Science
0-14-009250-1 PENGUIN PB $16.95

Hans **Lauwerier**
Fractals
The world of the controversial repeated geometrical figures, now considered a means to chart natural processes once thought random
0-691-08551-X PRINCETON $60.00
0-691-02445-6 PRINCETON PB $15.95

Benoit **Mandelbrot**
The Fractal Geometry of Nature
A work of unusual elegance and timely interest. Mandelbrot invented the term "fractals" to describe a class of highly irregular shapes, and then discusses various ways of calculating and measuring their dimension, with hundreds of illustrations
0-7167-1186-9 FREEMAN $39.95

H.O. **Peitgen** & P.H. **Richter**
The Beauty of Fractals
On a popular level, with many color pictures
0-387-15851-0 SPRINGER-VERLAG $49.95

Ilya **Prigogine** & Isabelle **Stengers**
Order Out of Chaos: Man's New Dialogue With Nature
0-553-34363-7 BANTAM PB $13.95

D. **Ruelle**
Chaotic Evolution and Strange Attractors: The Statistical Analysis For Time Series for Deterministic Nonlinear Systems
0-521-36830-8 CAMBRIDGE PB $18.95

David **Ruelle**
Chance and Chaos
0-691-02100-7 PRINCETON PB $9.95

Ian **Stewart**
Does God Play Dice?: The Mathematics of Chaos
1-55786-106-4 BLACKWELL PB $16.95

Geometry

H.S.M. **Coxeter**
Introduction to Geometry
Deserves special mention among the numerous geometry books because its central theme, symmetry, now plays such a major role in physics
0-471-50458-0 WILEY PB $54.43

David **Hilbert** & Stephan **Cohn-Vossen**
Geometry and the Imagination
A famous general work on geometry
0-8284-0087-3 CHELSEA $19.95

Dan **Pedoe**
Geometry and the Visual Arts
The crucial importance of geometry in the development of Western aesthetics
0-486-24458-X DOVER PB $8.95

Symmetry

Theodore **Cook**
The Curves of Life
The Golden Ratio plays a whimsical role in aesthetics and plant growth
0-486-23701-X DOVER PB $10.95

Michael **Field** & Martin **Golubitsky**
Symmetry in Chaos: A Search For Pattern in Mathematics, Art, and Nature
The notion that patterns occur naturally throughout the physical world has long been a mysterious frontier of science. Here the authors find order in what looks like chaos: processes such as the motion of rivers and patterns of weather
0-19-853689-5 OXFORD $39.95
0-19-853688-7 OXFORD PB $22.50

H.E. **Huntley**
Divine Proportion: Study in Mathematical Beauty
A bridge between science and art
0-486-22254-3 DOVER PB $6.95

Robert **Williams**
The Geometric Foundation of Natural Structure: A Source Book of Design
0-486-23729-X DOVER PB $14.95

Topology

Topology is a branch of modern geometry concerned with properties that remain the same regardless of how an object is continuously distorted. It has endless applications and has spawned hundreds of advanced books; those listed here are popularly written introductions.

Stephen **Barr**
Experiments in Topology
0-486-25933-1 DOVER PB $6.95

W.G. **Chinn** & N.E. **Steenrod**
First Concepts of Topology
0-88385-618-2 MATHEMATICAL ASSOC PB $15.00

Graph Theory

A branch of topology that has found applications in the social sciences as well as in many areas of mathematics is graph theory, which studies sets of points connected by lines.

Gary **Chartrand**
Introductory Graph Theory
0-486-24775-9 DOVER PB $8.95

Israel **Grossman** & Wilhelm **Magnus**
Groups and Their Graphs
Popularly written introduction
0-88385-614-X MATHEMATICAL ASSOC PB $16.00

Frank **Harary**
Graph Theory
The standard introductory book
0-201-02787-9 ADDISON-WESLEY PB $48.50

Oystein **Ore**
Graphs and Their Use
0-88385-635-2 MATHEMATICAL ASSOC PB $19.00

Richard **Trudeau**
Dots and Lines
An introductory work
0-87338-223-4 KENT STATE $9.95

Four-Color Theorem

The famous four-color map theorem of graph theory (which states that every planar map can be colored with as few as four colors) was finally solved with computer help in 1977.

A. K. **Dewdney**
The Planiverse: Computer Contact with a Two-Dimensional World
Destined to become a classic
0-7710-2742-7 MCCLELLAND & STEWART PB $16.95

Paul **Kainen**
The Four-Color Problem: Assaults and Conquests
An account of the combinatorial problem, its history and solution
0-486-65092-8 DOVER PB $6.95

Advanced Geometry

Edwin A. **Abbott**
Flatland
A two-dimensional world
See also **EARLY SCIENCE FICTION** under **SCIENCE FICTION AND FANTASY** in **POPULAR READING**
0-06-463573-2 BARNES & NOBLE PB $11.00
0-14-007615-8 PENGUIN PB $6.95
0-691-02525-8 PRINCETON PB $8.95

Branko **Grunbaum** & G.C. **Shephard**
Tilings and Patterns
The first attempt to bring together the newest development in tiling theory, including the

famous Penrose tiles, which have had surprising applications to quasicrystals
0-7167-1193-1 FREEMAN $59.95

Rudy **Rucker**
The Fourth Dimension: Toward a Geometry of Higher Reality
A good introduction, combining math, philosophy, and fantasy, including dozens of puzzles and problems
0-395-39388-4 HOUGHTON MIFFLIN PB $12.95

Calculus

David **Berlinski**
A Tour of the Calculus
This splendidly readable book manages to make sense of calculus while still representing it in its full complexity, no easy task. But still it is perhaps more impressive that, after elucidating the basic concepts of the calculus as a mathematical process, Berlinski moves on to show the strength of this tool in theorizing our place in the universe
0-679-42645-0 PANTHEON $27.50
0-679-74788-5 VINTAGE $14.00

Carl **Boyer**
History of the Calculus and Its Conceptual Development
The definitive modern history
0-486-60509-4 DOVER PB $9.95

Ivan **Niven**
Maxima and Minima Without Calculus
Many problems that seem to require calculus can be solved by more elementary means
0-88385-306-X MATHEMATICAL ASSOC $20.00

W.W. **Sawyer**
What Is Calculus About?
The best introduction for a beginner
0-394-01558-4 MATHEMATICAL ASSOC PB $16.50

Silvanus **Thompson**
Calculus Made Easy
0-312-11410-9 ST. MARTIN'S PB $8.95

Logic and Set Theory

Formal logic, once the domain of philosophy departments, is now considered part of mathematics, closely related to set theory.

Raymond **Smullyan**
Alice in Puzzleland: A Carrollian Tale For Children Under Eighty
Smullyan's books not only contain brilliant, unusual puzzles of his own invention, but also lead painlessly into modern logic and set theory, including Kurt Gödel's famous undecidability theorem
0-688-02197-2 MORROW $25.02

Clarence **Wylie**
101 Puzzles in Thought and Logic
A typical book on logic puzzles
0-486-20367-0 DOVER PB $3.95

Ernst **Nagel** & James **Newman**
Gödel's Proof
The best introduction to Gödel's theorem for non-specialists
0-8147-0325-9 NYU PB $10.50

Kurt Gödel

Recreational Mathematics

W.W. Rouse **Ball** & **H.S.M. Coxeter,**
Mathematical Recreations and Essays
The classic work in English
0-486-25357-0 DOVER PB $8.95

Martin **Gardner**
"In Gardner's writing, numbers break out of their gray procession toward infinity and take on personalities: the measured march of the square numbers; the primes in their unfathomable progression; the irrationals always a decimal place away from being captured; the imaginaries occupying the nonexistent gaps between the reals... Alone with his typewriter, he can find more excitement in the square root of 2 than most men could find in Faye Dunaway's whole telphone number"—Newsweek

Aha! Gotcha: Paradoxes to Puzzle & Delight
0-7167-1361-6 FREEMAN PB $14.95
0-7167-1361-7 FREEMAN PB $12.95

Aha! Insight
0-7167-1017-X FREEMAN PB $14.95

Entertaining Mathematical Puzzles
0-486-25211-6 DOVER PB $3.95

The Magic Numbers of Dr. Matrix
0-87975-282-3 PROMETHEUS PB $19.95

Mathematical Carnival: A New Round-Up of Tantalizers and Puzzles from Scientific American
0-88385-448-1 MATHEMATICAL ASSOC PB $15.00

Mathematics, Magic, and Mystery
0-486-20335-2 DOVER PB $5.95

The Second Scientific American Book of Mathematical Puzzles & Diversions
0-226-28253-8 CHICAGO PB $14.95

Time Travel & Other Mathematical Bewilderments
0-7167-1925-8 FREEMAN PB $14.95

The Unexpected Hanging & Other Mathematical Diversions
0-226-28256-2 CHICAGO PB $11.95

Wheels, Life, and Other Mathematical Amusements
One recreation stands above all others in the time consumed by computer buffs in debating its implications. Invented by Cambridge mathematician John Conway, who named it "Life", the game is closely related to a growing branch of mathematics called "cellular automata theory." This book devotes three chapters to the game
0-7167-1589-9 FREEMAN PB $14.95

Ross **Honsberger**
Ingenuity in Mathematics, 23
Honsberger has written five splendid books about recreational problems. Ingenious approaches to such topics as number theory, geometry, combinatrics, logic, and probability
0-88385-623-9 MATHEMATICAL ASSOC PB $17.50

Mathematical Gems
These three books contain dozens of mathematical vignettes from elementary combinatrics, number theory, and geometry
0-88385-301-9 MATHEMATICAL ASSOC $23.00

Mathematical Gems II
0-88385-302-7 MATHEMATICAL ASSOC PB $19.00

Mathematical Gems III
0-88385-318-3 MATHEMATICAL ASSOC PB $20.00

Mathematical Morsels
Solutions to problems from algebra, arithmetic, number theory, probability, and geometry
0-88385-303-5 MATHEMATICAL ASSOC $28.00

Joseph **Madachy**
Madachy's Mathematical Recreations
0-486-23762-1 DOVER PB $4.95

Isaac **Schoenberg**
Mathematical Time Exposures
0-88385-438-4 MATHEMATICAL ASSOC PB $10.00

Fred **Schuh**
The Master Book of Mathematical Puzzles and Recreations
0-486-22134-2 DOVER PB $9.95

Benjamin **Schwartz**, editor
Mathematical Solitaires and Games
0-89503-017-9 BAYWOOD PB $13.95

Dennis **Shasha**
Codes, Puzzles and Conspiracy
A highly entertaining (and illuminating) mathematical mystery story, starring Shasha's mathematical detective, Dr. Jacob Ecco, and featuring an array of puzzles that challenge the reader without demanding a background in mathematics
0-7167-2275-5 FREEMAN $19.95
0-7167-2314-X FREEMAN PB $12.95

Hugo **Steinhaus**
One Hundred Problems in Elementary Mathematics
0-486-23875-X DOVER PB $5.95

Special Topics

Albert **Beiler**
Recreations in the Theory of Numbers
The best reference on recreations involving numbers
0-486-21096-0 DOVER PB $7.95

Elwyn **Berlekamp**
Winning Ways Volume 2 Games in Particular
0-12-091102-7 ACADEMIC PRESS PB $53.00

Donald E. **Knuth**
Surreal Numbers
0-201-03812-9 ADDISON-WESLEY PB $16.25

David **Wells**
The Penguin Dictionary of Curious and Interesting Geometry
An illustrated feast of numerical oddities that would leave Euclid's head spinning. Toroids, fractals, moebius strips, and other geometric principles are laid bare herein
0-14-011813-6 PENGUIN PB $21.00

Puzzle Collections

Stephen **Barr**
Mathematical Brain Benders: Second Miscellany of Puzzles
0-486-24260-9 DOVER PB $6.95

Lewis **Carroll**
Pillow Problems & A Tangled Tale
See also **19TH-CENTURY FICTION** under **THE 19TH CENTURY** in **LITERATURE OF THE BRITISH ISLES**
0-486-20493-6 DOVER PB $7.95

Angela **Dunn**
Mathematical Bafflers
0-486-23961-6 DOVER PB $6.95

Second Book of Mathematical Bafflers
0-486-24352-4 DOVER PB $5.95

J.A. **Hunter**
Challenging Mathematical Teasers
0-486-23852-0 DOVER PB $3.95

Entertaining Mathematical Teasers and How to Solve Them
0-486-24500-4 DOVER PB $3.95

Mathematical Brain-Teasers
0-486-23347-2 DOVER PB $4.95

Ronnie **Shushan**, editor
The Games Magazine Big Book of Games
0-89480-806-0 WORKMAN PB $11.95

Charles **Trigg**
Mathematical Quickies: 270 Stimulating Problems with Solutions
0-486-24949-2 DOVER PB $6.95

Mechanical Puzzles

John **Beasley**
The Ins and Outs of Peg Solitaire
A special type of mechanical puzzle
0-19-286145-X OXFORD PB $10.95

Henry **Dudeney**
Amusements in Mathematics
England's greatest puzzle inventor
0-486-20473-1 DOVER PB $7.95

Sam **Loyd**
Best Mathematical Puzzles of Sam Loyd
America's greatest puzzle inventor
0-486-20498-7 DOVER PB $4.95

Ronald **Read**
Tangrams: 330 Puzzles
0-486-21483-4 DOVER PB $3.95

Magic Squares

William **Benson** & Oswald **Jacoby**
Magic Cubes: New Recreations
0-486-24140-8 DOVER PB $5.95

Rapid Calculation

Gerard **Kelly**
Short-Cut Math
A good book on arithmetic shortcuts
0-486-24611-6 DOVER PB $2.95

Henry **Sticker**
How to Calculate Quickly
Includes shortcuts to solving more than 8000 problems
0-486-20295-X DOVER PB $3.95

Steven **Smith**
The Great Mental Calculators: The Psychology, Methods, and Lives of Calculating Prodigies Past and Present
An admirable history of lightning calculators–human ones, that is
0-231-05640-0 COLUMBIA $52.50

Humor

John **Paulos**
Mathematics and Humor
0-226-65025-1 CHICAGO PB $12.95

Science and Technology

Most American adults don't know that electrons are smaller than atoms, and more than a quarter of all Americans 18 or older are unaware that the Earth revolves around the sun; almost one in five thinks sound travels faster than light. The extent of such basic ignorance was revealed in a recent survey, which concluded that perhaps no more than five percent of America's adults are "scientifically literate."

But at least one phenomenon suggests that we are not turning into a nation of technical dunces: an unprecedented number of popular science books are being bought and read by an apparently growing audience. Most science books were formerly written for adults who also happened to be scientists—books like *Microbial Degradation of Xenobiotics and Recalcitrant Compounds*. But popular science is now flourishing in works on such arcane topics as quantum physics, plate tectonics, and genetic engineering. Even books on cosmology and the mathematics of chaos now find their way to best-seller lists.

Isaac **Asimov**
Asimov's New Guide to Science
0-465-00473-3 BASIC $45.00

Charles **Cazeau**
Science Trivia: From Anteaters to Zeppelins
0-306-42353-7 PLENUM $19.95

Will **Curtis**
The Nature of Things: 200 Best Commentaries from NPR
9-997-28448-8 COUNTRYMAN $3.98

George **Gamow**
Mr. Tompkins in Paperback
0-521-44771-2 CAMBRIDGE PB $9.95

Martin **Gardner**
Science: Good, Bad and Bogus
0-87975-573-3 PROMETHEUS PB $18.95

Fritz **Goro**

On the Nature of Things: The Scientific Photography of Fritz Goro

A commemoration of the photojournalistic genius who, for nearly 50 years, recorded the most significant scientific and technological breakthroughs of our time. The splitting of the atom, the invention of the hologram, and the first forays into microsurgery are only a few of the many discoveries he captured on film. Presented here with brief explanations by leading scientists, "these images were sensational then as now. No one has done them better!"—Dr. Lennart Nilsson

INTRODUCTION BY STEPHEN JAY GOULD

0-89381-542-X APERTURE $40.00

Karl R. **Popper**

The most important contemporary philosopher of science, Popper argues that a hypothesis is scientific only if it can specify the results that would show it to be false. This allowed him to dismiss Marxism and similarly circular theories as pseudoscience, and to formulate an influential attack on totalitarian ideology

The Myth of the Framework: In Defense of Science & Rationality

An exploration of the meaning of science by one of the giants of 20th-century philosophy

TRANSLATED BY M.A. NOTTURNO

0415113203 ROUTLEDGE $22.95

Fritz **Rohrlich**

From Paradox to Reality: Basic Concepts of the Physical World

0-521-37605-X CAMBRIDGE PB $27.95

Robert Scott **Root-Bernstein**

Discovering

0-674-21175-8 HARVARD PB $35.00

Martin **Sherwood** & Christine **Sutton**, editors

The Physical World

A nontechnical, nonmathematical tour of physical phenomena, with nearly 500 illustrations, most in color

0-19-520632-0 OXFORD $40.00

Arthur N. **Strahler**

Understanding Science: An Introduction to Concepts and Issues

A wide-ranging tour of scientific issues including quantum mechanics, chaos, logic, religion, and aesthetics. Provides a comprehensive and illuminating guide to the world of science. "This volume merits a high place on the popular science reading list"—*Publishers Weekly*

0-87975-724-8 PROMETHEUS $28.95

Alfred North **Whitehead**

Science and the Modern World

Whitehead's approach, at once philosophical and scientific, yields many unique insights; physics, for example, was originally an anti-intellectual activity

See also **WHITEHEAD** under **PHILOSOPHY** in **RELIGION, SPIRITUALITY, AND PHILOSOPHY**

0-02-935190-1 FREE PRESS PB $16.95

M. Mitchell **Waldrop**

Complexity: The Emerging Science At the Edge of Order and Chaos

A journalistic profile of the iconoclastic thinkers involved with the new science of "complexity," a field that searches for order in systems previously thought to be chaotic. Waldrop explores their abiding fascination with such questions as why the stock market crashed in 1987, and how living organisms emerged from amino acids

See also **PARTICLE PHYSICS, COSMOLOGY, AND THE "NEW" PHYSICS** under **PHYSICS**

0-671-87234-6 TOUCHSTONE PB $12.00

History of Science and Technology

Margaret **Alic**

Hypatia's Heritage: A History of Women in Science from Antiquity Through the Nineteenth Century

Though Western society long proscribed women from entering scientific professions, this did not prevent gifted women (often outside the mainstream) from making distinguished contributions to astronomy

0-8070-6731-8 FS&G PB $14.00

Anthony **Alioto**

A History of Western Science

0-13-388513-5 PRENTICE HALL PB $47.88

Jeremy **Bernstein**

Cranks, Quarks, and the Cosmos: Writings on Science

As writer of the "Annals of Science" column in *New Yorker*, Bernstein has set new standards in his profiles of scientific thinkers. This is a collection of his essays, including one on Ernst Mach, who discovered the speed of sound but never believed in atoms; on Einstein, who hated quantum theory; and on Stephen Hawking, who grows peevish at theories of everything. "Drawn with lucidity, humanity and discreet intelligence"—*Publishers Weekly*

0-465-01449-6 BASIC PB $12.00

Peter **Coreney** & Roger **Highfield**

The Arrow of Time: A Voyage Through Science to Solve Time's Great Mystery

"A whirlwind tour of relativity, thermodynamics, quantum mechanics, chaos and more…" —*Boston Globe*

0-449-90723-6 FAWCETT PB $12.50

Facts On File

The History of Science and Technology: A Narrative Chronology

From prehistoric times to the mid-20th century; a two-volume set

0-87196-477-5 FACTS ON FILE $160.00

Helge **Kragh**

An Introduction to the Historiography of Science

One of the things that all the races of humankind have had in common is an attempt to account for the universe at large—to make a cosmology. (The brewing of alcoholic beverages is another)

0-521-38921-6 CAMBRIDGE PB $18.95

Jack **Meadows**

Great Scientists

Science through the lives of Aristotle, Galileo, Harvey, Newton, Lavoisier, Humboldt, Faraday, Darwin, Pasteur, Curie, Freud, and Einstein

0-19-520620-7 OXFORD $40.00

Dava **Sobel**

Longitude: The True Story of the Lone Genius Who Solved the Greatest Scientific Problem of His Time

0-140-25879-5 PENGUIN PB $10.95

David F. **Noble**

A World Without Women: The Christian Clerical Culture of Western Science

Suggests, among other things; that "defeminization" is at the core of the modern scientific enterprise

See also **WOMEN AND GENDER STUDIES** under **PERSPECTIVES IN HISTORY** under **THE VARIETIES OF CIVILIZATION** in **WORLD HISTORY AND CURRENT AFFAIRS**

0-19-508435-7 OXFORD PB $12.95

Marilyn **Ogilvie**

Women in Science: Antiquity Through the Nineteenth Century–A Biographical Dictionary

0-262-65038-X MIT PB $14.95

Arnold **Pacey**

Technology in World Civilization: A Thousand-Year History

A concise survey of the development of technology, from a global rather than Europe-centered viewpoint. Fascinating for its accounts of Islamic irrigation techniques, Chinese iron smelting, and the gunpowder empires of Asia. One of *Library Journal's* "Best Sci-Tech Books of 1990"

See also **TECHNOLOGY** under **SCIENCE AND TECHNOLOGY** under **THE VARIETIES OF CIVILIZATION** in **WORLD HISTORY AND CURRENT AFFAIRS**

0-262-66072-5 MIT PB $13.50

Paper-making also came to Europe via Spain…The paper was made from the same vegetable fibers as linen cloth (and usually from linen rags), which first had to be pounded in water until a pulp was formed. The process had been invented in China long before, where it replaced an even older method of making paper-like material from mulberry bark. Knowledge of the technique entered the Islamic world in A.D. 751 after a battle in Central Asia between Chinese forces and an Arab-led army. Chinese prisoners-of-war skilled in paper-making set up a workshop in Samarqand, and from there other workmen went to Baghdad…The manufacture of paper meant that books became more widely available. By A.D. 900 there were over a hundred shops in Baghdad employing scribes and binders to produce books for sale, and soon there were even some public libraries.

TECHNOLOGY IN WORLD CIVILIZATION: A THOUSAND-YEAR HISTORY

Roy **Porter**, editor

Man Masters Nature: 25 Centuries of Science

0-8076-1233-2 BRAZILLER PB........$9.95

Colin A. **Ronan**, editor

Science Explained: The World of Science in Everyday Life

Readers of all ages who are science-illiterate will appreciate the everyday examples and lucid writing of this fully illustrated volume. A unique cross-referencing system makes the book interactive by linking different areas of science, from outer space to artificial intelligence, providing an amazing guide to everyday life

See also **REFERENCE** under **SCIENTIFIC THOUGHT AND DISCOVERY**

0-8050-2551-0 HOLT........$45.00
0-8050-4236-9 HOLT PB........$22.50

R.S. **Westfall**

The Construction of Modern Science

0-521-21863-2 CAMBRIDGE........$57.95
0-521-29295-6 CAMBRIDGE PB........$15.95

L. Pearce **Williams** & Henry **Steffens**

The History of Science in Western Civilization

Volume 1
Antiquity and the Middle Ages

0-8191-0191-5 UNIV. PRESS OF AMERICA PB........$27.00

Volume 3
Modern Science, 1700-1900

0-8191-0333-0 UNIV. PRESS OF AMERICA PB........$29.00

Trevor **Williams**

The History of Invention: From Stone Axes to Silicon Chips

0-8160-1788-3 FACTS ON FILE........$40.00

Ancient and Medieval Science

Alan **Cromer**

Uncommon Sense: The Heretical Nature of Science

Contrasting the Greek practice of debate with the Judaic reliance on prophets for acquiring knowledge, Cromer shows how science was not an inevitable outgrowth of human development, as many believe, but the invention of a particular culture, Greece, at a particular historical moment. An illuminating book that examines, among other things, why science could not have developed in countries like India or China

0-19-508213-3 OXFORD........$27.50

Thomas **Goldstein**

The Dawn of Modern Science: From the Arabs to Leonardo Da Vinci

See also **THE SCIENTIFIC REVOLUTION** under **EARLY MODERN EUROPE** in **WORLD HISTORY AND CURRENT AFFAIRS**

0-306-80637-1 DA CAPO PB........$14.95

Joseph **Needham**

The Shorter Science and Civilisation in China: An Abridgement of Joseph Needham's Original Text

A useful abridgement of one of the masterpieces of 20th-century scholarship

Volume 1

0-521-29286-7 CAMBRIDGE........$29.95

Volume 2

0-521-31536-0 CAMBRIDGE PB........$31.95

Volume 3

0-521-33873-5 CAMBRIDGE PB........$34.95

Volume 4

0-521-46773-X CAMBRIDGE PB........$44.95

Richard **Olson**

Science Deified and Science Defied: The Historical Significance of Science in Western Culture from the Bronze Age to the Beginnings of the Modern Era, C. 3500 B.C. to C. A.D. 1640

0-520-20167-1 CALIFORNIA PB........$17.00

S. **Sambursky**

The Physical World of Late Antiquity

0-691-08476-9 PRINCETON........$27.95
0-691-02410-3 PRINCETON PB........$12.95

The Scientific Revolution

For related reading, see THE SCIENTIFIC REVOLUTION under EARLY MODERN EUROPE in WORLD HISTORY AND CURRENT AFFAIRS

Marie **Boas**

Scientific Renaissance, 1450-1630

Excellent on the relation of magic to science and in its treatment of Galileo's trial

0-486-28115-9 DOVER PB........$10.95

Amos **Funkenstein**

Theology and the Scientific Imagination from the Middle Ages to the Seventeenth Century

See also **RELIGIOUS HISTORY** under **MEDIEVAL AND RENAISSANCE EUROPE** in **WORLD HISTORY AND CURRENT AFFAIRS**

0-691-02425-1 PRINCETON PB........$22.50

Thomas **Hankins**

Science and the Enlightenment

0-521-28619-0 CAMBRIDGE PB........$16.95

Margaret **Jacob**

The Cultural Meaning of the Scientific Revolution

The road from the scientific to the industrial revolution

0-07-554361-3 MCGRAW HILL PB........$21.75

Thomas **Kuhn**

The Copernican Revolution

An outstanding account of the impact of the revolution in astronomy by the author of *The Structure of Scientific Revolutions*

See also **HISTORY OF ASTRONOMY** under **ASTRONOMY**

0-674-17103-9 HARVARD PB........$12.95

Pietro **Redondi**

Galileo Heretic

A deft and exciting blend of the scholarly and the popular, Redondi's book at times reads like a thriller, contending that Galileo ran afoul of the Roman Catholic Church not because of his astronomy, but because of the negative implications his ideas had for the religious doctrine of the Eucharist

TRANSLATED BY RAYMOND ROSENTHAL

069102427X PRINCETON PB........$16.95

Londa **Schiebinger**

Nature's Body: Gender in the Making of Modern Science

A strikingly original analysis of how 18th-century natural historians created the basic vocabulary that permeates scientific discourse today. Carl Linnaeus's choice of mammary glands as the distinguishing characteristic of Mammalia, for instance, was informed as much by the sexual politics of the day as by the animals he intended to describe. "Indispensable for all anthropologists, historians, philosophers, and practitioners of science"—Emily Martin, author of *The Woman in the Body*

0-8070-8901-X BEACON PB........$15.00

Steven **Shapin** & Simon **Schaffer**

Leviathan and the Air-Pump: Hobbes, Boyle, and the Experimental Life

A now-classic study of how unacknowledged social forces can shape the work of scientific experiment. "Highly original, meticulously researched, and stimulatingly controversial" —*Choice*

0-691-08393-2 PRINCETON........$70.00
0-691-02432-4 PRINCETON PB........$22.50

Modern Science

Stephen **Bush**

History of Modern Science: A Guide to the Second Scientific Revolution, 1800-1950

0-8138-0883-9 IOWA........$43.95

Thomas F. **Glick**

The Comparative Reception of Darwinism

The worldwide reaction to Darwin's *Origin of Species*

0-226-29977-5 CHICAGO PB........$17.95

Wolfgang **Schivelbusch**

Disenchanted Light: The Industrialization of Light in the Nineteenth Century

"Makes artificial illumination a historical subject of inquiry, I think for the first time,

giving an account that is interesting and imaginative, ranging through many countries and containing a number of striking apercus"
—Jerrold Seigel, Princeton University
TRANSLATED BY ANGELA DAVIES
0-520-05903-4 CALIFORNIA........$35.00

History of Science in America

For related reading, see HISTORY OF SCIENCE AND TECHNOLOGY under TOPICS IN AMERICAN STUDIES in HISTORY OF THE AMERICAS

Silvio A. **Bedini**
Thomas Jefferson: Statesman of Science
0-02-897041-1 MACMILLAN........$35.00

Peter **Kuznick**
Beyond the Laboratory: Scientist as Political Activist in 1930s America
0-226-46583-7 CHICAGO........$29.95

Steven **Lubar**
Engines of Change: An Exhibition on the American Industrial Revolution
0-8026-0020-4 UNIVERSITY PUBLICATIONS PB.....$23.00

Judith A. **McGaw**, editor
Early American Technology: Making & Doing Things from the Colonial Era to 1850
0-8078-2173-X NORTH CAROLINA........$49.95
0-8078-4484-5 NORTH CAROLINA PB........$19.95

Carroll W. **Pursell**, Jr.
The Machine in America: A Social History of Technology
From the medieval farm implements brought by the first colonists to the invisible links of the Internet, how technology has affected our lives
See also **TECHNOLOGY AND CULTURE** under **HISTORY OF SCIENCE AND TECHNOLOGY** under **TOPICS IN AMERICAN STUDIES** in **HISTORY OF THE AMERICAS**
0-8018-4817-2 JOHNS HOPKINS........$45.00
0-8018-4818-0 JOHNS HOPKINS PB........$15.95

Technology in America: A History of Individuals and Ideas
0-262-66067-9 MIT PB........$16.00

Nathan **Reingold** & Ida **Reingold**
Science in America: A Documentary History
0-226-70946-9 CHICAGO........$45.00

Science in Today's Society

Stewart **Brand**
The Media Lab: Inventing the Future At MIT
0-14-009701-5 PENGUIN PB........$15.95

David **Dickson**
The New Politics of Science
0-226-14763-0 CHICAGO PB........$15.95

Tom **Forester**, editor
The Materials Revolution: Superconductors, New Materials, and the Japanese Challenge
0-262-56043-7 MIT PB........$19.95

Richard **Golub** & Eric **Brus**, editors
Almanac of Science and Technology: What's New and What's Known
A useful, up-to-date guide to new discoveries and developments in science. "Remarkably fresh…An excellent resource and primer"
—*Kirkus Reviews*
0-15-105050-3 HARCOURT BRACE........$59.95
0-15-600049-0 HARCOURT BRACE PB........$29.95

George **Johnson**
Fire in the Mind: Science, Faith, and the Search for Order
After visiting scientific think tanks, the science writer considers the boundaries between chaos and order, belief and fact
See also **SCIENCE AND RELIGION** under **WORLD RELIGION** in **RELIGION, SPIRITUALITY, AND PHILOSOPHY**
0-679-41192-5 KNOPF........$30.00
0-679-74021-X VINTAGE PB........$14.00

Nicholas **Negroponte**
Being Digital
"Knowledgeable, argumentative, and entertaining, Nicholas Negroponte writes about the future with the authority of someone who has spent a great deal of time there"—Douglas Adams
0-679-76290-6 VINTAGE PB........$12.00

Arno **Penzias**
Ideas and Information: Managing in a High-Tech World
A Nobel Prize-winning physicist ruminates on a wide variety of topics, from the differences between human and machine intelligence and the prospects for artificial intelligence to microchip technology and the promise of superconducting ceramics
0-393-02649-3 NORTON........$17.95

John **Polkinghorne**
Beyond Science: The Wider Human Context
0-521-57212-6 CAMBRIDGE........$19.95

Carl **Sagan**
The Demon-Haunted World: Science as a Candle in the Darkness
Sagan looks at the pseudoscience and superstition that, ever more prevalent in our society, threaten our democratic institutions and technical civilization. In a personal account that intersperses rich stories of his childhood as well as tales of discovery while refuting the argument that science destroys spirituality, Sagan insists that a skeptical literacy in science can effectively challenge channeling, alien abduction, and what he calls "faith healer fraud," as well as providing a "baloney detection kit" for political and social issues
0-394-53512-X RANDOM HOUSE........$25.95

Robert B. **Silvers**, editor
Hidden Histories of Science
With contributions from such authors and scientists as Oliver Sacks and Stephen Jay Gould, these essays are science-writing at its best
0-940322-03-X NEW YORK REVIEW........$19.95
0-940322-05-6 NEW YORK REVIEW PB........$12.95

C.P. **Snow**
The Two Cultures
0-521-45730-0 CAMBRIDGE PB........$10.95

Scientific Thought and Discovery

Philosophers' efforts to describe the scientific process often reveal as much about the thinker as the thought. In the words of the British astronomer and physicist Arthur Eddington: "We have found a strange foot-print on the shores of the unknown. We have devised profound theories, one after another, to account for its origin. At last we have succeeded in reconstructing the creature that made the footprint. And lo! it is our own."

George **Basalla**
The Evolution of Technology
Argues that Darwin's theory can be applied to the development of human creativity and inventions
0-521-29681-1 CAMBRIDGE PB........$15.95

I. Bernard **Cohen**
Revolution in Science
A thorough historical analysis of revolution as a mechanism for explaining change in scientific theories
0-674-76777-2 HARVARD........$42.50

John **Cornwell**
Nature's Imagination: The Frontiers of Scientific Vision
Contributors, including some of the most distinguished and imaginitive scientists in the world, look beyond previous models to new, non-reductive paradigms
0-19-851775-0 OXFORD........$25.00

Philip **Davis** & David **Park**
No Way: The Nature of the Impossible
Explores the challenges, limits, and illusions at the frontiers of scientific discovery
0-7167-1966-5 FREEMAN PB........$14.95

Freeman **Dyson**
From Eros to Gaia
That rare combination of a brilliant writer and a distinguished scientist, Dyson's essays offer an unprecedented window into "the temple of science." Lucid, humorous, and readable, Dyson informs and entertains on subjects as diverse as astronomy and Tolstoy
0-14-017423-0 PENGUIN PB........$12.95

Paul **Feyerabend**

Against Method

Feyerabend, an Austrian-born American philosopher, remained the *enfant terrible* of the philosophy of science throughout his life, an iconoclast who relentlessly attacked the premises of modern science on behalf of a pluralist view of knowledge. This is his best-known book

See also **OTHER 20TH-CENTURY PHILOSOPHERS** under **PHILOSOPHY** in **RELIGION, SPIRITUALITY, AND PHILOSOPHY**

0-86091-481-X VERSO $64.95
0-86091-646-4 VERSO PB $19.00

Killing Time

The maverick philosopher's autobiography

See also **OTHER 20TH-CENTURY PHILOSOPHERS** under **PHILOSOPHY** in **RELIGION, SPIRITUALITY, AND PHILOSOPHY**

0-226-24531-4 CHICAGO $22.95
0-226-24532-2 CHICAGO PB $13.95

Gerald **Holton**

Introduction to Concepts and Theories in Physical Science

0-691-08384-3 PRINCETON PB $35.00

Thematic Origins of Scientific Thought: Kepler to Einstein

0-674-87748-9 HARVARD PB $16.95
0-674-87747-0 HARVARD PB $25.00

David **Hull**

Science as a Process: An Evolutionary Account of the Social and Conceptual Development of Science

0-226-36051-2 CHICAGO PB $27.95

Thomas S. **Kuhn**

Black-Body Theory and the Quantum Discontinuity, 1894-1912

0-226-45800-8 CHICAGO PB $23.00

The Structure of Scientific Revolutions

The classic study of the development and displacement of scientific "paradigms"

See also **HISTORICAL SOCIOLOGY** under **TOPICS IN MODERN SOCIOLOGY** under **SOCIOLOGY** in **SOCIAL STUDIES**

0-226-45803-2 CHICAGO $25.00
0-226-45804-0 CHICAGO PB $10.95

Pat **Langley**

Scientific Discovery: Computational Explorations of the Creative Processes

A fascinating study that shows how the discovery process can be described and modeled

0-262-62052-9 MIT PB $17.50

Henry **Petroski**

The Evolution of Useful Things: How Everyday Artifacts—from Forks and Pins to Paper Clips and Zippers—Came to be as They Are

Petroski, author of *The Pencil,* is a virtuoso when writing about everyday objects. Dredging up great anecdotes and unforeseen connections in the history of the invention of small things, Petroski shows how crazy ideas finally become accepted (cf. the man behind the pop-top lid)

See also **PERSPECTIVES IN HISTORY** under **THE VARIETIES OF CIVILIZATION** in **WORLD HISTORY AND CURRENT AFFAIRS**

0-679-41226-3 KNOPF $24.00
0-679-74039-2 VINTAGE PB $13.00

Karl **Popper**

The Logic of Scientific Discovery

A classic work on the philosophy of science

0-415-07892-X ROUTLEDGE PB $22.95

Karl Popper

Linda Jean **Shepherd**

Lifting the Veil: The Feminine Face of Science

A biochemist who has also studied Jung shows the salutary, sometimes enlightening influence of feminine principles on chaos theory, the new physics, and the new biology. A fresh attempt to point the way to restoring the lost soul of science

0-87773-656-1 SHAMBHALA PB $14.00

Reference

Robert **Bernhardt**

The American Heritage Dictionary of Science

0-395-48367-0 HOUGHTON MIFFLIN $29.95

William **Bynum**, editor

Dictionary of the History of Science

0-691-02384-0 PRINCETON PB $22.50

Harry **Judge**, editor

Oxford Illustrated Encyclopedia: The Physical World

See also **NATURE AND NATURAL HISTORY** under **NATURE STUDY**

0-19-869161-0 OXFORD $95.00

Peter **Lafferty** & Julian **Rowe**, editors

The Dictionary of Science

"This fine dictionary for students and general readers presents the rich world of science in an interesting, informative, and readily understandable manner while remaining concise and factual. Alphabetically arranged entries, while succinct, are really more like explanations, often placing terms in historical context and adding other tidbits of interesting information. Special features include chronologies, puzzles, and a thematic index. Brief articles describe momentous experiments and discoveries, while signed Progress Reports explore such topics as 'Genetic Engineering's Brave New World"—*Library Journal*

0-13-304718-0 SIMON & SCHUSTER $45.00

McGraw-Hill

McGraw-Hill Concise Encyclopedia of Science and Technology

Contains 7300 alphabetically arranged articles, 1600 illustrations, and a 30,000-entry index. An excellent reference book

0-07-045560-0 MCGRAW HILL $115.50

McGraw-Hill Dictionary of Scientific and Technical Terms

A 2200-page reference book comprising 100,100 terms, 117,500 definitions, and over 3000 illustrations

0-07-042333-4 MCGRAW HILL $125.00

McGraw-Hill Encyclopedia of Science and Technology

This sixth edition in 20 volumes includes 7,700 articles, 2,000 of them new or completely revised, covering 77 major subject areas; 15,000 illustrations. "A first-class tool without substitute"—*Scientific American*

0-07-079292-5 MCGRAW HILL $1600.00

Nina **Morgan**

Chemistry in Action: The Molecules of Everyday Life

An illustrated reference covering the basic and applied subjects of modern science

0-19-521086-7 OXFORD $35.00

Walter S. **Mossberg**

The Wall Street Journal Book of Personal Technology

Everything you've always wanted to know about the ever-changing, always-complex world of personal technology. Jargon-free and down-to-earth, Mossberg guides the reader from the Internet and multimedia to the latest in laptop and desktop computers and personal digital assistants. An essential roadmap to the electronic universe

0-8129-2602-1 TIMES BOOKS PB $15.00

Oxford University

The New Encyclopedia of Science

Volume I: Matter and Energy

Seasoned science journalists render this exhaustive collection readable; academic overseers ensure its accuracy

See also **ONE-VOLUME ENCYCLOPEDIAS** under **REFERENCE** in **BUSINESS AND REFERENCE**

0-19-521085-9 OXFORD $35.00

Volume II: Animal Life

See also **ONE-VOLUME ENCYCLOPEDIAS** under **REFERENCE** in **BUSINESS AND REFERENCE**

0-19-521084-0 OXFORD $35.00

Colin A. **Ronan**, editor

Science Explained: The World of Science in Everyday Life

Readers of all ages who are science-illiterate will appreciate the everyday examples and lucid writing of this fully illustrated volume. A unique cross-referencing system makes the book interactive by linking different areas of science, from outer space to artificial intelligence, providing an amazing guide to everyday life

See also **HISTORY OF SCIENCE AND TECHNOLOGY**

0-8050-2551-0 HOLT $45.00
0-8050-4236-9 HOLT PB $22.50

Kenneth Jon **Rose**

Quick Scientific Terminology: A Self-Teaching Guide

0-471-85763-7 WILEY PB $16.95

Physics

The revolution in physics that began in the '60s is based upon the discovery that "elementary particles" of matter are not really fundamental constituents after all, but are made up of even more basic particles. Physicists have used these findings to formulate a theory of nuclear forces, and are also making progress toward formulating a supertheory that would explain the four known forces of nature: gravity, electromagnetism, and the strong and weak nuclear forces. Such a unifying theory could not only explain all the properties of matter, but would also offer astonishing insights into the origin, structure, and evolution of the universe.

Highly technical books intended for professional scientists are not listed here; semi-technical books are identified as such. Most titles can be read by persons with no scientific or technical background. In fact, many readers may be surprised at how much they do understand; scientific popularizers are often skilled and entertaining authors, adept at explaining abstruse ideas.

General Works

John D. **Barrow**

Theories of Everything: The Quest for Ultimate Explanation

The author of *The World Within the World* and *The Anthropic Cosmological Principle* examines past and present attempts to explain the origin and purpose of the universe, from myths to contemporary physics

See also **OTHER 20TH-CENTURY PHILOSOPHERS** under **PHILOSOPHY** in **RELIGION, SPIRITUALITY, AND PHILOSOPHY**

0-19-853928-2 CLARENDON $30.00
0-449-90738-4 FAWCETT PB $12.00

The World Within the World

A look at some of the philosophical problems raised by modern physics, by the co-author of *The Anthropic Cosmological Principle*

0-19-851979-6 CLARENDON $30.00
0-19-286108-5 OXFORD PB $15.95

Albert **Einstein**

Einstein on Humanism: Collected Essays of Albert Einstein

Reveals the great scientist as an astute and critical observer of the social issues of his time—not protected by the ivory towers of research as often is the case with scholars. Among the topics in this book are "Why Socialism?" "On Military Service" and "The Goal of Human Existence." A testament to the workings of a conscientious and deeply human mind

0-8065-1436-1 CITADEL PB $8.95

The World as I See It

Einstein on good and evil, religion and science, Christianity and Judaism, pacifism and the Arabs. A witty and shrewd key to the great physicist's values and personality

0-8065-0711-X CITADEL PB $7.95

Richard P. **Feynman**

Six Easy Pieces: Essentials of Physics Explained by Its Most Brilliant Teacher

"If one book was all that could be passed on to the next generation of scientists it would undoubtedly have to be *Six Easy Pieces*" —John Gribbin in *New Scientist*

INTRODUCTION BY PAUL DAVIES

0-201-40825-2 ADDISON-WESLEY PB $12.00

Nick **Herbert**

Faster Than Light: Superluminal Loopholes in Physics

A quantum physicist explains how to take quantum leaps through space—and around Dr. Einstein's theory of relativity

0-452-26317-4 NEW AMERICAN LIBRARY PB $10.95

James **Jeans**

Science and Music

0-486-61964-8 DOVER PB $7.95

Lawrence M. **Krauss**

Fear of Physics: A Guide For the Perplexed

A master teacher to those uninitiated in the arcane ways of science, Krauss *(Cosmic Strings, The Fifth Essence)* illustrates the physicist's principle of simplifying the world in order to explain it. Rich with anecdotes and discussions of the ideas and tricks of everyone from Plato to Stephen Hawking

0-465-02367-3 BASIC PB $12.50

Russell **McCormmach**

Night Thoughts of a Classical Physicist

An absorbing novel set in early 20th-century Europe, concerning a physicist who has trouble coming to terms with new ideas

0-674-62461-0 HARVARD PB $9.95

Henry P. **Stapp**

Mind, Matter, & Quantum Mechanics

A collection of sharply written essays by a distinguished and articulate adherent of the idea that quantum mechanics and theories of consciousness can be combined in a grand synthesis

0-387-56289-3 SPRINGER-VERLAG $39.95

Hans Christian **von Baeyer**

Rainbows, Snowflakes, and Quarks: Physics and the World Around Us

An animated exploration of the science behind waves and whirlpools, snowflakes and colors, gravity, lightning, and motion. "Wonderfully wrought"—*Kirkus Reviews*

0-679-73976-9 RANDOM HOUSE PB $12.00

Steven **Weinberg**

Dreams of a Final Theory: The Scientist's Search for the Ultimate Laws of Nature

"Nobel Prize-winning physicist Weinberg's quest for a final loose explanation of the laws of nature displays a scientist's sense of wonder and an artist's love of beauty"—*Publishers Weekly*

0-679-74408-8 VINTAGE PB $13.00

Frank **Wilczek** & Betsy **Devine**

Longing For the Harmonies: Themes and Variations For Modern Physics

For scientists and laymen alike. "The explanations have an originality and a simplicity that come about through the deepest knowledge"—*New Yorker*

0-393-30596-1 NORTON PB $9.95

Essays

Physicists turned essayists are often quite entertaining. The following collection is especially recommended.

J. Robert **Oppenheimer**

Atom & Void: Essays on Science & Community

An anthology of essays by the physicist who spearheaded the development of the atomic bomb at Los Alamos and later became a proponent of strict controls on the use of nuclear energy

0-691-08547-1 PRINCETON $29.95
0-691-02434-0 PRINCETON PB $9.95

Robert Oppenheimer

Reference

Cesare **Emiliani**

Physical Sciences Dictionary

0-19-503651-4 OXFORD $19.95

Facts on File & John **Daintith**, editor

The Facts on File Dictionary of Physics: Revised and Expanded

"The most important and the most commonly used terms in the ever-expanding field of physics are explained. Line drawings enhance the text"—*Science News*

0-8160-1868-5 FACTS ON FILE $24.95

Larry **Gonick** & Art **Huffman**

The Cartoon Guide to Physics

0-06-279013-7 CD-ROM $39.99

McGraw-Hill

McGraw-Hill Encyclopedia of Physics

A 1,350-page reference containing 763 detailed articles spanning all of classic physics, modern physics, and related areas in mathematics

0-07-051400-3 MCGRAW HILL $99.95

The Philosophy of Physics

Many physicists like to speculate on the metaphysical implications of their theories, and they sometimes do so in a less rigorous manner than in their scientific work. Philosophers—who tend nowadays to be sceptical about metaphysical speculation—more often concern themselves with the logical structure of physical law.

David **Bohm**

Wholeness and the Implicate Order

0-7448-0000-5 ROUTLEDGE PB $14.95

Herbert **Butterfield**

The Origins of Modern Science

0-02-905070-7 FREE PRESS PB $16.95

Fritjof **Capra**

The Tao of Physics

This book has received so much attention that it can hardly be ignored; but most physicists are skeptical of a connection between physics and Eastern mysticism

0-87773-594-8 SHAMBHALA PB $14.00

Nancy **Cartwright**

How the Laws of Physics Lie

Argues that the regularities described by explanatory laws do not actually exist in nature

0-19-824704-4 OXFORD PB $24.95

Paul **Davies**

God and the New Physics

0-671-52806-8 SIMON & SCHUSTER PB $11.00

Pierre **Duhem**

The Aim & Structure of Physical Theory

TRANSLATED BY PHILIP P. WIENER

0-691-02524-X PRINCETON PB $14.95

Richard **Feynman**

The Character of Physical Law

0-262-56003-8 MIT PB $10.95

David **Goodstein** & others

Feynman's Lost Lecture

This extraordinary lecture from the Nobel Laureate physicist is teaching at its best: a proof of the discovery of the planets' elliptical movement around the sun that uses mathematics no more advanced than high school geometry. Delivered to the freshman class at Cal Tech, this text of Richard Feynman's lecture, accompanied by a CD recording, showcases a brilliant teacher explaining a watershed in human understanding of the universe

See also BIOGRAPHIES AND AUTOBIOGRAPHIES

0-393-03918-8 NORTON $35.00

Stephen **Hawking**

Black Holes and Baby Universes: And Other Essays

These essays are a distillation of Hawking's major scientific insights: that the universe is "neither created nor destroyed"; that space/time is finite but boundless, like the surface of a globe; and his newest discovery, that black holes are the generators of "baby universes" which branch off from our own universe and sometimes return. Also contains some revealing autobiographical essays about Hawking's youth as a mediocre student, and his triumph over Lou Gehrig's disease. His first new book since the widely read *A Brief History of Time*

0-553-37411-7 BANTAM PB $13.95

Werner **Heisenberg**

Physics and Philosophy: The Revolution in Modern Science

0-06-130549-9 HARPERCOLLINS PB $14.00

Werner Heisenberg

M. **Kafatos** & R. **Nadeau**

The Conscious Universe: Part & Whole in Modern Physical Theory

An argument that theories of consciousness are compatible with—and understandable in terms of—a scientific model of the physical universe

0-387-97262-5 SPRINGER-VERLAG PB $19.95

Martin H. **Krieger**

Doing Physics: How Physicists Take Hold of the World

A highly original study, less concerned with the concepts of physics *per se* than with how physicists organize and pursue their scientific exploration of the world

0-253-33123-4 INDIANA $29.95
0-253-20701-0 INDIANA PB $10.95

Henry **Margenau**

The Nature of Physical Reality: A Philosophy of Modern Physics

0-918024-02-1 OX BOW $35.00
0-918024-03-X OX BOW PB $17.00

Hermann **Weyl**

Symmetry

0-691-02374-3 PRINCETON PB $9.95

Relativity

Most of the following titles will be accessible to the lay reader.

Max **Born**

Einstein's Theory of Relativity

Probably the most easily understandable of these books

0-486-60769-0 DOVER PB $9.95

Nigel **Calder**

Einstein's Universe

A brief but cogent summary

0-517-38570-8 OUTLET $7.99
0-14-013516-2 VIKING PB $11.95

Eric **Chaisson**

Relatively Speaking: Relativity, Black Holes, and the Fate of the Universe

0-393-30675-5 NORTON PB $12.95

David **Darling**

Equations of Eternity: Speculations on Matter, Meaning, and the Mathematical Rules That Orchestrate the Cosmos

1-56282-875-4 HYPERION $19.95
0-7868-8072-4 HYPERION PB $10.95

Paul **Davies**

About Time: Einstein's Unfinished Revolution

0-671-79964-9 SIMON & SCHUSTER $24.00

Albert **Einstein**

The Collected Papers of Albert Einstein: The Early Years, 1879-1902

The first of approximately 40 projected volumes containing over 14,000 documents drawn from the Einstein archives

EDITED BY JOHN STACHEL

0-691-08407-6 PRINCETON $85.00

P.C. **Davies**

The Nature of Time

Like the title, it occupies a kind of no-man's-land between the popular and the semi-technical

0-631-16578-9 BLACKWELL PB $20.95

A.S. **Eddington**

Space, Time and Gravitation: An Outline of the General Relativity Theory

0-521-33709-7 CAMBRIDGE PB $21.95

The Collected Papers of Albert Einstein: Volume 2

0-691-08526-9 PRINCETON $85.00
0-691-08475-0 PRINCETON PB $35.00

Ideas and Opinions

0-679-60105-8 MODERN LIBRARY $15.50

The Principle of Relativity

0-486-60081-5 DOVER PB $6.95

Relativity

0-87975-979-8 PROMETHEUS PB $8.95

Relativity: The Special and the General Theory

0-517-88441-0 CROWN PB $7.00

The Theory of Relativity (And Other Essays)

0-8065-1765-4 CITADEL PB $8.95

Harald **Fritzsch**

An Equation That Changed the World: Newton, Einstein and the Theory of Relativity

In the style of Galileo's *Dialogues on Two Principal World Views,* Fritzsch offers us the chance to listen to an imaginary conversation among Newton, Einstein, and a present-day physicist. Created for readers without training in physics or higher mathematics, we learn the opposing theories of the two great scientists who founded classical physics and modern relativity and understand how they have revolutionized our view of the physical world. "A successful event in scientific communication, an area in which there is entirely too much babbling" —*Frankfurter Allgemeine Zeitung*

0-226-26557-9 CHICAGO $29.95

Robert **Geroch**

General Relativity from A to B

Somewhat difficult

0-226-28864-1 CHICAGO PB $12.95

Stanley **Goldberg**

Understanding Relativity: Origin and Impact of a Scientific Revolution

0-8176-3150-X BIRKHAUSER $46.50

Stephen W. **Hawking**

A Brief History of Time: From the Big Bang to Black Holes

"The basic ideas about the origin and fate of the universe can be stated without mathematics in a form that people without scientific education can understand. This is what I have attempted to do in this book"—Stephen Hawking

INTRODUCTION BY CARL SAGAN

0-553-05340-X BANTAM DOUBLEDAY DELL $26.95
0-553-34614-8 BANTAM PB $14.95

Stephen W. **Hawking** & G.F.R. **Ellis**

The Large-Scale Structure of Space-Time

An early work by Hawking published in 1973

0-521-09906-4 CAMBRIDGE PB $44.95

Stephen W. **Hawking** & Roger **Penrose**

The Nature of Space and Time

Two of the great scientific minds of our day offer their opposing views on key questions in physics. Why does time go forward, not backward? What are the physics of black holes, and the big bang, and how does the quantum gravity theory account for them? This unique collection of opposing views offers an unusually accessible view of current thinking on quantum theory and the nature of the universe

FOREWORD BY MICHAEL ATIYAH

0-691-03791-4 PRINCETON $24.95

Gerald **Holton** & Yehuda **Elkana**, editors

Albert Einstein, Historical and Cultural Perspectives: The Centennial Symposium in Jerusalem

0-691-08231-6 PRINCETON $65.00

Max **Jammer**

Concepts of Space: The History of Theories of Space in Physics

0-486-27119-6 DOVER PB $7.95

Delo **Mook** & Thomas **Vargish**

Inside Reality

Special and general relativity skillfully explained by a physicist and a professor of literature

0-691-08472-6 PRINCETON $60.00

David **Park**

The Image of Eternity: Roots of Time in the Physical World

0-87023-286-X MASSACHUSETTS $22.50

Hans **Reichenbach**

The Philosophy of Space and Time

0-486-60443-8 DOVER PB $7.95

Rudy **Rucker**

Geometry, Relativity and the Fourth Dimension

Another good introduction

0-486-23400-2 DOVER PB $5.95

Kip S. **Thorne**

Black Holes and Time Warps: Einstein's Outrageous Legacy

0-393-31276-3 NORTON PB $14.95

Kip S. **Thorne** & Richard H. **Price**

Black Holes: The Membrane Paradigm

0-300-03770-8 YALE PB $19.00

Robert M. **Wald**

Space, Time, and Gravity: The Theory of the Big Bang and Black Holes

0-226-87028-6 CHICAGO $29.00

John Archibald **Wheeler** & Ignazio **Ciufolini**

Gravitation and Inertia

0-691-03323-4 PRINCETON $49.50

Clifford **Will**

Was Einstein Right?: Putting General Relativity to the Test

"Of course Einstein was right! But this book tells you why. This is the best popular book describing the experimental basis for general relativity"—Heinz Pagels

0-465-09086-9 BASIC PB $16.00

Quantum Mechanics

Physicists are still arguing about the interpretation and philosophical implications of the theory of subatomic phenomena. No matter what interpretation one accepts, it seems impossible to avoid certain abiding questions about the nature of physical reality and the role of the observer.

David Z. **Albert**

Quantum Mechanics and Experience

With immense clarity, Albert explains how quantum mechanics—in which uncertainty is scientific fact—came to change the scientific world. His theories, explanations, and style make a previously obscure and difficult subject accessible and enjoyable

0-674-74112-9 HARVARD $32.00

Barbara **Cline**

The Ghost in the Atom: A Discussion of the Mysteries of Quantum Physics

Slightly more difficult than the others listed here. "A useful introduction to a variety of ideas and approaches about understanding quantum mechanics"—*Nature*

0-521-30790-2 CAMBRIDGE $47.95
0-521-45728-9 CAMBRIDGE PB $9.95

The Men Who Made a New Physics: Physicists and the Quantum Theory

A very readable history of the discovery of quantum mechanics

See also BIOGRAPHIES AND AUTOBIOGRAPHIES

0-226-11027-3 CHICAGO PB $12.95

Henry **Folse**, Jr.

The Philosophy of Niels Bohr: Framework of Complementarity

The most widely accepted approach to quantum mechanics was developed by Bohr and his colleagues at the Institute for Theoretical Physics in Copenhagen

0-444-86938-7 ELSEVIER PB $62.50

Richard **Feynman**
QED: The Strange Theory of Light and Matter
0-691-08388-6 PRINCETON....................$29.95
0-691-02417-0 PRINCETON PB....................$9.95

Richard Feynman

Arthur **Fine**
The Shaky Game: Einstein, Realism, and the Quantum Theory
A comprehensive account of Einstein's realism and his opposition to quantum theory—also examines the realism-antirealism debate in the philosophy of science, and proposes a bold and original solution to the "natural ontological attitude" with its emphasis on the actual practice of the sciences
0-226-24947-6 CHICAGO PB....................$13.95

A.P. **French** & others, editors
Niels Bohr: A Centenary Volume
The creative work, ideals, and life of the man who cracked the quantum code, as remembered by his students
0-674-62416-5 HARVARD PB....................$15.95

George **Gamow**
Thirty Years That Shook Physics: The Story of Quantum Theory
Another excellent historical survey
0-486-24895-X DOVER PB....................$7.95

John **Gribbin**
In Search of Schrödinger's Cat: Quantum Physics and Reality
0-553-34253-3 BANTAM PB....................$12.95

Schrödinger's Kittens and the Search for Reality: Solving the Quantum Mysteries
0-316-32838-3 LITTLE, BROWN....................$23.95
0-316-32819-7 LITTLE, BROWN PB....................$12.95

Werner **Heisenberg**
Physical Principles of the Quantum Theory
0-486-60113-7 DOVER PB....................$6.95

Nick **Herbert**
Quantum Reality
"Takes up the question of reality in the puzzling light of quantum theory and Bell's theorem. Be prepared for a rollercoaster ride that will stretch your mind and leave you gasping"
—Isaac Asimov
0-385-23569-0 ANCHOR PB....................$10.95

Anthony **Hey** & Patrick **Walters**
The Quantum Universe
A colorfully illustrated explanation of quantized properties
0-521-31845-9 CAMBRIDGE PB....................$31.95

Max **Jammer**
The Conceptual Development of Quantum Mechanics
0-88318-617-9 AMINP....................$90.00

David **Lindley**
Where Does the Weirdness Go?: Why Quantum Mechanics is Strange But Not as Strange as You Think
What is quantum physics, and can a non-scientist ever understand it? Lindley answers both questions in a resoundingly original way: quantum mechanics is strange, but not only can it be understood, it can also be enjoyed with readable, amusing, witty explanations, in which the weird behavior of subatomic effects becomes amazingly clear
0-465-06785-9 BASIC....................$24.95

Eugene **Wigner**
Symmetries and Reflections
A collection of essays, some more technical than others, that includes Wigner's celebrated writings on quantum mechanics and consciousness
0-918024-16-1 OX BOW PB....................$18.00

Particle Physics, Cosmology, and the "New" Physics

Theoretical research in cosmology and particle physics are intertwined. Particle physicists speculate about something that they have never observed, but whose existence is required by accepted theories. Energy of the magnitude necessary to create such particles existed in the Big Bang, the explosion that took place shortly after the creation of the universe. Similarly, the cosmologist—who cannot expect to see his theories confirmed in the laboratory—attempts to understand their consequences in relation to what is known about subnuclear particles. Of the books dealing with this combined field, the following place more emphasis on particle physics.

Robert K. **Adair**
The Great Design: Particles, Fields and Creation
0-19-504380-4 OXFORD....................$35.00

Richard E. **Carrigan**, Jr. & W. Peter **Trower**, editors
Particle Physics in the Cosmos: Readings from Scientific American
0-7167-1919-3 FREEMAN PB....................$16.95

Frank **Close**
The Particle Explosion
Interesting for its descriptions of numerous experiments, unlike most popular science books, which emphasize theory. "A pictorial feast"
—*Nature*
0-19-851965-6 OXFORD....................$39.95

Too Hot to Handle: The Race For Cold Fusion
An erudite examination of the recent furor over cold fusion's feasibility
0-691-08591-9 PRINCETON....................$35.00

P.C.W. **Davies**, editor
The New Physics
An accessible collection with contributions from 18 leading international physicists
0-521-43831-4 CAMBRIDGE PB....................$34.95

Murray **Gell-Mann**
The Quark and the Jaguar
0-7167-2725-0 FREEMAN PB....................$15.95

The quarks are basic building blocks of all matter. Every object we see is composed, more or less, of quarks and electrons. Even the jaguar, that ancient symbol of power and ferocity, is a bundle of quarks and electrons, but what a bundle! It exhibits an enormous amount of complexity, the result of billions of years of biological evolution. What exactly does complexity mean and how did it arise? Such questions are typical of the ones this book tries to answer.
THE QUARK AND THE JAGUAR

Michio **Kaku**
Hyperspace: A Scientific Odyssey Through Parallel Universes, Time Warps and the 10th Dimension
0-19-508514-0 OXFORD....................$25.00
0-385-47705-8 ANCHOR PB....................$14.95

Igor **Novikov**
Black Holes and the Universe
0-521-55870-0 CAMBRIDGE PB....................$8.95
0-521-36683-6 CAMBRIDGE PB....................$19.95

Barry **Parker**
The Search For a Supertheory: From Atoms to Superstrings
"This story is, indeed, physics for poets"—*NY Times*
0-306-42702-8 PLENUM....................$21.95

Andrew **Pickering**
Constructing Quarks: A Sociological History of Particle Physics
Though somewhat technical, long sections can be read by someone with no mathematical background. Pickering is interesting for his heretical view that quarks (the theoretical constituents of protons and neutrons) were "invented" rather than "discovered"
0-226-66799-5 CHICAGO PB....................$26.00

Sharon **Traweek**

Beamtimes and Lifetimes: The World of High Energy Physics

A cultural anthropologist looks at contemporary experimental physics and its practitioners

0-674-06348-1 HARVARD PB $12.95

James **Trefil**

From Atoms to Quarks: An Introduction to the Strange World of Particle Physics

0-385-47336-2 ANCHOR PB $12.95

M. Mitchell **Waldrop**

Complexity: The Emerging Science At the Edge of Order and Chaos

A journalistic profile of the iconoclastic thinkers involved with the new science of "complexity," a field that searches for order in systems previously thought to be chaotic. Waldrop explores their abiding fascination with such questions as why the stock market crashed in 1987, and how living organisms emerged from amino acids

See also **SCIENCE AND TECHNOLOGY**

0-671-87234-6 TOUCHSTONE PB $12.00

Steven **Weinberg**

The Discovery of Subatomic Particles

0-7167-1488-4 FREEMAN $32.95

Fred Alan **Wolf**

Parallel Universes: Worlds Within Our Present Senses

How recent advances in theoretical physics predict the existence of universes that are similar to—and perhaps even duplicates of—our own. "A remarkable bridge between the scientific intelligence and the creative imagination"—Norman Cousins

0-671-69601-7 TOUCHSTONE PB $12.00

History of Physics

The following historically significant texts have been included because of their accessibility to the lay reader

Aristotle

Aristotle's Physics

TRANSLATED BY RICHARD HOPE

0-9602870-3-5 PERIPATETIC PB $12.00

Aristotle's Physics Volume 1 Books 1 & 2

0-19-872026-2 CLARENDON PB $25.95

Volume 2 Books 3 & 4

0-19-872069-6 OXFORD PB $29.95

Jeremy **Bernstein**

The Tenth Dimension: An Informal History of High Energy Physics

0-07-005017-1 MCGRAW HILL PB $13.95

Albert **Einstein** & Leopold **Infeld**

The Evolution of Physics

0-671-20156-5 SIMON & SCHUSTER PB $12.00

Galileo **Galilei**

Dialogues Concerning Two New Chief World Systems, Ptolemaic and Copernican

See also **GALILEO AND NEWTON** under **THE SCIENTIFIC REVOLUTION** under **EARLY MODERN EUROPE** in **WORLD HISTORY AND CURRENT AFFAIRS**

0-520-00450-7 CALIFORNIA PB $17.95

Rupert **Hall**

From Galileo to Newton

0-486-24227-7 DOVER PB $9.95

P.M. **Harman**

Energy, Force and Matter: The Conceptual Development of Nineteenth-Century Physics

A history of 19th century "classical" physics

0-521-28812-6 CAMBRIDGE PB $17.95

Arthur I. **Miller**

Imagery in Scientific Thought: Creating Twentieth-Century Physics

0-8176-3196-8 BIRKHAUSER $36.50

0-262-63104-0 BIRKHAUSER $14.95

Isaac **Newton**

Opticks

FOREWORD BY ALBERT EINSTEIN

0-486-60205-2 DOVER PB $11.95

Isaac Newton

Ed **Regis**

Who Got Einstein's Office: Eccentricity and Genius At the Institute For Advanced Study

"I cannot praise this extraordinary book too highly. It signals the sudden entrance of Regis into the first rank of today's science writers" —Martin Gardner

0-201-12278-2 ADDISON-WESLEY PB $15.00

Philip **Sehle**

Order, Chaos, Order: The Transition from Classical to Quantum Physics

A history of physics from Galileo to the present, informatively based on direct and illuminating quotations from the work of the researchers who engineered each breakthrough

0-19-508473-X OXFORD PB $34.00

Stephen **Toulmin** & June **Goodfield**

The Architecture of Matter

0-226-80840-8 CHICAGO PB $21.00

Biographies and Autobiographies

David **Peat**

Infinite Potential: The Life and Times of David Bohm

Physicist, clarifier of human consciousness, friend to Robert Oppenheimer, opponent of the HUAC committee, David Bohm made lasting contributions not only to physics but to the understanding of consciousness, psychology, language, and education. This fascinating biography depicts a courageous human being in full intellectual range, from his refusal to bow before McCarthy to his work with the Indian philosopher Krishnamurti

0-201-40635-7 ADDISON-WESLEY $25.00

A.P. **French** & others, editors

Niels Bohr: A Centenary Volume

The creative work, ideals, and life of the man who cracked the quantum code, as remembered by his students

See also **QUANTUM MECHANICS**

Abraham **Pais**

Niels Bohr's Times: In Physics, Philosophy, and Polity

The widely acclaimed and award-winning biographer of Einstein presents a stunning biography of the father of quantum physics. Combines scientific achievement and physics theory with an in-depth portrait of the man's personal triumphs and tragedies. "As near to the ideal biographer as one can hope to find....A book for the general public that is cleverly nestled inside a second, bigger one for the specialist"—*Washington Post Book World*

0-19-852048-4 OXFORD PB $17.95

Susan **Quinn**

Marie Curie: A Life

"Certain to be this generation's definitive biography"—*Science*

0-201-88794-0 ADDISON-WESLEY PB $16.00

Barbara **Cline**

The Men Who Made a New Physics: Physicists and the Quantum Theory

A very readable history of the discovery of quantum mechanics

See also **QUANTUM MECHANICS**

0-226-11027-3 CHICAGO PB $12.95

Freeman **Dyson**

Disturbing the Universe: A Life in Science

0-465-01677-4 BASIC PB $16.00

Freeman Dyson

Jeremy **Bernstein**

Albert Einstein

Bernstein (Professor of Physics, Stevens Institute of Technology; and author of *Cranks, Quarks, and the Cosmos*) combines a scholar's erudition and a writer's elucidation to introduce us not only to Einstein's brain, but to his heart

0-19-509275-9 OXFORD $20.00

0-19-509896-X OXFORD PB $17.95

Ronald **Clark**

Einstein: The Life and Times

0-380-01159-X AVON PB $7.99

Einstein, Albert

Banesh **Hoffmann** & others

Albert Einstein, Creator and Rebel

0-452-26193-7 NEW AMERICAN LIBRARY PB $12.95

Albert **Einstein**

Albert Einstein: Philosopher-Scientist

Contains Einstein's own autobiographical notes, the only memoir he ever wrote, among other writings on his work

EDITED BY PAUL A. SCHILPP

0-87548-133-7 OPEN COURT $56.95

0-87548-286-4 OPEN COURT PB $29.95

Roger **Highfield** & others

The Private Lives of Albert Einstein

An eye-opening and far-from-flattering biography of the 20th century's most mythologized scientific figure, based on Einstein's private papers and revealing a number of hitherto well-kept secrets

0-312-13147-X ST. MARTIN'S PB $14.95

Abraham **Pais**

Subtle Is the Lord: The Science and Life of Albert Einstein

Fills many gaps, including Einstein's interest in philosophy, his concern with Jewish destiny, and his opinions of great figures from Newton to Freud. Winner of the 1983 American Book Award

0-19-520438-7 OXFORD PB $16.95

Einstein Lived Here: Essays for the Layman

Einstein's life outside of science: his personal life, the burden of his public image, his political and philosophical alliances, and the heartbreaking story of his immediate family

0-19-853994-0 OXFORD $25.00

Michael **White** & others

Einstein: A Life in Science

By the authors of *Stephen Hawking*, a vivid portrait of a paradoxical man, including several little-discussed stories: Einstein and the FBI, trouble with his marriages, and evidence that he may have suffered from schizophrenia early in his life

0-525-93750-1 DUTTON $21.95

Richard **Feynman**

What Do You Care What Other People Think?: Further Adventures of a Curious Character

0-553-34784-5 BANTAM PB $13.95

James **Gleick**

Genius: The Life and Science of Richard Feynman

Feynman left his mark on every area of modern science. An architect of quantum mechanics, he worked on the bomb project and criticized NASA's administration. Gleick shows how Feynman's passion and charm was integral to his work. A self-taught drummer, safe-cracker, and writer of Chinese, he ceaselessly questioned fundamental truths, and hugely reshaped our understanding of what science does.

"It achieves an almost perfect balance between the physicist's work and his life…Gleick [is a] consumate craftsman"–*Washington Post Book World*

0-679-40836-3 PANTHEON $27.50

0-679-74704-4 VINTAGE PB $14.00

David **Goodstein** & others

Feynman's Lost Lecture

This extraordinary lecture from the Nobel Laureate physicist is teaching at its best: a proof of the discovery of the planets' elliptical movement around the sun that uses mathematics no more advanced than high school geometry. Delivered to the freshman class at Cal Tech, this text of Richard Feynman's lecture, accompanied by a CD recording, showcases a brilliant teacher explaining a watershed in human understanding of the universe

See also **THE PHILOSOPHY OF PHYSICS**

0-393-03918-8 NORTON $35.00

Christopher **Sykes**

No Ordinary Genius: The Illustrated Richard Feynman

Feynman's passion for physics may have won him the Nobel Prize, but it was only a small part of his life. Irreverent and honest, Feynman's engagement with his family, friends, and colleagues was as passionate as was his work in physics, and the creativity of his mind was as engaged in play as in thought. A biography that gives "the reader…insight into the depth of Feynman's originality and gifts as a physicist" —*Washington Times*

0-393-31393-X NORTON PB $19.95

Richard **Feynman** & others

Surely You're Joking, Mr. Feynman!: Adventures of a Curious Character

Autobiographical musings by the late world-famous physicist who was probably the only Nobel Prize winner ever judged mentally deficient by the US Army. "Anyone who can read it without laughing is bad crazy"—*LA Times*

0-553-34668-7 BANTAM PB $13.95

0-674-62416-5 HARVARD PB $15.95

Stillman **Drake**

Galileo

A short biography that raises questions about the history of science and its relation to religion and philosophy

0-8020-2725-3 TORONTO $40.00

Maurice A. **Finocchiaro**, translator

The Galileo Affair: A Documentary History

Galileo was tried and condemned as a heretic by the Inquisition in 1633, an episode in the history of science that remains a subject of controversy

See also **GALILEO AND NEWTON** under **THE SCIENTIFIC REVOLUTION** under **EARLY MODERN EUROPE** in **WORLD HISTORY AND CURRENT AFFAIRS**

0-520-06662-6 CALIFORNIA PB $16.00

Pietro **Redondi**

Galileo: Heretic

"Redondi places before us not just Galileo but the entire milieu that surrounded the dispute of the 'new science' during a crucial twenty-year period of the 17th century"—Italo Calvino

See also **GALILEO AND NEWTON** under **THE SCIENTIFIC REVOLUTION** under **EARLY MODERN EUROPE** in **WORLD HISTORY AND CURRENT AFFAIRS**

TRANSLATED BY RAYMOND ROSENTHAL

0-691-08451-3 PRINCETON PB $49.50

0-691-02426-X PRINCETON PB $17.95

Jerome J. **Langford**

Galileo, Science, and the Church

The Galileo affair didn't end with his condemnation in 1633; it became the crucible for our understanding of the development of modern science. But Langford argues that most writing about it misses the point. He offers an account of the circumstances and consequences of the trial, and makes clear how much it still has to teach us about freedom and authority. "[Langford] has provided us with an account of enduring value"—Thomas P. McTighe

0-472-09510-2 MICHIGAN PB $32.50
0-472-06510-6 MICHIGAN PB $15.95

Michael **Segre**

In the Wake of Galileo

A thoroughgoing and original account of Galileo's intellectual milieu, especially informative on the subject of the great astronomer's disciples and followers

FOREWARD BY I. BERNARD COHEN

0-8135-1700-1 RUTGERS $35.00
0-8135-1701-X RUTGERS PB $14.00

Stephen Hawking: A Life in Science

A readable, compelling biography of the physicist whom many feel to be Einstein's successor. "A fascinating story…with the added plus that White and Gribbin are able to translate Hawking's bestselling *A Brief History Of Time* for those who…found it incomprehensible" —*Kirkus Reviews*

0-452-26988-1 PLUME PB $12.95

Gale **Christianson**

In the Presence of the Creator: Isaac Newton and His Times

See also **GALILEO AND NEWTON** under **THE SCIENTIFIC REVOLUTION** under **EARLY MODERN EUROPE** in **WORLD HISTORY AND CURRENT AFFAIRS**

0-02-905190-8 FREE PRESS $29.95

Richard S. **Westfall**

The Life of Isaac Newton

A condensed version of Westfall's classic biography *Never at Rest*. "That this is the best biography of Newton is easily and truthfully said..."—*New Scientist*

0-521-47737-9 CAMBRIDGE PB $12.95

Never At Rest: A Biography of Isaac Newton

A masterful rendering, from his absorption with Christian chronology to his tenure as master of the British Mint

See also **GALILEO AND NEWTON** under **THE SCIENTIFIC REVOLUTION** under **EARLY MODERN EUROPE** in **WORLD HISTORY AND CURRENT AFFAIRS**

0-521-27435-4 CAMBRIDGE PB $36.95

Peter **Goodchild**

Robert Oppenheimer: Shatterer of Worlds

0-88064-021-9 FROMM PB $16.95

Alice Kimball **Smith** & Charles **Weiner**, editors

Robert Oppenheimer: Letters and Recollections

FOREWORD BY MARTIN J. SHERWIN

0-8047-2620-5 STANFORD PB $14.95

Rudolf **Peierls**

Bird of Passage: Recollections of a Physicist

"Anybody with some interest in the way scientists live, feel and think, should read this book. They will be richly rewarded and entertained" —*Times Higher Education Supplement*

0-691-02416-2 PRINCETON PB $16.95

Walter **Moore**

The Life of Erwin Schrödinger

0-521-46934-1 CAMBRIDGE PB $11.95

Claudio G. **Segrè**

Atoms, Bombs, and Eskimo Kisses: A Memoir of Father and Son

0-670-86307-6 VIKING $23.95

Emilio **Segrè**

A Mind Always in Motion: The Autobiography of Emilio Segrè

0-520-07627-3 CALIFORNIA $30.00

William **Lanouette** & others

Genius in the Shadows: A Biography of Leo Szilard, the Man Behind the Bomb

Szilard's copious brainstorms made possible information theory, the atomic bomb, and Enrico Fermi's patent for CP-1. But General Groves, head of the Manhattan Project, considered him a "pushy Jew" and tried to get him interned during the war. "*Genius in the Shadows* leaves no doubt that this bizarre Hungarian was one of the great minds of our time, of any time…Mind-blowing Szilardian anecdotes make this one of the most entertaining stories in recent years" —Dick Teresi, *NY Times Book Review*

See also **BIOGRAPHIES** under **US HISTORY, 1945 TO THE PRESENT** in **HISTORY OF THE AMERICAS**

0-226-46888-7 CHICAGO PB $18.95

Astronomy

Meir **Degani**

Astronomy Made Simple

0-385-08854-X DOUBLEDAY PB $12.00

William **Liller** & Ben **Mayer**

The Cambridge Astronomy Guide: An Introduction to Practical Astronomy

For amateur photographers and astronomists

0-521-39915-7 CAMBRIDGE PB $22.95

Bernard **Lovell** & F. Graham **Smith**

Pathways to the Universe

A rich introduction with 70 black-and-white photos and 100 line drawings

0-521-32004-6 CAMBRIDGE $33.95

Patrick **Moore**

1996 Yearbook of Astronomy

An annual summary of findings and a schedule of what the next year will bring to astronomers, with monthly star charts for both hemispheres. This is the 27th edition of a "must" for both amateur and professional astronomers.

0-333-63702-X MCCLELLAND & STEWART PB $24.99

The Solar System

John **Brandt** & Robert **Chapman**

Introduction to Comets

0-521-27218-1 CAMBRIDGE PB $28.95

Andrew **Chaikin** & J. Kelley **Beatty**, editors

The New Solar System

INTRODUCTION BY CARL SAGAN

0-933346-55-7 SKY $39.95

Robert **Dodd**

Thunderstorms and Shooting Stars

"An excellent, up-to-date discussion of the nature and origin of meteorites"—*New Scientist*

0-674-89138-4 HARVARD PB $12.95

James **Elliot** & Richard **Kerr**

Rings: Discoveries from Galileo to Voyager

0-262-55013-X MIT PB $9.95

Kathleen **Mark**

Meteorite Craters

A nontechnical history of how scientists came to recognize craters as the result of meteoritic impact

0-8165-1568-9 ARIZONA PB $19.95

Harry Y. **McSween**, Jr.

Meteorites and Their Parent Planets

A comprehensive and readable introduction

0-521-32431-9 CAMBRIDGE $34.95

John **Postgate**

The Outer Reaches of Life

0-521-44010-6 CAMBRIDGE $23.95
0-521-55873-5 CAMBRIDGE PB $10.95

Fred **Whipple**

Orbiting the Sun: Planets and Satellites of the Solar System

0-674-64126-4 HARVARD PB $10.95

Laurel **Wilkening**

Comets

0-8165-0769-4 ARIZONA $51.00

Stars

Robert **Jastrow**

Red Giants and White Dwarfs

0-393-85004-8 NORTON PB $11.95

Ken **Croswell**

The Alchemy of the Heavens: Searching for Meaning in the Milky Way

"An excellent synthesis of current knowledge on the Milky Way, made all the more interesting by first-hand interviews"—*Astronomy*

0-385-47214-5 ANCHOR PB........................$14.95

Edward **Harrison**

Darkness At Night: A Riddle of the Universe

Why don't the billions of stars out there make the night sky bright as day? "It is refreshing to consider that so grand a matter as the boundaries of the universe can be investigated with only the unaided human eye"—Timothy Ferris

0-674-19271-0 HARVARD PB........................$12.95

In the twentieth century we have grown accustomed to the idea that our vision slices through space and time. When we gaze at the night sky, looking far out in space, we are fully aware that we see the apparitions of long ago. We find it difficult to understand why Descartes and other philosophers once viewed with alarm the prospect of slicing space and time together.

DARKNESS AT NIGHT: A RIDDLE OF THE UNIVERSE

Rudolf **Kippenhahn**

One Hundred Billion Suns: The Birth, Life, and Death of the Stars

TRANSLATED BY JEAN STEINBERG

0-691-08781-4 PRINCETON PB........................$16.95

Will **Kyselka** & Ray **Lanternman**

North Star to Southern Cross

0-8248-0419-8 HAWAII PB........................$7.95

Laurence **Marschall**

The Supernova Story

All about 1987A and earlier supernovas. "Everything you want to know about supernovas is here"—Heinz Pagels

0-306-42955-1 PLENUM........................$22.95

Jean-Pierre **Verdet**

The Sky: Mystery, Magic, and Myth

0-8109-2873-6 ABRAMS PB........................$12.95

Galaxies

Richard **Berendzen**

Man Discovers the Galaxies

0-231-05826-8 COLUMBIA........................$55.00
0-231-05827-6 COLUMBIA PB........................$18.00

Bart **Bok** & Priscilla **Bok**

The Milky Way

0-674-57503-2 HARVARD........................$41.50

Alan **Dressler**

Voyage to the Great Attractor: A Journey Through Intergalactic Space

"A riveting account of a major advance in astronomy by one of the key participants. Dressler does for astronomy what James D. Watson's *The Double Helix* did for molecular biology"—*Kirkus Reviews*

0-394-58899-1 KNOPF........................$25.00

Roman **Smoluchowski**, editor

The Galaxy and the Solar System

0-8165-0982-4 ARIZONA........................$41.00

R. Brent **Tully**

Nearby Galaxies Catalog

A companion to the *Atlas of Nearby Galaxies*, providing information on the 2,367 galaxies mapped in the atlas, including positions, morphological descriptions, sizes, luminosities, red shifts, and characteristics of each galaxy's environment

0-521-35299-1 CAMBRIDGE........................$65.00

R. Brent **Tully** & Richard J. **Fisher**

Nearby Galaxies Atlas

0-521-30136-X CAMBRIDGE PB........................$79.95

James **Wray**

Color Atlas of Galaxies

0-521-32236-7 CAMBRIDGE........................$99.95

The Universe and Cosmology

"The most incomprehensible thing about the Universe is that it is comprehensible."
—Albert Einstein

John D. **Barrow**

The Origin of the Universe

"As entertaining as any pure puzzle book"
—*Washington Post*

0-465-05354-8 BASIC........................$20.00

William **Calvin**

The River That Flows Uphill: A Journey from the Big Bang to the Big Brain

The log of an expedition down the Colorado River through the Grand Canyon

0-87156-719-9 SIERRA CLUB PB........................$18.00

Eric **Chaisson**

Cosmic Dawn: The Origins of Matter and Life

0-393-30587-2 NORTON PB........................$10.95

Stuart **Clark**

Stars and Atoms: From The Big Bang to the Solar System

A well-illustrated and clearly written account of current knowledge about the universe

0-19-521087-5 OXFORD........................$35.00

Nathan **Cohen**

Gravity's Lens: Views of the New Cosmology

Features 100 black-and-white photos and two four-page color inserts. An imaginative history of astronomy, methods of observing the universe, and the universe's future

0-471-63282-1 WILEY........................$19.95

James **Cornell**, editor

Bubbles, Voids and Bumps in Time: The New Cosmology

A "state of the universe" report from six leading cosmologists

0-521-42673-1 CAMBRIDGE PB........................$17.95

Philip M. **Dauber** & Richard A. **Muller**

The Three Big Bangs: Cosmic Crashes, Exploding Stars, and the Creation of the Universe

0-201-40752-3 ADDISON-WESLEY........................$25.00

Paul **Davies**

The Last Three Minutes: The Latest Thinking About the Ultimate Fate of the Universe

On Davies's *The Mind of God*: "The most powerful mind-bending experience you can have without violating the controlled substances act"—*Washington Post*

0-465-04892-7 BASIC........................$20.00

P.C. **Davies**

The Accidental Universe

0-521-28692-1 CAMBRIDGE PB........................$17.95

Timothy **Ferris**

Coming of Age in the Milky Way

"An exhilarating, wide-ranging journey that takes us from the shores of the Mediterranean, where the second-century astronomer Claudius Ptolemy fashioned his creaky celestial spheres, to modern-day research institutes, where theorists contemplate this and other universes bubbling out of a quantum vacuum"—*NY Times*

0-385-26326-0 ANCHOR PB........................$12.95

The Red Limit: The Search For the Edge of the Universe

INTRODUCTION BY CARL SAGAN

0-688-01836-X MORROW PB........................$12.95

Martin **Gardner**

The New Ambidextrous Universe: Symmetry and Asymmetry, from Mirror Reflections to Superstrings

A revised edition of a deservedly popular work exploring some of the most fascinating paradoxes of science and mathematics

0-7167-2092-2 FREEMAN PB........................$19.95

Edward **Harrison**

Cosmology: The Science of the Universe

0-521-22981-2 CAMBRIDGE........................$47.95

Nancy **Hathaway**

The Friendly Guide to the Universe: A Down-To-Earth Tour of Space, Time, and the Wonders of the Cosmos

Part of a refreshing series that takes the world's great discoveries very seriously indeed *and* maintains a sense of humor. Covers concepts of the major theorists, from Kepler to Hawking; debunks myths and other outdated frou-frou about

the heavens, provides a time-line history of the universe, and explains what a quark actually is
0-670-83944-2 VIKING $23.95

Michael D. **Lemonick**
The Light At the Edge of the Universe: Leading Cosmologists on the Brink of a Scientific Revolution
Cosmology, Lemonick says, remains "pretheoretic…like geology before tectonics, or physics before Newton—just a collection of facts." Yet theories do abound, and the author guides us through all of them. A fascinating tour. "Immensely informative—and lots of fun" —*Kirkus Reviews*
0-691-00158-8 PRINCETON PB $12.95

Patrick **Moore** & Iain **Nicolson**, editors
The Universe
0-02-922110-2 MACMILLAN $60.00

John **North**
Astronomy & Cosmology
A volume in Norton's distinguished *History of Science* series, richly detailed and authoritative, ranging from prehistoric times to the present, and including a discussion of the influence of astrology on early developments in the field
0-393-03656-1 NORTON $35.00
0-393-31193-7 NORTON PB $18.95

Barry **Parker**
Creation: The Story of the Origin and Evolution of the Universe
"A detailed look at the universe in all its mind-boggling aspects as well as personal glimpses of some of the people who have built our understanding"—Arno Penzias
0-306-42952-7 PLENUM $22.95

Einstein's Dream: The Search For a Unified Theory of the Universe
0-306-42343-X PLENUM $19.95

Richard **Preston**
First Light: The Search for the Edge of the Universe
Preston's recent bestseller, *The Hot Zone*, was a thrilling masterpiece of scientific reporting. Here, he makes equally exciting the efforts of astronomers at the Palomar Observatory to peer at the farthest edges of space and thereby solve the riddle of the creation of the universe. "The best popular account of astronomy in action" —*Kirkus Reviews*
0-679-44969-8 RANDOM HOUSE $24.00

Joseph **Silk**
The Big Bang: The Creation and Evolution of the Universe
0-7167-1997-5 FREEMAN $27.95
0-7167-1812-X FREEMAN PB $17.95

James **Trefil**
The Dark Side of the Universe: Searching For the Outer Limits of the Cosmos
An account of efforts to find the dark matter that many scientists think makes up at least 90 percent of the universe
0-385-26212-4 ANCHOR PB $10.95

Astronomical Observation

Bob **Berman**
Secrets of the Night Sky
0-688-12727-4 MORROW $23.00

Mark R. **Chartrand III**
The Audubon Society Field Guide to the Night Sky
A book to help all star gazers find and identify every major natural celestial object visible in the Northern Hemisphere. Sky charts are accompanied on the facing pages with a detailed map. 88 of the major constellations are labeled and keyed by page number to the text. 410 illustrations provide beautiful astrophotographic images of the celestial bodies
0-679-40852-5 KNOPF PB $19.00

Henry S. F. **Cooper**, Jr.
The Evening Star: Venus Observed
The veteran science and space reporter for the *New Yorker* tracks the Magellan spacecraft that has been mapping Venus since 1980. In vivid, accessible prose he lets us in on the latest mysteries and secrets of our almost identical planetary sister
0-374-15000-1 FS&G $22.00

Richard **Hirsh**
Glimpsing an Invisible Universe: The Emergence of X-Ray Astronomy
0-521-25121-4 CAMBRIDGE $65.00
0-521-31232-9 CAMBRIDGE PB $21.95

K. **Krisciunas**
Astronomical Centers of the World
Observatories ancient and recent, their major accomplishments, and the astronomers who made them famous
0-521-30278-1 CAMBRIDGE $34.95

James **Muirden**, editor
The Sky Watcher's Handbook: The Expert Reference Source for the Non-Professional Astronomer
0-7167-4502-X FREEMAN $34.95

Jay **Pasachoff**
A Field Guide to the Stars and Planets
This popular and completely up-to-date field guide maps and charts the sky, predicting the best times to view the moon, planets, nebulae, and stars. The best guide to the nighttime sky—perfect for gift giving
0-395-53764-9 HOUGHTON MIFFLIN $24.95
0-395-53759-2 HOUGHTON MIFFLIN PB $16.95

Wallace **Tucker** & Riccardo **Giacconi**
The X-Ray Universe
0-674-96285-0 HARVARD $25.00

Wallace **Tucker** & Karen **Tucker**
The Cosmic Inquirers: Modern Telescopes and Their Makers
0-674-17436-4 HARVARD PB $10.95

G.L. **Verschuur**
The Invisible Universe—Revealed
0-387-96280-8 SPRINGER-VERLAG $37.95

Guides

Richard **Berry**
Discovering the Stars: Star Watching Using the Naked Eye, Binoculars, Or a Telescope
0-517-56529-3 HARMONY PB $12.95

Guy J. **Consolmagno** & Daniel M. **Davis**
Turn Left At Orion: One Hundred Night Sky Objects to See in a Small Telescope—And How to Find Them
The guidebook for beginning astronomers
0-521-48211-9 CAMBRIDGE $24.95

Heather **Couper** & Nigel **Henbest**
How the Universe Works
0-89577-576-X READER'S DIGEST $24.00

Michael **Covington**
Astrophotography For the Amateur
"An up-to-date book for the budding astrophotographer, and a reference book that should be in your library"—*Reflector*
0-521-40984-5 CAMBRIDGE PB $19.95

Peter **Duffet-Smith**
Practical Astronomy With Your Calculator
0-521-35699-7 CAMBRIDGE PB $15.95

David J. **Eicher**
The Universe from Your Backyard: A Guide to Deep-Sky Objects from Astronomy Magazine
Over 150 color and-black-and-white photos and 116 telescopic sketches accompany the text
0-913135-13-5 KALMBACK $29.95

Svend **Laustsen**
Exploring the Southern Sky: A Pictorial Atlas from the European Southern Observatory
Ninety color and 147 black-and-white photos of the southern sky, including pictures of Supernova 1987A and Halley's Comet and a four-foot panoramic poster of the Milky Way
0-387-17735-3 SPRINGER-VERLAG $59.00

J.M. Levitt & Roy K. **Marshall**
Star Maps For Beginners
0-671-79187-7 SIMON & SCHUSTER PB $10.00

David **Levy**
Variable Star Observing
Includes a seasonal guide to observing the night sky in all latitudes
0-521-32113-1 CAMBRIDGE $27.95

James **Muirden**
How to Use an Astronomical Telescope
0-671-66404-2 SIMON & SCHUSTER PB $14.00

Fred W. **Price**
The Moon Observer's Handbook
What to look for, how to make observations, and how to record them
0-521-33500-0 CAMBRIDGE $42.50

I. **Ridpath** & W. **Tirion**
The Monthly Sky Guide
Help for beginning gazers in finding their way around the night sky
0-521-44865-4 CAMBRIDGE PB $14.95

Brad **Wallis** & Robert **Provin**
A Manual of Advanced Celestial Photography
This technical handbook for the serious astrophotographer includes detailed discussions of photographic optics, instrument design, techniques at the telescope, films and developers, advanced darkroom methods, sensitometry and film hyper-sensitization, and more
0-521-25553-8 CAMBRIDGE $49.95

Space Exploration

For related reading, see HISTORY OF SCIENCE AND TECHNOLOGY under TOPICS IN AMERICAN STUDIES in HISTORY OF THE AMERICAS

Henry S. **Cooper**, Jr.
Before Lift-Off: The Space Shuttle Crew
0-8018-3524-0 JOHNS HOPKINS $18.50

Ben **Finney** & Eric **Jones**, editors
Interstellar Migration and the Human Experience
Twenty-five scholars examine the technical and human side of our future beyond Earth. "New and important in bringing together for the first time the point of view of astronomers, space scientists, anthropologists, and humanists" —Freeman Dyson
0-520-05898-4 CALIFORNIA PB $16.00

Nigel **Henbest**
The Planets: A Guided Tour of Our Solar System Through the Eyes of America's Space Probes
Beautifully lighted and detailed photos of the nine planets, with their moons and satellites, by NASA probes: Mars's canyons, the volcanoes on Jupiter's moon, cloud formation on Neptune. "A pleasure tour"—*Publishers Weekly*
0-670-83384-3 PENGUIN PB $35.00

Harry **Hurt**, III
For All Mankind: Twenty-Four Men Went to the Moon, This Is Their Story
Based on interviews with Apollo astronauts
0-87113-351-2 ATLANTIC MONTHLY PB $12.95

Claus **Jensen**
No Downlink: A Dramatic Narrative about the Challenger Incident and Our Time
See also **THE REAGAN YEARS** under **US HISTORY, 1945 TO THE PRESENT** in **HISTORY OF THE AMERICAS**
0-374-12036-6 FS&G $25.00

Kevin **Kelley**, editor
The Home Planet
One hundred and fifty color photographs of Earth taken from space, selected from Soviet and American archives, with text by astronauts from 18 countries, adapted from interviews and air-to-ground transmissions
0-201-55095-4 ADDISON-WESLEY PB $22.95

Eugene F. **Mallove** & Gregory L. **Matloff**
The Starflight Handbook: A Pioneer's Guide to Interstellar Travel
A scholarly but accessible examination of the future of space travel. This is the cutting edge examined, from magnetic/electric scoops to solar sails. Extensively illustrated, and containing tables and charts for clarification of the principles discussed
0-471-61912-4 WILEY $29.95

The potential long duration of early interstellar voyages creates a glaring problem that has no parallel in human experience: A relatively slow vehicle dispatched too soon may be passed, long before it reaches its destination, by a more advanced technology, higher speed craft sent out much later. Would-be explorers of the New World may have been deterred by fears of sea monsters and falling off the edge of a flat Earth, but they did not hold back while anticipating a more efficient ride on the Queen Mary or hopping across the drink on the supersonic Concorde.
—*Eugen F. Mallove*
THE STARFLIGHT HANDBOOK: A PIONEER'S GUIDE TO INTERSTELLAR TRAVEL

Patrick **Moore**
Mission to the Planets: The Illustrated Story of Man's Exploration of the Solar System
Beginning with the first moon probe in 1959, Moore recounts in rich derail the steps in human exploration of the solar system
0-393-02872-0 NORTON $24.95

Harry L. **Shipman**
Humans in Space: 21st Century Frontiers
Prospects for the future
0-306-43171-8 PLENUM $22.95

Carl **Sagan**
Pale Blue Dot: A Vision of the Human Future in Space
"Mr. Sagan persuasively presents as the fundamental achievement of space science and exploration humanity's changing perception of the universe and, consequently, of itself"
—*NY Times Book Review*
0-679-76486-0 RANDOM HOUSE PB $22.00

Extraterrestrial Life

Joseph **Angelo**
The Extraterrestrial Encyclopedia: Our Search For Life in Outer Space
Four hundred entries cover recent information on such subjects as astrobiology, black holes, interstellar travel, robotics in space, and Voyagers I and II
0-8160-2276-3 FACTS ON FILE $40.00

Ronald N. **Bracewell**
The Galactic Club: Life in Outer Space
0-393-95022-0 NORTON PB $3.95

Paul **Davies**
Are We Alone?: Philosophical Implications of the Discovery of Extraterrestrial Life
0-465-00418-0 BASIC $20.00
0-465-00419-9 BASIC PB $12.00

History of Astronomy

Anthony **Aveni**
Conversing with the Planets: How Science and Myth Invented the Cosmos
An absorbing instance of "astronomical anthropology": the study of how cultures have viewed the stars across history. Aveni analyzes cosmic beliefs from the Mayans to today. Our view of the cosmos is not a matter of "scientific truth," but rather a long "conversation with the planets" dependent on time and belief. "Aveni writes with a mastery and polish that are wonderfully accessible"
—*NY Times Book Review*
1-56836-021-5 KODANSHA PB $14.00

Skywatchers of Ancient Mexico
Archaeoastronomy of Mesoamerica; illustrated
See also **MEXICO AND CENTRAL AMERICA: GENERAL WORKS** under **NATIVE AMERICAN CULTURES: CENTRAL AND SOUTH AMERICA** in **HISTORY OF THE AMERICAS**
0-292-77578-4 TEXAS PB $24.95

Donald **Goldsmith**
The Astronomers
An engaging illustrated overview of the rise of astronomy, published in conjunction with the public television series
0-312-09245-8 ST. MARTIN'S PB $14.95

Evan **Hadingham**

Early Man and the Cosmos

0-8027-0745-9 WALKER $22.50
0-8061-1919-5 OKLAHOMA PB $19.95

D.B. **Herrmann**

The History of Astronomy from Herschel to Hertzsprung

0-521-25733-6 CAMBRIDGE $34.95

Robert **Jastrow**

God & the Astronomers

A new edition of a classic first published in 1918, with an added section giving religious viewpoints on the significance of astronomical discovery

0-393-85005-6 NORTON $18.95

Rocky **Kolb**

Blind Watchers of the Sky: The People and Ideas That Shaped Our View of the Universe

0-201-48992-9 ADDISON-WESLEY $25.00

E.C. **Krupp**

Echoes of the Ancient Skies: The Astronomy of Lost Civilizations

0-19-508801-8 OXFORD PB $17.95

Thomas **Kuhn**

The Copernican Revolution

A outstanding account of the impact of the revolution in astronomy by the author of *The Structure of Scientific Revolutions*

See also **THE SCIENTIFIC REVOLUTION** under **HISTORY OF SCIENCE AND TECHNOLOGY** under **SCIENCE AND TECHNOLOGY**

See also **THE SCIENTIFIC REVOLUTION** under **EARLY MODERN EUROPE**

0-674-17103-9 HARVARD PB $12.95

Albert **Van Helden**

Measuring the Universe

Dimensions from Aristarchus to Halley

0-226-84882-5 CHICAGO PB $12.95

Biography

Joseph **Ashbrook**

The Astronomical Scrapbook: Skywatchers, Pioneers, and Seekers in Astronomy

0-521-30045-2 SKY $34.95

Gale E. **Christiansen**

This Wild Abyss: The Story of the Men Who Made Modern Astronomy

0-02-905660-8 FREE PRESS PB $15.95

Gale E. **Christianson**

Edwin Hubble: Mariner of the Nebulae

0-374-14660-8 FS&G $27.50
0-974-14660-8 FS&G $25.00

John **Banville**

Kepler

See also **THE MIDDLE GENERATION** under **20TH-CENTURY BRITISH AND IRISH FICTION** in **LITERATURE OF THE BRITISH ISLES**

0-679-74370-7 VINTAGE PB $12.00

Jean-Pierre **Maury**

Newton: The Father of Modern Astronomy

0-8109-2835-3 ABRAMS PB $12.95

Reference

Jean **Audouze** & Guy **Israel**

The Cambridge Atlas of Astronomy

Updated to include the 1986 appearance of Halley's Comet, Voyager's encounter in the same year with Uranus, 1987A Supernova, and more. Over 1,100 photos and illustrations

0-521-43438-6 CAMBRIDGE $90.00

McGraw-Hill

The McGraw-Hill Encyclopedia of Astronomy

Over 200 alphabetically arranged articles covering the latest advances, discoveries, models, and theories, and topics ranging from astronomical spectroscopy and the Big Bang theory to planetary physics, space probes, and stellar evolution

0-07-045314-4 MCGRAW HILL $75.50

Jacqueline **Mitton**

A Concise Dictionary of Astronomy

A compact yet comprehensive reference, clearly written and free of technical jargon

0-19-853967-3 OXFORD $30.00

Patrick **Moore**

Atlas of the Universe

Aimed at the lay reader, and including guidance and tips for the home astronomer

0-528-83704-4 RAND MCNALLY $29.95

Colin A. **Ronan**, editor

The Universe Explained: The Earth-Dweller's Guide to the Mysteries

"Drawing on telescopes, satellites, computer imagery, and intriguing current theories, this book examines the interlinked relationships of the cosmos. Ronan, a noted astronomy writer, has written a book that explains the marvel and mystery of the universe for all ages"—*Booklist*

0-8050-3488-9 HOLT $35.00

Carl **Sagan**

Cosmos

0-345-33135-4 BALLANTINE PB $5.99

Carl Sagan

Chemistry

There are few books on chemistry for the general reader. That situation, of course, could change—chaos theory on the best-seller lists today, perhaps quantum chemistry tomorrow. Biochemistry, on the other hand, is a popular topic; for books in this area see Life Sciences.

American Chemical Society Staff

Chemistry in Context: Applying Chemistry to Society

0-697-21951-8 BROWN PB $15.00

Leonard A. **Ford**

Chemical Magic, 2nd Edition

REVISED BY E.WINSTON GRUNDMEIER

0-486-67628-5 DOVER PB $5.95

Robert **Gardner**

Famous Experiments You Can Do

Allows older children and teenagers to duplicate (or at least approximate) classic experiments by celebrated figures like Faraday, William Harvey and Sir Isaac Newton

0-531-10883-X FRANKLIN WATTS $20.70

Richard **Graham**

The Problems of Chemistry

0-19-219191-8 OXFORD $19.95

Fred C. **Hess**

Chemistry Made Simple

REVISED BY ARTHUR L. THOMAS

0-385-18850-1 DOUBLEDAY PB $12.00

Roald **Hoffman**

The Same and Not the Same

0-231-10138-4 COLUMBIA $34.95

Rolf **Huisgen**

The Adventure Playground of Mechanisms & Novel Reactions

0-8412-1832-3 AMERICAN CHEMICAL SOCIETY ...$24.95

Muriel **Mandell**

Simple Kitchen Experiements: Learning Science with Everyday Foods

"For children from age 9 to 12. Mandell's raided the refrigerator and the pantry for the stuff of the experiments in this neat little book, which turns the kitchen into a chem lab with food as the focus. There's occasionally some chopping or cooking involved, but the experiments—running the gamut from mapping taste zones on the tongue to degassing beans—should be easy for middle-schoolers to manage"—*Booklist*

0-8069-8415-5 STERLING PB ...$4.95

B. **Parker**

Invisible Matter & the Fate of the Universe

A luminous study exploring the furthest frontiers of scientific inquiry, where chemistry, biology and physics overlap to reveal implications for the ultimate fate of the cosmos. "Absorbing, often astonishing"—*Booklist*

0-306-43294-3 PLENUM ...$23.50

Richard **Saferstein**

Criminalistics: An Introduction to Forensic Science, 5th Edition

0-13-307844-2 PRENTICE HALL ...$71.00

Carl H. **Snyder**

The Extraordinary Chemistry of Ordinary Things, 2nd Edition

A college-level text with an emphasis on the chemistry of everyday life

0-471-31042-5 WILEY ...$74.29

Textbooks

Molly M. **Bloomfield**

Chemistry & the Living Organism, 5th Edition

The latest edition of a widely used textbook, surveying chemistry for those interested in health-related fields

0-471-51292-3 WILEY ...$66.00

Dorothy M. **Feigl** & others

Foundations of Life, 3rd Edition

A comprehensive introductory textbook offering basic surveys of biochemistry as well as general and organic chemistry

0-02-336737-7 MACMILLAN ...$71.00
0-02-352845-1 MACMILLAN PB ...$34.58

John W. **Hill**

Chemistry For Changing Times

0-02-355070-8 MACMILLAN ...$61.00

Elizabeth **Kean** & Catherine **Middlecamp**

How to Survive (& Even Excel In) General Chemistry

A useful guide for students intimidated by the field

0-07-034033-1 MCGRAW HILL PB ...$12.95

Linus **Pauling** & Peter **Pauling**

Chemistry

The latest edition of a standard textbook

0-486-65622-5 DOVER PB ...$19.95

Ted **Goertzel** & Ben **Goertzel**

Linus Pauling: A Life in Science and Politics

Pauling's insights in applying quantum mechanics to complex molecules played a pivotal role in the development of modern chemistry and garnered him two Nobel Prizes. But Pauling's achievements reached far beyond the lab; he was also a political activist who heroically railed against McCarthyism and successfully campaigned to stop nuclear testing

0-465-00672-8 BASIC ...$27.50

There is a striking contrast between Pauling's scientific thinking, which was innovative and highly complex, and his political thought, which was simple and predictable. His political speeches were similar to those being given by thousands of other New Left radicals at the time. Even his examples and illustrations were constantly used in the rhetoric of the time. In his scientific work, he sought out difficult and unresolved problems. In his political rhetoric, he avoided the difficult issues.
LINUS PAULING: A LIFE IN SCIENCE AND POLITICS

Linus Pauling

Karen **Timberlake**

Chemistry, Fifth Edition

0-06-046696-0 HARPERCOLLINS ...$67.50
0-06-046577-8 HARPERCOLLINS PB ...$22.95

Reference

P.W. **Atkins**

The Periodic Kingdom

Oxford professor and acclaimed chemistry writer Atkins takes us on a journey through the periodic table, and from there, into the very nature of matter. Cleverly arranged like a travel guide, this book manages to be readable while introducing us not only to the fascinations of the elements, but to the history of chemistry

0-465-07265-8 BASIC ...$20.00

John **Daintith**

The Facts on File Dictionary of Chemistry

0-8160-1866-9 FACTS ON FILE ...$24.95
0-8160-2367-0 FACTS ON FILE PB ...$12.95

D.W. **Sharp**

The Penguin Dictionary of Chemistry, 2nd Edition

A capacious reference source, useful to the expert as well as the layperson

0-14-051232-2 PENGUIN PB ...$14.95

History of Chemistry

Cathy **Cobb** & Harold **Goldwhite**

Creations of Fire: Chemistry's Lively History from Alchemy to the Atomic Age

0-306-45087-9 PLENUM ...$28.95

Frederic L. **Holmes**

Lavoisier and the Chemistry of Life: An Exploration of Scientific Creativity

0-299-09984-9 WISCONSIN PB ...$19.50

Aaron **Ihde**

The Development of Modern Chemistry

A comprehensive history by an eminent authority

0-486-64235-6 DOVER PB ...$18.95

Bernard **Jaffee**

Crucibles: The Story of Chemistry from Ancient Alchemy to Nuclear Fission

Fourth, revised edition. Brief biographies primarily of physical chemists

0-486-23342-1 DOVER PB ...$8.95

David **Knight**

Ideas in Chemistry: A History of the Science

"Taking the view that chemistry has become today a service science, providing solutions to problems in other disciplines, Knight…recounts the transformations of the science, from occult alchemy through mechanistic materialism, experimental innovation, and other stages, to its reduced status. He emphasizes the interaction with other sciences, art, and society"
—*SciTech Book News*

0-8135-1835-0 RUTGERS ...$47.00
0-8135-1836-9 RUTGERS PB ...$18.00

J.R. **Partington**

Short History of Chemistry

0-486-65977-1 DOVER PB ...$11.95

Trevor H. **Levere**

Chemists & Chemistry in Nature & Society, 1770-1878

A collection of scholarly essays exploring the history of chemistry in England and Holland during one of its great formative epochs

0-86078-412-6 VARIORUM $89.95

Bruce **Merrifield**

Life During a Golden Age of Peptide Chemistry: The Concept & Development of Solid-Phase Peptide Synthesis

0-8412-1842-0 AM. CHEMICAL SOCIETY $34.95

John **Read**

Through Alchemy to Chemistry

1-56459-013-5 KESSINGER PB $19.95

Hugh W. **Salzburg**

From Caveman to Chemist: Circumstances & Achievements

0-8412-1786-6 AM. CHEMICAL SOCIETY $29.95
0-8412-1787-4 AM. CHEMICAL SOCIETY $14.95

Washington University Staff

Milestones in Analytical Chemistry

A collection of seminal 20th-century scientific papers, each carefully introduced, explained, and placed in its historical context

0-8412-2855-8 AM. CHEMICAL SOCIETY $74.95

Life Sciences

Until the 19th century most biologists tallied and described plants and animals, turning to philosophy and religion to explain almost everything they observed. The modern trend, by contrast, has been toward the experimental and analytical, not only in biology but in anatomy, natural history, and other fields as well.

A major landmark of modern biology was the discovery that living things are composed of large molecules. This led to the discovery of cellular respiration, energy metabolism, the functions of DNA and RNA, and the factors that promote cell growth and cancer. At the same time, geneticists created a formal explanation of how characteristics are transmitted from one generation to the next, how mutations occur, and how evolution might proceed. Neurobiologists located those regions of the brain and nervous system which are responsible for carrying out the tasks of motion, sensation, and cognition.

Many of these discoveries were made possible by the invention of new techniques. Whatever the object of study, the development of antibiotics, histological stains, the electron microscope, and X-ray crystallography permitted new and deeper observations and provided new answers to old questions.

Virology, cell biology, neurochemistry, and oncology are all younger than the century. Unfortunately, many descriptions of these disciplines are highly technical and unsuitable for the nonspecialist. Readers interested in immunology, cell biology, or embryology, for instance, are perhaps better off reading accounts of scientists who worked in those fields. The essays of such biologists as Peter Medawar, Lewis Thomas, and Stephen Jay Gould can also be highly recommended.

David **Attenborough**

The Atlas of the Living World

0-395-49481-8 HOUGHTON MIFFLIN $40.00

Adele E. **Clarke** & Joan H. **Fujimura**, editors

The Right Tools for the Job: At Work in Twentieth-Century Life Sciences

A stimulating collection of essays, each examining how scientists—esepcially biologists—actually perform the work that leads to discovery

0-691-08581-1 PRINCETON $39.50

Christian R. **De Duve**

Vital Dust: Life as A Cosmic Imperative

A Nobel-prize-winning physiologist explores the natural chemical and physical forces that produced life—yet without losing a sense of exhilarating amazement at the result

0-465-09044-3 BASIC $25.00

Manfred **Eigen** & Ruthild W. **Oswatitsch**

Steps Towards Life

A richly detailed and illuminating examination of how evolution works at the molecular level

0-19-854751-X OXFORD $35.00

Niles **Eldredge**

Dominion

The pioneering paleontologist, whose work on evolutionary theory with Stephen Jay Gould is today's accepted science, offers a startling insight into our species' cultural, as opposed to biological, adaptation. What does it mean for us to interact with the world's ecosystem, 10,000 years after we invented agriculture and stepped outside local ecosystems? Answering this question, Eldredge demonstrates, is key to our future survival

0-8050-2982-6 HOLT $25.00

Flora of North America Editorial Committee

Flora of North America

The first two of a projected 14 volumes in an already monumental series. The first volume includes an informative and wide-ranging series of introductory essays by more than twenty experts; the second covers ferns and cone-bearing plants

Volume I Introduction

0-19-505713-9 OXFORD $85.00

Volume II Ferns & Gymnosperms

See also **BOTANY** under **BIOLOGY**

0-19-508242-7 OXFORD $85.00

General Works

Connie **Barlow**

From Gaia to Selfish Genes: Selected Writings in the Life Sciences

An anthology of excerpts from the popular writings of the life sciences' leading theorists, highlighting controversies and novel contributions to contemporary research

0-262-02323-7 MIT $24.00
0-262-52178-4 MIT PB $16.00

Djerassi **Carl**

The Pill, Pygmy Chimps, and Degas' Horse

While in his 20s, Djerassi directed the small team in a Mexico City laboratory that synthesized the first steroid to become an effective birth control pill. In this eminently readable autobiography, he looks back at his life in science. "I found the first few pages so interesting that for two days I neglected my work in order to read the book from beginning to end"—Linus Pauling

0-465-05758-6 BASIC PB $14.00

William **Coleman**

Biology in the Nineteenth Century

0-521-29293-X CAMBRIDGE PB $16.95

Francis **Crick**

What Mad Pursuit: A Personal View of Scientific Discovery

"Crick…recounts his failures as well as his successes…But then the failures of a scientist of Crick's calibre are nearly as instructive as the successes"—*New Yorker*

0-465-09138-5 BASIC PB $13.00

Renato **Dulbecco**

The Design of Life

The state of the biological sciences, from a Nobel laureate and professor at the Salk Institute

0-300-04477-1 YALE PB $28.50

Francis Crick

A. Hunter **Dupree**

Asa Gray: American Botanist, Friend of Darwin

"Among the very finest scientific biographies I have read. The balance between the person and the career in science is unprecedented" —Thomas Kuhn

0-8018-3741-3 JOHNS HOPKINS PB $16.95

Mahlon **Hoagland** & Bert **Dodson**

The Way Life Works: From the Mysteries of DNA to the Miracle of Birth, Everything You Need to Know About the Way Life Grows, Develops, Reproduces and Gets By

In the tradition of *The Way Things Work*, this is a unique guide to the physical mechanics of life. From DNA to evolution, viruses to humans, this encyclopedic volume covers the variety of life in what amounts to a testament to the wondrous diversity of living forms

0-8129-2020-1 TIMES BOOKS $35.00

John **Janovy**, Jr.

On Becoming a Biologist

0-8032-7586-2 NEBRASKA PB $9.00

Ingrid **Johnson**

Why Can't You Tickle Yourself: And Other Bodily Curiosities

Can identical twins fool a bloodhound? How much valium would you have to take to equal the relaxant power of a single orgasm? These are among the many funny and fascinating questions that Johnson *(Why Do Clocks Run Clockwise?, Imponderables)* tackles in her new, highly entertaining book. "A wonderfully clever way of learning how your body works. I wish there were more books like this"—Dr. Frank Field, Senior Health and Science Editor, CBS

0-446-39395-9 WARNER PB $8.99

Elizabeth B. **Keeney**

The Botanizers: Amateur Scientists in Nineteenth-Century America

How botany, in the 19th century largely a hobby for avid amateurs, became a mature and exacting science

0-8078-2046-6 NORTH CAROLINA $37.50

Evelyn Fox **Keller**

A Feeling For the Organism: The Life and Work of Barbara McClintock

The Nobel Prize-winning geneticist who upset conventional wisdom by demonstrating that genes can spontaneously rearrange themselves

0-7167-1504-X FREEMAN PB $15.95

Stephen R. **Kellert** & Edward O. **Wilson**, editors

The Biophilia Hypothesis

1-55963-148-1 ISLAND $35.00
1-55963-147-3 ISLAND PB $17.95

R.C. **Lewontin**

Biology as Ideology: The Doctrine of DNA

A close look at how hard science is shaped and guided—sometimes very consciously—by social and political forces, and how it is packaged, often as a kind of religion, for general consumption. Lewontin shows how scientists are governed by such forces and the good work they sometimes manage in spite of it. "An important and timely book"—Stephen Jay Gould

0-06-097519-9 HARPERPERENNIAL PB $11.00

Edward **Lurie**

Louis Agassiz: A Life in Science

"By far the best work on this central figure in the history of American biology"— Stephen Jay Gould

0-8018-3743-X JOHNS HOPKINS PB $16.95

Lois **Magner**

A History of the Life Sciences

Excellent summaries of each branch of modern biology

0-8247-8942-3 MARCEL DEKKER $39.95

Ernst **Mayr**

Toward a New Philosophy of Biology: Observations of an Evolutionist

Reflections on evolutionary theory by the Harvard zoology professor

See also EVOLUTION AND THE ORIGINS OF LIFE under PALEONTOLOGY AND EVOLUTION

0-674-89666-1 HARVARD PB $18.95

Steve **Parker**

How the Body Works

0-89577-575-1 READER'S DIGEST $24.00

Erwin **Schrödinger**

What Is Life?

Schrödinger was one of the discoverers of quantum mechanics, and this is something of a classic, although much of it relates only marginally to physics. This edition also includes *Mind and Matter*

0-521-42708-8 CAMBRIDGE PB $10.95

Lewis **Thomas**

The Fragile Species

Thomas *(The Lives of a Cell, The Medusa and the Snail)* discusses such varied topics as evolutionary biology, the development of language, the therapeutic aspects of medicine, and his love for the planet Earth, "hanging there in space and so obviously alive." "What makes this book so ultimately valuable…is its wisdom. No one else writing about science and society speaks with such measured assurance and common good sense"—*Boston Globe*

0-02-054555-X COLLIER PB $10.00
0-02-054556-X MACMILLAN PB $10.00

Late Night Thoughts on Listening to Mahler's Ninth Symphony

0-14-024328-3 PENGUIN PB $10.95

John **Tyler Bonner**

Life Cycles: Reflections of an Evolutionary Biologist

"I have devoted my life to slime molds." So this fascinating book begins. And indeed, Bonner, a major participant in the development of biology as an experimental science, goes on to show how these common microscopic organisms revealed to him that living things *are* life cycles

0-691-03319-6 PRINCETON $35.00

Alexander **Rosenberg**

The Structure of Biological Science

0-521-25566-X CAMBRIDGE $75.00
0-521-27561-X CAMBRIDGE PB $22.95

Stephen **Vogel**

Vital Circuits: On Pumps, Pipes, and the Workings of Circulatory Systems

Here is everything you wanted to know about the human circulatory system explained in an…amusing vein. Using analogies such as hearing systems, balloons, and cocktail parties, Vogel tours readers through the complex network of "pipes" and "pumps" that keep the body functioning. "An elegant traversal of the whole shebang"—*Chicago Tribune.* "Leads us through the functions and regulation of heat and circulation…with extraordinary clarity and lightness of touch"—David Weatherall, *Nature*

ILLUSTRATED BY ROSEMARY ANNE CALVERT

0-19-508269-9 OXFORD PB $12.95

A. P. **Waterson** & L. **Wilkinson**

An Introduction to the History of Virology

The conceptual, experimental, and personal steps that elucidated the nature of virus particles

0-521-21917-5 CAMBRIDGE $49.95

Edward O. **Wilson**

Biophilia

Proposes that our natural affinity for life (biophilia) is the essence of our humanity and binds us to all other species. "Erudite, elegant, and poetic"—*Natural History*

See also BIOLOGY AND HUMAN BEHAVIOR under BIOLOGY

0-674-07441-6 HARVARD $23.00
0-674-07442-4 HARVARD PB $10.95

Textbooks

Karen **Arms** & Pamela **Camp**

Biology

0-03-003644-5 SAUNDERS $78.14

William **Keeton** & James **Gould**

Biological Science

0-393-96223-7 NORTON $67.95

Reference

M. **Abercrombie** & others

The New Penguin Dictionary of Biology

The latest edition of a capacious and well-illustrated reference tool, useful for both the expert and the generalist

0-14-051288-8 PENGUIN $13.95

Michael **Allaby**, editor

The Concise Oxford Dictionary of Zoology

"Some 6,000 entries…cover subjects such as animal behavior, physiology, genetics, cytology, evolution, earth history, and zoogeography. With biographical notes on important figures in the history of zoology, and reflecting the current

emphasis on ecology in the study of animals" —*SciTech Book News*
0-19-286093-3 OXFORD PB $12.95

Robert **King** & William **Stansfield**
Dictionary of Genetics
0-19-506371-6 OXFORD PB $19.95

William N. **Marchuk**
A Life Science Lexicon
A useful reference source on contemporary terminology in the health and biological sciences
0-697-12133-X BROWN PB $12.50

Peter **Medawar** & J.S. **Medawar**
Aristotle to Zoos: A Philosophical Dictionary of Biology
0-674-04537-8 HARVARD PB $12.50

Oxford University Press
Concise Dictionary of Biology
0-19-866144-4 OXFORD PB $17.95

Elizabeth **Toothill**, editor
The Facts on File Dictionary of Biology
Short and simple definitions for 31,000 common terms
0-8160-1865-0 FACTS ON FILE $24.95
0-8160-2368-9 FACTS ON FILE PB $12.95

Paleontology and Evolution

The orthodox conception of divine creation persisted in the 19th century but was increasingly challenged by conflicting evidence: the discovery of fossils of both extinct and living creatures, of strata overlaid with distinct flora, of disruptive breaks in the geological record, and of signs pointing to the Earth's immense age. Darwin's *Origin of the Species*, published in 1859, enriched these observations with insight into nature's evolutionary changes. Natural selection—the struggle among organisms for existence, and their adaptation to the environment—was the mechanism for evolution.

Paleontology and Fossils

Life has existed on Earth for at least 3.5 billion years, leaving behind an abundant fossil record as the visible trace of its grand procession. Paleontology seeks to re-create the progressive passage of life, and its practical endeavors concern the discovery of fossils and the study of the fossil record.

Paleontology embraces several disciplines, ranging from paleozoogeography to biostratigraphy, and contributes data to biomechanics, systematics, and geology. Thus, a balanced understanding of paleontology requires an overview of its principles, practices, and assumptions. Books dealing with the histories of specific fossil groups are enhanced by prior familiarity with a general text.

Perhaps the most satisfying reading in paleontology involves works that deal with fossils and with the lost ages in which magnificent creatures—now standing silent in a museum hall—once lived.

Audubon Society
The Audubon Society Field Guide to North American Fossils
0-394-52412-8 KNOPF PB $19.00

Derek E. **Briggs** & others
The Fossils of the Burgess Shale
"Although looking—as this book lets us, up close and in detail—at fossilized sponges, algae, worms, and such may not inspire another *Jurassic Park*, budding and armchair paleontologists will have a field day, even though the accompanying text is thick with technical talk"—*Booklist*
PHOTOGRAPHED BY CHIP CLARK
1-56098-364-7 SMITHSONIAN $39.95

Gerard **Case**
A Pictorial Guide to Fossils
0-89464-678-8 KRIEGER $65.63
0-89464-713-X KRIEGER PB $47.78

Lowell **Dingus**
Next of Kin: Great Halls of the American Museum of Natural History
Celebrating the renovation of the fossil halls at the American Museum of Natural History, and exploring the museum's enormous insights into the evolution of animal life, this splendidly illustrated volume is the first authoritative guide to the collection. From the smallest eggs to the mighty Barosaurus, this is a tour through the greatest fossil exhibit in the world by its chief paleontologist
0-8478-1929-9 RIZZOLI $40.00
0-8478-1992-2 RIZZOLI PB $42.00

Carroll **Fenton** & Mildred **Fenton**
The Fossil Book
A record of prehistoric life with over 1500 illustrations
0-486-29371-8 DOVER PB $29.95

Richard **Fortey**
Fossils: The Key to the Past
A well-illustrated practical guide for amateur fossil hunters, emphasizing where and how to find fossils and how to identify them
0-674-31136-1 HARVARD PB $18.95

Stephen Jay **Gould**
Bully For Brontosaurus: More Reflections in Natural History
A collection of 35 of Gould's most recent essays, covering everything from Kiwi eggs to a single-chromosomed ant
0-393-02961-1 NORTON $22.95
0-393-30857-X NORTON PB $13.95

Wonderful Life: The Burgess Shale and the Nature of History
Accepted classifications of the Cambrian creatures preserved in the Burgess Shale—a major fossil find discovered in British Columbia in 1909—were challenged in the '70s by scientists at Cambridge University, leading to an upheaval in fundamental theories of evolutionary development. For Stephen Jay Gould, the diversity found in the Burgess Shale provides important evidence for the improbability of human evolution. A fascinating book on the wonder and precariousness of life
0-393-02705-8 NORTON $19.95
0-393-30700-X NORTON PB $11.95

Finally, if you will accept my argument that contingency is not only resolvable and important, but also fascinating in a special sort of way, then the Burgess not only reverses our general ideas about the source of pattern—it also fills us with a new kind of amazement (also a *frisson* for the improbability of the event) at the fact that humans ever evolved at all. We came *this close* (put your thumb about a millimeter away from your index finger), thousands and thousands of times, to erasure by the veering of history down another sensible channel. Replay the tape a million times from a Burgess beginning, and I doubt that anything like *Homo sapiens* would ever evolve again. It is, indeed, a wonderful life.
WONDERFUL LIFE: THE BURGESS SHALE AND THE NATURE OF HISTORY

Björn **Kurten**
How to Deep-Freeze a Mammoth
0-231-05978-7 COLUMBIA $25.00

Our Earliest Ancestors
Respected paleontologist Kurten looks ahead in the evolutionary process by looking back via molecular biology and DNA sampling of our primitive ancestors. His extrapolations on what humans will look like in the distant future make for facinating reading. Fully illustrated. "One of the finest paleontologists of our times, Björn Kurten is a marvel"—Stephen Jay Gould
0-231-08061-1 COLUMBIA $24.50

David **Lambert**
A Field Guide to Prehistoric Life
An excellent introductory book that includes over 500 illustrations, maps, and charts
0-8160-1125-7 FACTS ON FILE $25.95
0-8160-1389-6 FACTS ON FILE PB $14.95

Url **Lanham**
The Bone Hunters: The Heroic Age of Paleontology in the American West
0-486-26917-5 DOVER PB $9.95

Helmut **Mayr**
A Guide to Fossils
A useful pictorial guide to European fossils
TRANSLATED BY D. DINALAY & A. G. WINDSOR
0-691-08789-X PRINCETON $29.95

Richard **Moody**
Fossils: How to Find and Identify Over 300 Genera
A how-to guide for the amateur
0-02-063370-X MACMILLAN PB $11.95

E.W. **Nield**
Drawing and Understanding Fossils: A Theoretical and Practical Guide For Beginners, with Self-Assessment
0-08-033941-7 PERGAMON $55.00

David **Raup** & Steven **Stanley**
Principles of Paleontology
0-7167-0022-0 FREEMAN $49.95

Martin **Rudwick**
The Meaning of Fossils: Episodes in the History of Paleontology
0-226-73103-0 CHICAGO PB $17.95

Martin J.S. **Rudwick**
Scenes from Deep Time: Early Pictorial Representations of the Prehistoric World
Scientists and artists have long been creating their own conception of the prehistoric past. Rudwick traces these attempts to re-create the Earth's early ages during the 18th and 19th centuries, showing (through over 100 reproduced illustrations) how the world gradually altered its notion of time, and how scientists and artists collaborated to overthrow biblical notions of the "deep past"
0-226-73104-9 CHICAGO $49.50
0-226-73105-7 CHICAGO PB $20.00

Dr. Karl **Shuker**
Dragons: A Natural History
0-684-81443-9 SIMON & SCHUSTER $22.50

George **Simpson**
Discoverers of the Lost World
The search for evidence of long-lost South American mammals
0-300-03188-2 YALE $35.00

George G. **Simpson**
Fossils & the History of Life
0-71-671564-4 FREEMAN $32.95

Ian **Tattersall**
The Fossil Trail: How We Know What We Think We Know About Human Evolution
0-19-506101-2 OXFORD $25.00

Paleobotany
Some of the best evidence of paleo-climatic change comes from fossil wood, seeds, and pollen. The great Sahara desert once held lush tropical rain forests, as fossil wood from sites in Libya and Egypt testifies. Pollen carried into marine sedimentary basins can often be traced to land origins, making it possible to re-create an earlier ecological scenario. The development of flowers, complex pollination strategies, growth mechanisms, and water retention schemes are other clues to the mystery of our planet's past.

Henry **Andrews**
The Fossil Hunters: In Search of Ancient Plants
0-8014-1248-X CORNELL $52.50

Wilson **Stewart**
Paleobotany and the Evolution of Plants
0-521-38294-7 CAMBRIDGE $52.95

Paleoanthropology
Unlike dinosaurs, early hominids have left only isolated traces in a fragmentary record of broken skeletons and scattered cultural remains. The history of their discovery is filled with eccentric characters and contested theories. The meagerness of the human fossil record, particularly at crucial evolutionary "jumps," and the scarcity of good diagnostic material, have led to a lack of consensus on virtually every theoretical and interpretive issue.

Michael **Day**
Guide to Fossil Man
Includes more than 140 illustrations
0-226-13889-5 CHICAGO $45.00

David **Lambert**
The Field Guide to Early Man
Traces man's growth from primitive primates to modern man, with 500 illustrations, diagrams, maps, and charts
0-8160-1517-1 FACTS ON FILE $25.95
0-8160-1801-4 FACTS ON FILE PB $14.95

Richard **Leakey**
The Origin of Humankind
A fascinating proof of the origins of human physicality, social organization, culture, and personal behavior
0-465-03135-8 BASIC $20.00

Richard **Leakey** & Roger **Lewin**
Origins Reconsidered: In Search of What Makes Us Human
In an original and brave account, the most famous paleoanthropologist alive reassesses both his own and others' work. Beginning with his 1984 discovery of "the Turkana boy," a million-and-a-half-year-old skull found at Lake Turkana, and extending his research, he theorizes how we became human and what that means. While bringing into his study the larger questions of consciousness and the human will to create, Leakey provides a personal and moving account of his lifetime in science
0-385-46792-3 ANCHOR PB $14.95

Roger **Lewin**
Bones of Contention: Controversies in the Search For Human Origins
0-671-52688-X SIMON & SCHUSTER $19.95

E. C. **Pielou**
After the Ice Age: The Return of Life to Glaciated North America
In his carefully crafted narrative, Pielou makes brilliantly clear what happened in North America as the glaciers melted, forming the continent as we see it today
0-226-66811-8 CHICAGO $29.95
0-226-66812-6 CHICAGO PB $14.95

Carl **Sagan** & Ann **Druyan**
Shadows of Forgotten Ancestors
This book sets out to restore the forgotten links in our chain of being, from strings in the primordial soup to our early hominid precursors, leading us on a fascinating botanical and biological mystery tour of evolutionary development. Popular science writing at its best
0-345-38472-5 BALLANTINE PB $14.00

Robert **Wenke**
Patterns in Prehistory: Humankind's First Three Million Years
See also **GENERAL ARCHAEOLOGY** under **ARCHAEOLOGY** in **WORLD HISTORY AND CURRENT AFFAIRS**
0-19-505522-5 OXFORD PB $28.00

Dinosaurs and Other Extinct Animals
Dinosaurs ruled the Earth for well over one hundred million years, only to vanish mysteriously in an event of spectacular magnitude. Possessing an array of spikes, horns, claws, and plated armor, these reptiles of the Mesozoic Era evoke images of monumental predatory battles and of true giants lumbering through primeval swamps and forests.

Flourishing during the great ice age that lasted some two and a half million years were such extinct beasts as the giant ground sloth and giant bear, the heavily insulated wooly mammoth and wooly rhinoceros, and the spectacular saber-toothed cats.

R. McNeill **Alexander**
The Dynamics of Dinosaurs and Other Extinct Giants
How did the biggest pterosaurs, the famous flying reptiles, take off and stay in the air? How fast could the biggest dinosaurs run? Could giant marine dinosaurs leap out of the water like today's dolphins? A biomechanics expert draws on mechanical engineering, aerodynamics, and heat-exchange theory for the answers and brings dinosaurs and extinct giant mammals back to life
0-231-06666-X COLUMBIA $58.50

Alan **Charig**
A New Look At the Dinosaurs
Examines long-held ideas and offers startling alternatives
0-87196-139-3 FACTS ON FILE $29.95

Edwin **Colbert**
The Great Dinosaur Hunters and Their Discoveries
0-486-24701-5 DOVER PB $8.95

The Little Dinosaur of Ghost Ranch
0-231-08236-3 COLUMBIA $29.95

Dougal **Dixon**
The Macmillan Illustrated Encyclopedia of Dinosaurs and Prehistoric Animals
For anyone who is fascinated, or was ever fascinated, by dinosaurs, this illustrated guide offers a complete listing of over 600 extinct species. Featuring full-color art based on the latest paleontological information available and entries that detail each critter's eating, hunting, and behavioral habits, this unique volume is a well-crafted work of science as well as art
FOREWORD BY DR. MALCOLM C. MCKENNA
0-02-042981-9 MACMILLAN PB $25.00

Dougal **Dixon**, editor

The Macmillan Illustrated Encyclopedia of Dinosaurs and Prehistoric Animals

A visual Who's Who of prehistoric life with full-color paintings based on the latest paleontological discoveries

0-02-580191-0 MACMILLAN $39.95

Björn **Kurten**

Before the Indians

A look at more than three million years of vertebrate animal life in the New World before the humans arrived at the end of the ice age

0-231-06583-3 COLUMBIA PB $21.50

Jean-Guy **Michard**

The Reign of the Dinosaurs

0-8109-2808-6 ABRAMS PB $12.95

Mark **Norell** & others

Discovering Dinosaurs: In the American Museum of Natural History

0-679-43386-4 KNOPF $35.00

Kevin **Padian**, editor

The Beginnings of the Age of Dinosaurs: Faunal Change Across the Triassic-Jurassic Boundary

0-521-36779-4 CAMBRIDGE PB $47.95

Rien **Poortvliet**

Journey to the Ice Age: Mammoths and Other Animals of the Wild

The acclaimed Dutch painter journeys, guided by his brush, to the Ice Age, and shows us a bestiary of its inhabitants, both real and imaginative. The mammoth, the giant deer, the woolly rhinoceros, as well as primitive humans. Over 220 pages of color illustrations make a world long lost come alive

0-8109-3648-8 ABRAMS $39.95

Louie **Psihoyas** & John **Knoebber**

Hunting Dinosaurs

Psihoyas and Knoebber travel the world in search of dinosaur fossils and fossil hunters. Richly illustrated with spectacular color photos

0-679-43124-1 RANDOM HOUSE $40.00

David **Raup**

The Nemesis Affair: A Story of the Death of Dinosaurs and the Ways Of Science

Does the sun have a companion star that passed close enough around 65 million years ago to have rained a shower of lethal comets on the Earth that ended the reign of the dinosaurs?

0-393-30409-4 NORTON PB $8.95

Zdenek V. **Spinar**

Life Before Man

From life's beginnings to the arrival of Homo sapiens, this beautiful book introduces us to the panorama of the prehistoric Earth. Beautifully illustrated and clearly written, *Life Before Man* covers the various theories of the solar system's birth, the first signs of single-cell life, the arrival of marine vertebrates—all the way to the emergence of human's ancestors. Authoritative and enlightening

ILLUSTRATED BY ZDENEK BURIAN

0-500-27796-6 THAMES & HUDSON PB $16.95

Steven M. **Stanley**

Extinction: A Scientific American Book

A reader-friendly yet scientifically rigorous introduction to why and how extinctions occur, particularly detailed on the role climate plays in the disappearance of species

0-7167-5014-8 FREEMAN $32.95

Evolution and the Origins of Life

One of the most intriguing questions suggested by the theory of evolution is when the first living organisms arose. Although Pasteur's experiments with fermentation toppled the doctrine of spontaneous generation, that idea has returned in a subtle form in the Soviet scientist Oparin's suggestion that organic chemicals in Earth's early seas may have formed a proto-organism by "happy chance." Other theories for the advent of life are almost as varied as life itself.

Natalie **Angier**

The Beauty of the Beastly: New Views of the Nature of Life

0-395-71816-3 HOUGHTON MIFFLIN $21.95

0-395-79147-2 HOUGHTON MIFFLIN PB $12.95

Isaac **Asimov**

Beginnings: the Story of Origins—Of Mankind, Life, the Earth, the Universe

0-425-11586-0 BERKLEY PB $5.99

Doug **Boucher**, editor

The Biology of Mutualism: Ecology and Evolution

Population biologists discuss the ecological strategies and evolutionary constraints that govern the maintenance of mutualistic relationships. "Required reading for everyone interested in species interactions"—*Ecology*

0-19-505392-3 OXFORD PB $29.95

Peter **Bowler**

Evolution: The History of an Idea from the 17th Century to the Present

0-520-06386-4 CALIFORNIA PB $18.00

A.G. **Cairns-Smith**

Genetic Takeover and the Mineral Origins of Life

Proposes that life and the genetic code might have first originated in the lattices of crystals

0-521-23312-7 CAMBRIDGE $110.00

Seven Clues to the Origin of Life: A Scientific Detective Story

An entertaining overview of the dominant theories

0-521-39828-2 CAMBRIDGE PB $8.95

A.G. **Cairns-Smith** & H. **Hartman**, editors

Clay Minerals and the Origin of Life

The continuation of a fascinating argument

0-521-32408-4 CAMBRIDGE $54.95

Helena **Cronin**

The Ant and the Peacock: Altruism and Sexual Selection from Darwin to Today

"The finest study of the evolution of Darwinian thought that we have to date"
—*New England Review of Books*

FOREWORD BY JOHN MAYNARD SMITH

0-521-45765-3 CAMBRIDGE PB $19.95

Richard **Dawkins**

The Blind Watchmaker: Why the Evidence of Evolution Reveals a Universe Without Design

A popular defense of Darwinian theory. Includes a computer model of how minute changes, such as those that occur in evolution, can lead to vastly divergent results

0-19-217773-7 OXFORD $30.00

0-393-30448-5 NORTON PB $10.95

Climbing Mount Improbable

0-393-03930-7 NORTON $25.00

The Extended Phenotype: The Gene as the Unit of Selection

A more technical sequel to *The Selfish Gene*

0-19-286088-7 OXFORD PB $15.95

River Out of Eden

Dawkins presents his model of evolutionary biology in terms of a flowing river of genes; his underlying purpose is to defend Darwinian theory against creationism by explaining how gradual, incremental changes can ultimately add up to dramatic forward leaps in evolution

0-465-01606-5 BASIC $20.00

The Selfish Gene

A controversial, entertaining discussion of what is "selected" during evolution

0-19-286092-5 OXFORD PB $11.95

Daniel C. **Dennett**

Darwin's Dangerous Idea: Evolution and the Meanings of Life

See also **OTHER 20TH-CENTURY PHILOSOPHERS** under **PHILOSOPHY** in **RELIGION, SPIRITUALITY, AND PHILOSOPHY**

0-684-80290-2 SIMON & SCHUSTER $30.00

Niles **Eldridge**

Unfinished Synthesis: Biological Hierarchies and Modern Evolutionary Thought

0-19-503633-6 OXFORD $29.95

Gerald M. **Edelman**

Topobiology: An Introduction to Molecular Embryology

Here, Edelman presents a comprehensive introduction to the field of molecular embryology, a necessary foundation for understanding recent work on the evolution of consciousness

0-465-08653-5 BASIC PB $17.00

Gerald M. Edelman

Maitland **Edey** & Donald **Johanson**

Blueprints: Solving the Mystery of Evolution

A history of the evidence of evolution by the authors of *Lucy: The Beginnings of Humankind.* "This book should be welcomed by anyone with a love of truth in a dark time" —Richard Dawkins, *NY Times Book Review*

0-14-013265-1 PENGUIN PB $14.95

Howard **Evans**

Life on a Little-Known Planet

The little-known planet is Earth

1-55821-249-3 LYONS & BURFORD PB $14.95

Stephen Jay **Gould**

Full House: The Spread of Excellence from Plato to Darwin

See also LATE ARRIVALS

0-517-70394-7 HARMONY $25.00

The Mismeasure of Man

A discussion of ideas about human intelligence in history

See also BIOLOGY

0-393-31067-1 NORTON PB $9.95

Ontogeny and Phylogeny

A classic on the relationship between individual development and the evolution of species and lineages

0-674-63940-5 BELKNAP $36.00
0-674-63941-3 BELKNAP PB $17.95

An Urchin in the Storm: Essays About Books and Ideas

Biological determinism, "cardboard Darwinism," evolutionary theory, and other subjects

0-393-30537-6 NORTON PB $8.95

François **Jacob**

The Possible and the Actual

0-295-95888-X WASHINGTON PB $20.00

Stuart A. **Kauffman**

The Origins of Order: Self-Organization & Selection in Evolution

How complexity theory can help to explain the workings of evolution

0-19-507951-5 OXFORD PB $32.00

Richard **Lewontin**

Human Diversity

The larger implications of evolutionary theory in terms of human values

0-7167-6013-4 FREEMAN PB $19.95

Lynn **Margulis**

Early Life

0-86720-005-7 JONES & BARTLETT PB $25.00

Symbiosis in Cell Evolution

A controversial theory

0-7167-7028-8 FREEMAN $50.95
0-7167-7029-6 FREEMAN PB $40.95

Ernst **Mayr**

The Growth of Biological Thought: Evolution and the Diversity of Life

One of the finest discussions of the evolutionary ideas that have given rise to modern biology

0-674-27104-1 HARVARD $45.00
0-674-36446-5 BELKNAP PB $18.95

Systematics and the Origin of Species

0-231-05449-1 COLUMBIA PB $24.50

Toward a New Philosophy of Biology: Observations of an Evolutionist

Reflections on evolutionary theory by the Harvard zoology professor

See also GENERAL WORKS

0-674-89666-1 HARVARD PB $18.95

H.M. **Morris**, editor

Scientific Creationism

The official statement of the defenders of creationism

0-89051-003-2 MASTER PB $10.95

J. Maynard **Smith**

Evolution and the Theory of Games

The importance of strategies in evolution

0-521-28884-3 CAMBRIDGE PB $21.95

Elliot **Sober**, editor

Conceptual Issues in Evolutionary Biology: An Anthology

0-262-19336-1 BRADFORD $55.00
0-262-69162-0 BRADFORD PB $29.50

Ken **Wilber**

Sex, Ecology, Spirituality: The Spirit of Evolution

The evolution of humankind is Wilber's passion—which way that evolution turns is Wilber's imperative concern in this original and innovative book

See also GENERAL BOOKS under SPIRITUALITY under SPIRITUALITY in RELIGION, SPIRITUALITY, AND PHILOSOPHY

1-57062-072-5 SHAMBHALA $39.50

George **Williams**

Sex and Evolution

0-691-08152-2 PRINCETON PB $19.95

Charles Darwin

Charles **Darwin**

Autobiography of Charles Darwin

See also CLASSIFICATION OF ORGANISMS under BIOLOGY

0-393-00487-2 NORTON PB $6.95

Charles Darwin's Beagle Diary

A fresh transcript of Darwin's diary, about half of which, together with material from his scientific notes, was used as the basis for his famous account of the Beagle voyage published in 1839

See also CLASSIFICATION OF ORGANISMS under BIOLOGY

EDITED BY R.D. KEYNES

0-521-23503-0 CAMBRIDGE $75.00

The Descent of Man & Selection in Relation to Sex

A facsimile of the first edition (1871)

See also CLASSIFICATION OF ORGANISMS under BIOLOGY

0-691-08278-2 PRINCETON $95.00
0-691-02369-7 PRINCETON PB $24.95

The Origin of Species

See also CLASSIFICATION OF ORGANISMS under BIOLOGY

0-14-043205-1 PENGUIN PB $8.95

The Voyage of the Beagle

The classic account of Darwin's voyage to South America and the Galapagos

See also CLASSIFICATION OF ORGANISMS under BIOLOGY
See also ESSAYS, MEDITATIONS, AND CLASSICS

0-14-043268-X PENGUIN PB $10.95

The natural history of the island is eminently curious, and well deserves attention. Most of the organic productions are aboriginal creations, found nowhere else; yet all show a marked relationship with those of America, though separated from that continent by an open space of ocean, between 500 and 600 miles in width. The archipelago is a little world within itself, or rather a satellite attached to America, whence it has derived a few stray colonists, and has received the general character of its indigenous productions. Considering the small size of these islands, we feel the more astonished at the number of their aboriginal beings, and at their confined range. Seeing every height crowned with its crater, and the boundaries of most of the lava-streams still distinct, we are led to believe that within a period, geologically recent, the unbroken ocean was here spread out. Hence, both in space and time, we seem to be brought somewhat near to that great first appearance of new beings on this Earth.

THE VOYAGE OF THE BEAGLE

Charles **Darwin** &
Frederick **Burkhardt**, editor

Charles Darwin's Letters: A Selection, 1825-1859

This selection of letters offers a wonderfully readable account of the daily experience, scientific observations, and personal concerns behind the founding work of evolutionary theory. "This is the human story behind the making of *The Origin of Species*. Frederick Burkhardt has selected the most fascinating letters, to reveal the private life of a minor squire's son whose dark secret was destined to shake the world. A perfect compendium"—Adrian Desmond

See also **CLASSIFICATION OF ORGANISMS** under **BIOLOGY**

FOREWORD BY STEPHEN JAY GOULD

0-521-56212-0 CAMBRIDGE $21.95

Charles Darwin

H.S. **Gruber**

Darwin on Man: A Psychological Study of Scientific Creativity

See also **CLASSIFICATION OF ORGANISMS** under **BIOLOGY**

0-226-31007-8 CHICAGO PB $10.00

David **Kohn**, editor

The Darwinian Heritage

This major collection of essays includes the proceedings of the Charles Darwin Centenary Conference held in 1982 in Florence

See also **CLASSIFICATION OF ORGANISMS** under **BIOLOGY**

0-691-02414-6 PRINCETON PB $35.00

Ernst **Mayr**

One Long Argument: Charles Darwin and the Genesis of Modern Evolutionary Thought

0-674-63906-5 HARVARD PB $14.00

Mark **Ridley**, editor

The Darwin Reader

"Ridley's artful selections...and entertaining introductions leave us in no doubt that Darwin's lesser achievements are all of a piece with his major discovery...Darwin is shown to be one of the 19th century's greatest geologists and biologists"—Richard Dawkins

See also **CLASSIFICATION OF ORGANISMS** under **BIOLOGY**

0-393-95673-3 NORTON PB $10.95

Keith Stewart **Thomson**

HMS Beagle: The Story of Darwin's Ship

Thomson's vivid and erudite portrait of the HMS Beagle, her crew, her captain, and her most famous passenger brings Darwin's historic journey to life

0-393-03778-9 NORTON $25.00

Genetics, Genetic Engineering, and Biotechnology

Alain F. **Corcos** & Floyd V. **Monaghan**

Gregor Mendel's Experiments on Plant Hybrids: A Guided Study

Mendel, thanks to high-school biology courses, has become a near-mythical figure in the history of evolution. Corcos and Monaghan, however, make him vividly real through a brief biography and a revealing and intriguing reconstruction of his pioneering experiments

ILLUSTRATED BY MARIA C. WEBBER

0-8135-1920-9 RUTGERS $34.00
0-8135-1921-7 RUTGERS PB $15.00

Claus **Emmeche**

The Garden in the Machine: The Emerging Science of Artificial Life

"Danish theorist Emmeche gives a far-ranging view of artificial life and related currents of thought, such as chaos theory and the study of emergence. He writes in a querying mode, not promoting any point of view but simply trying to ask the right questions. This is heady stuff that, far from being arcane, involves real issues about how human beings think about themselves" —*Library Journal*

TRANSLATED BY STEVEN SAMPSON

0-691-03330-7 PRINCETON $24.95

François **Jacob**

The Logic of Life: A History of Heredity

The Nobel Prize winner demonstrates the inappropriate application in earlier periods of nonbiological principles to heredity

0-691-00042-5 PRINCETON PB $14.95

Richard **Lewontin** & others

Not in Our Genes: Biology, Ideology, and Human Nature

An attack on the simplistic view that genes determine character, intelligence, and other traits

0-394-72888-2 PANTHEON PB $14.21

Jeff **Lyon** & Peter **Gorner**

Altered Fates: The Genetic Re-Engineering of Human Life

0-393-03596-4 NORTON $27.50
0-393-31528-2 NORTON PB $15.95

Lynn **Margulis**

The Origins of Sex: The Billion Years of Genetic Recombination

0-300-04619-7 YALE PB $19.00

Bruce **Wallace**

The Search for the Gene

"Wallace traces the intellectual development of genetics from its origins in antiquity to the Human Genome Project, and examines the work and thinking of the major contributors to genetics, such as Mendel, Morgan, Sturtevant, Avery, Watson and Crick. . . Since Wallace personally knew several of the key scientists covered, he is able to provide as well a valuable personal perspective to many of the discoveries....This book will be particularly interesting to the student who not only wishes to know the facts of genetics, but also the very interesting story behind those facts"—*Choice*

0-8014-2680-4 CORNELL $39.95
0-8014-9967-4 CORNELL PB $15.95

Biology

Tim M. **Berra**

Evolution and the Myth of Creationism: A Basic Guide to the Facts in the Evolution Debate

Berra debunks the claims of creationism and provides a compact layman's guide to current issues in evolutionary science

0-8047-1770-2 STANFORD PB $9.95

Stephen Jay **Gould**

The Mismeasure of Man

A discussion of ideas about human intelligence in history

See also **EVOLUTION AND THE ORIGINS OF LIFE** under **PALEONTOLOGY AND EVOLUTION**

0-393-31067-1 NORTON PB $9.95

Stephen Jay **Gould**, editor

The Book of Life: An Illustrated History of the Evolution of Life on Earth

This ambitious work of science and art uses more than 300 original paintings to illuminate and explain the history of life on Earth over 600 million years. A fascinating volume that depicts animals and plants from threads of bacteria to sharks, dinosaurs, camels, cats—and of course, human beings too

0-393-03557-3 NORTON $40.00

Stephen Jay Gould

Richard **Milner**

The Encyclopedia of Evolution: Humanity's Search for Its Origins

Did you know that early New England farmers believed that the fossilized "bird tracks" of the Connecticut Valley were made by Noah's ravens? Or that the sentimental movie classic *It's a Wonderful Life* reflects crucial evolutionary ideas? Trivia mixes with history mixes with theory and scholarship in this entertaining volume

See also **ONE-VOLUME ENCYCLOPEDIAS** under **REFERENCE** in **BUSINESS AND REFERENCE**

0-8050-2717-3 OWLET PB $25.00

John A. **Moore**

Science As a Way of Knowing: The Foundations of Modern Biology

An impeccably clear and concise history of discoveries about nature, genetics, evolution, and embryology, stressing the latest of current developments in each field

0-674-79481-8 HARVARD $36.00

Christopher **Vaughan**

How Life Begins: The Science of Life in the Womb

Enormous advances in the world of ultrasound technology and other imaging techniques have opened an unprecedented window into the pre-partum world of the fetus. What's revealed is a complex, sophisticated life, and an absolutely wondrous process of development from single cell to crying baby. Beautifully illustrated and readably written, this is a splendid book for the expectant parent or any person curious about the mysterious origins of human life in utero

0-8129-2103-8 TIMES BOOKS $23.00

Philip **Whitfield**, editor

The Human Body Explained: A Guide to Understanding the Incredible Living Machine

And none too soon! From a soccer-field sprint to the conversion of air molecule vibrations into music, this accessible volume leads us through the workings of the human body. Lavishly illustrated and impeccably researched, this is a wonderful reference book and a compelling read

0-8050-3752-7 HOLT $40.00

Classification of Organisms

Frederick **Burkhardt** & Sydney **Smith**, editors

The Correspondence of Charles Darwin

While all nine volumes of Darwin's correspondence are in print, they may be difficult to get. Please call for individual volumes

0-521-25587-2 CAMBRIDGE $60.00

Charles **Darwin**

Autobiography of Charles Darwin

See also **CHARLES DARWIN** under **PALEONTOLOGY AND EVOLUTION**

0-393-00487-2 NORTON PB $6.95

Charles Darwin's Beagle Diary

A fresh transcript of Darwin's diary, about half of which, together with material from his scientific notes, was used as the basis for his famous account of the Beagle voyage published in 1839

See also **CHARLES DARWIN** under **PALEONTOLOGY AND EVOLUTION**

EDITED BY R.D. KEYNES

0-521-23503-0 CAMBRIDGE $75.00

The Descent of Man & Selection in Relation to Sex

A facsimile of the first edition (1871)

See also **CHARLES DARWIN** under **PALEONTOLOGY AND EVOLUTION**

0-691-08278-2 PRINCETON $95.00

0-691-02369-7 PRINCETON PB $24.95

The NYU Press Edition of the Works of Charles Darwin

Volume 1

Diary of the Voyage of the H.M.S. Beagle

0-8147-1796-9 NYU $95.00

Volume 2

Journal Researches into the Geology and Natural History of the Various Countries Visited by H.M.S Beagle, Part 1

0-8147-1787-X NYU $95.00

Volume 3

Journal of Researches into the Geology and Natural History of the Various Countries Visited by H.M.S Beagle, Part 2

0-8147-1788-8 NYU $95.00

Volume 4

The Zoology of the Voyage of H.M.S. Beagle, Under the Command of Captain Fitzroy, During the Years 1832-1836—Fossil Mammalia, Mammalia

0-8147-1789-6 NYU $95.00

Volume 5

The Zoology of the Voyage of H.M.S. Beagle, Under the Command of Captain Fitzroy, During the Years 1832-1836—Birds

0-8147-1790-X NYU $95.00

Volume 6

The Zoology of the Voyage of H.M.S. Beagle, Under the Command of Captain Fitzroy, During the Years 1832-1836—Fish, Reptiles

0-8147-1791-8 NYU $95.00

Volume 7

The Structure and Distribution of Coral Reefs

0-8147-1792-6 NYU $95.00

Volume 8

Geological Observations on the Volcanic Island Visited During the Voyage of H.M.S. Beagle

0-8147-1793-4 NYU $95.00

Volume 9

Geological Observations on South America

0-8147-1794-2 NYU $95.00

Volume 10

The Foundations of the Origin of the Species

0-8147-1795-0 NYU $95.00

Volume 11

A Monograph on the Subclass Cirripedia, Vol.1

0-8147-1800-0 NYU $95.00

Volume 12

A Monograph on the Subclass Cirripedia

0-8147-1801-9 NYU $95.00

Volume 13

A Monograph on the Subclass Cirripedia, Vol. 1 Part 2

0-8147-1802-7 NYU $95.00

Volume 14

A Monograph on the Fossil Lepadidae

0-8147-1803-5 NYU $95.00

Volume 15

On the Origin of Species The first edition, written in 1859

0-8147-1804-3 NYU $95.00

Volume 16

On the Origin of Species

0-8147-1805-1 NYU $95.00

Volume 17

The Various Contrivances by which Orchides are Fertilized by Insects

0-8147-1806-X NYU $95.00

Volume 18

The Movements and Habits of Climbing Plants

0-8147-1807-8 NYU $95.00

Volume 19

The Variation of Animals and Plants Under Domestication, Vol. 1

0-8147-1808-6 NYU $95.00

Volume 20
The Variation of Animals and Plants Under Domestication, Vol. 2
0-8147-1809-4 NYU $95.00

The Origin of Species
See also **CHARLES DARWIN** under **PALEONTOLOGY AND EVOLUTION**
0-14-043205-1 PENGUIN PB $8.95

The Voyage of the Beagle
The classic account of Darwin's voyage to South America and the Galapagos
See also **ESSAYS, MEDITATIONS, AND CLASSICS** under **NATURE STUDY**
See also **CHARLES DARWIN** under **PALEONTOLOGY AND EVOLUTION**
0-14-043268-X PENGUIN PB $10.95

Charles **Darwin** & Frederick **Burkhardt**, editor
Charles Darwin's Letters: A Selection, 1825-1859
This selection of letters offers a wonderfully readable account of the daily experience, scientific observations, and personal concerns behind the founding work of evolutionary theory. "This is the human story behind the making of *The Origin of Species*. Frederick Burkhardt has selected the most fascinating letters, to reveal the private life of a minor squire's son whose dark secret was destined to shake the world. A perfect compendium"—Adrian Desmond
See also **CHARLES DARWIN** under **PALEONTOLOGY AND EVOLUTION**
FOREWORD BY STEPHEN JAY GOULD
0-521-56212-0 CAMBRIDGE $21.95

H.S. **Gruber**
Darwin on Man: A Psychological Study of Scientific Creativity
See also **CHARLES DARWIN** under **PALEONTOLOGY AND EVOLUTION**
0-226-31007-8 CHICAGO PB $10.00

David **Kohn**, editor
The Darwinian Heritage
This major collection of essays includes the proceedings of the Charles Darwin Centenary Conference held in 1982 in Florence
See also **CHARLES DARWIN** under **PALEONTOLOGY AND EVOLUTION**
0-691-02414-6 PRINCETON PB $35.00

Mark **Ridley**, editor
The Darwin Reader
"Ridley's artful selections…and entertaining introductions leave us in no doubt that Darwin's lesser achievements are all of a piece with his major discovery…Darwin is shown to be one of the 19th century's greatest geologists and biologists"—Richard Dawkins
See also **CHARLES DARWIN** under **PALEONTOLOGY AND EVOLUTION**
0-393-95673-3 NORTON PB $10.95

Biological Diversity

Gordon **Hendler** & others
Sea Stars, Sea Urchins, and Allies: Echinoderms of Florida and the Caribbean
See also **AQUATIC LIFE** under **ANIMALS** under **NATURE STUDY**
1-56098-450-3 SMITHSONIAN $39.95

Lynn **Margulis** & Dorion **Sagan**
What is Life?
Life, what is it but a dream? asks Lewis Carroll. In fact, answer the distinguished scientific authors of this remarkable book, it is something understandable only by deftly spanning astronomy, microbiology, physical anthropology, and the history of science. Then throw in 80 full-color photographs, much erudition and creativity, and we're almost there. This splendid volume, aptly using the title of Schrödinger's 1944 classic, revisits an ageless query from the most current scientific perspective
FOREWORD BY NILES ELDREDGE
0-684-81087-5 SIMON & SCHUSTER $40.00

Zoology

Birute M.F. **Galdikas**
Reflections of Eden: My Years With the Orangutans of Borneo
0-316-30186-8 LITTLE, BROWN PB $13.95

Nelson G. **Hairston**, Sr.
Vertebrate Zoology: An Experimental Field Approach
0-521-41703-1 CAMBRIDGE $38.95

Paul W. **Sherman** & John **Alcock**, editors
Exploring Animal Behavior: Readings from American Scientist
0-87893-762-5 SINAUR PB $16.50

Meredith F. **Small**
Female Choices: Sexual Behavior of Female Primates
According to the author, the battle between the sexes comes down to different mating strategies. In this intriguing book, Small uses female primates' reproductive strategies to show that, like their male counterparts, they search for good partners, enjoy sex, and have varied sexual habits and needs. "Filled with fascinating and compelling ideas about human behavior, *Female Choices* is superbly researched, very readable, and a splendid addition to any library"—Diane Ackerman
0-8014-8305-0 CORNELL PB $14.95

Botany

David **Attenborough**
The Private Life of Plants
0-691-00639-3 PRINCETON $26.95

Flora of North America Editorial Committee
Flora of North America
The first two of a projected 14 volumes in an already monumental series. The first volume includes an informative and wide-ranging series of introductory essays by more than twenty experts; the second covers ferns and cone-bearing plants

Volume II
Ferns & Gymnosperms
0-19-508242-7 OXFORD $85.00

Wendy **Zomlefer**
A Guide to Flowering Plant Families
Covers the temperate and tropical zones of the US. Full descriptions of leaves, flowers and fruits, supplemented by Zomlefer's elegant illustrative drawings
0-8078-2160-8 NORTH CAROLINA $55.00
0-8078-4470-5 NORTH CAROLINA PB $27.50

Microbiology

Wayne **Biddle**
A Field Guide to Germs
0-8050-3531-1 HOLT $22.50
0-385-48426-7 ANCHOR PB $12.95

Molecular Biology

David S. **Goodsell**
The Machinery of Life
"A fascinating introduction to biochemistry for the nonspecialist, combining a clear text with an abundance of drawings and computer graphics that vividly present the world of cells and their components"—*SciTech Book News*
0-387-97846-1 SPRINGER-VERLAG $29.00

Erwin **Schrödinger**
What Is Life?
Classic writings by a Nobel prize-winning German physicist
0-5242-708-8 CAMBRIDGE PB $9.95

Biology and Human Behavior

Edward O. Wilson and his fellow sociobiologists believe that genes influence behavior and that the theory of evolution applies not only to physical and structural characteristics but to social behavior as well. If a past behavioral pattern contributes to an organism's reproductive success, they argue that genes responsible for that behavior will be selected and transmitted to succeeding generations. Many critics disagree, especially when sociobiological thinking is applied to human behavior.

Richard **Coleman**
Wide Awake At 3:00 AM: By Choice Or by Chance?
0-7167-1796-4 FREEMAN PB $15.95

Philip **Kitcher**
Vaulting Ambition: Sociobiology and the Quest For Human Nature
"The best dissection ever published on the logic and illogic (mostly the latter) of sociobiology" —Stephen Jay Gould
0-262-11109-8 MIT $35.00

Marc **Lappe**

The Body's Edge: Our Cultural Obsession with Skin

See also **SKIN CARE AND DISORDERS** under **SPECIFIC HEALTH PROBLEMS** under **HEALTH** in **LIFESTYLES AND PRACTICAL ADVICE**

0-8050-4208-3 HOLT $22.50

J.A. **Michon** & J.L. **Jackson**

Time, Mind, and Behavior

0-387-15444-2 SPRINGER-VERLAG $59.00

Carol **Orlock**

Inner Time: The Science of Body Clocks and What Makes Us Tick

"Chronobiology" is the science that studies the innate wisdom and workings of the body clock in each of us. A broad look at a fascinating new field which explains the rhythms of aging, of energy, of weight fluctuation, and libido. And why *are* more babies born in the middle of the night?

1-55972-194-4 BIRCH LANE $18.95

Edward O. **Wilson**

Biophilia

Proposes that our natural affinity for life (biophilia) is the essence of our humanity and binds us to all other species. "Erudite, elegant, and poetic"—*Natural History*

See also **GENERAL WORKS**

0-674-07441-6 HARVARD $23.00

0-674-07442-4 HARVARD PB $10.95

On Human Nature

A popular discussion of sociobiology, one of the more controversial results of evolutionary theory

0-674-63441-1 HARVARD $27.50

0-674-63442-X HARVARD PB $13.95

Sociobiology: The New Synthesis, Abridged Edition

0-674-81624-2 HARVARD PB $24.95

The Neurosciences and the Brain

Much of the philosophical and scientific discussion of brain function is based on clinical observations and research.

For related reading, see PSYCHOLOGY in SOCIAL STUDIES

Peter **Baumgartner** & Sabine **Payr**, editors

Speaking Minds: Interviews with Twenty Eminent Cognitive Scientists

See also **THE COGNITIVE REVOLUTION** under **PSYCHOLOGY** in **SOCIAL STUDIES**

0-691-03678-0 PRINCETON $29.95

Colin **Blakemore** & Susan **Greenfield**, editors

Mindwaves: Thoughts on Intelligence, Identity, and Consciousness

Essays on the mind-body problem by noted researchers

0-631-14623-7 BLACKWELL PB $25.95

Edmund Blair **Bolles**

Remembering and Forgetting: An Inquiry Into the Nature of Memory

0-8027-1004-2 WALKER $22.95

William H. **Calvin** & George A. **Ojemann**

Conversations with Neil's Brain: Searching For the Narrator of Consciousness

Out of an absorbing drama comes a fascinating science book: the story of Neil, an epileptic patient, and his surgeon, Ojemann. The details of Neil's brain surgery (off by a millimeter, the knife could, for example, damage his ability to read, but not to write) make clear why language, memory, and decision-making are so complex and why learning disabilities are often so vexing. A study on par with the best of Oliver Sacks

0-201-48337-8 ADDISON-WESLEY PB $12.00

David J. **Chalmers**

The Conscious Mind: In Search of a Fundamental Theory

A provocative new dualist approach to the problem of consciousness

See also **OTHER 20TH-CENTURY PHILOSOPHERS** under **PHILOSOPHY** in **RELIGION, SPIRITUALITY, AND PHILOSOPHY**

0-19-510553-2 OXFORD $29.95

Jean-Pierre **Changeux** & Alain **Connes**

Conversations on Mind, Matter, & Mathematics

A dialogue between Changeux (a biologist) and Connes (a mathematician) on the relation between mathematics and the functioning of the human brain. Running through this often brilliant debate is a perennially fascinating question: do numbers exist independently of the human mind?

0-691-08759-8 PRINCETON $24.95

M. **Critchley**

The Divine Banquet of the Brain and Others Essays

An entertaining and unorthodox collection by an eminent clinician

0-89004-348-5 RAVEN $47.00

Antonio R. **Damasio**

Descartes' Error: Emotion, Reason, and the Human Brain

Damasio, a much-honored doctor and professor of neurology, draws on his treatment of brain-damaged patients to show, in direct contradiction to the durable Cartesian "mind-body duality," the interdependence of rationality and emotion. "Damasio's astonishing book takes us on a scientific journey into the brain that helps us see the source of our feelings, thoughts and desires, as well as our idiosyncratic creative and destructive behavior"—*Jonas Salk*

See also **DESCARTES** under **PHILOSOPHY** in **RELIGION, SPIRITUALITY, AND PHILOSOPHY**

0-399-13894-3 PUTNAM $24.95

0-380-72647-5 AVON PB $12.50

Daniel **Dennett**

Consciousness Explained

"An extraordinarily rich perspective so often brilliant, so witty, and so informed by contemporary culture as to make pleasurable the reading of what is truly a complex and demanding text"—*Kirkus Reviews*

See also **OTHER 20TH-CENTURY PHILOSOPHERS** under **PHILOSOPHY** in **RELIGION, SPIRITUALITY, AND PHILOSOPHY**

0-316-18065-3 LITTLE, BROWN $27.95

0-316-18066-1 LITTLE, BROWN PB $15.95

Daniel Dennett

Merlin **Donald**

Origins of the Modern Mind: Three Stages in the Evolution of Culture & Cognition

"Whereas countless philosophers since Aristotle have attempted to define what is quintessentially human, Donald brings new knowledge of neuropsychology, ethology, and archaeology to propose a tripartite theory of the transition from ape to man. Using the fossil evidence of braincase size and tool-kit remains, Donald concludes that the Australopithecines were limited to concrete/episodic minds: bipedal creatures able to benefit from pair-bonding, cooperative hunting, etc., but essentially of a seize-the-moment mentality. The first transition was to a "mimetic" culture: the era of Homo erectus in which mankind absorbed and refashioned events to create rituals, crafts, rhythms, dance, and other prelinguistic traditions. This was followed by the evolution to mythic cultures: the result of the acquisition of speech and the invention of symbols. The third transition carried oral speech to reading, writing, and an extended external memory store seen today in computer technology"
—*Kirkus Reviews*

See also **THE COGNITIVE REVOLUTION** under **PSYCHOLOGY** in **SOCIAL STUDIES**

0-674-64483-2 HARVARD $29.95

0-674-64484-0 HARVARD PB $16.95

J. **Eccles** & Karl R. **Popper**

The Self and Its Brain

0-7100-9584-8 ROUTLEDGE PB $22.50

Gerald M. **Edelman**

Bright Air, Brilliant Fire: On the Matter of the Mind

The Nobel laureate gives us a glimpse of the revolution in neuroscience that is leading us to an understanding of the most ancient mysteries about our nature. "Edelman is one of those lucky researchers who may be on the verge of answering some of the most profound questions in science today"—*LA Times Book Review*

See also **ARTIFICIAL INTELLIGENCE**

0-465-00764-3 BASIC PB $17.00

Michael **Gazzaniga**

The Integrated Mind

Uses clinical examples to explain brain function

0-306-31085-6 PLENUM.....$39.50

Mind Matters: How the Mind and Brain Interact to Create Our Conscious Lives

Cognitive neuroscience in an accessible survey

0-395-50095-8 HOUGHTON MIFFLIN PB.....$12.95

R.L. **Gregory**, editor

The Oxford Companion to the Mind

Fascinating reference work encompassing philosophical and psychological approaches to everything concerning the human, from perception to art to religion

See also **REFERENCE** under **PSYCHOLOGY** in **SOCIAL STUDIES**

0-19-866124-X OXFORD.....$60.00

Nick **Herbert**

Elemental Mind: Human Consciousness and the New Physics

"...Herbert scrutinizes recent brain research, reviews highly conjectural quantum models of mind, and outlines his own theory...which, if true, might help explain paranormal phenomena"—*Publishers Weekly*

See also **THE NEW PHYSICS** under **METAPHYSICS** under **SPIRITUALITY** in **RELIGION, SPIRITUALITY, AND PHILOSOPHY**

0-452-27245-9 PLUME PB.....$11.95

J. Allan **Hobson**

The Dreaming Brain

0-465-01702-9 BASIC BOOKS PB.....$17.00

Douglas **Hofstadter**

Fluid Concepts & Creative Analogies: Computer Models of Mental Fluidity & Creativity

0-465-05154-5 BASIC.....$30.00

0-465-02475-0 BASIC PB.....$18.00

David **Hubel**

Eye, Brain, and Vision

0-7167-5020-1 FREEMAN.....$32.95

George **Johnson**

In the Palaces of Memory: How We Build the Worlds Inside Our Heads

The author of *Machinery of the Mind* focuses on how contemporary biology, physics, and philosophy are revising the definition of memory. The author writes: "Whenever you read a book or have a conversation, the experience causes physical changes in your brain. In a matter of seconds, new circuits are formed, memories that can change forever the way you think about the world"

0-394-58348-5 VINTAGE PB.....$22.95

Kenneth **Klivington**

The Science of Mind

0-262-11141-1 MIT.....$45.00

Simon **Le Vay**

The Sexual Brain

The author, mostly known for his theory on the difference between hypothalamic structure in homosexual and heterosexual men, suggests that sexual behavior can be understood by exploring how the brain develops. A fascinating tour though the territory of evolutionary theory, molecular genetics, and developmental psychology

See also **GENDER AND SEXUALITY** under **PSYCHOLOGY** in **SOCIAL STUDIES**

0-262-12178-6 MIT.....$25.00

A.R. **Luria**

The Man with a Shattered World: The History of a Brain Wound

See also **CASE HISTORIES** under **DISORDERS AND TREATMENT** under **PSYCHOLOGY** in **SOCIAL STUDIES**

FOREWORD BY JEROME S. BRUNER

0-674-54625-3 HARVARD PB.....$11.95

The Mind of a Mnemonist: A Little Book About a Vast Memory

See also **CASE HISTORIES** under **DISORDERS AND TREATMENT** under **PSYCHOLOGY** in **SOCIAL STUDIES**

0-674-57622-5 HARVARD PB.....$12.95

The Working Brain: An Introduction to Neuropsychology

Somewhat technical but filled with fascinating observations

See also **NEUROPHYSIOLOGICAL APPROACHES** under **THE COGNITIVE REVOLUTION** under **PSYCHOLOGY** in **SOCIAL STUDIES**

0-465-09208-X BASIC BOOKS PB.....$17.00

R. **Ornstein** & R.F. **Thompson**

The Amazing Brain

0-395-58572-4 HOUGHTON MIFFLIN PB.....$15.95

Roger **Penrose**

The Emperor's New Mind: On Computers, Minds, and the Laws of Physics

A brilliant and controversial scientific argument on the nature of the mind, its relation to the laws of physics, and why computers may prove unable to duplicate its workings. "It is a book that I believe will become a classic...Penrose is one of an increasingly large band of physicists who think Einstein was not being stubborn or muddle-headed when he said his 'little finger' told him that quantum mechanics is incomplete. To support this contention, Penrose takes you on a dazzling tour that covers such topics as complex numbers, Turing machines, complexity theory, the bewildering paradoxes of quantum mechanics, formal systems, Gödel undecidability, phrase spaces, Hilbert spaces, black holes, white holes, Hawking radiation, entropy, the structure of the brain, and scores of other topics at the heart of current speculations"—Martin Gardner

0-14-014534-6 PENGUIN PB.....$15.95

Shadows of the Mind: A Search for the Missing Science of Consciousness

0-19-853978-9 OXFORD.....$25.00

0-19-510646-6 OXFORD PB.....$16.95

Richard **Restak**

Brainscapes: An Introduction to What Neuroscience Has Learned About the Structure, Function, and Abilties of the Brain

A world-renowned neurologist introduces us to the latest research about the structure, function, and abilities of the brain. In a concise and learned format, Restak covers the brain's conscious and unconscious operations, the astonishing pharmacological advances in controlling neurotransmitters and modifying personality, the new methods of study, and what all this knowledge does to our accepted ideas of personality and of morality. A riveting visit to a fascinating world

0-7868-6113-4 HYPERION.....$19.95

0-7868-8190-9 HYPERION PB.....$10.95

Israel **Rosenfield**

Strange, Familiar and Forgotten: An Anatomy of Consciousness

City University's Rosenfield has been trained as a mathematician, a physician, a philosopher and a historian of ideas. "Aspects of all four are reflected in this short and provocative work" —*Kirkus Reviews*

See also **MEMOIRS AND JOURNALS** under **20TH-CENTURY AMERICAN ESSAYS AND JOURNALISM** in **LITERATURE OF THE AMERICAS**

0-679-40259-4 KNOPF.....$20.00

0-679-74305-7 VINTAGE PB.....$10.00

Oliver **Sacks**

An Anthropologist on Mars

Seven narratives of neurological disorder allow Dr. Sacks to continue his humane, poetic, and wonder-filled exploration of what it is to be human

See also **CASE HISTORIES** under **DISORDERS AND TREATMENT** under **PSYCHOLOGY** in **SOCIAL STUDIES**

0-679-43785-1 KNOPF.....$24.00

0-679-75697-3 VINTAGE PB.....$13.00

Oliver Sacks

Oliver **Sacks**

Awakenings

A classic study

See also **CASE HISTORIES** under **DISORDERS AND TREATMENT** under **PSYCHOLOGY** in **SOCIAL STUDIES**

See also **MEMORY** under **SPECIAL TOPICS IN PSYCHOLOGY** under **PSYCHOLOGY** in **SOCIAL STUDIES**

0-8095-9035-2 BORGO $29.00
0-8446-6277-1 SMITH $21.30
0-06-097368-4 HARPERPERENNIAL PB $13.00

A Leg to Stand On

A superbly written, often gripping account of Sacks's experiences after breaking a leg while climbing a mountain in Norway

See also **CASE HISTORIES** under **DISORDERS AND TREATMENT** under **PSYCHOLOGY** in **SOCIAL STUDIES**

0-06-097082-0 HARPER & ROW PB $13.00
0-06-092544-2 HARPERPERENNIAL PB $12.50

The Man Who Mistook His Wife For a Hat & Other Clinical Tales

"Dr. Sacks's most absorbing book...His tales are so compelling that many of them serve as eerie metaphors not only for the condition of modern medicine but of modern man"—*New York*

See also **CASE HISTORIES** under **DISORDERS AND TREATMENT** under **PSYCHOLOGY** in **SOCIAL STUDIES**

0-06-097079-0 HARPERCOLLINS PB $13.00

I tried one final test. It was still a cold day, in early spring, and I had thrown my coat and gloves on the sofa.

"What is this?" I asked, holding up a glove.

"May I examine it?" he asked, and, taking it from me, he proceeded to examine it as he had examined the geometrical shapes.

"A continuous surface," he announced at last, "infolded on itself. It appears to have"—he hesitated—"five outpouchings, if this is the word."

"Yes," I said cautiously. "You have given me a description. Now tell me what it is."

"A container of some sort?"

"Yes," I said, "and what would it contain?"

"It would contain its contents!" said Dr. P., with a laugh. "There are many possibilities. It could be a change purse, for example, for coins of five sizes. It could..."

I interrupted the barmy flow. "Does it not look familiar? Do you think it might contain, might fit, a part of your body?"

No light of recognition dawned on his face.

THE MAN WHO MISTOOK HIS WIFE FOR A HAT & OTHER CLINICAL TALES

Migraine

"His commentary is so erudite, so gracefully written that even those people fortunate enough never to have had a migraine in their lives should find it compelling"—*NY Times*

See also **HEADACHES AND MIGRAINES** under **SPECIFIC HEALTH PROBLEMS** under **HEALTH** in **LIFESTYLES AND PRACTICAL ADVICE**

0-520-08101-3 CALIFORNIA $35.00
0-520-08223-0 CALIFORNIA PB $15.95

Carl **Sagan**

Broca's Brain

0-345-33689-5 BALLANTINE PB $5.99

John R. **Searle**

Minds, Brains, and Science

A leading philosopher gives us a restrained attack on Artificial Intelligence

0-674-57633-0 HARVARD PB $8.95

John Searle

Rediscovery of the Mind

Searle offers a philosophical perspective on the scientific debate about the relation between physical processes in the brain and subjective experience

See also **OTHER 20TH-CENTURY PHILOSOPHERS** under **PHILOSOPHY** in **RELIGION, SPIRITUALITY, AND PHILOSOPHY**

0-262-19321-3 MIT $30.00
0-262-69154-X BRADFORD PB $14.00

John **Spillane**

The Doctrine of the Nerves: Chapters in the History of Neurology

An excellent history, by a practicing neurologist, that uses extensive source material from Galen to the 19th century

0-19-261135-6 OXFORD $70.00

L. R. **Squire**

Memory and Brain

0-19-504208-5 OXFORD PB $19.95

Frank **Vertosick**, Jr., M.D.

When the Air Hits Your Brain: Tales of Neurosurgery

0-393-03894-7 NORTON $23.00

Arthur **Zajonc**

Catching the Light: The Entwined History of Light and Mind

Why don't blind people see shapes when they first regain sight? Zajonc, a noted professor of physics, asks. Because without a formative visual imagination we are blind—seeing is a metaphoric enterprise. In time we may learn, he says, that "the natural world... grows out of the moral world within us." "Brilliant study of the relationship miles apart"—*Kirkus Reviews*

0-19-509575-8 OXFORD PB $14.95

Artificial Intelligence

Jean-Pierre **Changeux**

Neuronal Man: The Biology of Mind

TRANSLATED BY LAURENCE GAREY

0-691-02666-1 PRINCETON PB $16.95

Patricia Smith **Churchland**

Neurophilosophy: Toward a Unified Science of Mind/Brain

0-262-03116-7 MIT $42.00
0-262-53085-6 BRADFORD PB $20.00

Patricia S. **Churchland** & Terrence J. **Sejnowski**

The Computational Brain

0-262-03188-4 MIT $50.00
0-262-53120-8 BRADFORD PB $19.95

Gerald M. **Edelman**

Bright Air, Brilliant Fire: On the Matter of the Mind

The Nobel laureate gives us a glimpse of the revolution in neuroscience that is leading us to an understanding of the most ancient mysteries about our nature. "Edelman is one of those lucky researchers who may be on the verge of answering some of the most profound questions in science today"—*LA Times Book Review*

See also **THE NEUROSCIENCES AND THE BRAIN**

0-465-00764-3 BASIC PB $17.00

Stephen M. **Kosslyn** & Olivier **Koenig**

Wet Mind: The New Cognitive Neuroscience

0-02-917595-X FREE PRESS $35.00
0-02-874085-8 FREE PRESS PB $19.95

Natural History

Natural history impinges on nearly every province of knowledge, inevitably creating something of a classification problem. The works listed here touch on aspects of literature, philosophy, biology, and anthropology, as well as more absolute sciences. In *Nature's Diary*, Mikhail Prishvin writes that "most plants and animals are closely connected with the life of man...but up to now science has done little to study this relationship, and that is where art comes in." There is a large part of art, as of science, in nearly every work here.

To understand the difficulty of selecting works of natural history, one need only consider the case of *Moby Dick*, probably the finest work of 19th-century cetology, or Virgil's *Georgics*, a superb example of early agrarian poetry. The boundaries we have chosen exclude both works, as well as others that belong more to American literature or the classics than to natural history. We have placed heavy emphasis on North America and have generally stopped short of highly technical works, choosing instead to include those of broadest appeal and greatest practicality.

For related reading, see NATURE STUDY

Bert **Hoelldobler** & Edward O. **Wilson**

The Ants

Winner of the 1991 Pulitzer Prize for General Nonfiction. "Although encyclopedic, the book is beautifully written, and has some of the most

stunning animal paintings and photographs I have seen"
—John Maynard Smith, *NY Review of Books*
See also **INSECTS** under **ANIMALS** under **NATURE STUDY**
0-674-04075-9 BELKNAP $75.00

Lyly **Rexer** & Rachel **Klein**
American Museum of Natural History: 100 Years of Expedition and Discovery
This beautifully illustrated book tells of the real-life adventurers who fought bandits and braved sandstorms, faced down elephants and conquered a leopard to bring home the specimens that made the museum famous
FOREWORD BY EDWARD O. WILSON
0-8109-1965-6 ABRAMS $49.50

Edward O. **Wilson**
Naturalist
"A mixture of loneliness, amusement, curiosity, and intellectual rigor makes the voice of this man unforgettable"—*NY Times*
0-446-67199-1 WARNER PB $11.99

Biological Diversity

Bryan **Norton**
Why Preserve Natural Variety?
A comprehensive rationale for preserving wild species and ecosystems
0-691-07762-2 PRINCETON PB $39.00

Bryan **Norton**, editor
The Preservation of Species: The Value of Biological Diversity
An important collection, resulting from a conference on the preservation of biological diversity held at the University of Maryland
0-691-08389-4 PRINCETON $60.00
0-691-02415-4 PRINCETON PB $19.95

Edward O. **Wilson**
Biodiversity
"The most comprehensive book, by the most distinguished group of scholars, ever published on one of the most important subjects of our (and all) time"—Stephen Jay Gould
0-309-03739-5 NATIONAL ACADEMY PB $24.50

Edward O. Wilson

The Diversity of Life
The two-time Pulitzer Prize-winning scientist unravels the complex evolutionary system that created diversity and illustrates why we now stand on the brink of catastrophe by creating man-made disasters in ecosystems around the world. "Stirring…an excellent guide to the broad movements of evolution"—*NY Times Book Review*. "Exhaustive, deftly written, and gorgeously illustrated"—*Newsweek*
0-674-21298-3 BELKNAP $29.95
0-393-31047-7 NORTON PB $14.95

Classification of Organisms

"At least three million and perhaps ten million species of living organisms are now alive…The effort to discern order in this incredible variety has given rise to systematics, the classification of the living world…This conceptual hierarchy grew gradually, in the course of about a century, from a solid base established by the Swede Carolus Linnaeus (1707-1778), who began the modern practice of binomial nomenclature. Every known organism is given a unique two-part name, Latin in form"—Lynn Margulis & Karlene Schwartz, *Five Kingdoms: An Illustrated Guide to the Phyla of life on Earth*

Lynn **Margulis** & Karlene **Schwartz**
Five Kingdoms: An Illustrated Guide to the Phyla of Life on Earth
The second edition of a standard textbook on the classification of living organisms
0-7167-1912-6 FREEMAN PB $38.95

Zoology

Durward L. **Allen**
Wolves of Minong: Isle Royale's Wild Community
An engaging and revealing account of the lives of a pack of wolves dwelling on a remote island in Lake Superior, between Michigan and Ontario
0-472-08237-X MICHIGAN PB $18.95

Lawrence **Elson**
The Zoology Coloring Book
For young readers
0-06-460301-6 BARNES & NOBLE PB $16.00

Jeffrey Moussaieff **Masson** & Susan **McCarthy**
When Elephants Sleep: The Emotional Lives of Animals
"A masterpiece, the most comprehensive and compelling argument for animal sensibility that I've yet seen "—Elizabeth Marshall Thomas, author of *The Hidden Life of Dogs*
See also **PETS** in **FOOD, TRAVEL, AND LEISURE**
0-385-31425-6 DOUBLEDAY $23.95

Botany

A. **Fahn**
Plant Anatomy
0-08-037490-5 PERGAMON $115.00
0-08-037491-3 PERGAMON PB $59.95

Janice **Glimn-Lacy** & Peter **Kaufman**
Botany Illustrated
0-442-22969-0 CHAPMAN & HALL PB $42.95

Edward **Greene**
Landmarks in Botanical History
A two-volume work
0-8047-1075-9 STANFORD $135.00

A.G. **Morton**
History of Botanical Science: An Account of the Development of Botany from the Ancient Time to the Present
0-12-508382-3 ACADEMIC PRESS PB $53.00

Dale **Pendell**
Pharmako/Poeia: Plant Powers, Poisons, and Herbcraft
"An ecological handbook, a dried-herb pastiche, a countercultural encyclopedia of ancient fact and lore"—Allen Ginsberg
1-56279-069-2 MERCURY HOUSE PB $16.95

Anthony **Robards**, editor
Botanical Microscopy
0-19-854587-8 OXFORD $32.50

Microbiology

The 16th-century Italian scholar Fracastorius first combined historical reports with his own observations to define the process of contagion, which transmits invisible "seeds" of disease from person to person. In the 17th century, the haberdasher Leeuwenhoek was astounded to discover such "beasts" in a drop of water by means of the newly invented microscope. However, it was not until the experiments of Pasteur and Koch that "germs" were identified as the microscopic causes of disease.

Johanna **Laybourn-Perry**
A Functional Biology of Free-Living Protozoa
0-520-05339-7 CALIFORNIA $47.50
0-520-05340-0 CALIFORNIA PB $30.00

Michael **Madigan** & Thomas **Brock**
The Biology of Microorganisms
A popular textbook
0-13-042169-3 PRENTICE HALL $80.00

Fergus **Priest** & Brian **Austin**
Modern Bacterial Taxonomy
0-412-46120-X CHAPMAN & HALL PB $34.50

Dorian **Sagan** & Lynn **Margulis**
A Garden of Microbial Delights: A Practical Guide to the Subvisible World
"With photographs, illustrations, or diagrams on almost every page, the authors present the beauty and complexity of these tiny creatures that perform jobs like transferring DNA and RNA, cleaning the air, and fertilizing the soil"
—*American Scientist*
0-8403-8529-3 KENDALL HUNT $38.95

John **Postgate**

Mirobes and Man

The revised edition of a classic

0-521-42355-4 CAMBRIDGE PB $17.95

Genetics

Chandler **Burr**

A Separate Creation: The Search for the Biological Origins of Sexual Orientation

"Burr's detailed, elegantly written report takes us to the front lines of research into a possible biological or genetic basis for homosexuality" —*Publishers Weekly*

See also **SEX AND SEXUALITY** under **GAY, LESBIAN, AND BISEXUAL STUDIES** in **SOCIAL STUDIES**

0-7868-6081-2 HYPERION $24.95

Steven **Fraser**, editor

The Bell Curve Wars

0-465-00693-0 BASIC PB $10.00

Joseph **Levine** & David **Suzuki**

The Secret of Life: Redesigning the Living World

The companion book to the PBS series discusses the role heredity plays in our lives as well as the ethical, medical, and political possibilities and consequences of genetic engineering

0-9636881-0-3 W.G.B.H. $24.95

Benjamin **Lewin**

Genes V

A popular textbook

0-19-854287-9 OXFORD $65.00

Robert **Olby**

The Origins of Mendelism

0-226-62592-3 CHICAGO PB $18.00

Norman **Rothwell**

Understanding Genetics

A reliable text

0-471-58822-9 WILEY-LISS $59.95

Genetic Engineering and Biotechnology

James **Coombs**, editor

Dictionary of Biotechnology

1-56159-074-6 STOCTON $90.00

O.J. **Crocomo**, editor

Biotechnology of Plants and Microorganisms

0-8142-0375-2 OHIO STATE $95.00

Karl **Drlica**

Understanding DNA and Gene Cloning: A Guide For the Curious

Genetic engineering made easier

0-471-62225-7 WILEY PB $35.30

John **Elkington**

The Gene Factory: The Science and Business of Biotechnology

0-88184-293-1 CARROLL & GRAF PB $8.95

Daniel J. **Kevles**

In the Name of Eugenics: Genetics and the Uses of Human Heredity

"It stands as a powerful warning against anyone today who would use the fruits of legitimate science to bolster arguments and policies that echo the social and racial prejudice of the past"—*Washington Post*

See also **SCIENCE AND MACHINES**

0-674-44557-0 HARVARD PB $16.95

Jean **Marx**, editor

A Revolution in Biotechnology

A survey by 26 eminent scientists of the major developments in the biotechnology revolution, sponsored by the International Council of Scientific Unions

0-521-32749-0 CAMBRIDGE $49.95

R.W. **Old** & S.B. **Primrose**

Principles of Gene Manipulation

0-632-02608-1 BLACKWELL PB $39.95

Molecular Biology

Watson and Crick's dramatic discovery of the double helix of DNA advanced the idea that a molecule's structure and function were intertwined. DNA's helical strands allow genetic information to be duplicated and passed on to the next generation.

Herrick **Baltscheffsky**, editor

The Molecular Evolution of Life

0-521-33642-2 CAMBRIDGE $89.95

Maclyn **McCarty**

The Transforming Principle: Discovering That Genes Are Made of DNA

The beginning of the story of the discovery of DNA. "The most interesting and portentous biological experiment of the 20th century authoritatively described by one of the three principal executants"— Peter Medawar

0-393-30450-7 NORTON PB $5.95

Peter **Medawar**

Memoir of a Thinking Radish: An Autobiography

Reflections on his role in the development of the new biology. "Has all the wonderful informality, immediacy and odd digressiveness that make this genre such a pleasure to read"—*NY Times*

0-19-217737-0 OXFORD $19.95

Anne **Sayre**

Rosalind Franklin and DNA

A version of the events surrounding the famous discovery of the DNA structure

0-393-00868-1 NORTON PB $9.95

Robert L. **Sinsheimer**

The Strands of Life: The Science of DNA and the Art of Education

0-520-08248-6 CALIFORNIA $30.00

James **Watson**

The Double Helix

A personal, candid memoir of the discovery of the structure of DNA. A good introduction

0-451-62787-3 NEW AMERICAN LIBRARY PB $6.99

James Watson

The Molecular Biology of the Gene

Explanation of the new technology

0-8053-9614-4 ADDISON-WESLEY $66.75

Recombinant DNA: A Short Course

A good short introduction that goes beyond standard popularizations

0-7167-2282-8 FREEMAN PB $45.95

Medicine

For related reading, see HEALTH in LIFESTYLES AND PRACTICAL ADVICE

Michael J. **Norden**

Beyond Prozac: Antidotes for Modern Times

Beyond Prozac, says Norden, lie many innovative natural remedies that combat depression in much the same way as the controversial drug. Light therapies, melatonin, specialized diets, acupuncture, and sleep deprivation are just some of the therapies that Norden discusses along with other alternative drugs and the successes and failures of Prozac itself

See also **DEPRESSION** under **SELF-HELP** in **LIFESTYLES AND PRACTICAL ADVICE**

0-06-039151-0 HARPERCOLLINS $23.00

History of Medicine

Erwin **Ackerknecht**
A Short History of Medicine
0-8018-2726-4 JOHNS HOPKINS PB $14.95

Kenneth J. **Carpenter**
A History of Scurvy and Vitamin C
0-521-34773-4 CAMBRIDGE PB $18.95

John **Duffy**
From Humors to Medical Science: A History of American Medicine
0-252-01736-6 ILLINOIS $44.95
0-252-06300-7 ILLINOIS PB $14.95

Sander **Gilman**
Disease and Representation: Images of Illness from Madness to AIDS
A pioneer in the study of stereotypes examines the images of disease and its victims that society creates
0-8014-2119-5 CORNELL $46.50
0-8014-9476-1 CORNELL PB $16.95

Richard **Gordon**
The Alarming History of Medicine: Amusing Anecdotes from Hippocrates to Heart Transplants
Rollicking and informative history, by the author of *Doctor in the House* and other novels
0-312-10411-1 ST. MARTIN'S $22.95

Anne **Hardy**
The Epidemic Streets: Infectious Diseases & the Rise of Preventive Medicine
It has become almost conventional wisdom to attribute the plunge in mortality from infectious disease in the West as much to advances in public health as to scientific breakthroughs in disease therapy. Hardy considers the question in a magnificently detailed study of eight communicable diseases that ravaged Victorian London: tuberculosis, whooping cough, measles, typhus, typhoid, diphtheria, smallpox and scarlet fever
0-19-820377-2 CLARENDON $69.00

Michael **Howell** & Peter **Ford**
The True History of The Elephant Man
A factual history of the case of John Merrick, made famous by John Pomerance's play and the popular film
0-8018-4427-4 JOHNS HOPKINS PB $18.95

James H. **Jones**
Bad Blood: The Tuskegee Syphilis Experiment
A scholarly exposition of one of the most disturbing—and most racially explosive—stories of human experimentation in the history of medicine
0-02-916676-4 FREE PRESS PB $14.95

Arno **Karlen**
Man and Microbes: Disease and Plagues in History and Modern Times
0-87477-759-3 TARCHER $24.95

J. William **Langston**
The Case of the Frozen Addicts
0-679-42465-2 PANTHEON $25.00

Christopher **Lawrence**
Medicine in the Making of Modern Britain: 1700-1920
0-415-09168-3 ROUTLEDGE PB $13.95

Judith Walzer **Leavitt** & Ronald **Numbers**, editors
Sickness and Health in America: Readings in the History of Medicine and Public Health
0-299-10274-2 WISCONSIN PB $16.95

Susan **Lederer**
Subjected to Science: Human Experimentation in America Before the Second World War
0-8018-4820-2 JOHNS HOPKINS $32.95

Albert **Lyons** & R. Joseph **Petrucelli**
Medicine: An Illustrated History
With over 1000 illustrations
0-8109-8080-0 ABRADALE $49.98
0-8016-3374-5 MOSBY $42.95

Matthew **Naythons**
The Face of Mercy: Medicine at War—A Photographic History
230 stunning photographs from archival sources, including the work of well-known photographers like Matthew Brady, but also including powerful work from lesser-known figures. Includes commentary by William Styron and Sherwin Nuland, among others
0-679-42744-9 RANDOM HOUSE $40.00

Sherwin B. **Nuland**
Doctors: The Biography of Medicine
"The heroes of [this] story (and there is even one heroine) are the great doctors…whose hunger to know carried the business of discovery forward"—*NY Times*
0-679-72215-7 VINTAGE PB $15.00

Ronald **Numbers**, editor
Medicine in the World: New Spain, New France, and New England
0-87049-517-8 TENNESSEE $25.00

Martin **Pernick**
A Calculus of Suffering: Pain, Professionalism, and Anesthesia in the 19th Century America
0-231-05186-7 COLUMBIA $57.50

William B. **Ober**
Boswell's Clap & Other Essays: Medical Analyses of Literary Men's Afflictions
Witty, learned, digressive, and gossipy essays by a doctor investigating the literary evidence for the medical and psychological problems of writers such as Lawrence, Swinburne, Johnson, and Rochester
0-8093-1433-9 SOUTHERN ILLINOIS PB $12.95

Charles E. **Rosenberg**
The Care of Strangers: The Rise of America's Hospital System
A groundbreaking study. Though it seems an eternal institution, Rosenberg traces it to its relatively recent rise in the medical turmoil of the 19th century. "The most ambitious historical work on the hospital and on American medicine generally"—*NY Times*
0-8018-5082-7 JOHNS HOPKINS PB $16.95

Edward **Shorter**
Bedside Manners: The Troubled History of Doctors and Patients
0-88738-871-X TRANSACTION PB $19.95
0-671-63309-0 TRANSACTION PB $9.95

Paul **Starr**
The Social Transformation of American Medicine
Highly influential, and now a standard work in its field, Starr's book documents the rise of American medicine, from its cottage-industry roots to the highly respected, lucrative semi-monopoly it became in the 20th century
See also **SCIENCE AND MACHINES** under **HISTORY OF SCIENCE AND TECHNOLOGY** under **TOPICS IN AMERICAN STUDIES** in **HISTORY OF THE AMERICAS**
0-465-07935-0 BASIC BOOKS PB $20.00

Susan N. **Terkel**
Colonial American Medicine
An intriguing, sometimes hair-raising introduction to the history of American medicine. For younger readers, but adults will find Terkel's account fascinating as well
0-531-12539-4 FRANKLIN WATTS $20.30

James W. **Trent**
Inventing the Feeble Mind: A History of Mental Retardation in the United States
An eye-opening history of the treatment—and mistreatment—of those with lower than "normal" intelligence, from the mid-19th century to the present. Trent ends with the controversial trend toward deinstitutionalization
0-520-08243-5 CALIFORNIA $30.00
0-520-20357-7 CALIFORNIA PB $14.95

George **Weisz**
The Medical Mandarins: The French Academy of Medicine in the Nineteenth and Early Twentieth Centuries
0-19-509037-3 OXFORD $57.50

Guy **Williams**

The Age of Agony: The Art of Healing, C. 1700-1800

A popular account

0-89733-202-4 ACADEMY CHICAGO $20.00

The Age of Miracles: Medicine and Surgery in the 19th Century

0-89733-285-7 ACADEMY CHICAGO PB $10.00

Disease and Research

Bernard **Asbell**

The Pill: The Untold Story of the Drug That Changed the World

Asbell "places the Pill in today's society by helping us understand all the players in its history"—Pepper Schwartz

0-679-41100-3 RANDOM HOUSE $25.00

Robert S. **Desowitz**

New Guinea Tapeworms and Jewish Grandmothers: Tales of Parasites and People

0-393-30426-4 NORTON PB $9.95

The Thorn in the Starfish: The Immune System and How It Works

0-393-30556-2 NORTON PB $9.95

Laurie **Garrett**

The Coming Plague: Newly Emerging Diseases in a World Out of Balance

A sobering reminder that infectious disease, aided and abetted by injudicious human activity, remains a potent worldwide threat

0-14-025091-3 PENGUIN PB $14.95

John **Last**, editor

A Dictionary of Epidemiology

The standard reference. "Consider this an essential companion to serious reading of the medical literature"
—*Yale Journal of Biology and Medicine*

0-19-505480-6 OXFORD PB $29.95
0-19-505481-4 OXFORD PB $14.95

Thomas **McKeown**

The Origins of Human Disease

A history drawing on archaeological, historical, and demographic evidence, and on the author's own work in the history of infection

0-631-17938-0 BLACKWELL PB $22.95

Eve **Nichols**

Human Gene Therapy

An examination of the potentials and pitfalls of an exciting and controversial new medical treatment

0-674-41480-2 HARVARD PB $12.95

Sherwin B. **Nuland**

How We Die: Reflections on Life's Final Chapter

A rare book that demythologizes death not with tired homilies but with an unflinching look at its reality. Rooted in both medical science and personal experience, Dr. Nuland's account, for instance, "of the decline and death of his grandmother—with whom he shared a bedroom until he was in his late teens and she was in her nineties—is unforgettable"—*Kirkus Reviews*

See also **DEATH AND MOURNING** under **SELF-HELP** in **LIFESTYLES AND PRACTICAL ADVICE**

0-679-41461-4 KNOPF $24.00
0-679-74244-1 VINTAGE PB $13.00

Bert E. **Park**

Ailing, Aging, Addicted: Studies of Compromised Leadership

The sequel to *The Impact of Illness on World Leaders*. Practicing neurological surgeon and historian, Park once again combines clinical diagnoses and scholarship to explain the behavioral patterns of historical figures—from Joan of Arc to Hitler and Stalin to Reagan. Syphilis, drug addiction, and senility are among the retrospective diagnoses he offers here

0-8131-1853-0 KENTUCKY $29.00

In appearance alone, one of the nation's youngest and ostensibly most vigorous presidents showed unequivocal manifestations of steroid excess. Press photographers were struck by the pudginess of Kennedy's face, which knowledgeable physicians of the day recognized as the telltale "moon face." More disconcerting still, word circulated in medical circles that he had suffered at least one psychological breakdown as a result of the drug.

AILING, AGING, ADDICTED: STUDIES OF COMPROMISED LEADERSHIP

Richard **Preston**

The Hot Zone

When a lethal virus carried by an African rainforest experimental monkey turned up in a Virginia laboratory, it became glaringly clear that African deforestation had unleashed extremely dangerous viruses into the human population. Preston recreates the efforts of a military biomedical SWAT team sent to arrest the spread of this dangerous near-runaway

0-679-43094-6 RANDOM HOUSE $23.00

Owsei **Temkin**

The Falling Sickness: A History of Epilepsy from the Greeks to the Beginnings of Modern Neurology

A new edition of a medical history classic

0-8018-4849-0 JOHNS HOPKINS PB $24.95

George **Vaillant**

The Natural History of Alcoholism Revisited

A revised and updated version of perhaps the most thorough, sophisticated, and readable exposition of the theory that alcoholism is a disease, based on Vaillant's long-term research

0-674-60378-8 HARVARD PB $16.95

Harold E. **Varmus** & Robert A. **Weinberg**

Cells, Development, and the Biology of Cancer

A textbook by two widely known and widely respected authorities that is invaluable for anyone seeking a clear and detailed understanding of the complex process by which normal cells can become malignant

0-7167-5037-6 FREEMAN $32.95

Joyce **Wadler**

My Breast: One Woman's Cancer Story

Based on widely acclaimed *New York Magazine* pieces, Wadler describes her horrified suspicion of breast cancer: its confirmation, her agonized decision about treatment, and her final recovery. This book contains insights of tremendous value to all women and it is also a highly readable, vivid, and inspiring true story

See also **BREAST CANCER** under **WOMEN'S HEALTH** under **HEALTH** in **LIFESTYLES AND PRACTICAL ADVICE**

0-671-87970-7 POCKET PB $5.50

Hans **Zinsser**

Rats, Lice and History

A bacteriologist on the struggle to conquer the scourge of typhus

See also **THE 14TH CENTURY: BLACK DEATH AND ECONOMIC DEPRESSION** under **MEDIEVAL AND RENAISSANCE EUROPE** in **WORLD HISTORY AND CURRENT AFFAIRS**

0-316-98896-0 LITTLE, BROWN PB $13.95

Medical Care and Health Policy

Robert **Blank**

Rationing Medicine

Who is to benefit from new medical technologies?

0-231-06536-1 COLUMBIA $45.00

Daniel **Callahan**

Setting Limits: Medical Goals in an Aging Society

Argues that society must limit the money spent on care that is merely life-extending and concentrate on relief for the suffering

See also **AGING** under **RITES OF PASSAGE** under **TOPICS IN AMERICAN STUDIES** in **HISTORY OF THE AMERICAS**

0-87840-572-0 GEORGETOWN PB $15.95

Jean **De Kervasdoue**, editor

The End of an Illusion: The Future of Health Policy in Western Industrialized Nations

Comparative studies of health systems and medical care

0-520-04726-5 CALIFORNIA $45.00

Charles **Dougherty**

American Health Care: Realities, Rights, and Reforms

A critical analysis, with arguments for creating a national health care system and health insurance

0-19-505271-4 OXFORD $35.00
0-19-505272-2 OXFORD PB $19.95

David **Eisenberg**

Encounters with Qi: Exploring Chinese Medicine

0-393-31213-5 NORTON PB $11.00

Daniel **Fox**

Health Policies, Health Politics: The British and American Experience, 1911-1965

0-691-04733-2 PRINCETON $34.00

Edward S. **Golub**

The Limits of Medicine: How Science is Reshaping Our Search for the Cure

Golub asserts that a new understanding of the place of medicine is needed in today's era of powerful, high-cost treatments for complex chronic diseases and degenerative conditions of aging. "Deft questioning of our basic assumptions about health, disease, and medicine"—*Kirkus Reviews*

0-8129-2141-0 TIMES BOOKS $23.00

Ruth **Hubbard** & Elijah **Wald**

Exploding the Gene Myth: How Genetic Information Is Produced and Manipulated by Scientists, Physicians, Employers, Insurance Companies, Educators, and Law Enforcers

Hubbard, Professor Emerita of Biology at Harvard, warns that the grandiose claims about the medical benefits of genetic research are grossly overinflated. The current hyperbole, she says, derives, in fact, from the old "scientific" rationale behind "ethnic cleansing." "Hubbard and Wald have given us an accessible yet scrupulously correct account of the truth about DNA and its real relation to human welfare" —R. C. Lewontin, Harvard University

0-8070-0419-7 BEACON PB $12.95

When the disastrous consequences of the Nazis' racist, hereditarian policies became widely known, they stood as a horrific warning of the dangers of assigning too much power to biological inheritance and using genetic means to improve humanity.

EXPLODING THE GENE MYTH: HOW GENETIC INFORMATION IS PRODUCED AND MANIPULATED BY SCIENTISTS, PHYSICIANS, EMPLOYERS, INSURANCE COMPANIES, EDUCATORS, AND LAW ENFORCERS

Ruth Hubbard

Ivan **Illich**

Medical Nemesis: The Expropriation of Health

A polemic on the limitations inherent in our traditional concepts of health and medical care

0-394-71245-5 PANTHEON PB $13.33

Melvin **Konner**

Medicine At the Crossroads: The Crisis in Health Care

In a passionate call to arms, this anthropologist provides an indictment of American medicine. Why does it cost $6,000 to have a baby? Why do other countries handle AIDS and care for the elderly better than we do? "Konner's arguments…are forceful, and his recommendations for change are specific" —*Kirkus Reviews*

See also HOSPITAL AND MEDICAL CARE under HEALTH in LIFESTYLES AND PRACTICAL ADVICE

0-679-41545-9 PANTHEON $23.00
0-679-74216-6 VINTAGE PB $13.00

National Academy of Sciences

The Future of Public Health

0-309-03831-6 NATIONAL ACADEMY $34.95
0-309-03830-8 NATIONAL ACADEMY PB $24.95

Lynn **Payer**

Medicine and Culture

A thought-provoking comparison of medical practice in the United States, West Germany, Britain, and France. "Deserves an audience beyond the medical community"—*NY Times*

See also THE MEDICAL PROFESSION

0-14-012404-7 PENGUIN PB $11.95

Edmund **Pellegrino** & David **Thomas**

For the Patient's Good: The Restoration of Beneficence in Health Care

Acting in the patient's best interest, examined in the context of current medical trends

0-19-504319-7 OXFORD $41.50

Robert N. **Proctor**

Cancer Wars: How Politics Shapes What We Know and Don't Know About Cancer

How acrimonious public debate can shape and sometimes distort medical research. "This forceful, scholarly study urges greater efforts to encourage cancer prevention, including a halt to tobacco subsidies, stiffer supervision of pesticides and federal support for alternatives to petrochemical agriculture"—*Publishers Weekly*

0-465-02756-3 BASIC $25.00
0-465-00859-3 HARPERCOLLINS PB $15.00

Medical Economics

David **Blumenthal**

Renewing the Promise: Medicare and Its Reform

Its history, current problems, and future

0-19-504304-9 OXFORD $37.95

Bryan **Jennett**

High Technology Medicine: Benefits and Burdens

0-19-261588-2 OXFORD PB $15.95

Kenneth **Lee** & Anne **Mills**, editors

The Economics of Health in Developing Countries

0-19-261385-5 OXFORD $39.95
0-19-261549-1 OXFORD PB $14.95

Carl J. **Schramm**, editor

Health Care and Its Costs

0-393-02437-7 NORTON $18.95
0-393-95671-7 NORTON PB $7.95

Anne **Stoline** & Jonathan **Weiner**

The New Medical Marketplace: A Physician's Guide to the Health Care Revolution

A guide for physicians to balancing medical care and medical costs

0-8018-4582-3 JOHNS HOPKINS $45.00
0-8018-4583-1 JOHNS HOPKINS PB $18.95

Medical Ethics

Tom **Beauchamp** & James **Childress**

Principles of Biomedical Ethics

0-19-508537-X OXFORD PB $23.95

Marshall **Cohen**, editor

Medicine and Moral Philosophy

0-691-07268-X PRINCETON $39.50

Diane **Dutton**

Worse Than the Disease: Pitfalls of Medical Progress

An assessment of the ethical and economic price we are paying—and will be paying—for medical progress

0-521-34023-3 CAMBRIDGE $44.95
0-521-39557-7 CAMBRIDGE PB $21.95

Abraham **Edel**

Morality, Philosophy, and Practice

0-07-554364-8 MCGRAW HILL PB $48.75

Joseph **Fletcher**

Morals and Medicine: The Moral Problem of the Patient's Right to Know the Truth

0-691-07234-5 PRINCETON $45.00
0-691-02004-3 PRINCETON PB $12.95

Carole **Joffe**

Doctors of Conscience: The Struggle to Provide Abortion Before and After Roe v. Wade

Despite the constitutionally mandated legality of abortion in America, access to safe medical abortions is rapidly narrowing. For this, Joffe argues in a novel and convincing thesis, the medical community is partly to blame. Even after *Roe v. Wade*, she demonstrates, mainstream medicine has failed to provide needed services and training and has stigmatized doctors who perform abortions. Doctors today who ensure safe abortions are subject to real threats to their professional standing and personal safety. "A book of major importance that looks at the abortion issue from a thoroughly fresh and critical perspective"—Rosalind Petchesky

See also **THE ABORTION DEBATE** under **THE FEMALE EXPERIENCE** under **WOMEN'S STUDIES** in **SOCIAL STUDIES**

0-8070-2100-8 BEACON $24.00

Robert **Levine**

Ethics and Regulation of Clinical Research

A review of federal regulations, ethical analyses, and case studies

0-300-04288-4 YALE PB $19.00

Ruth **Macklin**

Mortal Choices: Ethical Dilemmas in Modern Medicine

"A thoughtful and lively examination" —Sissela Bok

0-395-46847-7 HOUGHTON MIFFLIN PB $12.95

Kenneth **Vaux**, editor

Powers That Make Us Human: The Foundations of Medical Ethics

0-252-01187-2 ILLINOIS $21.95

Robert **Veatch**

Death, Dying, and the Biological Revolution: Our Quest For Responsibility

"One of the most comprehensive and useful examples of the literature born of [the] new interest in dying"—*Washington Post*

0-300-04364-3 YALE $40.00
0-300-04365-1 YALE PB $17.00

Ronald **Yezzi**

Medical Ethics

0-03-053256-6 HOLT RINEHART & WINSTON PB .. $32.59

The Medical Profession

Eliot **Freidson**

Medical Work in America

0-300-04157-8 YALE $30.00
0-300-04158-6 YALE PB $18.00

Jody **Heymann**

Equal Partners: A Physician's Call for a New Spirit of Medicine

Heymann, a Harvard faculty member, MacArthur Fellow, wife, and mother of two children recounts her harrowing experience at the other end of the medical profession when she was diagnosed with a brain tumor during her pediatric medical residency

0-316-35993-9 LITTLE, BROWN $22.95

Kathryn M. **Hunter**

Doctor's Stories: The Narrative Structure of Medical Knowledge

An illuminating and scholarly study, arguing that patients' narratives of their illnesses should form a more important part of diagnosis and treatment than is usually the case

0-691-06888-7 PRINCETON $37.50

Janet **Kraegel** & Mary **Kachoyeanos**

"Just a Nurse"

Two nurses use interviews with nurses from every area of the profession—burn units, cancer wards, AIDS wards, children's hospices, delivery rooms—to discuss the experiences and problems of nurses today and to dispose of myths and stereotypes

0-440-20763-0 DELL PB $5.99

William **Maples**

Dead Men Do Tell Tales

...to the Director of the Human Identification Laboratory of the University of Florida, at least. Maples has worked on the remains of Czar Nicholas II, Francisco Pizarro, and Vietnam MIAs. Reading the tales of death written on the bones of the deceased, he revisits his most interesting, strangest, and baffling cases. "When you think of all the horror movies you have seen in your entire life, you are visualizing only a dim, dull fraction of what I have seen in actual fact. "A fascinating account of forensic anthropology

0-385-47968-9 MAIN STREET PB $12.95

Robert **Mendelsohn**

Confessions of a Medical Heretic

0-8092-4131-5 CONTEMPORARY PB $14.95

Marcia **Millman**

The Unkindest Cut: Life in the Backrooms of Medicine

A not too kind behind-the-scenes account of surgeons and hospital personnel

0-688-08120-7 MORROW PB $7.95

Regina **Morantz-Sanchez**

Sympathy and Science: Women Physicians in American Medicine

See also **SCIENCE AND MACHINES** under **HISTORY OF SCIENCE AND TECHNOLOGY** under **TOPICS IN AMERICAN STUDIES** in **HISTORY OF THE AMERICAS**

0-19-503627-1 OXFORD $24.95
0-19-504985-3 OXFORD PB $12.95

Lynn **Payer**

Medicine and Culture

A thought-provoking comparison of medical practice in the United States, West Germany, Britain, and France. "Deserves an audience beyond the medical community"—*NY Times*

See also **MEDICAL CARE AND HEALTH POLICY**

0-14-012404-7 PENGUIN PB $11.95

Edward **Rosenbaum**

A Taste of My Own Medicine: When the Doctor Is the Patient

0-8041-0873-0 IVY PB $4.99

Richard **Selzer**

Letters to a Young Doctor

0-15-600399-6 HARVEST PB $12.00

Mortal Lessons: Notes on the Art of Surgery

0-15-600400-3 HARVEST PB $12.00

Rituals of Surgery

0-688-06490-6 MORROW PB $6.95

John **Stoeckle** & George Abbot **White**

Plain Pictures of Plain Doctoring: Vernacular Expression in New Deal Medicine and Photography

0-262-69138-8 MIT PB $17.50

Lewis **Thomas**

The Youngest Science: Notes of a Medicine Watcher

An informal, nostalgic autobiography reflecting the vast changes in medicine since the early part of the century

0-14-024327-5 PENGUIN PB $11.95

Medical Education

Thomas A. **Bonner**

Becoming a Physician: Students, Medicine, and National Cultures, 1750-1945

0-19-506298-1 OXFORD $45.00

Stephen **Hoffman**

Under the Ether Dome: One Doctor's Apprenticeship At Massachusetts General Hospital

0-8065-1207-5 CITADEL PB $9.95

Perri **Klass**

A Not Entirely Benign Procedure: Four Years as a Medical Student

0-452-27258-0 PLUME PB $11.95

Melvin **Konner**

Becoming a Doctor: A Journey of Initiation in Medical School

An anthropologist's career change

0-14-011116-6 PENGUIN PB $13.95

John **Langone**

Harvard Med: The Story Behind America's Premier Medical School and the Making of America's Doctors

0-517-59306-8 CROWN $25.00

AIDS

The most recent statistics on AIDS in the US, compiled by the Center for Disease Control in June of 1995, provide a quantitative measure of the massive toll the disease has taken on Americans of every race, age, and sex:

501,310 reported AIDS cases. 311,381 deaths. 630,000–897,000 Americans living with HIV.

One in 92 men ages 27–39 may be HIV infected. This number rises to 1 in 33 for black men.

One in every five deaths among black women ages 25–44 is due to HIV-related illness.

By the year 2000 there will be more than 60,000 AIDS orphans in New York City alone.

There is one AIDS-related death every 15 minutes.

The economy suffers a loss of $600,000 in medical costs and lost wages for each case of AIDS.

87% of all Americans believe the government should be devotiong more money to AIDS research, education, and prevention.

A 4% cut in cut in the requested military budget would finance the doubling of the biomedical research budget.

Barbara **Lazear Ascher**

Landscape Without Gravity: A Memoir of Grief

The intelligent, unflinching chronicle of the author's coming to terms with her wild, sometimes estranged brother's death from AIDS. "A warm, witty, very human voice" —Annie Dillard

See also **DEATH AND MOURNING** under **SELF-HELP** in **LIFESTYLES AND PRACTICAL ADVICE**

0-671-79676-3 DELPHINEUM $20.00
0-14-023495-0 PENGUIN PB $9.95

Susan **Bergman**

Anonymity

An unusually powerful and sophisticated AIDS memoir, by a daughter forced by AIDS to confront her father's homosexuality

0-374-25407-9 FS&G $20.00

Virginia **Berridge** & Philip **Strong**, editors

AIDS & Contemporary History

A thoroughgoing account with a British focus

0-521-41477-6 CAMBRIDGE $54.95

Elinor **Burkett**

The Gravest Show on Earth

From Jesse Helms to gay America, Burkett spares no one in her hard-hitting investigation of the age of AIDS. We meet playwright Larry Kramer and scientist Robert Gallo; MTV star Pedro Amora and a host of federally funded scientists—all the major players in the battle against the plague. Along the way, Burkett gives incisive accounts of AIDS in the African-American community, the fight of women to end the FDA practice of approving drugs tested only on men, as well as alarming anecdotes from the war between gay men and conservative Republicans. Vibrant, controversial, and informative, this is social history at its most compelling

0-395-74537-3 HOUGHTON MIFFLIN $24.95
0-312-14607-8 PICADOR PB $15.00

David B. **Feinberg**

Queer and Loathing: Rants and Raves of a Raging AIDS Clone

A collection of sulfurous, funny and heartbreaking essays on the AIDS crisis by the author of *Eighty-Sixed*. "Vibrant and caustic, this Eighties gonzo journalism from a New York, Jewish, HIV-positive gay perspective is a devastatingly powerful personal statement" —*Library Journal*

See also **CRITICAL COMMENTARY ON AMERICAN CULTURE** under **TOPICS IN MODERN SOCIOLOGY** under **SOCIOLOGY** in **SOCIAL STUDIES**

0-670-85766-1 VIKING $22.95

Mary **Fisher**

My Name is Mary: A Memoir

0-684-81305-X SCRIBNERS $24.00

Gregory **Flood**

I'm Looking for Mr. Right, But I'll Settle for Mr. Right Away: AIDS, True Love, the Perils of Safe Sex & Other Spiritual Concerns of the Gay Male

0-938407-02-3 READER'S CATALOG PB $12.00

Shelley **Geballe** & others, editors

Forgotten Children of the AIDS Epidemic

0-300-06270-2 YALE $25.00
0-300-06271-0 YALE PB $12.00

Mirko D. **Grmek**

History of AIDS: Emergence and Origin of a Modern Pandemic

A survey of the epidemic, its origins, and the scientific struggle to contain it

0-691-08552-8 PRINCETON $45.00
0-691-02477-4 PRINCETON PB $16.95

William G. **Hawkeswood** & Alex W. **Costley**

One of the Children: Gay Black Men in Harlem

0-520-08112-9 CALIFORNIA $40.00
0-520-20212-0 CALIFORNIA PB $15.00

James **Kinsella**

Covering the Plague: AIDS & the American Media

A pioneering scholarly treatment of the way the American media covered—or rather failed to cover—the epidemic in its early years

0-8135-1482-7 RUTGERS PB $14.95

Larry **Kramer**

Reports from the Holocaust: The Making of an AIDS Activist

A collection of essays on AIDS from 1978 to the present written by a leading gay activist and playwright, author of *The Normal Heart*

See also **AIDS AND HEALTH** under **GAY, LESBIAN, AND BISEXUAL STUDIES** in **SOCIAL STUDIES**

0-312-11419-2 ST. MARTIN'S PB $13.95

Paul **Monette**

Borrowed Time: An AIDS Memoir

Perhaps the most gripping, unsparing and moving account of a lover's illness and death

0-15-113598-3 HARCOURT BRACE $22.00
1-56956-198-2 READER'S CATALOG $52.64
0-380-70779-9 AVON PB $12.50

Jeanne **Moutoussamy-Ashe**

Daddy & Me

Text and photographs by Arthur Ashe's widow, documenting the tennis great's battle with AIDS and his relationship with Camera, his young daughter. A moving book, especially helpful for children dealing with a parent's illness

PHOTOGRAPHS BY JEANNE MOUTOUSSAMY-ASHE

0-679-95096-6 KNOPF $14.99

Randy **Shilts**

And the Band Played On: Politics, People, and the AIDS Epidemic

The groundbreaking masterpiece of investigative reporting reveals, in the mishandling of the AIDS epidemic, the inadequacies of a government obsessed with budget considerations, health authorities more interested in politics than public health, and scientists overly concerned with international prestige. "A heroic work of journalism on what must rank as one of the foremost catastrophes of modern history"—*NY Times*

See also **SCIENCE AND MACHINES** under **HISTORY OF SCIENCE AND TECHNOLOGY** under **TOPICS IN AMERICAN STUDIES** in **HISTORY OF THE AMERICAS**

See also **AIDS AND HEALTH** under **GAY, LESBIAN, AND BISEXUAL STUDIES** in **SOCIAL STUDIES**

0-14-023221-4 VIKING PB $15.00

Randy Shilts

Diane **Solway** & Tom **Miller**, editor

A Dance Against Time

A biography of Joffrey Ballet dancer and choreographer Edward Stierle, who died of AIDS in 1991; a powerful evocation both of Stierle's life and the devastating effect AIDS has had on the arts

0-671-78894-9 POCKET $23.00
0-671-78896-5 POCKET PB $14.00

Carter **Wilson**

Hidden in the Blood: A Personal Investigation of AIDS in The Yucatan

0-231-10190-2 COLUMBIA $29.95
0-231-10191-0 COLUMBIA PB $14.50

David **Wojnarowicz**

Close to the Knives: A Memoir of Disintegration

Wojnarowicz's dissident art has brought him to center of controversies involving AIDS and censorship. "The artist writes like a bestselling author...There's never a dull moment in Wojnarowicz' work...(It) depicts the terrain of heterosexual culture as quicksand for gays and lesbians"—*Village Voice*

0-679-73227-6 VINTAGE PB $11.00

Medical and Research Aspects

Ron **Brookmeyer** & Mitchell H. **Gail**

AIDS Epidemiology: A Quantitative Approach

A lucid exposition—by pioneers in the field—of how statistics help epidemiologists to track the spread of even a cryptic and often baffling agent like the HIV virus

0-19-507641-9 OXFORD $52.50

Consumer Reports

AIDS: Trading Fears for Facts

A guide for teenagers

See also **AIDS** under **SPECIFIC HEALTH PROBLEMS** under **HEALTH** in **LIFESTYLES AND PRACTICAL ADVICE**

See also **TEENAGE HEALTH** under **STAGES OF DEVELOPMENT** under **PARENTING** in **LIFESTYLES AND PRACTICAL ADVICE**

0-89043-269-4 CONSUMER REPORTS PB $4.95

Gena **Corea**

The Invisible Epidemic: The Story of Women and AIDS

The author, who has taken on the medical establishment before in her book *The Mother Machine,* interweaves factual research with personal narratives about AIDS sufferers, their relatives, professional experts, and activists to disclose many alarming truths about the effects of the disease on women. "A powerful report on the AIDS crisis...a long overdue exposé...and a heartfelt call to action"—*Kirkus Reviews*

See also **AIDS** under **SPECIFIC HEALTH PROBLEMS** under **HEALTH** in **LIFESTYLES AND PRACTICAL ADVICE**

0-06-016648-7 HARPERPERENNIAL PB $23.00

Peter H. **Duesberg**

Inventing the AIDS Virus

An impassioned argument by the best-known (and embattled) advocate of the idea that HIV is not the cause of AIDS

0-895-26470-6 REGNERY GATEWAY $29.95

John Nguyet **Erni**

Unstable Frontiers: Technomedicine and the Cultural Politics of "Curing" AIDS

See also **AIDS AND HEALTH** under **GAY, LESBIAN, AND BISEXUAL STUDIES** in **SOCIAL STUDIES**

0-8166-2380-5 MINNESOTA $39.95

0-8166-2381-3 MINNESOTA PB $15.95

Dr. Joseph **Feldschuh** & Doron **Weber**

Safe Blood: Purifying the Nation's Blood Supply in the Age of AIDS

Reveals the unreported risks of the average transfusion and assails the unsafe practices of some of America's leading blood services

0-02-910065-8 FREE PRESS $22.95

Robert C. **Gallo**

Virus Hunting: AIDS, Cancer, & the Human Retrovirus, A Story of Scientific Discovery

Both a personal and scientific account by the discoverer of HIV and the researcher who pioneered the detection of similar viruses in humans

0-465-09815-0 BASIC PB $16.00

Robert Gallo

Christine **Grady**

The Search for an AIDS Vaccine: Ethical Issues in the Development & Testing of a Preventive HIV Vaccine

Explains many of the problems, both ethical and scientific, that lie in the way of a safe and effective vaccine against AIDS

0-253-32619-2 INDIANA $26.50

Lorna **Greenberg**

AIDS: How It Works in the Body

A clear, sensitively written, yet admirably accurate introduction for children

0-531-20074-4 FRANKLIN WATTS $21.00

Judith **Grief** & Beth A. **Golden**

AIDS Care at Home: A Guide for Patients, Caregivers, Loved Ones, and People with AIDS

A useful practical manual. "The book opens with a brief overview of the disease, complete with the history of its spread and the ways in which HIV assaults immune systems and societies. Routine lab tests, treatments and alternative therapies are also explained. The body of the work, however, is much more specific, offering pragmatic techniques for living with AIDS day-to-day; protection against opportunistic infections is stressed, and the book is organized around specific subjects...The psychological and social issues of AIDS are also examined. This book is an invaluable tool to anyone undertaking the monumental task of wrestling with the terrible challenges of living with AIDS"—*Publishers Weekly*

0-471-58468-1 WILEY PB $17.95

Earvin **Johnson**

What You Can Do To Avoid AIDS

0-679-41616-1 RANDOM HOUSE $5.99

Elisabeth **Kübler-Ross** & Mal **Warshaw**

AIDS: The Ultimate Challenge

An expert on working with the terminally ill offers compassionate advice to those confronting AIDS

See also **AIDS** under **SPECIFIC HEALTH PROBLEMS** under **HEALTH** in **LIFESTYLES AND PRACTICAL ADVICE**

0-02-089143-1 COLLIER PB $10.00

Jay A. **Levy**

HIV & Pathogenesis of AIDS

A full, detailed and scholarly review of the state of AIDS science by a well-known researcher in the field. For the expert, but accessible to any serious reader

1-55581-076-4 AMERICAN SOCIETY FOR MICROBIOLOGY PB $49.00

Bettyclare **Moffatt**

When Someone You Love Has AIDS: A Book of Hope For Family and Friends

See also **AIDS** under **SPECIFIC HEALTH PROBLEMS** under **HEALTH** in **LIFESTYLES AND PRACTICAL ADVICE**

0-8095-6551-X BORGO $27.00

National Academy of Sciences

Mobilizing Against AIDS: The Unfinished Story of a Virus

See also **AIDS** under **SPECIFIC HEALTH PROBLEMS** under **HEALTH** in **LIFESTYLES AND PRACTICAL ADVICE**

0-674-57762-0 HARVARD PB $12.95

Monroe E. **Price**

Shattered Mirrors: Our Search For Identity and Community in the AIDS Era

0-674-80590-9 HARVARD $27.00

Scientific American

The Science of AIDS: Readings from Scientific American

0-7167-2036-1 FREEMAN PB $16.95

Marc **Vargo** & Claire **Zion**, editor

The HIV Test: What You Need to Know to Make an Informed Decision

"An exemplary roundup of AIDS knowledge and advice"—*Booklist*

0-671-77950-8 POCKET PB $9.00

Government and Health Policy

Ronald **Bayer**

Private Acts, Social Consequences: AIDS and the Politics of Public Health

A critical examination of the health establishment's response to the AIDS epidemic

0-02-901961-3 FREE PRESS $32.95

0-8135-1624-2 RUTGERS PB $16.00

Norman **Daniels**

Seeking Fair Treatment: From the AIDS Epidemic to National Health

0-19-505712-0 OXFORD $25.00

Douglas **Crimp**, editor

AIDS: Cultural Analysis, Cultural Activism

Essays on the cultural images that have emerged in the AIDS crisis and how they have affected public and private response

0-262-53079-1 MIT PB $17.95

Elizabeth **Fee** & Daniel **Fox**, editors

AIDS: The Making of a Chronic Disease

This collection of essays covers the AIDS virus and epidemiology, law, ethics and public policy, those afflicted, and international perspectives

See also **AIDS** under **SPECIFIC HEALTH PROBLEMS** under **HEALTH** in **LIFESTYLES AND PRACTICAL ADVICE**

0-520-07569-2 CALIFORNIA $50.00
0-520-07778-4 CALIFORNIA PB $15.95

Michael **Fumento**

Myth of Heterosexual AIDS: How a Tragedy Has Been Distorted by the Media & Partisan Politics

A highly controversial book. Fumento argues that AIDS, in the U.S. at least, is not a devastating threat to the heterosexual population, and criticizes the media for exaggerating the impact of the disease

0-89526-729-2 REGNERY PB $14.95

Stephen **Joseph**

The Dragon Within the Gates: The Once and Future AIDS Epidemic

As former NYC Health Commissioner, Joseph contends that AIDS is the first major public health issue of our time for which social and political values rather than health requirements have set the agenda. "Steve Joseph was a sane and courageous public official in a time of madness and cowardice. He has written a sane and courageous book"—*Newsweek*

See also **AIDS** under **SPECIFIC HEALTH PROBLEMS** under **HEALTH** in **LIFESTYLES AND PRACTICAL ADVICE**

0-7867-0033-5 CARROLL & GRAF PB $9.95

Susan **Kuklin**

Fighting Back

Focusing on volunteers in New York City who offer help and support to people with AIDS, this moving book shows what it is like to be part of the struggle against this disease

9-9921-5935-9 PUTNAM LIBRARY EDITION $5.00

Leon **McCusick**, editor

What to Do About AIDS: Physicians and Mental Health Professionals Discuss the Issues

A collection, first published in 1986, focusing on the effects of AIDS in San Francisco

0-520-05936-0 CALIFORNIA PB $14.00

Dorothy **Nelkin** & others

A Disease of Society: Cultural and Institutional Responses to AIDS

How AIDS is affecting the fabric of American society: a study of the disease's impact on popular culture, the legal and medical professions, and social norms and values

0-521-40411-8 CAMBRIDGE $57.95
0-521-40743-5 CAMBRIDGE PB $17.95

Thomas P. **McCormack**

The AIDS Benefits Handbook: Everything You Need to Know to Get Social Security, Welfare, Medicaid, Medicare, Food Stamps, Housing, Drugs, & Other Benefits

A reliable and wide-ranging practical guide to often-neglected and daunting problems, the solution of which is nonetheless of crucial importance to people with AIDS

0-300-04736-3 YALE $35.00
0-300-04721-5 YALE PB $12.00

Padraig **O'Malley**, editor

The AIDS Epidemic: Private Rights and the Public Interest

A handbook of articles on various aspects of the AIDS epidemic

0-8070-0601-7 BEACON PB $16.00

Sandra **Panem**

The AIDS Bureaucracy

An investigation into the efficacy of government efforts to deal with AIDS, focusing in particular on the U.S. Public Health Service

0-674-01270-4 HARVARD $28.00
0-674-01271-2 HARVARD PB $11.95

Charles **Perrow** & Mauro F. **Guillen**

The AIDS Disaster: The Failure of Organizations in New York and the Nation

The authors argue that, because the largest concentration of AIDS victims tend to be groups for which society has an aversion, care for these victims has been shockingly inadequate

0-300-04880-7 YALE PB $11.00

Robert S. **Root-Bernstein**

Rethinking AIDS: The Tragic Cost of Premature Consensus

Argues that HIV may only be a contributing factor in AIDS, and not its sole cause

0-02-926905-9 FREE PRESS $35.00

Earth Sciences

Geology has historically been hampered by conflicts between physical evidence and theological constraints. Leonardo da Vinci kept private his correct explanation of the fossilized seashells found on Italian mountain peaks; a century later a Vatican cataloger described them as having been created "as is" by God, simultaneously with everything else. The great boulders perched oddly across the European landscape, far from the original outcrop, were widely believed to have been displaced by Noah's flood until Louis Agassiz's theory that during the Ice Age glaciers had moved across the continents, dragging rocks along. Even the fashionable theory of continental drift (plate tectonics is the latest formulation) was ignored for decades after its initial publication early in this century.

History

Claude **Albritton**, Jr.

The Abyss of Time: Changing Conceptions of the Earth's Antiquity After the Sixteenth Century

0-87735-341-7 FREEMAN COOPER $30.00

Kenneth C. **Davis**

Don't Know Much About Geography

Davis offers an entertaining corrective measure to the widespread problem of geographical ignorance. In a format similar to his previous *Don't Know Much About History,* this is a compendium of geographical oddities, including bothersome blind spots in the popular consciousness like how has politics changed the world map? And where was Eden? Perfect for the consummate fact lover

0-688-10332-4 MORROW $23.00
0-380-71379-9 AVON PB $12.50

Gabriel **Gohau**

A History of Geology

A thorough history of Earth science from the very beginnings to the latest theories of plate tectonics

TRANSLATED BY ALBERT V. CAROZZI & MARGUERITE CAROZZI

0-8135-1665-X RUTGERS $40.00
0-8135-1666-8 RUTGERS PB $16.00

Stephen Jay **Gould**

Time's Arrow, Time's Cycle: Myth and Metaphor in the Discovery of Geological Time

A most engaging account of geology's discovery

0-674-89199-6 HARVARD PB $12.95

Mott **Greene**

Geology in the Nineteenth Century: Changing Views in a Changing World

0-8014-1467-9 CORNELL $49.95
0-8014-9295-5 CORNELL PB $17.95

Donald **Johanson** & James **Shreeve**

Lucy's Child: The Search For Our Beginnings

0-380-71234-2 AVON PB $12.50

Rachael **Laudan**

From Mineralogy to Geology

The Foundations of a Science, 1650-1830

0-226-46950-6 CHICAGO $33.00

Martin **Rudwick**

The Great Devonian Controversy: The Shaping of Scientific Knowledge Among Gentlemanly Specialists

Recounts the scientific debate of the 1830s and 1840s about the dating of puzzling rock strata and fossils. "[It] could become one of our century's key documents in understanding science and its history"—Stephen Jay Gould

0-226-73102-2 CHICAGO PB $24.95

Earth History

Claude **Allegre**

From Stone to Star: The Discovery of Interplanetary Geology

An English translation of a pioneering work that explores the borders between astronomy and Earth history

TRANSLATED BY DEBORAH K. VAN DAM

0-674-83866-1 HARVARD $42.50

Peter **Doyle** & others

The Key to Earth History: An Introduction to Stratigraphy

An introduction to the basic tools of geology

0-471-94845-4 WILEY PB $28.95

David **Fisher**

The Birth of the Earth: A Wanderlied Through Space, Time, and the Human Imagination

"A well-written, important, and novel history" —*New Scientist*

0-231-06043-2 COLUMBIA PB $17.50

John **Imbrie** & Katherine **Imbrie**

Ice Ages: Solving the Mystery

0-674-44075-7 HARVARD PB $14.00

Charles **Officer** & Jake **Page**

Tales of the Earth: Great Events in Geologic History

Officer and Page describe the catastrophic events of environmental history (the Black Plague, the Lisbon earthquake of 1755, Chernobyl, etc.) and how they have altered the course of the world. "A work of science that reads like a good mystery"—*Kirkus Reviews*

0-19-507785-7 OXFORD $27.50

Geology

Donald L. **Baars**

Navajo Country: A Geology & Natural History of the Four Corners

0-8263-1587-9 NEW MEXICO PB $19.95

John **Farndon**

How the Earth Works

0-89577-411-9 READER'S DIGEST $24.00

Stephen S. **Hall**

Mapping the Next Millennium: The Discovery of New Geographies

Computers and satellites have ushered in a new Age of Discovery, and like cartographers before them, the scientists using these new technologies have redefined our view of ourselves and the universe. Hall describes the terrains being mapped, from the bottom of the sea to the farthest reaches of the solar system, the hole in the ozone layer, and the chromosomes and atoms that are the very structure of life itself

0-394-57635-7 VINTAGE PB $30.00

David **Lambert**

The Field Guide to Geology

Includes 500 illustrations, diagrams, charts, and maps

0-8160-1697-6 FACTS ON FILE $25.95

0-8160-2032-9 FACTS ON FILE PB $14.95

John **McPhee**

Basin and Range

"McPhee has demonstrated that he is our best and liveliest writer about the Earth and Earth sciences. He overspreads his territory like an ice sheet, and yet his touch is light: he can distribute silt and sand as deftly as he wears down mountains"—Wallace Stegner, *LA Times*

0-374-10914-1 FS&G $23.00

0-374-51690-1 NOONDAY PB $10.00

On the geologic time scale, a human lifetime is reduced to a brevity that is too inhibiting to think about. The mind blocks the information. Geologists, dealing always with deep time, find that it seeps into their beings and affects them in various ways. They see the unbelievable swiftness with which one evolving species on the Earth has learned to reach into the dirt of some tropical island and fling 747s into the sky. They see the thin band in which are the all but indiscernible stratifications of Cro-Magnon, Moses, Leonardo, and now. Seeing a race unaware of its own instantaneousness in time, they can reel off all the species that have come and gone, with emphasis on those that have specialized themselves to death.

BASIN AND RANGE

John McPhee

In Suspect Terrain

0-374-17650-7 FS&G $23.00

0-374-51794-0 NOONDAY PB $11.00

Rising from the Plains

0-374-25082-0 FS&G $23.00

0-374-52065-8 NOONDAY PB $10.00

Plate Tectonics

Claude **Allegre**

The Behavior of the Earth: Continental and Seafloor Mobility

"Required reading for anyone interested in how science works and in the significance and benefits of its major breakthroughs"— Donald Turcotte

0-674-06458-5 HARVARD PB $15.95

Edwin **Colbert**

Wandering Lands and Animals: The Story of Continental Drift and Populations

0-486-24918-2 DOVER PB $9.95

Jon **Erickson**

Plate Tectonics: Unraveling the Mysteries of the Earth

0-8160-2588-6 FACTS ON FILE $24.95

H.E. **LeGrand**

Drifting Continents and Shifting Theories: The Modern Revolution in Geology and Scientific Change

A gracefully written introduction to plate tectonics and the theory of continental drift by a science historian

0-521-31105-5 CAMBRIDGE PB $24.95

Tjeerd H. **Van Andel**

New Views of an Old Planet: Continental Drift and the History of the Earth

0-521-44243-5 CAMBRIDGE $65.00

Earthquakes and Volcanoes

Bruce A. **Bolt**

Earthquakes

0-7167-2236-4 FREEMAN PB $19.95

Earthquakes & Geological Discovery

0-7167-5040-6 FREEMAN $32.95

Basil **Booth**

Earthquakes & Volcanoes

An introduction for children, showing how earthquakes and volcanoes are related

0-02-711735-9 CRESTWOOD EDITION. $13.95

James **Gere** & Haresh **Shah**

Terra Non Firma: Understanding and Preparing For Earthquakes

0-7167-1497-3 STANFORD ALUMNI PB $11.95

Carl **Johnson** & Charlotte **Stone**, editor
Fire on the Mountain: The Nature of Volcanoes
An introduction by a geologist, illustrated by color photos
PHOTOGRAPHED BY DORIAN WEISEL
0-8118-0493-3 CHRONICLE PB $18.95

Maurice **Kraff**
Volcanoes: Fire from the Earth
0-8109-2844-2 ABRAMS PB $12.95

David **Ritchie**
Encyclopedia of Earthquakes & Volcanoes
With 632 entries, illustrated by maps, diagrams and photographs
0-8160-2659-9 FACTS ON FILE $40.00

Andrew **Robinson**
Earthshock
The cataclysmic natural forces that have shaped the Earth—earthquakes, drought, floods—are dissected here in light of 20th-century science. What makes this book so innovative, however, is its discussion of the human influence on natural forces peculiar to modern times. Is global warming, for instance, a force of nature or of humanity? An enthralling, far-reaching synthesis by the creator of the six-part PBS series *The Shape of the World.* Photographs and diagrams
0-500-05067-8 THAMES & HUDSON $29.95
0-500-27738-9 THAMES & HUDSON PB $19.95

Meteorology

Michael **Allaby**
How the Weather Works: 100 Ways Parents and Kids Can Share the Atmosphere
0-89577-612-X READER'S DIGEST $24.00

William J. **Burroughs**
Weather Cycles: Real or Imaginary?
A skeptical and well-informed evaluation of the currently influential idea that long-term meteorological trends can be documented and predicted
0-521-47869-3 CAMBRIDGE PB $19.95

Rob **DeMillo**
How Weather Works
1-56276-228-1 ZIFF DAVIS PB $19.95

James R. **Fleming**
Meteorology in America, Eighteen Hundred to Eighteen Seventy
A highly original exploration of a field unjustly neglected by historians of science
0-8018-3958-0 JOHNS HOPKINS $45.00

William Price **Fox**
Lunatic Wind: Surviving Out the Storm of the Century
A writer of fiction and filmscripts, Fox puts his literary talents to the task of documenting the story of Hurricane Hugo
0-945575-42-4 ALGONQUIN $18.95

Robert M. **Friedman**
Appropriating the Weather: Vilhelm Bjerknes & the Construction of a Modern Meterology
A revealing account of the career of a pioneer of modern meteorological methods
0-8014-2062-8 CORNELL $39.95
0-8014-8160-0 CORNELL PB $16.95

David **Ludlum**
The Audubon Society Field Guide to North American Weather
In over 350 full-color photographs, the amateur scientist will be able to identify weather signs, understand their dynamics, and make educated predictions. Designed for use outdoors or from the window, this is absorbing reading for any nature lover
0-679-40851-7 KNOPF PB $19.00

McGraw-Hill
The Meteorology Source Book
Over 100 articles from the *Encyclopedia of Science and Technology* covering weather systems and meteorological phenomena, and the methods for studying, forecasting, and predicting weather
0-07-045511-2 MCGRAW HILL $49.50

Joseph M. **Moran** & Michael D. **Morgan**
Essentials of Atmosphere & Weather
0-02-383831-0 PRENTICE HALL PB $45.00

William **Reifsnyder**
Weathering the Wilderness: The Sierra Club Guide to Practical Meteorology
0-87156-266-9 SIERRA CLUB PB $12.00

Vincent **Schaefer** & John **Day**
A Field Guide to the Atmosphere
A Peterson Field Guide
0-395-33033-5 HOUGHTON MIFFLIN PB $16.95

Alan **Watts**
The Weather Handbook
0-924486-76-7 SHERIDAN $19.95

Jack **Williams**
USA Today Weather Book
USA Today's deservedly famous weather maps form the basis for an encyclopedic, informative, and entertaining reference source
0-679-73669-7 VINTAGE PB $19.00

Oceanography

Jurg **Alean**
Glaciers
"A beautiful publication with an exceptional collection of photographs, more than 80 in full color and a large number in black-and-white....The text is largely nontechnical and no bibliographic references mar the flow of the exquisite English language presentation—*Choice*
0-521-41915-8 CAMBRIDGE $39.95
0-521-46787-X CAMBRIDGE PB $16.95

Rachel L. **Carson**
Under The Sea Wind
0-14-025380-7 PENGUIN PB $11.95

G. **Ford** & others
The Future for Ocean Technology
Explores the future possibilities for engineering the world's oceans into a reliable source of energy and minerals
0-86187-522-2 PINTER $25.00

Nixon **Griffis**, editor
The Mariner's Guide to Oceanography
0-688-03976-6 MORROW $4.98

Robert **Sharp**
Living Ice: Understanding Glaciers and Glaciation
An introduction to glaciers with a clear description of how they form
0-685-47340-6 CAMBRIDGE PB $8.95

Jeremy **Stafford-Deitsch**
Reef: A Safari Through the Coral World
Veteran marine explorer and photographer Stafford-Deitsch takes readers on a remarkable journey to some of the world's most beautiful, mysterious, and environmentally fragile "undersea landscapes." More than 100 photographs, maps, and drawings as well as chapters on the formation of reefs, marine life, and environmental concerns. Awarded Best Science Book for General Readers by *Library Journal*
See also **TRAVEL PHOTOGRAPHY** in **FOOD, TRAVEL, AND LEISURE**
0-87156-541-2 SIERRA CLUB PB $20.00

Norbert **Wu**
Beneath the Waves: Exploring the World of the Kelp Forest
For children: a first-hand account of underwater research
ILLUSTRATED BY NORBERT WU
0-87701-835-9 CHRONICLE $12.95

Reference

Robert L. **Bates** & Julia A. **Jackson**, editors
Dictionary of Geological Terms
0-385-18101-9 DOUBLEDAY PB $14.00

Dorothy **Lapidus** & Donald **Coates**
The Facts on File Dictionary of Geology and Geophysics
0-87196-703-0 FACTS ON FILE $24.95

Sybil P. **Parker**, editor
McGraw-Hill Encyclopedia of Geological Sciences
0-07-045500-7 MCGRAW HILL $95.50

Nature Study

Thomas P. **Slaughter**

The Natures of John and William Bartram

See also **BIOGRAPHY** under **US HISTORY TO THE CIVIL WAR** in **HISTORY OF THE AMERICAS**

0-679-43045-8 KNOPF $27.50

Essays, Meditations, and Classics

Edward **Abbey**

"What entertains many and exasperates others is Abbey's unique prose voice. Alternately misanthropic and sentimental, enraged and hilarious, it is the voice of a full-blooded man airing his passions."—Peter Carlson

Abbey's Road: Take the Other on the Road in Australia, Mexico, and the United States

America's most famous former park ranger was an excellent writer and passionate conservationist

0-452-26564-9 DUTTON PB $11.95

Down the River

Among other things, Abbey on the Green River, contemplating Thoreau

See also **HISTORY, POLITICS, AND SOCIETY** under **20TH-CENTURY AMERICAN ESSAYS AND JOURNALISM** in **LITERATURE OF THE AMERICAS**

0-452-26563-0 DUTTON PB $11.95

Diane **Ackerman**

A Natural History of the Senses

Ackerman, a science-minded poet who previously wrote about aviation in *On Extended Wings,* explores the five senses in highly original fashion. "Rooted in science, enlivened by her own convincing sense of wonder, Ackerman's essays awaken us to a fresh awareness" —*Publishers Weekly*

See also **LITERATURE** under **20TH-CENTURY AMERICAN ESSAYS AND JOURNALISM** in **LITERATURE OF THE AMERICAS**

0-394-57335-8 RANDOM HOUSE $22.00
0-679-73566-6 VINTAGE PB $12.00

John James **Audubon**

Selected Journals and Other Writings

0-14-024126-4 PENGUIN PB $15.95

Robert **Baron** & Elizabeth **Junkin**, editors

Of Discovery and Destiny: An Anthology of American Writers and the American Land

1-55591-004-1 FULCRUM $17.95

William **Beebe**, editor

The Book of Naturalists: An Anthology of the Best Natural History

0-691-02408-1 PRINCETON PB $19.95

Wendell **Berry**

A Continuous Harmony: Essays Cultural and Agricultural

Berry's essays primarily concern land use and ecology; they are humane, poetic, and pragmatic all at once

0-15-622575-1 HARCOURT BRACE PB $8.95

Home Economics

0-86547-275-0 FS&G PB $11.00

Hugh **Brody**

Maps and Dreams: Indians and the British Columbia Frontier

0-88894-593-0 DOUGLAS & MCINTYRE PB $16.95

Harvey **Broome**

Faces of the Wilderness

Visits to various American wildernesses in the '50s and '60s

0-87842-027-4 MOUNTAIN $7.95

Erik **Brown**

Seat in a Wild Place

A retired businessman looks at life by a New Hampshire pond

0-87233-059-1 BAUHAN PB $8.95

John **Burroughs**

A Sharp Lookout: Selected Nature Essays of John Burroughs

0-87474-270-6 SMITHSONIAN $39.95
0-87474-271-4 SMITHSONIAN PB $19.95

David **Byrne**

How Nature Works

0-89577-391-0 READER'S DIGEST $24.00

John **Carey**, editor

The Faber Book of Science

Robert Hooke, Isaac Newton, Charles Darwin, Sigmund Freud, Richard Feynman, Henry David Thoreau, Mark Twain, Italo Calvino, John Updike, Carl Sagan, Stephen Jay Gould, Rachel Carson, Oliver Sacks… An extraordinary variety and number of scientists, novelists, and essayists are collected here in a single volume that charts virtually every facet of scientific history

0-571-16352-1 FABER $29.95

John **Clare**

Clare, who enjoyed brief celebrity as a "peasant poet" before succumbing to madness, is increasingly admired not so much for the Romantic coloring of his verse as for the meticulous natural observation at its core. This edition is the best available introduction to the full range of Clare's writing. "Although born in the Age of Enlightenment, Clare speaks in the tones of a more archaic culture. Much of the daily life he knew as a child would not have been out of place in a medieval Book of Hours…In the scurryings of Clare's birds and beasts we hear the cadences of the last medieval poet."—Village Voice

The Natural History Prose Writings of John Clare

Close observations of rural life by an early 19th Century English poet

0-19-818517-0 CLARENDON $89.00

Charles **Darwin**

The Voyage of the Beagle

The classic account of Darwin's voyage to South America and the Galapagos

See also **CLASSIFICATION OF ORGANISMS** under **BIOLOGY** under **LIFE SCIENCES**

See also **CHARLES DARWIN** under **PALEONTOLOGY AND EVOLUTION** under **LIFE SCIENCES**

0-14-043268-X PENGUIN PB $10.95

Annie **Dillard**

Holy the Firm: Essays/Nature

0-06-091543-9 HARPERCOLLINS PB $10.00

Pilgrim At Tinker Creek

Dillard's essays are masterpieces of terse observation

0-06-091545-5 HARPERCOLLINS PB $13.00

Teaching a Stone to Talk: Expeditions and Encounters

0-06-091541-2 HARPERCOLLINS PB $12.00

Loren **Eiseley**

The Immense Journey

Ranging from the history of science to anthropology, Eiseley's meditations include some famous essays in natural history

0-394-70157-7 RANDOM HOUSE PB $9.00

The Night Country

0-8446-6325-5 SMITH $22.05

The Star Thrower

INTRODUCTION BY W.H. AUDEN

0-15-684909-7 HARCOURT BRACE PB $8.95

The Unexpected Universe

0-15-692850-7 HARCOURT BRACE PB $11.00

John **Fowles**

The Tree

0-316-28957-4 BOOK SALES $7.98
0-88001-033-9 ECCO $13.50

Winifred **Gallagher**

The Power of Place: How Our Surroundings Shape Our Thoughts, Emotions, and Actions

What makes New Yorkers so different from Californians? Or are they so different after all? This book shows how strongly and subtly environment affects us—examining our reactions to light, heat, the seasons, and other natural phenomena, he explains how and why we are delighted in one place, depressed in another. "Restores place to its proper niche in the big picture"—*Kirkus Reviews*

0-06-097602-0 HARPERPERENNIAL PB $12.50

John **Gould**

Maine's Golden Road: A Memoir

0-393-03806-8 NORTON $21.00
0-940160-68-4 PARNASSUS PB $10.00

Stephen Jay **Gould**

Eight Little Piggies: More Reflections in Natural History

An original writer almost without peer in his field of natural history, Gould is an expert at writing elegently for a lay audience. Here he discusses extinction, the atmosphere, physiology, and other subjects, all the while gently advocating scientific awareness as a way to thwart crisis on Earth. "There is no scientist today whose books I look forward to reading with greater anticipation of enjoyment and enlightenment than Stephen Jay Gould" —Martin Gardner

0-393-31139-2 NORTON PB $10.95

John **Haines**

Living Off the Country: Essays on Poetry and Place

Meditations by a poet living in Alaska

See also LITERATURE under 20TH-CENTURY AMERICAN ESSAYS AND JOURNALISM in LITERATURE OF THE AMERICAS

0-472-06333-2 MICHIGAN PB $13.95

Digging in the soil, picking away the rock, uprooting stumps, I became in time a grower of things sufficient to feed myself and another. Slowly finding my way into the skills of hunter and trapper, I understand what blood and bone, hide and muscle, marrow and sinew really are; not as things read about, but as things touched and handled until they became as familiar to me as my own skin. Land itself came alive for me as it never had before, more alive sometimes than the people who moved about on it. I learned that it is land, *place*, that makes people, provides for them the possibilities they will have of becoming something more than mere lumps of sucking matter.

LIVING OFF THE COUNTRY: ESSAYS ON POETRY AND PLACE

Donald **Hall**

String Too Short to Be Saved: Recollections of Summers on a New England Farm

With an album of family snapshots and an added essay about returning 25 years later to spend the rest of his life on the farm

0-87923-282-X GODINE PB $12.95

Daniel **Halpern**, editor

On Nature

A superb collection of literary essays, with an invaluable bibliography

0-86547-284-X NORTH POINT PB $10.95

Linda **Hasselstrom**

Land Circle: Writings Collected from the Land

Rancher environmentalist Hasselstrom represents a new approach to both of her chosen pursuits—born of a love for the enduring values of the rancher, and a belief in her responsibility to the land. This collection of essays, meditations, and poems won the Mountains and Plains Booksellers Regional Book Award for 1992. "[It] explains so much; about the land, about death, about being a woman…It belongs on the top shelf of your bookcase with the very best"—Dan O'Brien

1-55591-082-3 FULCRUM $19.95

1-55591-142-0 FULCRUM PB $12.95

Jacquetta **Hawkes**

Nothing But Or Something More

A collection of essays and lectures by a distinguished British archaeologist

0-295-95231-8 WASHINGTON $10.00

Bernd **Heinrich**

A Year in the Maine Woods

From cutting logs to building a cabin to tracking deer; and night where the sound of a moth's wings seems utterly important, this is an exploration into the meaning of peace and quiet, and harmony with nature from "one of America's outstanding naturalists"(Stephen Jay Gould). The author spends a year alone and isolated, without electricity or telecommunications and with no company but his pet raven, Jack. It is a year in which he found that the "subtle matters, and the spectacular distracts. "A rediscovery of the meaning of life from a gifted writer

0-201-48939-2 ADDISON-WESLEY PB $13.00

Edward **Hoagland**

The Courage of Turtles

Hoagland's nature essays are among the best in recent decades

1-55821-215-9 LYONS & BURFORD PB $14.95

Red Wolves and Black Bears

1-55821-371-6 LYONS & BURFORD PB $14.95

Linda **Hogan**

Dwellings: Reflections on the Natural World

The award-winning Chickasaw poet writes about the nature of nature

See also GENERAL BOOKS under SPIRITUALITY under SPIRITUALITY in RELIGION, SPIRITUALITY, AND PHILOSOPHY

0-393-03784-3 NORTON $21.00

0-684-83033-7 TOUCHSTONE PB $11.00

Paul **Horgan**

Of America East and West: Selections from the Writings of Paul Horgan

INTRODUCTION BY HENRY STEELE COMMAGER

0-374-51896-3 FS&G PB $12.95

Aldo **Leopold**

The River of the Mother of God & Other Essays

0-299-12760-5 WISCONSIN $18.75

Round River: From the Journals of Aldo Leopold

Leopold was a pioneering, highly influential conservationist who wrote evocatively of flora, fauna, and seasonal changes in the Wisconsin countryside

0-19-501563-0 OXFORD PB $9.95

Meriwether **Lewis** & William **Clark**

The Journals of Lewis and Clark

The classic first glimpse of the Louisiana Purchase

EDITED WITH AN INTRODUCTION BY FRANK BERGON

0-14-017006-5 PENGUIN PB $12.95

Barry **Lopez**

Crossing Open Ground

A new collection of essays by the author of *Arctic Dreams*

0-679-72183-5 VINTAGE PB $10.00

Of Wolves and Men

Winner of the Burroughs Medal

0-684-16322-5 SCRIBNERS PB $18.00

Nick **Lyons**

Spring Creek

This richly humorous and perceptive account of the angler's passion explores the secrets and challenges of one of the continent's best trout rivers. "Spring Creek shows what fishing writing can be. Nick Lyons has written a genuinely literate and deeply felt book" —Thomas McGuane

See also TROUT, FLY-FISHING, AND FLY-TYING under FISHING under THE OUTDOORS in FOOD, TRAVEL, AND LEISURE

0-87113-612-0 GROVE PB $11.00

Nick Lyons (photo by Dave Whitlock)

Richard **Marey**, editor

The Oxford Book of Nature Writing

A collection of nature writing that manages to encompass Aristotle, Wordsworth, and Primo Levi in one volume

0-19-214172-4 OXFORD $25.00

Peter **Matthiessen**

The Cloud Forest: A Chronicle of the South American Wilderness

A journey through wild terrain from the Amazon rain forest to Tierra del Fuego

See also SOUTH AMERICA under TRAVEL LITERATURE in FOOD, TRAVEL, AND LEISURE

0-8446-6605-X SMITH $19.80

0-14-009549-7 PENGUIN PB $11.95

Peter Matthiessen

Under the Mountain Wall

Two seasons with tribesmen of New Guinea

See also **RESEARCH AND METHODOLOGY** under **GENERAL ANTHROPOLOGICAL STUDIES** under **ANTHROPOLOGY** in **SOCIAL STUDIES**

0-14-025270-3 PENGUIN PB $12.95

Thomas **McNamee**

Nature First: Keeping Our Wild Places and Wild Creatures Wild

A brief meditation on the meaning and preservation of nature

0-911797-33-5 ROBERTS RINEHART $12.95

Kathleen Dean **Moore**

Riverwalking: Reflections on Moving Water

Twenty elegant essays from the philosopher Moore on themes of love, loss, motherhood, happiness, music, and the relation of all these to the natural world. From rafting down rapids to walks along riverbanks, Moore ponders the philosophical and physical mysteries of life, observing the variety of landscapes sustained by moving water

1-55821-408-9 LYONS & BURFORD $19.95
0-15-600461-5 HARCOURT BRACE PB $12.00

John **Muir**

The Mountains of California

0-87156-663-X SIERRA CLUB PB $10.00

Arriving on the summit of this dividing crest, one of the most exciting pieces of pure wilderness was disclosed that I ever discovered in all my mountaineering. There, immediately in front, loomed the majestic mass of Mount Ritter, with a glacier swooping down its face nearly to my feet, then curving westward and pouring its frozen flood into a dark blue lake, whose shores were bound with precipices of crystalline snow; while a deep chasm drawn between the divide and the glacier separated the massive picture from everything else. I could see only the one sublime mountain, the one glacier, the one lake; the whole veiled with one blue shadow—rock, ice, and water close together without a single leaf or sign of life.

THE MOUNTAINS OF CALIFORNIA

My First Summer in the Sierra

Muir (1838-1914) is among the most romantic and sublime of American nature writers

0-86241-193-9 DAVID & CHARLES PB $9.95

A Thousand-Mile Walk to the Gulf

0-14-017017-0 PENGUIN PB $12.00

Travels in Alaska

0-14-017021-9 PENGUIN PB $12.00

The Yosemite

0-87156-782-2 RANDOM HOUSE PB $10.00

Should Hetch Hetchy be submerged for a reservoir, as proposed, not only would it be utterly destroyed, but the sublime canyon way to the heart of the High Sierra would be hopelessly blocked and the great camping ground, as the watershed of a city drinking system, virtually would be closed to the public... That any one would try to destroy such a place seems incredible; but sad experience shows that there are people good enough and bad enough for anything. The proponents of the dam scheme bring forward a lot of bad arguments to prove that the only righteous thing to do with the people's parks is to destroy them bit by bit as they are able.

THE YOSEMITE

John A. **Murray**, editor

Nature's New Voices

A splendid and readable collection of "nature nonfiction," the first to feature the younger voices of this ever more popular genre. Treating natural settings such as Alabama, Ohio, Hawaii, and North Dakota, this is sure to become one of the classics of nature writing

1-55591-117-X FULCRUM PB $15.95

Mary **Oliver**

Blue Pastures

See also **POETRY SINCE 1945** under **20TH-CENTURY AMERICAN POETRY** in **LITERATURE OF THE AMERICAS**

0-15-100190-1 HARCOURT BRACE $22.00
0-15-600215-9 HARVEST PB $13.00

Jake **Page**

Songs to Birds

In these delightful and witty essays, the sight of a cardinal leads to thoughts about our perceptions and experiences of the color red; the persistence of starlings is pondered, as are the author's observations of the deceitfulness of birds. "I envy his ability to start with the small particular observation, then make the leap to the large disturbing, or illuminating, or humorous thought, and always in such graceful, clean prose"—Russell Baker

0-87923-957-3 GODINE $18.95
1-56792-042-X GODINE PB $12.95

Brenda **Peterson**

Nature and Other Mothers: Personal Stories of Women and the Body of Earth

"Potent and poignant...Lively essays that mix politics, religion, nature, myth and memoir" —*San Francisco Chronicle*

See also **ANTHOLOGIES OF WOMEN'S WRITING** under **WOMEN'S STUDIES** in **SOCIAL STUDIES**

0-449-90967-0 FAWCETT PB $12.00

Duncan M. **Porter** &
Peter W. **Graham**, editors

The Portable Darwin

A generous and representative selection

0-14-015109-5 PENGUIN PB $13.95

David **Quammen**

Natural Acts

Essays collected from Quammen's column in *Outside* magazine; quirky, learned, amusing

1-55821-173-X LYONS & BURFORD $18.95
0-380-71738-7 AVON PB $11.00

Ann **Ronald**, editor

Words For the Wild: The Sierra Club Trailside Reader

0-87156-709-1 SIERRA CLUB PB $12.00

Theodore **Roosevelt**

Theodore Roosevelt: Wilderness Writings

0-306-80232-5 DA CAPO PB $16.95

Cheryl **Seal**

Thoreau's Maine Woods: Yesterday and Today

Inspired by his experiences in Maine, Thoreau wrote a plea for the preservation of our wilds. This book juxtaposes that plea with 51 beautiful Robert Bukaty photographs of Maine's woods today. Seal describes Thoreau's journey, sets Maine's wilderness in historical context, and makes the case for new efforts to save it

0-89909-314-0 YANKEE BOOKS $24.95

William H. **Shore**, editor

Mysteries of Life and the Universe: New Essays from America's Finest Writers on Science

Diane Ackerman on the Grand Canyon, Harold Klawans on stubbing his toe, Tim Ferris on the nature of time, and 27 others. The book's proceeds go to *Share our Strength*, a nonprofit hunger relief foundation. "A sense of wonder bonds these essays together, which means there's something for everyone and everything for those who love science"—*Kirkus Reviews*

0-15-163972-8 HARCOURT BRACE $24.95
0-15-600136-5 HARVEST PB $15.00

Wallace **Stegner**

All the Little Live Things

A novel drawing in part on the hippie culture of the late '60s

See also **SINCE 1945** under **20TH-CENTURY AMERICAN FICTION** in **LITERATURE OF THE AMERICAS**

9-99-354684-4 PENGUIN PB $11.00
0-14-015441-8 PENGUIN PB $11.95

John **Steinbeck**

The Log from the Sea of Cortez

0-14-004261-X PENGUIN PB $7.00

Edwin Way **Teale**

Autumn Across America

0-312-04455-0 ST. MARTIN'S PB $12.95

North with the Spring

0-312-04457-7 ST. MARTIN'S PB $12.95

Wandering Through Winter

Winner of the 1966 Pulitzer Prize

0-312-04458-5 ST. MARTIN'S PB $12.95

Henry David **Thoreau**

"In reading Henry Thoreau's journal, I am very sensible of the vigor of his constitution. That oaken strength which I noted whenever he walked or worked or surveyed wood lots, the same unhesitating hand with which a field-laborer accosts a piece of work which I should shun as a waste of strength, Henry shows in his literary task...In reading him, I find the same thought, the same spirit that is in me, but he takes a step beyond, & illustrates by excellent images that which I should have conveyed in a sleepy generality. 'Tis as if I went into a gymnasium, & saw youths leap, climb, & swing with a force unapproachable—though their feats are only continuations of my initial grapplings & jumps."—Ralph Waldo Emerson in his journal, June 1863

Cape Cod
Ten essays compose this journey of discovery in which Thoreau gained respect for the complex relationship between sea and shore
See also **THE 19TH CENTURY: TO THE CIVIL WAR** under **AMERICAN LITERATURE TO 1900** in **LITERATURE OF THE AMERICAS**
0-14-017002-2 PENGUIN PB..........$10.95

The Journal of Henry David Thoreau
Thoreau's works represent the heart of 19th-century American nature writing
Volume 1
0-486-20312-3 DOVER..........$65.00
Volume 2
0-486-20313-1 DOVER..........$65.00

The Maine Woods
"Here was traveling of the old heroic kind over the unaltered face of nature"—Henry David Thoreau
See also **THE 19TH CENTURY: TO THE CIVIL WAR** under **AMERICAN LITERATURE TO 1900** in **LITERATURE OF THE AMERICAS**
INTRODUCTION BY EDWARD HOAGLAND
0-14-017013-8 PENGUIN PB..........$12.95

Henry David Thoreau

Thoreau on Birds
This delightful new edition of the classic, originally published as *Thoreau's Bird Lore*, brings to life the literary naturalist's best nature writing with stunning illustrations, some by Thoreau
See also **BIRDS** under **ANIMALS**
INTRODUCTION BY JOHN HAY
ILLUSTRATIONS BY LOUIS AGASSIZ FUERTES
0-8070-8520-0 BEACON..........$25.00

Walden
First published in 1854, *Walden*, a chronicle of Thoreau's time spent alone on Walden pond in Massachussetts, remains one of the most influential books in American literature
See also **THE 19TH CENTURY: TO THE CIVIL WAR** under **AMERICAN LITERATURE TO 1900** in **LITERATURE OF THE AMERICAS**
0-679-41896-2 EVERYMAN'S..........$17.00
0-393-95905-8 NORTON PB..........$9.95

A Week, Walden, the Maine Woods & Cape Cod
See also **LIBRARY OF AMERICA** in **LITERATURE OF THE AMERICAS**
0-940450-27-5 LIBRARY OF AMERICA..........$30.00

A Writer's Journal
0-486-20678-5 DOVER PB..........$6.95

Faith in a Seed: The Dispersion of Seeds & Other Late Natural History Writings
A landmark edition of hitherto-unpublished notes and essays by America's greatest essayist and one of its most original naturalists
FOREWORD BY GARY P. NABHAN & INTRODUCTON BY ROBERT D. RICHARDSON, JR.
1-55963-181-3 ISLAND..........$27.50

Michael **Tobias**
A Vision of Nature: Traces of the Original World
This overview of "ecological aesthetics" examines the mark of nature on a multiplicity of images, stories, and religious systems
0-87338-483-0 KENT STATE..........$39.00

Yi-Fu **Tuan**
Passing Strange and Wonderful: Aesthetics, Nature, and Culture
1-55963-209-7 ISLAND..........$27.00

David Rains **Wallace**
The Untamed Garden & Other Personal Essays
0-8142-0423-6 OHIO STATE..........$35.00

Gilbert **White**
The Natural History of Selborne
An informal masterpiece of natural observation, first published in 1788
See also **PROSE** under **THE RESTORATION AND THE 18TH CENTURY** in **LITERATURE OF THE BRITISH ISLES**
0-14-043112-8 PENGUIN PB..........$8.95

Alfred North **Whitehead**
The Concept of Nature
An analysis of nature in terms of "events" and "objects" (which are recurrent patterns of events)
See also **WHITEHEAD** under **PHILOSOPHY** in **RELIGION, SPIRITUALITY, AND PHILOSOPHY**
0-521-09245-0 CAMBRIDGE PB..........$23.95

Nature and Natural History

Marcia M. **Bonta**, editor
American Women Afield: Writings by Pioneering Women Naturalists
0-89096-634-6 TEXAS A & M PB..........$15.95

Daniel B. **Botkin**
Our Natural History: The Lessons of Lewis and Clark
A biologist and naturalist revisits the famous trail, challenges the myth of a pristine natural past and offers environmental advice
0-399-14048-4 PUTNAM..........$25.95
0-399-52242-5 PERIGEE PB..........$14.00

Raymond D. **Bourroughs**, editor
The Natural History of the Lewis & Clark Expedition
0-87013-389-6 MICHIGAN STATE PB..........$19.95

Paul **Brooks**
Speaking For Nature: How Our Literary Naturalists Have Shaped America
0-87156-332-0 RANDOM HOUSE PB..........$8.95

Robert **Decker** & Barbara **Decker**
Volcanoes
0-7167-1851-0 FREEMAN PB..........$19.95

Arthur A. **Ekirch**, Jr.
Man and Nature in America
0-8032-5785-6 NEBRASKA PB..........$5.95

Antonello **Gerbi**
Nature in the New World: From Christopher Columbus to Gonzalo Fernandez De Oviedo
An account of the natural history of the New World as written by Columbus, Peter Martyr, and Oviedo
0-8229-3516-3 PITTSBURGH..........$49.95

Clarence J. **Glacken**
Traces on the Rhodian Shore: Nature and Culture in Western Thought from Ancient Times to the End of the 18th Century
An influential book now back in print. "One of the best and most important books published by a geographer in the English-speaking world in the last hundred years"
—*Professional Geographer*
9-990-97785-2 CALIFORNIA PB..........$25.00

Richard S. **Gottlieb**, editor
This Sacred Earth: Religion, Nature, Environment
0-415-91233-4 ROUTLEDGE PB..........$24.95

Stephen Jay **Gould**, editor
Finders, Keepers: Treasures & Oddities of Natural History Collectors from Peter the Great to Louis Agassiz
A photographic record of some of the worlds most remarkable collections of fossils, stuffed animals and artifacts. Essay by Stephen Jay Gould
PHOTOGRAPHY BY ROSAMOND W. PURCELL
0-393-31087-6 NORTON PB..........$24.95

Stephen Jay **Gould**
Dinosaur in a Haystack: Reflections in Natural History
0-517-88824-6 CROWN PB..........$15.00

Ever Since Darwin: Reflections in Natural History
Gould's provocative and witty columns in *Natural History* demonstrate the subtleties of evolution through concrete examples of the extraordinary
0-393-06425-5 NORTON..........$19.95
0-393-00917-3 NORTON PB..........$9.95

Stephen Jay **Gould**

Full House: The Spread of Excellence from Plato to Darwin

See also **EVOLUTION AND THE ORIGINS OF LIFE** under **PALEONTOLOGY AND EVOLUTION** under **LIFE SCIENCES**

0-517-70394-7 HARMONY $25.00

The Flamingo's Smile: Reflections in Natural History

0-393-30375-6 NORTON PB $12.95

Hen's Teeth and Horse's Toes: Further Reflections in Natural History

0-393-31103-1 NORTON PB $10.95

The Panda's Thumb: More Reflections in Natural History

0-393-30819-7 NORTON PB $11.95

John **Haines**

The Stars, the Snow, the Fire

1-55597-117-2 GRAYWOLF $17.95

Harry **Judge**, editor

Oxford Illustrated Encyclopedia: The Physical World

See also **REFERENCE** under **SCIENTIFIC THOUGHT AND DISCOVERY** under **SCIENCE AND TECHNOLOGY**

0-19-869161-0 OXFORD $95.00

Sally G. **Kohlstedt**, editor

The Origins of Natural Science in America: The Essays of George Brown Goode

Essays by a pioneering figure in the history of the Smithsonian Institution, and one of the originators of the concept of the science museum

1-56098-098-2 SMITHSONIAN $45.00

James L. **Larson**

Interpreting Nature: The Science of Living Form from Linnaeus to Kant

A penetrating intellectual history that explores how 18th-century philosophers and scientists shaped their—and our—investigations of the natural world

0-8018-4840-7 JOHNS HOPKINS $40.00

Katie **Lee**

A Visit to Galapagos

From seamen and early naturalists to Darwin, and continuing today, the fantastically rich biological diversity of the Galapagos Atoll has enthralled generations of nature lovers. Lee, widely acclaimed as among our finest nature illustrators, captures the zoological and botanical diversity of that unique place: the Galapagos tortoise, Darwin's 13 species of finches, seals, lizards, and fish. A stunning volume, a delight to own

0-8109-2597-4 ABRAMS PB $16.95

Roderick **Nash**

The American Environment: Reading in the History of Conservation

0-07-046059-0 KNOPF PB $22.50

George **Marsh**

Man and Nature: Or Physical Geography as Modified by Human Action

This 1869 book by an American statesman, scholar, and diplomat aroused great contemporary interest in conservation

0-674-54452-8 HARVARD PB $18.00

Sy **Montgomery**

Walking with the Great Apes: Jane Goodall, Dian Fossey, Birute Galdikas

The stories of three women naturalists, all trained by Louis Leakey. Montgomery's experience as both a journalist and an investigative scientist make her the ideal interpreter for Goodall, Fossey, and Galdikas, and the years they spent studying and gaining the trust of our nearest relatives in the animal world. "Montgomery's prose can be breathtaking…spellbinding"
—*San Francisco Chronicle*

0-395-61156-3 HOUGHTON MIFFLIN PB $13.95

Pat **Murphy**

By Nature's Design: An Exploratorium Book

This inspired collaboration between acclaimed nature photographer William Neill and San Francisco's famous Exploratorium Museum unveils nature's secrets, such as the heart of a daisy and spinal forms in seashells. "Few things are as beautiful to look at as a ripple, a spiral or a rosette. They are visually succulent. The mind savors them. It is a kind of comfort food. Feast here on some of the wonders of nature's pantry"—Diane Ackerman, from her Foreword

0-8118-0329-5 CHRONICLE PB $18.95

Alice **Outwater**

Water: A Natural History

0-465-03779-8 HARPERCOLLINS $23.00

Edward J. **Renehan**, Jr.

John Burroughs: An American Naturalist

Burroughs (1851-1921) was in equal parts litterateur and naturalist. He wrote the first biography of Walt Whitman and heightened the American appreciation of nature. "Renehan…has restored Burroughs to a well-deserved place in American literature and conservation"—*Publishers Weekly*

0-930031-59-8 CHELSEA GREEN $24.95

Frank **Stewart**

A Natural History of Nature Writing

1-55963-278-X ISLAND $34.00
1-55963-279-8 ISLAND PB $16.95

Richard **White**

The Organic Machine

The "organic machine" is the Columbia River. White's study shows how the crucial relationship between river and people has affected the history of the Pacific Northwest

0-8090-3559-6 HILL & WANG $17.95
0-8090-1583-8 HILL & WANG PB $7.95

Edward O. **Wilson**

In Search of Nature

1-55963-215-1 ISLAND $19.95

Animals

Vicki **Hearne**

Adam's Task: Calling Animals by Name

A philosophical work on the language shared by humans and animals

See also **PETS** in **FOOD, TRAVEL, AND LEISURE**

0-06-097634-9 HARPERPERENNIAL PB $13.00

Animal Happiness

See also **PETS** in **FOOD, TRAVEL, AND LEISURE**

0-06-092606-6 HARPERPERENNIAL PB $12.00

Bonnie L. **Hendricks**, editor

International Encyclopedia of Horse Breeds

See also **ONE-VOLUME ENCYCLOPEDIAS** under **REFERENCE** in **BUSINESS AND REFERENCE**

See also **HORSE BREEDS** under **HORSES** under **PETS** in **FOOD, TRAVEL, AND LEISURE**

FOREWORD BY ANTHONY A. DENT

0-8061-2753-8 OKLAHOMA $65.00

Gary **Indiana**, editor

Living With the Animals

0-571-19875-9 FABER PB $14.95

Susan **Middleton** & David **Liittschwager**

Witness: Endangered Species of North America

Beautiful and powerful, these photographs capture 100 North American species on the brink of extinction in 200 full-color and duotone photographs. "This eloquent and stirring book of photographs is an oasis for anyone who cares deeply about nature. The animals leap out of their two-dimensional frames; they are radiant with life"—Diane Ackerman

INTRODUCTION BY E.O. WILSON

0-8118-0282-5 CHRONICLE $50.00
0-8118-0258-2 CHRONICLE PB $35.00

Albert **Schweitzer**

The Animal World of Albert Schweitzer

EDITED AND TRANSLATED BY CHARLES R. JOY

0-88001-470-9 ECCO PB $14.00

Keith S. **Thomson**

The Common But Less Frequent Loon & Other Essays

"A provocative collection of essays, scientifically rich yet leisurely and meditative. Suffused with the sense of wonder that unites the wide-eyed child and the white-haired Nobel laureate: an uncommonly good collection"—*Kirkus Reviews*

ILLUSTRATED BY LINDA P. THOMSON

0-300-05630-3 YALE $25.00
0-300-06654-6 YALE PB $15.00

Mammals

Sydney **Anderson**, editor
The Simon & Schuster Guide to Mammals
0-671-42805-5 SIMON & SCHUSTER PB $15.00

David **Brown**
The Grizzly in the Southwest: Documentary of an Extinction
0-8061-1930-6 OKLAHOMA $29.95

William **Burt**
A Field Guide to the Mammals
0-395-24082-4 HOUGHTON MIFFLIN $24.95
0-395-24084-0 HOUGHTON MIFFLIN PB $16.95

Robert **Busch**
The Wolf Almanac
1-55821-351-1 LYONS & BURFORD $27.95

Douglas **Chadwick**
A Beast the Color of Winter: The Mountain Goat Observed
0-87156-568-4 SIERRA CLUB PB $12.00

Frank C. **Craighead**, Jr.
Track of the Grizzly
0-87156-322-3 RANDOM HOUSE PB $16.00

Robert **Delort**
The Life and Lore of the Elephant
0-8109-2848-5 ABRAMS PB $12.95

Charles **Fergus**
Swamp Screamer: At Large with the Florida Panther
0-86547-491-5 NORTH POINT $23.00

Jeremy **Gavron**
King Leopold's Dream: Travels in the Shadow of the African Elephant
For Gavron, the elephant's fight for survival is a metaphor for the broader battle of Old Africa to survive in the modern Africa of Coca-Cola and automatic weapons. This loyal and easily traumatized being, according to some, is even aware of the deadly value of its magnificent tusks
0-679-41998-5 PANTHEON $23.00

J. David **Henry**
Red Fox: The Catlike Canine
1-56098-635-2 SMITHSONIAN PB $15.95

Vincent **Maglio** & H.B. **Cooke**, editors
The Evolution of African Mammals
One of the best continental overviews of mammalian evolution; not for the novice
0-674-27075-4 HARVARD $88.00

Peter **Matthiessen**
The Snow Leopard
Matthiessen in the Himalayas in search of an endangered cat; winner of the National Book Award
See also **CENTRAL ASIA** under **ASIA** under **TRAVEL LITERATURE** in **FOOD, TRAVEL, AND LEISURE**
0-14-010266-3 PENGUIN PB $12.95

Gavin **Maxwell**
Ring of Bright Water
Maxwell among otters in the Scottish Highlands
0-14-003923-6 PENGUIN PB $9.95

Adolph **Murie**
The Grizzlies of Mount McKinley
0-295-96204-6 WASHINGTON PB $10.95

Mammals of Denali
0-9602876-6-3 ALASKA NAT. HIST. ASSOC. PB $4.50

Delia **Owens** & Mark **Owens**
The Eye of the Elephant: Life and Death in an African Wilderness
The Owenses sought a new Eden, and thought they'd discovered it in Zambia's Luanga Valley. But they soon learned of the tradition of killing 1,000 elephants a year by both villagers and big commercial poachers. After discovering that the villagers needed the poaching to survive, they started a development project that became a struggle for their own survival. "For anyone interested in animals or in real life adventure, this book is a must"—Jane Goodall
0-395-68090-5 TICKNOR & FIELDS PB $12.95

George **Schaller**
The Giant Pandas of Wolong
0-226-73643-1 CHICAGO $30.00

The Serengeti Lion: A Study of Predator-Prey Relations
Winner of the National Book Award 1973
0-226-73640-7 CHICAGO PB $27.50

George B. **Schaller**
The Last Panda
In 1980 the author became the first outsider ever permitted by the Chinese to study the panda in the wild. The result is this extraordinary book. "No scientist is better at letting the rest of us in on just how the natural world works; no poet sees that world with greater clarity or writes about it with more grace"—Geoffrey C. Ward, *NY Times Book Review.* "An absorbing account of the efforts to study (and to save) a very beautiful, near-mythic creature, filled with Mr. Schaller's fascinating information, shrewd commentary, and fine writing"—Peter Matthiessen
0-226-73628-8 CHICAGO $24.95

Paul **Schullery**
The Bears of Yellowstone
1-88101-900-4 HARBINGER PB $15.00

Robin **Schwartz**
Like Us: Primate Portraits
Over 60 provocative images that show how much we truly have in common with our fellow primates. A conceptual challenge and a visual delight
0-393-03499-2 NORTON $22.95
0-393-31044-2 NORTON PB $12.95

Shirley **Strum**
Almost Human: A Journey Into the World of Baboons
0-393-30708-5 NORTON PB $13.95

John O. **Whitaker**, Jr.
The Audubon Field Guide to North American Mammals
This classic guide (nearly 500,000 copies in print) is fully revised and expanded, with nearly 375 new photographs and up-to-date information on the characteristics, behavior, and habitats of 390 species that breed in the United States and Canada. Easy to use with thumb-tab keys, 135 drawings of tracks and anatomical features, and 300 range maps
0-394-50762-2 KNOPF PB $19.00

John James Audubon

Birds

Chuck **Bernstein**
The Joy of Birding: A Guide to Better Bird Watching
A "collection of anecdotes, love and knowledge"
INTRODUCTION BY ROGER TORY PETERSON
0-88496-220-2 CAPRA PB $8.95

Stephen **Bodio**
A Rage For Falcons
By a columnist and editor of *Gray's Sporting Journal*
See also **ESSAYS** under **THE OUTDOORS** in **FOOD, TRAVEL, AND LEISURE**
0-87108-826-6 PRUETT PB $12.95

John **Burroughs**
The Birds of John Burroughs
Eleven of Burroughs' classic essays
0-87951-312-8 OVERLOOK PB $9.95

Paul R. **Ehrlich** & others
The Birdwatcher's Handbook: A Field Guide to the Natural History of the Birds of Britian & Europe: Including 515 Species That Regularly Breed in Europe & Adjacent Parts of the Middle East & North Africa
A guide to 516 species resident in the Eastern hemisphere from Britain to North Africa; invaluable to the traveling birdwatcher or anyone interested in the birds of Europe
0-19-858407-5 OXFORD PB $25.00

Jack **Connor**

The Complete Birder: A Guide to Better Birding

Designed to upgrade your field skills

INTRODUCTION BY ROGER TORY PETERSON

0-395-46807-8 HOUGHTON MIFFLIN PB $13.95

Paul **Eriksson**, editor

Treasury of North American Birdlore

0-8397-8373-6 ERIKSSON PB $14.95

Paul **Eriksson** & Joseph Wood **Krutch**, editors

Songbirds in Your Garden

INTRODUCTION BY ROGER TORY PETERSON

1-56512-044-2 ALGONQUIN PB $14.95

Jon **Gerrard** & Gary **Bortolotti**

The Bald Eagle: Haunts and Habits of a Wilderness Monarch

0-87474-451-2 SMITHSONIAN PB $13.95

Frances **Hamerstrom**

Harrier, Hawk of the Marshes: The Hawk That Is Ruled by a Mouse

FOREWORD BY ROGER TORY PETERSON

0-87474-537-3 SMITHSONIAN PB $13.95

Peter **Harrison**

A Field Guide to Birds' Nests Found East of the Mississippi River

0-395-20434-8 HOUGHTON MIFFLIN $24.95

Bernd **Heinrich**

One Man's Owl

Life with a great horned owl, by a zoologist at the University of Vermont

0-691-08470-X PRINCETON $45.00

Joe **Hutto**

Illumination in the Flatwoods: A Season with the Wild Turkey

1-55821-390-2 LYONS & BURFORD $25.00

John **Marchant** & Tony **Prater**

Shorebird: An Identification Guide

FOREWORD BY ROGER TORY PETERSON

0-395-60237-8 HOUGHTON MIFFLIN PB $29.95

Roger Tory **Peterson**

A Field Guide to the Birds East of the Rockies

0-395-26619-X HOUGHTON MIFFLIN PB $15.95

A Field Guide to the Birds of Texas and Adjacent States

0-395-08087-8 HOUGHTON MIFFLIN $24.95
0-395-26252-6 HOUGHTON MIFFLIN PB $21.95

Roger Tory **Peterson** & Edward **Chalif**

A Field Guide to Mexican Birds

0-395-17129-6 HOUGHTON MIFFLIN $24.95
0-395-48354-9 HOUGHTON MIFFLIN PB $18.95

Roger Tory **Peterson** & others

Audubon's Birds of America

If the complete and revised hardcover "folio" edition of *Audubon's Birds of America* is too much to lug on an outing, try the paperback "tiny folio edition" also available

See also **THE 19TH CENTURY** under **AMERICAN ART** in **ART**
See also **WATERCOLORS** under **PAINTING** under **AMERICAN ART** in **ART**

1-55859-128-1 ABBEVILLE $250.00
1-55859-225-3 ABBEVILLE PB $11.95

Donald **Stokes**

A Guide to the Behavior of Common Birds

0-316-81725-2 LITTLE, BROWN PB $14.95

Donald **Stokes** & Lillian **Stokes**

A Guide to Bird Behavior: In the Wild and At Your Feeder

0-316-81729-5 LITTLE, BROWN PB $14.95

John **Terres**

The Audubon Society Encyclopedia of North American Birds

A comprehensive reference; highly recommended

0-517-03288-0 WINGS $44.99

How Birds Fly

0-8117-2443-3 STACKPOLE PB $16.95

Thoreau on Birds

This delightful new edition of the classic, originally published as *Thoreau's Bird Lore*, brings to life the literary naturalist's best nature writing with stunning illustrations, some by Thoreau

See also **ESSAYS, MEDITATIONS, AND CLASSICS**

INTRODUCTION BY JOHN HAY

ILLUSTRATIONS BY LOUIS AGASSIZ FUERTES AND HENRY DAVID THOREAU

0-8070-8520-0 BEACON $25.00

M.D. **Udvardy**

Audubon Society Guide to North American Birds: Western Region

0-394-41410-1 KNOPF PB $18.00

Reptiles and Amphibians

Hobart **Smith** & Edmund **Brodie**

Reptiles of North America

0-307-13666-3 GOLDEN PB $14.00

Aquatic Life

Richard **Ellis**

Monsters of the Sea

Mythological and real, the creatures that dwell in the deep have long enthralled the human imagination. Ellis, foremost writer on and painter of marine life, tours the world of man-eating octopuses, mermaids, leviathans, serpents and other legendary denizens of the sea. Along the way we learn the truth about mermaids and the facts of the Loch Ness monster. A fascinating and elegant account

0-679-40639-5 KNOPF $35.00
0-385-48233-7 MAIN STREET PB $12.95

Gordon **Hendler** & others

Sea Stars, Sea Urchins, and Allies: Echinoderms of Florida and the Caribbean

See also **BIOLOGICAL DIVERSITY** under **BIOLOGY** under **LIFE SCIENCES**

1-56098-450-3 SMITHSONIAN $39.95

John A. **Long**

The Rise of Fishes: 500 Million Years of Evolution

0-8018-4992-6 JOHNS HOPKINS $49.95

Joan **McIntyre Varawa**

The Delicate Art of Whale Watching

0-87156-550-1 SIERRA CLUB PB $10.00

Stefani **Paine**

The World of the Sea Otter

The life and times of this most playful and intelligent mammal, which spends its entire life in the water. Recounts the otter's unique relationship to humans, its range and skill in traveling long distances, its near extinction in the great 19th-century fur hunts, and its amazing resourcefulness. With 67 color photographs, many of them taken underwater

PHOTOGRAPHS BY JEFF FOOTT

0-87156-375-4 SIERRA CLUB PB $18.00

Roger **Payne** & Robin **Brown**

In the Company of Whales

With an eye toward the state of our own souls, the world's leading expert on cetacean creatures (or whales) recounts what we know about whales and dolphins—their culture, their music, their present status, and our future—together—on the planet. A brilliant work of literature and philosophy as well as science

0-02-595245-5 MACMILLAN $25.00

James **Prosek**

Trout: An Illustrated History

This prodigious celebration of the mysterious and beautiful trout captures, in over 70 original watercolors, varieties from the Apache to the rainbow, redband, golden, cutthroat, and other species and subspecies, of which some are already extinct. Passionate and accurate, this must-have for the serious angler is by a 20-year-old undergraduate at Yale who is already considered "a fair bid to become the Audubon of the fishing world"—*NY Times*

See also **TROUT, FLY-FISHING, AND FLY-TYING** under **FISHING** under **THE OUTDOORS** in **FOOD, TRAVEL, AND LEISURE**

0-679-44453-X KNOPF $27.50

John **Varley**

Fresh Water Wilderness: Yellowstone Fishes and Their World

0-934948-06-2 YELLOWSTONE PB $12.95
0-934948-04-6 YELLOWSTONE PB $12.95

Douglas **Whynott**

Giant Bluefin

The giant bluefin tuna can grow to 1,500 pounds and sell for more that $30,000 per fish. This account of the New England bluefin fishery brings a controversial industry to life

0-374-16208-5 FS&G $21.00
0-86547-497-4 NORTH POINT PB $12.00

Insects

Donald **Borror** & Richard **White**

A Field Guide to the Insects of America North of Mexico

0-395-07436-3 HOUGHTON MIFFLIN $24.95
0-395-18523-8 HOUGHTON MIFFLIN PB $15.95

Charles V. **Covell**, Jr.

A Field Guide to the Moths of Eastern North America

0-395-36100-1 HOUGHTON MIFFLIN PB $17.95

John **Crompton**

The Hunting Wasp

INTRODUCTION BY STEPHEN BODIO

0-941130-49-5 LYONS & BURFORD PB $8.95

Howard **Evans**

The Pleasures of Entomology: Portraits of Insects and the People Who Study Them

0-87474-421-0 SMITHSONIAN PB $16.95

Bernd **Heinrich**

Bumblebee Economics

0-674-08581-7 HARVARD PB $18.95

Bert **Hoelldobler** & Edward O. **Wilson**

The Ants

Winner of the 1991 Pulitzer Prize for General Nonfiction. "Although encyclopedic, the book is beautifully written, and has some of the most stunning animal paintings and photographs I have seen"
—John Maynard Smith, *NY Review of Books*

See also **NATURAL HISTORY** under **LIFE SCIENCES**

0-674-04075-9 BELKNAP $75.00

Alexander **Klots**

A Field Guide to the Butterflies of North America, East of the Great Plains

0-395-63279-X HOUGHTON MIFFLIN PB $16.95

Lotus **Milne** & Margery **Milne**

The Audubon Society Field Guide to North American Insects and Spiders

0-394-50763-0 KNOPF PB $19.00

Christopher **O'Toole**

Alien Empire: An Exploration of the Lives of Insects

The companion volume to the upcoming PBS/Nature mini-series, this fascinating book uses state-of-the-art technology to capture the world of insects in over 200 full-color photographs. The text illuminates every aspect of insect life: locomotion, eating habits, defenses, mating, parenting, and much more. An irresistible tour through this alien empire

0-06-270156-8 HARPERCOLLINS $25.00

Donald **Stokes**

A Guide to Observing Insect Lives

0-316-81727-9 LITTLE, BROWN PB $14.95

Gilbert **Waldbauer**

Insects Through the Seasons

0-674-45488-X HARVARD $24.95

Edward O. **Wilson**

Insect Societies

By the Pulitzer prize-winning sociobiologist

0-674-45495-2 HARVARD PB $26.50

Animal Behavior

Janine M. **Benyus**

Beastly Behaviors: What Makes Whales Whistle, Cranes Dance, Pandas Turn Somersaults, and Crocodiles Roar: a Watcher's Guide to How Animals Act and Why

Finally, sensible answers to many questions about animals that have continued to fascinate us since childhood (e.g, why do zebras have stripes?). Benyus's fun, illustrated field guide is an indispensable volume to bring to the zoo

0-201-62482-6 ADDISON-WESLEY PB $15.95

Paola **Cavalieri** & Peter **Singer**, editors

The Great Ape Project

"We demand the extension of the community of equals to include all great apes: human beings, chimpanzees, gorillas, and orangutans." And so begins Peter Singer's new manifesto, endorsed by 34 renowned scientists and writers who join in his impassioned and controversial plea. "May prove to be one of the most subversive books published in English this year"—*Independent*

0-312-10473-1 ST. MARTIN'S $21.95

Frans **de Waal**

Chimpanzee Politics: Power and Sex Among Apes

0-8018-3833-9 JOHNS HOPKINS PB $14.95

Michael **Ghiglieri**

East of the Mountains of the Moon: Chimpanzee Society in the African Jungle

0-02-911580-9 FREE PRESS $35.00

Donald **Griffin**

Animal Thinking

An important work on the "mental experiences" of animals

0-674-03713-8 HARVARD PB $14.50

Bert **Hoelldobler** & Edmund **Wilson**

Journey to the Ants

Myrmecologists have long known that tiny ants have everything to teach us about human society; Wilson's and Hoelldobler's *The Ants* brought this fascinating study to wide popular acclaim. Now, the authors take us on a mind-bending journey through one of the most complex and structured societies nature has created. A thoroughly compelling read

0-674-48525-4 BELKNAP $24.95

Konrad **Lorenz**

King Solomon's Ring

A seminal work by the founder of modern ethology

See also **BIRD WATCHING** under **CAMPING AND MOUNTAINEERING** under **THE OUTDOORS** in **FOOD, TRAVEL, AND LEISURE**

FOREWORD BY JULIAN HUXLEY

0-451-62831-4 NEW AMERICAN LIBRARY PB $3.99

On Aggression

A controversial theory of human violence and territoriality

0-15-668741-0 HARCOURT BRACE PB $10.95

Konrad Lorenz

David **McFarland**, editor

The Oxford Companion to Animal Behavior

0-19-866120-7 OXFORD $49.95

Desmond **Morris**

The Naked Ape

0-440-36266-0 DELL PB $5.99

Nan **Richardson** & Catherine **Chemayeff**

Wild Love

Granta, ArtNews, and *Mother Jones* contributor Richardson and Magnum Photos Director of Special Projects Chemayeff bring together a series of outstanding photos—from outstanding photojournalists—to depict the world of courtship and mating in the wild. From tortoises to praying mantises, these powerful and unexpected images show a universe of wild love

0-8118-0452-6 CHRONICLE $14.95

Trees, Plants, and Fungi

Boughton **Cobb**

A Field Guide to Ferns and Their Related Families

0-395-07560-2 HOUGHTON MIFFLIN $21.95
0-395-19431-8 HOUGHTON MIFFLIN PB $15.95

John **Craighead**
A Field Guide to Rocky Mountain Wildflowers
0-395-18324-3 HOUGHTON MIFFLIN PB $16.95

Jerry **Franklin**
Familiar Trees of North America, Eastern Region
0-394-74852-2 KNOPF PB $9.00
0-394-74851-4 KNOPF PB $9.00

Ronald **Lanner**
The Pinon Pine: A Natural and Cultural History
0-87417-065-6 NEVADA $21.95

Elbert L. **Little**, Jr.
Audubon Field Guide to North American Trees: Eastern Edition
0-394-50760-6 KNOPF PB $19.00

Chris **Maser**
Forest Primeval: The Natural History of an Ancient Forest
The biography of a forest: one of the ancient, and now endangered, forests of the Pacific Northwest, set in Oregon's Cascade Mountains. Writes the author: "I have not set out to write a litany of human blunders or a book about the future of forestry. I have instead…set out with you on a humble journey through a forest of a thousand years so you may see that the forest primeval represents our spiritual and historical roots as human beings"
0-87156-683-4 SIERRA CLUB PB $25.00

Kent **McKnight** & Vera **McKnight**
A Field Guide to Mushrooms
0-395-42102-0 HOUGHTON MIFFLIN PB $16.95

James B. **Nardi**
Once Upon a Tree: Life from Treetop to Root Tips
A nature book for children and adults, with handsome line drawings by the author, accompanied by observations designed to arouse an interest in the mushrooms, insects, songbirds and other wonders you can find on a walk near your house
0-8138-0917-7 IOWA STATE $17.95

Theodore **Niehaus**
A Field Guide to Pacific States Wildflowers
FOREWORD BY ROGER TORY PETERSON
0-395-21624-9 HOUGHTON MIFFLIN $24.95
0-395-31662-6 HOUGHTON MIFFLIN PB $15.95

William **Niering** & Nancy O **Olmstead**
The Audubon Society Field Guide to North American Wildflowers: Eastern Region
0-394-50432-1 KNOPF PB $19.00

Donald **Peattie**
A Natural History of Western Trees
0-395-58175-3 HOUGHTON MIFFLIN PB $19.95

Lee **Peterson**
A Field Guide to Eastern Edible Wild Plants
0-395-20445-3 HOUGHTON MIFFLIN $24.95
0-395-31870-X HOUGHTON MIFFLIN PB $15.95

Roger Tory **Peterson** & Margaret **McKenny**
A Field Guide to Wildflowers of Northeastern and North-Central North America
0-395-18325-1 HOUGHTON MIFFLIN PB $16.95

Richard **Preston**
North American Trees
The 4th edition of the most complete and up-to-date handbook on North American trees gives detailed descriptions of all the native trees and exotic species common in every region of the country. The trees are grouped by family, accompanied by line drawings, distribution maps, and a glossary of technical terms. This indispensable handbook is a convenient size for use in the field
0-8138-1171-6 IOWA STATE $41.95
0-8138-1172-4 IOWA STATE PB $22.95

Stanley **Schuler**, editor
The Simon & Schuster Guide to Trees
0-671-24125-7 SIMON & SCHUSTER PB $14.00

Richard **Spellenberg**
The Audubon Society Field Guide to North American Wildflowers: Western Region
0-394-50431-3 KNOPF PB $19.00

Donald **Stokes** & Lillian **Stokes**
A Guide to Enjoying Wildflowers
0-316-81731-7 LITTLE, BROWN PB $17.95

Regional Guides and Studies

Peter **Alden** & others
National Audubon Society Field Guide to African Wildlife
0-679-43234-5 KNOPF PB $19.00

Joseph **Barbato**
Heart of the Land: Essays on Last Great Places
0-679-75501-2 VINTAGE PB $13.00

Fodor
The Complete Guide to America's National Parks, 1994-1995
0-679-02676-2 FODOR'S PB $14.95

Joe **Kane**
Savages
New Yorker readers have long been familiar with Kane's brave and literate environmental reporting from the Amazon—indeed, his *Running the Amazon* was a *New York Times* best seller. This firsthand account of a small band of Amazonian warriors and their battle to preserve their traditional life against the encroachment of oil companies, missionaries, bureaucrats, and environmentalists is at once hilarious and heartbreaking, a tragic and fascinating story of the tenacious and delicate survival of a determinedly primitive people
See also **SOUTH AMERICA** under **NATIVE AMERICAN CULTURES: CENTRAL AND SOUTH AMERICA** in **HISTORY OF THE AMERICAS**
0-679-41191-7 KNOPF $25.00

Coastal

Jennifer **Ackerman**
Notes From the Shore
A perceptively written, lyrical, yet also richly factual evocation of the Delaware coast
0-670-84924-3 VIKING $21.95

Mary **Blocksma**
The Fourth Coast: From the St. Lawrence Seaway to the Boundary Waters of Minnesota
0-14-017881-3 PENGUIN PB $12.95

Rachel **Carson**
The Edge of the Sea
0-395-28519-4 HOUGHTON MIFFLIN PB $12.95

Rachel Carson

The Sea Around Us
A highly influential work which inspired a new consciousness of ocean ecology
0-19-506186-1 OXFORD $24.95

Deborah **Coulombe**
The Seaside Naturalist: A Guide to Study At the Seashore
0-671-76503-5 PRENTICE HALL PB $15.00

Jan **DeBlieu**
Hatteras Journal: Paradox of a Fragile Land
1-55591-010-6 FULCRUM $15.95

Kenneth **Gosner**
A Field Guide to the Atlantic Seashore
0-395-31828-9 HOUGHTON MIFFLIN PB $17.95

John **Hay**
The Great Beach
A walking trip along the Outer Beach of Cape Cod; winner of the John Burroughs Medal (1984)
0-393-00983-1 NORTON PB $7.95

Sandy Shore
0-9991530-2-1 CHATHAM $7.95

John **Hay** & Peter **Farb**
The Atlantic Shore
0-940160-14-5 PARNASSUS PB $7.95

George **Reiger**
Wanderer on My Native Shore
Tidewater essays by an ardent conservationist
1-55821-120-9 LYONS & BURFORD PB $14.95

Geerat J. **Vermeij**
A Natural History of Shells
0-691-00167-7 PRINCETON PB $14.95

William **Warner**
Beautiful Swimmers: Watermen, Crabs, and the Chesapeake Bay
A fine book on the crabmen of the Chesapeake Bay
INTRODUCTION BY JOHN BARTH
0-316-92335-4 LITTLE, BROWN PB $13.95

The East

Henry **Beston**
The Outermost House
Cape Cod in the '20s
0-8050-1966-9 HOLT PB $9.95

Alf **Evers**
The Catskills: From Wilderness to Woodstock
A massive natural and social history
0-87951-162-1 OVERLOOK $39.50

Robert **Finch**
Common Ground: A Naturalist's Cape Cod
0-393-31179-1 NORTON PB $10.95

Outlands: Journeys to the Outer Edges of Cape Cod
0-87923-619-1 GODINE $16.95

The Primal Place
Essays grounded largely in Brewster, Massachusetts
0-393-01623-4 NORTON $15.00

Jean **Gardner**
Urban Wilderness: Nature in New York City
A dramatic photographic survey of New York City's 50,000 acres of parklands and wilderness
PHOTOGRAPHS BY JOEL GREENBERG
FOREWORD BY BILL MOYERS
0-9621060-0-3 EARTH ENVIRONMENTAL GROUP $40.00

Paul **Jamieson**, editor
The Adirondack Reader
0-935272-21-6 ADIRONDACK $29.50
0-935272-22-4 ADIRONDACK PB $18.50

John **McPhee**
The Pine Barrens
An early McPhee book about a major natural area and New Jersey aquifer
0-374-51442-9 FS&G PB $10.00

John Hanson **Mitchell**
Walking Towards Walden: A Pilgrimage in Search of Place
A 15-mile walk on a brilliant October day through the woods to Thoreau's tomb serves as the occasion for the author and two friends to meditate on the land and the power of place: the forces that drew Ponce de Leon to Florida, and continue to draw tourists to Walden, artists to Tuscany, monarch butterflies to a few mountain acres in Mexico, and that, hopefully, draw each of us to a particular beloved spot. "John Mitchell speaks to that place inside us where we hope one day to be whole"—Tom McGuane
0-201-40672-1 ADDISON-WESLEY $23.00

Donald **Stokes**
A Guide to Nature in Winter: Northeast and North Central North America
0-316-81723-6 LITTLE, BROWN PB $14.95

W.D. **Wetherell**
Vermont River
An angler's appreciation
1-55821-261-2 LYONS & BURFORD PB $12.95

William **White**
Adirondack Country
An excellent natural portrait
0-8156-0193-X SYRACUSE PB $14.95

The South

Ken **Carey**
Flat Rock Journal: A Day in the Ozark Mountains
An extended nature essay that manages to be both whimsical and profound. "A model of moss-velvet nature writing, quite possibly a classic—*Kirkus Reviews*
0-06-250275-1 HARPERCOLLINS PB $10.00

Rose **Houk**
Great Smoky Mountains: A Natural History Guide
An illuminating guide to the natural history of Americas most-visited yet perhaps least fully appreciated national park
ILLUSTRATED BY MICHAEL COLLIER
0-395-59920-2 HOUGHTON MIFFLIN PB $14.95

William **Niering**
Wetlands
See also **AUDUBON NATURE GUIDES** under **GUIDES** under **THE OUTDOORS** in **FOOD, TRAVEL, AND LEISURE**
0-394-73147-6 KNOPF PB $19.00

John **Teal** & Mildred **Teal**
Portrait of an Island
0-8203-0581-2 GEORGIA PB $9.95

John **Terres**
From Laurel Hill to Siler's Bog: The Walking Adventures of a Naturalist
Observations in North Carolina wildlife preserves; winner of the Burroughs Medal 1971
0-8078-4426-8 NORTH CAROLINA PB $16.95

The Great Plains

Roy **Bedichek**
Adventures with a Texas Naturalist
0-292-70311-2 TEXAS PB $14.95

Karankaway Country
0-292-74304-1 TEXAS PB $12.95

John **Graves**
From a Limestone Ledge
Graves is a funny, observant, and down-to-Earth writer whose subject is rural Texas
0-932012-77-9 TEXAS MONTHLY PB $8.95

Goodbye to a River
0-394-42690-8 RANDOM HOUSE $22.50
0-932012-75-2 TEXAS MONTHLY PB $8.95

Hard Scrabble
0-932012-76-0 TEXAS MONTHLY PB $7.95

John **Janovy**, Jr.
Back in Keith County
Nebraska natural history by a parasitologist
0-8032-7560-9 NEBRASKA PB $5.95

Keith County Journal
0-8032-7588-9 NEBRASKA PB $10.00

Josephine **Johnson**
The Inland Island
Johnson won the Pulitzer Prize in 1934 for her first novel, *Now in November*. This is a collection of nature essays
0-8142-0450-3 OHIO STATE PB $16.95

David Rains **Wallace**
Idle Weeds: The Life of an Ohio Sandstone Ridge
Winner of the Ohioana Book Award for Science 1981
0-8142-0409-0 OHIO STATE PB $18.95

The North Woods

Anne **LaBastille**
Beyond Black Bear Lake
LaBastille is a biologist and ecologist
0-393-30539-2 NORTON PB $10.95

Woodswoman
LaBastille's account of her life in the Adirondacks, where she has lived since 1954
0-14-015334-9 DUTTON PB $11.95

Edward **Lueders**
The Clam Lake Papers: A Winter in the North Woods
0-940473-32-1 CAXTON $20.00

Sigurd **Olson**

Listening Point

Olson is an extremely popular writer on the Minnesota wilderness

0-394-43358-0 RANDOM HOUSE $27.50

The Singing Wilderness

0-394-44560-0 KNOPF $24.95

The Southwest and the Desert

Edward **Abbey**

"What entertains many and exasperates others is Abbey's unique prose voice. Alternately misanthropic and sentimental, enraged and hilarious, it is the voice of a full-blooded man airing his passions."—Peter Carlson

Desert Solitaire

See also **HISTORY, POLITICS, AND SOCIETY** under **20TH-CENTURY AMERICAN ESSAYS AND JOURNALISM** in **LITERATURE OF THE AMERICAS**

See also **ESSAYS** under **THE OUTDOORS** in **FOOD, TRAVEL, AND LEISURE**

0-8165-1057-1 ARIZONA $36.00
0-345-32649-0 BALLANTINE PB $5.95
0-671-69588-6 TOUCHSTONE PB $11.00

The Journey Home: Some Words in Defense of the American West

0-452-26562-2 DUTTON PB $11.95

Mary **Austin**

The Land of Little Rain

Stories of the western desert, published in 1903

INTRODUCTION BY EDWARD ABBEY

0-8263-0358-7 NEW MEXICO PB $11.95

Joseph Wood **Krutch**

The Desert Year

0-8165-0923-9 ARIZONA PB $15.95

The Forgotten Peninsula: A Naturalist's Interpretation

0-8165-0987-5 ARIZONA PB $15.95

Barry **Lopez**

Desert Notes: Reflections in the Eye of the Raven

0-380-71110-9 AVON PB $9.00

Gary **Nabhan**

The Desert Smells Like Rain: A Naturalist in Papago Indian Country

Nabhan is an important ethnobotanist and naturalist of the southwestern desert. He traces the relationship of the Papagos to their Sonora desert environment

0-86547-050-2 NORTH POINT PB $12.00

Gathering the Desert

0-8165-1014-8 ARIZONA PB $18.95

Saguaro: A Naturalist Looks At Saguaro National Monument and the Tucson Basin

0-911408-69-X SW PARKS PB $4.95

Jeremy **Schmidt**

The Grand Canyon National Park

A constantly surprising and richly informative guide to the natural history of a natural wonder

0-395-59932-6 HOUGHTON MIFFLIN PB $16.95

Terry **Tempest Williams** & Mary **Frank**

Desert Quartet

A meditation on the vastness and beauty of the desert and on the spiritual space that Williams, one of the West's most intense and popular writers, found there. Illuminated with drawings and paintings by Mary Frank, this is at once a guide, an offering, and a transfixing story of spiritual quest

0-679-43999-4 RANDOM HOUSE $17.00

Ann **Zwinger**

Wind in the Rock: Canyon of the Southeastern Utah

0-8165-0985-9 ARIZONA PB $14.95

The Mountain West

Mary **Back**

Seven Half Miles from Home

Detailed natural observations from short walks in Wyoming's Wind River region

0-933472-90-0 JOHNSON PB $9.95

Sally **Carrighar**

One Day on Beetle Rock

Beetle Rock is in Sequoia National Park in California

0-8032-6301-5 NEBRASKA PB $6.95

Gretel **Ehrlich**

The Solace of Open Spaces

Sparse, affecting prose about the steep plains of Wyoming

0-14-008113-5 VIKING PB $10.95

Steven **Meyers**, editor

Trails Among the Columbine, 1990: A Colorado High Country Anthology

0-913582-51-4 SUNDANCE $35.00

Wallace **Stegner**

This Is Dinosaur: Echo Park Country and Its Magic Rivers

0-911797-11-4 ROBERTS RINEHART $30.00
0-911797-12-2 ROBERTS RINEHART PB $8.95

David **Wallace**

The Klamath Knot

California's Trinity Alps; winner of the Burroughs Medal in 1984

0-87156-817-9 RANDOM HOUSE PB $10.00

Ann **Zwinger**

Beyond the Aspen Grove

0-8165-1054-7 ARIZONA PB $17.95

Run, River Run: A Naturalist's Journey Down One of the Great Rivers of the West

Winner of the Burroughs Medal (1976)

0-8165-0885-2 ARIZONA PB $15.95

Ann **Zwinger** & Beatrice **Willard**

Land Above the Trees: A Guide to American Alpine Tundra

0-06-091365-7 HARPERPERENNIAL PB $10.95

The Northwest and Alaska

Rockwell **Kent**

Wilderness: A Journal of Quiet Adventure in Alaska

0-8195-5293-3 WESLEYAN PB $12.95

Robert **Marshall**

Alaska Wilderness: Exploring the Central Brooks Range

0-520-01711-0 CALIFORNIA PB $14.00

John **McPhee**

Coming Into the Country

Alaska is the subject of what is perhaps McPhee's finest book

0-374-12645-3 FS&G $22.95
0-374-52287-1 NOONDAY PB $14.00

John **Muir**

Letters From Alaska

0-299-13950-6 WISCONSIN $30.00
0-299-13954-9 WISCONSIN PB $12.95

Richard **Nelson**

Hunters of the Northern Forest: Designs For Survival Among the Alaskan Kutchin

0-226-57181-5 CHICAGO PB $16.00

Make Prayers to the Raven: A Koyukon View of the Northern Forest

0-226-57163-7 CHICAGO PB $14.95

Robert **Pyle**

Wintergreen

Winner of the John Burroughs Medal; set in the state of Washington

0-395-46559-1 HOUGHTON MIFFLIN PB $12.95

David **Rockwell**

Glacier National Park: A Natural History Guide

0-395-69981-9 HOUGHTON MIFFLIN PB $16.95

The Arctic and Antarctica

David G. **Campbell**

The Crystal Desert: Summers in Antarctica

Campbell tells a tale of fantastic natural beauty, and of its imminent destruction—of penguins, terns, elephant seals, and whales, and of garbage, rusting oil drums, and the slaughter of both seals and whales. "His descriptions…are unforgettable"—*New Yorker*. "An elegantly brilliant pointillist compendium of maritime Antarctica….I reveled in it"—Edward M. Hoagland

0-395-58969-X HOUGHTON MIFFLIN $21.95
0-395-68082-4 HOUGHTON MIFFLIN PB $10.95

Bertrand **Imbert**

North Pole, South Pole: Journeys to the Ends of the Earth

See also **CANADA** under **TRAVEL GUIDES** in **FOOD, TRAVEL, AND LEISURE**

0-8109-2881-7 ABRAMS PB........$12.95

Sanford **Moss** & Lucia **Deleiris**

Natural History of the Antarctic Peninsula

By the author of *Sharks: An Introduction for the Amateur Naturalist*

0-231-06269-9 COLUMBIA PB........$19.50

Farming and Agriculture

"I have often thought that if heaven had given me a choice of my position and calling, it should have been on a rich spot of Earth, well watered, and near a good market for the products of the garden. No occupation is so delightful to me as the culture of the Earth."—Thomas Jefferson.

Histories and Personal Accounts

Joseph **Amato**

The Great Jerusalem Artichoke Circus: The Buying & Selling of the Rural American Dream

A compellingly written and intriguing history of a little-publicized American farming debacle, brought about by efforts in the '80s to promote cultivation of the Jerusalem artichoke as a food and energy source

0-8166-2344-9 MINNESOTA........$44.95
0-8166-2345-7 MINNESOTA PB........$16.95

Peggy F. **Bartlett**

American Dreams, Rural Realities: Family Farms in Crisis

A multifaceted, detailed, scholarly study of family farms in Dodge County, Georgia

0-8078-4399-7 NORTH CAROLINA PB........$19.95

Craig **Canine**

Dream Reaper: A Story of Modern Agriculture

See also **FARMING IN AMERICA** under **ECONOMIC HISTORY** under **TOPICS IN AMERICAN STUDIES** in **HISTORY OF THE AMERICAS**

0-679-41272-7 KNOPF........$25.00

Mark **Cohen**

The Food Crisis in Prehistory: Overpopulation and the Origins of Agriculture

0-300-02351-0 YALE PB........$19.00

Wendell **Berry**

The Gift of Good Land: Further Essays Cultural and Agricultural

0-86547-052-9 NORTH POINT PB........$13.00

Wendell Berry

The Unsettling of America: Culture and Agriculture

A collection of essays

0-87156-772-5 SIERRA CLUB PB........$10.00

Jane **Brox**

Here and Nowhere Else: Late Seasons of a Farm and Its Family

0-8070-6201-4 BEACON PB........$12.95

Gary **Comstock**, editor

Is There a Moral Obligation to Save the Family Farm?

Essays by farmers, journalists, politicians, economists, lawyers, academics, and religious leaders

0-8138-1000-0 IOWA STATE PB........$16.95

Stanley **Crawford**

A Garlic Testament: Seasons on a Small New Mexico Farm

0-06-098121-0 HARPERPERENNIAL PB........$11.00

Carl **Eicher** & John **Staatz**

Agricultural Development in the Third World

0-8018-4000-7 JOHNS HOPKINS PB........$19.95

Paul D. **Escott**

North Carolina Yeoman: The Diary of Basil Armstrong Thomasson, 1853-1962

0-8203-1755-1 GEORGIA........$50.00

Nelson **Foster** & Linda S. **Cordell**, editors

Chilies to Chocolate: Foods the Americas Gave the World

A cultural and agricultural history of foods native to the western hemisphere, from the potato to the tomato to chocolate

0-8165-1324-4 ARIZONA PB........$14.95

Mark **Friedberger**

Farm Families and Change in Twentieth-Century America

0-8131-1636-8 KENTUCKY........$32.00

Thomas **Isern**

Bull Threshers & Bindlestiffs: Harvesting & Threshing on the North American Plains

A fascinating and beautifully illustrated history of American harvesting techniques before the invention of modern machinery

0-7006-0468-5 KANSAS........$29.95

Wes **Jackson**

Altars of Unhewn Stone

Essays on sustainable agriculture and related topics

0-86547-287-4 NORTH POINT PB........$12.00

New Roots For Agriculture

0-8032-7562-5 NEBRASKA PB........$7.95

Thomas **Jefferson**

The Garden & Farm Books of Thomas Jefferson

EDITED BY ROBERT C. BARON & HENRY S. COMMAGER

1-55591-024-6 FULCRUM........$35.00
1-55591-013-0 FULCRUM........$20.00

Stanley **Joseph**

Maine Farm: A Year of Country Life

0-394-58464-3 RANDOM HOUSE........$32.50

M.G. **Kains** & J.E. **Oldfield**

Five Acres & Independence

0-486-20974-1 DOVER PB........$7.95

Verlyn **Klinkenborg**

Making Hay

A lyrical yet sharply defined evocation of life on a family farm

ILLUSTRATED BY GORDON ALLEN

0-941130-18-5 LYONS & BURFORD........$14.95

Andy **Lee**

Backyard Market Gardening: The Entrepreneur's Guide to Selling What You Grow

An authoritative handbook that treats virtually every aspect of the business, from planning crops to running a farm stand and a mail-order operation

0-9624648-0-5 GOOD EARTH PB........$19.95

Gene **Logsdon**

At Nature's Pace: Farming and the American Dream

A farmer who believes that healthy farming can only work "at nature's pace" lends his thoughts on single-crop megafarms, which, he believes, will eventually lead to economic and biological crisis. In Amish country he finds that care of the land and integration of business and family offer valuable lessons and finds inspiring his discovery of a renaissance in American agricultural awareness

0-679-75844-5 PANTHEON PB........$12.00

Gene **Logsdon**

The Contrary Farmer

A highly practical guide to the work of farming, enlivened by Logsdon's literate yet earthy sense of humor

0-930031-67-9 CHELSEA GREEN $21.95
0-930031-74-1 CHELSEA GREEN PB $16.95

Harry M. **Mason**

Life on the Dry Line: Working the Land, 1902-1944

Clear-sighted and unsentimental memoirs of farm life in Kansas in the early years of the 20th century

FOREWORD BY WES JACKSON
1-55591-122-6 FULCRUM $19.95

David Mas **Masumoto**

Epitaph for a Peach: Four Seasons on My Family Farm

See also **FARMING IN AMERICA** under **ECONOMIC HISTORY** under **TOPICS IN AMERICAN STUDIES** in **HISTORY OF THE AMERICAS**

0-06-251025-8 HARPERCOLLINS PB $12.00

Robert M. **Netting**

Smallholders, Householders: Farm Families & The Ecology of Intensive, Sustainable Agriculture

An argument—based on an extensive worldwide survey—that the small farm can survive, even thrive, in the era of agribusiness

0-8047-2061-4 STANFORD $49.50
0-8047-2102-5 STANFORD PB $16.95

Sonya **Salamon**

Prairie Patrimony: Family, Farming, & Community in the Midwest

An original and revealing scholarly study of contemporary farming in Illinois, exploring how different cultural ancestries (in this case British versus German) affect the way farmers operate their lands and their businesses

0-8078-2045-8 NORTH CAROLINA $49.95
0-8078-4553-1 NORTH CAROLINA PB $16.95

Hubert G. **Schmidt**

Agriculture in New Jersey: A 300-Year History

0-8135-0756-1 RUTGERS $40.00

Olive **Schreiner**

The Story of an African Farm

Nadine Gordimer has described this early feminist novel as the book to which all other South African work has to measure up

See also **CENTRAL AND SOUTHERN AFRICA** under **AFRICAN LITERATURE** in **LITERATURE OF EUROPE, AFRICA, AND ASIA**

0-19-282885-1 OXFORD PB $6.95

Otto T. **Solbrig** & Dorothy J. **Solbrig**

So Shall You Reap: Farming & Crops in Human Affairs

"The Solbrigs—he teaches biology at Harvard, she is librarian at Harvard's Biological Laboratories—emphasize the interdependence of farming and the environment. Their study proceeds from early hunter-gatherers to the development of sedentary agriculture and explores the connections between sugarcane, slavery and exploitation; the spread of coffee, grapes, tobacco, cotton, rubber; and the advent of biotechnology. Full of intriguing facts, this work shows how modern, chemicalized, industrialized agriculture threatens biodiversity, destroys topsoil and forests, and contaminates the food chain"—*Publishers Weekly*

1-55963-308-5 ISLAND $27.50
1-55963-309-3 ISLAND PB $16.95

Peter **Svenson**

Battlefield: Farming a Civil War Battleground

"Past and present interface as Svenson juxtaposes depictions of the battle with accounts of his struggle to produce a crop of hay. The death-grapples of blue and gray regiments echo in Svenson's modern-day war against mini-malls, pesticides and similar late-20th century detritus. This chronicle is a gem"—a moving military pastoral"—*Publishers Weekly*

0-345-38419-9 BALLANTINE PB $11.00

Allen M. **Young**

The Chocolate Tree: A Natural History of Cacao

An absorbing account of a crop that is of interest both as a natural phenomenon and a force in human history

1-56098-357-4 SMITHSONIAN $24.95

Technical and Practical Works

Miguel **Altieri**

Agroecology: The Scientific Basis of Alternative Agriculture

0-8133-7284-4 WESTVIEW PB $49.00

Jim **Bender**

Future Harvest: Pesticide-Free Farming

Bender argues that organic farming can be profitable, and that it doesn't merely constitute a turning away from modern methods

0-8032-1233-X NEBRASKA $25.00

M. **Buckett**

Introduction to Farm Organization and Management

How to run a farm by the book

0-08-034203-5 ELSEVIER $86.00
0-08-034202-7 PERGAMON PB $34.00

Larry **Connor**

Managing the Farm Business

0-13-550376-0 PRENTICE HALL $45.00

Kenneth **Dahlberg**, editor

New Directions For Agriculture and Agricultural Research: Neglected Dimensions and Emerging Alternatives

0-8476-7417-7 ROWMAN & LITTLEFIELD $72.75

J. Sholto **Douglas** & Robert **Hart**

Forest Farming: Towards a Solution to Problems of World Hunger and Conservation

See also **NATURAL RESOURCES AT RISK** under **THE ENVIRONMENT**

0-946688-30-3 INTERMEDIATE TECHNOLOGY PB. $19.50

Duane **Erickson**

Microcomputers on the Farm: Getting Started

0-8138-1157-0 IOWA STATE PB $9.95

Ronald D. **Kay** & William M. **Edwards**

Farm Management

The latest edition of a comprehensive and popular guide

0-07-033868-X MCGRAW HILL $63.15

Oscar A. **Lorenz** & Donald N. **Maynard**

Knott's Handbook for Vegetable Growers, Third Edition

"A classic reference offering current information on all aspects of vegetable growing, from planting to marketing—*SciTech Book News*

0-471-85240-6 WILEY PB $75.00

Marty **Strange**

Family Farming: A New Economic Vision

0-8032-9194-9 NEBRASKA PB $9.95

Stephen **Thomas** & George P. **Looby**

Backyard Livestock: Raising Good Natural Food for Your Family, Second Edition

0-88150-182-4 COUNTRYMAN PB $15.00

R.W. **Widdowson**

Towards Holistic Agriculture: A Scientific Approach

0-08-034211-6 PERGAMON $37.00

The Environment

Environmental History

Thomas **Allen**

Guardian of the Weld: The Story of the National Wildlife Federation, 1936-1986

0-253-32605-2 INDIANA $27.50

John **Bierhorst**

The Way of the Earth: Native America and the Environment

A book about the beliefs and practices regarding land use, conservation of species and wilderness, and population control

0-688-14349-0 QUILL PB $14.00

Christopher **Bosso**

Pesticides and Politics: The Life Cycle of a Public Issue

Traces the battle over control of pesticides through 40 years of technological and political changes

0-8229-3547-3 PITTSBURGH $49.95

Peter J. **Bowler** & Roy **Porter**, editor

Norton History of Environmental Sciences

A landmark volume in Norton's History of Science series, placing ecology and related fields in their social and cultural contexts

0-393-03535-2 NORTON $35.00

0-393-31042-6 NORTON PB $15.95

Anna **Bramwell**

Ecology in the 20th Century

0-300-04521-2 YALE PB $22.00

Jerry **Dennis**

The Bird in the Waterfall: A Natural History of the Oceans, Rivers, and Lakes

A celebration of the wonders of water and the natural history of rivers and lakes. The engaging text and evocative illustrations explore waterfalls and springs, waves and tides, mermaids and manatees, drawing on mythology, folklore, and science. From the team who brought us the innovative and acclaimed *It's Raining Frogs and Fishes*, which the *Houston Post* described as "A perfect choice for adults and kids alike who want to discover more about how the world is put together"

ILLUSTRATIONS BY GLENN WOLFF

0-06-017094-8 HARPERCOLLINS $26.00

Clarence **Glacken**

Traces of the Rhodian Shore: Nature and Culture in Western Thought from Ancient Times to the End of the 18th Century

0-520-03216-0 CALIFORNIA PB $32.50

Donald **Hughes**

Pan's Travail: Environmental Problems of the Ancient Greeks & Romans

A provocative and original study, which takes the study of man's interaction with nature back into ancient history

0-8018-4655-2 JOHNS HOPKINS $39.95

Hans **Huth**

Nature and the American: Three Centuries of Changing Attitudes

0-8032-7247-2 NEBRASKA PB $9.95

Martin **Melosi**

Garbage in the Cities: Refuse, Reform, and the Environment, 1880-1980

0-534-10714-1 DORSEY PB $26.75

Geoffrey **Jellicoe** & Susan **Jellicoe**

The Landscape of Man: Shaping the Environment from Prehistory to the Present Day

A brilliant and entertaining classic that ranges over philosophy, art, and literature as they pertain to landscape history

See also **LANDSCAPE AND GARDEN DESIGN** under **GARDENING** under **THE OUTDOORS** in **FOOD, TRAVEL, AND LEISURE**

0-500-27431-2 THAMES & HUDSON PB $24.95

Roderick **Nash**

Wilderness and the American Mind

See also **ESSAYS** under **THE OUTDOORS** in **FOOD, TRAVEL, AND LEISURE**

See also **INTELLECTUAL HISTORY** under **TOPICS IN AMERICAN STUDIES** in **HISTORY OF THE AMERICAS**

0-300-02910-1 YALE PB $16.00

Keith **Thomas**

Man and the Natural World: A History of the Modern Sensibility

0-19-511122-2 OXFORD PB $15.95

Donald **Worster**

Nature's Economy: A History of Ecological Ideas

0-521-45273-2 CAMBRIDGE $59.95

0-521-46834-5 CAMBRIDGE PB $15.95

The Wealth of Nature: Environmental History & the Ecological Imagination

A gathering of 16 eloquent essays on environmental issues facing the U.S., by scholars from a number of pertinent fields

0-19-507624-9 OXFORD $30.00

0-19-509264-3 OXFORD PB $13.95

Donald **Worster**, editor

The End of the Earth: Perspectives on Modern Environmental History

0-521-34846-3 CAMBRIDGE PB $15.95

The Environmental Movement

John H. **Adams**

An Environmental Agenda For the Future

Essays by the heads of Sierra Club, National Audubon Society, World Wildlife Fund, and the Conservation Foundation assess key issues of the past and future. "Environmentalists and their opponents alike will find this preview of ecological battles-to-come a useful blueprint for strategy"—*Washington Post*

0-933280-29-7 ISLAND PB $11.95

Ian **Barbour**

Technology, Environment, and Human Values

0-275-91483-6 PRAEGER PB $18.95

Peter **Borrelli**, editor

Crossroads: Environmental Priorities For the Future

Barry Commoner, Stewart Udall, and others evaluate the movement's successes and failures

0-933280-68-8 ISLAND $37.00

0-933280-67-X ISLAND PB $18.95

Daniel B. **Botkin**

Discordant Harmonies: A New Ecology For the 21st Century

How humans must reconceive their relation to nature. The author writes: "The changes that must take place are twofold: the recognition of the dynamic rather than the static properties of the Earth and its life-support system, and the acceptance of a global view of life on the Earth"

0-19-505491-1 OXFORD $25.00

0-19-507469-6 OXFORD PB $11.95

Lester **Brown**

State of the World 1989: A Worldwatch Institute Report on Progress Toward a Sustainable Society

0-393-30614-3 NORTON PB $9.95

Barry **Commoner**

Making Peace with the Planet

"An enlarged prescription for a technosphere brought into harmony with our ecosphere... Right and compassionate on nearly every major issue" —Stephen Jay Gould, *NY Times Book Review*

0-8446-6701-3 SMITH $23.00

Andrew **Dobson**, editor

The Green Reader: Essays Toward a Sustainable Society

Essays that explore the philosophy of environmentalism, the effort to move from a consumption-based society to one focused on the renewal of resources. Includes writings by Rachel Carson, E.F. Schumacher, Aldous Huxley, Kirkpatrick Sale, and Aldo Leopold

1-56279-017-X MERCURY HOUSE $24.95

1-56279-010-2 MERCURY HOUSE PB $11.95

Mark **Dowie**

Losing Ground: American Environmentalism at the Close of the 20th Century

0-262-04147-2 MIT $27.50

0-262-54084-3 MIT PB $12.50

Luc **Ferry**

The New Ecological Order

0-226-24482-2 CHICAGO $34.95

0-226-24483-0 CHICAGO PB $14.95

Daniel J. **Fiorino**

Making Environmental Policy

0-520-08918-9 CALIFORNIA PB $15.00

Bentley **Glass**

Progress Or Catastrophe: The Nature of Biological Science and Its Impact on Human Society

0-275-90107-6 PRAEGER $65.00

Al **Gore**

Earth in the Balance: Ecology and the Human Spirit

The reviews are in, and Gore's book is a great success. Most important, it shows how the roots of the environmental crisis reach into all aspects of our behavior. But instead of just setting off alarm bells, Gore offers a plan for change. "A work of intelligence and passionate authenticity… Gore has produced a labor of statesmanship, evangelism and scientific exposition.…His book is itself an act of leadership"—*Time*

0-395-57821-3 HOUGHTON MIFFLIN $22.95
0-452-26935-0 PLUME PB $13.95

Derrick **Jensen**

Listening to the Land: Nature, Culture, and Eros

Jensen seeks answers to the questions of why we are destroying the natural world, how we can stop it, and where can we find respect and compassion

0-87156-417-3 SIERRA CLUB PB $15.00

Lester **Milbrath**

Environmentalists: Vanguard For a New Society

0-87395-887-X SUNY $59.50
0-87395-888-8 SUNY PB $19.95

Joseph **Petulla**

Environmental Protection in the United States

0-936434-21-X SF STUDY CENTER $22.50
0-936434-22-8 SF STUDY CENTER PB $14.50

Tom **Regan**

Earthbound: An Introduction to Environmental Ethics

0-88133-568-1 WAVELAND PB $20.95

Charles T. **Rubin**

The Green Crusade: An Intellectual History of the Environmental Movement

A fair-minded account of the dawn and noon of the Green Revolution, through a careful evaluation of several influential environmentalist writers—including Rachel Carson, Paul Ehrlich, and Barry Commoner

0-02-927525-3 FREE PRESS $22.95

Geoffrey C. **Saign**

Green Essentials: What You Need to Know About the Environment

This unique, easy-to-use dictionary provides vital information on the myriad environmental problems we face each day. Concise, comprehensive, and extremely accessible, it guides the reader through definitions, solutions, and the probable impact of such problems as acid rain, ozone depletion, toxic waste, and tainted household water. Provides immediate literacy in one of the most complex and pressing issues of our time

1-56279-061-7 MERCURY HOUSE PB $16.95

George **Sessions**

Deep Ecology For the Twenty-First Century

Comprehensive readings on the environmentalist movement, on humankind's relationship with nature, and on the history and implications of "deep ecology." Sessions argues that a fundamental acknowledgment of the intrinsic value of nature must inform the way we think of our environment. A statement of an influential philosophical and political movement that has captured both Dave Foreman of "Earth First!" and Vice President Al Gore. Important and fascinating

0-87773-049-0 SHAMBHALA PB $20.00

Philip **Shabecoff**

A Fierce Green Fire: The American Environmental Movement

Environmentalism has become one of the hottest topics in America. This didn't just happen by accident—it is the result, as Shabecoff points out, of forces in political and literary life that have been slowly evolving for over a century. A social history of the environmental movement, this work documents the origins of today's highly politicized concerns over earth, air, and water

0-8090-8459-7 HILL & WANG $25.00
0-8090-1558-7 HILL & WANG PB $10.95

Christopher D. **Stone**

The Gnat Is Older Than Man: Global Environment & Human Agenda

A closely reasoned and compelling legal approach to environmental problems

0-691-03250-5 PRINCETON $39.50

Natural Resources at Risk

Rachel **Carson**

Silent Spring

"I particularly remember my mother's troubled response to Rachel Carson's classic book about DDT and pesticide abuse, Silent Spring*…She emphasized to my sister and me that this book was different—and important"*
—Al Gore, from Earth in Balance

INTRODUCTION BY AL GORE

0-395-68329-7 HOUGHTON MIFFLIN PB $11.95

Council on Environmental Quality

The Global 2000 Report to the President: Entering the 21st Century

0-14-006138-X VIKING PB $12.95

J. Sholto **Douglas** & Robert **Hart**

Forest Farming: Towards a Solution to Problems of World Hunger and Conservation

See also **TECHNICAL AND PRACTICAL WORKS** under **FARMING AND AGRICULTURE**

0-946688-30-3 INTERMEDIATE TECHNOLOGY PB $19.50

Mary **Douglas** & Aaron **Wildavsky**

Risk and Culture: An Essay on the Selection of Technologies and Environmental Dangers

0-520-05063-0 CALIFORNIA PB $14.95

Michael **Katakis**, editor

Sacred Trusts: Essays on Stewardship and Responsibility

Original essays by a diverse group of writers—including novelists, scientists, and sportsmen—on their personal approach to responsibility to the land

0-944439-52-7 MERCURY HOUSE PB $17.00

Bill **McKibben**

Hope, Human and Wild: True Stories of Living Lightly on the Earth

0-316-56064-2 LITTLE, BROWN $22.95

A.J. **McMichael**

Planetary Overload: Global Environmental Change and the Health of the Human Species

0-521-55871-9 CAMBRIDGE PB $11.95

William **Ramsay**

Bioenergy and Economic Development: Planning For Biomass Energy Programs in the Third World

0-8133-7037-X WESTVIEW PB $43.50

Air Pollution, Acid Rain, and the Greenhouse Effect

Dean E. **Abrahamson**, editor

The Challenge of Global Warming

An up-to-date, nontechnical compendium of research by scientists and policymakers on causes, effects, policies, and solutions

INTRODUCTION BY SENATOR TIMOTHY E. WIRTH

0-933280-87-4 ISLAND $40.00
0-933280-86-6 ISLAND PB $22.00

Bert **Bolin** & others

The Greenhouse Effect, Climate Change, and Ecosystems

0-471-92635-3 WILEY PB $75.00

John **Luoma**

The Air Around Us: An Air Pollution Primer

0-935577-10-6 ACID RAIN FOUNDATION PB $9.95

Robert A. **Mello**

Last Stand of the Bird Spruce

Written as a detective story, Mello's nontechnical assessment of the effects of acid rain on our forests and the role of the federal government is compelling

INTRODUCTION BY SENATOR PATRICK J. LEAHY

0-933280-37-8 ISLAND PB $14.95

National Academy of Sciences
Air Pollution, the Automobile, and the Public Health
0-309-03726-3 NATIONAL ACADEMY $69.95

Sandra **Postel**
Air Pollution, Acid Rain, and the Future of Forests
0-916468-57-7 WORLDWATCH INSTITUTE PB $5.00

Stephen H. **Schneider**
Global Warming
0-87156-693-1 SIERRA CLUB $20.00

Industrial Hazards and Solid Wastes

Tom **Athanasiou**
Divided Planet: The Ecology of Rich and Poor
Examining today's major threats to the environment, *Divided Planet* shows that the real issues of pollution, ozone depletion, deforestation, and the like can only be addressed with money, incentives, and the will to change an economic system
See also **CURRENT POLITICAL THOUGHT AND ISSUES** under **AMERICAN POLITICS AND FOREIGN POLICY** in **HISTORY OF THE AMERICAS**
0-316-05635-9 LITTLE, BROWN $24.95

Louis **Blumberg** & Robert **Gottlieb**
War on Waste: Can America Win Its Battle with Garbage?
0-933280-92-0 ISLAND $37.00
0-933280-91-2 ISLAND PB $21.95

Michael **Edelstein**
Contaminated Communities: The Social and Psychological Impacts of Residential Toxic Exposure
Love Canal and other toxic communities, and the physical and psychological effects of contamination
0-8133-7447-2 WESTVIEW $58.50

William **Rathje** & Cullen **Murphy**
Rubbish!: The Archeology of Garbage
The Garbage Project has been analyzing America's garbage for 20 years. An immensely readable account containing fascinating and detailed information on how America lives, while dispelling current myths about garbage and suggesting ways we can more responsibly deal with our garbage
0-06-092228-1 HARPERPERENNIAL PB $13.00

Nuclear Reactors

Luther J. **Carter**
Nuclear Imperatives and Public Trust: Dealing with Radioactive Waste
0-915707-47-0 RESOURCES FOR THE FUTURE PB $19.95

Anna **Gyorgy**
No Nukes: Everyone's Guide to Nuclear Power
0-89608-007-2 SOUTH END $40.00
0-89608-006-4 SOUTH END PB $10.00

Michio **Kaku** & Jennifer **Trainer**, editors
Nuclear Power: Both Sides (the Best Arguments For and Against the Most Controversial Technology)
"A clear and balanced representation of the complex issue of nuclear power"
—William Simon
0-393-30128-1 NORTON PB $11.95

Water Use and Pollution

Barbara **Graves**, editor
Radon, Radium, and Other Radioactivity in Ground Water: Hydrogeologic Impact and Application to Indoor Airborne Contamination
A compilation of conference papers presented by the EPA and Association of Ground Water Scientists and Engineers, with numerous case studies
0-87371-117-3 LEWIS $96.00

Jon A. **Kusler**
Our National Wetland Heritage: A Protection Guidebook
A comprehensive discussion of preservation, combined with a literature review, examination of statutes and cases, and a survey of protection programs; for both the professional and layperson
0-911937-11-0 ENVIRONMENTAL LAW PB $14.00

Ed **Marston**, editor
Western Water Made Simple
By focusing on the Colorado, the Columbia, and the Missouri rivers, this series of articles illustrates the most important issues affecting the conservation and management of our western water. George Polk Award for Environmental Reporting (1986)
0-933280-39-4 ISLAND PB $16.95

Practical Advice

Debra **Dadd**
The Nontoxic Home and Office: Protecting Yourself and Your Family from Everyday Toxics and Health Hazards
How to avoid toxins in cleaning products, food, tap water, and other dangers
0-87477-676-7 TARCHER PB $10.95

Howard **Rheingold**
The Millennium Whole Earth Catalog: Access to Tools and Ideas for the Twenty-First Century
The most up-to-date information for this century and beyond, by the cultural prophets of *The Whole Earth Catalog*. "A table of contents to the Zeitgeist—or the coolest Yellow Pages around"—*Kirkus Reviews*. "Implicit on every page is the…assumption that we're all intelligent, curious, and capable of educating ourselves, given access to the right tools"
—*Outside Magazine*
See also **ALMANACS AND BOOKS OF FACTS** under **GENERAL INFORMATION** under **REFERENCE** in **BUSINESS AND REFERENCE**
FOREWORD BY STEWART BRAND
0-06-251141-6 HARPERCOLLINS $50.00

Allan **Savory**
Holistic Resource Management
A comprehensive planning model for integrating environment and people in farming, ranching, and livestock management. "Savory's special genius is combining high-minded idealism with thoroughgoing practicality, and he has a nose for generating profit in the process"
—Gretel Ehrlich, *Time*
0-933280-62-9 ISLAND $47.50
0-933280-61-0 ISLAND PB $29.95

Sierra Club Legal Defense Fund
The Poisoned Well: New Strategies For Groundwater Protection
A useful guide for determining the existence of pollutants, protection against contamination, explanation of federal regulations, and legal strategies
0-933280-56-4 ISLAND $37.00
0-933280-55-6 ISLAND PB $21.95

Forestry and Land Conservation

Chris **Anderson**
Edge Effects: Notes from an Oregon Forest
A perceptive first-hand report from a forest preserve outside a medium-sized but fast-growing Oregon town—a zone where nature and human activity come into contact and conflict
FOREWORD BY WAYNE FRANKLIN
0-87745-419-1 IOWA $29.95
0-87745-438-8 IOWA PB $10.95

Russell L. **Brenneman** & Sarah M. **Bates**, editors
Land-Saving Action: A Written Symposium by Twenty-Nine Experts on Private Land Conservation in the 1980s
0-933280-23-8 ISLAND $35.00

Robert Pogue **Harrison**
Forests: The Shadow of Civilization
A unique new book, both a history of and a guide to the forest, that helps us to understand, as our woodlands disappear, their ecological and cultural importance. "This book is as deep with history as an ancient grove of trees, and as majestic, and open, and delightful"—Bill McKibben
0-226-31806-0 CHICAGO $24.95
0-226-31807-9 CHICAGO PB $14.95

Susan **Hecht** & Alexander **Cockburn**
The Fate of the Forest: Developers, Destroyers and Defenders of the Amazon
0-86091-261-2 VERSO $25.00

Nancy P. **Pittman**, editor
From "the Land": Articles Compiled from the Land, 1941-1954
Humor, science, short stories, and poetry; over 40 authors, including E.B. White and Aldo Leopold, on the subject of conservation
0-933280-66-1 ISLAND $38.00
0-933280-65-3 ISLAND PB $22.00

Paul B. **Sears**
Deserts on the March
Written in 1935, this book is a timely reminder of how mankind continues to unbalance nature
0-933280-46-7 ISLAND $35.00
0-933280-90-4 ISLAND PB $14.95

David J. **Simon**, editor
Our Common Lands: Defending the National Parks
Eighteen legal and environmental scholars discuss key environmental legislation. "This superb book contains all of the elements of a battle plan to preserve the national parks" —Stewart Udall
0-933280-58-0 ISLAND $47.50
0-933280-57-2 ISLAND PB $29.95

Jack **Westoby**
Introduction to World Forestry
0-631-16134-1 BLACKWELL PB $25.95

Tropical Forests

Brian **Alexander**
Green Cathedrals: A Rain Forest Pilgrimage
In this cold-eyed tour through seven rain forests throughout the world, Alexander fails to find eco-scholars and heroic natives, encountering instead Maori women in Elvis T-shirts and signs in the Malaysian airport threatening death to drug smugglers
1-55821-399-6 LYONS & BURFORD $22.95

Julie S. **Denslow** & Christine **Padoch**, editors
People of the Tropical Rain Forest
0-520-06351-1 CALIFORNIA PB $29.95

Philip **Fearnside**
The Human Carrying Capacity of the Brazilian Rainforests
0-231-06104-8 COLUMBIA $55.50

Adrian **Forsyth** & Ken **Miyata**
Tropical Nature: Life and Death in the Rain Forests of Central and South America
0-684-18710-8 MACMILLAN PB $13.00

Alain **Gheerbrant**
The Amazon: Past, Present, and Future
0-8109-2860-4 ABRAMS PB $12.95

Marius **Jacobs** & R.A.A. **Oldeman**
The Tropical Rain Forest: A First Encounter
"An outstanding 'first encounter' with tropical rain forests, and compelling plea—a *cri de coeur*—for conservation of large tracts of them"—*Nature*
0-387-17996-8 SPRINGER-VERLAG PB $59.95

C.F. **Jordan**
Amazonian Rainforests
0-387-96397-9 SPRINGER-VERLAG $66.00

Kenneth **Longman**
The Tropical Rainforest and Its Environment
0-470-20742-6 LONGMAN $69.95

Biological Diversity

Vaclav **Smil**
Cycles of Life: Civilization and the Biosphere
0-7167-5079-1 FREEMAN $32.95

Michael **Soule**
Conservation Biology: The Science of Scarcity and Diversity
0-87893-800-1 SINAUR PB $34.95

Colin **Tudge**, editor
The Environment of Life
Examines the setting shared by all flora and fauna—and the impact of one species on it
0-19-520621-5 OXFORD $40.00

Langdon **Winner**
The Whale and the Reactor: A Search For Limits in an Age of High Technology
0-226-90211-0 CHICAGO PB $12.95

Endangered Species

Diane **Ackerman**
The Rarest of the Rare: Vanishing Animals, Timeless Worlds
The renowned author of *A Natural History of the Senses* takes us on a search for "the rarest of the rare," several of the species most likely to become extinct before many of us have ever seen them. From the glorious monkey in Brazil to monk seals in the Pacific and on to the migration layovers of the monarch butterfly, Ackerman provides a magnificent chance, perhaps the last chance, to experience these species and thereby to understand, and appreciate, the work of those striving to save them
0-679-40346-9 RANDOM HOUSE $23.00
0-679-77623-0 VINTAGE PB $12.00

Raymond **Bonner**
At the Hand of Man: Peril and the Hope For Africa's Wildlife
Bonner brings some much-needed good sense to an emotional issue—the threat to African wildlife, especially the elephant. He makes it clear that unless we address the needs of African people, especially their poverty, they will of necessity destroy their wildlife. Controversial, and argumentative, he insists that to save African animals will require us to abandon naive romanticism
0-679-73342-6 VINTAGE PB $12.00

Joseph **Cone**
A Common Fate: Endangered Salmon & the People of the Pacific
0-8050-2388-7 HOLT $25.00
0-87071-391-4 OREGON PB $42.00

Thomas **Dunlap**
Saving America's Wildlife
Illustrates the shift in American attitudes toward preserving wildlife as we are faced with losing it
0-691-00613-X PRINCETON PB $14.95

Gerald **Durrell**
The Aye-Aye & I
A British naturalist on the trail of one of Madagascar's strangest and most elusive animals. "Another delightful excursion into nature by the always amusing Durrell" —*Kirkus Reviews*
1-55970-204-4 ARCADE $22.95

Errol **Fuller**
1988 IUCN Red List of Threatened Animals
2-8317-0031-0 ISLAND PB $15.00

Harold **Koopowitz** & Hilary **Kaye**
Plant Extinction: A Global Crisis
9-994115-16-2 AM. ORCHID SOCIETY $19.95
0-913276-44-8 STONE WALL $19.95

Charles C. **Mann** & Mark L. **Plummer**
Noah's Choice: The Future of Endangered Species
0-679-42002-9 KNOPF $27.50

John **Terborgh**
Where Have All the Birds Gone?
0-691-02428-6 PRINCETON PB $15.95

Animal Rights

Lawrence **Finsen** & Susan **Finsen**
Animal Rights Movement
"A readable history of the movement, from its beginning in early philosophy to more concerted and organized efforts in eighteenth-, nineteenth-, and twentieth-century Britain and the US"—*Booklist*
0-8057-3883-5 TWAYNE $27.95

Michael **Fox**

The Case For Animal Experimentation: An Evolutionary and Ethical Perspective

Argues that it is permissible for humans to experiment on animals, but only within carefully qualified ethical guidelines

0-520-06023-7 CALIFORNIA PB $12.00

Tom **Regan**

The Case For Animal Rights

"Makes any objections to the inclusion of animals in the moral community sound exactly like the feeble tenets that have supported racism, sexism, or antisemitism"—*Spectator*

0-520-05460-1 CALIFORNIA PB $15.00

Peter **Singer**

Animal Liberation

The first closely argued philosophical case for animal rights, Singer's 1979 book was a major inspiration for the animal rights movement

0-940322-00-5 NEW YORK REVIEW $19.95
0-380-71333-0 AVON PB $12.50

Susan **Sperling**

Animal Liberators: Research and Morality

A critical study of activists in the animal rights movement

0-520-06198-5 CALIFORNIA $28.00

Biographies

Rachel **Carson** & Martha **Freeman**, editor

Always, Rachel: The Letters of Rachel Carson & Dorothy Freeman, 1952-1964

A rich, quietly eloquent and often moving window into Carson's private life

INTRODUCTION BY PAUL BROOKS

0-8070-7010-6 BEACON $35.00
0-8070-7011-4 BEACON PB $18.00

Dan **Duane**

Lighting Out: A Vision of California and the Mountains

"[Duane] explores with fine irony and rare depth his awakening into manhood, love, and conquest"—Isabel Allende

1-55597-210-1 GRAYWOLF PB $14.00

Lewis **Gould**

Lady Bird Johnson and the Environment

0-7006-0336-0 KANSAS $29.95

Deanna **Kawatski**

Wilderness Mother

The story of a Canadian woman who raised a family without electricity or running water, 100 miles from a paved road. A brave, startling, and inspiring account of mothering without the safety and comforts of society

1-55821-201-9 LYONS & BURFORD $22.95
1-55110-168-8 LYONS & BURFORD PB $14.95

Curt **Meine**

Aldo Leopold: His Life and Work

Forester, scientist, sportsman, philosopher, writer, and conservation activist, Leopold advocated a "land ethic" to guide industrial man through the natural world. This biography offers an excellent personal view of the American conservation movement

0-299-11490-2 WISCONSIN $29.50

Michael **Cohen**

The Pathless Way: John Muir and American Wilderness

0-299-09720-X WISCONSIN $35.00

Linnie Marsh **Wolfe**

Son of the Wilderness: The Life of John Muir

0-299-07730-6 WISCONSIN $29.50
0-299-07734-9 WISCONSIN PB $14.95

The Computer Revolution

The Computer Revolution

The computer revolution, still in its infancy, has generated thousands of books, most of them about the latest hardware, the latest computer languages, how to write programs, and how to design faster, smaller, and more powerful machines. The following books are broad in scope: they discuss what the revolution is all about, its history, its philosophical implications, and how it is likely to affect our lives.

Apple Computer, Inc.

Demystifying Multimedia

The guide to the most-often-used, least-often-understood word in new technologies from the people who invented it. Case studies, checklists, and an astonishingly simple design explain the concept of multimedia with clarity. Covers each stage of multimedia product design and offers professional tips, interviews, and product reviews

0-679-75603-5 RANDOM HOUSE PB $30.00

Charles **Eames** & Ray **Eames**

A Computer Perspective

0-674-15626-9 HARVARD PB $17.95

Tom **Forester**, editor

Computers in the Human Context: Information Technology, Productivity, and People

0-262-06124-4 MIT $42.00
0-262-56050-X MIT PB $21.00

Herman **Goldstine**

The Computer from Pascal to Von Neumann

0-691-02367-0 PRINCETON PB $19.95

Tracy **Kidder**

The Soul of a New Machine

A book that defined a new genre of business writing. Kidder sketches a tale of heartache and exhilaration as a group of Data General engineers design a computer whose success may determine the fate of their company

See also COMPANIES AND INDUSTRIES under BUSINESS, INDUSTRY, AND FINANCE in BUSINESS AND REFERENCE

0-380-71115-X AVON PB $12.00

P. **Millican** & Andy **Clark**, editors

The Legacy of Alan Turing (Mind Association Occasional Series)

0-19-823594-1 CLARENDON $25.00

Brian **Randell**, editor

The Origins of Digital Computers

0-387-11319-3 SPRINGER-VERLAG $87.00

Donald **Sanders**

Computers in Society

0-07-054672-X MCGRAW HILL $43.95

Nancy **Stern** & Robert **Stern**

Computers in Society

0-13-165282-6 PRENTICE HALL PB $44.89

Biographies

Stephen **Manes** & others

Gates: How Microsoft's Mogul Reinvented an Industry—And Made Himself the Richest Man in America

Not the nebbish the public has taken him for, Bill Gates—the creator of Microsoft computer software and the youngest self-made billionaire in history—is a complex, brilliant businessman. The authors look at Gates's rapid rise to power, his position in the computer industry, and the nature of his ever-expanding company

0-671-88074-8 TOUCHSTONE PB $14.00

The Cybernetic Society

James **Brook** & Iain **Boal**, editors

Resisting the Virtual Life: The Culture and Politics of Information

0-87286-299-2 CITY LIGHTS PB $15.95

Bob **Cotton** & Richard **Oliver**

The Cyberspace Lexicon: An Illustrated Dictionary of Terms from Multimedia to Virtual Reality

New technologies emerge with pulsant quickness, and the infinitude of cyberspace becomes more chaotic daily. More than a dictionary, it is a meticulous, illustrated explanation of everything from interactive media to arcade games to virtual reality. "In addition to the 800 concise dictionary entries are illustrated features that range from computer animation, electronic books, and Nintendo to virtual sex. An essential guide"—*Library Journal*

See also REFERENCE
See also SPECIALIZED DICTIONARIES

0-714-83267-0 PHAIDON PB $29.99

Mark **Dery**
Flame Wars: The Discourse of Cyberculture
0-8223-6400-X DUKE PB......$10.00

Barbara **Garson**
The Electronic Sweatshop: How Computers Are Transforming the Office of the Future Into the Factory of the Past
0-14-012145-5 PENGUIN PB......$11.95

Linda M. **Harasim**, editor
Global Networks: Computers and International Communications
Once the realm of a handful of technocrats, international networks are now an everyday reality for millions, their scope expanding with every leap of imagination. Twenty-one experts explore the personal, business, cultural, and educational issues as well as the opportunities and pitfalls of this new technology
0-262-08222-5 MIT......$35.00
0-262-58137-X MIT PB......$16.95

O.B. **Hardison**, Jr.
Disappearing Through the Skylight: Culture and Technology in the 20th Century
A brilliant, intricate discussion of the disappearance of nature and what it means for us. "Fasten your cerebral seat belt…A contentious, infuriating, profound, and finally fascinating volume"—*Washington Post Book World*
0-14-011582-X PENGUIN PB......$16.95

In the nineteenth century, science presented nature as a group of objects set comfortably and solidly in the middle distance before the eyes of the beholder. In the work of D'Arcy Thompson, published around the turn of the century, nature has disappeared. It has become a set of geometric and mathematical relations that lie under the surface of the visible. It is still, however, indubitably there. Today, nature has slipped, perhaps finally, beyond our field of vision. We can imitate it in mathematics—we can even produce convincing images of it—but we can never know it. We can know only our own creations.
DISAPPEARING THROUGH THE SKYLIGHT: CULTURE AND TECHNOLOGY IN THE 20TH CENTURY

Steven **Holtzman**
Digital Mantras: The Languages of Abstract and Virtual Worlds
0-262-08228-4 MIT......$32.50

Kevin **Kelly**
Out of Control: The New Biology of Machines, Social Systems, and the Economic World
0-201-48340-8 ADDISON-WESLEY PB......$16.00

George P. **Landow**
Hypertext: The Convergence of Contemporary Critical Theory and Technology
0-8018-4280-8 JOHNS HOPKINS......$48.50
0-8018-4281-6 JOHNS HOPKINS PB......$16.95

Richard D. **Lanham**
The Electronic Word: Democracy, Technology and the Arts
0-226-46884-4 CHICAGO MAC......$19.95
0-226-46885-2 CHICAGO PB......$14.95

Timothy **Leary**
Chaos and Cyberculture
Leary and friends approach the boundaries of '90s computer culture and then give it a cerebral kick in the head. William Gibson, William S. Burroughs, David Byrne and special guests assist Leary in his encouragement of independent thinking and punching holes in society's barriers
See also **CULTURE ON THE EDGE** under **CUTTING EDGE** in **POPULAR READING**
0-914171-77-1 RONIN PB......$19.95

Les **Levidow** & Kevin **Robins**, editors
Cyborg Worlds: The Military Information Society
A collection of essays examining the disturbing links between computer culture and military paradigms, and what they imply about the function of human beings in the emerging cybernetic society
1-85343-092-7 FREE ASSOCIATION PB......$17.50

William J. **Mitchell**
City of Bits: Space, Place and the Infobahn
Entertaining and concise introduction to a new type of city—the virtual spaces of the information superhighway
See also **THEORY AND CRITICISM** under **20TH-CENTURY ARCHITECTURE** in **ARCHITECTURE, DESIGN, AND HOMES**
0-262-13309-1 MIT......$22.50
0-262-63176-8 MIT PB......$10.00

Ivars **Peterson**
Fatal Defect: Chasing Killer Computer Bugs
0-8129-2023-6 TIME BOOKS......$25.00

Theodore **Roszak**
The Cult of Information: The Folklore of Computers and the True Art of Thinking
A recent critique of computer enthusiasm
See also **THE HUMAN MIND AND ARTIFICIAL INTELLIGENCE** under **THE COGNITIVE REVOLUTION** under **PSYCHOLOGY** in **SOCIAL STUDIES**
See also **TECHNOLOGY AND EDUCATION** under **EDUCATION** in **SOCIAL STUDIES**
0-520-08584-1 CALIFORNIA PB......$12.00
0520085840 CALIFORNIA PB......$1.00

Winn **Schwartau**
Information Warfare: Chaos on the Electronic Superhighway
1-56025-132-8 THUNDER'S MOUTH PB......$16.95

Mark **Slouka**
War of the Worlds: Cyberspace and the High-Tech Assault on Reality
0-465-00486-5 BASIC......$20.00
0-465-00487-3 BASIC PB......$12.00

David **Sheff**
Game Over: How Nintendo Zapped an American Industry, Captured Your Dollars, and Enslaved Your Children
0-679-73622-0 VINTAGE PB......$13.00

Jonathan **Wallace** & Mark **Mangan**
Sex, Laws, and Cyberspace: Freedom and Regulation on the Frontiers of the Online Revolution
0-8050-4767-0 HOLT......$24.95

Sandy **Whiteley**
American Library Association Guide to Information Access
The first comprehensive guide to both print and electronic informafion services. The traditional: libraries, archives, newspapers, government agencies; and the new: CD-ROM databases, the Internet, electronic bulletin boards, electronic document delivery services, and the national catalogs (OCLC and RLIN). More than 3,000 print and electronic sources tame the information revolution
0-679-75075-4 RANDOM HOUSE PB......$19.00

Rob **Wittig**
Invisible Rendezvous: Connection and Collaboration in the New Landscape of Electronic Writing
0-8195-5275-5 WESLEYAN......$18.95

The Internet

Tom **Badgett** & Corey **Sandler**
Welcome To...Internet: From Mystery to Mastery
1-55828-308-0 MIT PB......$19.95

Eric **Braun**
The Internet Directory
0-449-90898-4 FAWCETT PB......$25.00

Mary J. **Cronin**
Doing Business on the Internet: How the Electronic Highway Is Transforming American Companies
0-442-01770-7 VAN NOSTRAND REINHOLD PB....$29.95

Daniel P. **Dern**
The Internet Guide For New Users
0-07-016511-4 MCGRAW HILL PB......$27.95

Katharine **English**, editor
Most Popular Web Sites: The Best of the Net from A2Z
Includes book and CD-ROM
0-7897-0792-6 QUE PB......$39.99

Adam C. **Engst**
Internet Starter Kit For Macintosh
1-56830-064-6 HAYDEN PB......$29.95

Bennett **Falk**
The Internet Roadmap
0-7821-1365-6 SYBEX PB $12.99

Sharon **Fisher**
Riding the Internet Highway
1-56205-192-X NEW RIDERS PB $16.95

Richard **Gibbs** & Richard **Smith**
Navigating the Internet
0-672-30485-6 SAMS PB $29.95

Laurel **Gilbert** & Crystal **Kile**, editors
SurferGrrrls: Look Ethel! An Internet Guide for Us!
1-87806-779-6 SEAL PB $15.00

Alfred **Glossbrenner**
Internet Slick Tricks
Tips, tricks, and techniques for beginners and intermediates on the Net. Features an easy-access interface, practical shortcuts, concise explanations to e-mail, information search and retrieval. Explains utilities such as Archie (software search), Gopher (information search), FTP (File Transfer Protocol), and much, much more. An indispensable guide to an indispensable service
0-679-75611-6 RANDOM HOUSE PB $16.00

The Little Online Book
1-56609-130-6 PEACHPIT PB $17.95

Katie **Hafner** & Matthew **Lyon**
Where the Wizards Stay Up Late: The Story Behind the Creation of the Internet
"...a clear readable history of the internet...Ms. Hafner and Mr. Lyon have done us a service by rescuing from oblivion the collection of geeks and nerds, bureaucrats and geniuses, who have changed everyday life for millions of people all across the planet"—*NY Times*
See also **LATE ARRIVALS**
0-684-81201-0 SIMON & SCHUSTER $24.00

Harley **Hahn** & Rick **Stout**
Internet: The Complete Reference
0-07-881980-6 OSBORNE PB $29.95

Harley **Hahn**
The Internet Yellow Pages
0-07-882182-7 OSBORNE PB $29.95

Angus J. **Kennedy**
The Internet & World Wide Web: The Rough Guide
1-85828-198-9 ROUGH GUIDES PB $8.00

J.C. **Herz**
Surfing on the Internet: A Nethead's Adventures On-Line
The book that captures the Internet for what it really is: not a corporate communication tool, not a research source, but an anarchic counterculture, strange and wonderful, where anything can happen—and often does. Hackers, Phreakers, Flame Wars and—of course—NetSex make up this amazing dispatch from Cyberspace
0-316-35958-0 LITTLE, BROWN $19.95
0-316-36009-0 LITTLE, BROWN PB $11.95

Brent **Heslop** & David **Angell**
The Instant Internet Guide: Hands-On Global Networking
0-201-62707-8 ADDISON WESLEY PB $14.95

Ed **Krol**
The Whole Internet: User's Guide & Catalog
1-56592-025-2 O'REILLY PB $24.95

Steve **Lambert** & Walt **Howe**
Internet Basics: Your Online Access to the Global Electronic Super Highway
0-679-75023-1 RANDOM HOUSE PB $27.00

Max **Lent**
Government Online
0-06-273301-X HARPERCOLLINS PB $15.00

John R. **Levine** & Carol **Baroudi**
Internet For Dummies
1-56884-024-1 I.D.G. PB $19.95

Douglas **Rushkoff**
Cyberia: Life in the Trenches of Hyperspace
"Rushkoff profiles the thinkers, technologies, sciences and philosophies that are moving our society to a new paradigm"—*Santa Cruz Sentinel*
0-06-251009-6 HARPERCOLLINS PB $11.00

Peter **Rutten** & Albert F. **Bayers**
Net Guide
A bestseller that covers commercial services, the Internet, and hundreds of bulletin boards, illustrated and cross-referenced. The first guide to offer free information updates online
0-679-75106-8 RANDOM HOUSE PB $19.00

William A. **Tolhurst** & others
Using the Internet, Special Edition
1-56529-353-3 QUE PB $39.95

Richard **Wiggins**
The Internet For Everyone: A Guide For Users and Providers
0-07-067019-6 MCGRAW HILL PB $29.95

Michael **Wolff**
Net Games
Easy-to-use guide to over 1,000 games on the Internet, including all the major services—CompuServe, Prodigy, America Online—as well as hundreds of bulletin boards. Each game is described with instructions and strategy tips, game sites, addresses, and the source of necessary shareware. *The* guide to fun on the Net
0-679-75592-6 RANDOM HOUSE PB $19.00

Reference

Computers have made it necessary to invent thousands of new terms. Although this terminology changes rapidly, it has stabilized enough to permit dozens of dictionaries and encyclopedias.

American Heritage
The American Heritage Dictionary of Computer Words: An A to Z Guide to Today's Computer
See also **COMPUTER DICTIONARIES** under **SPECIALIZED DICTIONARIES** under **REFERENCE** in **BUSINESS AND REFERENCE**
0-395-72834-7 HOUGHTON MIFFLIN PB $11.95

John A. **Barry**
Technobabble
An entertaining survey of computerspeak since its origins in the '50s, and the ways in which cybernetic lingo has penetrated areas far removed from computers
0-262-02333-4 MIT $27.50

William **Birnes** & others, editors
McGraw-Hill Personal Computer Programming Encyclopedia: Languages and Operating Systems
0-07-005393-6 MCGRAW HILL $109.50

Bob **Cotton** & Richard **Oliver**
The Cyberspace Lexicon: An Illustrated Dictionary of Terms from Multimedia to Virtual Reality
New technologies emerge with pulsant quickness, and the infinitude of cyberspace becomes more chaotic daily. More than a dictionary, it is a meticulous, illustrated explanation of everything from interactive media to arcade games to virtual reality. "In addition to the 800 concise dictionary entries are illustrated features that range from computer animation, electronic books, and Nintendo to virtual sex. An essential guide"—*Library Journal*
See also **THE CYBERNETIC SOCIETY**
See also **SPECIALIZED DICTIONARIES**
0714832670 PHAIDON PB $29.99

Douglas **Downing** & Michael **Covington**
Dictionary of Computer Terms
0-8120-4824-5 BARRONS PB $8.95

Philip E. **Margolis**
Random House Personal Computer Dictionary: Second Edition
0-679-76424-0 RANDOM HOUSE PB $15.00

Microsoft
Microsoft Press Computer Dictionary: Second Edition
More that 5,000 clearly written entries compiled by a team of computer and business professionals as well as academics
See also **COMPUTER DICTIONARIES** under **SPECIALIZED DICTIONARIES** under **REFERENCE** in **BUSINESS AND REFERENCE**
1-55615-597-2 MICROSOFT PB $19.95

Trevor **Owen** & others

The Learning Highway: A Student's Guide to Using the Internet in High School and College

How to learn to stop worrying and love the Internet. This unusually intelligent guide introduces practical operations on the Internet specifically for high school and college research. Divided into "electronic stacks"—Arts and Humanities, Social Sciences, and Pure and Applied Sciences— *The Learning Highway* offers solutions to practical research problems, accessing useful databases, finding periodicals, newspapers, maps, and photographs

1-55013-705-0 KEY PORTER PB $21.95
1-55013-615-1 NAT'L BOOK NETWORK PB $14.95

Computer Manuals

In the early 1900s, divers dredged up a puzzling clocklike mechanism from the hull of an ancient ship that had sunk near the Greek island of Antikythera. Certain calibrated elements showed it to be a measuring device of some kind, but it was years before archaeologists figured out that the Antikythera Device, dated at around 100 B.C., had been used to perform astronomical calculations *automatically*.

The modern term "computer" refers to high-speed electronic equipment capable of reading and writing data, executing various series of instructions (programs) to process such data and, finally, storing the results. At the end of the 17th century new kinds of calculating machines began to be invented as nascent capitalism demanded an accelerated rate of exchange. But it was Charles P. Babbage's visionary "Difference Engine" and "Analytical Engine" that definitively prefigured the modern computer. Both of his designs could have worked, except that the 19th century was incapable of making parts for them. Not until 1930 did anything comparable to Babbage's inventions appear. Over the next decades there appeared a "differential analyzer" built by the U.S. military for plotting artillery trajectories; the Mark I, the first fully automatic computer; and the first electronic computer, the ENIAC, produced by the University of Pennsylvania in 1946.

By today's standards the ENIAC was a hulking colossus which weighed over 30 tons. Its vacuum tubes threw off tremendous heat and required an elaborate cooling system. All that changed with the development of solid-state technology in the mid '60s. Transistorized circuitry miniaturized the computer, eliminated the heat problem, and greatly reduced production costs as well. Subsequently the silicon microprocessor "chip" or integrated circuit has permitted even smaller and cheaper designs, making possible today's "home" or "personal" computer, the PC.

When the PC first began to work its way into the everyday life of the American consumer, the need for information geared to the nonspecialist spawned a new field of publishing. Many of the books which meet this demand are instruction manuals written to augment or replace the often insufficient manuals of hardware and software vendors. Others are intended to improve the user's skills and techniques. Because most of these publications are linked to a rapidly changing technology, they offer fast-paced information open to continued revision. Accordingly, the following list is a broad survey of the field as a whole, not an exhaustive bibliography. It highlights major equipment and programs. But given the multiple functions of these, some overlapping between categories is inevitable.

Word Processing

Word processing first became popular in the early '70s with specialized, hardwired machines which enabled secretaries to correct and process text instead of having to type revised manuscripts from scratch. Today, powerful word-processing programs have made earlier systems like Exxon's Vydec totally obsolete; accordingly, the PC has become a standard writer's tool.

Sharon **Fisher-Larson**

Wordperfect 6.0 Made Perfectly Easy

0-02-802587-3 GLENCOE PB $27.95

Stephen **Harris**

Wordperfect 7 for Windows 95 Bible

With companion CD-ROM

1-56884-722-X I.D.G. PB $39.99

Jim **Heid**

Macworld Word 6.0 Companion

1-56884-082-9 I.D.G. PB $24.95

Julie Adair **King**

Wordperfect Suite 7 for Dummies

1-56884-946-X I.D.G. PB $19.99

Doug **Lowe**

Word 6.0 for Windows for Dummies

1-56884-628-2 I.D.G. PB $24.99

Microsoft Press

Microsoft Word for Windows 95: Step by Step

1-55615-828-9 MICROSOFT PB $29.95

Stephen L. **Nelson**

Field Guide to Microsoft Word for Windows 95

1-55615-832-7 MICROSOFT PB $9.95

William R. **Pasewark**

Clarisworks 4.0 Macintosh

0-538-71501-4 SOUTH-WESTERN PB $27.00

Charles **Rubin**

The Macintosh Bible Guide to Clarisworks 4

0-201-88406-2 PEACHPIT PB $24.95

Peter **Weverka**

Dummies 101: Word for Windows 95

1-56884-632-0 I.D.G. PB $24.99

Database Management

A data base can consist of subscription lists, inventories, personnel files, or any other data produced within a given system. Data base software allows the user to organize and recombine this information in a variety of ways.

Ken/ Litwin, Paul **Getz**

Microsoft Access 95 How-To: A Compendium of Dispensable Tips from Master Developers

1-57169-052-2 WAITE PB $44.99

Tamar E. **Granor** & others

Hacker's Guide to Visual Foxpro 3.0: An Irreverent Look at How Foxpro Really Works

0-201-48379-3 ADDISON WESLEY PB $44.95

Robert T. **Grauer** & Maryann **Barber**

Exploring Microsoft Access for Windows 95: Version 7.0

0-13-503393-4 PRENTICE HALL PB $31.92

Nelson **King**

Teach Yourself...Visual Foxpro 3.0 for the Mac

1-55828-496-6 M.I.S. PB $29.95

Stuart **Stuple**

QR-dBase 5.0 for Windows for Dummies

1-56884-953-2 I.D.G. PB $9.99

Spreadsheets and Money Management

Spreadsheet programs are the digital replacement for the traditional forecaster's columns, pad, and calculator. They are an invaluable tool for financial planners, accountants, statisticians, engineers, and scientists.

David **Bolocan** & Sandra J. **Bottomley**

Lotus 1-2-3 for Macintosh Simplifed

0-8306-3964-0 WINDCREST PB $18.95

Steve **Cummings**

Home Banking With Quicken

1-55828-477-X M.I.S. PB $16.95

Robert T. **Grauer** & Maryann **Barber**

Exploring Lotus 1-2-3 for Windows 95

0-13-503344-6 PRENTICE HALL PB $24.00

Greg **Harvey**
Excel 5.0 for Macs for Dummies
1-56884-186-8 I.D.G. PB $19.95

Robert **Machalow**
Using Lotus 1-2-3 for Windows
1-55570-187-6 SCHUMAN PB $39.95

Lawrence J. **Magid**
The Little Quicken Book: For Windows 3.1 and Windows 95
1-56609-185-3 PEACHPIT PB $18.95

Michael **Meadhra**
The ABCs of Online Banking With Quicken
0-7821-1886-0 SYBEX PB $19.99

Anne **Prince**
Excel 5.0 for Windows
0-911625-79-8 MURACH PB $25.00

Russell A. **Stultz**
Learn Microsoft Excel 7.0 for Windows 95 in a Day
1-55622-464-8 WORDWARE PB $15.95

Desktop Publishing

The development of low-cost laser printers and sophisticated page layout programs has radically affected the way that newsletters, magazines, newspapers, and business presentations are produced. The relative cheapness of electronic typography and graphics places them well within reach of small businesses and private individuals.

Ted **Alspach**
The Complete Idiot's Guide to Pagemaker for Windows 95
0-7897-0377-7 QUE PB $19.99

Linda **Chanda**
Xpress It!: A Step-by-Step Guide to Quark Express 3.0
0-697-14003-2 BROWN PB $31.90

Linnea **Dayton** & Janet **Ashford**
Aldus Pagemaker: A Visual Guide for the Macintosh
0-201-40724-8 ADDISON WESLEY PB $28.95

Nancy J. **McCarthy**
Quark Design: A Step-By-Step Approach to Page Layout Software
0-201-88376-7 PEACHPIT PB $34.95

Graphics, Presentation, Design, and Animation

Adobe Systems Staff
Adobe Illustrator for Windows
1-56830-053-0 HAYDEN PB $44.95

Michael **Beall** & Dennis **Balagtas**
AutoCAD for Beginners, New Version
1-56205-243-8 NEW RIDERS PB $30.00

David **Browne**
Teach Yourself...Pagemaker 6 for the Macintosh
1-55828-476-1 M.I.S. PB $24.95

Teach Yourself...Pagemaker 6 for Windows 95
1-55828-419-2 M.I.S. PB $24.95

Martin S. **Matthews**
Using PageMaker For the PC: Version 3
0-07-881422-7 OSBORNE PB $22.95

Deke **McClelland**
Drawing on the Macintosh: A Non-Artist's Guide to MacDraw, Illustrator, FreeHand, & Many Others
1-55623-909-2 BUSINESS ONE IRWIN PB $26.00

Yvonne **McCoy**
Quattro: The Complete Reference
0-07-881337-9 OSBORNE PB $24.95

Bert **Monroy** & David **Biedny**
Adobe Photoshop: A Visual Guide for the Mac
0-201-48993-7 ADDISON WESLEY PB $34.95

Katherine **Murray**
Mastering Powerpoint for Windows 95
0-7821-1787-2 SYBEX PB $29.99

Roger **Parker**
Harvard Graphics 2.0 for Windows for Dummies
1-56884-092-6 I.D.G. PB $19.95

Michael Todd **Peterson** & others
3D Studio Max Fundamentals
1-56205-625-5 NEW RIDERS PB $45.00

Que Development Staff
Easy Freelance Graphics 2.0 for Windows
1-56529-768-7 QUE PB $19.99

Sue **Reber** & Charles **Blum**
PC Learning Labs Teaches Microsoft Powerpoint for Windows 95
1-56276-379-2 ZIFF DAVIS PB $29.99

Tom **Reed**
Teach Yourself...Adobe Illustrator for Windows
1-55828-435-4 M & T BOOKS PB $21.95

Denise **Salles** & others
Adobe Photoshop Creative Techniques
1-56830-132-4 MACMILLAN PB $40.00

Gary **Shelly**
Microsoft Powerpoint 4.0 for Windows
0-87709-572-8 BOYD & FRASER PB $18.95

Bud **Smith**
AutoCAD for Dummies
1-56884-191-4 I.D.G. PB $19.95

Nadia Magnenat **Thalmann** & Daniel **Thalmann**, editors
Interactive Computer Animation
0-13-518309-X PRENTICE HALL $42.00

Elna **Tymes** & Charles **Prael**
Quattro For the Professional
0-8306-9378-5 TAB PB $19.95

Elaine **Weinmann** & Peter **Lourekas**
Illustrator 6 for Macintosh: Visual Quickstart Guide
0-201-88633-2 PEACHPIT PB $19.95

Photoshop 2.5 for Windows: Visual Quick Start Guide
1-56609-071-7 PEACHPIT PB $18.95

Photoshop 3 for Windows: Visual Quickstart Guide
0-201-88625-1 PEACHPIT PB $19.95

Communications and the Web

Telecommunications is the electronic transfer of data from one place to another via telephone lines. "Going online" allows users to access and transmit a wealth of information.

Charles **Bowen**
The Hitchhikers Guide to America Online
1-55828-396-X M.I.S. PB $21.95

Charles **Bowen** & David **Peyton**
How to Get the Most Out of Compuserve
0-553-34476-5 BDD PB $19.95

Ted **Coombs** & others
The Netscape Livewire Sourcebook: Create and Manage a Java-Based Web Site
0-471-15605-1 WILEY PB $29.95

Paul **Hoffman** & Paul E. **Hoffman**
Netscape and the World Wide Web for Dummies
1-56884-862-5 I.D.G. PB $19.99

David **Lawrence**
Learn HTML on the Macintosh
0-201-88793-2 ADDISON WESLEY PB $29.95

Julie **McKeehan**
Safe Surfing: A Family Guide to the Net
0-12-484834-6 APPRO PB $24.95

Michael **Miller**
Using Prodigy
0-7897-0323-8 QUE PB $24.99

Mike **Miller**
Using Compuserve
0-7897-0595-8 QUE PB $24.99

Bruce **Morris**
HTML in Action: Hot Tips for Cool Sites
See also PROGRAMMING
1-55615-948-X MICROSOFT PB $29.95

Shelley **O'Hara**
Official Netscape Beginner's Guide to the Internet
1-56604-522-3 VENAN PB $24.99

Dick **Oliver** & others
Netscape Unleashed: Covers Netscape Navigator 2, Java, and Javascript
1-57521-007-X SAMS PB $49.99

Jean **Polly**
The Internet Kids Yellow Pages: Special Edition
0-07-882197-5 OSBORNE PB $19.95

Mitchell **Shnier**
Dictionary of PC Hardware and Data Communications Terms
1-56592-158-5 O'REILLY PB $19.95

David **Siegel**
Creating Killer Web Sites: The Art of Third-Generation Site Design
1-56830-289-4 HAYDEN PB $45.00

Alan **Simpson**
Official Netscape Navigator Gold 3.0 Book, Windows Edition: The Official Guide to the Premiere Web Browser
1-56604-420-0 VENAN PB $39.95

Gene **Steinberg**
Using America Online With Windows 95
0-7897-0594-X QUE PB $24.99

Operating Systems

Microsoft Windows

Windows was Microsoft's attempt to introduce a Macintosh-like graphic interface to the IBM environment.

Doug/ Green, David W. **Azzarito**
The Os/2 Warp Survival Guide: Installing, Configuring, and Using Os/2 2.X
0-471-06083-6 WILEY PB $29.95

Lana K. **Bryan** & Robert E. **Whitsitt**
Illustrated Microsoft Windows 2.0
1-55622-069-3 WORDWARE PB $19.95

Jennifer **Fulton**
The Complete Idiot's Guide to DOS
1-56761-496-5 ALPHA PB $16.95

Jon **Haber** & Herbert R. **Haber**
Microsoft Windows 3.0 & 3.1, Word For Windows & Excel
1-55623-618-2 BUSINESSONE PB $19.00

Guy **Hart-Davis**
The ABCs of Microsoft Office for Windows 95
0-7821-1866-6 SYBEX PB $19.99

Doug **Lowe**
Microsoft Office for Windows 95 for Dummies: Quick Reference
1-56884-978-8 I.D.G. PB $12.99

Ron **Person**
Using Windows 95: Platinum Edition
0-7897-0797-7 QUE PB $60.00

Andy **Rathbone**
Windows 95 for Dummies
1-56884-240-6 I.D.G. PB $19.99

Barrie **Sosinsky**
The Warp Book: Your Definitive Guide to Installing and Using OS/2
0-7615-0034-0 PRIMA PB $24.95

DOS

Peter **Norton**
Peter Norton's DOS Guide: Special Edition Covering 6.2
1-56686-136-5 BRADY PB $24.95

Herbert **Schildt**
DOS 4 Made Easy
0-07-881448-0 OSBORNE PB $19.95

Van **Wolverton**
Running MS-DOS: Version 6.2
1-55615-633-2 MICROSOFT PB $19.95

Computer Systems and Hardware

Eric **Knorr**, editor
The PC Bible
1-56609-107-1 PEACHPIT PB $24.95

Scott **Mueller**
Upgrading and Repairing PCs
1-56529-467-X QUE PB $34.95

Programming

A programming language is a set of rules through which instructions are coded for the computer. "Machine language" refers to binary code, the most basic level at which data can be represented in memory. Assembly language is a low-level language that converts the numeric code of machine language into mnemonic code. Ordinarily, users employ more convenient, problem-oriented languages which serve as specialized, shorthand versions of assembly language. The American National Standard Institute (ANSI) insures the consistency of these high-level languages.

Mark **Andrews**
C++ Windows Nt Programming
1-55851-493-7 M & T BOOKS PB $44.95

Barry **Boone**
Java Essentials for C and C++ Programmers
0-201-47946-X ADDISON WESLEY PB $19.95

Steven **Holzner**
Java Workshop Programming
1-55851-491-0 M & T BOOKS PB $34.95

Andrew **Koenig**
Ruminations on C++: A Decade of Programming Insight and Experience
0-201-42339-1 ADDISON-WESLEY PB $29.25

David **Lawrence**
Learn HTML on the Macintosh
See also COMMUNICATIONS AND NETWORKING
0-201-88793-2 ADDISON WESLEY PB $29.95

Bruce **Morris**
HTML in Action: Hot Tips for Cool Sites
See also COMMUNICATIONS AND NETWORKING
1-55615-948-X MICROSOFT PB $29.95

Aaron E. **Walsh**
Java for Dummies
1-56884-641-X I.D.G. PB $24.99

Macintosh

Arnie H. **Abrams**

Educator's Guide to Macintosh Applications

0-205-16284-3 PRENTICE HALL PB $32.00

Darcy **DiNucci** & others, editors

The Macintosh Bible, 5th Edition

Without question, the single standard reference to the world of Macintosh operating systems, programs, hardware, and multimedia. The last word in Macintosh guides

1-56609-140-3 PEACHPIT PB $30.00

Hoyt **Hilsman**

Micro Doctor: Care, Troubleshooting, and Simple Repair For Your Apple Computer

0-673-39101-9 FORESMAN PB $13.95

Jeremy **Judson**, editor

The Macintosh Bible

Everything you need to know about your Mac

0-201-88636-7 PEACHPIT PB $29.95

Apple Computer Inc.

Guide to Macintosh Family Hardware

0-201-52405-8 ADDISON WESLEY PB $26.95

Part 6

Literature of the Americas

Wallace Stevens

The Nature of the New World

Bird Song
What is it
What is it
What is it —Paiute Indians

606

1716: A Place of Prayer
I with some of my schoolmates joined together and built a booth in a swamp, in a very retired spot, for a place of prayer.
—Jonathan Edwards (1704–1758)
A Personal Narrative

613

1827: Yankee Choppers
What will the Yankee choppers say when they have cut their path from the eastern to the western waters? They will turn on their tracks like a fox that doubles, and then the rank smell of their own footsteps will show them the madness of their waste.
—James Fenimore Cooper (1789–1851)
The Prairie

614

1847: Working the Land
Minott, Lee, Willard, Hosmer,
Meriam, Flint
Possessed the land which
rendered to their toil
Hay, corn, roots, hemp,
flax, apples, wool, and
wood.
—Ralph Waldo Emerson
(1803–1882)
"Hamatreya"

615

1864: A Crack
To my quick ear the Leaves — conferred —
The Bushes — they were Bells —
I could not find a Privacy
From Nature's sentinels —

In Cave if I presumed to hide
The Walls — begun to tell —
Creation seemed a mighty crack —
To make me visible —
—Emily Dickinson (1830–1886)

614

1930s: Questions
How can the water endure it?
What sky have the stones
dreamed?
—Pablo Neruda (1904–1973)
The Heights of Machu Picchu

777

1961: Abstraction
An abstraction grew around him—nothing else—the ruling abstraction of himself which he saw reflected nowhere. He was a ruler of men and a ruler of nothing. The sun rose into the blinding wall and river before him filling the stream and water with melting gold. He dipped his hand in but nothing was there. —Wilson Harris (1921–)
Palace of the Peacock

768

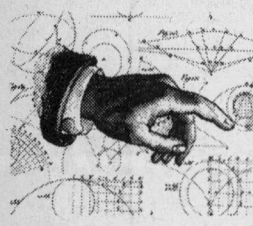

AD1700 AD1800 AD1850 AD1900 AD1950

1650: A True Vision
The trees all richly clad, yet void of pride,
Were gilded o'er by Phoebus' golden head;
Their leaves and fruits seemed painted, but were true…
—Anne Bradstreet (1612–1672)
"Contemplations"

612

1800: Westward Ho!
To western woods, and
lonely plains
Palemon from the
crowd departs,
Where Nature's wildest
genius reigns,
To tame the soil, and
plant the arts—
What wonders there shall freedom show,
What mighty states successive grow!
—Philip Freneau (1752–1832)
"On the Emigration to the Americas"

725

1838: A Conservationist
Woodman, spare that tree!
Touch not a single bough!
In youth it sheltered me,
And I'll protect it now.
—George Pope Morris (1802–1864)
"The Oak"

725

1856: Limitless
Limitless are leaves stiff or drooping in the fields,
And brown ants in the little wells beneath them,
And mossy scabs of the wormfence, and heaped
stones, and elder and mullen and pokeweed.
—Walt Whitman (1819–1892)
Song of Myself

619

1873: Fragments
Like fragments of an uncompleted
world
From icy bleak Alaska, white with
spray,
To where the peaks of Darien lie
curled
In clouds, the broken lands loom bold and
gray…
—Joaquin Miller (1837–1913)
"The Sierras"

724

1939: Pays Natal
Rise, phantoms, chemical-blue from a forest of hunted beasts
of twisted machines of jujube-trees of rotten flesh of a basket of
oysters of eyes of a lacework of lashes cut from a lovely sisal of
a human skin I would have words huge enough to contain you
all and you too
stretched earth
drunken earth
earth great sex raised in the sun
—Aimé Césaire (1913–)
Notebook of a Return to My Native Land

767

1963: The End
I lean back, as the evening darkens and comes on.
A chicken hawk floats over, looking for home.
I have wasted my life. —James Wright (1927–1980)
"Lying in a Hammock"

723

1 **The Cities of America**
are inexpressibly tedious. The Bostonians take their learning too sadly; culture with them is an accomplishment rather than an atmosphere; Baltimore is amusing for a week, but Philadelphia is dreadfully provincial. Chicago is a sort of monster shop, full of bustles and bores. Political life at Washington is like political life in a suburban vestry; and though one can dine in New York, one could not dwell there.
—Oscar Wilde
Aristotle at Afternoon Tea
815

2 **Port Townsend**
Sir, when I first came to this town I found three classes of people, Injuns, sailors and sons o' bitches. Now I find that the Injuns have all died and the sailors have sailed away.
—Ivan Doig
Winter Brothers
232

3 **St. Louis**
Old steamboats with their scrollwork more scrolled and withered by weathers sat in the mud inhabited by rats. Great clouds of afternoon overtopped the Mississippi Valley.
—Jack Kerouac
On The Road
659

4 **Chicago**
Later came the midsummer, with the stifling heat, when the dingy killing beds of Durham's became a very purgatory; one time in a single day three men fell dead from sunstroke. All day long the rivers of hot blood poured forth, until, with the sun beating down and the air motionless, the stench was enough to knock a man over; all the old smells of a generation could be drawn out by this heat.
—Upton Sinclair
The Jungle
634

5 **Albany**
Maybe this isn't the Chateaubriand or the filet mignon of American cities, but it certainly is one hell of a corned beef sandwich.
—William Kennedy
"O Albany: Remarks to the Publication Party"
658

6 **New York**
is the place where all the aspirations of the Western world meet to form one master aspiration as powerful as the suction of a steam dredge.
—H.L. Mencken
Prejudices
744

7 **Salem**
It is no matter that the place is joyless for him, that he is weary of the old wooden houses, the mud and dust, the dead level of site and sentiment, the chill east wind , and the chillest of social atmospheres —all these, and whatever faults besides he may see or imagine, are nothing to the purpose. The spell survives, and just as powerfully as if the natal spot were an earthly paradise.
—Nathaniel Hawthorne
The Scarlet Letter
615

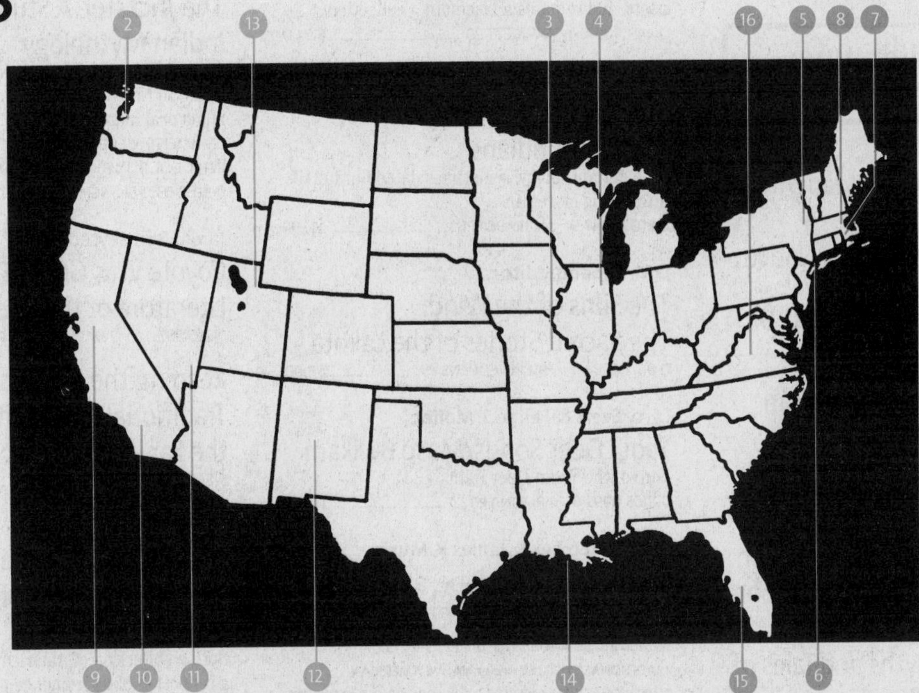

8 **Boston**
Boston runs to brains as well as to beans and brown bread. But she is cursed with an army of cranks whom nothing short of a straitjacket or a swamp elm club will ever control.
—William Cowper Brann
The Iconoclast, Beans and Blood
1543

9 **Oakland**
There's no there there.
—Gertrude Stein
The Autobiography of Alice B. Toklas
634

10 **L. A.**
Where the neon lights go when they die.
—Raymond Chandler
1062

11 **Las Vegas**
It started when I left Las Vegas that first time, skipping the hotel bill, driving off in that red convertible all alone, drunk and crazy, back to LA. That's exactly what I felt. Fear and loathing.
—Hunter S. Thompson
Songs of the Doomed
741

12 **Laguna–Acoma**
This mesa plain had an appearance of great antiquity, and an incompleteness, as if, with all the materials for world-making assembled, the Creator had desisted, gone away and left everything on the point of being brought together, on the eve of being arranged into mountain, plain, plateau. The country was still waiting to be made into a landscape.
—Willa Cather
Death Comes to the Archbishop
627

13 **Salt Lake City**
Salt Lake City was healthy—an extremely healthy city. They declared there was only one physician in the place, and he was arrested every week regularly and held to answer under the Vagrant Act for having "no visible means of support."
—Mark Twain
Roughing It
754

14 **New Orleans**
The ironwork on the balconies sags like rotting lace. Through deep sweating carriageways one catches glimpses of courtyards gone to jungle. —Walker Percy
The Moviegoer
668

15 **Eatonville, FL**
is what you might call hitting a straight lick with a crooked stick.
—Zora Neale Hurston
Dust Tracks on the Road
258

16 **Tinker Creek**
There is the mystery of the continuous creation and all that providence implies: the uncertainty of vision, the horror of the fixed, the dissolution of the present, the intricacy of beauty, the pressure of fecundity, the elusiveness of the free, the flawed nature of perfection.
—Annie Dillard
Pilgrim at Tinker Creek
578

Native American Literatures

"At the heart of the American Indian oral tradition is a deep and unconditional belief in the efficacy of language. Words are intrinsically powerful. They are magical. By means of words one can bring about physical change in the universe. By means of words one can quiet a raging weather, bring forth the harvest, ward off evil, rid the body of sickness and pain, subdue an enemy, capture the heart of a lover, live in the proper way, and venture beyond death. Indeed there is nothing more powerful…To be careless in the presence of words, on the inside of language, is to violate a fundamental morality."—N. Scott Momaday in *The Columbia Literary History of the United States*, edited by Emory Elliott

Traditional Literature: Poetry, Stories, Oratory

Paula Gunn **Allen**
Spider Woman's Granddaughters: Traditional Tales and Contemporary Writing by Native American Women
0-449-90508-X FAWCETT PB $12.50

John **Bierhorst**, editor
Four Masterworks of American Indian Literature
Includes *Quetzalcoatl*, *The Ritual of Condolence*, *Cuceb*, and *The Night Chant*
0-8165-0886-0 ARIZONA PB $19.95

In the Trail of the Wind: American Indian Poems and Ritual Orations
0-374-43576-6 FS&G PB $4.95

The Red Swan: Myths and Tales of the American Indians
"Bierhorst's brilliant selection of myths and tales—each representative, significant and interesting in itself—is designed to present a comprehensive view of the world"
—*Kirkus Reviews*
0-8263-1355-8 NEW MEXICO PB $15.95

The Sacred Path: Spells, Prayers, and Power Songs of the American Indians
0-688-02647-8 MORROW PB $10.00

William **Bright**, editor
A Coyote Reader
0-520-08062-9 CALIFORNIA PB $14.95

Ella E. **Clark**
Indian Legends from the Northern Rockies
Gathered from the traditions of 12 tribes, including the Nez Perces, the Kalispels, the Arapahoes, and the Blackfeet
0-8061-2087-8 OKLAHOMA PB $13.95

Indian Legends of the Pacific Northwest
A compendium of over 100 tales. "The vast amount of research the author has put into preparing this collection is obvious but never intrusive. The book remains…thoroughly readable"—*Indian Times*
0-520-00243-1 CALIFORNIA PB $13.95

George W. **Cronyn**, editor
American Indian Poetry: An Anthology of Songs and Chants
First published in 1918, this anthology, including versions by Frances Densmore, Mary Austin, and others, had an enormous influence on American poets, and remains a fascinating collection
0-449-90670-1 FAWCETT PB $10.00

Grove **Day**, editor
The Sky Clears: Poetry of the American Indians
An older anthology, sometimes dated but full of interesting materials
0-8032-5047-9 NEBRASKA PB $7.95

D.M. **Dooling**, editor
The Sons of the Wind: The Sacred Stories of the Lakota
0-06-250234-4 HARPERCOLLINS PB $11.00

Larry **Evers** & Felipe S. **Molina**
Yaqui Deer Songs/Maso Bwikam
Lore of the Yaqui Deer Dance
0-8165-0995-6 ARIZONA PB $16.95

Alice C. **Fletcher** & James R. **Murie**
The Hako: Song, Pipe, and Unity in a Pawnee Calumet Ceremony
See also **MUSIC AND DANCE** under **ASPECTS OF TRADITIONAL CULTURE** under **NATIVE AMERICAN CULTURES: NORTH AMERICA** in **HISTORY OF THE AMERICAS**
0-8032-6889-0 NEBRASKA PB $16.95

Virginia **Giglio**
Southern Cheyenne Women's Songs
0-8061-2605-1 OKLAHOMA $29.95

Jack F. **Kilpatrick** & Anna G. **Kilpatrick**
Friends of Thunder: Folktales of the Oklahoma Cherokees
0-8061-2722-8 OKLAHOMA PB $11.95

Karl **Kroeber**, editor
Traditional Literatures of the American Indian: Texts and Interpretations
0-8032-7753-9 NEBRASKA PB $10.00

Arnold **Krupat** & Brian **Swan**, editors
Recovering the Word: Essays on Native American Literature
0-317-44756-4 CALIFORNIA PB $14.95

Maureen E. **Mansell**
By the Power of Their Dreams: Songs, Prayers and Sacred Shields of the Plains Indians
0-8118-0460-7 CHRONICLE $16.95

Aileen **O'Bryan**
Navajo Indian Myths
0-486-27592-2 DOVER PB $5.95

Morris Edward **Opler**
Myths and Tales of Jicarilla Apache Indians
0-486-28324-0 DOVER PB $9.95

Paul **Radin**
The Trickster: A Study in American Indian Mythology
A psychological interpretation of an enduring figure in Native American mythology; contains much oral material
COMMENTARIES BY KARL KERENYI & C.G. JUNG
INTRODUCTION BY STANLEY DIAMOND
0-8052-0351-6 SCHOCKEN PB $13.00

Jarold **Ramsey**, editor
Coyote Was Going There: Indian Literature of the Oregon Country
0-295-95731-X WASHINGTON PB $17.95

Reading the Fire: Essays in the Traditional Indian Literatures of the Far West
0-8032-3864-9 NEBRASKA $25.00

Jerome **Rothenberg**, editor
Shaking the Pumpkin: Traditional Poetry of the Indian North Americas
Both a collection of American Indian poetry and a reflection of its influence on contemporary poets, as ethnological material is reworked by writers such as Armand Schwerner, Anselm Hollo, W.S. Merwin, and others. "Jerome Rothenberg is an exception to the general misuse of Native America…an example of the kind of borrowing that is possible: one that allows the dignity of giver and taker to remain not only undisturbed, but celebrated, illuminated, made clear"—Paula Gunn Allen
See also **ANTHOLOGIES** under **20TH-CENTURY AMERICAN POETRY**
0-8263-1246-2 NEW MEXICO PB $17.95

Greg **Sarris**
Keeping the Slug Woman Alive: A Holistic Approach to American Indian Texts
0-520-08006-8 CALIFORNIA $40.00
0-520-08007-6 CALIFORNIA PB $14.95

Brian **Swann**

Song of the Sky: Versions of Native American Songs and Poems, Revised Edition

0-87023-872-8 MASSACHUSETTS PB $16.95

Brian **Swann**, editor

Coming to Light: Contemporary Translations of Native American Literature of North America

An indispensable collection which brings together the best of contemporary translations of traditional poetry and stories, along with detailed and fascinating accounts of the linguistic background and the translation process. "By far the best anthology on the subject ever assembled"—Dr. Alfonso Ortiz

0-679-41816-4 RANDOM HOUSE $30.00
0-679-74358-8 VINTAGE PB $17.00

Smoothing the Ground: Essays on the Native American Oral Literature

0-520-04902-0 CALIFORNIA PB $42.50

Dennis **Tedlock**, translator

Finding the Center: Narrative Poetry of the Zuni Indians

Tedlock brilliantly captures the effect of traditional oral recitation through a range of poetic and typographic devices

0-8032-9400-X NEBRASKA PB $10.95

Frederick W. **Turner**, 3rd, editor

The Portable North American Indian Reader

0-14-015077-3 VIKING PB $14.95

W.C. **Vanderwert**, editor

Indian Oratory: A Collection of Famous Speeches by Noted Indian Chieftains

A comprehensive anthology ranging from the 18th to the 20th century

FOREWORD BY WILLIAM R. CARMACK

0-8061-1575-0 OKLAHOMA PB $14.95

Alan R. **Velie**, editor

American Indian Literature: An Anthology

Includes tales, songs, memoirs, oratory, poetry, and fiction by traditional and contemporary authors

0-8061-2345-1 OKLAHOMA PB $17.95

Gerald **Vizenor**

Earthdivers: Tribal Narratives on Mixed Descent

0-8166-1048-7 MINNESOTA $14.95

Gerald **Vizenor**, editor

Narrative Chance: Postmodern Discourse on Native American Literatures

0-8061-2561-6 OKLAHOMA PB $14.95

Bertrand N.O. **Walker**

Tales of the Bark Lodges

0-87805-794-3 MISSISSIPPI $35.00
0-87805-795-1 MISSISSIPPI PB $14.95

Paul G. **Zolbrod**

Dine Bahane: The Navajo Creation Story

"A brilliant rendering of a folk epic into a fascinating and highly literate work of art" —*NY Times*

0-8263-1043-5 NEW MEXICO PB $16.95

Mexico, Central, and South America

John **Bierhorst**, translator

Cantares Mexicanos: Songs of the Aztecs

The principal source of Aztec poetry in a complete English-Nahuatl edition

0-8047-1182-8 STANFORD $69.50

Marc **de Civrieux**

Watunna: An Orinoco Creation Cycle

One of the most complete mythic records available from a South American indigenous group, in this case the Yekuana Indians of Venezuela. Guss's translation maintains a high level of intensity

TRANSLATED AND EDITED BY DAVID GUSS

9-993-99246-1 NORTH ATLANTIC PB $10.95

There was Kahuna, the Sky Place. The Kahuhana lived there, just like now. They're good, wise people. And they were in the beginning too. They never died. There was no sickness, no evil, no war. The whole world was Sky. No one worked. No one looked for food. Food was always there, ready.

There were no animals, no demons, no clouds, no winds. There was just light. In the highest sky was Wanadi, just like now. He gave his light to the people, to the Kahuhana. He lit everything down to the very bottom, down to None, the Earth. Because of that light, the people were always happy. They had life. They couldn't die. There was no separation between Sky and Earth. Sky had no door like it does now. There was no night, like now. Wanadi is like a sun that never sets. It was always day. The Earth was like a part of the sky.

WATUNNA: AN ORINOCO CREATION CYCLE

Miguel **Leon-Portilla**

15 Poets of the Aztec World

0-8061-2441-5 OKLAHOMA $26.95

Pre-Columbian Literatures of Mexico

Early colonial Aztec and Maya song texts, myths, orations, and chronicles, examined for literary values

0-8061-1974-8 OKLAHOMA PB $14.95

Christopher **Sawyer-Laucanno**

The Destruction of the Jaguar: Poems from the Books of the Chilam Balam

Poetic adaptations from the ancient Mayan sacred text

0-87286-210-0 CITY LIGHTS PB $5.95

Dennis **Tedlock**, translator

Popol Vuh

The newest translation of the Quiche Maya classic combines anthropological and literary values

See also THE MAYA under NATIVE AMERICAN CULTURES: CENTRAL AND SOUTH AMERICA in HISTORY OF THE AMERICAS

0-8061-0205-5 OKLAHOMA $26.95
0-684-81845-0 TOUCHSTONE PB $15.00

Autobiographical Accounts

Luther Standing **Bear**

Land of the Spotted Eagle

Growing up among the Teton Sioux

0-8032-5890-9 NEBRASKA PB $10.95

My People the Sioux

"The account he gives us of his people… is one of the most engaging and voracious we have ever had"—Van Wyck Brooks

0-8032-5793-7 NEBRASKA PB $9.95

Elias **Boudinot**

Cherokee Editor: The Writings of Elias Boudinot

EDITED BY THEDA PERDUE

0-8203-1809-4 GEORGIA PB $15.95

Mary **Crow Dog** & Richard **Erdoes**

Lakota Woman

0-06-097389-7 HARPERPERENNIAL PB $13.00

Florence Edenshaw **Davidson**

During My Time

1-55054-024-6 WASHINGTON PB $14.95

Charles A. **Eastman**

From the Deep Woods to Civilization: Chapters in the Autobiography of an Indian

One of the best-known Native Americans of his time, Eastman witnessed the Wounded Knee massacre and devoted his life to helping Indians come to terms with the white world

0-8032-5873-9 NEBRASKA PB $9.95

The Soul of the Indian: An Interpretation

In this 1911 book Eastman set out "to paint the religious life of the typical American Indian as it was before he knew the white man"

0-8032-6701-0 NEBRASKA PB $6.95

Charles **Hamilton**, editor

Cry of the Thunderbird: The American Indian's Own Story

The voices gathered here include those of Black Elk, Tecumseh, Sitting Bull, and Geronimo. With paintings by George Catlin and sketches by American Indian artists

0-8061-1292-1 OKLAHOMA PB $17.95

Arnold **Krupat**

For Those Who Come After: A Study of Native American Autobiography

0-520-05307-9 CALIFORNIA PB $32.50

Arnold **Krupat**, editor

Native American Autobiography: An Anthology

0-299-14020-2 WISCONSIN $45.00
0-299-14024-5 WISCONSIN PB $19.95

Nancy O. **Lurie**, editor

Mountain Wolf Woman, Sister of Crashing Thunder: The Autobiography of a Winnebago Indian

FOREWORD BY RUTH UNDERHILL
0-472-06109-7 MICHIGAN PB $14.95

T.C. **McLuhan**

Touch the Earth: A Self Portrait of Indian Existence

0-671-22275-9 SIMON & SCHUSTER PB $14.00

Russell **Means** & Marvin J. **Wolf**

Where White Men Fear to Tread: The Autobiography of Russell Means

0-312-13621-8 ST. MARTIN'S $26.95

Rosalio **Moises**

A Yaqui Life: The Personal Chronicle of a Yaqui Indian

"The nightmare world of witchcraft and dream-dependence is one of the major fascinations of this strange and moving book"
—*Southern California Quarterly*
0-8032-8175-7 NEBRASKA PB $14.95

John G. **Neihardt**

Black Elk Speaks: Being the Life Story of a Holy Man of the Oglala Sioux

See also RELIGION AND MYTHOLOGY under ASPECTS OF TRADITIONAL CULTURE under NATIVE AMERICAN CULTURES: NORTH AMERICA in HISTORY OF THE AMERICAS
INTRODUCTION BY VINE DELORIA, JR.
0-8032-3301-9 NEBRASKA $25.00
0-8032-8359-8 NEBRASKA PB $9.95

Polingaysi (Elizabeth Q. White) **Qoyawayma**

No Turning Back: A Hopi Indian Woman's Struggle to Live in Two Worlds

A Hopi woman and her career as an educator
AS TOLD TO VADA F. CARLSON
0-8263-0439-7 NEW MEXICO PB $11.95

Paul **Radin**, editor

Crashing Thunder: The Autobiography of an American Indian

After many years of living among the Winnebago, Radin was able to elicit this autobiographical narrative
0-8032-8910-3 NEBRASKA PB $8.95

Joe **Starita**

The Dull Knifes of Pine Ridge: A Lakota Odyssey

0-399-14010-7 PUTNAM $24.95

Brian **Swann** & Arnold **Krupat**, editors

I Tell You Now: Autobiographical Essays by Native American Writers

0-8032-7757-1 BROMPTON PB $12.00

Contemporary Native American Writers

Sherman **Alexie**

Sherman Alexie was born in Spokane, Washington, in 1966. He is a Spokane/Coeur d'Alene Indian from the Spokane Indian Reservation, and is the recipient of grants from the Lila Wallace-Readers Digest Fund and the National Endowment for the Arts. He currently lives in Seattle.

The Business of Fancydancing: Stories and Poems

See also POETRY SINCE 1945 under 20TH-CENTURY AMERICAN POETRY
0-914610-00-7 HANGING LOOSE PB $10.00

Indian Killer

0-87113-652-X ATLANTIC MONTHLY $22.00

The Lone Ranger and Tonto Fistfight in Heaven

22 interlocking tales of life set on a Spokane reservation
See also NEW WRITERS OF THE '90S under 20TH-CENTURY AMERICAN FICTION
0-06-097624-1 HARPERPERENNIAL PB $12.50

Reservation Blues

A mythic tale of an all-Indian rock band traveling from reservation bars to Seattle and on to Manhattan. "Does for the American Indian what Richard Wright's *Native Son* did for the Black American in 1940"—*Chicago Tribune*
0-87113-594-9 ATLANTIC MONTHLY $21.00
0-446-67235-1 WARNER PB $12.99

The Summer of Black Widows

1-88241-335-0 HANGING LOOSE $20.00
1-88241-334-2 HANGING LOOSE PB $12.00

Paula Gunn **Allen**, editor

Song of the Turtle: American Indian Literature 1974-1994

0-345-37525-4 BALLANTINE $24.50

Louise **Erdrich**

Love Medicine

"A remarkable first novel...conveying unflinchingly the funkiness and great unspoken sadness of the Indian reservations"
—Peter Matthiessen
See also SINCE 1945 under 20TH-CENTURY AMERICAN FICTION
0-8050-1716-X HOLT $19.95

Patricia **Galvao**

Industrial Park

0-8032-2147-9 NEBRASKA $25.00
0-8032-7041-0 NEBRASKA PB $10.95

Diane **Glancy**

Claiming Breath

0-8032-2140-1 NEBRASKA $25.00

Firesticks: A Collection of Stories

0-8061-2490-3 OKLAHOMA $19.95

Monkey Secret

0-8101-5016-6 NORTHWESTERN $19.95

The Only Piece of Furniture in the House: A Novel

1-55921-183-0 MOYER BELL $18.95

Janet Campbell **Hale**

Bloodlines: Odyssey of a Native Daughter

0-06-097612-8 HARPERPERENNIAL PB $11.00

Joy **Harjo**

Joy Harjo is a member of the Muscogee Tribe. "I turn and return to Harjo's poetry for her breathtaking, complex witness and for her world-remaking language: precise, unsentimental, miraculous."—Adrienne Rich

She Had Some Horses

A poem cycle by a leading Native American poet. "Harjo's second major book of poetry rides an intense passion for survival through dangerous roads in America, in her own heart, in an Indian dream vision that can wrench and heal"—*Ms.*
0-938410-06-7 THUNDER'S MOUTH PB $8.95

The Woman Who Fell from the Sky

"I fell in love with these poems, with their clarity and light, their wisdom born somewhere between sky and earth"—Sandra Cisneros
See also POETRY SINCE 1945 under 20TH-CENTURY AMERICAN POETRY
0-393-03715-0 NORTON $21.00
0-393-31362-X NORTON PB $10.00

Jamake **Highwater**

Anpao: An American Indian Odyssey

0-06-022878-4 HARPERCREST LIBRARY EDITION $14.89

Beverly **Hungry Wolf**

The Ways of My Grandmother

0-688-00471-7 MORROW PB $10.00

Arnold **Krupat**, editor

New Voices in Native American Literary Criticism

1-56098-201-2 SMITHSONIAN $79.00
1-56098-226-8 SMITHSONIAN PB $34.95

N. Scott **Momaday**

House Made of Dawn

The conflicts of contemporary Native American culture
0-06-091633-8 HARPERCOLLINS PB $12.50

In the Presence of the Sun: Stories and Poems, 1961-1991

A superb collection of Momaday's poems, stories, and drawings, celebrating the beauty and mystery of the Native American past. "Scott Momaday is one of the most versatile and distinguished artists in America today"
—Peter Matthiessen
0-312-08222-3 ST. MARTIN'S $17.95

The Names: A Memoir
0-8165-1046-6 ARIZONA PB $11.95

Duane **Niatum**, editor

Harpers' Anthology of Twentieth Century Native American Poetry
A comprehensive survey of the Native American poetic renaissance, including work by Joy Harjo, Wendy Rose, James Welch, and many others
0-06-250666-8 HARPERCOLLINS PB $19.00

Alexander **Posey**

The Fus Fixico Letters
Posey, a Creek poet and journalist who died in 1908, wrote these satirical dialect pieces for *The Indian Journal*, the newspaper he edited in Oklahoma
0-8032-3704-9 NEBRASKA $40.00

Leslie Marmon **Silko**

Almanac of the Dead
"A brilliant, haunting, and tragic novel of ruin and resistance in the Americas…Leslie Silko dramatizes the often desperate struggle of native peoples in the Americas to keep, at all costs, the core of their culture"
—Larry McMurtry
0-14-017319-6 PENGUIN PB $14.95

Ceremony
0-14-008683-8 PENGUIN PB $10.95

Storyteller
Poetry and fiction intermingled, from an important Native American writer
1-55970-005-X ARCADE PB $16.95

Yellow Woman and a Beauty of the Spirit: Essays on Native American Life Today
From the Pueblo Indian language and literature to the injustice of the Anglo-American legal system, Silko offers a wonderful range of reasoned, impassioned, and devastating essays. A controversial collection on Native American life in contemporary America
0-684-81153-7 SIMON & SCHUSTER $23.00
0-684-82707-7 TOUCHSTONE PB $11.00

Alan R. **Velie**, editor

The Lightning Within: An Anthology of Contemporary American Indian Fiction
0-8032-4659-5 NEBRASKA $25.00
0-8032-9614-2 NEBRASKA PB $9.95

Gerald **Vizenor**

Manifest Manners: Postindian Warriors of Survivance
0-8195-5269-0 WESLEYAN $30.00
0-8195-6273-4 WESLEYAN PB $14.95

Velma **Wallis**

Two Old Women: An Alaska Legend of Betrayal, Courage, and Survival
This award-winning retelling of an ancient Indian legend marks the publishing debut of a new Native American writer. The tale chronicles the hardships and triumphs of two elderly women abandoned in the wilderness by their migrating tribe. "Full of adventure, suspense, and obstacles overcome—an octogenarian version of *Thelma and Louise* triumphant"
—*Kirkus Reviews*
0-945397-18-6 EPICENTER $16.95

Canadian Literature

Writing in English

Margaret **Atwood**

Alias Grace
0-385-47571-3 BDD $24.95

Bluebeard's Egg & Other Stories
"These tales expand in the mind until they become novels. The characters…take on lives of their own; they take over yours"
—Susan Schaeffer
0-449-21417-6 FAWCETT PB $5.95

Bodily Harm
0-553-37789-2 BANTAM PB $10.95

Cat's Eye
A successful artist relives painful episodes from her Toronto childhood
0-553-37790-6 BANTAM PB $10.95

Dancing Girls & Other Stories
0-553-37791-4 BANTAM PB $10.95

The Edible Woman
0-553-37792-2 BANTAM PB $10.95

Margaret Atwood

Good Bones and Small Murders
In over 20 books to date, Atwood has consistently delighted readers and impressed critics with her astonishing range: fiction, accomplished short fiction, poetry, and lyrical criticism. This collection of stories, parodies, and sketches is "[a] sparkling collection…She never fails to entertain"—*Sunday Times* [London]. "Atwood at her very best: concise, hilarious, agonizingly truthful, as in her finest poems"—*Canadian Press*
0-385-47110-6 DOUBLEDAY $20.00

The Handmaid's Tale
Atwood's most widely read book to date depicts a future society founded on the oppression of women
0-449-21260-2 FAWCETT PB $5.99

Lady Oracle
A writer fakes her own death to escape the success of a bestseller
0-553-37781-7 BANTAM PB $10.95

Life Before Man
Both parties to a slowly decaying marriage take lovers
0-553-37782-5 BANTAM PB $10.95

Morning in the Burned House
Atwood's first new poems in a decade are beautifully crafted, dark, playful, moving, tender, and intimate. "Margaret Atwood brings all the violence of mythology into the present world. She is the quiet Mata Hari, the mysterious, violent figure…who pits herself against the ordered, too-clean world like an arsonist"
—Michael Ondaatje
0-395-75591-3 HOUGHTON MIFFLIN $19.95
0-395-82521-0 HOUGHTON MIFFLIN PB $12.95

Murder in the Dark
0-88910-258-9 COACH HOUSE PB $10.95

The Robber Bride
From the bestselling literary author of *Cat's Eye* and *The Handmaid's Tale*, a subtle and spellbinding exploration of woman as villain. "Margaret Atwood deserves an adjective—Atwoodian—in recognition of her virtuoso wit and unmistakable style"—*Chicago Tribune*
0-385-26008-3 DOUBLEDAY $23.50
0-553-56905-8 BDD PB $6.50

Selected Poems, 1965-1975
0-395-40422-3 HOUGHTON MIFFLIN PB $12.95

Selected Poems II: Poems Selected and New, 1976-1986
0-395-45406-9 HOUGHTON MIFFLIN PB $12.95

Strange Things: The Malevolent North in Canadian Literature
0-19-811976-3 OXFORD $22.00

Surfacing
A woman's weekend excursion in quest of her father is enlivened by the complexities of a foursome
0-553-37780-9 BANTAM PB $10.95

Wilderness Tips
0-553-37793-0 BANTAM PB $10.95

Robin **Blaser**

The Holy Forest
Blaser, a longtime resident of Vancouver, was a close associate of Jack Spicer and Robert Duncan in San Francisco's poetry scene of the '50s. *The Holy Forest* is the definitive gathering of his poetry, luminous, brilliant, and sometimes unexpectedly comic. "Robin Blaser has become a touchstone for all his company, a bond in mind and heart"—Robert Creeley
0-88910-435-2 COACH HOUSE PB $19.95

Robin **Blaser**
Syntax
0-88922-209-6 TALONBOOKS PB ... $5.95

Robert **Bringhurst**
The Beauty of the Weapons: Selected Poems 1972-82
"Marked by sharpness, vigor and a timeless quality…a welcome introduction for U.S. readers to this Canadian poet" —*Publishers Weekly*
0-914742-90-6 COPPER CANYON PB ... $10.00

Pieces of Map, Pieces of Music
1-55659-003-2 COPPER CANYON PB ... $9.00

Leonard **Cohen**
Stranger Music: Selected Poems and Songs
0-679-75541-1 VINTAGE PB ... $14.00

Robertson **Davies**
High Spirits
Eighteen ghost stories, committed to paper exactly as originally told out loud
0-14-006505-9 PENGUIN PB ... $11.95

Leaven of Malice
0-14-016789-7 PUFFIN PB ... $11.95

The Lyre of Orpheus
0-14-011433-5 VIKING PB ... $12.95

The Mirror of Nature
0-8020-7939-3 TORONTO PB ... $12.95

Robertson **Davies**
The Deptford Trilogy
The same tale is told from three separate vantage points. This compendium volume is made up of the three titles listed below
0-14-014755-1 VIKING PB ... $19.95

Fifth Business
A rational man discovers that wonders are simply an aspect of reality
0-14-016794-3 VIKING PB ... $11.95

The Manticore
The manticore has the head of a man, the body of a lion, and the tail of a scorpion
0-14-016793-5 VIKING PB ... $11.95
0-14-009711-2 VIKING PB ... $10.95

World of Wonders
The tale of a master magician. "Among contemporary novelists only Graham Greene has trod this ground and gleaned it so successfully"—*New Republic*
0-14-016796-X VIKING PB ... $11.95

Murther & Walking Spirits
0-14-016884-2 PENGUIN PB ... $10.95

The Rebel Angels
0-14-006271-8 VIKING PB ... $11.95

The Salterton Trilogy
Includes *Tempest Tost, Leaven of Malice,* and *A Mixture Frailties*
0-14-015910-X VIKING PB ... $17.95

Robertson Davies (credit: ©Jerry Bauer)

What's Bred in the Bone
Portrait of an art expert with a stash of secrets. "Literary sleuthwork at its most inspired" —*Newsweek*

Christopher **Dewdney**
The Immaculate Perception
Dewdney is sometimes associated with the American "Language" poets
0-88784-151-1 HOUSE OF ANANSI PB ... $9.95

Marian **Engel**
Bear
0-7710-9958-4 GODINE PB ... $5.95

Brian **Fawcett**
Cambodia: A Book for People Who Find Television Too Slow
0-02-032150-3 MACMILLAN PB ... $8.95

Capital Tales
0-88922-221-5 TALONBOOKS PB ... $11.95

Secret Journal of Alexander MacKenzie
0-88922-227-4 TALONBOOKS PB ... $11.95

Mavis **Gallant**
The Collected Stories of Mavis Gallant
A new collection
0-679-44886-1 RANDOM HOUSE ... $40.00

Daryl **Hine**
Arrondissements
0-88984-130-6 PORCUPINE'S QUILL ... $16.95

Ovid's Heroines: A Verse Translation of the Heroides
0-300-05094-1 YALE PB ... $12.00

Postscripts: Poems
0-679-74274-3 KNOPF PB ... $12.00

Resident Alien
0-689-10651-3 ATHENEUM ... $6.95

Joy **Kogawa**
Obasan
0-385-46886-5 ANCHOR PB ... $9.95

Margaret **Laurence**
The Diviners
0-226-46935-2 CHICAGO PB ... $12.95

The Stone Angel
A disturbing study of senility set against the breadth of the Canadian prairie
0-226-46936-0 CHICAGO PB ... $12.95

Irving **Layton**
The Romanian-born Layton is one of Canada's most prolific and intellectually adventurous poets.

The Gucci Bag
0-88962-245-0 MOSAIC PB ... $8.95

Love Poems of Irving Layton
0-88962-246-9 MOSAIC PB ... $8.95

The Selected Poems of Irving Layton
INTRODUCTION BY HUGH KENNER
0-8112-0641-6 NEW DIRECTIONS ... $8.50
0-8112-0642-4 NEW DIRECTIONS PB ... $2.25

Sky **Lee**
Disappearing Moon Cafe
1-87806-712-5 SEAL PB ... $12.95

Steve **MacAffery**
North of Intention
Contemporary literary essays by a leading Canadian experimental poet
0-937804-23-1 ROOF PB ... $12.95

W.O. **Mitchell**
Since Daisy Creek
A later work by a writer greatly influenced by the world of the prairie
0-7715-7325-1 STODDART ... $6.99

Susanna **Moodie**
Roughing It in the Bush
An autobiographical work, published in 1852, which describes the life of early pioneers in the Canadian hinterland
INTRODUCTION BY MARGARET ATWOOD
0-8398-1266-3 IRVINGTON ... $56.50
0-7710-9975-4 MCCLELLAND & STEWART PB ... $8.95

Brian **Moore**
Black Robe
Jesuit priest Father LaForgue journeys through frozen Canadian wilderness in 1634 with the help of Algonquin Indians who become increasingly mistrustful of the man they call "Black Robe"
See also **THE MIDDLE GENERATION** under **20TH-CENTURY BRITISH AND IRISH FICTION** in **LITERATURE OF THE BRITISH ISLES**
0-449-20947-4 FAWCETT PB ... $5.99
0-586-08615-3 HARPERCOLLINS PB ... $10.00

The Colour of Blood
See also **THE MIDDLE GENERATION** under **20TH-CENTURY BRITISH AND IRISH FICTION** in **LITERATURE OF THE BRITISH ISLES**
0-586-08737-0 HARPERCOLLINS PB ... $10.00

The Statement

See also THE MIDDLE GENERATION under 20TH-CENTURY BRITISH AND IRISH FICTION in LITERATURE OF THE BRITISH ISLES

0-525-94128-2 DUTTON $22.95

Alice **Munro**

A gifted short story writer and novelist who tends to focus her realistic, minutely rendered tales on the lives of women in small rural towns.

The Beggar Maid

With her 10 stories of "Flo and Rose" she "manages to reproduce the vibrant practice of life while scrutinizing the workings of her own narrative art"—*NY Times*

0-679-73271-3 VINTAGE PB $11.00

Alice Munro

Dance of the Happy Shades & Other Stories

0-14-012408-X VIKING PB $10.95

Friend of My Youth

0-394-58442-2 KNOPF $18.95
0-679-72957-7 VINTAGE PB $11.00

Lives of Girls and Women

0-452-26184-8 PLUME PB $10.95

The Moons of Jupiter

Eleven stories on love, aging, and relationships

0-679-73270-5 VINTAGE PB $11.00

Open Secrets: Stories

A wonderfully evocative and accomplished collection of stories. "With a few strokes of her pen, Munro has the unerring ability to familiarize us with a foreign country or the entire life of another person. Even if you've already read these latest stories in the *New Yorker,* you'll want to luxuriate in their gorgeous prose again and again"—*Kirkus Reviews*

0-679-43575-1 KNOPF $23.00
0-679-75562-4 VINTAGE PB $13.00

The Progress of Love

0-14-010553-0 PENGUIN PB $11.95

Selected Stories

See also SHORT STORY COLLECTIONS under 20TH-CENTURY AMERICAN FICTION

0-679-44627-3 KNOPF $30.00

B.P. **Nichol**

Translating Apollinaire

0-87924-031-8 MEMBRANE PB $6.00

Truth: A Book of Fictions

0-920544-98-3 MERCURY PB $14.95

Michael **Ondaatje**

The Collected Works of Billy the Kid

A composite of eyewitness accounts, tall tales, facts, and photographic documents vividly construct the world of Billy the Kid

0-14-007280-2 PENGUIN PB $10.95
0-679-76786-X VINTAGE PB $10.00

Coming Through Slaughter

0-679-76785-1 VINTAGE PB $10.00

The English Patient

World War II has drawn to a close, and four people are suddenly brought face to face with history, with the consequences of the war, and with the sudden and terrible dawn of the nuclear age. A strange and original work of fiction

0-679-41678-1 KNOPF $24.00
0-679-74520-3 VINTAGE PB $12.00

In the Skin of a Lion

A country lad plunges into the world of immigrant workers in Toronto

0-14-011309-6 PENGUIN PB $10.95

Running in the Family

A fictional memoir of Ondaatje's family's "carefree but doomed" life in Sri Lanka

0-679-74669-2 VINTAGE PB $10.00

Michael Ondaatje

Mordecai **Richler**

A popular Montreal Jewish writer notable for his ability to elicit sympathy for unsympathetic characters.

The Incomparable Atuk

0-7710-9973-8 MCCLELLAND & STEWART PB $5.95

Sinclair **Ross**

As for Me and My House

This classic prairie novel about an artist turned priest gives a stark picture of rural desolation

INTRODUCTION BY DAVID STOUCK

1-55022-088-8 E.C.W. $18.95

Peter Dale **Scott**

Coming to Jakarta: A Poem About Terror

A long poem based on the 1965 massacre in Indonesia

0-8112-1095-2 NEW DIRECTIONS PB $8.95

Crossing Borders: Selected Shorter Poems

0-8112-1284-X NEW DIRECTIONS PB $11.95

Listening to the Candle: A Poem on Impulse

0-8112-1214-9 NEW DIRECTIONS PB $13.95

Elizabeth **Spencer**

Marilee

0-87805-141-4 MISSISSIPPI PB $5.95

Sharon **Thesen**

Aurora

"A wonderful book of light and dark daily things flowing outward into everything dark and light. In mind and heart and laughter, it's a big book, full of surprises"—Robin Blaser

0-88910-471-9 COACH HOUSE PB $12.95

Quebecois (French-Canadian) Literature

Quebec's literary production since the 1960s, rooted in the North American continent, also has powerful ties to France, resulting in unique tensions and a unique literary situation. This distinctive minority literature is notable for its political humor and satire and its lively linguistic play on the mixture of French, English, and Joual (the Quebec language).

Hubert **Aquin**

The Antiphonary

TRANSLATED BY ALAN BROWN

0-88784-426-X HOUSE OF ANANSI $9.95

Yves **Beauchemin**

The Alley Cat

TRANSLATED BY SHEILA FISCHMAN

0-7710-3451-2 MCCLELLAND & STEWART PB $8.95

Marie-Claire **Blais**

Deaf to the City

0-87951-296-2 OVERLOOK PB $10.95

A Season in the Life of Emmanuel

A grim saga of nastiness graduating to cruelty among the 16 offspring of a French-Canadian farming family, both at home and out in the world

TRANSLATED BY DEREK COLTMAN

INTRODUCTION BY EDMUND WILSON

0-7710-9880-4 MCCLELLAND & STEWART PB $6.95

Nicole **Brossard**

French Kiss: Or, A Pang's Progress

TRANSLATED BY PATRICIA CLAXTON
0-88910-158-2 COACH HOUSE PB $8.50

Mauve Desert

A woman travels through the Arizona desert, a journey at once literary and erotic. "Deserves a place of honor in any serious collection of modern fiction"—*Multicultural Review*
0-88910-389-5 COACH HOUSE PB $14.95

Picture Theory

0-920717-22-5 GUERNICA EDITIONS PB $15.00

Surfaces of Sense

Explores the relations between feminism, lesbian identity, and patriarchal culture
0-88910-372-0 COACH HOUSE PB $10.95

Under Tongue

TRANSLATED BY SUSANNE DE LOTHBINIERE-HARWOOD
0-921881-00-2 GYNERGY BOOKS PB $15.00

Louis **Caron**

The Draft Dodger

TRANSLATED BY DAVID TOBY
0-88784-085-X STODDART PB $9.95

Roche **Carrier**

Floralie, Where Are You?

TRANSLATED BY SHEILA FISCHMAN
0-88784-317-4 HOUSE OF ANANSI PB $6.95

The Garden of Delights

TRANSLATED BY SHEILA FISCHMAN
0-88784-066-3 HOUSE OF ANANSI PB $12.95

The Hockey Sweater & Other Stories

TRANSLATED BY SHEILA FISCHMAN
0-88784-078-7 TORONTO PB $11.95

Is This the Sun, Philibert?

TRANSLATED BY SHEILA FISCHMAN
0-88784-321-2 HOUSE OF ANANSI PB $6.95

La Guerre, Yes Sir!

TRANSLATED BY SHEILA FISCHMAN
0-88784-310-7 READER'S CATALOG PB $8.95

Lady with Chains

TRANSLATED BY SHEILA FISCHMAN
0-88784-139-2 HOUSE OF ANANSI PB $9.95

They Won't Demolish Me!

TRANSLATED BY SHEILA FISCHMAN
0-88784-328-X TORONTO PB $7.95

Jacques **Ferron**

Selected Tales

TRANSLATED BY BETTY BEDNARSKI
0-88784-140-6 HOUSE OF ANANSI PB $9.95

Madeleine **Gagnon**

Song for a Far Quebec

TRANSLATED BY HOWARD SCOTT
0-88910-465-4 COACH HOUSE PB $10.95

Jacques **Godbout**

An American Story

TRANSLATED BY YVES SAINT-PIERRE
0-8166-1709-0 MINNESOTA $19.95
0-8166-1710-4 MINNESOTA PB $8.95

The Golden Galarneaus

TRANSLATED BY PATRICIA CLAXTON
0-88910-487-5 COACH HOUSE PB $11.95

Anne **Hebert**

Day Has No Equal but Night

TRANSLATED BY A. POULIN, JR.
1-88023-805-5 BOA PB $12.50

Jacques **Poulin**

Spring Tides

TRANSLATED BY SHEILA FISCHMAN
0-88784-149-X HOUSE OF ANANSI PB $9.95

Volkswagen Blues

TRANSLATED BY STEILA FISCHMAN
0-7710-7160-4 MCCLELLAND & STEWART PB $14.95

Elise **Turcotte**

The Sound of Living Things

A novel about the daily lives of a 30-year-old librarian and her four-year-old daughter, centered around the role of language
0-88910-437-9 COACH HOUSE PB $11.95

Anthologies

Margaret **Atwood** & Robert **Weaver**, editors

The New Oxford Book of Canadian Short Stories in English

0-19-541025-4 OXFORD $30.00

The Oxford Book of Canadian Short Stories in English

0-19-540565-X OXFORD $27.95
0-19-540597-8 OXFORD $12.95

David **Lampe**, editor

Myths and Voices: Contemporary Canadian Fiction

1-87772-728-8 WHITE PINE PB $17.00

Richard **Teleky** & Marie-Claire **Blais**, editors

The Oxford Book of French-Canadian Short Stories

0-19-540298-7 OXFORD PB $16.95

Critical Studies

Madison J. **Davis**, editor

Conversations with Robertson Davies

0-87805-383-2 MISSISSIPPI $39.50
0-87805-384-0 MISSISSIPPI PB $15.95

Smaro **Kamboureli**, editor

Making a Difference: Canadian Multicultural Literature

0-19-541078-5 OXFORD PB $29.75

Carl F. **Klinck**, editor

Literary History of Canada: Canadian Literature in English Volume 4: From 1960 to 1974

0-8020-5685-7 TORONTO $60.00
0-8020-6610-0 TORONTO PB $24.95

B.W. **Powe**

A Climate Charged: Essays on Canadian Writers

0-88962-258-2 MOSAIC PB $9.95

David **Staines**

Beyond the Provinces: Literary Canada at Century's End

0-8020-0652-3 TORONTO $45.00
0-8020-7606-8 TORONTO PB $15.95

George **Woodcock**

The World of Canadian Writing: Critiques and Recollections

Insights into Canadian literary circles by a longtime member
0-295-95721-2 OLYMPIC $3.98

American Literature to 1900

The Early Colonial Period

William **Bradford**

Of Plymouth Plantation: 1620-1647

In his history of the Pilgrim settlement, Plymouth's governor aspired to "a plain style, with singular regard unto the simple truth in all things"
EDITED BY SAMUEL ELIOT MORISON
0-394-43895-7 RANDOM HOUSE $25.00

Anne **Bradstreet**

The Works of Anne Bradstreet

The first important American poet published her major collection, *The Tenth Muse Lately spring Up in America*, in 1650
EDITED BY JEANNIE HENSLEY
FOREWORD BY ADRIENNE RICH
0-674-95999-X BELKNAP PB $17.00

William **Penn**

The Peace of Europe, the Fruits of Solitude & Other Writings

The major works of the Quaker founder of Pennsylvania
EDITED BY EDWIN B. BRONNER
0-460-87302-4 EVERYMAN'S PB $6.95

John **Smith**

Captain John Smith: A Select Edition of His Writings

A rich collection of writings, arranged thematically, focusing on the founding of Jamestown and on Smith's relations with the Indians
See also **THE NEW COLONIES** under **US HISTORY TO THE CIVIL WAR** in **HISTORY OF THE AMERICAS**
EDITED BY KAREN ORDAHL KUPPERMAN
0-8078-1778-3 NORTH CAROLINA $45.00
0-8078-4208-7 NORTH CAROLINA PB $16.95

Edward **Taylor**

Poems of Edward Taylor

Taylor's medievil writings are very much in the tradition of metaphysical poets such as Herbert and Vaughan

0-8078-4248-6 NORTH CAROLINA PB........$19.95

Anthologies

Giles **Gunn**, editor

Colonial American Writing

0-14-039087-1 PENGUIN PB........$12.95

Alan **Heimert** & Andrew **Delbanco**, editors

The Puritans in America: A Narrative Anthology

0-674-74066-1 HARVARD PB........$16.95

Harrison T. **Meserole**, editor

American Poetry of the Seventeenth Century

The works of Bradstreet, Taylor, Wigglesworth, and others, presented in a well-designed scholarly edition

0-271-00418-5 PENN STATE PB........$18.95

Perry **Miller**, editor

The American Puritans: Their Prose and Poetry

Miller did more than anyone in this century to create new interest in America's Puritan inheritance

0-231-05419-X COLUMBIA PB........$19.00

The 18th Century

William **Bartram**

Travels and Other Writings

The most complete edition ever assembled of the writings of the great naturalist and, among other things, pioneer ethnographer. Includes a remarkable sampling of Bartram's drawings

EDITED BY THOMAS P. SLAUGHTER

1-88301-111-6 LIBRARY OF AMERICA........$37.50

William Bartram on the Southeastern Indians

"Among the most valuable primary historical sources on the Muscogulges—commonly known as the Creeks and Seminoles—and the Cherokees...Bartram's passionate regard for the natural world, his relative impartiality, and his keen scientist's eye make his writings unique and valuable resources"—from the Introduction

EDITED BY GREGORY A. WASELKOV AND KATHRYN E. HOLLAND-BRAUND

0-8032-4772-9 NEBRASKA........$50.00

Jonathan **Edwards**

Freedom of the Will

The major expression of Edwards's Calvinist doctrine, first published in 1754

EDITED BY ARNOLD S. KAUFMAN & WILLIAM K. FRANKENA

0-300-00848-1 YALE........$70.00

Charles Brockden **Brown**

As an American novelist, Brown could not be more prototypical, with his blending of Gothic plots and indigenous landscapes, scientific rationalism and superstitious dread.

Arthur Mervyn, Or Memoirs of the Year 1793

A novel revolving around Philadelphia's yellow fever epidemic of 1793

0-87338-241-2 KENT STATE........$35.00

Edgar Huntly: Memoirs of a Sleep Walker

A typically circuitous narrative of trance and violence, set against a wilderness background

EDITED BY NORMAN GRABO

0-14-039062-6 PENGUIN PB........$11.95

Ormond, Or the Secret Witness

Sexual conflict incites murder and attempted rape

0-87338-277-3 KENT STATE........$35.00

Wieland

Hypnotism and religious obsession propel a tale of murder and suicide in Pennsylvania

0-15-696680-8 HARCOURT BRACE PB........$10.95

Wieland & Memoirs of Carwin

EDITED BY SYDNEY J. KRAUS

0-87338-160-2 KENT STATE........$35.00
0-87338-220-X KENT STATE PB........$14.00

J. Hector St. John **de Crevecoeur**

Letters from an American Farmer & Sketches of Eighteenth-Century America

"Franklin is the real *practical* prototype of the American. Crevecoeur is the emotional. To the European, the American is first and foremost a dollar-fiend. We tend to forget the emotional heritage of Hector St. John de Crevecoeur" —D.H. Lawrence

EDITED BY ALBERT E. STONE

0-14-039006-5 VIKING PB........$12.95

A Jonathan Edwards Reader

The best available introduction to Edwards's work

EDITED BY JOHN E. SMITH AND HARRY S. STOUT

0-300-06204-4 YALE PB........$15.00

Selected Writings of Jonathan Edwards

EDITED BY HAROLD P. SIMONSON

0-88133-718-8 WAVELAND PB........$9.50

Benjamin **Franklin**

The Autobiography of Benjamin Franklin

EDITED BY KENNETH SILVERMAN

0-14-039052-9 PENGUIN PB........$6.95

Writings

The most complete one-volume collection ever published of this brilliant public figure, which includes *The Autobiography* and a new edition based on Franklin's manuscript. Also contains *Silence Dogood, Poor Richard's Almanac, Political Satires, Pamphlets, Letters and Bagatelles,* and *Journalism*

See also **LIBRARY OF AMERICA**

0-940450-29-1 LIBRARY OF AMERICA........$40.00

Thomas **Jefferson**

The Life and Selected Writings of Thomas Jefferson

0-679-60062-0 MODERN LIBRARY........$19.00

Notes on the State of Virginia

A new edition of Jefferson's 1781 survey, originally written as a response to the questions of a French diplomat

See also **SOUTHERN COLONIES** under **THE NEW COLONIES** under **US HISTORY TO THE CIVIL WAR** in **HISTORY OF THE AMERICAS**

EDITED BY WILLIAM PEDEN

0-8446-2321-0 SMITH........$11.30
0-8078-4588-4 NORTH CAROLINA PB........$14.95

Writings

A comprehensive gathering of Jefferson's remarkably varied writings, including *Autobiography, A Summary View of the Rights of British America, Public Papers, Miscellany*, and a large selection of letters. The letters in particular create a three-dimensional and often surprising portrait. Jefferson envisioned a nation of prosperous farmers whom he thought were far more likely than city-dwellers to cultivate the virtues of self-reliance, hard work, moderation, and common sense on which a free society depends

See also **CLASSICS** under **POLITICAL THOUGHT** in **SOCIAL STUDIES**

EDITED BY MERRIL D. PETERSON

0-940450-16-X LIBRARY OF AMERICA........$35.00

Thomas **Paine**

Common Sense

Paine's call to revolution sold over 100,000 copies in a three-month period in 1776

0-14-039016-2 PENGUIN PB........$6.95

The Rights of Man

A defense of the French Revolution against the attacks of Edmund Burke

0-14-039015-4 PENGUIN PB........$8.95

Thomas Paine: Collected Writings

1-88301-103-5 LIBRARY OF AMERICA........$35.00

The Thomas Paine Reader

Includes *Common Sense* and excerpts from *The Rights of Man, The American Crisis*, and *The Age of Reason*

EDITED BY MICHAEL FOOT & ISAAC KRAMNICK

0-14-044496-3 PENGUIN PB........$12.95

Susanna **Rowson**

Charlotte Temple

0-19-504238-7 OXFORD PB........$7.95

John **Woolman**

The Journal of John Woolman

A spiritual classic of Quakerism

INTRODUCTION BY FREDERICK B. TOLLES

0-8065-0294-0 CITADEL PB........$8.95

The 19th Century: To the Civil War

William Hill **Brown** & Hannah Webster **Foster**

The Power of Sympathy

0-14-043468-2 PENGUIN........$13.95

William Wells **Brown**

Clotel; Or, the President's Daughter

This story of a mulatto born to Jefferson's housekeeper was issued in the U.S. without references to the president as *Clotelle: A Tale of the Southern States* in 1864

INTRODUCTION BY WILLIAM EDWARD FARISON

1-56324-804-2 SHARPE PB $15.95

From Fugitive to Free Man: The Autobiographies of William Wells Brown

0-451-62860-8 MENTOR PB $4.99

James Fenimore **Cooper**

James Fenmore Cooper, once the most familiar of American writers, has by now become very nearly the strangest. He is an ancestor just remote enough to be impenetrable, the voice of an origin to which we no longer feel intimately linked. Only a generation separates him from Melville, but that generation marks a great divide: in our perspective Melville seems the first of the moderns, and Cooper the last of the ancients…The glades and rapids and rocky barricades of The last of the Mohicans *and* The Deerslayer *have served American literature as an internalized theme park, a terrain whose every cranny became absorbed into the collective unconscious."—Geoffrey O'Brien,* Village Voice

The American Democrat

Cooper became an increasingly outspoken and controversial political writer after establishing himself as America's best-known novelist

EDITED BY GEORGE DEKKER & LARRY JOHNSTON

0-913966-91-6 LIBERTY FUND $14.00

James Fenimore Cooper (photo by New York Historical Association)

The Bravo

A novel of political corruption in Renaissance Venice; one of the sharpest and most controlled of Cooper's works. "The manner in which the aristocrats themselves are corrupted by their fear of each other—the subtle inter-relation and inter-propagation among such vices as avarice, desire for power, and fear—offers a moral portrait worthy of Hawthorne"—Yvor Winters

0-8084-0065-7 NEW COLLEGE $21.95

The Deerslayer

The earliest adventures of Natty Bumppo, in what was actually the last of the *Leatherstocking Tales* to be written

INTRODUCTION BY DONALD PEASE

0-14-039061-8 PENGUIN PB $10.95

The Last of the Mohicans

Upstate New York in the throes of the French and Indian War

EDITED BY RICHARD SLOTKIN

0-14-039024-3 PENGUIN PB $9.95

The Last of the Mohicans

EDITED BY JAMES A. SAPPENFIELD & E.N. FELTSKOG

INTRODUCTION BY JAMES F. BEARD

0-87395-790-3 SUNY PB $19.95

The Leatherstocking Tales, Volume One

The five novels which make up the *Leatherstocking Tales* follow the exploits of Natty Bumppo from the French and Indian Wars to the early 19th century. They are here presented in their order of composition in two volumes. Volume One includes *The Pioneers, The Last of the Mohicans,* and *The Prairie*

See also **LIBRARY OF AMERICA**

0-940450-20-8 LIBRARY OF AMERICA $32.50

The Leatherstocking Tales, Volume Two

Volume Two includes *The Pathfinders* and *The Deerslayer*

0-940450-21-6 LIBRARY OF AMERICA $32.50

Lionel Lincoln: Or the Leaguer of Boston

0-87395-671-0 SUNY PB $19.95

The Oak Openings

Representative late Cooper, with the themes of wilderness becoming infused with religious allegory

INTRODUCTIONS BY DON BYRD, JOHN MORGAN & WILL BAKER

0-938190-33-4 NORTH ATLANTIC $40.00

The Pathfinder

The third installment of *The Leatherstocking Tales* is devoted largely to maritime exploits on Lake Ontario

0-14-039071-5 PENGUIN PB $7.95

The Pilot

EDITED BY KAY S. HOUSE

0-87395-791-1 SUNY PB $19.95

The Pioneers

Natty in discontented old age, a victim of progress in the rapidly developing frontier settlements

0-14-039007-3 PENGUIN PB $9.95

The Pioneers

EDITED BY JAMES F. BEARD

0-87395-359-2 SUNY $59.50

The Prairie

The last days of Natty, who is caught up in a conflict among the Sioux, the Pawnees, and a band of outlaw emigrants

INTRODUCTION BY BLAKE NEVIUS

0-14-039026-X PENGUIN PB $10.95

Sea Tales

Includes the romantic adventures *The Pilot* and *The Red Rover*

See also **LIBRARY OF AMERICA**

0-940450-70-4 LIBRARY OF AMERICA $35.00

Wynadotte

EDITED BY THOMAS PHILBRICK & MARIANNE PHILBRICK

0-87395-469-6 SUNY PB $19.95

Richard Henry **Dana**, Jr.

Two Years Before the Mast

"It is the story of a man pitted in conflict against the sea, the vast, almost omnipotent element…He comes out victorious, but not till the sea has tortured his living, integral body, and made him pay something for his triumph in consciousness…Dana's small book is a very great book"—D.H. Lawrence, *Studies in Classic American Literature*

EDITED BY THOMAS PHILBRICK

0-14-039008-1 PENGUIN PB $11.95

Emily **Dickinson**

Acts of Light

A small-format gift book reissue of 80 poems by Dickinson, illustrated by Nancy Ekholm Burkert's paintings and enriched by Jane Langton's essay

0-8212-2175-2 BULFINCH $19.95

Emily Dickinson

The Complete Poems of Emily Dickinson

EDITED BY THOMAS H. JOHNSON

0-316-18414-4 LITTLE, BROWN $29.95

0-316-18413-6 LITTLE, BROWN PB $16.95

The Essential Dickinson

EDITED BY JOYCE CAROL OATES

0-88001-494-6 ECCO $18.00

0-88001-520-9 ECCO PB $25.00

Final Harvest: Emily Dickinson's Poems

A selection from Johnson's edition of the complete poems

EDITED BY THOMAS H. JOHNSON

0-316-18416-0 LITTLE, BROWN $27.95

0-316-18415-2 LITTLE, BROWN PB $13.95

New Poems by Emily Dickinson

The "new poems" the editor purports to reveal are passages from Dickinson's letters, arranged in verse form

EDITED BY WILLIAM H. SHURR

0-8078-4416-0 NORTH CAROLINA PB $10.95

The Manuscript Books of Emily Dickinson: A Facsimile Edition

Given the contentiousness which still surrounds the proper way to edit Dickinson's poetry, the serious student will want to look at her original manuscripts. A two-volume set

EDITED BY RALPH W. FRANKLIN

0-674-54828-0 HARVARD $159.95

Selected Letters

Dickinson's poetry has to some extent overshadowed the range, inventiveness, and intensity of her letters

EDITED BY THOMAS H. JOHNSON

0-674-25070-2 BELKNAP PB $16.95

Frederick **Douglass**

Frederick Douglass: Autobiographies

These works help to illustrate the life of a slave who became an advisor to presidents, minister to Haiti, and one of the most powerful African-Americans in history. Includes *Narrative of the Life of Frederick Douglass, an American Slave*; *My Bondage and My Freedom*, and *Life and Times*

See also **LIBRARY OF AMERICA**

EDITED BY HENRY LOUIS GATES, JR.

0-940450-79-8 LIBRARY OF AMERICA $35.00

Frederick Douglass: The Narrative and Selected Writings

INTRODUCTION BY MICHAEL MEYER

0-07-554375-3 MCGRAW HILL PB $15.40

The Oxford Frederick Douglass Reader

EDITED BY WILLIAM L. ANDREWS

0-19-509118-3 OXFORD PB $16.95

Narrative of the Life of Frederick Douglass, an American Slave

First published in 1845, this became the most famous of all slave narratives

See also **CLASSIC AUTOBIOGRAPHIES** under **BLACK VOICES, BLACK LIVES** under **AFRICAN-AMERICAN STUDIES** in **HISTORY OF THE AMERICAS**

EDITED BY HOUSTON A. BAKER, JR.

0-14-039012-X PENGUIN PB $7.95

Ralph Waldo **Emerson**

"There was a strange charm in Emerson's eyes, which I felt then and always, something like that I saw in Lincoln's, but shyer, but sweeter and less sad. His smile was the very sweetest I have ever beheld ... It was his great fortune to have been mostly misunderstood, and to have reached the dense intelligence of his fellow-men after a whole lifetime of perfectly simple and lucid appeal, and his countenance expressed the patience and forbearance of a wise man content to bide his time."
—William Dean Howells

Collected Poems and Translations

The most comprehensive and accurate edition of Emerson's verse and his translations including versions of Rumi, Hafiz, Dante, and others

See also **LIBRARY OF AMERICA**

EDITED BY HAROLD BLOOM & PAUL KANE

0-940450-28-3 LIBRARY OF AMERICA $35.00

Emerson in His Journals

For many, Emerson's journals are his most important writings. Porte's selection, chosen from among the many volumes of the original journals, offers a graph of his incredibly wide-ranging concerns

EDITED BY JOEL PORTE

0-674-24861-9 HARVARD $42.50

Ralph Waldo Emerson

Emerson's Antislavery Writings

"Demonstrates Emerson's continuous involvement in protest against slavery and other forms of social oppression much more dramatically than has been done before"
—Lawrence Buell

EDITED BY LEN GOUGEON & JOEL MYERSON

0-300-05970-1 YALE $32.50

Essays and Lectures

Includes *Nature: Addresses and Lectures, Essays: First and Second Series, Representative Men, English Traits, The Conduct of Life,* addresses, lectures, and uncollected prose

0-940450-15-1 LIBRARY OF AMERICA $30.00

Essays and Poems

0-460-87677-5 EVERYMAN'S PB $6.95

The Portable Emerson

EDITED BY CARL BODE & MALCOLM COWLEY

0-14-015094-3 VIKING PB $14.95

Selected Essays

EDITED BY LARZER ZIFF

0-14-039013-8 PENGUIN PB $10.95

The Selected Writings of Ralph Waldo Emerson

EDITED BY BROOKS ATKINSON

0-679-60018-3 MODERN LIBRARY $21.00

Margaret **Fuller**

Essays in American Life and Letters

Writings by one of the major figures of the Transcendentalist circle

0-8084-0416-4 NEW COLLEGE PB $16.95

The Portable Margaret Fuller

EDITED BY MARY KELLEY

0-14-017665-9 PENGUIN PB $13.95

Summer on the Lakes in 1843

An important early travel journal

0-252-06164-0 ILLINOIS PB $10.95

These Sad but Glorious Days: Dispatches from Europe, 1846-1850

Fuller's letters from Europe offer a chronicle of revolutionary activism in which she herself was caught up

EDITED BY LARRY J. REYNOLDS AND SUSAN B. SMITH

0-300-05038-0 YALE $42.00

Woman in the Nineteenth Century

Fuller stresses in this 1845 work that men and women have a duty to fulfill their potential for the spiritual good of both sexes

See also **THE 19TH CENTURY AND THE INDUSTRIAL REVOLUTION** under **AMERICAN HISTORY** under **WOMEN'S STUDIES** in **SOCIAL STUDIES**

0-393-00615-8 NORTON PB $9.95

Woman in the Nineteenth Century & Other Writings

EDITED BY DONNA DICKENSON

0-19-283085-6 OXFORD PB $10.95

Nathaniel **Hawthorne**

"For spite of all the Indian-summer sunlight on the hither side of Hawthorne's soul, the other side—like the dark half of the physical sphere—is shrouded in a blackness, ten times black... Whether there really lurks in him, perhaps unknown to himself, a touch of Puritanic gloom,—this, I cannot altogether tell. Certain it is, however, that this great power of blackness in him derives its force from its appeals to that Calvinistic sense of Innate Depravity and Original Sin, from whose visitations, in some shape or other, no deeply thinking mind is always and wholly free free."—Herman Melville, reviewing Hawthorne's Mosses from an Old Manse *(1850)*

American Notebooks

EDITED BY CLAUDE M. SIMPSON

0-8142-0159-8 OHIO STATE $89.00

The Blithedale Romance

"*The Blithedale Romance*, long considered the least of his four mature romances, is yet the most actual, the most nervously alive, in its first-person voice and in its overwarm perversely shunned heroine... The novel in its smallest details conveys Hawthorne's instinctive tenet that matter and spirit are inevitably at war"
—John Updike

INTRODUCTION BY ANNETTE KOLODNY

0-14-039028-6 VIKING PB $7.95

The French and Italian Notebooks

EDITED BY THOMAS WOODSON

0-8142-0256-X OHIO STATE $75.00

The House of the Seven Gables

EDITED BY MILTON R. STERN

0-14-039005-7 PENGUIN PB $8.95

Nathaniel **Hawthorne**

The Marble Faun

The most neglected of Hawthorne's major novels is a dark allegory of art and innocence set in Rome

0-8142-0062-1 OHIO STATE $76.00
0-452-01012-8 NEW AMERICAN LIBRARY PB $4.95

Novels

Includes *Fanshawe, The Scarlet Letter, House of the Seven Gables, The Blithedale Romance,* and *The Marble Faun*

See also LIBRARY OF AMERICA

0-940450-08-9 LIBRARY OF AMERICA $37.50

The Scarlet Letter

"It is beautiful, admirable, extraordinary; it has in the highest degree that merit which I have spoken of as the mark of Hawthorne's best things—an indefinable purity and lightness of conception…One can often return to it; it supports familiarity and has the inexhaustible charm and mystery of great works of art"
—Henry James

ILLUSTRATED BY BARRY MOSER

0-679-41731-1 KNOPF $17.00

The Scarlet Letter

0-14-039019-7 PENGUIN PB $5.95

Nathaniel Hawthorne

Tales and Sketches

The most complete collection of Hawthorne's short fiction ever assembled

0-940450-03-8 LIBRARY OF AMERICA $37.50

John **Hollander**, editor

American Poetry: The Nineteenth Century

This extraordinary two-volume anthology redraws the map of a century of American poetry, with generous selections of major figures (Dickinson, Whitman, Melville, Emerson) side by side with popular verse, political satire, and brilliant lesser-known figures such as Tuckerman, and Stickney

1-88301-100-0
LIBRARY OF AMERICA BOXED SET $70.00

Volume 1 Freneau to Whitman

0-940450-60-7 LIBRARY OF AMERICA $35.00

Volume 2 Melville to Stickney, American Indian Poetry, Folk Songs, and Spirituals

0-940450-78-X LIBRARY OF AMERICA $35.00

Washington **Irving**

The Adventures of Captain Bonneville, U.S.A.: In the Rocky Mountains and the Far West

EDITED BY EDGELEY W. TODD

0-8061-2015-0 OKLAHOMA PB $14.95

Astoria

An idealized but robustly exciting chronicle of John Jacob Astor's great doomed fur-trading venture

EDITED BY RICHARD D. TRANS

0-7103-0255-X ROUTLEDGE PB $29.95

Bracebridge Hall, Tales of a Traveler & The Alhambra

Irving the cosmopolite gathers together Gothic ghost stories, observations of English daily life, and splendid romantic tales of the Moorish era in Spain

0-940450-59-3 LIBRARY OF AMERICA $35.00

History, Tales and Sketches

Includes *Letters of Jonathan Oldstyle Gent., Salmagundi, A History of New York,* and *The Sketch Book*. "His journalism contains delightful observations on the texture of the times"
—Boston Globe

0-940450-14-3 LIBRARY OF AMERICA $35.00

A Tour on the Prairies

Irving's rather sedate encounter with the wilderness makes for an interesting study in American sensibility

INTRODUCTION BY JOHN F. MCDERMOTT

0-8061-1958-6 OKLAHOMA PB $8.95

George **Lippard**

The Quaker City: Or, The Monks of Monk Hall

A lurid bestseller from 1845, exposing the social evils of Philadelphia. "The novel described fallen women and upper-class philanderers in such lip-smacking detail that it was widely condemned as filthy"—David S. Reynolds

0-87023-971-6 MASSACHUSETTS PB $19.95

Henry Wadsworth **Longfellow**

Evangeline & Selected Tales and Poems

EDITED BY HORACE GREGORY

0-451-52003-3 NEW AMERICAN LIBRARY PB $4.95

Selected Poems

Longfellow's immense reputation as the beloved poet of fireside and schoolroom has long since faded; now it is possible to discern other, more nuanced and sometimes darker sides of a writer who was remarkable for his wide literary culture

EDITED BY LAWRENCE BUELL

0-14-039064-2 PENGUIN PB $11.95

The Song of Hiawatha

Based on Ojibwa legends and making use of the meter of the Finnish folk epic *Kalevala,* Longellow's narrative poem was once universally familiar to American readers

EDITED BY DANIEL AARON

0-460-87268-0 EVERYMAN'S PB $2.95

Herman **Melville**

Battle-Pieces and Aspects of the War

Along with Whitman, Melville was the chief American poet of the Civil War, producing such masterpieces as "Shiloh" and "The House-top," his harsh monologue about the New York draft riots

0-306-80655-X DA CAPO PB $13.95

Billy Budd & Other Stories

0-14-039053-7 PENGUIN PB $7.95

Clarel

Clarel, an immensely long poem about a young man's loss of faith while on a tour of the Holy Land, is not, to put it mildly, an easy read; but Melville's crankiest work also contains many hidden beauties and surprises

EDITED BY WALTER E. BEZANSON

0-87532-011-2 HENDRICKS $29.95
0-8101-0907-7 NORTHWESTERN PB $29.95

Collected Poems

Includes all of Melville's poetry except for the epic *Clarel*

EDITED BY HOWARD P. VINCENT

0-8084-0417-2 NEW COLLEGE PB $14.95

The Confidence-Man: His Masquerade

0-8101-0324-9 NORTHWESTERN $59.95
0-8101-0325-7 NORTHWESTERN PB $18.95

The Confidence-Man: His Masquerade

The knottiest and perhaps most subversive of Melville's fiction, a dense verbal tapestry of deception and fraud

0-14-044547-1 PENGUIN PB $9.95

Correspondence

EDITED BY LYNN HORTH

0-8101-0995-6 NORTHWESTERN PB $29.95

The Essential Melville

A selection of the poetry, including excerpts from *Clarel*. "Melville's poetry belongs to that second half of his life after he had rounded his Horn and was trying to beat north to a latitude where peace might, at last, be possible…Melville had touched bottom, and he was now seeking a belief by which life could be considered and his own life rebuilt; and his poetry, in one dimension, may be read as a record of that search"—Robert Penn Warren

EDITED BY ROBERT PENN WARREN

0-88001-141-6 ECCO PB $6.00

Israel Potter

0-8101-0552-7 NORTHWESTERN $59.95
0-8101-0553-5 NORTHWESTERN PB $19.95

Journals

A little-known but fascinating aspect of Melville's writings emerges in these accounts of his travels in Europe and Asia. Fully annotated, with many illustrations

0-8101-0823-2 NORTHWESTERN PB $29.95

Mardi

0-8101-0015-0 NORTHWESTERN $79.95
0-8101-0014-2 NORTHWESTERN PB $29.95

Moby-Dick: Or, The Whale

"It is a book that is at once primitive, fatalistic, and merciless, like the very oldest books, and yet peculiarly personal, like so many 20th-century novels, in its significant emphasis on the subjective individual consciousness"
—Alfred Kazin

ILLUSTRATED BY ROCKWELL KENT
0-679-60010-8 MODERN LIBRARY $20.00

Champollion deciphered the wrinkled granite hieroglyphics, but there is no Champollion to decipher the Egypt of every man's and every being's face. Physiognomy, like every other human science, is but a passing fable. If then, Sir William Jones, who read in thirty languages, could not read the simplest peasant's face in its profounder and more subtle meanings, how may unlettered Ishmael hope to read the awful Chaldee of the Sperm Whale's brow? I but put that brow before you. Read it if you can.
MOBY-DICK: OR, THE WHALE

Herman Melville

Moby-Dick: Or, The Whale

A beautifully hand-set and illustrated edition first published by Arion Press
NOTES BY JAMES D. HART
DESIGNED BY ANDREW HOYEM
ILLUSTRATIONS BY BARRY MOSER
0-520-04354-5 CALIFORNIA $45.00
0-520-04548-3 CALIFORNIA PB $18.95

Moby-Dick: Or, The Whale

0-8101-0268-4 NORTHWESTERN $99.95
0-8101-0269-2 NORTHWESTERN PB $29.95

Moby-Dick: Or, The Whale

A new edition of Melville's masterpiece, with extensive notes, maps, and a glossary
INTRODUCTION BY ANDREW DELBANCO
0-14-039084-7 PENGUIN PB $10.95

Omoo

0-8101-0162-9 NORTHWESTERN $59.95
0-8101-0160-2 NORTHWESTERN PB $19.95

The Piazza Tales

0-87532-005-8 HENDRICKS $24.95
0-679-60198-8 MODERN LIBRARY $14.50

The Piazza Tales & Other Prose Pieces: 1839-1860

0-8101-0550-0 NORTHWESTERN $89.95
0-8101-0551-9 NORTHWESTERN PB $29.95

Pierre: Or, The Ambiguities

INTRODUCTION BY WILLIAM SPENGEMANN
0-14-043484-4 PENGUIN PB $12.95

Pierre, Israel Potter, The Confidence-Man & Billy Budd

EDITED BY G. THOMAS TANSELLE
0-940450-24-0 LIBRARY OF AMERICA $35.00

Pierre: Or, The Ambiguities

Melville's follow-up to *Moby-Dick* led some critics to charge him with insanity, and some modern readers have been hardly more kind. *Pierre* is the darkest and most disjointed book imaginable, written in a vein of nightmarish splendor; in many ways it prophesies the course of American literature in the 20th century
0-8101-0267-6 NORTHWESTERN PB $19.95

Pierre: Or, The Ambiguities

A curious publishing project: the editor (a distinguished Melville scholar) has "restored" Melville's original text by leaving out a chunk of it which he regards as an unfortunate afterthought. Sendak's illustrations are the chief attraction of this volume
DRAWINGS BY MAURICE SENDAK
0-06-118009-2 HARPERCOLLINS $30.00

Redburn

EDITED BY HAROLD BEAVER
0-14-043105-5 PENGUIN PB $10.95

Redburn

A largely autobiographical novel based on Melville's first voyage to England
0-8101-0013-4 NORTHWESTERN $69.95
0-8101-0016-9 NORTHWESTERN PB $19.95

Redburn, White-Jacket, & Moby-Dick

EDITED BY G. THOMAS TANSELLE
0-940450-09-7 LIBRARY OF AMERICA $35.00

Typee

0-8101-0159-9 NORTHWESTERN PB $19.95

Typee: A Peep at Polynesian Life

Melville's first book, based on his experiences among cannibals in the Marquesas, became a bestseller in 1846
See also **POLYNESIA** under **AUSTRALIA, NEW ZEALAND, AND POLYNESIA** in **WORLD HISTORY AND CURRENT AFFAIRS**
EDITED BY GEORGE WOODCOCK
0-14-043070-9 PENGUIN PB $9.95

Typee, Omoo, & Mardi

EDITED BY G. THOMAS TANSELLE
0-940450-00-3 LIBRARY OF AMERICA $37.50

White-Jacket

0-8101-0257-9 NORTHWESTERN $59.95
0-8101-0258-7 NORTHWESTERN PB $19.95

Francis **Parkman**

France and England in North America

Whatever its value as history, Parkman's chronicle of the French and English struggle for North America is an authentic American epic in which landscape and climate play as great a role as human personality
EDITED BY DAVID LEVINE
0-940450-10-0 LIBRARY OF AMERICA $30.00

Volume 1

Includes *Pioneers of France in the New World, The Jesuits in North America, La Salle and the Discovery of the Great West,* and *The Old Regime in Canada*

Volume 2

Includes *Count Frontenac* and *New France Under Louis XIV, Montcalm and Wolfe,* and *A Half-Century of Conflict*
EDITED BY DAVID LEVIN
See also **LIBRARY OF AMERICA**
0-940450-11-9 LIBRARY OF AMERICA $40.00

The Oregon Trail

A vivid account of Parkman's journey to Wyoming, published in 1849
See also **WESTERN EXPLORATIONS** under **AMERICAN REGIONAL HISTORY: THE WEST AND THE SOUTH** in **HISTORY OF THE AMERICAS**
EDITED BY DAVID LEVIN
0-451-52513-2 NEW AMERICAN LIBRARY PB $4.95
0-14-039042-1 VIKING PB $11.95

The Oregon Trail

EDITED BY BERNARD ROSENTHAL
0-19-282346-9 OXFORD PB $8.95

The Oregon Trail, The Conspiracy of Pontiac

See also **AMERICA MOVES WEST** under **AMERICAN REGIONAL HISTORY: THE WEST AND THE SOUTH** in **HISTORY OF THE AMERICAS**
See also **LIBRARY OF AMERICA**
0-517-14765-3 LIBRARY OF AMERICA $11.99
0-940450-54-2 LIBRARY OF AMERICA $35.00

Edgar Allan **Poe**

"The evident and most prominent aim of Mr. Poe is originality, either of idea, or the combination of ideas. He appears to think it a crime to write unless he has something novel to write about, or some novel way of writing about an old thing. He rejects every word not having a tendency to develop the effect...And he evidently holds whatever tends to the furtherance of the effect, to be legitimate material."—Edgar Allan Poe, reviewing his own work anonymously (1845)

The Complete Poetry of Edgar Allan Poe

0-451-52640-6 SIGNET PB $3.95

Complete Stories and Poems of Edgar Allan Poe

"All of Poe's fiction, and the poems as well, can be seen as one coherent piece—the work of one of the greatest ironists of world literature"
—G.R. Thompson
0-385-07407-7 DOUBLEDAY $19.95

Essays and Reviews

This collection shows Poe as a tireless critic and journalist, deeply involved in trying to influence the direction of American literature
0-940450-19-4 LIBRARY OF AMERICA $40.00

The Essential Poe

EDITED BY DAVE SMITH
0-8313-5001-6 LANTERN LIBRARY EDITION $19.95
0-88001-273-0 ECCO PB $8.00

Edgar Allan **Poe**

The Complete Tales and Poems

"The Murders in the Rue Morgue," "The Mystery of Marie Roget," "The Purloined Letter": these and other classic tales introduced the concept of *ratiocination*—detection through deduction—and the prototype for aristocratic amateur sleuths: the all-seeing C. Auguste Dupin

See also **PIONEERS AND LANDMARKS** under **RISE OF THE MYSTERY** under **CRIME FICTION** in **POPULAR READING**

0-679-60007-8 MODERN LIBRARY........$20.00
0-394-71678-7 VINTAGE PB........$15.00

Edgar Allan Poe

The Narrative of Arthur Gordon Pym of Nantucket

Poe's only novel-length work moves from the realism of a purported sea-log to a dizzying vista of emptiness

EDITED BY HAROLD BEAVER

0-14-043097-0 PENGUIN PB........$9.95

Poetry and Tales

The most comprehensive and scholarly one-volume edition

EDITED BY PATRICK F. QUINN

0-940450-18-6 LIBRARY OF AMERICA........$37.50

The Portable Poe

An intelligently edited anthology presents the many sides of Poe's work

EDITED BY PHILLIP V. STERN

0-14-015012-9 PENGUIN PB........$14.95

The Science Fiction of Edgar Allan Poe

EDITED BY HAROLD BEAVER

0-14-043106-3 PENGUIN PB........$10.95

The Unknown Poe

EDITED BY RAYMOND FOYE

0-87286-110-4 CITY LIGHTS PB........$7.95

Rebecca **Rush**

Kelroy

A new edition of a rare early American novel, not reprinted since its first appearance in 1812

0-19-507703-2 OXFORD PB........$11.95

Harriet Beecher **Stowe**

Oldtown Folks

A detailed portrait of New England village life in the post-revolutionary period

EDITED BY DOROTHY BERKSON

0-8135-1220-4 RUTGERS PB........$17.00

Poganuc People: Their Loves and Lives

0-917482-06-9 STOWE-DAY PB........$15.95

Three Novels

Includes *Uncle Tom's Cabin, The Minister's Wooing,* and *Oldtown Folks*

See also **LIBRARY OF AMERICA**

0-940450-01-1 LIBRARY OF AMERICA........$40.00

Uncle Tom's Cabin

0-679-60200-3 MODERN LIBRARY........$18.50

Uncle Tom's Cabin: Or, Life Among the Lowly

Stowe's masterpiece has a scope rare in 19th-century American literature

EDITED BY ANN DOUGLAS

0-14-039003-0 PENGUIN PB........$8.95

Tabitha Gilman **Tenney**

Female Quixotism

An early satirical novel, first published in 1801

0-19-507414-9 OXFORD PB........$11.95

Henry David **Thoreau**

"In reading Henry Thoreau's journal, I am very sensible of the vigor of his constitution. That oaken strength which I noted whenever he walked or worked or surveyed wood lots, the same unhesitating hand with which a field-laborer accosts a piece of work which I should shun as a waste of strength, Henry shows in his literary task…In reading him, I find the same thought, the same spirit that is in me, but he takes a step beyond, & illustrates by excellent images that which I should have conveyed in a sleepy generality. 'Tis as if I went into a gymnasium, & saw youths leap, climb, & swing with a force unapproachable—though their feats are only continuations of my initial grapplings & jumps."—Ralph Waldo Emerson in his journal, June 1863

Cape Cod

Ten essays compose this journey of discovery in which Thoreau gained respect for the complex relationship between sea and shore

See also **ESSAYS, MEDITATIONS, AND CLASSICS** under **NATURE STUDY** in **SCIENCE**

0-14-017002-2 PENGUIN PB........$10.95

The Illustrated "A Week on the Concord and Merrimack Rivers"

EDITED BY CARL F. BODE

0-940160-36-6 PARNASSUS PB........$9.95

The Maine Woods

"The Maine Woods is very much a book of the body and its limitations, a book that stays close to the ground with an ample stock of mud and rock and rainwater. In this context Thoreau is more aware of his dependence than his liberty"—*NY Review of Books*

INTRODUCTION BY RICHARD H. FLECK

0-691-06224-2 PRINCETON........$70.00

The Maine Woods

"Here was traveling of the old heroic kind over the unaltered face of nature"
—Henry David Thoreau

See also **ESSAYS, MEDITATIONS, AND CLASSICS** under **NATURE STUDY** in **SCIENCE**

INTRODUCTION BY EDWARD HOAGLAND

0-14-017013-8 PENGUIN PB........$12.95

Walden

First published in 1854, *Walden*, a chronicle of Thoreau's time spent alone on Walden Pond in Massachusetts, remains one of the most influential books in American literature

See also **ESSAYS, MEDITATIONS, AND CLASSICS** under **NATURE STUDY** in **SCIENCE**

0-679-41896-2 EVERYMAN'S........$17.00
0-393-95905-8 NORTON PB........$9.95

Walden & Civil Disobedience

INTRODUCTION BY MICHAEL MEYER

0-14-039044-8 PENGUIN PB........$9.95

Henry David Thoreau
(photo courtesy of Concord Free Public Library)

Walden & Other Writings

EDITED WITH AN INTRODUCTION BY BROOKS ATKINSON

0-679-60004-3 MODERN LIBRARY........$19.50
0-553-21246-X BDD PB........$3.95

A Week On The Concord and Merrimack Rivers, Walden, The Maine Woods, Cape Cod

EDITED BY ROBERT F. SAYRE

0-940450-27-5 LIBRARY OF AMERICA........$30.00

A Year in Thoreau's Journal

Rather than offering snippets, this valuable book gives a single year—1851—in all its profusion, as an emblematic example of the extraordinary project which was Thoreau's journal

0-14-039085-5 PENGUIN PB........$12.95

Jones **Very**

Jones Very: The Complete Poems

While much of Very's verse lapses into mediocrity, the poems of his visionary period are at once lucid and ecstatic, a remarkable American religious text

EDITED BY HELEN DEESE

0-8203-1481-1 GEORGIA........$65.00

Sojourner **Truth**

The Narrative of Sojourner Truth

A significant document of the anti-slavery movement

0-19-506638-3 OXFORD $35.00

Walt **Whitman**

"I am not blind to the worth of the wonderful gift of Leaves of Grass. *I find it the most extraordinary piece of wit & wisdom that America has yet contributed. I am very happy in reading it, as great power makes us happy…I give you joy of your free & brave thought. I have great joy in it. I find incomparable things said incomparably well, as they must be. I find the courage of treatment, which so delights us, & which large perception only can inspire. I greet you at the beginning of a great career, which yet must have had a long foreground somewhere, for such a start."—Ralph Waldo Emerson in a letter to Walt Whitman (July 21, 1855)*

Complete Poetry and Collected Prose

0-940450-02-X LIBRARY OF AMERICA $35.00

Earlier in the summer I occasionally saw the President and his wife toward the latter part of the afternoon, out in a barouche, on a pleasure ride through the city…They pass'd me once very close, and I saw the President in the face fully, as they were moving slowly, and his look, though abstracted happen'd to be directed steadily in my eye. He bow'd and smile but far beneath his smile I noticed well the expression I have alluded to. None of the artists or picture has caught the deep, though subtle and indirect expression of this man's face. There is something else there. One of the great painters of two or three centuries ago is needed.—From "Specimen Days"

COMPLETE POETRY AND COLLECTED PROSE

The Essential Whitman

EDITED BY GALWAY KINNELL

0-88001-137-8 ECCO PB $8.00

Leaves of Grass

"In the first edition everything belongs together and everything helps to exhibit Whitman at his best, Whitman at his freshest in vision and boldest in language, Whitman transformed by a new experience, so that he wanders among familiar objects and finds that each of them has become a miracle"—Malcolm Cowley

EDITED BY MALCOLM COWLEY

0-14-042199-8 PENGUIN PB $7.95

Leaves of Grass

0-679-60076-0 MODERN LIBRARY $19.50

The Neglected Walt Whitman: Vital Texts

Included in this collection is "Repondez," which Kenneth Burke called Whitman's one "outlaw moment," and three reviews in which the poet, writing under a pseudonym, assessed his own work

EDITED BY SAM ABRAMS

0-941423-90-5 FOUR WALLS $22.95

0-941423-97-2 FOUR WALLS PB $12.95

Harriet E. **Wilson**

Our Nig: Sketches from the Life of a Free Black

A lost 1855 novel rediscovered. What begins very much in the romantic style of the time leaps into an autobiographical recollection of a free black woman's servitude to an indifferent white family in Massachusetts

EDITED BY HENRY LOUIS GATES, JR.

0-394-71558-6 RANDOM HOUSE PB $11.00

The Nineteenth Century

The Schomburg Library of 19th-Century Black Women Writers

"The voices of these black women provide a stunning new collective portrait of the Afro-American rise from slavery to freedom …[The] project will dramatically change the landscape of Afro-American literature and American cultural history."—Eric J. Sundquist, *NY Times*

Octavia V. **Albert**

The House of Bondage, Or Charlotte Brooks and Other Slaves

INTRODUCTION BY FRANCES FOSTER

0-19-505263-3 OXFORD $24.00

Elizabeth **Ammons**, editor

Short Fiction by Black Women, 1900-1920

0-19-506195-0 OXFORD $39.95

William L. **Andrews**

Six Women's Slave Narratives

0-19-506083-0 OXFORD PB $12.95

Hallie Q. **Brown**

Homespun Heroines and Other Women of Distinction

INTRODUCTION BY RANDALL BURKETT

0-19-505237-4 OXFORD $29.95

0-19-507575-7 OXFORD PB $10.95

Olivia Ward **Bushbanks**

The Collected Works of Olivia Ward Bushbanks

0-19-506196-9 OXFORD $39.95

Anna Julia **Cooper**

A Voice from the South

Considered one of the original texts foretelling the black feminist movement, these essays offer unparalleled insight into the thought of black women writers in the 19th century. Originally published in 1892

See also **BLACK VOICES, BLACK LIVES** under **AFRICAN-AMERICAN STUDIES** in **HISTORY OF THE AMERICAS**

INTRODUCTION BY MARY HELEN WASHINGTON

0-19-505246-3 OXFORD $29.95

0-19-506323-6 OXFORD PB $12.95

Alice **Dunbar-Nelson**

The Works of Alice Dunbar-Nelson

Volume 1

0-19-505250-1 OXFORD $29.95

0-19-509055-1 OXFORD PB $12.95

Volume 2

0-19-505251-X OXFORD $29.95

Volume 3

0-19-505252-8 OXFORD $29.95

Hannah W. **Foster**

The Coquette

0-19-504239-5 OXFORD PB $7.95

Henry Louis **Gates**, Jr., editor

The Schomburg Library of 19th-Century Black Women Writers

0-19-507809-8 OXFORD $300.00

Angelina Weld **Grimke**

The Selected Works of Angelina Weld Grimke

EDITED BY CAROLIVIA HERRON

0-19-506199-3 OXFORD $42.00

Charlotte Forten **Grimke**

The Journals of Charlotte Forten Grimke

EDITED BY BRENDA STEVENSON

0-19-505238-2 OXFORD $39.95

0-19-506086-5 OXFORD PB $12.95

Frances E.W. **Harper**

Complete Poems of Frances E. W. Harper

INTRODUCTION BY MARYEMMA GRAHAM

0-19-505244-7 OXFORD $32.00

Iola Leroy, Or Shadows Uplifted

INTRODUCTION BY FRANCES FOSTER

0-19-505240-4 OXFORD $27.00

Pauline E. **Hopkins**

Contending Forces: A Romance Illustrative of Negro Life in the North and South

INTRODUCTION BY RICHARD YARBOROUGH

0-19-505258-7 OXFORD $29.95

0-19-506785-1 OXFORD PB $14.95

The Magazine Novels of Pauline Hopkins

Includes *Hagar's Daughter* and *Of One Blood*

INTRODUCTION BY HAZEL V. CARBY

0-19-505248-X OXFORD $35.00

Sue **Houchins**, editor

Spiritual Narratives

Includes writing by Jarena Lee, Zilipha Elaw, Virginia Broughton, Sara Mix, Julia Foote, Maria Stewart, and Rebecca Stewart

0-19-505266-8 OXFORD $27.00

0-19-506786-X OXFORD PB $13.95

Harriet **Jacobs**

Incidents in the Life of a Slave Girl

INTRODUCTION BY VALERIE SMITH

0-19-505243-9 OXFORD $27.00

0-19-506670-7 OXFORD PB $12.95

Amelia A.E. **Johnson**

Clarence and Corrine: Or God's Way

INTRODUCTION BY HORTENSE SPILLERS

0-19-505264-1 OXFORD $27.00

0-19-507574-9 OXFORD PB $10.95

The Hazeley Family

INTRODUCTION BY BARBARA CHRISTIAN

0-19-505257-9 OXFORD $24.00

0-19-507577-3 OXFORD PB $10.95

Elizabeth **Keckley**

Behind the Scenes: Or, Thirty Years a Slave, and Four Years in the House White

0-19-506084-9 OXFORD PB $12.95

Emma Dunham **Kelley**

Megda

INTRODUCTION BY MOLLY HITE

0-19-505245-5 OXFORD $29.95

0-19-507576-5 OXFORD PB $11.95

Four Girls at Cottage City

INTRODUCTION BY DEBORAH MCDOWELL

0-19-506787-8 OXFORD PB $10.95

C.W. **Larison**

Silvia Dubois: A Biografy of the Slav Who Whipt Her Mistres and Gand Her Fredom

INTRODUCTION BY JARED C. LOBDELL

0-19-505239-0 OXFORD $29.95

0-19-506671-5 OXFORD PB $9.95

N.F. **Mossell**

The Work of The Afro-American Woman

INTRODUCTION BY JOANNE BRAXTON

0-19-505265-X OXFORD $24.95

0-19-506326-0 OXFORD PB $9.95

Louisa **Picquet**

Collected Black Women's Narratives

Includes works by Louisa Picquet, Nancy Prince, Bethany Vaney, and Susie K. Taylor

INTRODUCTION BY ANTHONY BARTHOLOME

0-19-506669-3 OXFORD PB $13.95

Ann **Plato**

Essays

INTRODUCTION BY KENNY J. WILLIAMS

0-19-505247-1 OXFORD $26.00

Eliza **Potter**

A Hairdresser's Experience in High Life

0-19-506198-5 OXFORD $32.00

Mary **Prince**

Six Women's Slave Narratives, 1831-1909

Includes writings by Mary Prince, Mattie Jackson, Elizabeth Delaney, Lucy Delaney, and Kate Drumgoold

INTRODUCTION BY WILLIAM ANDREWS

0-19-505262-5 OXFORD $29.95

Mary **Seacole**

Wonderful Adventures of Mrs. Seacole in Many Lands

EDITED BY WILLIAM ANDREWS

0-19-505249-8 OXFORD $22.00

0-19-506672-3 OXFORD PB $11.95

Amanda Berry **Smith**

An Autobiography: The Story of the Lord's Dealing with Mrs. Amanda Smith the Colored Evangelist

INTRODUCTION BY JUALYNNE DODSON

0-19-505261-7 OXFORD $32.00

Effie Waller **Smith**

The Collected Works of Effie Waller Smith

EDITED BY HENRY LOUIS GATES, JR.

0-19-506197-7 OXFORD $35.00

Katherine Davis Chapman **Tillman**

The Works of Katherine Davis Chapman Tillman

EDITED BY CLAUDIA TATE

0-19-506200-0 OXFORD $42.00

Ida B. **Wells-Barnett**

The Selected Works of Ida B. Wells-Barnett

EDITED BY HARRIS TRUDIER

0-19-506202-7 OXFORD $42.00

Phillis **Wheatley**

Collected Works of Phillis Wheatley

EDITED BY JOHN SHIELDS

0-19-505241-2 OXFORD $32.00

0-19-506085-7 OXFORD PB $12.95

American Women Writers

This Rutgers University Press series is dedicated to bringing back into print "the most significant, influential, and popular American women writers from the 1820s to the 1920s." Joyce Carol Oates has described the series as "an ambitious, exciting, and highly valuable contribution to the reclamation of American women's lost literature."

Louisa May **Alcott**

The Alternative Alcott

Includes the "sensation story" *Behind a Mask*, *Transcendental Wild Oats*, and other works revealing unfamiliar aspects of the author of *Little Women*

EDITED BY ELAINE SHOWALTER

0-8135-1271-9 RUTGERS $45.00

0-8135-1272-7 RUTGERS PB $16.00

Louisa May Alcott

Moods

EDITED BY SARAH ELBERT

0-8135-1670-6 RUTGERS PB $15.00

Mary **Austin**

Stories from the Country of Lost Borders

Includes *The Land of Little Rain* (1903) and *Lost Borders* (1909), both set in the California desert

EDITED BY MARJORIE PRYSE

0-8135-1218-2 RUTGERS PB $13.00

Alice **Cary**

Clovernook Sketches & Other Stories

Cary, born in 1820 in a small Ohio town, was an early exponent of regional realism

EDITED BY JUDITH FETTERLY

0-8135-1251-4 RUTGERS PB $15.00

Lydia Maria **Child**

Hobomok & Other Writings on Indians

Hobomok, published in 1824, was an early and sympathetic treatment of Indian themes

EDITED BY CAROLYN L. KARCHER

0-8135-1163-1 RUTGERS $35.00

0-8135-1164-X RUTGERS PB $15.00

Rose Terry **Cooke**

How Celia Changed Her Mind & Selected Stories

Eleven stories covering Cooke's career from the 1850s to the 1890s, alternating between grim rural realism and playful humor

EDITED BY ELIZABETH AMMONS

0-8135-1166-6 RUTGERS PB $15.00

Maria **Cummins**

The Lamplighter

An enormously popular moralistic romance first published in 1854

EDITED BY NINA BAYM

0-8135-1333-2 RUTGERS PB $17.00

Fanny **Fern**

Ruth Hall and Other Writing

Fern was the first woman newspaper columnist in America; *Ruth Hall* (1855) reflects a spirit of practical feminism

EDITED BY JOYCE W. WARREN

0-8135-1168-2 RUTGERS PB $12.00

Margaret **Fuller**

The Essential Margaret Fuller

The best available sampling of Fuller's diverse work as critic, journalist, and poet

EDITED BY JEFFREY STEEL

0-8135-1778-8 RUTGERS PB $18.00

Gail **Hamilton**

Gail Hamilton: Selected Writings

EDITED BY SUSAN COULTRAP-MCQUIN

0-8135-1809-1 RUTGERS $44.00

0-8135-1810-5 RUTGERS PB $15.00

Nella **Larsen**

Quicksand & Passing

Novels of the black middle class, written in the '20s. "*Quicksand* and *Passing* are novels that I will never forget. They open up a whole world of experience that seemed to me, when I first read them years ago, absolutely absorbing, fascinating, and indispensable. They do that still"—Alice Walker

EDITED BY DEBORAH E. MCDOWELL

0-8135-1170-4 RUTGERS PB $10.00

Catharine Maria **Sedgwick**

Hope Leslie

A popular 1827 novel of Puritans and Indians

EDITED BY MARY KELLEY

0-8135-1222-0 RUTGERS PB $15.00

E.D.E.N. **Southworth**

The Hidden Hand

A popular 19th-century novel of comic intrigue

EDITED BY JOANNE DOBSON

0-8135-1296-4 RUTGERS PB $15.00

Harriet Prescott **Spoffard**

The "Amber Gods" and Other Stories

EDITED BY ALFRED BENDIXEN

0-8135-1401-0 RUTGERS PB $15.00

Cheryl **Walker**, editor

American Women Poets of the Nineteenth Century: An Anthology

An ample survey of such neglected figures as Alice Cary, Lucy Larcom, Helen Hunt Jackson, Ina Coolbrith, and Emma Lazarus

0-8135-1791-5 RUTGERS PB $17.00

Constance Fenimore **Woolson**

Women Artists, Women Exiles: "Miss Grief" and Other Stories

EDITED BY JOAN MYERS WEIMER

0-8135-1348-0 RUTGERS PB $15.00

The 19th Century: After the Civil War

Henry **Adams**

The Education of Henry Adams

A classic autobiography with an ironic analysis of the culture that formed this scion of a distinguished American family

EDITED BY ERNEST SAMUELS

0-395-08352-4 HOUGHTON MIFFLIN PB $14.95

At the rate of progress since 1800, every American who lived into the year 2000 would know how to control unlimited power. He would think in complexities unimaginable to an earlier mind. He would deal with problems altogether beyond the range of earlier society. To him the nineteenth century would stand on the same plane with the fourth—equally childlike—and he would only wonder how both of them, knowing so little, and so weak in force, should have done so much.

THE EDUCATION OF HENRY ADAMS

John Randolph

INTRODUCTION BY ROBERT MCCOLLEY

1-56324-653-8 SHARPE PB $15.95

Mont Saint-Michel and Chartres

A study of the medieval imagination through the religion, art, and architecture of the 12th century. "From beginning to end, it reads as from a man in the fresh morning of life, with a frolic power unusual to historic literature" —William James

See also **THE MEDIEVAL AESTHETIC** under **MEDIEVAL AND RENAISSANCE EUROPE** in **WORLD HISTORY AND CURRENT AFFAIRS**

INTRODUCTION BY RAYMOND CARNEY

0-14-039054-5 PENGUIN PB $11.95

Henry Adams

Novels and Other Writings

Contains *The Education of Henry Adams, Mont Saint-Michel and Chartres*, and the novels *Democracy* and *Esther*

0-940450-12-7 LIBRARY OF AMERICA $35.00

Louisa May **Alcott**

Behind a Mask: The Unknown Thrillers of Louisa May Alcott

EDITED BY MADELEINE STERN

0-688-00338-9 MORROW $22.50

From Jo March's Attic: Stories of Intrigue and Suspense

1-55553-177-6 NORTHEASTERN $21.95

Good Wives

0-14-035009-8 PUFFIN PB $3.99

Jo's Boys

AFTERWORD BY MADELEINE B. STERN

0-14-035015-2 PUFFIN PB $3.99

Life, Letters, and Journals

EDITED BY EDNAH D. CHENEY

0-517-12424-6 GRAMERCY $9.99

Little Men

0-451-52275-3 NEW AMERICAN LIBRARY PB $4.95

Little Women

The enduringly popular saga of the March sisters—Meg, Jo, Amy, and Beth—in Civil War New England. "There was one book in which I believed I had caught a glimpse of my future self: *Little Women* by Louisa May Alcott…I identified myself passionately with Jo, the intellectual"—Simone de Beauvoir

INTRODUCTION BY ELAINE SHOWALTER

0-14-039069-3 PENGUIN PB $6.95

A Long Fatal Love Chase

Deception, bigamy, domination, and murder characterize this strikingly modern novel, rejected by its contemporary 19th-century publishers as "too sensational" and published to tremendous acclaim today. This rediscovered thriller by the author of *Little Women* is an entirely grown-up story of a smart, strong-willed young woman who yearns for romance and adventure

0-679-44510-2 RANDOM HOUSE $21.00

Louisa May Alcott Unmasked: Collected Thrillers

1-55553-225-X NORTHEASTERN $55.00

1-55553-226-8 NORTHEASTERN PB $24.95

Modern Magic

More of Alcott's rediscovered Gothic fictions

EDITED BY MADELEINE B. STERN

0-679-60171-6 MODERN LIBRARY $14.50

A Modern Mephistopheles

EDITED BY OCTAVIA COWAN

0-8488-0412-0 AMEREON $17.95

0-553-37795-7 BANTAM PB $7.95

A Modern Mephistopheles & Taming a Tartar

0-275-92754-7 PRAEGER $49.95

Work: A Story of Experience

A significant ficitonal account of a woman looking for an independent life through work outside the home

EDITED BY JOY S. KASSON

0-14-039091-X PENGUIN PB $11.95

Horatio **Alger**, Jr.

Ragged Dick & Struggling Upward

Alger's optimistic tales of self-betterment sold in the tens of millions of copies

EDITED BY CARL BODE

0-14-039033-2 VIKING PB $9.95

Edward **Bellamy**

Looking Backward

A century later, Bellamy's mechanistic utopia looks more nightmarish than ever

EDITED BY CECELIA TICHI

0-14-039018-9 PENGUIN PB $9.95

Ambrose **Bierce**

Ambrose Bierce's Civil War

EDITED AND WITH AN INTRODUCTION BY WILLIAM MCCANN

0-89526-716-0 REGNERY PB $12.95

The Devil's Dictionary

A compendium of sardonic aphorisms, originally titled *The Cynic's Word Book*

0-89190-186-8 AEONIAN $21.95

Ghost and Horror Stories of Ambrose Bierce

EDITED BY E.F. BLEILER

0-486-20767-6 DOVER PB $6.95

In the Midst of Life

INTRODUCTION BY CLIFTON FADIMAN

0-8065-0551-6 CITADEL PB $8.95

Poems of Ambrose Bierce

EDITED BY M.E. GRENANDER

0-8032-6133-0 NEBRASKA PB $12.00

The Sardonic Humor of Ambrose Bierce

EDITED BY GEORGE BARKIN

0-486-20768-4 DOVER PB $6.95

George Washington **Cable**

The Grandissimes

A drama of social distinctions in Louisiana, by a sometimes controversial chronicler of Creole life

0-14-043322-8 PENGUIN PB $12.95

Charles W. **Chesnutt**

Chesnutt's gifts as a short story writer broke the color line around the turn of the century, but his editors waited 12 years before revealing his racial identity.

The Conjure Woman

Dialect stories of slavery days, published in 1899

INTRODUCTION BY ROBERT FARNSWORTH

0-472-06156-9 MICHIGAN PB $13.95

The Conjure Woman & Other Tales

0-8223-1378-2 DUKE $38.95

0-8223-1387-1 DUKE PB $12.95

The House Behind the Cedars

Two young African-Americans decide to pass for white

0-14-018685-9 PENGUIN PB $11.95

The Journals of Charles W. Chesnutt

0-8223-1379-0 DUKE $38.95

0-8223-1424-X DUKE PB $14.95

The Marrow of Tradition

A novel of Reconstruction based on violent events in Wilmington, N.C., in 1898

0-14-018686-7 PENGUIN PB $12.95

The Short Fiction of Charles W. Chesnutt

"The collection evinces Chesnutt's incisive humor, his narrative skill, his evocative characterizations, and his essential artistry"—*Choice*

0-88258-092-2 HOWARD PB $12.95

The Wife of His Youth & Other Stories

INTRODUCTION BY E.S. MIERS

0-472-06134-8 MICHIGAN PB $13.95

Kate **Chopin**

The Awakening & Selected Stories

The Awakening, a story about a woman who rebels against her bourgeois husband and falls in love with a younger man, created a scandal when it was first published in 1899

INTRODUCTION BY SANDRA GILBERT

0-394-32667-9 MCGRAW HILL PB $12.75

The Awakening and Selected Stories

0-679-42469-5 MODERN LIBRARY $15.50

0-8446-6229-1 SMITH $18.50

A Vocation and a Voice: Stories

EDITED BY EMILY TOTH

0-14-039078-2 PENGUIN PB $9.95

Stephen **Crane**

The Complete Poems of Stephen Crane

EDITED WITH AN INTRODUCTION BY JOSEPH KATZ

0-8014-9130-4 CORNELL PB $12.95

Maggie: A Girl of the Streets

0-449-30024-2 FAWCETT PB $5.99

Maggie: A Girl of the Streets & Other Short Fiction

INTRODUCTION BY JAYNE ANNE PHILLIPS

0-393-95024-7 NORTON PB $10.95

Prose and Poetry

Includes *Maggie: A Girl of the Streets*, *The Red Badge of Courage*, *George's Mother*, *The Third Violet*, journalism, tales and sketches, and poetry. "Crane's journalism and war dispatches ...disclose the complex interactions of history, journalism, and fiction"—*Boston Globe*

See also **LIBRARY OF AMERICA**

EDITED BY J.C. LEVENSON

0-940450-17-8 LIBRARY OF AMERICA $35.00

The Red Badge of Courage: An Episode of the American Civil War

"Crane was a brilliant Impressionist and has strong affinities with the Impressionist painters...He is aware of the ironical disparity between what imagination and tradition suggest and what in fact is seen"—V.S. Pritchett

INTRODUCTION BY PASCAL COVICI

0-14-035055-1 PENGUIN PB $2.99

The Red Badge of Courage: An Episode of the American Civil War

See also **YOUNG ADULT FICTION** in **BOOKS FOR YOUNG READERS**

0-679-60044-2 MODERN LIBRARY $13.50

0-679-73223-3 VINTAGE PB $9.50

Rebecca Harding **Davis**

A Rebecca Harding Davis Reader

EDITED BY JEAN PFAELZER

0-8229-3887-1 PITTSBURGH $35.00

Paul Laurence **Dunbar**

Dunbar, who died in 1906, preferred the poetry he wrote in standard English, and only at the insistence of his editors continued to turn out volumes of the dialect poetry that brought him fame. Nevertheless, among the black poets working in dialect around the turn of the century, Dunbar best evoked the voices and attitudes of real people.

The Complete Poems of Paul Laurence Dunbar

0-317-05269-1 HAKIMS BOOKSTORE PB $10.95

Lyrics of Lowly Life

INTRODUCTION BY WILLIAM DEAN HOWELLS

0-8065-0922-8 CITADEL PB $6.95

Harold **Frederic**

The Civil War Stories of Harold Frederic

EDITED BY THOMAS F. O'DONNELL

0-8156-2572-3 SYRACUSE PB $14.95

The Damnation of Theron Ware

This novel of a minister's loss of faith, subtly disturbing and subversively funny, remains a neglected masterpiece of American writing

0-14-039025-1 PENGUIN PB $11.95

Hamlin **Garland**

Main-Travelled Roads

Realistic stories of the Midwest, by a writer who later became a spokesman for Populism

0-8032-7058-5 NEBRASKA PB $10.00

A Son of the Middle Border

EDITED BY JOSEPH B. MCCULLOUGH

0-14-018796-0 PENGUIN PB $11.95

Henry Louis **Gates**, Jr., editor

Three Classic African American Novels

Includes *Clotel* by William Wells Brown, *Iola Leroy* by Frances E.W. Harper, and *The Marrow of Tradition* by Charles W. Chesnutt

0-679-72742-6 VINTAGE PB $15.00

Frances E.W. **Harper**

Iola Leroy

A sentimental novel interesting for the depiction of blacks in post-Civil War fiction

INTRODUCTION BY HAZEL CARBY

0-8070-6317-7 BEACON PB $12.00

Minnie's Sacrifice, Sowing and Reaping, Trial and Triumph: Three Rediscovered Novels

0-8070-8332-1 BEACON $22.00

0-8070-8333-X BEACON PB $12.95

Joel Chandler **Harris**

Uncle Remus: His Songs and His Sayings

EDITED BY ROBERT HEMENWAY

0-14-039014-6 VIKING PB $9.95

Bret **Harte**

The Outcasts of Poker Flat

In stories like "The Luck of Roaring Camp" and "Tennessee's Partner" Harte helped mythologize the Gold Rush era

0-89061-053-3 JAMESTOWN PB $7.32

Selected Stories and Sketches

EDITED BY DAVID WYATT

0-19-282354-X OXFORD PB $8.95

Lafcadio **Hearn**

Exotics and Retrospectives

0-8398-0774-0 IRVINGTON $36.50

Kwaidan: Stories and Studies of Strange Things

0-8048-0954-2 TUTTLE PB $12.95

Writings from Japan: An Anthology

After a life of Bohemian wandering, Hearn settled in Japan and wrote many still-popular volumes exploring Japanese culture and tradition

EDITED BY FRANCIS KING

0-14-043463-1 PENGUIN PB $10.95

O. **Henry**

The Best of O. Henry

EDITED BY IAN BELL AND CHRISTOPHER BIGSBY

0-460-87339-3 EVERYMAN'S PB $5.95

The Best Short Stories of O. Henry

EDITED BY BENNETT A. CERF AND VAN H. CARTMELL

0-679-60122-8 MODERN LIBRARY $20.50

Cabbages and Kings

EDITED BY GUY DAVENPORT

0-14-018689-1 PENGUIN PB $10.95

Selected Stories

EDITED BY GUY DAVENPORT

0-14-018688-3 PENGUIN PB $11.95

William Dean **Howells**

A Hazard of New Fortunes

A drama of capital versus militant labor which is also one of the most important novels about New York, filled with sharply observed scenes of public and private life

AFTERWORD BY BENJAMIN DEMOTT

0-452-00963-4 NEW AMERICAN LIBRARY PB $11.95

A Hazard of New Fortunes

0-452-00768-2 READER'S CATALOG PB $5.95

A Modern Instance

"Nothing could be more telling than Howells' description of the religious mood of the '70s and '80s, the movement from the last vestiges of faith to a genteel plausibility, the displacement of doctrine and moral strenuousness by a concern with 'social adjustment' and the amelioration of boredom"—Lionel Trilling

INTRODUCTION BY EDWIN CADY

0-14-039027-8 PENGUIN PB $10.95

Novels, 1875-1886

Includes *A Foregone Conclusion, A Modern Instance, Indian Summer*, and *The Rise of Silas Lapham*. "For those of us who are still able to read novels for pleasure, this is a marvelous book"—Gore Vidal, *NY Review of Books*

See also LIBRARY OF AMERICA

0-940450-04-6 LIBRARY OF AMERICA $35.00

Novels, 1886-1888

Includes *The Minister's Charge, April Hopes*, and *Annie Kilburn*. "A much neglected writer worth discovering or revisiting" —*Wall Street Journal*

0-940450-51-8 LIBRARY OF AMERICA $35.00

The Rise of Silas Lapham

Howell's most famous novel, published in 1885, offers a subtle portrait of a self-made businessman

INTRODUCTION BY KERMIT VANDERBILT

0-14-039030-8 PENGUIN PB $9.95

The Rise of Silas Lapham

0-19-282355-8 OXFORD PB $8.95

A Traveler from Altruria

0-312-11799-X BEDFORD PB $8.66

Henry **James**

"There is, I think, no more nutritive or suggestive truth...than that of the perfect dependence of the 'moral' sense of a work of art on the amount of felt life concerned in producing it. The question comes back thus, obviously, to the kind and degree of the artist's prime sensibility, which is the soil out of which his subject springs. The quality and capacity of that soil, its ability to 'grow' with due freshness and straightness any vision of life, represents, strongly or weakly, the projected morality. That element is but another name for the more or less close connexion of the subject with some mark made on the intelligence, with some sincere experience."—from the preface to the New York Edition of The Portrait of a Lady

The Ambassadors

James's classic "center of consciousness" novel, in which all the events are filtered through the mind of Lambert Strether as he struggles with his mission to bring back Chad Newsome from the lures of Paris

0-19-281703-5 OXFORD PB $4.95

0-14-043233-7 PENGUIN PB $5.95

The American

James's earliest foray into the international theme, introducing Christopher Newman, a wealthy, innocent American in Paris

EDITED BY WILLIAM SPENGEMANN

0-14-039082-0 PENGUIN PB $11.95

The American Scene

Returning to the United States after a lifetime of expatriation, James wrote this complex report on all that had changed for him and for the country

EDITED BY JOHN F. SEARS

0-14-043416-X PENGUIN PB $11.95

The Aspern Papers & The Turn of the Screw

Two of James's most concise and dramatically compelling novellas

EDITED BY ANTHONY CURTIS

0-14-043224-8 PENGUIN PB $5.95

Autobiography

0-691-06584-5 PRINCETON $65.00

The Awkward Age

"In no earlier novel had James called British society so to account. *The Awkward Age* records his complete disenchantment"—Leon Edel

EDITED BY RONALD BLYTHE

0-19-281654-3 OXFORD PB $6.95

The Bostonians

"As a representation of the American actuality, *The Bostonians* is in every way remarkable, the more so because it is so original...Manners have changed since James wrote, but not the peculiar tenuity of the fabric of American social life"—Lionel Trilling

EDITED BY R.D. GOODER

0-19-281639-X OXFORD PB $4.95

Collected Travel Writings: Great Britain and America

Includes *English Hours, The American Scene*, and other writings

EDITED BY RICHARD HOWARD

0-940450-76-3 LIBRARY OF AMERICA $35.00

Collected Travel Writings: The Continent

0-940450-77-1 LIBRARY OF AMERICA $35.00

The Complete Notebooks of Henry James

EDITED BY LEON EDEL AND H. POWERS LYALL

0-19-504397-9 OXFORD PB $13.95

Henry James

Complete Stories, 1892-1898

Part of what will be a five-volume series; 21 stories including "The Turn of the Screw," "The Figure in the Carpet," and "The Altar of the Dead"

EDITED BY JOHN HOLLANDER & DAVID BROMWICH

1-88301-109-4 LIBRARY OF AMERICA $35.00

Complete Stories, 1898-1910

The final phase of James's short fiction, including "The Best in the Jungle" and "The Jolly Corner"

EDITED BY DENIS DONOGHUE

1-88301-110-8 LIBRARY OF AMERICA $35.00

Daisy Miller

EDITED BY GEOFFREY MOORE

0-14-043262-0 PENGUIN PB $5.95

Eight Tales from the Major Phase

Includes *"The Altar of the Dead," "The Figure in the Carpet," "Brooksmith," "The Great Good Place,"* and others

INTRODUCTION BY MORTON DAUWEEN ZABEL

0-393-00286-1 NORTON PB $11.95

The Europeans

A pair of impoverished Continental sophisticates attempt to take advantage of American opportunities

EDITED BY TONY TANNER

0-14-043232-9 PENGUIN PB $6.95

Henry **James**

The Figure in the Carpet & Stories

Also includes *"The Author of Beltraffio," "The Lesson of the Master," "The Middle Years," "The Death of the Lion,"* and others

EDITED BY FRANK KERMODE

0-14-043255-8 PENGUIN PB $11.95

The Golden Bowl

A tragic drama of adultery and betrayal filtered through James's late prose at its most elaborate

EDITED BY GORE VIDAL

0-14-043235-3 PENGUIN PB $7.95

Great Short Works of Henry James

Includes *Washington Square, Daisy Miller, The Aspern Papers, The Pupil, The Turn of the Screw,* and *The Beast in the Jungle*

INTRODUCTION BY ALAN FLOWER

0-06-083040-9 HARPERCOLLINS PB $8.00

Henry James: Novels, 1886-1890

Includes *The Princess Casamassima, The Reverberator, The Tragic Muse*. "Reminds us of how James can surprise us by speaking directly to our present concerns"—*Chicago Tribune*

EDITED BY DANIEL MARK FOGEL

0-940450-56-9 LIBRARY OF AMERICA $37.50

An International Episode & Other Stories

Also includes *"The Pension Beaurepas"* and *"Lady Barberina"*

EDITED BY S. GORLEY PUTT

0-14-043227-2 PENGUIN PB $8.95

Italian Hours

0-271-00726-5 PENN STATE $32.50

Literary Criticism

the most comprehensive collection ever made of James's wide-ranging, superbly nuanced criticism. "Should help to establish James not only as our greatest novelist but also our most comprehensive and original critic"
—Leo Bersani, *The Atlantic Monthly*

EDITED BY LEON EDEL AND MARK WILSON

Volume 1
Essays, American and English Writers

1-940450-22-4 LIBRARY OF AMERICA $32.50

Volume 2
European Writers and Prefaces to the New York Edition

1-940450-23-2 LIBRARY OF AMERICA $32.50

A Little Tour in France

See also **EUROPE** under **TRAVEL LITERATURE** in **FOOD, TRAVEL, AND LEISURE**

0-374-18956-0 FS&G $18.95

The Notebooks of Henry James

EDITED BY F.O. MATTHIESSEN & KENNETH B. MURDOCK

0-226-51104-9 CHICAGO PB $13.50

The Portrait of a Lady

"No other American and few Europeans can match the superb feminine creations of the chief American master of the art of fiction"
—Oscar Cargill

0-19-282362-0 OXFORD PB $4.95

0-14-043223-X PENGUIN PB $9.95

The Princess Casamassima

"The Princess Casamassima, with its opening in the prison and its revolutionary exiles in London, deals with issues and social contrasts of a kind that James had never before attempted"
—Edmund Wilson

EDITED BY DEREK BREWER

0-14-043254-X PENGUIN PB $10.95

Roderick Hudson

A young American painter loses his way in Rome

EDITED BY GEOFFREY MOORE

0-14-043264-7 PENGUIN PB $9.95

The Sacred Fount

Perhaps the most esoteric and difficult of James's fictions, a work so convoluted in its abstraction that some have taken it for a form of self-parody, others for a purposely inscrutable confession

EDITED BY JOHN LYON

0-14-043350-3 PENGUIN PB $10.95

The Sacred Fount

INTRODUCTIONS BY LEON EDEL AND R.P. BLACKMUR

0-8112-1279-3 NEW DIRECTIONS PB $10.95

Selected Letters

EDITED BY LEON EDEL AND F.W. DUPEE

0-674-38793-7 HARVARD $42.50

The Spoils of Poynton

A novel centered on the valuable contents of an English country house

0-14-043288-4 PENGUIN PB $9.95

The Tragic Muse

0-14-043389-9 PENGUIN PB $12.95

The Turn of the Screw and Other Stories

0-19-282927-0 OXFORD PB $4.95

Washington Square

A plain heiress-to-be is courted by a fortune hunter

EDITED BY BRIAN LEE

0-14-043226-4 PENGUIN PB $6.95

Washington Square

0-19-281611-X OXFORD PB $3.95

What Maisie Knew

"If it were not for Henry James's art—his subtlety, his grace, his handy euphemisms—this very modern story about aimless lives and messy marriages would be practically untellable... It is most of all a novel about a small unselfish girl and the ways in which she is passionately victimized by adults"—Paul Theroux

0-19-282428-7 OXFORD PB $4.95

0-14-043248-5 PENGUIN PB $8.95

The Wings of the Dove

A novel of intrigue, guilt, and retribution, often considered the masterpiece of James's late period

EDITED BY JOHN BAYLEY

0-14-043263-9 PENGUIN PB $7.95

William **James**

Essays in Pragmatism

Including "The Will to Believe," "The Sentiment of Rationality," "The Dilemma of Determinism," and "What Pragmatism Means"

See also **WILLIAM JAMES** under **PHILOSOPHY** in **RELIGION, SPIRITUALITY, AND PHILOSOPHY**

0-02-847140-7 FREE PRESS PB $12.95

Essays in Radical Empiricism

0-8032-7589-7 NEBRASKA PB $12.00

The Varieties of Religious Experience

A wide-ranging masterpiece that highlights the personal, subjective, and mystical aspects of religion—an approach that coincides with contemporary tastes

See also **CLASSICS OF WESTERN RELIGIOUS THOUGHT** under **WORLD RELIGION** in **RELIGION, SPIRITUALITY, AND PHILOSOPHY**

0-14-039034-0 PENGUIN PB $10.95

Writings, 1878-1899

Includes *The Will To Believe and Other Essays in Popular Philosophy, Psychology: Briefer Course*, and excerpts from the monumental *Principles of Psychology*

EDITED BY GERALD MEYERS

0-940450-72-0 LIBRARY OF AMERICA $35.00

Writings, 1902-1910

Includes *The Varieties of Religious Experience, Pragmatism, A Pluralistic Universe, The Meaning of Truth, Some Problems of Philosophy,* and *Essays*

EDITED BY BRUCE KUKLICK

0-940450-38-0 LIBRARY OF AMERICA $37.50

Sarah Orne **Jewett**

A Country Doctor

INTRODUCTION BY JOY G. BOYUM & ANN SHAPIRO

0-452-00805-0 NEW AMERICAN LIBRARY PB $10.95

The Country of the Pointed Firs

Willa Cather wrote of this novel: "The young student of American Literature in far distant years to come will take up this book and say 'a masterpiece!'" Sarah Orne Jewett's realistic portrait of a coastal town in Maine, first published in 1896, is now reissued in a superbly illustrated edition, featuring 82 drawings that convey the serenity and emotional power of Jewett's work

ILLUSTRATED BY DOUGLAS ALVORD

0-87923-894-1 GODINE $24.95

0-7812-1313-4 REPRINT SERVICES $59.00

The Country of the Pointed Firs & Other Stories

"If I were to name the three American books which have the possibility of a long, long life, I would say at once *The Scarlet Letter, Huckleberry Finn,* and *The Country of the Pointed Firs*... The latter book seems to me fairly to shine with the reflection of its long, joyous future"—Willa Cather

0-385-09214-8 DOUBLEDAY PB $9.95

Sarah Orne Jewett: Novels and Stories

All of Jewett's best fiction, including her novels, *Deephaven, A Country Doctor,* and *The Country of the Pointed Firs*. "Descriptions so sharply etched you want to put them in your pocket like magic pebbles"—*Chicago Tribune*

EDITED BY MICHAEL DAVITT BELL

0-940450-74-7 LIBRARY OF AMERICA $35.00

Alice Ilgenfritz **Jones** & Ella **Merchant**

Unveiling a Parallel

An 1893 feminist utopian novel that has been out of print for decades, and an intriguing precursor to such titles as *Herland*. The book details two very different countries, discovered on the surface of Mars

See also **THE 19TH CENTURY AND THE INDUSTRIAL REVOLUTION** under **AMERICAN HISTORY** under **WOMEN'S STUDIES** in **SOCIAL STUDIES**

EDITED AND WITH AN INTRODUCTION BY CAROL KOLMERTEN

0-8156-2538-3 SYRACUSE......$34.50
0-8156-0259-6 SYRACUSE PB......$12.95

Frank **Norris**

McTeague: A Story of San Francisco

A pioneering naturalistic study of greed and moral decay, taking its hapless protagonist from San Francisco's Polk Street to the wastes of Death Valley

0-451-52421-7 NEW AMERICAN LIBRARY PB......$5.95
0-14-018769-3 PENGUIN PB......$10.95

Novels and Essays

Includes *Vandover and the Brute, McTeague, The Octopus,* and *Essays*

EDITED BY DONALD PIZER

0-940450-40-2 LIBRARY OF AMERICA......$35.00

The Octopus

"*The Octopus* has been described, justifiably, as the most ambitious novel up to its time since *Moby Dick:* ambitious in terms of its mighty social and philosophical themes—the clash of frontier and monopoly, the impersonal forces represented by technology and corporate structures, the problem of social justice, and the reconciling power of nature"—Kevin Starr

INTRODUCTION BY KEVIN STARR

0-14-039040-5 PENGUIN PB......$9.95

The Pit: A Story of Chicago

The second volume in Norris's uncompleted *Trilogy of the Wheat* evokes the murderous power struggles of 19th-century capitalism

EDITED BY GWENDOLYN JONES

0-14-018758-8 PENGUIN PB......$10.95

James Whitcomb **Riley**

Complete Poetical Works of James Whitcomb Riley

0-253-34989-3 INDIANA......$35.00
0-253-20777-0 INDIANA PB......$24.95

Harriet Prescott **Spofford**

The Amber Gods & Other Stories

The title novella is a symbolic fantasy first published in 1860

EDITED BY ALFRED BENDIXEN

0-8135-1400-2 RUTGERS......$40.00

Mark **Twain**

The Adventures of Huckleberry Finn

"The Mark Twain Library offers... new and accurate texts...sparingly annotated, and integrated once again with the illustrations Mark Twain considered essential to his books" —Robert H. Hirst, General Editor, The Mark Twain Project

EDITED BY WALTER BLAIR & VICTOR FISCHER
ILLUSTRATED BY EDWARD WINDSOR KEMBLE

0-520-05337-0 CALIFORNIA......$35.00
0-520-05520-9 CALIFORNIA PB......$12.95

Adventures of Huckleberry Finn

An edition based on the newly discovered complete manuscript of the novel, including a chapter later deleted by Twain

0-679-44889-6 RANDOM HOUSE......$25.00

The Adventures of Tom Sawyer

0-14-039083-9 VIKING PB......$5.95

The Adventures of Tom Sawyer

EDITED BY JOHN C. GERBER & PAUL BAENDER
ILLUSTRATED BY TRUE WILLIAMS

0-520-04558-0 CALIFORNIA......$35.00
0-520-04559-9 CALIFORNIA PB......$12.00

The Bible According to Mark Twain: Writings on Heaven, Eden, and the Flood

0-8203-1650-4 GEORGIA......$29.95
0-684-82439-6 TOUCHSTONE PB......$14.00

Collected Tales, Sketches, Speeches, and Essays, 1852-1890

0-940450-36-4 LIBRARY OF AMERICA......$35.00

Collected Tales, Sketches, Speeches, and Essays, 1891-1910

0-940450-73-9 LIBRARY OF AMERICA......$35.00

The Complete Short Stories of Mark Twain

EDITED BY CHARLES NEIDER

0-553-21195-1 BDD PB......$5.95

A Connecticut Yankee in King Arthur's Court

The famous fantasy of a factory foreman who wakes up in medieval England

0-14-043064-4 PENGUIN PB......$5.95

A Connecticut Yankee in King Arthur's Court

"To my mind the illustrations are better than the book—which is a good deal for me to say, I reckon"—Mark Twain

EDITED BY BERNARD L. STEIN
ILLUSTRATED BY DANIEL CARTER BEARD

0-520-05109-2 CALIFORNIA PB......$12.95

The Devil's Racetrack: Mark Twain's Great Dark Writings

Selections from *Which Was the Dream?* and *Fables of Man*

EDITED WITH AN INTRODUCTION BY JOHN S. TUCKEY

0-520-03780-4 CALIFORNIA......$35.00
0-520-03893-2 CALIFORNIA PB......$13.95

Following the Equator: A Journey Around the World

A travel classic that has been hard to find in recent years. In 1897 Mark Twain went around the world by steamship, and he recorded his impressions of India, Australia, South Africa, and many other places in this richly humorous, and sharply—sometimes harshly—observant book

0-486-26113-1 DOVER PB......$15.95

The Gilded Age: A Tale of To-Day

This satirical novel was written in collaboration with Charles Dudley Warner

0-452-00999-5 NEW AMERICAN LIBRARY PB......$11.95
0-940450-82-4 LIBRARY OF AMERICA......$35.00

Mark Twain

Historical Romances

Includes *The Prince and the Pauper, A Connecticut Yankee,* and the more serious, elaborately researched *Joan of Arc*

EDITED BY SUSAN K. HARRIS

0-94045-082-8 LIBRARY OF AMERICA......$35.00

Huck Finn and Tom Sawyer Among the Indians & Other Unfinished Stories

0-520-05090-8 CALIFORNIA......$35.00
0-520-05110-6 CALIFORNIA PB......$12.95

The Innocents Abroad

Shrewd observation and typical Twain humor in this familiar book about the New World encountering the Old on a trip to Europe and the Holy Land

See also **EUROPE** under **TRAVEL LITERATURE** in **FOOD, TRAVEL, AND LEISURE**

0-451-52502-7 NEW AMERICAN LIBRARY PB......$5.95

The Innocents Abroad & Roughing It

See also **LIBRARY OF AMERICA**

0-940450-25-9 LIBRARY OF AMERICA......$30.00

Letters from the Earth

EDITED BY BERNARD DE VOTO

0-06-092105-6 HARPERPERENNIAL PB......$12.00

Life on the Mississippi

INTRODUCTION BY JAMES M. COX

0-14-039050-2 PENGUIN PB......$8.95

Mississippi Writings

Includes *The Adventures of Tom Sawyer, Life on the Mississippi, Adventures of Huckleberry Finn,* and *Pudd'nhead Wilson*

0-940450-07-0 LIBRARY OF AMERICA......$30.00

The Mysterious Stranger & Other Stories

0-451-52458-6 NEW AMERICAN LIBRARY PB......$4.95

Mark Twain

Number Forty-Four: The Mysterious Stranger

The only authentic version of Twain's pessimistic fantasy

EDITED BY WILLIAM M. GIBSON & JOHN S. TUCKEY

0-520-04544-0 CALIFORNIA $35.00
0-520-04545-9 CALIFORNIA PB $12.95

A Pen Warmed Up in Hell: Mark Twain in Protest

EDITED WITH INTRODUCTION BY FREDERICK ANDERSON

0-8095-9043-3 BORGO $29.00
0-317-02692-5 HARPER & ROW PB $6.95

The Prince and the Pauper

Twin boys exchange identities in Tudor England

0-440-47186-9 BDD PB $3.50

The Prince and the Pauper

FOREWORD AND NOTES BY VICTOR FISCHER & MICHAEL B. FRANK

0-520-05108-4 CALIFORNIA PB $12.95

Pudd'nhead Wilson

A curious blend of detective novel and racial melodrama

EDITED BY MALCOLM BRADBURY

0-14-043040-7 PENGUIN PB $7.95

Roughing It

Twain out West, with satirical sidelights on Mormons, outlaws, and others

EDITED BY HAMLIN HILL

0-14-039010-3 PENGUIN PB $10.95

Roughing It

0-520-20559-6 CALIFORNIA PB $16.95

Tales, Speeches, Essays, and Sketches

EDITED BY TOM QUIRK

0-14-043417-8 PENGUIN PB $10.95

Tom Sawyer Abroad & Tom Sawyer, Detective

INTRODUCTION AND NOTES BY JOHN C. GERBER

0-520-04560-2 CALIFORNIA $35.00
0-520-04561-0 CALIFORNIA PB $11.95

20th-Century American Fiction

"This thing is an essentially American thing this sense of a space of time and what is to be done within this space of time not in any way excepting in the way that it is inevitable that there is this space of time and anybody who is an American feels what is inside this space of time and so well they do what they do within this space of time, and so ultimately it is a thing contained within ...Think of anything, of cowboys, of movies, of detective stories, of anybody who goes anywhere or stays at home and is an American and you will realize that it is something strictly American to conceive a space that is filled with moving, a space of time that is always filled with moving."—Gertrude Stein in "The Gradual Making of *The Making of Americans*"

From the Turn of the Century to World War II

Edward **Anderson**

Hungry Men

The boxcars and soup kitchens of the Depression, transcribed with deadpan precision

0-8061-2556-X OKLAHOMA PB $12.95

Thieves Like Us

An unforgettable novel of Oklahoma outlaws on the run, published in 1937

0-8061-2503-9 OKLAHOMA PB $14.95

Sherwood **Anderson**

Certain Things Last: The Selected Short Stories of Sherwood Anderson

EDITED BY CHARLES MOLDIN

1-56858-022-3 FOUR WALLS PB $14.95

Sherwood Anderson

Death in the Woods & Other Stories

"One of the very best and finest writers in the English language today"—F. Scott Fitzgerald

0-87140-140-1 NORTON PB $7.95

Poor White

0-8112-1242-4 NEW DIRECTIONS PB $12.95

The Teller's Tales: Short Stories

"Sherwood Anderson had a sweetness, and sweetness is rare"—Gertrude Stein

EDITED BY FRANK GADO

0-912756-08-X UNION COLLEGE PB $5.95

Windy McPherson's Son

0-252-06357-0 ILLINOIS PB $13.95

Winesburg, Ohio

Life in a small midwestern town at the beginning of the 20th century. "The only storyteller of his generation who left a mark on the style and vision of the generation that followed...Hemingway, Faulkner, Wolfe, Steinbeck, Caldwell, Saroyan, and Henry Miller...Each owes an unmistakable debt to Anderson"—Malcolm Cowley

INTRODUCTION BY MALCOLM COWLEY

0-14-018655-7 PENGUIN PB $8.95

Djuna **Barnes**

At the Roots of the Stars: The Short Plays

Hitherto largely unknown plays, experimental and naturalistic alike, by the author of *Nightwood*

See also **THE '20S, '30S, AND '40S** under **20TH-CENTURY AMERICAN DRAMA**

1-55713-160-0 SUN & MOON PB $12.95

The Book of Repulsive Women

1-55713-173-2 SUN & MOON PB $6.95

Collected Stories

EDITED BY PHILIP HERRING

1-55713-226-7 SUN & MOON $24.95

Ladies Almanack

0-916583-88-0 DALKEY ARCHIVE PB $9.95

New York

Journalistic pieces by the author of *Nightwood*, written between 1913 and 1919. "The great interviewer...explores the lives of tenement-dwellers, middle-class tangoers, squatters, suffragists, ordinary working men, and the literary Bohemians...In these still-fresh portraits, the city of New York is perceived by Barnes as an enormous landscape of theater, of circuses, operas, street performances, carneys, hawkers, con-men, clowns, and just a few saints"—Douglas Messerli

See also **REPORTING** under **20TH-CENTURY AMERICAN ESSAYS AND JOURNALISM**

0-940650-82-7 SUN & MOON $24.95
0-940650-99-1 SUN & MOON PB $12.95

Nightwood

"What I would leave the reader prepared to find is the great achievement of a style, the beauty of phrasing, the brilliance of wit and characterization, and a quality of horror and doom very nearly related to that of Elizabethan tragedy"—T.S. Eliot

INTRODUCTION BY T.S. ELIOT

0-8112-0005-1 NEW DIRECTIONS PB $9.95

Nightwood: The Original Version

Restores significant cuts made to Barnes's manuscript on first publication

1-56478-080-5 DALKEY ARCHIVE $23.95

Ryder

0-916583-55-4 DALKEY ARCHIVE PB $11.95

Smoke & Other Early Stories

"Fourteen stories, startlingly strange, cranky even, but also as raw and exciting as swigs of poteen"—Valentine Cunningham, *TLS*

EDITED BY DOUGLAS MESSERLI

1-55713-014-0 SUN & MOON PB $10.95

The Book of Repulsive Women: 8 Rhythms and 5 Drawings

Originally published as a chapbook in 1915

1-5571-3173-2 SUN AND MOON PB $6.95

Kay **Boyle**

The Crazy Hunter

0-8112-1233-5 NEW DIRECTIONS PB $6.00

Death of a Man
The relationship between a pro-Nazi doctor and a young American woman, set in the Tyrolean Alps in the mid-'30s
0-8112-1089-8 NEW DIRECTIONS PB $10.95

Fifty Stories
0-8112-1206-8 NEW DIRECTIONS PB $15.95

Life Being the Best & Other Stories
INTRODUCTION BY SANDRA W. SPANIER
0-8112-1053-7 NEW DIRECTIONS PB $8.95

Three Short Novels
INTRODUCTION BY MARGARET ATWOOD
0-8112-1149-5 NEW DIRECTIONS PB $10.95

Pearl S. **Buck**

The Good Earth
See also **THE '30s** under **THE GREAT FICTION BESTSELLERS 1930-1995** in **POPULAR READING**
0-89966-299-4 BUCCANEER $27.95

The House of Earth: The Good Earth Trilogy
1-55921-147-4 MOYER BELL $29.95

James Branch **Cabell**

The Cream of the Jest
A cunning literary game which plays with the line between fantasy and humdrum reality
EDITED BY JOSEPH M. FLORA
0-8084-0396-6 NEW COLLEGE PB $11.95

Jurgen: A Comedy of Justice
This ribald medieval fantasy had censorship problems when first published in the '20s
0-486-23507-6 DOVER PB $7.95

Abraham **Cahan**

The Rise of David Levinsky
The classic novel, by the editor of the *Jewish Daily Forward*, of material success and the elusive quest for happiness in the New World
0-06-131912-0 HARPERCOLLINS PB $21.60

Yekl and the Imported Bridegroom & Other Stories of the New York Ghetto
These stories of immigrant life on the Lower East Side reflect the Jewish struggle for acceptance in American society, which often conflicted with the desire to remain faithful to an ancient culture
0-486-22427-9 DOVER PB $6.95

James M. **Cain**
"A poet of the tabloid murder."—Edmund Wilson

Double Indemnity
Adultery, greed, and the perfect insurance policy: the ultimate in simmering cynicism
See also **AMERICA** under **RISE OF THE MODERN CRIME NOVEL** under **CRIME FICTION** in **POPULAR READING**
0-679-72322-6 BLACK LIZARD PB $8.00

Mildred Pierce
Not a crime novel, but stamped with Cain's deadpan, anti-heroic realism
0-679-72321-8 VINTAGE PB $8.95

The Postman Always Rings Twice
The stark death-row confession of an ordinary guy who became a killer, thanks to the lustful magnetism of a luncheonette owner's frustrated wife
0-679-72325-0 VINTAGE PB $8.00

Three by Cain
Includes *Serenade, Love's Lovely Counterfeit,* and *The Butterfly*
0-679-72323-4 VINTAGE PB $13.00

Erskine **Caldwell**

Call It Experience
FOREWORD BY ERIK BLEDSOE
0-8203-1849-3 GEORGIA PB $15.95

God's Little Acre
0-8203-1662-8 GEORGIA $25.00

Journeyman
FOREWORD BY EDWIN T. ARNOLD
0-8203-1848-5 GEORGIA PB $14.95

The Stories of Erskine Caldwell
0-8203-1693-8 GEORGIA $45.00
0-8203-1694-6 GEORGIA PB $24.95

Tobacco Road
Once-shocking saga of the shiftless and earthy Lester family. "A master illusionist who can create, as Hemingway did, an impression of absolute reality"—*Time*
0-8203-1661-X GEORGIA PB $9.95

Willa **Cather**
Cather is primarily known for novels that "celebrate the pioneer spirit so essential to our mythic notion of an ordained manifest American destiny." Her works also "explore the increasing social restrictions brought to bear on American society and on women in particular."—Sharon O'Brien

Alexander's Bridge
INTRODUCTION BY SHARON O'BRIEN
0-89968-491-2 LIGHTYEAR $16.95
0-8032-5863-1 NEBRASKA PB $8.00

Death Comes for the Archbishop
A novel of 19th-century mission life in New Mexico
0-679-60050-7 MODERN LIBRARY $13.50

Early Novels and Stories
Includes *O Pioneers!*, *Song of the Lark*, *My Antonia*, and *One of Ours*. "To reread Cather is to rediscover an arresting chapter in the national past"—*LA Times*
EDITED BY SHARON O'BRIEN
0-940450-39-9 LIBRARY OF AMERICA $35.00

Later Novels
Includes *A Lost Lady*, *The Professor's House*, *Death Comes for the Archbishop*, *Shadows on the Rock*, *Lucy Gayheart*, and *Sapphira and the Slave Girl*
EDITED BY SHARON O'BRIEN
0-940450-52-6 LIBRARY OF AMERICA $32.50

A Lost Lady
0-679-72887-2 VINTAGE PB $9.00

Lucy Gayheart
0-394-71756-2 RANDOM HOUSE PB $8.00

My Antonia
This portrait of a pioneer woman is generally considered to be Cather's greatest work
0-395-07514-9 HOUGHTON MIFFLIN $24.95
0-14-018764-2 PENGUIN PB $9.95

My Antonia
"No romantic novel ever written in America, by man or woman, is one half so beautiful as *My Antonia*"—H.L. Mencken
NEW FOREWORD BY KATHLEEN NORRIS
0-395-75514-X HOUGHTON MIFFLIN PB $5.95

My Mortal Enemy
0-679-73179-2 VINTAGE PB $8.95

O Pioneers!
The classic novel of pioneer life on the Nebraska prairie, first published in 1913, about which Cather said "this was the first time I walked off on my own feet"
0-14-018775-8 PENGUIN PB $7.95

One of Ours
0-679-73744-8 VINTAGE PB $12.00

The Professor's House
0-679-73180-6 VINTAGE PB $10.00

Sapphira and the Slave Girl
0-394-71434-2 VINTAGE PB $9.00

Shadows on the Rock
A chronicle of 17th-century Quebec
0-394-71680-9 VINTAGE PB $9.00

The Song of the Lark
A young woman artist attempts to escape from the restrictions of life in a small Colorado town, becoming a great Wagnerian soprano in the Metropolitan Opera
0-88411-288-8 AMEREON $32.95
0-395-34530-8 HOUGHTON MIFFLIN PB $9.95

The Troll Garden
This collection of short stories was Cather's first published book of fiction
AFTERWORD BY KATHERINE ANNE PORTER
0-553-21385-7 BDD PB $3.50

Stories, Poems, and Other Writings
Includes the novellas *Alexander's Bridge*, *My Mortal Enemy*, four short story collections, critical essays, and Cather's only book of poetry. "A treasury of riches, containing much that has been difficult to find"—*Chicago Tribune*
EDITED BY SHARON O'BRIEN
0-940450-71-2 LIBRARY OF AMERICA $35.00

Willa Cather's Collected Short Fiction, 1892-1912
EDITED BY VIRGINIA FAULKNER
INTRODUCTION BY M.R. BENNETT
0-8032-0770-0 NEBRASKA $45.00

Raymond **Chandler**

Later Novels & Other Writings
Includes *The Lady in the Lake*, *The Little Sister*, *The Long Goodbye*, and *Playback*, as well as the screenplay for *Double Indemnity* and selected articles and letters
See also **THE HARD-BOILED DETECTIVE** under **CRIME FICTION** in **POPULAR READING**
EDITED BY FRANK MACSHANE
1-88301-108-6 LIBRARY OF AMERICA $35.00

Raymond **Chandler**

Stories & Early Novels

Includes most of Chandler's pulp stories as well as *The Big Sleep*, *Farewell, My Lovely*, and *The High Window*

See also **THE HARD-BOILED DETECTIVE** under **CRIME FICTION** in **POPULAR READING**

EDITED BY FRANK MACSHANE

1-88301-107-8 LIBRARY OF AMERICA $35.00

e.e. **cummings**

The Enormous Room

Cumming's only novel is based on his experiences in a French jail during World WarI

EDITED BY GEORGE J. FIRMAGE

INTRODUCTION BY RICHARD S. KENNEDY

0-87140-150-9 NORTON PB $11.95

H.D. (Hilda Doolittle)

Bid Me to Live

"H.D.'s wit, sense of rhythm, and control of language prove the inadequacy of the imagist label that is so often applied to this writer" —*Library Journal*

0-933806-66-3 BLACK SWAN PB $13.95

Hermione

An autobiographical self-portrait. "In writing *Hermione* H.D. committed a daring act, the harbinger of her daringly unconventional life and a lifetime of unconventional works" —*Arizona Quarterly*

INTRODUCTION BY PERDITA SCHAFFNER

0-8112-0817-6 NEW DIRECTIONS PB $10.95

Kora & Ka

INTRODUCTION BY ROBERT SPOO

0-8112-1317-X NEW DIRECTIONS PB $7.00

Nights

INTRODUCTION BY PERDITA SCHAFFNER

0-8112-0979-2 NEW DIRECTIONS PB $19.95

John **Dos Passos**

1919

"Dos Passos reports all his characters' utterances to us in the style of a statement to the Press. Their words are thereby cut off from thought, and become pure utterances...Dos Passos' man is a hybrid creature, an interior-exterior being. We go on living with him and within him, with his vacillating, individual consciousness, when suddenly it wavers, weakens, and is diluted in the collective consciousness ...I regard Dos Passos as the greatest writer of our time"—Jean-Paul Sartre

0-88411-345-0 AMEREON $25.95

0-451-52468-3 NEW AMERICAN LIBRARY PB $6.95

The 42nd Parallel

"What Dos Passos created with *The 42nd Parallel* was in fact another American invention...the greatest possible homage to art as a new kind of 'practicality' in getting down the facts of human existence in our century" —Alfred Kazin

0-451-52457-8 NEW AMERICAN LIBRARY PB $7.95

The Big Money

"A furious and somber poem, written in a mood of revulsion even more powerful than that which T.S. Eliot expressed in *The Waste Land*" —Malcolm Cowley

INTRODUCTION BY ALFRED KAZIN

0-451-52401-2 NEW AMERICAN LIBRARY PB $7.95

U.S.A.

An annotated one-volume edition of Dos Passos's masterpiece

1-88301-114-0 LIBRARY OF AMERICA $40.00

Manhattan Transfer

A novel of New York City in the '20s, in many ways a preparation for the larger scale of *U.S.A.* "It may be the foundation for a whole new school of novel-writing"—Sinclair Lewis

0-8376-0433-8 BENTLEY $22.00

0-395-57423-4 HOUGHTON MIFFLIN PB $13.95

Three Soldiers

A realistic novel of World War I, published in 1921

0-88184-413-6 CARROLL & GRAF PB $9.95

Theodore **Dreiser**

An American Tragedy

Dreiser's masterpiece is a realistic look at the dark side of the American Dream

0-451-52465-9 NEW AMERICAN LIBRARY PB $7.95

The Financier

The first and best volume of the Frank Cowperwood trilogy is the closest thing to an epic of American business life

0-452-00825-5 PLUME PB $14.95

Jennie Gerhardt

FOREWOOD BY HELEN YGLESIAS

0-19-282743-X OXFORD PB $5.95

Sister Carrie

Dreiser's novel of a "fallen woman" was a literary scandal when first published in 1900

See also **YOUNG ADULT FICTION** in **BOOKS FOR YOUNG READERS**

0-451-52273-7 NEW AMERICAN LIBRARY PB $4.95

0-14-018828-2 PENGUIN PB $11.95

Sister Carrie, Jennie Gerhardt & Twelve Men

Dreiser's first two great novels, along with the non-fiction sketches *Twelve Men*

See also **LIBRARY OF AMERICA**

EDITED BY RICHARD LEHAN

0-940450-41-0 LIBRARY OF AMERICA $35.00

W.E.B. **DuBois**

Dark Princess

0-87805-764-1 MISSISSIPPI $40.00

0-87805-765-X MISSISSIPPI PB $16.95

John **Fante**

Fante began publishing his largely autobiographical novels in the late '30s; they are currently enjoying a rediscovery. Reissued by Black Sparrow in beautiful editions.

1933 Was a Bad Year

0-87685-656-3 BLACK SPARROW $20.00

0-87685-655-5 BLACK SPARROW PB $11.00

Ask the Dust

A young writer in California struggling for, and finding shreds of, literary success while falling in love with an older woman and dealing with the poverty inherent in his pursuits. A great book

0-87685-443-9 BLACK SPARROW PB $12.00

The Brotherhood of the Grape

0-87685-726-8 BLACK SPARROW PB $12.00

Dreams from Bunker Hill

0-87685-528-1 BLACK SPARROW PB $11.00

Full of Life

0-87685-719-5 BLACK SPARROW $20.00

0-87685-718-7 BLACK SPARROW PB $11.00

The Road to Los Angeles

0-87685-649-0 BLACK SPARROW PB $11.00

Wait Until Spring, Bandini

Fante's first novel, of which he later said, "all of the people of my writing life, all of my characters are to be found in this early work"

0-87685-555-9 BLACK SPARROW $25.00

0-87685-554-0 BLACK SPARROW PB $14.00

West of Rome

0-87685-677-6 BLACK SPARROW PB $13.00

The Wine of Youth: Selected Stories of John Fante

0-87685-582-6 BLACK SPARROW PB $14.00

Sui Sin **Far**

Mrs. Spring Fragrance and Other Writings

0-252-02133-9 ILLINOIS $39.95

0-252-06419-4 ILLINOIS PB $15.95

James T. **Farrell**

Studs Lonigan

Farrell's trilogy of working-class youth—originally published as *Young Lonigan, The Young Manhood of Studs Lonigan*, and *Judgement Day*—is a monument of social realism

0-252-02062-6 ILLINOIS $49.95

0-252-06282-5 ILLINOIS PB $17.95

William **Faulkner**

"Faulkner at his best—even sometimes at his worst—has a power, a richness of life, an intensity to be found in no other American writer of our time."—Malcolm Cowley

Absalom, Absalom!

Quentin Compson (from *The Sound and the Fury*) tells the story of the rise and fall of the Sutpen Family

EDITED BY NOEL POLK

0-394-55634-8 MODERN LIBRARY $25.00

0-679-73218-7 VINTAGE PB $11.00

William Faulkner

As I Lay Dying
The Bundrens—a backwoods family—trek into Jefferson (the seat of Faulkner's mythical Yoknapatawpha County) to bury their mother
EDITED BY NOEL POLK
0-679-73225-X VINTAGE PB $10.00

The Collected Stories
Includes 42 short stories
0-394-72257-4 RANDOM HOUSE PB $18.00

A Fable
A Second Coming parable set in World War I, which was awarded the Pulitzer Prize upon its publication in 1954
0-394-72413-5 VINTAGE PB $10.00

Flags in the Dust
Published in a much shorter version as *Sartoris* in 1929, this is the first of the Yoknapatawpha novels, tracing the history of the Sartoris clan from antebellum days through World War I
EDITED BY DOUGLAS DAY
0-394-71239-0 RANDOM HOUSE PB $9.00

Go Down, Moses
A collection of stories, including the great novella *The Bear*
0-679-73217-9 VINTAGE PB $10.00

The Hamlet
The first novel in the trilogy which includes *The Town* and *The Mansion. The Hamlet* chronicles the inexorable rise of the Snopes family
0-679-73653-0 VINTAGE PB $12.00

Intruder in the Dust
A black teenager, a white teenager, and a 70-year-old spinster clear a black man unjustly accused of murder
0-679-73651-4 VINTAGE PB $10.00

Knight's Gambit
"Six masterly whodunits"—*NY Times*
0-394-72729-0 VINTAGE PB $10.00

Light in August
Joe Christmas, a drifter of ambiguous race, plays out the doom of the South, while Lena Groves, serene and pregnant, seeks the father of her child
EDITED BY NOEL POLK
0-679-73226-8 VINTAGE PB $12.00

The Mansion
A tale of vengeance, the final volume in the Snopes trilogy
0-394-70282-4 VINTAGE PB $10.00

Mosquitoes
Faulkner's second novel is an uncharacteristic satire set in New Orleans
0-87140-167-3 NORTON PB $13.00

Novels, 1930-1935
The first volume in the Library of America's collected Faulkner, includes *As I Lay Dying, Sanctuary, Light in August*, and *Pylon*. "At last readers can enjoy and ponder these works in the form intended by their author. A distinguished addition to a distinctive series"
—*Library Journal*
EDITED BY JOSEPH BLOTNER AND NOEL POLK
0-940450-26-7 LIBRARY OF AMERICA $35.00

Novels, 1936-1940
America's greatest modern novelist at the height of his powers. Includes *Absalom, Absalom!, The Unvanquished, If I Forget Thee, Jerusalem (The Wild Palms)*, and *The Hamlet*. The second volume in the Library of America series
EDITED BY JOSEPH BLOTNER AND NOEL POLK
0-940450-55-0 LIBRARY OF AMERICA $35.00

Novels, 1942-1954
This third volume is comprised of *Go Down, Moses, Intruder in the Dust, Requiem for a Nun*, and *A Fable*, which earned a Pulitzer Prize
EDITED BY JOSEPH BLOTNER AND NOEL POLK
0-940450-85-2 LIBRARY OF AMERICA $35.00

The Portable Faulkner
This anthology, which weaves together stories and novel excerpts to create a portrait of Yoknaptawpha County, played a decisive role in rehabilitating Faulkner's reputation in the '40s
EDITED BY MALCOLM COWLEY
0-14-015018-8 VIKING PB $14.95

Pylon
The catch-as-catch-can lives of barn storming stunt pilots, based on the career and tragic early death of Faulkner's brother
EDITED BY NOEL POLK
0-394-74741-0 VINTAGE PB $7.00

The Reivers
Faulkner's last novel (a Pulitzer Prize winner in 1962) is a picaresque story about a car, a racehorse, and a prostitute
0-679-74192-5 VINTAGE PB $12.00

Requiem for a Nun
In this sequel to *Sanctuary*, written partially in dramatic form, Temple Drake undergoes a painful redemption. "Among the most successful of Faulkner's many experiments in narrative form"—Malcolm Cowley
0-394-71412-1 VINTAGE PB $10.00

Sanctuary
Temple Drake, a college girl, is kidnapped, raped, and systematically degraded by Popeye, a cold-blooded killer
EDITED BY NOEL POLK
0-679-74814-8 VINTAGE PB $10.00

Selected Short Stories of William Faulkner
0-679-42478-4 MODERN LIBRARY $14.50

Soldiers' Pay
Faulkner's first novel is the story of a wounded World War I vet's homecoming
0-8714-0166-5 NORTON PB $13.00

The Sound and the Fury
The fall of the Compson family, a story of suicide and incestuous desire told by three family members (including the retarded Benjy) and finally in a third-person account which focuses on the black servants
EDITED BY NOEL POLK
0-394-53241-4 RANDOM HOUSE $25.00
0-679-73224-1 VINTAGE PB $10.00

The Sound and the Fury
0-679-60017-5 MODERN LIBRARY $14.50

Three Famous Short Novels
Includes *Spotted Horses, Old Man*, and *The Bear*
0-394-70149-6 RANDOM HOUSE PB $9.00

The Town
The second volume of the Snopes trilogy traces the rise of Flem Snopes, who through treachery and trickery becomes Jefferson's leading citizen
0-394-70184-4 RANDOM HOUSE PB $9.00

The Uncollected Stories of William Faulkner
Forty-five stories
EDITED BY JOSEPH BLOTNER
0-394-74656-2 RANDOM HOUSE PB $18.00

The Unvanquished
An episodic novel of the Civil War
0-679-73652-2 VINTAGE PB $10.00

The Wild Palms
Two interwoven stories set during a flood on the Mississippi
0-394-60513-6 MODERN LIBRARY $20.00
0-394-70262-X RANDOM HOUSE PB $8.00

Jessie **Fauset**

The Chinaberry Tree
1-55553-207-1 NORTHEASTERN PB $15.95

Edna **Ferber**

So Big
0-252-06376-7 ILLINOIS PB $13.95

F. Scott **Fitzgerald**

Afternoon of an Author
Contains 14 uncollected stories and 6 essays
INTRODUCTION BY ARTHUR MIZENER
0-684-16469-8 SCRIBNERS $22.50

Babylon Revisited & Other Stories
Ten stories from Fitzgerald's most creative period, the years between 1920 and 1937
0-02-019980-5 MACMILLAN PB $5.95

The Basil and Josephine Stories
EDITED BY JOHN KUEHL & JACKSON R. BRYER
0-02-019870-1 MACMILLAN PB $6.00

The Beautiful and the Damned
An underrated and often overlooked early novel: a young man and woman are undermined by greed and destroyed by their own excesses
0-684-15153-7 MACMILLAN $55.00
0-02-019970-8 SCRIBNERS PB $8.00

The Crack-Up
A selection of later writings which becomes an autobiographical account of Fitzgerald's decline: "Sometimes I don't know whether I'm real or whether I'm a character in one of my own novels"
EDITED BY EDMUND WILSON
0-8112-1247-5 NEW DIRECTIONS PB $10.95

Flappers and Philosophers
INTRODUCTION BY ARTHUR MIZENER
0-671-55099-3 WASHINGTON SQUARE PB $4.99

The Last Tycoon
The unfinished last novel in which Fitzgerald drew upon his own Hollywood experiences to tell the story of a brilliant film producer, allegedly modeled on Irving Thalberg
0-684-15311-4 MACMILLAN $35.00
0-02-019950-3 SCRIBNERS PB $6.00

F. Scott **Fitzgerald**

The Great Gatsby

One of the great American works of this century. "There is a moment in any real author's career when he suddenly becomes capable of doing his best work. He has found a fable that expresses his central truth and everything falls into place around it, so that his whole experience of life is available for use in his fiction. Something like that happened to Fitzgerald when he invented the story of Jimmy Gatz, otherwise known as Jay Gatsby, and it explains the amazing richness and scope of a very short novel"—Malcolm Cowley

0-02-019881-7 SCRIBNERS PB $9.00

The Pat Hobby Stories

Stories of a struggling Hollywood scriptwriter. "[Fitzgerald's] last word from his last home, for much of what he felt about Hollywood and about himself permeated these stories"
—Arnold Gingrich

INTRODUCTION BY ARNOLD GINGRICH

0-02-019910-4 COLLIER PB $5.95

The Short Stories of F. Scott Fitzgerald

0-684-19160-1 SCRIBNERS $29.95

Six Tales of the Jazz Age & Other Stories

Nine stories, including "The Jelly-Bean," "The Camel's Back," and "Gretchen's Forty Winks"

0-684-71762-X SCRIBNERS PB $10.00

Stories of F. Scott Fitzgerald

Twenty-eight stories, including "Babylon Revisited" and "The Diamond as Big as the Ritz"

0-684-15366-1 MACMILLAN $50.00

Tender Is the Night

The gradual decline of psychiatrist Dick Diver mirrors Fitzgerald's own destiny

0-89190-600-2 AMEREON $23.95
0-684-71763-8 MICROSOFT PB $12.00

This Side of Paradise

Fitzgerald's first novel painted an influential picture of young collegians of the '20s

0-684-80072-1 SCRIBNERS PB $10.00

F. Scott **Fitzgerald** & Judith **Baughman**

F. Scott Fitzgerald on Authorship

EDITED BY MATTHEW JOSEPH BRUCCOLI AND JUDITH BAUGHMAN

1-57003-146-0 SOUTH CAROLINA $29.95

Daniel **Fuchs**

Summer in Williamsburg

0-88184-006-8 CARROLL & GRAF PB $8.95

Martha **Gellhorn**

Point of No Return

0-8032-7051-8 NEBRASKA PB $12.00

Inez Hayes **Gillmore**

Angel Island

A feminist fantasy first published in 1914

0-405-10979-2 AYER $36.95

Ellen **Glasgow**

Barren Ground

A woman's struggle to define herself in rural Virginia. "Glasgow's was a wit raised to the dignity of a style, a wit that peered through her affection for the life she described and summed up her exasperation with it"
—Alfred Kazin, *On Native Ground*

0-15-610685-X HARCOURT BRACE PB $15.00

The Romantic Comedians

0-8139-1615-1 VIRGINIA PB $14.95

The Sheltered Life

0-8139-1514-7 VIRGINIA PB $12.95

Vein of Iron

0-15-193497-5 HARCOURT BRACE PB $7.95

Virginia

0-14-039072-3 PENGUIN PB $12.95

Michael **Gold**

Jews Without Money

A 1935 novel about New York's Lower East Side

0-88184-026-2 CARROLL & GRAF PB $8.95

Caroline **Gordon**

Gordon is noted as a penetrating observer of the social values of her native Kentucky

Aleck Maury, Sportsman

0-8203-1866-3 GEORGIA PB $15.95

The Collected Stories

INTRODUCTION BY ROBERT PENN WARREN

0-8071-1630-0 LSU PB $16.95

Ernest **Hemingway**

Across the River and into the Trees

The love between an American colonel and an Italian countess during World War II

0-02-051920-6 MACMILLAN PB $7.00

The Complete Short Stories of Ernest Hemingway: The Finca Vigia Edition

0-684-18668-3 SCRIBNERS $40.00

A Farewell to Arms

A love story set on the Italian front of World War I

0-684-15562-1 SCRIBNERS $35.00
0-02-051900-1 SCRIBNERS PB $5.95

The Fifth Column & Four Stories of the Spanish Civil War

0-684-15815-9 MACMILLAN $40.00
0-684-12723-7 MACMILLAN PB $9.95

For Whom the Bell Tolls

A young American in an antifascist unit during the Spanish Civil War

0-684-10239-0 MACMILLAN $25.00
0-684-80335-6 SCRIBNERS PB $12.00

In Our Time

Short stories and vignettes, first published in 1925, that introduced readers to Nick Adams

0-684-16480-9 MACMILLAN $30.00

Islands in the Stream

0-684-16499-X MACMILLAN $50.00
0-684-14642-8 MACMILLAN PB $16.00

Men Without Women

This 1927 collection includes some of Hemingway's most celebrated stories, among them "Fifty Grand," "The Undefeated," and "The Killers"

0-02-051890-0 MACMILLAN PB $6.00

The Nick Adams Stories

0-684-16940-1 MACMILLAN PB $10.95

The Old Man and the Sea

An old Cuban fisherman and his battle with a giant marlin

0-684-80122-1 MACMILLAN PB $9.00

The Short Stories: The First Forty-Nine Stories

Includes a brief preface by Hemingway himself

0-684-80334-8 SIMON & SCHUSTER PB $14.00

Short Stories of Ernest Hemingway

Forty-nine stories, including "The Snows of Kilimanjaro" and "Soldier's Home"

0-684-15155-3 MACMILLAN $50.00

The Snows of Kilimanjaro & Other Stories

0-06-840444-1 SCRIBNERS PB $9.00

The Sun Also Rises

This classic portrait of the expatriate generation first appeared in 1926

0-684-10250-1 SCRIBNERS $20.00
0-684-80071-3 SCRIBNERS PB $10.00

Ernest Hemingway

To Have and Have Not

The story of Harry Morgan, who runs contraband between Key West and Cuba

0-684-81898-1 SCRIBNERS PB $11.00

The Torrents of Spring

Hemingway's first novel, a parody of Sherwood Anderson

0-02-550750-8 SCRIBNERS $30.00

Winner Take Nothing

Includes "A Clean, Well-Lighted Place," "The Gambler, the Nun, and the Radio," and 12 other stories; first published in 1933

0-02-051820-X MACMILLAN PB $8.00

Josephine **Herbst**

The Executioner Waits

"For sustained passion its excellence is unsurpassed"—William Carlos Williams

0-404-58440-3 AMS $34.00

John **Hersey**

Key West Tales

0-679-42992-1 KNOPF $23.00

Langston **Hughes**

The Langston Hughes Reader

See also **THE MODERNIST GENERATIONS** under **20TH-CENTURY AMERICAN POETRY**

0-8076-0057-1 BRAZILLER $17.50

Not Without Laughter

A novel of small-town Kansas life

0-02-052200-2 SCRIBNERS PB $6.95

The Ways of White Folks

0-679-72817-1 VINTAGE PB $11.00

Zora Neale **Hurston**

Zora Neale Hurston was a leading light of African-American writing in the '30s, but she died in obscurity and poverty in 1960, her books long out of print. Today Hurston's novels and folkloric studies are undergoing an extraordinary revival, making her more widely read than ever in her lifetime.

Jonah's Gourd Vine

Her first novel, published in 1934. "Hurston's language is superb, rich with wordplay and proverbs"—Rita Dove

0-06-091651-6 HARPERCOLLINS PB $13.00

Moses: Man of the Mountain

The Old Testament Moses and the Moses of black myth are combined in a reworking of Exodus. "One of Hurston's most fascinating books, clearly her most ambitious" —Kenneth Kinnamon

INTRODUCTION BY BLYDEN JACKSON

0-06-091994-9 HARPERCOLLINS PB $13.50

Seraph on the Suwanee

First published in 1948, this long, realistic novel of poor white "Florida Crackers" represented a departure for Hurston

0-06-097359-5 HARPERCOLLINS PB $13.00

Spunk: The Selected Stories of Zora Neale Hurston

FOREWORD BY BOB CALLAHAN

0-913666-79-3 TURTLE ISLAND PB $9.95

Tell My Horse

A fascinating glimpse into voodoo, folkways, politics, and other aspects of life in Jamaica and Haiti

0-06-091649-4 HARPERCOLLINS PB $13.00

Gods always behave like the people who make them. One can see the hand of the Haitian peasant in that boisterous god, Guede, because he does and says the things that the peasants would like to do and say. You can see him in the market women, in the domestic servant who now and then appears before her employer "mounted" by this god who takes occasion to say many stinging things to the boss…Guede is never visible. He manifests himself by "mounting" a subject as a rider mounts a horse, then he speaks and acts through his mount. The person mounted does nothing of his own accord. He is the horse of the loa until the spirit departs. Under the whip and guidance of the spirit-rider, the "horse" does and says many things that he or she would never have uttered un-ridden.

TELL MY HORSE

Their Eyes Were Watching God

This is Hurston's masterpiece, a gorgeous novel of a young woman's search for identity

0-06-091650-8 HARPERCOLLINS PB $13.00

Zora Neale Hurston: Complete Novels and Stories

Dedicated to Hurston the fiction-writer, this volume includes her celebrated novel *Their Eyes Were Watching God*

See also **LIBRARY OF AMERICA**

0-940450-83-6 LIBRARY OF AMERICA $35.00

Folklore, Memoirs, and Other Writings

Volume II draws on Hurston's work in anthropology with her ethnographical work, folklore, memoirs, and selected articles

See also **LIBRARY OF AMERICA**

0-940450-84-4 LIBRARY OF AMERICA $35.00

James Weldon **Johnson**

The Autobiography of an Ex-Coloured Man

0-14-018402-3 PENGUIN PB $8.95

Ring **Lardner**

A drinking companion of Fitzgerald, Lardner is, with Grantland Rice, one of the the foremost of American sports writers.

The Annotated Baseball Stories of Ring W. Lardner, 1914-1919

0-8047-2405-9 STANFORD $35.00

The Best Short Stories of Ring Lardner

0-89190-073-X AMEREON $21.95
0-684-14743-2 MACMILLAN $40.00

The Ring Lardner Reader

EDITED BY MAXWELL GEISMAR

0-451-52586-8 NEW AMERICAN LIBRARY PB $4.99

You Know Me Al: A Busher's Letters

The classic baseball novel. "With the surest touch, the sharpest insight, he lets Jack Keefe the baseball player cut his own outline, fill in his own depths, until the figure of the foolish, boastful, innocent athlete lives before us" —Virginia Woolf

See also **BASEBALL FICTION** under **BASEBALL** under **SPORTS** in **FOOD, TRAVEL, AND LEISURE**

INTRODUCTION BY WILFRID SHEED

0-02-022342-0 COLLIER PB $9.95

Margery **Latimer**

The Guardian Angel & Other Stories

0-935312-13-7 FEMINIST PRESS $8.95

Sinclair **Lewis**

Arrowsmith

The maturing of an idealistic young doctor

0-451-52225-7 NEW AMERICAN LIBRARY PB $5.95

Babbitt

"It is signed in every line with the unique personality of the writer. It is saturated with America's vitality"—Rebecca West

0-15-110421-2 HARCOURT BRACE $15.95
0-451-52366-0 NEW AMERICAN LIBRARY PB $5.95

Elmer Gantry

The life of a fundamentalist preacher traveling the revival meeting circuit

0-451-52251-6 NEW AMERICAN LIBRARY PB $5.95

It Can't Happen Here

Fascism comes to the U.S.A.

0-451-52582-5 SIGNET PB $4.95

Main Street

A young woman moves with her husband to a narrow-minded midwestern town. "A remarkable diary of the middle-class mind in America" —Maxwell Geismar

0-15-155547-8 HARCOURT BRACE $15.95
0-451-52461-6 NEW AMERICAN LIBRARY PB $5.95

Main Street and Babbitt

EDITED BY JOHN HERSEY

0-940450-61-5 LIBRARY OF AMERICA $35.00

Jack **London**

The Assassination Bureau, Ltd.

0-89190-655-X AMEREON $18.95

Before Adam

0-89190-651-7 AMEREON $18.95

The Call of the Wild, White Fang & Other Stories

EDITED BY ANDREW SINCLAIR
INTRODUCTION BY JAMES DICKEY

0-14-018651-4 PENGUIN PB $7.95

The Complete Short Stories of Jack London

0-8047-2058-4
STANFORD 3-VOLUME BOXED SET $180.00

The Iron Heel

A prophecy of 20th-century totalitarianism, sketched with the starkness of a violent comic book

INTRODUCTION BY H. BRUCE FRANKLIN

1-55652-071-9 LAWRENCE HILL PB $9.95

Novels and Stories

Includes his best-known novels, *The Call of the Wild*, *White Fang*, and *The Sea Wolf*, as well as selections from his Klondike tales, and previously uncollected short stories

EDITED BY JACK PIZER

0-940450-05-4 LIBRARY OF AMERICA $30.00

John Barleycorn

A memoir of London's struggle with alcoholism

EDITED BY JOHN SUTHERLAND

0-19-281804-X OXFORD PB $9.95

Martin Eden

A young writer struggles vainly against harsh circumstances, in what is often considered London's most mature work

INTRODUCTION BY ANDREW SINCLAIR

0-14-039036-7 PENGUIN PB $8.95

Mutiny on the Elsinore

0-935180-40-0 MUTUAL PUBLICATIONS PB $5.95

Novels and Social Writings

Includes *The People of the Abyss*, *The Road*, *The Iron Heel*, *John Barleycorn*, *Martin Eden*, and other works

EDITED BY DONALD PIZER

0-940450-06-2 LIBRARY OF AMERICA $37.50

Jack **London**

The People of the Abyss

A view of London's East End

1-55652-167-7 LAWRENCE HILL PB $14.95

The Portable Jack London

EDITED BY EARLE LABOR

0-14-017969-0 VIKING PB $13.95

The Sea Wolf

A sailor is shanghaied by a seal-hunting ship, captained by the legendary and brutal Sea Wolf

0-553-21225-7 BDD PB $3.95

The Star Rover

A novel of reincarnation

0-904526-10-0 PLUTO PB $13.50

To Build a Fire & Other Stories

0-553-21335-0 BDD PB $4.95

Anita **Loos**

But Gentlemen Marry Brunettes: The Illuminating Diary of a Professional Lady

The sequel to *Gentlemen Prefer Blondes*, this is "a masterpiece of comic literature"—*TLS*

0-14-018488-0 PENGUIN PB $7.95

Gentlemen Prefer Blondes: The Illuminating Diary of a Professional Lady

Loos's classic of the Jazz Age, which Edith Wharton called "the great American novel"

0-14-018487-2 PENGUIN PB $8.95

Kissing your hand may make you feel very, very good, but a diamond and saphire bracelet lasts forever.

GENTLEMEN PREFER BLONDES: THE ILLUMINATING DIARY OF A PROFESSIONAL LADY

John P. **Marquand**

H.M. Pulham, Esq.

See also **THE '40S** under **THE GREAT FICTION BESTSELLERS 1930-1995** in **POPULAR READING**

0-89733-231-8 ACADEMY CHICAGO PB $11.00

The Late George Apley: A Novel in the Form of a Memoir

1-56849-446-7 BUCCANEER $24.95

0-316-54652-6 LITTLE, BROWN $18.95

Point of No Return

An apparently successful banker re-evaluates his life after returning to his hometown in Massachusetts

See also **THE '40S** under **THE GREAT FICTION BESTSELLERS 1930-1995** in **POPULAR READING**

0-89733-174-5 ACADEMY CHICAGO PB $12.00

Wickford Point

See also **THE '80S** under **THE GREAT FICTION BESTSELLERS 1930-1995** in **POPULAR READING**

0-8446-2666-X SMITH $14.50

Horace **McCoy**

I Should Have Stayed Home

A doomed young couple tries to find a toehold in '30s Hollywood

1-852-42402-8 SERPENT'S TAIL PB $11.99

They Shoot Horses, Don't They?

The famous novel of a Depression-era dance marathon. "McCoy reveals himself as the real nihilist of the hardboiled school"
—Geoffrey O'Brien, *Hardboiled America*

See also **AMERICA** under **RISE OF THE MODERN CRIME NOVEL** under **CRIME FICTION** in **POPULAR READING**

1-85242-401-X SERPENT'S TAIL PB $9.99

Claude **McKay**

Banana Bottom

A Jamaican woman ignores the guidance of her white foster parents in order to search for her true self

0-15-610650-7 HARCOURT BRACE PB $9.00

Claude **Mckay**

Banjo

An international novel of black identity, set in 1920s Marseilles

0-15-610675-2 HARCOURT BRACE PB $9.95

Home to Harlem

Two black men struggle against the prejudice of America in the early years of the 20th century. "Here is realism, stark, awful but somehow beautiful. McKay has left no stone unturned, no detail unmentioned in this telling of things as they are"—*NY Herald Tribune*

FOREWORD BY WAYNE F. COOPER

1-55553-024-9 NORTHEASTERN PB $14.95

Long Way from Home

0-15-653145-3 HARCOURT BRACE PB $7.95

Henry **Miller**

Big Sur and the Oranges of Hieronymus Bosch

Miller's life on the famous stretch of California coast, a portrait of the place and many of the extraordinary people he knew there

See also **MEMOIRS AND JOURNALS** under **20TH-CENTURY AMERICAN ESSAYS AND JOURNALISM**

0-8112-0107-4 NEW DIRECTIONS PB $12.95

Black Spring

"What wonderful scenes of realism there are in *Black Spring*; what a marvelously vivid prose style used to describe them—what a great novelist, in the traditional sense, Henry Miller can be"—Maxwell Geismar

0-8021-3182-4 GROVE PB $12.00

Crazy Cock

An early novel, never before published. Using more orthodox fictional techniques, Miller deals here with much of the same autobiographical subject matter as in his later books

0-8021-3293-6 GROVE PB $10.95

0-8021-1412-1 GROVE PB $18.95

Moloch: Or This Gentile World

The earliest surviving novel, which was originally passed off as the work of Miller's wife, June, to gain the support of her wealthy, enamored patron. Based on Miller's first marriage and his years at Western Union, this is a full-fledged attempt at autobiographical fiction, a literary form he later perfected in Paris

0-8021-1419-9 GROVE PB $18.95

Quiet Days in Clichy

0-8021-3016-X GROVE PB $9.95

Henry Miller

The Rosy Crucifixion

An autobiographical trilogy

Volume 1: Sexus

0-8021-5180-9 GROVE PB $13.95

Volume 2:Plexus

0-8021-5179-5 GROVE PB $14.95

Volume 3:Nexus

0-8021-5178-7 GROVE PB $11.95

The Smile at the Foot of the Ladder

0-8112-0556-8 NEW DIRECTIONS PB $6.95

Tropic of Cancer

"Miller is at his best in *Tropic of Cancer*. There is an eager vitality and exuberance to the writing which is exhilarating"—William H. Gass

INTRODUCTION BY KARL SHAPIRO

0-8021-3178-6 GROVE PB $11.95

Tropic of Capricorn

The companion of *Tropic of Cancer*. "Miller has once and for all blasted the very foundation of human hypocrisy—moral, social, and political"—*The Nation*

0-8021-5182-5 GROVE PB $11.95

Margaret **Mitchell**

Gone with the Wind

"A remarkable book, a spectacular book, a book that will not be forgotten"—*Chicago Tribune*

0-446-36538-6 WARNER PB $6.99

Gone with the Wind

0-684-82625-9 SCRIBNERS $40.00

Lost Laysen: The Newly Discovered Story

0-684-82428-0 SCRIBNERS $18.00

Frances **Newman**

Dead Lovers Are Faithful Lovers

0-8203-1588-5 GEORGIA PB $17.95

The Hard-Boiled Virgin

0-8203-0526-X GEORGIA PB $17.95

Charles **Nordhoff** & James Norman **Hall**

Mutiny on the Bounty

0-316-61168-9 LITTLE, BROWN PB $13.95

John **O'Hara**

Appointment in Samarra
The country club is dissected in O'Hara's first and best novel
0-679-60110-4 MODERN LIBRARY $13.50

The Ewings
0-394-47404-X RANDOM HOUSE $14.95

From the Terrace
O'Hara's attempt at an epic of American life in the first half of the century. "A tremendous story about love, money, and war"—*NY Times*
0-88184-971-5 CARROLL & GRAF PB $7.95

John O'Hara

Gibbsville, Pa.
0-88184-899-9 CARROLL & GRAF $27.95
0-7867-0082-3 CARROLL & GRAF PB $17.95

Hope of Heaven
A short, sharp novel of Hollywood in the '30s
0-88184-149-8 CARROLL & GRAF PB $3.95

The Lockwood Concern
The story of an American dynasty
0-88184-217-6 CARROLL & GRAF PB $4.95

The Novellas of John O'Hara
0-679-60167-8 MODERN LIBRARY $19.00

A Rage to Live
0-88184-216-8 CARROLL & GRAF PB $4.95

Sermons and Soda Water
Three novellas. "No one has captured the relevant tones and shapes of American life with greater fidelity"—George Steiner
0-88184-271-0 CARROLL & GRAF PB $4.95

Ten North Frederick
0-88184-173-0 CARROLL & GRAF PB $4.50

Dorothy **Parker**
A prolific critic, a caustic wit, and a consummate literary insider—the Algonquin circle being her milieu—Parker is, unfortunately, better-known as an alchoholic than as the writer she was. "She has put into what she has written a voice, a state of mind, an era, a few moments of human experience that nobody else has conveyed."—Edmund Wilson

Complete Stories
EDITED BY COLLEEN BREESE
0-14-018939-4 PENGUIN PB $12.95

Poetry and Short Stories of Dorothy Parker
See also **THE MODERNIST GENERATIONS** under **20TH-CENTURY AMERICAN POETRY**
0-679-60132-5 MODERN LIBRARY $16.50

The Portable Dorothy Parker
Stories, poems, and criticism
See also **HUMOR WRITERS** under **HUMOR** in **POPULAR READING**
0-14-015074-9 VIKING PB $13.95

Katherine Anne **Porter**

The Collected Stories of Katherine Anne Porter
0-15-618876-7 HARCOURT BRACE PB $11.95

The Old Order
A selection of stories from *Flowering Judas, Pale Horse, Pale Rider,* and *The Leaning Tower*
0-15-668519-1 HARCOURT BRACE PB $8.00

Pale Horse, Pale Rider
0-15-170755-3 HARCOURT BRACE $17.00

Ship of Fools
An intensely wrought portrait of a group of misfits
0-316-71390-2 LITTLE, BROWN PB $13.95

Dawn **Powell**
"For decades Dawn Powell was always just on the verge of ceasing to be a cult and becoming a major religion. But despite the work of such dedicated cultists as Edmund Wilson and Matthew Josephson, John Dos Passos and Ernest Hemingway, Dawn Powell never became the popular writer that she ought to have been… Powell was that unthinkable monster, a witty woman who felt no obligation to make a single, much less a final, down payment on Love or the Family."—Gore Vidal

Angels on Toast
1-88364-240-X STEERFORTH PB $14.00

Dawn Powell: At Her Best
EDITED BY TIM PAGE
1-88364-216-7 STEERFORTH $28.00

The Locusts Have No King
1-88364-242-6 STEERFORTH PB $14.00

A Time to Be Born
A novel of "cynical New Yorkers stalking each other for various selfish ends" —*Publishers Weekly*
1-87827-406-6 STEERFORTH PB $9.95
1-88364-241-8 STEERFORTH PB $14.00

The Wicked Pavilion
1-88364-239-6 STEERFORTH PB $14.00

Marjorie Kinnan **Rawlings**

Cross Creek
An autobiographical novel set in the Florida Everglades
ILLUSTRATED BY EDWARD SHENTON
0-8488-0700-6 AMEREON $24.95

The Yearling
The enduringly popular novel of a boy and his pet deer; winner of the 1938 Pulitzer Prize
See also **THE '30S** under **THE GREAT FICTION BESTSELLERS 1930-1995** in **POPULAR READING**
0-02-044931-3 ALADDIN PB $5.95

Henry **Roth**

Call It Sleep
An immigrant youth's coming of age. "One of the few genuinely distinguished novels written by a 20th-century American"—*NY Times*
0-374-52292-8 NOONDAY PB $13.00

Mercy of a Rude Stream

Volume I: A Star Shines over Mt. Morris Park
0-312-10499-5 ST. MARTIN'S $23.00

Volume 2: A Diving Rock on the Hudson
0-312-14085-1 PICADOR PB $14.00

Volume 3: From Bondage
0-312-14341-9 ST. MARTIN'S $25.95

Shifting Landscape
A collection of later pieces which come to grips with Roth's long silence after writing *Call It Sleep*
0-8276-0292-8 JEWISH PUBLICATION SOCIETY $19.95

Damon **Runyon**

Guys and Dolls: The Stories of Damon Runyon
"It is the language, of course, that keeps Runyon's tall tales of Broadway con men and sporting ladies so vibrant and appealing. Every page drawls with that nasal slangy cool-guy voice"—*Washington Post Book World*
See also **HUMOR WRITERS** under **HUMOR** in **POPULAR READING**
0-670-84868-9 PENGUIN PB $27.50

George **Santayana**

The Last Puritan
An autobiographical novel
See also **SANTAYANA** under **PHILOSOPHY** in **RELIGION, SPIRITUALITY, AND PHILOSOPHY**
0-262-19328-0 MIT $52.50
0-262-69178-7 MIT PB $19.95

William **Saroyan**

Fresno Stories
0-8112-1282-3 NEW DIRECTIONS PB $5.00

The Human Comedy
Homer Macauley, a young telegraph messenger, and his family during World War II
0-15-142301-6 HARCOURT BRACE $15.95
0-440-33933-2 DELL PB $4.99

Madness in the Family
EDITED BY LEO HAMALIAN
0-8112-1064-2 NEW DIRECTIONS $16.95

My Name Is Aram
0-15-163827-6 HARCOURT BRACE $15.95

My Name Is Saroyan: A Collection
"Natural felicity of touch…instinctive sense of form"—Edmund Wilson
EDITED BY JAMES H. TASHJIAN
0-15-662333-1 HARCOURT BRACE PB $8.95

William **Saroyan**

The New Saroyan Reader: A Connoisseur's Anthology of the Writings of William Saroyan

EDITED BY BRIAN DARWENT

0-916870-80-4 CREATIVE ARTS $17.95

0-916870-81-2 CREATIVE ARTS PB $11.50

Evelyn **Scott**

Escapade

0-8139-1641-0 VIRGINIA PB $16.95

Upton **Sinclair**

The Jungle

The classic muckraking novel that exposed corrupt conditions in the Chicago meatpacking industry

INTRODUCTION BY MORRIS DICKSTEIN

0-553-21245-1 BDD PB $3.95

Lillian **Smith**

Killers of the Dream

The influential 1949 book about racism in the South and its connection to sexual oppression

0-393-31160-0 NORTON PB $9.95

Gertrude **Stein**

Stein (1874-1946) set out, almost singlehandedly, she believed, to invent and define modernist literature. A student of the pragmatic philosopher William James, Stein once said that "I was there to kill what was not dead."

The Autobiography of Alice B. Toklas

"Largely to amuse herself, [Gertrude Stein] wrote *The Autobiograpby of Alice B. Toklas* in 1932…The book is full of the most lucid and shapely anecdotes, told in a purer and more closely fitting prose… than even Gide or Hemingway have ever commanded"
—Donald Sutherland

0-679-72463-X VINTAGE PB $11.00

Fernhurst, Q.E.D., and Other Early Writings

0-87140-161-4 LIVERIGHT PB $11.00

The Geographical History of America

0-8018-5133-5 JOHNS HOPKINS PB $14.95

Geography and Plays

0-299-13470-9 WISCONSIN $40.00

0-299-13474-1 WISCONSIN PB $14.95

How to Write

See also **THE MODERNIST REVOLUTION** under **LITERARY CRITICISM** in **LITERATURE OF EUROPE, AFRICA, AND ASIA**

INTRODUCTION BY PATRICIA MEYEROWITZ

0-486-23144-5 DOVER PB $7.95

Ida

One of the most accessible and entrancing of Stein's fictions

0-394-71797-X RANDOM HOUSE PB $9.00

Last Operas and Plays

0-8018-4985-3 PAJ PUBLICATIONS PB $18.95

The Making of Americans

Stein's masterpiece finally back in print

1-56478-088-0 DALKEY ARCHIVE PB $16.95

Gertrude Stein

Mrs. Reynolds

An allegorical parable of World War II, with the title character interacting with surrogates for Adolf Hitler and Josef Stalin

1-55713-016-7 SUN & MOON PB $13.95

A Novel of Thank You

1-56478-049-X DALKEY ARCHIVE PB $9.95

Paris France

An affectionate memoir of Stein's adopted country

See also **LITERATURE** under **20TH-CENTURY AMERICAN ESSAYS AND JOURNALISM**

0871401600 LIVERIGHT PB $10.00

0-87140-231-9 NORTON PB $8.95

Selected Operas and Plays by Gertrude Stein

EDITED BY JOHN MALCOLM BRINNIN

0-8229-5501-6 PITTSBURGH PB $16.95

Selected Writings of Gertrude Stein

Stein is a writer who makes the distinction between "prose" and "poetry" meaningless; what cannot be questioned is the depth of her continuing influence on modern American poets. A longer selection of her works will be found under Modern American Fiction

See also **THE MODERNIST GENERATIONS** under **20TH-CENTURY AMERICAN POETRY**

0-8446-6633-5 SMITH $25.30

0-679-72464-8 VINTAGE PB $18.00

A Stein Reader

See also **THE MODERNIST GENERATIONS** under **20TH-CENTURY AMERICAN POETRY**

EDITED BY ULLA DYDO

0-8101-1083-0 NORTHWESTERN PB $24.95

Tender Buttons

The legendary classic of Cubist prose, photographed from the pages of the first edition published in 1914

1-55713-093-0 SUN & MOON PB $9.95

A Piano

If the speed is open, if the color is careless, if the selection of a strong scent is not awkward, if the button holder is held by all the waving color and there is no color, not any color. If there is no dirt in a pin and there can be none scarcely, if there is not then the place is the same as up standing.

This is no dark custom and it even is not acted in any such a way that a restraint is not spread. That is spread, it shuts and it lifts and awkwardly not awkwardly the centre is in standing.

TENDER BUTTONS

Three Lives

Portraits of three very different women. "Stein's most important and influential early work…A remarkable book for its time"—James Mellow

0-486-28059-4 DOVER PB $2.00

0-452-01006-3 NEW AMERICAN LIBRARY PB $4.95

0-14-018184-9 PENGUIN PB $8.95

Useful Knowledge

0-88268-075-7 STATION HILL $19.95

The Yale Gertrude Stein

INTRODUCTION BY RICHARD KOSTELANETZ

0-300-02609-9 YALE PB $22.00

John **Steinbeck**

The Acts of King Arthur and His Noble Knights

Steinbeck's modernization of the *Morte d'Arthur*, which he considered among the greatest challenges of his career, "embellishes Malory's spare legend with a richness of detail that transfers the vision, makes it no one but Steinbeck's"
—John Gardner, *NY Times Book Review*

See also **BRITISH AND CELTIC** under **EUROPEAN MYTHOLOGY** under **MYTHOLOGY AND FOLKLORE** in **RELIGION, SPIRITUALITY, AND PHILOSOPHY**

0-374-52378-9 NOONDAY PB $17.00

Burning Bright: A Play in Story Form

0-14-018742-1 PENGUIN PB $8.95

Cannery Row

Steinbeck's devasting portrait of cannery workers in Monterey, California

0-14-018737-5 PENGUIN PB $9.95

Cup of Gold

Steinbeck's first novel, based on the career of the pirate Henry Morgan

0-14-018743-X PENGUIN PB $10.95

East of Eden

Biblical parallels weigh heavily on this saga of a Salinas Valley rancher and his troubled family

0-670-28738-5 VIKING $27.95

0-14-004997-5 PENGUIN $7.95

The Grapes of Wrath

The epic story of the Joads, a family of Oklahoma farmers who flee from their farm to California during the dustbowl years of the '30s. *"The Grapes of Wrath is* the greatest American novel I have ever read"—Dorothy Parker

See also **YOUNG ADULT FICTION** in **BOOKS FOR YOUNG READERS**

0-670-82638-3 VIKING $25.00

0-14-018640-9 PENGUIN PB $11.95

In Dubious Battle

A novel of labor strife, considered Steinbeck's best book by some

0-14-018641-7 PENGUIN PB $11.95

The Grapes of Wrath and Other Writings, 1936 - 1941

Also includes *The Long Valley* and the travel account *The Log from the Sea of Cortez.* The text of *Grapes of Wrath* is newly corrected from the original typescript

EDITED BY ROBERT DEMOTT AND ELAINE STEINBECK

1-88301-115-9 LIBRARY OF AMERICA $35.00

John Steinbeck

The Long Valley
Thirteen short stories, including "The Red Pony" and "The Chrysanthemums"
0-14-008038-4 PENGUIN PB $6.00

The Moon Is Down
A novel set during the German invasion of Norway during World War II
0-14-018746-4 PENGUIN PB $9.95

Novels and Stories: 1932-1937
Includes *The Pastures of Heaven, To A God Unknown, Tortilla Flat, In Dubious Battle,* and *Of Mice and Men*
EDITED BY ROBERT DEMOTT & ELAINE STEINBECK
1-88301-101-9 LIBRARY OF AMERICA $35.00

Of Mice and Men
0-14-017739-6 PENGUIN PB $5.95

The Pastures of Heaven
Early stories of a California farming valley, first collected in 1932
0-14-004998-3 PENGUIN PB $6.95

The Short Reign of Pippin IV
0-14-018749-9 PENGUIN PB $9.95

Sweet Thursday
0-14-004889-8 PENGUIN PB $7.00

To a God Unknown
An early novel about the life of a California rancher, heavy with mythic overtones
0-14-004233-4 PENGUIN PB $6.95

Tortilla Flat
0-670-72109-3 VIKING $16.95
0-14-004240-7 PENGUIN PB $6.95

The Wayward Bus
0-14-005001-9 PENGUIN PB $7.00

Zapata
This is the original version of Steinbeck's narrative of the life of Emiliano Zapata, "the Little Tiger," a leader of the Mexican revolution, upon which he based his Academy Award-winning script for the Elia Kazan film *Viva Zapata!* Only recently discovered
See also **INDIVIDUAL FILMS** under **SCREENPLAYS** under **FILM** in **PERFORMING ARTS AND MEDIA**
0-14-017322-6 PENGUIN PB $12.95

Booth **Tarkington**

The Magnificent Ambersons
The basis of the Orson Welles film of the same name
0-253-35875-2 INDIANA $20.00
0-253-20546-8 INDIANA PB $11.95

Allen **Tate**

The Fathers
0-8071-2069-3 LSU PB $12.95

James **Thurber**

Writings and Drawings
The most comprehensive collection of the works of this American humorist available. Includes over 100 pieces and nearly 500 cartoons and drawings. "A comic continent unto itself" —Roy Blount, Jr.
See also **HUMOR WRITERS** under **HUMOR** in **POPULAR READING**
1-88301-122-1 LIBRARY OF AMERICA $35.00

Wallace **Thurman**

The Blacker the Berry
A satirical novel from the Harlem Renaissance
0-02-054750-1 MACMILLAN PB $7.00

Jean **Toomer**

Cane
Black life in Georgia during the early years of the 20th century. "No earlier volume of poetry or fiction or both had come close to expressing the ethos of the Negro in the Southern setting as *Cane* did. Even in today's ghettos astute readers are finding that its insights have anticipated and often exceeded their own"—Arna Bontemps
See also **THE MODERNIST GENERATIONS** under **20TH-CENTURY AMERICAN POETRY**
EDITED BY DARWIN T. TURNER
0-393-95600-8 NORTON PB $7.95

Cane
0-679-60109-0 MODERN LIBRARY $12.50

A Jean Toomer Reader: Selected and Unpublished Writings
EDITED BY FREDERICK L. RUSCH
0-19-507733-4 OXFORD $49.95
0-19-508329-6 OXFORD PB $17.95

The Wayward and the Seeking: A Collection of Writing by Jean Toomer
EDITED BY DARWIN T. TURNER
0-88258-028-0 HOWARD PB $12.95

B. **Traven**

The mysterious Traven wrote his legendary Jungle Novels, *which are about the birth of the Mexican Revolution, in the '30s.*

The Carreta
1-56663-045-2 DEE PB $11.95

The Cotton-Pickers
1-56663-075-4 DEE PB $12.95

The Death Ship
1-55652-110-3 LAWRENCE HILL PB $12.95

General from the Jungle
1-56663-076-2 DEE PB $13.95

Government
1-56663-038-X DEE PB $10.95

March to the Monteria
1-56663-046-0 DEE PB $10.95

The Night Visitor: And Other Stories
"B. Traven is coming to be recognized as one of the narrative masters of the twentieth century"—*NY Times Book Review*
0-89190-160-4 AMEREON $19.95
1-56663-039-8 DEE PB $10.95

The Treasure of the Sierra Madre
The source of John Huston's famous film remains a harshly compelling saga of greed and disintegration in the desert
0-374-52149-2 FS&G PB $12.00
0-8090-0160-8 HILL & WANG PB $12.00

Trozas
Trozas is a detailed description of conditions on a mahogany plantation in the remote southern province of Chiapas. Its unforgettable depiction of the relationship between the Spanish bosses and the subtle, highly cultured Mayan natives is eerily familiar. "A mastery of the politics of evil that is simply immense"—*Kirkus Reviews*
TRANSLATED BY HUGH YOUNG
1-56663-044-4 DEE $22.50

Carl **Van Vechten**

Novelist, photographer, socialite, promoter of the Harlem Renaissance and Gertrude Stein, Van Vechten was a crucial figure in the artistic world of his time. His novels are immensely sophisticated and frequently amusing.

Parties
1-55713-029-9 SUN & MOON PB $13.95

The Tattooed Countess: A Romantic Novel with a Happy Ending
0-87745-186-9 IOWA PB $12.95

The Tiger in the House
0-486-29129-4 DOVER PB $8.95

Nathanael **West**

"Putting down a book by West, a reader is not sure whether he has been presented with a nightmare endowed with the conviction of actuality or with actuality distorted into the semblance of a nightmare; but in either case, he has the sense that he has been presented with a view of a world in which, incredibly, he lives."—Leslie Fiedler

The Dream Life of Balso Snell & A Cool Million
0-374-50292-7 FS&G PB $11.00

Miss Lonelyhearts & The Day of the Locust
0-8112-0215-1 NEW DIRECTIONS PB $8.95

Edith **Wharton**

The first woman to win the Pulitzer Prize, Edith Wharton was an immensely popular writer in her day. She depicts the life of the American upper class—a class into which she was born—with irony and satire, exposing its lack of compassion and its stifling of human happiness.

The Age of Innocence

In the highest circle of New York society, a man falls in love with the wrong woman. Winner of the Pulitzer Prize in 1920

0-02-026476-3 COLLIER PB $9.00

The Buccaneers

Her classic saga of five young ladies who conspire to gain entrance into New York's fashionable society might have been Wharton's masterpiece. Unfortunately, she died before its completion. Now it has been completed by Wharton scholar Marion Mainwaring

0-670-86645-8 VIKING $15.95

The Custom of the Country

One of Wharton's most memorable characters, Undine Spragg, and her ruthless pursuit of social success in old New York and fashionable Paris

0-14-018190-3 PENGUIN PB $10.95

Ethan Frome

A simple tale about a poor New England farmer and his ill-fated bid for love. One of the foremost novellas of this century

0-684-18906-2 MACMILLAN PB $8.00

Fast and Loose & The Buccaneers

0-8139-1482-5 VIRGINIA $49.50
0-8139-1483-3 VIRGINIA PB $14.95

Ghost Stories of Edith Wharton

Eleven supernatural tales. "Flawlessly eerie"—*Ms.*

0-684-18382-X MACMILLAN PB $10.95

The Glimpses of the Moon

0-684-19693-X SCRIBNERS $25.00
0-02-038305-3 SCRIBNERS PB $10.00

The House of Mirth

Often considered her masterpiece, this is the tragic story of Lily Bart, born into New York society and a victim of its rigid code

INTRODUCTION BY CYNTHIA GRIFFIN WOLFF

0-14-018729-4 PENGUIN PB $8.95

Hudson River Bracketed

A satirical look at literary life in the '20s

0-684-18455-9 MACMILLAN $35.00

Madame de Treymes & Three Novellas

A brilliant novella about the life of Americans in French society during the Belle Epoque

INTRODUCTION BY SUSAN MARY ALSOP

0-02-055420-6 MACMILLAN PB $6.00

The Mother's Recompense

The bitter story of a woman who abandons her husband and child to live with the man she loves

PREFACE BY LOUIS AUCHINCLOSS

0-684-18737-X MACMILLAN PB $12.00

Novellas and Other Writings

Includes *Ethan Frome, Summer, Old New York, Madame de Treymes, The Mother's Recompense,* and the memoir *A Backward Glance*

See also **LIBRARY OF AMERICA**

0-940450-53-4 LIBRARY OF AMERICA $35.00

Novels

Includes *The House of Mirth, The Reef, The Custom of the Country*, and *The Age of Innocence*

See also **LIBRARY OF AMERICA**

0-940450-31-3 LIBRARY OF AMERICA $35.00

The Reef

Two Americans abandon society but find they are unable to live by their own rules

INTRODUCTION BY LOUIS AUCHINCLOSS

0-02-055410-9 MACMILLAN PB $5.00

Roman Fever & Other Stories

0-684-17011-6 SCRIBNERS $35.00
0-02-059880-7 COLLIER PB $5.95

A Son at the Front

0-87580-568-X NORTHERN ILLINOIS PB $15.00

Summer

Summer in the Berkshires, with passionate, young Charity Royal forced to marry her dour guardian to save her honor

INTRODUCTION BY CYNTHIA GRIFFIN WOLFF

0-06-080507-2 HARPERCOLLINS PB $6.50

Summer

0-14-018679-4 PENGUIN PB $9.95

Thornton **Wilder**

"I am not an innovator but a rediscoverer of forgotten goods and I hope a remover of obtrusive bric-a-brac. And as I look at the work of my contemporaries I seem to feel that I am an exception in one thing—I give (don't I) the impression of having enormously enjoyed it."—Thornton Wilder

The Bridge of San Luis Rey

Wilder's most famous novel ponders the significance of a random disaster

0-06-091341-X HARPERCOLLINS PB $10.00

The Cabala

Pagan gods linger on in modern Rome

0-88184-295-8 CARROLL & GRAF PB $3.95

The Eighth Day

Murder in a small Illinois mining town in 1902

0-88184-339-3 CARROLL & GRAF PB $4.95

The Ides of March

Intimate portrait of Caesar in the months before his assassination

See also **HISTORICAL FICTION** under **TOPICS IN ROMAN HISTORY** under **ANCIENT ROME** in **WORLD HISTORY AND CURRENT AFFAIRS**

1-56849-445-9 BUCCANEER $24.95

Theophilus North

Life among the wealthy and their servants in the Newport, Rhode Island of the '20s. "An extremely entertaining array of American life in a bygone era"—*New Yorker*

0-88184-382-2 CARROLL & GRAF PB $4.95

Tennessee **Williams**

Collected Stories

0-8112-1269-6 NEW DIRECTIONS PB $14.95

William Carlos **Williams**

"An American original... He stole time to create the most substantial one-man body of literature in our history. When he died at 79, he had no peer as the total American writer"
—Webster Scott, Life

The Build-Up

0-8112-0227-5 NEW DIRECTIONS PB $9.95

The Collected Stories

0-8112-1328-5 NEW DIRECTIONS PB $14.95

The Doctor Stories

Stories reflecting Williams's career as an obstetrician

EDITED BY ROBERT COLES

0-8112-0926-1 NEW DIRECTIONS PB $8.95

Imaginations

Contains some of Williams's greatest and most innovative writings, fusing poetry and prose in a variety of unpredictable ways: *Kora in Hell, Song and All, The Descent of Winter, The Great American Novel*, and others

See also **THE MODERNIST GENERATIONS** under **20TH-CENTURY AMERICAN POETRY**

EDITED BY WEBSTER SCHOTT

0-8112-0229-1 NEW DIRECTIONS PB $13.95

In the Money

0-8112-0231-3 NEW DIRECTIONS PB $7.45

A Voyage to Pagany

A fictional reworking of Williams's trip to Europe

0-8112-0237-2 NEW DIRECTIONS PB $8.25

White Mule

0-8112-0238-0 NEW DIRECTIONS PB $11.95

Edmund **Wilson**

Memoirs of Hecate County

0-374-52432-7 NOONDAY PB $16.00

Owen **Wister**

The Virginian

The original cowboy novel

INTRODUCTION BY MAX WESTBROOK

0-451-52325-3 NEW AMERICAN LIBRARY PB $5.95

Thomas **Wolfe**

The Complete Short Stories of Thomas Wolfe

EDITED BY FRANCIS E. SKIPP
FOREWARD BY JAMES DICKEY

0-684-18743-4 SCRIBNERS $27.50
0-02-040891-9 COLLIER PB $15.00

From Death to Morning

Fourteen short stories, including "Only the Dead Know Brooklyn" and "The Web of Earth"

0-684-17980-6 MACMILLAN $20.00

Look Homeward, Angel

Wolfe's best-known novel tells of a boy's coming of age in North Carolina

0-684-80443-3 SCRIBNERS PB $14.00

Of Time and the River

Eugene Gant, the hero of *Look Homeward, Angel,* leaves rural North Carolina for England and France

0-684-14739-4 SCRIBNERS $35.00

The Party at Jack's

0-8078-2206-X NORTH CAROLINA $19.95

The Short Novels of Thomas Wolfe

"What he gives is the feel, taste, smell, the very heartbeat of American life as no other modern writer has done"—*Atlanta Journal*

0-684-14554-5 MACMILLAN $40.00

Thomas Wolfe

You Can't Go Home Again
A testament to Wolfe's dense and magisterial prose, his last novel tells of successful author living in a city that cannot become his home
0-89966-294-3 BUCCANEER $39.95
0-06-080986-8 HARPERCOLLINS PB $7.50

Richard **Wright**

American Hunger
0-8095-9067-0 BORGO $29.00

Black Boy
The classic and scathing fictional portrait of ghetto life
0-06-081250-8 HARPERPERENNIAL PB $7.00

Early Works
Includes *Lawd Today!*, *Uncle Tom's Children*, and *Native Son*. "A major publishing event. Readers who think they know these works have some surprises in store for them"
—Henry Louis Gates, Jr.
EDITED BY ARNOLD RAMPERSAD
0-940450-66-6 LIBRARY OF AMERICA $35.00

Later Works
Includes *Black Boy* and *The Outsider*
EDITED BY ARNOLD RAMPERSAD
0-940450-67-4 LIBRARY OF AMERICA $35.00

The Long Dream
0-06-080869-1 HARPERCOLLINS PB $7.00

Native Son
This novel, about a young black man who commits murder during a moment of panic in 1930s Chicago, created a sensation when it appeared in 1940. It was an immediate best-seller and profoundly influenced an entire generation
0-06-081249-4 HARPERPERENNIAL PB $7.00

The Outsider
0-8095-9069-7 BORGO LIBRARY EDITION $25.00
0-06-081248-6 HARPERPERENNIAL PB $9.00

Savage Holiday
0-87805-749-8 MISSISSIPPI $37.50
0-87805-750-1 MISSISSIPPI PB $16.95

Uncle Tom's Children
Five stories on violence in the South
0-8095-9070-0 BORGO $23.00
0-06-081251-6 HARPERPERENNIAL PB $7.00

Since 1945

Edward **Abbey**

"What entertains many and exasperates others is Abbey's unique prose voice. Alternately misanthropic and sentimental, enraged and hilarious, it is the voice of a full-blooded man airing his passions."—Peter Carlson

Beyond the Wall
0-8050-0820-9 HOLT PB $11.95

The Brave Cowboy
0-380-71459-0 AVON PB $11.00

Fire on the Mountain
0-380-71460-4 AVON PB $10.00

The Fool's Progress
0-380-70856-6 AVON PB $12.00

Hayduke Lives!
0-316-00411-1 LITTLE, BROWN PB $17.95

The Monkey Wrench Gang
A band of ecologically-minded saboteurs wages war on Western land developers
0-380-71339-X AVON PB $12.50
0-380-00741-X AVON PB $5.99

Walter **Abish**

99: The New Meaning
The "new meaning" is what results when the author of *Alphabetical Africa* fuses together sentences and paragraphs from a wide range of sources—99 selections from 99 authors—to create altogether new combinations. With photographs by Cecile Abish
0-930901-66-5 BURNING DECK PB $8.00

Alphabetical Africa
Chapter by chapter, Abish lets in one letter of the alphabet; then, one at a time, he takes them all away. From this premise arises a mysteriously absorbing narrative of African adventures
0-8112-0533-9 NEW DIRECTIONS PB $8.95

Eclipse Fever
Set in high-gloss, contemporary Mexico, this long-awaited novel by the PEN/Faulkner Award-winning author of *How German Is It* provides a disturbing meditation on the modern world
0-679-41867-0 KNOPF $23.00

How German Is It
A Germany of the mind, reconstructed with brilliance and perverse humor
0-8112-0776-5 NEW DIRECTIONS PB $10.95

In the Future Perfect
7 short stories, all examining the nature of language
0-8112-0659-9 NEW DIRECTIONS $10.75

Paul **Ableman**

I Hear Voices
A comic novel in the mind and voice of a schizophrenic. "Arresting and brilliant"
—*NY Times Book Review*
0-929701-05-4 MCPHERSON $18.00
0-929701-04-6 MCPHERSON PB $10.00

Kathy **Acker**

Don Quixote
Don Quixote as a woman on a visionary quest
0-8021-3192-1 GROVE PB $9.95

Blood and Guts in High School
"A post-modern Colette with echoes of Cleland's *Fanny Hill*"—William Burroughs
0-8021-3193-X GROVE PB $10.95

Empire of the Senseless
0-8021-3179-4 GROVE PB $9.95

Great Expectations
"*Great Expectations* is Kathy Acker's most ambitious, most exciting, and masterful novel to date. Its influence will be long and strongly felt. The novel is as revolutionary in form as it is in content"—Steve Abbott, *Poetry Flash*
0-8021-3155-7 GROVE PB $8.95

Literal Madness
Includes *My Death, My Life By Pier Paolo Pasolini*, *Kathy Goes to Haiti*, and *Florida*
0-8021-3156-5 GROVE PB $12.00

Pussy, King of the Pirates
0-8021-1578-0 GROVE $21.00

Alice **Adams**

Almost Perfect
0-449-14892-0 GOLD MEDAL PB $5.99

A Southern Exposure
0-679-44452-1 KNOPF $23.00
0-449-91113-6 FAWCETT PB $12.00

Superior Women
Radcliffe, from the '40s to the '80s
0-449-20746-3 CREST PB $5.99

James **Agee**

A Death in the Family
A moving account of the aftermath of death, Agee's only novel is narrated by each of the bereaved family's member in turn
0-553-27011-7 BDD PB $5.99

Nelson **Algren**

"Algren can hit with both hands and move around and he will kill you if you are not awfully careful."—Ernest Hemingway

Chicago: City on the Make
0-226-01384-7 CHICAGO PB $9.95

The Man with the Golden Arm
The tough life of card-dealing drug addict Frankie machine
1-88836-318-5 SEVEN STORIES PB $10.95

The Neon Wilderness
A collection of short stories originally published in 1947
INTRODUCTION BY STUDS TERKEL
AFTERWORD BY TERRY SOUTHERN
0-8446-1014-3 SMITH $16.30
1-88836-321-5 SEVEN STORIES PB $10.95

Never Come Morning
INTRODUCTION BY KURT VONNEGUT, JR.
0-941423-00-X FOUR WALLS PB $8.95
1-88836-322-3 SEVEN STORIES PB $10.95

The Texas Stories
EDITED BY BETTINA DREW
0-292-70468-2 TEXAS PB $12.95

A Walk on the Wild Side
0-938410-80-6 THUNDER'S MOUTH PB $12.95

Lisa **Alther**

Bedrock

0-452-27776-0 PLUME PB $12.95

Five Minutes in Heaven

0-452-27613-6 PLUME PB $11.95

Kinflicks

Funny and explicit account of a woman growing up

0-452-27677-2 PLUME PB $12.95

Original Sins

0-452-27676-4 PLUME PB $13.95

Other Women

A woman and her therapist

0-452-27678-0 PLUME PB $11.95

Rudolfo **Anaya**

The Anaya Reader

0-446-67077-4 WARNER PB $11.99

Bless Me, Ultima

Most famous novel by the father of Mexican-American literature

0-446-60025-3 WARNER PB $5.99

Jalamanta: A Message from the Desert

0-446-52024-1 MYSTERIOUS $17.95

Raymond **Andrews**

Appalachee Red

The Deep South from the end of World War I to the beginning of the '60s

0-8203-0961-3 GEORGIA PB $10.95

Maya **Angelou**

I Know Why the Caged Bird Sings

Angelou's classic tale of her black girlhood in Arkansas, Chicago, and California, one of the finest coming-of-age novels ever written

See also **CLASSIC AUTOBIOGRAPHIES** under **BLACK VOICES, BLACK LIVES** under **AFRICAN-AMERICAN STUDIES** in **HISTORY OF THE AMERICAS**

0-394-42986-9 RANDOM HOUSE $20.00

0-553-27937-8 BDD PB $5.50

Carol **Anshaw**

Seven Moves

0-395-69131-1 HOUGHTON MIFFLIN $21.95

Harriet **Arnow**

The Dollmaker

0-380-00947-1 AVON PB $6.50

Louis **Auchincloss**

"Auchincloss's genius as a writer and chronicler of upper-class New York is to render even the prettiest of these American aristocrats as recognizably human figures."—Chicago Tribune

The Education of Oscar Fairfax

Three generations of a Wall Street law firm provide a revealing and fascinating portrait of the American upper classes throughout our century. From the distinguished American author, a new novel of ideals, ambition, conformism, and dissent. "Flawless prose, keen social observation, and a refined moral sensibility…Auchincloss ranks among the best in American literature"—*Kirkus Reviews*

0-395-73918-7 HOUGHTON MIFFLIN $22.95

Honorable Men

0-395-38812-0 HOUGHTON MIFFLIN $15.95

The House of the Prophet

The life of a distinguished man, from World War I to Vietnam. "The most accomplished book he has written to date"—*NY Times*

0-88738-857-4 TRANSACTION PB $19.95

Tales of Yesteryear

Spanning the century, a collection of stories that peer into the lives of the American elite with an attention that makes them universal. "Mr. Auchincloss's 'yesteryears' are far enough away to seem slightly exotic, but never so distant that we lose sight of their palpable human charm" —*NY Times Book Review.* "Vintage Auchincloss: moral tales that resonate with the history of our times….Auchincloss belongs among the masters of American short fiction, as this volume demonstrates"—*Kirkus Reviews*

0-395-69132-X HOUGHTON MIFFLIN $21.95

Paul **Auster**

City of Glass

A detective novelist makes a phone call and finds himself enmeshed in suddenly puzzling reality. Further espouses on Auster's preoccupation with, and always stunning rendering of, the theme of chance

0-14-009731-7 PENGUIN PB $10.95

Paul Auster

Ghosts

Blue, a student of Brown, has been hired by White to spy on Black. "Auster harnesses the inquiriring spirit any reader brings to a mystery, redirecting it from the grubby search for a wrongdoer to the more rarefied search for self"—Stephen Schiff, *NY Times Book Review*

0-940650-70-3 SUN & MOON $12.95

In the Country of Last Things

A postapocalyptic quest set against a backdrop of urban deprivation

0-14-009705-8 PENGUIN PB $11.95

Leviathan

A man recounting a tale of his friend's remarkable life and unlikely death. A stunning and gripping narrative. "Auster is a literary original who…has reaffirmed the dignity of elegant, intricate plots" —*The Wall Street Journal*

0-14-017813-9 PENGUIN PB $11.95

Moon Palace

0-14-011585-4 PENGUIN PB $11.95

Mr. Vertigo

A rollicking story of a child, his master, and the Vaudeville circuit, which serves as a canvas for the American experience in the 20th century

0-14-023190-0 PENGUIN PB $10.95

The Music of Chance

A Boston fireman and a young gambler become involved in an increasingly terrifying poker game on a vast Pennsylvania estate

0-14-015407-8 PENGUIN PB $10.95

The New York Trilogy: City of Glass/Ghosts/The Locked Room

Three novels in which Auster reinvents the detective story as a kind of philosophical endgame

1-55713-166-X SUN & MOON $21.95

0-14-013155-8 PENGUIN PB $14.95

Smoke & Blue in the Face: Two Films

Auster's warm homage to his home, Brooklyn. *Smoke* tells the story of Augie, a cigar-shop owner who comes into contact with the varieties of people who live in his neighborhood. *Blue in the Face* is a lighter, more improvised examination of the same characters and themes

See also **INDIVIDUAL FILMS** under **SCREENPLAYS** under **FILM** in **PERFORMING ARTS AND MEDIA**

0-7868-8098-8 HYPERION PB $12.95

Translations

French philosophers and poets translated by the acclaimed author of *Leviathan* and *New York Stories*

1-56886-032-3 MARSILIO $28.00

1-56886-033-1 MARSILIO PB $14.95

James **Baldwin**

Another Country

An ambitious novel of New York life, centered on a suicide and its repercussions

0-679-74471-1 VINTAGE PB $13.00

Giovanni's Room

A man torn between homosexual love and the love of a woman; set in Paris

0-440-32881-0 LAUREL LEAF PB $5.99

Go Tell It on the Mountain

Baldwin's first novel tells the story of two generations of a black American family

0-440-33007-6 LAUREL LEAF PB $5.99

Going to Meet the Man

A collection of stories

0-679-76179-9 VINTAGE PB $11.00

If Beale Street Could Talk

A pregnant young woman struggles to free her falsely imprisoned fiancé

0-440-34060-8 DELL PB $5.99

Just Above My Head

A harlem gospel singer seeks his place in the world

0-440-20599-9 DELL PB $5.95

Nicholson **Baker**

The Fermata

More erotica from Baker, this time on the fantasy of being able to suspend time

0-679-75933-6 VINTAGE PB $12.00

Nicholson Baker

The Mezzanine

This novel-sized look at an office worker's break crams an encyclopedia's worth of keenly observed minutia into one of fiction's longest hours ever

0-679-72576-8 VINTAGE PB $10.00

Room Temperature

0-679-73440-6 VINTAGE PB $9.00

Vox

The all-night conversation of a man and woman on an anonymous 900-number party line becomes not only wittily provocative, but also reveals the distance that seems to characterize postmodern sexuality

0-679-74211-5 VINTAGE PB $10.00

Toni Cade **Bambara**

Gorilla, My Love

A first collection of short stories

0-679-73898-3 VINTAGE PB $10.00

The Salt Eaters

A "tribal epic" about Southern blacks who seek out the healing properties of salt

0-679-74076-7 VINTAGE PB $11.00

The Sea Birds Are Still Alive

Short stories

0-394-71176-9 VINTAGE PB $11.00

Russell **Banks**

Affliction

"*Affliction* is a powerful, deeply troubling work of fiction, with a fiercely tender lyricism at its core that makes its outer drama—personal tragedy, sociological 'comedy'—the more memorable. This is realistic fiction at its most successful, with its ability to touch our lives in essential, if not always comprehensible, ways" —Joyce Carol Oates

0-06-016142-6 HARPERCOLLINS PB $18.95

This is the story of my brother's strange criminal behavior and his disappearance. No one urged me to reveal these things; no one asked me not to. We who loved him simply no longer speak of Wade, not among ourselves and not with anyone else, either. It is almost as if he never existed,or as if he were a member of some other family or from some other place and we barely knew him and never had occasion to speak him. So that by telling his story like this, as his brother, I am separating myself from the family and from all those who ever loved him.

AFFLICTION

Continental Drift

0-06-092574-4 HARPERCOLLINS $13.00

Family Life

A man's family becomes his mythical kingdom

0-06-097704-3 HARPERCOLLINS PB $10.00

1-55713-004-3 SUN & MOON $13.95

The Relation of My Imprisonment

0-940650-25-8 SUN & MOON $12.95

Rule of the Bone

An amazing journey of self-discovery through a world of magic and violence, betrayal and redemption

0-06-017275-4 HARPERCOLLINS $22.00

0-06-092724-0 HARPERCOLLINS PB $10.00

The Sweet Hereafter

A small town's response to numbing tragedy: the death of 14 children in a school bus accident. Banks examines human behavior in the face of the worst, finding unexpected deposits of warmth and even humor

0-06-016703-3 HARPERPERENNIAL PB $19.95

Russell Banks (photo by Nathan Farb)

John **Barth**

Chimera

0-449-21113-4 FAWCETT PB $5.95

The Floating Opera & The End of the Road

In the former, Barth's first novel, a man reviews his life as he ponders suicide; the latter involves a parody of a love triangle. Both are unmistakably from the hand that gave us "The Literature of Exhaustion" as a coda for high modernism

0-385-24089-9 ANCHOR PB $12.95

Giles Goat Boy: The Revised New Syllabus

The college campus as a satirical microcosm of the contemporary world

0-385-24086-4 ANCHOR PB $15.95

The Last Voyage of Somebody the Sailor

The story of a journalist escaping Baghdad, is "ingenious multi-story fiction in which every floor turns out to be a false bottom" —*NY Times Book Review*

0-316-08251-1 LITTLE, BROWN $22.95

Letters

1-56478-061-9 DALKEY ARCHIVE PB $14.95

Lost in the Funhouse

A collection of 14 pieces thematically linked by their self-conscious, playful concern with the act of writing and reading

0-385-24087-2 ANCHOR PB $9.95

On with the Story: Stories

A middle-aged couple on vacation decide to tell each other stories—and their dozen tales, deftly woven through "pillow talk" intermezzos, make up this collection

0-316-08263-5 LITTLE, BROWN $23.95

Once Upon a Time

0-316-08262-7 LITTLE, BROWN $23.95

Sabbatical: A Romance

1-56478-096-1 DALKEY ARCHIVE PB $12.95

The Sot-Weed Factor

Ribald, picaresque take-off of an 18th-century figure. "The book is a joke book, an endless series of gags … But the biggest joke of all is that Barth seems to have written something closer to the Great American Novel than any other book of the last decades"—Leslie Fiedler

0-385-24088-0 ANCHOR PB $16.00

The Tidewater Tales

0-449-90293-5 FAWCETT PB $15.00

Donald **Barthelme**

The Dead Father

A macabre tale of 19 children dragging the body of their father across a city

0-14-008667-6 PENGUIN PB $10.95

Forty Stories

0-14-011245-6 VIKING PB $11.95

Sixty Stories

0-14-015300-4 DUTTON PB $13.95

Snow White

His first novel, a contemporary fairy tale

0-689-70331-7 MACMILLAN PB $7.95

0-684-82479-5 SCRIBNERS PB $10.00

Frederick **Barthelme**

Moon Deluxe

"I admire his peculiar grasp of the slant side of human relationships. *Moon Deluxe* is something else entirely—superbly written and very funny"—Raymond Carver

0-8021-3437-8 GROVE PB $12.00

Frederick **Barthelme**

Painted Desert

The chronicler of postmodern middle-class life again picks up the characters of his recent *The Brothers*—but three years later, and this time probing deeper and deeper into their intense lives. An aging junior college professor and his "cybermuckraker" girlfriend are moved by the images of OJ's Bronco and the LA riots to make their own run from it all. "Barthelme's characters succeed in stepping beyond the generic…they emerge as real individuals, amusing and selfish, vexing yet somehow poignant"—*NY Times*

0-670-86469-2 VIKING $22.95

Tracer

"Frederick Barthelme is doing for the '80s what Raymond Chandler did for the '30s. He does for the 7-Eleven what Edward Hopper did for the all-night diner… *Tracer* crackles with dry wit"—*Baltimore Sun*

0-14-008969-1 PENGUIN PB $4.95

Two Against One

A 15-year marriage laid bare and examined in the light of a new triangle

0-8021-3460-2 GROVE PB $12.00

Rick **Bass**

In the Loyal Mountains

0-395-71687-X HOUGHTON MIFFLIN $21.95

Platte River

Haunting novellas set in remote Montana by "the best young writer to come along in many years"—Annie Dillard. "Three fascinating long stories from the greatly gifted avatar of the outdoors….Beautifully written and filled with radiant imagery and a powerful sense of the mysteries of nature—human and otherwise" —*Kirkus Reviews*

See also **TROUT, FLY-FISHING, AND FLY-TYING** under **FISHING** under **THE OUTDOORS** in **FOOD, TRAVEL, AND LEISURE**

0-395-68080-8 HOUGHTON MIFFLIN $19.95

The Watch

0-393-31135-X NORTON PB $9.95

John Calvin **Batchelor**

American Falls

The pursuit of a Confederate spy in the North crystallizes the Civil War as a duel between two. men

0-8050-3787-X HOLT PB $15.00

The Birth of the People's Republic of Antarctica

Deftly done yet bleak anti-utopian fable

0-8050-3786-1 HOLT PB $14.00

The Further Adventures of Halley's Comet

0-8050-3788-8 HOLT PB $14.00

Walking the Cat, by Tommy "Tip" Paine: Gordon Libby Is My Muse II

Adventures of a gleefully right-wing CIA black-ops specialist

0-8050-3789-6 HOLT PB $12.00

Richard **Bausch**

"To read the fiction of Richard Bausch is to be hugely moved, to be in touch with the depths of experience, to be present at the creation of a monument to human worth."—Newsday

The Last Good Time

0-679-75556-X VINTAGE PB $11.00

Rebel Powers

In his sixth novel, Bausch meticulously describes the disintegration of a family after the father is dishonorably discharged from the Air Force and sentenced to two years, labor in a federal prison in Wyoming

0-395-59508-8 HOUGHTON MIFFLIN $21.95
0-679-75253-6 VINTAGE PB $12.00

Nina **Bawden**

Familiar Passions

1-85381-414-8 VIRAGO PB $11.95

A Grain of Truth

1-85381-424-5 VIRAGO PB $11.95

Charles **Baxter**

Believers: A Novella and Stories

0-679-44267-7 PANTHEON $25.00

First Light

Sibling rivalry between a salesman and his astrophysicist sister. "An intricately reflective, simply beautiful book" —Elizabeth Tallent, *LA Times*

0-14-010091-1 PENGUIN PB $10.95

Harmony of the World: Stories

0-679-77651-6 VINTAGE $11.00

Shadow Play

"Baxter's true talent rests in a kind of pureness and sensibility, an uncanny lyrical wisdom that is as elegant and accurate as modern weaponry"—*Mirabella*

0-14-023510-8 PENGUIN PB $11.95

Ann **Beattie**

Another You

At the heart of this novel is an English teacher at a small New England college and his wife, their respective flirtations and affairs, a student charging rape, and a chain of events that force the couple to reexamine their marriage and themselves

0-679-40078-8 KNOPF $24.00

Chilly Scenes of Winter

Beattie's first novel, a portrait of disenchanted '70s youth

0-679-73234-9 VINTAGE PB $12.00

Distortions

"Nineteen stories as arresting as Diane Arbus photographs"—*Chicago Sun-Times*

0-679-73235-7 VINTAGE PB $13.00

Falling in Place

The misfortunes of a suburban Connecticut family. "What…*The Heart Is a Lonely Hunter* was to the early '40s and…*The Catcher in the Rye* was to the '50s"—*Vogue*

0-679-73192-X VINTAGE PB $12.00

Love Always

"The semi-beautiful people of late 20th-century media-fringe America"—Margaret Atwood

0-394-74418-7 RANDOM HOUSE PB $11.00

Secrets and Surprises

Fifteen stories

0-679-73193-8 VINTAGE PB $11.00

Louis **Begley**

About Schmidt

0-679-45033-5 KNOPF $22.50

As Max Saw It

The reunion of two men, years after their days together at Harvard, serves as the occasion to dramatize a magnificent tale of friendship and mortality

0-679-43307-4 KNOPF $21.00

Louis Begley

Wartime Lies

An unforgettable novel about a Jewish child hiding out in Nazi-occupied Poland, nominated for a National Book Award

0-8041-0990-7 IVY PB $5.99

Madison Smartt **Bell**

All Souls' Rising

A richly told story of the Haitian slave revolution of 1791

0-679-43989-7 PANTHEON $25.95

A Soldier's Joy

0-14-013359-3 PENGUIN PB $11.95

Straight Cut

"Bell is, quite simply, a virtuoso novelist. Imagine Graham Greene melding his 'entertainments' with his sober efforts and you'll have some idea of *Straight Cut*"—*Philadelphia Inquirer*

0-14-010471-2 SELECT PENGUIN PB $3.95

Ten Indians

0-679-44246-4 PANTHEON $24.00

Waiting for the End of the World

0-14-009330-3 PENGUIN PB $9.95

The Washington Square Ensemble

The denizens of New York's Washington Square Park in a portrait of that city's seedy underworld

0-14-007025-7 PENGUIN PB $11.95

The Year of Silence

0-14-011533-1 PENGUIN PB $11.95

Zero db & Other Stories

Eleven short stories. "Contemporary literature is receiving a welcome healthy impetus from the presence of Madison Smart Bell; and *Zero db*, this impressive book of short fiction, will likely stand as one of his best achievements" —*Washington Post*

0-14-010629-4 PENGUIN PB $6.95

Saul **Bellow**

The Adventures of Augie March

The life story of a Jewish Huck Finn, from the slums of Chicago to the glitzy capitals of the Continent

0-679-44460-2 EVERYMAN'S $20.00
0-14-018941-6 PENGUIN PB $12.95

Saul Bellow

Dangling Man

In Bellow's first novel, a young man is left dangling when the army snarls his induction in red tape

0-14-018935-1 PENGUIN PB $11.95

The Dean's December

"*The Dean's December* is renewed testament to a grand career, our greatest since Faulkner's and Frost's. At an age when most writers are hopelessly repeating themselves, Bellow is still finding good new things to do" —*Chicago Sun-Times*

0-671-60254-3 POCKET PB $4.50

Henderson the Rain King

Henderson tries to flee modern chaos in African jungles

0-14-007269-1 PENGUIN PB $11.95

Herzog

Moses Herzog deals with his personal crisis by writing erudite, compulsively readable letters to the living and the dead

0-14-018943-2 PENGUIN PB $11.95

Humboldt's Gift

A gifted, troubled writer (modeled on Delmore Schwartz) is torn apart by the conflicting demands of artistic purity and commercial success

0-14-007271-3 VIKING PB $12.95

Mosby's Memoir & Other Stories

A variety of stories, led off by Bellow's classic portrayal of a disaffected Jewish intellectual

0-14-018945-9 PENGUIN PB $11.95

Mr. Sammler's Planet

An elderly but vivacious man casts a skeptical eye on Manhattan in the radical '60s

See also **HOLOCAUST FICTION** under **ART AND LITERATURE** under **THE HOLOCAUST** in **WORLD HISTORY AND CURRENT AFFAIRS**

INTRODUCTION BY STANLEY CROUCH

0-393-30472-8 NORTON PB $7.95
0-14-018936-X PENGUIN PB $11.95

Seize the Day

A powerful novella in which a bewildered young New York man is defeated by an implacable father, estranged wife, and beguiling charlatan in one vertiginous day

INTRODUCTION BY CYNTHIA OZICK

0-14-018937-8 PENGUIN PB $10.95

The Victim

0-14-018938-6 PENGUIN PB $11.95

Thomas **Berger**

The Feud

0-385-29221-X DOUBLEDAY $13.95

Meeting Evil

0-316-09271-1 BULFINCH PB $9.95

Nowhere

0-385-29401-8 DIAL BOOKS $14.95

Regiment of Women

0-316-09242-8 LITTLE, BROWN PB $10.95

Suspect

0-688-11925-5 MORROW $23.00

Frank **Bergon**

Shoshone Mike

0-14-009876-3 NEVADA PB $7.95

Gina **Berriault**

Women in Their Beds: New and Selected Stories

1-88717-810-4 COUNTERPOINT $25.00

Wendell **Berry**

Nathan Coulter

The first in Berry's series of novels set in Port William, Kentucky

0-86547-184-3 NORTH POINT PB $11.00

Remembering

Berry's first novel in 14 years takes place in a single day in Port William

0-86547-331-5 FS&G PB $11.00

Watch with Me: And Six Other Stories of the Yet-Remembered Ptolemy Proudfoot and His Wife, Miss Minnie, Née Quinch

"A small treasure of a book…part of a long line that descends from Chaucer to Katherine Mansfield to William Trevor"—*Chicago Tribune*

0-679-75854-2 VINTAGE PB $11.00

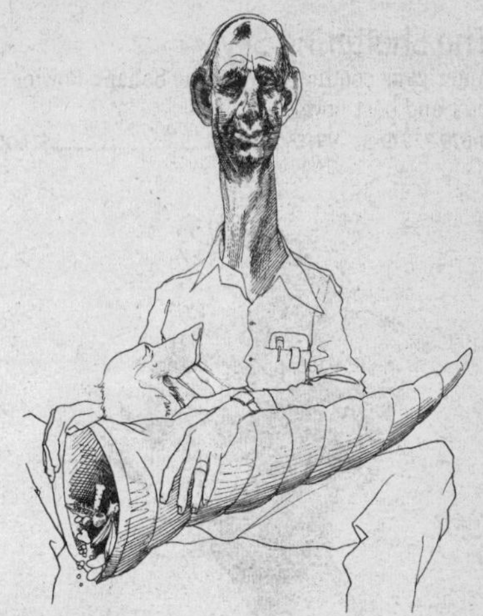

Wendell Berry

The Wild Birds: Six Stories of the Port William Membership

0-86547-217-3 NORTH POINT PB $9.00

Jane **Bowles**

My Sister's Hand in Mine: The Collected Works of Jane Bowles

Includes her novel *Two Serious Ladies,* her play *In the Summer House,* and other writings

0-374-50652-3 NOONDAY PB $16.00

Paul **Bowles**

Collected Stories of Paul Bowles

"A master of suggesting anxiety … Bowles has glimpsed what lies back of our sheltering sky … an endless flux of stars so like those atoms which make us see that in our apprehension of this terrible infinity, we experience not only horror but likeness"—Gore Vidal

INTRODUCTION BY GORE VIDAL

0-87685-396-3 BLACK SPARROW PB $16.00

The Delicate Prey

Seventeen stories. "One of the most profound, beautifully wrought, and haunting collections in our literatures"—Tobias Wolff

0-88001-263-3 ECCO PB $12.00

A Hundred Camels in the Courtyard

Four stories of contemporary Moroccan life, all dealing with kif-smokers

0-87286-002-7 SUBTERRANEAN PB $6.95

Let It Come Down

A mild-mannered American who goes to Morocco to find himself finds more than he bargained for

0-87685-479-X BLACK SPARROW PB $15.00

Midnight Mass

A collection of recent stories, some with considerably more humor than is generally attributed to Bowles

0-87685-476-5 BLACK SPARROW PB $12.50

Points in Time

The points in time are moments in the history of Morocco, imagined with precision and brevity

0-88001-044-4 ECCO $12.50
0-88001-117-3 ECCO PB $7.95

The Sheltering Sky

Americans coming apart in the Sahara: Bowles's first and best novel

0-679-72979-8 VINTAGE PB....$13.00

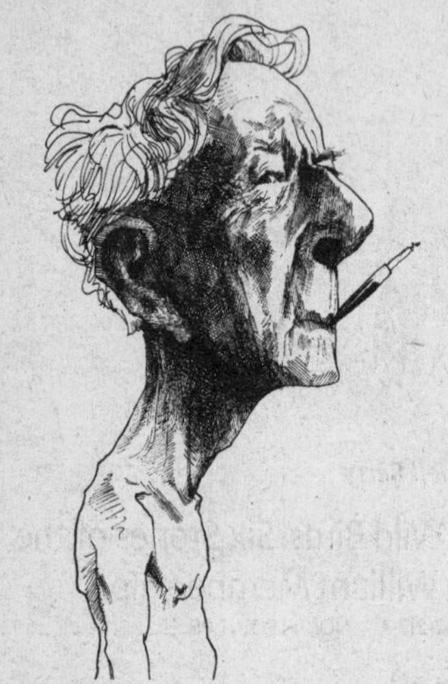

Paul Bowles

The Spider's House

This account of revolution in Fez in the 1950s is Bowles's most elaborate fiction

0-87685-545-1 BLACK SPARROW PB....$15.00

Too Far from Home: The Selected Writing of Paul Bowles

0-88001-295-1 ECCO....$29.95

0-88001-391-5 ECCO PB....$17.00

Unwelcome Words

Seven recent, frequently experimental stories

0-939180-44-8 TOMBOUCTOU PB....$8.00

Up Above the World

An American couple descends into drugs and violent death, courtesy of a charming South American psychopath

0-88001-302-8 ECCO PB....$10.95

Paul **Bowles** & Jane **Bowles**

The Portable Paul and Jane Bowles

EDITED BY MILLICENT DILLON

0-14-016960-1 VIKING PB....$13.95

T. Coraghessan **Boyle**

Budding Prospects

0-14-029996-3 VIKING PB....$11.95

T. Coraghessan Boyle (credit: ©Pablo Campos)

Descent of Man

Seventeen "wild and absurd stories that give new dimension to black humor"
—*Publishers Weekly*

0-14-029994-7 PENGUIN PB....$10.95

East Is East

0-14-013167-1 PENGUIN PB....$11.95

Greasy Lake & Other Stories

"Satirical fables of contemporary life, so funny and acutely observed that they might have been written by Evelyn Waugh as sketches for the old 'Saturday Night Live' "—*NY Times*

0-14-007781-2 PENGUIN PB....$10.95

If the River Was Whiskey

Boyle's most recent collection of short stories

0-14-011950-7 PENGUIN PB....$11.95

The Road to Wellville

A based-on-fact farce set in a health spa during the early part of the century

0-14-016718-8 PENGUIN PB....$10.95

The Tortilla Curtain

A rich and moving drama of the men and women who cross the Mexican border and muddy the complacent lives of those who think that they've attained the American Dream in a gated Los Angeles community. Two characters from each side of the fence lend their complex viewpoints to the story

0-670-85604-5 VIKING....$23.95

0-14-023828-X PENGUIN PB....$11.95

No one had moved. Not yet, not yet. They all turned back to the TV, hoping for a reprieve, hoping that they'd be been watching old footage, color-enhanced pictures of the Dresden bombing, anything but the real and actual.
THE TORTILLA CURTAIN

Water Music

0-14-006550-4 PENGUIN PB....$12.99

World's End

A man's search for his lost father spans many centuries of Hudson Valley history to reveal hidden family secrets. Winner of the PEN/Faulkner Award for American fiction

0-14-029993-9 PENGUIN PB....$12.95

John Ed **Bradley**

Smoke

"Monster Mart may have destroyed Smoke, but John Ed Bradley's entertaining narrative brings it right back to life"
—*Washington Post Book World*

0-14-024759-9 PENGUIN PB....$10.95

Harold **Brodkey**

Profane Friendship

0-374-23544-9 FS&G....$23.00

The Runaway Soul

Brodkey offers an intimate trip into "the runaway soul, flying and trying and crying and lying and dying" of his hero, growing up in St. Louis, through his adolescence and young adulthood

0-374-25286-6 FS&G....$30.00

This Wild Darkness: The Story of My Death

0-8050-4831-6 HOLT....$20.00

Harold Brodkey

Stories in an Almost Classical Mode

A collection of all his major stories. "For years, a small clutch of writers and critics not ordinarily given to breathtaking adoration has compared Brodkey to Freud, Wordsworth, and Whitman"
—*Washington Post*

0-394-50699-5 KNOPF....$24.95

0-679-72431-1 VINTAGE PB....$18.00

Michael **Brodsky**

***: A Novel

1-56858-000-2 FOUR WALLS....$26.95

1-56858-001-0 FOUR WALLS PB....$13.95

Southernmost

1-56858-064-9 FOUR WALLS....$25.00

1-56858-065-7 FOUR WALLS PB....$14.95

Larry **Brown**

Father and Son

1-56512-014-0 ALGONQUIN....$22.95

Joe

A novel of degradation and redemption in the back country of northern Mississippi, by a novelist whom the *Fort Lauderdale Sun-Sentinel* called "the most distinctive voice to emerge in Southern literature since Flannery O'Connor"

0-945575-61-0 ALGONQUIN....$19.95

On Fire

Brown writes of his 17 years of fighting fires for the Oxford, Miss., Fire Department

See also **MEMOIRS AND JOURNALS** under **20TH-CENTURY AMERICAN ESSAYS AND JOURNALISM**

1-56512-009-4 ALGONQUIN....$17.95

0446671140 ALGONQUIN PB....$17.95

Rita Mae **Brown**

Bingo

0-553-28220-4 BDD PB....$5.99

Rubyfruit Jungle

A witty autobiographical novel of a young lesbian's coming of age

0-553-27886-X BDD PB....$6.50

Six of One

Two sisters raise hell in the American South

0-553-27887-8 BDD PB....$6.50

Southern Discomfort
Interactions in early 20th-century Montgomery, Alabama, involving gay women, one macho man, and cocaine
0-553-27446-5 BDD PB $4.99

Starting from Scratch
0-553-34630-X BANTAM PB $11.95

Sudden Death
Lesbian love on the professional tennis circuit
0-553-26930-5 BDD PB $6.50

Rosellen **Brown**

Civil Wars
A white family living in a black neighborhood in mid-'60s Mississippi
0-440-21695-8 DELL PB $5.99

Cora Fry's Pillow Book
Brown returns after 20 years to her celebrated poetic character Cora Fry. Loss and bewildering challenge vie with redemption and wry humor in this portrait of a brave, ordinary woman in a small community. Brown is "full of humor, truth, anger, and tenderness [and] has given us a novel stripped down to essences in this remarkable set of poems and the critical evocations of a country woman's life"—May Sarton
0-374-14402-8 FS&G $15.00

Tender Mercies
A happy marriage is shattered when a man accidentally paralyzes his wife in a boating accident
0-440-21696-6 DELL PB $5.99

Wesley **Brown**

Darktown Strutters
0-943433-11-8 CANE HILL PB $11.95

Tragic Magic
0-88001-401-6 ECCO PB $13.00

Michael **Brownstein**

Self-Reliance
1-56689-018-7 COFFEE HOUSE PB $12.95

Charles **Bukowski**

The late, great chronicler of the down and out. "A professional disturber of the peace... Laureate of the Los Angeles netherworld."
—Newsweek

Factotum
0-87685-263-0 BLACK SPARROW PB $13.00

Ham on Rye
0-87685-557-5 BLACK SPARROW PB $14.00

Hollywood
0-87685-764-0 BLACK SPARROW $25.00
0-87685-763-2 BLACK SPARROW PB $13.50

The Most Beautiful Woman in Town
0-87286-156-2 SUBTERRANEAN PB $12.95

Notes of a Dirty Old Man
"Bukowski writes like a latter-day Celine, a wise fool talking straight from the gut about the futility and beauty of life"— *Publishers Weekly*
0-87286-074-4 CITY LIGHTS PB $11.95

Post Office
An autobiographical novel of a down-and-out, drinking, writing postman
0-87685-087-5 BLACK SPARROW $20.00
0-87685-086-7 BLACK SPARROW PB $12.00

Pulp
When you stop to think about it, who better than Bukowski, the late grand old man of L.A. letters, to set a potboiler in Chandler and Hammett's depression landscape? In his only venture into the form, Bukowski's alter ego, Hank Chinaski, is a gumshoe in the employ of Lady Death, on the trail of a missing writer, Céline
0-87685-927-9 BLACK SPARROW $25.00
0-87685-926-0 BLACK SPARROW PB $14.00

Run with the Hunted: A Charles Bukowski Reader
John Martin, Bukowski's editor and publisher at Black Sparrow for 25 years, has compiled the first anthology of his voluminous body of writing. Poems and stories are arranged chronologically by the period in Bukowski's life that they cover, making this a virtual autobiography told through his best work
0-87685-980-5 BLACK SPARROW $15.00

Tales of Ordinary Madness
Thirty-four autobiographical short stories
0-87286-155-4 CITY LIGHTS PB $12.95

Women
"I was fifty years old and hadn't been to bed with a woman for four years"—from *Women*
0-87685-390-4 BLACK SPARROW PB $14.00

James Lee **Burke**

The Convict
0-7868-8143-7 HYPERION PB $10.95

Half of Paradise
0-7868-8117-8 HYPERION PB $10.95

Lay Down My Sword and Shield
0-7868-8039-2 HYPERION PB $10.95

The Lost Get-Back Boogie
0-7868-8101-1 HYPERION PB $10.95

To the Bright and Shining Sun
0-7868-8012-0 HYPERION PB $10.95

Two for Texas
0-7868-8011-2 HYPERION PB $10.95

Olive **Burns**

A Cold Sassy Tree
"One of the best portraits of small-town Southern life ever written"—Pat Conroy
0-89919-309-9 TICKNOR & FIELDS $22.95
0-385-31258-X DELL PB $12.95

William S. **Burroughs**

"The only American novelist living today who could conceivably be possessed by genius."
—Norman Mailer

Cities of the Red Night
"Burroughs may be our only writer whose sociopolitical apocalyptica transcends both paranoia and triviality; his imagination is superb, his ear savagely satiric"
—Kirkus Reviews
0-8050-1763-1 HOLT PB $9.95

William S. Burroughs

Exterminator!
"Burroughs is the greatest satirical writer since Jonathan Swift"—Jack Kerouac
0-14-005003-5 VIKING PB $10.95

Ghost of Chance
1-85242-406-0 SERPENT'S TAIL $14.99

Interzone
A collection of hitherto unpublished early writings, some from the same period as *Naked Lunch*
EDITED BY JAMES GRAUERHOLZ
0-14-009451-2 PENGUIN PB $11.95

Junky
0-14-004351-9 PENGUIN $10.95

The Last Words of Dutch Schultz: A Fiction in the Form of a Film Script
1-55970-211-7 ARCADE PB $9.95

My Education: A Book of Dreams
"Mr. Burroughs has lost none of his irreverence or wit, but in recent years he has acquired an elegant, elegiac tone"—*NY Times*
0-670-81350-8 VIKING $21.95
0-14-009454-7 PENGUIN PB $10.95

Naked Lunch
"An absolutely devastating ridicule of all that is false, primitive, and vicious in current American life"—Terry Southern
0-8021-3295-2 GROVE PB $11.95

Nova Express
"*Nova Express*...is a sermon-blast of language...[Burroughs] is the Martin Luther of hipsterism, welding his decree onto the silicon doors of the solar system"—*Newsweek*
0-8021-3330-4 GROVE PB $9.95

The Place of Dead Roads
A surreal version of a 19th-century Western. "Bosch-like visions, extraordinarily precise vivid visualizations ... Outrageous ideas like mind bombs"— Allen Ginsberg
0-8050-3954-6 HOLT PB $12.00
0-8050-1541-8 HOLT PB $10.95

William S. **Burroughs**

Queer

The innovator of the cut up method donates another novel to the absurdist cache. Incomprehensible, yet oddly amusing, in the vein of *Naked Lunch,* but with less coherency, *The Soft Machine* is a fever-stream of semi-consciousness: the body as weak craver of sex, of junk, of any addiction available

0-14-008389-8 PENGUIN $10.95

The Soft Machine

0-8021-3329-0 GROVE PB $9.95

The Ticket that Exploded

A prophetic vision of a world in which technology has gone haywire. "His Swiftian vision of a processed, pre-packaged life, a kind of electro-chemical totalitarianism, often evokes the black laughter of hilarious horror"—*Playboy*

0-8021-5150-7 GROVE PB $9.95

The Western Lands

"In Mr. Burroughs' hands, writing reverts to acts of magic, as though he were making some enormous internal encyclopedia of all the black impulses and acts that, once made, would shut the fiends away forever"—*NY Times*

0-14-009456-3 PENGUIN PB $12.95

The Wild Boys

"An ethereally beautiful book"—*Rolling Stone*

0-8021-3331-2 GROVE PB $9.95

William S. **Burroughs,** Jr.

Speed/Kentucky Ham: Two Novels

0-87951-505-8 OVERLOOK PB $13.95

Frederick **Busch**

"Busch shows us why he ought to be a household name. His is the classic American style, ice-clear, dagger-sharp, with dialogue that slashes back and forth like a razor."—Seattle Times

The Children in the Woods: New and Selected Stories

From the winner of the 1991 PEN/Malamud Award for excellence in short fiction, a brilliant collection of stories about survival, abandonment, and vulnerability

0-395-64724-X TICKNOR & FIELDS $21.95

Manual Labor

0-8112-0535-5 NEW DIRECTIONS $8.50

0-8112-0536-3 NEW DIRECTIONS PB $3.95

Too Late American Boyhood Blues

0-87923-511-X GODINE $15.95

Octavia E. **Butler**

"What [William] Gibson does for young, disaffected persons of high tech and low life, Octavia E. Butler does for people of color. She gives us a future."—Vibe

Adulthood Rites

0-445-20903-8 QUEST PB $5.99

INTRODUCTION BY ROBERT CROSSLEY

0-8070-8305-4 BEACON PB $12.95

Bloodchild: Novellas and Stories

To say that Butler, a Hugo and Nebula Award winner, is the inventor of a genre—African-American-feminist science fiction—might imply that her stories are ideological excercises. Instead they are riveting prose dramas that bring universal experiences to life

See also **CONTEMPORARY SCIENCE FICTION** under **SCIENCE FICTION AND FANTASY** in **POPULAR READING**

1-56858-055-X FOUR WALLS $18.00

1-88836-336-3 SEVEN STORIES PB $10.00

Bloodchild is my pregnant man story. I've always wanted to explore what it might be like for a man to be put into that most unlikely of all positions. Could I write a story in which a man chose to become pregnant *not* through some sort of misplaced competitiveness to prove that a man could do anything a woman could do, not because he was forced to, not even out of curiosity? I wanted to see whether I could write a dramatic story of a man becoming pregnant as an act of love—choosing pregnancy in spite of as well as because of surrounding difficulties.

BLOODCHILD: NOVELLAS AND STORIES

Dawn

See also **CONTEMPORARY SCIENCE FICTION** under **SCIENCE FICTION AND FANTASY** in **POPULAR READING**

0-445-20779-5 POPULAR LIBRARY PB $5.99

Kindred

See also **CONTEMPORARY SCIENCE FICTION** under **SCIENCE FICTION AND FANTASY** in **POPULAR READING**

Wild Seed

See also **CONTEMPORARY SCIENCE FICTION** under **SCIENCE FICTION AND FANTASY** in **POPULAR READING**

0-445-20537-7 QUEST PB $5.99

Robert Olen **Butler**

Tabloid Dreams

0-8050-3131-6 HOLT $22.50

Hortense **Calisher**

Age

0-7145-3012-3 MARION BOYARS PB $13.95

In the Palace of the Movie King

From the esteemed author of *Mysteries of Motion,* a large-scale novel about a brilliant film director who is lured from his closed Balkan homeland to the fantastical kingdoms of California and New York

0-679-41574-2 RANDOM HOUSE $25.00

In the Slammer with Carol Smith

0-7145-3020-4 MARION BOYARS $24.95

Kissing Cousins

1-55584-194-5 WEIDENFELD & NICOLSON $14.95

Ethan **Canin**

Blue River

The complex, unresolved conflict between two brothers, one a doctor, the other a drifter

0-446-39447-5 WARNER PB $11.99

Emperor of the Air: Stories

1-55584-194-5 WEIDENFELD & NICOLSON $14.95

The Palace Thief

Four novellas with themes ranging from a boy's fascination with rebellion to a father trying to comprehend the patterns of relationships

0-060-97208-4 HARPERCOLLINS PB $12.00

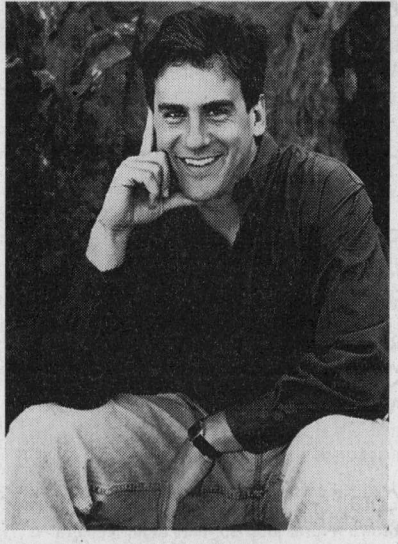

Ethan Canin (credit: ©Andy Freeberg)

Mary **Caponegro**

The Star Cafe & Other Stories

0-393-30791-3 NORTON PB $8.95

Truman **Capote**

Answered Prayers: The Unfinished Novel

Much discussed but never completed, Capote's last work stands as a bitter portrait of the beau monde on New York's Upper East Side

0-452-26483-9 NEW AMERICAN LIBRARY PB $11.95

Breakfast at Tiffany's

The novella about Holly Golightly, the backwoods girl on the fast track in Manhattan

0-679-74565-3 VINTAGE PB $11.00

Breakfast at Tiffany's: A Short Novel and Three Stories

0-679-60085-X MODERN LIBRARY $13.50

A Capote Reader

A varied sampling of Capote's work, including short stories, travel sketches, reportage, and the novellas *The Grass Harp* and *Breakfast at Tiffany's.* "When God hands you a gift, he also hands you a whip"—Truman Capote

See also **LITERATURE** under **20TH-CENTURY AMERICAN ESSAYS AND JOURNALISM**

0-394-55647-X RANDOM HOUSE $35.00

The Grass Harp, A Tree of Night & Other Short Stories

A novella and a group of stories that catch Capote in his early, elegiac, beautifully nostalgic mood

0-679-74557-2 VINTAGE PB $11.00

In Cold Blood

The original "nonfiction novel," first published in 1966, chronicling the murder of a Kansas family by two drifters

See also **MODERN CRIMINAL CASES** under **TRUE CRIME** in **POPULAR READING**

See also **REPORTING** under **20TH-CENTURY AMERICAN ESSAYS AND JOURNALISM**

0-679-60023-X MODERN LIBRARY $15.50

0-679-74558-0 VINTAGE PB $12.00

Music for Chameleons: New Writing
A collection of stories, interviews, and sketches, including the famous true-crime grotesque, "Handcarved Coffins"
0-679-74566-1 VINTAGE PB $12.00

Other Voices, Other Rooms
Capote's first novel, the story of a sensitive boy growing up in the American south
0-679-74564-5 VINTAGE PB $11.00

Philip **Caputo**

Del Corso's Gallery
0-06-098606-9 HARPERPERENNIAL PB $11.00

Equation for Evil
0-06-018360-8 HARPERCOLLINS $25.00

James **Carroll**

Mortal Friends
0-8070-6339-8 BEACON PB $16.95

Raymond **Carver**

Cathedral
"A dozen stories that overflow with the danger, excitement, mystery and possibility of life … Carver is a writer of astonishing compassion and honesty"—Jonathan Yardley, *Washington Post*
0-679-72369-2 VINTAGE PB $11.00

Fires
Selected essays, poems, and stories written between 1968 and 1983
0-679-72239-4 VINTAGE PB $11.00

Short Cuts: Selected Stories
The nine stories that Robert Altman adapted for the big screen. Includes an introduction by Altman. "Carver's stories can be counted among the masterpieces of American fiction" —Irving Howe, *NY Times Book Review*
0-679-74864-4 VINTAGE PB $10.00

Raymond Carver (credit: ©Marion Ettlinger)

Ultramarine
0-394-75535-9 VINTAGE PB $12.00

What We Talk About When We Talk About Love
Seventeen spare stories from the '70s. "Real as discount stores, time clocks, the franchises in small towns, bad marriages"— Stanley Elkin
0-679-72305-6 VINTAGE PB $9.00

Where I'm Calling From: New and Selected Stories
0-679-72231-9 VINTAGE PB $13.00

Will You Please Be Quiet, Please?: Stories
0-679-73569-0 VINTAGE PB $10.00

John **Casey**

Spartina
0-394-50098-9 KNOPF $18.95

John Casey (photo by Thomas Cogill)

Frederick Ted **Castle**

Gilbert Green: The Real Right Way to Dress for Spring
A dead-on evocation of the Warholian '60s, written on the spot
0-929701-23-2 MCPHERSON PB $11.00

Michael **Chabon**

A Model World and Other Stories
0-380-71099-4 AVON PB $10.00

The Mysteries of Pittsburgh
0-06-097212-2 HARPERCOLLINS PB $11.00

Wonder Boys
0-312-14094-0 PICADOR PB $13.00

Jerome **Charyn**

The Tar Baby
1-56478-078-3 DALKEY ARCHIVE PB $10.95

Joan **Chase**

The Evening Wolves
A poetic novel about American family life, seen through the eyes of two young sisters
0-374-15003-6 FS&G $18.95

Susan **Chase**

Intimacy
0-452-26375-1 PLUME PB $7.95

Barbara **Chase-Riboud**

The President's Daughter
The story of Jefferson's illegitimate daughter, her release from Monticello at 21, and her life in Philadelphia society. An enticing trip into the past
0-517-59861-2 CROWN $24.00

Sally Hemmings
0-345-38971-9 BALLANTINE PB $12.00

John **Cheever**

"Cheever is the celebrant of the grand poetry of life … The paradisiacal elixir … is served up sparkling."—John Updike, New Yorker

Falconer
A college professor is sentenced to prison for killing his brother
0-679-73786-3 VINTAGE PB $12.00

Oh What a Paradise It Seems
0-679-73785-5 VINTAGE PB $9.00

The Stories of John Cheever
"Some of the most wonderful stories any American has written"—*Boston Globe*
0-394-50087-3 KNOPF $40.00

The Wapshot Chronicle
A comic-elegiac account of an eccentric New England family
0-679-73899-1 VINTAGE PB $12.00

The Wapshot Scandal
A sequel to The *Wapshot Chronicle*. "John Cheever is one of the most urbane moralists of our time; he is also one of our most entertaining story tellers"—*NY Times*
0-679-73900-9 VINTAGE PB $13.00

John Cheever

Susan **Cheever**

Elizabeth Cole
0-374-14657-8 FS&G $18.95

Alfred **Chester**

Head of a Sad Angel
Since the late '60s, Chester's strange, outrageous fiction had been all but forgotten until this marvelous collection of his short stories was published. Includes critical essays by Gore Vidal and others
0-87685-804-3 BLACK SPARROW $25.00
0-87685-803-5 BLACK SPARROW PB $15.00

Frank **Chin**

The Chinaman Pacific and Frisco R.R. Co.
Acclaimed short fiction by one of America's most exciting playwrights. "The stories use fantasy, obscenity, slapstick and acute introspection to describe the frenzied search for identity of a Chinese-American artist" —*NY Times Book Review*
0-918273-44-7 COFFEE HOUSE PB $10.95

Frank **Chin**

Gunga Din Highway

1-56689-024-1 COFFEE HOUSE $24.95
1-56689-037-3 COFFEE HOUSE PB $14.95

Carolyn **Chute**

The Beans of Egypt, Maine

0-446-30010-1 WARNER PB $5.99

Merry Men

Another tale of Egypt, Maine, this time focusing on the Barringtons, a classic Egypt clan, and the hoity-toity family of newly deceased Dr. William Curry, whose wife and assorted children deal with loss in the most wondrous ways

0-15-159270-5 HARCOURT BRACE $24.95
0-15-600191-8 HARVEST PB $15.00

Carolyn Chute (photo by Joanna Eldredge Morrissey)

Walter Van Tilburg **Clark**

The Ox-Bow Incident

The famous novel of a lynching

See also **CLASSIC WESTERN WRITERS** under **WESTERNS** in **POPULAR READING**

0-88411-135-0 AMEREON $22.95
0-451-52525-6 NEW AMERICAN LIBRARY PB $4.95

The Track of the Cat

A mountain lion preys on an isolated ranchhouse

0-87417-230-6 NEVADA PB $14.95

Andrei **Codrescu**

The Blood Countess

The inimitable chronicler of American modernity turns his eye to his own past in a story about the roots of evil and violence

0-684-80244-9 SIMON & SCHUSTER $23.00
0-440-22191-9 DELL PB $6.99

Christopher **Coe**

I Look Divine

"A fascinating account of the relationship between two brothers"—*Village Voice*

0-394-75995-8 VINTAGE PB $8.00

Such Times

"May well be the gay novel of the decade" —*Publishers Weekly*

0-14-024143-4 PENGUIN PB $10.95

Cyrus **Colter**

A Chocolate Soldier

"Cyrus Colter tackles epic themes as though they were wild horses—and he tames them….A knockout!"—Studs Terkel

0-8101-5038-7 NORTHWESTERN PB $14.95

The Hippodrome

A Chicago man decapitates his wife and is discovered by two women who blackmail him into performing in a homosexual circus

0-8101-5036-0 NORTHWESTERN PB $13.95

The Rivers of Eros

0-252-06089-X ILLINOIS PB $9.95

Laurie **Colwin**

Another Marvelous Thing

Eight connected stories on love, marriage, and birth

0-14-009854-2 HARPERPERENNIAL PB $10.00

A Big Storm Knocked It Over

Posthumously published, this final novel is a "domestic fairy tale for adults….Colwin examines some traditional institutions with a laser-sharp eye and an offbeat sense of humor…in witty, accurate dialogue and graceful prose, and with inimitable charm" —*Publishers Weekly*

0-06-092546-9 HARPERPERENNIAL PB $12.00

Family Happiness

"A novel of a woman torn between her sense of family obligation and a wildly fulfilling love affair"—*NY Times*

0-06-097272-6 HARPERCOLLINS PB $12.00

Happy All the Time

0-14-007687-5 HARPERPERENNIAL PB $6.95

The Lone Pilgrim

"Laurie Colwin's witty, graceful stories convey both leisurely walks and sudden, unexpected springs…She is a remarkably cheerful messenger"—Paul Gray, *Time*

0-06-097270-X HARPERCOLLINS PB $10.00

Passion and Affect

"She gives the impression that she has single-handedly revitalized the short story" —Robert Kirsch, *LA Times*

0-14-007415-5 HARPERPERENNIAL PB $10.00

Shine On, Bright and Dangerous Object

0-14-007414-7 HARPERCOLLINS PB $10.00

Richard **Condon**

The Venerable Bead: A Deadly Serious Novel

America's master of satire mixes counter-espionage, rock superstardom, Washington lobbying law firms, arms dealing, and fast food empires in a wickedly funny new novel. "There's nobody quite like Richard Condon writing satirical novels today…May he go on forever" —*NY Times*

0-312-08331-9 ST. MARTIN'S $21.95

Evan S. **Connell**

The Alchemist's Journal

An imaginary collection of seven medieval alchemists' writings. "A banquet of ideas…Its surface resplendent with forgotten lore of alchemy, science, and love" —*Publishers Weekley*

0-86547-464-8 NORTH POINT $19.95

The Collected Stories of Evan S. Connell

1-88717-806-6 COUNTERPOINT $30.00

Diary of a Rapist

An obscure civil servant escapes from his dreary life through an obsession with a beautiful socialite

0-88001-408-3 ECCO PB $13.00

Mr. Bridge

The companion volume to *Mrs. Bridge*

0-86547-054-5 NORTH POINT PB $9.95

Mrs. Bridge

A brilliantly detailed and subtle portrait of a 1930s Kansas matron. "Funny, sad, touching and beautifully written, these sly yet sympathetic unfrockings of Kansas City's upper-bourgeoisie between the Depression and World War II seem even more readable and timely than when first published"—*San Francisco Chronicle*

0-86547-056-1 NORTH POINT PB $9.95

Frank **Conroy**

Body & Soul

The first novel by the author of the popular biography *Stop Time*. A child in post-World War II New York discovers his gift for music and rises from his less-than-prosperous surroundings to fame and riches. "Conroy pulls off one of the most difficult achievements imaginable in fiction—writing about an artist and making it seem authentic"—David Halberstam, *Vanity Fair*

0-440-21789-X BDD PB $5.99

Midair

0-14-008984-5 PENGUIN PB $10.00

Stop Time

0-14-004446-9 PENGUIN PB $11.95

Clarence **Cooper**, Jr.

The Scene

A harsh novel of the world of heroin addiction and prostitution, first published in 1960

0-393-31463-4 NORTON PB $11.00

Dennis **Cooper**

Closer

0-8021-3212-X GROVE PB $8.95

Frisk

0-8021-3289-8 GROVE PB $9.95

Try

"*Try* is a logical extension of what Cooper has been doing all along: trying to get under the skin, past the flesh, to figure out what's really inside"—*OUT Magazine*

0-8021-3338-X GROVE PB $11.00

Wrong

New and powerful stories by the author of *Safe* and *Frisk*. "Nobody since Genet has written with such lucid brutality"—*Mother Jones*

0-8021-1401-6 GROVE PB $18.95

J. California **Cooper**

Family

0-385-41171-5 DOUBLEDAY $21.00
0-385-41172-3 DOUBLEDAY PB $9.95

In Search of Satisfaction

0-385-46786-9 ANCHOR PB $10.00

A Piece of Mine
0-385-42087-0 ANCHOR PB $8.95

Robert **Coover**

John's Wife
Described by *The New York Times* as "probably the funniest and most malicious of all the postmodern writers," Coover presents in his newest novel a magical tale of small-town America in which a singular woman casts a spell on all around her
0-684-81841-8 SIMON & SCHUSTER $24.00

A Night at the Movies: Or, You Must Remember This
1-56478-016-3 DALKEY ARCHIVE PB $9.95

Pinocchio in Venice
0-8021-3485-8 GROVE $25.01

Spanking the Maid
A formalist variation on some traditional erotic motifs
0-394-17971-4 GROVE PB $4.95

The Universal Baseball Association, Inc.
In this tale of fate and imagination, a bachelor accountant brings a baseball league of his own creation to life every night on his kitchen table
See also **BASEBALL FICTION** under **BASEBALL** under **SPORTS** in **FOOD, TRAVEL, AND LEISURE**
0-452-26030-2 NEW AMERICAN LIBRARY PB $10.95

James Gould **Cozzens**

Guard of Honor
The Pulitzer Prize novel of 1949 is a long and painstaking account of an incident at a wartime army base
0-15-637609-1 HARCOURT BRACE PB $10.95

The Just and the Unjust
A murder trial in a small town
0-15-646578-7 HARCOURT BRACE PB $12.95

Stanley **Crawford**

Some Instructions to My Wife
A Swiftian satire on marriage manuals
0-916583-14-7 DALKEY ARCHIVE $20.00
0-916583-15-5 DALKEY ARCHIVE PB $11.95

Robert **Creeley**

The Collected Prose of Robert Creeley
Fiction by the distinguished poet
0-7145-2792-0 MARION BOYARS $26.00
0-520-06151-9 CALIFORNIA PB $15.95

Harry **Crews**

"What sticks in my mind about Crews's work is the voluminous hurdy-gurdy sweep of his comic and moral vision. He cracks open a southern-fried terrain that teems with heretofore unidentified life."—VLS

Body
0-671-75852-7 TOUCHSTONE PB $10.00

Classic Crews: A Harry Crews Reader
"Crews burns through the easy ways in which we would like to regard ourselves; what he leaves behind is something better, something touched by the refiner's fire"—*Newsday*. Includes his excellent *Autobiography of a Place*
0-671-86527-7 POSEIDON PB $15.00

A Feast of Snakes
The annual rattlesnake hunt brings a cast of eccentrics to Mystic, Georgia. "He begins where James Dickey left off"—Norman Mailer
0-689-70715-0 ATHENEUM PB $10.00

Florida Frenzy
0-8130-0726-7 FLORIDA PB $16.95

The Knockout Artist
0-06-091574-9 HARPERCOLLINS PB $11.00

The Mulching of America
The hilarious story of Hickum Looney, a door-to-door salesman who intends to outdo everyone in the annual sales contest. But his determination is no match for the forces against him: the overdeveloped masseur Russel Muscle, Bubba, the pit bull with a taste for human body parts, and above all, the Boss
0-684-80934-6 SIMON & SCHUSTER $22.00
0-684-82541-4 SCRIBNERS PB $11.00

It had been a good day, an unprecedented day, for Hickum Looney. As he eased his dirty yellow dented Dodge through bumper-to-bumper traffic, he whistled a gay little tune, his favorite. It had been a Coca-Cola kind of day and he was whistling a Coca-Cola commercial from a good while back—he couldn't remember how long—five or ten years, maybe even longer. And he loved it so much, he invariably saved it for those days when sickness, suffering, death, and the rankest kind of blasphemy—all subjects begging for confession and absolution—opened every door he knocked upon or responded to every bell he rang. But not one of his days over the last quarter of a century could match this one.
THE MULCHING OF AMERICA

Scar Lover
0-671-74489-5 TOUCHSTONE PB $19.00

John **Crowley**

Aegypt
0-553-34592-3 BANTAM PB $12.95

Love & Sleep
0-553-37468-0 BANTAM PB $12.95

Three Novels by John Crowley: The Deep/Beasts/Engine Summer
0-553-37398-6 BANTAM PB $12.95

James **Crumley**

One to Count Cadence
A novel of Vietnam
0-394-73559-5 VINTAGE PB $13.00

Guy **Davenport**

The Cardiff Team: Ten Stories
0-8112-1335-8 NEW DIRECTIONS $22.95

Eclogues
0-8018-4695-1 JOHNS HOPKINS PB $12.95

The Jules Verne Steam Balloon
"Guy Davenport mixes historical fact, a philosophical imagination, and an almost hallucinatory prose style to create short stories that are at once marvelous, frustrating, and original"—*Virginia Quarterly Review*
0-8018-4680-3 JOHNS HOPKINS PB $12.95

A Table of Green Fields: Ten Stories
0-8112-1251-3 NEW DIRECTIONS $21.95

Laurence **David**

Need
A love triangle between a New York therapist, her husband, and her suicidal patient steadily spirals into a confrontation that forces all three characters to examine their motivations, desires, and beliefs. "Each page pulls us deeper into a psychic spiral of loyalty, betrayal and eros. *Need* is addictive"
—Michael Drinkard, author of *Disobedience*
0-679-43433-X RANDOM HOUSE $21.00
0-312-95922-2 ST. MARTIN'S PB $6.99

Lydia **Davis**

Break It Down
0-374-52098-4 PENGUIN $6.95

The End of the Story
Obsession and redemption are the themes of this narrative, in which a thirtyish writer falls in love with a much younger man
0-374-14831-7 FS&G $20.00
1-85242-420-6 SERPENT'S TAIL PB $12.99

Fielding **Dawson**

Virginia Dare: Stories, 1976-1981
0-87685-618-0 BLACK SPARROW $14.00
0-87685-617-2 BLACK SPARROW PB $8.50

Tom **De Haven**

Derby Dugan's Depression Funnies
Novel inspired by both the spirit and telegraphic form of comic strips charts the screwball exploits of a 1930s cartoonist
0-8050-4445-0 HOLT $23.00

Frank **Deford**

Love and Infamy
A compulsively readable, large-scale novel about love and intrigue in the Pacific on the eve of Japan's attack on Pearl Harbor. "…the book rings with historical authenticity and vivid descriptions…Deford has created fresh characters and a consistently captivating story of romance, politics and the clash of two cultures"—*Publishers Weekly*
0-670-82995-1 VIKING $24.00

Nicholas **Delbanco**

As a NEA and Guggenheim Fellowship winner, the founder of the Bennington Writing Workshops, and the director of the prestigious Hopwood Writing Awards, Delbanco takes his place as one of the most accomplished men of letters writing today. "Delbanco wrestles with the abundance of his gifts as a novelist the way other men wrestle with their deficiencies."
—John Updike

In the Name of Mercy
A literary page-turner that innovates and fascinates all at once
0-446-51711-9 WARNER $21.95

Don **DeLillo**

End Zone

Football and nuclear war. "Like Groucho Marx on a faked end run"—*Bookworld*

0-14-008568-8 PENGUIN PB..............$11.95

Don DeLillo

Great Jones Street

A rock musician in New York's East Village. "Finally, a novel that understands rock and roll"—*Village Voice*

0-679-72303-X VINTAGE PB..............$13.00

Libra

A fictional look at Oswald, Ruby, and the Kennedy assassination

0-14-015604-6 PENGUIN PB..............$11.95

Mao II

0-14-015274-1 PENGUIN PB..............$11.95

The Names

An American in Europe becomes involved in international terrorism and intrigue. "The high-tech, jet-set variation of the American expatriates in *The Sun Also Rises*" —Steve Erickson, *LA Reader*

0-679-72295-5 VINTAGE PB..............$12.00

Players

Unsettling truths behind the attractive facade of an ideal modern couple

0-679-72293-9 VINTAGE PB..............$12.00

Ratner's Star

Astronomers trapped in an eerie sci-fi prison/wonderland

0-679-72292-0 VINTAGE PB..............$14.00

Running Dog

"The best Vietnam novel to appear so far" —*Houston Post*

0-679-72294-7 VINTAGE PB..............$13.00

White Noise

A dark comedy set at a liberal arts college in middle America. "One of DeLillo's funniest novels…eerie, brilliant, and touching" —*NY Times*

0-14-007702-2 PENGUIN PB..............$11.95

Rick **DeMarinis**

Coming Triumph of the Free World: Stories

0-393-30746-8 NORTON PB..............$7.95

The Mortician's Apprentice

18-year-old Ozzie Santee comes of age in blue-skies, Cold War America with a bright future as a mortician's apprentice—and a firm determination to escape it. A deadpan, incisive, intelligent view of Eisenhower's America by the American equivalent of Evelyn Waugh

0-393-03662-6 NORTON..............$21.00

Under the Wheat

0-88001-149-1 ECCO PB..............$7.50

Pete **Dexter**

Brotherly Love

Two Philadelphia boys are born into the violent world of organized labor and the mob

0-394-58573-9 RANDOM HOUSE..............$22.00

Deadwood

A gritty, pungent story of the Old West, complete with Wild Bill and Calamity Jane

0-14-012729-1 VIKING PB..............$11.95

God's Pocket

Dexter's portrait of the Philadelphia unions is informed by his stint as a Metro reporter in the city

0-446-32811-1 WARNER PB..............$3.95

The Paperboy

Dexter's latest and arguably his best novel, where the life and career of a journalist are seen through the eyes of his younger brother

0-679-42175-0 RANDOM HOUSE..............$23.00
0-385-31572-4 DELTA PB..............$11.95

Paris Trout

Winner of the National Book Award for 1988

0-14-012206-0 PENGUIN PB..............$11.95

Paul **Di Filippo**

Ribofunk

1-56858-062-2 FOUR WALLS..............$20.00

James **Dickey**

"Dickey is no ruminator or meditator. Perception with him is not a static matter. It is characteristically, whatever his subject, a clash, a confrontation, something that might happen in a cyclotron."—Wallace Stegner

Alnilam

An elaborate, myth-ridden novel about flight

1-55817-086-3 PINNACLE PB..............$4.95

Deliverance

Four suburban businessmen confront their own primitive impulses while canoeing down a Southern river. "A breathtaking adventure that is also an acute comment on America" —*New Yorker*

0-385-31387-X DELTA PB..............$10.95

To the White Sea

"A splendid tale…There are extraordinary passages of intense poetry…An intense, page-turning adventure" —*Atlanta Journal Constitution*

0-395-47565-1 HOUGHTON MIFFLIN..............$22.95
0-385-31309-8 DELTA PB..............$11.95

Charles **Dickinson**

Crows

0-380-71950-9 AVON PB..............$11.00

Waltz in Marathon

A moneylender in a small Michigan town finds his orderly life changing after he falls in love with an attractive attorney

0-380-71949-5 AVON PB..............$10.00

With or Without

Eleven short stories. "We come away from this collection sobered but enlightened… forced to look again, to discover at some deeper level what we thought we had already known" —*NY Times*

0-380-71951-7 AVON PB..............$9.00

Joan **Didion**

A Book of Common Prayer

"A completely knowing and sophisticated grasp of realities and all unrealities in our time and place, together with a lyrical treatment of them, strikes me as being the ultimate achievement of a contemporary novelist. Joan Didion has somehow accomplished this in *A Book of Common Prayer*"—Tennessee Williams

0-19-528706-1 OXFORD..............$34.95

Democracy

"The devastating personal and public consequences of the loss of history are Didion's theme… *Democracy* is absorbing, immensely intelligent, and witty"—*NY Review of Books*

0-88619-054-1 TORONTO..............$1.98

The Last Thing He Wanted

When reporter Elena McMahon leaves her life as a wife and mother to move to a Carribean island, she becomes embroiled in a world of secret political dealings

0-679-43331-7 KNOPF..............$23.00

Play It as It Lays

"A painful and exact novel about a young Hollywood actress whose balance is upset by a traumatic abortion, an impending divorce from her film-maker husband, and the hopeless future of her retarded daughter…Didion is at her best—her honesty, intelligence, and skill are wonders to behold"—*Newsweek*

0-374-52171-9 FS&G PB..............$9.00

Run River

0-679-75250-1 VINTAGE PB..............$12.00

Stephen **Dixon**

Frog

"Stephen Dixon's stories are talked to you right out of his head…full of infinite alternatives, tough facts, and humor"—Grace Paley

0-8050-4883-9 OWLET PB..............$16.00

Garbage

0-943433-00-2 CANE HILL PB..............$8.95

Gould: A Novel in Two Novels

0-8050-4424-8 HOLT..............$24.00

Interstate

The story of a man whose family is involved in a highway shooting, told in Dixon's wildly inventive prose and alternating first-person narratives

0-8050-2654-1 HOLT..............$25.00

The Play & Other Stories

0-918273-45-5 COFFEE HOUSE PB..............$9.95

Stephen **Dobyns**

The Two Deaths of Senora Puccini

0-14-010567-0 PENGUIN PB $7.95

E.L. **Doctorow**

Billy Bathgate

A young man's dealings with Dutch Schultz and others in '30s New York. "Billy Bathgate is the kind of book you find yourself finishing at three in the morning after promising at midnight that you'll stop after one more page. One scene glides into the next, and yet each is so complete in itself, so fully and precisely observed, that it seems to be encapsulated in a tiny glass paperweight"—Anne Tyler, *NY Times*

0-06-097595-4 HARPERPERENNIAL PB $12.00

The Book of Daniel

A fictional reconstruction of the Rosenberg case and its consequences

0-452-27566-0 PLUME PB $10.95

Loon Lake

0-452-27568-7 PLUME PB $11.95

Ragtime

The celebrated collage of turn-of-the-century America, with guest appearances by J.P. Morgan, Evelyn Nesbitt, and other iconic figures

0-452-27570-9 PLUME PB $9.95

The Waterworks

In post-Civil War New York, a young man recognizes his dead father passing on a horse-drawn omnibus. Following it leads him through a New York where mass misery vies with new industrial money. Mysterious and compelling, this historical retelling is marked by Doctorow's singular imagination and originality

0-394-58754-5 RANDOM HOUSE $23.00
0-451-18563-3 SIGNET PB $6.99

E.L. Doctorow

Welcome to Hard Times

A bitter little Western; Doctorow's first novel

0-452-27571-7 PLUME PB $10.95

World's Fair

"You get lost in *World's Fair* as if it were an exotic adventure. You devour it with the avidity usually provoked by a suspense thriller" —Christopher Lehmann-Haupt, *NY Times*

0-8446-6696-3 SMITH $22.00
0-452-27572-5 PLUME PB $10.95

Jim **Dodge**

Fup

0-933944-04-7 CITY MINER PB $5.95

Not Fade Away

0-87113-144-7 ATLANTIC MONTHLY PB $6.95

Harriet **Doerr**

Stones for Ibarra

An American couple move to a Mexican village to reopen an abandoned copper mine

0-14-007562-3 VIKING PB $10.95

The Tiger in the Grass: Stories and Other Inventions

0-8169-0675-0 VIKING $19.95

Ivan **Doig**

Bucking the Sun

0-684-81171-5 SIMON & SCHUSTER $23.00

Dancing at the Rascal Fair

A chronicle of two immigrants from Scotland who make their way to the American West during the first three decades of the 20th century

0-06-097181-9 HARPERCOLLINS PB $13.00

English Creek

0-8446-6608-4 SMITH $21.25
0-14-008442-8 PENGUIN PB $11.95

The Sea Runners

0-14-006780-9 PENGUIN PB $11.95

J.P. **Donleavy**

The Beastly Beatitudes of Balthazar B

A young man at prep school in England. "The prep school passages are wonderful, followed by one of the most perfect love affairs in modern literature. This romp of a novel is lush and lovely, bawdy and sad"—*NY Times*

0-87113-225-7 ATLANTIC MONTHLY PB $7.95

The Destinies of Darcy Dancer, Gentleman

"Tender, sexy, and tough by turns...His most enjoyable yet"—*Vogue*

0-87113-289-3 ATLANTIC MONTHLY PB $9.95

A Fairy Tale of New York

0-87113-264-8 ATLANTIC MONTHLY PB $7.95

Leila: Further in the Life and Destinies of Darcy Dancer, Gentleman

"A liltingly moving piece of writing from a wonderfully fruity romancer"—*Financial Times*

0-87113-288-5 ATLANTIC MONTHLY PB $9.95

A Singular Man

0-87113-265-6 ATLANTIC MONTHLY PB $7.95

Edward **Dorn**

By the Sound

See also **POETRY SINCE 1945** under **20TH-CENTURY AMERICAN POETRY**

0-87685-840-X BLACK SPARROW PB $12.50

Way West: Almost the Big Time

From his laconic, drifter-populated tales first published in *The Moderns* in 1963 to his later, satirical observations of cocktail-party gunslingers and crypto-mountainmen suffering from "neo-peckerwood madness," this essential roundup lights up unsuspected dimensions of the contemporay West

0-87685-906-6 BLACK SPARROW $25.00
0-87685-905-8 BLACK SPARROW PB $14.00

Michael **Dorris**

Paper Trail

"By turns charming, provocative, impassioned and deeply moving"—*NY Times Book Review*

0-06-092593-0 HARPERPERENNIAL PB $12.00

A Yellow Raft in Blue Water

Three generations of Native American women tell different versions of their family's story

0-8050-0045-3 HOLT $16.95
0-446-38787-8 WARNER PB $11.99

Rita **Dove**

Through the Ivory Gate

"Skillfully evokes the mood of a decade when social change seemed not only possible but imminent...An immensely gifted writer" —*Washington Post Book World*

0-679-41604-8 PANTHEON $21.00
0-679-74240-9 VINTAGE PB $11.00

Coleman **Dowell**

Island People

1-56478-093-7 DALKEY ARCHIVE PB $12.95

Mrs. October Was Here

0-8112-0519-3 NEW DIRECTIONS PB $3.75

Too Much Flesh and Jabez

A story within a story, in which a spinster schoolteacher writes a fantasy about a former student. "A meticulously and subtly composed tour de force of the 'imagination' " —Gilbert Sorrentino

0-916583-21-X DALKEY ARCHIVE PB $9.95

White on Black on White

1-85242-160-6 SERPENT'S TAIL PB $14.95

Andre **Dubus**

Dancing After Hours

"The stories in *Dancing After Hours* make up a compasionate, unsentimental portrait of the American soul at this hour...Andre Dubus is a master"—Tobias Wolff

0-679-43107-1 KNOPF $23.00
0-679-75114-9 VINTAGE $12.00

Finding a Girl in America

"Dubus is in top form in this new collection of ten stories and a novella as he continues to introduce us to ourselves, to see into the private worlds of everyday people as they live, dream and act, taking soundings that are deep and true"—*Publishers Weekly*

0-87923-393-1 GODINE PB $11.95

The Last Worthless Evening: Four Novellas and Two Short Stories

0-87923-642-6 GODINE $15.95
1-56792-067-5 NATIONAL BOOK NETWORK PB $12.95

Andre **Dubus**

Selected Stories of Andre Dubus

"Life goes on, and life's gallant, battered ongoingness, with its complicated fuelling by sex, religion, and liquor, constitutes his sturdy central subject"—John Uplike

0-679-72533-4 VINTAGE PB $12.00

The Times Are Never So Bad

A novella and eight short stories. "For the lyricism and directness of his language, the richness and precision of his observations, he is among the best short-story writers in America"—Judith Levine, *Village Voice*

0-87923-459-8 GODINE $14.95
0-87923-641-8 GODINE PB $11.95

Bruce **Duffy**

Last Comes the Egg

0-684-80883-8 SIMON & SCHUSTER $23.00

Henry **Dumas**

Goodbye, Sweetwater: New and Selected Stories

"A cult has grown up around Henry Dumas—a very deserved cult… He was brilliant. He was magnetic, and he was an incredible artist" —Toni Morrison

EDITED WITH A FOREWORD BY EUGENE B. REDMOND

0-938410-58-X THUNDER'S MOUTH PB $14.95

David **Duncan**

The River Why

A comic novel, whimsical yet serious, on man and nature as seen through the eyes of a fly-fishing fanatic

See also **ESSAYS** under **THE OUTDOORS** in **FOOD, TRAVEL, AND LEISURE**

0-87156-321-5 SIERRA CLUB $22.00
0-553-34486-2 BANTAM PB $11.95

Katherine **Dunn**

Attic

0-446-39152-2 WARNER PB $9.99

Geek Love

Tenderness and terror in the lives of a carnival family

0-394-56902-4 KNOPF $25.00
0-446-39130-1 WARNER PB $12.99

Truck

0-446-39153-0 WARNER PB $10.99

Dominick **Dunne**

A Season in Purgatory

After 20 years of covering up the peccadilloes of his wealthy, politically charismatic chum, Harrison Burns is exposed. A story of Kennedyesque privilege and power by the author of *An Inconvenient Woman* who knows this territory like few others

0-517-58386-0 CROWN $22.00
0-553-29076-2 BDD PB $6.99

An Inconvenient Woman

0-553-28906-3 BANTAM PB $6.99

Stuart **Dybek**

The Coast of Chicago

0-679-73334-5 VINTAGE PB $10.00

William **Eastlake**

Lyric of the Circle Heart: The Bowman Family Trilogy

1-56478-136-4 DALKEY ARCHIVE PB $14.95

Junius **Edwards**

If We Must Die

First published in 1963, Edwards's novel is the account of a young black veteran attempting to register to vote

0-88258-117-1 HOWARD PB $12.95

Janice **Eidus**

Urban Bliss

0-88064-159-2 FROMM $19.95

Vito Loves Geraldine

Eighteen stories about growing up in the Bronx and other rites of passage. "When she goes in deep and rides the treadmill of the psyche with her people, she makes marginality poignant and nervousness a gift. She is to be praised" —Paul West

0-87286-247-X CITY LIGHTS PB $7.95

Stanley **Elkin**

The McGuffin

0-14-017234-3 PENGUIN PB $10.00

Mrs. Ted Bliss

0-7868-6104-5 DISNEY $22.95

The Six-Year-Old-Man

0-917453-15-8 BAMBERGER PB $10.00

Van Gogh's Room at Arles: Three Novellas

0-14-023659-7 PENGUIN PB $10.95

Bret Easton **Ellis**

American Psycho

The book that caused much controversy due to its violent depictions of a Yuppie mass murderer

0-679-73577-1 RANDOM HOUSE PB $14.00

The Informers

0-679-74324-3 VINTAGE PB $11.00

Less than Zero

Wealthy young airheads on the prowl in L.A.

0-14-008894-6 VIKING PB $11.95

The Rules of Attraction

Alienated California youth at college in New England

0-14-011228-6 VIKING PB $11.95

Trey **Ellis**

Home Repairs

0-671-89070-0 WASHINGTON SQUARE PB $10.00

Platitudes

0-394-75439-5 VINTAGE PB $9.00

Ralph **Ellison**

Flying Home: And Other Stories

These stories were not discovered until after the author's death. They are now available for the first time and represent Ellison's first published fiction since *Invisible Man*

EDITED BY JOHN F. CALLAHAN

0-679-45704-6 RANDOM HOUSE $23.00

Invisible Man

Set in the immediate post-Depression era, Ellison's landmark novel is an unforgettable account of a black man's journey from South to North, from immaturity to terrible experience

0-679-60015-9 RANDOM HOUSE $16.50
0-679-73276-4 VINTAGE PB $11.00

Ralph Ellison (credit: ©Bern Schwartz)

Carol **Emshwiller**

Carmen Dog

A parable in which women turn into animals and animals into women. "This trenchant feminist fantasy-satire mixes elements of *Animal Farm, Rhinoceros,* and *The Handmaid's Tale*…Emshwiller is engaging even when most savage about male-female relationships" —*Booklist*

0-916515-77-X MERCURY HOUSE PB $9.95

Elizabeth **Engstrom**

Lizard Wine

0-385-31249-0 DELTA PB $11.95

Nora **Ephron**

Heartburn

0-679-76795-9 VINTAGE PB $11.00

Leslie **Epstein**

King of the Jews

See also **HOLOCAUST FICTION** under **ART AND LITERATURE** under **THE HOLOCAUST** in **WORLD HISTORY AND CURRENT AFFAIRS**

0-393-30959-2 NORTON PB $9.95

Pinto and Sons

0-393-30846-4 NORTON PB $9.95

Louise **Erdrich**

The Beet Queen

A brother and sister arrive in North Dakota by boxcar and stay for 40 years

0-553-34723-3 BANTAM PB $12.95

The Bingo Palace

"Magnificent…vitally alive and endearing. Few American authors write with more lyrical tenderness and magical power" —*Wall Street Journal*

0-06-092585-X HARPERPERENNIAL PB $13.00

The Blue Jay's Dance
"Astute, poetic reflections on the powerful mother-daughter relationship from conception through the baby's first year"—*Kirkus Reviews*
See also **MOTHERS** under **BEING A PARENT** under **PARENTING** in **LIFESTYLES AND PRACTICAL ADVICE**
0-06-017132-4 HARPERCOLLINS $21.00

Louise Erdrich

Love Medicine
"A remarkable first novel…conveying unflinchingly the funkiness and great unspoken sadness of the Indian reservations"
—Peter Matthiessen
See also **CONTEMPORARY NATIVE AMERICAN WRITERS** under **NATIVE AMERICAN LITERATURES**
0-8050-1716-X HOLT $19.95

Tales of Burning Love
Widely celebrated for colloquial familiarity and expert prose in novels of Native American life, Erdrich moves beyond the reservation in a novel in which five former wives of the same man tell their tales. Individual dreams and collective struggles wind through this narrative in a book that is finally a mystery of how hope and love are sustained
0-06-017605-9 HARPERCOLLINS $25.00

Tracks
North Dakota Chippewas fight for survival in the early 20th century
0-06-097245-9 HARPERCOLLINS PB $12.50

Steve **Erickson**

Amnesiascope
Anarchic, futuristic Los Angeles where sex is the last subversive act. "Steve Erickson has that rare and luminous gift for reporting back from the nocturnal side of reality"—Thomas Pynchon
0-8050-3503-6 HOLT $23.00

Arc D'X
A fictional account of Jefferson and his slave/mistress
0-8050-4882-0 OWLET PB $14.00

Lauren **Fairbanks**

Sister Carrie
1-56478-035-X DALKEY ARCHIVE $19.95
1-56478-070-8 DALKEY ARCHIVE PB $10.95

Howard **Fast**

April Morning
Coming of age during the American Revolution
0-553-27322-1 BDD PB $4.99

Freedom Road
INTRODUCTION BY ERIC FONER
1-56324-440-3 SHARPE PB $15.95

John **Faulkner**

Men Working
FOREWORD BY TRENT WATTS
0-8203-1827-2 GEORGIA PB $19.95

Jessie Redmon **Fauset**

There Is Confusion
1-55553-066-4 NORTHEASTERN PB $15.95

Raymond **Federman**

Smiles on Washington Square: A Love Story of Sorts
1-55713-181-3 SUN & MOON PB $10.95

David B. **Feinberg**

Spontaneous Combustion
0-14-014862-0 PENGUIN PB $10.95

Roberto **Fernandez**

Raining Backwards
A satirical look at the Cuban community in Miami
0-934770-79-4 ARTE PUBLICO PB $9.50

Jack **Finney**

Time and Again
Wonderfully researched time travel back to New York City in 1880
0-684-80117-5 SIMON & SCHUSTER $25.00
0-684-80105-1 SCRIBNERS PB $12.00

From Time to Time: A Novel
The sequal to *Time and Again*
0-684-81844-2 SCRIBNERS PB $12.00

M.F.K. **Fisher**

Not Now, But Now
Fisher's only novel charts a woman's devastating effect on those around her
0-86547-072-3 NORTH POINT PB $12.00

Rudolph **Fisher**

The City of Refuge: The Collected Stories of Rudolph Fisher
EDITED BY JOHN MCCLUSKEY, JR.
0-8262-0786-3 MISSOURI PB $16.95

Fannie **Flagg**

Daisy Fay and the Miracle Man
0-679-74947-0 RANDOM HOUSE PB $16.00

Fried Green Tomatoes at the Whistle Stop Cafe
A much-loved novel which was made into the immensely popular movie starring Jessica Tandy and Kathy Bates. "Flagg pours the heart of small-town life into her boisterous second novel"—*Booklist*
0-394-56152-X RANDOM HOUSE $25.00
0-07-021257-0 MCGRAW HILL PB $7.95

Patty L. **Floyd**

The Silver Desoto
0-933031-03-3 COUNCIL OAK $14.95

Shelby **Foote**

Follow Me Down
0-679-73617-4 VINTAGE PB $11.00

Love in a Dry Season
0-679-73618-2 VINTAGE PB $11.00

Shiloh
A realistic, close-up treatment of the Civil War battle
0-394-40873-X RANDOM HOUSE $21.00
0-679-73542-9 VINTAGE PB $11.00

Richard **Ford**

Granta 40: The Womanizer
Ford's novella, published here in *Granta*, is about Martin Austin, a salesman capable of persuading anyone of anything (the womanizer's character defined)
See also **GRANTA** under **LITERATURE** under **20TH-CENTURY AMERICAN ESSAYS AND JOURNALISM**
0-14-014054-9 PENGUIN PB $9.95

Independence Day
The Pulitzer Prize-winning sequel to Ford's celebrated *The Sportswriter*
0-679-49265-8 KNOPF $25.00
0-679-73518-6 VINTAGE PB $13.00

Richard Ford

A Piece of My Heart
Ford's first novel tells of two men in flight to an uncharted island in the Mississippi
0-394-72914-5 RANDOM HOUSE PB $12.00

Rock Springs
A collection of stories. "The finest of these stories achieve luminous moments, moments with the potential to change how the reader sees and thinks"—*NY Times Book Review*
0-394-75700-9 VINTAGE PB $12.00

The Sportswriter
"A book of life, full of life, and a grand achievement. The sport of this novel is the one all of us play—and win or lose at—every day"
—Frederick Exley
0-394-74325-3 VINTAGE PB $11.00

Richard **Ford**

The Ultimate Good Luck

A Vietnam vet mixes with soldiers, drug dealers, tourists, and Indians in Oaxaca. "So hardboiled and tough it might have been written on the back of a trenchcoat"—Stanley Elkin

0-394-75089-6 VINTAGE PB $12.00

Wildlife

The story of a young man coming out into the world as it is and not as he had it would be

0-679-73447-3 VINTAGE PB $11.00

Leon **Forrest**

There Is a Tree More Ancient than Eden

The first part of the Forrest County trilogy. An adolescent copes with the death of his mother and some 200 years of American history in this harrowing, dream-like narrative

0-9614644-5-3 ANOTHER CHICAGO PRESS PB $8.95

The Bloodworth Orphans

A mythical tale about the descendants of a Mississippi slave owner; the second of Forrest's novels. "How admirable the manner in which the great themes of life and literature are revealed in the black-white, white-black Americanness of his characters as dramatized in the cathedral-high and cloaca-low limits of his imaginative ranging"—Ralph Ellison

0-9614644-3-7 ANOTHER CHICAGO PRESS PB $8.95

Two Wings to Veil My Face

In the Forrest County trilogy's s final installment, a young man learns the secrets of his own family's past

0-9614644-4-5 ANOTHER CHICAGO PRESS PB $8.95

Divine Days

0-393-31221-6 NORTON PB $18.00

Paula **Fox**

King's Falcon

0-8446-6562-2 SMITH $22.30

A Place Apart

0-8446-6821-4 SMITH $17.50

A Servant's Tale

A Caribbean woman chooses to work as a maid for wealthy families

0-86547-164-9 NORTH POINT $16.50

Marilyn **French**

The Bleeding Heart

Middle-aged adultery in England

0-345-33284-9 BALLANTINE PB $6.99

The Mother's Daughter

0-345-35362-5 BALLANTINE PB $6.99

Our Father

The author of *The Women's Room* thrusts together four daughters at the deathbed of their father, one of the richest and most powerful men in America. The revelations that this crisis precipitates are bitterly charged, as the daughters, each born of a different mother, tell the gripping stories of their separate lives

0-316-29390-3 LITTLE, BROWN $22.95

0-345-38490-3 BALLANTINE PB $6.99

The Women's Room

A woman's journey to self-knowledge after her divorce, and a classic of the Women's Liberation movement

0-345-35361-7 BALLANTINE PB $6.99

Bruce Jay **Friedman**

About Harry Towns

0-87113-263-X ATLANTIC MONTHLY PB $8.95

A Father's Kisses

1-55611-499-0 FINE $22.95

William **Gaddis**

Carpenter's Gothic

0-670-69793-1 VIKING $16.95

A Frolic of His Own

0-684-80052-7 SCRIBNERS PB $12.00

JR

Told entirely in dialogue, *JR* is the 726-page chronicle of an 11-year-old entrepreneur operating on a mythical scale. "Behind the wild comedy, the frantic pace, the precise satire, the rigorous art, there is the somber mood of something that for want of a better word we might just as well call tragedy"—*NY Times*

0-14-018707-3 PENGUIN PB $13.95

William Gaddis (photo courtesy of Knopf)

The Recognitions

First published in 1955, Gaddis's long, complex novel of the varieties of forgery has been acclaimed by many as a masterpiece of American modern fiction

0-14-018708-1 PENGUIN PB $14.95

Ernest J. **Gaines**

The Autobiography of Miss Jane Pittman

The life of a black woman born a slave

0-553-26357-9 BDD PB $4.99

Catherine Carmier

A novel of Louisiana plantation country

0-679-73891-6 VINTAGE PB $11.00

A Gathering of Old Men

Murder on a Louisiana sugar cane plantation in the late '70s. "The best-written novel on Southern race relations in over a decade" —*Village Voice*

0-394-51468-8 KNOPF $22.00

0-679-73890-8 VINTAGE PB $10.00

In My Father's House

A minister and civil rights leader in a rural black community in the South. "A powerful, deeply probing novel…The Rev. Mr. Martin emerges as a complex, memorable character" —*NY Times*

0-679-72791-4 VINTAGE PB $10.00

A Lesson Before Dying

Jefferson, a humble, barely literate black man in Louisiana, witnesses a shootout in which a white store owner is killed. Jefferson is charged with the murder and condemned to death. Gaines has written an unusually authentic, deeply moving portrait of an American backwater in which the struggle for manhood is a struggle for life and death

0-679-41477-0 KNOPF $23.00

Of Love and Dust

0-679-75248-X VINTAGE PB $11.00

Mary **Gaitskill**

Bad Behavior

0-679-72327-7 VINTAGE PB $11.00

Because They Wanted To: Stories

0-684-80856-0 SIMON & SCHUSTER $22.00

Kenneth **Gangemi**

The Interceptor Pilot

The scenario for an imaginary Cold War adventure

0-7145-2765-3 RIZZOLI PB $7.95

Olt

"The style, the focus on one main character, and the cool listing of experiences tend to remind one of Meursault in *The Stranger*" —*Library Journal*

0-7145-0660-5 MARION BOYARS PB $5.95

John **Gardner**

Freddy's Book

"Gardner [was] one of our best novelists….You know you are in the presence of genius" —*Philadelphia Inquirer*

0-679-72194-0 VINTAGE PB $11.00

Grendel

The epic of Beowulf retold from the monster's viewpoint

0-679-72311-0 VINTAGE PB $8.00

John Gardner

Nickel Mountain
0-394-74393-8 VINTAGE PB $12.00

October Light
An elderly brother and sister in conflict in Vermont
0-679-72133-9 VINTAGE PB $15.00

The Sunlight Dialogues
0-394-74394-6 VINTAGE PB $16.00

George **Garrett**

Death of the Fox: A Novel of Elizabeth and Ralegh
An intricate and richly flavored novel of Sir Walter Ralegh, poet, adventurer, and political conniver, tracing his career from its origins to his eventual fall from power
0-15-625233-3 HARCOURT BRACE PB $14.95

Entered from the Sun: The Murder of Marlowe
In this third component of his Elizabeth triptych, an investigation into the murder of poet and playwright Christopher Marlowe reveals tortuous plots and counterplots. "The complexities, violences, sardonic humors, beauties, and deceptions of the Elizabethan age are fused in a manner which demands strictness of learning and imaginative daring"
—Thomas Flanagan
0-15-628795-1 HARCOURT BRACE PB $10.95

The King of Babylon Shall Not Come Against You
Garrett's latest novel looks back to the South of the '60s
0-15-157554-1 HARCOURT BRACE $24.00

The Succession: A Novel of Elizabeth and James
Another vivid recreation of the Elizabethan age which examines the dynastic intrigue surrounding the death of Elizabeth and the passing of the crown to James VI of Scotland
0-15-686303-0 HARCOURT BRACE PB $12.95

William **Gass**

In the Heart of the Heart of the Country & Other Stories
However cerebral in conception, Gass's virtuoso metafictions are naturalistic in their power, vividness, and grim humor
0-87923-374-5 GODINE PB $12.95

The Tunnel
A complex, endlessly self-reflexive novel about a scholar obsessed with Nazism
0-679-43767-3 KNOPF $30.00
0-06-097686-1 HARPERPERENNIAL PB $17.50

Willie Masters' Lonesome Wife
0-916583-46-5 DALKEY ARCHIVE PB $9.95

Reginald **Gibbons**

Sweetbitter
0-14-025242-8 PENGUIN PB $11.95

William **Gibson**

"Gibson distills a technopunk sensibility with a kick of white lightning and the clarity of white light."—Village Voice

Burning Chrome
See also **CONTEMPORARY SCIENCE FICTION** under **SCIENCE FICTION AND FANTASY** in **POPULAR READING**
0-441-08934-8 ACE PB $5.50

Idoru
0-399-14130-8 PUTNAM $24.95

Johnny Mnemonic
0-441-00234-X ACE PB $12.00

Mona Lisa Overdrive
0-553-28174-7 BDD PB $5.99

Neuromancer
A Hugo and Nebula winner. "State of the art"
—*Washington Post*
0-441-56959-5 ACE PB $6.50

Virtual Light
It's 2005, and in California the obscenely rich and the horribly poor live side by side in a grim dystopia. When a messenger steals a pair of "virtual light" glasses that stores secret data, a virtual reality hacker sets off to recover them—only to find that right and wrong are never simple in this surreal world. Gibson is "a genuine cultural phenomenon ...one of science fiction's chief visionaries"—*Publishers Weekly*
0-553-56606-7 SPECTRA PB $6.50

William **Gibson** & Bruce **Sterling**

The Difference Engine
0-553-29461-X SPECTRA PB $5.99

Barry **Gifford**

Night People
"Gifford's night people are pure American...pure in their madness, in their evil, and to read about...pure pleasure"
—Alan Cheuse, National Public Radio
0-8021-3369-X GROVE PB $11.00

Perdita Gurango
Just out in paperback
0-802-13483-1 PENGUIN $12.00

Port Tropique
A dreamlike recasting of *film noir* against the background of a corrupt waterfront
0-679-73492-9 VINTAGE PB $9.00

Wild at Heart: The Story of Sailor and Lula
"Gifford's book is a honey. It stuck to my fingers...Cuts right to the heart of what makes a good novel readable and entertaining: the voices of real people in it. The way Barry Gifford does it, it's high art"—Elmore Leonard.
0-8021-3453-X GROVE PB $12.00

The Wild Life of Sailor and Lula
0-8021-3454-8 GROVE PB $12.00

Dagoberto **Gilb**

The Last Known Residence of Mickey Acuna
0-8021-1554-3 ATLANTIC MONTHLY $21.00
0-8021-3419-X GROVE PB $11.00

Ellen **Gilchrist**

The Age of Miracles
"What sets Gilchrist's best work apart is honesty and clarity that appear in the form of deliberate artlessnesss. And the stories in this collection are among her best"—*Miami Herald*
0-316-31442-0 LITTLE, BROWN $22.95
0-316-31480-3 LITTLE, BROWN PB $11.95

Drunk with Love
Short stories. "Her stories are perceptive, her manner is both stylish and idiomatic—a rare and potent combination"—*TLS*
0-316-31314-9 LITTLE, BROWN PB $11.95

Falling Through Space: The Journals of Ellen Gilchrist
0-316-31317-3 LITTLE, BROWN PB $12.95

Light Can Be Both Wave and Particle
0-316-31318-1 LITTLE, BROWN $17.95

Victory over Japan: A Book of Stories
0-316-31307-6 LITTLE, BROWN PB $12.95

Gail **Godwin**

Father Melancholy's Daughter
A clergyman's daughter seeks to learn the truth about the mother who abandoned her
0-380-70314-9 AVON PB $5.99

The Finishing School
A young girl forms a disturbing friendship with an older woman
0-670-31494-3 VIKING $16.95

A Southern Family
0-380-70313-0 AVON PB $6.99

Donald **Goines**

Goines's violent novels of street life and ghetto crime have remained steadily in print since his murder in the '70s.

Black Gangster
0-87067-961-9 ALL AMERICA DISTRIBUTORS PB $4.95
0-87067-192-8 HOLLOWAY HOUSE PB $3.95

Black Girl Lost
0-87067-186-3 ALL AMERICA DISTRIBUTORS PB $3.50

Daddy Cool
0-87067-188-X ALL AMERICA DISTRIBUTORS PB $3.50

Dopefiend
0-87067-190-1 HOLLOWAY HOUSE PB $3.50

Eldorado Red
0-87067-194-4 HOLLOWAY HOUSE PB $3.50

Inner City Hoodlum
0-87067-193-6 HOLLOWAY HOUSE PB $3.50

Street Players
0-87067-960-0 HOLLOWAY HOUSE PB $4.95

White Man's Justice, Black Man's Grief
0-87067-184-7 HOLLOWAY HOUSE PB $3.50

Whoreson
0-87067-185-5 HOLLOWAY HOUSE PB $3.50

Herbert **Gold**

The Man Who Was Not With It

A man's journey south to Florida brings him in contact with a strange world of night clubs and carnivals

0-912697-69-5 ALGONQUIN PB $10.95

Rebecca **Goldstein**

The Dark Sister

0-14-017247-5 PENGUIN PB $11.95

Mazel

Winner of the National Jewish Book Award

0-670-85648-7 VIKING $23.95
0-14-023905-7 PENGUIN PB $11.95

The Mind-Body Problem

"Intelligent and perceptive, bawdy and witty—an articulate writer of great talent"—*LA Times*

0-14-017245-9 PENGUIN PB $11.95

Genaro **Gonzalez**

Rainbow's End

Three generations of a Mexican-American family residing in the Lower Rio Grande Valley Texas

0-934770-81-6 ARTE PUBLICO PB $9.50

Mitchell **Goodman**

The End of It

0-933256-10-8 PERMANENT $15.95

Paul **Goodman**

The Break-Up of Our Camp: Stories, 1932-1935

EDITED BY TAYLOR STOEHR

0-87685-330-0 BLACK SPARROW $20.00

A Ceremonial: Stories, 1936-1940

EDITED BY TAYLOR STOEHR

0-87685-353-X BLACK SPARROW PB $14.00

The Facts of Life: Stories, 1940-1949

EDITED BY TAYLOR STOEHR

0-87685-356-4 BLACK SPARROW PB $14.00

The Galley to Mytilene: Stories, 1949-1960

EDITED BY TAYLOR STOEHR

0-87685-359-9 BLACK SPARROW PB $14.00

Parents' Day

PREFACE BY TAYLOR STOEHR

0-87685-634-2 BLACK SPARROW PB $12.50

Mary **Gordon**

The Company of Women

A sheltered, religious girl goes to Columbia in the '60s

0-345-32972-4 BALLANTINE PB $5.99

Final Payments

A woman comes to terms with her father's death

0-345-32973-2 BALLANTINE PB $6.99

Men and Angels

Mother and children at the mercy of a born-again babysitter

0-345-32925-2 BALLANTINE PB $5.99

The Other Side

0-14-014408-0 PENGUIN PB $11.95

The Rest of Life

In each of these deceptively simple novellas, Gordon lets her first-person narrator tell the story of the lover who has most altered her life

0-14-014907-4 PENGUIN PB $9.95

Robert **Gover**

The One Hundred Dollar Misunderstanding

0-8021-3181-6 GROVE PB $10.95

William **Goyen**

Arcadio

0-8101-5006-9 TRIQUARTERLY PB $12.95

Come, the Restorer

0-8101-5064-6 TRIQUARTERLY PB $14.95

Had I a Hundred Mouths: New and Selected Stories, 1947-1983

Nineteen stories set mostly in East Texas

INTRODUCTION BY JOYCE CAROL OATES

0-89255-110-0 PERSEA PB $9.95

Half a Look of Cain: A Fantastical Narrative

0-8101-5031-X TRIQUARTERLY $22.50

The House of Breath

A young boy grows up in a small Texas town

0-89255-109-7 PERSEA PB $9.95

In a Farther Country

0-7206-4450-X DUFOUR $24.00

William Goyen: Selected Letters from a Writer's Life

0-292-72773-9 TEXAS $34.95

Shirley Ann **Grau**

The Black Prince and Other Stories

0-8203-1817-5 GEORGIA PB $19.95

George Dawes **Green**

The Caveman's Valentine

0-446-51722-4 WARNER $19.95
0-446-67151-7 WARNER PB $11.99

Eric Rolfe **Greenberg**

The Celebrant

0-8032-7037-2 NEBRASKA PB $9.95

Doris **Grumbach**

The Book of Knowledge

0-393-03770-3 NORTON $22.00

The Ladies

"Eloquently documents the existence of women who lived as they wished to, instead of as society expected them to"—Catherine Stimpson, *NY Times Book Review*

0-393-31092-2 NORTON PB $8.95

Life in a Day

0-8070-7088-2 BEACON $17.00

Albert J. **Guerard**

The Hotel in the Jungle

1-88090-945-6 BASKERVILLE $23.00

A.B. **Guthrie**

The Big Sky

One of the most famous Westerns ever written, a novel of early exploration on the Missouri

See also **CLASSIC WESTERN WRITERS** under **WESTERNS** in **POPULAR READING**

INTRODUCTION BY WALLACE STEGNER

0-553-26683-7 BDD PB $5.99
0-395-61153-9 HOUGHTON MIFFLIN PB $12.95

Fair Land, Fair Land

0-395-75519-0 HOUGHTON MIFFLIN PB $10.95

These Thousand Hills

0-395-75520-4 HOUGHTON MIFFLIN PB $11.95

Jessica **Hagedorn**

Danger and Beauty

0-14-017340-4 PENGUIN PB $14.00

Dogeaters

0-14-014904-X PENGUIN PB $11.95

The Gangster of Love

0-395-75412-7 HOUGHTON MIFFLIN $22.95

William **Hamilton**

The Lap of Luxury

A witty satire of the rich from the *New Yorker* cartoonist

0-87113-342-3 ATLANTIC MONTHLY PB $8.95

Barry **Hannah**

Bats Out of Hell

These wide-ranging stories jump from the Civil War to contemporary Mississippi, and confirm the author's status as "a writer of violent honesty and power in the creative Southern tradition"—Alfred Kazin

0-8021-3386-X GROVE PB $12.00

Boomerang

An autobiographical tour of the South

0-395-48882-6 HOUGHTON MIFFLIN $15.95

Ray

0-8021-3387-8 GROVE PB $10.00

The Tennis Handsome

0-8071-2008-1 LSU PB $9.95

Ron **Hansen**

Atticus

A grieving father travels to Mexico to investigate the death of his son and learns of his strange life

0-06-018217-2 HARPERCOLLINS $22.00

Nebraska: Stories

0-87113-349-0 ATLANTIC MONTHLY PB $9.95

Elizabeth **Hardwick**

The Ghostly Lover

A Kentucky family

0-88001-240-4 ECCO PB $8.95

The Simple Truth

The effects of a murder trial

0-912946-98-9 ECCO $12.95

Mark **Harris**

It Looked Like Forever

More about the baseball player Henry W. Wiggen

0-8032-7244-8 BROMPTON PB $9.50

Bang the Drum Slowly
A dying baseball player
See also **BASEBALL FICTION** under **BASEBALL** under **SPORTS** in **FOOD, TRAVEL, AND LEISURE**
0-8032-7221-9 NEBRASKA PB $8.95

Something About a Soldier
0-8032-7226-X NEBRASKA PB $6.50

The Southpaw
"By far the best 'serious' baseball novel published"—*San Francisco Chronicle*
0-8032-7220-0 NEBRASKA PB $12.95

A Ticket for a Seamstitch
Completes the baseball tetralogy begun by *The Southpaw, Bang the Drum Slowly*, and *It Looked Like Forever*
0-8032-7224-3 NEBRASKA PB $7.95

Robert **Harris**

Enigma
See also **HISTORICAL AND ROMANTIC FICTION** in **POPULAR READING**
0-679-42887-9 RANDOM HOUSE $23.00
0-8041-1548-6 IVY PB $6.99

Colin **Harrison**

Manhattan Nocturne
0-517-58492-1 CROWN $24.00

Jim **Harrison**
"For the last twenty years, Jim Harrison has been developing into one of our finest novelists…[He] gives his work a genuine mythopoetic quality that is rare, if not unique among contemporary American writers"
—Chicago Tribune

Dalva
0-671-74067-9 POCKET PB $14.00

Farmer
0-385-28228-1 DELTA PB $12.95

A Good Day to Die
0-385-28343-1 DOUBLEDAY PB $11.95

Julip
"A contemporary master of American storytelling. Typically, his humor tests the borders of the socially acceptable and the extremes of what is tolerable to a character; and there is pleasure to be had in this recklessness"—*Publishers Weekly*
0-395-48885-0 HOUGHTON MIFFLIN $21.95

Legends of the Fall
0-385-28596-5 DELACORTE PB $11.95

Sundog
0-671-74151-9 POCKET PB $12.00

Marianne **Hauser**

Prince Ishmael
A novel based on the legend of Casper Hauser, first published in 1963 and now brought back into print with great acclaim
1-55713-039-6 SUN & MOON PB $11.95

John **Hawkes**
Hawkes defines his writing in these terms: "I began to write fiction on the assumption that the true enemies of the novel were plot, character, setting, and theme, and having once abandoned these familiar ways of thinking about fiction, totality of vision or structure was really all that remained…I'm trying to hold in balance poetic and novelistic methods in order to make the novel a more valid and pleasurable experience."

The Blood Oranges
A comic variation on Ford Madox Ford's *The Good Soldier*. "Outrageous situations and unforgettable scenes refracted through a lens of rhetoric as beautiful as anything I know of in contemporary fiction"—John Barth
0-8112-0061-2 NEW DIRECTIONS PB $9.95

The Cannibal
INTRODUCTION BY ALBERT GUERARD
0-8112-0063-9 NEW DIRECTIONS PB $9.95

The Frog
A French child, asleep beside a lily pond shortly before the First World War, swallows a frog. Mysteriously, the creature survives within him, a companion for life and the source of a strange, exhilarating power. A brilliantly styled parable of violence and illusion, about nothing less than what makes us human, from "America's greatest living visionary"—Edmund White
0-670-86577-X VIKING $21.95

Humors of Blood and Skin: A John Hawkes Reader
"One has a wide choice of what to admire in the work of John Hawkes"—Donald Barthelme
INTRODUCTION BY WILLIAM GASS
0-8112-0907-5 NEW DIRECTIONS PB $12.95

The Lime Twig
"You suffer *The Lime Twig* like a dream. It seems to be something that is happening to you, that you want to escape from but can't"
—Flannery O'Connor
INTRODUCTION BY LESLIE A. FIEDLER
0-8112-0065-5 NEW DIRECTIONS PB $10.95

The Lime Twig, Second Skin, & Travesty
0-14-018982-3 PENGUIN PB $14.95

The Owl and the Goose on the Grave
1-55713-194-5 SUN & MOON PB $12.95

Second Skin
0-8112-0067-1 NEW DIRECTIONS PB $10.95

Sweet William: A Memoir of Old Horse
0-14-023616-3 PENGUIN PB $10.95

Virginie: Her Two Lives
"Hawkes' serene, inviolable prose is so precise, luminous and evocative as to make this novel seem dreamed rather than read"
—Angela Carter
0-88184-054-8 CARROLL & GRAF PB $7.95

Larry **Heinemann**

Paco's Story
The lone survivor of an attack that killed his 90-man company returns to civilian life as a Valium-popping dishwasher in a small-town cafe. Winner of the National Book Award (1987)
See also **LITERATURE: FICTION AND POETRY** under **THE VIETNAM WAR** in **HISTORY OF THE AMERICAS**
0-14-012761-5 VIKING PB $11.95

Joseph **Heller**

Catch-22
The celebrated novel of World War II. "One of the most bitterly funny books in the language"
—New Republic
0-440-20439-9 DELL PB $6.99

Closing Time
0-671-74604-9 SIMON & SCHUSTER $24.00
0-684-80450-6 SCRIBNERS PB $13.00

God Knows
An extended stand-up monologue by David, King of the Jews
0-440-20438-0 DELL PB $6.99

Something Happened
"Splendid, suspenseful, hypnotic, seductive …As clear and as hard-edged as a cut diamond"
—NY Times
0-440-20441-0 DELL PB $6.99

Mark **Helprin**

Ellis Island & Other Stories
A novella and ten stories. "A celebration of the transforming power of the imagination"
—Washington Post
0-15-628315-8 HARCOURT BRACE PB $10.00

Memoir from an Antproof Case
The story of an astounding life in a world that no longer exists: an ace pilot in World War II; a multimillionaire, a thief, murderer, lover
0-15-100097-2 HARVEST $24.00
0-380-72733-1 AVON PB $14.00

A Soldier of the Great War
An Italian professor of aesthetics looks back on his career as a soldier in World War I. "Vast, ambitious, spiritually lusty, all-guzzling, all-encompassing"
—Thomas Keneally, *NY Times Book Review*
0-15-183600-0 HARCOURT BRACE $24.95
0-380-72736-6 AVON PB $15.00

Mark Helprin

Winter's Tale
A long and intricate exercise in adventurous fantasia
0-15-197203-6 HARCOURT BRACE $26.95
0-671-72707-9 WASHINGTON SQUARE PB $14.00

Michael **Herr**

Walter Winchell

A fictionalized take, in screenplay form, on the life of the legendary gossip columnist. "It's as quick and catchy as a jazz melody, and its flair is all the more impressive for capturing the varied moods of its protagonist"
—Christopher Lehmann-Haupt, *NY Times*

0-394-58372-8 VINTAGE PB $18.95

Amy **Herrick**

At the Sign of the Naked Waiter

"[She] skates, almost Cheever-like, over the unbearable on the wit and shimmer of her prose"—*LA Times Book Review*

0-14-023189-7 PENGUIN PB $9.95

John **Hersey**

A Bell for Adano

American GIs in an Italian town liberated from the Nazis

See also **THE '40S** under **THE GREAT FICTION BESTSELLERS 1930-1995** in **POPULAR READING**

0-394-75695-9 RANDOM HOUSE PB $13.00

John Hersey

The Wall

The famous novel of life in the Warsaw ghetto during World War II

See also **HOLOCAUST FICTION** under **ART AND LITERATURE** under **THE HOLOCAUST** in **WORLD HISTORY AND CURRENT AFFAIRS**

0-394-75696-7 VINTAGE PB $14.00

Patricia **Highsmith**

"The most important crime novelist at present in practice."—Julian Symons

The Price of Salt

Highsmith is mostly known as genre writer. However, this book is universally considered the best of lesbian fiction and it has remained the most sought-out lesbian novel for over 30 years. This new edition from Naiad Press is well worth the price for Highsmith's new reflections on New York gay life in the '50s alone

1-56280-003-5 NAIAD PB $9.95

Oscar **Hijuelos**

The 14 Sisters of Emilio Montez O'Brian

0-374-15815-0 FS&G $22.00

The Mambo Kings Play Songs of Love

Two Cuban brothers come to America hoping to make the big time as popular musicians, and come to very different ends. Hijuelos won the Pulitzer Prize for this amazing recreation of an era and a milieu

0-374-20125-0 FS&G $18.95
0-06-097327-7 HARPERCOLLINS PB $13.00
0-06-097451-6 HARPERPERENNIAL PB $12.00

Mr. Ives' Christmas

0-06-017131-6 HARPERCOLLINS $23.00

Chester **Himes**

Best-known for his Harlem Detective series, which was the basis of films like Cotton Comes to Harlem, *Himes began writing while serving a prison term for jewel theft in the 1920s.*

All Shot Up

See also **POLICE PROCEDURAL** under **CRIME FICTION** in **POPULAR READING**

1-56025-103-4 THUNDER'S MOUTH PB $12.95

The Big Gold Dream

1-56025-104-2 THUNDER'S MOUTH PB $12.95

Blind Man with a Pistol

0-394-75998-2 VINTAGE PB $11.00

A Case of Rape

0-7867-0083-1 CARROLL & GRAF PB $8.95

The Collected Stories

All the surviving stories by an author whose work veered between bitter realism *(If He Hollers Let Him Go)* and unrestrained comic fantasy *(Cotton Comes to Harlem)*

1-56025-021-6 THUNDER'S MOUTH PB $14.95

Conversations with Chester Himes

EDITED BY ROBERT E. SKINNER AND MICHEL FABRE

0-87805-819-2 MISSISSIPPI PB $15.95

Cotton Comes to Harlem

0-394-75999-0 VINTAGE PB $10.00

The End of a Primitive

A disastrous interracial love affair culminates in violence

EDITED BY MARC GERALD AND SAMUEL BLUMENFELD

0-393-31540-1 NORTON PB $11.00

The Heat's On

See also **POLICE PROCEDURAL** under **CRIME FICTION** in **POPULAR READING**

0-394-75997-4 VINTAGE PB $10.00

If He Hollers Let Him Go

A young black encounters endemic racism at a California munitions plant during World War II. Himes's angry first novel is a tough, risky piece of work

INTRODUCTION BY GRAHAM HODGES

0-938410-32-6 THUNDER'S MOUTH PB $10.95
1-56849-386-X BUCCANEER $24.95
1-56025-097-6 THUNDER'S MOUTH PB $12.95

Lonely Crusade

A novel whose unflattering portrayals of white leftists provoked controversy in the late '40s

INTRODUCTION BY GRAHAM HODGES

0-938410-37-7 THUNDER'S MOUTH PB $13.95

Chester Himes

Pinktoes: A Novel

0-87805-887-7 MISSISSIPPI PB $16.95

Plan B

0-87805-645-9 MISSISSIPPI $27.50
0-87805-751-X MISSISSIPPI PB $14.95

A Rage in Harlem

Originally published as *For Love of Imabelle;* first in the Gravedigger and Coffin Ed series

0-679-72040-5 VINTAGE PB $10.00

The Real Cool Killers

0-679-72039-1 VINTAGE PB $10.00

Run Man Run

0-7867-0209-5 CARROLL & GRAF PB $8.95

The Third Generation

0-938410-73-3 THUNDER'S MOUTH PB $14.95

Rolando **Hinojosa**

Claros Varones de Belken/Fair Gentlemen of Belken County

"Hinojosa offers an epic survey of life in the Rio Grande Valley...a world filled with the everyday sights, sounds, smells, words, ironies, and sympathies that constitute a unique side of the Texas universe"—*Texas Observer*

0-916950-65-4 BILINGUAL PB $14.00

Dear Rafe

A bitter-comic story told in epistolary form

0-934770-38-7 ARTE PUBLICO PB $8.50

Klail City

0-934770-54-9 ARTE PUBLICO PB $9.00

This Migrant Earth

A montage of stories of migrant workers

0-934770-55-7 ARTE PUBLICO PB $9.00

Janet **Hobhouse**

Dancing in the Dark

Young professionals at large on Manhattan's Upper West Side

0-385-41570-2 ANCHOR PB $11.00

November

A middle-aged man flees New York City for London after being deserted by his wife

0-385-41571-0 ANCHOR PB $9.00

The Furies
Hobhouse's fourth novel, completed just before her untimely death, delineates one woman's Promethean struggle to come to terms with generations of female wealth and instability. "A tough, powerful, beautiful book, the memoir of a genuine heroine"—Philip Roth
0-385-47054-1 DOUBLEDAY PB $12.95

Alice **Hoffman**

Angel Landing
0-425-13952-2 BERKLEY PB $6.99

At Risk
0-425-11738-3 BERKLEY PB $6.99

The Drowning Season
0-451-17815-7 SIGNT PB $4.99

Fortune's Daughter
0-449-20976-8 CREST PB $5.99

Illumination Night
"Daringly mixing comedy with tragedy...she has created a narrative that somehow makes myth out of the sticky complexities of contemporary marriage...Her characters are branded onto one's memory"
—Christopher Lehmann-Haupt, *NY Times*
0-449-21594-6 FAWCETT PB $5.99

Practical Magic
Fairy tale more than magic realism, the 11th novel from bestselling Hoffman takes us back to the world of a Massachusetts family where spinster aunts cast spells and two nieces try to escape into normalcy only to learn that magic is strength, not affliction. "With vivid language and imperceptible plotting, Hoffman writes stories which take one back to the thrill of hearing, at bedtime, and now I will a tale unfold"
—Boston Review
0-399-14055-7 PUTNAM $22.95
0-425-15249-9 BERKLEY PB $6.99

Property of: A Novel
0-425-13903-4 BERKLEY PB $6.50

Second Nature
0-425-14681-2 BERKLEY PB $6.50

Seventh Heaven
0-449-22018-4 CREST PB $5.99

Turtle Moon
0-425-13699-X BERKLEY PB $5.99

White Horses
0-425-13980-8 BERKLEY PB $6.99

Andrew **Holleran**

The Beauty of Men
0-688-04857-9 MORROW $24.00

Dancer from the Dance
An evocation of gay life in the '70s. A male counterpart to *Rubyfruit Jungle*
0-452-26129-5 NEW AMERICAN LIBRARY PB $11.95

John Clellon **Holmes**

Go
The original novel of the Beat Generation
INTRODUCTION BY JAMES ATLAS
0-938410-60-1 THUNDER'S MOUTH PB $13.95

The Horn
A novel of the jazz world, first published in 1958. "Strongly reflects the history of jazz and many of its people are studies of jazz personalities (The Horn himself seems three parts Coleman Hawkins and one part Lester Young)"—*NY Times*
FOREWORD BY ARCHIE SHEPP
0-938410-51-2 THUNDER'S MOUTH PB $14.95

James **Houston**

Gig
0-88739-061-7 CREATIVE LEARNING PB $8.95

Maureen **Howard**

Natural History
Howard tells the story of an Irish-Catholic family in Bridgeport, Connecticut, through the "layering and dovetailing of fiction and history...that make reading this novel like watching a display of the aurora borealis"
—NY Times Book Review
0-06-097569-5 HARPERPERENNIAL PB $12.00

Fanny **Howe**

Deep North
1-55713-025-6 SUN & MOON $13.95
1-55713-105-8 SUN & MOON PB $9.95

Nod
1-55713-307-7 SUN & MOON $18.95

Saving History
1-55713-100-7 SUN & MOON PB $12.95

Josephine **Humphreys**

Dreams of Sleep
0-14-007787-1 VIKING PB $10.95

Rich in Love
0-14-017432-X PENGUIN PB $10.95

Kristin **Hunter**

God Bless the Child
The life and tragic early death of a black woman
INTRODUCTION BY PHIL PETRIE
0-88258-154-6 HOWARD PB $12.95

Siri **Hustvedt**

The Enchantment of Lily Dahl
A young woman becomes obsessed with a painter
0-8050-4920-7 HOLT $23.00

The Blindfold
Siri encounters the errie and strange realities of New York City
0-393-31013-2 NORTON PB $8.95

John **Irving**

John Irving "is more than popular. He is a populist, determined to keep alive the Dickensian tradition that revels in colorful set pieces and teaches moral lessons."—NY Times

The 158-Pound Marriage
0-345-36743-X BALLANTINE PB $5.99

The Cider House Rules
"The characters...break all the rules, and yet they remain noble and free-spirited. Victims of tragedy, violence, and injustice, their lives seem more interesting and full of thought-provoking dilemmas than the lives of many real people"
—Houston Post
0-345-38765-1 BALLANTINE PB $6.95

The Hotel New Hampshire
"Some of the most unforgettable characters in recent fiction...lively good fun"—*Newsday*
0-345-40047-X BALLANTINE PB $6.99

A Prayer for Owen Meany
"Its two main characters...are appealing, as are its themes—the persistence of friendship through adversity, the combat of conscience with mediocrity, and the search for the father and oneself"—*LA Times*
0-345-36179-2 BALLANTINE PB $6.99

John Irving (photo by Marion Ettlinger)

Setting Free the Bears
0-345-36741-3 BALLANTINE PB $5.99

A Son of the Circus
0-679-43496-8 RANDOM HOUSE $25.00

Trying to Save Piggy Sneed
Irving is at the top of his form in this collection of short fiction and nonfiction. Short stories include the O. Henry Award-winning "Interior Space," and essays include "An Introduction to *A Christmas Carol*"
1-55970-323-7 ARCADE $21.95

The Water Method Man
0-345-36742-1 BALLANTINE PB $5.99

The World According to Garp
Tragicomic account of an eccentric family
0-345-36676-X BALLANTINE PB $6.99

Charles **Jackson**

The Lost Weekend
The famous novel of alcoholism has a few surprises, even for those familiar with Billy Wilder's movie version
0-8156-0419-X SYRACUSE PB $14.95

Shirley **Jackson**

The Haunting of Hill House
An influential, disarmingly subtle novel about a lonely young woman driven to the brink of madness and beyond by a sinister, possibly haunted old mansion
0-14-007108-3 VIKING PB $9.95

Shirley **Jackson**

The Lottery

A well-crafted collection of stories that includes the universally read title story about a curious small-town ritual

0-374-51681-2 NOONDAY PB $12.00

The Sundial

Informed that the world will be destroyed and they alone spared, the eccentric Halloran family wait in their mansion for the comic and surprising end

0-8488-0370-1 AMEREON $22.95

Harold **Jaffe**

Beasts

Ten short works modeled on the medieval bestiary. "At times surreal, at times overtly political, these stories force us to reexamine our most basic human instincts"—Rochelle Ratner

0-915306-58-1 CURBSTONE $17.50

0-915306-52-2 CURBSTONE PB $9.00

Tama **Janowitz**

By the Shores of Gitchee Gumee

0-517-70298-3 CROWN $23.00

The Male Cross-Dresser Support Group

Humorous stories from the quintessential chronicler New York's downtown scene

0-671-87150-1 WASHINGTON SQUARE PB $12.00

Slaves of New York

Interrelated stories dealing with the artists and poseurs of downtown Manhattan

0-671-74524-7 POCKET PB $8.95

Randall **Jarrell**

Pictures from an Institution: A Comedy

A scintillating satirical novel of academic life

0-226-39374-7 CHICAGO PB $14.95

Len **Jenkin**

New Jerusalem

0-685-12126-7 SUN & MOON PB $10.95

Charles **Johnson**

Faith and the Good Thing

The fictional chronicle of an 18-year-old girl's journey from the backwoods of Georgia to the streets of Chicago, filled with remarkable characters and unforeseen adventures. "A brilliant novel of allegory, myth and folktales" —*Washington Post*

0-689-70720-7 PLUME PB $9.95

The Middle Passage

Winner of the 1991 National Book Award. A slave-trading captain, a petty criminal stowaway, and a host of undesirables make this adventure at sea unforgettable

0-689-11968-2 ATHENEUM $18.95

0-452-26638-6 PLUME PB $10.95

Denis **Johnson**

Denis Johnson was born in Munich, Germany, in 1949. "Denis Johnson speaks...with passion and wit...for every hushed or broken voice in America's cities of night."—David St. John

Angels

"I have not been so impressed by a first novel in years"—John le Carré

0-394-75987-7 VINTAGE PB $12.00

Fiskadoro

"The sort of book Herman Melville might have written had he lived today and studied such disparate works as the Bible, 'The Waste Land,' *Fahrenheit 451*, and *Dog Soldiers*, screened *Star Wars* and *Apocalypse Now* several times, dropped a lot of acid and listened to hours of Jimi Hendrix and the Rolling Stones" —*NY Times*

0-06-097609-8 HARPERPERENNIAL PB $11.00

Jesus' Son: Stories

Life among the very lost and very stoned, recounted with a horrific blank concision

0-06-097577-6 HARPERPERENNIAL PB $11.00

Resuscitation of a Hanged Man

0-374-24949-0 FS&G $19.95

0-14-016522-3 PENGUIN PB $10.95

The Stars at Noon

0-06-097610-1 HARPERPERENNIAL PB $11.00

Gayl **Jones**

Corregidora

0-8070-6315-0 BEACON PB $12.00

Eva's Man

0-8070-6319-3 BEACON PB $12.00

The Hermit-Woman

0-916418-43-X LOTUS PB $4.00

James **Jones**

From Here to Eternity

A naval base in Hawaii in the days preceding Pearl Harbor

See also **THE '50S** under **THE GREAT FICTION BESTSELLERS 1930-1995** in **POPULAR READING**

0-440-32770-9 DELL PB $6.99

Ward **Just**

The Congressman Who Loved Flaubert

0-88184-587-6 CARROLL & GRAF PB $8.95

In the City of Fear

0-393-30722-0 NORTON PB $10.95

Stringer

0-915308-61-4 GRAY WOLF PB $6.00

Steve **Katz**

43 Fictions

1-55713-069-8 SUN & MOON PB $12.95

Florry of Washington Heights

A half-Irish, half-Jewish boy growing up in pre-World War II upper Manhattan

0-940650-83-5 SUN & MOON $15.95

0-940650-84-3 SUN & MOON PB $10.95

Swanny's Ways

1-55713-209-7 SUN & MOON $22.95

Wier and Pouce

"A linguistic tour de force"—*Village Voice*

0-940650-33-9 SUN & MOON $17.95

0-940650-47-9 SUN & MOON PB $10.95

Janet **Kauffman**

Collaborators

A woman's relationship with her mother alters when the mother suffers a stroke. "A moving evocation of the real love between mother and daughter, and the burden it places on both of them"—*Cleveland Plain Dealer*

1-55597-185-7 GRAY WOLF PB $11.00

Joe **Keenan**

Blue Heaven

0-14-010764-9 PENGUIN PB $10.95

William Melvin **Kelley**

Dancers on the Shore

A collection of 16 short stories

0-88258-114-7 HOWARD PB $12.95

A Different Drummer

0-385-41390-4 ANCHOR PB $9.95

A Drop of Patience

0-88001-460-1 ECCO PB $13.00

Robert **Kelly**

Cat Scratch Fever

"Poet, novelist, storyteller, essayist, linguist, [Kelly] is the joker in the deck of post-modernist writing...*Cat Scratch Fever* is full of signs and wonders"—*NY Times Bobk Review*

0-929701-11-9 MCPHERSON PB $10.00

The Scorpions

0-88268-018-8 STATION HILL PB $7.95

A Transparent Tree: Fictions: Eleven Short Works

"Astonishing mix of intellect, romanticism, and daring imagination"—Robert Coover

0-914232-68-1 MCPHERSON $20.00

William **Kennedy**

Billy Phelan's Greatest Game

0-14-006340-4 VIKING PB $11.95

The Flaming Corsage

Opening on the "Love Nest Killing of 1908," Kennedy's new novel is a mystery of shifting sexual and personal interpretations that move back and forth between the 1880s and 1912. Albany's Irishtown and English-Dutch aristocracy are explored in Kennedy's evocative prose, and a world of joys, griefs, and furies is, once again inimitably, let loose

0-670-85872-2 VIKING $23.95

Ironweed

A former baseball player down and out in Albany, 20 years after the accidental killing of his son

0-14-007020-6 PENGUIN PB $11.95

Legs

The life and times of Prohibition-era gangster Legs Diamond

0-14-006484-2 VIKING PB $11.95

Quinn's Book

0-14-007737-5 PENGUIN PB $10.95

Very Old Bones

In this installment from of the "Albany Cycle" novels, Kennedy is at the height of his descriptive and narrative powers. "[Kennedy's] justly acclaimed *Albany Cycle* is one of the few

imperishable products of American literature since the Second World War"—Ward Just
0-670-83457-2 VIKING $22.00

William Kennedy (photo by Mariana Cook)

Susan **Kenney**

Graves in Academe
0-14-013349-6 SELECT PENGUIN PB $5.95

In Another Country
0-670-39486-6 VIKING $13.95

Sailing
0-670-81229-3 VIKING PB $18.95

Jack **Kerouac**

"Jack Kerouac, new Buddha of American prose, who spit forth intelligence … a spontaneous bop prosody and original classic literature."
—Allen Ginsberg

Big Sur
A late novel that confronts Kerouac's personal decline in the face of adulation and fame
0-14-016812-5 PENGUIN PB $11.95

Desolation Angels
"Kerouac was a breath of fresh air when he came on the literary scene. He was also a force, a tragedy, a triumph, and an ongoing influence, and that influence is still with us"
—Norman Mailer
1-57322-505-3 RIVERHEAD PB $12.00

The Dharma Bums
A novel of the Beat scene featuring thinly disguised portraits of Allen Ginsberg, Gary Snyder, Kenneth Rexroth, and others
0-14-004252-0 PENGUIN PB $11.95

Doctor Sax
Autobiographical novel of a French-Canadian growing up in Lowell, Massachusetts, haunted by the ghosts and demons of a fantasy world
0-8021-3049-6 GROVE PB $11.95

Lonesome Traveler
More life on the road. "There is nothing nobler than to put up with a few inconveniences like snakes and dust for the sake of absolute freedom"—Jack Kerouac
0-8021-3074-7 GROVE PB $9.95

Maggie Cassidy
0-14-017906-2 PENGUIN PB $11.95

On the Road
Kerouac's most famous novel
0-14-018521-6 PENGUIN PB $11.95

Satori in Paris & Pic: Two Short, Late Works
0-8021-3061-5 GROVE PB $11.00

The Town and the City
Kerouac's first novel
0-15-690790-9 HARCOURT BRACE PB $16.00

Tristessa
A strung-out Mexican prostitute
0-14-016811-7 PENGUIN PB $9.95

Visions of Cody
In part, a memoir of Kerouac's companion on the road, Neal Cassady
INTRODUCTION BY ALLEN GINSBERG
0-14-017907-0 PENGUIN PB $12.95

Visions of Gerard
The early childhood of Ti Jean Duluoz, Kerouac's alter ego, as reflected in the short life of his brother Gerard
0-14-014452-8 PENGUIN PB $9.95

Ann **Charters**, editor

The Portable Jack Kerouac
"[T]his volume may deal a fist in the face of the English sentence because Kerouac's revamping of the sentence is so song-filled and emotion-ridden that its properties could well do for American prose what Whitman did for verse: give it a new life"—*Publishers Weekly*
0-670-84957-X VIKING $27.95

Ken **Kesey**

Demon Box
0-14-008530-0 PENGUIN PB $13.95

One Flew over the Cuckoo's Nest
The moving story of a sane but rebellious man who is placed in an insane asylum, where he turns the very notion of insanity upside down. An eloquent statement of human individuality
0-14-015509-0 VIKING PB $13.95

Sailor Song
0-14-013997-4 PENGUIN PB $12.95

Sometimes a Great Notion
This social novel concerns itself with the economically depressed and claustrophobic culture of small family loggers in the Pacific Northwest
0-14-004529-5 PENGUIN PB $14.95

John Oliver **Killens**

An important figure in the Black Arts Movement of the '60s, Killens was a close friend of Martin Luther King and other civil rights activists.

And Then We Heard Thunder
Racism in the military during World War II
INTRODUCTION BY MEL WATKINS
0-88258-115-5 HOWARD PB $12.95

Youngblood
A generational novel from 1954
FOREWORD BY ADDISON GAYLE
0-8203-0602-9 GEORGIA PB $14.95

Jamaica **Kincaid**

Kincaid, an Antiguan writer now based in the US, uses a rich image of recollection to evoke coming of age in the Caribbean.

Annie John
See also **CARIBBEAN LITERATURE**
0-374-10521-9 HILL & WANG $18.95
0-452-26356-5 NEW AMERICAN LIBRARY PB $9.95

At the Bottom of the River
0-452-26754-4 PLUME PB $7.95

The Autobiography of My Mother
A 70-year-old West Indian woman looks back at her life, concentrating her memory on sex, human relations, and powerlessness
0-374-10731-9 FS&G $20.00

A Small Place
0-452-26235-6 PLUME PB $8.95

Lucy
0-452-26677-7 PLUME PB $10.95

Jamaica Kincaid

Barbara **Kingsolver**

Animal Dreams
0-06-092114-5 HARPERCOLLINS PB $13.00

The Bean Trees
0-06-091554-4 HARPERCOLLINS PB $13.00

Pigs in Heaven
Once again we encounter those memorable characters, Alice, Taylor, and Turtle, from Kingsolver's bestselling *The Bean Trees*. "The work of a visionary…It leaves you open-mouthed and smiling"—*LA Times*
0-06-092253-2 HARPERPERENNIAL $13.00

Maxine Hong **Kingston**

China Men
A follow-up into the minds of Chinese men in America. "It captures the emotional truth of the Chinese-American experience far better than any conventional history or biography ever could"—*Newsday*
See also **MEMOIRS AND JOURNALS** under **20TH-CENTURY AMERICAN ESSAYS AND JOURNALISM**
0-679-72328-5 VINTAGE PB $11.00

Maxine Hong **Kingston**

The Woman Warrior: Memoirs of a Girlhood Among Ghosts

A Chinese-American born in California describes her upbringing in a laundry amid the talk-stories of her mother, Brave Orchid. Winner of the National Book Critics Circle Award

0-394-40067-4 RANDOM HOUSE $24.95
0-679-72188-6 VINTAGE PB $11.00

John **Knowles**

Peace Breaks Out

0-553-27574-7 BDD PB $4.99

A Separate Peace

A boy's coming of age at a New England boarding school

0-553-28041-4 BDD PB $4.99

Christopher J. **Koch**

The Year of Living Dangerously

"A richly and fully realized work of fiction, well conceived and beautifully executed" —Larry McMurtry

0-14-006535-0 PENGUIN PB $10.95

Jerzy **Kosinski**

Being There

An uneducated gardener becomes a man of national influence

0-553-27930-0 BDD PB $5.99

The Painted Bird

A nightmarish vision of Eastern Europe during World War II

See also **HOLOCAUST FICTION** under **ART AND LITERATURE** under **THE HOLOCAUST** in **WORLD HISTORY AND CURRENT AFFAIRS**

0-8021-3422-X GROVE PB $10.00

Steps

A sequence of surreal episodes, with an emphasis on sadomasochistic situations

0-394-75716-5 VINTAGE PB $10.00

William **Kotzwinkle**

The Fan Man

0-679-75245-5 VINTAGE PB $10.00

Hearts of Wood: Timeless Tales

ILLUSTRATED BY JOE SERVELLO

0-87923-648-5 GODINE $12.95

The Midnight Examiner

Set in the insane world of tabloid newspapers

0-395-49859-7 HOUGHTON MIFFLIN $17.95

Eric **Kraft**

Herb 'n' Lorna: A Love Story

0-312-13509-2 PICADOR PB $13.00

Little Follies: The Personal History, Adventures, Experiences & Observations of Peter Leroy (So Far)

0-312-11928-3 PICADOR PB $13.00

What a Piece of Work I Am (A Confabulation)

0-517-59612-1 CROWN $22.00
0-312-13211-5 PICADOR PB $11.00

Where Do You Stop?: The Personal History, Adventures, Experiences & Observations of Peter Leroy

0-517-58544-8 CROWN $15.00
0-312-11932-1 ST. MARTIN'S PB $10.00

Larry **Kramer**

Faggots

0-452-26396-4 NEW AMERICAN LIBRARY PB $11.95

Anne **Lamott**

Hard Laughter

A young woman in northern California, coping with her father's terminal illness—while maintaining a sense of humor

0-86547-280-7 NORTH POINT PB $11.00

Ursula K. **Le Guin**

With 15 novels, 60 short stories, poetry, children's books, criticism, and screenplays to her name—as well as a National Book Award—Le Guin is the preeminent science fiction writer in America, as well as a major literary voice transcending genre classifications.

The Compass Rose

See also **CONTEMPORARY SCIENCE FICTION** under **SCIENCE FICTION AND FANTASY** in **POPULAR READING**

0-06-105607-3 HARPERCOLLINS PB $4.99

A Fisherman of the Inland Sea

0-06-105491-7 HARPERCOLLINS PB $4.99

Four Ways to Forgiveness

Four interlinked novellas from the only science fiction writer ever to win the National Book Award. Creating a nightmare world of slaves and owners, Le Guin studies the surprising and delicate forms that freedom can take: love, learning, compassion, and courage

0-06-105234-5 HARPER PRISM $20.00
0-06-105401-1 HARPER PRISM PB $5.99

The Lathe of Heaven

0-380-01320-7 AVON PB $5.50

Searoad: Chronicles of Klatsand

0-06-105400-3 HARPERCOLLINS PB $4.99

Unlocking the Air and Other Stories

"Lyric and luminous....A major imaginative vision"—*NY Times Book Review*. "Le Guin fashions ideas like a goldsmith; intricate, involved, and confident"—*Chicago Daily News*

0-06-017260-6 HARPERCOLLINS $22.00

Worlds of Exile and Illusion

0-312-86211-3 ST. MARTIN'S PB $14.95

David **Leavitt**

Equal Affections

1-55584-202-X PUBLISHERS GROUP WEST $18.95

Family Dancing

An acclaimed first collection of stories. "An astonishing collection...tender, funny, eloquent, and wise...Regardless of age, few writers so effortlessly achieve the sense of maturity and earned compassion so evident in these pages" —*NY Times*

0-394-53872-2 KNOPF $13.95

The Lost Language of Cranes

0-553-34465-X BANTAM PB $10.95

While England Sleeps

The story of a love affair between an aristocratic young British writer and a communist working-class employee of the London Underground

0-395-75286-8 DORLING KINDERSLEY PB $11.95

Brad **Leithauser**

Seaward

A perfectly logical Washington lawyer whose values are jolted to the core when his dead wife appears to him in an unmistakably real vision, swathed in a glow of light

0-394-58587-9 KNOPF $23.00

Life itself is a miracle—is it not?—and what additional miracle can possibly stand up to that? Life itself is a miracle, but so what? So what? The people find a way of going on with their lives all the same. As you will do, my friend.
SEAWARD

Madeleine **L'Engle**

Certain Women

"The gentle, rhythmic quality of L'Engle's prose is perfectly attuned to fictional aquatic cruise. A memorable work"—*Kirkus Reviews*

0-06-065207-1 HARPERCOLLINS PB $13.00

A Live Coal in the Sea

A mesmerizing tale of suspense and psychological complexity from the great L'Engle. The story of a family's struggle with loyalty, faith, and identity, shuttling through the distant past and troubled present

0-374-18989-7 FS&G $24.00

The Small Rain

"L'Engle's genteel exploration of the interior landscape of a sensitive young girl" —*Publishers Weekly*

0-374-51912-9 FS&G PB $13.00

Craig **Lesley**

River Song

A Nez Perce former rodeo rider and his father search for their personal and tribal heritage in Lesley's second novel, set in Oregon

0-385-31277-6 DELL PB $11.95

Mark **Leyner**

"With his pumped up prose and steroidal satire, it's easy to see why Leyner has become the new Hunter S. Thompson to the on-line generation. You could call him the Quentin Tarantino of cult fiction."—Newsweek

Et Tu, Babe

"Its rude, epic shriek...begs to be read aloud to friends and strangers alike"—*Village Voice*

0-679-74506-8 VINTAGE PB $10.00

I Smell Esther Williams: And Other Stories

0-679-75045-2 VINTAGE PB $11.00

My Cousin, My Gastroenterologist

"I really, really liked it. It's like nothing else. I laughed out loud in the bathroom" —David Byrne

0-679-74579-3 VINTAGE PB $10.00

Tooth Imprints on a Corn Dog

0-517-59384-X HARMONY $19.00
0-679-74521-1 VINTAGE PB $11.00

Gordon **Lish**

Dear Mr. Capote

1-56858-079-7 FOUR WALLS PB $12.95

Epigraph

1-56858-076-2 FOUR WALLS $22.00

My Romance

0-393-31104-X NORTON PB $8.95

What I Know So Far: Stories

1-56858-080-0 FOUR WALLS PB $10.95

Zimzum

0-679-42685-X PANTHEON $18.00

Ralph **Lombreglia**

Make Me Work

0-374-20004-1 FS&G $20.00
0-14-024222-8 PENGUIN PB $9.95

The Love Eaters and The Kiss of Kin: Two Books in One

The Love Eaters, Settle's first novel, is the story of a small-town theatrical troupe

1-57003-098-7 SOUTH CAROLINA PB $14.95

Alison **Lurie**

Foreign Affairs

Two Americans abroad, two love affairs; winner of the 1984 Pulitzer Prize

0-380-70990-2 AVON PB $12.00

Imaginary Friends

Two sociologists captivated by a teenage psychic

0-380-70073-5 AVON PB $8.95

The War Between the Tates

The breakup of a faculty marriage

0-380-71135-4 AVON PB $8.95

Nathaniel **Mackey**

Djbot Baghostus's Run

"At once a philosophical treatise on African-American art and culture; a rumination on the nature of eroticism, of dreams, of collective thought, and of the creative process; and a passionate love letter to African-American music"—*Utne Reader*

1-55713-055-8 SUN & MOON PB $12.95

Norman **Maclean**

A River Runs Through It

Subject of the acclaimed Ron Howard movie of the same title. "A collection of three passionately written autobiographical fiction pieces set in the Rocky Mountain wilderness of Maclean's childhood"—*Booklist*

0-226-50060-8 CHICAGO $24.95
0-671-77697-5 POCKET PB $5.99

Norman **Mailer**

Advertisements for Myself

A dissection of Mailer by Mailer in the form of excerpts from, and criticisms of, all of his early works

See also **LITERATURE** under **20TH-CENTURY AMERICAN ESSAYS AND JOURNALISM**

0-674-00590-2 HARVARD PB $15.95

An American Dream

The middle-aged Rojack murders his heiress wife in an act of madness

0-8050-0349-5 HOLT PB $12.95

Ancient Evenings

A portrait of Ramses II and ancient Egypt. "There is … power in Mailer's fantasy … and there is a relevance to current reality in America that actually surpasses that of Mailer's largest previous achievement"
—*NY Review of Books*

0-446-35769-3 WARNER PB $7.99

Norman Mailer

Barbary Shore

A metaphorical New York tenement houses the obsessed and dispossessed

0-686-65521-4 FERTIG $48.00

The Executioner's Song

Really two books: the first about the brutal life and death of convicted killer Gary Gilmore, the second about the media's no less savage fight for the story rights. "Not since *The Grapes of Wrath* has there been an American book that so discovered the voices in our culture"
—*Philadelphia Inquirer*

See also **SERIAL KILLERS** under **TRUE CRIME** in **POPULAR READING**

0-679-42471-7 MODERN LIBRARY $21.00

Harlot's Ghost

A sprawling CIA novel based on James Angleton's mole hunt through the catacombs of the Western power structure

0-345-37965-9 BALLANTINE PB $12.50

The Naked and the Dead

Mailer's first novel, a naturalistic account of a small fighting troop living and dying on a Pacific island in World War II

0-8050-0521-8 HOLT PB $14.95

Tough Guys Don't Dance

A thriller set on the East Coast, about a man who cannot remember whether or not he killed a girl

0-446-34521-0 WARNER PB $7.99

Why Are We in Vietnam

In a manic, amphetamine-like style, a young Texan D.J. relates the comic misadventures of a hunting trip with his father in Alaska; Mailer's funniest book

0-8050-1880-8 HOLT PB $9.95

Clarence **Major**

Poet, painter, teacher, lexicographer, and novelist, Major has been on the cutting edge of black fiction for 20 years. The Fiction Collective, a cooperative publishing house, was started by Major and a handful of colleagues in the early '70s.

Dirty Bird Blues

1-56279-085-4 MERCURY HOUSE PB $12.95

Reflex and Bone Structure

1-56279-084-6 MERCURY HOUSE PB $12.95

Bernard **Malamud**

The Assistant

The effect of a young man on an aging grocery store owner and his family

0-380-72085-X AVON PB $10.00

The Fixer

An ordinary man is accused of "ritual murder" in Czarist Russia

0-14-018515-1 PENGUIN PB $11.95

God's Grace

A prophetic novel examining humanity's dreams and failures. "Both somber and sometimes very funny … Malamud may have created his most lasting work"—*Wall Street Journal*

0-14-018491-0 PENGUIN PB $9.95

The Natural

"An allegory about the rise and fall of a baseball player who can't quite overcome his own pride or the chicanery of modern life"—*Booklist*

See also **BASEBALL FICTION** under **BASEBALL** under **SPORTS** in **FOOD, TRAVEL, AND LEISURE**

0-380-50609-2 AVON PB $5.99

Bernard Malamud

A New Life

S. Levin, a 30-year-old man, moves to the Pacific Northwest from New York. "Malamud has, among other gifts, a compassionate irony, and Levin's final desperation … is that rare fictional achievement, true tragi-farce"—*Newsweek*

0-374-52103-4 FS&G PB $8.95
0-14-018681-6 PENGUIN PB $9.95

The Stories of Bernard Malamud

0-374-27037-6 FS&G $17.95
0-452-26354-9 NEW AMERICAN LIBRARY PB $12.95

Clarence **Major**

The Tenants

Two writers, white and black, come into conflict on the Lower East Side

0-14-018516-X PENGUIN PB $9.95

Thomas **Mallon**

Henry and Clara

0-395-59071-X TICKNOR & FIELDS $22.95
0-312-13508-4 PICADOR PB $13.00

David **Mamet**

The Village

"Mamet's jolting, minimalist first novel has the hallmarks of his plays—sharply observed, fractured dialogue; characters who talk past each other; insight into a terrible emptiness at the core of American life"—*Publishers Weekly*

0-316-54572-4 LITTLE, BROWN $21.95

David **Markson**

Reader's Block

1-56478-132-1 DALKEY ARCHIVE PB $12.95

Wittgenstein's Mistress

A technically astonishing novel about a woman convinced that she is the only person left on earth. "As precise and dazzling as Joyce" —Ann Beattie

0-916583-50-3 DALKEY ARCHIVE PB $11.95

Paule **Marshall**

Brown Girl, Brownstones

AFTERWORD BY MARY H. WASHINGTON

1-55861-149-5 FEMINIST PRESS

The Chosen Place, the Timeless People

American anthropologists become entangled with inhabitants of a Caribbean island like Grenada. "A style remarkable for its courage, color, and its natural control"—*New Yorker*

0-394-72633-2 VINTAGE PB $14.00

Praisesong for the Widow

0-452-26711-0 PLUME PB $11.95

Soul Clap Hands and Sing

Four stories of middle age and despair ranging in location from Brooklyn to Barbados to Brazil

INTRODUCTION BY PHIL PETRIE

0-88258-155-4 HOWARD PB $12.95

Valerie **Martin**

Mary Reilly

A retelling of *Dr. Jekyll and Mr. Hyde* from a woman's viewpoint. "An astonishing tour de force"—Margaret Atwood

0-671-73150-5 POCKET PB $7.95

Max **Martinez**

Schoolland

The life of a Mexican-American family in rural Texas during the year of a great drought in the '50s

0-934770-87-5 ARTE PUBLICO PB $9.50

Bobbie Anne **Mason**

In Country

A girl comes to terms with her father's death in Vietnam two decades earlier

0-06-091350-9 HARPERPERENNIAL PB $12.00

Love Life

Short stories

0-06-091668-0 HARPERCOLLINS PB $11.00

Shiloh & Other Stories

Sixteen stories set in Kentucky. "A stunning debut"—Raymond Carver

0-06-091330-4 HARPERCOLLINS PB $12.00

Harry **Mathews**

The Journalist

1-56792-007-1 GODINE $21.95

Singular Pleasures

1-56478-024-4 DALKEY ARCHIVE $19.95

The Sinking of the Odradek Stadium

0-85635-572-0 CARCANET $11.25

Peter **Matthiessen**

At Play in the Fields of the Lord

A story of human frailty in a tropical rainforest written decades before the setting became a hot political topic

0-679-40874-6 RANDOM HOUSE $16.00
0-679-73741-3 VINTAGE PB $12.00

Far Tortuga

0-394-75667-3 VINTAGE PB $15.00

Killing Mr. Watson

A 1910 murder in the Florida Everglades. "A fiction in the tradition of Joseph Conrad, as fiercely incisive as the work of Sinclair Lewis, a virtuoso performance that powerfully indicts the heedlessness and hidden criminality that are part and parcel of America's devotion to the pursuit of wealth, to its cult of financial success"—Ron Hansen, *NY Times Book Review*

0-394-55400-0 RANDOM HOUSE $21.95

Armistead **Maupin**

Maybe the Moon

0-06-092434-9 HARPERCOLLINS PB $13.00

Tales of the City

A popular series, originally published serially in *The San Francisco Chronicle*, which follows the residents of a San Francisco apartment building from the promiscuous and carefree '70s to an increasingly conservative '80s and on to the era of safe sex. The characters include a former debutante-turned-lesbian mother, a marijuana-growing landlady, a swinging waiter, and girl from the heartland dropped into their midst

Volume 1: Tales of the City

0-06-096404-9 HARPERPERENNIAL PB $12.00

Volume 2: More Tales of the City

0-06-092479-9 HARPERPERENNIAL PB $12.00

Volume 3: Further Tales of the City

0-06-092492-6 HARPERPERENNIAL PB $13.00

Volume 4: Babycakes

0-06-092483-7 HARPERPERENNIAL PB $12.00

Volume 5: Significant Others

0-06-092481-0 HARPERPERENNIAL PB $13.00

Volume 6: Sure of You

0-06-092484-5 HARPERPERENNIAL PB $12.00

William **Maxwell**

All the Days and Nights: The Collected Stories

EDITED BY LUANN WALTHER

0-679-76102-0 VINTAGE PB $13.00

Ancestors: A Family History

Maxwell traces the history of his family, beginning in Ohio in 1818

0-679-75929-8 VINTAGE PB $12.00

Billie Dyer and Other Stories

0-679-40832-0 KNOPF $18.00

The Chateau

Americans in France after World War II

0-679-76156-X VINTAGE PB $13.00

The Folded Leaf

Two boys growing up in Chicago

0-404-61510-4 AMS $49.50
0-679-77256-1 VINTAGE PB $12.00

Over by the River & Other Stories

Twelve short stories. "These stories seem to tell themselves, with each precisely observed detail or snatch of talk tapped home like a design on tinware"—*NY Times*

0-87923-541-1 GODINE PB $10.95

So Long, See You Tomorrow

"A tale of inarticulate passion among innocent, middle-aged farming people...Maxwell's accomplishment is to present a fascinating tragedy enacted by sincere, gentle, reluctant participants—and to give his account the same inegrity that marks their deeds" —*Washington Post*

0-87923-754-6 GODINE PB $12.95
0-679-76720-7 VINTAGE PB $10.00

Time Will Darken It

Small-town Illinois in 1912

0-679-77258-8 VINTAGE PB $12.00

Bernadette **Mayer**

Proper Name & Other Stories

0-8112-1325-0 NEW DIRECTIONS PB $13.95

Cormac **McCarthy**

All the Pretty Horses

Set in West Texas and Mexico after the Second World War "*All the Pretty Horses* is a superb book, touching on matters that are never allowed access to serious (literary) novels. The prose is both raw and transcendentally lyric, and should gather Cormac McCarthy the attention he has long deserved"—Jim Harrison

0-394-57474-5 KNOPF $21.00

Blood Meridian: Or the Evening Redness in the West

The American West as continuous massacre: a stunningly visualized novel whose prose represents an original blend of dime novel and Old Testament

0-679-72875-9 VINTAGE PB $12.00

Child of God

A ballad-like piece of Southern Gothic, charting the hideous doings of a crazed loner

0-679-72874-0 VINTAGE PB $10.00

Cormac McCarthy (credit: ©Marion Ettlinger)

The Crossing
The long-awaited second part in *The Border Trilogy,* following the National Book Award-winning *All the Pretty Horses.* Not to be missed
0-394-57475-3 KNOPF $23.00

The Orchard Keeper
0-679-72872-4 VINTAGE PB $11.00

The Outer Dark
0-679-72873-2 VINTAGE PB $10.00

Suttree
Cornelius Suttree abandons his privileged life to live with outcasts on the banks of the Tennessee River. "McCarthy gives us a sense of river life that reads like a doomed *Huckleberry Finn*" —*NY Times Book Review*
0-8446-6792-7 SMITH $22.50
0-679-73632-8 VINTAGE PB $12.00

Mary **McCarthy**

Bird's of America
An American undergraduate in Paris in the '60s
0-15-612630-3 HARCOURT BRACE PB $10.95

Cannibals and Missionaries
A 1979 novel of terrorists and hostages
0-15-615386-6 HARCOURT BRACE PB $10.95

Cast a Cold Eye
Seven short stories
0-15-615444-7 HARCOURT BRACE PB $10.95

A Charmed Life
A New England artists's colony of the '50s
0-15-616774-3 HARCOURT BRACE PB $10.95

The Company She Keeps
McCarthy's first novel deals with adultery, careerism, and left-wing ideological wrangling in '30s New York
0-15-620085-6 HARCOURT BRACE PB $9.00

The Group
Eight Vassar girls of the class of 1933
See also **THE '60S** under **THE GREAT FICTION BESTSELLERS 1930–1995** in **POPULAR READING**
0-15-137281-0 HARCOURT BRACE $15.95
0-15-637208-8 HARCOURT BRACE PB $11.00

Stephen **McCauley**

The Object of My Affection
0-671-74350-3 POCKET PB $14.00

John A. **McCluskey**, Jr.

Mr. America's Last Season Blues
0-8071-1120-1 LSU $18.95

James **McConkey**

Court of Memory
0-87923-983-2 GODINE PB $13.95

Stories from My Life with the Other Animals
The third volume of McConkey's trilogy. "Searchingly honest, deeply stirring, highly original"—Eudora Welty
0-87923-967-0 GODINE $19.95

Jill **McCorkle**

Crash Diet
Eleven short stories by North Carolina's most respected novelist, in which 11 women paint a brilliant composite picture of their shared world. "Jill McCorckle renders it brilliantly" —*NY Times Book Review*
0-945575-75-0 ALGONQUIN $16.95

Carson **McCullers**

The Ballad of the Sad Cafe & Other Stories
Seven short stories, including the title story of a tall woman's love for a midget. "I have found in her work such intensity and nobility of spirit as we have not had in our prose-writing since Herman Melville"— Tennesse Williams
0-553-27254-3 BDD PB $4.99

The Heart Is a Lonely Hunter
Published when she was only 23, McCullers' first novel catapulted her to literary prominence
0-553-26963-1 BDD PB $5.99

The Member of the Wedding
A troubled, perceptive 12-year-old girl awaits her brother's wedding
See also **THE '50S AND '60S** under **20TH-CENTURY AMERICAN DRAMA**
0-8112-0093-0 NEW DIRECTIONS PB $7.95

Alice **McDermott**

That Night
Young love violently and irrevocably interrupted on Long Island. "Possesses the ability to make us remember our own youth"—*NY Times*
0-06-097141-X HARPERPERENNIAL PB $10.00

Joseph **McElroy**

McElroy's novels, complex and hybrid in form, explore late-20th-century crises of survival and personal power.

Plus
0-88184-289-3 CARROLL & GRAF PB $8.95

Women and Men
1-56478-023-6 DALKEY ARCHIVE PB $15.95

Dennis **McFarland**

The Music Room
"McFarland runs many risks, taking on some of the most difficult (and important) tasks a novelist can choose: the search into childhood for secrets of identity, the depiction of alcoholism and shocking parental failure, the interior landscape of a troubled mind, the mystery of self-knowledge. Yet even as the novel probes these various recesses, it retains a generous, hopeful and often comic underpinning, which does not falter" —Josephine Humphreys, *NY Times Book Review*
0-395-54417-3 HOUGHTON MIFFLIN $19.95

School for the Blind
0-395-64497-6 HOUGHTON MIFFLIN $21.95

Thomas **McGuane**

"It's time we recognized Thomas McGuane as a national resource."—The Boston Globe

The Bushwhacked Piano
0-394-72642-1 RANDOM HOUSE PB $11.00

Keep the Change
0-395-48887-7 VINTAGE PB $17.95

Nobody's Angel
An army man returns to Montana. "A thinking man's Western"—*LA Times*
0-394-74738-0 RANDOM HOUSE PB $11.00

Nothing but Blue Skies
A middle-aged man's sudden need to discover a reason to live. "Imagine Ernest Hemingway with a sense of humor. Imagine Franz Kafka journeying through Montana" —*Atlanta Journal & Constitution*
0-395-54540-4 HOUGHTON MIFFLIN $21.95

Panama
A fading, coked-up rock star goes to Key West seeking lost love
0-14-009908-5 VINTAGE PB $10.00

Something to Be Desired
"Nobody writes so well about the incongruities of modern western America"—*Chicago Tribune*
0-394-73156-5 RANDOM HOUSE PB $10.00

The Sporting Club
A mock duel escalates into bizarre and shocking violence
1-56849-401-7 BUCCANEER $24.95

To Skin a Cat
0-394-75521-9 VINTAGE PB $10.00

Vincent **McHugh**

I Am Thinking of My Darling
A classic from 1943 rediscovered: a mysterious virus makes New Yorkers euphorically happy. "To read it is a little like having a 1940s New York City taxicab in your living room, filled with early 1940s characters...The dialogue and the prose is spare, very fine, full of debonair reticences, yet punchy when it has to be. They don't make novels like this anymore"—Lawrence Ferlinghetti
1-87827-405-8 YARROW PB $9.95

As I started down the music came pouring up out of all the entrances and corridors of the subway, reverberating and clashing on itself. An astonishing music, Dixieland. *That Da Da Strain.* The two horns led it, the jostling timbres, pushing each other hard, the nervous-trigger phrasing of the cornet and the powerful thrusting, upward blurt of the trombone. Muggsy and George Brunis. The clarinet leaped high out of the melee, wriggling and flashing. A pure and balanced nimbleness. Fazola.
I AM THINKING OF MY DARLING

Jay **McInerney**

Bright Lights, Big City

An aspiring writer high on cocaine in the club scene of lower Manhattan

0-394-72641-3 VINTAGE PB $10.00

Brightness Falls

A roman à clef about the publishing world in New York. "Jay McInerney's delight in telling a story ... is contagious"—*NY Times Book Review*

0-679-74532-7 VINTAGE PB $13.00

The Last of the Savages

0-679-42845-3 KNOPF $24.00

Ransom

An American karate student in Japan

0-394-74118-8 VINTAGE PB $11.00

Larry **McMurtry**

All My Friends Are Going to Be Strangers

0-671-68103-6 TOUCHSTONE PB $7.95

Buffalo Girls

McMurtry follows up his earlier evocations of the Old West, *Lonesome Dove* and *Anything for Billy*, with a fictional recreation of the extraordinary life of Calamity Jane

See also **CONTEMPORARIES** under **WESTERNS** in **POPULAR READING**

0-671-53615-X POCKET PB $6.99

Cadillac Jack

A rodeo cowboy turned antique scout travels in his Cadillac between Texas and Washington, D.C.

0-671-63720-7 TOUCHSTONE PB $10.00

Dead Man's Walk

The prequel to *Lonesome Dove* concerns the legendary story of the Texas Republic, the Indian Wars, and the Texas Rangers' glory days

See also **CONTEMPORARIES** under **WESTERNS** in **POPULAR READING**

0-684-80753-X SIMON & SCHUSTER $26.00
0-671-00116-7 POCKET PB $6.99

The Desert Rose

A Las Vegas showgirl and her daughter

0-671-63721-5 TOUCHSTONE PB $8.00

The Evening Star

The aging of some of McMurtry's most familiar characters from *Terms of Endearment* make up the subject of this novel

See also **CONTEMPORARIES** under **WESTERNS** in **POPULAR READING**

0-671-00427-1 POCKET PB $7.99

Horseman, Pass By

0-671-75499-8 TOUCHSTONE PB $9.00

The Last Picture Show

Life in a small Texas town during the '50s

0-671-75487-4 TOUCHSTONE PB $10.00

Leaving Cheyenne

0-671-75490-4 TOUCHSTONE PB $11.00

Lonesome Dove

A long and constantly absorbing Western saga, full of humor and incident

See also **CONTEMPORARIES** under **WESTERNS** in **POPULAR READING**

0-671-50420-7 SIMON & SCHUSTER $24.95
0-671-68390-X POCKET PB $7.99

Moving On

Life in the American West in the '60s

0-671-63320-1 TOUCHSTONE PB $11.00

Some Can Whistle

0-671-64267-7 SIMON & SCHUSTER $19.95

Somebody's Darling

A woman director in Hollywood and the men in her life

0-671-63319-8 TOUCHSTONE PB $8.00

Terms of Endearment

The bittersweet relationship between a mother and daughter

0-671-75872-1 POCKET PB $6.50
0-671-68208-3 TOUCHSTONE PB $8.95

Larry **McMurtry** & Diana **Ossana**

Pretty Boy Floyd

The Pulitzer Prize-winning novelist and his screenwriting partner bring the life of Charley (Pretty Boy) Floyd in 1925 St. Louis to fast-paced life

0-671-89165-0 SIMON & SCHUSTER $24.00

David **Meltzer**

The Agency Trilogy

1-56333-216-7 MASQUERADE PB $12.95

James **Merrill**

The (Diblos) Notebook

A young man's inner and outer adventures on a Greek island, told through the revisions and repetitions of a work in progress

1-56478-064-3 DALKEY ARCHIVE PB $9.95

Leonard **Michaels**

The Men's Club

1-56279-039-0 MERCURY HOUSE PB $10.00

Sylvia: A Fictional Memoir

1-56279-029-3 MERCURY HOUSE PB $10.00

James A. **Michener**

Miracle in Seville

ILLUSTRATIONS BY JOHN FULTON

0-679-41822-9 RANDOM HOUSE $23.00

Arthur **Miller**

Homely Girl, A Life: And Other Stories

0-670-86541-9 VIKING $14.95

Sue **Miller**

The Good Mother

A woman torn between maternity and sexuality. "Goes straight to the dark heart of...modern sexual morality"—Russell Banks

0-385-31243-1 DELTA PB $12.95

Inventing the Abbotts & Other Stories

"Report from a frontier...The battlefields are the kitchen and the bedroom"—*NY Times*

0-440-54070-4 DELL PB $10.95

Steven **Millhauser**

Martin Dressler

0-517-70319-X CROWN $24.00

Edwin Mullhouse: The Life and Death of an American Writer, 1943-1954, by Jeffrey Cartwright

A tour de force

0-679-76652-9 VINTAGE PB $12.00

Susan **Minot**

Folly

A recreation of a woman's life in Boston society in the early part of this century

0-395-60339-0 HOUGHTON MIFFLIN $19.95
0-671-74951-X WASHINGTON SQUARE PB $10.00

Lust & Other Stories

0-671-70455-9 POCKET PB $10.00

Monkeys

"The seven children of a sorrowing alcoholic father and a blithe but most unoblivious mother are the viewpoint of a tale that has the compass of one of the great, 19th-century novels"—Penelope Gilliatt

0-671-70361-7 POCKET PB $10.00

N. Scott **Momaday**

House Made of Dawn

The conflicts of contemporary Native American culture

See also **CONTEMPORARY NATIVE AMERICAN WRITERS** under **NATIVE AMERICAN LITERATURES**

0-06-091633-8 HARPERCOLLINS PB $12.50

Susanna **Moore**

In the Cut

An erotic thriller, written in the wry voice of a smart, self-determined woman living in New York, in which murder and sex test the limits of safety, on one hand, and recklessness on the other

0-679-42258-7 KNOPF $21.00
0-451-40722-9 ONYX PB $6.99

My Old Sweetheart

0-14-006783-3 PENGUIN PB $10.95

Sleeping Beauties

0-679-75539-X VINTAGE PB $11.00

The Whiteness of Bones

0-14-013020-9 PENGUIN PB $10.95

Alejandro **Morales**

The Brick People

"Eloquently fuses the fantastic and the factual as he traces the growth of early California from 1892 to the late 1940s"—*Publishers Weekly*

0-934770-91-3 ARTE PUBLICO PB $10.50

Death of an Anglo

An idealistic young doctor's attempts to improve the lives of Chicano residents in a Texas town

0-916950-83-2 ARTE PUBLICO PB $13.00

Mary McGarry **Morris**

A Dangerous Woman

A young woman's odd behavior and obsession with truth make her vulnerable to abuse and betrayal in a small Vermont town

0-14-016764-1 PENGUIN PB $10.95

House Arrest

Travel writer's friendship with a Latin American revolutionary's daughter puts her in jeopardy while visiting a Caribbean island

0-385-47198-X DOUBLEDAY $22.95

Songs in Ordinary Time
0-14-024482-4 PENGUIN PB $12.95

Vanished
0-670-82216-7 VIKING $16.95

Wright **Morris**

Fire Sermon
A drama of old age giving way to youth
0-06-013066-0 HARPERCOLLINS $10.00

The Loneliness of the Long Distance Writer: The Works of Love and The Huge Season
0-87685-991-0 BLACK SPARROW $30.00
0-87685-990-2 BLACK SPARROW PB $17.50

Two for the Road
0-87685-946-5 BLACK SPARROW $40.00
0-87685-944-9 BLACK SPARROW PB $15.00

Toni **Morrison**

"The ordinary spars with the extraordinary in Morrison's books. What would be a classically tragic sensibility, with its implacable move toward crises and the extremes of pity and horror, is altered and illuminated by a thousand smaller, natural occurrences and circumstances."—Margo Jefferson

Beloved
Stunning. "A work that brings to the darkest corners of American experience the wisdom, and the courage, to know them as they are"
—*NY Review of Books*
0-452-26446-4 NEW AMERICAN LIBRARY PB $10.95

Toni Morrison

The Bluest Eye
"The novel becomes poetry...But *The Bluest Eye* is also history, sociology, folklore, nightmare, and music"—*NY Times*
0-679-43373-2 KNOPF $23.00
0-452-27305-6 PLUME PB $10.95

Jazz
0-679-41167-4 KNOPF $21.00
0-452-26965-2 PLUME PB $10.95

Song of Solomon
An allegorical novel blending the themes of family and conflict and the quest for the past
0-394-49784-8 RANDOM HOUSE $26.00

Sula
Two women, whose lives take sharply divergent paths, reaffirm the bonds of friendship. "A howl of love and rage, playful and funny as well as hard and bitter"—*NY Times*
0-394-48044-9 KNOPF $25.00
0-452-26349-2 NEW AMERICAN LIBRARY PB $10.95

Tar Baby
0-394-42329-1 KNOPF $26.00
0-452-26479-0 NEW AMERICAN LIBRARY PB $10.95

Toni Morrison: The Bluest Eye, Sula, Song of Solomon, Tar Baby, Jazz, and Beloved
A richly deserved celebration of the Nobel Prize-winning novelist, beautiful to read, to hold, and to own. Newly designed, with full-cloth bindings in a beautiful slip case
0-679-43436-4 KNOPF $125.00

Bradford **Morrow**

The Almanac Branch
0-393-30921-5 NORTON PB $8.95

Come Sunday
0-14-024756-4 PENGUIN PB $12.95

Trinity Fields
"Readable, compulsively so...Morrow sets up two wonderful young men, born on the same day in 1944...The unearthly beauty of *Trinity Fields* lies in the evocation of Los Alamos in the days of our lost, innocent past. Morrow is intelligent, compassionate and forgiving in this novel"
—*The Washington Post*
0-670-85728-9 VIKING $22.95

Bharati **Mukherjee**

Writing on the immigrant experience with wit and sensitivity, Mukherjee delineates a class of imperfectly assimilated Indians who never quite manage to break ties with their homeland.

The Holder of the World
When a New England woman discovers the record of a remote ancestor's 17th-century voyage to India, she begins a journey through "the barriers of time and geography" toward a powerful collision of cultures, past and present, history and imagination
See also **INDIAN LITERATURE IN ENGLISH** under **LITERATURES OF INDIA** in **LITERATURE OF EUROPE, AFRICA, AND ASIA**
0-394-58846-0 KNOPF $22.00
0-449-90966-2 FAWCETT PB $12.00

Jasmine
The critic Jonathan Raban has called Bharati Mukherjee's work "a romance with America itself, its infinitely possible geography, its license, sexiness, and violence." In this new novel, the appealing Indian-born heroine transforms herself from Jasmine to Jane Ripplemeyer, and explores American life at its fullest
0-449-21923-2 CREST PB $5.99

The Middlemen & Other Stories
0-449-21718-3 CREST PB $5.99

Albert **Murray**

The Seven League Boots
0-679-43986-2 PANTHEON $25.00
0-679-75858-5 VINTAGE $13.00

Vladimir **Nabokov**

Nabokov wrote his first nine novels in Russian, the last being The Gift, *written in the late '30s; thereafter he turned exclusively to English as his medium of expression.*

Ada or Ardor: A Family Chronicle
Nabokov's longest and perhaps most brilliant novel fuses his two worlds, Russia and America
0-679-72522-9 VINTAGE PB $16.00

The Annotated Lolita
A useful road map into the novel's erudite references
EDITED BY ALFRED APPEL, JR.
0-679-72729-9 VINTAGE PB $19.00

Bend Sinister
A stylized, nightmarish picture of life in an unnamed post-revolutionary state somewhere in Eastern Europe
0-679-72727-2 VINTAGE PB $14.00

Despair
0-679-72343-9 VINTAGE PB $12.00

The Enchanter
See also **FICTION AND OTHER PROSE** under **EARLY 20TH CENTURY** under **RUSSIAN LITERATURE** in **LITERATURE OF EUROPE, AFRICA, AND ASIA**
0-679-72886-4 VINTAGE PB $11.00

Glory
Written in 1932 but not published in English until 40 years later, *Glory* is perhaps Nabokov's most romantic novel
0-679-72724-8 VINTAGE PB $12.00

Invitation to a Beheading
See also **FICTION AND OTHER PROSE** under **EARLY 20TH CENTURY** under **RUSSIAN LITERATURE** in **LITERATURE OF EUROPE, AFRICA, AND ASIA**
0-679-72531-8 VINTAGE PB $12.00

King, Queen, Knave
A young German, seduced by his aunt, fails in his plot to kill the uncle for his money
See also **FICTION AND OTHER PROSE** under **EARLY 20TH CENTURY** under **RUSSIAN LITERATURE** in **LITERATURE OF EUROPE, AFRICA, AND ASIA**
0-679-72340-4 VINTAGE PB $11.00

Laughter in the Dark
"There is probably no more frangible encounter in the whole human gambit than the one between a sensitive, fiftyish man and a cretinous girl one-third his age, and in this short, swift, acrid novel originally published in 1938, the author of *Lolita* gives it as pitiless a treatment as it has ever had on paper"—*NY Sunday Tribune*
See also **FICTION AND OTHER PROSE** under **EARLY 20TH CENTURY** under **RUSSIAN LITERATURE** in **LITERATURE OF EUROPE, AFRICA, AND ASIA**
0-8112-1186-X NEW DIRECTIONS PB $10.95

Lolita
The modern classic about Humbert Humbert's passion for a twelve-year-old "nymphet"
0-679-72316-1 VINTAGE PB $12.00

Look at the Harlequins
A novel about a novelist not dissimilar to the author
0-679-72728-0 VINTAGE PB $12.00

Vladimir **Nabokov**

Nabokov's Dozen

A tart baker's dozen of short stories that dispatch Pushkin and word games with equal ease

0-8369-3078-9 AYER $18.95

Pale Fire

A novel in the form of footnotes to a poem whose formal inventiveness is matched only by its alternately comic and tragic brilliance

0-679-72342-0 VINTAGE PB $12.00

Vladimir Nabokov

Pnin

A befuddled Russian professor at a New England college

0-679-72341-2 VINTAGE PB $10.00

The Real Life of Sebastian Knight

The first of Nabokov's pseudo-biographies, about an author comically less gifted than his biographer

0-679-72726-4 VINTAGE PB $12.00

The Stories of Vladimir Nabokov

The collected stories—65 of them—of one of the 20th-century's greatest prose stylists. Written between the '20s and the '50s and edited by his son and translator Dmitri Nabokov, a masterfully published volume filled with surprise, wit, fancy, and inventiveness. A major literary event and a celebration of Nabokov's art

EDITED BY DMITRI NABOKOV

0-394-58615-8 KNOPF $35.00

Transparent Things

A 1972 novella about marriage and murder

0-679-72541-5 VINTAGE PB $10.00

Vladimir Nabokov, Novels, 1955 - 1962

Includes *Lolita, Pnin, Pale Fire,* and Nabokov's original screenplay for *Lolita*

EDITED BY BRIAN BOYD

1-88301-119-1 LIBRARY OF AMERICA $35.00

Novels 1969 - 1974

Includes *Ada, or Ardor, Transparent Things,* and *Look at the Harlequins*

EDITED BY BRIAN BOYD

1-88301-120-5 LIBRARY OF AMERICA $35.00

Vladimir Nabokov, Novels and Memoirs 1941 - 1951

Includes *The Real Life of Sebastian Knight, Bend Sinister,* and *Speak, Memory*

EDITED BY BRIAN BOYD

1-88301-118-3 LIBRARY OF AMERICA $35.00

Gloria **Nagy**

Marriage

1-575-66098-9 KENSINGTON PB $5.99

Leonard **Nathan**

Diary of a Left-Handed Birdwatcher

1-55597-250-0 GRAY WOLF PB $18.95

Gloria **Naylor**

Bailey's Cafe

A group of women—destitute all—gather as regulars in an urban coffee shop

0-15-110450-6 HARCOURT BRACE $19.95

Linden Hills

Life in an upper-class black community

0-14-008829-6 VIKING PB $10.95

Mama Day

0-679-72181-9 VINTAGE PB $12.00

The Women of Brewster Place

"The most refreshing voice in the black idiom since readers first discovered Toni Morrison" —Claude Brown

0-14-006690-X PENGUIN PB $10.95

John **Nichols**

A Ghost in the Music

0-393-31536-3 NORTON PB $13.00

The Nirvana Blues

0-345-30465-9 BALLANTINE PB $5.95

The Wizard of Loneliness

A young boy is sent to his father's family in Vermont during World War II

0-393-31073-6 NORTON PB $8.95

Anaïs **Nin**

Cities of the Interior

A five-volume novel cycle including *Ladders to Fire, Children of the Albatross, The Four-Chambered Heart, A Spy in the House of Love,* and *Seduction of the Minotaur*

0-8040-0666-0 OHIO PB $22.95

Collages

"Though written as a series of fugue studies, *Collages* spills over into a new and curious thematic relationship with the reality of American character and life"—Marguerite Young

ILLUSTRATED BY JEAN VERDE

0-8040-0045-X OHIO PB $8.95

Delta of Venus: Erotica

Seventeen erotic stories written by Nin in the '40s

See also **EROTICA** under **COURTSHIP, LOVE, SEX, AND MARRIAGE** in **LIFESTYLES AND PRACTICAL ADVICE**

0-671-74249-3 POCKET PB $6.99

House of Incest

A prose poem

0-8040-0148-0 OHIO PB $7.95

Little Birds: Erotica

More erotic stories

0-671-68011-0 POCKET PB $5.99

Winter of Artifice

A collection of novelettes. "Finely-wrought musical writing shot through with clear insights into the inner world of human beings" —Lawrence Durrell

0-8040-0322-X OHIO PB $8.95

Joyce Carol **Oates**

American Appetites

0-06-097278-5 HARPERCOLLINS PB $12.50

The Assignation: Stories

0-88001-200-5 ECCO $16.95

0-88001-440-7 ECCO PB $12.00

Because It Is Bitter, and Because It Is My Heart

0-452-26581-9 NEW AMERICAN LIBRARY PB $12.95

Bellefleur

Six generations of an aristocratic Adirondack family

0-452-26794-3 OBELISK PB $15.95

Black Water

A senator from a prominent family drunkenly drives off a bridge and drowns a girlfriend

0-525-93455-3 PLUME PB $17.00

Joyce Carol Oates

Expensive People

0-86538-069-4 ONTARIO REVIEW PB $10.95

First Love: A Gothic Tale

ILLUSTRATED BY BARRY MOSER

0-88001-457-1 ECCO $18.00

Foxfire: Confessions of a Girl Gang

Ever curious, ever resourceful, Oates turns her attention here to the story of five young women who, in the '50s, pool their rebellious rage in a secret and violent sisterhood

0-525-93632-7 DUTTON $21.00

Haunted: Tales of the Grotesque

0-452-27374-9 PLUME PB $10.95

Heat and Other Stories

0-452-26646-7 PLUME PB $13.95

I Lock My Door upon Myself

0-452-26708-0 PLUME PB $8.95

The Rise of Life on Earth
0-8112-1213-0 NEW DIRECTIONS PB $8.95

Them
The breakthrough novel that introduced Oates's characteristic themes of violence, passion, and madness underlying American family life. Winner of the 1969 National Book Award
0-449-20692-0 FAWCETT PB $6.99

We Were The Mulvaneys
0-525-94223-8 DUTTON $24.95

What I Lived For
0-452-27269-6 PLUME PB $14.95

Where Are You Going, Where Have You Been?: Selected Early Stories
0-86538-078-3 ONTARIO REVIEW PB $12.95

Where Is Here?: Stories
"I don't want to review this stunning collection of short stories because there is no way to convey their power, short of holding the book up in front of your nose and making you read it"
—*LA Times Book Review*
0-88001-283-8 ECCO $18.95

Will You Always Love Me? and Other Stories
0-525-93972-5 DUTTON $23.95

Wonderland
0-86538-075-9 ONTARIO REVIEW PB $12.95

You Must Remember This
0-06-097169-X HARPERCOLLINS PB $13.00

Zombie
Inside the mind of a serial killer
0-525-94045-6 DUTTON $19.95
0-452-27500-8 PLUME PB $10.95

Tim **O'Brien**

"[O'Brien's] landscapes have the breadth and scope of Tolstoy's and the essential American wonder and innocence of his vision deserves to stand beside that of Stephen Crane."
—*National Book Award Committee*

Going After Cacciato
A soldier dreams he and his platoon pursue a deserter on a fantastic voyage to Paris
See also **LITERATURE: FICTION AND POETRY** under **THE VIETNAM WAR** in **HISTORY OF THE AMERICAS**
0-385-28349-0 DELACORTE PB $11.95
0-440-21439-4 DELL PB $6.99

If I Die in a Combat Zone
O'Brien's first book, an account of Vietnam published in 1973
0-440-34311-9 DELL PB $5.99

In the Lake of the Woods
From the National Book Award winner, a powerful re-visiting to the legacy of the war in Southeast Asia and a buried memory of the infamous Thuan Yen massacre
See also **LITERATURE: FICTION AND POETRY** under **THE VIETNAM WAR** in **HISTORY OF THE AMERICAS**
0-395-48889-3 HOUGHTON MIFFLIN $21.95
0-14-025094-8 PENGUIN PB $10.95

The Nuclear Age
0-440-21586-2 DELL PB $6.99

The Things They Carried
Powerful, evocative Vietnam stories
0-14-014773-X PENGUIN PB $10.95

Edwin **O'Connor**

The Last Hurrah
The decline of an Irish-American political boss
See also **THE '50S** under **THE GREAT FICTION BESTSELLERS 1930–1995** in **POPULAR READING**
0-316-62659-7 LITTLE, BROWN PB $12.95

Flannery **O'Connor**

Collected Works
Includes *Wise Blood, A Good Man Is Hard to Find, The Violent Bear It Away, Everything that Rises Must Converge,* along with letters, essays, and uncollected stories. "Indispensable for the literary scholar and a joy for the general reader…a great book"—*Newsday*
See also **LIBRARY OF AMERICA**
EDITED BY SALLY FITZGERALD
0-940450-37-2 LIBRARY OF AMERICA $35.00

The Complete Stories
"She was not just the best 'woman writer' of this time and place; she expressed something secret about America, called 'the South,' with that transcendent gift for expressing the real spirit of a culture that is conveyed by those writers … who become nothing but what they see"—Alfred Kazin
0-374-51536-0 FS&G PB $14.00

Everything that Rises Must Converge
Nine short stories
INTRODUCTION BY ROBERT FITZGERALD
0-374-50464-4 FS&G PB $12.00

A Good Man Is Hard to Find
Ten stories of the South
0-15-636465-4 HARCOURT BRACE PB $8.95

The Violent Bear It Away
A boy tries to escape his tragic legacy in this novel of the interplay of cosmic and human forces
0-374-50524-1 FS&G PB $12.00

Wise Blood
The grotesque fate of itinerant preacher Hazel Motes
0-374-50584-5 FS&G PB $11.00

Tillie **Olsen**

Tell Me a Riddle
Four short pieces. "Explores the deep pain and real promise of fundamental American experience in a style of incomparable verbal richness and beauty"—Julian Moynihan
0-385-29010-1 DELACORTE PB $10.95

Toby **Olson**

Dorit in Lesbos
1-55713-214-3 SUN & MOON PB $14.95

The Life of Jesus: An Apocryphal Novel
A Catholic boyhood, interspersed with garishly fit Biblical fantasies
0-8112-0614-9 NEW DIRECTIONS PB $3.95

Seaview
0-8112-0828-1 NEW DIRECTIONS $15.95

Cynthia **Ozick**

Bloodshed
0-8156-0352-5 SYRACUSE PB $14.95

The Cannibal Galaxy
0-8156-0354-1 SYRACUSE PB $14.95

Cynthia Ozick (credit: ©Ricki Rosen)

Levitation: Five Fictions
0-8156-0353-3 SYRACUSE PB $14.95

The Messiah of Stockholm
0-394-75694-0 VINTAGE PB $11.00

The Shawl
See also **HOLOCAUST FICTION** under **ART AND LITERATURE** under **THE HOLOCAUST** in **WORLD HISTORY AND CURRENT AFFAIRS**
0-394-58199-7 KNOPF $12.95
0-679-72926-7 VINTAGE PB $7.95

Grace **Paley**

The Collected Stories
The complete stories from an American classic. "Paley makes me weep and laugh—and admire. She is that rare kind of writer, a natural, with a voice like no one else's: funny, sad, lean, modest, energetic, acute"—Susan Sontag. "A wonderful writer and troublemaker. We are fortunate to have her in our country"—Donald Barthelme
0-374-12636-4 FS&G $27.50
0-374-52431-9 FS&G PB $14.00

Grace Paley

Enormous Changes at the Last Minute
0-374-51524-7 FS&G PB $10.00

Grace **Paley**

Later the Same Day

Seventeen short stories written over the past ten years. "Technically, Grace Paley's work makes the novel as a form seem virtually redundant. Each one of her stories has more abundant inner life than most other people's novels" —Angela Carter, *London Review of Books*

0-14-008641-2 VIKING PB $11.00

Breece D'J **Pancake**

The Stories of Breece D'J Pancake

"An exceptional voice; gritty, mordant, invested with the texture of stroked reality; urgent and haunting"—Margaret Atwood

0-8050-0720-2 HOLT PB $9.95

Gwendolyn M. **Parker**

These Same Long Bones

Parker delivers an intimate view of a middle-class black community of Durham, N.C., on the eve of integration. "A wonderful book " —Ann Petry

0-395-67172-8 HOUGHTON MIFFLIN $21.95

T.R. **Pearson**

Cry Me a River

Firmly anchored as a murder mystery with a fallen cop and a wayward woman as its focus, Pearson's sixth novel is first and foremost the portrait of a contemporary small Southern town. A highly original writer with an engaging colloquial voice all his own, "Pearson writes sentences like a man peeling an apple in a single stroke"—*LA Times*

See also CRIMES AND CAPERS under CRIME FICTION TODAY under CRIME FICTION in POPULAR READING

0-8050-3187-1 OWLET PB $12.00

She could do that, could accomplish with some trifle, some gesture, some movement of her hand or inclination of her head an insinuation of comeliness and grace that would pass like a scent on the air and be gone before a fellow could even begin to know what it was that had…made him to look upon her with longing

CRY ME A RIVER

A Short History of a Small Place

0-8050-3320-3 OWLET PB $12.00

Walker **Percy**

Lancelot

A modern "knight" surveys the landscapes of contemporary America. "A funny and scarifying jeremiad on the modern age"—*Time*

0-8041-0380-1 IVY PB $5.99

The Last Gentleman

0-374-18372-4 NOONDAY $22.95

0-8041-0379-8 IVY PB $5.99

Love in the Ruins: The Adventures of a Bad Catholic at a Time Near the End of the World

0-374-19302-9 FS&G $27.95

The Moviegoer

In this first novel, which won the National Book Award, a New Orleans stockbroker finds the meaning for his life during Mardi Gras week

0-394-43703-9 RANDOM HOUSE $25.00

0-8041-0290-2 IVY PB $6.99

The Second Coming

Will Barrett, from *The Last Gentleman,* returns 25 years later

0-8041-0542-1 IVY PB $5.99

The Thanatos Syndrome

A paroled psychiatrist finds that a bizarre increase in sexual behavior is due to unauthorized additives in the water supply

0-374-27354-5 FS&G $17.95

Charles **Perry**

Portrait of a Young Man Drowning

0-393-31462-6 NORTON PB $11.00

Ann **Petry**

The Narrows

A novel of black life in a New England town

INTRODUCTION BY NELLIE MCKAY

0-8070-8303-8 BEACON PB $15.00

The Street

A realistic novel of Harlem, first published in 1946

0-395-57380-7 HOUGHTON MIFFLIN PB $10.95

Jayne Anne **Phillips**

Fast Lanes

0-931428-17-3 SMALL PRESS PB $18.00

Machine Dreams

An ordinary American family from the Depression to Vietnam. "One of the great books of this decade"—Robert Stone

0-671-74235-3 WASHINGTON SQUARE PB $10.00

Shelter

A girl's summer camp in the 1963 Virginia woods is the setting for an American drama, where two young sisters are transformed by love, violence, and the dark secrets of their family. "Powerful…brilliant…a legendary quest; a passage of exploits through dragons, demons, and dangerous enchantments, both within and and without"—*LA Times Book Review*

0-395-48890-7 HOUGHTON MIFFLIN $21.95

0-385-31389-6 BANTAM PB $11.95

Marge **Piercy**

Braided Lives

Growing up in 1950s Detroit

0-449-21300-5 CREST PB $5.95

Fly Away Home

A successful author reconstructs her life after a devastating divorce

0-449-20691-2 FAWCETT PB $5.95

Going Down Fast

A university's effect upon a depressed inner city neighborhood

0-449-24480-6 FAWCETT PB $5.99

Gone to Soldiers

World War II, as experienced by 10 people overseas and on the home front. "Piercy is the political novelist of our time"—Marilyn French

0-449-21557-1 FAWCETT PB $6.99

The High Cost of Living

A woman becomes involved in a romantic triangle with a virgin and a homosexual hustler

0-449-20879-6 FAWCETT PB $5.99

Small Changes

0-449-21083-9 FAWCETT PB $5.95

Woman on the Edge of Time

A Chicano woman in New York City is committed, against her will, to a mental hospital

0-449-21082-0 CREST PB $6.99

Sylvia **Plath**

The Bell Jar

Autobiographical account of a young woman's mental breakdown. "Its most notable quality is an astonishing immediacy, like a series of snapshots taken at high noon"—*Time*

0-553-27835-5 WINDSTONE PB $5.99

Carlene Hatcher **Polite**

The Flagellants

A lyrical novel about a modern-day love affair gone sour

INTRODUCTION BY CLAUDIA TATE

0-8070-6321-5 OLYMPIC PB $1.98

Chaim **Potok**

The Book of Lights

0-449-24569-1 FAWCETT PB $5.95

The Chosen

Potok's most widely read novel, a story of two Jewish boys in Brooklyn—one modern Orthodox and the other Hasidic—who form a friendship in the wake of Israel's war of independence

See also YOUNG ADULT FICTION in BOOKS FOR YOUNG READERS

0-449-21344-7 FAWCETT PB $6.99

Davita's Harp

0-449-20775-7 FAWCETT PB $6.99

The Gates of November: Chronicles of the Slepak Family

0-394-58867-3 KNOPF $25.00

The Gift of Asher Lev

0-449-21978-X CREST PB $5.95

In the Beginning

0-449-20911-3 FAWCETT PB $6.99

My Name Is Asher Lev

A gifted boy in New York begins to question his faith

0-449-20714-5 FAWCETT PB $6.99

The Promise

The sequel to *The Chosen* traces the characters' lives through college and young adulthood

0-449-20910-5 FAWCETT PB $6.99

Padgett **Powell**

Edisto

0-8050-1370-9 HOLT PB $9.95

Edisto Revisited

0-8050-4237-7 HOLT $20.00

Typical Stories

0-8050-2111-6 HOLT PB $9.95

Richard **Powers**

Galatea 2.2

"A splendid intellectual adventure, a heartbreaking love story, a brief tutorial on cognitive science, and the autobiography of one

of the most gifted writers of the younger generation"—*Washington Post*
0-374-19948-5 FS&G $23.00

The Gold Bug Variations
Two couples, separated by time, investigate related scientific mysteries
0-06-097500-8 HARPERPERENNIAL PB $15.00

Operation Wandering Soul
0-06-097611-X HARPERPERENNIAL PB $12.00

Prisoner's Dilemma
0-06-097708-6 HARPERPERENNIAL PB $13.00

Three Farmers on Their Way to a Dance
0-06-097509-1 HARPERPERENNIAL PB $12.00

John **Preston**

Franny, the Queen of Provincetown
"Achingly funny and sad, and chockablock with humanity"—*Publishers Weekly*
0-312-11792-2 ST. MARTIN'S $15.95
0-312-14106-8 ST. MARTIN'S PB $8.95

Reynolds **Price**

Blue Calhoun
0-345-37722-2 BALLANTINE PB $5.99

The Collected Stories
0-452-27218-1 PLUME PB $13.95

Kate Vaiden
A middle-aged woman's search for a son she abandoned when she was 17
0-345-34358-1 BALLANTINE PB $5.99

A Long and Happy Life
0-689-11947-X ATHENEUM $20.00

Michael Egerton
0-88682-591-1 CREATIVE EDUCATION $25.01

The Promise of Rest
0-684-80149-3 SCRIBNERS $24.00
0-684-82510-4 SCRIBNERS PB $13.00

The Source of Light
0-684-81338-6 SIMON & SCHUSTER PB $12.00

The Surface of Earth
0-684-81339-4 SIMON & SCHUSTER PB $14.00

Tongues of Angels
0-345-37102-X BALLANTINE PB $5.99

Richard **Price**

Clockers
A jaded homicide detective investigates a drug-related murder and is drawn into the complex world of street-corner cocaine dealers and the powerful family dynamics of the ghetto. "[*Clockers* is] one of those books that comes close to you, grabs you and takes you down like some heavy stone, convincing you with its unique and vivid details, its moral complexity and deep understanding that every word is true"—Scott Turow
0-380-72081-7 AVON PB $6.99

Ladies' Man
0-380-77475-5 AVON PB $9.00

Richard Price

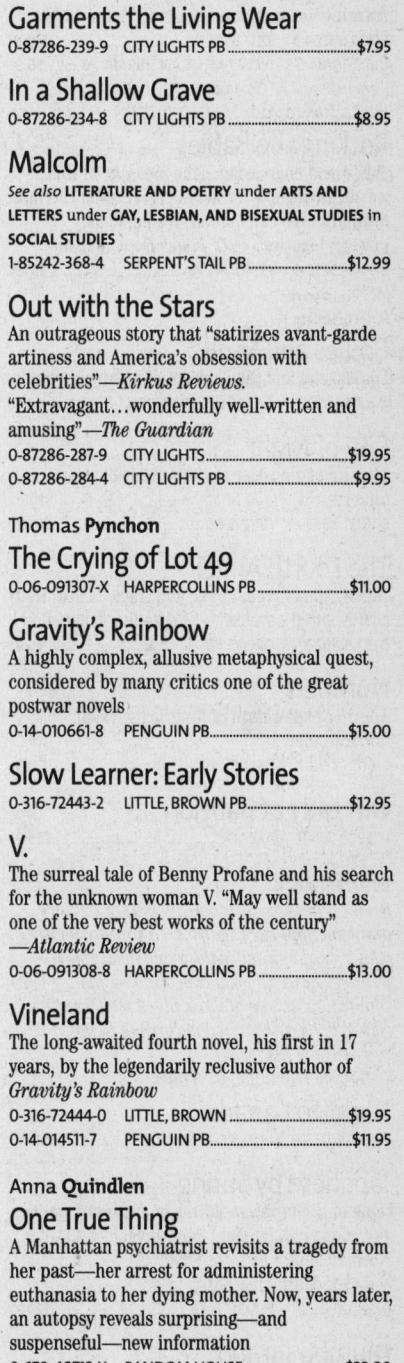

The Wanderers
0-380-77474-7 AVON PB $9.00

Francine **Prose**

Guided Tours of Hell: Novellas
0-8050-4861-8 HOLT $23.00

Household Saints
0-804-11165-0 IVY PB $4.99

Hunters and Gatherers
0-374-17371-0 FS&G $20.00

The Peaceable Kingdom
Short stories. A doting woman, on her honeymoon, finds her ideal husband to be less than she thought. A teenager is shocked when she comes to know the boy of her dreams. "Prose... works these tales of infidelity, envy, fear, and garden-variety confusion into a bright and memorable melody"—*Kirkus Reviews*
0-374-23042-0 FS&G $20.00

E. Annie **Proulx**

Accordion Crimes
The latest from Pulitzer Prize-winning Proulx relates the tale of an accordion from 19th-century Sicily as it is transported from Iowa to Texas, from Louisiana to Maine by immigrants from various homelands. Along the way the instrument's fate mirrors that of characters, recognizing the ambiguities of the mythic American dream
0-684-19548-8 SCRIBNERS $25.00

Heart Songs and Other Stories
0-02-036075-4 SCRIBNERS PB $10.00

Postcards
Proulx's first novel tells the story of a New England farming family confronting the loneliness and alienation of the 20th century. "E. Annie Proulx writes a sentence like a whip" —*Newsday*
0-684-80087-X SIMON & SCHUSTER PB $12.00

The Shipping News
Winner of the National Book Award for 1993, as well as the Pulitzer Prize for 1994. Quoyle, a second-rate journalist, moves with his two daughters back to his "home country" of Newfoundland
0-684-19337-X SCRIBNERS $20.00
0-671-51005-3 SIMON & SCHUSTER PB $12.00

James **Purdy**

63: Dream Palace & Other Stories
"Style as fluid and natural as a man thinking to himself in the dark, yet controlled, coherent, with an innate sense of form, and great powers of concentration"—Katherine Anne Porter
INTRODUCTION BY EDWARD ALBEE
0-87685-844-2 BLACK SPARROW PB $15.00

The Candles of Your Eyes: Stories
"A modern Book of Revelation, filled with prophecies, visions, and demonic landscapes" —Jerome Charyn
0-87286-256-9 CITY LIGHTS PB $7.95

Garments the Living Wear
0-87286-239-9 CITY LIGHTS PB $7.95

In a Shallow Grave
0-87286-234-8 CITY LIGHTS PB $8.95

Malcolm
See also **LITERATURE AND POETRY** under **ARTS AND LETTERS** under **GAY, LESBIAN, AND BISEXUAL STUDIES** in **SOCIAL STUDIES**
1-85242-368-4 SERPENT'S TAIL PB $12.99

Out with the Stars
An outrageous story that "satirizes avant-garde artiness and America's obsession with celebrities"—*Kirkus Reviews.* "Extravagant...wonderfully well-written and amusing"—*The Guardian*
0-87286-287-9 CITY LIGHTS $19.95
0-87286-284-4 CITY LIGHTS PB $9.95

Thomas **Pynchon**

The Crying of Lot 49
0-06-091307-X HARPERCOLLINS PB $11.00

Gravity's Rainbow
A highly complex, allusive metaphysical quest, considered by many critics one of the great postwar novels
0-14-010661-8 PENGUIN PB $15.00

Slow Learner: Early Stories
0-316-72443-2 LITTLE, BROWN PB $12.95

V.
The surreal tale of Benny Profane and his search for the unknown woman V. "May well stand as one of the very best works of the century" —*Atlantic Review*
0-06-091308-8 HARPERCOLLINS PB $13.00

Vineland
The long-awaited fourth novel, his first in 17 years, by the legendarily reclusive author of *Gravity's Rainbow*
0-316-72444-0 LITTLE, BROWN $19.95
0-14-014511-7 PENGUIN PB $11.95

Anna **Quindlen**

One True Thing
A Manhattan psychiatrist revisits a tragedy from her past—her arrest for administering euthanasia to her dying mother. Now, years later, an autopsy reveals surprising—and suspenseful—new information
0-679-40712-X RANDOM HOUSE $22.00
0-440-22103-X DELL PB $6.99

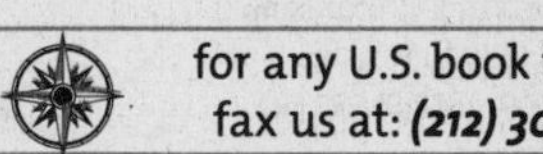

Ayn **Rand**

Atlas Shrugged

See also **THE '50S** under **THE GREAT FICTION BESTSELLERS 1930–1995** in **POPULAR READING**

0-525-93418-9 DUTTON $39.95
0-451-17192-6 SIGNET PB $7.99

The Fountainhead

The meteoric rise of a callous young architect (modeled on Frank Lloyd Wright) to the peaks of power; influential in its day

0-02-600910-2 BOBBS-MERRILL $40.00
0-451-17512-3 SIGNET PB $7.99

We the Living

An anti-Communist novel published in 1936

0-525-94054-5 DUTTON $25.95
0-451-18784-9 NEW AMERICAN LIBRARY PB $6.99

Linda **Raymond**

Rocking the Babies

"Vivid and engrossing…the message of this warm, earthy novel remains clear: even the most ordinary lives can contain tremendously powerful stories"—*NY Times Book Review*

0-14-023254-0 PENGUIN PB $10.95

John **Rechy**

Bodies and Souls

Los Angeles and the denizens of its fringe societies

0-88184-102-1 CARROLL & GRAF PB $4.50

City of Night

The life of a hustler in the American sexual underworld

0-8021-3083-6 GROVE PB $13.00

The Fourth Angel

"Rechy shows great comic and tragic talent. He is a truly gifted novelist"—Christopher Isherwood

0-8021-597-3 GROVE PB $6.95

Numbers

Another exploration of America's sexual underground

0-8021-5198-1 GROVE PB $11.95

Our Lady of Babylon

1-55970-335-0 ARCADE $23.95

Ishmael **Reed**

Reed's novels are fantastic blends of folklore and contemporary politics. "A prolific writer who…works in more than one medium. His novels…have already consolidated his reputation as one of those black writers who refuse to be categorized according to the relevance of his theme."
—George Lamming, *NY Times*

Flight to Canada

0-689-70733-9 ATHENEUM PB $11.00

Japanese by Spring

"One of the funniest satires of university politics I've ever read. Ishmael Reed is funnier than Norman Mailer or Gore Vidal"
—Leslie Marmon Silko

0-14-025585-0 PENGUIN PB $10.95

Mumbo Jumbo

"A novel about writing itself—not only in the figurative sense of the postmodern, self-reflexive text but also in a literal sense"
—Henry Louis Gates, Jr.

0-684-82477-9 SCRIBNERS PB $11.00

Ishmael Reed

The Terrible Twos

An elderly gent named St. Nicholas and a dwarf named Black Peter wreak havoc in the Oval Office and on Wall Street

0-689-70727-4 MACMILLAN PB $9.95

Laura **Riding**

Four Unposted Letters to Catherine

These four letters are the American equivalent of Rilke's *Letters to A Young Poet.* Written in the '30s to the sensitive eight-year-old daughter of Nancy Nicholson and Robert Graves, they explain in simple and luminous language the difference between learning and knowing, the value of thinking, and of not showing off. Sixty years later these private treasures endure as a moral and literary guideline for the young and for aspiring writers

See also **LITERATURE** under **20TH-CENTURY AMERICAN ESSAYS AND JOURNALISM**

0-89255-192-5 PERSEA $15.00

Lives of Wives

First published in 1939, Riding's work recounts ancient history from the perspective of the women who lived through it. "The great virtue of this book is that it sees life in a great pattern, and war, murder, sudden death and the 'domestic hearth of life' as part of the pattern"—Edwin Muir

0-85635-748-0 CARCANET $3.99

Progress of Stories

0-89255-203-4 PERSEA PB $15.00

Tomas **Rivera**

Y No Se lo Trago la Tierra/And the Earth Did Not Devour Him

Winner of the first national Chicano literature award in 1970. Stories told in English and Spanish, as witnessed through the eyes of a young boy, the child of migrant farm workers

1-55885-083-X ARTE PUBLICO PB $10.95

Anne **Rivers Siddons**

Fault Lines

0-06-017614-8 HARPERCOLLINS $24.00

Tom **Robbins**

Another Roadside Attraction

0-553-34948-1 BANTAM PB $10.95

Even Cowgirls Get the Blues

0-553-34949-X BANTAM PB $10.95

Jitterbug Perfume

0-553-34898-1 BANTAM PB $10.95

Still Life with Woodpecker

0-553-34897-3 BANTAM PB $10.95

Marilynne **Robinson**

Housekeeping

"A first novel that one reads as slowly as poetry—and for the same reason: the language is so precise, so distilled, so beautiful that one doesn't want to miss any pleasure it might yield up to patience"—*NY Times*

0-553-27872-X BDD PB $5.99

Michael Aaron **Rockland**

A Bliss Case

A professor of English leaves family and job to join a religious cult in India. "An irreverent wit that makes the sadness and seriousness strike home with greater force than they would in a more solemn book"—*NY Times Book Review*

0-918273-55-2 COFFEE HOUSE PB $9.95

Philip **Roth**

The Breast

A man wakes up to discover that he has become a woman's breast

0-679-74901-2 VINTAGE PB $9.00

The Counterlife

0-374-13026-4 FS&G $18.95
0-679-74904-7 VINTAGE PB $12.00

Goodbye, Columbus & Five Short Stories

The title story, Roth's first success, concerns a love affair between a poor boy from Newark and a rich girl from Radcliffe. Winner of the National Book Award for fiction

0-679-74826-1 VINTAGE PB $12.00

The Great American Novel

A ride through the mythical Patriot League, featuring unbeatable rookie hurler Gil Gamesh and iron-willed umpire Mike the Mouth Masterson

See also **BASEBALL FICTION** under **BASEBALL** under **SPORTS** in **FOOD, TRAVEL, AND LEISURE**

0-679-74906-3 VINTAGE PB $13.00

My Life as a Man

0-679-74827-X VINTAGE PB $11.00

Operation Shylock

A novel in which the author—and narrator—confronts his strange double. The lookalike espouses a mad plan to return Israeli Jews to Europe, drawing Roth into an international intrigue that involves the PLO and the Mossad. "Rarely have fact and fiction, personal confession and wild imaginings, led such a deeply, unnervingly comic dance"
—*Kirkus Reviews*

0-679-75029-0 VINTAGE PB $13.00

Philip **Roth**

The Ghost Writer

The first novel in the Zuckerman trilogy, in which a young writer thinks that he has met and fallen in love with Anne Frank. "A sensitive, deeply moving, exquisitely crafted portrait of the artist as a young man" —*Chicago Tribune*

0-679-74898-9 VINTAGE PB $10.00

Zuckerman Unbound

The second novel in the Zuckerman trilogy. "Nathan Zuckerman now struggles with the wealth, fame, intrusions, and estrangements bestowed upon him by the enormous success of his fourth novel...The comic diatribes seem almost engraved...and the polarities between id and superego, Jew and goy, artistic honesty and human decency are as beautifully played upon as the melodies in a Bach fugue"—*New Yorker*

0-679-74899-7 VINTAGE PB $11.00

The Anatomy Lesson

The final book in Roth's Zuckerman trilogy. "One finds in Zuckerman's self-doubt, guilt and quest for meaning the angst of much of 20th century humanity. *The Anatomy Lesson* is vintage Roth...His wildest, funniest—and darkest—novel yet" —*Publishers Weekly*

0-679-74902-0 VINTAGE PB $12.00

The Prague Orgy

The epilogue to the Zuckerman trilogy

0-679-74903-9 VINTAGE PB $9.00

Portnoy's Complaint

"No one has written so amusingly and yet so crassly about sex since Henry Miller"—*Time*

0-679-75645-0 VINTAGE PB $12.00

The Professor of Desire

0-679-74900-4 VINTAGE PB $10.00

Sabbath's Theater

Mickey Sabbath is the libidinous, outrageous, insatiable, raging, audacious, exuberant, gargantuan hero of Roth's new comic epic. In his sixties, beseiged by ghosts, bereft in the wake of his mistress's death, Sabbath embarks on a journey into his past that can only result in madness—or can it? Roth at the peak of his narrative powers

0-395-73982-9 DORLING KINDERSLEY $24.95
0-679-77259-6 VINTAGE PB $13.00

When She Was Good

0-679-75925-5 VINTAGE PB $12.00

Norman **Rush**

Mating

"A complex and moving love story... breathtaking in its cunningly intertwined intellectual sweep and brio"—*Chicago Tribune Books*

See also **CENTRAL AND SOUTHERN AFRICA** under **AFRICAN LITERATURE** in **LITERATURE OF EUROPE, AFRICA, AND ASIA**

0-679-73709-X VINTAGE PB $12.00

Whites

0-679-73816-9 VINTAGE PB $10.00

John **Russell**

Favorite Sons

Southern politics and passions are intertwined in this absorbing tale of power, history, ambition, hope, and alienation. *Favorite Sons* is "a splendidly ambitious and well thought out novel...richly evocative of Southern life in the all-transforming period from the '30s to the present"—Alfred Kazin

0-945575-36-X ALGONQUIN $19.95

Richard **Russo**

Mohawk

The poor of a small upstate New York town. "Offers a reader the authority of a documentary—yet the novel is full of comic invention"—John Irving

0-679-72577-6 VINTAGE PB $12.00

Nobody's Fool

In a novel of familial reconciliation, an unlucky man must both come to terms with his father and reconcile with his son. "What makes Richard Russo so admirable as a novelist is that his natural grace as a storyteller is matched by his compassion for his characters"—John Irving

0-394-57778-7 RANDOM HOUSE $23.00

The Risk Pool

0-679-75383-4 VINTAGE PB $14.00
0-679-72334-X VINTAGE PB $8.95

Jim **Sagel**

Tunomas Honey

Stories about youth in northern New Mexico

0-916950-40-9 BILINGUAL PB $11.00

Floyd **Salas**

What Now My Love

1-55885-112-7 ARTE PUBLICO PB $9.95

J.D. **Salinger**

The Catcher in the Rye

Probably the most famous novel of adolescence

See also **YOUNG ADULT FICTION** in **BOOKS FOR YOUNG READERS**

0-316-76953-3 LITTLE, BROWN $22.95
0-316-76948-7 LITTLE, BROWN PB $5.99

Franny and Zooey

Two long stories about the eccentric Glass family

See also **YOUNG ADULT FICTION** in **BOOKS FOR YOUNG READERS**

0-316-76954-1 LITTLE, BROWN $23.95
0-316-76949-5 LITTLE, BROWN PB $4.99

Nine Stories

See also **YOUNG ADULT FICTION** in **BOOKS FOR YOUNG READERS**

0-316-76956-8 LITTLE, BROWN $22.95
0-316-76950-4 LITTLE, BROWN PB $4.99

Raise High the Roof Beam, Carpenters & Seymour: An Introduction

More on the Glass family

0-316-76957-6 LITTLE, BROWN $22.95
0-316-76951-7 LITTLE, BROWN PB $4.99

James **Salter**

Dusk & Other Stories

"His is to ordinary prose what haiku is to cocktail chatter, what yoga is to mud wrestling"—*Providence Journal*

0-86547-389-7 NORTH POINT PB $12.00

Solo Faces

"Contrasts a devotion to mountain climbing with the earthbound tugs of love and ordinary life...A beautifully composed book that will remind readers of Camus and Saint-Exupery. It exemplifies the purity it describes" —Michael Dirda, *Washington Post*

0-86547-321-8 NORTH POINT PB $12.00

A Sport and a Pastime

0-679-60156-2 MODERN LIBRARY $12.50
0-86547-210-6 FS&G PB $10.95

William **Saroyan**

The Man with the Heart in the Highlands & Other Early Stories

0-8112-1115-0 NEW DIRECTIONS PB $15.95

May **Sarton**

Anger

0-393-30316-0 NORTON PB $4.95

As We Are Now

The old age of a schoolteacher

0-393-08372-1 NORTON $10.95
0-393-30957-6 NORTON PB $9.00

The Bridge of Years

Belgium between the wars

0-393-30239-3 NORTON PB $4.95

Crucial Conversations

The end of a marriage, filtered through the talk of those affected

0-393-31102-3 NORTON PB $8.95

Faithful Are the Wounds

0-393-30266-0 NORTON PB $4.95

The Fur Person

0-393-30131-1 NORTON PB $5.95

A Grain of Mustard Seed

0-393-04344-4 NORTON PB $6.95

Joanna and Ulysses

0-393-30414-0 NORTON PB $5.95

Kind of Love

0-393-31101-5 NORTON PB $9.95

The Magnificent Spinster

0-393-31249-6 NORTON PB $11.00

Mrs. Stevens Hears the Mermaids Singing

INTRODUCTION BY CAROLYN G. HEILBRUN

0-393-30929-0 NORTON PB $9.95

A Reckoning

A woman dying of cancer reassesses her relationship with the important women in her life

0-393-08828-6 NORTON $11.95
0-393-00075-3 NORTON PB $5.95

Shadow of a Man

The death of his mother enables a 26-year old man to see the world clearly and with a new maturity

0-393-30030-7 NORTON PB $4.95

The Small Room

A women's college in New England

0-393-00832-0 NORTON PB $9.00

John **Sayles**

Los Gusanos

The novelist and filmmaker sets his newest novel in Miami's Cuban community, where a range of characters struggle to make a life in a new land. "His characterizations are rich, his imagination boundless"—*Philadelphia Inquirer*

0-06-016653-3 HARPERPERENNIAL PB $22.95

Susan Fromberg **Schaeffer**

First Nights

Schaeffer's richly detailed novel juxtaposes the lives of a reclusive Swedish actress (read Greta Garbo) and her West Indian caretaker and maid

0-8041-0728-9 IVY PB $6.99

The Madness of a Seduced Woman

A tale of seduction, obsessive love, and murder. "A remarkable book…a riveting and intricate and altogether astonishing novel"—Alice Walker

0-452-26709-9 PLUME PB $13.95

Budd **Schulberg**

What Makes Sammy Run?

"Brilliantly effective. Sammy is a conquistador of the gutter…..His portrait is vitriolic, never dull, and the comic aspects are given full appreciation"—*NY Times Book Review*

0-394-47618-7 RANDOM HOUSE $19.95
0-679-73422-8 VINTAGE PB $13.00

Sarah **Schulman**

Empathy

Set on Manhattan's Lower East side, "sexual identity, gender trauma, and self-renewal are the elements of this gritty, funny, perceptive novel by America's enticingly transgressive lesbian writer"—*LA Times Book Review*

0-525-93521-5 DUTTON $18.00
0-452-27049-9 PLUME PB $10.00

Girls, Visions and Everything

A spirited romp through New York's Lower East Side, starring lesbian-at-large Lila Futuransky

0-931188-38-5 SEAL PB $9.95

People in Trouble

"Funny, street-sharp, gentle, graphic, sad, and angry…probably the first novel to focus on AIDS activists"—*Newsday*

0-452-26568-1 DUTTON PB $11.95

Rat Bohemia

0-525-93790-0 DUTTON $19.95
0-452-27182-7 PLUME PB $10.95

Delmore **Schwartz**

The Ego Is Always at the Wheel: Bagatelles

"Delmore Schwartz understood the world's inviolate sadness … Tacit in all he wrote was Kafka's parable of 'Infinite hope, but not for us' " —James Atlas

EDITED BY ROBERT PHILLIPS

0-8112-1028-6 NEW DIRECTIONS PB $8.95

In Dreams Begin Responsibilities

Eight short stories examining the world of New York intellectuals in the '30s and '40s

EDITED BY JAMES ATLAS
FOREWORD BY IRVING HOWE

0-8112-0680-7 NEW DIRECTIONS PB $10.95

Lynne Sharon **Schwartz**

Disturbances in the Field

0-553-34377-7 BANTAM PB $10.95

The Fatigue Artist

0-684-80247-3 SCRIBNERS $23.00

Sandra **Scofield**

Beyond Deserving

0-452-26907-5 PLUME PB $11.95

Walking Dunes

"A finely etched, sensitive portrait of an intelligent but flawed young man" —*Publishers Weekly*

1-87794-612-5 PERMANENT $21.95

Joanna **Scott**

Fading, My Parmacheene Belle

0-8050-3972-4 HOLT PB $14.00

Various Antidotes: Stories

0-8050-4176-1 HOLT PB $12.00

Hubert **Selby**, Jr.

The Demon

0-7145-2598-7 MARION BOYARS PB $19.95

Last Exit to Brooklyn

These interrelated and realistic stories of life in the New York borough created a sensation when they were first published in 1964

0-8021-3137-9 GROVE PB $11.95

The Room

0-7145-0888-8 MARION BOYARS $19.95

Hubert Selby, Jr.
(photo courtesy of Grove Press)

Song of the Silent Snow & Other Stories

Fifteen short stories. "Stories told with astonishing directness and energy [by an] occasionally brilliant and always fascinating writer of uncommon talent and integrity" —*Philadelphia Inquirer*

0-8021-3008-9 GROVE PB $10.95

Mary Lee **Settle**

The Beulah Quintet

Volume 1: Prisons

1-57003-114-2 SOUTH CAROLINA PB $12.95

Volume 2: O Beulah Land

1-57003-115-0 SOUTH CAROLINA PB $14.95

Volume 3: Know Nothing

1-57003-116-9 SOUTH CAROLINA PB $14.95

Volume 4: The Scapegoat

1-57003-117-7 SOUTH CAROLINA PB $12.95

Volume 5: The Killing Ground

1-57003-118-5 SOUTH CAROLINA PB $12.95

Blood Tie

Winner of the National Book Award

1-57003-097-9 SOUTH CAROLINA PB $12.95

Celebration

"Settle is such a thoughtful, generous narrator that this story of a slightly star-crossed quartet of loving friends wins us easily. In an era that honors novels for their fragility and self-consciousness, Settle has chosen another route: the great read"—*Newsweek*

1-57003-096-0 SOUTH CAROLINA PB $12.95

Charley Bland

0-88184-709-7 CARROLL & GRAF PB $8.95

Choices

0-385-47699-X DOUBLEDAY $24.95
0-15-600388-0 HARVEST PB $14.00

The Clam Shell

A young girl at a Southern woman's college is sexually assaulted. "Mary Lee Settle has a grand passion for what she's doing…and the instinct of the novelist for panorama"—E.L. Doctorow

1-57003-099-5 SOUTH CAROLINA PB $12.95

Fatima **Shaik**

The Mayor of New Orleans: Just Talking Jazz

Three novellas that capture the ambience of southern Louisiana

0-88739-071-4 CREATIVE ARTS PB $9.95

Ntozake **Shange**

Betsey Brown

Racial integration as experienced by a middle-class St. Louis family

0-312-13434-7 PICADOR PB $10.00

Liliane: Resurrection of the Daughter

"Extraordinary and wonderful…Miss Shange's prose and poetry is a lyric and tragic exploration into black women's awareness… [She] writes with such exquisite care and beauty that anyone can relate to her message" —Clive Barnes, *NY Times*

0-312-11310-2 ST. MARTIN'S $18.95
0-312-13559-9 PICADOR PB $12.00

Sassafras, Cypress, and Indigo

Three sisters growing up in the South

0-312-69972-7 ST. MARTIN'S PB $9.95

Aurelie **Sheehan**

Jack Kerouac Is Pregnant

1-56478-060-0 DALKEY ARCHIVE $19.95

Jim **Shepard**

Batting Against Castro: Stories

Shepard offers a virtuoso display of his fictive range in 13 stories spanning an immense landscape. From fighter pilots to Catholic school boys, Shepard offers a wise, witty, and original collection of truly American stories

0-679-44668-0 KNOPF $22.00

Kiss of the Wolf
0-15-600140-3 HARVEST PB $9.95

Sam **Shepard**

"It's a real thing, double nature. I think we're split in a much more devastating way than psychology can ever reveal."—Sam Shepard

Cruising Paradise: Tales
Tersely lyrical, reckless, stoic, and solitary, Pulitzer Prize-winning Shepard continues his exploration of American manhood in a collection of short stories, fictional diary excerpts, and dialogues
0-679-41564-5 KNOPF $23.00

Sam Shepard

Anita **Shreve**

Resistance
0-316-78999-2 LITTLE, BROWN $21.95
0-316-78984-4 LITTLE, BROWN PB $12.95

The Weight of Water
0-316-78997-6 LITTLE, BROWN $22.95

Alix Kates **Shulman**

On the Stroll
0-89733-243-1 ACADEMY CHICAGO PB $10.00

Leslie Marmon **Silko**

Almanac of the Dead
"A brilliant, haunting, and tragic novel of ruin and resistance in the Americas…Leslie Silko dramatizes the often desperate struggle of native peoples in the Americas to keep, at all costs, the core of their culture"—Larry McMurtry
0-14-017319-6 PENGUIN PB $14.95

Ceremony
See also **CONTEMPORARY NATIVE AMERICAN WRITERS** under **NATIVE AMERICAN LITERATURES**
0-14-008683-8 PENGUIN PB $10.95

Storyteller
Poetry and fiction intermingled, from an important Native American writer
1-55970-005-X ARCADE PB $16.95

Herbert **Simmons**

Corner Boy
0-393-31465-0 NORTON PB $11.00

Mona **Simpson**

Anywhere but Here
"There have been many novels about mothers and daughters…but Simpson has found a very special, achingly real, yet often funny way of portraying such a relationship that speaks directly to our times"—*Cleveland Plain Dealer*
0-679-73738-3 VINTAGE PB $12.00

The Lost Father
A young woman's search for her father
0-679-73303-5 VINTAGE PB $12.00

A Regular Guy
0-679-45091-2 KNOPF $25.00

Jane **Smiley**

The Age of Grief
0-449-90795-3 FAWCETT PB $10.00

At Paradise Gate
"A poignant recognition of ordinary lives that, of course, are never ordinary at all"—*LA Times*
0-671-88533-2 TOUCHSTONE PB $11.00

Barn Blind
0-449-90874-7 FAWCETT PB $12.00

Duplicate Keys
0-449-90879-8 FAWCETT PB $12.00

The Greenlanders
Calls up the barren, violent, heroic world of 14th-century Norsemen through the eyes of a Greenland maiden fascinated by a warrior who has learned courtly manners in the south
See also **HISTORICAL AND ROMANTIC FICTION** in **POPULAR READING**
0-8041-0453-0 IVY PB $6.99

Moo
A blackly comic send-up of a Midwestern agricultural college
0-679-42023-1 KNOPF $24.00

Ordinary Love and Good Will: Two Novellas
0-8041-0714-9 IVY PB $5.99

A Thousand Acres
Winner of the 1991 National Book Award. In a modern-day *King Lear*, an Iowa farmer decides to divide his enormous holdings among his three daughters. Mythic undercurrents power this major novel
0-449-90748-1 FAWCETT PB $12.00

Charlie **Smith**

Cheap Ticket to Heaven
Serial killers cut a bloody swath across the Midwest and South
0-8050-3797-7 HOLT $25.00

Lee **Smith**

Black Mountain Breakdown
A girl from Appalachia leaves home for college. "The most evocative book I have read in a long time…funny, tragic, and haunting"
—Mary Lee Settle
0-345-33849-9 BALLANTINE PB $4.99

Cakewalk
0-345-33950-9 BALLANTINE PB $5.99

Fair and Tender Ladies
0-345-38399-0 BALLANTINE PB $10.00

Family Linen
"A childhood memory relived through hypnosis, a funeral that brings about a family reunion, and the excavation of a swimming pool on the site of an old well uncover a family secret in this darkly humorous novel"—*Christian Science Monitor*
0-345-33642-9 BALLANTINE PB $5.99

Fancy Strut
Sesquicentennial Week in an Alabama town. "A Southland full of visionaries and dreamers whose illusions tell us enough about reality to drive us to laughter and tears"—*LA Herald Examiner*
0-345-34025-6 BALLANTINE PB $5.99

Oral History
"A novel as dark, winding, complicated as the hill country itself"—*Village Voice*
0-345-31607-X BALLANTINE PB $5.99

Saving Grace
0-399-14050-6 PUTNAM $22.95

Barbara Probst **Solomon**

Smart Hearts in the City
New York and the smart hearts of a middle-aged Jewish woman, an ambitious young black man, and a tough-guy millionaire are interwoven in a frenetic contemporary world of law and finance
0-15-183157-2 HARCOURT BRACE $21.95

Susan **Sontag**

The Benefactor
Sontag's first novel. "A major writer; I especially admired how she can make a real story out of dreams and thoughts"— Hannah Arendt
0-385-26710-X ANCHOR PB $11.00

Death Kit
A young man attempts to "perceive the inventory of the world"
0-385-26711-8 ANCHOR PB $12.00

I, Etcetera
Eight short stories
0-385-26707-X ANCHOR PB $9.95

The Volcano Lover: A Romance
Set in Naples in the late 18th century, Susan Sontag's novel is a triangular love story based on the lives of Sir William Hamilton, his wife Emma, and Lord Nelson. A historical novel about passion and revolution, the fare of nature and art, *The Volcano Lover* is "a treasury of pleasures, of a quality no reader should miss"
—Larry McMurtry
0-374-28516-0 FS&G $22.00
0-385-26713-4 ANCHOR PB $12.00

Gilbert **Sorrentino**

Aberration of Starlight
The same story told from four points of view: a formal *tour de force* which is also moving
1-56478-028-7 DALKEY ARCHIVE PB $9.95

Imaginative Qualities of Actual Things
The New York literary world of the '50s
0-916583-86-4 DALKEY ARCHIVE PB $11.95

Misterioso
0-916583-43-0 DALKEY ARCHIVE $19.95

Mulligan Stew
A novelist's personal life interferes with his work-in-progress, and the result is a playful literary "stew" of genres and characters
1-56478-087-2 DALKEY ARCHIVE PB $13.95

Gilbert **Sorrentino**

Red the Fiend
0-88064-163-0 FROMM $19.95

Rose Theatre
0-916583-23-6 DALKEY ARCHIVE $20.00

Splendide-Hotel
0-916583-01-5 DALKEY ARCHIVE PB $5.95

Steelwork
1-56478-004-X DALKEY ARCHIVE PB $9.95

Under the Shadow
0-916583-93-7 DALKEY ARCHIVE PB $9.95

Terry **Southern**

Blue Movie
0-8021-3466-1 GROVE PB $12.00

Flash and Filigree
"Southern is strikingly inventive… *Flash and Filigree* has an unfailing sense of the ridiculous, heightened by deadpan delivery"—*Time*
0-8021-3430-0 GROVE PB $12.00

The Magic Christian
Southern's most coherent satire recounts Guy Grand's savage practical jokes directed against the rest of humanity
0-8021-3465-3 GROVE PB $11.00

Terry **Southern** & Mason **Hoffenberg**

Candy
A pornographic comedy that helped break publishing barriers in the '60s
See also **THE '60S** under **THE GREAT FICTION BESTSELLERS 1930–1995** in **POPULAR READING**
0-8021-3429-7 GROVE PB $12.00

Elizabeth **Spencer**

The Light in the Piazza & Other Tales
0-87805-837-0 MISSISSIPPI PB $16.95

Scott **Spencer**

Men in Black
0-425-15379-7 BERKLEY PB $6.99

Jack **Spicer**

The Tower of Babel: Jack Spicer's Detective Novel
An unfinished novel that offers a sharply funny picture of the San Francisco poetry scene of the 1950s
1-88368-904-X TALISMAN PB $12.95

Matthew **Stadler**

The Dissolution of Nicholas Dee; His Researches
0-06-097627-6 HARPERPERENNIAL PB $12.00

The Sex Offender
0-06-092655-4 HARPERPERENNIAL PB $12.00

Jean **Stafford**

Boston Adventure
An impoverished ten-year-old girl dreams of escaping from her roots and entering the glittering world of Boston's Beacon Hill
0-15-613611-2 HARCOURT BRACE PB $7.95

The Collected Stories
"This collection will undoubtedly become a textbook for many students of short fiction. Jean Stafford can teach almost anything one could want to know about swiftly and deftly developing characters, balancing them in delicate counterpoint or wrenching conflict, and probing their thoughts and emotions"—*Newsweek*
0-374-12632-1 FS&G $30.00

The Mountain Lion
A beautifully written and disturbing story about the inevitable destruction of innocence. "[Stafford] creates a splendid sense of time, of the unending afternoons of youth, and of the actual color of noon and night"
—*Saturday Review*
0-292-75136-2 TEXAS PB $10.95

Johnny **Stanton**

Mangled Hands
A Burroughs-like collage of Jesuit missionaries and fantastic shape-changing Indians in an imaginary Canadian wilderness
0-940650-48-7 SUN & MOON PB $10.95

Ilan **Stavans**

One-Handed Pianist and Other Stories
0-8263-1645-X NEW MEXICO $22.50

Wallace **Stegner**

All the Little Live Things
A novel drawing in part on the hippie culture of the late '60s
See also **ESSAYS, MEDITATIONS, AND CLASSICS** under **NATURE STUDY** in **SCIENCE**
0-14-015441-8 PENGUIN PB $12.95

Angle of Repose
A novel based on the life of the 19th-century Western writer Mary Hallock Foote
0-14-016930-X PENGUIN PB $13.95

The Big Rock Candy Mountain
0-14-013939-7 PENGUIN PB $12.95

Recapitulation
A diplomat returns home to the West
0-8032-9165-5 NEBRASKA PB $9.95

Remembering Laughter
0-14-025240-1 PENGUIN PB $10.95

Second Growth
The inner conflicts of life in a New Hampshire village
0-8032-9157-4 NEBRASKA PB $10.00

A Shooting Star
0-14-025241-X PENGUIN PB $12.95

The Spectator Bird
This follow-up to *All the Little Live Things* won the National Book Award in 1976
0-14-013940-0 PENGUIN PB $11.95

Wolf Willow
"By combining history, fiction, and his own memories … Wallace Stegner has summarized the frontier story and interpreted it as only one who was a part of it could do"—*NY Times*
0-14-013439-5 PENGUIN PB $11.95

Michael **Stephens**

The Brooklyn Book of the Dead
1-56478-037-6 DALKEY ARCHIVE $19.95

Richard **Stern**

The Chaleur Network
0-933256-18-3 FRANKLIN WATTS $22.00
0-933256-19-1 FRANKLIN WATTS PB $15.95

Golk
0-226-77319-1 CHICAGO PB $9.95

Noble Rot: Stories 1949-1988
0-929968-30-1 ANOTHER CHICAGO PRESS PB $12.95

The Position of the Body
0-8101-0730-9 NORTHWESTERN $29.95
0-8101-0731-7 NORTHWESTERN PB $12.95

Robert **Stone**

Children of Light
Love, drugs, and alcohol on the Mexican set of a major motion picture
0-679-73593-3 VINTAGE PB $11.00

Dog Soldiers
Drug runners, Vietnam vets, and backwoods cultists in a violent panorama of late-'60s America
0-14-009835-6 PENGUIN PB $11.95

A Flag for Sunrise
"Gringos against Latins, Latins against Indians, Marxists against Christians, spies against innocents, women against men… all struggling in an oily whirlpool of betrayal"—*Chicago Sun-Times*
0-679-73762-6 VINTAGE PB $14.00

A Hall of Mirrors
"A surrealistic vision of a New Orleans rife with political paranoia"—*Newsweek*
0-14-009834-8 PENGUIN PB $11.95

Outerbridge Reach
0-06-097530-X HARPERPERENNIAL PB $13.00

William **Styron**

The Confessions of Nat Turner
The famous historical novel of a slave rebellion
0-679-60101-5 MODERN LIBRARY $15.50
0-679-73663-8 VINTAGE PB $13.00

Lie Down in Darkness
Styron's first novel tells of a troubled Virginia family
0-394-50659-6 RANDOM HOUSE $24.95
0-679-73597-6 VINTAGE PB $13.00

The Long March
A brutal novella of Marines in training
0-679-73675-1 VINTAGE PB $12.00

Sophie's Choice
The terrible secret of a 1940s immigrant in New York
See also **HOLOCAUST FICTION** under **ART AND LITERATURE** under **THE HOLOCAUST** in **WORLD HISTORY AND CURRENT AFFAIRS**
0-679-73637-9 VINTAGE PB $13.00

A Tidewater Morning: Three Tales from Youth
In Styron's first fictional book in over a decade, three stories visit a Pacific Marine division in World War II, a Depression-era Southern town, and a tidewater town in Virginia in 1938
0-679-42742-2 RANDOM HOUSE $17.00

Ronald **Sukenick**

Blown Away

"The reader who is interested in the future of fiction in this country should have a look at the writings of Sukenick"
—*San Francisco Bay Guardian*

0-940650-63-0 SUN & MOON $16.95
0-940650-64-9 SUN & MOON PB $10.95

Amy **Tan**

The Hundred Secret Senses

0-399-14114-6 PUTNAM $24.95
0-7451-3774-1 THORNDIKE PB $25.00

The Joy Luck Club

"Intensely poetic, startlingly imaginative and moving, this remarkable book will speak to many women, mothers and grown daughters"
—*Publishers Weekly*

0-399-13420-4 PUTNAM $22.95
0-679-72768-X VINTAGE PB $10.00

The Kitchen God's Wife

Amy Tan's novel of mothers and daughters brings a Chinese family's past into its present-day life in San Francisco

0-679-74808-3 VINTAGE PB $12.00

Peter **Taylor**

Taylor is noted for his nuanced portraits of privileged Southerners.

The Collected Stories of Peter Taylor

0-14-008361-8 PENGUIN PB $15.95

In the Miro District & Other Stories

0-345-36405-8 BALLANTINE PB $4.95

In the Tennessee Country

0-312-13521-1 PICADOR PB $10.00

The Old Forest & Other Stories

0-345-32778-0 BALLANTINE PB $5.99

A Summons to Memphis

0-345-34660-2 BALLANTINE PB $5.99

A Woman of Means

0-913720-44-5 FREDERICK BELL $16.95
0-312-14448-2 PICADOR PB $10.00

Alexander **Theroux**

Darconville's Cat

A professor at a Southern women's college falls in love with a student in a tale that is told in various forms, including diaries, sermons, poems, parodies, and fables

0-8050-4365-9 HOLT PB $16.00

Three Wogs

0-8050-4459-0 OWLET PB $14.00

Paul **Theroux**

The Black House

The Black House remains a suspenseful and often unnerving study of the irrational and instinctive forces in human nature… exceedingly well done"—*Houston Post*

0-14-008792-3 PENGUIN PB $10.95

Chicago Loop

0-8041-1161-8 IVY PB $5.99

The Family Arsenal

"Old-fashioned entertainment in the mode perfected by Graham Greene"—*Time*

0-14-004465-5 PENGUIN PB $11.95

Half Moon Street

Two novellas. " 'Doctor Slaughter' and 'Doctor Demarr,' the novellas that comprise *Half Moon Street*, are unrelated but well-paired, functioning as anima and animus, female and male versions of the title characters' double lives"—*Newsday*

0-395-36511-2 HOUGHTON MIFFLIN $14.95

Millroy the Magician

0-8041-1311-4 IVY PB $6.99

The Mosquito Coast

A man's attempt to escape from contemporary civilization

0-14-006089-8 PENGUIN PB $11.95

My Other Life

A semi-autobiographical novel—the protagonist shares the same name as the author—from the novelist and travel writer

0-395-82527-X HOUGHTON MIFFLIN $24.95

My Secret History

The story of a middle-aged writer, his career, travels, and love life

0-8041-0514-6 IVY PB $5.95

On the Edge of the Great Rift

0-14-024835-8 PENGUIN PB $14.95

O-Zone

America in the 21st century, a world of aliens, nuclear waste, and mutants

0-8041-0151-5 IVY PB $5.95

Sinning with Annie

0-8041-0517-0 IVY PB $3.95

Lawrence **Thornton**

Imagining Argentina

0-553-34579-6 BANTAM PB $12.95

Lynne **Tillman**

Haunted Houses

1-85242-400-1 SERPENT'S TAIL PB $12.99

Michael **Tolkin**

Among the Dead

The aftermath of a plane crash, told sharply and savagely, with a cynical eye for media exploitation

0-380-72299-2 AVON PB $11.00

The Player, The Rapture & The New Age: Three Screenplays

See also **COLLECTIONS** under **SCREENPLAYS** under **FILM** in **PERFORMING ARTS AND MEDIA**

0-8021-3392-4 GROVE PB $13.00

John Kennedy **Toole**

A Confederacy of Dunces

An obese, fractious, fastidious mama's boy cohabits with the denizens of New Orleans's lower depths

FOREWORD BY WALKER PERCY

0-8071-0657-7 LSU $22.95
0-8021-3020-8 GROVE PB $11.95

The Neon Bible

0-8021-1108-4 GROVE $15.95
0-8021-3207-3 GROVE PB $11.00

Lionel **Trilling**

Of this Time, of that Place & Other Stories

Five short stories

0-15-668062-9 HARCOURT BRACE PB $3.95

Frederic **Tuten**

Tintin in the New World: A Romance

Long a literary cult, Tintin, the comic-book boy reporter, is a man forever trapped in a teenager's body and a never-ending, adolescent adventure. Tuten's hip and literate fable breaks Tintin out of the frames of Herge's drawings and allows him an adventure of love and self-realization that his creator never dreamed of. "A complex delight…the clear bells of Tuten's prose linger after the book has been put down"—Larry McMurtry

0-688-12314-7 MORROW $22.00

Anne **Tyler**

The Accidental Tourist

A travel writer hates travel and change. "Tyler is not merely good, she is wickedly good"
—John Updike

0-394-54689-X KNOPF $25.00
0-425-09291-7 BERKLEY PB $6.99

Breathing Lessons

A moving portrait of a married couple caught in the normalcy of life's later years

0-425-11774-X BERKLEY PB $6.99

Celestial Navigation

A painter refuses to leave his rooftop studio fortress

0-8041-0888-9 IVY PB $5.99

The Clock Winder

A young woman is hired to care for an elderly woman and becomes involved with the matriarch's eccentric family

0-8041-0885-4 IVY PB $5.99

Dinner at the Homesick Restaurant

"Stunning psychological portrait of a family estranged from itself"—*Saturday Review*

0-394-52381-4 KNOPF $25.00
0-8041-0882-X IVY PB $5.99

Earthly Possessions

A wife leaving her husband is taken hostage by a bank robber

0-8041-0889-7 IVY PB $5.99

If Morning Ever Comes

A law student returns to a home overpopulated with women

0-8041-0884-6 IVY PB $5.99

Ladder of Years

A 40-year-old mother walks out on her marriage and children and hitchikes her way to a new life

0-679-44155-7 KNOPF $24.00
0-449-91057-1 FAWCETT PB $12.00

Anne Tyler (credit: ©Diana Walker)

Morgan's Passing
An unconventional hardware store proprietor crashes into middle age
0-8041-0881-1 IVY PB $5.99

Saint Maybe
Set in 1967, a powerful exploration of a man's sense of guilt for the death of his brother
0-679-40361-2 KNOPF $22.00

Searching for Caleb
Family saga spanning a century. "As hauntingly nostalgic as a glimpse into the lighted windows of a home in which you once lived"—*Detroit Free Press*
0-8041-0883-8 IVY PB $5.99

A Slipping Down Life
0-8041-0886-2 IVY PB $5.99

The Tin Can Tree
A family loses a young daughter
0-8041-0887-0 IVY PB $5.99

Sabine **Ulibarri**

The Condor & Other Stories/El Condor y Otros Cuentos
Stories about Mexican-Americans in an evolving political and economic environment in modern-day New Mexico
0-934770-92-1 ARTE PUBLICO PB $9.50

Primeros Encuentros/First Encounters
Stories about the interaction of Anglos and Hispanos
0-916950-27-1 BILINGUAL PB $9.00

John **Updike**

The Afterlife and Other Stories
The American master takes us into life beyond middle age where; from deaths of parents to births of grandchildren, beginnings are weighed against losses with wisdom and insight
0-679-43583-2 KNOPF $24.00
0-449-22391-4 CREST PB $6.99

Bech: A Book
Bech, the famous writer and Updike's alter ego, reflects upon his life
0-449-20277-1 FAWCETT PB $5.99

Bech Is Back
0-394-52806-9 KNOPF $25.00

Brazil
0-679-43071-7 KNOPF $23.00
0-449-91163-2 BALLANTINE PB $12.00

The Centaur
0-394-41881-6 KNOPF $24.95
0-449-21522-9 FAWCETT PB $5.95

Couples
Marriage and adultery in the suburbs
0-394-42066-7 RANDOM HOUSE $27.50

In the Beauty of the Lillies
0-679-44640-0 KNOPF $25.95

Marry Me: A Romance
0-449-20361-1 FAWCETT PB $5.99

Memories of the Ford Administration
An interweaving of two fascinating narratives and two periods—one highly personal and set in the '70s, one historic—to achieve a telling commentary on both the past and on the way we live now
0-679-41681-1 KNOPF $23.00
0-449-22188-1 CREST $5.99

A Month of Sundays
The Reverend Tom Marshfield and his indiscreet behavior with the women in his parish
0-394-49551-9 RANDOM HOUSE $16.95
0-449-20795-1 FAWCETT PB $4.95

Museums and Women & Other Stories
Twenty-nine short stories
0-394-48173-9 RANDOM HOUSE $25.00

The Music School
0-394-43727-6 KNOPF $25.00

Of the Farm
0-394-43898-1 FAWCETT PB $17.95

John Updike

Pigeon Feathers & Other Stories
0-394-44056-0 RANDOM HOUSE $19.95
0-449-21132-0 FAWCETT PB $5.99

The Poorhouse Fair
"A first novel of rare precision and real merit" —*Newsweek*
0-394-41050-5 RANDOM HOUSE $25.00

Rabbit at Rest
The fourth and final novel in Updike's 'Rabbit' series, taking his hero into the America of the late '80s
0-394-58936-X KNOPF $24.95

Rabbit Is Rich
Rabbit at midlife, circa 1979
0-394-52087-4 KNOPF $30.00
0-449-24548-9 FAWCETT PB $5.99

Rabbit Redux
Part two in the Rabbit series. "An anatomy of human life"—*Newsday*
0-394-47273-X RANDOM HOUSE $27.50
0-449-20934-2 FAWCETT PB $5.99

Rabbit Run
Part one in Updike's continuing saga of a Pennsylvania used-car dealer
0-394-44206-7 KNOPF $25.00
0-449-20506-1 FAWCETT PB $5.99

Roger's Version
Theological speculation and erotic intrigue in Boston
0-449-21288-2 CREST PB $6.99

S
A witty epistolary novel in which an affluent New England woman leaves her husband for a guru
0-394-56835-4 KNOPF $17.95
0-449-21652-7 CREST PB $6.99

Too Far to Go
"That a marriage ends is less than ideal; but all things end under heaven, and if temporality is held to be invalidating, then nothing real succeeds. The moral of these stories is that all blessings are mixed"—John Updike
0-449-20016-7 CREST PB $5.99

Trust Me
Twenty-two stories
0-449-21498-2 FAWCETT PB $5.95

The Witches of Eastwick
Three contemporary New England witches
0-449-20647-5 CREST PB $6.99

William **Van Wert**

What's It All About?: A Novel of Life, Love & Key Lime Pie
Trailer park retirees forge bonds against loneliness and impending death
0-684-81872-8 SIMON & SCHUSTER $20.00

Ed **Vega**

Mendoza's Dreams
Vega's clowning-gritty tales of barrio life
0-934770-56-5 ARTE PUBLICO PB $9.50

Gore **Vidal**

Vidal's novels include witty and iconoclastic fictional rewritings of American history and an imaginary autobiography of the emperor who tried to save Rome from Christianity.

Burr
One of the best of Vidal's historical novels, about the man who shot Alexander Hamilton
See also **HISTORICAL AND ROMANTIC FICTION** in **POPULAR READING**
0-345-33921-5 BALLANTINE PB $6.99

The City and the Pillar
A landmark novel, one of the first to deal openly with homosexuality
0-345-33271-7 BALLANTINE PB $6.99

Aaron Burr

The City and the Pillar & Seven Early Stories
Vidal's classic novel, republished with a new introduction by the author, plus seven early homoerotic stories the publication of which in 1948, depicting the "coming out" of a young man in California and New York, cut off Vidal's expected career in politics and launched him, instead, into a literary career
0-679-43699-5 RANDOM HOUSE $24.00

Creation
A fictional tour of the ancient world
0-345-34020-5 BALLANTINE PB $6.99

Dark Green, Bright Red
An early novel about revolution in Central America
0-345-33457-4 BALLANTINE PB $4.95

Duluth
Vidal's own favorite among his books, *Duluth* is an Orwellian tragedy set in a grotesque version of a typical American town
84-01-36053-6 LECTORUM PB $9.50

Empire
An epic of America in the Gilded Age. "In writing about how the US became an empire, Vidal gives us a rich and dazzling novel filled with more of the social observations, behavioral insights, political arguments, and personal quirks that have made him our most public of writers"
— Webster Schott, *Cleveland Plain Dealer*
0-394-56123-6 RANDOM HOUSE $2.98
0-345-35472-9 BALLANTINE PB $6.99

Julian
The 4th-century Roman emperor portrayed with sympathetic irony
0-345-32908-2 BALLANTINE PB $5.95

Lincoln
"The portrait is reasoned, judicious, straightforward and utterly convincing"
—Joyce Carol Oates, *NY Times*
0-679-60048-5 MODERN LIBRARY $19.00

Messiah
The creation of a cult of conformity. "Turns the Christian mythology and its attendant rituals inside out to create a religion based on death"
—P. Schuyler Miller
0-345-33917-7 BALLANTINE PB $4.99

Myra Breckinridge & Myron
Vidal's comic sendup of sexual mores
See also **THE '60S** under **THE GREAT FICTION BESTSELLERS 1930-1995** in **POPULAR READING**
0-394-55376-4 RANDOM HOUSE $19.95

A Search For the King
A poetic novel on the troubador Blondel. "A chaste, spare, intelligent, and essentially pictorial style, which frequently achieves a vividness equal to that of the best imagist poets"—*Chicago Tribune*
0-345-33272-5 BALLANTINE PB $4.95

A Thirsty Evil: Seven Short Stories
0-917342-84-4 BOOK PEOPLE PB $7.95

Two Sisters
0-345-33117-6 BALLANTINE PB $4.95

Washington, D.C.
Set in the late Depression, this skillful historical novel traces the parallel lives of a senator and a newspaper publisher joined by a startling marriage between the former's protégé and the latter's daughter
0-345-34236-4 BALLANTINE PB $5.99

Gore Vidal

Gerald **Vizenor**

The Heirs of Columbus
A fantastic variation on the legendary figure of Columbus, told as the story of Stone Columbus, a trickster healer who spreads his wisdom on talk radio. "Gerald Vizenor combines ancient American storytelling with space-age literary techniques. I don't know of anyone else who is doing this"—Ishmael Reed
0-8195-5241-0 WESLEYAN $22.95

William T. **Vollmann**

Vollmann's books "tower over the work of his contemporaries by virtue of their enormous range, huge ambition, stylistic daring, wide learning, audacious innovation, and sardonic wit."—Washington Post Book World

William T. Vollman (credit: ©Jerry Bauer)

The Atlas
"The most unconventional—and possibly also the most exciting and imaginative—novelist at work today" (*Newsday*) offers 53 stories capturing his last five years of travel: Phnom Penh, Sarajevo, Jerusalem, Berlin, Mogadishu. From an old walrus hunter to a drunken gypsy, Vollmann arranges his characters into richly imagined and incandescent stories
0-670-86578-8 VIKING $29.95

The Ice-Shirt: Volume One of A Book of North American Landscapes
0-14-013196-5 PENGUIN PB $12.95

Fathers and Crows: Volume Two of A Book of North American Landscapes
Vollmann continues his chronicle of America's native peoples and their colonization with this vivid account of how the Jesuits and Iroquois together destroyed Huron Indian civilization
0-670-84333-4 VIKING $30.00

The Rifles: Volume Six of A Book of North American Landscapes
Vollmann focuses his visionary historical optic on the white explorers of 150 years ago attempting to forge a Northwest Passage, then leaps to the contemporary Canadian north, where Inuit elders dream of the past while teenagers sniff gasoline. "In everything he writes, Vollman adamantly refuses to lie to himself or us. In an era saturated with political and commercial dishonesty and Disneyesque sentimentality, it is a quality as precious as diamonds"—*San Francisco Chronicle*
0-14-017623-3 PENGUIN PB $11.95

Thirteen Stories and Thirteen Epitaphs
This collection is populated with witch doctors, tramps, and other bizarre and disreputable figures
0-679-40439-2 PANTHEON $24.00

Whores for Gloria
0-14-023157-9 PENGUIN PB $9.95

You Bright and Risen Angels: A Cartoon
0-14-011087-9 PENGUIN PB $12.95

Kurt **Vonnegut**, Jr.

Bluebeard

0-440-20196-9 DELL PB $5.99

Breakfast of Champions

0-440-13148-0 BDD PB $6.50

Canary in a Cat House

0-89966-757-0 BUCCANEER $25.95

Cat's Cradle

A mixture of satire and fantasy that is "far more meaningful than the melodramatic tripe most critics seem to consider serious"
—Terry Southern

0-440-11149-8 DELL PB $6.50

Deadeye Dick

"A moving fable of passive resistance. Vonnegut, sweet cynic and ugly duckling, continues to write gentle swan songs for our uncivil society"—*Playboy*

0-440-11765-8 DELL PB $5.99

Galapagos

0-440-12779-3 DELL PB $6.50

God Bless You, Mr. Rosewater

"A hilariously wacky comedy. Its chief target is inherited wealth, but as in his earlier books, Vonnegut takes pot shots at many varieties of folly"—*Saturday Review*

0-440-12929-X BDD PB $6.50

Hocus Pocus

0-425-13021-5 BERKLEY PB $6.99

Jailbird

"*Jailbird* is an angry man's piercing look at America in the 1970s"—*People*

0-440-15473-1 DELL PB $6.50

Mother Night

A satirical look at a former American Nazi

0-440-15853-2 BDD PB $6.50

Palm Sunday

0-440-36906-1 DELL PB $5.99

Player Piano

A man runs away from a comfortable life in a timeless, excessively industrialized middle America

0-440-17037-0 LAUREL LEAF PB $6.50

The Sirens of Titan

The richest man in America takes a beautiful woman to outer space

0-440-17948-3 DELL PB $5.99

Slapstick: Or, Lonesome No More!

"Vonnegut's ongoing puppet show!...A saucy spaghetti of ideas...goes down like ice cream...The fabulous is reborn"
—John Updike, *New Yorker*

0-440-18009-0 DELL PB $6.50

Slaughterhouse Five: Or, the Children's Crusade

A former American prisoner of war relives the bombing of Dresden

0-385-28940-5 DELL PB $9.95

Wampeters, Foma and Granfalloons

0-440-18533-5 DELL PB $6.50

Welcome to the Monkey House

Twenty-five short works. "This volume gives everybody a chance to put Kurt Vonnegut, Jr. together"—*St. Louis Globe-Democrat*

0-440-19478-4 BDD PB $6.50

Chuck **Wachtel**

Because We Are Here: Stories and Novellas

0-670-83887-X VIKING $24.95

The Gates

"A story rarely told—of culture, the restraining collar of New York and Central America—is told by Wachtel with affection and with considerable anger"—Grace Paley

0-14-015231-8 PENGUIN PB $13.95

Joe the Engineer

0-14-015376-4 PENGUIN PB $10.95

Rosmarie **Waldrop**

The Hanky of Pippin's Daughter

"A novel rare for its evocation of the early experience of its protagonist, who grows up in the Germany of Hitler's era, and of the unique womanhood she gradually creates herself after the Second World War and far beyond her native Germany"—John Hawkes

0-88268-155-9 STATION HILL PB $10.95

Alice **Walker**

The Banned Works

1-87996-047-8 AUNT LUTE $10.95

The Color Purple

Epistolary novel of a black woman's life; winner of the Pulitzer Prize and the American Book Award in 1982

0-15-119154-9 HARCOURT BRACE $19.95
0-671-66878-1 POCKET PB $12.00

In Love and Trouble: Stories of Black Women

Thirteen short pieces

0-15-644450-X HARCOURT BRACE PB $6.95

Meridian

"A classic novel of both feminism and the Civil Rights Movement"—*Ms.*

0-15-159265-9 HARCOURT BRACE $18.95
0-671-72701-X POCKET PB $5.99

Alice Walker

Possessing the Secret of Joy

Set in Africa, this is a riveting story of the psychic imbalance and, eventually, murderous rage of a victim of female circumcision

0-671-78942-2 POCKET PB $5.99

The Third Life of Grange Copeland

A tenant farmer's life. "Almost no one has tried to tell us about the early lives, the *inner* lives, of black people...Alice Walker is a storyteller"
—Robert Coles, *New Yorker*

0-671-74588-3 POCKET PB $6.99

You Can't Keep a Good Woman Down

Fourteen short stories. "A major American writer, a cause for gratitude, delight, and celebration"—Tillie Olsen

0-15-699778-9 HARCOURT BRACE PB $8.00

David Foster **Wallace**

The Broom of the System

A switchboard operator in the Cleveland, Ohio, of 1990. "He often writes like a loquacious angel"—Richard Elman

0-380-71991-6 AVON PB $12.00

Girl with Curious Hair

0-380-71230-X AVON PB $9.95

Infinite Jest

Wallace's epic, vastly intelligent novel about tennis, AA, and the search for a fatally entertaining videotape, set in a near future of ecological disaster and rampant consumerism (even the years have sponsors)

0-316-92004-5 LITTLE, BROWN $29.95
0-316-92117-3 LITTLE, BROWN PB $14.95

Robert Penn **Warren**

All the King's Men

The saga of Willie Stark's political rise and fall

0-15-104772-3 HARCOURT BRACE $16.00
0-15-604762-4 HARCOURT BRACE PB $11.00

Paul **Watkins**

Archangel

Environmental terrorism in the forests of Maine gives Watkins the theme of his novel about the majesty of the wilderness and the passion of radicalism. "A wonderful literary adventure novel, squarely in the tradition of *Deliverance* and *Legends of the Fall*"
—Howard Frank Mosher

0-679-44391-6 RANDOM HOUSE $24.00

James **Welch**

The Death of Jim Loney

0-14-010291-4 PENGUIN PB $10.95

Fools Crow

The white man's effect upon the Blackfoot Indians in 1870s Montana. "A major contribution to Native American literature"—Wallace Stegner

0-14-008937-3 PENGUIN PB $12.95

The Indian Lawyer

0-14-011052-6 PENGUIN PB $11.95

Winter in the Blood

0-14-008644-7 PENGUIN PB $10.95

Eudora **Welty**

The Bride of the Innisfallen & Other Stories

0-15-614075-6 HARCOURT BRACE PB $7.95

The Collected Stories of Eudora Welty

0-15-118994-3 HARCOURT BRACE $29.95
0-15-618921-6 HARCOURT BRACE PB $14.00

A Curtain of Green & Other Stories

Welty's first collection of short stories. "Miss Welty's short stories are deceptively simple. They are concerned with ordinary people, but what happens to them and the manner of the telling are far from ordinary"—*New Yorker*

0-15-623492-0 HARCOURT BRACE PB $10.00

Delta Wedding

A Southern family on a Mississippi plantation in 1923. "Presents the essence of the deep South and does it with infinite finesse" —*Christian Science Monitor*

0-15-625280-5 HARCOURT BRACE PB $10.00

The Golden Apples

"I doubt that a better book about the South—one that more completely gets the feel of the particular texture of Southern life, and its special tone and pattern—has ever been written"—*New Yorker*

0-15-636090-X HARCOURT BRACE PB $10.00

Losing Battles

A Mississippi family in the '30s

0-394-72668-5 RANDOM HOUSE PB $11.00
0-679-72882-1 VINTAGE PB $13.00

The Optimist's Daughter

Winner of the 1972 Pulitzer Prize

0-8488-0660-3 AMEREON $19.95
0-679-72883-X VINTAGE PB $10.00

The Ponder Heart

A wealthy man is accused of murdering his 17-year-old bride in a small Southern town

0-15-672915-6 HARCOURT BRACE PB $7.00

The Robber Bridegroom

"A modern fairy tale, where irony and humor, outright nonsense, deep wisdom, and surrealistic extravaganzas become a poetic unity through the power of pure, exquisite style" —*NY Times*

0-15-178318-7 HARCOURT BRACE $19.95
0-15-676807-0 HARCOURT BRACE PB $8.00

Selected Stories

INTRODUCTION BY KATHERINE ANNE PORTER

0-679-60002-7 MODERN LIBRARY $14.50

Thirteen Stories

EDITED BY RUTH M. VANDE KIEFT

0-15-689969-8 HARCOURT BRACE PB $8.00

The Wide Net & Other Stories

Eight stories

0-15-696610-7 HARCOURT BRACE PB $7.95

Paul **West**

Love's Mansion

0-87951-503-1 OVERLOOK PB $13.95

Rat Man of Paris

0-87951-502-3 OVERLOOK PB $10.95

Sporting with Amaryllis

0-87951-666-6 OVERLOOK $19.95

Tenement of Clay

0-929701-27-5 MCPHERSON $20.00
0-929701-28-3 MCPHERSON PB $12.00

The Tent of Orange Mist

0-684-80031-4 SCRIBNERS $22.00

William **Wharton**

Birdy

A troubled youth retreats into a world of birds

0-679-73412-0 VINTAGE PB $13.00

Dad

1-55704-256-X NEWMARKET PB $14.95

Houseboat on the Seine

1-55704-272-1 NEWMARKET $23.95

A Midnight Clear

1-55704-257-8 NEWMARKET PB $12.95

Pride

A ten-year-old working-class boy growing up in South Philadelphia in the years just prior to World War II

1-55704-259-4 NEWMARKET PB $12.95

Scumbler

1-55704-258-6 NEWMARKET PB $12.95

Edmund **White**

The Beautiful Room Is Empty

"White is unquestionably the foremost American gay novelist"—*Newsweek*

0-679-75540-3 VINTAGE PB $11.00

A Boy's Own Story

A young gay man struggles against his own homosexuality. "This novel about seduction and maturity, about America and about 'homosexual fate,' is a large and happy accomplishment" —Susan Sontag

0-452-27300-5 PLUME PB $11.95

Caracole

"As a writer, White possesses the rare combination of a poetic sense of language and an ironic sense of humor"—*Newsweek*

0-679-76416-X VINTAGE PB $13.00

Forgetting Elena

White's first book was cited by Vladimir Nabokov as the American novel he most admired

0-679-75573-X VINTAGE PB $10.00

Nocturnes for the King of Naples

"A Baroque invention of quite startling brilliance and intensity"—Gore Vidal

0-312-02263-8 ST. MARTIN'S PB $7.95

Skinned Alive: Stories

Eight stories, several autobiographical, all exploring desire, the yearning to intimacy, the power of beauty, the effects of illness and loss

0-679-43476-3 KNOPF $23.00
0-679-75475-X VINTAGE PB $12.00

George **Whitmore**

Nebraska

0-671-67234-7 WASHINGTON SQUARE PB $6.95

John Edgar **Wideman**

All Stories Are True

0-679-73752-9 VINTAGE PB $10.00

The Cattle Killing

0-395-78590-1 HOUGHTON MIFFLIN $22.95

Damballah

0-679-72028-6 VINTAGE PB $11.00

A Glance Away

A confrontation between a black ex-addict and an alcoholic homosexual

0-911860-50-9 CHATHAM $15.90

Hiding Place

0-679-72027-8 RANDOM HOUSE PB $10.00

Sent for You Yesterday

"Hypnotic and deeply lyrical"—*NY Times*

0-679-72029-4 VINTAGE PB $11.00

The Stories of John Edgar Wideman

0-679-40719-7 PANTHEON $25.00

Marianne **Wiggins**

Bet They'll Miss Us When We're Gone

Wiggins, author of *John Dollar* and *Separate Checks,* presents 12 impeccable stories set in Virginia, Spain, London, Amsterdam, and "somewhere on the Welsh borders"—in a story that clearly reflects her period in hiding with Salman Rushdie, her former husband

0-06-016139-6 HARPERPERENNIAL PB $19.95

Diluted in me is John Wiggins as today's rain will be in summer's harvest. I wish that I could see him once again, hear his footfalls in the driveway, heavy on one foot: These dried leavings aren't complete in their remembrance, like the trimmings swept from green growth on a grocer's floor, they crumble on my fingertips and fly piecemeal to the wind.

BET THEY'LL MISS US WHEN WE'RE GONE

Eveless Eden

A love affair between a foreign correspondent for an American newspaper and the photographer he meets at the site of an ecological disaster in Africa

0-06-092760-7 HARPERPERENNIAL PB $13.00

John Dollar

A group of girls stranded on a desert island

0-06-091655-9 HARPERCOLLINS PB $12.00

Separate Checks

0-06-097207-6 HARPERCOLLINS PB $7.95

James **Wilcox**

Guest of a Sinner

0-06-092646-5 HARPERPERENNIAL PB $12.00

Modern Baptists

0-06-091985-X HARPERCOLLINS PB $12.00

Polite Sex

0-06-092165-X HARPERPERENNIAL PB $12.00

Sort of Rich

0-06-091707-5 HARPERCOLLINS PB $12.00

John A. **Williams**

The Angry Ones
A devastating novel of the New York publishing world, as reflected in the experiences of a talented black editor forced to work for a vanity press
0-393-31464-2 NORTON PB $11.00

The Berhama Account
0-88282-009-5 NEW HORIZON $16.95

Captain Blackman
A black soldier in Vietnam drifts in and out of a coma, hallucinating about past and present
0-938410-68-7 THUNDER'S MOUTH PB $10.95

!Click Song
"The 'private and public' vicissitudes of a black novelist trying to establish himself as a writer of distinction are chronicled in this revealing tale of the New York cultural scene from World War II to the present—told with directness of language and feeling"—*NY Times*
INTRODUCTION BY ISHMAEL REED
0-938410-43-1 THUNDER'S MOUTH PB $10.95

The Man Who Cried I Am
In Amsterdam in the spring of 1964, a black American writer is dying of cancer
0-938410-24-5 THUNDER'S MOUTH PB $12.95

Sissie
0-938410-66-0 THUNDER'S MOUTH PB $12.95

Joy **Williams**

Breaking and Entering
The travails of a pair of Florida drifters. "Funny, awful, and gruesomely Floridian" —Thomas McGuane
0-394-75773-4 VINTAGE PB $12.00

Taking Care
0-394-72912-9 RANDOM HOUSE PB $11.00

Lynna **Williams**

Things Not Seen and Other Stories
"Vibrant and shapely tales of disasters of the heart of people haunted by their unrelenting histories"—*NY Times Book Review*
0-316-94246-4 LITTLE, BROWN PB $9.95

Tennessee **Williams**

Collected Stories
"These stories are the true memoir of Tennessee Williams. Whatever happened to him, real or imagined, is here"—Gore Vidal
INTRODUCTION BY GORE VIDAL
0-8112-0952-0 NEW DIRECTIONS $19.95
0-345-33587-2 BALLANTINE PB $6.99

Hard Candy
Williams's second collection of short stories
0-8112-0221-6 NEW DIRECTIONS PB $9.95

One Arm & Other Stories
Williams' first collection of short fiction
0-8112-0223-2 NEW DIRECTIONS PB $9.95

The Roman Spring of Mrs. Stone
An older American actress and her obsession with a gigolo in Rome. "The Roman Spring is actually Mrs. Stone's Autumn. A sharp, witty, and moving novel"—*Chicago Tribune*
0-8112-1249-1 NEW DIRECTIONS PB $6.00

Geoffrey **Wolff**

The Age of Consent
0-312-14081-9 PICADOR PB $12.00

A Day at the Beach
A powerful collection of nine autobiographical essays by the author of *The Final Club,* describing his outlandish childhood, his Choate and Princeton days, and his life as a journalist and writer. "Wolff's eye is unfailingly sharp and his descriptions remarkable and glib" —*Kirkus Reviews*
0-679-40333-7 KNOPF $22.00
0-679-74449-5 VINTAGE PB $12.00

The Duke of Deception
0-679-72752-3 VINTAGE PB $13.00

The Final Club
0-679-73592-5 VINTAGE PB $13.00

Providence
0-679-73277-2 VINTAGE PB $10.00

Tobias **Wolff**

The Barracks Thief & Selected Stories
A novella and six short stories. "I have not read a book of stories in years that has given me such a shock of amazement and recognition—and such pleasure"—Raymond Carver
0-88001-049-5 ECCO PB $8.95

In Pharoah's Army: Memoirs of the Lost War
In this sequel to his celebrated *This Boy's Life* Wolff gives us an honest and unsparing tour of duty in Vietnam. A paratrooper and Green Beret who survived service in the Mekong Delta, Wolff documents, with biographical exactitude and literary grace, the price of survival
See also **MEMOIRS** under **THE VIETNAM WAR** in **HISTORY OF THE AMERICAS**
0-679-40217-9 KNOPF $23.00

In the Garden of the North American Martyrs
0-88001-245-5 ECCO PB $12.00

The Night in Question: Stories
Wolff is considered by many to be a master of the American short story
0-679-40218-7 KNOPF $23.00

This Boy's Life: A Memoir
The poignant portrait of a boy and his parents upon which the movie with Robert DeNiro is based
0-06-097277-7 HARPERPERENNIAL PB $12.00

Jack **Womack**

Random Acts of Senseless Violence
"With a street-slick future-speak worthy of *A Clockwork Orange* and an unflinching eye for the degeneration of our cities, Womack portrays a relentlessly convincing tomorrow that will leave no reader unmoved"—*Publishers Weekly*
0-8021-3424-6 GROVE PB $12.00

Douglas **Woolf**

Hypocritic Days & Other Tales
0-87685-912-0 BLACK SPARROW $25.00
0-87685-911-2 BLACK SPARROW PB $15.00

On Us
0-87685-284-3 BLACK SPARROW PB $10.00

The Timing Chain
The cross-country odyssey of a writer on the rebound from a soured love affair
0-939180-36-7 TOMBOUCTOU PB $7.00

Wall to Wall
"If you want to re-experience America as it might have been seen by a Smollett, a Sterne, a Fielding, or in places a Cervantes, don't miss *[Wall to Wall]*"—Robert R. Kirsch, *LA Times*
AFTERWORD BY EDWARD DORN
0-916583-06-6 DALKEY ARCHIVE $20.00
0-916583-07-4 DALKEY ARCHIVE PB $7.95

Stephen **Wright**

Going Native
0-374-16490-8 FS&G $22.00
0-385-31386-1 DELTA PB $11.95

M31: A Family Romance
0-385-31524-4 DELTA PB $11.95

Meditations in Green
The corruption and decay of Spec. 4 Griffin, who had planned to glide through the war untouched
See also **LITERATURE: FICTION AND POETRY** under **THE VIETNAM WAR** in **HISTORY OF THE AMERICAS**
0-385-31521-X DELTA PB $11.95

Rudolph **Wurlitzer**

Flats
1-85242-410-9 SERPENT'S TAIL PB $11.99

Nog
1-85242-423-0 SERPENT'S TAIL PB $11.99

Quake
1-85242-409-5 SERPENT'S TAIL PB $10.99

Richard **Yates**

Revolutionary Road
"Richard Yates is among the very truest of American writers. Each of his novels and each story unfalteringly traces our destinies and rescues us from the lost. He sees eye-to-eye with every one of us"—Gina Berriault
0-679-72191-6 VINTAGE PB $13.00

Al **Young**

Sitting Pretty
As the character Sit tells it, his life in and around San Francisco is based on this simple philosophy: "Play all the possibilities and stagger your bets"
0-88739-017-X CREATIVE ARTS PB $8.95

Marguerite **Young**

Miss MacIntosh, My Darling
1-56478-015-5 DALKEY ARCHIVE PB $30.00

Barry **Yourgrau**

The Sadness of Sex
0-385-31376-4 DELTA PB $11.95

Louis **Zukofsky**

Collected Fiction
0-916583-59-7 DALKEY ARCHIVE PB $9.95

New Writers of the '90s

Erica **Abeel**

Women Like Us

Abeel, a contributor to the popular *Hers* column in *The New York Times Magazine*, zeroes in on a group of four undergraduates at Sarah Lawrence College in the late '50s, and follows them through the adventures of marriage, career, "free love," and the feminist revolution

0-395-62150-X TICKNOR & FIELDS $21.95

Pearl **Abraham**

The Romance Reader

Rachel escapes the world of her strict Hasidic family by reading romance novels

1-57322-015-9 PUTNAM $21.95
1-57322-548-7 RIVERHEAD PB $12.00

Karen **Ackerman**

Song and Dance Man

See also **BOOKS FOR AGES FIVE, SIX, AND SEVEN** in **BOOKS FOR YOUNG READERS**

ILLUSTRATED BY STEPHEN GAMMELL

0-394-99330-6 RANDOM HOUSE $15.99

Meena **Alexander**

Nampally Road

0-916515-82-6 MERCURY HOUSE $15.95
0-916515-90-7 MERCURY HOUSE PB $9.95

Sherman **Alexie**

Sherman Alexie was born in Spokane, Washington in 1966. He is a Spokane/Coeur d'Alene Indian from the Spokane Indian Reservation, and is the recipient of grants from the Lila Wallace-Readers Digest Fund and the National Endowment for the Arts. He currently lives in Seattle.

The Business of Fancydancing: Stories and Poems

See also **CONTEMPORARY NATIVE AMERICAN WRITERS** under **NATIVE AMERICAN LITERATURES**
See also **POETRY SINCE 1945** under **20TH-CENTURY AMERICAN POETRY**

0-914610-00-7 HANGING LOOSE PB $10.00

Indian Killer

0-87113-652-X ATLANTIC MONTHLY $22.00

The Lone Ranger and Tonto Fistfight in Heaven

Twenty-two interlocking tales of life set on a Spokane reservation

0-06-097624-1 HARPERPERENNIAL PB $12.50

Reservation Blues

A mythic tale of an all-Indian rock band traveling from reservation bars to Seattle and on to Manhattan. "Does for the American Indian what Richard Wright's *Native Son* did for the Black American in 1940"—*Chicago Tribune*

0-87113-594-9 ATLANTIC MONTHLY $21.00
0-446-67235-1 WARNER PB $12.99

The Summer of Black Widows

1-88241-335-0 HANGING LOOSE $20.00
1-88241-334-2 HANGING LOOSE PB $12.00

Elizabeth **Berg**

The Pull of the Moon

0-679-44972-8 RANDOM HOUSE $21.00

Julia **Alvarez**

"Alvarez writes beautifully....[her] voice is her own, grounded in realism yet alive with the magic of everyday human beings who summon extraordinary courage and determination to fight for their beliefs."— Kirkus Reviews

In the Time of the Butterflies

Alvarez has created a fictional rendering of the tragic deaths of the sisters Mirabel, committed to revolution in the Dominican Republic, assassinated under the brutal Trujillo regime, and now reborn through Alvarez's lyrical fictional talent

See also **OTHER** under **FICTION** under **LATIN AMERICAN LITERATURE**

1-56512-038-8 ALGONQUIN $21.95
0-452-27442-7 PENGUIN PB $11.95

Donald **Antrim**

Elect Mr. Robinson for a Better World

"Entertaining and mischievously imagined...Antrim is a wonderful, truly original writer"—*San Francisco Chronicle*

0-14-023102-1 PENGUIN PB $9.95

The Hundred Brothers

0-517-70310-6 CROWN $20.00

Laura **Argiri**

The God in Flight

"A startling debut, a wildly idiosyncratic gay romance...a welcome successor to the novels of Gordon Merric and Patricia Nell Warren" —*Out Magazine*

0-14-025413-7 PENGUIN PB $12.95

Valerie Townsend **Bayer**

City of Childhood

A densely layered evocation of a Victorian girlhood, revealed by a pair of modern-day researchers. Bayer uses footnotes, quotations, and scholarly sleight-of-hand to penetrate the staid facades of the Forster family, the young heroine, Emma, and her cousins

0-312-06926-X ST. MARTIN'S $19.95

Paul **Beatty**

The White Boy Shuffle

Rap poet and slam champion satirizes race relations in this coming-of-age tale strewn with savvy pop culture winks and nods

0-395-74280-3 HOUGHTON MIFFLIN $19.95

Pinckney **Benedict**

Dogs of God

Set in rural West Virginia, this novel tells the story of Tannhauser, a crazed backwoodsman turned drug lord, and Goody, the young man who innocently stumbles into the company of his malevolent goons

0-385-42022-6 DOUBLEDAY $21.00
0-452-27370-6 PLUME PB $11.95

Talk Before Sleep

"Brilliantly funny...an illumination of some scarcely noticed corners of life in the oncoming glare of death. Berg is one of those rare souls who can play with truths as if swinging across the void from one trapeze to another" —Joan Gould

0-679-43299-X RANDOM HOUSE $18.00
0-440-22109-9 DELL PB $5.99

Lucia **Berlin**

Homesick: New and Selected Stories

A large selection of short stories by one of our best, least known writers

0-87685-816-7 BLACK SPARROW $25.00
0-87685-815-9 BLACK SPARROW PB $13.00

Wilton **Bernhardt**

Gospel

0-312-11924-0 PICADOR PB $15.00

R.C. **Binstock**

Tree of Heaven

Set in 1930s Nanking, the story of the love between a Japanese man and a Chinese woman

1-56947-038-3 SOHO $22.00

Peter **Blauner**

The Intruder

Can a good man go too far to protect his family when a mental patient begins stalking his wife and menacing his children? A New York thriller with headline immediacy

0-684-81094-8 SIMON & SCHUSTER $23.00
0-446-60505-0 WARNER PB $6.99

Amy **Bloom**

Come to Me

Bloom—whose work has appeared in *The Best American Short Stories* collections—brings psychological insight to the often purposely obscured complexities of life in this group of short stories

0-06-099514-9 HARPERPERENNIAL PB $11.00

Love Invents Us

0-679-44109-3 RANDOM HOUSE $21.00

Tom **Bodett**

The Free Fall of Webster Cummings

Cracker-barrel tale follows an Alaskan's adventures in the lower 48 states

0-7868-6209-2 HYPERION $22.95

Cindy **Bonner**

Lily: A Love Story

0-451-40439-4 ONYX PB $4.99

Looking After Lily

In 1880s Texas, when an outlaw is obliged to look after his jailed brother's pregnant wife, he finds, through a series of adventures, that it's becoming harder and harder to tell who's looking after whom. A self-contained sequel to Bonner's first novel, *Lily,* which was a runaway success, garnering prizes and an MGM production. "A finely evoked Texas landscape, a wide variety of mesmerizing and frightful villains, an absorbing story tempered with sweetness and good humor all triumph over...predictability in this romantic western"—*Publishers Weekly*

1-56512-045-0 ALGONQUIN $18.95
0-451-40587-0 SIGNET PB $4.99

The Passion of Dellie O'Barr

1-56512-103-1 ALGONQUIN $18.95

David **Bowman**

Let the Dog Drive

0-14-023724-0 PENGUIN PB $10.95

Duff **Brenna**

The Holy Book of the Beard

0-385-47962-X DOUBLEDAY $24.95

Connie **Briscoe**

Big Girls Don't Cry

A passionate portrayal of an African-American woman's search for purpose. From a solidly middle-class community in the '60s through a shocking personal confrontation between black and white America, Naomi Jefferson tries to negotiate a world whose emotional complexity is exacerbated by politics

0-06-017277-0 HARPERCOLLINS $23.00

Poppy Z. **Brite**

Drawing Blood

0-440-21492-0 DELL PB $5.99

Lost Souls

0-440-21281-2 DELL PB $5.99

Wormwood: A Collection of Short Stories

0-440-21798-9 DELL PB $5.50

Alan **Brown**

Audrey Hepburn's Neck

Clash of Japanese and American cultures as seen through the eyes of young sexual adventurer

0-671-52671-5 POCKET $21.00

John Gregory **Brown**

Decorations in a Ruined Cemetery

0-380-72447-2 AVON PB $11.00

Rebecca **Brown**

The Terrible Girls

"Haunting parables of betrayal and love, of loss and resurrection, of loneliness and solidarity… Brown creates a language of telling that is fiercely beautiful and honest"—Joan Nestle

0-87286-266-6 CITY LIGHTS PB $8.95

Jesse **Browner**

Turnaway

0-679-44788-1 VILLARD $23.00

James **Buchan**

High Latitudes: A Romance

0-374-16999-3 FS&G $25.01

Melvin Jules **Bukiet**

After

0-312-14536-5 ST. MARTIN'S $24.95

Catherine **Bush**

Minus Time

1-85242-408-7 SERPENT'S TAIL PB $12.99

Peter **Cameron**

Andorra

0-374-10505-7 FS&G $42.01

The Weekend

0-452-27411-7 PLUME PB $9.95

Kevin **Canty**

A Stranger in This World: Stories

0-679-76394-5 VINTAGE PB $10.00

Into the Great Wide Open

Emotionally troubled teenagers on the run

0-385-47388-5 DOUBLEDAY $21.95

Caleb **Carr**

The Alienist

A suspensful tale in which the search for the killer of child prostitutes takes the protagonist into the underbelly of early-20th-century New York society. Characters include a fictional Theodore Roosevelt who heads the investigation into the grisly murders

See also **THE '90S** under **THE GREAT FICTION BESTSELLERS 1930-1995** in **POPULAR READING**

0-553-57299-7 BDD PB $7.50

Jan **Carr**

Harem Wish

0-452-27118-5 PLUME PB $9.95

Elena **Castedo**

Paradise

"Ms. Castedo has brought off, with acid wit, the far from easy task of revealing arrogance, folly, injustice, and debauchery through the eyes of an observer who does not know what those qualities are"—*The Atlantic Monthly*

0-8021-3427-0 GROVE PB $13.00

Veronica **Chambers**

Mama's Girl

1-57322-030-2 PUTNAM $22.95

Vikram **Chandra**

Red Earth and Pouring Rain

Chandra creates a contemporary road novel about three college students in America. "Chandra's imagination is of a scale and a richness commensurate with his native India. A splendid novelistic debut"—John Barth

0-316-13276-4 LITTLE, BROWN $24.95

0-316-13293-4 LITTLE, BROWN PB $14.95

Sandra **Cisneros**

The House on Mango Street

The coming-of-age classic about a Latino girl in Chicago from the celebrated Cisneros. "Marvelous…spare yet luminous…The subtle power of Cisneros's storytelling is evident…She communicates all the rapture and rage of growing up in a modern world"
—*San Francisco Chronicle*

See also **YOUNG ADULT FICTION** in **BOOKS FOR YOUNG READERS**

0-679-43335-X KNOPF $21.00

0-679-73477-5 VINTAGE PB $9.00

Woman Hollering Creek and Other Stories

0-679-73856-8 VINTAGE PB $10.00

Joe **Coomer**

The Loop

"Deliciously quirky and perceptive"
—*Publishers Weekly*

0-571-19823-6 FABER PB $10.95

Clarence **Cooper, Jr.**

The Scene

0-393-31463-4 NORTON PB $11.00

Jennifer C. **Cornell**

Departures

Winner of the 14th Drue Heinz Literature Prize, Cornell sets her collection of stories in Belfast, where she explores the emotional and psychological consequences of violence and loss of belief. These are fictions that "seem to contain the heart of each story not in some single line or climactic scene, but in every careful sentence along the way, so that the final image always appears both inevitable and inspired"—Alice McDermott

0-8229-3855-3 PITTSBURGH $22.50

Douglas **Coupland**

Generation X: Tales for an Accelerated Culture

The book that defined the consumers of "McCulture" also served to saddle this youthful demographic with the most overused generational monicker since "baby-boomers." "Captures the listlessness that accompanies growing up in today's information-laden culture"—*Rolling Stone*

0-312-11814-7 ST. MARTIN'S $23.95

0-312-05436-X ST. MARTIN'S PB $13.95

Life After God

0-671-87434-9 POCKET PB $8.00

Microserfs

A group of Microsoft employees decides to turn off and tune out

0-06-039148-0 HARPERCOLLINS $21.00

Polaroids from the Dead

0-06-039149-9 HARPERCOLLINS $18.00

Shampoo Planet

0-671-75506-4 POCKET PB $14.00

Michael **Cunningham**

Flesh and Blood

Four generations of a Greek family travel from the past to the present in a novel about love, violence, and the changes wrought by time

0-374-18113-6 HILL & WANG $22.00

0-684-87431-8 SCRIBNERS PB $13.00

Michael Cunningham (photo by Sigrid Estrada)

Home at the End of the World

0-374-17250-1 FS&G $18.95

Susan **Daitch**

Storytown: Stories

Fifteen unsettling and tantalizing stories infused with a "downtown aesthetic" and a vivid historical imagination. "It is always a delight to discover a new voice as strong as Susan Daitch's" —Salman Rushdie. "Susan Daitch is a marvelous writer…I can't think of anyone else writing today who offers such proportionate measures of elan, erudition, and humor"—Mark Leyner

1-56478-094-5 DALKEY ARCHIVE PB $12.95

See your favorite characters come to life, billboards along the highway read. As a child Alice loved being taken to Storytown. Although she looked forward to each trip, when they actually arrived the park often turned out to be less wonderful than advertised.

STORYTOWN: STORIES

Edwidge **Danticat**

Breath, Eyes, Memory

From the much celebrated Haitian-American novelist comes "a lovely, poetic tale about loss and self discovery"—*The Bloomsbury Review*

See also CARIBBEAN LITERATURE

1-56947-005-7 SOHO $20.00
0-679-75661-2 VINTAGE PB $11.00

Krik? Krak!: Stories

From National Book Award-winning Danticat, intimate histories of Haitians and African Americans

1-56947-025-1 SOHO $20.00
0-679-76657-X RANDOM HOUSE PB $11.00

Diana **Darling**

The Painted Alphabet

"A vastly entertaining story, told with warmth, humor, and wisdom"—*NY Times Book Review*

0-395-59350-6 HOUGHTON MIFFLIN $19.95
1-555-9721-4 GRAY WOLF PB $12.00

Dayu Datu launched herself into the night sky on a scream of curses and grief, causing queer tides, earth tremors, power failures, viruses, landslides, traffic accidents, earaches, fat fires, miscarriages, an inexplicable proliferation of mosquitoes, and the disgorging from the earth of such a variety of stinging and flying ants that simple people everywhere said, "Witches."

THE PAINTED ALPHABET

1-55597-214-4 GRAY WOLF PB $12.00

Eric **Darton**

Free City

In this stylistic tour de force set in a European city like Antwerp in the 1660s, a polymath inventor and a ruthless merchant engage in devious political machinations

0-393-03980-3 NORTON $18.00

Carol **Dawson**

Body of Knowledge

0-671-53572-2 WASHINGTON SQUARE PB $12.00

Terri **de la Pena**

Latin Satins

"Brave writing…"—Alma Luz Villanueva

1-87806-752-4 SEAL PB $10.95

Junot **Diaz**

Drown

1-57322-041-8 PUTNAM $21.95
0-679-77657-5 VINTAGE $11.00

Irene **Dische**

Strange Traffic: Stories

An affluent American Jew returns to claim his patrimony in Germany. A homosexual restaurateur cooks a last meal for his first lover. A Viennese scientist in New York is haunted by ghosts from his past. Defectors, tourists, and travelers people Dische's stories—which have appeared in *New Yorker* and *The Nation*. "Irene Dische is an artist, a damned good writer, one of the very best now writing in English"—Harold Brodkey

0-8050-4172-9 HOLT $22.50

Melvin **Dixon**

Trouble the Water

This poet's first novel digs into the old wounds of African Americans' past in the South. "Melvin Dixon is a strong, new voice that at once charms and terrifies"—Maxine Hong Kingston

0-671-74187-X POCKET PB $8.00

Michael **Drinkard**

Disobedience

Drinkard delivers an apocalyptic comedy of a Californian family spanning five generations. Hilarious, innovative prose from *the* chronicler of Southern Californian lifestyle

0-393-03478-X NORTON $21.95

Tom **Drury**

The End of Vandalism

Eleven consecutive chapters of Drury's first novel were printed in *New Yorker* before its publication as a book, *The End of Vandalism* is "a brilliant, wonderfully funny novel about two men and a woman, in a place very like Iowa. It's hard to think of any novel—let alone a first novel—in which you can hear the people so well. This is indeed deadpan humor, and Tom Drury is its master"—Annie Dillard

0-395-62151-8 HOUGHTON MIFFLIN $21.95
0-449-90982-4 FAWCETT PB $11.00

Rikki **Ducornet**

Rikki Ducornet was born in New York, attended Bard College, and after living in North Africa, Canada, and France for many years now lives in Colorado, where she teaches creative writing at the University of Denver.

The Complete Butcher's Tales

1-56478-043-0 DALKEY ARCHIVE $19.95

Entering Fire

0-87286-207-0 CITY LIGHTS PB $6.95

The Fountains of Neptune

0-916583-96-1 DALKEY ARCHIVE $19.95

The Jade Cabinet

1-56478-031-7 DALKEY ARCHIVE PB $9.95

Phosphor in Dreamland

Set on the imaginary Caribbean island of Birdland, this novel takes the form of a series of letters about the island's history. The letters tell a story both dark and comic, ranging from the Inquisition to the modern extinction of the island's exotic fauna. Along the way a timeless yet modern love story is told in this complex and compelling meditation on power, creativity, and eroticism

1-56478-084-8 DALKEY ARCHIVE PB $12.95

The Stain

1-56478-085-6 DALKEY ARCHIVE PB $11.95

John **Dufresne**

Louisiana Power & Light

0-393-03648-0 NORTON $22.00
0-452-27502-4 PLUME PB $11.95

Tony **Earley**

Here We Are in Paradise: Stories

Earley, a North Carolinian journalist whose stories have appeared in *Harper's* and *Triquarterly*, offers a powerful collection of short stories from the modern South. From Charlotte to Gettysburg, from big cities to mountain hollows, Earley's extraordinary sense of place mixes with his deep understanding of the mysteries of human affairs, establishing him as foremost among today's Southern writers.

0-316-19962-1 LITTLE, BROWN $19.95

Louis **Edwards**

Ten Seconds

1-55597-150-4 GRAY WOLF PB $8.95

Jennifer **Egan**

Emerald City: Stories

0-385-48212-4 DOUBLEDAY $22.50

Barbara **Einzig**

"Einzig has invented another kind of novel—a novel which might also be read as a serial poem, travel journal, or philosophical investigation" —Geoffrey O'Brien

Distance Without Distance

0-932716-34-2 KELSEY ST. PB $10.00

Jeffrey **Eugenides**

The Virgin Suicides

Eugenides, who has received a Whiting Award, a Guggenheim Fellowship, and an NEA Fellowship, published this, his first novel, to tremendous acclaim. Mysterious and tragic, it is a provocative and wickedly funny story of five fatally doomed sisters

0-374-28438-5 FS&G $18.00
0-446-67025-1 WARNER PB $11.99

Eurydice

F/32

1-56333-350-3 MASQUERADE PB $10.95

Welch **Everman**

The Harry and Sylvia Stories

Harry loves Sylvia. Harry loses Sylvia. Lonely Harry names his parakeet Sylvia, his dog Sylvia, his prostitute Sylvia. But the dog bites the prostitute and they both run away. 13 stories

1-55713-052-3 SUN & MOON PB $12.95

Christopher John **Farley**

My Favorite War

0-374-21696-7 FS&G $20.00

Jonathan **Franzen**

Strong Motion

0-393-30996-7 NORTON PB $10.95

The Twenty-Seventh City

An imaginative novel set in St. Louis, where the newly appointed chief of police, a woman from Bombay, becomes involved in a political conspiracy

0-374-27972-1 FS&G $19.95

Jamie **Fuller**

The Diary of Emily Dickinson

Fuller blends fact and fiction to invent a diary of Emily Dickinson as convincing as—and perhaps more revealing than—the real thing

1-56279-048-X MERCURY HOUSE......$18.00
0-312-14586-1 ST. MARTIN'S......$10.95

Christina **Garcia**

Dreaming in Cuban

"Dazzling…Remarkable…Garcia stands revealed as a magical new writer….Fierce, visionary…completely original"
—Michiko Kakutani, *NY Times Book Review*

0-345-38143-2 BALLANTINE PB......$10.00

Kaye **Gibbons**

Charms for the Easy Life

0-380-72557-6 AVON PB......$12.00

A Cure for Dreams

0-679-73672-7 VINTAGE PB......$10.00

Ellen Foster

0-912697-52-0 ALGONQUIN......$14.95
0-679-72866-X VINTAGE PB......$9.00

Sights Unseen

0-380-72681-5 AVON PB......$6.99

A Virtuous Woman

0-945575-09-2 ALGONQUIN......$13.95
0-679-72844-9 VINTAGE PB......$9.00

Dagoberto **Gilb**

The Magic of Blood

0-8263-1436-8 NEW MEXICO......$24.95
0-8021-3399-1 ATLANTIC MONTHLY PB......$12.00

Francisco **Goldman**

The Long Night of White Chickens

0-8711-3541-8 ANTLANTIC MONTHLY PB......$12.00

Jeff **Gomez**

Our Noise

0-684-80099-3 SCRIBNERS PB......$12.00

Brad **Gooch**

The Golden Age of Promiscuity

Set in the gay club scene of New York in the '70s, Gooch's novel brilliantly captures the lifestyle and voice of a time long gone. Gooch constructs an erotic and fascinating narrative telling the story of one man's ambition in a cityscape of drugs and decadence

0-679-44708-3 KNOPF......$24.00

Allegra **Goodman**

The Family Markowitz

0-374-15321-3 FS&G......$22.00

Howard **Gordon**

The African in Me

Self-segregation on playgrounds at recess, divided families, and college students struggling with the vicissitudes of racism, "this book affectingly depicts black life in upstate New York over the past four decades"—*Publishers Weekly*

0-8076-1296-0 BRAZILLER......$19.95

Neil **Gordon**

Sacrifice of Isaac

When the son of a recently dead Israeli statesman sets out to find his brother in Paris, he becomes embroiled in a criminal and murderous world

0-679-43704-5 RANDOM HOUSE......$22.00

Stephanie **Grant**

The Passion of Alice

0-395-75518-2 HOUGHTON MIFFLIN......$19.95

Paul **Griner**

Follow Me

"His range of subject and technique are extraordinary. Patient, complex explorations of family life, flinty 'fabliaux noir,' stories about doctors and artists and outlaws, all told with with conviction and velocity"

0-679-44845-4 RANDOM HOUSE......$23.00

Kirsty **Gunn**

Rain

Luminous and sensuous prose by a writer who the London *Sunday Times* calls "a new author of undeniable talent"

0-87113-592-2 ATLANTIC MONTHLY......$15.00
0-8021-3447-5 GROVE PB......$10.00

David **Guterson**

The Country Ahead of Us,The Country Behind: Stories

"Guterson's tales are hard-won, stunning testimonials to the fact that unerring devotion to character and emotional honesty are at the very heart of memorable literature"
—Charles Johnson

0-679-76718-5 VINTAGE PB......$11.00

Snow Falling on Cedars

A surprise and unusually literate bestseller, Guterson's first novel was awarded the 1995 PEN/Faulkner Award for Fiction. Opening with a murder trial in a small town, Guterson constructs an innovative literary mystery in which compelling and complex suspense plotting allows entrance into a moral universe of character and motivation. "*Snow Falling on Cedars* is more than a mere murder mystery. It is so rich in its examination of the dark realities of jealousy, rage and racism that it's unfair to shackle it with a label. Much better to say that this is also a mystery, one which happens to be among the most insightful novels I've come across in years"—David Dawson

0-15-100100-6 HARCOURT BRACE......$21.95

Jane **Hamilton**

The Book of Ruth

0-385-26570-0 ANCHOR PB......$9.95

A Map of the World

0-385-47310-9 DOUBLEDAY......$22.00
0-385-47311-7 ANCHOR PB......$12.00

Brooks **Hansen**

The Chess Garden Or, The Twilight Letters of Gustav Uyterhoeven

0-374-16015-5 FS&G......$23.00
1-57322-563-0 RIVERHEAD PB......$14.00

Ron **Hansen**

Mariette in Ecstasy

An unusual examination of the inner life of a religious contemplative

0-06-092711-9 HARPERCOLLINS PB......$11.00

Kathryn **Harrison**

Poison

A story of two young women—one a silk-grower's daughter, one a queen—living in the poisonous atmosphere of the Spanish Inquisition. One is jailed under accusation of witchcraft; the other is under attack for failing to produce a royal heir. Between them, Harrison weaves a luminous tale of passion, punishment, and love

0-679-43140-3 RANDOM HOUSE......$23.00
0-380-72741-2 AVON PB......$12.00

David **Haynes**

Heathens

0-89823-166-3 NEW RIVERS......$21.95

Live at Five

A hilarious fictional media circus that focuses on class, color, and the American obsession with TV, was noted by *Publishers Weekly* for its "authentic characters, crisp dialogue, and brisk narration." *Booklist* writes that "Haynes' earlier novels...portray African American, middle-class family life. Here, he moves into a larger social arena, but without sacrificing his characters...A charming, intelligent, and significant comedy regarding the gap between image and reality"

1-57131-009-6 MILKWEED......$21.95

Right by My Side

0-89823-147-7 NEW RIVERS PB......$12.95

Somebody Else's Mama

0-15-600408-9 HARCOURT BRACE PB......$13.00

David **Hays** & Daniel **Hays**

My Old Man and The Sea

0-7862-0600-4 GK HALL......$24.95
0-06-097696-9 HARPERCOLLINS......$10.00

Julie **Hecht**

Do the Windows Open: And Other Inquiries

Readers of *The New Yorker* have been enjoying excerpts of Hecht's delightful novel for several years. Now a wider audience will be exposed to the quotidianly absurd exploits of a photographer who searches in vain for her elusive subjects: organically grown vegetables, a floorman who isn't intoxicated, and a bus with windows that open

0-679-45201-X RANDOM HOUSE......$21.00

Richard **Hell**

Go Now

A novel from the former punk rocker

0-684-82234-2 SCRIBNERS......$18.00

Robin **Hemley**

All You Can Eat: Stories

0-87113-261-3 ATLANTIC MONTHLY PB......$7.95

The Big Ear: Stories

0-89587-128-9 BLAIR......$18.95

The Last Studebaker

1-55597-200-4 GRAY WOLF PB......$12.00

A.M. **Homes**

The End of Alice

0-684-81528-1 SCRIBNERS $22.00
0-684-82710-7 SCRIBNERS PB $11.00

In a Country of Mothers

Explores the overlapping and profound relationships between mothers, daughters, therapists, and patients

0-679-74243-3 VINTAGE PB $12.00

Jack

A teenage boy must come to terms with his parents' divorce and his father's homosexuality. "Jack is such an engaging, attractive human being, it's a pleasure to believe in him" —David Foster Wallace

0-679-73221-7 VINTAGE PB $11.00

The Safety of Objects

0-679-73629-8 VINTAGE PB $11.00

Michael **Hornburg**

Bongwater

Under the low gray skies of Portland, Oregon, neo-Beats live and love in a demimonde of abandoned expectations and esoteric longings. The underworld that influenced all America with Nirvana, Pearl Jam, and Gus Van Sant, and became prevalent enough to put a style, "grunge," into the fashion spreads of *Vogue*

0-8021-1510-1 GROVE $17.00
0-8021-3456-4 GROVE PB $11.00

Deborah **Iida**

Middle Son

1-56512-119-8 WORKMAN $18.95

Gary **Indiana**

Gone Tomorrow

1-85242-336-6 SERPENT'S TAIL PB $11.99

Rent Boy

A hilarious, hardcore Indiana romp through the obsessive underside of New York with a beautiful—and all too obtainable—object of desire

1-85242-324-2 SERPENT'S TAIL PB $10.99

Susan **Isaacs**

Lily White

Set on Long Island, and peopled with con artists, lawyers, and lovers, this funny and poignant novel twists and turns its way through a story about social mobility, family, and betrayal

0-06-017607-5 HARPERCOLLINS $25.00

Michael Grant **Jaffe**

Dance Real Slow

0-374-13466-9 FS&G $20.00

Darius **James**

Negrophobia: An Urban Parable

"I was charmed, horrified…dazzled by the manic energy upholding this book from beginning to end"—*LA Times*. "With its feet firmly planted in the satiric tradition of Voltaire [and] John Kennedy Toole…James's book is both timely and necessary"—*VLS*

0-8065-1293-8 CITADEL $15.95

Kelvin Christopher **James**

Fling with a Demon Lover

James offers a story about a thirtysomething schoolteacher who meets a man 15 years her junior. An innocent fling, she thinks, under her control. But when, on a Greek island, she surrenders to her lover's temptation, she finds that her affair has a dark side and a complicated one that is spinning out of control

0-06-017350-5 HARPERCOLLINS $22.00

Kelvin Christopher James

Secrets

0-679-75546-2 VINTAGE PB $10.00

Gish **Jen**

Mona in the Promised Land

Gish Jen sets her novel in 1968, the dawn of the age of ethnicity. In Scarshill, New York, the Chang family is getting used to a new social landscape, and a new political world. An audacious, enthralling, and important new book by an emerging American voice

0-679-44589-7 KNOPF $24.00

Typical American

0-452-26774-9 PLUME PB $11.95

Matthew F. **Jones**

A Single Shot

0-374-26465-1 FS&G $22.00

Thom **Jones**

Cold Snap: Stories

"A striking, idiosyncratic gathering of stories...Reading Thom Jones's fiction is like speeding in an open car: the landscape blurs, the momentum is intoxicating" —Joyce Carol Oates, *NY Times Book Review*

0-316-47307-3 LITTLE, BROWN $19.95
0-316-47257-3 LITTLE, BROWN PB $10.95

The Pugilist at Rest

The references in these vivid stories of real, hard-bitten Americans range from rock 'n' roll to Schopenhauer, from Dostoevsky to Joe Louis. "One might have to reach back to Raymond Carver's *Will You Please Be Quiet, Please?* to find a debut collection that is so compelling and original"—*Publishers Weekly*

0-316-47302-2 LITTLE, BROWN $18.95
0-316-47304-9 LITTLE, BROWN PB $9.95

Elaine **Kagan**

Blue Heaven

0-679-43598-0 KNOPF $24.00

Susanna **Kaysen**

Asa, As I Knew Him

0-679-75377-X VINTAGE PB $12.00

Far Afield

0-679-75376-1 VINTAGE PB $12.00

John **Keene**

Annotations

An experimental novel about growing up in St. Louis. "These poetic meditations about private lives and public events are brilliant, polished and of considerable depth"—Ishmael Reed

0-811-21304-8 NEW DIRECTIONS PB $8.95

Randall **Kenan**

Let the Dead Bury Their Dead

0-15-650515-0 HARCOURT BRACE PB $11.00

A Visitation of Spirits: A Novel

0-385-41505-2 ANCHOR PB $11.00

Pagan **Kennedy**

Spinsters

1-85242-405-2 SERPENT'S TAIL PB $12.99

Binnie **Kirshenbaum**

A Disturbance in One Place

0-88064-164-9 FROMM PB $9.00

Brian **Kiteley**

I Know Many Songs, But I Cannot Sing

0-684-80905-2 SIMON & SCHUSTER $20.00

Still Life with Insects

1-55597-189-X GRAY WOLF PB $8.00

Kathe **Koja**

Kink

Sexual triangle set in seedy downtown nightclubs and the art scene

0-8050-4391-8 HOLT $23.00

Strange Angels

0-440-21498-X DELL PB $5.50

Allen **Kurzweil**

A Case of Curiosities

Nominated for both the Aer Lingus Prize and the Prix Medicis, and winner of the Premio Grinzane Cavour, this debut novel was described by Simon Schama as "an extraordinary and gripping work of the historical imagination, a novel of immense originality and creative power...It lives, breathes, and thinks the eighteenth century, especially the machine-obsessed world of the Enlightenment, but it re-creates this world in writing designed for the sensibillity of our own times. No one who opens *A Case of Curiosities* is likely to close it again unaffected by the ingenuity of its craft and the beauty of its writing"

0-345-38057-6 BALLANTINE PB $10.00

Frank **Lentricchia**

Johnny Critelli

0-684-81408-0 SCRIBNERS $21.00

Chang-rae **Lee**

Native Speaker

"Chang-rae Lee has composed a moving edgy new blues. His talent, compassion, and wisdom light up these pages, which are nothing less than brilliant"—Frederick Busch

1-57322-001-9 PUTNAM $22.95
1-57322-531-2 RIVERHEAD PB $12.00

Jonathan **Lethem**

Amnesia Moon

0-15-100091-3 HARCOURT BRACE $20.00
0-312-86220-2 ST. MARTIN'S PB $12.95

Jonathan **Lethem**

Gun, With Occasional Music

An original blend of science fiction and noir-ish detective fiction. "A brilliant postmodern romp"—James Morrow

0-312-85878-7 TOR PB $10.95

The Wall of the Sky, The Wall of the Eye: Seven Stories

0-151-00180-4 HARCOURT BRACE $23.00

Heather **Lewis**

House Rules

1-85242-413-3 SERPENT'S TAIL PB $12.99

Jim **Lewis**

Sister

1-55597-178-4 GRAY WOLF $20.00

Lewis **Libby**

The Apprentice

A group of strangers finds refuge from a blizzard in a mountain inn in northern Japan. "*The Apprentice* is a timeless tale of love, greed, and violence reminiscent of a Kurosawa film. A striking—utterly unusual—elegant novel" —Howard Norman

1-55597-245-4 GRAY WOLF $22.95

Alan **Lightman**

Einstein's Dreams

A re-creation of Einstein's discovery of the nature of time which "pulls the reader into a dream world like a powerful magnet"—*NY Times*

0-446-67011-1 WARNER PB $8.99

Good Benito

0-446-67160-6 WARNER PB $8.99

Michael **Lind**

Powertown: A Novel

0-06-017510-9 HARPERCOLLINS $23.00

Ralph **Lombreglia**

Men Under Water: Short Stories

0-671-73260-9 WASHINGTON SQUARE PB $7.95

Renee **Manfredi**

Where Love Leaves Us

0-87745-444-2 IOWA $22.95

Ben **Marcus**

The Age of Wire and String: Stories

0-679-42660-4 KNOPF $21.00

J. S. **Marcus**

The Captain's Fire

0-679-40184-9 KNOPF $24.00

Lee **Martin**

The Least You Need to Know: Stories

Winner of the 1995 Mary McCarthy Prize in Short Fiction. "Lee Martin's world is one of love gone true and astray, of power felt and misused and foolishly courted, and of forgiveness and the exhausting efforts toward happiness we cannot help making"—Amy Bloom

FOREWORD BY AMY BLOOM

0-9641151-3-1 SARABANDE PB $13.95

Jonathan **Maslow**

Torrid Zone: Seven Stories of the Gulf Coast

The peripatetic and erudite Guggenheim Fellow offers a collection of short stories unified by location—the Gulf Coast—and broad in scope: the 16th century to the present. We meet a one-legged Vietnam vet; an African slave; a famous pirate; and a Crystal Springs mermaid. A hilarious, touching, and erudite fictionalization of a vivid American locale

0-679-40876-2 RANDOM HOUSE $25.00

Carole **Maso**

The American Woman in the Chinese Hat

1-56478-045-7 DALKEY ARCHIVE $19.95
0-452-27507-5 PLUME PB $10.95

The Art Lover

0-88001-410-5 ECCO PB $13.00

Aureole

0-88001-482-2 ECCO $21.00

Ava

1-56478-029-5 DALKEY ARCHIVE $19.95
1-56478-074-0 DALKEY ARCHIVE PB $12.95

Ghost Dance

0-88001-409-1 ECCO PB $13.00

Elizabeth **McCracken**

Here's Your Hat, What's Your Hurry

"Maybe you wonder how a Jewish girl from Des Moines got a Jesus Christ tattooed on her three times...It wasn't religion that put them there: it was Tiny, my husband. I have a Buddha round back too. He was going to give me Moses parting the Red Sea, but I was running out of space." So McCracken introduces her offbeat, entirely original fictive voice in her first collection of short stories. Named a Notable Book of the Year in 1994 by the American Library Association, McCracken's novel introduces an imaginative universe in a unique and innovative contribution to American letters

0-679-40026-5 TURTLE BAY $20.00

T.M. **McNally**

Low Flying Aircraft

A collection of stories about a group of interconnected characters that won the prestigious Flannery O'Connor Prize

0-8203-1378-5 GEORGIA $17.95

Gita **Mehta**

Raj

See also **INDIAN LITERATURE IN ENGLISH** under **LITERATURES OF INDIA** in **LITERATURE OF EUROPE, AFRICA, AND ASIA**

0-449-90566-7 FAWCETT PB $12.50

Jane **Mendelsohn**

I Was Amelia Earhart

This fictional retelling of the famous aviator's life was propelled onto the bestseller list by Don Imus's on-the-air raves

0-679-45054-8 KNOPF $18.00
0-679-77636-2 VINTAGE $10.00

Claire **Messud**

When the World Was Steady

The story of two middle-aged sisters and the divergent paths of their lives. "Messud's technical hand is so sure, her psychological wisdom so ripe, her narrative so canny, that one imagines the ghosts of E.M. Forster and Barbara Pym somehow still at work, resident in a new generation"—Cynthia Ozick

0-9645611-0-7 GRANTA $19.95
0-9645611-3-1 GRANTA PB $9.95

Virginia tried to imagine what it would be to have such freedom, to glance across even such a modest expanse and know everything was in its place because she had put it there herself. Not only her body but her spirit would have run of the house, without being answerable to her mother, a lame, difficult old woman whose personality seemed to stretch by force of will into the corners of the London flat where her legs now refused to take her.

WHEN THE WORLD WAS STEADY

Jane **Miller**

August Zero

Winner of the Western States Book Award, *August Zero* is a movingly tender love story that takes place against a harsh, apocalyptic *fin de siècle* backdrop. "With skillful, irrepressible imagination, Jane Miller has written an intelligent, imaginative and evocative book about love. True in both thought and description, *August Zero* carries the author's sustained vision and intelligence from beginning to end" —Judges' Citation, Western States Book Awards

1-55659-060-1 COPPER CANYON $22.00
1-55659-061-X COPPER CANYON PB $11.00

Don't get me wrong, there's still a knowledge of freedom, a bath, a change of clothing, possession of a child's heart, a handshake, and the function of time, a detail—even in air language is a cross between an appetite and a mouth.

AUGUST ZERO

Lydia **Millet**

Omnivores

A father turns his home into an armed camp and secedes from the United States in this boisterous satire of American life, and especially the American male

1-56512-089-2 WORKMAN $17.95

Rick **Moody**

Garden State

Winner of Pushcart's Tenth Annual Editors' Book Award. "Extraordinary!...The ironies here are subtle, violent, terrifying and beautiful" —John Hawkes

0-916366-00-6 NORTON PB $15.00

The Ice Storm

Growing up suburban and dysfunctional in the '70s: a widely acclaimed portrait of a generation

0-316-57921-1 LITTLE, BROWN $19.95
0-446-67148-7 WARNER PB $10.99

The Ring of Brightest Angels Around Heaven: A Novella and Stories

The drug world of 1980s New York; the unhinging mind of an undergraduate who discovers that the Book of Revelations was written about him; an investigator spying on his wife. Moody offers 10 stories and a novella

0-316-57929-7 LITTLE, BROWN $21.95
0-446-67240-8 WARNER PB $11.99

Lorrie **Moore**

Anagrams

0-14-010328-7 PENGUIN PB $11.95

Like Life: Stories

0-452-26637-8 PLUME PB $10.95

Who Will Run the Frog Hospital?

Moore's work, which has appeared in *The New Yorker, Best American Short Stories*, and *Prize Stories: The O. Henry Award*, has garnered fellowships from the NEA and the Guggenheim Foundation. *Who Will Run the Frog Hospital?* is a story, told in retrospect, of a young girl working in an upstate New York amusement park, and learning life lessons of friendship and adulthood. "Exhilarating"—*NY Times Book Review,* "Funny and scalpel-sharp"—Jay McInerney, "She's a dazzler"—*Chicago Tribune*

0-679-43482-8 KNOPF $20.00
0-446-67191-6 WARNER PB $11.99

Frank **Moorhouse**

Grand Days

0-679-43362-7 PANTHEON $25.00

Seth **Morgan**

Homeboy

A violent, often hilarious, always original novel of the lower depths of San Francisco's criminal scene

0-394-57577-6 RANDOM HOUSE $19.95

Bill **Morrissey**

Edson

Well-known folk singer chronicles life in a decaying New England milltown

0-679-44629-X KNOPF $23.00

Walter **Mosley**

A Little Yellow Dog

The reluctant detective and natural existentialist Easy Rawlins returns in a new volume of Mosley's preeminent contribution to American crime writing. With signature suspense, style, and social observation, Mosley takes us to Watts, 1964, and a timeless tale of murder, investigation, and revenge

See also **HARD-BOILED DETECTIVES** under **CRIME FICTION TODAY** under **CRIME FICTION** in **POPULAR READING**

0-393-03924-2 NORTON $23.00

RL's Dream

In detective writer Mosley's first "non-genre" novel, aging bluesman Soupspoon Wise is dying in New York. Kiki Waters, a white Southerner, takes him in. Their story is one of pain and redemption

0-393-03802-5 NORTON $22.00
0-671-88428-X WASHINGTON SQUARE PB $12.00

Jess **Mowry**

Way Past Cool

Set in the violent urban streets of Oakland, this is a telling depiction of the fight for survival of young black men. "[Mowry] captures the strange mix of childishness and nihilism that the 1980s produced in so many young people" —*NY Times Book Review*

0-374-28669-8 FS&G $17.00

Elias Miguel **Munoz**

Crazy Love

An experimental novel reflecting the mosaic of Cuban-American culture

0-934770-83-2 ARTE PUBLICO PB $9.50

Eileen **Myles**

Chelsea Girls

A gritty, tender, and accomplished collection of stories by the popular poet dramatizes her '60s adolescence and '70s maturation as a writer. Drugs with Ted Berrigan, posing for Mapplethorpe, cruising for lesbian lovers: in stark, electrifying prose Myles brings a tough childhood and precarious adult urban existence to life

0-87685-933-3 BLACK SPARROW $25.00
0-87685-932-5 BLACK SPARROW PB $14.00

Lawrence **Naumoff**

Silk Hope, N.C.

When two sisters inherit their family house in Silk Hope they are forced to decide what exactly the house means to them

0-15-188900-7 HARCOURT BRACE $21.95
0-15-600207-8 HARVEST PB $11.00

Taller Women: A Cautionary Tale

"Naumoff creates a new genre—call it if you like the new male fiction of feeling. He is so funny, so clever, so disturbing, so un-put-downable about men and women [that] he seems, in *Taller Women,* to be summing up the fictional achievements of the last thirty years. His characters move in a nighmarish world (well, hasn't it so become?) yet run, jump, suffer, respond so vividly they quite give us hope for the next millennium, fictional and otherwise" —Fay Weldon

0-15-187991-5 HARCOURT BRACE $21.95
0-15-688162-4 HARVEST PB $10.95

At the moment Monroe was ready to unlock his front door, the girl next door called to him, and then fell in the grass, and a dog, coming from down the street, turned around, and went home.

Had the girl not yelled, Monroe would not have noticed her, because he had been lost in thought about how nice it would be to live with a woman who did not later turn out to be crazy, or sad, or depressed, or desperate, and in the middle of this, he saw the girl's legs fold up in the same helpless way his had when Lydia threw the rock at him.

TALLER WOMEN: A CAUTIONARY TALE

Fae Myenne **Ng**

Bone

Set in San Francisco's Chinatown, *Bone* chronicles the inextricably entangled lives of the Leong family as it explores the myths that pervade Chinese-American culture. "Tough and real, *Bone* marks the debut of a writer whose literary skills are fantastic"—Ishmael Reed

1-56282-944-0 HYPERION $19.95
0-06-097592-X HARPERPERENNIAL PB $11.50

William **Norwich**

Learning to Drive

Editor-at-large for *Vogue* and sharp commentator on contemporary life, Norwich offers the story of a fashion magazine staff member in the fabulous kaleidoscope of New York in the '80s. When he takes time out from his hectic schedule to visit his parents grave in Connecticut, he launches himself on a nightmare series of events. A dark satire of contemporary urban life (by one of its aficionados) and a moving examination of family and the loss of childhood

0-87113-631-7 ATLANTIC MONTHLY $22.00

Sigrid **Nunez**

Naked Sleeper

0-06-017276-2 HARPERCOLLINS $23.00

Robert **O'Connor**

Buffalo Soldiers

Specialist 4th Class Ray Elwood of "the fighting 57th" stationed in Germany writes requisition memos for his commanding officer, and sidelines in selling heroin and anything that might happen to fall off a truck

0-679-74203-4 VINTAGE PB $13.00

Mark **O'Donnell**

Getting over Homer

0-679-44590-0 KNOPF $21.00

Vertigo Park and Other Tall Tales

0-312-11363-3 ST. MARTIN'S PB $9.95

Chris **Offutt**

Kentucky Straight

A native of the Appalachian mountains of Eastern Kentucky, Offutt spent 10 years traveling and working over 50 jobs, including that of a circus hand, before publishing his first short story collection. He brings to his work a gift for hard-edged prose and the sort of rough-and-tumble dialogue that rings resoundingly true. "These are wild, tough, magical stories, often as shocking as real life, and every one a heartbreaker"—Josephine Humphreys

0-679-73886-X VINTAGE PB $12.00

Stewart **O'Nan**

O'Nan holds not only an MFA in fiction from Cornell but also a BS in Aerospace Engineering, and has worked on several projects for Grumman, including the Space Shuttle.

The Names of the Dead

A 30-year-old man living in upstate New York confronts his memories of Vietnam while enduring a myriad of family troubles. Add in a stalker from his Vietnam support group and the result is a gripping narrative that is at once thrilling and literary

See also **LITERATURE: FICTION AND POETRY** under **THE VIETNAM WAR** in **HISTORY OF THE AMERICAS**

0-385-48192-6 DOUBLEDAY $23.95

Snow Angels

A first novel of tremendous power and originality about the 15th year of Arty Parkinson's life in western Pennsylvania, when the murder of a baby-sitter and the breakup of his family draw the boy into a dark vortex of adulthood

0-14-025096-4 PENGUIN PB........$10.95

Steward O'Nan (photo by Dede Hatch)

Michael **Parker**

The Geographical Cure: Novellas and Stories

0-14-024390-9 PENGUIN PB........$10.95

Ann **Patchett**

The Patron Saint of Liars

0-8041-1151-0 IVY PB........$5.99

Taft

Father and son musicians in Memphis, Tennessee

0-8041-1388-2 IVY PB........$5.99

Jim **Paul**

Medieval in LA: A Fiction

1-88717-815-5 COUNTERPOINT........$21.00

Dale **Peck**

The Law of Enclosures

0-374-18419-4 FS&G........$23.00

Martin and John

An innovatively constructed novel of gay love, gay death, and the narrator's belief that "every fiction is opposed to some truth." "Dale Peck has written a powerful first novel, a book to be read not only for its promise of an impressive career, but also for its own stark and violet beauties" —Mona Simpson, *Chicago Tribune*

0-06-097588-1 HARPERPERENNIAL PB........$12.00

Fred **Pfeil**

What They Tell You to Forget: A Novella and Stories

Short story collection is winner of 1996 Editors Book Award

0-916366-49-9 PUSHCART........$25.00

Kate **Phillips**

White Rabbit

Minute-by-minute account of the very last day of a cantankerous 88-year-old woman

0-395-74285-4 DORLING KINDERSLEY........$21.95

Tom **Piazza**

Blues and Trouble: Twelve Stories

"Piazza is throwing his hat in the ring where *In Our Time* did its timeless tricks, or where *Go Down Moses* went for broke"—Stanley Crouch

0-312-13934-9 ST. MARTIN'S........$21.95

Felice **Picano**

Like People in History

"This is the big novel we've all been waiting for—the gay *Gone with the Wind*"—Edmund White

0-14-024525-1 PENGUIN PB........$12.95

Darryl **Pinckney**

High Cotton

A young black man's growing up in Midwestern America. "Pinckney has dared to treat his theme with excruciating honesty and the total freedom from restraint that Schiller said we find nowhere else but in authentic works of art"—*NY Times Book Review*

0-374-16998-5 FS&G........$21.00

Patricia **Powell**

Me Dying Trial

0-435-98935-9 HEINEMANN PB........$9.95

Geoffrey **Rees**

Sex with Strangers

A provocative and moving debut novel about passion, wordless sexual encounters, and failed relationships, as a young gay man struggles to combine sex and love

0-374-26165-2 FS&G........$20.00

Mark **Richard**

Fishboy

0-385-42568-6 ANCHOR PB........$10.95

The Ice at the Bottom of the World: Stories

0-385-41544-3 ANCHOR PB........$7.95

Ruthan **Robson**

Another Mother

The story of a lesbian mother in a committed relationship who becomes increasingly involved in her radical law practice, losing sight, temporarily, of that which is important to her: her child, her lover, and her mother

0-312-13431-2 ST. MARTIN'S........$21.95
0-312-14542-X ST. MARTIN'S PB........$10.95

Agnes **Rossi**

The Quick: A Novella & Stories

0-393-31470-7 NORTON PB........$11.00

Paul **Russell**

Sea of Tranquillity

0-452-27311-0 PLUME PB........$12.95

Sapphire

Push

The well-known poet offers a harrowing story of incest set in the inner city

0-679-44626-5 KNOPF........$20.00

Dori **Sanders**

Her Own Place

A striking work that follows the indomitable life of Mae Lee Barnes, war bride, abandoned wife, mother, farmer, and seeker of her family's African past

1-56512-027-2 ALGONQUIN........$16.95

George **Saunders**

Civilwarland in Bad Decline: Stories and a Novella

0-679-44812-8 RANDOM HOUSE........$22.00
1-57322-579-7 RIVERHEAD........$25.00

Cathleen **Schine**

Alice in Bed

The experiences of college student Alice, who is bedridden with a mysterious ailment and must cope with her hilariously dysfunctional family

0-452-27675-6 PLUME PB........$10.95

The Love Letter

A small bookstore owner falls passionately in love with a handsome college student who works for her, and this passion in the midst of books unites this delightful love story with the seduction of writing and bookselling

0-395-68996-1 HOUGHTON MIFFLIN........$19.95
0-451-18847-0 SIGNET PB........$6.99

Rameau's Niece

A young scholar who has unexpectedly gained recognition for an obscure literary study grows tired of her Whitman-esque professor husband and attempts to have an affair. A send-up of the literary and academic world

0-452-27161-4 PLUME PB........$10.95

To the Birdhouse

The further adventures of Alice, who is now married, but not free of her family's foibles

0-452-27662-4 PLUME PB........$10.95

Christine **Schutt**

Nightwork: Stories

0-679-40451-1 KNOPF........$20.00

Sandra **Scofield**

A Chance to See Egypt

0-06-017343-2 HARPERCOLLINS........$22.00

Joanna **Scott**

Various Antidotes: Stories

See also **SINCE 1945**

0-8050-4176-1 HOLT PB........$12.00

Robert J. **Seidman**

One Smart Indian

"Seidman is a good story teller and the suspenseful exciting moments in his narrative are fast paced and engrossing"—*LA Times Book Review.* "An astonishing act of empathy and imagination"—John Leonard, *NY Times*

0-87951-099-4 OVERLOOK PB........$13.95

Elizabeth **Shepard**

H

"Shepard is a reverse archaeologist, designing a tiny contemporary lost world for readers to excavate. Everything matters…Shepard gets everything right"—*New York Magazine*

0-670-85927-3 VIKING........$17.95
0-14-024389-5 PENGUIN PB........$9.95

Ann Allen **Shockley**

The Black and White of It

0-930044-96-7 NAIAD PB $7.95

Mark **Singer**

Citizen K: The Deeply Weird American Journey of Brett Kimberlin

0-679-42999-9 KNOPF $25.00

David **Sosnowski**

Rapture

0-679-45174-9 VILLARD $23.00

Susan **Straight**

The Gettin Place

Family tale spanning three generations, beginning with the Tulsa race riots of the '20s and climaxing amid the Los Angeles riots in 1992

0-7868-6086-3 HYPERION $22.95

Melanie **Sumner**

Polite Society

0-395-68998-8 HOUGHTON MIFFLIN $21.95

Terese **Svoboda**

Cannibal

0-8147-8012-1 NYU $19.95

Marly **Swick**

Paper Wings

0-06-017434-X HARPERCOLLINS $21.00

The Summer Before the Summer of Love

The new collection of short stories from the acclaimed author of *Monogamy* focuses, with signature perspicacity, on the characters and dynamics of family relationships: Anne Beattie and Amy Bloom are the comparisons for this author as she gains national attention. "Swick's deliciously bitter stories swing, metronomically, between life's almost unbearable barrenness and its sorrowful, sensual fullness"—*NY Times Book Review.* "Swick's characters are made real through fluid prose and generous servings of images and insight"—*Kirkus Reviews*

0-06-017254-1 HARPERCOLLINS $21.00

Marly A. **Swick**

Monogamy: Stories

0-06-097452-4 HARPERPERENNIAL PB $12.00

Jervey **Tervalon**

Understand This

"A gritty, haunting, *West Side Story*-esque ghetto romance of stunning violence yet overpowering beauty"—*The Philadelphia Inquirer*

0-385-47824-0 ANCHOR PB $10.95

Abigail **Thomas**

An Actual Life

1-56512-133-3 ALGONQUIN $17.95

Melanie Rae **Thon**

First, Body

0-395-78588-X HOUGHTON MIFFLIN $21.95

Girls in the Grass

0-571-12947-1 FABER PB $10.95

Iona Moon

An erotic and moving coming-of-age story that takes place in a small Idaho town, told in multiple and interchanging first-person narratives. "A dangerous and intricately drawn novel—rich and aching with desire" —*Washington Post*

0-452-27280-7 PLUME PB $10.95

Maria **Thomas**

Antonia Saw the Oryx First

Margaret Atwood describes Thomas's remarkable novel as a "complex, deeply written and finely wrought double portrait of two women; one black, one white, picking their way through the debris of a shattered colonialism, discovering unexpected treasures buried in the rubble"

0-939149-02-8 SOHO $17.95

0-939149-90-7 SOPHIA PB $12.00

Christopher **Tilghman**

Mason's Retreat

Family saga set on eastern shore of Maryland on the eve of World War II. "This first novel places him securely in the ranks of our most accomplished writers"—*Publishers Weekly*

0-679-42712-0 RANDOM HOUSE $22.00

Carla **Tomaso**

The House of Real Love

A comic and erotic look at a less than perfect lesbian relationship, complete with compassionate characters. "Tomaso takes an irreverent look at the attitudes and issues that affect lesbian relationships. A true lesbian farce, complete with costumes and mistaken identities and no shortage of ribald humor"—Lisa Donnelly

0-452-26826-5 PLUME PB $9.00

Bruce **Wagner**

Force Majeure

"If Jackie Collins was seduced by Dostoevsky on the floor of the William Morris mailroom, the literary offspring might read something like *Force Majeure*"—Carrie Fisher

0-312-09290-3 ST. MARTIN'S PB $14.95

I'm Losing You

A novel of surreal Hollywood by a disillusioned insider. Wagner is the author of the teleplay adaptation of the *Details* cartoon *Wild Palms*

0-679-41927-6 VILLARD $23.00

Katharine **Weber**

Objects in Mirror Are Closer than They Appear

0-312-14383-4 PICADOR PB $12.00

Diane **Williams**

The Stupefaction

Described by *The New York Times* as "a double agent in the house of fiction," Williams has long subverted the conventions of storytelling, creating an enchanted landscape of narrative. A longer work and 49 stories compose this innovative collection by a daring writer

0-679-44186-7 KNOPF $21.00

Jacqueline **Woodson**

Autobiography of a Family Photo: A Novel

0-452-27098-7 PLUME PB $9.95

Kate **Wheeler**

Not Where I Started From

South American bred, and briefly ordained a Buddhist nun in Rangoon, Wheeler reveals a stunning new fictive voice in her debut collection. Concentrating on Americans in alien cultures, Wheeler's characters include a teenager in Central America, a novitiate in a Burmese monastery, a New Yorker in Miami's Little Cuba, all seeking love, or enlightenment, or both. "Kate Wheeler has taken the post-imperial American condition as her theme and she sounds it with great skill. Her work is rich in observation and irony and her insights are reminiscent of the work of E.M. Forster or of the Doris Lessing of *African Stories*"—Robert Stone

0-395-66515-9 HOUGHTON MIFFLIN $19.95

Eric **Zencey**

Panama

A richly detailed historical novel that fictionalizes the life of the historian Henry Adams, placing him in a spinning plot of intrigue set in 19th-century Paris

0-374-22943-0 FS&G $24.00

0-425-15602-8 BERKLEY PB $6.99

Short Story Collections

Jack C. **Adrian** & Bill **Pronzini**, editors

Hard-Boiled: An Anthology of American Crime Stories

Covering 70 years of detective fiction, this volume includes classic work as well as hard-to-find stories by Chandler, Hammet, Cain, and others

See also THE HARD-BOILED DETECTIVE under CRIME FICTION in POPULAR READING

0-19-508499-3 OXFORD $30.00

Joyce **Antler**, editor

America and I: Short Stories by American Jewish Women Writers

Anthology of 20th-century American Jewish women writers including Cynthia Ozick, Edna Ferber, and Tillie Olsen

0-8070-3607-2 BEACON PB $15.00

David **Bergman**, editor

Men on Men 5: Best New Gay Fiction

"A ground-breaking collection" —*Lambda Book Report*

0-452-27244-0 PLUME PB $11.95

Daniel J. **Casey** & Robert E. **Rhodes**, editors

Modern Irish-American Fiction: A Reader

Short stories and novel excerpts from Peter Dunne, William Kennedy, Mary Gordon, and others

0-8156-2462-X SYRACUSE $34.95

0-8156-0234-0 SYRACUSE PB $14.95

John Edgar **Wideman** &
Katrina **Kenison**, editors

The Best American Short Stories, 1996

0-395-75290-6 HOUGHTON MIFFLIN PB.......$12.95

Jane **Smiley** & Katrina **Kenison**, editors

The Best American Short Stories, 1995

This 80th-anniversary edition of the preeminent anthology of short fiction—an annual bestseller—includes stories by Don DeLillo, Ellen Gilchrist, Thom Jones, Joy Williams, Stephen Dobyns, and Jamaica Kincaid. "Expect to be entertained, provoked, astonished—and to have plenty to think about"—*San Diego Tribune*. "As short story collections go, they don't get any better than this"—*Hartford Courant*

SERIES EDITED BY KATRINA KENISON

0-395-71179-7 HOUGHTON MIFFLIN PB.......$12.95

Tobias **Wolff** & Katrina **Kenison**, editors

The Best American Short Stories, 1994

The bestselling yearly source for the best short stories in America. "These are stories with unusual staying power"—*People Magazine*. "Bristling with the quickness of life's pain and pleasures"—*Hartford Courant*

0-395-68103-0 HOUGHTON MIFFLIN.........$24.95
0-395-68102-2 HOUGHTON MIFFLIN PB.......$11.95

Louise **Erdrich** & Katrina **Kenison**, editors

The Best American Short Stories, 1993

The premier collection of short fiction arrives annually like a bulletin from America's most profound imaginations. This year's editor, Erdrich (*The Beet Queen, Love Medicine*), presides over a dazzling group that includes Wendell Berry, Thom Jones, Mary Gaitskill, and Lorrie Moore. "Unforgettable characters, unexpected relationships, dramatic deeds, authentic voices"—*Washington Post Book World*

0-395-63627-2 HOUGHTON MIFFLIN PB.......$11.95

Robert **Stone** & Katrina **Kenison**, editors

The Best American Short Stories, 1992

This year's volume gathers 20 stories by such writers as Joyce Carol Oates, Reynolds Price, Mavis Gallant, Denis Johnson, and Alice Munro.
"The diverse voices of today's American short fiction create a bold and dramatic impact"—*Boston Globe*

0-395-59304-2 HOUGHTON MIFFLIN............$21.95

Richard **Ford**, editor

The Granta Book of the American Short Story

This unique selection contains the best of American short fiction from the last 40 years—from Robert Penn Warren and Paul Bowles to T. Coraghessan Boyle, Jamaica Kincaid, and David Leavitt. The editor, author of *The Sportswriter* and *Rock Springs*, has put together a superb introduction to the best of contemporary fiction

0-670-84527-2 PENGUIN.........................$27.50
0-14-014032-8 PENGUIN PB....................$15.95

Lilly **Golden**, editor

A Literary Christmas: Great Contemporary Christmas Stories

The Christmas season in all its psychological and emotional complexity viewed by some of today's best writers, from Toni Cade Bambara and Patricia Highsmith to Ann Beattie, Italo Calvino, Paul Auster, and Heinrich Boll

See also **FICTION ANTHOLOGIES** under **WORLD LITERATURE: WORLD LITERATURE SURVEYS AND ANTHOLOGIES** in **LITERATURE OF EUROPE, AFRICA, AND ASIA**

0-87113-583-3 GROVE PB.......................$15.00

James **Grady**, editor

Unusual Suspects: A Black Lizard Anthology

Some of the finest crime writers in America have lent their voices to this anthology of the celebrated Black Lizard series, from which the profits have been committed to benefit Share Our Strength in the fight against hunger, poverty, and illiteracy. Contributors include Jan Adins, David Corn, John Lutz, Joyce Carol Oates, Andrew Vachss, and John Weisman

See also **NEO-NOIR** under **CRIME FICTION TODAY** under **CRIME FICTION** in **POPULAR READING**

0-679-76788-6 VINTAGE PB....................$13.00

Jessica Tarahata **Hagedorn**, editor

Charlie Chan Is Dead: An Anthology of Contemporary Asian-American Fiction

0-14-023111-0 PENGUIN PB....................$14.95

Judith **Hamer** & Martin **Hamer**, editors

Centers of the Self: Stories by Black American Women

0-8090-1576-5 HILL & WANG PB..............$10.95

Robert **Drake** & Terry **Wolverton**, editors

Hers: Brilliant New Fiction by Lesbian Writers

Although the 21 submissions are written by lesbians, not all stories have lesbian themes or characters, but do often consider life's big question of identity

0-571-19867-8 FABER PB.......................$14.95

Rust **Hills** & Will **Blythe**, editors

Lust, Violence, Sin, Magic: Sixty Years of Esquire Fiction

From Flannery O'Connor, Ernest Hemingway, and John Dos Passos to Raymond Carver, Louise Erdrich, and Don DeLillo, *Esquire* has consistently published the finest new writing in each of its six decades. This 60th-anniversary anthology speaks volumes about the history of an American literary institution

0-87113-581-7 GROVE PB.......................$15.00

Langston **Hughes**, editor

The Best Short Stories by Black Writers

0-316-38031-8 LITTLE, BROWN PB............$12.95

Langston Hughes

Richard Glyn **Jones** &
Susan A. **Williams**, editors

The Penguin Book of Erotic Stories by Women

The 31 tales cover 103 years and six continents. "...In a compilation that includes such diverse authors as Edith Wharton and Kathy Acker, it's a safe bet that each reader will find some of these tales titillating, others curious and still others repulsive"—*Publishers Weekly*

See also **EROTICA** under **COURTSHIP, LOVE, SEX, AND MARRIAGE** in **LIFESTYLES AND PRACTICAL ADVICE**

0-670-86620-2 VIKING...........................$24.95

Charles **Jurrist**, editor

Shadows of Love: American Gay Fiction

1-55583-136-2 ALYSON PB........................$8.95

Marcy **Knopf**, editor

The Sleeper Wakes: Harlem Renaissance Stories by Women

0-8135-1945-4 RUTGERS PB....................$12.95

Susan **Koppelman**, editor

Women in the Trees: Stories of Battering and Resistance by U.S. Women, 1839-1994

See also **RAPE, INCEST, AND BATTERED WOMEN** under **THE FEMALE EXPERIENCE** under **WOMEN'S STUDIES** in **SOCIAL STUDIES**

0-8070-6777-6 BEACON PB....................$16.00

Adam **Mars-Jones**, editor

Mae West Is Dead: Recent Lesbian and Gay Fiction

A collection of short fiction from noted writers

0-571-14898-0 FABER PB.......................$10.95

Mark **Mitchell**, editor

The Penguin Book of Gay Short Stories

See also **ANTHOLOGIES AND REFERENCE** under **GAY, LESBIAN, AND BISEXUAL STUDIES** in **SOCIAL STUDIES**

0-670-85468-9 VIKING...........................$27.50

The Penguin Book of International Gay Writing

An unprecedentedly diverse collection of international gay writing, from Reinaldo Arenas to Balzac, Camus, Cocteau, Gide, Freud, Mishima, Popov, Yourcenar. "By the end of this collection, the reader feels that he or she has travelled over many different lands and lovescapes, and witnessed the width of possibilities, radiant and ugly, in gay desire" —*The Guardian*

INTRODUCTION BY DAVID LEAVITT

0-670-85369-0 VIKING............$27.95
0-14-023459-4 PENGUIN PB............$14.95

Ethan **Mordden**, editor

I've a Feeling We're Not in Kansas Anymore: Tales from Gay Manhattan

0-452-25929-0 NEW AMERICAN LIBRARY PB............$11.95

Joyce Carol **Oates**, editor

The Oxford Book of American Short Stories: 1991

A collection of classics and little-known stories by well-known writers of the American past and present. Oates contributes excellent introductions to each writer. A book full of surprises

0-19-507065-8 OXFORD............$30.00
0-19-509262-7 OXFORD PB............$15.95

Simon **Rae**, editor

The Faber Book of Murder

0-571-17494-9 FABER PB............$15.95

Shannon **Ravenel**, editor

Best of the South: From 10 Years of New Stories from the South

For years, Shannon Ravenel's splendid collections of the best stories from the South have brought a unique literary heritage north across the Mason-Dixon line and on to the world. In this volume, Anne Tyler combs the 10-year history of Ravenel's selections to bring forth 20 of her favorite stories, testing the theory that "a real Southern story remains Southern even if you change the name of the locale from Nashville to Boston, the name of the hero from Billy Bob to Kevin"—and finding that, decidedly, the theory holds

SELECTED AND INTRODUCED BY ANNE TYLER

1-56512-128-7 ALGONQUIN PB............$15.95

New Stories from the South: The Year's Best, 1994

"Maybe the best annual anthology around" —*Kirkus Reviews*

1-56512-053-1 ALGONQUIN PB............$11.95
0-912697-93-8 WORKMAN PB............$8.95

I guess in a way I'm waiting for the rarest breed of all, my sights set so high I have to squint to keep the sky in focus. I concentrate on migration habits. I keep in mind that owls fly silently at night. Some people (like Lorraine) might say I'm on a snipe hunt. But, call me an optimist. I'm sitting here in a pile of ashes, waiting for the phoenix to take shape and rise.
—*Jill McCorkle*
NEW STORIES FROM THE SOUTH: THE YEAR'S BEST, 1994

New Stories from the South: The Year's Best, 1996

1-56512-155-4 ALGONQUIN PB............$10.95

Robert **Shapiro** & James **Thomas**, editors

Sudden Fiction: American Short-Short Stories

0-87905-265-1 GIBBS SMITH PB............$12.95

Jerome **Sterne**, editor

Micro Fiction

The winners and finalists of "The World's Best Short Short Story Contest" in which each entry must be about 250 words long

0-393-31432-4 NORTON PB............$7.95

James **Thomas** & Denise **Thomas**, editors

The Best of the West: New Short Stories from the Wide Side of the Missouri

0-393-30962-2 NORTON PB............$9.95

Sue **Thomas**, editor

Wild Women: Contemporary Short Stories for Women Who Run with the Wolves

0-87951-514-7 OVERLOOK PB............$14.95

Anne **Turyn**, editor

Top Top Stories

Constance DeJong, Kathy Acker, Gary Indiana, Lynne Tillman, and Jenny Holzer are only some of the innovative writers and artists whose work has appeared in the series *Top Stories.* This retrospective collects some of the stories, graphics, and photography that have shaped the contemporary avant-garde

0-87286-258-5 CITY LIGHTS PB............$9.95

Sharon Oard **Warner**

The Way We Write Now: Short Stories From the AIDS Crisis

In chronological order from Susan Sontag's "The Way We Live Now" to Paul Monette's "Part One of Halfway Home"

INTRODUCTION BY ABRAHAM VERGHESE

0-8065-1638-0 CITADEL PB............$14.95

Tobias **Wolff**, editor

The Vintage Book of Contemporary American Short Stories

Includes stories written in the last fifteen years by such authors as Dorothy Allison, Raymond Carver, and Amy Tan. "Kafka spoke of literature as an ax, with which to break 'the frozen sea within us.' When you come to the end of…any number of the stories in this volume, you will know exactly what Kafka was talking about" —Tobias Wolff, from the Introduction

0-679-74513-0 VINTAGE PB............$13.00

20th-Century American Poetry

The Modernist Generations

"The first thing that strikes a reader about the best American poets is how utterly unlike each other they are. Where else in the world, for example, could one find seven poets of approximately the same generation so different as Ezra Pound, W.C. Williams, Vachel Lindsay, Marianne Moore, Wallace Stevens, e.e. cummings and Laura Riding?"—W.H. Auden

Poets such as John Berryman, Elizabeth Bishop, and George Oppen, who first made a reputation in the '30s and '40s are also listed in this section.

Conrad **Aiken**

Collected Poems, 1916-1970

"Aiken became aware of the broken nature of his world in a singularly brutal way: at the age of eleven he found his parents dead; his mother shot by his father, who then committed suicide…From that terrifying moment Aiken would search for 'an equivalent to it all, in terms of his own life, or work'…His reality was more chaotic, his ego more fragile, his need to grow in consciousness more acute than almost any other modern writer's"—Arthur Waterman, *Critique*

0-19-501258-5 OXFORD............$45.00

Conrad Aiken

Stephen Vincent **Benet**

John Brown's Body

One of the bestselling American books of poetry, this Civil War epic has found new audiences through a recent stage version. It is now restored to print after many years of neglect

0-929587-26-X DEE PB............$12.95

John **Berryman**

John Berryman (1914-1972) has remained, since he leaped to his death from a bridge in Minneapolis, one of the most elusive, yet enormously influential, writers of this century. As Ian Hamilton has observed, "his imaginative life seems, in retrospect, a ventriloquist's search for an appropriate dummy."

Collected Poems, 1937-1971

EDITED WITH AN INTRODUCTION BY CHARLES THORNBURY

0-374-12619-4 NOONDAY PB $25.00

The Dream Songs

Gathers together *77 Dream Songs* and *His Toy, His Dream, His Rest*. "Berryman is touting no theories, promoting no programme for Kulchur or society. The *Dream Songs* are, instead, the fragmentary inner biography, the perceptions by which he lives, of a character called Henry… Berryman is deliberately a mannerist who, out of his fraught nerviness, has made an original and remarkably flexible style"— A. Alvarez

0-374-51670-7 FS&G PB $16.00

Elizabeth **Bishop**

The poetic output of Elizabeth Bishop (1911-1979) is a small one by the standards of her day, but the few poems she wrote during the course of her life set her apart from her contemporaries.

The Complete Poems, 1927-1979

"From the moment Miss Bishop appeared on the scene it was apparent to everybody that she was a poet of strange, even mysterious, but undeniable and great gifts"—John Ashbery

0-374-51817-3 FS&G PB $13.00

Louise **Bogan**

"Behind the Bogan poems is a woman, intense, proud, strong-willed...Her poems can be read and reread: they keep yielding new meanings, as all good poetry should. The gound beat of great tradition can be heard, with the necessary and subtle variations. Bogan is one of the true inheritors."—Theodore Roethke

The Blue Estuaries: Poems 1923-1968

"Now that we can see the sweep of forty-five years' work in this collection of over a hundred poems, we can judge what a feat of character it has been...Hers is a language as supple as it is accurate, dealing with things in their own tones...reading this book with delight, I was struck...by a career of stubborn, individual excellence"

—William Meredith, *NY Review of Books*

0-374-52461-0 NOONDAY PB $12.00

Kay **Boyle**

Collected Poems of Kay Boyle

1-55659-039-3 COPPER CANYON PB $10.00

William **Bronk**

The Mild Day

Recent poems. "Bronk's work, I feel, is amongst the very few we will be remembered by, if we're remembered at all"—Gustaf Sobin

1-88368-900-7 TALISMAN PB $9.95

Our Selves

1-88368-914-7 TALISMAN PB $10.95

Selected Poems

A compact but essential collection of poems from the whole range of Bronk's career, including the now scarce early books. "The Bronk I love best is essentially a religious poet, in the sense of one committed to ultimate things, a poet of severe beauty and sudden tenderness"—from the editor's introduction

EDITED BY HENRY WEINFIELD

0-8112-1314-5 NEW DIRECTIONS PB $8.95

Gwendolyn **Brooks**

Blacks

A comprehensive gathering of Brooks's poetry

0-88378-139-5 THIRD WORLD $36.95
0-88378-105-0 THIRD WORLD PB $19.95

Selected Poems

0-06-090989-7 HARPERCOLLINS PB $11.50

Sterling A. **Brown**

The Collected Poems of Sterling A. Brown

"Sterling's poems reveal how in the struggle to exist the historic stands alongside the everyday…None of the characters in his ballads is treated sentimentally because his first duty was not to his sympathies but to the poem"

—Darryl Pinckney

EDITED BY MICHAEL S. HARPER

0-929968-07-7 ANOTHER CHICAGO PRESS PB $12.95

Witter **Bynner**

The Selected Witter Bynner: Poems, Plays, Translations, Prose, and Letters

EDITED BY JAMES KRAFT

0-8263-1607-7 NEW MEXICO $24.95

Hart **Crane**

The Bridge

0-87140-225-4 NORTON PB $9.95

The Complete Poems, Selected Letters & Prose

Includes *The Bridge* and *White Buildings*. "Essentially Crane …was using rhyme and meter and fantastic images to convey the emotional states that were induced in him by alcohol, jazz, machinery, laughter, intellectual stimulation, the shape and sound of words and the madness of New York in the late Coolidge era"—Malcolm Cowley

EDITED BY BROM WEBER AND MARK SIMON

0-87140-147-9 NORTON PB $12.95

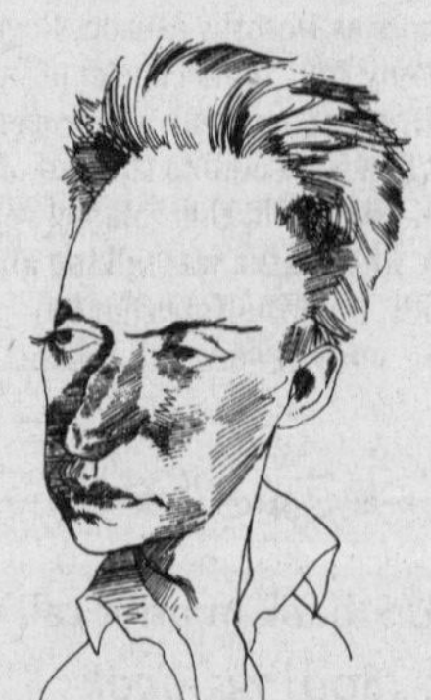

Hart Crane

Countee **Cullen**

My Soul's High Song: The Collected Writings of Countee Cullen, Voice of the Harlem Renaissance

The poetry and prose of a major black writer. "A generous introduction to new readers of Countee Cullen and a more than generous offering to those of us who hold the poet dear"—Maya Angelou

EDITED BY GERALD EARLY

0-385-41295-9 ANCHOR PB $16.95

e.e. **cummings**

Another Cummings

EDITED BY RICHARD KOSTELANETZ

0-87140-157-6 LIVERIGHT $25.00

e.e. cummings: Complete Poems, 1904-1962

Richard Kostelanetz has called him "the major American poet of the middle 20th century." There can be no argument that cummings's work altered the landscape of literary expression or that his brash, yet masterfully controlled experimentation is now all essential part of the accepted vernacular. Reissued for the e. e. cummings centennial year, this is the most complete, textually accurate edition of his work ever published

EDITED BY GEORGE J. FIRMAGE

0-87140-152-5 LIVERIGHT $50.00

e.e. cummings

may i feel said he

***may i feel said he/(i'll squeal said she/just once said he)/it's fun said she…*cummings's sensual, sweet, and funny poems, accompanied by the equally lyrical illustrations of Marc Chagall**

PAINTINGS BY MARC CHAGALL

1-55670-422-4 WELCOME ENTERPRISES $17.95

Selected Poems

0-87140-153-3 NORTON $25.00
0-87140-154-1 NORTON PB $9.95

Richard **Eberhart**

Collected Poems, 1930-1986

"Visionary intensity that throws caution to the winds in order to seize the given insight"

—Ralph J. Mills Jr., *Parnassus*

0-19-504055-4 OXFORD $35.00

The Long Reach: New and Uncollected Poems, 1948-1984

0-8112-0886-9 NEW DIRECTIONS PB $8.95

Maine Poems
0-19-505526-8 OXFORD PB $11.95

T.S. **Eliot**
Collected Poems, 1909-1962
"Any perspective which misses the abrupt discontinuities in Eliot's work has missed too much, for such discontinuities are the life of the poems. It is not simply that Eliot is a 'poet of fragments,' as Spender says, or that he sees the world as broken in pieces. Eliot specializes in putting fragments together in such a way that we see the wholeness that we lack"—Michael Wood, *NY Review of Books*
0-15-118978-1 HARCOURT BRACE $20.00

Selected Poems
0-15-680647-9 HARCOURT BRACE PB $6.95

William **Everson**
The Blood of the Poet: Selected Poems of William Everson
0-913089-42-7 BROKEN MOON PB $14.95

Charles Henri **Ford**
Out of the Labyrinth: Selected Poems
0-87286-251-8 CITY LIGHTS PB $6.95

Robert **Francis**
Collected Poems, 1936-1976
A compendium of a poet often compared to Robert Frost
0-87023-510-9 MASSACHUSETTS PB $17.95

Robert **Frost**
The Poetry of Robert Frost
"Frost, along with Stevens and Eliot, seems to me the greatest of the American poets of this century. Frost's virtues are extraordinary. No other living poet has written so well about the actions of ordinary men; his wonderful dramatic monologues or dramatic scenes come out of a knowledge of people that few poets have had, and they are written in a verse mastery, the rhythms of actual speech"—Randall Jarrell
EDITED BY EDWARD C. LATHEM
0-8050-0502-1 HOLT $30.00
0-8050-0501-3 HOLT PB $15.95

Robert Frost: Collected Poems, Prose, and Plays
A definitive collection, meticulously edited and annotated
EDITED BY RICHARD POIRIER AND MARK RICHARDSON
1-88301-106-X LIBRARY OF AMERICA $35.00
0-8047-1741-9 STANFORD $47.50

Versed in Country Things
PHOTOGRAPHS BY TONY KING
0-8212-2288-0 BULFINCH $22.50

Ramon **Guthrie**
Maximum Security Ward & Other Poems
"Guthrie belongs to that tragically small army of poets who have done superb in their seventies or beyond—poets with the power, and courage, to distill in their art their intimate experience of the trials and glories of old age"—M.L. Rosenthal
EDITED BY SALLY M. GALL
FOREWORD BY M.L. ROSENTHAL
0-89255-080-5 PERSEA PB $9.95

Marsden **Hartley**
The Collected Poems of Marsden Hartley, 1904-1943
Hartley's poems offer an interesting footnote to his career as a painter, and indicate the close connections between poetry and painting in the modernist epoch
EDITED BY GAIL R. SCOTT
0-87685-680-6 BLACK SPARROW PB $12.50

Robert **Hayden**
Collected Poems
Hayden's "Runagate Runagate," about Harriet Tubman and the Underground Railroad, is one of the most haunting of modern American poems. "[He] has always been a symbolist poet struggling with historical fact, his rigorous view of people and places providing a leap into the interior landscapes of the soul"
—Michael S. Harper
EDITED BY FREDERICK GLAYSHER
0-87140-138-X NORTON PB $10.95

Collected Poems
EDITED BY FREDERICK GHAYSHER
0-87140-651-9 NORTON $23.00
0-87140-159-2 NORTON PB $15.00

H.D. (Hilda Doolittle)
Collected Poems, 1912-1944
A landmark collection of the main body of H.D.'s work, including much poetry never before published
EDITED WITH AN INTRODUCTION BY LOUIS MARTZ
0-8112-0971-7 NEW DIRECTIONS PB $21.95

Hedylus
0-933806-00-0 BLACK SWAN $17.50

Helen in Egypt
A book-length poem playing out an alternate ending to the myth of Troy
INTRODUCTION BY HORACE GREGORY
0-8112-0544-4 NEW DIRECTIONS PB $11.95

Hermetic Definition
H.D.'s final poems, including sequences dedicated to Ezra Pound and St.-John Perse
INTRODUCTION BY NORMAN HOLMES PEARSON
0-8112-0453-7 NEW DIRECTIONS PB $8.95

Hippolytus Temporizes
0-933806-23-X BLACK SWAN $25.00

Ion: A Play After Euripides
0-933806-24-8 BLACK SWAN $25.00

Trilogy
Includes *The Walls Do Not Fall, Tribute to the Angels, and The Flowering of the Rod*. This sequence of visionary poems informed by science, Christian lore, and the World War II bombing of London is usually considered H.D.'s masterpiece
INTRODUCTION BY NORMAN HOLMES PEARSON
0-8112-0491-X NEW DIRECTIONS PB $8.95

Ernest **Hemingway**
Complete Poems
Revealing as his prose rarely was, Hemingway's verse blasts Dorothy Parker, Edmund Wilson, at least one of his ex-wives, and the sensibilities of his time. This edition includes previously unpublished poems and an updated bibliography
0-8032-7259-6 NEBRASKA PB $9.95

Langston **Hughes**
Hughes was the most important poet to come out of the Harlem Renaissance. He invented his own stanza forms or used blank verse to transcribe urban folk life, the mood of jazz and blues; he is probably the most widely read of all black poets, and by the time of his death in 1967 was known even by the man on the street as the poet laureate of the African-American people.
The Collected Poems of Langston Hughes
EDITED BY ARNOLD RAMPERSAD & DAVID ROSSELL
0-679-42631-0 KNOPF $30.00

The Langston Hughes Reader
See also **FROM THE TURN OF THE CENTURY TO WORLD WAR II** under **20TH-CENTURY AMERICAN FICTION**
0-8076-0057-1 BRAZILLER $17.50

The Panther and the Lash
A sampling of Hughes's political poems
0-679-73659-X VINTAGE PB $11.00

Selected Poems of Langston Hughes
"In Hughes's poetry, the oral tradition is perhaps strongest in those poems modeled on black music—the jazz and blues poems...The blues spirit in fact pervades Hughes's work—in all genres"—Onwuchekwa Jemie
0-679-72818-X VINTAGE PB $12.00

David **Ignatow**
Against the Evidence: Selected Poems, 1934-1994
0-8195-2211-2 WESLEYAN $30.00
0-8195-1214-1 WESLEYAN PB $14.95

I Have a Name
0-8195-2240-6 WESLEYAN PB $11.95

New and Collected Poems, 1970-1985
0-8195-6174-6 WESLEYAN PB $17.95

Randall **Jarrell**
"Randall Jarrell had his own peculiar and important excellence as a poet...His gifts, both by nature and by a lifetime of hard dedication and growth, were wit, pathos, and brilliance of intelligence."—Robert Lowell
The Complete Poems
0-374-12716-6 FS&G $45.00
0-374-51305-8 NOONDAY PB $16.00

Selected Poems
0-374-25867-8 FS&G $17.95

Robinson **Jeffers**
The Collected Poetry: 1928-1938
Jeffers's Californian landscapes and ecological pessimism continue to fascinate many poets
EDITED BY TIM HUNT
0-8047-1723-0 STANFORD $75.00

Dear Judas
INTRODUCTION BY ROBERT J. BROPHY
0-87140-113-4 LIVERIGHT PB $7.95

James Weldon **Johnson**
Saint Peter Relates an Incident: Selected Poems
0-14-018684-0 PENGUIN PB $8.95

James Weldon **Johnson**

God's Trombones

Diplomat, cultural observer, songwriter, lawyer, and novelist, Johnson was the most important figure in the transition from 19th-century gentility to the spirit of militant racial awareness

0-14-042217-X PENGUIN PB $6.95

Weldon **Kees**

The Collected Poems of Weldon Kees

All the poetry of a multitalented writer and artist who disappeared in San Francisco in 1955

EDITED BY DONALD JUSTICE

0-8032-5828-3 NEBRASKA PB $12.00

Stanley **Kunitz**

Passing Through: The Later Poems, New and Selected

0-393-03870-X NORTON $18.95

The Wellfleet Whale & Companion Poems

0-935296-37-9 SHEEP MEADOW $20.00

James **Laughlin**

Collected Poems of James Laughlin

The publisher of New Directions is also an accomplished poet

1-55921-067-2 MOYER BELL $34.95

The Country Road

0-944072-46-1 ZOLAND $22.95

The Man in the Wall

0-8112-1237-8 NEW DIRECTIONS PB $9.95

Phantoms

0-89381-613-2 APERTURE PB $12.95

The Secret Room

0-8112-1344-7 NEW DIRECTIONS PB $42.00

Janet **Lewis**

Poems Old and New, 1918-1978

0-8040-0372-6 OHIO PB $10.95

Robert **Lowell**

Collected Poems

0-374-12553-8 FS&G $25.00

Day by Day

Lowell's last book won the National Book Critics Circle prize in 1977

0-374-13525-8 FS&G $12.95
0-374-51471-2 FS&G PB $9.00

For Lizzie and Harriet

0-374-15729-4 FS&G PB $6.95

Imitations

0-374-50260-9 NOONDAY PB $11.00

Lord Weary's Castle & The Mills of the Kavanaughs

0-15-653500-9 HARCOURT BRACE PB $3.95

Notebook

0-374-50947-6 NOONDAY PB $12.00

Life Studies & For the Union Dead

Two of Lowell's most influential books. "There is no other poet writing at the moment who can match the dense visual accuracy of Lowell's best work...By an immensely subtle process of reverberation, his images seem to seek each other out, not to be wise so much as to be confirmed in tragedy"—Ian Hamilton

0-374-50628-0 FS&G PB $9.00

Poems: A Selection

0-571-10182-8 FABER PB $5.95

Robert Lowell

Selected Poems

0-374-51400-3 FS&G PB $14.00

Mina **Loy**

The Lost Lunar Baedeker: Poems of Mina Loy

Admired by Pound and other modernist luminaries, Mina Loy's poetry concentrates on subjects such as prostitution, destitution, and suicide, themes often too rich for her times. This edition is beautifully edited by Roger Conover (the biographer of Loy's husband, Arthur Craven)

EDITED BY ROGER L. CONOVER

0-374-25872-4 FS&G $22.00

Mina Loy

Archibald **MacLeish**

New and Collected Poems: 1917-1984

"His lyrics...unite the Romantic styles of the nineteenth century with the modern ones of his youth...His poetry is full of things seen, heard, touched, tasted, and smelled with pleasure" —David Perkins

PREFACE BY RICHARD MCADOO

0-395-39569-0 HOUGHTON MIFFLIN PB $16.95

Joseph Moncure **March**

The Wild Party: The Lost Classic

Spiegelman's brilliant tribute to 1920s illustration brings new life to March's celebrated doggerel epic of Hollywood decadence. As Spiegelman notes: "Maybe it's March's perfectly pitched tone of bewildered innocence curdled into worldly cynicism that resonates so well in our '90s"

ILLUSTRATED BY ART SPIEGELMAN

0-679-42450-4 PANTHEON $22.00

Don **Marquis**

Archy & Mehitabel

Began as a column for *The New York Sun* in 1916, Archy, literary cockroach who types out *vers libre* by banging his head against the keys (but can't reach the shift key), and Mehitabel, the sultry cat reincarnated from Cleopatra, have since gained a worldwide following

See also **HUMOR WRITERS** under **HUMOR** in **POPULAR READING**

0-385-09478-7 ANCHOR PB $8.95

Edgar Lee **Masters**

Spoon River Anthology

This edition of Masters's solitary masterpiece of Midwestern portraiture contains some additional poems

0-252-01561-4 ILLINOIS $29.95
0-252-06363-5 ILLINOIS PB $14.95
0-02-070010-5 MACMILLAN PB $7.00

Thomas **McGrath**

Death Song

The last book by an American poet who fused the personal and the political in original ways. "McGrath is major. If you don't know his work, you owe it to yourself to dive into it at the first opportunity"—*San Francisco Review of Books*

1-55659-036-9 COPPER CANYON PB $10.00

A Promise

All my life—noisy!
Walking around the world in my heavy shoes!
Now I grow lighter, And I begin to see
How, in that farther sunlight,
I shall move faster and faster
Until my shadow runs on alone
Without even an echo.

DEATH SONG

Letter to an Imaginary Friend: Parts 3 & 4

"Not since Pound's *Cantos* has any poet drawn upon such varied sources to make a personal and political statement"—*Library Journal*

0-914742-85-X COPPER CANYON $16.00
0-914742-86-8 SMALL PRESS PB $9.00

Selected Poems, 1938-1988

"Thomas McGrath has been writing remarkable poems of every size and form for nearly fifty years…His diction, with its vast word stock and multitude of language layers, is demotic to the core yet spiced with learned terms in Whitman's manner, a voice as richly American as any in our literature"—Terrence Des Pres

EDITED BY SAM HAMILL

1-55659-012-1 COPPER CANYON PB $10.00

Thomas **Merton**

The Collected Poems of Thomas Merton

"From his formal early poems to his late experiments in Surrealism, the voice remains vital and believable. It is seldom too religious, too metaphysical, too much the social critic; it is a combination of all of these, a large voice emerging to embody a large country" —Robert McDowell, *Hudson Review*

0-8112-0769-2 NEW DIRECTIONS PB $29.95

Thomas Merton

Josephine **Miles**

Collected Poems, 1930-1983

0-252-01017-5 ILLINOIS $24.95

Edna St. Vincent **Millay**

Collected Lyrics

Millay, an icon of the Greenwich village literary scene in its headiest days, was a surprisingly traditional lyricist whose best poems have proven enduringly popular

INTRODUCTION BY NORMA MILLAY

0-06-090863-7 HARPERCOLLINS PB $14.00

Collected Poems

0-89968-266-9 LIGHTYEAR $39.95

0-06-090889-0 HARPERCOLLINS PB $22.50

Collected Sonnets

0-06-091091-7 HARPERCOLLINS PB $11.00

Selected Poems

EDITED BY COLIN FALCK

0-06-092288-5 HARPERPERENNIAL PB $12.00

Marianne **Moore**

The Complete Poems of Marianne Moore

"With Miss Moore a word is a word most when it is separated out by science, treated with acid to remove the smudges, washed, dried and placed right sideup on a clean surface…In Miss Moore's work the purely stated idea has an edge exactly like a fruit or a tree or a serpent" —William Carlos Williams

0-14-058601-6 PENGUIN PB $12.00

Howard **Nemerov**

The Collected Poems

"He is at equal ease in the modes of epigram, comic poem, meditation, and narrative, yet his work in each is now clearly related to his work in all the rest. His style has great range" —Thom Gunn

0-226-57259-5 CHICAGO PB $18.95

A Howard Nemerov Reader

0-8262-0936-X MISSOURI PB $16.95

Trying Conclusions: New and Selected Poems, 1961-1991

0-226-57263-3 CHICAGO $18.95

Lorine **Niedecker**

Little known in her lifetime, Niedecker is now more widely read for the intensity and compression of her small body of verse.

Harpsichord & Salt Fish

"No one is so subtle with so few words" —Basil Bunting

1-85298-014-1 SMALL PRESS PB $15.00

George **Oppen**

Collected Poems

Contains the full texts of *Discrete Series, The Materials, This in Which, Of Being Numerous,* and *Seascape: Needle's Eye,* along with some late poems not elsewhere collected

0-8112-0615-7 NEW DIRECTIONS PB $11.95

Primitive

Oppen's last published book

0-87685-414-5 BLACK SPARROW PB $3.00

The Selected Letters of George Oppen

Oppen may be coming to be seen as the seminal poet of the second generation of American modernism. The letters add some necessary character highlights to the human face of a man whose poetry is known for its intellectual subtlety, formal austerity and deep moral commitment

EDITED BY RACHEL BLAU DUPLESSIS

0-8223-1024-4 DUKE PB $17.95

Dorothy **Parker**

Not Much Fun: The Lost Poems of Dorothy Parker

EDITED BY STUART Y. SILVERSTEIN

0-684-81855-8 SCRIBNERS $22.00

Poetry and Short Stories of Dorothy Parker

See also **FROM THE TURN OF THE CENTURY TO WORLD WAR II** under **20TH-CENTURY AMERICAN FICTION**

0-679-60132-5 MODERN LIBRARY $16.50

The Portable Dorothy Parker

Stories, poems, and criticism

See also **HUMOR WRITERS** under **HUMOR** in **POPULAR READING**

0-14-015074-9 VIKING PB $13.95

By the time you swear you are his,
Shivering and sighing,
And he swears his passion is
Infinite, undying—
Lady, make a note of this:
One of you is lying.

THE PORTABLE DOROTHY PARKER

Kenneth **Patchen**

Collected Poems

A huge influence on the Beats (although he did not relish the role), Patchen fused rage and lyricism in a heady atmosphere peopled with dream creatures and fabulous occurrences

0-8112-0140-6 NEW DIRECTIONS PB $16.95

Selected Poems

0-8112-0146-5 NEW DIRECTIONS PB $9.95

What Shall We Do Without Us?: The Voice and Vision of Kenneth Patchen

Examples of Patchen's "poem-paintings"

INTRODUCTION BY JAMES LAUGHLIN

0-87156-843-8 SIERRA CLUB $25.00

0-87156-818-7 RANDOM HOUSE PB $12.95

Ezra **Pound**

The Cantos

The complete work, for the first time in paperback, including a recently discovered English version of Canto LXXII, originally written in Italian

0-8112-1326-9 NEW DIRECTIONS PB $22.95

The Cantos, 1-117

Pound's great unfinished, unfinishable "poem containing history." "The poem is vigorous, bold, and packed with personality and diverse life…The sweep of the poem in time and geographical space brings into it an extraordinary diversity of settings, manners, and ways of speaking"—David Perkins

0-8112-0350-6 NEW DIRECTIONS $42.00

The Classic Anthology Defined by Confucius

Pound's version of the *Shih-ching* gave him the opportunity for some of his most purely musical writing

See also **EARLY CHINESE POETRY** under **POETRY** under **CLASSICAL CHINESE LITERATURE** in **LITERATURE OF EUROPE, AFRICA, AND ASIA**

0-674-13397-8 HARVARD PB $7.95

The Collected Early Poems of Ezra Pound

Includes the full text of *A Lume Spento, A Quinzaine for this Yule,* the 1909 *Personae, Canzon,* and other early work

EDITED BY MICHAEL KING

INTRODUCTION BY LOUIS MARTZ

0-8112-0843-5 NEW DIRECTIONS PB $12.95

Elektra: A Play

A significant work by Ezra Pound, written in 1949 when he was under indictment for treason, and published now for the first time. This free

adaptation of Sophocles characteristically mixes, in the editor's words, "transliterated Greek, jazzy slang, archaic English lyricism, Scots and Cockney and apparently Black American dialects," and casts new light on Pound's deep concern with Greek drama
EDITED AND ANNOTATED BY RICHARD REID
0-691-06778-3 PRINCETON $19.95

Personae
The essential gathering of Pound's work prior to *The Cantos*, including *Cathay*, *Homage to Sextus Propertius*, and *Hugh Selwyn Mauberly*
0-8112-1120-7 NEW DIRECTIONS $23.95

Selected Cantos
Pound made the selection, intended to touch on all the major motifs of his life work
0-8112-0160-0 NEW DIRECTIONS PB $7.95

Selected Poems
0-8112-0162-7 NEW DIRECTIONS PB $8.95

Translations
Pound's verse translations—from Chinese, Anglo-Saxon, Provencal, Japanese, Latin, and many other languages—imparted a new sense of context to American poetry
INTRODUCTION BY HUGH KENNER
0-8112-0164-3 NEW DIRECTIONS PB $12.95

Carl **Rakosi**

The Collected Poems
Early and late, Rakosi has been a mercurial poet offering abundant pleasures of sound, sight, and intellect
0-915032-35-X SUN & MOON $35.00
0-915032-36-8
NATIONAL POETRY FOUNDATION PB $15.95

Poems, 1923-1941
The early work of Rakosi, finally collected from the periodicals in which it appeared originally, reveals an extraordinary body of work, brillant and marvelously diverse. One of the essential books of recent years
EDITED BY ANDREW CROZIER
1-55713-185-6 SUN & MOON PB $12.95

John Crowe **Ransom**

Selected Poems
"The style in itself fascinates…There is the unusual structural clarity, the rightness of tone and rhythm, the brisk and effective ingenuity, the rhetorical fireworks of exposition, description, and dialogue; but even more: the sticking to concrete human subjects—the hardest; and a balanced temperament"
—Robert Lowell
0-679-40257-8 KNOPF $22.00

Naomi **Replansky**

The Dangerous World: New and Selected Poems, 1934-1994
"Has the fixity and power of experiences meditated on for a lifetime…Formal poetry in the best sense"—Harvey Shapiro
0-929968-34-4 ANOTHER CHICAGO PRESS PB $12.95

Kenneth **Rexroth**

Collected Shorter Poems
0-8112-0178-3 NEW DIRECTIONS PB $14.95

Flower Wreath Hill: Later Poems
0-8112-1178-9 NEW DIRECTIONS PB $9.95

Kenneth Rexroth (photo by Margo Moore)

The Morning Star
0-8112-0740-4 NORTON PB $4.95

Selected Poems
Philosophical, lyrical, erotic, and economical in its means, Rexroth's poetry is a varied and impressive body of work
EDITED BY BRADFORD MORROW
0-8112-0917-2 NEW DIRECTIONS PB $9.95

Charles **Reznikoff**

The Complete Poems
"No other poet, it strikes me, with perhaps the exception of Williams, has more thoroughly refused the artifices of style and chosen to let words have 'their daylight meanings,' to speak first of all, humanely and communicatively"
—Michael Heller

Poems

Volume 1: Poems 1918-1936
0-87685-262-2 BLACK SPARROW $17.50

Volume 2: Poems 1937-1975
0-87685-301-7 BLACK SPARROW $25.00

Testimony: The United States, 1885-1915
Incidents of American life reconstructed from old legal records

Volume 1
0-87685-321-1 BLACK SPARROW PB $13.00

Volume 2
0-87685-333-5 BLACK SPARROW $25.00
0-87685-332-7 BLACK SPARROW PB $13.00

Laura **Riding**

First Awakenings: The Early Poems of Laura (Riding) Jackson
The publication of Laura (Riding) Jackson's early poems is a true literary event. Written before she left the United States for England in 1925, many of these poems have never been published before. They attest to the power of a highly innovative poet who influenced such varied writers as Robert Graves and W.H. Auden. In 1991, the last year of her life, Laura (Riding) Jackson received the prestigious Bollingen Award for her achievement in poetry
0-89255-179-8 PERSEA $29.95

The Poems of Laura Riding
"Laura Riding is the greatest lost poet in American literature. W.H. Auden once called her the only living philosophical poet…The discoveries of Laura Riding's subtle ear escape analysis"—Kenneth Rexroth
0-89255-087-2 PERSEA PB $14.95

A Selection of the Poems of Laura Riding
0-89255-221-2 PERSEA PB $12.95

Laura Riding

Edwin Arlington **Robinson**

"Miniver Cheevy" and Other Poems
0-486-28756-4 DOVER PB $1.00

The Torrent & The Night Before
0-88448-183-2 TILBURY $12.95

Theodore **Roethke**

The Collected Poems
"His youthful experience around his father's greenhouse in Michigan provided just the vivid, squirmingly uncomfortable, and concrete focus his poetry needed to channel and concentrate this emotional tumult. The equally exuberant and disgusted earthiness of these poems, their violent rapport with plants and the slimy sublife of slugs and other such creatures, is unique"
—M.L. Rosenthal
0-385-08601-6 DOUBLEDAY PB $12.95

Edwin **Rolfe**

Trees Became Torches: Selected Poems
Rolfe's politically committed poetry has only recently been rediscovered
0-252-02131-2 ILLINOIS $13.95
0-252-06417-8 ILLINOIS PB $13.95

Muriel **Rukeyser**

A Muriel Rukeyser Reader
Passionately mixing the political and the erotic in poems of immense lyrical and historical sweep, Rukeyser wrote much of her best work in her final years in such underrated volumes as *Waterlily Fire* and *The Outer Banks*
0-393-03566-2 NORTON $25.00

Out of Silence: Selected Poems
EDITED BY KATE DANIELS
0-8101-5015-8 TRIQUARTERLY PB $14.95

Carl **Sandburg**
The Complete Poems of Carl Sandburg
"A marvelous prosody, a perfect ear for the beautiful potentials of common speech, something he learned from folk song, but mostly he learned from just listening"
—Kenneth Rexroth
0-15-120773-9 HARCOURT BRACE $29.95

Harvest Poems, 1910-1960
INTRODUCTION BY MARK VAN DOREN
0-15-639125-2 HARCOURT BRACE PB $8.00

The Selected Poems of Carl Sandburg
EDITED BY GEORGE HENDRICK & WILLENE HENDRICK
0-15-600396-1 HARVEST PB $15.00

May **Sarton**
Collected Poems
0-393-03493-3 NORTON $29.95

David **Schubert**
David Schubert, Works and Days
9-995-43985-9 QUARTERLY REVIEW $20.00

Delmore **Schwartz**
Late and Lost Poems: Revised Edition
Includes 17 recently discovered poems in addition to the contents of the first edition
0-8112-1096-0 NEW DIRECTIONS PB $9.95

Selected Poems: Summer Knowledge
"What renders his work so valuable…is Schwartz's profound historical consciousness…he relied on literature to explicate existence, much in the manner of a Talmudic scholar poring over some obscure text"—James Atlas
0-8112-0191-0 NEW DIRECTIONS PB $9.95

Gertrude **Stein**
Lifting Belly
A long erotic poem generally recognized as one of Stein's most moving and accessible works
0-941483-53-3 NAIAD $14.95

Gertrude Stein

Operas and Plays
0-88268-039-0 STATION HILL $29.95

Selected Writings of Gertrude Stein
Stein is a writer who makes the distinction between "prose" and "poetry" meaningless; what cannot be questioned is the depth of her continuing influence on modern American poets. A larger selection of her works will be found under Modern American Fiction
See also **FROM THE TURN OF THE CENTURY TO WORLD WAR II** under **20TH-CENTURY AMERICAN FICTION**
0-8446-6633-5 SMITH $25.30
0-679-72464-8 VINTAGE PB $18.00

Stanzas in Meditation
A rigorously abstract extended work written in 1932. "In the meditations consciousness focuses on abstract mental landscapes which do not cohere"—Ulla Dydo
1-55713-169-4 SUN & MOON PB $11.95

A Stein Reader
See also **FROM THE TURN OF THE CENTURY TO WORLD WAR II** under **20TH-CENTURY AMERICAN FICTION**
EDITED BY ULLA DYDO
0-8101-1083-0 NORTHWESTERN PB $24.95

Wallace **Stevens**
The Collected Poems
The 1954 gathering of Stevens's work, from *Harmonium* to the great late poems of *The Rock*. "His self and the sun were one / And his poems, although makings of his self, / Were no less makings of the sun"
0-394-40330-4 KNOPF $40.00

The Collected Poems of Wallace Stevens
0-679-72669-1 VINTAGE PB $15.00

Letters of Wallace Stevens
EDITED BY HOLLY STEVENS
0-520-20668-1 CALIFORNIA PB $24.95

Opus Posthumous: Poems, Plays, Prose
An enlarged, revised, and corrected edition of the companion volume to *The Collected Poems*
0-394-57792-2 KNOPF $30.00
0-679-72534-2 VINTAGE PB $17.00

The Palm at the End of the Mind: Selected Poems and a Play
"Here is the indispensable presentation of a central American poet, the best and most representative of our time"—Harold Bloom
EDITED BY HOLLY STEVENS
0-679-72445-1 VINTAGE PB $12.00

Allen **Tate**
Collected Poems, 1919-1976
0-8071-1533-9 LSU PB $9.95

Parker **Tyler**
The Granite Butterfly
The major poetic work of the film critic and pioneering avant-gardist
0-943373-27-1 NATIONAL POETRY $40.00

Robert Penn **Warren**
New and Selected Poems, 1923-1985
0-394-73848-9 RANDOM HOUSE PB $20.00

John **Wheelwright**
Collected Poems
The powerfully original work of the Boston poet who died at 43 in 1940. "I have always considered John Wheelwright to be one of the major poets of this century, on a level with Crane, Williams, Stevens, and others"—John Ashbery
EDITED BY ALVIN H. ROSENFELD
INTRODUCTION BY AUSTIN WARREN
0-8112-0849-4 NEW DIRECTIONS PB $10.00

William Carlos **Williams**
The Collected Poems of William Carlos Williams
Volume 1 1909-1939
0-8112-0999-7 NEW DIRECTIONS $35.00
Volume 2 1939-1963
0-8112-1063-4 NEW DIRECTIONS $37.00

William Carlos Williams

Imaginations
Contains some of Williams's greatest and most innovative writings, fusing poetry and prose in a variety of unpredictable ways: *Kora in Hell, Song and All, The Descent of Winter, The Great American Novel*, and others
See also **FROM THE TURN OF THE CENTURY TO WORLD WAR II** under **20TH-CENTURY AMERICAN FICTION**
EDITED BY WEBSTER SCHOTT
0-8112-0229-1 NEW DIRECTIONS PB $13.95

Paterson
All five books of Williams's personal and historical poem of his hometown in New Jersey. This edition includes Williams's notes on the sixth, unfinished book
0-8112-1225-4 NEW DIRECTIONS $38.00
0-8112-1298-X NEW DIRECTIONS PB $12.95

Before the grass is out the people are out
and bare twigs still whip the wind—
when there is nothing, in the pause between
snow and grass in the parks and at the street ends
—Say it, no ideas but in things—
nothing but the blank faces of the houses
  and cylindrical trees
bent, forked by preconception and accident
split, furrowed, creased, mottled, stained
secret—into the body of the light—
PATERSON

William Carlos **Williams**

Pictures from Brueghel: Collected Poems, 1950-1962

In addition to the title work, contains the late collections *The Desert Music* and *Journey to Love*

0-8112-0234-8 NEW DIRECTIONS PB $8.95

Selected Poems

"Although Williams has sometimes been labeled a Buddhist or Taoist, he's more like a Shintoist: the rocks vibrate, waterfalls are animate, the visible universe harbors deposits of magical energy. The ordinary is *not* ordinary; it's violent, explosive, outrageous"—*Village Voice*

EDITED BY CHARLES TOMLINSON

0-8112-0958-X NEW DIRECTIONS PB $9.95

Elinor **Wylie**

Last Poems of Elinor Wylie

0-89733-011-0 ACADEMY CHICAGO PB $8.00

Louis **Zukofsky**

"A"

Zukofsky's life work is a long poem of hermetic difficulty and frequent startling beauty

0-8018-4668-4 JOHNS HOPKINS PB $24.95

All: The Collected Short Poems, 1956-1964

"These poems are absolute clarification, crystal cabinets full of air and angels"
—Kenneth Rexroth

0-8018-4103-8 JOHNS HOPKINS $34.95

The New American Poetry

Donald Allen's *The New American Poetry*—published in 1960 and out of print at present—was a decisive event in American writing. It grouped together a variety of poets who had functioned under such rubrics as the Beats, the Black Mountain poets, the San Francisco Renaissance, and in the process revealed a new openness in structure, diction, and subject matter. Things have never been quite the same since

Helen **Adam**

Bells of Dis

0-915124-92-0 COFFEE HOUSE PB $10.00

Ghosts and Grinning Shadows

0-914610-10-4 HANGING LOOSE PB $8.00

John **Ashbery**

Ashbery's adoption by the critical establishment seems to have surprised even himself. He continues to work in the same absolutely individual voice whose echoes are everywhere in contemporary American poetry

And the Stars Were Shining

"Mr. Ashbery is the greatest original of his generation. He belongs to everyone interested in poetry or modern art, or just the possibility of change"—David Bromwich

0-374-10500-6 FS&G $18.00
0-374-52434-3 NOONDAY PB $11.00

As We Know

0-14-058591-5 PENGUIN PB $15.00

Can You Hear, Bird

A major new collection of 112 poems from the "dominant poetic voice in current American poetry"—*The Independent*. "We've come to expect the dazzle, the deadpan shifts from speed to languor, the jocular abutments of idiom, the teeming fluidities of tone....The key [is] genuine capaciousness of spirit, learning without pedantry—gifts to thank our lucky stars for"—*NY Times Book Review*

0-374-11831-0 FS&G $20.00

Flow Chart

An ambitious book-length poem published in 1992."Part of what the poetry does is stay ahead of what you might be thinking about it. By investigating the unfathomable connections between aesthetic and political domains, Ashbery creates an ever-new poetic space"
—Lawrence Joseph

0-679-74269-7 KNOPF PB $13.00

Hotel Lautréamont

This important new collection of Ashbery's poems is alive with the presences of Rimbaud, Raymond Roussel, and the pseudonymous Count de Lautréamont—the 19th-century French poet who spent his brief adult life in hotels in Paris. Tragic and playful, passionate and impersonal, these lyric poems reaffirm Ashbery as one of the most remarkable poets writing today

0-679-75276-5 KNOPF PB $13.00

John Ashbery

Rivers and Mountains

Contains the splendid long poems "Clepsydra" and "The Skaters"

0-88001-190-4 NORTON PB $9.95

Selected Poems

0-14-058553-2 VIKING PB $16.95

Self-Portrait in a Convex Mirror

"*Self-Portrait* is a laboratory in which past and present, yesterday and today, cross-fertilize each other. The alternating rhythm of withdrawal and arrival, the pendulum swing between past and present, is the mode of life that graphs the underlying blueprint of this poem's wave-like grand sweep"—Laurence Lieberman

0-14-058668-7 PENGUIN PB $12.95

Some Trees

First published in 1956. "These are amazing: each / Joining a neighbor, as though speech / Were a still performance"—from the title poem

0-88001-243-9 NORTON PB $9.95

Three Poems

Three long meditations in prose that have proven deeply influential. "Against Ashbery's, the work of most other poets seems dismally contingent. Somehow it is just the even weight he allows each thing, the possibility of blending 'in a union too subtle to cause any comment,' that accounts for its stature. This is a vision as simple to understand as it is impossible to learn"—John Koethe, *Parnassus*

0-88001-227-7 NORTON PB $8.95

Paul **Blackburn**

The Collected Poems of Paul Blackburn

"His poetry is joyous, gloomy, frisky, reflective and vulnerable to a sense of the living world that he never tried to master, but to inhabit as a kind of sad old citizen, a belonger filled with longing"—Clayton Eshleman

EDITED BY EDITH JAROLIM
FOREWORD BY M.L. ROSENTHAL

0-89255-086-4 PERSEA $37.50

Proensa: An Anthology of Troubadour Poetry

These brilliant, tensile translations of troubadour poetry contain some of Blackburn's finest work

See also **MEDIEVAL LITERATURE** in **LITERATURE OF EUROPE, AFRICA, AND ASIA**

EDITED BY GEORGE ECONOMOU

0-520-02985-2 CALIFORNIA $45.00

Selected Poems

EDITED WITH AN INTRODUCTION BY EDITH JAROLIM
FOREWORD BY M.L. ROSENTHAL

0-89255-123-2 PERSEA PB $14.95

Gregory **Corso**

"Corso is a great word-slinger, first naked sign of a poet, a scientific master of mad mouthfuls of language."—Allen Ginsberg

Elegiac Feelings American

0-8112-0026-4 NEW DIRECTIONS PB $8.95

Gasoline & The Vestal Lady on Brattle

9992762586 CITY LIGHTS PB $7.95

The Happy Birthday of Death

0-8112-0027-2 NEW DIRECTIONS PB $9.95

Long Live Man

0-8112-0025-6 NEW DIRECTIONS PB $8.95

Mindfield: New and Selected Poems

PREFACES BY WILLIAM BURROUGHS & ALLEN GINSBERG

0-938410-86-5 THUNDER'S MOUTH PB $12.95

Robert **Creeley**

The Collected Poems, 1945-1975

"From the first clear grounded 1940s insight snapshots of *For Love* through his recent decade experiments with syllable by syllable intelligence, Robert Creeley has created a noble life body of poetry that extends the work of his predecessors Pound, Williams, Zukofsky, and Olson"—Allen Ginsberg

0-520-04243-3 CALIFORNIA $45.00
0-520-04244-1 CALIFORNIA PB $15.95

Echoes
In this, his thirteenth collection of poems, Creeley continues to explore the limits and resonances, public and personal, of age.
0-8112-1263-7 NEW DIRECTIONS $17.95

Later
0-8112-0736-6 NEW DIRECTIONS PB $5.95

Memory Gardens
0-8112-0974-1 NEW DIRECTIONS PB $7.95

Places
9-991622-31-4 SMALL PRESS PB $7.50

Selected Poems
0-520-06936-6 CALIFORNIA PB $14.95

Windows
0-8112-1123-1 NEW DIRECTIONS PB $10.95

Diane **Di Prima**

Pieces of a Song: Selected Poems
Di Prima has been a consistently adventurous writer, and this survey charts the evolution of her work since the 1950s
0-87286-237-2 CITY LIGHTS PB $11.95

Seminary Poems
0-912449-34-9 FLOATING ISLAND PB $6.00

Robert **Duncan**

Bending the Bow
Initiates the long poem *Passages,* on which Duncan continued to work for the rest of his life
0-8112-0033-7 NEW DIRECTIONS PB $9.95

Ground Work II: In the Dark
Duncan's final work
0-8112-1042-1 NEW DIRECTIONS PB $9.95

The Opening of the Field
First published in 1960, this remarkable collection begins the "Structure of Rime" sequence, and contains such major works as "A Poem Beginning with a Line by Pindar" and "Often I Am Permitted to Return to a Meadow"
0-8112-0480-4 NEW DIRECTIONS PB $6.95

Selected Poems
Although tantalizingly brief (for such an expansive poet) and problematic in its selections, this is an indispensable retrospective of the writer who possessed one of the finest and most musical ears in American poetry—in Ferlinghetti's terms, "the finest ear this side of Dante." Duncan "is and will be always the magister, the singular Master of the Dance" —Robert Creeley
0-8112-1227-0 NEW DIRECTIONS $12.95

Larry **Eigner**

Areas; Lights; Heights
0-937804-33-9 SUN & MOON PB $12.00

Things Stirring Together or Far Away
"It is a full, complete world, even if, for most of the poems, the world extends no farther than his front porch.... Forced to spend most of his days in a wheel chair, he has learned to see and hear with a sensitive, untiring coherence" —Samuel Charters
0-87685-187-1 BLACK SPARROW PB $5.00

Waters; Places; A Time
A sensitively edited selection from the work of the poet who died in 1996
EDITED BY ROBERT GRENIER
0-87685-497-8 BLACK SPARROW PB $7.50

Windows; Walls; Yard; Ways
EDITED BY ROBERT GRENIER
0-87685-921-X BLACK SPARROW $25.00
0-87685-920-1 BLACK SPARROW PB $13.00

Lawrence **Ferlinghetti**

A Coney Island of the Mind
0-8112-0041-8 NEW DIRECTIONS PB $6.95

Pictures of the Gone World
An item for every basic Beat library: one of the early classics of the Pocket Poets series. This revised edition has 18 additional poems
0-87286-303-4 SUBTERRANEAN PB $6.95

These Are My Rivers: New and Selected Poems, 1955-1993
A unique figure in American letters, Ferlinghetti founded City Lights Press and introduced millions of readers to such unknown works as Allen Ginsberg's *Howl* and Gregory Corso's *Gasoline*—in editions that cost as little as half a dollar and fit in your pocket. But first and foremost he was a poet with a singular voice of unadorned lyricism that spoke straight to the heart. Here he selects the best work from his ten books, including the Beat landmark *A Coney Island of the Mind.* "Dynamic, verbose, alarming, charming, and unsettling poetry"—*Library Journal*
0-8112-1252-1 NEW DIRECTIONS $22.95

Allen **Ginsberg**

Collected Poems, 1947-1980
The full texts of *Howl, Kaddish, Reality Sandwiches, Planet News, The Fall of America, Mind Breaths,* and much else
0-06-091494-7 HARPERCOLLINS PB $23.00

Cosmopolitan Greetings: Poems, 1986-1992
0-06-092623-6 HARPERPERENNIAL PB $12.00

Howl and other Poems
0-872-86310-7 CITY LIGHTS $12.95

Illuminated Poems
ILLUSTRATED BY ERIC DROOKER
1-56858-045-2 FOUR WALLS $35.00
1-56858-070-3 FOUR WALLS PB $18.95

Reality Sandwiches, 1953-1960
0-872-86021-3 CITY LIGHTS PB $7.95

Selected Poems, 1947-1995
0-06-016457-3 HARPERCOLLINS $27.50

White Shroud: Poems, 1980-1985
0-06-055030-9 HARPERCOLLINS $50.00
0-06-091429-7 HARPERCOLLINS PB $13.00

Bob **Kaufman**

The Ancient Rain: Poems, 1956-1978
EDITED BY RAYMOND FOYE
0-8112-0790-0 NEW DIRECTIONS $5.95

Cranial Guitar: Selected Poems
EDITED BY GERALD NICOSIA
1-56689-038-1 COFFEE HOUSE PB $12.95

Solitudes Crowded with Loneliness
0-8112-0076-0 NEW DIRECTIONS PB $6.95

Jack **Kerouac**

"Jack Kerouac, new Buddha of American prose, who spit forth intelligence...a spontaneous bop prosody and original classic literature." —*Allen Ginsberg*

Book of Blues
0-14-058700-4 PENGUIN PB $12.95

Mexico City Blues: 242 Choruses
0-8021-3060-7 GROVE PB $12.00

Poems All Sizes
0-87286-269-0 CITY LIGHTS PB $10.95

Jack Kerouac

Kenneth **Koch**

On the Great Atlantic Rainway: Selected Poems, 1950-1988
Technician and farceur, Koch has experimented tirelessly with new forms and novel situations
0-679-76582-4 KNOPF PB $17.00

One Train
0-679-43417-8 KNOPF $20.00
0-679-76583-2 KNOPF PB $13.00

Denise **Levertov**

Breathing the Water
0-8112-1027-8 NEW DIRECTIONS PB $8.95

Collected Earlier Poems, 1940-1960
0-8112-0718-8 NEW DIRECTIONS PB $9.95

The Freeing of the Dust
0-8112-0582-7 NEW DIRECTIONS PB $7.95

Life in the Forest
0-8112-0693-9 NEW DIRECTIONS PB $7.95

Oblique Prayers: New Poems with 14 Translations
0-8112-0909-1 NEW DIRECTIONS PB $6.95

Poems, 1960-1967
Includes *The Jacob's Ladder, O Taste and See,* and *The Sorrow Dance*
0-8112-0859-1 NEW DIRECTIONS PB $9.95

Poems, 1968-1972
Includes *Relearning the Alphabet, To Stay Alive,* and *Footprints*
0-8112-1005-7 NEW DIRECTIONS PB $12.95

Sands of the Well
Here, Levertov is at the height of her considerable powers: "And then/once more the quiet mystery/is present to me, the throng's clamor/recedes: the mystery/that there is anything, anything at all,/let alone cosmos, joy, memory, everything,/rather than void: and that, O Lord,/Creator, Hallowed One, You still,/hour by hour sustain it." "Book by book, I have read her poems for their subtle music, for their deep compassionate intelligence, for their imagination, for the author's dignity and integrity and grace"—Sam Hamill
0-8112-1316-1 NEW DIRECTIONS $20.95

Michael **McClure**

Selected Poems
0-8112-0950-4 NEW DIRECTIONS $8.95
0-8112-0951-2 NEW DIRECTIONS PB $7.95

Simple Eyes & Other Poems
0-8112-1265-3 NEW DIRECTIONS PB $10.95

Three Poems: Dolphin Skull, Rare Angel, and Dark Brown
0-14-058709-8 PENGUIN PB $14.95

Frank **O'Hara**

The Collected Poems of Frank O'Hara
EDITED BY DONALD ALLEN
0-520-20166-3 CALIFORNIA PB $18.00

Meditations in an Emergency
0-8021-3452-1 GROVE PB $10.00

Selected Poems
Few styles have been more widely imitated than O'Hara's conversational lyricism, open to every passing influence in the inner and outer worlds
EDITED BY DONALD ALLEN
0-394-71973-5 RANDOM HOUSE PB $17.00

Charles **Olson**

The Collected Poems
Nearly all of Olson's poetry aside from *The Maximus Poems,* including much work never before published
EDITED BY GEORGE BUTTERICK
0-520-05764-3 CALIFORNIA $65.00

The Maximus Poems
"Olson's spiritual barometers and seismographs give readings that we have to live with for awhile before they begin to render up sense. His view of mankind reaches into the backward abysm. Geologically the world is in the Pleistocene still, the age that evolved the horse, elephant, and cow more or less as we know them. And man. And the arrangements of the continents as they now are…The severing of the continents is itself a comprehensive symbol of disintegration, of man's migratory fate, of the tragic restlessness of history"—Guy Davenport
EDITED BY GEORGE F. BUTTERICK
0-520-05595-0 CALIFORNIA PB $34.95

A Nation of Nothing but Poetry: Supplementary Poems
Work not included in the *Collected Poems*
0-87685-750-0 BLACK SPARROW PB $12.50

Selected Poems
0-520-07528-5 CALIFORNIA $25.00

Joel **Oppenheimer**

New Spaces: Poems, 1975-1983
0-87685-640-7 BLACK SPARROW PB $8.50

Why Not
"Spare and understated gems"—*Small Press*
0-934834-32-6 WHITE PINE PB $7.00

James **Schuyler**

Collected Poems
"There is no better way to come to [Schuyler's] poetry than to come to it all at once.... One sees at a sweep his life's work in all its comic elegance, its sad grandeur and wit, the gushing-forth of confessed love affairs and chemical addictions, as well as restraints and subtleties"—Liz Rosenberg, *Boston Globe*
0-374-12618-6 FS&G $35.00
0-374-52403-3 NOONDAY PB $14.00

Selected Poems
"One of the most original poets in America…He shares with Elizabeth Bishop…the knack of making the lyric dramatic"—Howard Moss
0-374-25878-3 FS&G $25.00

Gary **Snyder**

Axe Handles
0-86547-120-7 NORTH POINT PB $10.00

Left Out in the Rain: New Poems, 1947-1986
A revealing collection of outtakes and uncollected work that adds up to an informal graph of Snyder's evolution as a writer
0-86547-268-8 FS&G PB $12.00

Mountains and Rivers Without End
A book-length cycle of poems now completed decades after the earliest sections appeared. Taking its inspiration from Chinese scroll painting, it embodies Snyder's world-view
1-88717-820-1 COUNTERPOINT $20.00

Myths & Texts
A stunning poem cycle interweaving Buddhist and Native American elements with Snyder's own experience as a logger
0-8112-0686-6 NEW DIRECTIONS PB $6.95

No Nature: New and Selected Poems
Over a period of years Snyder has carved his own place in American writing—a charter member of the Beat generation, the model for Kerouac's *Dharma Bums*, a disciplined Buddhist, naturalist, etymologist, wanderer, a poet self-taught in the tradition of Ezra Pound. His poems are like Sung landscape paintings, deceptively simple meditations on what lies without. This book surveys his life's work, from the groundbreaking *Riprap* poems onward. "I have always found it difficult to imagine this century without the life and work of Gary Synder"—Wes Jackson
0-679-74252-2 PANTHEON PB $14.00

Regarding Wave
0-8112-0196-1 NEW DIRECTIONS PB $7.95

Riprap & Cold Mountain Poems
Snyder's brilliant first book, along with his translations from the Chinese Zen poet Han Shan
0-86547-455-9 NORTH POINT $19.95
0-86547-456-7 NORTH POINT PB $9.00

Turtle Island
0-8112-0546-0 NEW DIRECTIONS PB $7.95

Gary Snyder (photo by Virginia Schendler)

Gilbert **Sorrentino**

The Orangery
Reissue of Sorrentino's memorable set of variations on the word "orange," in wildly varying contexts. "In *The Orangery* Sorrentino makes things which are hard, gaudy and sometimes scary. They are stark artifacts of our world but not the world. They are made to last"—William Bronk
See also **SINCE 1945** under **20TH-CENTURY AMERICAN FICTION**
1-55713-225-9 SUN & MOON PB $10.95

Jack **Spicer**

The Collected Books of Jack Spicer
A poet-linguist who died prematurely in 1965, Spicer exercised a subterranean influence on American poetry for many years before his "serial poems" were finally gathered together. This extraordinary volume contains *After Lorca, Billy the Kid, The Heads of the Town On Up to the Aether, A Book of Music, Language, A Book of Magazine Verse,* and all the other late work
EDITED BY ROBIN BLASER
0-87685-241-X BLACK SPARROW PB $12.50

Lew **Welch**

Ring of Bone: Collected Poems, 1950-1971
EDITED BY DONALD ALLEN
0-912516-03-8 GREY FOX PB $12.95

Selected Poems
0-912516-20-8 GREY FOX PB $4.95

Philip **Whalen**

Clips: Buddhist Poems
0-938077-79-1 PARALLAX PB $12.00

Heavy Breathing: Poems, 1967-1980
0-87704-057-5 SUBTERRANEAN PB $9.95

Scenes of Life at the Capital
A book-length meditative poem; the capital in question is Kyoto
0-912516-00-3 SUBTERRANEAN PB $2.50

The New York School

The New York School is so called in homage to the great Abstract Expressionist painters of the '50s, and the poetry of Ashbery and O'Hara shares with the painting of de Kooning and Pollock a willingness to follow the unforeseen leads that arise in the very process of making art. In James Schuyler's work, and in the poems Frank O'Hara dashed off in the course of a day and happily called "lunch poems," another outstanding quality of the New York School emerges: unusual emotional intimacy and poise with an alert sense of humor.

John **Ashbery**
Rivers and Mountains
A volume from the '60s. In "Clepsydra" and "The Skaters," Ashbery first began to explore the potential of the long poem.

Frank **O'Hara**
Meditations in an Emergency
Few styles have been more widely imitated than O'Hara's conversational lyricism, open to every passing influence in the inner and outer worlds.

Edwin **Denby**
Collected Poems
Denby, a distinguished dance critic, was also a masterful and quirky writer of sonnets.

James **Schuyler**
The Collected Poems
"There is no better way to come to [Schuyler's] poetry than to come at all at once...One sees at a sweep his life's work in all its comic elegance, its sad grandeur and wit, the gushing-forth of confessed love affairs and chemical addictions, as well as restraints and subtleties."—*Boston Globe*

Kenneth **Koch**
Seasons on Earth
Includes the fanciful and inventive long poems *Ko, or a Season on Earth* and *The Duplications.*

Bernadette **Mayer**
A Bernadette Mayer Reader
"Love and the seasons and the exigencies and opportunities of daily survival are the inevitable occasions of a body of work that is as radical as it is Horatian, able as little else is both to delight and instruct."—*Boston Review*

Ron **Padgett**
Great Balls of Fire
Originally published in 1969, this volume established Padgett as one of the most comically inventive of the New York poets.

John **Wieners**
Cultural Affairs in Boston: Poetry and Prose, 1956-1985
0-87685-738-1 BLACK SPARROW PB $10.00

Selected Poems, 1958-1984
A thorough presentation of Wieners's work, beginning with the legendary *Hotel Wentley Poems.* "He presents emotion on the spot—despair, nostalgia, bliss of love, dissatisfaction, flesh pressing on flesh"—Allen Ginsberg
EDITED BY RAYMOND FOYE
FOREWORD BY ALLEN GINSBERG
0-87685-501-X BLACK SPARROW PB $12.50

Jonathan **Williams**
Eight Days in Eire: Or, Nothing So Urgent as Mañana
0-933598-14-9 NORTH CAROLINA WESLEYAN PB $10.00

Get Hot or Get Out: A Selection of Poems, 1957-1981
0-8108-1495-1 SCARECROW $13.50

Metafours for Mysophobes
1-87031-413-1 SMALL PRESS PB $12.00

Poetry Since 1945

Ai
Greed
0-393-03561-1 NORTON $17.95

Elizabeth **Alexander**
The Venus Hottentot
0-8139-1273-3 VIRGINIA PB $8.95

Night-Scene, The Garden
0-87376-074-3 RED DUST PB $3.00

Will **Alexander**
Asia & Haiti
Long poems which are at once surreal and historical, characterized by extraordinary flights of verbal invention
1-55713-189-9 SUN & MOON PB $11.95

Sherman **Alexie**
The Business of Fancydancing: Stories and Poems
See also **NEW WRITERS OF THE '90S** under **20TH-CENTURY AMERICAN FICTION**
See also **CONTEMPORARY NATIVE AMERICAN WRITERS** under **NATIVE AMERICAN LITERATURES**
0-914610-00-7 HANGING LOOSE PB $10.00

Miguel **Algarin**
Body Bee Calling from the 21st Century
An odyssey into the bionic 21st century
0-934770-17-4 ARTE PUBLICO PB $7.00

Time's Now/Ya Es Tiempo
Poetic travels from the most recondite corners of the soul through the streets of New York and to other battlefields—this time Central America
0-934770-33-6 ARTE PUBLICO PB $7.00

Heather **Allen**
Leaving a Shadow
1-55659-113-6 COPPER CANYON PB $12.00

A.R. **Ammons**
Brink Road
The latest collection from the winner of two National Book Awards, the Bollingen Prize, and the Robert Frost Medal from the Poetry Society of America. Elegance, wit, and ruminative gravity are the signature qualities embedded in this masterful collection. "No contemporary poet, in America, is likelier to become a classic than A.R. Ammons."—Harold Bloom
0-393-03958-7 NORTON $23.00

Garbage
0-393-03542-5 NORTON $17.95
0-393-31203-8 NORTON PB $9.00

The Really Short Poems of A.R. Ammons
0-393-30850-2 NORTON PB $9.95

The Selected Poems
0-393-30396-9 NORTON PB $9.95

Sphere: The Form of a Motion
0-393-31310-7 NORTON PB $8.95

Tape for the Turn of the Year
0-393-31204-6 NORTON PB $11.00

Worldly Hopes
0-393-00081-8 NORTON PB $5.95

Michael **Anania**
Selected Poems
1-55921-113-X MOYER BELL PB $14.95

The Sky at Ashland
Fluent poems of landscape and color
0-918825-32-6 MOYER BELL PB $7.95

Jon **Anderson**
The Milky Way: Poems, 1967-1982
Jon Anderson (1940-) is an elegiac writer focused and concentrated on the impermanent borderlines between solipsism, need, and community
0-88001-007-X ECCO PB $8.50

Bruce **Andrews**
Give 'Em Enough Rope
0-940650-73-8 SUN & MOON PB $10.95

I Don't Have Any Paper So Shut Up (or, Social Romanticism)
1-55713-077-9 SUN & MOON PB $13.95

Tom **Andrews**
Tom Andrews was born in Charleston, West Virginia in 1961. He currently teaches at Ohio University and lives in Lancaster, Ohio.
The Brother's Country
0-89255-151-8 PERSEA PB $9.95

The Hemophiliac's Motorcycle
0-87745-452-3 IOWA PB $10.95

Ralph **Angel**
Anxious Latitudes
0-8195-1125-0 WESLEYAN PB $7.95

Ralph **Angel**
Neither World
Plain, urgent speech is made to border on abstraction. "The poems say things you yourself wanted to say but left unsaid" —Michael Burkard
1-88116-313-X MIAMI PB $9.95

Maya **Angelou**
The Complete Collected Poems of Maya Angelou
The entire poetic opus, completely reset and beautifully presented, by the bestselling writer, accomplished poet and performer, and inaugural speaker
0-679-42895-X RANDOM HOUSE $23.00

I Shall Not Be Moved
0-553-35458-2 BANTAM PB $9.95

Just Give Me a Cool Dr.nk of Water 'fore I Die
0-394-47142-3 RANDOM HOUSE $18.00

On the Pulse of Morning: The Inaugural Poem
Angelou's ode to the diversity of America. For those moments it was the conscience of America, read at President Clinton's inauguration in 1993
0-679-42894-1 RANDOM HOUSE $13.00
0-679-74838-5 RANDOM HOUSE PB $6.00

Phenomenal Woman: Four Poems Celebrating Women
See also **CLASSIC AUTOBIOGRAPHIES** under **BLACK VOICES, BLACK LIVES** under **AFRICAN-AMERICAN STUDIES** in **HISTORY OF THE AMERICAS**
0-679-43924-2 RANDOM HOUSE $10.00

Maya **Angelou** & Jean-Michel **Basquiat**
Life Doesn't Frighten Me
An unusual mixture of forms, uniquely appropriate for children. The dynamic combination of the strength and courage of Angelou's poems and the daring of Basquiat's full-color artwork, together, in this unique book, compose a testament to courage
See also **BOOKS FOR AGES FIVE, SIX, AND SEVEN** in **BOOKS FOR YOUNG READERS**
EDITED BY SARA JANE BOYERS
1-55670-288-4 STEWART, TABORI $15.95

David **Antin**
Selected Poems, 1963-1973
Includes work from the early collections *Definitions, Autobiography, Code of Flag Behavior,* and others
1-55713-058-2 SUN & MOON PB $13.95

What It Means to Be Avant-Garde
0-8112-1238-6 NEW DIRECTIONS PB $15.95

James **Applewhite**
Lessons in Soaring
0-8071-1540-1 LSU PB $6.95

River Writing: An Eno Journal
"Applewhite has found his true subject as a poet, and has developed a stance and style wholly adequate to the philosophical and spiritual reach of his poignant concerns"—Harold Bloom
0-691-01442-6 PRINCETON PB $9.95

Rae **Armantrout**
Made to Seem
1-55713-220-8 SUN & MOON PB $9.95

Necromance
"At a time when experimental writing has lost at least some of its shock value, Rae Armantrout's *Necromance* could startle even the most jaded reader"—Elaine Equi
1-55713-096-5 SUN & MOON PB $8.95

Precedence
Small, deft constructions by one of the most original of the "language" poets
0-930901-24-X BURNING DECK PB $5.00

L. S. **Asekoff**
Dreams of a Work
"His eye employs the daily, surreal, Zen, dream properties of life; his gift for narrative and lyric and iron dialectic establishes presences as solid as any table or human face"—Stephen Berg
0-914061-47-X ORCHISES $18.95

Paul **Auster**
Disappearances: Selected Poems
Includes the collections *Wall Writing, White Spaces, Facing the Music,* and others, by the author of *The New York Trilogy*
0-87951-328-4 OVERLOOK $16.95
0-87951-341-1 OVERLOOK PB $12.95

Jimmy Santiago **Baca**
Black Mesa Poems
0-8112-1102-9 NEW DIRECTIONS PB $9.95

Martin & Meditations on the South Valley
Two long narrative poems of New Mexico. "He is far from being a naive realist; what makes his writing so exciting to me is the way in which it manifests both an intense lyricism and that transformative vision which perceives the mythic and archetypal significance of events" —Denise Levertov
INTRODUCTION BY DENISE LEVERTOV
0-8112-1032-4 NEW DIRECTIONS PB $8.95

Working in the Dark
1-87861-008-2 RED CRANE $19.95

John **Balaban**
Words for My Daughter
1-55659-037-7 COPPER CANYON PB $10.00

James **Baldwin**
Jimmy's Blues: Selected Poems
0-312-44247-5 ST. MARTIN'S $15.95

Amiri **Baraka**
Baraka, formerly known as LeRoi Jones, was an important voice in the 1960s, with his incendiary work calling for radical social change.

Transbluesency: Poems of Amiri Baraka/LeRoi Jones (1961-1995)
A major survey of Baraka's whole poetic work, through all its aesthetic and political phases
EDITED BY PAUL VANGELISTI
1-56886-013-7 MARSILIO $32.95
1-56886-014-5 MARSILIO PB $17.95

Amiri Baraka

Wise Why's Y's: The Griot's Tale
0-88378-150-6 THIRD WORLD $14.95
0-88378-047-X THIRD WORLD PB $12.00

Gerald **Barrax**
An Audience of One
0-8203-0500-6 GEORGIA $15.00
0-8203-0502-2 GEORGIA PB $7.95

The Deaths of Animals and Lesser Gods
0-912759-02-X CALLALOO JOURNAL PB $9.95

Leaning Against the Sun
1-55728-226-9 ARKANSAS $16.95
1-55728-227-7 ARKANSAS PB $8.95

Paul **Beatty**
Big Bank Take Little Bank
"Beatty's a poet for us kids who grew up on Saturday morning cartoons, video games, and rap, and have a jumble of media bites rattling in our brain cages....Beatty piles word play upon word play in a hyperstack of meaning" —Evelyn McDonnell, *Village Voice*
0-9627842-7-3 NUYORICAN POETS CAFE PB $9.95

Joker, Joker, Deuce
0-14-058723-3 PENGUIN PB $13.95

Robin **Becker**
All-American Girl
0-8229-5580-6 PITTSBURGH PB $10.95

Robin **Behn**
Robin Behn currently teaches at the University of Alabama.

Paper Bird
0-89672-163-9 TEXAS TECH PB $9.95

The Red Hour
0-06-096952-0 HARPERPERENNIAL PB $12.00

Erin **Belieu**
Infanta
1-55659-101-2 COPPER CANYON PB $12.00

Marvin **Bell**
"Bell's work is eclectic, domestic, personable, demotic in its sympathies and accent, busy with the quotidian yet with an ear out for the Undersong of Myself."—Poetry

The Book of the Dead Man
The poet's ninth collection, revolving around the admonition to "live as if you were already dead"
1-55659-063-6 COPPER CANYON PB $12.00

Iris of Creation
1-55659-032-6 COPPER CANYON PB $10.00

A Marvin Bell Reader
Collected works from Bell's 30-year career combine to form a unique and arresting composite
0-87451-670-6 MIDDLEBURY PB $17.95

Stars Which See, Stars Which Do Not See
0-88748-138-8 CARNEGIE-MELLON PB $10.95

April **Bernard**

Psalms
0-393-03569-7 NORTON $17.95
0-393-31304-2 NORTON PB $9.00

Charles **Bernstein**

The Absent Father in Dumbo
84-87467-03-2 SMALL PRESS PB $7.00

Dark City
1-55713-162-7 SUN & MOON PB $11.95

Islets/Irritations
0-937804-47-9 ROOF PB $9.95

The Lives of the Toll Takers
0-942433-14-9 SMALL PRESS PB $10.00

Republics of Reality: 1975-1995
1-55713-304-2 SUN & MOON PB $14.95

Rough Trades
"*Rough Trades* is Bernstein's most 'personalized' book. It is certainly his most readable book. And, I might add, for me it is his best"
—Keith Tuma, *Sulfur*
1-55713-080-9 SUN & MOON PB $10.95

The Sophist
"Yes, Bernstein is an elegant poet, and his work suggests to me that it is precisely a tradition of elegance which we can see evolving as we pass from Zukofsky to Creeley to, now Bernstein"
—Burton Hatlen, *Sagetrieb*
0-940650-78-9 SUN & MOON $16.96
0-940650-79-7 SUN & MOON PB $11.95

Ted **Berrigan**

Selected Poems
The Sonnets and more, by the quintessential poet of the East Village
0-14-058699-7 PENGUIN PB $12.50

Frank **Bidart**

In the Western Night: Collected Poems, 1965-90
0-374-52271-5 NOONDAY PB $13.95

Sophie Cabot **Black**

The Misunderstanding of Nature
A brilliant debut collection, and a winner of the Poetry Society of America's Norma Farber first book award. Among the poems in this collection is a lengthy poem about the pilgrim Dorothy Bradford, William Bradford's wife, who mysteriously drowned one night while the Mayflower was anchored off the coast of Massachusetts
1-55597-201-2 GRAY WOLF PB $12.00

Robert **Bly**

Light Around the Body
0-06-090786-X HARPERCOLLINS PB $9.95

The Man in the Black Coat Turns
0-06-097186-X HARPERCOLLINS PB $10.00

News of the Universe: Poems of Twofold Consciousness
0-87156-368-1 SIERRA CLUB PB $12.00

Selected Poems
"Robert Bly has, in his time, changed American poetry: opened up new directions it might move in, inspired some poets to explore those directions, others to react strongly against such prospects. His role, stature, and style seem to me equivalent to that of Ezra Pound in the early decades of this century"—Gregory Orr
0-06-096048-5 HARPERCOLLINS PB $12.00

Nina **Bogin**

In the North
Nina Bogin, an American poet long resident in France, has written a first book notable for its spare clarity and emotional directness: "The dark weeds, the drenched/ odor of lilacs./ It is the child come back/ to my arms, his skin/ humid, smelling of leaving./ He has been left outside/ and the flowers/ have grown up around him." A powerful simplicity distinguishes all of the poems in this promising collection
1-55597-121-0 GRAY WOLF $14.00

Catherine **Bowman**

Rock Farm
0-87905-745-9 GIBBS SMITH PB $12.95

George **Bradley**

Of the Knowledge of Good and Evil
The second book by a poet whose first was chosen for the Yale Series of Younger Poets Award by James Merrill
0-679-74273-5 KNOPF PB $12.00

Joe **Brainard**

I Remember
Artist-in-residence to the New York school of poets, Brainard was himself a writer of unique and underrated gifts. *I Remember* is his masterpiece, a sentence-by-sentence evocation of the past which has had wide influence
0-14-024521-9 PENGUIN PB $9.95

Lucie **Brock-Broido**

The Master Letters: Poems
From the distinguished professor of creative writing at Columbia University, a collection largely influenced by the manuscripts and letters of Emily Dickinson
0-679-44174-3 KNOPF $21.00

Karen **Brodine**

Illegal Assembly
0-914610-17-1 HANGING LOOSE PB $6.00

Woman Sitting at the Machine, Thinking
0-932323-01-4 RED LETTER PB $8.95

David **Bromige**

Desire: Selected Poems, 1963-1987
0-87685-724-1 BLACK SPARROW $20.00

Olga **Broumas**

Pastoral Jazz
"A lot of people these days write about love and nature, but none do it with Broumas's luminous language"—Susan Mernit
0-914742-70-1 INLAND PB $7.00

Perpetua
Emotionally and erotically direct poetry of great tenderness and strength
1-55659-025-3 COPPER CANYON PB $11.00

Christopher **Buckley**

Christopher Buckley is currently a professor of English at Westchester University in Pennsylvania.

Blue Autumn
0-914278-53-3 COPPER BEECH PB $9.95

Dark Matter
0-914278-62-2 COPPER BEECH PB $9.95

Charles **Bukowski**

Betting on the Muse: Poems and Stories
Bukowski battles on until his last breath, punching away at hypocrisy and fakery to lay bare essential truths. "I must soon declare my own war on their war/I must hold to my last piece of ground/I must protect the small space I have made that has allowed me life"
1-57423-002-6 BLACK SPARROW $27.50
1-57423-001-8 BLACK SPARROW PB $15.00

Burning in Water, Drowning in Flame
0-87685-191-X BLACK SPARROW PB $13.00

The Days Run Away Like Wild Horses Over the Hills
0-87685-005-0 BLACK SPARROW PB $12.00

The Last Night of the Earth Poems
0-87685-863-9 BLACK SPARROW PB $15.00

Love Is a Dog from Hell: Poems, 1974-1977
0-87685-362-9 BLACK SPARROW PB $14.00

Mockingbird Wish Me Luck
0-87685-138-3 BLACK SPARROW PB $11.00

Play the Piano Drunk Like a Percussion Instrument Until the Fingers Begin to Bleed a Bit
0-87685-437-4 BLACK SPARROW PB $12.00

The Roominghouse Madrigals: Early Selected Poems, 1946-1966
0-87685-732-2 BLACK SPARROW PB $14.00

You Get So Alone at Times that It Just Makes Sense
0-87685-683-0 BLACK SPARROW PB........$14.00

Gerald **Burns**
Shorter Poems
1-56478-026-0 DALKEY ARCHIVE PB........$9.95

Don **Byrd**
The Great Dimestore Centennial
An ambitious book-length poem mixing together everything from Wittgenstein to Bud Powell
0-88268-025-0 STATION HILL........$13.95

Marcus **Cafagna**
The Broken World
0-252-06550-6 ILLINOIS PB........$10.95

John **Cage**
Composition in Retrospect
1-87897-211-1 EXACT CHANGE PB........$13.95

Scott **Cairns**
Figures for the Ghost
0-8203-1601-6 GEORGIA PB........$9.95

The Theology of Doubt
0-914946-52-8 CLEVELAND STATE PB........$6.00

The Translation of Babel
0-8203-1200-2 GEORGIA PB........$8.95

Jim **Carroll**
Fear of Dreaming: The Selected Poems of Jim Carroll
0-14-058695-4 PENGUIN PB........$14.95

Living at the Movies
0-14-042290-0 PENGUIN PB........$12.95

Hayden **Carruth**
Asphalt Georgics
0-8112-0938-5 NEW DIRECTIONS PB........$6.95

The Collected Longer Poems
1-55659-058-X COPPER CANYON........$25.00
1-55659-059-8 COPPER CANYON PB........$14.00

Collected Shorter Poems, 1946-1991
1-55659-049-0 COPPER CANYON PB........$14.00

Scrambled Eggs & Whiskey: Poems, 1991-1995
1-55659-109-8 COPPER CANYON........$25.00
1-55659-110-1 COPPER CANYON PB........$14.00

The Sleeping Beauty
1-55659-033-4 COPPER CANYON PB........$10.00

Tell Me Again How the White Heron Rises and Flies Across the Nacreous River at Twilight Toward the Distant Islands
0-8112-0681-5 NEW DIRECTIONS........$15.00

Confessional Poetry

Confessional poetry emerged towards the end of, and in reaction to, what Robert Lowell called the "tranquilized fifties." Alternating between an extremist poetry of self-exposure and sober recitations of personal and family history, confessionalism became arguably the most influential poetic trend of the '60s and '70s and continues to define the work of such contemporaries as Sharon Olds.

John **Berryman**
Dream Songs
"The *Dream Songs* are...the fragmentary inner biography, the perceptions by which he lives, of a character called Henry... Berryman is deliberately a mannerist who, out of his fraught nerviness, had made an original and remarkably flexible style."—A. Alvarez

Robert **Lowell**
Life Studies
Beginning with poems that describe the poet's episodes of madness and continuing with a lengthy prose memoir of his childhood, *Life Studies* proved the model for much subsequent confessional poetry.

Sharon **Olds**
The Father
A sequence of poems about Olds' troubled relationship with her father.

Sylvia **Plath**
Ariel
Published just after her suicide in 1961, *Ariel* became the prototype of confessional extremism and remains one of most accomplished examples of the genre.

Adrienne **Rich**
Diving into the Wreck
"With 'Diving into the Wreck,' Rich completes her re-vision of woman as monster. It becomes a source of poetic/political identity extracted from the wreckage of self and society under patriachial rule. The old dispensation is displaced and a new 'book of myths' can be written."—Terrence Des Pres

Anne **Carson**
Glass, Irony and God
"Narratives as beguiling as good short stories...She commands a depth of field and a richness of emotion not often seen in contemporary verse"—Guy Davenport
0-8112-1302-1 NEW DIRECTIONS PB........$14.00

Plainwater: Essays and Poetry
0-679-43178-0 KNOPF........$23.00

Siv **Cedering**
Letters from the Floating World: New and Selected Poems
0-8229-5363-3 PITTSBURGH PB........$12.95

Joseph **Ceravolo**
The Green Lake Is Awake
Ceravolo, who died in 1988, is increasingly recognized as a poet of unique and exhilarating gifts. "He is one of those rare poets who make you want to sit down and write a thousand poems and who simultaneously make you feel nothing you've ever done or will ever do is good enough"—Charles North
1-56689-021-7 COFFEE HOUSE PB........$11.95

Fred **Chappell**
C: Poems
0-8071-1785-4 LSU PB........$8.95

Richard **Chess**
Tekiah
0-8203-1678-4 GEORGIA PB........$10.95

Nicholas **Christopher**
5 Degrees & Other Poems
0-14-058718-7 PENGUIN PB........$12.95

Desperate Characters: A Novella in Verse & Other Poems
The title work is an extended riff on the themes and recurrent images of film noir
0-14-012116-1 PENGUIN PB........$12.50

In the Year of the Comet
The fourth book of poetry by the winner of the prestigious Peter I.B. Lavan Award from the Academy of American Poets. "Everything here is luminous with accuracy of sight and delicacy of insight. He must now rank among the very best poets of his generation"—Anthony Hecht
0-14-058687-3 PENGUIN PB........$9.00

Sandra **Cisneros**
Loose Woman
The vibrant author of *The House on Mango Street* and *My Wicked Wicked Ways* regales us with her erotic survivor's voice from the barrio. Self-mocking, sincere, unbridled, rude—these intoxicating poems are exactly what Cisneros's many readers have come to expect from her
0-679-41644-7 KNOPF........$20.00

Sandra Cisneros (credit: ©Rubén Guzmán)

My Wicked Wicked Ways
The musical, radiant, passionate poems of Sandra Cisneros (*Woman Hollering Creek, The House on Mango Street*) are printed here for the first time in hardcover. Cisneros is "not only a gifted writer, but an absolutely essential one" —*NY Times Book Review*
0-679-41821-0 TURTLE BAY $16.00

Amy **Clampitt**
Archaic Figure
Of this collection, the author wrote: "The experience of attachment to another person or persons is a recurring theme in these poems, particularly those on George Eliot, Margaret Fuller and Dorothy Wordsworth; and the same theme is continued, sometimes metaphorically sometimes explicitly, in the final section. ...As before, there are evocations of Maine and other places, including Greece, England, Venice, and my native Midwest"
0-394-75090-X RANDOM HOUSE PB $12.95

The Kingfisher
"How to describe the delights of these poems? If Gerard Hopkins and Marianne Moore, those two uniquenesses, had married each other they might have borne Amy Clampitt, who brings to one in truly marvelous abundance, through metaphor, adjective and narrative, the burnished details of the world"—Mona Van Duyn
0-394-71251-X KNOPF PB $18.00

A Silence Opens
0-679-42997-2 KNOPF $20.00
0-679-75022-3 KNOPF PB $13.00

Westward
0-679-72867-8 KNOPF PB $15.00

What the Light Was Like
0-394-72937-4 KNOPF PB $15.00

Tom **Clark**
Like Real People
Drawing on private history and imaginative vision, Clark's new collection climaxes 30 years' experimental work in the lyric and shows a major American poet writing at the height of his powers. "Clark really flows and gambles and plays it loose. I like his guts. ...He's the raw gnawing end of the moon"—Charles Bukowski
0-87685-985-6 BLACK SPARROW $25.00
0-87685-984-8 BLACK SPARROW PB $13.50

David **Clewell**
Blessings in Disguise
0-14-058672-5 PENGUIN PB $12.50

Now We're Getting Somewhere
0-299-14410-0 WISCONSIN $17.95
0-299-14414-3 WISCONSIN PB $10.95

Lucille **Clifton**
The Book of Light
Clifton's poems are songs of the earth, of the spirit, of the self. In this new collection she begins by remembering her mother, and from that point of departure the poet reaches for the divine. "The poems here...are filled with a tangle of hot-to-the-touch cravings....There is a God in these poems, but that God is silent" —*NY Times Book Review*
1-55659-051-2 COPPER CANYON $21.00
1-55659-052-0 COPPER CANYON PB $11.00

Quilting: Poems, 1987-1990
"Ms. Clifton's poetry is big enough to accommodate sorrow and madness and yet her vision emerges as overwhelmingly joyous and calm"—*NY Times Book Review*
0-918526-81-7 BOA PB $10.00

Judith Ortiz **Cofer**
The Latin Deli
0-8203-1556-7 GEORGIA $19.95

Terms of Survival
0-934770-73-5 ARTE PUBLICO PB $7.00

Lisa **Coffman**
Likely
A first collection selected by Alicia Ostriker in the Stan and Tom Wick Poetry Prize sponsored annually by Kent State University Press. "*Likely* is a book brimming with surprises and beauty" —Alicia Ostriker
0-87338-554-3 KENT STATE $17.00
0-87338-555-1 KENT STATE PB $9.50

Peter **Cole**
Rift
Cole writes a nearly abstract poetry of air and light, informed by the physical presence of Jerusalem. The lyricism, despite its attenuated quality, is soaring and convincing
0-88268-087-0 STATION HILL PB $8.95

Wanda **Coleman**
Hand Dance
0-87685-896-5 BLACK SPARROW PB $13.00

Imagoes
0-87685-509-5 BLACK SPARROW PB $12.00

Evan S. **Connell**
Notes from a Bottle Found on the Beach at Carmel
0-88001-407-5 ECCO PB $13.00

Clark **Coolidge**
The Book of During
About sex, sort of
0-935724-49-4 FIGURES PB $25.00

The Crystal Text
"Coolidge's writing encroaches on the impossible language of dreams. ...He practices an ultimate naturalism, an endless home movie of raw thought"—*Village Voice*
1-55713-230-5 SUN & MOON PB $11.95

Mesh
About sex, sort of. Vivid new lyrics by a prolific and inventive writer
0-932597-05-X IN CAMERA PB $4.95

Own Face
A new edition of a major work first published in 1978
1-55713-120-1 SUN & MOON PB $10.95

Solution Passage: Poems, 1978-1981
Word-noise as lyric statement, from a young master who makes the concrete abstract and vice versa
0-940650-55-X SUN & MOON $18.95
0-940650-54-1 SUN & MOON PB $11.95

Dennis **Cooper**
The Dream Police
0-8021-3457-2 GROVE PB $11.00

William **Corbett**
Collected Poems, 1968-1984
0-915032-46-5
NATIONAL POETRY FOUNDATION PB $9.95

New and Selected Poems
"Taut, precise, lucid and unflinching" —Siri Hustvedt
0-944072-48-8 ZOLAND PB $18.75

Cid **Corman**
And the Word
0-918273-34-X COFFEE HOUSE PB $8.95

Of
A beautifully designed and printed two-volume edition representing nearly five decades of laconic, meditative work. Corman, a longtime resident of Japan and editor of the influential magazine *Origin*, is an important American poet
0-932499-61-9 LAPIS $55.00

Alfred **Corn**
Autobiographies
0-14-058690-3 PENGUIN PB $12.50

The West Door
0-14-058604-0 PENGUIN PB $8.95

Jayne **Cortez**
Coagulations: New and Selected Poems
0-938410-20-2 THUNDER'S MOUTH PB $8.95

Somewhere in Advance of Nowhere
1-85242-422-2 SERPENT'S TAIL PB $12.99

Henri **Coulette**
The Collected Poems of Henri Coulette
Gathers together *The War of the Secret Agents* and other work by a neglected poet who focused on public events in elegantly crafted verse. "A major poet...one who has seized upon thematic material of central importance to the modern world"—Zbigniew Herbert
1-55728-145-9 ARKANSAS PB $14.95

Victor Hernandez **Cruz**
By Lingual Wholes
A poet whose work is informed by intense musicality and the possibilities of Spanish-English bilingualism
0-917672-19-4 MOMO'S PB $5.95

Red Beans: Poems
0-918273-91-9 COFFEE HOUSE PB $11.95

Rhythm, Content and Flavor: New and Seleted Poems
0-934770-93-X ARTE PUBLICO PB $8.00

Alan **Davies**
Name
"See Doting. / Anxiety / settles / in the genitals. / So this will be most known / to you, who don't listen"
9-997226-32-1 SUN & MOON PB $5.00

Beverly **Dahlen**

A Reading 1-7

"Her writing abandons the notion of a focal point and deliberately spins off in all directions.... In a sense you cannot read it, because it has already usurped that function: you can only read with it, as if reading over something you just wrote"—*Village Voice*

0-917672-23-2 MOMO'S PB $12.50

A Reading 8-10

0-925904-08-2 CHAX PB $12.00

A Reading 11-17

0-937013-33-1 POTES & POETS PB $8.50

Edwin **Denby**

Collected Poems

0-916-19000-5 FULLCOUNT PB $17.95

Carl **Dennis**

Meetings with Time

0-670-84398-9 VIKING $21.00

The Outskirts of Troy

0-688-07756-0 MORROW PB $8.95

Signs and Wonders

0-691-01363-2 PRINCETON PB $9.95

Tory **Dent**

What Silence Equals

0-89255-196-8 PERSEA PB $9.95

W.S. **Di Piero**

The Restorers

0-226-15347-9 CHICAGO PB $9.95

James **Dickey**

"These are poems of darkness, darkness and a specialized light. Practically everything in them happens at night, by moonlight, starlight, firelight; or else in other conditions that will make ordinary daytime perception impossible."—Howard Nemerov

Buckdancer's Choice

0-8195-1028-9 WESLEYAN PB $11.95

The Eagle's Mile

0-8195-1187-0 WESLEYAN PB $11.95

Poems, 1957-1967

0-8195-6055-3 WESLEYAN PB $15.95

Sorties

0-8071-1140-6 LSU PB $9.95

The Whole Motion: Collected Poems, 1945-1992

"A career-spanning collection by National Book Award winner James Dickey, 'the high-flier of American poets' "—John Updike

0-8195-2202-3 WESLEYAN $29.95

0-8195-1218-4 WESLEYAN PB $19.95

William **Dickey**

The Education of Desire

0-8195-2235-X NEW ENGLAND $25.00

0-8195-2236-8 WESLEYAN PB $11.95

In the Dreaming: Selected Poems

1-55728-286-2 ARKANSAS PB $10.00

Deborah **Digges**

Rough Music: Poems

The Guggenheim Grant- and Delmore Schwartz Memorial Prize-winning poet presents a third collection of strong and sometimes bitter work. "Disparate images and details are yoked together to draw us through a rich, human 'story' whose closure often leaves us gasping with both surprise and grateful consent" —Mona Van Duyn

0-679-44176-X KNOPF $20.00

Tom **Disch**

Dark Verses and Light

0-8018-4192-5 JOHNS HOPKINS PB $12.95

Haikus of an Ampart

0-918273-68-4 COFFEE HOUSE PB $10.00

Yes, Let's: New and Selected Poems

0-8018-3851-7 JOHNS HOPKINS PB $8.95

Melvin **Dixon**

Change of Territory

0-912759-04-6 CALLALOO JOURNAL PB $8.95

Love's Instruments

1-88268-807-4 TIA CHUCHA PB $10.95

Stephen **Dobyns**

Common Carnage

0-14-058748-9 PENGUIN PB $14.95

Wayne **Dodd**

Wayne Dodd currently edits The Ohio Review.

Echoes of the Unspoken

0-8203-1198-7 GEORGIA PB $8.95

Of Desire and Disorder

0-88748-168-X CARNEGIE-MELLON $16.95

0-88748-169-8 CARNEGIE-MELLON PB $10.95

Sometimes Music Rises

0-8203-0824-2 GEORGIA PB $7.95

Joseph **Donahue**

Monitions of the Approach

"These poems root love, lineage, and loss in a physical world of desire, while manifesting the pleasures and subtleties of a mind at play in the language"—Hugh Seidman

0-87376-067-0 RED DUST PB $3.00

World Well Broken

Includes such major sequences as "Spectral Evidence" and "Christ Enters Manhattan." "Donahue's immense poetic gifts reveal themselves at the site of the tragic: we are found and surprised there"—Kathleen Fraser

1-88368-923-6 TALISMAN $29.95

1-88368-922-8 TALISMAN PB $9.95

Gregory **Donovan**

Calling His Children Home

0-8262-0895-9 MISSOURI $18.95

0-8262-0896-7 MISSOURI PB $10.95

Mark **Doty**

Atlantis

0-06-095106-0 HARPERPERENNIAL PB $12.00

My Alexandria

In part an homage to Cavafy, situated within the age of AIDS

0-252-02210-6 ILLINOIS $18.95

0-252-06317-1 ILLINOIS PB $10.95

Rita **Dove**

Mother Love

"This volume shows Dove—Pulitzer Prize winner, novelist, and 1993-95 U.S. Poet Laureate—at the height of her poetic powers"—*Publishers Weekly*

0-393-03808-4 NORTON $17.95

0-393-31444-8 NORTON PB $10.00

Museum

0-88748-147-7 PITTSBURGH PB $12.95

Lynne **Dreyer**

The White Museum

0-937804-21-5 ROOF PB $7.50

Norman **Dubie**

Radio Sky

0-393-30852-9 NORTON PB $8.95

Selected and New Poems

0-393-01817-2 NORTON $14.95

0-393-30140-0 NORTON PB $5.95

The Springhouse

0-393-30323-3 NORTON PB $6.95

Alan **Dugan**

New and Collected Poems, 1961-1983

0-88001-085-1 ECCO PB $9.50

Poems 6

0-88001-199-8 ECCO $17.95

Stephen **Dunn**

Between Angels

0-393-30658-5 NORTON PB $9.95

Loosestrife

0-393-03982-X NORTON $19.00

New & Selected Poems, 1974-1994

A generous sampling of poems by a poet

0-393-03618-9 NORTON $22.00

0-393-31300-X NORTON PB $15.00

Rachel Blau **DuPlessis**

Tabula Rosa

Poetry that is both steeped in lyrical tradition and deeply critical of its implications

0-937013-19-6 POTES & POETS PB $9.95

Barbara **Einzig**

Life Moves Outside

0-930901-42-8 BURNING DECK PB $7.00

Theodore **Enslin**

Synthesis

0-913028-36-3 NORTH ATLANTIC PB $6.00

Elaine **Equi**

Decoy

1-56689-026-8 COFFEE HOUSE PB $11.95

Clayton **Eshleman**

Fracture

0-87685-580-X BLACK SPARROW $14.00
0-87685-579-6 BLACK SPARROW PB $7.50

Hotel Cro-Magnon

0-87685-760-8 BLACK SPARROW PB $10.00

The Name-Encanyoned River: Selected Poems, 1960-1985

"As a result of his literal and imaginative explorations of the painted and gouged caves, Eshleman has constructed a myth, perhaps the first compelling post-Darwinian myth; that the Paleolithic represents the 'crisis' of the human 'separating out' of the animal, the original birth and the original fall of man"—Eliot Weinberger

INTRODUCTION BY ELIOT WEINBERGER
0-87685-652-0 BLACK SPARROW PB $12.50

Under World Arrest

0-87685-936-8 BLACK SPARROW $25.00
0-87685-935-X BLACK SPARROW PB $13.00

What She Means

0-87685-346-7 BLACK SPARROW PB $6.00

Dave **Etter**

Alliance, Illinois

A book-length sequence of Midwestern portraits
0-933180-43-8 SPOON RIVER $14.95

Carnival

0-944024-19-X PLAINS PB $5.95

Electric Avenue

0-944024-09-2 SPOON RIVER PB $5.95

Home State: A Prose Poem

0-933180-64-0 SPOON RIVER PB $4.95

Live at the Silver Dollar

0-933180-83-7 SPOON RIVER PB $4.95

George **Evans**

Sudden Dreams: New and Selected Poems

Finally: an American collection by an American poet whose first three books were published to great acclaim in England. "His poems, resembling him, have a hardy constitution.... Their observations are fresh, the imagination at work is bold without compromising reality, and they stand on a solid footing"—Carl Rakosi

0-918273-86-2 COFFEE HOUSE PB $8.95

Mari **Evans**

Nightstar: 1973-1978

0-934934-07-X CALIFORNIA PB $4.95

Roger **Fanning**

The Island Itself

0-14-058689-X PENGUIN PB $10.00

Candice **Favilla**

Cups

0-8203-1479-X GEORGIA PB $9.95

David **Ferry**

Dwelling Places: Poems and Translations

0-226-24478-4 CHICAGO $20.00
0-226-24479-2 CHICAGO PB $7.95

Formalists

The critical re-evaluation of the English Metaphysical Poets sponsored by T.S. Eliot and the New Critics together with the influence of the poetry of W.H. Auden led to an upsurge of interest in traditional verse forms in the decade after WWII. The '60s and '70s saw a turn to more emotionally and formally open poetry, but in the '80s formalism, taking its cue from the examples of Elizabeth Bishop and James Merrill, flourished anew.

Elizabeth **Bishop**

Collected Poems

"From the moment Miss Bishop appeared on the scene it was apparent to everybody that she was a poet of strange, even mysterious, but undeniable and great gifts."
—John Ashbery

Marilyn **Hacker**

Love, Death, and the Changing of the Seasons

"I don't see how anyone who knows versification can help but admire and relish her abilities."—Hayden Carruth

John **Hollander**

Harp Lake

Begins with the remarkable poem "Kinneret," a long *tour de force* that employs the Malaysian quatrain the *pantun*. "Hollander's *Harp Lake* is, with his *Powers of Thirteen*, the height of his poetic achievement so far."—Harold Bloom

James **Merrill**

The Scattering of Salts

Elegant, slangy, and witty, Merrill's last collection, published posthumously, transmutes autobiography into truth.

Gjertrud **Schnackenberg**

A Gilded Lapse of Time

"Schnackenberg has a control of line, of pace, and of tone that is rare in her generation."—John Hollander

Richard **Wilbur**

The Beautiful Changes

This book, published in the early '50s, and now included in his *Collected Poems*, epitomizes the elegaic elegance that Wilbur has cultivated throughout his career.

Edward **Field**

Counting Myself Lucky: Selected Poems, 1963-1992

0-87685-890-6 BLACK SPARROW PB $12.50

Norman **Finkelstein**

Restless Messengers

0-8203-1380-7 GEORGIA PB $8.95

Dennis **Finnell**

Beloved Beast

0-8203-1708-X GEORGIA PB $11.95

Lawrence **Fixel**

Truth, War, and the Dream-Game: Selected Prose Poems and Parables, 1966-1990

0-918273-88-9 COFFEE HOUSE PB $10.95

Paul **Fleischman**

Joyful Noise: Poems for Two Voices

ILLUSTRATED BY ERIC REDDOWS
0-06-021852-5 HARPERCOLLINS $19.95
0-06-446093-2 HARPERCOLLINS PB $3.95

Carolyn **Forché**

The Angel of History

0-06-017078-6 HARPERCOLLINS $20.00
0-06-092584-1 HARPERPERENNIAL PB $10.00

The Country Between Us

Poems dealing with, among other things, Forché's observations of political struggle in El Salvador
0-06-090926-9 HARPERCOLLINS PB $10.00

Kathleen **Fraser**

When New Time Folds Up

"The four series of poems in this collection are embedded in Italian history, culture, and artifact... Fraser is everywhere sensitive to marks and traces, the sounds of voices, of cries"—Susan Howe
0-925904-14-7 CHAX PB $11.00

Alice **Fulton**

Dance Script with Electric Ballerina

0-252-06576-X ILLINOIS PB $12.95

Palladium: Poems

0-252-01451-0 ILLINOIS $14.95

Powers of Congress

0-87923-867-4 GODINE PB $10.95

Sensual Math

0-393-03750-9 NORTON $17.95
0-393-31445-6 NORTON PB $12.00

Tess **Gallagher**

Amplitude: New and Selected Poems

1-55597-110-5 GRAY WOLF PB $12.00

Moon Crossing Bridge

1-55597-175-X GRAY WOLF PB $12.00

Portable Kisses: Expanded

Witty, mischievous, and moving, the poet observes "the kiss" in all its varied guises. "[Gallagher's] poems sometimes have a mythic quality, while at other times the poet all but steps aside to wink at us and to acknowledge the power of mind over matter as it intrudes itself into even the most romantic of myths. It's a book filled with beauty, energy, and surprise"
—Anne Beattie
0-8095-4091-6 BORGO $29.00
0-88496-387-X CAREY PB $10.95

James **Galvin**

Elements

1-55659-013-X COPPER CANYON PB $9.00

Lethal Frequencies

1-55659-069-5 COPPER CANYON PB $11.00

Forrest **Gander**

Deeds of Utmost Kindness

The backgrounds of Gander's poems range from Japan to the Ozarks to Moscow. "One of the most original and fascinating books of poetry I have seen in some time"—John Ashbery

0-8195-2209-0 WESLEYAN $25.00
0-8195-1212-5 WESLEYAN PB $11.95

Eggplants and Lotus Root

0-930901-78-9 BURNING DECK PB $5.00

Lynchburg

In this collection, Gander explores the landscape of the rural South. "There's a toughness, a hard edge of danger on the margins of these poems. Gander has a startling way of yoking beauty and violence"
—*Providence Sunday Journal*

0-8229-3746-8 PITTSBURGH $19.95
0-8229-5498-2 PITTSBURGH PB $10.95

Rush to the Lake

0-914086-79-0 JAMES PB $8.95

Amy **Gerstler**

The True Bride

0-932499-04-X LAPIS PB $9.50

John **Gery**

The Enemies of Leisure

1-88526-601-4 STORYLINE PB $10.95

Barry **Gifford**

Ghosts No Horse Can Carry: Collected Poems, 1967-1987

0-88739-064-1 CREATIVE ARTS PB $12.95

Jack **Gilbert**

The Great Fires: Poems, 1982-1992

0-679-42576-4 KNOPF $20.00
0-679-74767-2 KNOPF PB $13.00

Sandra **Gilbert**

Blood Pressure

0-393-30624-0 NORTON PB $7.95

Ghost Volcano

0-393-03783-5 NORTON $17.95
0-393-31447-2 NORTON PB $11.00

In the Fourth World

FOREWORD BY RICHARD EBERHART

0-8173-8528-2 ALABAMA PB $9.95

Dana **Gioia**

Daily Horoscope

0-915308-80-0 GRAY WOLF PB $9.95

The Gods of Winter

1-55597-147-4 GRAY WOLF $22.95
1-55597-148-2 GRAY WOLF PB $12.00

John **Giorno**

You Got to Burn to Shine: New and Selected Writings

A survey of the writing of a legendary figure in New York downtown culture. "His litanies from the underworld of the mind reverberate in your head and ventriloquize your own thoughts"
—William S. Burroughs

1-85242-321-8 SERPENT'S TAIL PB $11.99

Nikki **Giovanni**

"Talent is light, but mature talent is a beacon and Nikki Giovanni has…joined that small band of talented people who try to show us all the way to go home"—LA Times

Black Feeling, Black Talk, Black Judgment

0-688-25294-X MORROW PB $6.95

Cotton Candy on a Rainy Day

0-688-08365-X MORROW PB $7.00

My House

0-688-05021-2 MORROW PB $7.95

The Selected Poems

0-688-14047-5 MORROW $20.00

Those Who Ride the Night Winds

0-688-02653-2 MORROW PB $6.95

Greg **Glazner**

From the Iron Chair

0-393-30958-4 NORTON PB $8.95

Singularity

0-393-03992-7 NORTON $19.00

Louise **Glück**

Ararat

In this collection Glück focuses on the pain of family relationships

0-88001-247-1 ECCO PB $17.95

Descending Figure

"Her poetry is rock-bottom hard and final, jet-marked by a sentience next to clairvoyance, and subtle surprise, and strong beauty"
—Calvin Bedient

0-912946-72-5 NORTON PB $11.00

The First Four Books of Poems

0-88001-421-0 ECCO $22.00
0-88001-477-6 ECCO PB $15.00

The Triumph of Achilles

0-88001-082-7 ECCO PB $11.00

The Wild Iris

"[*The Wild Iris*] challenges the bulk of recent American poetry.... Glück asks: 'Is it enough/only to look inward?' Or mustn't poetry also 'force clarity' upon eternity and the whole of existence? In its visionary manner, *The Wild Iris* affirms the latter"
—*Washington Post Book World*

0-88001-334-6 ECCO PB $11.00

Albert **Goldbarth**

Across the Layers: Poems Old and New

0-8203-1547-8 GEORGIA $35.00
0-8203-1548-6 GEORGIA PB $16.95

The Gods

0-8142-0596-8 OHIO STATE PB $11.95

Heaven and Earth: A Cosmology

0-8203-1300-9 GEORGIA PB $9.95

Popular Culture

0-8142-0499-6 OHIO STATE PB $14.95

David **Graham**

Magic Shows

0-914946-58-7 CLEVELAND STATE PB $6.00

Jorie **Graham**

The Dream of the Unified Field: Selected Poems, 1974-1994

Winner of the 1996 Pulitzer Prize in poetry

0-88001-438-5 ECCO $23.00
0-88001-476-8 ECCO PB $15.00

The End of Beauty

"Graham, if we compare her with her Romantic predecessors, is nearest to Shelley in her creation of clouds of thought, accumulating and breaking open in a shower of consequences"
—Helen Vendler

0-88001-130-0 ECCO PB $9.95

Erosion

0-691-01405-1 PRINCETON PB $9.95

Materialism

"Jorie Graham is a poet of staggering intelligence. Her poems are constantly on the attack. She assays nothing less than the whole body of our history, reshaping myth in ways that risk new knowledge, fresh understanding of all that we might hope to be"—James Tate

0-88001-342-7 ECCO $22.00
0-88001-394-X ECCO PB $13.00

Region of Unlikeness

A meditation on the idea of history. "Her poetry though so fully at home in the mental, the imagined and the speculative, grounds itself nevertheless in that desire that is, as she says, the engine, the wind of the body"
—Helen Vendler

0-88001-271-4 ECCO $17.95
0-88001-290-0 ECCO PB $11.95

Debora **Greger**

The 1002nd Night

0-691-01492-2 PRINCETON PB $9.95

And

0-691-01423-X PRINCETON PB $9.95

Desert Fathers, Uranium Daughters

0-14-058774-8 PENGUIN PB $14.95

Movable Islands

0-691-01369-1 PRINCETON PB $13.95

Off-Season at the Edge of the World

0-252-06380-5 ILLINOIS PB $12.95

Robert **Grenier**

A Day at the Beach

0-937804-14-2 SUN & MOON PB $6.00

Pamela **Gross**

Birds of the Night Sky/Stars of the Field

0-8203-1776-4 GEORGIA PB $11.95

Allen **Grossman**

The Bright Nails Scattered on the Ground

0-8112-0976-8 NEW DIRECTIONS PB $8.95

Ether Dome and Other Poems: New and Selected, 1979-1991

0-8112-1177-0 NEW DIRECTIONS PB $10.95

Of the Great House: A Book of Poems

0-8112-0835-4 NEW DIRECTIONS PB $6.95

The Philosopher's Window

0-8112-1300-5 NEW DIRECTIONS PB $12.95

Barbara **Guest**

"Barbara Guest confirms that she is one of our finest poets.... Her images seem to feed from her hand like birds, and then take wing again."—James Schuyler

Defensive Rapture

1-55713-032-9 SUN & MOON PB $11.95

Fair Realism

1-55713-245-3 SUN & MOON PB $10.95

Selected Poems

1-55713-200-3 SUN & MOON $22.95

Maurice Kilwein **Guevara**

Postmortem

0-8203-1562-1 GEORGIA PB $9.95

Jeffrey **Gustavson**

Nervous Forces

"*Nervous Forces* is a feat of virtuosity—a lexical pressure-cooker of playful monologues, lyrical rants and shrewdly drawn portraits. Gustavson's poems are buoyed by an agitated sensibility. They are crafted with a sinewy style that is admirable for its intellectual breadth"—*Publishers Weekly*

1-88250-902-1 ALEF PB $12.00

Marilyn **Hacker**

Love, Death, and the Changing of the Seasons

0-393-31225-9 NORTON PB $11.00

Selected Poems, 1965-1990

0-393-03675-8 NORTON $22.00

Winter Numbers

0-393-31373-5 NORTON PB $10.00

Rachel **Hadas**

"Death, dying, and the radiant assurance of art—these are Rachel Hadas's passages of rite intercalated by pain. To read her poems is to be instructed in a life of dignity and conscience, hard to come by, worth the struggle." —Richard Howard

The Empty Bed

0-8195-2221-X WESLEYAN $25.00

0-8195-1225-7 WESLEYAN PB $11.95

Mirrors of Astonishment

0-8135-1900-4 RUTGERS PB $11.95

Pass It On

0-691-01454-X PRINCETON PB $9.95

Jessica **Hagedorn**

Pet Food and Tropical Apparitions

0-917672-14-3 MOMO'S PB $10.00

Susan **Hahn**

Confession

0-226-31274-7 CHICAGO PB $42.00

Harriet Rubin's Mother's Wooden Hand

0-226-31301-8 CHICAGO PB $8.95

Incontinence

0-226-31272-0 CHICAGO PB $8.95

John **Haines**

New Poems, 1980-88

Winner of the 1990 Western States Book Award. The jurors noted: "John Haines is a man of character in the most American sense—solitary; strong. He has spent much of his life in wild country, and he has written of the wilderness with profound wonder, perception, and thanksgiving"

0-934257-45-0 STORYLINE PB $9.95

The Owl in the Mask of the Dreamer: Collected Poems

"If Alaska had not existed, Haines might well have invented it, so much do the observed elements of landscape correspond to a harshly powerful inner mythology"—*Newsday*

1-55597-184-9 GRAY WOLF $25.00

Daniel **Hall**

Hermit with Landscape

0-300-04733-9 YALE PB $9.00

Strange Relation

This compelling new book from an emerging poet was chosen by Mark Doty in the 1995 National Poetry Series

0-14-058771-3 PENGUIN PB $13.95

Donald **Hall**

The Happy Man

0-394-74612-0 RANDOM HOUSE PB $8.95

Life Work

National Book Critics Circle Award winner for poetry, Hall presents a stirring memoir of his unusually prolific life in literature, which has included an outpouring of poetry, essays, short stories, biographies, and children's books. "If any living American writer deserves the description 'man of letters,' it is Donald Hall" —Richard Tillinghast, *NY Times Book Review*

0-8070-7054-8 BEACON $15.00

0-8070-7055-6 BEACON PB $9.00

The Museum of Clear Ideas

0-395-68085-9 TICKNOR & FIELDS PB $10.95

Old and New Poems

As poet, critic, and anthologist, Hall has been a force of lucid intelligence in American poetry for many years

0-89919-954-2 TICKNOR & FIELDS PB $14.95

The Old Life

0-395-78841-2 HOUGHTON MIFFLIN $19.95

Donald Hall

The One Day: A Poem in Three Parts

0-89919-816-3 HOUGHTON MIFFLIN PB $10.95

Judith **Hall**

To Put the Mouth To

0-688-11546-2 MORROW PB $8.00

Mark **Halliday**

Tasker Street

0-87023-777-2 MASSACHUSETTS PB $9.95

Kathleen **Halme**

Every Substance Clothed

0-8203-1762-4 GEORGIA PB $11.95

Daniel **Halpern**

Foreign Neon

0-679-74735-4 KNOPF PB $12.00

Selected Poems

0-679-76565-4 KNOPF PB $15.00

Tango

0-14-058588-5 VIKING PB $10.95

Joy **Harjo**

"I turn and return to Harjo's poetry for her breathtaking, complex witness and for her world-remaking language: precise, unsentimental, miraculous."—Adrienne Rich

She Had Some Horses

A poem cycle by a leading Native American poet. "Harjo's second major book of poetry rides an intense passion for survival through dangerous roads in America, in her own heart, in an Indian dream vision that can wrench and heal"—*Ms.*

See also **CONTEMPORARY NATIVE AMERICAN WRITERS** under **NATIVE AMERICAN LITERATURES**

0-938410-06-7 THUNDER'S MOUTH PB $8.95

The Woman Who Fell from the Sky

"I fell in love with these poems, with their clarity and light, their wisdom born somewhere between sky and earth"—Sandra Cisneros

See also **CONTEMPORARY NATIVE AMERICAN WRITERS** under **NATIVE AMERICAN LITERATURES**

0-393-03715-0 NORTON $21.00

0-393-31362-X NORTON PB $10.00

Michael S. **Harper**

Healing Song for the Inner Ear

0-252-01128-7 ILLINOIS $14.95
0-252-01099-X ILLINOIS PB $9.95

Honorable Amendments

0-252-06514-X ILLINOIS PB $12.95

Nightmare Begins Responsibility

0-252-00466-3 ILLINOIS $14.95
0-252-00226-1 ILLINOIS PB $9.95

Jeffrey **Harrison**

Signs of Arrival

0-914278-71-1 COPPER BEECH PB $10.00

Robert **Hass**

Human Wishes

0-88001-212-9 ECCO PB $11.00

Praise

0-88001-242-0 NORTON PB $11.00

Sun Under Wood: New Poems

0-88001-468-7 ECCO $22.00

Brooks **Haxton**

The Sun at Night: Poems

On Haxton's last book of poems, Eudora Welty wrote: "Extraordinary. I value their beauty and their strength, one by one, and their accumulating power to move their reader's own responding imagination"

0-679-44179-4 KNOPF $20.00

Vicki **Hearne**

In the Absence of Horses

0-691-01409-4 PRINCETON PB $9.95

The Parts of Light

0-8018-4939-X JOHNS HOPKINS $30.00
0-8018-4940-3 JOHNS HOPKINS PB $12.95

Anthony **Hecht**

Flight Among the Tombs

0-679-45095-5 KNOPF $23.00

Lyn **Hejinian**

The Cell

1-55713-021-3 SUN & MOON PB $11.95

The Cold of Poetry

Collects early works including *The Guard*, *Redo*, and *Gesualdo*

1-55713-063-9 SUN & MOON PB $12.95

My Life

A tour de force with heart, and one of the most influential texts out of the language movement

1-55713-024-8 SUN & MOON PB $9.95

Writing Is an Aid to Memory

0-685-99357-4 SUN & MOON PB $4.00

Michael **Heller**

In the Builded Place

0-918273-58-7 COFFEE HOUSE PB $8.95

David **Henderson**

De Mayor of Harlem

0-938190-39-3 DUTTON PB $7.95

Lance **Henson**

In a Dark Mist

0-89304-856-9 CROSS-CULTURAL PB $5.00

Selected Poems: 1970-1991

0-912678-62-3 GREENFIELD REVIEW PB $9.95

Calvin **Hernton**

Medicine Man

0-918408-05-9 REED CANNON & JOHNSON PB $4.95

Brenda **Hillman**

Bright Existence

0-8195-1207-9 WESLEYAN PB $12.95

Death Tractates

0-8195-1202-8 WESLEYAN PB $11.95

Fortress

0-8195-1168-4 WESLEYAN PB $11.95

Edward **Hirsch**

Earthly Measures

0-679-43070-9 KNOPF $20.00
0-679-76566-2 KNOPF PB $13.00

The Night Parade

0-679-72299-8 KNOPF PB $16.00

Wild Gratitude

0-394-74153-6 RANDOM HOUSE PB $16.00

Linda **Hogan**

The Book of Medicines

1-56689-010-1 COFFEE HOUSE PB $11.95

Savings

0-918273-41-2 COFFEE HOUSE PB $10.95

Jonathan **Holden**

American Gothic

0-8203-1409-9 GEORGIA PB $9.95

John **Hollander**

Hollander is a formalist of formidable talents, whose work is imbued with ecstatic and kabbalistic undertones.

Harp Lake

0-394-57247-5 KNOPF $16.95

Selected Poetry

0-679-41931-4 KNOPF $27.50
0-679-76198-5 KNOPF PB $15.00

Tesserae

0-679-42222-6 KNOPF $20.00
0-679-76200-0 KNOPF PB $12.00

Anselm **Hollo**

Corvus: Poems

1-56689-039-X COFFEE HOUSE PB $11.95

Near Miss Haiku: Praises, Laments, Aphorisms, Reports

0-916328-20-1 YELLOW PRESS PB $6.95

Outlying Districts

0-918273-76-5 COFFEE HOUSE PB $8.95

Pick Up the House: New and Selected Poems

0-918273-18-8 COFFEE HOUSE PB $8.95

Sojourner Microcosms: New and Selected Poems, 1959-1977

0-912652-38-1 BLUE WIND PB $12.95

Garrett Kaoru **Hongo**

The River of Heaven

Winner of the 1987 Lamont Poetry Prize

0-394-75785-8 KNOPF PB $16.00

Yellow Light

0-8195-1104-8 WESLEYAN PB $11.95

bell **hooks**

A Woman's Mourning Song

0-86316-318-1 WRITERS & READERS PB $8.00

Paul **Hoover**

Novel

0-8112-1153-3 NEW DIRECTIONS PB $9.95

Viridian

0-8203-1895-7 GEORGIA PB $25.00

Richard **Howard**

The poetry of Richard Howard (1929-) is characteristically witty, formally versatile, and reminiscent of Browning and Keats. A Pulitzer Prize winner in poetry, Howard is also one of America's best translators from French.

Like Most Revelations

Meditations on graffiti, Mozart, Beckett, and aging are among the subjects of this masterful collection from the Pulitzer Prize-winning poet. Howard's tenth book is already being hailed as his strongest and most moving to date

0-679-43163-2 PANTHEON $20.00

Fanny **Howe**

The End

1-55713-145-7 LITTORAL PB $9.95

The Lives of a Spirit

The author describes herself as having written in "a state of waiting-for-God which is passive yet alert, where everything matters, and there is no escape"

0-940650-95-9 SUN & MOON $10.95

Susan **Howe**

The Europe of Trusts

Collects in one volume *The Liberties*, *Pythagorean Silence*, and *The Defenestration of Prague*

1-55713-009-4 SUN & MOON PB $10.95

Frame Structures: Early Poems, 1974-1979

Includes *Hinge Picture*, *Chanting at the Crystal Sea*, *Cabbage Garden*, and *Secret History of the Dividing Line*. "Her work is a voyage of reconnaissance in language"—*Poetry Pilot*

0-8112-1322-6 NEW DIRECTIONS PB $12.95

The Nonconformists Memorial

One of our leading experimentalists whose work resonates back through Melville and Dickinson and forward again to T.S. Eliot and the abstract expressionists. "Howe searches for meaning like an alchemist searching for gold"
—*Publishers Weekly*

0-8112-1229-7 NEW DIRECTIONS PB $13.95

Singularities
Susan Howe's poetry is itself singular in its lyricism, its adventurousness, its haunting sense of the past caught in language. "She sounds the complex particulars of history's echoes with an intensity altogether her own. This is major work in every sense"—Robert Creeley
0-8195-1194-3 WESLEYAN PB $11.95

Richard **Hugo**
Making Certain It Goes On: The Collected Poems
0-393-01784-2 NORTON $25.00
0-393-30784-0 NORTON PB $10.95

Austin **Hummell**
The Fugitive Kind
0-8203-1885-X GEORGIA PB $14.95

Colette **Inez**
Getting Under Way: New and Selected Poems
0-934257-60-4 STORYLINE PB $18.95

Frances **Jaffer**
Alternate Endings
0-933539-00-2 SMALL PRESS PB $6.00

Mark **Jarman**
The Black Riviera
0-8195-2170-1 WESLEYAN $25.00

Iris
0-934257-88-4 STORYLINE PB $16.95

North Sea
0-914946-77-3 CLEVELAND STATE PB $6.00

Denis **Johnson**
"Denis Johnson speaks...with passion and wit...for every hushed or broken voice in America's cities of night. These are searing, unforgettable poems."—David St. John
The Incognito Lounge
0-88748-176-0 CARNEGIE-MELLON PB $12.95

Throne of the Third Heaven of the Nations Millennium General Assembly: Poems
This book collects in one volume Denis Johnson's four books of poetry from the last 25 years
0-06-092696-1 HARPERPERENNIAL PB $12.00

Ronald **Johnson**
Ark: The Foundations, 1-33
Johnson's monumental poem is an architectural tour de force, in intent something like a temple made of words
0-945953-07-0 NEW MEXICO PB $25.00

Stephen **Jonas**
Selected Poems
A mysterious figure on the Boston scene who died in 1970, Jonas has remained little known due to the unavailability of his work, including the legendary *Exercises for Ear*. "He was pushing the envelope when he wrote and a sense of risk and adventure distinguish his work today"—William Corbett
1-88368-907-4 TALISMAN $37.95

Rodney **Jones**
Apocalyptic Narrative and Other Poems
0-395-71087-1 HOUGHTON MIFFLIN PB $12.95

Things that Happen Once
0-395-77143-9 HOUGHTON MIFFLIN $19.95

Transparent Gestures
0-395-51063-5 HOUGHTON MIFFLIN PB $9.95

June **Jordan**
Haruko/Love Poems
1-85242-323-4 SERPENT'S TAIL PB $13.99

Living Room
0-938410-26-1 THUNDER'S MOUTH PB $8.95

Naming Our Destiny: New and Selected Poems
0-938410-84-9 THUNDER'S MOUTH PB $12.95

Lawrence **Joseph**
Before Our Eyes
"The rift between our public and private realms is where Joseph thrives.... These are idiosyncratic, off-kilter pieces, yet no less observant for being so"—Albert Mobilio, *VLS*
0-374-52404-1 NOONDAY PB $8.00

Donald **Justice**
A Donald Justice Reader
0-87451-626-9 MIDDLEBURY PB $14.95

New and Selected Poems
0-679-44173-5 KNOPF $25.00

Mary **Karr**
Devil's Tour
0-8112-1231-9 NEW DIRECTIONS PB $8.95

Claudia **Keelan**
The Secularist
0-8203-1802-7 GEORGIA PB $14.95

Brigit Pegeen **Kelly**
Song
1-88023-813-6 BOA PB $12.50

Robert **Kelly**
The Alchemist to Mercury
A selection surveying Kelly's prolific career
0-913028-83-5 NORTH ATLANTIC PB $7.95

The Flowers of Unceasing Coincidence
0-88268-054-4 STATION HILL PB $8.95

Kill the Messenger
0-87685-432-3 BLACK SPARROW PB $10.00

The Loom
0-87685-233-9 BLACK SPARROW PB $10.00

The Mill of Particulars
0-87685-172-3 BLACK SPARROW PB $7.00

Not This Island Music
0-87685-692-X BLACK SPARROW PB $10.00

Red Actions: Selected Poems, 1960-1993
At last, a large-scale survey of Kelly's career, drawing on such mostly out-of-print volumes as *Her Body Against Time, Finding the Measure,* and *Kali Yuga*: "Finding the measure is finding the mantram, / is finding the moon, as index of measure, / is finding the moon's source"
0-87685-977-5 BLACK SPARROW PB $17.50

A Strange Market
0-87685-875-2 BLACK SPARROW PB $12.50

Richard **Kenney**
The Evolution of the Flightless Bird
0-300-03152-1 YALE PB $11.00

The Invention of the Zero
0-679-74997-7 KNOPF PB $12.00

Maurice **Kenny**
Between Two Rivers: Selected Poems
0-934834-73-3 WHITE PINE PB $10.00

Myung Mi **Kim**
The Bounty
0-925904-21-X CHAX PB $12.00

Under Flag
"One is shaken by this severe and quiet telling—an assemblance of ongoing in the life of a child and her family"—Kathleen Fraser
0-932716-27-X KELSEY ST. PB $9.00

Galway **Kinnell**
The Avenue Bearing the Initial of Christ into the New World: Poems, 1946-1964
0-395-18628-5 HOUGHTON MIFFLIN PB $15.95

The Book of Nightmares
"Throughout his poetry there flows the awareness that growth involves a kind of dying…the attention burns through level after level, each vision catching up sparks and flashes from other sightings"—Charles Molesworth, *Western Humanities Review*
0-395-12098-5 HOUGHTON MIFFLIN PB $11.95

Imperfect Thirst
Recollections of youth; reflections on the relationship between human beings and other creatures; poems bearing on music, language, sex, and morality; love poems; a tender evocation of a daughter taking care of her old father; and five longer poems that show off the lyrical prowess of a poet whose lifetime achievements include 11 other collections, the Pulitzer Prize, and the American Book Award
0-395-71089-8 HOUGHTON MIFFLIN $22.95
0-395-75528-X DORLING KINDERSLEY PB $12.95

The Past
0-395-39385-X HOUGHTON MIFFLIN $13.95

Selected Poems
0-395-32046-1 HOUGHTON MIFFLIN PB $12.95

Galway **Kinnell**

Three Books: Body Rags; Mortal Acts, Mortal Words; The Past

0-395-68088-3 TICKNOR & FIELDS PB $18.95

When One Has Lived a Long Time Alone

0-679-73281-0 KNOPF PB $15.00

Carolyn **Kizer**

Carrying Over: Versions of Poems from Old and New China, Pakistan, Macedonian Yugoslavia and Mauritius, with Two Poems from the Yiddish

As a translator, Kizer is best known for her versions of Tu Fu, but this volume also introduces work by little-known poets such as Bogomil Gjuzel, Faiz Ahmed Faiz, and Shu Ting

1-55659-017-2 COPPER CANYON PB $9.00

Harping On: Poems, 1985-1995

1-55659-114-4 COPPER CANYON $22.00
1-55659-115-2 COPPER CANYON PB $12.00

Mermaids in the Basement: Poems for Women

"Collected new poems by a woman who was writing about women's concerns long before the movement began.... Much of the pilgrimage of these poems moves from reiteration of griefs to the good grace of letting go"—*NY Times*

0-914742-80-9 COPPER CANYON $14.00

The Nearness of You

0-914742-96-5 COPPER CANYON $15.00
0-914742-97-3 COPPER CANYON PB $10.00

August **Kleinzahler**

Earthquake Weather

"Kleinzahler is a poet in the Williams tradition... and is easily the most interesting of the younger poets to emerge from it"—Charles Tomlinson

0-918825-98-9 MOYER BELL PB $8.95

Red Sauce, Whiskey and Snow

Kleinzahler's most recent book

0-374-28924-7 FSG $19.00
0-374-52472-6 NOONDAY PB $10.00

Storm over Hackensack

"The poems make amazing sounds, weird and keen, for a dance joining other senses. Not a breath wasted, not a note in excess, Kleinzahler has converted Apollo's lyre into something like a cross between a Jew's harp and a catapult"
—Christopher Middleton

0-918825-06-7 MOYER BELL $16.95
0-918825-08-3 MOYER BELL PB $7.95

Etheridge **Knight**

The Essential Etheridge Knight

0-8229-5378-1 PITTSBURGH PB $12.95

Bill **Knott**

Outremer

0-87745-254-7 IOWA $17.95
0-87745-255-5 IOWA PB $10.95

Poems: 1963-1988

0-8229-5416-8 PITTSBURGH PB $10.95

The Quicken Tree

1-88023-824-1 BOA $20.00
1-88023-825-X BOA PB $12.95

John **Koethe**

The Late Wisconsin Spring

0-691-01414-0 PRINCETON PB $7.95

Yusef **Komunyakaa**

Magic City

0-8195-1208-7 WESLEYAN PB $11.95

Neon Vernacular: New and Selected Poems

A winner of the 1994 Pulitzer Prize and the Kingsley Tufts Award

0-8195-1211-7 WESLEYAN PB $14.95

Maxine **Kumin**

Connecting the Dots

In her 11th collection, Maxine Kumin expands themes that have engaged her most strongly: family connections, the shift of responsibility between generations, the narrow divide between human and animal, the cycle of seasons, and memories of youthful parties and lost friends. A winner of the Pulitzer Prize and countless awards, she lives on a farm in central New Hampshire. "Her poems become increasingly unforgettable, indispensable"
—*NY Times Book Review*

0-393-03962-5 NORTON $18.95

Looking for Luck: Poems

A new collection by the Pulitzer Prize-winning poet. "Unforgettable, indispensable...Thoreau would commend her honesty, the precision of her language and her occasional moral allegory"—*NY Times Book Review*

0-393-30947-9 NORTON PB $8.95

Joanne **Kyger**

Just Space: Poems, 1979-1989

0-87685-834-5 BLACK SPARROW PB $12.50

Gerrit **Lansing**

The Heavenly Tree Grows Downward

Poems erotic and mystical. "We celebrate Gerrit Lansing as the singer and pedagogue of an uncanny yet genial occultism"—Charles Stein

1-88368-913-9 TALISMAN $37.95
1-88368-912-0 TALISMAN PB $16.95

Ann **Lauterbach**

"Ann Lauterbach elevates the absence of presumption to a state of ecstasy. She protracts Rilkean moments of pure gaze to a point of nearly unbearable but vocal sympathy."
—Donald Revell

And for Example

"Ann Lauterbach's poetry goes straight to the elastic, infinite core of time"—John Ashbery

0-670-85883-8 PENGUIN $25.95
0-14-058715-2 PENGUIN PB $14.95

Before Recollection

0-691-06698-1 PRINCETON $21.95
0-691-01437-X PRINCETON PB $9.95

Clamor

0-14-058673-3 PENGUIN PB $11.00

Radicals

Beginning in the early '70s various younger poets began to react against the poetry of earnest self expression, tinged with surrealism, that was rapidly becoming the *lingua franca* of American poetry. Influenced by the work of Gertrude Stein and HD, and by such older contemporaries as Robert Creeley, Robert Duncan, and John Ashbery, their work manifested an impatience with received poetic conventions together with a consciously exploratory formal bent. Some of these poets were associated with the L-A-N-G-U-A-G-E writers, whose disjunctive verbal compostitions had a political basis, but as a whole they were united not so much by critical doctrine as by a shared belief that the disruptive and inventive energies unleased by the great Modernists were still far from exhausted.

Rae **Armantrout**

Necromance

One of the most deft and original of the "language" poets.

Clark **Coolidge**

Own Face

Word-noise as lyric statement by the most determined and inventive of verbal improvisors.

Susan **Howe**

The Europe of Trusts

A writer at once hypnotic and keenly attuned to historical circumstance.

Michael **Palmer**

Notes for Echo Lake

Palmer writes "so that unlikely combinations provoke new responses... He seems to permit the poem to connect as many diverse elements as possible, to propose rather than dictate... 'Content', as de Kooning said, 'is a slippery glimpse.' "
—William Corbett

Gustaf **Sobin**

The Earth as Air

"Sobin's world...is basic, stripped, often sundrenched, sometimes arid—and mysterious."—Charles Tomlinson

John **Taggart**

Loop

Meditative poems that share an impulse with minimalist, gospel, and soul music.

Barrett **Watten**

Complete Thought

An early collection from the obdurate and brilliant mastermind of "language" poetry. Now available in *Frame: 1971-1991.*

Marjorie **Welish**

The Windows Flew Open

"Explores the inner landscapes of psyche and dreams, but also the surface tensions and contradictory currents of the world before us."—Michael Palmer

Tato **Laviera**

AmeRican

"Laviera has two goals in mind…to pay homage to his city's ethnic diversity and to forge an 'AmeRican' identity out of mainland and island traditions"—*Hispania*

0-934770-31-X ARTE PUBLICO PB $7.00

Enclave

0-934770-11-5 ARTE PUBLICO PB $7.00

La Carreta Made a U-Turn

1-55885-064-3 ARTE PUBLICO PB $7.00

Mainstream Ethics

Laviera's poetry explores the geographic and linguistic imperatives of Hispanics in the United States

0-934770-90-5 ARTE PUBLICO PB $7.00

Robert **Lax**

Love Had a Compass: Journals and Poetry

Long resident in Greece, Lax is a master of the minimalist poem

0-8021-1587-X GROVE $22.00

Sydney **Lea**

The Blaineville Testament

0-934257-80-9 STORYLINE PB $11.95

To the Bone: New and Selected Poems

0-252-02223-8 ILLINOIS $29.95

0-252-06519-0 ILLINOIS PB $17.95

Joseph **Lease**

The Room

Taut, psychically charged poems. "Joseph Lease's work gives us the oldest shock, of authenticity, though he is a relentless craftsman of revisions. His triumphant sequences synthesize the pathos of naturalist description, historical perspective, and lyric intensity" —David Shapiro

1-88250-901-3 ALEF PB $12.00

Don L. **Lee**

We Walk the Way of the New World

0-910296-26-X BROADSIDE $6.00

9-992208-66-X BROADSIDE PB $1.50

Li-Young **Lee**

City in Which I Love You

0-918526-83-3 BOA PB $10.00

Rose

0-918526-53-1 BOA PB $10.00

The Winged Seed

0-671-70708-6 SIMON & SCHUSTER $20.00

Brad **Leithauser**

Cats of the Temple

Leithauser draws on his experiences of Japanese life in many of these poems

0-394-54806-X KNOPF $14.95

The Mail from Anywhere

0-679-73843-6 KNOPF PB $10.00

Philip **Levine**

The Look of Things

From the 1995 winner of the Pulitzer Prize

0-679-76593-X KNOPF PB $13.00

New Selected Poems

0-679-74056-2 KNOPF PB $15.00

Not This Pig

0-8195-1038-6 WESLEYAN PB $10.95

The Simple Truth

Levine uses elegy and prayer to paint a full picture of myth, history, family, and memory: basic truths, universal and simple. An affecting, accomplished work

0-679-43580-8 KNOPF $20.00

0-679-76584-0 KNOPF PB $13.00

A Walk with Tom Jefferson

0-394-75859-5 KNOPF PB $13.00

What Work Is

Levine won the 1991 National Book Award for this volume of darkly humorous poetry. Here are firefighters, auto assembly line workers, and polishers of plumbing parts whom the author presents with understanding, humor, and dignity. Levine "prefers difficulty to beauty, but manages to convey both"—*New Yorker*

0-679-40166-0 KNOPF $19.00

0-679-74058-9 KNOPF PB $13.00

Larry **Levis**

The Widening Spell of the Leaves

0-8229-5454-0 PITTSBURGH PB $10.95

Winter Stars

0-8229-3511-2 PITTSBURGH $19.95

0-8229-5368-4 PITTSBURGH PB $10.95

Joel **Lewis**

House Rent Boogie

0-916328-21-X YELLOW PRESS PB $5.95

Timothy **Liu**

Burnt Offerings

1-55659-104-7 COPPER CANYON PB $12.00

Vox Angelica

0-914086-97-9 JAMES PB $9.95

John **Logan**

The Collected Poems

0-918526-64-7 BOA $30.00

Audre **Lorde**

The Black Unicorn

0-393-31237-2 NORTON PB $9.00

Coal

0-393-31486-3 NORTON PB $10.00

The Marvelous Arithmetics of Distance

0-393-03513-1 NORTON $18.95

0-393-31170-8 NORTON PB $8.95

Our Dead Behind Us

0-393-30327-6 NORTON PB $7.95

Undersong: Chosen Poems

0-393-30975-4 NORTON PB $9.95

Jackson **Mac Low**

42 Merzegedichte in Memoriam Kurt Schwitters (February 1987-September 1989)

0-88268-145-1 STATION HILL PB $14.95

Barnesbook

1-55713-235-6 SUN & MOON PB $9.95

Bloomsday

PHOTOGRAPHS BY RICHARD GUMERRE

0-88268-008-0 STATION HILL PB $5.95

Pieces o' Six

1-55713-060-4 SUN & MOON PB $11.95

Representative Works, 1938-1985

"MacLow's Thoreau: he gives exact attention. No added flavor; just it… Musician, he introduced poetry to orchestra without syntax"—John Cage

0-937804-19-3 ROOF $18.95

Eroding Witness

"These poems are about prophecy and initiation; the uncompromising narratives that sing but *don't explain* are the sounds of a mythmaker-griot in the midst of ceremonial talk" —Michael S. Harper

0-252-01230-5 ILLINOIS PB $9.95

Nathaniel Mackey (photo courtesy of University of Illinois Press)

School of Udhra

"A book of haunted pleasure"—Wilson Harris

0-87286-278-X CITY LIGHTS PB $9.95

Elizabeth **Macklin**

A Woman Kneeling in the Big City

0-393-03400-3 NORTON $18.95

0-393-31105-8 NORTON PB $8.95

Tom **Mandel**

Letters of the Law

"His poems are grave, circuitous journeys toward truth, knowledge, eternity–journeys reaffirming that truth is not simple"—*Publishers Weekly*

1-55713-164-3 SUN & MOON PB $10.95

Clarence **Major**

Poet, painter, teacher, lexicographer, and novelist, Major has been on the cutting edge of black fiction for 20 years. The Fiction Collective, a cooperative publishing house, was started by Major and a handful of colleagues in the early 1970s.

Some Observations of a Stranger at Zuni in the Latter Part of the Century

"No writer to my knowledge has pushed the experimental wing of modernism to the structural limits achieved by Major" —Charles Johnson, *Callaloo*

1-55713-020-5 SUN & MOON PB $9.95

Surfaces with Masks

"Feeling is my foreground. Subject matter is my middle distance. I look for geometrical dramas in pictures and I try to create them in my poems"—Clarence Major

0-918273-43-9 COFFEE HOUSE PB $8.95

Paul **Mariani**

The Great Wheel

In a vigorous sequence of thirty-five poems, Mariani uses the trope of the great wheel, calling up by turns Hart Crane and Wilfred Owen, Stevens and Williams, Creeley and Levine, Whitman and Hopkins

0-393-03921-8 NORTON $18.95

Salvage Operations: New & Selected Poems

0-393-30759-X NORTON PB $9.95

Jack **Marshall**

Millennium Fever

1-56689-054-3 COFFEE HOUSE $11.95

Dionisio D. **Martinez**

Bad Alchemy

"Martinez's poems reflect poignantly on the poet's status as a Cuban exile destined to a perennial sense of dislocation"—David Lehman

0-393-31531-2 NORTON PB $12.00

History as a Second Language

0-8142-0592-5 OHIO STATE PB $10.95

David **Mason**

The Country I Remember

1-88526-620-0 STORYLINE $21.00
1-88526-623-5 TAYLOR PB $12.00

Harry **Mathews**

Armenian Papers: Poems, 1954-1984

0-691-01440-X PRINCETON PB $10.95

William **Matthews**

Sleek for the Long Flight

0-934834-22-9 WHITE PINE PB $8.00

Time & Money

0-395-71134-7 HOUGHTON MIFFLIN $19.95
0-395-82526-1 HOUGHTON MIFFLIN PB $11.95

Bernadette **Mayer**

A Bernadette Mayer Reader

0-8112-1203-3 NEW DIRECTIONS PB $11.95

Gail **Mazur**

The Common

0-226-51439-0 CHICAGO PB $11.95

J.D. **McClatchy**

The Rest of the Way

"A strong and elegant book…McClatchy emerges as one of the very finest poets of his generation"—John Hollander

0-679-74059-7 KNOPF PB $10.00

Heather **McHugh**

Hinge & Sign: Poems, 1968-1993

0-8195-1216-8 WESLEYAN PB $14.95

James **McMichael**

Each in a Place Apart

0-226-56107-0 CHICAGO PB $9.95

The World at Large: New and Selected Poems, 1971-1996

0-226-56104-6 CHICAGO $43.00
0-226-56105-4 CHICAGO PB $16.95

Sandra **McPherson**

Edge Effect: Trails and Portrayals

0-8195-2225-2 WESLEYAN $25.00
0-8195-2226-0 WESLEYAN PB $11.95

The God of Indeterminacy

0-252-06271-X ILLINOIS PB $11.95

Patron Happiness

0-88001-021-5 ECCO $12.95
0-88001-022-3 NORTON PB $6.50

The Spaces Between Birds: Mother/Daughter Poems, 1967-1995

0-8195-2228-7 WESLEYAN PB $11.95

Streamers

0-88001-214-5 ECCO PB $7.95

Jane **Mead**

The Lord and the General Din of the World

0-9641151-0-7 SARABANDE $19.95
0-9641151-1-5 SARABANDE PB $12.95

Peter **Meinke**

Liquid Paper

0-8229-5455-9 PITTSBURGH PB $12.95

Scars

0-8229-3935-5 PITTSBURGH $24.95
0-8229-5592-X PITTSBURGH PB $10.95

David **Meltzer**

Arrows: Selected Poetry 1957-1992

0-87685-939-2 BLACK SPARROW $25.00
0-87685-938-4 BLACK SPARROW PB $13.00

The Name: Selected Poetry, 1973-1983

0-87685-491-9 BLACK SPARROW PB $8.50

James **Merrill**

The Changing Light at Sandover

Merrill's major work takes both its matter and its manner from Ouija board communications, and incorporates the separately published "The Book of Ephraim" (from *Divine Comedies*), *Mirabell*, and *Scripts for the Pageant*

0-679-74736-2 KNOPF PB $20.00

The Inner Room

0-679-72049-9 KNOPF PB $15.00

A Scattering of Salts

Elegant, slangy, and witty, Merrill's last collection, published posthumously, transmutes autobiography into truth

0-679-44158-1 KNOPF $20.00
0-679-76590-5 KNOPF PB $14.00

James Merrill (credit: ©William Ball)

Selected Poems, 1946-1985

"Few writers approach his exquisite knowledge of the English language, its beauty and oddity—he breathes vigor into our most common words"—David Leavitt

0-679-74731-1 KNOPF PB $15.00

W.S. **Merwin**

Finding the Islands

A collection of haiku-like 3-line poems

0-86547-089-8 NORTH POINT PB $6.00

Flower & Hand: Poems, 1977-1983

1-55659-119-5 COPPER CANYON PB $15.00

The Miner's Pale Children: A Book of Prose

0-689-10356-5 HOLT PB $6.95

The Rain in the Trees

0-394-75858-7 KNOPF PB $15.00

The Second Four Books of Poems

1-55659-054-7 COPPER CANYON PB $15.00

Travels

Merwin is one of our most honored and read poets, and *Travels* is among "the most beautiful and moving collections of his career. [He]

displays his narrative gifts to provide us with a book of deep historical resonance and luminous poetic grace"—*LA Times Book Review*

See also **THE SUBCONTINENT AND THE HIMALAYAS** under **TRAVEL GUIDES** in **FOOD, TRAVEL, AND LEISURE**

0-679-41890-3 KNOPF $20.00
0-679-75277-3 KNOPF PB $14.00

The Vixen

0-679-44477-7 KNOPF $21.00

Ralph J. **Mills**

Living with Distance

Mills has mined richly the natural abstraction pioneered by William Carlos Williams

0-918526-17-5 BOA $18.00

A Window in Air

1-55921-073-7 PUBLISHERS GROUP WEST PB $9.95

Albert **Mobilio**

Bendable Siege

0-87376-068-9 RED DUST PB $3.00

The Geographics

"It's as if Humphrey Bogart were taking a good, if final, look at what's called the world"
—Robert Creeley

0-963-84332-X HARD PRESS PB $10.00

Carol **Moldaw**

Taken from the River

1-88250-900-5 ALEF PB $10.00

N. Scott **Momaday**

In the Presence of the Sun: Stories and Poems, 1961-1991

A superb collection of Momaday's poems, stories, and drawings, celebrating the beauty and mystery of the Native American past. "Scott Momaday is one of the most versatile and distinguished artists in America today"
—Peter Matthiessen

See also **CONTEMPORARY NATIVE AMERICAN WRITERS** under **NATIVE AMERICAN LITERATURES**

0-312-08222-3 ST. MARTIN'S $17.95

Pat **Mora**

Agua Santa: Holy Water

0-8070-6828-4 BEACON $17.95

Borders

"These are arduous expeditions…for both writer and reader….You don't plant your flag without earning the right"—*El Paso Times*

0-934770-57-3 ARTE PUBLICO PB $7.00

Laura **Moriarty**

Rondeaux

0-937804-39-8 ROOF PB $8.00

Hilda **Morley**

Cloudless at First

A new collection by a poet remarkable, among other things, for her flowing visual sense

0-918825-72-5 MOYER BELL PB $12.95

To Hold in My Hand: Selected Poems, 1955-1983

"Her touchstone for finding her way in the world is the recognition of common feeling, and she describes that recognition as a biological phenomenon…. We don't often find this much of a human life within a single volume of poetry"
—*Village Voice*

FOREWORD BY STANLEY KUNITZ

0-935296-46-8 SHEEP MEADOW $14.95

What Are Winds & What Are Waters

1-55921-089-3 MOYER BELL PB $9.95

Thylias **Moss**

Rainbow Remnants in Rock Bottom Ghetto Sky

0-89255-157-7 PERSEA PB $9.95

Small Congregations: New and Selected Poems

0-88001-363-X ECCO PB $12.00

Lisel **Mueller**

Alive Together: New and Selected Poems

0-8071-2128-2 LSU $17.95

Waving from Shore

0-8071-1576-2 LSU PB $7.95

Laura **Mullen**

The Surface

0-252-06187-X ILLINOIS PB $10.95

Carol **Muske**

Red Trousseau

0-14-058686-5 PENGUIN PB $12.00

Eileen **Myles**

Bread and Water

0-937815-02-0 HANUMAN PB $5.95

Larry **Neal**

Hoodoo Hollerin' Bebop Ghosts

Neal, who died in 1981, wrote of his work: "I've tried to select poems for this volume in which the polemic and poetic merge into an organic, personal statement"

0-88258-011-6 HOWARD $12.95

Claire **Needell**

Not a Balancing Act

0-930901-89-4 BURNING DECK PB $8.00

Charles **North**

New and Selected Poems

A survey of the career of a leading New York poet

1-55713-265-8 SUN & MOON PB $12.95

Alice **Notley**

At Night the States

0-916328-18-X SMALL PRESS PB $6.95

The Descent of Alette

A book-length narrative poem in which archaic myth and urban disorder cohabit

0-14-058764-0 PENGUIN PB $14.95

Selected Poems of Alice Notley

"Entertaining, moving, Notley's work engages ever-deepening areas of division and isolation while settling for nothing less than a restoration of wholeness"—Joseph Donahue

1-88368-902-3 TALISMAN PB $11.95

Naomi Shihab **Nye**

Red Suitcase

1-88023-815-2 BOA PB $12.50

The Words Under the Words: Selected Poems

0-933377-29-0 EIGHTH MOUNTAIN PB $13.95

Geoffrey **O'Brien**

Floating City: Selected Poems, 1978-1995

O'Brien's poetry has been anthologized in *The Best American Poetry, 1995* and elsewhere. He was a 1994 nominee for the National Book Critics Circle Award in criticism. "O'Brien writes with the eye of an historian and the ear of a cellist"—Gustaf Sobin

1-88368-938-4 TALISMAN PB $10.50

The Hudson Mystery

"Reincarnated 19th-century tales emerge renewed"—Marjorie Welish

0-873-76078-6 RED DUST PB $14.00

Michael **O'Brien**

The Floor and the Breath

A new collection of poems and prose poems

1-88604-403-1 CAIRN PB $7.50

Sharon **Olds**

The Dead and the Living

"Sharon Olds is enormously self-aware; her poetry is remarkable for its candor, its eroticism, and its power to move"—David Leavitt, *Village Voice*

0-394-71563-2 RANDOM HOUSE PB $13.00

Father

In her fourth book, Olds reflects on her father's illness and his death.

0-679-41127-5 KNOPF $20.00
0-679-74002-3 RANDOM HOUSE PB $13.00

The Gold Cell

0-394-74770-4 KNOPF PB $13.00

Satan Says

0-8229-5314-5 PITTSBURGH PB $10.95

The Wellspring: Poems

0-679-44592-7 KNOPF $21.00
0-679-76560-3 KNOPF PB $13.00

Mary **Oliver**

American Primitive

0-316-65004-8 LITTLE, BROWN PB $12.95

Blue Pastures

See also **ESSAYS, MEDITATIONS, AND CLASSICS** under **NATURE STUDY** in **SCIENCE**

0-15-100190-1 HARCOURT BRACE $22.00
0-15-600215-9 HARVEST PB $13.00

New and Selected Poems

0-8070-6818-7 BEACON $27.50
0-8070-6819-5 BEACON PB $16.00

White Pine

0-15-600120-9 HARCOURT BRACE PB $12.00

William **Olsen**

Vision of a Storm Cloud

"Captivating and charmingly unpredictable."
—*Publishers Weekly*

0-8101-5044-1 TRIQUARTERLY PB $12.95

Toby **Olson**

Unfinished Building
1-56689-009-8 COFFEE HOUSE PB $11.95

We Are the Fire: A Selection of Poems
0-8112-0914-8 NEW DIRECTIONS PB $7.50

Gregory **Orr**

City of Salt
0-8229-3876-6 PITTSBURGH $24.95
0-8229-5557-1 PITTSBURGH PB $10.95

New and Selected Poems
0-8195-2140-X WESLEYAN $22.50
0-8195-1141-2 WESLEYAN PB $11.95

Simon J. **Ortiz**

After and Before the Lightning
0-8165-1423-2 ARIZONA $36.95
0-8165-1448-8 ARIZONA PB $17.95

From Sand Creek
"A pained poet sees the My Lai massacre as a reflection of what happened to his own people…Truly moving"—*St. Louis Globe-Democrat*
0-938410-00-8 THUNDER'S MOUTH PB $6.95

Woven Stone
An epic by one of the leading Native American poets
0-8165-1294-9 ARIZONA $50.00
0-8165-1330-9 ARIZONA PB $21.50

Brenda Marie **Osbey**

Ceremony For Minneconjoux
0-912759-03-8 CALLALOO JOURNAL PB $7.95

In These Houses
0-8195-1147-1 WESLEYAN PB $11.95

Jacqueline **Osherow**

Conversations with Survivors
0-8203-1611-3 GEORGIA PB $9.95

With a Moon in Transit
0-8021-1599-3 GROVE $18.00

Jena **Osman**

Twelve Parts of Her
0-930901-63-0 BURNING DECK PB $4.00

Underwater Dive: Version One
0-945926-22-7 PARADIGM PB $4.00

Alicia **Ostriker**

The Crack in Everything
0-8229-3936-3 PITTSBURGH $24.95
0-8229-5593-8 PITTSBURGH PB $10.95

Green Age
0-8229-3624-0 PITTSBURGH $19.95
0-8229-5421-4 PITTSBURGH PB $10.95

A Woman Under the Surface: Poems and Prose Poems
0-691-01390-X PRINCETON PB $10.95

Maureen **Owen**

Imaginary Income
"Wit, exuberance, imagination…There is the real humor here of the unseen suddenly known, seen or speculated upon. Revelation!"
—Anne Waldman
0-914610-97-X HANGING LOOSE PB $9.00

Ron **Padgett**

The Big Something
0-935724-38-9 FIGURES PB $7.50

Great Balls of Fire
Originally published in 1969, this volume established Padgett as one of the most comically inventive of the New York poets
0-918273-80-3 COFFEE HOUSE PB $8.95

New & Selected Poems
1-56792-038-1 GODINE $20.95

Tulsa Kid
0-915990-17-2 Z PRESS PB $5.00

Michael **Palmer**

"Michael Palmer has been one of the most influential writers of recent years, perhaps because he fuses contemporary concerns about syntax and meaning-production with some very ancient poetic pleasures."—VLS

At Passages
0-8112-1294-7 NEW DIRECTIONS PB $11.95

Greg **Pape**

Storm Pattern
0-8229-5472-9 PITTSBURGH PB $10.95

Elise **Paschen**

Infidelities
The award-winning selection in the 1996 Nicholas Roerich Prize.
1-88526-628-6 STORYLINE PB $10.95

Linda **Pastan**

An Early Afterlife
0-393-03727-4 NORTON $17.95
0-393-31381-6 NORTON PB $10.00

Heroes in Disguise
0-393-30922-3 NORTON PB $8.95

The Imperfect Paradise
0-393-30524-4 NORTON PB $7.95

Molly **Peacock**

Original Love
"Accomplished and witty, this anatomy of 'original' love is not for the fainthearted; it's for those who believe that it is still possible to feel deeply"—*Library Journal.* "Peacock offers a new slant on the often misunderstood emotion, using rhyme, humor, and fierce honesty to convey passion for love and all love's trappings lyrical and beautiful"—*Booklist*
0-393-31466-9 NORTON PB $10.00

Take Heart
0-679-72196-7 VINTAGE PB $12.00

Richard **Peaver**

Night Talk & Other Poems
0-691-01342-X PRINCETON PB $9.95

John **Peck**

M and Other Poems
0-8101-5056-5 TRIQUARTERLY PB $12.95

Poems and Translations of Hi-Lo
Poems written through the persona of a Chinese medical student in Zurich. "Few poets are as witty as John Peck, few as erudite, and fewer still as skillful, and none except John Peck himself as witty, erudite, and skillful"
—Guy Davenport
1-87881-828-7 SHEEP MEADOW PB $12.95

Bob **Perelman**

Captive Audience
0-935724-36-2 FIGURES PB $7.50

Face Value
0-937804-26-6 ROOF PB $6.00

Virtual Reality
"Sharp-eyed ironic investigation of poetic language in the global information net of the 1990s"—Susan Howe
0-937804-49-5 ROOF PB $9.95

Robert **Peters**

The Gift to Be Simile: A Garland for Mother Ann Lee
0-87140-103-7 NORTON PB $4.95

New and Selected Poems, 1967-1991
1-87858-031-0 ASYLUM ARTS PB $11.95

Michael **Pettit**

American Light
0-8203-0677-0 GEORGIA PB $7.95

Cardinal Points
0-87745-206-7 IOWA PB $10.95

Carl **Phillips**

Cortége
"An unusually accomplished and innovative poet...Phillips has developed his own painful but luminous method for traveling trajectories, and it will be most interesting to see where it takes him from here"—*Publishers Weekly*
1-55597-230-6 GRAY WOLF PB $12.95

In the Blood
1-55553-135-0 NORTHEASTERN PB $10.95

Marge **Piercy**

Available Light
0-394-75691-6 KNOPF PB $12.00

Circles on the Water: Selected Poems
0-394-70779-6 RANDOM HOUSE PB $18.00

Mars and Her Children
0-679-73877-0 KNOPF PB $14.00

Pedro **Pietri**

Puerto Rican Obituary
Includes "Suicide Note from a Cockroach in a Low Income Housing Project"
0-85345-330-6 MONTHLY REVIEW PB $10.00

Miguel **Pinero**

La Bodega Sold Dreams
The only collection of poetry by the author of the acclaimed play *Short Eyes*. "Mixes ghetto invective and a feverish sentimentality, machismo swagger, and its reverse, a soft quality that is inadmissible to life except in art and has no proper name"—*Village Voice*
0-934770-02-6 ARTE PUBLICO PB $5.00

New Poets of the '80s and '90s

Some striking books from recent years.

Will **Alexander**

Asia and Haiti

Visions and tirades.

Anne **Carson**

Glass, Irony, and God

Carson, a Canadian poet who is also a scholar of classical Greek literature, writes poems that are at once essayistic and elliptical.

Joseph **Donahue**

World Well Broken

Includes such major sequences as "Spectral Evidence" and "Christ Enters Manhattan."

Martin **Edmunds**

The High Road to Taos

The first book of a pyrotechnical formalist whose work is also deeply felt.

Peter **Gizzi**

Periplum

The first full-length collection from a younger poet with a fine lyric sense who is unafraid to push the envelope of poetic form.

Barbara **Jordan**

Channel

An unusual and powerful collection of poems, many of which grapple with religious experience.

Myung Mi **Kim**

The Bounty

The latest volume of a much admired younger poet.

August **Kleinzahler**

Red Sauce, Whiskey, and Snow

Sharp, smart, and affecting poems from a poet with an ear for common speech.

Joseph **Lease**

The Room

"*The Room* is a terrific book."—John Yau

Nathaniel **Mackey**

School of Udhra

"A book of haunted pleasure."—Wilson Harris

C.D. **Wright**

Tremble

"The dramatic and emotional vitality of C.D. Wright's language, the authenticity and daring of her tone and speech make her poems, one after the other, surprising, outrageous, moving and funny."—W.S. Merwin

Robert **Pinsky**

An Explanation of America

0-691-01360-8 PRINCETON PB $9.95

The Figured Wheel: New and Collected Poems, 1966-1996

A gathering of four books of poetry plus a full section of new poems in a volume that reveals the courage and power of one of the finest poets of his generation. Human pain and imagination; an astonishing history of the saxophone; and a final section of Pinsky's translations, including the last canto of his award-winning version of the *Inferno*. "A mad, brilliant vortex that draws into itself gods, men, art, rags and bones, atoms and dust"—*San Francisco Chronicle*

See also **SINCE 1945** under **20TH-CENTURY AMERICAN FICTION**

0-374-15493-7 FS&G $30.00

The Inferno of Dante: A New Verse Translation

See also **THE MIDDLE AGES** under **ITALIAN LITERATURE** in **LITERATURE OF EUROPE, AFRICA, AND ASIA**

0-374-52452-1 NOONDAY PB $8.00

The Want Bone

0-88001-251-X ECCO PB $12.00

Sylvia **Plath**

Collected Poems

"She went to the extreme, far edge of the bearable and, in the end, slipped over. That is a risk in handling such touchy, violent material. Yet she turned it, too, to advantage; the courage it took to gamble in this way is reflected in the curious sense of creative optimism, of possibilities in the teeth of the impossible, that stirs in her poems like a moving bass"
—A. Alvarez

INTRODUCTION BY TED HUGHES

0-06-090900-5 HARPERCOLLINS PB $17.00

Stanley **Plumly**

Boy on the Step

0-88001-229-3 ECCO PB $9.95

Summer Celestial

0-88001-084-3 ECCO PB $7.50

Robert **Polito**

Doubles

"The narrative poems in *Doubles* are as if based in cinematic chiaroscuro.... The book's achievement is capped off in the remarkable long poem 'Evidence'"—David Lehman

0-226-67338-3 CHICAGO PB $8.95

Anne **Porter**

An Altogether Different Language: Poems, 1934-1994

Startling clear and fresh poetry by the wife of Fairfield Porter

0-944072-45-3 ZOLAND PB $10.95

Jim **Powell**

It Was Fever That Made the World

0-226-67706-0 CHICAGO $20.00
0-226-67707-9 CHICAGO PB $8.95

Thomas **Rabbitt**

Abandoned Country

0-88748-062-4 CARNEGIE-MELLON $14.95

Bin **Ramke**

The Erotic Light of Gardens

0-8195-1174-9 WESLEYAN PB $11.95

Massacre of the Innocents

0-87745-492-2 IOWA PB $10.95

Dudley **Randall**

A Litany of Friends: New and Selected Poems

0-916418-50-2 LOTUS PB $6.00

David **Rattray**

Opening the Eyelid

"Bright declarations, sardonic intimations, David Rattray's poems wheel and bob, loom, flash and dissipate; jubilate the Tantra!"—Gerrit Lansing

0-9627430-0-3 DIWAN PB $9.95

Liam **Rector**

American Prodigals

0-934257-22-1 STORYLINE PB $11.95

Pam **Rehm**

The Garment in Which No One Had Slept

0-930901-87-8 BURNING DECK PB $8.00

To Give It Up

1-55713-212-7 SUN & MOON PB $9.95

Donald **Revell**

Beautiful Shirt

Here the poet traverses the rocky terrain of innocence, memory, disillusion, and salvation in a voice at once haunted and elliptical

0-8195-2216-3 WESLEYAN $25.00
0-8195-1219-2 WESLEYAN PB $11.95

From the beginning,/sanctity yielded/to law that yielded/to history that yielded/to aphasia. Meridian of bitter cold and strings,/it never vanishes./Beloved, approachable zero never vanishes.
BEAUTIFUL SHIRT

Erasures

0-8195-1206-0 WESLEYAN PB $11.95

The Gaza of Winter

0-8203-0989-3 GEORGIA PB $6.95

New Dark Ages

0-8195-1186-2 WESLEYAN PB $11.95

Adrienne **Rich**

An Atlas of the Difficult World: Poems, 1988-1991

0-393-30831-6 NORTON PB $7.95

Collected Early Poems: 1950-1970

Collected here in one volume are all the poems from Rich's first six books of poetry plus a dozen other poems from those decades. Gathered together, these poems chart the development of one of the most unique and accomplished writers today

0-393-03418-6 NORTON $27.50
0-393-31385-9 NORTON PB $15.00

Dark Fields of the Republic: Poems, 1991-1995

Rich composes her new collection into a theater of voices, male and female, living and dead

0-393-03868-8 NORTON $25.00
0-393-31398-0 NORTON PB $10.00

Adrienne Rich

Diving into the Wreck: Poems, 1971-72
"With 'Diving into the Wreck,' Rich completes her re-vision of woman as monster. It becomes a source of poetic political identity extracted from the wreckage of self and society under patriarchal rule. The old dispensation is displaced and a new 'book of myths' can be written"—Terrence Des Pres
0-393-04384-3 NORTON PB $7.95

The Dream of a Common Language: Poems, 1974-1977
0-393-31033-7 NORTON PB $8.95

The Fact of a Doorframe: Poems Selected and New, 1950-1984
0-393-31075-2 NORTON PB $10.95

Time's Power: Poems, 1985-1988
0-393-30575-9 NORTON PB $9.95

A Wild Patience Has Taken Me This Far: Poems, 1978-1981
0-393-01494-0 NORTON $12.95
0-393-31037-X NORTON PB $8.95

Your Native Land, Your Life
0-393-31082-5 NORTON PB $8.95

James **Richardson**

As If
0-89255-171-2 PERSEA PB $9.95

Alberto **Ríos**

Five Indiscretions
0-935296-57-3 SHEEP MEADOW $14.95

The Lime Orchard Woman
0-935296-77-8 SHEEP MEADOW PB $10.95

Whispering to Fool the Wind
0-935296-31-X SHEEP MEADOW PB $10.95

David **Rivard**

Torque
0-8229-5410-9 PITTSBURGH PB $10.95

Ed **Roberson**

Voices Cast Out to Talk Us In
"A wrought, wry, entrancing, transportitive, strict, soul-sustaining book"—Nathaniel Mackey
0-87745-510-4 IOWA PB $10.95

Matthew **Rohrer**

"What Rohrer tells us about this world, in language that is both lush and exact, is likely to be a haunting experience."—Mary Oliver

A Hummock in the Malookas
A winner in the National Poetry Series selected by Mary Oliver
0-393-03798-3 NORTON $17.95
0-393-31548-7 NORTON PB $11.00

Alane **Rollings**

The Struggle to Adore
0-934257-97-3 STORYLINE PB $12.95

Leo **Romero**

Celso
"Celso is Everyman, his roles ranging from shabby Christ figure to buffoon, drunkard, and ladies' man, alternately unkempt, lascivious, pathetic, witty, cruel, curious, and outrageous" —*Literary Arts*
0-934770-36-0 ARTE PUBLICO PB $7.00

David **Romtvedt**

A Flower Whose Name I Do Not Know
1-55659-046-6 COPPER CANYON PB $10.00

William Pitt **Root**

Reasons for Going It on Foot
0-689-11138-X ATHENEUM $11.95

Wendy **Rose**

Bone Dance: New and Selected Poems, 1965-1993
0-8165-1428-3 ARIZONA PB $10.95

Going to War with All My Relations: New and Selected Poems
0-87358-556-9 NORTHLAND PB $9.95

The Halfbreed Chronicles & Other Poems
0-931122-39-2 WEST END PB $8.95

Now Poof She Is Gone
1-56341-048-6 FIREBRAND PB $8.95

Jerome **Rothenberg**

Gematria
Poems based on an ancient Jewish numerological method. "Words are placed in one another's neighborhood so that their respective powers act upon each other: light and stranger, song and scream, fountain and eye, god and blemish, dominion and parable"—*VLS*
1-55713-097-3 SUN & MOON PB $11.95

Khurbn & Other Poems
In his earlier *Poland/1931,* Rothenberg explored a Poland of the mind, the Poland from which his parents emigrated in 1920. *Khurbn* is the result of a journey to the real Poland and a confrontation of the reality of Nazi genocide; it is the most powerful poem of Rothenberg's career. He writes: "The poems that I first began to hear at Treblinka are the clearest message I have ever gotten about why I write poetry. They are an answer also to the proposition—by Adorno & others—that poetry cannot or, should not be written after Auschwitz"
0-8112-1109-6 NEW DIRECTIONS PB $9.95

The Lorca Variations
Versions, both faithful and free, of Lorca's lyrics: "Lorca," says Rothenberg, "was the first poet to open my mind to the contemporary poetry of Europe and of something possibly older and deeper that would surface for us later in America as well"
0-8112-1253-X NEW DIRECTIONS PB $10.95

New Selected Poems, 1970-1995
0-8112-0996-2 NEW DIRECTIONS $23.50
0-8112-0997-0 NEW DIRECTIONS PB $8.95

Poland/1931
A reinvention of ancestral landscape, wildly lyrical, funny, and moving
0-8112-0541-X NEW DIRECTIONS $7.50
0-8112-0542-8 NEW DIRECTIONS PB $3.25

Seedings & Other Poems
0-8112-1331-5 NEW DIRECTIONS $10.95

That Dada Strain
0-8112-0860-5 NEW DIRECTIONS PB $7.25

Vienna Blood & Other Poems
0-8112-0759-5 NEW DIRECTIONS PB $4.95

Mark **Rudman**

By Contraries & Other Poems
0-915032-93-7 NATIONAL POETRY FOUNDATION PB $12.95

The Millennium Hotel
0-8195-2229-5 NEW ENGLAND $35.00
0-8195-2230-9 WESLEYAN PB $14.95

The Nowhere Steps
0-935296-93-X SHEEP MEADOW $16.95
0-935296-90-5 SHEEP MEADOW PB $11.95

Rider
"A new departure in autobiographically confessional poetry...Relationships and characterizations are unfolded with brilliant boldness. It is striking the way this work evolves into a moving elegy for the stepfather, a rabbi *manqué*, in this brave, very American work" —M.L. Rosenthal
0-8195-1217-6 WESLEYAN PB $12.95

Vern **Rutsala**

Selected Poems
0-934257-61-2 STORYLINE PB $16.95

Luis Omar **Salinas**

The Sadness of Days: Selected and New Poems
0-934770-58-1 ARTE PUBLICO PB $8.00

Mary Jo **Salter**

Sunday Skaters
Praised by Joseph Brodsky for her "superb craftsmanship," Lamont Prize-winner Salter (*Henry Purcell in Japan, Unfinished Painting*) ponders two beautiful lovers on the Boulevard

de Montparnasse and starry-eyed ones on Rome's Gianicolo. The two longer poems in this luminous collection examine the troubled legends of Thomas Jefferson and Robert Frost

0-679-43109-8 KNOPF $20.00
0-679-76567-0 KNOPF PB $13.00

Sonia **Sanchez**

Homegirls and Handgrenades

Sanchez was one of the outstanding black poets to emerge in the 1960s

0-938410-23-7 THUNDER'S MOUTH PB $10.95

Under a Soprano Sky

0-86543-052-7 AFRICA WORLD $16.95
0-86543-053-5 AFRICA WORLD PB $8.95

Wounded in the House of a Friend

0-8070-6826-8 BEACON $15.00

Ed **Sanders**

Thirsting for Peace in a Raging Century: Poems, 1961-1985

"Restores Ed Sanders to his rightful place at the forefront of the poetry of his time, and reminds us that spending one's days in active pursuit of the betterment of all life on the planet isn't necessarily antithetical to the creation of first-rate writing"—*San Francisco Chronicle*

0-918273-24-2 COFFEE HOUSE PB $9.95

Sapphire

American Dreams

"Stunning…One of the strongest debut collections of the '90s"—*Publishers Weekly*

0-679-76799-1 VINTAGE PB $12.00

Leslie **Scalapino**

Crowd and Not Evening or Light

1-55713-141-4 SUN & MOON PB $9.00

The Front Matter, Dead Souls

0-8195-5290-9 WESLEYAN $25.00

Selected Writings

1-88368-936-8 TALISMAN PB $10.50

Gjertrud **Schnackenberg**

A Gilded Lapse of Time

Winner of the Rome Prize and Guggenheim Fellowships, Schnackenberg talks of themes of humanity, divinity, and remembrance. "What a superb poet she is, and what range of original sensibility, what private music, in the less well-worn emotions"
—Nadine Godimer

0-374-16226-3 FS&G $19.00
0-374-52399-1 NOONDAY PB $10.00

The Lamplit Answer

"Schnackenberg has a control of line, of pace, and of tone that is rare in her generation"
—John Hollander

0-374-18293-0 OLYMPIC $12.95
0-374-51978-1 FS&G PB $6.95

Portraits and Elegies

0-374-51981-1 OLYMPIC PB $1.98

Barry **Schwabsky**

Fate: Seen in the Dark

9-996-92379-7 BURNING DECK PB $4.00

Leonard **Schwartz**

Objects of Thought, Attempts at Speech

0-922792-00-3 GNOSIS PB $6.95

Armand **Schwerner**

Sounds of the River Naranjana

Includes *The Tablets,* Schwerner's ongoing series reflecting the formal influence of cuneiform fragments

0-930794-60-5 STATION HILL PB $6.95

Hugh **Seidman**

People Live, They Have Lives

Seidman's fourth book of poetry reworks some of the dominating themes of his earlier books, such as the torturous relationship of child to parent, the potential withdrawal of human love, and the booby trap of human wishes. The book also celebrates nature and human tenderness in a way not so palpably present in his work before

1-88116-302-4 MIAMI $16.95
1-88116-303-2 MIAMI PB $10.95

Selected Poems: 1965-1995

Precise and unblinking in his lyricism, Seidman is one of the most underrated of contemporaries

1-88116-310-5 MIAMI $20.95
1-88116-311-3 MIAMI PB $14.95

Robyn **Selman**

Directions to My House

"Robyn Selman's exact, hilarious, and often heartbreaking lyrics are anything but cool: I should say hot-headed, warm-hearted, astringent, peppery, and even, on her ardent, her tragic occasions, burning"—Richard Howard

0-8229-5568-7 PITTSBURGH PB $10.95

Vijay **Seshadri**

Wild Kingdom

1-55597-236-5 GRAY WOLF PB $12.95

Anne **Sexton**

Complete Poems, 1981

0-395-29475-4 HOUGHTON MIFFLIN $35.00
0-395-32935-3 HOUGHTON MIFFLIN PB $15.95

Love Poems

0-395-51760-5 HOUGHTON MIFFLIN PB $11.95

Selected Poems

0-395-47782-4 HOUGHTON MIFFLIN PB $13.95

Ntozake **Shange**

Ridin' the Moon in Texas: Word Paintings

0-312-02273-5 ST. MARTIN'S PB $9.95

See No Evil

0-917672-21-6 MOMO'S PB $5.95

Alan **Shapiro**

The Last Happy Occasion

0-226-75032-9 CHICAGO $22.95

Mixed Company

0-226-75031-0 CHICAGO PB $11.95

David **Shapiro**

After a Lost Original

"Endlessly experimental, David Shapiro's poetry manifests a never-resting mind, always questing after a formless form"—Harold Bloom. From the title poem: "When the translation and the original meet / The doubtful original and the strong mistranslation / The original feels lost like a triple pun / And the translation cries, Without me you are lost"

0-87951-527-9 OVERLOOK $19.95
0-87951-528-7 OVERLOOK PB $12.95

House (Blown Apart)

0-87951-331-4 OVERLOOK PB $9.95

To an Idea: A Book of Poems

0-87951-255-5 VIKING PB $8.95

Harvey **Shapiro**

A Day's Portion

1-88241-311-3 HANGING LOOSE $18.00
1-88241-310-5 HANGING LOOSE PB $10.00

The Light Holds

0-8195-6096-0 WESLEYAN PB $11.95

National Cold Storage Company: New and Selected Poems

Ironic, sensuous, meditative poems. "Shapiro is *the* American urban poet"—Cynthia Ozick

0-8195-1153-6 WESLEYAN PB $11.95

This World

0-8195-1057-2 WESLEYAN PB $12.95

Reginald **Shepherd**

Angel Interrupted

0-8229-3960-6 PITTSBURGH $24.95
0-8229-5614-4 PITTSBURGH PB $10.95

Some Are Drowning

This first collection enacts the struggle of a young black gay man in his search for identity. Many voices haunt these poems: black and white, male and female, the oppressor's voice as well as the oppressed. The poet's aim is to rescue some portion of the drowned and the drowning

0-8229-5547-4 PITTSBURGH PB $10.95

Aaron **Shurin**

The Graces

0-87704-060-5 FOUR SEASONS PB $4.95

Ron **Silliman**

Demo to Ink

0-925904-07-4 CHAX PB $11.00

Lit

0-937013-18-8 POTES & POETS PB $7.50

Paradise

A section from Silliman's long ongoing work *The Alphabet*

0-930901-32-0 BURNING DECK PB $7.00

Toner

0-937013-43-9 POTES & POETS PB $9.50

Charles **Simic**

Austerities

0-8076-1044-5 BRAZILLER PB $4.95

Charles **Simic**

Book of Gods and Devils
0-15-613546-9 HARCOURT BRACE PB $10.00

Hotel Insomnia
0-15-642182-8 HARCOURT BRACE PB $10.95

Selected Poems, 1963-1983
0-8076-1129-8 BRAZILLER $14.95
0-8076-1240-5 BRAZILLER PB $12.95

Walking the Black Cat
0-15-100219-3 HARCOURT BRACE $22.00
0-15-600481-X HARCOURT BRACE PB $13.00

Weather Forecast for Utopia and Vicinity: Poems, 1967-1982
0-930794-83-4 STATION HILL PB $7.95

A Wedding in Hell
0-15-100123-5 HARCOURT BRACE $19.95
0-15-600129-2 HARVEST PB $11.95

Maurya **Simon**

Days of Awe
1-55659-023-7 COPPER CANYON PB $9.00

The Enchanted Room
"An extraordinary first book of poetry…Almost every single poem is successful per se, includes at times fresh and surprising metaphors, and conveys a quiet, subtle, and crystal-clear view of the world"—Miroslav Holub
0-914742-98-1 COPPER CANYON PB $9.00

The Golden Labyrinth
0-8262-0995-5 MISSOURI PB $12.95

Speaking in Tongues
0-87905-082-9 GIBBS SMITH PB $9.95

Louis **Simpson**

There You Are
1-88526-615-4 STORYLINE $16.95
1-88526-617-0 STORYLINE PB $10.00

Adele **Slaughter**

What the Body Remembers
0-934257-99-X STORYLINE PB $11.95

Tom **Sleigh**

After One
0-395-34842-0 HOUGHTON MIFFLIN PB $6.95

The Chain
"Spirit,/in me accomplish your work," Sleigh writes to invoke memory's ineradicable work—the ways in which consciousness seeks to alter, in order to comprehend, the meaning of cultural inheritance. In a series of deeply moving portraits, Sleigh dramatizes the ambiguous nature of truth and the difficulties the moral imagination must overcome in recalling and judging the past. He is currently a professor at Dartmouth College. "Sleigh's precision marks him as the diamond cutter of poetry"
—NY Times Book Review
0-226-76240-8 CHICAGO $35.00
0-226-76241-6 CHICAGO PB $11.95

Waking
0-226-76239-4 CHICAGO PB $10.95

Charlie **Smith**

Before & After
0-393-31555-X NORTON PB $11.00

The Palms
0-393-31096-5 NORTON PB $8.95

Dave **Smith**

Fate's Kite: Poems, 1992-1995
0-8071-2041-3 LSU PB $12.95

Floating on Solitude: Three Volumes of Poetry
0-252-06584-0 ILLINOIS PB $16.95

Patti **Smith**

The Coral Sea
These elegant poems are a tribute to Smith's long-lasting friendship with the photographer Robert Mapplethorpe. For two decades, the two personified the creative forces of New York City, and Smith's retelling of her grief in these works recasts Mapplethorpe as a great and original artist whose death from AIDS is an enduring tragedy
0-393-03908-0 NORTON $18.00

Early Work: 1970-79
0-393-03605-7 NORTON $18.95
0-393-31301-8 NORTON PB $10.00

Wild Leaves
0-393-03743-6 NORTON $17.95

W.D. **Snodgrass**

Each in His Season
0-918526-99-X BOA PB $12.50

The Fuehrer Bunker: The Complete Cycle
Dramatic monologues recounting the fall of the Third Reich
1-88023-818-7 BOA $24.00
1-88023-819-5 BOA PB $15.00

Selected Poems
A collection spanning 30 years of the original "confessional" poet's life and work. Snodgrass was an inspiration to Robert Lowell, Anne Sexton, and Sylvia Plath, and the poems presented here are both humorous and moving. "Our first opportunity to see Snodgrass in perspective, and the view is impressive"
— Robert McDowell, *Hudson Review*
0-939149-61-3 SOPHIA PB $15.95
0-939149-04-4 SOHO $19.95

'Annah **Sobelman**

The Tulip Sacrament
In this astonishing first collection, the flesh becomes word: tough and iridescent. Whether addressing Jesus on the city sidewalks, her grandmother in the kitchen, dirt, rats, garlic, pigeons, or tulips, Sobelman's poetry vibrates between contradictions. Sobelman is a recent graduate of the University of Iowa Writers' Workshop
0-8195-2223-6 WESLEYAN $25.00
0-8195-1227-3 WESLEYAN PB $11.95

CRISTOBAL C.Z. JUL 29 1935 REGISTERED AIR MAIL

The Reader's Catalog
250 West 57th Street
New York, NY 10107

Gustaf **Sobin**
"Sobin is a landscape artist whose terrain is language…. The physicality which Sobin brings to poetry is not that of inert hunks of words on a page, but of organic matter in motion."—Geoffrey O'Brien, VLS

Breaths' Burials
"Many poems in *Breaths' Burials* exemplify the almost unutterable grace of long-legged shorebirds at dusk in a cove…. Gustaf Sobin is showing the sensory surface as he dives deep"
—Michael McClure
0-8112-1299-8 NEW DIRECTIONS PB $11.95

By the Bias of Sound: Selected Poems, 1972-1994
An indispensable collection covering the development of Sobin's work, including poems from the now rare early books
1-88368-921-X TALISMAN $33.95
1-88368-920-1 TALISMAN PB $13.95

The Earth as Air
"Sobin's world…is basic, stripped, often sun-drenched, sometimes arid—and mysterious"
—Charles Tomlinson
0-8112-0893-1 NEW DIRECTIONS PB $7.25

Voyaging Portraits
Visionary poetry by an American poet long resident in southern France.
0-8112-1061-8 NEW DIRECTIONS PB $9.95

Cathy **Song**

Frameless Windows, Squares of Light
0-393-30592-9 NORTON PB $7.95

School Figures
0-8229-3773-5 PITTSBURGH $19.95
0-8229-5517-2 PITTSBURGH PB $10.95

Gary **Soto**

New and Selected Poems
0-8118-0758-4 CHRONICLE PB $12.95

Who Will Know Us?: New Poems
0-87701-673-9 CHRONICLE PB $8.95

David **St. John**

The Orange Piano
0-89807-135-6 ILLUMINATI PB $5.95

Study for the World's Body: New and Selected Poems
0-06-095016-1 HARPERPERENNIAL PB $11.00

Timothy **Steele**

The Color Wheel: Poems
0-8018-4952-7 JOHNS HOPKINS PB $12.95

Sapphics and Uncertainties: Poems, 1970-1986
1-55728-375-3 ARKANSAS PB $12.00

Charles **Stein**

The Hat Rack Tree: Selected Poems, 1980-1993
0-88268-180-X STATION HILL PB $9.95

Horse Sacrifice
0-930794-30-3 STATION HILL PB $4.50

Gerald **Stern**

Gerald Stern (1925-) was born in Pittsburgh and taught for many years at Raritan Valley Community College in New Jersey before he settled in at the University of Iowa Writers' Workshop in 1982, where he taught for more than ten years.

Bread Without Sugar

Memory, survival, redemption, and secret joy are the major themes of Gerald Stern's eighth book of poetry. "Stern is one of those rare poetic souls who makes it almost impossible to remember what our world was like before his poetry came to exalt it"—C.K. Williams

0-393-03094-6 NORTON $18.95
0-393-31010-8 NORTON PB $8.95

Gerald Stern (photo by Star Black)

Odd Mercy: Poems

Love, hope, memory, faith: Stern writes from "the second half of [his] sixth decade on beautiful earth" of the long journey of mind and soul toward redemption and justice. "Stern's poems are musical transcriptions of the beauty and pain that define life itself"—*Library Journal*. "Stern is the most expansively celebratory poet in years—almost a spiritual reincarnation of Whitman"—*Georgia Review*

0-393-03879-3 NORTON $18.95

Two Long Poems

0-88748-100-0 CARNEGIE-MELLON PB $10.95

Sam **Stockwell**

Theater of Animals

0-252-06476-3 ILLINOIS PB $10.95

Ruth **Stone**

Simplicity

0-9638183-1-7 PARIS PB $12.95

Patricia **Storace**

Dinner with Persephone

0-679-42134-3 PANTHEON $25.00

Mark **Strand**

The Continuous Life

0-679-73844-4 KNOPF PB $15.00

Dark Harbor: A Poem

0-679-41886-5 KNOPF $19.00
0-679-75279-X KNOPF PB $13.00

Reasons for Moving, Darker, & The Sargentville Notebook

0-679-73668-9 KNOPF PB $11.00

Selected Poems

0-679-73301-9 KNOPF PB $15.00

Stephanie **Strickland**

The Red Virgin: A Poem of Simone Weil

0-299-13990-5 WISCONSIN $17.95
0-299-13994-8 WISCONSIN PB $10.95

Terese **Svoboda**

Laughing Africa

0-87745-272-5 IOWA PB $10.95

Mere Mortals

0-8203-1710-1 GEORGIA PB $14.95

Arthur **Sze**

Archipelago

Sze's poetry draws on both Japanese and Native American influences

1-55659-100-4 COPPER CANYON PB $12.00

John **Taggart**

Loop

1-55713-012-4 SUN & MOON PB $11.95

Nathaniel **Tarn**

The House of Leaves

0-87685-259-2 BLACK SPARROW PB $13.00

Lyrics for the Bride of God

A major sequence of poems drawing on Jewish spiritual themes

0-8112-0566-5 NEW DIRECTIONS PB $3.75

Seeing America First

Prose poems. "His work reveals a rich temperament and remarkable linguistic inventiveness"—Octavio Paz

0-918273-53-6 COFFEE HOUSE PB $8.95

James **Tate**

Constant Defender

0-88001-041-X ECCO PB $7.95

Distance from Loved Ones

0-8195-1191-9 WESLEYAN PB $11.95

Hints to Pilgrims

0-87023-347-5 MASSACHUSETTS PB $9.95

The Lost Pilot

0-912946-97-0 ECCO PB $5.95

The Oblivion Ha-Ha

0-87775-171-4 UNICORN PB $13.50

Selected Poems

0-8195-1192-7 WESLEYAN PB $15.95

Worshipful Company of Fletchers

Tate's most recent collection, and a winner of the National Book Award in poetry.

0-88001-380-X ECCO $20.00
0-88001-431-8 ECCO PB $13.00

Richard **Tillinghast**

Our Flag Was Still There

0-8195-6099-5 WESLEYAN PB $11.95

The Stonecutter's Hand

1-56792-011-X GODINE $19.95

Quincy **Troupe**

Avalanche

1-56689-045-4 COFFEE HOUSE $19.95
1-56689-044-6 COFFEE HOUSE PB $11.95

Snake-Back Solos

0-918408-11-3 REED CANNON & JOHNSON PB $5.95

Frederick **Turner**

April Wind & Other Poems

0-8139-1358-6 VIRGINIA $16.50

Genesis: An Epic Poem

A 10,000-line narrative poem about the exploration of Mars. "A prodigious work" —Brian Aldiss

0-933071-26-4 SAYBROOK PB $9.95

The New World

"*The New World* may be the first straight-forward heroic epic since Tennyson that really works. Turner's stroke of genius was to place the story in the future and tell it in a science-fiction mode. Suddenly all the epic form has become not only permissible again but credible" —Dana Gioia

0-691-06641-8 PRINCETON $35.00
0-691-01420-5 PRINCETON PB $10.95

Chase **Twichell**

The Ghost of Eden

0-86538-083-X ONTARIO REVIEW $17.95

Perdido

0-374-23073-0 FS&G $16.95

Leslie **Ullman**

Dreams by No One's Daughter

0-8229-5395-1 PITTSBURGH PB $10.95

John **Updike**

Collected Poems, 1953-1993

The earliest poems in this collection were written when Updike was 21, the latest after he had turned 60. Nimble meditations on ordinary life (the changing of a storm window, a sleepless trip to Spain) mix with anxious confessions of cruelty and love, tracing the writer's progress through the decades. Some of his wittiest and most knowing work can be found in this volume

0-679-42221-8 KNOPF $30.00
0-679-76204-3 KNOPF PB $15.00

Lee **Upton**

Approximate Darling

In these orchestral scores, in the stained glass of this lyric architecture, sonorous and multidimensional instrumentations "bow to a cooler judge": a Leonardo da Vinci cartoon, *Hamlet's* Gertrude, Beatrix Potter, Emily Dickinson, Louise Bogan, the "relentless experiment" of pregnancy, and the consequences of womanliness, the work "deepening into whatever we cannot avoid"

0-8203-1811-6 GEORGIA PB $14.95

Peter **Viereck**

Tide and Continuities: Last and First Poems, 1995-1938

1-55728-314-1 ARKANSAS PB $24.00

Evangelina **Vigil-Piñon**

The Computer Is Down

"Takes on a sophisticated sheen, at once celebrating the glittery image of the late 20th-century American city and taking a hard look at the human realities upon which the image rests"—*San Antonio Light*

0-934770-32-8 ARTE PUBLICO PB $7.00

Thirty And Seen a Lot

The first book of poems by this San Antonio native

0-934770-13-1 ARTE PUBLICO PB $7.00

Arthur **Vogelsang**

Cities and Towns

1-55849-021-3 MASSACHUSETTS PB $10.95

Twentieth-Century Women

0-8203-0996-6 GEORGIA PB $6.95

Ellen Bryant **Voigt**

Claiming Kin

0-8195-1083-1 WESLEYAN PB $11.95

Kyrie

0-393-31561-4 NORTON PB $11.00

Two Trees

0-393-31100-7 NORTON PB $8.95

Karen **Volkman**

Crash's Law

A winner of the 1995 National Poetry Series, judged and selected by Heather McHugh. "From its very first words, *Crash's Law* bespeaks a mind attuned no less to the accidents than to the orders of sensual life"—Heather McHugh. "A revelation of originality and invention" —Richard Howard

0-393-03956-0 NORTON $18.95

David **Wagoner**

Walt Whitman Bathing

0-252-06570-0 ILLINOIS PB $11.95

Diane **Wakoski**

The Collected Greed, Parts 1-13

0-87685-462-5 BLACK SPARROW PB $14.00

The Emerald City of Las Vegas

0-87685-972-4 BLACK SPARROW $25.00

0-87685-971-6 BLACK SPARROW PB $13.50

Emerald Ice: Selected Poems

0-87685-744-6 BLACK SPARROW PB $15.00

Medea the Sorceress: The Archaeology of Movies and Books, Vol. 1

0-87685-810-8 BLACK SPARROW $25.00

Jason the Sailor: The Archaeology of Movies and Books, Vol. 2

The second volume of an open-ended epic in which the poet, older and wiser, looks to her adolescence for the key to understanding desire

0-87685-903-1 BLACK SPARROW $25.00

0-87685-902-3 BLACK SPARROW PB $13.00

Anne **Waldman**

Fast Speaking Woman: Chants & Essays

An expanded edition revealing the centrality of chant to Waldman's work: "The performance of the text has power, and animation. I am the 'energumem.' The poem is the experience"

0-87286-316-6 CITY LIGHTS PB $10.95

Iovis: All Is Full of Jove

"A marvelous mytho-poetic collage of self-and-other, male and female…considers the role of Jove in detail, in cosmic gossip and multiple languages"—Gary Snyder

1-56689-005-5 COFFEE HOUSE PB $15.00

Kill or Cure

0-14-058708-X PENGUIN PB $14.95

Skin Meat Bones

0-918273-15-3 COFFEE HOUSE PB $8.95

Keith **Waldrop**

The Locality Principle

Recent work by a co-founder of Burning Deck Press. "Encounters whose meaning is suspect; illumination in darkness"—Barbara Guest

1-88071-303-9 AVEC PB $9.95

Potential Random

0-945926-32-4 PARADIGM PB $5.00

The Space of Half an Hour

0-930901-20-7 BURNING DECK PB $4.00

Rosemarie **Waldrop** & Keith **Waldrop**

Light Travels

0-930901-92-4 BURNING DECK PB $5.00

Rosmarie **Waldrop**

A Key into the Language of America

Variations on Roger Williams's 17th-century linguistic and spiritual treatise

0-8112-1287-4 NEW DIRECTIONS PB $10.95

Lawn of Excluded Middle

Prose poems that "stay deceptively close to the surface of language, poking at simple sentences until they yield glimpses of abysses within the ordinary"—*Newsday*

0-927920-04-2 SMALL PRESS PB $7.00

The Reproduction of Profiles

Prose poems derived from Wittgenstein: "I used Wittgenstein's phrases in an unsystematic way, sometimes quoting, sometimes letting them spark what they would, sometimes substituting different nouns within a phrase"

0-8112-1045-6 NEW DIRECTIONS PB $9.95

Streets Enough to Welcome Snow

0-88268-034-X STATION HILL PB $5.95

Alice **Walker**

Good Night, Willie Lee, I'll See You in the Morning

A boxed set of Walker's three earlier collections of poetry

0-15-636467-0 HARCOURT BRACE PB $5.95

Alice Walker

Her Blue Body Everything We Know: Earthling Poems, 1965-1990 Complete

Alice Walker gathers together more than a quarter of a century of her poetry from such volumes as *Good Night, Willie Lee,* and *Horses Make a Landscape Look More Beautiful.*

0-15-640093-6 HARVEST PB $14.95

Ronald **Wallace**

People and Dog in the Sun

0-8229-5388-9 PITTSBURGH PB $10.95

Time's Fancy

0-8229-5548-2 PITTSBURGH PB $10.95

Rosanna **Warren**

Stained Glass

0-393-31174-0 NORTON PB $8.95

Barrett **Watten**

Frame (1971-1991)

1-55713-239-9 SUN & MOON PB $13.95

Progress

0-937804-16-9 ROOF PB $7.50

Michael S. **Weaver**

My Father's Geography

0-8229-3706-9 PITTSBURGH $19.95

0-8229-5469-9 PITTSBURGH PB $10.95

Timber and Prayer: The Indian Pond Poems

0-8229-3873-1 PITTSBURGH $29.95

0-8229-5554-7 PITTSBURGH PB $15.95

Water Song

0-912759-05-4 CALLALOO JOURNAL PB $8.95

Bruce **Weigl**

The Monkey Wars

0-8203-0741-6 GEORGIA PB $7.95

Song of Napalm

0-87113-471-3 ATLANTIC MONTHLY PB $10.95

Sweet Lorain

"There is so much richness here that reading *Sweet Lorain* is like being a hungry boy first into the neighborhood bakery"—Dave Smith

0-8101-5054-9 TRIQUARTERLY PB $11.95

What Saves Us
0-8101-5013-1 TRIQUARTERLY PB $11.95

Marjorie **Welish**

Casting Sequences
"Welish demonstrates a mastery of abstraction in language, deploying an eclectic and playful vocabulary…in wiry constructions of unexpected starkness"—*Newsday*

0-8203-1512-5 GEORGIA PB $9.95

The Windows Flew Open
Welish explores language as a landscape full of cunning disguises and sudden unexpected openings in these beautiful new poems. "Explores the inner landscapes of psyche and dream, but also the surface tensions and contradictory currents of the world before us" —Michael Palmer

0-930901-74-6 BURNING DECK PB $8.00

Rachel **Wetzsteon**

The Other Stars
0-14-058728-4 PENGUIN PB $12.95

Susan **Wheeler**

Bag 'o' Diamonds
A winner of the Norma Farber First Book Award from the Poetry Society of America. "The wit, the deep humor, the friendly irony, the continuous eloquence of the book, presages a long and authentic career as a poet"—Harold Bloom

0-8203-1564-8 GEORGIA PB $9.95

Richard **Wilbur**

New and Collected Poems
Wilbur was established from the beginning of his career as a master of formal artifice

0-15-165206-6 HARCOURT BRACE $27.95
0-15-665491-1 HARCOURT BRACE PB $10.95

C.K. **Williams**

A Dream of Mind
0-374-28894-1 FS&G $16.00
0-374-52376-2 NOONDAY PB $12.00

Flesh and Blood
0-374-52090-9 FS&G PB $9.00

Poems, 1963-1983
0-374-23516-3 FS&G $19.95
0-374-52204-9 NOONDAY PB $14.00

Selected Poems
"No other contemporary poet...has given us a more textured or pressurized rendering of what it feels like to think—to try to think—through a situational or mental problem moment by moment: to bring the unconscious into the available light of language." —Edward Hirsch, *New Republic*

0-374-25881-3 FS&G $22.00
0-374-52455-6 NOONDAY PB $12.00

The Vigil: Poems
0-374-22653-9 FS&G $25.00

Alan **Williamson**

Love and the Soul
0-226-89933-0 CHICAGO PB $10.95

The Muse of Distance
0-394-75577-4 KNOPF PB $8.95

Elizabeth **Willis**

The Human Abstract
0-14-024935-4 PENGUIN PB $12.95

Edward W. **Wood**

On Being Wounded
1-55591-076-9 FULCRUM $19.95

C.D. **Wright**

Just Whistle: A Valentine
0-932716-32-6 KELSEY ST. PB $14.00

String Light: Poems
0-8203-1298-3 GEORGIA PB $8.95

Translations of the Gospel Back into Tongues: Poems
0-87395-652-4 SUNY $34.50

Tremble: Poems
0-88001-458-X ECCO $20.00

Charles **Wright**

Chickamauga
0-374-52481-5 NOONDAY PB $10.00

Country Music: Selected and Early Poems
0-8195-1201-X WESLEYAN PB $14.95

The World of the Ten Thousand Things: Poems, 1980-1990
0-374-52326-6 FS&G PB $13.00

Franz **Wright**

Entry in an Unknown Hand
0-88748-078-0 CARNEGIE-MELLON PB $10.95

The Night World and the Word Night
0-88748-155-8 CARNEGIE-MELLON PB $11.95

Rorschach Test
0-88748-209-0 CARNEGIE-MELLON PB $11.95

James **Wright**

"His poems are shorter, quieter, gentler than Roethke's; they usually present the poet in a specific Midwestern locale, contemplating a landscape which seems wholly alien until a sudden gesture or change in perspective momentarily unites poet and nature, self and other, in a muted epiphany." —*Marjorie Perloff,* Washington Post

Above the River: The Complete Poems
0-374-52282-0 NOONDAY PB $16.00

The Branch Will Not Break
0-8195-1018-1 WESLEYAN PB $11.95

Collected Poems
0-8195-4031-5 WESLEYAN $30.00
0-8195-6022-7 WESLEYAN PB $16.95

Saint Judas
0-8195-1110-2 WESLEYAN PB $11.95

Two Citizens
0-934834-09-1 WHITE PINE PB $7.00

Jay **Wright**

Boleros
0-691-01504-X PRINCETON PB $9.95

Selected Poems
Of his work, this southwestern poet has said: "A young man, hearing me read some of my poems, said that I seemed to be trying to weave together a lot of different things. My answer was that they are already woven, I'm just trying to uncover the weave"

0-691-06687-6 PRINCETON $29.95
0-691-01435-3 PRINCETON PB $12.95

John **Yau**

Edificio Sayonara
0-87685-887-6 BLACK SPARROW PB $13.00

Forbidden Entries
1-57423-017-4 BLACK SPARROW $25.01
1-57423-016-6 BLACK SPARROW PB $10.01

Hawaiian Cowboys
0-87685-957-0 BLACK SPARROW $25.00
0-87685-956-2 BLACK SPARROW PB $13.50

Radiant Silhouette: New and Selected Work, 1974-1988
Dream narratives, invented myths, visionary snapshots of the city: Yau's work invites us into a splendid and compelling universe all its own

0-87685-772-1 BLACK SPARROW PB $13.00

Al **Young**

Heaven: Collected Poems, 1958-1988
0-88739-069-2 CREATIVE ARTS PB $17.95

Kevin **Young**

Most Way Home
0-688-14765-8 MORROW PB $10.00

Peter **Zabelskis**

Loop: 50 Ideas for Pictures
"The fifty pieces are remarkable condensations…Beguilingly short and addictive"—Herbert Blau

0-9616193-1-7 SLATE PB $4.95

Paul **Zimmer**

Big Blue Train
1-55728-297-8 ARKANSAS PB $12.00

Crossing to Sunlight: Selected Poems
0-8203-1818-3 GEORGIA $29.95
0-8203-1829-9 GEORGIA PB $14.95

The Great Bird of Love
0-252-06060-1 ILLINOIS PB $9.95

Anthologies

A poetry anthology should function as a road map: not a substitute for journeying, but a guide to the available destinations. There is at present no one book that adequately describes modern American poetry; nor is that surprising, given the diversity of its practitioners and audiences, and the gradual splintering of whatever center might once have existed. Each of the books below presents a chunk, large or small, of the overall situation.

Miguel **Algarin** & Bob **Holman**, editors
Aloud!: Voices from the Nuyorican Poets' Cafe
0-8050-3257-6 OWLET PB $14.95

Donald **Allen** & George F. **Butterick**, editors
The Postmoderns: The New American Poetry
An updated version of Allen's influential (and now sadly out of print) *The New American Poetry*; the new book adds some important figures, but in some ways muddies the effect of the original
0-802-115035-7 GROVE PB $14.95

Joshua **Blum** & others, editors
The United States of Poetry
0-8109-3927-4 ABRAMS $29.95

Arna **Bontemps**, editor
American Negro Poetry
An update of the 1963 edition
0-374-52143-3 FS&G PB $10.00

Joseph **Brodsky** & others
Homage to Frost
See also **THE 20TH CENTURY** under **STUDIES OF INDIVIDUAL AUTHORS (ALPHABETICAL BY SUBJECT)** under **AMERICAN LITERATURE: ANTHOLOGIES AND CRITICAL STUDIES**
0-374-14814-7 FS&G $30.00

Joseph **Bruchac**, editor
Songs from This Earth on Turtle's Back: An Anthology of Poetry by American Indian Writers
0-912678-58-5 GREENFIELD REVIEW PB $14.95

Scott **Cairns** & W. Scott **Olsen**, editors
The Sacred Place
This unprecedented anthology brings together a provocative mix of new and well-known writers whose poetry and prose broaches the possibility of something "bigger" going on, something more significant at stake. What is the relation between what we call the sacred and what we witness as the apparent world?
0-87480-523-6 UTAH PB $19.95

Hayden **Carruth**, editor
The Voice that Is Great Within Us
One of the better anthologies of 20th-century American poetry: with a selection that is at once comprehensive, surprising, and judicious
0-553-26263-7 BDD PB $7.99

Ann **Charters**, editor
The Portable Beat Reader
0-14-015102-8 PENGUIN PB $14.95

Andrei **Codrescu**, editor
Up Late: American Poetry Since 1970
An informal assortment of some of the younger practitioners of the '70s and '80s. "This anthology does provide an earnestly comprehensive vita for the alternative poetry scene since 1970. Every tribe and its mutations are charted"—*Village Voice*
0-941423-26-3 FOUR WALLS PB $16.95

Andrei **Codrescu** & Laura **Rosenthal**, editors
American Poets Say Goodbye to the Twentieth Century
1-56858-071-1 FOUR WALLS $35.00
1-56858-068-1 FOUR WALLS PB $18.00

Michael **Collier**, editor
The Wesleyan Tradition: Four Decades of American Poetry
0-8195-2210-4 WESLEYAN $35.00
0-8195-1229-X WESLEYAN PB $14.95

Joel **Conarroe**, editor
Six American Poets
The compelling voices of Emily Dickinson, Walt Whitman, Langston Hughes, William Carlos Williams, Wallace Stevens, and Robert Frost are gathered here in one volume. Conarroe's lively essays highlight the life and works of each writer, and the 247 poems included are some of the nation's finest. A multifaceted portrait of American genius
0-679-74525-4 VINTAGE PB $13.00

Alison H. **Deming**, editor
Poetry of the American West
0-231-10386-7 COLUMBIA $24.95

Sascha **Feinstein** & Yusef **Komunyakaa**, editors
The Jazz Poetry Anthology
Jazz has always been an influence on modern American poetry, and this well-edited collection shows the astonishing variety of work that has paid tribute to that influence. The poems include Paul Blackburn on Sonny Rollins, Sterling Brown on Ma Rainey, Ted Joans on Lester Young, Nathaniel Mackey on John Coltrane. Not to mention Langston Hughes, Amiri Baraka, William Carlos Williams, Kenneth Rexroth, Mina Loy, Sonia Sanchez, and many others. "Essential for anyone who is interested in our music"—Dizzy Gillespie
0-253-20637-5 INDIANA PB $15.95

Lawrence **Ferlinghetti**, editor
City Lights Pocket Poets Anthology
The 40th-anniversary year of City Light's Pocket Poets Series offers a selection of its most potent poems. A virtual primer of international poetry from the second half of the century, including works by Ginsberg, Pasolini, Corso, Levertov, Duncan, Kerouac, Prevert, Mayakovsky, Rexroth, Lamantia, O'Hara, Picasso, and others
0-87286-311-5 CITY LIGHTS $18.95

Peter **Glassgold**, editor & translator
Hwaet!: A Little Old English Anthology of American Modernist Poetry
Glassgold renders William Carlos Williams, Marianne Moore, and others into Anglo-Saxon in this enormously entertaining book
0-940650-42-8 SUN & MOON PB $6.95

Ray **Gonzalez**, editor
After Aztlán: Latino Poetry of the Nineties
0-87923-932-8 GODINE PB $15.95

Donald **Hall**, editor
Contemporary American Poetry
An older book providing a brief but useful guide to some major tendencies of the postwar scene
0-14-058618-0 VIKING PB $9.95

Michael S. **Harper** & Anthony **Walton**, editors
Every Shut Eye Ain't Asleep: An Anthology of Poetry by African Americans Since 1945
0-316-34710-8 LITTLE, BROWN PB $12.95

Maureen **Honey**, editor
Shadowed Dreams: Women's Poetry of the Harlem Renaissance
Featuring the work of 34 poets including Angelina Weld Grimke, Jessie Fauset, and Alice Dunbar-Nelson and spanning the years between 1918 and 1931, this anthology focuses new attention on the role of women writers in the Harlem Renaissance
FOREWORD BY NELLIE Y. MCKAY
0-8135-1420-7 RUTGERS PB $16.95

Paul **Hoover**, editor
Postmodern American Poetry
0-393-31090-6 NORTON PB $24.95

James Weldon **Johnson**, editor
The Book of American Negro Poetry
First published in 1922, this volume includes critical and biographical notes by the author of *The Autobiograpby of an Ex-Colored Man*
0-15-613539-6 HARCOURT BRACE PB $12.00

Woodie **King**, editor
The Forerunners: Black Poets in America
Focuses on the middle generation between the Harlem Renaissance and the 1960s
0-88258-093-0 HOWARD PB $12.95

Michael **Klein**, editor
Poets for Life: 76 Poets Respond to AIDS
Features the work of James Merrill, Adrienne Rich, Allen Ginsberg, Jean Valentine, June Jordan, Paul Monette, Robert Creeley, and many others
0-89255-170-4 PERSEA PB $12.95

Art **Lange** & Nathaniel **Mackey**, editors
Moment's Notice: Jazz in Poetry and Prose
See also **THE JAZZ SCENE** under **JAZZ** in **PERFORMING ARTS AND MEDIA**
1-56689-001-2 COFFEE HOUSE PB $17.50

David **Lehman** & Adrienne **Rich**, editors
The Best American Poetry, 1996
0-684-81451-X TOUCHSTONE PB $13.00

David **Lehman** & Richard **Howard**, editors
The Best American Poetry, 1995
0-684-80151-5 TOUCHSTONE PB $13.00

David **Lehman** & A.R. **Ammons**, editors
The Best American Poetry, 1994
"A truly memorable anthology"
—*Chicago Tribune*
0-671-89948-1 TOUCHSTONE PB $13.00

David **Lehman** & Louise **Glück**, editors
The Best American Poetry, 1993
0-02-069846-1 COLLIER PB $13.00

Richard **Marius**, editor
The Columbia Book of Civil War Poetry
0-231-10002-7 COLUMBIA $24.95

J.D. **McClatchy**, editor
The Vintage Book of Contemporary Poetry
See also **POETRY ANTHOLOGIES** under **WORLD LITERATURE: WORLD LITERATURE SURVEYS AND ANTHOLOGIES** in **LITERATURE OF EUROPE, AFRICA, AND ASIA**
0-679-74115-1 VINTAGE PB $15.00

Douglas **Messerli**, editor
From the Other Side of the Century: A New American Poetry, 1960-1990
A jumbo anthology spanning a wide range of experimental work
1-55713-131-7 SUN & MOON PB $29.95

Language Poetries: An Anthology
"The most decisive exploration of poetry's resources and premises since the 1950s"
—Robert Creeley
0-8112-1006-5 NEW DIRECTIONS $21.95

Carl **Morse** & Joan **Larkin**, editors
Gay and Lesbian Poetry in Our Time
Some 200 poems by 94 writers. Contributions by W.H. Auden, James Baldwin, Judy Grahn, Susan Griffin, James Merrill, Adrienne Rich, and others
0-312-02213-1 ST. MARTIN'S $29.95

Jay **Parini**, editor
The Columbia Anthology of American Poetry
Parini's collection takes something of a Top-40 approach, restricting itself mostly to the already familiar
0-231-08122-7 COLUMBIA $29.95

The Columbia History of American Poetry
This superbly organized volume covers American poetry from the Puritans to the present day, with thorough discussions of African-American and Native American poets. Essays on such writers as T.S. Eliot, John Berryman, John Ashbery, Ezra Pound, Stephen Crane, Wallace Stevens, and Sylvia Plath
0-231-07836-6 COLUMBIA $59.95

Elise **Paschen** & others, editors
Poetry in Motion: 100 Poems from the Subways and Buses
A rich assemblage emanating from the immensely popular poetry placards displayed on the subways and buses in New York City.
0-393-03977-3 NORTON $18.95

Dudley **Randall**, editor
The Black Poets
A new anthology that spans the early folk idioms through the present
0-553-27563-1 BDD PB $5.95

Ishmael **Reed** & others, editors
The Before Columbus Foundation Poetry Anthology: Selections from the American Book Awards, 1980-1990
0-393-30833-2 NORTON PB $14.95

Bruce **Ross**, editor
Haiku Moment: An Anthology of Contemporary North American Haiku
0-8048-1820-7 TUTTLE PB $16.95

Jerome **Rothenberg**, editor
Shaking the Pumpkin: Traditional Poetry of the Indian North Americas
Both a collection of American Indian poetry and a reflection of its influence on contemporary poets, as ethnological material is reworked by writers such as Armand Schwerner, Anselm Hollo, W.S. Merwin, and others. "Jerome Rothenberg is an exception to the general misuse of Native America…an example of the kind of borrowing that is possible: one that allows the dignity of giver and taker to remain not only undisturbed, but celebrated, illuminated, made clear"—Paula Gunn Allen
See also **TRADITIONAL LITERATURE: POETRY, STORIES, ORATORY** under **NATIVE AMERICAN LITERATURES**
0-8263-1246-2 NEW MEXICO PB $17.95

Ron **Silliman**, editor
In the American Tree
A comprehensive gathering of such "language-centered" poets as Lyn Hejinian, Rae Armantrout, and Bruce Andrews; includes a selection of theoretical statements
0-915032-34-1
NATIONAL POETRY FOUNDATION PB $18.95

Erlene **Stetson**, editor
Black Sister: Poetry by Black American Women, 1746-1980
The best of the classics, as well as new voices. Includes Phyllis Wheatley, Anne Spencer, Gayle Jones, Ntozake Shange, and Colleen J. McElroy
0-253-20268-X INDIANA PB $13.95

Mark **Strand**, editor
Contemporary American Poets
Another collection from the vantage point of the '70s, although its range is narrower than its title would indicate
0-451-62780-6 NEW AMERICAN LIBRARY PB $6.99

Helen **Vendler**
Poems, Poets, Poetry: An Introduction and Anthology
0-312-08537-0 ST. MARTIN'S PB $29.99

Helen **Vendler**, editor
The Harvard Book of Contemporary American Poetry
A rather quirky selection of Vendler's favorite poets
0-674-37340-5 HARVARD $28.00

Eliot **Weinberger**, editor
American Poetry Since 1950: Innovators and Outsiders
The best anthology showing links in US poetry from the 60s to now
See also **POETRY** under **LITERARY CRITICISM** in **LITERATURE OF EUROPE, AFRICA, AND ASIA**
0-941419-92-4 MARSILIO PB $19.95

20th-Century American Drama

The 1920s, '30s, and '40s

Djuna **Barnes**
At the Roots of the Stars: The Short Plays
Hitherto largely unknown plays, experimental and naturalistic alike, by the author of *Nightwood*
See also **FROM THE TURN OF THE CENTURY TO WORLD WAR II** under **20TH-CENTURY AMERICAN FICTION**
1-55713-160-0 SUN & MOON PB $12.95

T.S. **Eliot**
The Complete Poems and Plays, 1909-1950
In addition to Eliot's poetry, includes *Murder in the Cathedral*, *The Family Reunion*, and *The Cocktail Party*
See also **THE 1920S, '30S, AND '40S** under **20TH-CENTURY BRITISH AND IRISH DRAMA** in **LITERATURE OF THE BRITISH ISLES**
0-15-121185-X HARCOURT BRACE $30.00

T.S. Eliot

Martha **Gellhorn** & Virginia **Cowles**

Love Goes to Press

A comedy co-written by two famous war correspondents

0-8032-2154-1 NEBRASKA $34.50

Lillian **Hellman**

Six Plays by Lillian Hellman

Includes *The Children's Hour, Days to Come, The Little Foxes, Watch on the Rhine, Another Part of the Forest,* and *The Autumn Garden*

0-394-74112-9 RANDOM HOUSE PB $15.00

Langston **Hughes**

Five Plays by Langston Hughes

Includes *Mulatto, Soul Gone Home, Little Ham, Simply Heaven,* and *Tambourines to Glory*

EDITED BY WEBSTER SMALLEY

0-253-32230-8 INDIANA $22.50

0-253-20121-7 INDIANA PB $9.95

Langston **Hughes** & Zora Neale **Hurston**

Mule Bone: A Comedy of Negro Life in Three Acts

Written in collaboration by two of the most important figures of the Harlem Renaissance, this folk comedy only received its premiere in 1991

0-06-096885-0 HARPERPERENNIAL PB $13.00

George S. **Kaufman**

George S. Kaufman and His Collaborators: Three Plays

Includes *June Moon* (written with Ring Lardner), *Bravo!* (inspired by Edna Ferber), and *The Late George Apley* (adapted from the John P. Marquand novel)

0-933826-66-4 OLYMPIC PB $3.98

Sidney **Kingsley**

Sidney Kingsley: Five Prizewinning Plays

EDITED BY NENA COUCH

0-8142-0665-4 OHIO STATE $42.50

Arthur **Miller**

"The suddenness of the '29 crash and the chaos that followed offered a pure instance of the impotence of individualist solutions to so vast a crisis. As a society we learned all over again that mass social organization does not necessarily weaken moral fiber but may set the stage for great displays of heroism and self-sacrifice and endurance."—Arthur Miller

After the Fall

A semi-autobiographical play touching on Miller's marriage to Marilyn Monroe

0-14-048162-1 PENGUIN PB $7.95

Broken Glass

0-14-024938-9 PENGUIN PB $7.95

The Crucible: Text and Criticism

The Salem witch-hunt trials as a parable of McCarthyism

EDITED BY GERALD WEALES

0-14-015507-4 VIKING PB $14.00

Danger: Memory!

Includes *I Can't Remember Anything* and *Clara*

0-8021-5176-0 GROVE PB $5.95

Death of a Salesman

A major American play, winner of the Pulitzer Prize and wide international acclaim

0-14-048134-6 PENGUIN PB $7.95

Incident at Vichy

0-14-048193-1 PENGUIN PB $8.95

The Last Yankee: With a New Essay About Theatre Language

0-14-048151-6 PENGUIN PB $7.50

The Portable Arthur Miller

EDITED BY CHRISTOPHER BIGSBY

0-14-024709-2 PENGUIN PB $14.95

The Price

Two brothers reunite after the death of their parents

0-14-048194-X PENGUIN PB $7.95

Two Plays

Includes *The Archbishop's Ceiling* and *The American Clock*

0-8021-3127-1 GROVE PB $8.95

A View from the Bridge

The clash of different "laws" concerning two Italian longshoremen illegally in the United States

0-14-048135-4 PENGUIN PB $7.95

Clifford **Odets**

Six Plays of Clifford Odets

Includes *Waiting for Lefty, Awake and Sing, Golden Boy, Rocket to the Moon, Till the Day I Die,* and *Paradise Lost*

INTRODUCTION BY HAROLD CLUMAN

0-8021-3220-0 GROVE PB $14.00

Eugene **O'Neill**

"To me the tragic alone has that significant beauty which is truth. It is the meaning of life—and the hope. The noblest is eternally the most tragic. The people who succeed and who do not push on to a greater failure are the spiritual middle classes. Their stopping at success is the proof of their compromising insignificance. How petty their dreams must have been."—Eugene O'Neill

See also **LIBRARY OF AMERICA**

The Complete Plays

The only complete and authoritative edition of all 50 plays

Volume 1: 1913-1920

0-940450-48-8 LIBRARY OF AMERICA $35.00

Volume 2: 1920-1931

0-940450-49-6 LIBRARY OF AMERICA $35.00

Volume 3: 1932-1943

0-940450-50-X LIBRARY OF AMERICA $35.00

The Emperor Jones, Anna Christie, The Hairy Ape

"In each play the central character is one of the insulted and injured: one a Negro, another a stoker, the third a prostitute. But whereas for most of us the plight of such people immediately evokes the social forces that have insulted and injured them, for O'Neill the social insult and injury are not so much facts in themselves as symbols of man's cosmic situation"—Lionel Trilling

0-679-76395-3 VINTAGE PB $11.00

The Iceman Cometh

A group of down-and-outers in a bar are forced to confront their flight from reality

0-394-70018-X VINTAGE PB $9.00

The Later Plays

"The view of America projected by O'Neill's last historical plays is not redeemed by any saving possibilities."—Travis Bogard.

Includes *Ah, Wilderness!, A Touch of the Poet, Hughie,* and *A Moon for the Misbegotten*

EDITED BY TRAVIS BOGARD

0-07-553664-1 VINTAGE PB $15.40

Long Day's Journey into Night

O'Neill's final, autobiographical masterpiece

0-300-04601-4 YALE PB $9.00

A Moon for the Misbegotten

0-394-71236-6 VINTAGE PB $8.00

More Stately Mansions

This play tracing a family from colonial times to the present is one of an unfinished nine-play cycle called *A Tale of Possessors Self-Dispossessed*

EDITED BY DONALD GALLUP

0-300-00177-0 YALE PB $11.00

Nine Plays

Includes *The Emperor Jones, The Hairy Ape, Desire Under the Elms, Marco Millions, The Great God Brown, All God's Chillun Got Wings, Lazarus Laughed, Strange Interlude,* and *Mourning Becomes Electra*

0-679-60045-0 MODERN LIBRARY $20.00

Seven Plays of the Sea

This volume of one-acts includes *The Long Voyage Home, Moon of the Caribbees, Bound East for Cardiff, In the Zone, The Rope, Ile,* and *Where the Cross Is Made*

0-394-71856-9 VINTAGE PB $9.00

Six Short Plays of Eugene O'Neill

Includes *The Dreamy Kid, Before Breakfast, Diff'rent, Welded, Straw,* and *Gold*

0-394-70276-X VINTAGE PB $9.00

Three Plays

Includes *Desire Under the Elms, Strange Interlude,* and *Mourning Becomes Electra*

EDITED BY LUANN WALTHER

0-679-76396-1 VINTAGE PB $11.00

The Unfinished Plays: Notes for the Visit

Includes three never-completed plays: *The Visit of Malatesta, The Last Conquest,* and *Blind Alley Guy*

INTRODUCTION BY VIRGINIA FLOYD

0-8044-2674-0 UNGAR $24.95

Sophie **Treadwell**

Machinal

An expressionist play from the 1920s whose vision of mechanization gone mad has found new favor in recent revivals

1-85459-211-4 CONSORTIUM PB $12.95

Mae **West**

Three Plays: Sex, The Drag and Pleasure Man

EDITED BY LILLIAN SCHLISSEL

0-415-90933-3 ROUTLEDGE PB $16.95

Thornton **Wilder**

"I am not an innovator but a rediscoverer of forgotten goods and I hope a remover of obtrusive bric-a-brac. And as I look at the work of my contemporaries I seem to feel that I am an exception in one thing—I give (don't I) the impression of having enormously enjoyed it."—Thornton Wilder

Our Town

When it opened on Broadway in 1938, *Our Town* met with mixed response. Over the next decades this play about "belonging" was to become the most popular American dramatic work of the century

0-06-080779-2 HARPERCOLLINS PB $6.00

Three Plays

"The theater has lagged behind the other arts in finding the 'new ways' to express how men and women think and feel in our time. I am not one of the new dramatists we are looking for. I wish I were. I hope I have played a part in preparing the way for them." Includes *Our Town, The Skin of Our Teeth,* and *The Matchmaker*

0-06-091293-6 HARPERCOLLINS PB $14.00

Tennessee **Williams**

"All my life I have been haunted by the obsession that to desire a thing or to love a thing intensely is to place yourself in a vulnerable position, to be a possible, if not a probable, loser of what you most want."—Tennessee Williams

Camino Real

0-8112-0218-6 NEW DIRECTIONS PB $10.95

Cat on a Hot Tin Roof

0-451-17112-8 NEW AMERICAN LIBRARY PB $5.99

Clothes for a Summer Hotel

A "ghost play" in which Scott and Zelda Fitzgerald inhabit one psyche

0-8112-0870-2 NEW DIRECTIONS $6.95

Dragon Country: Eight Plays

Includes *In the Bar of a Tokyo Hotel, Mutilated, Gnadiges Fraulein, I Rise in Flames, Cried the Phoenix, I Can't Imagine Tomorrow, Confessional, Frosted Glass Coffin,* and *A Perfect Analysis Given by a Parrot.* "Dragon Country, the country of pain, is an uninhabitable country which is inhabited"—Tennessee Williams.

0-8112-0219-4 NEW DIRECTIONS PB $10.95

The Glass Menagerie

His first major success, a powerful semi-autobiographical play that explores the fragility of private dreamworlds

0-451-16636-1 NEW AMERICAN LIBRARY PB $4.99

A Lovely Sunday for Creve Coeur

0-8112-0757-9 NEW DIRECTIONS PB $7.95

The Red Devil Battery Sign

A surreal Dallas is the setting for this late hallucinatory play

0-8112-1047-2 NEW DIRECTIONS PB $6.95

Small Craft Warnings

Mark Place, a bar on the California coast, and the people who gather there

0-8112-0461-8 NEW DIRECTIONS PB $7.95

Something Cloudy, Something Clear

0-8112-1310-2 NEW DIRECTIONS $19.95

Tennessee Williams (photo courtesy of New Directions Publishing Corporation)

A Streetcar Named Desire

Williams's most famous play has become part of American mythology

0-8112-0765-X NEW DIRECTIONS PB $8.95

Tennessee Williams: Four Plays

Includes *Summer and Smoke, Orpheus Descending, Suddenly, Last Summer,* and *Period of Adjustment*

0-451-52512-4 SIGNET PB $5.95

The Theatre of Tennessee Williams

Volume 1

0-8112-0417-0 NEW DIRECTIONS PB $35.00

Volume 2

0-8112-0418-9 NEW DIRECTIONS PB $35.00

Volume 3

0-8112-0419-7 NEW DIRECTIONS PB $35.00

Volume 4

0-8112-1257-2 NEW DIRECTIONS PB $19.95

Volume 5

0-8112-0593-2 NEW DIRECTIONS PB $35.00

Volume 6

0-8112-0794-3 NEW DIRECTIONS PB $35.00

Volume 7

0-8112-1286-6 NEW DIRECTIONS PB $19.95

Volume 8

0-8112-1201-7 NEW DIRECTIONS PB $35.00

Three by Tennessee Williams

Includes *Sweet Bird of Youth, The Rose Tattoo,* and *Night of the Iguana*

0-451-52149-8 SIGNET PB $6.95

Twenty-Seven Wagons Full of Cotton

Fourteen one-act plays

0-8112-0225-9 NEW DIRECTIONS PB $10.95

The Two-Character Play

Reality and illusion mix when two actors—a brother and a sister—are abandoned by their troupe in an unidentifiable location

0-8112-0729-3 NEW DIRECTIONS PB $8.95

Vieux Carré

An examination of various inhabitants of a rooming house, through a series of shifting memory scenes

0-8112-0728-5 NEW DIRECTIONS PB $8.95

The 1950s and '60s

Edward **Albee**

Albee began his career with brilliant absurdist one-act plays and made his Broadway debut with Who's Afraid of Virginia Woolf?, *a dissection of marital relationships that stands as a major American play. Calling himself a "demonic social critic," Albee has stated that "the role of the writer is to be, axiomatically, against any society he happens to be living in."*

The American Dream & The Zoo Story

In *The Zoo Story,* Albee's first play, a disaffected young man contrives to have himself killed by a stranger in Central Park. In *The American Dream,* conformist parents destroy their son because he fails to live up to their expectations

0-451-16643-4 NEW AMERICAN LIBRARY PB $5.99

A Delicate Balance

This dark variation on the drawing from comedy has been revived with great success

0-4522-7809-0 PLUME PB $9.95

The Plays, Volume 1

0-02-501761-6 MACMILLAN $75.00

The Plays, Volume 2

0-02-501762-4 MACMILLAN $75.00

The Plays, Volume 3

0-02-501763-2 MACMILLAN $75.00

The Sandbox & The Death of Bessie Smith

Two short plays commissioned for the Festival of Two Worlds in Italy

0-452-26083-3 NEW AMERICAN LIBRARY PB $8.95

Three Tall Women

0-452-27400-1 PLUMSTOCK PB $9.95

Who's Afraid of Virginia Woolf?

0-451-15871-7 NEW AMERICAN LIBRARY PB $5.99

Amiri **Baraka**

Dutchman & The Slave

Dutchman, a parable of murderous white rule, is about a black man on a subway and the white woman who provokes and finally kills him

0-688-21084-8 MORROW PB $7.95

The Sidney Poet Heroical

A play in 29 scenes

0-918408-12-1 REED CANNON & JOHNSON PB $5.95

Lee **Breuer**

The Gospel at Colonus
A gospel-inflected version of Sophocles' masterpiece
0-930452-94-1 THEATRE COMMUNICATIONS PB...$8.95

Paddy **Chayefsky**

The Collected Works

Volume 1: The Screenplays
1-557-83193-9 APPLAUSE PB $16.95

Volume 2: The Screenplays
1-557-83194-7 APPLAUSE PB $16.95

Volume 3: The Screenplays
1-557-83191-2 APPLAUSE PB $16.95

Volume 4: The Screenplays
1-557-83192-0 APPLAUSE PB $16.95

Maria Irene **Fornes**

Plays
Includes *Mud, The Danube, Sarita,* and *The Conduct of Life*
0-933826-83-4 PAJ PUBLICATIONS PB $13.95

Promenade & Other Plays
Includes *The Successful Life of Three, Tango Palace, Dr. Kheal, A Vietnamese Wedding,* and *Promenade*
1-55554-014-7 PAJ PUBLICATIONS PB $10.95

Bruce J. **Friedman**

A Mother's Kisses
INTRODUCTION BY STANLEY KAUFFMAN
0-917657-39-X FINE PB $8.95

William **Gibson**

The Miracle Worker
The story of Helen Keller and her teacher, Annie Sullivan
0-553-24778-6 BDD PB $4.99

William **Inge**

Four Plays
A popular Midwestern playwright of the 1950s, Inge wrote psychological dramas about average people coping with the stresses of life. Includes *Bus Stop, Come Back, Little Sheba, The Dark at the Top of the Stairs,* and *Picnic*
0-8021-3209-X GROVE PB $12.00

William Inge

Lorraine **Hansberry**

A Raisin in the Sun
This drama of a black family moving into a white neighborhood brought Hansberry overnight fame and success. "Never before in the history of the American theater had so much of the truth of Black people's lives been seen on the stage" —James Baldwin
0-451-16137-8 SIGNET PB $4.50

A Raisin in the Sun
INTRODUCTION BY ROBERT NEMIROFF
0-679-60172-4 MODERN LIBRARY $12.50
0-452-26776-5 PLUME PB $10.95

To Be Young, Gifted and Black
INTRODUCTION BY JAMES BALDWIN
0-451-15952-7 NEW AMERICAN LIBRARY PB $5.99

Arthur **Kopit**

The Day the Whores Came Out to Play Tennis & Other Plays
Includes *Chamber Music, The Questioning of Nick, Sing to Me Through an Open Window, The Hero,* and *The Conquest of Everest.*
"Like the absurdists before him, he chooses to depict a horrific world where logic holds no sway"—Gautam Dasgupta
0-8090-0736-3 FS&G PB $7.95

The End of the World: With a Symposium to Follow
"This play is the most accessible synthesis we've had of Nukespeak, and Kopit at the end has the courage to express his own view of the evil that may break through the circles of logic to unleash a nuclear apocalypse"—Jack Kroll, *Newsweek*
0-8090-1247-2 FS&G PB $8.95

Wings
An aviatrix battles her way back from a stroke
0-8090-1239-1 FS&G PB $7.95

Jerome **Lawrence**

The Night Thoreau Spent in Jail
A portrait of Thoreau as conscientious objector
0-553-27838-X BDD PB $4.99

Jerome **Lawrence** & Robert E. **Lee**

Inherit the Wind
The Scopes "monkey trial" of 1925
0-553-26915-1 BDD PB $4.99

Selected Plays of Jerome Lawrence and Robert E. Lee
0-8142-0646-8 OHIO STATE $45.00

Carson **McCullers**

The Member of the Wedding
A troubled, perceptive twelve-year-old girl awaits her brother's wedding
See also **SINCE 1945** under **20TH-CENTURY AMERICAN FICTION**
0-8112-0093-0 NEW DIRECTIONS PB $7.95

Neil **Simon**

One of America's most popular playwrights, Simon has weathered both commercial success and critical disdain. Of his own work, Simon has written: "When I was good, I was very, very good...and when I was bad, we folded."

The Collected Plays
0-679-40889-4 RANDOM HOUSE $35.00

The Collected Plays of Neil Simon

Volume 1
0-452-25870-7 NEW AMERICAN LIBRARY PB $17.95

Volume 2
0-452-26358-1 NEW AMERICAN LIBRARY PB $18.95

Biloxi Blues
In basic training in 1943, Eugene vows to become a writer, to lose his virginity, and to stay alive
0-394-55139-7 RANDOM HOUSE $11.95

Brighton Beach Memoirs
Eugene as a teenager, the first of Simon's autobiographical trilogy
0-394-53739-4 RANDOM HOUSE $14.95

Jake's Women
0-679-43019-9 RANDOM HOUSE $19.00

Laughter on the 23rd Floor
0-679-43906-4 RANDOM HOUSE $20.00

Lost in Yonkers
0-452-26883-4 PLUME PB $8.95

Plaza Suite
0-394-40667-2 RANDOM HOUSE $9.95

Rumors: A Farce
0-394-58799-5 RANDOM HOUSE $16.95

Megan **Terry** & Rochelle L. **Holt**

Two by Terry Plus One: An Anthology of Plays by Women
Includes *Pro Game* and *The Pioneer* by Megan Terry and Rochelle L. Holt's *Walking into the Dawn: A Celebration*
0-88680-218-0 CLARKE PB $4.50

The 1970s, '80s, and '90s

Ivan **Acosta**

El Super
A Cuban family living in exile in New York
0-89729-271-5 EDICIONES UNIVERSAL PB $9.95

Frank **Chin**

The Chickencoop Chinaman & The Year of the Dragon: Two Plays
0-295-95833-2 WASHINGTON PB $14.95

Mart **Crowley**

Three Plays
Includes *The Boys in the Band, A Breeze from the Gulf,* and *For Reasons that Remain Unclear*
1-55583-357-8 ALYSON PB $13.95

Christopher **Durang**

27 Short Plays
1-88039-989-X SMITH & KRAUS PB $19.95

Complete Full-Length Plays, 1975-1995, Vol. 2
1-57525-017-9 SMITH & KRAUS $35.00

Laughing Wild & Baby with the Bathwater
0-8021-3130-1 GROVE PB $8.95

Six Plays
0-8021-3232-4 GROVE PB $12.95

Horton **Foote**

Collected Plays, Vol. 2
1-57525-016-0 SMITH & KRAUS PB $17.95

Courtship, Valentine's Day, 1918: Three Plays from the Orphans' Home Cycle
INTRODUCTION BY REYNOLDS PRICE
0-8021-5155-8 GROVE PB $8.95

Cousins & The Death of Papa
0-8021-3152-2 GROVE PB $9.95

Four New Plays
1-88039-941-5 SMITH & KRAUS PB $16.95

The Young Man from Atlanta
0-452-27633-0 PLUME PB $9.95

Richard **Foreman**

My Head Was a Sledgehammer
Recent work by the visionary founder of the Hysteric-Ontological Theater
0-87951-575-9 OVERLOOK $24.95

My Head Was a Sledgehammer: Six Plays
0-87951-622-4 PENGUIN PB $14.95

Reverberation Machines: The Later Plays and Essays
0-88268-001-3 STATION HILL $19.95

Charles **Fuller**

A Soldier's Play
0-374-52148-4 FS&G PB $8.00

Herb **Gardner**

A Thousand Clowns
0-573-61657-4 SAMUEL FRENCH PB $4.50

Barry **Gifford**

Hotel Room Trilogy
0-87805-776-5 MISSISSIPPI $29.95
0-87805-777-3 MISSISSIPPI PB $12.95

Richard **Greenberg**

Eastern Standard
0-8021-3174-3 GROVE PB $9.95

John **Guare**

Four Baboons Adoring the Sun and Other Plays
0-679-74510-6 VINTAGE PB $12.00

Six Degrees of Separation
The story of a young man who uses lies and half-truths to ingratiate himself with a family of old money New Yorkers. "A hilarious and finally searing panorama of urban America in precisely our time"—Frank Rich, *NY Times*
0-679-73481-3 VINTAGE PB $10.00

The War Against the Kitchen Sink
1-57525-032-2 SMITH & KRAUS $35.00
1-57525-031-4 SMITH & KRAUS PB $17.95

A.R. **Gurney**

Love Letters & Two Other Plays
Also includes *The Golden Age* and *What I Did Last Summer*
0-452-26501-0 PLUME PB $10.95

Tina **Howe**

Approaching Zanzibar & Other Plays
Also includes *Birth and Afterbirth* and *One Shoe Off*
1-55936-104-2 THEATRE COMMUNICATIONS PB $13.95

Coastal Disturbances: Four Plays
0-930452-86-0 THEATRE COMMUNICATIONS PB $13.95

David Henry **Hwang**

Fob and Other Plays
0-452-26323-9 PLUME PB $9.95

M. Butterfly
0-452-27259-9 PENGUIN PB $9.00

Len **Jenkin**

Careless Love
1-55713-168-6 SUN & MOON PB $9.95

Dark Ride & Other Plays
Jenkin's plays have been described by the *New York Times* as "juxtapositions of the banal and the fabulous." Also includes *American Notes, My Uncle Sam, Limbo Tales,* and *Poor Folks' Pleasure*
1-55713-073-6 SUN & MOON PB $13.95

Tony **Kushner**

Angels in America: A Gay Fantasia on National Themes
"A vast, miraculous play… provocative, witty, and deeply upsetting"—Frank Rich, *NY Times*

Volume 1
Millenium Approaches
1-55936-061-5 THEATRE COMMUNICATIONS PB $10.95

Volume 2
Perestroika
1-55936-072-0 THEATRE COMMUNICATIONS $21.95
1-55936-073-9 THEATRE COMMUNICATIONS PB $10.95

A Bright Room Called Day
"Brash, audacious...and intoxicatingly visionary"—*Chicago Tribune*
1-55936-078-X THEATRE COMMUNICATIONS PB $10.95

Thinking About the Longstanding Problems of Virtue and Happiness: Slavs!, Essays, Poems and a Prayer
1-55936-100-X THEATRE COMMUNICATIONS PB $13.95

Romulus **Linney**

Six Plays
Linney is noted for his lyrical evocations of his native South
1-55936-053-4 THEATRE COMMUNICATIONS PB $14.95

Craig **Lucas**

Reckless & Blue Window
0-930452-95-X THEATRE COMMUNICATIONS PB $9.95

Collected Works
1-880-39917-2 SMITH & KRAUS PB $14.95

David **Mamet**

"Mamet deserves recognition for his careful, gorgeous, loving sense of language. He has the most acute ear for dialogue of any American writer since J.D. Salinger."—Village Voice

American Buffalo
0-8021-5057-8 GROVE PB $10.00

The Cryptogram
0-679-74653-6 VINTAGE PB $9.00

Glengarry Glen Ross
The patter of real estate sharks provides the music for this nightmarish, abbreviated melodrama
0-8021-3091-7 GROVE PB $8.95

Goldberg Street: Short Plays and Monologues
0-8021-5104-3 GROVE PB $12.00

Lakeboat
0-394-17925-0 GROVE PB $4.95

A Life in the Theatre
0-8021-5067-5 GROVE PB $10.95

Oh, Hell
0-573-69254-8 SAMUEL FRENCH PB $4.50

Oleanna
Issues of sexual harassment and political correctness inform this Strindbergian two-character play
0-679-42411-3 PANTHEON $20.00
0-679-74536-X VINTAGE PB $10.00

Reunion & Dark Pony: Two Plays
0-8021-5171-X GROVE PB $8.95

Sexual Perversity in Chicago & The Duck Variations
0-8021-5011-X GROVE PB $8.95

The Shawl & Prairie du Chien: Two Plays
0-8021-5172-8 GROVE PB $6.95

Speed-the-Plow
To greenlight or not to greenlight: Mamet explores the world of a newly powerful Hollywood producer
0-8021-3046-1 GROVE PB $8.95

Three Children's Plays
Includes *The Poet and the Rent, The Frog Prince,* and *The Revenge of the Space Pandas or Binky Rudich and the Two-Speed Clock*
0-8021-5173-6 GROVE PB $8.95

Three Plays
Includes *The Woods, Lakeboat,* and *Edmond*
0-8021-5109-4 GROVE PB $10.95

Cormac **McCarthy**

The Stonemason: A Play in Five Acts
0-88001-359-1 ECCO $19.95

Carlos **Morton**

Johnny Tenorio
0-88734-339-2 PLAYERS PB $5.00

Carlos **Morton**

Johnny Tenorio and Other Plays
1-55885-047-3 ARTE PUBLICO PB $13.00

The Many Deaths of Danny Rosales
0-88734-232-9 PLAYERS PB $6.00

The Many Deaths of Danny Rosales & Other Plays
Includes *El Jordan, Los Dorados,* and *Rancho Hollywood*
0-934770-16-6 PLAYERS PB $11.00

The Miser of Mexico
0-88734-270-1 PLAYERS PB $6.00

Pancho Diablo
0-88734-340-6 PLAYERS PB $5.00

The Savior
0-88734-271-X PLAYERS PB $6.00

Marsha **Norman**

Four Plays
Includes *Getting Out, Third and Oak, The Holdup,* and *Traveller in the Dark*
0-930452-84-4 THEATRE COMMUNICATIONS PB $12.95

'Night, Mother
0-374-52138-7 FS&G PB $8.95

Suzan-Lori **Parks**

The America Play & Other Works
"Parks has burst through every known convention to invent a new theatrical language, like a jive Samuel Backett"
—Alisa Solomon, *Theater*
1-55936-092-5 THEATRE COMMUNICATIONS PB $14.95

Imperceptible Mutabilities in the Third Kingdom
1-55713-134-1 SUN & MOON PB $10.95

Miguel **Piñero**

Outrageous One-Act Plays
0-934770-68-9 PLAYERS PB $10.00

Short Eyes
"An authentic, powerful theatrical piece that tells you more about the anti-universe of prison life than any play outside the work of Jean Genet"—*Newsweek*
0-374-52147-6 FS&G PB $10.00

The Sun Always Shines for the Cool, Midnight Moon at the Greasy Spoon & Eulogy for a Small Time Thief
0-934770-25-5 ARTE PUBLICO PB $11.00

David **Rabe**

Goose & Tom-Tom
0-8021-5193-0 GROVE PB $7.95

Hurlyburly
0-8021-3251-0 GROVE PB $9.95

In the Boom Boom Room
0-8021-5194-9 GROVE PB $9.95

Two Plays
Includes *Hurlyburly* and *Those the River Keeps*
0-8021-3351-7 GROVE PB $14.00

Ntozake **Shange**

Three Pieces
Includes *Spell #7, A Photograph: Lovers in Motion,* and *Boogie Woogie Landscapes*
0-312-07872-2 ST. MARTIN'S PB $10.95

Wallace **Shawn**

Aunt Dan and Lemon
0-8021-5103-5 GROVE PB $8.95

The Designated Mourner
0-374-13822-2 FS&G $25.00

The Fever
A moral self-interrogation by an American stranded in a Third World country. "If you come away feeling disturbed, angry, sore, confused, and eager to think, then Shawn's sneaky circuitous art is having its intended effect"
—*Village Voice*
0-374-52270-7 NOONDAY PB $8.95

Marie and Bruce
0-8021-3018-6 GROVE PB $5.95

Sam **Shepard**

"It's a real thing, double nature. I think we're split in a much more devastating way than psychology can ever reveal"—Sam Shepard

Chicago & Other Plays
0-87910-206-3 APPLAUSE THEATRE $18.95
0-87910-205-5 APPLAUSE THEATRE PB $9.95

Fool for Love & Other Plays
Also includes *Angel City, Geography of a Horse Dreamer, Action, Cowboy Mouth, Melodrama Play, Seduced,* and *Suicide in B-flat*
0-553-34590-7 BANTAM PB $11.95

Fool for Love & The Sad Lament of Pecos Bill on the Eve of Killing His Wife
0-87286-150-3 CITY LIGHTS PB $8.95

A Lie of the Mind
0-452-26357-3 PLUME PB $12.95

Seven Plays
Includes *Buried Child, Curse of the Starving Class, The Tooth of Crime, La Turista, Tongues, Savage Love,* and *True West*
0-553-34611-3 BANTAM PB $12.95

Simpatico: A Play in Three Acts
"Sam Shepard is phenomenal…the best practicing American playwright"
—*New Republic*
0-679-76317-1 VINTAGE PB $10.00

The Unseen Hand & Other Plays
Includes *Chicago, Icarus's Mother, Red Cross, Fourteen Hundred Thousand, Melodrama Play*
0-87910-203-9 APPLAUSE THEATRE PB $9.95

The Unseen Hand and Other Plays
Fourteen plays including *The Holy Ghostly, Red Cross* and *Back Bog Beast Bait*
0-679-76789-4 VINTAGE PB $14.00

Susan **Sontag**

Alice in Bed
In this dramatic fantasy the author merges the real-life Alice James, the brilliant but troubled sister of William and Henry, with Alice in Wonderland at a lively tea party that probes female imagination and grief
0-374-10273-2 NOONDAY $25.00
0-374-52385-1 NOONDAY PB $10.00

Susan Sontag

Wendy **Wasserstein**

The Heidi Chronicles and Other Plays
0-679-73499-6 VINTAGE PB $12.00

The Sisters Rosensweig
In the new play by the Pulitzer Prize-winning author of *The Heidi Chronicles,* three middle-aged sisters humorously reflect on love, sex, and the unexpected areas of their lives. This is "Wasserstein's most accomplished play to date"—*New York Magazine*
0-15-182692-7 HARCOURT BRACE $17.95
0-15-600013-X HARVEST PB $8.95

Mac **Wellman**

The Bad Infinity: Nine Plays
0-8018-4687-0 JOHNS HOPKINS $45.00
0-8018-4688-9 PAJ PUBLICATIONS PB $15.95

Bad Penny at Bow Bridge
1-55713-123-6 SUN & MOON PB $5.95

The Land Beyond the Forest
Includes *Dracula* and *Swoop*
1-55713-228-3 SUN & MOON PB $12.95

The Professional Frenchman
1-55713-115-5 SUN & MOON PB $7.95

Two Plays
Includes *A Murder of Crows* and *The Hyacinth Macaw*
1-55713-197-X SUN & MOON PB $11.95

August **Wilson**

Fences
0-452-26401-4 NEW AMERICAN LIBRARY PB $8.95

Joe Turner's Come and Gone
0-452-26009-4 NEW AMERICAN LIBRARY PB $8.95

Ma Rainey's Black Bottom
0-452-26113-9 NEW AMERICAN LIBRARY PB $9.95

The Piano Lesson
0-452-26534-7 PLUME PB $8.95

Seven Guitars
0-525-94196-7 PENGUIN $19.95

Three Plays
0-8229-3666-6 PITTSBURGH $29.95

Two Trains Running
0-452-26929-6 PLUME PB $8.95

Lanford **Wilson**

"From his earliest plays to his latest, Lanford Wilson has been firmly committed to the free expression of the individual spirit, no matter how nonconformist or even prodigal that spirit may seem to be."—Mel Gussow

21 Short Plays
1-88039-931-8 SMITH & KRAUS PB $16.95

Angels Fall
0-374-52231-6 FS&G PB $9.95

Burn This
0-374-52158-1 HILL & WANG PB $9.95

The Early Plays, 1965-1970
1-57525-025-X SMITH & KRAUS PB $17.95

The Fifth of July
0-374-52170-0 FS&G PB $10.00

Redwood Curtain
0-8090-8052-4 HILL & WANG $22.00

Talley's Folly
0-374-52157-3 FS&G PB $8.95

George C. **Wolfe**

The Colored Museum
"A bold new voice that is bound to shake up blacks and whites with separate-but-equal impartiality. True satire, fiercely funny"—Jack Kroll, *Newsweek*

0-8021-3048-8 GROVE PB $8.95

Paul **Zindel**

The Effect of Gamma Rays on Man-in-the-Moon Marigolds
See also **YOUNG ADULT FICTION** in **BOOKS FOR YOUNG READERS**

0-553-28028-7 BDD PB $5.50

Performance

Eric **Bogosian**

The Essential Bogosian: Talk Radio, Drinking in America, Funhouse & Men Inside
"What Lenny Bruce was to the 1950s, Bob Dylan to the 1960s, Woody Allen to the 1970s—that's what Eric Bogosian is to this frightening moment of drift in our history"—Frank Rich, *NY Times*

1-55936-082-8 THEATRE COMMUNICATIONS PB .. $11.95

Suburbia
1-55936-101-8 THEATRE COMMUNICATIONS PB . $10.95

Pounding Nails in the Floor with My Forehead
"The sharp-tongued, sharp-shooting Bogosian never misses"—Clive Barnes, *NY Post*

1-55936-096-8 THEATRE COMMUNICATIONS PB ... $8.95

Spalding **Gray**

Gray's Anatomy
0-679-75178-5 VINTAGE PB $9.00

Monster in a Box
Gray describes the monster he has carried with him for some time: the 1,600-page manuscript of a novel, and while detailing the symptoms of his writing block, detours to Nicaragua, a disastrous appearance at a Moscow film festival, and a journey to Los Angeles in search of the endangered few who have yet to write screenplays

0-679-73739-1 VINTAGE PB $9.00

Sex and Death to Age 14
0-394-74257-5 RANDOM HOUSE PB $12.00

Swimming to Cambodia
0-930452-50-X THEATRE COMMUNICATIONS PB ... $8.95

Holly **Hughes**

Clit Notes: A Sapphic Sampler
"Scrapes away decades of encrusted decorum from a subject (female sexuality) that is too often treated with a hushed sentimentality" —*NY Times*

0-8021-3333-9 GROVE PB $12.00

Denis **Leary**

No Cure for Cancer
0-385-42581-3 ANCHOR PB $8.00

Richard **Nelson**, editor

Strictly Dishonorable & Other Lost American Plays
The title work is by film director Preston Sturges

0-930452-55-0 THEATRE COMMUNICATIONS PB . $10.95

Claudia **Shear**

Blown Sideways Through Life
The actress/writer presents her job history while struggling through life. The play was a huge success

See also **HUMOR** under **ARTS AND LETTERS** under **WOMEN'S STUDIES** in **SOCIAL STUDIES**

0-385-31315-2 DELTA PB $8.95

Jane **Wagner**

The Search for Signs of Intelligent Life in the Universe
The script of the Broadway show which starred Lily Tomlin

AFTERWORD BY MARILYN FRENCH

0-06-092071-8 HARPERCOLLINS PB $13.00

The Musical Theater

Oscar **Hammerstein**

Lyrics by Oscar Hammerstein
EDITED BY WILLIAM HAMMERSTEIN

9-99188-702-4 LEONARD PB $40.00

The Sound of Music
0-88188-114-7 LEONARD PB $8.95

Alan Jay **Lerner** & Frederick **Loewe**

Camelot
0-88188-008-6 LEONARD PB $40.00

Cole **Porter**

The Complete Lyrics of Cole Porter
EDITED BY ROBERT KIMBALL

FOREWORD BY JOHN UPDIKE

0-306-80483-2 DA CAPO PB $22.50

George Bernard **Shaw** & others

Pygmalion & My Fair Lady
0-451-52476-4 NEW AMERICAN LIBRARY PB $4.95

Stephen **Sondheim** & James **Lapine**

Sunday in the Park with George
1-55783-067-3 APPLAUSE THEATRE $19.95

Stephen **Sondheim** & others

Sweeney Todd: The Demon Barber of Fleet Street
1-55783-065-7 APPLAUSE THEATRE $19.95

1-55783-066-5 APPLAUSE THEATRE PB $9.95

Anthologies

Bennett **Cerf**, editor

Four Contemporary American Plays
Includes Paddy Chayevsky's *The Tenth Man*, Lorraine Hansberry's *A Raisin in the Sun*, Lillian Hellman's *Toys in the Attic*, and Saul Levitt's *Andersonville Trial*

0-394-70203-4 RANDOM HOUSE PB $9.00

Allan G. **Halline**, editor

Six Modern American Plays
Includes Eugene O'Neill's *The Emperor Jones*, Maxwell Anderson's *Winterset*, George S. Kaufman and Moss Hart's *The Man Who Came to Dinner*, Lillian Hellman's *The Little Foxes*, and *Mister Roberts* by Joshua Logan and Thomas Heggen

0-07-553660-9 RANDOM HOUSE PB $15.40

Paul Carter **Harrison**, editor

Totem Voices: Eight Plays from the Black World Repertory
Includes Charles Fuller's *Zooman and the Sign*, Ntozake Shange's *For Colored Girls Who Have Considered Suicide When the Rainbow is Enuf*, Derek Walcott's *Ti Jean and His Brothers*, and Wole Soyinka's *The Strange Breed*

0-8021-3126-3 GROVE PB $15.95

Paul Carter **Harrison** & Gus **Edwards**, editors

Classic Plays from the Negro Ensemble Company
Ten plays, including *A Soldier's Play, Home*, and *The River Niger*

0-8229-3882-0 PITTSBURGH $65.00

0-8229-5560-1 PITTSBURGH PB $29.95

Henry **Hewes**, editor

Famous American Plays of the 1940s

Includes Thornton Wilder's *The Skin of Our Teeth*, *All My Sons* by Arthur Miller, Carson McCullers's *The Member of the Wedding*, Maxwell Anderson's *Lost in the Stars*, and *Home of the Brave* by Arthur Laurents

0-440-32490-4 DELL PB $6.99

Ted **Hoffman**, editor

Famous American Plays of the 1970s

Includes David Rabe's *The Basic Training of Pavlo Hummel*, Michael Weller's *Moonchildren*, Ed Bullins's *The Taking of Miss Janie*, Bernard Slade's *Same Time Next Year*, and Sam Shepard's *Buried Child*

0-440-32537-4 LAUREL LEAF PB $6.95

Morgan **Jenness** & Mac **Wellman**, editors

Slant Six: New Theater from Minnesota's Playwright's Center

0-89823-120-5 NEW RIVERS PB $9.95

Woodie **King** & Ron **Milner**, editors

Black Drama Anthology

Includes *Junebug Graduates Tonight* by Archie Shepp, Lonnie Elder's *Charades on East Fourth Street*, Elaine Jackson's *Toe Jam*, and *The Corner* by Ed Bullins, as well as selections by Amiri Baraka and others

0-452-00902-2 PLUME PB $11.95

James **Leverett**, editor

New Plays USA

Includes, among other plays, Jon Robin Baitz's *The Film Society* and George C. Wolfe's *The Colored Museum*

0-930452-80-1 THEATRE COMMUNICATIONS $24.95
0-930452-81-X THEATRE COMMUNICATIONS PB . $12.95

Joseph E. **Mersand**, editor

Three Comedies of American Family Life

Includes Lindsay Howard and Russell Crouse's *Life with Father*, John Van Druten's *I Remember Mama*, and *You Can't Take It with You* by George S. Kaufman and Moss Hart

0-671-66430-1 POCKET PB $5.50

Douglas **Messerli** & Mac **Wellman**, editors

From the Other Side of the Century II: A New American Drama, 1960-1995

A comprehensive, 1,200-page gathering of work by the innovators of recent decades, from Albee, Kopit, and Shepard to Len Jenkin and Suzan-Lori Parks

1-55713-247-X SUN & MOON PB $29.95

M. Elizabeth **Osborn**, editor

On New Ground: Contemporary Hispanic-American Plays

Playwrights represented include Maria Irene Fornes, José Rivera, Lynne Alvarez, Milcha Sanchez-Scott, John Jesurun, and Eduardo Machado

0-930452-68-2 THEATRE COMMUNICATIONS PB . $13.95

Coming to Terms: American Plays and the Vietnam War

Includes Emily Mann's *Still Life* and Amlin Gray's *How I Got that Story*. "The most accurate, most profound memory of Vietnam lies in the arts.... The playwright becomes more important than the historian"—James Reston, Jr.

INTRODUCTION BY JAMES RESTON, JR.

0-930452-44-5 THEATRE COMMUNICATIONS PB . $13.95

Michael **McClure**

Scratching the Beat Surface

0-14-023252-4 PENGUIN PB $10.95

Performance Arts Journal

Wordplays: New American Drama

Volume 1

0-933-82611-7 JOHNS HOPKINS $10.95

Volume 2 1920-1923

0-15-627248-2 JOHNS HOPKINS $12.95

Volume 3 1923-1927

0-15-627250-4 JOHNS HOPKINS $12.95

Volume 4 1927-1931

Includes Thomas Babe's *Kid Champion*, Charles L. Mee, Jr.'s *The Investigation into the Murder in El Salvador*, Philip Bosakowski's *Chopin in Space*, Jeffrey Jones's *Night Coil*, and JoAnne Akalaitis's *Dressed Like an Egg*

0-15-627251-2 JOHNS HOPKINS $14.95

Volume 5

Includes James Lapine and Stephen Sondheim's *Sunday in the Park with George*, Kathy Acker's *The Birth of the Poet*, Des McAnuff's *The Death of von Richthofen as Witnessed from Earth*, James Strah's *North Atlantic*, and John Jesurun's *Deep Sleep*

1-55554-007-4 JOHNS HOPKINS PB $15.95

Kathy A. **Perkins**, editor

Black Female Playwrights: An Anthology of Plays Before 1950

0-253-34358-5 INDIANA $39.95

Willis **Richardson**, editor

Plays and Pageants from the Life of the Negro

The earliest collection of plays by African-Americans

0-87805-657-2 MISSISSIPPI $40.00
0-87805-658-0 MISSISSIPPI PB $17.95

Ellen **Schiff**

Awake and Singing: 7 Classic Plays from the American Jewish Repertoire

0-451-62869-1 MENTOR PB $6.99

Don **Shewey**, editor

Out Front: Contemporary Gay and Lesbian Plays

Plays by Robert Chesley, Holly Hughes, Harry Kondoleon, Kathleen Tolan, and others serve what Shewey describes as "the primitive function of affirming the existence of a mistreated minority, confirming its convictions, and acting as a corrective to neglect or abuse by the culture-at-large"

0-8021-3025-9 GROVE PB $14.95

Howard **Stein** & Glenn **Young**, editors

The Best American Short Plays: 1992-1993

Dreamers by Shel Silverstein, *Jolly* by David Mamet, *The Drowning of Manhattan* by John Ford Noonan, and many more. This is the largest collection of Best American Short Plays in over half a century

1-55783-167-X APPLAUSE THEATRE $29.95
1-55783-166-1 APPLAUSE THEATRE PB $14.95

Roberta **Uno**, editor

Unbroken Thread: An Anthology of Plays by Asian American Women

Six recent plays give "further evidence that Asian American literature is not only alive but flourishing....The time is ripe for this fine volume"—Amy Ling, University of Wisconsin

0-87023-855-8 MASSACHUSETTS $45.00
0-87023-856-6 MASSACHUSETTS PB $19.95

Mac **Wellman**, editor

Theatre of Wonders: Six Contemporary American Plays

Includes selections from Len Jenkin, Jeffrey Jones, Des McAnuff, Elizabeth Wray, and Mac Wellman

0-940650-38-X SUN & MOON $16.95

20th-Century American Essays and Journalism

William **Safire**

In Love with Norma Loquendi

Norma loquendi: "The everyday voice of the native speaker." Long the preeminent chronicler for *The New York Times Magazine*, Safire sets a lively and contentious standard for the English language that opines elegantly on the advantages of "enthuse" over "emote," but does not disdain to show the difference between whom and who, and furthermore proves it. "Those who believe language is a delight as well as a necessity will happily while away the hours meandering through these pages"
—*Kirkus Reviews*

0-679-42386-9 RANDOM HOUSE $25.00

Memoirs and Journals

André **Aciman**

Out of Egypt: A Memoir

"With beguiling simplicity, Aciman recalls the life of Alexandria as his family knew it, and the seductiveness of that beautiful, polygot city permeates his book"—*New Yorker*

1-57322-534-7 RIVERHEAD PB $14.00

Hilton **Als**

The Women

A series of essays concerning the influence of race and gender on the works and lives of several prominent African Americans

0-374-29205-1 FS&G $21.00

Maya **Angelou**

Wouldn't Take Nothing for My Journey Now

Angelou relates the sexual abuse she endured as a child, the poverty, the challenge of being black in America, while also pondering her own sense of faith

See also **ARTISTS AND LITERARY FIGURES** under **BLACK VOICES, BLACK LIVES** under **AFRICAN-AMERICAN STUDIES** in **HISTORY OF THE AMERICAS**

0-679-42743-0 RANDOM HOUSE $17.00
0-553-56907-4 BDD PB $5.50

Paul **Auster**

The Invention of Solitude

The memoirs of an elusive author

0-14-010628-6 PENGUIN PB $11.95

Russell **Baker**

The Good Times

The second installment of Baker's memoirs, covering his early years as a reporter

See also **FIRST-PERSON ACCOUNTS** under **BIOGRAPHIES AND MEMOIRS** under **JOURNALISM** in **PERFORMING ARTS AND MEDIA**

0-451-17230-2 SIGNET PB $5.99

Growing Up

Baker's Pulitzer Prize-winning reminiscences of his childhood

0-451-16838-0 NEW AMERICAN LIBRARY PB $5.99
0-452-25550-3 PENGUIN PB $10.95

Rick **Bass**

The Deer Pasture

0-393-31435-9 NORTON PB $12.00

Mary Ellen **Barrett**

Irving Berlin: A Daughter's Memoir

Big surprise—his daughter can write, and she's probably more dependable than Lawrence Begreen

See also **SONGWRITERS** under **AMERICAN POPULAR MUSIC** in **PERFORMING ARTS AND MEDIA**

0-87910-078-8 LIMELIGHT PB $14.95

Paul **Bowles**

Days: Tangier Journal, 1987-1989

A characteristically deadpan and unblinking record of the novelist's life in his adopted city, punctuated by the comings and goings of a throng of international guests

0-88001-269-2 ECCO $15.95

Without Stopping

An idiosyncratic, strangely detached autobiography

0-88001-267-6 ECCO PB $14.95

In Touch: The Letters of Paul Bowles

EDITED BY JEFFREY MILLER

0-374-52459-9 NOONDAY PB $16.00

Bill **Bradley**

A Memoir

0-679-44488-2 KNOPF $26.00

Larry **Brown**

On Fire

Brown writes of his 17 years of fighting fires for the Oxford, Mississippi Fire Department

See also **SINCE 1945** under **20TH-CENTURY AMERICAN FICTION**

1-56512-009-4 ALGONQUIN $17.95
0-446-67114-0 WARNER PB $11.95

Charles **Bukowski**

Charles Bukowski: Screams from the Balcony, Selected Letters, 1960-1970

Bukowski at his best and most brutally candid. Beginning at the time of his first poetry chapbook, Bukowski sounds off on everything, from personal memories of public drunkenness to literary critiques. Filled with the same no-holds-barred humanity as his fiction and poetry, the consummate literary outsider corresponds with his publishers, friends, daughter, and her mother

EDITED BY SEAMUS COONEY

0-87685-915-5 BLACK SPARROW $25.00
0-87685-914-7 BLACK SPARROW PB $15.00

Living on Luck: Selected Letters, 1960s-1970s Volume 2

This second volume of Bukowski's letters picks up in 1960, when the author, on the strength of his publisher's promise to pay him 100 dollars per month, quit his job at the Post Office and began writing—literally—for his life. Always hilarious and moving, these letters provide a unique insight into the intellectual genesis of the great American writer and his work

0-87685-982-1 BLACK SPARROW $25.00
0-87685-981-3 BLACK SPARROW PB $15.00

William S. **Burroughs**

Junky

This laconic memoir, Burroughs's first book, was first published as a lurid paperback in 1953

0-14-004351-9 VIKING PB $10.95

Queer

An early work of autobiography, recently published for the first time

0-14-008389-8 VIKING PB $10.95

Erskine **Caldwell**

Deep South: Memory and Observation

The author of *Tobacco Road* and *God's Little Acre* draws on a wealth of anecdotes, memories, and interviews that, as an ensemble, create a unique portrait of Southern spirituality

0-8203-1716-0 GEORGIA PB $12.95

Philip **Caputo**

A Rumor of War

A powerful account of the author's experience in war

See also **MEMOIRS** under **THE VIETNAM WAR** in **HISTORY OF THE AMERICAS**

0-345-38656-6 BALLANTINE PB $12.00

James **Carroll**

An American Requiem: God, Vietnam, and the Struggle for My Father's Soul

Carroll grew up inside the Beltway, dating a vice president's daughter and waiting for the red telephone to ring in his father's house. But Martin Luther King, the civil rights movement, and Vietnam came between him and his father

0-395-77926-X HOUGHTON MIFFLIN $23.95

Jim **Carroll**

The Basketball Diaries

Carrol chronicles his transformation from a "good, Catholic school kid" to "junkie" and renders the recklessness of youth, the exhilaration of the basketball courts, and the cruelty of New York City with stark clarity

0-14-024999-0 PENGUIN PB $10.95

Forced Entries: The Downtown Diaries, 1971-1973

0-14-008502-5 PENGUIN PB $11.95

Stanley **Cavell**

A Pitch of Philosophy: Autobiographical Exercises

See also **OTHER 20TH-CENTURY PHILOSOPHERS** under **PHILOSOPHY** in **RELIGION, SPIRITUALITY, AND PHILOSOPHY**

0-674-66980-0 HARVARD $26.00
0-674-66981-9 HARVARD PB $14.95

John **Cheever**

The Journals of John Cheever

Cheever began to keep journals in the 1940s and continued for more than three decades, creating a painfully direct and unblinking picture of his inner life

INTRODUCTION BY BENJAMIN H. CHEEVER

0-394-57274-2 KNOPF $25.00

Susan **Cheever**

Home Before Dark

A memoir of her father, the novelist John Cheever

0-395-35297-5 HOUGHTON MIFFLIN $15.95

Thekla **Clark**

Wystan and Chester

A look at the relationship between W.H. Auden and Chester Kallman by a woman who knew them both as well as anyone. "Reading Mrs. Clark's memoir is likely to be an experience of undiluted pleasure"—*NY Times Book Review*

0-231-10706-4 COLUMBIA $42.00

Frank **Conroy**

Stop-Time

0-14-004446-9 PENGUIN PB $11.95

Douglas **Crase**

Amerifil.txt: A Commonplace Book

The highly regarded poet (*The Revisionist*) who has not published in many years gathers passages from his readings

0-472-09636-2 MICHIGAN $39.50
0-472-06636-6 MICHIGAN PB $13.95

Dennis **Covington**

Salvation on Sand Mountain: Snake Handling and Redemption in Southern Appalachia

A reporter's investigation of a case of attempted murder (by snake) among fundamentalist Protestants whose services include the handling of poisonous snakes leads to a spiritual reassessment of his life and to his own participation in the snake-handling rites

See also **RELIGION IN AMERICA TODAY** under **RELIGION IN AMERICA** under **TOPICS IN AMERICAN STUDIES** in **HISTORY OF THE AMERICAS**

0-14-025458-7 PENGUIN PB........$11.95

Harry **Crews**

A Childhood: The Biography of a Place

0-8203-1759-4 GEORGIA........$24.95

Diane **di Prima**

Memoirs of a Beatnik

First published by Olympia Press, this comic and erotic memoir provides a beguilingly chaotic portrait of the Beat scene in its formative stages

0-86719-346-8 LAST GASP PB........$8.95

Annie **Dillard**

An American Childhood

0-06-091518-8 HARPERCOLLINS PB........$13.00

J.P. **Donleavy**

The History of the Ginger Man

The autobiography of the American writer best known for the Darcy Dancer series who has lived most of his life in Ireland

0-395-51595-5 HOUGHTON MIFFLIN........$32.50

André **Dubus**

Broken Vessels

The novelist confronts, among other things, the aftermath of a disabling accident and the breakup of his marriage

0-87923-885-2 GODINE........$19.95

Peter **Duchin** & Charles **Michener**

Ghost of a Chance: A Memoir

Peter Duchin's enchanted life, from his childhood on the vast estate of Averell Harriman to his days living on a barge in the Seine with an editor from the *Paris Review*; from his presence at Capote's Black and White Ball to his private evenings with Fred Astaire. Now a renowned pianist, conductor, and composer, married to Brooke Hayward, he reflects on his life and its glamorous cast of characters

0-679-41418-5 RANDOM HOUSE........$27.50

Edward Robb **Ellis**

A Diary of the Century: Tales by America's Greatest Diarist, 1927-1995

Since 1927, Edward Robb Ellis, newspaperman and author, has maintained a daily journal of his journey through this century. It is peopled with the characters Ellis encountered during his life, some famous and some unknown

1-56836-080-0 KODANSHA........$25.00

James **Ellroy**

My Dark Places

See also **HARD-BOILED DETECTIVES** under **CRIME FICTION TODAY** under **CRIME FICTION** in **POPULAR READING**

0-679-44185-9 KNOPF........$25.00

Frederick **Exley**

A Fan's Notes

The drinking life, the New York Giants, and the beauty of women, distilled through an elegiac prose style. "No one should have had Exley's life, and no one who has read it can ever forget it" —James Dickey

0-679-72076-6 VINTAGE PB........$13.00

M.F.K. **Fisher**

Among Friends

An evocative account of an Episcopalian childhood in a Quaker town

0-86547-116-9 NORTH POINT PB........$14.00

Long Ago in France: The Years in Dijon

No one writes about France with the richness and verve of M.F.K. Fisher, as she proves once again in this memoir. "M.F.K. Fisher represents a type of American artist still cherished in the national imagination, one who has knocked around the world, and so understands lives lived under many different conditions" —Patricia Storace, *NY Review of Books*

See also **EUROPE SINCE 1945** under **EUROPE** under **TRAVEL LITERATURE** in **FOOD, TRAVEL, AND LEISURE**

0-671-75514-5 TOUCHSTONE PB........$10.00

Stay Me, Oh Comfort Me: Journals and Stories, 1933-1945

Completed just before her death in 1992, this last work picks up where *To Begin Again* ended. The author traces her California Depression years with her husband to their exile in Switzerland, where, in a complicated love triangle, she begins an affair with Dillwyn Parrish, whom she would later marry

See also **BOOKS ON FOOD** under **FOOD** in **FOOD, TRAVEL, AND LEISURE**

See also **AMERICAN FOOD WRITERS** under **AMERICAN COOKERY** under **FOOD** in **FOOD, TRAVEL, AND LEISURE**

0-679-75825-9 PANTHEON PB........$13.00

Suddenly all the men began to sing, and sing as Swiss all can, sweetly, truly, rather sadly: "Sur la haute montagne était un vieux chalet." We kept very still. Timmy's face got very red and crumpled, and he cried slightly, looking so much like his mother for a minute that I was startled.

STAY ME, OH COMFORT ME: JOURNALS AND STORIES, 1933-1945

M.F.K. Fisher

Thomas **Froncek**

Home Again, Home Again: A Memoir

"Thomas Froncek has written a marvelous book. Highly personal without being the least bit vainglorious, this memoir is simple, powerful, and compelling"—Benjamin Cheever

1-55970-332-6 ARCADE........$23.95

Allen **Ginsberg**

Journals: Early Fifties, Early Sixties

Here are journal entries, notes, dreams, and reflections from the period when Ginsberg and his fellow Beats led the insurrection that profoundly altered America's cultural landscape. "An utterly fascinating revelation of one of our most important poets. It is a remarkable work"—*Washington Post*

0-8021-3347-9 GROVE PB........$12.95

Allen Ginsberg

Mary **Gordon**

The Shadow Man

Gordon's singular quest for the truth about her father, whom she lost at the age of seven. When in mid-life, she undertakes a search to discover who he was, she finds a Jewish convert to Catholicism and right-wing politics, a literary critic, a pornographer, a loving parent, and a man desperate to hide his immigrant's past.

0-679-42885-2 RANDOM HOUSE........$24.00

Lucy **Grealy**

Autobiography of a Face

Of her disfigurement from cancer treatment, Grealy writes: "I've spent fifteen years being treated for nothing other than looking different from everyone else. It was the pain from that, from feeling ugly, that I'd always viewed as the great tragedy in my life. The fact that I had cancer seemed minor in comparison"

0-395-65780-6 HOUGHTON MIFFLIN........$19.95

0-06-097673-X HARPERPERENNIAL PB........$12.00

Doris **Grumbach**

Fifty Days of Solitude

Novelist and essayist Grumbach reports on 50 days of self-imposed solitude in the Maine countryside. She finds "the universal solitude in which we have all lived, try as we might to escape it"

0-8070-7060-2 BEACON........$15.00

0-8070-7061-0 BEACON PB........$10.00

Henry **Grunwald**

One Man's America: A Journalist's Search for the Heart of His Country

0-385-41408-0 DOUBLEDAY........$30.00

Rachel **Hadas**

The Double Legacy: Reflections on a Pair of Deaths

0-571-19878-3 FABER $19.95

Donald **Hall**

Life Work

"A spare and crafted memoir"
—*Publishers Weekly*

0-8070-7055-6 BEACON PB $9.00

String Too Short to Be Saved: Recollections of Summers on a New England Farm

With an album of family snapshots and an added essay about returning 25 years later to spend the rest of his life on the farm

See also **ESSAYS, MEDITATIONS, AND CLASSICS** under **NATURE STUDY** in **SCIENCE**

0-87923-282-X GODINE PB $12.95

Helene **Hanff**

84, Charing Cross Road

The now classic account of an American woman's love affair with a second-hand bookstore. "A real life love story…A timeless period piece. Do read it"—*Wall Street Journal*

See also **THE MIDDLE GENERATION** under **20TH-CENTURY BRITISH AND IRISH FICTION** in **LITERATURE OF THE BRITISH ISLES**

INTRODUCTION BY ANNE BANCROFT

1-55921-140-7 MOYER BELL $16.95
0-14-014350-5 PENGUIN PB $9.95

Keith **Haring**

Keith Haring: Journals

Haring's journals not only tell the story of his friendships with Warhol, Leary, and Burroughs, but also illuminate the development of his career from early subway chalk sketches to international exhibitions

See also **THE CONTEMPORARY SCENE** under **ART SINCE 1945** in **ART**

See also **ARTS AND LETTERS** under **GAY, LESBIAN, AND BISEXUAL STUDIES** in **SOCIAL STUDIES**

INTRODUCTION BY DAVID HOCKNEY

0-670-84774-7 VIKING $27.95

Barbara Grizzuti **Harrison**

An Accidental Autobiography

From the bestselling author of *Italian Days*, this memoir of the people, things, symbols, places, and feelings of Harrison's life reinvents the genre in a unique and spirited manner

0-395-78000-4 HOUGHTON MIFFLIN $24.95

William Least **Heat-Moon**

Blue Highways: A Journey nto America

0-395-58568-6 HOUGHTON MIFFLIN PB $12.95

Prairyerth (a Deep Map)

A personal "deep map" of the Great Plains by the author of *Blue Highways*. Heat-Moon delves into the essence of Chase County, Kansas, through geology, history, flora, fauna, legend, weather—and people. A highly original voyage of exploration into the apparently familiar

0-395-48602-5 HOUGHTON MIFFLIN $24.95

Ernest **Hemingway**

A Moveable Feast

Memoirs of Fitzgerald, Stein, and others

0-02-051960-5 MACMILLAN PB $5.95

Michael **Herr**

Dispatches

The ground war through the eyes of a first-time war correspondent; highly recommended

See also **THE BATTLEFIELD** under **THE VIETNAM WAR** in **HISTORY OF THE AMERICAS**

0-679-73525-9 VINTAGE PB $11.00

H.D. **(Hilda Doolittle)**

End to Torment: A Memoir of Ezra Pound

From their early days at the University of Pennsylvania through the founding days of the Imagist movement, Pound's and H.D.'s careers were inextricably and complexly intertwined

0-8112-0720-X NEW DIRECTIONS PB $6.95

The Gift

0-8112-0854-0 NEW DIRECTIONS PB $8.95

Tribute to Freud

A memoir of H.D.'s experiences as a patient of Freud

0-8112-0897-4 NEW DIRECTIONS PB $9.95

Chester **Himes**

The Autobiography of Chester Himes

A frank, sometimes bitter telling of Himes's extraordinary life, which encompassed a 7-year term in an Ohio state prison, a controversial career as a social novelist, a long residence in France, and belated acclaim as a writer of detective novels

Volume 1 The Quality of Hurt

1-56025-093-3 THUNDER'S MOUTH PB $13.95

Volume 2 My Life of Absurdity

1-56025-094-1 THUNDER'S MOUTH PB $13.95

Richard **Hoffman**

Half the House: A Memoir

0-15-100174-X HARCOURT BRACE $20.00

Garrett **Hongo**

Volcano: A Memoir of Hawaii

"Eloquent...Hongo has created a memoir as beautiful and endearing as the volcano itself"
—*San Francisco Chronicle*

0-679-76748-7 VINTAGE PB $14.00

Langston **Hughes**

The Big Sea

The first volume of his autobiography. *"The Big Sea* is a valuable segment in the history of Afro-American literature"—Ralph Ellison

INTRODUCTION BY AMIRI BARAKA

0-8090-1549-8 HILL & WANG PB $14.00

I Wonder as I Wander

Hughes's autobiography covers his travels to Cuba, Haiti, Russia, Japan, and civil-war Spain during the 1930s

See also **CLASSIC AUTOBIOGRAPHIES** under **BLACK VOICES, BLACK LIVES** under **AFRICAN-AMERICAN STUDIES** in **HISTORY OF THE AMERICAS**

0-8090-1550-1 HILL & WANG PB $14.00

Zora Neale **Hurston**

Dust Tracks on a Road: An Autobiography

"Warm, witty, imaginative, and down-to-earth by turns, *Dust Tracks on a Road* is a rich and winning book by one of our few, genuine Grade A folk writers"—*New Yorker*

See also **CLASSIC AUTOBIOGRAPHIES** under **BLACK VOICES, BLACK LIVES** under **AFRICAN-AMERICAN STUDIES** in **HISTORY OF THE AMERICAS**

0-06-092168-4 HARPERCOLLINS PB $13.00

Arthur Crew **Inman**

The Inman Diary: A Public and Private Confession

EDITED BY DANIEL AARON

0-674-45445-6 HARVARD $65.00

Erica **Jong**

Fear of Fifty

"This is the best book about being a woman I have read in years, and it's one of the best stories I have *ever* read. Erica Jong speaks for all of us in her most important book to date"
—Susan Cheever.

"With a quotable line on almost every page, Jong's story is more than flash and fire—there's poetry and wisdom, too"— *Kirkus Reviews*

0-06-109242-8 HARPERCOLLINS PB $5.99

Mary **Karr**

The Liar's Club

"Astonishing…one of the most dazzling and moving memoirs to come along in years"
—Michiko Kakutani, *NY Times*

0-14-017983-6 PENGUIN PB $11.95

Alfred **Kazin**

A Lifetime Burning in Every Moment

0-06-019037-X HARPERCOLLINS $26.00

Life is like that these days—a silent empty street, I stopping in the middle of it to be studied by a homely quiet mutt, and the new-colored edge of the world in golden flames of autumn. For how long will I live in this quietness, this newness, this positive strangeness?

A LIFETIME BURNING IN EVERY MOMENT

Alfred Kazin

Alfred **Kazin**

Starting Out in the Thirties

0-8014-9562-8 CORNELL PB $9.95

A Walker in the City

A lyrical memoir that uses New York as both literal setting and metaphor. "I was aware of being claimed by an extraordinary work of art"—Carson McCullers

0-15-694176-7 HARCOURT BRACE PB $10.00

Writing Was Everything

From one of America's most distinguished literary critics, this volume blends autobiography with history and criticism to tell the story of a writer's life, from New York in the '30s to the present. Along the way we meet Hart Crane and Allen Ginsberg, Simone Weil and Hannah Arendt, Robert Lowell and George Orwell. A fascinating summation of a long life in letters

0-674-96237-0 HARVARD $17.95

For many years now, academics high and low have preempted serious criticism, have been riding herd on students who are so unused to general reading that they have little taste of their own and are glad to be told how to read, especially what to discount. This will get them closer and closer to the work of art. What nonsense. What gets us closer to a work of art is not instruction but another work of art. Only a plurality of choices can open up the new *thinking* in a work of literature that excites and liberates us.

WRITING WAS EVERYTHING

Jack **Kerouac**

Jack Kerouac: Selected Letters, 1940-1956

Starting with correspondence to boyhood friends and continuing through to Neal Cassady, Ginsberg, Gary Snyder, and Burroughs, this volume presents a writer of startling talent and energy

EDITED BY ANN CHARTERS

0-670-84952-9 VIKING $29.95
0-14-023444-6 PENGUIN PB $15.95
0-88001-496-2 ECCO $23.00

Maxine Hong **Kingston**

China Men

A follow-up to *The Woman Warrior,* into the minds of Chinese men in America. "It captures the emotional truth of the Chinese-American experience far better than any conventional history or biography ever could"—*Newsday*

See also **SINCE 1945** under **20TH-CENTURY AMERICAN FICTION**

0-679-72328-5 VINTAGE PB $11.00

The Woman Warrior

A Chinese-American born in California describes her upbringing in a laundry amid the talk-stories of her mother, Brave Orchid. Winner of the National Book Critics Circle Award

0-679-72188-6 VINTAGE PB $11.00

Natalie **Kusz**

Road Song: A Memoir

When she was six, the author moved with her family from Los Angeles to Alaska; during their first winter there, she was attacked and severely mauled by a sled dog. *Road Song* is her moving account of the difficult years of surgery and reconstruction that followed

0-374-25121-5 FS&G $18.95

Anne **Lamott**

Operating Instructions: A Journal of My Son's First Year

A wry and witty look at the first year of single motherhood by the hilarious Lamott, author of *Hard No Laughter*

0-449-90928-X FAWCETT PB $9.50

Denise **Levertov**

Tesserae

A series of 25 memoirs, each complete and chronologically organized. "She can make yearnings and ideas seem almost physical, as if she held them in her hand"—*Village Voice*

0-8112-1292-0 NEW DIRECTIONS $18.95
0-8112-1337-4 NEW DIRECTIONS PB $9.95

Phillip **Levine**

The Bread of Time: Toward an Autobiography

0-679-42406-7 KNOPF $25.00

Portrait of My Body

0-385-47710-4 ANCHOR $22.95

Anne Morrow **Lindbergh**

A Gift for Life

Fascinating and essential...a convincing portrait of a gentle woman with the inner fiber of a piano wire, absolutely committed to a life within a love

0-14-023238-9 PENGUIN PB $12.50

Phillip **Lopate**

Bachelorhood: Tales of the Metropolis

Lopate has single-handedly set about to reinvent the personal essay, and succeeds marvelously well

0-671-67681-4 POSEIDON PB $8.95

Portrait of My Body

0-385-47710-4 ANCHOR $22.95H

David **Mamet**

The Cabin: Reminiscences and Diversions

In these autobiographical essays the Pulitzer Prize-winning playwright recollects stories of his youth in Chicago, his early years when he made his way in the New York theater, and his far-flung travels

0-679-41558-0 TURTLE BAY $20.00

Peter **Matthiessen**

Nine-Headed Dragon River: Zen Journals, 1969-1982

0-87773-401-1 SHAMBHALA PB $19.00

Mary **McCarthy**

How I Grew

Our "foremost liberal woman of letters" recalls her life between the ages of 13 and 21—from high school in Seattle to college at Vassar

0-15-142193-5 HARCOURT BRACE $16.95

Memories of a Catholic Girlhood

After an idyllic childhood, McCarthy was orphaned at six, then brought up by relatives of varied religious backgrounds

0-15-658650-9 HARCOURT BRACE PB $10.00

Intellectual Memoirs: New York 1936-1938

"An autobiography that does not tell something bad about the author," McCarthy quotes, "cannot be any good." "Vibrates with the wicked wit and moral astringency that made the author a giant of American belles-lettres"—*Kirkus Reviews*

0-15-144820-5 HARCOURT BRACE $15.95

H.L. **Mencken**

My Life as Author and Editor

This memoir was sealed in a vault upon Mencken's death, with the order that it not be read for 35 years. Now that the time is up, it's obvious why. Mencken serves up withering portraits of writers and colleagues (Dreiser, Alfred Knopf, Willa Cather) in his lively and inimitable style

0-679-41315-4 KNOPF $30.00

Thirty-Five Years of Newspaper Work: A Memoir

0-8018-4791-5 JOHNS HOPKINS $34.95

James **Merrill**

A Different Person: A Memoir

"Deeply intimate and funny"—*New Yorker*

0-06-251079-7 HARPERCOLLINS PB $14.00

Christina **Middlebrook**

Seeing the Crab: A Memoir of Dying Before I Do

A bestseller about living with cancer and its treatment

See also **CANCER** under **SPECIFIC HEALTH PROBLEMS** under **HEALTH** in **LIFESTYLES AND PRACTICAL ADVICE**

0-465-07493-6 BASIC $22.00

Henry **Miller**

Aller Retour New York

Miller always said that his best writing was in his letters, and this unbuttoned 80-page missive to his friend Alfred Perles bears him out. An exuberant, humorous account of his visit to New York in 1935, it was originally printed for private circulation only, and is a coveted favorite among Miller devotees

INTRODUCTION BY GEORGE WICKES

0-8112-1193-2 NEW DIRECTIONS $15.95
0-8112-1226-2 NEW DIRECTIONS PB $8.95

Big Sur and the Oranges of Hieronymus Bosch

Miller's life on the famous stretch of California coast, a portrait of the place and many of the extraordinary people he knew there

See also **FROM THE TURN OF THE CENTURY TO WORLD WAR II** under **20TH-CENTURY AMERICAN FICTION**

0-8112-0107-4 NEW DIRECTIONS PB $12.95

A Devil in Paradise

This portion of *Big Sur and the Oranges of Hieronymus Bosch* is one of Miller's least-known masterpieces, an extraordinary portrait of Conrad Moricand, astrologer and most difficult of house guests

0-8112-1244-0 NEW DIRECTIONS PB $6.50

The Hamlet Letters

0-8095-4058-4 BORGO $27.00

Henry **Miller** & Anaïs **Nin**

A Literate Passion: Letters of Anaïs Nin and Henry Miller, 1932-1953

See also **THE 20TH CENTURY** under **STUDIES OF INDIVIDUAL AUTHORS (ALPHABETICAL BY SUBJECT)** under **AMERICAN LITERATURE: ANTHOLOGIES AND CRITICAL STUDIES**

0-15-152729-6 HARCOURT BRACE....$19.95

Paul **Monette**

Becoming a Man

A moving description of the late Monette's secret life and subsequent self-discovery

0-15-111519-2 HARCOURT BRACE....$19.95

Forty-five now and dying by inches…I finally see how our lives align at the core, if not in the sorry details. I still shiver with a kind of astonished delight when a gay brother or sister tells of that narrow escape from the coffin world of the closet. *Yes yes yes,* goes a voice in my head, *it was just like that for me.* When we laugh together then and dance in the giddy circle of freedom, we are children for real at last, because we have finally grown up.

BECOMING A MAN

Last Watch of the Night: Essays Too Personal and Otherwise

Ten essays from the front: what endures and challenges, what falls away as AIDS makes time grow short

0-15-100071-9 HARCOURT BRACE....$21.95

Honor **Moore**

The White Blackbird: A Granddaughter's Life of the Painter Margaret Sargent

An icon of avant-garde art in the '20s, Sargent defied the Boston Brahmin strictures of her birth to become a major artist of her day, then abandoned her brushes for retirement at 40. Here, her granddaughter, the poet and playwright Honor Moore, documents a life of genius, alcoholism, and stubborn struggle for creative freedom against long odds, at the same time telling the story of the birth of modern art in America

See also **THE 1920S** under **AMERICAN ART BEFORE THE 1940S** under **20TH-CENTURY ART** in **ART**

0-670-80563-7 VIKING....$29.95

Willie **Morris**

My Dog Skip

The critically acclaimed Southern writer (*North Toward Home, New York Days*) and former *Harper's* editor brings the story of his youth in the '40s to life through his relationship with his dog

0-679-44144-1 RANDOM HOUSE....$15.00
0-679-76722-3 VINTAGE PB....$9.00

New York Days

0-316-58398-7 LITTLE, BROWN PB....$12.95

North Toward Home

0-916242-16-1 YOKNAPATAWPHA PB....$14.95

Wright **Morris**

Three Easy Pieces

"Expertly crafted, suggestive and mysterious" —*Library Journal*

0-87685-923-6 BLACK SPARROW PB....$15.00

David **Mura**

Turning Japanese: Memoirs of a Sansei

0-385-42344-6 ANCHOR PB....$12.00

Where the Body Meets Memory: An Odyssey of Race, Sexuality, and Identity

0-385-47183-1 ANCHOR....$22.95

Vladimir **Nabokov**

Speak,Memory: An Autobiography Revisited

"The finest autobiography written in our time"—*New Republic*

0-679-72339-0 VINTAGE PB....$13.00

The cradle rocks above an abyss, and common sense tells us that our existence is but a brief crack of light between two eternities of darkness. Although the two are identical twins, man, as a rule, views the prenatal abyss with more calm than the one he is heading for (at some forty-five hundred heartbeats an hour). I know, however, of a young chronophobiac who experienced something like panic when looking for the first time at homemade movies that had been taken a few weeks before his birth. He saw a world that was practically unchanged—the same house, the same people—and then realized that he did not exist there at all and that nobody mourned his absence.

SPEAK MEMORY: AN AUTOBIOGRAPHY REVISITED

Vladimir Nabokov: Selected Letters, 1940-1977

0-15-164190-0 HARCOURT BRACE....$29.95

Anaïs **Nin**

Nin's diaries, a remarkable lifelong undertaking, offer a unique record of self-discovery by a modern woman and writer who moved freely in the cosmopolitan world of art and society. "An extraordinary book...its egoism is redeemed and raised to a high standard of art by an extremely subtle sensibility, expressed in a prose style of astonishing beauty."—Herbert Read

The Diaries of Anaïs Nin

Volume 1, 1931-1934

0-15-626025-5 HARCOURT BRACE PB....$10.95

Volume 2, 1934-1939

0-15-626026-3 HARCOURT BRACE PB....$10.95

Volume 3, 1939-1944

0-15-626027-1 HARCOURT BRACE PB....$10.95

Volume 4, 1944-1947

0-15-626028-X HARCOURT BRACE PB....$10.00

Volume 5, 1947-1955

0-15-626030-1 HARCOURT BRACE PB....$10.95

Volume 6, 1955-1956

0-15-626032-8 HARCOURT BRACE PB....$12.00

Volume 7, 1966-1974

0-15-626035-2 HARCOURT BRACE PB....$12.00

Fire: "A Journal of Love," The Unexpurgated Diary of Anaïs Nin, 1934-1937

Starting in December 1934, when Nin arrived in New York from France to continue her marriage and dual affairs

0-15-100088-3 HARCOURT BRACE....$25.00

Henry and June: From the Unexpurgated Diary of Anäis Nin

0-15-640057-X HARCOURT BRACE PB....$11.00

Nearer the Moon: From "A Journal of Love," the Unexpurgated Diary of Anais Nin, 1937-1939

The diary of the famed expatriate, and the basis for the film *Henry and June*, details the author's relationship with Henry Miller

EDITED BY VICKI AUS

0-15-100089-1 HARCOURT BRACE....$28.00

Mary **Oppen**

Meaning a Life

A memoir of her life with poet George Oppen

0-87685-374-2 BLACK SPARROW PB....$12.50

Judith Hillman **Paterson**

Sweet Mystery

0-374-27226-3 FS&G....$23.00

Robert **Perkins**

Talking to Angels: A Life Spent at High Latitudes

0-8070-7078-5 BEACON....$18.00

Robert **Peters**

For You, Lilli Marlene

Drafted at 18 from a remote Wisconsin farm, Peters, now an acclaimed poet, has written a lyrical memoir of his coming-of-age in the middle of World War II. From the machismo of the barracks to his sexual awakening during the occupation of Germany, Peters grows from boy to man and from private to sergeant-major

See also **THE UNITED STATES AND WORLD WAR II** under **THE SECOND WORLD WAR** in **WORLD HISTORY AND CURRENT AFFAIRS**

0-299-14810-6 WISCONSIN....$19.95

Dawn **Powell**

The Diaries of Dawn Powell, 1931-1965

The novelist was a witness to the glory years of the New York literary world

EDITED BY TIM PAGE

1-88364-208-6 STEERFORTH....$32.00

Reynolds **Price**

A Whole New Life: An Illness and a Healing

Well-known writer documents his battle with a tumor in his spinal cord

See also **CANCER** under **SPECIFIC HEALTH PROBLEMS** under **HEALTH** in **LIFESTYLES AND PRACTICAL ADVICE**

0-452-27473-7 PENGUIN PB....$10.95

Kenneth **Rexroth**

An Autobiographical Novel

Rexroth's account of the first 21 years of his life encompasses a wide spectrum of radical and bohemian experience in the early 20th century

0-8112-1179-7 NEW DIRECTIONS PB....$14.95

Adele Crockett **Robertson**

The Orchard: A Memoir of the Great Depression

0-8050-4092-7 HOLT....$20.00

Philip **Roth**

The Facts: A Novelist's Autobiography

0-374-15212-8 FS&G PB $17.95

Patrimony

Roth's account of his father's life and death describes in detail "the agonized, sometimes comic labor of a family and a dying parent who must deal with all the loyalties of their past while coping with their transformed future" —Robert Pinsky, *NY Times Book Review*

0-679-75293-5 VINTAGE PB $12.00

Philip Roth

Pierre **Salinger**

P.S., A Memoir

0-312-13578-5 ST. MARTIN'S $24.95

Mark **Salzman**

Lost In Place: Growing Up Absurd

A delightful memoir of growing up in Connecticut, aspiring to be a Zen monk and kung fu black belt, wrecking cars, walking barefoot to school in the snow (a supposed Zen excercise—not a necessity), ingesting heroic quantities of marijuana, and other excesses of a privileged and tortured adolescence

0-679-43945-5 RANDOM HOUSE $22.00

May **Sarton**

At Seventy: A Journal

Chronicles the year that began on May 3, 1982, her 70th birthday, and the experience of being alive at her home in Maine

0-393-31030-2 NORTON PB $9.95

Journal of a Solitude

"On the surface it is a quiet book, but if you will read it carefully you will be aware of violent needs and a variant warrior who has battled every inch of the way to a share of serenity" —*Cleveland Plain Dealer*

0-393-30928-2 NORTON PB $10.00

Recovering: A Journal

"Sarton has fashioned her journals, 'sonatas' as she calls them, into a distinctive form: relaxed yet shapely, a silky weave of reflection, sensuous observation and record of her daily rounds, with the reader made companion to her inmost thoughts"—*Publishers Weekly*

0-393-01402-9 NORTON $14.95

At 82: A Journal

"Memory is full of riches, grief, and joy" reads one entry of Sarton's newest diary, the rich record of the rhythms, recollections, and routines of the celebrated poet and journalist in her 82nd year. "It has been one of Sarton's gifts never to pretend that a woman's life is easier or simpler than it is, but to record its austerity and richness"—Marge Piercy

See also **BIOGRAPHIES** under **GAY, LESBIAN, AND BISEXUAL STUDIES** in **SOCIAL STUDIES**

0-393-03889-0 NORTON $23.00

Alix Kates **Shulman**

Drinking the Rain

The memoirs of Shulman, who at the age of 50 left her busy political, literary, and family life for a summer of solitude on an island off the Maine coast. "A superb piece of work…It seems to encompass, in its narrow scope, all the anxieties and rewards, the political struggles and social changes of the American world" —Doris Grumbach, *The Boston Globe*

0-374-14403-6 FS&G $20.00
0-14-025584-2 PENGUIN PB $11.95

Elizabeth **Smart**

By Grand Street Station I Sat Down and Wept

A powerful memoir of a love affair

0-679-73804-5 VINTAGE PB $10.00

Gary **Snyder**

Passage Through India

A travel journal

0-912516-79-8 SUBTERRANEAN $12.95
0-912516-80-1 SUBTERRANEAN PB $8.95

Gertrude **Stein**

The Autobiography of Alice B. Toklas

This memoir, told through the voice of her lifelong companion, made Stein a bestselling author

1-679--72463-X VINTAGE PB $11.00

Everybody's Autobiography

Includes Stein's own account of her famous tour of America in the 30s

1-87897-208-1 EXACT CHANGE PB $15.95

Elaine **Steinbeck** & Robert **Wallsten**, editors

Steinbeck: A Life in Letters

"Surely his most interesting, plausibly his most memorable, and…arguably his best book" —*NY Times Book Review*

0-14-004288-1 PENGUIN PB $19.95

John **Steinbeck**

The Log From the Sea of Cortez

After completeing *The Grapes of Wrath*, Steinbeck took off on a marine biological expedition off the coast of Baja California. His journal is a prime statement of his personal philosophy

0-140-18744-8 PENGUIN PB $11.95

William **Styron**

Darkness Visible: A Memoir of Madness

The novelist writes of his descent into depression, and how he recovered

See also **DEPRESSION** under **DISORDERS AND TREATMENT** under **PSYCHOLOGY** in **SOCIAL STUDIES**

0-394-58888-6 RANDOM HOUSE $15.95

Mary **Swander**

Out of this World: A Journey of Healing

A woman's inspiring memoir of healing from a devastating environmental illness—and of creating a simpler life for herself—by living in rural Iowa

See also **LIVING SIMPLY** under **SPIRITUALITY** under **SPIRITUALITY** in **RELIGION, SPIRITUALITY, AND PHILOSOPHY**

0-14-024170-1 PENGUIN PB $11.95

Clifton L. **Taulbert**

When We Were Colored

"A bittersweet story about love, community and family—and the difference they made in the life of one young man"—*New Yorker*

0-14-024477-8 PENGUIN PB $8.95

Studs **Terkel**

Talking to Myself: A Memoir of My Times

"A magnificent book…It's a privilege to share Studs Terkel's experiences…Few autobiographies have been as equally moving and funny as this one"—Nora Sayre

1-56584-319-3 NEW PRESS PB $11.95

Studs Terkel (photo by Michael Weinstein)

Calvin **Trillin**

Messages from my Father

Author of 18 previous books and staff writer for the *New Yorker*, Trillin turns his vision of the American character toward a portrait of his father, a grocer in Kansas City with a western Missouri accent and a Russian-born vision of America's promise

0-374-20860-3 FS&G $18.00

Remembering Denny

In his most personal book to date, Trillin investigates the life of former Yale classmate Roger "Denny" Hansen, a boy so handsome, intelligent, and promising he was profiled in *Life* magazine, but whose life ended in suicide in early middle age

0-374-22607-5 FS&G $19.00
0-446-67032-4 WARNER PB $9.99

After all these years of poling around in other people's lives, I'm convinced that we can almost never know the precise motives of someone else, even old friends.

REMEMBERING DENNY

Calvin Trillin (credit: ©Sigrid Estrada 1993)

Diana **Trilling**

The Beginning of the Journey: The Marriage of Diana and Lionel Trilling

An intimate portrait of America's premier literary couple comes to life in this fascinating work. From the Trillings' early hardships to their mutual rise to literary prominence, this is a unique love story

0-15-111685-7 HARCOURT BRACE $24.95

John **Updike**

Self-Consciousness

"Raw material of an autobiography": six essays on childhood, psoriasis, writing, the Vietnam War, and other subjects

0-394-57222-X KNOPF $18.95

Gore **Vidal**

Palimpsest: A Memoir

Vidal tells of his boyhood in Washington, where he was page to his grandfather Senator Gore; homosexual life in the 40s and 50s; and on to Hollywood. Enriched with literary reflections, and the stellar host of characters (James Baldwin, Eleanor Roosevelt, Kerouac, Brando, Garbo, the Clintons), this is a writer's life in the very center of the century's culture and politics

0-679-44038-0 RANDOM HOUSE $27.50
0-14-026089-7 PENGUIN PB $13.95

Kurt **Vonnegut**, Jr.

Fates Worse Than Death: An Autobiographical Collage

0-425-13406-7 BERKELEY PB $12.00

Alice **Walker**

The Same River Twice: Honoring the Difficult

The autobiography of one of this century's most important African- American woman writers

See also **ARTISTS AND LITERARY FIGURES** under **BLACK VOICES, BLACK LIVES** under **AFRICAN-AMERICAN STUDIES** in **HISTORY OF THE AMERICAS**

0-684-81419-6 SCRIBNERS $24.00

Eudora **Welty**

One Writer's Beginnings

"Miss Welty presents her life as if it were one of her stories, so that the book is something more than a brief autobiography"—*NY Times*

0-674-63925-1 HARVARD $15.95

Paul **Watkins**

Stand Before Your God: A Boarding School Memoir

The first nonfiction work from the author of *Night over Day over Night* and *The Promise of Light*, about coming of age as an American in an English boarding school

0-679-42056-8 RANDOM HOUSE $22.00

And I knew that now I had arrived I could never leave this school behind. One look around me and I knew that you did not stop being an Etonian. Some people would use it as an insult and others as the highest praise they could find. Besides, it was one thing to wear a blue corduroy uniform like at the Dragon, but you couldn't come to Eton and dress up as a goddamn opera conductor for four years and not have that do something to you.

STAND BEFORE YOUR GOD: A BOARDING SCHOOL MEMOIR

Paul **West**

My Mother's Music

West (*Rat Man of Paris, Love's Mansion*) writes of his complicated, admiring, and somewhat ambivalent relationship to his mother, a woman he remembers for her "nimble uniqueness…her pell-mell profundity, her gentle enormity"

0-670-86757-8 VIKING $23.95

Words for a Deaf Daughter & Gala

"A heartbreaking, lyrical account of his 'retarded' daughter whose strange and beautiful presence in the world compelled her father to rethink and resee his own relation to the natural and human universe"—*Newsweek*

1-56478-036-8 DALKEY ARCHIVE PB $12.95

Margaret **Wettlin**

Fifty Russian Winters: An American Woman's Life in the Soviet Union

"A remarkable chunk of history that she writes about simply and elegantly"
—*NY Times Book Review*

0-471-02877-0 WILEY PB $14.95

Edith **Wharton**

A Backward Glance

0-684-15983-X SCRIBNERS $27.50

Thornton **Wilder**

The Journals of Thornton Wilder

EDITED BY DONALD GALLUP

0-300-03375-3 YALE $42.00

William Carlos **Williams**

The Autobiography of William Carlos Williams

0-8112-0226-7 NEW DIRECTIONS PB $12.95

I Wanted to Write a Poem

EDITED BY EDITH HEAL

0-8112-0707-2 NEW DIRECTIONS PB $7.95

Selected Letters of William Carlos Williams

EDITED BY JOHN C. THIRLWALL

0-8112-0934-2 NEW DIRECTIONS PB $9.95

John Edgar **Wideman**

Fatheralong: A Meditation on Fathers and Sons, Race and Society

Meditation on "fathers, color, roots, time, and language" that is also a summing up of a man's escape from the prison of racial ideology. "Our most powerful and accomplished artist of the urban black world"—*LA Times Book Review*

See also **ARTISTS AND LITERARY FIGURES** under **BLACK VOICES, BLACK LIVES** under **AFRICAN-AMERICAN STUDIES** in **HISTORY OF THE AMERICAS**

0-679-40720-0 PANTHEON $21.00

John Edgar Wideman

David **Wojnarowicz**

The Waterfront Journals

0-8021-1585-3 GROVE $20.00

Geoffrey **Wolff**

The Duke of Deception

Wolff examines his relationship with his father

0-679-72752-3 VINTAGE PB $13.00

Tobias **Wolff**

Back in the World

0-679-76796-7 VINTAGE PB $12.00

Elizabeth **Wurtzel**

Prozac Nation: Young and Depressed in America

This is a harrowing, if at times hilarious, account of what is becoming an all-too-common occurrence among today's young people

See also **DEPRESSION** under **SELF-HELP** in **LIFESTYLES AND PRACTICAL ADVICE**

0-395-68093-X HOUGHTON MIFFLIN $19.95
1-57322-512-6 RIVERHEAD PB $12.00

Al **Young**

Things Ain't What They Used to Be: Musical Memoirs

From the tango to the bossa nova, Young recaptures the past through the power of music

See also **ESSAYS AND REVIEWS** under **JAZZ** in **PERFORMING ARTS AND MEDIA**

0-88739-024-2 CREATIVE ARTS PB $8.95

Reporting

For related reading, see JOURNALISM in PERFORMING ARTS AND MEDIA

James **Agee**

James Agee: Selected Journalism

EDITED BY PAUL ASHDOWN

0-87049-466-X TENNESSEE $28.00

James **Agee** & Walker **Evans**

Let Us Now Praise Famous Men

The 1941 classic about cotton-farming tenantry among white sharecroppers, told through Agee's poetic prose and Evans's stark photographs

See also **PHOTOGRAPHERS** under **PHOTOGRAPHY** in **ART**

0-395-48897-4 HOUGHTON MIFFLIN PB $16.95

Djuna **Barnes**

New York

Journalistic pieces by the author of *Nightwood*, written between 1913 and 1919. "The great interviewer…explores the lives of tenement-dwellers, middle-class tangoers, squatters, suffragists, ordinary working men, and the literary Bohemians…In these still-fresh portraits, the city of New York is perceived by Barnes as an enormous landscape of theater, of circuses, operas, street performances, carneys, hawkers, con-men, clowns, and just a few saints"—Douglas Messerli

See also **FROM THE TURN OF THE CENTURY TO WORLD WAR II** under **20TH-CENTURY AMERICAN FICTION**

0-940650-82-7 SUN & MOON $24.95
0-940650-99-1 SUN & MOON PB $12.95

Jimmy **Breslin**

The World According to Breslin

EDITED BY WILLIAM BRINK & MICHAEL J. O'NEILL

0-89919-310-2 TICKNOR & FIELDS $15.95

Truman **Capote**

In Cold Blood

The original "nonfiction novel," first published in 1966, chronicling the murder of a Kansas family by two drifters

See also **MODERN CRIMINAL CASES** under **TRUE CRIME** in **POPULAR READING**

See also **SINCE 1945** under **20TH-CENTURY AMERICAN FICTION**

0-679-60023-X MODERN LIBRARY $15.50
0-679-74558-0 VINTAGE PB $12.00

Joan **Didion**

After Henry

Includes Didion's highly praised essays on the Central Park jogger case and her reflections on Los Angeles. "Out of the flickering images and layered fantasies of American public life she creates something hard, durable, and true" —*Mirabella*

0-679-74539-4 VINTAGE $13.00

Salvador

"Didion has that rare gift, the ability to take in the essence of a country through her pores" —Robert E. White, former ambassador to El Salvador

See also **EL SALVADOR** under **LATIN AMERICA AND THE CARIBBEAN** in **HISTORY OF THE AMERICAS**

0-679-75183-1 VINTAGE PB $10.00

Joan Didion

Slouching Towards Bethlehem

A collection from the mid-'60s, with the now classic title essay on Haight-Ashbury. "What most captivates the reader is discovering how her brittle sensibilities respond to events. Miss Didion suffers constantly, but compellingly and magically"—*Time*

0-374-52172-7 NOONDAY PB $10.00

The White Album

Includes the title essay plus "California Republic," "Women," "Sojourns," and "On the Morning After the Sixties"

0-374-52221-9 NOONDAY PB $10.00

Frederick **Exley**

Last Notes from Home

0-679-72456-7 VINTAGE PB $12.00

Michael **Kelly**

Martyr's Day: Chronicle of a Small War

Kelly was an eyewitness to almost every major event of the Gulf War: the bombing of Baghdad, the attacks on Israel, the American assault into Kuwait, and the tragic events in Kurdestan. His dispatches won him a National Magazine Award and an Overseas Press Club Award. This narrative covers the war in human terms, capturing Kelly's own extraordinary experiences as well as the political and social consequences of the war

See also **THE GULF CONFLICT, 1990-1991** under **IRAQ** under **THE CONTEMPORARY MIDDLE EAST** in **WORLD HISTORY AND CURRENT AFFAIRS**

0-679-75014-2 VINTAGE PB $12.00

Norman **Maclean**

Young Men and Fire

"A magnificent drama of writing, a tragedy that pays tribute to the dead and offers rescue to the living…"—*NY Times Book Review*

0-226-50062-4 CHICAGO PB $10.95

Norman **Mailer**

Miami and the Siege of Chicago

INTRODUCTION BY TOM WICKER

0-917657-85-3 FINE PB $9.95

The Prisoner of Sex

After the breakup of his fourth marriage, surrounded by his five children, Mailer's performing self takes on the issue of women's liberation

INTRODUCTION BY PETE HAMILL

0-917657-59-4 FINE PB $8.95

Janet **Malcolm**

The Purloined Clinic: Selected Writings

Harold Bloom called critic Malcolm "a calmly rational Alice in Wonderland," and in these essays on art, literature, and psychoanalysis she is at her witty, illuminating best. Malcolm's writings include reviews of Milan Kundera, Thomas Eakins, and Vaclav Havel as well as extended profiles of an unorthodox therapist, editor Ingrid Sischy, and a former Czech dissident negotiating the uncertainties of post-Velvet-Revolution Prague

0-679-74810-5 VINTAGE PB $13.00

John **McPhee**

The Deltoid Pumpkin Seed

A lively account about the deltoid-shaped Aeron, a modern hybrid of airship and airplane, and the strange cast of characters who tried to get it off the ground

0-374-13781-1 FS&G $18.95
0-374-51635-9 FS&G PB $9.00

Murray **Kempton**

Rebellions, Perversities, and Main Events

As a complex stylist with an unerring eye for the absurd details of life, Kempton has no equal in the newspaper trade

See also **THE PRACTITIONERS: A SAMPLER** under **JOURNALISM** in **PERFORMING ARTS AND MEDIA**

0-8129-2294-8 TIME BOOKS $27.50
0-8129-2528-9 TIME BOOKS PB $16.00

Murray Kempton

Encounters with the Archdruid: Narratives About a Conservationist and Three Natural Enemies
Classic encounters in the wilderness between David Brower ("the most militant conservationist in the world") and a mineral engineer, a real estate developer, and a dam builder

0-374-14822-8 FS&G $19.95
0-374-51431-3 NOONDAY PB $10.00

The Headmaster: Frank L. Boyden of Deerfield
0-374-16860-1 FS&G $16.95
0-374-51496-8 FS&G PB $10.00

The John McPhee Reader
An impressive gathering comprised of selections from the first twelve books published by "the most versatile journalist in America" (Edward Hoagland)

EDITED BY WILLIAM L. HOWARTH
0-374-17992-1 FS&G $25.00
0-374-51719-3 FS&G PB $14.00

La Place de la Concorde Suisse
"McPhee, in showing us as many aspects of the Swiss Army as their famous knife has blades, has produced one of his best books" —*Wall Street Journal*

0-374-18241-8 FS&G $18.95
0-374-51932-3 NOONDAY PB $10.00

Pieces of the Frame
McPhee's second collection of essays. "One has the sense always with McPhee of a man at a pitch of pleasure in his work, a natural at it, finding out on behalf of the rest of us how some portion of the world works"—Edward Hoagland

0-374-23281-4 FS&G $19.95
0-374-51498-4 FS&G PB $12.00

The Second John McPhee Reader
"McPhee's work has the quality of permanence ...He writes about geology and the reader is forever changed, more aware somehow of historical 'deep time', of the temporary state of the earth's surface and our fleeting stay on these shifting plates"—David Remnick

INTRODUCTION BY DAVID REMNICK
0-374-52463-7 NOONDAY PB $14.00

Table of Contents
A collection of eight essays written between 1981 and 1984, including "Heirs of General Practice" and "North of the C.P. Line"

0-374-27241-7 FS&G $19.95
0-374-52008-9 NOONDAY PB $12.00

Karl **Meyer**

Pundits, Poets and Wits: An Omnibus of American Newspaper Columns
An anthology of 72 of America's finest columnists. "An irresistibly oddball history of American life"—*Washington Post Book World*

See also **THE IMPACT OF THE MEDIA** under **TOPICS IN AMERICAN STUDIES** in **HISTORY OF THE AMERICAS**

0-19-507137-9 OXFORD PB $13.95

Henry **Miller**

The Air-Conditioned Nightmare
America in the '40s, seen with a deeply unsympathetic eye

0-8112-0106-6 NEW DIRECTIONS PB $10.95

Joseph **Mitchell**

The Bottom of the Harbor
0-679-60093-0 MODERN LIBRARY $12.50

Joe Gould's Secret
The portrait of a mysterious bohemian writer and his secret history

0-679-60184-8 MODERN LIBRARY $13.50

Up in the Old Hotel
0-679-41263-8 PANTHEON $27.50

Gay **Talese**

Fame and Obscurity
0-8041-1056-5 IVY PB $5.99

Honor Thy Father
Acclaimed portrayal of the Bonanno mafia dynasty

See also **ORGANIZED CRIME** under **TRUE CRIME** in **POPULAR READING**

0-8041-1058-1 IVY PB $5.99

The Kingdom and the Power
A report on the inner workings of *The New York Times*

0-8041-1057-3 IVY PB $5.99

The Neighbor's Wife
A first-hand, front line report on American sexuality

0-8041-1059-X IVY PB $5.99

Gay Talese

Hunter S. **Thompson**

The Curse of Lono
0-553-34354-8 BDD PB $12.95

Fear and Loathing in Las Vegas
"The best book on the Dope Decade"—*NY Times*

ILLUSTRATED BY RALPH STEADMAN
0-679-72419-2 VINTAGE PB $11.00

Fear and Loathing on the Campaign Trail '72
"The best account yet published of what it feels like to be out there in the middle of the American political process"—*NY Times*

0-446-31364-5 WARNER PB $6.99

The Great Shark Hunt
A collection of pieces written across two decades from anarchy's quintessential outlaw journalist, the "Duke of Gonzo"

0-446-31440-4 WARNER PB $7.99

E. B. White (photo by Jim Kalett)

Hell's Angels
"For all its uninhibited and sardonic humor, Thompson's book is a thoughtful piece of work"—*New Yorker*

0-345-33148-6 BALLANTINE PB $5.95

E.B. **White**

Writings from the New Yorker: 1927-1976
Short pieces and essays concerning everything from Khrushchev to cicadas, Thoreau to lipstick, and hyphens to sparrows. "There are enough sparkling gems here to show that White was one of the country's greatest literary treasures" —*NY Times*

0-06-092123-4 HARPERPERENNIAL PB $13.00

Edmund **White**

States of Desire: Travels in Gay America
A study of contemporary gay American life, written by the prominent novelist

See also **GAY LIFE AND CULTURE** under **GAY, LESBIAN, AND BISEXUAL STUDIES** in **SOCIAL STUDIES**

0-452-26689-0 PLUME PB $11.95

Tom **Wolfe**

The Electric Kool-Aid Acid Test
"*The Electric Kool-Aid Acid Test* is not only the best book on the hippies. It is the essential book"—*NY Times*

0-553-26491-5 BDD PB $6.50

In Our Time
ILLUSTRATED BY TOM WOLFE
0-374-17576-4 FS&G $12.95

The Kandy Kolored Tangerine-Flake Streamline Baby
His literary debut, a look at the early '60s and various exotic forms of status-seeking, including profiles of Phil Spector and Baby Jane Holzer

0-374-18064-4 FS&G $19.95
0-374-50468-7 FS&G PB $14.00

Mauve Gloves and Madmen, Clutter and Vine

Stories, essays, and sketches on the mood of the '70s, including "The Me Decade and the Third Great Awakening"

0-374-20424-1 FS&G $18.95
0-374-52092-5 FS&G PB $9.95

The Painted Word

A caustic essay on modern art

See also **CRITICISM** under **ART SINCE 1945** in **ART**

0-374-22878-7 FS&G $18.95
0-553-27379-5 BDD PB $5.99

Thomas Wolfe

The Pump House Gang

An early collection of essays; the title piece concerns a California surfing elite

0-374-23864-2 FS&G $18.95
0-374-52070-4 FS&G PB $13.00

The Purple Decades: A Reader

Includes "The Last American Hero," "The Pump House Gang," "The Me Decade and the Third Great Awakening," plus selections from *Radical Chic, The Right Stuff, The Electric Kool-Aid Acid Test*, and *From Bauhaus to Our House*

0-374-23927-4 FS&G $17.50

Radical Chic & Mau-Mauing the Flak Catchers

Two essays about political stances and social styles in a status-conscious world. Includes the famous account of Leonard Bernstein's party for the Black Panthers

0-374-24600-9 FS&G $16.95
0-374-52072-0 FS&G PB $11.00

The Right Stuff

The full, irreverent story of the first Americans in space

See also **THE SPACE AGE** under **HISTORY OF SCIENCE AND TECHNOLOGY** under **TOPICS IN AMERICAN STUDIES** in **HISTORY OF THE AMERICAS**

0-374-25033-2 FS&G $30.00
0-553-27556-9 BDD PB $6.99

History, Politics, and Society

Edward **Abbey**

"What entertains many and exasperates others is Abbey's unique prose voice. Alternately misanthropic and sentimental, enraged and hilarious, it is the voice of a full-blooded man airing his passions."—Peter Carlson

The Best of Edward Abbey

0-87156-786-5 SIERRA CLUB PB $15.00

Confessions of a Barbarian: Selections from the Journals, 1951-1989

EDITED BY DAVID PETERSEN

0-316-00415-4 LITTLE, BROWN $24.95

Desert Solitaire

See also **ESSAYS** under **THE OUTDOORS** in **FOOD, TRAVEL, AND LEISURE**

See also **THE SOUTHWEST AND THE DESERT** under **REGIONAL GUIDES AND STUDIES** under **NATURE STUDY** in **SCIENCE**

0-8165-1057-1 ARIZONA $36.00
0-345-32649-0 BALLANTINE PB $5.95
0-671-69588-6 TOUCHSTONE PB $11.00

Down the River

Among other things, "Abbey on the Green River", contemplating Thoreau

See also **ESSAYS, MEDITATIONS, AND CLASSICS** under **NATURE STUDY** in **SCIENCE**

0-452-26563-0 DUTTON PB $11.95

The Serpents of Paradise

A writer's duty, Abbey wrote, is "to defy the powerful, and to speak for the voiceless." Environmentalist, anarchist, guru to counterculturalists, and eloquent voice of reason against power, Abbey's death in 1989 deprived the world of a real individualist

0-8050-3132-4 HOLT $25.00

James **Baldwin**

Evidence of Things Not Seen

A report on the investigation into the Atlanta child murders

0-8050-0138-7 HOLT PB $7.95

The Fire Next Time

Prophetic warnings in the form of a "Letter to My Nephew on the 100th Anniversary of the Emancipation"

0-679-74472-X VINTAGE PB $9.00

Notes of a Native Son

His first nonfiction book, essays on life in Harlem, the protest novel, movies, and Americans abroad. "A straight-from-the-shoulder writer, writing about the troubled problems of this troubled earth, with an illuminating intensity that should influence for the better all who ponder on the things books say" —Langston Hughes

0-8070-6431-9 BEACON PB $11.00

The Price of the Ticket: Collected Nonfiction, 1948-1985

Includes the full text of "The Fire Next Time," "No Name in the Street," and "The Devil Finds Work," plus many selections

0-312-64306-3 ST. MARTIN'S $29.95

Wendell **Berry**

Another Turn of the Crank

1-88717-828-7 COUNTERPOINT PB $12.50

The Hidden Wound

An autobiographical meditation on racism and its effect on American society: "If the white man has inflicted the wound of racism upon black men, the cost has been that he would receive the mirror image of that wound himself"

0-86547-358-7 NORTH POINT PB $11.00

Sex, Economy, Freedom & Community: Eight Essays

0-679-75651-5 PANTHEON PB $11.00

Standing by Words: Essays

0-86547-122-3 NORTH POINT PB $12.00

The Unsettling of America: Culture & Agriculture

0-87156-877-2 SIERRA CLUB PB $12.00

Sven **Birkerts**

The Gutenberg Elegies: The Fate of Reading in the Electronic Age

0-449-91009-1 FAWCETT PB $12.50

Robert **Bly**

The Sibling Society

Bly looks to the psychic problems of our public life for an insight into why our culture is adrift. Using the psychological lessons of ancient folktales, Bly issues a condemnation of television, consumerism, and spiritual impoverishment

See also **WESTERN** under **20TH-CENTURY SPIRITUAL LEADERS** under **SPIRITUALITY** under **SPIRITUALITY** in **RELIGION, SPIRITUALITY, AND PHILOSOPHY**

0-201-40646-2 ADDISON-WESLEY $25.00

Talking All Morning

0-472-15760-4 MICHIGAN PB $13.95

Evan S. **Connell**

A Long Desire

A series of historical essays on the human quest for adventure and some of the strange forms it takes. "Quite simply, a great book…Combining a poet's vision and the narrative sweep of a born storyteller with painstaking historical research"—*LA Times*

0-86547-334-X FS&G PB $8.95

Son of the Morning Star: Custer and the Little Bighorn

"An unconventional, highly evocative retelling of the celebrated military disaster …One of the Ten Best of 1984"—*Time*

See also **GENERAL CUSTER** under **INDIAN WARS** under **NATIVE AMERICAN CULTURES: NORTH AMERICA** in **HISTORY OF THE AMERICAS**

0-06-097161-4 HARPERCOLLINS PB $10.95

Stanley **Crouch**

The All-American Skin Game, Or, The Decoy of Race: The Long and the Short of It, 1990-1994

As both writer and editor, Crouch specializes in undermining our accepted wisdom about race in America. "[Stanley Crouch] is the black writer whose unorthodox views and attacks on liberals,

feminists, and Black Power leaders often send ethnic militants into paroxysms of anger"—*NY Times*. "Behind his dissenter's rhetoric and hangman's mask, Stanley Crouch is actually a benign and eloquent provocateur"
—Ralph Ellison

See also **AFRICAN-AMERICANS** under **THE MELTING POT** under **AMERICAN PEOPLE AND PLACES** in **HISTORY OF THE AMERICAS**

0-679-44202-2 PANTHEON........$24.00
0-679-77660-5 VINTAGE PB........$13.00

Notes of a Hanging Judge

Some of the most controversial essays of recent years, on jazz, politics, and African-American culture, by a long-time music critic and contributor to *The Village Voice*

0-19-505591-8 OXFORD........$25.00

Mario R. **DiNunzio**, editor

Theodore Roosevelt: An American Mind: Selected Writings

"Controversial, but consistently provoking and entertaining"—*Publishers Weekly*

See also **THE GILDED AGE AND THE PROGRESSIVE ERA** under **US HISTORY, 1877-1945** in **HISTORY OF THE AMERICAS**

0-14-024520-0 PENGUIN PB........$13.95

Leslie **Fiedler**

Freaks: Myths and Images of the Secret Self

A social critic uses history, biology, psychology, literature, and pop culture to analyze our fascinations with and reactions to society's "freaks"

See also **CULTURE ON THE EDGE** under **CUTTING EDGE** in **POPULAR READING**

0-385-47013-4 ANCHOR PB........$14.00

Gustavo Perez **Firmat**

Life on the Hyphen: The Cuban-American Way

0-292-76551-7 TEXAS PB........$14.95

Next Year in Cuba: A Cubano's Coming of Age in America

0-385-47296-X ANCHOR........$22.95
0-385-47297-8 ANCHOR PB........$12.95

Leon **Forrest**

The Furious Voice for Freedom

Maya Angelou, Sandra Cisneros, Annie Dillard, Ursula Le Guin, Margaret Mead, Adrienne Rich, Gloria Steinem...A cornucopia of the most distinguished women's voices in America address ethnic identity, the natural world, rape, the joys of children, and a range of other contemporary issues

1-55921-080-X MOYER BELL PB........$14.95

Paul **Fussell**

Class: A Guide Through the American Status System

"Fussell identifies the class significance of not only clothes and houses but cars, food, language, vacations, reading habits and much more...Frighteningly acute"—Alison Lurie

See also **CLASS IN AMERICA** under **AMERICAN PEOPLE AND PLACES** in **HISTORY OF THE AMERICAS**

0-671-79225-3 TOUCHSTONE PB........$10.00

The Great War and Modern Memory

On the shattering of innocence in 1914-18 and the end of our concept that any war can be heroic. "An original and brilliant piece of cultural history and one of the most deeply moving books I have read in a long time"
—Lionel Trilling

See also **ARMAGGEDON: 1914-1918** under **THE 20TH CENTURY** under **GREAT BRITAIN AND IRELAND** in **WORLD HISTORY AND CURRENT AFFAIRS**

0-19-502171-1 OXFORD PB........$12.95

Wartime: Understanding and Behavior in the Second World War

Explores the psychological culture of Britons and Americans during World War II. Fussell frankly confronts the "euphemism and rationalization" needed to deal with the often unacceptable reality from 1939 to 1945. Chapters include "Chickenshit, An Anatomy," "Drinking Far Too Much, Copulating Too Little," "Reading in Wartime," and "The Real War Will Never Get in the Books"

See also **BRITAIN** under **THE WAR IN EUROPE** under **THE SECOND WORLD WAR** in **WORLD HISTORY AND CURRENT AFFAIRS**

0-19-503797-9 OXFORD........$27.50
0-19-506577-8 OXFORD PB........$12.95

Sue **Hubbell**

Far Flung Hubbell: Essays from The American Road

From the best homemade pies in the country to Elvis sightings and the Bowling Alley Hall of Fame, these offbeat essays inform and entertain

0-679-42833-X RANDOM HOUSE........$21.00

Jane **Jacobs**

The Economy of Cities

"This book is radiant with ideas about what makes cities rich or poor, how cities grow, and how city growth affects national economies"
—*New Yorker*

See also **CITIES AND CITY PLANNING** under **CRITICISM** under **20TH-CENTURY ARCHITECTURE** in **ARCHITECTURE, DESIGN, AND HOMES**

See also **URBAN ECONOMICS** under **SPECIAL TOPICS** under **ECONOMICS** in **SOCIAL STUDIES**

See also **URBAN SOCIOLOGY** under **TOPICS IN MODERN SOCIOLOGY** under **SOCIOLOGY** in **SOCIAL STUDIES**

0-394-70584-X RANDOM HOUSE PB........$10.00

Wendy **Kaminer**

True Love Waits: Essays and Criticism

The bestselling author of *I'm Dysfunctional, You're Dysfunctional* takes aim at sex and violence, pop psychology, the First Amendment, and more. "If a Nobel Prize were awarded for clarity and sanity in a world gone mad, lawyer and journalist Wendy Kaminer would be on her way to Stockholm...her crisp, witty prose is as engaging as it is logical"—*Newsday*

0-201-48914-7 ADDISON-WESLEY........$22.00

William **Kennedy**

O Albany!: An Urban Tapestry

"Kennedy celebrates his hometown in the rich and energetic prose that also distinguishes his fiction"—*Washington Post*

0-14-007416-3 VIKING PB........$12.95

Tracy **Kidder**

Old Friends

0-395-59303-4 HOUGHTON MIFFLIN........$22.95
0-395-71088-X HOUGHTON MIFFLIN PB........$10.95

Richard **Klein**

Eat Fat

0-679-44197-2 PANTHEON........$24.00

Jerzy **Kosinski**

Passing By: Selected Essays, 1960-1991

"This collection will rekindle interest in the mysteries of Kosinski's life and his suicide...Kosinski's vibrant, sexy, questioning voice is fully present"—*The Boston Globe*

0-8021-3423-8 GROVE PB........$12.00

Jane **Kramer**

Europeans

An elegant and witty series of essays by a *New Yorker* contributor. Chapters include "Being German," "Danton and Robespierre," and "Mitterand's Monarchy"

See also **COLD WAR EUROPE** under **EUROPE SINCE 1945** in **WORLD HISTORY AND CURRENT AFFAIRS**

0-374-14939-9 FS&G........$22.95

Wendy **Lesser**, editor

Hiding in Plain Sight: Essays in Criticism and Autobiography

Thirty provocative essays address what Randall Jarrell called "the terrible nakedness" of the critic who must expose his own inner values when standing in judgment on a work of art. Gore Vidal, Harold Brodkey, Susan Sontag, and Amy Tan are just a few of the contributors to this insightful and revelatory collection

1-56279-037-4 MERCURY HOUSE........$21.95

A.J. **Liebling**

Between Meals: An Appetite for Paris

The great journalist on his favorite subjects: wine, food and Paris

See also **AMERICAN FOOD WRITERS** under **AMERICAN COOKERY** under **FOOD** in **FOOD, TRAVEL, AND LEISURE**

0-679-60142-2 MODERN LIBRARY........$12.50
0-86547-236-X NORTH POINT PB........$11.00

A Neutral Corner: Boxing Essays

0-86547-450-8 NORTH POINT........$19.95

Dwight **Macdonald**

Against the American Grain: Essays on the Effects of Mass Culture

Critical essays on politics, literature, film, and popular writing—including the famous "Masscult and Midcult"—from a writer who believes that "a people which loses contact with its past becomes culturally psychotic"

INTRODUCTION BY JOHN SIMON

0-306-80205-8 OLYMPIC PB........$2.98

Discriminations: Essays and Afterthoughts

His last collection, with essays on Hemingway, the Constitution, Vietnam, and Hannah Arendt. "He had that rare gift of always speaking out of his own voice"—Norman Mailer

INTRODUCTION BY NORMAN MAILER

0-306-80252-X DA CAPO PB........$11.95

Peter **Matthiessen**

Indian Country

A harshly critical look at Federal policies toward Native Americans; one official brought suit in an unsuccessful attempt to suppress it

0-14-013023-3 PENGUIN PB $12.95

H.L. **Mencken**

A Choice of Days

Selections from the Sage of Baltimore's autobiographical volumes, including *Newspaper Days*

See also **FIRST-PERSON ACCOUNTS** under **BIOGRAPHIES AND MEMOIRS** under **JOURNALISM** in **PERFORMING ARTS AND MEDIA**

EDITED BY EDWARD L. GALLIGAN

0-394-74760-7 VINTAGE PB $7.95

A Mencken Chrestomathy

0-394-75209-0 VINTAGE PB $19.00

My Life as Author and Editor

0-679-74102-X VINTAGE PB $16.00

Prejudices: A Selection

These essays by the great American journalist include some of his sardonic writings on religion

See also **SKEPTICISM AND ATHEISM** under **WORLD RELIGION** in **RELIGION, SPIRITUALITY, AND PHILOSOPHY**

EDITED BY JAMES T. FARRELL

0-8018-5341-9 JOHNS HOPKINS PB $15.95

A Second Mencken Chrestomathy

EDITED BY TERRY TEACHOUT

0-679-42829-1 KNOPF $30.00

Vintage Mencken

A fine distillation

EDITED BY ALISTAIR COOKE

0-679-72895-3 VINTAGE PB $11.00

H.L. Mencken

Lewis **Mumford**

"Mumford is one of the most sensitive critics of the world we see about us; he has been one of the most energetic, sincere, and completely devoted apologists of modern architecture in both the US and Great Britain; a 20th-century Ruskin, he has educated a whole generation to the understanding of his enthusiasm and the appreciation of his prejudice"—Colin Rowe

The Brown Decades: A Study of the Arts in America, 1865-1895

See also **GENERAL WORKS** under **AMERICAN ARCHITECTURE TO 1900** in **ARCHITECTURE, DESIGN, AND HOMES**

0-486-20200-3 DOVER PB $6.95

Lewis Mumford

From the Ground Up: Observations on Contemporary Architecture, Housing, Highway Building, and Civic Design

0-15-634019-4 HARCOURT BRACE PB $12.95

The Myth of the Machine

Volume 1

Technics and Human Development

0-15-662341-2 HARCOURT BRACE PB $19.95

Volume 2

The Pentagon of Power

0-15-671610-0 HARCOURT BRACE PB $19.95

Sticks and Stones

Investigates the evolution of architectural style in the US and reveals its relationship to broader cultural trends

See also **GENERAL WORKS** under **AMERICAN ARCHITECTURE TO 1900** in **ARCHITECTURE, DESIGN, AND HOMES**

0-486-20202-X DOVER PB $5.95

Albert **Murray**

The Omni-Americans: Some Alternatives to the Folklore of White Supremacy

Usually considered the masterpiece of this erudite and original commentator on the American scene

0-306-80395-X DA CAPO PB $10.95

Camille **Paglia**

Sex, Art, and American Culture

Paglia, called everything from an "intellectual pin-up" to an "academic Rottweiler," lives up to all her reputations in this essay collection. Pieces on MTV, Anita Hill, the decline of education, and more

0-679-74101-1 VINTAGE PB $14.00

Madonna is the true feminist. She exposes the puritanism and suffocating ideology of American feminism, which is stuck in an adolescent whining mode. Madonna has taught young women to be fully female and sexual while still exercising control over their lives. She shows girls how to be attractive, sensual, energetic, ambitious, aggressive, and funny—all at the same time....Madonna has a far profounder vision of sex than do the feminists... Feminism says, "No more masks." Madonna says we are nothing but masks.

SEX, ART, AND AMERICAN CULTURE

Sexual Personae: Art and Decadence from Nefertiti to Emily Dickinson

This long and elaborately stylized discussion of androgyny in art has been admired and reviled, but no one has managed to ignore it. Walter Kendrick of the *Village Voice* calls it "quirky, sometimes outrageous...a down-and-dirty good time"

0-300-04396-1 YALE $40.00

Vamps and Tramps

Number three from the superstar intellectual, on subjects ranging from Madonna to D. H. Lawrence, Catherine MacKinnon, Howard Stern. "Paglia strikes with glorious insight that seduces even the most reluctant or argumentative reader" —*Washington Post Book World.* "Paglia writes with freshness and blithe arrogance"—*Time.* "A conspicuously gifted writer" —*NY Times Book Review*

0-679-75120-3 VINTAGE PB $15.00

Katha **Pollitt**

Reasonable Creatures: Essays on Women and Feminism

A collection of pieces from the prize-winning poet and essayist for *The Nation, New Yorker*, and *New York Times.* "[Pollitt] brings a lively wit and considerable erudition to analyzing topics ranging from date rape to media-bashing of Hillary Clinton, and she consistently sees past the ephemeral quality of specific newsmaking events to locate issues of enduring importance"—*Publishers Weekly*

See also **BIOGRAPHIES, AUTOBIOGRAPHIES, AND LETTERS** under **ANTHOLOGIES OF WOMEN'S WRITING** under **WOMEN'S STUDIES** in **SOCIAL STUDIES**

0-394-57060-X KNOPF $25.00

0-679-76278-7 VINTAGE PB $11.00

Anna **Quindlen**

Thinking Out Loud: On the Personal, Political, the Public, and the Private

Sharp and compassionate observations on the contemporary scene from the Pulitzer Prize-winning columnist and author (*Object Lessons, Living Out Loud*). "Anna Quindlen's beat is life, and she's one hell of a terrific reporter" —Susan Isaacs

See also **THE PRACTITIONERS: A SAMPLER** under **JOURNALISM** in **PERFORMING ARTS AND MEDIA**

0-449-90905-0 FAWCETT PB $12.00

David **Rattray**

How I Became One of the Invisible

A collection of Rattray's essays. His experiences in Mexico in the early sixties are particularly memorable, as is his essay on Holderlin

See also **LITERARY ESSAYISTS AND HISTORIANS** under **LITERARY CRITICISM** in **LITERATURE OF EUROPE, AFRICA, AND ASIA**

0-936756-98-5 SEMIATEXTEI PB........$6.00

Marilynne **Robinson**

Mother Country

A passionate condemnation of the British government's management of Sellafield, a plutonium waste plant on the Cumbrian coast

0-374-21361-5 FS&G........$18.95

Robert **Scheer**

Thinking Tuna Fish, Talking Death: Essays on the Pornography of Power

See also **THE PRESS AND GOVERNMENT** under **JOURNALISM TODAY** under **JOURNALISM** in **PERFORMING ARTS AND MEDIA**

0-8090-9316-2 HILL & WANG........$19.95
0-374-52214-6 NOONDAY PB........$11.95

Sarah **Schulman**

My American History: Lesbian and Gay Life During the Reagan/Bush Years

The prolific young novelist (*Empathy, People In Trouble*), activist (co-founder of Lesbian Avengers), and journalist (for *The Village Voice, The Nation, The New York Times*) has written an intensely personal political memoir of the '80s that chronicles the sometimes lonely progressive struggles of those bleak Reagan-Bush years

See also **BIOGRAPHIES** under **GAY, LESBIAN, AND BISEXUAL STUDIES** in **SOCIAL STUDIES**

See also **HISTORY** under **GAY, LESBIAN, AND BISEXUAL STUDIES** in **SOCIAL STUDIES**

0-415-90852-3 ROUTLEDGE........$49.95
0-415-90853-1 ROUTLEDGE PB........$18.95

Susan **Sheehan**

Is There No Place on Earth for Me?

Winner of the Pulitzer Prize for nonfiction, Sheehan's intense, close-up chronicle of a young woman's struggle with schizoprenia is also a penetrating study of mental health care

See also **SCHIZOPHRENIA** under **DISORDERS AND TREATMENT** under **PSYCHOLOGY** in **SOCIAL STUDIES**

FOREWORD BY ROBERT M. COLES

0-394-71378-8 RANDOM HOUSE PB........$13.00

Gary **Snyder**

Earth House Hold

Essays on poetry and ecology and their interconnections

0-8112-0195-3 NEW DIRECTIONS PB........$8.95

The Real Work: Interviews and Talks

EDITED BY SCOTT MCLEAN

0-8112-0761-7 NEW DIRECTIONS PB........$9.95

Studs **Terkel**

American Dreams: Lost and Found

Terkel practically invented oral history, using the words of ordinary men and women to illustrate the tenor of the times

0-345-32993-7 BALLANTINE PB........$6.99

Coming of Age: The Story of Our Century by Those Who've Lived It

The chronicler of our times has collected an extraordinary panorama of American life and work. Terkel records the stories of a vast and telling variety of Americans—an angry farmer in Nebraska, a New York bank president, trade union leaders, gay activists, artists—to construct a first-rate insight into how we work and live in the last years of our century

1-56584-284-7 NEW PRESS........$25.00
0-312-14573-X ST. MARTIN'S PB........$16.95

Division Street: America

Terkel's first oral history presents the voices of a highly diverse cross-section of Americans

1-56584-075-5 NEW PRESS PB........$12.95

Gore **Vidal**

At Home

Literary and political essays centering on America

0-679-72528-8 VINTAGE PB........$12.00

United States

America's finest, and most fearless, essayist by far, Vidal collects 100 of his best pieces in this indispensable volume. "American Plastic," "Sex Is Politics," "Theodore Roosevelt: An American Sissy," and "Remembering Orson Welles" are just a few of his memorable titles

0-679-41489-4 RANDOM HOUSE........$37.50
0-679-75572-1 RANDOM HOUSE PB........$23.00

Edmund **White**

The Burning Library: Essays

0-679-43475-5 KNOPF........$25.00
0-679-75474-1 VINTAGE PB........$14.00

George F. **Will**

Will, one of our best-known political commentators, has built a reputation based as much on his eloquence as his conservative outlook.

The Morning After: American Successes and Excesses, 1981-1986

See also **CURRENT POLITICAL THOUGHT AND ISSUES** under **AMERICAN POLITICS AND FOREIGN POLICY** in **HISTORY OF THE AMERICAS**

See also **THE REAGAN YEARS** under **US HISTORY, 1945 TO THE PRESENT** in **HISTORY OF THE AMERICAS**

0-02-934430-1 FREE PRESS........$24.95

Richard **Wright**

Black Power

0-06-092566-3 HARPERPERENNIAL PB........$12.00

The Color Curtain

0-87805-748-X MISSISSIPPI PB........$15.95

Pagan Spain

0-06-092565-5 HARPERPERENNIAL PB........$12.00

White Man, Listen!

0-06-092564-7 HARPERPERENNIAL PB........$12.00

Philip **Wylie**

Generation of Vipers

The famous exposé of "Momism" in American culture

1-56478-146-1 DALKEY ARCHIVE PB........$13.95

Literature

See also literary criticism and literary theory and separate sections devoted to national literatures.

Diane **Ackerman**

A Natural History of the Senses

Ackerman, a science-minded poet who previously wrote about aviation in *On Extended Wings*, explores the five senses in highly original fashion. "Rooted in science, enlivened by her own convincing sense of wonder, Ackerman's essays awaken us to a fresh awareness" —*Publishers Weekly*

See also **ESSAYS, MEDITATIONS, AND CLASSICS** under **NATURE STUDY** in **SCIENCE**

0-394-57335-8 RANDOM HOUSE........$22.00
0-679-73566-6 VINTAGE PB........$12.00

Nelson **Algren**

Nonconformity: Writing on Writing

Written in the '50s, *Nonconformity* is the author's meditation on the art of writing. "A certain ruthlessness and a sense of being alienated from society is as essential to creative writing as it is to armed robbery," writes Algren

1-56858-015-0 SEVEN STORIES........$16.00

Dorothy **Allison**

Skin: Talking About Sex, Class, and Literature

Allison delivers a courageous collection of essays that is the nonfiction equivalent to her breathtaking and bestselling *Bastard Out of Carolina*. An "exuberant volume by a writer who exposes even the most painful realities with reverence and awe"—*Publishers Weekly*

1-56341-045-1 FIREBRAND........$28.95
1-56341-044-3 FIREBRAND PB........$14.95

Paul **Auster**

The Art of Hunger

Essays on Kafka, Beckett, Laura Riding, John Ashbery, and others

0-14-017168-1 PENGUIN PB........$12.95

Mary **Austin**

Beyond Borders: The Essays of Mary Austin

EDITED BY REUBEN J. ELLIS

0-8093-1997-7 SOUTHERN ILLINOIS........$24.95

Nicholson **Baker**

The Size of Thoughts

Baker presents a collection of essays that celebrates the joy of the detailed, from library card catalogs to the significance of wine stains on a tablecloth

0-679-43932-3 RANDOM HOUSE........$25.00

U and I: A True Story

A candid recounting of Baker's long, strange fixation on John Updike

0-679-73575-5 VINTAGE PB........$10.00

Mary Catherine **Bateson**

Peripheral Visions

"Much truth streams behind the quiet elegance of these passages," wrote *The New York Times*

Book Review of Bateson's bestseller, *Composing a Life.* In this book she continues her reassessment of achievement and learning, taking us from a Persian garden to a bus full of Tibetan monks, and uses these instances to analyze our habits of inattention and blindness
0-06-092630-9 HARPERPERENNIAL PB $14.00

Mary Catherine Bateson

Saul **Bellow**

It All Adds Up: From a Dim Past to the Uncertain Future

This nonfiction collection of articles, essays, lectures, and travel pieces covers 40 years of an American literary giant. "Sentence by sentence, page by page, Bellow is simply the best writer we have"—*NY Times Book Review*
0-670-85331-3 VIKING $23.95

Elizabeth **Bishop**

The Collected Prose

EDITED BY ROBERT GIROUX
0-374-12628-3 FS&G $17.50
0-374-51855-6 FS&G PB $14.00

Elizabeth Bishop (photo by J. L. Castel)

One Art: Letters

Selected by her editor and friend, Robert Giroux, Bishop's letters vividly create an emotional and intellectual autobiography of one of our finest poets. Bishop's correspondents include such luminaries as Marianne Moore, Randall Jarrell, Edmund Wilson, Mary McCarthy, and her ill-fated lover, Lota Soares, whose life ended in suicide 15 years after their complicated relationship began. "When Elizabeth Bishop's letters are published she will be recognized as not only one of the best, but one of the most prolific writers of our century"—Robert Lowell
0-374-22640-7 FS&G $35.00
0-374-52445-9 NOONDAY PB $16.00

R.P. **Blackmur**

Selected Essays of R.P. Blackmur

Complex discussions of Emily Dickinson, Hart Crane, Henry James, Thomas Mann, and others
See also **THE NEW CRITICISM** under **LITERARY CRITICISM** in **LITERATURE OF EUROPE, AFRICA, AND ASIA**
EDITED BY DENIS DONOGHUE
0-88001-083-5 ECCO $17.50

Neal **Bowers**

Words for the Taking: The Hunt for a Plagiarist

0-393-04007-0 NORTON $17.00

Kay **Boyle** & Robert **McAlmon**

Being Geniuses Together: 1920-1930

A dual account of Paris in the '20s
See also **GENERAL STUDIES: THE 20TH CENTURY** under **AMERICAN LITERATURE: ANTHOLOGIES AND CRITICAL STUDIES**
0-86547-149-5 NORTH POINT PB $13.50

Joseph **Brodsky**

On Grief and Reason

A collection of essays on poetry, on his experience as an exile, and on the future of Europe by the late Poet Laureate of America
0-374-23415-9 FS&G $24.00

William **Bronk**

Vectors and Smoothable Curves: Collected Essays

1-88368-933-3 TALISMAN $37.95
1-88368-932-5 TALISMAN PB $16.95

Kenneth **Burke**

Counter-Statement

0-520-00196-6 CALIFORNIA PB $12.95

Language as Symbolic Action: Essays on Life, Literature, and Method

An "attempt" (in Burke's words) "to define and track down the implications of the term 'symbolic action' and how the marvels of language and literature look when considered from that point of view"
See also **AT MIDCENTURY: CRITICISM IN ENGLISH** under **LITERARY THEORY** in **LITERATURE OF EUROPE, AFRICA, AND ASIA**
0-520-00192-3 CALIFORNIA PB $18.00

Ralph **Ellison**

The Collected Essays of Ralph Ellison

EDITED BY JOHN CALLAHAN
INTRODUCTION BY SAUL BELLOW
0-679-60176-7 MODERN LIBRARY $20.00

Truman **Capote**

A Capote Reader

A varied sampling of Capote's work, including short stories, travel sketches, reportage, and the novellas *The Grass Harp* and *Breakfast at Tiffany's.* "When God hands you a gift, he also hands you a whip"—Truman Capote
See also **SINCE 1945** under **20TH-CENTURY AMERICAN FICTION**
0-394-55647-X RANDOM HOUSE $35.00

Robert **Coles**

A Robert Coles Omnibus

A first-rate, unusually accessible introduction to the writing of the author of the Pulitzer Prize-winning *The Moral Life of Children,* this paperback contains 20 previously uncollected essays from *The Red Wheelbarrow* and *Times of Surrender*
0-87745-411-6 IOWA PB $25.95

That Red Wheelbarrow: Selected Literary Essays

0-87745-208-3 IOWA $28.95

Edward **Dahlberg**

Can These Bones Live?

Original and eccentric essays on American literature
INTRODUCTION BY HERBERT READ
0-8112-0264-X NEW DIRECTIONS $6.50

The Sorrows of Priapus

See also **SINCE 1945** under **20TH-CENTURY AMERICAN FICTION**
ILLUSTRATED BY BEN SHAHN
0-7145-0670-2 MARION BOYARS PB $10.95

Guy **Davenport**

The Hunter Gracchus and Other Papers on Literature and Art

See also **LITERARY ESSAYISTS AND HISTORIANS** under **LITERARY CRITICISM** in **LITERATURE OF EUROPE, AFRICA, AND ASIA**
1-88717-824-4 COUNTERPOINT $25.00

David **Denby**

Great Books: My Adventures with Homer, Rousseau, Woolf and Other Indestructible Writers of the Western World

0-684-80975-3 SIMON & SCHUSTER $30.00

Annie **Dillard**

The Annie Dillard Reader

0-06-092660-0 HARPERPERENNIAL PB $14.00

Living by Fiction

0-06-091544-7 HARPERCOLLINS PB $12.00

The Writing Life

0-06-016156-6 HARPERCOLLINS PB $15.95

Robert **Duncan**

Fictive Certainties

Duncan was always an eloquent explicator of his "open field composition" and its spiritual roots
0-8112-0949-0 NEW DIRECTIONS PB $9.95

T.S. **Eliot**

T.S. Eliot: Essays from the Southern Review

EDITED BY JAMES OLNEY
0-19-818575-8 OXFORD $76.50

Ralph **Ellison**

Shadow and Act

0-394-71716-3 RANDOM HOUSE PB $11.00
0-679-76000-8 VINTAGE PB $13.00

Leslie **Fiedler**

Fiedler on the Roof: Essays on Literature and Jewish Identity

0-87923-949-2 GODINE PB $11.95

Tyranny of the Normal: Essays on Bioethics, Theology, and Myth

The brilliant literary and social critic presents a series of essays united by the common thread of bioethics. Abortion, removal of life support, the role of doctors in our society, old age and Eros—these frequently controversial and always fascinating essays bring freshness to the central social and philosophical questions of our culture

1-56792-003-9 NATIONAL BOOK NETWORK $22.95

F. Scott **Fitzgerald**

The Jazz Age

0-8112-1333-1 NEW DIRECTIONS PB $7.00

John **Gardner**

The Art of Fiction: Notes on Craft for Young Writers

0-679-73403-1 VINTAGE PB $10.00

On Becoming a Novelist

0-06-091126-3 HARPERCOLLINS PB $12.00

On Writers and Writing

Gardner's growing legacy as one of the most influential writing teachers of our time is reaffirmed in this superb collection of essays and reviews. Writing on Bellow, Nabokov, Joyce Carol Oates, John Cheever, and others, he explains his parameters for genuine fiction and deepens our understanding of his own writing

See also **CONTEMPORARY WRITERS ON WRITING** under **LITERARY CRITICISM** in **LITERATURE OF EUROPE, AFRICA, AND ASIA**

INTRODUCTION BY CHARLES JOHNSON

EDITED BY STEWART O'NAN

0-201-62672-1 ADDISON-WESLEY $25.00

William **Gass**

Fiction and the Figures of Life

0-87923-254-4 GODINE PB $11.95

On Being Blue: A Philosophical Inquiry

0-87923-237-4 GODINE PB $10.95

William Gass

The World Within the Word

0-87923-298-6 GODINE PB $11.95

Finding a Form: Essays

See also **CONTEMPORARY WRITERS ON WRITING** under **LITERARY CRITICISM** in **LITERATURE OF EUROPE, AFRICA, AND ASIA**

0-679-44662-1 KNOPF $26.00

Richard **Gilman**

Decadence: The Strange Life of an Epithet

0-374-51553-0 FS&G PB $5.95

Allen **Grossman** & Mark **Halliday**

The Sighted Singer: Two Works on Poetry for Readers and Writers

0-8018-4242-5 JOHNS HOPKINS $55.00

John **Haines**

Living Off the Country: Essays on Poetry and Place

Meditations by a poet living in Alaska

See also **ESSAYS, MEDITATIONS, AND CLASSICS** under **NATURE STUDY** in **SCIENCE**

0-472-06333-2 MICHIGAN PB $13.95

Digging in the soil, picking away the rock, uprooting stumps, I became in time a grower of things sufficient to feed myself and another. Slowly finding my way into the skills of hunter and trapper, I understand what blood and bone, hide and muscle, marrow and sinew really are; not as things read about, but as things touched and handled until they became as familiar to me as my own skin. Land itself came alive for me as it never had before, more alive sometimes than the people who moved about on it. I learned that it is land, *place*, that makes people, provides for them the possibilities they will have of becoming something more than mere lumps of sucking matter.

LIVING OFF THE COUNTRY: ESSAYS ON POETRY AND PLACE

Donald **Hall**

Principal Products of Portugal: Prose Pieces

0-8070-6203-0 BEACON PB $14.00

To Keep Moving: Essays 1959-1969

0-934888-02-7 HOBART & WILLIAM SMITH PB $5.95

Elizabeth **Hardwick**

A View of My Own: Essays on Literature and Society

0-912946-91-1 ECCO PB $6.95

Jim **Harrison**

Just Before Dark

A collection of Harrison's journalism from magazines as diverse as *Sports Illustrated* and *The Nation,* written over the past two decades

0-944439-30-6 CLARK CITY $24.95

Robert **Hayden**

The Collected Prose

EDITED BY FREDERICK GLAYSHER

0-472-06351-0 MICHIGAN PB $13.95

Patrick **Higgins**, editor

A Queer Reader

The New Press offers its contribution to this increasingly popular form of anthology, and as usual stands out above the crowd: Liberace, Christopher Isherwood, Virginia Woolf, James Dean, Susan Sontag, Roy Cohn, River Phoenix, Edmund White—and these are just a few. "Thoughtful, touching, and endearing… [with] huge laughs along the way" —*The Observer* [London]

1-56584-210-3 NEW PRESS $25.00

Irving **Howe**

"Irving Howe was one of the splendors of American culture and intellect, and the splendor was impeccably human"—New Yorker

A Critic's Notebook

Howe's distinguished literary criticism, his essays, and editorial work in the preeminent left-wing journal *Dissent* made him an American treasure. Collected here are the short pieces he left behind at his death in 1993. Including works on Dickens, Eliot, Gissing, Tolstoy, and many more. "A delightful potpourri in which Howe displays an essayist's ease, a critic's incisiveness, and, when necessary, an academic's scholarship"—*Kirkus Reviews*

See also **LITERARY ESSAYISTS AND HISTORIANS** under **LITERARY CRITICISM** in **LITERATURE OF EUROPE, AFRICA, AND ASIA**

INTRODUCTION BY NICHOLAS HOWE

0-15-119949-3 HARCOURT BRACE $27.95

0-15-600257-4 HARCOURT BRACE PB $14.00

Politics and the Novel

0-231-07994-X COLUMBIA $30.00

0-231-07995-8 COLUMBIA PB $16.00

Susan **Howe**

The Birth-Mark: Unsettling the Wilderness in American Literary History

Fiery, revisionist essays on early American literature

0-8195-5256-9 WESLEYAN $40.00

0-8195-6263-7 WESLEYAN PB $16.95

My Emily Dickinson

One-of-a-kind exploration of Dickinson's language and its historical and personal ramifications, written in prose that eschews the norms of academic analysis

See also **TO 1900** under **STUDIES OF INDIVIDUAL AUTHORS (ALPHABETICAL BY SUBJECT)** under **AMERICAN LITERATURE: ANTHOLOGIES AND CRITICAL STUDIES**

0-938190-53-9 NORTH ATLANTIC $25.00

0-938190-52-0 NORTH ATLANTIC PB $9.95

Henry **James**

Literary Criticism

Volume 1: Essays, American and English Writers

0-940450-22-4 LIBRARY OF AMERICA $40.00

Volume 2: European Writers & Prefaces to the New York Edition

0-940450-23-2 LIBRARY OF AMERICA $32.50

Randall **Jarrell**

No Other Book

Covering, in three parts, Jarrell's essays on poetry, on fiction, and on general subjects, the essays of *No Other Book* fully justify Robert Lowell's description of Jarrell as "a critic of genius"

EDITED BY BRAD LEITHAUSER

0-06-118012-2 HARPERCOLLINS $27.50

Poetry and the Age

0-912946-70-9 NORTON PB $8.50

Barbara **Kingsolver**

High Tide in Tucson: Essays from Now or Forever

A scientist's eye and a poet's voice characterize the author in this collection of 26 new essays about family, community, and the natural world. "Possessed of an extravagantly gifted narrative voice, Kingsolver blends a fierce and abiding moral vision with benevolent and concise humor. Her medicine is meant for the head, the heart, and the soul"—*NY Times Book Review*

0-06-017291-6 HARPERCOLLINS $22.00
0-7862-0630-6 THORNDIKE $25.95

Galway **Kinnell**

Walking Down the Stairs: Selections from Interviews

0-472-52530-1 MICHIGAN PB $13.95

Seymour **Krim**

What's this Cat's Story?: The Best of Seymour Krim

In the literary underground of the '50s and '60s, Seymour Krim was one of the electric presences, a keen observer of the scene with a flair for unrestrained self-revelation. His writings, long unavailable, evoke the energies of an entire era

EDITED BY PEGGY BROOKS

1-55778-470-1 PARAGON $21.95

Maxine **Kumin**

To Make a Prairie: Essays on Poets, Poetry, and Country Living

0-472-06306-5 MICHIGAN PB $13.95

Women, Animals, and Vegetables: Essays & Stories

This new prose collection by the Pulitzer Prize-winning poet offers stories and essays harvested from 17 years living on a New Hampshire farm. "Kumin's practical yet sensual New England reflections are a gift to any lover of the country"—*NY Times Book Review*

0-393-03655-3 NORTON $25.00
0-86538-084-8 ONTARIO REVIEW $12.95

Anne **Lamott**

Bird by Bird: Some Instructions on Writing and Life

0-385-48001-6 ANCHOR PB $11.95

Sara **Lawrence-Lightfoot**

I've Known Rivers: Lives of Loss and Liberation

"An invigorating and inspiring human document that adds depth to contemporary understanding…of the black professional class"—*NY Times*

0-14-024970-2 PENGUIN PB $14.95

Alan **Lightman**

Dance for Two: Essays

In a collection of essays from the author of *Einstein's Dreams*, the physics and writing teacher from MIT offers a glimpse into the creative compulsions of his two disciplines

0-679-75877-1 PANTHEON PB $12.00

Robert **Lowell**

Collected Prose

0-374-52267-7 NOONDAY PB $14.95

Norman **Mailer**

Advertisements for Myself

A dissection of Mailer by Mailer in the form of excerpts from, and criticisms of, all of his early works

See also **SINCE 1945** under **20TH-CENTURY AMERICAN FICTION**

0-674-00590-2 HARVARD PB $15.95

The Armies of the Night: History As a Novel/The Novel As History

The story of the author's 1968 march on the Pentagon with a cast including Robert Lowell, Dwight Macdonald, and the fugs

0-452-27279-3 PLUME PB $11.95

Oscar **Mandel**

The Book of Elaborations

0-8112-1023-5 NEW DIRECTIONS PB $12.95

Harry **Mathews**

Immeasurable Distances: The Collected Essays

0-932499-43-0 LAPIS $35.00

Twenty Lines a Day

The title was Stendhal's prescription for writers, and Mathews follows it to the letter, giving us a map of his gifts and preoccupations

0-916583-41-4 DALKEY ARCHIVE PB $8.95

Peter **Matthiessen**

The Tree Where Man Was Born

0-14-023934-0 PENGUIN PB $12.95

William **Maxwell**

The Outermost Dream: Essays and Reviews

0-394-57443-5 KNOPF $19.95

Mary **McCarthy**

The Writing on the Wall & Other Literary Essays

0-15-698390-7 HARCOURT BRACE PB $4.95

Paul **Metcalf**

Collected Works, 1956-1976

includes *Genoa, Apalache, The Middle Passage,* and other works

INTRODUCTION BY GUY DAVENPORT

1-56689-050-0 COFFEE HOUSE $35.00

Genoa

A classic of literary experiment, first published in 1965. Metcalf uses a collage technique to mix together many stories fictional and historical: his own life, that of his great-grandfather Herman Melville, and the influence of Christopher Columbus on Melville. The author writes: "Because of my relation to him, Melville was the monkey on my back…and I could never come to terms with myself until relieved of him. Much of the monstrosity, the 'telling of wonders' in *Genoa,* is withdrawal symptom"

0-8263-1300-0 NEW MEXICO PB $14.95

Henry **Miller**

The Books in My Life

Miller celebrates a mixed bag of favorites: H. Rider Haggard, Blaise Cendrars, Jean Giono, Marie Corelli, Jakob Wassermann, and others

0-8112-0108-2 NEW DIRECTIONS PB $11.95

The Cosmological Eye

The first book by Miller that an American publisher dared to print, this is a quintessential collection of stories, essays, and musings

0-8112-0110-4 NEW DIRECTIONS PB $12.95

Henry Miller on Writing

EDITED BY THOMAS H. MOORE

0-8112-0112-0 NEW DIRECTIONS PB $9.95

The Henry Miller Reader

Arranged by themes—"Places," "Stories," "Literary Essays," "Portraits," and "The Man Himself"—this selection from numerous books across many years reveals the underlying unity of the "single, endless autobiography" that is Miller's life work

EDITED BY LAWRENCE DURRELL

0-8112-0111-2 NEW DIRECTIONS PB $12.95

Stand Still Like the Hummingbird

Stories and essays including "Money and How It Gets That Way," "The Angel is My Watermark," and "First Love"

0-8112-0322-0 NEW DIRECTIONS PB $9.95

The Time of the Assassins: A Study of Rimbaud

"In Rimbaud I see myself as a mirror" —Henry Miller

0-8112-0115-5 NEW DIRECTIONS PB $8.95

The Wisdom of the Heart

Writings "from the heart" including "Reflections on Writing," "Balzac and His Double," "The Alcoholic Veteran with the Washboard Cranium," and "Creative Death"

0-8112-0116-3 NEW DIRECTIONS PB $10.95

Toni **Morrison**

Playing in the Dark

A powerful long essay on American literature and the influence of blackness on white writing. "Expressed with eloquence and fervor" —*NY Times Book Review*

0-674-67377-8 HARVARD $14.95
0-919627-83-8 QUARRY PB $12.95

Larry **Neal**

Visions of a Liberated Future

A posthumous collection of poetry and essays

0-938410-77-6 THUNDER'S MOUTH PB $10.95

Alicia **Ostriker**

Writing Like a Woman

0-472-06347-2 MICHIGAN PB $13.95

Cynthia **Ozick**

Fame and Folly: Essays

Many of the great Ozick essays here collected center on the perilous intersection of writers' lives with the public. Thus T.S. Eliot sympathizes with fascists, Isaac Babel rides with Red Cossacks, and Salman Rushdie is the victim of bitter public controversy

0-679-44690-7 KNOPF $26.00

Walker **Percy**

The Message in the Bottle

Philosophical reflections on language

0-374-51338-4 FS&G PB $14.00

Ezra **Pound**

ABC of Reading

The "Ezraversity" at work, laying down how and what to read, from Sappho to Laforgue

See also **THE MODERNIST REVOLUTION** under **LITERARY CRITICISM** in **LITERATURE OF EUROPE, AFRICA, AND ASIA**

0-8112-0151-1 NEW DIRECTIONS PB $9.95

Ezra Pound

Guide to Kulchur

See also **THE MODERNIST REVOLUTION** under **LITERARY CRITICISM** in **LITERATURE OF EUROPE, AFRICA, AND ASIA**

0-8112-0156-2 NEW DIRECTIONS PB $12.95

Literary Essays

Essays carefully selected to show the evolution of Pound's aesthetic

See also **THE MODERNIST REVOLUTION** under **LITERARY CRITICISM** in **LITERATURE OF EUROPE, AFRICA, AND ASIA**

0-8112-0157-0 NEW DIRECTIONS PB $13.95

Pavannes and Divagations

0-8112-0575-4 NEW DIRECTIONS PB $9.95

Selected Prose, 1909-1965

See also **THE MODERNIST REVOLUTION** under **LITERARY CRITICISM** in **LITERATURE OF EUROPE, AFRICA, AND ASIA**

EDITED BY WILLIAM COOKSON

0-8112-0574-6 NEW DIRECTIONS PB $12.95

Carl **Rakosi**

The Collected Prose

Rakosi's aphorisms have the same balance and wit as his poetry

0-915032-21-X

NATIONAL POETRY FOUNDATION PB $12.95

Kenneth **Rexroth**

Classics Revisited

Brief and lively essays on 60 literary classics, from *The Iliad* and *The Mahabharata* to the *Goncourt Journals* and *Huckleberry Finn*. "The talk is expansive, linking the archaic and the immediate…The books he loved he saw as emanations of living feelings, lines of communication miraculously kept open" —*Village Voice*

AFTERWORD BY BRADFORD MORROW

0-8112-0988-1 NEW DIRECTIONS PB $10.95

More Classics Revisited

The subjects include St. Thomas Aquinas, Ssuma Ch'ien's *Records of the Grand Historian of China*, and *Robinson Crusoe*

EDITED BY BRADFORD MORROW

0-8112-1083-9 NEW DIRECTIONS PB $10.95

World Outside the Window: The Selected Essays of Kenneth Rexroth

Twenty-seven essays written over 40 years by an extraordinarily versatile talent. "To define strangeness with no strain is the peculiar province of art; and it is as a master of this great art that Kenneth Rexroth defines and defends our earth for us"—*NY Times*

EDITED BY BRADFORD MORROW

0-8112-1025-1 NEW DIRECTIONS PB $12.95

Adrienne **Rich**

Lies, Secrets and Silence: Selected Prose, 1966-1978

Of the title essay of this collection: "An indispensable historical document of the women's movement"—Mary Daly

See also **FEMINIST CRITICISM** under **LITERARY THEORY** in **LITERATURE OF EUROPE, AFRICA, AND ASIA**

0-393-00942-4 NORTON PB $6.95

Laura **Riding**

Four Unposted Letters to Catherine

These four letters are the American equivalent of Rilke's *Letters To A Young Poet.* Written in the '30s to the eight-year-old daughter of Nancy Nicholson and Robert Graves, they explain the difference between learning and knowing, the value of thinking, and of not showing off

See also **SINCE 1945** under **20TH-CENTURY AMERICAN FICTION**

0-89255-192-5 PERSEA $15.00

Lynne Sharon **Schwartz**

Ruined by Reading: A Life in Books

0-8070-7082-3 BEACON $18.00

Duncan **Smith**

The Age of Oil

A psychoanalytic and linguistic critique of American pop culture. A fresh, witty comment on the pervasiveness of cars and oil in our society, and other topics

0-9616193-5-X SLATE PB $5.95

Gertrude **Stein**

How to Write

What is a sentence and what is a paragraph and why they are not the same and other matters

1-55713-204-6 SUN & MOON PB $12.95

Paris France

An affectionate memoir of Stein's adopted country

See also **FROM THE TURN OF THE CENTURY TO WORLD WAR II** under **20TH-CENTURY AMERICAN FICTION**

0871401600 LIVERIGHT PB $10.00

0-87140-231-9 NORTON PB $8.95

Louis **Sullivan**

Kindergarten Chats and Other Writings

In which Sullivan's theories about architecture, art, education, and life in general are presented in the classical form of dialogues or "chats" between an architect and a novice

See also **20TH-CENTURY INDIVIDUAL ARCHITECTS** under **20TH-CENTURY ARCHITECTURE** in **ARCHITECTURE, DESIGN, AND HOMES**

0-486-23812-1 DOVER PB $7.95

Nathaniel **Tarn**

Views from the Weaving Mountain: Selected Essays in Poetics and Anthropology

See also **POETRY** under **LITERARY CRITICISM** in **LITERATURE OF EUROPE, AFRICA, AND ASIA**

0-8263-1282-9 NEW MEXICO PB $19.95

Alexander **Theroux**

The Primary Colors

Three essays concerning color and its relation to literature

0-8050-4701-8 HOLT PB $11.00

The Secondary Colors

Reflections on literary works from *Moby Dick* to *A Clockwork Orange*, Mr.Spock's green blood, and Ted Williams's green eyes. "In an age of fifteen-minute foghorn fame, Theroux's voice is a silver trumpet. To neglect it is to miss out on a determining strain of that strong music Whitman would insist validated America"—James McCourt

0-8050-4458-2 HOLT $19.95

John **Updike**

Hugging the Shore

A generous collection of Updike's criticism, showing the curiosity and enthusiasm that make him an exemplary book reviewer

0-88001-398-2 ECCO PB $18.00

Odd Jobs: Essays and Criticism

Wide-ranging essays that once again display Updike's gifts as essayist and reviewer, as he tackles such disparate subjects as the Gospel of Matthew, Ted Williams, Gabriel García Màrquez, and contemporary fiction from Saudi Arabia and Albania

0-679-40414-7 KNOPF $35.00

Diane **Wakoski**

Towards a New Poetry

0-472-06307-3 MICHIGAN PB $13.95

David Foster **Wallace**

A Supposedly Fun Thing I'll Never Do Again: Essays and Ruminations

0-316-91989-6 LITTLE, BROWN $23.95

Eliot **Weinberger**

Outside Stories, 1987-1991

Salman Rushdie, Atlantis, Pol Pot, Chinese poetry, and much else. "His writing is passionate and clear"—*Boston Globe*

0-8112-1221-1 NEW DIRECTIONS PB $10.95

Works on Paper

Highly original takes on everything from tigers to nuclear war

0-8112-1001-4 NEW DIRECTIONS PB $9.95

Eliot **Weinberger**

Written Reaction: Poetics, Politics, Polemics, 1979-1995

1-56886-027-7 MARSILIO PB $12.95

E.B. **White**

Essays of E.B. White

A classic culled from 50 years, by a superb craftsman and master of English prose

0-06-090662-6 HARPERCOLLINS PB $13.50

One Man's Meat

A collection of White's essays for *Harper's*, written from his saltwater farm in Maine

0-06-091081-X HARPERCOLLINS PB $17.00

Tennessee **Williams**

Where I Live: Selected Essays

EDITED BY BOB WOODS AND CHRISTINE R. DAY

0-8112-0706-4 NEW DIRECTIONS PB $9.95

William Carlos **Williams**

In the American Grain

Meditations on American history and its myths, including chapters on Cotton Mather, Daniel Boone, Abraham Lincoln, and the conquest of Mexico

See also **THE MODERNIST REVOLUTION** under **LITERARY CRITICISM** in **LITERATURE OF EUROPE, AFRICA, AND ASIA**

0-8112-0230-5 NEW DIRECTIONS PB $10.95

William Carlos Williams (photo by John D. Schiff)

Selected Essays

0-8112-0235-6 NEW DIRECTIONS PB $12.95

Edmund **Wilson**

The American Earthquake

A chronicle of the Roaring Twenties, the Great Depression, and the dawn of the New Deal. Many consider this collection of social reporting one of Wilson's most important books

0-306-80696-7 DACAPO PB $17.95

Axel's Castle: A Study in the Imaginative Literature of 1870-1930

"Edmund Wilson was the first American critic to show that a single impulse persisted through eighty years of quarreling doctrines and self-devouring schools...His book was extraordinarily illuminating. Nobody before him had written a better exposition of Yeats, Joyce, Proust" —Malcolm Cowley

See also **LITERARY ESSAYISTS AND HISTORIANS** under **LITERARY CRITICISM** in **LITERATURE OF EUROPE, AFRICA, AND ASIA**

0-679-60233-X MODERN LIBRARY $16.50

The Fifties: From Notebooks and Diaries of the Period

"Contains some fine, brief intellectual portraiture—of Cyril Connolly, T.S. Eliot, Isaiah Berlin, André Malraux, W.H. Auden—of the sort one hopes for from the journals of literary men"—*NY Times*

EDITED WITH AN INTRODUCTION BY LEON EDEL

0-374-52066-6 FS&G PB $12.95

The Forties: From Notebooks and Diaries of the Period

EDITED BY LEON EDEL

0-374-51835-1 FS&G PB $9.25

The Sixties

"Of all critics of our time, the wisest and justest and best"— *Washington Post*

0-374-26554-2 FS&G $35.00

0-374-52414-9 NOONDAY PB $19.00

Upstate

0-8156-2499-9 SYRACUSE PB $15.95

From the Uncollected Edmund Wilson

EDITED BY JANET GROTH & DAVID CASTRONOVO

0-8214-1127-6 OHIO $32.95

The Shores of Light: A Literary Chronicle of the 1920s and 1930s

Essays on F. Scott Fitzgerald, Edna St. Vincent Millay, Sherwood Anderson, and Gertrude Stein in "a general history of the culture of a recklessly unspecialized era, when minds and imaginations were exploring in all directions" (Edmund Wilson)

See also **LITERARY ESSAYISTS AND HISTORIANS** under **LITERARY CRITICISM** in **LITERATURE OF EUROPE, AFRICA, AND ASIA**

INTRODUCTION BY DANIEL AARON

0-930350-68-5 NORTHEASTERN PB $16.95

The Thirties: From Notebooks and Diaries of the Period

EDITED BY LEON EDEL

0-374-27572-6 FS&G $17.50

Edmund Wilson

William **Zinsser**, editor

Paths of Resistance: The Art and Craft of the Political Novel

Revealing and varied essays from five masters of the genre: Robert Stone, Isabel Allende, Charles McCarry, Marge Piercy, and Gore Vidal. "Any novel of serious intent argues for the significance of its story. I think the key is to establish a connection between political forces and individual lives"—Robert Stone

0-395-51426-6 HOUGHTON MIFFLIN $19.95

Louis **Zukofsky**

Prepositions: The Collected Critical Essays of Louis Zukofsky

FOREWORD BY HUGH KENNER

0-520-04361-8 CALIFORNIA PB $10.95

Anthologies

Robert **Atwan** & Geoffrey C. **Ward**, editors

The Best American Essays 1996

0-395-71757-4 HOUGHTON MIFFLIN $24.95

0-395-71756-6 HOUGHTON MIFFLIN PB $12.95

Robert **Atwan** & Jamaica **Kincaid**, editors

The Best American Essays, 1995

This year's crop brings together pieces by Edward Hoagland, Grace Paley, William Gass, Joseph Brodsky, and many other exemplars of the essay form that appeared in magazines ranging from *The New Yorker* to *The Alaska Quarterly Review*

SERIES EDITED BY ROBERT ATWAN

0-395-69183-4 HOUGHTON MIFFLIN PB $12.95

Robert **Atwan** & Tracy **Kidder**, editors

The Best American Essays, 1994

"Essays that draw us into the quietly entertaining pleasures of contemplating what makes humans tick"—*Kirkus Reviews.* Kidder includes John McPhee, Jamaica Kincaid, Stanley Elkin, Louise Erdrich, David Denby, Ian Frazier, Nicholson Baker, Vicki Hearne...."If you've ever wanted to read essays and hesitated about where to begin, here is the place" — *Winston-Salem Journal*

0-395-69254-7 HOUGHTON MIFFLIN $24.95

0-395-69253-9 HOUGHTON MIFFLIN PB $11.95

Robert **Atwan** & Joseph **Epstein**, editors

The Best American Essays, 1993

0-395-63648-5 TICKNOR & FIELDS PB $12.95

Robert **Atwan** & Susan **Sontag**, editors

The Best American Essays, 1992

The essay is one of the liveliest genres in American writing, as this new collection amply demonstrates. Sontag has assembled a remarkable range of talent that includes Joan Didion, William Gass, John Updike, and Elizabeth Hardwick

0-395-59935-0 HOUGHTON MIFFLIN $21.95

0-395-59936-9 HOUGHTON MIFFLIN PB $11.95

Annie **Dillard** & Cort **Conley**, editors

Modern American Memoirs

0-06-017040-9 HARPERCOLLINS $27.50

Eric **Liu**

Next: Young American Writers on the New Generation

0-393-03585-9 NORTON........$21.00
0-393-31191-0 NORTON PB........$12.95

Wendy **Martin**, editor

The Beacon Book of Essays by Contemporary American Women

Publishers Weekly called this an "engrossing and lively collection" that features essays by women of differing ethnic backgrounds, religion, class, age, and sexual orientation. Included are Mary McCarthy, Adrienne Rich, Alice Walker, Margaret Mead, Mary Gordon, Carolyn Coma, Susan Faludi, Betty Friedan, and others

See also **ANTHOLOGIES OF WOMEN'S WRITING** under **WOMEN'S STUDIES** in **SOCIAL STUDIES**

0-8070-6346-0 BEACON........$26.00

Sara **Nickles**

Drinking, Smoking, & Screwing

...an anthology of hedonistic writing

0-8118-0784-3 CHRONICLE PB........$11.95

Gloria **Norris**, editor

The Seasons of Women: An Anthology

See also **ANTHOLOGIES OF WOMEN'S WRITING** under **WOMEN'S STUDIES** in **SOCIAL STUDIES**

0-393-03860-2 NORTON........$27.50

Joyce Carol **Oates**, editor

American Gothic Tales

An anthology

0-452-27489-3 PLUME PB........$14.95

Robert **Pack** & Jay **Parini**, editors

The Bread Loaf Anthology of Contemporary American Essays

0-87451-475-4 NEW ENGLAND PB........$19.95

Robert B. **Silvers**, Barbara **Epstein** & Rea S. **Hederman**, editors

The First Anthology: Thirty Years of the New York Review of Books

The preeminent American journal of politics and culture celebrates its 30th anniversary with a compendium of some of its finest pieces. Included are such landmark essays as Elizabeth Hardwick's report on the Watts Riots of LA in 1966, Gore Vidal's memorable portrait of Amelia Earhart, Hannah Arendt's "Reflections on Violence" as well as Joseph Brodsky, Robert Hughes, Dwight Macdonald, Susan Sontag, Isaiah Berlin, and more. A touchstone for the ideas that have shaped the past three decades, and an indispensable tutorial on the contemporary world

See also **THE PRACTITIONERS: A SAMPLER** under **JOURNALISM** in **PERFORMING ARTS AND MEDIA**

0-940322-01-3 NEW YORK REVIEW........$27.50
0-940322-02-1 NEW YORK REVIEW PB........$12.95

Ben **Sonnenberg**, editor

Performance and Reality: Essays from Grand Street

0-8135-1409-6 RUTGERS PB........$16.95

The Library of America

Henry **Adams**

History of the United States During the Administrations of Jefferson and Madison

See also **THE NEW NATION** under **US HISTORY TO THE CIVIL WAR** in **HISTORY OF THE AMERICAS**

0-940450-35-6 LIBRARY OF AMERICA........$40.00

The United States were supposed to have stabbed England in the back at the moment when her hands were tied, when her existence was in the most deadly peril and her anxieties were most heavy. England never could forgive treason so base and cowardice so vile. That Madison had been from the first a tool and accomplice of Bonaparte was thenceforward so fixed an idea in British history that time could not shake it. Indeed, so complicated and so historical had the causes of war become that no one even in America could explain or understand them, while Englishmen could see only that America required England as the price of peace to destroy herself by abandoning her naval power, and that England preferred to die fighting rather than to die by her own hand. The American party in England was extinguished; no further protest was heard against the war; and the British people thought moodily of revenge.
HISTORY OF THE UNITED STATES DURING THE ADMINISTRATIONS OF JEFFERSON AND MADISON

History of the United States During the Administrations of Jefferson and Madison

"All things considered, I suspect that it is the greatest historical work in English, with the probable exception of *The Decline and Fall of the Roman Empire*...The history is penetrated with precise intelligence in all its parts: it is in this quality, I think, that it surpasses any historical masterpiece with which I am acquainted"—Yvor Winters

0-940450-34-8 LIBRARY OF AMERICA........$35.00

Novels and Other Writings

Contains *The Education of Henry Adams, Mont Saint-Michel and Chartres*, and the novels *Democracy* and *Esther*

0-940450-12-7 LIBRARY OF AMERICA........$35.00

Bernard **Bailyn**, editor

The Debate on the Constitution

Employing newspaper articles, pamphlets, and letters, this collection captures the energy and the eloquence of Franklin, Madison, Jefferson, Washington, Patrick Henry, and other less recognized voices as they took part in the "bloodless revolution" that formed the government of the United States. Each volume includes the full texts of the Declaration of Independence, the Articles of Confederation, and the Constitution. "For Americans this is Shakespeare, and more. Not only is it wonderful writing, it is wonderful thinking"
—Nina Totenberg

Volume 1
September 17, 1787 to January 12, 1788

0-940450-42-9 LIBRARY OF AMERICA........$35.00

Volume 2
January 14, 1788 to August 9, 1788

0-940450-81-X LIBRARY OF AMERICA BOXED SET$70.00
0-940450-64-X LIBRARY OF AMERICA........$35.00

William **Bartram**

Travels & Other Writings

0-883011-11-6 LIBRARY OF AMERICA........$37.50

Willa **Cather**

Early Novels and Stories

Includes *O Pioneers!*, *Song of the Lark*, *My Antonia*, and *One of Ours*. "...To reread Cather is to rediscover an arresting chapter in the national past"—*LA Times*

EDITED BY SHARON O'BRIEN

0-940450-39-9 LIBRARY OF AMERICA........$35.00

Later Novels

Includes *A Lost Lady*, *The Professor's House*, *Death Comes for the Archbishop*, *Shadows on the Rock*, *Lucy Gayheart*, and *Sapphira and the Slave Girl*

EDITED BY SHARON O'BRIEN

0-940450-52-6 LIBRARY OF AMERICA........$32.50

Stories, Poems, and Other Writings

Includes the novellas *Alexander's Bridge*, and *My Mortal Enemy*, four short story collections, occassional pieces, critical essays, and Cather's only book of poetry. "A treasury of riches, containing much that has been difficult to find"—*Chicago Tribune*

EDITED BY SHARON O'BRIEN

0-940450-71-2 LIBRARY OF AMERICA........$35.00

James Fenimore **Cooper**

The Leatherstocking Tales, Volume 1

The five novels which make up the *Leatherstocking Tales* follow the exploits of Natty Bumppo from the French and Indian Wars to the early nineteenth century. They are here presented in their order of composition in two volumes. Volume One includes *The Pioneers, The Last of the Mohicans*, and *The Prairie*

0-940450-20-8 LIBRARY OF AMERICA........$32.50

The Leatherstocking Tales, Volume 2

Volume Two includes *The Pathfinders* and *The Deerslayer*

0-940450-21-6 LIBRARY OF AMERICA........$32.50

Sea Tales

Includes the romantic adventures *The Pilot* and *The Red Rover*

0-940450-70-4 LIBRARY OF AMERICA........$35.00

Stephen **Crane**

Prose and Poetry

Includes *Maggie: A Girl of the Streets*, *The Red Badge of Courage*, *George's Mother*, *The Third Violet*, journalism, tales and sketches, and poetry. "Crane's journalism and war dispatches...disclose the complex interactions of history, journalism, and fiction"—*Boston Globe*

EDITED BY J.C. LEVENSON

0-940450-17-8 LIBRARY OF AMERICA........$35.00

John **Dos Passos**

U.S.A.

1-88301-114-0 LIBRARY OF AMERICA $40.00

Frederick **Douglass**

Autobiographies

These works help to illustrate the life of a slave who became an advisor to presidents, minister to Haiti, and one of the most powerful African-Americans in history. Includes *Narrative of the Life of Frederick Douglass, an American Slave*; *My Bondage and My Freedom*, and *Life and Times*

EDITED BY HENRY LOUIS GATES, JR.

0-940450-79-8 LIBRARY OF AMERICA $35.00

Theodore **Dreiser**

Sister Carrie, Jennie Gerhardt & Twelve Men

Dreiser's first two great novels, along with the non-fiction sketches *Twelve Men*

EDITED BY RICHARD LEHAN

0-940450-41-0 LIBRARY OF AMERICA $35.00

W.E.B. **DuBois**

Writings

This volume contains DuBois' most important historical and autobiographical writings, including *The Suppression of the African Slave-Trade, The Souls of Black Folk,* and *Dusk of Dawn*

0-940450-33-X LIBRARY OF AMERICA $35.00

The history of the American Negro is the history of this strife—this longing to attain self-conscious manhood, to merge his double self into a better and truer self. In this merging he wishes neither of the older selves to be lost. He would not Africanize America, for America has too much to teach the world and Africa. He would not bleach his Negro soul in a flood of white Americanism, for he knows that Negro blood has a message for the world. He simply wishes to make it possible for a man to be both a Negro and an American, without being cursed and spit upon by his fellows, without having the doors of Opportunity closed roughly in his face.

WRITINGS

Ralph Waldo **Emerson**

Collected Poems and Translations

The most comprehensive and accurate edition of Emerson's verse and his translations, including versions of Rumi, Hafiz, Dante, and others

EDITED BY HAROLD BLOOM & PAUL KANE

0-940450-28-3 LIBRARY OF AMERICA $35.00

Essays and Lectures

Includes *Nature: Addresses and Lectures, Essays: First and Second Series, Representative Men, English Traits, The Conduct of Life,* addresses, lectures, and uncollected prose

0-940450-15-1 LIBRARY OF AMERICA $30.00

William **Faulkner**

Novels, 1930-1935

The first volume in the Library of America's collected Faulkner includes *As I Lay Dying*, *Sanctuary*, *Light in August*, and *Pylon*. "At last readers can enjoy and ponder these works in the form intended by their author. A distinguished addition to a distinctive series"
—*Library Journal*

EDITED BY JOSEPH BLOTNER AND NOAH POLK

0-940450-26-7 LIBRARY OF AMERICA $35.00

Novels, 1936-1940

America's greatest modern novelist at the height of his powers. Includes *Absalom, Absalom!, The Unvanquished, If I Forget Thee, Jerusalem (The Wild Palms),* and *The Hamlet*

EDITED BY JOSEPH BLOTNER AND NOAH POLK

0-940450-55-0 LIBRARY OF AMERICA $35.00

Novels, 1942-1954

This third volume is comprised of *Go Down, Moses*, *Intruder in the Dust*, *Requiem for a Nun*, and *A Fable*, which earned a Pulitzer Prize

EDITED BY JOSEPH BLOTNER AND NOAH POLK

0-940450-85-2 LIBRARY OF AMERICA $35.00

Benjamin **Franklin**

Writings

The most complete one-volume collection ever published of this brilliant public figure, which includes *The Autobiography* and a new edition based on Franklin's manuscript. Also contains *Silence Dogood, Poor Richard's Almanac, Political Satires, Pamphlets, Letters and Bagatelles,* and *Journalism*

0-940450-29-1 LIBRARY OF AMERICA $40.00

Robert **Frost**

Collected Poems, Prose, and Plays

EDITED BY RICHARD POIRIER AND MARK RICHARDSON

1-88301-106-X LIBRARY OF AMERICA $35.00

0-8047-1741-9 STANFORD $47.50

Ulysses S. **Grant**

Memoirs and Selected Letters

Grant's eloquently understated memoirs are an insufficiently recognized American literacy classic. "Perhaps the most revelatory autobiography of high command to exist in any language"—John Keegan

See also **CONFEDERATES AND YANKEES** under **THE LEADERS** under **THE CIVIL WAR AND RECONSTRUCTION** in **HISTORY OF THE AMERICAS**

0-940450-58-5 LIBRARY OF AMERICA $35.00

Nathaniel **Hawthorne**

"For in spite of all the Indian-summer sunlight on the hither side of Hawthorne's soul, the other side—like the dark half of the physical sphere—is shrouded in a blackness, ten times black… Whether there really lurks in him, perhaps unknown to himself, a touch of Puritanic gloom,—this, I cannot altogether tell. Certain it is, however, that this great power of blackness in him derives its force from its appeals to that Calvinistic sense of Innate Depravity and Original Sin, from whose visitations, in some shape or other, no deeply thinking mind is always and wholly free free."—Herman Melville reviewing Hawthorne's Mosses from an Old Manse *in 1850*

Novels

Includes *Fanshawe, The Scarlet Letter, House of the Seven Gables, The Blithedale Romance,* and *The Marble Faun*

0-940450-08-9 LIBRARY OF AMERICA $37.50

Tales and Sketches

The most complete collection of Hawthorne's short fiction ever assembled

0-940450-03-8 LIBRARY OF AMERICA $37.50

John **Hollander**, editor

American Poetry: The Nineteenth Century

Gathers 1,000 poems by nearly 150 poets. "For anyone whose love of poems is more than a decade deep, this is essential reading"—*Nation*

Volume 1
Freneau to Whitman

0-940450-60-7 LIBRARY OF AMERICA $35.00

Volume 2
Melville to Stickney, American Indian Poetry, Folk Songs, and Spirituals

0-940450-78-X LIBRARY OF AMERICA $35.00

1-88301-100-0 LIBRARY OF AMERICA BOXED SET$70.00

William Dean **Howells**

Novels, 1875-1886

Includes *A Foregone Conclusion, A Modern Instance, Indian Summer*, and *The Rise of Silas Lapham*. "For those of us who are still able to read novels for pleasure, this is a marvelous book"—Gore Vidal, *NY Review of Books*

0-940450-04-6 LIBRARY OF AMERICA $35.00

Novels, 1886-1888

Includes *The Minister's Charge, April Hopes,* and *Annie Kilburn*."A much neglected writer worth discovering or revisiting"—*Wall Street Journal*

0-940450-51-8 LIBRARY OF AMERICA $35.00

Zora Neale **Hurston**

Novels and Stories

Volume 1 is dedicated to Hurston the fiction writer, and includes her celebrated novel *Their Eyes Were Watching God*.

0-940450-83-6 LIBRARY OF AMERICA $35.00

Folklore, Memoirs, and Other Writings

Volume 2 draws on Hurston's work in anthropology, with her ethnographical work, folklore, memoirs, and selected articles

0-940450-84-4 LIBRARY OF AMERICA $35.00

Samuel **Hynes** and others, editors

Reporting World War II: American Journalism, 1938-1946

Volume 1

1-88301-104-3 LIBRARY OF AMERICA $35.00

Volume 2

1-88301-105-1 LIBRARY OF AMERICA $35.00

Washington **Irving**

Bracebridge Hall, Tales of a Traveler & The Alhambra

0-940450-59-3 LIBRARY OF AMERICA $35.00

History, Tales and Sketches

Includes *Letters of Jonathan Oldstyle Gent., Salmagundi, A History of New York,* and *The Sketch Book*. "His journalism contains delightful observations on the texture of times"
—*Boston Globe*

0-940450-14-3 LIBRARY OF AMERICA $35.00

Henry **James**

Complete Stories, 1892-1898

1-883011-09-4 LIBRARY OF AMERICA $35.00

Complete Stories, 1898-1910
1-883011-10-8 LIBRARY OF AMERICA $35.00

Literary Criticism
Volume 1
Essays, American and English Writers
"Few talents have ever combined a critical intelligence of this order with such luminous prose"—*Boston Globe*
EDITED BY LEON EDEL AND MARK WILSON
0-940450-22-4 LIBRARY OF AMERICA $40.00

Volume 2
European Writers & Prefaces to the New York Edition
0-940450-23-2 LIBRARY OF AMERICA $32.50

Henry James

Novels, 1871-1880
Contains the five early novels: *Watch and War*, *Roderick Hudson*, *The American*, *The Europeans*, and *Confidence*. They appear in their original versions without the changes James made in his later years
EDITED BY WILLIAM T. STAFFORD
0-940450-13-5 LIBRARY OF AMERICA $37.50

Novels, 1881-1886
The three major novels from James's early and middle years: *Washington Square*, *Portrait of a Lady*, and *The Bostonians*. "James beginning to realize the height of his powers"
—*Wall Street Journal*
EDITED BY WILLIAM T. STAFFORD
0-940450-30-5 LIBRARY OF AMERICA $35.00

Novels, 1886-1890
Includes *The Princess Casamassima*, *The Reverberator*, *The Tragic Muse*. "Reminds us of how James can suprise us by speaking directly to our present concerns"—*Chicago Tribune*
EDITED BY DANIEL MARK FOGEL
0-940450-56-9 LIBRARY OF AMERICA $37.50

Travel Writings: The Continent
"There are books in the hundreds ready to tell you where to eat, shop, sleep and be seen; I defy you to name any which will provide better company than these two"—*LA Times*
EDITED BY RICHARD HOWARD
0-940450-77-1 LIBRARY OF AMERICA $35.00

Travel Writings: Great Britain and America
Includes *English Hours*, *The American Scene*, and *Other Travels*
EDITED BY RICHARD HOWARD
0-940450-76-3 LIBRARY OF AMERICA $35.00

William **James**

Writings, 1878-1899
Includes *The Will To Believe and Other Essays in Popular Philosophy*, *Psychology: Briefer Course*, and excerpts from the monumental *Principles of Psychology*
EDITED BY GERALD MEYERS
0-940450-72-0 LIBRARY OF AMERICA $35.00

Writings, 1902-1910
Includes *The Varieties of Religious Experience*, *Pragmatism*, *A Pluralistic Universe*, *The Meaning of Truth*, *Some Problems of Philosophy*, and Essays
EDITED BY BRUCE KUKLICK
0-940450-38-0 LIBRARY OF AMERICA $37.50

One need only shut oneself in a closet and begin to think of the fact of one's being there, of one's queer bodily shape in the darkness (a thing to make children scream at, as Stevenson says), of one's fantastic character and all, to have the wonder steal over the detail as much as over the general fact of being, and to see that it is only familiarity that blunts it. Not only that *anything* should be, but that *this* very thing should be, is mysterious! Philosophy stares, but brings no reasoned solution for from nothing to being there is no logical bridge. From *Some Problems of Philosophy*
WRITINGS 1902-1910

Thomas **Jefferson**

Writings
A comprehensive gathering of Jefferson's remarkably varied writings, including *Autobiography*, *A Summary View of the Rights of British America*, *Public Papers*, *Miscellany*, and a large selection of letters. The letters in particular create a three-dimensional and often surprising portrait. Jefferson envisioned a nation of prosperous farmers who he thought were far more likely than city-dwellers to cultivate the virtues of self-reliance, hard work, moderation, and common sense on which a free society depends
0-940450-16-X LIBRARY OF AMERICA $35.00

Sarah Orne **Jewett**

Novels and Stories
Includes all of Jewett's best fiction including her three novels *Deephaven*, *A Country Doctor*, and *The Country of the Painted Firs*. "Descriptions so sharply etched you want to put them in your pocket like magic pebbles"—*Chicago Tribune*
EDITED BY MICHAEL DAVITT BELL
0-940450-74-7 LIBRARY OF AMERICA $35.00

Sinclair **Lewis**

Main Street & Babbitt
EDITED BY JOHN HERSEY
0-940450-61-5 LIBRARY OF AMERICA $35.00

Abraham **Lincoln**

Speeches and Writings, 1832-1858
A compact, comprehensive presentation of Lincoln's writings. Each volume includes a chronology of the president's life. "The greatest mystery of our most mysterious president is how, with almost no formal education and with no vast reading, he made himself a master of American prose, unique among our statesmen"—Gore Vidal. Includes *Speeches, Letters, and Miscellaneous Writings* and the complete text of *The Lincoln-Douglas Debates*
EDITED BY DON E. FEHRENBACHER
0-940450-43-7 LIBRARY OF AMERICA $35.00

Speeches and Writings, 1859-1865
Includes *Speeches, Letters, and Miscellaneous Writings* and *Presidential Messages and Proclamations*
0-940450-68-2 LIBRARY OF AMERICA BOXED SET $70.00
0-940450-63-1 LIBRARY OF AMERICA $35.00

Jack **London**

Novels and Social Writings
Includes *The People of the Abyss*, *The Road*, *The Iron Heel*, *John Barleycorn*, *Martin Eden*, and other works
EDITED BY DONALD PIZER
0-940450-06-2 LIBRARY OF AMERICA $37.50

Novels and Stories
Includes *The Call of the Wild*, *White Fang*, *The Sea Wolf*, and a selection of short stories
EDITED BY DONALD PIZER
0-940450-05-4 LIBRARY OF AMERICA $35.00

Herman **Melville**

Pierre, Israel Potter, The Confidence-Man & Billy Budd
EDITED BY HARRISON MAYFORD
0-940450-24-0 LIBRARY OF AMERICA $35.00

Redburn, White-Jacket, & Moby-Dick
EDITED BY G. THOMAS TANSELLE
0-940450-09-7 LIBRARY OF AMERICA $35.00

Typee, Omoo, & Mardi
EDITED BY G. THOMAS TANSELLE
0-940450-00-3 LIBRARY OF AMERICA $37.50

Vladimir **Nabokov**

Novels and Memoirs, 1941-1951
1-883011-18-3 LIBRARY OF AMERICA $35.00

Novels, 1955-1962
1-883011-19-1 LIBRARY OF AMERICA $35.00

Novelss, 1969-1974
1-883011-20-5 LIBRARY OF AMERICA $35.00

Frank **Norris**

Novels and Essays
Includes *Vandover and the Brute*, *McTeague*, *The Octopus*, and *Essays*
EDITED BY DONALD PIZER
0-940450-40-2 LIBRARY OF AMERICA $35.00

Flannery **O'Connor**

Collected Works
Includes *Wise Blood*, *A Good Man Is Hard to Find*, *The Violent Bear It Away*, *Everything that Rises Must Converge*, along with letters, essays, and uncollected stories. "Indispensable for the literary scholar and a joy for the general reader…a great book"—*Newsday*
EDITED BY SALLY FITZGERALD
0-940450-37-2 LIBRARY OF AMERICA $35.00

Eugene **O'Neill**

The Complete Plays

The only complete and authoritative edition of all 50 plays

Volume 1: 1913-1920

0-940450-48-8 LIBRARY OF AMERICA $35.00

Volume 2: 1920-1931

0-940450-49-6 LIBRARY OF AMERICA $35.00

Volume 3: 1932-1943

0-940450-50-X LIBRARY OF AMERICA $35.00

Thomas **Paine**

Collected Writings

EDITED BY ERIC FONER

1-883011-03-5 LIBRARY OF AMERICA $35.00

Francis **Parkman**

France and England in North America

Two great empires maneuver for dominance on hostile and unfamiliar terrain; a classic of 19th-century historical writing, despite its obvious biases

Volume 1

Includes *Pioneers of France in the New World, The Jesuits in North America in the Seventeenth Century, La Salle and the Discovery of the Great West,* and *The Old Regime in Canada*

0-940450-10-0 LIBRARY OF AMERICA $32.50

Volume 2

Includes *Count Frontenac* and *New France Under Louis XIV, Montcalm and Wolfe,* and *A Half-Century of Conflict*

0-940450-11-9 LIBRARY OF AMERICA $40.00

The Oregon Trail, The Conspiracy of Pontiac

0-940450-54-2 LIBRARY OF AMERICA $35.00

Edgar Allan **Poe**

Essays and Reviews

This collection shows Poe as a tireless critic and journalist, deeply involved in trying to influence the direction of American literature

0-940450-19-4 LIBRARY OF AMERICA $40.00

Poetry and Tales

EDITED BY PATRICK F. QUINN

0-940450-18-6 LIBRARY OF AMERICA $37.50

William Tecumseh **Sherman**

Memoirs of General W.T. Sherman

"Sherman's story of his march on the South must be one of the most articulate and engrossing ever written by an important general. It creates the appalled suspense of a kind of Grand Guignol horror, as we follow this intrepid and disciplined man, in many ways so sympathetic, going further and further in destructiveness, and recounting the process with the utmost exactitude and without the slightest compunction"—Edmund Wilson

EDITED BY CHARLES ROYSTER

0-940450-65-8 LIBRARY OF AMERICA $35.00

John **Steinbeck**

The Grapes of Wrath & Other Writings, 1936-1941

1-883011-15-9 LIBRARY OF AMERICA $35.00

Novels and Stories, 1932-1937

EDITED BY GARRISON KEILLOR

1-883011-22-1 LIBRARY OF AMERICA $35.00

Harriet Beecher **Stowe**

Three Novels

Includes *Uncle Tom's Cabin, The Minister's Wooing,* and *Oldtown Folks*

0-940450-01-1 LIBRARY OF AMERICA $40.00

Henry David **Thoreau**

A Week, Walden, The Maine Woods & Cape Cod

"In reading Henry Thoreau's journal, I am very sensible of the vigor of his constitution. That oaken strength which I noted whenever he walked or worked or surveyed wood lots, the same unhesitating hand with which a field-laborer accosts a piece of work which I should shun as a waste of strength, Henry shows in his literary task…In reading him, I find the same thought, the same spirit that is in me, but he takes a step beyond, & illustrates by excellent images that which I should have conveyed in a sleepy generality. 'Tis as if I went into a gymnasium, & saw youths leap, climb, & swing with a force unapproachable—though their feats are only continuations of my initial grapplings & jumps"—Ralph Waldo Emerson in his journal, June 1863

0-940450-27-5 LIBRARY OF AMERICA $30.00

James **Thurber**

Writings and Drawings

The most comprehensive collection of the works of this American humorist available. Includes over 100 pieces and nearly 500 cartoons and drawings. "A comic continent unto itself" —Roy Blount, Jr.

EDITED BY GARRISON KEILLOR

1-883011-22-1 LIBRARY OF AMERICA $35.00

Mark **Twain**

Collected Tales, Sketches, Speeches, and Essays, 1852-1890

0-940450-36-4 LIBRARY OF AMERICA $35.00

Collected Tales, Sketches, Speeches, and Essays, 1891-1910

0-940450-73-9 LIBRARY OF AMERICA $35.00

Historical Romances

0-940450-82-8 LIBRARY OF AMERICA $35.00

The Innocents Abroad & Roughing It

0-940450-25-9 LIBRARY OF AMERICA $30.00

Mississippi Writings

Includes *The Adventures of Tom Sawyer, Life on the Mississippi, Adventures of Huckleberry Finn, and Pudd'nhead Wilson*

0-940450-07-0 LIBRARY OF AMERICA $30.00

Edith **Wharton**

Novellas and Other Writings

0-940450-53-4 LIBRARY OF AMERICA $35.00

Novels

Includes *The House of Mirth, The Reef, The Custom of the Country,* and *The Age of Innocence*

0-940450-31-3 LIBRARY OF AMERICA $35.00

Walt **Whitman**

Poetry and Prose

0-940450-02-X LIBRARY OF AMERICA $35.00

1-88301-135-3 LIBRARY OF AMERICA PB....................$16.95

Richard **Wright**

Early Works

Includes *Lawd Today!, Uncle Tom's Children,* and *Native Son.* "A major publishing event. Readers who think they know these works have some surprises in store for them" —Henry Louis Gates, Jr.

EDITED BY ARNOLD RAMPERSAD

0-940450-66-6 LIBRARY OF AMERICA $35.00

Later Works

Includes *Black Boy* and *The Outsider*

EDITED BY ARNOLD RAMPERSAD

0-940450-67-4 LIBRARY OF AMERICA $35.00

American Literature: Anthologies and Critical Studies

Anthologies

General Anthologies

Nina **Baym**, editor

The Norton Anthology of American Literature

Volume 1

0-393-96461-2 NORTON PB $39.95

Volume 2

0-393-96462-0 NORTON PB $39.95

Richard **Ellmann**, editor

The New Oxford Book of American Verse

Gives much space to the moderns, but by sticking to the mainstream misses many aspects

0-19-502058-8 OXFORD $45.00

F.O. **Matthiessen**, editor

The Oxford Book of American Verse

0-19-500049-8 OXFORD $49.95

Specialized Anthologies

Jeffery **Chan**, editor

Aiiieeeee!: An Anthology of Asian-American Writers

0-451-62836-5 NEW AMERICAN LIBRARY PB....................$5.99

Shelby **Foote**, editor

Chickamauga: And Other Civil War Stories

0-385-31100-1 DELTA PB $12.95

Henry Louis **Gates** &
Nellie Y. **McKay**, editors
The Norton Anthology of African American Literature
0-393-04001-1 NORTON $39.95

William **Harmon**, editor
The Oxford Book of American Light Verse
0-19-502509-1 OXFORD $39.95

Bill **Henderson**, editor
The annual Pushcart Prize sets an American standard in its selection from the dazzling literary galaxy of small presses. Winner of Publishers Weekly*'s Carey-Thomas Award, often selected as an "outstanding book of the year" by* The New York Times Book Review, *this series brings the most distinguished short stories, essays, and poetry of the year to us in a single, compelling volume.*

The Pushcart Prize XX: 1995-1996
0-916366-63-4 PUSHCART PB $16.00

The Pushcart Prize XIX: Best of the Small Presses, 1994-1995
0-916366-98-7 PUSHCART PB $15.00

The Pushcart Prize XVIII: 1993-1994
0-916366-89-8 PUSHCART $29.00

The Pushcart Prize XVII: 1992-1993
0-916366-77-4 PUSHCART $29.50

The Pushcart Prize XVI: 1991-1992
0-916366-71-5 PUSHCART $28.50

Asuncion **Horno-Delgado**, editor
Breaking Boundaries: Latina Writing and Critical Reading
0-87023-636-9 MASSACHUSETTS PB $17.95

Paul **Kane**, editor
Poetry of the American Renaissance: A Diverse Anthology from the Romantic Period
0-8076-1398-3 BRAZILLER PB $14.95

Olga **Kenyon**, editor
800 Years of Women's Letters
"Here is the intimacy of heart and mind across distance and time"
—from the foreword by P.D. James
0-14-023389-X PENGUIN PB $12.95

David Levering **Lewis**
The Portable Harlem Renaissance Reader
"A fresh and brilliant portrait of African American art and culture in the 1920s"
—Arnold Rampersad, author of *The Life of Langston Hughes*
0-14-017036-7 PENGUIN PB $14.95

M. **Mark**, editor
Disorderly Conduct: The VLS Fiction Reader
The *VLS*, which enlivened the literary scene for the last ten years with its own brand of counter-cultural review, also published some of the finest short fiction in America. *Disorderly Conduct* collects the best stories from the VLS, by writers such as Russell Banks, Pagan Kennedy, Lynda Schor, and Janice Eidus. "Energized with quirky sensibility"
—*Publishers Weekly*
1-85242-245-9 SERPENT'S TAIL PB $12.95

James **McConkey**, editor
The Anatomy of Memory: An Anthology
From St. Augustine to Lewis Thomas, including along the way Yeats, Marianne Moore, James Baldwin, Nabokov, and Annie Dillard, McConkey's collection brings an astounding array of insights into the nature of consciousness. "Scientists, poets, essayists, philosophers, novelists, theologians parade through this anthology in a display of diverse perspectives and related insights that is dazzling in its coherent complexity"—Elizabeth Coleman
0-19-507841-1 OXFORD $30.00

Thomas **Pynchon**, editor
Deadly Sins
A collection of seven essays—one for each deadly sin—which originally appeared in *The New York Times Book Review* by such authors as Mary Gordon, John Updike, and William Trevor
0-688-14616-3 QUILL PB $10.00

Diane **Ravitch**
The American Reader: Words that Moved a Nation
An anthology of 200 poems, speeches, songs, essays, letters, photos, and documents
0-06-272016-3 HARPERCOLLINS PB $15.00

The Democracy Reader: Classic and Modern Speeches, Essays, Poems, Declarations, and Documents on Freedom and Human Rights Worldwide
EDITED BY ABIGAIL THERNSTROM
0062720350 HARPER & ROW PB $15.00

Ann A. **Schockley**, editor
Afro-American Women Writers, 1746-1933: An Anthology and Critical Guide
0-8161-8823-8 GK HALL $45.00

David **Seybold**, editor
Fathers and Sons: An Anthology
"Men would do well, after the literary polemic of *Iron John*, to turn to this evocative collection"—*Kirkus Reviews*
0-87113-602-3 GROVE PB $12.00

T.J. **Stiles**
The Citizen's Handbook: Essential Documents and Speeches from American History
Handy reference, from Paine's *Common Sense* to LBJ's "We Shall Overcome" speech
See also **SURVEYS OF US HISTORY** in **HISTORY OF THE AMERICAS**
0-425-14387-2 BERKELEY PB $12.00

Linda **Wagner-Martin** &
Cathy N. **Davidson**, editors
The Oxford Book of Women's Writing in the United States
This anthology includes short stories, poems, essays, plays, speeches, erotica, letters, and even some recipes to provide a comprehensive view of the best women's writing in America
See also **ANTHOLOGIES OF WOMEN'S WRITING** under **WOMEN'S STUDIES** in **SOCIAL STUDIES**
0-19-508706-2 OXFORD $30.00

General Studies and Reference

Lea **Baechler**
Modern American Women Writers: Profiles of Their Lives and Works—From the 1870s to the Present
Illuminates the lives and works of 32 of America's leading women writers, from Kate Chopin and Edith Wharton to Adrienne Rich and Susan Sontag. The paperback of the acclaimed 1991 Scribner Reference hardcover. "Highly recommended"—*Library Journal*
INTRODUCTION BY ELAINE SHOWALTER
0-02-082025-9 COLLIER PB $15.00

Kate Chopin

Sacvan **Bercovitch**, editor
Reconstructing American Literary History
0-674-75085-3 HARVARD $20.00

Richard **Chase**
The American Novel and Its Tradition
0-8018-2303-X JOHNS HOPKINS PB $14.95

Emory **Elliott**, editor
The Columbia Literary History of the United States
0-231-05812-8 COLUMBIA $69.50

James A. **Emanuel** &
Theodore L. **Gross**, editors
Dark Symphony: Negro Literature in America
0-02-909540-9 FREE PRESS PB $17.95

James D. **Hart**, editor

The Concise Oxford Companion to American Literature

Authors, books, poems, movements, theories, institutions: a copious reference book that explores the full range of writing in America, from the tribal chronicle of the Leni-Lenape to the Federal Writers' Project and *The Autobiography of Alice B. Toklas*

0-19-503074-5 OXFORD $48.00
0-19-504771-0 OXFORD PB $15.95

Annette **Kolodny**

The Lay of the Land: Metaphor as Experience and History in American Life and Letters

0-8078-4118-8 NORTH CAROLINA PB $12.95

Ronald E. **Martin**

American Literature and the Universe of Force

0-8223-0579-8 DUKE PB $17.50

Wendy **Martin**

An American Triptych: Anne Bradstreet, Emily Dickinson and Adrienne Rich

0-8078-4112-9 NORTH CAROLINA PB $12.95

Leo **Marx**

The Machine in the Garden: Technology and the Pastoral Ideal in America

0-19-500738-7 OXFORD PB $13.95

The Pilot and the Passenger: Essays on Literature, Technology and Culture in the United States

0-19-504875-X OXFORD $49.95

George **Plimpton**, editor

Women Writers at Work: The Paris Review Interviews

Edited by George Plimpton and introduced by Elizabeth Hardwick, this collection of the famed *Paris Review* interviews gathers classic discussions with Dorothy Parker, Isak Dinesen, and Lillian Hellman and modern conversations with Toni Morrison, P.D. James, Maya Angelou, and more. "The very model of the modern literary interview"—*Time*

WITH AN INTRODUCTION BY ELIZABETH HARDWICK
0-679-77129-8 RANDOM HOUSE PB $13.00

Richard **Poirier**

A World Elsewhere: The Place of Style in American Literature

0-299-09934-2 WISCONSIN PB $10.95

Richard **Ruland** & Malcolm **Bradbury**

From Puritanism to Postmodernism: A History of American Literature

Two leading literary critics offer a late-20th-century reassessment of American fiction. They address questions of literary and cultural nationalism and argue that American fiction has long been essentially modern. "Highly informative…a map of American literature that puts every writer in place"—*NY Times*

0-14-014435-8 PENGUIN PB $15.95

Elaine **Showalter**

Sister's Choice: Tradition and Change in American Women's Writing

New feminist criticism by the chairwoman of the English department at Princeton University. An astute reflection on American women's writing. "Ms. Showalter writes crisply and well, seldom lapsing into the jargon that makes much academic writing inaccessible to outsiders" —*NY Review of Books*

0-19-812383-3 OXFORD $25.00

Valerie **Smith**

Self-Discovery and Authority in Afro-American Narrative

0-674-80088-5 HARVARD PB $12.95

Werner **Sollors**

Beyond Ethnicity: Consent and Descent in American Culture

0-19-505193-9 OXFORD PB $19.95

Robert **Stepto**

From Behind the Veil: A Study of Afro-American Narrative

0-252-06211-6 ILLINOIS PB $11.95

General Studies to 1900

Jonathan **Arac**

Commissioned Spirits: The Shaping of Social Motion in Dickens, Carlyle, Melville, Hawthorne

0-231-07117-5 COLUMBIA PB $15.50

Lawrence **Buell**

The Environmental Imagination: Thoreau, Nature Writing and the Formation of American Culture

See also **CONTEMPORARY WRITERS ON WRITING** under **LITERARY CRITICISM** in **LITERATURE OF EUROPE, AFRICA, AND ASIA**

0-674-25861-4 HARVARD $36.50

Keith **Frome**, editor

Hitch Your Wagon to a Star: and Other Quotations from Ralph Waldo Emerson

"To be great is to be misunderstood." "It is better to be alone than in bad company." "To believe your own thought, to believe that what is true for you in your private heart is true for all men,—that is genius." Emerson's *aperçus* remain among the most insightful of American letters

0-231-10372-7 COLUMBIA $19.95

Myra **Jehlen**

American Incarnation: The Individual, the Nation, and the Continent

0-674-02427-3 HARVARD PB $15.95

D.H. **Lawrence**

Studies in Classic American Literature

Lawrence's pioneering studies of Cooper, Poe, Hawthorne, Melville, Dana, and Whitman have had an indelible effect on the way American literature is read

See also **20TH-CENTURY BRITISH ESSAYS AND OTHER PROSE** in **LITERATURE OF THE BRITISH ISLES**

0-14-018377-9 PENGUIN PB $10.95

Perry **Miller**

The New England Mind: From Colony to Province

One of the great books of American history written in this century. "The historical process whereby Puritan became Yankee—as part of that larger process whereby the Reformation became the Enlightenment" —*Christian Science Monitor*

See also **PURITAN LIVES** under **THE NEW COLONIES** under **US HISTORY TO THE CIVIL WAR** in **HISTORY OF THE AMERICAS**

0-674-61301-5 HARVARD PB $16.95

Kevin P. **Van Anglen**, editor

Simplify, Simplify: and Other Quotations from Henry David Thoreau

This distillation of Thoreau's massive body of work brings forth 750 of his most profound ideas on subjects from ecology to English literature, Confucius to Milton

0-231-10388-3 COLUMBIA $19.95

Peter **White**, editor

Puritan Poets and Poetics: Seventeenth-Century American Poetry in Theory and Practice

FOREWORD BY HARRISON T. MESEROLE
0-271-00413-4 PENN STATE $40.00

Bryan J. **Wolf**

Romantic Re-Vision: Culture and Consciousness in Nineteenth Century American Painting and Literature

0-226-90502-0 CHICAGO PB $19.50

Early American Literature

Sacvan **Bercovitch**

The American Jeremiad

0-299-07350-5 WISCONSIN $32.50
0-299-07354-8 WISCONSIN PB $15.95

The Puritan Origins of the American Self

0-300-02117-8 YALE PB $17.00

Andrew **Delbanco**

The Puritan Ordeal

Emphasizes that the Puritans left England to escape the acquisitive life and because, as immigrants, they believed their lives could be renewed. Winner of Columbia University's Lionel Trilling Award

See also **PURITAN LIVES** under **THE NEW COLONIES** under **US HISTORY TO THE CIVIL WAR** in **HISTORY OF THE AMERICAS**

0-674-74056-4 HARVARD PB $16.95

Jane D. **Eberwein**

Early American Poetry: Bradstreet, Taylor, Dwight, Freneau and Bryant

0-299-07444-7 WISCONSIN PB $16.50

Emory **Elliott**

Revolutionary Writers: Literature and Authority in the New Republic, 1725-1810

0-19-503995-5 OXFORD PB $18.95

Everett **Emerson**, editor

American Literature, 1764-1789: The Revolutionary Years

0-299-07270-3 WISCONSIN $32.50

Major Writers of Early American Literature: Introductions to Nine Major Writers

0-299-06194-9 WISCONSIN PB $14.50

Richard **Slotkin**

Regeneration Through Violence: The Mythology of the American Frontier, 1600-1860

0-06-097682-9 HARPERPERENNIAL PB $20.00

The 19th Century

Nina **Baym**

Woman's Fiction: A Guide to Novels by and About Women in America, 1820-1870

0-252-06285-X ILLINOIS PB $15.95

Warner **Berthoff**

The Ferment of Realism: American Literature, 1884-1919

0-521-28435-X CAMBRIDGE PB $22.95

Van Wyck **Brooks**

The Flowering of New England, 1815-1875

0-404-18007-8 AMS $45.00

Lawrence **Buell**

New England Literary Culture: From the Revolution to the Renaissance

0-521-30206-4 CAMBRIDGE $75.00

Irving **Howe**

The American Newness: Culture and Politics in the Age of Emerson

0-674-02640-3 HARVARD $18.95

John T. **Irwin**

American Hieroglyphics: The Symbol of the Egyptian Hieroglyphics in the American Renaissance

0-8018-2908-9 JOHNS HOPKINS PB $16.95

Jackson **Lears**

No Place of Grace: Antimodernism and the Transformation of American Culture, 1880-1920

0-226-46970-0 CHICAGO PB $16.95

Harry **Levin**

The Power of Blackness: Hawthorne, Poe, Melville

0-8214-0581-0 OHIO PB $14.95

F.O. **Matthiessen**

American Renaissance: Art and Expression in the Age of Emerson and Whitman

0-19-500759-X OXFORD PB $19.95

Donald **Pizer**

Realism and Naturalism in Nineteenth-Century American Literature

0-8093-1125-9 SOUTHERN ILLINOIS $19.95

David S. **Reynolds**

Beneath the American Renaissance: The Subversive Imagination in the Age of Emerson and Melville

See also **THE ROMANTIC AGE AND THE AMERICAN RENAISSANCE** under **US HISTORY TO THE CIVIL WAR** in **HISTORY OF THE AMERICAS**

0-674-06565-4 HARVARD PB $19.50

John L. **Thomas**

Alternative America: Henry George, Edward Bellamy, Henry Demarest Lloyd and the Adversary Tradition

0-674-01676-9 HARVARD $38.00

Edmund **Wilson**

Patriotic Gore: Studies in the Literature of the American Civil War

An immense and erudite collection of essays whose subjects include Harriet Beecher Stowe, Ulysses S. Grant, William T. Sherman, Mary Chesnut, George Washington Cable, and many lesser-known figures. "The richest and most many-sided book ever produced about the civil War"— Conor Cruise O'Brien

0-393-31256-9 NORTON PB $15.95

General Studies: The 20th Century

Daniel **Aaron**

Writers on the Left

0-231-08038-7 COLUMBIA $49.50
0-231-08039-5 COLUMBIA PB $14.95

Houston A. **Baker**, Jr.

Blues, Ideology, and Afro American Literature: A Vernacular Theory

0-226-03538-7 CHICAGO PB $12.95

The Journey Back: Issues in Black Literature and Criticism

0-226-03535-2 CHICAGO PB $14.00

Modernism and the Harlem Renaissance

See also **THE NORTH** under **HISTORY** under **AFRICAN-AMERICAN STUDIES** in **HISTORY OF THE AMERICAS**

0-226-03525-5 CHICAGO PB $10.95

Singers of Daybreak: Studies in Black American Literature

0-88258-025-6 HOWARD PB $12.95

Philip D. **Beidler**

Scriptures for a Generation: What We Were Reading in the '60s

A fresh look at influential favorites: Brautigan, Castaneda, Kesey, Hesse, *The Whole Earth Catalog,* and many more

0-8203-1787-X GEORGIA PB $12.95

Kay **Boyle** & Robert **McAlmon**

Being Geniuses Together: 1920-1930

A dual account of Paris in the '20s

See also **LITERATURE** under **20TH-CENTURY AMERICAN ESSAYS AND JOURNALISM**

0-86547-149-5 NORTH POINT PB $13.50

Malcolm **Cowley**

The Dream of the Golden Mountains: Remembering the 1930s

0-14-005919-9 PENGUIN PB $8.95

Exile's Return: A Literary Odyssey of the 1920s

0-8446-6053-1 SMITH $21.80
0-14-004392-6 PENGUIN PB $8.95

Arthur P. **Davis**

From the Dark Tower: Afro-American Writers, 1900-1960

0-88258-004-3 HOWARD $29.95
0-88258-058-2 HOWARD PB $14.95

Ursula B. **Davis**

Paris Without Regret: James Baldwin, Chester Himes, Kenny Clarke, and Donald Byrd

0-87745-147-8 IOWA $19.95

Mari **Evans**, editor
Black Women Writers, 1950-1980: A Critical Evaluation
INTRODUCTION BY STEPHEN HENDERSON
0-385-17125-0 DOUBLEDAY PB $14.95

Henry Louis **Gates**, Jr.
The Signifying Monkey: A Theory of American Literary Criticism
0-19-506075-X OXFORD PB $14.95

Henry Louis **Gates**, Jr., editor
Black Literature and Literary Theory
0-415-90334-3 ROUTLEDGE PB $18.95

Karen **Hinckley** & Barbara **Hinckley**
American Best Sellers: A Reader's Guide to Popular Fiction
0-253-32728-8 INDIANA $29.95

George **Hutchinson**
The Harlem Renaissance in Black and White
0-674-37262-X HARVARD $35.00

Charles **Johnson**
Being and Race: Black Writing Since 1970
See also **THE BLACK AESTHETIC** under **CULTURE** under **AFRICAN-AMERICAN STUDIES** in **HISTORY OF THE AMERICAS**
0-253-31165-9 INDIANA $20.00
0-253-20537-9 INDIANA PB $8.95

Bruce **Kellner**, editor
The Harlem Renaissance: A Historical Dictionary for the Era
0-313-23232-6 GREENWOOD $65.00

Hugh **Kenner**
The Pound Era
Kenner's major work is also a study of the many aspects of modernism on which Pound's career impinged
See also **LITERARY ESSAYISTS AND HISTORIANS** under **LITERARY CRITICISM** in **LITERATURE OF EUROPE, AFRICA, AND ASIA**
0-520-02427-3 CALIFORNIA PB $17.95

Elaine **Kim**
Asian-American Literature: An Introduction to the Writings and Their Social Context
0-87722-352-1 TEMPLE PB $19.95

Brenda **Knight**, editor
Women of the Beat: The Writers, Artists, and Muses at the Heart of Revolution
1-57324-061-3 CONARI $22.95

Kenneth **Lincoln**
Native American Renaissance
0-520-05457-1 CALIFORNIA PB $9.95

David **Madden**
Tough Guy Writers of the Thirties
0-8093-0912-2 SOUTHERN ILLINOIS PB $10.95

Frank N. **Magill**
Masterpieces of Latino Literature
0-06-270106-1 HARPERCOLLINS $45.00

Larry **McCaffery**, editor
Alive and Writing: Interviews with American Authors of the 1980s
0-252-06011-3 ILLINOIS PB $12.95

Donald **Pizer**
Twentieth-Century American Literary Naturalism: An Interpretation
0-8093-1027-9 SOUTHERN ILLINOIS $19.95

Roger **Rosenblatt**
Black Fiction
0-674-07622-2 HARVARD PB $11.50

Carl **Shirley** & Paula **Shirley**
Understanding Chicano Literature
0-87249-575-2 SOUTH CAROLINA $29.95

Robert **Siegle**
Suburban Ambush: Downtown Writing and the Fiction of Insurgency
A study of the writing that has emerged in recent years from New York's Lower East Side. Siegle looks at the work of Kathy Acker, Lynne Tillman, Ron Kolm, Joel Rose, and others
0-8018-3854-1 JOHNS HOPKINS PB $16.95

John **Tytell**
Naked Angels: Kerouac, Ginsberg, Burroughs
0-8021-3247-2 GROVE PB $12.95

Steven **Watson**
Circles of the Twentieth Century
Volume 1
The Harlem Renaissance: Hub of African American Culture, 1920-1930
0-679-75889-5 PANTHEON PB $16.00
Volume 2
The Birth of the Beat Generation, 1944-1960
An original view of the maverick poets and novelists whom history has dubbed "The Beats." An important, readable account of a brilliant group of radical artists
0-679-42371-0 PANTHEON $27.50

Edith **Wharton**
The Uncollected Critical Writings
EDITED BY FREDERICK WEGENER
0-691-04349-3 PRINCETON $29.95

John Hall **Wheelock**, editor
Editor to Author: The Letters of Maxwell E. Perkins
0-684-18840-6 SCRIBNERS PB $10.95

Whitney Museum of American Art
Beat Culture and the New America: 1950-1965
PROLOGUE BY ALLEN GINSBURG
2-08-013613-5 WHITNEY MUSEUM $55.00

Poetry

Houston A. **Baker**, Jr.
Afro-American Poetics: Revisions of Harlem and the Black Aesthetic
0-299-11500-3 WISCONSIN $21.95
0-299-11504-6 WISCONSIN PB $12.95

Charles **Bernstein**
Content's Dream: Essays, 1975-1984
Reflections on contemporary poetry, art, and philosophy by a leading "Language" poet
0-940650-57-6 SUN & MOON $17.95
0-940650-56-8 SUN & MOON PB $14.95

A Poetics
0-674-67857-5 HARVARD PB $16.95

Charles **Bernstein**, editor
The Politics of Poetic Form: Poetry and Public Policy
0-937804-35-5 SEGUE PB $12.95

Cordelia **Candelaria**
Chicano Poetry: A Critical Introduction
0-313-23683-6 GREENWOOD $42.95

Michael **Davidson**
The San Francisco Renaissance: Poetics and Community at Mid-Century
The best cultural history of the Beats
See also **CULTURAL AND SOCIAL HISTORY** under **TOPICS IN AMERICAN STUDIES** in **HISTORY OF THE AMERICAS**
0-521-25880-4 CAMBRIDGE $59.95
0-521-42304-X CAMBRIDGE PB $18.95

Frederick **Feirstein**, editor
Expansive Poetry: Essays on the New Narrative and the New Formalism
0-934257-27-2 STORYLINE PB $15.95

Dana **Gioia**
Can Poetry Matter? Essays on Poetry and American Culture
Gioia explores the role of the poet in today's world. "Gioia's challenging and valuable essays forcefully anatomize the situation of poetry today. No one since Randall Jarrell has talked more good sense on this subject"
—William H. Pritchard
1-55597-177-6 GRAY WOLF PB $12.00

One sees evidence of poetry's diminished statute even within the thriving subcultures. The established rituals of the poetry world—the readings, small magazines, workshops, and conferences—exhibit a surprising number of self-imposed limitations. Why for example, does poetry mix so seldom with music, dance, or theater? At most readings the program consists of verse only—and usually only verse by that night's author. Forty years ago, when Dylan Thomas read, he spent half the program reciting other poets' work. Hardly a self-effacing man, he was nevertheless humble before his art. Today most readings are celebrations less of poetry than of the author's ego. No wonder the audience for such events usually consists entirely of poets, would-be poets, and friends of the author.
CAN POETRY MATTER? ESSAYS POETRY AND AMERICAN CULTURE

Alan **Golding**
From Outlaw to Classic: Canons in American Poetry
0-299-14604-9 WISCONSIN PB $19.95

Laurence **Goldstein**
The American Poet at the Movies: A Critical History
Includes chapters on Vachel Lindsay, Hart Crane, Frank O'Hara, Jorie Graham, and others. "Influence of film on the forms, subjects and themes of modernist poetics…provocative and engaging"—*Choice*
0-472-08318-X MICHIGAN PB $14.95

Donald **Hall**
Death to the Death of Poetry: Essays, Reviews, Notes, Interviews
0-472-06571-8 MICHIGAN PB $13.95

Marie **Harris** & Kathleen **Aguero**, editors
A Gift of Tongues: Critical Challenges in Contemporary American Poetry
Essays on marginalized groups in American writing, studying the works of Chicano, Native American, Appalachian, black, gay, and prison writers
0-8203-0953-2 GEORGIA PB $15.00

George **Hartley**
Textual Politics and the Language Poets
0-253-32716-4 INDIANA $22.50

Robert **Hass**
Twentieth Century Pleasures: Prose on Poetry
0-88001-046-0 NORTON PB $14.00

Anthony **Hecht**
On the Laws of the Poetic Art
0-691-04363-9 PRINCETON $29.95

Michael **Heller**
Conviction's Net of Branches: Essays on the Objectivist Poets and Poetry
0-8093-1188-7 SOUTHERN ILLINOIS PB $9.95

John **Hollander**
The Gazer's Spirit: Poems Speaking to Silent Works of Art
0-226-34949-7 CHICAGO $39.95

David **Kalstone**
Becoming a Poet: Elizabeth Bishop, with Marianne Moore and Robert Lowell
EDITED WITH A PREFACE BY ROBERT HEMENWAY
AFTERWORD BY JAMES MERRILL
0-374-10960-5 FS&G $22.50

Mary **Kinzie**
The Cure of Poetry in an Age of Prose: Moral Essays on the Poet's Calling
The poet and director of the Creative Writing Program at Northwestern University diagnoses trends that have led to the unfortunate diminishing of truth and elegance in literature
0-226-43735-3 CHICAGO $49.00
0-226-43736-1 CHICAGO PB $16.95

Carolyn **Kizer**
Proses: Selected Essays, Reviews, and Conversations
With wit, grace, and the imaginative rigor that are her trademarks, Kizer reflects on the deification of Sylvia Plath, the work of Emily Dickinson, and her own passage in a major autobiographical essay, *The Stories of My Life*. An auspicious start to what promises to be a valuable and enduring series on poets writing about their work
1-55659-045-8 COPPER CANYON PB $12.00

Diane W. **Middlebrook** & Marilyn **Yalom**, editors
Coming to Light: American Women Poets in the Twentieth Century
0-472-08061-X MICHIGAN PB $16.59

Bill **Moyers**
Power of the Word: A Festival of Poets
In this companion volume to the PBS series, Moyers interviews an eclectic group of American poets from well-known figures as Adrienne Rich and Robert Bly to less familiar names
0-385-47917-4 DOUBLEDAY $29.95

Alicia Suskin **Ostriker**
Stealing the Language: The Emergence of Women's Poetry in America
0-8070-6303-7 BEACON PB $16.00

Jenny **Penberthy**
Lorine Niedecker and the Correspondence with Zukofsky, 1931-1970
These letters of poet Lorine Niedecker to Louis Zukofsky are essential to an understanding of the working methods of two great American poets
0-521-44369-5 CAMBRIDGE $65.00

David **Perkins**
A History of Modern Poetry
Volume 1
From the 1890s to the High Modernist Mode
A judicious and well-informed survey, gracefully written
See also **POETRY** under **SPECIALIZED STUDIES** under **ANTHOLOGIES AND STUDIES** in **LITERATURE OF THE BRITISH ISLES**
0-674-39945-5 HARVARD PB $20.00

Volume 2
Modernism and After
See also **POETRY** under **SPECIALIZED STUDIES** under **ANTHOLOGIES AND STUDIES** in **LITERATURE OF THE BRITISH ISLES**
0-674-39947-1 HARVARD PB $20.00

Marjorie **Perloff**
The Dance of the Intellect: Studies in the Poetry of the Pound Tradition
Ten essays addressing the problem of structure, mode, and genre in postmodernist and contemporary poetry
See also **POETRY** under **LITERARY CRITICISM** in **LITERATURE OF EUROPE, AFRICA, AND ASIA**
0-8101-1380-5 NORTHWESTERN PB $16.95

Robert **Pinsky**
The Situation of Poetry: Contemporary Poetry and Its Traditions
0-691-01352-7 PRINCETON PB $14.95

J. Saunders **Redding**
To Make a Poet Black
INTRODUCTION BY HENRY LOUIS GATES, JR.
0-8014-9438-9 CORNELL PB $9.95

Adrienne **Rich**
What Is Found There: Notebooks on Poetry and Politics
Through journals, letters, dreams, and close reading of the work of poets, Rich reflects on what it means to be a citizen of a country caught in the contradictions of its mythic past and its violent present. A passionate argument for poetry as an instrument for change and moral transcendence
0-393-03565-4 NORTON $20.00

Jerome **Rothenberg**
Pre-Faces & Other Writings
0-8112-0785-4 NEW DIRECTIONS $14.95
0-8112-0786-2 NEW DIRECTIONS PB $6.95

Mark **Rudman**
Diverse Voices: Essays on Poets and Poetry
Eighteen essays on poets as various as Yehuda Ammichai and Robert Duncan draw us into the act of writing in an original, extraordinarily revealing way. "Mark Rudman's criticism is a unique blend of passion, clarity, and disquiet"
—Paul Auster
0-934257-67-1 STORYLINE $26.95
0-934257-68-X STORYLINE PB $18.95

Martha E. **Sanchez**

Contemporary Chicano Poetry: A Critical Approach to an Emerging Literature

0-520-05888-7 CALIFORNIA PB $14.00

William **Stafford**

Writing the Australian Crawl

0-472-87300-8 MICHIGAN PB $13.95

Helen **Vendler**

The Breaking of Style: Hopkins, Heaney, Graham

See also **POETRY** under **LITERARY CRITICISM** in **LITERATURE OF EUROPE, AFRICA, AND ASIA**

0-674-08120-X HARVARD $29.95
0-674-08121-8 HARVARD PB $14.00

The Given and the Made: Strategies of Poetic Redefinition

See also **POETRY** under **LITERARY CRITICISM** in **LITERATURE OF EUROPE, AFRICA, AND ASIA**

0-674-35431-1 HARVARD $29.95
0-674-35432-X HARVARD PB $14.00

The Music of What Happens: Poems, Poets, Critics

See also **POETRY** under **LITERARY CRITICISM** in **LITERATURE OF EUROPE, AFRICA, AND ASIA**

0-674-59152-6 HARVARD $36.00

Part of Nature, Part of Us: Modern American Poets

0-674-65476-5 HARVARD PB $16.95

Soul Says: On Recent Poetry

See also **POETRY** under **LITERARY CRITICISM** in **LITERATURE OF EUROPE, AFRICA, AND ASIA**

0-674-82146-7 HARVARD $24.95
0-674-82147-5 HARVARD PB $14.00

Stephen **Vincent** & Ellen, **Zweig**, editors

The Poetry Reading: A Contemporary Compendium on Language and Performance

0-917672-11-9 MOMO'S $25.00

Robert **von Hallberg**

American Poetry and Culture, 1945-1980

0-674-03012-5 HARVARD PB $14.95

Gregory **Woods**

Articulate Flesh: Male Homoeroticism and Modern Poetry

A critical study of gay influences on modern poetry

0-300-03872-0 YALE $32.00

Drama

Ruby **Cohn**

New American Dramatists

0-312-04249-3 ST. MARTIN'S $19.95

Errol **Hill**, editor

The Theatre of Black Americans

See also **NORTH AMERICA** under **HISTORY** under **THEATER** in **PERFORMING ARTS AND MEDIA**

0-936839-27-9 APPLAUSE THEATRE PB $15.95

Nicholas **Kanellos**

Mexican American Theatre: Legacy and Realty

0-935480-22-6 LATIN AMERICAN LIT PB $10.00

Hispanic Theatre in the United States

0-934770-44-1 PLAYERS PB $9.00

Adrienne **Kennedy**

People Who Led to My Plays

1-55936-125-5 THEATRE COMMUNICATIONS PB $14.95

David **Savran**, editor

In Their Own Words: Contemporary American Playwrights

0-930452-70-4 THEATRE COMMUNICATIONS PB $13.95

Linda W. **Wagner-Martin**

Sylvia Plath: A Biography

0-312-02325-1 VERMILAN PB $12.95

Studies of Individual Authors

To 1900

Ernest **Samuels**

Henry Adams

A revised and abridged version of Samuels's monumental three-volume biography of the great scholar, historian, and novelist.

"One of the most powerful literary-intellectual biographies ever done of an American"
—R.W.B. Lewis

0-674-38735-X HARVARD $35.00

Louisa May **Alcott**

The Journals of Louisa May Alcott

EDITED BY JOEL MYERSON & DANIEL MYERSON

0-316-59362-1 LITTLE, BROWN $7.98

Sarah **Elbert**

A Hunger for Home: Louisa May Alcott's Place in American Culture

0-8135-1199-2 RUTGERS PB $16.00

Martha **Saxton**

Louisa May Alcott: A Modern Biography

"Martha Saxton's excellent biography is framed almost entirely in psychological terms…we discover the sources of her energy and determination and the scope of her imagination"—*The Boston Globe*

0-374-52460-2 NOONDAY PB $15.00

Per **Seyersted**

Kate Chopin: A Critical Biography

0-8071-0678-X LSU PB $9.95

Sharon **Cameron**

Lyric Time: Dickinson and the Limits of Genre

0-8018-2116-9 JOHNS HOPKINS PB $15.95

Jane D. **Eberwein**

Dickinson: Strategies of Limitation

0-87023-549-4 MASSACHUSETTS PB $17.05

Judith **Farr**

The Passion of Emily Dickinson

0-674-65665-2 HARVARD $29.95
0-674-65666-0 HARVARD PB $15.95

Susan **Howe**

My Emily Dickinson

See also **LITERATURE** under **20TH-CENTURY AMERICAN ESSAYS AND JOURNALISM**

0-938190-53-9 NORTH ATLANTIC $25.00
0-938190-52-0 NORTH ATLANTIC PB $9.95

Suzanne **Juhasz**, editor

Feminist Critics Read Emily Dickinson

0-253-32170-0 INDIANA $29.95

Vivian R. **Pollak**

Dickinson: The Anxiety of Gender

0-8014-9370-6 CORNELL PB $14.95

Cynthia Griffin **Wolff**

Emily Dickinson

0-201-16809-X ADDISON-WESLEY PB $15.95

Carlos **Baker**

Emerson Among the Eccentrics: A Group Portrait

Hawthorne, Thoreau, Margaret Fuller, Bronson Alcott, Walt Whitman, Abraham Lincoln: such was the circle of intellects surrounding Ralph Waldo Emerson, and such is the context in which Baker brings us to a new understanding of the American Renaissance and one of its primary figures

INTRODUCTION AND EPILOGUE BY JAMES R. MELLOW

0-670-86675-X VIKING $34.95

Joel **Porte**

Emerson: Prospect and Retrospect

0-674-24915-1 HARVARD $18.50
0-674-24917-8 HARVARD PB $7.95

Representative Man: Ralph Waldo Emerson in His Time

0-231-06740-2 COLUMBIA $67.50

Paula **Blanchard**

Margaret Fuller: From Transcendentalism to Revolution

INTRODUCTION BY CAROLYN HEILBRUN

0-201-10458-X ADDISON-WESLEY PB $12.95

Margaret Fuller

Joan **von Mehren**
Minerva and the Muse: A Life of Margaret Fuller
0-87023-941-4 MASSACHUSETTS $40.00
1-55849-015-9 MASSACHUSETTS PB $17.95

Edwin Haviland **Miller**
Salem Is My Dwelling Place: A Life of Nathaniel Hawthorne
"The best, and most thorough, biography yet of Hawthorne, setting the standard against which all others will be measured"—*Kirkus Reviews*
0-87745-332-2 IOWA $37.95

Philip **Young**
Hawthorne's Secret: An Un-Told Tale
Literary detective work disclosing the mysteries of Nathaniel Hawthorne's past
0-87923-515-2 GODINE $17.95

William **McMurray**
The Literary Realism of William Dean Howells
0-8093-0237-3 SOUTHERN ILLINOIS $12.95

R.W.B. **Lewis**
The Jameses: A Family Narrative
Novelist Henry, psychologist William, brilliant invalid Alice, and their extraordinary, mystically minded father play the central roles in this biography of a family crucial in American thought and writing
0-374-17861-5 FS&G $35.00

R.P. **Blackmur**
Studies in Henry James
EDITED BY VERONICA A. MAKOWSKY
0-8112-0864-8 NEW DIRECTIONS PB $9.25

Leon **Edel**
Henry James: A Life
0-691-06822-4 PRINCETON $37.00

Fred **Kaplan**
Henry James: The Imagination of Genius
Kaplan brings the formidable scholarly skills and narrative art that he displayed in his biographies of Dickens and Carlyle to this new study of Henry James. "Similar in its emotional complexity and cunning insights to James's own novels, this remarkably vivid biography offers a nuanced portrait of the author…who paid the price for his independence in loneliness and alienation"—*Publishers Weekly*
0-688-09021-4 MORROW PB $25.00

Edgar A. **Dryden**
Melville's Thematics of Form: The Great Art of Telling the Truth
0-8018-2619-5 JOHNS HOPKINS PB $12.95

Hershel **Parker**
Herman Melville: A Biography
0-8018-5428-8 JOHNS HOPKINS $39.95

Laurie **Robertson-Lorant**
Melville: A Biography
Drawing on over 500 newly discovered family letters, Robertson-Lorant brings to life the great American writer and the political and social climate of his century. From his impoverished childhood to his adventurous days on the sea, this major new biography takes us through Melville's life, chronicling his mixed fortunes as a writer and the alcoholism and violence that plagued his life. A highly readable, definitive account of this literary genius
0-517-59314-9 CLARKSON POTTER $40.00

Michael P. **Rogin**
Subversive Genealogy: The Politics and Art of Herman Melville
0-520-05178-5 CALIFORNIA PB $14.95

Gerald J. **Kennedy**
Poe, Death, and the Life of Writing
0-300-03773-2 YALE $32.50

Kenneth **Silverman** & others
Poe: Mournful and Never-Ending Remembrance
A look at the dark and tragic life of one of the most enigmatic of great American writers. "An engrossing literary biography"—Leon Edel
0-06-092331-8 HARPERPERENNIAL PB $15.00

Just what Poe did is known only through his own later and somewhat obscure allusions to "peccadilloes" committed after too much port and bourbon. When drunk he seems to have worn his cloak inside out, left a barber shop without paying, and insulted, acted petulantly toward, or otherwise offended his friend Thomas, as well as Dow and his wife, Rob Tyler, and several other persons…Poe suffered from his spree physically too. An old acquaintance who ran into him, and loaned him fifty cents for a meal, recalled that he seemed *"un homme blassé*—seedy in his appearance and woe-begone," trying to preserve a gentlemanly appearance but looking "used-up."
POE: MOURNFUL AND NEVER-ENDING REMEMBRANCE

Eric **Sundquist**, editor
New Essays on Uncle Tom's Cabin
0-521-31786-X CAMBRIDGE PB $12.95

Karl **Keller**
The Example of Edward Taylor
0-87023-174-X MASSACHUSETTS $35.00

Lawrence **Buell**
The Environmental Imagination
0-674-25862-2 HARVARD PB $16.95

Sharon **Cameron**
Writing Nature: Henry Thoreau's Journal
0-226-09228-3 CHICAGO PB $14.50

Stanley **Cavell**
The Senses of Walden: An Expanded Edition
0-226-09813-3 CHICAGO PB $12.95

Richard L. **Lebeaux**
Thoreau's Seasons
0-87023-401-3 MASSACHUSETTS $40.00

Robert D. **Richardson**, Jr.
Henry Thoreau: A Life of the Mind
0-520-05495-4 CALIFORNIA $35.00
0-520-06346-5 CALIFORNIA PB $14.95

Justin **Kaplan**
Mr. Clemens and Mark Twain
0-671-74807-6 TOUCHSTONE PB $15.00

Betsy **Erkkila**
Whitman the Political Poet
0-19-505438-5 OXFORD $49.95

James E. **Miller**, Jr
The American Quest for a Supreme Fiction: Whitman's Legacy in the Personal Epic
0-226-52612-7 CHICAGO PB $9.95

David S. **Reynolds**
Walt Whitman's America: A Cultural Biography
The life of the great American poet set in the social, cultural, and political context of his time by the noted professor of American literature and author of *Beneath the American Renaissance*
0-394-58023-0 KNOPF $35.00
0-679-76709-6 VINTAGE PB $19.00

The 20th Century

Irving **Howe**
Sherwood Anderson
0-8047-0237-3 STANFORD PB $14.95

Carol **Brightman**, editor
Between Friends: The Correspondence of Hannah Arendt and Mary McCarthy: 1949-1975
Twenty-six years of correspondence between the renowned political philosopher Arendt and the critic and novelist McCarthy not only provides brilliantly fresh insight into two of the century's greatest minds, but serves also as window into the most vibrant intellectual life of the century itself
0-15-100112-X HARCOURT BRACE $34.95

Dennis **Barone**, editor

Beyond the Red Notebook: Essays on Paul Auster

0-8122-3317-4 PENNSYLVANIA $36.95
0-8122-1556-7 PENNSYLVANIA PB $17.95

James **Baldwin**

Conversations with James Baldwin

EDITED BY FRED L. STANDLEY & LOUIS H. PRATT
0-87805-389-1 MISSISSIPPI PB $15.95

James Baldwin

Andrew **Field**

Djuna: The Formidable Miss Barnes

0-292-71546-3 TEXAS PB $10.95

Phillip **Herring**

Djuna: The Life and Work of Djuna Barnes

Witty and beautiful, friend of James Joyce and T.S. Eliot, Djuna Barnes frequented the most privileged circles of her time, and yet remains, despite her fame, the most elusive of modern writers
0-670-84969-3 VIKING $29.95

Billy **Altman**

Laughter's Gentle Soul: The Life of Robert Benchley

0-393-03833-5 NORTON $27.50

Gary **Fountain** & others

Remembering Elizabeth Bishop: An Oral Biography

This book interweaves more than 120 interviews with relatives, friends, colleagues, and students of Elizabeth Bishop, one of America's finest poets
0-87023-936-8 MASSACHUSETTS $40.00
1-55849-016-7 MASSACHUSETTS PB $17.95

Brett C. **Millier**

Elizabeth Bishop: Life and the Memory of It

The first full-length biography of the emotionally elusive poet who, after the death of her father when she was eight months old, endured the childhood of a virtual orphan. Her formative relationship at Vassar with mentor Marianne Moore is fascinatingly examined. "In the pages of this exemplary and highly readable biography, Elizabeth Bishop moves and speaks as the tragic and brilliant force for contemporary American poety she was"—Paul Mariani, author of *William Carlos Williams: A New World Naked*
0-520-07978-7 CALIFORNIA $30.00
0-520-20345-3 CALIFORNIA PB $16.95

Lee **Upton**

Obsession and Release: Rereading the Poetry of Louise Bogan

0-8387-5321-3 BUCKNELL $32.50

Richard F. **Patterson**

A World Outside: The Fiction of Paul Bowles

0-292-79035-X TEXAS PB $7.95

Christopher **Sawyer-Lauçanno**

An Invisible Spectator: A Biography of Paul Bowles

0-88001-257-9 ECCO PB $14.95

Joan **Mellen**

Kay Boyle: Author of Herself

The author of more than 30 books of fiction and poetry, Boyle practically invented what came to be known as the *New Yorker* style. A close friend to Joyce, Brancusi, and Duchamp in Paris, an anti-fascist activist in Austria and France, a victim of McCarthyism at home, and a US prisoner for her protests against the Vietnam War, she will be remembered as much for her life as for her work. Indeed, in this case, the two are truly inextricable
0-374-18098-9 FS&G $35.00

William S. **Burroughs**

The Job: Interviews by Daniel Odier

0-14-011882-9 PENGUIN PB $12.95

Ted **Morgan**

Literary Outlaw: The Life and Times of William S. Burroughs

0-380-70882-5 AVON PB $12.95

Robin **Lydenberg**

Word Cultures: Radical Theory and Practice in Williams S. Burroughs' Fiction

0-252-01413-8 ILLINOIS $24.95

Roy **Hoopes**

Cain: The Biography of James M. Cain

0-8093-1361-8 SOUTHERN ILLINOIS PB $16.95

Erskine **Caldwell**

Conversations with Erskine Caldwell

EDITED BY EDWIN T. ARNOLD
0-87805-344-1 MISSISSIPPI PB $15.95

Truman **Capote**

Conversations with Truman Capote

EDITED BY M.T. INGE
0-87805-275-5 MISSISSIPPI $14.95

With All My Might: An Autobiography

0-934601-11-9 PEACHTREE $19.95

Gerald **Clarke**

Capote: A Biography

See also **BIOGRAPHIES** under **GAY, LESBIAN, AND BISEXUAL STUDIES** in **SOCIAL STUDIES**
0-345-36078-8 BALLANTINE PB $12.95

Sharon **O'Brien**

Willa Cather: The Emerging Voice

0-19-504132-1 OXFORD $35.00
0-452-00874-3 NEW AMERICAN LIBRARY PB $9.95

James **Woodress**

Willa Cather: A Literary Life

0-8032-9708-4 BROMPTON PB $21.00

Frank **MacShane**, editor

Selected Letters of Raymond Chandler

See also **STUDIES OF INDIVIDUAL WRITERS** under **ABOUT CRIME FICTION** under **CRIME FICTION** in **POPULAR READING**
0-231-05080-1 COLUMBIA $49.50

John **Cheever**

Conversations with John Cheever

EDITED BY SCOTT DONALDSON
0-87805-331-X MISSISSIPPI $39.50
0-87805-332-8 MISSISSIPPI PB $15.95

Warner **Berthoff**

Hart Crane: A Re-Introduction

0-8166-1701-5 MINNESOTA PB $14.95

John **Unterecker**

Voyager: A Life of Hart Crane

0-87140-143-6 NORTON PB $14.95

Lawrence **Sutin**

Divine Invasions: A Life of Philip K. Dick

Dick's life was fully in keeping with the wildness of his writing, especially toward its delusion-ridden end. "A haunting, unforgettable, gripping narrative"—Timothy Leary
0-8065-1228-8 CITADEL PB $12.95

Rachel Blau **DuPlessis**

H.D.: The Career of that Struggle

0-253-32702-4 INDIANA $32.00
0-253-20400-3 INDIANA PB $9.95

Susan S. **Friedman**

Psyche Reborn: The Emergence of H.D.

0-253-20449-6 INDIANA PB $11.95

Richard **Lingeman**

Theodore Dreiser Volume 1: At the Gates of the City, 1871-1907 Volume 2: An American Journey, 1908-1945

0-399-13147-7 PUTNAM $22.95
0-399-13520-0 PUTNAM $39.95

Thomas P. **Riggio**, editor
The Dreiser-Mencken Letters: The Correspondence of Theodore Dreiser and H.L. Mencken, 1907-1945
Volume 1
0-8122-8008-3 PENNSYLVANIA $49.95
Volume 2
0-8122-8043-1 PENNSYLVANIA $49.95

Robert J. **Bertholf** & others
Robert Duncan: Scales of the Marvelous
0-8112-0735-8 NEW DIRECTIONS PB $5.95

Lawrence **Durrell** & Henry **Miller**
The Durrell-Miller Letters, 1935-1980
EDITED BY IAN S. MACNIVEN
0-8112-1043-X NEW DIRECTIONS $26.95

Ronald **Bush**
T.S. Eliot: A Study in Character and Style
0-521-39074-5 CAMBRIDGE $44.95
0-19-503376-0 OXFORD $35.00

Anthony **Julius**
T.S. Eliot, Anti-Semitism, and Literary Form
0-521-58673-9 CAMBRIDGE PB $18.95

Joseph **Blotner**
Faulkner: A Biography
0-679-73053-2 VINTAGE PB $24.00

Cleanth **Brooks**
William Faulkner: First Encounters
0-300-03399-0 YALE PB $15.00

Irving **Howe**
William Faulkner: A Critical Study
0-929587-69-3 DEE PB $12.95

David **Minter**
William Faulkner: His Life and Work
0-8018-2463-X SOFTSHELL PB $15.95

Carolyn W. **Sylvander**
Jessie Redmon Fauset: Black American Writer
0-87875-196-3 WHITSON $18.50

Matthew **Bruccoli**
Some Sort of Epic Grandeur: The Life of F. Scott Fitzgerald
0-88184-907-3 CARROLL & GRAF PB $16.95

F. Scott **Fitzgerald**
The Letters of F. Scott Fitzgerald
0-684-16476-0 MACMILLAN $60.00

F. Scott Fitzgerald

Zelda **Fitzgerald**
Zelda—An Illustrated Life: The Private Life of Zelda Fitzgerald
INTRODUCTION BY ELEANOR LANAHAN
ESSAYS BY PETER KURTH & JANE LIVINGSTON
0-8109-3983-5 ABRAMS $24.95

Nancy **Milford**
Zelda
Biography of Zelda Fitzgerald
0-06-091069-0 HARPERPERENNIAL PB $16.00

Joseph **Brodsky** & others
Homage to Frost
See also **ANTHOLOGIES** under **20TH-CENTURY AMERICAN POETRY**
0-374-14814-7 FS&G $30.00

Philip L. **Gerber**
Robert Frost
0-8057-7348-7 TWAYNE $21.95

Jeffrey **Meyers**
Robert Frost: A Biography
Perhaps the greatest American poet revealed in a startling new biographical interpretation. We meet a man who is neither the hayseed sage of his public persona nor the monster of his previous biographer, but an intense, impressive, and enormously sympathetic figure, destined to cast a long shadow over the poetic tradition of his country
0-395-72809-6 HOUGHTON MIFFLIN $30.00

Richard **Poirier**
Robert Frost: The Work of Knowing
0-8047-1742-7 STANFORD PB $15.95

William H. **Pritchard**
Frost: A Literary Life Reconsidered
"...deft, concise, and readable"
—*NY Times Book Review*
0-87023-838-8 MASSACHUSETTS PB $17.95

Lee **Upton**
Jean Garrigue: A Poetics of Plenitude
0-8386-3397-8 FAIRLEIGH DICKINSON $25.00

Julian **Symons**
Dashiell Hammett
More critical essay than biography
0-15-623956-6 HARCOURT BRACE PB $12.95

Joan **Mellen**
Hellman and Hammett
Eccentric, radical, and intriguing, the scandalous relationship of Lillian Hellman and Dashiell Hammett receives here its greatest rendering. Mellen draws on new material and in-depth interviews with Norman Mailer, Rose Styron, and Renata Adler, as well as diaries and love letters previously withheld. A splendid portrait of an American relationship and a fascinating era
0-06-018339-X HARPERCOLLINS $32.00

Carl **Rollyson**
Lillian Hellman: Her Legend and Her Legacy
0-312-03481-4 ST. MARTIN'S PB $13.95

Peter **Griffin**
Along with Youth: Hemingway, the Early Years
FOREWORD BY JACK HEMINGWAY
0-19-503680-8 OXFORD $22.95
0-19-505066-5 OXFORD PB $10.95

James R. **Mellow**
Hemingway: A Life Without Consequences
A major reassessment of Hemingway's life and work, revealing aspects of the writer's life previously unexplored and puncturing many of the myths Hemingway constructed about himself. Mellow pays special attention to Hemingway's friendships with men, his journalism, and his role as a central figure in the expatriate community in Paris between the wars
0-395-37777-3 HOUGHTON MIFFLIN $30.00
0-201-62620-9 ADDISON-WESLEY PB $17.00

Jeffrey **Meyers**
Hemingway: A Biography
0-7100-0929-1 ROUTLEDGE $85.00

Arnold **Rampersad**
The Life of Langston Hughes
Volume 1
I Too, Sing America, 1902-1941
0-19-504011-2 OXFORD $39.95
0-19-505426-1 OXFORD PB $15.95
Volume 2
I Dream a World, 1941-1967
See also **ARTISTS AND LITERARY FIGURES** under **BLACK VOICES, BLACK LIVES** under **AFRICAN-AMERICAN STUDIES** in **HISTORY OF THE AMERICAS**
0-19-506169-1 OXFORD PB $17.95

Robert E. **Hemenway**

Zora Neale Hurston: A Literary Biography

See also **SCIENTISTS AND EDUCATORS** under **BLACK VOICES, BLACK LIVES** under **AFRICAN-AMERICAN STUDIES** in **HISTORY OF THE AMERICAS**

FOREWORD BY ALICE WALKER

0-252-00807-3 ILLINOIS PB $12.50

Ralph F. **Voss**

A Life of William Inge: The Strains of Triumph

0-7006-0442-1 KANSAS PB $12.95

William H. **Pritchard**

Randall Jarrell: A Literary Life

0-374-24677-7 FS&G $25.00

Ann **Charters**

Kerouac: A Biography

0-312-00617-9 ST. MARTIN'S PB $13.95

Barry **Gifford** & others

Jack's Book: An Oral Biography of Jack Kerouac

0-312-01567-4 ST. MARTIN'S PB $9.95

Joyce **Johnson**

Minor Characters

A memoir of Jack Kerouac

0-671-72790-7 WASHINGTON SQUARE PB $7.95

Gerald **Nicosia**

Memory Babe: A Critical Biography of Jack Kerouac

"A splendid work, illuminating the pathos of a beautiful young novelist who, like Elvis Presley, became an object of derision when he dared to age"—*LA Times*

0-520-08569-8 CALIFORNIA PB $18.00

Jack Kerouac (photo courtesy of Grove Press, Inc.)

James Park **Sloan**

Jerzy Kosinski: A Biography

0-525-93784-6 DUTTON $27.95

William **Holtz**

The Ghost in the Little House: A Life of Rose Wilder Lane

Few people know that nearly every sentence of Laura Ingalls Wilder's classic *Little House* books were shaped at the hands of a gifted ghost writer: her daughter, Rose Wilder Lane. A promising young writer in her own right, Rose returned home to bail her parents out of financial difficulty with her rewrites. But the resulting emotional dependency on her mother plagued her for the rest of her life

0-8262-0887-8 MISSOURI $29.95

Sheldon N. **Grebstein**

Sinclair Lewis

0-8057-0448-5 TWAYNE $21.95
0-8084-0278-1 NEW COLLEGE PB $13.95

Tom **Dardis**

Firebrand: The Life of Horace Liveright

0-679-40675-1 RANDOM HOUSE $27.50

Paul **Mariani**

Lost Puritan: A Life of Robert Lowell

Elizabeth Bishop wrote of Lowell that "in the middle of our worst century so far, we have produced a magnificent poet." Mariani captures the poet as the final heir of a New England tradition and a man at the center of a revolution of American poetry: his friends William Carlos Williams, Adrienne Rich, T. S. Eliot, Sylvia Plath. Based on Lowell's unpublished letters and interviews: "A welcome volume about a Rabelaisian monster of a man and a poet" —*Kirkus Reviews*

0-393-03661-8 NORTON $27.50

Mark **Rudman**

Robert Lowell: An Introduction to the Poetry

0-231-04672-3 COLUMBIA $39.50

Richard **Tillinghast**

Robert Lowell's Life and Work: Damaged Grandeur

0-472-09570-6 MICHIGAN $39.50
0-472-06570-X MICHIGAN PB $13.95

Norman **Mailer**

Conversations with Norman Mailer

EDITED BY J. MICHAEL LENNON

0-87805-352-2 MISSISSIPPI PB $15.95

Joseph **Wenke**

Mailer's America

0-87451-393-6 NEW ENGLAND $35.00

Virginia S. **Carr**

The Lonely Hunter: A Biography of Carson McCullers

0-88184-123-4 CARROLL & GRAF PB $12.95

Brassai

Henry Miller: The Paris Years

Brassai, a lifetime friend, documents Miller's Paris life in photographs and essays

See also **PHOTOGRAPHERS** under **PHOTOGRAPHY** in **ART**

1-55970-287-7 ARCADE $23.95

Henry **Miller** & Anaïs Nin

A Literate Passion: Letters of Anaïs Nin and Henry Miller, 1932-1953

See also **MEMOIRS AND JOURNALS** under **20TH-CENTURY AMERICAN ESSAYS AND JOURNALISM**

0-15-152729-6 HARCOURT BRACE $19.95

Darden Asbury **Pyron**

Southern Daughter: The Life of Margaret Mitchell

A solidly researched, full-scale biography of the author of *Gone with the Wind*, emphasizing the influences of Southern culture on her work, and with full coverage of the filming of the book and Mitchell's later years

0-19-505276-5 OXFORD $30.00

Brian **Boyd**

Vladimir Nabokov: The American Years

0-691-02471-5 PRINCETON PB $19.95

Vladimir Nabokov: The Russian Years

Chosen as one of the best books of 1990 by the *New York Times Book Review*, this is the first volume of Boyd's biography. "A definitive life of the writer and a superbly documented chronicle of his time—from the brilliant last years of the czars through the 1917 Revolution and the decades of exile in Europe before Nabokov sailed for America in 1940" —*NY Times Book Review*

0-691-02470-7 PRINCETON $18.95

Jenny **Penberthy**, editor

Lorine Niedecker: Woman and Poet

A collection of essays which greatly enlarges our understanding of the life of a poet largely neglected in her lifetime

0-943373-39-5 READER'S CATALOG PB $14.00

Deirdre **Bair**

Anaïs Nin: A Biography

"A triumph of impartial reporting that never loses track of Nin's humanity—and the flesh-and-blood woman who emerges is far more engrossing than any saintly muse could be" —*San Francisco Examiner & Chronicle Book Review*

0-14-025525-7 PENGUIN PB $16.95

Noel Riley **Fitch**

Anaïs: The Erotic Life of Anaïs Nin

In this, the first biography of the famed diarist, sexual adventuress, and fabled femme fatale, the author explodes the myth Nin built around herself and her diaries. Meticulously researched, Fitch presents Nin as you've never seen her before, tracing a path that led her from childhood trauma to enduring sexual icon

0-316-28428-9 LITTLE, BROWN $24.95
0-316-28431-9 LITTLE, BROWN PB $14.95

Flannery **O'Connor**

The Habit of Being: Letters of Flannery O'Connor

EDITED BY SALLY FITZGERALD

0-374-16769-9 FS&G $30.00
0-374-52104-2 FS&G PB $20.00

Robert **Coles**

Flannery O'Connor's South

0-8203-1536-2 GEORGIA PB $12.95

Rosemary M. **Magee**, editor

Conversations with Flannery O'Connor

0-87805-265-8 MISSISSIPPI PB $15.95

Brad **Gooch**

City Poet: The Life and Times of Frank O'Hara

The first biography of O'Hara, the cultural catalyst and influential poet who, as curator at the Museum of Modern Art, was also one of the earliest champions of Abstract Expressionism. "Around him much of the best mid-century New York art revolved, played, feuded, splintered. Gooch misses none of these social complications"—*Kirkus Reviews*

0-394-57118-5 KNOPF $30.00

Frank O'Hara (photo by Ken Elmsue)

Don **Byrd**

Charles Olson's Maximus

0-252-00779-4 ILLINOIS $24.95

Charles **Stein**

The Secret of the Black Chrysanthemum

A study of Charles Olson

0-88268-017-X STATION HILL $27.50

Arthur **Gelb** & others

O'Neill

1-55783-186-6 APPLAUSE THEATRE PB $24.95

Eugene **O'Neill**

Selected Letters of Eugene O'Neill

EDITED BY TRAVIS BOGARD & JACKSON BRYER

0-300-04374-0 YALE $50.00

Louis **Sheaffer**

O'Neill, Son and Playwright

0-404-20321-3 AMS $82.50

Ronald H. **Wainscott**

Staging O'Neill: The Experimental Years, 1920-1934

0-300-04152-7 YALE $47.00

Tom **Teicholz**

Conversations with S.J. Perelman

0-87805-789-7 MISSISSIPPI $39.50
0-87805-790-0 MISSISSIPPI PB $15.95

Ted **Hughes** & others, editors

The Journals of Sylvia Plath

0-345-35168-1 BALLANTINE PB $5.99

Janet **Malcolm**

The Silent Woman: Sylvia Plath and Ted Hughes

Malcolm (*In the Freud Archives, The Journalist and the Murderer*) discusses the suicide and troubled legacy of Sylvia Plath—and of her husband, the poet Ted Hughes. Through this prism Malcolm explores her theme: the question of subjectivity in the biographer's craft. Totally gripping, its publication in *New Yorker* was a literary sensation

0-679-75140-8 VINTAGE PB $12.00

Joan **Givner**

Conversations with Katherine Anne Porter

0-87805-267-4 MISSISSIPPI PB $15.95

James **Laughlin**

Pound as Wuz: Essays on Ezra Pound

1-55597-097-4 GRAY WOLF $17.00
1-55597-098-2 GRAY WOLF PB $9.50

Gordon E. **Bigelow**

Frontier Eden: The Literary Career of Marjorie Kinnan Rawlings

0-8130-0672-4 FLORIDA PB $17.95

Bruce **Dick** & others, editors

Conversations with Ishmael Reed

0-87805-814-1 MISSISSIPPI $39.50
0-87805-822-2 MISSISSIPPI PB $14.95

Linda **Hamalian**

A Life of Kenneth Rexroth

A frank, sympathetic (although not always flattering) look at the private side of the poet, critic, and translator who dominated the San Francisco literary scene for decades

0-393-02944-1 NORTON $25.00
0-393-30915-0 NORTON PB $12.95

Soon after the Six Gallery reading, Rexroth invited Whalan, Ginsberg, Kerouac, and Snyder for dinner, but the hospitality he extended ended up by alienating him from them. After clowning around in North Beach, the younger poets, drunk and carefree, got to Eighth Avenue long after they were expected. Trying to make light of their rudeness, Kerouac asked for a drink. Rexroth exploded…Kerouac called Rexroth a "boche." And Ginsberg announced that he was a better poet than Rexroth, with youth on his side…Before Marthe could bring out the food, Rexroth ordered them to leave. They did so while Kerouac drunkenly shouted "Dirty German" repeatedly.

A LIFE OF KENNETH REXROTH

Milton **Hindus**, editor

Charles Reznikoff: Man and Poet

0-915032-60-0
NATIONAL POETRY FOUNDATION PB $15.95

Anne Sexton (photo courtesy of National Educational Television)

Susan **Sherman**, editor

May Sarton: Among the Unusual Days: A Portrait

Sarton's many admirers will revel in these unpublished journal excerpts, letters, and poems spanning six decades of her passionate life

0-393-03451-8 NORTON $25.00

Marita **Simpson** & others, editors

May Sarton: A Self-Portrait

0-393-30535-X NORTON PB $7.95

Delmore **Schwartz**

Letters of Delmore Schwartz

EDITED BY ROBERT PHILLIPS
FOREWORD BY KARL SHAPIRO

0-86538-044-9 BRAZILLER $24.95
0-86538-048-1 PERSEA PB $14.95

Diane Wood **Middlebrook**

Anne Sexton: A Biography

This biography of the celebrated "confessional poet" has created controversy through its liberal use of Sexton's psychiatric sessions. All in all, an indelible portrait of madness and creativity in uneasy partnership

0-395-35362-9 HOUGHTON MIFFLIN $24.95

Leland **Pogue**, editor

Conversations with Susan Sontag

0-87805-833-8 MISSISSIPPI $39.50
0-87805-834-6 MISSISSIPPI PB $15.95

Ann **Hulbert**

The Interior Castle: The Art and Life of Jean Stafford

"A model of honesty which reveals the life, both charmed and painful, of one of America's great women writers"—Maureen Howard

0-87023-870-1 MASSACHUSETTS PB $18.95

Jackson J. **Benson**

Wallace Stegner: His Life and Work

0-670-86222-3 VIKING $32.95

Marianne **DeKoven**

A Different Language: Gertrude Stein's Experimental Writing

0-299-09210-0 WISCONSIN $25.00

Gertrude **Stein**

Letters of Gertrude Stein and Thornton Wilder

EDITED BY EDWARD M. BURNS & ULLA DYDO WITH WILLIAM RICE

0-300-06774-7 YALE $35.00

Renate **Stendhal**

Gertrude Stein: In Words and Pictures

The "Mother and Muse of Modernism" entertained, at her famous Paris salon, the entirety of the Lost Generation: Picasso, Fitzgerald, Pound, Hemingway, Djuna Barnes, to name just a few. This photographic and literary portrait presents its readers with a complete experience of one of the century's most brilliant and unconventional lives

0-945575-99-8 ALGONQUIN PB $19.95

Linda **Wagner-Martin**

"Favored Strangers": Gertrude Stein and Her family

0-8135-2169-6 RUTGERS $34.95

Jayne L. **Walker**

The Making of a Modernist: Gertrude Stein from Three Lives to Tender Buttons

0-87023-323-8 MASSACHUSETTS $25.00

Brenda **Wineapple**

Sister Brother: Gertrude and Leo Stein

A perceptive and detailed examination of the tempestuous relationship between the siblings; particularly notable for its uncommonly fair treatment of Leo

0-399-14103-0 PUTNAM $35.00

Jackson J. **Benson**

The True Adventures of John Steinbeck, Writer: A Biography

0-14-014417-X PENGUIN PB $19.95

Harold **Bloom**

Wallace Stevens: The Poems of Our Climate

0-8014-9185-1 CORNELL PB $17.95

Glen **MacLeod**

Wallace Stevens and Modern Art: From the Armory Show to Abstract Expressionism

A brilliant book that shows how Stevens's involvement with artists, art dealers, artworks, and visual art theory played a central role in his poetry, his poetic theory, and the unusual character of his poetic development

0-300-05360-6 YALE $37.50

Helen **Vendler**

On Extended Wings: Wallace Stevens' Longer Poems

0-674-63436-5 HARVARD PB $12.95

James L. **West**, editor

Conversations with William Styron

0-87805-260-7 MISSISSIPPI $39.50

William Styron

William **Drake**

Sara Teasdale: Woman and Poet

0-87049-595-X TENNESSEE PB $16.95

Burton **Bernstein**

Thurber: A Biography

0-688-14772-0 MORROW PB $16.00

Thomas **Fensch**, editor

Conversations with James Thurber

0-87805-410-3 MISSISSIPPI PB $15.95

Neil A. **Grauer**

Remember Laughter: A Life of James Thurber

Grauer celebrates the great American humorist in this funny, readable biography. But he also delves below the surface to look at Thurber's misogyny, his alcoholism, to paint a complete picture of a complex man

0-8032-2155-X NEBRASKA $20.00

Cynthia E. **Kerman** & others

The Lives of Jean Toomer: A Hunger for Wholeness

0-8071-1548-7 LSU PB $12.95

Nellie Y. **McKay**

Jean Toomer, Artist: A Study of His Literary Life and Work, 1894-1936

0-8078-1583-7 NORTH CAROLINA $34.95

Ernst **Schurer** & others, editors

B. Traven: Life and Work

0-271-00382-0 PENN STATE $40.00

Jay **Martin**

Nathanael West: The Art of His Life

0-88184-030-0 CARROLL & GRAF PB $8.95

Eleanor **Dwight**

Edith Wharton: An Extraordinary Life

One of the most compelling things about Wharton was her highly developed aesthetic and social sensibility. This first fully illustrated biography is organized around the places Wharton lived and visited: Italy, France, Newport, Manhattan, and Lenox, Massachusetts. It shows her as gardener, artist, photographer, salon keeper, and literary star

0-8109-3971-1 ABRAMS $39.95

R.W.B. **Lewis**

Edith Wharton: A Biography

0-88064-020-0 FROMM PB $15.95

R.W.B. **Lewis** & others, editors

The Letters of Edith Wharton

0-02-034400-7 COLLIER PB $16.00

Albert J. **Devlin**

Conversations with Tennessee Williams

0-87805-263-1 MISSISSIPPI PB $15.95

Donald **Windham**, editor

Tennessee Williams' Letters to Donald Windham, 1940-1965

0-8203-1840-X GEORGIA PB $19.95

James **Laughlin**

Remembering William Carlos Williams

A memoir of the poet whose work Laughlin published for decades

0-8112-1307-2 NEW DIRECTIONS PB $7.95

Paul **Mariani**

William Carlos Williams: A New World Naked

0-393-30672-0 NORTON PB $14.95

Rosalind Baker **Wilson**

Near the Magician: A Memoir of My Father, Edmund Wilson

1-55584-342-5 GROVE $18.95

Addison **Gayle**

Richard Wright: Ordeal of a Native Son

0-8446-6000-0 SMITH $20.50

Margaret **Walker**

Richard Wright, Daemonic Genius: A Portrait of the Man, a Critical Look at His Work

1-56743-004-X AMISTAD PB $9.95

Caribbean Literature

The literature of Cuba and Puerto Rico will be found under Latin American Literature.

Peter **Abrahams**

Abrahams, a former broadcaster and news analyst, emigrated to Jamaica in 1955 from South Africa. His novels are concerned with relations between the races, and the political and social development of his adopted country.

Tell Freedom

The autobiography of a prominent writer who describes being caught between black and white culture and fitting into neither

See also **CENTRAL AND SOUTHERN AFRICA** under **AFRICAN LITERATURE** in **LITERATURE OF EUROPE, AFRICA, AND ASIA**

0-571-11777-5 FABER PB $12.95

The View from Coyaba

0-571-13289-8 FABER PB $8.95

Phyllis S. **Allfrey**

The Orchid House

The one published novel by the political activist, about a white family whose powers are waning

INTRODUCTION BY ELAINE CAMPBELL

0-8135-2332-X RUTGERS PB $16.95

Vernon F. **Anderson**

Sudden Glory

A tale centered around Mayan excavations in Guatemala

0-435-98808-5 HEINEMANN PB $9.95

Michael **Anthony**

All that Glitters: The Caribbean

See also **THE CARIBBEAN** under **THE CARIBBEAN AND CENTRAL AMERICA** under **TRAVEL LITERATURE** in **FOOD, TRAVEL, AND LEISURE**

0-435-98034-3 HEINEMANN PB $7.95

Cricket in the Road

0-435-98032-7 HEINEMANN PB $7.95

The Games Were Coming

The thrills and spills of a cycle race, and the importance of the finish for three characters in particular; Anthony's first novel

0-435-98033-5 HEINEMANN PB $7.95

Green Days by the River

0-435-98030-0 HEINEMANN PB $7.95

The Year in San Fernando

A classic novel of boyhood, in which a young servant gets a glimpse of grown-ups and their sometimes sordid doings

0-435-98031-9 HEINEMANN PB $7.95

Neil **Bissoondath**

Digging Up the Mountains

Fourteen stories concerned mainly with migration between the West Indies and North America. "Humorous and sad, observant and intuitive, it imparts a very vivid sense of place and how it shapes the lives of the people who live there"—Susan Hill

0-7715-9246-9

GENERAL DISTRIBUTION SERVICES PB $4.95

Kamau **Brathwaite**

A prominent Barbadian academic, historian, critic, and highly accomplished poet, Brathwaite has been a leader in experimental poetry and the use of indigenous speech patterns in Caribbean verse.

The Arrivants

A trilogy addressing the central themes of Caribbean history, consisting of *Rights of Passage, Masks,* and *Islands*

0-19-911103-0 OXFORD PB $14.95

Barabajan Poems, 1492-1992

0-9640424-3-6 SAVACOU NORTH PB $25.00

Black + Blues

A rich and beautiful collection of the internationally celebrated poet. "His dazzling, inventive language, his tragic yet unquenchable vision, make Kamau Brathwaite one of the most compelling of late 20th century poets"—Adrienne Rich. "This is just the kind of poetry Williams had in mind when he said that men die for the lack of what is to be found there"—*VLS*

0-8112-1313-7 NEW DIRECTIONS PB $9.95

Dreamstories

0-582-09340-6 ADDISON-WESLEY PB $8.95

Middle Passages

0-8112-1232-7 NEW DIRECTIONS PB $9.95

Roots

0-472-09544-7 MICHIGAN $34.50

0-472-06544-0 MICHIGAN PB $15.95

Trench Town Rock

0-918786-45-2 LOST ROADS PB $10.95

The Zea Mexican Diary

0-299-13640-X WISCONSIN $17.95

Aimé **Cesaire**

Cesaire, born in Martinique, was a founder of the Negritude movement. "More vividly perhaps than in the work of the Surrealists of France, Cesaire's poetry embodies the twin aspirations of political and aesthetic revolution, and in such a way that they are inseparably joined"—Paul Auster

The Collected Poetry

See also **POETRY** under **MODERN FRENCH LITERATURE** in **LITERATURE OF EUROPE, AFRICA, AND ASIA**

TRANSLATED BY CLAYTON ESHLEMAN & ANNETTE SMITH

0-520-04347-2 CALIFORNIA $45.00

0-520-05320-6 CALIFORNIA PB $18.00

Lost Body

TRANSLATED WITH AN INTRODUCTION BY CLAYTON ESHELMAN

ILLUSTRATED BY PABLO PICASSO

0-8076-1148-4 BRAZILLER PB $14.95

Lyric and Dramatic Poetry, 1946-82

0-8139-1244-X CARAF PB $14.95

A Tempest

A variation on Shakespeare's *Tempest*

TRANSLATED BY RICHARD MILLER

0-913745-15-4 UBU REPERTORY THEATER PB $8.95

Patrick **Chamoiseau**

Creole Folktales

TRANSLATED BY LINDA COVERDALE

1-56584-185-9 NEW PRESS $16.95

School Days: Chemin-d'Ecole

TRANSLATED BY LINDA COVERDALE

0-8032-6376-7 NEBRASKA $42.01

Texaco: A Novel

TRANSLATED BY ROSE-MYRIAM REJOUIS

0-679-43235-3 PANTHEON $25.01

Michelle **Cliff**

Abeng

0-14-015314-4 PENGUIN PB $10.95

0-452-27483-4 PLUME PB $10.95

Bodies of Water

0-452-27375-7 PLUME PB $9.95

Free Enterprise

0-452-27122-3 PLUME PB $9.95

The Land of Look Behind: Prose and Poetry

0-932379-09-5 FIREBRAND $18.95

0-932379-08-7 FIREBRAND PB $8.95

No Telephone to Heaven

In the period leading up to independence, a woman emigrates and wanders about Europe and North America

0-452-27569-5 PLUME PB $10.95

Merle **Collins**

Angel

A young woman's coming of age as she joins her country's move toward political autonomy

0-931188-64-4 SEAL PB $9.95

Rotten Pomerack

1-85381-556-X VIRAGO PB $13.95

Edwidge **Danticat**

Breath, Eyes, Memory

From the much celebrated Haitian-American novelist, "A lovely, poetic tale about loss and self discovery"—*The Bloomsbury Review*

See also **NEW WRITERS OF THE '90S** under **20TH-CENTURY AMERICAN FICTION**

1-56947-005-7 SOHO $20.00

0-679-75661-2 VINTAGE PB $11.00

Krik? Krak!: Stories

From National Book Award-winning Danticat, intimate histories of Haitians and African Americans

See also **NEW WRITERS OF THE '90S** under **20TH-CENTURY AMERICAN FICTION**

1-56947-025-1 SOHO $20.00

0-679-76657-X RANDOM HOUSE PB $11.00

René **Depestre**

The Festival of the Greasy Pole

0-8139-1282-2 CARAF PB $12.95

Geoffrey **Drayton**

Christopher

A white child's increasing involvement with the black world around him

0-435-98235-4 HEINEMANN PB $7.95

Edouard **Glissant**

Monsieur Toussaint: A Play

0-89410-128-5 THREE CONTINENTS $16.00

The Ripening

TRANSLATED BY MICHAEL J. DASH

0-435-98222-2 HEINEMANN PB $10.95

Wilson **Harris**

Using landscape as an aspect of his characters' consciousness, Harris deviates from the descriptive realism typical of much Caribbean fiction.

The Carnival Trilogy

0-571-15435-2 FABER PB $15.95

The Guyana Quartet

Harris's masterpiece, consisting of *Palace of the Peacock, The Far Journey of Oudin, The Whole Armor,* and *The Secret Ladder,* paints a comprehensive picture of contemporary Guyana through "a sacramental union of man and landscape" (John Hearne)

0-571-13451-3 FABER PB $14.95

The Infinite Rehearsal

0-571-14885-9 FABER $13.95

Palace of the Peacock

The first volume of *The Guyana Quartet,* written with the "staggering ebullience of language we begin to recognize in West Indian writers" —*The Times* [London]

0-571-08930-5 FABER PB $10.95

Resurrection at Sorrow Hill

0-571-16978-3 FABER $22.95

John **Hearne**

The Sure Salvation

0-571-13452-1 FABER PB $8.95

Voices Under the Window

"A tight, short, explosive book, remarkably polished" *(Spectator)* about a white islander orator who feels he doesn't really count as white

0-571-09985-8 FABER PB $5.95

Roy **Heath**

The Armstrong Trilogy

Includes *From the Heat of the Day, One Generation,* and *Genetha*

0-89255-199-2 PERSEA PB $15.00

From the Heat of the Day

0-89255-175-5 PERSEA $19.95

The Ministry of Hope

0-7145-3015-8 MARION BOYARS $24.95

The Murderer

0-89255-169-0 PERSEA PB $9.95

The Reasonable Adventurer

0-8229-5071-5 PITTSBURGH PB $14.95

The Shadow Bride

0-89255-213-1 PERSEA $24.95

Merle **Hodge**

Crick Crack Monkey

0-435-98401-2 HEINEMANN PB $7.95

A Fling with a Demon Lover

0-0601-7350-5 HARPERCOLLINS $22.00

C.L.R. **James**

The Black Jacobins: Toussaint l'Ouverture and the San Domingo Revolution

James's most famous book, an influential interpretation of the Haitian revolution of the 1790s

See also **HAITI** under **LATIN AMERICA AND THE CARIBBEAN** in **HISTORY OF THE AMERICAS**

0-679-72467-2 VINTAGE PB $14.00

The C.L.R. James Reader

0-631-18495-3 BLACKWELL PB $20.95

Bertene **Juminer**

The Bastards

The difficulties of reassimilation for a medical student studying in France

TRANSLATED WITH AN INTRODUCTION BY KEITH Q. WARNER

0-8139-1204-0 CARAF PB $12.95

Kwadwo Agymah **Kamau**

Flickering Shadows

1-56689-049-7 COFFEE HOUSE $21.95

Jamaica **Kincaid**

Kincaid, an Antiguan writer now based in the US, uses a rich image of recollection to evoke coming of age in the Caribbean.

Annie John

See also **SINCE 1945** under **20TH-CENTURY AMERICAN FICTION**

0-374-10521-9 HILL & WANG $18.95

0-452-26016-7 PLUME PB $8.00

Jamaica Kincaid

At the Bottom of the River

See also **SINCE 1945** under **20TH-CENTURY AMERICAN FICTION**

0-452-26754-4 PLUME PB $7.95

A Small Place

See also **SINCE 1945** under **20TH-CENTURY AMERICAN FICTION**

0-452-26235-6 PLUME PB $8.95

The Autobiography of My Mother

A 70-year-old West Indian woman looks back at her life, concentrating her memory on sex, human relations, and powerlessness

See also **SINCE 1945** under **20TH-CENTURY AMERICAN FICTION**

0-374-10731-9 FS&G $20.00

Dany **Laferriere**

An Aroma of Coffee

TRANSLATED BY DAVID HOMEL

0-88910-439-5 COACH HOUSE PB $11.95

Dining with the Dictator

TRANSLATED BY DAVID HOMEL

0-88910-480-8 COACH HOUSE PB $11.95

Eroshima

TRANSLATED BY DAVID HOMEL

0-88910-385-2 COACH HOUSE PB $10.95

How to Make Love to a Negro

TRANSLATED BY DAVID HOMEL

0-88910-305-4 COACH HOUSE PB $12.95

Why Must a Black Writer Write About Sex?

TRANSLATED BY DAVID HOMEL

0-88910-482-4 COACH HOUSE PB $11.95

George **Lamming**

Conversations: Essays, Addresses and Interviews, 1953-1990

EDITED BY RICHARD DRAYTON

0-472-09575-7 MICHIGAN $42.50

0-472-06575-0 MICHIGAN PB $14.95

The Emigrants

Of the disappointment and suffering that awaited hopeful West Indian immigrants in 1950s Britain

0-472-06470-3 MICHIGAN PB $14.95

In the Castle of My Skin

This major West Indian work of the 1950s focuses on the pains of adolescence

0-472-06468-1 MICHIGAN PB $15.95

Natives of My Person

The tale of a 17th-century voyage of discovery to the Caribbean leads to discussion of freedom, imperialism, and love

0-472-09467-X MICHIGAN $47.50

0-472-06467-3 MICHIGAN PB $15.95

The Pleasures of Exile

Collected essays and shorter pieces

0-472-09466-1 MICHIGAN $47.50

0-472-06466-5 MICHIGAN PB $15.95

Season of Adventure

A woman's quest for her Caribbean identity

0-8052-8011-1 SCHOCKEN PB $6.95

Paul **Laraque**

Camourade

Poems spanning 40 years. "Laraque's poems…fuse with the more intimately personal works to create a single body of revolutionary hope, the foundation of his every word" —Jack Hirschman

TRANSLATED BY ROSEMARY MANNO

0-915306-71-9 CURBSTONE PB $9.95

Liberty Drum: New and Selected Poems

1-88521-405-7 AZUL PB $11.95

Earl **Lovelace**

Brief Conversion and Other Stories

0-435-98882-4 HEINEMANN PB $7.50

The Schoolmaster

An idyllic village, untouched by big-city vices, is tarnished by the arrival of an avaricious schoolmaster

INTRODUCTION BY KENNETH RAMCHAND

0-435-98550-7 HEINEMANN PB $7.95

The Wine of Astonishment

Written in "richly demotic Caribbean patois (it) charts the struggles of a so-called 'Spiritual Baptist' sent to find toleration and freedom from persecutions"—*London Sunday Times*

0-435-98880-8 HEINEMANN PB $9.95

Roger **Mais**

Brother Man

The book about the birth of the Rastafarian movement that established Mais's early reputation as a social realist. "His best work because it brings together in one minor classic all of the author's varied talents"—Edward Brathwaite

0-435-98585-X HEINEMANN PB $8.95

The Hills Were Joyful Together

Under the bittersweet title from Psalm 98 he reveals the dire wretchedness of the slum class in Kingston

0-435-98586-8 HEINEMANN PB $9.95

Listen, the Wind

0-582-78551-0 LONGMAN PB $12.50

Edgar **Mittelholzer**

Corentyne Thunder

0-435-98593-0 HEINEMANN PB $8.95

Caryl **Phillips**

Based in Britain, Phillips is a leading and dynamic voice among the latest generation of Caribbean novelists and playwrights.

Cambridge

A highly inventive historical novel in which the intertwined stories of an Englishwoman and a slave are told in their own voices. "With *Cambridge*, Caryl Phillips takes a firm step toward joining the company of the literary giants of our time"—*NY Times Book Review*

See also **THE MIDDLE GENERATION** under **20TH-CENTURY BRITISH AND IRISH FICTION** in **LITERATURE OF THE BRITISH ISLES**

0-679-73689-1 VINTAGE PB $10.00

A State of Independence

A homecoming to the Caribbean after a 20-year absence creates a sharp sense of dislocation

0-374-26976-9 FS&G $13.95
0-679-75930-1 VINTAGE PB $10.00

V.S. **Reid**

The Leopard

The struggle of the Kenyan people during the Mau Mau era. "What the author has done is to give his story the quality of near myth to make the horror understandable"—*Time*

INTRODUCTION BY MERVYN MORRIS

0-435-98660-0 HEINEMANN PB $7.95

Jacques **Roumain**

Masters of the Dew

Born into an aristocratic family and a founder of the Haitian Communist party, Roumain is often considered Haiti's most important writer

0-435-98745-3 HEINEMANN PB $10.95

When the Tom-Tom Beats

0-9632363-8-5 AZUL PB $11.95

Sam **Selvon**

The Housing Lark

A jovial tale of Caribbean immigrant life in London, narrated wholly in Trinidadian dialect

0-89410-602-3 THREE CONTINENTS $20.00
0-89410-603-1 THREE CONTINENTS PB $11.00

The Lonely Londoners

0-920661-16-5 TSAR PB $10.95

Moses Ascending

A less merry account of the Caribbean experience in Britain, written a decade after *The Housing Lark*

INTRODUCTION BY MERVYN MORRIS

0-435-98750-X HEINEMANN PB $8.95

Michael **Smith**

It a Come

Dub poems combining folklore, biblical allusion, and international news items

PREFACE BY LINTON KWESI JOHNSON

0-87286-217-8 CITY LIGHTS PB $5.95

Garth **St. Omer**

Lights on the Hill

0-435-98964-2 HEINEMANN PB $8.95

Michael **Thelwell**

Duties, Pleasures, and Conflicts: Essays in Struggle

INTRODUCTION BY JAMES BALDWIN

0-87023-523-0 MASSACHUSETTS PB $17.95

The Harder They Come

An adaptation of the famous film that goes far beyond the usual "novelization," expanding the film's themes and characterizations

0-8021-3138-7 GROVE PB $11.95

Derek **Walcott**

Unlike many Caribbean writers of his generation, Walcott resisted for a long time the lure of emigration, preferring to help establish a strong Caribbean literary culture from within as both poet and dramatist. As such he is described as "a 20th century man with an Elizabethan sense of language"—G.E. Murray, Chicago Tribune

The Antilles

0-374-10530-8 FS&G $7.00

The Arkansas Testament

In his eighth collection of poetry, the two parts "Here" and "Elsewhere" reflect the problem of allegiance implicit in his recent move to the US

0-374-52099-2 FS&G PB $9.00

The Bounty

See also **POETRY SINCE 1945** under **20TH-CENTURY AMERICAN POETRY**

0-374-11556-7 FS&G $18.00

Collected Poems, 1948-1984

0-374-12626-7 FS&G $30.00
0-374-52025-9 FS&G PB $17.00

Conversations With Derek Walcott

0-87805-854-0 MISSISSIPPI $39.50
0-87805-855-9 MISSISSIPPI PB $16.95

Midsummer

A one-summer's-worth 54-poem sequence written in Trinidad by "the outsider, the poet of the periphery, but it may be time to center the compass at his position and draw the circle again"—Sven Birkerts, *New Republic*

0-374-51863-7 FS&G PB $10.00

The Odyssey: A Stage Version

0-374-17249-8 FS&G $25.00
0-374-52387-8 NOONDAY PB $12.00

Omeros

Derek Walcott's masterpiece is an expansive vision of Caribbean history cast in the form of an astonishingly inventive long poem

0-374-22591-5 FS&G $30.00
0-374-52350-9 NOONDAY PB $12.00

Denis **Williams**

Other Leopards

An abortive quest for origins set in Sudan, which represents for the author "the *alter ego* of ancestral times that I was sure quietly slumbered behind the cultured mask"

0-435-98590-6 HEINEMANN PB $8.95

Joseph **Zobel**

Black Shack Alley

TRANSLATED BY KEITH Q. WARNER

0-914478-67-2 THREE CONTINENTS PB $18.00

Anthologies

Paula **Barnett**, editor

The Penguin Book of Caribbean Verse in English

A comprehensive anthology including selections from the dub poets

0-14-058511-7 PENGUIN PB $13.95

Marcela **Breton**, editor

Rhythm and Revolt: Tales of the Antilles

0-452-27178-9 PLUMSTOCK PB $12.95

J. Edward **Chamberlin**

Come Back to Me My Language: Poetry and the West Indies

0-252-01973-3 ILLINOIS $44.95

O.R. **Dathorne**

Dark Ancestor: The Literature of the Black Man in the Caribbean

0-8071-0757-3 LSU $37.50

Carole B. **Davis** & Elaine **Fido**

Out of the Kumbla: Womanist Perspectives on Caribbean Literature

0-86543-042-X AFRICA WORLD $49.95
0-86543-043-8 AFRICA WORLD PB $15.95

Jean **D'Costa** & Barbara **Lalla**

Voices in Exile: A Collection of Archaic Jamaican Texts of the 18th and 19th Centuries

0-8173-0382-0 ALABAMA $32.50

Margarite Fernandez **Olmos** & Lizabeth **Paravisini-Gebert**, editors

Remaking a Lost Harmony: Stories from the Hispanic Caribbean

1-87772-736-9 WHITE PINE PB $17.00

Amon S. **Saakana**

The Colonial Legacy in Caribbean Literature

0-86543-059-4 AFRICA WORLD $24.95
0-86543-060-8 AFRICA WORLD PB $7.95

Patrick **Taylor**

The Narrative of Liberation

Perspectives on Afro-Caribbean literature, popular culture, and politics

0-8014-2193-4 CORNELL $34.95

Latin American Literature

"We must not forget that Spanish America has a very old literature, it has a great tradition I will just outline briefly. It starts in the Spanish language with the writing of Columbus and Amerigo Vespucci about the New World. But in the countries of Indian ancestry, such as Mexico and Central America, there was already a great deal of literature. So what we have is the full flowering of a tradition which doesn't culminate with the so-called Boom. It is not the writing of one generation; it includes writers as old as Borges, who died in his late eighties, or as young as Vargas Llosa, who is hardly in his fifties. So, it is not a generation but more a movement in which many strands of our tradition come together and transform the quality and the nature of narrative fiction in Latin America."—Carlos Fuentes in *Interviews With Latin American Writers* by Marie-Lise Gazarian Gautier (Dalkey Archive)

Fiction

Argentina

José **Bianco**

Shadow Play & The Rats: Two Novellas

Human and family relationships among the dead and the living

0-935480-11-0 LATIN AMERICAN LIT PB $9.50

Jorge Luis **Borges**

Dreamtigers

Poems, parables, stories, sketches, and aphorisms

TRANSLATED BY MILDRED BOYER & HAROLD MORLAND
INTRODUCTION BY MIGUEL ENGUIDANOS

0-292-71549-8 TEXAS PB $9.95

Ficciones

A collection containing many of Borges's most famous stories, including *The Circular Labyrinth* and *Pierre Menard, Author of Don Quixote*

EDITED BY ANTHONY KERRIGAN

0-679-42299-4 EVERYMAN'S $15.00
0-8021-3030-5 GROVE PB $9.95

Labyrinths: Selected Short Stories & Other Writings

EDITED BY DONALD A. YATES & JAMES E. IRBY
INTRODUCTION BY ANDRE MAUROIS

0-8112-0012-4 NEW DIRECTIONS PB $10.95

A Personal Anthology

An introductory volume compiled by the author

EDITED BY ANTHONY KERRIGAN

0-8021-3077-1 GROVE PB $11.00

Adolfo Bioy **Casares**

The Invention of Morel & Other Stories

The title novella, a cunning parable about illusion, is among Bioy Casares's best-known works

TRANSLATED BY NORMAN THOMAS DE GIOVANNI

0-292-73840-4 TEXAS PB $15.95

A Plan for Escape

A dreamlike novel of a penal colony. "This short novel, firmly rooted in the Borges tradition, reminiscent of H.G. Wells, and thoroughly weird by conventional standards, is an exceptionally ambitious, intellectual mystery woven with horror and science fiction"—*Village Voice*

TRANSLATED BY SUZANNE JILL LEVINE

1-55597-107-5 GRAY WOLF PB $7.50

Selected Stories

TRANSLATED BY SUZANNE JILL LEVINE

0-8112-1275-0 NEW DIRECTIONS $21.95

Julio **Cortazar**

Blow Up & Other Stories

Cortazar wrote some of the most original fantastic tales of this century, including *Axolotl, The Night Face Up,* and the title story, on which Antonioni's famous film is loosely based

TRANSLATED BY PAUL BLACKBURN

0-394-72881-5 RANDOM HOUSE PB $13.00

Hopscotch

Cortazar's most famous novel, set in Paris and Buenos Aires, is an exhilarating intellectual game that can be read either in linear fashion or by "hopscotching" according to the author's elaborate instructions

0-394-75284-8 PANTHEON PB $16.00

Unreasonable Hours

TRANSLATED BY ALBERTO MANGUEL

0-88910-494-8 COACH HOUSE PB $11.95

Julio Cortazar

Ezequiel Martinez **Estrada**

Holy Saturday and Other Stories

An important social critic's stories about small-town life, urban alienation, and bureaucracy

TRANSLATED BY LELAND H. CHAMBERS

0-935480-30-7 LATIN AMERICAN LIT PB $12.95

Ricardo **Guiraldes**

Don Segundo Sombra

0-8229-3851-0 PITTSBURGH $49.95
0-8229-5524-5 PITTSBURGH PB $22.95

Tomas Eloy **Martinez**

Santa Evita

TRANSLATED BY HELEN LANE

0-679-44704-0 KNOPF $23.00

Daniel **Moyano**

Flight of the Tiger

1-85242-174-6 SERPENT'S TAIL PB $13.99

Manuel **Puig**

Heartbreak Tango: A Serial

Two love triangles involving the adolescent of *Betrayed by Rita Hayworth*

TRANSLATED BY SUZANNE JILL LEVINE

0-14-018997-1 PENGUIN PB $11.95

Kiss of the Spider Woman

The story of two prisoners which unpredictably triggered a movie and an enormously successful musical

TRANSLATED BY THOMAS COLCHIE

0-8488-0614-X AMEREON PB $21.95
0-679-72449-4 VINTAGE PB $12.00

Pubis Angelical

TRANSLATED BY ELENA BRUNET

84-322-1379-9 LECTORUM PB $7.95

Luisa **Valenzuela**

He Who Searches

"Luisa Valenzuela is the heiress of Latin American fiction. She wears an opulent, baroque crown, but her feet are naked"—Carlos Fuentes

TRANSLATED BY HELEN LANE

0-916583-20-1 DALKEY ARCHIVE PB $8.00

The Lizard's Tail
A tale about power, politics, and magic, or how Isabel Peron's minister of social welfare, Lopez Rega, ruled Argentina through sorcery
TRANSLATED BY GREGORY RABASSA
1-85242-112-6 SERPENT'S TAIL PB $14.99

Brazil

Jorge **Amado**

Dona Flor and Her Two Husbands
"Reading *Dona Flor and Her Two Husbands* is like having a tropical jungle of scented flowers in blazing colors explode in your face" —*Cincinnati Enquirer*
0-380-75469-X AVON PB $11.00

Gabriela, Clove and Cinnamon
Perhaps the finest example of Amado's comic, sensuous fiction
TRANSLATED BY JAMES L. TAYLOR & WILLIAM L. GROSSMAN
0-380-75470-3 AVON PB $12.50

The Golden Harvest
TRANSLATED BY CLIFFORD E. LANDERS
0-380-76100-9 AVON PB $12.50

Home Is the Sailor
The misadventures of a magnificent sailor—or a magnificent liar
TRANSLATED BY HARRIET DE ONIS
0-380-75474-6 AVON PB $7.95

Pen, Sword, Camisole: A Fable to Kindle a Hope
The specter of Nazism shows its face in the Brazilian Academy of Letters during World War II
TRANSLATED BY HELEN R. LANE
0-380-75480-0 AVON PB $7.95

Tereza Batista Home from Wars
TRANSLATED BY BARBARA SHELBY
0-380-75468-1 AVON PB $9.95

Tieta
A hometown girl returns from the evil metropolis to rescue her people from big-time factories and pollution
TRANSLATED BY BARBARA SHELBY MERELLO
0-380-75477-0 AVON PB $9.95

The Violent Land
0-380-75475-4 AVON PB $10.00

The War of the Saints
TRANSLATED BY GREGORY RABASSA
0-553-37440-0 BANTAM PB $10.95

Adolpho **Caminha**

Bom Crioulo: The Black Man and the Cabin Boy
Latin America's first novel of homosexual relations
TRANSLATED BY E.A. LACEY
0-917342-88-7 BOOK PEOPLE PB $7.95

Euclydes **da Cunha**

Rebellion in the Backlands
The tragic story of the Canudos uprising of the late 1890s
TRANSLATED BY SAMUEL PUTNAM
0-226-12444-4 CHICAGO PB $19.95

Paulo **Coelho**

By the River Piedra I Sat Down and Wept
Coelho—Latin America's most widely read author after Márquez—has become an international sensation: a literary bestseller with over seven million copies in print. Here, he presents the story of Pilar, a young woman on a spiritual journey through the French Pyrenees, led by a mesmerizing and handsome miracle worker. A magical blend of action, exotic settings, vivid characters, and spiritual insight
TRANSLATED BY ALAN R. CLARKE
0-06-251398-2 HARPERCOLLINS $20.00

Joaquim Maria Machado **de Assis**

Counselor Ayres' Memorial
An old diplomat narrates this love story set on the eve of the abolition of slavery in 1888
TRANSLATED BY HELEN CALDWELL
0-520-02227-0 CALIFORNIA $32.50
0-520-04775-3 CALIFORNIA PB $12.00

The Devil's Church & Other Stories
TRANSLATED BY JACK SCHMITT & LORIE ISHIMATSU
0-292-71542-0 TEXAS PB $9.95

Dom Casmurro
Considered by many to be turn-of-the century Brazilian author de Assis's finest work, *Dom Casmurro* details a prosperous citizen of Rio's tragic love for his childhood sweetheart and wife. With chapters whose titles range from "The Cup of Coffee" to "Don't do it, my dear!"
INTRODUCTION BY CARLOS FUENTES
0-374-52303-7 NOONDAY PB $12.00

Dom Casmurro
TRANSLATED BY R.L. SCOTT-BUCCLEUCH
0-14-044612-5 PENGUIN PB $10.95

Epitaph of a Small Winner
From beyond the grave, Braz Cubes casts a disenchanted eye over his life; a dry masterpiece of comedy
0-374-52192-1 FS&G PB $12.00

Helena
A romantic tale of a proud and mysterious woman
TRANSLATED BY HELEN CALDWELL
0-520-04812-1 CALIFORNIA $37.50
0-520-06025-3 CALIFORNIA PB $12.00

Philosopher or Dog?
A simple philosophy clashes with the speculative business world in this excellent novel of late-19th-century Brazilian life
TRANSLATED BY CLOTILDE WILSON
0-374-52328-2 NOONDAY PB $12.00

The Wager: Buenos Aires Journal
0-7206-0772-8 DUFOUR $30.00

Rachel **de Queiroz**

The Three Marias
Woman's lot in traditional Brazil of the 1920s leads to demoralization and desperation
TRANSLATED BY FRED P. ELLISON
0-292-78079-6 TEXAS PB $11.95

Clarice **Lispector**

The Apple in the Dark
TRANSLATED BY GREGORY ROBASSA
0-292-70392-9 TEXAS PB $14.95

Ledo **Ivo**

Snake's Nest, or a Tale Badly Told
A dissertation on totalitarianism of the 1940s reflects the military repression of the 1970s
TRANSLATED BY KERN KRAPOHL
0-8112-0806-0 NEW DIRECTIONS $12.95
0-8112-0807-9 NEW DIRECTIONS PB $5.95

An Apprenticeship, or the Book of Delights
TRANSLATED BY RICHARD A. MAZZARA & LORRI A. PARRIS
0-292-79030-9 TEXAS $18.95

The Besieged City
TRANSLATED BY GIOVANNI PONTIERO
1-85754-061-1 CARCANET $39.95

Discovering the World
0-85635-954-8 SCHOLARLY $42.00

Family Ties
Marvelous short tales
TRANSLATED BY GIOVANNI PONTIERO
0-292-72448-9 TEXAS PB $10.95

The Hour of the Star
A woman from the northeast adrift in the big city
TRANSLATED BY GIOVANNI PONTIERO
0-85635-626-3 CARCANET $29.50
0-8112-1190-8 NEW DIRECTIONS PB $8.95

Near to the Wild Heart
A Joycean novel written in early youth
0-8112-1139-8 NEW DIRECTIONS $17.95

The Passion According to G.H.
An interior monologue in which a mundane event (killing a cockroach) provokes one woman's reinvestigation of language, values, and humanity itself. Unnerving yet beautiful
TRANSLATED BY RONALD W. SOUSA
0-8166-1711-2 MINNESOTA $24.95
0-8166-1712-0 MINNESOTA PB $10.95

Selected Cronicas
TRANSLATED BY GIOVANNI PONTIERO
0-8112-1340-4 NEW DIRECTIONS PB $12.95

Soulstorm: Stories
Twenty-nine stories. "Explores feminist issues on one level, class issues on another level, and the metaphysical issues of death and love on its most ambiguous level"—*Baltimore Sun*
0-8112-1091-X NEW DIRECTIONS PB $10.95

Graciliano **Ramos**

Barren Lives
The northeast's periodic drought reduces its victims to an animal existence
TRANSLATED BY RALPH E. DIMMICK
0-292-70133-0 TEXAS PB $9.95

Joao Ubaldo **Ribeiro**

An Invincible Memory
0-06-015622-8 HARPERCOLLINS $25.00

Moacyr **Scliar**

The One-Man Army
Mayer Ginsberg's narration of his rise to become the famous Captain Birobidjan
TRANSLATED BY ELOAH F. GIACOMELLI
0-345-32858-2 BALLANTINE PB $5.95

Chile

Marjorie **Agosin**

Dear Anne Frank
TRANSLATED BY RICHARD SCHAAF
0-9632363-6-9 AZUL PB $11.95

Happiness: Stories
TRANSLATED BY ELIZABETH HORAN
1-87772-734-2 WHITE PINE PB $14.00

Sargasso/Sargazo
TRANSLATED BY COLA FRANZEN
1-87772-727-X WHITE PINE PB $12.00

Toward the Splendid City
TRANSLATED BY RICHARD SCHAAF
0-927534-46-0 BILINGUAL PB $13.00

Women in Disguise: Stories
TRANSLATED BY DIANE RUSSEL-PINEDA
1-88521-401-4 AZUL PB $14.95

Fernando **Alegria**

Allende
TRANSLATED BY FRANK JANNEY
0-8047-1998-5 STANFORD $45.00
0-8047-2326-5 STANFORD PB $13.95

The Funhouse
A surrealistic vision of North American society during the Vietnam War
0-934770-52-2 ARTE PUBLICO PB $9.00

The Maypole Warriors
TRANSLATED BY CARLOS LOZANO
0-935480-58-7 LATIN AMERICAN LIT PB $16.95

Isabel **Allende**

Eva Luna
TRANSLATED BY MARGARET SAYERS PEDEN
0-553-28058-9 BDD PB $6.50

The House of the Spirits
Esteban Trueba's tale of political life from a distinctly feminist perspective
TRANSLATED BY MAGDA BOGIN
0-553-27391-4 BDD PB $6.50

The Infinite Plan
A rich and engrossing tale that follows the fortunes of one Gregory Reeves as he overcomes his childhood of poverty to make a place for himself in a violent and racist world. A bestseller in Latin America and Europe, this is the first novel to be set in the US by the author of *The House of the Spirits* and *Eva Luna*
TRANSLATED BY MARGARET SAYERS PEDEN
0-06-017016-6 HARPERPERENNIAL PB $23.00

Of Love and Shadows
"Allende skillfully evokes both the terrors of daily life under military rule and the subtler forms of resistance in the hidden corners"
—*NY Times*
TRANSLATED BY MARGARET S. PEDEN
0-553-27360-4 BDD PB $6.50

The Stories of Eva Luna
TRANSLATED BY MARGARET SAYERS PEDEN
0-553-57535-X BANTAM PB $6.99

Maria Luisa **Bombal**

House of Mist & The Shrouded Woman: Novels
0-292-70830-0 TEXAS PB $19.95

New Islands & Other Stories
TRANSLATED BY RICHARD CUNNINGHAM & LUCIA CUNNINGHAM
0-8014-9538-5 CORNELL PB $9.95

José **Donoso**

Curfew
TRANSLATED BY ALFRED MACADAM
1-55584-448-0 GROVE PB $9.95

The Garden Next Door
For a Chilean writer and his wife, the loan of a Madrid apartment for the summer promises an escape from their money problems, their fantasies, and a son gone wrong. But escape is not possible, as life grows progressively more complicated in this brilliant satire of the life of a writer. An adroit and bitterly comic novel about Latin Americans in Spain
TRANSLATED BY HARDIE ST. MARTIN
0-8021-1238-2 GROVE PB $18.95

The Obscene Bird of Night
TRANSLATED BY HARDIE ST. MARTIN AND LEONARD MADES
1-56792-046-2 GODINE PB $15.95

Taratuta & Still Life With Pipe: Two Novellas
0-393-31164-3 NORTON PB $8.95

Ariel **Dorfman**

Death and the Maiden
0-14-024684-3 PENGUIN PB $7.95

Hard Rain
0-930523-78-4 READERS INTERNATIONAL PB $10.95

Konfidenz
See also **DRAMA**
0-374-18218-3 FS&G $17.00
0-679-76716-9 VINTAGE PB $11.00

The Last Song of Manuel Sendero
0-14-008896-2 PENGUIN PB $8.95

Mascara
0-14-011253-7 PENGUIN PB $7.95

My House Is on Fire!: Short Stories
TRANSLATED BY GEORGE SHIVERS
0-14-014728-4 PENGUIN PB $7.95

Diamela **Eltit**

The Fourth World
0-8032-1817-6 NEBRASKA $30.00
0-8032-6723-1 NEBRASKA PB $10.00

Sacred Cow
TRANSLATED BY AMANDA HOPKINSON
1-85242-287-4 SERPENT'S TAIL PB $12.99

Antonio **Skarmeta**

I Dreamt the Snow Was Burning
Middle-class life in the 1950s
TRANSLATED BY MALCOLM COAD
0-930523-06-7 READERS INTERNATIONAL $14.95

Love-Fifteen
TRANSLATED BY JONATHAN TITTLER
0-935480-82-X LATIN AMERICAN LIT PB $13.95

The Postman
Originally published as *Burning Patience*
TRANSLATED BY KATHERINE SILVER
0-7868-8127-5 HYPERION PB $9.95

Mercedes **Valdivieso**

Breakthrough
This book, which appeared in Spanish in 1961, is regarded as the first feminist novel of Latin America
TRANSLATED BY GRACIELA DAICHMAN
0-935480-33-1 LATIN AMERICAN LIT PB $12.00

Luisa **Valenzuela**

Besides Manners
TRANSLATED BY MARGARET JULL COSTA
1-85242-313-7 SERPENT'S TAIL PB $12.99

The Censors
0-915306-12-3 CURBSTONE PB $12.95

Colombia

Gabriel **García Márquez**

The Autumn of the Patriarch
A thematically complex novel on the national roots of a "generic" Latin American dictator and his suffering people
TRANSLATED BY GREGORY RABASSA
0-06-091963-9 HARPERPERENNIAL PB $13.00

Chronicle of a Death Foretold
A prophetic tale of familial duty, honor, and murder
TRANSLATED BY GREGORY RABASSA
0-394-53074-8 KNOPF $22.00

Collected Stories
TRANSLATED BY GREGORY RABASSA & J.S. BERNSTEIN
0-06-091306-1 HARPERPERENNIAL PB $13.00

The General in His Labyrinth
A fictional exploration of the tumultuous inner life of Simón Bolivar, the iconic hero of South American political liberation
0-394-58258-6 KNOPF $19.95
0-14-014859-0 PENGUIN PB $12.95

In Evil Hour
Mysterious messages shake up the power structure in a Colombian village
TRANSLATED BY GREGORY RABASSA
0-06-091964-7 HARPERPERENNIAL PB $10.50

Innocent Erendira & Other Stories
Several early stories and a visit to the almost fairy-tale world of Erendira
TRANSLATED BY GREGORY RABASSA
0-8095-9052-2 BORGO $29.00
0-06-090701-0 HARPERCOLLINS PB $12.00

Leaf Storm & Other Stories
TRANSLATED BY GREGORY RABASSA
0-8095-9053-0 BORGO $27.00
0-06-090699-5 HARPERCOLLINS PB $11.00

Of Love and Other Demons
A bittersweet story of a doomed love affair set in the colonial era
0-679-43853-X KNOPF $21.00
0-14-025636-9 PENGUIN PB $11.95

Love in the Time of Cholera
A novel about love, old age, race, and social life in a 19th-century Colombian small town
TRANSLATED BY EDITH GROSSMAN
0-394-56161-9 KNOPF $27.50
0-14-011990-6 PENGUIN PB $12.95

Gabriel Garcia Márquez

One Hundred Years of Solitude
"The first piece of literature since the Book of Genesis that should be required reading for the entire human race. It takes up not long after Genesis left off and carries through to the air age, reporting on everything that happened in between with more lucidity, wit, wisdom, and poetry than is expected from 100 years of novelists, let alone one man…Mr. García Márquez has done nothing less than to create in the reader a sense of all that is profound, meaningful, and meaningless in life"
—William Kennedy
TRANSLATED BY GREGORY RABASSA
0-679-44465-3 KNOPF $20.00
0-06-091965-5 HARPERCOLLINS PB $13.50

Strange Pilgrims
0-679-42566-7 KNOPF $21.00
0-14-023940-5 PENGUIN PB $10.95

Alvaro **Mutis**

The Adventures of Maqroll
Includes *Amirbar; The Tramp Steamer's Last Port of Call; Abdul Bashur, Dreamer of Ships;* and *Triptych on Sea and Land*
0-06-092687-2 HARPERPERENNIAL PB $13.00

Maqroll: Three Novellas
Includes *The Snow of the Admiral, Ilona Comes with the Rain,* and *Un Bel Morir*
0-06-092444-6 HARPERPERENNIAL PB $12.00

Cuba

Reinaldo **Arenas**

The Assault
TRANSLATED BY ANDREW HURLEY
0-670-84066-1 VIKING $20.95
0-14-015718-2 PENGUIN PB $10.95

Before Night Falls
See also **CUBA** under **CRITICISM, MEMOIRS, AND OTHER PROSE**
TRANSLATED BY DOLORES M. KOCH
0-14-015765-4 PENGUIN PB $11.95

The Doorman
0-8021-3405-X ATLANTIC MONTHLY PB $10.00

The Ill-Fated Peregrinations of Fray Servando
TRANSLATED BY ANDREW HURLEY
0-14-024166-3 PENGUIN PB $11.95

Old Rosa: A Novel in Two Stories
TRANSLATED BY ANN TASHI SLATER & ANDREW HURLEY
0-8021-3406-8 ATLANTIC MONTHLY PB $10.00

Palace of the White Skunks
TRANSLATED BY ANDREW HURLEY
0-14-009792-9 PENGUIN PB $12.50

Singing from the Well
A child's life in the countryside of revolutionary Cuba
0-14-009444-X PENGUIN PB $7.95

Antonio **Benitez-Rojo**

Sea of Lentils
A stunning historical novel about the first encounters between Europe and the New World, which dismantles the heroic trapping of earlier accounts. Benitez-Rojo is a Cuban writer now resident in the US. "With the semi-millennial anniversary of Columbus' landfall almost upon us, this novel makes us sorry that America was discovered"—John Updike
TRANSLATED BY JAMES MARANISS
0-87023-754-3 MASSACHUSETTS PB $15.95

Guillermo **Cabrera Infante**

Now living in England in exile, Infante has a wit and inspired prose style that has positioned him as one of the greatest living writers of Spanish-language literature.

Three Trapped Tigers
A madcap linguistic romp through late 1950s Havana nightlife
TRANSLATED BY DONALD GARDNER & SUZANNE JILL LEVINE
0-571-15370-4 FABER PB $10.95

Alejo **Carpentier**

The Chase
First published in 1956, *The Chase* is regarded as a milestone in Latin American fiction. A richly atmospheric tale of Batista-era Havana, it exemplifies Carpentier's magnificently complex prose style. "Alejo Carpentier transformed the Latin American novel. He transcended naturalism and invented magic realism…We are all his descendants"—Carlos Fuentes
TRANSLATED BY ALFRED MACADAM
0-374-12083-8 FS&G $16.95

Explosion in a Cathedral
TRANSLATED BY JOHN STURROCK
0-374-52198-0 NOONDAY PB $14.00

The Harp and the Shadow
1-56279-024-2 MERCURY HOUSE PB $11.95

The Kingdom of this World
The Haitian Revolution recreated
TRANSLATED BY HARRIET DE ONIS
0-374-52197-2 NOONDAY PB $10.00

The Lost Steps
A modern man retraces a path into the tropical wilderness
TRANSLATED BY HARRIET DE ONIS
0-374-52199-9 NOONDAY PB $12.00

Jose Lezama **Lima**

Paradiso
84-00-06880-7 PITTSBURGH PB $41.95

Herberto **Padilla**

Self-Portrait of the Other: A Memoir
The autobiography of the exiled Cuban poet, admired and vilified for his opposition to the Castro regime
TRANSLATED BY ALEXANDER COLEMAN
0-374-26086-9 FS&G $19.95

Virgilio **Pinera**

Cold Tales
Stories by an influential writer whose homosexuality brought him into conflict with the Castro regime
TRANSLATED BY MARK SCHAFFER
INTRODUCTION BY GUILLERMO CABRERA INFANTE
0-941419-18-5 ERIDANOS PB $24.00

Rene's Flesh
A young boy's initiation into sexual cruelty at a boarding school. "Pinera's writing is far from any received notion of literature, for it comes from absolute alienation, where the shortest distance to hell is not through paradise but purgatory"
—Guillermo Cabrera Infante
TRANSLATED BY MARK SCHAFFER
1-56886-017-X MARSILIO PB $12.95

Severo **Sarduy**

Christ on the Rue Jacob
Sarduy's last major work before his death from AIDS
TRANSLATED BY SUZANNE JILL LEVINE AND CAROL MAIER
1-56279-075-7 MERCURY HOUSE PB $12.95

Cobra & Maitreya
TRANSLATED BY SUZANNE JILL LEVINE
1-56478-076-7 DALKEY ARCHIVE PB $13.95

From Cuba with a Song
1-55713-158-9 SUN & MOON PB $10.95

Maitreya
A journey toward revelation
TRANSLATED BY SUZANNE JILL LEVINE
0-910061-31-9 EDICIONES DEL NORTE PB $9.50

Ecuador

Jorge **Icaza**

The Villagers (Huasipungo)
A brutal confrontation of Indians and whites in one of the most moving novels of Latin American literature
TRANSLATED BY BERNARD M. DULSEY
0-8093-0653-0 SOUTHERN ILLINOIS PB $12.95

El Salvador

Claribel **Alegria**

Luisa in Realityland
TRANSLATED BY DARWIN J. FLAKOLL
0-915306-70-0 CURBSTONE $17.95
0-915306-69-7 CURBSTONE PB $9.95

Manlio **Argueta**

One Day of Life

"Does what virtually no other volume or newspaper story has even begun to do. It renders the Salvadoran peasant visible" —*New Republic*

TRANSLATED BY CLARK HANSEN

0-679-73243-8 VINTAGE PB $11.00

Guatemala

Miguel Angel **Asturias**

Men of Maize

TRANSLATED BY GERALD MARTIN

0-8229-5514-8 PITTSBURGH PB $19.95

The Mirror of Lida Sal: Tales Based on Mayan Myths and Guatemalan Legends

TRANSLATED BY GILBERT ALTER

0-935480-83-8 LATIN AMERICAN LIT PB $14.95

Augusto **Monterroseo**

Complete Works (and Other Stories)

TRANSLATED BY EDITH GROSSMAN

0-292-75183-4 TEXAS $27.50

0-292-75184-2 TEXAS PB $12.95

Mexico

Homero **Aridjis**

The Lord of the Last Days: Visions of the Year 1000

TRANSLATED BY BETTY FERBER

0-688-14342-3 MORROW $23.00

Ines **Arredondo**

Underground River and Other Stories

TRANSLATED BY CYNTHIA STEELE

0-8032-5927-1 NEBRASKA PB $12.00

Mariano **Azuela**

Three Novels by Mariano Azuela

The Trials of a Respectable Family, The Underdogs, and *The Firefly*

TRANSLATED BY FRANCES K. HENDRICKS & BEATRICE BERLER

0-911536-78-7 TRINITY $25.00

Two Novels of Mexico: The Flies & The Bosses

Satiric and somber novelettes of the Mexican Revolution

TRANSLATED BY LESLEY BYRD SIMPSON

0-520-00053-6 CALIFORNIA PB $12.00

The Underdogs

Azuela's classic work

TRANSLATED BY E. MUNGUIA

FOREWORD BY HARRIET DE ONIS

0-451-52625-2 SIGNET PB $4.95

Nellie **Campobello**

Cartucho/My Mother's Hand

The Mexican Revolution, from a child's perspective

TRANSLATED BY DORIS MEYER & IRENE MATTHEWS

INTRODUCTION BY ELENA PONIATOWSKA

0-292-71111-5 TEXAS PB $10.95

Rosario **Castellanos**

Another Way to Be: Selected Works of Rosario Castellanos

EDITED BY MYRALYN F. ALLGOOD

0-8203-1240-1 GEORGIA PB $13.95

The Book of Lamentations

TRANSLATED BY ESTHER ALLEN

1-56886-038-2 MARSILIO $24.00

City of Kings

0-935480-63-3 LATIN AMERICAN LIT PB $14.95

Meditation on the Threshold

One of Mexico's most important 20th-century poets and an exponent of feminism

See also **MEXICO** under **POETRY**

TRANSLATED BY JULIAN PALLEY

0-916950-80-8 BILINGUAL PB $13.00

The Nine Guardians

TRANSLATED BY IRENE NICHOLSON

0-930523-90-3 READERS INTERNATIONAL PB $11.95

A Rosario Castellanos Reader

0-292-77036-7 TEXAS PB $17.95

Fernando **del Paso**

Palinuro of Mexico

A satire of advertising, politics, pornography, and mythology, del Paso's massive novel has been compared not only to Fuentes and Márquez, but to Joyce, Sterne, and Rabelais. "At its deepest level, the narrative of *Palinuro of Mexico* embodies a totalizing ambition, reminiscent of Joyce, to investigate the conditions of culture and knowledge, to explore the relationship between myth and history, and to demonstrate the potential of literary language to revolutionize our ways of seeing the world" —*TLS*

1-56478-095-3 DALKEY ARCHIVE PB $14.95

Carlos **Fuentes**

Burnt Water

Life in modern-day Mexico City

TRANSLATED BY MARGARET SAYERS PEDEN

0-374-51988-9 FS&G PB $12.00

A Change of Skin

Fuentes' most sweeping novel—a search for individual truth on a journey from Mexico City to Vera Cruz

TRANSLATED BY SAM HILEMAN

0-374-51427-5 FS&G PB $14.95

Constancia & Other Stories for Virgins

A collection of five short stories from the author of *The Old Gringo*, which experiment with language and the treatment of time

0-374-12886-3 FS&G $19.95

The Death of Artemio Cruz

A peasant rises to power and importance

TRANSLATED BY SAM HILEMAN

0-374-52283-9 NOONDAY PB $11.00

Diana: The Goddess Who Hunts Alone

New Year's Eve, 1969. A novelist and self-proclaimed Don Juan meets an oddly elusive and beautiful movie actress. But this is not to be a practiced seduction for the writer, and his failure forces him to confront the foundations of his life. This new novel by Mexico's leading writer takes us on an extraordinary and original exploration of love, lust, betrayal, and humiliation

TRANSLATED BY ALFRED MACADAM

0-374-13903-2 FS&G $22.00

0-06-097712-4 HARPERPERENNIAL PB $12.50

Distant Relations

TRANSLATED BY MARGARET SAYERS PEDEN

0-374-14082-0 FS&G $11.95

0-374-51813-0 FS&G PB $12.00

The Glass Border

EDITED BY ANNE MESSITTE

0-679-77296-0 VINTAGE PB $14.95

The Good Conscience

A semibiographical novel of a youth coming to terms with his society

TRANSLATED BY SAM HILEMAN

0-374-50736-8 FS&G PB $10.00

The Hydra Head

A third world spy thriller: Mexico, the Middle East, and oil

TRANSLATED BY MARGARET SAYERS PEDEN

0-374-51563-8 FS&G PB $12.00

The Old Gringo

An American writer (modeled on Ambrose Bierce) disappears in Mexico during the Mexican Revolution

TRANSLATED BY MARGARET SAYERS PEDEN

0-06-097063-4 HARPERCOLLINS PB $12.00

The Orange Tree

Five new, insightful fictions by the Mexican grandmaster: "Could any image verify a Spaniard's identity better than the sight of a man eating an orange?" asks the dead narrator of *The Two Shores* after he is found by Cortes, shipwrecked in the New World. In *Apollo of the Whores* a famous American actor finds himself in Acapulco on a macabre ship of whores. "Exuberantly imaginative and unabashedly sensual, Fuentes...never fails to entertain, instruct—and, yes, provoke"—*Kirkus Reviews*

TRANSLATED BY ALFRED MACADAM

0-374-22683-0 FS&G $21.00

Terra Nostra

A fictional panorama of Spanish and Latin American history. *"Terra Nostra* implies taking the whole universe, which is all my past...I am trying to capture that cultural past, that richness of the civilization through a multitude of voices, a multitude of eyes"—Carlos Fuentes

TRANSLATED BY MARGARET SAYERS PEDEN

AFTERWORD BY MILAN KUNDERA

0-374-51750-9 FS&G PB $25.00

Where the Air Is Clear
A fast-paced expose of the foibles and decadence of the Mexican upper classes
TRANSLATED BY SAM HILEMAN
0-374-50919-0 FS&G PB............$14.00

Gregorio Lopez y **Fuentes**
El Indio
Mexican Indian life on the eve of the Revolution
TRANSLATED BY ANITA BRENNER
0-8044-6429-4 UNGAR PB............$11.95

Sergio **Galindo**
La Comparsa: A Mexican Masquerade
TRANSLATED BY JOHN BRUSHWOOD & CAROLYN BRUSHWOOD
0-935480-17-X LATIN AMERICAN LIT PB............$11.50

Otilia's Body
TRANSLATED BY JOHN BRUSHWOOD & CAROLYN BRUSHWOOD
0-292-72769-0 TEXAS............$37.50
0-292-72770-4 TEXAS PB............$15.95

Carlos **Montemayor**
Blood Relations
0-917635-16-7 ACADEMY CHICAGO............$17.95

Jose Emilio **Pacheco**
Battles in the Desert & Other Stories
TRANSLATED BY KATHERINE SILVER
0-8112-1020-0 NEW DIRECTIONS PB............$8.95

Juan Garcia **Ponce**
Encounters
Three short stories and a novella
TRANSLATED BY HELEN LANE
INTRODUCTION BY OCTAVIO PAZ
0-941419-25-8 ERIDANOS PB............$19.00

The House on the Beach
TRANLATED BY MARGARITA VARGAS & JUAN BRUCE NOVOA
0-292-72763-1 TEXAS............$30.00
0-292-72764-X TEXAS PB............$15.95

Juan **Rulfo**
The Burning Plain & Other Stories
Fifteen stories about guilt, poverty, and despair
TRANSLATED BY GEORGE D. SCHADE
ILLUSTRATED BY KERMIT OLIVER
0-292-70132-2 TEXAS PB............$10.95

Pedro Paramo: A Novel of Mexico
The moving story of the murder of a small-town tyrant
TRANSLATED BY LYSANDER KEMP
0-8021-3216-2 GROVE PB............$7.95

Paco Ignacio **Taibo II**
Four Hands
0-312-10987-3 ST. MARTIN'S............$22.95

Leonardo's Bicycle
0-446-40491-8 MYSTERIOUS PB............$5.99

Life Itself
See also **HARD-BOILED DETECTIVES** under **CRIME FICTION TODAY** under **CRIME FICTION** in **POPULAR READING**
TRANSLATED BY BETH HENSON
0-89296-518-5 MYSTERIOUS............$18.95
0-446-40331-8 WARNER PB............$5.99

No Happy Ending
0-446-40329-6 MYSTERIOUS PB............$5.50

Return to the Same City
0-89296-590-8 MYSTERIOUS............$19.95

Augustin **Yanez**
The Edge of the Storm
Religious oppression and Indian traditions in a small town just prior to the Revolution
TRANSLATED BY ETHEL BRINTON
0-292-70131-4 TEXAS PB............$16.95

Paraguay

Augusto Roa **Bastos**
Son of Man
TRANSLATED BY RACHEL CAFFYN
FOREWORD BY ARIEL DORFMAN
0-252-01059-0 ILLINOIS............$24.95
1-55597-160-1 GRAY WOLF PB............$12.00

Peru

Ciro **Alegria**
Broad and Alien Is the World
0-85036-282-2 DUFOUR PB............$23.00

Jose M. **Arguedas**
Deep Rivers
TRANSLATED BY FRANCES H. BARRACLOUGH
0-292-71533-1 TEXAS PB............$12.95

Yawar Fiesta
Social relations and influences between mestizo Indians and the upper classes of the Peruvian highlands of the 1920's and 1930's
0-292-79601-3 TEXAS............$22.50
0-292-79602-1 TEXAS PB............$11.95

Isaac **Goldemberg**
The Fragmented Life of Don Jacobo Lerner
TRANSLATED BY ROBERT PICCIOTTO
0-89255-003-1 PERSEA PB............$8.95

Mario Vargas **Llosa**
Conversation in the Cathedral
Two men from different social classes discuss Peruvian life, violence, and social decay in a bar called the Cathedral
TRANSLATED BY GREGORY RABASSA
0-374-51815-7 FS&G PB............$17.00

Julio **Ortega**
Ayacocho, Goodbye & Moscow's Gold
TRANSLATED BY EDITH GROSSMAN & ALITA KELLEY
0-935480-66-8 LATIN AMERICAN LIT PB............$13.95

Cesar **Vallejo**
Tungsten
A denunciation of the brutal treatment of Andean mine workers, written in an uncharacteristic vein of social realism by Peru's great modern poet
TRANSLATED BY ROBERT MESEY
0-8156-0226-X SYRACUSE............$29.95

Mario **Vargas Llosa**
Aunt Julia and the Scriptwriter
Reality and fantasy: can a real marriage be more than a soap opera?
TRANSLATED BY HELEN R. LANE
0-14-024892-7 PENGUIN PB............$11.95

Death in the Andes
In a rundown community in the Peruvian Andes, mysterious disappearances are linked to Shining Path guerrillas and local practitioners of canniabalistic sacrifice. Part detective novel and part political allegory, Llosa's narration paints a portrait of Peruvian society that also underscores the broadest themes of Latin America. "In the star-studded world of the Latin American novel, Mario Vargas Llosa is a supernova"—*Village Voice*
TRANSLATED BY EDITH GROSSMAN
0-374-14001-4 FS&G............$24.00

In Praise of the Stepmother
Vargas Llosa's erotic novel treats a romatic triangle between father, stepmother, and pre-pubescent son with subtlety and wit. Six full-color reproductions of paintings by Jordaens, Boucher, Titian, Bacon, and Fra Angelico accompany the text
TRANSLATED BY HELEN LANE
0-374-17583-7 FS&G............$18.95

The Storyteller
From the Peruvian novelist, the story of a Peruvian Jew and his conscience. "To me this is Mr. Vargas Llosa's most engaging and accessible book, for the urgency of the subject purifies and illuminates the writing"—Ursula LeGuin
TRANSLATED BY HELEN LANE
0-14-014349-1 PENGUIN PB............$11.95

The Time of the Hero
A military academy rife with corruption becomes a microcosm of Peruvian society's outdated social system
TRANSLATED BY LYSANDER KEMP
0-374-52021-6 FS&G PB............$15.00

Puerto Rico

Rosario **Ferre**
The House on the Lagoon
From Puerto Rico's preeminent literary figure, a multi-generational novel of love and death, privilege and servitude. This story of Quintin Mendizabal and his wife, Isabel, expertly uses a dual point of view to create a family history that begins in Spain and Corsica and involves central themes of racism, statehood, and identity. The themes ultimately come to shatter the marriage at the heart of the story. "Rosario Ferre shines, and it is high time for English-speakers to bask in her light"—*The Nation*
0-374-17311-7 FS&G............$22.00

Pedro J. **Soto**
Spiks
The struggle over assimilation versus acculturation among Nuyoricans (Puerto Ricans born or raised in New York City)
TRANSLATED WITH AN INTRODUCTION BY VICTORIA ORTIZ
0-85345-331-4 MONTHLY REVIEW PB............$8.00

Emilio Diaz **Valcarcel**

Schemes in the Month of March

"A brilliant comic novel about exile, the writer as outcast, the Puerto Rican as pariah, and the different languages of banishment he speaks" —*Washington Post*

TRANSLATED BY NANCY SEBASTIANI

0-916950-05-0 BILINGUAL PB $15.00

Uruguay

Felisberto **Hernandez**

Piano Stories

"He taught me that the most haunting mysteries are those of everyday life"—Gabriel Garcia

TRANSLATED BY LUIS HARSS

0-941419-54-1 MARSILIO PB $18.00

Antonio **Larreta**

The Last Portrait of the Duchess of Alba

A fictitious memoir of the duchess's affairs in Spanish society

TRANSLATED BY PAMELA CARMELL

9999696147 FS&G $1.98

Carlos Martinez **Moreno**

El Infierno

The rise and fall of the Tupamaro guerrillas, and the repression and dictatorship that followed

0-930523-48-2 CONSORTIUM PB $8.95

Juan Carlos **Onetti**

A Brief Life

1-85242-301-3 SERPENT'S TAIL PB $15.99

Let the Wind Speak

1-85242-196-7 SERPENT'S TAIL PB $14.99

The Shipyard

1-85242-191-6 SERPENT'S TAIL PB $14.99

Horacio **Quiroga**

The Decapitated Chicken & Other Stories

Tales of horror, madness, and death. "Full of pyschological shocks and eerie effects" —*New Yorker*

TRANSLATED BY MARGARET SAYERS PEDEN

INTRODUCTION BY GEORGE D. SCHADE

0-292-71541-2 TEXAS PB $12.95

The Exiles & Other Stories

Thirteen of the best stories by a writer who has been compared to Poe and Kipling

TRANSLATED BY J. DAVID DANIELSON

0-292-72050-5 TEXAS $17.95

Cristina Peri **Rossi**

Dostoevsky's Last Night

TRANSLATED BY LAURA DAIL

0-312-14322-2 PICADOR PB $11.00

A Forbidden Passion : Stories

TRANSLATED BY MARY JANE TREACY

0-939416-67-0 CLEIS $24.95

0-939416-68-9 CLEIS PB $9.95

The Ship of Fools

"Her great gift is the ability to project onto the high plains of the imagination the historical present in all its tragic reality"—Julio Cortazar

TRANSLATED BY PSICHE HUGHES

0-930523-54-7 READERS INTERNATIONAL PB $11.95

Venezuela

Romulo **Gallegos**

Canaima

A 1935 novel of a rough and adventurous life in the Guianan jungles

TRANSLATED BY JAIME TELLO

INTRODUCTION BY EFRAIN SUBERO

0-8061-9928-8 OKLAHOMA $22.95

0-8061-2119-X OKLAHOMA PB $9.95

Dominican Republic

Julia **Alvarez**

"Alvarez writes beautifully....[her] voice is her own, grounded in realism yet alive with the magic of everyday human beings who summon extraordinary courage and determination to fight for their beliefs"— Kirkus Reviews

Homecoming: New and Collected Poems

0-452-27567-9 PLUME PB $10.95

How the Garcia Girls Lost Their Accents

"A major achievement...family presented with such eloquence and such profound honesty you'll want to claim them as yours" —Gloria Naylor

0-452-26806-0 PLUME PB $11.95

In the Time of the Butterflies

Alvarez has created a fictional rendering of the tragic deaths of the sisters Mirabel, committed to revolution in the Dominican Republic, assassinated under the brutal Trujillo regime, and now reborn through Alvarez's lyrical fictional talent

See also **NEW WRITERS OF THE '90S under 20TH-CENTURY AMERICAN FICTION**

1-56512-038-8 ALGONQUIN $21.95

0-452-27442-7 PENGUIN PB $11.95

The Other Side

0-452-27341-2 PLUME PB $10.95

Yo

1-56512-157-0 ALGONQUIN $18.95

Honduras

Roberto **Quesada**

The Ships

A widely praised novel about a young writer working on a pineapple plantation in Honduras in the midst of poverty, US military exercises, and, to the south, the stirrings of the Nicaraguan revolution

0-941423-65-4 FOUR WALLS $17.95

Poetry

Argentina

Jose **Hernandez**

The Gaucho Martin Fierro

Civilization versus barbarism in this epic of 19th-century Argentine life

TRANSLATED BY FRANK G. CARRINO

0-87395-284-7 SUNY PB $9.95

Roberto **Juarroz**

Vertical Poetry: Recent Poems

"Each of Roberto Juarroz's poems is a surprising verbal crystallization: language reduced to a drop of light. A great poet of absolute instants"—Octavio Paz

TRANSLATED BY W.S. MERWIN

1-87772-708-3 WHITE PINE PB $11.00

Brazil

Elizabeth **Bishop** & Brasil **Emanuel**, editors

An Anthology of Twentieth-Century Brazilian Poetry

Selection of poems by members of the modernist generation

TRANSLATED BY PAUL BLACKBURN

0-8195-6023-5 WESLEYAN PB $16.95

Joao **Cabral de Melo Neto**

Selected Poetry 1937-1990

0-8195-2231-7 WESLEYAN PB $14.95

Basilio **da Gama**

The Uruguay: A Historical Romance of South America

An epic narration of the 18th-century Seven Missions Wars, which pitted the Spanish and Portuguese against the Jesuits and their Indian flock

TRANSLATED BY SIR RICHARD F. BURTON

EDITED BY FREDERICK G.H. GARCIA & EDWARD STANTON

0-520-04524-6 CALIFORNIA $45.00

Mario **de Andrade**

Hallucinated City

This outcry against the unrestrained urbanization of Sao Paulo in the 1920s is a masterpiece of Brazilian modernism

TRANSLATED BY JACK E. TOMLINS

0-8265-1113-9 VANDERBILT $7.95

Carlos **Drummond de Andrade**

The Minus Sign

A collection of verse interpretations of 54 poems by Brazil's greatest poet

EDITED AND TRANSLATED BY VIRGINIA DE ARAUJO

0-933806-03-5 BLACK SWAN $22.50

Travelling in the Family: Selected Poems

EDITED BY THOMAS COLCHIE AND MARK STRAND

0-88001-434-2 ECCO PB $13.00

Chile

Marjorie **Agosin**

Brujas y Algo Mas/Witches and Other Things

TRANSLATED BY COLAN FRANZEN

0-935480-16-1 LATIN AMERICAN LIT PB $10.50

Fernando **Alegria**

Changing Centuries: Selected Poems

TRANSLATED BY STEPHEN KESSLER

0-935480-37-4 LATIN AMERICAN LIT PB $11.95

Ariel **Dorfman**

Last Waltz in Santiago & Other Poems of Exile and Disappearance

TRANSLATED BY EDITH GROSSMAN WITH THE AUTHOR

0-14-058608-3 PENGUIN PB $8.95

Oscar **Hahn**

The Art of Dying

0-935480-32-3 LATIN AMERICAN LIT PB $10.00

Vincente **Huidobro**

One of the most lively and controversial Chilean poets was the flamboyant, gifted, and quarrelsome Vincente Huidobro (1893-1948), the inventor of an extreme form of Cubist poetry.

Altazor

A long poem published in 1931, "*Altazor's* space voyage becomes a voyage into language…Its words begin to mimic and devour each other; sounds and meanings break away and fuse again in new combinations; waves of punning go on for pages"—*Village Voice*

TRANSLATED BY ELIOT WEINBERGER

1-55597-106-7 GRAY WOLF PB $8.50

The Selected Poetry of Vincente Huidobro

A sample of Huidobro's intensely personal and autobiographical poetry revealing his continual experimentation with language and the poetic tradition

TRANSLATED BY ELIOT WEINBERGER, MICHAEL PALMER, AND OTHERS

0-8112-0805-2 NEW DIRECTIONS PB $6.95

Pablo **Neruda**

Art of Birds

TRANSLATED BY JACK SCHMITT

0-292-70371-6 TEXAS $19.95

The Book of Questions

A biligual edition

TRANSLATED BY WILLIAM O'DALY

1-55659-041-5 COPPER CANYON PB $11.00

Canto General

The first complete translation of Neruda's epic vision of South American history, from the pre-human to the post-industrial, incorporating jaguars, Machu Picchu, conquistadors, Bolivar, the United Fruit Company, and the Pacific Ocean. "Neruda was a kind of King Midas. Everything he touched turned to poetry" —Gabriel García Márquez

TRANSLATED BY JACK SCHMITT

INTRODUCTION BY ROBERTO GONZALEZ ECHEVARRIA

0-520-08279-6 CALIFORNIA PB $15.95

Pablo Neruda

The Captain's Verses

Poetry chronicling a love affair united by dedication to political and social struggle

TRANSLATED WITH AN INTRODUCTION BY DONALD D. WALSH

0-8112-0457-X NEW DIRECTIONS PB $9.95

Ceremonial Songs

TRANSLATED BY MARIA JACKETTI

0-935480-80-3 LATIN AMERICAN LIT PB $13.95

Extravagaria

An English/Spanish edition

TRANSLATED BY ALASTAIR REID

0-292-72083-1 TEXAS PB $14.95

Five Decades: Poems, 1925-1970

TRANSLATED AND EDITED BY BEN BELITT

0-8021-3035-6 GROVE PB $15.00

Fully Empowered

TRANSLATED BY ALASTAIR REID

0-8112-1281-5 NEW DIRECTIONS PB $10.95

The Heights of Machu Picchu

This meditation on the Inca ruin, a section from Neruda's epic of the Americas *Canto General*, is one of his most sustained and powerful works

TRANSLATED BY NATHANIEL TARN

0-374-50648-5 FS&G PB $10.00

Isla Negra: A Notebook

TRANSLATED BY ALASTAIR REID

0-374-51734-7 FS&G PB $15.00

Late and Posthumous Poems: 1968-1974

0-8021-3145-X GROVE PB $11.95

Neruda's Garden: An Anthology of Odes

TRANSLATED BY MARIA JACKETTI

0-935480-68-4 LATIN AMERICAN LIT PB $17.95

Ode to Common Things

0-8212-2080-2 BULFINCH $22.50

Odes to Opposites

TRANSLATED BY KENNETH KRABBENHOFT

0-8212-2227-9 BULFINCH $22.50

Pablo Neruda: Selected Poems

A bilingual edition

TRANSLATED BY ANTHONY KERRIGAN

0-395-54418-1 HOUGHTON MIFFLIN PB $15.95

Residence on Earth & Other Poems

Neruda's early surrealist poetry, which for many represents his highest achievement

TRANSLATED WITH AN INTRODUCTION BY DONALD O. WALSH

0-8112-0467-7 NEW DIRECTIONS PB $12.95

Selected Odes of Pablo Neruda

TRANSLATED BY MARGARET SAYERS PEDEN

0-520-07172-7 CALIFORNIA PB $13.95

A Separate Rose

A posthumously published collection; the poet in total communion with nature

TRANSLATED BY WILLIAM O'DALY

0-914742-88-4 COPPER CANYON PB $9.00

Still Another Day

TRANSLATED BY WILLIAM O'DALY

0-914742-77-9 COPPER CANYON PB $10.00

The Stones of Chile

TRANSLATED BY DENNIS MALONEY

0-934834-01-6 WHITE PINE PB $10.00

Stones of the Sky

TRANSLATED BY JAMES NOLAN

1-55659-006-7 COPPER CANYON $15.00

1-55659-007-5 COPPER CANYON PB $10.00

Twenty Love Poems and a Song of Despair

TRANSLATED BY W.S. MERWIN

0-8118-0320-1 CHRONICLE $12.95

0-14-018648-4 PENGUIN PB $8.95

Winter Garden

Another posthumously published collection

TRANSLATED BY WILLIAM O'DALY

0-914742-93-0 CONSORTIUM PB $10.00

Pablo **Neruda** & Cesar **Vallejo**

Neruda and Vallejo: Selected Poems

See also **PERU**

EDITED BY ROBERT BLY

0-8070-6489-0 BEACON PB $14.00

Nicanor **Parra**

Antipoems: New and Selected

Parra works consciously against the lyrical and rhetorical traditions of Spanish-language poetry, creating a purposely flat and deadpan style

TRANSLATED BY MILLER WILLIAMS

EDITED BY DAVID UNGER

0-8112-0960-1 NEW DIRECTIONS PB $8.95

Emergency Poems

TRANSLATED AND EDITED BY MILLER WILLIAMS

0-8112-0340-9 NEW DIRECTIONS $8.75

Sermons and Homilies of the Christ of Elqui

TRANSLATED BY SANDRA REYES

FOREWORD BY MILLER WILLIAMS

0-8262-0451-1 MISSOURI $19.95

Cecilia **Vicuna**

Unraveling Words & The Weaving of Water

TRANSLATED BY ELIOT WEINBERGER AND OTHERS

1-55597-166-0 GRAY WOLF PB $12.00

Raúl **Zurita**

Anteparadise: A Bilingual Edition

"The only meaning of art, its only purpose …is to make life more humanly livable. In brief, we should keep on proposing Paradise even if the evidence might indicate that such a pursuit is folly"—Raúl Zurita

TRANSLATED BY JACK SCHMITT

0-520-05434-2 CALIFORNIA $30.00

0-520-05926-3 CALIFORNIA PB $13.95

Purgatorio, 1970-1977

"Zurita's quest for redemption results in a sustained sequence of great power and beauty on the Atacama desert, a spiritual exercise that recalls the experience of fellow poet and countryman Pablo Neruda at Machu Picchu" —*Choice*

TRANSLATED BY JEREMY JACOBSON

0-935480-21-8 LATIN AMERICAN LIT PB $11.95

Cuba

Nicolas **Guillen**

The Daily Daily

TRANSLATED BY VERA M. KUTZINSKI

0-520-06218-3 CALIFORNIA $30.00

Legacies: Selected Poems

TRANSLATED BY ALASTAIR REID & ANDREW HURLEY

0-374-51736-3 FS&G PB $9.95

New Love Poetry

TRANSLATED BY KEITH ELLIS

0-8020-0427-X TORONTO $45.00

Herberto **Padilla**

A Fountain, a House of Stone

A bilingual edition

0-374-15781-2 FS&G $19.95

Selected Poems

0-374-25877-5 FS&G $15.95

El Salvador

Claribel **Alegria**

Ashes of Izalco

TRANSLATED BY DARWIN FLAKOLL

0-915306-83-2 CONSORTIUM $17.95

0-915306-84-0 CURBSTONE PB $9.95

Family Album

0-915306-94-8 CURBSTONE PB $10.95

Flowers from the Volcano

Memories of torture and death in El Salvador

TRANSLATED BY CAROLYN FORCHE

0-8229-3469-8 PITTSBURGH $19.95

Fugues

TRANSLATED BY DARWIN FLAKOLL

1-88068-410-1 CURBSTONE PB $10.95

Umbrales, Thresholds: Poems

TRANSLATED BY DARWIN FLAKOLL

1-88068-436-5 CURBSTONE $10.95

Woman of the River

0-8229-5409-5 PITTSBURGH PB $10.95

Roque **Dalton**

Clandestine Poems

0-915306-91-3 CURBSTONE PB $7.95

Poems

Popular poetry in support of revolution

TRANSLATED BY RICHARD SCHAAF

0-915306-43-3 CURBSTONE PB $7.50

Small Hours of the Night: Selected Poems

TRANSLATED BY HARDIE ST. MARTIN AND JONATHAN COHEN

1-88068-435-7 CURBSTONE PB $14.95

Hugo **Lindo**

Ways of Rain/Maneras de Llover

"A song of praise to his tropical homeland. Although inspired by the *Popul Vuh*, Lindo's cosmogony of 28 cantos transcends its locale to become a song to human perseverance generally"—*Choice*

0-935480-24-2 LATIN AMERICAN LIT PB $14.95

Gabriela **Yanes**, editor

Mirrors of War: Literature and Revolution in El Salvador

A collection of prose and poetry of the revolutionary movement in El Salvador

TRANSLATED BY KEITH ELLIS

0-85345-687-9 MONTHLY REVIEW PB $10.00

Mexico

Homero **Aridjis**

Exaltation of Light

Lyricism verges on crystalline abstraction in this effective translation

TRANSLATED BY ELIOT WEINBERGER

0-918526-28-0 BOA $20.00

Rosario **Castellanos**

Meditation on the Threshold

One of Mexico's most important 20th-century poets and an exponent of feminism

See also MEXICO under FICTION

TRANSLATED BY JULIAN PALLEY

0-916950-80-8 BILINGUAL PB $13.00

Sor Juana Ines **de la Cruz**

A Sor Juana Anthology

New translations of work by the 17th-century nun who was the first great poet of Latin America, including her baroque masterpiece *First Dream*. "Of all the major poets of the Americas, Sor Juana Ines de la Cruz has until recently been the most neglected…[Alan S.] Trueblood has now managed, in the case of Sor Juana's poems, without being unfaithful to them, to create texts in English which have a poetic value of their own"—Octavio Paz

TRANSLATED BY ALAN TRUEBLOOD

0-674-82121-1 HARVARD PB $14.95

Sor Juana Ines de La Cruz: Poems

A bilingual anthology

TRANSLATED BY MARGARET SAYERS PEDEN

0-916950-60-3 BILINGUAL PB $12.00

Isabel **Fraire**

Poems in the Lap of Death

A bilingual edition

TRANSLATED BY THOMAS HOEKSEMA

0-935480-04-8 LATIN AMERICAN LIT PB $8.50

Jose **Gorostiza**

Death Without End

TRANSLATED BY LAURA VILLASENOR

0-87959-057-2 RANSOM HUMANITIES $15.00

Acosta **Juvenal**, editor

Light from a Nearby Window: Contemporary Mexican Poetry

0-87286-281-X CITY LIGHTS PB $12.95

Marco Antonio **Montes de Oca**

Twenty-One Poems

"A talented poet of inner experience whose verse is rich in metaphor and devoid of social commentary"—*Choice*

TRANSLATED BY LAURA VILLASENOR

PROLOGUE BY OCTAVIO PAZ

0-935480-09-9 LATIN AMERICAN LIT PB $9.00

Jose Emilio **Pacheco**

City of Memory and Other Poems

0-87286-324-7 CITY LIGHTS $25.00

Selected Poems

"The poetry of Jose Emilio Pacheco is not inscribed in the world of nature, but in culture, and within that in shadow in the midst of it. Each poem by Pacheco is a homage to the No; for Jose Emilio time is the agent of universal destruction, and history—the passage of ruins"—Octávio Paz

EDITED BY GEORGE MCWHIRTER

TRANSLATED BY THOMAS HOEKSEMA & OTHERS

0-8112-1022-7 NEW DIRECTIONS PB $11.95

Octavio **Paz**

Mexico's great modern poet has explored the same themes over many decades, fusing autobiography and metaphysical speculation, eroticism and politics, vibrant imagery and formal experimentation.

The Collected Poems, 1957-1987

A bilingual edition

TRANSLATED BY ELIOT WEINBERGER & OTHERS

EDITED BY ELIOT WEINBERGER

0-8112-1037-5 NEW DIRECTIONS $37.50

0-8112-1173-8 NEW DIRECTIONS PB $21.00

Configurations

TRANSLATED BY MURIEL RUKEYSER & OTHERS

0-8112-0150-3 NEW DIRECTIONS PB $9.95

A Draft of Shadow & Other Poems

The title poem is a long autobiographical meditation

TRANSLATED BY ELIOT WEINBERGER

0-8112-0738-2 NEW DIRECTIONS PB $10.95

Eagle or Sun?

Prose poems

TRANSLATED BY ELIOT WEINBERGER

0-8112-0623-8 NEW DIRECTIONS PB $8.95

Selected Poems of Octavio Paz

EDITED BY ELIOT WEINBERGER

TRANSLATED BY ELIOT WEINBERGER & OTHERS

0-8112-0899-0 NEW DIRECTIONS PB $8.95

Octavio Paz

A Tree Within
A recent long poem
TRANSLATED BY ELIOT WEINBERGER
0-8112-1071-5 NEW DIRECTIONS PB $9.95

Manuel **Ponce**
Some of My Poems
Views of life, death, and God
TRANSLATED BY MARIA LUISA RODRIGUEZ-LEE
0-935480-28-5 LATIN AMERICAN LIT PB $11.50

Jaime **Sabines**
Pieces of Shadow: Selected Poems of Jaime Sabines
TRANSLATED BY W.S. MERWIN
INTRODUCTION BY MARIO DEL VALLE
1-56886-023-4 MARSILIO $24.00

Ramon Lopez **Velarde**
Song of the Heart
TRANSLATED BY MARGARET SAYERS PEDEN
0-292-74685-7 TEXAS $19.95

Xavier **Villaurrutia**
Nostalgia for Death & Heiroglyphs of Desire
The only book by a pioneering, openly homosexual modernist Mexican poet. Also includes the essay "Hieroglyphs of Desire" by Octavio Paz
TRANSLATED BY ELIOT WEINBERGER AND OTHERS
1-55659-053-9 COPPER CANYON PB $12.00

Nicaragua

Ernesto **Cardenal**
Apocalypse & Other Poems
Protest poetry by the committed revolutionary priest turned politician
0-8112-0662-9 NEW DIRECTIONS PB $7.95

Cosmic Canticle
TRANSLATED BY JOHN LYONS
1-88068-407-1 CURBSTONE $24.95

The Gospel in Solentiname
0-88344-176-4 ORBIS PB $18.95

Zero Hour & Other Documentary Poems
Poetry of the struggle that "debunks, corroborates and mediates" reality. Includes the post-revolutionary work *Lights*
TRANSLATED BY PAUL W. BORGESON
EDITED BY DONALD D. WALSH
0-8112-0767-6 NEW DIRECTIONS PB $6.95

Peru

Pablo **Neruda** & Cesar **Vallejo**
Neruda and Vallejo: Selected Poems
See also CHILE
EDITED BY ROBERT BLY
0-8070-6489-0 BEACON PB $14.00

Cesar **Vallejo**
Cesar Vallejo: The Complete Posthumous Poetry
The definitive translation of a great 20th-century poet
TRANSLATED BY CLAYTON ESHLEMAN & JOSE R. BARCIA
0-520-04099-6 CALIFORNIA PB $16.95

Selected Poems of Cesar Vallejo
Selections from his four most important collections: *The Black Messengers, Trilce, Human Poem*, and *Spain, Take This Cup from Me*
TRANSLATED BY H.R. HAYS
0-937584-01-0 SACHEM $13.50

Trilce
First published in 1922, *Trilce* is a masterpiece of high modernism, a landmark work that had a profound impact on poetry in this century. "Among all existing translations, this is without doubt the one that touches the hidden nerve of Vallejo's work most directly, the one that best carries on the movement and the gesture of freedom from which it was born"—Americo Ferrari, Introduction
TRANSLATED BY CLAYTON ESHLEMAN
0-941419-50-9 MARSILIO $28.00
0-941419-51-7 MARSILIO PB $14.00

Drama

Ariel **Dorfman**
Death and the Maiden
0-140-24684-3 PENGUIN PB $7.95

Konfidenz
See also CHILE under FICTION
0-374-18218-3 FS&G $17.00
0-679-76716-9 VINTAGE PB $11.00

Octavio **Paz**
Rappaccini's Daughter
TRANSLATED BY SEBASTIAN DOGGART
1-56886-034-X MARSILIO $24.00
1-56886-035-8 MARSILIO PB $14.95

Manuel **Puig**
Kiss of the Spider Woman and Two Other Plays
0-393-31148-1 NORTON PB $10.95

Manuel Puig (photo by J. E. Lamarca)

Under a Mantle of Stars
A heavy dramatic mixture of politics and fantasy with a dash of eroticism
TRANSLATED BY RONALD CHRIST
0-930829-32-8 LUMEN PB $10.00

Severo **Sarduy**
For Voice
Sarduy is noted for the brilliance of his linguistic play
TRANSLATED BY PHILIP BARNARD
EDITED BY YVETTE E. MILLER
0-935480-20-X LATIN AMERICAN LIT PB $12.95

Rodolfo **Usigli**
Two Plays: Crown of Light & One of These Days
An "antihistorical comedy" and a "nonpolitical fantasy" by a leading Mexican playwright
TRANSLATED BY THOMAS BLEDSOE
0-8093-0494-5 SOUTHERN ILLINOIS $14.95

George W. **Woodyard**, translator
Dramacontemporary: Latin America
Includes Carlos Fuentes' *Orchids in the Moonlight*, Mario Vargas Llosa's *Kathie and the Hippopotamus*, Antonio Skarmeta's *Burning Patience*, and Manuel Puig's *Kiss of the Spider Woman*
1-55554-005-8 PAJ PUBLICATIONS PB $16.95

Criticism, Memoirs, and Other Prose

Argentina

Jorge Luis **Borges**
Borges on Writing
See also CONTEMPORARY WRITERS ON WRITING under LITERARY CRITICISM in LITERATURE OF EUROPE, AFRICA, AND ASIA
0-88001-368-0 ECCO PB $12.00

Seven Conversations with Jorge Luis Borges
0-87875-214-5 WHITSON $18.50

Jorge Luis **Borges**

Other Inquisitions: 1937-1952

Literary and speculative essays fully as enthralling as Borges's fiction; the topics include Coleridge, Whitman, Kafka, time, dreams, and the Great Wall of China

See also ARGENTINA under FICTION

TRANSLATED BY RUTH L. SIMMS

0-292-76002-7 TEXAS PB $14.95

Seven Nights

Seven lectures on *The Divine Comedy*, nightmares, *The Thousand and One Nights*, Buddhism, poetry, blindness, and the Kabbalah

See also CONTEMPORARY WRITERS ON WRITING under LITERARY CRITICISM in LITERATURE OF EUROPE, AFRICA, AND ASIA

TRANSLATED BY ELIOT WEINBERGER

INTRODUCTION BY ALASTAIR REID

0-8112-0905-9 NEW DIRECTIONS PB $7.95

Eduardo **Mallea**

History of an Argentine Passion

An essay on the two Argentinas: Buenos Aires and the interior, where the author believed the nation's future lay

TRANSLATED BY MYRON I. LICHTBLAU

EDITED BY YVETTE E. MILLER

0-935480-10-2 LATIN AMERICAN LIT PB $13.95

Brazil

Antonio **Candido**

Antonio Candido: On Literature and Society

0-691-03629-2 PRINCETON $49.50

0-691-03630-6 PRINCETON PB $16.95

Clarice **Lispector**

The Foreign Legion

Lispector's views of literature and her own working methods

TRANSLATED BY GIOVANNI PONTIERO

0-8112-1189-4 NEW DIRECTIONS PB $10.95

Chile

Marjorie **Agosin**

A Cross and a Star: Memoirs of a Jewish Girl in Chile

0-8263-1573-9 NEW MEXICO $19.95

Isabel **Allende**

Paula

In 1991 when her daughter fell ill and then into a coma, Allende began to write for her the story of her ancestors, her mother, and of Chile during the 1973 military coup and the ensuing dictatorship

0-06-017253-3 HARPERCOLLINS $24.00

0-06-092721-6 HARPERCOLLINS PB $12.50

Julio **Cortazar**

Nicaraguan Sketches

See also PERU

TRANSLATED BY KATHLEEN WEAVER

0-393-30642-9 NORTON PB $7.95

Pablo **Neruda**

Memoirs

TRANSLATED BY HARDIE ST. MARTIN

0-14-018628-X VIKING PB $11.95

Colombia

Gabriel **García Márquez**

Clandestine in Chile: The Adventures of Miguel Littin

Littin, a Chilean exile, secretly returned to Chile to film; García Márquez narrates his experience

TRANSLATED BY ASA ZATZ

0-8050-0945-0 HOLT PB $9.95

The Story of a Shipwrecked Sailor

"Who drifted on a life raft for ten days without food or water, was proclaimed a national hero, kissed by beauty queens, made rich through publicity, and then spurned by the government and forgotten for all time"

TRANSLATED BY RANDOLPH HOGAN

0-679-72205-X VINTAGE PB $9.00

Cuba

Reinaldo **Arenas**

Before Night Falls

See also CUBA under FICTION

TRANSLATED BY DOLORES M. KOCH

0-14-015765-4 PENGUIN PB $11.95

Guillermo **Cabrera Infante**

Mea Cuba

"An enduringly original literary presence, unquestionably Cuba's most important living writer…His view of Cuba is as clear as it is relentless, and he has Cuba at heart"
—Alastair Reid, *NY Review of Books*

See also CUBA UNDER COMMUNISM under CUBA under LATIN AMERICA AND THE CARIBBEAN in HISTORY OF THE AMERICAS

TRANSLATED BY KENNETH HALL

0-374-20497-7 FS&G $23.00

0-374-52446-7 NOONDAY PB $15.00

Roberto Fernandez **Retamar**

Caliban & Other Essays

TRANSLATED BY EDWARD BAKER

0-8166-1742-2 MINNESOTA $14.95

Severo **Sarduy**

Written on a Body

TRANSLATED BY CAROL MAIER

0-930829-11-5 SUN & MOON PB $10.95

El Salvador

Roque **Dalton**

Poetry and Militancy in Latin America

TRANSLATED BY ARLENE & JAMES SCULLY

0-915306-26-3 CURBSTONE PB $4.00

Mexico

Carlos **Fuentes**

Don Quixote, or the Critique of Reading

0-86728-015-8 TEXAS PB $2.00

Myself with Others: Selected Essays

Fuentes on his writing, Cervantes, García Márquez, Bunuel's films, and Borges

0-374-21750-5 FS&G $19.95

A New Time for Mexico

Mexico's leading novelist addresses the challenge facing that lush and beautiful country: the crisis of its political system and the transition to democracy. This timely study treats the origins of Mexico's political system and the watershed events of 1994: the rebellion in Chiapas, the break between Presidents Salinas and Zedillo, and the trauma of the quest for democratic self-rule. An urgent and personal assessment from one of Mexico's—and the world's—greatest thinkers

See also LATE ARRIVALS in HISTORY OF THE AMERICAS

See also CONTEMPORARY MEXICO under MEXICO under LATIN AMERICA AND THE CARIBBEAN in HISTORY OF THE AMERICAS

0-374-22170-7 FS&G $22.00

Frank **Gonzalez-Crussi**

The Day of the Dead: And Other Moral Reflections

This rare and fluent essayist (*Notes of an Anatomist, On the Nature of Things Erotic*) whom *New Yorker* called "a writer of precision and originality" turns his sharp eye on human mortality. He discusses the indestructible corpse of Evita Perón with an embalmer, the demystifying "celebration" of death in his native Mexico, and, most eloquently, the haunting relationship between death and art

0-15-181192-X HARCOURT BRACE $19.95

0-15-600142-X HARVEST PB $8.95

Martin L. **Guzman**

The Eagle and the Serpent

The national polarities reflected in the Mexican Revolution

TRANSLATED BY HARRIET DE ONIS

0-8446-0668-5 SMITH $17.00

Sor Juana **Ines Dela Cruz**

The Answer/La Respuesta

An important early essay on women's rights, with extensive commentary. "Essential reading for anyone who wishes to understand not only this remarkable woman but also the whole world in which she forged her identity"
—Stephen Greenblatt

TRANSLATED BY ELECTA ARENAL AND AMANDA POWELL

1-55861-077-4 FEMINIST PRESS PB $12.95

Octavio **Paz**

Alternating Current

See also ASPECTS OF MEXICAN CULTURE under MEXICO under LATIN AMERICA AND THE CARIBBEAN in HISTORY OF THE AMERICAS

1-55970-136-6 ARCADE PB $9.95

Children of the Mire: Modern Poetry from Romanticism to the Avant-Garde

The underlying myths of modern poetry, explored by the great Mexican poet in brilliant aphoristic style

See also **POETRY** under **LITERARY CRITICISM** in **LITERATURE OF EUROPE, AFRICA, AND ASIA**

0-674-11625-9 HARVARD $18.00

Convergences: Essays on Art and Literature

TRANSLATED BY HELEN LANE

0-15-122585-0 HARCOURT BRACE $19.95

The Double Flame: Essays on Love and Eroticism

0-15-100103-0 HARCOURT BRACE $22.00

The Labyrinth of Solitude: Life and Thought in Mexico

Paz's famous essay on the Mexican character

See also **ASPECTS OF MEXICAN CULTURE** under **MEXICO** under **LATIN AMERICA AND THE CARIBBEAN** in **HISTORY OF THE AMERICAS**

TRANSLATED BY LYSANDER KEMP

0-8021-5042-X GROVE PB $13.95

Marcel Duchamp: Appearance Stripped Bare

TRANSLATED BY RACHEL PHILLIPS & DONALD GARDNER

1-55970-138-2 ARCADE PB $9.95

The Monkey Grammarian

Essays prompted in part by Paz's residence in India

TRANSLATED BY HELEN R. LANE

1-55970-135-8 ARCADE PB $9.95

On Poets and Others

TRANSLATED BY MICHAEL SCHMIDT

1-55970-139-0 ARCADE PB $9.95

One Earth, Four or Five Worlds: Reflections on Contemporary History

TRANSLATED BY HELEN LANE

0-15-668746-1 HARCOURT BRACE PB $5.95

The Other Voice: Essays in Modern Poetry

An erudite and passionate discourse on the uses of poetry in the modern world, by the Nobel Prize winner

See also **POETRY** under **LITERARY CRITICISM** in **LITERATURE OF EUROPE, AFRICA, AND ASIA**

0-15-170449-X HARCOURT BRACE $16.95

Sor Juana: Or, The Traps of Faith

"Octavio Paz's book on Sor Juana displays an extraordinary sweep of imagination and intelligence, and it is many things: a biography, a critical study, a re-creation of an era, a meditation on Mexican history, a dialogue of poet with poet, a reflection on the role of the intellectual in the modern world—the world on whose threshold Sor Juana lived and died, and which she often seems to predict"
—Michael Wood, *NY Review of Books*

TRANSLATED BY MARGARET SAYERS PEDEN

0-674-82105-X BELKNAP $44.00

0-674-82106-8 BELKNAP PB $16.95

Nicaragua

Ernesto **Cardenal**

In Cuba

TRANSLATED BY DONALD D. WALSH

0-8112-0538-X NEW DIRECTIONS PB $9.95

Peru

Julio **Cortazar**

Nicaraguan Sketches

See also **CHILE**

TRANSLATED BY KATHLEEN WEAVER

0-393-30642-9 NORTON PB $7.95

Cesar **Vallejo**

The Mayakovsky Case

TRANSLATED BY RICHARD SCHAAF

EDITED BY JAMES SCULLY

0-915306-31-X CURBSTONE PB $4.00

Mario **Vargas Llosa**

A Fish in the Water: A Memoir

0-374-15509-7 FS&G $25.00

0-14-024890-0 PENGUIN PB $14.95

The Madness of Things Peruvian: Democracy Under Siege

1-56000-114-3 TRANSACTION $32.95

Anthologies

Marjorie **Agosin**, editor

Landscapes of a New Land: Short Fiction by Latin American Women

"The best anthology of Latin American women's literature in translation. Highly recommended"—*Choice*

0-934834-96-2 WHITE PINE PB $12.00

These Are Not Sweet Girls: Latin American Women Poets

Fifty poets are represented, including Gabriela Mistral and Violeta Parra

1-87772-738-5 WHITE PINE PB $17.00

What Is Secret: Stories by Chilean Women

1-87772-741-5 WHITE PINE PB $17.00

Mary **Crow**, editor

Woman Who Has Sprouted Wings: Poems by Contemporary Latin American Poets

0-935480-35-8 LATIN AMERICAN LIT PB $13.95

Victor Hernandez **Cruz**, editor

Paper Dance: 54 Latino Poets

0-89255-201-8 PERSEA PB $13.95

Claudio **Freoxas**, editor

Afro-Cuban Poetry

A bilingual critical study, with a selection of poems by Jose Sanchez Boudy

0-89729-192-1 EDICIONES UNIVERSAL PB $6.00

C.L.R. **James**

Beyond a Boundary

0-8223-1383-9 DUKE PB $15.95

Alberto **Manguel**, editor

Other Fires: Short Fiction by Latin American Women

Stories by Brazilian, Argentinian, Colombian, Mexican, Cuban, and Uruguayan writers

See also **ANTHOLOGIES OF WOMEN'S WRITING** under **WOMEN'S STUDIES** in **SOCIAL STUDIES**

0-517-55870-X CLARKSON POTTER PB $12.00

Emir R. **Monegal**, editor

The Borzoi Anthology of Latin American Literature

Volume 1

0-394-73301-0 KNOPF PB $19.95

Volume 2

0-394-73366-5 KNOPF PB $19.95

Barbara **Paschke** &
David **Volpendesta**, editors

Clamor of Innocence: Stories from Central America

Includes works by Manlio Argueta, Miguel Angel Asturias, Ernesto Cardenal, Carmen Naranjo, and others. "These stories have the ring of truth, the sound of having been lived in the heart of the beast"—Lawrence Ferlinghetti

0-87286-227-5 CITY LIGHTS PB $9.95

Raúl **Zurita**

Poems of Chile: A Bilingual Anthology, 1965-1985

TRANSLATED BY STEVEN F. WHITE

0-87775-180-3 UNICORN PB $16.95

Critical Studies

Michael **Bell**

Gabriel García Márquez: Solitude and Solidarity

0-312-09988-6 ST. MARTIN'S $29.95

J. Ann **Duncan**

Voices, Visions, and a New Reality: Mexican Fiction Since 1970

0-8229-3815-4 PITTSBURGH $49.95

Roberto **Gonzalez Echevarria**

The Voice of the Masters: Writing and Authority in Modern Latin American Literature

A study of Cabrera Infante, Cortazar, Fuentes, García Márquez, and others

0-292-78709-X TEXAS PB $10.95

John **King**, editor

On Modern Latin American Fiction

0-374-52178-6 FS&G PB $9.95

Christopher T. **Leland**
The Last Happy Men: The Generation of 1922, Fiction, and the Argentine Reality
0-8156-2376-3 SYRACUSE..$29.95

Marvin A. **Lewis**
Treading the Ebony Path: Ideology and Violence in Contemporary Afro-Colombian Prose Fiction
0-8262-0638-7 MISSOURI..$24.95

Part 7

Literature of the British Isles

William Blake

1 Samuel Beckett (1906–1989)
"What matter whether I was born or not, have lived or not, am dead or merely dying, I shall go on doing as I have always done, not knowing what it is I do, nor who I am, nor where I am, nor if I am. Yes, a little creature, I shall try and make a little creature, to hold in my arms, a little creature in my image, no matter what I say. And seeing what a poor thing I have made, or how like myself, I shall eat it."
—*Malone Dies*

818

2 Thomas Carlyle (1795–1881)
Born and educated in Glasgow, Carlyle was at once conservative and radical, bigoted and visionary; he was for all that a profound thinker and a remarkable literary stylist. "[Carlyle] reasserted a prophetic understanding of history and human nature in opposition to the reigning celebration of progress." (Christopher Lasch)

816

3 James Hogg (1770–1835)
"The Ettrick Shepherd" was a farmer for many years before his popular rural songs and ballads made him famous. In 1824 he published his masterpiece, the novel *Confessions of a Justified Sinner,* about a Calvinist youth who believes himself to be among the elect and therefore permitted to do whatever he likes. "Hogg's portrayal of the stages by which a human spirit can descend into darkness is somber, truthful, and unforgettable." (John Wain)

812

4 Patrick Kavanagh (1904–1967)
Poet of rural Ireland, most acclaimed for his powerful long poem *The Great Hunger.* "His authority and oddity derive from the fact that he wrested his idiom barehanded out of literary nowhere." (Seamus Heaney)

"Clay is the word and clay is the flesh
Where the potato-gatherers like mechanized scarecrows move
Along the side-fall of the hill—MacGuire and his men."
—*The Great Hunger*

853

5 Hugh MacDiarmid (1892–1978)
Founder of the Scottish Nationalist Party and a committed communist as well as a great poet. In his early masterpiece, *A Drunk Man Looks at a Thistle,* MacDiarmuid fused European high modernism with a rich rhyming Scots of his own concoction. "My job," he once said, "is to erupt like a volcano, emitting not only flame, but a lot of rubbish."

850

1

2

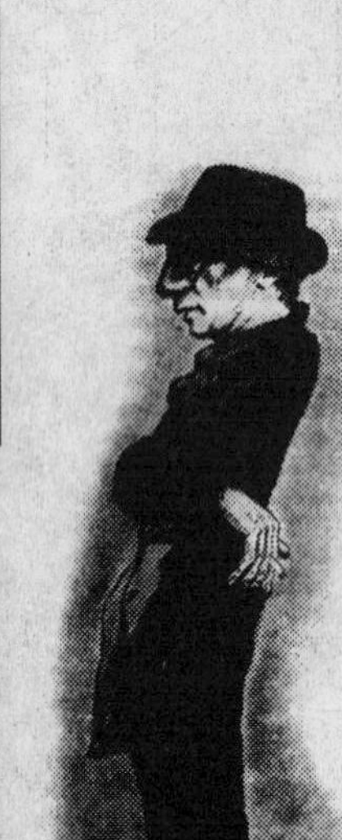
4

8

3

5

7

9

10

6 Sorley MacLean (1911–)
MacLean grew up speaking Gaelic in a family that still kept the memory of the old Gaelic songs. A leader of Scotland's Gaelic renaissance, he also translated his work into English. "The full-time professional poet is not for me. I brood over something till a rhythm comes, as a more or less tight rope across an abyss of silence. I go on it, as far as I can see, unconsciously."

872

7 Louis MacNeice (1907–1963)
Born in Belfast, the son of an Anglican priest, MacNeice became friends with W.H. Auden in college. His formally polished yet intimate poems reflect his knowledge of classical literature.

"Inside the tang of a tiny oil lamp. Outdoors
The winking signal and the waste sea.
Indoors the sound of the wind. Outdoors the wind.
Indoors the locked heart and the lost key."
—"House on a Cliff"

853

8 Edwin Muir (1887–1959)
Born in the Orkneys, Muir was a novelist, a translator (of Kafka, Broch, and others), and a fine, lyrically reflective poet. In Muir "there is something which is neither English nor Scottish, but Orcadian: the sensibility of a remote islander." (T.S. Eliot)

"What saves us from the raging desolations
And tells us we shall walk through peace to peace?"
—"The Desolations"

851

9 Flann O'Brien (1910–1966)
O'Brien's brilliant, bitter, and very funny novels, written in English and Gaelic, at once satirize and celebrate Irish exceptionalism while describing the bleak lot of all humankind. "When you are writing about the world of the dead—and the damned—where none of the rules and laws (not even the law of gravity) holds good, there is any amount of scope for backchat and funny cracks."

825

10 R.S. Thomas (1913–)
Thomas spent many years as a Welsh parish priest.

"When I was a child and the soft flesh was forming
Quietly as snow on the bare boughs of bone,
My father brought me trout from the green river
From whose chill lips the water song had flown.
Dull grew their eyes, the beautiful, blithe garland
Of stipples faded, as light shocked the brain;
They were the first sweet sacrifice I tasted,
A young god, ignorant of the blood's stain."
—"Song for Gwydion"

852

London: Unreal City

1 Camden Town

Everywhere were bridges that led nowhere; temporary wooden houses and enclosures, in the most unlikely situations; carcasses of ragged tenements, and fragments of unfinished walls and arches, and piles of scaffolding, and wildernesses of bricks, and giant forms of cranes, and tripods straddling above nothing. The Railroad was in progress; and from the very core of all this dire disorder, trailed smoothly away, upon its mighty course of civilization and improvement.

—Charles Dickens
Dombey and Son

810

2 Covent Garden

The authors and supporters of this secret institution would, in the height of their humour, style themselves the restorers of the liberty of the golden age and its simplicity of pleasures, before their innocence became so unjustly branded with the names of guilt and shame.

—John Cleland
Fanny Hill

798

3 Camberwell

Here you may see how men have multiplied toil for toil's sake. The energy, the ingenuity daily put forth in these grimy burrows task the brain's power of wondering. But that those who sit here through the livelong day, through every season, do it all without prospect or hope of reward save the permission to eat and sleep and bring into the world other creatures to strive with them for bread, surely that is yet more marvelous.

—George Gissing
The Nether World

811

4 Brett Street

Branched off, narrow, from the side of an open triangular space surrounded by dark and mysterious houses, temples of petty commerce emptied of traders for the night. Only a fruiterer's stall on the corner made a violent blaze of light and colour. Beyond, all was black, and a few people passing in that direction vanished at one stride beyond the glowing heaps of oranges and lemons. No footsteps echoed. They would never be heard of again.

—Joseph Conrad
The Secret Agent

820

5 London Bridge

Unreal City
Under the brown fog of a
winter dawn,
A crowd flowed over London
Bridge, so many,
I had not thought death had
undone so many.

—T.S. Eliot
The Waste Land

693

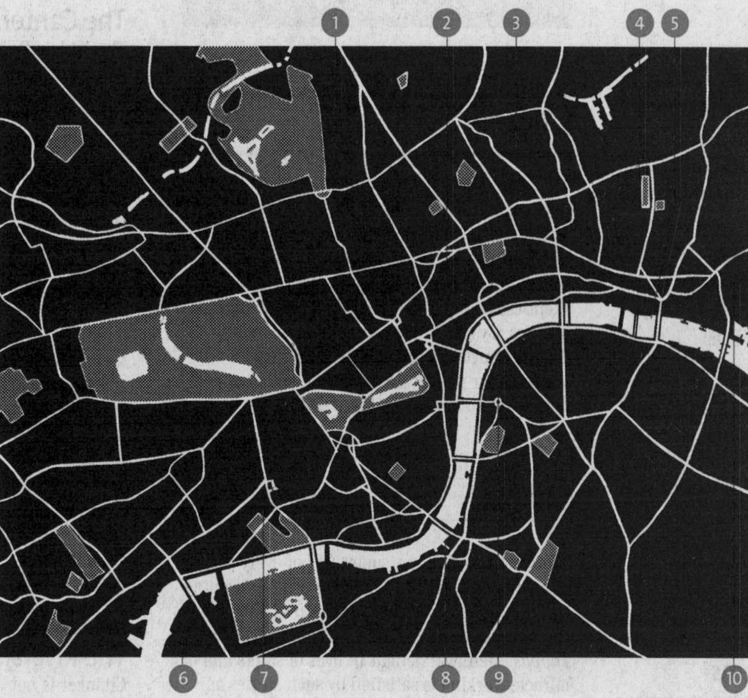

6 Barnes Common

Her notion of life was perfectly clear and perfectly simple; it was to be out with me all day on the towing-path or Barnes Common and to be always on the move. I gratified her wishes in everything; it was, after all, what I had brought her away to do; but it must be added that I derived from it all a sense of personal satisfaction also, for it was a long time, I thought sourly, since anyone had seemed to want my company so much.

—J.R. Ackerley
We Think the World of You

818

7 Sloane Square

I would travel either to Sloane Square or to Liverpool Street to have a drink in the station buffet. In the whole extension of the Underground system those two stations are, as far as I've been able to discover, the only ones which have bars actually upon the platform. These two bars were not just a cosy after-the-office treat, they were the source of a dark excitement, places of profound communication with London, with the sources of life, with the caverns of resignation to grief and to mortality.

—Iris Murdoch
A Word Child

837

8 Vauxhall Gardens

Here on the site where thousands of lights once sparkled; where sweet sounds of music made night tuneful till morning dawned; where the beauty and fashion of London feasted and danced through the summer seasons of a century—spreads, at this day, an awful wilderness of mud and rubbish; the deserted dead body of Vauxhall Gardens mouldering in the open air.

—Wilkie Collins
No Name

809

9 Waterloo Station

He recalled the figure of a man he had seen on the steps outside Waterloo Station. It was an English face; and it was also a Chinese face, a Russian face, an Indian face. It was just the face of a man, a mortal man, against whom Providence had grown as malignant as a mad dog. And the woe upon the face was of such a character that Wolf knew at once that no conceivable social readjustments or ameliorative revolutions could ever atone for it—could ever make up for the single irremediable fact that it had been as it has been!

—John Cowper Powys
Wolf Solent

826

10 Whitechapel

"I should like very much to know if I am wrong in believing that he has gone about with you in the bar-quarters—in Saint Giles's and Whitechapel."

"We've certainly inquired and explored together," the Princess admitted, "and in the depths of this huge luxurious wandering wasteful city we've seen sights of unspeakable misery and horror. But we've been not only in the slums; we've been to the music hall and the penny-reading."

—Henry James
The Princess Casamassima

624

The Anglo-Saxon Period

The Anglo-Saxon (or Old English) period extends from the dawn of English literary culture in the 5th-century AD through the Norman Conquest in the 11th-century. Though many of its seminal texts, like *Beowulf*, are at least nominally Christian, both the poetry and prose of this period reflect an older and darker culture, by turns fatalistic, brutal, and elegaic. Stark and often strange, these works are the bedrock of English literature, and their influence on later writing, though often hidden, is pervasive.

Michael **Alexander**, translator

Beowulf

Beowulf is the great native English epic, overlaid with Christian elements but imbued with the brooding pessimism of the pagan culture behind it. Alexander has made a powerful attempt to approximate the textures of the Anglo-Saxon verse

0-14-043377-5 PENGUIN PB $10.95

Gliding through the shadows
came the walker in the night; the warriors slept
whose task was to hold the horned building,
all except one. It was well-known to men
that the demon could not drag them to the shades
without God's willing it; yet the one man kept
unblinking watch. He awaited, heart swelling
with anger against his foe, the ordeal of battle.
Down off the moorlands' misting fells came
Grendel stalking; God's brand was on him.
The spoiler meant to snatch away
from the high hall some of human race.
BEOWULF

The Earliest English Poems

Another outstanding fusion of Modernist poetics with Anglo-Saxon tonalities by Michael Alexander

0-14-044594-3 PENGUIN PB..............................$8.95

Howell D. **Chickering**, Jr., translator

Beowulf: A Dual Language Edition

The Anglo-Saxon text with Chickering's excellent translation on facing pages

0-385-06213-3 DOUBLEDAY PB.......................$14.00

S.A.J. **Bradley**, editor

Anglo-Saxon Poetry

Clear prose translations of virtually all the surviving corpus of Anglo-Saxon verse

0-460-87507-8 EVERYMAN'S PB.......................$11.50

Michael **Swanton**, editor & translator

Anglo-Saxon Prose

Religious, legal, narrative, and other writings giving a cross-section of Anglo-Saxon life

0-460-87341-5 EVERYMAN'S PB $7.95

Kevin **Crossley-Holland**, editor

The Anglo-Saxon World: An Anthology

A compact collection of documents and poems, including a complete translation of *Beowulf*

See also **BRITISH AND CELTIC** under **EUROPEAN MYTHOLOGY** under **MYTHOLOGY AND FOLKLORE** in **RELIGION, SPIRITUALITY, AND PHILOSOPHY**

See also **EARLY BRITISH HISTORY: FROM PREHISTORY TO 1066** under **GREAT BRITAIN AND IRELAND** in **WORLD HISTORY AND CURRENT AFFAIRS**

0-19-281632-2 OXFORD PB $9.95

The Exeter Book of Riddles

0-14-043367-8 PENGUIN PB.............................$11.95

Medieval Literature

Poetry

Though much of medieval poetry is uncomplicated lyricism, the major poets—such as Chaucer, Gower, and the anonymous author of *Sir Gawain and the Green Knight*— are remarkable for their sophistication and their skeptical (though tolerant) rendering of human frailties. By the 14th-century London and the English court had both a discriminating audience for poetry and a wide selection of targets for social analysis and satire.

Chaucer

"Chaucer has given us something of every variety of medieval story. The romances are represented by the *Knight's Tale*, and the *Squire's Tale*, while their decadence is satirized in the *Tale of Sir Thopas*. Medieval delight in lives of saints and of miracle working is satisfied by such stories as those of the Prioress, the Second Nun, and the Monk. The tales of the Man of Law or of the Clerk, of Melibeus or of the Franklin, dealt with various attitudes to life full of interest to Chaucer's audience. Again, the *Wife of Bath's Tale* delighted them with a story of 'faerye,' and the *Nun's Priest's Tale* and the *Pardoner's Tale* amused while they instructed. And besides these Chaucer gave, in good measure, that body of 'churl's tales' which bring us so close to '*l'homme moyen sensuel*.' In the tales of the Miller, Reeve, Shipman, Summoner, Merchant or Friar the brilliance of the telling makes us condone the coarse nature of the tale."
—H.S. Bennett, *Chaucer and the Fifteenth Century*

Geoffrey **Chaucer**

The Canterbury Tales

The most enduringly popular translation; an idiomatic but accurate rendering

See also **MEDIEVAL LITERATURE** in **LITERATURE OF EUROPE, AFRICA, AND ASIA**

TRANSLATED BY NEVILL COGHILL

0-14-044022-4 PENGUIN PB $7.95

Geoffrey Chaucer

The Canterbury Tales

The Middle English text, in the famous Skeat edition, with brief but useful glosses

0-679-60125-2 MODERN LIBRARY....................$17.50

The Canterbury Tales

See also **MEDIEVAL LITERATURE** in **LITERATURE OF EUROPE, AFRICA, AND ASIA**

0-679-40989-0 KNOPF $20.00

0-19-281597-0 OXFORD PB...............................$4.95

The Canterbury Tales: The First Fragment

See also **MEDIEVAL LITERATURE** in **LITERATURE OF EUROPE, AFRICA, AND ASIA**

EDITED BY MICHAEL ALEXANDER

0-14-043409-7 PENGUIN PB...............................$8.95

Love Visions

Modern English versions of *The Book of the Duchess, The Parliament Birds, The Legend of Good Women,* and *The House of Fame*

TRANSLATED BY BRIAN STONE

0-14-044408-4 PENGUIN PB $9.95

The Riverside Chaucer

Chaucer is not difficult to read in the original. The impeccably edited *Riverside Chaucer* has full and convenient annotations which make the Middle English text highly accessible

EDITED BY LARRY D. BENSON

0-395-29031-7 HOUGHTON MIFFLIN $61.96

Troilus and Criseyde

An incomparable, novelistic love story, at once romantic and sardonic

See also **MEDIEVAL LITERATURE** in **LITERATURE OF EUROPE, AFRICA, AND ASIA**

TRANSLATED BY NEVILL COGHILL

0-14-044239-1 PENGUIN PB $9.95

Other Medieval Poets

Marie **Boroff**, translator

Pearl: A New Verse Translation

Perhaps the most tantalizing mysterious and moving of medieval English religious allegories

0-393-09144-9 NORTON PB $7.95

William **Dunbar**

The Poems of William Dunbar

"Dunbar is professional through and through; the accomplished master of one tradition that goes back to *Beowulf* and of another that goes back to the Troubadours ...When you are in the mood for it, his poetry has a sweep and volume of sound and an assured virility which (while the mood lasts) makes most other poets seem a little faint and tentative and half-hearted"—C.S. Lewis

EDITED BY JAMES KINSLEY

0-403-01321-6 SCHOLARLY $29.00

Casey **Finch**, translator

The Complete Works of the Pearl Poet

0-520-07871-3 CALIFORNIA PB $22.50

John **Gardner**, editor

The Alliterative Morte d'Arthur, The Owl and The Nightingale & Five Other Middle English Poems

0-8093-0648-4 SOUTHERN ILLINOIS PB $19.95

Eric V. **Gordon**

Pearl

0-19-812675-1 OXFORD PB..............................$19.95

John **Gower**

Confessio Amantis

A debate on the nature of love, supplemented by a vast collection of romantic tales in polished verse, by Chaucer's sometime friend and most accomplished rival

EDITED BY RUSSELL A. PECK

0-8020-6438-8 TORONTO PB............................$15.95

Robert **Henryson**

The Moral Fables of Aesop

Henryson's recastings of Aesop are realistic and elegant; at his best he is fully worthy of comparison with Chaucer. This edition has a modern English translation on the facing page

EDITED BY GEORGE D. GOPEN

0-268-01361-6 NOTRE DAME PB......................$22.95

The Poems of Robert Henryson

"Critical studies will henceforth be able to utilize the wealth of information that Fox provides on the literal meaning of the poems. The strength of the new edition, and it is great, lies in its clarification of Henryson's text" —*Speculum*

EDITED BY DENTON FOX

0-19-812324-8 CLARENDON PB......................$26.00

Selected Poems

0-85635-301-9 CARCANET PB............................$7.50

Thomas **Hoccleve**

Selected Poems

Hoccleve's poetry has an autobiographical dimension unusual among medieval writers

EDITED BY BERNARD O'DONOGHUE

0-85635-321-3 CARCANET PB..........................$11.25

William **Langland**

Piers Plowman

The "B" text of the poem, generally regarded as the most authoritative, with notes and glossary

EDITED BY JACK A. BENNETT

0-19-871090-9 OXFORD PB..............................$14.95

Piers the Ploughman

A modern prose rendering of the most sweeping (and ambiguous) of medieval allegories; the masterpiece of the so called "alliterative" tradition

TRANSLATED BY J.F. GOODRIDGE

0-14-044087-9 PENGUIN PB $9.95

Lawman

Brut

Lawman, or Layamon, drew this early verse chronicle of Britain's legendary founding by the Roman Brutus from the 12th-century French version by Wace

TRANSLATED BY ROSAMUND ALLEN

0-460-87021-1 EVERYMAN'S PB $12.95

Brian **Stone**, translator

King Arthur's Death: The Alliterative Morte d'Arthure & the Stanzaic Le Morte d'Arthur

New translations of two great medieval poems

0-14-044445-9 PENGUIN PB $10.95

Sir Gawain and the Green Knight

A modern English verse translation

0-14-044092-5 PENGUIN PB $7.95

J.J. **Anderson**, editor

Sir Gawain and the Green Knight

0-460-87510-8 EVERYMAN'S PB $6.95

J.A. **Burrow**, editor

Sir Gawain and the Green Knight

The original text of a linguistically difficult but endlessly fascinating poem, a deft and entertaining yet serious allegory of love, pleasure, and responsibility

0-14-042295-1 PENGUIN PB $9.95

Anthologies

J.A.W. **Bennett** & G.V. **Smithers**, editors

Early Middle English Verse and Prose

A large-scale collection spanning all the genres and styles of the period

0-19-871101-8 OXFORD PB..............................$34.00

R.T. **Davies**, editor

Early Middle English Lyrics: A Critical Anthology

A rich sampling of the early English tradition

See also **MEDIEVAL LITERATURE** in **LITERATURE OF EUROPE, AFRICA, AND ASIA**

0-571-06571-6 FABER PB $15.95

Robert D. **Stevick**, editor

One Hundred Middle English Lyrics

A standard college text and a useful introduction to the medieval lyric in all its variety

0-252-06379-1 ILLINOIS PB $14.95

Drama

Of all medieval genres, drama is perhaps the most accessible. The English mystery plays performed during religious festivals are exhilarating blends of piety, awe, storytelling vigor, and high spirits that sometimes border on the scatological. Because drama was a folk genre, even the more sophisticated morality plays—for all their elaborate allegorical underpinnings—share the immediacy of the mysteries.

David **Bevington**, editor

Medieval Drama

The most comprehensive generally available anthology

0-395-13915-5 HOUGHTON MIFFLIN................$57.16

A.C. **Cawley**, editor

Everyman & Medieval Miracle Plays

0-460-87280-X EVERYMAN'S PB $5.95

John **Gassner**, editor

Medieval and Tudor Drama

A selection of English mystery and miracle plays including *Everyman*, Tudor interludes and comedies, and some interesting source materials

0-936839-84-8 APPLAUSE THEATRE PB.............$12.95

Peter **Happe**, editor

English Mystery Plays

A generous selection indicating the range of subject matter of the mysteries

0-14-043093-8 PENGUIN PB $12.95

Martial **Rose**, editor

The Wakefield Mystery Plays

A complete cycle, including examples of raucous comedy and genuine folk piety

0-393-00483-X NORTON PB $12.95

Prose

Malory's *Morte d'Arthur* is the great monument of late Middle English prose, a digest of Arthurian material as well as a compendium of late medieval attitudes toward ethics, chivalry, and even romantic love. Among shorter prose works, the most memorable are contemplative treatises like the anonymous *Cloud of Unknowing* and Julian of Norwich's *Revelations of Divine Love*. They bear witness to an enduring tradition of medieval spirituality, an intensely private, often mystical sensibility that did not always tamely accept the yoke of the medieval church.

Richard **Barber**, editor

The Pastons: A Family in the Wars of the Roses

A fascinating, uniquely detailed portrait of daily life in England during the 15th-century

See also **THE TUDORS: 1485-1603** under **GREAT BRITAIN AND IRELAND** in **WORLD HISTORY AND CURRENT AFFAIRS**

0-85115-338-0 BOYDELL & BREWER PB $23.00

Norman **Davis** & James **Girdner**, editors

The Paston Letters: Selection

0-312-01210-1 ST. MARTIN'S...........................$59.95

Walter **Hilton**

The Ladder of Perfection

Hilton remains the most accessible of the 14th-century mystics; this book of advice to a female hermit is his best-known work

See also **CHRISTIAN MYSTICISM** under **CHRISTIANITY** in **RELIGION, SPIRITUALITY, AND PHILOSOPHY**

0-14-044511-0 PENGUIN PB $6.95

Andrea **Hopkins**, editor

Chronicles of King Arthur

The most resonant, durable, and interpreted tale of medieval Europe is revitalized in this volume. Drawing on the masterpieces of Geoffrey of Monmouth, Chrétien de Troyes, and Sir Thomas Malory, Hopkins recounts the myths of this great story cycle in an authentically medieval voice

0-670-85232-5 STUDIO $25.00

Julian of Norwich

Revelations of Divine Love

Perhaps the best-known of medieval mystical meditations. It includes the phrase made famous by T.S. Eliot's *Four Quartets:* "All shall be well and all shall be well and all manner of thing shall be well"

See also **CHRISTIAN MYSTICISM** under **CHRISTIANITY** in **RELIGION, SPIRITUALITY, AND PHILOSOPHY**

TRANSLATED BY CLIFTON WOLTERS

0-14-044177-8 PENGUIN PB $9.95

Margery **Kempe**

The Book of Margery Kempe

A religious work with a fascinating autobiographical dimension, including an unforgettable account of Kempe's trial for heresy

See also **WOMEN** under **GENERAL TOPICS** under **CHRISTIANITY** in **RELIGION, SPIRITUALITY, AND PHILOSOPHY**

See also **MEDIEVAL LITERATURE** in **LITERATURE OF EUROPE, AFRICA, AND ASIA**

TRANSLATED BY BARRY WINDEATT

0-14-043251-5 PENGUIN PB $10.95

Sir Thomas **Malory**

Le Morte d'Arthur

See also **BRITISH AND CELTIC** under **EUROPEAN MYTHOLOGY** under **MYTHOLOGY AND FOLKLORE** in **RELIGION, SPIRITUALITY, AND PHILOSOPHY**

0-679-60099-X MODERN LIBRARY $21.00

Le Morte d'Arthur

The complete text of Malory's monumental compilation of Arthurian legend, one of the most influential books in English

Volume 1

0-14-043043-1 PENGUIN PB $9.95

Volume 2

0-14-043044-X PENGUIN PB $9.95

Works

The standard scholarly edition, first published in 1947

EDITED BY EUGENE VINAVER

0-19-281217-3 OXFORD PB $18.95

0-19-254163-3 OXFORD PB $24.95

Richard **Rolle**

The Fire of Love

Rolle is among the most fervently rapturous of the medieval English mystics

TRANSLATED BY CLIFTON WOLTERS

0-14-044256-1 PENGUIN PB $9.95

Hugh **White**, translator

Ancrene Wisse: Guide for Anchoresses

A devotional manual for women entering on a life of solitary religious contemplation

0-14-044585-4 PENGUIN PB $10.95

Clifton **Wolters**, editor

The Cloud of Unknowing & Other Works

A classic mystical work, written anonymously in England in the 14th-century

See also **CHRISTIAN MYSTICISM** under **CHRISTIANITY** in **RELIGION, SPIRITUALITY, AND PHILOSOPHY**

See also **MEDIEVAL LITERATURE** in **LITERATURE OF EUROPE, AFRICA, AND ASIA**

0-14-044385-1 PENGUIN PB $10.95

The 16th Century

The rather uncertain productions characteristic of the first decades give only occasional promise of the imaginative explosion that was to take place during the reign of Elizabeth. Voracious in its interests, bountifully (at times carelessly) exuberant in its expression, Elizabethan lyric poetry is by turns delicately sensuous, ribald, anguished. Drama, though it was yet to attain the self-confident mastery of Shakespeare, gave evidence in Marlowe and Kyd of a new inventiveness and energy.

Poetry

With the generation of Spenser and his contemporaries in the 1570s, a new and more avowedly gorgeous poetic vernacular emerged, sensuous and musical. Nowhere is it better illustrated than in the period's acknowledged masterpiece, Spenser's *The Faerie Queene*.

Thomas **Campion**

The Essential Campion

"Campion was not rediscovered until the late nineteenth century. Since then, it's been difficult to imagine the history of poetry without him. Whoever dreams of a poem where language begins to resemble music, thinks of him" —Charles Simic

EDITED BY CHARLES SIMIC

0-88001-172-6 ECCO PB $6.00

The Selected Songs of Thomas Campion

A selection of Campion's poems accompanied by his original musical settings

EDITED BY W.H. AUDEN

INTRODUCTION BY JOHN HOLLANDER

0-87923-091-6 GODINE PB $10.00

The Works of Thomas Campion

The complete poetry of one of the most musical poets in the language; also includes Campion's theoretical writings on the art of poetry

EDITED BY WALTER R. DAVIS

0-393-00439-2 NORTON PB $2.95

Michael **Drayton**

Selected Poems

Drayton was the most urbane of Elizabethan poets; contemporary readers will find his combination of sardonic humor and light sensuousness surprisingly modern

0-85635-225-X CARCANET $7.50

Henry Howard, **Earl of Surrey**

Selected Poems

Surrey virtually invented the mellifluous iambic line that became the standard of later English poetry. His verse is remarkable for its urbanity; his love poems to Geraldine made her into the near-proverbial lady-love of the 16th-century

EDITED BY DENNIS KEENE

0-85635-552-6 CARCANET PB $16.25

Fulke **Greville**

Selected Poems

0-85635-856-8 SCHOLARLY PB $16.95

Christopher **Marlowe**

The Complete Poems and Translations

Though less well known than Shakespeare's *Venus and Adonis,* Marlowe's *Hero and Leander* is one of the high points of English erotic poetry, poised elegantly between the sensous and the comic, with overtones of dark melancholy. This edition also includes Marlowe's deft versions of Ovid's love poems

EDITED BY STEPHEN ORGEL

0-14-042267-6 PENGUIN PB $11.95

Philip **Sidney**

The Oxford Authors: Sir Philip Sidney

EDITED BY KATHERINE DUNCAN-JONES

0-19-282024-9 OXFORD PB $22.00

Selected Writings

EDITED BY RICHARD DUTTON

0-85635-625-5 SCHOLARLY PB $15.95

John **Skelton**

Selected Poems

Skelton, who died in 1529, is one of the great eccentrics of English poetry, remarkable for the improvisational wordplay and untrammeled rhyme of such poems as "Philip Sparrow" and "The Tunnyng of Elynour Rummyng"

EDITED BY GERALD HAMMOND

0-85635-308-6 CARCANET PB $10.95

Edmund **Spenser**

Edmund Spenser's Poetry

Includes a generous selection of the shorter poems, and excerpts from *The Faerie Queene*

EDITED BY RICHARD S. SYLVESTER & HUGH MACLEAN

0-393-96299-7 NORTON PB $15.95

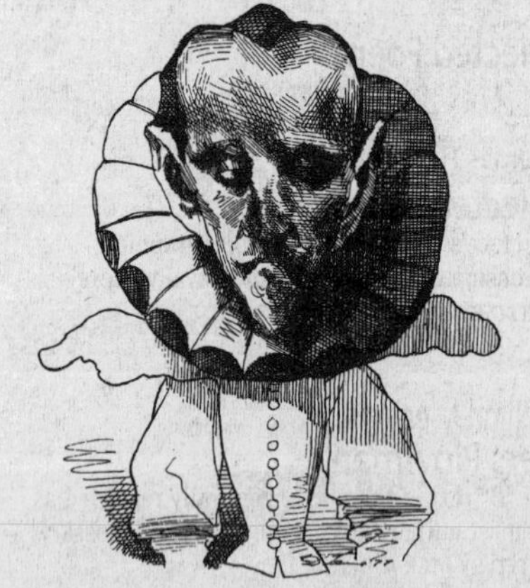

Edmund Spenser

Edmund **Spenser**
The Faerie Queene
A highly readable edition of the quintessential English Renaissance poem, with convenient notes
EDITED BY THOMAS P. ROCHE & C.P. O'DONNELL
0-14-042207-2 PENGUIN PB $16.95

The Fairy Queen
EDITED BY DOUGLAS BROOKS-DAVIES
0-460-87572-8 EVERYMAN'S PB $7.95

The Shorter Poems of Edmund Spenser
A handsome and comprehensive edition incorporating the most recent scholarship. "This is a book that will have a powerful impact on future study of English Renaissance literature"—Donald Cheney, University of Massachusetts
EDITED BY WILLIAM A. ORAM
0-300-04244-2 YALE $65.00
0-300-04245-0 YALE PB $22.00

Thomas **Wyatt**
The Complete Poems
Wyatt wrote some of the greatest and most complex lyrics in English, including "They Flee from Me that Sometime Did Me Seek" and "Awake, My Lute"
EDITED BY R.A. REBHOLZ
0-14-042227-7 PENGUIN PB $12.95

The Essential Wyatt
EDITED BY W.S. MERWIN
0-88001-180-7 ECCO PB $6.00

Anthologies

Norman **Ault**, editor
Elizabethan Lyrics
A pleasant collection of lyrics, arranged chronologically
0-686-02251-3 SCHOLARLY $49.00

Sandra Clark **Birkbeck**, editor
Amorous Rites: Elizabethan Erotic Narrative Verse
A useful gathering of Shakespeare's *Venus and Adonis*, Marlowe's *Hero and Leander*, and Beaumont's *Salmacis and Hermaphroditus*, three poems which have their roots in Ovid
0-460-87530-2 EVERYMAN'S PB $8.50

Douglas **Brooks-Davies**, editor
Silver Poets of the Sixteenth Century
Includes the work of Wyatt, Surrey, Ralegh, and John Davies' long philosophical poems *Orchestra* and *Nosce Teipsum*
0-460-87103-X EVERYMAN'S PB $10.95

Sukanta **Chaudhuri**, editor
An Anthology of Elizabethan Poetry
0-19-563204-4 OXFORD PB $8.95

Maurice **Evans**, editor
Elizabethan Sonnets
Collects not merely individual poems, but entire sonnet sequences by Drayton, Daniel, Spenser, and Sidney, along with selections from other poets
0-460-87363-6 EVERYMAN'S PB $7.50

William B. **Hunter**, Jr., editor
The English Spenserians
An unusual and typographically elegant anthology that includes work by Phineas and Giles Fletcher, Michael Drayton, George Wither, and Henry More
0-87480-110-9 UTAH $15.00

Emrys **Jones**, editor
The New Oxford Book of 16th-Century Verse
The classics of the period are fully represented here, including works by Shakespeare, Spenser, and Donne, but an expanded view of the significant poems of the 16th-century has prompted the inclusion of an unparalleled variety of work
0-19-214126-0 OXFORD $45.00

Hugh **MacDonald**, editor
England's Helicon
Perhaps the most typical, certainly one of the most delightful, of the poetical miscellanies—the collections of short lyrics by various hands that were a staple of Elizabethan literary taste
0-674-25551-8 HARVARD PB $8.95

David **Norbrook** & H.R. **Woudhuysen**, editors
The Penguin Book of Renaissance Verse: 1509-1659
Differs from the lyric emphasis of previous anthologies in its wide range of genres and styles, encompassing regional, satirical, and popular works rarely represented
0-14-042346-X PENGUIN PB $22.95

Hyder E. **Rollins**
Phoenix Nest (1593)
0-674-66610-0 HARVARD $16.50

Hyder E. **Rollins**, editor
A Handful of Pleasant Delights
0-486-21382-X DOVER PB $4.95

Richard S. **Sylvester**, editor
English Sixteenth Century Verse: An Anthology
0-393-30206-7 NORTON PB $14.95

Prose

The achievement of 16th-century prose writers is considerable, although less familiar to modern readers than that of their 17th-century successors. Richard Hooker's *Laws of Ecclesiastical Polity* is a magisterial paean to high Elizabethan values, an eloquent plea for the virtues and the beauties of civilization. And in Sir Philip Sidney's *Arcadia* the reader can discern an early precursor of the novel.

Muriel **Byrne** & Bridget **Boland**, editors
The Lisle Letters: An Abridgment
A collection of early-16th-century letters written to and from Arthur Plantagenet, Viscount Lisle, offering a revealing mirror of life at the beginning of the Renaissance
See also **THE TUDORS: 1485-1603** under **GREAT BRITAIN AND IRELAND** in **WORLD HISTORY AND CURRENT AFFAIRS**
0-226-08810-3 CHICAGO PB $12.95

Richard **Hakluyt**
Voyages and Discoveries
The most complete first-hand record of England's voyages (and occasional piracies) in the northern and western seas during the great age of exploration. This selection also includes such powerful narratives as Walter Raleigh's "Discoverie of Guiana," the story of the shipwrecked sailor Miles Phillips, and dramatic narratives of Martin Frobisher's Arctic voyages
EDITED BY JACK BEACHING
0-14-043073-3 PENGUIN PB $10.95

Guiana is a country that hath yet her maidenhead, never sacked, turned, nor wrought, the face of the earth hath not been torn, nor the virtue and salt of the soil spent by manurance, the graves have not been opened for gold, the mines not broken with sledges, nor their images pulled down out of their temples. It hath never been entered by any army of strength, and never conquered by any Christian prince.
VOYAGES AND DISCOVERIES

Richard **Hooker**
Ecclesiastical Polity: Selections
0-85635-860-6 SCHOLARLY PB $18.75

Of the Laws of Ecclesiastical Polity
Includes the preface as well as books I and VIII
EDITED BY ARTHUR STEPHEN MCGRADE
0-521-37908-3 CAMBRIDGE PB $18.95

Hugh **Latimer**
Selected Sermons of Hugh Latimer
A collection of sermons especially striking for Latimer's homely but telling similes
EDITED BY ALLAN CHESTER
0-918016-43-6 FOLGER $29.50

Thomas **More**
The Apology
More's famous defense of his conduct in relation to Henry VIII and the English church
EDITED BY J.B. TRAPP
0-300-02067-8 YALE $70.00

A Dialogue of Comfort Against Tribulation
A strong and moving treatise on coping with adversity
0-300-01609-3 YALE $85.00

The History of King Richard III & Selections from the English and Latin Poems
The *History of King Richard III* popularized and helped to perpetuate the view of Richard as a deformed, inhuman monster that became a fixture of Tudor propaganda and the basis of Shakespeare's dramatic portrait
0-300-01840-1 YALE $37.50

Utopia
The ancestor of all later ideal commonwealths, and a subtle expression both of More's idealism and his penchant for satire
EDITED & TRANSLATED BY ROBERT M. ADAMS
0-393-09256-9 NORTON PB $6.95

Utopia
More invented the word utopia (a pun in Greek on "good place"), and described a rational and

tolerant communistic society that reflected his humanist sympathies and was very remote from the 16th-century England of Henry VIII in which he was eventually beheaded

See also **CLASSICS** under **POLITICAL THOUGHT** in **SOCIAL STUDIES**

TRANSLATED BY PAUL TUMOR

0-14-044165-4 PENGUIN PB $6.95

Thomas **Nashe**

The Unfortunate Traveller & Other Works

Nashe's inexhaustible imagination—hilarious, surrealistic, and at times deeply unsettling—foreshadows (and sometimes outdoes) Dickens

EDITED BY J.B. STEANE

0-14-043067-9 PENGUIN PB $11.95

Paul **Salzman**, editor

An Anthology of Elizabethan Prose Fiction

0-19-281744-2 OXFORD PB $10.95

Philip **Sidney**

Arcadia

Sidney's greatly expanded version of his pastoral novel

EDITED BY MAURICE EVANS

0-14-043111-X PENGUIN PB $12.95

The Countess of Pembroke's Arcadia (The Old Arcadia)

The original version of Sidney's epic romantic fiction, much simpler and more classical in plot structure than his more-often-read reworking

EDITED BY KATHERINE DUNCAN-JONES

0-19-811855-4 OXFORD PB $89.00

Betty **Travitsky**, editor

The Paradise of Women: Writing by Englishwomen of the Renaissance

See also **ANTHOLOGIES OF WOMEN'S WRITING** under **WOMEN'S STUDIES** in **SOCIAL STUDIES**

0-231-06885-9 COLUMBIA PB $17.50

William **Tyndale**, translator

The New Testament

Tyndale completed his translation in 1525. The first vernacular English version of any part of the Bible to be published, it seems the basis for the King James version

See also **BIBLES AND COMMENTARY** under **CHRISTIANITY** in **RELIGION, SPIRITUALITY, AND PHILOSOPHY**

EDITED AND INTRODUCED BY DAVID DANIELL

0-300-05211-1 YALE $45.00

0-300-06580-9 YALE PB $15.00

Drama

By the late 1580s, London's stages had become famous throughout Europe, and the drama that flourished there during the years before Shakespeare had immense imaginative vitality. At its best, as in Kyd's *Spanish Tragedy* and Marlowe's *Tamburlaine* and *Dr.Faustus*, it could be a powerful combination of ravishing poetry and overpowering dramatic action.

Thomas **Dekker**

The Shoemaker's Holiday

A drama with an engaging tradesman as its hero, and aimed expertly at an audience of common Londoners; perhaps the most winning of the Elizabethan popular comedies

EDITED BY ANTHONY PARR

0-393-90062-2 A&C BLACK PB $6.95

Thomas **Kyd**

The Spanish Tragedy

A searing drama of revenge, and the play most often credited (or blamed) for the potent doses of dramatic violence so frequent in Elizabethan and Jacobean plays

EDITED BY J.R. MULRYNE

0-393-90057-6 NORTON PB $5.95

Christopher **Marlowe**

The Complete Plays

Contains *Dr. Faustus, Tamburlaine the Great, The Jew of Malta, Edward II, Dido Queen of Carthage*, and *The Massacre at Paris*

EDITED BY STEPHEN J. ORGEL

0-14-043037-7 PENGUIN PB $12.95

Anthologies

Bernard **Beckerman**, editor

Five Plays of the English Renaissance

Includes *Dr. Faustus, Volpone, The Duchess of Malfi, Women Beware Women*, and *'Tis Pity She's a Whore*

0-452-00881-6 NEW AMERICAN LIBRARY PB... $13.95

William **Tydeman**, editor

Two Tudor Tragedies

Contains *Gorboduc* and *The Spanish Tragedy*, two of the most influential forerunners of Shakespeare's work

0-14-044531-5 PENGUIN PB $12.95

Shakespeare

No writer's work has been as universally appreciated or as variously (and often contentiously) interpreted as Shakespeare's, and virtually every opinion expressed has also been authoritatively, sometimes violently, confuted. If Shakespeare's plays elude easy characterization, it may be precisely because they were written at an unsettled time, by a writer whose genius turned ambiguity to advantage. Teasing, mysterious, and endlessly fascinating, they hold an undiminished interest for the contemporary reader.

Below we have listed all the plays that are currently available in four different multi-volume editions. Other plays can reasonably be expected to become available in the future.

Charlton **Hinman**, editor

Norton Facsimile of the First Folio of Shakespeare

0-393-03985-4 NORTON $150.00

William **Shakespeare**

The Complete Non-Dramatic Poetry with New Literary Criticism

EDITED BY SYLVAN BARNET

0-451-52314-8 SIGNET PB $5.95

The Complete Oxford Shakespeare: Comedies

EDITED BY STANLEY WELLS AND GARY TAYLOR

0-19-818273-2 OXFORD PB $13.95

The Complete Oxford Shakespeare: Histories

EDITED BY STANLEY WELLS AND GARY TAYLOR

0-19-818272-4 OXFORD PB $11.95

Complete Tragedies

0-19-818274-0 OXFORD PB $13.95

The Complete Pelican Shakespeare

An attractive, durable one-volume edition

EDITED BY ALFRED HARBAGE

0-14-071449-9 PENGUIN $55.00

The Poems

EDITED BY JOHN ROE

0-521-22231-1 CAMBRIDGE $39.95

0-521-29411-8 CAMBRIDGE PB $11.95

Riverside Shakespeare

Includes the complete plays and poetry, thoroughly annotated and fully introduced

0-395-04402-2 HOUGHTON MIFFLIN $59.16

The Sonnets

0-451-52262-1 SIGNET PB $4.95

The Sonnets and a Lover's Complaint

EDITED BY JOHN KERRIGAN

0-14-070732-8 PENGUIN PB $9.95

The Sonnets and Narrative Poems

0-679-41741-9 KNOPF $15.00

Arden

These standard scholarly editions provide lengthy introductions with full coverage of textual and interpretive issues, as well as detailed line-by-line annotations.

William **Shakespeare**

All's Well that Ends Well

0-416-47560-4 ARDEN $45.00

0-415-02679-2 ARDEN PB $9.95

Antony and Cleopatra

EDITED BY JOHN WILDERS

0-415-01102-7 ARDEN $45.00

0-415-01103-5 ARDEN PB $9.95

As You Like It

0-416-17830-8 ARDEN $45.00

0-415-02681-4 ARDEN PB $9.95

Comedy of Errors

0-416-47460-8 ARDEN $49.95

0-415-02749-7 ARDEN PB $9.95

Coriolanus

EDITED BY PHILIP BROCKBANK

0-415-02682-2 ARDEN $9.95

Cymbeline
0-416-47350-4 ARDEN $49.95
0-415-02689-X ARDEN PB $9.95

Hamlet
0-416-17910-X ARDEN $45.00
0-415-02683-0 ARDEN PB $9.95

Julius Caesar
0-415-02719-5 ARDEN $45.00
0-415-02684-9 ARDEN PB $9.95

King Henry IV, Part 1
0-416-47420-9 ARDEN $45.00
0-415-02750-0 ARDEN PB $9.95

King Henry IV, Part 2
0-416-47430-6 ARDEN $45.00
0-415-02688-1 ARDEN PB $9.95

King Henry V
EDITED BY T.W. CRAIK
0-415-01413-1 ARDEN $45.00
0-415-01414-X ARDEN PB $9.95

King Henry VI, Part 1
0-416-47200-1 ARDEN $55.00
0-415-02687-3 ARDEN PB $9.95

King Henry VI, Part 2
EDITED BY ANDREW S. CAIRNCROSS
0-416-47210-9 ARDEN $55.00
0-415-02685-7 ARDEN PB $9.95

King Henry VI, Part 3
0-416-47220-6 ARDEN $49.95
0-415-02711-X ARDEN PB $9.95

King Henry VIII
0-416-47230-3 ARDEN $49.95
0-415-02690-3 ARDEN PB $9.95

King John
0-416-47370-9 ARDEN $49.95
0-415-02691-1 ARDEN PB $9.95

King Lear
EDITED BY KENNETH MUIR
0-415-02728-4 ARDEN $49.95
0-415-02692-X ARDEN PB $9.95

King Richard II
0-416-47520-5 ARDEN $45.00
0-415-00882-4 ARDEN PB $9.95

King Richard III
0-416-17970-3 ARDEN $45.00
0-415-02694-6 ARDEN PB $9.95

Love's Labour's Lost
EDITED BY RICHARD DAVID
0-416-47310-5 ARDEN $49.95
0-415-02695-4 ARDEN PB $9.95

Macbeth
0-416-47320-2 ARDEN $45.00
0-415-02696-2 ARDEN PB $9.95

Measure for Measure
0-416-47530-2 ARDEN $49.95
0-415-02697-0 ARDEN PB $9.95

The Merchant of Venice
0-416-47500-0 ARDEN $55.00
0-415-02751-9 ARDEN PB $9.95

The Merry Wives of Windsor
0-416-47690-2 ARDEN $45.00
0-415-02698-9 ARDEN PB $9.95

A Midsummer Night's Dream
0-416-17930-4 ARDEN $45.00
0-415-02699-7 ARDEN PB $9.95

I have had a dream, past the wit of man to say what dream it was: man is but an ass, if he go about to expound this dream. Methought I was—there is no man can tell what. Methought I was,—and methought I had,—but man is but a patched fool, if he will offer to say what methought I had. The eye of man hath not heard, the ear of man hath not seen, man's hand is not able to taste, his tongue to conceive, nor his heart to report, what my dream was. I will get Peter Quince to write a ballad of this dream: it shall be called Bottom's Dream, because it hath no bottom.

A MIDSUMMER NIGHT'S DREAM

Much Ado About Nothing
EDITED BY A.R. HUMPHREYS
0-416-17990-8 ARDEN $59.95
0-415-02700-4 ARDEN PB $9.95

Othello
0-416-47440-3 ARDEN $45.00
0-415-02701-2 ARDEN PB $9.95

Pericles
0-416-47570-1 ARDEN $45.00
0-415-02702-0 ARDEN PB $9.95

Romeo and Juliet
0-416-17850-2 ARDEN $45.00
0-415-02753-5 ARDEN PB $9.95

The Taming of the Shrew
0-416-47580-9 ARDEN $45.00
0-415-02703-9 ARDEN PB $9.95

The Tempest
EDITED BY FRANK KERMODE
0-416-47360-1 ARDEN $45.00
0-415-02704-7 ARDEN PB $9.95

Timon of Athens
0-416-47250-8 ARDEN $55.00
0-415-02705-5 ARDEN PB $9.95

Titus Andronicus
EDITED BY JONATHAN BATE
0-415-04868-0 ARDEN PB $9.95

Troilus and Cressida
EDITED BY KENNETH PALMER
0-416-47680-5 ARDEN $55.00
0-415-02707-1 ARDEN PB $9.95

Twelfth Night
0-415-02747-0 ARDEN $45.00
041602708X ARDEN PB $9.95

The Two Gentlemen of Verona
0-416-47490-X ARDEN $49.95
0-415-02709-8 ARDEN PB $9.95

The Two Noble Kinsmen
0-415-01666-5 ARDEN $42.00
0-415-01667-3 ARDEN PB $15.00

The Winter's Tale
0-416-47470-5 ARDEN $55.00
0-415-02710-1 ARDEN PB $9.95

Complete Arden Set of Shakespeare
0-415-91498-1 ARDEN PB $378.00

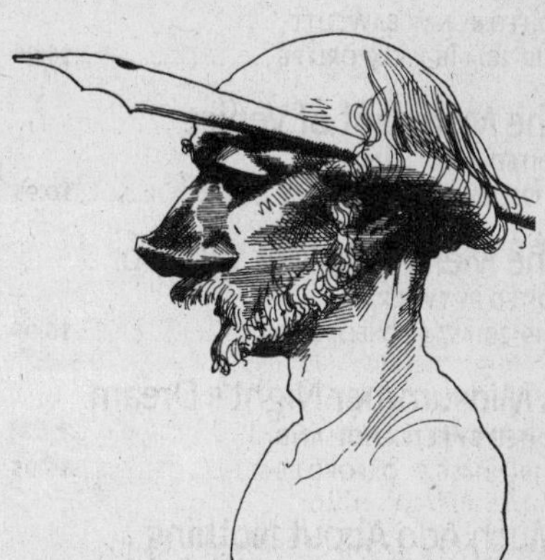

William Shakespeare

Oxford

The Oxford Shakespeare provides a level of textual sophistication more likely to appeal to the specialist, and incorporates sometimes controversial innovations in the establishment of a definitive text.

William **Shakespeare**

All's Well that Ends Well
EDITED BY SUSAN SNYDER
0-19-281459-1 OXFORD PB $6.95

Antony and Cleopatra
EDITED BY MICHAEL NEILL
0-19-281447-8 OXFORD PB $6.95

As You Like It
EDITED BY ALAN BRISSENDEN
0-19-281955-0 OXFORD PB $6.95

Coriolanus
0-19-281452-4 OXFORD PB $6.95

Hamlet
EDITED BY G.R. HIBBARD
0-19-281448-6 OXFORD PB $6.95

Julius Caesar
EDITED BY ARTHUR HUMPHREYS
0-19-281445-1 OXFORD PB $6.95

King Henry IV, Part 1
EDITED BY DAVID BEVINGTON
0-19-281449-4 OXFORD PB $6.95

King Henry V
EDITED BY GARY TAYLOR
0-19-281438-9 OXFORD PB $6.95

King John
EDITED BY A.R. BRAUNMULLER
0-19-812930-0 CLARENDON $75.00

King Lear
EDITED BY ROMA GILL
0-19-831977-0 OXFORD PB $7.50

Love's Labour's Lost
EDITED BY G.R. HIBBARD
0-19-812947-5 CLARENDON $59.00

Macbeth
EDITED BY NICHOLAS BROOKE
0-19-281441-9 OXFORD PB $6.95

Measure for Measure
EDITED BY N.W. BAWCUTT
0-19-281446-X OXFORD PB $6.95

The Merchant of Venice
EDITED BY JAY L. HALIO
0-19-281454-0 OXFORD PB $6.95

The Merry Wives of Windsor
EDITED BY T.W. CRAIK
0-19-281457-5 OXFORD PB $6.95

A Midsummer Night's Dream
EDITED BY PETER HOLLAND
0-19-281456-7 OXFORD PB $6.95

Much Ado About Nothing
EDITED BY SHELDON P. ZITNER
0-19-282620-4 OXFORD PB $6.95

Othello
0-19-831922-3 OXFORD PB $7.95

The Taming of the Shrew
EDITED BY H.J. OLIVER
0-19-281440-0 OXFORD PB $6.95

The Tempest
EDITED BY STEPHEN ORGEL
0-19-281450-8 OXFORD PB $6.95

Titus Andronicus
EDITED BY EUGENE M. WAITH
0-19-281442-7 OXFORD PB $6.95

Troilus and Cressida
EDITED BY KENNETH MUIR
0-19-281439-7 OXFORD PB $6.95

Twelfth Night
0-19-283140-2 OXFORD PB $6.95

The Two Noble Kinsmen
0-19-812939-4 OXFORD $81.00

The Winter's Tale
0-19-281956-9 OXFORD PB $6.95

Penguin

Inexpensive and accessible to the nonspecialist, the New Penguin Shakespeare offers more elaborate commentary than before and a pleasing typographical style.

William **Shakespeare**

All's Well that Ends Well
0-14-070720-4 PENGUIN PB $5.50

Antony and Cleopatra
EDITED BY EMRYS JONES
0-14-070731-X PENGUIN PB $5.50

As You Like It
0-14-070714-X PENGUIN PB $5.50

The Comedy of Errors
0-14-070725-5 PENGUIN PB $5.50

Coriolanus
0-14-070703-4 PENGUIN PB $5.95

Cymbeline
0-14-071428-6 PENGUIN PB $5.95

Hamlet
0-14-070734-4 PENGUIN PB $5.50

Henry V
0-14-070708-5 PENGUIN PB $5.95

Julius Caesar
0-14-070704-2 PENGUIN PB $5.50

King Henry IV, Part 1
0-14-070718-2 PENGUIN PB $5.50

King Henry IV, Part 2
0-14-070728-X PENGUIN PB $5.50

King Henry VI, Part 2
0-14-070736-0 PENGUIN PB $5.50

King Henry VIII
0-14-070722-0 PENGUIN PB $5.50

King John
0-14-070727-1 PENGUIN PB $5.50

King Lear
EDITED BY G.K. HUNTER
0-14-070724-7 PENGUIN PB $5.50

King Richard II
0-14-070719-0 PENGUIN PB $5.50

King Richard III
0-14-070712-3 PENGUIN PB $5.95

Love's Labour's Lost
0-14-070738-7 PENGUIN PB $5.95

Macbeth
0-14-071401-4 PENGUIN PB $3.95

Measure for Measure
EDITED BY JIM NOSWORTHY
0-14-070715-8 PENGUIN PB $5.50

The Merchant of Venice
EDITED BY BRENTS STIRLING
0-14-071421-9 PENGUIN PB $3.95

The Merry Wives of Windsor
0-14-070726-3 PENGUIN PB $5.95

A Midsummer Night's Dream
0-14-070702-6 PENGUIN PB $5.50

Much Ado About Nothing
EDITED BY R.A. FOAKES
0-14-070709-3 PENGUIN PB $5.50

Othello
0-14-070707-7 PENGUIN PB $5.50

Pericles
0-14-070729-8 PENGUIN PB $5.50

Romeo and Juliet
0-14-070701-8 PENGUIN PB $5.50

The Taming of the Shrew
0-14-070710-7 PENGUIN PB $5.50

The Tempest
0-14-070713-1 PENGUIN PB $5.50

Timon of Athens
EDITED BY G.R. HIBBARD
0-14-070721-2 PENGUIN PB $5.50

Troilus and Cressida
EDITED BY R.A. FOAKES
0-14-070741-7 PENGUIN PB $5.95

Twelfth Night
0-14-070711-5 PENGUIN PB $5.50

Two Gentlemen of Verona
0-563-20277-7 PENGUIN PB $5.95

The Winter's Tale
0-14-070716-6 PENGUIN PB $5.50

Signet

The Signet Shakespeare (published by NAL) is an economical choice for the beginning student, with clear notes particularly well-tailored to American readers.

William **Shakespeare**

All's Well that Ends Well
0-451-52261-3 NEW AMERICAN LIBRARY PB $3.95

Antony and Cleopatra
0-451-52264-8 NEW AMERICAN LIBRARY PB $3.95

As You Like It
0-451-52460-8 NEW AMERICAN LIBRARY PB $3.95

The Comedy of Errors
0-451-52311-3 SIGNET PB $4.95

Coriolanus
0-451-52296-6 NEW AMERICAN LIBRARY PB $4.95

Hamlet
EDITED BY EDWARD HUBLER
0-451-52128-5 NEW AMERICAN LIBRARY PB $3.95

William Shakespeare

Henry VI, Parts 1, 2 & 3
EDITED BY SYLVAN BARNET
0-451-52312-1 SIGNET PB $5.95

Julius Caesar
0-451-52124-2 NEW AMERICAN LIBRARY PB $3.95

King Henry IV, Part 2
0-451-52253-2 NEW AMERICAN LIBRARY PB $3.95

King Henry IV, Part I
0-451-52405-5 NEW AMERICAN LIBRARY PB $3.95

King Henry V
0-451-52286-9 NEW AMERICAN LIBRARY PB $3.95

King John
0-451-52299-0 NEW AMERICAN LIBRARY PB $5.95

King Lear
EDITED BY RUSSELL FRASER
0-451-52410-1 NEW AMERICAN LIBRARY PB $3.95

King Richard II
0-451-52268-0 NEW AMERICAN LIBRARY PB $3.95

King Richard III
EDITED BY MARK ECCLES
0-451-52266-4 NEW AMERICAN LIBRARY PB $3.95

Love's Labour's Lost
0-451-52267-2 NEW AMERICAN LIBRARY PB $3.95

Macbeth
EDITED BY SYLVAN BARNET
0-451-52444-6 NEW AMERICAN LIBRARY PB $3.95

Measure for Measure
0-451-52409-8 NEW AMERICAN LIBRARY PB $3.95

The Merchant of Venice
EDITED BY KENNETH MYRICK
0-451-52133-1 NEW AMERICAN LIBRARY PB $3.95

A Midsummer Night's Dream
EDITED BY WOLFGANG CLEMEN
0-451-52494-2 NEW AMERICAN LIBRARY PB $3.95

Much Ado About Nothing
EDITED BY DAVID L. STEVENSON
0-451-52298-2 NEW AMERICAN LIBRARY PB $3.95

Othello
0-451-52132-3 NEW AMERICAN LIBRARY PB $3.95

Pericles, Cymbeline & The Two Noble Kinsmen
0-451-52265-6 NEW AMERICAN LIBRARY PB $5.95

Romeo and Juliet
0-451-52438-1 NEW AMERICAN LIBRARY PB $3.95

The Taming of the Shrew
EDITED BY ROBERT B. HEILMAN
0-451-52126-9 NEW AMERICAN LIBRARY PB $3.95

The Tempest
EDITED BY ROBERT LANGBAUM
0-451-52125-0 NEW AMERICAN LIBRARY PB $3.95

Titus Andronicus
0-451-52034-3 SIGNET PB

Troilus and Cressida
0-451-52297-4 NEW AMERICAN LIBRARY PB $4.95

Twelfth Night
EDITED BY HERSCHEL BAKER
0-451-52129-3 NEW AMERICAN LIBRARY PB $3.95

The Winter's Tale
0-451-52260-5 NEW AMERICAN LIBRARY PB $3.95

The Early 17th Century

With the turn of the 17th-century, the great Elizabethan consensus began to break down, and a new spirit of doubt and pessimism became evident. Seventeenth-century literature reflects the uneasiness as well as the exhilaration of its times, from the restless, supercharged imagination of John Donne to the meditative inwardness of Thomas Browne and George Herbert.

Poetry

Donne's name and style tend to dominate discussions of 17th-century poetry. Indeed, the "metaphysical" style that he pioneered, with its startling imagery and exhilarating pursuit of wit, remained widely influential throughout his own century. Yet the era produced other kinds of poetry as well: religious and meditative, light and deftly entertaining, even cheerfully obscene. As England slid toward civil war, writers often turned inward. Seventeenth-century poetry is a study in surprise, rich in personal and sometimes idiosyncratic voices.

John **Donne**

The Complete English Poems
A useful inexpensive edition, with reliable texts and succinct notes
EDITED BY A.J. SMITH
0-14-042209-9 PENGUIN PB $12.95

The Complete English Poems
0-460-87441-1 EVERYMAN'S PB $9.50

The Complete Poetry and Selected Prose
EDITED BY CHARLES M. COFFIN
0-679-60102-3 MODERN LIBRARY $18.50

John Donne: Selected Poetry
EDITED BY JOHN CAREY
0-19-282499-6 OXFORD $8.95

John Donne's Poetry
An annotated text with critical essays
EDITED BY ARTHUR L. CLEMENTS
0-393-96062-5 NORTON PB $10.95

Poems
0-679-40558-5 EVERYMAN'S $20.00

George **Herbert**

The Complete English Poems
Though he is often labeled a Metaphysical poet, the intense, tortured, yet finally serene tenor of Herbert's religious poetry places him in a class by himself. One of the most accomplished lyric poets of any century
EDITED BY JOHN TOBIN
0-14-042348-6 PENGUIN PB $11.95

The Essential Herbert
"The formal originality and individuality of these poems seem to emphasize the freshness, uniqueness and novelty of each spiritual experience the poet presents, to enhance the excitement of unprecedentedness that belongs to any new experience. The forms themselves are witty, exacting from the poet elaborate pains and planning; but they are also an index of the care he takes in his dealings with his God"
—Anthony Hecht
EDITED BY ANTHONY HECHT
0-88001-159-9 ECCO PB $6.00

Poems and Other Writings
0-679-44359-2 EVERYMAN'S $20.00

Robert **Herrick**

Selected Poems
EDITED BY DAVID JESSON-DIBLEY
0-85635-320-5 CARCANET PB $15.95

Ben **Jonson**

The Alchemist and Other Plays
An intricate and explosive satirical comedy that makes bravura use of alchemical terms and other contemporary jargon
EDITED BY DOUGLAS BROWN
0-19-282252-7 OXFORD PB $7.95

Ben Jonson

Ben Jonson's Plays and Masques
Includes *Volpone, Epicoene, The Alchemist, The Sad Shepherd,* four masques, and a selection of critical essays
EDITED BY ROBERT M. ADAMS
0-393-09035-3 NORTON PB $14.95

The Complete Masques
The masques contain some of Jonson's most magnificent verse, and introduce the modern reader to an extravagant theatrical form long since vanished from the stage
EDITED BY STEPHEN ORGEL
0-300-01181-4 YALE $62.00

The Complete Poems
Jonson's genius as a playwright has sometimes obscured his greatness as a poet; he is by turns acerbic, sensual, musical, political, and passionate
EDITED BY GEORGE PARFITT
0-14-042277-3 PENGUIN PB $12.95

Every Man in His Humour
A pathbreaking comedy that exemplifies Jonson's theory of character
EDITED BY MARTIN SEYMOUR-SMITH
0-393-90015-0 NORTON PB $5.95

Five Plays
Includes *Every Man in His Humour, Sejanus, Volpone, The Alchemist,* and *Bartholomew Fair*
EDITED WITH AN INTRODUCTION BY G.A. WILKES
0-19-281782-5 OXFORD PB $7.95

The Oxford Authors: Ben Jonson
EDITED BY IAN DONALDSON
0-19-281339-0 OXFORD PB $19.95

He [Jonson] dissuaded me from poetry, for that she had beggared him, when he might have been a rich lawyer, physician, or merchant…

In his merry humour he was wont to name himself The Poet…

He is a great lover and praiser of himself, a contemner and scorner of others, given rather to lose a friend than a jest, jealous of every word and action of those about him (especially after drink, which is one of the elements in which he liveth), a dissembler of ill parts which reign in him, a bragger of some good that he wanteth, thinketh nothing well but what either he himself or one of his friends and countrymen hath said or done…

Oppressed with fantasy, which hath ever mastered his reason, a general disease in many poets.—*William Drummond*
THE OXFORD AUTHORS: BEN JONSON

Three Comedies
Includes *Volpone, The Alchemist,* and the riotous London comedy *Bartholomew Fair*
0-14-043013-X PENGUIN PB $9.95

Volpone
Unquestionably the greatest satiric play in English. "The characters are named after creatures that feed on carrion; thus Jonson drives home Dante's point—the worship of money is life-denying"—Kenneth Rexroth
EDITED BY ALVIN B. KERNAN
PREFACE BY RICHARD B. YOUNG
0-300-00139-8 YALE PB $15.00

Andrew **Marvell**

Andrew Marvell
EDITED BY FRANK KERMODE AND KEITH WALKER
0-19-282271-3 OXFORD PB $7.95

The Complete Poems
The last of the great Metaphysical poets, author of some of the greatest and most complex lyrics in English
EDITED BY ELIZABETH S. DONNO
0-14-042213-7 PENGUIN PB $9.95

The Complete Poems
0-679-42038-X KNOPF $15.00

The Essential Marvell
EDITED BY DONALD HALL
0-88001-312-5 ECCO PB $8.00

Thomas **Traherne**

Selected Poems and Prose
0-14-044543-9 PENGUIN PB $12.95

Selected Writings
Traherne's poetry was not discovered until the 20th-century; he now stands as one of England's most remarkable poets of religious ecstasy
EDITED BY DICK DAVIS
0-85635-231-4 SCHOLARLY PB $16.00

Henry **Vaughan**

The Complete Poems
One of the great religious lyricists of the 17th-century; his mystical view of nature influenced Wordsworth
EDITED BY ALAN RUDRUM
0-300-02680-3 YALE $55.00
0-14-042208-0 PENGUIN PB $14.95

Selected Poems
EDITED BY ROBERT SHAW
0-85635-139-3 CARCANET PB $11.25

Anthologies

Thomas **Crofts**, editor

The Cavalier Poets: An Anthology
0-486-28766-1 DOVER PB $1.00

Alastair **Fowler**, editor

The New Oxford Book of Seventeenth Century Verse
In this new compilation, popular and minor poets are grouped with recognized masters of the greatest century of English literary achievement. Included, for the first time, is a generous portion of poetry by women, as well as a sampling of American colonial verse
0-19-214164-3 OXFORD $45.00

Helen **Gardner**, editor

The Metaphysical Poets
Intelligent selections from Donne, Herbert, Vaughan, Traherne, Cowley, and others
0-14-042038-X PENGUIN PB $8.95

Germaine **Greer**, editor

Kissing the Rod: An Anthology of 17th-Century Women's Verse
See also **POETRY ANTHOLOGIES** under **ANTHOLOGIES OF WOMEN'S WRITING** under **WOMEN'S STUDIES** in **SOCIAL STUDIES**
0-374-52164-6 FS&G PB $15.00

Herbert J. **Grierson**

Metaphysical Lyrics and Poems of the Seventeenth Century: Donne to Butler
0-19-282290-X OXFORD PB $10.95

Hugh **MacLean**, editor

Ben Jonson and the Cavalier Poets: Authoritative Texts, Criticism
0-393-09308-5 NORTON PB $14.95

Louis L. **Martz**, editor

English Seventeenth-Century Verse
0-393-00675-1 NORTON PB $16.95

Alexander M. **Witherspoon** & Frank J. **Warnke**

Seventeenth-Century Prose and Poetry
0-15-580237-2 HARCOURT BRACE $61.18

Drama

Francis **Beaumont** & John **Fletcher**

The Maid's Tragedy
A romantic tragedy typifying the popular taste of the early 17th-century
EDITED BY T. W. CRAIK
0-7190-1636-3 MANCHESTER PB $17.95

George **Chapman**

Bussy d'Ambois
A difficult, impressive political tragedy
EDITED BY ROBERT J. LORDI
0-7190-1616-9 MANCHESTER PB $12.95

The Plays of George Chapman: The Comedies
EDITED BY ALAN HOLADAY
0-85991-243-4 BOYDELL & BREWER $130.00

John **Ford**

Three Plays
Includes *'Tis Pity She's a Whore, The Broken Heart,* and *Perkin Warbeck*
0-14-043059-8 PENGUIN PB $10.95

'Tis Pity She's a Whore & Other Plays
Also includes *The Lover's Melancholy, The Broken Heart,* and *Perkin Warbeck*
0-19-282253-5 OXFORD PB $10.95

Philip **Massinger**

A New Way to Pay Old Debts
Long one of the most popular English plays, notable for its characterization of the grasping Sir Giles Overreach
0-393-90009-6 NORTON PB $6.95

Thomas **Middleton**

Five Plays
Includes *A Trick to Catch the Old One, The Revenger's Tragedy, A Chaste Maid in Cheapside, Women Beware Women,* and *The Changeling*
0-140-43219-2 PENGUIN PB $9.95

Thomas **Middleton** & William **Rowley**

The Changeling
EDITED BY N.W. BAWCUTT
0-7190-1610-X MANCHESTER PB $14.95

Cyril **Tourneur**

The Atheist's Tragedy
EDITED BY BRIAN MORRIS & ROMA GILL
0-393-90030-4 NORTON PB $4.95

The Revenger's Tragedy
The most splendidly horrific of Jacobean revenge plays; its conceits include a fatal kiss administered to a skull with poisoned lips; the play is often now attributed to Thomas Middleton
EDITED BY R.A. FOAKES
0-393-90060-6 NORTON PB $6.95

John **Webster**

Three Plays
After Shakespeare, perhaps the most powerful of Jacobean tragedians. Includes *The Duchess of Malfi, The White Devil,* and *The Devil's Law Case*
EDITED BY D.C. GUNBY
0-14-043081-4 PENGUIN PB $10.95

John **Webster**

The Duchess of Malfi

0-393-90066-5 NORTON PB $6.95

The White Devil, The Duchess of Malfi, The Devil's Law-Case & A Cure for a Cuckold

0-19-282247-0 OXFORD PB $8.95

Anthologies

David **Lindley**, editor

Court Masques: Jacobean and Caroline Entertainments, 1605-1640

Eighteen works by Jonson, Davenant, and others trace the brief flourishing of this extravagant genre blending mythology, lyricism, and political allegory

0-19-282569-0 OXFORD PB $13.95

Katharine Eisaman **Maus**, editor

Four Revenge Tragedies

Includes Kyd's *The Spanish Tragedy*, Middleton's *The Revenger's Tragedy* (sometimes attributed to Tourneur), Chapman's *The Revenge of Bussy D'Ambois*, and Tourneur's *The Atheist's Tragedy*

0-19-282633-6 OXFORD PB $10.95

Gamini **Salgado**, editor

Three Jacobean Tragedies

Includes Tourneur's *The Revenger's Tragedy*, Webster's *The White Devil*, and Middleton and Rowley's *The Changeling*

0-14-043006-7 PENGUIN PB $9.95

Prose

Lancelot **Andrewes**

Selected Writings

EDITED BY P.E. HEWISON

1-85754-118-9 CARCANET PB $36.95

Francis **Bacon**

The Advancement of Learning

See also **BACON** under **PHILOSOPHY** in **RELIGION, SPIRITUALITY, AND PHILOSOPHY**

EDITED BY G.W. PITCHER

INTRODUCTION BY ARTHUR JOHNSTON

1-56459-436-X KESSINGER PB $16.95

The Essays

A few years after Montaigne invented the essay in French, Bacon composed his terse, epigrammatic, and shrewdly perceptive meditations, introducing the form into English

See also **BACON** under **PHILOSOPHY** in **RELIGION, SPIRITUALITY, AND PHILOSOPHY**

EDITED BY JOHN PITCHER

0-14-043216-7 PENGUIN PB $10.95

Essays

EDITED BY MICHAEL J. HAWKINS

0-460-87433-0 EVERYMAN'S PB $7.50

Francis Bacon

EDITED BY BRIAN VICKERS

0-19-282025-7 OXFORD PB $21.00

The New Organon & Related Writings

Bacon's revolutionary philosophy of science

See also **BACON** under **PHILOSOPHY** in **RELIGION, SPIRITUALITY, AND PHILOSOPHY**

EDITED BY FULTON H. ANDERSON

0-02-303380-0 BOBBS-MERRILL PB $17.40

Thomas **Browne**

The Major Works

Browne's ornate, darkly meditative prose, in such works as *Urn-Burial* and *Religio Medici*, is one of the wonders of 17th-century literature

0-14-043109-8 PENGUIN PB $12.95

To see our selves again, we need not look for Plato's year: every man is not only himself; there hath been many Diogenes, and as many Timons, though but few of that name: men are liv'd over again, the world is now as it was in Ages past; there was none then, but there hath been some one since that parallels him, and is, as it were, his revived self. From *Urn-Burial*

THE MAJOR WORKS

John **Bunyan**

Grace Abounding to the Chief of Sinners

Bunyan's spiritual autobiography; an epic of ceaselessly tested faith

EDITED BY W.R. OWENS

0-14-043280-9 PENGUIN PB $9.95

The Pilgrim's Progress

After the Bible, the most-read book in the history of English literature

See also **CLASSICS** under **CHRISTIANITY** in **RELIGION, SPIRITUALITY, AND PHILOSOPHY**

EDITED BY ROGER SHATTUCK

0-14-043004-0 PENGUIN PB $7.95

John **Donne**

Selected Prose

EDITED WITH AN INTRODUCTION BY NEIL RHODES

0-14-043239-6 PENGUIN PB $9.95

Sermons on the Psalms and Gospels: With a Selection of Prayers & Meditations

EDITED WITH AN INTRODUCTION BY EVELYN M. SIMPSON

0-520-00340-3 CALIFORNIA PB $13.00

Thomas **Traherne**

Centuries

Meditations on divine benevolence

EDITED BY H.M. MARGOLIOUTH

0-8192-1397-7 MOREHOUSE PB $10.95

Izaak **Walton**

The Compleat Angler

Walton's treatise on fishing is one of the most treasured books in English

See also **FISHING** under **THE OUTDOORS** in **FOOD, TRAVEL, AND LEISURE**

0-88001-406-7 ECCO $23.00

The Compleat Angler

This edition also includes Charles Cotton's additions to Walton's original text

EDITED BY JOHN BUXTON

0-19-281511-3 OXFORD PB $5.95

The Restoration and the 18th Century

In the period following the restoration of Charles II, the neoclassical strain pioneered nearly 60 years before by Ben Jonson acquired new polish with Dryden, Pope, Prior, and Gay. Judicious, economically expressed wit became the lingua franca of poetry and the intellectual coin of a newly vigorous urban culture.

Poetry

Aphra **Behn**

Behn, a highly successful playwright and novelist, was England's first professional woman of letters.

The Poems of Aphra Behn: A Selection

EDITED BY JANET TODD

0-8147-8216-7 NYU $50.00

Robert **Burns**

A Choice of Burns's Poems and Songs

Among the most beloved poets in English, a master of both broad sentiment and low comedy

0-571-06835-9 FABER PB $12.95

The Essential Burns

EDITED BY ROBERT CREELEY

0-88001-194-7 ECCO PB $6.00

Poems and Songs

EDITED BY JAMES KINSLEY

0-19-281114-2 OXFORD PB $21.00

Robert Burns: Selected Poems

EDITED BY CAROL MCGUIRK

0-14-042382-6 PENGUIN PB $11.95

Thomas **Chatterton**

Selected Poems

Chatterton remains one of the most bizarre figures in English literary history. His forged pseudomedieval poems reflect a precocious talent cut short at the age of 18

EDITED BY GRAVEL LINDOP

0-85635-694-8 SCHOLARLY PB $13.50

Thomas Chatterton

Charles **Cotton**

Selected Poems

A friend of Walton and Lovelace, Cotton celebrated his native Staffordshire landscapes

EDITED BY KEN ROBINSON

0-85635-413-9 CARCANET PB $11.95

William **Cowper**

The Poems of William Cowper

Cowper is surely, and undeservedly, the least-read major poet in English. The first volume in this series is currently out of print

Volume 2
1782-1785

0-19-812339-6 OXFORD $110.00

Volume 3
1785-1800

0-19-818296-1 OXFORD $98.00

George **Crabbe**

Selected Poems

EDITED BY GAVIN EDWARDS

0-14-042365-6 PENGUIN PB $12.95

John **Dryden**

"Dryden's performances were always hasty, extorted by domestic necessity; he composed without consideration, and published without correction. What his mind could supply at call, or gather in one excursion, was all that he sought, and all that he gave. The dilatory caution of Pope enabled him to condense his sentiments, to multiply his images, and to accumulate all that study might produce, or chance might supply. If the flights of Dryden therefore are higher, Pope continues longer on the wing. If of Dryden's fire the blaze is the brighter, of Pope's the heat is more regular and constant. Dryden often surpasses expectation, and Pope never falls below it. Dryden is read with frequent astonishment, and Pope with perpetual delight."
—Samuel Johnson, *Lives of the Poets (1781)*

John Dryden

EDITED BY KEITH WALKER

0-19-282264-0 OXFORD PB $7.95

The Oxford Authors: Dryden

Includes, along with much else, the complete *Fables Ancient and Modern, Religio Laici,* and a generous selection from the translations

EDITED BY KEITH WALKER

0-19-281402-8 OXFORD PB $21.00

Poems

EDITED BY DOUGLAS GRANT

0-14-058503-6 VIKING PB $10.00

Selected Poetry and Prose

0-07-553553-X RANDOM HOUSE PB $11.25

Anne **Finch**, Countess of Winchilsea

Selected Poems

A poet of minor lyric gifts, nonetheless significant in the emergence of women in literature

EDITED BY DENYS THOMPSON

0-85635-624-7 CARCANET PB $11.25

John **Gay**

Selected Poems

EDITED BY MARCUS WALSH

0-85635-280-2 CARCANET PB $11.25

Oliver **Goldsmith**

Poems and Plays

EDITED BY TOM DAVIS

0-460-87390-3 EVERYMAN'S PB $8.95

Thomas **Gray**

Selected Poems

Gray's reputation rests largely on the familiar "Elegy in a Country Churchyard," obscuring the satirical wit and originality of poems like "On the Death of a Favorite Cat"

EDITED BY JOHN HEATH-STUBBS

0-85635-317-5 CARCANET PB $13.95

Samuel **Johnson**

The Complete English Poems

Though better known for his prose, as a poet Johnson was one of the most accomplished English moralists, as evident in his masterpiece, "The Vanity of Human Wishes"

EDITED BY J.D. FLEEMAN

0-14-042296-X PENGUIN PB $11.95

John **Milton**

"Milton...always labours and almost always succeeds. He strives hard to say the finest things in the world, and he does say them. He adorns and dignifies his subject to the utmost: he surrounds it with every possible association of beauty or grandeur, whether moral, intellectual, or physical. He refines on his descriptions of beauty; loading sweets on sweets, till the sense aches at them; and raises his images of terror to a gigantic elevation."
—William Hazlitt, *Lectures on the English Poets (1818)*

The Complete Poems and Major Prose

The best and most comprehensive one-volume edition, with useful if occasionally pedantic notes

EDITED BY MERRITT Y. HUGHES

0-02-358290-1 PRENTICE HALL $77.00

Complete Poetry of John Milton

A well-edited and typographically attractive edition

EDITED BY JOHN T. SHAWCROSS

0-385-02351-0 DOUBLEDAY PB $15.00

Paradise Lost

EDITED BY SCOTT ELLEDGE

0-393-09230-5 NORTON PB $9.95

Paradise Lost and Other Poems

0-451-62826-8 NEW AMERICAN LIBRARY PB ... $6.99

Paradise Lost and Paradise Regained

0-451-52474-8 NEW AMERICAN LIBRARY PB $6.95

The Portable Milton

EDITED BY DOUGLAS BUSH

0-14-015044-7 VIKING PB $14.95

Alexander **Pope**

"Of his intellectual character, the constituent and fundamental principle was good sense, a prompt and intuitive perception of consonance and propriety. He saw immediately, of his own conceptions, what was to be chosen, and what to be rejected; and, in the works of others, what was to be shunned, and what was to be copied. But good sense alone is a sedate and quiescent quality, which manages its possessions well, but does not increase them; it collects few materials for its own operations, and preserves safety, but never gains supremacy. Pope had likewise genius: a mind active, ambitious, and adventurous, always investigating, always aspiring; in its widest searches still longing to go forward, in its highest flights still wishing to be higher."
—Samuel Johnson, *Lives of the Poets (1781)*

Alexander Pope: Selected Poetry

EDITED BY PAT ROGERS

0-19-283276-X OXFORD PB $42.00

0-19-282270-5 OXFORD PB $7.95

Poems and Prose

EDITED BY DOUGLAS GRANT

0-14-058508-7 VIKING PB $9.95

The Poems of Alexander Pope

A one-volume edition of the famous Twickenham text, with selected annotations

EDITED BY JOHN BUTT

0-300-00030-8 YALE PB $22.00

Poetical Works

EDITED BY HUBERT DAVIS

0-19-281246-7 OXFORD PB $21.00

Christopher **Smart**

The Poetical Works of Christopher Smart: Jubilate Agno

Jubilate Agno, written in a madhouse and imitative of Hebrew verse forms, is an extraordinarily original outpouring of ecstatic poetry. While much of the poem was lost, this scholarly edition contains the still sizeable remainder of Smart's *magnum opus*

0-19-811869-4 OXFORD $65.00

Selected Poems

An admirably comprehensive survey of Smart's poetic career, including along with the complete *Jubilate Agno* and *A Song to David* such lesser-known works as the Seatonian Poems, the *Hymns and Spiritual Songs, Hymns for the Amusement of Children,* and selections from the translations of Horace

EDITED BY KATRINA WILLIAMSON & MARCUS WALSH

0-14-042367-2 PENGUIN PB $10.95

Edward **Young**

Night Thoughts, Or the Complaint and the Consolation

Blake's engravings serve as a tribute to a poet who deeply influenced him

ILLUSTRATIONS BY WILLIAM BLAKE

0-521-34185-X CAMBRIDGE $110.00

0-8446-5261-X SMITH $14.75

Selected Poems

Perhaps the best-known figure in the Graveyard school, remarkable for his searching melancholic meditations

EDITED BY BRIAN HEPWORTH

0-85635-140-7 SCHOLARLY $11.25

Jonathan **Swift**

The Complete Poems

Swift's genius as a prose writer has overshadowed his poetic accomplishments. He wrote some of the greatest and most savage (and occasionally scatological) satirical verse in the language

EDITED BY PAT ROGERS

0-14-042261-7 PENGUIN PB $16.95

Jonathan Swift: Selected Poems

EDITED BY PAT ROGERS

0-85635-134-2 CARCANET PB $7.50

Jonathan Swift

Anthologies

Roger **Lonsdale**, editor

Eighteenth-Century Women Poets

More than a hundred poets are featured in this groundbreaking collection, ranging in social status from the Countess of Winchilsea to the washerwoman Mary Collier, and including both well-known figures such as Lady Mary Wortley Montagu and Ann Radcliffe and hitherto obscure writers like Elizabeth Thomas, Mary Leapor, and Hannah More. The detailed biographical notes and scholarly introduction open up new perspectives on 18th-century literature

See also **POETRY ANTHOLOGIES** under **ANTHOLOGIES OF WOMEN'S WRITING** under **WOMEN'S STUDIES** in **SOCIAL STUDIES**

0-19-811769-8 OXFORD PB $35.00

Angela **Leighton**, editor

Victorian Women Poets: A Critical Reader

0-631-19756-7 BLACKWELL $49.95

0-631-19757-5 BLACKWELL PB $21.95

The New Oxford Book of Eighteenth Century Verse

0-19-214122-8 OXFORD $29.95

Drama

Restoration and 18th-century plays seem divided by more than a mere century from the brutal world of late Elizabethan and Jacobean tragedy. Comedy was the chosen mode for Congreve, Wycherley, and Sheridan, and though heroic tragedy survived (notably in Dryden's *All for Love*), it was overshadowed by a keenly observed world of rakes, fools, jealous husbands, lecherous dowagers, and wayward ladies' maids. With Sheridan, the satire grew less bitter, but the unblinking observation of folly no less acute.

Aphra **Behn**

Behn, a highly successful playwright and novelist, was England's fist professional woman of letters.

The Rover

EDITED BY FREDERICK M. LINK

0-8032-5350-8 NEBRASKA PB $5.95

The Rover and Other Plays

Also includes *The Feigned Courtesans*, *The Lucky Chance*, and *The Emperor of the Moon*

EDITED BY JANE SPENCER

0-19-282248-9 OXFORD PB $8.95

William **Congreve**

The Comedies of William Congreve

Includes *The Old Bachelor, The Double Dealer, Love for Love*, and *The Way of the World*

EDITED BY ERIC S. RUMP

0-14-043231-0 PENGUIN PB $10.95

Love for Love

EDITED BY EMMETT L. AVERY

0-393-90003-7 NORTON PB $4.95

The Way of the World

One of the great English comedies, relentless and unsparing

EDITED BY BRIAN GIBBONS

0-393-90004-5 NORTON PB $6.95

I like her with all her Faults; nay, like her for her Faults. Her Follies are so natural, or so artful, that they become her; and those Affectations which in another Woman wou'd be odious, serve but to make her more agreeable. I'll tell thee, Fainall, she once us'd me with that Insolence, that in Revenge I took her to pieces; sifted her, and separated her Failings; I study'd 'em, and got 'em by Rote. The Catalogue was so large, that I was not without Hopes, one Day or other to hate her heartily: To which end I so us'd my self to think of 'em, that at length, contrary to my Design and Expectation, they gave me ev'ry Hour less and less Disturbance; 'till in a few Days it became habitual to me, to remember 'em without being displeas'd. They are now grown as familiar to me as my own Frailties; and in all probability in a little time longer I shall like 'em as well.

THE WAY OF THE WORLD

John **Dryden**

All for Love

Antony and Cleopatra in a surprisingly romantic treatment from the great neoclassicist

EDITED BY NICHOLAS J. ANDREW

0-393-90006-1 NORTON PB $5.95

John Dryden

Marriage a La Mode

EDITED BY MARK S. AUBURN

0-8032-6556-5 NEBRASKA PB $7.95

George **Etherege**

The Man of Mode

EDITED BY W.B. CARNOCHAN

0-8032-5356-7 NEBRASKA PB $9.95

George **Farquhar**

The Recruiting Officer

EDITED BY MICHAEL SHUGRUE

0-8032-5357-5 NEBRASKA PB $9.95

The Recruiting Officer and Other Plays

Four plays of frank and sometimes brutal wit, including *The Constant Couple*, *The Twin Rivals*, and *The Recruiting Officer*

EDITED BY WILLIAM MYERS

0-19-282249-7 OXFORD PB $11.95

Henry **Fielding**

The Grub-Street Opera

EDITED BY EDGAR V. ROBERTS

0-8032-5359-1 NEBRASKA $18.95

John **Gay**

The Beggar's Opera

The famous ballad opera of the outlaw Macheath and the whores, cutpurses, and corrupt officials who surround him became the basis for Brecht's *The Threepenny Opera*

0-14-043220-5 PENGUIN PB $7.95

Oliver **Goldsmith**

She Stoops to Conquer

One of the gentlest and most enduringly popular comedies of the English stage

EDITED BY J.A. LAVIN

0-393-90046-0 NORTON PB $6.95

George **Lillo**

Fatal Curiosity

EDITED BY WILLIAM H. MCBURNEY

0-8032-0364-0 NEBRASKA $10.95

The London Merchant

A bourgeois tragedy of a London clerk gone wrong

EDITED BY WILLIAM H. MCBURNEY

0-8032-5365-6 NEBRASKA PB $6.95

Richard Brinsley **Sheridan**

The Rivals

EDITED BY J. LAVIN

0-393-90044-4 NORTON PB $6.95

The School for Scandal

EDITED BY C.J. PRICE

0-19-911008-5 OXFORD PB $9.95

William **Wycherley**

The Country Wife

EDITED BY THOMAS H. FUJIMURA

0-8032-5371-0 NEBRASKA PB $7.95

The Plain Dealer

An adaptation of Molière's *The Misanthrope*

EDITED BY JAMES L. SMITH

0-393-90042-8 NORTON PB $7.95

Anthologies

Michael **Cordner**, editor

Four Restoration Marriage Plays

Includes Otway's *The Soldier's Fortune*, Lee's *The Princess of Cleves*, Dryden's *Amphitryon*, and Southerne's *The Wives' Excuse*

0-19-812163-6 OXFORD $65.00

0-19-282570-4 OXFORD PB $12.95

Jeffrey N. **Cox**, editor

Seven Gothic Dramas, 1789-1825

Explores the flamboyant entertainments of a little-known period in English drama

See also **ANTHOLOGIES** under **19TH-CENTURY DRAMA** under **THE 19TH-CENTURY**

0-8214-1065-2 OHIO PB $24.95

Brice **Harris**, editor

Restoration Plays

Includes Villiers's *The Rehearsal*, Wycherley's *The Country Wife*, Etherege's *The Man of Mode*, Otway's *Venice Preserv'd*, Vanbrugh's *The Relapse*, Congreve's *The Way of the World*, and Farquhar's *The Beaux' Stratagem*

0-07-553658-7 MCGRAW HILL PB $15.40

Robert G. **Lawrence**, editor

Restoration Plays

Includes *All for Love*, *The Country Wife*, *The Way of the World*, *Venice Preserv'd*, *The Beaux' Stratagem*, *The Provok'd Wife*, and *The Man of Mode*

0-460-87432-2 EVERYMAN'S PB $14.95

David **Lindsay**, editor

The Beggar's Opera and Other Eighteenth-Century Plays

Also includes *Cato*, *The Tragedy of Jane Shore*, *The Tragedy of Tragedies*, *or Tom Thumb the Great*, *The London Merchant*, *The Clandestine Marriage*, and *The West Indian*

0-460-87314-8 EVERYMAN'S PB $5.95

Paddy **Lyons** & Fidelis **Morgan**, editors

Female Playwrights of the Restoration: Five Comedies

Includes *The Feigned Courtesans*, *She Ventures and He Wins*, *The Beau Defeated*, *The Basset Table*, and *The Busybody*

0-460-87427-6 EVERYMAN'S PB $9.95

Katharine M. **Rogers**, editor

The Meridian Anthology of Restoration and Eighteenth-Century Plays by Women

0-452-01110-8 MERIDIAN PB $15.95

Fiction

The informality and frequent eccentricity of the 18th-century novel make it a constant source of surprise and delight—from the moral analysis of Richardson's *Clarissa* to the picaresque verve of Fielding and Smollett and the Gothic fiction of Beckford, Walpole, and Radcliffe.

William **Beckford**

Vathek

Among the most delightfully perverse books in English, a Gothic romance in Arabian dress

EDITED BY ROGER LONSDALE

0-19-281645-4 OXFORD PB $7.95

Aphra **Behn**

Love Letters Between a Nobleman and His Sister

INTRODUCTION BY MAUREEN DUFFY

0-14-043537-9 PENGUIN PB $12.95

Oroonoko: Or, the Royal Slave

A Rousseauan evocation of the Noble Savage, and a condemnation of the slave trade—which draws on Behn's experiences in Surinam, and which is regarded as the first anti-slave fiction

0-393-00702-2 NORTON PB $6.95

Oroonoko, The Rover & Other Works

0-14-043338-4 PENGUIN PB $9.95

Fanny **Burney**

Camilla

EDITED BY EDWARD A. BLOOM & LILLIAN D. BLOOM

0-19-281662-4 OXFORD PB $10.95

Cecilia

EDITED BY PETER SABOR

0-19-281742-6 OXFORD PB $8.95

Evelina

An entertaining epistolary novel that combines humor and satire with strong moralism

EDITED BY EDWARD A. BLOOM

0-393-00294-2 NORTON PB $11.95

0-451-52560-4 SIGNET PB $6.95

Margaret **Cavendish**

The Blazing World and Other Writings

The title work can be seen as an early example of science fiction, depicting an imaginary realm ruled by a woman

EDITED BY KATE LILLEY

0-14-043372-4 PENGUIN PB $10.95

John **Cleland**

Fanny Hill: Or, Memoirs of a Woman of Pleasure

Cleland's use of elaborate and elegant figurative language to describe explicit sexual episodes sets his book apart from most erotic literature

EDITED BY PETER WAGNER

0-14-043249-3 PENGUIN PB $8.95

Daniel Defoe

Daniel **Defoe**

A Journal of the Plague Year

A classic early text in the literature of disease; a harrowing blend of fiction and fact

EDITED BY ANTHONY BURGESS

0-14-043015-6 PENGUIN PB $7.95

The Life, Adventures, and Pyracies of the Famous Captain Singleton

0-19-282200-4 OXFORD PB $6.95

Moll Flanders

"It is most popularly thought of as a tale of thievery and prostitution, of crime, punishment and worldly success: a lively account of an attractive, independent and wicked woman who eventually makes good—both morally and economically. In fact *Moll Flanders* is throughout as much about financial investment as about theft, as much about marriage as about prostitution"—Juliet Mitchell

EDITED BY JULIET MITCHELL

0-14-043313-9 PENGUIN PB $8.95

Robinson Crusoe

"*Robinson Crusoe* falls most naturally into place, not with other novels, but with the great myths of Western civilization, with *Faust*, *Don Juan*, and *Don Quixote*"—Ian Watt

0-679-40585-2 KNOPF $15.00

0-14-035072-1 PUFFIN PB $3.50

Roxana

EDITED BY DAVID BLEWETT

0-14-043149-7 PENGUIN PB $9.95

Roxana

EDITED BY JOHN MULLAN

0-19-282459-7 OXFORD PB $8.95

Henry **Fielding**

Amelia

An uncharacteristically sentimental novel about a virtuous wife, modeled on the author's spouse

EDITED BY DAVID BLEWETT

0-14-043229-9 PENGUIN PB $8.95

Jonathan Wild

The law and the criminal underworld intermingle in this story of a doomed rake

EDITED BY DAVID NOKES

0-14-043151-9 PENGUIN PB $9.95

In the histories of Alexander and Caesar, we are frequently, and indeed impertinently, reminded of their benevolence and generosity, of their clemency and kindness. When the former had with fire and sword overrun a vast empire, had destroyed the lives of an immense number of innocent wretches, had scattered ruin and desolation like a whirlwind, we are told, as an example of his clemency, that he did not cut the throat of an old woman and ravish her daughters, but was content with only undoing them.

JONATHAN WILD

Joseph Andrews

Fielding's first full-fledged novel features the great comic creations Lady Booby and Mrs. Slipslop

EDITED BY R.F. BRISSENDEN

0-14-043114-4 PENGUIN PB $8.95

Joseph Andrews, Shamela & Related Writings

Shamela (a takeoff on Richardson's *Pamela*) is perhaps the most skillful extended parody in English

EDITED BY HOMER GOLDBERG

0-393-95555-9 NORTON PB $14.95

Tom Jones

0-394-60519-5 MODERN LIBRARY $10.95

0-393-09394-8 NORTON PB $12.95

Tom Jones

EDITED BY REG MUTTER

0-14-043009-1 PENGUIN PB $8.95

Tom Jones

0-19-283110-0 OXFORD PB $5.95

The History of Tom Jones, a Foundling

Fielding's masterpiece, in a splendidly designed scholarly edition

EDITED BY FREDSON BOWERS

INTRODUCTION BY MARTIN C. BATTESTIN

0-8195-6048-0 WESLEYAN PB $22.95

William **Godwin**

Caleb Williams

Godwin's 1794 forerunner of the crime novel is part murder mystery, part hunted-man adventure—with an underlying skepticism about the rule of law that foreshadows everyone from Hammett to Highsmith

See also **PIONEERS AND LANDMARKS** under **RISE OF THE MYSTERY** under **CRIME FICTION** in **POPULAR READING**

EDITED BY MAURICE HINDLE

0-14-043256-6 PENGUIN PB $10.95

St. Leon

EDITED BY PAMELA CLEMIT

0-19-282833-9 OXFORD PB $12.95

Oliver **Goldsmith**

The Vicar of Wakefield

0-14-043159-4 PENGUIN PB $6.95

Elizabeth **Inchbald**

A Simple Story

"Daring in theme, elegant in style, *A Simple Story* is one of the most remarkable novels of the late eighteenth century… Inchbald's concise, ironic narrative style anticipates Austen, while the passionate heroine she creates to disrupt the world of social comedy looks further forward, to the work of the Brontës"—Jane Spencer

EDITED BY J.M.S. TOMPKINS

INTRODUCTION BY JANE SPENCER

0-19-281849-X OXFORD PB $7.95

Samuel **Johnson**

The History of Rasselas, Prince of Abissinia

Johnson's characters, searching for a "choice of life," encounter only the endless vanity of human pretensions

EDITED BY D.J. ENRIGHT

0-140-43108-X PENGUIN PB $9.95

The History of Rasselas, Prince of Abissinia

0-19-281778-7 OXFORD PB $5.95

Samuel Johnson

A Voyage to Abyssinia

EDITED BY JOEL J. GOLD

0-300-03003-7 YALE $55.00

Charlotte **Lennox**

The Female Quixote

"Dr. Johnson, Samuel Richardson and Henry Fielding all thought she merited the label 'genius,' with Henry Fielding rating her *Female Quixote* as surpassing Cervantes' work" —Dale Spender

INTRODUCTION BY SANDRA SHULMAN

0-19-281765-5 OXFORD PB $9.95

Matthew **Lewis**

The Monk

Murder, rape, torture, the Inquisition, and a diabolical pact are some of the ingredients of Lewis's archetypal Gothic novel, which shocked his contemporaries

EDITED BY HOWARD ANDERSON

0-19-281524-5 OXFORD PB $8.95

Robert **Mack**

Oriental Tales

0-19-282764-2 OXFORD PB $9.95

Henry **Mackenzie**

The Man of Feeling

An example of the "Novel of Sentiment"

EDITED BY BRIAN VICKERS

0-393-00214-4 NORTON PB $7.95

Delariver **Manley**

The New Atlantis

A roman à clef of political and social life which created a scandal when published in 1709

0-14-043370-8 PENGUIN PB $11.95

Ann **Radcliffe**

Radcliffe, the most talented of the Gothic novelists, was remarkable for her ability to transform the creaky melodramatics of her plots through the expressive use of landscape and supernaturally charged imagery.

The Castles of Athlin and Dunbayne

EDITED BY ALISON MILBANK

0-19-282357-4 OXFORD PB $7.95

The Italian

EDITED BY FREDERICK GARBER

0-19-281572-5 OXFORD PB $8.95

The Mysteries of Udolpho

EDITED BY BONAMY DOBREE

0-19-281502-4 OXFORD PB $8.95

The Romance of the Forest

EDITED WITH AN INTRODUCTION BY CHLOE CHARD

0-19-281712-4 OXFORD PB $8.95

A Sicilian Romance

0-19-282212-8 OXFORD PB $8.95

Ann **Radcliffe** & Jane **Austen**

Two Gothic Classics by Women: The Italian & Northanger Abbey

0-451-52607-4 SIGNET PB $6.95

Samuel **Richardson**

Clarissa: Or the History of a Young Lady

A complete text of Richardson's immensely long epistolary novel of threatened but ultimately triumphant virtue

EDITED BY ANGUS ROSS

0-395-05164-9 HOUGHTON MIFFLIN PB $11.16

Pamela: Or Virtue Rewarded

A shorter, earlier novel prefiguring *Clarissa's* moral drama

EDITED BY PETER SABOR

INTRODUCTION BY MARGARET DOODY

0-14-043140-3 PENGUIN PB $6.95

Pamela

0-460-87064-5 EVERYMAN'S PB $7.95

Frances **Sheridan**

Memoirs of Miss Sidney Bidulph

A significant work of moral fiction exploring questions of female conduct in marriage

EDITED BY PATRICIA KOSTER

0-19-282308-6 OXFORD PB $12.95

Tobias **Smollett**

Smollett's picaresque novels are rougher and more episodic than Fielding's; they are also closer to the ugly realities of 18th-century urban squalor.

The Adventures of Ferdinand Count Fathom

EDITED BY PAUL-GABRIEL BOUCE

0-14-043307-4 PENGUIN PB $10.95

The Adventures of Roderick Random

This masterpiece contains one of the earliest descriptions of English naval life

EDITED BY PAUL-GABRIEL BOUCE

0-19-281261-0 OXFORD PB $7.95

Roderick Random

EDITED BY DAVID BLEWETT

0-14-043332-5 PENGUIN PB $8.95

The Expedition of Humphrey Clinker

The inimitable dyspepsia of Matthew Bramble, reflecting Smollett's own temperament, meets its match in the maddening provocations supplied by his sister Tabitha

EDITED BY ANGUS ROSS

0-14-043021-0 PENGUIN PB $7.95

The Life and Adventures of Sir Launcelot Greaves

A lesser-known Smollett novel modeled on *Don Quixote*

0-14-043306-6 PENGUIN PB $10.95

Laurence **Sterne**

The Life and Opinions of Tristram Shandy, Gentleman

The first antinovel: an uproarious attack on the conventions of fiction and a celebration of unbridled eccentricity

EDITED BY IAN C. ROSS

0-19-281566-0 OXFORD PB $6.95

The Life and Opinions of Tristram Shandy, Gentleman

EDITED BY GRAHAM PETRIE

0-14-043019-9 PENGUIN PB $8.95

Tristram Shandy

0-679-40560-7 EVERYMAN'S $20.00

0-393-95034-4 NORTON PB $17.95

Jonathan **Swift**

"The true greatness of Swift as a prose stylist lies in the taut, nervous energy of his sentences; he was a man whose every word was alive with the instincts of attack and defense. Very often the severe conformist values for which he stood are deeply concealed behind the complacent masks of his bland and superficial narrators, but they give edge and bite to his writing…Swift was not really a black humorist in our modern sense; most of his jokes were against despair, not expressions of despair."—Robert M. Adams, The Land and Literature of England

Gulliver's Travels

0-679-60188-0 MODERN LIBRARY $14.00

0-14-43022-5 PENGUIN PB $5.95

Gulliver's Travels

EDITED BY PAUL TURNER

0-19-281755-8 OXFORD PB $3.95

A Modest Proposal and Other Satires

0-87975-919-4 PROMETHEUS PB $7.95

Horace **Walpole**

The Castle of Otranto

Historically important as the first Gothic novel

EDITED BY W.S. LEWIS & JOSEPH W. REED, JR.

0-19-282351-5 OXFORD PB $6.95

Mary **Wollstonecraft**

Mary & The Wrongs of Woman

EDITED BY GARY KELLY

0-19-281527-X OXFORD PB $5.95

Mary **Wollstonecraft** & Mary **Shelley**

Mary/Maria/Matilda

Three short novels by mother and daughter

See also **19TH-CENTURY FICTION** under **THE 19TH-CENTURY**

0-14-043371-6 PENGUIN PB $11.95

Prose

John **Aubrey**

Brief Lives

EDITED BY RICHARD BARBER

0-85115-206-6 BOYDELL & BREWER PB $23.00

James **Boswell**

Life of Johnson

In this monumental work Boswell invented the modern art of biography and supplied posterity with a gold mine of anecdotal information about the 18th-century's leading man of letters

EDITED BY R.W. CHAPMAN & J.E. FLEEMAN

INTRODUCTION BY PAT ROGERS

0-19-281537-7 OXFORD PB $16.95

James Boswell

Life of Johnson

0-679-60204-6 MODERN LIBRARY $22.00

The Life of Samuel Johnson

0-679-41717-6 KNOPF $25.00

Edmund **Burke**

A Philosophical Enquiry into the Origin of Our Ideas of the Sublime and Beautiful

0-19-281807-4 OXFORD PB $8.95

Reflections on the Revolution in France

Burke, who had supported the American Revolution as a vindication of traditional English liberties, produced in *Reflections on the Revolution in France* (1790) the most influential arguments against the French Revolution and in the process invented conservatism as a distinct political philosophy. He favored gradual reform based on experience and local tradition, which distinguishes his conservatism from the more iron-handed and pessimistic variety developed on the Continent by De Maistre and others

See also **INTERPRETING THE REVOLUTION** under **THE FRENCH REVOLUTION AND NAPOLEON** in **WORLD HISTORY AND CURRENT AFFAIRS**

See also **CLASSICS** under **POLITICAL THOUGHT** in **SOCIAL STUDIES**

0-14-043204-3 PENGUIN PB $9.95

It is now sixteen or seventeen years since I saw the queen of France, then the dauphiness, at Versailles; and surely never lighted on this orb, which she hardly seemed to touch, a more delightful vision…Oh! What a revolution! and what an heart must I have, to contemplate without emotion that elevation and that fall!…I thought ten thousand swords must have leaped from their scabbards to avenge even a look that threatened her with insult.—But the age of chivalry is gone.—That of sophisters, economists, and calculators, has succeeded; and the glory of Europe is extinguished for ever. Never, never more, shall we behold that generous loyalty to rank and sex, that proud submission, that dignified obedience, that subordination of the heart, which kept alive, even in servitude itself, the spirit of an exalted freedom.

REFLECTIONS ON THE REVOLUTION IN FRANCE

William **Cowper**

Letters and Prose Writings of William Cowper

Volume 1, 1748-1782

0-19-811863-5 OXFORD $98.00

Volume 2, 1782-1785

0-19-812607-7 OXFORD $149.00

Volume 3, 1785-1800

0-19-818296-1 OXFORD $98.00

Volume 4, Prose 1756-1798 and Cumulative Index

0-19-812690-5 OXFORD $72.00

Daniel **Defoe**

A Tour Through the Whole Island of Great Britain

Businessman, journalist, soldier, and spy, Defoe toured Britain from 1724 to 1726. "Far the best authority for early 18th-century England" —Dorothy George

See also **THE 18TH-CENTURY** under **GREAT BRITAIN AND IRELAND** in **WORLD HISTORY AND CURRENT AFFAIRS**

0-14-043066-0 PENGUIN PB $13.95

Henry **Fielding**

The Journal of a Voyage to Lisbon

EDITED BY TOM KEYMER

0-14-043487-9 PENGUIN PB $10.95

Edward **Gibbon**

Eighteenth-century prose style reached its apogee in the limpid ironies of the narration that Gibbon composed out of his vast researches into the fall of Rome. "The style is as smooth as a Flemish picture and the muscles are concealed and only for natural uses, not exaggerated like Michelangelo's to show the painter's skill in anatomy"—Horace Walpole

The Decline and Fall of the Roman Empire

Whet your appetite with this one-volume abridgment, but don't miss the main course

See also **ANCIENT ROME** in **WORLD HISTORY AND CURRENT AFFAIRS**

EDITED BY DERO A. SAUNDERS & CHARLES A. ROBINSON, JR.

0-14-043189-6 PENGUIN PB $13.95

The Decline and Fall of the Roman Empire

Volume 1

0-679-60148-1 MODERN LIBRARY $22.00

Volume 2

0-679-60149-X MODERN LIBRARY $22.00

Volume 3

0-679-60150-3 MODERN LIBRARY $22.00

The History of the Decline and Fall of the Roman Empire

This convenient edition contains the complete original work

Volume 1

See also **ANCIENT ROME** in **WORLD HISTORY AND CURRENT AFFAIRS**

0-14-043393-7 PENGUIN PB $24.95

Volume 2

0-14-043394-5 PENGUIN PB $24.95

Volume 3

0-14-043395-3 PENGUIN PB $24.95

Memoirs of My Life

"Decency and ignorance cast a veil over the mystery of generation, but I may relate that after floating nine months in a liquid element I was painfully transported into the vital air." Gibbon's autobiography offers a glimpse into the cool, poised mind of the 18th-century. "Intelligent, entertaining, dignified and often amusing…One of the minor masterpieces of its century"—E.M. Forster

EDITED BY BETTY RADICE

0-14-043217-5 PENGUIN PB $10.95

Samuel **Johnson**

Diaries, Prayers & Annals

EDITED BY E.L. MCADAM, JR.

0-300-00733-7 YALE $65.00

The Idler & The Adventurer

EDITED BY W.J. BATE

0-300-00294-7 YALE $65.00

Johnson on Shakespeare

A 2-volume set

EDITED BY ARTHUR SHERBO

INTRODUCTION BY BERTRAND BRONSON

0-300-00605-5 YALE $120.00

The Journey to the Western Islands of Scotland

Johnson's piece of travel writing is the occasion of an unlikely outpouring of sympathy

INTRODUCTION BY J.D. FLEEMAN

0-19-812766-9 OXFORD $85.00

Journey to the Western Islands of Scotland

EDITED BY MARY LASCELLES

0-300-01251-9 YALE $45.00

0-395-05181-9 HOUGHTON MIFFLIN PB $10.36

The Letters of Samuel Johnson with Mrs. Thrale's Genuine Letters to Him

Volume 1: 1731-1772

0-691-06881-X PRINCETON $39.50

Volume 2: 1773-1776

0-691-06928-X PRINCETON $39.50

Volume 3: 1777-1781

0-691-06929-8 PRINCETON $39.50

The Oxford Authors: Samuel Johnson

A generous and well-chosen selection illustrating the enormous range of Johnson's output

EDITED BY DONALD GREENE

0-19-281340-4 OXFORD PB $21.00

Political Writings

EDITED BY DONALD J. GREENE

0-300-01593-3 YALE $65.00

The Rambler

A 3-volume set

EDITED BY W.J. BATE

0-300-01157-1 YALE $125.00

Selected Essays from the Rambler, Adventurer & Idler

EDITED BY W.J. BATE

0-300-00364-1 YALE $60.00

0-300-00016-2 YALE PB $16.00

Selected Writings

EDITED BY PATRICK CRUTTWELL

0-14-043033-4 PENGUIN PB $12.95

Sermons

EDITED BY JEAN H. HAGSTRUM AND JAMES GRAY

0-300-02104-6 YALE $55.00

Samuel **Johnson** & James **Boswell**

A Journey to the Western Islands of Scotland & The Journal of a Tour to the Hebrides

Johnson's account of the Hebrides paired with Boswell's; the latter focuses more on Johnson himself than on their surroundings

EDITED BY PETER LEVI

0-14-043221-3 PENGUIN PB $11.95

Charles **Miller-Kerby**, editor

The Memories of the Extraordinary Life, Works and Discoveries of Martinus Scriblerus

A satire of educational and artistic practices, produced by a club whose members included Pope, Swift, Gay, and Arbuthnot

0-19-520648-7 OXFORD PB $22.00

Samuel **Pepys**

The Diary of Samuel Pepys

The only complete and unexpurgated edition of Pepys's incomparable diary. Perhaps no other human being has ever recorded his own life in such compulsively honest detail

Volume 1: 1660

0-00-499021-8 HARPERCOLLINS PB $16.00

Volume 2: 1661

0-00-499022-6 HARPERCOLLINS PB $16.00

Volume 3: 1662

0-00-499023-4 HARPERCOLLINS PB $16.00

Volume 4: 1663

0-00-499024-2 HARPERCOLLINS PB $16.00

Volume 5: 1664

0-00-499025-0 HARPERCOLLINS PB $16.00

Volume 6: 1665

0-00-499026-9 HARPERCOLLINS PB $16.00

Volume 7: 1666

0-00-499027-7 HARPERCOLLINS PB $16.00

Volume 8: 1667

0-00-499028-5 HARPERCOLLINS PB $18.00

Volume 9: 1668-1669

0-00-499029-3 HARPERCOLLINS PB $18.00

Volume 10: The Companion

0-00-499030-7 HARPERCOLLINS PB............$20.00

Samuel Pepys

The Shorter Pepys

"Pepys's diary is the cheerful self-report, not of the man eminent in naval history, nor of the historical witness, but of the unobjectionable hedonist"—Geoffrey Grigson

See also **SOURCES** under **THE CENTURY OF REVOLUTION** under **GREAT BRITAIN AND IRELAND** in **WORLD HISTORY AND CURRENT AFFAIRS**

EDITED BY ROBERT LATHAM

0-520-03426-0 CALIFORNIA $50.00

January 21, 1664. Up; and after sending my wife to my aunt Wight's to get a place to see Turner hanged, I to the office, where we sat all the morning. And at noon, going to the Change and seeing people flock in that, I enquired and found

that Turner was not yet hanged; and so I went among them to Leadenhall street at the end of Lyme street, near where the robbery was done, and to St. Mary Axe, where he lived; and there I got for a shilling to stand upon the wheel of a Cart, in great pain, above an hour before the execution was done—he delaying the time by long discourses and prayers one after another, in hopes of a reprieve; but none came, and at last was flung off the lather in his cloak. A comely-looking man he was, and kept his countenance to the end—I was sorry to see him. It was believed there was at least 12 or 14000 people in the street.
THE SHORTER PEPYS

Laurence **Sterne**

A Sentimental Journey, The Journal to Eliza & A Political Romance

This edition includes several of Sterne's lesser-known works
0-19-281685-3 OXFORD PB $4.95

A Sentimental Journey Through France and Italy

A travel book whose open structure captures the spontaneity and unpredictability of travel
EDITED BY GRAHAM PETRIE
INTRODUCTION BY A. ALVAREZ
0-14-043026-1 PENGUIN PB $4.95

Jonathan **Swift**

A Tale of a Tub & Related Pieces

EDITED BY ANGUS ROSS & DAVID WOOLLEY
0-19-281689-6 OXFORD PB $4.95

Horace **Walpole**

Horace Walpole's Miscellany, 1786-1795

EDITED BY LARS TROIDE
0-300-02105-4 YALE $35.00

Gilbert **White**

The Natural History of Selborne

An informal masterpiece of natural observation, first published in 1788
See also **ESSAYS, MEDITATIONS, AND CLASSICS** under **NATURE STUDY** in **SCIENCE**
0-14-043112-8 PENGUIN PB $8.95

The 19th-century

The Romantic Movement

Thomas Lovell **Beddoes**

Selected Poems

Beddoes' morbid lyricism—extreme even by the standards of the Romantic movement—was profoundly influenced by Jacobean writers such as Webster and Tourneur
EDITED BY JUDITH HIGGENS
0-85635-192-X CARCANET $11.25

William **Blake**

America, a Prophecy & Europe, a Prophecy

Facsimile editions of two of Blake's major prophetic poems
0-486-24548-9 DOVER PB $8.95

The Book of Urizen

A facsimile of what is perhaps the most strikingly designed—and accessible—of Blake's shorter prophetic poems
0-87024-065-X MIAMI PB $7.95

The Complete Poems

An up-to-date scholarly edition, in a convenient format
EDITED BY ALICIA OSTRIKER
0-14-042215-3 PENGUIN PB $14.95

The Complete Poetry and Prose

The standard scholarly edition of Blake's writings; the typography is clumsy, but the texts are authoritative
EDITED BY DAVID V. ERDMAN
0-385-15213-2 DOUBLEDAY PB $21.00

The Early Illuminated Books

0-691-03387-0 PRINCETON $75.00

The Essential Blake

0-88001-502-0 ECCO PB $10.00

Jerusalem: The Emanation of the Giant Albion

The famous William Blake Trust edition, with its painstaking reproduction of Blake's 100 illuminated plates, is now made more widely available. Features a new transcription of the text along with notes and plate-by-plate commentaries
0-691-06935-2 PRINCETON $75.00

Lambeth Prophecies

0-691-03674-8 PRINCETON $85.00

The Marriage of Heaven and Hell

A facsimile of Blake's most concise exposition of his symbolic system, including some of his most celebrated aphorisms ("Energy is Eternal Delight")
INTRODUCTION AND COMMENTARY BY GEOFFREY KEYNES
0-19-281167-3 OXFORD PB $13.95

Milton, A Poem

0-691-03393-5 PRINCETON $65.00

The Oxford Authors: Blake

An annotated and modernized selection, including most of Blake's poetry and prose works; the prophetic poems *Milton* and *Jerusalem* are presented in full
EDITED BY MICHAEL MASON
0-19-282001-X OXFORD PB $22.00

Poems and Prophecies

0-679-40552-6 EVERYMAN'S $20.00

Songs of Innocence and Experience

Blake's popular early poems are presented here in a facsimile edition
INTRODUCTION BY GEOFFREY KEYNES
0-19-281089-8 OXFORD PB $13.95

Songs of Innocence and Experience

Blake's best-known poems, as prepared for publication by the William Blake Trust, reproduced from the finest surviving copy, preserved at King's College, Cambridge
0-691-06936-0 PRINCETON $75.00
0-486-25264-7 DOVER PB $9.90

William Blake: Selected Poetry

EDITED BY MICHAEL MASON
0-19-282305-1 OXFORD PB $7.95

William Blake: Selected Works

EDITED BY DAVID STEVENS
0-521-48546-0 CAMBRIDGE PB $6.95

The Essential Blake

EDITED BY STANLEY KUNITZ
0-88001-138-6 ECCO PB $12.50

Emily **Brontë**

The Complete Poems

"Her poems need to be read not merely for their passing felicities of melody… but for the profoundly original conceptions that propel them, hidden at times in the most deceptively simple forms. Hers is the poetry of a refusal to mediate between her vision and the world, a refusal to modify or compromise or translate into more accessible terms"—*Village Voice*
EDITED BY C.W. HATFIELD
0-231-01222-5 COLUMBIA $39.50

The Complete Poems

A new edition with an illuminating introduction and notes
EDITED BY JANET GEZARI
0-14-042352-4 PENGUIN PB $11.95

Poems

0-679-44725-3 EVERYMAN'S $12.50

Lord **Byron**

Byron's Letters and Journals

This definitive edition clearly establishes Byron as one of the great prose writers of the 19th-century. Volumes two, three, and ten are currently out of print

Volume 1
In My Hot Youth: 1798-1810

0-674-08940-5 HARVARD $22.50

Volume 4
Wedlock's the Devil: 1814-1815

0-674-08944-8 HARVARD $25.00

Volume 5
So Late the Night: 1816-1817

0-674-08945-6 HARVARD $13.50

Volume 6
The Flesh Is Frail: 1818-1819

0-674-08946-4 HARVARD $25.00

Volume 7
Between Two Worlds: 1820

0-674-08947-2 HARVARD $25.00

Volume 8
Born for Opposition: 1821

0-674-08948-0 HARVARD $27.50

Lord **Byron**

Byron's Letters and Journals (cont')

Volume 9

In the Wind's Eye: 1821-1822

0-674-08949-9 HARVARD $25.00

Volume 11

For Freedom's Battle: 1824

0-674-08953-7 HARVARD $25.00

Volume 12

The Trouble of an Index

0-674-08954-5 HARVARD $25.00

Don Juan

Byron's masterpiece, alternately hilarious, indignant, savage, and tender, yet uniformly readable. "What had been Byron's defect as a serious poet, his lack of reverence for words, was a virtue for the comic poet. Serious poetry requires that the poet treat words as if they were persons, but comic poetry demands that he treat them as things and few, if any, English poets have rivaled Byron's ability to put words through the hoops"—W.H. Auden

EDITED BY T.G. STEFFAN

0-14-042216-1 PENGUIN PB $13.95

Lord Byron

The Oxford Authors: Lord Byron

EDITED BY JEROME MCGANN

0-19-281349-8 OXFORD PB $21.00

Poems

A compact selection from the Penguin Poets series

0-14-058507-9 VIKING PB $9.95

Poetical Works

EDITED BY FREDERICK PAGE & JOHN JUMP

0-19-281068-5 OXFORD PB $21.00

Selected Letters and Journals

EDITED BY LESLIE A. MARCHAND

0-674-53915-X HARVARD $32.00

John **Clare**

Clare, who enjoyed brief celebrity as a "peasant poet" before succumbing to madness, is increasingly admired not so much for the Romantic coloring of his verse as for the meticulous natural observation at its core. This edition is the best available introduction to the full range of Clare's writing. "Although born in the Age of Enlightenment, Clare speaks in the tones of a more archaic culture. Much of the daily life he knew as a child would not have been out of place in a medieval Book of Hours…In the scurryings of Clare's birds and beasts we hear the cadences of the last medieval poet."—Village Voice

Autobiographical Writings

Includes the famous "Journey Out of Essex," Clare's harrowing account of his escape from the madhouse

EDITED BY ERIC ROBINSON

0-19-211774-2 OXFORD $19.95

The Essential Clare

A well-chosen short selection

EDITED BY CAROLYN KIZER

0-88001-157-2 ECCO PB $8.00

John Clare's Birds

EDITED BY ERIC ROBINSON & RICHARD FITTER

0-19-212977-5 OXFORD $17.95

The Shepherd's Calendar

The complete text of a long poem describing the cycles of rural life

EDITED BY ERIC ROBINSON & GEOFFREY SUMMERFIELD

0-19-211249-X OXFORD $29.95

0-19-281142-8 OXFORD PB $9.95

Samuel Taylor **Coleridge**

Biographia Literaria

A scholarly, well-designed edition of Coleridge's critical masterpiece

0-691-01861-8 PRINCETON PB $35.00

The Oxford Authors: Samuel Taylor Coleridge

Contains a generous selection of poetry and the complete *Biographia Literaria*

EDITED BY H.J. JACKSON

0-19-281383-8 OXFORD PB $19.95

Poems

The format is rather crabbed, but this is the fullest readily available edition of Coleridge's verse

EDITED BY E.H. COLERIDGE

0-19-281051-0 OXFORD PB $21.00

Poems and Prose

SELECTED BY KATHLEEN RAINE

0-14-058501-X VIKING PB $8.95

The Portable Coleridge

EDITED BY I.A. RICHARDS

0-14-015048-X PENGUIN PB $13.95

Selected Letters of Samuel Taylor Coleridge

EDITED BY H.J. JACKSON

0-19-282140-7 OXFORD PB $13.95

Samuel Taylor Coleridge

Thomas **De Quincey**

Confessions of an English Opium Eater

De Quincey's narration of his long-term addiction combines florid Romantic style with unexpected moments of psychological realism

EDITED BY ALETHEA HAYTER

0-14-043061-X PENGUIN PB $9.95

Confessions of an English Opium-Eater and Other Writings

0-19-281675-6 OXFORD PB $8.95

William **Hazlitt**

Liber Amoris: Or, The New Pygmalion 1823

A painful account of Hazlitt's obsessive and unrequited love for a young girl

1-85477-119-1 WOODSTOCK $48.00

Selected Writings

Hazlitt is perhaps the most underestimated major critic in English

0-19-281734-5 OXFORD PB $10.95

William Hazlitt

John **Keats**

Complete Poems

EDITED BY JOHN BERNARD

0-14-042210-2 PENGUIN PB $12.95

Complete Poems

The definitive scholarly edition

EDITED BY JACK STILLINGER

0-674-15431-2 HARVARD PB $14.95

The Complete Poems of John Keats

0-679-60108-2 MODERN LIBRARY $17.00

The Essential Keats

EDITED BY PHILIP LEVINE

0-88001-135-1 ECCO PB $8.00

John Keats: Selected Poetry

EDITED BY ELIZABETH COOK

0-19-283275-1 OXFORD $42.00

0-19-282291-8 OXFORD PB $7.95

Letters of John Keats

"In the history of literature the letters of John Keats are unique…Because of the letters it is impossible to think of Keats only as a poet—inevitably we think of him as something more interesting than a poet, we think of him as a man, and as a certain kind of a man, a hero" —Lionel Trilling

EDITED BY ROBERT GIDDINGS

0-19-281081-2 OXFORD PB $19.95

We hate poetry that has a palpable design upon us—and if we do not agree, seems to put its hand in its breeches pocket. Poetry should be great and unobtrusive, a thing which enters into one's soul, and does not startle it or amaze it with itself, but with its subject.—John Keats to John Hamilton Reynolds, February 3, 1818
SELECTED LETTERS

John Keats

Poems

0-679-43319-8 KNOPF $10.95

Poems

0-679-40553-4 EVERYMAN'S $17.00

Selected Poems

EDITED BY JOHN BARNARD

0-14-058598-2 PENGUIN PB $9.95

Philip **Levine**, editor

The Essential Keats

0-88001-134-3 ECCO PB $14.50

Charles **Lamb** & Mary **Lamb**

Tales from Shakespeare

See also **YOUNG ADULT FICTION** in **BOOKS FOR YOUNG READERS**

0-451-52391-1 NEW AMERICAN LIBRARY PB $5.95

0-14-036677-6 PUFFIN PB $3.99

Charles Lamb

Walter Savage **Landor**

Selected Poems and Prose

Landor is today better known for his "imaginary conversations" in prose than for his poetry, but he is nonetheless an occasionally gifted lyricist

EDITED BY KEITH HANLEY

0-85635-272-1 CARCANET $21.25

Walter **Scott**

Selected Poems

EDITED BY THOMAS CRAWFORD

0-85635-958-0 SCHOLARLY PB $18.95

Percy Bysshe **Shelley**

A Choice of Shelley's Verse

EDITED BY STEPHEN SPENDER

0-571-08790-6 FABER PB $10.95

The Complete Poems of Percy Bysshe Shelley

0-679-60111-2 MODERN LIBRARY $20.00

Poems

SELECTED BY ISABEL QUIGLY

0-14-058504-4 PENGUIN PB $11.95

Poems and Prose

EDITED BY TIMOTHY WEBB

0-460-87449-7 EVERYMAN'S PB $7.95

Poetical Works

This is the standard scholarly edition of a poet whose reputation has shifted dramatically in the 20th-century

0-395-18461-4 HOUGHTON MIFFLIN $40.00

0-19-281070-7 OXFORD PB $22.00

Edward J. **Trelawny**

Records of Shelley, Byron, and the Author

An anecdotal memoir by a hanger-on of the great Romantics

EDITED BY DAVID WRIGHT

0-405-09031-5 AYER $36.95

Dorothy **Wordsworth**

The Grasmere Journals

In recent years the singularity of Dorothy Wordsworth's talent has generated new interest

EDITED BY JONATHAN WORDSWORTH

0-19-817001-7 OXFORD $65.00

0-19-283130-5 OXFORD PB $13.95

Journals of Dorothy Wordsworth

Edited by Mary Moorman

0-19-281103-7 OXFORD PB $13.95

Dorothy **Wordsworth** & William **Wordsworth**

Home at Grasmere

Extracts from Dorothy Wordsworth's journal are juxtaposed with the poems William was writing on the days described, to telling effect

EDITED BY CLARK COLETTE

0-14-043136-5 PENGUIN PB $11.95

April 15, 1802: When we were in the woods beyond Gowbarrow Park we saw a few daffodils close to the water-side. We fancied that the lake had floated the seeds ashore, and that the little colony had so sprung up. But as we went along there were more and yet more; and at last, under the boughs of the trees, we saw that there was a long belt of them along the shore, about the breadth of a country turnpike road. I never saw daffodils so beautiful. They grew among the mossy stones about and about them; some rested their heads upon these stones as on a pillow for weariness; and the rest tossed and reeled and danced, and seemed as if they verily laughed with the wind, that blew upon them over the lake; they looked so gay, ever glancing, ever changing.
HOME AT GRASMERE

William **Wordsworth**

The Essential Wordsworth

EDITED BY SEAMUS HEANEY

0-88001-169-6 ECCO PB $14.50

Guide to the Lakes

EDITED BY ERNEST DE SELINCOURT

0-19-281219-X OXFORD PB $14.95

The Letters of William Wordsworth: A New Selection

EDITED BY ALAN G. HILL

0-19-818529-4 OXFORD $45.00

The Oxford Authors: William Wordsworth

An abundant selection of poetry, including the complete 1805 text of *The Prelude*

EDITED BY STEPHEN GILL

0-19-281333-1 OXFORD PB $22.00

Poems

0-679-44369-X EVERYMAN'S $10.95

The Prelude, Or, Growth of a Poet's Mind

The 1805 text, in a revised version of Selincourt's classic edition

EDITED WITH AN INTRODUCTION BY ERNEST DE SELINCOURT

0-19-281074-X OXFORD PB $17.95

The Prelude: A Parallel Text

EDITED BY J.C. MAXWELL

0-14-042214-5 PENGUIN PB $12.95

The Prelude: The Four Texts (1798, 1799, 1805, 1850)
0-14-043369-4 PENGUIN PB $19.95

Selected Prose Writings
EDITED BY JOHN O. HAYDEN
0-14-043292-2 PENGUIN PB $10.95

William **Wordsworth** & Samuel Taylor **Coleridge**

Lyrical Ballads, 1798
The book that launched the Romantic movement in England
EDITED BY W.J. OWEN
0-19-911006-9 OXFORD PB $13.95

Later 19th-Century Poetry

Matthew **Arnold**

Matthew Arnold
EDITED BY MIRIAM ALLOTT
0-19-282273-X OXFORD PB $7.95

The Oxford Authors: Matthew Arnold
This excellent selection shows the many sides of Arnold's accomplishment, both as poet and critic
EDITED BY MIRIAM ALLOTT & ROBERT H. SUGAR
0-19-281376-5 OXFORD PB $19.95

Selected Poems
EDITED BY TIMOTHY PELTASON
0-14-042376-1 PENGUIN PB $9.95

Elizabeth Barrett **Browning**

Aurora Leigh
A "novel in verse" about the life of a woman writer. "One of the longest in the world, and there is not a dead line in it"
—Algernon Swinburne
0-8214-0956-5 OHIO $69.95

Aurora Leigh and Other Poems
0-14-043412-7 PENGUIN PB $11.95

Selected Poems
"In all her poetry from 1844 feminist themes are strong…She wanted, above all, to 'tell the truth' and to tell it in particular for women"
—Margaret Forster
EDITED BY MARGARET FORSTER
0-460-87425-X EVERYMAN'S PB $7.50
0-8018-3754-5 JOHNS HOPKINS PB $15.95

Sonnets from the Portuguese: Illuminated by the Love Letters
EDITED BY JULIA MARKUS
0-88001-451-2 ECCO $22.00

Robert **Browning**

The Complete Works of Robert Browning: With Variant Readings and Annotations
EDITED BY ALLAN DOOLEY AND JOHN BERKEY
0-8214-1137-3 OHIO $65.00

Robert Browning

The Essential Browning
EDITED BY DOUGLAS DUNN
0-88001-195-5 ECCO PB $8.00

Poems
Browning's energy and vast intellectual interests make him perhaps the most engaging, occasionally even shocking, of the major Victorian poets. This excellent two-volume edition includes all of his poems except *The Ring and the Book.* Unfortunately, Volume 2 is out of print

Volume 1
0-14-042259-5 PENGUIN PB $16.95

The Ring and the Book
A long narrative poem told from a series of different viewpoints, reconstructing the events surrounding a 17th-century Italian murder case
EDITED BY RICHARD D. ALTICK
0-14-042294-3 PENGUIN PB $11.95

Robert Browning
EDITED BY ADAM ROBERTS
0-19-254203-6 OXFORD $42.00
0-19-282372-8 OXFORD PB $25.00

Robert Browning: Selected Poetry
0-14-058615-6 PENGUIN PB $10.95

Lewis **Carroll**

Humorous Verse of Lewis Carroll
0-486-20654-8 DOVER PB $9.95

Arthur Hugh **Clough**

Selected Poems
EDITED BY SHIRLEY CHEW
0-85635-622-0 CARCANET PB $12.18

Selected Poems
EDITED BY JIM MCCUE
0-14-042374-5 PENGUIN PB $10.95

Samuel **Ferguson**

Poems of Sir Samuel Ferguson
0-404-13807-1 AMS $43.75

Edward **Fitzgerald**

The Rubaiyat of Omar Khayyam
The classic statement of hedonism that influenced a generation; the sardonic music of Fitzgerald's verse remains impressive
ILLUSTRATED BY EDMUND DULAC
0-8317-1582-0 SMITHMARK $7.98

The Rubaiyat of Omar Khayyam
See also CLASSICAL LITERATURE under PERSIAN LITERATURE in LITERATURE OF EUROPE, AFRICA, AND ASIA
TRANSLATED BY EDWARD FITZGERALD
0-8139-1689-5 VIRGINIA $42.00
0-14-005954-7 PENGUIN PB $11.95

W.S. **Gilbert**

The Bab Ballads
Masterpieces of humorous verse
EDITED BY JAMES ELLIS
0-674-05801-1 HARVARD PB $15.95

Thomas **Hardy**

The Essential Hardy
EDITED BY JOSEPH BRODSKY
0-88001-405-9 ECCO PB $10.00

Thomas Hardy: Selected Poetry
EDITED BY SAMUEL HYNES
0-19-282268-3 OXFORD PB $7.95

Gerard Manley **Hopkins**

Gerard Manley Hopkins
EDITED BY CATHERINE PHILLIPS
0-19-282303-5 OXFORD PB $8.95

The Oxford Authors: Gerard Manley Hopkins
"He wrote religious lyrics that are thoroughly of the 19th-century and yet are unsurpassed by anything written in the great ages of religion"
—Robert Lowell
EDITED BY CATHERINE PHILLIPS
0-19-254190-0 OXFORD PB $15.95

Poems and Prose of Hopkins
EDITED BY W.H. GARDNER
0-14-042015-0 PENGUIN PB $12.95

A.E. **Housman**

Collected Poems of A.E. Housman
Housman's chief work, the nostalgic neoclassical *A Shropshire Lad,* is filled with homoerotic feeling
0-8050-0547-1 HOLT PB $14.95

Rudyard **Kipling**

A Choice of Kipling's Prose
Kipling's verse is more varied, subtle, and politically sophisticated than is generally imagined.
EDITED BY T.S. ELIOT
0-571-14703-8 FABER PB $8.95

Complete Verse
0-385-26089-X ANCHOR PB $17.95

Edward **Lear**

The Complete Nonsense of Edward Lear
Includes "The Pobble Who Has No Toes," "The Dong with the Luminous Nose," and Lear's other great comic creations
0-486-20167-8 DOVER PB $6.95

George **Meredith**

Modern Love
EDITED BY GILLIAN BEER
0-14-038909-1 PENGUIN PB $3.95

Selected Poems
Contains selections from the moving sonnet sequence *Modern Love* — the story of a disintegrating marriage
EDITED BY KEITH HANLEY
0-313-22034-4 GREENWOOD $42.50

Alice C. **Meynell**
Poems
EDITED BY FREDERICK PAGE
0-88355-704-5 HYPERION $27.00

Christina **Rossetti**
A Choice of Christina Rossetti's Verse
Rossetti's odd metrical patterns and hidden refinement have recently stimulated new interest in her work
EDITED BY ELIZABETH JENNINGS
0-571-09018-4 FABER PB $9.95

Poems: Feasts and Fasts
0-679-42908-5 KNOPF $10.95
0-00-627995-3 HARPERCOLLINS PB $6.00

Poems and Prose
EDITED BY JAN MARSH
0-460-87536-1 EVERYMAN'S PB $7.95

Selected Poems
EDITED WITH AN INTRODUCTION BY C.H. SISSON
0-85635-533-X CARCANET PB $16.25

Christina Rossetti

Dante Gabriel **Rossetti**
The Essential Rossetti
EDITED BY JOHN HOLLANDER
0-88001-196-3 ECCO PB $6.00

Robert Louis **Stevenson**
A Child's Garden of Verses
An attractive edition of poetry that has retained undiminished appeal for the young
ILLUSTRATED BY TASHA TUDOR
0-684-20949-7 ATHENEUM $19.00
0-02-788365-5 SIMON & SCHUSTER $14.00

Essays and Poems
EDITED BY CLAIRE HARMAN
0-460-87224-9 EVERYMAN'S PB $7.95

Charles Algernon **Swinburne**
Selected Poems
The great master of English metrics and a lyricist of exceptional morbidity
EDITED BY L.M. FINDLEY
0-85635-728-6 SCHOLARLY PB $17.75

Alfred Lord **Tennyson**
Idylls of the King
The perennially popular poetic retelling of the Arthurian legends
EDITED BY J.M. GRAY
0-14-042253-6 PENGUIN PB $8.95

In Memoriam
Tennyson's masterful account of the cycles of grief and spiritual doubt occasioned by the death of a close friend
EDITED BY ROBERT H. ROSS
0-393-09379-4 NORTON PB $10.95

Poems
EDITED BY W.E. WILLIAMS
0-14-058502-8 VIKING PB $8.95

The Poems of Tennyson
A new 3-volume edition that has been hailed for its scholarship
EDITED BY CHRISTOPHER RICKS
0-520-06012-1 CALIFORNIA $385.00

Selected Poems
EDITED BY MICHAEL MILLGATE
0-19-911056-5 OXFORD PB $12.95

Selected Poems
EDITED BY AIDAN DAY
0-14-044545-5 PENGUIN PB $11.95

Selected Poems
0-486-27282-6 DOVER PB $1.00

Tennyson: A Selected Edition
A comprehensive, annotated selection of Tennyson's major poetry, based on Ricks's acclaimed 3-volume complete edition. Includes the long poems *The Princess, In Memoriam,* and *Idylls of the King* in their entirety, along with a generous gathering of the shorter work
0-520-06588-3 CALIFORNIA $55.00
0-520-06666-9 CALIFORNIA PB $18.95

The Letters of Alfred Lord Tennyson
0-674-52583-3 HARVARD $42.50

Francis **Thompson**
The Hound of Heaven
A classic of fervent although reluctant Catholic spirituality
0-8192-1205-9 MOREHOUSE PB $2.50

Anthologies

W.H. **Auden** &
Norman Holmes **Pearson**, editors
Romantic Poets: Blake to Poe
An outstanding collection, the only part of the multivolume *Portable Poets of the English Language* currently in print
0-14-015052-8 VIKING PB $14.95

Harold **Bloom** & Lionel **Trilling**, editors
Romantic Poetry and Prose
0-19-501615-7 OXFORD PB $23.00

Jennifer **Breen**, editor
Women Romantic Poets, 1785-1832: An Anthology
The full artistic achievement of women Romantic poets revealed for the first time in this new anthology, which presents the work of Joanna Baillie, Jane Taylor, Anna Seward, Hannah More, Charlotte Smith, Anna Letitia Barbauld, and many others
0-460-87078-5 EVERYMAN'S PB $7.95

George **MacBeth**, editor
Victorian Verse
"It is the great and crucial merit of this volume that it changes one's attitude to contemporary poetry, as well as to that of the period it sets out to cover"—Edward Lucie-Smith
0-14-042110-6 PENGUIN PB $10.95

Jerome J. **McGann**, editor
The New Oxford Book of Romantic Period Verse
0-19-214158-9 OXFORD $45.00
0-19-282329-9 OXFORD PB $16.95

Christopher **Ricks**
The New Oxford Book of Victorian Verse
An idiosyncratic and carefully conceived anthology that sheds light on a great many obscure figures and on relatively obscure poems by major poets. "It is the great and crucial merit of this volume that it changes one's attitude to contemporary poetry, as well as to that of the period it sets out to cover"
—Edward Lucie-Smith
0-19-282778-2 OXFORD PB $14.95

David **Wright**, editor
English Romantic Verse
Traces the movement from its 18th-century roots (Thomson, Collins, Cowper) through its major figures, finding room also for such less familiar poets as Elliot, Darley, and Mangan
0-14-042102-5 PENGUIN PB $7.95

19th-Century Drama

By comparison with the Elizabethan and Restoration periods, the theater of Victoria's age has left us a short roster of plays that are still viable. Aside from the comedies of Wilde and the early plays of Shaw (which will be found under Modern English and Irish Drama), the century's chief theatrical legacy was the ever-popular work of Gilbert and Sullivan.

Michael R. **Booth**, editor
The Lights o' London and Other Victorian Plays
Also includes such once-popular favorites as *The Inchcape Bell, Did You Ever Send Your Wife to Camberwell?, The Games of Speculation,* and *The Middleman*
0-19-282736-7 OXFORD PB $11.95

W.S. **Gilbert**
The Complete Plays of Gilbert and Sullivan
0-393-00828-2 NORTON PB $16.95

Henry Arthur **Jones**

Plays

Jones helped to rescue the English theater of his day from trivial melodramas. This volume includes *The Silver King, The Case of Rebellious Susan*, and *The Liars*

EDITED BY RUSSELL JACKSON

0-521-29936-5 CAMBRIDGE PB $22.95

Arthur Wing **Pinero**

Plays

Includes *The Schoolmistress, The Second Mrs. Tanqueray, Trelawny of the Wells,* and *The Thunderbolt*

0521 284406 CAMBRIDGE PB $21.95

Anthologies

Jeffrey N. **Cox**, editor

Seven Gothic Dramas, 1789-1825

Explores the flamboyant entertainments of a little-known period in English drama

See also **ANTHOLOGIES** under **DRAMA** under **THE RESTORATION AND THE 18TH-CENTURY**

0-8214-1065-2 OHIO PB $24.95

Gerald B. **Kauvar** &
Gerald C. **Sorensen**, editors

Nineteenth Century English Verse Drama

0-8386-7631-6 ASSOCIATED UNIVERSITIES....$45.00

George **Rowell**, editor

Nineteenth Century Plays

0-19-281104-5 OXFORD PB $13.95

19th-Century Fiction

Jane **Austen**

Catherine and Other Writings

0-19-282823-1 OXFORD PB $9.95

The Complete Novels, Volume I: Sense and Sensibility, Pride and Prejudice, Mansfield Park

0-679-60025-6 MODERN LIBRARY $22.00

The Complete Novels Volume II: Emma, Northanger Abbey, Persuasion

0-679-60026-4 MODERN LIBRARY $21.00

Emma

"In *Emma* the heroine is made to stand at bay to our adverse judgment through virtually the whole novel, but we are never permitted to close in for the kill—some unnamed quality in the girl, some trait of vivacity or will, erects itself into a moral principle, or at least a vital principle, and frustrates our moral blood-lust" —Lionel Trilling

EDITED BY RONALD BLYTHE

0-14-043010-5 PENGUIN PB $6.95

Emma

EDITED BY FIONA SHAW

0-451-52627-9 NEW AMERICAN LIBRARY PB....$4.95

Emma

EDITED BY JAMES KINSLEY

0-19-282432-5 OXFORD PB $3.95

Jane Austen: The Complete Shorter Works

Splendidly introduced and annotated, this collection gathers important shorter works together for the first time. From the whimsical satires of "Love and Friendship" and the "History of England by a partial, prejudiced and ignorant author" to the unfinished novels "Lady Susan" and "Sanditon," we meet here a new view of Austen: formidably articulate, light-hearted, satirical, and enormously mature

EDITED BY JULIAN THOMPSON

0-19-282284-5 OXFORD PB $17.95

Jane Austen's History of England

By her own admission "a partial, prejudiced, ignorant historian," the future author of *Pride and Prejudice* set out, at 16, to satirize her dull schoolbooks for the amusement of herself and her sister. Includes a complete facsimile along with a typeset version of the text, and Cassandra Austen's illustrations

INTRODUCTON BY A. S. BYATT

1-56512-055-8 ALGONQUIN $14.95

Lady Susan, the Watsons & Sanditon

Three fragmentary novels unpublished in Austen's lifetime but fascinating to enthusiasts of her work

EDITED BY MARGARET DRABBLE

0-14-043102-0 PENGUIN PB $7.95

Mansfield Park

Fanny Price is Austen's most difficult protagonist, and *Mansfield Park* her darkest—but to some readers her finest—novel

EDITED BY TONY TANNER

0-14-043016-4 PENGUIN PB $6.95

Mansfield Park

EDITED BY JAMES KINSLEY

0-19-282757-X OXFORD PB $5.95

Northanger Abbey

A genial parody of Gothic melodrama

EDITED BY ANNE EHRENPRIES

0-8488-1244-1 AMEREON $18.95

Northanger Abbey

EDITED BY MARILYN BUTLER

0-14-043413-5 PENGUIN PB $6.95

Northanger Abbey, Lady Susan, The Watsons & Sanditon

0-19-282758-8 OXFORD PB $4.95

The Oxford Illustrated Jane Austen

All of Austen's major and minor novels as a 6-volume set, with 19th-century illustrations and R.W. Chapman's notes

EDITED BY R.W. CHAPMAN

0-19-254707-0 OXFORD $100.00

0-19-254704-6 OXFORD PB $16.95

The Penguin Complete Novels of Jane Austen

0-14-010649-9 PENGUIN PB $16.95

Persuasion

In Austen's last completed novel she explores emotion (including problems of conscience) without her characteristic skeptical edge

EDITED BY D.W. HARDING

0-140-43005-9 PENGUIN PB $5.95

Persuasion

0-19-282759-6 OXFORD PB $4.50

Pride and Prejudice

In Elizabeth Bennet and Fitzwilliam Darcy, Austen draws a masterful portrait of love as the play of intelligence and good sense

EDITED BY TONY TANNER

0-14-043072-5 PENGUIN PB $7.95

Pride and Prejudice

EDITED BY JAMES KINSLEY

0-19-283225-5 OXFORD PB $10.00

Sanditon and Other Stories

0-679-44719-9 EVERYMAN'S $20.00

Selected Letters, 1796-1817

EDITED BY R.W. CHAPMAN

INTRODUCTION BY MARILYN BUTLER

0-19-281485-0 OXFORD PB $10.95

Sense and Sensibility

In this, her first mature novel, Austen contrasts the personalities of the sisters Elinor and Marianne Dashwood

EDITED BY TONY TANNER

0-14-043425-9 PENGUIN PB $6.95

Sense and Sensibility

0-19-282761-8 OXFORD PB $4.95

Charlotte laughed heartily to think that her husband could not get rid of her, and exultingly said, she did not care how cross he was to her, as they must live together. It was impossible for any one to be more thoroughly good-natured or more determined to be happy than Mrs. Palmer. The studied indifference, insolence, and discontent of her husband gave her no pain; and when he scolded or abused her, she was highly diverted.

"Mr. Palmer is so droll!" said she, in a whisper, to Elinor. "He is always out of humour."

SENSE AND SENSIBILITY

Jane **Austen** & Charlotte **Brontë**

The Juvenilia of Jane Austen and Charlotte Brontë

"These juvenilia are, of course, sometimes crude and sometimes childish. But they also serve to demonstrate their authors' originality and freedom of spirit, their delight in the very process of creation, their changing attitudes towards character and style…Both sets of juvenilia provide us with an extraordinary opportunity to watch the growth and coalescence of the creative consciousness" —Frances Beer

EDITED BY FRANCES BEER

0-14-043267-1 PENGUIN PB $7.95

Mary Elizabeth **Braddon**

Lady Audley's Secret

An ancestor of the modern detective novel, and still fascinating; an evil adventuress, a spectacular fire, murder, and a grisly denouement

EDITED BY DAVID SKILTON

0-19-281741-8 OXFORD PB $8.95

Anne **Brontë**

Agnes Grey

A modest portrait of the life of a 19th-century governess

INTRODUCTION BY ANNE SMITH

0-14-043210-8 PENGUIN PB $7.95

The Brontë sisters

Agnes Grey

EDITED BY ROBERT INGLESFIELD AND HILDA MARSDEN

0-19-282711-1 OXFORD PB $5.95

The Tenant of Wildfell Hall

A Byronic hero and a passionate denunciation of the ravages of drink

EDITED BY G.D. HARGREAVES

INTRODUCTION BY WINIFRED GERIN

0-14-043137-3 PENGUIN PB $6.95

The Tenant of Wildfell Hall

EDITED BY HERBERT ROSENGARTEN AND MARGARET SMITH

0-19-282989-0 OXFORD PB $6.95

Charlotte **Brontë**

High Life in Verdopolis: A Story from the Glass Town Saga

EDITED BY CHRISTINE ALEXANDER

0-7123-0408-8 BRITISH LIBRARY $24.95

Jane Eyre

"One and all are full of praise of this great, unknown genius, which suddenly appeared amongst us. Conjecture as to the authorship ran about like wild-fire. People in London…were astonished and delighted to find that a fresh sensation, a new pleasure, was in reserve for them in the uprising of an author, capable of depicting with accurate and Titanic power the strong, self-reliant, racy, and individual characters which were not, after all, extinct species but lingered still in existence in the North"—Elizabeth Gaskell

EDITED BY Q.D. LEAVIS

0-14-043011-3 PENGUIN PB $5.95

Jane Eyre

0-89966-493-8 BUCCANEER $27.95

0-679-40582-8 EVERYMAN'S $20.00

Jane Eyre

0-19-281513-X OXFORD PB $4.95

The Professor

A novel whose materials were later reworked into the more ambitious *Villette*

0-14-043311-2 PENGUIN PB $7.95

The Professor

EDITED BY HERBERT ROSENGARTEN AND MARGARET SMITH

0-19-282741-3 OXFORD PB $5.95

Shirley

A novel of industrialism and labor strife in the Yorkshire mills; Brontë's realism will surprise some readers of *Jane Eyre*

EDITED BY ANDREW HOOK & JUDITH HOOK

0-14-043095-4 PENGUIN PB $6.95

Shirley

0-19-281562-8 OXFORD PB $6.95

Villette

By many accounts Charlotte Brontë's best novel; a low-keyed and remarkably subtle study of frustrated passion in a Belgian boarding school

INTRODUCTION BY TONY TANNER

0-14-043118-7 PENGUIN PB $9.95

Villette

0-19-281836-8 OXFORD PB $6.95

Charlotte **Brontë** & others

The Brontës: Three Great Novels: Jane Eyre, Wuthering Heights, The Tenant of Wildfell Hall

0-19-282285-3 OXFORD PB $14.95

Emily **Brontë**

Wuthering Heights

EDITED BY DAVID DAICHES

0-14-043001-6 PENGUIN PB $4.95

Wuthering Heights

0-679-40543-7 EVERYMAN'S $17.00

Wuthering Heights

EDITED BY IAN JACK

0-19-282350-7 OXFORD PB $3.95

Samuel **Butler**

Erewhon

A curious satire on Darwinism, industrialism, and other matters, set in an alternate world

0-14-043057-1 PENGUIN PB $9.95

The Way of All Flesh

Perhaps the most harrowing account of father-fixation and Victorian religiosity ever recorded

EDITED BY JAMES COCHRANE

INTRODUCTION BY RICHARD HOGGART

0-14-043012-1 PENGUIN PB $10.95

Lewis **Carroll**

Alice's Adventures in Wonderland

A masterpiece of children's literature, this classic remains fresh and whimsically magical generation after generation

See also **YOUNG ADULT FICTION** in **BOOKS FOR YOUNG READERS**

ILLUSTRATED BY JOHN TENNIEL

0-14-035038-1 PUFFIN PB $2.99

Alice's Adventures in Wonderland & Through the Looking-Glass

See also **YOUNG ADULT FICTION** in **BOOKS FOR YOUNG READERS**

EDITED BY ROGER L. GREEN

ILLUSTRATED BY JOHN TENNIEL

0-19-281620-9 OXFORD PB $4.95

The Collected Works

0-679-42475-X MODERN LIBRARY $21.50

The Hunting of the Snark

EDITED BY R. EUGENE JACKSON & DAVID ELLIS

0-88680-273-3 CLARK PB $3.00

More Annotated Alice

Gardner's original but now out of print *Annotated Alice* has long been a classic; now he has put together an altogether new book to supplement it, with yet more of the strange speculative byways leading off from Lewis Carroll's *Alice* books (whose complete texts are included)

EDITED BY MARTIN GARDNER

0-394-58571-2 RANDOM HOUSE $35.00

Pillow Problems & A Tangled Tale

See also **PUZZLE COLLECTIONS** under **RECREATIONAL MATHEMATICS** under **MATHEMATICS** in **SCIENCE**

0-486-20493-6 DOVER PB $7.95

Lewis Carroll

Wilkie **Collins**

Armadale

Collins's most memorable villainess, Lydia Gwilt, dominates this baroque melodrama involving a pair of long-separated twins and culminating in an experimental madhouse

0-19-281802-3 OXFORD PB $10.95

Blind Love

A neglected novel from Collins's late period

0-486-25189-6 DOVER PB $8.95

The Dead Secret

An early novel of suspense involving a harrowing search for a lost document

0-486-23775-3 DOVER PB $8.95

The Haunted Hotel

A late novella memorable for one of Collins's edgiest adventuresses

0-486-24333-8 DOVER PB $4.95

Hide and Seek

INTRODUCTION BY NORMAN DONALDSON

0-486-24211-0 DOVER PB $8.95

The Law and the Lady

EDITED BY JENNY BOURNE TAYLOR

0-19-282847-9 OXFORD PB $10.95

The Legacy of Cain

0-7509-0453-4 ALAN SUTTON PB $10.95

Wilkie **Collins**

Man and Wife

EDITED BY NORMAN PAGE

0-19-283146-1 OXFORD PB $11.95

The Moonstone

A tale of theft, drugs, an apparently cursed Indian gem, enriched by Collins's knack for Dickensian caricature

See also **PIONEERS AND LANDMARKS** under **RISE OF THE MYSTERY** under **CRIME FICTION** in **POPULAR READING**

0-451-52394-6 NAL $5.95

0-13-600677-9 PRENTICE HALL PB $5.33

The light that streamed from it was like the light of the harvest-moon. When you looked down into the stone, you looked into a yellow deep that drew your eyes into it so that they saw nothing else. It seemed unfathomable; this jewel, that you could hold between your finger and thumb, seemed unfathomable as the heavens themselves.

THE MOONSTONE

The Moonstone

0-19-581378-2 OXFORD PB $4.95

No Name

Often considered Collins's best novel, a protofeminist tale of prim Victorian maidens cast on the mercy of cruel and opportunistic strangers

EDITED BY VIRGINIA BLAIN

0-19-281648-9 OXFORD PB $9.95

Poor Miss Finch

A blind girl and a pair of identical twins who both love her are the principal figures of this late novel

EDITED BY CATHERINE PETERS

0-19-282322-1 OXFORD PB $10.95

Tales of Terror and the Supernatural

EDITED WITH AN INTRODUCTION BY HERBERT VAN THAL

0-486-20307-7 DOVER PB $8.95

The Woman in White

A great novel that is also a landmark in romantic suspense

See also **PIONEERS AND LANDMARKS** under **RISE OF THE MYSTERY** under **CRIME FICTION** in **POPULAR READING**

0-679-40563-1 EVERYMAN'S $20.00

0-14-043096-2 PENGUIN PB $6.95

The Woman in White

EDITED BY JOHN SUTHERLAND

0-19-282403-1 OXFORD PB $6.95

Marie **Corelli**

The Sorrows of Satan: Or the Strange Experience of One Geoffrey Tempest, Millionaire

0-19-283220-4 OXFORD PB $10.95

Charles **Dickens**

"Chesterton asserted that time would show that Dickens was not merely one of the Victorians, but incomparably the greatest English writer of his time; and Shaw coupled his name with that of Shakespeare. It is the conviction of the present writer that both these judgments were justified. Dickens—though he cannot of course pretend to the rank where Shakespeare has few companions—was nevertheless the greatest dramatic writer that the English had had since Shakespeare, and he created the largest and most varied world"—Edmund Wilson in The Wound and the Bow

Barnaby Rudge

The anti-Catholic Gordon riots of 1780 provide the turbulent backdrop for one of Dickens's most neglected novels

0-14-043090-3 PENGUIN PB $8.95

Bleak House

Dicken's assault on the British court system in which he stresses the interconnectedness of all levels of society—from Lord and Lady Deadlock to orphaned (and saintly) Esther Sommerson to Jo the street-sweeper

0-679-40568-2 EVERYMAN'S $23.00

0-393-09332-8 NORTON PB $18.95

Charles Dickens

Bleak House

EDITED BY STEPHEN CHARLES GILL

0-19-282985-8 OXFORD PB $7.95

The Christmas Books

Includes *A Christmas Carol* and *The Chimes*

Volume 1

0-14-043068-7 PENGUIN PB $6.95

Volume 2

0-14-043069-5 PENGUIN PB $8.95

A Christmas Carol

0-14-007120-2 PENGUIN PB $6.95

A Christmas Carol

A new edition of the yuletide favorite with fine watercolor illustrations. Awarded first place in the New York Book Show in 1991 and two critics' prizes at the Bologna Children's Fair. "One of the year's best children's book"—*NY Times*

See also **FICTION** under **BOOKS FOR EIGHTS, NINES, AND UP** in **BOOKS FOR YOUNG READERS**

ILLUSTRATED BY ROBERTO INNOCENTI

0-15-100200-2 CREATIVE EDUCATION $19.95

David Copperfield

0-19-585337-7 OXFORD PB $5.25

Dombey and Son

A somber dramatization of the corrupting influence of money, and—in Florence and Paul Dombey—the transfiguring power of innocence

0-14-043048-2 PENGUIN PB $7.95

Great Expectations

This late masterpiece is, perhaps, Dickens's most penetrating treatment of adolescence

EDITED BY ANGUS CALDER

0-14-043003-2 PENGUIN PB $6.95

Great Expectations

EDITED BY MARGARET CARDWELL AND KATE FLINT

0-19-282926-2 OXFORD PB $5.95

Hard Times

An unusually spare novel of protest against the harshness of utilitarianism and industrialism, as espoused by the humorless schoolmaster Gradgrind and the fraudulent capitalist Bounderby

EDITED BY DAVID CRAIG

0-14-043042-3 PENGUIN PB $5.95

The Life of Our Lord

Originally written as a gift for Dickens's own children and not intended for publication, this book was meant to convey an abiding appreciation of Jesus, of whom Dickens wrote: "No one ever lived, who was so good, so kind, so gentle"

0-8407-9126-7 NELSON $15.99

0-8317-1568-5 SMITHMARK $6.98

Little Dorrit

"The whole book is much gloomier than *Bleak House,* where the fog is external to the characters and represents something removable, the obfuscatory elements of the past. The murk of *Little Dorrit* permeates the souls of the people…The fable is here presented from the point of view of imprisoning states of mind as much as from that of oppressive institutions" —Edmund Wilson

EDITED BY JOHN HOLLOWAY

0-14-043025-3 PENGUIN PB $8.95

Little Dorrit

0-19-281592-X OXFORD PB $5.95

Martin Chuzzlewit

Dickens's "American" novel, today one of his less popular books but nonetheless containing such unforgettable figures as Mr. Pecksniff, Sairey Gamp, and Poll Sweedlepipes

EDITED BY P.N. FURBANK

0-14-043574-3 PENGUIN PB $10.95

Martin Chuzzlewit

0-19-281676-4 OXFORD PB $6.95

The Mystery of Edwin Drood

Dickens's last novel, a melodrama of murder and opium addiction that even in its tantalizingly unfinished rate ranks as one of his most original novels

See also **PIONEERS AND LANDMARKS** under **RISE OF THE MYSTERY** under **CRIME FICTION** in **POPULAR READING**

INTRODUCTION BY ANGUS WILSON

0-88411-276-4 AMEREON $20.95

0-14-043092-X PENGUIN PB $7.95

Nicholas Nickleby

A grim exposé of maltreated schoolboys under the tutelage of the brutal Wackford Squeers and a wonderful evocation of Vincent Crummles's traveling players are the highlights of this homage to the picaresque novel

EDITED BY MICHAEL SLATER

0-14-043113-6 PENGUIN PB $7.95

Nicholas Nickleby
EDITED BY PAUL SCHLICKE
0-19-281794-9 OXFORD PB $6.95

The New Oxford Illustrated Dickens
Oxford offers a handsome complete edition of Dickens' work with illustrations by Phiz, George Cruikshank, and others. It is available as a whole or in individual volumes. Along with those listed below the set includes *Sketches by Boz, The Uncommercial Traveller & Reprinted Pieces, Master Humphrey's Clock & A Child's History of England, Barnaby Rudge, Nicholas Nickleby, American Notes & Pictures from Italy, Christmas Books, Martin Chuzzlewit, The Mystery of Edwin Drood, Hard Times,* and *The Old Curiosity Shop*
0-19-254522-1 OXFORD $240.00

Bleak House
0-19-254503-5 OXFORD $13.95

David Copperfield
0-19-254502-7 OXFORD $13.95

Dombey and Son
0-19-254507-8 OXFORD $13.95

Great Expectations
0-19-254511-6 OXFORD $13.95

Oliver Twist
0-19-254505-1 OXFORD $13.95

Our Mutual Friend
0-19-254510-8 OXFORD $13.95

Little Dorrit
0-19-254512-4 OXFORD $13.95

The Pickwick Papers
0-19-254501-9 OXFORD $13.95

A Tale of Two Cities
0-19-254504-3 OXFORD $13.95

The Old Curiosity Shop
The epitome of Dickens's sentimental strain, featuring the tragic Little Nell and a host of characters, including Mr. Quilp, Dick Swiveller, and Miss Wackles
EDITED BY ANGUS EASSON
0-14-043075-X PENGUIN PB $8.95

Oliver Twist
The novel in which Dickens broke decisively with the good cheer of *The Pickwick Papers*, producing a violent melodrama of child abuse and the criminal underworld
EDITED BY PETER FAIRCLOUGH
0-14-043017-2 PENGUIN PB $6.95

Our Mutual Friend
Dickens's last completed work is perhaps his darkest vision of urban decay and corruption, centering on a garbage heap in which various characters scavenge for hidden treasure
EDITED BY STEPHEN GILL
0-14-043060-1 PENGUIN PB $10.95

Our Mutual Friend
EDITED BY MICHAEL COTSELL
0-19-281795-7 OXFORD PB $6.95

The Pickwick Papers
Dickens's first great comic triumph immediately became part of English literary mythology
EDITED BY ROBERT L. PATTEN
0-14-043078-4 PENGUIN PB $9.95

The Pickwick Papers
EDITED BY JAMES KINSLEY
0-19-281775-2 OXFORD PB $5.95

Selected Short Fiction
A gathering of supernatural tales, impressionistic sketches, and dramatic monologues
EDITED BY DEBORAH THOMAS
0-14-043103-9 PENGUIN PB $7.95

Sikes and Nancy & Other Public Readings
These are Dickens's adaptations of episodes from his novels, which he read to fantastic acclaim in his later years; the nervous exhaustion induced by these readings probably shortened his life
EDITED BY PHILIP COLLINS
0-19-281617-9 OXFORD PB $7.95

A Tale of Two Cities
The famous historical novel of the French Revolution, inspired by Carlyle
EDITED BY GEORGE WOODCOCK
0-14-043054-7 PENGUIN PB $5.95

A Tale of Two Cities
0-19-281771-X OXFORD PB $4.95

Benjamin **Disraeli**

Coningsby
The Tory creed forms the basis for one of the most memorable Victorian political novels
EDITED BY THOM BRAUN
0-14-043192-6 PENGUIN PB $7.95

Sybil
A fresco of social conditions in the 1840s, with a memorable evocation of the Chartist movement
INTRODUCTION BY R.A. BUTLER
0-14-043134-9 PENGUIN PB $9.95

George **Douglas**

The House with Green Shutters
A tale of greed and ambition set in a Scottish village
EDITED BY DOROTHY PARKER
0-14-018278-0 VIKING PB $9.95

Arthur Conan **Doyle**

The Lost World
The scientist-hero Professor Challenger discovers a realm of living dinosaurs
See also EARLY SCIENCE FICTION under SCIENCE FICTION AND FANTASY in POPULAR READING
0-19-283186-0 OXFORD PB $7.95

The Oxford Sherlock Holmes
In 9 volumes; the most complete Holmes available
See also SHERLOCK HOLMES under RISE OF THE MYSTERY under CRIME FICTION in POPULAR READING
0-19-212329-7 OXFORD........................$99.00

George **Du Maurier**

Trilby
The famous tale of the poor artist's model who becomes a singing star under the influence of the sinister Svengali; this international bestseller of its day is also marked by vicious anti-Semitism
0-14-043403-8 PENGUIN PB $7.95

Maria **Edgeworth**

The Absentee
This comic novel about absentee landownership in Ireland was first published in 1812
EDITED WITH AN INTRODUCTION BY W.J. MCCORMACK & KIM WALKER
0-19-281682-9 OXFORD PB $9.95

Belinda
INTRODUCTION BY EVA FIGES
0-460-87228-1 EVERYMAN'S PB $9.95

Castle Rackrent
A rich and boisterous anecdotal picture of the decayed Irish gentry of the 18th-century; a pioneering historical novel, first published in 1800
EDITED BY GEORGE WATSON
0-393-00288-8 NORTON PB........................$6.95

Castle Rackrent
0-19-282394-9 OXFORD PB $7.95

George **Eliot**

Adam Bede
An unflinching depiction of English village life and of the consequences of seduction
INTRODUCTION BY STEPHEN GILL
0-14-043121-7 PENGUIN PB........................$8.95

Daniel Deronda
One of Eliot's masterpieces; Gwendolen Harleth is perhaps her most intriguing heroine
EDITED WITH AN INTRODUCTION BY BARBARA HARDY
0-14-043020-2 PENGUIN PB $7.95

Goodness is a large, often a prospective word; like harvest, which at one stage when we talk of it lies all underground, with an indeterminate future: is the germ prospering in the darkness? at another, it has put forth delicate green blades, and by-and-by the trembling blossoms are ready to be dashed off by an hour of rough wind or rain. Each stage has its peculiar blight, and may have the healthy life choked out of it by a particular action of the foul land which rears or neighbours it, or by damage brought from foulness afar.

DANIEL DERONDA

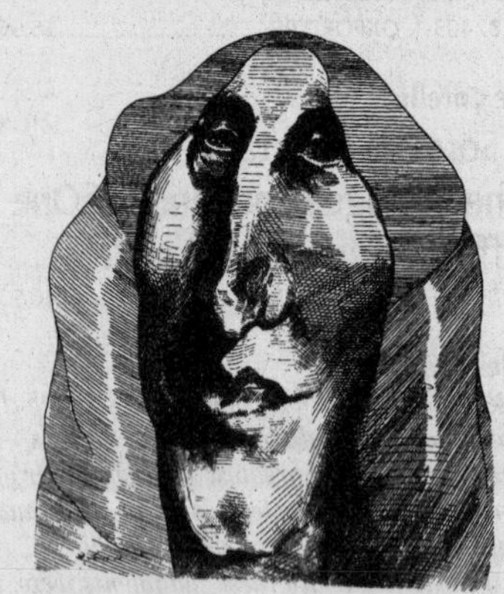

George Eliot

George **Eliot**

Felix Holt, the Radical
George Eliot's most political novel; the crowd scenes are masterful
EDITED BY PETER COVENEY
0-14-043084-9 PENGUIN PB $6.95

The Impressions of Theophrastus Such
Eighteen sketches inspired by the character studies of the ancient Greek Theophrastus
0-460-87550-7 EVERYMAN'S PB $6.95

The Lifted Veil
0-14-016116-3 PENGUIN PB $8.95

Middlemarch
One of the greatest Victorian novels; a magisterial and multilayered recreation of English life
EDITED WITH AN INTRODUCTION BY W.J. HARVEY
0-14-043002-4 PENGUIN PB $6.95

Middlemarch
0-679-40567-4 EVERYMAN'S $22.00
0-679-60019-1 MODERN LIBRARY $19.00
0-393-09210-0 NORTON PB $17.95

The Mill on the Floss
An almost nightmarish evocation of a spirited woman's childhood and its destructive consequences
EDITED BY GORDON S. HAIGHT
0-19-281567-9 OXFORD PB $5.95

Romola
Although somewhat mannered, this novel convincingly recreates Renaissance Florence
EDITED BY ANDREW SANDERS
0-14-043139-X PENGUIN PB $8.95

Scenes from Clerical Life
The unpromising title belies three engaging, realistic tales dealing with such themes as alcoholism and romance among the aged
EDITED BY DAVID LODGE
0-14-043087-3 PENGUIN PB $7.95

Silas Marner
Eliot's most familiar tale, and a high point of 19th-century pastoral fiction
0-14-043030-X PENGUIN PB $6.95

John Meade **Falkner**

The Lost Stradivarius
EDITED BY EDWARD WILSON
0-19-282848-7 OXFORD PB $7.95

Moonfleet
A rousing adventure story about smugglers and an ancient curse, set in Cornwall
0-19-282617-4 OXFORD PB $8.95

Elizabeth **Gaskell**

Cousin Phillis & Other Tales
EDITED BY ANGUS EASSON
0-19-281554-7 OXFORD PB $3.95

Cranford
A charming tale of English village life
EDITED BY ELIZABETH WATSON
0-19-281531-8 OXFORD PB $5.95

Mary Barton
A vivid picture of life in working-class Victorian Manchester
EDITED BY STEPHEN GILL
0-14-043053-9 PENGUIN PB $6.95

The Moorland Cottage and Other Stories
A short novel and eight stories not elsewhere available
EDITED BY SUZANNE LEWIS
0-19-282321-3 OXFORD PB $10.95

My Lady Ludlow and Other Stories
0-19-281838-4 OXFORD PB $9.95

North and South
The story revolves around a contrast between England's bucolic South and the grim industrial conditions of the North
EDITED BY PATRICIA INGHAM
0-14-043424-0 PENGUIN PB $8.95

Ruth
EDITED BY ALAN SHELSTON
0-19-281669-1 OXFORD PB $6.95

Sylvia's Lovers
EDITED BY ANDREW SANDERS
0-19-281571-7 OXFORD PB $8.95

Wives and Daughters
EDITED BY FRANK G. SMITH
INTRODUCTION BY LAURENCE LERNER
0-14-043046-6 PENGUIN PB $9.95

George **Gissing**

After a long period of neglect, George Gissing's powerfully realistic, relentlessly pessimistic novels have been rediscovered.

Born in Exile
EDITED BY DAVID GRYLLS
0-460-87241-9 EVERYMAN'S PB $6.95

The Day of Silence and Other Stories
EDITED BY PIERRE COUSTILLAS
0-460-87242-7 EVERYMAN'S PB $6.95

In the Year of Jubilee
EDITED BY PAUL DELANY
A satirical look at the middle classes
0-460-87533-7 TUTTLE PB $7.95

The Nether World
EDITED BY STEPHEN GILL
0-19-281769-8 OXFORD PB $9.95

New Grub Street
A brilliant and complex novel about literary failure
EDITED BY BERNARD BERGONZI
0-14-043032-6 PENGUIN PB. $11.95

New Grub Street
EDITED BY JOHN GOODE
0-19-282963-7 OXFORD PB $6.95

The Odd Women
A unusually subtle view of London society that has stirred much recent interest among feminist critics
INTRODUCTION BY ELAINE SHOWALTER
0-452-01014-4 NEW AMERICAN LIBRARY PB $7.00

The Odd Women
0-14-043379-1 PENGUIN PB $10.95

The Private Papers of Henry Ryecroft
Gissing's fictional alter ego muses on books, poverty, solitude, and nature
0-7812-7535-0 REPRINT SERVICES $79.00

Sleeping Fires
0-8032-7011-9 NEBRASKA PB $7.95

H. Rider **Haggard**

Allan Quartermain
The hunter discovers a lost white race in central Africa
EDITED BY DENNIS BUTTS
0-19-282297-7 OXFORD PB $8.95

Ayesha: The Return of She
A Himalayan reincarnation of She-Who-Must-Be-Obeyed
0-486-23649-8 DOVER PB $6.95

King Solomon's Mines
Haggard's first novel, introducing the character of the hunter Allan Quartermain, made him one of the most popular writers of his day. The archetypal British imperialist adventure story, and perhaps Haggard's most entertaining book
EDITED BY DENNIS BUTTS
0-19-282204-7 OXFORD PB $4.95

She
This mystical fantasy first published in 1887, about an immortal woman in a lost African city, retains its fascination far more than any of Haggard's other works
0-19-282767-7 OXFORD PB $6.95

Thomas **Hardy**

A Changed Man
A collection of twelve tales of fate originally published in magazines. Hardy called them "minor novels"
0-404-60748-9 AMS $38.00

Desperate Remedies
A strongly plotted suspense novel, enriched by Hardy's eye for the detail of English rural life
0-404-60745-4 AMS $32.50

The Distracted Preacher and Other Tales
0-14-043124-1 PENGUIN PB $9.95

Far from the Madding Crowd
Perhaps Hardy's most affecting and explosive mixture of tragedy and comedy; the troubled love affair of the hero, Gabriel Oak, is the focus for a melodrama of seduction and desertion, set against the eternal cycles of the country year
EDITED BY RONALD BLYTHE
0-14-043126-8 PENGUIN PB $5.95

Far from the Madding Crowd
0-679-40576-3 EVERYMAN'S $20.00

The Hand of Ethelberta
The tale of an opportunistic yet ultimately loyal adventuress, who begins humbly and ends as the wife of a rakish aristocrat
0-404-60746-2 AMS $32.50

Jude the Obscure
Hardy's bleakest and greatest novel of fate
0-14-043131-4 PENGUIN PB $6.95

A Laodicean
A minor novel about the dying aristocracy, giving way to the onslaught of a new generation of self-made men
INTRODUCTION BY JANE GATEWOOD
0-19-282783-9 OXFORD PB $8.95

Life's Little Ironies
A collection of short stories, some grimly fatalistic, others broadly comic
0-19-2831-77-1 OXFORD PB $7.95

The Mayor of Casterbridge
One of Hardy's masterpieces, and perhaps his most purely tragic novel
0-14-043125-X PENGUIN PB $6.95

A Pair of Blue Eyes
A love triangle set in Cornwall, in which the heroine's innocence ironically leads to tragedy
EDITED BY ROGER EBBATSON
0-14-043266-3 PENGUIN PB $6.95

The Return of the Native
Egdon Heath is one of Hardy's most striking pieces of landscape painting, providing a brooding backdrop for the story of Clym Yeobright and Eustacia Vye
0-14-043122-5 PENGUIN PB $7.95

Tess of the d'Urbervilles
A harrowing novel of seduction and abandonment. Tess is Hardy's most memorable heroine
EDITED BY A. ALVAREZ & DAVID SKILTON
1-393-95903-1 NORTON PB $11.95

Thomas Hardy

The Trumpet-Major
A suspenseful but ultimately happy love story, set during the reign of George III, and a welcome relief from Hardy's habitual fatalism
0-14-043273-6 PENGUIN PB $6.95

Under the Greenwood Tree
The first of Hardy's Wessex novels is a largely comic peasant love story
0-14-043123-3 PENGUIN PB $5.95

The Well-Beloved
An artist pursues his ideal woman through three generations
EDITED BY TOM HETHERINGTON
0-19-281721-3 OXFORD PB $5.95

Wessex Tales
Six stories, including "The Three Strangers," "The Withered Arm," "Interlopers at the Knap," "Fellow Townsmen," and "The Distracted Preacher"
EDITED BY KATHRYN R. KING
0-19-282720-0 OXFORD PB $4.95

The Woodlanders
A tale of destructive passions, set in Dorsetshire
EDITED BY DALE KRAMER
0-19-281600-4 OXFORD PB $5.95

James **Hogg**

The Private Memoirs and Confessions of a Justified Sinner
First published in 1824, this morbidly exact portrait of a self-righteous religious fanatic and his diabolical alter ego is surprisingly modern in its depiction of alienation and split personality
EDITED BY JOHN WAIN
0-14-043198-5 PENGUIN PB $8.95

Anthony **Hope**

Rupert of Hentzau
A sequel to *The Prisoner of Zenda*
0-89966-227-7 BUCCANEER $21.95

W.H. **Hudson**

Green Mansions
The tragic romance of Rima the bird-girl in the jungles of Venezuela
INTRODUCTION BY N.R. TEITEL
0-486-25993-5 DOVER PB $7.95

Jerome K. **Jerome**

Three Men in a Boat
A popular comic novel about a trio of young men idling on the Thames
0-14-001213-3 VIKING PB $6.95

Three Men on the Bummel
A sequel to *Three Men in a Boat*
0-86299-029-7 ALAN SUTTON PB $8.00

Charles **Kingsley**

Alton Locke, Tailor and Poet: An Autobiography
A fictional exposition of Kingsley's doctrine of Christian socialism
EDITED BY ELIZABETH A. CRIPPS
0-403-01056-X SCHOLARLY $39.00

The Water Babies
A favorite children's book of the Victorian era
0-14-035035-7 PUFFIN PB $2.95

The Water Babies
EDITED BY BRIAN ALDERSON
0-19-282238-1 OXFORD PB $7.95

Rudyard **Kipling**

Captains Courageous
0-88411-818-5 AMEREON $18.95
0-451-51751-2 NEW AMERICAN LIBRARY PB $2.95

Collected Stories
0-679-43592-1 KNOPF $23.00

The Day's Work
Twelve stories from the 1890s, written at the height of Kipling's powers and demonstrating the range of his subject matter. Includes "The Bridge-Builders," "The Tomb of His Ancestors," ".007," "The Brushwood Boy," and others
EDITED BY THOMAS PINNEY
0-19-281714-0 OXFORD PB $7.95

The Jungle Books
The saga of the lost boy Mowgli and his animal brothers, and other tales
EDITED BY DANIEL KARLIN
0-14-018316-7 PENGUIN PB $7.95

Just So Stories
Animal fables that retain their magic
EDITED WITH AN INTRODUCTION BY PETER LEVI
0-679-41797-4 KNOPF $12.95

Just So Stories
See also **FICTION** under **BOOKS FOR EIGHTS, NINES, AND UP** in **BOOKS FOR YOUNG READERS**
0-688-13957-4 MORROW $22.00

The Light that Failed
0-14-018512-7 PENGUIN PB $8.95

The Man Who Would Be King & Other Stories
A good selection containing many of Kipling's most famous stories
EDITED BY LOUIS L. CORNELL
0-19-281674-8 OXFORD PB $7.95

Plain Tales from the Hills
The early tales that made Kipling famous
EDITED BY H.R. WOUDHUYSEN
0-19-281652-7 OXFORD PB $6.95

Puck of Pook's Hill
A fantasy journey through English history
EDITED BY SARAH H. WINTLE
0-14-018353-1 PENGUIN PB $9.95

Rewards and Fairies
A sequel to *Puck of Pook's Hill*
EDITED BY ROGER LEWIS
0-14-018437-6 PENGUIN PB $8.95

Selected Stories
0-460-87220-6 EVERYMAN'S PB $8.95

Traffics and Discoveries
EDITED BY SARAH WINTLE
0-14-018375-2 PENGUIN PB $9.95

Joseph Sheridan **Le Fanu**

"He took great pleasure in ghost stories, and was fascinated by hints of the supernatural... He was a writer of remarkable power in creating suspense, at his best a master of plot, and the creator of some of the most satisfying villains in Victorian literature."—Julian Symons

Best Ghost Stories
Includes "Carmilla" (one of the best—and most erotic—of vampire stories) and the brief shocker "Green Tea," among others
See also **SUPERNATURAL FANTASY AND HORROR** under **SCIENCE FICTION AND FANTASY** in **POPULAR READING**
EDITED BY E.F. BLEILER
0-486-20415-4 DOVER PB $8.95

Ghost Stories & Mysteries
See also **SUPERNATURAL FANTASY AND HORROR** under **SCIENCE FICTION AND FANTASY** in **POPULAR READING**
EDITED WITH AN INTRODUCTION BY E.F. BLEILER
0-486-20715-3 DOVER PB $8.95

Joseph Sheridan **Le Fanu**

In a Glass Darkly

EDITED BY ROBERT TRACY

0-19-282805-3 OXFORD PB $10.95

Uncle Silas

A terrifying novel of a young girl in the hands of a ruthless and greedy relative

See also **PIONEERS AND LANDMARKS** under **RISE OF THE MYSTERY** under **CRIME FICTION** in **POPULAR READING**

EDITED BY W.J. MCCORMACK

0-19-281541-5 OXFORD PB $9.95

Wylder's Hand

See also **PIONEERS AND LANDMARKS** under **RISE OF THE MYSTERY** under **CRIME FICTION** in **POPULAR READING**

0-405-09246-6 AYER $87.95

George **MacDonald**

At the Back of the North Wind

Part children's story, part religious meditation, with indelible descriptions of nature

1-55661-196-X BETHANY $10.99

0-14-035030-6 VIKING PB $3.50

Lilith

0-8028-6061-3 EERDMANS PB $8.00

Phantastes

0-8028-6060-5 EERDMANS PB $8.00

Arthur **Machen**

The Great God Pan

Occult fiction by a true believer

0-8369-3628-0 BOOKS FOR LIBRARIES $24.95

Charles **Maturin**

Melmoth the Wanderer

A Gothic novel of diabolical wanderings that reads in parts like a fever dream

EDITED BY DOUGLAS GRANT

0-19-282199-7 OXFORD PB $9.95

Frederick **Marryat**

Mr. Midshipman Easy

The first of Marryat's classic sea stories (which are unfortunately out of print), which have greatly influenced Patrick O'Brian

0-848-81678-1 AMEREON $22.95

George **Meredith**

The Egoist

Probably Meredith's masterpiece, featuring the inimitably vacuous Willoughby Patterne, of whom the most complimentary thing that can be said is "he has a leg"

EDITED BY MARGARET HARRIS

0-393-09171-6 NORTON PB $14.95

0-19-28187-1 OXFORD PB $9.95

Merlin

0-060-9183-5 HARPER & ROW PB $15.00

George **Moore**

Esther Waters

This story of the wretched life of a servant girl seduced and abandoned is a landmark of English naturalism

EDITED BY DAVID SKILTON

0-19-281578-4 OXFORD PB $9.95

William **Morris**

News from Nowhere

Morris was a Victorian Renaissance man, a fine poet, a major innovator in visual design, and a tireless socialist-activist. This 1891 novel describes an ideal socialist community

See also **CLASSICS** under **POLITICAL THOUGHT** in **SOCIAL STUDIES**

0-7100-6756-9 ROUTLEDGE PB $14.95

Arthur **Morrison**

A Child of the Jago

Slum life in the streets of East London; first published in 1896

0-89733-392-6 ACADEMY CHICAGO PB $10.00

The Hole in the Wall

Another of Morrison's explorations of the lives of London's poorest

0-89733-393-4 BOYDELL & BREWER PB $10.00

Tales of Mean Streets

0-8369-3633-7 AYER $17.00

John Henry **Newman**

Loss and Gain

A fictionalized retelling of Newman's conversion to Catholicism

EDITED WITH AN INTRODUCTION BY ALAN G. HILL

0-19-281687-X OXFORD PB $6.95

Margaret **Oliphant**

A Beleaguered City & Other Stories

The title novella is a haunting supernatural story about the dead coming to life

EDITED BY MERRYN WILLIAMS

0-19-281835-X OXFORD PB $7.95

Salem Chapel: Chronicles of Carlingford

INTRODUCTION BY PENELOPE FITZGERALD

0-14-016152-X OLYMPIC PB $2.98

Baroness **Orczy**

The Scarlet Pimpernel

The stirring adventures of an English aristocrat during the French Revolution

0-451-52315-6 NEW AMERICAN LIBRARY PB $4.95

Ouida

Under Two Flags

0-19-282328-0 OXFORD PB $12.95

Walter **Pater**

Marius the Epicurean

An elaborately written philosophical novel of ancient Rome which incorporates a retelling of Apuleius' story of Cupid and Psyche

EDITED BY MICHAEL LEVY

0-948166-02-9 DUFOUR PB $18.95

Thomas Love **Peacock**

Nightmare Abbey & Crotchet Castle

Unique, good-natured satirical novels in dialogue form, featuring a cast of memorably eccentric characters, some of them modeled on famous acquaintances like Shelley and Byron

0-14-043045-8 PENGUIN PB $10.95

Thomas Love Peacock

Mark **Rutherford**

Clara Hopgood

EDITED BY LORRAINE DAVIES

0-460-87771-2 EVERYMAN'S PB $7.95

Walter **Scott**

The Black Dwarf

0-231-08474-9 COLUMBIA $39.50

The Bride of Lammermoor

EDITED BY FIONA ROBERTSON

0-19-281791-4 OXFORD PB $8.95

The Heart of Midlothian

The tragic story of Effie Deans is the center of this most widely praised of Scott's novels, remarkable for its portrait of humble Scottish life in the 18th-century

EDITED BY CLARE LAMOT

0-19-281583-0 OXFORD PB $11.95

The Heart of Mid-Lothian

EDITED BY TONY INGLIS

0-14-043129-2 PENGUIN PB $11.95

Ivanhoe

The famous novel of England under Norman rule

EDITED BY A.N. WILSON

0-14-043143-8 PENGUIN PB $7.95

Ivanhoe

EDITED BY IAN DUNCAN

0-19-283172-0 OXFORD PB $5.95

Kenilworth

0-231-08472-2 COLUMBIA $45.00

Old Mortality

A novel concerning the Covenanters' rebellion of 1685

EDITED BY ANGUS CALDER

0-14-043098-9 PENGUIN PB $6.95

Quentin Durward

0-19-282658-1 OXFORD PB $11.95

Redgauntlet

A novel of Jacobite conspiracy that includes the famous "Wandering Willie's Tale"

EDITED BY KATHRYN SUTHERLAND

0-19-281668-3 OXFORD PB $7.95

Rob Roy
0-679-44362-2 EVERYMAN'S $20.00
0-460-87594-9 EVERYMAN'S PB $7.95
0-14-043554-9 PENGUIN PB $6.95

Waverley
The novel that initiated Scott's long series of historical romances
0-14-043071-7 PENGUIN PB............................$8.95

Mary **Shelley**

Frankenstein
Those who know the story only from the film versions will be amazed by the depth and sophistication of the novel

See also **EARLY SCIENCE FICTION** under **SCIENCE FICTION AND FANTASY** in **POPULAR READING**

EDITED BY MAURICE HINDLE
0-679-40999-8 EVERYMAN'S $15.00
0-553-21247-8 BDD PB $2.95
0-14-043362-7 PENGUIN PB............................$6.95

It was on a dreary night of November, that I beheld the accomplishment of my toils. With an anxiety that almost amounted to agony, I collected the instruments of life around me, that I might infuse a spark of being into the lifeless thing that lay at my feet. It was already one in the morning; the rain pattered dismally against the panes, and my candle was nearly burnt out, when, by the glimmer of the half-extinguished light, I saw the dull yellow eye of the creature open; it breathed hard, and a convulsive motion agitated its limbs.
FRANKENSTEIN

The Last Man
EDITED BY MORTON D. PALEY
0-19-283152-6 OXFORD PB............................$10.95

The Last Man
An odd, variegated account of a worldwide plague

See also **EARLY SCIENCE FICTION** under **SCIENCE FICTION AND FANTASY** in **POPULAR READING**

0-8032-5182-3 NEBRASKA PB............................$5.95

Robert Louis **Stevenson**

The Black Arrow: A Tale of the Two Roses
Vigorous adventure tale of medieval England
ILLUSTRATED BY N.C. WYETH
0-684-18877-5 ATHENEUM............................$25.00
0-8049-0020-5AIRMONT PB $2.95

Catriona
1-86046-012-7 HARPERCOLLINS PB $12.00

The Complete Shorter Fiction
9-992-93745-9 CARROLL & GRAF $38.00

Dr. Jekyll and Mr. Hyde
One of the most controlled and powerful of Stevenson's works
EDITED BY JENN CALDER
0-14-043117-9 PENGUIN PB $6.95

Kidnapped
0-002730-17-0 HARPERCOLLINS PB $12.00

The Master of Ballantrae
Stevenson's most complex novel experiments with point of view and chronology to tell an already fractured story of conflict between two brothers
EDITED BY EMMA LETLY
0-19-281635-7 OXFORD PB $6.95

Treasure Island
The novel that revolutionized popular fiction by inventing a more realistic style of adventure story
EDITED BY EMMA LETLEY
0-19-281681-0 OXFORD PB............................$5.95

Weir of Hermiston & Other Stories
Many consider *Weir of Hermiston*, unfinished at the author's death, to be Stevenson's finest work
EDITED BY PAUL BINDING
0-14-043138-1 PENGUIN PB............................$10.95

Robert Louis **Stevenson** & Lloyd **Osborne**

The Wrong Box
0-19-282426-0 OXFORD PB $8.95

Bram **Stoker**

Dracula
The definitive literary incarnation of the undead

See also **SUPERNATURAL FANTASY AND HORROR** under **SCIENCE FICTION AND FANTASY** in **POPULAR READING**

EDITED BY A.N. WILSON
0-19-281598-9 OXFORD PB $4.95

Robert Smith **Surtees**

Mr. Sponge's Sporting Tour
ILLUSTRATED BY JOHN LEECH
INTRODUCTION BY JOYCE CAREY
0-7022-1419-1 UNIV OF QUEENSLAND $27.95

Mary **Taylor**

Miss Miles: Or, A Tale of Yorkshire Life 60 Years Ago
0-19-506492-5 OXFORD PB............................$11.95

William Makepeace **Thackeray**

The Book of Snobs
EDITED BY JOHN SUTHERLAND
0-86299-636-8ALAN SUTTON PB $9.50

The History of Henry Esmond
A historical novel of the early 18th-century
EDITED BY JOHN SUTHERLAND
0-14-043049-0 PENGUIN PB $7.95

The History of Pendennis
A novel of London life, much influenced by Fielding and containing many autobiographical elements
EDITED BY DONALD HAWES
INTRODUCTION BY J.M. STEWART
0-14-043076-8 PENGUIN PB $7.95

The Memoirs of Barry Lyndon
The life of an Irish adventurer, source of the Stanley Kubrick film
EDITED BY ANDREW SANDERS
0-19-281667-5 OXFORD PB $8.95

The Newcomes: The Memoirs of a Most Respectable Family
0-19-283173-9 OXFORD PB............................$13.95

Vanity Fair
By far the most popular of Thackeray's novels: Becky Sharp remains one of the great comic creations of the 19th-century
EDITED BY J.M. STEWART
0-14-043035-0 PENGUIN PB............................$8.95

Vanity Fair
0-679-40566-6 EVERYMAN'S $20.00

Anthony **Trollope**

The Palliser Novels
Trollope's six-volume panorama of the political life of Victorian England is now available in an illustrated set from Oxford. The Palliser novels chronicle the upper echelons of society with meticulous realism and unwavering narrative verve
0-19-520901-X OXFORD............................$120.00

Can You Forgive Her?
EDITED BY STEPHEN WALL
0-14-043086-5 PENGUIN PB $10.95

Phineas Finn
0-14-043085-7 PENGUIN PB............................$6.95

The Eustace Diamonds
0-14-043832-7 PENGUIN PB............................$8.95

Phineas Redux
0-14-043833-5 PENGUIN PB............................$8.95

The Prime Minister
0-14-043837-8 PENGUIN PB............................$9.95

The Duke's Children
0-14-043843-2 PENGUIN PB $9.95

Anthony **Trollope**

The American Senator
An American politician visits, and is comically puzzled by English social and political mores
EDITED WITH AN INTRODUCTION BY JOHN HALPERIN
0-19-281739-6 OXFORD PB $8.95

An Autobiography
0-14-043811-4 PENGUIN PB $9.95

Ayala's Angel
A young girl must choose among three suitors, each with his own disadvantages
0-14-043845-9 PENGUIN PB............................$8.95

The Belton Estate
0-14-043819-X PENGUIN PB............................$8.95

The Bertrams
0-14-043807-6 PENGUIN PB............................$8.95

Anthony Trollope

Anthony **Trollope**

Can You Forgive Her?
0-19-520895-1 OXFORD $16.95

Castle Richmond
0-14-043808-4 PENGUIN PB $9.95

The Claverings
A novel of conflicting choices in love, often accounted one of Trollope's best
EDITED WITH AN INTRODUCTION BY DAVID SKILTON
0-19-281727-2 OXFORD PB $8.95

Collected Short Stories
0-405-14117-3 AYER $30.00

The Complete Short Stories
Volumes 1 and 3 in this series are out of print

Volume 2
Editors and Writers
0-912646-57-8 TEXAS A & M....................$17.50

Volume 4
Courtship and Marriage
0-912646-75-6 A&M....................$17.50

Dr. Thorne
0-14-043326-0 PENGUIN PB $10.95

An Editor's Tales
0-14-043828-9 PENGUIN PB $7.95

The Fixed Period
0-14-043849-1 PENGUIN PB....................$8.95

The Golden Lion of Granpere
0-14-043831-9 PENGUIN PB $6.95

Harry Heathcote of Gangoil: A Tale of Australian Bush Life
A novella of Australian bush life, with a hero more complex than he at first appears
0-14-043835-1 PENGUIN PB $6.95

He Knew He Was Right
A novel of obsessive jealousy and the disintegration of a marriage
0-14-043826-2 PENGUIN PB $9.95

Is He Popenjoy?
0-19-250492-4 OXFORD $7.50

John Caldigate
A man who made his fortune in Australian gold fields is threatened by a scandal out of his past
0-14-043841-6 PENGUIN PB....................$8.95

The Kellys and the O'Kellys: Or Landlords and Tenants
An early novel of Irish life
0-14-043801-7 PENGUIN PB....................$8.95

La Vendee: An Historical Romance
0-405-14122-X AYER $105.00

Lady Anna
0-486-24669-8DOVER PB $8.95

The Landleaguers
0-19-282891-6 OXFORD PB....................$10.95

Marion Fay
0-14-043848-3 PENGUIN PB $9.95

Miss Mackenzie
0-14-043818-1 PENGUIN PB....................$8.95

Mr. Scarborough's Family
0-14-043850-5 PENGUIN PB....................$8.95

Nina Balatka
0-14-043820-3 PENGUIN PB....................$8.95

An Old Man's Love
0-14-043852-1 PENGUIN PB $6.95

Orley Farm
An intricate plot revolving around a complex law case and troubled family relations. Lady Mason is among Trollope's most successful female characters
EDITED BY DAVID SKILTON
0-19-281713-2 OXFORD PB $9.95

Rachel Ray
0-486-23930-6 DOVER PB....................$7.95
0-14-043815-7 PENGUIN PB $7.95

Ralph the Heir
0-14-043830-0 PENGUIN PB $9.95

Sir Harry Hotspur of Humblethwaite
0-486-24953-0 DOVER PB....................$6.95

The Struggles of Brown, Jones, and Robinson: By One of the Firm
0-14-043813-0 PENGUIN PB $7.95

Tales of All Countries
0-14-043810-6 PENGUIN PB $6.95

The Three Clerks
A novel of civil-service life
0-14-043805-X PENGUIN PB....................$8.95

The Vicar of Bullhampton
A heroic clergyman attempts to clear an innocent man charged with murder
0-14-043827-0 PENGUIN PB....................$8.95

The Way We Live Now
One of Trollope's darkest novels: a panoramic fictional overview of English life, rural and urban, high and low, with a plot that moves easily from business and politics to romance
EDITED BY JOHN SUTHERLAND
0-19-281576-8 OXFORD PB....................$10.95

Oscar **Wilde**

Complete Short Fiction
EDITED BY IAN SMALL
0-14-043423-2 PENGUIN PB $9.95

The Complete Shorter Fiction of Oscar Wilde
EDITED BY ISOBEL M. MURRAY
0-19-281500-8 OXFORD PB....................$5.95

Lord Arthur Savile's Crime & Other Stories
Also includes "The Canterville Ghost" and such morbid children's stories as "The Happy Prince" and "The Birthday of the Infanta"
0-14-001021-1 VIKING PB $6.95

The Oxford Authors: Oscar Wilde
A large-scale collection that includes *The Picture of Dorian Gray, Lady Windermere's Fan, The Importance of Being Earnest,* "The Critic as Artist," "The Ballad of Reading Goal," as well as other, less familiar works
EDITED BY ISOBEL MURRAY
0-19-281978-X OXFORD PB....................$19.95

The Picture of Dorian Gray
A masterpiece that examines the relationship between art and artist, the muse and inspirations's material
EDITED BY PETER ACKROYD
0-14-043187-X PENGUIN PB $6.95

The Picture of Dorian Gray
0-679-60001-9 MODERN LIBRARY....................$13.50

Plays, Prose Writings, and Poems
EDITED BY ANTHONY FOTHERGILL
0-460-87655-4 EVERYMAN'S PB $8.95

The Portable Oscar Wilde
Includes *The Picture of Dorian Gray, De Profundis, Salome, The Importance of Being Earnest,* selections from three comedies, letters, reviews, poems, "Phrases and Philosophies for the Young," and "The Critic as Artist"
See also **THE EARLY 20TH-CENTURY** under **20TH-CENTURY BRITISH AND IRISH DRAMA**
EDITED BY STANLEY WEINTRAUB
0-14-015093-5 VIKING PB $14.95

Anthony **Trollope**
In these, the Barsetshire novels, Trollope invented a wholly fictional yet beautifully complete West Country. "I had it all in my mind," he wrote, "its roads and railroads, its towns and parishes, its members of Parliament, and the different hunts which rode over it."

The Warden
0-14-043214-0 PENGUIN PB....................$8.95

Barchester Towers
EDITED BY JAMES R. KINCAID
ILLUSTRATED BY EDWARD ARDIZZONE
0-19-281507-5 OXFORD PB $4.95

Doctor Thorne
EDITED BY DAVID SKILTON
0-19-281508-3 OXFORD PB....................$7.95

Framley Parsonage
0-14-043809-2 PENGUIN PB....................$5.95

The Small House at Allington
0-19-281552-0 OXFORD PB....................$6.95

The Last Chronicle of Barset
EDITED BY PETER FAIRCLOUGH
0-14-043024-5 PENGUIN PB $9.95

Henry **Wood**

East Lynne
First published in 1861, this intense melodrama of illicit passion and motherly love became one of the most popular stories of the 19th-century
EDITED BY SALLY MITCHELL
0-8135-1042-2 RUTGERS $15.00

East Lynne
0-460-87430-6 EVERYMAN'S PB $8.95

19th-Century Prose

The ambitious mid-19th-century pundits—Carlyle, Mill, Arnold, Ruskin, and Pater—have aptly been called "Victorian Sages," writers who included everything within their purview. They were literary critics, moralists, sociologists, economists, whose interests ranged from the culture of the urban factory to the craftsmanship of the Gothic cathedral.

Unlike modern cultural critics, they were unhampered by the restraints of academic specialization; seeing human culture as ultimately seamless, they felt a responsibility to confront it as a whole rather than in fragments.

Matthew **Arnold**

Culture and Anarchy

An attack on the narrow-minded cultural provincialism that Arnold labeled "philistine"

0-300-05866-7 YALE $35.00
0-300-05867-5 YALE PB $14.00
0-521-09103-9 CAMBRIDGE PB $16.95

The Letters of Matthew Arnold

0-8139-1651-8 VIRGINIA $60.00

Selected Prose

EDITED BY P.J. KEATING
0-14-043058-X PENGUIN PB $12.95

Jane **Austen**

Jane Austen's Letters

0-19-811764-7 OXFORD $49.95

Hilaire **Belloc**

The Path to Rome

An account of Belloc's journey from France to Rome on foot. In later years he wrote, "I hate writing. I wouldn't have written a word if I could have helped it. I only wrote for money. *The Path to Rome* is the only book I ever wrote for love"

See also **EUROPE** under **TRAVEL LITERATURE** in **FOOD, TRAVEL, AND LEISURE**

0-89526-784-5
REGIONAL LABORATORY FOR EDUCATION PB ... $8.95

Hilaire Belloc

Thomas **Carlyle**

The French Revolution

A great work of literature and history

See also **THE REVOLUTION: 1789-1799** under **THE FRENCH REVOLUTION AND NAPOLEON** in **WORLD HISTORY AND CURRENT AFFAIRS**

EDITED BY K.J. FIELDING & DAVID SORENSEN
0-19-281843-0 OXFORD PB $14.95

His hands are tied, his head bare; the fatal moment is come. He advances to the edge of the Scaffold, his face very red, and says: 'Frenchmen, I die innocent: it is from the Scaffold and near appearing before God that I tell you so. I pardon by enemies; I desire that France—' A General on horseback, Santerre or another, prances out, with uplifted hand: *'Tambours!'* The drums drown the voice. 'Executioners, do your duty!' The Executioners, desperate lest themselves be murdered (for Santerre and his Armed Ranks will strike, if they do not), seize the hapless Louis: six of them desperate, him singly desperate, struggling there; and bind him to their plank. Abbé Edgeworth, stopping, bespeaks him: 'Son of Saint Louis, ascend to Heaven.' The Axe clanks down; a King's Life is shorn away. It is Monday, the 21st of January 1793. He was aged Thirty-eight years four months and twenty-eight days.

THE FRENCH REVOLUTION

On Heroes, Hero-Worship and the Heroic in History

First delivered as a series of lectures in 1840, included here are essays on Dante, Rousseau, Cromwell, and Napoleon

EDITED BY CARL NIEMEYER
0-8032-5030-4 NEBRASKA PB $12.00

Past and Present

"It is a moral, political, historical, and a most questionable red hot indignant thing," Carlyle wrote of this volume, "for my heart is sick to look at the things now going on in England." Carlyle's principal contemporary social criticism, first published in 1843

See also **PROTEST, REFORM, AND THE NEW ECONOMIC THOUGHT** under **THE 19TH-CENTURY AND THE INDUSTRIAL REVOLUTION** under **GREAT BRITAIN AND IRELAND** in **WORLD HISTORY AND CURRENT AFFAIRS**

EDITED BY RICHARD D. ALTICK
0-8147-0562-6 NYU PB $16.00

Sartor Resartus

Carlyle's spiritual autobiography, written in a powerful metaphorical style

EDITED BY PETER SABOR & KERRY MCSWEENEY
0-19-281757-4 OXFORD PB $8.95

Selected Writings

In the highly rhetorical prose of such works as *Chartism* and *The French Revolution* (excerpted here), Carlyle established himself as a kind of official moral opposition to his era. The excitement and power of his finest works exerted a profound influence on writers as diverse as Mill and Emerson, Dickens and George Eliot, Thackeray and Whitman

See also **PROTEST, REFORM, AND THE NEW ECONOMIC THOUGHT** under **THE 19TH-CENTURY AND THE INDUSTRIAL REVOLUTION** under **GREAT BRITAIN AND IRELAND** in **WORLD HISTORY AND CURRENT AFFAIRS**

EDITED BY A. SHELSTON
0-14-043065-2 PENGUIN PB $12.95

Madame Lafarge

Charles **Dickens**

American Notes

WITH AN INTRODUCTION BY CHRISTOPHER HITCHENS
0-679-60185-6 MODERN LIBRARY $15.50
0-7812-5121-4 REPRINT SERVICES $69.00

Dickens' Journalism

Volume I

Sketches by Boz and Other Early Papers 1833-39

0-8142-0629-8 OHIO STATE $39.50

Volume II

The Amusements of the People and Other Papers

0-8142-0724-3 OHIO STATE $39.50

Charles M. **Doughty**

Travels in Arabia Deserta

Doughty's wanderings in Arabia are recorded in a unique prose style rich in archaisms and poetic figures

Volume 1

0-486-23825-3 DOVER PB $17.95

Volume 2

0-486-23826-1 DOVER PB $17.95

Elizabeth **Gaskell**

The Life of Charlotte Brontë

A classic biography by a close friend of the novelist

EDITED BY ALAN SHELSTON
0-14-043099-7 PENGUIN PB $9.95

The Life of Charlotte Brontë

EDITED BY ANGUS EASSON
0-19-282809-6 OXFORD PB $8.95

Edmund **Gosse**

Father and Son

Gosse's account of his conflicts with his father's allegiance to a narrow religious sect: "This book is the record of a struggle between two temperaments, two consciences, and almost two epochs. It ended, as was inevitable, in disruption. Of the two human beings here described, one was born to fly backward, the other could not help being carried forward…But, at least, it is some comfort to the survivor that neither, to the very last hour, ceased to respect the other, or to regard him with a sad indulgence"—from the first chapter

0-14-018276-4 PENGUIN PB $10.95

John Stuart **Mill**

The Autobiography

One of the most penetrating accounts of depression and recovery ever written

0-395-05120-7 HOUGHTON MIFFLIN PB $11.16

William **Morris**

The Ideal Book: Essays and Lectures on the Art of the Book

EDITED BY WILLIAM S. PETERSON

0-520-04563-7 CALIFORNIA $50.00

News from Nowhere & Selected Writings and Design

Morris, a key figure in the revival of interest in medieval culture and traditional crafts, was also the author of utopian fiction and heroic poetry

EDITED BY ASA BRIGGS

0-14-043115-2 PENGUIN PB $6.95

John Henry **Newman**

Apologia Pro Vita Sua

A humane and intellectually incisive testament to Newman's fervent yet independent-minded Catholic faith

See also **CLASSICS** under **CHRISTIANITY** in **RELIGION, SPIRITUALITY, AND PHILOSOPHY**

See also **CLASSICS OF WESTERN RELIGIOUS THOUGHT** under **WORLD RELIGION** in **RELIGION, SPIRITUALITY, AND PHILOSOPHY**

EDITED BY DAVID DELAURA

0-393-09766-8 NORTON PB $14.95

Apologia Pro Vita Sua

See also **CLASSICS** under **CHRISTIANITY** in **RELIGION, SPIRITUALITY, AND PHILOSOPHY**

0-460-87232-X EVERYMAN'S PB $10.95

0-14-043374-0 PENGUIN PB $12.95

An Essay in Aid of a Grammar of Assent

A theological classic on the nature of faith and knowledge

See also **CLASSICS** under **CHRISTIANITY** in **RELIGION, SPIRITUALITY, AND PHILOSOPHY**

INTRODUCTION BY NICHOLAS LASH

0-268-01000-5 NOTRE DAME PB $16.50

The Idea of a University

EDITED BY MARTIN J. SVAGLIC

0-268-01150-8 NOTRE DAME PB $12.95

Florence **Nightingale**

Ever Yours, Florence Nightingale: Selected Letters

"Along with letters to family, friends, politicians, medical men, reformers … the editors have printed many of the letters that Nightingale habitually wrote to herself, expressing feelings or examining perplexities she could confide only to paper …Her letters arc succinct—sometimes funny, sometimes biting… Yet always, in her verbal glitter, you feel Florence's driving intelligence"—Naomi Bliven, *New Yorker*

EDITED BY MARINA VICINUS & BEA NERGAARD

0-674-27020-7 HARVARD $32.00

Walter **Pater**

Essays on Literature and Art

0-460-87009-2 DENT PB $7.95

The Renaissance

A touchstone of aestheticism

EDITED BY ADAM PHILIPS

0-19-281737-X OXFORD PB $6.95

The Renaissance: Studies in Art and Poetry

A scholarly edition

EDITED BY DONALD H. HILL

0-520-03664-6 CALIFORNIA PB $16.95

John **Ruskin**

"He was one of those rare men who think with their hearts, and so he thought and said not only what he himself had seen and felt, but what everyone will think and say in the future."—Leo Tolstoy

Art Criticism

Ruskin endowed criticism with a moral fervor, demanding of art that it speak eloquently to the human condition

EDITED BY R.L. HERBERT

0-8446-0694-4 SMITH $14.50

The King of the Golden River, or the Black Brother

A fairy tale that achieved great popularity

ILLUSTRATED BY RICHARD DOYLE

0-486-20066-3 DOVER PB $3.50

The Lamp of Beauty: Writings on Art

See also **THE PRE-RAPHAELITES** under **ENGLAND** under **EUROPEAN ART: 1750-1900** in **ART**

0-7148-3358-4 PHAIDON PB $14.95

Selected Writings

Includes selections from *Modern Painters, The Stones of Venice, The Seven Lamps of Architecture,* and *Praeterita*

EDITED BY PHILIP DAVIS

0-460-87460-8 EVERYMAN'S PB $8.50

The Seven Lamps of Architecture

0-374-50188-2 FS&G PB $8.95

The Stones of Venice

Ruskin's most accessible exposition of his principles, only available in this heavily abridged edition

EDITED BY J.G. LINKS

0306802440 DA CAPO PB $10.95

Unto this Last & Other Writings

Also includes *The King of the Golden River* and excerpts from *The Stones of Venice, Sesame and Lilies,* and *Fors Clavigera*

EDITED BY CLIVE WILMER

0-14-043211-6 PENGUIN PB $11.95

Mary **Shelley**

The Journals of Mary Shelley

EDITED BY PAULA FELDMAN & DIANE SCOTT-KILVERT

0-8018-5088-6 JOHNS HOPKINS PB $29.95

Mary Shelley

Selected Letters of Mary Wollstonecraft Shelley

EDITED BY BETTY T. BENNETT

0-8018-4885-7 JOHNS HOPKINS $49.95

0-8018-4886-5 JOHNS HOPKINS PB $19.95

Robert Louis **Stevenson**

In the South Seas

Firsthand impressions of the Marquesas and the Paumotus and Gilbert Islands

See also **AUSTRALIA, NEW ZEALAND, AND THE SOUTH PACIFIC** under **TRAVEL LITERATURE** in **FOOD, TRAVEL, AND LEISURE**

See also **POLYNESIA** under **AUSTRALIA, NEW ZEALAND, AND POLYNESIA** in **WORLD HISTORY AND CURRENT AFFAIRS**

0-7103-0140-5 ROUTLEDGE PB $25.50

Travels in Hawaii

EDITED WITH AN INTRODUCTION BY A. GROVE DAY

0-8248-0257-8 HAWAII PB $12.95

Travels with a Donkey in the Cevennes & Selected Travel Writings

0-19-282629-8 OXFORD PB $9.95

John Addington **Symonds**

Selected Writings

EDITED BY R.V. HOLDSWORTH

0-85635-059-1 CARCANET PB $16.25

Anthony **Trollope**

Autobiography

EDITED BY P.D. EDWARDS

0-19-281509-1 OXFORD PB $6.95

Oscar **Wilde**

The Artist as Critic: Critical Writings of Oscar Wilde

EDITED BY RICHARD ELLMANN

0-226-89764-8 CHICAGO PB $18.95

20th-Century British and Irish Fiction

The Early 20th-century

J.R. **Ackerley**

We Think the World of You

A fine short novel about a bureaucrat and a petty criminal and their common passion for an untrainable dog.

0-671-67811-6 POSEIDON PB $7.95

T.H. **White**

The Once and Future King

This retelling of King Arthur was the basis for *Camelot*, and contains fascinating information about living in the Middle Ages

See also YOUNG ADULT FICTION in BOOKS FOR YOUNG READERS
See also FANTASY under SCIENCE FICTION AND FANTASY in POPULAR READING
See also BRITISH AND CELTIC under EUROPEAN MYTHOLOGY under MYTHOLOGY AND FOLKLORE in RELIGION, SPIRITUALITY, AND PHILOSOPHY

0-441-62740-4 ACE PB $6.99

Daisy **Ashford**

The Young Visiters

An immensely amusing novel of manners written by an Edwardian child. Found in a drawer, it was published in 1919 and has since gained recognition as a masterpiece of naive comedy

INTRODUCTION BY WALTER KENDRICK

0-89733-365-9 ACADEMY CHICAGO $15.00

H.E. **Bates**

Elephant's Nest in a Rhubarb Tree & Other Stories

0-8112-1088-X NEW DIRECTIONS PB $9.95

A Month by the Lake & Other Stories

"Nearly perfect stories…He is as adept at the seductive rise and fall of his narrative voice as he is cunning with naturalistic dialogue. Comparisons to Joyce, Chekhov, and Mansfield are inevitable"—*Publishers Weekly*

INTRODUCTION BY ANTHONY BURGESS

0-8112-1036-7 NEW DIRECTIONS PB $9.95

My Uncle Silas

"Bates understood the power of the short story form perfectly, and these pieces must not be missed by anyone who favors short fictions"
—*Booklist*

INTRODUCTION BY V.S. PRITCHETT

0-915308-63-0 GRAY WOLF PB $7.00

A Party for the Girls: Six Stories

Six long stories. "He achieved such sovereignty of what literary land he inherited that he deserves the homage of our uncomplicated enjoyment"—Anthony Burgess

0-8112-1051-0 NEW DIRECTIONS PB $10.95

Samuel **Beckett**

Disjecta

The first publication of these miscellaneous criticisms, reviews, and selected letters sheds new light on Beckett's work

EDITED BY RUBY COHN

0-8021-1189-0 GROVE $17.50
0-7145-3974-0 RIVERRUN $14.95

Dream of Fair to Middling Women

1-55970-217-6 ARCADE $21.95
0-7145-4213-X ARCADE PB $15.95

First Love & Other Shorts

The two outcasts of *First Love* succeed in making a mockery of the title

0-8021-5131-0 GROVE PB $9.95

How It Is

"What *is* the story? Well, it is spoken by a nameless man face down in mud, and apart from him its principal character is called Pim. Three sections describe how it was before, with and after this Pim, who is therefore a measure of time and history"—Frank Kermode

0-8021-5066-7 GROVE PB $10.95

Samuel Beckett

I Can't Go On, I'll Go On: A Selection from Samuel Beckett's Work

EDITED BY RICHARD W. SEAVER

0-8021-3287-1 GROVE PB $15.95

The Lost Ones

A compressed and very powerful late work. *"The Lost Ones* imagines the death of imagination, the end of life on the planet"
—Christopher Ricks

0-8021-3092-5 GROVE PB $9.95

Mercier and Camier

An early work of fiction

0-8021-3235-9 GROVE PB $7.95

Molloy

The first novel of Beckett's trilogy (which also includes the out-of-print *Malone Dies* and *The Unnamable*) is, for all its austerity, one of the richest of his fictions

TRANSLATED BY SAMUEL BECKETT & PATRICK BOWLES

0-8021-5136-1 GROVE PB $12.95

But in the end I understood this language. I understood it, I understood it, all wrong perhaps. That is now what matters. It told me to write the report. Does this mean I am freer now than I was? I do not know. I shall learn. Then I went back into the house and wrote, It is midnight. The rain is beating on the windows. It was not midnight. It was not raining.

MOLLOY

More Pricks Than Kicks

A collection of stories that first appeared in 1934

0-8021-5137-X GROVE PB $11.00

Murphy

Beckett's first novel, published in 1938

0-8021-5037-3 GROVE PB $12.00

Nohow On

0-8021-3426-2 GROVE PB $11.00

Samuel Beckett: The Complete Short Prose 1929-1989

This definitive short prose collection from the Nobel Prize winner and perhaps the most original writer of our century includes not only the work that Beckett himself spoke of as his most "important writing" but, in addition, a number of never-before-published pieces

See also EUROPEAN DRAMA SINCE 1945 under MODERN EUROPEAN DRAMA in LITERATURE OF EUROPE, AFRICA, AND ASIA

EDITED BY S.E. GONTARSKI

0-8021-1577-2 GROVE $23.00
0-521-35775-6 CAMBRIDGE PB $10.95

Stories and Texts for Nothing

"This art often casts a cold eye of contempt over that which is the supreme mark of humanity: curiosity about the world and about the undiscovered possibilities of human life. Saint Beckett records with supreme skill the solipsist visions of the pillar and the desert, instead of preaching to the birds"
—Matthew Hodgart, *NY Review of Books*

0-8021-5062-4 GROVE PB $11.00

The Unnamable

The last volume of Beckett's trilogy. "You must say words, as long as there are any, until they find me, until they say me…"

0-8021-5091-8 GROVE PB $14.00

Watt

A richly—and darkly—comic early novel

0-8021-5140-X GROVE PB $11.95

Worstward Ho!

"Focuses to a pinpoint one of the great sensibilities in modern world literatures"
—*Washington Post*

0-8021-5141-8 GROVE PB $8.95

Sybille **Bedford**

A Legacy

"A book of entirely delicious quality. Two families, vastly dissimilar, the one Jewish inartistic millionaires, the other slightly decadent Catholic aristocrats, become joined in marriage. Everything is new, cool, witty, elegant, and some scenes are uproariously funny"
—Evelyn Waugh

See also THE '80S under THE GREAT FICTION BESTSELLERS 1930-1995 in POPULAR READING

0-912946-26-1 NORTON PB $8.50

Max **Beerbohm**

A Christmas Garland

Perhaps one of the greatest parodies ever written, as Beerbohm uncannily assumes the voices of Henry James, Conrad, Kipling, Hardy, and others

0-300-05809-8 YALE $27.50

Zuleika Dobson

An elegant pastiche of the highly proper decadence of the British Empire

INTRODUCTION BY N. JOHN HALL

0-8488-0914-9 AMEREON $20.95

Arnold **Bennett**

Anna of the Five Towns

Anna's choice between love with a bankrupt or marriage to a bore is sketched against the provincial background of Britain's pottery industry

INTRODUCTION BY FRANK SWINNERTON

0-14-018015-X PENGUIN PB $9.95

The Card

0-14-003826-4 PENGUIN PB $5.95

The Old Wives' Tale

The contrasting life-stories of two sisters—a stay-at-home and a wanderer—form the basis for Bennett's best novel

EDITED BY JOHN WAIN

0-14-018255-1 PENGUIN PB $11.95

Riceyman Steps

A book dealer and his marriage provide the basis for a strong realistic novel

0-89733-093-5 ACADEMY CHICAGO PB $11.95

E.F. **Benson**

Desirable Residences and Other Stories

0-19-212304-1 OXFORD $25.00

Fine Feathers and Other Stories

0-19-282416-3 OXFORD PB $9.95

Make Way For Lucia

A one-volume edition of the complete Lucia cycle, one of the peaks of modern comic writing. Includes *Queen Lucia, Miss Mapp, Mapp and Lucia, Lucia in London, Trouble for Lucia,* and *The Worshipful Lucia.* "The most enchantingly malicious works written by the hand of man"
—Gilbert Seldes

INTRODUCTION BY NANCY MITFORD

0-06-091508-0 HARPERCOLLINS PB $30.00

Elizabeth **Bowen**

"She is what happened after Bloomsbury…the link that connects Virginia Woolf with Iris Murdoch and Muriel Spark."
—Victoria Glendinning

The Collected Stories of Elizabeth Bowen

"To see anew these bright stars set among their own constellations…is to experience in its full force that concentration of imaginative power which was hers"—Eudora Welty

INTRODUCTION BY ANGUS WILSON

0-394-51666-4 KNOPF $25.00

The Collected Stories of Elizabeth Bowen

0-88001-493-8 ECCO PB $17.00

Elizabeth Bowen

The Death of the Heart

Sensitive observation of the adolescence of the orphaned Portia, whose caretakers' indifference propels her into an affair with a cad

0-14-018300-0 VIKING PB $11.95

Eva Trout

0-14-018298-5 PENGUIN PB $10.95

Friends and Relations

0-14-018299-3 VIKING PB $9.95

The Hotel

0-14-018302-7 PENGUIN PB $11.95

The House in Paris

0-14-018303-5 PENGUIN PB $10.95

The Last September

0-14-018304-3 VIKING PB $9.95

The Little Girls

"We might conceivably be reminded of Wallace Stevens's poetry with its pure crystalline exterior and its metaphysical interior"
—Allen E. Austen

0-14-018305-1 PENGUIN PB $10.95

Mary **Butts**

The Classical Novels

Contains *The Macedonian* and *Scenes from the Life of Cleopatra* along with three classical short stories

0-929701-43-7 MCPHERSON $24.00
0-929701-42-9 MCPHERSON PB $14.00

From Altar to Chimney Piece: Selected Stories

0-929701-19-4 MCPHERSON $22.00
0-929701-20-8 MCPHERSON PB $12.00

Scenes from the Life of Cleopatra

1-55713-140-6 SUN & MOON PB $13.95

The Taverner Novels: Armed with Madness & Death of Felicity Taverner

English expatriate writer from the 20s and 30s; a notable stylist. Introduction to this volume by Paul West

0-929701-17-8 MCPHERSON $25.00
0-929701-18-6 MCPHERSON PB $15.00

Joyce **Cary**

Except the Lord

The second volume in the Chester Nimmo trilogy, which began with *Prisoner of Grace*

0-8112-0965-2 NEW DIRECTIONS PB $7.95

Herself Surprised

A picaresque tale of the femme moyenne sensuelle Sarah Munday, told in her own words with verve and vivacity

0-89244-070-8 AMEREON $21.95

The Horse's Mouth

The Blake-quoting old reprobate Gulley Jimson struggles for his art against the wiles of his discarded mistress and his skinflint patron

0-06-092021-1 HARPERPERENNIAL PB $13.00

A House of Children

An evocation of the Ireland of Cary's childhood. "The organization—the progress of children toward maturity by means of sudden epiphanies—is remarkable. The characters, based on Cary's cousins and aunts and the author himself, are charming. The language is intoxication"—Edwin Christian

0-8112-1008-1 NEW DIRECTIONS PB $8.95

Mister Johnson

0-8112-1174-6 NEW DIRECTIONS PB $8.95

Not Honour More

The third volume of the Nimmo trilogy consists of the less-than-contrite confession of the messianic reformer's assassin

0-8112-0966-0 NEW DIRECTIONS PB $7.95

Prisoner of Grace

The first volume of a trilogy presents the career of Chester Nimmo, a mixture of radical politician and religious charlatan, through the eyes of his wife

0-8112-0964-4 NEW DIRECTIONS PB $7.95

G.K. **Chesterton**

"He is as much a political writer as George Orwell. Politics, in the narrow, as well as the widest, sense, informs and inspires his writing, which is why he remained all his life a journalist, to the despair of those who recognized the enormous scale of his gifts. But that is what Chesterton wanted to be, a 'jolly journalist'…because he thought his message important, and from Fleet Street it could reach the people who needed it most, and who perhaps had the best chance of understanding it."—P.J. Kavanagh

G.K. **Chesterton**

The Man Who Was Thursday

A whimsical morality play with no fewer than six detectives

See also **CRIME FICTION AFTER CONAN DOYLE** under **RISE OF THE MYSTERY** under **CRIME FICTION** in **POPULAR READING**

0-486-25121-7 DOVER PB $3.95
0-14-018388-4 PENGUIN PB $8.95

Ivy **Compton-Burnett**

Compton-Burnett's tales of manorhouse intrigue are told almost exclusively in knife-sharp, ultra-sophisticated dialogue.

A Heritage and Its History

1-85381-281-1 VIRAGO PB $11.95

The Mighty and Their Fall

1-85381-177-7 VIRAGO PB $11.95

Mother & Son

1-85381-291-9 VIRAGO PB $11.95

Two Worlds & Their Ways

1-85381-176-9 VIRAGO PB $11.95

Joseph **Conrad**

Almayer's Folly

Conrad's first novel traces the downfall of a young Dutchman at a remote trading outpost in Borneo

0-14-018030-3 VIKING PB $9.95

Chance

The romantic tale of Flora de Barral was Conrad's first great popular success

0-19-281709-4 OXFORD PB $5.95

Chance: A Tale in Two Parts

EDITED BY JACQUES BERTHOUD

0-14-018654-9 PENGUIN PB $5.95

The Collected Letters of Joseph Conrad, 1912-1916

EDITED BY LAURENCE DAVIES

0-521-32389-4 CAMBRIDGE $120.00

The Collected Stories of Joseph Conrad

EDITED BY SAMUEL HYNES

0-88001-464-4 ECCO PB $18.00

The Collected Tales of Joseph Conrad

EDITED BY SAMUEL HYNES

0-88001-439-3 ECCO PB $18.00

The Complete Short Fiction of Joseph Conrad

Volume I
The Stories

0-88001-307-9 ECCO $24.95

Volume II
The Stories

0-88001-308-7 ECCO $24.95

Volume III
The Tales

0-88001-287-0 ECCO $24.95

Volume IV
The Tales

0-88001-288-9 ECCO $24.95

Heart of Darkness

The horrors perpetrated in the name of civilization by the 19th-century rush to colonize attain symbolic power in the narrative of an innocent young naval officer

0-14-018090-7 PENGUIN PB $3.50

Going up that river was like travelling back to the earliest beginnings of the world, when vegetation rioted on the earth and the big trees were kings. An empty stream, a great silence, an impenetrable forest. The air was warm, thick, heavy, sluggish. There was no joy in the brilliance of sunshine. The long stretches of the waterway ran on, deserted, into the gloom of overshadowed distances. On silvery sandbanks hippos and alligators sunned themselves side by side. The broadening water flowed through a mob of wooded islands; you lost your way on that river as you would in a desert, and butted all day long against shoals, trying to find the channel, till you thought yourself bewitched and cut off for ever from everything you had known once—somewhere—far away—in another existence perhaps.

HEART OF DARKNESS

Heart of Darkness and Other Tales

EDITED BY CEDRIC WATTS

0-19-282651-4 OXFORD PB $4.95

Heart of Darkness, with the Congo Diary

0-14-018652-2 PENGUIN PB $6.95

Lord Jim

His romantic self-image shattered by momentary cowardice, Jim seeks to recoup his lost honor through an act of heroism

0-19-281625-X OXFORD PB $3.95
0-14-018092-3 PENGUIN PB $5.95

The Mirror of the Sea and a Personal Record

EDITED BY ZDZISLAW NAJDER

0-19-281729-9 OXFORD PB $8.95

The Nigger of the "Narcissus"

0-19-281623-3 OXFORD PB $4.95

Nostromo

A hero of the people breaks under the conflicting demands of a South American revolution that preserves the silver-producing province for an Anglo-American consortium

0-679-60202-X MODERN LIBRARY $18.50
0-19-281624-1 OXFORD PB $5.95
0-14-018371-X VIKING PB $6.95

An Outcast of the Islands

A tale of self-destruction in the tropics, in the lush and clotted style of Conrad's early novels

0-14-018032-X VIKING PB $8.95

An Outcast of the Islands

0-460-87773-9 EVERYMAN'S PB $6.95

The Portable Conrad

EDITED BY MORTON DAUWEN ZABEL

0-14-015033-1 VIKING PB $14.95

The Rescue: A Romance of the Shallows

0-14-018034-6 PENGUIN PB $9.95

The Rover

0-19-282623-9 OXFORD PB $4.99

The Secret Agent

Idealistic anarchists in London destroy their own association by an act of terrorism

0-679-41723-0 KNOPF $17.00
0-14-018096-6 PENGUIN PB $9.95

The Shadow Line

0-19-281686-1 OXFORD PB $6.95

Tales of Unrest

Early stories, including "The Lagoon," in the rich prose typical of Conrad's first period

0-14-018036-2 PENGUIN PB $7.95

Typhoon & Other Stories

Typhoon's central character, Captain MacWhirr, "is not," Conrad wrote, "an acquaintance of a few hours, or a few weeks, or a few months. He is the product of twenty years of life. My own life"

INTRODUCTION BY CEDRIC WATTS

0-19-281711-6 OXFORD PB $3.95

Typhoon and Other Stories

0-679-40547-X EVERYMAN'S $17.00

Under Western Eyes

The psychological self-destruction of Razumov among prerevolutionary Russian exiles in Geneva

0-679-40554-2 EVERYMAN'S $20.00
0-14-018287-X VIKING PB $9.95
0-19-281619-5 OXFORD PB $7.95

Victory

INTRODUCTION BY CHRISTOPHER HITCHENS

0-460-87478-0 EVERYMAN'S PB $6.95

Victory

0-19-281708-6 OXFORD PB $5.95
0-14-018978-5 PENGUIN PB $8.95

Youth & The End of the Tether

0-14-018038-9 VIKING PB $7.95

Youth, Heart of Darkness, The End of the Tether

EDITED BY JOHN LYON

0-14-018513-5 PENGUIN PB $7.95

Joseph **Conrad** & Ford Madox **Ford**

The Inheritors

0-7509-0011-3 ALAN SUTTON PB $7.50

Romance

0-88184-166-8 CARROLL & GRAF PB $8.95

Daphne **Du Maurier**

Rebecca

The famous Gothic novel of an aristocrat's ingenuous second wife struggling against the malevolent influence of her dead predecessor

See also **ENGLAND** under **RISE OF THE MODERN CRIME NOVEL** under **CRIME FICTION** in **POPULAR READING**

See also **THE '30S** under **THE GREAT FICTION BESTSELLERS 1930-1995** in **POPULAR READING**

0-385-04380-5 DOUBLEDAY $20.00
0-380-77855-6 AVON PB $6.50

Ronald **Firbank**

Complete Short Stories

Written between the ages of 16 and 22, these stories range in genre from impressionistic prose poem to sardonic high-society vignette, and shed new light on Firbank's distinctive talent

0-916583-61-9 DALKEY ARCHIVE PB $9.95

Ronald **Firbank**

Concerning the Eccentricities of Cardinal Pirelli

0-7156-1095-3 OLYMPIC PB $3.98

Five Novels

Includes *Valmouth, Artificial Princess, The Flower Beneath the Foot, Prancing Nigger*, and *Concerning the Eccentricities of Cardinal Pirelli.* Plots constantly on the verge of expiring breathe the purest spirit of persiflage in these late blooms of imperial decadence

0-8112-0799-4 NEW DIRECTIONS PB $12.95

Santal

1-55713-174-0 SUN & MOON PB $7.95

Three More Novels

Includes *Vainglory, Inclinations,* and *Caprice*

INTRODUCTION BY ERNEST JONES

0-8112-0975-X NEW DIRECTIONS PB $9.95

Penelope **Fitzgerald**

The Gate of Angels

0-88184-960-X CARROLL & GRAF PB $9.95

Ford Madox **Ford**

"There is no novelist of this century more likely to live than Ford Madox Ford…In an age of increasing carelessness among good writers, Ford was an artist. No one in our century except Henry James has been more attentive to the craft of letters."—Graham Greene

The Fifth Queen

A trilogy about the life of Catherine Howard, the fifth of Henry VIII's six wives

0-88001-101-7 NORTON PB $12.95

The Ford Madox Ford Reader

A large and well-stocked collection that demonstrates the many aspects of Ford's talent, as evidenced in stories, excerpts from novels, essays, and poems

INTRODUCTION BY GRAHAM GREENE

0-88001-122-X ECCO PB $13.50

The Good Soldier

A tragic quartet of cross-purposes and ambiguous motivations; a meticulously told and ultimately horrifying tale, which many consider Ford's masterpiece

0-679-40665-4 EVERYMAN'S $15.00

0-14-018081-8 PENGUIN PB $8.95

0-679-72218-1 VINTAGE PB $11.00

No Enemy

The aftereffects of World War I on a single personality

0-88001-062-2 NORTON PB $8.50

Parade's End

The complete Tietjens tetralogy, consisting of *Some Do Not, No More Parades, A Man Could Stand Up,* and *Last Post.* The misadventures of a public-school Candide during World War I expose the hypocrisy and corruption of military and civilian alike, and provide an elegy for a lost era

0-679-41728-1 KNOPF $20.00

0-394-74108-0 RANDOM HOUSE PB $20.00

The Rash Act

"The Rash Act ought to be bought and read by all interested in the novel as an art form…The action takes place in the French South which Ford loved, but man no longer sustains the tradition of myth and history which that region once represented"—Anthony Burgess

INTRODUCTION BY C.H. SISSON

0-85635-529-1 SCHOLARLY PB $12.50

E.M. **Forster**

The Celestial Omnibus & Other Stories

A blind alley is the departure point for a tour of heaven conducted by Sir Thomas Browne; a lonely soul breaks out of the automated world of the future and once again sees the stars

0-394-72176-4 RANDOM HOUSE PB $8.00

The Eternal Moment & Other Stories

0-15-629125-8 HARCOURT BRACE PB $7.00

E.M. Forster

Great Novels of E.M. Forster

Four of Forster's finest works of fiction are brought together here in a single volume: *Howard's End, A Room with a View, The Longest Journey*, and *Where Angels Fear to Tread*. "The shapeliness of his prose and his plotting still satisfies. The wit remains piercing and seemingly painless"—*NY Times*

0-88184-908-1 CARROLL & GRAF PB $17.95

Howard's End

Forster contrasts the inner lives of the half-German Schlegels and the robust English Wilcoxes

0-553-21208-7 BDD PB $4.50

The Life to Come & Others Stories

INTRODUCTION BY OLIVER STALLYBRASS

0-393-30442-6 NORTON PB $11.95

The Longest Journey

The contrast of the lives of two half-brothers elevates a crude zest for life over public-school stuffiness

0-679-74815-6 VINTAGE PB $12.00

Maurice

In this posthumous publication, Forster draws on his own experiences as a homosexual in an unforgiving society

0-393-31032-9 NORTON PB $8.95

A Passage to India

The social chasm between ruled and ruler in British India contributes to bitterly ironic misunderstandings when an attempt is made to bridge the gap

0-15-171141-0 HARCOURT BRACE $15.95

0-15-671142-7 HARCOURT BRACE PB $11.00

A Room with a View

Lucy Honeychurch is torn between a vibrant railway clerk and a desiccated intellectual

0-553-21323-7 BDD PB $4.95

0-679-72476-1 VINTAGE PB $10.00

Where Angels Fear to Tread

British priggishness in conflict with Italian ardor over the offspring of a misalliance between two families

0-89968-224-3 LIGHTYEAR $21.95

0-553-21444-6 BDD PB $4.95

John **Galsworthy**

The Forsyte Saga

The fortunes of an English family from 1886 to the 1920s pivot on the contrast between Soames, the man of property, and his artistic cousin Jolyon. Originally published separately as *The Man of Property, In Chancery,* and *To Let*

0-684-17653-X MACMILLAN PB $18.00

A Modern Comedy

A continuation of the Forsyte saga, encompassing *The White Monkey, The Silver Spoon,* and *Swan Song*

0-02-542370-3 SCRIBNERS $50.00

William **Gerhardie**

Futility

A black comedy of love and revolution, by a writer of whom Graham Greene wrote: "To those of my generation he was the most important new novelist to appear in our young lives"

0-8112-1176-2 NEW DIRECTIONS PB $10.95

Stella **Gibbons**

Cold Comfort Farm

London socialite descends on her eccentric country relatives in this wry satire of rural life

0-14-025813-2 PENGUIN PB $9.95

0-14-018869-X PENGUIN PB $9.95

Rumer **Godden**

Kingfishers Catch Fire

0-915943-81-6 MILKWEED PB $12.95

Robert **Graves**

Graves combines stunning powers of characterization and storytelling with deep historical knowledge of such diverse areas as mythical Greece, classical Rome, Byzantium, and colonial America.

Claudius the God and His Wife Messalina

The sequel to *I, Claudius,* in which the new emperor and his wife, the infamous Messalina, fall prey to the evils of power

See also **HISTORICAL FICTION** under **TOPICS IN ROMAN HISTORY** under **ANCIENT ROME** in **WORLD HISTORY AND CURRENT AFFAIRS**

0-679-72573-3 VINTAGE PB $14.00

Collected Short Stories

0-14-018484-8 PENGUIN PB $11.95

Robert Graves

I, Claudius
The pedantic ugly duckling of the imperial family survives mad rulers and political purges to inherit the Roman Empire
See also **HISTORICAL FICTION** under **TOPICS IN ROMAN HISTORY** under **ANCIENT ROME** in **WORLD HISTORY AND CURRENT AFFAIRS**
0-394-60811-9 MODERN LIBRARY $15.00
0-679-72477-X VINTAGE PB $13.00

Sergeant Lamb's America
0-89733-213-X ACADEMY CHICAGO PB $13.95

They Hanged My Saintly Billy
A Victorian fresco, based on a murder trial of the era
0-89733-030-7 ACADEMY CHICAGO PB $20.00

Henry **Green**
Green's terse, elliptical, and utterly serious comedies are among the most original creations of modern British fiction. Unfortunately, several of his best books are out of print.

Concluding
In a state dystopia of the future, two girls escape from a soulless institution to seek out other free spirits
FOREWORD BY EUDORA WELTY
0-678-03158-4 AUGUSTUS KELLY $25.00

Loving, Living, and Party Going
An omnibus of three novels
0-14-018691-3 PENGUIN PB $14.95

Nothing, Doting & Blindness
Another package of three novels
0-14-018692-1 PENGUIN PB $14.95

Pack My Bag: A Self-Portrait
A literary memoir
0-14-018793-6 PENGUIN PB $10.95

Graham **Greene**

Brighton Rock
In this precursor of *A Clockwork Orange,* an alienated teenage gang leader at a holiday resort waits for his enemies to catch up with him
0-14-018492-9 PENGUIN PB $10.95

A Burnt-Out Case
A celebrity and philanderer ends up working at an African leper colony
0-14-018539-9 PENGUIN PB $10.95

Captain and the Enemy
0-14-012418-7 PENGUIN PB $7.95

Collected Stories
0-14-018612-3 VIKING PB $10.95

The Comedians
A tense drama of foreigners caught up in the violence of Papa Doc Duvalier's Haiti
0-14-018494-5 PENGUIN PB $10.95

The Confidential Agent
An anti-Fascist emissary in London encounters a nightmare world of betrayal and murder
See also **MODERN SPY NOVEL** under **SPY FICTION** in **POPULAR READING**
0-14-018538-0 VIKING PB $7.95

The End of the Affair
An adulterous affair ends tragically in one of Greene's best novels, which hinges ultimately on Catholic doctrine
0-14-018495-3 PENGUIN PB $10.95

England Made Me
"The fragments of reality are wonderfully magnified through the glass of a strange powerful imagination"—Julian Symons
0-14-018551-8 PENGUIN PB $9.95

A Gun for Sale
A suspense novel about a hit man, also known as *This Gun for Hire*
See also **ENGLAND** under **RISE OF THE MODERN CRIME NOVEL** under **CRIME FICTION** in **POPULAR READING**
0-14-018540-2 PENGUIN PB $9.95

The Heart of the Matter
Scobie, a West African police commissioner during the war, allows compassion for his wife and his mistress to overcome his sense of duty. Many find this Greene's most powerful book
0-14-018496-1 PENGUIN PB $10.95

The Honorary Consul
A British derelict in Argentina tries to maintain tone throughout terrorist activity
1-56849-285-5 BUCCANEER LIBRARY EDITION..$29.95

The Human Factor
An ironic novel of espionage. "The most near-perfect novel in English of the last ten years and his own best"—Don Coles
0-679-40992-0 EVERYMAN'S $17.00

It's a Battlefield
0-14-018541-0 PENGUIN PB $9.95

The Last Word & Other Stories
A collection of stories spanning 60 years of Greene's career, only four of which have appeared in book form. "Serves admirably well as a microcosmic view of Greene's entire body of work to date"—*Publishers Weekly*
1-87106-123-7 VIKING $18.95

Loser Takes All
0-14-018542-9 VIKING PB $8.95

The Man Within
Greene's first novel
0-14-003283-5 PENGUIN PB $4.95

May We Borrow Your Husband? & Other Comedies of the Sexual Life
0-14-018537-2 PENGUIN PB $9.95

The Ministry of Fear
A thriller about a network of Nazi spies in wartime London
See also **MODERN SPY NOVEL** under **SPY FICTION** in **POPULAR READING**
0-14-018536-4 VIKING PB $9.95

Graham Greene

Our Man in Havana
An ironic touch alleviates the tragic consequences of a vacuum salesman's unwitting involvement in spy games between great powers
See also **MODERN SPY NOVEL** under **SPY FICTION** in **POPULAR READING**
0-14-018493-7 PENGUIN PB $10.95

The Portable Graham Greene
EDITED BY PHILIP STRATFORD
0-14-023359-8 VIKING PB $13.95

The Power and the Glory
An alcoholic priest in poverty-stricken Mexico struggles to vindicate the kingdom of heaven within and without
0-14-001791-7 PENGUIN PB $6.95

The Quiet American
A prescient novel of Vietnam, published in 1955: cynical British opium addict's resentment against American inheritors of French colonialism leads to betrayal and murder
See also **LITERATURE: FICTION AND POETRY** under **THE VIETNAM WAR** in **HISTORY OF THE AMERICAS**
0-679-60014-0 MODERN LIBRARY $13.50
0-14-018500-3 PENGUIN PB $10.95

Stamboul Train
Greene's first successful novel, a thriller published in 1932; also known as *Orient Express*
0-14-018532-1 PENGUIN PB $9.95

The Third Man & The Fallen Idol
The sources for two outstanding British films of the late '40s
0-14-018533-X PENGUIN PB $9.95

Travels with My Aunt
0-14-003221-5 PENGUIN PB $4.95

Twenty-One Stories
0-14-003093-X VIKING PB $3.95

Neil **Gunn**

Morning Tide

Set in a fishing village, *Morning Tide* captures unforgettably a world long gone. "In the hands of this masterful writer, a simple story becomes a flash of poetry, at once violent and gentle, poignant in its tone and unique in its narrative"—*Publishers Weekly*.

0-8027-1228-2 WALKER $19.95

Radclyffe **Hall**

The Well of Loneliness

This classic novel of lesbianism provoked a storm of opposition when it was published in 1928

0-385-41609-1 ANCHOR PB $10.95

L.P. **Hartley**

The Go-Between

0-14-018307-8 PENGUIN PB $9.95

Winifred **Holtby**

The Land of Green Ginger

A young woman outgrows her illusions

0-915864-25-8 ACADEMY CHICAGO PB $9.00

Aldous **Huxley**

After Many a Summer Dies the Swan

Huxley's entry in the Britisher-in-Hollywood firework display against the backdrop of a hilarious burlesque of Hearst's San Simeon

1-56663-018-5 DEE PB $14.95

Brave New World

The most famous dystopia of them all satirizes a rationalist paradise where genetic and social control breeds out creativity and passion, and breeds in hygienic promiscuity

0-8095-9046-8BORGO $23.00

0-06-012037-1 HARPER & ROW $12.95

0-06-080983-3HARPERCOLLINS PB $7.00

Brave New World & Brave New World Revisited

0-06-090101-2 HARPERCOLLINS PB $14.00

Crome Yellow

0-88184-588-4 CARROLL & GRAF PB $10.95

Eyeless in Gaza

0-89244-045-7 QUEEN'S HOUSE $24.95

0-88184-460-8 CARROLL & GRAF PB $10.95

Island

A late novel of a utopian society founded on the benefits of a mystical drug

0-06-080985-X HARPERCOLLINS PB $7.00

Point Counter Point

A brilliant novel containing thinly disguised portraits of some of Huxley's contemporaries

1-56478-131-3 DALKEY ARCHIVE PB $13.95

Time Must Have a Stop

0-8488-0536-4 AMEREON $20.95

Christopher **Isherwood**

All the Conspirators

0-8112-0725-0 NEW DIRECTIONS PB $7.95

The Berlin Stories

Includes *Goodbye to Berlin* and *The Last of Mr. Norris.* Portrays more sensitively than its musical offshoot, *Cabaret*, the erosion and decadence of the last years of the Weimar Republic

0-8112-0070-1 NEW DIRECTIONS PB $9.95

Diaries

EDITED BY KATHERINE BUCKNELL

0-06-118000-9 HARPERCOLLINS $40.00

Down There on a Visit

"It belongs with Rousseau's *Confessions* and Gide's *Journal* and it has about it the authentic ring of a small offbeat classic"—William Peden, *Saturday Review*

0-374-52052-6 FS&G PB $8.95

The Memorial: Portrait of a Family

0-374-52067-4 FS&G PB $8.95

The Mortmere Stories

1-87061-269-8 DUFOUR PB $15.95

Prater Violet

The tragic aura of events from the Reichstag fire to the Anschluss darkens this satire about a Viennese producer's frothy movie project

0-374-52053-4 FS&G PB $10.00

A Single Man

The Britisher-in-Hollywood genre receives a twist in the novel of a day in the life of an older man who has just lost his male lover

0-374-52038-0 FS&G PB $11.00

Where Joy Resides: A Christopher Isherwood Reader

0-374-12332-2 FS&G $25.00

The World in the Evening

0-374-52088-7 FS&G PB $8.95

James **Joyce**

Dubliners

Joyce described these stories as chapters in the moral history of Dublin. "In calling his original jottings 'epiphanies,' Joyce underscored the ironic contrast between the manifestation that dazzled the Magi and the apparitions that manifest themselves on the streets of Dublin; he also suggested that those pathetic and sordid glimpses…offer a kind of revelation"
—Harry Levin

0-679-60049-3 MODERN LIBRARY $13.50

0-312-09790-5 ST. MARTIN'S $35.00

0-14-018647-6 PENGUIN PB $8.95

0-14-004222-9 VIKING PB $7.95

A few light taps upon the pane made him turn to the window. It had begun to snow again. He watched sleepily the flakes, silver and dark, falling obliquely against the lamplight. The time had come for him to set out on his journey westward. Yes, the newspapers were right, snow was general all over Ireland. It was falling on every part of the dark central plain, on the treeless hills, falling softly upon the Bog of Allen and, farther westward, softly falling into the dark mutinous Shannon waves. It was falling, too, upon every part of the lonely churchyard on the hill where Michael Furey lay buried. It lay thickly drifted on the crooked crosses and headstones, on the spears of the little gate, on the barren thorns. His soul swooned slowly as he heard the snow falling faintly through the universe and faintly falling, like the descent of their last end, upon all the living and the dead.

"THE DEAD," DUBLINERS

Finnegans Wake

"It is a strange book, a compound of fable, symphony, and nightmares, monstrous enigma beckoning imperiously from the shadowy pits of sleep"—Joseph Campbell & Henry Morton Robinson

0-14-006286-6 PENGUIN PB $15.95

Giacomo Joyce

EDITED BY RICHARD ELLMANN

0-571-13164-6 FABER PB $9.95

James Joyce's Letters to Sylvia Beach, 1921-1940

EDITED BY MELISSA BANTA & OSCAR A. SILVERMAN

0-253-32334-7 INDIANA $39.95

The Portable James Joyce

A useful collection that includes the lyrics and verse satires as well as selections from the major works

INTRODUCTION BY HARRY LEVIN

0-14-015030-7 VIKING PB $14.95

A Portrait of the Artist as a Young Man

In writing the story of the growth of a human soul and of an artist, Joyce sought to portray the past as what he called a "fluid succession of presents." "The first page, which looks like a long passage of baby talk, is an elaborate construct that relates the development of the senses to the development of the arts"
—Frank O'Connor

EDITED BY RICHARD ELLMANN

0-14-004221-0 PENGUIN PB $7.00

A Portrait of the Artist as a Young Man

0-679-40575-5 EVERYMAN'S $17.00

0-14-018683-2 PENGUIN PB $8.95

Stephen Hero

A discarded early version of *A Portrait of the Artist*, couched in the realistic manner of the late 19th-century

INTRODUCTION BY THEODORE SPENCER

0-8112-0074-4 NEW DIRECTIONS PB $10.95

Ulysses

"On nothing is *Ulysses* more insistent than on the fact that there is no Bloom there, no Stephen there, no Molly there, no Dublin there, simply language. To say this is by no means to surrender to the artificer's whimsical virtuosity. We and he are co-creators; characters and city have their existence in our minds"
—Hugh Kenner

0-679-60011-6 MODERN LIBRARY $20.00

0-679-72276-9 VINTAGE PB $17.00

Ulysses: The Corrected Text

This new text, claiming to correct many errors that crept into previous editions, has provoked a storm of controversy

INTRODUCTION BY RICHARD ELLMANN

0-394-55373-X MODERN LIBRARY $29.95

0-394-74312-1 RANDOM HOUSE PB $19.00

Ulysses: The Dublin Edition

EDITED BY JOHN KIDD

0-393-03390-2 NORTON $35.00

Arthur **Koestler**

Darkness At Noon

The complicated dance of idealism and falsehood in the thoughts of an imprisoned former commissar who is required to distort his own lifework for the good of the regime

0-02-565210-9 MACMILLAN $35.00
0-553-26595-4 BDD PB $6.50

D.H. **Lawrence**

The intemperate, tubercular coal miner's son looked like a satyr, at times filled his writing with crazed messianism, was accused by Bertrand Russell and others of espousing fascism, and—by loosening the sexual clamp on the English novel of the 1910s, '20s, and '30s—excited the imaginations of several generations of readers. Among the editions listed below, the Cambridge series presents new texts incorporating recent research.

Aaron's Rod

"If *Aaron's Rod* can be said to have a theme it is the gratification of [Lawrence's] always frustrated longing for power…We have a dilution of what he called his philosophy, but chiefly we have the satirical Lawrence, not at his best, but almost at the level of spiteful gossip"—Richard Aldington

0-521-25250-4 CAMBRIDGE $95.00
0-14-018196-2 VIKING PB $9.95

Collected Stories

0-679-43135-7 KNOPF $25.00

The Complete Short Stories of D.H. Lawrence

Volume 1

0-14-004382-9 VIKING PB $8.95

Volume 2

0-14-004255-5 VIKING PB $8.00

Volume 3

0-14-004383-7 VIKING PB $8.00

England, My England and Other Stories

EDITED BY BRUCE STEELE

0-14-018791-X PENGUIN PB $11.95

Kangaroo

Lawrence's brilliant evocation of the strange life forms of the Antipodes overwhelms the somewhat dubious political intentions of his novel

0-14-018201-2 PENGUIN PB $9.95

Lady Chatterley's Lover

The gamekeeper and the lady celebrate the triumph of sexual love in Lawrence's most programmatic novel

0-8021-3334-7 GROVE PB $9.95
0-451-52498-5 NEW AMERICAN LIBRARY PB $4.95

Lady Chatterley's Lover

EDITED BY MICHAEL SQUIRES

0-14-018786-3 PENGUIN PB $9.95

The Lost Girl

0-553-21448-9 BDD PB $5.95

Love Among the Haystacks and Other Stories

EDITED BY JOHN WORTHEN

0-14-018818-5 PENGUIN PB $10.95

Mr. Noon

Not discovered until 1972, *Mr. Noon* is a semiautobiographical sequel to *Sons and Lovers* in which a young schoolmaster's love affair causes him to break with provincial life. "For anyone interested in the derivation and interpretation of Lawrence's sexual doctrine, it is mandatory reading"—Diana Trilling

0-14-008341-3 VIKING PB $8.95

The Plumed Serpent

The mythic undertones of Aztec Mexico revitalize the tired blood of Western tourists. "For sheer magnificence of writing, Lawrence has surpassed himself"—Katherine Anne Porter

0-521-22262-1 CAMBRIDGE $115.00
0-521-29422-3 CAMBRIDGE PB $32.95
0-679-73493-7 VINTAGE PB $12.00

The Prussian Officer and Other Stories

EDITED BY ANTONY ATKINS

Rebellious spontaneity against the rigidity of domination in a love/hate clash between a martinet and his valet

0-19-283181-X OXFORD PB $8.95

The Rainbow

Three generations of the Brangwen family struggle with love and marriage. The story continues in *Women in Love*

0-679-42305-2 KNOPF $20.00
0-14-018218-7 VIKING PB $7.95
0-14-018813-4 PENGUIN PB $8.95

Selected Letters

Lawrence's letters offer readers an interesting means of understanding his works

EDITED BY RICHARD ALDINGTON

0-14-018950-5 PENGUIN PB $16.99

Sons and Lovers

The talents of a sensitive young man are liberated from a coal-mining background by an intelligent but dominating mother

0-393-95758-6 NORTON $14.95
0-14-018832-0 PENGUIN PB $9.95

Sons and Lovers

EDITED BY DAVID TROTTER

0-19-283107-0 OXFORD PB $7.95

The Trespasser

0-14-018210-1 PENGUIN PB $6.95

The Virgin and the Gipsy

0-679-74077-5 VINTAGE PB $10.00

The White Peacock

EDITED BY ANDREW ROBERTSON

0-14-018778-2 PENGUIN PB $10.95

The Woman Who Rode Away and Other Stories

EDITED BY DIETER MEHL AND CHRISTA JANSOHN

0-521-22270-2 CAMBRIDGE $89.95

Women in Love

Love for the Brangwen sisters breaks Gerald Crich, the masterful man of affairs, but enhances the life of the artist Rupert Birkin

0-679-40995-5 KNOPF $20.00
0-14-004260-1 VIKING PB $7.95
0-451-52591-4 SIGNET PB $4.95

D.H. **Lawrence** & M.L. **Skinner**

The Boy in the Bush

0-14-018817-7 PENGUIN PB ....

C.S. **Lewis**

Lewis' space trilogy, with its peculiar mix of theology and science, is unique in science fiction.

Out of the Silent Planet

Ransom struggles against interplanetary rationalist science to keep the cosmos safe for Christian fundamentalism

See also **EARLY SCIENCE FICTION** under **SCIENCE FICTION AND FANTASY** in **POPULAR READING**

0-684-83364-6 SCRIBNERS $22.00

Perelandra

0-02-570845-7 MACMILLAN $40.00
0-684-83365-4 SCRIBNERS $22.00

That Hideous Strength: A Modern Fairy-Tale for Grown-Ups

0-684-82385-3 SCRIBNERS PB $6.95

The Space Trilogy

0-02-022360-9 COLLIER BOXED SET $16.95

Till We Have Faces

Transposes into Tolkienlike fantasy the Greek myth of Cupid and Psyche while retaining its allegorical force

0-15-690436-5 HARCOURT BRACE PB $10.00

Wyndham **Lewis**

Publisher, novelist, painter, and ferocious critic, Lewis was described by Ezra Pound as "the only English writer who can be compared to Dostoevsky." His work, much of it long out of print, has been revived in recent years.

Wyndham Lewis

Blasting and Bombardiering

0-7145-0130-1 RIVERRUN PB $11.95

Wyndham **Lewis**

The Apes of God

"No satire in English is more comprehensive and unrelenting than that in *The Apes of God.* The reader looks in vain for a character who embodies the positive values against which the rest are measured"—Paul Edwards

AFTERWORD BY PAUL EDWARDS

0-87685-512-5 BLACK SPARROW PB $15.00

The Complete Wild Body

Lewis' major collection of short fiction

EDITED BY BERNARD LAFOURCADE

0-87685-551-6 BLACK SPARROW PB $15.00

Malign Fiesta

0-7145-0355-X RIVERRUN PB $7.95

Monstre Gai

0-7145-0386-X RIVERRUN PB $7.95

The Revenge for Love

A savage novel, ranging in setting from London cocktail parties to the front lines of the Spanish Civil War, which dissects the uses of political ideology. First published in 1937, this is one of Lewis's most accessible works

0-87685-828-0 BLACK SPARROW PB $15.00

Rotting Hill

EDITED BY PAUL EDWARDS

0-87685-647-4 BLACK SPARROW $20.00

0-87685-646-6 BLACK SPARROW PB $14.00

Self-Condemned

A bitter, revealing novel that reflects the personal failures of Lewis's later life

AFTERWORD BY ROWLAND SMITH

0-87685-575-3 BLACK SPARROW PB $15.00

Snooty Baronet

EDITED BY BERNARD LAFOURCADE

0-87685-599-0 BLACK SPARROW PB $12.50

Tarr: The 1918 Version

0-87685-784-5 BLACK SPARROW PB $15.00

The Vulgar Streak

One of the more entertaining and formally conventional of Lewis's novels

AFTERWORD BY PAUL EDWARDS

0-87685-628-8 BLACK SPARROW PB $14.00

Malcolm **Lowry**

Hear Us O Lord from Heaven Thy Dwelling Place

0-88184-281-8 CARROLL & GRAF PB $9.95

Malcolm Lowry

Sursum Corda!: The Collected Letters of Malcolm Lowry, 1926-1946

Lowry's letters listed here for convenience

EDITED BY SHERRILL E. GRACE

0-8020-0748-1 TORONTO $49.95

Under the Volcano

Lowry's masterpiece renders the last day in the life of an alcoholic Englishman in Mexico with linguistic splendor that transfigures its essentially self-pitying subject matter

0-452-25595-3 NEW AMERICAN LIBRARY PB ... $12.95

W. Somerset **Maugham**

Maugham's talent flourished best in the short story; a number of his tales have virtually become part of 20th-century mythology

Cakes and Ale

One of Maugham's most entertaining novels, a satirical *roman à clef* about the literary life

0-14-018588-7 VIKING PB $9.95

The Collected Short Stories

Volume 1

Thirty stories set in Europe and the Pacific, including the famous "Rain"

0-14-018589-5 PENGUIN PB $11.95

Volume 2

0-14-018590-9 PENGUIN PB $12.95

Volume 3

Originally published as *Ashenden: The British Agent,* this collection contains the first starkly contemporary spy stories: downbeat, less than heroic, derived from Maugham's own experience in the Secret Service. "After the easy, absurd assumptions made by Buchan, Sapper, and Oppenheim, the Ashenden stories have the reality of a cold bath"—Julian Symons

0-14-018591-7 PENGUIN PB $11.95

Volume 4

0-14-018592-5 PENGUIN PB $12.95

Liza of Lambeth

An early naturalistic novel of Cockney poverty

0-14-018593-3 VIKING PB $8.95

The Magician

A melodramatic tale based on the career of the sinister magus Aleister Crowley

See also **MAGIC** under **THE OCCULT** under **SPIRITUALITY** in **RELIGION, SPIRITUALITY, AND PHILOSOPHY**

0-14-018595-X VIKING PB $11.95

The Moon and Sixpence

Paul Gauguin was the basis for the character of Charles Strickland, who gives up his family and his job in the city to paint in Tahiti

0-14-018597-6 VIKING PB $9.95

Mrs. Craddock

0-14-018594-1 VIKING PB $10.95

The Narrow Corner

An atmospheric tale of seedy adventures in the South Pacific

0-14-018598-4 PENGUIN PB $10.95

Of Human Bondage

Semiautobiographical novel follows the crippled Philip Carey from his lonely childhood in Blackstable through medical school. The fascinating, cruel waitress Mildred was immortalized on film by Bette Davis

0-14-018522-4 PENGUIN PB $10.95

The Razor's Edge

A splendid novel of spiritual awakening in which Larry Darrell's training at a Tibetan ashram gives him a unique perspective on the struggle for fun and status in Paris and Chicago in the 1920s

0-14-018523-2 PENGUIN PB $10.95

Up at the Villa

A brief and ultimately violent novella of sexual passion

0-405-07824-2 AYER $23.95

Nancy **Mitford**

Christmas Pudding

0-88184-342-3 CARROLL & GRAF PB $4.95

Highland Fling

0-88184-390-3 CARROLL & GRAF PB $3.95

Olive **Moore**

Spleen

1-56478-148-8 DALKEY ARCHIVE PB $10.95

Flann **O'Brien**

At Swim-Two-Birds

A phantasmagoria of a comic novel, first published in 1939, in which multiple plots intrude on each other with maddening unpredictability, and language runs wild on every page

0-452-25913-4 PLUME PB $12.95

The Dalkey Archive

James Joyce returns to Ireland under bizarre circumstances

1564780190 DALKEY ARCHIVE PB $9.95

The Hard Life

1-56478-019-8 DALKEY ARCHIVE PB $9.95

The Poor Mouth: A Bad Story about the Hard Life

Some Irish readers had trouble forgiving O'Brien for this savagely parodistic novel, originally written in Gaelic, which depicts traditional Irish peasant life in less than idyllic terms

TRANSLATED BY PATRICK C. POWER

1-56478-091-0 DALKEY ARCHIVE PB $10.95

The Third Policeman

O'Brien depicts—with wild humor masking ultimate horror—a circular Hell inhabited largely by semihuman bicycles

0-452-25912-6 NEW AMERICAN LIBRARY PB ... $12.95

Liam **O'Flaherty**

Famine

A chronicle of the Great Hunger of the 1840s

AFTERWORD BY THOMAS FLANAGAN

0-87923-434-2 GODINE PB $18.95

The Informer

A drunkard is destroyed by his own guilt after betraying an IRA leader to the authorities

0-15-644356-2 HARCOURT BRACE PB $9.00

George **Orwell**

1984

Orwell's bleak 1948 vision of a totalitarian England under Big Brother

See also **CLASSICS** under **POLITICAL THOUGHT** in **SOCIAL STUDIES**

0-451-52493-4 NEW AMERICAN LIBRARY PB $5.95

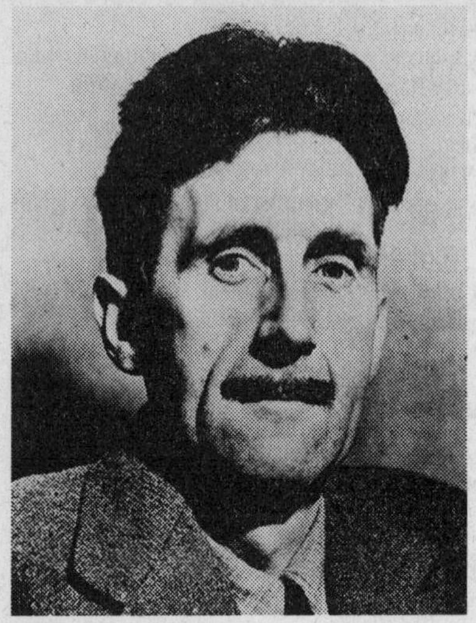

George Orwell

Animal Farm
The famous satire on Soviet communism depicted as a revolutionized barnyard in which "some animals are more equal than others"
See also **CLASSICS** under **POLITICAL THOUGHT** in **SOCIAL STUDIES**
0-452-26490-1 NEW AMERICAN LIBRARY PB $9.95

Animal Farm: A Fairy Story
ILLUSTRATED BY RALPH STEADMAN
0-15-100217-7 HARCOURT BRACE..................$26.00
0-451-52466-7 NEW AMERICAN LIBRARY PB $4.95

Burmese Days
An early novel based on Orwell's experiences in the colonial service
See also **BURMA (MYANMAR)** under **SOUTHEAST ASIA AND THE PHILIPPINES** in **WORLD HISTORY AND CURRENT AFFAIRS**
0-15-614850-1 HARCOURT BRACE PB $8.95

A Clergyman's Daughter
A mysterious relocation into London's lower depths transforms the quiet life and orthodox views of a proper young lady
0-15-618065-0 HARCOURT BRACE PB $13.00

Coming Up For Air
An insurance salesman breaks out of his daily routine to revisit his native village
0-15-619625-5 HARCOURT BRACE PB $8.95

Keep the Aspidistra Flying
0-15-646899-9 HARCOURT BRACE PB $10.00

John Cowper **Powys**

A Glastonbury Romance
A monumental novel first published in 1932, set in the modern era but drawing on the supernatural legends associated with Glastonbury
0-87951-282-2 OVERLOOK $35.00
0-87951-681-X PENGUIN PB $19.95

Maiden Castle
0-912568-18-6 COLGATE PB $19.95

Porius: A Romance of the Dark Ages
0-912568-16-X SYRACUSE $48.95

Three Fantasies
AFTERWORD BY GLEN CAVALIERO
0-85635-693-X CARCANET PB $11.25

Wolf Solent
0-912568-09-7 SYRACUSE $35.95

V.S. **Pritchett**

A Careless Window
A new collection of short stories from one of England's most distinguished men of letters. "Pritchett combines charm and wit, kindness and satire, to write some of the best social comedy of our time. No one alive writes a better English sentence"—Irving Howe
0-394-57612-8 RANDOM HOUSE.....................$16.95

Collected Stories
"Pritchett remains one of the few writers who can discern in the distances between the pieces of furniture a story as dramatic as a divorce" —*Boston Globe*
0-679-73892-4 VINTAGE PB $22.00

Dead Man Leading
INTRODUCTION BY PAUL THEROUX
0-19-281469-9 OXFORD PB $6.95

V. S. Pritchett (photo by Elliott Erwitt)

Herbert **Read**

The Green Child
INTRODUCTION BY KENNETH REXROTH
0-8112-0365-4 NEW DIRECTIONS $8.95

Mary **Renault**

Renault uses her wide knowledge of the ancient world, from the historical reality to the great Athenian myths, to depict daily life during the war with Sparta and the conquests of Alexander.

The Bull from the Sea
See also **HISTORICAL AND ROMANTIC FICTION** in **POPULAR READING**
0-394-71504-7 RANDOM HOUSE PB $8.00

The Charioteer
A young man who discovers his homosexuality when convalescing after Dunkirk must choose between a heroic naval officer and a conscientious objector. One of Renault's few contemporary novels
0-15-616768-9 HARVEST PB.............................$10.95

Fire from Heaven
See also **HISTORICAL AND ROMANTIC FICTION** in **POPULAR READING**
0-394-72291-4 RANDOM HOUSE PB $10.00

The King Must Die
Fascinating story set in the Minoan period as Theseus, mythical king of Athens, saves the city from its annual tribute of young men and maidens for sacrifice to the Minotaur
See also **HISTORICAL AND ROMANTIC FICTION** in **POPULAR READING**
0-394-75104-3 VINTAGE PB $11.00

The Last of the Wine
A young Athenian actor tells of his troupe's exciting travels through Greece during the Peloponnesian War
See also **HISTORICAL AND ROMANTIC FICTION** in **POPULAR READING**
0-394-71653-1 RANDOM HOUSE PB $8.95

The Persian Boy
A first-person account by a beautiful young captive of the Macedonian army who becomes the catamite of the conqueror Alexander
See also **HISTORICAL AND ROMANTIC FICTION** in **POPULAR READING**
0-394-75101-9 VINTAGE PB $13.00

Jean **Rhys**

John Updike has described Jean Rhys's fiction as "amazing in its resolute economy of style and in its illusionless portrait of a drifting heroine, a portrait…stunningly honest and severe."

After Leaving Mr. MacKenzie
0-393-31547-9 NORTON PB..............................$11.00

The Collected Short Stories
0-393-02375-3 NORTON $19.95
0-393-30625-9 NORTON PB $12.95

Good Morning, Midnight
Rhys searingly depicts the vulnerability of a young woman adrift in Paris and at the mercy of a predatory male
0-393-30394-2 NORTON PB................................$9.95

Letters, 1931-1966
Provides fine insights into Rhy's fiction
EDITED BY FRANCIS WYNDHAM AND DIANA MELLY
0-14-018906-8 PENGUIN PB $12.95

Quartet
0-393-31546-0 NORTON PB..............................$11.00

Smile Please: An Unfinished Autobiography
An interesting look at Rhy's life
0-14-018405-8 PENGUIN PB $9.95

Tigers Are Better-Looking, with a Selection from the Left Bank
0-14-018346-9 PENGUIN PB.............................$11.95

Voyage in the Dark
0-393-31146-5 NORTON PB................................$8.95

Wide Sargasso Sea
Derived from *Jane Eyre,* this tour de force about the adolescence and marriage of Rochester's first wife turns the tropical landscape of the West Indies into an image for her tormented soul
0-393-31048-5 NORTON PB................................$8.95

Frederick **Rolfe**

The Desire and Pursuit of the Whole
0-8076-1331-2 BRAZILLER..............................$20.00

Frederick **Rolfe**

The Desire and Pursuit of the Whole: A Romance of Modern Venice

INTRODUCTION BY W.H. AUDEN
0-306-80258-9 DA CAPO PB....................$9.95

Hadrian the Seventh

Unemployed writer is elected Pope in this bizarre camp classic
0-486-22323-X DOVER....................$1.00

S.P. **Rosenbaum**, editor

A Bloomsbury Group Reader

0-631-17318-8 BLACKWELL....................$57.95
0-631-19059-7 BLACKWELL PB....................$22.95

Rafael **Sabatini**

The Fortunes of Casanova and Other Stories

0-19-212319-X OXFORD....................$30.00

Saki

"The Edwardian era, in spite of its political idiocies and a sinister sense of foreboding which, to intelligent observers, underlay the latter part of it, must have been, socially at least, very charming. It is this evanescent charm that Saki so effortlessly evoked."
—Noel Coward

The Chronicles of Clovis

The scourge of the country-house set: no bridge game, no hunting party, no children's game is safe from Clovis's clever pranks
INTRODUCTION BY AUBERON WAUGH
0-14-018349-3 VIKING PB....................$5.95

The Complete Saki

INTRODUCTION BY NOEL COWARD
0-14-018420-1 PENGUIN PB....................$13.95

Siegfried **Sassoon**

Though published as fiction, Sassoon's Sherston series is in fact an undisguised autobiography of his experiences in the Great War.

Complete Memoirs of George Sherston

Sassoon traces the career of the author's fictional alter ego from his privileged early manhood through his protest against the militaristic folly of the conduct of the Great War
0-571-09913-0 FABER PB....................$16.95

Stevie **Smith**

Novel on Yellow Paper

0-8112-1239-4 NEW DIRECTIONS PB....................$10.95

C.P. **Snow**

The Light and the Dark

Roy Calvert's search for meaning among the political ideologies of the 1930s reveals the spiritual emptiness of a generation
0-684-14841-2 MACMILLAN....................$20.00

Time of Hope

From a modest background, Lewis Eliot struggles to establish himself in professional life and free himself from an unhappy affair
0-684-15315-7 MACMILLAN....................$20.00

James **Stephens**

The Crock of Gold

A lilting, sentimental novel that takes a fantasy journey into the heart of Irish folklore
0-89190-616-9 AMEREON....................$19.95

Dylan **Thomas**

Adventures in the Skin Trade & Other Stories

The semiautobiographical title piece was never completed, but contains the quintessence of Thomas's humor
0-8112-0202-X NEW DIRECTIONS PB....................$8.95

Dylan Thomas

A Child's Christmas in Wales

An evocation of childhood that has long been one of Thomas's most popular works. This 1980 edition was chosen as one of the year's ten best illustrated books by *The New York Times* and *Time*
ILLUSTRATED BY EDWARD ARDIZZONE
0-87923-339-7 GODINE....................$14.95
0-87923-529-2 GODINE PB....................$9.95

The Collected Stories

INTRODUCTION BY LESLIE NORRIS
0-8112-0998-9 NEW DIRECTIONS PB....................$11.95

Eight Stories

0-8112-1245-9 NEW DIRECTIONS PB....................$5.00

Portrait of the Artist as a Young Dog

The amusing and whimsical adventures of a provincial young man's first days in London
0-8112-0207-0 NEW DIRECTIONS PB....................$7.95

Quite Early One Morning

A collection of short stories
0-8112-0208-9 NEW DIRECTIONS PB....................$9.95

Rebecca's Daughters

A 19th-century adventure about the midnight raids of Welsh saboteurs against villainous landlords
ILLUSTRATED BY FRITZ EICHENBERG
0-8112-0852-4 NEW DIRECTIONS....................$8.50

Flora **Thompson**

Lark Rise to Candleford: A Trilogy

0-14-018850-9 PENGUIN PB....................$12.95

Over to Candleford

0-7089-0231-6 ULVERSCROFT....................$15.95

Rex **Warner**

The Aerodrome

1-56663-025-8 DEE PB....................$12.95

Sylvia Townsend **Warner**

After the Death of Don Juan

1-85381-057-6 VIRAGO PB....................$11.95

Lolly Willowes

"The witty, eerie, tender but firm life history of a middle-class Englishwoman who politely declines to make the expected connection with the opposite sex and becomes a witch instead"—John Updike
INTRODUCTION BY ANITA MILLER
0-915864-91-6 ACADEMY CHICAGO PB....................$10.00

Selected Stories

1-85381-159-9 VIRAGO PB....................$11.95

Evelyn **Waugh**

Black Mischief

Satire and Grand Guignol whimsy in postcolonial Africa as a band of British colonists flees revolution
0-316-92609-4 LITTLE, BROWN PB....................$10.95

Brideshead Revisited

Roman Catholic aristocrats succumb to age and alcohol, but bequeath their spirit to the middle-class narrator
0-679-42300-1 KNOPF....................$17.00
0-316-92634-5 LITTLE, BROWN PB....................$11.95

Charles Ryder's Schooldays & Other Stories

The title story tells more about the protagonist of *Brideshead Revisited*
0-316-92639-6 LITTLE, BROWN PB....................$11.95

A Handful of Dust

"Waugh treats society as a wonderland in which he plays the part of a rude, libellous, yet domestic Alice"—V.S. Pritchett
0-316-92605-1 LITTLE, BROWN PB....................$12.95

Evelyn Waugh (photo courtesy of Little, Brown and Company)

The Loved One

This classic Britisher-in-Hollywood novel inters the burlesque fantasia of L.A. funeral customs with mordant wit
0-316-92608-6 LITTLE, BROWN PB....................$10.95

Waugh's "Sword of Honor Trilogy" is one of the outstanding fictional accounts of the Second World War

Men At Arms
0-316-92628-0 LITTLE, BROWN PB $12.95

Officers and Gentlemen
0-316-92630-2 LITTLE, BROWN PB $12.95

The End of the Battle
0-316-92620-5 LITTLE, BROWN PB $11.95

The Sword of Honour Trilogy
0-679-43136-5 KNOPF $20.00

Put Out More Flags
An acerbic description of the Bright Young Things at war includes vignettes of Auden and Isherwood
0-316-92615-9 LITTLE, BROWN $15.95
0-316-92612-4 LITTLE, BROWN PB $11.95

Remote People
0-88001-256-0 ECCO PB $8.95

Scoop
An error that assigns an eccentric birdwatcher to cover an African revolution provides the basis for this satire of the newspaper business
0-316-92617-5 LITTLE, BROWN PB $15.95
0-316-92610-8 LITTLE, BROWN PB $10.95

Vile Bodies
The amusing effects of an American revivalist carnival on the habitués of the society pages in the London papers.
"Derisive, staccato, slightly cockeyed, and somehow heartbreaking…The defiant hilarity of a dance on a sinking ship"—Alexander Woolcott
0-316-92611-6 LITTLE, BROWN PB $11.95

Mary **Webb**

Gone to Earth
The spirits of a violated earth struggle against the triumphant aggressors in this tale of a half-wild Gypsy girl and her fox cub
0-86068-143-2 VIRAGO PB $11.95

Precious Bane
0-268-01538-4 NOTRE DAME PB $14.00

H.G. **Wells**

Ann Veronica
EDITED BY SYLVIA HARDY
0-4608-7306-7 EVERYMAN'S PB $7.95

The Complete Short Stories of H.G. Wells
0-312-15855-6 ST. MARTIN'S $19.95

History of Mister Polly
Sick of the routine of modern existence, a shopkeeper burns down his shop and finds fulfillment in returning to an older way of life
EDITED BY GORDON N. RAY
0-395-05149-5 HOUGHTON MIFFLIN PB $10.36

Kipps
Artie Kipps struggles to survive in a more rarefied society when sudden wealth lifts him above his station in the world
INTRODUCTION BY BENNY GREEN
EDITED BY PETER VAN SITTART
0-460-87277-X EVERYMAN'S PB $7.95

Love and Mr. Lewisham
INTRODUCTION BY BENNY GREEN
0-460-87420-9 EVERYMAN'S PB $6.95

The New Machievelli
0-4608-7422-5 TUTTLE PB $7.95

Selected Short Stories
0-14-018188-1 PENGUIN PB $9.95

Tono-Bungay
EDITED BY JOHN HAMMOND
0-460-87259-1 EVERYMAN'S PB $7.95

The War of the Worlds
See also **EARLY SCIENCE FICTION** under **SCIENCE FICTION AND FANTASY** in **POPULAR READING**
AFTERWORD BY ISAAC ASIMOV
0-451-52276-1 NEW AMERICAN LIBRARY PB $4.95

Rebecca **West**

Cousin Rosamund
AFTERWORD BY VICTORIA GLENDINNING
0-14-010130-6 PENGUIN PB $6.95

Rebecca West

The Judge
0-86068-136-X VIRAGO PB $11.95

The Judge
"A brilliant piece of work. Through its pages there shines the clear, unmistakable light of genius"—*NY Times*
0-7867-0287-7 CARROLL & GRAF PB $13.95

The Return of the Soldier
0-7867-0347-4 CARROLL & GRAF PB $10.95

Sunflower
A posthumously published early novel. "This unfinished novel, written in the mid-1920s, is a study in frustration—for its readers, in that the problems it poses remain unresolved, and for Sunflower and her creator in that it is about the unsatisfied physical desire of a woman for a man, unusual for the period and unusual for Rebecca West"—Victoria Glendinning
AFTERWORD BY VICTORIA GLENDINNING
0-670-81386-9 VIKING PB $18.95

Young Rebecca: Writings of Rebecca West, 1911-17
EDITED BY JANE MARCUS
0-253-23101-9 INDIANA PB $6.95

Antonia **White**

Antonia White: Diaries, 1926-1957
EDITED BY SUSAN CHITTY
0-670-83970-1 VIKING $25.00

Beyond the Glass
0-86068-097-5 VIRAGO PB $11.95

The Lost Traveller
0-86068-095-9 VIRAGO PB $11.95

Strangers
0-860-68171-8 VIRAGO PB $11.95

P.G. **Wodehouse**

If I Were You
This richly comic 1931 novel is one of the master's rarest works and one of the most sought after. Other books by P.G. Wodehouse can be found in the Humorous Writers section of Popular Reading
1-55882-058-2 INT'L POLYGONICS PB $11.95

Virginia **Woolf**

"Virginia Woolf stands as the chief figure of modernism in England and must be included with Joyce and Proust in the realization of experiments that have completely broken with tradition."—NY Times

Between the Acts
Woolf's last novel moves between eras while describing a pageant on a country estate
0-15-611870-X HARCOURT BRACE PB $7.95

The Complete Shorter Fiction of Virginia Woolf
A gathering of nearly 50 stories
EDITED BY SUSAN DICK
0-15-621250-1 HARCOURT BRACE PB $11.00

A Haunted House & Other Short Stories
FOREWORD BY LEONARD WOOLF
0-15-639401-4 HARCOURT BRACE PB $6.95

Jacob's Room
An elegiac early novel about a young man who becomes a casualty of the First World War
0-15-645742-3 HARCOURT BRACE PB $7.95

Monday or Tuesday: Eight Stories
0-486-29453-6 DOVER PB $1.00

Mrs. Dalloway
A 1925 landmark of modernist fiction that follows an MP's wife on an outing, tracing the shifting consciousness of herself and others, including a shell-shocked veteran whose destiny briefly intersects with hers
0-15-662863-5 HARCOURT BRACE PB $5.95

Through all ages—when the pavement was grass, when it was swamp, through the age of tusk and mammoth, through the age of silent sunrise, the battered woman—for she wore a skirt—with her right hand exposed, her left clutching at her side, stood singing of love—love which has lasted a million years, she sang, love which prevails, and millions of years ago, her

lover, who had been dead these centuries, had walked, she crooned, with her in May; but in the course of ages, long as summer days, and flaming, she remembered, with nothing but red asters, he had gone; death's enormous sickle had swept those tremendous hills, and when at last she laid her hoary and immensely aged head on the earth, now become a mere cinder of ice, she implored the Gods to lay by her side a bunch of purple heather, there on her high burial place which the last rays of the last sun caressed; for then the pageant of the universe would be over.
MRS. DALLOWAY

Mrs. Dalloway's Party: A Short Story Sequence
Seven stories related to Mrs. Dalloway
INTRODUCTION BY STELLA MCNICHOL
0-15-662900-3 HARCOURT BRACE PB $4.95

Night and Day
EDITED BY JULIA BRIGGS
0-14-018568-2 PENGUIN PB $12.95

Orlando: A Biography
A historical fantasy following a single hero/heroine through sexual metamorphoses from Elizabethan times to the present
0-15-670160-X HARCOURT BRACE PB $12.00

The Pargiters
A restoration of Woolf's originally projected form for the first section of *The Years*
0-87104-268-1
PUBLISHERS CENTER CULTURAL RESOURCES.. $25.00

A Room of One's Own
Woolfe's graceful manifesto about women, their place in the world and their writing
EDITED BY JENIFER SMITH
0-521-48590-8 CAMBRIDGE PB $6.95

To the Lighthouse
"One of few books which are filled with goodness and genuine love but also, in its feminine way, with irony, amorphous sadness, and doubt of life"—Auerbach
0-15-690739-9 HARCOURT BRACE PB $7.95

The Virginia Woolf Reader
An abundant selection from Woolf's fiction and non-fiction
See also **20TH-CENTURY BRITISH ESSAYS AND OTHER PROSE**
EDITED BY MITCHELL A. LEASKA
0-15-693590-2 HARCOURT BRACE PB $12.95

The Voyage Out
EDITED BY LORNA SAGE
0-19-281834-1 OXFORD PB $8.95

The Waves
Woolf interweaves six interior voices in one of her most complex works. "In each soliloquy in this pattern of soliloquies we ourselves are at the centre. We are Bernard, we are Susan, but with this difference: that we have borrowed, for a moment, the lamp of genius, and by its light may read the secrets of our private universe"
—Gerald Bullett
0-15-694960-1 HARCOURT BRACE PB $9.00

The Years
A generational novel spanning half a century, from 1880 to the 1930s
0-15-699701-0 HARCOURT BRACE PB $12.95

The Middle Generation

Peter **Ackroyd**

Chatterton
A fictional exploration of the strange career of the short-lived 18th-century poet
0-8021-3480-7 GROVE PB $12.00

English Music
0-345-37613-7 BALLANTINE PB $12.50

First Light
0-8021-3481-5 GROVE PB $12.00

Trial of Elizabeth Cree: A Novel of the Limehouse Murders
0-385-47707-4 DOUBLEDAY $22.00

Richard **Adams**

The Girl in a Swing
0-451-16306-0 NEW AMERICAN LIBRARY PB $5.95

Watership Down
The quest of a band of Berkshire rabbits for a new home has allegorical overtones but treats the conditions of wildlife with astonishing fidelity. "His true achievement lies in the altogether enchanting civilization he has created"—Peter S. Prescott
See also **YOUNG ADULT FICTION** in **BOOKS FOR YOUNG READERS**
See also **THE '70S** under **THE GREAT FICTION BESTSELLERS 1930-1995** in **POPULAR READING**
0-02-700030-3 MACMILLAN $40.00
0-380-00293-0 AVON PB $5.99

Kingsley **Amis**

The Green Man
A philandering innkeeper struggles with his addictions and a chthonic presence in his pub
0-89733-220-2 ACADEMY CHICAGO PB $6.95

Lucky Jim
Amis's widely hailed first novel about an Angry Young Man at a provincial university in England
0-14-018630-1 PENGUIN PB $10.95

The Russian Girl
"Sex, booze and Russian intrigue have never gone as well together as they do in this brilliant, mordant and quite funny new novel"
—*NY Times Book Review*
0-670-85329-1 VIKING $22.95
0-14-025172-3 PENGUIN PB $10.95

Martin **Amis**

Dead Babies
A futuristic satire. "Rather as I hope for society that this is no true prophecy, I hope for Martin Amis that the nightmare of this vision will rapidly become part of his past. In the meanwhile, it is a remarkable fantasy"
—Elaine Feinstein, *New Statesman*
0-679-73449-X VINTAGE PB $12.00

Einstein's Monsters
Five pieces dealing with nuclear madness
0-679-72996-8 VINTAGE PB $10.00

London Fields
0-679-73034-6 VINTAGE PB $13.00

The Information
Biting portrait of the literary life as one writer hits the bestseller list while his corrosively envious college chum bottoms out
0-517-58516-2 HARMONY $24.00
0-679-73573-9 VINTAGE PB $13.00

Money: A Suicide Note
A fresco of contemporary greed. "A highly original and often dazzling piece of work"
—John Gross, *NY Times*
0-14-008891-1 VIKING PB $11.95

Other People
"Amis is a born comic novelist, in the tradition that ranges from Dickens to Waugh... [His] mercurial style can rise to Joycean brilliance"
—*Newsweek*
0-679-73589-5 VINTAGE PB $10.00

The Rachel Papers
A first novel about youthful naughtiness
0-679-73458-9 VINTAGE PB $11.00

Success
0-679-73448-1 VINTAGE PB $15.95

Time's Arrow: Or the Nature of the Offense
0-679-73572-0 VINTAGE PB $11.00

Beryl **Bainbridge**

"Short, laconic and rich in black comedy, her novels deal with the lives of characters at once deeply ordinary and highly eccentric, in a world where violence and the absurd lurk beneath the daily routine of urban domesticity."
—Oxford Companion to English Literature

An Awfully Big Adventure
0-7867-0184-6 CARROLL & GRAF PB $8.95

The Bottlefactory Outing
A day out for workers at a wine bottle factory irrevocably changes the lives of two women
0-7867-0146-3 CARROLL & GRAF PB $9.95

The Dressmaker
0-7867-0322-9 CARROLL & GRAF PB $8.95

Every Man for Himself
0-7867-0349-0 CARROLL & GRAF $21.00

Weekend with Claude
A country sojourn with an art dealer, interrupted by the mysterious wounding of a female guest, leads to some tense reevaluations among friends
0-8076-1031-3 BRAZILLER $10.95

Young Adolf
0-7867-0258-3 CARROLL & GRAF PB $9.95

J.G. **Ballard**

The Atrocity Exhibition
See also **CONTEMPORARY SCIENCE FICTION** under **SCIENCE FICTION AND FANTASY** in **POPULAR READING**
0-940642-18-2 V/SEARCH PB $13.99

Concrete Island
0-374-52413-0 NOONDAY PB $12.00

Crash
0-374-52412-2 NOONDAY PB $12.00

J.G. **Ballard**

Empire of the Sun
Ballard's autobiographical novel about his capture and imprisonment by the Japanese following the fall of Shanghai became the basis for Steven Spielberg's movie
0-671-64877-2 POCKET PB $5.99

Rushing to Paradise
See also **CONTEMPORARY SCIENCE FICTION** under **SCIENCE FICTION AND FANTASY** in **POPULAR READING**
0-312-13415-0 PICADOR PB $12.00

John **Banville**

Athena
Darkly comic tale mixes gangsters, bizarre sexual encounters, and 17th- century Flemish paintings
0-679-40521-6 KNOPF $22.00
0-679-73685-9 VINTAGE PB $12.00

Book of Evidence
0-446-39253-7 WARNER PB $8.99

Doctor Copernicus
0-679-73799-5 VINTAGE PB $11.00

Ghosts
The talented author of *Doctor Copernicus* and *Kepler* takes a grounded boat, its eccentric passengers, the island of the eminent recluse upon which they are stranded, and mixes them all together to produce this brilliant novel of ideas where even the motives of the nameless narrator are enticingly suspect
0-679-40519-4 KNOPF $21.00
0-679-75512-8 VINTAGE PB $12.00

Kepler: A Novel
0-679-74370-70 VINTAGE PB $10.00

Mefisto
0-446-39282-0 WARNER PB $8.99

The Newton Letter
0-446-39283-9 WARNER PB $8.99

Pat **Barker**

The Eye in the Door
0-452-27272-6 PLUME PB $10.95

The Ghost Road
"Calls to mind such early Modernists as Hemingway and Fitzgerald…some of the most powerful anti-war literature in modern English literature"—*Boston Globe*
0-452-27672-1 PLUME PB $11.95

Regeneration
Fictional characters share the stage with Siegfried Sassoon, Wilfred Owen, and Robert Graves in this look at the First World War's effect on the homefront
0-452-27007-3 PLUME PB $10.95

Julian **Barnes**

Before She Met Me
A middle-aged academic becomes obsessed with his beautiful second wife's premarital affairs
0-679-73609-3 VINTAGE PB $11.00

Cross Channel: Stories
The first collection of Barnes's stories showcases his uncommon sophistication and wit. Concentrating on the strange rapport that unites and divides England and France across the English Channel, 10 stories move from the 17th-century to the future in a historical and emotional panorama. "Barnes's literary energy and daring are nearly unparalleled"—*The New Republic*
0-679-44691-5 KNOPF $21.00
0-679-76755-X VINTAGE $11.00

Flaubert's Parrot
A charming and digressive entertainment—erudite, ironical, and amusing—that hinges on a biographer's obsession with Flaubert. "A most brilliant and impressive book"—James Fenton
0-679-73136-9 VINTAGE PB $10.00

A History of the World in 10 1/2 Chapters
An audacious fictional history of the world from one of Britain's most brilliant young novelists, which begins aboard Noah's Ark and continues in separate but connected stories. "Barnes is an accomplished equilibrist; a reader who appreciates being made to work for his sense of balance will find in *A History of the World* special pleasures, special perils"—*NY Review of Books*
0-679-73137-7 VINTAGE PB $12.00

Metroland
The sophisticated attitudes of two schoolboys prevent them from coming to terms with their feelings. "Its crisp oneliners, cultural jokes and lyrical *aperçus* are organized with the tension of poetry"—Angela Carter
0-679-73608-5 VINTAGE PB $10.00

The Porcupine
The trial of a deposed Communist Party leader provides the frame for this powerful and unsettling novel about Eastern Europe's political transformation, by the author of *Flaubert's Parrot, Talking It Over,* and other novels. "Barnes probably is the finest practitioner of a new hybrid form of journalism-fiction. His elegant intelligence skims and swoops and repeatedly scores"—*Kirkus Reviews*
0-679-74482-7 VINTAGE PB $9.00

Staring at the Sun
Barnes traces the course of a woman's life and the philosophical issues she encounters
0-679-74820-2 VINTAGE PB $11.00

Talking It Over
A love triangle involving three young Londoners—two of them just married to each other—spins out into jealousy, deceit, divorce, anger, and atonement
0-679-40525-9 KNOPF $21.00
0-679-73687-5 VINTAGE PB $11.00

Simi **Bedford**

Yoruba Girl Dancing
A story of a young African who is sent to post-World War II England to be educated at an upper-class boarding school. "*Yoruba Girl Dancing* fingers the pain of exile and exclusion with a feather-light touch"
—*The Guardian* (London)
0-14-023293-1 PENGUIN PB $9.95

John **Berger**

A celebrated Marxist art critic, John Berger is also a novelist, screenwriter, and painter.

Corker's Freedom
Freedom, for the elderly owner of an employment agency, is a world of fantasy that may, in the end, be as shabby as his real life. A disturbing and witty examination of the private, hidden space in public human life. "In contemporary English letters [Berger] seems to me peerless….He is a wonderful artist and thinker"—Susan Sontag
0-679-42722-8 PANTHEON $21.00
0-904613-40-2 WRITERS & READERS PB $5.95

Once in Europa
The second volume of the trilogy *Into Their Labours*, Berger's indelibly original evocation of rural France as the site of a battle between archaic patterns and new technologies
0-679-73716-2 VINTAGE PB $13.00

Photocopies
Berger's latest collection of stories
0-679-43525-5 PANTHEON $22.00

Pig Earth
Stories, essays, and poems about French peasant life dramatize the struggle between the sons of the soil and heartless bureaucrats; the initial volume of the projected trilogy *Into Their Labours*
0-679-73715-4 VINTAGE PB $12.00

To the Wedding
0-679-43981-1 PANTHEON $22.00
0-679-76777-0 VINTAGE PB $11.00

Maeve **Binchy**

Circle of Friends
Spunky young woman confronts the hard realities of social class in this popular coming-of-age novel set in 1960s Dublin
0-440-21126-3 DELL PB $6.99

The Glass Lake
0-385-31354-3 DELACORTE $23.95
0-440-22159-5 BDD PB $7.50

London Transports
0-440-21235-9 DELL PB $6.99

William **Boyd**

The Blue Afternoon
0-679-43295-7 KNOPF $23.00
0-679-77260-X VINTAGE $13.00

Brazzaville Beach
0-380-78049-6 AVON PB $11.00

The Destiny of Nathalie "X" and Other Stories
0-679-44705-9 KNOPF $25.00

A Good Man in Africa
The comic misadventures of a bumbling but decent British diplomat in West Africa. "A sweaty tropical setting in which dead bodies rapidly become unapproachable and live ones, even if lusted for, have a certain grotesquerie"
—Alan Hollinghurst
0-380-71566-X AVON PB $9.00

Malcolm **Bradbury**

Cuts
0-14-023154-4 PENGUIN PB $9.95

Eating People Is Wrong
A spirited satire of British and Commonwealth university types
0-89733-189-3 ACADEMY CHICAGO PB $6.95

Rates of Exchange
A barbed account of an English academic in Eastern Europe
0-14-007631-X PENGUIN PB $10.00

Stepping Westward
0-14-002865-X PENGUIN PB $11.95

Melvyn **Bragg**

The Maid of Buttermere
A love story set against the Cumbrian lakes
0-340-40173-7 TRAFALGAR SQUARE $24.95

Mary **Breasted**

Why Should You Doubt Me Now?
A biting, hilarious sendup of contemporary Irish life. Ultra-Catholic columnist Rupert Penrose is about to seduce a young woman in his Dublin flat when an apparition of the Virgin Mary interrupts the action. It's all uphill from there. "Breasted not only offers right-on-the-button humor, but she's an acute observer of life in that often aggravating but always appealing Emerald Isle"—*Kirkus Reviews*
0-374-29007-5 FS&G $23.00

If there is a fate that can befall a man worse than having the Virgin Mary appear in his bedroom just as he is about to seduce the most beautiful apprentice horoscope writer in Dublin, Rupert Penrose did not know of one. When the apparition came he suddenly knew nothing at all except that he dared not move a muscle. His heart, which had been pounding wildly ever since Attracta Dorris had climbed naked under his duvet, now threatened to break out of his rib cage and catapult itself onto the floor.
WHY SHOULD YOU DOUBT ME NOW?

Christine **Brooke-Rose**
Brooke-Rose is one of England's leading fictional experimentalists.

Amalgamemnon
1-56478-050-3 DALKEY ARCHIVE PB $9.95

The programme-cuts will one by one proceed apace, which will entail laying off paying off with luck all the teachers of dead languages like literature philosophy history, for who will want to know about ancient passions divine royal middle class or working in words and phrases and structures that will continue to spark out inside the techne that will soon be silenced by the high technology? Who will still want to read at night some utterly other discourse that will shimmer out of a minicircus of light upon a page of say Agamemnon returning to his murderous wife the glory-gobbler with his new slave Cassandra princess of fallen Troy...
AMALGAMEMNON
DALKEY ARCHIVE

Textermination
0-8112-1230-0 NEW DIRECTIONS $21.95
0-8112-1216-5 NEW DIRECTIONS PB $10.95

Anita **Brookner**
"These are novels for a disciplined sensibility—not the excesses of the groaning board but the light sufficiency of the luncheon table."—Frances Taliaferro

Altered States
0-679-44973-6 RANDOM HOUSE $23.00

A Closed Eye
A shattered marriage of convenience, and a vivid portrait of pretension, loss, materialism, and regret. "Anita Brookner works a spell on the reader; being under it is both an education and a delight"—*Washington Post Book World*
0-679-40447-3 VINTAGE PB $21.00

Anita Brookner

The Debut
0-679-72712-4 VINTAGE PB $10.00

Dolly
0-679-74578-5 VINTAGE PB $11.00

Fraud
Anna Durrant, a compliant, intelligent, self-sacrificing spinster, has been missing for months by the time the police are called in to find her. Brookner probes not only the mystery of her protagonist's disappearance, but that of her smothered heart as well. "If Henry James were around, the only writer he'd be reading with complete approval would be Anita Brookner"
—*NY Times*
0-679-41606-4 RANDOM HOUSE $21.00
0-679-74308-1 VINTAGE PB $11.00

Hotel du Lac
EDITED BY ROBIN DESSER
0-679-75932-8 VINTAGE PB $11.00

Incidents in the Rue Laugier
0-679-76512-3 VINTAGE PB $12.00

Latecomers
0-679-72668-3 VINTAGE PB $11.00

Look at Me
After her mother's death, a woman tends a collection of medical prints while casting around for an escape from her depressing self-absorption
0-679-73813-4 VINTAGE PB $12.00

A Private View
"Brookner is back once again at her uncompromising and understated best...There is no doubt that she is one of very few contemporary authors whose novels deserve to live on well into the next century"
—*Washington Post Book World*
0-679-43444-5 RANDOM HOUSE $23.00
0-679-75443-1 VINTAGE PB $12.00

Providence
0-679-73814-2 VINTAGE PB $11.00

Anthony **Burgess**

A Clockwork Orange
An original, futuristic vision of authoritarian society and teenage gangs on the loose. "Much more than a linguistic tour de force. It is also the most devastating piece of satire since Zamiatin's *We*"—Geoffrey Aggeler
0-393-31283-6 NORTON PB $10.00

The Complete Enderby: Inside Mr. Enderby, Enderby Outside, The Clockwork Testament, and Enderby's Dark Lady
"With the most offhand, scurrilous charm, Burgess illustrates [how Enderby the artist] is the man who expresses for all men their unbuttoned true selves"—*Time*
0-7867-0248-6 CARROLL & GRAF PB $15.95

A Dead Man in Deptford
Burgess's last, posthumously published novel re-creates the world of Elizabethan England with the life of Christopher Marlowe
0-7867-0192-7 CARROLL & GRAF $21.00
0-7867-0321-0 CARROLL & GRAF PB $11.95

The Doctor Is Sick
A philologist in the throes of a dissolving marriage embarks on a burlesque quest through the seamy side of '50s London
0-393-00959-9 NORTON PB $9.95

Earthly Powers
Roman à clef charting the final years of an English writer very much like W. Somerset Maugham. "Remarkable! Bursts with manic erudition, garlicky puns, and omnilingual jokes"—Martin Amis
0-7867-0026-2 CARROLL & GRAF PB $15.95

Honey for the Bears
0-393-31441-3 NORTON PB $12.00

The Kingdom of the Wicked
0-671-72955-1 POCKET PB $5.95

The Long Day Wanes: A Malayan Trilogy
Victor Crabbe, the hero of Burgess's first published novel, is a comic, victimized colonial administrator caught up in the decay of empire in Malaya during the Second World War
0-393-30943-6 NORTON PB $10.95

Nothing Like the Sun
Shakespeare's lusty and turbulent affair with the Dark Lady of the sonnets, rendered in a lusty, turbulent pastiche of Elizabethan prose
0-393-00795-2 NORTON PB $9.95

Anthony **Burgess**

The Wanting Seed

A witty vision of an overpopulated futuristic state whose ideology oscillates between pessimistic Augustinianism and optimistic Pelagianism

0-393-00808-8 NORTON PB $10.95

Gordon **Burn**

Alma

An unusual and marvelously written reinvention of the life of one of the famous English pop stars of the '50s, *Alma* won the 1991 Whitbread Award, Britain's highest honor for a first novel. "I simply couldn't stop reading this book" —Richard Ford.
"An extraordinary, unprecedented novel....Audacious, innovative and totally compelling"—William Boyd

0-395-63414-8 HOUGHTON MIFFLIN $19.95

A.S. **Byatt**

Babel Tower

New from the Booker Prize-winning author of *Possession,* an inventive story set in the decade of the Berlin Wall, the Cuban Missile Crisis, *Lady Chatterly,* and the Beatles. Revolving around two bitter law cases, peopled with vivid characters, this novel is charted with brilliant imaginative sympathy

0-679-40513-5 RANDOM HOUSE $25.95

The Game

A compelling novel that offers a darkly convincing portrait of sibling rivalry while forcing us to reconsider the uses—and misuses—of the imagination. "Byatt is the most formidably equipped of contemporary novelists...The great merit of her writing...is that it continually engages the reader's mind"—*Daily Telegraph*

0-679-74256-5 VINTAGE PB $11.00

The Matisse Stories

Byatt peels away the quotidian to expose the pain, desire, and joy in the lives of ordinary women

0-679-43882-3 RANDOM HOUSE $17.00
0-679-76223-X VINTAGE PB $10.00

Possession: A Romance

A bestselling tale of young scholars researching the lives of two Victorian poets. "A masterpiece of wordplay and adventure, a novel that compares with Stendhal and Joyce"—*LA Times.* "Gorgeously written...dazzling"—*NY Times*

0-679-73590-9 VINTAGE PB $13.00

The Shadow of the Sun

For the first time in paperback, Byatt's remarkable debut novel: the coming-of-age story of a sensitive 17-year-old girl who emerges from under the shadow of her powerful father by embarking on a love affair with one of his colleagues

0-15-681416-1 HARCOURT BRACE PB $13.00

Still Life

A stunning group portrait of an extended family and the different paths they follow in life and in art. "I am, as always, amazed and rewarded by her intelligence and sensitivity. When it comes to probing characters her scalpel is sure but gentle. She is a loving surgeon"—Toni Morrison

0-02-017855-7 COLLIER PB $12.00

Sugar and Other Stories

0-679-74227-1 VINTAGE PB $12.00

A.S. Byatt

Angels & Insects: Two Novellas

0-679-75134-3 VINTAGE PB $13.00

The Virgin in the Garden

Combines Victorian romanticism with mystery, humor, and intellectual depth. "The stories, skillfully alternated, are linked by cunning echoes"—*TLS*

0-679-73829-0 VINTAGE PB $13.00

Angela **Carter**

Burning Your Boats: The Collected Short Stories

INTRODUCTION BY SALMAN RUSHDIE

0-8050-4462-0 HOLT $30.00

Heroes and Villains

0-14-023464-0 PENGUIN PB $9.95

The Infernal Desire Machines of Doctor Hoffman

Metaphysical fantasy of a magic land where Desiderio, detailed by the logical Minister of Determination to destroy the wizard of dreams, falls in love with the latter's beautiful daughter

0-14-023519-1 PENGUIN PB $10.95

The Magic Toyshop

"A magic novel, sexy and eccentric, romantic and tricky"—*VLS*

0-14-025640-7 PENGUIN PB $10.95

Nights at the Circus

Fevvers and Lizzie are performers of almost magical skills in this 19th-century circus fantasy spanning every country in Europe. "A couple of sexual revolutionaries taking over the male illusion game"—Valerie Cunningham, *Observer*

0-14-007703-0 VIKING PB $11.95

Saints and Strangers

0-14-008973-X PENGUIN PB $10.95

Shadow Dance

Carter's first novel: "[She] has remarkable descriptive gifts, a powerful imagination, and...a capacity for looking at the mess of contemporary life without totally flinching"—Anthony Burgess

0-14-025524-9 PENGUIN PB $10.95

Wise Children

Carter's last book is the story of four generations of theater personalities, told from the perspective of Nora and Dora, septuaganerian twin sisters. "A gala production...told with extravagant humor"—*New Yorker*

0-374-29133-0 FS&G $21.00

Bruce **Chatwin**

On the Black Hill

A novel about a rural Welsh community

0-14-006896-1 PENGUIN PB $11.95

The Songlines

This fascinating picture of the interaction between the Aborigine and Anglo cultures in Australia is also a philosophical meditation on the human potential of "nomadism"

See also **AUSTRALIA, NEW ZEALAND, AND THE SOUTH PACIFIC** under **TRAVEL LITERATURE** in **FOOD, TRAVEL, AND LEISURE**

0-14-009429-6 PENGUIN PB $12.95

Utz

Chatwin's final novel

See also **AUSTRALIA, NEW ZEALAND, AND THE SOUTH PACIFIC** under **TRAVEL LITERATURE** in **FOOD, TRAVEL, AND LEISURE**

0-14-011576-5 PENGUIN PB $10.00

The Viceroy of Ouidah

The colorful life of a Spanish slave merchant in Africa and his impact on the culture and customs of the local peoples

0-14-011290-1 VIKING PB $10.95

Barbara **Comyns**

Who Was Changed and Who Was Dead

0-86068-677-9 VIRAGO PB $11.95

Cyril **Connolly** & Peter **Levi**

Shade Those Laurels

A literary whodunit by the eminent Cyril Connolly, left unfinished at his death in 1974, has now been completed by Oxford's Peter Levi, who learned the denouement from Connolly himself. "Like the final bottle of a rare and unrepeatable vintage"—*The Spectator*

0-679-40433-3 PANTHEON $20.00

In this house wine takes precedence. Let's see what we're drinking: with the turtle, an old Solera that was of age when Rimbaud and Verlaine played boy in Howland Street—a Montrachet, discreet as Docteur Blanche, to keep a flinty eye on the fish—a Romanee Saint Vivant as old as *Prufrock* that should hold your attention, Mr. Kemble—and when the birds are stomached and while the cheese souffle exhales its brief "Coronemeus," the last—or almost the last—of my Yquem '21. *Reverentia!* And with the dessert we shall listen to the deplorable confessions of a magnum of dear Hugh Walpole's pink champagne.

SHADE THOSE LAURELS

Catherine **Cookson**

The Golden Straw

0-684-81177-4 SIMON & SCHUSTER $23.00

Jim **Crace**

Arcadia

A virtuoso performance by one of England's most celebrated young writers, *Arcadia* is a brilliant novel on the fate of the postmodern city. Having been compared to Borges, Coetzee, Calvino, and Kafka, Crace with his new book establishes himself as one of the most distinctive writers of fiction in the English language today. "Jim Crace is a new writer who is gifted almost beyond belief"—John Hawkes

0-689-12158-X ATHENEUM $20.00

Continent

0-88001-498-9 ECCO PB $12.00

The Gift of Stones

0-88001-450-4 ECCO PB $13.00

Signals of Distress

See also **AMERICAN MILITARY HISTORY** under **MILITARY HISTORY** under **MILITARY AFFAIRS** in **WORLD HISTORY AND CURRENT AFFAIRS**

0-374-26379-5 FS&G $22.00
0-88001-486-5 ECCO PB $15.00

Roald **Dahl**

The Best of Roald Dahl

Dahl, a master of the bizarre, creates terrifying effects by combining the mundane with the grotesque

0-679-72991-7 VINTAGE PB $15.00

My Uncle Oswald

0-14-005577-0 PENGUIN PB $10.95

Roald Dahl's Tales of the Unexpected

0-679-72989-5 VINTAGE PB $15.00

Anita **Desai**

Clear Light of Day

"A wonderful novel about silence and music, about the partition of a family as well as a nation"—*NY Times*

See also **INDIAN LITERATURE IN ENGLISH** under **LITERATURES OF INDIA** in **LITERATURE OF EUROPE, AFRICA, AND ASIA**

0-14-010859-9 PENGUIN PB $10.95

Anita Desai

Margaret **Drabble**

The Gates of Ivory

0-14-016719-6 PENGUIN PB $12.00

The Millstone

A young woman working on a dissertation decides to keep the baby conceived in a casual love affair

0-452-26126-0 NEW AMERICAN LIBRARY PB.....$7.95

A Natural Curiosity

0-14-012228-1 PENGUIN PB $10.00

The Radiant Way

0-8041-0365-8 IVY PB $5.99

Lawrence **Durrell**

The Alexandria Quartet

Includes *Justine, Balthazar, Mountolive,* and *Clea.* "People are always saying—inaccurately—that something or another is like a dream, but Durrell's Alexandria is actually like the landscape of a dream. A hot, dry city, surrounded by desert, raked by winds and by contradictions. A relentless yet voluptuous city, beautiful and squalid, overcivilized and primitive"—Anatole Broyard, *Times* [London]

0-14-015317-9 PENGUIN PB $47.80

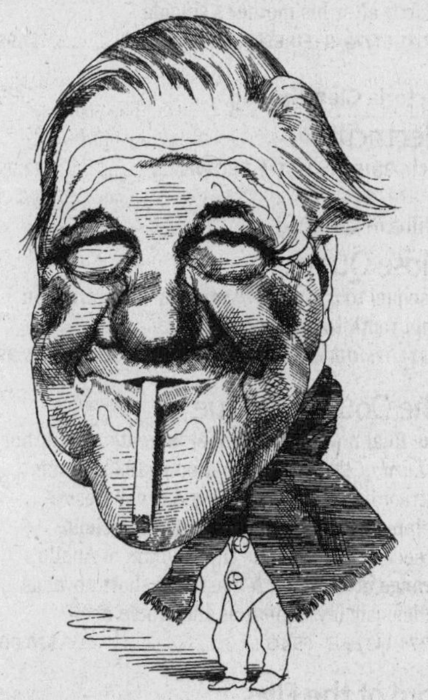

Lawrence Durrell

Balthazar

0-14-015321-7 PENGUIN PB $11.95

Clea

0-14-015322-5 VIKING PB $11.95

Justine

0-14-015319-5 VIKING PB $11.95

Mountolive

0-14-015320-9 PENGUIN PB $11.95

Pope Joan

0-87951-964-9 VIKING PB $12.95

Quinx: The Ripper's Tale

0-670-80658-7 VIKING PB $15.95

White Eagles Over Serbia

1-55970-312-1 ARCADE $19.95

G.B. **Edwards**

The Book of Ebenezer Le Page

Edwards's only novel, written in old age and published posthumously, chronicles an isolated life on the island of Guernsey. "Like Proust, Edwards can make us feet the passage of time as a tragic force. Like Proust, he has a surprise for us that can only be convincingly revealed in the fullness of time. For this is a novel you must read every word of, or miss the deeply human meaning altogether"—Guy Davenport, *NY Times*

INTRODUCTION BY JOHN FOWLES

1-55921-142-3 MOYER BELL PB $12.95

Penelope **Farmer**

Charlotte Sometimes

0-440-41261-7 YEARLING PB $3.50

J.G. **Farrell**

Singapore Grip

0-88184-124-2 CARROLL & GRAF PB $4.95

Troubles

In the decaying Majestic Hotel in Dublin, the disintegrating remnants of the Anglo-Irish aristocracy slowly live out their last days

0-88184-269-9 CARROLL & GRAF PB $4.95

Penelope **Fitzgerald**

Innocence

0-88184-537-X CARROLL & GRAF PB $7.95

Offshore

Richly eccentric characters in a houseboat community in Battersea Reach during the 1960s

0-88184-476-4 CARROLL & GRAF PB $7.95

Nina **Fitzpatrick**

Fables of the Irish Intelligentsia

Populated by lunatics, poets, and visionaries, these wonderful stories poke sly fun at the English tendency to regard the Irish as infantile and naive. "Beautiful without being mannered or precious, it is Irish in the best sense" —*TLS* [London]

0-14-017324-2 PENGUIN PB $9.00

The Loves of Faustyna

0-14-024132-9 PENGUIN PB $9.95

Ken **Follett**

The 3rd Twin

See also **CONTEMPORARY SPY FICTION** under **SPY FICTION** in **POPULAR READING**

0-517-70296-7 CROWN $25.95

The Pillars of the Earth

0-451-16689-2 NEW AMERICAN LIBRARY PB.....$7.99

A Place Called Freedom

See also **CONTEMPORARY SPY FICTION** under **SPY FICTION** in **POPULAR READING**

0-517-70176-6 CROWN $25.00
0-449-22515-1 CREST PB $6.99

John **Fowles**

The Ebony Tower

This collection of stories ranges from a study of the subtle eroticism of a French master-painter's old age to the vivid retelling of a medieval "lay"

0-452-26710-2 PLUME PB $12.95

John **Fowles**

The French Lieutenant's Woman

Ostensibly a Victorian romance, this novel's own narrative ploys are analogs of the male desire to rationalize and manipulate the enigma of woman

0-316-29099-8 LITTLE, BROWN $29.95
0-451-16375-3 NEW AMERICAN LIBRARY PB $5.99

A Maggot

An unusual historical novel, with Fowles's characteristic blend of the magical and the erotic

0-316-28994-9 LITTLE, BROWN $19.95

John Fowles

The Magus

A popular novel set on a Greek island, in which a local magician leads a young Englishman to self-knowledge through a series of fantastic adventures

0-440-35162-6 DELL PB $6.99

Mantissa

One of Fowles's more experimental works, with an emphasis on erotic and mythic elements

0-316-28980-9 LITTLE, BROWN $16.95
0-452-27094-4 PLUME PB $13.95

George Macdonald **Fraser**

The Flashman novels are a rollicking series of historical adventures set in the 19th-century

Flash for Freedom!

0-452-26089-2 NEW AMERICAN LIBRARY PB ... $11.95

Flashman

In the first novel of the series, the drunken bully deservedly expelled from Harrow in *Tom Brown's Schooldays* begins a sidesplitting career of unparalleled success in Victorian England

0-452-25961-4 NEW AMERICAN LIBRARY PB ... $11.95

Flashman and the Dragon

See also **HISTORICAL AND ROMANTIC FICTION** in **POPULAR READING**

0-452-26191-0 NEW AMERICAN LIBRARY PB .. $10.95

Flashman and the Redskins

0-452-26487-1 NEW AMERICAN LIBRARY PB ... $11.95

Flashman at the Charge

0-452-26413-8 NEW AMERICAN LIBRARY PB ... $11.95

Flashman's Lady

0-452-26489-8 NEW AMERICAN LIBRARY PB ... $11.95

Michael **Frayn**

A Landing on the Sun

A civil servant's disappearance leads to a Cabinet official's discovery of a secret science underground in England

0-14-017700-0 PENGUIN PB $10.00

Now You Know

"As intricately worked out as a Joe Orton play... Frayn seems bent on a single-handed crusade to restore plotting to a central place in the British novel"—*Kirkus Reviews*

0-670-84554-X VIKING $21.00
0-14-023235-4 PENGUIN PB $9.95

Carlo **Gebler**

The Cure

0-316-29038-6 LITTLE, BROWN PB $12.95

The Eleventh Summer

Middle-aged Paul Weisman recalls his adolescence during a fateful summer in Ireland shortly after his mother's suicide

0-671-67779-9 FIRESIDE PB $7.95

Victoria **Glendinning**

Electricity

0-316-30159-0 LITTLE, BROWN $22.95

William **Golding**

Close Quarters

A sequel to *Rites of Passage,* on the transition from youth to manhood

0-374-12510-4 FS&G $16.95

The Double Tongue

The final novel of the Nobel laureate and author of *Lord of the Flies*, who died in 1993. In this extraordinary fiction, an aged prophetess at Delphi looks back over her life in ancient Greece, a life spent as the medium of Apollo's strange utterances. A masterful short novel as deliciously mysterious as the oracle itself

0-374-14329-3 FS&G $20.00

Lord of the Flies

Golding's best-known book: schoolboys marooned on a desert island revert to primitive savagery and superstition

0-399-50148-7 PERIGEE PB $6.95

Alasdair **Gray**

The Fall of Kelvin Walker

0-8021-3004-6 OLYMPIC PB $1.98

A History Maker

A sci-fi yarn full of poetry, courage, and sex, set in Scotland's Ettrick Forest in the 23rd century. Gray has once again "found a way to evoke a cracked, slightly out-of-balance sense of our reality. And although he warrants comparison to Laurence Sterne, to William Blake, to Flan O'Brien, you can't put him in any choir. He's a soloist first and last, a glorious one-man band"—*Newsweek*

0-15-100207-X HARVEST $25.00

Lanark: A Life in Four Books

"The saga of a city where reality is about as reliable as a Salvador Dali watch"—Brian Aldiss

0-15-600361-9 HARVEST PB $16.00

Poor Things

A witty sendup of Victorian mytho-scientific obsessions. Gray gives us the tale of two doctors and a drowned woman who, with the help of body transplants, is brought back to life. The picaresque adventures of this female Frankenstein turn our preconceptions of the period on their heads. Winner of the Whitbread Novel Award for 1992

0-15-173076-8 HARCOURT BRACE $21.95
0-15-600068-7 HARVEST PB $10.95

Ten Tales Tall & True

Ten illustrated tales, tender and uproarious, from the preeminent Scottish writer who the *Chicago Tribune* said "would not disgrace the pen of the great Voltaire." "Gray may be the most interesting and extraordinary author working in English today"
—*Atlanta Journal Constitution*

0-15-100090-5 HARCOURT BRACE $19.95

Peter **Green**

The Laughter of Aphrodite: A Novel About Sappho at Lesbos

"I very much admire *The Laughter of Aphrodite,* one of the best novels set in the classical world"—Gore Vidal

0-520-07966-3 CALIFORNIA $29.95
0-520-20340-2 CALIFORNIA PB $13.95

George **Grossmith**

The Diary of a Nobody

0-460-87227-3 EVERYMAN'S PB $8.95

Romesh **Gunesekera**

Monkfish Moon

Nine graceful stories that take place in the luxuriant, tropical environment of Sri Lanka, suddenly disoriented by violence and civil war. "The delicate firmness with which Gunesekera portrays the dilemmas living in a spoiled paradise gives this collection a haunting, eye-opening quality"—*The London Observer*

See also **INDIAN LITERATURE IN ENGLISH** under **LITERATURES OF INDIA** in **LITERATURE OF EUROPE, AFRICA, AND ASIA**

1-56584-077-1 NEW PRESS $16.95
1-57322-550-9 RIVERHEAD PB $11.00

Reef

See also **INDIAN LITERATURE IN ENGLISH** under **LITERATURES OF INDIA** in **LITERATURE OF EUROPE, AFRICA, AND ASIA**

1-56584-219-7 NEW PRESS $20.00
1-57322-533-9 RIVERHEAD PB $10.00

Brion **Gysin**

The Process

0-87951-277-6 OVERLOOK $22.95

James **Hamilton-Paterson**

Gerontius

0-939149-69-9 SOPHIA PB $10.95

Ghosts of Manila

0-374-16190-9 FS&G $22.00

James **Hamilton-Paterson**

Griefwork

0-374-16699-4 FS&G $22.00

That Time in Malomba

0-939149-68-0 SOPHIA PB $9.95

Helene **Hanff**

84, Charing Cross Road

The now classic account of an American woman's love affair with a second-hand bookstore. "A real life love story…A timeless period piece. Do read it"—*Wall Street Journal*

See also **MEMOIRS AND JOURNALS** under **20TH-CENTURY AMERICAN ESSAYS AND JOURNALISM** in **LITERATURE OF THE AMERICAS**

INTRODUCTION BY ANNE BANCROFT

1-55921-140-7 MOYER BELL $16.95

The Duchess of Bloomsbury Street

1-55921-144-X MOYER BELL PB $11.95

Aidan **Higgins**

Balcony of Europe

Semiautobiographical story of an adulterous love affair among artistic expatriates in Spain. "The underwater love-scene is the literary equivalent of Esther Williams in its virtuosity" —John Montague

0-7145-0103-4 RIVERRUN PB $9.95

Langrishe Go Down

Pre-war tale of a young German who brings cruelty and passion to one of the daughters of a remote, decaying Irish country house

0-7145-0328-2 M.S.I. $10.95

Scenes from a Receding Past

A novel of childhood set in Ireland, in which Higgins captures the protagonist's evolving consciousness through corresponding stylistic changes

0-7145-3753-5 RIVERRUN PB $7.95

Richard **Hughes**

A High Wind in Jamaica

0-06-091627-3 HARPERCOLLINS PB $11.00

Isla Grande

1-88372-110-5 SILMT PB $12.50

Legends of the Heart

1-88372-145-8 SILMT $25.01

Clive **James**

The Man from Japan

James is a lively, irreverent critic, as iconoclastic about his adopted home (England) and its more voguish enclaves as he is about his birthplace.

0-679-41172-0 RANDOM HOUSE $20.00

P.D. **James**

These are dense, implacably serious whodunnits from a "writer who is not going to shirk anything."—H.R.F. Keating

The Children of Men

In her twelfth book P.D. James unexpectedly turns from her usual mystery genre to a novel of futuristic dystopia. The year is 2021, the infirm are encouraged to commit group suicide, immigrants are slaves, and, for reasons unknown, the worldwide sperm count has reached zero. How England and the human race survive this state of affairs is the harrowing business at hand. "The departure from her usual formula is brilliantly conceived—the note of sad mortality so powerfully sustained that James's benediction of hope is almost unbearable"—*Kirkus Reviews*

0-679-41873-3 KNOPF $22.00

Ruth Prawer **Jhabvala**

Heat and Dust

The best-known work of the expatriate writer Ruth Prawer Jhabvala, this novel was awarded the Booker Prize in 1975

See also **INDIAN LITERATURE IN ENGLISH** under **LITERATURES OF INDIA** in **LITERATURE OF EUROPE, AFRICA, AND ASIA**

0-8446-6335-2 SMITH $22.00

0-671-64657-5 SIMON & SCHUSTER PB $11.00

The Householder

A young teacher in New Delhi has just become a householder and is finding his responsibilities perplexing. "The detail of Prem's daily round, school and domestic, is beautifully done" —*New Statesman*

See also **INDIAN LITERATURE IN ENGLISH** under **LITERATURES OF INDIA** in **LITERATURE OF EUROPE, AFRICA, AND ASIA**

0-393-00851-7 NORTON PB $8.95

Poet and Dancer

The author of *Heat and Dust* and of the screenplay for *Howard's End, The Europeans*, and other Merchant Ivory productions dissects the relationship between two unusual cousins who remain psychologically entwined for life after an early sexual encounter. "A masterful portrait of good people trying to do all right and the bad ones that pull them down and win, from a writer of remarkably acute sensitivity and perception"—*Kirkus Reviews*

See also **INDIAN LITERATURE IN ENGLISH** under **LITERATURES OF INDIA** in **LITERATURE OF EUROPE, AFRICA, AND ASIA**

0-385-46869-5 DOUBLEDAY $19.95

0-385-46887-3 ANCHOR PB $9.00

Shards of Memory

Jhabvala's tale of a family's multigenerational relationship with a mysterious and charismatic spiritual leader

0-385-47722-8 DOUBLEDAY $22.95

0-385-47723-6 ANCHOR PB $11.00

Neil **Jordan**

A Neil Jordan Reader

Selected writings of the prominent novelist, screenwriter, and director best known in America for *The Crying Game*

0-679-74834-2 VINTAGE PB $12.00

Nightlines

A young Irish man caught between political strife in Ireland and Spain during the civil war

0-679-44439-4 RANDOM HOUSE $21.00

Alan **Judd**

The Devil's Own Work

0-679-74745-1 VINTAGE PB $9.00

Anna **Kavan**

Kavan's fragmented, sometimes surrealistic ficiton, stemming from a troubled life, has won her a cult following.

Asylum Piece and Other Stories

0-935576-02-9 KESEND $16.95

Charmed Circle

0-7206-0928-3 DUFOUR $29.00

Ice

0-393-02273-0 NORTON $14.95

My Soul in China: A Novella and Stories

EDITED BY RHYS DAVIES

0-7206-0786-8 OWEN PB $16.95

The Parson

0-7206-0962-3 DUFOUR PB $24.00

Sleep Has His House

0-935576-00-2 KESEND $16.95

A Stranger Still

0-7206-0955-0 OWEN $30.00

Anna **Kavan** & Doris **Lessing**

Mercury

0-7206-0940-2 DUFOUR $28.00

John B. **Keane**

The Bodhran Makers

A story of conflict between farmers celebrating ancient Celtic rituals and the Catholic Church in a dirt-poor Irish village. "For those who wear the green, this book will provide a bounty of laughs and tears"—*Publishers Weekly*

0-941423-80-8 FOUR WALLS $18.95

1-57098-063-2 ROBERTS RINEHART PB $14.95

Durango

1-57098-038-1 ROBERTS RINEHART $22.95

The Ram of God and Other Stories

1-85635-017-7 DUFOUR PB $12.95

Philip **Larkin**

A Girl in Winter

"He wrote these books like poems. Fastidiousness is everywhere and flamboyance non-existent; the touch is unfaltering" —Clive James

0-87951-217-2 PENGUIN PB $12.95

Jill

Student life at Oxford during World War II sets the background for this first novel, which explores themes of class and sexuality later taken up in Larkin's poetry

0-87951-961-4 OVERLOOK PB $12.95

Doris **Lessing**

Briefing for a Descent into Hell

A nightmare in the form of a medical report, exploring themes of individual and collective breakdown and violence

0-394-74662-7 RANDOM HOUSE PB $9.00

Children of Violence

The first volume of Lessing's *Children of Violence* quintet is currently out of print

Volume 2

A Proper Marriage

Martha suffers the pains of a conventional marriage and awakens to political consciousness

0-060-97663-2 HARPER PERENNIAL PB $14.00

Doris **Lessing**

Children of Violence

Volume 3

A Ripple from the Storm

A liberated Martha, remarried to a Communist Party member, finds that ideals can be turned to jargon and personal advantage

0-060-97664-0 HARPER PERENNIAL PB..........$13.00

Volume 4

Landlocked

The scene changes to England as Martha's activism wanes

0-060-97665-9 HARPER PERENNIAL PB.......$13.00

Volume 5

The Four-Gated City

A brilliant conclusion to the *Children of Violence* series, exploring the corruptions of postwar London

0-060-97667-5 HARPER PERENNIAL PB..........$15.00

Doris Lessing

The Fifth Child

A powerful novel of horror within the family

0-679-72182-7 VINTAGE PB..............................$9.00

The Golden Notebook

"Her most important work has left its mark upon the ideas and feelings of a whole generation of women"—Elizabeth Hardwick

0-8095-9146-4 BORGO....................................$31.00

0-06-097590-3 HARPERPERENNIAL PB............$13.00

The Good Terrorist

A tale of a young female activist turned terrorist, set in London

0-394-74629-5 VINTAGE PB............................$10.00

The Grass Is Singing

Lessing's first novel, set in Africa, concerns a white farmer's wife and her relationship with an African servant

0-452-26119-8 PLUME PB...................................$12.95

Love, Again

Lessing's first novel in seven years promises to be her most brilliant and most controversial since *The Golden Notebook*. The story of a 65-year-old woman who is surprised to revisit the amatory provinces of her youth, *Love, Again* is a brilliant anatomy of love, desire, and grief. It is as complex and memorable as anything Lessing has ever written

0-06-017687-3 HARPERCOLLINS.....................$24.00

The Marriages Between Zones Three, Four, and Five

0-394-74978-2 VINTAGE PB.............................$10.00

The Memoirs of a Survivor

Visions of a grim and anarchic near future

0-394-75759-9 VINTAGE PB.............................$12.00

Particularly Cats...and Rufus

ILLUSTRATED BY JAMES MCMULLAN

0-394-58671-9 KNOPF......................................$20.00

The Real Thing: Stories and Sketches

0-06-092417-9 HARPERPERENNIAL PB............$12.00

Stories

0-394-74249-4 RANDOM HOUSE PB...............$24.00

The Summer Before the Dark

A middle-aged housewife leaves her home and family for a summer, only to encounter her own invisibility in a world where she has no role

0-394-71095-9 RANDOM HOUSE PB.................$8.00

Penelope **Lively**

Cleopatra's Sister

0-06-092217-6 HARPERPERENNIAL PB............$12.00

Heat Wave

0-06-017476-5 HARPERCOLLINS......................$22.00

Judgement Day

0-06-097198-3 HARPERCOLLINS PB................$10.00

Moon Tiger

0-06-097200-9 HARPERCOLLINS PB................$12.00

Passing on

0-06-097370-6 HARPERCOLLINS PB.................$12.00

The Road to Lichfield

0-06-097461-3 HARPERPERENNIAL PB............$12.00

David **Lodge**

The British Museum Is Falling Down

0-14-012419-5 PENGUIN PB............................$10.95

Changing Places

A sequel to *Small World*

0-14-017098-7 VIKING PB...............................$10.95

Nice Work

0-14-013396-8 PENGUIN PB............................$11.95

Paradise News

The worlds of academics and of Catholicism have each provided Lodge with plentiful material for his witty satires. In *Paradise News*, both are combined when an anthropologist and a teacher of theology are thrown together on a packaged tour to Hawaii

0-14-016521-5 PENGUIN PB............................$11.95

Small World

A clever roman à clef exposing highjinks on the international academic conference circuit

0-446-39327-4 WARNER PB..............................$10.99

Souls & Bodies

0-14-013018-7 PENGUIN PB............................$11.95

Therapy

Tubby Passmore eases through his midlife crisis with the aid of, among other things, aromatherapy and Kierkegaard. "*Therapy* is a delicious read" —Jane Smiley, *LA Times Book Review*

0-670-86358-0 VIKING.....................................$22.95

0-14-024900-1 PENGUIN PB............................$11.95

Hilary **Mantel**

An Experiment in Love

A story of class, place, family, and faith is set in motion when an Irish Catholic girl is urged by her parents to penetrate the class barriers of England. "A profoundly original storyteller in full control of her material. Funny, tragic, and wonderfully perceptive"—*The Independent*

0-8050-4427-2 HOLT.......................................$23.00

Peter **Mayle**

A Dog's Life

Recounts a dog's life in the French countryside

DRAWINGS BY EDWARD KOREN

0-679-44122-0 KNOPF......................................$20.00

0-679-76267-1 VINTAGE PB.............................$11.00

Hotel Pastis

A British advertising tycoon drops out and escapes to Provence, from the bestselling author of *A Year in Provence* and *Toujours Provence*

0-679-40229-2 KNOPF......................................$23.00

John **McGahern**

Amongst Women

Winner of the Irish Times Literary Award. "A wonderful writer...his spare but luminous prose evokes a severely repressed life and the aching passion that lies beneath its stony surface" —*Chicago Tribune*

0-14-009255-2 PENGUIN PB............................$10.95

Collected Stories

0-679-41913-6 KNOPF......................................$24.00

0-679-74401-0 VINTAGE PB.............................$12.00

Ian **McEwan**

Black Dogs

Poland's Majdanek concentration camp, Berlin during the dismantling of the Wall, a remote area of the French countryside—these are some of the powerfully evoked setting in this suspenseful, probing novel.

0-553-37367-6 BDD PB.......................................$9.95

The Cement Garden

Disturbing and laconic tale of four London children who conceal their mother's death to avoid appropriation by the state apparatus

0-679-75018-5 VINTAGE PB.............................$10.00

A Child in Time

0-14-011246-4 PENGUIN PB............................$11.95

The Comfort of Strangers

"Convincing and clinging as a nightmare...McEwan [is] an alluringly gifted writer"—*NY Times Book Review*

0-679-74984-5 VINTAGE PB...............................$9.00

Ian **McEwan**

In Between the Sheets
"Pure, vicious entertainments"—*Village Voice*
0-679-74983-7 VINTAGE PB $10.00

The Innocent
Berlin, 1955: British and American espionage technicians begin an uneasy collaboration, preparing to burrow into the heart of the Soviet communications system. A young Englishman, politically and sexually naive, undergoes a series of initiations which lead him into the heart of horror and betrayal. McEwan's swift, sharp novel is far from a conventional thriller
0-553-55000-4 BDD PB $6.95

Glass pulled to the side of the tract and stopped. Up ahead was a barrier, and a sentry standing beside it, watching them. "Let me tell you about level one. The Army engineer who built this place is told he's putting up a warehouse, a regular Army warehouse. Now, his instructions specify a basement with a twelve-foot ceiling. That's deep. That means shifting a hell of a lot of earth, dump truck to take it away, finding a site, and so on. And it isn't the way the Army builds a warehouse. So the commander refuses to do it till he has confirmation direct from Washington. He's taken aside, and at this point he discovers there are clearance levels, and he's being up-graded to level two. He's not really building a warehouse at all, he's told, it's a radar station, and the deep basement is for special equipment. So he gets to work, and he's happy. He's the only guy on site who knows what the building is really for. But he's wrong. If he had level three clearance, he'd know it wasn't a radar station at all.
THE INNOCENT

Brian **Moore**

Black Robe
Jesuit priest Father LaForgue journeys through frozen Canadian wilderness in 1634 with the help of Algonquin Indians who become increasingly mistrustful of the man they call "Black Robe"
See also **WRITING IN ENGLISH** under **CANADIAN LITERATURE** in **LITERATURE OF THE AMERICAS**
0-449-20947-4 FAWCETT PB $5.99
0-586-08615-3 HARPERCOLLINS PB $10.00

The Colour of Blood
0-586-08737-0 HARPERCOLLINS PB $10.00

The Lonely Passion of Judith Hearne
The Irish-Canadian's first novel. "A penetrating, comic, tragic tale of a plain woman… It is a novel that occasionally sings with the lilt of the Irish greats"—*San Francisco Chronicle*
0-316-57966-1 LITTLE, BROWN PB $9.95

The Statement
0-525-94128-2 DUTTON $22.95

John **Mortimer**

Dunster
"A delicious read"
—Jane Smiley, *NY Times Book Review*
0-14-023270-2 PENGUIN PB $10.95

The Narrowing Stream
0-670-81930-1 VIKING $17.95

Summer's Lease
0-14-015827-8 PENGUIN PB $10.95

Nicholas **Mosley**

Accident
0-916583-10-4 DALKEY ARCHIVE $20.00
0-916583-11-2 DALKEY ARCHIVE PB $9.95

Catastrophe Practice
0-916583-35-X DALKEY ARCHIVE $19.95

Hopeful Monsters
A young English physicist and German-Jewish anthropologist pursue one another from Hitler's Germany to Los Alamos. "An expansive and liberating adventure of tests, quests, miracles, and coincidences"—*The Observer*
0-916583-85-6 DALKEY ARCHIVE $21.95

Imago Bird
0-916583-36-8 DALKEY ARCHIVE $19.95

Impossible Object
0-916583-08-2 DALKEY ARCHIVE $20.00

Judith
0-916583-69-4 DALKEY ARCHIVE $19.95
0-916583-77-5 DALKEY ARCHIVE PB $10.95

Natalie Natalia
Mosley's new novel is a brilliant examination of political life, centering on Anthony Greville, a conservative Member of Parliament tormented by ambivalence about his career, religious doubts, and an adulterous affair
1-56478-086-4 DALKEY ARCHIVE PB $12.95

Serpent
0-916583-49-X DALKEY ARCHIVE $19.95

Iris **Murdoch**

Murdoch's novels are carefully plotted works whose layers of intricacy reflect the author's philosophical training. They are kept buoyantly afloat by the lucid, ironic language of her upper-middle-class characters. "What an incorrigible, irresistible conjurer-up this woman is!… Let it be asked now: what other living novelist in the language is the peer of Iris Murdoch at inventing characters and moving them fascinatingly, at least as long as the book is in our hands?"—John Updike

The Bell
The inhabitants of a monastery find themselves trapped between a desire for a higher order and an inability to lead normal lives
0-14-001688-0 VIKING PB $11.95

The Black Prince
A kind of psychological whodunit involving an older man's love for a young woman and a murder
0-14-003934-1 VIKING PB $12.95

The Book and the Brotherhood
A student reunion reveals a shift from radical energy to languor, and awakens sleeping passions
0-14-010470-4 PENGUIN PB $10.95

Fairly Honourable Defeat
A Machiavellian intruder into a conventional group of people forces them to reconsider their lives by destroying their complacency
0-14-003332-7 VIKING PB $10.95

The Flight from the Enchanter
0-14-001770-4 PENGUIN PB $10.00

The Good Apprentice
0-14-009815-1 PENGUIN PB $10.95

The Green Knight
0-14-024337-2 PENGUIN PB $12.95

Iris Murdoch (photo by Tom Blau)

Jackson's Dilemma
0-670-86815-9 VIKING $22.95

The Nice and the Good
"Sweeps up black magic, science fiction, thriller and half-a-dozen kinds of novel into the wittiest sort of concoction"—*NY Times*
0-14-003034-4 PENGUIN PB $11.95

Nuns and Soldiers
"She has perfected her technique and pulled off the big one: a book that unwinds with all the sinuous inevitability of a contortionist to rise into the higher spheres of myth"
—*Atlantic Monthly*
0-14-005757-9 PENGUIN PB $12.95

The Philosopher's Pupil
A renowned philosopher goes home to an English spa. "The author does what old-fashioned novelists did when they could; she makes us gods, observing, weighing, rebuking, forgiving, and happy with our omniscience… It is one of the most difficult and rewarding things a novelist can do for us"—Robertson Davies, *Washington Post*
0-14-006695-0 PENGUIN PB $11.95

The Red and the Green
A novel set in Dublin in 1916, the year of the Easter Rising
0-14-002756-4 PENGUIN PB $10.95

The Sacred and Profane Love Machine
A man must choose between wife and mistress. "*The Sacred and Profane Love Machine* reads like a breeze, a whirlwind of deepening surprise, a provocation to the intellect and an invitation to the heart"—John Updike
0-14-004111-7 PENGUIN PB $11.95

The Sea, the Sea
This study of a theater director's obsessive passion for a childhood sweetheart won the Booker Prize
0-14-005199-6 PENGUIN PB $12.95

A Severed Head
A satirical portrait of the variously adulterous and incestuous liaisons of a Bloomsbury-like social set
0-14-002003-9 PENGUIN PB $10.95

The Time of the Angels
A wasteland rectory beset by evil
0-14-002848-X PENGUIN PB $10.95

Under the Net
Murdoch's first novel describes a writer's search for a place to live in London, and much more
0-14-001445-4 PENGUIN PB $10.95

The Unicorn
0-14-002476-X PENGUIN PB $10.95

A Word Child
Hilary Brede, nursing guilt and disappointment in a dull civil service job, discovers that a man he hurt and betrayed has become his superior
0-14-008153-4 PENGUIN PB $12.00

Shiva **Naipaul**

Fireflies
The first novel of V.S. Naipaul's younger brother deals with the decline of Hindu culture in the Caribbean
0-14-018824-X PENGUIN PB $11.95

A Hot Country
0-14-018834-7 PENGUIN PB $10.95

A Man of Mystery and Other Stories
0-14-018835-5 PENGUIN PB $10.95

V.S. **Naipaul**

A Bend in the River
A powerful later work, set in a fictional African state, about the damage inflicted by the West on the Third World
0-679-72202-5 VINTAGE PB $12.00

The Enigma of Arrival
A semi-autobiographical portrait of an author getting on in years in the West Country
0-394-75760-2 VINTAGE PB $13.00

A Flag on the Island
"So good you'll be tempted to read them straight through, and so full of vitality"—*Sunday Times*
0-14-002939-7 PENGUIN PB $10.00

Guerrillas
Three would-be revolutionaries in search of a cause
0-679-73174-1 VINTAGE PB $12.00

A House for Mr. Biswas
A large novel in which a mild man's struggle for ownership of his own home represents a higher striving toward individual autonomy
0-679-44458-0 KNOPF $20.00
0-14-018604-2 PENGUIN PB $12.95

In a Free State
0-394-72205-1 RANDOM HOUSE PB $9.00

Middle Passage
A satirical version of Caribbean life
See also **THE CARIBBEAN** under **THE CARIBBEAN AND CENTRAL AMERICA** under **TRAVEL LITERATURE** in **FOOD, TRAVEL, AND LEISURE**
0-14-002920-6 PENGUIN PB $10.00

Miguel Street
Naipaul's first novel portrays both the vibrancy and the limitations of a small Trinidadian community
0-14-003302-5 PENGUIN PB $11.95

The Mimic Men
Post-independence politicking in the Third World: an intellectual assumes power, is toppled, and finds time for reappraisal as a recluse in London
0-14-002940-0 PENGUIN PB $11.95

The Mystic Masseur
A fictitious biography of a masseur who connives his way to political power
0-14-002156-6 PENGUIN PB $10.95

The Suffrage of Elvira
A comedy about rural council elections in Trinidad, animated by much hustling and bargaining
0-14-002938-9 PENGUIN PB $11.95

Way in the World
Naipaul works on a majestic canvas to tell a tale of inheritance, the legacy of imperialism in the Caribbean, and the post-colonial experience
0-394-56478-2 KNOPF $23.00
0-679-76166-7 VINTAGE PB $14.00

Philip **Norman**

Everyone's Gone to the Moon
6679443814 RANDOM HOUSE $25.00

Robert **Nye**

Tales I Told My Mother
Rabelaisian and poetic variations on the theme of literary biography turn Chatterton, the Rossettis, and others into something rich and strange
0-7145-2954-0 MARION BOYARS PB $12.95

Edna **O'Brien**

The Country Girls Trilogy & Epilogue
A saga of escape from girlhood, countryside, and convent to the big city. Includes *Country Girls, The Lonely Girl,* and *Girls in Their Married Bliss.* "Despite feminist efforts on behalf of their kind, Miss O'Brien's sex-dazzled heroines continue to race like lemmings towards unhappiness"—Julia O'Faolain
0-452-26394-8 NEW AMERICAN LIBRARY PB ... $14.95

An Edna O'Brien Reader
0-446-39516-1 WARNER PB $11.99

A Fanatic Heart: Selected Stories of Edna O'Brien
A recent choice of her best stories, with four new ones
FOREWORD BY PHILIP ROTH
0-374-15342-6 FS&G $17.95
0-452-26116-3 NEW AMERICAN LIBRARY PB ... $12.95

The High Road
0-374-29273-6 FS&G $18.95

House of Splendid Isolation
0-374-17309-5 FS&G $21.00

Lantern Slides
0-452-26628-9 PLUME PB $11.95

Night
Erotic memories of Irishwoman recalling her awakening to maturity in the odyssey from rural Ireland to London
0-374-52051-8 FS&G PB $8.00

Time and Tide
0-446-39510-2 WARNER PB $10.99

Joe **Orton**

Head to Toe
"To him nothing was sacred, but the fury of his attack, its peculiar combination of joy and horror, was not without a broader spiritual motive. Orton wanted to shock the society but also to reform it"—John Lahr
0-7493-9029-8 HEINEMANN PB $7.95

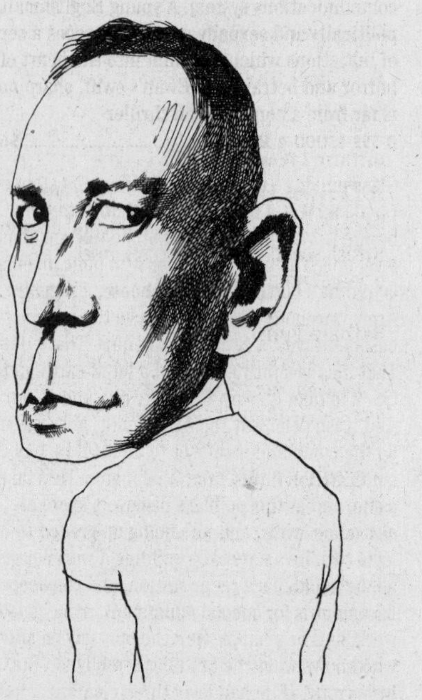

Joe Orton

Charles **Palliser**

Betrayals
0-345-36959-9 BALLANTINE $23.00

The Quincunx
This 800-page tour de force is a first novel from Palliser, an English professor living in Scotland. Filled with adventure and excitement, the story, modeled on *Bleak House,* centers around a young man's attempts to solve the mysteries of his family
0-345-37113-5 BALLANTINE PB $16.00

Mervyn **Peake**

The Gormenghast Trilogy
An extraordinary mix of the Gothic and the Dickensian
See also **FANTASY** under **SCIENCE FICTION AND FANTASY** in **POPULAR READING**
INTRODUCTION BY ANTHONY BURGESS
0-87951-628-3 OVERLOOK PB $23.95

Caryl **Phillips**

Based in Britain, Phillips is a leading and dynamic voice among the latest generation of Caribbean novelists and playwrights.

Cambridge
A highly inventive historical novel in which the intertwined stories of an Englishwoman and a slave are told in their own voices. "With *Cambridge*, Caryl Phillips takes a firm step toward joining the company of the literary giants of our time"—*NY Times Book Review*
See also **CARIBBEAN LITERATURE** in **LITERATURE OF THE AMERICAS**
0-679-73689-1 VINTAGE PB $10.00

Caryl **Phillips**

Crossing the River

0-679-40533-X KNOPF $22.00
0-679-75794-5 VINTAGE PB $12.00

The Final Passage

The story of a young woman adrift in despair, set against the upheaval of Caribbean emigration and its impact on British society

0-679-75931-X VINTAGE PB $10.00

Higher Ground: A Novel in Three Parts

0-679-76376-7 VINTAGE PB $11.00

Anthony **Powell**

A Dance to the Music of Time

Powell's life work and a monumental account of British social life. A four-volume set

0-226-67719-2 CHICAGO PB $72.80

Barbara **Pym**

"In her novels the reader is always on the verge of smiling. Amusement is constantly foiling more pretentious emotion, but emotion is there all the same."—Philip Larkin, TLS

Excellent Women

Mildred Lathburn, a clergyman's daughter, observes with a penetrating but sympathetic eye the Napiers' marriage, and yearns discreetly for Everard Bone

0-452-26730-7 PLUME PB $11.95

No Fond Return of Love

0-452-26934-2 DUTTON PB $10.95

Some Tame Gazelle

0-452-26919-9 PLUME PB $10.95

Salman **Rushdie**

East, West: Stories

"Poignant and intimate, boisterously inventive, and gently provocative"—*NY Times Book Review*

See also **INDIAN LITERATURE IN ENGLISH** under **LITERATURES OF INDIA** in **LITERATURE OF EUROPE, AFRICA, AND ASIA**

0-679-75789-9 VINTAGE PB $11.00

Haroun and the Sea of Stories

"Salman Rushdie has in his own veins the flow of the Sea of Stories, fantastical, funny, whooping through drama and comedy, good and evil, personified in creatures delightful or frightening"—Nadine Gordimer

See also **FICTION** under **BOOKS FOR EIGHTS, NINES, AND UP** in **BOOKS FOR YOUNG READERS**
See also **INDIAN LITERATURE IN ENGLISH** under **LITERATURES OF INDIA** in **LITERATURE OF EUROPE, AFRICA, AND ASIA**

0-14-015737-9 PENGUIN PB $11.95

And in the depths of the city, beyond an old zone of ruined buildings that looked like broken hearts, there lived a happy young fellow by the name of Haroun, the only child of the storyteller Rashid Khalifa, whose cheerfulness was famous throughout that unhappy metropolis, and whose never-ending stream of tall, short and winding tales had earned him not one but two nicknames. To his admirers he was Rashid the Ocean of Notions, as stuffed with cheery stories as the sea was full of glumfish; but to his jealous rivals he was the Shah of Blah.

HAROUN AND THE SEA OF STORIES

Midnight's Children

A fantastic epic of Indian independence and its aftermath. "Dense with passion, intelligence, excitement, and every vocal and literary effect conceivable"—Margo Jefferson, *Village Voice*

See also **INDIAN LITERATURE IN ENGLISH** under **LITERATURES OF INDIA** in **LITERATURE OF EUROPE, AFRICA, AND ASIA**

0-679-44462-9 KNOPF $20.00
0-14-013270-8 PENGUIN PB $14.95

Salman Rushdie

The Moor's Last Sigh

0-679-42049-5 PANTHEON $25.00
0-679-74466-5 VINTAGE $13.00

Mine is the story of the fall from grace of a high-born crossbreed—me, Moraes Zogoiby, called "moor," for most of my life the only heir to the spice-trade-'n'-big-business millions of the Gama-Zogoiby dynasty of Cochin—and of my banishment by mother Aurora.

THE MOOR'S LAST SIGH

The Satanic Verses

"What is being expressed is a discomfort with plural identity…We are increasingly becoming a world of migrants, made up of bits and fragments from here, there. We are here. And we have never really left anywhere we have been"
—Salman Rushdie

See also **INDIAN LITERATURE IN ENGLISH** under **LITERATURES OF INDIA** in **LITERATURE OF EUROPE, AFRICA, AND ASIA**

0-670-82537-9 VIKING $19.95

Paul **Scott**

The Birds of Paradise

The scion of an Anglo-Indian family recalls life's vicissitudes—from adviser to nabobs to Japanese POW

0-88184-232-X CARROLL & GRAF PB $4.50

The Chinese Love Pavilion

Brent of military intelligence and the guerrilla leader Saxby play a homicidal game in the Malayan jungle

0-88184-190-0 CARROLL & GRAF PB $4.50

A Division of the Spoils

The last volume of Scott's Raj Quartet, of which the first three (*The Jewel in the Crown*, *The Day of the Scorpion*, and *The Towers of Silence*) are out of print

0-380-71811-1 AVON PB $11.00

The Mark of the Warrior

A contest of wills between the introspective and inept C.O. of a British army unit and an efficient subordinate

0-88184-189-7 CARROLL & GRAF PB $3.95

Tom **Sharpe**

Indecent Exposure

"Banning cricket tours may be one way of civilizing South Africa, but Tom Sharpe's remorseless mockery is a lot more fun"
—Stanley Reynolds, *Punch*

0-87113-142-0 ATLANTIC MONTHLY PB $10.95

Porterhouse Blue

0-87113-279-6 ATLANTIC MONTHLY PB $11.00

Riotous Assembly

Slapstick but ultimately serious farce about police power and racism in South Africa

0-87113-143-9 ATLANTIC MONTHLY PB $10.95

Wilt

0-394-72418-6 RANDOM HOUSE PB $9.00

Wilt on High

0-394-54480-3 RANDOM HOUSE $13.95

Alan **Sillitoe**

The Loneliness of the Long-Distance Runner

A juvenile delinquent at reform school deliberately sacrifices the goodwill of the authorities when he realizes the dehumanizing effect of "finding his niche"

0-452-26908-3 PLUMSTOCK PB $9.95

Saturday Night and Sunday Morning

Sillitoe's first novel introduced the prototype of the Angry Young Man, in a chronicle of petty victories and defeats in the north of England. "His people are alive, lusty, and vigorous"
—*San Francisco Chronicle*

0-452-26909-1 PLUMSTOCK PB $11.95

Muriel **Spark**

The Abbess of Crewe: A Modern Morality Tale

0-8112-1296-3 NEW DIRECTIONS PB $6.00

Muriel Spark (photo by Jerry Bauer)

The Ballad of Peckham Rye

A bizarre story of the London underworld

0-380-70936-8 AVON PB $7.95

The Comforters
0-8112-1285-8 NEW DIRECTIONS PB $10.95

The Driver's Seat
0-8112-1271-8 NEW DIRECTIONS PB $6.00

Loitering with Intent
0-380-70935-X AVON PB $9.00

Memento Mori
A macabre study of the lives of a set of octogenarians victimized by a mysterious phone caller who tells them to "remember death"
0-380-70938-4 AVON PB $9.00

The Prime of Miss Jean Brodie
An Edinburgh schoolmistress who tries to dispel provincial ideas is betrayed by a student
0-8095-9144-8 BORGO...$27.00
0-06-092398-9 HARPERPERENNIAL PB $11.00

The Public Image
0-8112-1246-7 NEW DIRECTIONS PB................$9.95

Symposium
0-380-71553-8 AVON PB $9.00

Graham **Swift**

Ever After
0-679-74026-0 VINTAGE PB......................................$12.00

Last Orders
About friendship and love among a group of men whose lives have been intertwined since World War II. When one dies, the survivors are brought together and are forced to take stock of the paths their lives have taken, by choice and by accident, since the war
0-679-41224-7 KNOPF..$23.00

Learning to Swim & Other Stories
0-679-73978-5 VINTAGE PB..$9.00

Shuttlecock
0-679-73933-5 VINTAGE PB......................................$10.00

The Sweet-Shop Owner
0-679-73980-7 VINTAGE PB......................................$10.00

Waterland
A novel that earned Swift acclaim as one of the most promising younger English writers
0-679-73979-3 VINTAGE PB......................................$12.00

Elizabeth **Taylor**

At Mrs. Lippincote's
0-14-016226-7 VIKING PB $9.95

A View of the Harbour
Love and passion at a drab seaside spa
INTRODUCTION BY ROBERT LIDDELL
0-404-20252-7 AMS..$30.00

The Wedding Group
The foolish but pretty wife of a weak man becomes subordinated to his domineering mother
0-14-016114-7 VIRAGO PB $6.95

D.M. **Thomas**

Eating Pavlova
1939, and in London Sigmund Freud waits to die, tended by his devoted—neurotically devoted—daughter Anna. Thomas takes us through the last moments, conscious and unconscious, of Freud's life, and along with Anna into his diaries, where she discovers damning secrets. Powerful, provocative. "Thomas is a terrific writer of high intelligence and integrity, acute sensitivity and sustained seriousness…He writes haunting novels that are put forth with brilliance and complexity" *—Boston Globe*
0-7867-0270-2 CARROLL & GRAF PB $10.95

Flying into Love
"The complexity is richly astonishing…few will fail to be mesmerized"—*Publishers Weekly*
0-7867-0208-7 CARROLL & GRAF PB...................$9.95

A Lady with a Laptop
A decidedly second-rate novelist is invited to a third-rate writer's colony in which the quest for sex is as compelling, to the participants, as the call of creativity. From this setup D.M. Thomas constructs a marvelous comedy of manners, and a sublime entertainment
0-7867-0308-3 CARROLL & GRAF.......................$22.00

Pictures at an Exhibition
Thomas's return to the themes of *The White Hotel* is unmercifully suspenseful in this tale of the strange rapport between a Nazi doctor and a Czech prisoner at Auschwitz. A moving, shocking, stunning reprise of Thomas's most powerful writing
0-7867-0147-1 CARROLL & GRAF PB $10.95

The White Hotel
"The diagnosis of an epoch through the experience of an individual. The opening sentences are so authoritative and imaginatively daring that I quickly came to the conclusion that I had found that mythical book that would explain us to ourselves"—Leslie Epstein
0-14-023173-0 PENGUIN PB...............................$11.95

Sue **Townsend**

Adrian Mole: The Lost Years
The third volume in the enormously popular Adrian Mole series (the second, *The Growing Pains of Adrian Mole*, is out of print). "I not only wept, I howled and hooted and had to get up and walk around the room and wipe my eyes so that I could go on reading"—Tom Sharpe
1-56947-014-6 SOHO...$22.00
1-56947-055-3 SOHO PB..$14.00

Sue Townsend (photo courtesy of Soho Press)

The Queen and I
The Queen and her family are deposed by a new republican government and allocated housing in a Midlands housing project
See also **THE 1970S, '80S, AND '90S under 20TH-CENTURY BRITISH AND IRISH DRAMA**
0-413-68970-0 METHUEN PB $11.95
1-56947-015-4 SOHO PB.......................................$11.00

The Secret Diary of Adrian Mole, Aged 13 3/4
0-7451-4333-4 CHIVERS NORTH AMERICA.....$39.95

Rose **Tremain**

Restoration: A Novel of 17th Century England
A physician to the royal dogs of Charles II gets a vast estate for marrying the king's mistress, yet he makes the mistake of falling in love with his own life
0-14-024488-3 PENGUIN PB $10.95

Sacred Country
0-671-88609-6 WASHINGTON SQUARE PB $10.00

William **Trevor**

After Rain: Stories
0-670-87007-2 VIKING...$22.95

The Boarding-House
0-14-010749-5 PENGUIN PB...................................$10.95

Children of Dynmouth
Mocking, malicious, fatherless Timothy Gedge brings trouble to everyone he meets in a seaside town
0-14-004718-2 PENGUIN PB $10.95

The Collected Stories
The crafted humor and compassion of the Irish master William Trevor *(Two Lives, The Day We Got Drunk on Cake)* have been cherished by fans of his 19 books for almost 30 years. Throughout his career, short fiction has been Trevor's most passionate pursuit, and this invaluable book gathers together the best of his seven collections. "Work of impeccable strength and piercing profundity"—Reynolds Price, *NY Times Book Review*. "Trevor is probably the greatest living writer of short stories in the English language"—*New Yorker*
0-14-023245-1 PENGUIN PB $16.00

Elizabeth Alone
0-14-009756-2 PENGUIN PB...................................$11.95

Felicia's Journey
0-670-85745-9 VIKING $21.95
0-14-025360-2 PENGUIN PB...................................$10.95

Fools of Fortune
The love between an Irish and an English cousin is frustrated by civil violence
0-14-011181-6 PENGUIN PB...................................$10.95

The Love Department
0-14-003130-8 PENGUIN PB...................................$11.95

Miss Gomez and the Brethren
0-14-025264-9 PENGUIN..$25.00

William **Trevor**

Mrs. Eckdorf in O'Neill's Hotel
A German photographer, who intends to expose the drunks of a gritty Dublin hotel, falls prey herself to the prevailing Celtic madness
0-14-010748-7 PENGUIN PB $11.95

Old Boys
0-14-002428-X PENGUIN PB $11.95

Other People's Worlds
0-140-10669-3 PENGUIN PB $9.95

The Silence in the Garden
The latest of Trevor's stories, about the last scions of an Anglo-Irish house facing up to the ghost of the distant and not-so-distant past
0-14-012065-3 PENGUIN PB $10.95

Two Lives: Reading Turgenev & My House in Umbria
Two narratives which mirror each other: one about a young Irish girl who escapes from an unhappy marriage through reading, and the other about a writer whose life is more horrific than her own books
0-670-83933-7 VIKING $21.95
0-14-017263-7 PENGUIN PB $11.95

Alexander **Trocchi**

Cain's Book
A lean and unsentimental novel of adultery, murder, and addiction in Trocchi's native Scotland
INTRODUCTION BY RICHARD W. SEAVER
0-8021-3314-2 GROVE PB $9.95

Helen and Desire
1-56201-088-3 BLUE MOON PB $6.96

Invisible Insurrection of a Million Minds: A Trocchi Reader
0-7486-6108-5 SMALL PRESS PB $18.95

Thongs
0-922233-11-X BLASB PB $9.95

White Thighs
0-922233-14-4 BLASB PB $9.95

Joanna **Trollope**

The Choir
The best selling British novelist offers a story set in an English cathedral town that is divided over the question of whether or not to dissolve the expensive boys' choir. From this premise, Trollope creates a schism in which fabulous characters are revealed in ever more complex dimensions
0-679-44454-8 RANDOM HOUSE $22.00

The Rector's Wife
0-425-15529-3 BERKELEY PB $6.99

The Men and the Girls
0-380-72408-1 AVON PB $12.00

Barry **Unsworth**

The Hide
0-393-03955-2 NORTON $22.00

Morality Play
0-385-47953-0 DOUBLEDAY $22.50
0-393-31560-6 NORTON PB $11.00

Mooncranker's Gift
Tale of innocence corrupted set in a Turkish spa. "Intense and quite readable, reminding one of Paul Bowles's exotic tropical novels"
—Library Journal
0-393-31478-2 NORTON PB $11.00

The Rage of Vultures
0-393-31308-5 NORTON PB $12.00

Sacred Hunger
1994 Booker Prize winner. "This brilliantly suspenseful period piece about the slave trade in the 18th-century is also a meditation on how avarice dehumanizes the oppressor as well as the oppressed"*—Chicago Tribune*
0-393-31114-7 NORTON PB $11.95

Stone Virgin
0-393-31309-3 NORTON PB $13.00

Umbrian Mosaic
Unsworth's latest
0-385-48651-0 DOUBLEDAY $25.00

Fay **Weldon**

The Cloning of Joanna March
From the feminist author of *The Life and Loves of a She-Devil*, the story of a millionaire's cloning of his unsuspecting wife, who is confronted with four younger versions of herself
0-670-83090-0 VIKING $18.95

Down Among the Women
"Her major subject is the experience of women. But she is not tedious about the rich texture of everyday female existence. She most often selects the telling and the funny, the absurd and the horrifying"—Agate Nesaule Krouse
0-89733-116-8 ACADEMY CHICAGO PB $8.95

Female Friends
Three friends survive the various catastrophes of their private lives
0-89733-290-3 ACADEMY CHICAGO PB $10.95

Growing Rich
0-14-015915-0 PENGUIN PB $9.95

The Heart of the Country
0-14-010397-X PENGUIN PB $9.95

The Life and Loves of a She-Devil
The humble Ruth reveals her true nature, ousts her husband's mistress, turns him into a doormat, and has plastic surgery that makes her irresistible to men
0-345-32375-0 BALLANTINE PB $5.99

Moon over Minneapolis: Or Why She Couldn't Stay
A collection of Weldon's punchy, deft short fiction. Whether she's chronicling the thoughts of a woman awaiting her turn in an abortion clinic or the separate dialogues of four patients with their silent therapist, the author defies categorization
0-670-83646-X PENGUIN $19.95
0-14-014542-7 PENGUIN PB $10.00

Splitting
"Weldon's greatest marvel is probably not her fast pace or brilliant asides but her wit and wisdom about sex"*—Ms.*
0-87113-636-8 GROVE PB $12.00

Trouble
0-14-015916-9 PENGUIN PB $10.95

Worst Fears
When an actress returns from her stint as Ibsen's Nora to find her real husband dead, she's struck by the extent to which her friends are covering up the mystery of his demise. The result is a furious adventure of discovery about her husband's adultery and her own worst fears
0-87113-635-X ATLANTIC MONTHLY $21.00

A.N. **Wilson**

Hearing Voices
Part mystery, part comedy of manners, the acclaimed biographer of Tolstoy and C.S. Lewis has written a strange and fascinating novel in which a biographer's research yields clues to forgery, fraud, and murder. A gripping story at the heart of which lies a perfectly realized riddle
0-393-03875-0 NORTON $22.50

The Vicar of Sorrows
0-393-31294-1 NORTON PB $12.00

A Watch in The Night: Being the Conclusion of the Lampitt Chronicles
See also LATE ARRIVALS
0-393-04042-9 NORTON $23.00

Angus **Wilson**

Anglo-Saxon Attitudes
0-312-14275-7 ST. MARTIN'S PB $14.95

Late Call
A retired manager is forced to live with her widowed son in a chillingly described New Town
0-586-04895-2 ACADEMY CHICAGO PB $8.00

Patrick O'Brian's Aubrey/Maturin Novels and Other Fiction

An irresistible naval adventure series set during the Napoleonic Wars, the novels also paint English society with an exactitude worthy of Jane Austen and develop characters with the sensitivity of Henry James. Seasoned O'Brian fans will grab the first copy they can—all other have the great pleasure of starting at the beginning. "Literate, leisurely, and as charming as the rest of the series. The illustrated guide to sails and masts is worth the price by itself"
—Kirkus Reviews.
"They're funny, they're exciting, they're informative…there are legions of us who gladly ship out time and time again under Captain Aubrey"*—New Yorker*

Dean **King** & others, editors

A Sea of Words: A Lexicon Companion for Patrick O'Brian's Seafaring Tales
The vocabulary not only of the British Navy, but also of the medical, political, and scientific terms O'Brian uses, is explained in this companion
0-8050-3812-4 HOLT $27.50
0-8050-3816-7 HOLT PB $14.00

Patrick **O'Brian**

The Aubrey-Maturin Novels
0-393-03749-5 NORTON $360.00

Master and Commander
0-393-03701-0 NORTON $22.50
0-393-30705-0 NORTON PB $11.95

Post Captain
0-393-03702-9 NORTON $22.50
0-393-30706-9 NORTON PB $11.95

H.M.S. Surprise
0-393-03703-7 NORTON $22.50
0-393-30761-1 NORTON PB $11.95

The Mauritius Command
0-393-03704-5 NORTON $22.50
0-393-30762-X NORTON PB $11.95

Desolation Island
0-393-03705-3 NORTON $22.50
0-393-30812-X NORTON PB $11.95

The Fortune of War
0-393-03706-1 NORTON $22.50
0-393-30813-8 NORTON PB $11.95

The Surgeon's Mate
0-393-03707-X NORTON $22.50
0-393-30820-0 NORTON PB $11.95

The Ionian Mission
0-393-03708-8 NORTON $22.50
0-393-30821-9 NORTON PB $11.95

Treason's Harbour
0-393-03709-6 NORTON $22.50
0-393-30863-4 NORTON PB $11.95

The Far Side of the World
0-393-03710-X NORTON $22.50
0-393-30862-6 NORTON PB $11.95

The Reverse of the Medal
0-393-03711-8 NORTON $22.50

The Letter of Marque
0-393-02874-7 NORTON $22.50

The Thirteen-Gun Salute
0-393-02974-3 NORTON $22.50

The Nutmeg of Consolation
0-393-03032-6 NORTON $22.50
0-393-30906-1 NORTON PB $11.95

The Truelove
Called *Clarrissa Oakes* in English Edition
0-393-03109-8 NORTON $22.50
0-393-31016-7 NORTON PB $11.95

The Wine-Dark Sea
0-393-03558-1 NORTON $22.50
0-393-31244-5 NORTON PB $11.00

The Commodore
0-393-03760-6 NORTON $22.50
0-393-31459-6 NORTON PB $11.95

The Yellow Admiral
0-393-04044-5 NORTON $24.00

Other Novels

Men-of-War: Life in Nelson's Navy
Concise, richly illustrated, and beautifully written, this volume is a splendid companion to all of O'Brian's work. What was daily life like in Nelson's navy? What did sailors eat, how did they work, what were they paid? All these questions and more are answered in this anecdotal, erudite, and altogether readable account of Nelson's navy. "You will meet nothing like O'Brian in all literature"—Stephen Becker
0-393-03858-0 NORTON $23.00

The Rendezvous and Other Stories
In O'Brian's first published collection of short stories he shows new scope for old and practiced talents. "Heir to the greatness of Melville and Conrad"—*Wall Street Journal*
0-393-03685-5 NORTON $22.00
0-393-31380-8 NORTON PB $11.00

The Golden Ocean
See also **HISTORICAL AND ROMANTIC FICTION** in **POPULAR READING**
0-393-03630-8 NORTON $22.50
0-393-31537-1 NORTON PB $12.00

The Unknown Shore
This reissue of his second novel, the immediate precursor to the Aubrey/Maturin series, follows the fates of the *Wager*, a ship that was parted from Commodore Anson's fateful circumnavigation in 1740 and was shipwrecked on the coast of Chile. A story of survival and friendship written by the master himself
See also **HISTORICAL AND ROMANTIC FICTION** in **POPULAR READING**
0-393-03859-9 NORTON $23.00
0-393-31538-X NORTON PB $12.00

Testimonies
In 1952, Delmore Schwartz called this novel "a triumph [in which the reader] discovers the riddle of existence itself." This sinister tale of love and death in Wales by the masterful author of the *Aubrey/ Maturin* series is available to American readers again. "O'Brian is blessed by the two greatest gifts any storyteller could ask for: an irresistible narrative drive, and an equally irresistible sense of humor"
—*Chicago Sun Times*
0-393-03483-6 NORTON $20.95

New Writers of the '90s

Julia **Blackburn**

The Book of Colour
0-679-43983-8 RANDOM HOUSE $22.00

Louis **de Bernières**

Corelli's Mandolin
Against a background of natural beauty, mythic past, and modern barbarism, de Bernières chronicles five decades in a Greek island's life, from the eve of German invasion to the present. "Heartbreaking, beautiful and deeply moving…this soaring novel glows with a wise humanity that is rare in contemporary fiction"
—*Publishers Weekly*
0-679-43644-8 PANTHEON $24.00
0-679-76397-X VINTAGE PB $13.00

Alain **de Botton**

On Love
"A tour-de-force pleasure of a novel that takes a conventional love story and textures it with philosophical ruminations, ironic subtitles, and various sorts of playfulness, including pencil drawings…Both intellectually stimulating and emotionally touching. A very promising debut"
—*Kirkus Reviews*
0-8021-3409-2 GROVE PB $10.00

Roddy **Doyle**

The Barrytown Trilogy: The Commitments, The Snapper, The Van
"Earthy and exuberant…with brash energy, cheerful irreverence, and a street idiom that reads like poetry"—Fay Weldon
0-14-025262-2 PENGUIN PB $16.95

Paddy Clarke Ha Ha Ha
Told in the voice of Paddy, a young boy growing up in an Irish Catholic town, in trouble and grappling with the inconsistencies of the adult world. Winner of the Booker Prize
0-14-023390-3 PENGUIN PB $10.95

The Snapper
"The dialogue of *The Snapper* crackles with wit and authenticity. The characterization is superbly accomplished"—*The Times* [Londonn]
0-14-017167-3 PENGUIN PB $10.95

The Woman Who Walked into Doors
Booker Prize-winning Doyle reaches new heights with a heart-rending story of a woman struggling to reclaim her dignity after an abusive husband and a worsening drinking problem. A portrait of vulnerability and strength in a real, tough, and poignant novel
0-670-86775-6 VIKING $22.95

Roddy Doyle

Tibor **Fischer**

Under the Frog
1-56584-149-2 NEW PRESS PB $11.00

Esther **Freud**

Hideous Kinky
0-15-140216-7 HARCOURT BRACE $18.95

Esther **Freud**

Peerless Flats

Through the eyes of a 16-year-old girl we see the life of a London homeless shelter and the drug-infested, crime-ridden world in which she must come of age. An "unusual book…like a beautiful, disturbing painting that renders, on an intuitive level, a troubled young girl's soul"
—*Publishers Weekly*

0-15-171608-0 HARCOURT BRACE....................$19.95

Lisa had always been good at keeping secrets. She was so good at it that no one even suspected she had any to keep. She had often found herself having to listen to something she had been holding sacred and to herself for years
PEERLESS FLATS

Stephen **Fry**

The Hippopotamus

1-56947-054-5 SOHO PB....................$14.00

The Liar

1-56947-012-X SOHO PB....................$11.00

Alison **Habens**

Dreamhouse

"Both cruel and amusing, it reads like Lewis Carroll on acid"—*Cosmopolitan*

0-312-14086-X PICADOR....................$23.00

Josephine **Hart**

Damage

A man falls obsessively in love with his son's girlfriend, with violent consequences

See also **THE MIDDLE GENERATION**

0-8041-0841-2 IVY PB....................$5.99

Oblivion

The internationally best selling author of *Damage* and *Sin* offers a third novel, in which a dead woman cannot be forgotten by her husband. Caught between the living and the memory of his beloved, he must confront the fact of her second death, her passage not out of life but out of memory and into oblivion. A sensual, ethereal novel

0-670-86612-1 VIKING....................$19.95

Sin

0-8041-1097-2 IVY PB....................$5.99

Alan **Hollinghurst**

The Folding Star

0-679-43605-7 PANTHEON....................$24.00

The Swimming Pool Library

"Beautifully welds the standard conventions of fiction to a tale of modern transgressions. It talks of impurities with shimmering elegance, and of complexities with camp-fired wit"
—Catherine R. Stimpson

0-394-57025-1 VINTAGE PB....................$16.95

Nick **Hornby**

High Fidelity

"It is rare that a book so hilarious is also so sharp about sex and manliness, memory and music"—*New Yorker*

1-57322-016-7 PUTNAM....................$21.95
1-57322-551-7 RIVERHEAD PB....................$12.00

Is it so wrong, wanting to be at home with your record collection?…There's a whole world in there, a nicer, dirtier, more violent, more peaceful, more colorful, sleazier, more dangerous, more loving world than the world I live in; there is history, and geography, and poetry, and countless other things I should have studied at school, including music.
HIGH FIDELITY

Elizabeth Jane **Howard**

Cazalet Chronicles

A family saga detailing upper-middle class life in England just before and during World War II spans these three novels

Volume I
The Light Years

0-671-52793-2 WASHINGTON SQUARE PB.....$12.00

Volume II
Marking Time

0-671-52794-0 WASHINGTON SQUARE PB.....$12.00

Volume III
Confusion

0-671-52796-7 WASHINGTON SQUARE PB.....$12.00

James **Kelman**

How Late It Was, How Late

1994 Booker Prize winner. The story of a fist-fighting alcoholic whose beating by the police initiates a harrowing descent in Glasgow's netherworld

0-385-31560-0 DELTA PB....................$11.95

James Kelman

Kazuo **Ishiguro**

An Artist of the Floating World

A subtle psychological novel. Examines a Japanese artist's career in relation to the rise of Japanese fascism. Recommended

0-679-72266-1 VINTAGE PB....................$10.00

A Pale View of the Hills

A Japanese woman living in England contemplates her daughter's suicide and the destruction of Japan in World War II in this ruminative first novel

0-679-72267-X VINTAGE PB....................$11.00

The Remains of the Day

"Brilliant and deeply moving. Beneath the simple and compelling narrative, Ishiguro has run a line into the core of history and the English mind"—Michael Herr

0-394-57343-9 KNOPF....................$22.00
0-394-25134-2 VINTAGE PB....................$11.00

The Unconsoled

When an internationally renowned pianist arrives in a European city he cannot name, he finds himself expected to perform a concert he cannot remember, surrounded by people who have inexplicable knowledge and expectations of him. From this starting point, Ishiguro takes us on a seamless fictional adventure across physical and emotional landscapes, endlessly strange, of a public self that has taken leave of its owner

0-679-40425-2 KNOPF....................$25.00

John **Lanchester**

The Debt to Pleasure

0-8050-4388-8 HOLT....................$20.00

Margot **Livesey**

Criminals

"This fascinating, disturbing and beautiful novel haunts us like a visitation from every suspect thing we've ever done, with the best intentions"—Francine Prose

0-679-44487-4 KNOPF....................$23.00

Sara **Maitland**

Ancestral Truths

0-8050-3779-9 HOLT PB....................$12.00

Angel Maker: The Short Stories of Sara Maitland

0-8050-4412-4 HOLT....................$25.00

A Daughter of Jerusalem

0-8050-3810-8 HOLT PB....................$12.00

Three Times Table

A paleontologist, her mathematician daughter, and her 15-year-old granddaughter share a house and confront cancer, aging, and the end of childhood together

0-8050-2923-0 OWLET PB....................$12.95

Adam **Mars-Jones**

Monopolies of Loss

"A formidably intelligent writer, issuing civilized, if urgent, invitations for the straight world to reconcile itself with the gay…"—*LA Times*

0-679-74415-0 VINTAGE PB....................$11.00

The Waters of Thirst

The brilliant, digressive narrator of this novel prepares elaborate meals that he cannot eat, is obsessed with motorcycle riders and with Peter Hunter, famous American porn star. His monogamous lover moves in and out of his consciousness—as do his debilitating illness and his intense evaluations of love and desire

0-679-41941-1 KNOPF....................$20.00
0-679-75960-3 VINTAGE PB....................$11.00

Patrick **McCabe**

The Butcher Boy

Irish criminal's *bildungsroman* slashes at church and state. "Stunning…Part Huck Finn, part Holden Caulfield, part Hannibal Lecter"
—*NY Times Book Review*

0-385-31237-7 DELTA PB....................$10.95

The Dead School

0-385-31420-5 DIAL BOOKS....................$21.95
0-385-31423-X DELTA PB....................$11.95

Colum **McCann**

Fishing the Sloe-Black River: Stories

0-8050-4106-0 HOLT $22.00

Songdogs

0-8050-4104-4 HOLT $22.50
0-312-14741-4 PICADOR PB $12.00

John **McGahern**

Amongst Women

Winner of the Irish Times Literary Award. "A wonderful writer…his spare but luminous prose evokes a severely repressed life and the aching passion that lies beneath its stony surface" —*Chicago Tribune*

See also THE MIDDLE GENERATION

0-14-009255-2 PENGUIN PB $10.95

Collected Stories

See also THE MIDDLE GENERATION

0-679-41913-6 KNOPF $24.00
0-679-74401-0 VINTAGE PB $12.00

High Ground

0-14-017708-6 PENGUIN PB $10.00

Ferdinand **Mount**

Of Love and Asthma

Two asthmatics and would-be philanderers pursue the same girl. "English comedy writing at its best"—*Scotsman*

0-7493-1064-2 TRAFALGAR SQUARE PB $13.95

Umbrella

The quixotic rise and fall of Byron's cousin and English Prime Minister, Lord Aberdeen. "Quite simply the best historical novel in years" —*Daily Mail*

0-7493-2193-8 R.B.H.P. PB $8.99

Lawrence **Norfolk**

Lemprière's Dictionary

While writing a dictionary of classical allusions in the 18th-century, a young scholar discovers a 150-year conspiracy against his family. "Deftly merging history, classical allusions and fabulous fantasy in a style that merits comparison to Dickens as well as Gilbert and Sullivan" —*Kirkus Reviews*

0-345-38423-7 BALLANTINE PB $12.50

The Pope's Rhinoceros

Picaresque fictional tapestry spun around the 16th-century attempt to procure a rhinoceros for the amusement of Pope Leo X

0-517-59532-X HARMONY $25.00

Will **Self**

Cock & Bull

Fantastical meditation on gender has a mousy wife growing a penis and a jock lawyer growing a vagina behind his knee

0-679-75092-4 VINTAGE PB $11.00

Grey Area

0-87113-620-1 GROVE $22.00

My Idea of Fun

0-679-75093-2 VINTAGE PB $12.00

The Quantity Theory of Insanity

"If a manic J.G. Ballard and a depressed David Lodge got together, they might produce something like *The Quantity Theory of Insanity*. But Will Self's world is all his own; it is both exotic and institutionalized, full of dread and dowdiness and entirely unsuspected comedy"—Martin Amis

See also HUMOR WRITERS under HUMOR in POPULAR READING

0-87113-585-X GROVE $21.00
0-679-75094-0 VINTAGE PB $12.00

Adam **Thorpe**

Ulverton

The history of a fictional village on the Wessex Downs of England, from a soldier's homecoming after Cromwell's campaigns to a real-estate scandal during the '80s economic boom. "A superb and moving meditation on history, fate, and the nature of time, *Ulverton* is at once a traditional fiction and a daring and wholly successful testing of the limits of literary art" —John Banville

0-374-28031-2 FS&G $23.00

Colm **Toíbín**

The South

0-670-83870-5 VIKING $18.95

Irvine **Welsh**

The Acidhouse

Stories by the "Scottish Céline of the 90s"

0-393-31280-1 NORTON PB $13.00

Trainspotting

Welsh's slangy prose may be slightly off-putting to those not accustomed to the peculiar dialect of working-class Edinburgh twenty-somethings, but his alternately bleak and hilarious portrait of '80s heroin subculture is imbued with a lyric grace and sensitivity that rises above any provincial categorization

0-393-31480-4 NORTON PB $13.00

Jeanette **Winterson**

"Winterson has the ability to fuse seamlessly the historical and the imaginary. Her lyrical prose penetrates to the heart of things without apparent effort. She knows how to speak plain truth and at the same time satisfy our longing for the fabulous."—Washington Post

Art & Lies

Handel, Picasso, and Sappho meet on a high-speed train. Their discussion ranges over the centuries and freely through art, philosophy, and personal confession

0-679-44181-6 KNOPF $22.00
0-679-76270-1 VINTAGE PB $11.00

Oranges are not the Only Fruit

Winterson's fabulous first novel in which a young girl becomes a child preacher in an Evangelical church, only to be later cast out for her burgeoning "deviant" sexuality. Winner of England's Whitbread Award

0-87113-163-3 ATLANTIC MONTHLY PB $10.95

The Passion

"We can't help recalling Gabriel García Márquez. Magical touches dance like highlights over the fairy-tale about passion, gentility, madness and androgynous ecstasy"—Edmund White

0-679-72437-0 RANDOM HOUSE PB $10.00

Sexing the Cherry

0-679-73316-7 VINTAGE PB $10.00

Jeanette Winterson

Written on the Body

A meditation on both the metaphysics and the very physical nature of longing, on sexuality beyond gender's confines. "Jeanette Winterson has once again proved to be a storyteller of compelling interest and exceptional grace" —*New Yorker*

0-679-42007-X KNOPF $20.00
0-679-74447-9 VINTAGE PB $11.00

Granta

Granta

1. New American Writing

Some of the most accomplished American writers of the seventies many published for the first time in Britain. John Hawkes, William Gass, Joyce Carol Oates, Leonard Michaels, Donald Barthelme, James Purdy, Tillie Olsen, Stanley Elkin, Susan Sontag, Ronald Sukenick

0-920-13432-1 GRANTA PB 11.95

2. The Portage to San Cristobal of A.H.

A novella by George Steiner a fantasy (or not?) of Hitler alive in the Amazon, waiting for us. Plus Robert Coover, Walter Abish and John Barth. "Questions on a large human scale are being asked, and if these are not very English questions for a novelist to be asking, then so much the worse for us"—Elaine Feinstein, *The Times*

0-920-13432-2 GRANTA PB 11.95

3. The End of the English Novel

Is it the end of the English novel? Has it grown predictable and unadventurous? Granta collects work from writers and critics which suggests it might be the end of the English novel, but also the beginning of British fiction. Contributors include Salman Rushdie, Angela Carter, Desmond Hogan, Alan Sillitoe, Emma Tennant, Russell Hoban and Lorna Sage

0-920-13432-3 GRANTA PB 11.95

4. Beyond the Crisis

Arguments for the future of publishing from Brigid Brophy, John Sutherland, David Caute, Blake Morrison, Per Gedin, David Godine and Walter Abish. Plus fiction from Martin Amis, Guy Davenport, Mario Vargas Llosa on the sexuality of shoes and the first British publication of Raymond Carver. "A must for anyone who wants the goods on the state of contemporary writing"—*City Limits*

0-920-13432-4 GRANTA PB 11.95

5. The Modern Common Wind

The earth and the question of human survival: with contributions from Don Bloch, Russell Hoban, Susan Sontag, Jonathan Schell, T. Coraghessan Boyle, Lisa St Aubin de Tern, Ted Mooney, Jorge Ibarguengoitia and Leonard Michaels

0-920-13432-5 GRANTA PB 11.95

6. A Literature for Politics

Interviews with the Argentine soldiers who fought in the Falklands war; the transcript of Eichmann interrogated. Plus Gregor von Rezzori, Nadine Gordimer, Ariel Dorfman and Milan Kundera

0-920-13432-6 GRANTA PB 11.95

First Six Issues: Boxed Set

The only way to get your hands on the first six issues of Granta

0-920-13432-X GRANTA BX 70.00

7. Best of Young British Novelists 1

Martin Amis, William Boyd, Maggie Gee, Kazuo Ishiguro, Adam Mars-Jones, Salman Rushdie, Julian Barnes, Ursula Bentley, Pat Barker, Buchi Emecheta, Ian McEwan, Shiva Naipaul, Graham Swift, Rose Tremain, Clive Sinclair, Alan Judd, Philip Norman, A.N. Wilson, Christopher Priest, Lisa St. Aubin de Teran

014-01-4082-4 GRANTA PB 11.95

8. Dirty Realism

The issue of Granta that defined a new school of American writers. Featuring Richard Ford, Jayne Anne Phillips, Raymond Carver, Elizabeth Tallent, Tobias Wolff, Bobbie Anne Mason and others. "For the first time in two decades, something interesting is once again happening in American literature"— Gordon Burn, *The Face*

014-00-6869-4 GRANTA PB 11.95

9. John Berger, BORIS

Boris: a story of love and pain and self-destruction. Also a chronicle of an obsession with political and historical implications that extend far beyond its seemingly straightforward, spartan narrative. Plus Gabriel Garcià Màrquez on 'The Solitude of Latin America', with Mario Vargas Llosa and José Donoso. "A cause for congratulation"—*Guardian*

014-00-6880-5 GRANTA PB 11.95

10. Travel Writing

The most popular issue of Granta, now in its fifth printing. Including Jonathan Raban, James Fenton, Colin Thubron, Martha Gellhorn, Bruce Chatwin, Norman Lewis, Saul Bellow, Jan Morris, Paul Theroux, Redmond O'Hanlon and others. "One of the best numbers of this magazine to date"—*Sunday Times*

014-00-7052-4 GRANTA PB 11.95

11. Milan Kundera

'In November 1956, the director of the Hungarian News Agency, shortly before his office was flattened by artillery fire, sent a telex to the entire world with a desperate message announcing that the Russian attack against Budapest had begun. The dispatch ended with these words: "We are going to die for Hungary and for Europe." What did this sentence mean?' Milan Kundera, 'A Kidnapped West'

014-00-7383-3 GRANTA PB 11.95

12. The Rolling Stones

Stanley Booth's 'The True Adventures of the Rolling Stones' is only in part about the musicians it depicts. It is also a social history and a confession a chronicle, of a people committed to their own destruction. Plus: Günter Grass, Breyten Breytenbach, Richard Ford, Raymond Carver and the inside story of—*The Guardian* and Sarah Tisdall

014-00-7565-8 GRANTA PB 11.95

13. After the Revolution The Soviet Union, Czechoslovakia, East Germany, China, Cuba.

What has happened to the nineteenth-century dream of revolution? John Berger, Milan Kundera, Orville Schell, Anita Brookner, James Fenton, Doris Lessing, Martin Amis and Edward Said. "It represents the pinnacle of literary and political writing. Granta is surprising and pointed, often funny, never dry"—*Vogue*

014-00-7566-9 GRANTA PB 11.95

14. Autobiography

'The Americans call photography an art. But what I'm doing is not art. How can I talk of these photographs as art objects? These are real people. I have inhaled their suffering.' Don McCullin, 'A Life in Photographs'. Plus: Beryl Bainbridge, Michael Ignatieff, William Boyd, Eddie Limonov, Todd McEwen, Jaroslav Seifert, Doris Lessing and others

014-00-7567-4 GRANTA PB 11.95

15. James Fenton, The Fall of Saigon

Witty, bizarre and verging on the lunatic who in his right mind would gatecrash an embassy on the back of an invading army's tank James Fenton's account of the fall of Saigon is an extraordinary record of the collapse of a city at war. Plus: Nadine Gordimer, George Steiner and Ryszard Kapuscinski's 'Warsaw Diary'. "One of the finest pieces of reportage I've ever seen" —*Sunday Times*

014-00-7581-X GRANTA PB 11.95

16. Science

Oliver Sacks on excess, Italo Calvino on love-making turtles, Stephen Jay Gould, Primo Levi and William Broad on the scientists of Star Wars. Plus: Germaine Greer, David Hare, David Mamet, Mary Gordon and others. "Here is scientific literature at its very best"—*New Scientist*

014-00-8479-7 GRANTA PB 11.95

17. Graham Greene, While Waiting for a War

'I find myself in 1985 refreshing my memory of 1937 and 1938 in an old commonplace book and very fragmentary diary. There are verses copied there which I must have chosen for their significance at these moments of my life; literary gossip, bizarre crimes and divorces wrenched from newspapers—and then suddenly the digging of trenches on Clapham Common.' Plus Alice Munro, John Updike, Doris Lessing, Kazuo Ishiguro, Marianne Wiggins'

014-00-8480-0 GRANTA PB 11.95

18. James Fenton, The Snap Revolution

'We had found our way, we realized, into the Marcoses' private rooms. It seemed to me that in every room I saw, practically on every available surface, there was a signed photograph of Nancy Reagan. But this can hardly be true. It just felt as if there was a lot of Nancy in evidence.' Also in this issue: Seamus Deane, Primo Levi, David Hare, and John Berger

014-00-8482-7 GRANTA PB 11.95

19. More Dirt

The companion volume to 'Dirty Realism' (Granta 8): unillusioned, spare fiction of the belly-side of American life: with Richard Ford, Ellen Gilchrist, Louise Erdrich, Jayne Anne Phillips and others. Plus: John Updike, Adam Mars-Jones and Primo Levi

014-00-8595-5 GRANTA PB 11.95

20. In Trouble Again: A Special Issue of Travel Writing

Redmond O'Hanlon in the Amazon jungle, Salman Rushdie in Nicaragua, Colin Thubron in China, Ryszard Kapuscinski in Angola, Martha Gellhorn in Cuba, Peregrine Hodson in Afghanistan. Plus: Amitav Ghosh, Norman Lewis, Timothy Garton Ash, Hanif Kureishi, Orville Schell

014-00-8597-1 GRANTA PB 11.95

21. The Story-Teller

Bruce Chatwin in the outback, Ryszard Kapuscinski carrying a coffin through the Polish 'bush' and John Berger defining the story-teller: detached, sceptical and intensely compassionate. With stories from Richard Ford, Isabel Allende, Raymond Carver, Oliver Sacks and Primo Levi on weightlessness one of the last pieces he wrote before his suicide

014-00-8599-8 GRANTA PB 11.95

22. With Your Tongue Down My Throat

Hanif Kureishi's first novella: a tale of Nadia and Nina, of two sisters, two cities, two worlds, two passions. Plus: 'An Escape from Kampala', the story Graham Greene called 'an illustration of how politics can turn insane', Leslie Cockburn on the Contras' cocaine trail, Nadine Gordimer, Doris Lessing, Carlos Fuentes, and James Fenton's 'The Truce'

014-00-8602-1 GRANTA PB..................................11.95

23. Home

Prague, Beirut, Des Moines, Derry and the ugliest village in Essex. What is home for an Arab in Israel? Or for an exile returning to the Iowa county fair? Plus: Nicholas Shakespeare in Peru in search of the leader of the Shining Path, Abimael Guzmán, and Ian Hamilton in pursuit of J.D. Salinger

014-00-8604-8 GRANTA PB 11.95

24. Inside Intelligence

Philip Roth, Peter Carey, Tobias Wolff, Bruce Chatwin, E.L. Doctorow and Jay McInerney

014-00-8606-4 GRANTA PB 11.95

25. Murder
Martin Amis's tale of Nicola Six, a girl who's been trouble all her life. Plus: 'Gibraltar', Ian Jack's award-winning investigation into the Death on the Rock, Raymond Carver, Tess Gallagher, Todd McEwen, John Berger, Angela Carter and Don DeLillo. "An extraordinary success"—*NY Times*
014-00-8608-0 GRANTA PB 11.95

26. Travel
This travel issue is dedicated to the memory of Bruce Chatwin with three unpublished pieces by one of the world's greatest travel writers, plus contributions from Ryszard Kapuscinski, Colin Thubron, Ian Buruma, Norman Lewis, Hans Magnus Enzensberger, Amitav Ghosh, Timothy Garton Ash, and Bill Bryson with More Fat Girls
014-01-2356-3 GRANTA 11.95

27. Death
A story becomes a story once it has an ending, and there is no ending more powerful than death. But what of death itself? Here, fourteen writers and photographers set out to look at death: John Gregory Dunne, Adam Mars-Jones, Mary McCarthy, Edmund White, Louise Erdrich, Michael Ignatieff, John Treherne and eerie death faces by photographer Rudolph Schñfer. "The quality and variety of its contributors is stunning Granta is, quite simply, the most impressive literary magazine of its time"
—*Daily Telegraph*
014-01-2358-X GRANTA 11.95

28. Birthday Special!
A merry miscellany, a mad editorial tea-party of some of the writers who, since 1979, have made Granta the most widely-read magazine in the English language. John Simpson, Salman Rushdie, Ian Jack, Ryszard Kapuscinski, Nadine Gordimer, David Goldblatt, Guy Davenport, Jeanette Winterson, Richard Rayner, George Steiner, Walter Abish, William Boyd, Russell Hoban, Marketa Luskacova, Eugene Richards, Joy Williams, Leonard Michaels, Jay McInerney, John Updike, Peregrine Hodson, Mario Vargas Llosa and Colin Thubron
014-01-2360-1 GRANTA 11.95

29. Jonathan Raban, New World
Is it possible, by travelling to a new world, to become a new person? A year ago, Jonathan Raban crossed the Atlantic by ship and, like the immigrants before him, made for America in search of a new language, a new name, a new identity. Plus: Rian Malan, Robert Fisk, Roger Garfitt, Josef Skvoreck y, Paul Theroux, Patricia Highsmith, Tim O'Brien and Patrick McGrath's 'A Boy's Broadmoor'
014-01-2863-8 GRANTA 11.95

30. New Europe!
Nineteen eighty-nine was the most important year in Europe since the end of World War Two; Europe will never be the same. Granta sets out to describe how it has changed. Contributors include Graham Swift, Neal Ascherson, Michael Ignatieff, Josef Skvorecky, George Steiner, Isaiah Berlin, Hans Magnus Enzensberger, Czeslaw Milosz, Noel Annan, Andrei Sinyavsky, Ivan Klima, Stephen Spender and Joseph Brodsky
014-01-3299-6 GRANTA 11.95

31. The General
Nobody has ever got through to the 'General' General Alfredo Stroessner who, until deposed in 1989, was one of the world's longest reigning dictators. Nobody had ever got an interview: nobody, that is, until Isabel Hilton, following the suggestions of the General's former mistresses, tracked him down to his hiding place in Brazil. Plus: Salman Rushdie, Richard Ford, Jonathan Raban, Gabriel Garcià Màrquez, Christopher Hitchens and Margaret Atwood
014-01-3431-X GRANTA 11.95

32. History
An issue of stories, about the ways in which we make sense of the past. Contributors include Gore Vidal, Simon Schama, Julian Barnes, Richard Holmes, Allan Gurganus, plus Jonathan Raban and Martha Gellhorn. "At once curiously old-fashioned and profoundly subversive"
—*Observer*
014-01-3856-0 GRANTA 11.95

33. What Went Wrong?
The first chilling account of the darker side of Europe's Revolution of 1989. William McPherson in Romania during the brutal six months 'after' communism. Plus: Victoria Tokareva, Hans Magnus Enzensberger, Isabel Allende, Christa Wolf, Ryszard Kapuscinski, and Martin Amis, Time's Arrow (part one)
014-01-3858-7 GRANTA 11.95

34. Death of a Harvard Man
Simon Schama sets out to discover which story, if any story, is the story of the many stories of the disappearance of Doctor George Parkman, the perfect Yankee. Plus: William Boyd, Geoffrey Wolff, Louise Erdrich, Don DeLillo, Amitav Ghosh and Martin Amis (part two)
014-01-3860-9 GRANTA 11.95

35. The Unbearable Peace
John le Carré's story about the Swiss, money and democracy and about our own unbearable peace. Plus: Max Frisch, Friedrich Durrenmatt, John Berger, Jayne Anne Phillips, Nadine Gordimer, Patrick Süjskind and Allan Gurganus
014-01-4846-9 GRANTA 11.95

36. Vargas Llosa for President
The novelist's personal account of his campaign for the presidency of Peru. Plus: Alvaro Vargas Llosa as his father's press officer, Sergio Ramirez on the end of the Sandinistas, George Steiner on the end of the dream of communism, Graham Swift, T. Coraghessan Boyle and Martin Amis (part three)
014-01-5208-3 GRANTA 11.95

37. The Family
The controversial issue about the most important, powerful and potentially destructive relationship of our lives. Contributors include Mikal Gilmore on his brother, the murderer; Sappho Durrell on her father, the novelist. Plus: William Wharton, Geoffrey Wolff, Seamus Deane, Mona Simpson, Harold Pinter and Giorgio Pressburger
014-01-5209-1 GRANTA 11.95

38. We're So Happy!
Featuring the fictional debut of Bill Morris, set in the design department of General Motors, between New Year's Day and New Year's Eve 1954: the year (Elvis Presley, Marilyn Monroe, Dwight Eisenhower and Edgar Hoover) when America changed. Plus: Jeremy Rifkin, Ivan Klima, Tracy Kidder, Eugene Richards, Louise Erdrich, Adam Mars-Jones and Sue Halpern
014-01-5211-3 GRANTA 11.95

39. The Body
Is it us or is it nothing more than the container of what we really are? Contributors include Abraham Verghese, Jeanette Winterson, Michael Dibdin, Geoffrey Biddle, Todd McEwen, Hanif Kureishi, Giorgio Pressburger, Anchee Min, Antonin Kratochvil, John Conroy, Peregrine Hodson and Victoria Tokareva. Plus: fiction by Salman Rushdie, and Redmond O'Hanlon in the Congo
014-01-4049-2 GRANTA 11.95

40. The Womanizer
Richard Ford's womanizer is an insistently ordinary man until he goes abroad. Paul Theroux's 'imaginary' young American novelist loses his self-control in London. William T. Vollmann, alone in the wilderness with Erica, risks losing his life for her. Plus: Nadine Gordimer, André Brink and Richard Rayner.
014-01-4054-9 GRANTA 11.95

41. Biography
Is it merely a form of gossip (the affairs, the drinking, the public rows), or does it satisfy an important curiosity? Saul Bellow (on his father), James Atlas (on Saul Bellow), Gabriel Garcià Màrquez (on the mysterious Frau Frida) and Lorna Sage, Louise Erdrich, Andrew Motion and Luc Sante
014-01-4055-7 GRANTA 11.95

42. Krauts!
What is the new Germany? 'Krauts!' seeks the uncomfortable answer to this simple question. With Günter Grass on neo-Nazis, Hans Magnus Enzensberger on the new European the immigrant, Ian Buruma on Buchenwald, and Martha Gellhorn on why she'll never return to Germany
014-01-4056-5 GRANTA 11.95

43. Best of Young British Novelists 2
The second generation: Kazuo Ishiguro, Hanif Kureishi, Ben Okri, Esther Freud, Caryl Phillips, Will Self, Iain Banks, Adam Lively, Helen Simpson, Tibor Fischer, Nicholas Shakespeare, Philip Kerr, Lawrence Norfolk, Louis de Berniäres, A.L. Kennedy, Alan Hollinghurst, Candia McWilliam, Anne Billson, Adam Mars-Jones, Jeanette Winterson
014-01-4059-X GRANTA 11.95

44. The Last Place on Earth
When the time comes our appointment, our dark hour what thoughts will we have? Tracy Kidder's fable-like account of old age; new novelist Mary Karr on her terrifying Grandma Moore; and the first publication of Bruce Chatwin's notebooks. Plus: Paul Auster, T. Coraghessan Boyle, Ivan Klima and Tobias Wolff
014-01-4062-X GRANTA 11.95

45. Gazza Agonistes
Ian Hamilton's story of soccer superstar Paul Gascoigne: at play, on show, in the press, in pain, in distress. This is a fan's account of a player's life and of a fan's obsession, of a sports celebrity and of our apparent need to have one. Also in this issue: Jonathan Raban on the flooded Mississippi, Timothy Garton Ash with Erich Honecker
014-01-4065-4 GRANTA 11.95

46. Crime

An issue devoted exclusively to criminal behaviour, a testimony to social deviance. With James Ellroy on the dark, manic, sexed-up world of Los Angeles in the 1950s; Allan Gurganus on necrophilia; the extraordinary stories of two murderers told by the murderers themselves. Plus Paul Auster, Italo Calvino and Tibor Fischer. "The decidedly unpulpish Granta takes on "Crime" with an oblique, sometimes coy touch Ellroy's piece is soaked in seedy and peppered with jive"—*Voice Literary Supplement*

014-01-4067-0 GRANTA 11.95

47. Losers

A hymn to humiliation–unmitigated public humiliation. With Martin Amis on a writer who can't write; Neil Steinberg on the stress of the National Spelling Bee. Plus, Beverly Lowry on two boys who kill their daddy; Jean Hatzfeld with dispatches from the Yugoslav war (photos by Gilles Peress), Jayne Anne Phillips, Julian Barnes and Bret Easton Ellis

014-01-4083-2 GRANTA 11.95

48. Africa

Twelve writers describe the profound changes this continent is undergoing. With Lynda Schuster in Liberia as Doe falls; Gilles Peress in Rwanda after the massacres; Paul Theroux at a leper colony in Malawi; Sousa Jamba in Angola; Ryszard Kapuscinski and Abraham Verghese in Ethiopia; William Finnegan in South Africa

014-01-4084-0 GRANTA 11.95

49. Money

Get it, spend it. Save it, lose it. Risk it, win it. Lose it again, get it again. What is money? With Richard Rayner on becoming a thief; Steve Pyke's portraits of the very rich; Jonathan Raban on the consequences of dreaming in America, and James Buchan on the psychology of money. Plus short stories by Seamus Deane and John McGahern

014-01-4085-9 GRANTA 11.95

50. Fifty

In 1985, Granta published James Fenton's extraordinary account of the fall of Saigon. Twenty years after the first tank entered the city, Philip Gourevitch, Tran Vu, Paul Eggers and Bao Ninh examine the aftermath of that terrible war. Also: work from some of our finest contributors Redmond O'Hanlon, Norman Lewis, Germaine Greer, Timothy Garton Ash, Julian Barnes, and more. "Granta's heart is where it has always been: good writing and, more importantly, a fantastic range of good writing, is given a worthy showcase"—*Daily Telegraph*

014-01-4104-9 GRANTA 11.95

51. Big Men

Big as in substantial, tall, powerful, famous; men as in weak, wicked, cruel and notorious. With Gitta Sereny on Albert Speer, the tyrant as survivor, Caroline Alexander on a classical tyrant, Hastings Banda, Andrea Ashworth on the tyrant in the next room (her stepfather). Blake Morrison considers failing manhood, John Sweeney investigates the myth and mystery of Hitler's missing testicle, and Douglas Brooker photographs the young some may say strange women of L.A.

014-01-4108-1 GRANTA 1.95

52. Food

Food as indulgence, certainly, but also food as a taboo, a cruelty, a desperate need, a failed sex aid, and a means of making a living. Including Graham Swift on the life and death of a butcher, J.M. Coetzee's attempt at vegetarianism in Texas, Giles Foden at Idi Amin's dinner table, and Sean French on the delights of Icelandic cuisine (including roast puffin and whale sushi). Plus Georges Perec, Romesh Gunesekera, John Lanchester, Jane Rogers, Margaret Visser and Joan Smith

014-01-4113-8 GRANTA 11.95

53. News

Who makes it? Who owns it? Should we believe it? With Phillip Knightley on his life in journalism (the scoops, the groundwork, the kangaroos), Lynda Schuster on a reporter killed by an anti-tank mine her husband, Zoë Heller inside tabloid television, David Xiao on personal losses in the Kobe earthquake, Tom Pilston's visual vocabulary of selling murder. Plus fiction by Paul Theroux, and the scorching, hilarious debut of Paul Beatty

014-01-4113-2 GRANTA 11.95

54. Best of Young American Novelists

The twenty best American novelists under forty: Sherman Alexie, Madison Smartt Bell, Ethan Canin, Edwidge Danticat, Tom Drury, Tony Earley, Jeffrey Eugenides, Jonathan Franzen, David Guterson, David Haynes, Allen Kurzweil, Elizabeth McCracken, Lorrie Moore, Fae Myenne Ng, Robert O'Connor, Stewart O'Nan, Chris Offutt, Mona Simpson, Melanie Rae Thon, and Kate Wheeler. Judged by Robert Stone, Anne Tyler, Tobias Wolff and Granta's editor, Ian Jack

014-01-4135-9 GRANTA 11.95

55. Children

014-01-4141-3 GRANTA 11.95

20th-Century British and Irish Poetry

British Poets

Modern British poetry has been heavily influenced by external events and trends. The First World War, the ideological struggles of the 1930s, the decline of the British Empire, and the postwar economic austerity form the historical backdrop. In purely literary terms, the native tradition found itself more open to foreign influences—to international modernism and the new poetics of American verse—than at any time in four centuries. As a result, the 20th-century has been a time of movements and countermovements (the New Apocalypse, the Movement, the Liverpool Poets, the Martians), of poets judged as much by their politics as by their poetry, and of a general lack of consensus. Many of the greatest figures (David Jones, Hugh MacDiarmid, D.H. Lawrence, Basil Bunting) worked in isolation from the literary establishments of London, Oxford, and Cambridge, and this splendid individualism persists in many latter-day practitioners.

Dannie **Abse**

Remembrance of Crimes Past: Poems

A leading Welsh poet of the postwar years, who is also a practicing physician

0-89255-176-3 PERSEA PB $9.95

Fleur **Adcock**

The Inner Harbour

0-19-211888-9 OXFORD PB $8.95

Meeting the Comet

1-85224-054-7 DUFOUR PB $6.95

Time Zones

0-19-282831-2 OXFORD PB $9.95

John **Agard**

Lovelines for a Goat-Born Lady

1-85242-201-7 SERPENT'S TAIL PB $12.95

Mangoes and Bullets: Selected and New Poems, 1972-84

"John Agard, from Guyana, is an outstanding luminary of the exploding galaxy of West Indian British troubadours, hilarious and moving by turns"—Michael Horovitz

1-85242-124-X SERPENT'S TAIL PB $12.95

Simon **Armitage**

Zoom

1-85224-078-4 DUFOUR PB $14.95

John **Ash**

The Branching Stairs

"This may be the most auspicious debut of its kind since Auden's"—Carolyn Kizer, *NY Times*

0-85635-501-1 SCHOLARLY PB $11.25

The Burnt Pages

An English poet currently residing in New York City, Ash has been praised for the elegance and highly colored imagination of his work

0-679-40175-X RANDOM HOUSE $19.00

Disbelief

"Ash's poetry is…resonant with gorgeous imagery. It seems both familiar and strange, noble and funny, romantic and level-headed" —John Ashbery

0-85635-695-6 SCHOLARLY PB $14.75

W.H. **Auden**

Collected Poems

0-394-40895-0 RANDOM HOUSE $39.95

Collected Poems

A thick, compact collection of Auden's poetry, available in paperback for the first time

EDITED BY EDWARD MENDELSON

0-679-73197-0 VINTAGE PB $22.50

The Complete Works: Prose and Travel Books in Prose and Verse, 1926-1938

EDITED BY EDWARD MENDELSON

0-691-06803-8 PRINCETON $59.50

The English Auden: Poems, Essays, and Dramatic Writings, 1927-1959

EDITED BY EDWARD MENDELSON

The original texts of the electrifying early work that Auden later revised and toned down

0-571-11502-0 FABER PB $24.95

W.H. Auden

Juvenilia: 1922-1928

Just what the title says

0-691-03415-X PRINCETON $29.95

Poems

0-679-44367-3 EVERYMAN'S $10.95

Selected Poems of W.H. Auden

EDITED BY EDWARD MENDELSON

0-679-72483-4 VINTAGE PB $13.00

W.H. **Auden** & Chester **Kallman**

Libretti and Other Dramatic Writings, 1939-1973

0-691-03301-3 PRINCETON $55.00

Owen **Barfield**

A Barfield Sampler: Poetry and Fiction by Owen Barfield

0-7914-1587-2 SUNY $59.50
0-7914-1588-0 SUNY PB $12.95

George **Barker**

Anno Domini

0-571-13026-7 FABER PB $8.95

Selected Poems by George Barker

Barker, a skillful metricist and a great romantic, was a preeminent figure in postwar British poetry

0-571-17285-7 FABER PB $14.95

Street Ballads

0-571-16609-1 FABER PB $8.95

James **Berry**

Chain of Days

Poetry that draws on the cultures of the Old World and the New, and on the relationship between the colonizers and the colonized

0-19-211964-8 OXFORD PB $8.95

John **Betjeman**

A Nip in the Air

Betjeman, who was appointed Poet Laureate in 1972, was one of the most widely read postwar poets

0-393-04423-8 NORTON PB $2.50

Edmund **Blunden**

Selected Poems

Blunden wrote memorable poetry of the First World War and survived to flourish as a poet of landscape and a distinguished scholar

EDITED BY ROBYN MARSACK

0-85635-425-2 CARCANET PB $12.50

Rupert **Brooke**

The Poetical Works of Rupert Brooke

0-571-04704-1 FABER PB $11.95

George MacKay **Brown**

Following a Lark

0-7195-5620-1 MURRAY PB $14.95

Selected Poems, 1954-1983

Much-admired poetry which evokes the desolate landscape of the author's native Orkneys

0-87745-555-4 IOWA PB $12.95

Basil **Bunting**

A close associate of Ezra Pound, Bunting did not become widely known until he published his magnificent autobiographical poem "Briggflatts" in the 1960s. "Bunting compresses immensities of experience into clipped, tightly stitched lines. The miniature epic 'Briggflatts' is only 22 pages long, but in the mind it expands to infinitely greater length…The poet makes himself an instrument of the world, constructs a summing-up of earthly elements, a catalogue of smells and colors, the distillation of a life into essential—and often microscopic—perceptions."—The Village Voice

The Complete Poems

Bunting was Britain's outstanding Modernist poet

EDITED BY RICHARD CADDEL

0-19-282282-9 OXFORD PB $17.95

Uncollected Poems

0-19-282870-3 OXFORD PB $11.95

Wendy **Cope**

Making Cocoa for Kingsley Amis

A witty collection that was immensely popular on its first publication

0-571-13747-4 FABER PB $10.95

Serious Concerns

0-571-16705-5 FABER PB $8.95

Adam **Cornford**

Animations

0-87286-208-9 CITY LIGHTS PB $5.95

Donald **Davie**

Collected Poems

Davie, also a distinguished literary critic, was a leading figure in the Movement, the anti-Romantic group of the 1950s

0-226-13760-0 CHICAGO $48.00
0-226-13761-9 CHICAGO PB $17.95

Selected Poems

0-85635-595-X CARCANET PB $11.25

Keith **Douglas**

The Complete Poems

"The *Complete Poems* of Keith Douglas… confirms that when Douglas was killed in Normandy, three days after D-day, at the age of 24, we lost the finest poet to come out of the Second World War"—Robert Nye

0-19-281964-X OXFORD PB $11.95

Douglas **Dunn**

Dante's Drum Kit

0-571-17055-2 FABER PB $9.95

Elegies

0-571-13469-6 FABER PB $8.95

New & Selected Poems, 1966-1968

A fine poet whose work combines metrical sophistication, political passion, and an acute awareness of the limitations of ordinary life

0-88001-177-7 ECCO $17.95

Terry Street

0-571-09713-8 FABER PB $8.95

Lawrence **Durrell**

The Ikons & Other Poems

Poems imbued with the spirit of the Greek islands

0-933806-01-9 BLACK SWAN $15.00

D.J. **Enright**

Collected Poems, 1987

"Often he seems to be quite simply the funniest writer alive. But his humor is tempered by his very large compassion, which is always directed to living particulars"
—John W. Aldridge, *NY Times*

0-19-282061-3 OXFORD PB $12.95

Old Men and Comets

0-19-283176-3 OXFORD PB $10.95

Under the Circumstances

0-19-282834-7 OXFORD PB $10.95

Gavin **Ewart**

Selected Poems, 1933-1988

A survey of the work of England's best-known comic poet, who died in 1995. "The most remarkable phenomenon of the English poetic scene during the last ten years has been the advent, or perhaps I should say the irruption, of Gavin Ewart"—Philip Larkin

0-8112-1055-3 NEW DIRECTIONS PB $8.95

Elaine **Feinstein**

Selected Poems

1-85754-097-2 CARCANET PB $19.09

James **Fenton**

Children in Exile: Poems, 1968-1984

0-374-52406-8 NOONDAY PB $12.00

Out of Danger

0-374-22831-0 FS&G $23.00

Roy **Fisher**

Birmingham River

An extraordinarily gifted British poet who is just beginning to get recognition

0-19-282342-6 OXFORD PB $10.95

The Dow Low Drop: New and Selected Poems

1-85224-340-6 BLOODAXE PB $21.00

Poems, 1955-1987

Fisher has a jazz pianist's ear and the chiseled line of a modernist poet. His collected poems reveal him as one of the most powerful English poets of recent decades. "Fisher's work has always been an original mixture of real experiment and physical observations" —*Observer*

0-19-282230-6 OXFORD PB $14.95

Roy **Fuller**

Collected Poems

"Has all the qualities—formal control, rationality, social awareness—that the Movement poets were demanding in the fifties...He is a calm, sad, intelligent moralist and a very good poet"—*Guardian*

0-8023-1046-X DUFOUR $18.95

New Poems

0-8023-1180-6 DUFOUR $10.95

David **Gascoyne**

Collected Poems

Gascoyne was a precocious writer who initiated a Surrealist strain in modern English poetry

0-19-211801-3 OXFORD PB $12.95

Selected Poems

1-87061-234-5 ENITH PB $18.95

W. S. **Graham**

Selected Poems

The Scottish poet's early work is much influenced by Dylan Thomas; he later developed a striking, stripped-down, meditative idiom of his own

0-571-17659-3 FABER PB $15.95

Jonathan **Griffin**

Collected Poems Two-Volume Set

0-943373-05-0
NATIONAL POETRY FOUNDATION $62.50

0-943373-06-9
NATIONAL POETRY FOUNDATION PB $22.50

Thom **Gunn**

The Man with Night Sweats

"A poet at the top of his form, gathering his world into art without ever choking off passion"—*Boston Globe*

0-374-52381-9 NOONDAY PB $8.00

Collected Poems

"With their undemonstrative viruosity, their slightly corrupt openness, their atmosphere of unfathomable secrets and their intimacy, so like that of a reticent friend who has something crucial to confess, these poems strike a chord at once insinuatingly familiar and infinitely alien"—M.L. Rosenthal, *NY Times*

0-374-52433-5 NOONDAY PB $14.00

Thom Gunn

Shelf Life: Essays, Memoirs, and an Interview

0-472-09541-2 MICHIGAN $39.50

0-472-06541-6 MICHIGAN PB $13.95

Ivor **Gurney**

Gurney was a gifted musician and composer of songs as well as a poet. He emerged from the trenches of World War I with a bad case of shell-shock and spent the remainder of his life in a mental hospital. His poems, which reflect the influence of Whitman without in any way seeming imitations, are among the most moving in modern British literature.

Best Poems & The Book of Five Makings

1-85754-200-2 CARCANET PB $18.95

Collected Letters

Provides insights into the poet's work

EDITED BY R.K.R. THORNTON

0-85635-941-6 CARCANET $67.50

Selected Poems

0-19-282636-0 OXFORD PB $10.95

Ian **Hamilton**

Fifty Poems

0-571-14920-0 FABER PB $8.95

Tony **Harrison**

Harrison is a poet and translator whose realistic vision and technical skill have attracted much attention in recent years.

A Cold Coming: Gulf War Poems

1-85224-186-1 DUFOUR PB $6.95

The Mysteries

0-571-13790-3 FABER PB $10.95

V. and Other Poems

Hard-hitting poems in traditional meters that expose the fissures of British class society

0-374-52273-1 NOONDAY PB $12.95

John **Heath-Stubbs**

Game of Love and Death

1-87061-295-7 DUFOUR PB $13.95

Selected Poems

0-85635-900-9 PAUL & CO PB $12.95

Watchman's Flute

0-85635-245-4 CARCANET PB $8.50

Geoffrey **Hill**

The Enemy's Country: Words, Contexture, and Other Circumstances of Language

0-8047-2368-0 STANFORD PB $14.95

The Lords of Limit: Essay on Literature and Ideas

Essays by a leading poet of the postwar period

0-19-503517-8 OXFORD PB $8.95

The Mystery of the Charity of Charles Peguy

A meditation on the work and political career of the French poet

0-19-503515-1 OXFORD PB $7.95

New & Collected Poems, 1952-1992

A profound and passionate poet—contemporary England's greatest. Includes the acclaimed sequences *For the Unfallen*, *King Log*, *Merciam Hymns*, *Tenebrae*, and *The Mystery of the Charity of Charles Peguy*

0-395-68086-7 HOUGHTON MIFFLIN PB $17.95

Michael **Hofmann**

K.S. in Lakeland: New and Selected Poems

0-88001-197-1 ECCO $17.95

Ted **Hughes**

"Ted Hughes seems to me quite simply the best living English poet...Ted Hughes is not the only poet whose books are events in my life, but there are none whose works I anticipate with greater excitement and few who give me more consistent pleasure"—Dave Smith

The Hawk in the Rain

0-571-08614-4 FABER PB $7.95

Lupercal

0-571-09246-2 FABER PB $9.95

New Selected Poems

0-06-090925-0 HARPERCOLLINS PB $17.00

Rain-Charm for the Duchy and Other Laureate Poems
0-571-16713-6 FABER PB $8.95

River
9-998-13933-3 OLYMPIC $12.98

Wodwo
0-571-09714-6 FABER PB $8.95

Wolfwatching
0-374-52325-8 NOONDAY PB $9.00

Elizabeth **Jennings**

Collected Poems
A poet whose work often deals intimately with her own troubled life
0-85635-721-9 CARCANET PB....................$18.95

Selected Poems
0-85635-282-9 CARCANET PB $7.40

David **Jones**

The Anathemata
A difficult and extraordinarily beautiful orchestration of paleolithic, Christian, and ancient British themes; W.H. Auden called it "very probably the finest long poem written in English in this century"
0-571-10127-5 FABER PB....................$16.95

In Parenthesis
This 1937 masterpiece, written in a combination of verse and prose, is a palimpsest in which Jones's World War I combat experiences merge with layers of mythic association
0-571-05661-X FABER PB $12.95

The Roman Quarry & Other Sequences
An extension of the themes of *The Anathemata*, recovered from manuscripts arranged after Jones's death
0-935296-24-7 TILBURY PB $14.95

The Sleeping Lord: And Other Fragments
0-571-17449-3 FABER PB $14.95

Philip **Larkin**

Collected Poems
Larkin was the leading figure associated with the Movement. "Larkin is a moral poet, an honest one, who hated grandeur and the posing that encourages experiment. This is not conservatism, it is, purely devotion"
—Derek Walcott, *NY Review of Books*
EDITED BY ANTHONY THWAITE
0-374-12623-2 FS&G....................$30.00
0-374-52275-8 NOONDAY PB....................$15.00

High Windows
"The total impression of *High Windows* is of despair made beautiful. Real despair and real beauty, with not a trace of posturing"
—Clive James, *Encounter*
0-374-51212-4 FS&G PB $9.00

The North Ship
0-571-10503-3 FABER PB $8.95

The Whitsun Weddings
0-571-09710-3 FABER PB $9.95

Selected Letters of Philip Larkin: 1940-1985
This book generated much controversy with its often unflattering revelations
EDITED BY ANTHONY THWAITE
0-374-25829-5 FS&G....................$40.00

James **Lasdun**

Woman Police Officer in Elevator
0-393-04043-7 NORTON $19.00

D.H. **Lawrence**

Birds, Beasts and Flowers
See also **THE EARLY 20TH-CENTURY** under **20TH-CENTURY BRITISH AND IRISH FICTION**
0-87685-866-3 BLACK SPARROW PB....................$13.00

The Complete Poems of D.H. Lawrence
A work of scholarship which provides for the first time a fair estimate of Lawrence's stature as one of the major poets of the century
EDITED BY VIVIAN DE SOLA PINTO & F. WARREN ROBERTS
0-14-058644-X PENGUIN PB $19.50

Laurie **Lee**

Selected Poems
Lee's writing often evokes the natural world of the Cotswolds
0-233-97503-9 DAVID & CHARLES PB....................$11.95

C. Day **Lewis**

The Complete Poems of C. Day Lewis
0-8047-2585-3 STANFORD PB $24.95

Christopher **Logue**

The Husbands: An Account of Books III and IV of Homer's Iliad
The third installment of Logue's epic retelling of the *Iliad*, dangerously modern and hauntingly powerful. In language at once musical, tender, and graphic, Logue brings to us "the best translation of Homer since Pope's"—*NY Review of Books*
See also **HOMER** under **THE ARCHAIC PERIOD** under **ANCIENT GREEK LITERATURE** in **LITERATURE OF EUROPE, AFRICA, AND ASIA**
0-374-17391-5 FS&G $19.00

Kings: An Account of Books One to Four of Homer's Iliad
Continuing in his unique vein of Homeric adaptation as explored in *War Music,* Logue writes his version of the first four books of the *Iliad.* "Homer is reexperienced, is given the mystery of creative echo"
—George Steiner, *The Times* [London]
See also **HOMER** under **THE ARCHAIC PERIOD** under **ANCIENT GREEK LITERATURE** in **LITERATURE OF EUROPE, AFRICA, AND ASIA**
0-374-18151-9 FS&G....................$16.95

War Music
Logue's *Iliad*, books Ten to Twelve
0-374-52494-7 FS&G PB....................$14.00

Malcolm **Lowry**

Selected Poems of Malcolm Lowry
0-87286-030-2 SUBTERRANEAN PB....................$3.95

George **MacBeth**

Poems of Love and Death
0-689-11049-9 SCRIBNERS....................$9.95

Norman **MacCaig**

Collected Poems
0-7011-3713-4 CHATTO & WINDOWS $39.95

Hugh **MacDiarmid**

MacDiarmid began by reinventing the Scottish language and ended up writing long verse discourses on science and politics. "Once he got beyond his early lyrics, MacDiarmid was no longer interested in just the sliver of moonlight on the ocean, but in the tidal pull, the contours of the shoreline, the position and philosophical prejudices of the observer, the chemical components of the brine, and the profusion of sea life below the water's surface…He dilates syntax, finds spacious unforeseen cavities within clauses, slows down the rhythm of the poem until each syllable seems enormous."
—Village Voice

Selected Poetry
0-8112-1248-3 NEW DIRECTIONS....................$25.00

Walter de la **Mare**

Collected Poems
A poet of often striking effects, whose work is tinged with the supernatural and the perverse
0-571-11382-6 FABER PB....................$19.95

Selected Poems
0-571-10401-0 FABER PB $6.95

Charlotte **Mew**

Collected Poems and Prose
Mew, who committed suicide in 1928, has found an increasing number of appreciative readers
EDITED BY VAL WARNER
0-85635-260-8 CARCANET....................$67.50

Christopher **Middleton**

The Balcony Tree
The newest collection of poetry by one of the best poets around
0-85635-981-5 CARCANET PB....................$11.95

Intimate Chronicles
1-87881-847-3 SHEEP MEADOW PB....................$10.95

Two Horse Wagon Going By
"Middleton is easily the most intelligent and serious of our innovators, a poet with a disconcerting knack of making it new in almost every poem"—*New Statesman*
0-85635-661-1 CARCANET PB....................$12.50

Edwin **Morgan**

Poems of Thirty Years
0-85635-365-5 SCHOLARLY....................$41.95

Selected Poems
0-85635-596-8 CARCANET PB $8.50

Andrew **Motion**

The Pleasure Steamers
0-85635-247-0 CARCANET PB....................$13.50

Andrew **Motion**

The Price of Everything
0-571-16900-7 FABER PB....................$10.95

Edwin **Muir**

Selected Poems

A sampling of the work of a Scottish poet deeply influenced by psychoanalysis and German literature. Unfortunately, his poems are currently out of print

0-571-06342-X FABER PB....................................$4.95

Douglas **Oliver**

Kind: Collected Poems

This volume was cited by Peter Ackroyd in the London *Times* as "the finest poetry of the year"

0-907954-05-7 SMALL PRESS PB....................$12.00

Selected Poems

1-88368-934-1 TALISMAN PB..............................$10.50

Wilfred **Owen**

Collected Poems

Owen's trench poems are now indelibly part of our conception of the First World War

EDITED BY C. DAY LEWIS

0-8112-0132-5 NEW DIRECTIONS PB.................$9.95

Tom **Pickard**

Typing Errors: New and Selected Poems

A selection of poems by the best British poet of his generation

1-85224-130-6 BLOODAXE PB.............................$16.95

Harold **Pinter**

Harold Pinter: Collected Poems and Prose

0-8021-3434-3 GROVE PB..................................$11.00

F.T. **Prince**

Collected Poems: 1935-1992

"Undervalued at home and abroad, F.T. Prince ranks with Auden and Spender as one of the major English poets of his generation"
—John Ashbery

1-87881-816-3 SHEEP MEADOW PB.................$13.95

Walks in Rome

0-935296-72-7 SHEEP MEADOW PB..................$7.95

Craig **Raine**

History: A Home Movie

Raine first made a splash as a leader of the so-called "Martian" school. His latest work is a novel in verse that counterpoints the author's family history (he is married to a Pasternak) with that of the century

0-38547660-4 ANCHOR PB.................................$12.95

Kathleen **Raine**

The Inner Journey of the Poet

With a naturalistic, Scottish-inspired "sense of the sacred"

0-8076-1039-9 BRAZILLER.................................$20.00

The Presence: Poems 1984-87

Raine, a Blake scholar, writes a poetry grounded in mystical awareness and a powerful sense of the forces of nature

0-89281-082-3 LINDISFARNE..............................$14.95

Selected Poems

0-940262-19-3 LINDISFARNE PB.......................$12.95

Tom **Raworth**

Eternal Sections

A recent volume by the most inventive of England's experimental poets

1-55713-129-5 SUN & MOON PB.........................$9.95

Peter **Reading**

C: Poems

0-436-40984-4 DAVID & CHARLES....................$13.95

Collected Poems 1: Poems, 1970-1984

1-85224-321-X BLOODAXE PB...........................$23.00

Evagatory

0-7011-3924-2 CHATTO & WINDOWS PB.........$13.95

Last Poems

0-7011-6100-0 CHATTO & WINDOWS PB.........$15.95

Ukulele Music: Perduta Gente

0-8101-5005-0 TRIQUARTERLY PB....................$11.95

Oliver **Reynolds**

The Player Queen's Wife

0-571-14999-5 FABER PB....................................$6.95

Skevington's Daughter

0-571-13697-4 FABER...$17.95

0-571-13546-3 FABER PB....................................$7.95

Edgell **Rickword**

Collected Poems

0-85635-919-X CARCANET..................................$50.95

Carol **Rumens**

Direct Dialing

0-7011-2911-5 TRAFALGAR SQUARE PB...........$13.95

From Berlin to Heaven

0-7011-3524-7 CHATTO & WINDOWS PB.........$13.95

Thinking of Skins: New & Selected Poems

1-85224-280-9 DUFOUR PB................................$18.95

Siegfried **Sassoon**

Collected Poems, 1908-1956

Sassoon is especially notable for his unsparingly harsh poems of the First World War

0-571-13262-6 FABER PB..................................$18.95

Selected Poems

0-571-08540-7 FABER PB..................................$10.95

The War Poems of Siegfried Sassoon

EDITED BY RUPERT HART-DAVIS

0-571-13015-1 FABER PB..................................$12.95

E.J. **Scovell**

Selected Poems

0-85635-922-X CARCANET PB...........................$15.95

Penelope **Shuttle**

Adventures with My Horse

Shuttle's sensually vibrant poetry has attracted a growing number of readers

0-19-282218-7 OXFORD PB.................................$8.95

Jon **Silkin**

The Little Time-Keeper

Poems ranging geographically and historically through the Hebrides, Australia, and the Third Reich

0-393-04486-6 OLYMPIC......................................$2.98

Selected Poems

0-415-00219-2 ROUTLEDGE PB........................$16.95

Matt **Simpson**

Catching Up with History

"If one of the tasks of poetry is to build monuments to the ephemeral, Simpson is in there with his spade"
—George Szirtes, *Critical Survey*

1-85224-324-4 DUFOUR PB...............................$16.95

C.H. **Sisson**

One of the finest of British contemporary poets

Antidotes

0-85635-908-4 CARCANET PB..........................$18.75

God Bless Karl Marx

0-85635-710-3 CARCANET PB..........................$14.25

Selected Poems

0-8112-1327-7 NEW DIRECTIONS PB................$9.95

Stevie **Smith**

Collected Poems

"Stevie Smith was an artist of the utmost sophistication…calculating her linguistic effects with such precision that they sound as innocently commanding as a baby's cry in the night"—Clive James, *New Yorker*

EDITED BY JAMES MACGIBBON

0-8112-0882-6 NEW DIRECTIONS PB..............$18.95

New Selected Poems

A new chronological selection containing 165 poems and many drawings

0-8112-1068-5 NEW DIRECTIONS PB................$9.95

Some Are More Human than Others

Stevie Smith's poetry is a strange mix of whimsy, black humor, and serious speculation. *Some Are More Human Than Others* presents another side of what Robert Lowell described as her "unique and cheerfully gruesome voice": her off-the-cuff, off-kilter drawings, with handwritten captions that sometimes cut to the bone. These deceptively casual sketches are at once funny, plaintive, and often unexpectedly nightmarish

0-8112-1110-X NEW DIRECTIONS PB................$7.95

Stephen **Spender**

Collected Poems, 1928-1985

0-571-13666-4 FABER PB....................................$6.99

Dolphins

0-312-11264-5 ST. MARTIN'S..........................$18.95

Selected Poems

0-8045-0953-0 SPOKEN ARTS........................$10.95

Jon **Stallworthy**

The Anzac Sonata: New and Selected Poems

0-393-02449-0 NORTON....................................$15.95

0-393-30422-1 NORTON PB...............................$7.95

From the Life
0-393-03809-2 NORTON $17.95

Grete **Tartler** & Fleur **Adcock**
Orient Express: Poems
0-19-282699-9 OXFORD PB $10.95

Dylan **Thomas**
A Child's Christmas in Wales
ILLUSTRATED BY FRITZ EICHENBERG
0-8112-1309-9 NEW DIRECTIONS PB $6.00

The Collected Poems: 1934-1954
Thomas's surreal lyricism decisively marked postwar poetry, while his reckless career made him the preeminent icon of the self-destroying poet
0-8112-0205-4 NEW DIRECTIONS PB $10.95

The Poems of Dylan Thomas
This collection adds 102 poems to those already gathered in the *Collected Poems*
EDITED BY DANIEL JONES
0-8112-0398-0 NEW DIRECTIONS....................$19.95

Under Milk Wood
A radio play written for the BBC. "It was lyrical, impassioned and funny, an *Our Town* given universality: by comparison with anything broadcast for a very long time, it exploded on the air like a bomb—but a life-giving bomb" —*New Statesman & Nation*
See also THE 1920S, '30S, AND '40S under 20TH-CENTURY BRITISH AND IRISH DRAMA
0-8112-0209-7 NEW DIRECTIONS PB....................$6.95

R.S. **Thomas**
Collected Poems, 1945-1990
0-460-86080-1 DENT $55.00

Mass for Hard Times
1-85224-229-9 BLOODAXE PB $14.95

Poems of R.S. Thomas
A deeply religious poet whose work is imbued with the spirit of the Welsh countryside
0-938626-47-7 ARKANSAS PB $12.00

Charles **Tomlinson**
Annunciations
0-19-282680-8 OXFORD PB....................$10.95

The Door in the Wall
0-19-282939-4 OXFORD PB....................$11.95

The Return
0-19-282079-6 OXFORD PB $8.95

Vernon **Watkins**
Selected Poems
One of the leading Welsh poets of his generation, Watkins was a close friend of Dylan Thomas
0-8112-0214-3 NEW DIRECTIONS PB $2.25

Peter **Whigham**
Things Common, Properly: Selected Poems, 1942-1982
Whigham (praised by William Carlos Williams as "the most delightful translator of Catullus") lived in Italy and California; this collection reflects his wide sense of poetic tradition, and includes translations of Sappho and Ronsard, among others
0-933806-21-3 BLACK SWAN $25.00

Irish Poets

Samuel **Beckett**
Collected Poems in English and French
0-8021-3096-8 GROVE PB $9.95

Eavan **Boland**
In a Time of Violence
0-393-31298-4 NORTON PB $9.00

Object Lessons: The Life of the Woman and the Poet in Our Times
0-393-03716-9 NORTON....................$23.00
0-393-31437-5 NORTON PB $13.00

An Origin Like Water: Collected Poems, 1967-1987
0-393-03852-1 NORTON $25.00

Outside History: Selected Poems, 1980-1990
"The best possible introduction to her work" —J.D. McClatchy
0-393-30822-7 NORTON PB $10.95

Eavan Boland

Austin **Clarke**
The Selected Poems
Overshadowed by his contemporaries Joyce and Yeats, Clarke was nonetheless a highly significant figure in the Irish Renaissance
EDITED BY THOMAS KINSELLA
0-916390-50-0 WAKE FOREST $20.00

Selected Poems
An annotated collection
EDITED BY W.J. MCCORMACK
0-14-018649-2 PENGUIN PB....................$11.95

Greg **Delanty**
American Wake
"This shapely book revolves around emigration seen from both sides of the Atlantic, and then goes back to Irish literary and mythic figures to find buried resonance"—*Books Ireland*
0-85640-549-3 DUFOUR PB $12.95

Desmond **Egan**
Selected Poems
1-88187-103-7 FORDHAM PB....................$17.50

Eamon **Grennan**
As If It Matters
"Contains some of his most telling work, and with so fine a poet that is saying a great deal" —W.S. Merwin
1-55597-155-5 GRAY WOLF PB....................$11.00

So It Goes: Poems
Grennan's work has been described as "verbal equivalents of 17th-century Dutch paintings"
1-55597-232-2 GRAY WOLF PB....................$14.00

Seamus **Heaney**
Crediting Poetry: The Nobel Lecture
0-374-13138-4 FS&G $12.00

Death of a Naturalist
0-571-09024-9 FABER PB....................$10.95

Field Work
"A superb book, the most eloquent and far-reaching book he has written, a perennial poetry offered at a time when many of us have despaired of seeing such a thing"—Denis Donoghue
0-374-51620-0 FS&G PB $8.00

The Haw Lantern
"Heaney is keyed and pitched unlike any significant poet now at work in the language, anywhere"—Harold Bloom
0-374-16837-7 FS&G....................$12.95

North
0-571-10813-X FABER PB....................$10.95

Poems: 1965-1975
A comprehensive gathering of the Nobel Prize-winning poet, including work from *Death of a Naturalist, Door into the Dark, Wintering Out,* and *North*
0-374-51652-9 FS&G PB $12.00

Preoccupations: Selected Prose, 1968-1978
Heaney discusses, among others, Wordsworth, Keats, Hopkins, Yeats, Kavanagh, and Robert Lowell
0-374-51650-2 FS&G PB....................$11.00

The Redress of Poetry
The poet's ten Oxford lectures explore a wide range of writers, from Christopher Marlowe to Oscar Wilde, the 18th-century poet Brian Merriman to Elizabeth Bishop. Eloquent and insightful, Heaney presents his argument that poetry's special spiritual power can oppose hostile and oppressive forces with conviction and poetic force of its own
0-374-24853-2 FS&G....................$22.00
0-19-951332-5 OXFORD....................$2.95

Seeing Things
"Heaney's new work represents a maturer lyricism than anything he has done before...it reaches for a poetry in which images are left to speak for themselves" —Douglas Dunn, *The Irish Times*
0-374-25776-0 FS&G $19.00
0-374-52389-4 NOONDAY PB....................$10.00

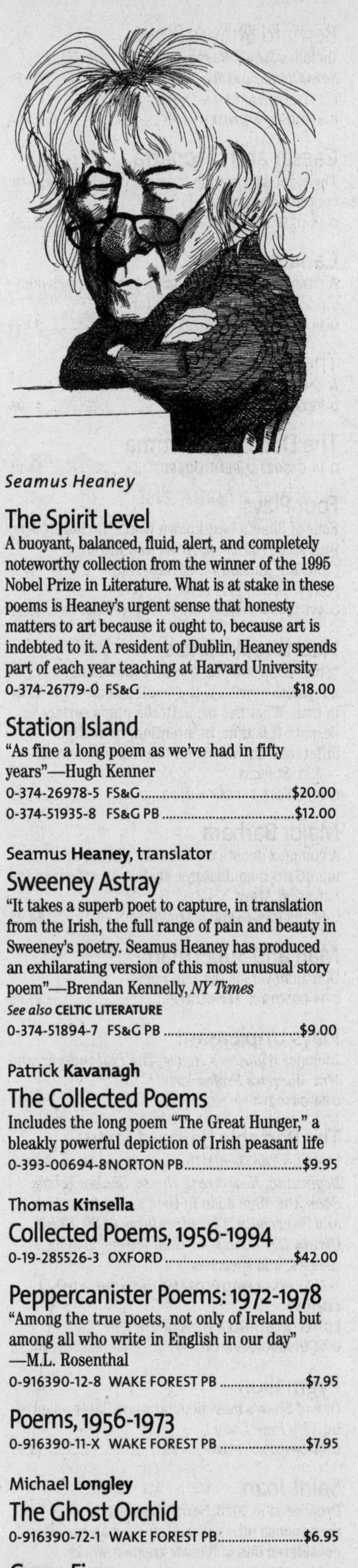

Seamus Heaney

The Spirit Level

A buoyant, balanced, fluid, alert, and completely noteworthy collection from the winner of the 1995 Nobel Prize in Literature. What is at stake in these poems is Heaney's urgent sense that honesty matters to art because it ought to, because art is indebted to it. A resident of Dublin, Heaney spends part of each year teaching at Harvard University

0-374-26779-0 FS&G $18.00

Station Island

"As fine a long poem as we've had in fifty years"—Hugh Kenner

0-374-26978-5 FS&G..$20.00
0-374-51935-8 FS&G PB $12.00

Seamus **Heaney**, translator

Sweeney Astray

"It takes a superb poet to capture, in translation from the Irish, the full range of pain and beauty in Sweeney's poetry. Seamus Heaney has produced an exhilarating version of this most unusual story poem"—Brendan Kennelly, *NY Times*

See also CELTIC LITERATURE

0-374-51894-7 FS&G PB $9.00

Patrick **Kavanagh**

The Collected Poems

Includes the long poem "The Great Hunger," a bleakly powerful depiction of Irish peasant life

0-393-00694-8NORTON PB...............................$9.95

Thomas **Kinsella**

Collected Poems, 1956-1994

0-19-285526-3 OXFORD.....................................$42.00

Peppercanister Poems: 1972-1978

"Among the true poets, not only of Ireland but among all who write in English in our day" —M.L. Rosenthal

0-916390-12-8 WAKE FOREST PB $7.95

Poems, 1956-1973

0-916390-11-X WAKE FOREST PB $7.95

Michael **Longley**

The Ghost Orchid

0-916390-72-1 WAKE FOREST PB.......................$6.95

Gorse Fires

0-916390-48-9 WAKE FOREST PB.......................$6.95

Poems, 1963-1983

0-916390-28-4 WAKE FOREST PB.......................$8.95

Derek **Mahon**

The Hunt by Night

Mary Kinzie in *American Poetry Review* has written of Mahon's "multiple gift of cultivation, verbal sophistication, rhetorical daring, high descriptive subtlety and accuracy, and public conscience"

0-916390-17-9 WAKE FOREST PB.......................$4.95

Selected Poems

"Mahon is uparalleled in his metrical and formal virtuosity"—*Publishers Weekly*

0-14-058704-7 PENGUIN PB...............................$12.00

Medbh **McGuckian**

Captain Lavender

0-916390-67-5 WAKE FOREST.............................$15.95

Marconi's Cottage

0-916390-51-9 WAKE FOREST PB.......................$8.95

Louis **MacNeice**

Collected Poems

An outstanding—and moving—poetic formalist. Unfortunately the *Collected Poems* are currently out of print

0-571-11353-2 FABER PB..................................$18.95

John **Montague**

About Love

1-87881-823-6 SHEEP MEADOW PB $13.95

Collected Poems

0-916390-68-3 WAKE FOREST PB.......................$19.95

Selected Poems

"In Mr. Montague's fine, firm poems... loving force is always made real by being felt as threatened by the angers of Ireland and of this Irishman"—Christopher Ricks, *NY Times*

0-916390-15-2 WAKE FOREST PB.......................$9.95

Paul **Muldoon**

The Annals of Chile

0-374-10518-9 FS&G $21.00
0-374-52456-4 NOONDAY PB.............................$10.00

Madoc: A Mystery

A book-length poem revolving around the legendary Welsh prince who discovered America

0-374-19557-9 FS&G..$19.95

Quoof

0-916390-19-5 WAKE FOREST PB $5.95

Selected Poems

0-374-52374-6 NOONDAY PB.............................$12.00

Selected Poems, 1968-1986

Gathered from six previous volumes. "Muldoon seems to me unusually gifted, endowed with an individual sense of rhythm, a natural and copious vocabulary, a technical accomplishment and intellectual boldness that mark him as the most promising poet to appear in Ireland for years"—Seamus Heaney

0-88001-154-8 ECCO..$16.50

Nuala **Ni Dhomhnaill**

The Astrakhan Cloak

"The poems read like spells set to invigorate and intrigue"—*Sunday Tribune*

TRANSLATED BY PAUL MULDOON

0-916390-54-3 WAKE FOREST PB $10.95

Pharaoh's Daughter

Ni Dhomhnaill is a leading contemporary poet writing in Gaelic, and is here translated by a group of Irish poets

0-916390-53-5 WAKE FOREST PB $10.95

Tom **Paulin**

Liberty Tree

0-571-13025-9 FABER PB $7.95

Minotaur: Poetry and the Nation State

0-674-57637-3 HARVARD...................................$29.95

The Strange Museum

0-571-11511-X FABER PB $7.95

Walking a Line

0-571-17081-1 FABER PB $9.95

William Butler **Yeats**

The Collected Poems

"Early and late he has the simple, indispensable gift of enchanting the ear ...Though he plunged deep into arcane studies, his themes are most clearly the general ones of life and death, love and hate, man's condition, and history's meanings...He grew at last into the boldest, most vigorous voice of this century" —M.L. Rosenthal

EDITED BY RICHARD J. FINNERAN

0-684-80731-9 SCRIBNERS PB..........................$18.00

Early Poems

0-486-27808-5 DOVER PB..................................$1.50

Selected Poems and Four Plays

EDITED BY M.L. ROSENTHAL

0-684-82646-1 SCRIBNERS PB..........................$16.00

Under the Moon: The Unpublished Early Poetry

EDITED BY GEORGE BORNSTEIN

0-684-80254-6 SCRIBNERS................................$22.00

Anthologies

Anthony **Braley**, editor

Contemporary Irish Poetry

0-520-05874-7 CALIFORNIA PB........................$16.00

Chris **Brooks** & Peter **Faulkner**, editors

The White Man's Burdens: An Anthology of British Poetry of the Empire

0-85989-492-4 EXETER $50.00
0-85989-450-9 EXETER PB...............................$19.95

Patrick **Crotty**, editor

Modern Irish Poetry: An Anthology

0-85640-561-2 BLACKSTAFF PB........................$19.95

Gabriel **Fitzmaurice**, editor
Irish Poetry Now
0-86327-379-3 DUFOUR PB $17.95

Joyce **Fullard**, editor
British Women Poets, 1660-1800: An Anthology
0-87875-370-2 WHITSON $55.00

Edward B. **Germain**, editor
Surrealist Poetry in English
Includes such now-neglected figures as David Gascoyne and Henry Treece, along with Americans working in the same tradition
0-14-018486-4 PENGUIN PB $13.95

John **Heath-Stubbs**, editor
Faber Book of 20th-century Verse: An Anthology of Verse in Britain
0-7812-0287-6 REPRINT SERVICES $69.00

A.A. **Kelly**, editor
Pillars of the House: An Anthology of Irish Women's Poetry
0-86327-143-X IRISH BOOKS & MEDIA PB $15.95

Thomas **Kinsella**, editor & translator
The New Oxford Book of Irish Verse
See also CELTIC LITERATURE
0-19-211868-4 OXFORD $30.00
0-19-282643-3 OXFORD PB $14.95

Philip **Larkin**, editor
The Oxford Book of Twentieth-Century English Verse
0-19-812137-7 OXFORD $35.00

Frank **Ormsby**, editor
The Long Embrace: 20th-century Irish Love Poems
0-571-12988-9 FABER PB $9.95

Carol **Rumens**, editor
New Women Poets
1-85224-145-4 DUFOUR PB $17.95

Jon **Silkin**, editor
The Penguin Book of First World War Poetry
A superb collection that includes generous selections from Isaac Rosenberg, Wilfred Owen, Herbert Read, Siegfried Sassoon, Edmund Blunden, Edward Thomas, Ivor Gurney, and other English poets, as well as a sampling of work by such European writers as Heym, Trakl, Goll, Ungaretti, and Blok
0-14-018367-1 PENGUIN PB $12.95

Carl **Woodring** & others, editors
The Columbia Anthology of British Poetry
0-231-10180-5 COLUMBIA $29.95

20th-Century British and Irish Drama

The Early 20th-century

J. M. **Barrie**
Peter Pan and Other Plays
Also includes *The Admirable Cricthon*, *When Wendy Grew Up*, *What Every Woman Knows*, and *Mary Rose*
EDITED BY PETER HOLLINDALE
0-19-282572-0 OXFORD PB $12.95

Ronald **Firbank**
Complete Plays
1-56478-047-3 DALKEY ARCHIVE $19.95

Lady **Gregory**
Collected Plays of Lady Gregory
Lady Augusta Gregory was a pioneer of Irish theater, collaborating with Yeats and championing the work of Synge and O'Casey. Her own plays include the famous one-acters *The Rising of the Moon*, *The Workhouse Ward*, and *Spreading the News*

Volume 1 Comedies
0-86140-016-X DUFOUR PB $9.95

Volume 2 Tragedies and Tragic Comedies
0-86140-017-8 DUFOUR PB $15.95

Volume 3 Wonder and Supernatural Plays
0-86140-018-6 DUFOUR PB $13.95

Volume 4 Collaborations, Adaptations, and Translations
0-86140-019-4 DUFOUR PB $16.95

Selected Writings
0-14-018955-6 PENGUIN PB $13.95

George Bernard **Shaw**
"It was clear from the start that Bernard Shaw was a man of ideas. Later it turned out that he was a fabulous entertainer. But few have granted that the two Shaws were one… The shock of that long career in the theater has still not been absorbed. Shaw has not yet been seen in perspective"—Eric Bentley

Androcles and the Lion
The fable of the lion and the thorn provides the opportunity for an unidealized depiction of martyrs
0-88734-247-7 PLAYERS PB $6.00

Arms and the Man
A satire on the romantic glorification of war
0-14-045035-1 PENGUIN PB $7.95

Bernard Shaw's Plays
Includes *Major Barbara*, *Heartbreak House*, *Saint Joan*, and *Too True to Be Good*
EDITED BY WARREN S. SMITH
0-393-09942-3 NORTON PB $14.95

Caesar and Cleopatra
The legendary couple dramatized with an eye to contemporary parallels
0-14-045036-X PENGUIN PB $7.95

Candida
A triangle in which a woman is caught between cleric husband and poet suitor
0-14-045037-8 PENGUIN PB $7.95

The Devil's Disciple
A comedy of the American Revolution
0-88734-229-9 PLAYERS PB $7.00

The Doctor's Dilemma
0-14-045027-0 PENGUIN PB $6.95

Four Plays
Four of Shaw's best-known works, including *Mrs. Warren's Profession*, *Arms and the Man*, *Candida*, and *Man and Superman*
FOREWORD BY ERIC BENTLEY
0-451-52434-9 NEW AMERICAN LIBRARY PB $5.95

Heartbreak House
"Shaw confronts, for the first time in his imaginative writing, the small extent of his faith in man. What lies beneath the play's surface is despair. It is thus, in intention, radically different from almost all the rest of his work" —J.M. Stewart
0-14-045017-3 PENGUIN PB $7.95

Major Barbara
A complex debate on morality, pitting a munitions manufacturer against an officer in the Salvation Army
0-88295-088-6 HARLAN DAVIDSON PB $4.95

Man and Superman
Don Juan versus the Life Force
0-14-045019-X PENGUIN PB $7.95

Plays Unpleasant
Includes *Widower's House*, *The Philanderer*, and *Mrs. Warren's Profession*
0-14-045021-1 PENGUIN PB $9.95

The Portable Bernard Shaw
Includes *The Devil's Disciple*, *Pygmalion*, *In the Beginning*, *Heartbreak House*, *Shakes Versus Shav*, the "Don Juan in Hell" scene from *Man and Superman*, *The Adventures of the Black Girl in Her Search for God*, letters, articles, reviews, and speeches
See also 19TH-CENTURY DRAMA under THE 19TH-CENTURY
EDITED BY STANLEY WEINTRAUB
0-14-015090-0 VIKING PB $14.95

Pygmalion
One of Shaw's most popular plays, later adapted into *My Fair Lady*
0-14-045022-X PENGUIN PB $7.95

Saint Joan
Premiered in 1923, *Saint Joan* was a tremendous international success and is often considered one of Shaw's greatest works
0-14-045023-8 PENGUIN PB $7.95

John Millington **Synge**

The Collected Works of John Millington Synge

Volume 1: The Poems

0-8132-0562-X CATHOLIC UNIVERSITY PB $8.95

Volume 2: The Prose

0-8132-0564-6 CATHOLIC UNIVERSITY PB $10.95

Volume 3: The Plays (Book 1)

Includes *Riders to the Sea, The Shadow of the Glen, The Well of the Saints,* and the previously unpublished *When the Moon Has Set*

0-8132-0566-2 CATHOLIC UNIVERSITY PB $10.95

Volume 4: The Plays (Book 2)

Includes *The Tinker's Wedding, The Playboy of the Western World,* and *Deirdre of the Sorrow*

0-8132-0568-9 CATHOLIC UNIVERSITY PB $10.95

Complete Plays of John Millington Synge

All of these plays were produced at the Abbey Theatre, which Synge founded with Lady Gregory and W.B. Yeats. The predominant style of the Abbey Theatre was split between Yeats's mythic poeticism and Gregory's domestic realism. Synge fused the two into powerful and often extremely controversial drama. Includes *The Playboy of the Western World, Riders to the Sea, In the Shadow of the Glen, The Well of the Saints, The Tinker's Wedding,* and *Deirdre of the Sorrows*

0-394-70178-X VINTAGE PB $10.00

The Playboy of the Western World

Synge was accused of insulting the Irish national character in this play about a man who becomes a town hero after boasting how he murdered his own father. Also includes *Riders to the Sea*

0-88295-097-5 HARLAN DAVIDSON PB.............$3.95

Oscar **Wilde**

The Importance of Being Earnest

"It is exquisitely trivial, a delicate bubble of fancy, and it has its philosophy…that we should treat all the trivial things of life seriously, and all the serious things of life with sincere and studied triviality"—Oscar Wilde

INTRODUCTION BY ADELINE HARTCUP

0-413-31000-0 METHUEN PB $8.95

Lady Windermere's Fan

EDITED BY IAN SMALL

0-393-90048-7 NORTON PB $6.95

The Plays of Oscar Wilde

Includes *Salome, The Importance of Being Earnest, Lady Windemere's Fan, An Ideal Husband,* and *A Woman of No Importance.* "A work of art is useless as a flower is useless. A flower blossoms for its own joy. We gain a moment of joy by looking at it"—Oscar Wilde

INTRODUCTION BY JOHN LAHR

0-394-75788-2 VINTAGE PB $13.00

The Portable Oscar Wilde

Includes *The Picture of Dorian Gray, De Profundis, Salome, The Importance of Being Earnest,* selections from three comedies, letters, reviews, poems, "Phrases and Philosophies for the Young," and "The Critic as Artist"

See also **19TH-CENTURY PROSE** under **THE 19TH-CENTURY**

EDITED BY STANLEY WEINTRAUB

0-14-015093-5 VIKING PB $14.95

Salome

"Few English plays have such a peculiar history. Written in French in 1893, it was in full rehearsal by Madame Bernhardt at the Palace Theatre when it was prohibited by the Censor. Oscar Wilde immediately announced his intention of changing his nationality, a characteristic jest which was only taken seriously, oddly enough, in Ireland. The interference of the Censor has seldom been more popular or more heartily endorsed by English critics"—from "Note on Salome" by Robert Ross

ILLUSTRATED BY AUBREY BEARDSLEY

0-8283-1467-5 BRANDEN PB...............................$4.95

Selected Plays

Includes *The Importance of Being Earnest, An Ideal Husband, Lady Windermere's Fan, A Woman of No Importance,* and *Salome*

0-14-048209-1 PENGUIN PB $7.95

William Butler **Yeats**

Eleven Plays of William Butler Yeats

Of his verse plays, Yeats wrote, "I wanted all of my poetry to be spoken on a stage or sung." Includes *On Baile's Strand, Deirdre, The Player Queen, Resurrection, Words Upon the Window Pane, A Full Moon in March, Herne's Egg, Cathleen Ni Houlihan, The Only Jealousy of Emer, Purgatory,* and *The Death of Cuchulain*

EDITED BY A. NORMAN JEFFARES

0-02-012970-X MACMILLAN PB $7.00

The 1920s, '30s, and '40s

Agatha **Christie**

The Mousetrap & Other Plays

In addition to the title work—the longest-running play in history—includes *Ten Little Indians, Appointment with Death, The Hollow, Witness for the Prosecution, Towards Zero, Verdict,* and *Go Back for Murder*

0-06-100374-3 HARPERCOLLINS PB..................$6.99

Noel **Coward**

The Lyrics of Noel Coward

"Mad Dogs and Englishmen," "Don't Put Your Daughter on the Stage, Mrs. Worthington," and other songs

0-87951-187-7 VIKING PB $10.95

Three Plays

Includes *Blithe Spirit, Hay Fever,* and *Private Lives*

0-8021-5108-6 GROVE PB $11.95

T.S. **Eliot**

Cats

The book of the musical, based on *Old Possum's Book of Practical Cats*

0-15-615582-6 HARCOURT BRACE PB..............$14.95

The Cocktail Party

"By using very little imagery, by his language which is so idiomatic that one accepts his rhythm as that of ordinary speech with an insistent beat pulsing through it…Eliot really does portray real-seeming characters. He cuts down his poetic effects to a minimum, and then finally rewards us with most beautiful poetry" —Stephen Spender

0-15-618289-0 HARCOURT BRACE PB $7.00

The Complete Poems and Plays, 1909-1950

In addition to Eliot's poetry, includes *Murder in the Cathedral, The Family Reunion,* and *The Cocktail Party*

0-15-121185-X HARCOURT BRACE...................$30.00

T.S. Eliot

The Confidential Clerk

0-15-622015-6 HARCOURT BRACE PB $6.95

The Family Reunion

"Mr. Eliot has re-created a Greek tragedy in an English country house…the crowding ideas behind the rhythmic power of verse soon raise to great drama"—*Catholic World*

0-15-630157-1 HARCOURT BRACE PB $8.00

Murder in the Cathedral

0-15-663277-2 HARCOURT BRACE PB $5.95

Christopher **Fry**

Selected Plays

Includes *The Boy with a Cart, A Sleep of Prisoners, The Lady's Not for Burning, A Phoenix Too Frequent,* and *Curtmantle*

0-19-281873-2 OXFORD PB...............................$19.95

Sean **O'Casey**

Seven Plays

Includes *The Shadow of a Gunman, Juno and the Paycock, The Plough and the Stars, The Silver Tassie, Red Roses for Me, Cock-a-Doodle Dandy,* and *The Bishop's Bonfire*

EDITED BY RONALD AYLING

0-312-71323-1 ST. MARTIN'S..............................$32.50

Three Plays

Three of the major works of O'Casey's early realist phase: *Juno and the Paycock, The Shadow of a Gunman,* and *The Plough and the Stars*

0-312-80290-0 ST. MARTIN'S PB $7.95

Dylan **Thomas**

Under Milk Wood

A radio play written for the BBC. "It was lyrical, impassioned and funny, an *Our Town* given universality: by comparison with anything broadcast for a very long time, it exploded on the air like a bomb—but a life-giving bomb" —*New Statesman & Nation*

See also **BRITISH POETS** under **20TH-CENTURY BRITISH AND IRISH POETRY**

0-8112-0209-7 NEW DIRECTIONS PB $6.95

The 1950s and '60s

John **Arden**

"Arden is a genuine original, and far more important than the differences between his plays and those of his contemporaries is the internal consistency which makes them a logical coherent progession, all first, foremost, and unmistakable the product of one exceptional mind."—John Russell Taylor

Pearl
"The time is the late 1630s, the political and religious climate is deeply troubled, the moment could be right for something extraordinary to happen which will change the course of history"—Gillian Reynolds, *Daily Telegraph*

0-413-40100-6 METHUEN PB $9.95

Plays: One
Includes *Armstrong's Last Goodnight, Serjeant Musgrave's Dance,* and *The Workhouse Donkey. Plays: Two* is not yet available

0-413-68800-3 HEINEMANN PB $15.95

John **Arden** & Margaretta **D'Arcy**

The Little Gray Home in the West: An Anglo-Irish Melodrama
0-86104-221-2 METHUEN PB $8.95

Royal Pardon
0-413-33410-4 METHUEN PB $8.95

Vandaleur's Folly: An Anglo-Irish Melodrama
"Vandaleur was an Irish landowner in the 1830s who turned his estate into an agriculture cooperative. His folly was to lose it again as a gambling debt. It is an ideal subject for Margareta D'Arcy and John Arden" —Jeremy Treglown, *Times* (London)

0-413-48540-4 METHUEN PB $8.95

Alan **Bennett**

Plays
Includes *Forty Years On, Getting On, Habeas Corpus,* and *Enjoy*

0-571-17745-X FABER PB $13.95

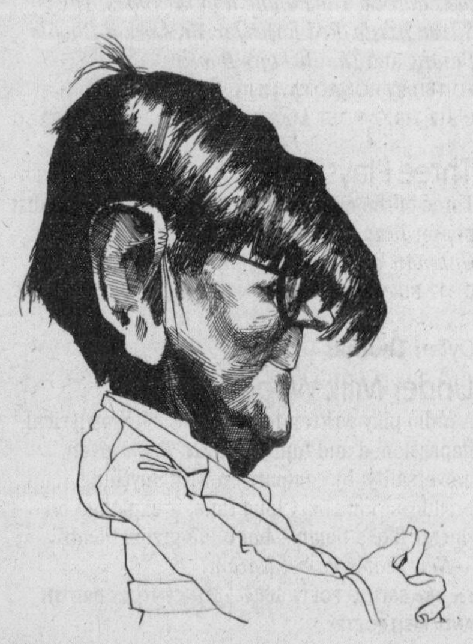

Alan Bennett

Brendan **Behan**

The Complete Plays
Includes *The Hostage, The Quare Fellow, Richard's Cork Leg* and *Three One Act Plays for Radio.* "It seems to be Ireland's function, every twenty years or so, to provide a playwright who will kick English drama from the past into the present. Brendan Behan may well fill the place vacated by Sean O'Casey"—Kenneth Tynan

INTRODUCTION BY ALAN SIMPSON

0-8021-3070-4 GROVE PB $14.00

Robert **Bolt**

A Man for All Seasons
Sir Thomas More against Henry VIII. "An extraordinarily lucid play about an extraordinarily difficult subject: the authority of the individual consciences"—Walter Kerr

0-679-72822-8 VINTAGE PB $8.00

Edward **Bond**

A-A-America & Stone
A double bill of plays offering a stunning indictment of American racism

0-413-48320-7 METHUEN PB $8.95

The Bundle
"I've tried to demystify the use of moral argument so that we can't be morally blackmailed anymore. In order to change society structurally, you may find yourself doing what is, in quotes, wrong"—Edward Bond

0-413-39360-7 METHUEN PB $9.95

Coffee: A Tragedy
0-413-69710-X HEINEMANN PB $11.95

Derek & Choruses from After the Assassinations
In *Derek*, an aristocrat too stupid even for a career in politics tricks a working-class genius into swapping brains with him. The second piece is a series of choral pieces from an as-yet-unpublished play

0-413-54700-0 METHUEN PB $9.95

Early Morning
A play populated by such figures as Florence Nightingale, Queen Victoria, and Benjamin Disraeli

0-7145-0206-5 RIVERRUN $9.95

The Fool & We Come to the River
Based on the life of the 19th-century poet John Clare. Also included is the libretto from the opera *We Come to the River*

0-413-34770-2 METHUEN PB $9.95

Human Cannon
Charts the struggle against Fascism in Spain through the stories of the village community of Estarobon and one of its members, Agustina, who becomes the most dangerous weapon in the arsenal of revolution—the human cannon

0-413-57250-1 METHUEN PB $7.95

Olly's Prison
A portrayal of the violence inherent in the prison system and in police practice as a savage mirror image of the violence of a domestic killer

0-413-67610-2 HEINEMANN PB $11.95

Plays: One
Saved, Early Morning, and *The Pope's Wedding*

0-413-45410-X METHUEN PB $9.95

Plays: Two
Includes *Lear, The Sea, Narrow Road to the Deep North, Black Mass,* and *Passion*

0-413-39270-8 HEINEMANN PB $9.95

Plays: Four
0-413-64830-3 METHUEN PB $13.95

Plays: Five
0-413-70390-8 HEINEMANN PB $15.95

Restoration & The Cat
Restoration is a satirical comedy about social injustice in 18th-century England. *The Cat* is a view of turn-of-the-century London with cats as the main characters, and a mouse, a fox, and a few dogs completing the cast

0-413-48840-3 METHUEN $20.00

0-413-49920-0 METHUEN PB $9.95

Tuesday
A young girl's reaction to sudden and violent change in her life

0-413-68220-X HEINEMANN PB $11.95

Two Post-Modern Plays
Includes *Jackets* and *In the Company of Men*

0-413-62650-4 HEINEMANN PB $13.95

The War Plays
A presentation of the horror of nuclear holocaust and, springing from that horror, a vision of hope in a post-nuclear age. All three parts are published together for the first time in this volume

0-413-64600-9 HEINEMANN PB $19.95

Shelagh **Delaney**

A Taste of Honey
Written when Delaney was 17, this realistic drama about the life of a working-class girl made a tremendous impact when produced in 1958

0-8021-3185-9 GROVE PB $8.95

Stephen **Lacey**

British Realist Theatre: The New Wave in Its Context, 1956-1965
0-415-07782-6 ROUTLEDGE $49.95

David **Mercer**

After Haggerty
While trying to escape his own past, a man is forced to confront the past of his new apartment's previous occupants

0-413-39860-9 METHUEN PB $8.95

No Limits to Love
"The play says a great deal about what people have become through the great social and economic disintegration of the '70s" —David Mercer

0-413-48260-X METHUEN PB $8.95

Plays: One
Contains *Where the Difference Begins, A Suitable Case for Treatment, The Governor's Lady, On the Eve of Publication, The Cellar and the Almond Tree, Emma's Time,* and *After Haggerty*

0-413-63450-7 HEINEMANN PB $13.95

0-413-65200-9 HEINEMANN PB $15.95

Peter **Nichols**

Joe Egg

"A remarkable play about…living with a child born so hopelessly crippled as to be, as the father in it says brutally, 'a human parsnip.' For all that, it has to be described as a comedy, one of the funniest and most touching I've seen" —Ronald Bryden, *Observer*

0-8021-5115-9 GROVE PB $9.95

Passion Play

About marriage and how to function within it

0-413-47800-9 METHUEN PB $5.95

A Piece of My Mind

"A witheringly funny play about middle-aged failure"—John Peter, *Times* (London)

0-413-17360-7 METHUEN PB $9.95

Plays: One

Contents: *Forget-Me-Not Lane, Hearts and Flowers, Neither Up Nor Down, Chez Nous, The Common,* and *Privates on Parade*

0-413-64870-2 HEINEMANN PB $17.95

Plays: Two

0-413-65070-7 HEINEMANN PB $13.95

Poppy

Pantomime and spectacle are essential elements in a play based on the 19th-century Opium Wars

0-413-49490-X HEINEMANN PB $6.95

Joe **Orton**

The Complete Plays

Includes every radio, television, and stage play that Orton wrote during his brief career: *Entertaining Mr. Sloane, Loot, What the Butler Saw, The Ruffian on the Stair, The Erpingham Camp, Funeral Games,* and *The Good and Faithful Servant*

INTRODUCTION BY JOHN LAHR

0-8021-3215-4 GROVE PB $14.00

John **Osborne**

Dejavu

In this transposition of his widely celebrated *Look Back in Anger*, John Osborne carries his explosive, searing original into the present day. It is not 1956, but a generation later. The setting is no longer an attic apartment with a cold-water tank in the corner, but the comfy kitchen of a large country house. And Alison is Jimmy's daughter, up for the weekend with a week's worth of ironing in tow

0-571-14345-8 FABER PB $8.95

Look Back in Anger

"Presents post-war youth as it really is. It is a minor miracle"—Kenneth Tynan, *Observer*

0-14-048175-3 PENGUIN PB $7.95

Look Back in Anger & Other Plays

In 1956 John Osborne changed the course of British theater with *Look Back in Anger*. This volume contains that play as well as *Epitaph for George Dillon, The World of Paul Slickey,* and *Dejavu*. "Savage drama…Most vivid play of the decade"—*NY Times* on *Look Back in Anger*

0-571-16908-2 FABER PB $16.95

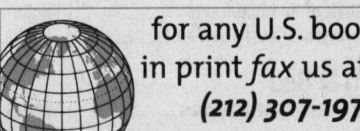

A Patriot for Me & A Sense of Detachment

In the first play, a homosexual officer in the Austro-Hungarian army is blackmailed into becoming a spy

0-571-13041-0 FABER PB $8.95

Harold **Pinter**

"There are two silences. One when no word is spoken. The other when perhaps a torrent of language is employed. This speech is speaking a language locked beneath it. That is its continual reference. The speech we hear is an indication of what we don't hear."—Harold Pinter

Betrayal

A drama of adultery in which time runs backwards

0-8021-3080-1 GROVE PB $11.00

The Caretaker

Pinter's most celebrated work. Also includes *The Dumb Waiter*

0-8021-5087-X GROVE PB $8.95

Complete Works

Volume 1

Includes *The Birthday, The Black and White, The Dumb Waiter, The Examination, A Night Out, The Room,* and *A Slight Ache*

0-8021-5096-9 GROVE PB $12.00

Volume 2

Includes *The Caretaker, The Collection, The Dwarfs, Five Revue Sketches, The Lover,* and *Night School*

0-8021-3237-5 GROVE PB $10.95

Volume 3

Includes *The Basement, Landscape, Silence, Six Revue Sketches, Tea Party* (a Play), and *Tea Party* (a Short Story)

0-8021-5049-7 GROVE PB $10.95

Volume 4

Includes *Old Times, No Man's Land, Betrayal, Monologue,* and *Family Voices*

0-8021-5050-0 GROVE PB $12.00

The Homecoming

A man returns with his wife to his cloistered, male-dominated family

0-8021-5105-1 GROVE PB $7.95

Moonlight

0-8021-3393-2 GROVE PB $12.00

No Man's Land

"A masterly summation of all the themes that have long obsessed Pinter" —Michael Billington, *Arts Guardian*

0-8021-5187-6 GROVE PB $9.95

Old Times

A couple are reunited with an old friend after an absence of twenty years. The ensuing conversation threatens the present with intimations of an unknown and disturbing past

0-8021-5029-2 GROVE PB $7.95

One for the Road

"One for the Road is an expression of a series of events where we are looking at people who have been tortured or will be tortured. It's brutally real: my earlier plays were perhaps metaphors for states of affairs in various respects. This is not a metaphor about anything—it's just a brutal series of facts"—Harold Pinter

0-8021-5188-4 GROVE PB $7.95

Other Places: Three Plays

Includes *A Kind of Alaska, Victoria Station,* and *Family Voices*

0-8021-5189-2 GROVE PB $6.95

Party Time & The New World Order

0-8021-3352-5 GROVE PB $11.00

Harold **Pinter** & Mel **Gussow**

Conversations with Pinter

0-8021-3467-X GROVE PB $12.00

Harold Pinter

The 1970s, '80s, and '90s

Alan **Ayckbourn**

A tireless experimenter who takes the logic of the "well-made play" and puts it through unforeseeable transmutations, Ayckbourn has produced a body of work of remarkable scope and ambition, in which the precepts of classical comedy are pushed to sometimes brutal conclusions

A Chorus of Disapproval

A tough-minded comedy centering on an amateur production of *The Beggar's Opera*

0-571-13917-5 FABER PB $9.95

Communicating Doors

A time-travelling thriller set in 1974, 1994, and 2014, when British cities are at war with one another and brothels are state-registered.

0-571-17682-8 FABER PB $9.95

Confusions

Five interlocking one-act plays

0-413-53270-4 METHUEN PB $9.95

Invisible Friends

A very ordinary teenager resorts to extraordinary measures in her quest for a perfect companion

0-571-14476-4 FABER PB $9.95

The Norman Conquests

Includes *Table Manners, Living Together,* and *Round and Round the Garden.* Three full-length plays that take place simultaneously in three different parts of the same house: an extraordinary technical accomplishment

0-8021-3134-4 GROVE PB $8.95

Plays
A generous sampling of plays from one of Britain's most popular and prolific comic playwrights. Includes *A Chorus of Disapproval, A Small Family Business, Henceforward*, and *Man of the Moment*
0-571-17680-1 FABER PB $13.95

The Revengers' Comedies
Two strangers meet on a London bridge at midnight. Both have been cheated and are preparing to jump to their deaths until, deciding that revenge is sweeter than suicide, they join forces, with rich, vintage Ayckbourn results
0-571-14358-X FABER PB $10.95

A Small Family Business
0-571-14970-7 FABER PB $8.95

Three Plays
Includes *Absurd Person Singular, Absent Friends*, and *Bedroom Farce*
0-8021-3157-3 GROVE PB $9.95

Time of My Life
Charts the decline and fall of a successful family business founded and nurtured by Gerry and Laura Stratton. It is Laura's 54th birthday and Gerry has organized a family dinner for the couple and their two sons at their favorite restaurant. Domestically all seems well but, as we suspect, this is merely the surface—as the evening proceeds, the play reveals skeletons from the past and a specter of the future
0-571-16990-2 FABER PB $8.95

Wildest Dreams
The story of Stanley, Haze, Warren, and Rick as they make their weekly escape from their real-life nightmares into a role-playing board game peopled by dragons and monsters. They enter a safe world where the dangers are of their own imagining; where they are free to become heroes of their own devising
0-571-17304-7 FABER PB $8.95

Woman in Mind
A wife's "vitality is directed into an active fantasy life, peopling the play with an idealized family, invisible to others, which positively mirrors the negative gaps in her own reality"—*Guardian*
0-571-14520-5 FABER PB $8.95

Howard **Barker**

Stripwell & Claw
Stripwell's characters include a judge, his son, a drug dealer, his lover, and a go-go dancer. "The social, psychological, sexual and political are interwoven with an unnerving dexterity"
—John Ford, *Plays and Players*
0-7145-3572-9 RIVERRUN PB $7.95

Two Plays for the Right
Includes *The Loud Boys' Life* and *Birth on a Hard Shoulder*
0-7145-3896-5 RIVERRUN PB $8.95

Peter **Barnes**

Lulu: A Sex Tragedy
Brilliant adaptation of Frank Wedekind's powerful dramas of destructive sexuality, *Earth Spirit* and *Pandora's Box*
0-413-61390-9 METHUEN PB $9.95

Plays: One
0-413-62180-4 HEINEMANN PB $12.95

Plays: Two
0-413-68030-4 HEINEMANN PB $15.95

Plays: Three
0-413-69980-3 HEINEMANN PB $17.95

Revolutionary Witness & Nobody Here but Us Chickens
Written to mark the bicentennial of Bastille Day, *Revolutionary Witness* is a set of four monologues voiced by relatively unknown characters whose lives were transformed by the French Revolution. *Nobody Here but Us Chickens* is a collection of three short plays about being handicapped
0-413-62170-7 HEINEMANN PB $9.95

The Spirit of Man
A remarkable trilogy of plays about the sometimes wayward power of faith
0-413-63130-3 HEINEMANN PB $9.95

Alan **Bennett**

Writing Home
0-679-44489-0 RANDOM HOUSE $25.00

Steven **Berkoff**

The Collected Plays, Volume 1
Includes *East, West, Greek, Sink the Belgrano!, Massage*, and *Lunch*
0-571-16903-1 FABER PB $14.95

The Collected Plays, Volume 2
Includes *Decadence, Kvetch, Acapulco, Harry's Christmas, Brighton Beach Scumbags, Darling You Were Marvellous, Pitbull*, and *Actor*
0-571-17102-8 FABER PB $15.95

Nicolas **Bloomfield** & Neil **Bartlett**

Night After Night
"*Night After Night* is that great rarity: a successful theatre piece about life in the theatre"—Irving Wardle, *Independent on Sunday*
0-413-68500-4 HEINEMANN PB $11.95

Howard **Brenton**

13th Night & A Short Sharp Shock
0-413-48500-5 METHUEN PB $7.95

Bloody Poetry
An artist in conflict with middle-class English society
0-413-58350-3 METHUEN PB $9.95

Epsom Downs
"Brenton's portrait of Derby Day is...an exuberant documentary about a secular English festival"—Michael Billington, *Guardian*
0-413-38930-8 METHUEN PB $8.95

The Genius
Written as a counter to Brecht's *Galileo*, which Brenton had just translated, about the modern scientist's responsibility to society
0-413-54650-0 METHUEN PB $7.95

Magnificence: A Play
In a violent collision of two worlds, a group of protesters run up against a Cabinet minister, and what began as a demonstration becomes an assassination plot
0-413-46750-3 METHUEN PB $8.95

Plays: One
Includes *Christie in Love, Magnificence, The Churchill Play, Weapons of Happiness, Epsom Downs*, and *Sore Throats*
0-413-61490-5 HEINEMANN PB $12.95

Plays: One
Includes *The Romans in Britain, Thirteenth Night, The Genius, Bloody Poetry*, and *Greenland*
0-413-61490-5 HEINEMANN PB $12.95

Revenge
0-413-50010-1 METHUEN PB $8.95

The Romans in Britain
"The first part concerns the period before the Roman conquest, the brief and unimportant second raid by Julius Caesar in 54 BC; while the second part oscillates between a date a century after the departure of the Romans (515 AD) and the present day. The play therefore turns out to be about imperialism in a rather special sense"—*TLS*
9990481504 HEINEMANN PB $9.95

Howard **Brenton** & David **Hare**

Pravda: A Fleet Street Comedy
This is the bitingly hilarious play about a newspaper magnate and his effect on the papers and people around him
0-413-58480-1 METHUEN PB $9.95

Howard **Brenton** & Tunde **Ikoli**

Sleeping Policemen
0-413-55660-3 METHUEN PB $8.95

Simon **Burke**

The Lodger
A forked-tongued thriller set in the underbelly of contemporary England, as well as an exciting new drama in the best tradition of film noir
0-413-68620-5 HEINEMANN PB $11.95

John **Byrne**

Colquhoun and MacBryde
The true story of two Scottish painters and lovers, contemporaries of Francis Bacon and Lucien Freud, whose careers take off with a bang, only to fizzle out again soon after
0-571-16959-7 FABER PB $8.95

Ken **Campbell**

The Bald Trilogy
Includes *The Recollections of a Furtive Nudist, Pigspurt*, and *Jamais Vu*
0-413-69080-6 HEINEMANN PB $16.95

Jim **Cartwright**

The Rise and Fall of Little Voice
This play follows the fortunes of a young singer who escapes the clutches of her mother and manager to find her true voice
0-413-67130-5 METHUEN PB $9.95

Road
The story of a derelict, Lancashire streets, and the lives of its inhabitants
0-413-14550-6 METHUEN PB $9.95

Two & Bed
0-413-68330-3 HEINEMANN $13.95

Caryl **Churchill**

"A playwright of genuine audacity and assurance, able to use her considerable wit and intelligence in ways at once unusual, resonant and dramatically riveting."
—Benedict Nightingale, New Statesman

Cloud Nine
"Miss Churchill has found a theatrical method that is easily as dizzying as her theme. Not only does she examine a cornucopia of sexual permutations—from heterosexual adultery right up to bisexual incest—but she does so with a wild array of dramatic styles and tricks"
—Frank Rich, *NY Times*
1-55936-099-2 THEATRE COMM PB $9.95

Lives of Great Poisoners
0-413-67070-8 HEINEMANN PB $18.95

Mad Forest: A Play from Romania
1-55936-114-X THEATRE COMM PB $9.95

Plays: One
Includes *Owners, Traps, Vinegar Tom, Light Shining in Buckinghamshire,* and *Cloud Nine*
0-415-90196-0 METHUEN PB $10.95

Plays: Two
0-413-62270-3 HEINEMANN PB $12.95

Serious Money
A comedy in rhymed verse about high finance
0-413-16660-0 METHUEN PB $9.95

The Skriker
1-55936-097-6 THEATRE COMM PB $9.95

Softcops & Fen
Softcops uses as its basis the memoirs of two notorious 19th-century French criminals to explore the themes of law and order; *Fen* scrutinizes the lives and loves of the low-paid potato pickers of East Anglia
0-413-41200-8 METHUEN PB $9.95

Top Girls
"In this bold and original play, Caryl Churchill...forces brilliant women of history into the context of their less brilliant sisters' timeless struggle against poverty and oppression"—*City Limits*
0-413-55480-5 METHUEN PB $9.95

Sarah **Daniels**

Beside Herself
The chronicler of women's lives in modern times, Daniels looks at the usually taboo topic of childhood sexual abuse
0-413-62400-5 HEINEMANN PB $9.95

Masterpieces
Deals with pornography and its wide-ranging effects as a cause of violence against women
0-413-55470-8 METHUEN PB $9.95

Plays: One
Contains *Ripen Our Darkness, The Devil's Gateway, Masterpieces, Neaptide,* and *Byrthrite*
0-413-64930-X HEINEMANN PB $14.95

Plays: Two
Includes *The Gut Girls, Beside Herself, Head-Rot Holiday,* and *The Madness of Esme and Shaz*
0-413-69040-7 HEINEMANN PB $15.95

Nick **Dear**

The Art of Success & In the Ruins
The Art of Success follows "Rake's Progress" artist William Hogarth on a kind of artist's progress from his club and his home to the cell of a woman condemned to hang for murder. *In the Ruins* offers mad King George III musing in the prison of his own mind
0-413-68230-7 HEINEMANN PB $13.95

Zenobia
A third-century queen of Palmyra makes a stand for independence against the empire in this play about love and adventure set during the decline of Imperial Rome
0-571-17676-3 FABER PB $9.95

David **Edgar**

Destiny
A play about the rise of fascism in modern Britain
0-413-38910-3 METHUEN PB $8.95

Entertaining Strangers
Centers on the battle of wills between an unbending churchman and the independent spirited proprietress of a local brewery, both of whom are challenged and changed by the cholera epidemic of 1854
0-413-40770-5 METHUEN PB $6.95

Maydays
An epic view of political life since 1945 told through the interconnected stories of an ex-middle-class Trotskyite, an ex-Communist right winger, and an ex-Soviet army dissident
0-413-57080-0 METHUEN PB $8.95

Pentecost
1-85459-292-0
THEATRE COMMUNICATIONS PB $14.95

Plays: One
Contains *Destiny, Mary Barnes, The Jail Diary of Albi Sachs, Saigon Rose,* and *O Fair Jerusalem*
0-413-15220-0 METHUEN PB $9.95

Plays: Two
0-413-63050-1 HEINEMANN PB $13.95

Plays: Three
Includes *Our Own People, Teendreams, Maydays, That Summer*
0-413-64850-8 HEINEMANN PB $15.95

Strange Case of Dr Jekyll and Mr Hyde
1-85424-145-1 HERN PB $11.91

That Summer
A middle-class couple take two miner's daughters on a vacation during the great strike of 1984
0-413-17450-6 METHUEN PB $9.95

Wreckers
An intense, highly dramatic piece concerning industrial strife
0-413-38510-8 METHUEN PB $6.95

Michael **Frayn**

Balmoral
This farce takes place in 1937 in a hypothetical Britain that has become a Soviet republic. The play centers around the occupants of the "State Home for Writers"
0-413-17180-9 METHUEN PB $8.95

Michael Frayn

First and Last
An examination of the courage of old age and the prickly affection which can knit a family together
0-413-17190-6 HEINEMANN PB $11.95

Plays: One
Includes *Alphabetical Order, Donkey's Years, Clouds, Make and Break,* and *Noises Off*
0-413-59280-4 METHUEN PB $9.95

Plays: Two
Contains Frayn's adaptation of Chekhov's *Wild Honey* and the two comedies *Balmoral* and *Benefactors*
0-413-66080-X HEINEMANN PB $11.95

Brian **Friel**

Dancing at Lughnasa
The Olivier Award-winning play about the interior landscape of a group of human beings trapped in a domestic situation, and the wider Christian and pagan landscape of which they are a part
0-571-14479-9 FABER PB $8.95

Molly Sweeney
0-452-27508-3 PLUME PB $9.95

Philadelphia, Here I Come!
"A funny play, a prickly play, finally a most affecting play and the pleasure it gives is of a most peculiar kind. Brian Friel has written a play about an ache, and he has written it so simply and so honestly that the ache itself becomes a warming fire"—*New York Herald Tribune*
0-571-08586-5 FABER PB $8.95

Selected Plays
0-8132-0626-X CATHOLIC UNIVERSITY $33.50

Selected Plays of Brian Friel
INTRODUCTION BY SEAMUS DEANE
0-8132-0627-8 CATHOLIC UNIVERSITY PB $16.95

Translations
0-571-11742-2 FABER PB $9.95

Wonderful Tennessee
On a pier in northwest Donegal, three middle-aged couples congregate in anticipation of a trip to a mysterious, unoccupied island. But the ferryman never shows up, and the six people are left to spend the night confronting their stalled careers, terminal illness, discontent, and depression. "Friel is a master"—*New Yorker*
0-571-17123-0 FABER PB $8.95

Pam **Gems**

Deborah's Daughter

1-85459-247-5 HERN PB $12.95

John **Godber**

Lucky Sods & Passion Killers

Lucky Sods is a satirical and candid black comedy about the topic of the lottery. It revolves around Jean and Morris, a couple who have nothing on Friday and four million pounds on Saturday. *Passion Killers* is a bittersweet comedy about temptation and passion

0-413-70170-0 METHUEN PB $11.95

Simon **Gray**

After Pilkington

A brilliant play in which what starts out as a light-hearted fling at adultery turns into murder and intrigue

0-413-15290-1 METHUEN PB $8.95

Close of Play & Pig in a Poke

A black comedy about a family reunion, and a television play about a couple who buy a house in the country and get more than they bargained for with the tenant in the basement

0-413-46960-3 METHUEN PB $8.95

The Common Pursuit

The lives of six friends, from college days to middle age

0-413-55990-4 METHUEN PB $8.95

Fat Change

0-571-17792-1 FABER PB $9.95

Hidden Laughter

A witty, wicked, and diabolically comic attack on the pretensions of the new, young, rich middle class.

0-571-14433-0 FABER PB $10.95

Homesick

This play takes as its central characters the spy George Blake and the Irish petty criminal Sean Bourke, who sprang Blake from Wormwood Scrubs prison. It tracks their relationship from their first meeting behind bars to their hideout in London and the apartment they shared in Moscow. Here, Gray is concerned with ambition and betrayal, mutual dependence, self-imprisonment, and the struggle for inner freedom

0-571-17402-7 FABER PB $10.95

Melon

A middle-aged publisher goes through a mental breakdown—as seen from his point of view so that it seems as though all around him are going mad

0-413-16550-7 METHUEN PB $9.95

Old Flames & A Month in the Country

0-571-14229-X FABER PB $8.95

The Rear Column & Other Plays

Includes *The Rear Column*, based on an incident in the Congo in 1887; *Molly*, based on the Alma Rottenberg murder case in the 1930s; and *Man in a Sidecar*, charting the breakdown of a marriage and the bystander who is drawn into it

0-413-39170-1 METHUEN PB $8.95

Simply Disconnected

0-571-17972-X FABER PB $10.95

Trevor **Griffiths**

Comedians

"The subject of Trevor Griffith's serious and funny play is laughter....How and why it is engineered, what dark secrets within us trigger mirthful responses to shaped remarks about sex, ethnic groups and physical disabilities"
—Michael Coveney, *Financial Times*

0-571-04986-9 FABER PB $8.95

The Gulf Between Us: Or the Truth and Other Fictions

Trevor Griffiths wrote this play to mark the first anniversary of the 1991 war in the Persian Gulf. It follows two men living in the Gulf and working for its community of British builders and engineers

0-571-16728-4 FABER PB $8.95

Hope in The Year Two & Thatcher's Children

A charismatic exploration of the fundamental questions that confronted the makers of the French Revolution in their search to create a better world and that, still unanswered, continue to confront us two centuries later

0-571-17308-X FABER PB $10.95

The Party

This play takes place in 1968 and contains a British discussion of the possibilities of socialism and the Paris student riots

0-571-10647-1 FABER PB $6.95

Piano: A New Play for Theatre Based on the Film

Summer, 1904: a Russian general's widow is entertaining two generations of friends and relations. On display is the full gamut of human behavior—comic, pathetic, dignified, visionary, obtuse—in a society to which history is about to speak. Trevor Griffiths based *Piano* on the Russian film *Unfinished Piece for a Mechanical Piano* and on themes from Chekhov

0-571-16176-6 FABER PB $8.95

Plays

Includes *Occupations, The Party, Comedians,* and *Real Dreams*

0-571-17742-5 FABER PB $13.95

Trevor **Griffiths** & Jeremy **Pikser**

Real Dreams & Revolution in Cleveland

0-571-14677-5 FABER PB $7.95

Christopher **Hampton**

Alice's Adventures Under Ground

"Hampton's haunting and enchanting new play resurrects Lewis Carroll and his haunting, enchanted world...Hampton shows that Carroll's unforgettable characters embody the inscrutable banalities of the grown-up world, full of childish, evasive, oversensitive adults with their incomprehensible logic and menacing joviality, as seen by a precocious, observant child...Sheer uninterrupted magic"—*Sunday Times*

0-571-17601-1 FABER PB $11.95

Carrington

0-571-15336-4 FABER PB $12.95

Les Liaisons Dangereuses

An adaptation of the 1782 Laclos novel about the decadence of the French aristocracy

0-571-13724-5 FABER PB $9.95

The Philanthropist with Total Eclipse and Treats

Deals with the relationship between Arthur Rimbaud and Paul Verlaine

0-571-16218-5 FABER PB $10.95

Savages

"A play that delicately, with cumulative power, transcribes Mr. Hampton's sorrow and indignation at the gradual extinction of the Brazilian Indians, and his reluctant but inexorable disillusionment with freedom fighters and liberal champions of good causes"
—Howard Hobson, *Sunday Times* (London)

0-571-10348-0 FABER PB $8.95

Total Eclipse

See also under INDIVIDUAL FILMS in SCREENPLAYS under FILM in PERFORMING ARTS and MEDIA

0-571-17873-1 FABER PB $10.95

White Chameleon

A semifictional play based on Hampton's own memories of his life in Egypt between 1952 and 1956. It opened at the National Theatre in London in 1991

0-571-16305-X FABER PB $9.95

David **Hare**

The Absence of War

"Quite simply, drama at its athletic and magisterial best"—*London Sunday Times*

0-571-17071-4 FABER PB $9.95

The Asian Plays

Includes *Fanshen, Saigon*, and *A Map of the World*

0-571-13990-6 FABER PB $14.95

The Early Plays

Includes *Slag, The Great Exhibition,* and *Teeth 'N' Smiles*

0-571-16220-7 FABER PB $10.95

Heading Home, Wetherby, & Dreams of Leaving

0-571-16244-4 FABER PB $16.95

The History Plays

0-571-13132-8 FABER PB $11.95

Murmuring Judges

0-571-17219-9 FABER PB $9.95

Plays: One

Includes *Slag, Teeth 'N' Smiles, Knuckle, Licking Hitler,* and *Plenty*

0-571-17741-7 FABER PB $13.95

Plays: Two

Includes *Fanshen, A Map of the World, Saigon, The Bay at Nice,* and *The Secret Rapture*

0-571-17835-9 FABER PB $13.95

Racing Demon

0-571-16106-5 FABER PB $9.95

The Secret Rapture

0-8021-3175-1 GROVE PB $9.95

David **Hare**

Skylight

A characteristically distinctive and contemporary play that revolves around a sharply contrasted couple trying to reconcile their confused desires within and beyond their own volatile relationship. From the writer described by the *London Times* as "Britain's leading contemporary playwright"

0-571-17612-7 FABER PB $9.95

Tony **Harrison**

Square Rounds

A play directly inspired by events during the Gulf War, the history of relations between East and West, the creative and destructive powers of science, and warfare in particular

0-571-16868-X FABER PB $8.95

David **Harrower**

Knives in Hens

In this sparse and poetic play about lust, love, and order, the lives of three people—the ploughman, his young wife, and the village miller—are dangerously woven together

0-413-70510-2 HEINEMANN PB $9.95

Jonathan **Harvey**

Babies

A hilarious comedy by a latter-day Joe Orton, a warm, funny comedy by the author of the 1993 hit *Beautiful Thing*

0-413-69220-5 METHUEN PB $11.95

Beautiful Thing

"Deliciously upbeat…seldom has there been a play which so exquisitely and joyously depicts what it's like to be sixteen, in the first flush of love and full optimism. Truly a most unusual and beautiful thing"—*Guardian*

0-413-69590-5 HEINEMANN PB $11.95

Rupert Street Lonely Hearts Club & Boom Bang-A-Bang

Boom Bang-a-Bang is a hilarious examination of trust and communication among a group of predominantly gay friends. In *Rupert Street Lonely Hearts Club*, Dean loves Marti who loves Shaun who loves Juliet who's in Barbados, and George is in love with Malcolm who has left the Lonely Hearts Club

0-413-70450-5 METHUEN PB............................$13.95

Ronald **Harwood**

Taking Sides

"A brave, wise, and deeply moving play about the fatal confrontation between culture and power, between art and politics, between irresponsible freedom and responsible compromise. A gripping moral challenge in a cocksure and self-seeking age"—*Sunday Times*

0-571-17772-7 FABER PB $9.95

The Collected Plays

This collection brings together four of Ronald Harwood's most successful plays—*A Family, J.J. Farr, Another Time,* and *The Dresser*, the film version of which went on to receive five Academy Award nominations, including one for Best Screenplay

0-571-17001-3 FABER PB $14.95

Plays: Two

Includes *Taking Sides, Poison Pen, Tramway Road, The Ordeal of Gilbert Pinfold, After the Lions,* and *The Guests. Plays: One* is not in print

0-571-17401-9 FABER PB $13.95

Seamus **Heaney**

The Cure at Troy: A Version of Sophocles' Philoctetes

A free, highly theatrical adaptation of *Philoctetes*. "A purifying play, in the great tradition of modern Irish drama: think of Synge's *Playboy,* O'Casey's early work, or even some of Yeats's Cuchulain plays"—John Peters, *The Sunday Times* (London)

See also **SOPHOCLES** under **TRAGEDY** under **THE CLASSICAL PERIOD** under **ANCIENT GREEK LITERATURE** in **LITERATURE OF EUROPE, AFRICA, AND ASIA**

0-374-13355-7 FS&G..$20.00
0-374-52289-8 NOONDAY PB..............................$10.00

Seamus Heaney

Iain **Heggie**

An Experienced Woman Gives Advice

Exploring matters of love and lust and set in the back garden of a block of flats on two sunny Sunday mornings, this is a sharply observed comic tale of experience and innocence, insecurities and prejudices, all explored in Heggie's trademark raw and eloquent style

0-413-70340-1 METHUEN PB $11.95

Robert **Holman**

Across Oka

A lyrical play set half in England and half in Russia, about conservation and modern attitudes toward it

0-413-19360-8 METHUEN PB $8.95

Making Noise Quietly

Three thematically linked plays about "the dark sense of history in general and 20th-century war in particular"—*Observer*

0-413-15250-2 METHUEN PB $8.95

The Overgrown Path

A British scientist and his wife retreat to a Greek island where they try to forget their separate memories of the first atom bombs

0-413-59760-1 METHUEN PB $5.95

Today

A group of men journey to and from the Spanish Civil War

0-413-59490-4 METHUEN PB..............................$6.95

Kevin **Hood**

Hammett's Apprentice

This original and funny play uses the historical figure of James Hammett, one of the Tolpuddle Martyrs, to explore a contemporary family's relationship with the past, with each other, and with the outside world

0-413-68640-X HEINEMANN PB $11.95

Stephen **Jeffreys**

A Going Concern

1-85459-270-X CONSORTIUM PB $12.95

Stephen **Jeffreys** & Mickey **Gallagher**

The Libertine

1-85459-277-7 HERN PB $12.95

Terry **Johnson**

Cries from the Mammal House

"A cry of despair masquerading as a droll allegory about the closing down of a small English zoo"—*City Limits*

0-413-56250-6 METHUEN PB $5.95

Dead Funny

The death of Benny Hill provides the impetus for the story about Eleanor, who wants what Richard won't give her; Richard, who wants to be left in peace; and Benny, who would rather rest in peace, but, for tonight at least, his fans won't let him

0-413-68340-0 HEINEMANN PB $11.95

Hysteria

Sigmund Freud's possessions, and Sigmund Freud himself, have been shipped from Nazi-occupied Vienna to a quiet Hampstead studio where he hopes to spend his last days in peace. Then Salvador Dali suddenly appears…

0-413-70360-6 HEINEMANN PB $11.95

Imagine Drowning

An investigative journalist disappears after uncovering a major story about the massive abuse of nuclear power. His wife sets out on his trail only to discover a more disturbing and intimate horror

0-413-65250-5 METHUEN PB $11.95

Unsuitable for Adults

0-571-13773-3 FABER PB $8.95

Manfred **Karge**

Conquest of the South Pole & Man to Man

Two hits from the Edinburgh Fringe that subsequently transferred to the Royal Court Theatre, London

0-413-61200-7 HEINEMANN PB $3.50

Charlotte **Keatley**

My Mother Said I Never Should

"A warm and poignant elegy about growing up, growing old, and growing or not growing wise, this play concerns four generations of women living and partly living in Manchester and London. It's about debts, responsibilities, and the burden of a Puritan inheritance"
—*Sunday Times*

0-413-61720-3 HEINEMANN PB $9.95

Barrie **Keeffe**

Barbarians

A Trilogy comprising *Killing Time, Abide With Me,* and *In the City*

0-413-38990-1 METHUEN PB $8.95

My Girl & Frozen Assets

My Girl is a love story set in East London. *Frozen Assets* is a modern morality play

0-413-62200-2 HEINEMANN PB $11.95

Wild Justice, Not Fade Away & Gimme Shelter

Barrie Keeffe has been called "one of the best chroniclers of working class life"—*The Observer*

0-413-64180-5 HEINEMANN PB $13.95

Paul **Kember**

Not Quite Jerusalem

A clash of preconceptions occurs when 3 English lads looking for sand, sun, and sex go to work on a kibbutz

0-413-50280-5 METHUEN PB $6.95

Hanif **Kureishi**

Outskirts and Other Plays

Includes *The King and Mem, Outskirts, Borderline,* and *Birds of Passage*

0-571-16307-6 FABER PB $13.95

David **Lan**

The Ends of the Earth

While working on a dam somewhere in the Balkans, Daniel, a young geologist, begins to crack up. Back home in London, his wife is looking after their dangerously ill child. Told of an old man who can cure his daughter, Daniel sets off on a journey into the mountains where he is asked to make a simple yet nearly impossible sacrifice: to give up smoking

0-571-17910-X FABER PB $10.95

Flight

The story of three generations of the Levine family fleeing from a pogrom in Lithuania in the '30s, settling in Rhodesia in the '50s, and hitting the road for Capetown in the '80s

0-413-14590-5 METHUEN PB $7.95

Hugh **Leonard**

Selected Plays of Hugh Leonard

EDITED BY S.F. GALLAGHER

0-8132-0759-2 CATHOLIC UNIVERSITY $49.95
0-8132-0760-6 CATHOLIC UNIVERSITY PB $16.95

David **Lodge**

The Writing Game

David Lodge is best known for his comic novels, but his first play is an equally witty, satirical look at courses on creative writing and the motives of those who teach them

9-99-118795-2 HEINEMANN PB $9.95

Sharman **MacDonald**

All Things Nice

Moira's parents have moved to the Middle East and sent her to stay with Gran and the Captain, Gran's paying guest. Moira is left to explore adolescent pain and adult responsibilites amidst new family dynamics. First performed by the Royal Court Theatre in 1991

0-571-16429-3 FABER PB $9.95

Plays: One

Includes *When I Was a Girl, I Used to Scream and Shout, When We Were Women,* and *The Brave,* among others

0-571-17621-6 FABER PB $13.95

Shades

Shades opens as the widowed mother of a 10-year-old boy prepares for a night out. The evening eventually brings changes that neither mother nor son expect

0-571-16884-1 FABER PB $8.95

Patrick **Marber**

Dealer's Choice

Poker, money, men, power, compulsion, fathers, sons, and toilets—an exhuberant first play by this award-winning writer/comedian

0-413-69210-8 METHUEN PB $11.95

Rona **Munro**

The Maiden Stone

1-85459-243-2 THEATRE COMMUNICATIONS PB .$14.95

Your Turn to Clean the Stair & Fugue

1-85459-248-3 THEATRE COMMUNICATIONS PB .$14.95

Phyllis **Nagy**

Neverland

0-413-70140-9 HEINEMANN PB $11.95

The Strip

1-85459-223-8 HERN PB $12.95

Weldon Rising & Disappeared

A bitterly funny and chillingly surreal look at the soulless poverty of urban life

0-413-70150-6 METHUEN PB $15.95

Joseph **O'Connor**

Red Roses & Petrol

0-413-69990-0 METHUEN PB $11.95

Louise **Page**

Diplomatic Wives

When a high-flying diplomat is offered a new posting in another country, she must choose between her husband and career

0-413-61430-1 METHUEN PB $9.95

Plays: One

Contains *Golden Girls, Tissue, Salonika,* and *Real Estate*

0-413-64500-2 HEINEMANN PB $13.95

Real Estate

Jenny, a 38-year old pregnant career woman, returns home to the mother and stepfather she abandoned 20 years before

0-413-57950-6 METHUEN PB $7.95

Salonika

Hauntingly conjures up the ghosts of the First World War on a beach in present-day Greece

0-413-52180-X METHUEN PB $6.95

Joe **Penhall**

Pale Horse

A look at the fiery relationship between a wine bar owner who has recently lost his wife under suspicious circumstances and a woman working in his bar who inadvertently kills an abusive customer

0-413-70410-6 METHUEN PB $9.95

Winsome **Pinnock**

The Rebirth of Robert Samuels

0-571-17662-3 FABER PB $9.95

Stephen **Poliakoff**

Breaking the Silence

An autobiographical play about the effects of World War II on a Russian family

0-413-57210-2 HEINEMANN PB $8.95

Coming in to Land

A hit from the National Theatre, this play is about the attempt of a Polish woman to deceive the sharpest minds in the Immigration Service and remain in Britain

0-413-15430-0 METHUEN PB $8.95

Plays: One

Includes *Clever Soldiers, Hitting Town, City Sugar, Shout Across the River, American Days,* and *Strawberry Fields*

0-413-62460-9 HEINEMANN PB $13.95

Plays: Two

0-413-368660-4 HEINEMANN PB $15.95

She's Been Away & Hidden City

0-413-62210-X HEINEMANN PB $13.95

Sienna Red

"Poliakoff always has an eye fixed on where society and fashion is going. His plays are evolutionary reflections of the social scene, on a much wider spectrum than Alan Ayckbourn"
—Peter Hall

0-413-66430-9 HEINEMANN PB $9.95

The Summer Party

The stars of an outdoor music festival receive a surprise visit from the police

0-413-47600-6 METHUEN PB $6.95

Bernard **Pomerance**

The Elephant Man

0-8021-3041-0 GROVE PB $8.95

David **Rudkin**

The Saxon Shore

Set in northern Britain in the fifth century AD, a play that looks at the effect of the fall of Rome on a community on the fringes of the empire and suggests parallels with current-day Ireland

0-413-14100-4 METHUEN PB $8.95

Peter **Shaffer**

Amadeus

The rise and fall of Mozart through the eyes (and psyche) of his rival Salieri

0-06-090783-5 HARPERCOLLINS PB $11.00

Peter **Shaffer**

Equus

A psychiatrist analyzes a boy who has blinded six horses

0-14-048185-0 PENGUIN PB $7.95

Tom **Stoppard**

Arcadia

An award-winning investigation into the nature of truth and time, the difference between the Classical and the Romantic temperament, and the disruptive influence of sex on our orbits in life. An intricate play on gothic themes, and one of his greatest successes

0-571-16934-1 FABER PB $9.95

Enter a Free Man

One of Stoppard's earliest plays concerning George Riley, the man who invented indoor rain

0-571-08794-9 FABER PB $8.95

Hapgood

A play about physics, espionage, thriller novels, superpower paranoia, Star Wars technology, defectors, homelife, and three sets of twins. "Stoppard, whose plays at minimum offer glorious wordplay and the simmering surface of what seems to be Big Ideas, is at his funniest and saddest in *Hapgood*"—*Time*

0-571-19857-0 FABER PB $10.95

In the Native State

0-571-16464-1 FABER PB $8.95

Indian Ink

0-571-17556-2 FABER PB $10.95

Jumpers

"The New Radical Liberal Party has made the ex-Minister of Agriculture Archbishop of Canterbury, British astronauts are scrapping with each other on the moon, and spritely academics steal about London by night engaging in murderous gymnastics"
—Michael Billington, *Guardian*

0-8021-5100-0 GROVE PB $8.95

The Real Inspector Hound and Other Entertainments

A new collection of serious fun from the ingenious author of *The Real Thing* and *Rosencrantz and Guildenstern Are Dead*. "Mr. Stoppard has never been the sort of writer to resist the temptation of a naughty good time"
—*NY Times*

0-571-16569-9 FABER $19.95
0-571-16571-0 FABER PB $9.95

The Real Inspector Hound & After Magritte

0-8021-5205-8 GROVE PB $8.95

The Real Thing

"An intelligent play about love"—*Guardian*

0-571-12529-8 FABER PB $8.95

Rosencrantz and Guildenstern Are Dead

Hamlet viewed from an oblique angle; the play that made Stoppard's reputation

0-8021-3275-8 GROVE PB $8.95

Rough Crossing & On the Razzle

0-571-16400-5 FABER $18.95

Tom Stoppard

Stoppard: The Plays for Radio, 1964-1991

A reflection of the full range of the playwright's gifts, as well as his theatrical and literary craftsmanship and versatility. This edition includes *The Dissolution of Dominic Boot, "M" Is for Moon Among Other Things, If You're Glad I'll Be Frank, Albert's Bridge, Where Are They Now?, Artist Descending a Staircase, The Dog It Was that Died,* and *In the Native State*

0-571-17208-3 FABER $22.95
0-571-17209-1 FABER PB $13.95

The Television Plays, 1965-1984

0-571-16570-2 FABER PB $11.95

Travesties

"Tom Stoppard is not the first man to have noticed that Lenin, James Joyce, and the Dadaist Tristan Tzara were all living in Zurich during the Great War ...From this obscure footnote to *Ulysses* Stoppard has spun out a fantastically elaborate web to snare his three giants in the same play"—Irving Wandle, *Times* (London)

0-8021-5089-6 GROVE PB $7.95

Tom **Stoppard** & Mel **Gussow**

Conversations with Stoppard

0-8021-3468-8 GROVE PB $12.00

David **Storey**

The Changing Room

The play takes us into the world of a Rugby League changing room on a wintry Saturday afternoon, as a disparate group of men change themselves gradually into a team. Thirteen players, two trainers, a physiotherapist, a club secretary, a referee, a cleaner, and a club chairman—a cross-section of classes and types—are each transformed by the beauty and cruelty of the game

0-413-70370-3 METHUEN PB $11.95

Plays: Two

Contains three of his most famous works: *The Restoration of Arnold Middleton, In Celebration*, and *The March on Russia. Plays: One* is not available

0-413-68610-8 HEINEMANN PB $15.95

C.P. **Taylor**

Good

"An original and intelligent play...that tries to work out how decent, liberal, humane men came to be swept up by the Nazi juggernaut"
—Michael Billington, *Guardian*

0-413-63910-X HEINEMANN PB $12.95

Sue **Townsend**

Bazaar and Rummage, Womberang & Groping for Words

Bazaar and Rummage brings together a neurotic do-gooder, a trainee social worker, and three agoraphobics who have been persuaded to venture out of the security of their homes to run a rummage sale. *Groping for Words* is set in an adult literacy class, where the students' fear of admitting ignorance is as much a handicap as their inability to read. *Womberang* is a terrific, life-affirming play

0-413-64620-3 METHUEN PB $11.95

The Great Celestial Cow

When Sita and her children leave India to join her husband in England, she is forced to sell her cow, but keeps her milking bucket in the hope that she will buy another cow in Leicester. Sita clings to her dream of the cow, just as she tries to cling to some sense of her own identity

0-413-64630-0 METHUEN PB $9.95

The Queen and I

The Queen and her family are deposed by a new republican government and allocated housing in a Midlands housing project. Based on Townsend's best-selling book

See also **THE MIDDLE GENERATION** under **20TH-CENTURY BRITISH AND IRISH FICTION**

0-413-68970-0 METHUEN PB $11.95
1-56947-015-4 SOHO PB $11.00

Sue Townsend
(photo courtesy of Soho Press)

Judy **Upton**

Bruises & The Shorewatchers' House

Bruises centers on the complicated relationships between a father and son, the father's lover, the son's lover, the son's lover's mother, the son's former lover—now the father's lover. *The Shorewatchers' House* premiered in England late in 1995

0-413-70430-0 METHUEN PB $13.95

Nick **Ward**

Apart from George

0-413-19230-X ROUTLEDGE PB $3.50

Plays: One

Includes *The Present, Apart from George, The Strangeness of Others,* and *Trouble Sleeping.* "An artist with two priceless gifts: the ability to play the stage like a musical instrument, and to make the theatre speak through inarticulate characters"—*London Times*

0-571-17681-X FABER PB $13.95

Timberlake **Wertenbaker**

The Break of Day

0-571-17679-8 FABER PB $9.95

The Love of the Nightingale & The Grace of Mary Traverse

The Love of the Nightingale is a dramatization of the Greek myth of Procne and Philomel in which Philomel is deceived and seduced by her sister's husband Tereus, who silences her by tearing out her tongue. Also contains the revised text of *The Grace of Mary Traverse*

0-571-15383-6 FABER PB $10.95

Our Country's Good

Australia. 1789. A young lieutenant is directing rehearsals of the first play ever to be staged in that country. With only two copies of the text, a cast of largely illiterate convicts, and one leading lady who may be about to be hanged, conditions for what will be the antipodean premiere of *The Recruiting Officer* are hardly ideal

0-413-65900-3 HEINEMANN PB $9.95

Plays

Contains *New Anatomies, The Grace of Mary Traverse, Our Country's Good,* and *The Love of the Nightingale*

0-571-17743-3 FABER PB $13.95

Three Birds Alighting on a Field

An artist confronts the fact that galleries and auctioneers artificially inflate the prices of artworks according to the standards of fashion and high finance—and in so doing undermine the idea of intrinsic artistry and the very concept of value

0-571-16105-7 FABER PB $8.95

Nigel **Williams**

Class Enemy

The portrayal of every teacher's living nightmare: confronting a group of anarchic teenage boys on a daily basis. "Extraordinary wit, lyricism and orginality…manages to subsist on the frontiers of fun and horror, sadness and exhilaration"—*New York Magazine*

0-571-17474-4 FABER PB $10.95

Harry and Me

0-571-17819-7 FABER PB $10.95

Anthologies

K.A. **Berney**, editor

Contemporary British Dramatists

1-55862-213-6 ST. JAMES $55.00

Yvonne **Brewster**, editor

Black Plays

Talking in Tongues by Winsome Pinnock explores the tangled racial and sexual issues of modern-day Britain and was premiered at the Royal Court Theatre. *A Jamaican Airman Foresees His Death*, based on a Yeats poem, is a rhapsody on a colonial theme, set in World War II Scotland. Paul Boakye's *Boy with Beer* is a funny and sexy story of a *Guardian*-reading gay photographer who finds his fantasy African prince. *Scrape off the Black* by Tunde Ikoli is an East End mixed-race drama. Bonnie Greer's examination of the heart of darkness in *Western Civilization, Munda Negra*, premiered in the US

0-413-69130-6 METHUEN PB $17.95

Ian **Brown** & Mark **Fisher**, editors

Made in Scotland: An Anthology of New Scottish Plays

These prize-winning plays, produced in Scotland, celebrate the tremendous wealth and creativity of Scottish writing for the theatre. The plays in this collection are Simon Donald's *The Life of Stuff*; Sue Glover's *Bondagers*; Duncan McLean's *Julie Allardyce*; and *The Cut* by ex-miner Mike Cullen

0-413-69180-2 HEINEMANN PB $19.95

Roger **Cornish** & Violet **Ketels**, editors

Landmarks of Modern British Drama: The Plays of the 1960s

"Angry Young Men" was a label pegged to many of the playwrights represented here. Included are John Arden's *Serjeant Musgrave's Dance*, Harold Pinter's *The Caretaker*, John Osborne's *A Patriot for Me*, Joe Orton's *Loot*, Arnold Wesker's *Roots*, Edward Bond's *Saved*, and Peter Barnes's *The Ruling Class*

0-413-59090-9 METHUEN $29.95

0-413-57260-9 METHUEN PB $12.95

Stephen **Daldry** & Dominic **Tickell**, editors

Coming on Strong: New Writing from the Royal Court Theatre

A collection of short plays by new and promising British playwrights from the renowned Royal Court Theatre. Includes *Peaches* by Nick Grosso, *The Knocky* by Michael Wynne, *Essex Girls* by Rebecca Pritchard, and *Corner Boys* by Kevin Coyle. "A restorative cocktail of fresh talent and warm humanity"—*Daily Telegraph*

0-571-17678-X FABER PB $14.95

Linda **Fitzsimmons** & Viv **Gardner**, editors

New Woman Plays

This anthology contains Elizabeth Robins's *Alan's Wife, Diana of Dobson's* by Cicely Hamilton, Elizabeth Baker's *Chains*, and Githa Sowerby's *Rutherford and Son*

0-413-64200-3 METHUEN PB $17.95

Trevor R. **Griffiths** & Margaret **Llewellyn-Jones**, editors

British and Irish Women Dramatists Since 1958: A Critical Handbook

0-335-09602-6 OOPEN UNIVERSITY PB $29.95

Michael P. **Harding** & Christopher **Fitz-Simon**, editors

New Plays from the Abbey Theatre, 1993-1995

0-8156-2699-1 SYRACUSE $39.95

0-8156-0345-2 SYRACUSE PB $17.95

Jan **McDonald**

New Drama, 1900-1914

0-394-55138-9 GROVE $27.50

0-394-62112-3 GROVE PB $11.95

Brooks **McNamera**, editor

Plays from the Contemporary British Theater

Includes major works by Joe Orton, David Hare, David Storey, Harold Pinter, and others, including David Edgar's famous adaptation of *Nicholas Nickleby*

0-451-62851-9 MENTOR PB $6.99

Anthony **Roche**

Contemporary Irish Drama: From Beckett to McGuinness

0-312-12325-6 ST. MARTIN'S $39.95

0-312-12326-4 ST. MARTIN'S PB $17.95

20th-Century British Essays and Other Prose

Anour **Abdallah**

For Rushdie—In Defense of Free Speech: Essays by 100 Arab and Muslim Writers

0-8076-1354-1 BRAZILLER $27.50

0-8076-1355-X BRAZILLER PB $14.95

A. **Alvarez**

The Biggest Game in Town

Alvarez's take on gambling

0-948353-02-3 OLDCASTLE PB $10.95

Night: Night Life, Night Language, Sleep, and Dreams

0-393-03724-X NORTON $23.00

0-393-31434-0 NORTON PB $13.00

The Savage God: A Study of Suicide

0-393-30657-7 NORTON PB $8.95

Martin **Amis**

The Moronic Inferno

0-14-012719-4 PENGUIN PB $11.95

Visiting Mrs. Nabokov and Other Excursions

0-679-75793-7 VINTAGE PB $12.00

W.H. **Auden**

The Dyer's Hand

This most substantial of his prose collections is an essential book of modern criticism, varied in its themes and unfailingly brilliant in its perceptions

See also **LITERARY ESSAYISTS AND HISTORIANS** under **LITERARY CRITICISM** in **LITERATURE OF EUROPE, AFRICA, AND ASIA**

0-679-72484-2 VINTAGE PB $17.00

I have always found the atmosphere of *Twelfth Night* a bit whiffy. I get the impression that Shakespeare wrote the play at a time when he was in no mood for comedy, but in a mood of puritanical aversion to all those pleasing illusions which men cherish and by which they lead their lives. The comic convention in which the play is set prevents him from giving direct expression to this mood, but the mood keeps disturbing, even spoiling, the comic feeling. One has a sense, and nowhere more strongly than in the songs, of there being inverted commas around the "fun."

THE DYER'S HAND

The Enchafed Flood

A study in the Romantic sensibility, exploring at length the images encountered in a single passage by Wordsworth

0-8139-0827-2 VIRGINIA........................$16.50

0-8139-0828-0 VIRGINIA PB........................$7.50

Forewords and Afterwords

Brief occasional essays on a range of subjects illustrating Auden's extraordinarily eclectic interests

See also **LITERARY ESSAYISTS AND HISTORIANS** under **LITERARY CRITICISM** in **LITERATURE OF EUROPE, AFRICA, AND ASIA**

0-679-72485-0 VINTAGE PB $15.00

The Prolific and the Devourer

Written in 1939 when Auden fled the European tragedy for America, this collection of aphorisms and reflections on politics, on religion, and on aesthetics provides new insights into the poet's psyche, and by extension into the psyche of that pivotal historical moment

INTRODUCTION BY EDWARD MENDLESON

0-88001-344-3 ECCO........................$27.50

Julian **Barnes**

Letters from London

Observations from the author of *Flaubert's Parrot* and *Cross Channel*

0-679-76161-6 VINTAGE PB........................$13.00

John **Berger**

A celebrated Marxist art critic, John Berger is also a novelist, screenwriter, and painter.

And Our Faces, My Heart, Brief as Photos

A short, poetic essay that uses Berger's own experience—"What draws me to love?"—as a springboard for larger investigations, from Van Gogh to 20th-century homelessness

0-394-72427-5 VINTAGE PB $9.00

Keeping a Rendezvous

Berger's acute observations and lucid prose continually delight and impress us. A true Renaissance man. "[His] ability to see something clearly, with fresh surprise yet profound understanding, makes his writing singularly moving and informative"
—Michael Welzenbach, *The Washington Times*

0-679-40632-8 VINTAGE PB $21.00

Permanent Red: Essays in Seeing

0-904613-92-5 WRITERS & READERS PB $6.95

The Sense of Sight

A wide-ranging collection of essays spanning three decades. Includes the classic "Moment of Cubism"

0-8446-6612-2 SMITH........................$22.30

0-394-74206-0 RANDOM HOUSE PB $12.00

0-679-73722-7 VINTAGE PB........................$14.00

The Three Lives of Lucie Cabrol

See also **THEORY AND CRITICISM** under **ART HISTORY: GENERAL STUDIES** in **ART**

0-413-69690-1 METHUEN PB $11.95

Ways of Seeing

An essay on the ideological and technological conditioning of our ways of seeing both art and the world, based on the acclaimed BBC series

0-8446-6175-9 SMITH........................$21.25

0-14-013515-4 VIKING PB........................$10.95

John **Berger** & Jean **Mohr**

A Fortunate Man: The Story of a Country Doctor

0-679-73726-X VINTAGE $13.00

Quentin **Bell**

Bloomsbury Recalled

The nephew and acclaimed biographer of Virginia Woolf, and one of the last members of the Bell family, presents candid recollections of the intellectual giants that gathered around Gordon Square, Bloomsbury. Woolf, E.M. Forster, Vita Sackville-West, John Maynard Keynes, Roger Fry, Lytton Strachey

0-231-10564-9 COLUMBIA $24.95

Vanessa Bell

Anthony **Burgess**

A Mouthful of Air: Languages, Languages, Especially English

In one of his most important books, the author of *A Clockwork Orange*, less well known as an accomplished linguist and polyglot, tackles the subject of the spoken word. A fascinating exploration of how language evolved to reach its present form, how it operates in society, and how it is likely to be transformed in the future. "As you could guess in anything from Burgess, this is a rich and succulent study of languages and literatures, sounds and music, poetry and the demotic"—*The Times* [London]

0-688-13789-X QUILL PB $13.00

A.S. **Byatt**

Passions of the Mind: Selected Writing

Supple, writerly essays on Iris Murdoch, Saul Bellow, Toni Morrison, Sylvia Plath, social politics, and herself. The author of *Possession* actively contemplates the alliance of literature and life. "Erudite…her insights [are] both elegant and commanding"
—*NY Times Book Review*

0-679-73678-6 VINTAGE PB........................$14.00

Robert **Byron**

The Road to Oxiana

Persia and Afghanistan in the early 1930s, described in a rich mixture of scholarship and adventure narrative

See also **THE NEAR AND MIDDLE EAST** under **ASIA** under **TRAVEL LITERATURE** in **FOOD, TRAVEL, AND LEISURE**

0-19-503067-2 OXFORD PB $13.95

Bruce **Chatwin**

Anatomy of Restlessness: Selected Writings, 1969-1989

See also **TRAVEL ESSAYS** under **TRAVEL LITERATURE** in **FOOD, TRAVEL, AND LEISURE**

0-670-86859-0 VIKING........................$23.95

G.K. **Chesterton**

"He is as much a political writer as George Orwell. Politics, in the narrow, as well as the widest, sense, informs and inspires his writing, which is why he remained all his life a journalist, to the despair of those who recognized the enormous scale of his gifts. But that is what Chesterton wanted to be, a 'jolly journalist'…because he thought his message important, and from Fleet Street it could reach the people who needed it most, and who perhaps had the best chance of understanding it."—P.J. Kavanagh

Criticisms & Appreciations of the Works of Charles Dickens

0-460-87084-X EVERYMAN'S PB $7.95

The Everlasting Man

0-89870-444-8 IGNATIUS PB........................$12.95

Saint Francis of Assisi

0-385-02900-4 IMAGE PB $9.95

Cyril **Connolly**

Enemies of Promise

Essays on the writer in modern society, and the forces that conspire to bring him down

0-89255-078-3 PERSEA PB $6.95

The Evening Colonnade

A collection of later literary essays. "Remember that the object of the critic is to revenge himself on the creator"—Cyril Connolly

0-15-629060-X HARCOURT BRACE PB...............$9.95

The Unquiet Grave

A series of meditative essays originally published in 1944 under the pseudonym Palinurus

0-89255-058-9 PERSEA PB $9.95

Joseph **Conrad**

The Collected Letters Volume 1: 1861-1897

0-521-24216-9 CAMBRIDGE $95.00

Volume 2: 1898-1902
0-521-25748-4 CAMBRIDGE $95.00

Volume 3: 1903-1907
0-521-32387-8 CAMBRIDGE $95.00

The Mirror of the Sea
A memoir of Conrad's life as a sailor: "I have attempted here," he wrote, "to lay bare with the unreserve of a last hour's confession the terms of my relation to the sea"
0-910395-34-9 MARLBORO PB $10.95

A Personal Record
0-910395-46-2 MARLBORO PB $8.95

Artemis **Cooper**

The Letters of Evelyn Waugh and Diana Cooper
An effervescent collection of letters, lost for some 15 years, is here published for the first time. Waugh and Lady Diana first met in 1932, when he was depressed and between marriages, and the two shared an intimate though platonic relationship until his death. The editor, Lady Diana's granddaughter, has produced a volume that is sure to intrigue both Waugh fans and scholars. Includes a number of black-and-white photos
0-395-56265-1 TICKNOR & FIELDS $27.50

Denis **Donoghue**

Warrenpoint
An autobiographical account of Northern Ireland by the distinguished literary critic
0-8156-0303-7 SYRACUSE PB $14.95

Lawrence **Durrell**

Bitter Lemons
A book about Cyprus
1-56924-839-7 MARLOWE PB $10.95

Prospero's Cell: A Guide to the Landscape and Manners of the Island of Corfu
See also **EUROPE SINCE 1945** under **EUROPE** under **TRAVEL LITERATURE** in **FOOD, TRAVEL, AND LEISURE**
1-56924-766-8 MARLOWE PB $10.95

Reflections on a Marine Venus: A Companion to the Landscape of Rhodes
1-56924-791-9 MARLOWE PB $10.95

T. S. **Eliot**

The Use of Poetry and the Use of Criticism
See also **THE MODERNIST REVOLUTION** under **LITERARY CRITICISM** in **LITERATURE OF EUROPE, AFRICA, AND ASIA**
0-674-93150-5 HARVARD PB $11.95

To Criticize the Critic and Other Writings
0-8032-6721-5 NEBRASKA PB $8.95

The Varieties of Metaphysical Poetry
0-15-100096-4 HARCOURT BRACE $29.95

D.J. **Enright**

Memoirs of a Mendicant Professor
0-85635-859-2 CARCANET PB $21.95

Caradoc **Evans**

Nothing to Pay
0-8112-1290-4 NEW DIRECTIONS PB $11.95

James **Fenton**

All the Wrong Places: Adrift in the Politics of the Pacific Rim
Fenton, one of the most acclaimed English poets of his generation, writes about the fall of Saigon, the upheaval in the Philippines, and other events
0-87113-204-4 ATLANTIC MONTHLY PB $9.95

Ford Madox **Ford**

"There is no novelist of this century more likely to live than Ford Madox Ford... In an age of increasing carelessness among good writers, Ford was an artist. No one in our century except Henry James has been more attentive to the craft of letters."—Graham Greene

It Was the Nightingale
Ford's not-quite-trustworthy reminiscences of the literary world of the early modernists
0-88001-034-7 NORTON PB $9.50

The March of Literature: From Confucius' Day to Our Own
See also **GENERAL STUDIES** under **WORLD LITERATURE: WORLD LITERATURE SURVEYS AND ANTHOLOGIES** in **LITERATURE OF EUROPE, AFRICA, AND ASIA**
1-56478-051-1 DALKEY ARCHIVE PB $16.95

Provence: From Minstrels to the Machine
"The expansiveness and exuberance of spirit, the embracing knowledge of the place, that show forth in Ford's love affair with Provence will always give this book a joyous life of its own"—Eudora Welty
See also **EUROPE SINCE 1945** under **EUROPE** under **TRAVEL LITERATURE** in **FOOD, TRAVEL, AND LEISURE**
0-88001-413-X ECCO PB $13.00

Ford Madox Ford

Return to Yesterday
0-87140-563-6 LIVERIGHT $12.95
0-87140-271-8 LIVERIGHT PB $7.95

The Soul of London
0-460-87621-X EVERYMAN'S PB $7.95

E.M. **Forster**

Abinger Harvest
0-15-602610-4 HARCOURT BRACE PB $10.00

Aspects of the Novel
A classic discussion of the techniques and structure of fiction, with a focus on craft
See also **GENERAL HISTORIES AND STUDIES** under **ANTHOLOGIES AND STUDIES**
0-15-609180-1 HARCOURT BRACE PB $7.95

A Commonplace Book
EDITED BY PHILIP GARDNER
0-8047-1280-8 STANFORD $45.00

The Hill of Devi
Life in India as private secretary to the Maharajah of Dewas
See also **INDIA** under **ASIA** under **TRAVEL LITERATURE** in **FOOD, TRAVEL, AND LEISURE**
0-8419-5828-9 HOLMES & MEIER $55.00
0-15-640265-3 HARCOURT BRACE PB $4.95

Selected Letters of E.M. Forster
Volume 1: 1879-1920
0-674-79825-2 HARVARD $35.00

Volume 2: 1921-1970
0-674-79827-9 HARVARD $35.00

William **Golding**

An Egyptian Journal
The novelist takes a trip down the Nile
See also **NORTH AFRICA** under **AFRICA** under **TRAVEL LITERATURE** in **FOOD, TRAVEL, AND LEISURE**
0-571-12547-6 FABER PB $12.95

Robert **Graves**

Goodbye to All That
Graves's "bitter leave-taking of England" at 33, in a classic autobiography (first published in 1929) about coming of age in the trenches of World War I
See also **ARMAGGEDON: 1914-1918** under **THE 20TH-CENTURY** under **GREAT BRITAIN AND IRELAND** in **WORLD HISTORY AND CURRENT AFFAIRS**
0-385-09330-6 DOUBLEDAY PB $10.95

In Broken Images: Selected Correspondence of Robert Graves
0-918825-82-2 MOYER BELL PB $9.95

The White Goddess: A Historical Grammar of Poetic Myth
An eccentric and engaging study of poetry and its relation to muses and myths, mainly Celtic and Greek; in the author's words, "a very difficult book, as well as a very queer one"
See also **GENERAL INTRODUCTIONS** under **MYTHOLOGY AND FOLKLORE** in **RELIGION, SPIRITUALITY, AND PHILOSOPHY**
0-374-50493-8 FS&G PB $15.00

Robert **Graves** & Alan **Hodge**

The Long Weekend: A Social History of Great Britain, 1918-1939
0-393-00217-9 NORTON PB $10.95

Henry **Green**

Green's terse, elliptical, and utterly serious comedies are among the most original creations of modern British fiction. Unfortunately, several of his best books are out of print.

Pack My Bag: A Self-Portrait
0-8112-1234-3 NEW DIRECTIONS $18.95

Surviving: The Uncollected Writings of Henry Green
0-670-80476-2 VIKING $24.00

Graham **Greene**

Collected Essays

Over 80 miscellaneous pieces, divided into "The Lost Childhood," "Novels and Novelists," and "Some Characters"

0-14-018576-3 VIKING PB $10.95

In Search of a Character

Two journals of two trips Greene made to Africa—which resulted in two novels, *The Heart of the Matter* and *A Burnt-Out Case*

0-14-002822-6 PENGUIN PB....................................$4.95

Journey Without Maps

A record of Greene's first trip outside Europe, into the heart of Liberia

0-14-018579-8 PENGUIN PB $10.95

A World of My Own: A Dream Diary

Obsessively recording the private world of his dreams during the last third of his long and productive writing life, Greene allows us a look at his personal life and creative processes

0-670-85279-1 VIKING $21.95

Richard **Holmes**

Footsteps: Adventures of a Romantic Biographer

0-679-77004-6 VINTAGE PB $13.00

Aldous **Huxley**

Brave New World Revisited

An explicit, as opposed to the fictionalized, warning about freedom and its enemies, how we must fight to protect ourselves

0-8095-9047-6 BORGO $23.00

0-06-080984-1 HARPERCOLLINS PB....................$6.00

The Devils of London

Huxley's engrossing account of sex and demonic possession in a late medieval French town

0-786-70368-7 CARROLL & GRAF PB $12.95

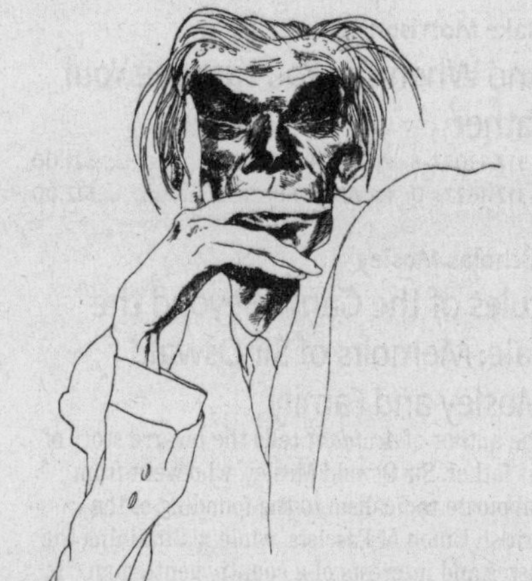

Aldous Huxley

The Doors of Perception & Heaven and Hell

Huxley's exploration of mescaline and LSD paved the way for much of the hallucinogenic experimentation that followed in the '60s and '70s

0-06-090007-5 HARPERCOLLINS PB $12.00

Grey Eminence

A biography of Father Joseph, Cardinal Richelieu's principal associate and collaborator, becomes, in Huxley's hands, a bold look at the antecedents of modern war and terror. "A brilliant study of politics, morals, mysticism"—*TLS*

0-8371-7508-9 GREENWOOD $65.00

The Perennial Philosophy

A collection of aphorisms and brief extracts relating to mystical experience. "It is both an anthology and an interpretation of the supreme mystics, East and West...This is the first time that anybody has adequately covered the field and showed an equal familiarity with all fields. It is a magnificent achievement"—Rufus Jones

0-8095-9001-8 BORGO $33.00

0-06-090191-8 HARPERCOLLINS PB $13.50

Christopher **Isherwood**

My Guru and His Disciple

"A sweetly modest and honest portrait of Isherwood's spiritual instructor, Swami Prabhavananda, the Hindu guru who guided Isherwood for some years. It is also a book about the often amusing and sometimes painful counterpoint between worldliness and holiness in Isherwood's own life"—Edmund White

0-374-52087-9 FS&G PB $13.00

Christopher and His Kind

A partial autobiography covering the years from his first visit to Germany in 1929 to his move to the United States ten years later includes vignettes of Auden and Forster

See also **BIOGRAPHIES** under **GAY, LESBIAN, AND BISEXUAL STUDIES** in **SOCIAL STUDIES**

0-374-52036-4 FS&G PB $13.00

Frank **Kermode**

Not Entitled: A Memoir

One of the great critics of English literature turns his wry attention to a new subject: his own life.

0-374-18103-9 FS&G $23.00

D.H. **Lawrence**

D.H. Lawrence and Italy

A collection of three of his most evocative books on Italy: *Twilight in Italy, Sea and Sardinia,* and the posthumously published *Etruscan Places*

See also **EUROPE** under **TRAVEL LITERATURE** in **FOOD, TRAVEL, AND LEISURE**

0-14-009520-9 VIKING PB....................................$13.99

The dancers on the right wall move with a strange, powerful alertness onwards. They are men dressed only in a loose coloured scarf, or in the gay handsome chlamys draped as a mantle. The subulo plays the double flute the Etruscans loved so much, touching the stops with big, exaggerated hands, the man behind him touches the seven-stringed lyre, the man in front turns round and signals with his left hand, holding a big wine-bowl in his right. And so they move on, on their long, sandalled feet, past the little berried olive-trees, swiftly going with their limbs full of life, full of life to the tips.

D.H. LAWRENCE AND ITALY

Reflections on the Death of a Porcupine & Other Essays

EDITED BY MICHAEL HERBERT

0-521-35847-7 CAMBRIDGE PB $38.95

Apocalypse: Definitive Text

"It protests against the dehumanizing of men and women by Christianity...and it protests against their dehumanization by science, which has taken the gods out of heaven and the heart out of man"—Richard Aldington

0-8488-0558-5 AMEREON PB $13.95

0-14-018197-0 PENGUIN PB....................................$8.95

Studies in Classic American Literature

Lawrence's pioneering studies of Cooper, Poe, Hawthorne, Melville, Dana, and Whitman have had an indelible effect on the way American literature is read

See also **GENERAL STUDIES TO 1900** under **AMERICAN LITERATURE: ANTHOLOGIES AND CRITICAL STUDIES** in **LITERATURE OF THE AMERICAS**

0-14-018377-9 PENGUIN PB $10.95

T.E. **Lawrence**

The Essential T.E. Lawrence: A Selection of His Finest Writings

EDITED BY DAVID GARNETT

0-19-282962-9 OXFORD PB....................................$14.95

Lawrence of Arabia, Strange Man of Letters: The Literary Criticism and Correspondence of T.E. Lawrence

EDITED BY HAROLD ORLANS

0-8386-3508-3 FAIRLEIGH DICKINSON $47.50

Seven Pillars of Wisdom

"The revolt in Arabia against the Turks, as it appeared to an Englishman who took part. Round this tentpole of a military chronicle T.E. has hung an unexampled fabric of portraits, descriptions, philosophies, emotions, adventures, dreams"—E.M. Forster

0-385-41895-7 ANCHOR PB....................................$15.95

T.E. **Lawrence** & Malcolm **Brown**, editor

T.E. Lawrence: The Selected Letters

1-56924-995-4 MARLOWE PB $16.95

Hugh **Lee**, editor

A Cézanne in the Hedge and Other Memories of Charleston and Bloomsbury

0-226-47004-0 CHICAGO PB....................................$11.95

Doris **Lessing**

Doris Lessing: Conversations

0-86538-080-5 ONTARIO REVIEW PB $13.95

Going Home

0-06-097630-6 HARPERPERENNIAL PB $13.00

Prisons We Choose to Live Inside

Five lectures on the art of thinking for oneself

0-06-039077-8 HARPERCOLLINS PB $10.00

Under My Skin: Volume One of My Autobiography—to 1949 Volume I

Other volumes of Lessing's autoiography are forthcoming

0-06-092664-3 HARPERPERENNIAL PB $14.00

C.S. **Lewis**

A Grief Observed

Lewis's effort to console himself after the death of his wife—and to defend against his loss of belief in God. "The author has done something I believed impossible—assuaged his own grief by conveying it"—Anne Freemantle

See also **DEATH OF A SPOUSE** under **DEATH AND MOURNING** under **SELF-HELP** in **LIFESTYLES AND PRACTICAL ADVICE**

0-553-27486-4 BDD PB $5.50
0-06-065284-5 HARPERCOLLINS PB $10.00

The Letters of C.S. Lewis

EDITED BY W.H. LEWIS

0-15-650871-0 HARVEST PB $14.95

On Stories & Other Essays on Literature

"If wit and wisdom, style and scholarship, are requisites to passage through the pearly gates, then Mr. Lewis will be among the angels" —*New Yorker*

0-15-668788-7 HARCOURT BRACE PB $7.00

The Problem of Pain

"A theologian for everyman"—Anthony Burgess

See also **CLASSICS** under **CHRISTIANITY** in **RELIGION, SPIRITUALITY, AND PHILOSOPHY**

0-02-086850-2 MACMILLAN PB $4.95

The Screwtape Letters

A classic satiric work consisting of a series of letters from Screwtape, an elderly devil, advising his nephew Wormwood, an apprentice devil, how to corrupt his earthly "patient"

See also **WESTERN** under **20TH-CENTURY SPIRITUAL LEADERS** under **SPIRITUALITY** in **RELIGION, SPIRITUALITY, AND PHILOSOPHY**

INTRODUCTION BY RICHARD GILMAN

0-553-26369-2 BDD PB..$4.50
0-451-62821-7 MENTOR PB $4.99

The Seeing Eye & Other Selected Essays

Selected essays from *Christian Reflections.* "Lewis is the ideal persuader for the half-convinced, the man who would like to be a Christian but finds his intellect getting in the way"—Anthony Burgess, *NY Times Book Review*

0-345-32866-3 BALLANTINE PB $4.99

Surprised by Joy: The Shape of My Early Life

Lewis's spiritual journey from Christianity to atheism and back again to Christianity. "Anyone approaching this book as a study in the psychology of conversion will find the greatest interest in the dual paths—intellectual and intuitive—which converged at last"—*Saturday Review*

0-15-100185-5 HARCOURT BRACE $16.00
0-15-687011-8 HARCOURT BRACE PB $9.00

Wyndham **Lewis**

Publisher, novelist, painter, and ferocious critic, Lewis was described by Ezra Pound as "the only English writer who can be compared to Dostoevsky." His work, much of it long out of print, has been revived in recent years.

The Caliph's Design

An essay in art criticism

AFTERWORD BY PAUL EDWARDS

0-87685-665-2 BLACK SPARROW $20.00
0-87685-664-4 BLACK SPARROW PB $12.50

Journey into Barbary

Morocco in 1931: the writer and painter's escape from "dying European society" into a search for "the mirages of the great electric desert"

See also **NORTH AFRICA** under **AFRICA** under **TRAVEL LITERATURE** in **FOOD, TRAVEL, AND LEISURE**

See also **THE EARLY 20TH-CENTURY** under **20TH-CENTURY BRITISH AND IRISH FICTION**

EDITED BY C.J. FOX

0-87685-519-2 BLACK SPARROW......................$25.00
0-87685-518-4 BLACK SPARROW PB $14.00

Wyndham Lewis

Men Without Art

"*Men Without Art* is Wyndham Lewis' defense of his second calling, literature. It is also his liveliest and most accessible book of literary criticism. For its sustained analyses of individual major figures—alone the essays on Hemingway, Faulkner, Virginia Woolf and (above all) T.S. Eliot—it deserves a permanent place in the criticism of modern literature"—Seamus Cooney

EDITED BY SEAMUS COONEY

0-87685-687-3 BLACK SPARROW $20.00
0-87685-686-5 BLACK SPARROW PB $14.00

Pound/Lewis: The Letters of Ezra Pound and Wyndham Lewis

EDITED BY TIMOTHY MATERER

0-8112-0932-6 NEW DIRECTIONS......................$37.50

Rude Assignment: An Intellectual Autobiography

EDITED BY TOBY FOSHAY

0-87685-604-0 BLACK SPARROW......................$25.00
0-87685-603-2 BLACK SPARROW PB $14.00

Time and Western Man

This is Lewis's most important work of criticism, long unobtainable. In it, he turns on fellow-modernists Pound, Stein, and Joyce to assert that they made their "revolutionary" creative strategies vehicles for ideologies that undermine real creativity and progress. "One of the dozen or so most important books of the 20th-century"—Hugh Kenner

EDITED BY PAUL EDWARDS

0-404-17125-7 AMS $36.00
0-87685-878-7 BLACK SPARROW PB.................$17.50

Nigel **Lewis**

The Book of Babel: Words and the Way We See Things

0-87745-496-5 IOWA PB $19.95

David **Lodge**

The Art of Fiction

Fifty pieces from the acclaimed series that appeared in the *Washington Post* and the London *Independent.* A valuable book for anyone who enjoys literary fiction and would like to understand better how it works

See also **LITERARY ESSAYISTS AND HISTORIANS** under **LITERARY CRITICISM** in **LITERATURE OF EUROPE, AFRICA, AND ASIA**

0-14-017492-3 PENGUIN PB...............................$11.95

W. Somerset **Maugham**

The Summing Up

"In this book I am going to sort out my thoughts on a number of subjects that have chiefly interested me during the course of my life" —W. Somerset Maugham

0-14-018600-X VIKING PB $10.95

A Writer's Notebook

Selections from the journals he kept from 1912 to 1949 that show Maugham's evolution as his literary professionalism takes over

0-14-002644-4 PENGUIN PB $6.95

Nancy **Mitford**

Love from Nancy: The Letters of Nancy Mitford

The acerbic wit and charm of the acclaimed author of *Love in a Cold Climate* and *The Sun King* was never more on display than in her brilliant correspondence with the likes of Evelyn Waugh, Harold Acton, Robert Byron, et al. A unique portrait of a fascinating era in literary history

EDITED BY CHARLOTTE MOSLEY

0-395-57041-7 HOUGHTON MIFFLIN $35.00

Blake **Morrison**

And When Did You Last See Your Father

0-312-13023-6 PICADOR.....................................$21.00
0-312-14273-0 PICADOR PB.................................$12.00

Nicholas **Mosley**

Rules of the Game Beyond the Pale: Memoirs of Sir Oswald Mosley and Family

The author of *Accident* tells the bizarre story of his father, Sir Oswald Mosley, who went from Labourite radicalism to the founding of the British Union of Fascists, while maintaining the tastes and interests of a country gentleman. "It is as a serene and sustained attempt by a son to understand a strange father that this book is chiefly remarkable...Lucky the father who has such a son to plead his cause" —*The Sunday Times* (London)

0-916583-75-9 DALKEY ARCHIVE $27.50

Malcolm **Muggeridge**

Something Beautiful for God

Memoirs

0-8027-2474-4 WALKER PB $9.95

V.S. **Naipaul**

Among the Believers: An Islamic Journey

A foremost novelist, essayist, and frequently controversial sociopolitical critic, born of Indian parents in Trinidad, but a British resident since the 1950s, provides commentary conducted through Iran, Pakistan, Malaysia, and Indonesia to the "Islamic Winter" of the final chapter

See also **FUNDAMENTALISM** under **CONTEMPORARY POLITICS AND SOCIETY** under **THE CONTEMPORARY MIDDLE EAST** in **WORLD HISTORY AND CURRENT AFFAIRS**

0-394-71195-5 RANDOM HOUSE PB $15.00

An Area of Darkness

Harsh observation of the subcontinent that met with little Indian popularity in the late 1960s

See also **INDIA** under **ASIA** under **TRAVEL LITERATURE** in **FOOD, TRAVEL, AND LEISURE**

0-14-002895-1 PENGUIN PB $11.95

India: A Million Mutinies Now

Naipaul's impassioned account of India, his ancestral country. Shaped by his obsession with the subcontinent, to him at once a homeland and an alien nation, this landmark achievement follows up on the book he wrote on first venturing there 30 years ago. "Naipaul's book partakes of the excellence of every category and fulfills itself in one of the oldest and rarest forms—prophecy. It bears witness, in unforgettable language, to the best of hopes in the worst of times"—*Christian Science Monitor*

See also **CURRENT AFFAIRS** under **NATIONALISM AND INDEPENDENCE** under **THE INDIAN SUBCONTINENT** in **WORLD HISTORY AND CURRENT AFFAIRS**

0-670-83702-4 VIKING $24.95

0-14-015680-1 PENGUIN PB $14.95

To awaken to history was to cease to live instinctively. It was to begin to see oneself and one's group the way the outside world saw one; and it was to know a kind of rage. India was now full of this rage. There had been a general awakening. But everyone awakened first to his own group or community; every group thought itself unique in its awakening; and every group sought to separate its rage from the rage of other groups.

INDIA: A MILLION MUTINIES NOW

V.S. Naipaul

Patrick **O'Brian**

Joseph Banks: A Life

O'Brian's 18th-century sea novels have been lionized by Delmore Schwartz, Iris Murdoch, Eudora Welty, and thousands of readers. But Sir Joseph Banks, the botanist and explorer whose eventful life included the discovery of Australia with Captain Cook, was O'Brian's true passion. Ten years in the writing, this fine biography "combines scholarship with a masterly gift" —Mary Renault

0-87923-930-1 GODINE $29.95

Blew fresh all last night which has given us a good deal of westing. This morn some sea weed floated past the ship and my servant declares that he saw a large beetle fly over her: I do not believe he would deceive me…

JOSEPH BANKS: A LIFE

George **Orwell**

A Collection of Essays

Includes such classics as "Such, Such Were the Joys," "Shooting an Elephant," "Politics and the English Language," and "Why I Write"

See also **NON-MARXIST SOCIALISM** under **POLITICAL THOUGHT** in **SOCIAL STUDIES**

0-15-618600-4 HARCOURT BRACE PB $11.00

Dickens, Dali and Others

0-15-626053-0 HARCOURT BRACE PB $8.95

Down and Out in Paris and London

Orwell's first published work, a worm's-eye-view of life as a kitchen hand in Paris and a tramp in London, peppered with some hard-earned insights on poverty

0-15-626224-X HARCOURT BRACE PB $7.95

Homage to Catalonia

Memoirs of fighting for the left-wing Spanish republican government

See also **THE SPANISH CIVIL WAR** under **20TH-CENTURY EUROPE TO THE SECOND WORLD WAR** in **WORLD HISTORY AND CURRENT AFFAIRS**

INTRODUCTION BY LIONEL TRILLING

0-15-642117-8 HARCOURT BRACE PB $8.00

The Road to Wigan Pier

A powerful account of unemployment and proletarian life in the north of England

See also **BRITAIN BETWEEN THE WARS** under **THE 20TH-CENTURY** under **GREAT BRITAIN AND IRELAND** in **WORLD HISTORY AND CURRENT AFFAIRS**

FOREWORD BY VICTOR GOLLANCZ

0-15-676750-3 HARCOURT BRACE PB $9.00

In Wigan I stayed for a while with a miner who was suffering from nystagmus. He could see across the room but not much further. He had been drawing compensation of twenty-nine shilling a week for the past nine months, but the colliery company were now talking of putting him on "partial compensation" of fourteen shilling a week … Watching this man go to the colliery to draw his compensation, I was struck by the profound differences that are made by status. Here was a man who had been half blinded in one of the most useful of all jobs and was drawing a pension to which he had a perfect right, if anybody has a right to anything. Yet he could not, so to speak, demand this pension—he could not, for instance, draw it when and how he wanted it. He had to go to the colliery once a week at a time named by the company, and when he got there he was kept waiting about for hours in the cold wind. For all I know he was also expected to touch his cap and show gratitude to whomever paid him; at any rate he had to waste an afternoon and spend sixpence in bus fares. It is very different for a member of the bourgeoisie, even such a down- at-heel member as I am. Even when I am on the verge of starvation I have certain rights attaching to my bourgeois status. I do not earn much more than a miner earns, but I do at least get it paid into my bank in a gentlemanly manner and can draw it out when I choose. And even when my account is exhausted the bank people are still passably polite.

THE ROAD TO WIGAN PIER

V.S. **Pritchett**

A Cab at the Door & Midnight Oil

0-679-60103-1 MODERN LIBRARY $16.00

Complete Collected Essays

Gore Vidal called Pritchett the "greatest English-language critic" of this century, Anthony Burgess hailed him "our best literary critic," and Frank Kermode believes Pritchett is "the finest English writer alive." This book of his memorable and important essays is indispensable to anyone interested in literature

0-679-41112-7 RANDOM HOUSE $35.00

Richard **Rayner**

The Blue Suit: A Memoir of Crime

This memoir by the *Granta* and *NY Times Magazine* writer tells the story of Rayner's strange and hilarious life of crime by which he supported his studies at Cambridge: stealing first-edition books, forging checks, and housebreaking

0-395-75288-4 HOUGHTON MIFFLIN $19.95

Richard Rayner

Jonathan **Raban**

Bad Land: An American Romance

See also **NORTH AMERICA** under **TRAVEL LITERATURE** in **FOOD, TRAVEL, AND LEISURE**

0-679-44254-5 PANTHEON $25.00

For Love and Money: A Writing Life

0-06-016166-3 HARPERCOLLINS $22.50

God, Man, and Mrs Thatcher

0-7011-3470-4 CHATTO & WINDUS PB $8.95

Salman **Rushdie**

Imaginary Homelands: Essays, Criticism, 1981-1991

Intense and elegant essays. "How literature of the highest order can serve the interests of our common humanity is freshly illustrated here" —Michael Foot, *The London Observer*

See also **INDIAN LITERATURE IN ENGLISH** under **LITERATURES OF INDIA** in **LITERATURE OF EUROPE, AFRICA, AND ASIA**

0-14-014036-0 PENGUIN PB $13.95

It may be that writers in my position, exiles or emigrants or expatriates, are haunted by some sense of loss, some urge to reclaim, to look back, even at the risk of being mutated into pillars of salt. But if we do look back, we must also do so in the knowledge—which gives rise to profound uncertainties—that our physical alienation from India almost inevitably means that we will not be capable of reclaiming precisely the thing that was lost; that we will, in short, create fictions, not actual cities or villages, but invisible ones, imaginary homelands, Indias of the mind.

IMAGINARY HOMELANDS: ESSAYS, CRITICISM 1981-1991

0-14-016894-X PENGUIN PB $12.50

Bertrand **Russell**

Mysticism and Logic & Other Essays

0-389-20135-9 BARNES & NOBLE PB $14.00

Philosophical Essays

See also **RUSSELL** under **PHILOSOPHY** in **RELIGION, SPIRITUALITY, AND PHILOSOPHY**

0-415-10579-X ROUTLEDGE PB $10.95

Why I Am Not a Christian & Other Essays on Religion and Related Subjects

Essays, 1899-1954, all centering on one deeply held belief: "I am as firmly convinced that religions do harm as I am that they are untrue"—Bertrand Russell

See also **SKEPTICISM AND ATHEISM** under **WORLD RELIGION** in **RELIGION, SPIRITUALITY, AND PHILOSOPHY**

0-671-20323-1 SIMON & SCHUSTER PB $12.00

Stevie **Smith**

A Very Pleasant Evening with Stevie Smith

0-8112-1295-5 NEW DIRECTIONS PB $8.95

Muriel **Spark**

Curriculum Vitae: An Autobiography

The celebrated author of 20 novels *(The Prime of Miss Jean Brodie, A Far Cry from Kensington)* remembers her disastrous marriage in Africa, wartime London, and the grim yet hopeful austerity in which she began her writing career. "A short cracker of a book, full of love and malice, black wit, intelligence and sharp perceptions and judgments" —*The Times* [London]

0-395-71093-6 HOUGHTON MIFFLIN PB.........$12.95

Stephen **Spender**

Journals: 1939-1983

0-19-505209-9 OLYMPIC PB $4.98

Letters to Christopher: Stephen Spender's Letters to Christopher Isherwood, 1929-1939

Includes *The Line of the Branch*

EDITED BY LEE BARTLETT

0-87685-470-6 BLACK SPARROW.....................$25.00

George Bernard **Shaw**

"It was clear from the start that Bernard Shaw was a man of ideas. Later it turned out that he was a fabulous entertainer. But few have granted that the two Shaws were one...The shock of that long career in the theater has still not been absorbed. Shaw has not yet neen seen in perspective."—Eric Bentley

Major Critical Essays

Includes *The Quintessence of Ibsenism, The Perfect Wagnerite,* and *The Sanity of Art*

INTRODUCTION BY MICHAEL HOLROYD

0-7812-0175-6 REPRINT SERVICES.................$79.00

George Bernard Shaw

World Within World: An Autobiography

Back in print after 12 years—and after the controversy over David Leavitt's appropriation of Spender's life story—this is a powerful classic and one of the most illuminating pictures of literary life in the '20s and '30s. We meet Virginia Woolf, Eliot, Auden, Isherwood, and many other now near-mythical luminaries, and come away with a fresh understanding of a fantastically fertile period of literary and cultural history

0-312-11358-7 ST. MARTIN'S PB $14.95

George **Steiner**

The Death of Tragedy

See also **LITERARY ESSAYISTS AND HISTORIANS** under **LITERARY CRITICISM** in **LITERATURE OF EUROPE, AFRICA, AND ASIA**

0-300-06916-2 YALE PB....................................$17.00

Lytton **Strachey**

Biographical Essays

Thirty-five essays, whose subjects include Frederick the Great, Voltaire, Gibbon, and Rousseau

0-15-612616-8 HARCOURT BRACE PB $6.95

Eminent Victorians

Quietly devastating thumbnail biographies of five quintessential high Victorians (Cardinal Manning, Dr. Arnold, Florence Nightingale, General Gordon, and of course Queen Victoria)

See also **EMINENT VICTORIANS: BIOGRAPHICAL STUDIES** under **GREAT BRITAIN AND IRELAND** in **WORLD HISTORY AND CURRENT AFFAIRS**

INTRODUCTION BY MICHAEL HOLROYD

0-15-628697-1 HARCOURT BRACE PB $10.00

Edward **Thomas**

The South Country

0-460-87291-5 EVERYMAN'S PB $6.95

William **Trevor**

Excursions in the Real World: Memoirs

Twenty-nine autobiographical vignettes that possess the craft and insight you would expect from this masterful writer

ILLUSTRATIONS BY LUCY WILLIS

0-679-43029-6 KNOPF $23.00

0-14-024029-2 PENGUIN PB $10.95

Kenneth **Tynan**

Letters

See also **ESSAYS AND CRITICISM** under **DRAMATIC THEORY AND CRITICISM** under **THEATER** in **PERFORMING ARTS AND MEDIA**

0-679-42610-8 RANDOM HOUSE.......................$30.00

Profiles

0-679-75639-6 RANDOM HOUSE PB $20.00

Denton **Welch**

A Voice Through a Cloud

An extraordinary book about the author's incomplete recovery after being hit by a car

1-87897-215-4 D.A.P. PB.......................................$13.95

Raymond **Williams**

The Country and the City

"A critical history of English literature from a stimulatingly original point of view"—*Nation*

See also **RECENT MARXIST CRITICISM** under **CULTURAL CRITICISM** under **LITERARY THEORY** in **LITERATURE OF EUROPE, AFRICA, AND ASIA**

0-19-519810-7 OXFORD PB $12.95

Culture and Revolution

0-86091-943-9 VERSO PB $19.95

Colin **Wilson**

The Essential Colin Wilson

0-89087-472-7 CELESTIAL ARTS PB $9.95

Colin **Wilson**

The Outsider

A work of popular philosophy, heavily influenced by Existentialism, which established Wilson's reputation when it appeared in 1956

0-87477-206-0 TARCHER PB $11.95

Jeanette **Winterson**

Art Objects: Essays on Ecstasy and Effrontery

Ten interlocking essays from "one of our most important writers in English" (*Washington Post*) center on the importance of the arts in our lives. From pieces on modernism, painting, autobiography, and the future of fiction to intimate reflections on her own work and books, *Art Objects* shows Winterson, again, as "a brilliant and deeply feeling artist at work"
—*San Francisco Chronicle*

0-679-44644-3 KNOPF....$21.00
0-679-76820-3 VINTAGE....$11.00

Leonard **Woolf**

The Autobiography of Leonard Woolf

Volume 1
Sowing, 1890-1904

0-15-683945-8 HARCOURT BRACE PB....$8.95

Volume 2
Growing, 1904-1911

0-15-637215-0 HARCOURT BRACE PB....$8.95

Volume 3
Beginning Again, 1911-1918

0-15-611680-4 HARCOURT BRACE PB....$8.95

Volume 4
Downhill All the Way, 1919-1939

0-15-626145-6 HARCOURT BRACE PB....$8.95

Volume 5
The Journey Not the Arrival Matters, 1939-1969

0-15-646523-X HARCOURT BRACE PB....$8.95

The Letters of Leonard Woolf

"Frederic Spotts, who has judiciously edited this volume, describes Woolf as a Briton 'whose scope and variety of accomplishments were equaled by few other Englishmen of the century.' To read these brilliant letters, 600 of them, selected from the 8,000 that survive, is to find confirmation of this view…He could be sharp or gentle; above all, we see him trying to be fair. He was a man who insisted on speaking the truth as he saw it"—Leon Edel, *NY Times Book Review*

EDITED BY FREDERIC SPOTTS
0-15-150915-8 HARCOURT BRACE PB....$32.95

Virginia **Woolf**

"Virginia Woolf stands as the chief figure of modernism in England and must be included with Joyce and Proust in the realization of experiments that have completely broken with tradition."—NY Times

Books and Portraits

0-15-613560-4 HARCOURT BRACE PB....$4.95

The Captain's Death Bed & Other Essays

Includes essays on Ruskin, Goldsmith, Turgenev, and Conrad. "Perhaps the greatest gift which Woolf possessed was the gift of stimulation. Everything that she touches shines with a fresh iridescence"—Harold Nicholson, *Observer*

0-15-615395-5 HARCOURT BRACE PB....$9.95

The Death of the Moth & Essays

"There is warmth and wit in her writing and at moments, as in the shorter papers on Shelley and Coleridge, a rare wondering tenderness towards great men of whom she could not quite approve"—*Saturday Review*

0-15-625234-1 HARCOURT BRACE PB....$7.95

The Diary of Virginia Woolf

Woolf's journal has already taken its place as one of the great English literary diaries, an unrivaled record of the growth of a writer's mind, and a crystalline portrait of the society of high modern English culture

Volume 1: 1915-1919

0-15-626036-0 HARCOURT BRACE PB....$15.00

Volume 2: 1920-1924

0-15-626037-9 HARCOURT BRACE PB....$14.00

Volume 3: 1925-1930

0-15-626038-7 HARCOURT BRACE PB....$11.95

Volume 5: 1936-1941

0-15-125603-9 HARCOURT BRACE....$19.95

Flush: A Biography

In this highly original exercise in point of view, Woolf undertakes to write the biography of Elizabeth Barrett Browning's cocker spaniel

0-15-631952-7 HARCOURT BRACE PB....$9.00

The Letters of Virginia Woolf

Volume 1: 1888-1912

0-15-650881-8 HARCOURT BRACE PB....$12.95

Volume 2: 1912-1922

0-15-650882-6 HARCOURT BRACE PB....$5.95

Volume 3: 1923-1928

0-15-650883-4 HARCOURT BRACE PB....$5.95

Volume 4: 1929-1931

0-15-650884-2 HARCOURT BRACE PB....$15.00

Volume 6: 1936-1941

0-15-650887-7 HARCOURT BRACE PB....$9.95

A Moment's Liberty: The Shorter Diary

A compact condensation of the original five-volume edition of Woolf's journals, written between 1915 and 1941. "The self-charting of an extraordinarily vibrant personality—fresh, alive, restless, brilliant"—*Publishers Weekly*

EDITED BY ANNE OLIVIER BELL
0-15-661912-1 HARCOURT BRACE PB....$18.00

A Passionate Apprentice: Early Journals, 1897-1909

Woolf's seven journals, written before she began to keep a regular diary, date from 1897, when she was fourteen and recovering from a breakdown following her mother's death. These writings are important not only for what they reveal of her early life, but for their documentation of her beginnings as an author

0-15-171287-5 HARCOURT BRACE....$24.95
0-15-671160-5 HARCOURT BRACE PB....$14.95

A Room of One's Own

"Future historians will place Mrs. Woolf's little book beside Mary Wollstonecraft's *A Vindication of the Rights of Women* and John Stuart Mill's *The Subjection of Women.* It does for the intellectual and spiritual liberation of women what these works did for their political emancipation. But *A Room of One's Own* outshines them both in genius"—*Spectator*

0-15-178733-6 HARCOURT BRACE....$16.00

The First Common Reader

See also **THE MODERNIST REVOLUTION** under **LITERARY CRITICISM** in **LITERATURE OF EUROPE, AFRICA, AND ASIA**

0-15-619806-1 HARCOURT BRACE PB....$10.00

The Second Common Reader

On English literature, with a special interest in women writers. "As nearly perfect as Heaven grants it to a critic to be"—*NY Times*

See also **THE MODERNIST REVOLUTION** under **LITERARY CRITICISM** in **LITERATURE OF EUROPE, AFRICA, AND ASIA**

0-15-619808-8 HARCOURT BRACE PB....$7.95

Three Guineas

0-15-690177-3 HARCOURT BRACE PB....$8.00

The Virginia Woolf Reader

An abundant selection from Woolf's fiction and non-fiction

See also **THE EARLY 20TH-CENTURY** under **20TH-CENTURY BRITISH AND IRISH FICTION**

EDITED BY MITCHELL A. LEASKA
0-15-693590-2 HARCOURT BRACE PB....$12.95

Women and Writing

EDITED BY MICHELE BARRETT
0-15-693658-5 HARCOURT BRACE PB....$11.00

A Writer's Diary: Being Extracts from the Diary of Virginia Woolf

"I have never read any book that conveyed more truthfully what a writer's life was like"
—W.H. Auden

EDITED BY LEONARD WOOLF
0-15-698380-X HARCOURT BRACE PB....$13.00

Celtic Literature

The British Isles are home to literary traditions independent of, but often influential upon, English. The Celtic languages dominated Britain for centuries before the ascendancy of English, and (with some exceptions) they continue not only to exist but also to support thriving and highly distinctive literatures.

In the early Middle Ages, Ireland had perhaps the most accomplished and sophisticated literature in Europe, with a rich tradition of lyric poetry and highly developed narratives, at once heroic and sardonic, like the stories in the *Tain*. By the 9th-century Welsh literature had produced the epic *Gododdin*, several complete cycles of bardic poetry, the wealth of narrative material that would form the basis of the King Arthur stories, and the beginnings of the collection of prose tales later famous as the *Mabinogion*. Welsh, Irish, and Scottish Gaelic all boast important contemporary writers who continue to work in these languages.

Gerald of Wales

The History and Topography of Ireland

Realism and fantasy alternate in this none-too-flattering early description of Ireland

0-14-044423-8 PENGUIN PB....$10.95

Seamus **Deane**, editor

The Field Day Anthology of Irish Writing

Three beautiful volumes capture the best of Irish literature from the seventh century to the present. "If you're interested in Ireland, forgo two meals on the town and buy the set" —Hugh Kenner, *NY Times Book Review*

0-393-03046-6 NORTON $150.00

Jeffrey **Gantz**, translator

Early Irish Myths and Sagas

See also **BRITISH AND CELTIC** under **EUROPEAN MYTHOLOGY** under **MYTHOLOGY AND FOLKLORE** in **RELIGION, SPIRITUALITY, AND PHILOSOPHY**

0-14-044397-5 PENGUIN PB $9.95

The Mabinogion

The classic collection of medieval Welsh tales, ranging from very early and rather primitive stories to elaborate Arthurian romances

See also **MEDIEVAL LITERATURE** in **LITERATURE OF EUROPE, AFRICA, AND ASIA**

0-14-044322-3 PENGUIN PB $6.95

Seamus **Heaney**, translator

Sweeney Astray

"It takes a superb poet to capture, in translation from the Irish, the full range of pain and beauty in Sweeney's poetry. Seamus Heaney has produced an exhilarating version of this most unusual story poem"—Brendan Kennelly, *NY Times*

See also **IRISH POETS** under **20TH-CENTURY BRITISH AND IRISH POETRY**

0-374-51894-7 FS&G PB $9.00

Kenneth Hartstone **Jackson**, editor

A Celtic Miscellany

Prose and verse from six Celtic languages, including bardic elegies, heroic tales, and the literature of love

0-14-044247-2 PENGUIN PB $12.95

Gwyn **Jones**, editor

The Oxford Book of Welsh Verse in English

0-19-211858-7 OXFORD $35.00

Brendan **Kennelly**, editor

The Penguin Book of Irish Verse

Includes translations from Gaelic and English-language writing

0-14-058526-5 VIKING PB $12.95

Thomas **Kinsella**, editor & translator

The New Oxford Book of Irish Verse

See also **ANTHOLOGIES** under **20TH-CENTURY BRITISH AND IRISH POETRY**

0-19-211868-4 OXFORD $30.00
0-19-282643-3 OXFORD PB $14.95

Thomas **Kinsella**, translator

The Tain

An elegantly designed edition of the early Irish heroic tales, in a translation by a leading contemporary poet

0-19-281090-1 OXFORD PB $14.95

John **MacQueen** & Tom **Scott**, editors

The Oxford Book of Scottish Verse

0-19-282600-X OXFORD PB $14.95

Sorley **MacLean**

From Wood to Ridge: Collected Poems in Gaelic and English

0-85635-844-4 CARCANET $51.95

Alywn **Rees** & Brinley **Rees**

Celtic Heritage: Ancient Tradition in Ireland and Wales

"What the Grimm brothers are to fairy tales and philology, the Rees brothers are to Celtic culture"—*Seattle Post Intelligencer*

0-500-27039-2 THAMES & HUDSON PB $12.95

W.B. **Yeats**, editor

Fairy and Folk Tales of Ireland

Fairies, leprechauns, ghosts, witches, princesses, devils, and others, compiled by Yeats in the 1880s

See also **FOLKLORE** under **MYTHOLOGY AND FOLKLORE** in **RELIGION, SPIRITUALITY, AND PHILOSOPHY**

FOREWORD BY BENEDICT KIELY

0-02-055640-3 MACMILLAN PB $11.00

Anthologies and Studies

General Anthologies

M. H. **Abrams**, editor

The Norton Anthology of English Literature: The Major Authors

0-393-96803-0 NORTON $41.95
0-393-96808-1 NORTON PB $39.95

Frank **Kermode** & John **Hollander**, editors

The Oxford Anthology of English Literature

Volume 1: The Middle Ages Through the Eighteenth Century

0-19-501657-2 OXFORD PB $32.00

Volume 2: 1800 to the Present

0-19-501658-0 OXFORD PB $32.00

Poetry

Kingsley **Amis**, editor

The New Oxford Book of Light Verse

0-19-211862-5 OXFORD $35.00

W.H. **Auden**, editor

The Oxford Book of Light Verse

0-19-282075-3 OXFORD PB $12.95

Donald **Davie**, editor

The New Oxford Book of Christian Verse

0-19-213426-4 OXFORD PB $30.00

Helen **Gardner**, editor

The New Oxford Book of English Verse

0-19-812136-9 OXFORD $45.00

John **Gross**, editor

The Oxford Book of Comic Verse

0-19-214207-0 OXFORD $30.00
0-19-283207-7 OXFORD PB $13.95

Francis T. **Palgrave** & John **Press**, editors

The Golden Treasury of the Best Songs and Lyrical Poems in the English Language

A classic anthology from the 19th-century. Updated.

0-19-282035-4 OXFORD PB $10.95

Francis T. **Palgrave**, editor

The Golden Treasury of the Best Songs and Lyrical Poems in the English Language

0-14-042364-8 PENGUIN PB $11.95

Drama

Sylvan **Barnet**, editor

The Genius of the Early English Theatre

Includes *Abraham and Isaac, The Second Shepherd's Play, Everyman, Doctor Faustus, Macbeth, Volpone,* and *Samson Agonistes*

0-452-01164-7 NEW AMERICAN LIBRARY PB ... $14.95

Janet M. **Morrell**, editor

Four English Comedies

Includes *Volpone, The Way of the World, She Stoops to Conquer,* and *The School for Scandal*

0-14-043158-6 PENGUIN PB $9.95

Fiction

Malcolm **Bradbury**, editor

The Penguin Book of Modern British Short Stories

0-14-006306-4 PENGUIN PB $12.95

John **Sutherland**, editor

The Oxford Book of English Love Stories

Love in all its guises—marital, adulterous, platonic, religious, and erotic—is the unifying principle for this collection of stories by Mary Shelley, Anthony Trollope, V.S. Pritchett, Sylvia Plath, Paul Theroux, and many, many others. A delightful, mysterious, and complex compilation

0-19-214237-2 OXFORD $25.00

William **Trevor**, editor

The Oxford Book of Irish Short Stories

0-19-214180-5 OXFORD $35.00
0-19-282845-2 OXFORD PB $13.95

William Trevor

General Histories and Studies

Robert M. **Adams**
The Land and Literature of England: A Historical Account
0-393-30343-8 NORTON PB $17.95

Douglas **Bush**
Mythology and the Romantic Tradition in English Poetry
0-674-59825-3 HARVARD $35.00

Denis **Donoghue**
We Irish: Essays on Irish Literature and Society
See also **IRELAND** under **GREAT BRITAIN AND IRELAND** in **WORLD HISTORY AND CURRENT AFFAIRS**
0-520-06425-9 CALIFORNIA PB $14.00

Margaret Anne **Doody**
The True Story of the Novel
See also **NARRATIVE** under **LITERARY CRITICISM** in **LITERATURE OF EUROPE, AFRICA, AND ASIA**
0-8135-2168-8 RUTGERS $44.95

Dorothy **Eagle** & Carnell **Hilary**, editors
The Oxford Literary Guide to the British Isles
0-19-283133-X OXFORD PB $13.95

Margaret **Drabble**, editor
The Oxford Companion to English Literature
The fifth edition of the reference book that every book lover needs: revised, updated, expanded to include topics ranging from comic strips and children's literature to the Beat Generation and Saussurean linguistics
0-19-866221-1 OXFORD $55.00

Philip **Edwards**
Threshold of a Nation: A Study in English and Irish Drama
0-521-27695-0 CAMBRIDGE PB $17.95

Avrom **Fleishman**
The English Historical Novel: Walter Scott to Virginia Woolf
0-8018-1433-2 JOHNS HOPKINS PB $14.95

Ford Madox **Ford**
The English Novel
0-85635-480-5 CARCANET PB $12.50

E.M. **Forster**
Aspects of the Novel
A classic discussion of the techniques and structure of fiction, with a focus on craft
See also **20TH-CENTURY BRITISH ESSAYS AND OTHER PROSE**
0-15-609180-1 HARCOURT BRACE PB $7.95

C.S. **Lewis**
Studies in Words
0-521-39831-2 CAMBRIDGE PB $11.95

Ian **Ousby**, editor
The Cambridge Guide to Literature in English
0-521-44086-6 CAMBRIDGE $49.95

John **Richetti**, editor
The Columbia History of the British Novel
0-231-07858-7 COLUMBIA $69.95

Christopher **Ricks**
The Force of Poetry
"Exactly the kind of critic every poet dreams of finding"—W.H. Auden
See also **POETRY** under **LITERARY CRITICISM** in **LITERATURE OF EUROPE, AFRICA, AND ASIA**
0-19-282046-X OXFORD PB $12.95

Christopher **Ricks**, editor
English Drama to 1710
A volume in the New History of Literature series
0-87226-127-1 BEDRICK LIBRARY EDITION $39.50

Pat **Rogers**, editor
The Oxford Illustrated History of English Literature
0-19-812816-9 OXFORD $49.95

George **Sampson**
The Concise Cambridge History of English Literature
0-521-09581-6 CAMBRIDGE PB $34.95

James **Sutherland**, editor
The Oxford Book of Literary Anecdotes
0-19-281936-4 OXFORD PB $8.95

Robert **Welch**, editor
The Oxford Companion to Irish Literature
0-19-866158-4 CLARENDON $55.00

Carl **Woodring**, editor
The Columbia History of British Poetry
0-231-07838-2 COLUMBIA $59.95

Specialized Studies

Anglo-Saxon and Medieval

C.S. **Lewis**
Studies in Medieval and Renaissance Literature
0-521-29701-X CAMBRIDGE PB $19.95

A.C. **Spearing**
Medieval to Renaissance in English Poetry
0-521-31533-6 CAMBRIDGE PB $27.95

From the Elizabethan Age to the Commonwealth

Julia **Briggs**
This Stage Play World: English Literature and Its Background, 1580-1625
0-19-289134-0 OXFORD PB $17.95

C.S. **Lewis**
Poetry and Prose in the Sixteenth Century
0-19-812231-4 CLARENDON $65.00

Christopher **Ricks**, editor
English Prose and Poetry: 1540-1674
0-87226-126-3 BEDRICK LIBRARY EDITION $39.50

E.M. **Tillyard**
The Elizabethan World Picture
0-394-70162-3 RANDOM HOUSE PB $5.31

Basil **Willey**
The Seventeenth Century Background: Studies in the Thought of the Age in Relation to Poetry and Religion
0-231-01395-7 COLUMBIA $53.50

The Restoration and the 18th-Century

Marilyn **Butler**
Romantics, Rebels, and Reactionaries: English Literature and Its Background, 1760 to 1830
0-19-520384-4 OXFORD $27.00
0-19-289132-4 OXFORD PB $19.95

Leopold **Damrosch**, editor
Modern Essays on Eighteenth-Century Literature
0-19-504924-1 OXFORD PB $19.95

Roger **Lonsdale**, editor

Dryden to Johnson

A volume in the New History of Literature series

0-87226-128-X BEDRICK LIBRARY EDITION.....$39.50

The 19th-century

Meyer H. **Abrams**

The Correspondent Breeze: Essays on English Romanticism

0-393-01837-7 NORTON $22.50

The Mirror and the Lamp: Romantic Theory and the Critical Tradition

See also **POSTWAR TO POSTMODERNISM** under **LITERARY THEORY** in **LITERATURE OF EUROPE, AFRICA, AND ASIA**

0-19-501471-5 OXFORD PB $14.95

Harold **Bloom**

The Visionary Company: A Reading of English Romantic Poetry

0-8014-9117-7 CORNELL PB $16.95

C. Maurice **Bowra**

The Romantic Imagination

0-19-281006-5 OXFORD PB $17.95

Julie A. **Carlson**

In the Theatre of Romanticism: Coleridge, Nationalism, Women

0-521-44428-4 CAMBRIDGE $52.95

Richard **Foulkes**, editor

British Theatre in the 1890's: Essays on Drama and the Stage

0-521-41478-4 CAMBRIDGE $65.00

George **Levine**

Darwin and the Novelists: Patterns of Science in Victorian Fiction

0-674-19285-0 HARVARD $35.00

0-226-47574-3 CHICAGO PB $19.50

Anthony **Jenkins**

The Making of Victorian Drama

0-521-40205-0 CAMBRIDGE $69.95

Debra N. **Mancoff**

The Return of King Arthur: The Legend Through Victorian Eyes

See also **THE PRE-RAPHAELITES** under **ENGLAND** under **EUROPEAN ART: 1750-1900** in **ART**

0-8109-3782-4 ABRAMS $35.00

Arthur **Pollard**, editor

The Victorians

A volume in the New History of Literature series

0-87226-130-1 BEDRICK LIBRARY EDITION.....$39.50

Daniel P. **Watkins**

A Materialist Critique of English Romantic Drama

0-8130-1240-6 FLORIDA $49.95

0-8130-1241-4 FLORIDA PB $18.95

The 20th-century

Noel **Annan**

Our Age: English Intellectuals Between the World Wars—a Group Portrait

A fresh look at the impact "the war to end all wars" and the Depression had on Britain's intellectuals

0-394-54295-9 RANDOM HOUSE $30.00

John **Bull**

Stage Right: Crisis and Recovery in British Contemporary Mainstream Theatre

0-312-12026-5 ST. MARTIN'S $39.95

0-312-12029-X ST. MARTIN'S PB $16.95

Richard **Ellman**

Four Dubliners: Wilde, Yeats, Joyce and Beckett

0-8076-1185-9 BRAZILLER $12.95

Paul **Fussell**

The Great War and Modern Memory

A classic study of the First World War and its literature

0-19-501918-0 OXFORD $27.50

Shusha **Guppy**

Looking Back: A Panoramic View of a Literary Age by the Grandes Dames of European Letters

A quirky, highly entertaining series of interviews, in the style of *The Paris Review* with such figures as Molly Keane, Rosamond Lehmann, Kathleen Raine, Lesley Blanch, P.L. Travers (the creator of Mary Poppins), and Diana Mosley (wife of England's leading Fascist)

0-945167-30-X BRITISH AMERICAN $23.95

Suddenly there she was—plain, vain, capricious, able to perform miracles for the children. But despite her plainness, she appeals to men. A friend once said to me: "Don't expect me to read *Mary Poppins,* I hate children's books!" Nevertheless I sent the book to him. "Why didn't you *tell* me!" he wrote, "Mary Poppins with her cool, green core of sex has enthralled me for ever!"—*P.L. Travers*

LOOKING BACK: A PANORAMIC VIEW OF A LITERARY AGE BY THE GRANDES DAMES OF EUROPEAN LETTERS

Robert **Hewison**

In Anger: British Culture in the Cold War, 1945-1960

0-19-520238-4 OLYMPIC $5.98

Samuel **Hynes**

The Auden Generation: Literature and Politics in England in the 1930s

0-691-06516-0 PRINCETON $52.00

Hugh **Kenner**

A Colder Eye: The Modern Irish Writers

0-8018-3838-X JOHNS HOPKINS PB $13.95

S.P. **Rosenbaum**, editor

The Bloomsbury Group: A Collection of Memoirs, Commentary and Criticism

0-8020-6268-7 TORONTO PB $21.95

John I. **Stewart**

Writers of the Early 20th Century

Studies of Hardy, James, Shaw, Conrad, Kipling, Yeats, Joyce, and Lawrence

0-19-812240-3 OXFORD $59.00

Poetry

Cleanth **Brooks**

The Well Wrought Urn: Studies in the Structure of Poetry

Detailed commentaries on ten British poets from Elizabethan times to the 20th-century, including Donne, Shakespeare, Milton, Pope, Wordsworth, Keats, and Yeats

See also **POETRY** under **LITERARY CRITICISM** in **LITERATURE OF EUROPE, AFRICA, AND ASIA**

See also **THE NEW CRITICISM** under **LITERARY CRITICISM** in **LITERATURE OF EUROPE, AFRICA, AND ASIA**

0-15-695705-1 HARCOURT BRACE PB $12.00

John **Hollander**

Rhyme's Reason: A Guide to English Verse

An introduction to verse forms, with clever examples

0-300-04306-6 YALE $25.00

William K. **Wimsatt**

The Verbal Icon: Studies in the Meaning of Poetry

Combines theoretical vigor with precise case studies

See also **THE NEW CRITICISM** under **LITERARY THEORY** in **LITERATURE OF EUROPE, AFRICA, AND ASIA**

0-8131-0111-5 KENTUCKY PB $15.95

David **Perkins**

A History of Modern Poetry Volume 1: From the 1890s to the High Modernist Mode

A judicious and well-informed survey, gracefully written

See also **POETRY** under **GENERAL STUDIES: THE 20TH-CENTURY** under **AMERICAN LITERATURE: ANTHOLOGIES AND CRITICAL STUDIES** in **LITERATURE OF THE AMERICAS**

0-674-39945-5 HARVARD PB $20.00

Volume 2: Modernism and After

0-674-39947-1 HARVARD PB $20.00

Christopher **Ricks**

The Force of Poetry

0-19-818326-7 OXFORD PB $18.95

The Reader's Catalog
250 West 57th Street
New York, NY 10107

Studies of Individual Authors

Medieval and Renaissance

H.S. **Bennett**

Chaucer and the Fifteenth Century

0-19-812229-2 OXFORD $60.00

Derek **Pearsall**

The Life of Geoffrey Chaucer

1-55786-665-1 BLACKWELL PB $19.95

D.W. **Robertson**, Jr.

Preface to Chaucer: Studies in Medieval Perspective

0-691-01294-6 PRINCETON PB $27.95

Amy M. **Charles**

A Life of George Herbert

0-8014-1014-2 CORNELL $29.95

David **Riggs**

Ben Jonson: A Life

0-674-06625-1 HARVARD $37.50
0-674-06626-X HARVARD PB $16.95

Charles **Nicholl**

The Reckoning: The Murder of Christopher Marlowe

0-226-58024-5 CHICAGO PB $14.95

Anthony **Kenny**

Thomas More

A biography of the humanist and Catholic martyr by a prolific and wide-ranging British philosopher

See also **SAINTS** under **BIOGRAPHIES** under **CHRISTIANITY** in **RELIGION, SPIRITUALITY, AND PHILOSOPHY**

0-19-287573-6 OXFORD PB $7.95

Shakespeare

Jonathan **Bate** & others, editors

Shakespeare: An Illustrated Stage History

0-19-812372-8 OXFORD $39.95

Samuel **Johnson**

On Shakespeare

Johnson contradicted 18th-century critical opinion which had compared Shakespeare unfavorably to classical drama in these works—originally introductions to his own annotated edition of Shakespeare. He also advised readers to skip the lengthy notes when first reading the plays

0-14-053020-7 PENGUIN PB $8.95

Eric **Sams**

The Real Shakespeare: Retrieving the Early Years, 1564-1594

0-300-06129-3 YALE $32.50

Jan **Kott**

Shakespeare Our Contemporary

This important political interpretation of Shakespeare's plays has influenced Peter Brook and a host of Eastern European directors active in America today

See also **ESSAYS AND CRITICISM** under **DRAMATIC THEORY AND CRITICISM** under **THEATER** in **PERFORMING ARTS AND MEDIA**

INTRODUCTION BY MARTIN ESSLIN

0-393-00736-7 NORTON PB $13.95

A.C. **Bradley**

Shakespearean Tragedy: Lectures on Hamlet, Othello, King Lear, Macbeth

A classic of Shakespearean criticism

INTRODUCTION BY JOHN R. BROWN

0-7812-7298-X REPRINT SERVICES $99.00
0-312-07923-0 ST. MARTIN'S $45.00

Anthony **Burgess**

Shakespeare

1-56663-056-8 DEE PB $13.95

John **Drakakis**, editor

Alternative Shakespeare

0-415-02528-1 ROUTLEDGE PB $17.95

Terry **Eagleton**

William Shakespeare

0-631-14554-0 BLACKWELL PB $16.95

Philip **Edwards**

Shakespeare: A Writer's Progress

0-19-219184-5 OXFORD $35.00
0-19-289166-9 OXFORD PB $13.95

Russell **Fraser**

Shakespeare: The Later Years

The follow-up to Fraser's eloquent volume on Shakespeare's early life. It opens with the bard's completion of *Romeo and Juliet* at the age of 30, and chronicles his most productive years as a playwright. "Russell Fraser lifts William Shakespeare out of time-encrusted mosaics of 'little facts' to create a flesh and blood late Renaissance man"—Leon Edel

0-231-06766-6 COLUMBIA $34.50

Young Shakespeare

0-231-06764-X COLUMBIA $39.50

Northrop **Frye**

Frye was one of the most distinguished literary theorists of the second half of the 20th century

A Natural Perspective: The Development of Shakespearean Comedy and Romance

0-231-08271-1 COLUMBIA PB $12.00
0-15-665414-8 HARCOURT BRACE PB $6.95

Northrop Frye on Shakespeare

EDITED BY ROBERT SANDLER

0-300-03711-2 YALE $32.00
0-300-04208-6 YALE PB $12.00

René **Girard**

A Theatre of Envy: William Shakespeare

A distinguished critic's often surprising new interpretation of the emotional meanings of Shakespeare's plays

0-19-505339-7 OXFORD $29.95

Stephen **Greenblatt**

Shakespearean Negotiations: The Circulation of Social Energy in Renaissance England

0-520-06160-8 CALIFORNIA PB $14.95

Germaine **Greer**

Shakespeare

0-19-287538-8 OXFORD PB $8.95

Graham **Holderness**, editor

The Shakespearean Myth

0-7190-1488-3 MANCHESTER $49.95

Dennis **Kay**

Shakespeare: His Life, Work, and Era

"[A] masterly study…All that is known about William Shakespeare can be found in this volume"—*New Yorker*

0-688-13225-1 QUILL PB $12.00

G. Wilson **Knight**

The Wheel of Fire: Interpretations of Shakespearean Tragedy

An influential study of Shakespeare's use of symbolism

0-416-67620-0 ROUTLEDGE PB $14.95

Jan **Kott**

The Bottom Translation: Marlowe and Shakespeare and the Carnival Traditions

TRANSLATED BY DANIELA MIEDZYRZECKA & LILLIAN VALLEE

0-8101-0737-6 NORTHWESTERN $32.95
0-8101-0738-4 NORTHWESTERN PB $14.95

Samuel **Schoenbaum**

William Shakespeare: A Compact Documentary Life

0-19-505161-0 OXFORD PB $16.95

Marvin **Spevack**, editor

The Harvard Concordance to Shakespeare

3-487-04852-3 LUBRECHT & CRAMER $225.00

Caroline **Spurgeon**

Shakespeare's Imagery

0-521-09258-2 CAMBRIDGE PB $29.95

Gary **Taylor**

Reinventing Shakespeare: A Cultural History, 1642-1986

How Shakespeare came to dominate the canon

0-19-506679-0 OXFORD PB $14.95

Garry **Wills**

Witches and Jesuits: Shakespeare's Macbeth

Reconsiders the tragedy in light of the politics of Shakespeare's time

0-19-508879-4 OXFORD $23.00
0-19-510290-8 OXFORD PB $11.95

Louis **Zukofsky**
Bottom: On Shakespeare
0-520-04851-2 CALIFORNIA PB $17.00

The Restoration and the 18th-Century

Conor Cruise **O'Brien**
The Great Melody: A Thematic Biography of Edmund Burke
See also **BIOGRAPHY** under **THE 18TH-CENTURY** under **GREAT BRITAIN AND IRELAND** in **WORLD HISTORY AND CURRENT AFFAIRS**
0-226-61651-7 CHICAGO PB $24.95

Paula **Backscheider**
Daniel Defoe: His Life
0-8018-3785-5 JOHNS HOPKINS $60.00
0-8018-4512-2 JOHNS HOPKINS........................$19.95

John **Carey**
John Donne: Life, Mind and Art
0-571-14337-7 FABER PB $9.95

George **McFadden**
Dryden the Public Writer, 1660-1685
0-691-06350-8 PRINCETON..............................$39.50

James A. **Winn**
John Dryden and His World
0-300-02994-2 YALE $50.00
0-300-04591-3 YALE PB $23.00

Maynard **Mack**
Alexander Pope: A Life
0-393-02208-0 NORTON $25.95
0-393-30529-5 NORTON PB $14.95

Patricia B. **Craddock**
Edward Gibbon: Luminous Historian, 1772-1794
The long-awaited second volume of this masterly biography relates the 20 years of work on the *Decline and Fall* to the incidents of Gibbon's own life
See also **ANCIENT ROME** in **WORLD HISTORY AND CURRENT AFFAIRS**
0-8018-3720-0 JOHNS HOPKINS $39.95

Young Edward Gibbon
See also **ANCIENT ROME** in **WORLD HISTORY AND CURRENT AFFAIRS**
0-8018-2714-0 JOHNS HOPKINS $42.50

Walter Jackson **Bate**
Samuel Johnson
Unfortunately, this landmark biography of Johnson is currently out of print
0-15-679259-1 HARCOURT BRACE PB $10.95

Richard **Holmes**
Dr. Johnson & Mr. Savage
A fascinating examination of the often misunderstood, affectionate relationship between the rakish poet and an upstanding critic
0-679-75770-8 VINTAGE PB $13.00

Christopher **Ricks**
Milton's Grand Style
0-19-812090-7 OXFORD PB...............................$16.95

Daniel **Danielson**, editor
The Cambridge Companion to Milton
0-521-33402-0 CAMBRIDGE.............................$59.95
0-521-36885-5 CAMBRIDGE PB.........................$17.95

Arthur **Cash**
Laurence Sterne: The Early and Middle Years
0-415-08033-9 ROUTLEDGE PB $24.95

Laurence Sterne: The Later Years
0-415-08032-0 ROUTLEDGE PB $22.95

Claire **Tomalin**
The Life and Death of Mary Wollstonecraft
A biography of Wollstonecraft (1759-1797), whose *A Vindication of the Rights of Women* remains a feminist classic, and whose unconventional life led her from the most exalted literary circles of the day, to revolutionary France, to an early death giving birth to her daughter, Mary Wollstonecraft Shelly
0-14-016761-7 PENGUIN PB $12.95

The 19th-century

Park **Honan**
Matthew Arnold: A Life
0-674-55465-5 HARVARD PB $17.95

Lionel **Trilling**
Matthew Arnold
0-15-657734-8 HARCOURT BRACE PB...............$6.95

Tony **Tanner**
Jane Austen
0-674-47174-1 HARVARD PB $15.50

Peter **Ackroyd**
Blake: A Biography
The renowned biographer of Dickens and T.S. Eliot brings William Blake to life. Born in 1757, the artist's strange aloofness and tendency toward the supernatural left many in his own time and since doubting his sanity, all the while admitting the brilliance of his poetic and artistic visions. Now, Ackroyd places Blake in the context of an 18th-century London inflamed with radicalism and mysticism, and proposes a new understanding of his life and art. Includes 16 pages of black-and-white and 24 pages of color illustrations
0-679-40967-X KNOPF $35.00

S. Foster **Damon**
A Blake Dictionary: Ideas and Symbols of William Blake
FOREWORD BY MORRIS EAVES
0-87451-436-3 BROWN PB...............................$24.00

David V. **Erdman**
Blake: Prophet Against Empire
0-486-26719-9 DOVER PB $15.95

Northrop **Frye**
Fearful Symmetry: A Study of William Blake
0-691-01291-1 PRINCETON PB..........................$17.95

William Blake

Kathleen **Raine**
William Blake
A brief but informative introduction; the visionary artist viewed in the context of the Greek revival
See also **ENGLAND** under **EUROPEAN ART: 1750-1900** in **ART**
0-500-20107-2 THAMES & HUDSON PB $14.95

E.P. **Thompson**
Witness Against the Beast: William Blake and the Moral Law
The great historian of the English working class examines Blake's relation to the world of religious and political dissent
1-56584-058-5 NEW PRESS $30.00
1-56584-099-2 NEW PRESS PB.........................$17.00

E.P. Thompson (credit: ©Michael Bennett)

Juliet **Barker**
The Brontës
A mad father, a wastrel brother, and three gifted sisters: this much of the Brontës's story is well

known. Here, Juliet Barker looks behind this familiar picture to provide an unprecedented psychological portrait of a unique family. "An outstanding achievement, a magnificent portrait which not only contains a wealth of new material, but is also a delight to read"—*The Times* [London]. "The finest biography I have read for many years"—*The Literary Review*

0-312-13445-2 ST. MARTIN'S....$35.00
0-312-14555-1 ST. MARTIN'S PB....$24.95

The very ordinariness of the surroundings makes the Brontës' achievements all the more extraordinary. They had neither wealth nor power and therefore lacked the richness and diversity of experience which these can bring; what they did have was the vicarious experience of books and an irrepressible creativity which more than supplied their place. More than any thing else, however, they had each other.
THE BRONTËS

Lyndall **Gordon**
Charlotte Brontë: A Passionate Life
A good concise biography
0-393-31448-0 NORTON PB....$17.00

Edward **Chitham**
A Life of Emily Brontë
0-631-18629-8 BLACKWELL PB....$19.95

Phyllis **Bentley**
The Brontës
0-8383-2096-1 HASKELL....$75.00

Rebecca **Fraser**
The Brontës
0-449-90465-2 FAWCETT PB....$14.00

Clyde de L. **Ryals**
The Life of Robert Browning: A Critical Biography
0-631-20093-2 BLACKWELL PB....$19.95

Fred **Kaplan**
Thomas Carlyle: A Biography
0-8014-1508-X CORNELL....$54.50
0-520-08200-1 CALIFORNIA PB....$17.95

Michael **Bakewell**
Lewis Carroll: A Biography
This new biography of the Reverend Charles Lutwidge Dodgson—Lewis Carroll—reveals the complex and contradictory character of Alice's creator. Relentlessly active, Carroll lived in a world of puzzles, mathematical and logical problems, tricks and games, and the original genius of Alice's adventures came almost effortlessly from his fertile mind. Meanwhile, his love of little girls was the joy and tragedy of his life. A fascinating account of a mysterious and mythical figure
0-393-03906-4 NORTON....$27.50

Morton N. **Cohen**
Lewis Carroll: A Biography
0-87745-231-8 IOWA....$32.95
0-679-42298-6 KNOPF....$35.00

Robert **Gittings** & others
Claire Clairemont and the Shelleys
The story of Clairemont, Mary Shelly's step-sister, who had a affairs with both Byron and Shelley
0-19-818351-8 OXFORD PB....$21.00

Basil **Willey**
Samuel Taylor Coleridge
0-393-00696-4 NORTON PB....$2.95

William M. **Clarke**
The Secret Life of Wilkie Collins
The author of *The Moonstone* and *The Woman in White* also led a private life calculated to shock Victorian sensibilities. "A literary coup...Casts a fresh beam of light on the great, dark seam of Victorian sexual mores"—*The Observer*
0-929587-51-0 DEE....$24.95

Catherine **Peters**
The King of Inventors: A Life of Wilkie Collins
The most thorough and informative biography of this enigmatic figure
0-691-03392-7 PRINCETON....$35.00

Michael **Allen**
Charles Dickens' Childhood
0-312-01275-6 ST. MARTIN'S....$39.95

Edgar **Johnson**
Charles Dickens: His Tragedy and Triumph
The standard account
0-14-058027-1 VIKING....$12.95

Gordon S. **Haight**
George Eliot
0-14-016632-7 PENGUIN PB....$12.95

Frederick **Karl**
George Eliot: Voice of a Century
Linking her energetic and controversial life with the themes of her work, Karl shows an obsessively curious writer who precisely captured the ethos of Victorian England
0-393-03785-1 NORTON....$30.00
0-393-31521-5 NORTON PB....$18.00

Marghanita **Laski**
George Eliot
0-500-26023-0 THAMES & HUDSON PB....$9.95

Jenny **Uglow**
Elizabeth Gaskell: A Habit of Stories
Although she was the perfect minister's wife, Gaskell's stories were shocking tales of fallen women and class wars in Victorian England. This thoroughly readable biography, using Gaskell's own extensive correspondence, presents not only the picture of a literary activist, but a woman's view of Victorian culture
0-374-14751-5 FS&G....$35.00

L.J. **Butler**
Thomas Hardy
0-521-21743-1 CAMBRIDGE....$34.50
0-521-29271-9 CAMBRIDGE PB....$16.95

Michael **Millgate**
Thomas Hardy: A Biography
0-312-12233-0 ST. MARTIN'S PB....$17.95

Martin **Seymour-Smith**
Hardy
0-312-11819-8 ST. MARTIN'S....$35.00

Stanley **Jones**
Hazlitt: A Life from Winterstow to Frith Street
A clear and well-rounded portrait of a major literary figure of the Romantic period, based on 25 years of research. Letters, personal documents, and other contemporary material add new depth to our knowledge of the author of some of the most important criticism in English
0-19-812840-1 OXFORD....$84.00

Norman **White**
Hopkins: A Literary Biography
0-19-818350-X OXFORD PB....$24.00

John **Barnard**
John Keats
0-521-31806-8 CAMBRIDGE PB....$16.95

Walter Jackson **Bate**
John Keats
0-674-47825-8 HARVARD PB....$24.95

Robin **Mayhead**
John Keats
0-521-05706-X CAMBRIDGE....$27.95

Christopher **Ricks**
Keats and Embarrassment
0-19-812829-0 OXFORD PB....$19.95

Helen **Vendler**
The Odes of John Keats
0-674-63075-0 HARVARD....$34.00

Kingsley **Amis**
Rudyard Kipling
0-500-26019-2 THAMES & HUDSON PB....$9.95

Fiona **MacCarthy**
William Morris
See also **THE PRE-RAPHAELITES** under **ENGLAND** under **EUROPEAN ART: 1750-1900** in **ART**
0-394-58531-3 KNOPF....$45.00

Denis **Donoghue**
Walter Pater: Lover of Strange Souls
The distinctively voiced literary critic sets his sights on the 19th-century aesthetician who ushered in modernism
0-679-43753-3 KNOPF....$27.50

Jan **Marsh**
Christina Rossetti
0-670-83517-X VIKING....$29.95

visit our
web site at:
www.nybooks.com

John Ruskin

Tim **Hilton**
John Ruskin: The Early Years, 1819-1859
0-300-03298-6 YALE $35.00

Marcel **Proust**
"Supremely sensitive, and with a prodigious memory for recording sensations, he laid his own mind and body open like an intricate musical instrument for experience to play on, studying every note, always searching for a mysterious underlying theme half-perceived from the first. This theme he was to discover was Time."—William Sansom
On Reading Ruskin
See also **ESSAYS: PERSONAL, LITERARY, PHILOSOPHICAL** under **MODERN FRENCH LITERATURE** in **LITERATURE OF EUROPE, AFRICA, AND ASIA**
0-300-03513-6 YALE $13.00

Frank **McLynn**
Robert Louis Stevenson.
0-679-41284-0 RANDOM HOUSE $30.00

Donald **Thomas**
Swinburne: The Poet of His World
0-19-520136-1 OXFORD $25.00

Christopher **Ricks**
Tennyson
0-8240-4225-5 GARLAND $117.00

Michael **Thorn**
Tennyson
0-312-10414-6 ST. MARTIN'S $30.00

Winifred G. **Gerould** & others
A Guide to Trollope: An Index to Characters and Places, and Digests of the Plots, in All of Trollope's Work
0-691-06053-3 PRINCETON $45.00

N. John **Hall**
Trollope: A Biography
0-19-812627-1 OXFORD $35.00
0-19-283071-6 OXFORD PB $17.95

Victoria **Glendinning**
Anthony Trollope: A Biography
The admired biographer of Vita Sackville-West and Edith Sitwell turns her eye on the Victorian giant, a writer emblematic. "So rich and sweet, so beautifully told that it manages to catch our attention, not as news, certainly, but as a ballad sung once more…Brilliant social history…unfailingly acute"
—James R. Kincaid, *NY Times Book Review*
0-394-58268-3 KNOPF $30.00

Richard **Ellman**
Oscar Wilde
0-394-75984-2 VINTAGE PB $20.00

H. Montgomery **Hyde**
Oscar Wilde
0-306-80147-7 DA CAPO PB $11.95

Edouard **Roditi**
Oscar Wilde
0-8112-0995-4 NEW DIRECTIONS PB $10.95

Oscar Wilde

Robert **Gittings** & others
Dorothy Wordsworth
0-19-818519-7 OXFORD $25.00
0-19-282048-6 OXFORD $12.95

Jonathan **Wordsworth**
William Wordsworth: The Borders of Vision
0-19-812831-2 OXFORD PB $24.95

The 20th-century

Edward **Callan**
Auden: A Carnival of Intellect
0-19-503168-7 OXFORD $30.00

Richard **Davenport-Hines**
Auden
Davenport-Hines (*Sex, Death, and Punishment, The MacMillans*) offers the first biography in 15 years of a central poetic figure of the 20th-century. Following Wystan Hugh Auden from the birth of his ambition in England to 30 years of literary preeminence in New York, this study not only dramatizes the life—the ambitions, addictions, and lusts—but succeeds in taking the full measure of Auden's tremendous accomplishments
0-679-42633-7 PANTHEON $30.00

Anthony **Hecht**
The Hidden Law: The Poetry of W.H. Auden
0-674-39006-7 HARVARD $39.95
0-674-39007-5 HARVARD PB $16.95

Edward **Mendelson**
Early Auden
0-674-21986-4 HARVARD PB $15.95

Lois **Gordon**
The World of Samuel Beckett, 1906-1946
This new perspective on Beckett challenges the image of him as reclusive and disturbed. Peering into the first 40 years of the artist's life, Gordon finds a kind, generous, even heroic man, aware of and engaged with the tumultuous political and cultural world—from Dublin during the Easter uprising to Paris in the 20s and Germany in the 30s—that formed him. "Not strictly a biography, this book draws a forceful, enormously informative and compelling portrait of Beckett"—Robert Scanlan, president, the Samuel Beckett Society
0-300-06409-8 YALE $28.50

Boris **Conrad**
My Father Joseph Conrad
0-7145-0018-6 RIVERRUN $12.95

Ford Madox **Ford**
Joseph Conrad
0-88001-176-9 ECCO PB $9.95

Geoffrey Galt **Harpham**
One of Us: The Mastery of Joseph Conrad
0-226-31695-5 CHICAGO $35.00

Norman **Sherry**

Conrad

0-500-26028-1 THAMES & HUDSON PB $9.95

Philip **Hoare**

Bitter Sweet: A Biography of Noel Coward

When we think of Noel Coward, we think of effortless sophistication. To the contrary, writes Hoare, this socially adept and scathingly witty artist crafted his life as carefully as he did his plays in his rise from a middle-class suburban childhood to the zenith of urbanity. An extraordinary work revealing the gulf between the image and reality of Coward

See also **SONGWRITERS** under **AMERICAN POPULAR MUSIC** in **PERFORMING ARTS AND MEDIA**

See also **SELECTED MEMOIRS AND BIOGRAPHIES** under **THEATER** in **PERFORMING ARTS AND MEDIA**

0-684-80937-0 SIMON & SCHUSTER................$30.00

Alan **Judd**

Ford Madox Ford

The eventful life and literary career of the author of *The Good Soldier* and *Parade's End* receive expert treatment in this full-scale biography

0-674-30815-8 HARVARD $29.95

Nicola **Beauman**

E.M. Forster: A Biography

0-394-58381-7 KNOPF......................................$30.00

Francis **King**

E.M. Forster

0-500-26029-X THAMES & HUDSON PB $9.95

Richard P. **Graves**

Robert Graves: The Assault Heroic, 1895-1926

The second volume in this biography written by Graves's nephew is primarily concerned with his long-term and turbulent relationship with the American poet Laura Riding

0-670-81327-3 PENGUIN PB $24.95

Robert Graves and The White Goddess, 1940-1985

The fluid volume of the much acclaimed biography by Graves's son. The first volume is out of print

0-297-817671-1 WEIDENFELD PB.......................$24.95

Frank **Kersnowski**, editor

Conversations with Robert Graves

0-87805-414-6 MISSISSIPPI PB..........................$15.95

Amanda **Seymour**

Robert Graves: Life on the Edge

Perhaps the finest poet of our time, Graves was a man both arrogant and pugnacious, generous and sustained, impulsive and careless. Novelist Seymour has succeeded brilliantly in compiling this complete and intimate portrait of a hugely complex, enormously talented man

0-8050-3055-7 HOLT..$37.50

Michael **Shelden**

Graham Greene: The Enemy

A radical reinterpretation of the novelist. Shelden draws on previously secret documents and many interviews to peer behind Greene's literary reputation

0-679-42883-6 RANDOM HOUSE.....................$27.50

Martin **Seymour-Smith**

Robert Graves: His Life and Work

0-913729-18-3 MARLOWE PB $10.95

Norman **Sherry**

The Life of Graham Greene: 1904-1939

The authorized and exhaustive two-volume examination of Greene's enigmatic life

0-14-014450-1 PENGUIN PB $18.95

The Life of Graham Greene: 1939-1955

The second volume of the definitive Greene biography. A third has yet to appear

0-14-024526-X PENGUIN PB.............................$17.95

John **Lehmann**

Christopher Isherwood: A Personal Memoir

0-8050-0435-1 OLYMPIC....................................$4.98

0-8050-1029-7 HOLT PB $9.95

James Joyce

Anthony **Burgess**

Re Joyce

Arguing that "the appearance of difficulty is part of Joyce's big joke," Burgess provides a readable, accessible guide. "Mr. Burgess has written a study of the most brilliant and humane of twentieth-century humanists"—Philip Toynbee, *Observer*

0-393-00445-7 NORTON PB $12.95

Joseph **Campbell** & others

A Skeleton Key to Finnegans Wake

A guide to Joyce's daunting final work

1-56849-168-9 BUCCANEER $28.95

Peter **Costello**

James Joyce: The Years of Growth 1882-1915

In this compelling biography, Costello, using newly available sources, delves more deeply than ever before into Joyce's Irish background. Some fascinating revelations surface—one of them is the discovery that Leopold Bloom derives not from a Jew, but from a Belfast Presbyterian. "A work of major importance that deserves to stand on the shelf beside Ellmann's great book which it supplements and, in many significant areas, supersedes. Brilliant and indispensable"—*Dublin Sunday Press*

0-679-42201-3 PANTHEON $30.00

Richard **Ellmann**

James Joyce

A classic of modern biography

0-19-503381-7 OXFORD PB..............................$25.95

Gisele **Freund**

Three Days with Joyce

A photographic record

PREFACE BY RICHARD ELLMANN

9-993-58087-2 PERSEA......................................$17.95

Don **Gifford**

Ulysses Annotated

0-520-06745-2 CALIFORNIA PB $21.95

Hugh **Kenner**

Dublin's Joyce

0-231-06632-5 COLUMBIA $46.50

0-231-06633-3 COLUMBIA PB.........................$18.50

James **Knowlson**

Damned to Fame: The Life of Samuel Beckett

0-684-80872-2 SIMON & SCHUSTER $35.00

Andrew **Motion**

Philip Larkin: A Writer's Life

In his lifetime, Larkin vowed that as soon as he saw "the Grim Reaper coming up the path" he would burn all his papers. Fortunately, he broke this vow, enabling his friend and fellow poet, Andrew Motion, to create this engrossing and detailed portrait

0-374-23168-0 FS&G $35.00

0-374-52407-6 NOONDAY PB $13.00

F.R. **Leavis**

D.H. Lawrence: Novelist

0-226-46971-9 CHICAGO PB $6.95

Anaïs **Nin**

D.H. Lawrence: An Unprofessional Study

INTRODUCTION BY H.T. MOORE

0-8040-0067-0 SWALLOW PB $8.95

D.H. Lawrence

Brenda **Maddox**

D. H. Lawrence: The Story of a Marriage

The paradoxical contrast between Lawrence's misogyny, racism, and repressed homosexuality and his piercing understanding of female sexuality. Maddox documents Lawrence's adultery, his fascism, and examines his life through the optic of his marriage. A monumental work

0-671-68712-3 SIMON & SCHUSTER $30.00

Harry T. **Moore**

D.H. Lawrence

0-500-26030-3 THAMES & HUDSON PB $9.95

A.N. **Wilson**

C.S. Lewis: A Biography

From the British novelist and biographer of Tolstoy, an engrossing critical biography of the Christian apologist, Oxford scholar, and writer of children's tales

0-393-02813-5 NORTON $25.00
0-449-90609-4 FAWCETT PB $14.00

Jane **Farrington**

Wyndham Lewis

FOREWORD BY TIMOTHY CLIFFORD
INTRODUCTION BY SIR JOHN ROTHENSTEIN

0-85331-434-9 LUND HUMPHRIES PB $25.00

Robert **Calder**

Willie: The Life of W. Somerset Maugham

A sympathetic and well-documented account of the complex life of the British author, which dispels many of the accusations of earlier biographers

0-312-03954-9 ST. MARTIN'S $22.95

Jon **Stallworthy**

Wilfred Owen

0-19-282211-X OXFORD PB $18.95

Fredric **Jameson**

Fables of Aggression: Wyndham Lewis, the Modernist as Fascist

0-520-03792-8 CALIFORNIA $37.50
0-520-04398-7 CALIFORNIA PB $12.00

Mel **Gussow**

Conversations with Pinter

0-87910-179-2 LIMELIGHT $18.00

Harold Pinter (photo by R. Jones)

Hugh **Kenner**

The Pound Era

0-5200-2427-3 CALIFORNIA PB $17.95

Ezra **Pound** & Ford Madox **Ford**

Pound-Ford: The Story of a Literary Friendship

EDITED BY BRITA L. SEYERSTED

0-8112-0833-8 NEW DIRECTIONS $22.95

David **Sweetman**

Mary Renault: A Biography

One of the first novelists to depict homosexual love in an open and sympathetic fashion, Renault was so private and reclusive many still believed her to be a man at the time of her death. This biography, developed from a rare interview she granted the author shortly before she died, details her harsh upbringing, her belief that the gay liberation movement was a misguided form of "sexual tribalism," and her own life long romance with Julie Mullard

0-15-193110-0 HARCOURT BRACE $24.95

Victoria **Glendinning**

Vita: The Life of Vita Sackville-West

"In Glendinning's stunning biography, Vita Sackville-West finally emerges as a major personality, a woman who embodies all the virtues and faults of her class and time"—*Booklist*

0-688-04111-6 MORROW PB $12.00

Michael **Holroyd**

Bernard Shaw

Volume 1: Search for Love, 1856-1898

0-674-85830-1 VINTAGE $15.95

Volume 2: The Pursuit of Power, 1898-1918

"Hell," Shaw wrote, "is not working." And judging from his output in this period, GBS enjoyed a piece of creative heaven. Holroyd's acclaimed study portrays its subject at the height of his powers, amid the world of Chesterton, Beerbohm, Wells, Russell, Ellen Terry, and Mrs. Patrick Campbell

0-679-73132-6 VINTAGE PB $16.00

Volumes 3 & 4: The Lure of Fantasy & The Last Laugh, 1918-1991

Volume three is a tumultuous account of the last three decades of the playwright's life, from the international triumphs of *Heartbreak House* and *Saint Joan* through his often perplexing and curmudgeonly political stands, to his death at 95. Volume four is an epilogue about Shaw's diputed estate, his chimeric (and squandered) dream for a simple, phonetic English alphabet, and, most important, the special tone of irony GBS left us with his alternative view of the world

0-679-72507-5 VINTAGE PB $18.00

Michael **Holroyd**

Lytton Strachey

When this biography was orginally published in 1967, it was limited by the fact that so many of Strachey's friends and lovers were still alive. Now, newly available material allows the eminent biographer to represent, in uncompromising detail, Strachey's life

0-374-19439-4 FS&G $35.00

Philip **Hoare**

Serious Pleasures: The Life of Stephen Tennant

Tennant made a career out of the cultivation of his own beauty and wit, and effortlessly dominated a circle of friends that included Cecil Beaton, E.M. Forster, and such far-flung admirers as Greta Garbo and Willa Cather

0-241-12416-6 VIKING $29.95

George **Tremlett**

Dylan Thomas: In the Mercy of His Means

The definitive portrait of one of the 20th-century's most highly mythologized, admired, and tormented writers. Tremlett is the first biographer whom Thomas's widow, Caitlin, agreed to work with, and his book examines the life and work of the poet in far greater depth than previous studies have done

0-312-06957-X ST. MARTIN'S $21.95

Margaret **Drabble**

Angus Wilson

0-312-14276-5 ST. MARTIN'S $35.00

Lyndall **Gordon**

Virginia Woolf: A Writer's Life

"A very readable and lively book….in its way, her book is a masterpiece of the kind of intuitive biography in which Virginia Woolf believed" —*London Times Higher Education Supplement*

0-393-31061-2 NORTON PB $11.95

Selina **Hastings**

Evelyn Waugh: A Biography

With unrestricted access to Waugh's personal papers, Hastings paints a perceptive, fascinating, and expansive portrait of *Brideshead Revisited's* author

0-395-71821-X HOUGHTON MIFFLIN $40.00

Evelyn Waugh

Martin **Stannard**

Evelyn Waugh: The Early Years, 1903-1939

A life of wit, bravado, and colorful escapades; but in Waugh's own phrase, a "sad story" of one who was melancholy at heart

See also **20TH-CENTURY BIOGRAPHY** under **GREAT BRITAIN AND IRELAND** in **WORLD HISTORY AND CURRENT AFFAIRS**

0-393-02450-4 NORTON $24.95
0-393-30605-4 NORTON PB $10.95

Harold **Bloom**

Yeats

0-19-501603-3 OXFORD PB $15.95

A. Norman **Jeffares**

W.B. Yeats: A New Biography

0-374-28588-8 FS&G $30.00

Richard **Ellmann**

Yeats: The Man and the Masks

0-393-00859-2 NORTON PB $12.95

Ian **Fletcher**

W.B. Yeats and His Contemporaries

0-312-85306-8 ST. MARTIN'S $32.50

R. F. **Foster**

W.B. Yeats

0-19-211735-1 OXFORD $25.00

David **Lynch**

Yeats: The Poetics of the Self

0-226-49812-3 CHICAGO PB $2.98

Kathleen **Raine**

Yeats the Initiate: Essays on Certain Themes in the Work of William Butler Yeats

0-389-20951-1 BARNES & NOBLE $83.00
0-8076-1073-9 BRAZILLER $30.00

Late Arrivals

Mel **Gussow**, editor

Conversations with and About Beckett

0-8021-1593-4 GROVE $21.00

Harold **Orel**, editor

The Brontës: Interviews and Recollections

0-87745-537-6 IOWA $24.95

Terry **Castle**

Noel Coward and Radclyffe Hall: Kindred Spirits

0-231-10596-7 COLUMBIA $19.95
0-231-10597-5 COLUMBIA PB $10.00

Oliver Lawson **Dick**

Aubrey's Brief Lives

1-56792-063-2 NAT'L BOOK NETWORK PB $17.95

Ian **Hamilton**

Walking Possession: Essays and Reviews, 1968-93

0-201-48397-1 ADDISON-WESLEY $25.00

London Review of Books

An Anthology

FORWARD BY ALAN BENNET
INTRODUCTION BY PERRY ANDERSON

1-85984-860-5 VERSO $60.00
1-85984-121-X VERSO PB $18.00

Eoin **McNamee**

Resurrection Man

0-312-14716-3 PICADOR PB $12.00

Andrew **O'Hagan**

The Missing

1-56584-335-5 NEW PRESS $20.00

Caradog **Prichard**

One Moonlit Night

TRANSLATED BY PHILIP MITCHELL

0-8112-1342-0 NEW DIRECTIONS PB $12.95

Irvine **Welsh**

Ecstasy

0-393-31581-9 NORTON PB $13.00

Literature of Europe, Africa & Asia

C.P. Cavafy

Tales of the Tribe

800 BC

800 BC: Book of Songs, China
The 305 Odes are as familiar to literate Chinese as the Homeric poems were to the ancient Greeks.
"The morning's over and I've picked less than a handful of green lu grass.
My hair's in a tangle, I'd better go wash."
1014

800 BC: The Odyssey and The Iliad

200 BC: The Mahabarata

AD 1: The Aeneid

AD 1

100: Lucan, The Civil Wars
"Wars worse than civil on the Thessalian plains,
And outrage strangling law and people strong
We sing…"
"Lucan may be called the father of yellow journalism and the costume-film"—Robert Graves
896

AD 500

500: Kalidasa, The Origin of the Young God

An epic of sacred eroticism from the great Gupta kingdom in India.
"She with her eyes like dark waterlilies
had full breasts
and they were of a light color, with
black nipples,
and pressed so closely together not
even
the fiber of a lotus could find a space
between them."
1008

900: The Arabian Nights
Have their origin in a lost 9c Persian collection, *A Thousand Legends,* which featured a framework story (with ancient roots in Indian folklore) similar to that of Scheherazade. Over the subsequent centuries, the compilation picked up stories from a range of Arabic cultures, mixing idioms high and low in a fantastic mélange that finally assumed its current form near the end of the 18c.
1003

AD 1000

1000: Njal's Saga
The Icelandic epics are at once romantic, heroic, and historical documents. This, the greatest of them, tells of a grim world in which justice means vengeance and all men are either lucky or doomed.
965

1300: The Divine Comedy

AD 1500

1532: Ludovico Ariosto, Orlando Furioso
This frivolous and pyrotechnic story of Knights of Arms and ladies in armor, of monsters, Saracens, and crusaders, rejoices in the absurdities of the chivalric tradition even as it punctures romantic illusions.
945

1650: Paradise Lost

1796: J. W. v. Goethe, Wilhelm Meister's Apprenticeship
The prototypical bildungsroman, Goethe's great novel is less a story of growing up than a picaresque, realistic, and mysterious tale that changes character in the course of its telling.
954

AD 1800

1850: Elias Lönnrot, The Kalevala
Lönnrot collected, transcribed, and fabricated traditional Finnish folk tales to compose a shamanistic national epic, "in which great deeds are accomplished, not by feats of arms, but by the magical power of word and incantations." (Felix Oinas)
966

c. 1875: Gustave Flaubert, Bouvard and Pécuchet
Flaubert's last, unfinished novel is a mock epic of the modern mania for information. The title characters are provincial clerks who set out to learn everything there is to know. Ultimately, fruitless studies at an end, they return with relief to the business of copying.
919

1890s: Stéphane Mallarmé, Le Livre

"Everything exists to end up as a book," Mallarmé declared. He spent his last years preparing the singular work that was to be "the Orphic explanation of the Earth, the poet's only duty." Only fragments remain.
920

AD 1900

1996: The Griots of Mali
Continue the ancient tradition of oral recitation.
996

1 Baie des Dépassés
"The people of Armorica had the task of conducting the dead. In the middle of the night they heard a knocking on the door and a low voice calling. They went to the seashore without knowing what force drew them there. They found boats which seemed empty, but which were laden with the souls of the dead. In less than an hour they reached the end of their voyage and heard a voice which numbered the passengers, calling each by his name." —Millicent Dillon and Nora Chadwick
The Celtic Realms
872

2 Banaras
"People come from all over India to live in Banaras until they die. Dying in Banares, they make the final crossing which ends the pilgrimage of this life, and all lives. Death in Banaras is liberation."
—Diana Eck
Banaras: City of Light
371

3 Cumae
After consulting the oracle here, Aeneas descended into the underworld.
"The way downward is easy
from Avernus,
Black Dis's door stands open
night and day.
But to retrace your steps to
heaven's air,
This is the trouble, this is
the toil." —Virgil
The Aeneid
896

4 Doctor's Island
Near Tierra del Fuego, in 1520, Magellan discovered this island, which soon became known for its unhealthy climate and its numerous medicinal plants and mineral springs. The inhabitants are chiefly doctors and pharmacists: the Doctors' Palace is built all of black marble with black tapestries. The island's vast cemeteries are also famous. The shortest passage from Earth to Hell is said to lie nearby.
33

5 Fujiyama
This traditional goal of Japanese pilgrims is known as "the mountain of the voyage beyond the tomb."
336

6 Ganges
The river Ganges plummets down from Heaven into the Himalayas, oozing through Shiva's locks out onto the Indian plain until it reaches Calcutta, the mouth of Hell.
1007

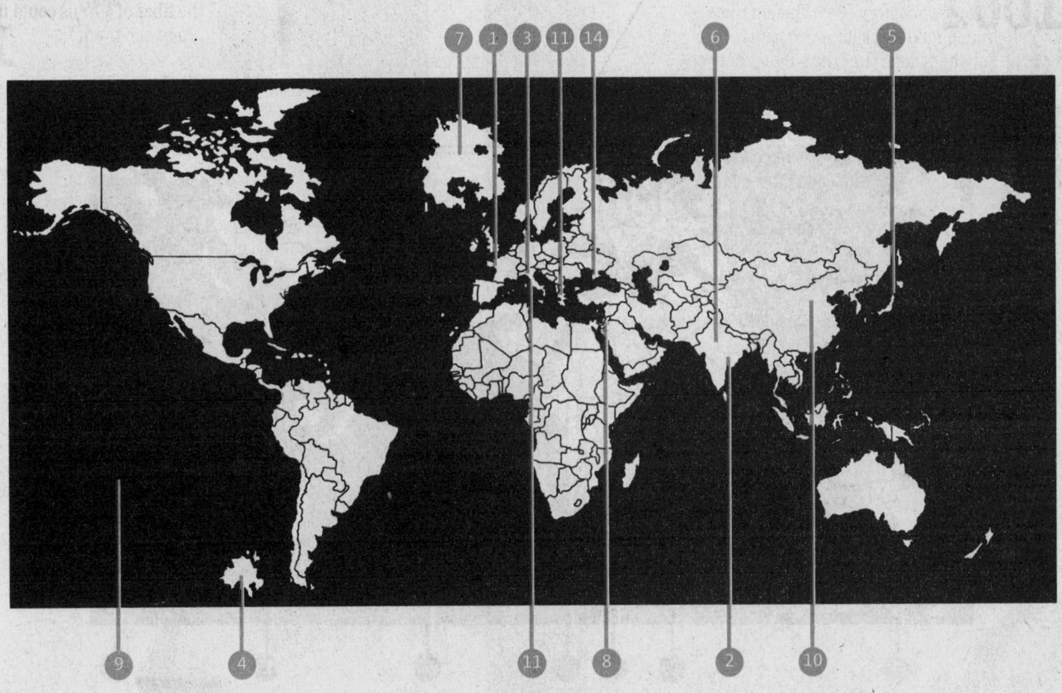

7 Hyperborea
Located somewhere north of Scotland, this heavenly land can be reached only through a narrow strait surrounded by high cliffs in the shape of women, which come alive at night and destroy passing ships. The sun rises once in midsummer and sets once in midwinter. Inhabitants choose the day of their death and leap to it from a special rock. Sorrow there is unknown.
899

8 Jordan
"And it came to pass, as they still went on, and talked, that, behold, there appeared a chariot of fire, and horses of fire, and parted them both asunder; and Elijah went up by a whirlwind into heaven."
—II Kings 2:11
340

9 Purgatory
The great mountain where the contrite soul atones for its past sins before ascending to Heaven. Dante locates it in the southern hemisphere of oceans, directly opposite Jerusalem.
944

10 Taishan
From China's most sacred mountain, "the god of Taishan presided over human destinies. He maintained an account of the life of each man in a kind of ledger. It was believed that the dead went to reside in Taishan."
—Yves Bonnefoy
Mythologies
325

11 Styx
"A small stream in Arcadia, the waters of which were supposed to be deadly poison. Tartarus seems to be a reduplication of the pre-Hellenic word *tar,* which occurs in the names of places lying to the West."
—Robert Graves
The Greek Myths
893

12 Hell
Located at the dead-center of the Earth; reached by way of a dark wood.
—Dante
The Divine Comedy
944

1 Johann Wolfgang von Goethe (1749–1832)

"What pleasure, God! of like a flame to born,
A virteous fire, that ne'er to vice can turn.
What volupty! when trembling in my arms,
The bosom of my maid my bosom warmeth!"

954

2 Olive Schreiner (1855–1920)

This South African feminist wrote under the pseudonym Ralph Iron. Her powerful novel *The Story of an African Farm,* about two children in the veldt, has been compared to *Wuthering Heights.*

1002

3 Joseph Conrad (1857-1924)

"Conrad didn't learn English until the age of twenty and had contempt for it as a language for writing prose. He explained, '"Oaken" in French means "made of oak wood"—nothing more. "Oaken" in English connotes innumerable moral attributes. No English word has clean edges.' He would have preferred to have been a French novelist, he said, but it was too late to change." (Paul O'Prey)

820

4 Constantine Cavafy (1863–1933)

The Greek poet lived in Liverpool from his 9th to his 16th year, published his first verse in English, and is said to have spoken Greek with a British accent all through his life. His initial recognition as a poet also occurred in England, thanks to his friendship with E.M. Forster.

985

5 Fernando Pessoa (1885–1935)

The Portuguese modernist master wrote under numerous "heteronyms" representing different characters, and as Alexander Search he even wrote and published in English:

"This is all the story of Salomon Waste
Always hurrying yet never in haste
He fussed and worked and toiled all frothing
And at the end of it did nothing.
This is all the story of Salomon Waste."

942

6 Isak Dinesen (1885–1962)

Baroness Karen Blixen, who used the pseudonym Dinesen, moved from her native Denmark to a Kenyan plantation after marrying her cousin. In the 1930s she returned to Denmark, where she wrote *Out of Africa.* Her other writings revolve around the supernatural.

965

7 R.K. Narayan (1906–)

Narayan's many novels are set in Malgudi, a fictionalized version of the southern Indian town of Mysore. His stories of ordinary life are full of sympathy, wisdom, and humor.

1011

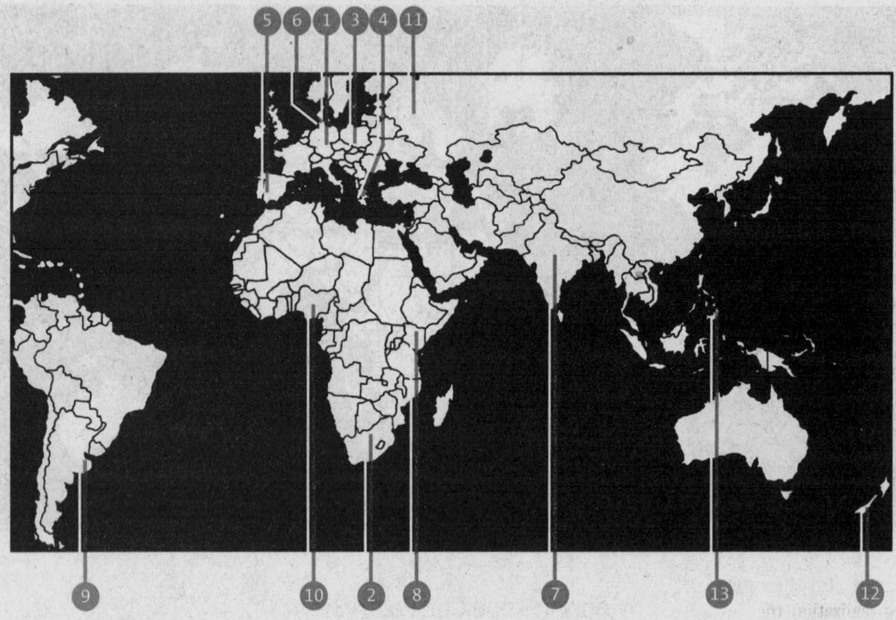

8 G.V. Desani (1909–)

Born in Kenya, Desani fashioned the rhythms and locutions of Indian English into an instrument of the imagination in *All About H. Hatterr,* his whimsical portrait of intellectual eccentricity, much admired by T.S. Eliot and Salman Rushdie, among others.

1010

9 Jorge Luis Borges (1899–1986)

The Argentinian master, proud of having come from English stock, was obsessed with English and American themes and writers.

"I come back on the far shore of a great river
Never reached by the Norsemen's long ships
To the harsh and work-wrought words
Which, with a tongue now dust,
I used in the days of Northumbria and Mercia
Before becoming Haslam or Borges."

—"On Embarking on the Study of Anglo-Saxon Grammar"

770

10 Amos Tutuola (1920–)

Tutuola's novels draw on Yoruba folk traditions and the rhythms of Nigerian English. "The Description of the Creature: he was a beautiful complete gentleman, he dressed with the finest and most costly clothes, all the parts of his body were completed, he was a tall man but stout. As this gentle man came to market on that day, if he had been an article or an animal for sale, he would be sold at least for 2000."

—*The Palm-Wine Drinkard*

999

11 Joseph Brodsky (1940–1996)

Exiled for political reasons from the Soviet Union, Brodsky moved to the US. He claimed that it was to please the ghost of W. H. Auden, whom he passionately admired, that he began to write essays, and eventually poetry, in the language of his adopted country. "Composed in a rather heroically determined English, clumsily phrased and idiomatically challenged, Brodsky's essays are still inventive and alive."

—*Boston Review*

982

12 Keri Hulme (1947–)

The New Zealand novelist's *The Bone People* won the 1986 Booker Prize. Controversial and ambitious, it is a mystery and love story that explores the uncertain territory in which Maori and European New Zealanders encounter each other, clash, and sometimes arrive at an understanding.

1033

13 Jessica Hagedorn (1949–)

Hagedorn was born and raised in the Phillipines before moving to the US. Her first novel, *Dogeaters,* is a surrealistic and lyrical tale of Manila under the Marcos dictatorship.

654

Literature of the Ancient Near East

Michael D. **Coogan**, editor
Stories from Ancient Canaan
Four principal works of Ugaritic literature
0-664-24184-0 KNOX PB $12.00

Stephanie **Dalley**, editor
Myths from Mesopotamia
0-19-814397-4 OXFORD PB $55.00

David **Ferry**
Gilgamesh: A New Rendering in English Verse
0-374-52383-5 NOONDAY PB $10.00

John **Gardner** & John **Maier**, translators
Gilgamesh
0-394-74089-0 RANDOM HOUSE PB $13.00

Alexander **Heidel**
The Gilgamesh Epic and Old Testament Parallels
Literary and religious themes held in common by these two ancient texts
0-226-32398-6 CHICAGO PB $13.95

Maureen Gallery **Kovacs**, translator
The Epic of Gilgamesh
0-8047-1711-7 STANFORD PB $7.95

N.K. **Sandars**, translator
The Epic of Gilgamesh
The story of Gilgamesh, ruler of Uruk (Biblical Erech) in the mid-3rd millennium BC. "*The Epic of Gilgamesh* dates from the beginnings of civilization in Mesopotamia… It is a spiritual adventure, a story of self-realization, the discovery of the meaning of the personality, of a type that would never change down the four-thousand-year-long history of human imagination. Its figures have the cogency of symbols that will never alter. It is modern because it is like a dream of a modern man" —Kenneth Rexroth, *Classics Revisited*
0-14-044100-X PENGUIN PB $7.95

Utnapishtim said, "There is no permanence. Do we build a house to stand for ever, do we seal a contract to hold for all time? Do brothers divide an inheritance to keep for ever, does the flood-time of rivers endure? It is only the nymph of the dragon-fly who sheds her larva and sees the sun in his glory. From the days of old there is no permanence. The sleeping and the dead, how alike they are, they are like a painted death. What is there between the master and the servant when both have fulfilled their doom? When the Annunaki, the judges, come together, and Mammetun the mother of destinies, together they decree the fates of men. Life and death they allot but the day of death they do not disclose."
THE EPIC OF GILGAMESH

Alexander **Heidel**
The Babylonian Genesis
A translation of creation stories from cuneiform tablets
0-226-32399-4 CHICAGO PB $7.95

Thorkild **Jacobsen**
The Harps that Once…: Sumerian Poetry in Translation
A generous selection of the poetry preserved in the Sumerian tablets, including a number of works never before translated
0-300-03906-9 YALE $47.00

Samuel Noah **Kramer**
History Begins at Sumer: Thirty-Nine "Firsts" in Man's Recorded History
Classic introduction to Sumerian literary and religious texts
0-8122-1276-2 PENNSYLVANIA PB $20.95

In the World of Sumer: An Autobiography
Kramer's autobiography is also the story of the recovery of Sumerian literature
0-8143-2121-6 WAYNE STATE PB $15.95

James B. **Pritchard**, editor
The Ancient Near East: An Anthology of Texts and Pictures, Volume 1
The most important documents in the literature and history of Egypt, Mesopotamia, and the Levant from the third to the first millennium BC
0-691-00200-2 PRINCETON PB $18.95

Erica **Reiner**
Your Thwarts in Pieces, Your Mooring Rope Cut: Poetry from Babylonia and Assyria
Translations and analytical essays which, though sometimes technical, are fascinating for the light they throw on the function of poetry in ancient Near Eastern societies
0-936534-04-4 MICHIGAN PB $10.00

N.K. **Sandars**, translator
Poems of Heaven and Hell from Ancient Mesopotamia
Among the important works in this collection are the Babylonian creation epic *Enuma Elish* and the Sumerian account of Inanna's journey to the underworld
0-14-044249-9 PENGUIN PB $10.95

Diane **Wolkstein** & Samuel Noah **Kramer**
Inanna: Queen of Heaven and Earth
Kramer's translations reworked by a folklorist
0-06-090854-8 HARPERCOLLINS PB $14.00

Ancient Egyptian Literature

Carol **Andrews** & Raymond **Faulkner**
The Ancient Egyptian Book of the Dead
A recent edition, with an illuminating introduction
0-292-70425-9 TEXAS PB $24.95

E.A. Wallis **Budge**
The Egyptian Book of the Dead: The Papyrus of Ani in the British Museum
The collection of religious documents for the guidance of the soul in the world after death
0-486-21866-X DOVER PB $9.95

The Liturgy of Funerary Offerings: The Egyptian Texts with English Translations
0-486-28335-6 DOVER PB $7.95

W.V. **Davies**
Egyptian Hieroglyphs
Explanation of their principles, origins, development, and use, as well as the history of their decipherment
See also **LANGUAGE AND WRITING** under **ARCHAEOLOGY** in **WORLD HISTORY AND CURRENT AFFAIRS**
0-520-06287-6 CALIFORNIA PB $11.00

Ancient Egyptian occupies a special position among the languages of the world. It is not only one of the very oldest recorded languages (probably only Sumerian is older) but it also has a documented history longer by far than that of any other. It was first written down toward the end of the fourth millennium BC and thereafter remained in continuous recorded use down to about the eleventh century AD, a period of over 4,000 years… Although it can only be a minute fraction of what was actually produced, the body of written material to have survived in Egyptian is, nevertheless, enormous. It consists, in large part, of religious and funerary texts, but it also includes secular documents of many different types—administrative, business, legal, literary and scientific—as well as private and official biographical and historical inscriptions. This record is our most important single source of evidence on ancient Egyptian society.
EGYPTIAN HIEROGLYPHS

John L. **Foster**, translator
Love Songs of the New Kingdom
Poems of courtship and desire, in modern translations. "An unusual and handsomely printed collection demonstrating that at least some things are relatively unchanged since the time of the pharaohs…These translations are as lusty, humorous and sometimes sentimental as though they were written yesterday" —*Washington Post*
0-292-72476-4 TEXAS $20.00
0-292-72477-2 TEXAS PB $9.95

Barbara Hughes **Fowler**, translator

Love Lyrics of Ancient Egypt

0-8078-2159-4 NORTH CAROLINA $19.95
0-8078-4468-3 NORTH CAROLINA PB $10.95

Ogden **Goelet** & others, editors

The Egyptian Book of the Dead

0-8118-0792-4 CHRONICLE $40.00
0-8118-0767-3 CHRONICLE PB $24.95

Miriam **Lichtheim**

Ancient Egyptian Literature: A Book of Readings

The most comprehensive collection of Egyptian literature

Volume 1
The Old and the Middle Kingdoms

0-520-02899-6 CALIFORNIA PB $14.00

Volume 2
The New Kingdom

0-520-03615-8 CALIFORNIA PB $14.00

Volume 3
The Late Period

0-520-04020-1 CALIFORNIA PB $14.00

R.B. **Parkinson**

Voices from Ancient Egypt: An Anthology of Middle Kingdom Writings

0-8061-2362-1 OKLAHOMA PB $21.95

William Kelley **Simpson**

The Literature of Ancient Egypt: An Anthology of Stories, Instructions, and Poetry

0-300-01711-1 YALE PB $18.00

Ancient Greek Literature

The Archaic Period

Greek literature from the period before the Persian invasion of 480 BC differs in fundamental ways from what follows. The bards at the beginning of the tradition (Homer, Hesiod, Orpheus, and Musaeus) were personae rather than poets, legendary identities that stood for the creators of poetic traditions, rather than individuals with biographies. Their lives were continually reinvented. Even such an undoubtedly historic figure as the Athenian poet-politician Solon is steeped in legend. But whatever their origins, these earliest voices laid the foundation for a tradition that had taken to heart the principle later enunciated by Aristotle that "that which is oldest is likewise most honored."

Homer

George **Steiner**, editor

Homer in English

An anthology which brings together a wide variety of translations of the works of Homer

0-14-044621-4 PENGUIN PB $14.95

The Iliad

Homer

The Iliad

TRANSLATED BY ROBERT FITZGERALD

0-385-05941-8 ANCHOR PB $7.95

The Iliad

Pope's translation is a masterpiece of neoclassical verse, although far removed from today's conceptions of Homer's poetry

TRANSLATED BY ALEXANDER POPE
EDITED BY STEVEN SHANKMAN

0-14-044504-8 PENGUIN PB $22.95

The Iliad of Homer

An "Iliad of woes" that does remarkable justice to the somber majesty of the original. Lattimore, an accomplished scholar and a fine poet in his own right, attempts to match the length of the Homeric line and, to some extent, the formulaic nature of the language, rendering the Greek with astonishing immediacy

See also **ANCIENT GREEK CLASSICS** under **ANCIENT GREECE** in **WORLD HISTORY AND CURRENT AFFAIRS**

TRANSLATED BY RICHMOND LATTIMORE

0-226-46940-9 CHICAGO PB $9.95

The Iliad of Homer

Fagles's excellent version is geared to the poetics of the late 20th century, fast-moving and so compressed that Lattimore's version seems positively prolix by comparison

TRANSLATED BY ROBERT FAGLES
INTRODUCTION AND NOTES BY BERNARD KNOX

0-670-83510-2 VIKING $40.00
0-14-044592-7 PENGUIN PB $8.95

The Odyssey

Homer

The Odyssey

Faithfulness to the repetitive use of formulaic phrases helps recapture the cadence of oral poetry

TRANSLATED BY RICHMOND LATTIMORE

0-06-090479-8 HARPERCOLLINS PB $13.00

The Odyssey

A prose translation that presents the *Odyssey* as a novel

TRANSLATED BY E. V. RIEU

0-14-044556-0 PENGUIN PB $8.95

The Odyssey

An elegant translation into an English prose that no one would confuse with American

TRANSLATED BY WALTER SHEWRING

0-19-281542-3 OXFORD PB $6.95

The Odyssey

The work of a poet thoroughly in sympathy with the poet of the original; Fitzgerald's pentameter trips along at a speed perfectly adapted to the twists and turns of the hero's wanderings

TRANSLATED BY ROBERT FITZGERALD

0-679-41047-3 KNOPF $20.00

The Odyssey

A new and highly acclaimed translation with a significant introduction by Bernard Knox

TRANSLATED BY ROBERT FAGLES

0-670-82162-4 VIKING $35.00

The Homeric Hymns

Homer

The Homeric Hymns

Traditionally attributed to Homer, this collection of prologues to epic performances is basic for understanding archaic Greek theology. A vigorous verse translation with helpful notes

TRANSLATED BY APOSTOLOS N. ATHANASSAKIS

0-8018-1792-7 JOHNS HOPKINS PB $9.95

Christopher **Logue**

War Music

A transmutation of Homer into contemporary language. "Logue's miniature epic is a remarkable achievement, and one that justifies its title. The war it portrays is real, and harsh, and horrible; but the music is real, too"—John Gross, *NY Times*

See also **BRITISH POETS** under **20TH-CENTURY BRITISH AND IRISH POETRY** in **LITERATURE OF THE BRITISH ISLES**

0-374-52494-7 FS&G PB $14.00

Kings: An Account of Books I and II of Homer's Iliad

Continuing in his unique vein of Homeric adaptation as explored in *War Music*, Logue writes his version of the first two books of *The Iliad*. "Homer is reexperienced, is given the mystery of creative echo"—George Steiner, *The Times* [London]

0-374-18151-9 FS&G $16.95

The Husbands: An Account of Books III and IV of Homer's Iliad

The third installment of Logue's epic retelling of the Iliad, dangerously modern and hauntingly powerful. In language at once musical, tender, and graphic, Logue brings to us "the best translation of Homer since Pope's"—*NY Review of Books*

0-374-17391-5 FS&G $19.00

Hesiod

As Homer founded the heroic epic tradition, Hesiod, the shepherd of Ascra, wrote the earliest Greek wisdom poetry (*Works and Days*) and theological poetry (*Theogony*). Much "Hesiodic" poetry is lost, but we do have the mannered and lovely *Shield of Herakles*.

Hesiod

Hesiod & Theognis

A solid, credible blank verse translation. The unlovely Theognis is good to have for comparison and contrast

TRANSLATED BY DOROTHEA WENDER

0-14-044283-9 PENGUIN PB $9.95

Theogony & Works and Days
A verse translation with very generous notes. Remarkable for its use of parallels from modern Greek folklore
TRANSLATED BY APOSTOLOS N. ATHANASSAKIS
0-8018-2999-2 JOHNS HOPKINS PB $9.95

Theogony & Works and Days
This newest translation, with concise and valuable notes, by the greatest living expert on Hesiod, is a peculiar, often fascinating mix of styles and diction. West keeps the promise of his prefatory note: "If I have sometimes made Hesiod sound a little quaint and stilted, that is not unintentional: he is"
TRANSLATED WITH NOTES BY M. L. WEST
0-19-281788-4 OXFORD PB $7.95

The Works and Days
An excellent verse translation of *Works and Days*, *Theogony*, and *The Shield of Herakles*, with a useful introduction. This is arguably the greatest accomplishment of Lattimore's career as a translator
TRANSLATED BY RICHMOND LATTIMORE
0-472-08161-6 MICHIGAN PB $12.95

Lyric Poetry

Greek lyric begins in the archaic period and extends into the classical; certain types, notably the epigram, continued to be created into the Byzantine period. Here more than anywhere, the reader is at the mercy of the translator. Fortunately, many scholar-poets and poet-scholars have successfully rethought and re-created the originals as living poetry.

Willis **Barnstone**, translator
Sappho and the Greek Lyric Poets
The most inclusive anthology
PREFACE BY WILLIAM MCCULLOUGH
0-8052-0831-3 SCHOCKEN PB $16.00

Peter **Bing**, translator
Games of Venus: An Anthology of Greek and Roman Erotic Verse from Sappho to Ovid
An engaging distillation of the erotic vein in classical poetry
TRANSLATED BY RIP COHEN
0-415-90260-6 ROUTLEDGE $44.95
0-415-90261-4 ROUTLEDGE PB $15.95

Guy **Davenport**, translator
7 Greeks
Davenport's translations are notably pithy and energetic. The Greeks in question are poets and philosophers: Archilochus, Sappho, Aleman, Anakraeon, Herakleitos, Diogenes, and Herondas. "It is astonishing how Davenport has been able to invent an idiosyncratic style for each poet, distinguishable even in scraps of a few words"—Eliot Weinberger, *American Poet*
0-8112-1288-2 NEW DIRECTIONS PB $16.95

Richmond **Lattimore**, translator
Greek Lyrics
Contains over 100 poems and fragments in first-class verse translations. Includes the more substantial fragments of Archilochus, Callinus, Semonides, Hipponax, Tyrtaeus, Mimnermus, Solon, Xenophanes, Alcman, Ibycus, Sappho, Alcaeus, Anacreon, and Simonides, some fragments of Pindar, and five poems of Bacchylides
0-226-46944-1 CHICAGO PB $6.95

Pindar
The Odes of Pindar
TRANSLATED BY C.M. BOWRA
0-14-044209-X PENGUIN PB $10.95

Pindar

Diane **Rayor**, translator
Sappho's Lyre: Archaic Lyric and Women Poets of Ancient Greece
New translations of Sappho and other archaic Greek poets, with a special emphasis on the women poets whose surviving works are presented here in their entirety. "These works surpass any translations of the archaic lyricists that I have seen"—John Herington
0-520-07336-3 CALIFORNIA PB $13.95

Sappho
Sappho
These sensitive, accomplished translations do true justice to the enduring lyricism of the celebrated—and mysterious—poet of the sixth century BC. Everything Sappho left behind (two intact poems and nearly 100 fragments) can be found in this lovely miniature edition
TRANSLATED BY MARY BARNARD
0-87773-991-9 SHAMBHALA PB $6.00

Sappho: A Garland: The Poems and Fragments of Sappho
Superb new translations by a gifted poet
TRANSLATED BY JIM POWELL
0-374-25393-5 FS&G $15.00
0-374-52421-1 NOONDAY PB $9.00

Sappho: A New Translation
This early translation by Barnard (herself an excellent and underrated poet) remains outstanding
TRANSLATED BY MARY BARNARD
0-520-01117-1 CALIFORNIA PB $10.00

Sappho: Poems and Fragments
TRANSLATED BY JOSEPHINE BALMER
0-8216-2000-2 LYLE STUART PB $7.95

The Greek Anthology

This Byzantine compilation brings together thousands of short poems from the 7th century BC to the High Middle Ages. A complete prose translation takes up five volumes of the Loeb Classical Library, but a substantial number of the jewels can be found in the following selections.

Peter **Jay**, editor
The Greek Anthology
A selection in modern verse translation
See also **ANCIENT GREEK CLASSICS** under **ANCIENT GREECE** in **WORLD HISTORY AND CURRENT AFFAIRS**
0-14-044285-5 PENGUIN PB $10.95

Kenneth **Rexroth**, translator
Poems from the Greek Anthology
0-472-06063-5 MICHIGAN PB $9.95

The Classical Period

The century and a half from the Persian Wars to the death of Alexander the Great in 323 BC stands out as the "classical" period. The process of canonization began quickly. Even before Alexander, the Athenian plays of the 5th century were enjoying revivals. All the surviving tragedies as well as the earliest historical writing belong to that period.

University of Chicago Tragedy Series

David **Grene** &
Richmond **Lattimore**, editors
For countless modern readers the voices of Aeschylus, Sophocles, and Euripides have been heard through the brilliant translations of David Grene, Richmond Lattimore, William Arrowsmith, and other contributors to the University of Chicago tragedy series.

The Complete Greek Tragedies: A Centennial Edition
The series is now available in an attractive four-volume slipcased edition.
0-226-30763-8 CHICAGO $140.00

Aeschylus One: The Oresteia
Includes *The Oresteia*, consisting of *Agamemnon, The Libation Bearers,* and *The Eumenides*
TRANSLATED WITH AN INTRODUCTION BY RICHMOND LATTIMORE
0-226-30778-6 CHICAGO PB $8.95

Aeschylus Two: Four Tragedies
Includes *Prometheus Bound* and *Seven Against Thebes* (translated by David Grene), *The Persians,* and *The Suppliant Maidens* (translated by Seth Benardete)
0-226-30794-8 CHICAGO PB $8.95

Sophocles One: Three Tragedies
Includes *Oedipus the King* (translated by David Grene), *Oedipus at Colonus* (translated by Robert Fitzgerald), and *Antigone* (translated by Elizabeth Wykoff)
0-226-30792-1 CHICAGO PB $8.95

Sophocles Two: Four Tragedies
Includes *Ajax* (translated by John Moore), *Women of Trachis* (translated by Michael Jameson), *Electra*, and *Philoctetes* (translated by David Grene)
0-226-30786-7 CHICAGO PB $8.95

Euripides One: Four Tragedies
Includes *Alcestis* (translated by Richmond Lattimore), *Medea* (translated by Rex Warner), *Heracleidae* (translated by Ralph Gladstone), and *Hippolytus* (translated by David Grene)
0-226-30780-8 CHICAGO PB $8.95

Euripides Two: Four Tragedies
Includes *Cyclops* and *Heracles* (translated by William Arrowsmith), *Iphigenia in Tauris* (translated by Witter Bynner), and *Helen* (translated by Richmond Lattimore)
0-226-30781-6 CHICAGO PB $8.95

Euripides Three: Four Tragedies
Includes *Hecuba* and *Andromache* (translated by William Arrowsmith), *The Trojan Women* (translated by Richmond Lattimore), and *Ion* (translated by Ronald Willetts)
0-226-30782-4 CHICAGO PB $8.95

Euripides Four: Four Tragedies
Includes *Rhesus* (translated by Richmond Lattimore), *The Suppliant Women* (translated by Frank Jones), *Orestes* (translated by William Arrowsmith), and *Iphigenia in Aulis* (translated by Charles Walker)
0-226-30783-2 CHICAGO PB $8.95

Euripides Five: Three Tragedies
Includes *Electra*, *The Phoenician Women*, and *The Bacchae*
See also **ANCIENT GREEK CLASSICS** under **ANCIENT GREECE** in **WORLD HISTORY AND CURRENT AFFAIRS**
TRANSLATED BY EMILY VERMEULE, ELIZABETH WYCKOFF & WILLIAM ARROWSMITH
EDITED BY DAVID GRENE & RICHMOND LATTIMORE
0-226-30784-0 CHICAGO PB $8.95

Aeschylus

Aeschylus
The Oresteia
Includes *Agamemnon*, *The Libation Bearers*, and *The Eumenides*. A verse translation in a more modern idiom than Lattimore's. Highly recommended
See also **ANCIENT GREEK CLASSICS** under **ANCIENT GREECE** in **WORLD HISTORY AND CURRENT AFFAIRS**
TRANSLATED BY ROBERT FAGLES
0-14-044333-9 PENGUIN PB $8.95

Oresteia
TRANSLATED BY HUGH LLOYD-JONES
0-520-08328-8 CALIFORNIA PB $12.00

The Persians
TRANSLATED BY JANET LEMBKE & C. JOHN HERINGTON
0-19-507008-9 OXFORD PB $7.95

Prometheus Bound
TRANSLATED BY JAMES SCULLY & C. JOHN HERINGTON
0-19-506165-9 OXFORD PB $7.95

Sophocles

Sophocles
Antigone
TRANSLATED BY RICHARD BRAUN
0-19-506167-5 OXFORD PB $7.95

Electra & Other Plays
Also includes *Ajax*, *Women of Trachis*, and *Philoctetes*
TRANSLATED BY E.F. WATLING
0-14-044003-8 PENGUIN PB $9.95

Philoktetes
TRANSLATED BY GREGORY MCNAMEE
1-55659-002-4 COPPER CANYON PB $8.00

The Three Theban Plays
Includes *Antigone*, *Oedipus the King*, and *Oedipus at Colonus*. This highly readable translation has many advantages over the Grene/Fitzgerald/Wyckoff translations in the Chicago series: the plays are arranged in the order in which they were written, and Bernard Knox has contributed introductions and notes about the plays' relationship to the audience that first viewed them in the Theater of Dionysus
TRANSLATED BY ROBERT FAGLES
0-14-044425-4 PENGUIN PB $8.95

Women of Trachis
TRANSLATED BY C.K. WILLIAMS & GREGORY DICKERSON
0-19-507009-7 OXFORD PB $6.95

Women of Trachis
A quirky, purposefully rough-hewn version in which Sophocles provides Pound with the scope to affirm that "it all coheres"
TRANSLATED BY EZRA POUND
0-8112-0948-2 NEW DIRECTIONS PB $6.95

Seamus **Heaney**
The Cure at Troy: A Version of Sophocles' Philoctetes
A free, highly theatrical adaptation of *Philoctetes*. "A purifying play, in the great tradition of modern Irish drama: think of Synge's *Playboy*, O'Casey's early work, or even some of Yeats's Cuchulain plays"—John Peters, *The Sunday Times* (London)
See also **THE '70S, '80S, AND '90S** under **20TH-CENTURY BRITISH AND IRISH DRAMA** in **LITERATURE OF THE BRITISH ISLES**
0-374-13355-7 FS&G $20.00
0-374-52289-8 NOONDAY PB $10.00

Euripides

Euripides
Alcestis
TRANSLATED BY WILLIAM ARROWSMITH
0-19-506166-7 OXFORD PB $7.95

Alcestis & Other Plays
TRANSLATED BY JOHN DAVIE
0-14-044643-5 PENGUIN PB $9.95

Alcestis & Other Plays
Also includes *Hippolytus* and *Iphigenia in Tauris*
TRANSLATED BY PHILIP VELLACOTT
0-14-044031-3 PENGUIN PB $8.95

The Bacchae & Other Plays
Also includes *Ion*, *The Women of Troy*, and *Helen*
TRANSLATED BY PHILIP VELLACOTT
0-14-044044-5 PENGUIN PB $9.95

The Children of Herakles
TRANSLATED BY HENRY TAYLOR & ROBERT BROOKS
0-19-507288-X OXFORD PB $7.95

Electra
TRANSLATED BY JANET LEMBKE
0-19-508576-0 OXFORD PB $7.95

Helen
TRANSLATED BY JAMES MICHIE & COLIN LEACH
0-19-507710-5 OXFORD PB $6.95

Hippolytus
TRANSLATED BY ROBERT BAGG
0-19-507290-1 OXFORD PB $7.95

Ion
TRANSLATED BY W.S. DI PIERO
0-19-509451-4 OXFORD PB $7.95

Iphigeneia at Aulis
TRANSLATED BY W.S. MERWIN & GEORGE DIMOCK, JR.
0-19-507709-1 OXFORD PB $7.95

Iphigeneia in Tauris
TRANSLATED BY RICHMOND LATTIMORE
0-19-507291-X OXFORD PB $7.95

Medea & Other Plays
Includes *Hecuba*, *Electra*, and *Heracles*
TRANSLATED BY PHILIP VELLACOTT
0-14-044129-8 PENGUIN PB $8.95

Orestes
TRANSLATED BY JOHN PECK
0-19-509659-2 OXFORD PB $7.95

Orestes & Other Plays
Also includes *The Children of Heracles*, *Andromache*, *The Suppliant Women*, *The Phoenician Women*, and *Iphigenia in Aulis*
TRANSLATED BY PHILIP VELLACOTT
0-14-044259-6 PENGUIN PB $7.95

Phoenician Women
TRANSLATED BY PETER BURIAN & BRIAN SWANN
0-19-507708-3 OXFORD PB $6.95

Rhesos
TRANSLATED BY RICHARD BRAUN
0-19-507289-8 OXFORD PB $6.95

Suppliant Women
TRANSLATED BY ROSANNA WARREN
0-19-504553-X OXFORD PB $7.95

Comedy

Athenian Old and Middle Comedy are known only through the 11 surviving plays of Aristophanes, which date between 425 and 388 BC. Because of its pervasive obscenity, this drama has not been given adequate translation until quite recently.

Aristophanes

The Complete Plays of Aristophanes

Includes *The Acharnians, The Birds, The Clouds, Ecclesiazusae, The Frogs, The Knights, Lysistrata, Peace, Plutus, Thesmophoriazusae,* and *The Wasps.* This handy volume has the virtue of completeness but cannot seriously be compared with the Arrowsmith series

TRANSLATED BY MOSES HADAS & OTHERS

0-553-321343-1 BDD PB $4.75

Four Comedies

Includes *Lysistrata, The Congresswomen,* and *The Frogs.* This and the following volume contain all the translations from the William Arrowsmith edition currently in print. They are far and away the best English translations ever made

TRANSLATED BY RICHMOND LATTIMORE & DOUGLAS PARKER

EDITED BY WILLIAM ARROWSMITH

0-472-06152-6 MICHIGAN PB $13.95

Three Comedies

Includes *The Birds, The Clouds,* and *The Wasps*

EDITED BY WILLIAM ARROWSMITH

0-472-06153-4 MICHIGAN PB $13.95

The Frogs

TRANSLATED BY KENNETH J. DOVER

0-19-815071-7 OXFORD PB $15.00

The Frogs & Other Plays

Also includes *The Wasps* and *The Poet and the Women*

TRANSLATED BY DAVID BARRETT

0-14-044152-2 PENGUIN PB $9.95

The Knights, Peace, The Birds, The Assemblywomen & Wealth

TRANSLATED BY DAVID BARRETT & ALAN SOMMERSTEIN

0-14-044332-0 PENGUIN PB $9.95

Lysistrata & Other Plays

Also includes *The Acharnians* and *The Clouds*

TRANSLATED BY ALAN SOMMERSTEIN

0-14-044287-1 PENGUIN PB $7.95

History

The classical historians whose work survives substantially intact are Herodotus (who researched the background of the Persian invasions of Greece in 490 and 480 BC), Thucydides (who explored the war between Athens and Sparta that dominated the latter part of the 5th century), and Xenophon (whose supplement to Thucydides' narratives extends down into the 4th century).

Herodotus

The Histories

An uncompromising modern prose version

TRANSLATED BY GEORGE RAWLINSON

0-460-87170-6 EVERYMAN'S PB $12.95

The Histories

Father of history; father of lies—Herodotus has both reputations. The new translation upholds the reputation of this bestiary of ancient customs, which becomes a history of Greek resistance to the invasion of the Persian king Xerxes in 480 BC

TRANSLATED BY DAVID GRENE

0-226-32770-1 CHICAGO $35.00

0-226-32772-8 CHICAGO PB $13.95

Thucydides

The History of the Peloponnesian War

Seapower was the key to Greek victory in the Persian War, and the Athenians used the navy to dominate other Greek states until the tragic conflict with Sparta destroyed her empire. This unflinching record by an exiled Athenian general established a standard for accurate history writing

TRANSLATED BY REX WARNER

0-14-044039-9 PENGUIN PB $10.95

The Peloponnesian War

TRANSLATED BY RICHARD CRAWLEY

REVISED BY T.E. WICK

0-07-554372-9 MCGRAW HILL PB $15.40

The Peloponnesian War: The Complete Hobbes Translation

Thucydides' great history as translated by philosopher Thomas Hobbes and first published in 1629. "Thomas Hobbes' translation of Thucydides brings together the magisterial prose of one of the greatest writers of the English language and the depth of mind and experience of one of the greatest writers of history in any language"—David Grene

WITH NOTES AND INTRODUCTION BY DAVID GRENE

0-226-80106-3 CHICAGO PB $17.95

Xenophon

A History of My Times

Life in the defeated Athenian empire, with personal reminiscences of Plato and Socrates

TRANSLATED BY REX WARNER

0-14-044175-1 PENGUIN PB $10.95

The Persian Expedition

Stranded in the heart of the Persian empire, a Greek contingent fights its way north from Babylon to the Black Sea: an excellent translation of the *Anabasis*

0-14-044007-0 PENGUIN PB $9.95

Oratory

Oratory was central to Athenian society. Sophists charged high fees to teach the art of public speaking and successful orators used language to exert influence, whether in the assembly, the law court, or the theater.

W. Robert **Connor**, editor

Greek Orations: Fourth Century BC

0-88133-282-8 WAVELAND PB $7.95

A.N. **Saunders**, translator

Greek Political Oratory

0-14-044223-5 PENGUIN PB $9.95

Philosophy

Greek thought forged the fundamental concepts that form the root of European philosophical inquiry. The beginnings of Greek philosophy, up to the time of Socrates (who died in 399 BC), reach us only in remarkably accessible fragments.

See also **WESTERN PHILOSOPHY**

Aristotle

Basic Works of Aristotle

EDITED BY RICHARD P. MCKEON

0-394-41610-4 RANDOM HOUSE $40.00

The Complete Works of Aristotle

The revised Oxford translation in a two-volume set

See also **ARISTOTLE** under **PHILOSOPHY** in **RELIGION, SPIRITUALITY, AND PHILOSOPHY**

EDITED BY JONATHAN BARNES

0-691-09950-2 PRINCETON $79.00

Jonathan **Barnes**, editor

Early Greek Philosophy

Collects the extant writings of the pre-Socratics

See also **THE PRESOCRATICS** under **PHILOSOPHY** in **RELIGION, SPIRITUALITY, AND PHILOSOPHY**

0-14-044461-0 PENGUIN PB $10.95

Plato

The Collected Dialogues of Plato

EDITED BY EDITH HAMILTON & HUNTINGTON CAIRNS

See also **PLATO** under **PHILOSOPHY** in **RELIGION, SPIRITUALITY, AND PHILOSOPHY**

0-691-09718-6 PRINCETON $37.50

Plato's Republic

The best overall translation, with just enough notes to make it accessible

TRANSLATED BY G.M.A. GRUBE

0-915144-04-2 HACKETT $32.50

0-915144-03-4 HACKETT PB $5.95

The Republic

TRANSLATED BY ROBIN WATERFIELD

0-19-212604-0 OXFORD $30.00

0-19-282909-2 OXFORD PB $5.95

Plato

Xenophon

Conversations of Socrates

See also **SOCRATES** under **PHILOSOPHY** in **RELIGION, SPIRITUALITY, AND PHILOSOPHY**

0-14-044517-X PENGUIN PB $11.95

The Hellenistic and Roman Periods

During the 3rd and 2nd centuries BC, there was a great burst of literary activity in Alexandria, Alexander's new city on the edge of the Egyptian desert. With the coming of Roman military and economic dominance in the East, Greek wisdom, oratory, and literature spread throughout the Mediterranean world. Divorced from the world that had given it birth, Greek literature became the international standard of clear thought and articulate speech.

Drama

We have only scant examples of Attic New Comedy from the period around 300 BC, all of them by Menander. This drama was imitated by the Roman writers Plautus and Terence and became the foundation of comedy in the West. With Menander, Greek drama turns away from the divine and achieves dignity in human scale.

Menander

The Dyskolos

The only, essentially intact play (though others can be credibly restored to near-completeness)

TRANSLATED BY CAROLL MOULTON

0-452-00865-4 NEW AMERICAN LIBRARY PB $6.00

The Girl from Samos

The pioneering reconstruction of this beautiful play

TRANSLATED BY ERIC TURNER

0-485-12019-4 HUMANITIES PB $17.50

Plays and Fragments

The revised Penguin Menander makes available to a general audience the recently recovered Menander plays and fragments

TRANSLATED BY NORMA MILLER

0-14-044501-3 PENGUIN PB $10.95

Alexandrian Poetry

In the 3rd century BC, Alexandria saw the birth of a new genre, pastoral poetry, whose belated influence on Western European literature from the Middle Ages to the 18th century was to be decisive. Alexandria also saw the extension of earlier genres, such as the epic and the hymn.

Callimachus

Hymns, Epigrams, Select Fragments

TRANSLATED BY STANLEY LOMBARDO & DIANE RAYOR

FOREWORD BY D.S. CARNE-ROSS

0-8018-3281-0 JOHNS HOPKINS PB $8.95

Barbara Hughes **Fowler**, translator

Hellenistic Poetry: An Anthology

A comprehensive presentation of the range and varying moods of Hellenistic poetry, including work by Theocritus, Callimachus, Bion, Moschus, selections from *The Greek Anthology*, and a complete translation of the *Argonautica* of Apollonius of Rhodes

0-299-12534-3 WISCONSIN PB $14.95

Apollonius **of Rhodes**

The Voyage of Argo

This richly ironic epic is the principal bridge from Homer to Virgil

TRANSLATED BY E.V. RIEU

0-14-044085-2 PENGUIN PB $9.95

Theocritus

Idylls

TRANSLATED BY ROBERT WELLS

0-14-044523-4 PENGUIN PB $10.95

Greek Knowledge

Apollodorus

Gods and Heroes of the Greeks: The "Library" of Apollodorus

When the Greeks started collecting the old stories for their own sake, the results were compilations like this one—pedantic, pedestrian, and systematic. Apollodorus is the least unreadable of the Greek mythographers

TRANSLATED BY MICHAEL SIMPSON

ILLUSTRATED BY LEONARD BASKIN

0-87023-206-1 MASSACHUSETTS PB $17.95

Hans Dieter **Betz**, editor

The Greek Magical Papyri in Translation, Including the Demotic Spells

0-226-04446-7 CHICAGO $49.50

0-226-04447-5 CHICAGO PB $24.95

Hippocrates

Hippocratic Writings

A fascinating introduction to Greek medicine in theory and practice

TRANSLATED BY J. CHADWICK & W.N. NANN

EDITED WITH AN INTRODUCTION BY G.E.R. LLOYD

0-14-044451-3 PENGUIN PB $10.95

Pausanias

Guide to Greece

Volume 1 Northern Greece

A selection from the 2nd-century BC description by Pausanias, reorganized around a geographical pattern more useful to the tourist than that of the original

See also **ANCIENT GREEK CLASSICS** under **ANCIENT GREECE** in **WORLD HISTORY AND CURRENT AFFAIRS**

0-14-044225-1 PENGUIN PB $13.95

Volume 2 Southern Greece

0-14-044226-X PENGUIN PB $13.95

Plutarch

Essays

Not only a biographer, Plutarch was a prolific essayist with an encyclopaedic grasp of the Greek tradition and an easy-going style which served as a model for Montaigne. The topics here include "How to Distinguish a Flatterer from a Friend" and "On the Avoidance of Anger"

0-14-044564-1 PENGUIN PB $12.95

Plutarch

Plutarch's Lives

The great monument of ancient biography, comparing the accomplishments of Greece and Rome

Volume 1

0-679-60008-6 MODERN LIBRARY $19.00

Volume 2

0-679-60009-4 MODERN LIBRARY $20.00

Selected Essays and Dialogues

0-19-283094-5 OXFORD PB $10.95

Prose Fiction, Fables, and Romances

Aesop

Aesop's Fables

TRANSLATED BY JACK ZIPES

0-451-52565-5 NEW AMERICAN LIBRARY PB $4.95

Fables of Aesop

TRANSLATED BY S.A. HANDFORD

0-14-044043-7 PENGUIN PB $7.95

Longus

Daphnis and Chloe

A widely influential novel of erotic awakening and youthful adventure

TRANSLATED BY PAUL TURNER

0-14-044059-3 PENGUIN PB $9.95

Lucian

Satirical Sketches

Lucian, one of the great debunkers of religious and philosophical absolutes, wrote in the 2nd century AD. His influence on Western writers, from Erasmus and Rabelais to Swift and Voltaire, has been immense, and his uproarious humor makes him as readable as ever

TRANSLATED BY PAUL TURNER

0-253-20581-6 INDIANA PB $6.95

Selected Satires of Lucian

TRANSLATED AND EDITED BY LIONEL CASSON

0-393-00443-0 NORTON PB $12.95

B.P. **Reardon**, editor

Collected Ancient Greek Novels

Scholars are showing renewed respect for the seriousness and structural importance of these

earliest novels, once dismissed as lightweight escapism
0-520-04306-5 CALIFORNIA PB $29.95

Richard **Stoneman**, editor
Legends of Alexander the Great
Examples of the enormous fanciful literature that swirled around the life of the conqueror
0-460-87514-0 EVERYMAN'S PB $8.50

Xenophon
The Education of Cyrus
A political romance about the early training of the Persian king
TRANSLATED BY H.G. DAKYNS
0-460-87154-4 EVERYMAN'S PB $10.95

Greek Literary Criticism

T.S. **Dorsch**, translator
Classical Literary Criticism
Includes Aristotle's *Poetics,* Horace's *Ars Poetica,* and Longinus's *On the Sublime*
0-14-044155-7 PENGUIN PB $9.95

D.A. **Russell** & M. **Winterbottom**, editors
Classical Literary Criticism
A compact gathering of crucial works by Plato, Longinus, Horace, Tacitus, Plutarch, and Dio of Prusa
0-19-281830-9 OXFORD PB $6.95

Anthologies

W.H. **Auden**, editor
The Portable Greek Reader
With an illuminating introduction
0-14-015039-0 VIKING PB $14.95

Michael **Grant**, editor
Greek Literature: An Anthology
A collection of excerpts from the whole range of Greek writing, interesting primarily for its sampling of translations, including many now out of print
0-14-044323-1 PENGUIN PB $10.95

Robert **Graves**
The Greek Myths
Drawn from the definitive classic, this condensed edition cites the legends of birth and the lives of the great Olympians, from Andromeda and Aphrodite to Narcissus and Zeus. Illustrated by the artists of ancient Greece
See also **CLASSICAL MYTHOLOGY: ANCIENT GREECE AND ROME** under **MYTHOLOGY AND FOLKLORE** in **RELIGION, SPIRITUALITY, AND PHILOSOPHY**
0-918825-80-6 MOYER BELL $27.95
0-14-007602-6 PENGUIN PB $17.95

Adrian **Poole** & Jeremy **Maule**, editors
The Oxford Book of Classical Verse in Translation
Ben Jonson, Alexander Pope, Alfred Lord Tennyson, and Ezra Pound are among the poets assembled here to display the rich tradition of classical translation in English
See also **ANTHOLOGIES** under **LATIN LITERATURE**
0-19-214209-7 OXFORD $29.95

Bernard **Knox**, editor
The Norton Book of Classical Literature
0-393-03426-7 NORTON $29.95

Critical Studies

The enduring critical engagement with the classical world is not only stimulated by the continuous discovery of archaeological material but also reflects new approaches that derive from modern theory, from modern concern with the histories of minorities, and from new scholarship in linguistics, anthropology, and other disciplines.

For example, Homeric studies have been revolutionized by Milman Parry's attempt to demonstrate that "Homer" was an illiterate poet (or poets); Eric Havelock's thesis that the Greeks did not become truly literate until well into the 4th century BC has raised controversial issues about the origin and nature of extant texts and, whereas Victorian scholars emphasized the resemblances between Western democratic man and his Greek forbears, historians now stress the difference, the strangeness of many aspects of the ancient world.

General Studies

P.E. **Easterling** & Bernard **Knox**, editors
The Cambridge History of Classical Literature: Greek Literature
An ingeniously organized group effort, offering a coherent and highly credible survey. Tremendously valuable for bibliography
See also **ANCIENT GREEK CLASSICS** under **ANCIENT GREECE** in **WORLD HISTORY AND CURRENT AFFAIRS**
0-521-21042-9 CAMBRIDGE $125.00

Charles Rowan **Beye**
Ancient Greek Literature and Society
Vigorous and irreverent—an account that takes the Greeks off their pedestals and finds values in them for our time
0-8014-1874-7 CORNELL $44.95
0-8014-9444-3 CORNELL PB $15.95

Fritz **Graf**
Greek Mythology: An Introduction
See also **CLASSICAL MYTHOLOGY: ANCIENT GREECE AND ROME** under **MYTHOLOGY AND FOLKLORE** in **RELIGION, SPIRITUALITY, AND PHILOSOPHY**
0-8018-4657-9 JOHNS HOPKINS $35.95

Eric **Havelock**
Preface to Plato
Perhaps the most influential discussion of the oral nature of early Greek literature
See also **PLATO** under **PHILOSOPHY** in **RELIGION, SPIRITUALITY, AND PHILOSOPHY**
0-674-69906-8 HARVARD PB $16.95

Bernard **Knox**
Backing into the Future: The Classical Tradition and Its Renewal
The renowned classicist and author of *The Oldest Dead White European Males* and *Essays Ancient and Modern* opens his new collection with a group of essays on heroes and poets, including one on Achilles and another on Ovid in exile
See also **KULTURKAMPF: THE WAR OVER THE CANON** under **THE STATE OF THE SCHOOLS** under **EDUCATION** in **SOCIAL STUDIES**
0-393-03595-6 NORTON $25.00

The Oldest Dead White European Males
0-393-03492-5 NORTON $15.95
0-393-31233-X NORTON PB $9.95

Greek Tragedy

H.D. F. **Kitto**
Greek Tragedy: A Literary Study
Cogent and passionately argued essays about the meaning of drama in the mid-20th century
See also **ANCIENT** under **HISTORY** under **THEATER** in **PERFORMING ARTS AND MEDIA**
0-416-68900-0 ROUTLEDGE PB $16.95

Bernard **Knox**
Word and Action: Essays on the Ancient Theater
Essays and reviews full of rich analyses and insights
0-8018-3409-0 JOHNS HOPKINS PB $15.95

Nicole **Loraux**
Tragic Ways of Killing a Woman
A single class of tragic episodes unexpectedly reveals much about Athenian life
0-674-90225-4 HARVARD $23.00

Charles **Segal**
Interpreting Greek Tragedy: Myth, Poetry, Text
Important essays by an insightful contemporary interpreter
0-8014-1890-9 CORNELL $47.50

Oliver **Taplin**
Greek Tragedy in Action
Concentrates on the *Oresteia* and six other plays, reconstructing staging conventions and acting styles
0-520-03949-1 ROUTLEDGE PB $11.00

Jean-Pierre **Vernant** & Pierre **Vidal-Naquet**
Myth and Tragedy in Ancient Greece Volumes 1 & 2
A major contribution from the anthropological wing of contemporary French scholarship
0-942299-18-3 ZONE $32.95

Comedy

R.L. **Hunter**
The New Comedy of Greece and Rome
New comedy and its Latin adaptations, treated as an integral body
0-521-31652-9 CAMBRIDGE PB $19.95

Lyric Poetry

Page du **Bois**
Sappho Is Burning
0-226-16755-0 CHICAGO $24.95

Ellen **Greene**, editor
Reading Sappho: Contemporary Approaches
0-520-20601-0 CALIFORNIA PB $15.00

Re-Reading Sappho: Reception and Transmission
0-520-20603-7 CALIFORNIA PB $10.00

Margaret **Williamson**
Sappho's Immortal Daughters
0-674-78912-1 HARVARD $24.95

Lyn Hatherly **Wilson**
Sappho's Sweetbitter Songs: Configurations of Female and Male in Ancient Greek Lyric
0-415-12671-1 ROUTLEDGE PB $42.00

Studies of Individual Authors

D.J. **Conacher**
Aeschylus' Oresteia: A Literary Commentary
On the model of Conacher's earlier *Prometheus* commentary
0-8020-6747-6 TORONTO PB $18.95

Aeschylus' Prometheus Bound: A Literary Commentary
"Should be extremely profitable to any student of the *Prometheus,* at any level"—C.J. Herington, *Phoenix*
0-8020-2391-6 TORONTO $30.00
0-8020-6416-7 TORONTO PB $12.95

John **Herington**
Aeschylus
The best available introduction
0-300-03643-4 YALE PB $14.00

Thomas **Rosenmeyer**
The Art of Aeschylus
A rich introductory study
0-520-04608-0 CALIFORNIA PB $15.00

Kenneth J. **Dover**
Aristophanic Comedy
Play-by-play analysis by a major scholar
0-520-02211-4 CALIFORNIA PB $14.95

Rosemary **Harriott**
Aristophanes: Poet and Dramatist
0-8018-3279-9 JOHNS HOPKINS $28.00

Ann **Michelini**
Euripides and the Tragic Tradition
0-299-10760-4 WISCONSIN $32.75

J.A.S. **Evans**
Herodotus
"A balanced and thoughtful account of Herodotus as a working historian"—*American Journal of Philology*
0-691-06871-2 PRINCETON $29.50

Robert **Lamberton**
Hesiod
"Combines the sophistication of cultural anthropology with a refined sense for the mechanics and aesthetics of archaic Greek literature and gives Hesiod a fresh and original reading"—Gregory Nagy, Harvard University
0-300-04069-5 YALE PB $14.00

Mark **Edwards**
Homer: Poet of the Iliad
0-8018-3329-9 JOHNS HOPKINS $48.00

M.I. **Finley**
The World of Odysseus
The revision of Finley's 1956 book locating the world of the *Odyssey* in the early Dark Age of Greece. A pioneering application of sociological and anthropological insights. "Finley's magnificent work has long been one of the treasures of my library"—Mary Renault
See also **EARLY GREEK AND MINOAN PERIODS** under **ANCIENT GREECE** in **WORLD HISTORY AND CURRENT AFFAIRS**
0-14-013686-X PENGUIN PB $10.95

Jasper **Griffin**
Homer on Life and Death
"Restores to Homer the humanity he had steadily lost in recent years to the computer and the microphilologists of formulaic analysis" —*American Journal of Philology*
0-19-814026-6 OXFORD PB $19.95

Ralph **Hexter**
A Guide to the Odyssey: A Commentary on the English Translation of Robert Fitzgerald
0-679-72847-3 VINTAGE PB $12.00

G.S. **Kirk**
Homer and the Epic
A concise, focused account of the relationship of the *Iliad* and the *Odyssey* to oral tradition
0-521-09356-2 CAMBRIDGE PB $23.95

Robert **Lamberton**
Homer the Theologian: Neoplatonist Allegorical Reading and the Growth of the Epic Tradition
0-520-06607-3 CALIFORNIA PB $16.00

Milman **Parry**
The Making of Homeric Verse: The Collected Papers of Milman Parry
Parry's demonstration of the structural similarities between Homeric epic and living oral epic was a watershed in Homeric scholarship
EDITED BY ADAM PARRY
0-19-520560-X OXFORD PB $29.95

Seth **Schein**
The Mortal Hero: An Introduction to Homer's Iliad
The best recent introduction
0-520-05626-4 CALIFORNIA PB $14.95

Simone **Weil**
The Iliad, Or the Poem of Force
Intelligence, insight, and compassion combine to make this brief essay the most moving reading of the *Iliad* in our time
See also **ESSAYS: PERSONAL, LITERARY, PHILOSOPHICAL** under **MODERN FRENCH LITERATURE**
0-87574-091-X PENDLE HILL PB $3.00

Malcolm **Willcock**
A Companion to the Iliad
A commentary based on the Lattimore translation
0-226-89855-5 CHICAGO PB $10.95

Albert Bates **Lord**
The Singer of Tales
A classic account of the relationship between Homeric epic poetry and living traditions of oral epic
See also **POETRY** under **LITERARY CRITICISM**
0-674-80881-9 HARVARD PB $15.95

Gregory **Nagy**
The Best of the Achaeans: Concepts of the Hero in Archaic Greek Poetry
"Learned, clever, and disturbing"—*TLS*
0-8018-2388-9 JOHNS HOPKINS PB $16.95

D.S. **Carne-Ross**
Pindar
Readings of twelve odes that bring home much of this evasive poet's richness
0-300-03383-4 YALE $30.00
0-300-03393-1 YALE PB $12.00

Julia **Annas**
An Introduction to Plato's Republic
A remarkable achievement. Presents Plato as a philosophical educator rather than a dogmatist and discusses various problems raised by this difficult text
See also **PLATO** under **PHILOSOPHY** in **RELIGION, SPIRITUALITY, AND PHILOSOPHY**
0-19-827429-7 OXFORD PB $18.95

David **Halperin**
Before Pastoral: Theocritus and the Ancient Tradition of Bucolic Poetry
Pastoral theory and the originality of Theocritus
0-300-02582-3 YALE $37.00

Thomas **Rosenmeyer**
The Green Cabinet: Theocritus and the European Pastoral Lyric
"Many brilliant insights"—P.V. Marinelli, *Phoenix*
0-520-02362-5 CALIFORNIA PB $14.00

Bernard M. **Knox**

The Heroic Temper: Studies in Sophoclean Tragedy

An essential introduction to the craggy, intractable Sophoclean hero

0-520-04957-8 CALIFORNIA PB $14.00

Bernard Knox

W. Robert **Connor**

Thucydides

An insightful evocation of the somber, threatening worldview of the historian whose panoramic presentation of the Peloponnesian War is an indictment not only of the failures of democracy but also of human nature

0-691-10239-2 PRINCETON PB $17.95

Latin Literature

Latin literature is a strange anomaly: an imitation which has itself been abundantly imitated. From its earliest appearance in the 3rd century BC, the literature of ancient Rome drew on the subject matter, plots, and even specific lines of Greek drama, comedy, and epic. But the Roman authors transformed these models into their own ways of seeing, and Western literary traditions owe more to this hybrid than to the Greek sources. The poised satire of Horace rather than the vigorous iambs of Archilochus; the melodrama of Seneca rather than the restraint of the Greek tragedians; Virgil's teleological epic rather than Homer's naturalism: these have been primary influences on the great European poets and dramatists, Shakespeare and Milton among them.

E.J. **Kenney** & W.V. **Clausen**, editors

The Cambridge History of Classical Literature: Latin Literature

Part 1
The Early Republic

0-521-27375-7 CAMBRIDGE PB $22.95

Part 2
The Late Republic

0-521-27374-9 CAMBRIDGE PB $22.95

Part 3
The Age of Augustus

0-521-27373-0 CAMBRIDGE PB $22.95

Part 4
The Early Principate

0-521-27372-2 CAMBRIDGE PB $22.95

Part 5
The Later Principate

0-521-27371-4 CAMBRIDGE PB $22.95

The Early Period

Most of the literature of the older republic has been lost, depriving us of the important dramas and epics of Ennius and others. But the works of two comic playwrights from the late 3rd and early 2nd century BC are treasures of world literature. Plautus, who rose from miller's apprentice to popular dramatist, and Terence, a freed North African slave, added a robust Roman quality to their adaptations of Greek plays while retaining the cleverness of the original models.

Plautus

Four Comedies

TRANSLATED BY ERICH SEGAL

0-19-283108-9 OXFORD PB $8.95

Plautus: The Comedies

Volume 1

0-8018-5070-3 JOHNS HOPKINS $45.00

0-8018-5071-1 JOHNS HOPKINS PB $15.95

Volume 2

0-8018-5056-8 JOHNS HOPKINS $45.00

0-8018-5057-6 JOHNS HOPKINS PB $15.95

The Pot of Gold & Other Plays

Includes *The Brothers Menaechmus, The Prisoner, The Swaggering Soldier,* and *Pseudolus.* Rough farce and exuberant word-play give new life to standardized Greek plots. *The Brothers Menaechmus* is the basis for Shakespeare's *Comedy of Errors,* and the title play influenced Molière's *L'Avare*

TRANSLATED BY E.F. WATLING

0-14-044149-2 PENGUIN PB $9.95

The Rope & Other Plays

Includes *The Ghost, The Three-Dollar Day,* and *Amphitryon.* In *The Rope,* low comedy rises to genuine romance, while Jupiter Almighty becomes the humorous butt of *Amphitryon*

TRANSLATED BY E.F. WATLING

0-14-044136-0 PENGUIN PB $9.95

Terence

The Comedies

Includes the complete plays: *The Girl from Andros, The Mother-in-Law, The Self-Punisher, The Eunuch, Phormio,* and *The Brother.* More refined and original than the works of his older contemporary Plautus, Terence's plays are among the earliest comedies of manners

TRANSLATED BY BETTY RADICE

0-14-044324-X PENGUIN PB $11.95

The Comedies

TRANSLATED BY PALMER BOVIE & OTHERS

0-8018-4353-7 JOHNS HOPKINS $45.00

0-8018-4354-5 JOHNS HOPKINS PB $15.95

The Golden Age

Usually taken to refer to the years from the Social War in 70 BC to the end of the reign of Augustus in AD 14, this period encompasses a heterogeneous group of Rome's most brilliant writers. Preeminent among poets in the late republic were the passionate lyricist Catullus and the moody optimist Lucretius, while the principate triumphant produced the stabilizing synthesis of Virgil's epic and the civilized verse forms of Horace and Ovid.

A.J. **Boyle** & J.P. **Sullivan**, editors

Roman Poets of the Early Empire

Ambitious in its attempt to take a fresh look at the aesthetic issues of Roman poetry, not only Ovid, Martial, and Juvenal, but underappreciated figures like Seneca, Lucan, and Statius, not to mention Calpurnius Siculus and Valerius Flaccus

0-14-044544-7 PENGUIN PB $10.95

Catullus

Odi et Amo: The Complete Poetry of Catullus

TRANSLATED BY ROY SWANSON

0-02-418490-X PRENTICE HALL PB $13.00

The Poems of Catullus

A sharp-edged and colloquial translation by an English poet of modernist bent

TRANSLATED BY PETER WHIGHAM

0-14-044180-8 PENGUIN PB $10.95

Catullus

The Poems of Catullus

"Charles Martin has captured what other translators of Catullus have missed—his perpetual modernity"—Dana Gioia

TRANSLATED BY CHARLES MARTIN

0-8018-3925-4 JOHNS HOPKINS $35.00

0-8018-3926-2 JOHNS HOPKINS PB $13.95

The Poems of Catullus

0-19-282850-9 OXFORD PB $8.95

Cicero

Orator and statesman, lawyer and philosopher, Marcus Tullius Cicero was the consummate Roman, whose intellectual abilities were always at the service of public affairs. He transmitted Greek thought to Rome, and in the Renaissance his oratorical style was a model for great Italian scholars and writers.

The Nature of the Gods
An elegant discussion of the popular Greek philosophies of Epicureanism, Stoicism, and the new Academic skepticism
TRANSLATED BY HORACE MCGREGOR
INTRODUCTION BY J.M. ROSS
0-14-044265-0 PENGUIN PB........$10.95

On the Good Life
0-14-044244-8 PENGUIN PB........$10.95

Selected Letters
Cicero's correspondence gives an intimate portrait of the man and his times
TRANSLATED BY D.R. SHACKLETON-BAILEY
0-14-044458-0 PENGUIN PB........$10.95

Selected Political Speeches
Decisions in the contentious Roman Senate were often based on persuasive speech-making, of which Cicero was a master
TRANSLATED BY MICHAEL GRANT
0-14-044214-6 PENGUIN PB........$10.95

Selected Works
Includes *Against Verres, Twenty-Three Letters, Second Philippic Against Antony, On Duties,* and *On Old Age.* A wide-ranging selection of speeches, letters, and essays, from Cicero's prosecution of corrupt colonial administrators and his scathing denunciation of Mark Antony, to his placid and witty encomium on old age
TRANSLATED BY MICHAEL GRANT
0-14-044099-2 PENGUIN PB........$10.95

Horace

Carpe Diem: Horace Odes I
TRANSLATED BY DAVID WEST
0-19-872161-7 OXFORD PB........$19.95

Complete Odes and Epodes
The son of a freedman whose poetic talents gained him fame and fortune at the court of Augustus, Horace appears in this collection in all his extraordinary variety
TRANSLATED BY W.G. SHEPHERD
INTRODUCTION BY BETTY RADICE
0-14-044422-X PENGUIN PB........$9.95

Horace & Persius

The Satires of Horace and Persius
A generation apart, these two social commentators display the contrasting qualities of smooth bonhomie and crabbed erudition
TRANSLATED BY NIALL RUDD
0-14-044279-0 PENGUIN PB........$9.95

Lucan

Civil War
TRANSLATED BY SUSAN H. BRAUND
0-19-282994-7 OXFORD PB........$9.95

Lucan's Civil War
A new translation of the *Pharsalia,* the chief Roman epic after *The Aeneid*
TRANSLATED BY P.F. WIDDOWS
0-253-31399-6 INDIANA........$52.95

Pharsalia
TRANSLATED BY JANE WILSON JOYCE
0-8014-2907-2 CORNELL........$39.95
0-8014-8137-6 CORNELL PB........$17.95

Lucretius

On the Nature of the Universe
A straightforward prose version
TRANSLATED BY R.E. LATHAM
0-14-044610-9 PENGUIN PB........$11.95

On the Nature of Things: De Rerum Natura
TRANSLATED BY ANTHONY M. ESOLEN
0-8018-5054-1 JOHNS HOPKINS........$35.95
0-8018-5055-X JOHNS HOPKINS PB........$14.95

The Way Things Are: The De Rerum Natura of Titus Lucretius Carus
An excellent verse translation of the philosophical poem which exults in the freedom from tyrannical gods conferred by Epicurean materialism
See also **STOICS AND EPICUREANS** under **PHILOSOPHY** in **RELIGION, SPIRITUALITY, AND PHILOSOPHY**
TRANSLATED BY ROLFE HUMPHRIES
0-253-20125-X INDIANA PB........$8.95

Ovid

The Art of Love
Another fine verse translation by Humphries
TRANSLATED BY ROLFE HUMPHRIES
0-253-10391-6 INDIANA........$25.00
0-253-20002-4 INDIANA PB........$8.95

The Erotic Poems
Ovid's manuals on the art of love have influenced poets and lovers ever since
TRANSLATED BY PETER GREEN
0-14-044360-6 PENGUIN PB........$10.95

Heroides
A series of epistolary poems in which Ovid recreates the myths of Hero and Leander, Helen and Paris, and others
TRANSLATED BY HAROLD ISBELL
0-14-042355-9 PENGUIN PB........$10.95

The Love Poems
TRANSLATED BY A.D. MELVILLE
0-19-282194-6 OXFORD PB........$8.95

The Metamorphoses
This retelling of the Greek myths, held together by the theme of physical transformation, has provided Western writers with innumerable plots and images
TRANSLATED BY ROLFE HUMPHRIES
0-253-33755-0 INDIANA........$31.95
0-253-20001-6 INDIANA PB........$7.95

The Metamorphoses
A superbly fluent verse rendering
TRANSLATED BY HORACE GREGORY
0-451-62622-2 NEW AMERICAN LIBRARY PB........$5.99

The Metamorphoses
TRANSLATED BY DAVID R. SLAVITT
0-8018-4797-4 JOHNS HOPKINS........$45.00
0-8018-4798-2 JOHNS HOPKINS PB........$14.95

The Metamorphoses
TRANSLATED BY A.D. MELVILLE
0-19-281691-8 OXFORD PB........$6.95

The Metamorphoses of Ovid
From the National Book Award-winning translator of Virgil
TRANSLATED BY ALLEN MANDELBAUM
0-156-00126-8 HARVEST PB........$15.00

Ovid's Fasti: Roman Holidays
TRANSLATED BY BETTY ROSE NAGLE
0-253-20933-1 INDIANA PB........$8.95

Ovid's Poetry of Exile
A new translation of the poems in which Ovid directly describes his exile by Emperor Augustus to the remote Black Sea town of Tomis. Includes *Tristia, Epistulae ex Ponto,* and *Ibis.* "Witty, affecting, and occasionally grand... If Ovid were writing his complaints from exile today, this, one ends up feeling, is what he would sound like" —Bernard M. Knox
TRANSLATED BY DAVID SLAVITT
0-8018-3916-5 JOHNS HOPKINS PB........$12.95

The Poems of Exile
TRANSLATED BY PETER GREEN
0-14-044407-6 PENGUIN PB........$10.95

Sorrows of an Exile
TRANSLATED BY A.D. MELVILLE
0-19-282452-X OXFORD PB........$10.95

Michael **Hofmann** & James **Lasdun**, editors

After Ovid: New Metamorphoses
Contemporary poets, including Seamus Heaney, Jorie Graham, and Ted Hughes, rework Ovid to new effect
See also **ANTHOLOGIES** under **20TH-CENTURY AMERICAN POETRY** in **LITERATURE OF THE AMERICAS**
0-374-10197-3 FS&G........$25.00
0-374-52478-5 NOONDAY PB........$14.00

Propertius

Charm
Colloquial translations of the great lyrics, at once sophisticated and sincere, of a poet who was a friend of Ovid
TRANSLATED BY VINCENT KATZ
1-55713-224-0 SUN & MOON PB........$11.95

Statius

The Thebaid
A turbulent and complex epic concerning the internecine wars of the sons of Oedipus, by a poet who had seen his share of civil conflict
TRANSLATED BY A.D. MELVILLE
0-19-282453-8 OXFORD PB........$12.95

Virgil

The Aeneid
Virgil's great epic transforms the Homeric tradition into a triumphal statement of the Roman civilizing mission. Fitzgerald's version is up to the high standard established by his Homer translations
TRANSLATED BY ROBERT FITZGERALD
0-679-41335-9 KNOPF........$17.00
0-679-72952-6 VINTAGE PB........$8.00

The Aeneid of Virgil: A Verse Translation
TRANSLATED BY ALLEN MANDELBAUM
0-553-21041-6 BDD PB........$3.95
0-520-04550-5 CALIFORNIA PB........$15.95

The Eclogues
Virgil's earliest work brings an apocalyptic element to the pastoral tradition of Theocritus
TRANSLATED WITH AN INTRODUCTION BY GUY LEE
0-14-044419-X PENGUIN PB $10.95

The Georgics
Gibbon claimed that this poem in praise of rural life was designed to help Augustus's discharged veterans adjust to conditions on the farm
TRANSLATED BY L.P. WILKINSON
0-14-044414-9 PENGUIN PB $8.95

Virgil in English
EDITED BY K.W. GRANSDEN
0-14-042386-9 PENGUIN PB $14.95

The Works of Virgil in English (1697)
Dryden's 17th-century versions have not been surpassed for clarity and power

Eclogues, Georgics, Aeneid I-IV
0-520-02121-5 CALIFORNIA $75.00

Aeneid VII-XIII
0-520-02122-3 CALIFORNIA $75.00

The Silver Age

Appian
The Civil Wars
0-14-044509-9 PENGUIN PB $13.95

Lucius **Apuleius**
The Golden Ass
A humorous, first-person account of one man's "conversion" to the worship of the goddess Isis and his initiation into her mysteries in the second-century Roman empire
See also **ANCIENT MEDITERRANEAN RELIGIONS** under **WORLD RELIGION** in **RELIGION, SPIRITUALITY, AND PHILOSOPHY**
TRANSLATED BY ROBERT GRAVES
0-374-50532-2 FS&G PB $11.00

The Golden Ass
A new translation of Apuleius's endlessly fascinating masterpiece
TRANSLATED BY P.G. WALSH
0-19-282492-9 OXFORD PB $11.95

Juvenal
The Satires of Juvenal
Humphries's translation is full-bodied and rhythmically alive
TRANSLATED BY ROLFE HUMPHRIES
0-253-20020-2 INDIANA PB $8.95

The Sixteen Satires
The most savage of Roman satirists lashes out at the corruption of Antonine Rome
TRANSLATED BY PETER GREEN
0-14-044194-8 PENGUIN PB $10.95

Martial
The Epigrams
Witty miniatures from the Rome of Domitian, ranging from pathos to burlesque
TRANSLATED BY JAMES MICHIE
0-14-044350-9 PENGUIN PB $8.95

J.P **Sullivan** & A.J. **Boyle**, editors
Martial in English
0-14-042389-3 PENGUIN PB $14.95

Petronius
The Satyricon
A 1996 translation of the first-century novel. A chronology, introduction, and commentary provide background on Petronius's social milieu
See also **SOCIAL LIFE** under **TOPICS IN ROMAN HISTORY** under **ANCIENT ROME** in **WORLD HISTORY AND CURRENT AFFAIRS**
TRANSLATED & EDITED BY R. BRACHT BRANHAM & DANIEL KINNEY
0-520-20599-5 CALIFORNIA $28.00

Caligula

The Satyricon
A picaresque account of the vices high and low of Nero's Rome, by the arbiter of elegance who turned his enforced suicide into a triumph of Epicurean indifference. Arrowsmith's translation is outstanding
TRANSLATED BY WILLIAM ARROWSMITH
0-452-01005-5 NEW AMERICAN LIBRARY PB $10.95

The Satyricon
Also includes Seneca's *Apocolocyntosis,* in which he mocks the deification of emperors
TRANSLATED BY J.P. SULLIVAN
0-19-815012-1 OXFORD $55.00

Pliny the Elder
Natural History: A Selection
The major source of ancient belief on subjects from agriculture to zoology, this is the first century AD's answer to the *Encyclopædia Britannica* text
TRANSLATED BY JOHN F. HEALY
0-14-044413-0 PENGUIN PB $12.95

Changes of sex

That women have changed into men is not a myth. We find in historical records during the consulship of Publius Licinius Crassus and Gaius Cassius Longinus, a girl at Casinum became a boy before her parent's very eyes, and, on the order of the augurs, was taken away to an uninhabited island. Licinius Mucianus records that at Argos he saw a man called Areseon, who, as Arescusa, had married a husband, but had subsequently grown a beard, developed male characteristics and had married a wife. He had also seen a boy at Smyrna who had experienced the same fate. In Africa, I myself saw someone who became a man on his wedding-day.
NATURAL HISTORY: A SELECTION

Pliny the Younger
The Letters of the Younger Pliny
An autobiography through personal letters that shows the best side of the civilized Roman aristocrat
TRANSLATED BY BETTY RADICE
0-14-044127-1 PENGUIN PB $9.95

Seneca
Four Tragedies & Octavia
These unrestrained melodramas were a prime influence on the Elizabethan tragedians
TRANSLATED BY E.F. WATLING
0-14-044174-3 PENGUIN PB $11.95

Letter from a Stoic
The austere ideal of passionless virtue developed by the Stoics was never more eloquently urged than by the Roman essayist and dramatist Seneca
See also **STOICS AND EPICUREANS** under **PHILOSOPHY** in **RELIGION, SPIRITUALITY, AND PHILOSOPHY**
EDITED BY ROBIN CAMPBELL
0-14-044210-3 PENGUIN PB $9.95

The Stoic Philosophy of Seneca: Essays and Letters
EDITED BY MOSES HADAS
0-393-00459-7 NORTON PB $9.95

The Tragedies
Volume I
Trojan Women, Thyestes, Phaedra, Medea, Agamemnon
TRANSLATED BY DAVID R. SLAVITT
0-8018-4308-1 JOHNS HOPKINS $38.50
0-8018-4309-X JOHNS HOPKINS PB $12.95

Volume II
Oedipus, Hercules Furens, Hercules Oetaeus, Octavia, The Phoenician Women
TRANSLATORS INCLUDE RACHEL HADAS, DANA GIOIA, & STEPHEN SANDY
0-8018-4931-4 JOHNS HOPKINS $45.00
0-8018-4932-2 JOHNS HOPKINS PB $15.95

Suetonius
The Twelve Caesars: An Illustrated Edition
Madness and perversity among the supremely powerful
See also **ANCIENT ROMAN SOURCES** under **ANCIENT ROME** in **WORLD HISTORY AND CURRENT AFFAIRS**
TRANSLATED BY ROBERT GRAVES
0-14-044072-0 PENGUIN PB $11.95

Tacitus

Annals of Imperial Rome

This ironic depiction of the gradual loss of freedom among Romans under the first emperors includes memorable vignettes of Messalina's career and the failed plot against Nero. Tacitus's influence on later European writers is incalculable

TRANSLATED BY MICHAEL GRANT

0-14-044060-7 PENGUIN PB $9.95

Late Writers

Saint **Augustine**

The City of God

See also CLASSICS OF WESTERN RELIGIOUS THOUGHT under WORLD RELIGION in RELIGION, SPIRITUALITY, AND PHILOSOPHY

TRANSLATED BY HENRY BETTENSON

0-14-044426-2 PENGUIN PB $15.95

The City of God

The first Christian philosophy of history. A monumental response to pagan interpretations of the decline of Rome

TRANSLATED BY MARCUS DODDS

0-679-60087-6 MODERN LIBRARY $20.00

The Confessions

"The *Confessions* is more than a narrative of conversion. It is a work of rare sophistication and intricacy, in which even the apparently simple autobiographical narrative often carries harmonics of deeper meaning"—from the translator's introduction

TRANSLATED BY HENRY CHADWICK

0-19-281779-5 OXFORD $30.00

0-19-281774-4 OXFORD PB $6.95

And so step by step I ascended from bodies to the soul which perceives through the body, and from there to its inward force, to which bodily senses report external sensations, this being as high as the beasts go. From there again I ascended to the power of reasoning to which is to be attributed the power of judging the deliverances of the bodily senses. This power, which in myself I found to be mutable, raised itself to the level of its own intelligence, and led my thinking out of the ruts of habit. It withdrew itself from the contradictory swarms of imaginative fantasies, so as to discover the light by which it was flooded.

THE CONFESSIONS

Avianus

The Fables of Avianus

TRANSLATED BY DAVID R. SLAVITT

0-8018-4684-6 JOHNS HOPKINS $19.95

Boethius

The Consolation of Philosophy

The Roman adviser to the Gothic king Theodoric wrote this amalgamation of Roman and Christian wisdom while awaiting execution

See also EARLY CHRISTIAN WRITINGS under CLASSICS under CHRISTIANITY in RELIGION, SPIRITUALITY, AND PHILOSOPHY

TRANSLATED BY V.E. WATTS

0-14-044208-1 PENGUIN PB $10.95

Peter **Glassgold**

Boethius: The Poems from On The Consolation of Philosophy

Glassgold's experimental work is a curious palimpsest drawing on centuries of earlier English translations

1-55713-109-0 SUN & MOON PB $10.95

Ammianus **Marcellinus**

The Later Roman Empire (AD 353-378)

A pagan historian writes a florid and somber account of the early Christian empire. Gibbon praised him as "an accurate and faithful guide, who has composed the history of his own times without indulging the prejudices and passions which usually affect the mind of a contemporary"

See also ANCIENT ROMAN SOURCES under ANCIENT ROME in WORLD HISTORY AND CURRENT AFFAIRS

EDITED BY WALTER HAMILTON

INTRODUCTION BY ANDREW WALLACE-HADRILL

0-14-044406-8 PENGUIN PB $14.95

Anthologies

Basil **Davenport**, editor

The Portable Roman Reader

A pleasing anthology enriched by many early translations: here are Horace by Herrick, Ovid by Addison, and Juvenal by Dryden, among others

0-14-015056-0 VIKING PB $13.95

Michael **Grant**, editor

Latin Literature: An Anthology

An anthology of relatively brief excerpts which offers a rich sampling of all eras of English translation

0-14-044389-4 PENGUIN PB $10.95

Adrian **Poole** & Jeremy **Maule**, editors

The Oxford Book of Classical Verse in Translation

Ben Jonson, Alexander Pope, Alfred Lord Tennyson, and Ezra Pound are among the poets assembled here to display the rich tradition of classical translation in English

See also ANTHOLOGIES under ANCIENT GREEK LITERATURE

0-19-214209-7 OXFORD $29.95

Critical Studies

David **Armstrong**

Horace

0-300-04579-4 YALE $35.00

0-300-04573-5 YALE PB $12.00

Jasper **Griffin**

Virgil

A compact introduction, from the Past Masters series

9-99-006873-1 OXFORD $14.95

Moses **Hadas**

A History of Latin Literature

Hadas's conversational style draws the reader deep into the recesses of the Roman literary world

0-231-01848-7 COLUMBIA $70.00

Gilbert **Highet**

The Classical Tradition: Greek and Roman Influences in Western Tradition

0-19-500206-7 OXFORD PB $17.95

Sara **Mack**

Ovid

A study aimed at the general reader, focusing on the originality of Ovid's narrative techniques

0-300-04295-7 YALE PB $14.00

Paul **Veyne**

Roman Erotic Elegy: Love, Poetry, and the West

Veyne applies contemporary critical theory to the work of Propertius, Tibullus, Catullus, and Ovid

TRANSLATED BY DAVID PELLANER

0-226-85432-9 CHICAGO PB $13.95

The Loeb Classics

The Loeb Classics is the only existing series of books which gives access to all that is important in Greek and Latin literature in convenient pocket-sized volumes, with an up-to-date text and an English translation on the facing page. Each volume is annotated and is prefaced by a brief biography, and most contain a bibliography. Greek authors are bound in green; Latin, in red.

Greek Literature

Achilles Tatius

Achilles Tatius

0-674-99050-1 HARVARD $16.95

Aelian

On the Characteristics of Animals

Volume 1 Books 1-5

0-674-99491-4 HARVARD $18.95

Volume 2 Books 6-11

0-674-99493-0 HARVARD $16.95

Volume 3 Books 12-17

0-674-99494-9 HARVARD $16.95

Aelian & others

Letters

0-674-99421-3 HARVARD $16.95

Aenias Tacticus & others

Aenias Tacticus, Aslepiodotus, and Onasander

0-674-99172-9 HARVARD $16.95

Aeschines

Speeches

0-674-99118-4 HARVARD $18.95

Aeschylus

Aeschylus

Volume 1

Includes *Suppliant Maidens, Persians, Prometheus,* and *Seven Against Thebes*

0-674-99160-5 HARVARD $18.95

Volume 2

Includes *Agamemnon, Libation-Bearers, Eumenides,* and *Fragments*

0-674-99161-3 HARVARD $18.95

Apollodorus

The Library

Volume 1

Books 1-3 (9)

0-674-99135-4 HARVARD $16.95

Volume 2

Book 3 (10-16) & Epitome

0-674-99136-2 HARVARD $16.95

Apollonius Rhodius

Apollonius Rhodius

0-674-99001-3 HARVARD $18.95

Apostolic Fathers

Apostolic Fathers

Volume 1

I Clement, II Clement, Ignatius, Polycarp, Didache, and Barnabas

0-674-99027-7 HARVARD $16.95

Volume 2

Shepherd of Hermas, Martyrdom of Polycarp, and Epistle to Diognetus

0-674-99028-5 HARVARD $18.95

Appian

Roman History

Volume 1

Books 1-8, Part 1

0-674-99002-1 HARVARD $18.95

Volume 2

Book 8, Parts 2-12

0-674-99004-8 HARVARD $16.95

Volume 3

Civil Wars, Books 1-3 (26)

0-674-99005-6 HARVARD $16.95

Volume 4

Civil Wars, Book 3 (27-5)

0-674-99006-4 HARVARD $16.95

Aristides

Panathenaicus, In Defense of Oratory

0-674-99505-8 HARVARD $16.95

Aristophanes

Aristophanes

Volume 1

Includes *Acharnians, Knights, Clouds,* and *Wasps*

0-674-99197-4 HARVARD $18.95

Volume 2

Includes *Peace, Birds,* and *Frogs*

0-674-99198-2 HARVARD $18.95

Volume 3

Includes *Lysistrata, Thesmorphoriazusae, Ecclesiazusae,* and *Plutus*

0-674-99199-0 HARVARD $18.95

Aristotle

Aristotle

Volume 1

Includes *Categories, On Interpretation,* and *Prior Analytics*

0-674-99359-4 HARVARD $18.95

Volume 2

Posterior Analytics, Topica

0-674-99430-2 HARVARD $18.95

Volume 3

Includes *On Sophistical Refutations, On Coming-to-Be and Passing Away,* and *On the Cosmos*

0-674-99441-8 HARVARD $18.95

Volume 4

Physics, Books 1-4

0-674-99251-2 HARVARD $16.95

Volume 5

Physics, Books 5-8

0-674-99281-4 HARVARD $18.95

Volume 6

On the Heavens

0-674-99372-1 HARVARD $18.95

Volume 7

Meteorologica

0-674-99436-1 HARVARD $18.95

Volume 8

Includes *On the Soul, Parva Naturalia,* and *On Breath*

0-674-99318-7 HARVARD $18.95

Volume 9

History of Animals, Books 1-3

0-674-99481-7 HARVARD $18.95

Volume 10

History of Animals, Books 4-6

0-674-99482-5 HARVARD $18.95

Volume 11

History of Animals, Books 7-10

0-674-99483-3 HARVARD $18.95

Volume 12

Parts of Animals

0-674-99357-8 HARVARD $18.95

Volume 13

Generation of Animals

0-674-99403-5 HARVARD $18.95

Volume 14

Minor Works

Includes *On Colours, On Things Heard, Physiognomics, On Plants, On Marvellous Things Heard, Mechanical Problems, On Indivisible Lines, The Situations and Names of Winds, On Melissus, Xenophanes,* and *Georgias*

0-674-99338-1 HARVARD $18.95

Volume 15

Problems, Books 1-21

0-674-99349-7 HARVARD $18.95

Volume 16

Problems, Books 22-38 & Rhetorica ad Alexandrum

0-674-99350-0 HARVARD $18.95

Volume 17

Metaphysics, Books 1-9

0-674-99299-7 HARVARD $18.95

Volume 18

Metaphysics, Books 10-14, Oeconomica & Magna Moralia

0-674-99317-9 HARVARD $18.95

Volume 19

Nicomachean Ethics

0-674-99081-1 HARVARD $18.95

Volume 20

Includes *Athenian Constitution, Eudemian Ethics,* and *Virtues and Vices*

0-674-99315-2 HARVARD $18.95

Volume 21

Politics

0-674-99291-1 HARVARD $18.95

Volume 22

Art of Rhetoric

0-674-99212-1 HARVARD $18.95

Volume 23

Includes *Poetics,* Longinus's *On the Sublime,* and Demetrius's *On Style*

0-674-99563-5 HARVARD $18.95

Arrian

History of Alexander

Volume 1

Anabasis, Books 1-4

0-674-99260-1 HARVARD $18.95

Volume 2

Anabasis, Books 5-7

0-674-99297-0 HARVARD $18.95

Athenaeus

Deipnosophists

Volume 1

Books 1-3 (106c)

0-674-99224-5 HARVARD $16.95

Volume 2

Book 3 (106c)-5

0-674-99229-6 HARVARD $16.95

Volume 3

Books 6-7

0-674-99247-4 HARVARD $16.95

Volume 4

Books 8-10

0-674-99259-8 HARVARD $16.95

Volume 5

Books 11-12

0-674-99302-0 HARVARD $16.95

Volume 6
Books 13-14 (653b)
0-674-99361-6 HARVARD $16.95

Volume 7
Book 14 (653b)-15
0-674-99380-2 HARVARD $16.95

Marcus Aurelius

Marcus Aurelius
0-674-99064-1 HARVARD $18.95

Babrius & Phaedrus

Babrius & Phaedrus
Translated, with an historical introduction and a comprehensive survey of Greek and Latin fables in the Aesopic tradition
See also LATIN LITERATURE
0-674-99480-9 HARVARD $18.95

St. Basil

Letters

Volume 1
Letters 1-58
0-674-99209-1 HARVARD $16.95

Volume 2
Letters 59-185
0-674-99237-7 HARVARD $15.50

Volume 3
Letters 186-248
0-674-99268-7 HARVARD $16.95

Volume 4
Letters 249-368 & Address to Young Men on Greek Literature
0-674-99298-9 HARVARD $18.95

Callimachus

Callimachus
Includes *Aetia, Iambi, Hecale, Other Fragments,* and Musaeus's *Hero and Leander*
0-674-99463-9 HARVARD $18.95

Hymns and Epigrams
Also includes the works of Lycophron and Aratus
0-674-99143-5 HARVARD $18.95

Dio Cassius

Roman History

Volume 1
Fragments of Books 1-11
0-674-99036-6 HARVARD $18.95

Volume 2
Fragments of Books 12-35 & Fragments of Uncertain Reference
0-674-99041-2 HARVARD $18.95

Volume 3
Books 36-40
0-674-99059-5 HARVARD $18.95

Volume 4
Books 41-45
0-674-99073-0 HARVARD $18.95

Volume 5
Books 46-50
0-674-99091-9 HARVARD $18.95

Volume 6
Books 51-55
0-674-99092-7 HARVARD $18.95

Volume 7
Books 56-60
0-674-99193-1 HARVARD $18.95

Volume 8
Books 61-70
0-674-99195-8 HARVARD $18.95

Volume 9
Books 71-80 & General Index
0-674-99196-6 HARVARD $18.95

Chariton

Callirhoe: Love Story in Syracuse
0-674-99530-9 HARVARD $18.95

Dio Chrysostom

Dio Chrysostom

Volume 1
Discourses 1-11
0-674-99283-0 HARVARD $18.95

Volume 2
Discourses 12-30
0-674-99374-8 HARVARD $16.95

Volume 3
Discourses 31-36
0-674-99395-0 HARVARD $16.95

Volume 4
Discourses 37-60
0-674-99414-0 HARVARD $16.95

Volume 5
Discourses 61-80, Fragments, Letters
0-674-99424-8 HARVARD $16.95

Clement of Alexandria

Clement of Alexandria
Includes *Exhortations to the Greeks, Rich Man's Salutation, To the Newly Baptized*
0-674-99103-6 HARVARD $18.95

St. John Damascene

Barlaam and Ioasaph
0-674-99038-2 HARVARD $16.95

Demosthenes

Demosthenes

Volume 1
Includes ***Olynthiacs 1-3, Philippic 1, On the Peace, Philippic 2, On the Halonnesus, On the Chersonese, Philippics 3 and 4, Philip's Letter, Answer to Philip's Letter, On Organization, On the Navy-Boards, For the Liberty of the Rhodians, For the People of Megalopolis, On the Treaty with Alexander, Against Leptines*** (1-17 and 20)
0-674-99263-6 HARVARD $16.95

Volume 2
De Corona & De Falsa Legatione (18-19)
0-674-99171-0 HARVARD $18.95

Volume 3
Includes *Against Meidias, Against Androtion, Against Aristocrates, Against Timocrates, Against Aristogeiton* (1-2, 21-26)
0-674-99330-6 HARVARD $16.95

Volume 4
Private Orations (27-40)
0-674-99351-9 HARVARD $16.95

Volume 5
Private Orations (41-49)
0-674-99381-0 HARVARD $16.95

Volume 6
Private Orations (50-58) & In Neaeram (59)
0-674-99386-1 HARVARD $16.95

Volume 7
Includes *Funeral Speech* (60), *Erotic Essay* (61), *Exordia, Letters,* and General Index
0-674-99412-4 HARVARD $18.95

Diogenes Laertius

Lives of Eminent Philosophers

Volume 1
Books 1-5
0-674-99203-2 HARVARD $18.95

Volume 2
Books 6-10
0-674-99204-0 HARVARD $18.95

Dionysius of Halicarnassus

Critical Essays

Volume 1
Includes *Ancient Orators, Lysias, Isocrates, Isaeus, Demosthenes,* and *Thucydides*
0-674-99512-0 HARVARD $16.95

Volume 2
Includes *On Literary Composition, Dinarchus,* and *Letters to Ammaeus and Pompeius*
0-674-99513-9 HARVARD $16.95

Roman Antiquities

Volume 1
Books 1-2
0-674-99352-7 HARVARD $16.95

Volume 2
Books 3-4
0-674-99382-9 HARVARD $18.95

Volume 3
Books 5-6 (48)
0-674-99394-2 HARVARD $16.95

Volume 4
Book 6 (49)-7
0-674-99401-9 HARVARD $16.95

Volume 5
Books 8-9 (24)
0-674-99410-8 HARVARD $16.95

Volume 6
Book 9 (25)-10
0-674-99416-7 HARVARD $16.95

Volume 7
Book 11, Fragments of Books 12-20 & General Index
0-674-99427-2 HARVARD $16.95

Sextus Empiricus

Sextus Empiricus

Volume 1
Outlines of Pyrrhonism
0-674-99301-2 HARVARD $16.95

Volume 2
Against the Logicians
0-674-99321-7 HARVARD $16.95

Volume 3
Against the Physicists & Against the Ethicists
0-674-99344-6 HARVARD $16.95

Volume 4
Against the Professors
0-674-99420-5 HARVARD $18.95

Epictetus

Epictetus

Volume 1
Discourses, Books 1-2
0-674-99145-1 HARVARD $18.95

Volume 2
Includes *Discourses* (Books 3-4), *Fragments*, and *Encheiridion*
0-674-99240-7 HARVARD $18.95

Euripides

Euripides

Volume 1
Includes *Iphigeneia at Aulis, Rhesus, Hecuba, Daughters of Troy,* and *Helen*
0-674-99010-2 HARVARD $18.95

Volume 2
Includes *Electra, Orestes, Iphigeneia in Taurica, Andromache,* and *Cyclops*
0-674-99011-0 HARVARD $18.95

Volume 3
Includes *Bacchanals, Madness of Hercules, Children of Hercules, Phoenician Maidens,* and *Suppliants*
0-674-99012-9 HARVARD $18.95

Volume 4
Includes *Cyclops, Alcestis,* and *Medea*
0-674-99013-7 HARVARD $16.95
0-674-99560-0 HARVARD $16.95

Eusebius

Ecclesiastical History

Volume 1
Books 1-5
0-674-99169-9 HARVARD $16.95

Volume 2
Books 6-10
0-674-99293-8 HARVARD $18.95

Galen

On the Natural Faculties
0-674-99078-1 HARVARD $18.95

Greek Anthology

Greek Anthology

Volume 1
Books 1-6
Includes *Christian Epigrams, Christodorus of Thebes in Egypt, The Cyzicene Epigrams, The Poems of the Different Anthologies, The Amatory Epigrams,* and *The Dedicatory Epigrams*
0-674-99074-9 HARVARD $16.95

Volume 2
Books 7-8
Includes *Sepulchral Epigrams* and *The Epigrams of St. Gregory the Theologian*
0-674-99075-7 HARVARD $18.95

Volume 3
Book 9
Includes *The Declamatory Epigrams*
0-674-99093-5 HARVARD $18.95

Volume 4
Books 10-12
Includes *The Hortatory and Admonitory Epigrams, The Convivial and Satirical Epigrams,* and Strato's *Musa Puerilis*
0-674-99094-3 HARVARD $18.95

Volume 5
Books 13-16
Includes *Epigrams in Various Metres, Arithmetical Problems, Riddles, Oracles, Miscellanea,* and *Epigrams of the Planudean Anthology Not in the Palatine Manuscript*
0-674-99095-1 HARVARD $18.95

Greek Bucolic Poets

Greek Bucolic Poets: Theocritus, Bion & Moschus
0-674-99031-5 HARVARD $18.95

Greek Elegy and Iambus

Greek Elegy and Iambus

Volume 1
Elegiac Poets from Callinus to Critias
Includes works by Tyrtaeus, Mimnermus, Solon, Phocylides, Xenophanes, and Theognis
0-674-99284-9 HARVARD $16.95

Volume 2
Elegiac Poetry of the Fourth Century, Iambic Poets
Includes Archilochus and Semonides, *Anonymous Inscriptions,* and *Fragments*
0-674-99285-7 HARVARD $16.95

Greek Lyric

Greek Lyric

Volume 1: Sappho and Alcaeus
0-674-99157-5 HARVARD $18.95

Volume 2: Anacreon, Anacreontea, Choral Lyric from Olympus to Alcman
0-674-99158-3 HARVARD $18.95

Volume 3: Stesichorus, Ibycus, Simonides, and Others
0-674-99525-2 HARVARD $18.95

Volume 4: Bacchylides, Corinna, and Others
0-674-99508-2 HARVARD $18.95

Volume 5
The New School of Poetry and Anonymous Songs and Hymns
0-674-99559-7 HARVARD $18.95

Greek Mathematical Works

Greek Mathematical Works

Volume 1
From Thales to Euclid
0-674-99369-1 HARVARD $18.95

Volume 2
From Aristarchus to Pappus
0-674-99399-3 HARVARD $18.95

Herodian

Herodian

Volume 1
Books 1-4
0-674-99500-7 HARVARD $18.95

Volume 2
Books 5-8
0-674-99501-5 HARVARD $18.95

Herodotus

The Persian Wars

Volume 1
Books 1-2
0-674-99130-3 HARVARD $18.95

Volume 2
Books 3-4
0-674-99131-1 HARVARD $18.95

Volume 3
Books 5-7
0-674-99133-8 HARVARD $16.95

Volume 4
Books 8-9
0-674-99134-6 HARVARD $18.95

Hesiod

Homeric Hymns, Fragments of the Epic Cycle, Homerica
0-674-99063-3 HARVARD $18.95

Hippocrates

Hippocrates

Volume 1
Includes *Ancient Medicine, Airs, Waters, Places, Epidemics 1-2, Oath, Precepts,* and *Nutriment*
0-674-99162-1 HARVARD $18.95

Volume 2
Includes *Prognostic, Regimen in Acute Diseases, Sacred Disease, Art, Breaths, Law, Decorum, Physician (Chapter 1),* and *Dentition*
0-674-99164-8 HARVARD $16.95

Volume 3
Includes *On Wounds in the Head, In the Surgery, On Fractures, On Joints,* and *Mochlikon*
0-674-99165-6 HARVARD $18.95

Volume 4
Includes *Nature of Man, Regimen in Health, Humours, Aphorisms, Regimen 1-3, Dreams,* Heracleitus's *On the Universe,* and General Index
0-674-99166-4 HARVARD $16.95

Volume 5
Includes *Affections, Diseases I,* and *Diseases II*
0-674-99520-1 HARVARD $18.95

Volume 6
Includes *Diseases III, Internal Affections,* and *Regimen in Acute Diseases*
0-674-99522-8 HARVARD $18.95

Volume 7
Includes *Epidemics 2, 4-7*
0-674-99526-0 HARVARD $18.95

Volume 8
Includes *Places in Man, Glands, Fleshes, Prorrhetic 1-2, Physician, Use of Liquids, Ulcers,* and *Haemorrhoids and Fistulas*
0-674-99531-7 HARVARD $18.95

Homer

The Iliad

Volume 1
Books 1-12
0-674-99188-5 HARVARD $18.95

Volume 2
Books 13-24
0-674-99189-3 HARVARD $18.95

The Odyssey

Volume 1
Books 1-12
0-674-99561-9 HARVARD $18.95

Volume 2
Books 13-24
0-674-99562-7 HARVARD $18.95

Isaeus

Isaeus
0-674-99222-9 HARVARD $16.95

Isocrates

Isocrates

Volume 1
Includes *To Demonicus, To Nicocles, Nicocles or Cyprians, Panegyricus, To Philip,* and *Archidamus*
0-674-99231-8 HARVARD $18.95

Volume 2
Includes *On the Peace, Areopagiticus, Against the Sophists, Antidosis,* and *Panathenaicus*
0-674-99252-0 HARVARD $16.95

Volume 3
Includes *Evagoras, Helen, Busiris, Plataicus, Concerning the Team of Horses, Trapeziticus, Against Callimachus, Aegineticus Against Lochites, Against Euthynus, Letters* 1-9, and General Index
0-674-99411-6 HARVARD $16.95

Josephus

Josephus

Volume 1
Against Apion
0-674-99205-9 HARVARD $18.95

Volume 2
Jewish War, Books 1-3
0-674-99223-7 HARVARD $18.95

Volume 3
Jewish War, Books 4-6 & Indexes to Volumes 2-3
0-674-99232-6 HARVARD $18.95

Volume 4
Antiquities, Books 1-4
0-674-99267-9 HARVARD $16.95

Volume 5
Antiquities, Books 5-8
0-674-99310-1 HARVARD $18.95

Volume 6
Antiquities, Books 9-11
0-674-99360-8 HARVARD $16.95

Volume 7
Antiquities, Books 12-14
0-674-99402-7 HARVARD $16.95

Volume 8
Antiquities, Books 15-17
0-674-99451-5 HARVARD $16.95

Volume 9
Antiquities, Books 18-20 & General Index
0-674-99477-9 HARVARD $18.95

Volume 10
Jewish Antiquities, Book 20
0-674-99502-3 HARVARD $18.95

Julian

Julian

Volume 1
Orations 1-4
0-674-99014-5 HARVARD $18.95

Volume 2
Includes *Orations 6-8, Letters to Themistius, To the Senate and People of Athens, To a Priest, The Caesars,* and *Misopogon*
0-674-99032-3 HARVARD $18.95

Volume 3
Includes *Letters, Epigrams, Against the Galilaeans,* and *Fragments*
0-674-99173-7 HARVARD $16.95

Libanius

Autobiography and Selected Letters

Volume 1
Autobiography, Letters 1-50
0-674-99527-9 HARVARD $18.95

Volume 2
Letters 51-193
0-674-99528-7 HARVARD $18.95

Selected Orations

Volume 1
Julianic Orations
0-674-99496-5 HARVARD $16.95

Volume 2
Orations 2, 19-23, 30, 33, 45, 47-50
0-674-99497-3 HARVARD $16.95

Longinus

Daphnis and Chloe
Includes Parthenius's *Love Romances, Fragments of the Ninus Romance,* and *Poetical Fragments*
0-674-99076-5 HARVARD $18.95

Lucian

Lucian

Volume 1
Includes *Phalaris 1-2, Hippias or Bath, Dionysus, Heracles, Amber or Swans, Fly, Nigrinus, Demonax, Hall, My Native Land, Octogenarians, True Story 1-2, Slander, Consonants at Law,* and *The Carousal or The Lapiths*
0-674-99015-3 HARVARD $18.95

Volume 2
Includes *The Downward Journey or The Tyrant, Zeus Catechized, Zeus Rants, The Dream or The Cock, Prometheus, Icaromenippus or The Sky-Man, Timon or The Misanthrope, Charon or The Inspectors,* and *Philosophies for Sale*
0-674-99060-9 HARVARD $18.95

Volume 3
Includes *The Dead Come to Life or The Fisherman, The Double Indictment or Trials by Jury, On Sacrifices, The Ignorant Book Collector, The Dream or Lucian's Career, The Parasite, The Lover of Lies, The Judgement of the Goddesses,* and *On Salaried Posts in Great Houses*
0-674-99144-3 HARVARD $18.95

Volume 4
Includes *Anacharsis or Athletics, Menippus or The Descent into Hades, On Funerals, A Professor of Public Speaking, Alexander the False Prophet, Essays in Portraiture, Essays in Portraiture Defended,* and *The Goddesses of Surrye*
0-674-99179-6 HARVARD $18.95

Volume 5
Includes *The Passing of Peregrinus, The Runaways, Toxaris or Friendship, The Dance, Lexiphanes, The Eunuch, Astrology, The Mistaken Critic, The Parliament of the Gods, The Tyrannicide,* and *Disowned*
0-674-99333-0 HARVARD $18.95

Volume 6
Includes *How to Write History, The Dipsads, Saturnalia, Herodotus or Aetion, Zeuxis or Antiochus, A Slip of the Tongue in Greeting, Apology for the Salaried Posts in Great Houses, Harmonides, A Conversation with Hesiod, The Scythian or The Consul, Hermotimus or Concerning the Sects, To One Who Said "You're a Prometheus in Words,"* and *The Ship or The Wishes*
0-674-99474-4 HARVARD $18.95

Volume 7
Includes *Diologues of the Dead, Dialogues of the Sea-Gods, Dialogues of the Gods,* and *Dialogues of the Courtesans*
0-674-99475-2 HARVARD $18.95

Volume 8
Includes *Soloecista, Lucius or The Ass, Amores, Halcyon, Demosthenes, Podagra, Ocypus, Cyniscus, Philopatris, Charidemus,* and *Nero*
0-674-99476-0 HARVARD $18.95

Lysias
Lysias
0-674-99269-5 HARVARD $18.95

Manetho
Aegyptiaca & Other Works
0-674-99385-3 HARVARD $18.95

Menander
Includes *Aspis, Georgos, Dis Exapaton, Dyskolos, Encheiridion,* and *Epitrepontes*
0-674-99147-8 HARVARD $18.95

Minor Attic Orators
Minor Attic Orators
Volume 1
Antiphon & Andocides
0-674-99340-3 HARVARD $16.95

Volume 2
Lycurgus, Dinarchus, Demades & Hyperides
0-674-99434-5 HARVARD $16.95

Nonnos
Dionysiaca
Volume 1
Books 1-15
0-674-99379-9 HARVARD $18.95

Volume 2
Books 16-35
0-674-99391-8 HARVARD $18.95

Volume 3
Books 36-48
0-674-99393-4 HARVARD $18.95

Oppian & others
Oppian, Colluthus, and Tryphiodorus
0-674-99241-5 HARVARD $16.95

Papyri
Papyri
Volume 1
Non-Literary Papyri
Includes private documents (agreements, receipts, wills, letters, memoranda, accounts, and lists)
0-674-99294-6 HARVARD $16.95

Volume 2
Non-Literary Papyri
Includes public documents (codes and regulations, edicts and orders, public announcements, reports of meetings, judicial business, petitions and applications, declarations to officials, contracts, receipts, accounts and lists, and correspondence)
0-674-99312-X HARVARD $15.50

Volume 3
Literary Papyri
Includes poetry
0-674-99397-7 HARVARD $16.95

Pausanias
Description of Greece
Volume 1
Books 1-2 (Attica & Corinth)
0-674-99104-4 HARVARD $18.95

Volume 2
Books 3-5
(Laconia, Messenia, Elis 1)
0-674-99207-5 HARVARD $18.95

Volume 3
Books 6-8
(21) (Elis 2, Achaia, Arcadia)
0-674-99300-4 HARVARD $18.95

Volume 4
Books 8
(22)-10 (Arcadia Boeotia, Phocis & Ozolian Locris)
0-674-99328-4 HARVARD $16.95

Volume 5
Maps, Plans, Illustrations & General Index
0-674-99329-2 HARVARD $18.95

Philo
Philo
Volume 1
Includes *On the Creation* and, *Allegorical Interpretation*
0-674-99249-0 HARVARD $18.95

Supplement 1
Questions and Answers on Genesis
0-674-99418-3 HARVARD $18.95

Volume 2
Includes *On the Cherubim, The Sacrifices of Abel and Cain, The Worse Attacks the Better, On the Posterity and Exile of Cain,* and *On the Giants*
0-674-99250-4 HARVARD $18.95

Supplement 2
Questions and Answers on Exodus
0-674-99442-6 HARVARD $18.95

Volume 3
Includes *On the Unchangeableness of God, On Husbandry, Concerning Noah's Work as a Planter, On Drunkenness,* and *On Sobriety*
0-674-99272-5 HARVARD $16.95

Volume 4
Includes *On the Confusion of Tongues, On the Migration of Abraham, Who is the Heir of Divine Things?,* and *On Mating, with the Preliminary Studies*
06749928703 HARVARD $16.95

Volume 5
Includes *On Flight and Finding, On the Change of Names,* and *On Dreams*
0-674-99303-9 HARVARD $18.95

Volume 6
Includes *On Abraham, On Joseph,* and *On Moses*
0-674-99319-5 HARVARD $18.95

Volume 7
Includes *On the Decalogue* and *On the Special Laws (Books I-III)*
0-674-99353-5 HARVARD $18.95

Volume 8
Includes *On the Special Laws (Book IV), On the Virtues,* and *On Rewards and Punishments*
0-674-99376-4 HARVARD $18.95

Volume 9
Includes *Every Good Man Is Free, On the Contemplative Life, On the Eternity of the World, Against Flaccus, Apology for the Jews,* and *On Providence*
0-674-99287-3 HARVARD $18.95

Volume 10
On the Embassy to Gaius, General Index
0-674-99417-5 HARVARD $16.95

Philostratus
Life of Apollonius of Tyana
Volume 1
Books 1-4
0-674-99018-8 HARVARD $18.95

Volume 2
Books 6-8
Includes *Epistles of Apollonius* and Eusebius' *Treatise*
0-674-99019-6 HARVARD $18.95

Lives of the Sophists
Includes Eunapius' *Lives of the Philosophers and Sophists*
0-674-99149-4 HARVARD $18.95

Philostratus the Elder
Imagines, Books I and 2
Includes Philostratus the Younger's *Imagines* and Callistratus' *Descriptions*
0-674-99282-2 HARVARD $18.95

Pindar
Pindar
0-674-99062-5 HARVARD $18.95

Pindar

Plato
Plato
Volume 1
Includes *Euthyphro, Apology, Crito, Phaedo,* and *Phaedrus*
0-674-99040-4 HARVARD $18.95

Volume 2
Includes *Laches, Protagoras, Meno,* and *Euthydemus*
0-674-99183-4 HARVARD $18.95

Volume 3
Includes *Lysis, Symposium,* and *Georgias*
0-674-99184-2 HARVARD $18.95

Volume 4
Includes *Cratylus, Parmenides, Greater Hippias,* and *Lesser Hippias*
0-674-99185-0 HARVARD $18.95

Volume 5
Republic, Books 1-5
0-674-99262-8 HARVARD $18.95

Volume 6
Republic, Books 6-10
0-674-99304-7 HARVARD $16.95

Volume 7
Theaetetus & Sophist
0-674-99137-0 HARVARD $15.50

Volume 8
Includes *Statesman, Philebus,* and *Ion*
0-674-99182-6 HARVARD $16.95

Volume 9
Includes *Timaeus, Critias, Cleitophon, Menexenus,* and *Epistles*
0-674-99257-1 HARVARD $18.95

Volume 10
Laws, Books 1-6
0-674-99206-7 HARVARD $18.95

Volume 11
Laws, Books 7-12
0-674-99211-3 HARVARD $16.95

Volume 12
Includes *Charmides, Alcibiades 1-2, Hipparchus, The Lovers, Theages, Minos,* and *Epinomis*
0-674-99221-0 HARVARD $18.95

Plotinus

Plotinus

Volume 1
Porphyry's Life of Plotinus, Ennead 1
0-674-99484-1 HARVARD $16.95

Volume 2
Ennead 2
0-674-99486-8 HARVARD $18.95

Volume 3
Ennead 3
0-674-99487-6 HARVARD $18.95

Volume 4
Ennead 4
0-674-99488-4 HARVARD $16.95

Volume 5
Ennead 5
0-674-99489-2 HARVARD $16.95

Volume 6
Ennead 6, 1-5
0-674-99490-6 HARVARD $18.95

Volume 7
Ennead 6, 6-9
0-674-99515-5 HARVARD $18.95

Plutarch

Moralia

Volume 1
Includes *Education of Children, How the Young Man Should Study Poetry, On Listening to Lectures, How to Tell a Flatterer from a Friend,* and *How a Man May Become Aware of His Progress in Virtue*
0-674-99217-2 HARVARD $18.95

Volume 2
Includes *How to Profit by One's Enemies, On Having Many Friends, Chance, Virtue and Vice, Letter of Condolence to Apollonius, Advice About Keeping Well, Advice to Bride and Groom, The Dinner of the Seven Wise Men,* and *Superstition*
0-674-99245-8 HARVARD $16.95

Volume 3
Includes *Sayings of Kings and Commanders, Sayings of Romans, Sayings of Spartans, The Ancient Customs of the Spartans, Sayings of Spartan Women,* and *Bravery of Women*
0-674-99270-9 HARVARD $18.95

Volume 4
Includes *Roman Questions, Greek Questions, Greek and Roman Parallel Stories, On the Fortune of the Romans, On the Fortune or the Virtue of Alexander,* and *Were the Athenians More Famous in War or in Wisdom?*
0-674-99336-5 HARVARD $18.95

Volume 5
Includes *Isis and Osiris, The E at Delphi, The Oracles at Delphi No Longer Given in Verse,* and *The Obsolescence of Oracles*
0-674-99337-3 HARVARD $18.95

Volume 6
Includes *Can Virtue Be Taught?, On Moral Virtue, On the Control of Anger, On Tranquility of Mind, On Brotherly Love, On Affection for Offspring, Whether Vice Be Sufficient to Cause Unhappiness, Whether the Affections of the Soul Are Worse than Those of the Body, Concerning Talkativeness,* and *On Being a Busybody*
0-674-99371-3 HARVARD $16.95

Volume 7
Includes *On Love of Wealth, On Compliancy, On Envy and Hate, On Praising Oneself Inoffensively, On the Delays of the Divine Vengeance, On Fate, On the Sign of Socrates, On Exile,* and *Consolation to His Wife*
0-674-99446-9 HARVARD $18.95

Volume 8
Table-Talk, Books 1-6
0-674-99466-3 HARVARD $18.95

Volume 9
Table-Talk, Books 7-9 & Dialogue on Love
0-674-99467-1 HARVARD $18.95

Volume 10
Includes *Love Stories, That a Philosopher Ought to Converse Especially with Men in Power, To an Uneducated Ruler, Whether an Old Man Should Engage in Public Affairs, Precepts of Statecraft, On Monarchy, Democracy, and Oligarchy, That We Ought Not to Borrow, Lives of the Ten Orators,* and *Summary of a Comparison Between Aristophanes and Menander*
0-674-99354-3 HARVARD $18.95

Volume 11
Includes *On the Malice of Herodotus* and *Causes of Natural Phenomena*
0-674-99469-8 HARVARD $18.95

Volume 12
Includes *Concerning the Face Which Appears in the Orb of the Moon, On the Principle of Cold, Whether Fire or Water is More Useful, Whether Land or Sea Animals Are Cleverer, Beasts are Rational,* and *On the Eating of Flesh*
0-674-99447-7 HARVARD $18.95

Volume 13, 2
Stoic Essays
0-674-99517-1 HARVARD $18.95

Volume 14
Includes *That Epicurus Actually Makes a Pleasant Life Impossible, Reply to Colotes in Defence of the Other Philosophers, Is Life Unknown a Wise Precept?,* and *On Music*
0-674-99472-8 HARVARD $15.50

Volume 15
Fragments
0-674-99473-6 HARVARD $18.95

Parallel Lives

Volume 1
Includes *Theseus and Romulus, Lycurgus and Numa,* and *Solon and Publicola*
0-674-99052-8 HARVARD $18.95

Volume 2
Includes *Themistocles and Camillus, Aristides and Cato Major,* and *Cimon and Lucullus*
0-674-99053-6 HARVARD $16.95

Volume 3
Includes *Pericles and Fabius Maximus* and *Micias and Crassus*
0-674-99072-2 HARVARD $18.95

Volume 4
Includes *Alcibiades and Coriolanus* and *Lysander and Sulla*
0-674-99089-7 HARVARD $16.95

Volume 5
Includes *Agesilaus and Pompey* and *Pelopidas and Marcellus*
0-674-99097-8 HARVARD $18.95

Volume 6
Includes *Dion and Brutus* and *Timoleon and Aemilius Paulus*
0-674-99109-5 HARVARD $15.50

Volume 7
Includes *Demosthenes and Cicero* and *Alexander and Caesar*
0-674-99110-9 HARVARD $18.95

Volume 8
Includes *Sertorius and Eumenes* and *Phocion and Cato the Younger*
0-674-99111-7 HARVARD $18.95

Volume 9
Includes *Demetrius and Antony* and *Pyrrhus and Gaius Marius*
0-674-99112-5 HARVARD $18.95

Volume 10
Includes *Agis and Cleomenes, Tiberius and Gaius Gracchus,* and *Philopoemen and Flamininus*
0-674-99113-3 HARVARD $18.95

Volume 11
Includes *Aratus, Artaxerxes, Galba, Otho,* and General Index
0-674-99114-1 HARVARD $18.95

Polybius
Histories
Volume 1
Books 1-2
0-674-99142-7 HARVARD $18.95
Volume 2
Books 3-4
0-674-99152-4 HARVARD $18.95
Volume 3
Books 5-8
0-674-99153-2 HARVARD $18.95
Volume 4
Books 9-15
0-674-99175-3 HARVARD $18.95
Volume 5
Books 16-27
0-674-99176-1 HARVARD $18.95
Volume 6
Books 28-39
0-674-99178-8 HARVARD $18.95

Procopius
History of the Wars & Secret History
Volume 1
Books 1-2, Persian War
0-674-99054-4 HARVARD $16.95
Volume 2
Books 3-4, Vandalic War
0-674-99090-0 HARVARD $16.95
Volume 3
Books 5-6 (15), Gothic War
0-674-99119-2 HARVARD $18.95
Volume 4
Books 6, (16)-7, 35, Gothic War
0-674-99191-5 HARVARD $18.95
Volume 5
Book 7, (36)-8, Gothic War
0-674-99239-3 HARVARD $18.95
Volume 6
Anecdota or Secret History
0-674-99320-9 HARVARD $16.95
Volume 7
On Buildings & General Index
0-674-99378-0 HARVARD $16.95

Ptolemy
Tetrabiblos
0-674-99479-5 HARVARD $18.95

Diodorus Siculus
Library of History
Volume 1
Books 1-2 (34)
0-674-99307-1 HARVARD $18.95

Volume 2
Books 2 (35)-4 (58)
0-674-99334-9 HARVARD $18.95
Volume 3
Books 4 (59)-8
0-674-99375-6 HARVARD $18.95
Volume 4
Books 9-12 (40)
0-674-99413-2 HARVARD $18.95
Volume 5
Books 12 (41)-13
0-674-99422-1 HARVARD $18.95
Volume 6
Books 14-15 (19)
0-674-99439-6 HARVARD $16.95
Volume 7
Books 15 (20)-16 (65)
0-674-99428-0 HARVARD $18.95
Volume 8
Books 16 (66)-17
0-674-99464-7 HARVARD $18.95
Volume 9
Books 18-19 (65)
0-674-99415-9 HARVARD $18.95
Volume 10
Books 19 (66)-20
0-674-99429-9 HARVARD $18.95
Volume 11
Fragments of Books 21-32
0-674-99450-7 HARVARD $18.95
Volume 12
Fragments of Books 33-40 & General Index
0-674-99465-5 HARVARD $18.95

Quintus Smyrnaeus
Fall of Troy
0-674-99022-6 HARVARD $16.95

Sophocles
Sophocles
Volume 1
Includes *Ajax, Electra,* and *Oedipus Tyrannus*
0-674-99557-0 HARVARD $18.95
Volume 2
Includes *Antigone, The Women of Trachis, Philoctetes,* and *Oedipus at Colonus*
0-674-99558-9 HARVARD $18.95

Strabo
Geography
Volume 1
Books 1-2
0-674-99055-2 HARVARD $18.95
Volume 2
Books 3-5
0-674-99056-0 HARVARD $18.95
Volume 3
Books 6-7
0-674-99201-6 HARVARD $18.95

Volume 4
Books 8-9
0-674-99216-4 HARVARD $18.95
Volume 5
Books 10-12
0-674-99233-4 HARVARD $16.95
Volume 6
Books 13-14
0-674-99246-6 HARVARD $16.95
Volume 7
Books 15-16
0-674-99266-0 HARVARD $18.95
Volume 8
Book 17 & General Index
0-674-99295-4 HARVARD $18.95

Theophrastus
De Causis Plantarum
Volume 1
Books 1-2
0-674-99519-8 HARVARD $16.95
Volume 2
Books 3-4
0-674-99523-6 HARVARD $16.95
Volume 3
0-674-99524-4 HARVARD $16.95

Enquiry into Plants
Volume 1
Books 1-5
0-674-99077-3 HARVARD $16.95
Volume 2
Books 6-9
0-674-99088-9 HARVARD $16.95

Thucydides
History of the Peloponnesian War
Volume 1
Books 1-2
0-674-99120-6 HARVARD $18.95
Volume 2
Books 3-4
0-674-99121-4 HARVARD $18.95
Volume 3
Books 5-6
0-674-99122-2 HARVARD $18.95
Volume 4
Books 7-8, General Index
0-674-99187-7 HARVARD $18.95

Xenophon
Xenophon
Volume 1
Hellenica, Books 1-4
0-674-99098-6 HARVARD $18.95
Volume 2
Hellenica, Books 5-7
0-674-99099-4 HARVARD $18.95

Volume 3
Anabasis
0-674-99100-1 HARVARD $18.95

Volume 4
Memorabilia, Oeconomicus
0-674-99186-9 HARVARD $18.95

Volume 5
Cyropaedia, Books 1-4
0-674-99057-9 HARVARD $18.95

Volume 6
Cyropaedia, Books 5-8
0-674-99058-7 HARVARD $18.95

Volume 7
Includes *Scripta Minora* and *Constitution of the Atheneans*
0-674-99202-4 HARVARD $16.95

Latin Literature

Apuleius

Apuleius: Metamorphoses

Volume 1
Books 1-6
0-674-99049-8 HARVARD $18.95

Volume 2
Books 7-11
0-674-99498-1 HARVARD $18.95

Ausonius

Ausonius

Volume 1
Books 1-17
0-674-99107-9 HARVARD $15.50

Volume 2
Books 18-20
Also includes Paulinus Pellaeus's *Eucharisticus*
0-674-99127-3 HARVARD $15.50

Babrius & Phaedrus

Babrius & Phaedrus
Translated, with a historical introduction and a comprehensive survey of Greek and Latin fables in the Aesopic tradition
See also GREEK LITERATURE
0-674-99480-9 HARVARD $18.95

Bede

Historical Works

Volume 1
Ecclesiastical History, Books 1-3
0-674-99271-7 HARVARD $18.95

Volume 2
Ecclesiastical History, Books 4-5
Also includes *Lives of the Abbots* and *Letter to Egbert*
0-674-99273-3 HARVARD $18.95

Boethius

Boethius
Includes *Theological Tractates* and *The Consolation of Philosophy*
See also BOETHIUS under OTHER MEDIEVAL PHILOSOPHERS under PHILOSOPHY in RELIGION, SPIRITUALITY, AND PHILOSOPHY
0-674-99083-8 HARVARD $18.95

Caesar

Caesar

Volume 1
Gallic War
0-674-99080-3 HARVARD $18.95

Volume 2
Civil Wars
0-674-99043-9 HARVARD $18.95

Volume 3
Alexandrian, African and Spanish Wars
0-674-99443-4 HARVARD $18.95

Cato & Varro

On Agriculture
0-674-99313-6 HARVARD $18.95

Catullus

Tibullus & Pervigilium Veneris
0-674-99007-2 HARVARD $18.95

Celsus

On Medicine

Volume 1
Books 1-4
0-674-99322-5 HARVARD $18.95

Volume 2
Books 5-6
0-674-99335-7 HARVARD $16.95

Volume 3
Books 7-8
0-674-99370-5 HARVARD $18.95

Cicero

Letters

Volume 22
Letters to Atticus, Books 1-6
0-674-99008-0 HARVARD $15.50

Volume 23
Letters to Atticus, Books 7-11
0-674-99009-9 HARVARD $15.50

Volume 24
Letters to Atticus, Books 12-16
0-674-99108-7 HARVARD $18.95

Volume 25
Letters to His Friends, Books 1-6
0-674-99225-3 HARVARD $18.95

Volume 26
Letters to His Friends, Books 7-12
0-674-99238-5 HARVARD $18.95

Volume 27
Letters to His Friends, Books 13-16
0-674-99253-9 HARVARD $16.95

Volume 28
Letters to His Brother Quintus
0-674-99509-0 HARVARD $18.95

Orations

Volume 6
Includes *Pro Quinctio, Pro Roscio Amerino, Pro Roscio Comoedo*, and *Three Speeches on the Agrarian Law Against Rullus*
0-674-99265-2 HARVARD $16.95

Volume 7
The Verrine Orations 1
Includes *Against Caecillius, Against Verres, Part 1; Part 2, Books 1-2*
0-674-99243-1 HARVARD $18.95

Volume 8
The Verrine Orations 2
Includes *Against Verres, Part 2, Books 3-5*
0-674-99323-3 HARVARD $18.95

Volume 9
Includes *Pro Lege Manilia, Pro Caecina, Pro Cluentio*, and *Pro Rabirio Perduellionis Reo*
0-674-99218-0 HARVARD $18.95

Volume 10
Includes *In Catilinam 1-4, Pro Murena, Pro Sulla*, and *Pro Flacco*
0-674-99358-6 HARVARD $18.95

Volume 11
Includes *Pro Archia, Post Reditum in Senatu, Post Reditum ad Quirites, De Domo Sua, De Haruspicum Responsis*, and *Plancio*
0-674-99174-5 HARVARD $18.95

Volume 12
Pro Sestio & In Vatinium
0-674-99341-1 HARVARD $16.95

Volume 13
Includes *Pro Caelio, De Provinciis Consularibus*, and *Pro Balbo*
0-674-99492-2 HARVARD $18.95

Volume 14
Includes *Pro Milone, In Pisonem, Pro Scauro, Pro Fonteio, Pro Rabirio Postumo, Pro Marcello, Pro Ligario*, and *Pro Rege Deiotaro*
0674 992784 HARVARD $15.50

Volume 15
Philippics
0-674-99208-3 HARVARD $18.95

Philosophical Treatises

Volume 16
De Re Publica & De Legibus
0-674-99235-0 HARVARD $18.95

Volume 17
De Finibus
0-674-99044-7 HARVARD $16.95

Volume 18
Tusculan Disputations
0-674-99156-7 HARVARD $18.95

Volume 19
De Natura Deorum & Academica
0-674-99296-2 HARVARD $18.95

Volume 20
De Senectute, De Amicitia, De Divinatione
0-674-99170-2 HARVARD $18.95

Volume 21
De Officiis
0-674-99033-1 HARVARD $18.95

Rhetorical Treatises
Volume 1
Rhetorica ad Herennium
0-674-99444-2 HARVARD $18.95

Volume 2
Includes *De Inventione, De Optima Genere Oratorum,* and *Topica*
0-674-99425-6 HARVARD $18.95

Volume 3
De Oratore, Books 1-2
0-674-99383-7 HARVARD $18.95

Volume 4
Includes *De Oratore Book 3, De Fato, Paradoxa Stoicorum,* and *De Partitione Oratoria*
0-674-99384-5 HARVARD $18.95

Volume 5
Brutus, Orator
0-674-99377-2 HARVARD $18.95

Claudian
Claudian
Volume 1
Includes *Panegyric on Probinus and Olybrius, Against Rufinus 1-2, War Against Gildo, Against Eutropius 1-2, Fescennine Verses on the Marriage of Honorius, Epithalamium of Honorius and Maria, Panegyrics on the Third and Fourth Consulships of Honorius, Panegyric on the Consulship of Manlius,* and *On Stilicho's Consulship 1*
0-674-99150-8 HARVARD $14.50

Volume 2
Includes *On Stilicho's Consulship 2-3, Panegyric on the Sixth Consulship of Honorius, The Gothic War, Shorter Poems,* and *Rape of Proserpina 1-3*
0-674-99151-6 HARVARD $15.50

Columella
De Re Rustica
Volume 1
Books 1-4
0-674-99398-5 HARVARD $15.50

Volume 2
Books 5-9
0-674-99448-5 HARVARD $18.95

Volume 3
Books 10-12
0-674-99449-3 HARVARD $16.95

Cornelius Nepos
Cornelius Nepos
0-674-99514-7 HARVARD $18.95

Curtius & Quintus
History of Alexander
Volume 1
Books 1-5
0-674-99405-1 HARVARD $18.95

Volume 2
Books 6-10
0-674-99407-8 HARVARD $18.95

Valerius Flaccus
Argonautica
0-674-99316-0 HARVARD $18.95

Florus
Florus
0-674-99254-7 HARVARD $18.95

Frontinus
Stratagems & Aqueducts
0-674-99192-3 HARVARD $18.95

Fronto
Correspondence
Volume 1
0-674-99124-9 HARVARD $18.95

Volume 2
0-674-99125-7 HARVARD $16.95

Gellius
Attic Nights
Volume 1
Books 1-5
0-674-99215-6 HARVARD $18.95

Volume 2
Books 6-8
0-674-99220-2 HARVARD $18.95

Volume 3
Books 14-20
0-674-99234-2 HARVARD $18.95

Horace
Odes & Epodes
0-674-99037-4 HARVARD $18.95

Satires, Epistles & Ars Poetica
0-674-99214-8 HARVARD $18.95

Silius Italicus
Punica
Volume 1
Books 1-8
0-674-99305-5 HARVARD $15.50

Volume 2
Books 9-17
0-674-99306-3 HARVARD $15.50

Juvenal & Persius
Juvenal & Persius
0-674-99102-8 HARVARD $18.95

Livy
Roman History
Volume 1
Books 1-2
0-674-99126-5 HARVARD $18.95

Volume 2
Books 3-4
0-674-99148-6 HARVARD $18.95

Volume 3
Books 5-7
0-674-99190-7 HARVARD $18.95

Volume 4
Books 8-10
0-674-99210-5 HARVARD $18.95

Volume 5
Books 21-22
0-674-99256-3 HARVARD $18.95

Volume 6
Books 23-25
0-674-99392-6 HARVARD $15.50

Volume 7
Books 26-27
0-674-99404-3 HARVARD $15.50

Volume 8
Books 28-30
0-674-99419-1 HARVARD $16.95

Volume 9
Books 31-34
0-674-99326-8 HARVARD $16.95

Volume 10
Books 35-37
0-674-99332-2 HARVARD $49.95

Volume 11
Books 38-39
0-674-99346-2 HARVARD $18.95

Volume 12
Books 40-42
0-674-99366-7 HARVARD $18.95

Volume 13
Books 43-45
0-674-99435-3 HARVARD $18.95

Volume 14
Summaries, Fragments, Julius Obsequens, Index
0-674-99445-0 HARVARD $18.95

Lucan
Civil War (Pharsalia)
0-674-99242-3 HARVARD $18.95

Lucretius
Lucretius
0-674-99200-8 HARVARD $18.95

Manilius
Astronomica
0-674-99516-3 HARVARD $18.95

Ammianus **Marcellinus**
Roman History
Volume 1
Books 14-19
0-674-99331-4 HARVARD $18.95

Volume 2
Books 20-26
0-674-99348-9 HARVARD $18.95

Volume 3
Books 27-31
0-674-99365-9 HARVARD $18.95

Martial

Epigrams

Volume 1
Spectacles, Books 1-5
0-674-99555-4 HARVARD $18.95

Volume 2
Books 6-10
0-674-99556-2 HARVARD $18.95

Volume 3
Books 11-14
0-674-99529-5 HARVARD $18.95

Minor Latin Poets

Minor Latin Poets

Volume 1
Includes *Publilius Syrus, Elegies on Maecenas, Gratitius, Calpurnius Ciculus, Laus Pisonis, Einsiedeln Eclogues,* and *Aetna*
0-674-99314-4 HARVARD $18.95

Volume 2
Includes *Florus, Hadrian, Nemesianus, Reposianus, Tiberianus, Dicta Catonis, Phoenix, Avianus, Rutilius Namatianus,* and others
0-674-99478-7 HARVARD $18.95

Ovid

Ovid

Volume 1
Heroides & Amores
0-674-99045-5 HARVARD $18.95

Volume 2
Includes *Art of Love, Cosmetics, Remedies for Love, Ibis, Walnut-Trees, Sea Fishing,* and *Consolation*
0-674-99255-5 HARVARD $18.95

Volume 3
Metamorphoses, Books 1-8
0-674-99046-3 HARVARD $18.95

Volume 4
Metamorphoses, Books 9-15
0-674-99047-1 HARVARD $16.95

Volume 5
Fasti
0-674-99279-2 HARVARD $18.95

Volume 6
Tristia & Ex Ponto
0-674-99167-2 HARVARD $18.95

Velleius Paterculus

Res Gestae Divi Augusti
0-674-99168-0 HARVARD $18.95

Petronius

Satyricon
Also includes Seneca's *Apocolocyntosis*
0-674-99016-1 HARVARD $18.95

Plautus

Plautus

Volume 1
Includes *Amphitryon, Comedy of Asses, Pot of Gold, Two Bacchises,* and *Captives*
0-674-99067-6 HARVARD $16.95

Volume 2
Includes *Casina, The Casket Comedy, Curculio, Epidicus,* and *The Two Menaechmuses*
0-674-99068-4 HARVARD $18.95

Volume 3
Includes *The Merchant, The Braggart Warrior, The Haunted House,* and *The Persian*
0-674-99181-8 HARVARD $18.95

Volume 4
Includes *The Little Carthaginian, Pseudolus,* and *The Rope*
0-674-99286-5 HARVARD $18.95

Volume 5
Includes *Stichus, Three Bob Day, Truculentus, The Tale of a Travelling Bag,* and *Fragments*
0-674-99362-4 HARVARD $18.95

Pliny

Natural History

Volume 1
Books 1 and 2
0-674-99364-0 HARVARD $18.95

Volume 2
Books 3-7
0-674-99388-8 HARVARD $18.95

Volume 3
Books 8-11
0-674-99389-6 HARVARD $16.95

Volume 4
Books 12-16
0-674-99408-6 HARVARD $18.95

Volume 5
Books 17-19
0-674-99409-4 HARVARD $18.95

Volume 6
Books 20-23
0-674-99431-0 HARVARD $16.95

Volume 7
Books 24-27
0-674-99432-9 HARVARD $18.95

Volume 8
Books 28-32
0-674-99460-4 HARVARD $18.95

Volume 9
Books 33-35
0-674-99433-7 HARVARD $18.95

Volume 10
Books 36-37
0-674-99461-2 HARVARD $18.95

Pliny the Younger

Letters and Panegyricus

Volume 1
Books 1-7
0-674-99061-7 HARVARD $18.95

Volume 2
Books 7-10, Panegyricus
0-674-99066-8 HARVARD $18.95

Propertius

Elegies
0-674-99020-X HARVARD $18.95

Prudentius

Prudentius

Volume 1
Includes *Preface, Daily Round, Divinity of Christ, Origin of Sin, Fight for Mansoul,* and *Against Symmachus I*
0-674-99426-4 HARVARD $18.95

Volume 2
Includes *Against Symmachus II, Crowns of Martyrdom, Scenes from History,* and *Epilogue*
0-674-99438-8 HARVARD $18.95

Quintilian

Training of an Orator

Volume 1
Books 1-3
0-674-99138-9 HARVARD $18.95

Volume 2
Books 4-6
0-674-99139-7 HARVARD $16.95

Volume 3
Books 7-9
0-674-99140-0 HARVARD $15.50

Volume 4
Books 10-12
0-674-99141-9 HARVARD $15.50

Remains of Old Latin

Remains of Old Latin

Volume 1
Ennius, Caecilius
0-674-99324-1 HARVARD $16.95

Volume 2
Livius Andronicus, Naevius, Pacuvius, Accius
0-674-99347-X HARVARD $15.50

Volume 3
Lucilius, Laws of the 12 Tables
0-674-99363-2 HARVARD $16.95

Volume 4
Archaic Inscriptions
0-674-99396-9 HARVARD $18.95

Saint Augustine

The City of God

Volume 1
Books 1-3
0-674-99452-3 HARVARD $18.95

Volume 2
Books 4-7
0-674-99453-1 HARVARD $16.95

Volume 3
Books 8-11
0-674-99455-8 HARVARD $16.95

Volume 4
Books 12-15
0-674-99456-6 HARVARD $18.95

Volume 5
Books 16-18 (35)
0-674-99457-4 HARVARD $14.50

Volume 6
Books 18 (36)-20
0-674-99458-2 HARVARD $16.95

Volume 7
Books 21-22, Index
0-674-99459-0 HARVARD $15.50

The Confessions
Volume 1
Books 1-8
0-674-99029-3 HARVARD $18.95

Volume 2
Books 9-13
0-674-99030-7 HARVARD $18.95

Select Letters
0-674-99264-4 HARVARD $18.95

Saint Jerome

Select Letters
0-674-99288-1 HARVARD $18.95

Sallust

Sallust
Includes *War with Catiline, War with Jugurtha, Selections from the Histories,* and *Doubtful Works*
0-674-99128-1 HARVARD $16.95

Scriptores Historiae Augustae

Historia Augusta
Volume 1
Includes works on Hadrian, Aelius, Antoninus Pius, Marcus Aurelius, L. Verus, Avidius Cassius, Commodus, Pertinax, Didius Julianus, Septimius Severus, Pescennius Niger, and Clodius Albinus
0-674-99154-0 HARVARD $18.95

Volume 2
Includes works on Caracalla, Geta, Opellius Macrinus, Diadumenianus, Elagabalus, Severus Alexander, the Two Maximini, the Three Gordians, and Maximus and Balbinus
0-674-99155-9 HARVARD $18.95

Volume 3
Includes works on the two Valerians, the two Gallieni, the thirty Pretenders, the deified Claudius, the deified Aurelian, Tacitus, Probus, Firmus, Saturninus, Proculus and Bonosus, Carus, Carinus, and Numerian
0-674-99290-3 HARVARD $18.95

Seneca

Seneca
Volume 1
Moral Essays
Includes *De Providentia, De Constantia, De Ira, De Clementia*
0-674-99236-9 HARVARD $18.95

Volume 2
Moral Essays
Includes *De Consolatione ad Marciam, De Vita Beata, De Otio, De Tranquillitate Animi, De Brevitate Vitae, De Consolatione ad Polybium,* and *De Consolatione ad Helvm*
0-674-99280-6 HARVARD $18.95

Volume 3
Moral Essays
Includes *De Beneficus*
0-674-99343-8 HARVARD $18.95

Volume 4
Epistles 1-65
0-674-99084-6 HARVARD $18.95

Volume 5
Epistles 66-92
0-674-99085-4 HARVARD $18.95

Volume 6
Epistles 93-124
0-674-99086-2 HARVARD $18.95

Volume 7
Naturales Quaestiones, Books 1-3
0-674-99495-7 HARVARD $16.95

Volume 8
Tragedies
Includes *Hercules Furens, Troades, Medea, Hippolytus or Phaedra,* and *Oedipus*
0-674-99069-2 HARVARD $18.95

Volume 9
Tragedies
Includes *Agamemnon, Thyestes, Hercules Oetaeus, Phoenissae,* and *Octavia*
0-674-99087-0 HARVARD $18.95

Volume 10
Naturales Quaestiones, Books 4-7
0-674-99503-1 HARVARD $18.95

Seneca the Elder

Declamations
Volume 1
Controversiae, Books 1-6
0-674-99510-4 HARVARD $18.95

Volume 2
Controversiae, Books 7-10, Suasortiae
0-674-99511-2 HARVARD $18.95

Sidonius

Poems and Letters
Volume 1
Poems, Letters (Books 1-2)
0-674-99327-6 HARVARD $18.95

Volume 2
Letters (Books 3-4)
0-674-99462-0 HARVARD $18.95

Statius

Statius
Volume 1
Includes *Silvae Books 1-4, Thebaid Books 1-4*
0-674-99226-1 HARVARD $18.95

Volume 2
Includes *Thebaid Books 5-7* and *Achilleid*
0-674-99228-8 HARVARD $18.95

Suetonius

Suetonius
Volume 1
Includes *Lives of the Caesars* from Deified Julius to Gaius Caligula
0-674-99035-8 HARVARD $18.95

Volume 2
Includes *The Lives of the Caesars* (continued), Claudius, Nero, Galba, Otho, and Vitellius, Vespasian, Titus, Domitian, *The Lives of Illustrious Men: Grammarians and Rhetoricians, Poets* (Terence, Virgil, Horace, Tibullus, Persius, Lucan), *The Lives of Pliny the Elder,* and *Passienus Crispus*
0-674-99042-0 HARVARD $18.95

Tacitus

Tacitus
Volume 1
Agricola, Germania & Dialogus
0-674-99039-0 HARVARD $18.95

Volume 2
Histories 1-3
0-674-99123-0 HARVARD $18.95

Volume 3
Histories 4-5, Annals 1-3
0-674-99274-1 HARVARD $16.95

Volume 4
Annals 4-6, 11-12
0-674-99345-4 HARVARD $16.95

Volume 5
Annals 13-16
0-674-99355-1 HARVARD $16.95

Terence

Terence
Volume 1
Includes *Lady of Andros, Self-Tormenter,* and *Eunuch*
0-674-99025-0 HARVARD $16.95

Volume 2
Includes *Phormio, The Mother-in-Law,* and *The Brothers*
0-674-99026-9 HARVARD $16.95

Tertullian

Apology & De Spectaculis
Includes Minucius Felix's *Octavius* .
0-674-99276-8 HARVARD $18.95

Varro

De Lingua Latina
Volume 1
Books 5-7
0-674-99367-5 HARVARD $18.95

Volume 2
Books 8-10, Fragments
0-674-99368-3 HARVARD $16.95

Virgil

Virgil
Volume 1
Includes *Eclogues, Georgics Books 1-4,* and *Aeneid Books 1-6*
0-674-99070-6 HARVARD $18.95

Volume 2
Includes *Aeneid Books 7-12* and *Minor Poems*
0-674-99071-4 HARVARD $18.95

Vitruvius

On Architecture

Volume 1
Books 1-5

0-674-99277-6 HARVARD $18.95

Volume 2
Books 6-10

0-674-99309-8 HARVARD $18.95

Medieval Literature

In this catalog, writings of the Middle Ages will be found within each of the national literatures. The following list offers for convenience a selective sampling of some of the high points of medieval literature, along with some useful critical studies.

Adomnan of Iona

Life of St. Columba

A devout telling of the life of the great sixth-century Irish religious leader

0-14-044462-9 PENGUIN PB $12.95

Michael **Alexander**, translator

Beowulf

Beowulf is the great native English epic, overlaid with Christian elements but imbued with the brooding pessimism of the pagan culture behind it. Alexander has made a powerful attempt to approximate the textures of the Anglo-Saxon verse

See also **THE ANGLO-SAXON PERIOD** in **LITERATURE OF THE BRITISH ISLES**

0-14-043377-5 PENGUIN PB $10.95

Bede

The Ecclesiastical History of the English People

Includes Bede's "Letter to Egbert" and Cuthbert's "Letter on the Death of Bede"

EDITED BY D.H. FARMER

0-14-044565-X PENGUIN PB $11.95

Paul **Blackburn**

Proensa: An Anthology of Troubador Poetry

These brilliant, tensile translations of troubador poetry contain some of Blackburn's finest work

See also **POETRY SINCE 1945** under **20TH-CENTURY AMERICAN POETRY** in **LITERATURE OF THE AMERICAS**

EDITED BY GEORGE ECONOMOU

0-520-02985-2 CALIFORNIA $45.00

Giovanni **Boccaccio**

The Decameron

Boccaccio's Decameron*—a series of 100 tales told by ten Florentines during the plague of 1348 at the rate of one each over ten days—became the first classic of European prose fiction, a book that has been said to herald the passage of Western civilization out of the Middle Ages. It has proved an enduring sourcebook into which other writers and artists have been dipping for centuries.*

TRANSLATED BY G.H. MCWILLIAM

0-14-044629-X PENGUIN PB $12.95

Geoffrey **Chaucer**

The Canterbury Tales

The most enduringly popular translation; an idiomatic but accurate rendering

See also **CHAUCER** under **POETRY** under **MEDIEVAL LITERATURE** in **LITERATURE OF THE BRITISH ISLES**

TRANSLATED BY NEVILL COGHILL

0-14-044022-4 PENGUIN PB $7.95

The Canterbury Tales

0-679-40989-0 KNOPF $20.00
0-19-281597-0 OXFORD PB $4.95

Troilus and Criseyde

An incomparable, novelistic love story, at once romantic and sardonic

TRANSLATED BY NEVILL COGHILL

0-14-044239-1 PENGUIN PB $9.95

Anna **Comnena**

The Alexiad of Anna Comnena

A biography of Alexius I (1081-1118) by his daughter, who demonstrates a gift for fast-moving narrative and shrewd character sketches

See also **BYZANTIUM** under **THE EARLY MIDDLE AGES** under **MEDIEVAL AND RENAISSANCE EUROPE** in **WORLD HISTORY AND CURRENT AFFAIRS**

TRANSLATED BY E.R.A. SEWTER

0-14-044215-4 PENGUIN PB $10.95

Dante

The Divine Comedy

A definitive prose version with facing Italian text and extensive commentary. "What a triumphant joy it is to see the honest light of literality take over again, after ages of meretricious paraphrases"—Vladimir Nabokov

TRANSLATED BY CHARLES SINGLETON

Volume 1
Inferno

See also **THE MIDDLE AGES** under **ITALIAN LITERATURE**

0-691-01896-0 PRINCETON PB $14.95

Commentary

0-691-01895-2 PRINCETON PB $24.95

Text and Commentary

0-691-09855-7 PRINCETON $110.00
0-691-01897-9 PRINCETON PB $34.00

Volume 2
Purgatorio

0-691-01909-6 PRINCETON PB $15.95

Commentary

0-691-01910-X PRINCETON PB $29.95

Text and Commentary

0-691-09887-5 PRINCETON $125.00
0-691-01911-8 PRINCETON PB $40.50

Volume 3
Paradiso

0-691-01912-6 PRINCETON PB $15.95

Commentary

0-691-01913-4 PRINCETON PB $24.95

Text and Commentary

0-691-09888-3 PRINCETON $110.00
0-691-01914-2 PRINCETON PB $49.50

The Divine Comedy

TRANSLATED BY JOHN CIARDI

Volume 1
Inferno

0-679-60209-7 MODERN LIBRARY $15.50

Volume 2
Purgatorio

0-679-60210-0 MODERN LIBRARY $15.50

Volume 3
Paradiso

0-679-60211-9 MODERN LIBRARY $15.50

R.T. **Davies**, editor

Early Middle English Lyrics: A Critical Anthology

A rich sampling of the early English tradition

See also **ANTHOLOGIES** under **POETRY** under **MEDIEVAL LITERATURE** in **LITERATURE OF THE BRITISH ISLES**

0-571-06571-6 FABER PB $15.95

Jean **Froissart**

Chronicles

Froissart's book is a triumph both of literary art and reportorial skill. To read his firsthand accounts of the Hundred Years' War, the Black Death, or the court of Richard II is to breathe the air of the 14th century

See also **WARS AND REVOLTS** under **THE 14TH CENTURY: BLACK DEATH AND ECONOMIC DEPRESSION** under **MEDIEVAL AND RENAISSANCE EUROPE** in **WORLD HISTORY AND CURRENT AFFAIRS**

See also **MIDDLE AGES** under **FRENCH LITERATURE TO 1900**

TRANSLATED BY GEOFFREY BRERETON

0-14-044200-6 PENGUIN PB $11.95

Jeffrey **Gantz**, translator

The Mabinogion

The classic collection of medieval Welsh tales, ranging from very early and rather primitive stories to elaborate Arthurian romances

See also **CELTIC LITERATURE** in **LITERATURE OF THE BRITISH ISLES**

0-14-044322-3 PENGUIN PB $6.95

Geoffrey of Monmouth

The History of the Kings of Britain

An almost entirely fanciful history, and an early source of Arthurian lore

See also **THE FEUDAL PRINCIPALITIES OF ENGLAND AND FRANCE** under **THE HIGH MIDDLE AGES: EMPIRE AND PAPACY** under **MEDIEVAL AND RENAISSANCE EUROPE** in **WORLD HISTORY AND CURRENT AFFAIRS**

TRANSLATED BY LEWIS THORPE

0-14-044170-0 PENGUIN PB $11.95

Gregory of Tours

The History of the Franks

An absorbing chronicle of the violent lives and reigns of the long-haired Merovingian kings

01400442952 VIKING PB $9.95

Robert **Harrison** &
Glyn **Burgess**, translators

The Song of Roland

A lucid and energetic poetic translation of the great medieval epic, which tells of the death in battle of Charlemagne's commander in the Pyrenées

See also **CHARLEMAGNE AND THE MAKING OF EUROPE** under **THE EARLY MIDDLE AGES** under **MEDIEVAL AND**

RENAISSANCE EUROPE in **WORLD HISTORY AND CURRENT AFFAIRS**

See also **MIDDLE AGES** under **FRENCH LITERATURE TO 1900**

0-451-62822-5 NEW AMERICAN LIBRARY PB $4.99

0-14-044532-3 PENGUIN PB $8.95

The battle rages, spreads throughout the hosts: Count Roland pays no heed to his own but plies his lance as long as its shaft holds—with fifteen blows it's splintered and is useless—and then unsheathes his good sword Durendal. He spurs his horse and goes against Chernuble: he breaks the helmet on which rubies gleam; he slices downward through the coif and hair and cuts between the eyes, down through his face the shiny hauberk made of fine-linked mail, entirely through the torso to the groin, and through the saddle trimmed with beaten gold. The body of the horse slows down the sword, which, seeking out no joint, divides the spine: both fall down dead upon the field's thick grass. He says then: "Coward, you have come in vain! Mohammed will not give you any help; no glutton such as you will win this fight."

THE SONG OF ROLAND

A.T. **Hatto**, editor

The Nibelungenlied

Often regarded as a national epic (though based on the Norse Edda tales), this anonymous 13th-century poem has been read both as a celebration of military heroism and as an urbane critique of an anachronistic warrior's code

See also **MEDIEVAL AND BAROQUE LITERATURE** under **GERMAN LITERATURE**

0-14-044137-9 PENGUIN PB $10.95

Margery **Kempe**

The Book of Margery Kempe

A religious work with a fascinating autobiographical dimension, including an unforgettable account of Kempe's trial for heresy

See also **WOMEN** under **GENERAL TOPICS** under **CHRISTIANITY** in **RELIGION, SPIRITUALITY, AND PHILOSOPHY**

TRANSLATED BY BARRY WINDEATT

0-14-043251-5 PENGUIN PB $10.95

Thomas **Kinsella**, translator

The Tain

An elegantly designed edition of the early Irish heroic tales, in a translation by a leading contemporary poet

0-19-281090-1 OXFORD PB $14.95

Guillaume **de Lorris** & Jean **de Meun**

The Romance of the Rose

This immense dream allegory, written over 50 years by two poets, is the culminating work of the medieval courtly tradition. The first half is an idealistic account of a lover's adventures, the second a cynical satire against love and the church

TRANSLATED BY CHARLES DAHLBERG

0-691-04456-2 PRINCETON PB $18.95

Magnus **Magnusson** & Hermann **Palsson**, translators

Laxdaela Saga

A complex family saga in which the central issue is a love triangle

See also **OLD NORSE AND ICELANDIC LITERATURE** under **SCANDINAVIAN LITERATURE**

0-14-044218-9 PENGUIN PB $9.95

Njal's Saga

This much-praised translation gives new life to the greatest of the Icelandic sagas. *"Njal's Saga* is one of the most complex and dramatic novels ever written. It teems with characters: each sharply, however briefly, drawn; all presented in the most dramatic contexts. The narrative is carried by dialogue and by action of maximum concreteness"—Kenneth Rexroth

0-14-044103-4 PENGUIN PB $11.95

John **Mandeville**

The Travels of Sir John Mandeville

0-14-044435-1 PENGUIN PB $9.95

W.S. **Merwin**, translator

The Poem of the Cid

A verse translation by a leading American poet

See also **THE MIDDLE AGES** under **SPANISH LITERATURE**

0-452-01060-8 NEW AMERICAN LIBRARY PB $10.95

Christine de **Pisan**

The Book of the City of Ladies

The author, often called the first French woman of letters, responded in prose and poetry to the prevailing misogyny of her time

See also **MEDIEVAL HISTORY** under **EUROPEAN HISTORY** under **WOMEN'S STUDIES** in **SOCIAL STUDIES**

See also **MIDDLE AGES** under **FRENCH LITERATURE TO 1900**

TRANSLATED BY EARL RICHARDS

0-89255-066-X PERSEA PB $11.95

Marco **Polo**

The Travels of Marco Polo

The Italian trader who followed the Silk Road opened by the Mongol invasion and became the advisor of Kublai Khan

Volume 1

See also **EUROPE AND THE REST OF THE WORLD** under **MEDIEVAL AND RENAISSANCE EUROPE** in **WORLD HISTORY AND CURRENT AFFAIRS**

0-486-27587-6 DOVER PB $17.95

Volume 2

0-486-27586-8 DOVER PB $17.95

The Travels of Marco Polo

TRANSLATED BY RONALD LATHAM

0-14-044057-7 PENGUIN PB $10.95

Betty **Radice**, translator

The Letters of Abelard and Heloise

Includes Abelard's *History of My Misfortunes*, four personal letters, two hymns, and other correspondences

0-14-044297-9 PENGUIN PB $10.95

James B. **Ross** & Mary M. **McLaughlin**, editors

The Portable Medieval Reader

A well-edited collection drawing on many rare sources

See also **SOURCES AND DOCUMENTS** under **GENERAL HISTORIES** under **MEDIEVAL AND RENAISSANCE EUROPE** in **WORLD HISTORY AND CURRENT AFFAIRS**

0-14-015046-3 VIKING PB $14.95

Brian **Stone**, translator

Sir Gawain and the Green Knight

A modern English verse translation

See also **OTHER MEDIEVAL POETS** under **POETRY** under **MEDIEVAL LITERATURE** in **LITERATURE OF THE BRITISH ISLES**

0-14-044092-5 PENGUIN PB $7.95

Patricia **Terry**, translator

Renard the Fox: The Misadventures of an Epic Hero

This cycle of animal fables uses the sly Renard, the powerful wolf Isengrim, and other beasts to depict the classes and character types of medieval France

0-520-07683-4 CALIFORNIA $35.00

0-520-07684-2 CALIFORNIA PB $14.95

Chrétien **de Troyes**

Yvain: The Knight of the Lion

A verse translation that admirably captures the narrative cadences of this Arthurian romance

TRANSLATED BY BURTON RAFFEL

0-300-03838-0 YALE PB $13.00

François **Villon**

The Poems of François Villon

The felonious career and literary brilliance of this 15th-century rogue and vagabond calls to mind the 20th century's Jean Genet. Villon's highly personal and technically accomplished poetry has always presented a challenge to translators. Kinnell's version is outstanding

TRANSLATED BY GALWAY KINNELL

0-87451-236-0 NEW ENGLAND PB $15.95

Wolfram **von Eschenbach**

Parzival

This long and complex narrative variation on the Grail legend is the crowning masterpiece of medieval German literature

See also **MEDIEVAL AND BAROQUE LITERATURE** under **GERMAN LITERATURE**

TRANSLATED BY A.T. HATTO

0-14-044361-4 PENGUIN PB $10.95

Gottfried **von Strassburg**

Tristan

Strassburg's version of the Tristan and Isolde story imparts a mystical dimension to the concept of courtly love

TRANSLATED BY A.T. HATTO

0-14-044098-4 PENGUIN PB $10.95

Jacobus **de Voragine**

The Golden Legend: Readings on the Saints

TRANSLATED BY WILLIAM GRANGER RYAN

0-691-00162-6 PRINCETON PB $29.95

The Golden Legend: Readings on the Saints

A new and complete translation of the collection of saints' lives that, after the Bible, was perhaps the most widely read work of the late Middle Ages. "A treasure-house of European culture, crammed full of the things which everyone, once upon a time, used to know"
—Noel Malcolm, *Sunday Telegraph*

Volume One

0-691-00153-7 PRINCETON PB $16.95

Volume Two

0-691-00154-5 PRINCETON PB $16.95

Winthrop **Wetherbee**, translator

The Cosmographia of Bernardus Silvestris

An example of full-scale medieval allegory at its most elaborate. A volume in the excellent *Records of Western Civilization* series

0-231-09625-9 COLUMBIA PB....$14.50

Clifton **Wolters**, editor

The Cloud of Unknowing & Other Works

A classic mystical work, written anonymously in England in the 14th century

See also **CHRISTIAN MYSTICISM** under **CHRISTIANITY** in **RELIGION, SPIRITUALITY, AND PHILOSOPHY**

0-14-044385-1 PENGUIN PB....$10.95

Histories and Critical Studies

Erich **Auerbach**

Literary Language and its Public in Late Latin Antiquity and in the Middle Ages

An extraordinary tour de force of scholarship, tracing the "inner history" of changes in literary style. "It is seldom that a work dealing with style, especially Latin style, should have the flair of an adventure-book. But Auerbach magically relates the story of Christian transformation of the... style of classical pagan antiquity, with the lowly style accepted as standard in the Middle Ages until the reemergence of the sublime style through Dante's *Divine Comedy*" —*Virginia Quarterly Review*

0-691-02468-5 PRINCETON PB....$19.95

There was virtually no possibility of obtaining even an elementary education except in the Church schools; only in rare and exceptional cases did these schools accept students who were not destined for an ecclesiastical career; the education there administered had as its instrument a foreign language which was nowhere in use as the language of daily life; the mother tongues had no culture, it was not even possible to write them. By far the greater number of the small and medium landholders and, indeed, most of the great lords could neither read nor write; laymen who could do so with ease were very rare until far into the twelfth century.

LITERARY LANGUAGE AND ITS PUBLIC IN LATE LATIN ANTIQUITY AND IN THE MIDDLE AGES

Norman F. **Cantor**

Inventing the Middle Ages: The Lives, Works, and Ideas of the Great Medievalists of the Twentieth Century

A tale of how nearly all of our ideas about the Middle Ages were actually created in this century by 20 scholars—including J.R.R. Tolkein and C.S. Lewis. It is both an artful description of a group of fascinating people and an intellectual history of our century. "A highly impassioned and personal book"—*Washington Post Book World*

See also **NEW DIRECTIONS** under **HISTORIOGRAPHY** in **WORLD HISTORY AND CURRENT AFFAIRS**

0-688-09406-6 QUILL....$28.00
0-688-12302-3 QUILL PB....$12.00

Rita **Copeland**

Rhetoric, Hermeneutics and Translation in the Middle Ages

0-521-38517-2 CAMBRIDGE....$65.00
0-521-48365-4 CAMBRIDGE PB....$22.95

Ernst Robert **Curtius**

European Literature and the Latin Middle Ages

A legendary work of scholarship and literary-historical analysis. "A powerfully presented and richly informative study of medieval standards, values, assumptions and literary conventions" —*The Virginia Quarterly Review*

0-691-01793-X PRINCETON PB....$16.95

Norris J. **Lacy**, editor

The Arthurian Encyclopedia

See also **BRITISH AND CELTIC** under **EUROPEAN MYTHOLOGY** under **MYTHOLOGY AND FOLKLORE** in **RELIGION, SPIRITUALITY, AND PHILOSOPHY**

0-87226-164-6 BEDRICK PB....$16.95

Helen **Waddell**

The Wandering Scholars

This eloquent study, first published in 1927, brings to life the vanished world of the medieval Latin poet: "There is no beginning, this side of the classics, to a history of medieval Latin; its roots take hold too firmly on the kingdoms of the dead. The scholar's lyric of the twelfth century seems as new a miracle as the first crocus; but its earth is the leafdrift of centuries of forgotten scholarship"—from *The Wandering Scholars*

0-472-06412-6 MICHIGAN PB....$18.95

French Literature to 1900

Middle Ages

French freed itself from the dominance of Latin to emerge as a literary language in the 11th century. Among the earliest surviving works are the *chansons de geste*—epic paeans to the heroic deeds of knights in Carolingian times, of which the most famous is the early-12th-century *Song of Roland*.

The medieval period also produced a strong current of lyric poetry in French as well as in the Provençal of the troubadours. In addition there evolved a cycle of courtly romances based on Arthurian legend.

Two very different types of "verse tales" flourished: the *fabliau*—ranging in tone from satirical banter to bawdy irreverence—and the *fable* such as *Renard the Fox*, in which animal characters expose the vagaries of feudal society.

Joseph **Bedier**

The Romance of Tristan and Iseult

A compelling amalgam of several versions of the Tristan story

0-394-70271-9 VINTAGE PB....$7.29

James **Cable**, translator

The Death of King Arthur

0-14-044255-3 PENGUIN PB....$9.95

Marie de **France**

Fables

EDITED AND TRANSLATED BY HARRIET SPIEGAL

0-8020-7636-X TORONTO PB....$17.95

The Lais of Marie de France

Short narrative poems by a late-12th-century Anglo-Norman poet, based on Celtic tales and often containing supernatural elements. These translations are in prose

TRANSLATED BY GLYN S. BURGESS & KEITH BUSBY

0-14-044476-9 PENGUIN PB....$8.95

Jean **Froissart**

Chronicles

Froissart's book is a triumph both of literary art and reportorial skill. To read his firsthand accounts of the Hundred Years' War, the Black Death, or the court of Richard II is to breathe the air of the 14th century

See also **WARS AND REVOLTS** under **THE 14TH CENTURY: BLACK DEATH AND ECONOMIC DEPRESSION** under **MEDIEVAL AND RENAISSANCE EUROPE** in **WORLD HISTORY AND CURRENT AFFAIRS**

TRANSLATED BY GEOFFREY BRERETON

0-14-044200-6 PENGUIN PB....$11.95

Frederick **Goldin**, editor & translator

Lyrics of the Troubadours and Trouvères: An Anthology and a History

A generous and finely translated selection of the lyrics of these balladeers, writing respectively in the *langue d'oc* of Provence and the *langue d'oil* of the North

0-8446-5036-6 SMITH....$19.75

Robert **Harrison**, translator

Gallic Salt: Eighteen Fabliaux Translated from the Old French

Funny, bawdy tales of peasant life

0-520-02418-4 CALIFORNIA....$47.50

Robert **Harrison** & Glyn **Burgess**, translators

The Song of Roland

A lucid and energetic poetic translation of the great medieval epic, which tells of the death in battle of Charlemagne's commander in the Pyrenées

See also **CHARLEMAGNE AND THE MAKING OF EUROPE** under **THE EARLY MIDDLE AGES** under **MEDIEVAL AND RENAISSANCE EUROPE** in **WORLD HISTORY AND CURRENT AFFAIRS**

0-451-62822-5 NEW AMERICAN LIBRARY PB....$4.99
0-14-044532-3 PENGUIN PB....$8.95

Jacques **LeGoff**

The Medieval Imagination

See also **CULTURAL AND INTELLECTUAL HISTORY** under **MEDIEVAL AND RENAISSANCE EUROPE** in **WORLD HISTORY AND CURRENT AFFAIRS**

TRANSLATED BY ARTHUR GOLDHAMMER

0-226-47084-9 CHICAGO....$29.95

Guillaume **de Lorris** & Jean **de Meun**

The Romance of the Rose

0-452-01083-7 DUTTON PB....$14.00
0-19-282689-1 OXFORD PB....$13.95

The Romance of the Rose
This immense dream allegory, written over 50 years by two poets, is the culminating work of the medieval courtly tradition. The first half is an idealistic account of a lover's adventures, the second a cynical satire against love and the church
TRANSLATED BY CHARLES DAHLBERG
0-691-04456-2 PRINCETON PB $18.95

Roger Sherman **Loomis**
Grail: From Celtic Myth to Christian Symbol
See also **BRITISH AND CELTIC** under **EUROPEAN MYTHOLOGY** under **MYTHOLOGY AND FOLKLORE** in **RELIGION, SPIRITUALITY, AND PHILOSOPHY**
0-691-02075-2 PRINCETON PB $12.95

P.M. **Matarasso**, translator
The Quest of the Holy Grail
A cycle of journeys in which evil enchantresses lay traps for Christian knights
0-14-044220-0 PENGUIN PB $9.95

Christine **de Pisan**
The Book of the City of Ladies
The author, often called the first French woman of letters, responded in prose and poetry to the prevailing misogyny of her time
See also **MEDIEVAL HISTORY** under **EUROPEAN HISTORY** under **WOMEN'S STUDIES** in **SOCIAL STUDIES**
TRANSLATED BY EARL RICHARDS
0-89255-066-X PERSEA PB $11.95

The Book of the Duke of True Lovers
A beguiling chivalric romance by France's first woman of letters: the third in a distinguished series of translations which have made this important writer's work widely available in English for the first time
TRANSLATED BY THELMA S. FENSTER
0-89255-166-6 PERSEA PB $11.95

A Medieval Woman's Mirror of Honor: The Treasury of the City of Ladies
A companion volume to *The Book of the City of Ladies*
TRANSLATED WITH AN INTRODUCTION BY CHARITY CANNON WILLARD
0-89255-144-5 BARD HALL $24.95
0-89255-135-6 BARD HALL PB $11.95

The Writings of Christine de Pisan
0-89255-180-1 PERSEA $35.00

Patricia **Terry**, translator
Renard the Fox: The Misadventures of an Epic Hero
This cycle of animal fables uses the sly Renard, the powerful wolf Isengrim, and other beasts to depict the classes and character types of medieval France
0-520-07683-4 CALIFORNIA $35.00
0-520-07684-2 CALIFORNIA PB $14.95

Chrétien **de Troyes**
Erec and Enide
TRANSLATED BY BURTON RAFFEL
0-300-06770-4 YALE $30.00
0-300-06771-2 YALE PB $15.00

Perceval: Or, the Story of the Grail
An accurate translation of Chrétien's greatest work, a highly original treatment of Arthurian legend
TRANSLATED BY RUTH CLINE
0-8203-0812-9 GEORGIA PB $12.00

Yvain: The Knight of the Lion
A verse translation that admirably captures the narrative cadences of this Arthurian romance
See also **MEDIEVAL LITERATURE**
TRANSLATED BY BURTON RAFFEL
0-300-03838-0 YALE PB $13.00

Geoffrey **de Villehardouin** & Jean **de Joinville**
Chronicles of the Crusades
Firsthand accounts by two French noblemen who took part in the Crusades
See also **THE CRUSADES** under **THE HIGH MIDDLE AGES: EMPIRE AND PAPACY** under **MEDIEVAL AND RENAISSANCE EUROPE** in **WORLD HISTORY AND CURRENT AFFAIRS**
TRANSLATED BY MARGARET R.B. SHAW
0-14-044124-7 PENGUIN PB $12.95

François **Villon**
The Poems of François Villon
The felonious career and literary brilliance of this 15th-century rogue and vagabond calls to mind the 20th century's Jean Genet. Villon's highly personal and technically accomplished poetry has always presented a challenge to translators. Kinnell's version is outstanding
TRANSLATED BY GALWAY KINNELL
0-87451-236-0 NEW ENGLAND PB $15.95

The Renaissance

The 16th century in France was marked by a revival of interest in classical antiquity that created a climate for new ideas and a more humanistically centered worldview. This new orientation manifested itself in the urbane and contemplative writings of Montaigne, Rabelais' boisterous celebration of human life, and the works of the seven poets of the *Pléade*, led by Ronsard and du Bellay, who were eager to free the French language from pedantic dependence on Italian literary forms.

Joachim **du Bellay**
The Regrets
A sequence of poems lamenting the ruins (real and figurative) of Rome, and satirizing the corruption of the modern city, translated with flair by a contemporary British poet
TRANSLATED BY C.H. SISSON
0-85635-471-6 CARCANET PB $8.50

Hélisenne **de Crenne**
The Torments of Love
EDITED AND INTRODUCTION BY LISA NEAL
TRANSLATED BY LISA NEAL & STEVEN RENDALL
0-8166-2788-6 MINNESOTA $47.95
0-8166-2789-4 MINNESOTA PB $18.95

Michel **de Montaigne**
The Complete Essays
The most recent translation of the complete body of Montaigne's essays, by a distinguished scholar
TRANSLATED BY M.A. SCREECH
0-14-044604-4 PENGUIN PB $22.50

Michel de Montaigne

An Apology for Raymond Sebond
A new translation of Montaigne's eloquent disquisition on human ignorance and the folly of fanaticism
TRANSLATED BY M. SCREECH
0-14-044493-9 PENGUIN PB $9.95

The Complete Essays of Montaigne
"A perfect translation of Montaigne appears impossible, yet Donald Frame has accomplished this feat"—André Maurois, *NY Times*
TRANSLATED BY DONALD M. FRAME
0-8047-0485-6 STANFORD $65.00
0-8047-0486-4 STANFORD PB $22.50

The Complete Works of Montaigne: Essays, Travel Journal,
A sturdy and complete edition of the definitive versions
TRANSLATED BY DONALD M. FRAME
0-8047-0484-8 STANFORD $85.00

Essays
TRANSLATED BY M.A. SCREECH
0-14-017897-X PENGUIN PB $10.95

Travel Journal
In 1580 Montaigne began a 17-month journey to Rome by way of Austria and Switzerland, compiling this account along the way
TRANSLATED BY DONALD M. FRAME
FOREWORD BY GUY DAVENPORT
0-86547-123-1 NORTH POINT PB $11.50

Marguerite **de Navarre**
The Heptameron
These 72 stories, inspired by Boccaccio's *Decameron*, range from the courtly to the ribald
TRANSLATED BY PAUL A. CHILTON
0-14-044355-X PENGUIN PB $14.95

François **Rabelais**

"Gargantua and Pantagruel *is the great epic of energy expended for its own sake. Its hero isn't the amiable father-and-son team of giants, Gargantua and Pantagruel, or the mercurial trickster Panurge, or the combative and hard-drinking monk Brother John, but Rabelais himself as the master of ceremonies who announces that he has no aim except to heal through laughter, and no method except to write while eating and drinking, 'which is the right time for writing about such exalted matters, such profound truths.'* "
—Geoffrey O'Brien, VLS

The Complete Works of François Rabelais

A translation of the exuberant genius of the French Renaissance by the famed Montaigne scholar Donald M. Frame. This volume contains both the five books of *Gargantua and Pantagruel* and the remainder of Rabelais' known writings, including his letters

0-520-06400-3 CALIFORNIA $75.00

Gargantua and Pantagruel

Rabelais drew on all levels of society to create his literary carnival. Cohen's translation rarely captures the bravura of the original

TRANSLATED BY J.M. COHEN

0-14-044047-X PENGUIN PB $11.95

Gargantua and Pantagruel

Another recent version of Rabelais' masterpiece

TRANSLATED BY BURTON RAFFEL

0-393-30806-5 NORTON PB $18.95

Now, with that out of the way, I can go back to my barrel. Drink up, my friends! …And there's no need to worry about the wine running out, the way it did at the wedding feast at Cana, in Galilee. Whatever you pull out through the spigot, I'll put right back in through the bung hole. And the barrel will be forever inexhaustible. It has a living source; it will flow eternally—like the liquid in Tantalus' cup, as portrayed by Brahman wise men, or that Spanish mountain of salt celebrated by Cato, or that golden branch sacred to the goddess of the underworld made famous by Virgil. It's a true cornucopia of happiness and good cheer. Sometimes you'll think it's drained right down to the bottom, but it will never go dry.

GARGANTUA AND PANTAGRUEL

Gargantua and Pantagruel

TRANSLATED BY DONALD M. FRAME

0-987-67898-7 CALIFORNIA $1.00

Gargantua and Pantagruel

This sometimes quite free 17th-century translation does offer a linguistic richness appropriate to Rabelais

TRANSLATED BY PIERRE LE MOTTEUX & THOMAS URQUHANT

0-679-43137-3 KNOPF $23.00

François Rabelais

The Age of Classicism

The 17th century—*le grand siècle*—established the norms destined to dominate—or oppress—French literature ever after. The animated conflict between champions of creative freedom and advocates of literary dogma was eventually resolved in favor of the formal, elegant aesthetic of classicism.

No external cause or principles however, can account for the period's extraordinary procession of writers: France's three greatest dramatists, Corneille, Racine, and Molière; the first "analytical" novelist in French literature, Mme. de La Fayette; the fabulist La Fontaine; and the mathematician and philosopher Pascal.

Pierre **Corneille**

The father of French tragedy, rivaled only by Racine, Corneille exalts man's freedom to fashion his fate in the age-old duel between duty and inclination. Such grandeur and heroism tend to sound bombastic in English, but the translations by John Cairncross work hard to do justice to the exuberant theatricality of these dramas.

The Cid, Cinna & The Theatrical Illusion

Two early tragedies (*The Cid* marks the true birth of French classical tragedy) and a comedy

TRANSLATED BY JOHN CAIRNCROSS

0-14-044312-6 PENGUIN PB $9.95

The Illusion

A recent adaptation of Corneille's comedy by the author of *Angels in America*

TRANSLATED BY TONY KUSHNER

1-55936-089-5 THEATRE COMMUNICATIONS $22.50

1-55936-090-9 THEATRE COMMUNICATIONS PB $8.95

Madame **de La Fayette**

The Princesse de Clèves

This subtle and notably unsentimental work has been called the first French psychological novel, or "novel of character"

TRANSLATED BY NANCY MITFORD

0-19-282687-5 OXFORD PB $8.95

Jean **de La Fontaine**

Selected Fables

The charms and hidden depths of La Fontaine, so dependent on quicksilver shifts in tone, are resistant to translation. Michie, however, does well by the challenge

TRANSLATED BY JAMES MICHIE

0-14-044376-2 PENGUIN PB $4.95

Selected Fables

TRANSLATED BY CHRISTOPHER WOOD

0-19-282440-6 OXFORD PB $8.95

Molière

The master of French high comedy, Molière appealed to many levels of sophistication and was equally skilled at classical verse and rough farce.

Amphitryon

A mythological comedy showing Molière at his most courtly

TRANSLATED BY RICHARD WILBUR

0-15-600211-6 HARVEST PB $12.00

The Misanthrope & Other Plays

Includes *Tartuffe, The Imaginary Invalid, The Doctor in Spite of Himself,* and *The Sicilian*

TRANSLATED BY JOHN WOOD

0-14-044089-5 PENGUIN PB $8.95

The Misanthrope & Tartuffe

The cantankerous idealist and the religious hypocrite; invigoratingly translated

TRANSLATED BY RICHARD WILBUR

0-15-660517-1 HARCOURT BRACE PB $10.00

The Miser & Other Plays

Includes *The Would-Be Gentleman, That Scoundrel Scapin, Don Juan,* and *Love's the Best Doctor*

TRANSLATED BY JOHN WOOD

0-14-044036-4 PENGUIN PB $8.95

The School for Husbands & Sganarelle, or the Imaginary Cuckold

TRANSLATED BY RICHARD WILBUR

0-15-679500-0 HARVEST PB $12.95

Tartuffe & Other Plays

Includes *Ridiculous Precieuses, School for Husbands, School for Wives, Critique for the School for Wives, Versailles Impromptu,* and *Don Juan*

TRANSLATED BY DONALD M. FRAME

0-451-52454-3 NEW AMERICAN LIBRARY PB $6.95

Blaise **Pascal**

Pensées

See also **CLASSICS OF WESTERN RELIGIOUS THOUGHT** under **WORLD RELIGION** in **RELIGION, SPIRITUALITY, AND PHILOSOPHY**

TRANSLATED BY A.J. KRAILSHEIMER

0-14-044645-1 PENGUIN PB $9.95

Pensées and Other Writings

TRANSLATED BY HONOR LEVI

0-19-282990-4 OXFORD PB $8.95

The Provincial Letters

A theological debate on Jansenism, revealing Pascal's mastery of polemic

0-14-044196-4 PENGUIN PB $7.95

Jean **Racine**

Though Racine presents enormous difficulties of translation, Richard Wilbur and C.H. Sisson have recently had some notable successes.

Andromache

A new translation of Racine's first major tragedy

TRANSLATED BY RICHARD WILBUR

0-15-607510-5 HARCOURT BRACE PB $6.95

Andromache & Other Plays

Also includes *Britannicus* and *Berenice*

TRANSLATED BY JOHN CAIRNCROSS

0-14-044195-6 PENGUIN PB $8.95

Britannicus, Phaedra & Athaliah

TRANSLATED BY C.H. SISSON

0-19-281758-2 OXFORD PB $6.95

Phaedra

A passionate drama that shocked 17th-century audiences, this profound study of adulterous love and murderous jealousy is based on Euripides' *Hippolytus*

TRANSLATED BY RICHARD WILBUR

0-15-675780-X HARCOURT BRACE PB $8.00

Phaedra
More Lowell than Racine, but fascinating
TRANSLATED BY ROBERT LOWELL
0-88734-266-3 PLAYERS PB $6.50

Phaedra & Other Plays
Also includes *Iphigenia* and *Athaliah*
TRANSLATED BY JOHN CAIRNCROSS
0-14-044122-0 PENGUIN PB $9.95

La Rochefoucauld

Maxims
Penetrating, acerbic aphorisms on the harsh truths of self-love, self-interest, and self-deceit
TRANSLATED BY LEONARD TANCOCK
0-14-044095-X PENGUIN PB $9.95

Madame **de Sevigné**

Selected Letters
Much of our direct knowledge of social and literary life in the age of Louis XIV comes from these witty and perspicacious letters
TRANSLATED BY LEONARD TANCOCK
0-14-044405-X PENGUIN PB $10.95

The Enlightenment

The 18th century was stirred by a new spirit of scientific inquiry; and consequently much of 18th-century literature is inherently didactic, veering away from *belles lettres* toward philosophy, and from the orthodoxies of Versailles toward the more liberal, frequently libertine salons of Paris.

For related reading, see EARLY MODERN EUROPE in WORLD HISTORY AND CURRENT AFFAIRS

For related reading, see POLITICAL THOUGHT in SOCIAL STUDIES

Pierre-Augustin **de Beaumarchais**

Barber of Seville & The Marriage of Figaro
An adventurer in life as well as art, Beaumarchais is remembered primarily for these two comedies of intrigue, with their bold strokes of social satire
0-14-044133-6 PENGUIN PB $8.95

Jacques **Cazotte**

The Devil in Love
Long unavailable in English: a classic tale of the fantastic in which the devil takes the form of a woman
TRANSLATED BY STEPHEN SARTARELLI
0-941419-78-9 MARSILIO $28.00
0-941419-79-7 MARSILIO PB $14.00

Isabelle **de Charrière**

Letters of Mistress Henley Published by Her Friend
EDITED BY PHILIP STEWART & JEAN VACHE
0-87352-776-3 MLA PB $3.95

Denis **Diderot**
Philosopher and critic, novelist and playwright, Diderot was one of the century's most influential figures. As editor of the Encyclopédie, *he was instrumental in the popularization of science and philosophy.*

The Indiscreet Jewels
A satirical blend of erotic and philosophical fiction
TRANLSATED BY SOPHIE HAWKES
0-941419-82-7 MARSILIO $32.00
0-941419-83-5 MARSILIO PB $16.00

Jacques the Fatalist and His Master
This rambling picaresque novel is structured around the highly animated, wide-ranging dialogue between Jacques and his master
TRANSLATED BY MICHAEL HENRY
0-14-044472-6 PENGUIN PB $10.95

Memoirs of a Nun
TRANSLATED BY FRANCIS BIRRELL
0-679-41324-3 KNOPF $15.00

The Nun
A reluctant nun's sufferings in the cloister form the basis for a virulent condemnation of the hypocrisy of religiosity
TRANSLATED BY LEONARD TANCOCK
0-14-044300-2 PENGUIN PB $7.95

Rameau's Nephew & d'Alembert's Dream
Two of Diderot's most famous works in one volume
See also **THE ENLIGHTENMENT: A SAMPLER** under **THE AGE OF ENLIGHTENMENT** under **EARLY MODERN EUROPE** in **WORLD HISTORY AND CURRENT AFFAIRS**
TRANSLATED BY LEONARD TANCOCK
0-14-044173-5 PENGUIN PB $10.95

Selected Writings On Art and Literature
Diderot was also a brilliant art critic
TRANSLATED BY GEOFFREY BREMNER
0-14-044588-9 PENGUIN PB $12.95

This is Not a Story and Other Stories
TRANSLATED BY P.N. FURBANK
0-19-282958-0 OXFORD PB $7.95

Claire **de Duras**

Ourika: An English Translation
TRANSLATED BY JOHN FOWLES
0-87352-780-1 MLA PB $5.95

Francoise **de Graffigny**

Letters from a Peruvian Woman
TRANSLATED BY DAVID KORNACKER
0-87352-778-X MLA PB $5.95

Choderlos **de Laclos**

Les Liaisons Dangereuses
The famous epistolary novel of systematic seduction has obviously struck a chord, to judge by its many stage and screen adaptations
TRANSLATED BY P.W.K. STONE
0-14-044116-6 PENGUIN PB $8.95

Charles **de Montesquieu**

The Persian Letters
A satire on French institutions, thinly disguised as the observations of two Persians visiting Paris
See also **THE CLASSICS** under **HISTORIOGRAPHY** in **WORLD HISTORY AND CURRENT AFFAIRS**
TRANSLATED BY C.J. BETTS
0-14-044281-2 PENGUIN PB $10.95

Abbé **Prévost**

Manon Lescaut
Those who know the heroine only from the operatic versions will be surprised at the unsparing sharpness of the original character
TRANSLATED BY DONALD M. FRAME
0-88355-600-6 HYPERION $30.00

Jean-Jacques **Rousseau**
Some of the profound contradictions in Rousseau's life found their way into his political philosophy, which is meant to show the way to freedom and equality but finds true freedom in the submission of the individual to the "general will." Rousseau has been seen as both the champion of revolution and individual liberty and the harbinger of 20th-century totalitarianism.

The Confessions
This *philosophe* shared with his colleagues a loathing of the Old Regime, yet he also opposed certain of the Enlightenment's principal tenets. The keystone of Rousseau's writings: a self-portrait preserving the author's contradictions and self-doubts
See also **ROUSSEAU** under **PHILOSOPHY** in **RELIGION, SPIRITUALITY, AND PHILOSOPHY**
TRANSLATED BY J.M. COHEN
0-14-044033-X PENGUIN PB $8.95

Discourse on Political Economy and the Social Contract
TRANSLATED BY CHRISTOPHER BETTS
0-19-282750-2 OXFORD PB $5.95

A Discourse on the Origins of Inequality
The book that made Rousseau famous, on the happiness of a state of nature and the miseries of civilized sophistication
TRANSLATED BY MAURICE CRANSTON
0-14-044439-4 PENGUIN PB $8.95

Discourse on the Origins of Inequality
TRANSLATED BY FRANKLIN PHILIP
0-19-282947-5 OXFORD PB $7.95

Discourse on the Sciences and Arts
EDITED BY ROGER D. MASTERS AND C. KELLY
0-87451-580-7 NEW ENGLAND $40.00

Emile
Rousseau's treatise on education, advocating a return to nature and rural values
See also **CLASSICS** under **THEORY AND PHILOSOPHY** under **EDUCATION** in **SOCIAL STUDIES**
TRANSLATED BY ALLAN BLOOM
0-465-01931-5 BASIC BOOKS PB $20.00

The Essential Rousseau
Includes Rousseau's *Social Contract, Discourse on Inequality, Discourse on Arts and Sciences* and *The Creed of a Savoyard Priest*
TRANSLATED BY LOWELL BAIR
ILLUSTRATED BY MATTHEW JOSEPHSON
0-452-01031-4 NEW AMERICAN LIBRARY PB $12.95

La Nouvelle Héloise: Julie, Or the New Eloise
A portrayal of idealized conjugal fidelity set against a joyous rustic backdrop
TRANSLATED BY JUDITH MCDOWELL
0-271-00602-1 PENN STATE PB $15.00

First and Second Discourse, Together with Replies to the Critics, & Essay on the Origin of Languages

The philosopher of the state of nature draws on travelers' tales to ponder "savage man." Includes *On the Origin and Foundations of Inequality Among Men*

See also **PRECURSORS** under **GENERAL ANTHROPOLOGICAL STUDIES** under **ANTHROPOLOGY** in **SOCIAL STUDIES**

TRANSLATED BY VICTOR GOUREVITCH

0-8095-9091-3 BORGO....$37.00

0-06-132083-8 HARPERCOLLINS PB....$16.00

On the Origin of Language

0-226-73012-3 CHICAGO PB....$9.95

Reveries of the Solitary Walker

Evocations of wild natural beauty and the moral implications of solitude and independence

TRANSLATED BY PETER FRANCE

0-14-044363-0 PENGUIN PB....$7.95

The Social Contract

The chief work of Rousseau's political philosophy, in which the individual attains true freedom by submitting to the "general will"

See also **CLASSICS** under **POLITICAL THOUGHT** in **SOCIAL STUDIES**

TRANSLATED BY MAURICE CRANSTON

0-14-044201-4 PENGUIN PB....$7.95

The Social Contract and Discourses

TRANSLATED BY G.D.H. COLE

0-679-42302-8 KNOPF....$17.00

Marquis **de Sade**

Crimes of Love

These five morality tales, here translated into English for the first time, show a philosophical side to his work completely different from his infamous pornography

TRANSLTED BY MARGARET CROSLAND

0-7206-0957-7 DUFOUR....$28.95

Juliette

The alternative title—*Or the Benefits of Vice*—makes clear de Sade's advocacy in this volume written behind bars

TRANSLATED BY AUSTRYN WAINHOUSE

0-8021-3085-2 GROVE PB....$21.95

Justine, Philosophy in the Bedroom, and Other Writings

TRANSLATED BY AUSTRYN WAINHOUSE & RICHARD SEAVER

0-8021-3218-9 GROVE PB....$17.95

The Misfortunes of Virtue and Other Early Tales

EDITED AND TRANSLATED BY DAVID COWARD

0-19-282863-0 OXFORD PB....$8.95

The Mystified Magistrate: Four Stories

TRANSLATED BY MARGARET CROSLAND

0-7206-0849-X OWEN PB....$17.95

The Passionate Philosopher: A Marquis de Sade Reader

TRANSLATED BY MARGARET CROSLAND

0-7206-0826-0 DUFOUR....$40.00

Voltaire

Philosopher, poet, tragedian, and man of letters, Voltaire is the emblematic figure of his age. Unfortunately only a small selection of his works is represented in English.

Candide

A "philosophical tale" of human calamity intended as a satirical counterpoint to the bland optimism of Leibniz

TRANSLATED BY JOHN BUTT

0-14-044004-6 PENGUIN PB....$5.95

Candide & Philosophical Letters

TRANSLATED BY RICHARD ALDINGTON & ERNEST DILWORTH

0-679-60003-5 MODERN LIBRARY....$13.50

Letters on England

Also known as the *Philosophical Letters*: a description of English society and politics written during Voltaire's exile there

TRANSLATED BY LEONARD TANCOCK

0-14-044386-X PENGUIN PB....$8.95

Philosophical Dictionary

Principally a mordant onslaught on religious dogma

TRANSLATED BY THEODORE BESTERMAN

0-14-044257-X PENGUIN PB....$12.95

The Portable Voltaire

Including *Candide* (Part 1), *Zadig, Micromegas, The Story of a Good Brahmin,* selections from the *Philosophical Dictionary, The English Letters, The Lisbon Earthquake, Essay on the Manners and Spirit of Nations,* and 35 selected letters

See also **THE ENLIGHTENMENT: A SAMPLER** under **THE AGE OF ENLIGHTENMENT** under **EARLY MODERN EUROPE** in **WORLD HISTORY AND CURRENT AFFAIRS**

EDITED BY BEN R. REDMAN

0-14-015041-2 VIKING PB....$14.95

Selected Writings

EDITED BY CHRISTOPHER THACKER

0-460-87624-4 EVERYMAN'S PB....$8.50

Zadig & l'Ingenu

Two "philosophical tales," the first hitting out at the clergy and Catholic dogma, the second a thinly veiled attack on the powers-that-be

TRANSLATED BY JOHN BUTT

0-14-044126-3 PENGUIN PB....$8.95

The 19th Century: Romanticism and Realism

The period following the Napoleonic era saw the novel come into its own as an instrument for registering social upheaval. A radical change in direction was signaled by the extreme subjectivity and rich rhetoric of Romanticism; unfortunately such leading figures as Chateaubriand remain inaccessible in English translation.

Honoré **de Balzac**

Balzac's is a literature of vigorous documentation and powerful obsession, moving from dreamlike melodrama to drab photo-realism and forming one of the great exceptions to the French tradition of concision and balance. La Comédie humaine, *with its cast of thousands, written over the best part of a decade, must be viewed as a whole to be fully appreciated.*

The Bureaucrats

The tyranny of the clerks: an eerily modern analysis of Parisian power politics at their most subtle

TRANSLATED BY MARCO DIANI

0-8101-0973-5 NORTHWESTERN....$39.95

0-8101-0987-5 NORTHWESTERN PB....$14.95

The Chouans

An early highly Romantic novel of anti-revolutionary guerrilla warfare in Brittany

0-14-044260-X PENGUIN PB....$11.95

Cousin Bette

The celebrated study of the tumult ensuing from unbridled jealousy and licentiousness

TRANSLATED BY MARION CRAWFORD

0-679-40671-9 KNOPF....$20.00

0-19-282606-9 OXFORD PB....$7.95

Cousin Pons

A classic portrait of the "poor relation"

TRANSLATED BY HERBERT HUNT

0-14-044205-7 PENGUIN PB....$9.95

Eugenie Grandet

The colorful study of a rich miser and the almost improbable goodness of his daughter

TRANSLATED BY MARION CRAWFORD

0-14-044050-X PENGUIN PB....$8.95

A Harlot High and Low

A swirling, intrigue-ridden panorama of Parisian life, embracing the worlds of high finance and low crime, and dominated by the sinister figure of Vautrin

TRANSLATED BY RAYNER HEPPENSTALL

0-14-044232-4 PENGUIN PB....$9.95

History of the Thirteen

These "Scenes of Parisian Life," loosely linked by the activities of a powerful secret society, include *Farragus, The Duchess of Langeais,* and *The Girl with the Golden Eyes*

TRANSLATED BY HERBERT HUNT

0-14-044301-0 PENGUIN PB....$11.95

Only a few devotees, people who never walk along in heedless inattention, sip and savour their Paris and are so familiar with its physiognomy that they know its every wart, every spot or blotch on its face. For all others, Paris is still the same monstrous miracle, an astounding assemblage of movements, machines and ideas, the city of a thousand different romances, the world's thinking-box. But, for the devotees, Paris is sad or gay, ugly or beautiful, living or dead; for them Paris is a sentient being; every individual, every bit of a house is a lobe in the cellular tissue of that great harlot whose head, heart and unpredictable behaviour are perfectly familiar to them.

HISTORY OF THE THIRTEEN

The Lily of the Valley

0-88184-482-9 CARROLL & GRAF PB....$9.95

Lost Illusions

A provincial poet attempts to rise in Parisian high society in this relentlessly detailed account of the French publishing world at its seamiest

TRANSLATED BY HERBERT HUNT

0-14-044251-0 PENGUIN PB....$10.95

A Murky Business

Political intrigue in the Napoleonic era

0-14-044271-5 PENGUIN PB....$10.95

Old Goriot
The poignant and Lear-like tale of ungrateful daughters and the thanklessness of parental sacrifice
TRANSLATED BY MARION CRAWFORD
0-14-044017-8 PENGUIN PB........$10.95

Père Goriot
A new translation of Balzac's most famous novel
TRANSLATED BY BURTON RAFFEL
0-393-03620-0 NORTON........$29.95
0-451-52190-0 NEW AMERICAN LIBRARY PB........$5.95

The Rise and Fall of César Birotteau
A scent-merchant falls prey to dreams of wealth and pomp—and the nightmare of debt. "A study in morals, the picture of a world which Balzac knew from top to bottom because he came from it"—André Maurois
TRANSLATED BY FRANCIS FUREY
0-88184-448-9 CARROLL & GRAF PB........$8.95

Selected Short Stories
Includes "A Study in Feminine Psychology," "An Incident in the Reign of Terror," "The Atheists' Mass," and nine others
TRANSLATED AND EDITED BY SYLVIA RAPHAEL
0-14-044325-8 PENGUIN PB........$8.95

Seraphita
A fantastic novel reflecting Balzac's interest in the mystical theories of Swedenborg
0-8369-3691-4 AYER........$20.95

Ursule Mirouet
A novel demonstrating Balzac's deep involvement in occult lore
TRANSLATED BY DONALD ADAMSON
0-14-044316-9 PENGUIN PB........$9.95

The Wild Ass's Skin
A Faustian tale of magic and damnation, set against a backdrop of garrets and gambling halls
TRANSLATED BY HERBERT HUNT
0-14-044330-4 PENGUIN PB........$9.95

Francois-René **de Chateaubriand**

Atala & René
These romanticized novellas of American Indian life (which the author had observed at first hand) give only a small idea of Chateaubriand's talents
TRANSLATED BY IRVING PUTTER
0-520-00223-7 CALIFORNIA PB........$13.95

Benjamin **Constant**

Adolphe
Although his work is classical in style, Constant gave the Romantic age an idealized image of itself in his portrait of the self-doubting, world-weary Adolphe
TRANSLATED BY LEONARD TANCOCK
0-14-044134-4 PENGUIN PB........$8.95

Alphonse **Daudet**

Letters from my Windmill
Genial evocations of Provence
TRANSLATED BY FREDERICK DAVIES
0-14-044334-7 PENGUIN PB........$9.95

Alexandre **Dumas**

Dumas was not only the great yarn-spinner of 19th-century literature, an effortless storyteller with a sure instinct for melodramatic excitement, but a writer able to weave subtler moods into his relentlessly paced stories.

The Black Tulip
An uncharacteristic foray into 17th-century Dutch history
TRANSLATED BY DAVID COWARD
0-19-283079-1 OXFORD PB........$10.95

The Three Musketeers
Countless movie versions later, Dumas' great adventure novel remains fresh and often startling
See also **YOUNG ADULT FICTION** in **BOOKS FOR YOUNG READERS**
0-14-044025-9 PENGUIN PB........$8.95

Twenty Years After
The three musketeers make a surprisingly ironic and elegiac return appearance
TRANSLATED BY DAVID COWARD
0-19-283074-0 OXFORD PB........$12.95

The Count of Monte Cristo
A masterpiece of melodramatic plotting, in which a wronged sailor accomplishes his revenge through the power of unlimited capital
TRANSLATED BY DAVID COWARD
0-19-282715-4 OXFORD PB........$11.95

Queen Margot
A turbulent saga of 16th-century France and its savage factional warfare
0-7868-8082-1 HYPERION PB........$14.95

The Vicomte de Bragelonne
First in a trilogy featuring, once more, D'Artagnan and his musketeer comrades
EDITED BY DAVID COWARD
0-19-282390-6 OXFORD PB........$13.95

Louise de La Vallières
Second in the "Vicomte de Bragelonne" trilogy
EDITED BY DAVID COWARD
0-19-282389-2 OXFORD PB........$14.95

The Man in the Iron Mask
The final and most famous installment of the "Bragelonne" trilogy
TRANSLATED BY DAVID COWARD
0-19-282752-9 OXFORD PB........$11.95

Alexandre **Dumas fils**

La Dame aux Camelias
This tale of doomed love is important if only for the material it provided for Verdi and Garbo
TRANSLATED BY DAVID COWARD
0-19-281736-1 OXFORD PB........$8.95

Victor **Hugo**

The grand old man of the Romantic movement embarked at an early age on his prolific literary career, which spanned almost the entire 19th century.

The Last Day of a Condemned Man
Hugo's passionate plea against capital punishment has a contemporary ring for Americans in view of the resurgence of the death penalty
TRANSLATED BY GEOFF WOLLEN
0-19-282890-8 OXFORD PB........$8.95

Les Misérables
Hugo's immense, powerful novel is one of the 19th century's most representative creations; Denny's excellent translation trims a few marginal passages
TRANSLATED BY NORMAN DENNY
0-14-044430-0 PENGUIN PB........$10.95

Les Misérables
A complete translation revised from an 1863 edition
0-451-52157-9 NEW AMERICAN LIBRARY PB........$7.95

Les Misérables
TRANSLATED BY CHARLES WILBOUR
0-679-60012-4 MODERN LIBRARY........$22.00

Ninety-Three
A novel of the counterrevolutionary Vendé uprising
0-88184-405-5 CARROLL & GRAF PB........$8.95

Notre-Dame of Paris
The hunchback Quasimodo, the gypsy Esmeralda, and the sinister priest Frollo are set against the minutely drawn tumult of medieval Paris
0-14-044353-3 PENGUIN PB........$10.95

Toilers of the Sea
0-9626854-7-X ATLANTEAN PB........$17.95

Joan C. **Kessler**, editor

Demons of the Night: Tales of the Fantastic, Madness, and the Supernatural from 19th-Century France
See also **ANTHOLOGIES** under **SUPERNATURAL FANTASY AND HORROR** under **SCIENCE FICTION AND FANTASY** in **POPULAR READING**
0-226-43207-6 CHICAGO........$45.00
0-226-43208-4 CHICAGO PB........$14.95

Jules **Michelet**

Michelet, the great Romantic historian, used magnificent, unrestrained rhetoric and picturesque narrative in his evocations of the past.

Joan of Arc
A rhetorically superb distillation of the Maid of Orleans as French national archetype
TRANSLATED BY ALBERT GUERARD
0-472-06122-4 MICHIGAN PB........$12.95

The People
Michelet's famous study of the French peasantry is fervently nationalistic in tone
TRANSLATED WITH AN INTRODUCTION BY JOHN MCKAY
0-252-00321-7 ILLINOIS........$24.95
0-252-00331-4 ILLINOIS PB........$11.95

Satanism and Witchcraft
In effect, a long prose poem on the darker side of the Middle Ages as distilled through a Romantic consciousness
0-8065-0059-X CITADEL PB........$12.95

Alfred **de Musset**

Comedies and Proverbs
TRANSLATED BY DAVID SICES
0-8018-4682-X JOHNS HOPKINS........$45.00
0-8018-4683-8 PAJ PUBLICATIONS PB........$14.95

Historical Dramas of Alfred de Musset
0-8204-3143-5 LANG........$42.00

George **Sand**

Sand's reputation is now being reevaluated in light of feminist criticism, and her novels, long unavailable, are again finding many readers.

Horace

TRANSLATED BY ZACK ROGOW

1-56279-082-X MERCURY HOUSE PB $15.95

George Sand

Indiana

A beautiful Creole flees a sadistic husband

TRANSLATED BY GEORGE IVES

0-915864-57-6 ACADEMY CHICAGO PB $10.00

Indiana

TRANSLATED BY ELEANOR DUNCAN

0-451-52572-8 SIGNET PB $5.95

Lavinia

TRANSLATED BY GEORGE IVES

AFTERWORD BY DANIEL SKARRY

0-915288-28-1 SHAMELESS HUSSY PB $2.95

Lettres d'un Voyageur

An account of Sand's liaison with Musset, including their visit to Italy

TRANSLATED BY SACHA RABINOVITCH

0-14-044411-4 PENGUIN PB $11.95

Lucrezia Floriani

TRANSLATED BY JULIUS EKER

0-89733-143-5 ACADEMY CHICAGO PB $20.00

The Miller of Angibault

0-19-283084-8 OXFORD PB $9.95

Valentine

TRANSLATED BY GEORGE BURNHAM IVES

0-915864-59-2 ACADEMY CHICAGO PB $14.00

A Woman's Version of the Faust Legend: The Seven Strings of the Lyre

TRANSLATED BY GEORGE A. KENNEDY

0-8078-1856-9 NORTH CAROLINA $45.00

Germaine **de Staël**

Delphine

TRANSLATED BY AVRIEL GOLDBERGER

0-87580-200-1 NORTHERN ILLINOIS $50.00

0-87580-567-1 NORTHERN ILLINOIS PB $22.95

Major Writings of Germaine de Staël

TRANSLATED BY VIVIAN FOLKENFLIK

0-231-05587-0 COLUMBIA PB $18.00

Stendhal

Barely appreciated in his own lifetime, Stendhal evolved a style combining elegant aphorism and realistic psychological description.

The Charterhouse of Parma

A novel of intrigue at the court of Parma in the early 19th century

TRANSLATED BY C. K. MONCRIEFF

0-679-41743-5 KNOPF $20.00

The Life of Henry Brulard

A thinly disguised autobiography, posthumously published, that details the author's bitterly unhappy youth

TRANSLATED BY JEAN STEWART

0-226-77251-9 CHICAGO PB $12.95

The Life of Henry Brulard

TRANSLATED BY JOHN STURROCK

0-14-044611-7 PENGUIN PB $12.95

Lucien Leuwen

0-8112-0388-3 NEW DIRECTIONS PB $5.00

The Pink and the Green

An unfinished novel, published in English for the first time. This edition also includes the story *Mina de Vanghel*

TRANSLATED WITH AN AFTERWORD BY RICHARD HOWARD

0-8112-1062-6 NEW DIRECTIONS $17.95

The Red and the Black

0-679-60162-7 MODERN LIBRARY $17.50

Scarlet and Black

An excellent translation of *Le Rouge et le Noir*, Stendhal's most celebrated book, notable for its portrait of the frustrated rebel Julien Sorel and the post-Napoleonic conformity that oppresses him

TRANSLATED BY MARGARET SHAW

0-14-044030-5 PENGUIN PB $7.95

Three Italian Chronicles

Three tales of passion and intrigue—*The Cenci, The Abbess of Castro,* and *Vanina Vanini*—available again in the *Revived Modern Classics* series

TRANSLATED BY C.K. SCOTT-MONCRIEFF

0-8112-1150-9 NEW DIRECTIONS PB $9.95

Eugène **Sue**

The Mysteries of Paris

Sue's melodramatic novel of the Parisian underworld was enormously popular and influential

09466263081 DAEDALUS PB $9.95

0-946626-30-8 HIPPOCRENE PB $11.95

The Wandering Jew

A labyrinthine novel in which seemingly unrelated people all over the world become the victims of a fiendish Jesuit plot. Sue's contraption feels like the blueprint for 20th-century conspiracy theories at their most paranoid

0-87052-816-5 HIPPOCRENE PB $22.50

The Later 19th Century: Symbolism, Naturalism, and the Roots of Modernism

With the later 19th century we are on familiar ground. The great writers—Baudelaire, Flaubert, Mallarmé, Rimbaud—are very much a part of our own world; indeed, they played a major part in creating it.

Charles **Baudelaire**

Baudelaire's verse technique was classical, but his themes and point of view could not have been less so. He defined the role of the modern poet, even as he railed against the modern age.

Intimate Journals

TRANSLATED BY CHRISTOPHER ISHERWOOD

0-87286-146-5 CITY LIGHTS PB $6.95

Intimate Journals

TRANSLATED BY NORMAN CAMERON

0-14-038911-3 PENGUIN PB $3.95

La Fanfarlo

Baudelaire's only novella, based on his complicated relationship with his mistress, Jeanne Duval. A bilingual edition

TRANSLATED BY GREG BOYD

0-88739-003-X CREATIVE ARTS PB $6.95

Les Fleurs du Mal

This widely praised translation of the complete text won the American Book Award in 1983. Bilingual edition

TRANSLATED BY RICHARD HOWARD

0-87923-462-8 GODINE PB $16.95

The Flowers of Evil

A selection by a variety of translators. Bilingual edition

EDITED BY JACKSON MATHEWS & MARTHIEL MATHEWS

0-8112-0006-X NEW DIRECTIONS PB $9.95

The Painter of Modern Life & Other Essays

Baudelaire was a controversial and imaginative art critic whose work still excites interest

EDITED BY JONATHAN MAYNE

0-306-80279-1 DA CAPO PB $13.95

Paris Spleen

Prose poems of the metropolis

TRANSLATED BY LOUISE VARESE

0-8112-0007-8 NEW DIRECTIONS PB $7.95

Parisian Prowler

An outstanding new translation of *Le Spleen de Paris* and *Petits Poemes en Prose,* the works in which Baudelaire explored the prose poem as a poetic form and pioneered a new strain of harsh urban imagery

TRANSLATED BY EDWARD KAPLAN

0-8203-1162-6 GEORGIA $19.95

0-8203-1163-4 GEORGIA PB $11.95

Selected Letters of Charles Baudelaire: The Conquest of Solitude

"Unable to excel in virtue, he made himself a legend in vice"—Morris Bishop

TRANSLATED AND EDITED BY ROSEMARY LLOYD

0-226-03928-5 CHICAGO $29.95

Selected Poems
EDITED BY CAROL CLARK
0-14-044624-9 PENGUIN PB $12.95

Twenty Prose Poems
A bilingual edition
TRANSLATED WITH AN INTRODUCTION BY MICHAEL HAMBURGER
0-87286-216-X CITY LIGHTS PB $6.95

Georges **Feydeau**

Feydeau, First to Last: Eight One-Act Comedies
Feydeau's genius for plot construction has given his lively farces remarkable durability.
TRANSLATED BY NORMAN SHAPIRO
0-8014-9271-8 CORNELL PB $13.95

Gustave **Flaubert**

"Flaubert's aloof, melancholic temperament caused some of the bleakness of his vision, as any writer's negations or affirmations owe something to his temperament. Yet the bleakness is also inherent in an Old World skepticism concerning human nature as manifested in society, the only form in which human nature can be known."—F.W. Dupee

The Dictionary of Accepted Ideas
Flaubert's extraordinary catalog of clichés and banalities was intended as part of the unfinished *Bouvard and Pecuchet*, to which it now forms a sort of addendum
TRANSLATED BY JACQUES BARZUN
0-8112-0054-X NEW DIRECTIONS PB $6.95

ABELARD. No need to have any notion of his philosophy, nor even to know the titles of his works. Just refer discreetly to his mutilation by Fulbert. The grave of Abelard and Heloise: if someone tells you it is apocryphal, exclaim: "You rob me of my illusions!" ABSINTHE. Extra-violent poison: one glass and you're dead. Newspaper-men drink it as they write copy. Has killed more soldiers than the Bedouin. ACCIDENT. Always "regrettable" or "unlucky"—as if a mishap might sometimes be a cause for rejoicing. ACTRESSES. The ruin of young men of good family. Are fearfully lascivious; engage in "nameless orgies," run through fortunes; end in the poorhouse. "I beg to differ, sir: some are excellent mothers!" AFFAIRS (BUSINESS). Come first. A woman must not refer to hers. The most important thing in life. Be-all and end-all. AIR. Beware of drafts of air. The depths of the air are invariably unlike the surface. If the former are warm, the latter is cold and vice versa.
THE DICTIONARY OF ACCEPTED IDEAS

Dictionary of Received Ideas
A more complete translation of Flaubert's masterpiece of glossing
TRANSLATED BY GEOFFREY WALL
0-14-038904-0 PENGUIN PB $3.95

Flaubert in Egypt
A compilation of Flaubert's travel notes and letters from his Egyptian journey of 1849-50. "By turns beautiful, rapturous, bawdy, hideous and brutal…also from time to time quite funny" —William Styron
EDITED AND TRANSLATED BY FRANCIS STEEGMULLER
0-89733-018-8 ACADEMY CHICAGO PB $8.95

The Letters of Gustave Flaubert, 1857-1880
0-674-52640-6 HARVARD $29.00

Madame Bovary
Flaubert's meticulous, superbly controlled study of the romantic reveries and less-than-romantic adventures of a provincial doctor's wife
TRANSLATED BY ALAN RUSSELL
0-14-044015-1 PENGUIN PB $3.95

Madame Bovary
Steegmuller's is generally acknowledged to be the finest English translation of Flaubert's masterpiece
TRANSLATED BY FRANCIS STEEGMULLER
0-679-60013-2 MODERN LIBRARY $15.50
0-679-73636-0 VINTAGE PB $12.00

November
A short coming-of-age novel
0-88184-334-2 CARROLL & GRAF PB $7.95

Salâmmbo
Flaubert's penchant for decadent Romanticism emerges in full splendor in this violent and erotic novel of Carthage
TRANSLATED BY A.J. KRAILSHEIMER
0-14-044328-2 PENGUIN PB $9.95

The Sentimental Education
"If one rereads it in middle age, one finds that the author's tone no longer seems quite so acrid, that one is listening to a muted symphony of which the varied instrumentation and the pattern, the marked rhythms and the melancholy sonorities, had been hardly perceptible before. There are no heroes, no villains, to arouse us, no clowns to entertain us, no scenes to wring our hearts. Yet the effect is deeply moving"—Edmund Wilson
TRANSLATED BY ROBERT BALDICK
0-14-044141-7 PENGUIN PB $5.95

A Simple Heart
TRANSLATED BY ARTHUR MCDOWALL
0-8112-1318-8 NEW DIRECTIONS PB $6.00

The Temptation of Saint Anthony
A fluid dramatization of the anchorite's ordeal in the desert; Flaubert displays his pedantic knowledge with great gusto
TRANSLATED BY KITTY MROSOVSKY
0-14-044410-6 PENGUIN PB $9.95

Three Tales
Includes *A Simple Heart, The Legend of Saint Julian Hospitalor,* and *Herodias:* three very different examples of Flaubert's skill in narrative
TRANSLATED BY ROBERT BALDICK
0-14-044106-9 PENGUIN PB $8.95

Rémy **de Gourmont**

Angels of Perversity
TRANSLATED BY FRANCIS AMERY
0-7818-0004-8 HIPPOCRENE PB $11.95

Rémy **de Gourmont**, editor

The Book of Masks: French Symbolist and Decadent Writing of the 1890s
An important collection of *fin-de-siècle* writing including hard-to-find works by such figures as Leon Bloy, Rachilde, Gustave Kahn, Villiers de l'Isle-Adam, Marcel Schwob, and the American expatriate Stuart Merrill. With illustrations by Felix Vallotton
EDITED AND TRANSLATED BY ANDREW MANGRAVITE
0-947757-81-3 SERPENT'S TAIL PB $19.99

J.K. **Huysmans**

Against Nature
A textbook of decadence (sometimes translated as *Against the Grain)*, with a somewhat cheerless aftertaste
TRANSLATED BY ROBERT BALDICK
0-14-044086-0 PENGUIN PB $10.95

Against the Grain
INTRODUCTION BY HAVELOCK ELLIS
0-486-22190-3 DOVER PB $6.95

Becalmed
TRANSLATED BY TERRY HALE
0-947757-30-9 SERPENT'S TAIL PB $13.99

The Cathedral
0-87052-615-4 HIPPOCRENE PB $11.95

En Route
0-87052-616-2 HIPPOCRENE PB $9.95

La-Bàs
This largely autobiographical work charts the progress of a young man embracing Catholicism after a skirmish with Satanism
0-946626-19-7 HIPPOCRENE PB $11.95

La-Bàs (Down There)
TRANSLATED BY KEENE WALLACE
0-486-22837-1 DOVER PB $7.95

Marthe: The Story of a Woman
1-55713-138-4 SUN & MOON PB $10.95

Eugene **Labiche**

A Slap in the Farce
Includes *A Matter of Wife and Death*
TRANSLATED BY NORMAN SHAPIRO
0-936839-82-1 APPLAUSE THEATRE PB $7.95

Jules **Laforgue**

Moral Tales
Elaborately composed satirical versions of old stories, including a parody of Flaubert's *Hérodias*
TRANSLATED BY WILLIAM JAY SMITH
0-8112-0943-1 NEW DIRECTIONS PB $8.95

Comte **de Lautréamont**

Maldoror
Lautréamont's dreamlike prose poetry had a profound effect on modern French writers
TRANSLATED BY GUY WERNHAM
0-8112-0082-5 NEW DIRECTIONS PB $11.95

Villiers **de l'Isle-Adam**

Axel
TRANSLATED BY M. GADDIS ROSE
0-948166-05-3 DUFOUR PB $11.95

Pierre **Loti**

Azyade
0-7103-0316-5 KEGAN & PAUL PB $14.95

The Desert/Le Desert
TRANSLATED BY JAY PAUL
0-87480-427-2 UTAH PB $14.95

Madam Chrysanthemum
Loti describes Japanese life in his patented vein of richly colored exoticism
TRANSLATED BY LAURA ENSOR
0-7103-0138-3 KEGAN & PAUL PB $25.50

The Marriage of Loti
A romance of the South Pacific
TRANSLATED BY CLARA BELL
0-7103-0231-2 ROUTLEDGE PB $25.50

Pierre **Louys**

The Songs of Bilitis
In an Ossianic literary hoax, Louys claimed that these prose poems were translated from a Greek poetess contemporary with Sappho
0-486-25670-7 DOVER PB $5.95

Two Erotic Tales: Aphrodite, The Songs of Bilitis
"Although certain he would die young from tuberculosis, he was never without a cigarette dangling from his mouth; known for his sense of humor and practical jokes, he also suffered from suicidal depressions; he was a homophobe who advocated lesbianism; an anti-semite, who made the female protagonist of his first novel Jewish; a scholar, whose research was disregarded because his first work feigned to be a translation from the Greek; a libertine who squandered his inheritance"—from the translator's introduction
EDITED BY DOROTHY KAVKA
1-87926-024-7 EVANSTON PB $18.00

Stephane **Mallarmé**

"Hero, prophet, magus, and tragedian, it was fitting that this feminine little man, discreet and not much drawn to women, should die on the brink of our century: he announces it. More and better than Nietzsche, he lived the Death of God; well before Camus, he realized that suicide is the primary question that man must ask himself; his daily battle against chance will be taken up by others, but none will surpass his lucidity. For in essence he asked himself: Can one find, within determinism, a means by which to exit from it?"
—Jean-Paul Sartre

Collected Poems
"The gaping empty space on the shelf has now been filled, handsomely, almost miraculously, by Henry Weinfeld's magnificent version of Mallarmé's *Collected Poems*"
—Washington Post Book World
TRANSLATED BY HENRY WEINFELD
0-520-08188-9 CALIFORNIA $30.00

Stephane Mallarmé

Selected Poems
The abstraction and musicality of Mallarme's poetry make it border on the untranslatable. This older edition has the French text on facing pages
TRANSLATED BY C.F. MACINTYRE
0-520-00801-4 CALIFORNIA PB $10.95

Guy **de Maupassant**

Bel-Ami
A journalist fights and inveigles his way to the top of Parisian society
TRANSLATED BY DOUGLAS PARMEE
0-14-044315-0 PENGUIN PB $10.95

Pierre and Jean
Considered his best novel. A preface sets out Maupassant's concept of the novelist's function and describes the instruction received from his mentor, Flaubert
TRANSLATED BY LEONARD TANCOCK
0-14-044358-4 PENGUIN PB $7.95

A Woman's Life
Depicts a woman's lonely life in Normandy, the author's home ground
TRANSLATED BY H.N. SLOMAN
0-14-044161-1 PENGUIN PB $9.95

Octave **Mirbeau**

The Torture Garden
"The most sickening work of art of the nineteenth century" is back in print thanks to the fearless geniuses at RE/SEARCH. Originally published in 1899, this story was far ahead of its time. A bourgeois Frenchman submits to the wiles of an Englishwoman who leads him to a garden in China where all his dreams and nightmares of degradation are realized
See also **RE/SEARCH** under **CUTTING EDGE** in **POPULAR READING**
0-9651042-6-5 JUNO PB $13.99

Gérard **de Nerval**

Aurelia & Sylvie
TRANSLATED BY KENDALL LAPPIN
1-87858-007-8 ASYLUM ARTS PB $9.95

The Chimeras
A sensitive and painstaking rendering of the twelve celebrated sonnets, written a year before Nerval's suicide
TRANSLATED BY PETER JAY
0-933806-34-5 BLACK SWAN $20.00

Arthur **Rimbaud**

"No one else has ever had the faith, the hope, and the lack of charity to attack poetry the way Rimbaud did. No one else with so much strength and intelligence has ever had the innocence to take all of its most extravagant claims with complete seriousness. Rimbaud tried to do with poetry what others only pretended to be able to do. Poetry has never recovered. To say it has never been the same since is not slang, but simple fact."
—Kenneth Rexroth

Collected Poems
TRANSLATED BY OLIVER BERNARD
0-14-042064-9 PENGUIN PB $11.95

Complete Works with Selected Letters
TRANSLATED BY WALLACE FOWLIE
0-226-71973-1 CHICAGO PB $13.95

Illuminations
Rimbaud's prose poems, compressed and infinitely suggestive, have exerted extraordinary influence on 20th-century poetics
0-8112-0184-8 NEW DIRECTIONS PB $9.95

A Season in Hell
Also includes the long poem *The Drunken Boat*
TRANSLATED BY LOUISE VARESE
0-8112-0185-6 NEW DIRECTIONS PB $8.95

A Season in Hell & Illuminations
TRANSLATED BY ENID PESCHEL
INTRODUCTION BY HENRI PEYRE
0-19-501760-9 OXFORD PB $8.95

A Season in Hell & Illuminations
0-918526-89-2 BOA PB $12.50

Selected Poems
Perhaps the best translation of Rimbaud's poetry yet achieved
TRANSLATED BY PAUL SCHMIDT
0-679-43321-X EVERYMAN'S $10.95

Georges **Rodenbach**

Bruges-la-Morte
TRANSLATED BY THOMAS DUNCAN
0-947757-58-9 CONSORTIUM PB $12.99

Marcel **Schwob**

The King in the Golden Mask
Steeped in the exotic and the decadent, Schwob's stories meditate on strange moments in history. This excellent collection includes his masterful *The Children's Crusade*
TRANSLATED BY IAN WHITE
0-85635-403-1 CARCANET $14.95
0-85635-579-8 CARCANET PB $16.95

Paul **Verlaine**

Selected Poems
Bilingual edition
TRANSLATED BY C.F. MACINTYRE
0-520-01298-4 CALIFORNIA PB $12.95

Jules **Verne**

Verne was a varied and profound writer whose obsession with scientific, geographical, and political information combines with a capacity for broad and potent—and often unconscious—symbolism.

Around the World in Eighty Days
TRANSLATED BY GEORGE TOWLE
0-553-21356-3 BDD PB $2.95

The Fur Country
TRANSLATED BY EDWARD BAXTER
0-920053-82-3 TORONTO PB $9.95

A Journey to the Center of the Earth
Verne's first great, popular success describes a geological descent that takes on dreamlike fascination
See also **YOUNG ADULT FICTION** in **BOOKS FOR YOUNG READERS**
See also **EARLY SCIENCE FICTION** under **SCIENCE FICTION AND FANTASY** in **POPULAR READING**
0-8049-0060-4 AIRMONT PB $3.50
0-19-585460-8 OXFORD PB $4.95

The Mysterious Island
Captain Nemo's last stand
0-451-52491-8 NEW AMERICAN LIBRARY PB $5.95

Paris in the Twentieth Century
TRANSLATED BY RICHARD HOWARD
0-679-44434-3 RANDOM HOUSE $21.00

Twenty Thousand Leagues Under the Sea
Notable for the powerful archetypal figure of Captain Nemo
0-14-036721-7 PUFFIN PB 3.99

Emile **Zola**

It was Emile Zola (1840-1902) who influenced the reading public to accept harrowing descriptions of poverty, disease, and other largely industrial or urban phenomena in the place of romantic fiction. In his writing he reflected the true nature of 19th-century faith in science, and illustrated the principle of determinism.

The Attack on the Mill & Other Stories
Includes *The Way People Die, Dead Men Tell No Tales, Priest and Sinners,* and others
EDITED BY DOUGLAS PARMEE
0-19-281599-7 OXFORD PB $7.95

The Belly of Paris
Inside the markets of Les Halles
1-55713-066-3 SUN & MOON PB $14.95

The Debacle
A novel of the Franco-Prussian War
TRANSLATED BY LEONARD TANCOCK
0-14-044280-4 PENGUIN PB $11.95

The Earth
The extremely naturalistic focus here is on the grimmer aspects of peasant existence
TRANSLATED BY DOUGLAS PARMEE
0-14-044387-8 PENGUIN PB $9.95

Germinal
Zola's most celebrated work, depicting a failed strike, is deeply informed by his sympathies for the workers' cause
TRANSLATED BY LEONARD TANCOCK
0-14-044045-3 PENGUIN PB $7.95

Germinal
0-679-40556-9 EVERYMAN'S $17.00
0-679-75430-X VINTAGE PB $9.00

La Bête Humaine
TRANSLATED BY ROGER PEARSON
0-19-282261-6 OXFORD PB $8.95

The Ladies' Paradise
The world of a fashionable Parisian department store
0-520-07867-5 CALIFORNIA PB $13.95

The Ladies' Paradise
TRANSLATED BY BRIAN NELSON
0-19-283180-1 OXFORD PB $11.95

L'Assommoir
A vivid portrait of working-class life
0-14-044231-6 PENGUIN PB $9.95

L'Assommoir
TRANSLATED BY MARGARET MAULDON
0-19-282983-1 OXFORD PB $6.95

The Masterpiece
The central character was modeled on Cézanne—the painter never forgave Zola
0-472-06145-3 MICHIGAN PB $16.95

Nana
This tale of a call-girl permits Zola to delve into the seamy side of Second Empire society
TRANSLATED BY GEORGE HOLDEN
0-14-044263-4 PENGUIN PB $6.95

Nana
TRANSLATED BY DOUGLAS PARMEE
0-19-282674-3 OXFORD PB $6.95

The Sin of Father Mouret
Priestly temptation and self-betrayal
TRANSLATED BY SANDY PETREY
0-8032-9901-X NEBRASKA PB $14.00

Thérèse Raquin
A powerful early realist novel culminating in a lovers' joint suicide
TRANSLATED BY LEONARD TANCOCK
0-14-044120-4 PENGUIN PB $9.95

Anthologies

Eric **Bentley**, editor

The Misanthrope & Other French Classics
Includes Racine's *Phaedra,* Corneille's *The Cid,* and Beaumarchais' *Figaro's Marriage,* in well-chosen translations
0-936839-19-8 APPLAUSE THEATRE PB $10.95

Morris **Bishop**

Survey of French Literature
Volume 1
The Middle Ages to 1800
0-15-584963-8 H.B.J. $39.90

Volume 2
The 19th and 20th Centuries
0-15-584964-6 H.B.J. $39.90

Stephen S. **Stanton**, editor

Camille & Other Plays
Includes Augustin Scribe's *A Peculiar Position* and *The Glass of Water,* Victorien Sardou's *A Scrap of Paper,* and *Olympe's Marriage* by Emile Augier
0-8090-0706-1 FS&G PB $10.95

Critical Studies

James **Allen**

Popular French Romanticism: Authors, Readers, and Books in the 19th Century
0-8156-2232-5 OLYMPIC $5.98

Geoffroy **Atkinson** & Abraham **Keller**

Prelude to the Enlightenment: French Literature, 1690-1740
0-295-95082-X WASHINGTON $20.00

Morris **Bishop**

The Middle Ages
0-8281-0487-5 AMERICAN HERITAGE PB $13.95

Victor **Brombert**

The Hidden Reader: Stendhal, Balzac, Hugo, Baudelaire, Flaubert
0-674-39012-1 HARVARD $38.00

Peter **France**, editor

The New Oxford Companion to Literature in French
0-19-866125-8 OXFORD $55.00

Denis **Hollier**, editor

A New History of French Literature
Not a conventional reference book: this elaborate volume focuses on mentalities and those points where the cultural and political intersect. "This grandly imagined and executed history of French literature is without precedent in any language...Here are many of the best contemporary critics and theorists, writing with vivid originality, always in a personal accent" —Richard Poirier
0-674-61565-4 HARVARD $62.50
0-674-61566-2 HARVARD PB $29.95

Lynette R. **Muir**

Literature and Society in Medieval France: The Mirror and the Image, 1100-1500
0-312-48748-7 ST. MARTIN'S $29.95

Roger L. **Williams**

The Horror of Life: Charles Baudelaire, Jules de Goncourt, Gustave Flaubert, Guy de Maupassant, Alphonse Daudet
0-226-89919-5 CHICAGO PB $15.95

Studies of Individual Writers

André **Maurois**

Prometheus: The Life of Balzac
0-88184-023-8 CARROLL & GRAF PB $11.95

Graham **Robb**

Balzac: A Biography
0-393-03679-0 NORTON $35.00

Roland **Barthes**

S/Z
A scrupulous literary analysis of *Sarrasine,* a short story by Balzac
See also **ROLAND BARTHES** under **CRITICAL TEXTS** under **SEMIOTICS AND STRUCTURALISM AND AFTER** under **LITERARY THEORY**
TRANSLATED BY RICHARD MILLER
0-374-52167-0 FS&G PB $11.95

Jean-Paul **Sartre**

Baudelaire
Sartre's study of Baudelaire is not quite like anyone else's, but brings the poet to life
TRANSLATED BY MARTIN TURNELL
0-8112-0189-9 NEW DIRECTIONS PB $9.95

Mario **Vargas Llosa**
The Perpetual Orgy: Flaubert and Madame Bovary
0-374-23077-3 FS&G $17.95
0-374-52062-3 FS&G PB $8.95

David **Arkell**
Looking for Laforgue: A Biography of Jules Laforgue
0-89255-042-2 PARSES $20.00

Austin **Gill**
The Early Mallarmé: Parentage, Early Years and Juvenilia
0-19-815790-8 CLARENDON $68.00
0-19-815726-6 OXFORD $59.00

Jean-Paul **Sartre**
Mallarmé, Or the Poet of Nothingness
TRANSLATED BY ERNEST STURM
0-271-00755-9 PENN STATE $22.50

Frances **Mossiker** & Marie **de Sevigné**
Madame de Sevigné: A Life and Letters
0-231-06153-6 COLUMBIA PB $22.50

Mikhail **Bakhtin**
Rabelais and His World
Discusses the world of carnival in Rabelais as symbolic of popular culture and the destruction of authority—and links this with the age of revolution in Russia

See also **MIKHAIL BAKHTIN** under **RUSSIAN FORMALISTS AND THE PRAGUE SCHOOL** under **SEMIOTICS AND STRUCTURALISM AND AFTER** under **LITERARY THEORY**

TRANSLATED BY HELENE ISWOLSKY
0-253-34830-7 INDIANA $39.95
0-253-20341-4 INDIANA PB $16.95

Jean-Claude **Carron**
François Rabelais: Critical Assessments
0-8018-5028-2 JOHNS HOPKINS $38.50

Roland **Barthes**
On Racine
A personal view of theater arranged in three long essays exploring space, erotics, and human relations in Racine's plays
0-520-07824-1 CALIFORNIA PB $12.95

Robert G. **Cohn**
The Poetry of Rimbaud
See also **STUDIES OF INDIVIDUAL AUTHORS** under **CRITICAL STUDIES** under **MODERN FRENCH LITERATURE**
0-691-06462-8 PRINCETON $49.50

Henry **Miller**
The Time of the Assassins: A Study of Rimbaud
0-8112-0115-5 NEW DIRECTIONS PB $9.95

Pierre **Petitfils**
Rimbaud
TRANSLATED BY ALAN SHERIDAN
0-8139-1142-7 VIRGINIA $34.95

Enid **Starkie**
Arthur Rimbaud
0-8112-0197-X NEW DIRECTIONS PB $16.95

Arthur Rimbaud

Maurice **Lever**
Sade: A Biography
A superbly researched biography that definitively reconstructs the life and times of the author of *Justine,* and *The 120 Days of Sodom.* Demonstrates how the sensibilities of the day spawned the philosophical justification for sexual cruelty with which Sade is inextricably identified
TRANSLATED BY ARTHUR GOLDHAMMER
0-374-20298-2 FS&G $35.00

Frederick **Brown**
Zola: A Life
Brown's biography offers an unprecedentedly complete life through an exploration of Zola's artistic circle of Flaubert, Manet, and Cézanne as well as his works, cultural contexts, and political battles
0-374-29742-8 FS&G $37.50

Modern French Literature

Much modern French writing does not lend itself to convenient categorizing. Indeed, questioning the notion of genre itself is fundamental to much of it: one finds memoir as fiction, poem as analytical essay, novel as collage.

For related reading, see MODERN EUROPEAN DRAMA

Poetry

Anne-Marie **Albiach**
État
First published in 1971, this volume helped usher in a new and rigorous abstraction in French poetry
TRANSLATED BY KEITH WALDROP
0-942433-13-0 SMALL PRESS PB $10.00

Mezza Voce
Albiach, who has translated American writers such as Louis Zukofsky and Frank O'Hara, is one of the most striking of contemporary French poets
TRANSLATED BY JOSEPH SIMAS & OTHERS
0-942996-11-9 POST APOLLO PB $12.95

Vocative Figure
"There is a passionate intelligence set into motion here, but at the same time a new depth of feeling"—Paul Auster
0-907954-18-9 SMALL PRESS PB $5.00

Pierre **Alferi**
Natural Gaits
Recent poetry by the son of Jacques Derrida
TRANSLATED BY COLE SWENSEN
1-55713-231-3 SUN & MOON PB $10.95

Guillaume **Apollinaire**
This tirelessly inquisitive intellectual was not only involved with Cubism and Futurism but is also credited with coining the terms "Orphism" and "Surrealism."

Alcools: Poems
A major translation from a leading voice in contemporary American poetry. "It is an unfussy version—personal yet not eccentric—that will give readers the chance to taste the source" —Mark Rudman
TRANSLATED BY DONALD REVELL
0-8195-2224-4 WESLEYAN $30.00
0-8195-1228-1 WESLEYAN PB $15.95

Calligrammes
Shaped compositions that foreshadow the work of the concrete poets. A bilingual edition
TRANSLATED BY ANNE HYDE GREET
0-520-07390-8 CALIFORNIA PB $19.95

Selected Writings
Includes poems, criticism, and fiction
TRANSLATED BY ROGER SHATTUCK
0-8112-0003-5 NEW DIRECTIONS PB $12.95

Paul **Auster**, editor
The Random House Book of Twentieth-Century French Poetry
A dual-language edition with translations by American and British poets; unsurpassed in its breadth and the outstanding quality of its translations
0-394-71748-1 RANDOM HOUSE PB $24.00

Yves **Bonnefoy**
Early Poems, 1947-1959
0-8214-1048-2 OHIO PB $16.95

New and Selected Poems
Defining his work, Bonnefoy has written: "Poetry does not interest itself in the shape of the world itself, but in the world that this universe will become"
0-226-06460-3 CHICAGO PB $14.95

Words in Stone: Pierre Écrite

TRANSLATED BY SUSANNA LANG

0-87023-203-7 MASSACHUSETTS $22.50

André **Breton**

Earthlight

TRANSLATED BY ZACH ROGOW

1-55713-095-7 SUN & MOON PB $12.95

Poems of André Breton: A Bilingual Anthology

A rich selection of the poetry of the pope of the Surrealist movement. A bilingual edition

TRANSLATED BY JEAN-PIERRE CAUVIN & MARY ANNA CAWS

0-292-76476-6 TEXAS PB $35.50

André Breton

Blaise **Cendrars**

Complete Poems

A magnificent translation of the most adventurous of modern French poets

TRANSLATED BY RON PADGETT

0-520-06579-4 CALIFORNIA $50.00

0-520-06580-8 CALIFORNIA PB $16.00

Complete Postcards from the Americas: Poems of Road and Sea

This precursor of Apollinaire and the Surrealist poets introduced syncopated jazz and African rhythms into his poetry

0-520-02716-7 CALIFORNIA $42.50

Aimé **Césaire**

Césaire, born in Martinique, was a founder of the Negritude movement. "More vividly perhaps than in the work of the Surrealists of France, Césaire's poetry embodies the twin aspirations of political and aesthetic revolution, and in such a way that they are inseparably joined"—Paul Auster

The Collected Poetry

See also **CARIBBEAN LITERATURE** in **LITERATURE OF THE AMERICAS**

TRANSLATED BY CLAYTON ESHLEMAN & ANNETTE SMITH

0-520-04347-2 CALIFORNIA $45.00

0-520-05320-6 CALIFORNIA PB $18.00

René **Char**

Poems of René Char

The work of this sometimes elliptical, unwaveringly humanistic poet reflects a profound preoccupation with man in nature

TRANSLATED BY JONATHAN GRIFFIN & MARY ANNE CAWS

0-691-06297-8 PRINCETON $55.00

Selected Poems of René Char

0-8112-1191-6 NEW DIRECTIONS $19.95

Jean **Daive**

A Lesson in Music

TRANSLATED BY JULIE KALENDEK

0-930901-80-0 BURNING DECK PB $6.00

Michel **Deguy**

Given Giving: Selected Poems of Michel Deguy

"Always present in Deguy's work are his wit, his experimentation, his sensuous intellectuality, the seeming urgency of what he has to say about what moves him to write"—Kenneth Koch

TRANSLATED BY CLAYTON ESHLEMAN

INTRODUCTION BY KENNETH KOCH

0-520-06458-5 CALIFORNIA PB $13.95

Jacques **Dupin**

Selected Poems

TRANSLATED BY PAUL AUSTER, STEPHEN ROMER, AND DAVID SHAPIRO

0-916390-52-7 WAKE FOREST PB $10.95

Paul **Eluard**

Selected Poems

Shifting from Surrealism to an engaged Marxist stance in his work, Eluard is notable above all for his very pure and intense love poetry

TRANSLATED BY GILBERT BOWEN

0-7145-3995-3 RIVERRUN PB $10.95

Shadows and Sun: Poems & Prose of 1913-1952

0-9617481-7-6 OYSTER RIVER PB $24.95

Jean **Follain**

D'Après Tout: Poems by Jean Follain

Follain's work has a concrete sharpness rare in modern French poetry. Characteristically, he takes a real or imagined moment in history and, in a few lines, enters it completely. A bilingual edition

TRANSLATED BY HEATHER MCHUGH

0-681-01372-1 PRINCETON PB $8.50

Jean **Genet**

Treasures of the Night: Collected Poems of Jean Genet

TRANSLATED BY STEVEN FINCH

0-917342-76-3 GAY SUNSHINE PB $6.95

Eugène **Guillevic**

Selected Poems

The stark materiality of Guillevic's poetry is influenced by both his Communist convictions and his Breton origins

TRANSLATED BY DENISE LEVERTOV

0-8112-0283-6 NEW DIRECTIONS $5.95

Emmanuel **Hocquard**

A Day in the Strait

Hocquard is also an influential publisher of contemporary poetry; his own work is steeped in Mediterranean landscapes and historical echoes

TRANSLATED BY MARYANN DEJULIO & JANE STAW

0-87376-045-X RED DUST PB $4.95

Edmond **Jabès**

In 1972 Jacques Derrida wrote: "In the last ten years nothing of interest has been written in France that does not have its precedent somewhere in the texts of Jabès." Since that time, the influence of the Egyptian Jewish poet, who fled to France because of political persecution during the Nasser regime and died in 1991 at the age of 78, has extended to English-language poets. The Book of Questions *and its successor,* The Book of Dialogue, *and* The Book of Resemblances, *are extraordinary probings into the nature of language, Kabbalistic in their openness to multiple layers of meaning. Waldrop's version is one of the great translations of recent years. "It is impossible to think about writing, the book, the relation of man and language without taking Edmond Jabès into account"—Yves Bonnefoy*

The Book of Dialogue

TRANSLATED BY ROSEMARIE WALDROP

0-8195-5147-3 WESLEYAN $25.00

The Book of Margins: Religion and Post-Modernism

TRANSLATED BY ROSEMARIE WALDROP

0-226-38888-3 CHICAGO $35.50

0-226-38889-1 CHICAGO PB $13.95

The Book of Questions

Volume 1

The Book of Questions; The Book of Yukel; Return to the Book

0-8195-6247-5 WESLEYAN PB $24.00

Volume 2

Yaël; Elya; Aëly; El, or the Last Book

0-8195-6248-3 WESLEYAN PB $24.00

The Book of Resemblances

TRANSLATED BY ROSEMARIE WALDROP

Volume 1

0-819-55232-1 WESLEYAN $19.95

Volume 2

Intimations, the Desert

0-819-55240-2 WESLEYAN $19.95

Volume 3

Ineffaceable, the Unperceived

0-819-55245-3 WESLEYAN $19.95

A Foreigner Carrying in the Crook of His Arms a Tiny Book

TRANSLATED BY ROSEMARIE WALDROP

0-8195-5259-3 NEW ENGLAND $35.00

0-8195-6266-1 WESLEYAN PB $14.95

The Little Book of Unsuspected Subversion

TRANSLATED BY ROSEMARIE WALDROP

0-8047-2684-1 STANFORD PB $12.95

If There Were Anywhere but Desert: The Selected Poems of Edmond Jabès
The earlier, more lyrical work preceding *The Book of Questions*
TRANSLATED BY KEITH WALDROP
0-88268-052-8 STATION HILL $16.95

Philippe **Jaccottet**
"Jaccottet is one of a group of poets who turned away from the Surrealists' sometimes abstruse experiments with form in favor of a muted lyrical expression born of a quasi-fraternal bonding with the wonder of earth, light, water, sky. This lyricism is steeped in an ambiguous sense of our planet's vulnerability in this nuclear age"—Germaine Brée

Seedtime
TRANSLATED BY ANDRÉ LEFEVRE & MICHAEL HAMBURGER
0-8112-0637-8 NEW DIRECTIONS PB $3.25

Selected Poems
A selection that surveys Jaccottet's whole career, translated by a leading Irish poet
TRANSLATED BY DEREK MAHON
0-916390-31-4 WAKE FOREST PB $8.95

Jean **Joubert**
Black Iris
TRANSLATED BY DENISE LEVERTOV
1-55659-015-6 COPPER CANYON PB $9.00

Paol **Keineg**
Boudica
Keineg evokes ancient Celtic themes
TRANSLATED BY KEITH WALDROP
0-930901-94-0 BURNING DECK PB $6.00

Claire **Malroux**
Edge
Edge offers a selection of poems from Claire Malroux's previous volumes, published under her *nom de plume* Claire Sara Roux, with new poems all translated by Marilyn Hacker. A highly esteemed translator, Malroux won the Grand Prix National de la Traduction in 1995
TRANSLATED BY MARILYN HACKER
0-916390-74-8 WAKE FOREST PB $10.95

Henri **Michaux**
Darkness Moves: An Henri Michaux Anthology, 1927-1984
TRANSLATED BY DAVID BALL
0-520-07231-6 CALIFORNIA $30.00

Selected Writings of Henri Michaux
Michaux, who traveled widely in Africa, Asia, and the Americas, was both a painter and a poet; he is noted especially for his exploration of the prose poem
TRANSLATED BY RICHARD ELLMANN
0-8112-0105-8 NEW DIRECTIONS PB $10.95

Oscar V. **de Lubicz Milosz**
Fourteen Poems
TRANSLATED BY KENNETH REXROTH
0-914742-71-X INLAND PB $6.95

The Noble Traveller: The Life and Selected Writings of Oscar V. de Lubicz Milosz
A Lithuanian writer and diplomat who had become a French citizen by the time of his death in 1939, Milosz explores occult themes in much of his poetry
TRANSLATED BY DAVID GASCOYNE, KENNETH REXROTH, EDOUARD RODITI & OTHERS
INTRODUCTION BY CZESLAW MILOSZ
0-89281-064-5 LINDISFARNE PB $14.95

Charles **Péguy**
The Mystery of the Charity of Joan of Arc
This work illustrates Péguy's almost obsessive veneration for Joan of Arc
TRANSLATED BY JEFFREY WAINWRIGHT
0-85635-690-5 CARCANET PB $9.50

The Portal of the Mystery of Hope
0-8028-0899-9 EERDMANS PB $15.00

Benjamin **Péret**
From the Hidden Storehouse: A Selection of Poems
Péret was a poet absolutely committed to Surrealism, as well as to the political ideals for which he fought in the Spanish Civil War
TRANSLATED BY KEITH HOLLAMAN
INTRODUCTION BY CHARLES SIMIC
0-932440-10-X FIELD TRANSLATIONS $10.95
0-932440-11-8 OBERLIN PB $5.95

A Marvelous World
TRANSLATED BY ELIZABETH JACKSON
0-8071-0664-X LSU $25.00

Saint-John **Perse**
Diplomat, traveler, scholar and Nobel laureate, Saint-John Perse wrote large-scale, metaphysical, fundamentally optimistic poetry celebrating the wonders of the physical world and human resilience.

Anabasis
A long prose poem describing ancient nomadic wanderings and conquests, written while Saint-John Perse was serving as a diplomat in China. A bilingual edition
TRANSLATED BY T.S. ELIOT
PREFACE BY VALERY LARBAUD
0-15-607406-0 HARCOURT BRACE PB $2.95

Birds
A bilingual edition
TRANSLATED BY ROBERT FITZGERALD
0-691-09713-5 PRINCETON $50.00

Selected Poems
TRANSLATED WITH AN INTRODUCTION BY MARY ANN CAWS
EDITED BY T.S. ELIOT
0-8112-0855-9 NEW DIRECTIONS PB $9.95

Song for an Equinox
TRANSLATED BY RICHARD HOWARD
0-691-09938-3 PRINCETON $14.50

Jacques **Prévert**
Paroles: Selected Poems
0-87286-249-6 CITY LIGHTS PB $5.95

Blood and Feathers: Selected Poems
Prévert's work is marked by a blend of brisk satire and languid sentimentality, couched in an accessible style that has made him one of the most popular modern poets
1-55921-056-7 MOYER BELL PB $11.95

Selections from Paroles
Ferlinghetti's translations of Prévert have been popular ever since they appeared in the '50s
TRANSLATED BY LAWRENCE FERLINGHETTI
0-87286-042-6 SUBTERRANEAN PB $8.95

Francis **Ponge**
Selected Poems
Ponge's dismantling of language in order to get at objects themselves has made him an influential figure for more recent French poets
TRANSLATED BY MARGARET GUITON & JOHN MONTAGUE
0-916390-59-4 WAKE FOREST $18.95
0-916390-58-6 WAKE FOREST PB $12.95

Pierre **Reverdy**
Selected Poems
"Reverdy's strange landscapes, which combine an intense inwardness with a proliferation of sensual data, bear in them signs of a continual search for an impossible totality. Almost mystical in effect, his poems are nevertheless anchored in the minutiae of the everyday world"—Paul Auster
TRANSLATED BY KENNETH REXROTH
0-8112-0373-5 NEW DIRECTIONS $6.50

Selected Poems
TRANSLATED BY JOHN ASHBERY, MARY ANN CAWS, & DAVID SHAPIRO
0-916390-47-0 WAKE FOREST $16.95
0-916390-46-2 WAKE FOREST PB $10.95

Jacques **Roubaud**
The Plurality of Worlds of Lewis
TRANSLATED BY ROSEMARIE WALDROP
1-56478-069-4 DALKEY ARCHIVE PB $9.95

Some Thing Black
A contemporary French writer's wrenching meditation on the early death of his wife. "To cling to death as such, to recognize it as a real hunger, has meant admitting that there is in language, in all of its constructions, something over which I have no control"
TRANSLATED BY ROSEMARIE WALDROP
0-916583-48-1 DALKEY ARCHIVE $19.95

Victor **Segalen**
Steles
Segalen, who spent much time in China in the early 20th century, embodied in these haunting and strangely impersonal poems his sense of the essence of Chinese tradition
TRANSLATED BY MICHAEL TAYLOR
0-932499-21-X LAPIS PB $12.50

Philippe **Soupault**
I'm Lying: Selected Poems
Soupault was a prominent Surrealist until he was expelled from the movement for political reasons
TRANSLATED BY PAULETTE SCHMIDT
0-918786-30-4 LOST ROADS PB $5.95

Jules **Supervielle**

Selected Writings

This witty humanist expressed what he called a "pansympathy" with nature, as well as a mindfulness of death

0-8112-0389-1 NEW DIRECTIONS $7.50

Tristan **Tzara**

Primele Poeme: First Poems

A founder of Dada, Tzara was one of the movement's most radically experimental poets

TRANSLATED BY MICHAEL IMPEY & BRIAN SWANN

0-88910-307-0 COACH HOUSE PB $12.95

Paul **Valéry**

Selected Writings

See also **ESSAYS: PERSONAL, LITERARY, PHILOSOPHICAL**

0-8112-0213-5 NEW DIRECTIONS PB $12.95

Fiction

Henri **Alain-Fournier**

Le Grand Meaulnes

This influential novel of innocence and first love, published in 1913, ran counter to the naturalist approach then prevalent

TRANSLATED BY FRANK DAVISON

0-14-018282-9 VIKING PB $8.95

Guillaume **Apollinaire**

The Heresiarch and Co.

EDITED BY REMI INGLIS

1-87897-203-0 EXACT CHANGE PB $11.95

Les Onze Mille Verges

In addition to being a poet and art critic, Apollinaire was a writer of erotic fiction, tempering his violent fantasies with considerable humor

TRANSLATED BY NINA ROOTES

INTRODUCTION BY RICHARD N. COE

0-7206-0735-3 OWEN PB $17.95

Louis **Aragon**

The Adventures of Telemachus

A satirical antinovel, rich in verbal play, based on the didactic 17th-century work by Fenelon. "Essential for the understanding of Aragon, and of his concept of art and of the surrealist undertaking"—Mary Ann Caws

TRANSLATED BY RENEE HUBERT & JUDD HUBERT

0-8032-1021-3 NEBRASKA $27.50

Paris Peasant

TRANSLATED BY SIMON WATSON TAYLOR

1-87897-210-3 D.A.P. PB $13.95

Emmanuelle **Arsan**

Emmanuelle

A celebrated work of philosophical erotica

TRANSLATED BY LOWELL BAIR

0-8021-3069-0 GROVE PB $11.00

Henri **Barbusse**

Hell

1-88598-301-8 TURTLE POINT PB $12.95

Christophe **Bataille**

Annam

0-8112-1330-7 NEW DIRECTIONS $15.95

Georges **Bataille**

"One of the most original and unsettling of those thinkers who, in the wake of Sade and Nietzsche, have confronted the possibility of thought in a world that has lost its myth of transcendence" —Peter Brooks, NY Times Book Review

Blue of Noon

In a prewar novel now attracting new attention, Bataille describes a dark journey through the psyche of the '30s French intelligentsia

TRANSLATED BY HARRY MATHEWS

0-7145-2850-1 MARION BOYARS PB $12.95

Guilty

The first English translation of one of Bataille's masterpieces, a combination fiction, confession, and philosophical meditation. Written during World War II, this is a clarified expression of the author's belief that desire is the only constant available to humankind

TRANSLATED BY BRUCE BOONE

INTRODUCTION BY DENIS HOLLIER

0-932499-60-0 LAPIS PB $12.95

The Impossible

TRANSLATED BY ROBERT HURLEY

0-87286-262-3 CITY LIGHTS PB $10.95

L'Abbé C

Depicts the intense relationship between twin brothers, one an unabashed libertine, the other an improbably devout priest. "Bataille speaks about man's condition, not his nature. Bataille has survived the death of God"—Jean-Paul Sartre

TRANSLATED BY PHILIP A. FACEY

0-7145-2848-X MARION BOYARS PB $11.95

My Mother, Madame Edwarda, The Dead Man

TRANSLATED BY AUSTRYN WAINHOUSE

0-7145-2886-2 MARION BOYARS $19.95

Story of the Eye

The centerpiece of the Surrealist movement's erotic literature, *Eye* was published in 1928 anonymously and follows the sexual awakening of a young man as he quickly discovers that only those acts which can be described as "dirty" are worthy of his attention. Fortunately, he finds Simone, a woman who shares his appetites and knocks down more boundaries than the young man knew existed. Shocking even by '90s standards

See also **WRITING FROM THE EDGE** under **CUTTING EDGE** in **POPULAR READING**

See also **EROTICA** under **COURTSHIP, LOVE, SEX, AND MARRIAGE** in **LIFESTYLES AND PRACTICAL ADVICE**

0-87286-209-7 CITY LIGHTS PB $7.95

Tears of Eros

TRANSLATED BY PETER CONNORS

0-87286-222-4 CITY LIGHTS PB $14.95

Tahar **Ben Jelloun**

Corruption

Against the backgrounds of Casablanca and Tangier, this is the tale of an honest man in Morocco finally succumbing to the prevalent corruption of his materialistic society. "Poetic and analytical...Ben Jelloun's genius lies in evoking through language the grammar of existence, and the possibility of transforming with words the grimness of life's narratives"—*TLS*

See also **MODERN LITERATURE** under **ARABIC LITERATURE**

TRANSLATED BY CAROL VOLK

1-56584-295-2 NEW PRESS $17.95

1-56584-296-0 NEW PRESS PB $10.00

Georges **Bernanos**

The Diary of a Country Priest

An austere Catholic drama of spirituality in the face of materialistic values. "A strange and sad, yet beautiful and triumphant story"—*NY Times*

TRANSLATED BY PAMELA MORRIS

0-88184-013-0 CARROLL & GRAF PB $10.95

Mr. Ouine

0-525-24492-1 DUTTON $17.95

Maurice **Blanchot**

Often likened to the work of Kafka and Beckett, Blanchot's writing paints a sharp picture of an absurd world and points forward to the antinovel. His fiction, which has only recently become widely available in English, has begun to exert its influence on American writers.

A Blanchot Reader

TRANSLATED BY PAUL AUSTER

1-88644-917-1 BARRYTOWN PB $24.95

Death Sentence

"A transumptive romance of the erotic triangle of death, consciousness and the possible world of narrative"—John Hollander

TRANSLATED BY LYDIA DAVIS

0-930794-04-4 STATION HILL PB $5.95

The Most High

0-8032-1240-2 NEBRASKA $35.00

André **Breton**

Immaculate Conception

0-947757-22-8 SERPENT'S TAIL PB $13.99

The Magnetic Fields

TRANSLATED BY DAVID GASCOYNE

0-947757-03-1 SERPENT'S TAIL PB $13.99

Nadja

A Surrealist romance describing the author's relationship with a girl who is not so much a person as a state of mind

TRANSLATED BY RICHARD HOWARD

0-8021-5026-8 GROVE PB $9.95

Michel **Butor**

Portrait of the Artist as a Young Ape

1-56478-089-9 DALKEY ARCHIVE PB $10.95

Albert **Camus**

Exile and the Kingdom

0-679-73385-X VINTAGE PB $11.00

The Fall

A late work whose pessimistic view of man caused some surprise after the more positive final note of *The Plague*, written a decade earlier

TRANSLATED BY JUSTIN O'BRIEN

0-679-72022-7 VINTAGE PB $10.00

The First Man

Discovered in the wrecked car in which Camus was killed, this opening of a projected epic novel was a bestseller in France for months. Covering the years of Camus's poverty-stricken childhood in Algeria, this is a book filled with detail and provocative emotions that define both Camus's life and work

EDITED BY SARAH BURNS

0-679-43937-4 KNOPF $23.00

0-679-76816-5 VINTAGE PB $12.00

A Happy Death
An early version of *The Stranger*
TRANSLATED BY RICHARD HOWARD
0-679-76400-3 VINTAGE PB $11.00

The Plague
An epidemic serves as a telling symbol for the Nazi occupation of France and, by extension, for human existence as a whole. The characters rediscover dignity and meaning through collective endeavor
TRANSLATED BY STUART GILBERT
0-679-72021-9 VINTAGE PB $11.00

Albert Camus

The Stranger
Among the most widely read novels of the century, this study of individual alienation in a bourgeois society is still remarkable for its resonant tone of understatement. A new translation that comes close to the directness of Camus' style
TRANSLATED BY MATTHEW WARD
0-679-72020-0 VINTAGE PB $9.00

Louis-Ferdinand **Céline**

Death on the Installment Plan
A "creative confession" that continues Céline's litany of disgust with his follow creatures
TRANSLATED BY RALPH MANHEIM
0-8112-0017-5 NEW DIRECTIONS PB $14.95

Guignol's Band
TRANSLATED BY BERNARD FRECHTMAN & JACK T. NILE
0-8112-0018-3 NEW DIRECTIONS PB $12.95

Journey to the End of Night
Céline's misanthropic 1932 novel broke radically with French literary traditions in both style and subject matter. "Céline often said that he regarded himself primarily as a stylist. He held that the French literary language was stiff and spent with age, that classicism and academicism had emasculated the language of Villon and Rabelais, and that in our age emotion could be captured only in the spoken tongue"—Ralph Manheim
TRANSLATED BY RALPH MANHEIM
0-8112-0847-8 NEW DIRECTIONS PB $12.95

London Bridge
TRANSLATED BY DOMINIC DI BERNARDI
1-56478-071-6 DALKEY ARCHIVE $23.95

North
Europe at the end of World War II, as Céline and others on the losing side scramble for cover
TRANSLATED BY RALPH MANHEIM
1-56478-142-9 DALKEY ARCHIVE PB $13.95

Jean **Cocteau**

The Holy Terrors
The perverse loyalties and passions of childhood; also well known under its French title, *Les Enfants Terribles*
TRANSLATED BY ROSAMOND LEHMANN
0-8112-0021-3 NEW DIRECTIONS PB $8.95

The Impostor
TRANSLATED BY DOROTHY WILLIAMS
0-7206-0843-0 OWEN PB $19.95

The White Book
0-87286-238-0 SUBTERRANEAN PB $7.95

Albert **Cohen**

Belle du Seigneur
Set in '30s Geneva, Cohen's tale takes us through a world of middle-class manners in which the League of Nations intersects with a world of larger-than-life Jews. A mock-epic that has been compared to Joyce and acclaimed as a great Jewish comic work
0-670-82187-X VIKING $34.95

Colette

Break of Day
A reminiscence of the writer's girlhood, and a portrait of her mother
TRANSLATED BY ENID MCLEOD
0-374-51221-3 FS&G PB $9.00

Chance Acquaintances & Julie de Carneilhan
0-14-010032-6 PENGUIN PB $10.95

Cheri & The Last of Cheri
0-14-018317-5 PENGUIN PB $9.95

The Claudine Novels
Includes *Claudine at School*, *Claudine in Paris*, *Claudine Married*, and *Claudine and Annie*
0-14-018322-1 PENGUIN PB $9.95

The Collected Stories of Colette
One hundred stories written between 1908 and 1945. "No other woman seems to have had as much lived experience to draw upon or as much sexual sophistication"—Phyllis Rose, *NY Times*
EDITED WITH AN INTRODUCTION BY ROBERT PHELPS
TRANSLATED BY MATTHEW WORD & OTHERS
0-374-51865-3 FS&G PB $18.00

Gigi & The Cat
0-14-018319-1 PENGUIN PB $8.95

My Mother's House & Sido
Two autobiographical works dealing with Colette's childhood
TRANSLATED BY UNA V. TROUBRIDGE & ENID MCLEOD
0-374-51218-3 FS&G PB $10.00

Retreat from Love
The first novel in the Claudine series offers bucolic impressions of rural life and "reflections on the heights and depths of Claudine's narcissism"—*New Yorker*
TRANSLATED BY MARGARET CROSLAND
0-15-676588-8 HARCOURT BRACE PB $6.95

The Ripening Seed
0-14-018321-3 PENGUIN PB $9.95

The Vagabond
A portrait of music-hall life
0-14-018325-6 PENGUIN PB $9.95

Cyril **Collard**

Savage Nights
An unflinching portrait of French youth; the author died of AIDS shortly after directing the film version of this novel
0-87951-534-1 OVERLOOK $18.95
0-87951-580-5 PENGUIN PB $11.95

René **Crevel**

Putting My Foot in It
TRANSLATED BY THOMAS BUCKLEY
1-56478-002-3 DALKEY ARCHIVE $19.95
1-56478-017-1 DALKEY ARCHIVE PB $9.95

René **Daumal**

You've Always Been Wrong
A *roman á clef* about post war French intellignesia
0-8032-1699-8 NEBRASKA $25.00

Simone **de Beauvoir**

All Men Are Mortal
TRANSLATED BY LEONARD M. FRIEDMAN
0-393-30845-6 NORTON PB $13.00

The Mandarins
0-393-30745-X NORTON PB $15.00

Antoine **de Saint-Exupéry**

Flight to Arras
A pilot's experiences in wartime. "A flight not only of an airplane but of a spirit"
—William Rose Benet, *Saturday Review*
TRANSLATED BY LEWIS GALANTIERE
0-15-631880-6 HARCOURT BRACE PB $5.95

The Little Prince
A children's story that has achieved worldwide popularity
TRANSLATED BY KATHERINE WOODS
0-15-246503-0 HARCOURT BRACE $15.00
0-15-646511-6 HARCOURT BRACE PB $7.00

Night Flight
A spare and riveting tale of adventure, published in 1931
TRANSLATED BY STUART GILBERT
0-15-665605-1 HARCOURT BRACE PB $5.95

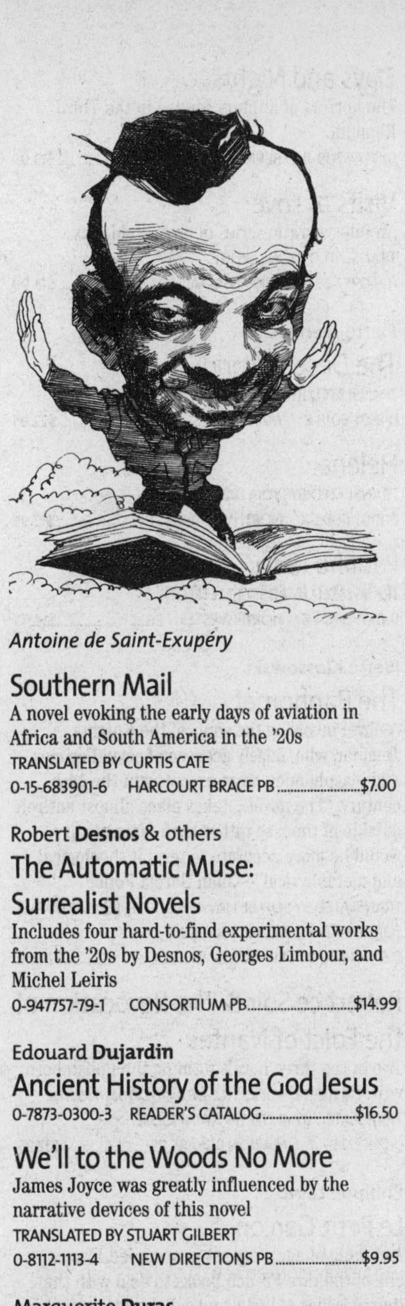

Antoine de Saint-Exupéry

Southern Mail
A novel evoking the early days of aviation in Africa and South America in the '20s
TRANSLATED BY CURTIS CATE
0-15-683901-6 HARCOURT BRACE PB $7.00

Robert **Desnos** & others
The Automatic Muse: Surrealist Novels
Includes four hard-to-find experimental works from the '20s by Desnos, Georges Limbour, and Michel Leiris
0-947757-79-1 CONSORTIUM PB $14.99

Edouard **Dujardin**
Ancient History of the God Jesus
0-7873-0300-3 READER'S CATALOG $16.50

We'll to the Woods No More
James Joyce was greatly influenced by the narrative devices of this novel
TRANSLATED BY STUART GILBERT
0-8112-1113-4 NEW DIRECTIONS PB $9.95

Marguerite **Duras**
Duras, one of the foremost exponents of the nouveau roman, *describes a world in which banal surfaces are constantly ruffled by an agitated inner world of spontaneous impulse.*
Agatha & Savannah Bay
0-942996-16-X POST APOLLO PB $14.00

Four Novels
Includes *The Afternoon of Mr. Andesmas, Ten-Thirty on a Summer Night, Moderato Cantabile,* and *The Square*
TRANSLATED BY RICHARD SEAVER
0-8021-5111-6 GROVE PB $12.00

The Lover
Vietnam in the '30s, an 18-year-old French girl, and lyrical memories of love with a Chinese man
0-06-097521-0 HARPERPERENNIAL PB $11.00

The Malady of Death
TRANSLATED BY BARBARA BRAY
0-8021-3036-4 GROVE PB $7.95

The Man Sitting in the Corridor
1-56201-006-9 BLUE MOON PB $5.95

The North China Lover
"Neither her worldly success nor the fuss about *The Lover* have caused this novelist to deviate an inch from her desire to tell all about the freshness of desire, the violence of loving, which make us understand the work. Everything is here, immediate, sensual. It's utterly stunning and diabolical"—*Le Point*
TRANSLATED BY LEIGH HAFREY
1-56584-018-6 NEW PRESS $19.95
1-56584-043-7 NEW PRESS PB $10.00

Practicalities
0-8021-3311-8 GROVE PB $9.95

The Ravishing of Lol Stein
A young woman recreates a past tragedy of abandonment; then she voyeuristically spies on the characters she has called back into play
TRANSLATED BY RICHARD SEAVER
0-394-74304-0 PANTHEON PB $11.00

Summer Rain
TRANSLATED BY BARBARA BRAY
0-02-073040-3 COLLIER PB $9.00

Two by Duras
In *The Slut of the Normandy Coast* Duras writes of her older self, grown to maturity now, but still grappling with the same passions of the young girl from *The Lover*. In *The Atlantic Man* she exposes the male side of a broken affair. The first English translation of these erotic, intimate works
TRANSLATED BY ALBERTO MANGUEL
0-88910-441-7 COACH HOUSE PB $9.95

Annie **Ernaux**
Cleaned Out
TRANSLATED BY CAROL SANDERS
0-916583-65-1 DALKEY ARCHIVE $19.95
1-56478-139-9 DALKEY ARCHIVE PB $10.95

Exteriors
TRANSLATED BY TANYA LESLIE
1-88836-331-2 SEVEN STORIES $16.00

A Frozen Woman
A 30-year-old mother's struggle to maintain her identity under the weight of her household routine
TRANSLATED BY LINDA COVERDALE
1-56858-029-0 FOUR WALLS $17.00
1-88836-338-X SEVEN STORIES PB $9.95

Simple Passion
The unflinching account of the love affair between a woman and the nameless, married businessman to whom, during one enthralled year, she gives up her heart. "A stunning story...that pulsates with the very passion Ernaux so truthfully describes"—*Kirkus Reviews*
1-88836-326-6 SEVEN STORIES $15.00

Anatole **France**
When Anatole France won the Nobel Prize in 1921 he was one of the world's best-known writers, but since then his reputation has languished. The brilliance and control of his style and the ferocity of his satire make him overdue for a revival.
The Gods Will Have Blood
A novel of the Terror, in which a young idealist is transformed by slow stages into a merciless Jacobin
TRANSLATED BY FREDERICK DAVIES
0-14-044352-5 PENGUIN PB $6.95

Penguin Island
A parody of French history, culminating in a savagely satirical treatment of the Dreyfus case
TRANSLATED BY A.W. EVANS
0-918172-09-8
INDEPENDENT PUBLISHERS GROUP PB $6.95

Romain **Gary**
The Life Before Us: Madame Rosa
An orphaned Arab boy's devotion to a dying Auschwitz survivor forms the basis for a macabre tale of love, with a supporting cast of pimps, shamans, and transvestites
TRANSLATED BY RALPH MANHEIM
0-8112-0961-X NEW DIRECTIONS PB $7.95

Promise at Dawn
An autobiographical novel chronicling Gary's childhood in Russia, Poland, and on the French Riviera, and telling above all of his mother's love and support
TRANSLATED BY JOHN M. BEACH
0-8112-1016-2 NEW DIRECTIONS PB $10.95

Jean **Genet**
Thief, recidivist, homosexual, and poet, Genet is the modern French writer who most thoroughly and compellingly rejects accepted social values, in both his art and his life.
Funeral Rites
Genet's grief for his lover, killed during the liberation of Paris, is matched by his perverse attraction to a collaborator
TRANSLATED BY BERNARD FRECHTMAN
0-8021-3087-9 GROVE PB $9.95

Miracle of the Rose
Portraits of men encountered behind bars merge to become extensions of Genet himself, a rootless figure in total revolt
TRANSLATED BY BERNARD FRECHTMAN
0-8021-3088-7 GROVE PB $10.95

Our Lady of the Flowers
Genet's first and perhaps greatest novel, an autobiographical work written in prison
TRANSLATED BY BERNARD FRECHTMAN
INTRODUCTION BY JEAN-PAUL SARTRE
0-8021-3013-5 GROVE PB $12.00

Prisoners of Love
0-8195-5246-1 WESLEYAN $35.00
0-8195-6274-2 WESLEYAN PB $15.95

Querelle
Taking the Dostoevskian theme of murder as an act of absolute liberation, this book is "a confrontation with the basest of angels...sailor, assassin, dealer in opium, homosexual, thief and traitor"—Michael Levenson, *Harper's*
TRANSLATED BY ANSELM HOLLO
0-394-62368-1 GROVE PB $7.95

The Selected Writings of Jean Genet
Excerpts from the controversial writer's most famous works, including novels, poetry, plays, letters, autobiography, and essays. Also included is a rare, recently discovered interview with Genet. "Only a handful of twentieth Century writers such as Kafka and Proust have as important, as authoritative, as irrevocable a voice and style"—Susan Sontag
EDITED BY EDMUND WHITE
0-88001-331-1 ECCO $27.50
0-88001-420-2 ECCO PB $17.00

Splendid's
0-571-17613-5 FABER PB $6.99

The Thief's Journal
The record, worthy of Rimbaud, of a pilgrimage in quest of the deepest imaginable state of evil. "The most beautiful book that Genet has written"—Jean-Paul Sartre
TRANSLATED BY BERNARD FRECHTMAN
FOREWORD BY JEAN-PAUL SARTRE
0-8021-3014-3 GROVE PB $10.95

André **Gide**

The Counterfeiters
A novel whose innovative structure presents an apparently haphazard series of events encompassing several generations of characters—one of whom is a novelist at work on a book called *The Counterfeiters*
TRANSLATED BY DOROTHY BUSSY
0-394-71842-9 RANDOM HOUSE PB $10.00

The Immoralist
The famous novella of a man who pursues every impulse regardless of moral consequence; his "immorality" resides in his languid duty to be happy
TRANSLATED BY RICHARD HOWARD
0-679-74191-7 VINTAGE PB $11.00

Lafcadio's Adventures
In this novel of farcical intrigue, Gide's preoccupation with the unmotivated crime receives its most thorough treatment
TRANSLATED BY DOROTHY BUSSY
0-8376-0452-4 BENTLEY $18.00
0-394-70096-1 RANDOM HOUSE PB $10.00

Jean **Giono**

Giono is renowned for his pastoral, pagan studies of Provençal life. The existence he paints is hard but rewardingly simple and contrasts with his distaste for most of the modern world.

Blue Boy
An autobiographical novel of Giono's childhood in pre-World War I Provence
TRANSLATED BY KATHERINE A. CLARKE
0-86547-037-5 NORTH POINT PB $9.50

Harvest
A brief, intensely poetic novel based on the seasonal rhythms of peasant life
TRANSLATED BY HENRI FLUCHERE & GEOFFREY MYERS
0-86547-124-X NORTH POINT PB $9.00

The Horseman on the Roof
A young man journeys through southern France during the cholera epidemic of 1838. This repetitive and relentless chronicle has a cumulative hypnotic power
TRANSLATED BY JONATHAN GRIFFIN
0-614-97777-0 FS&G PB $12.00

The Man Who Planted Trees
A lyrical novella of the French countryside
0-930031-06-7 CHELSEA GREEN PB $6.95

Julien **Gracq**

Balcony in the Forest
A second-generation Surrealist, Gracq advocates the joys of political noninvolvement in resolutely anti-Sartrian fashion
TRANSLATED WITH A PREFACE BY RICHARD HOWARD
0-231-06673-2 COLUMBIA PB $12.50

The Opposing Shore
A novel set in a mythical nation that has been at war for three centuries
TRANSLATED BY RICHARD HOWARD
0-231-05789-X COLUMBIA PB $16.00

Julien **Green**

This French-American novelist explores the theme of anguish issuing from the conflict between spirit and flesh.

Adrienne Mesurat
0-8419-1193-2 HOLMES & MEIER $27.95

The Distant Lands
Exploring a landscape reminiscent of *Gone with the Wind,* Julian Green's 906-page novel, originally a huge success in Europe, focuses on the destructive passions of a young Englishwoman who becomes involved with the plantation culture of the old American South
See also **HISTORICAL AND ROMANTIC FICTION** in **POPULAR READING**
TRANSLATED BY BARBARA BEAUMONT
0-7145-2909-5 MARION BOYARS $24.95

Hervé **Guibert**

Blindsight
0-8076-1414-9 BRAZILLER $20.00

The Compassion Protocol
TRANSLATED BY JAMES KIRKUP
0-8076-1352-5 BRAZILLER $20.00

The Gangsters
A novel of Paris which evokes the moods of film noir
TRANSLATED BY IAN WHITE
1-85242-224-6 SERPENT'S TAIL PB $10.99

Ghost Images
TRANSLATED BY ROBERT BONANNO
1-55713-267-4 SUN & MOON PB $13.95

My Parents
TRANSLATED BY LIZ HERON
1-85242-286-6 SERPENT'S TAIL PB $12.99

To the Friend Who Did Not Save My Life
"An insightful, quirky, alternately humorous and distraught account of how AIDS affects friendships...The painful, ironic record of a young man's reckoning with the disease that becomes his closest companion"—*NY Times Book Review*
TRANSLATED BY LINDA COVERDALE
1-85242-328-5 SERPENT'S TAIL PB $11.99

Emmanuel **Hocquard**

Aerea in the Forests of Manhattan
TRANSLATED BY LYDIA DAVIS
0-910395-88-8 MARLBORO $16.95

Max **Jacob**

The Story of King Kabul the First and Gawain the Kitchen-Boy
TRANSLATED BY MOISHE BLACK & MARIA GREEN
0-8032-2577-6 NEBRASKA $20.00

Alfred **Jarry**

Caesar Antichrist
Jarry's variation on the themes of the Book of Revelations
TRANSLATED BY ANTHONY MELVILLE
0-947757-46-5 CONSORTIUM PB $13.99

Days and Nights
The horrors of military service in the Third Republic
0-947757-19-8 SERPENT'S TAIL PB $13.99

Visits of Love
An idiosyncratic series of erotic tableaux
TRANSLATED BY IAN WHITE
0-947757-63-5 SERPENT'S TAIL PB $13.99

Pierre-Jean **Jouve**

The Desert World
TRANSLATED BY LYDIA DAVIS
0-8101-6018-8 MARLBORO $22.95

Helène
TRANSLATED BY LYDIA DAVIS
0-8101-6003-X NORTHWESTERN PB $12.95

Paulina 1880
TRANSLATED BY ROSETTE LETELLIER
0-8101-6004-8 NORTHWESTERN PB $14.95

Pierre **Klossowski**

The Baphomet
A novel involving the souls of the Knights Templar, who, falsely accused of sexual crimes and blasphemies, were executed in the 14th century. "The novel…takes place almost entirely outside of time, so rather than fantastic, it would be more accurate to term it theological and metaphysical"—Juan Garcia Ponce
TRANSLATED BY SOPHIE HAWKES & STEPHEN SARTARELLI
FOREWORD BY MICHEL FOUCAULT
0-941419-16-9 ERIDANOS PB $24.00

Robert ce Soir & The Revocation of the Edict of Nantes
Two of the three novels forming the Polish-born writer's major work, *The Laws of Hospitality*
TRANSLATED BY AUSTRYN WAINHOUSE
0-7145-2739-4 MARION BOYARS PB $12.95

Philippe **Labro**

Le Petit Garcon
A coming-of-age story set in occupied France, one of the rare French books to deal with the thorny issues of Vichy and collaboration. "Labro tells tenderly and with humor the story of a small boy's encounter with lawlessness, brutality and treason in wartime Vichy. His treatment of the boy's heroic father and the values he personifies is masterful"—Louis Begley
0-374-18448-8 FS&G $23.00

Valéry **Larbaud**

Childish Things
TRANSLATED BY CATHERINE WALD
1-55713-119-8 SUN & MOON PB $13.95

The Diary of A.O. Barnabooth
A wealthy cosmopolite travels from capital to capital—Venice, Moscow, Sarajevo, London—in search of self-realization in this 1924 novel
TRANSLATED BY GILBERT CANNAN
0-929701-14-3 MCPHERSON $18.00
0-929701-15-1 MCPHERSON PB $10.00

An Homage to Jerome, Patron Saint of Translators
0-910395-09-8 MARLBORO PB $6.95

Michel **Leiris**

Aurora

TRANSLATED BY ANNA WARBY

0-947757-25-2 CONSORTIUM PB $12.50

Scratches

TRANSLATED BY LYDIA DAVIS

0-8018-5485-7 JOHNS HOPKINS $42.00

0-8018-5486-5 JOHNS HOPKINS PB $15.00

Simon **Leys**

The Death of Napoleon

A fantasy chronicle of Napoleon after his fall. Leaving a dying look alike behind, Napoleon is smuggled away from St. Helena, in a plot designed to restore him to the throne—but misses his connection in Bordeaux, and instead is left to drift through the world he brought about

0-374-13565-7 FS&G $15.00

Amin **Maalouf**

The First Century After Beatrice

TRANSLATED BY DOROTHY BLAIR

0-8076-1373-8 BRAZILLER $18.50

The Rocks of Tanois

0-8076-1365-7 BRAZILLER $18.50

Samarkand

TRANSLATED BY RUSSELL HARRIS

1-56656-194-9 INTERLINK PB $14.95

André **Malraux**

The Conquerors

A fictional presentation of the struggle between the Communists and Chiang's Kuomintang in '20s China, based on Malraux's first-hand observation

TRANSLATED BY STEPHEN BECKER

FOREWORD BY HERBERT R. LOTTMAN

0-226-50290-2 CHICAGO PB $12.95

Man's Fate

Malraux's most famous work, a panoramic novel of the failed Communist uprising in Shanghai in 1927

TRANSLATED BY HAAKON CHEVALIER

0-679-72574-1 VINTAGE PB $13.00

Man's Hope

A novel of the Spanish Civil War

TRANSLATED BY STUART GILBERT & ALASTAIR MACDONALD

0-394-60478-4 RANDOM HOUSE $10.95

The Temptation of the West

Malraux's first novel is a series of fictional letters between a young Chinese visiting Europe and a young Frenchman in China. "One of the important works of the twentieth century. Sixty years after its publication, it maintains a relevance to current events that is astonishing"— Claude Tannery

TRANSLATED BY ROBERT HOLLANDER

FOREWORD BY JONATHAN D. SPENCE

0-226-50291-0 CHICAGO PB $12.95

The Walnut Trees of Altenberg

TRANSLATED BY A.W. FIELDING

0-226-50289-9 CHICAGO PB $13.95

François **Mauriac**

The Desert of Love

The work of this Nobel laureate is stamped by Catholicism, although he makes a consistent separation between religious and sociopolitical life.

TRANSLATED BY GERARD HOPKINS

0-88184-485-3 CARROLL & GRAF PB $7.95

Thérèse

Mauriac's best-known work is a four-part study of a provincial who attempts to murder her husband and spends the rest of her life living with the consequences

TRANSLATED BY GERARD HOPKINS

0-14-018153-9 PENGUIN PB $10.95

The Woman of the Pharisees

A self-righteous Catholic attempts to dominate the lives of those around her

TRANSLATED BY GERARD HOPKINS

0-88184-371-7 CARROLL & GRAF PB $8.95

Patrick **Modiano**

Honeymoon

In a fugue to the Parisian suburb of his origins, a man, tired of his present, takes a solitary trip into his past

TRANSLATED BY BARBARA WRIGHT

0-87923-947-6 GODINE $19.95

Paul **Morand**

Fancy Goods, Open All Night

An impressionistic picture of European night-life in the '20s

TRANSLATED BY EZRA POUND

PREFACE BY MARCEL PROUST

0-8112-0889-3 NEW DIRECTIONS PB $7.50

Paul **Nizan**

Aden & Arabie

Unflattering depictions of colonial, capitalist Aden in the late '20s

TRANSLATED BY JOAN PINKHAM

INTRODUCTION BY JEAN-PAUL SARTRE

0-231-06357-1 COLUMBIA PB $11.50

Marcel **Pagnol**

Jean de Florette & Manon of the Springs: Two Novels

A tale of legendary vengeance exacted by a mysterious shepherdess, enhanced by Pagnol's keen understanding of the rugged hinterland near Marseilles

TRANSLATED BY W.E. VAN HEYNINGEN

0-86547-312-9 NORTH POINT PB $16.00

Georges **Perec**

Life: A User's Manual

Perec's masterpiece combines the highest level of structural gamesmanship and a delirious vision of the recombinatory possibilities of human life. Bellos's translation is a remarkable feat

TRANSLATED BY DAVID BELLOS

0-87923-751-1 GODINE PB $19.95

Things: A Story of the Sixties

Perec's first novel, published in 1965, concerns a young middle-class couple who attempt to abandon material things for "a calm and frugal life" in Tunisia

0-87923-857-7 GODINE $19.95

A Void

Adair has done the nearly impossible: create an English equivalent to Perec's *La Disparition,* in which a narrative of complex intrigue manages to do without the letter "e"—and the result, in both French and English, is much more than a stunt

TRANSLATED BY GILBERT ADAIR

1-86046-098-4 HARPERCOLLINS PB $12.00

Georges Perec (photo by Anne de Brunhoff)

The Winter Journey

A tiny volume containing a story whose reverberations are, in the Perec manner, quite vast: a scholar stumbles upon an unknown book which seems to predict everything that came after it

TRANSLATED BY JOHN STURROCK

0-14-038912-1 PENGUIN PB $3.95

Benjamin **Péret**

Death to the Pigs & Other Writings

This first authorized collection of the work of the writer most admired by the Surrealists includes the title novel, poetry, critical pieces, and miscellany such as "The Round-the-World Calendar of Tolerable Inventions"

TRANSLATED BY RACHEL STELLA & OTHERS

0-8032-8721-6 NEBRASKA PB $8.95

Robert **Pinget**

A prolific practitioner of the nouveau roman, *Pinget has been well served in English by the remarkable translations of Barbara Wright.*

The Apocrypha

The story of a shepherd becomes the story of several people, with voices, fragments, and notes from earlier texts linked in a succession of seasons

TRANSLATED BY BARBARA WRIGHT

0-87376-050-6 RED DUST $12.95

Baga

TRANSLATED BY JOHN STEVENSON

0-7145-0099-2 RIVERRUN PB $9.95

Between Fantoine and Agapa

TRANSLATED BY BARBARA WRIGHT

0-87376-040-9 RED DUST $8.95

Fable

TRANSLATED BY BARBARA WRIGHT

0-87376-036-0 RED DUST $6.95

0-7145-3792-6 RIVERRUN PB $5.95

The Inquisitory
The interrogation of a servant opens a window on provincial life, in Pinget's longest and best-known novel
TRANSLATED BY DONALD WATSON
0-7145-3911-2 RIVERRUN PB $11.95

The Libera Me Domine
The anatomy of a tragedy that occurred a decade earlier is pieced together through hearsay and a network of gossip and absurd remarks—resulting in a powerful uncertainty about everything
TRANSLATED BY BARBARA WRIGHT
0-87376-025-5 RED DUST $10.50
0-7145-0339-8 RIVERRUN $9.95

Monsieur Songe
Pinget's brilliantly experimental novels, often compared to Beckett's, have made him one of the most respected French writers of the postwar period. *Monsieur Songe* presents a lighter side of his writing, chronicling the reveries and misadventures of a provincial bachelor. Barbara Wright's translation is skillful, as always
TRANSLATED BY BARBARA WRIGHT
0-87376-060-3 RED DUST PB $10.95

Passacaglia
A fragmentary, oblique story of a mysterious death, possibly a murder, in a small village
TRANSLATED BY BARBARA WRIGHT
0-87376-033-6 RED DUST $6.95

Someone
A writer's tryst with writing, portrayed as a hateful but almost involuntary occupation
TRANSLATED BY BARBARA WRIGHT
0-87376-043-3 RED DUST $12.95

That Voice
A tale of death and disintegration in a French village
TRANSLATED BY BARBARA WRIGHT
0-87376-041-7 RED DUST $10.95

Marcel **Proust**
"Supremely sensitive, and with a prodigious memory for recording sensations, he laid his own mind and body open like an intricate musical instrument for experience to play on, studying every note, always searching for a mysterious underlying theme half-perceived from the first. This theme he was to discover was Time."—William Sansom

In Search of Lost Time
The publication of this revised translation of Proust's masterpiece is a major literary event. D.J. Enright's revision of the Scott-Moncrieff translation is based on the new French edition that corrects many errors and omissions in the original

Volume I
Swann's Way
0-679-60005-1 MODERN LIBRARY $18.50

Volume II
Within a Budding Grove
0-679-60006-X MODERN LIBRARY $18.50

Volume III
The Guermantes Way
0-679-60028-0 MODERN LIBRARY $18.50

Volume IV
Sodom and Gomorrah
0-679-60029-9 MODERN LIBRARY $18.50

Volume V
The Captive and the Fugitive
0-679-42477-6 MODERN LIBRARY $19.50

Marcel Proust

Volume VI
Time Regained
0-679-42476-8 MODERN LIBRARY $18.50

Remembrance of Things Past
A 3-volume set
TRANSLATED BY C. SCOTT MONCRIEFF & TERENCE KILMARTIN
0-394-71243-9 RANDOM HOUSE PB $64.00

Raymond **Queneau**

The Blue Flowers
TRANSLATED BY BARBARA WRIGHT
0-8112-0945-8 NEW DIRECTIONS PB $8.95

Exercises in Style
Queneau's most famous text consists of a single banal incident on a bus, recounted in 99 different styles. Barbara Wright works wonders with material that at first glance might appear untranslatable
TRANSLATED BY BARBARA WRIGHT
0-8112-0789-7 NEW DIRECTIONS PB $10.95

The Last Days
0-916583-40-6 DALKEY ARCHIVE PB $9.95

Odile
0-916583-34-1 DALKEY ARCHIVE $19.95

Oulipo Laboratory: Texts from the Bibliothèque Oulipienne
0-947757-89-9 SMALL PRESS PB $15.99

Pataphysical Poems
An expanded version that includes many new poems
TRANSLATED BY TEO SAVORY
0-87775-172-2 UNICORN $29.95

Pierrot Mon Ami
0-91658-340-0 DALKEY ARCHIVE PB $7.95

Pierrot Mon Ami & Saint Glinglin: Two Novels
1-56478-059-7 DALKEY ARCHIVE $13.95

Saint Glinglin
A novel set in a strange land where it never rains. "By turns strange, beautiful, ludicrous, and intellectually stimulating"—Vivian Mercier
TRANSLATED BY JAMES SALLIS
1-56478-027-9 DALKEY ARCHIVE $19.95

The Sunday of Life
TRANSLATED BY BARBARA WRIGHT
0-8112-0645-9 NEW DIRECTIONS $5.95

We Always Treat Women Too Well
TRANSLATED BY BARBARA WRIGHT & VALERIE CATON
0-8112-0792-7 NEW DIRECTIONS $14.95

Zazie in the Metro
A country girl's disjointed jaunt to Paris, rendered even zanier by Queneau's use of phonetic transcription as part of his program to introduce a "neo-French" incorporating argot and other jargon
TRANSLATED BY BARBARA WRIGHT
0-7145-3872-8 RIVERRUN $13.95

Pascal **Quignard**

All the World's Mornings
This novel of the conflict between the baroque composer Marin Marais and the Maitre de St. Colombe became the basis for a successful film
TRANSLATED BY JAMES KIRKUP
1-55597-203-9 GRAY WOLF PB $9.00

Rachilde

The Juggler
A "decadent classic" from 1900 by a writer whose reputation has been revived recently in Europe; now available for the first time in English
TRANSLATED BY MELANIE C. HAWTHORNE
0-8135-1625-0 RUTGERS PB $12.95

Raymond **Radiguet**

Count D'Orgel's Ball
Though he died of typhoid fever at 20, this talented protegé of Cocteau produced two powerful and erotic analytical novels. This is the story of an unusual love triangle
TRANSLATED BY ANNAPAOLO CANCOGNI
FOREWORD BY JEAN COCTEAU
0-941419-30-4 ERIDANOS PB $11.00

The Devil in the Flesh
A 14-year-old boy is propelled by wartime circumstances into precocious maturity
TRANSLATED BY A.M. SMITH
0-7145-0193-X MARION BOYARS PB $10.95

Marie **Redonnet**

Candy Story
0-8032-8958-8 NEBRASKA PB $10.00

Hotel Splendid
TRANSLATED BY JORDAN STUMP
0-8032-8953-7 NEBRASKA PB $10.00

Nevermore
TRANSLATED BY JORDAN STUMP
0-8032-3912-2 NEBRASKA $32.00
0-8032-8959-6 NEBRASKA PB $12.00

Rose Mellie Rose with 'The Story of the Triptych'
TRANSLATED BY JORDAN STUMP
0-8032-8952-9 NEBRASKA PB $10.00

Alain **Robbe-Grillet**
"Forerunner of a revolution in the novel"
—Claude Mauriac

The Erasers
Twenty-four hours in a Flemish town where, for eight days, a murder a day has been committed. One of the most influential *nouveaux romans*
TRANSLATED BY RICHARD HOWARD
0-8021-5086-1 GROVE PB $12.95

La Belle Captive
TRANSLATED BY BEN STOLTZFUS
0-520-20707-6 CALIFORNIA PB $17.95

Recollections of the Golden Triangle
A literary thriller mingling fantasy, dream, and erotic invention; the reader is challenged to play detective
TRANSLATED BY J.A. UNDERWOOD
0-8021-5200-7 GROVE PB $11.00

Snapshots
Six short pieces that represent the "new novelist's" most accessible fiction
TRANSLATED BY BRUCE MORRISSETTE
0-8101-0728-7 NORTHWESTERN PB $9.95

The Voyeur
Inside the mind of an unsuccessful traveling salesman turned homicidal maniac. But did the crime really occur, and if so, when?
TRANSLATED BY RICHARD HOWARD
0-8021-3165-4 GROVE PB $9.95

Romain **Rolland**

Jean-Christophe
This monumental novel of a musician's development against a backdrop of war and social change enjoyed international fame in the early part of the century
0-7867-0307-5 CARROLL & GRAF $35.00

Jacques **Roubaud**

The Great Fire of London
Roubaud's most ambitious book. "In writing a book that implicitly supercedes the 'book,' the object of his self-proclaimed intellectual love, he parallels his major thematic concern: constructing a literary project centered on the memory of a dead, beloved wife, and in the process fashioning a prose whose chief effect, echoing the Platonic injunction against writing, is the destruction of all memory"—Dominic Di Bernardi
TRANSLATED BY DOMINIC DI BERNARDI
0-916583-89-9 DALKEY ARCHIVE PB $12.95
0-936-42990-6 CUMBERLAND PB $8.95

I read every day: I read by day, I read by night; I read more than I ought to; I spend perhaps more of my time doing this than anything else. If the days of my life are few and far between when I have gone without reading (and they certainly number among the grimmest), countless are those when that's all I did. I can read at any time, in any place. Nevertheless (and this is why I have a passion for *reading*, not for the prolonged sequential viewing of printed lines) I can't read just anything.
THE GREAT FIRE OF LONDON

Hortense in Exile
TRANSLATED BY DOMINIC DI BERNARDI
1-56478-001-5 DALKEY ARCHIVE $19.95

The Princess Hoppy, or the Tale of Labrador
TRANSLATED BY BERNARD HOEPFFNER
1-56478-032-5 DALKEY ARCHIVE PB $9.95

Raymond **Roussel**
Committed as he was to linguistic experimentation in pre-Surrealist days, Roussel had a considerable influence on later writers.

Raymond Roussel: Life, Death and Works
EDITED BY ALAISTER BROTCHIE, MALCOM GREEN, AND ANTHONY MELVILLE
0-947757-14-7 SMALL PRESS PB $13.00

Raymond Roussel: Selections from Certain of His Books
An excellent introduction to one of the most influential (and bizarre) of modern French writers. Includes *Documents to Serve as an Outline* (translated by John Ashbery), the plays *The Dust of Suns* and *The Star on the Forehead*, and the poem *The View*. "Genius in its pure state"—Jean Cocteau
0-947757-26-0 CONSORTIUM PB $14.95

Raymond **Roussel** & Ron **Padgett**

Among the Blacks
A clear insight into Roussel's special vision, in a perceptive translation. Also included is an autobiographical essay by Padgett
0-939691-03-5 SUN & MOON PB $7.50

Raymond Roussel

Nathalie **Sarraute**
One of the leading theorists and exponents of the nouveau roman, *Sarraute stripped her fiction of realistic and didactic elements in order to construct a world out of "sensations."*

Between Life and Death
0-7145-0122-0 CALDER $14.95

The Planetarium
0-7145-0444-0 RIVERRUN PB $9.95

Portrait of a Man Unknown
0-7145-0484-X CALDER PB $11.95

Tropisms
A collection of shorter pieces built around evanescent sensations that trigger emotional responses
TRANSLATED BY MARIA JOLAS
0-8076-0412-7 BRAZILLER PB $5.95

Tropisms & The Age of Suspicion
0-7145-0046-1 RIVERRUN PB $11.95

Jean-Paul **Sartre**

Nausea
Sartre's famous 1938 novel, with its relentless analysis of the consciousness of its protagonist, did much to popularize the concepts of existentialism
TRANSLATED BY LLOYD ALEXANDER
0-8112-0188-0 NEW DIRECTIONS PB $9.95

The Age of Reason
The first part of the trilogy *The Roads to Freedom*, which charts the period from Munich to the fall of France in 1940. The *Age of Reason* describes events in 1938, already darkened by the shadow of war
0-679-73895-9 VINTAGE PB $14.00

The Reprieve
Part two of the trilogy depicts the critical eight days before the German annexation of Czechoslovakia in 1938
TRANSLATED BY ERIC SUTTON
0-679-74078-3 VINTAGE PB $15.00

Troubled Sleep
The final volume of *The Roads to Freedom* describes the fall of France to the Nazis and its repercussions on the lives of a small group of French men and women
TRANSLATED BY GERARD HOPKINS
0-679-74079-1 VINTAGE PB $15.00

The Wall
These five stories, including *Intimacy* and *The Childhood of a Leader*, deal broadly with the dilemma generated by commitment to a chosen political action. Sartre presents many instances of his concept of "bad faith"
TRANSLATED BY LLOYD ALEXANDER
0-8112-0190-2 NEW DIRECTIONS PB $8.95

André **Schwarz-Bart**

The Last of the Just
A novel of the Holocaust. "Transcends the definition of fiction. It's part history, part vision, forged into a single echoing, terrifying outcry"
—NY Times
See also **HOLOCAUST FICTION** under **ART AND LITERATURE** under **THE HOLOCAUST** in **WORLD HISTORY AND CURRENT AFFAIRS**
TRANSLATED BY STEPHEN BECKER
0-689-70365-1 MACMILLAN PB $15.95

Victor **Serge**

Resistance
TRANSLATED BY JAMES BROOK
0-87286-225-9 CITY LIGHTS PB $5.95

Victor **Segalen**

René Leys

Segalen's novel of China circa 1909 is itself a maddening Chinese box. The austere and brilliant European youth René Leys has penetrated the most intimate mysteries of the Forbidden City—or has he? A meditation on exoticism and the nature of truth, with the kick of a well-told ghost story

TRANSLATED BY J.A. WUNDERWOOD

0-87951-350-0 OVERLOOK PB $10.95

Claude **Simon**

A major proponent of the nouveau roman, *Simon has experimented with stream of consciousness, working outside of ordinary linear structures. He won the Nobel Prize in 1985.*

The Flanders Road

0-7145-3994-5 RIVERRUN PB $11.95

The Georgics

A major novel that moves through different historical periods

TRANSLATED BY JOHN FLETCHER

0-7145-3897-3 RIVERRUN PB $13.95

The Grass

TRANSLATED BY RICHARD HOWARD

0-8076-1156-5 BRAZILLER PB $8.95

The Invitation

0-916583-79-1 DALKEY ARCHIVE $15.95

Triptych

0-7145-3609-1 RIVERRUN $17.95

0-7145-3787-X RIVERRUN PB $11.95

The Wind

A novel of pedestrian lives caught up in a tide of clashing emotional forces when a wayfarer claims his inheritance, a vineyard

TRANSLATED BY RICHARD HOWARD

0-8076-1155-7 BRAZILLER PB $8.95

Philippe **Sollers**

The Park

The literary theorist's early novel is rooted in a keen appreciation of the process of writing

TRANSLATED BY A. SHERIDAN SMITH

0-87376-013-1 RED DUST PB $4.95

Philippe **Soupault**

Last Nights of Paris

TRANSLATED BY WILLIAM CARLOS WILLIAMS

1-87897-205-7 D.A.P. PB $13.95

Michel **Tournier**

Gilles & Jeanne

Currently out of print, as with all of his novels. A novel based on the strange relationship between Joan of Arc and the child-murderer Gilles de Rais. "In a few quick images, Tournier brings the historic Jeanne and Gilles alive…The book is a master's twisting of history into dark ethical questions, a work of spare elegance and icy power"—Toby Olson

TRANSLATED BY ALAN SHERIDAN

0-8021-0021-X GROVE $3.98

Antoine **Volodine**

Naming the Jungle

A tale of psychological and political intrigue set in the Latin American jungle. Fabian Golpiez is being investigated by the revolutionary secret police, and in order to avoid torture and interrogation, he takes refuge in madness. "Volodine's fiction is pure and visionary, making him one of the most forceful personalities of the new generation"—*La Croix*

TRANSLATED BY LINDA COVERDALE

1-56584-274-X NEW PRESS $18.95

Monique **Wittig**

Les Guerillères

TRANSLATED BY DAVID LE VAY

0-8070-6301-0 FS&G PB $12.95

The Lesbian Body

TRANSLATED BY DAVID LE VAY

INTRODUCTION BY MARGARET CROSLAND

0-8070-6307-X BEACON PB $12.95

Marguerite **Yourcenar**

The Abyss

A novel about an alchemist in 16th-century France

TRANSLATED BY GRACE FRICK

0-374-51666-9 FS&G PB $15.00

Alexis

Set in Austria-Hungary just before the outbreak of the First World War, this early novel takes the form of a lengthy letter of confession

TRANSLATED BY WALTER KAISER

0-374-51906-4 FS&G PB $6.95

A Blue Tale and Other Stories

0-226-96530-9 CHICAGO $14.95

0-226-96531-7 CHICAGO PB $7.95

Coup de Grace

The tale of an unhappy youthful triangle, set in the Baltics in the aftermath of World War I

TRANSLATED BY GRACE FRICK

0-374-51631-6 FS&G PB $11.00

Fires

Nine monologues and narratives based on classical Greek stories, interspersed with personal notations

TRANSLATED BY DORI KATZ

0-226-96528-7 CHICAGO PB $9.95

Memoirs of Hadrian

Yourcenar's major work, which presents the fictitious memoirs of the Roman emperor, earned her a place among the great contemporary French writers

See also **HISTORICAL FICTION** under **TOPICS IN ROMAN HISTORY** under **ANCIENT ROME** in **WORLD HISTORY AND CURRENT AFFAIRS**

0-374-50348-6 FS&G PB $14.00

The slightest and most superficial of contacts are enough for us with most persons, or prove even too much. But when these contacts persist and multiply about one unique being, to the point of embracing him entirely, when each fraction of a body becomes laden for us with meaning as overpowering as that of the face itself, when this one creature haunts us like music and torments us like a problem (instead of inspiring in us, at most, mere irritation, amusement, or boredom), when he passes from the periphery of our universe to its center, and finally becomes for us more indispensable than ourselves, then the astonishing prodigy takes place where I see much more an invasion of the flesh by the spirit than a simple play of the body alone.

MEMOIRS OF HADRIAN

Oriental Tales

Something of a tour of China, Japan, the Balkans, and India, showing "the fabulist as mythographer and sage"—Stephen Koch, *NY Times Book Review*

0-374-51997-8 FS&G PB $11.00

Two Lives and a Dream

Three late tales

TRANSLATED BY WALTER KAISER

0-374-28019-3 FS&G $16.95

0-226-96529-5 CHICAGO PB $14.95

Essays: Personal, Literary, Philosophical

Louis **Althusser**

The Future Lasts Forever

A memoir written after the Marxist philosophers mental collapse and murder of his wife

1-56584-087-9 NEW PRESS $25.00

1-56584-278-2 NEW PRESS PB $14.95

Robert **Antèlme**

The Human Race

A memoir of a Nazi concentration camp

TRANSLATED BY JEFFREY HAIGHT & ANNIE MAHLER

0-910395-77-2 MARLBORO $23.95

0-910395-78-0 MARLBORO PB $13.95

Antonin **Artaud**

Anthology

EDITED BY JACK HIRSCHMAN

0-87286-000-0 SUBTERRANEAN PB $12.95

The Theater and Its Double

These major statements of dramatic theory, influenced by Balinese and Mexican Indian culture, focus on restoring myth and mystery to the stage. They deeply influenced the absurdists, and inspired the Theater of Cruelty in the '60s

See also **DRAMATIC THEORY AND CRITICISM** under **THEATER** in **PERFORMING ARTS AND MEDIA**

TRANSLATED BY MARY C. RICHARDS

0-8021-5030-6 GROVE PB $9.95

Watchfiends and Rack Screams: Works from the Final Period

TRANSLATED BY CLAYTON ESHLEMAN & BERNARD BADOR

1-87897-218-9 D.A.P. PB $15.95

Roland **Barthes**

A principal exponent of the application of structuralism and semiotics to the study of literature and society, Barthes is widely regarded as a central intellectual figure of our era.

A Barthes Reader

An excellent introduction to Barthes' thinking as applied to such diverse topics as Gide, Garbo, striptease, photography, and the Eiffel Towel

See also **ROLAND BARTHES** under **CRITICAL TEXTS** under **SEMIOTICS AND STRUCTURALISM AND AFTER** under **LITERARY THEORY**

EDITED BY SUSAN SONTAG

0-374-52144-1 FS&G PB $16.95

A Lover's Discourse: Fragments

"Barthes surprises us by making love, in its most absurd and sentimental forms, an object of interest"—Jonathan Culler

TRANSLATED BY RICHARD HOWARD

0-374-52161-1 FS&G PB $10.95

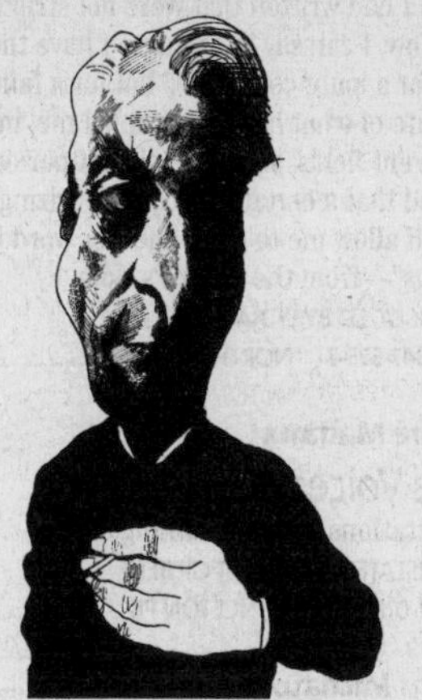

Roland Barthes

The Pleasure of the Text
Barthes' brilliant effort to define an erotics of reading
TRANSLATED BY RICHARD MILLER
0-374-52160-3 FS&G PB $8.95

The text you write must prove to me *that it desires me*. This proof exists: it is writing. Writing is: the science of the various blisses of language, its Kama Sutra (this science has but one treatise: writing itself).
THE PLEASURE OF THE TEXT

Georges **Bataille**

The Absence of Myth: Writings on Surrealism
TRANSLATED BY MICHAEL RICHARDSON
0-86091-419-4 VERSO $29.95

Erotism: Death and Sensuality
Originally published in 1957, this book provides Bataille's perspective on sacrifice, language, taboos, cruelty, and "mystical ecstasy"
See also **WRITING FROM THE EDGE** under **CUTTING EDGE** in **POPULAR READING**
TRANSLATED BY MARY DALWOOD
0-87286-190-2 CITY LIGHTS PB $14.95

Literature and Evil
Essays about Blake, Emily Brontë, Baudelaire and others
See also **OTHER FRENCH THEORISTS** under **POSTSTRUCTURALISM** under **LITERARY THEORY**
TRANSLATED BY ALASTAIR HAMILTON
0-7145-0346-0 MARION BOYARS PB $13.95

Visions of Excess: Selected Writings, 1927-1939
Essays on fascism, Marxism, de Sade, Nietzsche, Breton, Hegel
TRANSLATED BY ALLAN STOEKL
0-8166-1283-8 MINNESOTA PB $17.95

Simone **de Beauvoir**

All Said and Done: Autobiography, 1962-1972
The fourth and final installment of de Beauvoir's evaluation of her extraordinary life. This one is written from the bittersweet vantage point of her later years, when she had become a feminist icon, and the old warriors of Existentialism had died
TRANSLATED BY PATRICK O'BRIAN
1-55778-525-2 MARLOWE PB $16.95

The Ethics of Ambiguity
0-8065-0160-X LYLE STUART PB $9.95

Memoirs of a Dutiful Daughter
This autobiographical work is "a record of the emotional and intellectual birth pangs of a fascinating woman"—*Time*
0-06-090351-1 HARPERCOLLINS PB $13.00

The Second Sex
One of the most significant minds of the 20thcentury, de Beauvoir began this book to find out who and what she was as a woman, and ended up producing a masterpiece of feminist thought
See also **FEMINIST THEORY** under **WOMEN'S STUDIES** in **SOCIAL STUDIES**
0-679-42016-9 KNOPF $20.00
0-679-72451-6 VINTAGE PB $14.00

Simone de Beauvoir

A Very Easy Death
A stark yet warm account of the struggle of the author's mother against terminal illness
TRANSLATED BY PATRICK O'BRIAN
0-394-72899-8 RANDOM HOUSE PB $11.00

Samuel **Beckett**

Proust
A guide to "that double-headed monster of damnation and salvation—Time"—Samuel Beckett
0-8021-5025-X GROVE PB $10.95

Marcel **Benabou**

Why I Have Not Written Any of My Books
Like Queneau, Perec, and Roubaud, Benabou is a product of the OuLiPo group, and this work is marked by playful humor
TRANSLATED BY DAVID KORNACKER
0-8032-1239-9 NEBRASKA $25.00

Maurice **Blanchot**

The Space of Literature
TRANSLATED BY ANN SMOCK
0-8032-6092-X NEBRASKA PB $12.00

The Work of Fire
0-8047-2432-6 STANFORD $45.00
0-8047-2493-8 STANFORD PB $16.95

The Writing of the Disaster
A treatment of the notion that, in Blanchot's words, "disaster belongs to a past that never ceases to impend"
See also **OTHER FRENCH THEORISTS** under **POSTSTRUCTURALISM** under **LITERARY THEORY**
TRANSLATED WITH AN INTRODUCTION BY ANN SMOCK
0-8032-1186-4 NEBRASKA $30.00
0-8032-6077-6 NEBRASKA PB $9.95

André **Breton**

Anthology of Black Humor
Breton's explanation of *l'humeur noir*—a defining characteristic of Surrealism
TRANSLATED BY MARK POLIZZOTTI
0-87286-321-2 CITY LIGHTS PB $16.95

Arcanum 17
"A fluid and dynamic work by one of the most influential thinkers of the century"
—*Publishers Weekly*
1-55713-170-8 SUN & MOON PB $12.95

Free Rein
0-8032-1241-0 NEBRASKA $35.00

The Lost Steps: Les Pas Perdus
0-8032-1242-9 NEBRASKA $30.00

Mad Love
A primary text of Surrealism. "I have wanted to show above all what precautions and what ruses desire takes, in search of its object and evading it"—André Breton
TRANSLATED BY MARY ANN CAWS
0-8032-1200-3 NEBRASKA $27.50
0-8032-6072-5 NEBRASKA PB $9.00

What Is Surrealism? Selected Writings
EDITED BY FRANKLIN ROSEMONT
0-8383-1709-X HASKELL $75.00
0-913460-60-5 MONAD PRESS PB $30.95

Manifestoes of Surrealism
See also **DADA AND SURREALISM** under **20TH-CENTURY ART** in **ART**
TRANSLATED BY RICHARD SEAVER & HELEN R. LANE
0-472-06182-8 MICHIGAN PB $15.95

Michel **Butor**

The Spirit of Mediterranean Places
Unusual travel essays—on Cordoba, Istanbul, Salonika, Delphi, and other places—by a leading experimental novelist. "These essays, demanding and wonderful, convey a profound sense of places and the people who have inhabited them, what they have created and what they have destroyed"—Gail Pool, *Christian Science Monitor*
TRANSLATED BY LYDIA DAVIS
0-910395-17-9 MARLBORO PB $9.00

Albert **Camus**

American Journals
1-56924-823-0 MARLOWE PB $12.95

The Myth of Sisyphus & Other Essays
In the famous title essay, Camus "analyzes a contemporary malady: the recognition of the absurdity of human life"—Justin O'Brien
0-679-73373-6 VINTAGE PB $11.00

Between Hell and Reason: Essays from the Resistance Newspaper Combat, 1944-1947

Forty-one eloquent pieces—most of them never before published in English—that grapple with questions of revolutions, violence, ethics, and the emerging social order directly after the war. A unique testimonial to a watershed period in history, as well as all important link to the great existentialist's prewar and postwar works

0-8195-5189-9 WESLEYAN PB $15.95

Notebooks, 1935-1942

1-56924-993-8 MARLOWE PB $12.95

Notebooks, 1942-1951

A self-portrait of Camus from the period in which he wrote his most famous works: *The Stranger, The Plague,* and *The Rebel.* The notebooks provide an intimate view of inner ideological struggles and eventual disillusionment

TRANSLATED BY JUSTIN O'BRIEN

1-55778-413-2 MARLOWE PB $10.95

The Rebel

"The logbook of the intellectual's pilgrimage to paradise on earth, the biography of that European rebellion which was born with the French Revolution"—Manes Sperber, *NY Times*

0-679-73384-1 VINTAGE PB $11.00

Youthful Writings

TRANSLATED BY ELLEN CONROY KENNEDY

1-56924-968-7 MARLOWE PB $12.95

Hélène **Cixous**

Coming to Writing & Other Essays

EDITED BY DEBORAH JENSON

0-674-14436-8 HARVARD $28.00

Jean **Cocteau**

Beauty and the Beast: Diary of a Film

INTRODUCTION BY GEORGE AMBERG

0-486-22776-6 DOVER PB $6.95

Jean Cocteau

The Difficulty of Being

Cocteau's most personal statement

0-306-80633-9 DA CAPO PB $13.95

Opium

0-7206-0800-7 DUFOUR PB $17.95

Rene **Daumal**

The Powers of the Word: Selected Essays and Notes, 1927-1943

0-87286-259-3 CITY LIGHTS PB $12.95

Rasa, Or Knowledge of the Self

Writings on Indian culture, by the poet and scholar of Sanskrit

TRANSLATED BY LOUISE LANDES LEVI

0-8112-0825-7 NEW DIRECTIONS PB $5.95

Marguerite **Duras**

The War: A Memoir

Paris during the Nazi occupation and the first month of liberation

See also **FRANCE** under **THE WAR IN EUROPE** under **THE SECOND WORLD WAR** in **WORLD HISTORY AND CURRENT AFFAIRS**

TRANSLATED BY BARBARA BRAY

1-56584-221-9 NEW PRESS PB $10.00

Michel **Foucault**

The Foucault Reader

Presents many aspects of Foucault's investigation of the nature of power in society

See also **MICHEL FOUCAULT** under **POSTSTRUCTURALISM** under **LITERARY THEORY**

EDITED BY PAUL RABINOW

0-394-71340-0 RANDOM HOUSE PB $15.00

André **Gide**

Travels in the Congo

TRANSLATED BY DOROTHY BUSSY

0-88001-365-6 ECCO PB $13.00

Simone **Weil**

The Iliad, Or the Poem of Force

Intelligence, insight, and compassion combine to make this brief essay the most moving reading of the *Iliad* in our time

0-87574-091-X PENDLE HILL PB $3.00

Julia **Kristeva**

"Julia Kristeva changes the places of things: she always destroys the latest preconception, the one we thought we could be comforted by, the one of which we could be proud; what she displaces is the illusion that it has all been said already."—Roland Barthes

A Kristeva Reader

See also **CRITICAL TEXTS** under **SEMIOTICS AND STRUCTURALISM AND AFTER** under **LITERARY THEORY**

EDITED BY TORIL MOI

0-231-06324-5 COLUMBIA $55.00

0-231-06325-3 COLUMBIA PB $18.50

Laure

Laure: The Collected Writings

TRANSLATED BY JEANINE HERMAN

0-87286-293-3 CITY LIGHTS PB $13.95

Michael **Leiris**

Brisées: Broken Branches

"Back in 1949, Maurice Saillet and I conceived the plan of collecting in a single volume a number of texts I had written that were not strictly literary ... Now, I can say in any case I have the material, not for a 'pure collection,' but for a fairly complete picture of what has preoccupied me, in very different fields, since the distant period at which I hoped that a certain way of pulverizing words would allow me to grasp the last word in all things"—from the Author's Note

TRANSLATED BY LYDIA DAVIS

0-86547-375-7 NORTH POINT $3.98

André **Malraux**

The Voices of Silence

Meditations on the meaning of art

TRANSLATED BY STUART GILBERT

0-691-01821-9 PRINCETON PB $29.95

Henri **Michaux**

A Barbarian in Asia

Impressions of the Far East, in a classic translation

TRANSLATED BY SYLVIA BEACH

0-8112-0991-1 NEW DIRECTIONS PB $7.95

Adrienne **Monnier**

The Very Rich Hours of Adrienne Monnier

TRANSLATED BY RICHARD MCDOUGALL

0-8032-8227-3 NEBRASKA PB $23.00

Marcel **Pagnol**

My Father's Glory & My Mother's Castle: Marcel Pagnol's Memories of Childhood

Rich evocations of life as it once was in Provence, by the novelist and filmmaker

TRANSLATED BY RITA BARISSE

0-86547-257-2 FS&G PB $13.00

Georges **Perec**

W: Or the Memory of Childhood

Childhood memories and childhood fantasies are juxtaposed, in this reconstruction of Perec's childhood under Nazi occupation, until in a devastating conclusion memory and fantasy merge. This is in many ways his most profound and moving book

TRANSLATED BY DAVID BELLOS

0-87923-756-2 GODINE $16.95

Georges **Perec** & Robert **Bober**

Ellis Island

An illustrated edition of the script and other materials related to a documentary film about the immigration center

1-56584-318-5 NEW PRESS PB $16.95

Jose **Pierre**, editor

Investigating Sex: Surrealist Discussions, 1928-1932

Leading surrealists happily reveal themselves as juvenile, silly, and afraid of women

See also **PORNOGRAPHY** under **FEMINIST THEORY** under **WOMEN'S STUDIES** in **SOCIAL STUDIES**

TRANSLATED BY MALCOM IMRIE

0-86091-378-3 NORTON $24.95

0-86091-603-0 NORTON PB $16.95

Marcel **Proust**

Selected Letters Volume 1, 1880-1903

0-226-68459-8 CHICAGO PB $16.95

Selected Letters
Volume 2, 1904-1909
TRANSLATED BY TERENCE KILMARTIN
0-19-505961-1 OXFORD $35.00

Marcel Proust on Art and Literature
See also THE MODERNIST REVOLUTION under LITERARY CRITICISM
0-88184-114-5 CARROLL & GRAF PB $8.95

On Reading
A profound essay originally written in response to John Ruskin, and printed here in an elegant miniature edition
TRANSLATED BY JOHN STURROCK
0-14-038903-2 PENGUIN PB $3.95

We feel very clearly that our own wisdom begins where that of the author leaves off, and would like him to provide us with desires. And he can only awaken these desires in us by making us contemplate the supreme beauty to which the utmost efforts of his art have enabled him to attain. But by a singular and moreover providential law of mental optics (a law which signifies perhaps that we cannot receive the truth from anyone else, but must create it for ourselves), the end-point of their wisdom appears to us as only the beginning of our own, such that it is at the moment when they have told us everything they could have told us that they give rise in us to the feeling that they have as yet told us nothing.
ON READING

On Reading Ruskin
See also THE 19TH-CENTURY under STUDIES OF INDIVIDUAL AUTHORS under ANTHOLOGIES AND STUDIES in LITERATURE OF THE BRITISH ISLES
0-300-03513-6 YALE $13.00

Alain **Robbe-Grillet**

"Forerunner of a revolution in the novel."
—Claude Mauriac

For a New Novel: Essays on Fiction
TRANSLATED BY RICHARD HOWARD
0-8369-1844-4 AYER $19.95
0-8101-0821-6 NORTHWESTERN PB $14.95

Ghosts in the Mirror
Robbe-Grillet recounts his childhood in the first volume of his memoirs
TRANSLATED JO LEVY
0-8021-1036-3 GROVE $2.98

Antoine **de Saint-Exupéry**

Wartime Writings, 1939-1944
0-15-694740-4 HARCOURT BRACE PB $8.95

Nathalie **Sarraute**

Childhood
Writing in old age, Sarraute sets out to remember her childhood as accurately as possible. The result is a work of uncanny surprise and disturbing beauty
TRANSLATED BY WRIGHT BARBARA
0-8076-1116-6 BRAZILLER PB $10.95

However much I huddle up, roll myself into a bell, hide my head under blankets, fear, a fear such as I never remember having known since, creeps up on me, insinuates itself…That's where it comes from…I don't even need to look, I can sense it in everything there…it gives that light its greenish tinge…it is fear, that avenue of pointed, rigid, sombre trees with livid trunks, that procession of ghosts attired in long white robes advancing in a lugubrious file towards the grey flagstones…it flickers in the flames of the tall pallid candles they are carrying…it spreads all around, fills my room…I would like to escape, but I haven't the courage to cross the space impregnated with it that separates my bed from the door.
CHILDHOOD

Jean-Paul **Sartre**

Anti-Semite and Jew
A challenge to anti-Semitism from a non-Jewish point of view. "One of the most brilliant psychological analyses of the marginal Jew and the fanatical anti-Semite that has ever been published"—Sidney Hook
See also SARTRE under PHILOSOPHY in RELIGION, SPIRITUALITY, AND PHILOSOPHY
See also ANTI-SEMITISM under JEWISH HISTORY in WORLD HISTORY AND CURRENT AFFAIRS
0-8052-1047-4 SCHOCKEN PB $12.00
0-8052-0102-5 SCHOCKEN PB $12.00

Jean-Paul Sartre

Mallarmé, or the Poet of Nothingness
TRANSLATED BY ERNEST STURM
0-271-00498-3 PENN STATE $22.50

Politics and Literature
Discusses relations between politics and literature, the intellectual and the revolution, and myth and reality in theatre, with essays and interviews on language and its uses
0-7145-0823-3 RIVERRUN $12.95

The Words
An autobiography in which Sartre describes his earliest encounters with language
TRANSLATED BY BERNARD FRECHTMAN
0-394-74709-7 VINTAGE PB $10.00

Michel **Serres**

Conversations on Science, Culture and Time
0-472-09548-X MICHIGAN $39.50

Genesis
0-472-10592-2 MICHIGAN $29.95

The Natural Contract
0-472-09549-8 MICHIGAN $39.50
0-472-06549-1 MICHIGAN PB $14.95

Philippe **Sollers**

Writing and the Experience of Limits
TRANSLATED BY PHILLIP BARNARD
EDITED BY DAVID HAYMAN
0-231-05292-8 COLUMBIA $40.50

Tristan **Tzara**

Seven Dada Manifestos and Lampisteries
0-7145-3762-4 RIVERRUN PB $8.95

Paul **Valéry**

The Art of Poetry
"These essays should come into the hands of everyone interested not only in the now almost mythical figure of Valéry but in the evolving situation of poetry and poetic theory in our time"—*New Yorker*
See also THE MODERNIST REVOLUTION under LITERARY CRITICISM
TRANSLATED BY DENISE FOLLIOT
EDITED BY MATHEWS JACKSON
0-691-09838-7 PRINCETON $43.00
0-691-01880-4 PRINCETON PB $15.95

The Collected Works of Paul Valéry
Plays
0-691-09844-1 PRINCETON $55.00

Dialogues
0-691-09840-9 PRINCETON $35.00
0-691-01878-2 PRINCETON PB $12.95

Masters and Friends
0-691-09843-3 PRINCETON $60.00

Degas, Manet, Morisot
0691013320 PRINCETON PB $9.95

Moi
0-691-09936-7 PRINCETON $47.50

Selected Writings
See also POETRY
0-8112-0213-5 NEW DIRECTIONS PB $12.95

Simone **Weil**

Formative Writings, 1929-1941
TRANSLATED BY DOROTHY MCFARLAND
0-87023-632-6 MASSACHUSETTS PB $17.95

Lectures on Philosophy
TRANSLATED BY H. PRICE
0-521-29333-2 CAMBRIDGE PB $20.95

Oppression and Liberty
TRANSLATED BY ARTHUR WILLS & JOHN PETRIE
0-87023-251-7 MASSACHUSETTS PB $15.95

Two Moral Essays: Human Personality & On Human Obligations
0-87574-240-8 PENDLE HILL PB $3.00

Waiting for God
Searching spiritual autobiography by a brilliant and austere writer of Jewish origins who was drawn to an existentialist Christianity

influenced by Pascal, Kierkegaard, and her own mystical experience
See also CLASSICS OF WESTERN RELIGIOUS THOUGHT under WORLD RELIGION in RELIGION, SPIRITUALITY, AND PHILOSOPHY
See also CLASSICS under CHRISTIANITY in RELIGION, SPIRITUALITY, AND PHILOSOPHY
TRANSLATED BY EMMA CRAUFURD
0-06-090295-7 HARPERPERENNIAL PB $12.00

Marguerite **Yourcenar**
The Dark Brain of Piranesi: And Other Essays
Seven critical studies ranging from Agrippa d'Aubigné and the *Historia Augusta* to Mann and Cavafy
TRANSLATED BY RICHARD HOWARD
0-374-17709-0 FS&G $16.95

That Mighty Sculptor, Time
A posthumous collection of essays on Tantrism, Albrecht Durer, Andalusia, Christian feasts, and the Sanskrit erotic poem *Gita Govinda*, among other subjects
TRANSLATED BY WALTER KAISER & THE AUTHOR
0-374-27358-8 FS&G $22.00

Marguerite Yourcenar (photo by Carlos Freire)

Critical Studies

General Studies

Anna **Balakian**
Surrealism: The Road to the Absolute
"One of the clearest, as well as one of the earliest studies of the Surrealist movement…" —Mary Ann Caws
0-226-03560-3 CHICAGO PB $13.95

Germaine **Brée**
Twentieth Century French Literature
0-226-07196-0 CHICAGO PB $11.95

Wallace **Fowlie**
Dionysus in Paris: A Guide to Contemporary French Literature from Valéry to Sartre
See also EUROPE under HISTORY under THEATER in PERFORMING ARTS AND MEDIA
0-8446-0096-2 SMITH $11.55

Wilbur M. **Frohock**
Image and Theme: Studies in Modern French Fiction
Includes Georges Bernanos, André Malraux, Nathalie Sarraute, André Gide, and Roger Martin du Gard
EDITED BY SUSAN KEANE
0-674-44395-0 HARVARD PB $4.50

Tony **Judt**
Past Imperfect: French Intellectuals, 1944-1956
0-520-07921-3 CALIFORNIA $35.00
0-520-08650-3 CALIFORNIA PB $14.00

Jean-Philippe **Mathy**
Extrême-Occident: French Intellectuals and America
0-226-51063-8 CHICAGO $49.00
0-226-51064-6 CHICAGO PB $16.95

Lois **Oppenheim**, editor
Three Decades of the French New Novel
0-252-01158-9 ILLINOIS $28.95

Melinda **Porter**
Through Parisian Eyes: Reflections on Contemporary French Arts and Culture
0-19-504104-6 OXFORD $4.98

Roger **Shattuck**
The Banquet Years: The Origins of the Avant-Garde in France, 1885 to World War I
0-394-70415-0 VINTAGE PB $13.00

Martin **Sorrell** & Lawrence **Sail**, editors
Modern French Poetry: A Bilingual Anthology Covering Seventy Years
1-85610-005-7 FOREST PB $24.00

Tzvetan **Todorov**
On Human Diversity: Nationalism, Racism, and Exoticism in French Thought
0-674-63438-1 HARVARD $55.00
0-674-63439-X HARVARD PB $16.95

Mary Ann **Witt**
Existential Prisons: Captivity in Mid-20th Century French Literature
0-8223-0631-X DUKE $34.50

Studies of Individual Authors

Bettine **Knapp**
Antonin Artaud: Man of Vision
0-8040-0809-4 SWALLOW PB $14.95

Claude **Francis** & Fernandale **Gontier**
Simone de Beauvoir: A Life—A Love
0-312-02324-3 ST. MARTIN'S PB $12.95

Toril **Moi**
Simone de Beauvoir: The Making of an Intellectual Woman
0-631-19181-X BLACKWELL PB $22.95

Mark **Polizzotti**
Revolution of the Mind: The Life of André Breton
0-374-24982-2 FS&G $35.00

David **Sprintzen**
Camus: A Critical Examination
0-87722-544-3 TEMPLE $37.95

Albert Camus (photo courtesy of Knopf)

Merlin **Thomas**
Louis-Ferdinand Céline
0-8112-0754-4 NEW DIRECTIONS $16.50

Francis **Steegmuller**
Cocteau: A Biography
0-87923-606-X GODINE PB $17.95

Genevieve **Dormann**
Colette: A Passion for Life
0-89659-583-8 ABBEVILLE $49.95

Alain **Vircondelet**
Duras
1-56478-065-1 DALKEY ARCHIVE $24.95

Edmund **White**
Genet
0-394-57171-1 KNOPF $35.00
0-679-75479-2 VINTAGE PB $17.00

George **Painter**

Marcel Proust: A Biography

0-394-57669-1 RANDOM HOUSE $39.95

David **Bellos**

Georges Perec: A Life in Words

In Calvino's words, Perec was "so singular a literary personality that he bears absolutely no resemblance to anyone else." A tormented genius whose mother was killed in Auschwitz, Perec devoted his own truncated life (he died at 46) to such unprecedented literary experiments as *Life: A User's Manual*, *A Void*, and *W or The Memory of Childhood*: Bellos has written a biography as obsessively fascinating as the life and work it depicts

0-87923-980-8 GODINE $45.00

Wallace **Fowlie**

A Reading of Proust

0-8446-0627-8 SMITH $14.50

Julia **Kristeva**

Proust and the Sense of Time

See also **CRITICAL TEXTS** under **SEMIOTICS AND STRUCTURALISM AND AFTER** under **LITERARY THEORY**

0-231-08478-1 COLUMBIA $19.50

William **Sansom**

Proust

0-500-26020-6 THAMES & HUDSON PB $9.95

Roger **Shattuck**

Proust's Binoculars: A Study of Memory, Time and Recognition in *À la Recherche du temps perdu*

0-691-01403-5 PRINCETON PB $12.95

Stacy **Schiff**

Saint-Exupéry: A Biography

The beloved author of *The Little Prince* was, Schiff shows, a fantastic character himself: a French aristocrat, a pioneer aviator, and a swashbuckling international hero. But he was also broke, touchy, promiscuous, and difficult. Schiff brings us an uncommonly readable portrait of a legend

0-679-40310-8 KNOPF $30.00

Annie **Cohen-Solal**

Sartre: A Life

TRANSLATED BY ANNA CANCONGI

0-394-52525-6 PANTHEON $24.95

Jean-Paul Sartre

Elie **Wiesel**

All the Rivers Run to the Sea: Memoirs

See also **ELIE WIESEL** under **ART AND LITERATURE** under **THE HOLOCAUST** in **WORLD HISTORY AND CURRENT AFFAIRS**

0-679-43916-1 KNOPF $30.00

Josyane **Savigneau**

Marguerite Yourcenar: Inventing a Life

TRANSLATED BY JOAN E. HOWARD

0-226-73544-3 CHICAGO $25.00

Spanish Literature

The Middle Ages

Cola **Franzen**, editor

Poems of Arab Andalusia

0-87286-242-9 CITY LIGHTS PB $8.95

Rita **Hamilton** & Janet **Perry**, translators

The Poem of the Cid

The Spanish national epic of the Christian reconquest, in a prose translation with the original Spanish text on facing pages

0-14-044446-7 PENGUIN PB $9.95

W.S. **Merwin**, translator

The Poem of the Cid

A verse translation by a leading American poet

See also **MEDIEVAL LITERATURE**

0-452-01060-8 NEW AMERICAN LIBRARY PB $10.95

Fernando **de Rojas**

The Celestina: A 15th-Century Spanish Novel in Dialogue

A long play of emotional intrigue which, although it is written in dialogue form, is often considered the first great Spanish realist novel

TRANSLATED BY LESLEY BYRD SIMPSON

0-520-01177-5 CALIFORNIA PB $10.95

Juan **Ruiz, Archpriest of Hita**

The Book of True Love (El Libro de Buen Amor): A Bilingual Edition

"Well-executed, readable, and informative. The volume has an assured place among translations of the Spanish masterpieces"
— *Hispanic American Historical Review*

ORIGINAL TEXT EDITED BY ANTHONY ZAHAREAS

TRANSLATED BY SARALYN DALY

0-271-00523-8 PENN STATE $14.95

The Golden Age

Michael **Alpert**, translator

Two Spanish Picaresque Novels

Includes *Lazarillo de Tormes* and Francisco de Quevedo's *The Swindler (El Buscón)*

0-14-044211-1 PENGUIN PB $11.95

Eric **Bentley**, editor

Life Is a Dream & Other Spanish Classics

Includes, in addition to the title play by Calderón, Lope de Vega's *Fuente Ovejuna* and Tirso de Molina's *The Trickster of Seville*. Campbell's verse translations are infused with energy; they are also eminently accessible

TRANSLATED BY ROY CAMPBELL

1-55783-006-1 APPLAUSE THEATRE PB $10.95

Pedro **Calderón de la Barca**

"Calderón owes his great place in literature to his being the last heir in the direct line of the inheritance of the Middle Ages. Though he was trained by the Jesuits, and though his plays are full of classical allusions, and the subjects are often borrowed from heathen mythology or Roman history, he was in no sense a child of the Renaissance. His Latin quotations and his allusions to pagan mythology are like Ionic cornices or Corinthian pilasters placed upon the front of a building of the thirteenth century… Only in Spain was such a treatment possible in the middle of the seventeenth century."—Norman MacColl

Four Comedies by Pedro Calderón de la Barca

Includes *From Bad to Worse, The Secret Spoken Aloud, The Worst Is Not Always Certain,* and *The Advantages and Disadvantages of a Name.* "If some of the poetic quality of the plays is inevitably lost in translation, Calderón's mastery of stagecraft is everywhere apparent. He is as expert as Feydeau in developing dramatic complications from initial situations. One of Calderón's contemporaries praised him for having given to drama the logical form of the syllogism"— Kenneth Muir

TRANSLATED BY KENNETH MUIR

0-8131-1409-8 KENTUCKY $30.00

Guardate de la Agua Mansa

A lesser-known Calderon comedy, in a bilingual edition

TRANSLATED BY DAVID GITLITZ

0-939980-08-8 TRINITY PB $15.00

The Painter of His Dishonour

EDITED BY ALAN K.G. PATERSON

0-948230-88-6 BROWN PB $12.95

Three Comedies

0-8131-1546-9 KENTUCKY $30.00

Miguel **de Cervantes**

"Many people, not all of them Spanish, are on record as believing that Don Quixote *is the greatest prose fiction ever produced in the Western world...It epitomizes the spiritual world of European man at mid-career as* The Odyssey *and* The Iliad *do at his beginnings and as* The Brothers Karamazov *does in his decline. It is so vast, so ecumenical, that it serves only inadequately as the epic of Spain—a role better played by the more national* Poem of the Cid. Don Quixote *represents only a part of Spain, but a part that is far greater than the whole."—Kenneth Rexroth in* Classics Revisited

The Adventures of Don Quixote

TRANSLATED BY J. M. COHEN

0-14-044010-0 PENGUIN PB $8.95

The Adventures of Don Quixote de La Mancha

TRANSLATED BY TOBIAS SMOLLETT
INTRODUCTION BY CARLOS FUENTES
0-374-51943-9 FS&G PB........$18.00

Don Quixote de La Mancha

TRANSLATED BY CHARLES JARVIS
0-19-282726-X OXFORD PB........$7.95

Exemplary Stories

Cervantes' tales of pirates, gypsies, passion, and romance, with their realistic depictions of life in Toledo and Madrid, are supreme examples of his later fiction
TRANSLATED BY C. A. JONES
0-14-044248-0 PENGUIN PB........$9.95

The Trials of Persiles and Sigismunda

This baroque adventure novel, first published in 1617 and considered by Cervantes to be superior to *Don Quixote*, is now available for the first time in a modern English translation. Pirates, barbarians, sea serpents, and witches are among the participants in the highly eventful plot
TRANSLATED BY CELIA RICHMOND WELLER & CLARK A. COLAHAN
0-520-06315-5 CALIFORNIA........$45.00

Luis **de Gongora**

Polyphemus and Galatea

An elaborate mythological poem by Spain's master of Baroque verse
TRANSLATED BY GILBERT CUNNINGHAM
COMMENTARY BY ALEXANDER PARKER
0-292-72421-7 TEXAS........$17.95

Tirso **de Molina**

Tamar's Revenge

A revenge play on a Biblical theme, by the author of *The Trickster of Seville*
EDITED BY J.E. LYON
0-85668-324-8 ARIS & PHILLIPS PB........$22.00

Lope **de Vega**

The Duchess of Amalfi's Steward

EDITED AND TRANSLATED BY CYNTHIA RODRIGUEZ-BADENDYCK
0-919473-53-9 DOVEHOUSE PB........$8.00

Fuente Ovejuna

EDITED BY VICTOR DIXON
0-85668-328-0 ARIS & PHILLIPS PB........$22.00

The Knight of Olmedo (El Caballero de Olmedo)

A bilingual edition of one of Lope's great dramas of honor
TRANSLATED BY WILLARD KING
84-376-0309-9 LECTORUM PB........$6.50

La Dorotea

A unique mix of forms and genres: an autobiographical novel in the form of a multi-act play interspersed with poems, depicting the progress of a courtship in moods ranging from coarse farce to romantic tragedy
TRANSLATED BY ALAN TRUEBLOOD & EDWIN HONIG
0-674-50590-5 HARVARD........$32.50

Peribañez

EDITED BY J.M. LOYD
0-85668-439-2 ARIS & PHILLIPS PB........$19.95

Francisco **de Quevedo**

Dreams and Discourses

Baroque prose of almost Surrealist density
EDITED BY R.K. BRITTON
0-85668-353-1 ARIS & PHILLIPS PB........$25.00

St. John of the Cross

The poems of St. John of the Cross run to fewer than a thousand lines, yet their compressed fervor and lyricism establish him as one of the great mystical poets in any language. His prose works, taking the form of commentary on the poems, are major treatises on mystical theology

The Dark Night of the Soul

A prose elaboration on the significance of one of St. John's greatest poems
TRANSLATED BY ALLISON PEE
0-385-02930-6 DOUBLEDAY PB........$9.95

The Poems of St. John of the Cross

TRANSLATED WITH AN INTRODUCTION BY WILLIS BARNSTONE
0-8112-0449-9 NEW DIRECTIONS PB........$6.95

The Poems of St. John of the Cross

TRANSLATED BY JOHN FREDERICK NIMS
0-226-40111-1 CHICAGO PB........$12.95

The spring that brims and ripples—oh I know
  in dark of night.

Waters that flow forever and a day
through a lost country—oh I know the way
  in dark of night.

Its origin no knowing, for there's none.
But well I know, from here all sources run
  in dark of night.

No other thing, has such delight to give.
Here earth and wide heavens drink to live
  in dark of night.

SONG OF THE SOUL

St. Teresa of Avila

The Interior Castle

0-385-03643-4 DOUBLEDAY PB........$10.95

The Life of Saint Teresa of Avila by Herself

The autobiography of the great Carmelite mystic
TRANSLATED BY J. M. COHEN
0-14-044073-9 PENGUIN PB........$9.95

19th-Century Fiction

Leopoldo **Alas**

La Regenta

This realistic novel of provincial society is now acknowledged as a masterpiece
TRANSLATED BY JOHN RUTHERFORD
0-14-044346-0 PENGUIN PB........$12.95

The city of heroes was having a nap. The south wind, warm and languid, was coaxing grey-white clouds through the sky breaking them up as they drifted along. The streets of the city were silent, except for the rasping whispers of whirls of dust, rags, straw and paper on their way from gutter to gutter, pavement to pavement, street corner to street corner, now hovering, now chasing after one another, like butterflies which the air envelops in its invisible folds, draws together, and pulls apart. This miscellany of left-overs, remnants of refuse, would come together like throngs of gutter urchins, stay still for a moment as if half asleep, and then jump up and scatter in alarm, scaling walls as far as the loose panes of street lamps or the posters daubed up at street corners; and a feather might reach a third floor, and a grain of sand be stuck for days, or for years, in a shop window, embedded in lead.

LA REGENTA

Benito **Perez Galdós**

Fortunata and Jacinta: Two Stories of Married Women

Galdós' masterpiece is a panoramic view of 19th-century Spanish life
TRANSLATED BY AGNES MONCY GULLON
0-8203-0783-1 GEORGIA........$35.00
0-14-043305-8 PENGUIN PB........$13.95

Misericordia

TRANSLATED BY CHARLES DE SALIS
0-7818-0378-0 HIPPOCRENE PB........$16.95

Nazarin

A priest aspires to imitate Christ while wandering through the most poverty-stricken regions of Spain: the source for Bunuel's classic film
TRANSLATED BY JO LABANYI
0-19-282878-9 OXFORD PB........$9.95

Our Friend Manso

A poignant tale about a gentle, self-deceived soul
TRANSLATED BY ROBERT RUSSELL
0-231-06404-7 COLUMBIA........$30.50

That Bringas Woman

EDITED AND TRANSLATED BY CATHERINE JAGOE
0-460-87636-8 EVERYMAN'S PB........$7.95

The Generation of 1898

Antonio **Machado**

Selected Poems

A large-scale selection of the work of one of the greatest Spanish poets; the translations are excellent
TRANSLATED WITH AN INTRODUCTION BY ALAN TRUEBLOOD
0-674-04065-1 HARVARD........$28.00
0-674-04066-X HARVARD PB........$16.95

Selected Poems of Antonio Machado

TRANSLATED BY BETTY CRAIGE
0-8071-0456-6 LSU........$25.00

Times Alone: Selected Poems of Antonio Machado

TRANSLATED BY ROBERT BLY
0-8195-6081-2 WESLEYAN PB........$14.95

José **Ortega y Gasset**

History as a System

0-393-00122-9 NORTON PB........$10.95

Man and Crisis

TRANSLATED BY MILDRED ADAMS
0-393-00121-0 NORTON PB........$9.95

Man and People

TRANSLATED BY WILLARD R. TRASK
0-393-00123-7 NORTON PB........$9.95

The Revolt of the Masses
Ortega's renowned study of the forces society brings to bear on the individual
TRANSLATED BY ANTHONY KERRIGAN
FOREWORD BY SAUL BELLOW
0-268-01609-7 NOTRE DAME $33.50

What Is Philosophy?
0-393-00126-1 NORTON PB $9.95

Miguel **de Unamuno**

Abel Sanchez & Other Stories
0-89526-707-1 REGNERY PB $12.95

Three Exemplary Novels
Includes *The Marquis of Lumbria, Nothing Less than a Man,* and *Two Mothers.* Unamuno described these novellas as "glimpses of the deep mystery of man's soul and conscience"
TRANSLATED BY ANGEL FLORES
0-8021-5153-1 GROVE PB $7.95

The Tragic Sense of Life
TRANSLATED BY J. CRAWFORD FLITCH
0-486-20257-7 DOVER PB $8.95

The Tragic Sense of Life in Men and Nations
Unamuno argues that the only common ground for humanity is the abyss of tragic despair that threatens each individual life
See also **UNAMUNO** under **PHILOSOPHY** in **RELIGION, SPIRITUALITY, AND PHILOSOPHY**
TRANSLATED BY ANTHONY KERRIGAN
0-691-01820-0 PRINCETON PB $19.95

From Republicanism to the Spanish Civil War

Rafael **Alberti**

Concerning the Angels
Visionary poem-cycle by a leading member of the "Generation of 1927"
TRANSLATED BY CHRISTOPHER SAWYER-LAUCANNO
0-87286-297-6 CITY LIGHTS PB $12.95

The Lost Grove: The Autobiography of a Spanish Poet in Exile
TRANSLATED BY GABRIEL BERNS
0-520-04265-4 CALIFORNIA PB $12.00

Vicente **Aleixandre**

A Longing for the Light: Selected Poems
Often associated with Surrealism in the '20s and '30s, Aleixandre won the Nobel Prize for Literature in 1977
0-914742-89-2 COPPER CANYON PB $10.00

Shadow of Paradise
TRANSLATED BY HUGH A. HARTER
0-520-05599-3 CALIFORNIA $40.00
0-520-08257-5 CALIFORNIA PB $16.00

Felipe **Alfau**

Chromos
A late work, written in English, by the author of *Locos*
0-916583-52-X DALKEY ARCHIVE $19.95

Locos: A Comedy of Gestures
Although this Surreal classic was first published in 1936, Alfau's contribution to modern fiction is only now being recognized. "A witty, fantastic novel of modern Spain…demanding comparison not with literature but with art…the modernist novel as detective story"—Mary McCarthy
0-679-72846-5 VINTAGE PB $8.95

Sentimental Songs: La Poesia Cursi
TRANSLATED BY ILAN STAVANS
0-916583-98-8 DALKEY ARCHIVE $15.95
0-916583-99-6 DALKEY ARCHIVE PB $9.95

Luis **Cernuda**

Selected Poems of Luis Cernuda
Cernuda's poetry is delicate, sometimes Surrealist, always intensely personal
TRANSLATED BY REGINALD GIBBONS
0-520-02984-4 CALIFORNIA $37.50

Rosa **Chacel**

Acropolis
84-322-0488-9 PLANETA PB $14.20

The Maravillas District
TRANSLATED BY D.A. DEMERS
0-8032-6353-8 NEBRASKA PB $14.95

Memoirs of Leticia Valle
TRANSLATED BY CAROL MAIER
0-8032-6360-0 NEBRASKA PB $12.95

Miguel **Hernandez**

The Unending Lightning: The Selected Poems of Miguel Hernandez
Edwin Honig, the magisterial translator of Calderón, Lorca, and Pessoa, addresses himself to the work of Miguel Hernandez, the powerful lyrical poet who died at 32 in one of Franco's prisons. As the critic Timothy Baland has written: "Two centuries after Goya, Miguel Hernandez etched once again the disasters of war in poems bordered with the dark color of blood and silenced longings"
TRANSLATED BY EDWIN HONIG
0-935296-86-7 SHEEP MEADOW PB $10.95

Juan Ramón **Jiménez**

Platero and I
Prose poems about a companionable donkey
TRANSLATED BY ANTONIO DE NICOLAS
0-913729-06-X MARLOWE PB $9.95

Federico García **Lorca**

Blood Wedding & Yerma
Two of Lorca's most famous verse dramas, translated by leading poets
TRANSLATED BY LANGSTON HUGHES AND W.S. MERWIN
1-55936-080-1 THEATRE COMMUNICATIONS PB $12.95

Collected Poems
The first complete gathering in English of Lorca's poetry, this 800-page collection features the Spanish text on facing pages and a distinguished roster of translators including Alan Trueblood, Jerome Rothenberg, and William B. Logan
EDITED BY CHRISTOPHER MAURER
0-374-12624-0 FS&G $50.00

The Cricket Sings
Poems and songs for children
TRANSLATED BY WILL KIRKLAND
ILLUSTRATED BY MARIA HORVATH
0-8112-0734-X NEW DIRECTIONS PB $6.95

Federico García Lorca

Deep Song & Other Prose
The poet states his identification with the traditional Andalusian *canto jondo*
EDITED BY CHRISTOPHER MAURER
0-8112-0764-1 NEW DIRECTIONS $10.00

Four Puppet Plays, Play Without a Title, The Divan Poems, Prose Poems & Dramatic Pieces
TRANSLATED BY EDWIN HONIG
0-935296-94-8 SHEEP MEADOW PB $11.95

Ode to Walt Whitman & Other Poems
TRANSLATED BY CARLOS BAUER
0-87286-212-7 SUBTERRANEAN PB $8.95

Poem of the Deep Song
Sad poems of death and loss based on folk ballads of Andalusia, but with a surprisingly playful tone
TRANSLATED BY CARLOS BAUER
0-87286-205-4 SUBTERRANEAN PB $9.95

The Poet in New York
One of the most influential poetic sequences of the 20th century, in a new translation
TRANSLATED BY GREG SIMON
EDITED BY CHRISTOPHER MAURER
0-374-23539-2 FS&G $25.00
0-374-52083-6 FS&G PB $14.00

Selected Letters
EDITED AND TRANSLATED BY DAVID GERSHATOR
0-8112-0873-7 NEW DIRECTIONS PB $6.95

Selected Poems
The most complete collection in paperback of the great Spanish poet whose lyrical intensity takes readers straight to what he describes as "the dark root of the scream"
EDITED BY CHRISTOPHER MAURER
0-374-52352-5 NOONDAY PB $16.00

Three Plays: Blood Wedding, Yerma, & The House of Bernarda Alba

See also **EARLY 20TH-CENTURY** under **MODERN EUROPEAN DRAMA**

TRANSLATED BY MICHAEL DEWELL AND CARMEN ZAPATA

0-374-52332-0 NOONDAY PB.....$16.00

Ramón **Pérez de Ayala**

Belarmino and Apolonio

This truly Spanish but universal novel, published in 1921, centers on a dialogue between two philosophical shoemakers

TRANSLATED BY MURRAY BAUMGARTEN & GABRIEL BERNS

0-520-04958-6 CALIFORNIA PB.....$11.00

Pedro **Salinas**

My Voice Because of You

Salinas is best known for these poems of love and desire

TRANSLATED BY WILLIS BARNSTONE

PREFACE BY JORGE GUILLEN

0-87395-285-5 SUNY.....$19.50

The Franco Era and After

Francisco **Ayala**

Usurpers

Seven short stories about power and corruption, set in the Spanish Golden Age but reflecting events of the Civil War

INTRODUCTION AND TRANSLATION BY CAROLYN RICHMOND

0-14-018977-7 PENGUIN PB.....$10.95

Juan **Benet**

Return to Region

In this challenging novel, the mythical Region represents all that is paradoxical and mysterious about Spain

TRANSLATED BY GREGORY RABASSA

0-231-05456-4 COLUMBIA.....$39.50

0-231-05457-2 COLUMBIA PB.....$12.50

Julieta **Campos**

The Fear of Losing Eurydice

TRANSLATED BY LELAND H. CHAMBERS

1-56478-020-1 DALKEY ARCHIVE.....$19.95

1-56478-030-9 DALKEY ARCHIVE PB.....$8.95

Juan Luis **Cebrián**

Red Doll

A tale of political intrigue and passion in the post-Franco democratic government

TRANSLATED BY PHILIP SILVER

1-55584-145-7 GROVE.....$15.95

Camilo José **Cela**

The Family of Pascual Duarte

Life in the Franco era at its grimmest, in this confessional tale by the 1989 Nobel Prize winner

0-316-13432-5 LITTLE, BROWN PB.....$17.95

0-316-13431-7 LITTLE, BROWN PB.....$10.95

The Hive

Banned in Spain upon publication in 1951, this influential novel depicts the suffering postwar nation in a cinematic narrative style often imitated during the Franco years

INTRODUCTION BY ARTURO BAREA

0-374-17155-6 FS&G PB.....$19.95

Journey to the Alcarria

A traveler escaping the city's tumult discovers a surprising inner resilience among the rural poor

TRANSLATED BY FRANCES M. LOPEZ-MORILLAS

0-87113-379-2 ATLANTIC MONTHLY PB.....$8.95

Mazurka for Two Dead Men

This powerful novel of the Spanish Civil War is Cela's culminating achievement. Set in a remote rural community in Galicia (the author's home province), Cela's masterpiece is by turns melancholy and humorous, lyrical and earthy

0-8112-1222-X NEW DIRECTIONS.....$21.95

0-8112-1277-7 NEW DIRECTIONS PB.....$10.95

Mrs. Caldwell Speaks to Her Son

TRANSLATED BY J.S. BERNSTEIN

0-8014-9783-3 CORNELL PB.....$11.95

San Camilo, 1936: The Eve, Feast, and Octave of St. Camillus of the Year 1936 in Madrid

TRANSLATED BY JOHN H. POLT

0-8223-1196-8 DUKE PB.....$15.95

Gabriel **Celaya**

The Poetry of Gabriel Celaya

A bilingual edition of the works of an important modern poet concerned with social questions

TRANSLATED BY BETTY JEAN CRAIGE

0-8387-5062-1 BUCKNELL.....$29.50

Miguel **Delibes**

Five Hours with Mario

In a tour-de-force monologue, a middle-aged, middle class woman reflects on her existence as she contemplates her husband's corpse

TRANSLATED BY FRANCES LOPEZ-MORILLAS

0-231-06828-X COLUMBIA.....$35.00

The Hedge

"Delibes' evocation of totalitarianism is brilliantly convincing and the translation never misses a beat"—*Publishers Weekly*

TRANSLATED BY FRANCES LOPEZ-MORILLAS

0-231-05460-2 COLUMBIA.....$59.00

Jaime **Gil de Biedma**

Longing: Selected Poems

0-87286-277-1 CITY LIGHTS PB.....$9.95

Juan **Goytisolo**

Makabara

1-85242-266-1 SERPENT'S TAIL PB.....$14.99

Quarantine

TRANSLATED BY PETER BUSH

1-56478-044-9 DALKEY ARCHIVE.....$19.95

Space in Motion

TRANSLATED BY HELEN LANE

0-930829-03-4 LUMEN PB.....$9.95

The Virtues of the Solitary Bird

A man in a hospital is haunted by visions of St. John of the Cross. "Like all great imaginative writers, Goytisolo demands to be read with what William Blake called 'the burning fires of thought' "—*Boston Phoenix*

TRANSLATED BY HELEN LANE

1-85242-175-4 SERPENT'S TAIL PB.....$16.95

Marks of Identity

The first volume of the great trilogy which also includes *Count Julian* and *Juan the Landless*

1-85242-134-7 SERPENT'S TAIL PB.....$12.95

Count Julian

A masterpiece by one of the great writers of modern Spain. "*Count Julian* is the most terrible attack against the oppressive forces of a nation that I have ever read. Nothing that black has written against white, or woman against man, or poor against rich, or son against father, reaches quite the peak of intense hatred and horror that Goytisolo achieves in this novel"—Carlos Fuentes

TRANSLATED BY HELEN LANE

1-85242-158-4 SERPENT'S TAIL PB.....$12.95

Juan the Landless

1-85242-192-4 SERPENT'S TAIL PB.....$14.95

Almudena **Grandes**

The Ages of Lulu

A novel of sexual awakening which became an international bestseller. "Leads us into profound questions about the nature of sexuality and the morality of pleasure. Deeply disturbing" —*Seattle News*

0-8021-3348-7 GROVE PB.....$10.00

Julian **Rios**

Larva: Midsummer Night's Babel

Spain's answer to *Finnegans Wake*: a welter of puns and uproarious wordplay rendered into English with amazing faithfulness in this remarkable translation

TRANSLATED BY RICHARD ALAN FRANCIS WITH SUZANNE JILL LEVINE AND THE AUTHOR

0-916583-66-X DALKEY ARCHIVE.....$27.50

Poundemonium

TRANSLATED BY JOHN E. WOODS

1-56478-138-0 DALKEY ARCHIVE PB.....$13.50

Jesús Fernandez **Santos**

Extramuros

Two nuns are determined to rescue their convent from ruin during the Inquisition

TRANSLATED BY HELEN LANE

0-231-05552-8 COLUMBIA.....$34.50

9995711303 PLANETA PB.....$14.00

Esther **Tusquets**

The Same Sea as Every Summer

The inner journey of a disillusioned middle-aged woman. A powerful example of contemporary Spanish fiction, first published in 1978

0-8032-9416-6 NEBRASKA PB.....$9.95

Stranded

A woman whose husband has left her comes to terms with her abandonment. "Tusquets has opted courageously for the more dangerous path, that of shutting herself up alone with the theme of love and recovery from love…And she has succeeded without a doubt in creating her best work"—Carmen Martin Gaite

0-916583-83-X DALKEY ARCHIVE.....$19.95

0-916583-91-0 DALKEY ARCHIVE PB.....$9.95

Irene **Vilar**

A Message from God in the Atomic Age

TRANSLATED FROM THE SPANISH BY GREGORY RABASSA

0-679-42281-1 PANTHEON $24.00

Catalán Literature

The literary traditions of Catalonia have produced masterpieces in both the medieval and the modern era. This body of work is only beginning to make its appearance in English translation.

Medieval

Ramon **Llull**

Blanquerna

A late-13th-century novel. "[Llull's] fictional works contain such startling and imaginative conceptions that they have become an imperishable part of early Spanish literature. Chief of these books is *Blanquerna,* a kind of Catholic *Pilgrim's Progress*"—Martin Gardner

TRANSLATED WITH AN INTRODUCTION BY E. A. PEERS

0-87052-376-7 HIPPOCRENE PB $14.95

Doctor Illuminatus: A Ramon Llull Reader

EDITED BY ANTHONY BONNER

0-691-03406-0 PRINCETON $69.50

0-691-00091-3 PRINCETON PB $17.95

The New Rhetoric of Ramon Llull (1232-1316): Text and Translation of his Rhetorica Nova

EDITED BY MARK D. JOHNSTONE

1-88039-303-4 HERMAGORAS PB $12.95

Selected Works of Ramon Llull (1232-1316)

Theologian, philosopher, novelist and martyr, Ramon Llull is one of Catalonia's major medieval writers. A two-volume set

TRANSLATED & EDITED BY ANTHONY BONNER

0-691-07288-4 PRINCETON $225.00

Joanot **Martorell** & Marti Joan **De Galba**

Tirant lo Blanc: The Complete Translation

A classic of medieval chivalric literature in a splendid translation by David Rosenthal

TRANSLATED WITH AN INTRODUCTION BY DAVID ROSENTHAL

0-8204-1688-6 LANG PB $39.95

Modern

While Catalán letters flourished during the late 19th and early 20th centuries, the language as a literary idiom was suppressed throughout the Franco regime. In recent years, it has once again been at the forefront of innovation in peninsular literature.

Salvadore **Espriu**

La Pell de Brau

The foremost among the Catalán postwar poets, Espriu in this work views Spanish life through images from Jewish history

TRANSLATED BY BURTON RAFFEL

0-910395-28-4 MARLBORO PB $9.00

J. V. **Foix**

When I Sleep, Then I See Clearly: Selected Poems

The selection spans the entire career of Catalonia's major avant-garde poet, who won Spain's 1985 National Prize for Literature

TRANSLATED BY DAVID ROSENTHAL

0-89255-130-5 PERSEA PB $12.95

Kathleen **McNerney**, editor

On Our Own Behalf: Women's Tales from Catalonia

0-8032-3122-9 NEBRASKA $35.00

Merce **Rodoreda**

Camellia Street

With scenes of hallucinatory intensity, this unforgettable novel tells the story of a woman's life in war-torn Barcelona of the '40s and '50s. "What scares me about this book is that it means what it says and never wavers; it scares me and steals me and delights me. Merce Rodoreda is the writer I cannot stop talking about"—Alberto Rios

TRANSLATED BY DAVID H. ROSENTHAL

1-55597-192-X GRAY WOLF $20.00

It was my laugh that won them over, and since they were old and childless they took in me. One lady who lived nearby said maybe my father was a murderer and adopting an unknown child was a big responsibility. The gentleman of the house let the ladies talk.

CAMELLIA STREET

My Christina & Other Stories

TRANSLATED BY DAVID ROSENTHAL

0-915308-65-7 GRAY WOLF PB $11.00

The Time of the Doves

This major work of modern Catalán fiction presents a powerful narration of a woman's life in postwar Barcelona

TRANSLATED BY DAVID ROSENTHAL

0-915308-75-4 GRAY WOLF PB $12.00

Anthologies

Linton **Barrett**, editor

Five Centuries of Spanish Literature: From The Cid Through the Golden Age

0-8384-3754-0 HEINLE & HEINLE PB $31.95

J.M. **Cohen**, editor

The Penguin Book of Spanish Verse

The Spanish texts, with literal prose transitions on facing pages

0-14-058570-2 PENGUIN PB $14.95

Angel **Flores**, editor

Great Spanish Plays in English Translation

A good standard survey, from the middle ages to the 20th century

0-486-26898-5 DOVER PB $10.95

Louis **Hammer** & Sarah **Sarashyiffer**, translators

Recent Poetry of Spain: A Bilingual Anthology

0-937584-08-8 SACHEM PB $11.95

Studies in Spanish Literature

General Studies

Richard **Chandler** & Kessel **Schwartz**

New History of Spanish Literature

0-8071-1699-8 LSU $45.00

Andrew P. **Debicki**

Spanish Poetry of the 20th Century: Modernity and Beyond

0-8131-0835-7 KENTUCKY PB $14.95

Marie-Lise Gazarian **Gautier**

Interviews with Spanish Writers

0-916583-81-3 DALKEY ARCHIVE PB $14.95

Paul **Ilie**

Literature and Inner Exile: Authoritarian Spain, 1939-1975

0-8018-2424-9 OLYMPIC $3.98

Marshall **Schneider** & Irwin **Stern**, editors

Modern Spanish and Portuguese Literatures

Selections from criticism on 65 Spanish, Catalán, and Galician writers of the 20th century

See also **CRITICAL STUDIES** under **PORTUGUESE LITERATURE**

0-8044-3280-5 UNGAR $85.00

Studies of Individual Authors

Edwin **Honig**

Calderòn and the Seizures of Honor

0-674-09075-6 HARVARD $25.00

Robert **Horst**

Calderòn: The Secular Plays

0-8131-1440-3 KENTUCKY $29.00

Vladimir **Nabokov**

Lectures on Don Quixote

0-15-649540-6 HARCOURT BRACE PB $7.95

Ian **Gibson**

Federico Garcìa Lorca: A Life

0-679-77401-7 PANTHEON PB $18.00

Francisco Garcìa **Lorca**

In the Green Morning: Memories of Federico

Lorca remembered by his brother

TRANSLATED BY CHRISTOPHER MAURER

0-8112-0969-5 NEW DIRECTIONS $23.50

0811-09709 NEW DIRECTIONS PB $12.95

Martin **Nozick**

Miguel de Unamuno: The Agony of Belief

0-691-01366-7 PRINCETON PB $14.95

Donald R. **Larson**

The Honor Plays of Lope de Vega

0-674-40628-1 HARVARD $24.95

Portuguese Literature

Although Portugal has produced major writers who have garnered fame within Europe, little attention has been paid to them in the United States and few translations exist. Writers such as Camões, Eça de Queiroz, and Fernando Pessoa deserve to be more widely known and appreciated.

Medieval and Renaissance

Portugal took form as a nation during the long period of the Christian reconquest of the Iberian peninsula and became totally unified by the end of the 13th century, although Castilian threats to the new country's independence continued throughout the 14th century. In the age of exploration, Portugal acquired a far-flung empire, which by the mid-16th century included parts of Africa, Asia, and the Americas. Lisbon was Europe's emporium.

Luis **de Camões**

The Lusiads

Portugal's national poem, an extraordinary epic blending the voyages of Vasco da Gama with elements from classical mythology. Atkinson's straightforward prose version emphasizes Camões' masterful gifts as a storyteller

TRANSLATED BY WILLIAM ATKINSON

0-14-044026-7 PENGUIN PB $8.95

The Lusiads

TRANSLATED WITH AN INTRODUCTION BY LEONARD BACON

9-9916-3239-5 HISPANIC SOCIETY PB $10.00

T.F. **Earle**

The Muse Reborn: The Poetry of Antonio Ferreira

Selections from and an analysis of the works of a great poet who defended the use of the Portuguese language at a time when Castilian was the fashionable peninsular idiom

0-19-815856-4 CLARENDON $59.00

Barbara Hughes **Fowler**, translator

Songs of a Friend: Love Lyrics of Medieval Portugal

0-8078-2271-X NORTH CAROLINA $29.95

0-8078-4574-4 NORTH CAROLINA PB $13.95

Fernão **Lopes**

The English in Portugal

Selections from this important medieval historian's vivid chronicles of court intrigues during the reigns of Dom Fernando and Dom Joao I

TRANSLATED WITH AN INTRODUCTION BY D.W. LOMAX & R.J. OAKLEY

0-85668-341-8 ARIS & PHILLIPS $49.95

0-85668-342-6 ARIS & PHILLIPS PB $25.00

The 19th Century

The cost to Portugal of the glorious empire was centuries of decadence. The Napoleonic invasions and liberal revolutions of the early 19th century and the independence of Brazil in 1822 gave rise to a new understanding of the nation's identity—and a preoccupation with the nation's very existence.

João **Almeida Garrett**

Travels in My Homeland

In the style of Sterne's *Tristram Shandy*, Garrett takes us on a psychological "voyage" through rural Portugal during the era of the liberal revolutions

TRANSLATED WITH AN INTRODUCTION BY JOHN M. PARKER

0-7206-0663-2 DUFOUR $22.50

Eça de Queiroz

The Illustrious House of Ramires

0-8112-1264-5 NEW DIRECTIONS PB $14.95

The Mandarin and Other Stories

0-7818-0214-8 HIPPOCRENE PB $11.95

Relic

0-946626-94-4 HIPPOCRENE PB $16.95

The 20th Century

The 40-year dictatorship of Antonio de Oliveira Salazar kept Portugal an undeveloped, inward-looking nation. African liberation movements, which began in the early '60s, eventually led to the downfall of the regime in 1974 and the subsequent loss of the colonial empire. A new democratic government is gradually healing old wounds and participating in European affairs through membership in the European Economic Community.

Eugenio **de Andrade**

The Inhabited Heart: The Selected Poems of Eugenio de Andrade

A bilingual edition of poems by a leading contemporary poet

TRANSLATED BY ALEXIS LEVITIN

INTRODUCTION BY PILAR GOMEZ BEDATE

0-912288-24-8 PERIVALE PB $7.95

Antonio Lobo **Antunes**

Act of the Damned

TRANSLATED BY RICHARD ZENITH

0-8021-1575-6 GROVE $22.00

0-8021-3476-9 GROVE PB $12.00

An Explanation of the Birds

TRANSLATED BY RICHARD ZENITH

0-8021-3420-3 GROVE PB $11.00

Fado Alexandrino

"A mad amalgam of Dos Passos and Céline" —*NY Times Book Review*

TRANSLATED BY GREGORY RABASSA

0-8021-3421-1 GROVE PB $14.00

José Rodrigues **Migueis**

Steerage & Ten Other Stories

Compassionate, witty tales of immigrants and the unfortunate by a Portuguese writer self-exiled in New York

EDITED WITH A FOREWORD BY GEORGE MONTEIRO

0-943722-06-3 GAVEA-BROWN PB $6.00

Fernando **Pessoa**

Always Astonished: Selected Prose

TRANSLATED BY EDWIN HONIG

0-87286-228-3 CITY LIGHTS PB $8.95

The Book of Disquiet

TRANSLATED BY MARGARET COSTA

1-85242-204-1 SERPENT'S TAIL PB $15.99

Message-Mensagem

TRANSLATED BY JONATHAN GRIFFIN

0-9513753-8-5 SMALL PRESS PB $16.00

Poems of Fernando Pessoa

One of the greatest and least-known of modern poets, Pessoa created a series of personalities—heteronyms—for himself, each with its own style and vision

TRANSLATED BY SUSAN BROWN & EDWIN HONIG

0-88001-123-8 ECCO PB $10.50

The Surprise of Being

Poems that Pessoa published under his own name; many are characteristically reflexive considerations on the art of poetry

TRANSLATED BY JAMES GREENE & CLARA DE MAFRA AZEVEDO

0-946162-23-9 DUFOUR $25.00

Jose **Saramago**

The Stone Raft

TRANSLATED BY GIOVANNI PONTIERO

0-15-185198-0 HARCOURT BRACE $23.00

Jorge **de Sena**

By the Rivers of Babylon & Other Stories

A collection of stories written between 1946 and 1964, many involving historical figures

EDITED BY DAPHNE PATAI

0-8135-1388-X RUTGERS $19.95

Metamorphoses

TRANSLATED BY FRANCESCO COTA FAGUNDES & JAMES HOULIHAN

0-914278-55-X COPPER BEECH PB $9.95

Critical Studies

Alfred **Hower** & Richard **Preto-Rodas**, editors

Empire in Transition: The Portuguese World at the Time of Camões

Essays on many aspects of Portuguese, Brazilian, African, and European culture

0-8130-0790-9 FLORIDA PB $39.95

George **Monteiro**, editor

The Man Who Never Was: Essays on Fernando Pessoa

0-943722-07-1 LUSO BRAZILIAN $17.50
0-943722-08-X GAVEA-BROWN PB $7.50

Marshall **Schneider** & Irwin **Stern**, editors

Modern Spanish and Portuguese Literatures

Selections from criticism on 65 Spanish, Catalán, and Galician writers of the 20th century

See also **GENERAL STUDIES** under **STUDIES IN SPANISH LITERATURE** under **SPANISH LITERATURE**

0-8044-3280-5 UNGAR $85.00

Ronald **Sousa**

The Rediscoverers: Major Writers in the Portuguese Literature of National Regeneration

Essays on Camões, Eça de Queiroz, Pessoa and others

0-271-00300-6 PENN STATE $22.50

Italian Literature

The Middle Ages

The troubadour inspired love lyrics of the so-called Sicilian school of the 13th century represent the first literature to be written in Italian rather than Latin. But it was the Florentine Dante who properly forged a new national literary language at the beginning of the 14th century by electing to write in his native Tuscan dialect. In refining and strengthening the vernacular, the great Italian writers of the 14th century—Dante, Cavalcanti, Petrarch, Boccaccio—established one of the great European literatures.

Giovanni **Boccaccio**

Boccaccio's Decameron*—a series of 100 tales told by ten Florentines during the plague of 1348 over ten days—became the first classic of European prose fiction, a book that has been said to herald the passage of Western civilization out of the Middle Ages. It has proved an enduring sourcebook into which other writers and artists have been dipping for centuries.*

The Corbaccio

A misogynistic satire, influential in its day

TRANSLATED BY ANTHONY CASSELL

0-86698-154-3 MRTS/LNG 99 PB $8.95

The Decameron

EDITED BY MARK MUSA & PETER BONDANELLA

0-393-09132-5 NORTON PB $10.95

The Elegy of Lady Fiammetta

EDITED AND TRANSLATED BY MARIANGELA CAUSA-STEINDLER AND THOMAS MAUCH

0-226-06276-7 CHICAGO PB $11.95

Dante

"If we start from his predecessors, Dante's language is a well-nigh incomprehensible miracle. There were great poets among them. But compared with theirs, his style is so immeasurably richer in directness, vigor, and subtlety, he knows and uses such an immeasurably greater stock of forms, he expresses the most varied phenomena and subjects with such immeasurably superior assurance and firmness, that we come to the conclusion that this man used his language to discover the world anew."
—Erich Auerbach in Mimesis

The Portable Dante

This anthology features Lawrence Binyon's outstanding translation of *The Divine Comedy,* of which Ezra Pound wrote: "Binyon sheds more light on Dante than any translation I have ever seen. Almost more than any translation sheds on *any* original." Also included are Dante Gabriel Rossetti's version of *The New Life* and a selection of prose writings

EDITED BY PAOLO MILANO

0-14-015032-3 PENGUIN PB $12.50

The Portable Dante

TRANSLATED BY MARK MUSA

0-14-023114-5 PENGUIN PB $14.95

The Inferno of Dante

A new verse translation by an important American poet

TRANSLATED BY ROBERT PINSKY

See also **POETRY SINCE 1945** under **20TH-CENTURY AMERICAN POETRY** in **LITERATURE OF THE AMERICAS**

0-374-52452-1 NOONDAY PB $8.00

Dante's Rime

TRANSLATED BY PATRICK DIEHL

0-691-06409-1 PRINCETON $38.00

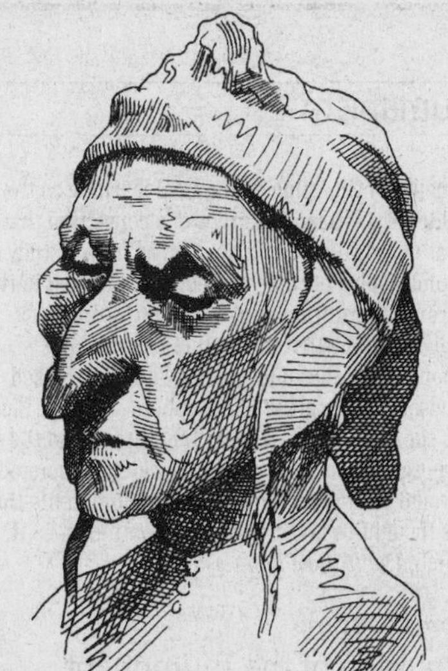

Dante

De Vulgari Eloquentia: Dante's Book of Exile

A translation, with lengthy commentary, of Dante's treatise (written in Latin) on the proper use of vernacular Italian as a literary language. "In all literary history we can find no more full or significant document concerning vernacular writing in the Middle Ages"—from the translator's introduction

TRANSLATED BY MARIANNE SHAPIRO

0-8032-4211-5 NEBRASKA $40.00

The Divine Comedy

John Ciardi's eminently readable translation, loose at times but full of narrative drive, was admired by Archibald MacLeish and John Crowe Ransom

TRANSLATED BY JOHN CIARDI

Volume 1 Inferno

See also **MEDIEVAL LITERATURE**

0-679-60209-7 MODERN LIBRARY $15.50

Volume 2 Purgatorio

0-679-60210-0 MODERN LIBRARY $15.50

Volume 3 Paradiso

0-679-60211-9 MODERN LIBRARY $15.50

The Divine Comedy

A definitive prose version with facing Italian text and extensive commentary. "What a triumphant joy it is to see the honest light of literality take over again, after ages of meretricious paraphrase"—Vladimir Nabokov

TRANSLATION AND COMMENTARY BY CHARLES SINGLETON

Volume 1 Inferno

See also **MEDIEVAL LITERATURE**

0-691-01896-0 PRINCETON PB $14.95

Commentary

0-691-01895-2 PRINCETON PB $24.95

Text and Commentary

0-691-09855-7 PRINCETON $110.00
0-691-01897-9 PRINCETON PB $34.00

Volume 2 Purgatorio

0-691-01909-6 PRINCETON PB $15.95

Commentary

See also **MEDIEVAL LITERATURE**

0-691-01910-X PRINCETON PB $29.95

Text and Commentary

0-691-09887-5 PRINCETON $125.00
0-691-01911-8 PRINCETON PB $40.50

Volume 3 Paradiso

0-691-01912-6 PRINCETON PB $15.95

Commentary

0-691-01913-4 PRINCETON PB $24.95

Text and Commentary

0-691-09888-3 PRINCETON $110.00
0-691-01914-2 PRINCETON PB $49.50

The Divine Comedy

An inexpensive paperback edition with facing Italian text

TRANSLATED BY ALLEN MANDELBAUM

Volume 1 Inferno

0-553-21339-3 BDD PB $5.95

Volume 2 Purgatorio

0-553-21344-X BDD PB $5.95

Volume 3 Paradiso

0-553-21204-4 BDD PB $5.95

The Divine Comedy

Mark Musa's iambic version is clear and musical

Volume 1 Inferno

0-14-044441-6 PENGUIN PB $9.95

Volume 2 Purgatory

0-14-044442-4 PENGUIN PB $9.95

Volume 3 Paradise

0-14-044443-2 PENGUIN PB $9.95

The Divine Comedy of Dante Alighieri

"A Dante with clarity, eloquence, terror, and profoundly moving depths"—Robert Fagles. The artwork and typography of this edition have also received much praise

TRANSLATED BY ALLEN MANDELBAUM
ILLUSTRATED BY BARRY MOSER

Volume 1 Inferno

0-520-02712-4 CALIFORNIA $50.00

Volume 2 Purgatorio

0-520-04516-5 CALIFORNIA $50.00

Volume 3 Paradiso

0-520-04517-3 CALIFORNIA $50.00

The Divine Comedy

A strong translation by one of contemporary Britain's best poets—succeeds in capturing the terse, aphoristic qualities of Dante's style

TRANSLATED BY C.H. SISSON

0-19-283073-2 OXFORD PB $17.95

La Vita Nuova

A spiritual autobiography, interspersed with poems, in which Dante—writing some years after his beloved Beatrice's death—charts his devotion to her

TRANSLATED BY BARBARA REYNOLDS

0-14-044216-2 PENGUIN PB $8.95

Petrarch

"Petrarch's example aroused in poets all over Europe the hope of achieving classic expressiveness in the mother tongue. The deepest tributes to Petrarch's influence are in poets great enough to make his lessons their own, poets like Ariosto, Michelangelo, Ronsard, Garcilaso de la Vega, Gongora, Camões, Sidney, and Donne. He stood for a new sensibility that could combine aristocratic reserve and elegance, wit, allusiveness, Virgilian evocativeness and emotional depth, symbolic complexity—in classically balanced, perfected form."—Robert Durling in Petrarch's Lyric Poems

Petrarch's Lyric Poems: The Rime Sparse & Other Lyrics

A complete prose translation of Petrarch's major collection of more than 350 lyrics, with Italian text

EDITED & TRANSLATED BY ROBERT M. DURLING

0-674-66345-4 HARVARD $46.50
0-674-66348-9 HARVARD PB $17.95

Selections from the Canzoniere & Other Works

A fluently translated selection of love lyrics which Petrarch titled *Rerum vulgarium fragmenta*—"short pieces in the vernacular," and which became a standard model for love poetry; also includes an interesting autobiographical fragment addressed to Laura, the poet's Beatrice

EDITED & TRANSLATED BY MARK MUSA

0-19-281707-8 OXFORD PB $6.95

In my younger days I struggled constantly with an overwhelming but pure love-affair—my only one, and I would have struggled with it longer had not premature death, bitter but salutary for me, extinguished the cooling flames. I certainly wish I could say that I have always been entirely free from desires of the flesh, but I would be lying if I did. I can, however, surely say this: that, while I was being carried away by the ardour of my youth and by my temperament, I always detested such sins from the depths of my soul. When I was nearing the age of forty, and my vigour and passions were still strong, I renounced abruptly not only those bad habits, but even the very recollection of them—as if I had never looked at a woman. This I consider to be among my greatest blessings, and I thank God, who freed me while I was still sound and vigorous from that vile slavery which I always found hateful. But let us turn to other matters now.—From "Letter to Posterity"

SELECTIONS FROM THE CANZONIERE & OTHER WORKS

The Renaissance

Humanism

"A belief in the value of classical learning as the molder of a citizen's character, a conviction that great moral value could be derived from a study of its philosophy, became as deeply embedded in the Florentine tradition as it did in 19th-century England. And when the Medici founded and encouraged a Platonic academy and patronized handsomely the great philosophers—Ficino, Pico, and the rest—they were no innovators, and the purpose of their patronage was widely understood. It would strengthen an attitude to human life that was thought to be singularly Florentine."— J.H. Plumb, *The Italian Renaissance*

Giordano **Bruno**

Expulsion of the Triumphant Beast

EDITED BY ARTHUR D. IMERTI

0-8032-6104-7 NEBRASKA PB $12.95

The Ash Wednesday Supper

Dialogues on the Copernican heliocentric theory, on magic, and on Bruno's concept of an animated cosmos

See also **GIORDANO BRUNO** under **RENAISSANCE PHILOSOPHERS** under **PHILOSOPHY** in **RELIGION, SPIRITUALITY, AND PHILOSOPHY**

EDITED AND TRANSLATED BY EDWARD A. GOSSELIN & LAWRENCE S. LERNER

0-8020-7469-3 TORONTO PB $20.95

Niccolò **Machiavelli**

The radical innovation of Machiavelli was to base political theory on experience rather than edifying ideals; in his work he drew on history as well as on his own career as a Florentine diplomat. His ambiguous legacy includes both modern empirical political science and the realpolitik of the nation state as a law unto itself.

Discourses on Livy

See also **CLASSICS** under **POLITICAL THOUGHT** in **SOCIAL STUDIES**

TRANSLATED BY HARVEY C. MANSFIELD

0-226-50035-7 CHICAGO $34.95

The Portable Machiavelli

Contains *The Prince*, excerpts from *The Discourses* (Machiavelli's commentary on Roman history), and other writings

TRANSLATED BY MARK MUSA & PETER BONDANELLA

0-14-015092-7 VIKING PB $14.95

Angelo **Poliziano**

The Stanze of Angelo Poliziano

A picturesque celebration of a courtly jousting tournament and the landscape in which it took place

TRANSLATED BY DAVID QUINT

0-271-00937-3 PENN STATE PB $14.95

Antonia **Pulci**

Florentine Drama for Convent and Festival: Seven Sacred Plays

EDITED AND TRANSLATED BY JAMES WYATT COOK

0-226-68516-0 CHICAGO $33.00
0-226-68517-9 CHICAGO PB $14.00

Artists

Benvenuto **Cellini**

The Autobiography of Benvenuto Cellini

A vivid picture of the Renaissance sculptor and metalsmith, and an unforgettable evocation of high life and low life in 16th-century Italy

EDITED BY GOERGE BULL

0-14-044049-6 PENGUIN PB $9.95

Leonardo da Vinci

The Notebooks of Leonardo da Vinci

A one-volume selection from Leonardo's voluminous journals

EDITED BY IRMA RICHTER

0-19-281538-5 OXFORD PB $6.95

Michelangelo **Buonarotti**

Life, Letters and Poetry

An anthology of sonnets and other writings, with a contemporary biography

See also **ARTISTS ON ART** under **ART HISTORY: GENERAL STUDIES** in **ART**

EDITED BY GEORGE BULL

0-19-281603-9 OXFORD PB $8.95

The Poetry of Michelangelo: An Annotated Translation

The best available translation

See also **CONTEMPORARY SOURCES** under **ITALY** under **EUROPEAN ART: THE RENAISSANCE** in **ART**

TRANSLATED BY JAMES M. SASLOW

0-300-04960-9 YALE $55.00

0-300-05509-9 YALE PB $22.00

Giorgio **Vasari**

Lives of the Artists

Perhaps the most entertaining work of art history ever written. This generous selection includes an appendix correcting some of Vasari's attributions and biographical data. Impresario and Michelangelo-idolater, Vasari writes candidly and engagingly

Volume 1

See also **CONTEMPORARY SOURCES** under **ITALY** under **EUROPEAN ART: THE RENAISSANCE** in **ART**

0-14-044500-5 PENGUIN PB $10.95

Volume 2

0-14-044460-2 PENGUIN PB $11.95

Lives of the Painters, Sculptors, and Architects

A complete edition

TRANSLATED BY GASTON DE VERE

0-679-45101-3 KNOPF $60.00

Epic Poets of the Renaissance

Ludovico **Ariosto**

Cinque Canti/Five Cantos

TRANSLATED BY ALEXANDER SHEERS AND DAVID QUINT

0-520-20009-8 CALIFORNIA PB $18.00

Orlando Furioso

"The *Furioso* is a book unique in its kind, and can be—or should I say, must be?—read without reference to any other book either before or after it. It is a world of its own that one can travel the length and breadth of, going in, coming out again, and losing oneself in it"—Italo Calvino. A straightforward prose version

TRANSLATED BY GUIDO WALDMAN

0-19-281636-5 OXFORD PB $15.95

Orlando Furioso

Alive with self-mockery and mockery of its audience, this famous work, depicting a world sparkling with chivalry, magic, and romance, greatly influenced Elizabethan and 17th-century English writers. Barbara Reynolds' skillful translation employs rhymed octaves

Volume 1

0-14-044311-8 PENGUIN PB $15.95

Volume 2

0-14-044310-X PENGUIN PB $14.95

Matteo **Boiardo**

Orlando Innamorato

The classic tale of Charlemagne's knight, Orlando

TRANSLATED BY CHARLES ROSS

0-19-282438-4 OXFORD PB $13.95

Torquato **Tasso**

A great poet of the Italian High Renaissance and one of its most tragic figures, Tasso was also a distinguished critic.

Tasso's Dialogues: A Selection, with the Discourse of the Art of the Dialogue

The subjects covered include philosophy, morality, literature, and aesthetics

TRANSLATED BY CARNES LORD & DAIN TRAFTON

0-520-04464-9 CALIFORNIA $35.00

0-520-04985-3 CALIFORNIA PB $12.95

Fiction

Pietro **Aretino**

Aretino's Dialogues

An erotic classic in the form of a dialogue between two women. "Aretino is an extraordinary storyteller…He possessed an exceptionally quick, clear, sharp and precise eye"—Alberto Moravia

0-941419-96-7 MARSILIO PB $16.95

Pamela Joseph **Benson**, editor

Italian Tales from the Age of Shakespeare

0-460-87551-5 EVERYMAN'S PB $12.50

Laura **Martines**, editor

An Italian Renaissance Sextet

Six 15th-century tales, including the brilliant and cruel story of "The Fat Woodcarver"

1-56886-011-0 MARSILIO PB $18.95

The Tradition of Italian Theater

Eric **Bentley**, editor

The Servant of Two Masters & Other Italian Classics

The title play by Goldoni plus Gozzi's *The King Stag,* Machiavelli's *The Mandrake,* and Beolco's *Ruzzante Returns from the Wars*

0-936839-20-1 APPLAUSE THEATRE PB $10.95

Carlo **Goldoni**

The Coffee House

A comic masterpiece from 1750

TRANLSATED BY JEREMY PARZAN

0-941419-85-1 MARSILIO PB $17.00

The Holiday Trilogy

A satirical portrait of Venetian society. "Oldcorn has finally given us a text that transports the Venetian scene to the ear and psyche of an English-speaking audience"—Jackson Cope

TRANSLATED BY ANTHONY OLDCORN

0-941419-60-6 MARSILIO $28.00

0-941419-61-4 MARSILIO PB $17.00

Niccolò **Machiavelli**

The Comedies of Machiavelli

A bilingual edition including *The Woman from Andros, The Mandrake,* and *Clizia.* Machiavelli's talents were not limited to history and political theory. His trenchant *Mandragola (The Mandrake)* is considered by many to be *the* great Italian play

TRANSLATED BY DAVID SICES & JAMES ATKINSON

0-87451-330-8 NEW ENGLAND PB $19.95

Pietro **Metastasio**

Three Melodramas

Includes *Dido Abandoned, Demetrius,* and *The Olympiad.* Metastasio was the chief literary architect of *opera seria,* and his librettos were set to music by Mozart, Gluck, Handel, and Scarlatti

TRANSLATED BY JOSEPH FUCILLA

0-8131-1400-4 KENTUCKY $18.00

Henry F. **Salerno**, editor & translator

Scenarios of the Commedia del l'Arte: Flaminio Scala's Il Teatro delle Favole Rappresentative

A fascinating 1611 treatise which provides a meticulous cataloguing of all the stock situations of Italian comedy

0-87910-133-4 LIMELIGHT PB $22.50

The 19th Century

The 19th century witnessed a decisive literary rebirth, even though its major figures are still insufficiently known and some (Foscolo, Carducci, Pascoli) are barely represented in English. The stylistic distance covered in a single century can be measured by the differences between the disenchanted classicism of Leopardi at its outset, the epic historical pageantry of Manzoni at mid-century, and finally the Sicilian *verismo*—realism—of Verga, signaling a breakthrough of regional elements and harsh economic realities. Curiously enough it is Leopardi, with his clear-eyed contemplation of nothingness, who strikes the most modern note.

Gabriele **d'Annunzio**

The Flame

A sensational novel based on the author's love affair with actress Eleonora Duse. "The sexual conflict, mythified and aestheticized, is played out against a sumptuous evocation of Venice in autumn"—Peter Hainsworth

TRANLSATED BY SUSAN BASSNETT

0-941419-89-4 MARSILIO $24.00

L'Innocente (The Victim)

TRANSLATED BY GEORGINA HARTING

0-781-80006-4 HIPPOCRENE $14.95

Giuseppe Giocchinio **Belli**

The Sonnets of Giuseppe Belli

A scholarly and comprehensive version

TRANSLATED BY MILLER WILLIAMS

0-8071-0762-X LSU $22.50

Giacomo **Leopardi**

Italy's greatest 19th-century lyric poet and philosopher who saw a pressing need for human brotherhood to counter the brutality of

life and nature

The Moral Essays

Leopardi's masterpiece, a book which creates its own genre: in tones at once lyrical and bitterly lucid, he invents a mythology of the death of mythology, a hymn of non-belief

TRANSLATED BY PATRICK CREAGH

0-231-05707-5 COLUMBIA PB $18.00

Poems

TRANSLATED BY ARTURO VIVANTE

0-962-03050-3 DELPHINIUM PB $12.00

Alessandro **Manzoni**

The Betrothed

A national institution in Italy, Manzoni's masterwork contains much penetrating political realism along with its captivating narrative of two lovers struggling against war, famine, plague, and feudal abuse. Bruce Penman's translation is exceptionally good. *"The Betrothed* gives us a vision of history as a constant confrontation with catastrophe"—Italo Calvino

TRANSLATED BY BRUCE PENMAN

0-14-044274-X PENGUIN PB $12.95

On the Historical Novel

0-8032-3084-2 NEBRASKA $20.00

0-8032-8226-5 NEBRASKA PB $10.00

I.U. **Tarchetti**

Fantastic Tales

Gothic tales by a writer sometimes called "the Italian Edgar Allan Poe"

EDITED AND TRANSLATED BY LAWRENCE VENUTI

1-56279-020-X MERCURY HOUSE $25.00

Passion

The source for the Stephen Sondheim musical. "Tarchetti's striking novel has it all—obsession, deception, sex, death, and passion in many ineluctable forms"—*Kirkus Reviews*

TRANSLATED BY LAWRENCE VENUTI

1-56279-064-1 MERCURY HOUSE PB $12.95

Giovanni **Verga**

The late-19th-century novelist, whose verismo *often earns him comparisons with Flaubert and Zola, starkly depicts the oppressive impoverishment of the Sicilian peasant class.*

The House by the Medlar Tree

Verga's masterpiece describes the tragic futility of the life of fisherfolk

TRANSLATED BY RAYMOND ROSENTHAL

0-520-04850-4 CALIFORNIA PB $14.00

Mastro Don Gesualdo

A study of an arriviste whose social and material success ends in emotional bankruptcy and isolation

TRANSLATED BY RAYMOND ROSENTHAL

0-520-05077-0 CALIFORNIA PB $11.95

The 20th Century

Fiction

American readers became keenly aware of Italian fiction in the postwar period when they began to encounter translations of writers such as Elio Vittorini, Mario Soldati, Curzio Malaparte, and Alberto Moravia. The so-called neo-realist style of these novelists—deeply influenced by both Verga's *verismo* and American naturalism—developed within the constraints of Fascist censorship, and reached its full flowering in the war's aftermath.

The realist tendency has remained evident in the work of Natalia Ginzburg, Giorgio Bassani, Elsa Morante, and (in his own idiosyncratic fashion) Pier Paolo Pasolini. On the other hand, a distinctive vein of fantastic fiction has been explored by Dino Buzzati, Tommaso Landolfi, and Italo Calvino. The popularity of Calvino's work in America has been such that a great many other Italian writers are now being translated, making it possible to encounter the younger, often more experimental, voices of Andrea de Carlo, Ferdinando Camon, Antonio Tabucchi, and others.

Anna **Banti**

Artemisia

A fictional portrayal, first published in 1947, of the 17th-century Neapolitan portraitist Artemisia Gentileschi

TRANSLATED BY SHIRLEY D'ARDIA

0-8032-6119-5 NEBRASKA PB $10.00

Giorgio **Bassani**

A rigorous stylist, Bassani focuses on the world of his native Ferrara and its Jewish community during the Nazi persecution.

The Heron

The killing of a heron triggers a variety of reactions in a Jewish survivor of Mussolini's Italy

TRANSLATED BY WILLIAM WEAVER

0-15-640085-5 HARCOURT BRACE PB $5.95

Stefano **Benni**

Terra!

Comic science fiction by a political journalist and humorist

TRANSLATED BY ANNA-PAOLA CANCAGNI

0-394-54353-X PANTHEON $12.95

Mario **Brelich**

The Holy Embrace

TRANSLATED BY JOHN SHEPLEY

1-56897-002-1 MARLBORO $22.95

0-8101-6029-3 MARLBORO PB $13.95

The Work of Betrayal

Poe's hero, C. Auguste Dupin, tackles "The Case of Judas Iscariot," the one case he has been forever unable to resolve. In what way did Judas specifically betray Christ, and what was his motive? "At once a compelling detective story, a creative hermeneutic enterprise and a tour de force of biblical deconstruction"—*NY Times Book Review*

TRANSLATED BY RAYMOND ROSENTHAL

0-910395-44-6 MARLBORO $29.95

0-910395-45-4 MARLBORO PB $12.00

Gesualdo **Bufalino**

The Keeper of Ruins: And Other Inventions

TRANSLATED BY PATRICK CREAGH

0-00-271335-7 HARPERCOLLINS PB $14.00

Night's Lies

TRANSLATED BY PATRICK CREAGH

0-00-271122-2 HARPERCOLLINS PB $12.00

The Plague-Sower

A powerful novel of a sanitarium in postwar Italy, written over a period of 30 years and published to great acclaim in 1981

TRANSLATED BY STEPHEN SARTARELLI

INTRODUCTION BY LEONARDO SCIASCIA

0-941419-13-4 ERIDANOS PB $13.00

Dino **Buzzati**

Buzzati was a prolific writer of allegorical and surrealistic fiction.

A Love Affair

"A rollicking, lyric, and delightful account of a respectable middle-aged man's devotion to a vulgar, lying, and unfaithful young trollop" —*New Yorker*

TRANSLATED BY JOSEPH GREEN

0-85635-586-0 CARCANET $34.95

The Tartar Steppe

Soldiers at a remote outpost spend their lifetime waiting for an enemy to appear

TRANSLATED BY STUART HOOD

0-87923-992-1 GODINE PB $13.95

Italo **Calvino**

"Calvino does what very few writers can do: he describes imaginary worlds with the most extraordinary precision and beauty"—Gore Vidal

The Baron in the Trees

In this widely admired book, an aristocratic rebel defies parental authority and takes to an arboreal perch from which he watches the Age of Voltaire unfold

TRANSLATED BY ARCHIBALD COLQUHOUN

0-15-610680-9 HARCOURT BRACE PB $8.00

The Castle of Crossed Destinies

A series of short, fantastic narratives inspired by 15th-century tarot cards and their archetypal images

TRANSLATED BY WILLIAM WEAVER

0-15-615455-2 HARCOURT BRACE PB $10.00

Cosmicomics

Fantasies on the evolution of the universe

TRANSLATED BY WILLIAM WEAVER

0-15-622600-6 HARCOURT BRACE PB $6.95

Difficult Loves

The intricate inner worlds of ordinary people. "A certain lovable nuttiness makes this collection well worth reading" —Margaret Atwood, *NY Times*

TRANSLATED BY WILLIAM WEAVER

0-15-626055-7 HARCOURT BRACE PB $8.95

If on a Winter's Night a Traveler

Ten different novels interwoven into one. Each chapter begins a new book, a new plot, and a different writing style

TRANSLATED BY WILLIAM WEAVER

0-15-643961-1 HARCOURT BRACE PB $10.00

Marcovaldo: The Seasons in the City

Twenty short stories, in settings ranging from the poverty of a northern industrial city in the '50s to the illusory economic boom of the '60s

TRANSLATED BY WILLIAM WEAVER

0-15-657204-4 HARCOURT BRACE PB $6.00

The Nonexistent Knight & The Cloven Viscount

Two novellas: a parody of medieval knighthood and "a dark-hued Gothic gem" *(NY Times)* about a nobleman bisected into his good and evil halves

TRANSLATED BY ARCHIBALD COLQUHOUN

0-15-665975-1 HARCOURT BRACE PB $8.00

Numbers in the Dark and Other Stories

An enchanting and diabolically brilliant collection of stories, fables, and "impossible interviews" by the masterful writer. Written between 1943 and 1984, these whimsical, horrifying, hilarious, wry stories cover an enormous range of ideas and concerns: politics, power, technology, truth, and the elusive promise of human connection

TRANSLATED BY TIM PARKS

0-679-44205-7 PANTHEON $24.00

0-679-74353-7 VINTAGE PB $12.00

The Path to the Nest of Spiders

The hero of Calvino's first, neo-realistic novel is a cobbler's apprentice turned partisan who makes common cause with his fellow outcasts

0-88001-327-3 ECCO PB $11.00

T-Zero

Evolutionary and space-time tales blending higher mathematics with higher comedy and poetic imagination

TRANSLATED BY WILLIAM WEAVER

0-15-692400-5 HARCOURT BRACE PB $6.95

Under the Jaguar Sun

0-15-692794-2 HARCOURT BRACE PB $8.00

The Watcher and Other Stories

Contains *Smog* and *The Argentine Ant*

TRANSLATED BY WILLIAM WEAVER & ARCHIBALD COLQUHON

0-15-694952-0 HARCOURT BRACE PB $5.95

Ferdinando **Camon**

"A writer of such importance that one does not know where or with whom to place him in the literature of our time."—Philippe Guilhon, Le Monde des Livres

The Fifth Estate

The chronicle of a postwar childhood in a peasant community near Padua

TRANSLATED BY JOHN SHEPLEY

0-910395-29-2 MARLBORO $16.95

0-910395-30-6 MARLBORO PB $9.95

Life Everlasting

A novel of the Resistance, of which the author has said: "On the part of the peasantry the Resistance was a visceral, furious and chaotic reaction against the violence of the invaders…They knew nothing about communism or capitalism. They had no ideas at all about creating a new Italy for after the war"

TRANSLATED BY JOHN SHEPLEY

0-910395-31-4 MARLBORO $17.95

0-910395-32-2 MARLBORO PB $10.95

Memorial

In writing of the death of his mother, Camon also confronts another kind of death: the end of peasant civilization

TRANSLATED BY DAVID CALICCHIO

0-8101-6013-7 MARLBORO PB $13.95

0-910395-07-1 MARLBORO PB $8.95

The Sickness Called Man

TRANSLATED BY JOHN SHEPLEY

0-8101-6015-3 MARLBORO PB $14.95

Giorgio **de Chirico**

Hebdomeros: With Monsieur Dudron's Adventure and Other Metaphysical Writings

1-87897-206-5 D.A.P. PB $15.95

Gabriella **de Ferrari**

A Cloud on Sand

A strong-willed mother and her equally strong-willed daughter work out their destinies in Italy and South America. "A classically assured, quietly enthralling masterpiece…With its rich, unerring sense of history, class, and culture and its subtle social comedy, *A Cloud on Sand* can be honorably mentioned in the same breath as another first novel with an evocative Italian background, Giuseppe di Lampedusa's classic *The Leopard*"

—L.S. Klepp, *Entertainment Weekly*

0-394-55145-1 KNOPF $19.95

Grazia **Deledda**

Deledda, winner of the Nobel Prize in 1926, wrote intense character studies rooted in Sardinian life, of which D.H. Lawrence remarked: "What she does do is create the passionate complex of a primitive populace."

After the Divorce

0-8101-1248-5 NORTHWESTERN $39.95

La Madre (The Woman and the Priest)

A study of a cleric's spontaneous passion "which only the blind instinct of mother obedience, the child passion, can overcome"—D.H. Lawrence

0-946626-20-0 HIPPOCRENE PB $7.95

Paola **Drigo**

Maria Zef

TRANSLATED WITH AN INTRODUCTION BY BLOSSOM STEINBERG KIRSCHENBAUM

0-8032-6577-8 NEBRASKA PB $9.95

Umberto **Eco**

Foucault's Pendulum

Knights Templar, Illuminati, and a host of other secret orders figure in a novel that is also a dizzying compendium of occult and conspiratorial lore

TRANSLATED BY WILLIAM WEAVER

0-15-132765-3 HARCOURT BRACE $22.95

The Island of the Day Before

Eco turns his voluminous knowledge and imagination to a novel of science and navigation set in the 17th century. When Roberto della Griva finds himself, after a violent storm, alone on a fully provisioned but abandoned ship, he is left to experience an adventure of remembrance that spans the history and knowledge of his century

TRANSLATED BY WILLIAM WEAVER

0-15-100151-0 HARCOURT BRACE $25.00

0-14-025919-8 PENGUIN PB $13.95

Is it possible—as anyone would ask himself—that Roberto had not reflected on the fact that this rescue would be granted him only if he were to reach the Island within that day, or at most by the early hours of the following morning: an exploit that his most recent experiments hardly made probable? Is it possible he did not realize that he was planning to land in reality on the Island to rescue a woman who was arriving there only through his narrative?

THE ISLAND OF THE DAY BEFORE

The Name of the Rose

The surprise bestseller of the '80s: a medieval version of Agatha Christie, densely interlarded with contemporary semiotic and political references

TRANSLATED BY WILLIAM WEAVER

0-15-144647-4 HARCOURT BRACE $29.95

Carlo Emilio **Gadda**

Acquainted with Grief

A "potpourri of linguistic flights, puns, literary allusions, phonetic tricks and endlessly proliferating verbosity"—*Library Journal*

TRANSLATED BY WILLIAM WEAVER

0-8076-1115-8 BRAZILLER PB $8.95

That Awful Mess on Via Merulana

Another stylistically innovative work. "Bawdy, obscene, punning, enormously learned. Gadda explodes language"—*Newsweek*

TRANSLATED BY WILLIAM WEAVER

INTRODUCTION BY ITALO CALVINO

0-8076-1093-3 BRAZILLER PB $8.95

Natalia **Ginzburg**

"A brilliant eccentric; she is almost certainly Italy's best woman writer today."—TLS

All Our Yesterdays

TRANSLATED BY ANGUS DAVIDSON

1-55970-026-2 LITTLE, BROWN PB $8.95

The City and the House

TRANSLATED BY DICK DAVIS

1-55970-029-7 LITTLE, BROWN PB $8.95

The Little Virtues

TRANSLATED BY DICK DAVIS

1-55970-028-9 LITTLE, BROWN PB $7.95

Voices in the Evening

"Her simplicity is an achievement hard-won and remarkable, and the more welcome in a literary world where the cloak of omniscience is all too readily donned"—William Weaver, *NY Times Book Review*

0-85635-818-5 CARCANET $32.75

1-55970-016-5 LITTLE, BROWN $16.95

Giuseppe Tomasi **di Lampedusa**

The Leopard

The decline of the Sicilian aristocracy traced in a classic novel that is both an indictment and a lament

See also **THE '60S** under **THE GREAT FICTION BESTSELLERS 1930-1995** in **POPULAR READING**

TRANSLATED BY ARCHIBALD COLQUHOUN

0-679-40757-X EVERYMAN'S $16.50

0-679-73121-0 PANTHEON PB $12.00

Tommaso **Landolfi**

Landolfi, a master of the fantastic tale and a major influence on Italo Calvino, has been compared with Kafka, Joyce, Borges, and Poe

Gogol's Wife & Other Stories

0-8112-0080-9 NEW DIRECTIONS PB $8.95

An Autumn Story
One of the great love stories of modern Italian literature incorporates elements of gothic horror
TRANSLATED BY JOACHIM NEUGROSCHEL
0-941419-27-4 MARSILIO $20.00
0-941419-26-6 MARSILIO PB $11.00

Primo **Levi**
If Not Now, When?
A novel of Jewish resistance to the Nazis
See also **HOLOCAUST FICTION** under **ART AND LITERATURE** under **THE HOLOCAUST** in **WORLD HISTORY AND CURRENT AFFAIRS**
TRANSLATED BY WILLIAM WEAVER
0-14-008492-4 PENGUIN PB $11.00

The Monkey's Wrench
Often quirky tales of the joys and passions of work, as told by a structural engineer
0-14-018892-4 PENGUIN PB $10.95

Curzio **Malaparte**
Kaputt
In these novels of World War II and its aftermath Malaparte shows the demoralization of Italy in the face of foreign invaders: Germans in *Kaputt*, Americans in *The Skin*
TRANSLATED BY CESARE FOLIGNO
0-910395-01-2 MARLBORO PB $12.95

The Skin
This sequel to *Kaputt* depicts the Italy of 1943-45 against a canvas of "vast landscapes and seething cities as full of extravagant detail as a crowd sequence directed by Griffith"—*Observer*
TRANSLATED BY DAVID MOORE
0-910395-37-3 MARLBORO PB $12.95

Giorgio **Manganelli**
All the Errors
Stories translated by Henry Martin. The only English language book of the late great Italian meta-fabulist's work
0-929701-07-0 MCPHERSON $20.00
0-929701-06-2 MCPHERSON PB $10.00

Filippo T. **Marinetti**
The Untameables
The Futurist poet described this novel as follows: "Nude crude symbolizing. Simultaneous polychromatic polyhumorous. Vast violent dynamic"
1-55713-064-7 SUN & MOON PB $10.95

Anna Maria **Ortese**
The Iguana
A fantasy novel, published in the late '60s, concerning an uncharted island off the coast of Portugal. "A satiric fable dense with echoes of Shakespeare's *Tempest* and Kafka's *Metamorphosis*"—*NY Times*
TRANSLATED BY HENRY MARTIN
0-914232-95-9 MCPHERSON PB $9.00

A Music Behind the Wall
The celebrated stories of the author of *The Iguana*
TRANSLATED BY HENRY MARTIN
0-929701-39-9 MCPHERSON $20.00

Goffredo **Parise**
Abecedary
TRANSLATED BY JAMES MARCUS
0-910395-60-8 MARLBORO $17.95
0-910395-61-6 MARLBORO PB $10.95

Solitudes
Short stories by a young Italian writer
TRANSLATED BY ISABEL QUIGLY
INTRODUCTION BY NATALIA GINZBURG
0-394-72994-3 OLYMPIC PB $2.98

Pier Paolo **Pasolini**
Susan Sontag described Pasolini, who was murdered in 1975, as "indisputably the most remarkable figure to have emerged in Italian arts and letter since the Second World War." In addition to his fiction his prolific output includes poetry, essays, and screenplays.

Petrolio
TRANSLATED BY ANN GOLDSTEIN
0-679-42990-5 PANTHEON $25.00

The Ragazzi
TRANSLATED BY EMILE CAPOUYA
0-85635-605-0 CARCANET $34.95

Roman Nights & Other Stories
"Several of the stories are so strong, so raw in their homoeroticism, that one is dumbfounded to discover that the earliest was written more than 30 years ago"—Peter Brunette, *NY Times*
TRANSLATED BY JOHN SHEPLEY
0-910395-20-9 MARLBORO PB $9.00

Cesare **Pavese**
Stories
These tales reflect the often unhappy experiences of Pavese's own life: his inadequacy with women, his political exile, and his musings on suicide
TRANSLATED BY A.E. MURCH
0-88001-124-6 ECCO PB $12.95

Cesare Pavese

Luigi **Pirandello**
Awarded the Nobel Prize in 1934, Pirandello was a prolific writer of fiction before he embarked on his career as a dramatist.

The Late Mattia Pascal
Pirandello's best novel, published in 1904, tells of a small-town librarian who is erroneously declared dead and tries to make a new life for himself: "For the moment (and God knows how much it pains me), I have died already twice, but the first time was a mistake, and the second…well, you may read for yourself"
TRANSLATED BY WILLIAM WEAVER
0-941419-44-4 MARSILIO PB $12.00

One, No One, and One Hundred Thousand
A typically wry meditation on identity by the great playwright and novelist: a man suddenly discovers that he is not seen by others as he sees himself, and everything changes for him
TRANSLATED BY WILLIAM WEAVER
0-941419-35-5 MARSILIO $17.95

Tales of Madness
TRANSLATED BY GIOVANNI BUSSINO
0-937832-26-X BRANDEN $17.95

Tales of Suicide
TRANSLATED BY GIOVANNI BUSSINO
0-937832-31-6 DANTE UNIVERSITY PB $14.95

Giorgio **Pressburger**
The Law of White Spaces
A doctor loses his memory on the occasion of having to say Kaddish for his dead brother. An American physician develops a morbid, semi-erotic attachment to a mute 16-year old girl, and destroys his marriage and career in order to break her perpetual silence. "Pressburger, a Hungarian-born film director who lives in Italy, provides a fascinating and often frightening look at the human condition in these elegantly translated tales"—*Publishers Weekly*
TRANSLATED BY PIERS SPENCE
0-679-42048-7 PANTHEON $19.00

Umberto **Saba**
Ernesto
A novel of a young man's homosexual awakening, written by an outstanding lyric poet
TRANSLATED BY MARK THOMPSON
0-85635-559-3 CARCANET $34.50

Stories and Recollections of Umberto Saba
Touching, tensile short stores and non-fiction by one of the three greatest Italian poets of this century. All of these pieces in English for the first time
TRANSLATED BY ESTELLE GILSON
1-87881-821-X SHEEP MEADOW $22.50

Alberto **Savinio**
Childhood of Nivasio Dolcemare
An autobiographical novel set in Athens at the turn of the century. Savinio was the brother of the painter Giorgio de Chirico
TRANSLATED BY RICHARD PEVERAR
INTRODUCTION BY DORE ASHTON
0-941419-05-3 GODINE PB $3.98

Lives of the Gods
A Surrealist reworking of classical mythology. "The whole of the modern myth still in the process of formation is founded on Alberto Savinio's work"—André Breton
TRANSLATED BY JAMES BROOK & SUSAN ETLINGER
PREFACE BY EDOUARD RODITI
0-947757-28-7 SERPENT'S TAIL PB $12.99

Operatic Lives
TRANSLATED BY JOHN SHEPLEY
0-910395-42-X MARLBORO........$21.95
0-910395-43-8 MARLBORO PB........$13.95

Leonardo **Sciascia**
Sciascia frequently employs the techniques and motifs of detective fiction to illuminate, in unpredictable ways, the social landscape of Italy. "Sciascia…invents for us a world quite as real as any that Dreiser ever dealt with, rendered in a style that is, line by line, as jolting as an exposed electrical wire."—Gore Vidal

The Council of Egypt
Political and literary intrigue in 18th-century Sicily
TRANSLATED BY ADRIENNE FOULKE
0-85635-740-5 CARCANET........$18.95

One Way or Another
An odd sort of murder mystery, foreshadowing recent Italian political scandals
TRANSLATED BY SACHA RABINOVITCH
0-85635-664-6 CARCANET........$25.86

The Wine-Dark Sea: Thirteen Stories
"The well-translated collection is an ideal introduction for anyone who hasn't yet come across one of the major writers of the age" —*TLS*
TRANSLATED BY AVRIL BARDONI
0-85635-556-9 CARCANET........$34.95
0-85635-783-9 SCHOLARLY PB........$6.95

Ignazio **Silone**
Silone's literary reputation has faded somewhat but his novels remain primary documents of anti-Fascism.

Bread and Wine
TRANSLATED BY HARVEY FERGUSON
0-451-52500-0 NEW AMERICAN LIBRARY PB........$5.95

Fontamara
0-460-87494-2 EVERYMAN'S PB........$7.50

Italo **Svevo**

As a Man Grows Older
This earlier Svevo novel is a penetrating analysis of the discomfiture of a bachelor from Trieste
TRANSLATED BY BERYL DE ZOETE
1-55713-128-7 SUN & MOON PB........$12.95

The Confessions of Zeno
An experimental novel exploring an old man's consciousness. It was a favorite of James Joyce
0-679-72234-3 VINTAGE PB........$12.00

Further Confessions of Zeno
Includes a variety of posthumously published fragments
TRANSLATED BU BEN JOHNSON & P.N. FURBANK
0-520-01436-7 CALIFORNIA........$28.50

Antonio **Tabucchi**
Of the short stories which make up the collections below, Tabucchi has written: "Misunderstandings, uncertainties, belated understandings, useless remorse, treacherous memories, stupid and irredeemable mistakes, all these irresistibly fascinate me"

Letter from Casablanca
TRANSLATED BY JANICE THRENSHER
0-8112-0985-7 NEW DIRECTIONS........$17.95
0-8112-0986-5 NEW DIRECTIONS PB........$7.95

Little Misunderstandings of No Importance
TRANSLATED BY FRANCES FRENAYE
0-8112-1029-4 NEW DIRECTIONS........$16.95

Pereira Declares
An inhibited man's awakening, against the backdrop of Salazar's Portugal in the late 30s
TRANSLATED BY P. CREAGH
0-8112-1319-6 NEW DIRECTIONS........$19.95

Requiem: A Hallucination
TRANSLATED BY MARGARET JULL COSTA
0-8112-1270-X NEW DIRECTIONS........$15.95

Elio **Vittorini**
Influenced by Hemingway and other American novelists, Vittorini was a leading practicioner of literary neorealism.

Men and Not Men
This tale of the Resistance in Milan at the end of World War II is "an unsparing analysis of the moral ambiguities inherent in political violence"—*LA Times*
0-910395-13-6 MARLBORO........$16.95
0-910395-14-4 MARLBORO PB........$11.00

Women of Messina
TRANSLATED BY FRANCES FRENAYE & FRANCES KEENE
0-8112-0496-0 NEW DIRECTIONS........$9.50

Poetry

Modern Italian poetry has known its share of contending schools, ranging from the crepuscularism of the 1880s (which in response to earlier bombast sought a more restrained approach) to the futurism associated with Marinetti and the hermeticism explored by Giuseppe Ungaretti. Ungaretti has been perhaps the most influential Italian poet of this century, although unfortunately his work is currently hard to come by in English. His influence can be traced in the work of Quasimodo, Luzi, Sereni, Sinisgalli, and Erba, all of whom share a certain elusive, almost aristocratic privacy of expression. The other great figures of the era are Eugenio Montale—who won the Nobel Prize in 1975 and whose work represents, among other things, a profound meditation on Italy's experience under Fascism—and the short-lived Cesare Pavese, in whose poems realism achieves the mysteriousness of a dream.

Recent years have witnessed an extravagant variety of stylistic modes. Out of the welter of the "Roman School," the "neo-avant-garde," and other groupings, a few major voices have emerged: Sandro Penna, the experimentalist Antonio Porta, the more traditional Andrea Zanzotto, and the filmmaker and novelist Pier Paolo Pasolini, whose poetry, some of it written in his native Friulian dialect, is considered by many his most important work.

Milo **de Angelis**

Finite Intuition: Selected Poetry and Prose
A survey of the work of a major figure of the '70s and '80s
TRANSLATED BY LAWRENCE VENUTI
1-55713-068-X SUN & MOON PB........$11.95

Dino **Campana**

Orphic Songs
Campana spent much of his life in mental hospitals, and this passionately imagistic collection, written in 1913, is his only book
TRANSLATED BY CHARLES WRIGHT
0-932440-16-9 FIELD TRANSLATIONS........$11.50

Alfredo **Giuliani**, editor

I Novissimi
Presents the work of five poets who pushed the limits of experimentation in the '60s
TRANSLATED BY LUIGI BALLERINI AND OTHERS
1-55713-137-6 SUN & MOON PB........$14.95

Guido **Gozzano**

The Colloquies & Selected Letters
Described as reluctantly in love with his bourgeois world, this influential "crepuscular" poet "made his debut in a quite casual way, with his hands in his pockets"—Eugenio Montale
TRANSLATED WITH AN INTRODUCTION BY J.G. NICHOLS
0-85635-628-X SCHOLARLY PB........$23.00

Primo **Levi**

The Collected Poems
Levi's poetry engages the same themes of Holocaust and survival as his prose work
TRANSLATED BY RUTH FELDMAN & BRIAN SWANN
0-571-16539-7 FABER PB........$10.95

Primo Levi

Mario **Luzi**

In the Dark Body of Metamorphosis & Other Poems
A religious poet somewhat in the tradition of Ungaretti
TRANSLATED BY I.L. SALOMON
0-393-04391-6 NORTON........$6.95

Filippo Tommaso **Marinetti**

Selected Poems and Related Prose
0-300-04103-9 YALE........$42.00

Eugenio **Montale**
"Montale speaks to us of a spinning world driven by a wind of destruction, with no solid ground to stand on...It is the world of the First and Second World Wars, and perhaps even of the Third."—Italo Calvino

Cuttlefish Bones
TRANSLATED BY WILLIAM ARROWSMITH
0-393-02803-8 NORTON $25.00
0-393-31171-6 NORTON PB $10.95

It Depends: A Poet's Notebook
A bilingual edition of Montale's last collection, published at age 82
TRANSLATED BY G. SINGH
0-8112-0774-9 NEW DIRECTIONS PB $4.95

Mottetti: Poems of Love
Montale's *Motets* are one of the most stunning lyrical sequences in modern poetry. "The power of Montale's poetic effects depends on the dramatic concentration of the visionary moments… The sequence recreates isolated moments of insight, stripped of their nonessential elements"—Dana Gioia
TRANSLATED BY DANA GIOIA
1-55597-123-7 GRAY WOLF $14.95

New Poems
Written after the death of the poet's wife, this collection includes witty and ironical pieces which clearly display his acute critical intelligence
TRANSLATED BY G. SINGH
ESSAY BY F.R. LEAVIS
0-8112-0598-3 NEW DIRECTIONS $7.95
0-8112-0599-1 NEW DIRECTIONS PB $2.95

Eugenio Montale

The Occasions
Montale's second book, published in 1939, contains many of his greatest poems, including "Dora Markus" and *Motets*
TRANSLATED BY WILLIAM ARROWSMITH
0-393-30324-1 NORTON PB $9.95

The Storm and Other Things
Published in 1956 and often considered Montale's masterpiece. "One of the truly distinguished renderings of modern Italian poetry. Arrowsmith is an authentically *poetic* translator surpassed by none of our contemporaries"—Harold Bloom. This book is unfortunately out of print at present
TRANSLATED BY WILLIAM ARROWSMITH
0-393-30249-0 NORTON PB $6.95

Pier Paolo **Pasolini**

Pier Paolo Pasolini: Poems
SELECTED AND TRANSLATED BY NORMAN MACAFEE
0-374-52469-6 NOONDAY PB $14.00

Roman Poems
The "infernal" aspect of modern Italian life as witnessed by a poet passionately involved in his country's political upheaval
TRANSLATED BY LAWRENCE FERLINGHETTI & FRANCESCA VALENTE
0-87286-187-2 SUBTERRANEAN PB $7.95

Sandro **Penna**

This Strange Joy: Selected Poems of Sandro Penna
Poems dealing largely with homosexual love
TRANSLATED BY W.S. DI PIERO
0-8142-0328-0 OHIO STATE $22.50

John **Picchione** & Lawrence R. **Smith**, editors

Twentieth Century Italian Poetry
0-8020-7368-9 TORONTO PB $36.00

Antonio **Porta**

Kisses from Another Dream
Bittersweet, defiant lyrics from a leading figure of the *Gruppo 63* movement that was committed to politically subversive and formally innovative poetry
TRANSLATED BY ANTHONY MOLINO
0-87286-206-2 CITY LIGHTS PB $5.95

Gian Paolo **Renello**, editor

Italian Poetry: 1950-1990
TRANSLATED BY GAYLE RIDINGER
0-937832-34-0 DANTE UNIVERSITY PB $18.95

Amelia **Roselli**

War Variations
Poems of madness by the daughter of a wartime resistance hero
TRANSLATED BY LUCIA RE AND PAUL VANGELISTI
1-55713-208-9 SUN & MOON PB $11.95

Umberto **Saba**

The Dark of the Sun: Selected Poems
TRANSLATED BY CHRISTOPHER MILLIS
0-8191-9330-5 UNIVERSITY PRESS OF AMERICA $37.50

Rocco **Scotellaro**

The Dawn Is Always New: Poetry of Rocco Scotellaro
A village mayor at 23, imprisoned for embezzlement, released thanks to the interventions of Carlo Levi and Alberto Moravia, and dead in 1953 at age 30, Scotellaro has received widespread posthumous recognition as a poet who speaks for the peasant culture of Southern Italy
TRANSLATED BY RUTH FELDMAN & BRIAN SWANN
0-691-01370-5 PRINCETON PB $12.95

Lawrence R. **Smith**, editor

The New Italian Poetry: 1945 to the Present
Twenty-one realist, hermetic, and avant-garde poets, with an account of each school's development. A bilingual edition
0-520-03859-2 CALIFORNIA $45.00
0-520-04411-8 CALIFORNIA PB $14.95

Adriano **Spatolo** & Paul **Vangelisti**, editors

Italian Poetry, 1960-1980: From Neo to Post Avant-Garde
The cutting edge of poetic experimentation
0-88031-061-8 SMALL PRESS $12.50
0-88031-060-X SMALL PRESS PB $7.50

Giuseppe **Steiner**

Drawn States of Mind
Visual poems by a contemporary experimentalist
TRANSLATED BY GUY BENNETT
1-55713-171-6 SUN & MOON PB $8.95

Diego **Valeri**

My Name on the Wind: Selected Poems
TRANSLATED BY MICHAEL PALMA
0-691-01462-0 PRINCETON PB $12.95

Andrea **Zanzotto**

Selected Poetry of Andrea Zanzotto
Radical linguistic experimentation combined with multiple layers of literary reference
TRANSLATED BY RUTH FELDMAN & BRIAN SWANN
0-691-01323-3 PRINCETON PB $17.95

Essays, Memoirs, and Other Prose

Roberto **Calasso**

The Marriage of Cadmus and Harmony
A beautifully written recounting of and meditation on Greek myths
See also **CLASSICAL MYTHOLOGY: ANCIENT GREECE AND ROME** under **MYTHOLOGY AND FOLKLORE** in **RELIGION, SPIRITUALITY, AND PHILOSOPHY**
0-394-58154-7 KNOPF $25.00
0-679-73348-5 VINTAGE PB $13.00

Dionysus's phallus is more hallucinogenic than coercive. It is close to a fungus, or a parasite in nature, or to the toxic grass stuffed in the cavity of the thýrsus. It has none of the faithfulness of the farmer's crop, it won't stretch out in the plowed furrow where Iasion made love to Demeter, nor does it push its way up amid flourishing harvest fields, but rather in the most intractable woodland. It is a metallic tip concealed beneath innocuous green leaves. It doesn't intoxicate to promote growth; yet, growth sustains intoxication, as the stem of a goblet holds up the wine. Dionysus is not a useful god who helps weave or knot things together, but a god who loosens and unties.
THE MARRIAGE OF CADMUS AND HARMONY

The Ruin of Kasch
The author of *The Marriage of Cadmus and Harmony* brings his enormous erudition and unique stylistic skills to the period immediately preceding and following the French Revolution and charts the downfall of "The Modern." "This book has two subjects: one is Talleyrand; and the other is everything else"—Italo Calvino
0-674-78026-4 HARVARD $24.95

Italo **Calvino**

The Road to San Giovanni

TRANSLATED BY TIM PARKS

0-679-41523-8 PANTHEON $19.00

0-679-74348-0 VINTAGE PB $10.00

Italo Calvino (photo by Jerry Bauer)

Six Memos for the Next Millennium

TRANSLATED BY PATRICK CREAGH

0-679-74237-9 VINTAGE PB $10.00

Benedetto **Croce**

Aesthetic

See also **CROCE** under **PHILOSOPHY** in **RELIGION, SPIRITUALITY, AND PHILOSOPHY**

TRANSLATED BY DOUGLAS AINSLIE

1-56000-818-0 TRANSACTION PB $29.95

Aesthetic

Croce's most famous and influential work: a classic treatise on the theory of art and the origins of language, published in 1909

TRANSLATED BY COLIN LYAS

0-521-35216-9 CAMBRIDGE $69.95

0-521-35996-1 CAMBRIDGE PB $19.95

Umberto **Eco**

How to Travel with a Salmon and Other Essays

TRANSLATED BY WILLIAM WEAVER

0-15-100136-7 HARCOURT BRACE $18.95

0-15-600125-X HARVEST PB $11.00

The Limits of Interpretation

0-253-31852-1 INDIANA $35.00

0-253-20869-6 INDIANA PB $15.95

The Search for the Perfect Language

Traces the complex history of European attempts to rediscover or invent a pure primordial language: "We shall see that the dream of a perfect language has always been invoked as a solution to religious or political strife…The history of the reasons why Europe thought that it needed a perfect language can thus tell us a good deal about the cultural history of that continent"

See also **LANGUAGE AND WRITING** under **ARCHAEOLOGY** in **WORLD HISTORY AND CURRENT AFFAIRS**

0-631-17465-6 BLACKWELL $24.95

Six Walks in the Fictional Woods

The renowned semiotician and novelist (*The Name of the Rose*) takes us into the deep woods of fiction's basic mechanisms. How does text signal the type of reader it wants? Who is the "model reader" and how does he or she get deliciously lost? Eco answers these questions with examples from Flaubert and Poe, Mickey Spillane and fairy tales

See also **UMBERTO ECO** under **CRITICAL TEXTS** under **SEMIOTICS AND STRUCTURALISM AND AFTER** under **LITERARY THEORY**

0-674-81050-3 HARVARD $18.95

0-674-81051-1 HARVARD PB $10.00

Natalia **Ginzburg**

Family Sayings

A collection of autobiographical essays spanning the Fascist era and the war years in Turin

1-55970-027-0 LITTLE, BROWN PB $7.95

Carlo **Levi**

Christ Stopped At Eboli

A memoir of the author's internal exile under Mussolini in the impoverished Basilicata region

TRANSLATED BY FRANCES FRENAYE

0-374-50316-8 FS&G PB $10.00

Primo **Levi**

The Drowned and the Saved

TRANSLATED BY RAYMOND ROSENTHAL

0-679-72186-X VINTAGE PB $10.00

Moments of Reprieve

TRANSLATED BY RUTH FELDMAN

0-14-009370-2 PENGUIN PB $10.00

The Periodic Table

"The best introduction to the psychological world of one of the most important and gifted writers of our time"—*Newsweek*

TRANSLATED BY RAYMOND ROSENTHAL

0-679-44463-7 RANDOM HOUSE $17.00

0-8052-0811-9 SCHOCKEN PB $10.00

Survival in Auschwitz

"Documentary evidence of the first order of the inhumanity of man to man in our time"
—*American Journal of Sociology*

TRANSLATED BY STUART WOOLF

See also **FIRST-PERSON ACCOUNTS** under **THE HOLOCAUST** in **WORLD HISTORY AND CURRENT AFFAIRS**

0-684-82680-1 COLLIER PB $11.00

Now everyone is busy scraping the bottom of his bowl with his spoon so as not to waste the last drops of the soup; a confused, metallic clatter, signifying the end of the day. Silence slowly prevails and then, from my bunk on the top row, I see and hear old Kuhn praying aloud, with his beret on his head swaying backwards and forwards violently. Kuhn is thanking God because he has not been chosen. Kuhn is out of his senses. Does he not see Beppo the Greek in the bunk next to him, Beppo who is twenty years old and is going to the gas chamber the day after tomorrow and knows it and lies there looking fixedly at the light without saying anything and without even thinking any more? Can Kuhn fail to realize that next time it will be his turn? Does Kuhn not understand that what has happened today is an abomination, which no propitiatory prayer, no pardon, no expiation by the guilty, which nothing at all in the power of man can ever clean again? If I was God, I would spit at Kuhn's prayer.

SURVIVAL IN AUSCHWITZ

Filippo T. **Marinetti**

Let's Murder the Moonshine: Selected Writings

A survey of the career of the preeminent Futurist

See also **FUTURISM** under **20TH-CENTURY ART** in **ART**

EDITED BY R.W. FLINT

1-55713-101-5 SUN & MOON PB $13.95

Eugenio **Montale**

The Second Life of Art: Selected Essays

EDITED BY JONATHAN GALASSI

0-912946-84-9 ECCO $17.50

Pier Paolo **Pasolini**

Heretical Empiricism

EDITED BY LOUISE K. BARNETT

0-253-32717-2 INDIANA $15.95

Lutheran Letters

Late essays, whose tone can be gauged from this excerpt: "All middle-class persons are, in fact, fascist, always, everywhere"

TRANSLATED BY STUART HOOD

0-85635-410-4 CARCANET $27.50

Luigi **Pirandello**

Pirandello's Love Letters to Mara Abba

EDITED BY BENITO ORTOLANI

0-691-03499-0 PRINCETON $35.00

Antonio **Porta**

Melusine: A Ballad and a Diary (1982-1987)

TRANSLATED BY ANTHONY MOLINO

0-920717-58-6 GUERNICA EDITIONS PB $10.00

Alberto **Savinio**

Speaking to Clio

A contemplative travel journal concerning Etruscan burial places and the Abruzzi highlands

TRANSLATED BY JOHN SHEPLEY

0-910395-22-5 MARLBORO $14.95

0-910395-23-3 MARLBORO PB $9.00

Anthologies

Herman W. **Haller**, editor

The Hidden Italy: A Bilingual Edition of Italian Dialect Poetry

Poetry in ten dialects, from the Middle Ages to the present, reflecting a new broadening of linguistic tolerance

0-8143-1802-9 WAYNE STATE $45.00

Katherine **Jason**, editor

Name and Tears & Other Stories: Forty Years of Italian Fiction

More than 30 short stories give an overview of Italian fiction from the 40s to the present day. Includes work by Calvino, Ginzburg, Sciascia, Eco, and others

1-55597-132-6 GRAY WOLF $17.95

1-55597-126-1 GRAY WOLF PB $10.00

Critical Studies

General Studies

Alba **Amoia**
Twentieth Century Italian Women Writers: The Feminine Experience
0-8093-2027-4 SOUTHERN ILLINOIS PB $15.95

Gregory **Lucente**
Beautiful Fables: Self-Consciousness in Italian Narrative from Manzoni to Calvino
0-8018-3331-0 JOHNS HOPKINS $44.00

Ernest H. **Wilkins**
A History of Italian Literature
A readable and authoritative overview
0-674-39701-0 HARVARD $49.00

Studies of Individual Authors

Frances **Yates**
Giordano Bruno and the Hermetic Tradition
A pioneering, sympathetic study of Renaissance uses of ancient magical traditions
0-226-95007-7 CHICAGO PB $19.95

Joan **Ferrante**
The Political Vision of the Divine Comedy
An exploration of political issues and ideas relating the poem to the turbulence of Dante's Florence
0-691-06603-5 PRINCETON $60.00

Rachel **Jacoff**, editor
The Cambridge Companion to Dante
Some of the world's greatest Dante scholars are within reach with this collection of 15 new essays
0-521-42742-8 CAMBRIDGE PB $19.95

Giuseppe **Mazzotta**
Dante, Poet of the Desert: History and Allegory in the Divine Comedy
Special emphasis on Dante's source materials
0-691-10233-3 PRINCETON PB $18.95

Charles **Singleton**
An Essay on the Vita Nuova
An erudite commentary on Dante's early masterwork
0-8018-2004-9 JOHNS HOPKINS PB $12.95

Journey to Beatrice
An acclaimed study by a preeminent Dante scholar
0-8018-2005-7 JOHNS HOPKINS PB $15.95

Glauco **Cambon**
Ugo Foscolo: Poet of Exile
0-691-06424-5 PRINCETON $39.50

Sebastian **de Grazia**
Machiavelli in Hell
Winner of the Pulitzer Prize in biography: a stunningly intimate approach to the great political philosopher. "Complex, brilliant, attractive, at times profound"
—*Christian Science Monitor*
See also **RENAISSANCE ITALY AND THE COMING OF HUMANISM** under **MEDIEVAL AND RENAISSANCE EUROPE** in **WORLD HISTORY AND CURRENT AFFAIRS**
0-691-00861-2 VINTAGE PB $14.95

Glauco **Cambon**
Michelangelo's Poetry: Fury of Form
0-691-06648-5 PRINCETON $39.50

Eugenio Montale's Poetry: A Dream in Reason's Presence
0-691-06520-9 PRINCETON $39.50

Davide **Lajolo**
An Absurd Vice: A Biography of Cesare Pavese
0-8112-0850-8 NEW DIRECTIONS $18.50

Brian **Moloney**
Italo Svevo
0-85224-248-4 COLUMBIA $18.00

Dutch Literature

A. **Alberts**
The Islands
TRANSLATED BY HANS KONING
0-87023-385-8 MASSACHUSETTS $22.50

E.R. **Beekman**, editor & translator
Fugitive Dreams: An Anthology of Dutch Colonial Literature
0-87023-575-3 MASSACHUSETTS $40.00

J. **Bernlef**
Out of Mind
A gripping novel about the onset of senility
TRANSLATED BY ADRIENNE DIXON
0-87923-734-1 GODINE $17.95

Gerbrand A. **Bredero**
The Spanish Brabanter: A 17th-Century Dutch Social Satire in Five Acts
TRANSLATED BY H. DAVID BRUMBLE III
0-86698-018-0 SUNY $20.00

Jeroen **Brouwers**
Sunken Red
A 1981 novel of a man's relationship with his mother and their imprisonment in a Japanese prisoner-of-war camp
TRANSLATED BY ADRIENNE DIXON
0-941533-19-0 NEW AMSTERDAM $15.95
1-56131-025-5 NEW AMSTERDAM PB $9.95

Hugo **Claus**
The Sorrow of Belgium
Belgium under Nazi rule, through the eyes of a ten-year-old boy
TRANSLATED BY ARNOLD J. POMERANS
0-14-018801-0 PENGUIN PB $11.95

Louis **Couperus**
The Hidden Force
TRANSLATED BY ALEXANDER T. DEMATTOS
0-87023-715-2 MASSACHUSETTS PB $17.95

Maria **Dermout**
The Ten Thousand Things
A novel of Indonesia under Dutch rule
0-87023-384-X MASSACHUSETTS $35.00

Carl **Friedman**
Nightfather
TRANSLATED BY ARNOLD & ERICA POMERANS
0-89255-193-3 PERSEA $18.50

Peter **Glassgold**, editor
Living Space: Poems of the Dutch Fiftiers
Includes work by Schierbeek, Elburg, Kouwenaar, Lucebert, Polet, Campert, and Claus
INTRODUCTION BY PETER GLASSGOLD
0-8112-0747-1 NEW DIRECTIONS PB $3.95

Arnon **Grunberg**
Blue Mondays
TRANSLATED BY ARNOLD & ERICA POMERANS
0-374-11485-4 FS&G $25.00

Hella **Haasse**
Forever a Stranger and Other Stories
983-56-0003-1 OXFORD PB $17.95

In a Dark Wood Wandering
The larger-than-life characters in this historical novel of the Hundred Years War include Charles VI, Louis of Orleans, Richard II, and Henry V. "The great colorful pageant of events here unfolded... [is] described with scholarship and admirable lucidity. The characters really come to life"—*TLS*
See also **THE '90S** under **THE GREAT FICTION BESTSELLERS 1930-1995** in **POPULAR READING**
TRANSLATED BY LEWIS KAPLAN & ANITA MILLER
0-89733-336-5 ACADEMY CHICAGO $22.95

The Scarlet City
The author of *In a Dark Wood Wandering* brings to life the world of the Borgias, Machiavelli, Michelangelo, and Aretino, the strange mix of the savage and the civilized that marked the 16th century in Italy
See also **HISTORICAL AND ROMANTIC FICTION** in **POPULAR READING**
TRANSLATED BY ANITA MILLER
0-89733-349-7 ACADEMY CHICAGO $22.95
0-89733-372-1 ACADEMY CHICAGO PB $12.95

Threshold of Fir: A Novel of Fifth-Century Rome
0-89733-390-X ACADEMY CHICAGO $19.95

Etty **Hillesum**
Etty Hillesum: An Interrupted Life and Letters from Westerbork
0-8050-4894-4 HOLT $27.50
0-8050-5087-6 HOLT PB $15.95

An Interrupted Life: The Diaries of Etty Hillesum, 1941-1943
TRANSLATED BY ARNOLD POMERANS
0-671-74555-7 POCKET PB $5.99

Harry **Mulisch**
The Assault
The sole young survivor of a family slaughtered in a Nazi vendetta massacre confronts the reasons for the incident many years later, despite his efforts to steer clear of the whole affair
TRANSLATED BY CLAIRE WHITE
0-394-74420-9 RANDOM HOUSE PB $13.00

The Discovery of Heaven
0-670-85668-1 VIKING $34.95

Multatuli
Max Havelaar: Or, the Coffee Auctions of the Dutch Trading Company
A fierce literary onslaught directed at the Dutch colonial masters in the East Indies, by Holland's major 19th-century novelist
TRANSLATED BY ROY EDWARDS
INTRODUCTION BY D. H. LAWRENCE
0-87023-359-9 MASSACHUSETTS $40.00
0-14-044516-1 PENGUIN PB $12.95

Cees **Nooteboom**
The Following Story
TRANSLATED BY INA RILKE
0-15-100098-0 HARCOURT BRACE $14.95

Cees Nooteboom

In the Dutch Mountains
TRANSLATED BY ADRIENNE DIXON
0-8071-1425-1 LSU $14.95

Philip and the Others
In this first, surrealistic novel, a young man pursues his identity on a hitch-hiking odyssey of self-discovery, but ends up alone
TRANSLATED BY ADRIENNE DIXON
0-8071-1376-X LSU $14.95

Rituals
TRANSLATED BY ADRIENNE DIXON
0-8071-1081-7 LSU $14.95
0-15-600394-5 HARVEST PB $11.00

The Roads to Santiago: Essays
Twenty-five essays by the winner of the 1993 European Literary Prize recount explorations of Spain over three decades. Noteboom describes the shrine of the Black Madonna of Guadalupe, reflects on the life and work of Velazquez from the Prado, and admires the under-appreciated Zurbaran
See also **EUROPE SINCE 1945** under **EUROPE** under **TRAVEL LITERATURE** in **FOOD, TRAVEL, AND LEISURE**
TRANSLATED BY INA RILKE
0-15-100197-9 HARCOURT BRACE $24.00

A Song of Truth and Semblance
TRANSLATED BY ADRIENNE DIXON
0-8071-1176-7 LSU $12.95

Bert **Schierbeek**
Cross Roads
"For outsiders like me, who have sometimes managed a glimpse of contemporary Dutch poetry, Schierbeek has long appeared as the dominant figure, energetic and graceful. This poem-novel goes beyond anything we've seen, to place him among the masters of an art that breaks distinctions between genres"
—Jerome Rothenberg
TRANSLATED BY CHARLES MCGEEHAN
0-942668-11-1 KATYDID PB $14.95

Stijn **Streuvels**
The Flaxfield
TRANSLATED BY PETER GLASSGOLD & ANDRÉ LEFEVERE
1-55713-050-7 SUN & MOON PB $11.95

Adriaan **van Dis**
My Father's War
The story of a part-Indonesian man struggling to understand his family's wartime experience in a Japanese concentration camp and to come to grips with the origins of his father's endurance, charm, and cruelty. "A settling-of-accounts so raw the reader almost forgets he's dealing with language and composition.... A beautiful book"—*Vrij Nederland*
TRANSLATED BY CLAIRE NICOLAS WHITE
1-56584-033-X NEW PRESS $23.00

Paul **van Ostaijen**
Feasts of Fear and Agony
An example of the Flemish poet's experimental, expressionist writing, originally published in 1921
TRANSLATED BY HIDDE VAN AMEYDEN VAN DUYM
0-8112-0600-9 NEW DIRECTIONS $5.95

The First Book of Schmoll
TRANSLATED BY THEO HERMAN AND OTHERS
1-55713-266-6 SUN & MOON PB $11.95

German Literature

Medieval and Baroque Literature

Germanic peoples are recorded as a distinct tribal presence in the first century, and by the ninth century Old High German was established as the earliest written form of their language. However, no continuous literary tradition emerges until the late 12th century, with the work of the medieval poets Hartmann von Aue, Wolfram von Eschenbach, and Gottfried von Strassburg.

Reinhard **Becker**, translator
German Humanism and Reformation
Includes writings by von Tepl, Erasmus, Luther, Muntzer, and Brant
0-8264-0251-8 CONTINUUM $17.50

Francis G. **Gentry**, editor
German Medieval Tales
Includes *The Unfortunate Lord Henry, Reinhart the Fox, The Tale of Doctor Johannes Faustus,* and others
0-8264-0273-9 CONTINUUM PB $14.95

A.T. **Hatto**, editor
The Nibelungenlied
Often regarded as a national epic (though based on the Norse Edda tales), this anonymous 13th-century poem has been read both as a celebration of military heroism and as an urbane critique of an anachronistic warrior's code
See also **MEDIEVAL LITERATURE**
0-14-044137-9 PENGUIN PB $10.95

Martin **Luther**
Table Talk
0-00-627937-6 HARPERCOLLINS PB $11.00

Ronald G. **Murphy**, translator
The Heiland: The Saxon Gospel
The story of Jesus recast as heroic saga
0-19-507376-2 OXFORD PB $15.95

Paul **Oppenheimer**, translator
Till Eulenspiegel
The life and misdeeds of a celebrated medieval trickster figure
0-19-282343-4 OXFORD PB $8.95

Hartmann **von Aue**
Erec
This long poem from the late 12th century introduced Arthurian romance into German literature
TRANSLAED BY J.W. THOMAS
0-8122-8074-1 PENNSYLVANIA $33.95

Wolfram **von Eschenbach**
Parzival
This long and complex narrative variation on the Grail legend is the crowning masterpiece of medieval German literature
See also **MEDIEVAL LITERATURE**
TRANSLATED BY A.T. HATTO
0-14-044361-4 PENGUIN PB $10.95

Hans Jakob **von Grimmelshausen**
Adventures of a Simpleton
Grimmelshausen's grotesque realism is the primary literary testimony of the Thirty Years' War—and the human folly implicit in it—by an errant soldier of fortune. Influenced by the Spanish picaresque novel, the saga of Simplicius takes its hero through wars, marriages, and travels that culminate on an uncharted South Atlantic island
TRANSLATED BY WALTER WALLICH
0-8044-6229-1 UNGAR PB $9.95

Gottfried **von Strassburg**

Tristan

Strassburg's version of the Tristan and Isolde story imparts a mystical dimension to the concept of courtly love

See also **MEDIEVAL LITERATURE**

TRANSLATED BY A.T. HATTO

0-14-044098-4 PENGUIN PB....................$10.95

Enlightenment, Sturm und Drang, and Classicism

Emerging a century after the devastation of the Thirty Years' War, the German Enlightenment was committed to rationalism, tolerance, and human progress. That ostensible serenity, however, gave way during the 1770s to a radical protest of the sentiments: this was the *Sturm und Drang* (Storm and Stress) literary movement, which embraces the plays of Lenz and the early works of Goethe (especially *The Sorrows of Young Werther*) and Schiller.

Led by Goethe and Schiller, German classicism was largely an attempt to achieve through art what the French Revolution had failed to achieve through bloodshed.

Johann Wolfgang **von Goethe**

The Collected Works

Princeton's 12-volume edition of Goethe's major writings—in new translations into modern English, and including a number of works never before translated—is a remarkable achievement that makes Goethe newly accessible to the English-language reader

Volume 1
Selected Poems

Translators include Michael Hamburger, Christopher Middleton, and David Luke

EDITED BY CHRISTOPHER MIDDLETON

TRANSLATED BY MICHAEL HAMBURGER AND OTHERS

0-691-03658-6 PRINCETON PB....................$15.95

Volume 2
Faust 1 and 2

"Atkins's lively translation will most certainly assume a place of importance among the numerous English versions currently available"—*Choice*

EDITED AND TRANSLATED BY STUART ATKINS

0-691-03656-X PRINCETON PB....................$14.95

Volume 3
Essays on Art and Literature

"This third volume of the Goethe edition responsibly and fully responds to our questions in an age of theoretical reflection"—Peter Demetz

EDITED BY JOHN GEARY

0-691-03657-8 PRINCETON PB....................$14.95

Volume 4
From My Life: Poetry and Truth, Parts 1 to 3

EDITED BY THOMAS P. SAINE AND JEFFREY L. SAMMONS

0-691-03797-3 PRINCETON PB....................$14.95

Volume 5
From My Life: Poetry and Truth, Part 4; Campaign in France 1792/Siege of Mainz

Goethe's autobiography, along with a military chronicle not translated since the 19th-century

EDITED BY THOMAS P. SAINE AND JEFFREY L. SAMMONS

TRANSLATED BY ROBERT HEITNER AND THOMAS SAINE

0-691-03798-1 PRINCETON PB....................$15.95

Volume 6
Italian Journey

Goethe's midlife sojourn in Italy was the wellspring of his subsequent writing

TRANSLATED BY ROBERT R. HEITNER

EDITED BY THOMAS SAINE AND JEFFREY SAMMONS

0-691-03799-X PRINCETON PB....................$15.95

Volume 7
Early Verse Drama and Prose Plays

Includes *Goetz von Berlichingen, Egmont, Clavigo, Stella, Brother and Sister, Prometheus, Jery and Betty,* and *Proserpina*

EDITED BY CYRUS HAMLIN AND FRANK RYDER

TRANSLATED BY ROBERT BROWNING AND OTHERS

0-691-04342-6 PRINCETON PB....................$17.95

Volume 8
Verse Plays and Epic

Includes the plays *Iphigenia in Tauris, Torquato Tasso, The Natural Daughter, Pandora* (the latter two appearing in English for the first time), and the epic poem *Hermann and Dorothea*

EDITED BY CYRUS HAMLIN AND FRANK RYDER

TRANSLATED BY MICHAEL HAMBURGER AND OTHERS

0-691-04343-4 PRINCETON PB....................$16.95

Volume 9
Wilhelm Meister's Apprenticeship

EDITED AND TRANSLATED BY ERIC A. BLACKALL

0-691-04344-2 PRINCETON PB....................$16.95

Volume 10
Conversations of German Refugees; Wilhelm Meister's Journeyman Years, or the Renunciants

The final volume of *Wilhelm Meister* and the earlier *Conversations,* a cycle of novellas reflecting the events of the French Revolution

EDITED BY JANE K. BROWN

TRANSLATED BY KRISHNA WINSTON AND JAN VAN HERUCK

0-691-04345-0 PRINCETON PB....................$16.95

Volume 11
The Sorrows of Young Werther; Elective Affinities; Novella

Three of Goethe's major works

EDITED BY DAVID E. WELLBERY

TRANSLATED BY VICTOR LANGE AND JUDITH RYAN

0-691-04346-9 PRINCETON PB....................$13.95

Volume 12
Scientific Studies

Writings on anatomy, botany, physics, chemistry, zoology, meteorology, and geology

EDITED AND TRANSLATED BY DOUGLAS MILLER

0-691-04347-7 PRINCETON PB....................$16.95

Egmont

A great political tragedy based on an incident in the 16th-century Dutch rebellion against Spanish rule

TRANSLATED BY WILLARD TRASK

0-8120-0060-9 BARRONS PB....................$5.95

Elective Affinities

A novel that attempts a scientific analysis of two couples and their interlocking passions

0-14-044242-1 PENGUIN PB....................$10.95

Faust: Part 1

A nimble version in the original meters

TRANSLATED BY DAVID LUKE

0-19-281666-7 OXFORD PB....................$4.95

Faust: Part 2

TRANSLATED BY DAVID LUKE

0-19-282616-6 OXFORD PB....................$7.95

Faust: Parts 1 and 2

The second part is abridged

TRANSLATED BY LOUIS MACNIECE

0-19-500410-8 OXFORD PB....................$14.95

Faust: Part 1

TRANSLATED BY MARTIN GREENBERG

0-300-05656-7 YALE PB....................$12.00

Italian Journey: 1786-1788

"*Italian Journey* is not only a description of places, persons and things, but also a psychological document of the first importance dealing with a life crisis which, in various degrees of intensity, we all experience somewhere between the ages of thirty-five and forty-five"—W.H. Auden

See also **EUROPE** under **TRAVEL LITERATURE** in **FOOD, TRAVEL, AND LEISURE**

TRANSLATED BY W.H. AUDEN & ELIZABETH MAYER

0-14-044233-2 PENGUIN PB....................$11.95

Johann Wolfgang von Goethe

The Sorrows of Young Werther

This self-dramatizing epistolary novel of a young man's fatal love for a married woman became one of the most influential statements of European Romanticism

TRANSLATED BY LOUISE BOGAN, ELIZABETH MAYER & W.H. AUDEN

0-394-71958-1 VINTAGE PB....................$10.00

Tales of Transformation

Contains "Fairy Tale," "The New Melusine," and other stories tinged with alchemical imagery

TRANSLATED BY SCOTT THOMPSON

0-87286-211-9 CITY LIGHTS PB....................$8.95

Wilhelm Meister
This seminal *Bildungsroman* was an instrumental link in the tradition that embraces Dickens, Joyce, and Mann

Volume 1
The Years of Apprenticeship, Books 1-3
0-7145-3675-X RIVERRUN $11.95

Volume 2
The Years of Apprenticeship, Books 4-6
0-7145-4218-0 RIVERRUN PB $19.95

Volume 3
The Years of Apprenticeship, Books 7-8
0-7145-3702-0 RIVERRUN $7.95

Volume 4
The Years of Travel, Book 1
0-7145-3827-2 RIVERRUN $12.95

Volume 5
The Years of Travel, Book 2
0-7145-3838-8 RIVERRUN $12.95

Volume 6
The Years of Travel, Book 3
0-7145-3934-1 RIVERRUN PB $7.95

Friedrich **Hölderlin**

Hölderlin—who immersed himself in Greek classicism and translated Sophocles and Pindar—set the stage for German Romanticism and is now widely regarded as the precursor of poetic modernism.

Hymns and Fragments
The prophetic late work brilliantly translated and introduced

TRANSLATED BY RICHARD SIEBURTH

0-691-01412-4 PRINCETON PB $14.95

Hyperion and Selected Poems
0-8264-0334-4 CONTINUUM PB $14.95

Heinrich **von Kleist**

Before his suicide at 34 in 1811, Kleist had written a series of novellas and tales, plays (of which the greatest was Prince Frederick of Homburg*), essays, and letters—expressing, with unwavering formal control, themes of emotional devastation.*

Heinrich von Kleist

Five Plays
A new and excellent translation of Kleist's major dramatic works, *Amphitryon, The Broken Jug, Penthesilea, The Prince of Homburg,* and *The Tragedy of Robert Guiscard*

TRANSLATED BY MARTIN GREENBERG

0-300-04905-6 YALE PB $25.00

The Marquise of O. & Other Stories
Includes *Michael Kohlhaas, The Earthquake in Chile,* and *The Foundling*

TRANSLATED BY DAVID LUKE & NIGEL REEVES

0-14-044359-2 PENGUIN PB $9.95

Plays
Includes the one-act *The Broken Pitcher*, the blank-verse comedy *Amphitryon,* the Amazon tragedy *Penthesilea,* and Kleist's masterpiece *Prince Frederick of Homburg*

EDITED BY WALTER HINDERER

FOREWORD BY E.L. DOCTOROW

0-8264-0263-1 CONTINUUM PB $14.95

Prince Friedrich of Homburg
TRANSLATED BY DIANA PETERS

0-8112-0694-7 NEW DIRECTIONS PB $7.95

J.M. **Lenz**

The Tutor & The Soldiers
A didactic comedy of manners and a technically innovative tragedy that influenced Büchner

TRANSLATED BY WILLIAM YUILL

0-226-47221-6 CHICAGO PB $1.95

Gotthold **Lessing**

Laocoon: An Essay on the Limits of Painting and Poetry
An enormously influential 18th-century essay about the fundamental difference between poetry and the plastic arts

See also **THEORY** under **ART HISTORY: GENERAL STUDIES** in **ART**

TRANSLATED BY EDWARD MCCORMICK

0-8018-3139-3 JOHNS HOPKINS PB $14.95

Nathan the Wise, Minna von Barnhelm and Other Plays and Writings
EDITED BY PETER DEMETZ

0-8264-0706-4 CONTINUUM $29.50
0-8264-0707-2 CONTINUUM PB $14.95

Georg Christoph **Lichtenberg**

Aphorisms
The reflections of this 18th-century German mathematician and scientist were admired by Goethe, Schopenhauer, Nietzsche, and many others

TRANSLATED WITH AN INTRODUCTION BY R.J. HOLLINGDALE

0-14-044519-6 PENGUIN PB $10.95

I once lodged in Hanover in a room whose window gave on to a narrow street which formed a communicating link between two bigger streets. It was very pleasant to see how people's faces changed when they entered the little street, where they thought they were less observed; how here one pissed, there another fixed her garter, one gave way to private laughter and another shook his head. Girls thought with a smile of the night before and adjusted their ribbons for conquests in the big street ahead.

APHORISMS

Friedrich **Schiller**

Poet and philosopher, dramatist and historian, Schiller is notable above all for his lofty verse tragedies on themes of individual liberty and human dignity.

Mary Stuart
Perhaps his finest tragedy, in a 19th-century translation considerably streamlined by Bentley

TRANSLATED BY ERIC BENTLEY & JOSEPH MELLISH

0-936839-00-7 APPLAUSE THEATRE PB $7.95

Plays I
Includes *Intrigue and Love,* an antidespotic domestic tragedy, and *Don Carlos,* a drama of incestuous love and political sacrifice

0-8264-0274-7 CONTINUUM $27.50

The Robbers & Wallenstein
The Robbers, an early work, was a popular Romantic melodrama; *Wallenstein,* a trilogy of the Thirty Years' War, was Schiller's most ambitious dramatic epic

TRANSLATED BY F.J. LAMPORT

0-14-044368-1 PENGUIN PB $11.95

Wilhelm Tell
Schiller uses the Tell legend to epitomize the struggle for freedom

TRANSLATED BY WILLIAM MAINLAND

0-226-73801-9 CHICAGO PB $11.50

The 19th Century: Romanticism

Dismissed by Goethe on occasion as a "disease," German Romanticism nonetheless shared classicism's yearning for the "purity" of ancient Greek culture. German Romanticism derived much of its momentum from the thinking of Kant and Fichte and influenced every aspect of culture and art.

Folktales were a primary influence on the Romantics, in whose hands the novella became the quintessential 19th-century German genre.

Georg **Büchner**

Complete Plays, Lenz, and Other Writings
TRANSLATED BY JOHN REDDICK

0-14-044586-2 PENGUIN PB $10.95

Danton's Death, Leonce and Lena & Woyzeck
0-19-281827-9 OXFORD PB $6.95

Jacob **Grimm** & Wilhelm **Grimm**

The Complete Grimm's Fairy Tales
ILLUSTRATED BY JOSEF SCHARL

0-394-70930-6 RANDOM HOUSE PB $18.00

Selected Tales
The Grimms' collection of 210 fairytales is one of the great monuments of Romantic scholarship

TRANSLATED BY DAVID LUKE

0-14-044401-7 PENGUIN PB $9.95

E.T.A. **Hoffmann**

Tales of E.T.A. Hoffmann
A major Romantic author, Hoffmann is now famous chiefly for his weird and often comic tales.

EDITED BY LEONARD KENT

0-226-34789-3 CHICAGO PB $12.95

The Tales of Hoffmann

0-14-044392-4 PENGUIN PB $9.95

Novalis

Hymns to the Night

Six hymns inspired by the death of his fiancée

TRANSLATED BY DICK HIGGINS

0-914232-90-8 MCPHERSON PB $5.95

Philosophical Writings

0-7914-3271-8 SUNY PB $10.00

Frank **Ryder** & Robert **Browning**, editors

Romantic Novellas

Four works by Kleist and two by Jean Paul

0-8264-0295-X CONTINUUM PB $10.95

V. **Sanders**, editor

German Romantic Criticism

Includes writings by Schleiermacher, Jean Paul, Novalis, Schlegel, Hölderlin, Kleist, and Grimm

0-8264-0262-3 CONTINUUM PB $14.95

Ronald **Taylor**, editor

Six German Romantic Tales

Contains work by Heinrich von Kleist, Ludwig Tieck, and E.T.A. Hoffmann

0-8023-1295-0 DUFOUR PB $13.95

Adelbert **von Chamisso**

Peter Schlemiel

TRANSLATED BY PETER WORTSMAN

0-88064-142-8 FROMM $16.95

Late Romanticism

Heinrich **Heine**

Heine's work evolves from exquisitely crafted lyricism to an equally exquisite irony. He was also a great satirist and polemicist.

The Harz Journey

A bilingual edition of Heine's masterpiece of travel writing

TRANSLATED BY CHARLES GODFREY LELAND

1-56886-003-X MARSILIO PB $12.95

Heinrich Heine

Poetry and Prose

Includes 47 poems in German and English, *The Harz Journey*, *Ideas—Book Le Grand*, and *Germany: A Winter's Tale*, a mordant critique of social conditions in Germany

EDITED BY JOST HERMAND & ROBERT HOLUB

0-8264-0265-8 CONTINUUM PB $14.95

The Romantic School & Other Essays

EDITED BY VOLKMAR SANDER

0-8264-0291-7 CONTINUUM PB $14.95

Selected Prose

TRANSLATED BY RITCHIE ROBERTSON

0-14-044555-2 PENGUIN PB $11.95

Selected Verse

German text with literal prose translations

0-14-042098-3 PENGUIN PB $11.95

Songs of Love and Grief

TRANSLATED BY WALTER ARNDT

0-8101-1323-6 NORTHWESTERN $49.95

0-8101-1324-4 NORTHWESTERN PB $13.95

Richard **Wagner**

The Ring of the Nibelung

TRANSLATED BY ANDREW PORTER

0-393-00867-3 NORTON PB $13.95

Tristan and Isolde

TRANSLATED BY ANDREW PORTER

0-7145-3849-3 RIVERRUN PB $9.95

The 19th Century: Realist Fiction

No 19th-century German novelist commands the stature of a Balzac or a Tolstoy; indeed, Thomas Mann once remarked that Wagner's operas represented the German corollary to the great realist novels of France and Russia. Nevertheless, many late 19th-century writers did investigate contemporary social and moral problems. Foremost among them were Theodor Fontane (whose *Before the Storm* and *Effi Briest* scrutinize Prussian society and the emerging metropolis in Berlin) and the Swiss writer Gottfried Keller.

Theodor **Fontane**

Effi Briest

In this richly delineated portrait of stuffy provincial life, Effi is something of a German counterpart to Emma Bovary

TRANSLATED BY DOUGLAS PARMEE

0-14-044190-5 PENGUIN PB $10.95

Short Novels & Other Writings

Includes *A Man of Honor*, *Jenny Treibel*, and *The Eighteenth of March*

EDITED BY PETER DEMETZ

FOREWORD BY PETER GAY

0-8264-0260-7 CONTINUUM PB $14.95

Two Novellas: The Woman Taken in Adultery and The Poggenpuhl Family

TRANSLATED BY GABRIELE ANNAN

0-14-043524-7 PENGUIN PB $10.95

Johann Peter **Hebel**

The Treasure Chest

A collection of humorous and sensational stories, first published in 1811

TRANSLATED BY JOHN HIBBERD

0-14-044639-7 PENGUIN PB $10.95

Gottfried **Keller**

Green Henry

The Swiss storyteller and master of the novella offers a good example of poetic realism in this autobiographical work

TRANSLATED BY A.M. HOLT

0-7145-0265-0 RIVERRUN PB $16.95

Stories

Ten village tales in novella form including *A Village Romeo and Juliet* and *The Banner of the Upright Seven*

EDITED BY FRANK RYDER

FOREWORD BY MAX FRISCH

0-8264-0266-6 CONTINUUM PB $14.95

Adalbert **Stifter**

Brigitta and Other Tales

Psychologically realistic stories by an Austrian master

TRANSLATED BY HELEN WATANABE-O'KELLY

0-14-044630-3 PENGUIN PB $10.95

Humor

Wilhelm **Busch**

German Satirical Writings

Busch's ironic, illustrated poems can be seen as precursors of the comic strip. This collection also contains work by Christian Morgenstern, Kurt Tucholsky, and Erich Kastner

TRANSLATED BY WILHELM LOTZE & VOLKMAR SANDER

0-8264-0285-2 CONTINUUM PB $9.95

Max and Moritz

A celebrated German work of illustrated humor

0-486-20181-3 DOVER PB $5.95

Christian **Morgenstern**

The Gallows Songs: Christian Morgenstern's Galgenlieder

Morgenstern cultivated a highly original brand of nonsense poetry with serious undertone. "An amazingly good job of rewording Morgenstern's puns, idioms, neologisms, making the English lines dance to the metrics of the German" —Babette Deutsch

TRANSLATED WITH AN INTRODUCTION BY MAX KNIGHT

0-520-00884-7 CALIFORNIA PB $12.00

Songs from the Gallows: Galgenlieder

TRANSLATED BY WALTER ARNDT

0-300-05278-2 YALE $25.00

Modern German Literature: To 1945

The apparent linguistic unity of German literature encompasses a variety of cultural, geographic, and political fragmentations. In the first half of the 20th century, for example, a number of distinct literary cultures can be discerned, among them *fin-de-siècle* Vienna (Schnitzler, Kraus, Musil, Canetti), the German-speaking minority of Prague (Kafka, Rilke), and Berlin between the wars (Brecht, Benn, Döblin).

For related reading, see MODERN EUROPEAN DRAMA

Poetry

Gottfried **Benn**

Benn ranks as the great German Expressionist poet. Something of his tone can be gauged from the titles of his collections: Morgue, Rubble, Narcosis, *and* Split.

Poems, 1937-1947
0-943045-06-1 PLUTARCH PB $4.95

Primal Vision
EDITED BY E.B. ASHTON
0-7145-2500-6 MARION BOYARS $18.00

I saw the ego, the look in its eyes. I dilated its pupil, looked far into it, looked far out of it; the gaze from such eyes is almost expressionless, more like scenting, scenting danger, an age-old danger. From disasters that were latent, disasters that antedated the word, come dreadful memories of the race, hybrid, beast-shaped, sphinx-pouched features of the primal face. I recalled the dicta of certain profoundly experienced men, that evil would come of their telling all they knew. I thought of the strange adages, that one should give up searching for the ultimate words that need only be spoken to unhinge heaven and earth. I sniffed in masks, I rattled in runes, I dove into demons with sleep-craving brutality, with mythical instincts, in the ante-verbal, instinctual threat of prehistoric neura; I began to grasp, I saw the vision: monism in rhythms, mass in intoxications, compulsion and repression, Ananke of the I.
PRIMAL VISION

Prose, Essays, Poems
EDITED BY RICHARD BECKER & WOLKMAR SANDER
FOREWORD BY JOHN SIMON
0-8264-0310-7 CONTINUUM $29.50
0-8264-0311-5 CONTINUUM PB $14.95

Else **Lasker-Schüler**

Lasker-Schuler, an eccentric and visionary Jewish poet closely associated with the Expressionist movement who used much Oriental imagery in her work, settled in Palestine in the late '30s.

Your Diamond Dreams Cut Open My Arteries
TRANSLATED BY ROBERT NEWTON
0-8078-8100-7 NORTH CAROLINA $32.50

Rainer Maria **Rilke**

"Rilke's special gift as a poet is that he does not seem to speak from the middle of life, that he is always calling us away from it. His poems have the feeling of being written from a great depth in himself. What makes them so seductive is that they also speak to the reader so intimately. They seem whispered or crooned into our inmost ear, insinuating us toward the same depth in ourselves. The effect can be hypnotic..."—Robert Hass in the introduction to The Selected Poetry of Rainer Maria Rilke.

Between Roots: Selected Poems
TRANSLATED BY RIKA LESSER
0-691-01429-9 PRINCETON PB $9.95

The Complete French Poems of Rainer Maria Rilke
TRANSLATED BY A. POULIN, JR.
FOREWORD BY W.D. SNODGRASS
0-915308-83-5 GRAY WOLF PB $14.00

The Duino Elegies
Young adopts a stanzaic format of triplets modelled on William Carlos Williams. A bilingual edition
TRANSLATED BY DAVID YOUNG
0-393-30931-2 NORTON PB $8.95

Rainer Maria Rilke

The Duino Elegies & The Sonnets to Orpheus
A bilingual edition. "Now, because of Mr. Poulin's translations, I experience the *Elegies* almost as English. He gives Rilke the crisp speed of English, and yet seems to remain very close to the original meaning"—Robert Lowell
TRANSLATED BY A.B. POULIN, JR.
0-395-25058-7 HOUGHTON MIFFLIN PB $12.95

Letters on Cézanne
See also **CRITICS AND WRITERS ON ART** under **ART HISTORY: GENERAL STUDIES** in **ART**
TRANSLATED BY JOEL AGEE
0-88064-022-7 FROMM PB $14.95

Letters to a Young Poet
A passionate exposition of the poetic vocation, addressed to a correspondent Rilke had never met
TRANSLATED BY STEPHEN MITCHELL
0-394-74104-8 RANDOM HOUSE PB $9.00

New Poems [1907]
This bilingual volume, together with its companion *New Poem: The Other Part,* offers the first complete English translation of what many consider Rilke's most radically original work. The *New Poems* attempt to find a linguistic equivalent to the objective and tactile qualities Rilke discovered in the work of Rodin and Cézanne: "Somehow I too must come to make things; not plastic, but written things—*realities* that emerge from handwork. Somehow I too must discover the smallest basic, element, the cell of my art, the tangible immaterial means of representation for everything"
TRANSLATED BY EDWARD SNOW
0-86547-415-X NORTH POINT PB $12.00

New Poems [1908]: The Other Part
TRANSLATED BY EDWARD SNOW
0-86547-416-8 NORTH POINT PB $12.00

Center of all centers, core of cores,
almond, that closes in and sweetens,—
this entire world out to all the stars
is your fruit-flesh: we greet you.

Look, you feel how nothing any longer
clings to you; your husk is in infinity,
and there the strong juice stands and presses.
And from outside a radiance assists it,

for high above, your suns in full splendor
have wheeled blazingly around.
Yet already there's begun inside you
what lasts beyond the suns.
BUDDHA IN GLORY

The Notebooks of Malte Laurids Brigge
"Each reading of this timeless modern classic stirs the imagination with a new remembrance of its richness, originality of design and purity of language"—Elizabeth Hardwick
0-393-30881-2 NORTON PB $9.95

Poems from the Book of Hours
An early work, tendered in Rilke's rhyme scheme
TRANSLATED WITH AN INTRODUCTION BY BABETTE DEUTSCH
0-8112-0595-9 NEW DIRECTIONS PB $5.95

Selected Poetry of Rainer Maria Rilke
Mitchell's bilingual edition is by far the best selection currently available. It spans the whole of Rilke's career and includes along with much else the complete *Duino Elegies*
EDITED AND TRANSLATED BY STEPHEN MITCHELL
INTRODUCTION BY ROBERT HASS
0-679-72201-7 VINTAGE PB $13.00

The Sonnets to Orpheus
Another superior translation by Mitchell, filling out the *Selected Poetry* listed above. Bilingual edition
TRANSLATED BY STEPHEN MITCHELL
0-393-30932-0 NORTON PB $8.95

Sonnets to Orpheus
A bilingual edition. "An artful and sensitive translation of this most elusive of Rilke's poetry"—Stanley Plumly
TRANSLATED BY DAVID YOUNG
0-8195-6165-7 WESLEYAN PB $13.95

Two Stories of Prague: "King Bohush" and "The Siblings"
TRANSLATED BY ANGELA ESTERHAMMER
0-87451-661-7 NEW ENGLAND $25.00
0-87451-789-3 NEW ENGLAND PB $12.95

Uncollected Poems
TRANSLATED BY EDWARD SNOW
0-86547-482-6 NORTH POINT $22.00

Where Silence Reigns: Selected Prose
0-393-20697-1 NORTON PB $8.95

Georg **Trakl**

Autumn Sonata: Selected Poems
One of the most successful attempts ever made to bring into English the stark imagistic power of the great modern Austrian poet who died in 1914
TRANSLATED BY DANIEL SIMKO
0-918825-94-6 MOYER BELL PB $9.95

Fiction and Other Prose

Walter **Benjamin**

This incisive critic and cultural historian, who strove to balance the conflicting influences of Marxism and Jewish theology, committed suicide rather than fall into the hands of the Gestapo.

The Correspondence of Walter Benjamin, 1910-1940

See also THE FRANKFURT SCHOOL under CULTURAL CRITICISM under LITERARY THEORY

EDITED BY THEODOR ADORNO

0-226-04237-5 CHICAGO $45.00

The Correspondence of Walter Benjamin and Gershom Scholem, 1932-1940

TRANSLATED BY GARY SMITH

0-674-17415-1 HARVARD PB $16.50

Illuminations

Benjamin was the foremost writer to emerge from the Frankfurt school; he has been called the finest critic of the 20th century. Whether talking about Baudelaire, photography, storytelling, or unpacking a library, Benjamin always touches a nerve

INTRODUCTION BY HANNAH ARENDT

0-8052-0241-2 SCHOCKEN PB $14.00

Moscow Diary

TRANSLATED BY RICHARD SIEBURTH
EDITED BY GARY SMITH
FOREWORD BY GERSHOM SCHOLEM

0-674-58743-X HARVARD $30.00
0-674-58744-8 HARVARD PB $14.00

Reflections: Essays, Aphorisms, Autobiographical Writings

See also BIOGRAPHY under JEWISH HISTORY in WORLD HISTORY AND CURRENT AFFAIRS

TRANSLATED BY EDMUND JEPHCOTT
EDITED BY PETER DEMETZ

0-8052-0802-X SCHOCKEN PB $15.00

Walter Benjamin: Selected Writings

A new selection from the work of this enormously influential critic and writer

0-674-94585-9 HARVARD $35.00

Bertolt **Brecht**

Journals, 1934-1955

0-415-91282-2 ROUTLEDGE PB $22.95

Hermann **Broch**

The Death of Virgil

Close to despair over the impotence of art and about to burn his *Aeneid*, Virgil receives a deathbed illumination. This highly experimental book owes much to Broch's own close encounter with death following the Anschluss

TRANSLATED BY JEAN UNTERMEYER

0-86547-115-0 NORTH POINT PB $16.95

The Guiltless

A study of "shared guilt" showing how European apathy nurtured the growth of fascism

TRANSLATED BY RALPH MANHEIM

0-86547-305-6 FS&G PB $12.50

The Sleepwalkers

A philosophical novel on the deterioration of moral values culminating in Nazism

TRANSLATED BY EDWIN AND WILLA MUIR

0-679-76406-2 VINTAGE PB $16.00

The Unknown Quantity

Broch's second novel, published in 1933, is another meditation on decaying values

TRANSLATED BY WILLA AND EDWIN MUIR

0-910395-36-5 MARLBORO PB $10.95

Elias **Canetti**

The theme underlying the work of this 1981 Nobel Laureate—who was born in Bulgaria, emigrated to Manchester, and came to rest in German-speaking Europe—is the relationship of the intellectual to the mass, and the relevance of this to fascism

Auto-da-Fé

A scholarly recluse marries and is destroyed by his brutish housekeeper

TRANSLATED BY D.V. WEDGEWOOD

0-374-51879-3 FS&G PB $17.00

Crowds and Power

A monumental study of crowd psychology, ranging from the Bushmen and the Pueblo Indians to Christianity and industrial societies

TRANSLATED BY CAROL STEWART

0-374-51820-3 FS&G PB $17.00

The Play of the Eyes

The third volume of Canetti's memoirs, set in Vienna in the '30s, describes his relations with Broch, Musil, Berg, and Alma Mahler

TRANSLATED BY RALPH MANHEIM

0-374-52075-5 FS&G PB $9.95

The Secret Heart of the Clock

Collected "notations" present reflections on death and aging

TRANSLATED BY JOEL AGEE

9-993-58078-3 FS&G $19.95

The Torch in My Ear

The second volume of the memoirs. *The Tongue Set Free,* the first volume is presently out-of-print

TRANSLATED BY JOACHIM NEUGROSCHEL

0-374-27847-4 FS&G $16.50

Alfred **Döblin**

"I am greatly indebted to Alfred Döblin...He will unsettle you; he will trouble your dreams; you will have difficulty swallowing him; you will find him unsavory; he is indigestible, gristly. He changes his readers. The self-complacent are hereby cautioned against Döblin"—Gunter Grass

A People Betrayed: November 1918, a German Revolution

Part One of Doblin's magnum opus. "A panoramic vision of disaster and betrayal that blends realism and fantasy to stunning effect" —Ernst Pawel

TRANSLATED BY JOHN E. WOODS

0-88064-008-1 FROMM PB $16.95

Karl and Rosa: November 1918, a German Revolution

The second half of Döblin's revolutionary epic pursues the careers of the revolution's leaders, Karl Liebknecht and Rosa Luxemburg

TRANSLATED BY JOHN WOODS

0-88064-011-1 FROMM PB $15.95

Berlin Alexanderplatz: The Story of Franz Biberkopf

0-80446-121-X UNGER PB $16.95

Hermann **Hesse**

Hesse's absorption in Eastern religion and Jungian psychology and his criticism of European bourgeois values has made him a great favorite with several generations of young readers.

The Fairy Tales of Herman Hesse

TRANSLATED AND WITH AN INTRODUCTION BY JACK ZIPES

0-553-37776-0 BANTAM PB $12.95

The Journey to the East

An allegorical pilgrimage toward enlightenment

TRANSLATED BY HILDA ROSNER

0-374-50036-3 FS&G PB $9.00

Magister Ludi: The Glass Bead Game

A study of how the quest for freedom necessarily conflicts with tradition

0-8446-6524-X SMITH $23.00
0-8050-1246-X HOLT PB $13.95

Narcissus and Goldmund

Hesse's protagonists express a polarity between artistic revolt and the continuity of social structures

TRANSLATED BY URSULA MOLINARO

0-374-50684-1 FS&G PB $12.00

Siddhartha

The famous novel of spiritual growth

TRANSLATED BY HILDA ROSNER

0-553-20884-5 BDD PB $4.99
0-8112-0068-X NEW DIRECTIONS PB $5.95

Steppenwolf

A Surrealist narrative recounted by an artist-outsider who eventually comes to believe that misfits may find harmony with each other

0-8050-1247-8 HOLT PB $7.95

Hugo **von Hofmannsthal**

The Lord Chandos Letters

TRANSLATED BY RUSSELL STOCKMAN

0-910395-18-7 MARLBORO PB $7.25

Ernst **Jünger**

Aladdin's Problem

TRANSLATED BY JOACHIM NEUGROSCHEL

0-941419-58-4 ERIDANOS $19.00

A Dangerous Encounter

Jünger *(On the Marble Cliffs)* was the most decorated German soldier of the First World War. Later, he developed into one of the major European writers of the 20th century. *A Dangerous Encounter,* with its brilliant interweaving of philosophy, sexual obsession, politics, and crime, is a perfect introduction to his huge and influential body of work, largely untranslated in the U.S. until now

TRANSLATED BY HILARY BARR

0-941419-37-1 MARSILIO $21.00

The Storm of Steel: From the Diary of a German Stormtroop Officer on the Western Front

0-865-27423-1 HOWARD FERTIG PB $13.95

Eumeswil

TRANSLATED BY JOACHIM NEUGROSCHEL

0-941419-97-5 MARSILIO........................$29.95

Franz **Kafka**

"Had one to name the author who comes nearest to bearing the same kind of relation to our age as Dante, Shakespeare, and Goethe bore to theirs, Kafka is the first one would think of."—W.H. Auden

Amerika

A comic masterpiece about a young immigrant's attempt to find a niche in an incomprehensible country

TRANSLATED BY EDWIN & WILLA MUIR

0-8112-0075-2 NEW DIRECTIONS PB........................$10.95

Franz Kafka

Amerika

0-8052-1064-4 SCHOCKEN PB $13.00

The Blue Octavo Notebook

TRANSLATED BY ERNST KAISER & EITHNE WILKINS

1-87897-204-9 EXACT CHANGE PB........................$13.95

The Castle

Allegory of a man's hopeless attempt to "reach the Castle" and have his identity acknowledged by its inhabitants

TRANSLATED BY EDWIN & WILLA MUIR

COMMENTARY BY THOMAS MANN

0-679-41735-4 KNOPF $17.00

0-8052-1039-3 SCHOCKEN PB........................$15.00

The Complete Stories

EDITED BY ARTHUR SAMUELSON

0-8052-1055-5 SCHOCKEN PB........................$15.00

The Metamorphosis, In the Penal Colony, and Other Stories

TRANSLATED BY EDWIN AND WILLA MUIR

0-8052-1057-1 SCHOCKEN PB $12.00

The Metamorphosis, In the Penal Colony, and Other Stories

TRANSLATED BY JOACHIM NEUGROSCHEL

0-02-021807-9 SCRIBNERS PB........................$10.00

Selected Short Stories of Franz Kafka

TRANSLATED BY EDWIN & WILLA MUIR

INTRODUCTION BY PHILIP RAHV

0-679-60061-2 MODERN LIBRARY $14.50

The Transformation and Other Stories: Works Published During Kafka's Lifetime

TRANSLATED BY MALCOLM PASLEY

0-14-018478-3 PENGUIN PB........................$10.95

The Trial

"We are taken to the limits of human thought. Indeed, everything in this work is, in the true sense, essential. It states the problem of the absurd in its entirety"—Albert Camus

0-679-40994-7 KNOPF $17.00

0-8052-1040-7 SCHOCKEN PB $11.00

Erich **Kastner**

Fabian: The Story of a Moralist

TRANSLATED BY CYRUS BROOKS

0-8101-1137-3 NORTHWESTERN PB $14.95

Karl **Kraus**

This Austrian critic has been described as "probably the greatest satirist of the 20th century."—Christian Science Monitor

Half-Truths and One-and-a-Half Truths: Selected Aphorisms

TRANSLATED WITH AN INTRODUCTION BY HARRY ZOHN

0-226-45268-9 CHICAGO PB $11.95

In These Great Times: A Karl Kraus Reader

A selection of prose satires (including "The Good Conduct Medal," "Promotional Trips to Hell," and "Psychoanalysis"), poems, and excerpts from *The Last Days of Mankind*

TRANSLATED BY JOSEPH FABRY

EDITED BY HARRY ZOHN

0-226-45265-4 CHICAGO........................$29.95

No Compromise: Selected Writings of Karl Kraus

TRANSLATED BY SHEEMA BUEHNE

EDITED BY FREDERICK UNGAR

0-8044-6373-5 UNGAR PB........................$9.95

Alexander **Lernet-Holenia**

Baron Bagge & Count Luna

Two novellas by an acclaimed Austrian stylist

TRANSLATED BY RICHARD & CLARA WINSTON

0-941419-20-7 ERIDANOS........................$23.00

0-941419-21-5 GODINE PB........................$3.98

The Resurrection of Maltravers

TRANSLATED BY JOACHIM NEUGROSCHEL

0-941419-23-1 GODINE PB........................$3.98

Heinrich **Mann**

Young Henry of Navarre

The first installment of a two-volume historical epic dealing with the career of Henry IV

TRANSLATED BY ERIC SUTTON

0-87951-206-7 VIKING PB $19.95

Henry, King of France

Henry's story continued. "Fictional history in the grand manner"—*New Republic*

0-87951-224-5 OVERLOOK PB $15.95

Man of Straw

This 1918 satire of German militarism led to Mann's imprisonment

0-14-018137-7 PENGUIN PB........................$10.95

Klaus **Mann**

Mephisto

A famous actor is corrupted by Nazism

TRANSLATED BY ROBYN SMYTH

0-14-018918-1 PENGUIN PB........................$11.95

Thomas **Mann**

Heinrich's younger brother, the foremost German novelist of the 20th century, was awarded the Nobel Prize in 1929 for what many consider his masterpiece, The Magic Mountain.

The Black Swan

An unflattering portrait of an American woman

TRANSLATED BY WILLARD TRASK

0-520-07009-7 CALIFORNIA PB........................$12.95

Buddenbrooks

A partly autobiographical account of the decline of a patrician family

TRANSLATED BY H.T. LOWE-PORTER

0-679-73646-8 VINTAGE PB $14.00

Thomas Mann

Buddenbrooks: The Decline of a Family

The first new translation since 1924 of Mann's monumental first book

TRANSLATED BY JOHN E. WOODS

0-679-41994-2 KNOPF........................$35.00

0-679-75260-9 VINTAGE PB $16.00

Confessions of Felix Krull, Confidence Man

Mann's last novel presents its picaresque hero in a tone of serene cynicism

TRANSLATED BY DENVER LINDLEY

0-679-73904-1 VINTAGE PB $14.00

Death in Venice & Seven Other Stories

Includes "Tonio Kroger," "Tristan," "Disorder and Early Sorrow," "Mario and the Magician," "Felix Krull," "The Blood of the Walsungs," and "A Man and His Dog"

TRANSLATED BY H.T. LOWE-PORTER

0-679-72206-8 VINTAGE PB $10.00

Doctor Faustus
A great composer makes a pact with the devil to achieve release from sterility and decadence; Mann's story is filled with echoes of the Hitler era
TRANSLATED BY H.T. LOWE-PORTER
0-679-73905-X VINTAGE PB $14.00

The Holy Sinner
Mann's rendering of the "birth of the blessed Pope Gregory," modeled on Hartmann von Aue's *Gregorius*
TRANSLATED BY H.T. LOWE-PORTER
0-520-07671-0 CALIFORNIA PB $14.95

Joseph and His Brothers
In the Joseph tetralogy Mann explores a more optimistic mode
0-394-43132-4 KNOPF $65.00

Very deep is the well of the past. Should we not call it bottomless? Bottomless indeed, if—and perhaps only if—the past we mean is the past merely of the life of mankind, that riddling essence of which our own normally unsatisfied and quite abnormally wretched existences form a part; whose mystery, of course, includes our own and is the alpha and omega of all our questions, lending burning immediacy to all we say, and significance to all our striving. For the deeper we sound, the further down into the lower world of the past we probe and press, the more do we find that the earliest foundations of humanity, its history and culture, reveal themselves unfathomable.
JOSEPH AND HIS BROTHERS

Lotte in Weimar: The Beloved Returns
A reissue of one of Mann's most complex and self-revealing novels. "Mann's most daring work…*Lotte in Weimar* stands out as the work in which Mann took the most risks and exposed most completely his deepest feelings about himself and his art"—Hayden White
TRANSLATED BY H.T. LOWE-PORTER
0-520-07007-0 CALIFORNIA PB $14.95

The Magic Mountain
This large-scale novel set in a sanatorium charts the ills of Western civilization, while offering hope for the future
TRANSLATED BY JOHN E. WOODS
0-679-44183-2 KNOPF $35.00
0-679-77287-1 VINTAGE PB $17.00

On Myself & Other Princeton Lectures
0-8204-2996-1 LANG $42.00

Royal Highness
A subtly ironic celebration of Mann's own marriage, the groom a German princeling, the bride an American heiress
TRANSLATED BY A. CECIL CURTIS
0-520-07673-7 CALIFORNIA PB $14.95

The Transposed Heads
"At once the quintessence and the *reductio ad absurdum* of all love triangles"—Lionel Trilling
0-394-70086-4 RANDOM HOUSE PB $8.00

Robert **Musil**

Five Women
Five short stories representing "elaborate attempts to use fiction for its true purposes, the discovery and regeneration of the human world"—Frank Kermode
TRANSLATED BY EITHNE WILKINS & ERNST KAISER
0-87923-603-5 GODINE PB $12.95

The Man Without Qualities
This new translation of Musil's monumental unfinished novel, in two volumes, is the only complete version ever available in English. It confirms the extraordinary reputation of Musil's comic and philosophical meditation on modern history
TRANSLATED BY BURTON PIKE AND SOPHIE WILKINS
0-394-51052-6 KNOPF $60.00
0-679-76787-8 VINTAGE PB $20.00

Robert Musil

Posthumous Papers of a Living Author
"This collection's appearance is a major literary event…Wortsman's translation is splendid" —*NY Times Book Review*
TRANSLATED BY PETER WORTSMAN
0-14-018915-7 PENGUIN PB $11.95

Precision and Soul: Essays and Addresses
TRANSLATED BY DAVID S. LUFT
0-226-55409-0 CHICAGO PB $16.95

Selected Writings
Contains *Young Törless* (Musil's harsh study of sadism among military cadets), four stories, and *Posthumous Papers and Other Prose*
TRANSLATED BY EITHNE WILKINS
0-8264-0304-2 CONTINUUM PB $14.95

Max **Nordau**

Degeneration
A cranky but vigorous and influential attack on the founders of modernism—including Nietzsche, Ibsen, and the French Symbolists—by a founder of Zionism. Nordau was a prolific writer and a physician who claimed to find evidence of psychopathology throughout *fin-de-siècle* literature
0-8032-8367-9 NEBRASKA PB $18.00

Leo **Perutz**

The Master of the Day of Judgement
A mysterious book exerts a disastrous influence on everyone who reads it
1-55970-171-4 ARCADE $19.95

The Swedish Cavalier
TRANSLATED BY JOHN BROWNJOHN
1-55970-170-6 ARCADE $19.95

Erich Maria **Remarque**

All Quiet on the Western Front
Incinerated by the Nazis in 1933, this famous war novel depicts the horror of the front with deliberately brutal realism
See also **THE GREAT WAR** under **WORLD WAR I** under **20TH-CENTURY EUROPE TO THE SECOND WORLD WAR** in **WORLD HISTORY AND CURRENT AFFAIRS**
TRANSLATED BY A.W. WHEEN
0-316-73992-8 LITTLE, BROWN $21.95
0-449-21394-3 FAWCETT PB $5.99

Joseph **Roth**

Confession of a Murderer: Told in One Night
A tale of collaboration, deception, and exile. "Worthy to sit beside Conrad's and Dostoevsky's excursions into the twisted world of secret agents"—*Times* (London)
0-87951-989-4 OVERLOOK $22.50
0-87951-287-3 OVERLOOK PB $9.95

The Emperor's Tomb
TRANSLATED BY JOHN HOARE
0-87951-270-9 OVERLOOK PB $12.95

Flight Without End
"An important chronicle of the disintegration of early twentieth-century Europe"—*NY Times*
TRANSLATED BY DAVID LE VAY
0-87951-279-2 OVERLOOK PB $8.95

Hotel Savoy
TRANSLATED BY JOHN HOARE
0-87951-211-3 OVERLOOK $22.95

The Radetzky March
Roth's best novel surveys the waning of the Hapsburg Empire
TRANSLATED BY JOACHIM NEUGROSCHEL
0-87951-548-1 OVERLOOK $25.00
0-87951-558-9 OVERLOOK PB $14.95

Arthur **Schnitzler**

Schnitzler epitomized the elegance and pessimism of Viennese culture at the turn of the centuy. His plays and ficiton have enjoyed a revival in recent years.

Dream Story
1-55713-081-7 SUN & MOON PB $11.95

Lieutenant Güstl
An extraordinary inner monologue traces the unraveling of a military officer
1-55713-176-7 SUN & MOON PB $9.95

The Road to the Open
A 1908 novel that offers a vibrant chronicle of Vienna at the turn of the century, focusing on the encounters of an aristocratic musician with the world of Jewish intellectuals and artists. Schnitzler pioneered the use of inner monologues in his dissection of social conflicts and identity crises
0-8101-0996-4 CALIFORNIA PB $12.95

Anna **Seghers**

The Excursion of the Dead Young Girls
TRANSLATED BY ALBERTO MANGUEL
0-88910-486-7 COACH HOUSE PB $12.95

Robert **Walser**

Masquerade & Other Stories

Walser's peculiar blend of comedy, terror, and verbal experimentation is concentrated to a hypnotic intensity in his dazzling, brief stories. This collection presents 64 works written between 1899 and 1933 by a writer whom William Gass has called "post-modernist well before the fashion"

0-8018-3977-7 JOHNS HOPKINS PB $12.95

Kurt was a boorish fellow, at least he was seen as such. He bettered himself and became a snob. As a snob he was more boorish than as a boor. Still, I don't want to tell anecdotes, but rather practice analysis. Somewhere there's a revue where only married couples may show up. I must hurry and get married. Kunigunde sits lonely in the coffeehouse, crying her eyes out on account of my unrelentingness. I believe the following: in the nuptial bed my spirit will celebrate its resurrection. Not long ago I received a letter. What was in it? The touching request that I not follow Gottfried Keller's bad example, and that it was so nice to be cock of the walk. I replied: "As a voluptuous village girl is at my disposal as well as a wife, I'll gain a work of art. The best thing will be to beget a child and offer the product to a publisher, who's hardly likely to reject it. Daily my wife will cloak me in reproaches, I could use a good dressing down anyhow. I'll learn from this child. What a promising future!" [1925]

MASQUERADE & OTHER STORIES

The Walk

Obsessive and fantastically inventive, Walser is like no other writer. "He is truly a wonderful, heartbreaking writer"—Susan Sontag

1-85242-276-9 SERPENT'S TAIL PB $15.99

Jack **Zipes**, editor

Utopian Tales from Weimar

0-87451-501-7 NEW ENGLAND $30.00

Postwar Literature

In a short story by Heinrich Böll, a wounded young soldier in the final days of World War II is carried into a makeshift hospital. Gradually he comes to recognize his surroundings as the high school he had recently been forced to leave. From his stretcher he catches a glimpse of his own handwriting on the blackboard—just as the surgeon begins to amputate his limbs. This might be a symbol of the modern German writer, whose literary traditions were dismembered by the Nazis and who is now forced to confront the consequences of war and the Holocaust.

For ease of reference, postwar Austrian, German, and Swiss writers are grouped together here in alphabetical order.

Alfred **Andersch**

The Father of a Murderer

TRANSLATED BY LEILA VENNEWITZ

0-8112-1261-0 NEW DIRECTIONS $17.95

Ingeborg **Bachmann**

Bachmann has been claimed as a major influence by Peter Handke and Christa Wolf.

Malina

Bachmann's only novel is a complex study of postwar consciousness and sexual conflict

0-8419-1192-4 HOLMES & MEIER $24.95

Songs in Flight: The Collected Poems of Ingeborg Bachmann

"Eloquent translations (and an excellent essay and notes by the translator)"—Susan Sontag

TRANSLATED BY PETER FILKINS

1-56886-010-2 MARSILIO PB $19.95

Three Paths to the Lake

TRANSLATED BY MARY FRAN GILBERT

0-8419-1070-7 HOLMES & MEIER $29.95

Jurek **Becker**

Jacob the Liar

TRANSLATED BY LEILA VENNEWITZ

1-55970-315-6 ARCADE $21.95

Sleepless Days

Becker, a concentration camp survivor, left East Germany in 1977 after this book was rejected for publication

0-15-682765-4 HARCOURT BRACE PB $5.95

Thomas **Bernhard**

Concrete

In this macabre tale of failure, a musicologist strives for ten years to produce the perfect opening sentence. "A book of mysterious, dark beauty"—John Rechy, *LA Times*

TRANSLATED BY DAVID MCLINTOCK

0-226-04398-3 CHICAGO PB $12.95

Correction

A surviving friend becomes progressively more absorbed in the manuscripts left by a brilliant mathematician and philosopher who has committed suicide. The shadow of Wittgenstein looms over this novel by the author of *Gargoyles, Woodcutters,* and *The Lime Works*

TRANSLATED BY SOPHIE WILKINS

0-226-04393-2 CHICAGO PB $15.95

We're up to something, as we know, it's invariably something stupendous, even our most insignificant, unimpressive brainchild is always the most stupendous thing, and we feel we must speak of it, go into it, and we're disappointed, either we're not understood, no matter how clearly and forcefully we put our case, or else we don't want to be understood. We're always left without an answer, and of course in a more debilitated state than before, because no one, no expert or person, whichever, wants to help us. And so we naturally have to depend entirely on ourselves all our lives and we go our way alone, depending on ourselves only, working to earn everything ourselves, with no outside help. And so we're always full up and never come to rest…

CORRECTION

Extinction

TRANSLATED BY DAVID MCLINTOCK

0-394-57253-X KNOPF $24.00

0-226-04383-5 CHICAGO PB $14.95

Gargoyles

A doctor's rounds take him through a panorama of human suffering, ending with a schizophrenic "whose uninterrupted monologue for a hundred pages is a virtuoso verbal performance" —A.C. Foote, *Book World*

TRANSLATED BY RICHARD & CLARA WINSTON

0-226-04399-1 CHICAGO PB $14.95

Gathering Evidence: A Memoir

TRANSLATED BY DAVID MCLINTOCK

0-679-73809-6 VINTAGE PB $14.00

The Lime Works

A nameless insurance salesman recounts the life and crime of a tormented recluse

TRANSLATED BY SOPHIA WILKINS

0-226-04397-5 CHICAGO PB $16.95

The Loser

In *Wittgenstein's Nephew* Bernhard offered a fictionalized version of a real friendship; in *The Loser* he wrote of an entirely imaginary friendship with pianist Glenn Gould. The depiction of a relationship that never occurred is suffused with Bernhard's characteristic themes of the pain of loss and the difficulty of memory

0-394-57239-4 KNOPF $19.00

0-679-74179-8 VINTAGE PB $10.00

Old Masters: A Comedy

TRANSLATED BY EWALD OSERS

0-226-04391-6 CHICAGO PB $12.95

On the Mountain: Rescue Attempt, Nonsense

TRANSLATED BY RUSSELL STOCKMAN

0-910395-76-4 MARLBORO PB $10.95

Wittgenstein's Nephew: A Friendship

A mordant memoir about Bernhard's friendship with the philosopher's mentally troubled nephew

TRANSLATED BY DAVID MCLINTOCK

0-226-04392-4 CHICAGO PB $9.95

Woodcutters

A savagely funny demolition of the cultural elite of Vienna, told through the moment-to-moment reactions of an unhappy guest at a dinner party

TRANSLATED BY DAVID MCLINTOCK

0-226-04396-7 CHICAGO PB $12.95

Yes

TRANSLATED BY EWALD OSERS

0-226-04390-8 CHICAGO PB $10.95

Horst **Bienek**

Selected Poems, 1957-1987

Bienek spent four years as a political prisoner in the Urals in the '50s before being granted amnesty and settling in West Germany

0-87775-207-9 UNICORN PB $14.95

Johannes **Bobrowski**

Bobrowski, an outstanding East German poet, explored throughout his work a visionary geography typified by the title Shadow Lands.

Darkness and a Little Light

TRANSLATED BY LEILA VENNEWITZ

0-8112-1259-9 NEW DIRECTIONS $19.95

Levin's Mill

A novel set in West Prussia in 1874, about a plot to dispossess a Jewish mill-owner

TRANSLATED BY JANET CROPPER

0-8112-1329-3 NEW DIRECTIONS PB $12.00

Shadow Lands: Selected Poems

Bobrowski, who served with Hitler's armies on the Eastern Front and was afterward a Russian prisoner of war until 1949, became the most important of East German poets. His haunting landscapes are charged with unspoken tragedy

TRANSLATED BY RUTH AND MATTHEW MEAD

INTRODUCTION BY MICHAEL HAMBURGER

0-8112-1276-9 NEW DIRECTIONS PB $10.95

Heinrich **Böll**

Awarded the Nobel Prize in 1972, Böll was an outspoken critic of modern society who focused on institutional structures that demand mindless conformity

Absent Without Leave: Two Novellas

0-8101-1209-4 NORTHWESTERN PB $13.95

And Never Said a Word

TRANSLATED BY LEILA VENNEWITZ

0-8101-1153-5 NORTHWESTERN $29.95
0-8101-1147-0 NORTHWESTERN PB $10.95

And Where Were You, Adam?

0-8101-1164-0 NORTHWESTERN PB $10.95

Billiards at Half-Past Nine

0-14-018724-3 PENGUIN PB $11.95

The Bread of Those Early Years

TRANSLATED BY LEILA VENNEWITZ

0-8101-1163-2 NORTHWESTERN PB $10.95

The Casualty

TRANSLATED BY LEILA VENNEWITZ

0-374-11967-8 FS&G $16.95
0-393-30599-6 NORTON PB $8.95

Children Are Civilians Too

Stories written in the aftermath of World War II

TRANSLATED BY LEILA VENNEWITZ

0-14-018725-1 PENGUIN PB $10.95

The Clown

The life of a professional clown, during and after the Hitler era

TRANSLATED BY LEILA VENNEWITZ

0-14-018726-X PENGUIN PB $11.95

End of a Mission

TRANSLATED BY LEILA VENNEWITZ

0-8101-1154-3 NORTHWESTERN $29.95
0-8101-1148-9 NORTHWESTERN PB $10.95

Group Portrait With Lady

TRANSLATED BY LEILA VENNEWITZ

0-14-018727-8 PENGUIN PB $11.95

Irish Journal

TRANSLATED BY LEILA VENNEWITZ

0-8101-1155-1 NORTHWESTERN $29.95
0-8101-1149-7 NORTHWESTERN PB $9.95

The Lost Honor of Katharina Blum: Or How Violence Develops and Where It Can Lead

An innocent woman, driven to murder, is destroyed by slanderous journalism

TRANSLATED BY LEILA VENNEWITZ

0-14-018728-6 PENGUIN PB $10.95

Missing Persons and Other Essays

TRANSLATED BY LEILA VENNEWITZ

0-8101-1162-4 NORTHWESTERN PB $13.95

The Safety Net

TRANSLATED BY LEILA VENNEWITZ

0-8101-1210-8 NORTHWESTERN PB $15.95

The Silent Angel

0-312-13171-2 PICADOR PB $12.00
0-312-11064-2 ST. MARTIN'S $19.95

A Soldier's Legacy

TRANSLATED BY LEILA VENNEWITZ

0-8101-1198-5 NORTHWESTERN $35.00
0-8101-1202-7 NORTHWESTERN PB $10.95

The Stories of Heinrich Böll

These 63 stories and novellas, embracing the previous collections, mount a dogged assault on the hypocrisies of modern Germany

TRANSLATED BY LEILA VENNEWITZ

0-8101-1207-8 NORTHWESTERN PB $19.95

Tomorrow and Yesterday

0-8101-1206-X NORTHWESTERN PB $16.95

The Train Was on Time

TRANSLATED BY LEILA VENNEWITZ

0-8101-1156-X NORTHWESTERN $29.95
0-8101-1123-3 NORTHWESTERN PB $9.95

What's to Become of the Boy?: Or, Something to Do With Books

A memoir of childhood in the Third Reich

TRANSLATED BY LEILA VENNEWITZ

0-8101-1208-6 NORTHWESTERN PB $13.95

Women in a River Landscape: A Novel in Dialogues and Soliloquies

0-8101-1205-1 NORTHWESTERN PB $14.95

Paul **Celan**

Breathturn

A complete translation of the late collection *Atemwende*

TRANSLATED BY PIERRE JORIS

1-55713-217-8 SUN & MOON $21.95
1-55713-218-6 SUN & MOON PB $12.95

Collected Prose

0-935296-92-1 SHEEP MEADOW $15.95

Correspondence

1-87881-837-6 SHEEP MEADOW $19.95

Poems of Paul Celan

Celan, a concentration camp survivor for whom German remained the speech of the Other, pushes against the limits of language in his disturbing and profoundly influential poems. This is the most extensive collection available, in a bilingual edition

TRANSLATED BY MICHAEL HAMBURGER

0-89255-140-2 PERSEA $24.95
0-89255-134-8 PERSEA PB $15.95

Threadsuns

TRANSLATED BY PIERRE JORIS

1-55713-295-X SUN & MOON $21.95
1-55713-294-1 SUN & MOON PB $13.95

Heimito **von Doderer**

The Demons

An immense novel, the masterpiece of this Austrian novelist

TRANSLATED BY RICHARD AND CLARA WINSTON

1-55713-030-2 SUN & MOON PB $29.95

Every Man a Murderer

An early novel centering around a sensational murder case

TRANSLATED BY RICHARD AND CLARA WINSTON

1-55713-183-X SUN & MOON PB $14.95

The Merovingians

TRANSLATED BY VINAL OVERING BINNER

1-55713-250-X SUN & MOON PB $15.95

The Waterfalls of Slunj

A family chornicle set in turn-of-the-century Vienna. "The forgotten moods of the nineteenth century, the sly, subtle telling of one of our master narrators"—Sven Birkerts

TRANSLATED BY ERNST KAISER AND EITHNE WILKINS

0-941419-11-8 RIZZOLI PB $15.00

Friedrich **Dürrenmatt**

The Assignment: Or, On Observing the Observer of the Observers

"Misanthropically funny...Dark and devious" —*Chicago Tribune*

0-679-72233-5 VINTAGE PB $7.95

Gunter **Eich**

Valuable Nail: The Selected Poems of Gunter Eich

Good examples of the terse lyrical expression of this Austrian "apostle of brevity"

TRANSLATED BY DAVID WALKER

0-932440-08-8 FIELD TRANSLATIONS $9.95
0-932440-09-6 FIELD TRANSLATIONS PB $4.95

Max **Frisch**

Homo Faber

What it means to be human in the age of technology

TRANSLATED BY MICHAEL BULLOCK

0-15-642135-6 HARCOURT BRACE PB $9.95

I'm Not Stiller

The first complete English translation of Frisch's best-known novel

0-15-684990-9 HARVEST PB $12.95

Man in the Holocene

Many consider this short novella to be the Swiss writer's masterpiece

TRANSLATED BY GEOFFREY SKELTON

0-15-656952-3 HARCOURT BRACE PB $8.95

Sketchbook: 1966-1971

99904-999-2-6 SMITH $16.75

Günter **Grass**

"The greatest living German novelist"—Newsweek. *"A virtuoso, a vastly intelligent, sensitive, and humane writer with a zany eye for the preposterous."*—Washington Post

The Call of the Toad

Writing with the wit and savage energy that have made him famous, Grass skewers the commercial imperialism of German reunification in his provocative new novel. "Reconciliation," cemeteries, environmentally friendly rickshaws in the streets of Gdansk, and the hazards of middle-aged love are all part of the mix in this riotous, macabre tale

0-15-125743-4 HARCOURT BRACE $19.95
0-15-615340-8 HARVEST PB $10.95

Dog Years

TRANSLATED BY RALPH MANHEIM

0-15-626112-X HARCOURT BRACE PB $12.95

In the Egg & Other Poems

TRANSLATED BY MICHAEL HAMBURGER AND CHRISTOPHER MIDDLETON

0-15-672239-9 HARCOURT BRACE PB $5.95

Headbirths: Or, the Germans Are Dying Out
A satirical discussion of the problems facing the industrialized world: energy, nuclear war, and Third World poverty
0-15-639995-4 HARCOURT BRACE PB $8.95

Local Anaesthetic
A fragmented portrait of modern Germany
0-15-652940-8 HARCOURT BRACE PB $9.95

The Meeting at Telgte
The most potent minds of 17th-century Germany convene in somewhat disorderly fashion to ponder cosmic paradoxes
TRANSLATED BY RALPH MANHEIM
0-15-658575-8 HARCOURT BRACE PB $8.95

Novemberland: Selected Poems, 1956-1993
Half-mad women lament the ruins of Berlin; nuns on a beach resemble the Spanish Armada; scarecrows multiply in a field; a glove washed up on a beach prophesizes the fate of humanity's rebellion. A bilingual volume of his selected poems from the last four decades
TRANSLATED BY MICHAEL HAMBURGER
0-15-100177-4 HARVEST $25.00
0-15-600331-7 HARVEST PB $15.00

The Rat
TRANSLATED BY RALPH MANHEIM
0-15-175920-0 HARCOURT BRACE $17.95
0-15-675830-X HARCOURT BRACE PB $13.00

The Tin Drum
Grass's exuberant prose epic, narrated by a dwarf drummer, presents a kaleidoscopic vision of the war years and the postwar period
TRANSLATED BY RALPH MANHEIM
0-679-72575-X VINTAGE PB $15.00

Peter **Handke**
"The best writer, altogether, in his language." —John Updike

Across
TRANSLATED BY RALPH MANHEIM
0-374-10054-3 FS&G $14.95

The Afternoon of a Writer
Fear besets a writer and sends him on an afternoon odyssey
TRANSLATED BY RALPH MANHEIM
0-374-10207-4 FS&G $14.95

Repetition
A search for a missing brother turns into an investigation of language
TRANSLATED BY RALPH MANHEIM
0-374-24934-2 FS&G $18.95

Slow Homecoming
0-374-26635-2 FS&G $16.95

Voyage to the Sonorous Land: The Art of Asking & The Hour We Knew Nothing of Each Other
Two plays
See also **EUROPEAN DRAMA SINCE 1945** under **MODERN EUROPEAN DRAMA**
TRANSLATED BY GITTA HONEGGER
0-300-06274-5 YALE PB $12.00

Walk About the Villages: A Dramatic Poem
1-57241-000-0 ARIADNE $25.00

The Weight of the World
TRANSLATED BY RALPH MANHEIM
0-374-28745-7 FS&G $16.95

Gert **Hofmann**

The Parable of the Blind
Taking Brueghel's painting as his starting point, Hofmann recounts the fable of six blind beggars who are brought to an artist's home to pose for a painting
TRANSLATED BY CHRISTOPHER MIDDLETON
0-88064-113-4 FROMM PB $7.95

The Spectacle at the Tower
Horrible events in a decaying Sicilian village bring together an estranged couple.
"Unnerving…Vivid and compelling" —*Chicago Tribune*
TRANSLATED BY CHRISTOPHER MIDDLETON
0-88064-114-2 FROMM PB $8.95

Uwe **Johnson**

Anniversaries II
A sequel to *Speculations about Jakob,* in which Germany is surveyed from the United States. The East German author again uses an innovative montage technique
TRANSLATED BY LEILA VENNEWITZ & WALTER ARNDT
0-15-107562-X HARCOURT BRACE $29.95

Speculations About Jakob
An experimental novel dealing with the problematic coexistence of the two Germanies
TRANSLATED BY URSULE MOLINARO
0-15-684719-1 HARCOURT BRACE PB $4.95

Gert **Jonke**

Geometric Regional Novel
TRANSLATED BY JOHANNES W. VAZUILIK
1-56478-048-1 DALKEY ARCHIVE $19.95

Erland **Josephson**

A Story About Mr. Silberstein
0-8101-1277-9 NORTHWESTERN $24.95

Michael **Kruger**

Diderot's Cat: Selected Poems
TRANSLATED BY RICHARD DOVE
0-8076-1343-6 BRAZILLER PB $14.95

Siegfried **Lenz**

The German Lesson
A juvenile delinquent writes down his life, describing the clash of father against son and duty against loyalty in wartime Germany
TRANSLATED BY ERNST KAISER & EITHNE WILKINS
0-8112-0982-2 NEW DIRECTIONS PB $15.95

The Selected Stories of Siegfried Lenz
0-8101-1314-7 NORTHWESTERN PB $15.95

Jakov **Lind**

Soul of Wood
A collection of darkly comic stories exploring the atrocities and distortions of wartime
TRANSLATED BY RALPH MANHEIM
0-8090-1526-9 FS&G PB $1.98

Christoph **Ransmayr**

The Last World
0-8021-3458-0 GROVE PB $12.00

The Terrors of Ice and Darkness
0-8021-3459-9 GROVE PB $12.00

Gregor **von Rezzori**

Memoirs of an Anti-Semite: A Novel in Five Stories
0-679-73182-2 VINTAGE PB $12.00

Arno **Schmidt**

Collected Novellas: Collected Early Fiction 1949-1964
1-56478-066-X DALKEY ARCHIVE $22.95

The Collected Stories of Arno Schmidt
1-56478-135-6 DALKEY ARCHIVE $32.00
1-56478-134-8 DALKEY ARCHIVE PB $13.50

The Egghead Republic
A science fiction parable set in 2008 in the International Republic of Artists and Scientists—a jet-propelled island where the world's geniuses have been installed to preserve world culture
TRANSLATED BY MICHAEL HOROVITZ
EDITED BY ERNST KRAWEHL
0-7145-2592-8 MARION BOYARS PB $7.95

Nobodaddy's Children: A Trilogy
1-56478-090-2 DALKEY ARCHIVE PB $13.95

Scenes from the Life of a Faun
Small-town life in provincial Germany before and during World War II, transcribed in lively experimental fashion
TRANSLATED BY JOHN E. WOODS
0-7145-2763-7 MARION BOYARS PB $8.95

Peter **Schneider**

Couplings
TRANSLATED BY PHILIP BOEHM
0-374-13053-1 FS&G $24.00

W. G. **Sebald**

The Emigrants
A recent German novel, by an author long resident in England, which deals with the Holocaust and the Nazi era in an oblique yet powerfully disturbing way. The book's form, tracing how four lives intersected with historical events, purposely blurs the line between fact and fiction. The photographic illustrations add to the effect
TRANSLATED BY MICHAEL HULSE
0-8112-1338-2 NEW DIRECTIONS $22.95

Manes **Sperber**

Until My Eyes Are Closed with Shards
0-8419-1033-2 HOLMES & MEIER $34.95

Uwe **Timm**

Headhunter
TRANSLATED BY PETER TEGEL
0-8112-1254-8 NEW DIRECTIONS $22.95

The Invention of Curried Sausage
0-8112-1297-1 NEW DIRECTIONS $19.95

The Snake Tree
A German engineer working on a construction project in the South American rain forest runs afoul of his workers, local superstition, and nature itself. "Tension that drips with jungle and cakes with soil…A book of subtle evocative power"—*Sunday Times*
TRANSLATED BY PETER TEGEL
0-8112-1121-5 NEW DIRECTIONS PB........................$10.95

Christa **Wolf**

Accident: A Day's News
How an accident, in this instance the nuclear disaster at Chernobyl, affects a writer's daily routine
TRANSLATED BY HEIKE SCHWARZBAUER AND RICK TAKVORIAN
0-374-10046-2 FS&G........................$15.95
0-374-52254-5 NOONDAY PB........................$7.95

The Author's Dimension: Selected Essays
0-226-90494-6 CHICAGO PB........................$14.95

Cassandra: A Novel and Four Essays
A retelling of the Trojan War from Cassandra's perspective
TRANSLATED BY JAN VAN HEURCK
0-374-51904-8 FS&G PB........................$11.00

Patterns of Childhood
Complex account of growing up in Nazi Germany; originally titled *A Model Childhood* in the hardcover edition
TRANSLATED BY URSULA MOLINARO & HEDWIG RAPPOLT
0-374-51844-0 FS&G PB........................$15.00

The Quest for Christa T.
TRANSLATED BY CHRISTOPHER MIDDLETON
0-374-51534-4 FS&G PB........................$10.00

What Remains: And Other Stories
The eminent (formerly East) German writer explores a wide range of topics and styles in these eight stories. In the title story she explores censorship, both external and internal. In another a female research scientist takes a drug that changes her into a man. "Christa Wolf has set herself nothing less than the task of exploring what it is to be conscious human being alive in a moment of history"
—Mary Gordon, *NY Times Book Review*
TRANSLATED BY HEIKE SCHWARZBAUER & RICK TAKVOIRAN
0-374-28888-7 FS&G........................$25.00

Christa Wolf

What Remains and Other Stories
TRANSLATED BY HEIKE SCHWARZBAUER & RICH TAKVORIAN
0-226-90495-4 CHICAGO PB........................$14.95

Anthologies

Robert **Browning**, editor

German Poetry: 1750-1900
0-8264-0283-6 CONTINUUM PB........................$14.95

Leonard **Forster**, editor

The Penguin Book of German Verse
German texts with literal prose translations
0-14-058546-X PENGUIN PB........................$13.95

Margaret **Herzfeld-Sander**, editor

Essays on German Theater
Includes essays by Lessing, Schiller, Buchner, Wagner, Nietzsche, Brecht, Lukács, and Dürrenmatt
0-8264-0297-6 CONTINUUM PB........................$10.95

Frank **Ryder** & Robert **Browning**, editors

German Literary Fairy Tales
Includes work by Goethe, Tieck, Wackenroder, Novalis, Hoffmann, Eichendorff, Brentano, Hauff, Mörike, Storm, Hofmannsthal, and Kafka
0-8264-0277-1 CONTINUUM PB........................$14.95

Harry **Steinhauser**, editor & translator

Twelve German Novellas
0-520-03002-8 CALIFORNIA PB........................$17.95

Critical Studies

Russell **Berman**

The Rise of the Modern German Novel: Crisis and Charisma
0-674-77165-6 HARVARD........................$39.95

Robert **Browning**

German Baroque Poetry: 1618-1723
0-271-01146-7 PENN STATE........................$24.50

German Poetry in the Age of the Enlightenment: From Brockes to Klopstock
0-271-00541-6 PENN STATE........................$40.00

Henry **Garland** & Mary **Garland**

The Oxford Companion to German Literature
0-19-866139-8 OXFORD........................$55.00

Michael **Hamburger**

After the Second Flood: Essays on German Post-War Literature
0-312-00087-1 ST. MARTIN'S........................$35.00
0-312-00088-X ST. MARTIN'S PB........................$12.95

A Proliferation of Prophets: Essays on German Writers from Nietzsche to Brecht
0-312-65117-1 ST. MARTIN'S........................$29.95

Henry **Hatfield**

Clashing Myths in German Literature: From Heine to Rilke
0-674-13375-7 HARVARD........................$21.95

Anthony **Heilbut**

Exiled in Paradise: German Refugee Artists and Intellectuals from the '30s to the Present
0-8070-5411-9 OLYMPIC PB........................$2.98

Carl **Schorske**

Fin-de-Siècle Vienna: Politics and Culture
0-394-74478-0 RANDOM HOUSE PB........................$19.00

John **Willett**

Art and Politics in the Weimar Period: The New Sobriety, 1917-1933
From the German typographic revolution to the Brecht-Weill partnership. "An original and challenging book, thoroughly researched and aptly illustrated"—*Times* (London)
See also **EXPRESSIONISM AND THE BLUE RIDER** under **20TH-CENTURY ART** in **ART**
See also **PORTRAITS OF WEIMAR** under **THE THIRD REICH** under **20TH-CENTURY EUROPE TO THE SECOND WORLD WAR** in **WORLD HISTORY AND CURRENT AFFAIRS**
0-306-80724-6 DA CAPO PB........................$17.95

The Theatre of the Weimar Republic
An account by an English critic of the Weimar period (1920-33), from Reinhardt to the Expressionists, from the Bauhaus to Piscator, Brecht, and Kurt Weill
See also **EUROPE** under **HISTORY** under **THEATER** in **PERFORMING ARTS AND MEDIA**
0-8419-0759-5 HOLMES & MEIER........................$79.50

Studies of Individual Authors

Gershom **Scholem**

Walter Benjamin: The Story of a Friendship
Memoir of the friendship between two noted scholars
See also **BIOGRAPHY** under **JEWISH HISTORY** in **WORLD HISTORY AND CURRENT AFFAIRS**
TRANSLATED BY HARRY ZOHN
0-8276-0197-2 JEWISH PUBLICATION SOCIETY......$17.95

Isaiah **Berlin**

The Magus of the North: J.G. Hamann and the Origins of Modern Irrationalism
An elegant essay on an obscure German thinker whose peculiar secular mysticism helped prepare the way for intellectual fascism
0-374-19657-5 FS&G........................$21.00

Eric **Bentley**

The Brecht Commentaries
0-8021-5142-6 GROVE PB........................$9.95

Martin **Esslin**

Brecht: A Choice of Evils—A Critical Study of the Man, His Work, and His Opinions

0-413-54750-7 METHUEN PB $12.95

John **Fuegi**

Brecht and Company: Sex, Politics, and the Making of the Modern Drama

A controversial study that depicts Brecht's relations with his (purportedly unacknowledged) collaborators in less than flattering terms

See also **SELECTED MEMOIRS AND BIOGRAPHIES** under **THEATER** in **PERFORMING ARTS AND MEDIA**

0-8021-1529-2 GROVE $32.50

M.B. **Benn**

The Drama of Revolt: A Critical Study of George Büchner

0-521-29415-0 CAMBRIDGE PB $25.95

John **Felstiner**

Paul Celan: Poet, Survivor, Jew

A close and useful biographical reading of Celan's poetry

0-300-06068-8 YALE $30.00

Aris **Fioretos**, editor

Word Traces: Readings of Paul Celan

0-8018-4767-2 JOHNS HOPKINS PB $24.95

Ronald **Gray**

Goethe: A Critical Introduction

0-521-09404-6 CAMBRIDGE PB $23.95

George **Lukács**

Goethe and His Age

TRANSLATED BY ROBERT ANCHOR

0-391-01983-X HUMANITIES PB $19.95

George Lukács

John **Ellis**

One Fairy Story Too Many: The Brothers Grimm and Their Tales

0-226-20547-9 CHICAGO PB $8.95

Julien **Hervier**

The Details of Time: Conversations with Ernst Jünger

0-941419-95-9 MARSILIO $17.95

Max **Brod**

Franz Kafka: A Biography

0-306-80670-3 DA CAPO PB $13.95

Frederick **Karl**

Franz Kafka, Representative Man: Prague, Germans, Jews, and the Crisis of Modernism

A masterful biography of the writer who created the most enduring symbolic vision of the 20th century. Karl's 768-page book places Kafka within the context of a crisis-ridden central Europe to show how he became the emblematic figure of modern man and modern artist

0-395-56143-4 TICKNOR & FIELDS $40.00

0-88064-146-0 FROMM PB $17.95

Ernst **Pawel**

The Nightmare of Reason: A Life of Franz Kafka

0-374-52335-5 NOONDAY PB $15.00

Robert **Helbling**

Heinrich von Kleist: The Major Works

0-8112-0563-0 NEW DIRECTIONS $13.50

0-8112-0564-9 NEW DIRECTIONS PB $3.95

Joachim **Maass**

Kleist: A Biography

TRANSLATED BY RALPH MANHEIM

0-374-18162-4 FS&G $3.98

Ronald **Hayman**

Thomas Mann: A Biography

0-684-19319-1 SCRIBNERS $35.00

Anthony **Heilbut**

Thomas Mann: Eros and Literature

0-394-55633-X KNOPF $40.00

Erich **Heller**

Thomas Mann: The Ironic German

0-911858-29-6 APPEL $15.00

Scandinavian Literature

Old Norse and Icelandic Literature

Magnus **Magnusson** & Hermann **Palsson**, translators

Laxdaela Saga

A complex family saga in which the central issue is a love triangle

See also **MEDIEVAL LITERATURE**

0-14-044218-9 PENGUIN PB $9.95

Njal's Saga

This much-praised translation gives new life to the greatest of the Icelandic sagas. *"Njal's Saga* is one of the most complex and dramatic novels ever written. It teems with characters: each sharply, however briefly, drawn; all presented in the most dramatic contexts. The narrative is carried by dialogue and by action of maximum concreteness"—Kenneth Rexroth

See also **MEDIEVAL LITERATURE**

0-14-044103-4 PENGUIN PB $11.95

The Vinland Sagas: The Norse Discovery of America

Two chronicles from which derives most of our knowledge of the Norse incursions into North America

0-14-044154-9 PENGUIN PB $9.95

Hermann **Palsson**

Eyrbyggja Saga

"Of all the various records of Icelandic history and literature, there is none more interesting than *Eyrbyggja Saga*"—Sir Walter Scott

TRANSLATED BY PAUL EDWARDS

0-14-044530-7 PENGUIN PB $8.95

Hermann **Palsson** & Paul **Edwards**, translators

Egil's Saga

0-14-044321-5 PENGUIN PB $10.95

Seven Viking Romances

0-14-044474-2 PENGUIN PB $11.95

Snorri **Sturluson**

King Harald's Saga

An account of the Norwegian king which culminates in the conflict between Norway and England in 1066

TRANSLATED BY MAGNUS MAGNUSSON & HERMANN PALSSON

0-14-044183-2 PENGUIN PB $8.95

The Prose Edda of Snorri Sturluson: Tales from Norse Mythology

Originally penned as a manual in skaldic (courtly) poetry

See also **NORSE** under **EUROPEAN MYTHOLOGY** under **MYTHOLOGY AND FOLKLORE** in **RELIGION, SPIRITUALITY, AND PHILOSOPHY**

TRANSLATED BY JEAN YOUNG

0-520-01232-1 CALIFORNIA PB $12.00

Danish Literature

Hans Christian **Andersen**

Tales & Stories

TRANSLATED BY PATRICIA CONROY & SVEN ROSSELL

ILLUSTRATED BY VILHELM PEDERSEN & LORENZ FROLICH

0-295-95936-3 WASHINGTON PB $18.95

Isak **Dinesen**

Somewhat paradoxically, Denmark's best-known 20th-century author lived in Africa and wrote her major works in English.

Carnival: Entertainments & Posthumous Tales

0-226-15304-5 CHICAGO PB $14.95

Letters from Africa, 1914-1931
Covering the entire period when Dinesen owned a coffee plantation in British colonial Kenya
EDITED BY FRANS LESSON
TRANSLATED BY ANNE BORN
0-226-15311-8 CHICAGO PB $18.95

Out of Africa
The celebrated account of her years running a plantation in Kenya
0-679-60021-3 MODERN LIBRARY $15.50

Seven Gothic Tales
This collection of highly colored, sometimes melodramatic stories was an international bestseller in the '40s
INTRODUCTION BY DOROTHY CANFIELD
0-679-60086-8 MODERN LIBRARY $17.50

Winter's Tales
0-679-74334-0 VINTAGE PB $13.00

Tove **Ditlevsen**

Early Spring
TRANSLATED BY TIINA NUNNALLY
0-931188-28-8 SEAL PB $8.95

Peter **Hoeg**

Borderliners
"The Catcher in the Rye meets *A Brief History of Time*...Brilliantly tormenting and philosophically haunting"—*Glamour*
0-374-11554-0 FS&G $22.00

The History of Danish Dreams
TRANSLATED BY BARBARA HAVELAND
0-374-17138-6 FS&G $24.00
0-385-31591-0 DELTA PB $12.95

Smilla's Sense of Snow
Expert writing and intricate plotting make this tale of a remarkable woman's search for the killer of a small boy compelling. An international bestseller
See also **ODD ONES OUT: EXPERIMENTS AND MIXED GENRES** under **CRIME FICTION TODAY** under **CRIME FICTION** in **POPULAR READING**
0-374-26644-1 FS&G $21.00

The Woman and the Ape
A modern-day *Beauty and the Beast* in which the alcoholic wife of a behavioral scientist falls in love with her husband's newest discovery
TRANLATED BY BARBARA HAVELAND
0-374-29203-5 FS&G $23.00

Martin Anderson **Nexø**

Pelle the Conqueror
Volume 1: Childhood
0-940242-40-0 FJORD PB $9.95

Volume 2: Apprenticeship
0-940242-48-6 FJORD PB $9.95

Klaus **Rifbjerg**

Witness to the Future
TRANSLATED BY STEVE MURRAY
0-940242-18-4 FJORD PB $8.95

Villy **Sorensen**

Another Metamorphosis and Other Fictions
0-940242-43-5 FJORD $17.95

Harmless Tales
TRANSLATED BY PAULA HISTRUO-JESSEN
1-87004-115-1 DUFOUR PB $18.95

Finnish Literature

Elias **Lonnrot**

The Kalevala
See also **NORSE** under **EUROPEAN MYTHOLOGY** under **MYTHOLOGY AND FOLKLORE** in **RELIGION, SPIRITUALITY, AND PHILOSOPHY**
TRANSLATED BY KEITH BOSLEY
0-19-281700-0 OXFORD PB $13.95

The Kalevala: Epic of the Finnish People
TRANSLATED BY EINO FRIBERG
EDITED BY JAN GEORGE C. SCHOOLFIELD
951-1-10137-4 ILLINOIS $39.95

Kalevala: The Land of the Heroes
The Finnish national epic, compiled in the 19th-century from folk materials still current at the time, centers around three semi-divine brothers who live in Kaleva, a mythical land of plenty and happiness
EDITED BY MICHAEL BRANCH
TRANSLATED BY W.F. KIRBY
0-485-12048-8 ATHLONE $14.95

The Kalevala: or Poems of the Kaleva District
Regarded as a more scholarly and readable edition than the "rather antiquated language" (Kenneth Rexroth) of the Kirby translation
TRANSLATED BY FRANCIS P. MAGOUN, JR.
0-674-50010-5 HARVARD PB $16.95

The Kanteletar: Lyrics and Ballads after the Oral Tradition
TRANSLATED BY KEITH BOSLEY
0-19-282862-2 OXFORD PB $8.95

Icelandic Literature

Gunnar **Gunnarsson**

Black Cliffs
A novel revolving around themes of isolation and faith
TRANSLATED BY CECIL WOOD
0-299-04471-8 WISCONSIN $8.00

Halldor **Laxness**

The Atom Station
A satirical account by this Nobel laureate of the decline of Icelandic culture, represented by the admission of US bases to the country
0-933256-31-0 PERMANENT PB $16.95

Norwegian Literature

For Ibsen's plays see Modern European Drama

Knut **Hamsun**

Dreamers
A lively and humorous portrait of a remote Norwegian fishing village
TRANSLATED BY TOM GEDDES
0-8112-1321-8 NEW DIRECTIONS PB $9.95

Growth of the Soil
A family struggles for survival in the Norwegian wilderness
0-394-71781-3 RANDOM HOUSE PB $12.00

Hunger
Hamsun's masterpiece, published in 1890, focuses with remarkable intensity on a few days in the life of a young man at the end of his economic and psychological resources
TRANSLATED BY ROBERT BLY
INTRODUCTION BY ISAAC BASHEVIS SINGER
0-374-50520-9 FS&G PB $10.00

Mysteries
An investigation of the mysterious forces at work in the human psyche
0-88184-031-9 CARROLL & GRAF PB $8.95

Pan: From Lieutenant Thomas Glahn's Papers
TRANSLATED BY JAMES W. MCFARLANE
0-374-50016-9 FS&G PB $10.00

Victoria
A lyrical story of young love
TRANSLATED BY OLIVER STALLYBRASS
1-55713-177-5 SUN & MOON PB $10.95

Wayfarers
A village boy attaches himself to a vagabond and sets out on years of wandering
TRANSLATED BY JAMES MCFARLANE
1-55713-211-9 SUN & MOON PB $13.95

The Women at the Pump
TRANSLATED BY OLIVER & GUNNVOR STALLYBRASS
0-374-29280-9 FS&G $10.95
1-55713-244-5 SUN & MOON PB $14.95

Paal Espolin **Johnson**

For Love of Norway
TRANSLATED BY CONRAD ROYKSUND
0-8032-7571-4 NEBRASKA PB $11.95

Torborg **Nedreaas**

Nothing Grows by Moonlight
"This glowing, elegantly translated novel has already earned a wide audience in Europe and a rising reputation for its author"
—*Publishers Weekly*
TRANSLATED BY BIBBI LEE
0-8032-3313-2 NEBRASKA $21.00

O. E. **Rolvaag**

Giants in the Earth
A translation of the first two novels in the tetralogy depicting the family of Per Hansa
0-06-083047-6 HARPERPERENNIAL PB $8.00

Peder Victorious, A Tale of the Pioneers: Twenty Years Later
The third title in the Per Hansa sequence
TRANSLATED BY NORA SOLUM & THE AUTHOR
0-8032-8906-5 NEBRASKA PB $10.95

Their Fathers' God
The final installment in the Per Hansa tetralogy
TRANSLATED BY TRYGVE AGER
0-8032-8911-1 NEBRASKA PB $12.00

O. E. **Rolvåag**

The Boat of Longing

A stark portrait of the hardships of the immigrant experience by a Norwegian-American who immigrated to the US in 1896

TRANSLATED BY NORA O. SOLUM

0-87351-184-0 MINNESOTA HISTORICAL PB..........$10.95

Cora **Sandel**

Alberta Alone

TRANSLATED BY ELIZABETH ROKKAN

INTRODUCTION BY LINDA HUNT

0-8214-0760-0 OHIO..........$15.95

0-8214-0761-9 OHIO PB..........$9.95

Alberta and Freedom

First title of the Alberta trilogy which unhurriedly charts the growing pains and pleasures of a provincial Norwegian girl who comes of age in Paris

TRANSLATED BY ELIZABETH ROKKAN

INTRODUCTION BY LINDA HUNT

0-8214-0758-9 OHIO..........$15.95

0-8214-0759-7 OHIO PB..........$9.95

Alberta and Jacob

TRANSLATED BY ELIZABETH ROKKAN

INTRODUCTION BY LINDA HUNT

0-8214-0756-2 OHIO..........$15.95

Selected Short Stories

TRANSLATED WITH AN INTRODUCTION BY BARBARA WILSON

0-931188-30-X SEAL PB..........$8.95

The Silken Thread

TRANSLATED BY ELIZABETH ROKKAN

0-8214-0865-8 OHIO PB..........$8.95

0-8214-0864-X OHIO PB..........$17.95

Sigrid **Undset**

Kristin Lavransdatter

A trilogy set in medieval Norway, tracing the protagonist's evolution from girlhood to maturity against a vividly detailed historical backdrop

Volume 1
The Bridal Wreath

0-394-75299-6 VINTAGE PB..........$11.00

Volume 2
The Mistress of Husaby

0-394-75293-7 VINTAGE PB..........$12.00

Volume 3
The Cross

0-394-75291-0 VINTAGE PB..........$12.00

The Master of Hestviken

The Nobel laureate's other literary masterpiece and monument to medieval Scandinavian history. It was written after her conversion to Catholicism—a bold step in Lutheran Norway—and clearly shows her greater preoccupation with matters religious

Volume 1
The Axe

0-679-75273-0 VINTAGE PB..........$11.00

Volume 2
The Snake Pit

0-679-75554-3 VINTAGE PB..........$12.00

Volume 3
In the Wilderness

0-679-75553-5 VINTAGE PB..........$10.00

Volume 4
The Son Avenger

0-679-75552-7 VINTAGE PB..........$10.00

Tarjei **Vesaas**

The Birds

TRANSLATED BY TORBJORN STOVERUD AND MICHAEL BARNES

0-7206-0952-6 OWEN PB..........$24.00

The Ice Palace

Vesaas, who died in 1970, was a major Norwegian novelist. "The narrative is urgent, the description relentless, beautiful"

TRANSLATED BY ELIZABETH ROKKAN

1-55713-094-9 SUN & MOON PB..........$11.95

Selected Poems: 100 Poems Translated from the Norwegian with 8 Poems in the Original Nynorsk

A collection of 100 poems, with the original Norwegian text provided for eight of them. Vesaas' poetry is full of stark landscapes, to which he imparts moods ranging from domestic warmth to violent anxiety

0-907954-12-X SMALL PRESS PB..........$15.00

Swedish Literature

Ingmar **Bergman**

The Best Intentions

Bergman continues, in fiction, the exploration of his childhood that he began in his movie masterpiece *Fanny and Alexander.* A re-enactment of his parents' courtship and marriage, *The Best Intentions* was also written as a script for the film by Bille August that won the 1992 Golden Palm Award at Cannes

TRANSLATED BY JOAN TATE

1-55970-207-9 ARCADE..........$22.95

Private Confessions

TRANSLATED BY JOAN TATE

1-55970-364-4 ARCADE..........$19.95

Sunday's Children

Since his "retirement" in 1986, Bergman has written two volumes of memoirs and two novels. In this we see through the skewed and adventuresome eyes of the couple's eight-year-old son, Pu, who ruminates on what he has to look forward to in sex and love, and frets over his parents' fragile marriage

TRANSLATED BY JOAN TATE

1-55970-244-3 ARCADE..........$16.95

1-55970-292-3 ARCADE PB..........$9.95

Gunnar **Ekelöf**

Guide to the Underworld

Ekelöf is widely considered the most distinguished modern Swedish poet

TRANSLATED BY RIKA LESSER

0-87023-306-8 MASSACHUSETTS..........$20.00

A Molna Elegy

TRANSLATED BY MURIEL RUKEYSER & LEIF SJOBERG

0-87775-163-3 UNICORN PB..........$25.00

Jan **Fridegard**

The Holme Trilogy: Volume 1, Land of Wooden Gods

This is the only volume currently available

TRANSLATED BY ROBERT E. BJORK

0-8032-6870-X NEBRASKA PB..........$8.95

Lars **Gustafsson**

Bernard Foy's Third Castling

0-8112-1086-3 NEW DIRECTIONS..........$19.95

Funeral Music for Freemasons

TRANSLATED BY YVONNE L. SANDSTOREM

0-8112-1018-9 NEW DIRECTIONS PB..........$9.95

Sigismund

A novel in which various historical periods intermingle

TRANSLATED BY JOHN WEINSTOCK

0-8112-0924-5 NEW DIRECTIONS PB..........$7.95

The Stillness of the World Before Bach: New Selected Poems

TRANSLATED BY CHRISTOPHER MIDDLETON

0-8112-1058-8 NEW DIRECTIONS PB..........$9.95

Stories of Happy People

TRANSLATED BY YVONNE L. SANDSTROEM & JOHN WEINSTOCK

0-8112-0978-4 NEW DIRECTIONS PB..........$7.95

The Tennis Players

TRANSLATED BY YVONNE L. SANDSTROEM

0-8112-0862-1 NEW DIRECTIONS PB..........$6.25

A Tiler's Afternoon

TRANSLATED BY TOM GEDDES

0-8112-1240-8 NEW DIRECTIONS PB..........$8.95

Reidar **Jonsson**

My Father, His Son

In this sequel to *My Life as a Dog,* Ingemar stands at the threshold of adulthood. Struggling to find his place in the world, he follows his father's footsteps and enlists in the merchant marine

TRANSLATED BY MARIANNE RUUTH

1-55970-117-X ARCADE..........$19.95

1-55970-201-X ARCADE PB..........$9.95

My Life as a Dog

A poignant Swedish novel of a 13-year-old's coming of age under difficult circumstances. The film version was a great international success

TRANSLATED BY EIVOR MARTINUS

0-374-52379-7 NOONDAY PB..........$11.00

She smiled strangely at my question and I could see the hatred toward the man who had ruined her life.

MY LIFE AS A DOG

Pär **Lagerkvist**

Lagerkvist's spare symbolic words earned him the Nobel Prize in 1951.

Barabbas

Lagerkvist explores the fate of Barabbas after his liberation

TRANSLATED BY ALAIN BLAIR

0-679-72544-X VINTAGE PB..........$9.00

The Dwarf
TRANSLATED BY ALEXANDRA DICK
0-8090-1303-7 FS&G PB $9.95

The Sibyl
TRANSLATED BY NAOMI WALFORD
0-394-70240-9 RANDOM HOUSE PB $9.00

August **Strindberg**
By the Open Sea
A naturalistic novel about the destruction of a divided personality
TRANSLATED BY MARY SANDBACH
0-14-044488-2 PENGUIN PB $8.95

Inferno & From an Occult Diary
Inferno is Strindberg's extraordinary account of a spiritual crisis he underwent in Paris in the 1890s
TRANSLATED BY MARY SANDBACH
0-14-044364-9 PENGUIN PB $11.95

The Roofing Ceremony & The Silver Lake
The Roofing Ceremony, a novella first published in 1906, concerns a man's experiences as he approaches death. "Strindberg's most experimental, most modern work of fiction" —Eric O. Johannesson, *The Novels of August Strindberg*
TRANSLATED BY DAVID MEL PAUL & MARGARETA PAUL
0-8032-4171-2 NEBRASKA $16.95

Selected Essays by August Strindberg
TRANSLATED BY MICHAEL ROBINSON
0-521-56375-5 CAMBRIDGE $49.95

Tomas **Tranströmer**
Selected Poems 1954-1986
The translators include Robin Fulton, Robert Bly, May Swenson, and Samuel Charters
EDITED BY ROBERT HAAS
0-88001-403-2 ECCO PB $13.00

Truth Barriers: Poems by Tomas Transtromer
TRANSLATED BY ROBERT BLY
0-87156-235-9 SIERRA CLUB $9.95

Critical Studies

Michael **Robinson**
Strindberg and Autobiography: Writing and Reading a Life
1-87004-100-3 DUFOUR PB $19.95

Elias **Bredsdorff**
Hans Christian Andersen: The Story of His Life and Work, 1805-75
0-374-52397-5 NOONDAY PB $17.50

Eastern European Literature

Albanian Literature

Ismail **Kadare**
Broken April
Blood feuds on the high plateaus of Albania in the early 20th-century, told by a writer gaining recognition as a major voice in European fiction
0-941533-57-3 NEW AMSTERDAM $17.95

Chronicle in Stone
A city in World War II, as filtered through a child's imagination. "A thoroughly enchanting novel—sophisticated and accomplished in its poetic prose and narrative deftness, yet drawing resonance from its roots in one of Europe's most primitive societies"—John Updike
0-941533-00-X NEW AMSTERDAM $19.95
0-941533-50-6 NEW AMSTERDAM PB $10.95

Doruntine
A novel of medieval Albania. "The great modern Albanian writer, Ismail Kadare, has given us a masterpiece…an age-old legend transformed into a splendid fable"—Alain Bosquet
TRANSLATED BY JON ROTHSCHILD
0-941533-20-4 NEW AMSTERDAM $15.95

The Pyramid
TRANSLATED BY JUSUF VRIONI & DAVID BELLOS
1-55970-314-8 ARCADE $21.95

The Three-Arched Bridge
1-55970-368-7 ARCADE $19.95

Czech Literature

Karel **Capek**
Capek was a major playwright, novelist, and essayist, the leading Czech writer of the post-World War I period. In his play R.U.R. *hee coined the word "robot"; the satirical science-fiction novel* War with the Newts *was a remarkable blend of political and ecological vision. His works also include travel books, essays on gardening, and philosophical mystery stories. "Fifty years after his death, Capek's work has lost nothing of its freshness and luster … He is as great a delight to read today as he ever was"*—NY Times Book Review

The Absolute at Large
An early satirical romance in which the "Absolute" is liberated like a gas and runs amok among the populace
INTRODUCTION BY WILLIAM HARKINS
0-88355-104-7 HYPERION $28.00

The Gardener's Year
Humorous pieces on the joys and frustrations of gardening, with delightful illustrations by the author's brother Josef
0-299-10020-0 WISCONSIN $14.95
0-299-10024-3 WISCONSIN PB $8.95

Nine Fairy Tales: And One More Thrown in for Good Measure
TRANSLATED BY DAGMAR HERRMANN
0-8101-1464-X NORTHWESTERN PB $14.95

Three Novels: Hordubal, Meteor, and Ordinary Life
This trilogy of meditative novels, casting a speculative eye over apparently banal occurrences, is considered Capek's masterpiece
0-945774-08-7 CATBIRD PB $13.95

Toward the Radical Center: A Karel Capek Reader
A fine introduction to Capek's work, including stories, essays on travel and gardening, and three of his best-known plays: *R.U.R., The Makropoulos Secret,* and *The Mother*
0-945774-07-9 CATBIRD PB $12.95

War with the Newts
TRANSLATED BY M. WEATHERALL
0-8101-1468-2 NORTHWESTERN PB $14.95

Clayton **Eshelman**, translator
Conductors of the Pit: Major Works by Rimbaud, Vallejo, Césaire, Artaud and Holan
Includes the only English translation of Vladimir Holan's masterpiece *"A Night with Hamlet"*
1-55778-058-7 PARAGON $24.95

Jaroslav **Hasek**
The Good Soldier Svejk and His Fortunes in the World War
A major satirical epic about the archetypal little man caught up in the horror and idiocy of war. An important influence on writers like Bertolt Brecht and Joseph Heller
TRANSLATED BY CECIL PARROTT
ILLUSTRATED BY JOSEF LADA
0-14-003568-0 VIKING PB $10.95
0-679-42036-3 KNOPF $20.00

Vaclav **Havel**
The Garden and Other Plays
0-8021-3307-X GROVE PB $13.00

Vaclav Havel

Letters to Olga: June 1979 to September 1982
Havel's letters to his wife during three years of imprisonment on charges of subversion
TRANSLATED BY PAUL WILSON
0-8050-0973-6 HOLT PB $16.95

The Memorandum
A satiric comedy in which an artificial language is created to mask the foibles of the bureaucracy
TRANSLATED BY VERA BLACKWELL
0-394-17653-7 GROVE PB $5.95

Open Letters: Selected Writings 1965-1990
EDITED BY PAUL WILSON
0-679-73811-8 VINTAGE PB $15.00

Vladimir **Holan**

Mirroring: Selected Poems of Vladimir Holan
Holan is perhaps the most powerful of modern Czech poets; this translation effectively conveys the varied aspects of his prolific output and includes excerpts from the long poem *A Night with Hamlet*
TRANSLATED BY C.G. HANZLICEK & DANA HABOVA
0-8195-6119-3 WESLEYAN PB $14.95

Miroslav **Holub**

Interferon: or, On Theater
"One of the sanest voices of our time"—A. Alvarez
0-932440-12-6 FIELD TRANSLATIONS $10.95

Bohumil **Hrabal**

Closely Watched Trains
This novel was adapted into one of the most influential Czech films of the '60s "Prague Spring." "A Chaplinesque blend of black humor and pathos"—*Columbia Dictionary of Modern European Literature*
0-8101-0857-7 NORTHWESTERN PB $9.95

Dancing Lessons for the Advanced in Age
0-15-123810-3 HARCOURT BRACE $14.00

I Served the King of England
A playful tale of a waiter turned millionaire
0-15-145745-X HARCOURT BRACE $17.95
0-679-72786-8 VINTAGE PB $12.00

The Little Town Where Time Stood Still
The story of a free-spirited woman whose scandalous behavior shocks her prewar Czech village. When the war comes and the new order sets in, the social standards she so offended are inexorably torn apart
TRANSLATED BY JAMES NAUGHTON
0-679-42225-0 PANTHEON $23.00

Too Loud a Solitude
TRANSLATED BY MICHAEL HENRY HEIM
0-15-690458-6 HARCOURT BRACE PB $9.00
0-15-190491-X HARCOURT BRACE $16.95

Eva **Kanturkova**

My Companions in the Bleak House
Reminiscences of the author's years in a political prison, and the women she met there
0-87951-289-X OVERLOOK $19.95

Ivan **Klima**

"Ivan Klima is a writer of enormous power and originality. His work is a sort of alchemy; it makes gold out of the base metals of state repression and the spiritual constriction it spawns"—NY Times

Judge on Trial
0-679-73756-1 VINTAGE PB $14.00

Love and Garbage
TRANSLATED BY EWALD OSERS
0-679-73755-3 VINTAGE PB $12.00

My First Loves
First US publication of four short pieces
0-393-30601-1 NORTON PB $9.95

My Merry Mornings
A series of stories about Prague. "That rare genre of a funny—sometimes hilariously funny—surface with a sad and serious iceberg below"—Josef Skvorecky
0-930523-05-9 READERS INTERNATIONAL PB $11.95

The Spirit of Prague and Other Essays
A collection of essays charting five critical decades in the history of Czechoslovakia. From his early witnessing of Nazi occupation to his life in the Stalinist regimes of the '50s from the celebrations of Prague Spring to the Velvet Revolution, Klima offers a keen and sensitive view of a life in his country's tumultuous history
See also **EASTERN EUROPE** under **EUROPE SINCE 1945** in **WORLD HISTORY AND CURRENT AFFAIRS**
0-9645611-2-3 GRANTA PB $10.95

Waiting for the Dark, Waiting for the Light
The story of a dissident artist living through the Velvet Revolution
TRANSLATED BY PAUL WILSON
0-8021-1574-8 GROVE $21.00

Milan **Kundera**

The Art of the Novel
Kundera develops his conception of the European novel and looks closely at such writers as Broch, Kafka, Cervantes, and Flaubert. Incites us to reflect on fiction and philosophy, knowledge and truth, and brilliantly illustrates the art of the essay"—*The New Republic*
TRANSLATED BY LINDA ASHER & DAVID BELLOS
0-8021-0011-2 HARPERCOLLINS PB $17.95

The Book of Laughter and Forgetting
An experimental mixture of history, philosophy, journalism, and fiction; it led to the revocation of Kundera's Czech citizenship in 1979. "A work of social realism and protest co-exists with a brittleness, an angelic mockery that, amid such melancholy remembrance and shrewd psychology, makes *us*, the respectful Western readers, uncomfortable"—John Updike
TRANSLATED BY LINDA ASHER
0-06-092608-2 HARPERCOLLINS PB $13.00

The Farewell Party
Life in a small Czech resort town
INTRODUCTION BY ELIZABETH POCHODA
0-14-009694-9 VIKING PB $11.95

Immortality
TRANSLATED BY PETER KUSSI
0-06-097448-6 HARPERPERENNIAL PB $13.00

The Joke
Kundera's first novel concerns a student's innocent joke and the hard price he pays for it in Stalinist Czechoslovakia
TRANSLATED BY MICHAEL HEIM
0-06-099505-X HARPERCOLLINS PB $13.00

Laughable Loves
0-140-09691-4 PENGUIN $12.95

Life Is Elsewhere
A novel about a young poet who collaborates with the Stalinist regime and brings about his own downfall
0-14-006470-2 PENGUIN PB $11.95

Slowness
Kundera's first novel written in French—beautifully translated by Linda Asher—is an entertaining, wickedly funny satire. The story is of two seductions, one a delicious night of pleasure by an 18th-century nobleman, the other—less successful—by a 20th-century academic
0-06-017369-6 HARPERCOLLINS $21.00

Testaments Betrayed: An Essay in Nine Parts
Following his brilliant and acclaimed *The Art of the Novel*, the author of *The Unbearable Lightness of Being* offers here a reflection on the history of the novel from its birth with Rabelais and Cervantes through its demonization by the fundamentalist persecutors of Salman Rushdie
0-06-017145-6 HARPERCOLLINS $24.00

The Unbearable Lightness of Being
A novel about two lovers in Prague in 1968. "Kundera has raised the novel of ideas to a new level of dream-like lyricism and emotional intensity"—*Newsweek*
TRANSLATED BY MICHAEL HEIM
0-06-091465-3 HARPERCOLLINS PB $13.00

To ensure that erotic friendship never grew into the aggression of love, he would meet each of his long-term mistresses only at intervals. He considered this method flawless and propagated it among his friends: "The important thing is to abide by the rule of threes. Either you see a woman three times in quick succession and then never again, or you maintain relations over the years but make sure that the rendezvous are at least three weeks apart."
THE UNBEARABLE LIGHTNESS OF BEING

Arnost **Lustig**

Children of the Holocaust
0-8101-1279-5 NORTHWESTERN PB $19.95

Dita Saxova
0-8101-1132-2 NORTHWESTERN PB $17.95

Indecent Dreams
Three stories emerging from World War II and the Holocaust. "I know of very few stories that express so vividly the madness of the stream-of-consciousness of people living on the brink of death"—Josef Skvorecky
0-8101-0909-3 NORTHWESTERN PB $12.95

Arnost **Lustig**

Street of Lost Brothers
0-8101-0960-3 NORTHWESTERN PB $13.95

The Unloved: From the Diary of Perla
0-8101-1347-3 NORTHWESTERN PB $14.95

T. G. **Masaryk**

Talks with T.G. Masaryk
TRANSLATED BY MICHAEL HEIM
0-945774-26-5 CATBIRD PB $13.95

Jan **Neruda**

Prague Tales
TRANSLATED BY MICHAEL HEIM
1-85866-058-0 OXFORD PB $14.95

Jan **Patocka**

Heretical Essays in the Philosophy of History
TRANSLATED BY ERAZIM KOHAK
0-8126-9336-1 LIBPR $39.95
0-8126-9337-X LIBPR PB $16.95

Iva **Pekarkova**

Truck Stop Rainbows
TRANSLATED BY DAVID POWELSTOCK
0-679-74675-7 VINTAGE PB $12.00
0-374-24065-5 FS&G $22.00

The World Is Round
TRANSLATED BY DAVID POWELSTOCK
0-374-29287-6 FS&G $22.00

Martin M. **Simecka**

The Year of the Frog
TRANSLATED BY PETER PETRO
0-684-81367-X SCRIBNERS PB $12.00

Josef **Skvorecky**

The Bass Saxophone: Two Novellas
Two novellas: Skvorecky's young hero plays illegal jazz under the Nazis. This is the second volume of the World War II trilogy, which also includes *The Swell Season*
0-88001-370-2 ECCO PB $12.00

The Bride of Texas
TRANSLATED BY KACA POLACKOVA HENLEY
0-679-44411-4 KNOPF $27.00

Dvorák in Love
A biographical novel about the Czech composer's life in the US in the 1890s
0-393-30548-1 NORTON PB $10.00

Headed for the Blues
0-88001-462-8 ECCO $23.00

The Miracle Game
0-393-30849-9 NORTON PB $10.95

Miss Silver's Past
A largely comic novel featuring hilarious anecdotes about Czech publishing and censorship under communism
INTRODUCTION BY GRAHAM GREENE
0-88001-074-6 NORTON PB $7.50

The Mournful Demeanour of Lieutenant Boruvka: Detective Tales
The Czech translator of Hemingway, Faulkner and Dashiell Hammett tries his own hand in the detective genre
TRANSLATED BY ROSEMARY KAVAN
0-393-02470-9 NORTON $15.95
0-393-30786-7 NORTON PB $8.95

The Republic of Whores: A Fragment from the Time of the Cults
TRANSLATED BY PAUL WILSON
0-88001-428-8 ECCO PB $15.00

Sins for Father Knox
A collection of Skvorecky's detective tales, with Lieutenant Boruvka as the investigator. The stories are attributed to a certain Father Knox, faintly echoing Chesterton's Father Brown
TRANSLATED BY PAUL WILSON
0-393-30787-5 NORTON PB $8.95

The Swell Season
The first part of the war trilogy, concerning the young musician Danny's life under Nazi occupation
TRANSLATED BY PAUL WILSON
0-88001-090-8 ECCO PB $8.50

Ludvik **Vaculik**

The Axe
0-8101-1018-0 NORTHWESTERN PB $12.95

A Cup of Coffee with My Interrogator
By the Czech political novelist and author, the manifesto which may have helped precipitate the Soviet invasion. "Vaculik is the night watchman at a temporarily shut-down enterprise whose product is the national soul"—*LA Times*
TRANSLATED BY GEORGE THEINER
0-930523-34-2 READERS INTERNATIONAL $14.95

The Guinea Pigs
0-8101-0726-0 NORTHWESTERN PB $13.95

Michal **Viewegh**

Bringing Up Girls in Bohemia
A comic novel of life in Prague
TRANSLATED BY A.G. BRAIN
1-88737-804-9 READERS INTERNATIONAL $27.95
1-88737-805-7 READERS INTERNATIONAL PB $12.95

Jiri **Weil**

Life with a Star
A novel based on Weil's experience escaping and hiding from the Nazis. "The book is, without a doubt, one of the outstanding novels I've read about the fate of a Jew under the Nazis. I don't know another like it"—Philip Roth,in his Preface
TRANSLATED BY R. KLIMA
PREFACE BY PHILIP ROTH
0-374-18737-1 FS&G $22.95

Mendelssohn is on the Roof
TRANSLATED BY MARIE WINN
0-374-20810-7 FS&G $23.95

Estonian Literature

Jaan **Kaplinski**

The Same Sea in Us All
The first book of poems to appear in English by the gifted Estonian poet. "He is re-thinking Europe, revisioning history, in these poems of our times…Poems of gentle politics and love that sometimes scare you"—Gary Snyder
TRANSLATED BY SAM HAMILL
INTRODUCTION BY GARY SNYDER
0-932576-29-X FAR CORNER $14.95

The Wandering Border
TRANSLATED BY RIINA TAMM & SAM HAMILL
1-55659-010-5 COPPER CANYON PB $9.00

Jaan **Kross**

The Czar's Madman
Estonia's "national novel," is reminiscent in its scope and complexity of *War and Peace*
TRANSLATED BY ANSELM HOLLO
1-56584-121-2 NEW PRESS PB $13.95

Hungarian Literature

Sandor **Csoori**

Selected Poems of Sandor Csoori
Csoori is a major and very popular Hungarian poet who has also written for the screen
TRANSLATED BY LEN ROBERTS
1-55659-047-4 COPPER CANYON PB $11.00

Peter **Esterhazy**

The Book of Hrabal
TRANSLATED BY JUDITH SOLLOSY
0-8101-1192-6 NORTHWESTERN $22.50
0-8101-1199-3 NORTHWESTERN PB $15.95

A Little Hungarian Pornography
TRANSLATED BY JUDITH SOLLOSY
0-8101-1340-6 NORTHWESTERN $24.95

Milan **Fust**

The Story of My Wife
The finest novel from the influential Hungarian poet, novelist, and aesthetic theorist
TRANSLATED BY IVAN SANDERS
0-679-72217-3 VINTAGE PB $8.95

Jascha **Keller**, editor

The Face of Creation: Contemporary Hungarian Poetry
"Evident throughout is a high level of craftsmanship, even as a diverse range of poetic voices are presented: the elegiac Sandor Csoori, the sarcastic Laszlo Kalnoky, the surrealistic Anna Kiss and the violent Laszlo Nagy"
—*Publishers Weekly*
0-918273-20-X COFFEE HOUSE PB $11.95

George **Konrad**

The City Builder
0-14-009947-6 PENGUIN PB $6.95

A Feast in the Garden
0-15-130548-X HARCOURT BRACE $23.95
0-15-630454-6 HARVEST PB $14.95

The Melancholy of Rebirth: Essays from Post-Communist Central Europe, 1989-1994
0-15-600252-3 HARCOURT BRACE PB $12.00

Miklos **Radnoti**
Foamy Sky: The Major Poems of Miklos Radnoti
TRANSLATED BY FREDERICK TURNER
0-691-06954-9 PRINCETON $24.95
0-691-01530-9 PRINCETON PB $10.95

Under Gemini: The Selected Poems of Miklos Radnoti with a Prose Memoir
From the major Hungarian poet of the war years, a man obsessed in his work by the inevitability of violent death, which he himself met in 1944
TRANSLATED BY JASCHA KESSLER
0-8214-0763-5 OHIO $18.00
0-8214-0764-3 OHIO PB $11.95

Dezso **Tandori**
Birds and Other Relations: Selected Poetry of Dezso Tandori
TRANSLATED BY BRUCE BERLIND
0-691-01433-7 PRINCETON PB $9.95

Albert **Tezla**, editor
Ocean at the Window: Hungarian Prose and Poetry Since 1945
0-8166-0992-6 MINNESOTA $34.95

Polish Literature

Janusz **Anderman**
The Edge of the World
"An urgent dispatch to the outer world…An outcry, an expose, brimming with talent and frustrated passion"—NY *Times*
TRANSLATED BY NINA TAYLOR
0-930523-50-4 READERS INTERNATIONAL PB $7.95

Poland Under Black Light
A collection of short stories depicting Polish life after the imposition of martial law
TRANSLATED BY NINA TAYLOR & ANDREW SHORT
0-930523-13-X READERS INTERNATIONAL $12.50

Jerzy **Andrzejewski**
Ashes and Diamonds
The source for Wajda's celebrated film: chronicle of the anti-Nazi resistance
0-8101-0856-9 NORTHWESTERN PB $11.95

Stanislaw **Baranczak**
View with a Grain of Sand: Selected Poems
TRANSLATED BY CLARE CAVANAGH
0-15-600216-7 HARVEST PB $12.00

Polish Poetry of the Last Two Decades of Communist Rule: Spoiling Cannibals' Fun
EDITED BY CLARE CAVANAGH
0-8101-0968-9 NORTHWESTERN $29.95
0-8101-0982-4 NORTHWESTERN PB $12.95

Tadeusz **Borowski**
This Way for the Gas, Ladies and Gentlemen
Writings of a legendary Polish writer, who began writing in Nazi-occupied Warsaw, spent two years in Auschwitz, and committed suicide at age 29 in 1951
0-14-004114-1 PENGUIN PB $9.95

Adam **Czerniawski**, editor & translator
The Burning Forest
A personal selection of modern Polish poetry
1-85224-009-1 DUFOUR PB $18.95

Witold **Gombrowicz**
Several generations of Polish writers have seen Gombrowicz as their master. "Gombrowicz's provocative writing was a rebellion against all values in literature, against the accepted rules in social life, and the conventional attitudes toward national tradition. But under the mask of grotesque and sarcastic humor Gombrowicz poses the most important questions about the freedom of man."—Columbia Dictionary of Modern European Literature

Cosmos and Pornografia: Two Novels
0-8021-5159-0 GROVE PB $10.00

Diary: Volume 1
"It is an autobiography and at the same time an autobiographical novel, a discussion of literary and philosophical problems, and a commentary on cultural and social life, his own works, points of view, doubts and obsessions"—Samuel Fiszman
TRANSLATED BY LILLIAN VALLEE
INTRODUCTION BY WOJCIECH KARPINSKI
0-8101-0715-5 NORTHWESTERN PB $14.95

Witold Gombrowicz

Diary: Volume 2, 1957-1961
Charts the exile's life in Argentina
TRANSLATED BY LILLIAN VALLEE
0-8101-0717-1 NORTHWESTERN PB $14.95

Diary: Volume 3, 1961-1966
TRANSLATED BY LILLIAN VALLEE
0-8101-0719-8 NORTHWESTERN PB $14.95

A Kind of Testament
TRANSLATED BY ALASDAIR HAMILTON
0-7145-0916-7 MARION BOYARS PB $8.95

Possessed: Or the Secret of Myslotch
TRANSLATED BY J.A. UNDERWOOD
0-7145-2738-6 MARION BOYARS PB $10.95

Trans-Atlantyk
TRANSLATED BY CAROLYN FRENCH & NINA KARSOV
0-300-05384-3 YALE $23.00

Helena **Goscilo**, editor
Russian and Polish Women's Fiction
TRANSLATED BY HELENA GOSCILO
0-87049-472-4 TENNESSEE PB $20.00

Zbigniew **Herbert**
Herbert is widely regarded as the greatest Polish poet who actually lives in Poland; his background in philosophy, law, and art history gives his work an intellectual tone which has led to comparisons with T.S. Eliot.

Mr. Cogito
TRANSLATED BY JOHN AND BOGDANA CARPENTER
0-88001-330-3 ECCO $22.95
0-88001-381-8 ECCO PB $12.00

Report from the Besieged City
TRANSLATED BY JOHN CARPENTER & BOGDANA CARPENTER
0-88001-094-0 NORTON PB $8.50

Selected Poems
TRANSLATED BY CZESLAW MILOSZ & PETER SCOTT
INTRODUCTION BY A. ALVAREZ
0-88001-099-1 ECCO PB $12.00

Still Life with a Bridle: Essays and Apocryphas
See also **CONTEMPORARY WRITERS ON WRITING** under **LITERARY CRITICISM**
TRANSLATED BY JOHN CARPENTER & BOGDANA CARPENTER
0-88001-320-6 ECCO PB $9.95

Gustaw **Herling**
The Island: Three Tales
TRANSLATED BY RONALD STROM
0-14-023279-6 PENGUIN PB $9.95

Volcano and Miracle: A Selection of Fiction and Nonfiction from the Journal Written at Night
Considered by many to be Poland's greatest living writer, Herling offers here selections of his fiction and essays, written in his self-described ideal of "free and lucid thinking…ceaseless moral tension…words alive with the whole being of the person who utters them as his long meditation and suffered truth."
SELECTED AND TRANSLATED BY RONALD STROM
0-670-85482-4 VIKING $24.95

A World Apart
TRANSLATED BY ANDRZEJ CIOLKOSZ
0-14-025184-7 PENGUIN PB $11.95

Ryszard **Kapuscinski**

A practitioner of the "new journalism" whose writings were often interpreted allegorically under the Communist regime.

The Emperor: Downfall of an Autocrat

The Polish journalist's depiction of the outrageous pomp and decadence at the Ethiopian court, through interviews with Haile Selassie's servants

See also **ETHIOPIA** under **A NATIONAL FOCUS** under **AFRICA** in **WORLD HISTORY AND CURRENT AFFAIRS**

TRANSLATED BY WILLIAM R. BRAND & KATARZYNA MROCZKOWSKA-BRAND

0-679-72203-3 VINTAGE PB $10.00

Imperium

A report on the many long-buried identities now emerging from the fall of the Soviet Empire

See also **AFTER THE END OF THE SOVIET UNION** under **RUSSIAN STUDIES** in **WORLD HISTORY AND CURRENT AFFAIRS**

0-679-42619-1 KNOPF $24.00
0-679-74780-X VINTAGE PB $13.00

Shah of Shahs

Verbal snapshots capture the theater of the popular Islamic revolution that toppled the Shah

See also **THE IRANIAN REVOLUTION** under **IRAN** under **THE CONTEMPORARY MIDDLE EAST** in **WORLD HISTORY AND CURRENT AFFAIRS**

TRANSLATED BY W.R. BRAND & K. MROCZKOWSKA-BRAND

0-679-73801-0 VINTAGE PB $11.00

Shah of Iran

The Soccer War

TRANSLATED BY WILLIAM BRAND

0-679-73805-3 VINTAGE PB $12.00

Jan **Kochanowski**

Laments

A masterpiece of 16th-century Polish poetry, superbly translated

TRANSLATED BY STANLISAW BARANCZAK & SEAMUS HEANEY

0-374-18290-6 FS&G $17.50

Leszek **Kolakowski**

God Owes Us Nothing: A Brief Remark on Pascal's Religion and on the Spirit of Jansenism

0-226-45051-1 CHICAGO $22.50

Modernity on Endless Trial

0-226-45045-7 CHICAGO $29.95

Tadeusz **Konwicki**

The Anthropos-Specter-Beast

0-87599-218-8 PHILLIPS $21.95

New World Avenue and Vicinity

0-374-22182-0 FS&G $24.95

Jan **Kott**

The Memory of the Body: Essays on Theater and Death

TRANSLATED BY JADWIGA KOSICKA

0-8101-1043-1 NORTHWESTERN PB $16.95

Still Alive: An Autobiographical Essay

TRANSLATED BY JADWIGA KOSICKA

0-300-05276-6 YALE $32.50

Stanislaw **Lem**

The prolific Lem is an internationally renowned writer of science fiction with a strong philosophical dimension.

Chain of Chance

"Written in 1975, as an Eastern European's speculation upon some possible short-term extensions of such Western topical developments as terrorism, space exploration, and chemical pollution"—John Updike

0-15-616500-7 HARCOURT BRACE PB $7.95

The Cyberiad: Fables for the Cybernetic Age

Robots roam the cosmos creating beasts and machines

See also **CONTEMPORARY SCIENCE FICTION** under **SCIENCE FICTION AND FANTASY** in **POPULAR READING**

TRANSLATED BY MICHAEL KENDAL

0-15-623550-1 HARCOURT BRACE PB $9.00

Fiasco

A saga of warfare in space

TRANSLATED BY MICHAEL KANDEL

0-15-630630-1 HARCOURT BRACE PB $8.95

Highcastle: A Remembrance

TRANSLATED BY MICHAEL KANDEL

0-15-140218-3 HARCOURT BRACE $22.00
0-15-600472-0 HARCOURT BRACE PB $11.00

Hospital of the Transfiguration

A novel set in a mental hospital in 1939 Poland

TRANSLATED BY WILLIAM BRAND

0-15-142186-2 HARCOURT BRACE $17.95

The Investigation

A metaphysical variation on the traditional whodunit

TRANSLATED BY ADELE MILCH

0-15-645158-1 HARCOURT BRACE PB $8.00

Memoirs Found in a Bathtub

The destruction of all paper leads to the downfall of a worldwide bureaucracy

TRANSLATED BY MICHAEL KANDEL & CHRISTINE ROSE

0-15-658585-5 HARCOURT BRACE PB $9.00

Peace on Earth

TRANSLATED BY ELINOR FORD & MICHAEL KANDEL

0-15-600242-6 HARVEST PB $11.00

Solaris

A Polish masterpiece: planet as intelligent organism. Later filmed by Andrei Tarkovsky

0-15-683750-1 HARCOURT BRACE PB $9.00

Adam **Mickiewicz**

Pan Tadeusz

Includes the text in both Polish and English

TRANSLATED BY KENNETH MACKENZIE

0-7818-0033-1 HIPPOCRENE PB $19.95

Czeslaw **Milosz**

Probably the best-known contemporary Polish writer, Milosz began his literary career before World War II; he left Poland in 1951 and subsequently settled in the United States. He won the Nobel Prize in 1980.

Bells in Winter

TRANSLATED BY LILLIAN VALLEE

0-912946-56-3 NORTON $15.95
0-88001-456-3 ECCO PB $13.00

The Captive Mind

An analysis of the influence of Stalinist dogma on creativity

See also **FASCISM AND TOTALITARIANISM** under **POLITICAL THOUGHT** in **SOCIAL STUDIES**

0-8446-6615-7 SMITH $21.30
0-679-72856-2 VINTAGE PB $12.00

The Collected Poems

"These poems anchor themselves in the memory in a way so unusual that it cannot be simply the effect of discreet and gifted translations … Even in English, the poems have a structural contour so strong that it strikes with the force of an originally conceived shape … It is as though Milosz were at once Chardin, Rembrandt, Matisse, Gericault, and Cézanne, or—to turn to poetic analogues—as though he were from moment to moment Clare, Whitman, Lawrence, Auden, and Marvell"—Helen Vendler, *New Yorker*

0-88001-174-2 NORTON PB $17.00

Emperor of the Earth: Modes of Eccentric Vision

0-520-04503-3 CALIFORNIA PB $12.95

Facing the River: New Poems

TRANSLATED BY ROBERT HASS

0-88001-404-0 ECCO $22.00
0-88001-454-7 ECCO PB $13.00

The Issa Valley

A Wordsworthian novel about childhood

TRANSLATED BY LOUIS IRIBARNE

0-374-51695-2 FS&G PB $13.00

The Land of Ulro

TRANSLATED BY LOUIS IRIBARNE

0-374-51937-4 FS&G PB $9.95

Native Realm: A Search for Self-Definition

TRANSLATED BY CATHERINE LEACH

0-520-04474-6 CALIFORNIA PB $14.95

Provinces: Poems, 1987-1991

A collection by "One of the greatest poets of our time, perhaps the greatest…The core of the major themes of Milosz's poetry is the unbearable realization that a human being is not able to grasp his experience, and the more that time separates him from this experience,

the less become his chances to comprehend it"—Joseph Brodsky
TRANSLATED BY ROBERT HASS & CZESLAW MILOSZ
0-88001-317-6 ECCO $19.95
0-88001-321-4 ECCO PB $9.95

Czeslaw Milosz

Selected Poems
0-88001-455-5 ECCO PB $13.00

The Separate Notebooks
TRANSLATED BY ROBERT HASS
0-88001-116-5 NORTON PB $12.50

Unattainable Earth
0-88001-098-3 ECCO $17.95
0-88001-102-5 ECCO PB $10.95

Visions from San Francisco Bay
A collection of essays comparing Europe and America
TRANSLATED BY RICHARD LOURIE
0-374-28488-1 FS&G $14.95

The Witness of Poetry
The Charles Eliot Norton lectures
See also **CONTEMPORARY WRITERS ON WRITING** under **LITERARY CRITICISM**
0-674-95383-5 HARVARD PB $7.95

A Year of the Hunter
"A wonderful addition to his other autobiographical writing"
—Ian Buruma, *LA Times Book Review*
TRANSLATED BY MADELINE G. LEVINE
0-374-29344-9 FS&G $27.50
0-374-52444-0 NOONDAY PB $12.00

Czeslaw **Milosz**, editor

Postwar Polish Poetry: An Anthology
0-520-04476-2 CALIFORNIA PB $13.95

Jan **Potocki**

The Manuscript Found in Saragossa
Written in French in the 18th century, this haunting work is a masterpiece of fantastic literature
TRANSLATED BY IAN MACLEAN
0-670-83428-9 VIKING $27.95

0-14-044580-3 PENGUIN PB $13.95

Bruno **Schulz**

Schulz made his name with only two books before he was murdered by a German army officer in 1942. "Bruno Schulz was one of the great writers, one of the great transmogrifiers of the world into words."—John Updike

The Complete Fiction of Bruno Schulz: The Street of Crocodiles, Sanatorium Under the Sign of the
TRANSLATED BY CELINA WIENIEWSKA
0-8027-1091-3 WALKER $22.95

The Drawings of Bruno Schulz
0-8101-0965-4 NORTHWESTERN PB $13.95

The Street of Crocodiles
A phantasmagoric recreation of life in the Polish city of Drogobych
INTRODUCTION BY JERZY FICOWSKI
0-14-018625-5 PENGUIN PB $11.95

Henryk **Sienkiewicz**

Fire in the Steppe
TRANSLATED BY W.S. KUNICZAK
0-7818-0025-0 HIPPOCRENE $24.95

In Desert and Wilderness
EDITED BY MIROSLAW LIPINSKI
0-7818-0235-0 HIPPOCRENE $19.95

Quo Vadis?
TRANSLATED BY STANLEY F. CONRAD
0-7818-0100-1 HIPPOCRENE $22.50

With Fire and Sword
The national historical epic of Poland, by the author of *Quo Vadis,* available for the first time in a modern translation
See also **HISTORICAL AND ROMANTIC FICTION** in **POPULAR READING**
0-02-082044-5 COLLIER $20.00

Wislawa **Szymborska**

Sounds, Feelings, Thoughts: 70 Poems
Szymborska won the Nobel Prize in 1996
TRANSLATED BY MAGNUS J. KRYNSKI & ROBERT A. MAGUIRE
0-691-06469-5 PRINCETON $35.00

View with a Grain of Sand: Selected Poems
0-15-100153-7 HARVEST $20.00

Tomas **Venclova**

Aleksander Wat: Life and Art of an Iconoclast
0-300-06406-3 YALE $35.00

Aleksander **Wat**

Lucifer Unemployed
TRANSLATED BY LILLIAN VALLEE
0-8101-0840-2 NORTHWESTERN PB $9.95

My Century: The Odyssey of a Polish Intellectual
TRANSLATED BY RICHARD LOURIE
INTRODUCTION BY CZESLAW MILOSZ
0-520-04425-8 CALIFORNIA $50.00

With the Skin
A selection of poems
TRANSLATED BY CZESLAW MILOSZ & LEONARD NATHAN
0-88001-183-1 ECCO $17.95

Adam **Zagajewski**

Canvas
0-374-52398-3 NOONDAY PB $8.00
0-374-11867-1 FS&G $20.00

Solidarity, Solitude: Essays
See also **CONTEMPORARY WRITERS ON WRITING** under **LITERARY CRITICISM**
TRANSLATED BY LILLIAN VALLEE
0-88001-186-6 ECCO $19.95

Two Cities: On Exile, History, and the Imagination
TRANSLATED BY LILLIAN VALLEE
0-374-28016-9 FS&G $24.00

Romanian Literature

Luican **Blaga**

At the Court of Yearning
TRANSLATED WITH AN INTRODUCTION BY ANDREI CODRESCU
0-8142-0489-9 OHIO STATE $40.00
0-8142-0496-1 OHIO STATE PB $19.50

Joan P. **Couliano**

Eros and Magic in the Renaissance
Magic as a manipulative psychology of motives, especially erotic ones
See also **THE OCCULT, WITCHCRAFT, AND THE DEVIL** under **WORLD RELIGION** in **RELIGION, SPIRITUALITY, AND PHILOSOPHY**
TRANSLATED BY MARGARET COOK
FOREWORD BY MIRCEA ELIADE
0-226-12315-4 CHICAGO $34.95
0-226-12316-2 CHICAGO PB $14.95

Ioan **Culianu**

Psychanodia I: A Survey of the Evidence Concerning the Ascension of the Soul and Its Relevance
90-04-06903-8 E.J. BRILL PB $29.50

Ted **Anton**

Eros, Magic and the Murder of Professor Culianu
Much useful information not only on Culianu, but also on Romanian intelligentsia, abroad and at home
0-8101-1396-1 NORTHWESTERN $24.95

Mircea **Eliade**

Born in Bucharest, educated in Calcutta, and a professor at the Sorbonne before settling at the University of Chicago, Eliade was considered the foremost authority on religion in the world. He was also an original writer of fiction and short stories, blending philosophy, mythology, fantasy, and personal narrative.

Fantastic Tales
0-948259-92-2 DUFOUR PB $17.95

The Myth of the Eternal Return
An influential study of history and mythical time; using Eastern European folk materials, Eliade traces the transmutation of historical events into myths
See also **MIRCEA ELIADE** under **WORLD RELIGION** in **RELIGION, SPIRITUALITY, AND PHILOSOPHY**
TRANSLATED BY WILLARD R. TRASK
0-691-09798-4 PRINCETON $37.50
0-691-01777-8 PRINCETON PB $9.95

Myths, Dreams and Mysteries
0-8446-6625-4 SMITH $26.25

The Old Man and the Bureaucrats
A short novel set in the author's native Romania
TRANSLATED BY MARY STEVENSON
0-268-01497-3 NOTRE DAME $15.00

Patterns in Comparative Religion
TRANSLATED BY ROSEMARY SHEED
0-8032-6733-9 NEBRASKA PB $17.95

Rites and Symbols of Initiation
0-88214-358-1 SPRING PB $16.00

Symbolism, the Sacred and the Arts
EDITED BY DIANE APOSTOLOS-CAPPADONA
0-8245-0723-1 CROSSROAD $18.95

Mircea **Eliade**
Bengal Nights
0-226-20418-9 CHICAGO $22.50
0-226-20419-7 CHICAGO PB $12.95

Maltreyi **Devi**
It Does Not Die: A Romance
A response to Mircea Eliade's novel *Bengal Nights*, by the Indian woman on whom the central character is based, protesting Eliade's distortion of their relationship
0-226-14363-5 CHICAGO $22.50
0-226-14365-1 CHICAGO PB $14.95

Norman **Manea**
The Black Envelope
In Bucharest in the '80s, a man searches for the truth of his father's death and is drawn into a web of intrigue left over from the days of communism
0-374-11397-1 FS&G $25.00

Compulsory Happiness
These four superbly observed novellas demonstrate why Manea's depiction of everyday life in the police state of his native Romania has been compared to Kafka, Robert Musil, and Bruno Schulz. "A writer of acute conscience and formidable originality…Manea displays a gift for seeing the familiar world in a new and utterly astonished way"—Richard Burgin, *Washington Post Book World*
TRANSLATED BY LINDA COVERDALE
0-374-12785-9 FS&G $22.00

October, Eight O'clock: Stories
"The reader becomes absorbed at once. The background is dreamlike but terribly familiar…. Manea's prose treads the edge of the poetry of nightmare"—John Bayley, *NY Times Book Review*
0-8021-3371-1 GROVE PB $12.00

Liviu **Rebreanu**
Ion
In his major, landmark novel Rebreanu tells the story of a ruthless peasant thwarted by his own ambition in pre-World War I Transylvania
0-7206-4650-2 DUFOUR $26.00

Uprising
The tale of a Romanian peasant revolt
0-7206-9382-9 DUFOUR $26.00

Mihail **Sadoveaunu**
Evening Tales
Stories about ordinary folk which illuminate the Romanian national spirit
TRANSLATED BY E. FARCIA & L. MARINESCU
0-8057-5172-6 IRVINGTON $26.00

The Mud-Hut Dwellers
Perhaps the finest Romanian prose stylist, Sadoveanu here evokes 19th century peasant life with a deep feeling for the bond between man and nature
0-8057-5195-5 IRVINGTON $25.00

Tales of War
An early historical novel about the 1877 War of Independence against the Ottoman Empire
0-8057-5208-0 IRVINGTON $27.00

Marin **Sorescu**
The Biggest Egg in the World
1-85224-021-0 DUFOUR PB $14.95

Hands Behind My Back: Selected Poems
0-932440-57-6 FIELD TRANSLATIONS PB $12.95

Selected Poems
0-906427-48-7 DUFOUR PB $17.95

Vladimir **Tismaneanu**
Political Culture and Civil Society in Russia and the New States of Eurasia
9-995-09385-5 SHARPE PB $22.95

Reinventing Politics: Eastern Europe from Stalin to Havel
0-02-932606-0 FREE PRESS PB $16.95

Uprooting Leninism, Cultivating Liberty
0-8191-8729-1 FOREIGN POLICY $35.00
0-8191-8730-5 FOREIGN POLICY PB $9.50

Literature of the Balkans

Ivo **Andric**
Bosnian Chronicle
This epic story of the struggle for supremacy in a small Bosnian town set during the Napoleonic era is eerily relevant today. A timely reissue of the Nobel laureate's masterpiece
TRANSLATED BY JOSEPH HITRECK
1-55970-236-2 ARCADE PB $10.95

The Bridge on the Drina
The most famous work from the only Yugoslav writer to win the Nobel Prize, this teeming chronicle spans centuries of life in a fictionalized Bosnia
TRANSLATED BY LOVETT EDWARDS
0-226-02045-2 CHICAGO PB $11.95

The Damned Yard and Other Stories
1-85610-022-7 DUFOUR PB $24.00

Dobrica **Cosic**
This Land, This Time
Volume 1
Into the Battle
0-15-644991-9 HARCOURT BRACE PB $8.95
Volume 2
Reach to Eternity
0-15-676012-6 HARCOURT BRACE PB $7.95

Ales **Debeljak**
Anxious Moments: Poems
TRANSLATED BY CHRISTOPHER MERRILL
1-87772-735-0 WHITE PINE PB $12.00

Milovan **Djilas**
Djilas played leading roles in the prewar Yugoslav Communist Party and the resistance and held several high positions in Tito's government, making his scathing study of the new privileged ruling class that had developed in communist societies all the more devastating (it earned him years of confinement in Tito's prisons).

Conversations with Stalin
Memoir by one of Tito's top aides, ousted from the Communist Party in 1954
See also **PORTRAITS OF STALIN** under **THE STALIN ERA** under **RUSSIAN STUDIES** in **WORLD HISTORY AND CURRENT AFFAIRS**
TRANSLATED BY MICHAEL B. PETROVICH
0-15-622591-3 HARCOURT BRACE PB $8.95

The New Class: An Analysis of the Communist System
See also **FASCISM AND TOTALITARIANISM** under **POLITICAL THOUGHT** in **SOCIAL STUDIES**
0-15-665489-X HARCOURT BRACE PB $8.95

Rise and Fall
TRANSLATED BY JOHN LOUD
0-15-676708-2 HARCOURT BRACE PB $8.95

Wartime
0-15-694712-9 HARCOURT BRACE PB $7.95

Danilo **Kis**
Garden, Ashes
0-15-634548-X HARVEST PB $10.95

Homo Poeticus: Essays and Interviews
WITH SUSAN SONTAG
0-374-25791-4 FS&G $25.00

Hourglass
TRANSLATED BY RALPH MANHEIM
0-374-17287-0 FS&G $22.95

A Tomb for Boris Davidovich
0-8101-0855-0 NORTHWESTERN PB $9.95

Danilo **Kis** & Michael **Heim**

Encyclopedia of the Dead

TRANSLATED BY HENRY MICHAEL HEIM

0-374-14826-0 FS&G $17.95

Miroslav **Krleza**

On the Edge of Reason

A bitterly satirical novel of the destruction of an honest individual, by a leading Croatian writer. "One of the greatest novels of the first half of the twentieth century"—Susan Sontag

TRANSLATED WITH AN INTRODUCTION BY JEREMY CATTO

0-8112-1306-4 NEW DIRECTIONS PB $10.95

Josip **Novakovich**

Apricots from Chernobyl

See also **NUCLEAR REACTORS** under **NATURAL RESOURCES AT RISK** under **THE ENVIRONMENT** in **SCIENCE**

1-55597-212-8 GRAY WOLF PB $12.95

Fiction Writer's Workshop

1-88491-003-3 STORY $17.99

Yolk: Short Stories

1-55597-229-2 GRAY WOLF PB $12.95

Milorad **Pavic**

Dictionary of the Khazars: A Lexicon Novel in 100,000 Words

The first novel by the distinguished Yugoslav poet comes in two versions, male and female, which differ by 15 crucial lines. "Pavic is a 20th-century Scheherazade spinning a series of interconnected folk tales, drawing on a vast source of literary references, eventually metamorphosing his narrative into a murder mystery"—*Publishers Weekly*

Female Version

0-679-72754-X VINTAGE PB $13.00

Male Version

0-679-72461-3 VINTAGE PB $13.00

Vasko **Popa**

Homage to the Wolf: Selected Poems

From the Serbian poet who led the modernist rebellion in the '50s

TRANSLATED BY CHARLES SIMIC

0-932440-22-3 FIELD TRANSLATIONS PB $9.00

Vasko Popa

Tomaz **Salamun**

The Selected Poems of Tomaz Salamun

Salamun is a leading Slovene poet

0-88001-161-0 ECCO PB $12.95

The Shepherd, The Hunter

TRANSLATED BY SANJA KRAVANJA

1-88161-302-X READER'S CATALOG PB $8.95

Charles **Simic**, Editor & Translator

The Horse Has Six Legs: An Anthology of Serbian Poetry

1-55597-165-2 GRAY WOLF PB $12.00

Critical Studies

General Studies

Antun **Barac**

A History of Yugoslav Literature

0-930042-49-2 MICHIGAN PB $10.00

Dmitrij **Cizevskij**

Comparative History of Slavic Literatures

TRANSLATED BY RICHARD PORTER & MARTIN RICE

0-8265-1159-7 VANDERBILT $17.50

Emery **George**, editor

Contemporary East European Poetry: An Anthology

0-19-508636-8 OXFORD PB $16.95

Adam **Gillon** & Ludwik **Krzyzanowski**, editors

Introduction to Modern Polish Literature

0-88254-516-7 HIPPOCRENE PB $6.95

Czeslaw **Milosz**

The History of Polish Literature

0-520-04477-0 CALIFORNIA PB $14.95

Studies of Individual Writers

Stanislaw **Baranczak**

A Fugitive from Utopia: The Poetry of Zbigniew Herbert

The author is himself an outstanding younger Polish poet

0-674-32685-7 HARVARD $32.00

Donald **Davie**

Czeslaw Milosz and the Insufficiency of Lyric

0-87049-483-X TENNESSEE $9.50

Alexander **Fiut**

The Eternal Moment: The Poetry of Czeslaw Milosz

0-520-06689-8 CALIFORNIA $35.00

Russian Literature

Before the 20th Century

Although Russian literature dates from the Christianization of Kiev Rus in 988, the earliest texts (mostly chronicles, hagiographies, and other quasi-historical writings) are of interest primarily to specialists. By the end of the 18th century, however, an independent tradition of secular literature had evolved, following the importation and assimilation of a variety of Western genres. It was the life and work of the great poet Alexander Pushkin, born in 1799, that marked Russia's entrance into the community of world literature. Following his death in 1837 a spectacular blossoming of fiction occurred, with Lermontov, Gogol, Dostoevsky, Turgenev, Tolstoy, and Chekhov producing the body of work that made Russian literature internationally respected and influential.

Anton **Chekhov**

"One must have Chekhov...He is not only a great writer, but even rarer, a liberating one."
—Susan Sontag

Anton Chekhov's Life and Thought: Selected Letters and Commentary

TRANSLATED BY SIMON KARLINSKY & MICHAEL HEIM

0-520-02684-5 CALIFORNIA PB $12.00

The Fiancée & Other Stories

Chekhov's shorter short stories, including *On Official Business, Rothschild's Fiddle, Peasant Women, Three Years, The Bet,* and others

TRANSLATED BY RONALD WILKS

0-14-044470-X PENGUIN PB $5.95

The Kiss & Other Stories

In the same volume are *Peasant, The Bishop, The Russian Master, Man in a Case, Gooseberries, Concerning Love, A Case History, In the Gully,* and *Anna Around the Neck*

0-14-044336-3 PENGUIN PB $5.95

Lady with Lapdog & Other Stories

Chekhov's most celebrated short story, as well as *The Grasshopper, Ward 6, Ariadne, The House with an Attic, Ionych,* and *The Darling*

TRANSLATED BY DAVID MAGARSHACK

0-14-044143-3 PENGUIN PB $8.95

The Notebook of Anton Chekhov

A look at Chekhov's thoughts and sketches for his work

0-88001-145-9 ECCO PB $8.50

She fed her dog on the best caviare.

Our self-esteem and conceit are European, but our culture and actions are Asiatic.

A Russian's only hope to win two hundred thousand rubles in a lottery.

She is wicked, but taught her children good.

Every one has something to hide.

THE NOTEBOOK OF ANTON CHEKHOV

The Tales of Chekhov

A uniform set of Chekhov's short fiction, in 13 volumes, along with the two companion volumes *The Notebook of Anton Chekhov* and *The Unknown Chekhov.* "Our gratitude to the Ecco Press for its publication of *The Tales of Chekhov* series can never be too great"—Eudora Welty

Volume 1
The Darling & Other Stories
0-88001-038-X ECCO PB $9.50

Volume 2
The Duel & Other Stories
0-88001-039-8 ECCO PB $9.95

Volume 3
The Lady with the Dog & Other Stories
0-88001-050-9 ECCO PB $13.00

Volume 4
The Party & Other Stories
0-88001-051-7 ECCO PB $9.50

Volume 5
The Wife & Other Stories
0-88001-052-5 ECCO PB $8.50

Volume 6
The Witch & Other Stories
0-88001-053-3 ECCO PB $8.50

Volume 7
The Bishop & Other Stories
0-88001-054-1 ECCO PB $9.95

Volume 8
The Chorus Girl & Other Stories
0-88001-055-X ECCO PB $9.95

Volume 9
The Schoolmistress & Other Stories
0-88001-056-8 ECCO PB $9.95

Volume 10
The Horse-Stealers & Other Stories
0-88001-057-6 ECCO PB $9.95

Volume 11
The Schoolmaster & Other Stories
0-88001-058-4 ECCO PB $9.50

Volume 12
The Cook's Wedding & Other Stories
0-88001-059-2 ECCO PB $9.50

The Party & Other Stories

Includes *A Woman's Kingdom, My Life: A Provincial Story, An Unpleasant Business,* and *A Nervous Breakdown*

TRANSLATED BY RONALD WILKS

0-14-044452-1 PENGUIN PB $7.95

The Selected Letters of Anton Chekhov

Chekhov's funny, intense, compassionate letters show him to be a supreme realist in life as well as in literature

TRANSLATED BY SIDONIE K. LEDERER
EDITED BY LILLIAN HELLMAN
9-993-23671-3 ECCO PB $12.95

The Unknown Chekhov

TRANSLATED BY AVRAHM YARMOLINSKY
0-88001-142-4 ECCO PB $9.50

Nikolai **Chernyshevsky**

Prologue

0-8101-1165-9 NORTHWESTERN PB $19.95

What Is to Be Done?

This novel of love and sacrifice by one of the Old Regime's most famous radical critics is a primary text of Russian feminism and socialism

See also **LEFTISM AND MARXISM** under **POLITICAL THOUGHT** in **SOCIAL STUDIES**

TRANSLATED BY MICHAEL R. KATZ
0-8014-1744-9 CORNELL $46.50
0-8014-9547-4 CORNELL PB $14.95

Joshua **Cooper**, translator

The Government Inspector and Other Russian Plays

In addition to Gogol's play, includes *The Infant* by Fonvizin, *Chatsky* by Griboyedov, and *Thunder* by Ostrovsky

0-14-044579-X PENGUIN PB $9.95

Fyodor **Dostoevsky**

An Accidental Family

A new translation of the late novel also known as *The Adolescent* and *A Raw Youth*

TRANSLATED BY RICHARD FREEBORN
0-19-282836-3 OXFORD PB $10.95

The Adolescent

A powerful study of the psychology of avarice, also translated as *A Raw Youth*

TRANSLATED BY ANDREW MACANDREW
0-393-00995-5 NORTON PB $17.95

The Best Short Stories of Dostoevsky

0-679-60020-5 MODERN LIBRARY $14.50

The Brothers Karamazov

Dostoevsky's crowning achievement, planned as the first volume of a never-written trilogy. "I'd die happy if I could finish this final novel, for I would have expressed myself completely" —Dostoevsky

TRANSLATED BY RICHARD PEVEAR AND LARISSA VOLOKHONSKY
0-679-41003-1 EVERYMAN'S $20.00
0-679-72925-9 VINTAGE PB $17.00
0-553-21216-8 BDD PB $5.95

The Brothers Karamazov

TRANSLATED BY CONSTANCE GARNETT
0-394-60415-6 MODERN LIBRARY $17.00

Crime and Punishment

"*Crime and Punishment* has upon most readers an impact as immediate and obvious and full as the news of murder next door; one *almost* participates in the crime, and the trivial details become obsessively important"—R.P. Blackmur

TRANSLATED BY CONSTANCE GARNETT
0-394-60450-4 RANDOM HOUSE $15.00

Crime and Punishment

A new translation

TRANSLATED BY JESSIE COULSON
0-19-281549-0 OXFORD PB $7.95

Crime and Punishment

A brilliant new translation. "[Compared] with other translations of *Crime and Punishment*, the Pevear-Volokhonsky version is in every way more accurate...The energy of Dostoevsky's style, its disturbing rhythms and rough edges, are all perceptible here"—William Mills Todd III, Harvard University

TRANSLATED BY RICHARD PEVEAR & LARISSA VOLOKHONSKY
0-553-21175-7 BDD PB $3.95

Crime and Punishment

The translator writes: "A detective novel, a religious epic, a study in criminal psychology, an indictment of urban social conditions in 19th-century Russia, and a proto-Nietzschean analysis of the will to power...*Crime and Punishment* is all these things—but it is more"

TRANSLATED BY DAVID MCDUFF
0-670-83640-0 PENGUIN $30.00

Demons

Pevear and Volokhonsky continue their acclaimed series of Dostoevsky translations with this new version of the novel also known as *The Demons* and *The Possessed*

TRANSLATED BY RICHARD PEVEAR AND LARISSA VOLOKHONSKY
0-679-42314-1 KNOPF $27.50
0-679-73451-1 KNOPF PB $16.00

The Devils

In this novel of nihilism, conspiracy, madness, and suicide (also known as *The Possessed*), Dostoevsky fully anticipated the political paranoia of the 20th-century

TRANSLATED BY DAVID MAGARSHACK
0-14-044035-6 PENGUIN PB $8.95

The Double

Golyadkin and his "double," one of Dostoevsky's first studies in split personality

TRANSLATED BY EVELYN HARDEN
0-88233-757-2 ARDIS PB $10.95

The Gambler

Dostoevsky's own mania for gambling was the basis for this vivid psychological portrait

TRANSLATED BY ANDREW MACANDREW
0-393-00044-3 NORTON PB $7.95

The Gambler, Bobok & A Nasty Story

Three of Dostoevsky's best-known short works

TRANSLATED BY JESSIE COULSON
0-14-044179-4 PENGUIN PB $9.95

Great Short Works of Fyodor Dostoevsky

Includes *The Double, White Nights, Notes from Underground, The Dream of a Ridiculous Man,* and others

TRANSLATED BY GEORGE BIRD
EDITED BY RONALD HINGLEY
0-06-083081-6 HARPERCOLLINS PB $9.50

The House of the Dead
The fictional transposition of Dostoevsky's experiences as a prisoner in Siberia
TRANSLATED BY DAVID MCDUFF
0-14-044456-4 PENGUIN PB $8.95

The Idiot
TRANSLATED BY HENRY & OLGA CARLYLE
0-451-52492-6 NEW AMERICAN LIBRARY PB $6.95

The Idiot
In the epileptic Prince Myshkin, Dostoevsky undertook to create a truly good character
TRANSLATED BY DAVID MAGARSHACK
0-14-044054-2 PENGUIN PB $8.95

Netochka Nezvanova
Unfinished owing to the author's arrest in 1849, *Netochka Nezvanova* exhibits Dostoevsky's early penchant for irrationality and caprice, this time in the memoir of a girl brought up among aristocrats and struggling musicians
TRANSLATED BY JANE KENTISH
0-14-044455-6 PENGUIN PB $9.95

Notes from Underground & The Double
"Still, I firmly believe that not only too much consciousness, but any sort of consciousness is a disease. I insist upon that"
—*The Underground Man*
TRANSLATED BY JESSIE COULSON
0-14-044252-9 PENGUIN PB $8.95

Poor Folk
Dostoevsky's debut, *Poor Folk* caused a sensation when it came out in 1846, eliciting high praise from Russia's radical critics for it depiction of the downtrodden and destitute
TRANSLATED BY ROBERT DESSAIX
0-88233-755-6 ARDIS PB $12.50

Uncle's Dream & Other Stories
TRANSLATED WITH AN INTRODUCTION BY DAVID MCDUFF
0-14-044518-8 PENGUIN PB $9.95

Nikolai **Gogol**

The Complete Tales of Nikolai Gogol

Volume 1
Contains *Evenings on a Farm Near Dikanka* (1 & 2) and *Arabesques*
0-226-30068-4 CHICAGO PB $12.95

Volume 2
0-226-30069-2 CHICAGO PB $14.95

Dead Souls
Arguably the most enigmatic of the Russian classics, *Dead Souls* relates the errant quest of its hero for dead serfs, which he buys up as collateral for a mortgage on the estate he hopes someday to own
TRANSLATED BY ANDREW MACANDREW
0-14-044113-1 PENGUIN PB $9.95

The Chief of Police, sure enough, turned out to be a miracle worker... The Chief was, in a way, the father and benefactor of the town. He was in the midst of the citizens altogether as if in the bosom of his own family, and as for the shops and the marketplace, he dropped in on them as if into his own pantry. In general, he had found his proper niche, as they say, and had mastered his job to perfection. It was even hard to decide whether he had been made for the job or the job for him. So cleverly did he handle it that he made twice as much of a good thing out of it as his predecessors had done, and yet at the same time he had earned the love of the whole town. The merchants, first of all, loved him very much precisely because there was nothing stuck up about him; he stood godfather to their children, he was on hail-fellow-well-met terms with them and although at times he did take a powerful chunk out of their hides, yet he did it somehow with exceeding adroitness.
DEAD SOULS

Dead Souls
This translation, offered here in a slightly revised version to conform to the most recent textual scholarship, was praised by the hard-to-please Vladimir Nabokov as "an extraordinarily fine piece of work"
TRANSLATED BY BERNARD GUILBERT GUERNEY
REVISED AND EDITED BY SUSANNE FUSSO
0-300-06099-8 YALE PB $14.00

Dead Souls
TRANSLATED BY RICHARD PEVEAR & ELENA VOLOKHONSKY
0-679-43022-9 PANTHEON $27.50

The Diary of a Madman
Gogol's best short works in an excellent translation. Includes *The Nose, The Overcoat, Taras Bulba,* and others
TRANSLATED BY ANDREW MACANDREW
0-451-52403-9 NEW AMERICAN LIBRARY PB $4.95

Diary of a Madman and Other Stories
The fictional memoir of a self-styled king of Spain—a psychologist's case study in literary form
TRANSLATED BY RONALD WILKS
0-14-044273-1 PENGUIN PB $8.95

Gogol: Plays and Selected Writings
0-8101-1159-4 NORTHWESTERN PB $13.95

The Inspector & Other Plays
Also includes Gogol's brilliant comedies *Marriage, Gamblers,* and a dramatization of *Diary of a Madman*
TRANSLATED WITH AN INTRODUCTION BY ERIC BENTLEY
0-936839-12-0 APPLAUSE THEATRE PB $10.95

The Overcoat & Other Tales of Good and Evil
"When, as in his immortal *The Overcoat*, he really let himself go...Gogol became the greatest artist that Russia has yet produced"
—Vladimir Nabokov
TRANSLATED BY DAVID MAGARSHACK
0-393-00304-3 NORTON PB $8.95

Petersburg Tales, Marriage, and The Government Inspector
TRANSLATED BY CHRISTOPHER ENGLISH
0-192-82881-9 OXFORD PB $6.95

Ivan **Goncharov**

Oblomov
Goncharov's masterpiece is an extended portrait of an obsessively indolent landowner
TRANSLATED BY DAVID MAGARSHACK
0-14-044040-2 PENGUIN PB $10.95

Alexander **Herzen**

My Past and Thoughts
This brilliant synthesis of personal memoir and social criticism by a great 19th-century Russian agitator and man of letters is an essential text
See also **LEFTISM AND MARXISM** under **POLITICAL THOUGHT** in **SOCIAL STUDIES**
TRANSLATED BY J. D. DUFF
INTRODUCTION BY ISAIAH BERLIN
0-520-04191-7 CALIFORNIA $52.50
0-520-04210-7 CALIFORNIA PB $13.95

Alexander Herzen (photo courtesy of The Bettmann Archives)

Who Is to Blame?
Herzen's novel of social convention and its stultifying effects on three characters caught in a love triangle
TRANSLATED BY MICHAEL KATZ
0-8014-9286-6 CORNELL PB $15.95

Mikhail **Lermontov**

A Hero of Our Time
Lermontov's greatest prose work is a masterful examination of the superfluous man of the 1830s: Byronic, alienated, egotistical, and self-absorbed
TRANSLATED BY VLADIMIR & DMITRI NABOKOV
0-679-41327-8 KNOPF $15.00

Nikolai **Leskov**

The Enchanted Wanderer: Selected Tales
The title story traces the wild adventures of a runaway serf and his ultimate sanctuary in a monastery. Also includes *Lady Macbeth, The Left-Handed Craftsman, The Sentry*, and *The White Eagle*
TRANSLATED BY DAVID MAGARSHACK
0-948166-04-5 DUFOUR PB $13.95

Five Tales
Includes *Chasing Out the Devil, A Spiteful Fellow, A Shameless Rascal, The Robber,* and *An Iron Will*
TRANSLATED BY MICHAEL SHOTTON
0-946162-12-3 DUFOUR $25.00
0-946162-13-1 DUFOUR PB $13.95

Lady Macbeth of the Mtsensk District & Other Stories
The title story was the basis for the libretto of Shostakovich's opera
TRANSLATED BY DAVID MCDUFF
9-99378-842-2 PENGUIN PB $10.95

Alexander **Ostrovsky**
The Storm
Ostrovsky's most noted play, on which Janacek's opera *Katya Kabanova* was based
0-88233-551-0 ARDIS PB $9.95

A.F. **Pisemsky**
Nina, The Comic Actor & An Old Friend
Overshadowed during his lifetime by the works of Dostoevsky and Tolstoy, Pisemsky's stories provide a vivid, often satirical view of provincial life and social inequality
TRANSLATED BY MAYA JENKINS
0-88233-986-9 ARDIS $17.50

Alexander **Pushkin**
The Captain's Daughter & Other Stories
Contains also *The Tales of Belkin, The Queen of Spades, Kirdjali,* and *The Negro of Peter the Great*
0-679-41331-6 KNOPF $15.00

Collected Poetry
An excellent translation of Pushkin's finest poems
TRANSLATED BY WALTER ARNDT
0-88233-826-9 ARDIS PB $18.95

The Complete Prose Tales of Pushkin
Includes *The Tales of Belkin, Queen of Spades, The Captain's Daughter*, and others
0-393-00465-1 NORTON PB $13.95

Eugene Onegin
Pushkin's masterpiece, a novel in verse about rejected love
TRANSLATED BY WALTER ARNDT
0-87501-106-3 ARDIS PB $12.95

Eugene Onegin
This deftly rendered version, employing Pushkin's original rhyme scheme and meter, is preferred by many readers
TRANSLATED BY CHARLES JOHNSTON
0-14-044394-0 PENGUIN PB $9.95

Alexander Pushkin

Eugene Onegin: A Novel in Verse
With annotations and commentary by Vladimir Nabokov; for the serious student of Pushkin
TRANSLATED BY VLADIMIR NABOKOV
0-691-01905-3 PRINCETON PB $15.95
0-691-01904-5 PRINCETON PB $35.00

Mozart and Salieri: The Little Tragedies
Four studies of human weakness: *The Covetous Knight, Mozart and Salieri, The Stone Guest,* and *A Feast During the Plague*
TRANSLATED BY ANTONY WOOD
0-8023-1282-9 DUFOUR PB $15.95

The Queen of Spades & Other Stories
Also includes *The Negro of Peter the Great, Dubrowsky,* and *The Captain's Daughter*
TRANSLATED BY ROSEMARY EDMONDS
0-14-044119-0 PENGUIN PB $10.95

Secret Journal: 1836-1837
A chronicle of Pushkin's troubled last years
0-916201-03-1 M.I.P. PB $19.00

F.D. **Reeve**, editor & translator
Nineteenth-Century Russian Plays
0-393-00683-2 NORTON PB $13.95

M.E. **Saltykov-Shchedrin**
The Golovlyov Family
The best-known novel of this fierce satirist traces the disintegration of a family through hypocrisy, greed, and alcoholism
TRANSLATED BY RONALD WILKS
0-14-044490-4 PENGUIN PB $6.95

The Pompadours
A satire of the provincial bureaucrats who governed the countryside like little czars
TRANSLATED WITH AN INTRODUCTION BY DAVID MAGARSHACK
0-88233-743-2 ARDIS PB $8.95

Leo **Tolstoy**
Anna Karenina
"We are not to take *Anna Karenina* as a work of art; we are to take it as a piece of life. A piece of life as it is"—Matthew Arnold
TRANSLATED BY LOUISE & AYLMER MAUDE
0-19-281510-5 OXFORD PB $5.95

Anna Karenina
The standard translation for many years
TRANSLATED BY CONSTANCE GARNETT
0-394-60448-2 EVERYMAN'S $19.00
0-07-553632-3 MCGRAW HILL PB $15.40

Anna Karenina
TRANSLATED BY ROSEMARY EDMONDS
0-14-044041-0 PENGUIN PB $7.95

Childhood, Boyhood, Youth
This trilogy (an intended fourth volume was never written) set the standard for the psychological memoir in 19th-century Russian fiction
TRANSLATED BY ROSEMARY EDMONDS
0-14-044139-5 PENGUIN PB $10.95

Childhood, Boyhood, and Youth
0-679-40578-X EVERYMAN'S $17.00

A Confession & Other Religious Writings
Key texts in the author's spiritual development, essential for understanding Tolstoy's moral and ethical concerns
INTRODUCTION BY JANE KENTISH
0-14-044473-4 PENGUIN PB $9.95

The Cossacks
0-679-43131-4 KNOPF $15.00

Great Short Works of Leo Tolstoy
Includes *The Cossacks, Family Happiness, The Death of Ivan Ilych, The Devil, The Kreutzer Sonata*, and others
INTRODUCTION BY JOHN BAYLEY
0-06-083071-9 HARPERCOLLINS PB $7.50

How Much Land Does a Man Need? And Other Stories
TRANSLATED BY RONALD WILKS
0-14-044506-4 PENGUIN PB $9.95

The Kreutzer Sonata & Other Stories
Includes *The Devil, The Forged Coupon*, and *After the Ball*
TRANSLATED BY DAVID MCDUFF
0-14-044469-6 PENGUIN PB $8.95

Master and Man & Other Stories
Also includes *Father Sergius* and *Hadji Murat*
TRANSLATED BY PAUL FOOTE
0-14-044331-2 PENGUIN PB $10.95

The Portable Tolstoy
EDITED BY JOHN BAYLEY
0-14-015091-9 VIKING PB $15.95

The Raid & Other Stories
Tolstoy collaborated with Aylmer and Louise Maude on this translation
EDITED BY AYLMER & LOUISE MAUDE
INTRODUCTION BY P.N. FURBANK
0-19-281584-9 OXFORD PB $7.95

Resurrection
Tolstoy's last long novel was written to raise money for the Dukhobors, a Christian sect he admired. Considered inferior to his other works, it remains an interesting source for Tolstoy's views of society
TRANSLATED BY ROSEMARY EDMONDS
0-14-044184-0 PENGUIN PB $10.95

The Sebastopol Sketches
TRANSLATED BY DAVID MCDUFF
0-14-044468-8 PENGUIN PB $8.95

Tolstoy: Plays, 1856-1886
TRANSLATED BY MARVIN KANTOR & TANYA TULCHINSKY
0-8101-1109-8 NORTHWESTERN $49.95
0-8101-1110-1 NORTHWESTERN PB $14.95

War and Peace
Considered by many the greatest novel ever written
TRANSLATED BY ANN DUNNIGAN
0-451-52326-1 NEW AMERICAN LIBRARY PB $8.95

War and Peace
TRANSLATED BY ROSEMARY EDMONDS
0-14-044417-3 PENGUIN PB $12.95

War and Peace
An excellent translation by a friend of Tolstoy's, with notes and useful critical essays
TRANSLATED BY AYLMER MAUDE
0-393-09672-6 NORTON PB $16.95

War and Peace
Long the standard translation
TRANSLATED BY CONSTANCE GARNETT
0-679-60084-1 MODERN LIBRARY $23.00

What Is Art?
TRANSLATED BY RICHARD PEVEAR AND LARISSA VOLOKHONSKY
0-14-044642-7 PENGUIN PB $11.95

Ivan **Turgenev**

Diary of a Superfluous Man
Early exposure of the superfluous type in Russian society, later embodied in Goncharov's idle hero, Oblomov
TRANSLATED BY DAVID PATTERSON
0-393-30306-3 NORTON PB $4.95

The Essential Turgenev
0-8101-1085-7 NORTHWESTERN PB $24.95

Fathers and Children
0-679-40536-4 EVERYMAN'S $15.00
0-03-009650-2 HOLT RINEHART & WINSTON PB $20.95

Fathers and Sons
Turgenev's classic exposition of the generation gap of the 1860s, with his brilliant portrait of the would-be nihilist Evgeny Bazarov. A key work in Russian intellectual history
TRANSLATED BY ROSEMARY EDMONDS
0-14-044147-6 PENGUIN PB $6.95

First Love
A subtle and lyrical story of love and its betrayal from a boy's perspective
TRANSLATED BY ISAIAH BERLIN
INTRODUCTION BY V.S. PRITCHETT
0-14-044335-5 PENGUIN PB $6.95

Home of the Gentry
A middle-aged landowner returns to Russia after a long residence in Western Europe to find and then lose the love of a young girl
TRANSLATED BY RICHARD FREEBORN
0-14-044224-3 PENGUIN PB $8.95

A Month in the Country
Turgenev's one memorable play. An outsider upsets the status quo of a country family—a persistent motif in Turgenev's novels
TRANSLATED BY ISAIAH BERLIN
0-14-044436-X PENGUIN PB $8.95

On the Eve
TRANSLATED BY GILBERT GARDINER
0-14-044009-7 PENGUIN PB $9.95

Rudin
Turgenev's first full-length novel, depicting an ineffectual hero whose death on the barricades of Paris is emblematic of the failures of Russia's radical intelligentsia
TRANSLATED BY RICHARD FREEBORN
0-14-044304-5 PENGUIN PB $9.95

Smoke
TRANSLATED BY CONSTANCE GARNETT
1-88598-300-X D.A.P. PB $12.95

Sketches from a Hunter's Album
Early stories that may have hastened the emancipation of the serfs in 1861
TRANSLATED BY RICHARD FREEBORN
0-14-044522-6 PENGUIN PB $9.95

Ivan Turgenev

Spring Torrents
Written during the Franco-Prussian War, this short novel—unlike most of Turgenev's other work—does not specifically concern Russia and its political problems but focuses instead on the international crisis of mid-19th-century Europe
TRANSLATED BY LEONARD SHAPIRO
0-14-044369-X PENGUIN PB $9.95

The Torrents of Spring
0-8021-1594-2 GROVE $25.00

Early 20th Century

Poetry

Anna **Akhmatova**

Poems
Akhmatova was the great proponent of Acmeism, a movement focused on precision and emotional clarity
TRANSLATED BY LYN COFFIN
0-393-30014-5 NORTON PB $9.95

Selected Poems
A sound translation
TRANSLATED BY ROBIN KENDALL & CARL PROFFER
EDITED BY WALTER ARNDT
0-88233-180-9 ARDIS PB $7.95
1-85224-063-6 DUFOUR PB $21.00

Selected Poems
TRANSLATED BY D.M. THOMAS
0-14-018617-4 PENGUIN PB $11.95

A Stranger to Heaven and Earth
The selected poems of Russia's great poet, a singular witness to the resilience of the human spirit. Illustrated by Mikhail Dorokhov
TRANSLATED BY JUDITH HEMSCHEMEYER
0-87773-894-7 SHAMBHALA PB $9.00

Velimir **Khlebnikov**

The King of Time: Selected Writings of the Russian Futurian
An excellent collection of works by one of Russia's Futurist poets
TRANSLATED BY PAUL SCHMIDT
EDITED BY CHARLOTTE DOUGLAS
0-674-50515-8 HARVARD $21.00

How can we free ourselves from being dominated by people from the past who still retain a shadow of power in the world of space, without soiling ourselves by coming into contact with their lives (we can use the soap of word-creation), and leave them to drown in the destiny they have earned for themselves, that of malicious termites? We are fated to fight with *rhythm and time* for our right to be free from the filthy habits of people from past centuries, and to win that right.
THE KING OF TIME: SELECTED WRITINGS OF THE RUSSIAN FUTURIAN

Osip **Mandelstam**
"In Mandelstam Russian poetry at last has a poet of a stature comparable to Pushkin's—a claim that even the most fanatical admirers of Blok, Mayakovsky or Pasternak would not dream of making."—Simon Karlinksy

Fifty Poems
0-89255-006-6 PERSEA PB $8.95

The Moscow Notebooks
TRANSLATED BY RICHARD AND ELIZABETH MCKANE
1-85224-126-8 DUFOUR PB $14.95

A Necklace of Bees: Selected Poems
0-9513753-6-9 SMALL PRESS PB $10.00

Selected Poems
Selections from *Stone, Tristia*, and other collections of the '20s and '30s
TRANSLATED BY CLARENCE BROWN AND W.S. MERWIN
0-02-579401-9 MACMILLAN $27.50

The Voronezh Notebooks: Poems, 1935-1937
1-85224-205-1 BLOODAXE PB $16.95

Vladimir **Mayakovsky**

The Bedbug & Selected Poetry
The Bedbug is a satirical verse play by the experimental Soviet poet
See also **EARLY 20TH-CENTURY** under **MODERN EUROPEAN DRAMA**
TRANSLATED BY MAX HAYWARD & GEORGE REAVEY
0-253-20189-6 INDIANA PB $13.95

Listen! Early Poems
A selection from the innovative, irreverent early poetry of Mayakovsky
TRANSLATED BY MARIA ENZENSBERGER
0-87286-255-0 CITY LIGHTS PB $5.95

Boris **Pasternak**

My Sister, Life
A cycle of poems that won Pasternak wide acclaim, this celebration of life was written in the aftermath of war and revolution
TRANSLATED WITH AN INTRODUCTION BY MARK RUDMAN
0-8101-1090-3 EXILE EDITIONS PB $12.95

Selected Poems

TRANSLATED BY PETER FRANCE AND JON STALLWORTHY

0-14-018466-X PENGUIN PB $8.95

Marina **Tsvetaeva**

Selected Poems

"[Pasternak] was immediately overcome by the immense lyrical power of her poetic form…personal, and neither narrow-chested nor short of breath from line to line but rich and compact and enveloping"
—George Steiner, *New Yorker*

1-85224-025-3 DUFOUR PB $18.95

0-14-018759-6 PENGUIN PB $11.95

Fiction and Other Prose

Anna **Akhmatova**

The Akhmatova Journals, 1938-41

0-374-22342-4 FS&G $27.50

Leonid **Andreyev**

The Little Angel And Other Stories

0-946626-42-1 HIPPOCRENE PB $8.95

The Red Laugh

TRANSLATED BY ALEXANDRA LINDEM

0-946626-41-3 HIPPOCRENE PB $8.95

Isaac **Babel**

Collected Stories

Some of Babel's best stories, including the *Red Cavalry* series and *Tales of Odessa*. Terse and violent, they present an ironic and stylized view of the Russian Civil War

TRANSLATED & EDITED BY WALTER MORISON

INTRODUCTION BY LIONEL TRILLING

0-452-00798-4 NEW AMERICAN LIBRARY PB $12.50

Collected Stories

TRANSLATED BY DAVID MCDUFF

0-14-018462-7 PENGUIN PB $11.95

The Lonely Years, 1925-1939: The Unpublished Stories and Private Correspondence of Isaac Babel

EDITED BY NATHALIE BABEL

0-87923-978-6 GODINE PB $15.95

Andrei **Bely**

Petersburg

The first definitive edition of what Nabokov considered one of the four greatest novels of the 20th century

TRANSLATED BY ROBERT A. MAGUIRE & JOHN E. MALMSTAD

0-253-20219-1 INDIANA PB $15.95

Petersburg: A Novel in Eight Chapters

TRANSLATED BY DAVID MCDUFF

0-14-018696-4 PENGUIN PB $14.95

Nina **Berberova**

The Italics Are Mine

TRANSLATED BY PHILIPPE RADLEY

0-679-74537-8 VINTAGE PB $16.00

The Tattered Cloak

Six short novels by the 90-year-old Russian émigré detail the lives of expatriots in exile. These are White Russians who become cabbies, waiters, and governesses; all of whom are living abroad and at the mercy of the 20th century

0-679-73366-3 VINTAGE PB $11.00

Mikhail **Bulgakov**

Heart of a Dog

An unusual transplant has surprising results

TRANSLATED BY MIRRA GINSBURG

0-8021-5059-4 GROVE PB $8.95

The Life of Monsieur de Molière

TRANSLATED BY MIRRA GINSBURG

0-8112-0984-9 NEW DIRECTIONS $17.95

0-8112-0956-3 NEW DIRECTIONS PB $8.95

The Master and Margarita

TRANSLATED BY MIRRA GINSBURG AND MICHAEL GLENNY

0-679-41046-5 EVERYMAN'S $17.00

0-8021-3011-9 GROVE PB $11.95

The White Guard

TRANSLATED BY MICHAEL GLENNY

0-897-33246-6 ACADEMY CHICAGO PB $12.95

Ivan **Bunin**

The Gentleman from San Francisco & Other Stories

The title story, about the lonely death of a man of wealth, is Bunin's most celebrated work

TRANSLATED BY DAVID RICHARDS AND SOPHIE LUND

0-14-018552-6 PENGUIN PB $9.95

In a Far Distant Land

Bunin's stories arc best known for their evocative visual imagery and shifting moods

TRANSLATED BY ROBERT BOWIE

0-938920-27-8 HERMITAGE PB $8.50

Wolves and Other Stories

TRANSLATED BY MARK SCOTT

0-88496-303-9 CAPRA PB $9.95

Lydia **Chukovskaya**

Sofia Petrovna

0-8101-1150-0 NORTHWESTERN PB $12.95

Fyodor Vasilievich **Gladkov**

Cement

The acknowledged prototype for all subsequent "production" novels—a Soviet classic

0-8101-1175-6 NORTHWESTERN $49.95

0-8101-1160-8 NORTHWESTERN PB $14.95

Maxim **Gorky**

Decadence

Also known under the title *The Artamonov Business*, this story traces the dissolution of a middle-class family

TRANSLATED BY VERONICA DEWEY

0-8032-7012-7 NEBRASKA PB $8.95

Mother

Gorky's revolutionary novel of 1906 remains one of the most frequently cited works in the Soviet canon

TRANSLATED BY ISADORE SCHNEIDER

0-8065-0890-6 CITADEL PB $10.95

My Apprenticeship

TRANSLATED BY RONALD WILKS

0-8464-0660-8 BEEKMAN $24.95

Maxim Gorky

My Childhood

This account of Gorky's tumultuous and often difficult life contains some of his most vivid writing

TRANSLATED BY RONALD WILKS

0-14-018285-3 VIKING PB $10.95

My Universities

TRANSLATED BY RONALD WILKS

0-14-044302-9 PENGUIN PB $8.95

V.I. **Ivanov** & M.O. **Gershenzon**

Correspondence Across a Room

TRANSLATED BY LISA SERGIO

0-910395-11-X MARLBORO PB $7.25

Roman **Jakobson**

Language in Literature

Highly influential literary theory based on linguistics, by the cofounder of the Prague School

See also **PIONEERS IN LINGUISTICS** under **LINGUISTICS** in **SOCIAL STUDIES**

EDITED BY KRYSTYNA POMORSKA & STEPHEN RUDY

0-674-51027-5 HARVARD $40.00

On Language

"An accessible collection of theoretical works by one of the most important and versatile linguists of the century"—*Russian Review*

See also **RUSSIAN FORMALISTS AND THE PRAGUE SCHOOL** under **SEMIOTICS AND STRUCTURALISM AND AFTER** under **LITERARY THEORY**

EDITED BY LINDA R. WAUGH & MONIQUE MONVILLE-BURSTON

0-674-63536-1 HARVARD PB $22.95

Russian Epic Studies

0-527-01094-4 KRAUS $23.00

Roman **Jakobson** & Krystyna **Pomorska**

Dialogues

Intimate and casual interviews between the linguist and his wife give their thought a charming accessibility

0-262-60016-1 MIT PB $9.95

Roman **Jakobson** & Linda R. **Waugh**

The Sound Shape of Language

0-89925-335-0 MOUTON DE GRUYBER PB............$36.95

Velimir **Khlebnikov**

Prose, Plays, and Supersagas

TRANSLATED BY PAUL SCHMIDT
EDITED BY RONALD VROON
0-674-14046-X HARVARD............$44.00

Letters and Theoretical Writings

Russian Futurism explained
TRANSLATED BY PAUL SCHMIDT
EDITED BY CHARLOTTE DOUGLAS
0-674-14045-1 HARVARD............$35.00

Osip **Mandelstam**

Complete Critical Prose

0-679-77541-2 VINTAGE PB............$16.00

Vladimir **Nabokov**

Nabokov wrote his first nine novels in Russian, the last being The Gift, *written in the late '30s; thereafter he turned exclusively to English as his medium of expression.*

The Enchanter

See also **SINCE 1945** under **20TH-CENTURY AMERICAN FICTION** in **LITERATURE OF THE AMERICAS**
0-679-72886-4 VINTAGE PB............$11.00

The Gift

TRANSLATED BY MICHAEL SCAMMEL
0-679-72725-6 VINTAGE PB............$13.00

Invitation to a Beheading

0-679-72531-8 VINTAGE PB............$12.00

King, Queen, Knave

A young German, seduced by his aunt, fails in his plot to kill the uncle for his money
0-679-72340-4 VINTAGE PB............$11.00

Laughter in the Dark

"There is probably no more frangible encounter in the whole human gambit than the one between a sensitive, fiftyish man and a cretinous girl one-third his age, and in this short, swift, acrid novel originally published in 1938, the author of *Lolita* gives it as pitiless a treatment as it has ever had on paper"—*NY Sunday Tribune*
0-8112-1186-X NEW DIRECTIONS PB............$10.95

Yury **Olesha**

No Day Without a Line

A compilation of Olesha's later writing, forming something of an autobiography
0-88233-211-2 ARDIS............$17.50

Boris **Pasternak**

Doctor Zhivago

Pasternak's lyrical novel of the Russian Revolution and Civil War won him the Nobel Prize in 1958, but he relinquished the award under government pressure
See also **THE '50S** under **THE GREAT FICTION BESTSELLERS 1930-1995** in **POPULAR READING**
0-679-40759-6 EVERYMAN'S............$20.00
0-345-34100-7 BALLANTINE PB............$5.95

I Remember: Sketch For an Autobiography

TRANSLATED BY DAVID MAGARSHACK
0-674-43950-3 HARVARD PB............$11.95

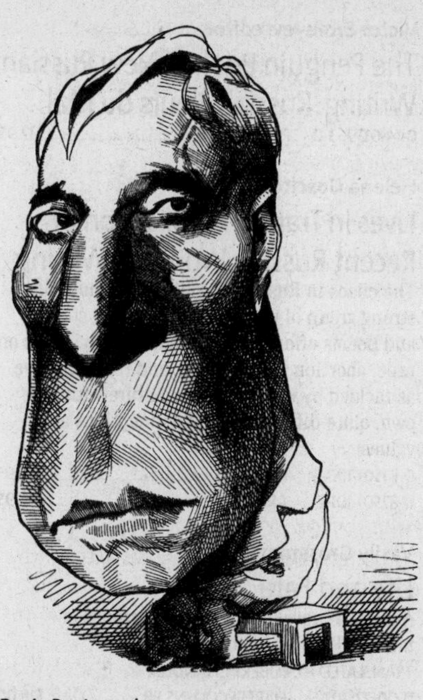

Boris Pasternak

Safe Conduct

This account of Scriabin, Mayakovsky, Rilke, and others presents Pasternak's views on poetic creation and the artistic personality
INTRODUCTION BY BABETTE DEUTSCH
0-8112-0135-X NEW DIRECTIONS PB............$6.95

Andrei **Platonov**

Chevengur

0-88233-309-7 ARDIS............$17.50

Mikhail **Sholokhov**

And Quiet Flows the Don

The greatest work of the Nobel laureate
TRANSLATED BY STEVEN GARY
0-679-72521-0 VINTAGE PB............$17.00

Fyodor **Sologub**

The Little Demon

TRANSLATED BY RONALD WILKS
0-14-018638-7 PENGUIN PB............$10.95

The Petty Demon

A provincial schoolteacher's paranoid visions enliven his otherwise dull surroundings
TRANSLATED BY SAM CIORAN
0-88233-808-0 ARDIS PB............$13.95

Aleksei N. **Tolstoy**

Aëlita, Or the Death of Mars

A sci-fi classic about the Russians landing on Mars
0-88233-788-2 ARDIS............$15.00

Jindrich **Toman** & Roman **Jakobson**

Letters and Other Materials from the Moscow and Prague Linguistic Circles, 1912-1945

0-930042-75-1 MICHIGAN PB............$19.00

Marina **Tsvetaeva**

Art in the Light of Conscience: Eight Essays on Poetry

TRANSLATED BY ANGELA LIVINGSTONE
0-674-04802-4 HARVARD............$30.00

Yevgeny **Zamyatin**

Yevgeny Zamyatin (1884-1937) was the moving spirit behind the Serapion Brothers, a literary group and movement formed in 1921 whose initial aim was to reject the spirit of philistinism in the Proletkult school and interpret the Russian Revolution in an individual way.

A Soviet Heretic: Essays by Yevgeny Zamyatin

Incisive criticism of early Soviet literature and society
TRANSLATED & EDITED BY MIRRA GINSBURG
0-8101-1091-1 NORTHWESTERN PB............$15.95

We

The inspiration for Orwell's *1984* presents a futuristic dystopia with wit and black humor
TRANSLATED BY MIRRA GINSBURG
0-380-63313-2 AVON PB............$5.99

We

See also **EARLY SCIENCE FICTION** under **SCIENCE FICTION AND FANTASY** in **POPULAR READING**
TRANSLATED BY CLARENCE BROWN
0-14-018585-2 PENGUIN PB............$10.95

Mikhail **Zoshchenko**

Nervous People & Other Satires

Contains the short novels *What the Nightingale Sang, The Lilacs Are Blooming,* and *Michael Sinyagin,* as well as the short stories *Nervous People* and *The Bathhouse*
TRANSLATED BY HUGH MCLEAN & MARIA GORDON
EDITED BY HUGH MCLEAN
0-253-20192-6 INDIANA PB............$13.95

Scenes from the Bathhouse & Other Stories of Communist Russia

TRANSLATED BY SIDNEY MONAS
0-472-06070-8 MICHIGAN PB............$14.95

Contemporary Russian Writers

Chingiz **Aitmatov**

The Day Lasts More Than a Hundred Years

A native of Soviet Kirghizia, Aitmatov is widely acclaimed in the Soviet Union. His persistent theme is the clash of Soviet and local culture
TRANSLATED BY JOHN FRENCH
0-253-20482-8 INDIANA PB............$13.95

Vassily **Aksyonov**

The Burn

An insider's view of the Moscow intelligentsia during the '60s and early '70s
TRANSLATED BY MICHAEL GLENNY
0-394-74174-9 RANDOM HOUSE PB............$10.95

The Destruction of Pompeii: And Other Stories

0-679-73441-4 VINTAGE PB............$9.95

Generations of Winter

0-679-76182-9 VINTAGE PB............$15.00

The Winter's Hero

0-679-43274-4 RANDOM HOUSE............$27.50

Quest for an Island
A collection of Aksyonov's stories and plays, including *Destruction of Pompeii, Looking for Climatic Asylum, The Hollow Herring, Quest for an Island, The Four Temperaments,* and *The Heron*
1-55554-020-1 PAJ PUBLICATIONS $17.95

Joseph **Brodsky**
Less Than One: Selected Essays
The poet explains himself in subtle and elegant essays on childhood, poetry, criticism, Dante, and tyranny
See also CONTEMPORARY WRITERS ON WRITING under LITERARY CRITICISM
0-374-18503-4 FS&G $30.00
0-374-52055-0 FS&G PB $15.00

A Part of Speech
Containing his poems written in exile from 1972 to 1976, *A Part of Speech* was largely responsible for Brodsky's winning of the Nobel Prize for literature in 1986. The translators include Anthony Hecht, Howard Moss, and Richard Wilbur
0-374-22987-2 FS&G $15.95
0-374-51633-2 FS&G PB $11.00

Place as Good as Any: Essays
See also CONTEMPORARY WRITERS ON WRITING under LITERARY CRITICISM
0-374-26649-2 FS&G $20.00

So Forth: Poems
Four dozen of the Nobel Laureate's poems, some translated by the author and others originally written in English
0-374-26641-7 FS&G $18.00

To Urania
0-374-17253-6 FS&G $14.95

Watermark
0-374-14812-0 FS&G $15.00
0-374-52382-7 NOONDAY PB $11.00

Arkadii **Dragomoschenko**
Description
A formally radical contemporary Russian poet, translated by a gifted American counterpart
TRANSLATED BY LYN HEJINIAN AND ELENA BALASHOVA
1-55713-075-2 SUN & MOON PB $11.95

Xenia
TRANSLATED BY LYN HEJINIAN
1-55713-107-4 SUN & MOON PB $12.95

Venedikt **Erofeyev**
Moscow to the End of the Line
A fine comic novel about going on a train trip and a suicidal bender
0-8101-1078-4 NORTHWESTERN PB $12.95

Victor **Erofeyev**
Moscow Beauty
A Rabelaisian novel about the adventures of a bisexual beauty who is ostracized when one of her lovers—a Communist state icon—dies in her arms. Erofeyev is "a dynamo…the best of the Russian writers working now"
—*Kirkus Reviews*
TRANSLATED BY ANDREW REYNOLDS
0-670-83606-0 VIKING $22.00

Victor **Erofeyev**, editor
The Penguin Book of New Russian Writing: Russia's Fleurs du Mal
0-14-015963-0 PENGUIN PB $12.95

Helena **Goscito**, editor
Lives in Transit: A Collection of Recent Russian Women's Writing
The chaos in Russia has yielded an unusually strong group of women writers. These stories and poems offer Western readers fresh angles on rape, abortion, motherhood, and romantic love as tackled by women from a culture with its own, quite different, set of assumptions and values
0-87501-100-4 ARDIS $39.95
0-87501-101-2 ARDIS PB $18.95

Vasily **Grossman**
Life and Fate
A massive novel about the misfortunes of modern Russian history
TRANSLATED BY ROBERT CHANDLER
0-00-271207-5 HARPERCOLLINS PB $18.00

Fazil **Iskander**
The Goatibex Constellation
A comic attack on the Khrushchev bureaucracy and Lysenko's bogus school of agrobiology
TRANSLATED BY H. BURLINGAME
0-88233-072-1 ARDIS PB $3.95

Mark **Kharitonov**
Lines of Fate
This philosophical mystery explores a world of artists, criminals, and drug addicts in Russia at the height of Gorbachev's power. "With an intellectual insight rare in any novelist, Kharitonov invents and imagines a great but long-forgotten Russian writer whose destiny foretells the coming shape and being of Russian culture, the smell of its consciousness, the prison of its history"
—John Bayley, *TLS*
TRANSLATED FROM THE RUSSIAN BY HELENA GOSCILO
1-56584-230-8 NEW PRESS $25.00

Alesandr **Kushner**
Apollo in the Snow: Selected Poems
0-374-10549-9 FS&G $19.95
0-374-52321-5 NOONDAY PB $10.00

Inger Thorup **Lauridsen** & Per **Dalgaard**, editors
The Beat Generation and the Russian New Wave
Like the Beat Generation, the Russian New Wave came to maturity during the Cold War. Their confessional literature is reflected here in interviews with writers Allen Ginsberg, Andrei Voznesensky, Vassily Aksyonov, Gary Snyder, Lawrence Ferlinghetti, and Bella Akhmadulina
0-87501-034-2 ARDIS $21.95

Victor **Pelevin**
Omon Ra
A cosmonaut fantasy, by one of the most imaginatively unfettered of current Russian writers
TRANSLATED BY ANDREW BROMFIELD
0-374-22592-3 FS&G $21.00

The Yellow Arrow
A long-distance train to nowhere provides a metaphor for the Soviet Union in decay. "Indifferent to their fate, the passengers carry on as usual—trading in nickel melted down from carriage doors, attending the Upper Bunk avant-garde dramas, leafing through Pasternak's *Early Trains,* or disposing of their dead through the compartment windows"—*The Observer*
TRANSLATED BY ANDREW BROMFIELD
0-8112-1324-2 NEW DIRECTIONS $17.95

Ludmilla **Petrushevskaya**
Immortal Love
A winner of the Pushkin Prize and a short-list nominee for the first Russian Booker Prize, Petrushevskaya with *Immortal Love* confirms her reputation as the most powerful Russian writer at work today. Her stories are set in a world of cramped apartments, short rations, long lines, and diminished expectations, exploring the harsh lives of women in Russia and offering universal insight through personal tales of struggle and hope
TRANSLATED FROM THE RUSSIAN BY SALLY LAIRD
0-679-42257-9 PANTHEON $25.00

The Time: Night
EDITED BY ROBIN DESSER
0-679-75768-6 VINTAGE PB $11.00

Evgeny **Popov**
The Soul of a Patriot
TRANSLATED BY ROBERT PORTER
0-8101-1203-5 NORTHWESTERN $49.95
0-8101-1193-4 NORTHWESTERN PB $14.95

Felix **Roziner**
A Certain Finkelmeyer
0-8101-1263-9 NORTHWESTERN PB $16.95

Anatoli **Rybakov**
Children of the Arbat
A major event in the post-Brezhnev era, this novel signaled the beginning of greater freedom in the arts under Gorbachev
0-316-76372-1 LITTLE, BROWN $19.95

Fear
The follow-up to this Soviet author's acclaimed *Children of the Arbat.* The second volume traces the life of student Sasha Pankratov following his arrest in 1934—from his Siberian exile to his return in the midst of Stalin's Great Purge
0-316-76377-2 LITTLE, BROWN $24.95

Dust and Ashes
The third volume in Rybakov's *Arbat* trilogy
TRANSLATED BY ANTONINA BOUIS
0-316-76379-9 LITTLE, BROWN $24.95

Victor **Serge**
The Case of Comrade Tulayev
TRANSLATED BY ROGER TRASK
1-85172-052-9 JOURNEYMAN PB $19.00

Aleksandr **Shaginyan**
Pogrom: A Novel of Armenian History
1-88369-500-7 EDITION Q $21.95

Varlam **Shalamov**

Graphite

The sequel to *Kolyma Tales*
TRANSLATED BY JOHN GLAD
0-393-01476-2 NORTON $14.95

Kolyma Tales

A fictional recreation of the gulag based on Shalamov's 17 years in Siberian labor camps
0-14-018695-6 PENGUIN PB $12.95

Andrei **Sinyavsky (Abram Tertz)**

Fantastic Stories

A collection of stories steeped in the tradition of Gogol, reflecting Sinyavsky's advocacy of a "phantasmagoric art, with hypotheses instead of purpose"
TRANSLATED BY MAX HAYWARD & OTHERS
0-8101-0727-9 NORTHWESTERN PB $13.95

Strolls with Pushkin

0-300-05279-0 YALE $30.00

The Trial Begins

Essential for understanding modern Soviet policy in the arts. Includes *On Socialist Realism*
TRANSLATED BY MAX HAYWARD & GEORGE DENIS
INTRODUCTION BY CZESLAW MILOSZ
0-520-04677-3 CALIFORNIA PB $12.95

Aleksandr **Solzhenitsyn**

August, 1914

Conceived as the first part of *The Red Wheel,* a vast historical novel exploring the meaning of the Bolshevik Revolution
TRANSLATED BY HARRY T. WILLETTS
0-374-51999-4 NOONDAY PB $19.95

The Cancer Ward

Death and moral responsibility, examined in the setting of a provincial hospital
TRANSLATED BY NICHOLAS BETHELL & DAVID BURG
0-394-60499-7 MODERN LIBRARY $20.00
0-374-51199-3 NOONDAY PB $16.00

The Gulag Archipelago

A monumental exposé of the Stalinist period, based on the author's experience in forced labor camps and in exile
See also **DISSIDENTS** under **THE SOVIET UNION: FROM KRUSHCHEV TO GORBACHEV** under **RUSSIAN STUDIES** in **WORLD HISTORY AND CURRENT AFFAIRS**
TRANSLATED BY THOMAS WHITNEY & HARRY WILLETTS
0-06-092104-8 HARPERPERENNIAL PB $17.50

One Day in the Life of Ivan Denisovich

Personally sanctioned by Khrushchev for publication in 1963, this grim work made Solzhenitsyn famous overnight
TRANSLATED BY H.T. WILLETS
0-374-22643-1 FS&G $24.95
0-374-52195-6 FS&G PB $13.00

We Never Make Mistakes

TRANSLATED BY PAUL W. BLACKSTOCK
0-393-00598-4 NORTON PB $7.95

Vladimir **Sorokin**

The Queue

A comic account of days and nights spent waiting on line in Moscow
TRANSLATED WITH AN INTRODUCTION BY SALLY LAIRD
0-930523-45-8 READERS INTERNATIONAL PB $8.95

Tatyana **Tolstaya**

On the Golden Porch

TRANSLATED BY ANTONINA W. BOUIS
0-394-57798-1 KNOPF $17.95
0-679-72843-0 VINTAGE PB $12.00

Tatyana Tolstaya

Sleepwalker in a Fog

A brilliant collection of short stories from one of the best of living Russian writers. "The most original, tactile, luminous voice in Russian prose today"—Joseph Brodsky
TRANSLATED BY JAMEY GAMBRELL
0-394-58731-6 KNOPF $19.00
0-679-73063-X VINTAGE PB $11.00

Yuri **Trifonov**

The Long Goodbye: A Trilogy

TRANSLATED BY HELEN BURLINGAME & ELLEN PROFFER
0-88233-281-3 ARDIS PB $7.95

Vladimir **Voinovich**

The Fur Hat

0-15-139100-9 HARCOURT BRACE PB $17.95

The Life & Extraordinary Adventures of Private Ivan Chonkin

A hilarious Russian version of *The Good Soldier Svejk*
TRANSLATED BY RICHARD LOURIE
0-8101-1243-4 NORTHWESTERN PB $15.95

Moscow 2042

An immensely enjoyable story of a flight into the future, destination Moscow
TRANSLATED BY RICHARD LOURIE
0-15-662165-7 HARCOURT BRACE PB $12.95

Pretender to the Throne: The Further Adventures of Private Ivan Chonkin

TRANSLATED BY RICHARD LOURIE
0-374-23715-8 FS&G $17.95

Yevgeny **Yevtushenko**

Almost at the End

Poetry and prose on censorship, freedom, and the East-West divide
TRANSLATED BY ANONINA BOUIS & ALBERT TODD
FOREWORD BY HARRISON SALISBURY
0-8050-0785-7 HOLT PB $8.95

The Collected Poems, 1952-1990

EDITED BY JAMES RAGAN
0-8050-2378-X HOLT PB $18.95

Don't Die Before You're Dead

A memoir by a poet who as the most visible of Soviet poets walked a fine line between free expression and government restraint
TRANSLATED BY ANTONIA W. BOUIS
0-679-44574-9 RANDOM HOUSE $25.00

The Face Behind the Face

"Readers will be mistaken if they imagine that the hero of this book is called Yevgeny Yevtushenko. I myself am, of course, that hero, but it has never been enough for me to be merely myself"—Yevgeny Yevtushenko
TRANSLATED BY ARTHUR BOYARS & SIMON FRANKLIN
0-7145-2616-9 MARION BOYARS $12.00

Wild Berries

TRANSLATED BY ANTONINA BOUIS
0-8050-1178-1 HOLT PB $12.95

Zinovy **Zinik**

One-Way Ticket: Stories

0-8112-1341-2 NEW DIRECTIONS $19.95

Anthologies

Nicholas **Luker**, editor

An Anthology of Socialist Realism

0-87501-037-7 ARDIS PB $17.95

Carl **Proffer** & Ellen **Proffer**, editors

The Twenties: An Anthology

A representative collection from an interesting and creative epoch
0-88233-821-8 ARDIS PB $22.95

Christine **Rydel**, editor & translator

The Ardis Anthology of Russian Romanticism

Poetry, prose, and verse narratives from the Golden Age of 19th-century Russian poetry
AFTERWORD BY JOHN MERSEREAU, JR.
0-88233-741-6 ARDIS $42.50

Fiction

Clarence **Brown**, editor

The Portable Twentieth Century Russian Reader

0-14-015107-9 VIKING PB $14.95

Vytas **Dukas**, editor & translator

Twelve Contemporary Russian Stories

0-8386-1491-4 ASSOCIATED UNIVERSITIES $25.00

Masha **Gessen**, editor

Half a Revolution: Contemporary Fiction by Russian Women

1-57344-006-X CLEIS PB $12.95

George **Gibian**, editor
The Portable Nineteenth Century Russian Reader
0-14-015103-6 VIKING PB $13.95

Helena **Goscilo** & Byron **Lindsey**, editors
Glasnost: The New Soviet Prose
Important works by 19 writers
0-679-73008-7 VINTAGE PB $15.95

Poetry

Dimitri **Obolensky**, editor
The Heritage of Russian Verse
A collection of some of the finest Russian poetry that includes such ancient monuments as *The Tale of Igor's Campaign* as well as a wide selection of modern verse. A dual-language edition, with commentary
0-253-32736-9 INDIANA PB $15.95

Gerald S. **Smith**, editor
Contemporary Russian Poetry: A Bilingual Anthology
0-253-20769-X INDIANA PB $18.95

Yevgeny **Yevtushenko**
Twentieth Century Russian Poetry: Silver and Steel, An Anthology
EDITED BY MAX HAYWARD
0-385-05264-2 ANCHOR PB $19.95

Critical Studies

General Studies

Isaiah **Berlin**
Russian Thinkers
This collection of essays includes the famous "The Hedgehog and the Fox," as well as comparisons of Herzen and Bakunin
See also **ROOTS OF REVOLUTION** under **THE OLD REGIME** under **RUSSIAN STUDIES** in **WORLD HISTORY AND CURRENT AFFAIRS**
0-8446-6604-1 SMITH $19.80
0-14-013625-8 VIKING PB $10.95

Joseph **Frank**
Through the Russian Prism: Essays on Literature and Culture
0-691-01456-6 PRINCETON PB $12.95

Maurice **Friedberg**
Literary Translation in Russia: A Cultural History
0-271-01600-0 PENN STATE $25.00

Robert A. **Maguire**
Red Virgin Soil: Soviet Literature in the '20s
0-8014-9447-8 CORNELL PB $16.95

Dmitry S. **Mirsky**
A History of Russian Literature from Its Beginnings to 1900
0-394-70720-6 RANDOM HOUSE PB $8.87

Charles A. **Moser**, editor
The Cambridge History of Russian Literature
0-521-30994-8 CAMBRIDGE $79.50

Vitaly **Shentalinsky**
Arrested Voices: Resurrecting the Disappeared Writers of the Soviet Regime
0-684-82776-X FREE PRESS $25.00

Victor **Terras**
Handbook of Russian Literature
0-300-04868-8 YALE PB $26.00

Studies of Individual Writers

Konstantin **Polivanov**
Anna Akhmatova and Her Circle
TRANSLATED BY PATRICIA BERIOZKINA
1-55728-308-7 ARKANSAS $32.00
1-55728-309-5 ARKANSAS PB $20.00

Roberta **Reeder**
Anna Akhmatova: Poet and Prophet
0-312-11241-6 ST. MARTIN'S $35.00

Nina **Berberova**
Alexander Blok: A Life
TRANSLATED BY ROBYN MARSACK
0-8076-1408-4 BRAZILLER $22.50

J.A.E. **Curtis**
Manuscripts Don't Burn: Mikhail Bulgakov: A Life in Letters and Diaries
In the pantheon of 20th-century Russian literature, Bulgakov ranks with Pasternak and Solzhenitsyn. Derived from diaries and papers seized by the secret police, this biography provides insight into the nightmarishly precarious existence of a writer struggling against the Stalinist regime
0-87951-462-0 OVERLOOK $25.00

Ed **Sanders**
Chekhov
Sanders puts his notion of "investigative poetics" to work in this evocation of the life of Anton Chekhov
0-87685-966-X BLACK SPARROW $25.00
0-87685-965-1 BLACK SPARROW PB $13.50

V.S. **Pritchett** & Anton **Chekhov**
Chekhov: A Spirit Set Free
0-394-54650-4 RANDOM HOUSE $17.95
0-679-72546-6 VINTAGE PB $8.95

Joseph **Frank**
Frank's biography of Dostoevsky is in itself an extraordinary piece of literary reconstruction, evoking the political and social context with novelistic density

Dostoevsky: The Seeds of Revolt, 1821-1849
0-691-01355-1 PRINCETON PB $16.95

Dostoevsky: The Years of Ordeal, 1850-1859
0-691-06576-4 PRINCETON $55.00
0-691-01422-1 PRINCETON PB $16.95

Dostoevsky: The Stir of Liberation, 1860-1865
0-691-06652-3 PRINCETON $65.00
0-691-01452-3 PRINCETON PB $16.95

Dostoevsky: The Miraculous Years, 1865-1871
0-691-04364-7 PRINCETON $35.00

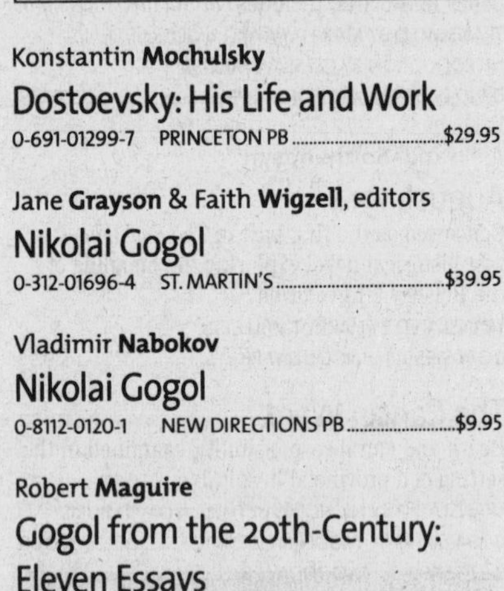

Konstantin **Mochulsky**
Dostoevsky: His Life and Work
0-691-01299-7 PRINCETON PB $29.95

Jane **Grayson** & Faith **Wigzell**, editors
Nikolai Gogol
0-312-01696-4 ST. MARTIN'S $39.95

Vladimir **Nabokov**
Nikolai Gogol
0-8112-0120-1 NEW DIRECTIONS PB $9.95

Robert **Maguire**
Gogol from the 20th-Century: Eleven Essays
0-691-01326-8 PRINCETON PB $19.95

Anton Chekhov

Ernest **Simmons**
Pushkin
0-8446-0259-0 SMITH $14.50

John **Bayley**

Tolstoy and the Novel

0-226-03960-9 CHICAGO PB $16.95

Isaiah **Berlin**

The Hedgehog and the Fox

An essay on Tolstoy's theory of history

1-56663-019-3 DEE PB $6.95

Richard F. **Gustafson**

Leo Tolstoy: Resident and Stranger

0-691-06674-4 PRINCETON $60.00

George **Steiner**

Tolstoy or Dostoevsky

0-300-06917-0 YALE PB $17.00

Viktoria **Schweitzer**

Tsvetaeva

TRANSLATED BY ROBERT CHANDLER & H.T. WILLETTS

0-374-27945-4 FS&G $35.00

Elaine **Feinstein**

Marina Tsvetayeva

0-14-008733-8 PENGUIN PB $5.95

Viktoria **Schweitzer**

Tsvetayeva

0-374-52402-5 NOONDAY PB $14.00

V.S. **Pritchett**

The Gentle Barbarian: The Life and Work of Turgenev

0-88001-120-3 ECCO PB $9.50

Leonard **Shapiro**

Turgenev: His Life and Times

0-674-91297-7 HARVARD PB $15.95

Modern Greek Literature

Poetry

C.P. **Cavafy**

Collected Poems

"Cavafy combined a unique voice and a unique sensibility. He is for me not only the great poet of the Levant, but of all culture in decline—which makes him universal in this century"
—John Fowles

TRANSLATED BY EDMUND KEELEY & PHILIP SHERRARD
EDITED BY GEORGE SAVIDIS

0-691-01320-9 PRINCETON PB $10.95

Complete Poems of Cavafy

Sixty-three poems have been added to the 1963 edition, helping to complete Cavafy's body of work

TRANSLATED BY RAE DALVEN
INTRODUCTION BY W.M. AUDEN

0-15-619820-7 HARCOURT BRACE PB $12.00

Odysseas **Elytis**

Axion Esti

The title of this symphonic poem is Greek for "worthy it is." The complex structure is divided into three main parts: Genesis, The Passions, and Gloria

TRANSLATED BY EDMUND KEELEY & GEORGE SAVIDIS
FOREWORD BY SAMUEL HAZO

0-8229-5318-8 PITTSBURGH PB $10.95

The Sovereign Sun: Selected Poems

Elytis won the Nobel Prize in 1979. "His poems are spells"—Lawrence Durrell

TRANSLATED BY KIMON FRIAT

1-85224-120-9 DUFOUR PB $18.95

Yannis **Ritsos**

Exile and Return

"This collection contains powerful selections from eight volumes of poetry...In a surreal landscape, outer and inner terrains merge, showing how the consciousness of a 'country in exile' affects the individual psyche"
—*Bloomsbury Review*

TRANSLATED BY EDMUND KEELEY

0-88001-017-7 ECCO $17.50
0-88001-018-5 ECCO PB $8.50

The Fourth Dimension

0-691-06940-9 PRINCETON $49.50
0-691-02465-0 PRINCETON PB $14.95

Selected Poems, 1938-1988

0-918526-67-1 BOA PB $17.00

George **Seferis**

Collected Poems

A revised edition, compact and in English only, of the expanded bilingual edition of 1981

TRANSLATED BY EDMUND KEELEY & PHILIP SHERRARD

0-691-06861-5 PRINCETON $39.50
0-691-01491-4 PRINCETON PB $14.95

Prose

Odysseas **Elytis**

Open Papers: Selected Essays

1-55659-070-9 COPPER CANYON PB $12.00

Nikos **Kazantzakis**

Japan-China: A Journal of Two Voyages to the Far East

A diary of Asian explorations before and after World War II brings the culture, history, and literature of these two countries into vivid perspective

TRANSLATED BY GEORGE C. PAPPAGEOTES
EPILOGUE BY HELEN KAZANTZAKIS

0-916870-40-5 CREATIVE ARTS PB $9.95

The Last Temptation of Christ

A fictional reinterpretation of the story of the Gospels explores the human component of Christ's being

TRANSLATED BY P.A. BIEN

0-671-67257-6 TOUCHSTONE PB $10.95

Zorba the Greek

An English writer's life is transformed by his encounter with a Greek laborer

TRANSLATED BY CARL WILDMAN

0-671-21132-3 SIMON & SCHUSTER PB $11.00

Anthologies and Critical Studies

Edmund **Keeley**

Cavafy's Alexandria

A critical study by the outstanding translator of Cavafy, Seferis, and other Greek poets

0-691-04498-8 PRINCETON PB $15.95

Edmund **Keely** & Philip **Sherrad**

Voices of Modern Greece

Translations of poems by Sikelianos, Seferis, Cavafy, and Elytis. The poems were selected according to how well they translated into English and how representative they were of each particular poet's work

0-691-01382-9 PRINCETON PB $13.95

Modern European Drama

For critical works on major dramatists see the relevant national literatures.

Ibsen

"An intellectual pioneer can never gather a majority about him...The majority, the masses, the mob, will never catch him up; he can never rally them behind him. I myself feel a similarly unrelenting compulsion to keep pressing forward. A crowd now stands where I stood when I wrote my earlier books. But I myself am there no longer. I am somewhere else—far ahead of them—or so I hope. At present I am struggling with the draft of a new play in four acts. As time passes, various odd ideas settle in one's head, and one must find some outlet for them."—Henrik Ibsen, from a letter to Georg Brandes, June 12, 1883

Henrik **Ibsen**

Complete Major Prose Plays of Ibsen

Twelve prose plays in chronological order with introductions and stage histories of productions for each. Fjelde's translations are admirably clear and accurate. "Only by grasping and comprehending my entire production as a continuous and coherent whole will the reader be able to receive the precise impression I sought to convey in the individual parts...I therefore appeal to the reader that he not put any play aside, and not skip anything, but that he absorb the plays...in the order in which I wrote them"—Henrik Ibsen

TRANSLATED BY ROLF FJELDE

0-452-25797-2 NEW AMERICAN LIBRARY PB $16.95

Correspondence

0-8383-1098-2 HASKELL $75.00

Henrik Ibsen

An Enemy of the People
TRANSLATED BY ARTHUR MILLER
0-14-048140-0 PENGUIN PB $7.95

Four Major Plays
Includes *Ghosts, An Enemy of the People, The Lady from the Sea,* and *John Gabriel Borkman*
0-451-52515-9 NEW AMERICAN LIBRARY PB $4.95

From Ibsen's Workshop: Notes, Scenarios, and Drafts of the Modern Plays
TRANSLATED BY A.G. CHATER
EDITED BY WILLIAM ARCHER
FOREWORD BY JOHN GUARE
0-306-80090-X DA CAPO PB $7.95

Peer Gynt
Ibsen's last verse play, based on motifs from Norwegian folklore, follows the light-hearted Peer, who escapes conflict by avoiding self-knowledge
TRANSLATED BY PETER WATTS
0-14-044167-0 PENGUIN PB $8.95

Peer Gynt
A fluent verse translation which has been successfully performed
TRANSLATED BY CHRISTOPHER FRY & JOHAN FILINGER
0-19-282227-6 OXFORD PB $6.95

Strindberg

"It was reading his [Strindberg's] plays when I first started to write, back in the winter of 1913-14; that, above all else, first gave me the vision of what modern drama could be, and first inspired me with the urge to write for the theatre myself. If there is anything of lasting worth in my work, it is due to that original impulse from him, which has continued as my inspiration down all the years since then." —Eugene O'Neill, in his 1936 Nobel Prize acceptance speech

August **Strindberg**

Apologia & Two Folk Plays
Also includes the folk plays *The Crownbride* and *Swanwhite*
TRANSLATED BY WALTER JOHNSON
0-295-95760-3 WASHINGTON $30.00

The Chamber Plays
Includes *The Ghost Sonata, The Pelican, Burned House,* and *Storm Weather*. "These chamber plays occupy roughly the same place in Strindberg's oeuvre as do the last quartets in Beethoven's"—Evert Sprinchorn
TRANSLATED BY EVERT SPRINCHORN
0-948230-41-X THEATRE COMMUNICATIONS PB $14.95

Dramas of Testimony
Includes *The Dance of Death I & II, Advent, Easter,* and *There Are Crimes and Crimes*
TRANSLATED BY WALTER JOHNSON
0-295-95433-7 WASHINGTON $20.00

A Dream Play & Four Chamber Plays
Includes the chamber plays *Storm Weather, The House that Burned, The Ghost Sonata,* and *The Pelican*
TRANSLATED BY WALTER JOHNSON
0-393-00791-X NORTON PB $10.95

Five Plays
Translated into fresh colloquial English, these plays continue Strindberg's tradition of "poetry spoken." Included are his most frequently performed works: *The Father, Miss Julie, A Dream Play, The Dance of Death,* and *The Ghost Sonata*
TRANSLATED BY HARRY CARLSON
0-520-04698-6 CALIFORNIA PB $14.95
0-451-51862-4 NEW AMERICAN LIBRARY PB $6.95

Miss Julie
0-486-27281-8 DOVER PB $1.50

Plays from the Cynical Life
Includes the early one-acters *Debit and Credit, Facing Death, The First Warning, Mother Love, Pariah, Playing with Fire,* and *Simoon*
TRANSLATED BY WALTER JOHNSON
0-295-95980-0 WASHINGTON $25.00

Plays of Confession and Therapy: To Damascus I, II & III
The plays *To Damascus* dramatically chart Strindberg's conversion from atheism to a "Strindbergian" brand of Christianity
TRANSLATED BY WALTER JOHNSON
0-295-95567-8 WASHINGTON $25.00

August Strindberg

Pre-Inferno Plays
Includes *The Father, Lady Julie, Creditors, The Stronger,* and *The Bond*. The term "inferno" refers to a disastrous period in Strindberg's emotional life in the 1890s
TRANSLATED WITH AN INTRODUCTION BY WALTER JOHNSON
0-393-00834-7 NORTON PB $7.95

Selected Plays
Containing *Master Olof, The Father, Miss Julie, Creditors, The Stronger, Playing with Fire, To Damascus, Crime and Crime, The Dance with Death, A Dream Play, The Ghost Sonata,* and *The Pelican*. "Our leading Strindberg critic and biographer has given us some splendid translations of Strindberg's most playable works. His unerring theatrical sense makes these volumes invaluable for both scholars and practitioners"—Robert Brustein
TRANSLATED BY EVERT SPRINCHORN
0-8166-1506-3 MINNESOTA $49.95
0-8166-1507-1 MINNESOTA PB $21.90

Chekhov

"In Chekhov's plays, as in his stories, however bewildering the reflections may be, the reflecting surface is cool, shadowless, perfectly clear. It neither judges nor analyzes nor comments, yet the things that show in it will serve as well as anything in literature as the images of truth."—Wallace Stegner

Anton **Chekhov**

The Brute & Other Farces: Seven Short Plays
Containing *Apologia, The Harmfulness of Tobacco, Swansong, A Marriage Proposal, Summer in the Country, A Wedding,* and *The Celebration*
EDITED AND TRANSLATED BY ERIC BENTLEY
0-87910-224-1 APPLAUSE THEATRE $14.95
0-87910-233-0 APPLAUSE THEATRE PB $5.95

Chekhov: The Major Plays
TRANSLATED BY JEAN CLAUDE VAN ITALLIE
1-55783-162-9 APPLAUSE THEATRE PB $7.95

Five Plays
Includes *Ivanov, The Seagull, Uncle Vanya, Three Sisters,* and *The Cherry Orchard*
0-19-281548-2 OXFORD PB $4.95

The Oxford Chekhov—Short Plays
0-19-211349-6 OXFORD $49.95

The Portable Chekhov
0-14-015035-8 VIKING PB $14.95

Uncle Vanya
Mamet's compressed translation was the basis for the André Gregory production of the play that was filmed by Louis Malle as *Vanya on 42nd Street*
TRANSLATED BY DAVID MAMET
0-8021-3151-4 GROVE PB $8.95

The Cherry Orchard
"Nobody in the play gives a damn about the cherry orchard…The play is a series of scenes

about sexuality, and, particularly, frustrated sexuality"—David Mamet
TRANSLATED BY DAVID MAMET
0-8021-3002-X GROVE PB $8.95

The Cherry Orchard
TRANSLATED BY MICHAEL FRAYN
0-413-39340-2 METHUEN PB $9.95

The Major Plays
Includes *Ivanov, The Sea Gull, Uncle Vanya, The Three Sisters,* and *The Cherry Ochard*
TRANSLATED BY ANN DUNNIGAN
AFTERWORD BY ROBERT BRUSTEIN
0-451-52270-2 NEW AMERICAN LIBRARY PB $5.95

The Sea Gull
After the disastrous opening of this play in 1898 Chekhov vowed to give up playwriting. Two years and two plays later, *The Sea Gull* was revived by Konstantin Stanislavsky and enjoyed a critical success
TRANSLATED BY OLIVER MURPHY
0-8283-1454-3 BRANDEN PB $4.95

The Three Sisters
"Full of those little liberties and intimacies of ordinary speech which override grammar and syntax and betray moods of ordinary people and impulses of the heart"
—John Barber, *Daily Telegraph*
TRANSLATED BY DAVID MAMET & VLADA CHERNOMORBIK
0-8021-3276-6 GROVE PB $10.95

Wild Honey
This play, sometimes known as *Platonov,* was discovered in 1920
TRANSLATED BY MICHAEL FRAYN
0-413-55160-1 METHUEN PB $8.95

Early 20th Century

Bertolt **Brecht**

Brecht on Theatre
Selected writings on epic theater and the alienation effect and how these concepts apply to Brecht's own work
See also **DRAMATIC THEORY AND CRITICISM** under **THEATER** in **PERFORMING ARTS AND MEDIA**
TRANSLATED BY JOHN WILLETT
0-8090-0542-5 HILL & WANG PB $14.00

Bertolt Brecht (photo by Fred Stein)

The Caucasian Chalk Circle
1-55970-253-2 ARCADE PB $8.95

Galileo
A critical treatment of Galileo's struggle with the church and his eventual recantation
TRANSLATED BY CHARLES LAUGHTON
EDITED WITH AN INTRODUCTION BY ERIC BENTLEY
0-8021-3059-3 GROVE PB $6.95

The Good Woman of Seszuan
An eloquent play on the near impossibility of virtue in a rapacious society
1-55970-235-4 ARCADE PB $8.95

Mother Courage and Her Children
As the owner of a canteen during the Thirty Years' War, Mother Courage tries to make the war serve her own ends
TRANSLATED AND ADAPTED BY ERIC BENTLEY
0-8021-3082-8 GROVE PB $6.95

Mr. Puntila and His Man Matti
1-55970-280-X ARCADE PB $9.95

The Rise and Fall of the City of Mahogany & The Seven Deadly Sins
These works, an opera and a cantata both set in a mythical and savage America, were the culmination of Brecht's collaborations with Kurt Weill. Auden's translations are designed to be sung
TRANSLATED BY W.H. AUDEN & CHESTER KALLMAN
1-55970-279-6 ARCADE PB $8.95

Saint Joan of the Stockyards
Another stylized Brechtian foray into the wilds of capitalist America
TRANSLATED BY FRANK JONES
0-253-20127-6 INDIANA PB $8.95

The Threepenny Opera
This best-known of Brecht's works, based on John Gay's *The Beggar's Opera,* broke box office records during its original run in Berlin in the '30s, and became a long-running Off-Broadway success of the '50s
TRANSLATED BY DESMOND VESEY
LYRICS TRANSLATED BY ERIC BENTLEY
INTRODUCTION BY LOTTE LENYA
0-8021-5039-X GROVE PB $5.95
1-55970-252-4 ARCADE PB $8.95

Mikhail **Bulgakov**

Flight & Bliss
TRANSLATED BY MIRRA GINSBURG
0-8112-0941-5 NEW DIRECTIONS PB $9.95

Elias **Canetti**

Comedy of Vanity & Life Terms
Comedy of Vanity, a satire on mass movements, constructs a world where all mirrors, photographs, and films are taken away. In *Life Terms,* all people are assigned a specific number of years to live and value is determined solely by age
TRANSLATED BY GITTA HONEGGER
0-933826-30-3 PAJ PUBLICATIONS $18.95

The Wedding
Written in 1932, this social allegory is based around an apartment which collapses in the midst of a wild celebration
TRANSLATED BY GITTA HONEGGER
1-55554-008-2 PAJ PUBLICATIONS PB $8.95

Karel **Capek**

R.U.R. & The Insect Play
Capek's science-fiction play *R.U.R.* introduced the word "robot"; *The Insect Play,* written in collaboration with his brother Josef, is an entomological allegory much influenced by Maeterlinck's nature writings
0-19-281010-3 OXFORD PB $14.95

Jean **Cocteau**

Five Plays
Includes *Orpheus, The Holy Terrors, Intimate Relations,* and other plays exhibiting Cocteau's theatrical range, from poeticized myth to searing boulevard melodrama
0-8090-0722-3 HILL & WANG PB $14.00

The Infernal Machine & Other Plays
The title play recreates the Oedipus myth, while *Bacchus, Orpheus,* and *Knights of the Round Table* transform other familiar stories. Also includes the short play *The Eiffel Tower Wedding Party* and the text for the Stravinsky opera *Oedipus Rex*
0-8112-0022-1 NEW DIRECTIONS PB $12.95

Jean **Giraudoux**

Four Plays
Includes *Ondine, The Enchanted, The Madwoman of Chaillot,* and *The Apollo of Bellac*
ADAPTED WITH AN INTRODUCTION BY MAURICE VALENCY
0-8090-0712-6 FS&G PB $9.95

Maxim **Gorky**

The Lower Depths & Other Plays
Contains *Enemies* and *The Zykovs*
TRANSLATED BY ALEXANDER BAKSHY & PAUL S. NATHAN
0-300-00100-2 YALE PB $13.00

Gerhart **Hauptmann**

Three Plays
The socially aware dramas of this Nobel laureate influenced many writers including Eugene O'Neill. This volume includes *The Weavers, Hannele*, and *The Beaver*
TRANSLATED BY HORST FRANZ & MILES WAGGONER
0-88133-540-1 WAVELAND PB $9.95

Odon **von Horvath**

Odon von Horvath
Includes *Kasmir & Karoline, Faith, Hope and Charity, Figaro Gets a Divorce*, and *Judgement Day*. Martin Esslin has called Horvath "the most important, next to Brecht, of the dramatists who wrote in German in this century"
TRANSLATED BY MARTIN ESSLIN
1-55554-003-1 OLYMPIC PB $3.98

Alfred **Jarry**

Ubu Roi
In its handwritten presentation, and with accompanying drawings by Bonnard and Jarry, this volume captures the ferociously irreverent tone of Jarry's play
TRANSLATED BY BARBARA WRIGHT
0-8112-0072-8 NEW DIRECTIONS PB $8.95

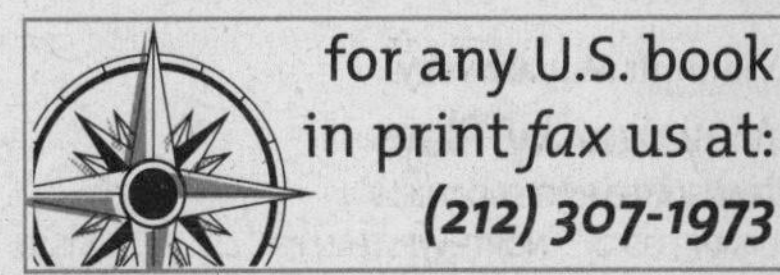

Georg **Kaiser**

Plays

The principal works of the leading German Expressionist playwright

Volume 1

Includes *From Morning to Midnight, The Burghers of Calais,* and the trilogy consisting of *The Coral, Gas One* and *Gas Two*

0-7145-0242-1 RIVERRUN PB $9.95

Volume 2

0-7145-3899-X RIVERRUN PB $11.95

Federico García **Lorca**

Five Plays: Comedies and Tragicomedies

Includes *The Shoemaker's Prodigious Wife, Don Perlimplin, Dona Rosita the Spinster, Billy-Club Puppets, The Butterfly's Evil Spell.* These comedies range from poet puppet-farce to highly realistic tragi-comedy

TRANSLATED BY RICHARD O'CONNELL & JAMES GRAHAM-LUJAN

INTRODUCTION BY FRANCISCO GARCIA LORCA

0-8112-0090-6 NEW DIRECTIONS PB $9.95

Four Major Plays

0-19-282370-1 OXFORD PB $11.00

Once Five Years Pass & Other Dramatic Works

0-88268-070-6 STATION HILL $24.95

Plays: One

Includes *Blood Wedding, Dona Rosita, The Spinster,* and *Yerma*

0-413-15780-6 METHUEN PB $11.95

The Public & Play Without a Title: Two Posthumous Plays

These plays draw on varied traditions that include Surrealism, folk theatre, Symbolist poetry, and black humor

TRANSLATED WITH AN INTRODUCTION BY CARLOS BAUER

0-8112-0881-8 NEW DIRECTIONS PB $5.25

Three Plays: Blood Wedding, Yerma, & The House of Bernarda Alba

Includes *Blood Wedding, Yerma,* and *The House of Bernarda Alba*

See also **FROM REPUBLICANISM TO THE SPANISH CIVIL WAR** under **SPANISH LITERATURE**

TRANSLATED BY MICHAEL DEWELL AND CARMEN ZAPATA

0-374-52332-0 NOONDAY PB $16.00

Three Tragedies

Includes Lorca's three major poetic plays: *Blood Wedding, Yerma,* and *The House of Bernarda Alba*

TRANSLATED BY RICHARD L. O'CONNELL & JAMES GRAHAM-LUJAN

0-8112-0092-2 NEW DIRECTIONS PB $9.95

Two Plays of Misalliance

Includes *The Love of Don Perlimplin* and *The Prodigious Cobbler's Wife*

0-85668-402-3 ASIA SPECIALTY BOOK CO. PB $22.00

Vladimir **Mayakovsky**

Mayakovsky: Plays

TRANSLATED BY GUY DANIELS

0-8101-1339-2 NORTHWESTERN PB $15.95

The Bedbug & Selected Poetry

The Bedbug is a satirical verse play by the experimental Soviet poet

See also **POETRY** under **EARLY 20TH-CENTURY** under **RUSSIAN LITERATURE**

TRANSLATED BY MAX HAYWARD & GEORGE REAVEY

0-253-20189-6 INDIANA PB $13.95

Luigi **Pirandello**

Naked Masks: Five Plays

Includes *It Is So If You Think So, Henry IV, Six Characters in Search of an Author, Each in His Own Way,* and *Liola*

EDITED BY ERIC BENTLEY

0-452-01082-9 DUTTON PB $12.95

Collected Plays

Includes *Right You Are, Lazarus,* and *The Man with the Flower in His Mouth*

0-7145-4110-9 RIVERRUN PB $10.95

Six Characters in Search of an Author & Other Plays

0-14-018922-X PENGUIN PB $11.95

Frank **Wedekind**

The Lulu Plays & Other Sex Tragedies

In the devouring Lulu (herself ultimately prey for Jack the Ripper) Wedekind created a figure who inspired an opera by Alban Berg and a famous silent move by G.W. Pabst

0-7145-0868-3 RIVERRUN PB $13.95

Spring Awakening

Wedekind's masterpiece, written in a mixture of harsh colloquialisms and lyrical speech, was a radically realistic treatment of adolescent sexual anguish. "Edward Bond seems the right translator for Wedekind in that his laconic style exactly suits the original's innovatory one-sentence line"—*Guardian*

TRANSLATED BY TOM OSBORN

0-413-47620-0 METHUEN PB $8.95

European Drama Since 1945

Jean **Anouilh**

Becket

"Anouilh's essential theme—the portrayal of a life that ends by championing the honor of God, no matter what the cost—has nobility and exaltation"—*NY Times*

0-399-51354-X PERIGEE PB $9.00

Five Plays

Containing *Antigone, Eurydice, The Ermine, The Rehearsal,* and *Romeo and Jeanette*

0-374-52229-4 FS&G PB $9.95

Plays: One

Includes *Leocadia, Antigone, The Waltz of the Toreadors, The Lark,* and *Poor Bites*

0-413-14030-X METHUEN PB $9.95

Samuel **Beckett**

Cascando & Other Short Dramatic Pieces

Also includes *Words and Music, Eh Joe, Play, Come and Go,* and *Film (Original Version)*

0-8021-5099-3 GROVE PB $8.95

The Collected Shorter Plays

Includes *Krapp's Last Tape,* mimes, radio and television plays, the screenplay for *Film,* and much more

0-8021-5055-1 GROVE PB $15.95

Eleutheria

Quite different in style from Beckett's mature plays, this early play features a large cast and a complex dramatic action

0-9643740-0-5 FOUR WALLS $20.00

1-56858-067-3 FOUR WALLS PB $12.95

Endgame & Act Without Words

The austere and somber *Endgame* is often considered Beckett's greatest play

0-8021-5024-1 GROVE PB $8.95

Ends and Odds: Dramatic Pieces

Eight pieces, including *Footfalls, That Time,* and *Not I,* which A. Alvarez described by saying that it "focuses in one final, unanswerable image all Beckett's lifelong obsessions"

0-8021-5046-2 GROVE PB $8.95

Happy Days

The horror of mutual dependency is personified in the relations between Winnie—buried in a mound of dirt—and the frustratingly silent Willie

0-8021-3076-3 GROVE PB $7.95

Krapp's Last Tape & Other Dramatic Pieces

Also includes *All That Fall, Acts Without Words I & II,* and the radio play *Embers*

0-8021-5134-5 GROVE PB $7.95

Ohio Impromptu, Catastrophe, & What Where

0-8021-5116-7 GROVE PB $6.95

Rockaby & Other Works

0-394-51953-1 GROVE $12.50

0-8021-5138-8 GROVE PB $8.95

Waiting for Godot

The play that transformed postwar theater

0-8021-3034-8 GROVE PB $8.95

Samuel Beckett

Joseph **Brodsky**

Marbles: A Play in Three Acts

Two prisoners discuss freedom, reality and illusion, and literature and politics

TRANSLATED BY ALAN MYERS & THE AUTHOR

0-374-52116-6 NOONDAY PB $11.00

Albert **Camus**

Caligula & Three Other Plays

Also includes *The Misunderstanding, State of Siege*, and *The Just Assassins*

TRANSLATED BY STUART GILBERT

0-394-70207-7 RANDOM HOUSE PB $8.87

Eduardo **de Filippo**

Saturday, Sunday, Monday

"Shows a touching understanding not of Italians merely, but of the comic, complex predicaments of family life everywhere"—*Daily Telegraph*

TRANSLATED BY KEITH WATERHOUSE & WILLIS HALL

0-435-23201-0 HEINEMANN PB $6.50

Friedrich **Dürrenmatt**

The Physicists

Dürrenmatt uses the metaphor of three nuclear scientists in an insane asylum to explore the nuclear predicament

TRANSLATED BY JAMES KIRKUP

0-8021-5088-8 GROVE PB $8.95

Plays, Fiction & Essays

Includes *Romulus the Great, The Visit, The Judge and His Hangman, Problems of the Theater,* and *A Monster Lecture on Justice and Law*

EDITED BY VOLKMAR SANDER

FOREWORD BY MARTIN ESSLIN

0-8264-0267-4 CONTINUUM PB $14.95

The Visit

A millionairess visits the small town of Guellen and offers to pull it out of bankruptcy on one condition: that they kill someone for her

TRANSLATED BY PAUL BOWLES

0-8021-3066-6 GROVE PB $9.00

Max **Frisch**

The Firebugs

A German couple entertain two arsonists in the hope that their hospitality will save their house and themselves

TRANSLATED BY MICHAEL BULLOCK

0-8090-1248-0 HILL & WANG PB $9.95

Jean **Genet**

The Balcony

The Balcony is a brothel where the customers enact their fantasies of power and self-abasement. "A theatrical experience as startling as anything since Ibsen"—Kenneth Tynan

TRANSLATED BY BERNARD FRECHTMAN

0-8021-5034-9 GROVE PB $8.95

The Blacks: A Clown Show

TRANSLATED BY BERNARD FRECHTMAN

0-8021-5028-4 GROVE PB $8.95

The Maids & Deathwatch

Two astonishing one-act plays: the first an ultimate presentation of role-playing and exchange of identities, the second a portrayal of prisoners awaiting execution

TRANSLATED BY BERNARD FRECHTMAN

INTRODUCTION BY JEAN-PAUL SARTRE

0-8021-5056-X GROVE PB $9.95

The Screens

Genet's last play is set during the Algerian War and its 17 scenes are populated by over 50 characters; the world of the dead is differentiated from the world of the living by the manipulation of screens

TRANSLATED BY BERNARD FRECHTMAN

0-8021-5158-2 GROVE PB $7.95

Peter **Handke**

"The best writer, altogether, in his language." —John Updike

Voyage to the Sonorous Land: The Art of Asking & The Hour We Knew Nothing of Each Other

Two plays

See also **POSTWAR LITERATURE** under **GERMAN LITERATURE**

TRANSLATED BY GITTA HONEGGER

0-300-06273-7 YALE $25.00

0-300-06274-5 YALE PB $12.00

Peter Handke

Vaclav **Havel**

Largo Desolato

A philosopher and human rights activist in a totalitarian state is persecuted for one paragraph in his book and charged with "disturbing the intellectual peace"

0-8021-5163-9 GROVE PB $8.95

The Memorandum

In Havel's satiric comedy, an artificial language is created to mask the foibles of the bureaucracy

TRANSLATED BY VERA BLACKWELL

INTRODUCTION BY TOM STOPPARD

0-8021-3229-4 GROVE PB $7.95

Temptation

A provocative twist to the Faust legend, set in "The Institute," whose mission is to combat "irrational tendencies" in society through its scientific work

TRANSLATED BY MARIE WINN

0-8021-3100-X GROVE PB $9.95

Eugène **Ionesco**

Exit the King, The Killer, & Macbett

TRANSLATED BY DONALD WATSON

0-8021-5110-8 GROVE PB $13.95

Four Plays

Includes *The Bald Soprano, The Lesson, The Chairs,* and *Jack, or the Submission.* "The language, made up of clichés and ready made phrases, which is our daily speech...once it is spoken by actors and exposed on the stage, finds its focus, and acquires the force of revelation" —*France-Observateur*

TRANSLATED BY DONALD M. ALLEN

0-8021-3079-8 GROVE PB $9.95

Rhinoceros & Other Plays

Ionesco's satire on conformism was one of his most successful plays. Also includes *The Leader* and *The Future Is in Eggs*

TRANSLATED BY DEREK PROUSE

0-8021-3098-4 GROVE PB $8.95

Three Plays

Includes *Amedée*, *The New Tenant,* and *Victims of Duty*. "In his greatest plays—*Amedée* and *Victims of Duty*—Ionesco has written works of the same solidity, fullness and permanence as his predecessors in the dramatic revolution that began with Ibsen and is still going on" —Ricard Gilman

TRANSLATED BY DONALD WATSON

0-8021-3101-8 GROVE PB $12.00

Milan **Kundera**

Jacques and His Master

Kundera's stage adaptation of Diderot's 18th-century philosophical novel

TRANSLATED BY MICHAEL H. HEIM

0-06-091222-7 HARPERCOLLINS PB $12.00

Heiner **Muller**

Hamlet Machine & Other Texts for the Stage

Also *Quartet, Correction, The Task, Despoiled Shore,* and *Gundling's Life*

0-933826-45-1 PAJ PUBLICATIONS PB $14.95

Nathalie **Sarraute**

Collected Plays

These plays bring Sarraute's nouveau roman style to the stage. Includes *It Is There, It's Beautiful, Izzum, The Life,* and *Silence*

TRANSLATED BY MARIA JOLAS & BARBARA WRIGHT

0-8076-0940-4 BRAZILLER PB $5.95

Jean-Paul **Sartre**

No Exit & Three Other Plays

Also includes *Dirty Hands, The Respect Prostitute*, and *The Flies*

0-679-72516-4 VINTAGE PB $11.00

Jean-Paul Sartre and Simone de Beauvoir

Peter **Weiss**

The Persecution and Assassination of Jean-Paul Marat as Performed by the Inmates of the Asylum of Charenton Under the Direction of the Marquis de Sade

The problem of revolution, the gap between the masses and their leaders, and the question of modern-day sanity are among the themes touched upon in this touchstone of '60s dramatic radicalism, usually referred to as *Marat/Sade*

ENGLISH VERSION BY GEOFFREY SKELTON

VERSE ADAPTATION BY ADRIAN MITCHELL

0-689-70568-9 ATHENEUM PB $6.95

Anthologies

Michael **Glenny**, editor

The Golden Age of Soviet Theatre

Includes *The Bedbug* by Vladimir Mayakovsky, *Marya* by Isaac Babel, and *The Dragon* by Yevgeny Zamyatin

0-14-048143-5 PENGUIN PB $6.95

Mel **Gordon**, editor

Expressionist Texts

Includes Oskar Kokoschka's *Sphinx and Strawman*, August Stramm's *Sancta Susanna*, Gottfried Benn's *Ithaka*, Georg Kaiser's *From Morn to Midnight*, Ernst Toller's *Transfiguration*, Walter Hasenclever's *The Son*, and Lothar Schreyer's *Crucifixion*

1-55554-013-9 PAJ PUBLICATIONS PB $14.95

Michael **Green**, translator

The Russian Symbolist Theatre: An Anthology of Plays and Critical Texts

0-686-82225-0 ARDIS $37.50

Marion **Holt**, editor

Dramacontemporary: Spain

Includes Jaime Salom's *The Cock's Short Flight*, Antonio Buero-Vallejo's *The Foundation*, Francisco Nieva's *Coranada and the Bull*, and José Martin Recuerda's *The Inmates of the Convent of Saint Mary Egyptian*

0-933826-86-9 PAJ PUBLICATIONS PB $13.95

Michael **Kirby** & Victoria Nes **Kirby**, editors

Futurist Performance

An anthology of theatrical texts and manifestoes by Marinetti, Balla, Boccioni, and others

1-55554-009-0 PAJ PUBLICATIONS PB $13.95

Walter **Sokel**, editor

Anthology of German Expressionist Drama

Includes plays by Oskar Kokoschka, Reinhard Sorge, Carl Sternheim, Walter Hasenclever, Georg Kaiser, Yvon Goll, Rolf Lauckner, and Bertolt Brecht. Also included are four essays by writers of the period

0-8014-9296-3 CORNELL PB $14.95

Phillipa **Wehle**, editor

Dramacontemporary: France

Includes Marguerite Duras' *Vera Baxter*, Nathalie Sarraute's *Over Nothing at All*, Michel Vinaver's *Chamber Theatre*, Enzo Cormann's *Exiles*, and Gildas Bourdet's *The Gas Station*. With an introduction that sets the plays in their historical and political context

0-933826-94-X PAJ PUBLICATIONS PB $16.95

Hebrew Literature

The classical age of Hebrew literature, commonly known as the biblical period, began 3200 years ago; biblical poems like "The Song of Deborah" and "The Song of the Sea"—which schoolchildren in Israel can still understand—were first set down in the 11th century BCE.

Hebrew ceased to be a spoken language around the 6th century BCE and was used primarily for religious and legal purposes. By the Middle Ages it was known as "the sacred tongue" and was proscribed for colloquial use. Beginning in the 10th century, however, Spain, Provence, and then Italy witnessed a unique flowering of secular Hebrew poetry and philosophy. This Spanish-Arabic period, or "Hebrew Golden Age," was largely a Sephardic phenomenon, confined to the southern Mediterranean, and was already waning by the 15th century. Unfortunately, this work is not widely available in good English translations.

The Medieval Period

Shmuel **Ha-Nagid**

Selected Poems of Shmuel Ha-Nagid

Warrior, prime minister of the Muslim state of Granada, Shmuel Ha-Nagid was also the first of the great medieval Jewish poets. "These very fine translations of the work of a remarkable medieval poet gain their authority as much from the literary gifts of the poet-translator as from his linguistic and historical knowledge"
—John Hollander

TRANSLATED BY PETER COLE

0-691-01121-4 PRINCETON $39.95

0-691-01120-6 PRINCETON PB $14.95

Raymond P. **Scheindlin**, translator

The Gazelle: Medieval Hebrew Poems on God, Israel, and the Soul

0-8276-0384-3 JEWISH PUBLICATION SOCIETY $24.95

The 18th and 19th Centuries

Modern Hebrew literature, which began to emerge during the late 18th and 19th centuries, mirrored and in some sense shaped the emergence of the Jews from the ghetto into the modern age.

The early proponents of the *Haskalah*, or Enlightenment, embarked on a mission to use literature to educate and transform the Jewish masses. They chose Hebrew as a means of creating a Jewish culture that might take its place with the cultures of other peoples: Yiddish was a "low jargon" associated with the ghetto, while German was considered too "foreign."

In the later 19th century, some Hebrew writers attacked the early, idealistic enlightenment and called for a more realistic literature, which would reflect the true character of the Jewish people and lead to economic and social reform. At the same time, the violent pogroms of 1881-82 shattered any remaining faith in reformism and impelled the first wave of Jews to leave for Palestine.

Hayyim Nachman **Bialik**

Knight of Onions and Knight of Garlic

A brief, comic elaboration of an Eastern European anecdote; illustrated with woodcuts

0-88482-734-8 HEBREW $5.95

Moses **Luzzato**

Moses Luzzato (known in Hebrew as Moshe Chaim) was an 18th-century Italian-born Hebrew poet and mystic. He is often called the "father of modern Hebrew literature."

The Path of the Just

Moral guidelines from a major Hebrew poet, kabbalist, and ethical thinker of the 18th century

See also **MODERN THEOLOGY AND PHILOSOPHY** under **JUDAISM** in **RELIGION, SPIRITUALITY, AND PHILOSOPHY**

1-56821-596-7 ARONSON $30.00

0-87306-114-4 FELDHEIM $14.95

Moses **Mendelssohn**

It was with Mendelssohn—"the second Moses"—that the real movement toward the Enlightenment and the outside world began in the early 19th century. He became accepted as a symbol of the new type of Jew.

Jerusalem: Or, on Religious Power and Judaism

Mendelssohn attempts to reconcile Jewish tradition with the philosophical rationalism of his age

0-87451-264-6 NEW ENGLAND PB $19.95

The Pioneer Period

After the First World War, Palestine became the base for Hebrew writers. An indigenous literature had been developing since the first migration of the 1880s, but with the third emigration in 1920-24, a younger, more radical literary generation came to the fore.

These were mostly socialist-minded pioneers who had come to build a new society. They challenged Bialik and the old classicism, and were influenced by Russian revolutionary poets and French symbolists.

S.Y. **Agnon**

The first and only Hebrew writer to win the Nobel Prize for literature, Agnon used the resources of midrashic, Hasidic, and folk literature to create a unique prose style. Edmund Wilson called him "a man of unquestionable genius."

A Book that Was Lost and Other Stories

This collection brings Nobel laureate Agnon's English readers into his chronicles of Eastern European Jewry and the society of modern Israel

0-8052-1066-0 SCHOCKEN PB $15.00

Days of Awe: A Treasury of Tradition, Legends and Learned Commentaries Concerning Rosh Ha-Shanah, Yom Kippur and the Days Between

See also **SABBATH AND HOLIDAYS** under **HOW-TO: RITUAL AND PRACTICE** under **JUDAISM** in **RELIGION, SPIRITUALITY, AND PHILOSOPHY**

INTRODUCTION BY JUDAH GOLDIN

0-8052-0100-9 SCHOCKEN PB $15.00

S.Y. Agnon

Shira

Agnon's final novel, published posthumously, involves the adulterous affair in Jerusalem of the '30s of a middle-aged professor with the enigmatic woman he calls "Shira" (which means "poetry")

TRANSLATED BY ZEVA SHAPIRO

0-8156-0425-4 SYRACUSE $42.00

Israeli Literature

Since the establishment of the state of Israel, there have been two main movements in Hebrew literature. The *Palmach*, or '48 generation, writers were the first for whom Hebrew was a natural—rather than a literary—language. They subscribed to the collectivist pioneering ideology of their day and wrote social novels in which the individual was defined by his relations to the community.

In the late '50s and early '60s, Hebrew writers began to express their disillusionment with the collectivist ideology and turned to more introspective, alienated characters. The Eichmann trial in 1961 was a national event, opening up the Holocaust as a subject for public debate and private imaginings.

If there is a third "movement" today, it may be characterized by a return to social and psychological realism; the marginal character has moved back to the center of Israeli life in keeping with the society as a whole, which has lost some of its old certainties and self-confidence and become more alienated itself.

Fiction

Gila **Almagor**

Under the Domin Tree

Orphaned children of the Holocaust come of age in an Israeli youth village in this exceptional tale of friendship and love

TRANSLATED BY HILLEL SCHENKER

0-671-89020-4 SIMON & SCHUSTER $15.00

Yehudah **Amichai**

Not of This Time, Not of This Place

An experimental novel about the split consciousness of a contemporary Israeli, haunted by the Holocaust and the past, lured by love and the present

TRANSLATED BY SHLOMO KATZ

0-85303-180-0 MITCHELL $15.00

The World Is a Room & Other Stories

An original collection of short stories more reliant on metaphor than on plot

0-8276-0234-0 JEWISH PUBLICATION SOCIETY $19.95

Aharon **Appelfeld**

Deported to a concentration camp at the age of eight, Appelfeld escaped and wandered the forests for several years, finally reaching Palestine in 1946. His short stories and novels dwell on the Holocaust, although it is never mentioned by name or depicted directly

The Age of Wonders

A Jewish intellectual and his family cling to their Austrian homeland during the Final Solution—as recorded through the "innocent" eyes of a child who returns years later

TRANSLATED BY DALYA BILU

0-87923-798-8 GODINE PB $11.95

Badenheim, 1939

"This fable-like novel is an eerie controlled experiment in silence that makes its readers supply the horrors it never mentions"
—Bill Buford, *Time Out*

TRANSLATED BY DALYA BILU

0-87923-799-6 GODINE PB $10.95

For Every Sin

A Holocaust survivor attempts to walk across Europe

0-8021-3446-7 GROVE PB $11.00

The Immortal Bartfuss

TRANSLATED BY JEFFREY M. GREEN

0-8021-3358-4 GROVE PB $11.00

Katerina

0-393-31110-4 NORTON PB $9.95

To the Land of the Cattails

A Jewish woman and her half-gentile son travel eastward across Europe on the brink of the Holocaust

TRANSLATED BY JEFFREY M. GREEN

1-55504-279-1 CURLEY $18.95

1-55504-370-4 CURLEY PB $16.95

Tzili

A moving and tender tale of a young girl abandoned by her family during the Holocaust. Alone, she hides in the forest and survives the war

0-8021-3455-6 GROVE PB $11.00

David **Grossman**

The Book of Intimate Grammar

0-374-11547-8 FS&G $22.00

See Under: Love

Hailed in Israel as the first novel to deal with the Holocaust from the standpoint of the children of the survivors

TRANSLATED BY BETSY ROSENBERG

0-374-25731-0 FS&G $22.95

The Yellow Wind

A nonfictional account of relations between Arab and Jew in Israel's occupied territories

See also **ARABS, ISRAELIS, AND THE PALESTINIAN QUESTION** under **THE CONTEMPORARY MIDDLE EAST** in **WORLD HISTORY AND CURRENT AFFAIRS**

TRANSLATED BY HAIM WATZMAN

0-374-29345-7 FS&G $17.95

Shulamith **Hareven**

City of Many Days

"A volatile and aromatic book…bursting with the sensuous images, pungent smells, street noices and tensions of Jerusalem"
—*NY Times Book Review*

TRANSLATED BY HILLEL HALKIN

1-56279-050-1 MERCURY HOUSE PB $11.95

Thirst: The Desert Trilogy

Haraven's major work, a modern variation on Biblical stories

TRANSLATED BY HILLEL HALKIN

1-56279-088-9 MERCURY HOUSE PB $16.95

Twilight & Other Stories

"Lyrical, compassionate stories on modern life. Her women characters, especially, are not easily forgettable"—*Ms.*

TRANSLATED BY HILLEL HALKIN AND OTHERS

1-56279-012-9 MERCURY HOUSE PB $10.95

Yehoshua **Kenaz**

After the Holidays

TRANSLATED BY DALYA BILU

0-15-103959-3 HARCOURT BRACE $16.95

Musical Moment and Other Stories

Stories and novellas by the celebrated Israeli writer concentrate on rites of passage and the loss of innocence as young men discover the beauty of sin

1-88364-218-3 STEERFORTH $19.50

1-88364-247-7 STEERFORTH PB $12.00

Never in my life had I heard such beautiful playing, almost terrifing in its purity, provocative, utterly dispassionate, both cool and ecstatic. And as the rhythm accelerated, the tall boy in the white shirt, blue trousers and grown-up shoes appeared to be wrestling with mysterious forces. Sometimes he looked troubled, but it was only the exertion of a flawless performance, sounding the quickening sequence of chords with his nimble fingers.

MUSICAL MOMENT AND OTHER STORIES

The Way to the Cats

A *New York Times Book Review*-recommended novel, called "[A] throbbing hymn to life" by *Publishers Weekly*

1-88364-220-5 STEERFORTH $20.00

1883-6342485 STEERFORTH PB $14.00

Sammi **Michael**

Refuge

A wartime tale of conflicting loyalties—both sexual and political—involving a communist Iraqi couple in Israel and the Arab comrade to whom the wife gives refuge

0-8276-0308-8 JEWISH PUBLICATION SOCIETY $22.50

Amos **Oz**

Oz was the first contemporary Israeli writer to earn an international reputation. The kibbutz as an emblem of Israeli society—with its morals and ideals as well as the secret passions and seething hatreds—has informed much of his fiction. As a Zionist on the Israeli moderate left, he has become a leading spokesman for reconciliation with the Arabs.

Black Box

A happily married woman obsessively attached to her former husband writes to him about her troubles with their adolescent son

0-679-72185-1 VINTAGE PB $12.00

Don't Call It Night

0-15-100152-9 HARCOURT BRACE $22.00

Elsewhere, Perhaps

Life in the kibbutz and its web of relationships

TRANSLATED BY NICHOLAS DE LANGE

0-15-628475-8 HARCOURT BRACE PB $11.00

Fima

A comedy of ideas about a Jerusalem man who has lived the life of the mind—written poetry, theorized, fantasized—but who now, in his early 50s, realizes that he has done virtually nothing

TRANSLATED BY NICHOLAS DE LANGE

0-15-189851-0 HARCOURT BRACE $22.95

A Perfect Peace

A novel about attempted flight from the constricting pressures of life in Israel and, finally, a kind of reconciliation

TRANSLATED BY HILLEL HALKIN

0-15-671683-6 HARVEST PB $11.95

The Slopes of Lebanon

TRANSLATED BY MAURIE GOLDBERG BARTURA

0-15-183090-8 HARCOURT BRACE $18.95

To Know a Woman

After his wife's death, a veteran of the Israeli secret service attempts to build a new life in retirement. "Oz touches a universal chord in one man's anguished search for meaning in a country that is a microcosm of a chaotic, dangerous world"—*Publishers Weekly*

0-15-190499-5 HARCOURT BRACE $19.95

0-15-690680-5 HARCOURT BRACE PB $8.95

Under this Blazing Light: Essays

"A wondrous collection of essays that reveal to us the heart and mind of one of the great writers of our time"—Chaim Potok

0-521-44367-9 CAMBRIDGE $19.95

0-521-57622-9 CAMBRIDGE PB $9.95

Yaakov **Shabtai**

Past Continuous

One of the outstanding achievements in Israeli fiction, an epochal stream-of-consciousness novel about three intellectual, bohemian Tel Aviv friends

TRANSLATED BY DALYA BILU

0-8276-0239-1 JEWISH PUBLICATION SOCIETY $16.95

Nathan **Shaham**

The Other Side of the Wall: Three Novellas

"Vivid refractions of Israeli society as experienced through the prism of the kibbutz"—*Judaic Book News*

TRANSLATED BY LEONARD GOLD

0-8276-0223-5 JEWISH PUBLICATION SOCIETY $13.95

Moshe **Shamir**

One of Israel's most important and popular novelists, Shamir started out as a characteristic writer of the Palmach generation and later turned to historical epics based on the biblical past.

The Hittite Must Die

TRANSLATED BY MARGARET BENAYA

0-85222-231-9 HEBREW PB $6.95

King of Flesh and Blood

Shamir's popular historical novel about the political folly of the ambitious King Alexander Yannai

0-85222-220-3 HEBREW $7.95

A.B. **Yehoshua**

Like Amos Oz, Yehoshua explores the ambivance of the Israeli attitude toward the Arab conflict. He began by writing surreal, parable-like stories under the influence of Agnon and Kafka but has lately moved to more realistic, psychological novels.

A Late Divorce

A brilliant psychological novel about nine days in the lives of the Kaminka family, narrated through a series of interior monologues

0-15-649447-7 HARCOURT BRACE PB $12.95

The Lover

The Yom Kippur War and its aftermath, structured around a husband's obsessive search for his wife's lover; an instant bestseller in Israel

0-15-653912-8 HARCOURT BRACE PB $14.00

Mr. Mani

From the acclaimed Hebrew novelist, this is an epic of six generations of an Israeli family. Told entirely in conversation, *Mr. Mani* is "one of the most remarkable pieces of fiction I have ever read. [It] convinced me more than ever of A.B. Yehoshua's very great gift"—Alfred Kazin

0-15-662769-8 HARCOURT BRACE PB $12.95

Poetry

Early Israeli poets were all connected in some way with revolutionary Zionist ideology. Led by Yehudah Amichai, a "New Wave" in poetry in the '50s helped introduce a more natural, colloquial idiom, often employing slang and conversational language.

Yehuda **Amichai**

Amichai was born in Germany but emigrated to Israel at the age of 12 in 1936. His main contribution has been in poetry, although he has written some important fiction. Amichai's insistence on the personal life of the dislocated citizen-soldier, who wants to love but must go instead to war, heralded the rebellion against the generation of '48.

Poems of Jerusalem and Love Poems

1-87881-819-8 SHEEP MEADOW PB $12.95

The Selected Poetry of Yehuda Amichai: Newly Revised and Expanded Edition with Forty New Poems

TRANSLATED BY STEPHEN MITCHELL

0-520-20538-3 CALIFORNIA PB $14.95

Songs of Jerusalem and Myself

Jerusalem has been Amichai's home for 50 years, and no one knows it more intimately

INTRODUCTION BY TED HUGHES

0-06-010097-4 HARPERCOLLINS $6.95

0-06-010101-6 HARPER & ROW PB $2.95

Travels

Amichai's longest, most ambitious work is a series of 56 poems conceived as both poetic autobiography and fiction

TRANSLATED BY RUTH NEVO

0-935296-62-X SHEEP MEADOW $13.95

0-935296-63-8 SHEEP MEADOW PB $11.95

Yehuda Amichai: A Life of Poetry 1948-1994

0-06-092666-X HARPERPERENNIAL PB $15.00

T. **Carmi**

At the Stone of Losses

Carmi, the pseudonym of Carmi Charny, was born in New York City and emigrated to Palestine in 1947 in time to fight in the War of Independence. He was one of the earliest new poets to draw upon American and French modernist techniques

TRANSLATED BY GRACE SCHULMAN

0-520-05107-6 CALIFORNIA PB $11.95

Abba **Kovner**

As the partisan leader of the Vilna ghetto and later a high-ranking commander of the resistance, Kovner was transformed by the Holocaust. His poetry deals in a highly personal way with themes of national struggle and anti-Nazi resistance.

My Little Sister & Selected Poems

In the award-winning title poem, an ironic travesty on a world without love pity, a brother narrates a few episodes in the life of his "little sister," who was shielded from the Nazis in a convent

TRANSLATED WITH PREFACE BY SHIRLEY KAUFMAN

0-932440-20-7 FIELD TRANSLATIONS $13.50

0-932440-21-5 FIELD TRANSLATIONS PB $7.95

Dan **Pagis**

Points of Departure

The Holocaust and the various strategies and displacements necessary to survive it are central themes in the daring poetry of this Romanian-born writer, himself a Holocaust survivor

TRANSLATED BY STEPHEN MITCHELL

0-8276-0200-6 JEWISH PUBLICATION SOCIETY $12.95

The Selected Poetry of Dan Pagis

A good introduction to the work of Pagis, who died in 1986. "One of the best Hebrew poets of his generation, exhibiting a rare combination of acerbic wit and understated poignance"
—Robert Alter

TRANSLATED BY STEPHEN MITCHELL

0-520-20539-1 CALIFORNIA PB $14.95

Gabriel **Preil**

Sunset Possibilities & Others Poems

TRANSLATED BY ROBERT FRIEND

0-8276-0240-5 JEWISH PUBLICATION SOCIETY $12.95

Esther **Raizen**, translator

No Rattling of Sabers: An Anthology of Israeli War Poetry

0-292-77071-5 TEXAS PB $13.95

Dalia **Ravikovitch**

A Dress of Fire

One of the country's leading "New Wave" poets, Ravikovitch employs ungrammatical language and unfinished sentences with a stylized slang to produce a new syntax. Desolation and loss are her subjects: what happens "when people break" is her preoccupation

TRANSLATED BY CHANA BLOCH

0-8180-1545-4 TILBURY $11.95

Avoth **Yeshurun**

The Syrian-African Rift & Other Poems

One of the most striking statements of the "spiritual earthquake" that Israel experienced in the '70s

TRANSLATED BY HOWARD SCHIMMEL

0-8276-0181-6 JEWISH PUBLICATION SOCIETY $11.95
0-8276-0182-4 JEWISH PUBLICATION SOCIETY PB . $7.95

Anthologies

Robert **Alter**, editor

Modern Hebrew Literature

Excellent, scholarly introductions and selections from Seforim, Peretz, Bialik, Brenner, Barash, Agnon, Amichai, Oz, and Yehoshua

0-87441-235-8 BEHRMAN PB $15.95

Warren **Bargad** &
Stanley F. **Chyet**, translators

Israeli Poetry: A Contemporary Anthology

0-253-33140-4 INDIANA $32.50
0-253-20356-2 INDIANA PB $14.95

T. **Carmi**, editor

The Penguin Book of Hebrew Verse

0-14042-197-1 PENGUIN PB $18.95

Myra **Glazer**, editor

Burning Air and a Clear Mind: Contemporary Israeli Women Poets

Selections from 18 women poets

ILLUSTRATED BY SHIRLEY FAKTOR

0-8214-0572-1 OHIO $17.95

Curt **Leviant**

Masterpieces of Hebrew Literature: A Treasury of 2000 Years of Jewish Creativity

0-87068-079-X KTAV PB $22.95

Jerome **Rothenberg**

Exiled in the Word: Poems & Other Visions of the Jews from Tribal Times to Present

The poetic anthologies of Jerome Rothenberg—*Technicians of the Sacred, Shaking the Pumpkin,* and many others—have been among the most influential of our time. In this new, more compact version of the long-out-of-print *A Big Jewish Book,* he and Harris Lenowitz create a highly personal collage of Jewish traditions both orthodox and heretical, focusing, in Rothenberg's words, "on a poetic/visionary continuum & on the mystical & magical."

See also **JEWISH CULTURE** under **JEWISH HISTORY** in **WORLD HISTORY AND CURRENT AFFAIRS**

1-55659-026-1 COPPER CANYON PB $12.00

Ted **Solotaroff** & **Nessa Rapoport**, editors

The Shocken Book of Contemporary Jewish Fiction

0-8052-1065-2 SCHOCKEN PB $14.00

History and Criticism

General Studies

Robert **Alter**

Hebrew and Modernity

The development of a modern Israeli literature in Hebrew, as seen by a distinguished American critic

0-253-20856-4 INDIANA PB $12.95

Nehema **Aschkenasy**

Eve's Journey: Feminine Images in Hebraic Literary Tradition

0-8122-8033-4 WAYNE STATE PB $42.95

Warren **Bargad**

From Agnon to Oz: Studies in Modern Hebrew Literature

0-788-50094-1 SCHOLARS $79.95

Dan **Pagis**

Hebrew Poetry of the Middle Ages and the Renaissance

Engaging lectures on the great tradition of medieval poetry and how it balanced individual expression and preestablished formulae. "Pagis was the great expert in medieval Hebrew literature, and this book reflects his customary mastery of the field. It is informed by a far more literary spirit than most of what has been written on the subject by specialists"
—Raymond Scheindlin

0-520-06547-6 CALIFORNIA $27.50

Eisig **Silberschlag**

From Renaissance to Renaissance: Hebrew Literature, 1492-1967

0-87068-184-2 KTAV $35.00

Yiddish Language and Literature

Yiddish developed among Jews in the Rhine region between the 10th and 12th centuries as a spoken vernacular adapted mainly from Middle High German and transliterated into Hebrew characters. Over the years, this "fusion language" assimilated words and expressions from many European and Near Eastern languages, yet it always managed to preserve its distinctive identity. While Hebrew remained the language of the Jewish religion, Yiddish became its vernacular counterpart.

Though early Yiddish produced many works of interest, it was not until the rise of Hasidism and the Jewish Enlightenment of the 18th and early 19th centuries that a renaissance in Yiddish literature began. Hasidic leaders and poets such as Baal Shem Tov and Rabbi Nachman of Breslov helped legitimize the literary use of Yiddish and set new standards with their inspired handling of folk material and their unique art of traditional storytelling.

The 19th and early 20th centuries were the "golden age" of Yiddish literature, followed by a period of experimentation. But all this intense creative activity was brutally snuffed out by Nazism and Stalinism, which eliminated over half of all Yiddish-speaking Jews. At its height before 1939 Yiddish was spoken by more than 11 million people; today there are no more than two to three million speakers and the language is slowly dying out. Yet the past decade has seen a renewed interest in the language and the literature.

Early Yiddish

Miriam **Zaikon**, editor

Tz'enah Ur'enah

These endearingly popular biblical paraphrases and wise sayings from contemporary sages, first published in 1622, were compiled by a serious scholar and itinerant preacher

Volume 1 Bereishis with Haftoros

Focuses on the stories and lessons of the book of Genesis

0-89906-926-6 MESORAH PB $11.95

Volume 2 Bamidbar-Devarim with Haftoros

0-89906-929-0 MESORAH $15.95

Gluckel of Hameln

The Memoirs of Gluckel of Hameln

This fascinating diary of a 17th-century German-Jewish mother and businesswoman is the only document of its kind. Though this edition omits some important material, overall it offers an unparalleled literary and historical view of the author's times

0-8052-0572-1 SCHOCKEN PB $15.00

The Golden Age

By the late 19th and early 20th centuries, Yiddish entered its classical phase, producing three writers of genius: Mendel Mokher Seforim (the pen name of S.Y. Abramovitsch); I.L. Peretz; and Sholom Aleichem (the pen name of S. Rabinowitz). Drawing from both traditional and modern sources, these pioneers fused the vitality of folk and Hasidic tales with the literary sophistication of the Russian novel.

S.Y. **Abramovitsh**

Tales of Mendele the Book Peddler

0-8052-4136-1 SCHOCKEN $25.00

Sholom **Aleichem**

The Bloody Hoax

0-253-30401-6 INDIANA $29.95

Sholom Aleichem

Tevye the Dairyman & The Railroad Stories

The tales of Tevye and his daughters were the basis of *Fiddler on the Roof* but, according to the translator, they are "more reckless, giddy, wildly funny and wrenchingly painful—and far less sentimental"

TRANSLATED BY HILLEL HALKIN
EDITED BY RUTH R. WISSE
0-8052-0905-0 SCHOCKEN PB $16.00

I.L. **Peretz**

Peretz, who initially looked down on Yiddish as "jargon," became one of its great innovative stylists. His folk-like yet sophisticated tales introduced a terse, fast-paced prose that helped bring Yiddish out of the shtetl and into the modern world.

The I.L. Peretz Reader

"This volume presents some of the finest and most interesting of Peretz's works…"
—From the Introduction

EDITED BY RUTH R. WISSE & ARTHUR SAMUELSON
0-8052-1071-7 SCHOCKEN PB $15.00

The 20th Century

In the 20th century, Yiddish literature underwent a rapid series of experiments and movements. In America, Yiddish was introduced by the "sweatshop" or labor poets like Morris Rosenfeld, champion of the immigrant working masses. Abraham Cahan turned his Yiddish *Jewish Daily Forward* into the largest foreign-language daily newspaper in America. A talented group of Yiddish poets known as *Di Yunge* flourished in New York around the First World War, linking Yiddish to the mainstream of European modernism.

S. **Ansky**

The Dybbuk

Ansky's highly wrought symbolic drama about the primacy of spirit over force in Judaism is based on the folk belief in possessed souls

TRANSLATED BY S. MORRIS ENGEL
0-89526-904-X REGNERY PB $8.95

The Dybbuk: And Other Writings

0-8052-1070-9 SCHOCKEN PB $14.00

The Dybbuk and Other Writings

"An excellent anthology that offers a superior introduction to the brilliant works of a Yiddish master"—*Publishers Weekly*

08052100113 PANTHEON PB $13.00

Meir **Blinkin**

Stories by Meir Blinkin

Blinkin died at 36, a promising member of the *Di Yunge* (The Young) literary group, which rebelled against the social emphasis of the older generation and insisted on a more personal, inward-looking art. These stories are of the *shtetl* and the Lower East Side of New York

TRANSLATED BY MAX ROSENFELD
INTRODUCTION BY RUTH R. WISSE
0-87395-818-7 SUNY $10.95

Moyshe-Leyb **Halpern**

In New York: A Selection

A leading member of the *Di Yunge,* Halpern established a new kind of verse narrative, combining folk and didactic elements with American poetry, particularly that of Whitman

TRANSLATED BY KATHRYN HELLERSTEIN
0-8276-0209-X JEWISH PUBLICATION SOCIETY $14.95

Samuel **Lewin**

A Distant Voice: An Autobiography of Samuel Lewin

0-8453-4854-X CORNWALL $42.00

Between Two Abysses

The first novel of a trilogy set in a Polish *shtetl* between the wars covers the collapse of the old way of life and the resulting scramble for survival, the generational struggle, and the moral and political issues that dominated the Jewish community

TRANSLATED BY JOSEPH LEFTWICH
0-8453-4795-0 CORNWALL $12.95

Dark Mountains and Blue Valleys

Part two of the trilogy

TRANSLATED BY JOSEPH LEFTWICH
0-8453-4804-3 CORNWALL $12.95

Shining Through the Clouds

Part three of the trilogy

TRANSLATED BY JOSEPH LEFTWICH
0-8453-4805-1 CORNWALL $12.95

Israel **Rabon**

The Street

A surrealistic novel about a Jewish soldier who returns to Lodz at the end of World War I and joins the ranks of the unemployed transients

TRANSLATED BY LEONARD WOLF
0-8052-3981-2 ALLISON & BUSBY $14.95

I.J. **Singer**

The brother of I.B. Singer, Israel Joshua Singer is himself an important literary figure, the author of massive social novels about Jewish life in Eastern Europe as well as numerous short stories and plays.

The Brothers Ashkenazi

0-14-018777-4 PENGUIN PB $11.95

Isaac Bashevis Singer

"In the years I have been writing I have heard many discouraging words about my themes and languages. I was told that Jewishness and Yiddishness were dying, the short story was out of vogue and about to disappear from the literary market. Some critics decided that the art of telling stories with a beginning, middle and end—as Aristotle demanded—was archaic, a primitive form of fiction. I heard similar degrading opinions about the value of folklore in the literature of our times. I was living in a civilization which despised the old and worshipped the young. But somehow I never took these dire threats seriously. I belong to an old tribe and I know that literature thrives best on ancient faith, timeless hopes and illusions."—I.B. Singer

Isaac Bashevis **Singer**

The Certificate

A young Jewish writer living in Warsaw is offered a certificate permitting him to emigrate to Palestine—but only if he will enter into a fictitious marriage. This early novel by the 1976 Nobel laureate, now translated for the first time, reveals again Singer's mastery at re-creating the vanished world of Polish Jewry between the world wars. "Vintage Singer, a welcome addition to his oeuvre"—*Publishers Weekly*

0-374-12029-3 FS&G $22.00

The Collected Stories of Isaac Bashevis Singer

Forty-seven of his finest. A cornucopia of invention

0-374-12631-3 FS&G $30.00
0-374-51788-6 FS&G PB $18.00

The Death of Methusaleh & Other Stories

0-452-26215-1 PLUME PB $10.95

Enemies, a Love Story

This farcical comedy of Herman Broder and his three wives is also a subtle exploration of the experience of refugees from the Holocaust

0-374-51522-0 FS&G PB $12.00

The Family Moskat

Life in the Warsaw ghetto from the beginning of the century to Hitler; the third of a trilogy beginning with the out-of-print *The Manor* and *The Estate*

0-374-50392-3 FS&G PB $16.00

Gimpel the Fool & Other Stories

TRANSLATED BY SAUL BELLOW
0-374-50052-5 NOONDAY PB $12.00

The Image & Other Stories

0-374-52079-8 FS&G PB $11.00

Meshugah

A posthumous gift from the Nobel laureate and master Yiddish storyteller. A tale of mad poets, beautiful, troubled women, and inextricable love triangles on Manhattan's Upper West Side in the '50s, when, "no sooner did one free oneself of a neurosis, then another rushed in to take its place." "Wherever Singer touched pen to paper there sprang up a village—of ghosts, of survivors, of all of us"—*Kirkus Reviews*

TRANSLATED BY NILI WACHTEL
0-374-20847-6 FS&G $22.00
0-452-27384-6 PLUME PB $10.95

Lovers of Singer will enjoy his children's books—illustrated by such outstanding artists as Uri Shulevitz and Maurice Sendak—because they combine the same fluent storytelling and curious humanity.

A Day of Pleasure: Stories of a Boy
Growing up in Warsaw
PHOTOGRAPHS BY ROMAN VISHNIAC
0-374-41696-6 FS&G PB $7.95

Elijah the Slave
The Hebrew legend—possibly the most significant for Yiddish writers—retold with transparent simplicity
ILLUSTRATED BY ANTONIO FRASCONI
0-374-32084-5 FS&G $16.00
0-374-42047-5 FS&G PB $4.95

Naftali the Storyteller and His Horse, Sus
ILLUSTRATED BY MARGOT ZEMACH
0-374-45487-6 FS&G PB $3.50

Stories for Children
See also **SUGGESTED READ ALOUDS** in **BOOKS FOR YOUNG READERS**
0-374-37266-7 FS&G $22.95
0-374-46489-8 SUNBURST PB $13.00

The Fools of Chelm and Their History
TRANSLATED BY ELIZABETH SHUB
ILLUSTRATED BY URI SHULEVITZ
0-374-42429-2 FS&G PB $3.95

Mazel and Shlimazel Or the Milk of a Lioness
ILLUSTRATED BY MARGOT ZEMACH
0-374-44786-1 SUNBURST PB $6.95

The Power of Light: Eight Stories of Hanukkah
The late Nobel Prize-winning author presents eight autobiographically inspired tales, one for each night of Hanukkah
See also **SABBATH AND HOLIDAYS** under **HOW-TO: RITUAL AND PRACTICE** under **JUDAISM** in **RELIGION, SPIRITUALITY, AND PHILOSOPHY**
ILLUSTRATED BY IRENE LIEBLICH
0-374-36099-5 SUNBURST $15.00
0-374-45984-3 FS&G PB $8.95

When Shlemiel Went to Warsaw & Other Stories
Eight stories, several based on traditional Jewish tales
TRANSLATED BY ELIZABETH SHUB
ILLUSTRATED BY MARGOT ZEMACH
0-374-38316-2 FS&G $16.00
0-374-48365-5 FS&G PB $4.95

Why Noah Chose the Dove
TRANSLATED BY ELIZABETH SHUB
ILLUSTRATED BY ERIC CARLE
0-374-38420-7 FS&G $16.00
0-374-48382-5 FS&G PB $5.95

Zlateh the Goat & Stories
TRANSLATED BY ELIZABETH SHUB
0-06-025699-0 HARPERCREST LIBRARY ED $15.89

Satan in Goray
A multilayered historical tale of religious hysteria in a Polish *shtetl* in the mid-17th century, based on the false Messianism of Sabbatai Zevi
0-374-52479-3 NOONDAY PB $12.00

Scum
"A work of genius…*Scum* has about it a simple, genuine naturalness, which impells both belief and attention" —Francis King
TRANSLATED BY ROSALINE DUKALSKY SCHWARTZ
0-14-018842-8 PENGUIN PB $10.95

Isaac Bashevis Singer (credit: ©1991 Jerry Bauer)

Shosha
A compelling novel, favored by the author himself, about the love between a Yiddish writer and his childhood sweetheart against the backdrop of World War II
0-374-52480-7 NOONDAY PB $12.00

In My Father's Court
A beautiful, evocative memoir of growing up in Warsaw as the son of a famous rabbi
See also **EASTERN EUROPE** under **MODERN EUROPE** under **JEWISH HISTORY** in **WORLD HISTORY AND CURRENT AFFAIRS**
0-374-50592-6 NOONDAY PB $12.00

The Language

These books range from the scholarly to the frolicsome, but all have a similar purpose: to preserve this much-loved language and to convey its salty, racy, flavor and the culture for which it speaks.

Nathan **Ausubel**, editor

A Treasury of Jewish Folklore
A compendium of stories, traditions, legends, humor, wisdom, and folk songs
See also **JEWISH CULTURE** under **JEWISH HISTORY** in **WORLD HISTORY AND CURRENT AFFAIRS**
0-517-50293-3 CROWN $22.00

Gene **Bluestein**

Anglish-Yinglish: Yiddish in American Life and Literature
0-8203-1084-0 GEORGIA PB $11.95

David **Goldberg**

Yidish Af Yidish: Grammatical, Lexical and Conversational Materials for the Second and Third Years of Study
0-300-06414-4 YALE $35.00

Emmanuel **Goldsmith**

Modern Yiddish Culture: The Story of the Yiddish Language Movement
EDITED BY MALCOLM J. ROBINSON
0-933503-95-4 SURE SELLERS PB $10.95

Fred **Kogos**

1,001 Yiddish Proverbs
Brief, pungent and illustrated. "In it can be described the longings and strivings, the trials and tribulations, the joys and griefs of the Jewish people"—Fred Kogos
0-8065-0455-2 CITADEL PB $6.95

Instant Yiddish
0-8065-1154-0 CITADEL PB $6.95

Ausubel **Nathan**, editor

A Treasury of Jewish Humor
0-87131-546-7 EVANS PB $14.95

Leo **Rosten**

The Joys of Yiddish
"A cheerful lexicon of Yiddish words which have become part of the English language, plus English words and phrases which have been transformed into Yinglish; the whole garnished with stories, jokes, parables, revered quotations from the Talmud and a glittering gallery of writers, rabbis, sages, wits, with impulsive side trips into the faith, folklore, genius and history of the Jews—from their servitude in Babylon to their magnitude in Beverly Hills"—Leo Rosten
0-452-26543-X PLUME PB $14.95
0-671-72813-X POCKET PB $6.50

Uriel **Weinreich**

College Yiddish: An Introduction to the Yiddish Language and to Jewish Life and Culture
Intended for a one-year college course or for learning on one's own. "Strange as it seems, a rational, practical textbook of Yiddish happens to be a pioneering work"—Roman Jakobson
INTRODUCTION BY ROMAN JAKOBSON
0-914512-04-8 YIVO INSTITUTE $25.00

Uriel **Weinreich**, editor

The Field of Yiddish: Studies in Yiddish Language, Folklore, and Literature
A scholarly collection of essays for the specialist; a milestone in the launch of serious study of Yiddish following the Holocaust
0-8101-1012-1 NORTHWESTERN $49.95

Uriel **Weinreich** & Beatrice **Weinreich**

Say It in Yiddish
0-486-20815-X DOVER PB $3.95

Anthologies

Benjamin **Harshav** & Barbara **Harshav**, editors
American Yiddish Poetry: A Bilingual Anthology
0-520-04842-3 CALIFORNIA $65.00

Irving **Howe** & Eliezer **Greenberg**, editors
A Treasury of Yiddish Stories
An excellent collection from the 19th and 20th centuries
ILLUSTRATED BY BEN SHAHN
0-670-83037-2 VIKING $29.95
0-14-014419-6 PENGUIN PB $17.95

Joseph **Landis**, editor & translator
Three Great Jewish Plays
Ansky's *The Dybbuk*, Asch's *God of Vengeance*, and Leivick's *The Golem*
0-936839-04-X APPLAUSE THEATRE PB $8.95

Joseph **Leftwich**, editor
An Anthology of Modern Yiddish Literature
Includes 42 Yiddish writers, with biographical notes, glossary, and bibliography
90-279-3496-7 WALTER DE GRUYTER PB $24.30

Mani **Leib**
Yingl Tsingl Khvat
Poems for children from a famous Yiddish writer
0-918825-52-0 MOYER BELL $11.95
0-918825-54-7 MOYER BELL $11.75

David **Lifson**, translator
Epic and Folk Plays from the Yiddish Theatre
Includes *Favorfn Vinkl* by Hirshbein, *Hirsh Lekert* by Leivick, *Yanke Boyla* by L. Kobrin, and *Recruits* by Aksenfeld
0-8386-1082-X ASSOCIATED UNIVERSITIES $36.50

Beatrice Silverman **Weinreich**, editor
Yiddish Folktales
A collection of nearly 200 tales
0-679-73097-4 PANTHEON PB $18.00

Ruth R. **Wisse**, editor
A Shtetl & Other Yiddish Novellas
Includes *At the Depot* by Bergelson, *Romance of a Horsethief* by Opatoshu, *Behind a Mask* by Ansky, and *Of Bygone Days* by Sforim
0-8143-1848-7 WAYNE STATE $34.95
0-8143-1849-5 WAYNE STATE PB $17.95

History and Criticism

Ruth **Alder**
Women of the Shtetl: Through the Eye of I.L. Peretz
0-8386-2336-0 FAIRLEIGH DICKINSON $26.50

Sol **Gittleman**
Sholum Aleichem: A Non-Critical Introduction
90-279-2606-9 WALTER DE GRUYTER PB $31.15

Janet **Hadda**
Passionate Women, Passive Men: Suicide in Yiddish Literature
A provocative work of literary criticism, with some debt to psychoanalysis but an altogether original approach
0-88706-597-X SUNY PB $16.95

Sanford **Pinsker**
Schlemiel as Metaphor: Studies in the Yiddish and American Jewish Novel
Includes a look at the work of Seforim, Sholom Aleichem, and I.B. Singer
0-8093-1581-5 SOUTHERN ILLINOIS $29.95

Nahma **Sandrow**
Vagabond Stars: A World History of Yiddish Theater
A comprehensive history of the Yiddish Theater in America and the world. "I recommend *Vagabond Stars* to all who are interested in Yiddish theater"—Isaac Bashevis Singer
0-8156-0329-0 USYRT PB $16.95

Meyer **Waxman**
A History of Jewish Literature
From biblical times to the 20th century, with generous portions on Yiddish literature; in six volumes
0-8453-8640-9 CORNWALL $50.00

Shimon **Wincelberg** & Anita **Wincelberg**, editors
The Samurai of Vishogrod: The Notebooks of Jacob Marateck
TRANSLATED BY ANITA WINCELBERG
0-8276-0074-7 JEWISH PUBLICATION SOCIETY PB $8.95

Ruth R. **Wisse**
A Little Love in Big Manhattan: Two Yiddish Poets
A double biography of two opposing personalities, Mani Leib and Moishe Leib Halpern, two of the most prominent figures of the *Di Yunge* group
0-674-53659-2 HARVARD $34.00

Israel **Zamir**
Journey to My Father, Isaac Bashevis Singer
I.B. Singer, the Nobel Prize-winning novelist, left his wife and five-year-old son in Poland when he immigrated to America before the war. Despite his promise to send for them, he never did, and the wife and son ended up on a kibbutz in Israel. It was not until 20 years had passed that the now-grown son was reunited with his father, beginning a 35-year relationship that lasted until the writer's death. This candid, personal account of a unique relationship is as revealing of the life of the preeminent Yiddish writer as it is of the relationship between all fathers and sons
TRANSLATED BY BARBARA HARSHAV
1-55970-309-1 ARCADE $21.95

African Literature

Africa has a long tradition—or, more precisely, many distinct traditions—of epics, praise songs, riddles, and proverbs, in some cases committed to memory and recited by generations of carefully trained bard/historians known as *griots*. The written literature is, however, mostly a 20th-century phenomenon. This literature is influenced by both Western literature and Africa's own oral tradition.

African writers are not yet widely read in the United States, but they are taken very seriously in their own countries. Almost all of the major writers—Soyinka, Achebe, Ngugi, and Laye, to name a few—have been banned or jailed for extended periods in their homelands.

West Africa

Chinua **Achebe**
The Nigerian novelist Chinua Achebe, a fine stylist and an astute social critic, is one of the best-known African writers in the West and his novels are often assigned in university courses. He casts a cold eye on the British colonial administration, post-Independence corruption, and the ravages of civil war.

Anthills of the Savannah
Achebe's book deals with three friends who have come to play major roles in the fictional African nation of Nangan, one as the country's corrupt president, another as a troubled statesman, and the third as an opposition journalist. A riveting portrayal of an educated elite losing touch with the common people
0-385-01664-6 ANCHOR PB $16.95

Things Fall Apart
Achebe's most famous novel, the first in a trilogy, brilliantly portrays the impact of colonialism on a traditional Nigerian village at the turn of the century. Its hero, Obi Okonkwo, epitomizes both the nobility and the rigidity of the traditional culture
0-679-41714-1 KNOPF $15.00
0-385-47454-7 ANCHOR PB $5.95

Arrow of God
The second book in the trilogy examines life under colonialism in early years of the 20th century. The protagonist is a head priest who scores a series of psychological victories over the British administration but is eventually defeated
0-385-01480-5 DOUBLEDAY PB $9.95

No Longer at Ease
The trilogy concludes with this fine novel about how a high-ranking and respected villager's Western education ends up separating him from his tribal culture
0-449-30023-4 FAWCETT PB $4.95

Beware, Soul Brother
0-435-90120-6 HEINEMANN PB $8.95

Chike and the River

0-521-04003-5 CAMBRIDGE PB $4.50

Girls at War & Other Stories

Tales from the Biafran war and the period of disintegration that followed

0-385-41896-5 ANCHOR PB $8.95

Chinua Achebe

Hopes and Impediments: Selected Essays

0-385-24730-3 ANCHOR PB $16.95

Ama Ata **Aidoo**

Changes: A Love Story

1-55861-064-2 FEMINIST PRESS $35.00

Ayi K. **Armah**

Ghana's greatest novelist, Armah combines a tremendous versatility of language with deep-rooted social concerns. Although Armah has written few books, his impact on African letters has been considerable.

The Beautyful Ones Are Not Yet Born

A remarkable portrait of corruption in post-independence Ghana and of the disillusionment of the idealistic "been-tos." The graphic description of physical corruption merges with a powerful and detailed portrait of the morally bankrupt officialdom

0-435-90540-6 HEINEMANN PB $9.95

Mongo **Beti**

The Cameroonian writer Mongo Beti (a pseudonym for Alexandre Biyidi) is known for his lively and scathingly funny attacks on quasi-Westernized Africans and on the role of the church in Africa.

Mission to Kala

Jean-Marie Medza goes to the distant country town of Kala to rescue his aunt and incidentally teach the ignorant villagers about the joys of civilization, with hilarious results

0-435-90013-7 HEINEMANN PB $8.95

The Poor Christ of Bomba

The weakness of the Christian mission in Africa is revealed by the actions of a well-intentioned but confused black acolyte, an obtuse Reverend Father Superior, and a salacious cook who profits by the general chaos

0-435-90088-9 HEINEMANN PB $9.95

John P. **Clark**

Casualties: Poems, 1966-1968

Clark is a leading Nigerian playwright and poet whose work has been performed in England by Soyinka's troupe, Masks. His poems are concise, powerful, and imagistic

0-8419-0041-8 HOLMES & MEIER PB $9.50

Bernard **Dadie**

The best-known writer from Côte d'Ivoire (and his country's Director of Cultural Affairs), Dadie wrote about the daily life of the common people.

Climbie

An autobiographical novel about a young Ivorian's growing awareness of the evils of colonialism

TRANSLATED BY KAREN CHAPMAN

0-8419-0080-9 HOLMES & MEIER $14.50

M.S. **Dipoko**

Because of Women

Dipoko writes frankly about love and the unfortunate destinies of lovers who swim against society's tide. In this novel, a man is torn between two women who love him—a traditional woman who was pregnant with his child and a seductive modern one

0-435-90057-9 HEINEMANN PB $8.95

Cyprian **Ekwensi**

This Nigerian writer is one of the most popular and prolific of African novelists. His work has been praised for its insights into the problems faced by rural Africans when circumstances force them into the towns and for his vibrant descriptions of town life.

Jagua Nana

The most acclaimed of Ekwensi's novels tells the story of Jagua Nana, a socially ambitious prostitute who has taken her name from the automobile, the Jaguar

0-435-90678-X HEINEMANN PB $9.95

Buchi **Emecheta**

Kehinde

0-435-90985-1 HEINEMANN PB $9.95

The Rape of Shavi

Foreigners who drop from the sky into the mythic and idyllic kingdom of Shavi prove to be the downfall of the local citizens who come to their rescue

0-8076-1118-2 BRAZILLER PB $8.95

Second-Class Citizen

A Nigerian woman's search for independence. "One of the most informative books about contemporary African life that I have read" —Alice Walker

0-8076-1066-6 BRAZILLER PB $8.95

Olaudah **Equiano**

Equiano's Travels: His Autobiography

The classic narrative of a West African who was brought as a slave boy to England and educated there. First published in London in 1745, Equiano's narrative proved so popular it went into 17 consecutive printings

EDITED BY PAUL EDWARDS

0-435-90010-2 HEINEMANN PB $10.95

The Interesting Narrative and Other Writings

EDITED BY VINCENT CARRETTA

0-14-043485-2 PENGUIN PB $9.95

John **Johnson** & Fa-Digi **Sisoko**

The Epic of Son-Jara: A West African Tradition

The life of the legendary 13th-century Malian ruler Sundiata (or Son-Jara) became the basis for an oral epic that *griots* have kept alive to the present day. A careful transcription and translation of a recitation by the Malian griot Fadigi Sisoko, along with a detailed essay on the nature of the epic in Africa

0-253-33102-1 INDIANA $32.00

Sheikh Hamidou **Kane**

Ambiguous Adventure

Kane seeks to capture the somber beauty of the Koran in this exquisitely written novel about a young man's Islamic education, his subsequent estrangement from both Islamic and Western thought, and his fear of mortality

0-435-90119-2 HEINEMANN PB $10.95

Camara **Laye**

One of the most influential francophone African writers, the Guinean novelist Laye created a highly personal vision of Africa, reflecting an organic world view that gives equal weight to African deities, nature, and the thoughts and observations of humankind.

Enfant Noir

This lyrical tale beautifully depicts the hero's youth in a traditional Senegalese village and his eventual confrontation with colonial culture. The descriptions of the hero's father's goldsmithing craft are particularly moving

0-8090-1548-X NOONDAY PB $9.00

René **Maran**

Batouala

Originally published in 1921, *Batouala* was the first of many novels by Africans to criticize the colonial regimes, in this case, the French in what is now the Central African Republic. "You smell the smells of the village, you eat its food, you see the white man as the black man sees him, and after you have lived in the village, you die there…When you read it, you have been to Batouala, and that means that it is a great novel"—Ernest Hemingway

0-435-90135-4 HEINEMANN PB $8.95

D.T. **Niane**

Sundiata: An Epic of Old Mali

Niane's retelling of the Sundiata story focused new attention on traditional African literature when it appeared in 1960

0-582-64259-0 LONGMAN PB $9.95

Flora **Nwapa**

A major woman writer, Nwapa frequently uses Nigerian myths to create essentially modern stories.

Efuru

A distinguished woman who cannot fit into village life and who loses two husbands and her child is nevertheless respected by the people around her

0-435-90026-9 HEINEMANN PB $8.95

Never Again
0-86543-318-6 AFRICA WORLD $24.95
0-86543-319-4 AFRICA WORLD PB $9.95

One Is Enough
0-86543-323-2 AFRICA WORLD PB $9.95

Wives at War & Other Stories
0-86543-328-3 AFRICA WORLD PB $9.95

Christopher **Okigbo**

Labyrinths with Path of Thunder
The posthumously collected works of one of Nigeria's leading poets, whose career was tragically cut short during the Biafran war
0-8419-0045-0 HOLMES & MEIER $12.50
0-8419-0016-7 HOLMES & MEIER PB $10.00

Ben **Okri**

The Famished Road
0-385-42476-0 DOUBLEDAY $22.50
0-385-42513-9 ANCHOR PB $12.00

Songs of Enchantment
0-385-47157-2 ANCHOR PB $12.00

Stars of the New Curfew
0-14-011602-8 PENGUIN PB $11.95

Sembene **Ousmane**

A great Senegalese writer and Africa's best known filmmaker, Ousmane delineates social themes while creating memorable, lovingly detailed characters.

God's Bits of Wood
A novel about a bitter railroad strike in 1947. Although the colonial administration eventually defeats the strikers, it is clear that their life force will triumph in the end. A beautifully drawn, fully realized portrayal of an African people
TRANSLATED BY FRANCIS PRICE
0-435-90892-8 HEINEMANN PB $10.95

Xala
When a corrupt businessman becomes afflicted with impotence *(xala)* he seeks refuge in superstition and folk remedies. A wickedly funny book with a powerful social message
TRANSLATED BY CLIVE WAKE
1-55652-070-0
INDEPENDENT PUBLISHERS GROUP PB $8.95

Ferdinand **Oyono**

Houseboy
A portrait of a houseboy who gradually loses his naive faith in the benevolence of his masters. A witty exposé of the deceptions of colonialism
TRANSLATED BY JOHN REED
0-435-90532-5 HEINEMANN PB $9.95

The Old Man and the Medal
Old Meka is awarded a medal for years of devoted service to the colonial government; all he has given up in return are his lands and his heritage. Oyono creates a first-class satire out of the reactions of the villagers, the colonial official who presents the medal, and the old man himself
TRANSLATED BY JOHN REED
0-435-90039-0 HEINEMANN PB $8.95

Road to Europe
TRANSLATED BY RICHARD BJORNSON
0-89410-590-6 THREE CONTINENTS $24.00

Ken **Saro-Wiwa**

A Month and a Day: A Detention Diary
The writings of the tribal spokesman who was executed by the Nigerian government despite international protests
0-14-025914-7 PENGUIN PB $10.95

Leopold S. **Senghor**

One of the founders of the Negritude movement, Senghor eventually became president of Senegal.

Collected Poetry
TRANSLATED BY MELVIN DIXON
0-8139-1275-X VIRGINIA $45.00

Nocturnes
0-89388-015-9 THIRD PRESS REVIEW PB $9.95

Leopold S. Senghor

Wole **Soyinka**

Winner of the Nobel Prize for Literature in 1986, Soyinka's work is complex and wide-ranging. His plays are a sophisticated blend of African dance rhythms, Yoruba mythology, and oral storytelling combined with Western imagery. Many of these plays have been performed by Soyinka's own company, Masks. Soyinka was jailed by the Nigerian government for 27 months for his criticism of their policies, and his experiences are chillingly narrated in The Man Died. *He is currently living in exile.*

Wole Soyinka (credit: ©Rex Collings Ltd.)

Ake: The Years of Childhood
An extraordinarily vivid recreation of a happy, middle-class, quintessentially African childhood. "I know of few better illustrations of Baudelaire's statement about the child: for him, everything is new; he is always exhilarated" —*New Society*
0-679-72540-7 VINTAGE PB $12.00

Art, Dialogue, and Outrage: Essays on Literature and Culture
0-679-40065-6 PANTHEON $25.00

The Bacchae of Euripides: A Communion Rite
0-393-00789-8 NORTON PB $7.95

Collected Plays
Volume 1
Theater of the Mind
0-89410-134-X THREE CONTINENTS PB $12.00

Volume 2
Theater of Society
0-89410-280-X THREE CONTINENTS $25.00

Dance of the Forest
Possibly Soyinka's most difficult play, it tells the story of a Council member who calls upon the spirits of the dead, expecting to hear tales of the glorious past. Instead, he calls forth two unknown, ordinary shades who criticize the empire that destroyed their lives
0-19-911082-4 OXFORD PB $9.95

The Essential Soyinka: A Reader
0-679-43990-0 PANTHEON $27.50

Idanre & Other Poems
The title work is a long poem based on the fierce and terrible god Ogun's role in the Yoruba myth of creation
0-8090-5725-5 HILL & WANG $16.95

The Interpreters
Soyinka's first novel is a complex account of the disintegration of a group of intellectuals in search of their identity
0-8419-0121-X HOLMES & MEIER $29.50
0-435-90076-5 HEINEMANN PB $9.95

Isara, a Voyage Around "Essay"
A tribute by Soyinka to his father and to the small Nigerian town where he grew up. "A touching portrait of a man of principle, great loyalty, and love, who longs for greatness and wide experience but is wise enough to recognize what blessings he does have"—*Kirkus Reviews*
0-679-73246-2 VINTAGE PB $13.00

Kongi's Harvest
A corrupt politician and his effect on those around him
0-19-911085-9 OXFORD PB $9.95

The Lion and the Jewel
A farce about a schoolteacher and a wily, older chieftain who are in love with the same woman
0-19-911083-2 OXFORD PB $8.95

Madmen and Specialists
Written after Soyinka's incarceration, this play takes a more serious political stance than his earlier work
0-8090-6708-0 FS&G $16.95

The Open Sore of a Continent
Soyinka makes his case against the current Nigerian regime

See also CURRENT AFFAIRS IN AFRICA under AFRICA in WORLD HISTORY AND CURRENT AFFAIRS

0-19-510557-5 OXFORD $19.95

Amos **Tutuola**

Combining non-standard pidgin English, oral narrative techniques, and his own deliberately naive forms of expression, Tutuola, a Nigerian, has created a delightfully idiosyncratic version of the English language for his wildly imaginative adventure stories based on African myth.

Feather Woman of the Jungle
"A *Pilgrim's Progress* of the devil-world" —*Manchester Guardian*

0-87286-215-1 CITY LIGHTS PB $6.95

The Palm-Wine Drinkard and My Life in the Bush of Ghosts
0-8021-3363-0 GROVE PB $12.95

Pauper, Brawler and Slanderer
0-571-14765-8 FABER PB $8.95

Simbi and the Satyr of the Dark Jungle
A wealthy and beautiful woman sets out to experience poverty

0-87286-214-3 CITY LIGHTS PB $6.95

The Wild Hunter in the Bush of the Ghosts
0-89410-452-7 THREE CONTINENTS $20.00

0-89410-453-5 THREE CONTINENTS PB $10.00

The Witch-Herbalist of the Remote Town
0-571-11704-X FABER PB $8.95

East Africa

Nuruddin **Farah**

Sweet and Sour Milk
A man investigates his brother's violent death in this first volume of a trilogy by the Somali novelist. "A chilling exploration of corruption and terror" —*NY Times Book Review*

1-55597-159-8 GRAY WOLF PB $12.00

Sardines
The second volume in Farah's trilogy of political oppression

1-55597-161-X GRAY WOLF PB $12.00

Close Sesame
The third volume of the trilogy takes a turn into the mystical

1-55597-162-8 GRAY WOLF PB $12.00

Lee **Haring**, translator

Ibonia: Epic of Madagascar
0-8387-5284-5 BUCKNELL $32.50

Meja **Mwangi**

Striving for the Wind
0-435-90979-7 HEINEMANN PB $8.95

Going Down River Road
The powerful and gritty story of a Kenyan day laborer's drinking, womanizing, friendships, and troubles at work

0-435-90176-1 HEINEMANN PB $8.95

Okot **P'Bitek**

Song of Lawino and Song of Ocol
These most famous of his works are complementary narrative poems that take the form of a song by a traditional African woman saddened that her husband has become Westernized, and her husband's response

INTRODUCTION BY G.A. HERON

0-435-90266-0 HEINEMANN PB $9.95

Ngugi-Wa **Thiong'O**

The finest Kenyan novelist, Ngugi has had a powerful impact on all African literature. His novels have a broad historical and political sweep, ranging from the struggle against colonialism to the new ravages committed by an African elite. Imprisoned by the Kenyan government for 18 months, he currently lives in exile in London.

Devil on the Cross
This novel was written in Gikuyu while Ngugi was imprisoned

0-435-90844-8 HEINEMANN PB $11.95

A Grain of Wheat
Ngugi's best-known work tells the stories of four characters looking back with regret on their failure to act in accordance with ideals during Kenya's "Emergency." A powerful vision of salvation through suffering

0-435-90836-7 HEINEMANN PB $8.95

I Will Marry When I Want
The play that triggered Ngugi's jailing by the Kenyan authorities

0-435-90246-6 HEINEMANN PB $9.95

Matigari
Ngugi's latest work is a visionary imagining of political struggle in post-independence Kenya

0-435-90546-5 HEINEMANN PB $11.95

Petals of Blood
A portrayal of the corrupting power of the new African elite who work with the colonials from whom they wrested power

0-14-015351-9 DUTTON PB $13.95

The River Between
Ngugi has called this novel an attempt to remove the Christian doctrine from its Western dress and incorporate it into African mythology

0-435-90548-1 HEINEMANN PB $10.95

Central and Southern Africa

Olive Schreiner's *The Story of an African Farm*, published in 1883, set the stage for all subsequent South African literature. The novel takes a clear-sighted look at racial inequality, the role of religion in an unjust society, and the difficulties faced by an individual who does not fit in with the country's rigidly conservative social mores. These themes form the dynamic of what is the largest body of literature from any one African country.

Peter **Abrahams**

Abrahams, a former broadcaster and news analyst, emigrated to Jamaica in 1955 from South Africa. His novels are concerned with relations between the races, and the political and social development of his adopted country.

Mine Boy
The difficulties faced by a rural African who seeks work in the city. One of the first novels to take the reader behind the scenes in the daily life of an African laborer

0-435-90562-7 HEINEMANN PB $9.95

Path of Thunder
A tragic love affair between a "coloured" man and a white woman and their eventual defeat and destruction by the pressures of a racist society

0-911860-43-6 CHATHAM $17.95

Tell Freedom
An autobiography that describes the experience of being caught between black and white culture and fitting into neither

See also CARIBBEAN LITERATURE in LITERATURE OF THE AMERICAS

0-571-11777-5 FABER PB $12.95

Breyten **Breytenbach**

Breytenbach was a leading figure in Die Sestigers, *the Afrikaans-speaking writers who criticized the policies of the Afrikaner nationalists in their own language. Scion of a powerful family, Breytenbach was a thorn in the government's side, and when he returned to South Africa clandestinely he was arrested and sentenced to seven years in prison.*

In Africa Even the Flies Are Happy
Selected poems

TRANSLATED BY THE AUTHOR & DENIS HIRSON

0-7145-3696-2 RIVERRUN $13.95

The Memory of Birds in Time of Revolution: Essays
These searing new essays by the acclaimed South African author include penetrating insights on the release of Mandela and controversial comments on the early days of the ANC leadership of South Africa as well as essays on the writer's imagination, death, and the philosophical implications of reform and reconciliation. "An immensely gifted writer" —J.M. Coetzee

0-15-100168-5 HARCOURT BRACE $22.00

The True Confessions of an Albino Terrorist
A masterpiece of prison memoir that earned Breytenbach the sobriquet "South Africa's Solzhenitsyn"

0-374-27935-7 FS&G $18.95

André **Brink**

A Chain of Voices
0-14-006538-5 PENGUIN PB $12.95

A Dry White Season
A man's life is destroyed when he tries to find out why his gardener disappeared after being arrested

0-14-006890-2 PENGUIN PB $12.95

Imaginings of Sand
0-15-100224-X HARCOURT BRACE $24.00

On the Contrary
Brink revisits the past of his native South Africa with an illuminating tale of an 18th-century rebel awaiting execution by the Dutch authorities for fomenting rebellion. With characteristic subtlety, be explores his tormented country in the person of this ambiguous adventurer, and delivers a novel that teaches volumes about oppression and rebellion
0-316-10884-7 LITTLE, BROWN $22.95

André **Brink** & J. M. **Coetzee**, editors
A Land Apart: A South African Reader
0-14-010004-0 PENGUIN PB $9.95

Dennis **Brutus**
Possibly South Africa's most influential black poet, Brutus was instrumental in having the country banned from the Olympic Games. He was a political prisoner on Robben Island for many years.
A Simple Lust
Poems of jail and exile
0-435-90115-X HEINEMANN PB $11.95

Stubborn Hope: Poems
0-435-90208-3 HEINEMANN PB $9.95

J.M. **Coetzee**
Increasingly recognized as one of South Africa's finest writers, Coetzee is a brilliant and experimental stylist, and his profound and increasingly chilling vision (in the words of Nadine Gordiner) "goes to the nerve center of being. What he finds there is more than most people will ever know about themselves."
Age of Iron
A dying South African woman, a classics professor, is forced to come to terms with the apartheid system and its consequences
0-679-73292-6 VINTAGE PB $12.00

J.M. Coetzee

Foe
Robinson Crusoe's story as told by his abandoned lover provides new insights into imperialism. "A small miracle of a book... of marvelous intricacy and almost overwhelming power"—Russell Banks, *Washington Post*
0-14-011032-1 PENGUIN PB $10.00

In the Heart of the Country
A woman's journal describes an individual in retreat from sexual and moral imperialism
0-14-006228-9 VIKING PB $9.95

Life and Times of Michael K
Winner of the 1983 Booker McConnell Prize, this powerful Kafkaesque novel portrays a desolate South Africa after the outbreak of civil war
0-14-007448-1 VIKING PB $10.95

The Master of Petersburg
0-670-85587-1 VIKING $21.95

Waiting for the Barbarians
A magistrate in the outer territories comes to identify with the tortured victims of the government he serves
0-14-006110-X VIKING PB $11.95

Tim **Couzens** & Essop **Patel**, editors
The Return of the Amasi Bird: Black South African Poetry, 1891-1981
0-86975-195-6 OHIO PB $12.95

Jeni **Couzyn**
Life by Drowning: Selected Poems
Poems by a young Afrikaner
0-88784-098-1 HOUSE OF ANANSI PB $8.95

H.I.E. **Dhlomo**
Collected Works
Heroic plays about Dingane, Cetewayo, and Shaka by one of the first Zulu writers. Includes the long autobiographical poem "Valley of a Thousand Hills"
EDITED BY TIM COUZENS & NICK VISSER
0-86975-271-5 RAVAN PB $25.95

Modikwe **Dikobe**
The Marabi Dance
The first inside picture of African daily life depicts the chaos of the slums outside Johannesburg and the dilemma of a woman caught between two worlds
0-435-90124-9 HEINEMANN PB $8.95

Ahmed **Essop**
Hajji Musa and the Hindu Firewalker
Stories and a novella about the Asians of South Africa. "The vivid aromatic world of Johannesburg's Indian community...adds a new world to those already represented in South African fiction"—Lionel Abrahams
0-930523-52-0 READERS INTERNATIONAL PB $8.95

Athol **Fugard**
A world-renowned playwright, Fugard explores the limits of the human condition—people pushed to the breaking point.
A Lesson from Aloes
A visit from a black friend brings to the surface the tensions of a white couple. The wife is still traumatized by a police raid years before, and the question remains: Who betrayed their friends in the movement? A disturbing work about the fear and distrust created by a police state
1-55936-001-1 THEATRE COMMUNICATIONS PB $6.95

Master Harold and the Boys
When young Harold returns to his mother's hotel and visits his old friends he finds that things are not the same
0-14-048187-7 PENGUIN PB $7.95

Notebooks: 1960-1977
Fugard's diaries provide an insight into his creative process. Many entries offer poignant descriptions of South African daily life
1-55936-012-7 THEATRE COMMUNICATIONS PB $10.95

The Road to Mecca
An independent and eccentric woman artist refuses well-intentioned attempts to put her in an old-age home
0-930452-79-8 THEATRE COMMUNICATIONS PB $7.95

Statements: Three Plays
Includes *Statements After an Arrest Under the Immorality Act, The Island,* and *Sizwe Bansi Is Dead*
0-930452-61-5 THEATRE COMMUNICATIONS PB $8.95

Valley Song
1-55936-119-0 THEATRE COMMUNICATIONS PB $10.95

Arthur N. **Fula**
The Golden Magnet
Fula is one of the few black South Africans to write in Afrikaans. He describes life in the townships and the confusion experienced by rural blacks when they first come to the city
TRANSLATED BY CARROL LASKER
0-89410-291-5 THREE CONTINENTS $17.00
0-89410-292-3 THREE CONTINENTS PB $7.00

Nadine **Gordimer**
"Nadine Gordimer is one of the world's finest writers," wrote Joyce Carol Oates in the New York Times Book Review, *expressing a widely held opinion about the woman who has dominated the South African literary scene for the past 30 years. Gordimer's work reflects her growing political involvement, her earliest stories deal predominantly with the lives of liberal whites and their oblique relationship with blacks.*
Burger's Daughter
A woman seeks an identity beyond that of being the daughter of a famous activist who died in prison
0-14-005593-2 PENGUIN PB $12.95

The Conservationist
A convincing portrait of an Afrikaner industrialist, a man at once ambitious, cynical, sensual, and sharply observant
0-14-004716-6 PENGUIN PB $11.95

The Essential Gesture: Writing, Politics and Places
0-14-012212-5 PENGUIN PB $12.00

A Guest of Honour
A liberal white tries to come to terms with the increasing divisions in the black African country whose independence he fought for
0-14-003696-2 VIKING PB $11.95

July's People
A household servant rescues the white family he works for when the city becomes a battleground
0-14-006140-1 PENGUIN PB $10.95

Jump and Other Stories
Fifteen poignant and vital new stories by the Nobel Prize winner, set in London, Mozambique, South Africa, and on an imaginary island. This is fiction with a universal scope that examines everything from family dynamics to murder, racism, illicit love, children, and fear
0-374-18055-5 FS&G $20.00

The Late Bourgeois World
After her ex-husband betrays the revolutionary movement and then commits suicide, a woman faces involvement in a perilous mission for a black activist
0-14-005614-9 PENGUIN PB $9.95

The Lying Days
Gordimer's first novel, originally published in 1953, tells the story of Helen Shaw, daughter of white middle-class parents in a small gold mining town in South Africa. As Helen comes of age, so does her awareness grow of the African life around her. Her involvement with young blacks as a bohemian student leads her into complex relationships of emotion and action in a culture of dissension
0-14-023367-9 PENGUIN PB $10.95

My Son's Story
"It's an old story—ours. My father's and mine. Love, love/hate are the most common and universal of experiences. But no two are alike. Each is a fingerprint of life." A poignant study of the intersection of the political and the personal
0-374-21751-3 FS&G $19.95

None to Accompany Me
"This post-Nobel, post-apartheid novel—Gordimer's least political and most emotionally intricate—may well be the finest she has ever produced"—*Washington Post Book World*
0-374-22297-5 FS&G $22.00
0-14-025039-5 PENGUIN PB $11.95

Occasion for Loving
"One feels that it is life itself that absorbs her—the infinite variety of human character, the rich and surprising drama inherent in individual personality and in the clash of personalities"
—*NY Times*
0-14-023362-8 PENGUIN PB $10.95

Selected Stories
"A magnificent collection, worthy of all homage"—Graham Greene
0-14-006737-X PENGUIN PB $12.95

Nadine Gordimer

Six Feet of Country
The title story recounts the difficulties of a liberal white farmer who helps his servant to get her brother buried
0-14-006559-8 PENGUIN PB $8.95

Something Out There
A collection of short stories
0-14-007711-1 PENGUIN PB $10.00

A Sport of Nature
A white woman falls in love with a revolutionary who becomes the first black president of South Africa
0-14-008470-3 PENGUIN PB $11.95

A World of Strangers
0-14-001704-6 PENGUIN PB $11.95

Writing and Being
A brilliant discussion published in collaboration with the Charles Eliot Norton Lecture Series at Harvard University
0-674-96232-X HARVARD $18.95
0-674-96233-8 HARVARD PB $10.95

Bessie **Head**

Although Head was South African by birth, most of her work is set in neighboring Botswana, where she lived until her death in 1986. Among her favorite themes were the adaptation of villages to change, and individuals to prejudice.

The Cardinals: With Meditations and Short Stories
0-435-90967-3 HEINEMANN PB $10.95

The Collector of Treasures
Beautifully drawn stories about women in Botswana and township life in South Africa
0-435-90182-6 HEINEMANN PB $9.95

A Question of Power
Written from the viewpoint of a "coloured" woman exiled to Botswana while undergoing a nervous breakdown, this is a compelling psychological study of African life
0-435-90720-4 HEINEMANN PB $11.95

Serowe: Village of the Rain-Wind
A panoramic view of daily life in a Botswanan village
INTRODUCTION BY RONALD BLYTHE
0-435-90220-2 HEINEMANN PB $11.95

Denis **Hirson**

The House Next Door to Africa
An experimental work about childhood in South Africa
0-85635-720-0 CARCANET $28.25

Luis Bernardo **Honwana**

We Killed Mangy-Dog & Other Stories
After the boys in a small village in Mozambique stone a stray dog to death they confront the brutal conditions of their own lives
0-435-90060-9 HEINEMANN PB $8.95

A.C. **Jordan**, editor

Tales from Southern Africa
ILLUSTRATED BY FENI DUMILE
0-520-03638-7 CALIFORNIA PB $7.95

Mazisi **Kunene**

Emperor Shaka the Great
Kunene is the best-known interpreter of traditional Zulu poems and stories. Here, he has set the epic of the great Zulu conqueror into English
0-435-90211-3 HEINEMANN PB $14.95

Ellen **Kuzwayo**

Call Me Woman
PREFACE BY NADINE GORDIMER
1-87996-009-5 AUNT LUTE PB $9.95

Alex **La Guma**

Walk in the Night & Other Stories
Apartheid meticulously exposed by one of South Africa's finest writers
0-8101-0139-4 NORTHWESTERN PB $10.95

Rian **Malan**

My Traitor's Heart: A South African Exile Returns to Face His Country
An Afrikaner exile returns to South Africa. "His stories are haunting the way bad dreams are. They fascinate us, and only in retrospect do we realize their horror"—Vincent Crapanzano, *NY Times Book Review*
See also **SOUTH AFRICA SINCE 1948** under **AFRICA** in **WORLD HISTORY AND CURRENT AFFAIRS**
0-679-73215-2 VINTAGE PB $14.00

Mark **Mathabane**

Kaffir Boy: The True Story of a Black Youth's Coming of Age in Apartheid South Africa
See also **SOUTH AFRICA SINCE 1948** under **AFRICA** in **WORLD HISTORY AND CURRENT AFFAIRS**
0-02-034530-5 COLLIER PB $10.00

Thomas **Mofolo**

Chaka: An Historical Romance
Written in Sotho in 1925, this breakthrough novel uses the techniques of the oral tradition to create a complex psychological portrait of the great chief who founded the Zulu nation
TRANSLATED BY F.H. DUTTON
0-435-90229-6 HEINEMANN PB $9.95

Es'kia **Mphahlele**

Mphahlele's insightful fiction and criticism have made him one of the most important African literary figures. He has rendered the joys and horrors of growing up black in South Africa in his extraordinary autobiographies.

Afrika My Music: An Autobiography, 1957-1983
Describes a period of exile and homelessness
0-86975-237-5 RAVAN PB $13.95

Chirundu
A novel about black South African expatriates in an independent African country
0-88208-122-5 RAVAN PB $7.95

Down Second Avenue: Growing Up in a South African Ghetto
A brilliant autobiographical novel. "Mphahlele's writing is like the taste of blood on the tongue"
—Gerald Moore, *Seven African Writers*
0-571-09716-2 FABER PB $10.95

Percy **Mtwa** & others

Woza Albert!

When Jesus arrives in South Africa, he is welcomed by the government until he reveals why he chose to come. This play was a popular hit on Broadway

0-413-53000-0 METHUEN PB $9.95

V.Y. **Mudimbe**

The Rift

Mudimbe is an award-winning poet and novelist born in Zaire; *The Rift* is his best-known novel

0-8166-2312-0 MINNESOTA $16.95

Nat **Nakasa**

The World of Nat Nakasa: Selected Writings of the Late Nat Nakasa

Writing by the celebrated journalist and founder of the influential *Classic Magazine*

EDITED BY ESSOP PATEL

0-86975-050-X RAVAN PB $12.95

Njabulo S. **Ndebele**

Fools & Other Stories

Vivid tales of contemporary township and village life

0-930523-20-2 READERS INTERNATIONAL PB $11.95

Duma **Ndlovu**, editor

Woza Afrika!: A Collection of South African Plays

Also includes Nongema's *Asinamali!*

INTRODUCTION BY WOLE SOYINKA

0-8076-1170-0 BRAZILLER PB $14.95

Mike **Nicol**

Horseman

0-679-76039-3 VINTAGE PB $12.00

This Day and Age

Filled with folklore, magic, history, and romance, Nicol's new novel tells the story of a black messiah in the parched South African veld. "A dreamlike, darkly prophetic meditation on the savagery of South African political history, and on the impossibility of historical knowledge in general"—*Kirkus Reviews*

0-679-41682-X KNOPF $22.00

Essop **Patel**, editor

The World of Can Themba: Selected Writings

0-86975-145-X RAVAN PB $12.95

Alan **Paton**

Often considered the greatest South African writer, Paton was unflagging in his efforts to encourage racial harmony based on Christian ideas of brotherly love and the dignity of man. This pious vision has been criticized by other African writers as unrealistic, but few would deny his courage.

Ah, But Your Land Is Beautiful

A novel depicting the courageous self-sacrifice of those who fight apartheid and the triumph of human dignity over oppression

0-684-17336-0 SCRIBNERS $12.95

Cry, the Beloved Country

Paton's famous 1948 novel traces a Zulu minister's journey into Johannesburg's underworld in search of his son. A passionate exposure of apartheid, the book has sold more than 17 million copies

0-89966-788-0 BUCCANEER $25.95

0-684-81894-9 SCRIBNERS PB $12.00

Too Late the Phalarope

A lyrically written novel that conveys the full tragedy of the Immorality Act, the law forbidding sex between races

0-89190-392-5 AMEREON $21.95

0-684-81895-7 SCRIBNERS PB $11.00

Towards the Mountain: An Autobiography

0-8446-6322-0 SMITH $20.05

Norman **Rush**

An American novelist whose acclaimed novels and short stories are set in Central Africa

Mating

"A complex and moving love story…breath taking in its cunningly intertwined intellectual sweep and brio"—*Chicago Tribune Books*

See also **SINCE 1945** under **20TH-CENTURY AMERICAN FICTION** in **LITERATURE OF THE AMERICAS**

0-679-73709-X VINTAGE PB $12.00

Whites

Rush's sensitive stories show the bewilderment of American expatriates faced with the mysteries of Botswanan culture. "I found these stories wonderfully well written. Their wry humor and compassion bring to life middle-class Americans trying to lead a normal life in the back of beyond"
—J. M. Coetzee

0-679-73816-9 VINTAGE PB $10.00

Norman Rush

Olive **Schreiner**

Dream Life and Real Life

0-915864-32-0 ACADEMY CHICAGO $12.00

The Story of an African Farm

Nadine Gordimer has described this early feminist novel as the book to which all other South African work has to measure up

See also **HISTORIES AND PERSONAL ACCOUNTS** under **FARMING AND AGRICULTURE** in **SCIENCE**

0-19-282885-1 OXFORD PB $6.95

0-14-043184-5 PENGUIN PB $10.95

Sipho **Sepamla**

A Ride on the Whirlwind

A novel about the maelstrom that was the Soweto Uprising, by an important young black poet

0-435-90268-7 HEINEMANN PB $8.95

Mongane **Serote**

To Every Birth Its Blood

"This is a major literary landmark…In the jagged, fragmented narration, combined with syncopated jazz-rhythms in the language, Serote has pulled off a brilliant *tour de force*"—Dennis Brutus

0-435-90263-6 HEINEMANN PB $10.95

Sony Labou **Tansi**

The Antipeople

A Zairean novel

TRANSLATED BY J.A. UNDERWOOD

0-7145-2845-5 MARION BOYARS $18.95

0-7145-2901-X MARION BOYARS PB $9.95

Tchicaya **u-Tam'si**

A major voice from Zaire and an important figure in the Negritude movement, u-Tam'si has had his work translated into many different languages.

The Madman and the Medusa

TRANSLATED BY SONJA HAUSSMANN SMITH & WILLIAM JAY SMITH

0-8139-1205-9 CARAF PB $12.95

Laurens **Van der Post**

A widely traveled writer who states that he has walked over more of Africa than anyone else alive, Van der Post spent many years among the bushmen and writes feelingly of their myths and legends.

A Far-Off Place

In the sequel to *A Story Like the Wind*, a young white boy and girl, accompanied by their bushman friend, flee war by crossing a thousand miles of desert. "The author creates an enchanted world to go with his enchanted hero. The Africa through which his characters move is vivid and palpable"—*NY Times*

0-15-630198-9 HARCOURT BRACE PB $10.95

The Heart of the Hunter

A beautifully written if somewhat romanticized version of bushman myths and stories

1-85089-042-0 ISIS $16.95

A Story Like the Wind

The history of a liberal white family and their relationships with the Africans and the land

0-15-685261-6 HARCOURT BRACE PB $12.00

Uanhenga **Xitu**

The World of "Mestre" Tamoda: Angolan Stories

Written while its author was imprisoned by the colonial authorities, these stories are "outrageously funny…the stuff of which modern African comedy is made: equal parts African oral

narrative tradition and philosophy, garnished with European manners"—*NY Times*
TRANSLATED BY ANNELLA MCDERMOTT
0-930523-42-3 READERS INTERNATIONAL $16.95
0-930523-43-1 READERS INTERNATIONAL PB $8.95

Anthologies and Critical Studies

Roger D. **Abrahams**, editor
African Folktales: Traditional Stories of the Black World
0-394-72117-9 PANTHEON PB $17.00

Chinua **Achebe** & C. L. **Innes**, editors
African Short Stories
Includes selections by Gordimer, Ngugi, Kenyatta, Marechera, and Head
0-435-90270-9 HEINEMANN PB $8.95

Chidi **Amuta**
The Theory of African Literature: Implications for Practical Criticism
0-86232-546-3 ZED $55.00

B.W. **Andrzejewski**
An Anthology of Somali Poetry
0-253-30462-8 INDIANA $25.00
0-253-30463-6 INDIANA PB $9.95

Ulli **Beier**
The Origin of Life and Death
0-435-90023-4 HEINEMANN PB $7.95

Ulli Beier **Beier** & Gerald **Moore**, editors
The Penguin Book of Modern African Poetry
0-14-058573-7 PENGUIN PB $12.95

Brenda **Berrian**
Bibliography of African Women Writers and Journalists
PREFACE BY FLORA NWAPA
0-89410-226-5 THREE CONTINENTS $24.00

J. M. **Coetzee**
Doubling the Point: Essays and Interviews
EDITED BY DAVID ATTWELL
0-674-21517-6 HARVARD $49.95
0-674-21518-4 HARVARD PB $19.95

Giving Offense: Essays on Censorship
0-226-11174-1 CHICAGO $24.95

Bernard B. **Dadie**
The Black Cloth: A Collection of African Folk Tales
Stories rich in humor and inventiveness, retold by the distinguished Ivory Coast poet, novelist, and statesman
See also **AFRICAN** under **THE NON-WESTERN WORLD** under **MYTHOLOGY AND FOLKLORE** in **RELIGION, SPIRITUALITY, AND PHILOSOPHY**
TRANSLATED BY KAREN C. HATCH
0-87023-557-5 MASSACHUSETTS PB $13.95

Samba **Gadjigo** & others
Ousmane Sembene: Dialogues with Critics and Writers
0-87023-889-2 MASSACHUSETTS PB $13.95

Judith **Gleason**, translator
Leaf and Bone: African Praise Poems
0-14-058722-5 PENGUIN PB $14.95

Kenneth **Harrow**, editor
The Marabout and the Muse: New Aspects of Islam in African Literature
0-435-08983-8 HEINEMANN PB $22.00

Janheinz **Jahn**
Muntu: African Culture and the Western World
A pioneering study of traditional African culture and its contemporary impact
TRANSLATED BY MARJORIE GRENE
0-8021-3208-1 GROVE PB $12.95

Bernth **Lindfors**, editor
Contemporary Black South African Literature: A Symposium
0-89410-454-3 THREE CONTINENTS $22.00
0-89410-455-1 THREE CONTINENTS PB $14.00

Lee **Nichols**
African Writers at the Microphone
PREFACE BY ES'KIA MPHAHLELE
0-89410-164-1 THREE CONTINENTS $25.00
0-89410-165-X THREE CONTINENTS PB $12.00

Jeff **Opland**
Xhosa Oral Poetry: Aspects of a Black South African Tradition
0-521-24113-8 CAMBRIDGE $69.95

Oyekan **Owomoyela**, editor
A History of 20th Century African Literature
0-8032-3552-6 NEBRASKA $60.00
0-8032-8604-X NEBRASKA PB $25.00

Cosmo **Pieterse** & Donald **Munro**, editors
Protest and Conflict in African Literature
0-8419-0005-1 HOLMES & MEIER PB $15.00

Ngugi-Wa **Thiong'O**
Decolonising the Mind: The Politics of Language in African Literature
0-435-08016-4 HEINEMANN PB $15.00

Janet G. **Vaillant**
Black, French, and African: A Life of Leopold Sedar Senghor
A biography of the poet and intellectual who became the first president of Senegal
See also **OTHER** under **A NATIONAL FOCUS** under **AFRICA** in **WORLD HISTORY AND CURRENT AFFAIRS**
0-674-07623-0 HARVARD $32.50

Piniel **Viriri Shava**
A People's Voice: Black South African Writing in the 20th Century
An exploration of fiction, poetry, township theater, and autobiography from World War I to now, via the Soweto uprising
0-8214-0931-X ZED $24.95
0-8214-0932-8 SWALLOW PB $12.95

Dennis **Walder**
Athol Fugard
0-333-30904-9 ST. MARTIN'S PB $11.95

Arabic Literature

Arabic is a particularly difficult language to translate into English, not just because its grammatical concepts are fundamentally different, but also because of the cultural gulf that exists between Arabic and European culture. Few of the classic works of Arabic literature are available in English, but a glimpse of this great canon can be obtained in the titles listed below.

For related reading, see ISLAM in RELIGION, SPIRITUALITY, AND PHILOSOPHY

Classical Literature

Ghazi **Algosaibi**, translator
Lyrics from Arabia
A bilingual collection of classical poetry, including pre-Islamic work
0-89410-379-2 THREE CONTINENTS $17.00
0-89410-447-0 THREE CONTINENTS PB $10.00

Shah **Amin**
Assemblies of Al-Hariri
0-900860-86-3 ISHK $25.00

N.J. **Dawood**, translator
Tales from the Thousand and One Nights
0-14-044289-8 PENGUIN PB $10.95

Husain **Haddawy**, translator
The Arabian Nights
The most authentic translation of the classic of Oriental storytelling. "Haddawy's *Arabian Nights* is … indispensable. He has given us not a new version of an old favorite, but a work we've never known"— *Village Voice*
See also **ARAB** under **THE NON-WESTERN WORLD** under **MYTHOLOGY AND FOLKLORE** in **RELIGION, SPIRITUALITY, AND PHILOSOPHY**
0-393-02707-4 NORTON $27.95
0-393-31367-0 NORTON PB $14.95

The Arabian Nights II: Sinbad and Other Popular Stories
Haddaway follows up his remarkable earlier translations with these versions of tales interpolated later in the story-cycle, including

"Ali Baba and the Forty Thieves" and "Ala al-Din and the Magic Lamp"
See also **ARAB** under **THE NON-WESTERN WORLD** under **MYTHOLOGY AND FOLKLORE** in **RELIGION, SPIRITUALITY, AND PHILOSOPHY**
0-393-03815-7 NORTON $27.50

Lena **Jayyusi**, editor
The Adventures of Sayf Ben Dhi Yazan: An Arab Folk Epic
0-253-33034-3 INDIANA $39.95

James **Kritzeck**, editor
Anthology of Islamic Literature: From the Rise of Islam to Modern Times
The best introduction to classical Arabic, Persian, and Turkish literature. From the poetry of pre-Islamic Arabia to the popular dramas of the Ottoman era
0-452-00783-6 NEW AMERICAN LIBRARY PB $14.00

Omar **Pound**, editor
Arabic and Persian Poems in English
Free and very convincing translations from a dozen poets
See also **ANTHOLOGIES** under **MODERN LITERATURE**
See also **ANTHOLOGIES AND CRITICAL STUDIES**
0-8112-0358-1 NEW DIRECTIONS $7.50

Charles G. **Tuetey**, translator
Classic Arabic Poetry: 160 Poems from Imrulkais to Ma'arri
0-7103-0110-3 KEGAN & PAUL $76.50

Modern Literature

Adonis
An Introduction to Arab Poetics
A fascinating theoretical discussion of a tradition largely unknown to Western readers, by a leading contemporary poet
TRANSLATED BY CATHERINE COBHAM
0-292-73860-9 TEXAS PB $14.95

The Pages of Day and Night
TRANSLATED BY SAMUEL HAZO
0-910395-96-9 MARLBORO $22.95

Hanan **Al-Shaykh**
Beirut Blues
TRANSLATED BY CATHERINE COBHAM
0-385-47381-8 ANCHOR $22.95
0-385-47382-6 ANCHOR PB $12.95

The Story of Zahra
A 1980 novel of Beirut. "A haunting and chilling study of the fatal fascination of violence"
—*The Observer*
0-385-47206-4 ANCHOR PB $11.00

Hanna **Al-Shaykh**
Women of Sand and Myrrh
TRANSLATED BY CATHERINE COBHAM
0-385-42358-6 ANCHOR PB $10.00

Halim **Barakat**
Days of Dust
A novel about the Six Day War, viewed from an Arab perspective
TRANSLATED BY TREVOR LE GASSICK
0-89410-360-1 THREE CONTINENTS PB $11.00

Tahar Ben **Jelloun**
Corruption
Against the backgrounds of Casablanca and Tangier, this is the tale of an honest man in Morocco finally succumbing to the prevalent corruption of his materialistic society. "Poetic and analytical…Ben Jelloun's genius lies in evoking through language the grammar of existence, and the possibility of transforming with words the grimness of life's narratives"—*TLS*
See also **FICTION** under **MODERN FRENCH LITERATURE**
TRANSLATED BY CAROL VOLK
1-56584-295-2 NEW PRESS $17.95
1-56584-296-0 NEW PRESS PB $10.00

Mohamed **Choukri**
For Bread Alone
TRANSLATED BY PAUL BOWLES
0-87286-196-1 CITY LIGHTS PB $6.95

Driss **Chraibi**
Birth at Dawn
A sequel to *The Mother of Spring*, concerning the arrival of Islam in the Maghreb
TRANSLATED BY SHEENA CHRAIBI
0-89410-576-0 THREE CONTINENTS $22.00

The Mother of Spring
A Moroccan novel exploring the world of the Berbers in pre-Islamic times
TRANSLATED BY HUGH HARTER
0-89410-402-0 THREE CONTINENTS PB $11.00

Fathy **Ghanem**
The Man Who Lost His Shadow
TRANSLATED BY DESMOND STEWART
0-89410-207-9 THREE CONTINENTS PB $12.00

Fuad S. **Haddad**, translator
From the Vineyards of Lebanon: Poems by Khalil Hawi & Nadeem Naimy
0-8156-6085-5 SYRACUSE PB $11.95

Khalil **Hawi**
Naked in Exile: Khalil Hawi's "The Threshing Floors of Hunger"
The major work by a poet who committed suicide in 1982 during the Israeli invasion of Lebanon
TRANSLATED BY ADRIAN HAYDAR & MICHAEL BEARD
0-89410-366-0 THREE CONTINENTS $20.00

Taha **Hussein**
An Egyptian Childhood
Egypt's leading man of letters. This is the first volume of his autobiography, one of the great works of modern Arabic literature
INTRODUCTION BY PIERRE CACHIA
977-424-246-7 CAIRO PB $9.95

Jabra I. **Jabra**
The Ship
TRANSLATED BY ADRIAN HAYDER & ROGER ALLEN
0-89410-328-8 THREE CONTINENTS $24.00

Elias **Khoury**
Little Mountain
TRANSLATED BY MAIA TABET
FOREWORD BY EDWARD SAID
0-8166-1770-8 MINNESOTA PB $9.95

Naguib **Mahfouz**
The only Arabic writer to be awarded the Nobel Prize, which he won in 1988, Mahfouz published his first novel in 1939. His renoun as the leading figure in contemporary Arabic letters was established with the publication of his Cairo Trilogy *in 1956. He recently survived an assassination attempt by Islamic fundamentalists.*

Adrift on the Nile
A group of young Egyptian professionals spend their evenings aimlessly floating in a houseboat on the Nile, until tragedy strikes their group and they're brought powerfully to earth
TRANSLATED BY JEAN LIARDET
0-385-42333-0 ANCHOR PB $10.95

Naguib Mahfouz

Arabian Nights and Days
TRANSLATED BY DENYS JOHNSON-DAVIES
0-385-46901-2 ANCHOR PB $12.00

Autumn Quail
A bureaucrat runs afoul of political change, and the bottom drops out of his world
0-385-26454-2 ANCHOR PB $10.95

The Beggar
TRANSLATED BY KRISTIN HENRY
0-385-26456-9 ANCHOR PB $9.95

The Beginning and the End
TRANSLATED BY RAMSES AWAD
0-385-26458-5 ANCHOR PB $11.00

Children of Gebelaawi
0-89410-818-2 THREE CONTINENTS PB $20.00

Children of the Alley
TRANSLATED BY PETER THEROUX
0-385-42094-3 DOUBLEDAY $24.95
0-385-26473-9 ANCHOR PB $11.00

Echoes of an Autobiography
0-385-48555-7 DOUBLEDAY $19.95

Fountain and Tomb
A complex, cinematic novel about a child's initiation into the life of modern Cairo
TRANSLATED BY JAMES KENNESON
0-89410-581-7 THREE CONTINENTS PB $10.00

The Harafish
TRANSLATED BY CATHERINE COBHAM
0-385-42335-7 ANCHOR PB $11.00

Midaq Alley
The best-known work by the Nobel Prize-winner focuses on a young girl growing up in a poor Cairo neighborhood
0-385-26476-3 DOUBLEDAY PB $9.95

Miramar
A hotel in Alexandria provides the setting for one of Mahfouz's best works
TRANSLATED BY FATMA MOUSSA-MAHMOUD
INTRODUCTION BY JOHN FOWLES
0-89410-693-7 THREE CONTINENTS PB $11.00

Palace Walk
The first volume in *The Cairo Trilogy*, considered Mahfouz's major work. First published in 1956, *Palace Walk* is only now available in English. "It is a masterwork because it is not just a social portrayal but penetrates the psyche, the intellect and the soul of the Egyptian people"—Sasson Somekh, Tel Aviv University
0-385-26465-8 DOUBLEDAY $22.95
0-385-26466-6 DOUBLEDAY PB $11.95

Palace of Desire
The second volume of *The Cairo Trilogy* takes us into the world of Egypt in the '20s, with its new currents of modernity. "Rich in psychological insight and cultural observation"—*Boston Globe*
0-385-26467-4 DOUBLEDAY $22.95

Sugar Street
The third volume of *The Cairo Trilogy*
TRANSLATED BY WILLIAM MAYNARD HUTCHINS AND ANGELE BOTROS SAMAAN
0-385-26470-4 ANCHOR PB $11.95

The Search
0-385-26460-7 ANCHOR PB $9.95

The Thief and the Dogs
A stream-of-consciousness account of a self-destructive and embittered man who embarks on a vengeful rampage after serving a jail sentence
TRANSLATED BY M.M. BADAWI & TREVOR LE GASSICK
0-385-26461-5 ANCHOR PB $16.95

Wedding Song
A story of emotional conflicts within the theater world of Cairo, told from multiple viewpoints
TRANSLATED BY OLIVE KENNEDY
0-385-26464-X ANCHOR PB $9.95

Fatima **Mernissi**

Dreams of Trespass: Tales of a Harem in Girlhood
Today a prominent feminist scholar, Mernissi grew up behind the iron gates of a domestic harem in Morocco. Removed from the outside world, the women there understood the mysteries of time and place out of sheer imagination. "A remarkable book…its good humor is unwavering; it tempers judgmentalism with understanding; and it provides a vivid portrait of a world that most Westerners can scarcely comprehend"
—*Washington Post Book World*
0-201-48937-6 ADDISON-WESLEY PB $12.00

Mohammed **Mrabet**

The Boy Who Set the Fire
Seventeen tales by the Maghrebi storyteller. "Part folklore, part magic, part braggadocio, these sometimes autobiographical, sometimes traditional tales are filled with Mediterranean light, crazy kif wisdom and vivid characters"
—Andrei Codrescu
TRANSLATED BY PAUL BOWLES
0-87286-230-5 CITY LIGHTS PB $8.95

Abdelrahman **Munif**

Cities of Salt
The impact of American oil workers on an impoverished Persian Gulf community in the '30s. "It opens up new vistas to the imagination"
—Graham Greene
TRANSLATED BY PETER THEROUX
0-394-75526-X VINTAGE PB $17.00

The Trench
0-679-74533-5 VINTAGE PB $14.00

Variations on Night and Day
"Abdelrahman Munif's monumental cycle of novels dealing with the history of oil ought to be regarded as a work of immense significance"
—*New Republic*
0-394-57673-X PANTHEON $24.00
0-679-75551-9 VINTAGE PB $12.00

Nawal **el Saadawi**

The Innocence of the Devil
0-520-08889-1 CALIFORNIA $20.00

Memoirs from the Women's Prison
TRANSLATED BY MARILYN BOOTH
0-520-08888-3 CALIFORNIA PB $12.00

Memories of a Woman Doctor
A novel of a young Egyptian woman in rebellion against social constraints
0-87286-223-2 CITY LIGHTS PB $8.95

Two Women in One
A young Egyptian woman's sexual and political awakening
TRANSLATED BY OSMAN NUSAIRI & JANA GOUGH
1-87967-901-9 WOMEN IN TRANSLATION PB $9.95

Woman at Point Zero
TRANSLATED BY SHERIF HETATA
0-86232-110-7 ZED PB $7.95

Tayeb **Salih**

Season of Migration to the North
The story of a talented Sudanese whose life goes to waste in the chasm between East and West
TRANSLATED BY DENYS JOHNSON-DAVIES
0-89410-199-4 THREE CONTINENTS PB $11.00

The Wedding of Zein
A masterwork of modern Arabic fiction that has been neglected in favor of Salih's more popular *Season of Migration to the North*
0-89410-201-X THREE CONTINENTS PB $10.00

Rafik **Schami**

Damascus Nights
Once upon a time, Salim, the most famous storyteller in Damascus, was mysteriously struck dumb. Seven of his friends gathered on seven nights, each in turn reciting a story, all hoping thereby to cure their dear friend. On this ancient tale, Schami builds a modern masterpiece of Middle Eastern literature, combining ancient art with 20th-century settings, unfolding his tale with grace, wit, and wise charm
0-374-13446-4 FS&G $20.00

Bahaa' **Taher**

Aunt Safiyya and the Monastery
TRANSLATED BY BARBARA ROMAINE
0-520-20075-6 CALIFORNIA PB $12.95

Anthologies

Abu Bakr Ahmed **Bagader**

Assassination of Light: Modern Saudi Fiction
0-89410-599-X THREE CONTINENTS PB $11.00

Ben **Bennani**, editor

Bread, Hashish and Moon: Four Modern Arab Poets
Selected poems of Nizar Qabbani, Badr Shakir al-Sayyab, Adonis, and Mahmud Darwish
0-87775-135-8 UNICORN PB $9.95

Marilyn **Booth**, editor & translator

My Grandmother's Cactus: Stories by Egyptian Women
0-292-70803-3 TEXAS PB $10.95

Kamal **Boullata**, translator & editor

Women of the Fertile Crescent: An Anthology of Arab Women's Poems
0-914478-42-7 THREE CONTINENTS PB $16.00

Abdel **Elmessiri**, editor

The Palestinian Wedding: A Bilingual Anthology of Contemporary Palestinian Resistance Poetry
TRANSLATED BY ABDEL ELMESSIRI
ILLUSTRATED BY KERNEL BOULLATA
0-89410-095-5 THREE CONTINENTS $28.00

Salma K. **Jayyusi**, editor
Modern Arabic Poetry: An Anthology
0-231-05273-1 COLUMBIA PB $17.50

The Literature of Modern Arabia
0-292-74662-8 TEXAS PB $24.95

Denys **Johnson-Davies**
Arabic Short Stories
0-520-08944-8 CALIFORNIA PB $12.00

Mahmoud **Manzaloui**, editor
Arabic Short Stories: 1945-1965
977-424-121-5
AMERICAN UNIVERSITY OF CAIRO PB $20.00

Omar **Pound**, editor
Arabic and Persian Poems in English
Free and very convincing translations from a dozen poets
See also **CLASSICAL LITERATURE**
See also **ANTHOLOGIES AND CRITICAL STUDIES**
0-8112-0358-1 NEW DIRECTIONS $7.50

Background Studies

Lila **abu-Lughod**
Veiled Sentiments: Honor and Poetry in a Bedouin Society
0-520-06327-9 CALIFORNIA PB $15.95

Krishna **Chaitanya**
A History of Arabic Literature
0-8364-1045-9 SOUTH ASIA $18.00

Rasheed **El-Enany**
Naguib Mahfouz: The Pursuit of Meaning
0-415-07395-2 ROUTLEDGE PB $17.95

Naguib Mahfouz (photo by R. Neil Hewison)

Robert **Irwin**
The Arabian Nights: A Companion
See also **ARAB** under **THE NON-WESTERN WORLD** under **MYTHOLOGY AND FOLKLORE** in **RELIGION, SPIRITUALITY, AND PHILOSOPHY**
0-7139-9105-4 ALLEN LANE $24.95

Louis **Massignon**
Essay on the Origins of the Technical Language of Islamic Mystics
See also **SUFISM** under **ISLAM** in **RELIGION, SPIRITUALITY, AND PHILOSOPHY**
0-268-00928-7 NOTRE DAME $34.95

Matti **Moosa**
Origins of Modern Arabic Fiction
0-89410-683-X THREE CONTINENTS $32.00
0-89410-684-8 THREE CONTINENTS PB $16.00

Reynold A. **Nicholson**
Literary History of the Arabs
0-7007-0261-X CURZON $70.00

Saad Abdullah **Sowayan**
Nabati Poetry: The Oral Poetry of Arabia
0-520-04882-2 CALIFORNIA $45.00

Suzanne Pinckney **Stetkevych**, editor
Reorientations: Arabic and Persian Poetry
0-253-35493-5 INDIANA $16.95

Persian Literature

Iran has often been called the France of the premodern Middle East—the source and standard-bearer of what people from Constantinople to Delhi considered high culture. But little of its enormous literary output has been translated for Western readers. Having escaped occupation by an imperial power, Iran never had a large number of foreign scholars, civil servants, and missionaries exploring its literature. While it is true that the image of Persia has been a powerful one in the West since the time of the Achmaenid dynasty, the job of making the best of the Persian tradition available to Europeans remains largely uncompleted. As a result the list that follows is necessarily partial and unrepresentative.

Classical Literature

Farid al-Din **Attar**
The Conference of the Birds
A stunning English rendering of a classic mystical allegory
TRANSLATED BY AFKHAM DARBANDI & DICK DAVIS
0-14-044434-3 PENGUIN PB $10.95

Muslim Saints and Mystics: Episodes from the Tadhkirat al-Auliya (Memorial of the Saints)
The biographical dictionary of saints was a common form of literature in the Islamic world, and this work is considered the finest example of the genre
TRANSLATED BY A.J. ARBERRY
0-14-019264-6 ARKANA PB $9.95

Ferdowsi
The Legend of Seyavash
A graceful translation of a crucial episode from the Persian national epic, the *Shahnameh*
TRANSLATED WITH AN INTRODUCTION BY DICK DAVIS
0-14-044566-8 PENGUIN PB $8.95

The Tragedy of Sohrab and Rostam
Another famous episode from the epic, translated with somewhat less panache but with Persian on the facing page
TRANSLATED BY JEROME W. CLINTON
0-295-96582-7 WASHINGTON PB $12.50

Hafiz
Fifty Poems of Hafiz
Although the selection is fairly small, this is the best introduction to the greatest Persian lyric poet
EDITED AND TRANSLATED BY A.J. ARBERRY
0-7007-0275-X CURZON PB $18.50

The Green Sea of Heaven: Fifty Ghazals from the Diwan of Hafiz
1-88399-106-4 S.C.B. PB $14.95

Hafez: Dance of Life
Translations of Hafez's poetry accompanied by beautiful illuminations by the Iranian artist Hossein Zenderoudi
TRANSLATED BY MICHAEL BOYLAN & WILBERFORCE CLARKE
EDITED BY M. BATMANGLIJ
0-934211-04-3 MAGE $32.95
0-934211-13-2 MAGE PB $19.95

Omar **Khayyam**
The Rubaiyat of Omar Khayyam
After the King James Bible, Fitzgerald's rather free version of Omar's quatrains is perhaps the most familiar translation in the English language
TRANSLATED BY EDWARD FITZGERALD
0-14-005954-7 PENGUIN PB $11.95

Nasir-i Khusraw
Make a Shield from Wisdom: Selected Verses from Nasir-i Khusraw's Divan
TRANSLATED WITH AN INTRODUCTION BY ANNEMARIE SCHIMMEL
0-7103-0455-2 COLUMBIA $49.95

Nizami
Haft Paykar: A Medieval Persian Romance
EDITED & TRANSLATED BY JULIE S. MEISAMI
0-19-283184-4 OXFORD PB $11.95

Rumi
The Essential Rumi
TRANSLATED BY COLEMAN BARKS
0-06-250958-6 HARPERCOLLINS $20.00
0-06-250959-4 HARPERCOLLINS PB $12.00

A Garden Beyond Paradise: The Mystical Poetry of Rumi
0-553-08221-3 BANTAM PB $22.50

Look! This Is Love: Poems of Rumi
TRANSLATED BY ANNEMARIE SCHIMMEL
1-57062-224-8 SHAMBHALA PB $10.00

Love Is a Stranger: Selected Lyric Poetry

TRANSLATED BY KABIR EDMUND HELMINSKI

0-939660-32-6 THRESHOLD PB $10.00

Mystical Poems of Rumi

The prolific orientalist's translation of 200 of Rumi's shorter poems

TRANSLATED BY A.J. ARBERRY

0-226-73151-0 CHICAGO PB $12.95

Signs of the Unseen: The Discourses of Jalaluddin Rumi

TRANSLATED BY W. M. THACKSON

0-939660-34-2 THRESHOLD PB $15.00

These Branching Moments: 40 Odes

TRANSLATED BY COLEMAN BARKS & JOHN MOYNE

0-914278-50-9 COPPER BEECH PB $6.95

Sadi

The Rose Garden

This work is the greatest example of the Persian genre that mixed prose and poetry for the purposes of edification and entertainment. In various translations it has had a continuous influence on literature in Europe

TRANSLATED BY EDWARD EASTWICK

0-900860-65-0 ISHK $25.00

Modern Persian Literature

Mahshid **Amirshahi**

Suri & Co.: Tales of a Persian Teenage Girl

TRANSLATED BY J.E. KNORZER

0-292-70463-1 TEXAS PB $9.95

Simin **Daneshvar**

A Persian Requiem

This was the first book by an Iranian woman ever to have been published. Set in a small Persian town during the British occupation in World War II, the book contemplates women's roles in Iranian society and the corrupting weight of colonialism. "A novel that touched an entire nation and is credited with planting some of the seeds of the Iranian revolution"
—*The Independent*

0-8076-1273-1 BRAZILLER $22.50
0-8076-1274-X BRAZILLER PB $12.50

Forugh **Farrokhzad**

A Rebirth: Poems

TRANSLATED BY DAVID C. MARTIN

0-939214-30-X MAZDA PB $9.95

Dilip **Hiro**

Three Plays

Includes *To Anchor a Cloud, Apply, No Reply*, and *A Clean Break*

0-946013-01-2 THREE CONTINENTS PB $10.00

Parvin E'tesami

Divane Parvin E'tesami

Parvin is an important woman poet of the first half of the century in whom the transition from classical to modern concerns is clearly represented

EDITED BY HESHMAT MOAYYAD

0-939214-38-5 MAZDA PB $14.95

Anthologies and Critical Studies

Coleman **Barks**, translator

The Hand of Poetry: Five Mystic Poets of Persia

Includes work by Inayat Khan, Sanai, Attar, Rumi, Saadi, and Hafiz

0-930872-47-9 OMEGA PB $12.00

Omar **Pound**, editor

Arabic and Persian Poems in English

Free and very convincing translations from a dozen poets

See also **CLASSICAL LITERATURE** under **ARABIC LITERATURE**

0-8112-0358-1 NEW DIRECTIONS $7.50

Annemarie **Schimmel**

The Triumphal Sun: A Study of the Works of Rumi

0-7914-1636-4 SUNY PB $21.95

A Two-Colored Brocade: The Imagery of Persian Poetry

0-8078-2050-4 NORTH CAROLINA $75.00

Literatures of India

Readers educated in the secular literary traditions of the West tend to experience bewilderment when confronted with the writing of the Indian subcontinent. Literature in India has historically been bound to religious life, and literary artifacts are only imperfectly understood if one forgets that they serve as aids to worship and piety. Secular traditions—such as the court poetry of the Guptas and the Mughals—have developed, but even they acquiesce in crucial ways to the religious institutions that surround them.

Included in this section are a large number of modern works written in English and most of the available translations of modern literature in the vernacular.

Sanskrit Literature

The Vedas and the Great Epics

William **Buck**, translator

The Mahabharata

A highly readable abridgement of the massive epic poem that defines the Indian identity

ILLUSTRATED BY SHIRLEY TRIESTE

0-520-04393-6 CALIFORNIA PB $15.00

The Ramayana

A prose condensation of the epic

0-520-04394-4 CALIFORNIA PB $15.00

Barbara Stoler **Miller**, translator

Bhagavad-Gita: Krishna's Counsel in Time of War

A very precise translation. Unlike Zaehner's work, which reflects the subtle influence of its translator's Roman Catholicism, this version maintains a rigorous neutrality with respect to interpretation

See also **CLASSIC TEXTS** under **HINDUISM** under **ASIAN RELIGION AND PHILOSOPHY** in **RELIGION, SPIRITUALITY, AND PHILOSOPHY**

0-231-06468-3 COLUMBIA $29.50
0-553-21365-2 BDD PB $4.95

Robert C. **Zaehner**, translator & editor

The Bhagavad-Gita

India's most sacred text, translated by a distinguished student of comparative religion

See also **CLASSIC TEXTS** under **HINDUISM** under **ASIAN RELIGION AND PHILOSOPHY** in **RELIGION, SPIRITUALITY, AND PHILOSOPHY**

0-19-501666-1 OXFORD PB $15.95

G.D. **Khosla**, translator

Tales of Love & War from the Mahabharata

0-19-563466-7 OXFORD PB $7.95

R.K. Narayan

R.K. **Narayan**

The Mahabharata

81-7094-001-X SOUTH ASIA PB $8.00

The Ramayana: The Indian Epic

A fluent retelling of the story by India's foremost contemporary writer

See also **INDIAN** under **THE NON-WESTERN WORLD** under **MYTHOLOGY AND FOLKLORE** in **RELIGION, SPIRITUALITY, AND PHILOSOPHY**

0-14-018700-6 PENGUIN PB $9.95

Wendy Doniger **O'Flaherty**, editor

The Rig Veda

The standard contemporary English version of one of the world's oldest religious texts, containing a beautiful version of the Vedic hymn to creation, the earliest extant lyric poem

See also **CLASSIC TEXTS** under **HINDUISM** under **ASIAN RELIGION AND PHILOSOPHY** in **RELIGION, SPIRITUALITY, AND PHILOSOPHY**

0-14-044402-5 PENGUIN PB $11.95

Valmiki

The Ramayana of Valmiki: An Epic of Ancient India

A translation-in-progress of the complete Ramayana, the "original poem" of India. This hardbound edition contains notes on the translation and on problems with the original

Volume 1 Balakanda

The complete poem, in a new and definitive translation

0-691-06561-6 PRINCETON $67.50

Volume 2 Ayodhyakanda

0-691-06654-X PRINCETON $85.00

Volume 3 Aranyakanda

0-691-06660-4 PRINCETON $72.50

Volume 4 Kiskindhakanda

0-691-06661-2 PRINCETON $65.00

Volume 5 Sundarakanda

0-691-06662-0 PRINCETON $89.50

J.A.B. **van Buitenen**, translator

The Mahabharata

Although left incomplete by Professor Van Buitenen at his death, this translation provides the most direct experience of the epic an English reader can have

Part 1, The Book of the Beginning

0-226-84663-6 CHICAGO PB $24.95

Part 2, The Book of the Assembly Hall & Part 3, The Book of the Forest

0-226-84664-4 CHICAGO PB $27.50

Part 4, The Book of Virata & Part 5, The Book of the Effort

0-226-84665-2 CHICAGO PB $27.50

Tales

Roy C. **Amore** & Larry D. **Shinn**

Lustful Maidens and Ascetic Kings: Buddhist and Hindu Stories of Life

Anecdotes from the Buddhist and Hindu folk traditions

ILLUSTRATED BY SHARON WALLACE

0-19-502839-2 OXFORD PB $10.95

R.K. **Narayan**

Gods, Demons, and Others

Narayan's version of the Hindu myths are exceptionally engaging

0-226-56825-3 CHICAGO PB $12.95

Visnu **Sarma**

The Panchatantra

0-14-044596-X PENGUIN PB $12.95

Pandit V. **Sharma**

The Panchatantra

These old-fashioned versions give an idea of the charm of a corpus of stories that is regarded as the principal source for the *Arabian Nights*

81-7167-065-2 SOUTH ASIA PB $9.50

J.A.B. **van Buitenen**, translator

Tales of Ancient India

A very entertaining sampling of the enormous body of ancient Indian narratives

0-226-84647-4 CHICAGO PB $11.95

Heinrich **Zimmer**

The King and the Corpse: Tales of the Soul's Conquest of Evil

Tales of the soul's conquest of evil, culled fron Eastern and Western folk literature and retold by the renowned Indologist and Jungian

See also **FOLKLORE** under **MYTHOLOGY AND FOLKLORE** in **RELIGION, SPIRITUALITY, AND PHILOSOPHY**

EDITED BY JOSEPH CAMPBELL

0-691-01776-X PRINCETON PB $12.95

Poetry and Drama

John **Brough**, translator

Poems from the Sanskrit

0-14-044198-0 PENGUIN PB $9.95

Robert A. **Hueckstedt**

The Style of Bana: An Introduction to Sanskrit Prose Poetry

0-8191-4999-3

UNIVERSITY PRESS OF AMERICA PB $25.50

Daniel H.H. **Ingalls**, translator

The Dhvanyaloka of Anandavardhana with the Locana of Abhinavagupta

This is a revision by Ingalls of the Ph.D. thesis of Jeffrey Moussaieff Masson. It shows the development of a theory of poetic suggestion which may be of greater interest to modern readers in the West than is the more familiar sytem of rasas, or moods, borrowed from dramatic arts. Ingalls's translations of the mostly Prakit verses used as examples by Anandavardhana and his commentator Abhinavagupta are also excellent

0-674-20278-3 HARVARD $50.00

Jayadeva

Love Song of the Dark Lord: Jayadeva's Gitagovinda

A sensual and highly influential medieval devotional poem in a beautiful translation. "Miller's volume is an essential contribution to Indian study and to poetry in translation in general. She has given us the Indian equivalent of the *Song of Songs* without the usual sentimentality"—David Shapiro, *Parabola*

TRANSLATED BY BARBARA STOLER MILLER

0-231-04028-8 COLUMBIA $24.00

0-231-04029-6 COLUMBIA PB $15.00

Kalidasa

The Origin of the Young God: Kalidasa's Kumarasambhava

An epic of sacred eroticism, superbly translated. "This remarkable translation of a previously inaccessible text holds its active authority as poetry throughout, never relaxing into simply prosaic patterns nor the all too usual paraphrase. Hank Heifetz has managed a compelling unity of resources, which I consider an exceptional literary accomplishment" —Robert Creeley

TRANSLATED BY HANK HEIFETZ

0-520-05304-4 CALIFORNIA $40.00

The Theater of Memory: Three Plays of Kalidasa

These translations succeed in giving the reader a sense of why Kalidasa holds a position in Sanskrit literature comparable to that of Shakespeare in English

TRANSLATED BY BARBARA STOLER MILLER & OTHERS

0-231-05838-1 COLUMBIA $59.00

0-231-05839-X COLUMBIA PB $21.50

Barbara Stoler **Miller**, translator

The Hermit and the Love-Thief: Sanskrit Poems of Bhartrihari and Bilhana

Lyric poems from the devotional tradition

0-14-044584-6 PENGUIN PB $6.95

Andrew **Schelling**

Dropping the Bow: Poems from Ancient India

Outstanding translations offering a fresh impression of the Sanskrit tradition of classical poetry. "Like the erotic moods they investigate, these versions shimmer and startle with a palpable desire to be heard, and a mystical sense of impermanence. They are exactly tough and tender to the right degree, bold and shy in the loves they evoke"—Anne Waldman

0-913089-18-4 BROKEN MOON PB $10.00

Now that the rainy
season is on us,
restless wild mountain tribe couples
no longer descend
the paths to make love here.
The bamboo thickets
flanking these hillside
creeks have grown quiet.
Along the banks, fresh
shoots are emerging,
tips clad in soft bark,
black as the skin
of a kid-goat's ear.

DROPPING THE BOW: POEMS FROM ANCIENT INDIA

Andrew **Schelling** & Anne **Waldman**, editors

Songs of the Sons and Daughters of the Buddha: Versions from the Theragatha and Therigatha

1-57062-172-1 SHAMBHALA PB $11.00

Vidyakara

An Anthology of Sanskrit Court Poetry: Vidyakara's Subhasitaratnakosa

Far and away the best translations of classical Sanskrit poetry into English verse

TRANSLATED BY DANIEL H. INGALLS

0-674-03950-5 HARVARD $40.00

Pali and Tamil Literature

Margaret **Cone** & Richard **Gombrich**, editors

The Perfect Generosity of Prince Vessantara: A Buddhist Epic

This version of the birth of the Buddha is one of the few translations from the vast Buddhist literature of Sri Lanka

0-19-826530-1 OXFORD $48.00

A.K. **Ramanujan**, translator

The Interior Landscape: Love Poems from a Classical Tamil Anthology

Ramanujan deftly clarifies the stock characters and situations of the Tamil lyrical tradition in these excellent translations

0-19-563501-9 OXFORD PB $7.95

Poems of Love and War: From the Eight Anthologies and the Ten Songs of Classical Tamil

Dramatic poems from the secular Tamil tradition

0-231-05107-7 COLUMBIA PB $20.00

Merchant-Prince Shattan

Manimekhalai: The Dancer with the Magic Bowl

A 4th-century Tamil verse epic which portrays that age through the story of a dancer who dedicates her life to charity

TRANSLATED BY ALAIN DANIELOU

0-8112-1098-7 NEW DIRECTIONS PB $11.95

South Indian Literature

Edward C. **Dimock** & Denise **Levertov**, translators

In Praise of Krishna: Songs from the Bengali

The ecstatic nature of Bengali devotion is well captured by this volume, a collaboration between a scholar and a leading American poet

ILLUSTRATED BY ANJU CHAUDHURI

0-226-15231-6 CHICAGO PB $10.95

Richard A. **Frasca**

The Theater of the Mahabharata: Terukkuttu Performances in South India

0-8248-1290-5 HAWAII $45.00

Hank **Heifetz** & Velcheru N. **Rao**, translators

For the Lord of the Animals: Poems from the Telugu—The Kalabastisvara of Satakamu of Dhurjati

Devotional poems of great intimacy and psychological penetration, sensitively translated

0-520-05669-8 CALIFORNIA $35.00

A.K. **Ramanujan**

A Flowering Tree and Other Indian Oral Tales from the Kannada Region

0-520-20398-4 CALIFORNIA $42.00
0-520-20399-2 CALIFORNIA PB $25.00

A.K. **Ramanujan**, translator

Speaking of Siva

Devotional poems originally composed in the South Indian language Kannada, and emanating from the *bhakti* movement of spiritual protest which originated in the 10th century. This is arguably the single best set of translations from an Indian language into English

0-14-044270-7 PENGUIN PB $9.95

Does it matter how long
a rock soaks in the water:
will it ever grow soft?

Does it matter how long
I've spent in worship,
when the heart is fickle?

Futile as a ghost
I stand guard over hidden gold,

O lord of the meeting rivers.

SPEAKING OF SIVA

When God Is a Customer: Telugu Courtesan Songs by Ksetrayya and Others

0-520-08068-8 CALIFORNIA $25.00
0-520-08069-6 CALIFORNIA PB $12.00

Hindi and Urdu Literature

Kenneth E. **Bryant**

Poems to the Child-God: Structures and Strategies in the Poetry of Sur Das

Translations and a study of the poems of Sur Das, the greatest of the sectarian medieval poets

0-520-03540-2 CALIFORNIA $45.00

Ghalib

Urdu Letters of Mirza Asadullah Khan Ghalib

0-88706-412-4 SUNY $49.50

Ralph **Russell** & Khurshidul **Islam**

Ghalib, 1797-1869: Life and Letters

A biography of the 19th-century poet based on letters which are themselves regarded as the highwater mark of Urdu prose

0-19-563506-X OXFORD PB $12.95

Ann Grodzins **Gold**

A Carnival of Parting: The Tales of King Bharthari and King Gopi Chand as Sung and Told by Madhu Natisar Nath of Ghatiyali, Rajasthan

These unabridged literal translations of performances tape-recorded in Rajasthan give an idea of how the epic style has continued in India

0-520-07535-8 CALIFORNIA PB $17.00

John S. **Hawley**

Sur Das: Poet, Singer, Saint

A study with translations, from the perspective of a student of religions

0-295-96102-3 WASHINGTON $25.00

John S. **Hawley** & Mark **Juergensmeyer**, translators

Songs of the Saints of India

Examples of the movement of medieval poet-saints exemplified by Kabir

0-19-505221-8 OXFORD PB $15.95

Kabir

The Bijak of Kabir

Lucid, precise, and faithful translations which also have a great deal of poetic merit. "Kabir has the unusual distinction of being claimed by both Muslims and Hindus as a great teacher…His teasing verses, authentic and ascribed, were and still are sung all over the vast subcontinent, forming an integral part of its rich oral tradition"—*Booklist*

TRANSLATED BY LINDA HESS & SHUKDEV SINGH
COMMENTARY BY LINDA HESS

0-86547-114-2 NORTH POINT PB $12.50

The Kabir Book: Forty-Four of the Ecstatic Poems of Kabir

Robert Bly's versions, based on Tagore's English text, bear the stamp of his distinctive poetic sensibility

TRANSLATED BY ROBERT BLY

0-8070-6379-7 BEACON PB $10.00

Songs of Kabir

Tagore's highly personal translations are based on Bengali versions of Kabir's poems

TRANSLATED BY RABINDRANATH TAGORE

0-87728-695-7 WEISER PB $7.95

R.P. **Prasad**, translator

Tulsidasa's Shriramacharitamanasa (The Holy Lake of the Acts of Rama)

A compact edition of the translation of the hugely popular Hindi version of the Valmiki Ramayana

81-208-0680-8 SOUTH ASIA $42.00

Ralph **Russell** & Khurshidul **Islam**

Three Mughal Poets: Mir, Sauda, Mir Hasan

An acknowledged classic, this book provides an illuminating introduction to the first great period of classical Urdu poetry

INTRODUCTION BY ANNEMARIE SCHIMMEL

0-19-562850-0 OXFORD $14.95

20th-Century Literature of the Indian Subcontinent

Ahmed **Ali**

Twilight in Delhi
0-8112-1267-X NEW DIRECTIONS PB........$12.95

Mulk Raj **Anand**

Along with R.K. Narayan, Anand is one of India's best-known novelists. His most successful novels, like Untouchable *and* The Sword and the Sickle, *often reveal his strong commitment to socialist values.*

Across the Black Waters
0-86578-081-1 IND-US PB........$5.95

Apology for Heroism
0-86578-074-9 IND-US PB........$3.60

The Barber's Trade Union & Stories
0-86578-145-1 IND-US PB........$3.00

The Big Heart
0-86578-144-3 IND-US PB........$3.95

Confession of a Lover
0-86578-073-0 IND-US PB........$5.75

Coolie
The adventures of a young boy forced to leave his village
0-14-018680-8 PENGUIN PB........$10.95

Morning Face
0-86578-062-5 IND-US PB........$5.75

Seven Summers
0-88253-124-7 IND-US PB........$3.00

Untouchable
This exposure of the horrors of the caste system was Anand's most famous work
0-14-018395-7 PENGUIN PB........$9.95

Mulk Raj **Anand** & S. Balu **Rao**

Panorama: An Anthology of Modern Indian Short Stories
81-207-0611-0 STOSIUS/ADVENT........$27.50

Aditya **Behl** & David **Nicholls**, editors

The Penguin Book of New Writing in India
0-14-023340-7 PENGUIN PB........$11.95

Anita **Desai**

Baumgartner's Bombay
The compelling story of a German Jew who flees the Holocaust and finds refuge in India
0-14-013176-0 PENGUIN PB........$9.00

Clear Light of Day
"A wonderful novel about silence and music, about the partition of a family as well as a nation"—*The NY Times*
See also **THE MIDDLE GENERATION** under **20TH-CENTURY BRITISH AND IRISH FICTION** in **LITERATURE OF THE BRITISH ISLES**
0-14-010859-9 PENGUIN PB........$10.95

Anita Desai

Fire on the Mountain
0-8364-1455-1 SOUTH ASIA........$7.50

Games at Twilight
Set in Bombay and other cities, these short stories are peopled with intensely individual characters
0-14-011907-8 PENGUIN PB........$9.95

In Custody
A lecturer in a small northern town is unexpectedly asked to interview India's greatest living poet. "She tells a touching and moral story supremely well"—*Guardian*
0-14-023932-4 PENGUIN PB........$9.95

Journey to Ithaca
Three superbly realized characters during the '70s flight of young Europeans to India take us through a world of swamis, gurus, ashrams, and holy women
0-679-43900-5 KNOPF........$23.00
0-14-025818-3 PENGUIN PB........$12.95

Voices in the City
0-88253-250-2 IND-US PB........$7.95

Where Shall We Go This Summer?
0-86578-125-7 IND-US PB........$8.95

G.V. **Desani**

All About H. Hatterr
This brilliant novel, highly praised by T.S. Eliot when it was first published, is one of the neglected treasures of 20th-century literature
0-914232-79-7 MCPHERSON........$20.00
0-914232-78-9 MCPHERSON PB........$12.00

Hali and Collected Stories
Stories, sacred and profane
0-929701-12-7 MCPHERSON........$20.00

Vinay **Dharwadker** & A.K. **Ramanujan**, editors

The Oxford Anthology of Modern Indian Poetry
0-19-562865-9 OXFORD........$18.95

Faiz Ahmed **Faiz**

The Rebel's Silhouette: Selected Poems
Well-informed, though free, translations of an excellent selection
TRANSLATED BY AGHA SHAHID ALI
0-87023-975-9 MASSACHUSETTS PB........$14.95

The True Subject: Selected Poems
Superb translations of the greatest Urdu poet of the 20th century
TRANSLATED BY NAOMI LAZARD
0-691-06704-X PRINCETON........$35.00
0-691-01438-8 PRINCETON PB........$13.95

Amitav **Ghosh**

The Circle of Reason
0-670-80984-5 VIKING........$17.95

In an Antique Land
A vivid account of ancient and modern Egypt, in which the author-historian uncovers the life of a slave who lived 800 years ago. Combining history with cultural investigation, travel writing with storytelling, Ghosh explains the strange and intense relationship that developed across centuries between his subject and himself
See also **EGYPT** under **THE CONTEMPORARY MIDDLE EAST** in **WORLD HISTORY AND CURRENT AFFAIRS**
0-679-72783-3 VINTAGE PB........$13.00

By the time the trading nations of the Indian Ocean began to realize that their old understandings had been rendered defunct by the Europeans it was already too late. In 1509 AD the fate of that ancient trading culture was sealed in a naval engagement that was sadly, perhaps pathetically, evocative of its ethos: a transcontinental fleet, hastily put together by the Muslim potentate of Gujarat, the Hindu ruler of Calicut, and the Sultan of Egypt was attached and defeated by a Portuguese force off the shores of Diu, in Gujarat. As always, the determination of a small, united band of soldiers triumphed easily over the rich confusions that accompany a culture of accommodation and compromise.
IN AN ANTIQUE LAND

The Shadow Lines
With subtly crisscrossing lines of narration, Ghosh examines the lives of two families, one Indian, one English, and how they interconnect over three generations in both Calcutta and London against a background of war and political violence. The remarkably sustained tone—conversational and attentive to the minutest surfaces—distills a cumulative sense of the patterns of family life. "Ghosh has found his own distinctive voice—polished and profound...His work, like that of Chekhov, allows the flow of life to follow its own form in art"—*TLS*
0-02-516001-X SOUTH ASIA PB........$17.95

Romesh **Gunesekera**

Monkfish Moon
Nine graceful stories that take place in the luxuriant, tropical environment of Sri Lanka, suddenly disoriented by violence and civil war. "The delicate firmness with which Gunesekera portrays the dilemmas of living in a spoiled

paradise gives this collection a haunting, eye-opening quality"—*London Observer*
See also **THE MIDDLE GENERATION** under **20TH-CENTURY BRITISH AND IRISH FICTION** in **LITERATURE OF THE BRITISH ISLES**
1-56584-077-1 NEW PRESS $16.95
1-57322-550-9 RIVERHEAD PB $11.00

Reef
1-56584-219-7 NEW PRESS $20.00
1-57322-533-9 RIVERHEAD PB $10.00

Ruth Prawer **Jhabvala**

Heat and Dust
The best-known work of this expatriate writer was awarded the Booker Prize in 1975
See also **THE MIDDLE GENERATION** under **20TH-CENTURY BRITISH AND IRISH FICTION** in **LITERATURE OF THE BRITISH ISLES**
0-8446-6335-2 SMITH $22.00
0-671-64657-5 SIMON & SCHUSTER PB $11.00

The Householder
A young teacher in New Delhi has just become a householder and is finding his responsibilities perplexing. "The detail of Prem's daily round, school and domestic, is beautifully done" —*New Statesman*
0-393-00851-7 NORTON PB $8.95

Poet and Dancer
The author of *Heat and Dust* and of the screenplay for *Howard's End, The Europeans,* and other Merchant-Ivory productions dissects the relationship between two unusual cousins who remain psychologically entwined for life after an early sexual encounter. "A masterful portrait of good people trying to do all right and the bad ones that pull them down and win, from a writer of remarkably acute sensitivity and perception"—*Kirkus Reviews*
0-385-46869-5 DOUBLEDAY $19.95
0-385-46887-3 ANCHOR PB $9.00

Jayanta **Mahapatra**

Selected Poems
0-19-562051-8 OXFORD PB $8.95

Saadat Hasan **Manto**
Manto is the most celebrated practitioner of the Chekhovian realism that characterizes short fiction in Urdu.

Kingdom's End and Other Stories
TRANSLATED BY KHALID HASAN
0-14-011774-1 PENGUIN PB $7.95

Ameena **Meer**

Bombay Talkie
The world of Bombay movie stars, in a novel that moves from India to London and New York. "While the story concludes tragically, it still leaves you breathless with laughter"—*Paper*
1-85242-325-0 SERPENT'S TAIL PB $12.99

Gita **Mehta**

Raj
See also **NEW WRITERS OF THE '90S** under **20TH-CENTURY AMERICAN FICTION** in **LITERATURE OF THE AMERICAS**
0-449-90566-7 FAWCETT PB $12.50

A River Sutra
A bureaucrat retires to India's holiest river in search of tranquility, only to encounter a teacher who confesses to murder, a girl fleeing her kidnapper, and a naked ascetic who teaches him that "a man who cannot suffer is not alive"
0-385-47007-X DOUBLEDAY $20.00
0-679-75247-1 VINTAGE PB $12.00

Ved **Mehta**

The Ledge Between the Streams
0-393-01828-8 NORTON $17.50

Sound-Shadows of the New World
"As a record of self-reliance and tenacity *Sound-Shadows* is extraordinarily moving; but as an account of one boy's ambition, it is equally remarkable"—Peter Ackroyd
0-393-30437-X NORTON PB $8.95

Vedi
"His objective world is intensely remote from ours, but his inner world…is as close as art can make it. His is obviously a singular life…I urge you to catch up with it"—Clark Blaise, *NY Times*
0-393-30417-5 NORTON PB $7.95

Rohinton **Mistry**

A Fine Balance
The second novel by this elegant writer has augmented his already high reputation
0-679-44608-7 KNOPF $26.00
0-679-77645-1 VINTAGE $14.00

Such a Long Journey
0-679-73871-1 VINTAGE PB $14.00

Swimming Lessons
Short stories mainly set in a Parsi neighborhood in Bombay
0-679-77632-X VINTAGE $25.00

Bharati **Mukherjee**
Writing on the immigrant experience with wit and sensitivity, Mukherjee delineates a class of imperfectly assimilated Indians who never quite manage to break ties with their homeland.

Darkness
"Bharati Mukherjee's stories of contemporary Indian inmmigrants painfully recreating their lives and selves on this continent are astounding and simply brilliant"—Lynne Sharon Schwartz
0-449-22099-0 CREST PB $5.99

The Holder of the World
When a New England woman discovers the record of a remote ancestor who in the late 17th century traveled to India, she begins a journey through "the barriers of time and geography" toward a powerful collision of cultures, past and present, history and imagination
See also **SINCE 1945** under **20TH-CENTURY AMERICAN FICTION** in **LITERATURE OF THE AMERICAS**
0-394-58846-0 KNOPF $22.00
0-449-90966-2 FAWCETT PB $12.00

Jasmine
The critic Jonathan Raban has called Bharati Mukherjee's work "a romance with America itself, its infinitely possible geography, its license, sexiness, and violence." In this new novel, the appealing Indian-born heroine transforms herself from Jasmine to Jane Ripplemeyer, and explores American life at its fullest
0-449-21923-2 CREST PB $5.99

The Middlemen & Other Stories
0-449-21718-3 CREST PB $5.99

The Tiger's Daughter
0-449-22100-8 FAWCETT PB $5.99

Wife
0-449-22098-2 CREST PB $5.99

R.K. **Narayan**
Many of Narayan's novels center around Malgudi, a sleepy South Indian town of his own creation. Its inhabitants—civil servants, merchants, artisans—are excellent fodder for rich social satire. Narayan's prose, simple but elegant, describes an unchanging India reluctantly being dragged into the 20th century.

An Astrologer's Day & Other Stories
0-88253-105-0 IND-US PB $4.95

The Bachelor of Arts
A youth is caught between his Western education and the traditional values of the Hindu Orthodoxy
INTRODUCTION BY GRAHAM GREENE
0-226-56833-4 CHICAGO PB $10.95

The Dark Room
A woman tries to leave her abusive husband
0-226-56837-7 CHICAGO PB $10.95

The English Teacher
The hero receives supernatural visitations from his dead wife
0-226-56835-0 CHICAGO PB $11.95

The Financial Expert
0-226-56841-5 CHICAGO PB $11.95

The Guide
A peasant mistakes Raju, one of India's most corrupt tourist guides, for a holy man. "The best of R.K. Narayan's enchanting novels" —*New Yorker*
0-14-018547-X PENGUIN PB $11.95

Malgudi Days
A collection of short stories
0-14-018543-7 PENGUIN PB $10.95

The Printer of Malgudi
0-87013-025-0 MICHIGAN STATE $6.00

Talkative Man
Bizarre happenings at Malgudi are heralded by the arrival of a stranger on the Delhi train. "His lean, matter-of-fact prose has lost none of its chuckling sparkle mixed with melancholy" —*Spectator*
0-14-018546-1 PENGUIN PB $9.95

A Tiger for Malgudi
0-14-018545-3 PENGUIN PB $8.95

Under the Banyan Tree & Other Stories
0-14-018544-5 VIKING PB $8.95

The Vendor of Sweets
Jagan's patience begins to fray when his son descends on the sleepy town of Malgudi full of modern notions
0-14-018550-X PENGUIN PB $10.95

Waiting for the Mahatma

0-226-56826-1 CHICAGO $18.00
0-226-56828-8 CHICAGO PB $12.95

Taslima **Nasrin**

The Game in Reverse

Poems by a writer who was forced to leave Bangladesh after she came under fierce attack by Islamic fundamentalists for her defense of women's rights

TRANSLATED BY CAROLYNE WRIGHT

0-8076-1392-4 BRAZILLER PB $11.95

A. K. **Ramanujan**

The Collected Poems of A. K. Ramanujan

0-19-563561-2 OXFORD $25.00

Raja **Rao**

Kanthapura

The story of the impact of Gandhi's ideas on a village on the tea-growing Malabar coast

0-8112-0168-6 NEW DIRECTIONS PB $10.95

Satyajit **Ray**

Phatik Chand

TRANSLATED BY LILA RAY

0-86578-230-X IND-US PB $6.00

Salman **Rushdie**

East, West: Stories

"Poignant and intimate, boisterously inventive, and gently provocative"
—*NY Times Book Review*

See also **THE MIDDLE GENERATION** under **20TH-CENTURY BRITISH AND IRISH FICTION** in **LITERATURE OF THE BRITISH ISLES**

0-679-75789-9 VINTAGE PB $11.00

Haroun and the Sea of Stories

"Salman Rushdie has in his own veins the flow of the Sea of Stories, fantastical, funny, whooping through drama and comedy, good and evil, personified in creatures delightful or frightening"—Nadine Gordimer

See also **SUGGESTED READ ALOUDS** in **BOOKS FOR YOUNG READERS**

0-14-015737-9 PENGUIN PB $11.95

Imaginary Homelands: Essays, Criticism, 1981-1991

Intense and elegant essays. "How literature of the highest order can serve the interests of our common humanity is freshly illustrated here"
—Michael Foot, *The London Observer*

See also **20TH-CENTURY BRITISH ESSAYS AND OTHER PROSE** in **LITERATURE OF THE BRITISH ISLES**

0-14-014036-0 PENGUIN PB $13.95

It may be that writers in my position, exiles or emigrants or expatriates, are haunted by some sense of loss, some urge to reclaim, to look back, even at the risk of being mutated into pillars of salt. But if we do look back, we must also do so in the knowledge—which gives rise to profound uncertainties—that our physical alienation from India almost inevitably means that we will not be capable of reclaiming precisely the thing that was lost; that we will, in short, create fictions, not actual cities or villages, but invisible ones, imaginary homelands, Indias of the mind.

IMAGINARY HOMELANDS: ESSAYS, CRITICISM 1981-1991

The Jaguar Smile: A Nicaraguan Journey

Vivid literary journalism and "the view from underneath" based on a three-week trip in 1986 by the renowned Anglo-Indian author

See also **CENTRAL AMERICA** under **THE CARIBBEAN AND CENTRAL AMERICA** under **TRAVEL LITERATURE** in **FOOD, TRAVEL, AND LEISURE**

0-670-81757-0 VIKING $12.95

Midnight's Children

A fantastic epic of Indian independence and its aftermath. "Dense with passion, intelligence, excitement, and every vocal and literary effect conceivable"—Margo Jefferson, *Village Voice*

0-679-44462-9 KNOPF $20.00
0-14-013270-8 PENGUIN PB $14.95

The Moor's Last Sigh

0-679-74466-5 VINTAGE PB $13.00

Salman Rushdie

The Satanic Verses

"What is being expressed is a discomfort with plural identity...We are increasingly becoming a world of migrants, made up of bits and fragments from here, there. We are here. And we have never really left anywhere we have been"
—Salman Rushdie

0-670-82537-9 VIKING $19.95
0-9632707-0-2 CONSORTIUM PB $14.00

The Wizard of Oz

See also **BFI FILM CLASSICS** under **FILM** in **PERFORMING ARTS AND MEDIA**

0-85170-300-3 BRITISH FILM INST PB $9.95

Nayantara **Sahgal**

Mistaken Identity

"Many levels of meaning are unfolded—not least the questionable role of the Rajas; through it all, Sahgal sustains the note of suspense while cleverly suggesting the contrast between cultural synthesis and the divide-and-rule of recent, fractured times"—*TLS*

0-8112-1093-6 NEW DIRECTIONS $16.95
0-8112-1207-6 NEW DIRECTIONS PB $10.95

Rich Like Us

0-8112-1078-2 NEW DIRECTIONS PB $8.95

Vikram **Seth**

The Golden Gate

A deftly executed verse novel about contemporary Californians taking its inspiration from Byron and Pushkin

0-679-73457-0 VINTAGE PB $13.00

Love and Longing in Bombay

0-316-13307-8 LITTLE, BROWN $21.95

A Suitable Boy

A quest of a widowed mother to find a proper match for her youngest daughter. "In the tradition of the 19th century's monumental European novels, this worthy successor sprawls with events and characters, unrolls at a stately pace and takes the pulse of every nuance of emotional life"—*The Observer* [London]

0-06-017012-3 HARPERPERENNIAL PB $30.00

Khushwant **Singh**

Train to Pakistan

A novel that examines the effects of partition on a small Punjabi village. A classic in the literature

0-8021-3221-9 GROVE PB $8.95

Sara **Suleri**

Meatless Days

An odd, sensual, unsettling memoir of living in the shadow of British colonialism by the daughter of a prominent Pakistani polemicist

See also **COLONIALISM** under **SPECIALIZED STUDIES** under **ANTHROPOLOGY** in **SOCIAL STUDIES**

0-226-77980-7 CHICAGO $21.95
0-226-77981-5 CHICAGO PB $11.95

Rabindranath **Tagore**

Gitanjali: A Collection of Prose Translations Made by the Author from the Original Bengali

Tagore's beautiful English translations of his own poems, with an introduction by W.B. Yeats

INTRODUCTION BY W.B. YEATS

0-02-089630-1 MACMILLAN PB $5.95

Gora

A great novel

0-318-36928-1 ASIA BOOK CORPORATION PB $9.50

The Home and the World

0-14-018187-3 PENGUIN PB $10.95

I Won't Let You Go: Selected Poems

These are the only English versions of Tagore's poetry that give some hint of why he is so loved in Bengal

TRANSLATED BY KETAKI KUSHARI DYSON

81-85944-17-2 SOUTH ASIA PB $10.00

Quartet

0-435-95086-X HEINEMANN PB $9.95

Selected Poems

EDITED BY WILLIAM RADICE

0-14-018366-3 PENGUIN PB $10.95

Shashi **Tharoor**

The Five Dollar Smile and Other Stories

1-55970-225-7 ARCADE $18.95

The Great Indian Novel
Tharoor rewrites India's great poetic epic *The Mahabharata* as a satirical account of modern Indian history. "A tour-de-force of considerable brilliance"—*VLS*
1-55970-116-1 ARCADE $19.95

Show Business
A splendid satirical view of India through the ails of "Bollywood"—the Bombay center of the Hindi movie industry
1-55970-181-1 ARCADE $19.95

Mahadevi **Varma**
Sketches from My Past: Encounters with India's Oppressed
TRANSLATED BY NEERA K. SAHANI
1-55553-198-9 NORTHEASTERN $21.95

Nirmal **Verma**
The World Elsewhere
Stories by a leading Hindi writer
0-930523-46-6 READERS INTERNATIONAL $16.95

Critical Studies

J.L. **Brockington**
Righteous Rama: The Evolution of an Epic
An engrossing study of the smaller of the two Indian epic poems
0-19-561710-X OXFORD $36.00

Edward **Dimock**, Jr.
The Place of the Hidden Moon: Erotic Mysticism in the Vaisnava-Sahajiya Cult of Bengal
With a new foreword by Wendy Doniger O'Flaherty
0-226-15237-5 CHICAGO PB $18.00

The Sound of Silent Guns & Other Essays
0-19-562308-8 OXFORD $19.95

Kali for Women, editors
The Slate of Life: More Contemporary Stories by Women Writers of India
"Dense with...customs, manners, and objects" —*NY Review of Books*
1-55861-088-X FEMINIST PRESS PB $12.95

Richard **Lannoy**
The Speaking Tree: A Study of Indian Culture and Society
A highly praised work of cultural criticism
0-19-519754-2 OXFORD PB $14.95

Barbara Stoler **Miller**
The Powers of Art: Patronage in Indian Culture
See also **INDIA** under **EAST ASIAN ART** in **ART**
0-19-562842-X OXFORD $16.95

Meenakshi **Mukherjee**
Realism and Reality: The Novel and Society in India
A discussion of the uses to which the novel, an imported art form, has been put in modern India
0-19-561648-0 OXFORD PB $11.95

Frances **Pritchett**
Nets of Awareness: Urdu Poetry and Its Critics
0-520-08386-5 CALIFORNIA PB $17.00

David **Rubin**
After the Raj: British Novels of India Since 1947
A discussion of current fictional attitudes to India. The sections on Paul Scott and Ruth Prawer Jhabvala are particularly illuminating
0-87451-383-9 NEW ENGLAND $25.00

Lee **Siegel**
Fires of Love, Waters of Peace
An excellent introduction to the themes and archetypes of Indian civilization
0-8248-0828-2 HAWAII $12.50

Rashna **Singh**
The Imperishable Empire: A Study of British Fiction on India
A reliable guide to a subject that extends well beyond Forster and Kipling
0-89410-342-3 THREE CONTINENTS $28.00

Sara **Suleri**
The Rhetoric of English India
0-226-77983-1 CHICAGO PB $12.95

Andrew **Robinson** & Krishna **Dutta**
Rabindranath Tagore: The Myriad-Minded Way
These biographers attempt to give Western readers a context for Tagore's work that is broader than the rather shallow celebrity he briefly enjoyed with Yeats, Pound, and others
0-312-14030-4 ST. MARTIN'S $35.00

Heinrich **Zimmer**
Myths and Symbols in Indian Art and Civilization
See also **INDIAN** under **THE NON-WESTERN WORLD** under **MYTHOLOGY AND FOLKLORE** in **RELIGION, SPIRITUALITY, AND PHILOSOPHY**
0-691-01778-6 PRINCETON PB $10.95

Classical Chinese Literature

China has one of the world's oldest continuous literary traditions, going back more than 3000 years. Poetry and historical writing have traditionally been its most esteemed genres. The Chinese poetic voice has made use of certain recurrent themes: the beauty of nature, political and social strife, the joys of wine and friendship, the grief of separation and war. Written predominantly by scholar-officials educated in the classics and the intricacies of the literary language, Chinese poetry has also been composed by Buddhist monks, emperors, and dancing girls.

Drama and fiction, which originated with traveling performers, developed comparatively late and was created by storytellers writing in both the literary and vernacular languages. Chinese drama developed a variety of forms, from dramatic romances and detective stories to the stylized Peking opera. The works of the professional storytellers grew in sophistication, culminating in novels of great complexity and length, such as *The Dream of the Red Chamber* (or *The Story of the Stone*), first published in 1792.

Traditionally, Chinese surnames are given first. In the case of long known figures the names appear in the traditional order, otherwise the surname appears in bold type. Chinese names and titles (except for some modern works) are give in Wade-Giles Romanization.

General Anthologies

Cyril **Birch**, editor
Anthology of Chinese Literature
An excellent introduction encompassing poetry, prose, and drama, with brief prefaces placing the selections in their historical context. The translations have been chosen with care, and many were commissioned especially for this collection. "It is a remarkable Chinese banquet indeed—drinking poems and didactic biographies, cynical love stories and operatic plays, philosophical letters and lyrical religious tracts—it is all a delight"—*New Yorker*

Volume 1
From Early Times to the 14th Century
0-8021-5038-1 GROVE PB $15.95

Volume 2
From the 14th Century to the Present
0-8021-5090-X GROVE PB $14.95

William T. **De Bary**, editor
Sources of Chinese Tradition
This invaluable survey of Chinese intellectual history is a collection of translated sources with introductions

Volume 1
See also **THE CHINESE TRADITIONS** under **ASIAN RELIGION AND PHILOSOPHY** in **RELIGION, SPIRITUALITY, AND PHILOSOPHY**
0-231-08602-4 COLUMBIA PB $19.50

Volume 2
See also **THE CHINESE TRADITIONS** under **ASIAN RELIGION AND PHILOSOPHY** in **RELIGION, SPIRITUALITY, AND PHILOSOPHY**
0-231-08603-2 COLUMBIA PB $17.00

Victor H. **Mair**, editor
The Columbia Anthology of Traditional Chinese Literature
0-231-07428-X COLUMBIA $65.00
0-231-07429-8 COLUMBIA PB $30.00

Stephen **Owen**, editor
An Anthology of Chinese Literature: Beginnings to 1911
0-393-03823-8 NORTON $39.95

Eliot **Weinberger** & Octavio **Paz**
Nineteen Ways of Looking at Wang Wei
Weinberger's remarkable comparison of 19 translations of a single poem by the T'ang dynasty poet, with further commentary by Paz
See also **T'ANG POETRY** under **CRITICAL STUDIES OF CLASSICAL CHINESE LITERATURE**
0-918825-14-8 MOYER BELL PB $6.95

Poetry

Poetry has generally been regarded as the glory of the Chinese literary tradition, and certain characteristics make it particularly accessible to non-Chinese readers. The intensely concrete and visual qualities of classical poetry have had wide appeal for 20th-century poets and translators, whose versions have greatly influenced modern poetry in the West.

Chinese poetry is primarily lyrical rather than narrative or dramatic. It generally avoids abstraction and seeks to be concise and suggestive rather than expansive and descriptive.

David **Lattimore**, translator
The Harmony of the World: Chinese Poems
A small volume with an interesting essay on translation
0-914278-31-2 COPPER BEECH PB $4.50

Wu-Chi **Liu** & Irving Yucheng **Lo**, editors
Sunflower Splendor
The most comprehensive single-volume anthology in English, containing some 1000 poems. It includes introductions, biographies of the poets, and bibliographies
0-253-20607-3 INDIANA PB $19.95

Kenneth **Rexroth**, translator
One Hundred Poems from the Chinese
Rexroth's translations are loose but they are memorable American poetry in themselves
0-8112-0180-5 NEW DIRECTIONS PB $8.95

100 More Poems from the Chinese: Love and the Turning Year
0-8112-0179-1 NEW DIRECTIONS PB $9.95

Kenneth **Rexroth** & **Ling Chun**, translators
Women Poets of China
Focuses on a neglected area; the translations are not always reliable
0-8112-0821-4 NEW DIRECTIONS PB $8.95

P. **Seaton** & Dennis **Maloney**, editors
A Drifting Boat: An Anthology of Chinese Zen Poetry
Covers over 1500 years of Zen-inspired poetry, including translations by Seaton, Sam Hamill, and many others
1-87772-737-7 WHITE PINE PB $15.00

Lucien **Stryk**, editor & Takashi **Ikemoto**, translator
The Penguin Book of Zen Poetry
Includes both Chinese and Japanese poets
See also **POETRY** under **THE MIDDLE PERIOD (1200-1600)** under **JAPANESE LITERATURE**
0-14-058599-0 PENGUIN PB $10.95

Burton **Watson**, translator & editor
The Columbia Book of Chinese Poetry: From Early Times to the 13th Century
A comprehensive anthology by a pre-eminent scholar and translator
0-231-05683-4 COLUMBIA PB $19.50

Early Chinese Poetry

Several poetic genres were practiced in the Han dynasty (202 BC-AD 220). *Fu*, or rhyme-prose, is characterized by long descriptive poetic passages occasionally interspersed with prose. It was used especially to describe palaces, cities, and imperial hunts. *Shih*, or lyrical poetry, developed the major formal characteristics found in later poetry.

David **Hawkes**, translator
The Songs of the South: An Ancient Chinese Anthology of Poems
The second collection of Chinese poetry, very different from *The Book of Songs*. There is much controversy on the attribution of poems to the statesman Ch'u Yuan. The ostensibly autobiographical poem "Li Sao" (On Encountering Sorrow) is at once a political allegory and a quasi-shamanistic account of a spiritual quest, laden with exotic imagery and empassioned language
0-14-044375-4 PENGUIN PB $11.95

Ezra **Pound**
The Classic Anthology Defined by Confucius
Pound's version of the *Shih-ching* gave him the opportunity for some of his most purely musical writing
See also **THE MODERNIST GENERATIONS** under **20TH-CENTURY AMERICAN POETRY** in **LITERATURE OF THE AMERICAS**
0-674-13397-8 HARVARD PB $7.95

T'ao Ch'ien
The Selected Poems of T'ao Ch'ien
The philosophical nature poems of T'ao Ch'ien have profoundly influenced all subsequent Chinese poetry. "David Hinton is one of the most impressive of the younger translators of classical Chinese poetry"—Burton Watson
TRANSLATED BY DAVID HINTON
1-55659-056-3 COPPER CANYON PB $11.00

Arthur **Waley**, translator
The Book of Songs
The *Book of Songs*, compiled in the 7th century BCE, is the oldest collection of Chinese poetry and one of the Five Classics. It includes folk songs, court songs, and sacrificial songs. Its simple style (four-character meter) and sincere emotional expressiveness greatly influenced later poetry
0-8021-3021-6 GROVE PB $11.95

Yu Hsin
The Lament for the South: Yu Hsin's Ai Chiang Nan Fu
Yu Hsin was a preeminent Six Dynasties (220-581) literary figure whose work describes his elegant life and the events of the time
TRANSLATED BY WILLIAM GRAHAM
0-521-22713-5 CAMBRIDGE $69.95

T'ang Dynasty

Of the T'ang era, traditionally regarded as the most glorious period of Chinese poetry, Cyril Birch has written: "A renaissance was ushered in whose equation with the Italian would not be too misleading. Even the old rites of artificiality were turned to good account in the supreme artistry now sought and attained by the poets."

A.C. **Graham**, translator
Poems of the Late T'ang
Graham's fine translations of poetry and essays on poetry by some of the major figures — including Tu Fu, Wang Wei, Li Ho, and Li Shang-Yin—offer the best introduction to the subject
0-14-044157-3 PENGUIN PB $8.95

Poetry presents the thing in order to convey the feeling. It should be precise about the thing and reticent about the feeling, for as soon as the mind responds and connects with the thing the feeling shows in the words; this is how poetry enters deeply into us. If the Poet presents directly feelings which overwhelm him, and keeps nothing back to linger as an aftertaste, he stirs us superficially; he cannot start the hands and feet involuntarily waving and tapping in time, far less strengthen morality and refine culture, set heaven and earth in motion and call up the spirits!—*Wei T'ai* (11th century)
POEMS OF THE LATE T'ANG

Li Po
Selected Poems
TRANSLATED BY DAVID HINTON
0-8112-1323-4 NEW DIRECTIONS PB $11.95

Li Po & Tu Fu
Li Po & Tu Fu
An introduction to China's two most celebrated poets. Li Po is admired for his simple, direct style and spontaneous compositions on nature. Of Tu Fu, Burton Watson has written: "Tu Fu's originality is evident not only in the way he handled poetic form, but in his wide choice of subject matter…[He] worked to broaden the definition of poetry by demonstrating that no subject, if properly handled, need be unpoetic"
TRANSLATED BY ARTHUR COOPER
0-14-044272-3 PENGUIN PB $8.95

Wang Wei
Laughing Lost in the Mountains: Poems of Wang Wei
TRANSLATED BY TONY BARNSTONE
0-87451-563-7 NEW ENGLAND $30.00

Han Shan

Cold Mountain: 100 Poems by the T'ang Poet Han Shan

Nothing is known of the Buddhist recluse Han Shan beyond what we can learn from these vivid poems of spiritual pilgrimage

TRANSLATED BY BURTON WATSON

0-231-03450-4 COLUMBIA PB $13.00

Tu Fu

The Selected Poems of Tu Fu

"Written largely in poverty and at a time of great political upheaval, Tu Fu's work shows above all its author's persistent humility and humanity"
—*American Poetry Review*

TRANSLATED BY DAVID HINTON

0-8112-1100-2 NEW DIRECTIONS PB $10.95

Sung Dynasty

The 10th century saw the full development of a new verse form, the *tz'u*, lyrics written to pre-established musical melodies. Often concerned with love and separation, these lyrics are characterized by delicacy of sentiment, sensuous imagery, and elegant diction.

Fan Ch'eng-Ta

Five Seasons of a Golden Year: A Chinese Pastoral

A series of 60 poems depicting the seasons; with original Chinese text

TRANSLATED BY GERALD BULLETT

0-295-95834-0 CHINESE UNIVERSITY $14.50

Lois **Fusek**, translator

Among the Flowers: A Translation of the 10th-Century Anthology of Tz'u Lyrics, the Hua-Chien Chi

A major Five Dynasties anthology gracefully and accurately translated

0-231-04986-2 COLUMBIA $50.00
0-231-04987-0 COLUMBIA PB $17.50

Li Ching-Chao

The Complete Poems

Considered China's most accomplished woman poet. Poetically exciting although not always trustworthy translations

TRANSLATED BY KENNETH REXROTH & LING CHUNG

0-8112-0745-5 NEW DIRECTIONS PB $7.95

Ou-Yang Hsiu

Love and Time: Poems of Ou-Yang Hsiu

"He was an idealist; he was a pragmatist; pioneering epigraphist and major historian; lover of women, lover of wine. He was friend to many men, patron to the finest literary minds of his time; masterful and innovative poet, and founder of a school of prose writing...which was to remain the dominant form of expression from his own eleventh into the present century"
—from the translator's introduction

EDITED AND TRANSLATED BY J.P. SEATON

1-55659-024-5 COPPER CANYON PB $9.00

Su Tung-P'o

Selected Poems of Su Tung-P'o

Watson's superb translations of the greatest poet of the Sung dynasty won the 1995 PEN translation award. "Commemorating the ordinary—family difficulty, neighborhood tragedy, personal insecurity, or seasonal beauty—Su Tung-P'o voices perennial human concerns"—*Parabola*

TRANSLATED BY BURTON WATSON

1-55659-064-4 COPPER CANYON PB $12.00

Later Poetry

Jonathan **Chaves**, translator & editor

The Columbia Book of Later Chinese Poetry: Yuan, Ming, and Ch'ing Dynasties (1279-1911)

A companion to the Watson anthology by an excellent translator who has championed the lesser-known later periods of Chinese poetry

0-231-06149-8 COLUMBIA PB $21.50

J. I. **Crump**

Songs from Xanadu: Studies in Mongol Dynasty Song-Poetry (san-ch'u)

The Yuan dynasty (1260-1368), the period of Mongol rule in China, saw the emergence of a new form of lyric, the *san-ch'u*, which explored new colloquial areas of language and developed new narrative and descriptive techniques

0-89264-047-2 MICHIGAN PB $15.00

Irving Yucheng **Lo** &
William **Schultz**, editors

Waiting for The Unicorn: Poems and Lyrics of China's Dynasty, 1644-1911

Poems of the Ch'ing; Lo coedited *Sunflower Splendor*

0-253-36321-7 INDIANA $37.95

J.P. **Seaton**, translator

The Wine of Endless Life: Taoist Drinking Songs

The third printing of a unique collection of 13th- and 14th-century Chinese poems. "The poems...are imbued with a warm, disarming humor, with a deep sense of understanding and human feeling"—William Schultz

0-934834-59-8 WHITE PINE PB $9.00

Yuan Hung-Tao

Pilgrim of the Clouds: Poems and Essays from Ming China by Yuan Hung-Tao and His Brothers

Yuan and his brothers were leaders of the individualistic school that flourished in the Ming

TRANSLATED BY JONATHAN CHAVES

0-8348-0134-5 WEATHERHILL PB $6.95

I often see strange people in the cities and regret that I know nothing about their lives. And I regret that of the strange people holed up in the forests and mountains, probable only one out of ten appears in the cities! As for the strange people recorded in the official records and unofficial books, surely they represent no more than one-tenth of those who do appear in the cities. Since these are people with no ambition to become known, and since they associate only with butchers, wine merchants, shop owners, wandering monks and beggars, how many worthy scholar-officials even get to know about them and hand down their stories? In the past, I have heard of a woman known as the Cap-wearing Immortal, and a Taoist of the Single Gourd, both living in Feng-chou. Recently, several people in the Wu-han area have been acting quite strange, and one of them seems to know a thing or two about the Tao. Yes, it appears that this is what is meant by the old saying: "Though he possesses the powers of a dragon, he remains hidden."

PILGRIM OF THE CLOUDS: POEMS AND ESSAYS FROM MING CHINA BY YUAN HUNG-TAO AND HIS BROTHERS

Drama

Chinese drama blends music, dance, song, and speech. Its first great age was the Yuan dynasty, often considered the peak of the tradition, although many individual masterpieces were written later. Chinese drama is stylized and self-consciously theatrical; its texts consist largely of arias, many of them fine poetry in their own right. The longer dramatic works that flourished in the Ming Dynasty, such as *Peach Blossom Fan* and *The Peony Pavilion*, are notable for their elaborate narrative structure.

George **Hayden**, translator

Crime and Punishment in Medieval Chinese Drama: Three Judge Pao Plays of the Yuan and Ming Dynasties

Crime and punishment was an important theme in Chinese drama. These have fascinating plots and are written in bawdy language

0-674-17608-1 HARVARD $20.00

Kao Ming

The Lute

A 14th-century play on the dilemma of filial piety. The translation and introduction are excellent

TRANSLATED BY JEAN MULLIGAN

0-231-04760-6 COLUMBIA $40.00

Kung Shang-jen

The Peach Blossom Fan

A famous story of love and political strife by an important Ch'ing playwright. Read in this superb translation, it is as absorbing as a novel. Unfortunately, this book is currently out-of-print

TRANSLATED BY S.H. CHEN, HAROLD ACTON & CYRIL BIRCH

0-520-02928-3 CALIFORNIA $50.00

Liu Jung-En, translator

Six Yuan Plays

Includes *The Orphan of Chao, Autumn in Han Palace, A Stratagem of Interlocking Rings*, and other classic 13th-century plays

0-14-044262-6 PENGUIN PB $10.95

T'ang Hsien-Tsu

The Peony Pavilion

A well-known play by the most talented Ming playwright. The story concerns the heroine's return to earth after her death

TRANSLATED BY CYRIL BIRCH

0-253-35723-3 INDIANA........$49.95

Wang Shifu

The Story of the Western Wing

A new translation of the classic drama of romantic love

EDITED AND TRANSLATED BY STEPHEN H. WEST & WILT L. IDEMA

0-520-20184-1 CALIFORNIA PB........$15.00

Fiction

Short Stories

The earliest colloquial works of fiction were the orally transmitted tales. By the Sung dynasty (960-1279), professional storytellers had become so wellestablished that they had their own union. By the Ming dynasty, the tales of the marvelous were a popular genre. The more polished later stories of Feng Meng-Lung and the great Chinese novels derive from these heroic fantastic tales told in the marketplace.

H.C. **Chang**, editor

Tales of the Supernatural

0-231-05794-6 COLUMBIA........$36.00

Feng Meng-Lung

Stories from a Ming Collection

Richly entertaining stories ranging over all the basic genres

TRANSLATED BY CYRIL BIRCH

0-8021-5031-4 GROVE PB........$10.95

Moss **Roberts**, editor

Chinese Fairy Tales and Fantasies

See also **CHINESE** under **THE NON-WESTERN WORLD** under **MYTHOLOGY AND FOLKLORE** in **RELIGION, SPIRITUALITY, AND PHILOSOPHY**

0-394-73994-9 RANDOM HOUSE PB........$14.00

Novels

David **Top Roy**, translator

The Plum in the Golden Vase, or, Chin P'ing Mei

Beautiful two-volume translation of this racy, Dickensian novel with original woodcut illustrations

See also **MEMOIRS AND JOURNALS** under **20TH-CENTURY AMERICAN ESSAYS AND JOURNALISM** in **LITERATURE OF THE AMERICAS**

TRANSLATED BY DAVID TOD ROY

0-691-06932-8 PRINCETON........$45.00

Li Yu

The Carnal Prayer Mat

"This strange and delightful book, one of the most vivid texts on the shelf of Chinese erotica, shows Chinese society in a state of undress. Patrick Hanan's translation is illuminating, fluent, and exhaustive—not only scholarly but sexy"—Paul Theroux

TRANSLATED BY PATRICK HANAN

0-8248-1798-2 HAWAII PB........$12.95

Lo Kuan-Chung

The Romance of the Three Kingdoms

The classic Chinese novel of the civil wars following the fall of the Han dynasty. Written in the 14th century, it shows the full flowering of China's storytelling tradition. A two-volume edition

0-8048-1649-2 TUTTLE PB........$39.95

Shih Nai-An & Luo Guanzhong

Outlaws of the Marsh

A modern translation, complete in four volumes, of the great saga otherwise known as *Water Margin*

TRANSLATED BY SIDNEY SHAPIRO

0-8351-2289-1 CHANG & TSUI........$29.95

Ts'ao Hsueh-Ch'in

The Story of the Stone

China's greatest novel, also known as *The Dream of the Red Chamber*, tells of the decline and disintegration of a rich, aristocratic family. It mixes sophisticated psychological analysis, a dense and robustly realistic description of social structures, and a layer of religious speculation. The Hawkes-Minford translation is itself a superbly modulated piece of English writing

TRANSLATED BY DAVID HAWKES & JOHN MINFORD

0-253-19266-8 INDIANA........$92.00

Volume 1
The Golden Days

0-14-044293-6 PENGUIN PB........$12.95

Volume 2
The Crab-Flower Club

0-14-044326-6 PENGUIN PB........$12.95

Volume 3
The Warning Voice

0-14-044370-3 PENGUIN PB........$11.95

Volume 4
The Debt of Tears

0-14-044371-1 PENGUIN PB........$10.95

Volume 5
The Dreamer Wakes

0-14-044372-X PENGUIN PB........$12.95

Robert **Van Gulik**, translator

Celebrated Cases of Judge Dee

An early Chinese crime novel, recounting the criminal cases of a T'ang judge. Van Gulik used it as the starting point for his own series of detective novels based on the same character

0-486-23337-5 DOVER PB........$6.95

Wu Ch'eng-En

Journey to the West

"Imagine a combination of picaresque novel, fairy tale, fabliau, Mickey Mouse, Davy Crockett, and *Pilgrim's Progress;* and then imagine if you can all these elements welded into an artistic whole so that no matter how fantastic the adventure or how enigmatic the allegory, the characterization and meaning remain always human and realizable" —*The Nation*

Volume 1

0-226-97145-7 CHICAGO........$45.00

Volume 2

0-226-97146-5 CHICAGO........$37.50

Volume 3

0-226-97147-3 CHICAGO........$37.50

Monkey

Abridged; a superb translation

TRANSLATED BY ARTHUR WALEY

0-8021-3086-0 GROVE PB........$10.95

Other Prose

Shih S. **Liu**, translator

Chinese Classical Prose: The Eight Masters of the T'ang-Sung Period

Essays in the classical or literary language, as distinct from the colloquial of the great fiction masterpieces

0-295-95662-3 CHINESE UNIVERSITY........$24.95

Shen Fu

Six Records of a Floating Life

A moving autobiographical account of the author's marriage

TRANSLATED BY LEONARD PRATT

0-14-044429-7 PENGUIN PB........$9.95

Critical Studies of Classical Chinese Literature

General Studies and Reference Works

Robert E. **Hegel** &
Richard C. **Hessney**, editors

Expressions of Self in Chinese Literature

0-231-05829-2 COLUMBIA PB........$19.00

James J. Y. **Liu**

Language-Paradox-Poetics: A Chinese View

See also **GENERAL STUDIES OF POETRY**

EDITED BY RICHARD JOHN LYNN

0-691-06741-4 PRINCETON........$37.50

William H. **Nienhauser**, Jr., editor

The Indiana Companion to Traditional Chinese Literature

A monumental volume, this reference work is indispensable for knowledgeable readers

0-253-32983-3 INDIANA........$95.00

Stephen **Owen**

Remembrances: The Experience of the Past in Classical Chinese Literature

0-674-76015-8 HARVARD........$24.50

Laurence A. **Schneider**

A Madman of Ch'u: The Chinese Myth of Loyalty and Dissent

0-520-03685-9 CALIFORNIA $45.00

Burton **Watson**

Early Chinese Literature

An excellent guide

0-231-02579-3 COLUMBIA $48.00
0-231-08671-7 COLUMBIA PB $17.50

General Studies of Poetry

Hans H. **Frankel**

The Flowering Plum and the Palace Lady: Interpretations of Chinese Poetry

Poems grouped by themes and styles, plus an extensive bibliography

0-300-02242-5 YALE PB $14.00

James J. Y. **Liu**

Language-Paradox-Poetics: A Chinese View

See also **GENERAL STUDIES AND REFERENCE WORKS**

EDITED BY RICHARD JOHN LYNN

0-691-06741-4 PRINCETON $37.50

Arthur **Waley**

Yuan Mei: 18th-Century Chinese Poet

A vivid picture of a celebrated Ch'ing man of letters. The text includes translations of some 100 poems, prose works, and letters

0-8047-0718-9 STANFORD $37.50

Pauline **Yu**

Reading of Imagery in the Chinese Poetic Tradition

0-691-06682-5 PRINCETON $32.50

Early Chinese Poetry

Chang Kang-I Sun

Six Dynasties Poetry

0-691-06669-8 PRINCETON $33.50

Lin Shuen-Fu & Stephen **Owen**

The Vitality of the Lyric Voice: Shih Poetry from the Late Han to the T'ang

0-691-03134-7 PRINCETON $65.00

T'ang Poetry

David **Hawkes**

A Little Primer of Tu Fu

962-7255-02-5 CHANG & TSUI PB $14.95

Edward H. **Schaefer**

The Golden Peaches of Samarkand: A Study of T'ang Exotics

Schaefer's studies on various aspects of T'ang cultural life, including many examples of poetry, are impeccable and a delight to read.

0-520-05462-8 CALIFORNIA PB $18.95

The Vermilion Bird: T'ang Images of the South

See also **GENERAL HISTORIES** under **CHINA** in **WORLD HISTORY AND CURRENT AFFAIRS**

0-520-05463-6 CALIFORNIA PB $17.00

Burton **Watson**

Chinese Lyricism: Shih Poetry from the Second to Twelfth Century

Watson traces the critical and historical development of *shih*, the main form of Chinese poetry, with some 200 poems as examples. The text and translations are both outstanding

0-231-03465-2 COLUMBIA PB $18.50

Delicate grasses, faint wind on the bank;
stark mast, a lone night boat;
stars hang down, over broad fields sweeping;
the moon boils up, on the great river flowing.
Fame—how can my writings win me that?
Office—age and sickness have brought it to an end.
Fluttering fluttering—where is my likeness?
Sky and earth and one sandy gull.
—Tu Fu

CHINESE LYRICISM: SHIH POETRY FROM THE SECOND TO TWELFTH CENTURY

Eliot **Weinberger** & Octavio **Paz**

Nineteen Ways of Looking at Wang Wei

See also **GENERAL ANTHOLOGIES**

0-918825-14-8 MOYER BELL PB $6.95

Sung Poetry

Chang Kang-I Sun

The Evolution of Chinese Tz'u Poetry: From Late T'ang to Northern Sung

A careful analysis of the *tz'u* tradition, interspersed with skillful translations

0-691-06425-3 PRINCETON $45.00

Lin Shuen-Fu

The Transformation of a Chinese Lyrical Tradition: Chiang K'uei and Southern Sung Tz'u Poetry

0-691-06351-6 PRINCETON $34.50

Drama

Colin **Mackerras**, editor

Chinese Theater: From Its Origins to the Present Day

A recommended history

0-8248-1220-4 HAWAII PB $15.00

Richard **Strassberg**

The World of K'ung Shang-Jen: A Man of Letters in Early Ch'ing China

The world of a Confucian scholar-official

See also **BIOGRAPHIES AND MEMOIRS** under **TOPICS IN IMPERIAL CIVILIZATION** under **CHINA** in **WORLD HISTORY AND CURRENT AFFAIRS**

INTRODUCTION BY CYRIL BIRCH

0-231-05530-7 COLUMBIA $59.00

Fiction

Shelley Hsueh-lun **Chang**

History and Legend: Ideas and Images in the Ming Historical Novels

0-472-10117-X MICHIGAN $37.50

The Four Masterworks of the Ming Novel: Ssu Ta Ch'i-Shu

0-691-06708-2 PRINCETON $70.00

David L. **Rolston**

How to Read the Chinese Novel

0-691-06753-8 PRINCETON $69.50

Modern Chinese Literature

By the 20th century, exposure to Western culture had introduced many new themes to Chinese literature. Spoken plays (without music) were written, and the novels of the '30s showed great sophistication. The colloquial written style replaced the traditional literary language, and literature reached large audiences.

The most drastic change in Chinese literature came about as a result of the May 4th Movement in 1919. Acceptance of the vernacular language had several consequences: a dramatic increase in literacy and a new adventurousness on the part of an intellectual class liberated from historical precedent.

Fiction 1917-1949

Fu Lin

The Sea of Regret

TRANSLATED BY PATRICK HANAN

0-8248-1666-8 HAWAII $32.00
0-8248-1709-5 HAWAII PB $15.95

Hsiao Hung

Market Street: A Chinese Woman in Harbin

Hsiao Hung is known for her vivid accounts of rural poverty and oppression

TRANSLATED BY HOWARD GOLDBLATT

0-295-96266-6 WASHINGTON $17.50

Lao She

Rickshaw

A bitter tale of social struggle; Lao She's most popular novel was an American bestseller in the '40s

TRANSLATED BY JEAN M. JAMES

08248061.66 HAWAII $12.00
0-8248-0655-7 HAWAII PB $5.95

Lu Hsun

Selected Stories of Lu Hsun

Considered one of the great modern Chinese writers, Lu Hsun is best known for his short stories and essays

TRANSLATED BY YANG HSIEN-YI & GLADYS YANG

0-393-00848-7 NORTON PB $10.95

Pa Chin

The Family

A popular novel dealing with family struggles

0-917056-40-X CHANG & TSUI PB $5.95

Wang Wen-Hsing

Family Catastrophe: A Modernist Novel

0-8248-1618-8 HAWAII $36.00
0-8248-1710-9 HAWAII PB $14.95

From 1949 to the Present

Mainland Literature Since 1949

Chinese Communist literature has been characterized by party control, socialist realism, the influence of folk literature, and the overwhelming view that literature should serve the people and the revolution. However, since 1980 there has been a loosening of control, producing a body of increasingly experimental works.

Tony **Barnstone**, editor

Out of the Howling Storm: The New Chinese Poetry

0-8195-2207-4 WESLEYAN $30.00
0-8195-1210-9 WESLEYAN PB $14.95

Bei Dao

The August Sleepwalker

Bei, China's foremost younger poet, is one of the most controversial writers to emerge from the political upheavals of recent decades

TRANSLATED BY BONNIE S. MCDOUGALL

0-8112-1132-0 NEW DIRECTIONS PB $8.95

Forms of Distance

TRANSLATED BY DAVID HINTON

0-8112-1266-1 NEW DIRECTIONS $16.95

Landscape over Zero

TRANSLATED BY DAVID HINTON & YANBING CHEN

0-8112-1334-X NEW DIRECTIONS PB $9.95

Old Snow

A bilingual edition of works written in exile by one of China's premier underground poets, a former Red Guard. Divided into three sections of poems completed in Berlin, Oslo, and Stockholm, where the poet has resided, separated from his wife and child, since he left China in 1989

0-8112-1182-7 NEW DIRECTIONS $16.95
0-8112-1183-5 NEW DIRECTIONS PB $8.95

When heavy snow revives an ancient language
maps of national territories change shape
on this continent snow shows deep concern
for a foreigner's small room
OLD SNOW

Can Xue

Dialogues in Paradise

Stories, often phantasmagorically dislocated, of life in post-Mao China. "A simplicity and directness reminiscent of the Russian novelists of the last century. Can Xue captures both the miserable hardships of rural poverty and its fleeting, unpredictable oddity—*Booklist*

0-8101-0831-3 NORTHWESTERN PB $10.95

Ch'en Jo-Hsi

The Execution of Mayor Yin & Other Stories from the Great Proletarian Cultural Revolution

These stories by a woman now living in Canada depict disillusion among peasants, students, and party members

TRANSLATED BY NANCY ING & HOWARD GOLDBLATT

0-253-20231-0 INDIANA PB $12.95

Ding Ling

I Myself Am a Woman: Selected Readings of Ding Ling

TRANSLATED BY TANI BARLOW

0-8070-6736-9 BEACON $24.95

Michael **Duke**, editor

Contemporary Chinese Literature

An anthology of post-Mao fiction and poetry

0-87332-340-8 SHARPE PB $28.95

Liu Heng

Black Snow

TRANSLATED BY HOWARD GOLDBLATT

0-8021-3389-4 GROVE PB $11.00

Lucien **Miller** & others, editors

South of the Clouds: Tales from Yunnan

0-295-97293-9 WASHINGTON $40.00

Mo Yan

The Garlic Ballads

Mo Yan is the author of four novels, dozens of novellas, and numerous short stories. He has won virtually every national literary prize and is the most highly praised Chinese writer of his generation

TRANSLATED BY HOWARD GOLDBLATT

0-14-023391-1 PENGUIN PB $11.95

Red Sorghum

"Mo Yan deserves a place in world literature" —Amy Tan

0-14-016854-0 PENGUIN PB $10.95

Nieh Hua-Ling

Literature of the Hundred Flowers

Selected literary works and political essays from the One Hundred Flowers Campaign of 1956-57

0-231-05264-2 COLUMBIA $150.00

Wang Anyi

Lapse of Time

Six stories and a novella by a leading woman writer from Shanghai

0-8351-2032-5 CHINA BOOKS PB $8.95

Yang Jiang

Six Chapters from My Life "Downunder"

A harsh depiction of reeducation during the Cultural Revolution, modeled on the classic *Six Chapters from a Floating Life*

TRANSLATED BY HOWARD GOLDBLATT

0-295-96644-0 WASHINGTON PB $9.95

Zhai Zhenhua

Red Flower of China

Born two years after the Communist Party seized power in China, Zhu Zhenhua grew up in the movement. When the Red Guards sprang to power at Mao's behest she was a young student, passionately loyal to the party. Now she recounts her days within the Red Guard, the violence of "home raids," the purging, during which time she was sent to a peasant labor camp

See also **THE CULTURAL REVOLUTION** under **THE COMMUNIST REVOLUTION** under **CHINA** in **WORLD HISTORY AND CURRENT AFFAIRS**

0-939149-83-4 SOHO $24.00
1-56947-009-X SOHO PB $13.00

Zhu Hong, translator & editor

The Chinese Western: Short Fiction from Today's China

New realistic prose about China's outlying regions. "What's interesting about these exciting Chinese westerns is the way the folk tales, myths, and traditions have remained a part of the story of the political life of all China: the Great Leap Forward, the Cultural Revolution, the end of the Gang of Four happen in the wastes of the Gobi, in the icy Western mountains"—Grace Paley

0-345-37358-8 BALLANTINE PB $4.99

Literature in Taiwan since 1949

Dominic **Cheung**, translator & editor

The Isle Full of Noises: Modern Chinese Poetry from Taiwan

0-231-06402-0 COLUMBIA $45.00

Joseph S. **Lau** & Timothy A. **Ross**, editors

Chinese Stories from Taiwan, 1960-1970

The best anthology in English features works of the second-generation writers, less nostalgic than their predecessors, focusing on city life and the conflicts between Western and Chinese values

0-231-04007-5 COLUMBIA $55.50

Lilian Lee

Farewell My Concubine

A novel of the passionate private lives of Chinese opera stars. This work by a popular Taiwanese writer became the basis for Chen Kaige's film

0-06-097644-6 HARPERCOLLINS PB $10.00

Critical Studies of Modern Chinese Literature

Marston **Anderson**

The Limits of Realism: Chinese Fiction in the Revolutionary Period

0-520-06436-4 CALIFORNIA $42.00

Merle **Goldman**

Literary Dissent in Communist China

Profiles the major revolutionary writers and discusses their conflict with the Communist party

See also **DEMOCRACY AND DISSENT** under **CHINA AFTER MAO** under **CHINA** in **WORLD HISTORY AND CURRENT AFFAIRS**

0-674-53625-8 HARVARD $25.50

Merle **Goldman**, editor

Modern Chinese Literature in the May Fourth Era

This important collection of essays is especially useful as so many English translations of the great works of this period are now out of print

0-674-57911-9 HARVARD PB $17.95

Jianying Zha

China Pop: How Soap Operas, Tabloids, and Bestsellers Are Transforming China

A unique account of how drastically Chinese popular culture has been transformed in the period since Tiananmen Square. "What *China Pop* so brilliantly chronicles is the commercialization of China's cultural world and the anxiety that change is causing in China's intellectuals"—*Christian Science Monitor*

See also **CONTEMPORARY CHINESE SOCIETY** under **CHINA** in **WORLD HISTORY AND CURRENT AFFAIRS**

1-56584-249-9 NEW PRESS $20.00

1-56584-250-2 NEW PRESS PB $12.00

George **Kao**, editor

Two Writers and the Cultural Revolution: Lao She and Chen Jo-Hsi

Translations and essays about Lao She and Chen Jo-Hsi, two important writers deeply affected by the Cultural Revolution

0-295-95747-6 WASHINGTON $25.00

Jeffrey **Kinkley**, editor

After Mao: Chinese Literature and Society, 1978-1981

0-674-00885-5 HARVARD PB $18.00

Julia C. **Lin**

Modern Chinese Poetry: An Introduction

0-295-95281-4 WASHINGTON PB $10.00

Perry **Link**

Roses and Thorns: The Second Blooming of the Hundred Flowers in Chinese Fiction, 1979-1980

0-520-04980-2 CALIFORNIA PB $15.00

William **Lyell**, Jr.

Lu Hsun's Vision of Reality

Detailed study for the general reader

0-520-02940-2 CALIFORNIA $50.00

Colin **Mackerras**

The Chinese Theatre in Modern Times: From 1840 to the Present Day

0-87023-196-0 MASSACHUSETTS $30.00

Bonnie **McDougall**, editor

Popular Chinese Literature and Performing Arts in the People's Republic of China, 1949-1979

0-520-04852-0 CALIFORNIA $60.00

James R. **Pusey**

Wu Han: Attacking the Present Through the Past

After his Peking opera *Hai Jui Dismissed from Office* was condemned during the Cultural Revolution, the playwright Wu Han committed suicide

0-674-96275-3 HARVARD PB $11.00

Ránbir **Vohra**

Lao She and the Chinese Revolution

A discussion of Lao She's major novels, placed in their social context

0-674-51075-5 HARVARD $24.00

David Der-Wei **Wang** & Jeanne **Tai**, editors

Running Wild: New Chinese Writers

0-231-09649-6 COLUMBIA PB $16.00

Japanese Literature

Japanese literature dates from AD 712, when the *Kojiki (Record of Ancient Matters)*, a semi-mythological account of the nation's history, was compiled. Since then Japanese writers have created a rich and increasingly varied tradition of poems, stories, diaries, novels, and dramas. By comparison with other non- Western literatures, a large proportion of this work is available in English.

When Japan ended its isolation in the 19th century, a small band of Western scholars began to explore the byways of Japanese literature. Their perspective was often limited, however, by preconceptions and insufficient knowledge. Since World War II, Japanese studies in English have taken a more systematic turn, largely under the influence of Donald Keene, who remains the outstanding historian and popularizer in the field. Increasingly, translators seem more willing to take Japanese writers on their own terms rather than attempting to fit them into Western aesthetic schemes.

General Anthologies

Donald **Keene**

Travelers of a Hundred Ages

See also **CRITICAL STUDIES AND HISTORIES**

0-8050-1655-4 HOLT PB $24.95

Donald **Keene**, editor

Anthology of Japanese Literature from the Earliest Era to the Mid-Nineteenth Century

When this collection first appeared in 1955, it opened up to English-language readers the full range and beauty of Japanese writing; three decades later it remains reliable and endlessly readable

0-8021-5058-6 GROVE PB $13.95

Modern Japanese Literature: From 1868 to the Present Day

A follow-up to the previous title, published in 1957; excellent as far as it goes

0-8021-5095-0 GROVE PB $15.95

Hiroaki **Sato** & Burton **Watson**, editors

From the Country of Eight Islands: Anthology of Japanese Poetry

By far the most generous collection of Japanese poetry in English, with special attention paid to hitherto unfamiliar genres

0-231-06395-4 COLUMBIA PB $19.00

The Ancient Period (To AD 794)

Donald **Philippi**

Kojiki

Philippi, a brilliant scholar and translator, casts fresh light on this somewhat forbidding work, with its blend of mythology and archaic dynastic politics

0-86008-320-9 COLUMBIA PB $44.50

The Heian Period (794-1185)

The court society of the Heian period was virtually a world unto itself, producing masterpieces which continue to dominate Japanese literature: Lady Murasaki's *Tale of Genji*, the *Pillow Book* of Sei Shonagon, and the classical tanka of the imperial anthologies. Much of this literature was written by women, practicing a native style which counteracted the formal influence of Chinese.

Poetry

Robert H. **Brower** & Earl **Miner**

Japanese Court Poetry

A pioneering attempt to understand Japanese court poetry from a Japanese viewpoint; contains many translations

0-8047-0536-4 STANFORD $65.00

Edwin A. **Cranston**, translator

A Waka Anthology Volume I The Gem Glistening Cup

0-8047-1922-5 STANFORD $99.50

Ono no **Komachi** & Izumi **Shikibu**

The Ink Dark Moon: Love Poems by Ono No Komachi and Izumi Shikibu

New versions of the work of two great poets of the Heian period

TRANSLATED BY JANE HIRSHFIELD & MARIKO ARATANI

0-679-72958-5 VINTAGE PB $13.00

Helen C. **McCullough**, translator

Kokin Wakashu: The First Imperial Anthology of Japanese Poetry

Another complete translation; this edition also includes *Tosa Nikki* (the earliest of Japanese diaries, written by the anthology's editor, Ki no Tsurayuki) and the smaller collection *Shinsen Waka*

0-8047-1258-1 STANFORD $57.50

Earl **Miner**

An Introduction to Japanese Court Poetry

A condensed version of *Japanese Court Poetry*

0-8047-0636-0 STANFORD PB $11.95

Yasuhiko **Moriguchi** & David **Jenkins**, translators

The Dance of the Dust on the Rafters: Selections from Ryojin-Hisho

"I have the most profound respect for the nameless folksingers who honed these songs through centuries of Japanese oral tradition. I take joy in their subtle, unexpected turns of thought…A book to treasure"—Robert Aitken

0-913089-10-9 BROKEN MOON PB $10.00

There is fine music
by the sea.
The pines
in the wood by the beach
sound like a harp
while waves come drumming in
and fish-hawks and plovers
dance and swoop and play.

THE DANCE OF THE DUST ON THE RAFTERS: SELECTIONS FROM RYOJIN-HISHO

Princess Shikishi

A String of Beads: Complete Poems of Princess Shikishi

A translation of all the 400 tanka attributed to Princess Shikishi

TRANSLATED BY HIROAKI SATO

0-8248-1483-5 HAWAII $34.00

Kenneth **Rexroth**, translator

One Hundred Poems from the Japanese

Relatively free translations by a great American lyric poet, drawn mostly from the repertoire of classical tanka

0-8112-0181-3 NEW DIRECTIONS PB $8.95

One Hundred More Poems from the Japanese

A sequel to Rexroth's earlier very popular collection

0-8112-0619-X NEW DIRECTIONS PB $9.95

Tales, Diaries, and Essays

Helen Craig **McCullogh**, translator

Genji and Heike: Selections from the Tale of Genji and the Tale of the Heike

0-8047-2257-9 STANFORD $69.50
0-8047-2258-7 STANFORD PB $19.95

The Tales of Ise: Lyrical Episodes from 10th-Century Japan

An early collection of brief tales, mostly about love, interwoven with poems; attributed to the poet Ariwara no Narihara

0-8047-0653-0 STANFORD $39.50

Ivan **Morris**, translator

As I Crossed a Bridge of Dreams: Recollections of a Woman in Eleventh-Century Japan

0-14-044282-0 PENGUIN PB $7.95

Edward G. **Seidensticker**, translator

The Gossamer Years: The Diary of a Noblewoman of Heian Japan

An account of the restricted life of a 10th-century aristocrat, predating *The Tale of Genji*

0-8048-1123-7 TUTTLE PB $12.95

Murasaki **Shikibu**

The Diary of Lady Murasaki

The doings of the Heian court as observed by the author of *The Tale of Genji*

TRANSLATED BY RICHARD BOWRING

0-14-043576-X PENGUIN PB $9.95

The Tale of Genji

"The great masterpiece of Japanese literature… The translation by Arthur Waley is a marvelous recreation of the original, capturing its beauty and its unique evocative power"—Donald Keene

TRANSLATED BY ARTHUR WALEY

0-679-42467-9 MODERN LIBRARY $22.00

Their room was in front of the house. Genji got up and opened the long, sliding shutters. They stood together looking out. In the courtyard near them was a clump of fine Chinese bamboos; dew lay thick on the borders, glittering here no less brightly than in the great gardens to which Genji was better accustomed. There was a confused buzzing of insects. Crickets were chirping in the wall. He had often listened to them, but always at a distance; now, singing so close to him, they made a music which was unfamiliar and indeed seemed far lovelier than that with which he was acquainted.

THE TALE OF GENJI

The Tale of Genji

The Lady Murasaki's epic romance chronicles the court life of Heian Japan from the 10th century into the 11th. For the Everyman Library edition, this spellbinding novel is introduced by Edward Seidensticker, whose translation is the fullest and most accurate English version of the Japanese classic

TRANSLATED BY EDWARD G. SEIDENSTICKER

0-679-41738-9 KNOPF $25.00

Sei **Shonagon**

The Pillow Book of Sei Shonagon

An inside view of Heian court life and amusements. "One of the most delightful works of Japanese literature. The author, a near contemporary of Murasaki Shikibu, was a woman of remarkable talent and wit, and her book is perhaps the closest approach to high comedy in Japanese literature"—Donald Keene

TRANSLATED BY IVAN MORRIS

0-231-07337-2 COLUMBIA PB $16.00

Sparrows feeding their young. To pass a place where babies are playing. To sleep in a room where some fine incense has been burnt. To notice that one's elegant Chinese mirror has become a little cloudy. To see a gentleman stop his carriage before one's gate and instruct his attendants to announce his arrival. To wash one's hair, make one's toilet, and put on scented robes; even if not a soul sees one, these preparations still produce an inner pleasure. It is night and one is expecting a visitor. Suddenly one is startled by the sound of rain-drops, which the wind blows against the shutters.—*Sixteen. Things that Make One's Heart Beat Faster*

THE PILLOW BOOK OF SEI SHONAGON

Royall **Tyler**

Japanese Tales

The most extensive Japanese folk tale collection available

See also **JAPAN** under **THE NON-WESTERN WORLD** under **MYTHOLOGY AND FOLKLORE** in **RELIGION, SPIRITUALITY, AND PHILOSOPHY**

0-394-75656-8 PANTHEON PB $17.00

The Middle Period (1200-1600)

This era is notable for three literary developments: the linked poetry called renga, in which two or more persons strung together units of 17 and 14 syllables; the war tales attesting to the new dominance of the military class; and the Nō (or Noh) drama, which combined poetic texts with music and dance.

Poetry

Steven **Carter**

Three Poets at Yuyama

A full translation of one of the most famous sequences of linked poetry

0-912966-61-0 CALIFORNIA PB $6.00

Waiting for the Wind: 36 Poets of Japan's Late Medieval Age

0-231-06854-9 COLUMBIA $49.50
0-231-06855-7 COLUMBIA PB $16.50

Lady **Daibu**

The Poetic Memoirs of Lady Daibu

TRANSLATED BY PHILLIP T. HARRIES

0-8047-1077-5 STANFORD $37.50

Earl **Miner**
Japanese Linked Poetry
A detailed description of the renga form, with translations of six sequences—two of them "orthodox," four "humorous" (with the poet Basho a participant in three of the latter)
0-691-01368-3 PRINCETON PB $16.95

Yasuhiko **Moriguchi**
The Song in the Dream of the Hermit: Selections from the Kanginshu
TRANSLATED BY DAVID JENKINS
0-913089-35-4 BROKEN MOON PB $12.95

Fujiwara **no Teika**
Fujiwara Teika's "Superior Poems of Our Time": A 13th-Century Poetic Treatise and Sequence
Teika was both the greatest poet of his time and an influential anthologist
TRANSLATED BY ROBERT BROWER & EARL MINER
0-8047-0171-7 STANFORD $27.50

Ryokan
Ryokan: Zen Monk-Poet of Japan
A Zen monk who was also one of the greatest of tanka poets
TRANSLATED BY BURTON WATSON
0-231-04415-1 COLUMBIA PB $11.95

Saigyo
Poems of a Mountain Home
Saigyo, a Buddhist priest, wrote some of the most remarkable meditative poems in the Japanese tradition
TRANSLATED BY BURTON WATSON
0-231-07492-1 COLUMBIA $24.95
0-231-07493-X COLUMBIA PB $14.95

Hiroaki **Sato**
One Hundred Frogs
A serious delight: a hundred versions of Basho's most famous haiku ("Old pond, frog jumps in, water sound") by poets and scholars including Lafcadio Hearn, Allen Ginsberg, Harold Henderson, and Robert Aitken
0-8348-0335-6 WEATHERHILL PB $7.95

Lucien **Stryk**, editor &
Takashi **Ikemoto**, translator
The Penguin Book of Zen Poetry
Includes both Chinese and Japanese poets
See also **POETRY** under **CLASSICAL CHINESE LITERATURE**
0-14-058599-0 PENGUIN PB $10.95

Prose

Thomas **Cogan**, translator
The Tale of the Soga Brothers
The most famous vendetta in early Japanese history
0-86008-411-6 UNIVERSITY OF TOKYO $39.50

Kamo-No-Chomei
Hojoki: Visions of a Torn World
The vicissitudes and sufferings of the material world, as observed in Kyoto in the early 13th century
TRANSLATED BY YASUHIKO MORIGUCHI & DAVID JENKINS
1-88065-622-1 STONE BRIDGE PB $9.95

Yoshida **Kenko**
Essays in Idleness: The Tsurezuregusa of Kenko
Humorous and philosophical reflections of a poet and official who became a Buddhist monk
TRANSLATED BY DONALD KEENE
0-231-08308-4 COLUMBIA PB $16.00

Helen C. **McCullough**, translator
Yoshitsune: A 15th-Century Japanese Chronicle
The life of Minamoto no Yoshitsune, a brilliant, tragic military leader in the war between the Taira and Minamoto clans
0-8047-0270-5 STANFORD $42.50

Lady **Nijo**
The Confessions of Lady Nijo
TRANSLATED BY KAREN BRAZELL
0-8047-0929-7 STANFORD $45.00
0-8047-0930-0 STANFORD PB $15.95

Drama: Noh and Kyogen

Zeami **Motokiyo**
On the Art of the Noh Drama: The Major Treatises of Zeami
Zeami was Noh's greatest playwright and subtlest theoretician; his elucidation of the term *yugen* (mysterious elegance) is crucial to Japanese aesthetics
TRANSLATED BY J. THOMAS RIMER & YAMAZAKI MASAKAZU
0-691-10154-X PRINCETON PB $27.50

Ezra **Pound**
The Classic Noh Theatre of Japan
Pound, who knew no Japanese, worked from Fenollosa's notes to create these influential early versions
NOTES BY ERNEST FENOLLOSA
INTRODUCTION BY W.B. YEATS
0-8112-0152-X NEW DIRECTIONS PB $10.95

Royall **Tyler**, translator
Japanese Noh Dramas
New translations of 24 classic plays, with detailed background information
0-14-044539-0 PENGUIN PB $13.95

Arthur **Waley**
The Noh Plays of Japan
Waley's Noh translations may have been surpassed on the level of scholarship, but their poetic force is undiminished. Nineteen plays are translated in full, and 16 others summarized with excerpts
0-8048-1198-9 TUTTLE PB $14.95

Kenneth **Yasuda**, translator
Masterworks of the Noh Theater
0-253-36805-7 INDIANA $89.95

The Edo Period (1600-1850)

The literature created during Japan's isolation from the outside world is dominated by three writers and three genres: Matsuo Basho and the 17-syllable haiku form; Ihara Saikaku and the fiction reflecting the concerns of the city-dwelling merchant class; and Chikamatsu Monzaemon and the plays written for the puppet theater (and later, in many cases, adapted for the Kabuki).

Poetry

Matsuo **Basho**
Back Roads to Far Towns
Cid Corman, an American poet who has lived for many years in Japan, hews as closely as possible to Basho's syntax, creating an eloquent if at times cryptic effect
TRANSLATED BY KAMAIKE SUSUMU AND CID CORMAN
0-88001-467-9 ECCO PB $18.00

Basho's Narrow Road: Spring & Autumn Passages: Narrow Road to the Interior and the Renga Sequence
Includes Basho's *Narrow Road to the Interior* and the renga sequence *A Farewell Gift to Sora*; this is the first extensively annotated translation, with emphasis on the renga composed during the journey. "In this remarkable translation by Hiroaki Sato, we find the elliptical, allusive, suggestive richness of the original"—Cor van den Heuvel
TRANSLATED BY HOROAKI SATO
1-88065-620-5 STONE BRIDGE PB $15.00

The Narrow Road to the Deep North & Other Travel Sketches
Basho's travel writings mingle prose and poetry to create a startlingly telegraphic record of his experiences
TRANSLATED BY NOBUYUKI YUASA
0-14-044185-9 PENGUIN PB $9.95

Narrow Road to the Interior
A new translation of Basho's classic of *haibun* (a fusion of haiku and prose) recounting a journey through 18th-century Japan. "Hamill achieves a kind of luminosity of language that I find unparalleled in other translations" —Burton Watson
TRANSLATED BY SAM HAMILL
0-87773-644-8 SHAMBHALA PB $10.00

On Love and Barley: Haiku of Basho
Stryk emphasizes the influence of Zen on Basho's writing
TRANSLATED BY LUCIEN STRYK
0-8248-1012-0 HAWAII $11.95
0-14-044459-9 PENGUIN PB $8.95

Cid **Corman**, translator

One Man's Moon: 50 Haiku By Basho, Buson, Issa, Hakuin, Shiki, Santaka

0-917788-26-5 GNOMON PB $7.50

Robert **Hass**, editor

The Essential Haiku: Versions of Basho, Buson, and Issa

Substantial assemblage of the haiku triumvirate, translated by several hands. Part of the *Essential Poets* series

0-88001-372-9 ECCO $25.00
0-88001-351-6 ECCO PB $15.00

Yoel **Hoffman**, translator & editor

Japanese Death Poems: Written by Zen Monks and Haiku Poets on the Verge of Death

A large collection of traditional *jisei*, verses written at the point or in anticipation of death, with commentary by the translator

0-8048-1505-4 TUTTLE $21.95

Sojun **Ikkyu**

Crow with Noh Mouth: Ikkyu

TRANSLATED BY STEPHEN BERG

1-55659-022-9 COPPER CANYON PB $10.00

Kobayashi **Issa**

The Dumpling Field: Haiku of Issa

Issa (1763-1827) is one of the greatest haiku poets, and for the warmth and humor of his work perhaps the best loved. This collection by a poet steeped in the traditions of haiku and Zen presents over 360 of Issa's brief, compassionate poems

TRANSLATED BY LUCIEN STRYK WITH NOBORU FUJIWARA

0-8040-0953-8 SWALLOW PB $14.95

Makoto **Ueda**

Basho and his Interpreters: Selected Hokku with Commentary

0-8047-2526-8 STANFORD PB $19.95

Kenneth **Yasuda**

The Japanese Haiku: Its Essential Nature, History and Possibilities in English, with Examples

0-8048-1096-6 TUTTLE PB $12.95

Prose

Howard **Hibbett**

The Floating World in Japanese Fiction

A survey of the pleasures of the merchant class, with lengthy excerpts from Saikaku and his contemporary Kiseki

0-8048-1154-7 TUTTLE PB $12.95

Genroku fashion required a very large wardrobe. At a picnic to look at flowers, for instance, a lady would not only dress as elegantly as possible, and see that her attendants did so, in their way; but she would also have servants bring along a carpet, a wind curtain to be hung between the trees, a set of lacquer boxes for food, cosmetics, and other supplies, and a few extra gowns so that she need not spend a whole afternoon in the same costume. The spare kimono, which were no less luxurious, would be draped casually over the curtain, or in place of it, presumably to help screen her from public view as she sat admiring some especially pretty blossoms.

THE FLOATING WORLD IN JAPANESE FICTION

Jippensha **Ikku**

Shank's Mare

A broadly humorous picaresque novel which was immensely popular in 18th-century Japan

0-8048-1580-1 TUTTLE PB $14.95

Ihara **Saikaku**

Five Woman Who Loved Love

Saikaku's tales of love and money reflect the same "floating world" depicted in the prints and paintings of Utamaro and Kiyonaga

TRANSLATED BY WILLIAM THEODORE DE BARY

0-8048-0184-3 TUTTLE PB $12.95

The Great Mirror of Male Love

The first complete translation of Saikaku's tales of homosexual love among the samurai and kabuki actors of 17th-century Japan, illustrated with 58 drawings from the original edition

TRANSLATED WITH AN INTRODUCTION BY PAUL GORDON SCHALOW

0-8047-1895-4 STANFORD PB $18.95

The Life of an Amorous Man

TRANSLATED BY HAMADA KENGI

0-8048-0381-1 TUTTLE PB $9.95

The Life of an Amorous Woman & Other Writings

The best introduction to Saikaku's prolific writings

TRANSLATED & EDITED BY IVAN MORRIS

0-8112-0187-2 NEW DIRECTIONS PB $12.95

Drama: Kabuki and Bunraku

Takeda **Izumo**, II

Chushingura: The Treasury of Loyal Retainers, a Puppet Play

A complete translation of the original puppet version of the 47 ronin story, Japan's ever-popular drama of loyalty and revenge

TRANSLATED BY DONALD KEENE

0-231-03531-4 COLUMBIA PB $15.50

Chikamatsu **Monzaemon**

Major Plays of Chikamatsu

Keene's Chikamatsu translations are a monument of scholarship and skill, revealing the poetic splendor and realistic shadings of these merchant-class tragedies

TRANSLATED BY DONALD KEENE

0-231-02490-8 COLUMBIA $55.50

The Modern Period: Since 1850

Poetry

Of all Japanese literary forms, the 17-syllable haiku has had the greatest worldwide influence, and has been adopted by many poets writing in English and other languages.

As Japan absorbed Western culture in the 19th century, sweeping changes took place. Among literary genres, poetry underwent the most remarkable transformation because the earlier formal and stylistic constraints on it had been the greatest. Poets such as Hagiwara, Miyazawa, and Takamura invented new kinds of poetry—open in length and free in structure—without precedent in the Japanese tradition.

Amy **Heinrich**

Fragments of Rainbows: The Life and Poetry of Saito Mokichi, 1882-1993

The biography of a poet-psychologist, including translations of 219 tanka

0-231-05428-9 COLUMBIA $35.00

Hosea **Hirata**

The Poetry and Poetics of Nishiwaki Junzaburo: Modernism in Translation

The first scholarly treatment of an important poet, Nishiwaki Junzaburo (1894-1982)

0-691-06981-6 PRINCETON $37.50

Takuboku **Ishikawa**

Romaji Diary & Sad Toys

This tanka poet who died in 1912 is still widely read

TRANSLATED BY SANFORD GOLDSTEIN & SHINODA SEISHI

0-8048-1494-5 TUTTLE PB $12.95

Shimpei **Kusano**

Asking Myself/Answering Myself

The secret life of frogs and other matters, in poems full of fantasy and humor

TRANSLATED BY CID CORMAN & KAMAIKE SUSUMU

0-8112-0887-7 NEW DIRECTIONS PB $5.95

Leza **Lowitz** & Miyuki **Aoyama**

A Long Rainy Season: Haiku & Tankas

A selection of 20th century women writers of haiku and tanka

1-88065-615-9 WEATHERHILL PB $12.00

Hosai **Ozaki**

Right Under the Big Sky, I Don't Wear a Hat: The Haiku and Prose of Hosai Ozaki

About 500 haiku of Hosai Ozaki (1885-1926) translated in one line. He is among the most important Japanese poets who wrote haiku without seasonal references and ignoring the 5-7-5 syllabic pattern. The title itself is a haiku

TRANSLATED BY HIROAKI SATO

1-88065-605-1 STONE BRIDGE PB $12.00

Makoto **Ooka** &
Thomas **Fitzsimmons**, editors

A Play of Mirrors: Eight Major Poets of Modern Japan

0-942668-08-1 KATYDID PB $21.95

Sanki **Saito**

The Kobe Hotel

A substantial selection of prose and haiku of a prominent modern haiku poet, Saito Sanki (1900-1962)

0-8348-0274-0 WEATHERHILL PB $12.95

Nanao **Sakaki**

Break the Mirror

Sakaki, who has spent much time in America, writes in both Japanese and English

INTRODUCTION BY GARY SNYDER

0-86547-298-X NORTH POINT PB $9.95

Kazuko **Shiraishi**

Seasons of Sacred Lust

An outstanding contemporary woman poet, in some ways comparable to America's Beats

EDITED WITH AN INTRODUCTION BY KENNETH REXROTH

0-8112-0678-5 NEW DIRECTIONS PB $7.95

Mutsuo **Takahashi**

A Bunch of Keys: Selected Poems

Powerful homoerotic poetry by an important contemporary

TRANSLATED BY HIROAKI SATO

0-89594-144-9 CROSSING $8.95

Sleeping Sinning Falling

TRANSLATED BY HIROAKI SATO

0-87286-268-2 CITY LIGHTS PB $8.95

Shinkichi **Takahashi**

Triumph of the Sparrow: Zen Poems of Shinkichi Takahashi

A great poet of modern Japan who combines early surrealist and Dada interests with a serious Zen discipline

0-252-01253-4 ILLINOIS $24.95
0-252-01229-1 ILLINOIS PB $9.95

Kotaro **Takamura**

A Brief History of Imbecility: Poetry and Prose of Takamura Kotaro

A comprehensive survey of the stage of Takamura's unusual career, from the Parisian poems of his youth, the love poems about his wife Chieko, the intensely nationalistic work of the war years, and the self-critical title work

TRANSLATED BY HIROAKI SATO

0-8248-1456-8 HAWAII PB $17.00

Ryuichi **Tamura**

Dead Languages: Selected Poems, 1946-1984

A postwar poet who has been compared to T.S. Eliot

TRANSLATED BY CHRISTOPHER DRAKE

9-994-18693-0 KATYDID PB $14.95

Santoka **Taneda**

Mountain Tasting: Zen Haiku

Free-form haiku by a mendicant Zen monk, translated with feeling and precision

TRANSLATED BY JOHN STEVENS

0-8348-0151-5 WEATHERHILL PB $12.50

Akiko **Yosano**

Tangled Hair: Selected Tanka from Midaregami

First published in 1901, these frank, romantic poems marked a radical break with traditional tanka

TRANSLATED BY SANFORD GOLDSTEIN & SHINODA SEICHI
EDITED BY FLORENCE SAKADE & LORA SHARNOFF

0-8048-1522-4 TUTTLE PB $11.95

Fiction and Other Prose

Kobo **Abe**

The Ark Sakura

"A large, ambitious work about the lives of outcasts in modern Japan and such troubling themes as ecological destruction, old age, violence and nuclear war"
—Edmund White, *NY Times*

TRANSLATED BY JULIET WINTERS CARPENTER

0-679-72161-4 VINTAGE PB $15.00

Beyond the Curve

"Beyond the Curve consists of superb gems of the storyteller's art, many of which stand on their own as pure tale but which also work on a metaphorical level: the fright of human beings, alone, facing their most inner—and outer—demons"—*San Francisco Chronicle*

TRANSLATED BY JULIET WINTERS CARPENTER

4-7700-1465-1 KODANSHA $18.95
4-7700-1690-5 KODANSHA PB $9.00

The Box Man

0-86547-461-3 NORTH POINT PB $11.00

Kangaroo Notebook

The last novel Abe completed before his death tells a funny and terrifyingly surreal story. When the nameless narrator discovers that radish sprouts are growing from his shins, he enters a hell of bizarre and unpredictable forces

TRANSLATED BY MARYELLEN T. MORI

0-679-42412-1 KNOPF $22.00

The Ruined Map

"A compelling tour de force...A horror story of such magnitude it stuns the mind"
—*NY Times Book Review*

TRANSLATED BY E. DALE SAUNDERS

4-7700-1635-2 KODANSHA PB $13.00

The Woman in the Dunes

0-679-73378-7 VINTAGE PB $11.00

Ryunosuke **Akutagawa**

Rashomon & Other Stories

Some of Akutagawa's greatest short works, including *In a Grove* (source of Kurosawa's *Rashomon*) and *Kesa and Morita* (on which *Gate of Hell* was based)

TRANSLATED BY KOJIMA TAKASHI

0-8048-1457-0 TUTTLE PB $9.95

Sawako **Ariyoshi**

The Doctor's Wife

TRANSLATED BY WAKAKO HIRONAKA & ANN S. KOSTANT

0-87011-465-4 KODANSHA PB $9.00

The River Ki

TRANSLATED BY MILDRED TAHARA

0-87011-514-6 KODANSHA PB $10.00

The Twilight Years

TRANSLATED BY MILDRED TAHARA

0-87011-852-8 KODANSHA PB $10.00

Osamu **Dazai**

No Longer Human

TRANSLATED WITH AN INTRODUCTION BY DONALD KEENE

0-8112-0481-2 NEW DIRECTIONS PB $9.95

Return to Tsugaru: Travels of a Purple Tramp

TRANSLATED BY JAMES WESTERHOVEN

0-87011-841-2 KODANSHA PB $5.95

Self Portraits: Stories

TRANSLATED BY RALPH MCCARTHY

4-7700-1689-1 KODANSHA PB $8.00

The Setting Sun

Dazai was the classic exponent of postwar alienation

TRANSLATED BY DONALD KEENE

0-8112-0032-9 NEW DIRECTIONS PB $9.95

Fumiko **Enchi**

The Waiting Years

Chronicle of an upper-class family in the years following the Meiji Restoration of 1868

TRANSLATED BY JOHN BESTER

0-87011-424-7 KODANSHA PB $9.00

Shusaku **Endo**

Deep River

TRANSLATED BY VAN C. GESSEL

0-8112-1320-X NEW DIRECTIONS PB $10.95

The Final Martyrs

TRANSLATED BY VAN G. GESSEL

0-8112-1272-6 NEW DIRECTIONS $21.95

The Girl I Left Behind

An early Endo novel translated for the first time, about a student and the country girl he abandons

TRANSLATED BY MARK WILLIAMS

0-8112-1303-X NEW DIRECTIONS $21.95

The Samurai

Brilliant historical novel of four samurai who leave 17th-century Japan to explore the Western world

TRANSLATED BY VAN C. GESSEL

0-06-859852-1 HARPERCOLLINS $12.95

Scandal

A famous writer confronts the darker side of his nature

TRANSLATED BY VAN C. GESSEL

0-7206-0682-9 DUFOUR $30.00

The Sea and Poison

TRANSLATED BY MICHAEL GALLAGHER

0-8112-1198-3 NEW DIRECTIONS PB $10.95

Silence

Christian martyrs under the Tokugawa shogunate

TRANSLATED BY WILLIAM JOHNSTON

0-8008-7186-3 PARKWEST PB $9.95

Stained Glass Elegies: Stories

TRANSLATED BY VAN C. GESSEL

0-8112-1142-8 NEW DIRECTIONS PB $10.95

Wonderful Fool

TRANSLATED BY FRANCIS MATHY
0-7206-0979-8 OWEN PB $28.00

Masuji **Ibuse**

Black Rain

A devastating, detailed account of the day the bomb drops on Hiroshima, told from the perspective of a minor local official

See also **THE ATOMIC BOMB** under **FROM THE MEIJI RESTORATION TO THE END OF THE EMPIRE: 1868-1945** under **JAPAN** in **WORLD HISTORY AND CURRENT AFFAIRS**

TRANSLATED BY JOHN BESTER
0-87011-364-X KODANSHA PB $10.00

Salamander & Other Stories

TRANSLATED BY JOHN BESTER
0-87011-458-1 KODANSHA PB $8.00

Yasushi **Inoue**

The Hunting Gun

TRANSLATED BY YOKOO SADAMICHI & SANFORD GOLDSTEIN
0-8048-0257-2 TUTTLE PB $8.95

The Roof Tiles of Tempyo

A historical novel set in ancient China
TRANSLATED BY JAMES T. ARAKI
0-86008-307-1 TOKYO PB $17.50

Takeshi **Kaiko**

Into a Black Sun

"At last the sights, sounds and smells of wartime Vietnam have been tendered by a master. Writing from the point of view of a neutral Japanese journalist, Takeshi Kaiko filters his tale through an idiosyncratic but deeply compassionate sensibility"—Edmund White
TRANSLATED BY CECILIA SEGAWA SEIGLE
0-87011-609-6 KODANSHA PB $8.00

Yasunari **Kawabata**

Beauty and Sadness

From the Nobel Prize-winning novelist
TRANSLATED BY HOWARD HIBBETT
0-679-76105-5 VINTAGE PB $11.00

The House of the Sleeping Beauties & Other Stories

"*The House of the Sleeping Beauties* is most certainly an esoteric masterpiece...While in the grip of this story, the reader sweats and grows dizzy, and knows with the greatest immediacy the terror of lust urged on by the approach of death"—Yukio Mishima
TRANSLATED BY EDWARD G. SEIDENSTICKER
INTRODUCTION BY YUKIO MISHIMA
0-87011-426-3 KODANSHA PB $10.00

The Lake

"Readers who have inferred from previously translated novels that everything Kawabata is delicate and understated will be surprised and perhaps even shocked at the brutal sensuality of some of the scenes"—Donald Keene
TRANSLATED BY REIKO TSUKIMURA
0-87011-365-8 KODANSHA PB $10.00

The Master of Go

Austere even by Kawabata's standards, this early novel has the abstract fascination of a game of go
TRANSLATED BY EDWARD SEIDENSTICKER
0-679-76106-3 VINTAGE PB $11.00

The Old Capital

Two generations of traditional artists confront the disorienting changes of postwar Japan
TRANSLATED BY J. MARTIN HOLMAN
0-86547-411-7 NORTH POINT PB $8.95

Thousand Cranes

0-679-76265-5 RANDOM HOUSE PB $11.00

Taeko **Kono**

Toddler-Hunting & Other Stories

Stories by the first woman writer in Japan to explicitly address sexuality. "At once the most carnally direct and the most lucidly intelligent woman writing in Japan"—Kenzaburo Oe
TRANSLATED BY LUCY NORTH WITH LUCY LOWER
0-8112-1305-6 NEW DIRECTIONS $21.95

Seicho **Matsumoto**

Points and Lines

The most famous of Japanese crime novels
0-87011-456-5 KODANSHA PB $9.95

Yukio **Mishima**

Acts of Worship: Seven Stories

Despite the impact that Mishima's work—and the flamboyance of his life and death—have made, much of his work has remained untranslated. These seven stories reveal new facets of his meticulous psychological observation and stylistic elegance
TRANSLATED WITH AN INTRODUCTION BY JOHN BESTER
0-87011-937-0 KODANSHA $17.95
0-87011-824-2 KODANSHA PB $9.00

Yukio Mishima

Confessions of a Mask

The autobiographical novel which established Mishima's reputation
TRANSLATED BY MEREDITH WEATHERBY
0-8112-0118-X NEW DIRECTIONS PB $9.95

Patriotism

A pivotal work in its author's career, this novella of an army officer and his wife committing suicide marks his turn toward the values which culminated in his own violent death
TRANSLATED BY GEOFFREY W. SARGENT
0-8112-1312-9 NEW DIRECTIONS PB $6.00

The Sailor Who Fell from Grace with the Sea

TRANSLATED BY JOHN NATHAN
0-679-75015-0 VINTAGE PB $10.00

This tetralogy, Mishima's final work (he mailed the last volume to his publisher on the day of his violent death), constructs an elaborate plot spanning decades of Japanese history and involving reincarnation and confusion of identity

Spring Snow

0-679-72241-6 VINTAGE PB $13.00

Runaway Horses

0-679-72240-8 VINTAGE PB $14.00

The Temple of Dawn

0-679-72242-4 VINTAGE PB $14.00

The Decay of the Angel

0-679-72243-2 VINTAGE PB $13.00

The Temple of the Golden Pavilion

One of Mishima's masterpieces: based on the true story of an acolyte monk who burned down a famous Zen temple
TRANSLATED BY IVAN MORRIS
0-679-43315-5 EVERYMAN'S $17.00

Kenji **Miyazawa**

Milky Way Railroad

A children's story by a great modern Japanese poet
TRANSLATED BY JOSEPH SIGRIST AND D.M. STROUD
1-88065-626-4 STONE BRIDGE PB $11.95

Ogai **Mori**

Saiki Koi & Other Stories

A collection of historical fiction focused on samurai vendettas
TRANSLATED & EDITED BY DAVID DILWORTH & J. THOMAS RIMER
0-8248-0454-6 HAWAII $14.95

Vita Sexualis

Banned when it appeared in 1909, this novel pioneered new levels of sexual frankness
TRANSLATED BY NINOMIYA KAZUJI & SANFORD GOLDSTEIN
0-8048-1048-6 TUTTLE PB $9.95

The Wild Geese

A famous and melancholy novel of frustrated love
TRANSLATED BY OCHIAI KINGO & SANFORD GOLDSTEIN
0-8048-1070-2 TUTTLE PB $8.95

Wild Goose

A new and more accurate translation of the classic Meiji-era novel
TRANSLATED BY BURTON WATSON
0-939512-70-X MICHIGAN $28.95

Soseki **Natsume**

Botchan

A young man's rebellion against the system. "Soseki's lightest and funniest work"
—Donald Keene
TRANSLATED BY ALAN TURNEY
0-87011-367-4 KODANSHA PB $8.00

I Am a Cat
A famous satirical novel: the life of a Japanese professor of English, seen through a cat's eyes
TRANSLATED BY SHIBATA KATSUE
0-8048-1621-2 TUTTLE PB.........$12.95

Kokoro
The best introduction to Natsume's writings
TRANSLATED BY EDWIN MCCLELLAN
0-89526-951-1 REGIONAL LABORATORY PB.........$12.95

Kenzaburo **Oe**

The Crazy Iris and Other Stories of the Atomic Aftermath
0-8021-5184-1 GROVE PB.........$11.00

An Echo of Heaven
TRANSLATED BY MARGARET MITSUTANI
4-7700-1986-6 KODANSHA.........$25.00

Hiroshima Notes
0-8021-3464-5 GROVE PB.........$12.00

Japan, the Ambiguous, and Myself: The Nobel Prize Speech and Other Lectures
4-7700-1980-7 KODANSHA.........$15.00

Nip the Buds, Shoot the Kids
Reform-school boys are trapped by plague during wartime
0-7145-2997-4 MARION BOYARS.........$22.95
0-8021-3463-7 GROVE PB.........$11.00

A Personal Matter
Wrenching postwar novel centering around the birth of a retarded son
TRANSLATED BY JOHN NATHAN
0-8021-5061-6 GROVE PB.........$10.00

The Pinch Runner Memorandum
TRANSLATED BY MICHAEL K. WILSON
1-56324-183-8 SHARPE.........$50.95
1-56324-184-6 SHARPE PB.........$22.95

Seventeen (The Political Being) and I (The Sexual Being)
1-56201-091-3 BLUE MOON PB.........$16.95

The Silent Cry
TRANSLATED BY JOHN BESTER
0-87011-466-2 KODANSHA PB.........$8.00

Shohei **Ooka**

Fires on the Plain
A Japanese soldier in the Philippines during World War II
TRANSLATED BY IVAN MORRIS
0-8048-1379-5 TUTTLE PB.........$12.95

Taken Captive
A compelling account of a Japanese POW in a US prison camp
TRANSLATED BY WAYNE LAMMERS
0-471-14285-9 WILEY.........$27.95

Jiro **Osaragi**

Homecoming
A popular novel about the end of the war
TRANSLATED BY BREWSTER HORWITZ
0-8371-9369-9 GREENWOOD.........$59.75
0-8224-6438-1 LAKE PB.........$8.71

Naoya **Shiga**

A Dark Night's Passing
TRANSLATED BY EDWIN MCCLELLAN
0-87011-362-3 KODANSHA PB.........$10.00

The Paper Door & Other Stories
Seventeen stories demonstrating the range of an author who has been called "the god of the Japanese short story"
TRANSLATED BY LANE DUNLOP
0-8048-1893-2 TUTTLE PB.........$12.95

Toson **Shimazaki**

Before the Dawn
A monumental novel dealing with the turbulence before and after Japan's opening to the West
TRANSLATED BY WILLIAM NAFF
0-8248-0914-9 HAWAII.........$30.00

The Broken Commandment
Breakthrough novel about the sufferings of the outcast class
TRANSLATED WITH AN INTRODUCTION BY KENNETH STRONG
0-86008-191-5 COLUMBIA PB.........$22.50

The Family
TRANSLATED BY CECILIA SEGAWA SEIGLE
0-86008-254-7 COLUMBIA PB.........$22.50

Junichiro **Tanizaki**

A Cat, a Man, and Two Women
A novella and two short stories illustrating a more lighthearted side of Tanizaki's genius
TRANSLATED BY PAUL MCCARTHY
0-87011-755-6 KODANSHA.........$18.95

Childhood Years
0-87011-863-3 KODANSHA.........$17.95

Diary of a Mad Old Man
Tanizaki's final, grotesquely humorous examination of sexuality in the face of imminent death
TRANSLATED BY HOWARD HIBBETT
0-679-73024-9 VINTAGE PB.........$12.00

The Key
TRANSLATED BY HOWARD HIBBETT
0-679-73023-0 VINTAGE PB.........$11.00

The Makioka Sisters
A long, meticulously detailed account of the decline of a genteel merchant family in prewar Osaka focusing on the women who must negotiate both traditional expectations and modern desires
TRANSLATED BY EDWARD G. SEIDENSTICKER
0-679-76164-0 VINTAGE PB.........$13.00

Naomi
A novel from the '20s: a Japanese man becomes obsessed with a foreign-looking woman. "Tanizaki writes with an unabashed sensuality rare in the often hectic, guilt-ridden annals of modernism"—John Updike, *New Yorker*
TRANSLATED BY ANTHONY CHAMBERS
0-86547-457-5 NORTH POINT PB.........$11.00

Quicksand
TRANSLATED BY HOWARD HIBBETT
0-394-58547-X KNOPF.........$22.00
0-679-76022-9 VINTAGE PB.........$11.00

The Reed Cutter & Captain Shigemoto's Mother: Two Novellas
0-679-42010-X KNOPF.........$22.00
0-679-75791-0 VINTAGE PB.........$11.00

The Secret History of the Lord of Musashi & Arrowroot: Two Novellas
"These fictions, subversive and self-referential, join the already dazzling canon of Tanizaki's work in English…I believe they are masterpieces"—Richard Howard, *Nation*
TRANSLATED BY ANTHONY CHAMBERS
0-86547-470-2 NORTH POINT PB.........$10.95

Seven Japanese Tales
TRANSLATED BY HOWARD HIBBETT
0-679-76107-1 VINTAGE PB.........$13.00

Some Prefer Nettles
0-679-75269-2 VINTAGE PB.........$11.00

Inoue **Yasushi**

Wind and Waves
A novel of the Mongols in 13th-century Korea as they prepare their invasion of Japan
TRANSLATED BY JAMES T. ARAKI
0-8248-1178-X HAWAII.........$20.00

Eiji **Yoshikawa**

Musashi: An Epic Novel of the Samurai Era
A sample of popular fiction: an immensely long and complicated chronicle of a celebrated swordsman
TRANSLATED BY CHARLES TERRY
0-87011-966-4 KODANSHA.........$30.00

Fiction Anthologies

Lane **Dunlop**, translator & editor

A Late Chrysanthemum: 21 Stories from the Japanese
0-8048-1578-X TUTTLE PB.........$12.95

Van C. **Gessel** & Tomone **Matsumoto**, editors

The Showa Anthology: Modern Japanese Short Stories, 1929-1984
4-7700-1708-1 KODANSHA PB.........$13.00

Noriko **Lippit** & Kyoko **Selden**, editors

Japanese Women Writers: Twentieth Century Short Fiction
0-87332-859-0 SHARPE.........$56.95
0-87332-860-4 SHARPE PB.........$21.95

Yukiko **Tanaka**, editor

To Live and to Write: Selections by Japanese Women Writers, 1913-1938
Stories and essays by early feminists
TRANSLATED BY YUKIKO TANAKA & OTHERS
0-931188-43-1 SEAL PB.........$12.95

Drama

Kobo **Abe**

The Secret Rendezvous

TRANSLATED BY JULIET WINTERS CARPENTER
1-56836-003-7 KODANSHA PB $12.00

Three Plays

TRANSLATED BY DONALD KEENE
0-231-08280-0 COLUMBIA $32.50

Shusaku **Endo**

The Golden Country: A Play About Martyrs in Japan

Endo, a Japanese Christian, returns to the subject matter of his novel *Silence*
TRANSLATED BY FRANCIS MATHY
0-7206-0758-2 DUFOUR $27.00

Shusako Endo

Thomas J. **Rimer**, editor

Mask and Sword: Two Plays for the Contemporary Japanese Theater

0-231-04932-3 COLUMBIA $47.50

Robert T. **Rolf** & John K. **Gillespie**, translators

Alternative Japanese Drama: Ten Plays

A sampling of contemporary Japanese playwrights, with an emphasis on the experimental
0-8248-1347-2 HAWAII $38.00
0-8248-1379-0 HAWAII PB $14.95

Ted **Takaya**, translator

Modern Japanese Drama: An Anthology

0-231-04684-7 COLUMBIA $52.50
0-231-04685-5 COLUMBIA PB $20.00

New Japanese Writers

Alfred **Birnbaum**, editor

Monkey Brain Sushi: New Tastes in Japanese Fiction

Sexy, deviant, cybernetic stories from the new generation of writers, revealing more about Japan today than 1,000 pages of cultural analysis. "The authors tend toward near-zero emotional chill, stunned urbanity, and a shiny kind of violence. But unlike, say, Bret Easton Ellis, they also have wit and something to say about their society"—*NY Times Book Review*
4-7700-1688-3 KODANSHA PB $10.00

Haruki **Murakami**

Dance Dance Dance

A hack journalist returns to a seedy Hokkaido hotel where his true love disappeared four and a half years before. With his sidekick, a 13-year-old psychic named Yuki, our hero moves fearlessly through the world of movies, murder, and power. A first-class yarn from the phenomenal author of *A Wild Sheep Chase* and *Norwegian Wood* that have sold more than 4,000,000 copies in Japan. "[His] bold willingness to go straight-over-the-top has always been a signal indication of his genius" —*Washington Post*
TRANSLATED BY ALFRED BIRNBAUM
4-7700-1683-2 KODANSHA $22.00

Hard-Boiled Wonderland and the End of the World

Japan's most popular novelist has little in common with his more tradition-minded predecessors, as he explores a new global landscape of shifting identities and uncertain codes of behavior
4-7700-1544-5 KODANSHA $21.95

A Wild Sheep Chase

Murakami, born in 1949, speaks for a new generation of Japanese, and his whimsical and ingenious novels have made him a bestselling author in Japan. A *Wild Sheep Chase*, his first work translated into English, has been received enthusiastically for its unique blend of comedy, fantasy, and mystery
TRANSLATED BY ALFRED BIRNBAUM
0-87011-905-2 KODANSHA $18.95

Ryu **Murakami**

Coin Locker Babies

A novel of nihilistic youth which created controversy in Japan
TRANSLATED BY STEPHEN SNYDER
4-7700-1590-9 KODANSHA $23.00

Junzo **Shono**

Still Life and Other Stories

An exquisite translation of an elegant writer. Lammers has already won two awards, the 1993 PEN West Literary Award and the 1993-94 Japan-U.S. Friendship Commission Prize for the translation of Japanese literature
TRANSLATED BY WAYNE LAMMERS
1-88065-602-7 STONE BRIDGE PB $11.95

Amy **Yamada**

Trash

Yamada casts a female Japanese protagonist into New York, caught between two worlds—with her boyfriend in Harlem and downtown, with her cosmopolitan, fast-paced friends. "One of Japan's brightest young literary stars, whose sexually explicit prose makes Tama Janowitz read like Mary Poppins [and] has earned Yamada a reputation as one of Japan's most liberated women writers"—*Washington Post*
TRANSLATED BY SONYA JOHNSON
1-56836-018-5 KODANSHA $18.00

Gozo **Yoshimasu**

Osiris, the God of Stone

Yoshimasu, one of the most striking figures of contemporary Japanese literature, writes a visionary, almost shamanistic poetry
TRANSLATED BY HIROAKI SATO
0-932662-70-6 SAINT ANDREWS $14.00

Banana **Yoshimoto**

Kitchen

A bestseller in Japan, where it won two prestigious literary prizes, *Kitchen* is a daringly original yet deeply moving work by one of today's most talented young Japanese writers. In this book Yoshimoto juxtaposes two stories about mothers, transsexuality, kitchens, love, and tragedy, as seen through the eyes of a pair or free-spirited young women in contemporary Japan
0-671-88018-7 WASHINGTON SQUARE PB $10.00

The place I like best in this world is the kitchen. No matter where it is, no matter what kind, if it's a kitchen, if it's a place where they make food, it's fine with me. Ideally it should be well broken in. Lots of tea towels, dry and immaculate. White tile catching the light (ting! ting!).
KITCHEN

Lizard

Stories from the Japanese writer who in two books has established herself as an international bestseller and prominent voice of comic postmodernism. "Ms. Yoshimoto's writing is lucid, earnest and disarming, as emotionally observant as Jane Smiley's, as fluently readable as Anne Tyler's"—*NY Times*
0-8021-1564-0 GROVE $18.00

NP

TRANSLATED BY ANN SHERIF
0-8021-1545-4 GROVE $18.00

The Water Buddha Drinks

Yoshimoto (*Kitchen*, *NP*, *Lizard*) has established herself as the most acclaimed of Japan's young novelists. "Here she tells of a journey in which a sister, brother, and fiancé of a dead actress travel to confront the spirits of the dead on a remote island in the Pacific. "Yoshimoto confirms that art is perhaps the best ambassador among nations"—*Library Journal*
0-8021-1590-X GROVE $20.00

Banana Yoshimoto (photo by Eiichiro Sakata)

Akira **Yoshimura**

Shipwrecks

TRANSLATED BY MARK EALEY

0-15-100211-8 HARCOURT BRACE $21.00

Critical Studies and Histories

Shuichi **Kato**

A History of Japanese Literature

Volume 1 The First Thousand Years

0-87011-491-3 KODANSHA PB $10.00

Volume 2 The Years of Isolation

4-7700-1546-1 KODANSHA PB $8.95

Volume 3 The Modern Years

4-7700-1547-X KODANSHA PB $8.95

Donald **Keene**

Dawn to the West: Japanese Literature in the Modern Era

Volume 1 Fiction

0-03-062814-8 HOLT RINEHART & WINSTON $60.00

0-8050-0607-9 HOLT PB $29.95

Volume 2 Poetry, Drama, Criticism

0-03-062816-4 HOLT RINEHART & WINSTON $40.00

0-8050-0608-7 HOLT PB $19.95

Japanese Literature: An Introduction for Western Readers

Still the most concise survey of the periods and genres of Japanese literature

0-03-013626-1 HOLT $22.95

The Pleasures of Japanese Literature

Everyone should have Keene's brief elegant monograph on the Japanese aesthetic

0-231-06736-4 COLUMBIA $25.00

Seeds in the Heart: Japanese Literature from Earliest Times to the Late Sixteenth Century

0-8050-1999-5 HOLT $50.00

Some Japanese Portraits

Lively essays on 21 writers, covering a span of five centuries

0-87011-575-8 KODANSHA PB $5.95

Travelers of a Hundred Ages

See also **GENERAL ANTHOLOGIES**

0-8050-1655-4 HOLT PB $24.95

Thomas J. **Rimer**

Pilgrimages: Aspects of Japanese Literature and Culture

Eight essays on modern Japanese fine arts, fiction, drama, and poetry, showing links with older traditions

0-8248-1148-8 HAWAII $17.00

A Reader's Guide to Japanese Literature

The former Chief of the Asian Division of the Library of Congress explores fifty of the greatest Japanese literary works

4-7700-1477-5 KODANSHA PB $10.00

Burton **Watson**

The Rainbow World: Japan in Essays and Translations

Watson, a distinguished translator and interpreter of Chinese and Japanese literature, writes of his long experience in Japan, beginning with his first glimpses of it in 1945. "A fresh and insightful miscellany from the mature experience of a great and graceful scholar" —Gary Snyder

See also **GENERAL STUDIES** under **JAPAN** in **WORLD HISTORY AND CURRENT AFFAIRS**

0-913089-06-0 BROKEN MOON PB $10.00

Languages like English or Chinese achieve a scurrilous effect by the addition of epithets or expletives that serve to suggest all sorts of awful things about the parentage or moral habits of the person addressed. Japanese, on the other hand, gets the same effect by purely formal means. Just as there is an elaborate set of honorific pronouns, verbs, and verb endings which are used to express varying degrees of respect…so there is a complementary set for expressing varying degrees of contempt. The sting of the latter comes not from any scurrility explicit in the words themselves, but from the insulting implication of inferior social status they carry.

THE RAINBOW WORLD: JAPAN IN ESSAYS AND TRANSLATIONS

Poetry

Robert **Aitken**

A Zen Wave: Basho's Haiku and Zen

An American Zen master's commentaries on a selection of Basho's haiku. "Illuminates the angles and corners of lone-ness and community, plainness and beauty, in the homey, homeless way of Zen"—Gary Snyder

FOREWORD BY W.S. MERWIN

0-8348-0137-X WEATHERHILL PB $16.95

William J. **Higginson**

The Haiku Handbook

A meticulous and comprehensive guide to haiku in Japanese and other languages

4-7700-1430-9 KODANSHA PB $12.00

Makoto **Ueda**

Matsuo Basho

A biography of the great haiku poet

0-87011-553-7 KODANSHA PB $10.00

Drama

James R. **Brandon**

Studies in Kabuki: Its Acting, Music, and Historical Context

0-8248-0452-X HAWAII PB $14.00

Barbara C. **Adachi**

Backstage at Bunraku: A Behind-the-Scenes Look at Japan's Puppet Theatre

Members of the Osaka Bunraku Troupe reveal secrets of puppet theater; many photographs and stage diagrams

PHOTOGRAPHS BY JOEL SACKETT

0-8348-0199-X WEATHERHILL PB $25.00

Earle **Ernst**

The Kabuki Theatre

The social niche occupied by Kabuki performers entailed ramifications as fascinating as the plot of a Kabuki play. This is only one of the aspects that Ernst touches on in this rich account

0-8248-0319-1 HAWAII PB $20.00

Masakatsu **Gunji**

Kabuki

An authoritative book featuring hundreds of photos of famous scenes, stock characters, special effects, backstage maneuvers, makeup traditions, and classic performances

INTRODUCTION BY DONALD KEENE

0-87011-732-7 KODANSHA $80.00

Heinz **Horioka** & Miyoko **Sasaki**

Rakugo: The Popular Narrative Art of Japan

0-674-74725-9 HARVARD $35.00

Kunio **Komparu**

The Noh Theater: Principles and Perspectives

An absolutely thorough, sometimes quite technical description of the many elements involved in a Noh performance

See also **ASIA** under **HISTORY** under **THEATER** in **PERFORMING ARTS AND MEDIA**

0-8348-1529-X WEATHERHILL $32.50

Akiko **Miyake** & others, editors

A Guide to Ezra Pound and Ernest Fenollosa's Classic Noh Theatre of Japan

0-943373-31-X NATIONAL POETRY FOUND PB $25.00

Ivan **Morris**

The World of the Shining Prince

A splendid re-creation of the court society that created *The Tale of Genji* and other literary masterpieces

See also **HEIAN PERIOD: 794–1185** under **JAPAN TO 1600** under **JAPAN** in **WORLD HISTORY AND CURRENT AFFAIRS**

1-56836-029-0 KODANSHA PB $15.00

Modern Fiction

Robert L. **Danly**

In the Shade of Spring Leaves: The Life and Writings of Higuchi Ichiyo, a Woman of Letters in Meiji Japan

0-393-30913-4 NORTON PB $10.95

Henry **Scott Stokes**
The Life and Death of Yukio Mishima
"Humane, intelligent and, for the moment, probably as close as a Western reader is likely to get to the subject...Scott Stokes never sensationalizes...a literate examination of the man's work"—*Time*
0-374-52464-5 NOONDAY PB $15.00

Edward G. **Seidensticker**
Kafu the Scribbler: The Life and Writings of Nagai Kafu, 1879-1959
The curious career of the chronicler of geisha life
0-8047-0267-5 STANFORD $47.50

Makoto **Ueda**
Modern Japanese Writers and the Nature of Literature
0-8047-0904-1 STANFORD $42.50

Other Asian Literatures

Indonesian Literature

Kratini Raden **Adjeng**
Letters of a Javanese Princess
Letters of a young noblewoman, now beloved as an early advocate of feminist and nationalist ideas
TRANSLATED BY AGNES L. SYMMERS
0-8191-4758-3 AMERICA PB $22.00

James R. **Brandon**
On Thrones of Gold: Three Javanese Shadow Plays
0-8248-1425-8 HAWAII PB $28.00

Burton **Raffel**, editor
Anthology of Modern Indonesian Poetry
0-87395-024-0 SUNY $49.50

Pramoedya Ananta **Toer**
Pramoedya Ananta Toer is the preeminent Indonesian writer of this century. He has spent many years under detention by the government.

Child of All Nations
0-14-025633-4 PENGUIN PB $12.95

Footsteps
0-14-025634-2 PENGUIN PB $12.95

This Earth of Mankind
0-14-025635-0 PENGUIN PB $12.95

Korean Literature

So **Chongju**
Selected Poems
TRANSLATED BY DAVID MCCANN
0-231-06794-1 COLUMBIA $40.50

Chongwha Chung, editor
Korean Classical Literature: An Anthology
See also **CULTURE** under **KOREA DIVIDED** under **KOREA** in **WORLD HISTORY AND CURRENT AFFAIRS**
0-7103-0279-7 ROUTLEDGE $42.50

Love in Mid-Winter Night: Korean Sijo Poetry
0-7103-0104-9 ROUTLEDGE $34.00

Yun Heung-gil
The House of Twilight
A collection of stories by an iconoclastic chronicler of today's Korea
EDITED WITH AN INTRODUCTION BY J. MARTIN HOLMAN
0-930523-60-1 READERS INTERNATIONAL PB $9.95

Ahn Junghyo
White Badge
"The first major book about Korean involvement in the Vietnam War"—*LA Times*
1-56947-004-9 SOPHIA PB $13.00

Chong-un **Kim**, editor
Postwar Korean Short Stories: An Anthology
0-8248-0833-9 HAWAII $18.00

Jaihiun **Kim**
Modern Korean Poetry
0-87573-057-4 JAIN PB $30.00

Peter H. **Lee**
Songs of Flying Dragons: A Critical Reading
0-674-82075-4 HARVARD $22.50

Peter H. **Lee**, editor
Anthology of Korean Literature: From Early Times to the 19th Century
0-8248-0756-1 HAWAII PB $13.00

Pine River and Lone Peak: An Anthology of Three Chosen Dynasty Poets
This collection makes available the complete works of three great Korean poets of the 16th and 17th centuries, revealing a great poetic tradition little known in the West
0-8248-1298-0 HAWAII $24.00

Peter H. **Lee**, translator
Lives of Eminent Korean Monks: The Haedong Kosung Chon
0-674-53662-2 HARVARD PB $7.00

David R. **McCann**, editor
Black Crane: An Anthology of Korean Literature
0-939657-14-7 CORNELL PB $7.00

O **Sukkwon**
A Korean Storyteller's Miscellany: The P'aegwan Chapki of O Sukkwon
TRANSLATED BY PETER H. LEE
0-691-06771-6 PRINCETON $40.00

Hwang Sun-won
Masks & Other Stories
Outstanding late stories by a leading figure of modern Korean literature
EDITED WITH AN INTRODUCTION BY J. MARTIN HOLMAN
0-930523-58-X READERS INTERNATIONAL PB $9.95

Myung-Ho **Sym**
The Making of Modern Korean Poetry: Foreign Influences and Native Creativity
0-8248-0935-1 HAWAII $18.00

Agnita **Tennant**
The Star, and Other Korean Short Stories
0-7103-0533-8 ROUTLEDGE $29.00

In-sob **Zong**
Folk Tales from Korea
"These 99 examples are as various as they are enjoyable, some fantastic, some ironic, others with morality as their aim. All are presented in clear and comfortable English"—TLS
0-930878-26-4 HOLLYM $27.95

A Guide to Korean Literature
0-930878-29-9 HOLLYM $29.95

Filipino Literature

F. Sionil **José**
Sins
0-679-42018-5 RANDOM HOUSE $22.00

Wilfrido D. **Nolledo**
But for the Lovers
1-56478-067-8 DALKEY ARCHIVE PB $12.95

Linda **Ty-Casper**
Awaiting Trespass
Ty-Casper has been publishing her realistic novels of contemporary Philippine life and politics since the early '60s. "This deeply moving book is full of good people, good talk, and a wisdom regarding the inner life"
—*Kirkus Reviews*
0-930523-12-1 READERS INTERNATIONAL PB $7.95

Wings of Stone
A novel set against the chaotic backdrop of the Marcos regime in its final years
0-930523-26-1 READERS INTERNATIONAL $16.95

Southeast Asian Literature

John **Balaban**, editor

Vietnam: A Traveler's Literary Companion

See also **VIETNAM** under **SOUTHEAST ASIA AND THE PHILIPPINES** in **WORLD HISTORY AND CURRENT AFFAIRS**

1-88351-302-2 WHEREABOUTS PRESS PB $12.95

John **Balaban**, translator & editor

Cadao Vietnam: Bilingual Anthology of Vietnamese Folk Poetry

0-87775-129-3 UNICORN PB $13.95

Ming **Cher**

Spider Boys

0-688-12858-0 MORROW $22.00

Duong Thu **Huong**

Novel Without a Name

"If it is a crime to take an unflinching look at the reality of war and of life under a totalitarian regime, and to do it with great art and mastery, then Duong Thu Huong is gloriously guilty"
—*NY Times Book Review*

0-688-12782-7 MORROW $23.00
0-14-025510-9 PENGUIN PB $11.95

Paradise of the Blind

Duong Thu Huong is the most popular novelist in Vietnam, even though her work is banned there. Here is the moving story of three women struggling to affirm their existence in a society where subservience to men is expected and official corruption crushes every dream. The first Vietnamese novel to be published in the US. "Intricately wrought, this is a literary jewel dripping with political nitroglycerine"
Entertainment Weekly

0-688-11445-8 MORROW $20.00

Jade Ngoc Quang **Huynh**

South Wind Changing

1-55597-198-9 GRAY WOLF $20.00

Sanh Thong **Huynh**, editor

An Anthology of Vietnamese Poems: From the Eleventh Through the Twentieth Centuries

0-300-06410-1 YALE $37.50

Bao **Ninh**

The Sorrow of War

"A brutal and emotionally daring portrayal of the war in the jungle"—*NY Times*

1-57322-543-6 RIVERHEAD PB $12.00

Burton **Raffel**, translator

From the Vietnamese: Ten Centuries of Poetry

0-8079-0053-2 OCTOBER HOUSE PB $7.95

Alice M. **Terada**, editor

Under the Starfruit Tree: Folktales from Vietnam

0-8248-1252-2 HAWAII PB $15.95

Nguyen Huy **Thiep**

The General Retires and Other Stories

0-19-588580-5 OXFORD PB $11.95

Turkish Literature

Melih **Anday**

Rain One Step Away

Poems by a modern Turkish writer who has excelled in many genres

TRANSLATED BY TALAT HALMAN & BRIAN SWANN

0-910350-00-0 CHARIOTEER $7.50

Fazil Huznu **Daglarca**

The Bird and I

A chapbook of poetry by a prolific and highly esteemed contemporary writer

TRANSLATED BY TALAT HALMAN

0-89304-803-8 CROSS-CULTURAL PB $5.00

Nazim **Hikmet**

Hikmet, who wrote in many genres and suffered long periods of imprisonment for his political views, is the major figure of modern Turkish literature, and a poet of world stature.

Rubaiyat

TRANSLATED BY RANDY BLASING & MUTLU KONUK

0-914278-48-7 COPPER BEECH PB $4.95

Selected Poems

TRANSLATED BY RANDY BLASING & MUTLU KONUK

0-89255-198-4 PERSEA PB $12.95

Bilge **Karasu**

Night

TRANSLATED BY GUNELI GUN

0-8071-1849-4 LSU $19.95

Yashar **Kemal**

Memed, My Hawk

TRANSLATED BY EDOUARD RODITI

1-86046-103-4 HARPERCOLLINS PB $14.00

Geoffrey **Lewis**, translator

The Book of Dede Korkut

Twelve traditional stories set in the heroic age of the Oghuz Turks

0-14-044298-7 PENGUIN PB $8.95

Orhan **Pamuk**

The Black Book

TRANSLATED BY GUNELI GUN

0-374-11394-7 FS&G $25.00
0-15-600329-5 HARVEST PB $15.00

New Life

0-374-22129-4 FS&G $25.00

The White Castle

0-8076-1264-2 BRAZILLER $17.50
0-85635-882-7 CARCANET $34.25

Orhan **Veli**

I, Orhan Veli

Humorous and sensual poems by a writer who introduced everyday language into Turkish poetry

TRANSLATED BY MURAT NEMET-NEJAT

0-914610-64-3 HANGING LOOSE PB $8.00

Other (Including Pacific Islands)

Ulli **Beier**

Words of Paradise: Poetry of Papua New Guinea

0-87775-031-9 UNICORN $15.00

Ruth **Finnegan** & Margaret **Orbell**, editors

South Pacific Oral Traditions

0-253-32868-3 INDIANA $29.95
0-253-20958-7 INDIANA PB $12.95

Albert **Wendt**, editor

Nuanua: Pacific Writing in English Since 1980

0-8248-1731-1 HAWAII PB $16.00

Australian Literature

The Australian Aboriginal oral tradition, with its myths of ancestral "dreamtime," endured uninterrupted until the intrusion of European settlers in the late 18th century. Gradually an émigré literature began to record often astonished impressions of the exoticism of Australia (designed chiefly for European consumption). Convict themes frequently played a large part, as in the work of Marcus Clarke. By the end of the 19th century a new literature imbued with political nationalism gave rise to more positive images of Australian life, typified by the notion of "outback individualism." This genre of local writing, often colored by social realism, persisted between the wars.

In the postwar period a less parochial, more introspective tone becomes evident, along with a broadening of subject matter and the tempering of pride and self-confidence with self-criticism. The Australian historical experience—with its imagery of isolation, exile, and escape—remains important but often in a more symbolic fashion. Most of the works listed below are relatively recent, an indication of the continuing vitality and expansion of Australian writing.

Jessica **Anderson**

Tirra Lirra by the River

An old woman recalls her past. "A wry, romantic story that should make Anderson's American reputation"—*Washington Post*

0-14-099705-9 PENGUIN PB $6.95

Thea **Astley**

The Acolyte

A penetrating study of the damage wrought by obsessive egotism

0-7022-1540-6 UNIV OF QUEENSLAND PB $14.95

A Descant for Gossips

A vivid portrait of a small-minded small town

0-7022-1843-X UNIV OF QUEENSLAND PB $14.95

Barbara **Baynton**

The Portable Barbara Baynton

Best-known for her 19th-century publication *Bush Studies,* Baynton depicts the bush as a malevolent force—and a theater for fear and loneliness

EDITED BY SALLY KRIMMER & ALAN LAWSON

0-7022-1469-8 UNIV OF QUEENSLAND PB $16.95

Martin **Boyd**

The Cardboard Crown

A turn-of-the-century, upper-middle-class family never feels completely at home either in Australia or England

0-14-006904-6 VIKING PB $4.95

A Difficult Young Man

A study in ambition and the forces that trigger a young man's mutiny. "A subtle and beautifully observed social comedy"—*TLS*

0-14-006906-2 VIKING PB $4.95

Peter **Carey**

Carey is an important young novelist, often described as a Borgesian fabulist whose tone ranges from macabre to realistic.

Bliss

The momentary "deaths" of a salesman interrupt the 39-year bell of his life and lead him on to some very unusual happenings

0-571-13729-6 FABER PB $11.95

Peter Carey

Oscar and Lucinda

Set in 1864 aboard a ship, Carey's most recent novel links a gambling seminarian with an Australian heiress

0-06-091592-7 HARPERPERENNIAL PB $13.00

The Tax Inspector

The fortunes of an extremely unusual family are brought to a head when they are audited by the tax department in a wild, dark, hilarious novel by one of Australians' best-known chroniclers of the absurd. "*The Tax Inspector* is glorious entertainment, storytelling at its best, a piece of richly comic invention"—*The Boston Globe*

0-679-40434-1 KNOPF $25.00

Miles **Franklin**

Miles Franklin was the pseudonym of Stella Franklin, who escaped from the humble origins of her squatter family to become a journalist and early feminist.

Bring the Monkey

0-7022-1817-0 UNIV OF QUEENSLAND $15.95
0-7022-1809-X UNIV OF QUEENSLAND PB $11.95

My Brilliant Career: My Career Goes Bung

Rightly regarded as a classic, this 1901 *Bildungsroman* traces the evolution of a bright country girl struggling against prejudice in the late-19th-century outback

0-207-18695-2 HARPERCOLLINS PB $14.00

On Dearborn Street

A spirited woman-executive in Chicago is not inclined to wedlock

0-7022-1954-1 UNIV OF QUEENSLAND PB $14.95

Joseph **Furphy**

The Portable Joseph Furphy

Alias "Tom Collins," the self-styled "half bushman, half bookworm" achieved renown with a single volume, *Such Is Life,* a vivid turn-of-the-century picture of what he calls "offensively Australian" country life

EDITED BY JOHN BARNES

0-7022-1612-7 UNIV OF QUEENSLAND PB $16.95

Kate **Grenville**

Albion's Story

0-15-100122-7 HARCOURT BRACE $21.95
0-15-600241-8 HARVEST PB $13.00

Bearded Ladies

Selected stories that have earned Grenville comparison with Hemingway

0-7022-1716-6 UNIV OF QUEENSLAND PB $14.95

Lilian's Story

A daughter escapes from her well-to-do family and her old-fashioned despotic father

0-15-600123-3 HARVEST PB $10.95

Rodney **Hall**

Hall is known for both his poetry and his fiction.

The Most Beautiful World: Fictions and Sermons

0-7022-1588-0 UNIV OF QUEENSLAND PB $7.50

A Place Among People

0-7022-0963-5 UNIV OF QUEENSLAND PB $11.95

The Second Bridegroom

0-374-25668-3 FS&G $19.95

Selected Poems

0-7022-0994-5 UNIV OF QUEENSLAND $19.95

The Yandilli Trilogy

0-374-52439-4 NOONDAY PB $16.00

Barbara **Hanrahan**

Hanrahan's work shows a pervasive concern with the choices women confront.

Dove

A generational study of the relationship between a mother and daughter

0-7022-1890-1 UNIV OF QUEENSLAND PB $14.95

The Frangipani Garden

Respectable Adelaide society—and its dark secrets—in the '20s

0-7022-1563-5 UNIV OF QUEENSLAND PB $14.95

The Peach Groves

The setting switches between Adelaide and New Zealand in the 1880s

0-7022-1458-2 UNIV OF QUEENSLAND $24.95
0-7022-1459-0 UNIV OF QUEENSLAND PB $12.95

Where the Queens All Strayed

0-7022-1305-5 UNIV OF QUEENSLAND PB $14.95

Shirley **Hazzard**

The Evening of the Holiday

An encounter in Italy develops into an overwhelming, doomed love

0-14-010451-8 VIKING PB $6.95

Dorothy **Hewett**

Bobbin Up

A novel based on the factory experiences of a card-carrying Communist and radical—Hewett herself

0-86068-686-8 VIRAGO PB $11.95

Michael **Heyward**

The Ern Malley Affair

Diverting account of how a poetic hoax—the publication of poems by an imaginary experimentalist—created a storm in Australia

0-571-17154-0 FABER PB $12.95

Clive **James**

James is a lively, irreverent critic, as iconoclastic about his adopted home (England) and its more voguish enclaves as he is about his birthplace.

Falling Towards England: Unreliable Memoirs II

An autobiographical account of James's arrival, early adventures in, and first impressions of England

1-85089-556-2 ISIS $21.95

Elizabeth **Jolley**

Palomino

The love of two women, one decades older than the other. "The hypnotic style and emotional richness make it clear that Jolley is very much…a voice that can pierce right to the heart of emotion"—*San Francisco Chronicle*

0-89255-136-4 PERSEA PB $8.95

Thomas **Keneally**

Bring Larks and Heroes

0-14-010929-3 PENGUIN PB $10.95

The Chant of Jimmie Blacksmith

Racism in 19th-century Australia leads to rebellion and murder

0-14-003620-2 VIKING PB $10.00

Confederates

A stirring tale set in the United States in 1862 and culminating in the battle of Antietam. "The best Civil War novel since *The Killer Angel*" —*Library Journal*

0-06-091446-7 HARPERPERENNIAL PB $13.00

A Family Madness
"A disturbing look at obsessions and their impact on the human spirit"
—*Toronto Globe and Mail*
0-671-88512-X TOUCHSTONE PB........$12.00

Gossip from the Forest
A re-creation of the making of the armistice that ended World War I
0-15-636469-7 HARCOURT BRACE PB........$8.95

The Playmaker
To mark the King's birthday in 1789, an officer stages a play with a group of convicts who in time cast a weird spell over their director. "A world so rich and strange that we experience it as if in a dream"—*Chicago Tribune*
0-671-88511-1 TOUCHSTONE PB........$12.00

River Town
0-385-47696-5 DOUBLEDAY........$24.00
0-452-27655-1 PLUME PB........$12.95

Schindler's List
The story of a Catholic director of a Nazi factory—and prison camp—who saved many Jewish lives, reconstructed from the testimony of those who came to be known as *Schindlerjuden*
See also **RESCUE AND RESISTANCE** under **THE HOLOCAUST** in **WORLD HISTORY AND CURRENT AFFAIRS**
0-671-51688-4 SIMON & SCHUSTER........$25.00
0-671-88031-4 TOUCHSTONE PB........$12.00

A Season in Purgatory
In the struggle against the Nazis in Yugoslavia two lovers—a British doctor and an empassioned partisan—also struggle to retain their humanity
0-15-679850-6 HARCOURT BRACE PB........$8.95

The Survivor
The survivor of a polar expedition confronts doubt and guilt when the body of the dead leader is exhumed 40 years later
1-86340-066-4 XS BOOKS PB........$17.95

Victim of the Aurora
Murder adds spice to a 1910 expedition to the South Pole. "Edwardian innocence and stuffiness crashing against the Antarctic void"
—*Washington Post*
0-15-693534-1 HARCOURT BRACE PB........$8.95

Christopher J. **Koch**

Highways to a War
"A gripping tale, a convincing, page-turning evocation of recent history full of compelling characters, tumultuous events, and just plain excitement"—*NY Times*
0-14-024757-2 PENGUIN PB........$12.95

Ern **Malley**

The Poems of Ern Malley
The notorious poems that sparked the uproar chronicled by Michael Heyward in *The Ern Malley Affair*
0-04-150088-1 UNWIN HYMAN........$35.00

David **Malouf**

Child's Play: The Bread of Time to Come
A terrorist sets a trap to assassinate a famous author, and finds himself ensnared by the writer's plot
0-8076-1032-1 BRAZILLER........$10.95

First Things Last
0-7022-1564-3 UNIV OF QUEENSLAND........$16.95
0-7022-1565-1 OLYMPIC PB........$1.98

The Great World
A bestseller in England and his native Australia, Malouf's newest novel is set against 70 years of modern history, with its pivot point the meeting of two men in a Japanese POW camp during World War II
0-679-74836-9 VINTAGE PB........$13.00

An Imaginary Life
"A daring novel...Malouf has a gift for phrases and an eye for the evocation of murky and mystical places"—*New Republic*
0-679-76793-2 VINTAGE PB........$11.00

Remembering Babylon
From one of Australia's greatest living writers, the story of a 13-year-old castaway who is taken in by Aborigines on an otherwise unsettled island. "Full of wisdom and magic—the most delicate tracing of a profound and elliptical history, thrilling in its style and in its adventurousness. The story is universal—it contains the violence of the world equal to Goya's and also, alongside it, the most honorable and human gentleness"—Michael Ondaatje
0-679-74951-9 VINTAGE PB........$11.00

David Malouf (photo by Jane Brown)

Colleen **McCullough**

A Creed for the Third Millennium
0-380-70134-0 AVON PB........$5.99

An Indecent Obsession
A psychiatric hospital is the setting for an odd mixture of romance, violence, and paranoia
See also **THE '80S** under **THE GREAT FICTION BESTSELLERS 1930-1995** in **POPULAR READING**
0-380-60376-4 AVON PB........$6.99

The Ladies of Missalonghi
See also **HISTORICAL AND ROMANTIC FICTION** in **POPULAR READING**
0-380-70458-7 AVON PB........$4.99

The Thorn Birds
See also **THE '70S** under **THE GREAT FICTION BESTSELLERS 1930-1995** in **POPULAR READING**
0-380-01817-9 AVON PB........$6.99

Tim
A feeble-minded but Adonis-like laborer strikes up a relationship with a plain spinster
0-380-71196-6 AVON PB........$6.99

Les **Murray**

Murray is the preeminent figure among contemporary Australian poets, a writer of great range and verbal inventiveness.

The Boys Who Stole the Funeral
0-374-11603-2 FS&G........$20.00

The Daylight Moon & Other Poems
"It would be as myopic to regard Mr. Murray as an Australian poet as to call Yeats an Irishman. He is, quite simply the one by whom the language lives"—Joseph Brodsky
0-89255-138-0 PERSEA PB........$9.95

Dog Fox Field: Poems
0-374-14314-5 FS&G........$19.00

The Rabbiter's Bounty: Collected Poems
0-374-12622-4 FS&G........$25.00

The Vernacular Republic
"One of the greatest poets, in my opinion, in the English-speaking world. What he gives is enormous and quite beyond price"
—Thomas Keneally
0-89255-063-5 PERSEA PB........$8.95

Hal **Porter**

The Extra
0-7022-2052-3 UNIV OF QUEENSLAND PB........$14.95

Tilted Cross
0-7022-2183-X UNIV OF QUEENSLAND PB........$14.95

Peter **Porter**

The Automatic Oracle
0-19-282088-5 OXFORD PB........$8.95

Collected Poems
0-19-211965-6 OXFORD PB........$7.95

Fast Forward
0-19-211967-2 OXFORD PB........$7.95

Thomas **Shapcott**

Shapcott, an important anti-establishment poet, came to prominence in the '60s.

The City of Home
0-7022-2782-X UNIV OF QUEENSLAND PB........$16.95

Hotel Bellevue
0-7011-3139-X RANDOM HOUSE........$15.95

Shabbytown Calendar
0-7022-0959-7 UNIV OF QUEENSLAND PB........$9.95

Thomas Shapcott: Selected Poems, 1956-1988
0-7022-2243-7 UNIV OF QUEENSLAND PB........$18.95

Travel Dice
0-7022-2077-9 UNIV OF QUEENSLAND PB........$9.95

Nevil **Shute**

On the Beach

A suspenseful, apocalyptic novel in which Australia becomes the last haven in a world devastated by nuclear holocaust

See also **THE '50S** under **THE GREAT FICTION BESTSELLERS 1930-1995** in **POPULAR READING**

0-89968-365-7 LIGHTYEAR $18.95
0-345-31148-5 BALLANTINE PB $5.99

A Town Like Alice

A classic story of survival concerning a Japanese death march through Malaya during the Second World War

0-345-35374-9 BALLANTINE PB $5.99

Christina **Stead**

Rebecca West described Stead as "one of the few people really original since the war." Her powerfully realistic novels, set in Australia, England, and the United States, reflect her involvement with feminist and left-wing issues.

Little Hotel

A cross-section of human life under the roof of a Swiss hotel

0-8050-2412-3 HOLT PB $12.95

The Man Who Loved Children

Stead's most famous book, a masterpiece of modern fiction, is a chilling novel of family life filled with loathing, manipulation, and madness

INTRODUCTION BY RANDALL JARRELL

0-8050-0499-8 HOLT PB $14.95
0-679-44364-9 EVERYMAN'S $22.00

Christina Stead
(photo courtesy of Henry Holt and Company)

Patrick **White**

The Aunt's Story

The journey of an independent lady from rugged Australia to crazy prewar Europe and on to the United States

0-14-018653-0 PENGUIN PB $10.95

The Eye of the Storm

A callous woman on her deathbed elicits varying waves of love and hate from those gathered around her

0-670-30374-7 VIKING $13.95

Patrick White

A Fringe of Leaves

White's version of a classic Australian adventure story, involving shipwreck, escaped convicts, and Aborigines

0-14-018610-7 PENGUIN PB $11.95

The Living and the Dead

0-14-018526-7 PENGUIN PB $10.95

Riders in the Chariot

0-14-018634-4 PENGUIN PB $11.95

The Twyborn Affair

0-14-018606-9 PENGUIN PB $11.95

The Vivisector

Incapable of love, a painter assiduously dissects the weaknesses of others

0-14-018527-5 PENGUIN PB $11.95

David **Marr**, editor

Patrick White: Letters

0-226-89503-3 CHICAGO $35.00

Donna **Williams**

Like Color to the Blind: Soul Searching and Soul Finding

Williams (*Nobody Nowhere*, *Somebody Somewhere*) has previously chronicled her autistic childhood and her growth out of the sheltered bubble of autism into the real world. Here she tells the powerful sequel to the story, the emotional transformation of love and marriage that followed her emergence. "Donna Williams isn't just teaching us what it is like to be autistic. She is teaching us what it is like to be human"—*NY Times Book Review*

See also **OTHER PROBLEMS** under **DISORDERS AND TREATMENT** under **PSYCHOLOGY** in **SOCIAL STUDIES**

0-8129-2640-4 TIME BOOKS $24.00

Nobody Nowhere: The Extraordinary Autobiography of an Autistic

A challenging, wrenching, and disturbing memoir. Williams is attached to the outside world firmly enough to evoke for the reader the disjointed, phantasmagoric, yet intensely vivid nature of her experiences as an autistic

See also **OTHER PROBLEMS** under **DISORDERS AND TREATMENT** under **PSYCHOLOGY** in **SOCIAL STUDIES**

0-8129-2042-2 TIME BOOKS $21.00
0-380-72217-8 AVON PB $10.00

Somebody Somewhere: Breaking Free from the World of Autism

"Williams continues to build a bridge between 'my' world and 'the' world"—*Publishers Weekly*

See also **OTHER PROBLEMS** under **DISORDERS AND TREATMENT** under **PSYCHOLOGY** in **SOCIAL STUDIES**

0-8129-2287-5 TIME BOOKS $23.00
0-8129-2524-6 TIME BOOKS PB $14.00

B. **Wongar**

"B. Wongar" is the pseudonym of a Yugoslavian anthropologist who writes with a profound understanding of Aboriginal culture.

Bilma

0-8142-0370-1 OHIO STATE $22.50

Gabo Djara: A Novel of Australia

0-8076-1243-X BRAZILLER PB $9.95

Karan: A Novel of the Australian Hinterland

0-8076-1242-1 BRAZILLER PB $9.95

The Track to Bralgu

0-207-17148-3 ANGUS & ROBERTSON PB $10.00

Walg: A Novel of Australia

FOREWORD BY SIMONE DE BEAUVOIR

0-8076-1241-3 BRAZILLER PB $9.95

Anthologies

Murray **Bail**, editor

The Faber Book of Contemporary Australian Short Stories

0-571-15083-7 FABER PB $13.95

Leon **Cantrell**, editor

The '80s: Stories, Verses & Essays

Includes pieces by Henry Lawson and Christopher Brennan

0-7022-2019-1 UNIV OF QUEENSLAND PB $16.95

Brian **Elliott**, editor

The Jindyworobaks

Selections from the nationalist poetry movement of the '30s

0-7022-1297-0 UNIV OF QUEENSLAND PB $17.95

Laurie **Hergenhan**, editor

The Australian Short Story: An Anthology from the 1890s to the '80s

0-7022-1787-5 UNIV OF QUEENSLAND PB $18.95

Sally **Morgan**

My Place

An exploration of the author's Aboriginal roots. "Sally Morgan's extraordinary work is about a quest for the past of one person and one family, an individual past which turns out to be a communal past, which is, in turn, the history of a people"—Janette Turner Hospital, *NY Times*

See also **ABORIGINAL HISTORY** under **AUSTRALIA, NEW ZEALAND, AND POLYNESIA** in **WORLD HISTORY AND CURRENT AFFAIRS**

0-316-58289-1 LITTLE, BROWN PB $13.95

Les **Murray**, editor

The New Oxford Book of Australian Verse

0-19-554618-0 OXFORD $39.95

Thomas **Shapcott**, editor

Consolidation: The Second Poets Anthology

0-7022-1676-3 OLYMPIC PB $2.98

New Zealand Literature

Sylvia **Ashton-Warner**

Teacher

0-671-61768-0 SIMON & SCHUSTER PB $9.95

Janet **Frame**

The Carpathians

0-8076-1298-7 BRAZILLER PB $11.95

Daughter Buffalo

0-8076-1284-7 BRAZILLER PB $8.95

The Edge of the Alphabet

An exploration of fantasy, isolation, and the difficulties of communication by the New Zealand writer whose fiction and memoirs have received fresh attention recently

0-8076-1270-7 BRAZILLER PB $10.95

And I have changed. I must touch the surface. I must encircle what is dead. I must think in this way, shuttled over and under… I, Zoe Bryce, on my working tour of New Zealand, spending my day crying out in the white kitchens, Soup two, roast beef one, a lady, corned beef one, a gent, to follow!…the rhythm of my demands alive in my mind beside the composite historical cries of my own country—victory, rag-and-bone pleadings, church music of ice cream, disaster, bring out your dead.

THE EDGE OF THE ALPHABET

Faces in the Water

Ostensibly about the insane, the semi-autobiographical *Faces in the Water* "is especially brilliant in its descriptions of what happens inside the patient's mind"—*Time*

0-8076-0957-9 BRAZILLER PB $10.95

Intensive Care

0-8076-1341-X BRAZILLER PB $12.95

Janet Frame: An Autobiography

The New Zealand writer Janet Frame endured long periods of confinement in mental institutions, powerfully narrated in this memoir. "One of the greatest autobiographies written this century"—Michael Holroyd

0-8076-1259-6 BRAZILLER PB $17.50

Living in the Maniototo

The tale of a ventriloquist, "full of wordplays, cameo portraits and deliberate mystery" —*Publishers Weekly*

0-8076-0926-9 BRAZILLER $8.95
0-8076-0958-7 BRAZILLER PB $7.95

The Pocket Mirror: Poems

0-8076-1272-3 BRAZILLER PB $6.95

The Reservoir: Stories and Sketches

0-8076-1305-3 BRAZILLER PB $10.95

Scented Gardens for the Blind

0-8076-0985-4 BRAZILLER PB $10.95

A State of Siege

0-8076-0986-2 BRAZILLER PB $10.95

To the Island

The first part of Frame's autobiography. "My life had been for many years in the power of words. I was driven now by a constant search and need for what was, after all, only a word—imagination"

0-8076-1042-9 BRAZILLER $10.95

Yellow Flowers in the Antipodean Room

0-8076-1340-1 BRAZILLER PB $11.95

Patricia **Grace**

The Dream Sleepers & Other Stories

Of Maori descent, Grace's persistent theme is the status of the Maori—and Maori culture—in white New Zealand society. Tales of Maoris in a society where the prevalent values are alien to them

0-582-71779-5 THREE CONTINENTS PB $7.00

Potiki

0-8248-1706-0 HAWAII PB $10.95

Keri **Hulme**

Bait

0-14-017037-5 VIKING PB $12.00

The Bone People

The prize-winning tale of a strange trio—an artist-cum-anchorite, her boy lover, and the boy's foster father—"reminding us of things in heaven and earth we too often forget or provincially ignore"—*Houston Post*

0-14-008922-5 VIKING PB $12.95

Robin **Hyde**

Selected Poems

Robin Hyde was the pseudonym of Iris Wilkinson, an anguished and peripatetic writer who took her own life on the eve of World War II

EDITED BY LINDA WAVERS

0-19-558114-8 OXFORD PB $14.95

Katherine **Mansfield**

The Collected Letters of Katherine Mansfield: 1920-1921

EDITED BY VINCENT O'SULLIVAN AND MARGARET SCOTT

0-19-818532-4 OXFORD $80.00
0-19-812614-X OXFORD PB $34.00

Stories

Twenty-seven thoughtfully selected tales. "Katherine Mansfield was not a rebel, she was an innovator…simply, she passed beyond the English tradition of prose narrative" —Elizabeth Bowen

EDITED BY ELIZABETH BOWEN

0-679-73374-4 VINTAGE PB $13.00

Maurice **Shadbolt**

Monday's Warriors

0-87923-915-8 GODINE $21.95

Season of the Jew

0-87923-753-8 GODINE PB $12.95

Ian **Wedde**

Survival Arts

0-14-010503-4 PENGUIN PB $6.95

Anthologies

Vincent **O'Sullivan**, editor

An Anthology of Twentieth Century New Zealand Poetry

0-19-558163-6 OXFORD PB $22.95

Lydia **Wevers**, editor

Yellow Pencils: Contemporary Poetry by New Zealand Women

0-19-558178-4 OXFORD PB $13.95

Literary Criticism

Literary Essayists and Historians

Robert **Alter**

The Pleasures of Reading in an Ideological Age

0-393-31499-5 NORTON PB $13.00

W.H. **Auden**

The Dyer's Hand

This most substantial of his prose collections is an essential book of modern criticism, varied in its themes and unfailingly brilliant in its perceptions

See also **20TH-CENTURY BRITISH ESSAYS AND OTHER PROSE** in **LITERATURE OF THE BRITISH ISLES**

0-679-72484-2 VINTAGE PB $17.00

Forewords and Afterwords

Brief occasional essays on a range of subjects illustrating Auden's extraordinarily eclectic interests

0-679-72485-0 VINTAGE PB $15.00

Jacques **Barzun**

Use and Abuse of Art

0-691-01804-9 PRINCETON PB $10.95

Alan **Bloom**

Love and Friendship

Bloom argues that we have lost the language of love, and with it, the imaginative fuel that transforms sex into Eros.

0-671-67336-X TOUCHSTONE PB $25.00

Guy **Davenport**

The Hunter Gracchus and Other Papers on Literature and Art

See also **LITERATURE** under **20TH-CENTURY AMERICAN ESSAYS AND JOURNALISM** in **LITERATURE OF THE AMERICAS**

1-88717-824-4 COUNTERPOINT $25.00

Leon **Edel**

Writing Lives: Principia Biographica

"Edel has brilliantly provided for the art of biography a much-needed statement of first principles"—Louis Auchincloss

0-393-30382-9 NORTON PB $6.95

Richard **Ellman**

Golden Codgers: Biographical Speculations

0-19-211827-7 OXFORD PB $1.98

Joseph **Epstein**

A Line Out for a Walk: Familiar Essays

0-393-30854-5 NORTON PB $10.95

Once More Around the Block: Familiar Essays

0-393-30633-X NORTON PB $8.95

Partial Payments: Essays on Writers and Their Lives

0-393-30716-6 NORTON PB $12.95

With My Trousers Rolled: Familiar Essays

0-393-03757-6 NORTON $25.00

Geoffrey H. **Hartman**

Minor Prophecies: The Literary Essay in the Culture Wars

0-674-57636-5 HARVARD $34.50

Irving **Howe**

"Irving Howe was one of the splendors of American culture and intellect, and the splendor was impeccably human."
—New Yorker

A Critic's Notebook

Howe's distinguished literary criticism, his essays, and his editorial work in the preeminent left-wing journal *Dissent* made him an American treasure. Collected here are the short pieces he left behind at his death in 1993. Including works on Dickens, Eliot, Gissing, Tolstoy, and many more. "A delightful potpourri in which Howe displays an essayist's ease, a critic's incisiveness, and, when necessary, an academic's scholarship"—*Kirkus Reviews*

See also **LITERATURE** under **20TH-CENTURY AMERICAN ESSAYS AND JOURNALISM** in **LITERATURE OF THE AMERICAS**

INTRODUCTION BY NICHOLAS HOWE

0-15-119949-3 HARCOURT BRACE $27.95
0-15-600257-4 HARCOURT BRACE PB $14.00

Randall **Jarrell**

Kipling, Auden and Co.: Essays and Reviews, 1935-1964

0-374-18153-5 FS&G $17.95
0-374-51668-5 FS&G PB $9.95

Alfred **Kazin**

An American Procession

See also **ANTHOLOGIES** under **20TH-CENTURY AMERICAN DRAMA** in **LITERATURE OF THE AMERICAS**

0-674-03143-1 HARVARD PB $15.95

Hugh **Kenner**

The Counterfeiters: An Historical Comedy

ILLUSTRATED BY GUY DAVENPORT

0-8018-2981-X JOHNS HOPKINS $22.50
0-8018-2983-6 JOHNS HOPKINS PB $9.95

The Mechanic Muse

How such inventions as the linotype and the subway altered the literary imaginations of Eliot, Pound, Joyce, and Beckett

0-19-504142-9 OXFORD $17.95

Founded on faith in the possibility of insight—the Joycean epiphany, the Poundian image that can flash in an instant of time; on faith, too, that technology need not consign the arts to irrelevance, the Modernist enterprise evolved its verbal technologies, its poem- and novel-machines of intricate interacting discrete pieces. The technology on which it drew for tacit analogies is largely obsolescent now: as much so as, say, Dante's Earth-centered cosmos. The Dublin trams are long gone, and the linotype machine; the typewriter is going; Bloom's watch with hands will some day need a footnote. Already students need the explanation that when a telephone whirs and a man says "Twentyeight. No. Twenty. Double four, yes" [7.385] he has cranked the magneto and is now requesting a number. That world survives now, like Dante's world, in art. Its assumptions survive in the structures of its art: complex artifacts we even sometimes take apart for maintenance.

THE MECHANIC MUSE

The Pound Era

Kenner's major work is also a study of the many aspects of modernism on which Pound's career impinged

See also **GENERAL STUDIES: THE 20TH-CENTURY** under **AMERICAN LITERATURE: ANTHOLOGIES AND CRITICAL STUDIES** in **LITERATURE OF THE AMERICAS**

0-520-02427-3 CALIFORNIA PB $17.95

The Stoic Comedians: Flaubert, Joyce and Beckett

0-520-02584-9 CALIFORNIA PB $9.95

David **Lodge**

The Art of Fiction

Fifty pieces from the acclaimed series which appeared in the *Washington Post* and the London *Independent*. A valuable book for anyone who enjoys literary fiction and would like to understand better how it works

See also **20TH-CENTURY BRITISH ESSAYS AND OTHER PROSE** in **LITERATURE OF THE BRITISH ISLES**

0-14-017492-3 PENGUIN PB $11.95

The Novelist at the Crossroads: And Other Essays on Fiction and Criticism

0-7448-0039-0 ROUTLEDGE PB $16.50

Leonard **Michaels** & Christopher **Ricks**, editors

The State of the Language

A collection of essays, with contributions from M.F.K. Fisher, Anthony Burgess, Angela Carter, and Ishmael Reed, among others

See also **ABOUT LANGUAGE** under **REFERENCE** in **BUSINESS AND REFERENCE**

0-520-05906-9 CALIFORNIA $40.00

Richard **Poirier**

The Performing Self: Compositions and Decompositions in the Languages of Contemporary Life

0-8135-1795-8 RUTGERS PB $15.00

Poetry and Pragmatism

0-674-67991-1 HARVARD PB $13.95

Anthony **Powell**

Writings on Writers

Essays from the author of *A Dance to the Music of Time*

Volume 1
Miscellaneous Verdicts, 1946-1989

0-226-67710-9 CHICAGO $38.50

Volume 2
Under Review, 1946-1990

0-226-67712-5 CHICAGO $34.95

Mario **Praz**

The Flaming Heart: Essays on Crashaw, Machiavelli, and Other Studies from Chaucer to T.S. Eliot

0-393-00669-7 NORTON PB $3.95

Burton **Raffel**

The Art of Translating Prose

0-271-01080-0 PENN STATE $29.95

David **Rattray**

How I Became One of the Invisible

A collection of Rattray's essays. His experiences in Mexico in the early sixties are particularly memorable, as is his essay on Holderlin

See also **HISTORY, POLITICS, AND SOCIETY** under **20TH-CENTURY AMERICAN ESSAYS AND JOURNALISM** in **LITERATURE OF THE AMERICAS**

0-936756-98-5 SEMIOTEXTET PB $6.00

F.D. **Reeve**

The White Monk: An Essay on Dostoevsky and Melville

0-8265-1234-8 VANDERBILT $22.50

Christopher **Ricks**

Essays in Appreciation

0-19-818344-5 OXFORD $29.95

Susan **Sontag**

Against Interpretation

Selections from her early writings about the arts and contemporary culture, including "Notes on Camp" and "The Imagination of Disaster"

0-385-26708-8 ANCHOR PB $9.95

Illness as Metaphor & AIDS and Its Metaphors

See also **AIDS** under **SPECIFIC HEALTH PROBLEMS** under **HEALTH** in **LIFESTYLES AND PRACTICAL ADVICE**

0-385-26705-3 ANCHOR PB $9.95

Susan Sontag

Styles of Radical Will

Extends her investigations to film, literature, politics, and pornography

0-385-26709-6 ANCHOR PB $9.95

A Susan Sontag Reader

An interview, three short stories, an excerpt from "On Photography," two novels, and a selection of essays including "Notes on Camp," "On Style," "The Pornographic Imagination," and "Fascinating Fascism"

INTRODUCTION BY ELIZABETH HARDWICK

0-374-27216-6 FS&G $60.00

Jean **Starobinski**

Blessings in Disguise; Or, the Morality of Evil

From one of our greatest living critics comes a discussion on the nature of art, criticism, and civilization. What role does art play in countering barbarism in society? How closely does 17th- and 18th-century thinking mirror current condemnation of art and criticism as being immoral and perverse? Starobinski uses ideas in 17th- and 18th-century French cultural thought to chart criticism's historic and intellectual limits

TRANSLATED BY ARTHUR GOLDHAMMER

0-674-07647-8 HARVARD $45.00

The Living Eye

0-674-53664-9 HARVARD $37.00

George **Steiner**

After Babel: Aspects of Language and Translation

"Great erudition brought to bear on linguistics...celebrates the beauty and mystery of the subject"—*NY Times*

0-19-282874-6 OXFORD PB $17.95

Antigones: How the Antigone Legend Has Endured in Western Literature, Art and Thought

0-300-06915-4 YALE PB $17.00

The Death of Tragedy

See also **20TH-CENTURY BRITISH ESSAYS AND OTHER PROSE** in **LITERATURE OF THE BRITISH ISLES**

0-300-06916-2 YALE PB $17.00

George Steiner: A Reader

A rich sampling of Steiner's ideas

0-19-505068-1 OXFORD PB $16.95

In Bluebeard's Castle: Some Notes Toward the Redefinition of Culture

0-300-01710-3 YALE PB $14.00

No Passion Spent: Essays, 1978-1995

See also **THEOLOGY** under **THEOLOGY AND DOCTRINE** under **CHRISTIANITY** in **RELIGION, SPIRITUALITY, AND PHILOSOPHY**

0-300-06630-9 YALE $30.00

Lionel **Trilling**

The Last Decade: Essays and Reviews, 1965-1975

EDITED BY DIANA TRILLING

0-15-148421-X HARCOURT BRACE $19.95

0-15-648892-2 HARCOURT BRACE PB $7.95

The Opposing Self

This 1955 collection includes essays on *Little Dorrit, Anna Karenina, The Bostonians, Bouvard and Pechuchet,* and *Mansfield Park*

0-15-170068-0 HARCOURT BRACE $10.95

Prefaces to the Experience of Literature

0-15-673810-4 HARCOURT BRACE PB $8.95

Sincerity and Authenticity

How sincerity—being true to oneself—came to occupy a place of supreme importance in moral life and how it was replaced by the more strenuous ideal of authenticity. Ranges over the whole of Western literature

0-674-80861-4 HARVARD PB $10.50

Paul **West**

Sheer Fiction

Literary essays and reviews from the past thirty years by a major writer

0-929701-38-0 MCPHERSON $22.00

Edmund **Wilson**

The American Earthquake

0-306-80696-7 DA CAPO PB $17.95

Axel's Castle: A Study in the Imaginative Literature of 1870-1930

"Edmund Wilson was the first American critic to show that a single impulse persisted through eighty years of quarreling doctrines and self-devouring schools...His book was extraordinarily illuminating. Nobody before him had written a better exposition of Yeats, Joyce, Proust" —Malcolm Cowley

See also **LITERATURE** under **20TH-CENTURY AMERICAN ESSAYS AND JOURNALISM** in **LITERATURE OF THE AMERICAS**

0-679-60233-X MODERN LIBRARY $16.50

The Shores of Light: A Literary Chronicle of the '20s and '30s

Essays on F. Scott Fitzgerald, Edna St. Vincent Millay, Sherwood Anderson, and Gertrude Stein in "a general history of the culture of a recklessly unspecialized era, when minds and imaginations were exploring in all directions" (Edmund Wilson)

See also **LITERATURE** under **20TH-CENTURY AMERICAN ESSAYS AND JOURNALISM** in **LITERATURE OF THE AMERICAS**

INTRODUCTION BY DANIEL AARON

0-930350-68-5 NORTHEASTERN PB $16.95

Edmund Wilson

To the Finland Station

The roots of modern radicalism, from Fourier and Saint-Simon to Marx and Lenin. "A work of the historical imagination at its most creative...puts us in touch with the revolutionary dreams and visions of our past" —*NY Times*

See also **CLASSICS** under **POLITICAL THOUGHT** in **SOCIAL STUDIES**

0-374-51045-8 FS&G PB $16.00

The Modernist Revolution

T.S. **Eliot**

Selected Prose of T.S. Eliot

Includes the influential essay "Traditions and the Individual Talent"

EDITED BY FRANK KERMODE

0-15-680654-1 HARCOURT BRACE PB $11.00

The Use of Poetry and the Use of Criticism

See also **20TH-CENTURY BRITISH ESSAYS AND OTHER PROSE** in **LITERATURE OF THE BRITISH ISLES**

0-674-93150-5 HARVARD PB $11.95

The Varieties of Metaphysical Poetry

See also **20TH-CENTURY BRITISH ESSAYS AND OTHER PROSE** in **LITERATURE OF THE BRITISH ISLES**

0-15-100096-4 HARCOURT BRACE $29.95

John **Gross**, editor

The Modern Movement: A TLS Companion

0-226-30985-1 CHICAGO $49.50

0-226-30987-8 CHICAGO PB $14.95

T. E. **Hulme**

The Collected Writings of T.E. Hulme

EDITED BY KAREN CSENGERI

0-19-811234-3 OXFORD $85.00

Notes on Language and Style

0-8383-2017-1 HASKELL $29.95

Ezra **Pound**

ABC of Reading

The "Ezraversity" at work, laying down how and what to read, from Sappho to Laforgue

See also **LITERATURE** under **20TH-CENTURY AMERICAN ESSAYS AND JOURNALISM** in **LITERATURE OF THE AMERICAS**

0-8112-0151-1 NEW DIRECTIONS PB $9.95

Ezra Pound

Guide to Kulchur

0-8112-0156-2 NEW DIRECTIONS PB $12.95

Literary Essays

Essays carefully selected to show the evolution of Pound's aesthetic

0-8112-0157-0 NEW DIRECTIONS PB $13.95

Selected Prose, 1909-1965

Gathers Pound's political and economic animadversions

EDITED BY WILLIAM COOKSON

0-8112-0574-6 NEW DIRECTIONS PB $12.95

The Spirit of Romance

0-8112-0163-5 NORTON PB $12.95

Marcel **Proust**

"Supremely sensitive, and with a prodigious memory for recording sensations, he laid his own mind and body open like an intricate musical instrument for experience to play on, studying every note, always searching for a mysterious underlying theme half-perceived from the first. This theme he was to discover was Time."—William Sansom

Marcel Proust on Art and Literature

See also **ESSAYS: PERSONAL, LITERARY, PHILOSOPHICAL** under **MODERN FRENCH LITERATURE**

0-88184-114-5 CARROLL & GRAF PB $8.95

Gertrude **Stein**

Stein (1874-1946) set out, almost singlehandedly, she believed, to invent and define modernist literature. A student of the pragmatic philosopher William James, Stein once said that "I was there to kill what was not dead."

How to Write

See also **FROM THE TURN OF THE CENTURY TO WORLD WAR II** under **20TH-CENTURY AMERICAN FICTION** in **LITERATURE OF THE AMERICAS**

INTRODUCTION BY PATRICIA MEYEROWITZ

0-486-23144-5 DOVER PB $7.95

Paul **Valéry**

The Art of Poetry

"These essays should come into the hands of everyone interested not only in the now almost mythical figure of Valéry but in the evolving situation of poetry and poetic theory in our time"—*New Yorker*

See also **ESSAYS: PERSONAL, LITERARY, PHILOSOPHICAL** under **MODERN FRENCH LITERATURE**

TRANSLATED BY DENISE FOLLIOT

EDITED BY MATHEWS JACKSON

0-691-09838-7 PRINCETON $43.00

0-691-01880-4 PRINCETON PB $15.95

William Carlos **Williams**

"An American original... He stole time to create the most substantial one-man body of literature in our history. When he died at 79, he had no peer as the total American writer."
—Webster Scott, Life

In the American Grain

Meditations on American history and its myths, including chapters on Cotton Mather, Daniel Boone, Abraham Lincoln, and the conquest of Mexico

See also **LITERATURE** under **20TH-CENTURY AMERICAN ESSAYS AND JOURNALISM** in **LITERATURE OF THE AMERICAS**

0-8112-0230-5 NEW DIRECTIONS PB $10.95

William Carlos Williams (photo by John D. Schiff)

Virginia **Woolf**

The Collected Essays of Virginia Woolf

The first volume of this series is currently out of print

Volume 2: 1904-1912

0-15-129056-3 HARCOURT BRACE $22.95

Volume 3: 1919-1924

0-15-629056-1 HARCOURT BRACE PB $18.95

The Common Reader, First Series

See also **20TH-CENTURY BRITISH ESSAYS AND OTHER PROSE** in **LITERATURE OF THE BRITISH ISLES**

0-15-619806-1 HARCOURT BRACE PB $10.00

The Second Common Reader

On English literature, with a special interest in women writers. "As nearly perfect as Heaven grants it to a critic to be"—*NY Times*

See also **20TH-CENTURY BRITISH ESSAYS AND OTHER PROSE** in **LITERATURE OF THE BRITISH ISLES**

0-15-619808-8 HARCOURT BRACE PB $7.95

Contemporary Writers on Writing

Though critics profess to unravel the workings of a writer's mind, authors themselves frequently offer quite a different view of the creative process.

Charles **Bernstein**

Content's Dream: Essays, 1975-1984

Reflections on contemporary poetry, art, and philosophy by a leading "Language" poet

See also **POETRY** under **GENERAL STUDIES: THE 20TH-CENTURY** under **AMERICAN LITERATURE: ANTHOLOGIES AND CRITICAL STUDIES** in **LITERATURE OF THE AMERICAS**

0-940650-57-6 SUN & MOON $17.95

0-940650-56-8 SUN & MOON PB $14.95

A Poetics

0-674-67857-5 HARVARD PB $16.95

Jorge Luis **Borges**

Borges on Writing

See also **ARGENTINA** under **CRITICISM, MEMOIRS, AND OTHER PROSE** under **LATIN AMERICAN LITERATURE** in **LITERATURE OF THE AMERICAS**

0-88001-368-0 ECCO PB $12.00

Seven Nights

Seven lectures on *The Divine Comedy*, nightmares, *The One Thousand and One Nights*, Buddhism, poetry, blindness, and the Kabbalah

TRANSLATED BY ELIOT WEINBERGER

INTRODUCTION BY ALASTAIR REID

0-8112-0905-9 NEW DIRECTIONS PB $7.95

Joseph **Brodsky**

Less Than One: Selected Essays

The poet explains himself in subtle and elegant essays on childhood, poetry, criticism, Dante, and tyranny

See also **CONTEMPORARY RUSSIAN WRITERS** under **RUSSIAN LITERATURE**

0-374-18503-4 FS&G $30.00

0-374-52055-0 FS&G PB $15.00

On Grief and Reason

A collection of essays on poetry, on his experience as an exile, and on the future of Europe by the late Poet Laureate of America

See also **LITERATURE** under **20TH-CENTURY AMERICAN ESSAYS AND JOURNALISM** in **LITERATURE OF THE AMERICAS**

0-374-23415-9 FS&G $24.00

Place as Good as Any: Essays
See also **CONTEMPORARY RUSSIAN WRITERS** under **RUSSIAN LITERATURE**
0-374-26649-2 FS&G $20.00

John **Gardner**
On Writers and Writing
Gardner's growing legacy as one of the most influential writing teachers of our time is reaffirmed in this superb collection of essays and reviews. Writing on Bellow, Nabokov, Joyce Carol Oates, John Cheever, and others, he explains his parameters for genuine fiction and deepens our understanding of his own writing
See also **LITERATURE** under **20TH-CENTURY AMERICAN ESSAYS AND JOURNALISM** in **LITERATURE OF THE AMERICAS**
INTRODUCTION BY CHARLES JOHNSON
EDITED BY STEWART O'NAN
0-201-62672-1 ADDISON-WESLEY $25.00

William H. **Gass**
Finding a Form: Essays
See also **LITERATURE** under **20TH-CENTURY AMERICAN ESSAYS AND JOURNALISM** in **LITERATURE OF THE AMERICAS**
0-679-44662-1 KNOPF $26.00

Seamus **Heaney**
Crediting Poetry: The Nobel Lecture
See also **IRISH POETS** under **20TH-CENTURY BRITISH AND IRISH POETRY** in **LITERATURE OF THE BRITISH ISLES**
0-374-13138-4 FS&G $12.00

The Government of the Tongue: Selected Prose, 1978-1987
0-374-52220-0 FS&G PB $10.00

Preoccupations: Selected Prose, 1968-1978
Heaney discusses, among others, Wordsworth, Keats, Hopkins, Yeats, Kavanagh, and Robert Lowell
See also **THE MIDDLE GENERATION** under **20TH-CENTURY BRITISH AND IRISH FICTION** in **LITERATURE OF THE BRITISH ISLES**
0-374-51650-2 FS&G PB $11.00

The Redress of Poetry
The poet's ten Oxford lectures explore a wide range of writers, from Christopher Marlowe to Oscar Wilde, the 18th-century poet Brian Merriman to Elizabeth Bishop. Eloquent and insightful, Heaney presents his argument that poetry's special spiritual power can oppose hostile and oppressive forces with conviction and poetic force of its own
See also **IRISH POETS** under **20TH-CENTURY BRITISH AND IRISH POETRY** in **LITERATURE OF THE BRITISH ISLES**
0-374-24853-2 FS&G $22.00
0374-52488-2 FS&G PB $12.00

Zbigniew **Herbert**
Herbert is widely regarded as the greatest Polish poet who actually lives in Poland; his background in philosophy, law, and art history gives his work an intellectual tone which has led to comparisons with T.S. Eliot.

Still Life with a Bridle: Essays and Apocryphas
See also **POLISH LITERATURE** under **EASTERN EUROPEAN LITERATURE**
TRANSLATED BY JOHN AND BOGDANA CARPENTER
0-88001-320-6 ECCO PB $9.95

Geoffrey **Hill**
The Enemy's Country: Words, Contexture, and Other Circumstances of Language
See also **BRITISH POETS** under **20TH-CENTURY BRITISH AND IRISH POETRY** in **LITERATURE OF THE BRITISH ISLES**
0-8047-2368-0 STANFORD PB $14.95

Czeslaw **Milosz**
Beginning with My Streets: Essays and Recollections
TRANSLATED BY MADELINE G. LEVINE
0-374-11010-7 FS&G $30.00

The Witness of Poetry
The Charles Eliot Norton lectures
See also **POLISH LITERATURE** under **EASTERN EUROPEAN LITERATURE**
0-674-95383-5 HARVARD PB $7.95

Vladimir **Nabokov**
Nabokov wrote his first nine novels in Russian, the last being The Gift, *written in the late '30s; thereafter he turned exclusively to English as his medium of expression.*

Lectures on Literature: British, French and German Writers
0-15-649589-9 HARCOURT BRACE PB $14.00

Octavio **Paz**
Mexico's great modern poet has explored the same themes over many decades, fusing autobiography and metaphysical speculation, eroticism and politics, vibrant imagery and formal experimentation.

Alternating Current
See also **MEXICO** under **CRITICISM, MEMOIRS, AND OTHER PROSE** under **LATIN AMERICAN LITERATURE** in **LITERATURE OF THE AMERICAS**
See also **ASPECTS OF MEXICAN CULTURE** under **MEXICO** under **LATIN AMERICA AND THE CARIBBEAN** in **HISTORY OF THE AMERICAS**
1-55970-136-6 ARCADE PB $9.95

Children of the Mire: Modern Poetry from Romanticism to the Avant-Garde
The underlying myths of modern poetry, explored by the great Mexican poet in brilliant aphoristic style
See also **MEXICO** under **CRITICISM, MEMOIRS, AND OTHER PROSE** under **LATIN AMERICAN LITERATURE** in **LITERATURE OF THE AMERICAS**
0-674-11629-1 HARVARD PB $12.50

Convergences: Essays on Art and Literature
See also **MEXICO** under **CRITICISM, MEMOIRS, AND OTHER PROSE** under **LATIN AMERICAN LITERATURE** in **LITERATURE OF THE AMERICAS**
TRANSLATED BY HELEN LANE
0-15-122585-0 HARCOURT BRACE $19.95

On Poets and Others
See also **MEXICO** under **CRITICISM, MEMOIRS, AND OTHER PROSE** under **LATIN AMERICAN LITERATURE** in **LITERATURE OF THE AMERICAS**
TRANSLATED BY MICHAEL SCHMIDT
1-55970-139-0 ARCADE PB $9.95

The Other Voice: Essays in Modern Poetry
An erudite and passionate discourse on the uses of poetry in the modern world, by the Nobel Prize winner
See also **MEXICO** under **CRITICISM, MEMOIRS, AND OTHER PROSE** under **LATIN AMERICAN LITERATURE** in **LITERATURE OF THE AMERICAS**
0-15-170449-X HARCOURT BRACE $16.95

John **Updike**
Hugging the Shore
See also **LITERATURE** under **20TH-CENTURY AMERICAN ESSAYS AND JOURNALISM** in **LITERATURE OF THE AMERICAS**
0-88001-398-2 ECCO PB $18.00

Odd Jobs: Essays and Criticism
Wide-ranging essays that once again display Updike's gifts as essayist and reviewer, as he tackles such disparate subjects as the Gospel of Matthew, Ted Williams, Gabriel García Màrquez, and contemporary fiction from Saudi Arabia and Albania
See also **LITERATURE** under **20TH-CENTURY AMERICAN ESSAYS AND JOURNALISM** in **LITERATURE OF THE AMERICAS**
0-679-40414-7 KNOPF $35.00

Adam **Zagajewski**
Solidarity, Solitude: Essays
See also **POLISH LITERATURE** under **EASTERN EUROPEAN LITERATURE**
TRANSLATED BY LILLIAN VALLEE
0-88001-186-6 ECCO $19.95

Two Cities: On Exile, History, and the Imagination
See also **POLISH LITERATURE** under **EASTERN EUROPEAN LITERATURE**
TRANSLATED BY LILLIAN VALLEE
0-374-28016-9 FS&G $24.00

The Bible

Robert **Alter**
The Art of Biblical Narrative
A commentary on the Bible as a literary work. "Alter's book may open up the Bible to those who usually avoid it, and offer new insights to those who know it well"
—Elaine Pagels, *New Republic*
See also **BIBLICAL COMMENTARY** under **THE BIBLE** under **JUDAISM** in **RELIGION, SPIRITUALITY, AND PHILOSOPHY**
0-465-00427-X BASIC BOOKS PB $13.00

Robert **Alter** & Frank **Kermode**
The Literary Guide to the Bible
"A veritable thesaurus of literary and human evaluation of the Scriptures, both absorbing and authoritative"—Amos N. Wilder, Harvard University
See also **BIBLICAL COMMENTARY** under **THE BIBLE** under **JUDAISM** in **RELIGION, SPIRITUALITY, AND PHILOSOPHY**
0-674-87530-3 HARVARD $46.95
0-674-87531-1 HARVARD PB $16.95

Harold **Bloom** & David **Rosenberg**
"It will probably turn out that, in his understanding of the patterns of misreading, as in his understanding of Romanticism, Harold Bloom has been ahead of everybody else all along"—Paul De Man

The Book of J
Harold Bloom's idiosyncratic and controversial interpretation of the earliest stratum of the Hebrew Bible, or Old Testament, accompanied by David Rosenberg's new translation. Bloom speculates that the author of the earliest Jewish scriptures was a woman
See also **BIBLICAL COMMENTARY** under **THE BIBLE** under **JUDAISM** in **RELIGION, SPIRITUALITY, AND PHILOSOPHY**
See also **HAROLD BLOOM** under **POSTWAR TO POSTMODERNISM: CRITICISM IN ENGLISH** under **LITERARY THEORY**
0-679-73624-7 VINTAGE PB..............$13.00

Northrop **Frye**
Frye was one of the most distinguished literary theorists of the second half of the 20th Century.
The Great Code: The Bible in Literature
"May be one of the most provocative books ever written about the Bible. No one has ever stated so broadly the literary debt we owe it"
—*Cleveland Plain Dealer*
0-15-636480-8 HARCOURT BRACE PB..............$11.00

John B. **Gabel** & Charles B. **Wheeler**
The Bible as Literature
0-19-505932-8 OXFORD PB..............$32.50

David **Rosenberg**, editor
Congregation: Contemporary Writers Read the Jewish Bible
The continuing relevance of the Bible to the life and work of contemporary writers, including Isaac Bashevis Singer, Mordecai Richler, and Cynthia Ozick
See also **BIBLICAL COMMENTARY** under **THE BIBLE** under **JUDAISM** in **RELIGION, SPIRITUALITY, AND PHILOSOPHY**
0-15-146350-6 HARCOURT BRACE PB..............$29.95

Poetry

Derek **Attridge**
Poetic Rhythm: An Introduction
0-521-42369-4 CAMBRIDGE PB..............$15.95

Jacques **Barzun**
An Essay on French Verse for Readers of English
0-8112-1157-6 NEW DIRECTIONS..............$12.95

Cleanth **Brooks**
The Well Wrought Urn: Studies in the Structure of Poetry
Detailed commentaries on ten British poets from Elizabethan times to the 20th century, including Donne, Shakespeare, Milton, Pope, Wordsworth, Keats, and Yeats
See also **POETRY** under **SPECIALIZED STUDIES** under **ANTHOLOGIES AND STUDIES** in **LITERATURE OF THE BRITISH ISLES**
See also **THE NEW CRITICISM** under **LITERARY THEORY**
0-15-695705-1 HARCOURT BRACE PB..............$12.00

Donald **Davie**
Articulate Energy: An Inquiry into the Syntax of English Poetry
9-990-92873-8 REPRINT SERVICES..............$49.00

Edward Halsey **Foster**
Postmodern Poetry: The Talisman Interviews
1-88368-911-2 TALISMAN..............$33.95

Paul **Fussell**
Poetic Meter and Poetic Form
0-07-553606-4 MCGRAW HILL PB..............$20.65

Harvey **Gross** & Robert **McDowell**
Sound and Form in Modern Poetry
0-472-09517-X MICHIGAN..............$44.50
0-472-06517-3 MICHIGAN PB..............$17.95

Harvey **Gross**, editor
The Structure of Verse: Modern Essays on Prosody
0-912946-58-X NORTON..............$17.50

Charles O. **Hartman**
Free Verse: An Essay on Prosody
0-8101-1316-3 NORTHWESTERN PB..............$14.95

Albert Bates **Lord**
The Singer of Tales
A classic account of the relationship between Homeric epic poetry and living traditions of oral epic
See also **STUDIES OF INDIVIDUAL AUTHORS** under **CRITICAL STUDIES** under **ANCIENT GREEK LITERATURE**
0-674-80881-9 HARVARD PB..............$15.95

The Singer Resumes the Tale
EDITED BY MARY LOUISE LORD
0-8014-3103-4 CORNELL..............$39.50

Maria Rosa **Menocal**
Shards of Love: Exile and the Origins of the Lyric
0-8223-1405-3 DUKE..............$49.95
0-8223-1419-3 DUKE PB..............$18.95

Marjorie **Perloff**
The Dance of the Intellect: Studies in the Poetry of the Pound Tradition
Ten essays addressing the problem of structure, mode, and genre in postmodernist and contemporary poetry
See also **POETRY** under **GENERAL STUDIES: THE 20TH-CENTURY** under **AMERICAN LITERATURE: ANTHOLOGIES AND CRITICAL STUDIES** in **LITERATURE OF THE AMERICAS**
0-8101-1380-5 NORTHWESTERN PB..............$16.95

Poetic License: Essays on Modernist and Postmodernist Lyric
Essays on the canon debate, "Language" poetry, D.H. Lawrence, Samuel Beckett, Gertrude Stein, Susan Howe, and others
0-8101-0844-5 NORTHWESTERN PB..............$18.95

Radical Artifice: Writing Poetry in the Age of Media
0-226-65734-5 CHICAGO PB..............$13.95

Wittgenstein's Ladder: Poetic Language and the Strangeness of the Ordinary
0-226-66058-3 CHICAGO..............$27.95

Alex **Preminger** & T. V. F. **Brogan**
The New Princeton Encyclopedia of Poetry and Poetics
Updated and revised, this definitive volume deals with all aspects of its subject: history, types, movements, prosody, and critical terminology. "An extraordinarily helpful volume that will save untold hours of reference time for the student, the general reader, and the literary scholar"—*The Modern Language Journal*
0-691-03271-8 PRINCETON..............$135.00
0-691-02123-6 PRINCETON PB..............$29.95

Christopher **Ricks**
The Force of Poetry
"Exactly the kind of critic every poet dreams of finding"—W.H. Auden
See also **GENERAL HISTORIES AND STUDIES** under **ANTHOLOGIES AND STUDIES** in **LITERATURE OF THE BRITISH ISLES**
0-19-282046-X OXFORD PB..............$12.95

M. L. **Rosenthal** & Sally M. **Gall**
The Modern Poetic Sequence: The Genius of Modern Poetry
"The most useful critical book in years"
—Hugh Kenner
0-19-503170-9 OXFORD..............$39.95

M.L. **Rosenthal**
Essays of Four Decades
0-89255-149-6 PERSEA..............$47.50

Poetry and the Common Life
Explores the sources of poetry in our daily lives and reintroduces those elements of poetry which speak of our daily preoccupations
0-89255-118-6 PERSEA PB..............$8.95

Nathaniel **Tarn**
Views from the Weaving Mountain: Selected Essays in Poetics and Anthropology
See also **LITERATURE** under **20TH-CENTURY AMERICAN ESSAYS AND JOURNALISM** in **LITERATURE OF THE AMERICAS**
0-8263-1282-9 NEW MEXICO PB..............$19.95

Helen **Vendler**
The Breaking of Style: Hopkins, Heaney, Graham
See also **POETRY** under **GENERAL STUDIES: THE 20TH-CENTURY** under **AMERICAN LITERATURE: ANTHOLOGIES AND CRITICAL STUDIES** in **LITERATURE OF THE AMERICAS**
0-674-08120-X HARVARD..............$29.95
0-674-08121-8 HARVARD PB..............$14.00

The Given and the Made: Strategies of Poetic Redefinition
See also **POETRY** under **GENERAL STUDIES: THE 20TH-CENTURY** under **AMERICAN LITERATURE: ANTHOLOGIES AND CRITICAL STUDIES** in **LITERATURE OF THE AMERICAS**
0-674-35431-1 HARVARD..............$29.95
0-674-35432-X HARVARD PB..............$14.00

The Music of What Happens: Poems, Poets, Critics

See also **POETRY** under **GENERAL STUDIES: THE 20TH-CENTURY** under **AMERICAN LITERATURE: ANTHOLOGIES AND CRITICAL STUDIES** in **LITERATURE OF THE AMERICAS**

0-674-59152-6 HARVARD.......$36.00

Soul Says: On Recent Poetry

See also **POETRY** under **GENERAL STUDIES: THE 20TH-CENTURY** under **AMERICAN LITERATURE: ANTHOLOGIES AND CRITICAL STUDIES** in **LITERATURE OF THE AMERICAS**

0-674-82146-7 HARVARD.......$24.95
0-674-82147-5 HARVARD PB.......$14.00

Yvor **Winters**

Forms of Discovery: Critical and Historical Essays on the Forms of the Short Poem in English

0-8040-0119-7 OHIO PB.......$12.95

George T. **Wright**

Shakespeare's Metrical Art

0-520-07642-7 CALIFORNIA PB.......$14.95

Narrative

Erich **Auerbach**

Mimesis: The Representation of Reality in Western Literature

This legendary work has lost none of its power. "There is no other work in contemporary literary criticism, known to me, that is comparable…in scope, in analytical and historical richness; it is actually a history of European literature from the *Odyssey* to *Ulysses* and shows a quiet mastery of all the literatures of the West"—Alfred Kazin

TRANSLATED BY WILLARD R. TRASK

0-691-06078-9 PRINCETON PB.......$55.00

Abraham, Jacob, or Moses produces a more concrete, direct and historical impression than the figures of the Homeric world—not because they are better described in terms of sense (the contrary is the case) but because the confused, contradictory multiplicity of events, the psychological and factual cross-purposes, which true history reveals, have not disappeared in the representation but still remain clearly perceptible.

MIMESIS: THE REPRESENTATION OF REALITY IN WESTERN LITERATURE

0-691-01269-5 PRINCETON PB.......$16.95

Wayne C. **Booth**

The Rhetoric of Fiction

0-226-06558-8 CHICAGO PB.......$16.95

Malcolm **Bradbury**

Dangerous Pilgrimages: Trans-Atlantic Mythologies and the Novel

"Malcolm Bradbury, in this highly entertaining book, tracks Henry James from New England to Rye, England; Evelyn Waugh to a Hollywood as grotesque as he expected; Gertrude Stein to Spain to be mistaken for a bishop; Oscar Wilde to a rickety stage in Leadville, Colorado… Bradbury is an excellent guide and orchestrator... diversifying the march of his subject with side-lights on critical theory or advantageous hits of nonliterary history"—*The Guardian*

0-670-86625-3 VIKING.......$32.95

Peter **Brooks**

Body Work: Objects of Desire in Modern Narrative

"Uncovering," "discerning," "revealing"—Brooks says the modern story is motivated by desire to *expose.* Discussing dozens of familiar works of modernism, he shows how and why narrative is a strip-tease, an unveiling (primarily of the female body) that holds out the promise of forbidden knowledge. "A fascinating and most thought-provoking book"—Juliet Mitchell

0-674-07725-3 HARVARD PB.......$21.50

Peter Brooks

Reading for the Plot

Plots and plotting, and our desire and need for them

0-674-74892-1 HARVARD PB.......$14.95

Margaret Anne **Doody**

The True Story of the Novel

See also **GENERAL HISTORIES AND STUDIES** under **ANTHOLOGIES AND STUDIES** in **LITERATURE OF THE BRITISH ISLES**

0-8135-2168-8 RUTGERS.......$44.95

Gerard **Genette**

Narrative Discourse: An Essay in Method

0-8014-9259-9 CORNELL PB.......$13.95

Narrative Discourse Revisited

0-8014-9535-0 CORNELL PB.......$10.95

Georg **Lukács**

The Historical Novel

See also **THE GREAT TRADITION** under **HISTORIOGRAPHY** in **WORLD HISTORY AND CURRENT AFFAIRS**

TRANSLATED BY HANNAH & STANLEY MITCHELL

0-8032-7910-8 NEBRASKA PB.......$13.00

Theory of the Novel

Written during WWI, this early work of theory is still important

TRANSLATED BY ANNA BOSTOCK

0-262-62027-8 MIT PB.......$11.95

Tzvetan **Todorov**

Poetics of Prose

TRANSLATED BY RICHARD HOWARD

0-8014-0857-1 CORNELL.......$39.95
0-8014-9165-7 CORNELL PB.......$14.95

Ian **Watt**

Myths of Modern Individualism: Faust, Don Quixote, Don Juan, Robinson Crusoe

0-521-48011-6 CAMBRIDGE.......$27.95

The Rise of the Novel

0-520-01318-2 CALIFORNIA PB.......$14.95

Literary Theory

General Histories and Anthologies

Hazard **Adams**

Critical Theory Since Plato

0-15-516143-1 H.B.J.......$61.00

Hazard **Adams** & Leroy **Searle**, editors

Critical Theory Since 1965

0-8130-0844-1 FLORIDA PB.......$39.95

Chris **Baldick**

The Social Mission of English Criticism, 1848-1932

0-19-812979-3 OXFORD PB.......$22.00

Walter J. **Bate**

Criticism: The Major Texts

0-15-516148-2 H.B.J.......$47.88

Terry **Eagleton**

Function of Criticism: From the Spectator to Post-Structuralism

1-85984-151-1 VERSO PB.......$15.00

Gerald **Graff**

Professing Literature: An Institutional History

Wide-ranging and provocative

0-226-30604-6 CHICAGO PB.......$12.95

Michael **Groden** & Martin **Kreiswirth**, editors

The Johns Hopkins Guide to Literary Theory and Criticism

0-8018-4560-2 JOHNS HOPKINS.......$65.00

J. Hillis **Miller**

Theory Now and Then

0-8223-1112-7 DUKE.......$54.95

René **Wellek**

A History of Modern Criticism, 1750-1950

Unfortunately, only the last two volumes of this important work are currently in print

Volume 7 German, Russian and Eastern European Criticism, 1900-1950

0-300-05039-9 YALE.......$47.50

Volume 8
French, Italian, and Spanish Criticism, 1900-1950
0-300-05451-3 YALE $47.50

The New Criticism

Under the influence of modernism, criticism became professionalized as an academic discipline. The so-called New Criticism of the '40s and '50s, which helped establish modernist literature in academia, has been seen both as modernism's apotheosis and as its betrayal.

R.P. **Blackmur**

Selected Essays of R.P. Blackmur
Complex discussions of Emily Dickinson, Hart Crane, Henry James, Thomas Mann, and others
See also **LITERATURE** under **20TH-CENTURY AMERICAN ESSAYS AND JOURNALISM** in **LITERATURE OF THE AMERICAS**
EDITED BY DENIS DONOGHUE
0-88001-083-5 ECCO $17.50

Cleanth **Brooks**

The Well Wrought Urn: Studies in the Structure of Poetry
Detailed commentaries on ten British poets from Elizabethan times to the 20th century, including Donne, Shakespeare, Milton, Pope, Wordsworth, Keats, and Yeats
See also **POETRY** under **LITERARY CRITICISM**
See also **POETRY** under **SPECIALIZED STUDIES** under **ANTHOLOGIES AND STUDIES**
0-15-695705-1 HARCOURT BRACE PB $12.00

William **Empson**

Argufying: Essays on Literature and Culture
0-87745-199-0 IOWA PB $22.50

Essays on Renaissance Literature: Donne and the New Philosophy
EDITED BY JOHN HAFFENDEN
0-521-48360-3 CAMBRIDGE PB $19.95

Essays on Renaissance Literature: The Dramas
EDITED BY JOHN HAFFENDEN
0-521-44044-0 CAMBRIDGE $52.95

Seven Types of Ambiguity
Revised twice since 1930, this remains one of the most widely read and quoted works of literary analysis
0-8112-0037-X NEW DIRECTIONS PB $11.95

Some Versions of Pastoral
"Unquestionably one of the keenest, most independent and most imaginative books of criticism"—Kenneth Burke
0-8112-0038-8 NEW DIRECTIONS PB $8.95

The Structure of Complex Words
Difficult and rewarding essays on the way writers use words
0-674-84375-4 HARVARD PB $17.50

C.K. **Ogden** & I.A. **Richards**

The Meaning of Meaning: A Study of the Influence of Language upon Thought and of the Science of Symbolism
0-15-658446-8 HARCOURT BRACE PB $8.95

I.A. **Richards**

Mencius on the Mind: Experiments in Multiple Definition
0-7007-0434-5 CURZON $49.00

Principles of Literary Criticism
0-15-674592-5 HARCOURT BRACE PB $7.95

Richards on Rhetoric: I.A. Richards: Selected Essays, 1929-1974
EDITED BY ANN E. BERTHOFF
0-19-506950-1 OXFORD $35.00

René **Wellek**

The Attack on Literature and Other Essays
0-8078-4090-4 NORTH CAROLINA PB $12.95

Theory of Literature
0-15-689084-4 HARCOURT BRACE PB $12.00

William K. **Wimsatt**

The Verbal Icon: Studies in the Meaning of Poetry
Combines theoretical vigor with precise case studies
See also **POETRY** under **SPECIALIZED STUDIES** under **ANTHOLOGIES AND STUDIES** in **LITERATURE OF THE BRITISH ISLES**
0-8131-0111-5 KENTUCKY PB $15.95

At Mid-Century: Criticism in English

Kenneth **Burke**

Counter-Statement
See also **LITERATURE** under **20TH-CENTURY AMERICAN ESSAYS AND JOURNALISM** in **LITERATURE OF THE AMERICAS**
0-520-00196-6 CALIFORNIA PB $12.95

A Grammar of Motives
0-520-01544-4 CALIFORNIA PB $15.00

Language as Symbolic Action: Essays on Life, Literature, and Method
An "attempt," in Burke's words, "to define and track down the implications of the term symbolic action' and how the marvels of language and literature look when considered from that point of view"
0-520-00192-3 CALIFORNIA PB $18.00

Permanence and Change: An Anatomy of Purpose
0-520-04144-5 CALIFORNIA $45.00

The Philosophy of Literary Form
A brilliant selection of his work from the '30s in the field of poetic theory
0-520-02483-4 CALIFORNIA PB $18.00

A Rhetoric of Motives
Burke as the philosopher of language and human conduct, with an analysis of persuasion and identification and what lies behind them
0-520-01546-0 CALIFORNIA PB $16.00

Northrop **Frye**

"No doubt the most distinguished literary theorist writing in English today."
—NY Review of Books

Anatomy of Criticism
A synoptic view of the scope, theory, principles, and techniques of literary criticism
0-691-01298-9 PRINCETON PB $14.95

The Eternal Act of Creation: Essays, 1979-1990
EDITED BY ROBERT D. DENHAM
0-253-32516-1 INDIANA $12.95

Fables of Identity: Studies in Poetic Mythology
0-15-629730-2 HARCOURT BRACE PB $12.95

Northrop Frye, Myth and Metaphor: Selected Essays, 1974-1988
EDITED BY ROBERT D. DENHAM
0-8139-1369-1 VIRGINIA PB $18.50

The Secular Scripture: A Study of the Structure of Romance
How the simplest stories work and rework archetypal themes. "*The Secular Scripture* is in fact the most sophisticated study of popular culture, considered on a world scale, that we have yet had"—*Washington Post*
0-674-79676-4 HARVARD PB $11.95

Yvor **Winters**

Function of Criticism: Problems and Exercises
0-8040-0130-8 OHIO PB $11.95

In Defense of Reason
Includes *Primitivism and Decadence, Maule's Curse*, and *The Anatomy of Nonsense*
EDITED WITH A PREFACE BY KENNETH FIELDS
0-8040-0151-0 OHIO PB $19.95

Postwar to Postmodernism: Criticism in English

M.H. **Abrams**

Doing Things with Texts: Essays in Criticism and Critical Theory
0-393-30747-6 NORTON PB $14.95

Paul J. **Alpers**

What Is Pastoral?
0-226-01516-5 CHICAGO $34.95

Walter Jackson **Bate**

The Burden of the Past and the English Poet

0-674-08587-6 HARVARD PB $11.95

Marshall **Blonsky**

American Mythologies

A semiotically informed look at the tastemakers of popular culture, based on interviews with a diverse collection of influential people including Stephen King, Giorgio Armani, Vanna White, and Helmut Newton

0-19-505062-2 OXFORD $30.00

Wayne C. **Booth**

The Company We Keep: An Ethics of Fiction

0-520-06210-8 CALIFORNIA PB $16.95

Now Don't Try to Reason With Me: Essays and Ironies for a Credulous Age

0-226-06579-0 CHICAGO $9.50

A Rhetoric of Irony

0-226-06553-7 CHICAGO PB $15.95

Frederick **Crews**

The Critics Bear It Away: American Fiction and the Academy

0-679-40413-9 RANDOM HOUSE $20.00

Thomas **Docherty**, editor

Postmodernism: A Reader

0-231-08220-7 COLUMBIA $57.50

0-231-08221-5 COLUMBIA PB $19.50

Terry **Eagleton**

The Ideology of the Aesthetic

A useful overview of various post-modern and post-structuralist modes of analysis, by a writer often critical of their aims and methods

See also **RECENT MARXIST CRITICISM** under **CULTURAL CRITICISM**

0-631-16302-6 BLACKWELL PB $22.95

Joel **Fineman**

Shakespeare's Perjured Eye: The Invention of Poetic Subjectivity in the Sonnets

0-520-06331-7 CALIFORNIA PB $15.00

Angus **Fletcher**

Allegory: The Theory of a Symbolic Mode

"An encyclopaedic storehouse of theory… which no one in my generation is likely to surpass" —Harold Bloom

0-8014-9238-6 CORNELL PB $21.95

Colors of the Mind: Conjectures on Thinking in Literature

0-674-14312-4 HARVARD $42.50

Gerald **Graff**

Literature Against Itself: Literary Ideas in Modern Society

1-56663-097-5 DEE PB $12.95

Stephen J. **Greenblatt**

Learning to Curse: Essays in Early Modern Culture

0-415-90352-1 ROUTLEDGE PB $16.95

Marvelous Possessions: The Wonder of the New World

An imaginative scholar's reconstruction of the way Europeans represented non-Europeans and took possession of their lands. Studying travel narratives, legal documents, and official reports, Greenblatt shows how the sense of wonder was harnessed to the process of appropriation

See also **THE COLONIAL EMPIRES** under **THE EXPANSION OF EUROPE: EMPIRE AND COMMERCE** under **EARLY MODERN EUROPE** in **WORLD HISTORY AND CURRENT AFFAIRS**

0-226-30651-8 CHICAGO $28.95

0-226-30652-6 CHICAGO PB $12.95

Renaissance Self-Fashioning: From More to Shakespeare

0-226-30654-2 CHICAGO PB $13.95

Stephen **Greenblatt**, editor

New World Encounters

See also **THE COLONIAL EMPIRES** under **THE EXPANSION OF EUROPE: EMPIRE AND COMMERCE** under **EARLY MODERN EUROPE** in **WORLD HISTORY AND CURRENT AFFAIRS**

0-520-08021-1 CALIFORNIA PB $15.95

Stephen J. **Greenblatt** & Giles B. **Gunn**

Redrawing the Boundaries: The Transformation of English and American Literary Studies

0-87352-396-2 MLA PB $19.75

Geoffrey H. **Hartman**

Criticism in the Wilderness: The Study of Literature Today

0-300-02085-6 YALE $33.00

The Unremarkable Wordsworth

0-8166-1176-9 MINNESOTA PB $14.95

Andreas **Huyssen**

After the Great Divide: Modernism, Mass Culture, Postmodernism

0-253-10057-7 INDIANA $35.00

0-253-20399-6 INDIANA PB $11.95

Frank **Kermode**

The Art of Telling: Essays on Fiction

0-674-04829-6 HARVARD PB $13.50

The Classic: Literary Images of Permanence and Change

0-674-13398-6 HARVARD PB $10.95

The Sense of an Ending: Studies in the Theory of Fiction

The relationship of fiction to age-old conceptions of chaos and crisis. "An impressively learned, eloquent and brilliant defense of a non-schismatic use of human time"—Leo Bersani, *NY Times*

0-19-500770-0 OXFORD PB $10.95

The Uses of Error

0-674-93152-1 HARVARD $32.00

Frank **Lentricchia**

After the New Criticism

An inviting overview

0-226-47198-5 CHICAGO PB $18.95

Ariel and the Police: Michel Foucault, William James, Wallace Stevens

0-299-11540-2 WISCONSIN $27.50

0-299-11544-5 WISCONSIN PB $14.95

Criticism and Social Change

0-226-47200-0 CHICAGO PB $12.95

Modernist Quartet

0-521-46975-9 CAMBRIDGE PB $17.95

Nathaniel **Mackey**

Discrepant Engagement: Dissonance, Cross-Culturality and Experimental Writing

0-521-44453-5 CAMBRIDGE $65.00

Jerome J. **McGann**

Black Riders: The Visible Language of Modernism

Discusses modernist innovations in how poems appear on the page

0-691-06985-9 PRINCETON $35.00

0-691-01544-9 PRINCETON PB $12.95

Walter Benn **Michaels**

The Gold Standard and the Logic of Naturalism: American Literature at the Turn of the Century

0-520-05981-6 CALIFORNIA $45.00

J. Hillis **Miller**

Ariadne's Thread: Story Lines

0-300-06309-1 YALE PB $18.00

The Ethics of Reading: Kant, De Man, Eliot, Trollope, James and Benjamin

Explores the question of the ethical dimension in the act of reading

See also **POSTSTRUCTURALISM**

0-231-06335-0 COLUMBIA PB $15.50

Fiction and Repetition: Seven English Novels

0-674-29926-4 HARVARD PB $12.95

The Linguistic Moment: From Wadsworth to Stevens

0-691-01439-6 PRINCETON PB $19.95

Topographies

0-8047-2379-6 STANFORD PB $16.95

Victorian Subjects

0-8223-1110-0 DUKE $54.95

David **Perkins**
Is Literary History Possible?
0-8018-4274-3 JOHNS HOPKINS $25.95
0-8018-4715-X JOHNS HOPKINS PB $12.95

Bruce **Robbins**, editor
The Phantom Public Sphere
0-8166-2124-1 MINNESOTA $49.95
0-8166-2126-8 MINNESOTA PB $18.95

Edward **Said**
Beginnings: Intention and Method
0-231-05937-X COLUMBIA PB $18.50

Barbara **Spackman**
Decadent Genealogies: The Rhetoric of Sickness from Baudelaire to D'Annunzio
0-8014-2290-6 CORNELL $33.95

Patricia Meyer **Spacks**
Boredom: The Literary History of a State of Mind
0-226-76854-6 CHICAGO PB $16.95

Harold **Veeser**, editor
The New Historicism Reader
0-415-90781-0 ROUTLEDGE $49.95
0-415-90782-9 ROUTLEDGE PB $17.95

Lawrence **Venuti**
The Translator's Invisibility: A History of Translation
0-415-11537-X ROUTLEDGE $69.95
0-415-11538-8 ROUTLEDGE PB $18.95

Nicholas **Zurbrugg**
The Parameters of Postmodernism
0-8093-1852-0 SOUTHERN ILLINOIS $19.95
0-8093-1887-3 SOUTHERN ILLINOIS PB $12.95

Harold Bloom

Harold **Bloom**
Agon: Towards a Theory of Revisionism
"Readers…will be unsettled by Bloom's deliberately provocative sentences on anxiety, knowledge, evasion, negation, rhetoric" —Helen Vendler
0-19-503354-X OXFORD PB $11.95

The American Religion
In a nation boasting of 1,200 religious denominations, the brilliant and controversial literary critic Harold Bloom argues that there is an underlying "American Religion" characterized by a sense of divinity within the solitary individual which he relates to the ancient heresy of Gnosticism. He pays special attention to such original American sects as Christian Science and Mormonism. "The end result is a novel analysis of the American soul"—*NY Times Book Review*
See also **NORTH AMERICA** under **HISTORY** under **CHRISTIANITY** in **RELIGION, SPIRITUALITY, AND PHILOSOPHY**
0-671-86737-7 TOUCHSTONE PB $12.00

The Anxiety of Influence: A Theory of Poetry
How strong poets make history by "misreading" one another so as to clear imaginative space for themselves—and how they wrestle with their precursors and with their anxieties of indebtedness
0-19-501896-6 OXFORD PB $9.95

The Breaking of the Vessels
0-226-06044-6 CHICAGO PB $7.95

A Map of Misreading
"It will probably turn out that, in his understanding of the patterns of misreading, as in his understanding of Romanticism, Harold Bloom has been ahead of everybody else all along"—Paul De Man
0-19-502809-0 OXFORD PB $10.95

All literary tradition has been necessarily elitist, in every period, if only because the Scene of Instruction always depends upon a primal choosing and a being chosen, which is what "elite" means. Teaching, as Plato knew, is necessarily a branch of erotics, in the wide sense of desiring what we have not got, of redressing our poverty, of compounding without our fantasies. No teacher, however impartial he or she attempts to be, can avoid choosing among students, or being chosen by them, for this is the very nature of teaching. Literary teaching is precisely like literature itself; no strong writer can choose his precursors until first he is chosen by them, and no strong student can fail to be chosen by his teachers. Strong students, like strong writers, will find the sustenance they must have. And strong students, like strong writers, will rise in the most unexpected places and times, to wrestle with the internalized violence pressed upon them by their teachers and precursors.
A MAP OF MISREADING

Harold Bloom

Omens of Millennium: The Gnosis of Angels, Dreams and Resurrection
"A dazzling account of the Gnostic, Jewish, and Islamic roots of American spirituality by our most prominent literary and religious critic. *Omens of the Millennium* is one of those magnificent works of religious interpretation and synthesis that appear only once in a generation"—Bentley Layton, Pofessor of Religious Studies, Yale
See also **GNOSTICISM** under **HISTORY** under **CHRISTIANITY** in **RELIGION, SPIRITUALITY, AND PHILOSOPHY**
1-57322-045-0 PUTNAM $24.95

Poetics of Influence: New and Selected Criticism
Twenty-one essays ranging in method from close reading to comprehensive theory
INTRODUCTION BY JOHN HOLLANDER
0-939681-01-3 SCHWAB PB $24.95

Ruin the Sacred Truths: Poetry and Belief from the Bible to the Present
0-674-78027-2 HARVARD $32.00

The Visionary Company: A Reading of English Romantic Poetry
See also **THE 19TH-CENTURY** under **SPECIALIZED STUDIES** under **ANTHOLOGIES AND STUDIES** in **LITERATURE OF THE BRITISH ISLES**
0-8014-9117-7 CORNELL PB $16.95

Wallace Stevens: The Poems of Our Climate
See also **THE 20TH-CENTURY** under **STUDIES OF INDIVIDUAL AUTHORS (ALPHABETICAL BY SUBJECT)** under **AMERICAN LITERATURE: ANTHOLOGIES AND CRITICAL STUDIES** in **LITERATURE OF THE AMERICAS**
0-8014-9185-1 CORNELL PB $17.95

The Western Canon: The Books and Schools of the Ages
The outstanding contemporary literary critic speaks up for the canon and names his candidates for inclusion
See also **KULTURKAMPF: THE WAR OVER THE CANON** under **THE STATE OF THE SCHOOLS** under **EDUCATION** in **SOCIAL STUDIES**
0-15-195747-9 HARCOURT BRACE $29.95
1-57322-514-2 RIVERHEAD PB $15.00

Yeats
0-19-501603-3 OXFORD PB $15.95

Harold **Bloom** & David **Rosenberg**
The Book of J
Harold Bloom's idiosyncratic and controversial interpretation of the earliest stratum of the Hebrew Bible, or Old Testament, accompanied by David Rosenberg's new translation. Bloom speculates that the author of the earliest Jewish scriptures was a woman
See also **BIBLICAL COMMENTARY** under **THE BIBLE** under **JUDAISM** in **RELIGION, SPIRITUALITY, AND PHILOSOPHY**
0-679-73624-7 VINTAGE PB $13.00

Harold **Bloom** & Lionel **Trilling**, editors
Romantic Poetry and Prose
See also **ANTHOLOGIES** under **LATER 19TH-CENTURY POETRY** under **THE 19TH-CENTURY** in **LITERATURE OF THE BRITISH ISLES**
0-19-501615-7 OXFORD PB $23.00

Semiotics and Structuralism and After

Narrative became central to literary theory in the '60s. Since then, semiotics (the study of sign systems) and anthropology (the study of culture in the broadest sense) have been enlisted, along with other disciplines, to offer a global perspective on literature that makes much traditional criticism seem narrow in scope.

Overviews

Marshall **Blonsky**, editor
On Signs
A witty and elegant anthology that offers a good sampling of diverse tendencies
0-8018-3007-9 JOHNS HOPKINS PB $16.95

Jonathan **Culler**
On Deconstruction: Theory and Criticism After Structuralism
Deconstruction as the principal source of energy and innovation in contemporary criticism
0-8014-1322-2 CORNELL $39.95
0-8014-9201-7 CORNELL PB $13.95

The Pursuit of Signs: Semiotics Literature, Deconstruction
0-8014-1417-2 CORNELL PB $35.00

Structuralist Poetics: Structuralism, Linguistics and the Study of Literature
A good introduction to the field
0-8014-9155-X CORNELL PB $13.95

Geoffrey H. **Hartman**
Easy Pieces
"Delightful flippant 'communications' from one of today's best critics"—*Publishers Weekly*
0-231-06018-1 COLUMBIA $29.50
0-231-06019-X COLUMBIA PB $16.00

Edith **Kurzweil**
The Age of Structuralism: Lévi-Strauss to Foucault
1-56000-879-2 TRANSACTION PB $24.95

Christopher **Norris**
Deconstruction: Theory and Practice
0-415-06174-1 ROUTLEDGE PB $14.95

Madan **Sarup**
An Introductory Guide to Post-Structuralism and Postmodernism
The second edition
0-8203-1538-9 GEORGIA $30.00
0-8203-1531-1 GEORGIA PB $15.95

Russian Formalists and the Prague School

Victor **Erlich**
Russian Formalism: History-Doctrine
0-300-02635-8 YALE PB $17.00

Roman **Jakobson**
My Futurist Years
A memoir of friendships with Khlebnikov, Mayakovsky, and other major figures of the Russian avant-garde
TRANSLATED BY STEPHEN RUDY
0-941419-81-9 MARSILIO $24.95

On Language
"An accessible collection of theoretical works by one of the most important and versatile linguists of the century"—*Russian Review*
See also **FICTION AND OTHER PROSE** under **EARLY 20TH-CENTURY** under **RUSSIAN LITERATURE**
See also **PIONEERS IN LINGUISTICS** under **LINGUISTICS**
EDITED BY LINDA R. WAUGH & MONIQUE MONVILLE-BURSTON
0-674-63536-1 HARVARD PB $22.95

Fredric **Jameson**
The Prison-House of Language: A Critical Account of Structuralism and Russian Formalism
0-691-01316-0 PRINCETON PB $13.95

Daniel P. **Lucid**, editor
Soviet Semiotics: An Anthology
0-8018-1980-6 JOHNS HOPKINS $32.00

Vladimir **Propp**
Morphology of the Folktale
TRANSLATED BY LAURENCE SCOTT
0-292-78376-0 TEXAS PB $8.95

Viktor **Shklovsky**
Theory of Prose
0-916583-64-3 DALKEY ARCHIVE PB $14.95

Peter **Steiner**, editor
The Prague School: Selected Writings, 1929-1946
0-292-78043-5 TEXAS $27.50

Mikhail Bakhtin

Mikhail **Bakhtin**
The Dialogic Imagination: Four Essays
Examines the difficulty of arriving at a generic definition of the novel
TRANSLATED BY CARYL EMERSON
EDITED BY MICHAEL HOLQUIST
0-292-71534-X TEXAS PB $16.95

Rabelais and His World
Discusses the world of carnival in Rabelais as symbolic of popular culture and the destruction of authority—and links this with the age of revolution in Russia
See also **STUDIES OF INDIVIDUAL WRITERS** under **CRITICAL STUDIES** under **FRENCH LITERATURE TO 1900**
TRANSLATED BY HELENE ISWOLSKY
0-253-34830-7 INDIANA $39.95
0-253-20341-4 INDIANA PB $16.95

Toward a Philosophy of the Act
0-292-76534-7 TEXAS $25.00
0-292-70805-X TEXAS PB $10.95

Speech Genres and Other Late Essays
Essays on Dostoevsky, Rabelais, Saussure, and the theory of the novel
TRANSLATED BY VERN W. MCGEE
EDITED BY CARYL EMERSON & MICHAEL HOLQUIST
0-292-72046-7 TEXAS $25.00
0-292-77560-1 TEXAS PB $12.95

Mikhail **Bakhtin** & P.N. **Medvedev**
The Formal Method in Literary Scholarship: A Critical Introduction to Sociological Poetics
A critique of formalism, first published in 1928
TRANSLATED BY ALBERT J. WEHRLE
0-8018-4318-9 JOHNS HOPKINS PB $13.95

Tzvetan **Todorov**
Mikhail Bakhtin: The Dialogical Principle
0-8166-1291-9 MINNESOTA PB $12.95

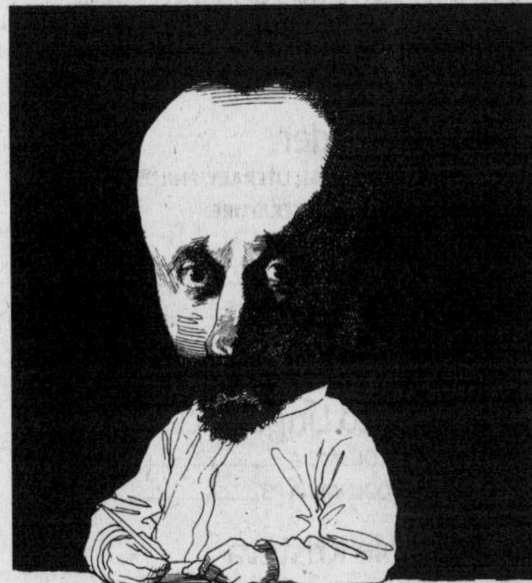

Mikhail Bakhtin

Pam **Morris**, editor
The Bakhtin Reader: Selected Writings of Bakhtin, Medvedev and Voloshinov
0-340-59267-2 ARNOLD PB $16.95

Critical Texts

Emile **Benveniste**
Problems in General Linguistics
0-87024-132-X MIAMI PB $17.95

Vincent **Crapanzano**
Hermes' Dilemma and Hamlet's Delight: On the Epistemology of Interpretation
Thought-provoking essays which trace the intricacies of language and cultural forces as they insinuate themselves in social practices and the formation of the self
0-674-38981-6 HARVARD PB $17.95

Gerard **Genette**

The Architext: An Introduction
TRANSLATED BY JANE E. LEWIN
0-520-07661-3 CALIFORNIA PB $11.95

Fiction and Diction
TRANSLATED BY CATHERINE PORTER
0-8014-2832-7 CORNELL $29.95
0-8014-8086-8 CORNELL PB $10.95

Mimologics
TRANSLATED BY THAIS E. MORGAN
0-8032-7044-5 NEBRASKA PB $25.00

Paratexts: The Thresholds of Textuality
TRANSLATED BY JANE E. LEWIN
0-521-42406-2 CAMBRIDGE PB $19.95

Julia **Kristeva**

"Julia Kristeva changes the places of things: she always destroys the latest preconception, the one we thought we could be comforted by, the one of which we could be proud; what she displaces is the illusion that it has all been said already"—Roland Barthes

Desire in Language: A Semiotic Approach to Literature and Art
0-231-04806-8 COLUMBIA PB $15.00

A Kristeva Reader
See also **ESSAYS: PERSONAL, LITERARY, PHILOSOPHICAL** under **MODERN FRENCH LITERATURE**
EDITED BY TORIL MOI
0-231-06324-5 COLUMBIA $55.00
0-231-06325-3 COLUMBIA PB $18.50

Language: The Unknown: An Initiation into Linguistics
0-231-06106-4 COLUMBIA $49.50
0-231-06107-2 COLUMBIA PB $17.00

The Portable Kristeva
EDITED BY KELLY OLIVIER
0-231-10505-3 COLUMBIA PB $25.00

Powers of Horror
0-231-05347-9 COLUMBIA PB $17.00

The Revolution in Poetic Language
TRANSLATED BY MARGARET WALLER
0-231-05642-7 COLUMBIA $55.00
0-231-05643-5 COLUMBIA PB $18.00

Proust and the Sense of Time
See also **STUDIES OF INDIVIDUAL AUTHORS** under **CRITICAL STUDIES** under **MODERN FRENCH LITERATURE**
0-231-08478-1 COLUMBIA $19.50

Michael **Riffaterre**

Fictional Truth
0-8018-3934-3 JOHNS HOPKINS PB $11.95

Text Production
0-231-05334-7 COLUMBIA $37.00

Tzvetan **Todorov**

The Fantastic: A Structural Approach to a Literary Genre
0-8014-9146-0 CORNELL PB $10.95

French Literary Theory Today
0-521-29777-X CAMBRIDGE PB $19.95

Genres in Discourse
0-521-34999-0 CAMBRIDGE PB $16.95

Introduction to Poetics
0-8166-1011-8 MINNESOTA PB $9.95

Literature and Its Theorists: A Personal View of Twentieth-Century Criticism
TRANSLATED BY CATHERINE PORTER
0-8014-1816-X CORNELL $34.95

The Morals of History
TRANSLATED BY ALYSON WATERS
0-8166-2298-1 MINNESOTA PB $18.95

Symbolism and Interpretation
0-8014-1269-2 CORNELL $32.95

Theories of the Symbol
TRANSLATED BY CATHERINE PORTER
0-8014-9288-2 CORNELL PB $15.95

Roland Barthes

"Roland Barthes must be counted the most characteristic and important French intellectual of the structuralist generation that gained worldwide attention starting in the '60s."
—Peter Brooks

Roland **Barthes**

A principal exponent of the application of structuralism and semiotics to the study of literature and society, Barthes is widely regarded as a central intellectual figure of our era.

A Barthes Reader
An excellent introduction to Barthes' thinking as applied to such diverse topics as Gide, Garbo, striptease, photography, and the Eiffel Towel
See also **ESSAYS: PERSONAL, LITERARY, PHILOSOPHICAL** under **MODERN FRENCH LITERATURE**
EDITED BY SUSAN SONTAG
0-374-52144-1 FS&G PB $16.95

Roland Barthes

Camera Lucida: Reflections on Photography
In a book both highly personal and speculative, Barthes explores in depth the various ways in which the viewer perceives a photographed image. The second half is a meditation on a photograph of the author's mother
See also **HISTORIES AND GENERAL WORKS** under **PHOTOGRAPHY** in **ART**
TRANSLATED BY RICHARD HOWARD
0-374-52134-4 HILL & WANG PB $9.95

Elements of Semiology
A fairly technical analysis of writing's relation to a general science of signs
TRANSLATED BY ANNETTE LAVERS & COLIN SMITH
0-374-52146-8 FS&G PB $9.95

The Empire of Signs
The semiotics of Japan, from simple food to sumptuous gift wrapping
See also **SYMBOLS AND SEMIOTICS** under **SPECIALIZED STUDIES** under **ANTHROPOLOGY** in **SOCIAL STUDIES**
TRANSLATED BY RICHARD HOWARD
0-374-52207-3 FS&G PB $8.95

The Fashion System
TRANSLATED BY MATTHEW WARD & RICHARD HOWARD
0-520-07177-8 CALIFORNIA PB $13.95

The Grain of the Voice
A collection of interviews
TRANSLATED BY LINDA COVERDALE
0-520-07237-5 CALIFORNIA PB $13.95

Image-Music-Text
TRANSLATED BY STEPHEN HEATH
0-374-52136-0 FS&G PB $13.95

A Lover's Discourse: Fragments
"Barthes surprises us by making love, in its most absurd and sentimental forms, an object of interest"—Jonathan Culler
TRANSLATED BY RICHARD HOWARD
0-374-52161-1 FS&G PB $10.95

Michelet
Recovers the "structure of an existence" of France's great 19th-century romantic historian
TRANSLATED BY RICHARD HOWARD
0-8090-6926-1 HILL & WANG $18.95

Mythologies
Barthes brings a highly literary anthropological technique to bear in these meditations on stripping and other Parisian activities
See also **SYMBOLS AND SEMIOTICS** under **SPECIALIZED STUDIES** under **ANTHROPOLOGY** in **SOCIAL STUDIES**
TRANSLATED BY ANNETTE LAVERS
0-374-52150-6 FS&G PB $9.95

On Racine
A personal view of theater arranged in three long essays exploring space, erotics, and human relations in Racine's plays
0-520-07824-1 CALIFORNIA PB $12.95

The Pleasure of the Text
Barthes' brilliant effort to define an erotics of reading
TRANSLATED BY RICHARD MILLER
0-374-52160-3 FS&G PB $8.95

The text you write must prove to me *that it desires me*. This proof exists: it is writing. Writing is: the science of the various blisses of language, its Kama Sutra (this science has but one treatise: writing itself).
THE PLEASURE OF THE TEXT

The Responsibility of Forms
Barthes's essays on Cy Twombly are among the best on any contemporary artist
See also **PHILOSOPHY AND ART** under **ART SINCE 1945** in **ART**
TRANSLATED BY RICHARD HOWARD
0-8090-8075-3 HILL & WANG $22.95

Roland Barthes
TRANSLATED BY RICHARD HOWARD
0-520-08783-6 CALIFORNIA PB $11.00

The Rustle of Language
Forty-five essays on literature and teaching, from Brecht to Proust and Jakobson to Kristeva
See also **LOVE AND ROMANCE** under **COURTSHIP, LOVE, SEX, AND MARRIAGE** in **LIFESTYLES AND PRACTICAL ADVICE**
TRANSLATED BY RICHARD HOWARD
0-520-06629-4 CALIFORNIA PB $13.95

Sade-Fourier-Loyola
TRANSLATED BY RICHARD MILLER
0-8018-5526-8 JOHNS HOPKINS PB $14.95

The Semiotic Challenge
"A grave, poker-faced parody of conventional scholarship whose serene, fastidious tones barely conceal the most impudently subversive of intents"—Terry Eagleton, *TLS*
TRANSLATED BY RICHARD HOWARD
0-520-08784-4 CALIFORNIA PB $15.00

S/Z
A scrupulous literary analysis of *Sarrasine*, a short story by Balzac
See also **STUDIES OF INDIVIDUAL WRITERS** under **CRITICAL STUDIES** under **FRENCH LITERATURE TO 1900**
TRANSLATED BY RICHARD MILLER
0-374-52167-0 FS&G PB $11.95

Louis-Jean **Calvet**
Roland Barthes: A Biography
0-253-34987-7 INDIANA $35.00

Umberto Eco

Umberto **Eco**
Apocalypse Postponed
0-253-31851-3 INDIANA $14.95

The Role of the Reader: Explorations in the Semiotics of Texts
Addresses musical composition, contemporary art, and aesthetic manipulations of language
0-253-20318-X INDIANA PB $13.95

Six Walks in the Fictional Woods
The renowned semiotician and novelist (*The Name of the Rose*) takes us into the deep woods of fiction's basic mechanisms. How does text signal the type of reader it wants? Who is the "model reader" and how does he or she get deliciously lost? Eco answers these questions with examples from Flaubert and Poe, Mickey Spillane and fairy tales
See also **ESSAYS, MEMOIRS, AND OTHER PROSE** under **THE 20TH-CENTURY** under **ITALIAN LITERATURE**
0-674-81050-3 HARVARD $18.95
0-674-81051-1 HARVARD PB $10.00

A Theory of Semiotics
"In many respects it constitutes the greatest contribution to this field since the pioneering work of C.S. Peirce and Charles Morris" —Robert Scholes, *Journal of Aesthetics and Art Criticism*
0-253-20217-5 INDIANA PB $13.95

Umberto **Eco** & Anna **Cancogni**
The Open Work
0-674-63975-8 HARVARD $42.50
0-674-63976-6 HARVARD PB $17.95

Poststructuralism

Originating in the '60s, in Jacques Derrida's critique of Western metaphysics, deconstruction became the most influential and controversial literary-critical method of the '70s and '80s, thanks to the work of Derrida, Paul De Man, J. Hillis Miller, and others.

Paul **De Man**
Aesthetic Ideology
EDITED BY ANDRZEJ WARMINSKI
0-8166-2203-5 MINNESOTA $49.95
0-8166-2204-3 MINNESOTA PB $19.95

Allegories of Reading: Figural Language in Rousseau, Nietzsche, Rilke, Proust
Examines the unreliability of language and argues that all writing concerns itself with its own activity
0-300-02845-8 YALE PB $17.00

Blindness and Insight: Essays in the Rhetoric of Contemporary Criticism
Questions the problematic nature of reading itself
INTRODUCTION BY WLAD GODZICH
0-8166-1135-1 MINNESOTA PB $16.95

The Resistance to Theory
0-8166-1294-3 MINNESOTA PB $14.95

Wartime Journalism, 1939-43
Facsimile reprints of all De Man's articles for the pro-Nazi Brussels *Le Soir:* music and literary reviews, newspaper, interviews, and pieces on cultural politics
EDITED BY WERNER HAMACHER
0-8032-6576-X NEBRASKA PB $20.00

Werner **Hamacher**, editor
Responses: On Paul De Man's Wartime Journalism
Contributors include Yves Bonnefoy, Jacques Derrida, and Barbara Johnson
0-8032-7243-X NEBRASKA PB $19.95

Barbara **Johnson**
The Critical Difference: Essays in the Contemporary Rhetoric of Reading
0-8018-2728-0 JOHNS HOPKINS PB $13.95

J. Hillis **Miller**
The Ethics of Reading: Kant, De Man, Eliot, Trollope, James and Benjamin
Explores the question of the ethical dimension in the act of reading
See also **POSTWAR TO POSTMODERNISM: CRITICISM IN ENGLISH**
0-231-06335-0 COLUMBIA PB $15.50

Christopher **Norris**
The Truth About Postmodernism
0-631-18717-0 BLACKWELL $54.95
0-631-18718-9 BLACKWELL PB $22.95

Mark C. **Taylor**
Altarity
A quirky geneology of otherness and a challenging reading of a range of post-structuralist thinkers and cultural critics
0-226-79137-8 CHICAGO $42.50
0-226-79138-6 CHICAGO PB $17.95

Michel Foucault

Foucault's emphasis on history and politics takes him well beyond the limits of literary studies, and has produced great excitement among younger critics.

Michel **Foucault**
A vivid writer of studies on how Western societies develop rational systems of control to order themselves, Foucault also wrote the following two theoretical volumes, which examine Western rationalism as a whole and attempt to describe how universalist schemes of knowledge determine our understanding of what is meaningful. Foucault has been the single greatest influence on postmodern and poststructural descriptions of society.

Discipline and Punish
A dizzying treatment of modern methods of social regulation, focused on criminology and penology
0-679-75255-2 VINTAGE PB $12.00

Michel Foucault

The Foucault Reader
Presents many aspects of Foucault's investigation of the nature of power in society
See also **OTHER 20TH-CENTURY PHILOSOPHERS** under **PHILOSOPHY** in **RELIGION, SPIRITUALITY, AND PHILOSOPHY**
EDITED BY PAUL RABINOW
0-394-71340-0 RANDOM HOUSE PB $15.00

The History of Sexuality

Volume 1

An Introduction

An examination of how rationalist social systems attempt to control the human body

See also **HISTORICAL SOCIOLOGY** under **TOPICS IN MODERN SOCIOLOGY** under **SOCIOLOGY** in **SOCIAL STUDIES**

0-679-72469-9 VINTAGE PB $10.00

Volume 2

The Use of Pleasure

Foucault's last major project changed direction in the writing. Volume two alone addresses the sexual mores of the Ancients. "Required reading for those who cling to stereotyped ideas about our difference from the Greeks in terms of pagan license versus Christian austerity or their hedonism versus our anxiety"
—*LA Times Book Review*

0-394-75122-1 VINTAGE PB $13.00

Volume 3

The Care of the Self

0-394-74155-2 RANDOM HOUSE PB $12.00

Madness and Civilization: A History of Insanity in the Age of Reason

This 1961 study of madness—from the medieval "ship of fools" to 19th-century efforts to correct insanity through moral instruction—was Foucault's first major work

See also **HISTORIES AND INTRODUCTIONS** under **PSYCHOLOGY** in **SOCIAL STUDIES**

See also **HISTORICAL SOCIOLOGY** under **TOPICS IN MODERN SOCIOLOGY** under **SOCIOLOGY** in **SOCIAL STUDIES**

0-679-72110-X VINTAGE PB $12.00

The Order of Things: An Archaeology of the Human Sciences

See also **HISTORICAL SOCIOLOGY** under **TOPICS IN MODERN SOCIOLOGY** under **SOCIOLOGY** in **SOCIAL STUDIES**

See also **OTHER 20TH-CENTURY PHILOSOPHERS** under **PHILOSOPHY** in **RELIGION, SPIRITUALITY, AND PHILOSOPHY**

0-679-75335-4 VINTAGE PB $13.00

Power/Knowledge: Selected Interviews & Other Writings, 1972-1977

Investigations of prisons, schools, factories, and other social institutions that control our bodies and minds

0-394-73954-X PANTHEON PB $14.00

Michel **Foucault** & Ludwig **Binswanger**

Dream & Existence

An important document in the history of existential psychology

See also **EXISTENTIAL PSYCHOLOGY** under **PSYCHOLOGY** in **SOCIAL STUDIES**

EDITED BY KEITH HOELLER

0-391-03783-8 HUMANITIES PB $12.50

Jonathan **Arac**

Critical Genealogies: Historical Situations for Postmodern Literary Studies

A remarkable application of Foucault's theories

0-231-06254-0 COLUMBIA $50.00

Paul **Bove**

Intellectuals in Power: A Genealogy of Critical Humanism

A brilliant extension of Foucault

0-231-06010-6 COLUMBIA PB $34.00

Didier **Eribon**

Michel Foucault

The life and career of one of the most influential modern French intellectuals, recounted by a close acquaintance who interviewed Foucault and his associates extensively. "Lively, lucid, and fast paced...Eribon's book is structured like a novel"—Paul Veyne, *Le Nouvel Observateur*

0-674-57287-4 HARVARD $36.50

David **Macey**

The Lives of Michel Foucault

A good, chronological account of Foucault's public life and works

0-679-43074-1 PANTHEON $30.00

0-679-75792-9 VINTAGE PB $16.00

David Macey (photo courtesy of David Macey)

David M. **Halperin**

Saint Foucault: Towards a Gay Hagiography

0-19-509371-2 OXFORD $23.00

James **Miller**

The Passion of Michael Foucault

0-385-47240-4 ANCHOR PB $15.95

Jacques Derrida

Jacques **Derrida**

Derrida's philosophy has brought the influence of Nietzsche and Heidegger to bear on questions of semiotics and literary language. He has been the chief philosophical exponent of deconstrutionism, which has had a pervasive influence on contemporary literary theory and confines itself to unmasking hidden assumptions and the prejudices of language.

Aporias

On death as limit and the limits of truth, with reflections on Seneca and Heidegger, among others

See also **OTHER 20TH-CENTURY PHILOSOPHERS** under **PHILOSOPHY** in **RELIGION, SPIRITUALITY, AND PHILOSOPHY**

0-8047-2233-1 STANFORD $32.50

0-8047-2252-8 STANFORD PB $12.95

Archive Fever: A Freudian Impression

0-226-14336-8 CHICAGO $17.95

Cinders

Discusses the German poet and Holocaust survivor Paul Celan

TRANSLATED BY NED LUKACHER

0-8032-1689-0 NEBRASKA $35.00

Dissemination

TRANSLATED BY BARBARA JOHNSON

0-226-14334-1 CHICAGO PB $17.95

The Gift of Death

0-226-14306-6 CHICAGO PB $10.95

Given Time: Counterfeit Money

TRANSLATED BY PEGGY KAMUF

0-226-14314-7 CHICAGO PB $13.95

Glas

TRANSLATED BY JOHN P. LEAVEY JR. & RICHARD RAND

0-8032-6581-6 NEBRASKA PB $35.00

Limited, Inc

Derrida's reply to American philosopher John Searles's criticisms

TRANSLATED BY SAMUEL WEBER & JEFFREY MEHLMAN

0-8101-0788-0 NORTHWESTERN PB $13.95

Margins of Philosophy

Dismantles the philosophic tradition of Plato, Kant, Hegel, and Nietzsche, among others

See also **OTHER 20TH-CENTURY PHILOSOPHERS** under **PHILOSOPHY** in **RELIGION, SPIRITUALITY, AND PHILOSOPHY**

TRANSLATED BY ALAN BASS

0-226-14326-0 CHICAGO PB $15.95

Of Grammatology

TRANSLATED BY GAYATRI C. SPIVAK

0-8018-1879-6 JOHNS HOPKINS PB $16.95

On the Name

EDITED BY THOMAS DUTOIT

0-8047-2555-1 STANFORD PB $14.95

Points...Interviews, 1974-1994

EDITED BY ELISABETH WEBER

TRANSLATED BY PEGGY KAMUF

0-8047-2488-1 STANFORD PB $18.95

The Post Card: From Socrates to Freud and Beyond

A systematic deconstruction of Western metaphysics

TRANSLATED BY ALAN BASS

0-226-14322-8 CHICAGO PB $23.95

Specters of Marx: The State of the Debt, the Work of Mourning, and the New International

TRANSLATED BY PEGGY KAMUF

0-415-91045-5 ROUTLEDGE PB $17.95

Speech and Phenomena & Other Essays on Husserl's Theory of Signs

The fashionable Derrida acknowledges his debt to the monkish professor

See also **HUSSERL** under **PHILOSOPHY** in **RELIGION, SPIRITUALITY, AND PHILOSOPHY**

TRANSLATED BY DAVID B. ALLISON

0-8101-0397-4 NORTHWESTERN $24.95

0-8101-0590-X NORTHWESTERN PB $16.95

The Truth of Painting
"Calling into question every certain conclusion, Derrida exposes the impossibility of all final solutions"—*NY Times*
0-226-14323-6 CHICAGO $49.95
0-226-14324-4 CHICAGO PB $23.95

Writing and Difference
Derrida brings Hegel, Heidegger, Husserl, and Foucault to bear on the project of deconstructing the Western philosophical tradition and discloses what that tradition has supressed
See also **OTHER 20TH-CENTURY PHILOSOPHERS** under **PHILOSOPHY** in **RELIGION, SPIRITUALITY, AND PHILOSOPHY**
TRANSLATED BY ALAN BASS
0-226-14329-5 CHICAGO PB $14.95

Richard **Beardsworth**
Derrida and the Political
0-415-10966-3 ROUTLEDGE $49.95
0-415-10967-1 ROUTLEDGE PB $15.95

Mark **Edmundson**
Literature Against Philosophy, Plato to Derrida: A Defence of Poetry
0-521-41093-2 CAMBRIDGE $59.95
0-521-48532-0 CAMBRIDGE PB $17.95

Joseph H. **Smith** & William **Kerrigan**, editors
Taking Chances: Derrida, Psychoanalysis, and Literature
Essays by Derrida, J. Hillis Miller, Samuel Weber, and others
0-8018-3749-9 JOHNS HOPKINS PB $10.95

Geoffrey H. **Hartman**
Saving the Text: Literature, Derrida, Philosophy
0-8018-2452-4 JOHNS HOPKINS $26.00

Other French Theorists

The resurgence of French thought has brought to the fore some previously neglected writers who in many ways prefigured current preoccupations.

Concurrently, some younger figures continue to challenge the assumptions of their immediate predecessors.

Georges **Bataille**
"One of the most original and unsettling of those thinkers who, in the wake of Sade and Nietzsche, have confronted the possibility of thought in a world that has lost its myth of transcendence."—Peter Brooks, NY Times Book Review

Inner Experience
TRANSLATED WITH AN INTRODUCTION BY LESLIE A. BOLDT
0-88706-634-8 SUNY $54.50
0-88706-635-6 SUNY PB $18.95

Literature and Evil
See also **ESSAYS: PERSONAL, LITERARY, PHILOSOPHICAL** under **MODERN FRENCH LITERATURE**
TRANSLATED BY ALASTAIR HAMILTON
0-7145-0346-0 MARION BOYARS PB $13.95

Visions of Excess: Selected Writings, 1927-1939
Essays on fascism, Marxism, de Sade, Nietzsche, Breton, Hegel
TRANSLATED BY ALLAN STOEKL
0-8166-1283-8 MINNESOTA PB $17.95

Jean **Baudrillard**
For a Critique of the Political Economy of the Sign
TRANSLATED BY CHARLES LEVIN
0-914386-23-9 TELOS $24.00
0-914386-24-7 TELOS PB $14.00

The Gulf War Did Not Take Place
0-253-32946-9 INDIANA $25.00
0-253-21003-8 INDIANA PB $11.95

The Mirror of Production
TRANSLATED BY MARK POSTER
0-914386-06-9 TELOS PB $12.00

Selected Writings
TRANSLATED BY JACQUES MOURRAIN
EDITED BY MARK POSTER
0-8047-1480-0 STANFORD PB $12.95

Maurice **Blanchot**
The Space of Literature
TRANSLATED BY ANN SMOCK
0-8032-6092-X NEBRASKA PB $12.00

The Writing of the Disaster
A treatment of the notion that, in Blanchot's words, "disaster belongs to a past that never ceases to impend"
TRANSLATED WITH AN INTRODUCTION BY ANN SMOCK
0-8032-1186-4 NEBRASKA $30.00
0-8032-6077-6 NEBRASKA PB $9.95

Guy **Debord**
Society of the Spectacle
In this influential work, the house philosopher of the elusive Situationist International, which came to public attention with the French student rebellion of 1968, analyzes modern capitalist society as a hypnotic show
See also **LEFTISM AND MARXISM** under **POLITICAL THOUGHT** in **SOCIAL STUDIES**
TRANSLATED BY DONALD NICHOLSON-SMITH
0-942299-80-9 ZONE $21.95
0-942299-79-5 ZONE PB $10.95

Gilles **Deleuze**
Difference and Repetition
0-231-08158-8 COLUMBIA $49.50
0-231-08159-6 COLUMBIA PB $17.00

Gilles **Deleuze** & Felix **Guattari**
Anti-Oedipus: Capitalism and Schizophrenia
0-8166-1225-0 MINNESOTA PB $16.95

Denis **Hollier**, editor
The College of Sociology
Founded by Georges Bataille, Roger Caillois, and Michel Leiris, the prewar "College of Sociology" examined contemporary society with an emphasis on the formation of close-knit communities—brotherhoods, orders, secret societies, churches, and armies. A valuable glimpse of the '30s as well as of some of the forerunners of poststructuralism
0-8166-1592-6 MINNESOTA PB $21.95

Henri **LeFebvre**
The Production of Space
0-631-18177-6 BLACKWELL PB $22.95

Jean-François **Lyotard**
Libidinal Economy
TRANSLATED BY IAIN HAMILTON GRANT
0-253-33614-7 INDIANA $51.95
0-253-20728-2 INDIANA PB $18.95

The Postmodern Condition: A Report on Knowledge
Literary theory that art critics have found applicable to contemporary aesthetics. "Lyotard's thought is as original and as important as those two influential *maîtres penseurs* of the new human sciences, Derrida and Foucault"—Ihab Hassan
0-8166-1173-4 MINNESOTA PB $12.95

Georges **Poulet**
Exploding Poetry: Baudelaire, Rimbaud
0-226-67650-1 CHICAGO $16.95

Reader-Response Criticism

As theory has shaken the authority of the author and the text, it has often relocated meaning in the reader's own interpretive activities. But this approach serves less to anchor meaning than to open up new ways for it to drift—as the diversity of reader-response theories testifies.

Stanley **Fish**
Doing What Comes Naturally: Change, Rhetoric, and the Practice of Theory in Literary and Legal Studies
0-8223-0995-5 DUKE PB $19.95

Is There a Text in This Class?: The Authority of Interpretive Communities
"It is a great...pleasure these days to find a critic willing to discuss language, literature, reading, writing, and the community of readers on the understanding that the reader plays a real part in the production of his experience" —Denis Donoghue
0-674-46726-4 HARVARD PB $16.00

Professional Correctness: Literary Studies and Political Change
0-19-812373-6 CLARENDON $22.00

Robert C. **Holub**
Reception Theory: A Critical Introduction
0-7870-0006-X
NATIONAL ASSOCIATION OF COLLEGE STORES PB ... $16.38

Roman **Ingarden**

The Literary Work of Art

TRANSLATED BY GEORGE G. GRABOWICZ

0-8101-0537-3 NORTHWESTERN PB $22.95

Wolfgang **Iser**

The Act of Reading: A Theory of Aesthetic Response

An important work that analyzes the relation between reader and text

0-8018-2371-4 JOHNS HOPKINS PB $14.95

The Implied Reader: Patterns of Communication in Prose Fiction from Bunyan to Beckett

"When the present flurry of works on the theory of narrative fiction comes to an end ...this seems likely to be one of the survivors"
—Frank Kermode

0-8018-2150-9 JOHNS HOPKINS PB $15.95

Hans Robert **Jauss**

Toward an Aesthetic of Reception

TRANSLATED BY TIMOTHY BAHTI
INTRODUCTION BY PAUL DE MAN

0-8166-1037-1 MINNESOTA PB $15.95

Jane P. **Tompkins**, editor

Reader-Response Criticism: From Formalism to Post-Structuralism

0-8018-2401-X JOHNS HOPKINS PB $13.95

Psychoanalytic Criticism

Psychoanalytic criticism has come a long way from decoding texts into phallic symbols and traumatized childhoods. Diagnosis of the author has been displaced by examination of the reader and self-examination of the critic. Under the influence of feminism and the French psychoanalyst Jacques Lacan, critics today take Freud's writings as an object of, rather than a guide to, analysis.

Rudolf **Arnheim**

Baudelaire and Freud

0-520-03402-3 CALIFORNIA $32.50

The Freudian Body: Psychoanalysis and Art

0-231-06219-2 COLUMBIA PB $15.00

Leo **Bersani**

A Future for Astyanax

0-231-05938-8 COLUMBIA $57.00
0-231-05939-6 COLUMBIA PB $19.50

Homos

The widely respected literary and cultural critic looks toward homosexuality in America

See also **GAY LIFE AND CULTURE** under **GAY, LESBIAN, AND BISEXUAL STUDIES** in **SOCIAL STUDIES**

0-674-40619-2 HARVARD $22.95

Bruno **Bettelheim**

The Uses of Enchantment: The Meaning and Importance of Fairy Tales

A classic study by this distinguished psychologist and interpreter of childhood who links folk tales to children's most pressing emotional needs

See also **FOLKLORE** under **MYTHOLOGY AND FOLKLORE** in **RELIGION, SPIRITUALITY, AND PHILOSOPHY**

See also **CHILD PSYCHOLOGY** under **PSYCHOLOGY** in **SOCIAL STUDIES**

0-679-72393-5 VINTAGE PB $13.00

Bruno Bettelheim

Shoshana **Felman**

Writing and Madness: Literature, Philosophy, Psychoanalysis

TRANSLATED BY MARTHA N. EVANS & BRIAN MASSUMI

0-8014-1285-4 CORNELL $37.95
0-8014-9394-3 CORNELL PB $16.95

Geoffrey H. **Hartman**, editor

Psychoanalysis and the Question of the Text

0-8018-3160-1 JOHNS HOPKINS PB $10.95

Jacques **Lacan**

Television

The texts of a series of French television appearances

TRANSLATED BY DENIS HOLLIER

0-393-02496-2 NORTON $24.95

Cultural Criticism

Like psychoanalysis, Marxism has been carried along on the wave of European theory and significantly transformed in the process. Current "post-Marxist" thinking coexists uneasily with poststructuralism and with earlier versions of cultural critique.

John **Guillory**

Cultural Capital: The Problem of Literary Canon Formation

0-226-31044-2 CHICAGO PB $16.95

Andreas **Huyssen**

Twilight Memories: Marking Time in a Culture of Amnesia

0-415-90935-X ROUTLEDGE PB $17.95

Edward W. **Said**

Representations of the Intellectual: The 1993 Reith Lectures

Said calls for the rehabilitation of an intellectual vision, resistant to the seduction of money, power, and specialization. He attacks government by the few, the ascendance of special interest over common interest, and the heavily compromised media—a passionate challenge to today's intellectuals

0-679-76127-6 VINTAGE PB $11.00

The World, the Text, and the Critic

"The book issues from a remarkable sharp intelligence, forcing us to face questions and possiblities that literary theorists on the whole prefer not even to raise"—*New Republic*

0-674-96187-0 HARVARD PB $15.95

Culture and Imperialism

Said, author of the bestselling *Orientalism*, here investigates the connections between culture and imperialism. Analyzing the classics—among them Austen's *Mansfield Park*, Verdi's *Aida*, and Camus's *The Stranger*—Said demonstrates how many Western artists have encouraged and justified imperialism. The result, he says, suggested both a right and *obligation* to rule—and similar assumptions continue to influence Western politics and art right up to the recent Gulf War

0-394-58738-3 KNOPF $25.00
0-679-75054-1 VINTAGE PB $13.00

Orientalism

While not strictly speaking anthropology, Said's discussion of how "the Orient" was constructed by Westerners as an explanation of the nature of the West has had enormous influence on how people write about non-Western cultures

See also **COLONIALISM** under **SPECIALIZED STUDIES** under **ANTHROPOLOGY** in **SOCIAL STUDIES**

0-394-74067-X RANDOM HOUSE PB $14.00

Edward Said

John **Storey**

An Introductory Guide to Cultural Theory and Popular Culture

0-8203-1590-7 GEORGIA $30.00
0-8203-1591-5 GEORGIA PB $14.95

The Frankfurt School

The most powerful influence on American Marxist criticism has been the Frankfurt school, a group of German-Jewish expatriates whose diagnosis inverted the privileging of economic base over cultural superstructure. For the Frankfurt school, culture and aesthetics have become central Marxist concerns.

Theodor **Adorno**

The leading figure of the postwar German Frankfurt school of philosophy and social theory, Adorno combined Marxism and Freudianism in an attemt to vindicate an ideal of enlighteded human freedom. A gifted musicologist and composer, he made several notable contributions to aesthetics.

Minima Moralia: Reflections from a Damaged Life

These fragmentary reflections and essays on contemporary society were composed in America during and just after World War II. Adorno's most characteristic book and a brilliant stylistic achievement

See also **MARXISM AND THE FRANKFURT SCHOOL** under **SOCIOLOGY AFTER WEBER** under **SOCIOLOGY** in **SOCIAL STUDIES**

0-86091-704-5 VERSO PB $19.00

Prisms

Essays on sundry subjects

See also **OTHER 20TH-CENTURY PHILOSOPHERS** under **PHILOSOPHY** in **RELIGION, SPIRITUALITY, AND PHILOSOPHY**

TRANSLATED BY SAMUEL & SHERRY WEBER

0-262-51025-1 MIT PB $13.95

Theodor **Adorno**, editor

Notes to Literature

Volume 1

Includes Adorno's wonderful and self-revealing essay on "the essay"

0-231-06333-4 COLUMBIA PB $16.00

Volume 2

0-231-06912-X COLUMBIA $49.50
0-231-06913-8 COLUMBIA PB $15.50

Walter **Benjamin**

This incisive critic and cultural historian, who strove to balance the conflicting influences of Marxism and Jewish theology, committed suicide rather than fall into the hands of the Gestapo.

The Correspondence of Walter Benjamin, 1910-1940

See also **FICTION AND OTHER PROSE** under **MODERN GERMAN LITERATURE: TO 1945** under **GERMAN LITERATURE**

EDITED BY THEODOR ADORNO

0-226-04237-5 CHICAGO $45.00

The Correspondence of Walter Benjamin and Gershom Scholem 1932-1940

TRANSLATED BY GARY SMITH

0-674-17415-1 HARVARD PB $16.50

Illuminations

Benjamin was the foremost writer to emerge from the Frankfurt school; he has been called the finest critic of the 20th century. Whether talking about Baudelaire, photography, storytelling, or unpacking a library, Benjamin always touches a nerve

INTRODUCTION BY HANNAH ARENDT

0-8052-0241-2 SCHOCKEN PB $14.00

Moscow Diary

TRANSLATED BY RICHARD SIEBURTH
EDITED BY GARY SMITH
FOREWORD BY GERSHOM SCHOLEM

0-674-58743-X HARVARD $30.00
0-674-58744-8 HARVARD PB $14.00

Reflections: Essays, Aphorisms, Autobiographical Writings

See also **BIOGRAPHY** under **JEWISH HISTORY**

TRANSLATED BY EDMUND JEPHCOTT
EDITED BY PETER DEMETZ

0-8052-0802-X SCHOCKEN PB $15.00

Walter Benjamin: Selected Writings

A new selection from the work of this enormously influential critic and writer

See also **FICTION AND OTHER PROSE** under **MODERN GERMAN LITERATURE: TO 1945** under **GERMAN LITERATURE**

0-674-94585-9 HARVARD $35.00

Susan **Buck-Morss**

The Dialectics of Seeing: Walter Benjamin and the Arcades Project

Now available in paperback: An intellectually adventurous reconstruction of the project on which Walter Benjamin worked for years but never brought to completion. The "arcades project" was an attempt to create a new kind of cultural archaeology, drawing heavily on visual imagery and the artifacts of mass production

0-262-52164-4 MIT PB $19.95

Jeffrey **Mehlman**

Walter Benjamin for Children: An Essay on His Radio Years

From 1929 to 1933 the legendary cultural theorist delivered a regular 20-minute radio program for children. He talked about whatever was on his mind: the destruction of Pompeii, a railroad disaster, bootlegging, Faust. By tuning in to the most telling psychological aspects of these programs, Mehlman is able to pick up signals from some of the least understood corners of Benjamin's thought

0-226-51865-5 CHICAGO $17.50

Martin **Jay**

The Dialectical Imagination: A History of the Frankfurt School and the Institute of Social Research, 1923-1950

Jay is the leading American historian and analyst of the Frankfurt school, and this book is its leading history. "A fascinating and indispensable contribution to the understanding of modern European thought"
—Raymond Williams

0-520-20423-9 CALIFORNIA PB $13.95

Alvin **Kernan**

The Death of Literature

A penetrating look at the demise of "literature" as known in the past, and the encroachments of a new electronic culture

0-300-04783-5 YALE $32.50

Herbert **Marcuse**

An exponent of the Frankfurt school of critical philosophy, Marcuse became a major influence on the New Left. He argues that capitalism enslaves individuals through advertising and consumerism.

The Aesthetic Dimension: Toward a Critique of Marxist Aesthetics

0-8070-1519-9 FS&G PB $12.00

Walter J. **Ong**

Orality and Literacy: The Technologizing of the World

The intellectual, literary, and social effects of writing

0-415-02796-9 ROUTLEDGE PB $14.95

Bruce **Robbins**

Secular Vocations: Intellectuals, Professionalism, Culture

0-86091-430-5 VERSO $59.95
0-86091-630-8 VERSO PB $18.95

Recent Marxist Criticism

Terry **Eagleton**

The Ideology of the Aesthetic

A useful overview of various postmodern and poststructuralist modes of analysis, by a writer often critical of their aims and methods

See also **POSTWAR TO POSTMODERNISM: CRITICISM IN ENGLISH**

0-631-16302-6 BLACKWELL PB $22.95

The Illusions of Postmodernism

0-631-20322-2 BLACKWELL $44.95
0-631-20323-0 BLACKWELL PB $15.95

Marxism and Literary Criticism

0-520-03243-8 CALIFORNIA PB $12.95

Fredric **Jameson**

The Geopolitical Aesthetic: Cinema and Space in the World System

0-253-20966-8 INDIANA PB $12.95

Late Marxism: Adorno, or the Persistence of the Dialectic

1-85984-156-2 VERSO PB $15.00

Marxism and Form: 20th-Century Dialectical Theories of Literature

0-691-01311-X PRINCETON PB $18.95

The Political Unconscious: Narrative as a Socially Symbolic Act

0-8014-9222-X CORNELL PB $14.95

Postmodernism, or the Cultural Logic of Late Capitalism

0-8223-1090-2 UDUKT PB $19.95

The Seeds of Time

0-231-08058-1 COLUMBIA $22.95
0-231-08059-X COLUMBIA PB $16.50

Signatures of the Visible
0-415-90012-3 ROUTLEDGE PB $15.95

Raymond **Williams**
The Country and the City
"A critical history of English literature from a stimulatingly original point of view"—*Nation*
See also **20TH-CENTURY BRITISH ESSAYS AND OTHER PROSE** in **LITERATURE OF THE BRITISH ISLES**
0-19-519810-7 OXFORD PB $12.95

Culture and Revolution
0-86091-943-9 VERSO PB $19.95

Culture and Society: 1780-1950
From Edmund Burke and William Cobbett to F.R. Leavis and George Orwell. Written from an independent Left standpoint, this critical history…is exactly to the point of contemporary discussions of value"—Harold Rosenberg
See also **THE 19TH-CENTURY AND THE INDUSTRIAL REVOLUTION** under **GREAT BRITAIN AND IRELAND** in **WORLD HISTORY AND CURRENT AFFAIRS**
0-231-02287-5 COLUMBIA $91.00
0-231-05701-6 COLUMBIA PB $19.00

Keywords: A Vocabulary of Culture and Society
Focuses on the sociology of language, showing how it reflects the political bent and values of society
0-19-520469-7 OXFORD PB $13.95

Marxism and Literature
0-19-876061-2 OXFORD PB $9.95

Raymond Williams on Television: The Culture of Television
A collection of Williams' essays for *The Listener*
See also **TELEVISION AND SOCIETY** under **TELEVISION** in **PERFORMING ARTS AND MEDIA**
EDITED BY ALAN O'CONNOR
0-415-02627-X ROUTLEDGE PB $20.50

The Sociology of Culture
An influential Marxist literary theorist and Cambridge professor who developed a sociological approach to this subject
See also **POSTWAR FRENCH AND BRITISH THOUGHT** under **SOCIOLOGY AFTER WEBER** under **SOCIOLOGY** in **SOCIAL STUDIES**
0-226-89921-7 CHICAGO PB $14.95

Television
0-8195-6259-9 WESLEYAN PB $14.95

Writing in Society
0-86091-772-X VERSO PB $18.95

Literature, Ethnicity, and Multiculturalism

Peter **Bishop**
The Myth of Shangri-La: Tibet, Travel Writing and the Western Creation of Sacred Landscape
How Western travelers and writers turned Tibet into an archetype of the mysterious and sacred. "An important contribution to the rapidly developing fields of 'imaginative geography,' 'the poetics of space,' and the ideology of exoticism"—Hayden White
0-520-06686-3 CALIFORNIA $40.00

Henry Louis **Gates**, Jr.
Figures in Black: Words, Signs and the Racial Self
0-19-506074-1 OXFORD PB $13.95

Henry Louis **Gates**, Jr., editor
Race, Writing, and Difference
0-226-28435-2 CHICAGO PB $19.50

David Theo **Goldberg**
Multiculturalism: A Critical Reader
0-631-18912-2 BLACKWELL PB $20.95

Peter **Hulme**
Colonial Encounters: Europe and the Native
0-416-41860-0 ROUTLEDGE $74.95

Gayatri Chakravorty **Spivak**
In Other Worlds: Essays in Cultural Politics
0-415-90002-6 ROUTLEDGE PB $16.95

The Spivak Reader: Selected Works of Gayatri Chakravorty Spivak
EDITED BY DONNA LANDRY AND GERALD MACLEAN
0-415-91001-3 ROUTLEDGE PB $17.95

Raymond **Williams**
Politics of Modernism: Against the New Conformists
1-85984-161-9 VERSO PB $15.00

Raymond Leslie **Williams**
The Postmodern Novel in Latin America: Politics, Culture and the Crisis of Truth
0-312-16458-0 ST. MARTIN'S PB $16.95

Feminist Criticism

Salvaging neglected writing by women, revising accepted views of the classics, and rethinking the meaning of literature and interpretation have made feminist criticism among the most exciting branches of literary studies today.

Henry **Abelove**, editor
The Lesbian and Gay Studies Reader
Forty-two groundbreaking essays that explore a multitude of sexual, racial, ethnic, and socioeconomic experiences. Contributors include Kobena Mercer, Adrienne Rich, and Judith Butler. The most comprehensive multidisciplinary anthology of critical work in lesbian/gay studies
See also **ANTHOLOGIES AND REFERENCE** under **GAY, LESBIAN, AND BISEXUAL STUDIES** in **SOCIAL STUDIES**
0-415-90518-4 ROUTLEDGE $65.00
0-415-90519-2 ROUTLEDGE PB $24.95

Nina **Auerbach**
Romantic Imprisonment: Women and Other Glorified Outcasts
0-231-06004-1 COLUMBIA $45.50

Judith **Butler**
Excitable Speech: Contemporary Scenes of Politics
0-415-91588-0 ROUTLEDGE PB $16.95

Gender Trouble: Feminism and the Subversion of Identity
See also **FEMINIST THEORY** under **WOMEN'S STUDIES** in **SOCIAL STUDIES**
0-415-90043-3 ROUTLEDGE PB $16.95

Barbara **Christian**
Black Feminist Criticism: Perspectives on Black Women Writers
0-8077-6253-9 ELSEVIER PB $19.95

Hélène **Cixous**
Three Steps on the Ladder of Writing
TRANSLATED BY SARAH CORNELL & SUSAN SELLERS
0-231-07658-4 COLUMBIA $21.50
0-231-07659-2 COLUMBIA PB $12.00

Hélène **Cixous** & Catherine **Clement**
The Newly Born Woman
TRANSLATED BY BETSY WING
0-8166-1465-2 MINNESOTA $34.95
0-8166-1466-0 MINNESOTA PB $13.95

Mary **Eagleton**
Feminist Literary Theory: A Reader
0-631-14805-1 BLACKWELL PB $20.95

Sandra M. **Gilbert** & Susan **Gubar**
The Madwoman in the Attic: A Study of Women and the Literary Imagination in the Nineteenth Century
"Like gnostic heretics who claim to have found the secret code that unlocks the mysteries in old texts, the authors force us to take a new look at the grandes dames of English literature, and the result is that they will never seem quite the same again"—LeAnne Schreiber, *NY Times*
0-300-02596-3 YALE PB $22.00

No Man's Land: The Place of the Woman Writer in the 20th-Century
Volume 1
The War of the Words
0-300-04005-9 YALE $35.00

Volume 2
Sexchanges
0-300-05025-9 YALE PB $22.00

Volume 3
Letters from the Front
0-300-06660-0 YALE PB $18.00

Carolyn G. **Heilbrun**

Reinventing Womanhood

"Ranks with de Beauvoir's *The Second Sex* as a landmark work"—Claudia Dreifus

0-393-31076-0 NORTON PB $9.95

In the past those women who have made their way successfully into the male-dominated worlds of business, the arts, or the professions have done so as honorary men, neither admiring nor bonding with other women, offering no encouragement to those who might come after them, preserving the socially required "feminity," but sacrificing their womanhood.

REINVENTING WOMANHOOD

0-393-00997-1 NORTON PB $8.95

Luce **Irigaray**

Sexes and Genealogies

TRANSLATED BY GILLIAN C. GILL

0-231-07032-2 COLUMBIA $49.50

0-231-07033-0 COLUMBIA PB $15.00

Speculum of the Other Woman

Posits that masculine ideology is implicit in psychoanalytic theory and in Western discourse in general

TRANSLATED BY GILLIAN C. GILL

0-8014-9330-7 CORNELL PB $16.95

This Sex Which Is Not One

Reconsiders the question of female sexuality in a variety of contexts

TRANSLATED BY CATHERINE PORTER & CAROLYN BURKE

0-8014-1546-2 CORNELL $39.95

0-8014-9331-5 CORNELL PB $14.95

Juliet **Mitchell** & Jacqueline **Rose**, editors

Feminine Sexuality: Jacques Lacan and the Ecole Freudienne

0-393-01633-1 NORTON $19.50

0-393-30211-3 NORTON PB $12.95

Toril **Moi**

Sexual-Textual Politics

Weighs the strengths and limitations of the Anglo-American and the French strands in feminist criticism

0-416-35360-6 ROUTLEDGE $25.00

0-416-35370-3 ROUTLEDGE PB $13.95

Janice A. **Radway**

Reading the Romance: Women, Patriarchy, and Popular Literature

0-8078-4349-0 NORTH CAROLINA PB $12.95

Adrienne **Rich**

Blood, Bread and Poetry: Selected Prose, 1979-1985

Essays on feminism, heterosexism, and racism from a major American poet

0-393-02376-1 NORTON $15.95

0-393-30397-7 NORTON PB $7.95

Lies, Secrets and Silence: Selected Prose, 1966-1978

Of the title essay of this collection: "An indispensable historical document of the women's movement"—Mary Daly

See also **LITERATURE** under **20TH-CENTURY AMERICAN ESSAYS AND JOURNALISM** in **LITERATURE OF THE AMERICAS**

0-393-00942-4 NORTON PB $6.95

Eve Kosofsky **Sedgwick**

Epistemology of the Closet

"Sedgwick's brilliant *Epistemology of the Closet* will have many lives: as a work of literary criticism, a cultural study, a political analysis; as a text for gay and straight, academic and nonacademic readers, and potentially as a landmark in the development of lesbian and gay studies…An extraordinary book"—Julie Abraham, *Women's Review of Books*

See also **GAY LIFE AND CULTURE** under **GAY, LESBIAN, AND BISEXUAL STUDIES** in **SOCIAL STUDIES**

0-520-07874-8 CALIFORNIA PB $14.95

Tendencies

See also **GENDER STUDIES** in **SOCIAL STUDIES**

0-8223-1408-8 DUKE $44.95

0-8223-1421-5 DUKE PB $16.95

Elaine **Showalter**

Sister's Choice: Tradition and Change in American Women's Writing

New feminist criticism by the chairwoman of the English department at Princeton University. An astute reflection on American women's writing. "Ms. Showalter writes crisply and well, seldom lapsing into the jargon that makes much academic writing inaccessible to outsiders" —*NY Review of Books*

See also **GENERAL STUDIES AND REFERENCE** under **AMERICAN LITERATURE: ANTHOLOGIES AND CRITICAL STUDIES** in **LITERATURE OF THE AMERICAS**

0-19-812383-3 OXFORD $25.00

Speaking of Gender

0-415-90027-1 ROUTLEDGE PB $17.95

Elaine **Showalter**, editor

Daughters of Decadence: Women Writers from the Fin-de-Siècle

A splendid collection of the best innovative fiction about, and often by, the "New Women" from turn-of-the-century America and Britain. Included are short stories by Charlotte Perkins Gilman, Edith Wharton, Kate Chopin, and Charlotte Mew, women whose works led to their being reviled as "literary degenerates" and "erotomaniacs." An important contribution to the study of women's fiction

See also **ANTHOLOGIES OF WOMEN'S WRITING** under **WOMEN'S STUDIES** in **SOCIAL STUDIES**

0-8135-2015-0 RUTGERS $30.00

0-8135-2018-5 RUTGERS PB $14.95

The New Feminist Criticism: Essays on Women, Literature, and Theory

0-394-72647-2 RANDOM HOUSE PB $14.21

Marina **Warner**

From the Beast to the Blonde: On Fairy Tales and Their Tellers

Richly illustrated and beautifully written, Warner's fresh interpretation of fairy tales from Charles Perrault and the Brothers Grimm to Angela Carter is "brilliant work: wise, witty, and as magisterially omniscient as any Sibylline oracle."—*The New Statesman*. "A landmark book. Warner [is] a terrific writer and original scholar"—Victoria Glendinning

0-374-15901-7 FS&G $35.00

The Debate on Pornography

Murray S. **Davis**

Smut: Erotic Reality, Obscene Ideology

0-226-13792-9 CHICAGO PB $17.95

Pamela Church **Gibson** & Roma **Gibson**

Dirty Looks: Women, Pornography, Power

0-85170-404-2 BRITISH FILM INST PB $18.95

Susan **Griffin**

Pornography and Silence: Culture's Revolt Against Nature

0-06-090915-3 HARPERCOLLINS PB $13.00

Susan **Gubar** & Joan **Hoff**, editors

For Adult Users Only: The Dilemma of Violent Pornography

0-253-32365-7 INDIANA $42.00

0-253-20508-5 INDIANA PB $13.95

Lynn **Hunt**, editor

The Invention of Pornography: Obscenity and the Origins of Modernity, 1500-1800

Includes "The Libertine Whore: Prostitution in French Pornography from Margot to Juliette" by Kathryn Norberg; "Pornography and the French Revolution" by Lynn Hunt; and "Truth and the Obscene World in Eighteenth-Century Pornography" by Lucienne Frappier-Mazur

0-942299-68-X ZONE $30.00

0-942299-69-8 ZONE PB $18.00

The Marquis De Sade

Laura **Kipnis**

Bound and Gagged: Pornography and the Politics of Fantasy in America

Five essays by a "lively and engaging writer who argues, often convincingly, that we would be better off simply thinking of pornography as just another form of science fiction" —*Publishers Weekly*

See also **CULTURE ON THE EDGE** under **CUTTING EDGE** in **POPULAR READING**

0-8021-1584-5 GROVE $22.00

Nadine **Strossen**

Defending Pornography: Free Speech and the Fight for Women's Rights

0-684-19749-9 SCRIBNERS $22.00
0-385-48173-X ANCHOR PB $14.00

Sallie **Tisdale**

Talk Dirty to Me

A defense of pornography by a pornography user

See also **PORNOGRAPHY** under **FEMINIST THEORY** under **WOMEN'S STUDIES** in **SOCIAL STUDIES**

0-385-46854-7 DOUBLEDAY $22.95

Reference

M. H. **Abrams**

A Glossary of Literary Terms

0-03-054982-5 H.B.J. PB $23.61

Frank **Lentricchia** & Thomas **McLaughlin**

Critical Terms for Literary Study

0-226-47203-5 CHICAGO PB $17.95

Irena R. **Makaryk**, editor

Encyclopedia of Contemporary Literary Theory: Approaches, Scholars, Terms

0-8020-6860-X TORONTO PB $39.95

Robert **Pinsky**

The Situation of Poetry: Contemporary Poetry and Its Traditions

See also **POETRY** under **GENERAL STUDIES: THE 20TH-CENTURY** under **AMERICAN LITERATURE: ANTHOLOGIES AND CRITICAL STUDIES** in **LITERATURE OF THE AMERICAS**

0-691-01352-7 PRINCETON PB $14.95

World Literature: Surveys and Anthologies

Elsewhere in *The Reader's Catalog*, literary works have been classified according to an essentially geographical scheme, with three main sections: Literature of Europe, Africa, and Asia; Literature of the British Isles; and Literature of the Americas.

Under the present heading we have grouped together those general works which do not fit easily into that scheme.

General Studies

Willis **Barnstone**

The Poetics of Translation: History, Theory, Practice

0-300-06300-8 YALE PB $18.00

Nicholas A. **Basbanes**

A Gentle Madness: Bibliophiles, Bibliomanes, and the Eternal Passion for Books

0-8050-3653-9 HOLT $35.00

T. V. F. **Brogan**

The Princeton Handbook of Multicultural Poetries

0-691-00168-5 PRINCETON PB $17.95

T.V.F. **Brogan**

The New Princeton Handbook of Poetic Terms

0-691-03671-3 PRINCETON $45.00
0-691-03672-1 PRINCETON PB $17.95

Colin **Campbell**

The Romantic Ethic and the Spirit of Modern Consumerism

0-631-16941-5 BLACKWELL PB $23.95

W. Theodore **de Bary** & others, editors

A Guide to Oriental Classics

0-231-06674-0 COLUMBIA PB $32.50

Elizabeth **Diefendorf**, editor

The New York Public Library's Books of the Century

0-19-510897-3 OXFORD $14.95

Johanna **Drucker**

The Alphabetic Labyrinth: The Letters in History and Imagination

0-500-01608-9 THAMES & HUDSON $45.00

Dorothy M. **Figueira**

The Exotic: A Decadent Quest

0-7914-1630-5 SUNY PB $16.95

Ford Madox **Ford**

The March of Literature: From Confucius' Day to Our Own

See also **20TH-CENTURY BRITISH ESSAYS AND OTHER PROSE** in **LITERATURE OF THE BRITISH ISLES**

1-56478-051-1 DALKEY ARCHIVE PB $16.95

Michael **Gitter** & Sylvie **Anapol**

Do You Remember: The Book that Takes You Back

0-8118-1304-5 CHRONICLE PB $9.95

Ian **Hamilton**, editor

The Oxford Companion to Twentieth-Century Poetry in English

Hamilton, the acclaimed biographer of Salinger and Robert Lowell, has assembled this comprehensive guide to modern English-language poetry. The works of 1,500 poets from New Zealand to Zimbabwe are discussed in the context of the literary and cultural movements that spawned them. Seamus Heaney writes on Lowell and Ann Stevenson weighs in on Sylvia Plath, while the works of such writers as Chinua Achebe, Maya Angelou, and Carolyn Forche are extensively covered

0-19-866147-9 OXFORD $45.00

Edwin **Honig**

The Poet's Other Voice: Conversations on Translating Poetry

0-87023-477-3 MASSACHUSETTS PB $16.95

William **Hornstein**, editor

The Reader's Companion to World Literature

0-451-62816-0 MENTOR PB $7.95

Guida M. **Jackson**

Encyclopedia of Traditional Epics

0-87436-724-7 ABC CLIO $65.00

Alberto **Manguel**

A History of Reading

0-670-84302-4 VIKING $26.95

Barbara Stoler **Miller**, editor

Masterworks of Asian Literature in Comparative Perspective: A Guide for Teaching

1-56324-257-5 SHARPE $79.95
1-56324-258-3 SHARPE PB $28.95

Geoffrey **Nunberg**, editor

The Future of the Book

AFTERWORD BY UMBERTO ECO

0-520-20451-4 CALIFORNIA PB $14.95

Peter **Parker** & Frank **Kermode**, editors

A Reader's Guide to Twentieth-Century Writers

The distinguished critics Parker and Kermode offer over 1,000 biographical entries of all the major literary figures of the century the world over. Each entry offers biography, critical assessment, a full bibliography, and other essential information, such as literary brawls, libel actions, honors, and difficulties with drink, drugs, lovers, and publishers. A splendid, lively, and readable guide to the literature and writers of our century

See also **BIOGRAPHICAL DICTIONARIES** under **GENERAL INFORMATION** under **REFERENCE** in **BUSINESS AND REFERENCE**

0-19-521215-0 OXFORD $35.00

Daniel **Pennac**

Better than Life

0-88910-484-0 COACH HOUSE $16.95

John R. **Reed**

Decadent Style

0-8214-0793-7 OHIO $35.00

Jerome **Rothenberg** & Diane **Rothenberg**

Symposium of the Whole: A Range of Discourse Toward an Ethnopoetics

0-520-04531-9 CALIFORNIA PB $16.00

Thomas **Simmons**

Erotic Reckonings: Mastery and Apprenticeship in the Work of Poets and Lovers

0-252-02120-7 ILLINOIS $27.50

General Anthologies

John **Gross**, editor

The Oxford Book of Essays

By turns profound or whimsical, personal or learned, this selection perfectly captures the range and elasticity of this grand form. Contributors range from Jonathan Swift to Joan Didion. "Every essay here is a pleasure to read. It must be the best Oxford anthology so far" —John Bayley, *TLS*. "Gross has provided something for every mood and fancy....Delightful"—Roger Kimball, *The New Criterion*

0-19-214185-6 OXFORD $30.00

Daniel **Halpern**, editor

The Autobiographical Eye

A collection of autobiographical essays as varied as the people who wrote them. Tennessee Williams spends his mornings trying to think of one sentence to say to his father; Annie Dillard journeys through tunnels of snow to see an eclipse, only to leave before the show is over. Plus, equally surprising and intimate autobiographical writings by Derek Walcott, James Wright, Calvino, Fowles, and others

0-88001-329-X ECCO PB $12.95

Philip **Lopate**, editor

The Art of the Personal Essay: An Anthology from the Classical Era to the Present

This paperback publication brings to readers 75 carefully chosen essays from ancient Greece through the present

0-385-42298-9 ANCHOR $30.00
0-385-42339-X ANCHOR PB $16.95

Ian P. **McGreal**, editor

Great Literature of the Eastern World

Following his celebrated *Great Thinkers of the Eastern World*, McGreal presents a rich tour of ancient classics, modern novels, drama, poetry, and prose of China, India, Japan, Korea, and the Middle East. Lao She, the *Bhagavadgita*, Rabindranath Tagore, Yukio Mishima: this is a splendid introduction to the world of Eastern literature, in which critical studies and references guide the reader with a sure hand

0-06-270104-5 HARPERCOLLINS $50.00

John **Miller**, editor

On Suicide: Great Writers on the Ultimate Question

Only a fifth of the contributors to this fascinating volume actually committed the act. But every one of them is in their own way qualified to discuss it. "A most generous collection, broad and deep and touching and provocative"—Robert Coles, from the Introduction

0-8118-0231-0 CHRONICLE PB $10.95

The courage of the suicide, like that of the pirate, is not incompatible with a selfish disregard for the rights of others

ON SUICIDE: GREAT WRITERS ON THE ULTIMATE QUESTION

Roy **Porter**, editor

The Faber Book of Madness

Includes excerpts from some of the world's greatest, and/or "mad" writers such as Auden, Brontë, Nietzsche, Pope, Plath, Rhys, Sexton, and Voltaire. "Salutary in what it reveals not so much about the mad, but about the way the sane think of them, treat them and usually fail to love them"—Jeanette Winterson

See also REFERENCE under PSYCHOLOGY in SOCIAL STUDIES

0-571-14388-1 FABER PB $14.95

James B. **Ross** & Mary M. **McLaughlin**, editors

The Portable Renaissance Reader

See also RENAISSANCE ITALY AND THE COMING OF HUMANISM under MEDIEVAL AND RENAISSANCE EUROPE in WORLD HISTORY AND CURRENT AFFAIRS

0-14-015061-7 VIKING PB $14.95

Barney **Rosset**, editor

Evergreen Review Reader, 1957-1966

1-55970-273-7 ARCADE PB $16.95

Poetry Anthologies

Fleur **Adcock**, editor

The Faber Book of Twentieth Century Women's Poetry

Includes Stevie Smith, Edna St. Vincent Millay, Gwendolyn Brooks, and Denise Levertov

See also POETRY ANTHOLOGIES under ANTHOLOGIES OF WOMEN'S WRITING under WOMEN'S STUDIES in SOCIAL STUDIES

0-571-13693-1 FABER PB $13.95

The New York Public Library

The Hand of the Poet: 100 Great Poems in Manuscript

0-8478-1958-2 RIZZOLI $40.00

Keith **Bosley**, editor

The Poetry of Asia: Five Millenniums of Verse from 33 Languages

0-8348-0139-6 WEATHERHILL $17.50

Carol **Cosman**, editor

The Penguin Book of Women Poets

0-14-058533-8 VIKING PB $12.95

David **Curzon**, editor

The Gospels in Our Image: An Anthology of Twentieth-Century Poetry Based on Biblical Texts

0-15-100161-8 HARCOURT BRACE $30.00

Richard **Ellmann** & Robert **O'Clair**, editors

Modern Poems: A Norton Introduction

0-393-95907-4 NORTON PB $34.95

Carolyn **Forché**, editor

Against Forgetting: Twentieth Century Poetry of Witness

0-393-03372-4 NORTON $35.00
0-393-30976-2 NORTON PB $19.95

Geoffrey **Grigson**, editor

The Faber Book of Love Poems

Shakespeare, Dickinson, Lawrence, and others on love, from early expectations to final renunciation

See also LOVE AND ROMANCE under COURTSHIP, LOVE, SEX, AND MARRIAGE in LIFESTYLES AND PRACTICAL ADVICE

0-571-13118-2 FABER PB $12.95

William **Harmon**, editor

The Classic Hundred: All Time Favorite Poems

0-231-08239-8 COLUMBIA PB $14.95

The Top 500 Poems

0-231-08028-X COLUMBIA $29.95

John **Hollander**

Garden Poems

0-679-44726-1 EVERYMAN'S $12.50

The Gazer's Spirit: Poems Speaking to Silent Works of Art

Hollander's critical commentaries accompany an anthology of poems about works of art

See also CRITICS AND WRITERS ON ART under ART HISTORY: GENERAL STUDIES in ART

0-226-34949-7 CHICAGO $39.95

John **Hollander**, editor

Animal Poems

0-679-43631-6 KNOPF $10.95

Carolyn **Kizer**, editor

The Golden Ecco Anthology: 100 Poems by Women

0-88001-422-9 ECCO $22.00

J.D. **McClatchy**, editor

The Vintage Book of Contemporary Poetry

See also ANTHOLOGIES under 20TH-CENTURY AMERICAN POETRY in LITERATURE OF THE AMERICAS

0-679-74115-1 VINTAGE PB $15.00

Peter **Opie** & Iona **Opie**, editors

The Oxford Book of Narrative Verse

0-19-214131-7 OXFORD $35.00
0-19-282243-8 OXFORD PB $12.95

Michael **Roberts**, editor

The Faber Book of Modern Verse

0-571-18017-5 FABER PB $12.95

Jerome **Rothenberg**, editor

Technicians of the Sacred: A Range of Poetries from Africa, America, Asia, Europe and Oceania

A revised edition of the profoundly influential anthology that focused attention on ethnopoetics

0-520-04912-8 CALIFORNIA PB $17.95

Jerome **Rothenberg** & Pierre **Joris**, editors

Poems for the Millennium

This first volume offers three "galleries" of individual poets—figures such as Mallarmé, Stein, Rilke, Tzara, Mayakovsky, Pound, H.D., Vallejo, Artaud, Cesaire, and Tsvetayeva—along with a sampling of the most significant pre-World War II movements in poetry and the other arts: Futurism, Expressionism, Dada, Surrealism, "Objectivism," *Negritude.* The projected second volume will extend the gathering to the present day

0-520-07227-8 CALIFORNIA PB........$24.95

Jerome Rothenberg (photo by Diane Rothenberg)

Jon **Stallworthy**, editor

The Oxford Book of War Poetry

0-19-214125-2 OXFORD........$30.00

Fiction Anthologies

Chris **Baldick**, editor

The Oxford Book of Gothic Tales

This collection of horror, suspense, and moody doom includes works by Edgar Allan Poe, Thomas Hardy, William Faulkner, Arthur Conan Doyle, as well as Joyce Carol Oates, Jorge Luis Borges, Isak Dinesen, and Isabel Allende. "A sumptuous spread of eeriness, horror, and decay"—*The Sunday Times* [London]

See also **ANTHOLOGIES** under **SUPERNATURAL FANTASY AND HORROR** under **SCIENCE FICTION AND FANTASY** in **POPULAR READING**

0-19-283117-8 OXFORD PB........$14.95

Stephen **Brook**, editor

The Penguin Book of Infidelities

"A sinfully delectable anthology of extramarital dirty laundry through the ages written by literary masters from Chaucer to Updike" —*Vanity Fair*

0-14-024373-9 PENGUIN PB........$12.95

Italo **Calvino**, editor

Fantastical Tales

The late modern Italian master (*Invisible Cities, If on a Winter's Night a Traveler*) counts these tales among the most significant products of the 19th century. Includes work by Balzac, Walter Scott, Gogol, Hawthorne, and others, whose supernatural fictions, Calvino says, speak to us "like the rebellion of the unconscious." "Calvino possesses the power of seeing into the deepest recesses of human minds and then bringing their dreams to life"—Salman Rushdie

0-679-41526-2 PANTHEON........$25.00

Patricia **Craig**, editor

The Oxford Book of Modern Women's Stories

A welcome collection of 40 gems with themes from South African racism to American rootlessness, representing both the mainstream and the more esoteric, a wide-ranging representation of the finest women's voices of our time: Willa Cather, Katherine Anne Porter, Eudora Welty, Jean Stafford, Cynthia Ozick, Ruth Prawer Jhabvala, Patricia Highsmith, Amy Tan

0-19-214232-1 OXFORD........$30.00
0-19-283204-2 OXFORD PB........$13.95

Larry **Dark**, editor

The Literary Lover: Great Contemporary Stories of Passion and Romance

Harold Brodkey, John Updike, Laurie Colwin, Nadine Gordimer, and Charles Bukowski are just some of the contributors to this stunning volume of...well, passion and romance. "A collection sure to tempt the choosiest lover of literature"—*The Boston Sunday Herald*

0-14-017164-9 PENGUIN PB........$12.95

Howard **Goldblatt**, editor

Chairman Mao Would Not Be Amused: Fiction from Today's China

0-8021-1573-X GROVE........$21.00
0-8021-3449-1 GROVE PB........$13.00

Lilly **Golden**, editor

A Literary Christmas: Great Contemporary Christmas Stories

The Christmas season in all its psychological and emotional complexity viewed by some of today's best writers, from Toni Cade Bambara and Patricia Highsmith to Ann Beattie, Italo Calvino, Paul Auster, and Heinrich Boll

See also **SHORT STORY COLLECTIONS** under **20TH-CENTURY AMERICAN FICTION** in **LITERATURE OF THE AMERICAS**

0-87113-583-3 GROVE PB........$15.00

Granta Books

The Granta Book of the Family

Saul Bellow writes of his immigrant parents trying to make it in America; William Wharton tells the tale of a tragic car accident; Doris Lessing relates the troublesome facts of her birth and her youth; Mona Simpson tells of a daughter searching for her father... This collection from *Granta* showcases 22 exciting and gritty essays and stories that plumb the depths of the family, by contemporary American and British writers including Bret Easton Ellis, Louise Erdrich, Mikal Gilmore, and Geoffrey Wolff

0-14-014124-3 PENGUIN PB........$11.95

Edward M. **Gunn**, editor

Twentieth-Century Chinese Drama: An Anthology

0-253-36109-5 INDIANA........$35.00
0-253-20310-4 INDIANA PB........$15.00

Daniel **Halpern**, editor

The Art of the Tale: An International Anthology of Short Stories, 1945-1985

0-14-007949-1 PENGUIN PB........$15.95

Joseph S.M. **Lau** & Howard **Goldblatt**, editors

The Columbia Anthology of Modern Chinese Literature

0-231-08002-6 COLUMBIA........$39.00
0-231-08003-4 COLUMBIA PB........$25.00

Alberto **Manguel**, editor

Black Water 2: More Tales of the Fantastic

Includes work by Isabel Allende, Gabriel García Márquez, V.S. Naipaul, Boris Vian, Amos Tutuola, and others

0-517-57559-0 CLARKSON POTTER PB........$17.50

Everything (he kept saying) is something it isn't. And everybody is always somewhere else. Maybe it was the city, being in the city, that made him feel how queer everything was and that it was something else. Maybe (he kept thinking) it was the names of things. The names were tex and frequently koid. Or they were flex and oid, or they were duroid (sani) or flexsan (duro), but everything was glass (but not quite glass) and the thing that you touched (the surface, washable, crease-resistant) was rubber, only it wasn't quite rubber and you didn't quite touch it but almost.—*E.B. White,* "The Door"

BLACK WATER 2: MORE TALES OF THE FANTASTIC

V.S. **Pritchett**, editor

The Oxford Book of Short Stories

0-19-214116-3 OXFORD........$30.00
0-19-282113-X OXFORD PB........$13.95

Lucy **Rosenthal**, editor

The World Treasury of Love Stories

0-19-509361-5 OXFORD........$30.00

Marsha **Rowe**, editor

Sex and the City: A Serpent's Tail Compilation

An anthology of short fiction that keeps pace with the jagged rhythms of contemporary urban life. Includes work by Luisa Valenzuela, Lynne Tillman, Steve Katz, Rita Dove, Janice Eidus, and many others

1-85242-165-7 SERPENT'S TAIL PB........$9.95

Robert **Shapard** & James **Thomas**, editors

Sudden Fiction International: 60 Short-Short Stories

This follow-up to the enormously popular *Sudden Fiction* offers more exciting examples of very short fiction (no story is more than five pages long) from Colette, Doris Lessing, Gabriel García Márquez, Isak Dinesen, Italo Calvino, and 55 others. "These stories can do in a page what a novel can do in 200"—Mark Strand

0-393-30613-5 NORTON PB........$11.95

Part 9

Popular Reading

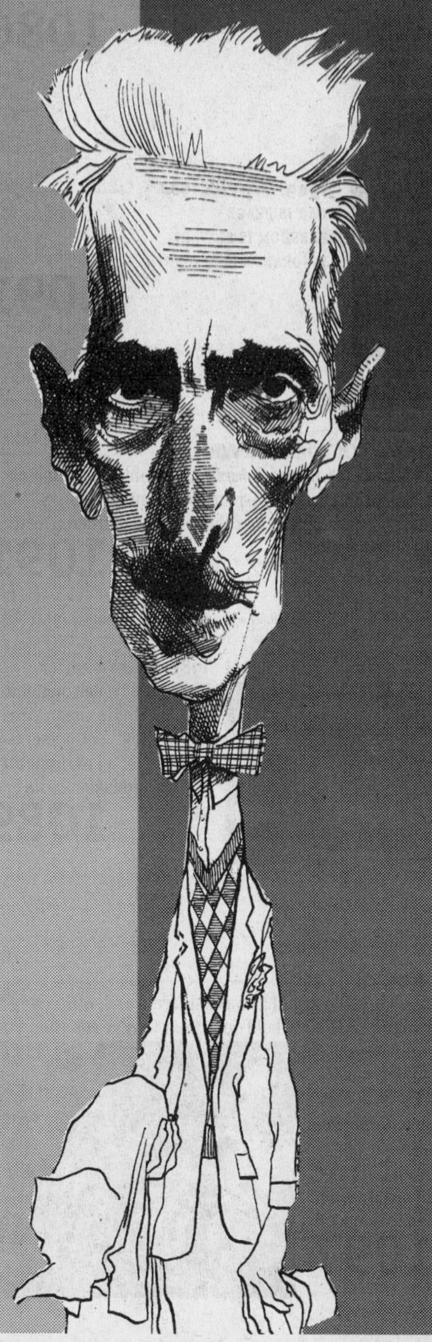

Dashiell Hammett

Science Fiction's Troubled Mirror

1900 · 1910 · 1920 · 1930 · 1940 · 1950 · 1960 · 1970 · 1980 · 1990

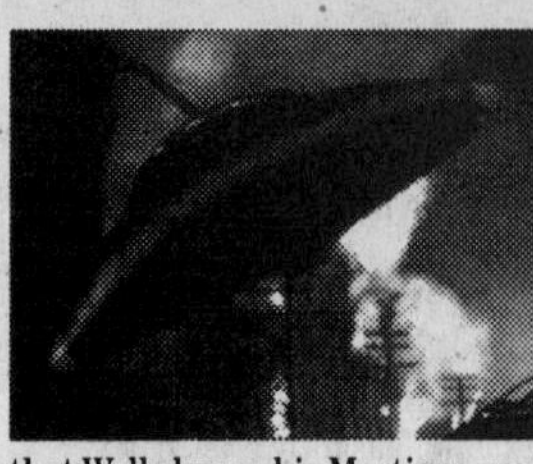

1898: The Colonialists' Nightmare: "Do Unto Others..."
In *The War of the Worlds,* "the Martian is all too familiar. We know its planet, we know its lust for territory, and we recognize its methods. Like the British that Wells knew, his Martians are born imperialists. It is appropriate that Wells's Martians landed in Britain, but those in the 1953 film take on America."
—John Clute
Science Fiction: The Illustrated Encyclopedia

1097

1920: Too Good to Be True: Karel Čapek's *R.U.R.*
Rossum's Universal Robots are mechanical slaves, capitalism's ideal workers in an age of industrial unrest. Until they too begin to organize...

1085

1924: Lenin Goes Galactic
"You will subjugate the unknown beings on other planets, who may still be living in the primitive state of freedom, to the beneficent yoke of reason. If they fail to understand that we bring them mechanically infallible happiness, it will be our duty to compel them to be happy."
—Yevgeny Zamyatin
We

1086

1926: *Metropolis*
Fritz Lang's fizzy brew of industrial nightmare, class warfare, and Eros both sentimental and sinister–with a premonition of imminent nastiness in Germany.

1330

1949: Orwell's *1984*
WAR IS PEACE
FREEDOM IS SLAVERY
IGNORANCE IS STRENGTH

1091

1956: Worse than Commies!
It's *The Invasion of the Bodysnatchers,* there's a pod person growing in the garage, and it looks just like you.

1087

1961: Beware Of What You Wish For
On Stanislaw Lem's planet *Solaris,* a sentient ocean creates almost human simulacra of explorers' absent loved ones—embodiments of yearning and fear that must be murdered again, and again, and again...

1091

1965: *Dune*
Creepy, effeminate tyrants rule the galaxy with big machines; formerly dead savants with metal eyeballs search for who they really are; manly desert campers teach a kid to take drugs and kill people, then help him avenge his Dad.

1090

1973: *Beneath The Planet of The Apes*
The ape general exhorts his troops: "I don't say all humans are evil simply because their skin is white; no! But our Great Lawgiver tells us that never, never, will the human have the ape's divine ability to tell evil from good. The only good human is a dead human!"

1097

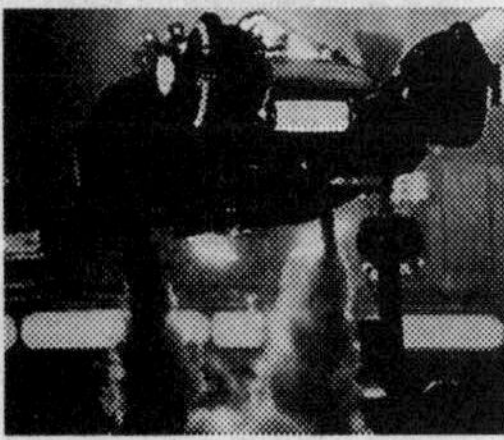

1982: *Blade Runner*
Time to get tough on immigration. On the mean streets of P.K. Dick's poisoned anthill, L.A.'s finest put undocumented labor in its place.

1089

1984: Arnold!
Computers rule the ruin that was California and, with a very human determination to hold on to what they've got, they dispatch sci-fi's most memorable robot into the past to seal our doom. *Terminator* appears in our dreams just as computers appear on our desks. Coincidence?

1097

1990: *Neuromancer*
We'll say it again: William Gibson coined the word "cyberspace." "I was looking for a meaningless buzzword that sounded hot. I found my buzzword, and so did the rest of the world."

1090

Now or Never: The World of Popular Fiction

1 **Five Points, New York City**
Police Commissioner Teddy Roosevelt and Dr. Kreizler examine the mutilated corpse of a young boy in women's clothes.
1077

2 **Arkham, Massachussetts**
The tall Whately twin heads over to the Miscatonic University library to fetch a copy of the *Necronomicon.*
1095

3 **The Center of the Earth**
2,250 miles below Reykjavik, on the shores of the underground Lidenbrock Sea, the Professor and Axel contemplate just how far they have come.
1086

4 **Scotland**
Hopelessly drunk on Loch Lomond whisky, Snowy trails Tintin down a craggy slope.
1117

5 **England**
Toad blazes toward Toad Hall in his roadster, yelling "Clear the way!"
1635

6 **Switzerland**
Dr. Watson nods off as Holmes reads from his latest treatise on the properties of cigar ash.
1058

7 **Rome**
Claudius lies awake in bed while his stout wife, Urgulanilla, strangles a cousin in the hall.
822

8 **Transylvania**
Jonathan Harker settles into his mirrorless quarters at Castle Dracula after an unpleasantly brisk carriage ride.
814

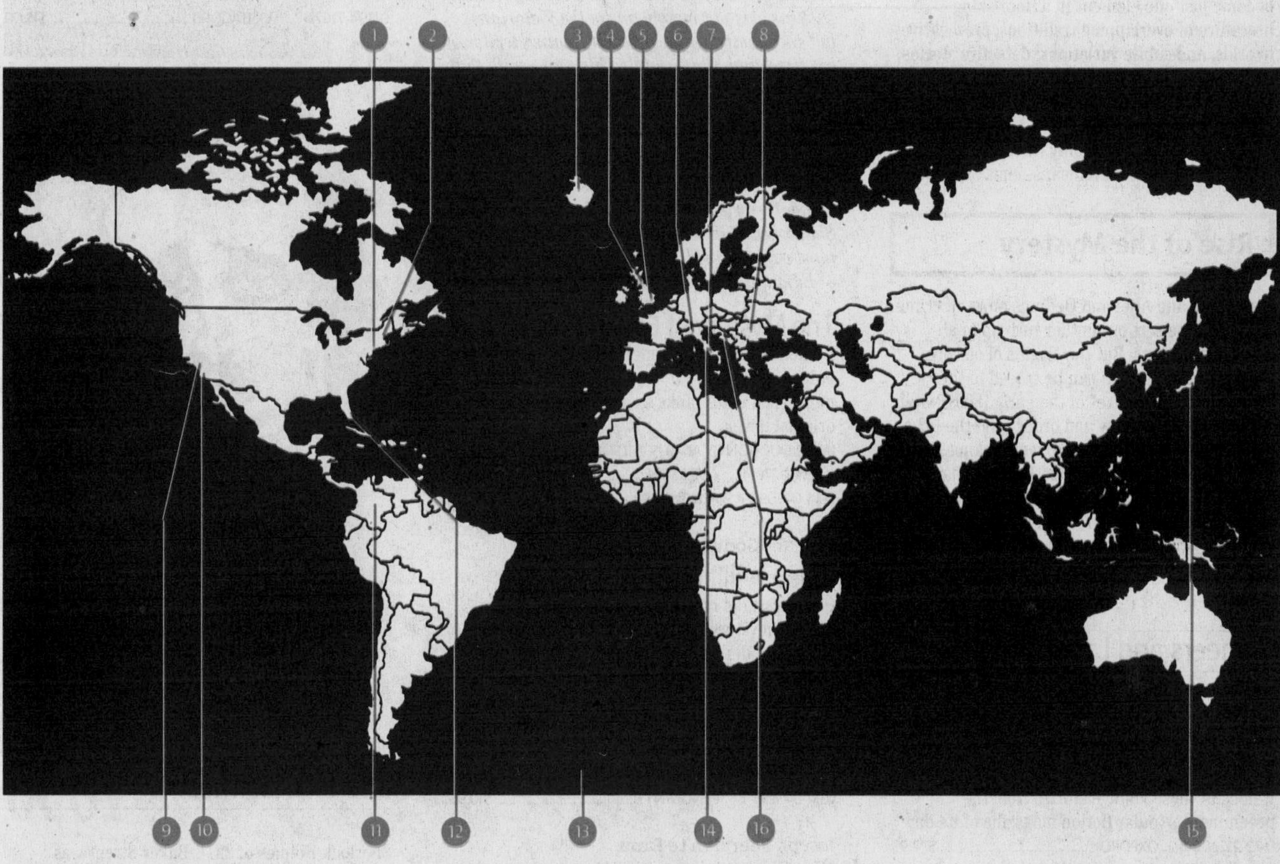

9 **San Luis Obispo, California**
Kinsey Milhone slips an automatic into her handbag and steps out of her Volkswagen into the night.
1068

10 **Los Angeles, California**
Easy Rawlins stares at the barroom ceiling and downs another shot.
1068

11 **Colombia**
Gripping his Glock, Jack Ryan reflects on life, death, and the structural integrity of Chinook helicopters.
1107

12 **Miami, Florida**
US Marshal Raylan Givens guns down The Zip across a café table in a South Beach hotel.
1073

13 **Desolation Island**
Dr. Maturin squeezes bitter drops of laudanum onto his tongue before another long subarctic night.
1102

14 **San Remo, Italy**
Ripley studies the large oar lying on the floor of the outboard, as Dickie Greenleaf steers them out of the harbor.
1064

15 **Japan**
Blackthorne is sleeping on the tatami mat beside Kiku; in the fortress above, Shogun Toranaga prepares for war.
1100

16 **Syldavia**
Tintin averts World War II.
1117

Crime Fiction

"Who cares who killed Roger Ackroyd?" Literary critic Edmund Wilson emphatically answered "not I" in his notorious 1943 *New Yorker* essay, dismissing nearly all crime fiction as unreadable rubbish. Yet millions of readers continue to care who committed *The Murder of Roger Ackroyd*; Agatha Christie's classic 1926 puzzler remains one of publishing's all-time, worldwide best-sellers. Moreover, in the decades since Wilson and Christie's heyday, the pure "whodunit" has become just one element in a flourishing literature of overlapping traditions, provocative hybrids, and subtle variations: detective stories, thrillers, spy novels, hard-boiled crime fiction, romantic suspense, studies in psychopathology. The lines between genres have blurred, and the readership—caring not only whodunit but how and why and what it all means—has expanded.

Rise of the Mystery

From Cain and Abel and Oedipus onward, crime stories of one sort or another turn up in all literary traditions. But the origins of our own brand of crime fiction can be traced to the "sensational literature" of the early 1800s, when modern notions of law and order (and the urban police as an organized force) were taking shape in Europe and America. From Poe to Conan Doyle, the rise of the mystery was essentially the rise of the detective-hero: enforcer of social good and brilliant solver (through logic, science, and perseverance) of baffling puzzles.

Pioneers and Landmarks

Jack **Adrian**, editor

Detective Stories from the Strand

Period atmosphere doesn't get much riper than it does in these vintage stories from the preeminent popular fiction magazine of its day

0-19-212306-8 OXFORD $22.95

Wilkie **Collins**

The Moonstone

A tale of theft, drugs, an apparently cursed Indian gem, enriched by Collins's knack for Dickensian caricature

See also **19TH-CENTURY FICTION** under **THE 19TH CENTURY** in **LITERATURE OF THE BRITISH ISLES**

0-14-043014-8 PENGUIN PB $4.95
0-13-600677-9 PRENTICE HALL PB $5.33

The light that streamed from it was like the light of the harvest-moon. When you looked down into the stone, you looked into a yellow deep that drew your eyes into it so that they saw nothing else. It seemed unfathomable; this jewel, that you could hold between your finger and thumb, seemed unfathomable as the heavens themselves.
THE MOONSTONE

The Woman in White

A great novel that is also a landmark in romantic suspense

0-679-40563-1 EVERYMAN'S $20.00
0-14-043096-2 PENGUIN PB $6.95

Michael **Cox**, editor

Victorian Detective Stories

0-19-283150-X OXFORD PB $14.95

Victorian Tales of Mystery and Detection

The Victorian era saw the first great flowering of the detective story. Cox provides a chronological sampling—from Poe to Dickens through Wilkie Collins and Conan Doyle—of the finest examples, both familiar and previously unknown, written from the 1840s to the present

0-19-212308-4 OXFORD $25.00

Charles **Dickens**

"Chesterton asserted that time would show that Dickens was not merely one of the Victorians, but incomparably the greatest English writer of his time; and Shaw coupled his name with that of Shakespeare. It is the conviction of the present writer that both these judgments were justified. Dickens—though he cannot of course pretend to the rank where Shakespeare has few companions—was nevertheless the greatest dramatic writer that the English had had since Shakespeare, and he created the largest and most varied world."
—Edmund Wilson in The Wound and the Bow

The Mystery of Edwin Drood

Dickens's last novel, a melodrama of murder and opium addiction that even in its tantalizingly unfinished state ranks as one of his most original novels

INTRODUCTION BY ANGUS WILSON

0-88411-276-4 AMEREON $20.95
0-14-043092-X PENGUIN PB $7.95

William **Godwin**

Caleb Williams

Godwin's 1794 crime-novel forerunner is part murder mystery, part hunted-man adventure—with an underlying skepticism about the rule of law that foreshadows everyone from Hammett to Highsmith

See also **FICTION** under **THE RESTORATION AND THE 18TH CENTURY** in **LITERATURE OF THE BRITISH ISLES**

EDITED BY MAURICE HINDLE

0-14-043256-6 PENGUIN PB $10.95

Joseph Sheridan **Le Fanu**

"He took great pleasure in ghost stories, and was fascinated by hints of the supernatural...He was a writer of remarkable power in creating suspense, at his best a master of plot, and the creator of some of the most satisfying villains in Victorian literature."—Julian Symons

Uncle Silas

A terrifying novel of a young girl in the hands of a ruthless and greedy relative

EDITED BY W.J. MCCORMACK

0-19-281541-5 OXFORD PB $9.95

Wylder's Hand

0-405-09246-6 AYER $87.95

Edgar Allan **Poe**

"The evident and most prominent aim of Mr. Poe is originality, either of idea, or the combination of ideas. He appears to think it a crime to write unless he has something novel to write about, or some novel way of writing about an old thing. He rejects every word not having a tendency to develop the effect...And he evidently holds whatever tends to the futherance of the effect, to be legitimate material"—Edgan Allan Poe reviewing his own work anonymously (1845)

The Complete Tales and Poems

"The Murders in the Rue Morgue," "The Mystery of Marie Roget," "The Purloined Letter": these and other classic tales introduced the concept of *ratiocination*—detection through deduction—and the prototype for aristocratic amateur sleuths: the all-seeing C. Auguste Dupin

See also **THE 19TH CENTURY: TO THE CIVIL WAR** under **AMERICAN LITERATURE TO 1900** in **LITERATURE OF THE AMERICAS**

0-679-60007-8 MODERN LIBRARY $20.00
0-394-71678-7 VINTAGE PB $15.00

Edgar Allan Poe

Sherlock Holmes

Sherlock Holmes of 221B Baker Street was begotten from the ratiocination of Poe's Dupin, the logic and legwork of Emile Gaboriau's Lecoq, the inscrutability of Wilkie Collins's Sergeant Cuff. Yet Holmes transcended all that had gone before, with the wry textures and fine quirks of his personality, the demonstrable genius of his moment-by-moment deductions, and his evolving relationships with stubborn policeman Lestrade, arch-villain Moriarty, and—above all—the loyal, plucky, and mildly confused Dr. Watson.

Arthur Conan **Doyle**

The Adventures of Sherlock Holmes

0-19-282378-7 OXFORD PB $5.95

The Case-Book of Sherlock Holmes

0-19-282374-4 OXFORD PB $5.95

The Complete Sherlock Holmes

0-385-00689-6 DOUBLEDAY $25.00

His Last Bow
0-19-282381-7 OXFORD PB $5.95

The Hound of the Baskervilles
0-19-282377-9 OXFORD PB $5.95

The Memoirs of Sherlock Holmes
0-19-282375-2 OXFORD PB $5.95

The Oxford Sherlock Holmes 9 volumes
See also 19TH-CENTURY FICTION under THE 19TH CENTURY in LITERATURE OF THE BRITISH ISLES
0-19-212329-7 OXFORD $99.00

The Return of Sherlock Holmes
EDITED BY RICHARD LANCELYN GREEN
0-19-282376-0 OXFORD PB $5.95

Sherlock Holmes: The Complete Novels and Stories
Volume 1
0-553-21241-9 BDD PB $5.95

Volume 2
0-553-21242-7 BDD PB $5.95

The Sign of the Four
0-19-282379-5 OXFORD PB $5.95

A Study in Scarlet
0-19-282380-9 OXFORD PB $5.95

The Valley of Fear
0-19-282382-5 OXFORD PB $5.95

Crime Fiction After Conan Doyle

Between 1890 and 1920, Holmes's immense popularity inspired an outpouring of similar mystery tales from writers such as R. Austin Freeman and A.E.W. Mason. The Holmesian supersleuths were complemented by heroic criminals like Raffles and Arsène Lupin.

E.C. **Bentley**
Trent's Last Case
In its day, this was among the most famous of detective stories, urbane and elaborate
0-19-282422-8 OXFORD PB $7.95

G.K. **Chesterton**
Four Faultless Felons
0-486-25852-1 DOVER PB $6.95

The Man Who Was Thursday
A whimsical morality play with no fewer than six detectives
See also THE EARLY 20TH CENTURY under 20TH-CENTURY BRITISH AND IRISH FICTION in LITERATURE OF THE BRITISH ISLES
0-486-25121-7 DOVER PB $3.95
0-14-018388-4 PENGUIN PB $8.95

The Penguin Complete Father Brown
The metaphysical sleuthings of an intuitive priest. "Pungent, paradoxical, and romantic" —Julian Symons
0-14-009766-X VIKING PB $13.95

R. Austin **Freeman**
Freeman's solidly built mysteries center on the scientific detection of Dr. Thorndyke, physician and criminologist.

The Red Thumb Mark
0-88184-240-0 CARROLL & GRAF PB $3.95

E.W. **Hornung**
The Collected Raffles
The gentleman-thief who inspired a long line of debonair criminals
0-460-87393-8 EVERYMAN'S PB $8.95

Marie Belloc **Lowndes**
The Lodger
Could the man upstairs be a Jack-the-Ripper-like killer? Genteel shivers and chills from 1913
0-89733-299-7 ACADEMY CHICAGO PB $5.95

A.E.W. **Mason**
The first true police detective since Gaboriau: Hanaud of the Sureté—whose adventures are brightened by mordant humor and wry psychology

At the Villa Rose
0-88184-111-0 CARROLL & GRAF PB $3.50

Mary Roberts **Rinehart**
The Circular Staircase
Noises in the night, ghostly lurking, and a feisty spinster-heroine: a 1908 prototype for gothic suspense
0-89968-181-6 LIGHTYEAR $19.95

Three Complete Novels
The Bat, *The Haunted Lady*, and *The Yellow Room* by a leading practioner of the "had-I-but-known" school
1-57566-114-4 ZEBRA PB $13.00

The Golden Age

England

Despite the popularity of Holmes and his followers, the traditional English detective story didn't really hit its stride as a popular form until after World War I. During the '20s and '30s—the so-called "Golden Age"—mystery novels, produced in great quantities by a new generation of specialists, became the "light reading" of choice. The figure of the Great Detective was filled out with charm and humor, sometimes even emerging as a credible hero. The who, how, and why of the murder puzzles became (in Agatha Christie's work especially) unnervingly elaborate and clever. In some ways this perfection of the form was a triumph of tunnel vision: escapist, elitist, rarely concerned with social issues. At its best and on its own genteel terms, the English Golden Age mystery represents a high point in the history of popular reading.

Margery **Allingham**
Dancers in Mourning
0-7867-0384-9 CARROLL & GRAF PB $4.95

Deadly Duo
0-7867-0335-0 CARROLL & GRAF PB $4.50

The Fashion in Shrouds
0-7867-0224-9 CARROLL & GRAF PB $4.95

Flowers for the Judge
0-7867-0291-5 CARROLL & GRAF PB $4.50

More Work for the Undertaker
Allingham at her most baroque and Dickensian
0-89190-180-9 AMEREON $20.95

The Oaken Heart
1-56723-126-8 AMEREON $24.95

Pearls Before Swine
0-7867-0338-5 CARROLL & GRAF PB $4.95

Tether's End
0-7867-0383-0 CARROLL & GRAF PB $4.95

The Tiger in the Smoke
A homicidal escaped prisoner at loose in foggy postwar London. "One of the peaks of crime fiction"—H.R.F. Keating
0-89190-198-1 AMEREON $19.95
0-7867-0225-7 CARROLL & GRAF PB $4.95

Agatha **Christie**
The ABC Murders
A classic Poirot showing Christie's mastery of crime novel as pure puzzle
0-425-13024-X BERKLEY PB $5.50

And Then There Were None
A one-of-a-kind, detectiveless landmark (also known as *Ten Little Indians*): ten strangers stranded in an island manse, being murdered one after another
0-425-12958-6 BERKLEY PB $5.50

The Body in the Library
A classic Jane Marple novel
0-06-100364-6 HARPERCOLLINS PB $4.99

Cards on the Table
0-425-10567-9 BERKLEY PB $4.99

Cat Among the Pigeons
0-06-100284-4 HARPERCOLLINS PB $4.99

Crooked House
0-06-100277-1 HARPERCOLLINS PB $4.99

Curtain
Hercule's downbeat, ironic adieu
0-06-100366-2 HARPERCOLLINS PB $4.99

Agatha Christie

Agatha **Christie**

Endless Night

A late Christie novel quite different in structure and tone from her other work, but very effective

0-06-100334-4 HARPERCOLLINS PB $4.99

Evil Under the Sun

Filmed with Peter Ustinov as Poirot and also starring Maggie Smith

0-425-12960-8 BERKLEY PB $4.99

The Hollow

Christie at her most novelistic: Poirot's "little grey cells" share the stage with tense close-ups of character and motive

0-399-13727-0 PUTNAM $24.95

9-995-60803-0 BERKLEY PB $4.99

The Mirror Crack'd from Side to Side

Basis of the movie starring Elizabeth Taylor, Rock Hudson, and with Angela Lansbury as Miss Marple

0-06-100285-2 HARPERCOLLINS PB $4.99

Mrs. McGinty's Dead

0-06-100375-1 HARPERCOLLINS PB $4.99

Murder at the Vicarage

Miss Jane Marple at her best—in a gently comic, ultimately somber study of evil forces at work in picturesque English-village surroundings

9-995-76314-1 BERKLEY PB $4.99

The Murder of Roger Ackroyd

The 1926 Hercule Poirot mystery that made Christie famous remains as fresh, readable, and shrewdly shocking as ever

0-06-100286-0 HARPERCOLLINS PB $4.99

Murder on the Orient Express

0-06-100274-7 HARPERCOLLINS PB $4.99

The Mysterious Affair at Styles

0-425-12961-6 BERKLEY PB $5.50

The Pale Horse

Supernatural elements come into play in one of Christie's more somber thrillers

0-06-100377-8 HARPERCOLLINS PB $4.99

Peril at End House

0-425-13025-8 BERKLEY PB $4.99

Towards Zero

Countdown to inevitable murder at a family gathering: no Poirot, no Marple, but sturdy Superintendent Battle copes admirably

0-425-12959-4 BERKLEY PB $4.99

The Witness for the Prosecution and Other Stories

The title story was the basis for Christie's enormously successful play, later filmed twice

0-425-06809-9 BERKLEY PB $5.50

Edmund **Crispin**

The Moving Toyshop

This comical cultivated adventure of Oxford don Gervase Fen is a bit bizarre and more than a bit rococo

0-14-008817-2 PENGUIN PB $6.95

Cyril **Hare**

Hare's amusingly observant explorations of murder in fascinating settings frequently hinge on esoteric points of law.

Suicide Excepted

0-486-24245-5 DOVER PB $4.95

Georgette **Heyer**

Heyer, known for her Regency romances, was also a quintessential Golden Age writer.

Behold Here's Poison

Scotland Yard's Inspector Hannasyde stalks a diabolically clever murderer

0-89190-639-8 AMEREON $22.95

The Unfinished Clue

0-89190-648-7 AMEREON $22.95

C.H.B. **Kitchin**

The Death of My Aunt

0-88184-549-3 CARROLL & GRAF PB $3.50

Philip **MacDonald**

The Rasp

"Golden Age" plotting at its most endearingly tricky: utterly unconvincing, but fun

0-486-23864-4 DOVER PB $5.95

Ngaio **Marsh**

Part satire, part charm, part mystery; the low-key investigations of upper-class cop Roderick Alleyn—in theatrical milieu, in picturesque villages, and sometimes in tandem with artist-wife Troy

Alleyn and Others: The Collected Short Fiction of Ngaio Marsh

EDITED BY DOUGLAS G. GREENE

1-55882-028-0 INTL POLYGONICS PB $10.95

Artists in Crime

0-88411-471-6 AMEREON $22.95

Colour Scheme

0-425-14651-0 BERKLEY PB $5.99

Death in Ecstasy

0-88411-478-3 AMEREON $22.95

Enter a Murderer

0-88411-483-X AMEREON $20.95

Final Curtain

0-88411-485-6 AMEREON $24.95

Night at the Vulcan

0-88411-490-2 AMEREON $22.95

The Nursing Home Murder

0-425-14242-6 BERKLEY PB $4.50

Spinsters in Jeopardy

0-88411-495-3 AMEREON $21.95

Tied Up in Tinsel

0-88411-496-1 AMEREON $21.95

Vintage Murder

0-88411-497-X AMEREON $20.95

When in Rome

0-425-14656-1 BERKLEY PB $4.99

Eden **Phillpotts**

The Red Redmaynes

A classic detective novel about the systematic extermination of a set of siblings

0-486-24255-2 DOVER PB $6.95

Dorothy **Sayers**

"Dorothy Sayers made two great contributions to the art of crime writing. She moved the conventional detective story, the pure puzzle, forward towards being a book in which a whole social milieu could be examined and chronicled with characters much more than cardboard cut-outs. And she created Lord Peter Wimsey."—H.R.F. Keating

Clouds of Witness

0-06-104353-2 HARPERCOLLINS PB $4.99

The Documents in the Case

0-06-104360-5 HARPERCOLLINS PB $4.99

The Five Red Herrings

0-06-104363-X HARPERCOLLINS PB $4.99

Gaudy Night

Fear and suspicion at a women's college

0-06-104349-4 HARPERCOLLINS PB $4.99

Hangman's Holiday

0-06-055033-3 HARPERPERENNIAL PB $21.95

Have His Carcase

0-06-104352-4 HARPERCOLLINS PB $4.99

In the Teeth of the Evidence

0-06-104356-7 HARPERCOLLINS PB $4.99

Lord Peter: The Complete Lord Peter Wimsey Stories

0-06-104361-3 HARPERCOLLINS PB $4.99

Murder Must Advertise

Sayers at her most brightly satirical, as Wimsey sleuths in and about a London ad agency circa 1933

0-06-104355-9 HARPERCOLLINS PB $4.99

0-06-092388-1 HARPERCOLLINS PB $8.00

The Nine Tailors

0-15-665899-2 HARCOURT BRACE PB $6.95

Strong Poison

When Lord Peter first meets Harriet Vane, she is under accusation of murder

0-06-104350-8 HARPERCOLLINS PB $4.99

Unnatural Death

0-06-104358-3 HARPERCOLLINS PB $4.99

The Unpleasantness at the Bellona Club

0-06-104354-0 HARPERCOLLINS PB $4.99

Josephine **Tey**

Brat Farrar

0-02-008822-1 COLLIER PB $6.00

The Daughter of Time

Was Richard III a murderer? A contemporary sleuth tackles the case—and the nature of historical "truth"—from his sickbed

0-02-054550-9 MICROSOFT PB $6.00

The Franchise Affair

False accusations of kidnapping destroy a respectable family: a powerful blend of courtroom drama, suspense, and psychology

0-02-008823-X COLLIER PB $6.00

The Man in the Queue

0-02-008824-8 MICROSOFT PB $6.00

0-684-81502-8 SCRIBNERS PB $9.00

Miss Pym Disposes
0-8376-0447-8 BENTLEY $16.00

A Shilling for Candles
A body on the beach leads to a call for Scotland Yard—and for Inspector Alan Grant, Tey's gentle, empathetic hero (here at his Scottish best)
0-02-054530-4 MACMILLAN PB $6.00

The Singing Sands
0-02-008825-6 COLLIER PB $6.00

Arthur W. **Upfield**

An Author Bites the Dust
0-02-054900-8 MACMILLAN PB $5.00

The Bachelors of Broken Hill
0-684-18246-7 SCRIBNERS PB $6.00

The Bone Is Pointed
0-684-18247-5 SCRIBNERS PB $6.00

Bony and the Kelly Gang
0-02-025880-1 COLLIER PB $4.95

The Bushman Who Came Back
0-02-025911-5 COLLIER PB $5.95

Man of Two Tribes
0-02-025950-6 MACMILLAN PB $6.00

The New Shoe
0-684-18020-0 MACMILLAN PB $4.95

No Footprints in the Bush
0-02-025940-9 MACMILLAN PB $4.95

The Sands of Windee
0-89190-570-7 AMEREON $19.95

Venom House
0-8488-1212-3 AMEREON $20.95

The Widows of Broome
0-684-18389-7 MACMILLAN PB $5.95

Winds of Evil
0-89190-563-4 AMEREON $18.95

Arthur William **Upfield**

The Will of the Tribe
0-684-18141-X MACMILLAN PB $5.95

Patricia **Wentworth**

On a par with Miss Marple is Wentworth's governess turned private investigator, Miss Maud Silver.

The Clock Strikes Twelve
0-89190-923-0 AMEREON $19.95

The Fingerprint
0-88411-727-8 AMEREON $21.95

The Ivory Dagger
0-88411-735-9 AMEREON $19.95

The Watersplash
0-88411-741-3 AMEREON $20.95

America

In America, the classic detective story peaked in the mid-'20s with the advent of S.S. Van Dine's phenomenally popular mysteries featuring Philo Vance, the posh British amateur-sleuth with a snobbish New York City veneer. But the best of those who followed—Ellery Queen and Rex Stout above all—were thoroughly American in idiom and approach: more casual, more Twain-laconic than Oxford-droll in humor, more democratic in outlook. And many of those writing in the '30s were of course influenced by the hard-boiled revolution in crime fiction spearheaded by Dashiell Hammett.

Earl Derr **Biggers**

The House Without a Key
The 1925 debut of Honolulu police-detective Charlie Chan—and more shrewdly humorous than the old Chan movies would suggest
1-88340-223-9 PENZLER $35.00

John Dickson **Carr**

Macabre, delightfully improbable sleuthings, mostly conducted by bibulous Dr. Gideon Fell.

The Bride of Newgate
0-7867-0102-1 CARROLL & GRAF PB $4.95

The Burning Court
0-930330-27-7 INTL POLYGONICS PB $4.95

Dark of the Moon
0-7867-0222-2 CARROLL & GRAF PB $4.95

The Devil in Velvet
0-7867-0101-3 CARROLL & GRAF PB $4.95

The Eight of Swords
0-8217-3649-3 ZEBRA PB $3.99

The Emperor's Snuff-Box
0-7867-0223-0 CARROLL & GRAF PB $4.95

Fire, Burn!
0-7867-0175-7 CARROLL & GRAF PB $4.50

The Ghosts' High Noon
0-88184-673-2 CARROLL & GRAF PB $4.50

The Hollow Man
0-7451-8637-8 CHIVERS NORTH AMERICA $18.50

The Nine Wrong Answers
0-7867-0174-9 CARROLL & GRAF PB $3.95

Patrick Butler for the Defense
1-55882-131-7 INTL POLYGONICS PB $5.95

The Problem of the Green Capsule
0-930330-51-X INTL POLYGONICS PB $5.95

The Problem of the Wire Cage
0-8217-3384-2 ZEBRA PB $3.95

The Three Coffins
Generally regarded as the most ingenious of all locked-room mysteries
0-89966-048-7 BUCCANEER $16.95

Lillian **de la Torre**

Dr. Sam Johnson, Detector
Historical crime stories, with Dr. Johnson as sleuth, Boswell as Watson
0-930330-08-0 INTL POLYGONICS PB $6.95

Carter **Dickson**

The more openly comic side of John Dickson Carr, featuring Sir Henry Merrivale, solver of impossible mysteries.

Behind the Crimson Blind
0-86220-768-1 PRSCT $12.95

Curse of the Bronze Lamp
0-88184-101-3 CARROLL & GRAF PB $3.50

The Judas Window
0-930330-62-5 INTL POLYGONICS PB $5.95

Merrivale Holds the Key
1-55882-027-2 INTL POLYGONICS PB $14.95

Nine and Death Makes Ten
0-86220-797-5 CURLEY $12.95

Peacock Feather Murders
0-930330-68-4 INTL POLYGONICS PB $5.95

The Reader Is Warned
1-55882-019-1 INTL POLYGONICS PB $5.95

The Skeleton in the Clock
1-55882-103-1 INTL POLYGONICS PB $5.95

Mignon G. **Eberhart**

Another Man's Murder
0-446-34930-5 WARNER PB $5.50

Death in the Fog
0-8032-6730-4 NEBRASKA PB $13.00

From this Dark Stairway
0-8032-6729-0 NEBRASKA PB $13.00

The House on the Roof
0-8032-6734-7 NEBRASKA PB $13.00

Man Missing
0-446-35212-8 WARNER PB $5.50

The Patient in Room 18
0-8032-6727-4 NEBRASKA PB $9.95

Postmark Murder
0-446-31181-2 MYSTERIOUS PB $5.50

While the Patient Slept
0-8032-6726-6 NEBRASKA PB $9.95

Wolf in Man's Clothing
0-8032-6732-0 NEBRASKA PB $13.00

Erle Stanley **Gardner**

These titles are early, superior Perry Mason—with taut courtroom drama and authentic, science-oriented detection.

The Case of the Borrowed Brunette
0-345-34374-3 BALLANTINE PB $4.99

The Case of the Calendar Girl
0-345-34375-1 BALLANTINE PB $4.99

The Case of the Careless Cupid
0-345-39226-4 BALLANTINE PB $4.99

The Case of the Caretaker's Cat
0-345-32156-1 BALLANTINE PB $4.99

Erle Stanley **Gardner**

The Case of the Cautious Coquette
0-345-35202-5 BALLANTINE PB $4.99

The Case of the Fenced-In Woman
0-345-39223-X BALLANTINE PB $4.99

The Case of the Horrified Heirs
0-345-39227-2 BALLANTINE PB $4.99

The Case of the Lame Canary
0-345-90796-5 BALLANTINE PB $4.99

The Case of the One-Eyed Witness
0-345-39225-6 DEL RAY PB $4.99

The Case of the Postponed Murder
0-345-39229-9 BALLANTINE PB $4.99

The Case of the Screaming Woman
0-345-37875-X DEL RAY PB $4.99

The Case of the Stuttering Bishop
0-345-35680-2 BALLANTINE PB $3.99

The Case of the Sulky Girl
0-345-37145-3 BALLANTINE PB $4.99

The Case of the Troubled Trustee
0-345-39224-8 BALLANTINE PB $4.99

Ellery **Queen**

The Dutch Shoe Mystery
1-88340-212-3 PENZLER PB $6.95

The Player on the Other Side
0-89340-107-2 CURLEY PB $16.95

The Siamese Twin Mystery
1-88340-211-5 PENZLER PB $6.95

The Tragedy of X
Fetching backgrounds (New York circa 1932), a nasty murder method, and a dandy sleuth: retired Shakespearean actor Drury Lane. The series continues with *Drury Lane's Last Case*
0-930330-43-9 INTL POLYGONICS PB $5.95

The Tragedy of Z
0-930330-58-7 INTL POLYGONICS PB $4.95

Rex **Stout**

Nero Wolfe of 35th Street is fat, brilliant, crabby, a connoisseur of beer and orchids—a sedentary legend. But his breezy, slangy assistant Archie Goodwin is, as Howard Haycraft put it, "the one example in history...of a Watson who steals the play from his Holmes, and a first-rate Holmes to boot."

And Be a Villain
0-553-23931-7 BDD PB $4.99

Champagne for One
0-553-24438-8 BDD PB $4.99

Curtains for Three
0-553-24498-1 BDD PB $4.99

Death of a Dude
0-553-24730-1 BDD PB $4.99

Double for Death
0-553-26059-6 BDD PB $4.99

Fer-de-Lance
1-88340-217-4 PENZLER $35.00
0-553-27819-3 BDD PB $4.99

The Golden Spiders
0-553-27780-4 BDD PB $4.99

In the Best Families
0-553-27776-6 BDD PB $4.99

Over My Dead Body
0-553-23116-2 BDD PB $4.99

A Prize for Princes
0-7867-0104-8 CARROLL & GRAF PB $4.95

Red Threads
0-553-22530-8 BDD PB $4.99

A Right to Die
0-553-24032-3 BDD PB $4.99

The Second Confession
0-553-24594-5 BDD PB $4.99

The Silent Speaker
0-553-23497-8 BDD PB $4.99

Three at Wolfe's Door
0-553-23803-5 BDD PB $4.99

Three Doors to Death
0-553-25127-9 BDD PB $4.99

Phoebe Atwood **Taylor**

The Cape Cod Mystery
New England atmosphere and Yankee shrewdness, in the homespun company of the "Codfish Sherlock": taciturn Asey Mayo of Welfleet, Mass.
0-88150-046-1 BACKCOUNTRY PB $6.00

Cold Steal
0-88150-269-3 FOUL PLAY PB $6.00

The Cut Direct
0-88150-270-7 FOUL PLAY PB $6.00

Octagon House
0-88150-194-8 FOUL PLAY PB $5.95

Punch with Care
0-88150-229-4 FOUL PLAY PB $6.00

The Six Iron Spiders
0-88150-230-8 FOUL PLAY PB $6.95

The Tinkling Symbol
0-88150-263-4 FOUL PLAY PB $6.50

S.S. **Van Dine**

The most popular American mystery novels of the mid-20s—starring suave, erudite Philo Vance, the much-parodied prototype of the amateur New York City detective.

The Benson Murder Case
0-89190-511-1 AMEREON $22.95

The Bishop Murder Case
0-89190-512-X AMEREON $23.95

The Canary Murder Case
0-89190-513-8 AMEREON $22.95

The Dragon Murder Case
1-88340-221-2 PENZLER $35.00

The Gracie Allen Murder Case
1-88340-209-3 PENZLER PB $6.95

The Winter Murder Case
1-88340-208-5 PENZLER PB $6.95

The Hard-Boiled Detective

By the time that Ogden Nash wrote that: "Philo Vance needs a kick in the pance" in the '30s, S.S. Van Dine and the elegant world of the traditional detective story had already received a firm and decisive kick: the rise of the American "pulp" adventure magazines, with their contemporary slang, racy and violent exploits, rapid pacing, and heroes more notable for toughness than for "little grey cells." The best of the pulps, *Black Mask*, featured the melodramatic yet seedily realistic investigations of professional private detectives. And the best of these "hard-boiled" adventures were written by Dashiell Hammett, a former Pinkerton operative who became—in the words of Ross Macdonald—"the first American writer to use the detective-story for the purposes of a major novelist." In Hammett and his finest successors this view of a corrupt society is mirrored in street-wise, darkly poetic language.

Jack C. **Adrian** & Bill **Pronzini**, editors

Hard-Boiled: An Anthology of American Crime Stories
Covering 70 years of detective fiction, this volume includes classic work as well as hard-to-find stories by Chandler, Hammet, Cain, and others
See also **SHORT STORY COLLECTIONS** under **20TH-CENTURY AMERICAN FICTION** in **LITERATURE OF THE AMERICAS**
0-19-508499-3 OXFORD $30.00

Fredric **Brown**

The Lenient Beast
0-88184-444-6 CARROLL & GRAF PB $3.50

Murder Can Be Fun
0-88184-504-3 CARROLL & GRAF PB $3.95

The Screaming Mimi
A peculiar statue plays a crucial role in this typically inventive Brown thriller
0-88184-449-7 CARROLL & GRAF PB $3.50

What Mad Universe?
0-89968-333-9 LIGHTYEAR $18.95

Paul **Cain**

Seven Slayers
Pulp stories don't get much more swift and stripped down than these
0-679-75185-8 VINTAGE PB $9.00

Raymond **Chandler**

The Big Sleep
The prototypical Southern California mystery—corrupt wealth, secret vices, family scandal—and the debut of Philip Marlowe
0-394-75828-5 VINTAGE PB $10.00

The Big Sleep & Farewell, My Lovely
0-679-60140-6 MODERN LIBRARY $16.50

Farewell, My Lovely
Marlowe stumbles upon a murder in '30s L.A., taking in the city's gambling circuit and three deadly beauties en route
0-394-23907-5 BLACK LIZARD PB $10.00

The High Window
Marlowe seeks a priceless gold coin and becomes entangled in the shady dealings of a dead collector
0-394-75826-9 VINTAGE PB $11.00

The Lady in the Lake
Betrayed husband, mising wife—and Marlowe, impeded by a few vicious cops, on the maze-like trail
1-88340-294-8 PENZLER $35.00

Later Novels & Other Writings
Includes *The Lady in the Lake*, *The Little Sister*, *The Long Goodbye*, *Playback*, as well as the screenplay for *Double Indemnity* and selected articles and letters
See also **FROM THE TURN OF THE CENTURY TO WORLD WAR II** under **20TH-CENTURY AMERICAN FICTION** in **LITERATURE OF THE AMERICAS**
EDITED BY FRANK MACSHANE
1-88301-108-6 LIBRARY OF AMERICA $35.00

The Little Sister
A rising movie star, her blackmailing brother, agents, prostitutes, and studio heads. Marlowe sardonically takes on the interlocking levels of Hollywood society
0-394-75767-X VINTAGE PB $10.00

The Long Goodbye
Why did Terry Lennox—drunken war hero, victim of Nazism, apparent wife killer—commit suicide? Chandler's most ambitious blend of genre sleuthing and serious fiction
9-992-82404-2 BLACK LIZARD PB $10.00
0-394-75768-8 VINTAGE PB $12.00

Playback
0-394-75766-1 VINTAGE PB $9.00

The Simple Art of Murder
The best of Chandler's pulp stories—plus his notorious attack on Britain's "Golden Age" eminences
0-394-75765-3 VINTAGE PB $12.00

Stories & Early Novels
Includes most of Chandler's pulp stories as well as *The Big Sleep*, *Farewell, My Lovely*, and *The High Window*
EDITED BY FRANK MACSHANE
1-88301-107-8 LIBRARY OF AMERICA $35.00

Trouble Is My Business
0-394-75764-5 VINTAGE PB $10.00

Carroll John **Daly**
Daly, a Black Mask *regular, was in his day one of the most popular of the hardboiled writers, although today his work has a primarily nostalgic appeal.*

The Adventures of Race Williams
0-89296-959-8 MYSTERIOUS PB $9.95

The Adventures of Satan Hall
0-89296-938-5 MYSTERIOUS PB $8.95

Murder from the East: A Race Williams Story
EDITED BY TONY SPARAFUCILE
0-930330-01-3 INTL POLYGONICS PB $5.00

Erle Stanley **Gardner**

The Adventures of Paul Pry
0-89296-976-8 MYSTERIOUS PB $9.95

Dashiell **Hammett**

The Big Knockover
Nine standout stories, most featuring the Continental Op
0-679-72259-9 VINTAGE PB $13.00

The Continental Op
Introducing the nameless Continental Op, fat and living by the code of the fat, brutish and living by the code of the Continental Detective Agency, in *Black Mask* stories that are landmarks in the history of hardboiled style
0-679-72258-0 VINTAGE PB $12.00

The Hambletons had been for several generations a wealthy and decently prominent New York family. There was nothing in the Hambleton history to account for Sue, the youngest member of the clan. She grew out of childhood with a kink that made her dislike the polished side of life, like the rough. By the time she was twenty-one, in 1926, she definitely preferred Tenth Avenue to Fifth, grifters to bankers, and Hymie the Riveter to the Honorable Cecil Windown, who had asked her to marry him.
THE CONTINENTAL OP

Dashiell Hammett (photo by Eileen Darby, Graphic House)

The Dain Curse
Stolen diamonds, sexual obsessions, religious cults, as the Continental Op encounters the accursed Dain clan of San Francisco
0-679-72260-2 VINTAGE PB $10.00

The Glass Key
A corrosive study of big-city corruption—with a politico's loyal (yet ambivalent) henchman as sleuth
0-394-71773-2 VINTAGE PB $10.00

The Maltese Falcon
The definitive hard-boiled private-eye novel
0-679-72264-5 VINTAGE PB $9.00

Red Harvest
Warring gangs and crooked cops in Montana's "Poisonville"—a rotten town that needs a clean-up visit from the Op. Total violence, raw poetry
0-679-72261-0 VINTAGE PB $10.00

The Thin Man
A missing inventor and a murdered secretary, investigated in an urbane wash of booze and wisecracks, by ex-gumshoe Nick Charles and his wife Nora
0-679-72263-7 VINTAGE PB $9.00

Woman in the Dark
A novella recently republished for the first time in decades
0-679-72265-3 VINTAGE PB $8.00

Maxim **Jakubowski**, editor

The Mammoth Book of Pulp Fiction
A jumbo-size collection of rarities by writers including Dashiell Hammett, Jim Thompson, John Macdonald, and many more
0-7867-0300-8 CARROLL & GRAF PB $9.95

Jonathan **Latimer**

The Dead Don't Care
Latimer's hardboiled sleuths in Key West, circa 1938
1-55882-082-5 INTL POLYGONICS PB $7.95

The Lady in the Morgue
Farcical hardboiled goings-on, heavily laced with alcohol
0-930330-79-X INTL POLYGONICS PB $4.95

Murder in the Madhouse
The first of Latimer's raucous, often bawdy crime novels
1-55882-023-X INTL POLYGONICS PB $7.95

Solomon's Vineyard
Sex, violence, and a warped religious cult; written in the '40s but only now printed in unexpurgated form
0-930330-91-9 INTL POLYGONICS PB $4.95

Ross **Macdonald**
The bleak, past-haunted investigations of Lew Archer take him through a corrupted southern California full of confused adolescents, hints of incest, family secrets.

Archer in Jeopardy
A set containing three of the best Archers: *The Doomsters*, *The Zebra-Striped Hearse*, and *The Instant Enemy*
0-394-50804-1 KNOPF $24.95

Black Money
0-7862-0464-8 THORNDIKE PB $20.95

Black Money
0-679-76810-6 VINTAGE PB $11.00

The Blue Hammer
0-89190-095-0 AMEREON $21.95

Ross **Macdonald**

The Chill

Many consider this the greatest of all the Archer novels: baroque in the architecture of its plotting, devastating in its emotional fallout

0-679-76807-6 VINTAGE PB $11.00
0-679-65807-6 VINTAGE PB $11.00

The Drowning Pool

0-679-76806-8 VINTAGE PB $11.00

The Far Side of the Dollar

The death of a Hollywood starlet is the pivot for another Macdonald masterpiece

0-679-76865-3 VINTAGE PB $11.00

The Galton Case

For Macdonald, this novel—filled with autobiographical elements derived from his own unsettled youth—was the turning point in his career

0-679-76864-5 VINTAGE PB $11.00

The Underground Man

0-679-76808-4 VINTAGE PB $11.00

Rise of the Modern Crime Novel

America

The hardboiled style and outlook—lean, raw, darkly skeptical—helped foster a new focus on crime from the viewpoint of criminals and victims, with the detective either on the sidelines or entirely absent. The major players were instead gangsters, psychopaths, or semi-innocent bystanders, driven to violence by greed, lust, or fateful circumstance. Crime novelists of the '30s like James M. Cain and Horace McCoy most often placed their antiheroes in a nightmarish socioeconomic landscape. By the late '40s, with the ascent of Patricia Highsmith, Margaret Millar, and Jim Thompson, the traumas were more likely to be Freudian—or existential.

W.R. **Burnett**

Little Caesar

Knowledgeable gangster melodrama from 1929

0-88184-235-4 CARROLL & GRAF PB $3.50

James M. **Cain**

"A poet of the tabloid murder."
—Edmund Wilson

Double Indemnity

Adultery, greed, and the perfect insurance policy: the ultimate in simmering cynicism

See also **FROM THE TURN OF THE CENTURY TO WORLD WAR II** under **20TH-CENTURY AMERICAN FICTION** in **LITERATURE OF THE AMERICAS**

0-679-72322-6 VINTAGE PB $8.00

Mildred Pierce

Not a crime novel, but stamped with Cain's deadpan, anti-heroic realism

0-679-72321-8 VINTAGE PB $8.95

The Postman Always Rings Twice

The stark death-row confession of an ordinary guy who became a killer—thanks to the lustful magnetism of a luncheonette owner's frustrated wife

0-679-72325-0 VINTAGE PB $8.00

Three by Cain

Includes *Serenade, Love's Lovely Counterfeit*, and *The Butterfly*

0-679-72323-4 VINTAGE PB $13.00

Steve **Fisher**

I Wake Up Screaming

0-679-73677-8 VINTAGE PB $8.00

David **Goodis**

Pure noir: downbeat evocations of an urban underworld where nobody wins.

Shoot the Piano Player

Originally published as *Down There*: one of Goodis's best

0-679-73254-3 VINTAGE PB $10.00

Richard **Hallas**

You Play the Black and the Red Comes Up

A parodic approach to the hardboiled novel, set in Hollywood

INTRODUCTION BY DAVID FEINBERG

0-88748-058-6 CARNEGIE-MELLON $19.95

Patricia **Highsmith**

"The most important crime novelist at present in practice."—Julian Symons

The Boy Who Followed Ripley

0-679-74567-X VINTAGE PB $11.00

A Game for the Living

0-87113-210-9 ATLANTIC MONTHLY PB $7.95

Ripley Under Ground

0-679-74230-1 VINTAGE PB $11.00

Ripley Under Water

Gore Vidal calls Highsmith one of the century's most interesting writers. "It's been twelve long years since *The Boy Who Followed Ripley*: welcome back, Tom"—*Kirkus Reviews*

0-679-74809-1 VINTAGE PB $11.00

Ripley's Game

0-679-74568-8 VINTAGE PB $11.00

The Talented Mr. Ripley

Liar, psychopath, killer—and hero: the first of Highsmith's creepy, funny novels featuring Tom Ripley, cosmopolitan seeker of the good life—and the embodiment of the criminal as free spirit

0-679-74229-8 VINTAGE PB $11.00

Those Who Walk Away

A violent encounter by a Venetian canal is the starting point for a strange war of nerves

0-87113-259-1 ATLANTIC MONTHLY PB $12.00

The Two Faces of January

0-87113-209-5 ATLANTIC MONTHLY PB $7.95

Tony **Hillerman** &
Rosemary **Herbert**, editors

The Oxford Book of American Detective Stories

Thirty-four tales illustrate the evolution of crime fiction in America from its roots in "locked room" mysteries through the hardboiled '30s and '40s to the contemporary range of styles. Earle Stanley Gardner, Raymond Chandler, Rex Stout, Ed McBain, Sara Paretsky, Sue Grafton: all the greats of the genre are here, along with surprising selections from the likes of Faulkner and Brett Harte

0-19-508581-7 OXFORD $25.00

Charlotte **Jay**

Beat Not the Bones

Winner of the 1954 Edgar Award for Best Novel

1-56947-047-2 SOHO PB $11.00

John D. **MacDonald**

Many fans feel that MacDonald was even more convincing in his many non-Travis McGee books.

Barrier Island

MacDonald's last book is an absorbing intrigue involving Florida real estate swindles

0-449-13179-3 FAWCETT PB $5.99

Cape Fear

Originally published as *The Executioners*, and filmed twice: a searing novel of how a victim turns the tables

0-449-13190-4 FAWCETT PB $5.99

A Flash of Green

An ambitious novel involving the dark side of land development

0-449-12692-7 FAWCETT PB $5.99

Horace **McCoy**

I Should Have Stayed Home

A downbeat tale of Hollywood in the '30s by a protagonist who is "...alone and friendless in the most terrifying town in the world"

1-85242-402-8 SERPENT'S TAIL PB $11.99

They Shoot Horses Don't They?

The famous novel of a Depression-era dance marathon. "McCoy reveals himself as the real nihilist of the hardboiled school"
—Geoffrey O'Brien, *Hardboiled America*

See also **FROM THE TURN OF THE CENTURY TO WORLD WAR II** under **20TH-CENTURY AMERICAN FICTION** in **LITERATURE OF THE AMERICAS**

1-56849-241-3 BUCCANEER $19.95
1-85242-401-X SERPENT'S TAIL PB $9.99

Margaret **Millar**

An Air that Kills

0-930330-23-4 INTL POLYGONICS PB $4.95

The Fiend

0-930330-10-2 INTL POLYGONICS PB $5.95

Fire Will Freeze

0-930330-59-5 INTL POLYGONICS PB $5.95

The Listening Walls

0-930330-52-8 INTL POLYGONICS PB $5.95

A Stranger in My Grave

How does a living person's name come to appear on a tombstone? And whose body is really buried there?

1-55882-066-3 INTL POLYGONICS PB $7.95

Joel Townsley **Rogers**

The Red Right Hand

Teetering on the edge of madness, Dr. Harry Riddle struggles to make sense of the grim funhouse he has stumbled into: a cleverly executed nightmare novel

0-88184-008-4 CARROLL & GRAF PB $3.50

Jim **Thompson**

Thompson is one of the great literary resurrections of our time—a powerful, scary, obsessive writer capable of both extreme violence and wild humor.

After Dark, My Sweet
An alcoholic, a schizophrenic, and a bunko artist plan a kidnapping
0-679-73247-0 VINTAGE PB $7.95

The Alcoholics
0-679-73313-2 VINTAGE PB $9.00

The Criminal
A murder case told from multiple viewpoints, with an ambiguous outcome
0-679-73314-0 VINTAGE PB $9.00

Cropper's Cabin
A young Okie sharecropper is penned up with his malicious father and amorous stepmother in a fevered cabin. When he falls in love with a rich girl, we enter the nightmare world where Thompson is such an exquisitely brutal guide
0-679-73315-9 VINTAGE PB $9.00

The Getaway
A charming psychopath on the run
0-679-73250-0 VINTAGE PB $10.00

The Grifters
A con-man caught up in spiraling violence with his mother and mistress
0-679-73248-9 VINTAGE PB $10.00

Jim Thompson

Heed the Thunder
An atypical attempt at regional realism which veers off into some unexpected byways
0-679-74014-7 VINTAGE PB $10.00

A Hell of a Woman
Thompson takes us inside his hero's mind as it begins to split apart
0-679-73251-9 VINTAGE PB $10.00

The Killer Inside Me
Under the corny, folksy facade of a Texas sheriff seethes the cold and brilliant mind of a homicidal psychopath
0-679-73397-3 VINTAGE PB $10.00

Nothing More than Murder
Adultery and murder among small-time movie exhibitors
0-679-73309-4 VINTAGE PB $9.00

Now and On Earth
Thompson's first novel is also his most transparently autobiographical: an uncomfortable, unblinkingly realistic portrait of a family devastated by economic and psychological pressures
0-679-74013-9 VINTAGE PB $9.00

Pop. 1280
"The great merit of the novels of Jim Thompson is that they are completely without good taste. And *Pop. 1280* has the least good taste of them all"—H.R.F. Keating
0-679-73249-7 VINTAGE PB $9.00

Well, sir, I should have been sitting pretty, just about as pretty as a man could sit. Here I was, the high sheriff of Potts County, and I was drawing almost two thousand dollars a year—not to mention what I could pick up on the side. On top of that, I had free living quarters on the second floor of the courthouse, just as nice a place as a man could ask for; and it even had a bathroom so that I didn't have to bathe in a washtub or tramp outside to a privy, like most folks in town did. I guess you could say that Kingdom Come was really here as far as I was concerned. I had it made, and it looked like I could go on having it made—being high sheriff of Potts County—as long as I minded my own business and didn't arrest no one unless I just couldn't get out of it and they didn't amount to nothin'.

POP. 1280

Recoil
Convict Pat Cosgrove is released from the most vile of state prisons by Doc Luther, who then provides him with two mistresses (one of them Mrs. Luther). Cosgrove, like so many other Thompson characters, neglects to examine the fine print
0-679-73308-6 VINTAGE PB $10.00

Savage Night
A pint-sized hit man comes to a grotesquely violent end
0-679-73310-8 VINTAGE PB $9.00

South of Heaven
A fictionalized memoir of Thompson's youthful experiences in Texas oil fields
0-679-74017-1 VINTAGE PB $9.00

A Swell-Looking Babe
Behind the scenes at a seedy hotel
0-679-73311-6 VINTAGE PB $9.00

Texas by the Tail
A comedy of conmen and oil millionaires, with some characteristically rough touches
0-679-74011-2 VINTAGE PB $9.00

The Transgressors
0-679-74016-3 VINTAGE PB $8.00

Wild Town
Murder and madness in Texas oil country
0-679-73312-4 VINTAGE PB $9.00

Charles **Willeford**

High Priest of California
0-9651042-4-9 JUNO PB $10.99

Miami Blues
The darkly comic tribulations of Miami cop Hoke Mosley—as he deals with psychos, drug dealers, the housing shortage, his ex-wife, his teenage daughters, and midlife crisis.
0-440-21883-7 DELL PB $4.99

New Hope for the Dead
0-440-21884-5 DELL PB $4.99

Pick-Up
Fifties-style alienation relentlessly explored, with a surprise ending
0-679-73253-5 VINTAGE PB $9.00

The Shark-Infested Custard
0-440-21881-0 DELL PB $4.99

Sideswipe
0-440-21882-9 DELL PB $4.99

The Way We Die Now
0-440-21885-3 DELL PB $4.99

Wild Wives
0-940642-29-8 RE-SEARCH PB $10.99

The Woman Chaser
0-88184-556-6 CARROLL & GRAF PB $3.95

Paula L. **Woods**, editor

Spooks, Spies, and Private Eyes: Black Mystery, Crime, and Suspense Fiction
0-385-47827-5 DOUBLEDAY $23.95

Cornell **Woolrich**

I Married a Dead Man
Woolrich, one of the most influential of American mystery writers, purveyed an authentically dark and paranoid vision. In this, one of his best (first published in 1948), a woman changes her identity with catastrophic results
0-14-023427-6 PENGUIN PB $5.95

Rear Window and Other Stories
Woolrich was at his best in the short story form, notably the title story: the source for Hitchcock's film
0-14-023426-8 PENGUIN PB $5.95

Waltz into Darkness
Doom-laden romance in old Louisiana: the source of Truffaut's film *Mississippi Mermaid*
0-14-023973-1 PENGUIN PB $6.95

England

British writers were also drawn to the unsettling notion of a killer as a curious sort of hero, but their tone tended to be sly and droll rather than grim or fiercely poetic. Murder as black comedy—which would become a popular element in postwar fiction on both sides of the Atlantic—had its first flowering in the British crime novel of the '30s.

Christianna **Brand**

Cat and Mouse
"The whole gamut of human terror…A first-rate chiller"—Patricia Highsmith
0-930330-18-8 INTL POLYGONICS PB $5.95

Patricia **Craig**, editor

The Oxford Book of English Detective Stories
From the intricate trickery of R. Austin Freeman and Ngaio Marsh to the darker strains of Ruth Rendell and Julian Symons: an invariably entertaining feast of mysteries
0-19-214187-2 OXFORD $30.00
0-19-282968-8 OXFORD PB $13.95

Daphne **Du Maurier**

The Glass Blowers

1-56849-561-7 BUCCANEER $24.95

The House on the Strand

0-89968-424-6 LIGHTYEAR $27.95

Rebecca

The famous Gothic novel of an aristocrat's ingenuous second wife struggling against the malevolent influence of her dead predecessor

See also **THE '30S** under **THE GREAT FICTION BESTSELLERS 1930-1995**

0-385-04380-5 DOUBLEDAY $20.00
0-380-77855-6 AVON PB $6.50

The Scapegoat

0-89190-154-X AMEREON $23.95
1-56849-550-1 BUCCANEER $24.95

Graham **Greene**

A Gun for Sale

A suspense novel about a hit man, also known as *This Gun for Hire*

See also **THE EARLY 20TH CENTURY** under **20TH-CENTURY BRITISH AND IRISH FICTION** in **LITERATURE OF THE BRITISH ISLES**

0-14-018540-2 PENGUIN PB $9.95

Richard **Hull**

The Murder of My Aunt

Repeated attempts at homicide by an effete, despicable antihero

0-930330-02-1 INTL POLYGONICS PB $4.95

Raymond **Postgate**

Verdict of Twelve

A woman stands trial for her nephew's murder, but the jurors, and their hidden motives, take center stage

0-89733-198-2 ACADEMY CHICAGO PB $5.95

Continental Europe

In Europe, the crime novel offered writers a vehicle for dramatizing social tensions, questions of class and politics—and especially after World War II, philosophical nightmares involving guilt, justice, and responsibility.

Leo **Perutz**

The Master of the Day of Judgement

A mysterious book has lethal consequences down the ages

TRANSLATED BY ERIC MOSBACHER

1-55970-334-2 ARCADE PB $10.95

Police Procedural

Policemen have been an important part of crime fiction since *The Moonstone*. But not until the late '40s did American and British mystery writers begin to take serious interest in the authentic evocation of nuts-and-bolts policework. The early "procedurals" owed something to the hardboiled school, something to crime journalism and radio's *Dragnet*, and something to Simenon's purposely drab Maigret novels.

Chester **Himes**

Best known for his Harlem Detective series, which was the basis of films like* Cotton Comes to Harlem, *Himes began writing while serving a prison term for jewel theft in the '40s.

All Shot Up

See also **SINCE 1945** under **20TH-CENTURY AMERICAN FICTION** in **LITERATURE OF THE AMERICAS**

1-56025-103-4 THUNDER'S MOUTH PB $12.95

The Big Gold Dream

1-56025-104-2 THUNDER'S MOUTH PB $12.95

Blind Man with a Pistol

0-394-75998-2 VINTAGE PB $11.00

Cotton Comes to Harlem

0-394-75999-0 VINTAGE PB $10.00

Chester Himes

The Heat's On

0-394-75997-4 VINTAGE PB $10.00

A Rage in Harlem

Originally published as *For Love of Imabelle*; first in the Gravedigger and Coffin Ed series

See also **SINCE 1945** under **20TH-CENTURY AMERICAN FICTION** in **LITERATURE OF THE AMERICAS**

0-679-72040-5 VINTAGE PB $10.00

The Real Cool Killers

0-679-72039-1 VINTAGE PB $10.00

Run Man Run

0-7867-0209-5 CARROLL & GRAF PB $8.95

Ed **McBain**

An imaginary city—very much like New York. A multiethnic team of detectives, juggling caseloads and unsettled personal lives. Welcome to the gritty world of the 87th Precinct, where, according to Julian Symons, "the most consistently skillful writer of police novels" keeps low-key humor, authentic dialogue, and grim suspense in perfect balance.

And All Through the House

The illustrious McBain takes us back to the 87th Precinct for Christmas. All is quiet until detectives bring in a kid who has stolen a sheep, a pawnshop owner with a bagful of gold, and a couple of guys fighting over a dimebag of frankincense…yes, there's a birth. "It's hard to think of anyone better at what he does. In fact, it's impossible"—Robert B. Parker

0-446-51845-X WARNER $12.95

Doll

0-446-60146-2 WARNER PB $5.99

Doors

0-446-60148-9 WARNER PB $5.99

Downtown

0-380-70761-6 AVON PB $5.99

The Eighty-Seventh Precinct Companion

0-89296-989-X MYSTERIOUS PB $25.01

Gladly the Cross-Eyed Bear

0-446-51989-8 WARNER $23.00

Goldilocks

0-446-60305-8 WARNER PB $5.99

Hail, Hail, the Gang's All Here

0-451-15609-9 SIGNET PB $3.99

He Who Hesitates

0-446-60147-0 WARNER PB $5.99

Heat

0-451-17078-4 SIGNET PB $4.99

Ice

0-446-60390-2 WARNER PB $5.99

Jigsaw

0-451-15480-0 SIGNET PB $4.50

Lightning

0-694-51547-7 HARPER AUDIO $17.00

Like Love

0-451-16383-4 SIGNET PB $4.50

Mischief

0-380-71384-5 AVON PB $5.99

Mischief

0-7927-2014-8 CHIVERS NORTH AMERICA PB $23.95

The Mugger

0-446-60143-8 WARNER PB $5.99

Romance

0-446-60280-9 WARNER PB $6.50

Sadie When She Died

0-451-15366-9 SIGNET PB $3.99

The Sentries

0-446-60145-4 WARNER PB $5.99

There Was a Little Girl

With an astounding 100 million books in print, McBain is the master of American mystery writing. Here, the famed Matthew Hope returns for the 11th time in a riveting story of murder, sex, and drugs in which the search for the guilty leads inexorably to the strange world of the local circus. "McBain…is a superior stylist, a spinner of artfully designed and sometimes macabre plots"—*Newsweek*

0-446-51739-9 WARNER $21.95
0-446-60214-0 WARNER PB $6.50
1-57042-197-8 TIME BOOKS $17.00

Vespers
The murder of a Catholic priest, a satanic cult, and racial tensions are the elements of this new episode in McBain's long-running series
0-380-70385-8 AVON PB $5.99

Georges **Simenon**
The Maigret series offers police procedure of a very idiosyncratic, very French sort: the patient stares and oblique interrogations of Inspector Maigret, alive to every nuance in people, places, and weather.

Maigret Afraid
0-15-655142-X HARCOURT BRACE PB $6.00

Maigret and the Apparition
0-15-655127-6 HARCOURT BRACE PB $5.95

Maigret and the Bum
0-15-655130-6 HARVEST PB $3.95

Maigret and the Calame Report
0-15-655153-5 HARVEST PB $6.00

Maigret and the Flemish Shop
0-15-655118-7 HARCOURT BRACE PB $6.00

Maigret and the Fortuneteller
0-15-655163-2 HARCOURT BRACE PB $5.95

Maigret and the Headless Corpse
0-15-655144-6 HARCOURT BRACE PB $6.00

Maigret and the Hotel Majestic
0-15-655133-0 HARCOURT BRACE PB $5.95

Maigret and the Killer
0-15-655124-1 HARCOURT BRACE PB $5.95

Maigret and the Madwoman
0-15-655122-5 HARCOURT BRACE PB $5.95

Maigret and the Man on the Bench
0-15-655123-3 HARCOURT BRACE PB $5.95

Maigret and the Millionaires
0-15-655150-0 HARCOURT BRACE PB $5.95

Maigret and the Nahour Case
0-15-655149-7 HARVEST PB $5.95

Maigret and the Pickpocket
0-156-55145-4 HARCOURT BRACE $6.00

Maigret and the Reluctant Witnesses
0-15-655159-4 HARCOURT BRACE PB $5.95

Maigret and the Saturday Caller
0-15-655175-6 HARCOURT BRACE PB $6.00

Maigret and the Spinster
0-15-655129-2 HARCOURT BRACE PB $6.00

Maigret and the Tavern by the Seine
0-15-655164-0 HARCOURT BRACE PB $6.00

Maigret and the Toy Village
0-15-655154-3 HARVEST PB $5.95

Maigret and the Yellow Dog
0-15-655157-8 HARVEST PB $6.00

Georges Simenon
(photo courtesy of Harcourt Brace)

Maigret at the Gai-Moulin
0-15-655176-4 HARCOURT BRACE PB $6.00

Maigret Bides His Time
0-15-655151-9 HARCOURT BRACE PB $5.95

Maigret Goes to School
9993744980 HARCOURT BRACE PB $25.00

Maigret Hesitates
0-15-655152-7 HARVEST PB $5.95

Maigret in Exile
0-15-655136-5 HARCOURT BRACE PB $5.95

Maigret in Holland
Inspector Maigret arrives in the toylike town of Delfzijl to investigate the murder of a teacher. The amusing cast of suspects is vintage Simeon
TRANSLATED BY GEOFFREY SAINSBURY
0-15-155159-6 HARCOURT BRACE $18.95
0-15-600084-9 HARVEST PB $5.95

Maigret in Vichy
0-15-655140-3 HARVEST PB $6.00

Maigret Loses His Temper
0-15-655128-4 HARVEST PB $5.95

Maigret Sets a Trap
0-15-655126-8 HARCOURT BRACE PB $5.95

Maigret's Boyhood Friend
0-15-655131-4 HARCOURT BRACE PB $6.00

Maigret's Mistake
0-15-655155-1 HARCOURT BRACE PB $3.95

Maigret's Pipe: Seventeen Stories
0-15-655146-2 HARVEST PB $8.95

Crime Fiction Today

"We are all murderers, we are all spies, we are all criminals." So writes Nicolas Freeling, creator of Dutch police inspector Piet Van der Valk, in describing the pervasive skepticism and ambivalence of crime fiction in the '60s and after. The influence of the genre's radicals—Hammett, Cain, Simenon, and their followers—has been dramatic, profound, virtually universal.

Few suspense novels in any category still offer the Great Detective's comforting scenario: clear good triumphing over alien evil, restoring the untainted status quo. Today's detective most likely doubts himself or his client or both. The heroes of police fiction mistrust their partners, their captains, the commissioner. Spies fear their masters as much as their enemies. Nearly everyone is suspicious of the System.

Hard-Boiled Detectives

Linda **Barnes**

Snapshot
"Unhackneyed dialogue, vivid characters, carefully crafted, tension-filled, never predictable plotting and the savviest, most spirited of three-dimensional heroines—*Snapshot* has them all. Another bull's-eye for Barnes"—*Kirkus Reviews*
0-440-21220-0 DELL PB $5.99

Lawrence **Block**

Ariel
0-7867-0385-7 CARROLL & GRAF PB $4.95

Eight Million Ways to Die
An alcoholic ex-cop "hustling for a buck" in New York City's grimiest precinct
0-380-71573-2 AVON PB $5.99

Even the Wicked
0-688-14181-1 MORROW $25.00

Keller on Horseback
1-56740-974-1 BRILLIANCE $4.99

Like a Lamb to Slaughter: Stories
0-380-78806-3 AVON PB $5.99

No Score
0-451-18796-2 SIGNET PB $5.50

Not Comin' Home to You
0-7867-0388-1 CARROLL & GRAF PB $4.95

Out on the Cutting Edge
Scudder investigates the death of a fellow member of Alcoholics Anonymous in Hell's Kitchen
0-380-70993-7 AVON PB $5.99

You Could Call It Murder
0-7867-0342-3 CARROLL & GRAF PB $4.95

Jerome **Charyn**, editor

The Crime Lover's Casebook
42 new and classic stories from the world's foremost mystery writers
0-451-18679-6 SIGNET PB $5.99

James **Crumley**

Dancing Bear
0-394-72576-X RANDOM HOUSE PB $11.00

The Last Good Kiss
The detective novel as alcoholic odyssey into the American heartland, violent and richly humorous by turns
0-394-75989-3 VINTAGE PB $11.00

The Mexican Tree Duck
0-446-40407-1 MYSTERIOUS PB $5.99

James **Crumley**

The Wrong Case

0-394-73558-7 RANDOM HOUSE PB $11.00

Loren D. **Estleman**

Edsel

0-89296-552-5 MYSTERIOUS $21.95

Sugartown

A wry, dour, Chandleresque P.I. in Detroit

0-317-57641-0 ULTRA MARINE $25.00

Joe **Gores**

Dead Skip

Tracing debtors and repossessing cars in San Francisco

0-446-40312-1 MYSTERIOUS PB $4.99

Sue **Grafton**

Grafton's series of "alphabetic" mysteries involving female private eye Kinsey Millhone has attracted tremendous fan interest. "The best of the new breed of female mystery writers" —People

"A" Is for Alibi

A convincing (and funny) female private eye in Southern California

0-553-27991-2 BDD PB $6.99

"B" is for Burglar

0-553-28034-1 BDD PB $6.50

"C" Is for Corpse

0-553-28036-8 BDD PB $6.99

"D" Is for Deadbeat

0-553-27163-6 BDD PB $6.99

"E" Is for Evidence

0-553-27955-6 BDD PB $6.99

"F" Is for Fugitive

0-553-28478-9 BDD PB $6.99

"G" Is for Gumshoe

0-449-21936-4 CREST PB $6.99

"H" Is for Homicide

California sleuth Kinsey Millhone returns, in a case involving street gangs and insurance scams. "Wit is the most versatile weapon in Sue Grafton's well-stocked arsenal, and she uses it with disarming precision"—*Newsweek*

0-449-21946-1 CREST PB $6.99

"I" Is for Innocent

Another clever, irresistible mystery for P.I. Kinsey Millhone, whose "wonderful first-person narration makes these books addictive. Full of idiosyncracies and sharp simile, it's a voice that might draw an appreciative snort from Raymond Chandler"—*Wall Street Journal*

0-449-22151-2 CREST PB $6.99

"J" Is for Judgment

"Grafton has moved the private eye story closer to real life than did either Hammett or Chandler."—*LA Times* "The most satisfying mystery series going"—*Wall Street Journal*

0-449-22148-2 CREST PB $6.99

"K" Is for Killer

0-449-22150-4 FAWCETT PB $6.99

"L" Is for Lawless

0-8050-1937-5 HOLT $24.00

0-449-22149-0 FAWCETT PB $6.99

"M" Is for Malice

0-8050-3637-7 HOLT $25.00

Joseph **Hansen**

Low-key, serious, laconically eloquent: the California cases of gay insurance-investigator Dave Brandstetter.

Death Claims

0-8050-0622-2 HOLT PB $5.95

The Man Everybody Was Afraid Of

0-8050-0723-7 HOLT PB $5.95

Skinflick

0-8050-0197-2 HOLT PB $5.95

Troublemaker

0-8050-0812-8 HOLT PB $5.95

George V. **Higgins**

Swan Boats at Four

A wealthy couple crossing the Atlantic is joined by a charming shipmate. The couple has problems with money and marriage, and the shipmate has a plan…

0-8050-3077-8 HOLT $23.00

Arthur **Lyons**

Nasty, glitzy doings in Southern California—as exposed by ex-reporter Jake Asch, the only genuinely hard-boiled Jewish P.I.

Other People's Money

0-89296-218-6 MYSTERIOUS $17.95

John D. **MacDonald**

In the best pulp tradition, with a running commentary on modern American business mores: the adventures of Florida's Travis McGee, private avenger and salvage expert.

Darker than Amber

0-449-13339-7 GOLD MEDAL PB $4.95

The Deep Blue Goodbye

0-449-13252-8 FAWCETT PB $4.95

Dress Her in Indigo

0-449-13293-5 FAWCETT PB $4.95

The Lonely Silver Rain

0-449-22485-6 FAWCETT PB $5.99

0-449-12509-2 GOLD MEDAL PB $5.95

Nightmare in Pink

0-449-22414-7 FAWCETT PB $5.99

One Fearful Yellow Eye

0-449-13292-7 FAWCETT PB $4.95

Pale Gray for Guilt

0-449-13331-1 FAWCETT PB $4.95

Walter **Mosley**

Black Betty

0-393-03644-8 NORTON $19.95

0-671-88427-1 POCKET PB $6.50

Devil in a Blue Dress

In the late '40s, a black private eye probes the many intersecting worlds of postwar Los Angeles. "Amazing…The social commentary is sly, the dialogue fabulous, the *noir* atmosphere so real you could touch it"—*Cosmopolitan*

0-671-51142-4 POCKET PB $5.99

A Little Yellow Dog

With signature suspense, style, and social observation, Mosley takes us to Watts, 1964, and a timeless tale of murder, investigation, and revenge

0-393-03924-2 NORTON $23.00

A Red Death

Easy Rawlins, the hard-luck hero of *Devil in a Blue Dress,* is back in a mystery set in Los Angeles in the early '50s, an era of Red-baiting and blacklisting in which Rawlins finds himself targeted by a racist IRS agent

0-393-02998-0 NORTON $19.95

0-671-74989-7 POCKET PB $5.99

White Butterfly

0-671-86787-3 POCKET PB $5.99

Sara **Paretsky**

Guardian Angel

"Paretsky's work does more than turn the genre upside-down: her books are beautifully paced and plotted, and the dialogue is fresh and smart"—*Newsweek*

0-385-29931-1 DELACORTE $20.00

Indemnity Only

Specializing in white-collar crime but no stranger to violence: Chicago's V.I. (Vicky) Warshawski

0-440-21069-0 DELL PB $6.99

Walking Shadow

0-385-29932-X DELACORTE $21.95

Robert B. **Parker**

Spenser, Boston's enlightened macho man, engages in confrontational sleuthing, hip repartee, and solemn musings on relationships.

All Our Yesterdays

0-385-30437-4 DELACORTE $22.95

0-440-22146-3 DELL PB $6.99

Chance

0-399-14134-0 PUTNAM $21.95

Double Deuce

Spenser and his sidekick Hawk solve a gang-related murder while Spenser debates whether or not to move in with his longstanding girlfriend, the psychotherapist Susan Silverman. "Pure adrenaline…pure satisfaction" —*Kirkus Reviews*

0-425-13793-7 BERKLEY PB $6.99

God Save the Child

0-440-12899-4 DELL PB $6.50

The Godwulf Manuscript

0-440-12961-3 DELL PB $5.99

Looking for Rachel Wallace

0-440-15316-6 DELL PB $5.99

Thin Air

Spencer has a beautiful woman to find, and her trail is littered not only with obsession and violence, but with questions about boozy law enforcers and the meaning of justice

0-399-14020-4 PUTNAM $21.95

0-425-15290-1 BERKLEY PB $6.99

Andrew **Vachss**

Batman: The Ultimate Evil
0-446-51912-X WARNER $19.95

Blossom
0-679-77261-8 VINTAGE PB $12.00

Blue Belle
0-679-76168-3 VINTAGE PB $11.00

Down in the Zero
0-679-76066-0 VINTAGE PB $12.00

False Allegations: A Burke Novel
0-679-45109-9 KNOPF $23.00

Footsteps of the Hawk
0-679-44500-5 KNOPF $23.00
0-679-76663-4 VINTAGE PB $12.00

Hard Candy
0-679-76169-1 VINTAGE PB $11.00

Hard Looks
1-56971-209-3 DARK HORSE COMICS PB $17.95

Sacrifice
"Vachss waves a powerful light across a city landscape that few writers go near and none portray so convincingly...*Sacrifice* is mesmerizing in its intensity"—*LA Times*
0-679-76410-0 VINTAGE PB $11.00

Strega
"Vachss's writing is as gritty as ever"—*Newsday*
0-679-76409-7 VINTAGE PB $11.00

Neo-Noir

James **Ellroy**

Because the Night
0-380-70063-8 AVON PB $5.99

The Big Nowhere
Starkly realistic, often disturbingly violent evocations of America in the '40s and '50s
0-445-40832-4 POPULAR LIBRARY PB $5.99

James Ellroy

The Black Dahlia
9-993-96827-7 MYSTERIOUS PB $5.99

Blood on the Moon
0-380-69851-X AVON PB $4.99

Brown's Requiem
0-380-78741-5 AVON PB $4.99

Hollywood Nocturnes
1-88340-254-9 PENZLER $20.00
0-440-22098-X DELL PB $5.50

L.A. Confidential
0-446-40010-6 MYSTERIOUS PB $5.99

Suicide Hill
0-445-40852-9 POPULAR LIBRARY PB $5.99

White Jazz
0-449-14841-6 GOLD MEDAL PB $5.99

Ed **Gorman**, editor

Dark Crimes 2: Modern Masters of Noir
"The writing throughout this outstanding anthology is direct, blunt, tough. There is an attitude here and its label is 'no nonsense.' This is a fine book, showcasing some very dark thoughts, deeds and people you might not always like, but they're fascinating all the same"
—*Coast Book Review Service*
0-88184-919-7 CARROLL & GRAF PB $12.95

James **Grady**, editor

Unusual Suspects: A Black Lizard Anthology
Some of the finest crime writers in America have lent their voices to this anthology of the celebrated Black Lizard series, from which the profits have been committed to benefit Share Our Strength in the fight against hunger, poverty, and illiteracy. Contributors include Jan Adins, David Corn, John Lutz, Joyce Carol Oates, Andrew Vachss, and John Weisman
See also **SHORT STORY COLLECTIONS** under **20TH-CENTURY AMERICAN FICTION** in **LITERATURE OF THE AMERICAS**
0-679-76788-6 VINTAGE PB $13.00

Colin **Harrison**

Manhattan Nocturne
See also **SINCE 1945** under **20TH-CENTURY AMERICAN FICTION** in **LITERATURE OF THE AMERICAS**
0-517-58492-1 CROWN $24.00

Vicki **Hendricks**

Miami Purity
Splendid stuff from the classic chronicler of "American trash culture" (Robert Polito, *NY Times Book Review*). Sexual enslavement and homicidal social climbing start with a job at Miami-Purity Dry Cleaners, of all places, in an explosive *noir* tale. "An instant classic: so gruesome and funny and deadpan outlandish that you wind up baying at the moon like a Florida coondog"—James Ellroy
0-679-76800-9 VINTAGE PB $10.00

Stephen **Hunter**

Dirty White Boys
0-440-22179-X BDD PB $6.99

Ellis **Peters**

Mystery meets sinewy costume drama; the detections of a Benedictine monk and herbalist in 12th-century Shrewsbury

Death and the Joyful Woman
0-446-40068-8 MYSTERIOUS PB $5.50

Fallen into the Pit
0-446-40318-0 MYSTERIOUS PB $5.99

Heretic's Apprentice
0-446-40000-9 MYSTERIOUS PB $5.99

The Piper on the Mountain
0-446-40071-8 MYSTERIOUS PB $5.99

Sin **Soracco**

Edge City
"Dark and sultry...An illuminating view of hell as a nightclub that never closes"
—*NY Times Book Review*
0-452-27034-0 PLUME PB $10.00

Julian **Symons**

Playing Happy Families
0-446-40412-8 MYSTERIOUS PB $5.50

Traditional Mysteries, English-Style

The heyday of the gentleman sleuth and the "Great Detective" is long gone. The work of P.D. James, Ruth Rendell, or Peter Dickinson is open to new worlds of psychological depth and social detail; the days of pure escapism are over. But "Golden Age" values—richness of language, intricacies of plot, atmospheric charm, and droll humor—remain very much in evidence.

Robert **Barnard**

The most consistently witty and cheerfully misanthropic British mystery talent of the '80s.

The Bad Samaritan
0-684-81334-3 SCRIBNERS $21.00
0-14-025730-6 PENGUIN PB $5.95

The Case of the Missing Bronte
0-14-023785-2 PENGUIN PB $5.95

The Cherry Blossom Corpse
0-14-023789-5 DELL PB $5.95

Corpse in a Gilded Cage
0-14-023788-7 DELL PB $5.95

Death of a Mystery Writer
0-14-023786-0 PENGUIN PB $5.95

Fête Fatale
0-88150-319-3 FOUL PLAY PB $6.00

The Habit of Widowhood
0-684-82648-8 SCRIBNERS $21.00

A Little Local Murder
0-88150-325-8 FOUL PLAY PB $6.00

The Masters of the House
0-380-72511-8 AVON PB $4.99

Out of the Blackout
0-88150-327-4 FOUL PLAY PB $6.00

Political Suicide
0-88150-326-6 FOUL PLAY PB $6.00

School for Murder
0-88150-320-7 FOUL PLAY PB $6.00

Robert **Barnard**

Too Many Notes, Mr. Mozart
0-7867-0315-6 CARROLL & GRAF $21.00

Colin **Dexter**

Service of All the Dead
The setting is Oxfordshire; the detective is sardonic, boozy Inspector Morse, a rough-edged intellectual

0-8041-1485-4 IVY PB $5.99

The Wench Is Dead
The latest outing for Inspector Morse involves the temporarily bedridden detective in a crime dating back to the 19th century. "Stylish...A taxing brainteaser"
—Marilyn Stasio, *NY Times Book Review*

0-553-29120-3 BDD PB $5.99

Michael **Dibdin**

The Dying of the Light
A darkly humorous variation on the drawing-room mystery. "Horribly, monstrously funny... a merry and maddening *jeu d'esprit*"
—*The Independent on Sunday*

0-679-75310-9 VINTAGE PB $10.00

The Last Sherlock Holmes Story
0-679-76658-8 VINTAGE PB $10.00

Dick **Francis**

The stoic heroes are jockeys, horse owners, trainers. The action is visceral. The storytelling is lean, crafty, briskly sentimental.

Blood Sport
0-449-21262-9 FAWCETT PB $5.95

Come to Grief
0-399-14082-4 PUTNAM $23.95

Decider
0-515-11617-3 JOVE PB $5.99

Driving Force
A young ex-jockey must unravel a conspiracy that threatens his business—and his life. "Few things are more convincing than Dick Francis at full gallop"—*Chicago Tribune*

0-449-22139-3 CREST PB $5.99

Forfeit
0-449-21272-6 FAWCETT PB $5.95

Straight
0-449-21720-5 CREST PB $5.99

Whip Hand
0-449-21274-2 FAWCET PB $5.99

Wild Horses
Yet another visit to the world of British horse racing society; yet another satisfying read from the addictive, readable mystery master. A film director learns a deadly secret from a dying scion of the racing world, and wild horses are nothing compared to the forces that try to make him tell. But telling, too, has its risks..."Any mention of Dick Francis to one of his readers brings unrestrained eruptions of enthusiasm"
—J.P Donleavy

0-515-11723-4 JOVE PB $5.99

Elizabeth **George**

In the Presence of the Enemy
0-553-09265-0 BDD $23.95

Payment in Blood
0-553-28436-3 BDD PB $6.50

Playing for the Ashes
0-553-57251-2 BDD PB $6.50

A Suitable Vengeance
Inspector Lynley of Scotland Yard returns in this traditional mystery set in a quiet Cornwall village

0-553-29560-8 BDD PB $6.50

Michael **Gilbert**

The Crack in the Teacup
0-88184-988-X CARROLL & GRAF PB $3.95

Into Battle: A Novel
0-7867-0398-9 CARROLL & GRAF $21.00

Roller-Coaster
0-7867-0220-6 CARROLL & GRAF PB $4.95

Thomas **Godfrey**, editor

English Country House Murders
0-445-40845-6 MYSTERIOUS PB $6.99

Martha **Grimes**

With mysteries named after British pubs and featuring Inspector Jury of Scotland Yard, "Martha Grimes...is winning the hearts of readers who long to return to the golden age of the dagger beneath the tea cozy and the butler lurking at the drawing-room door."
—San Francisco Chronicle

The Anodyne Necklace
0-440-10280-4 DELL PB $5.99

The Deer Leap
0-440-11938-3 DELL PB $5.99

Dirty Duck
0-440-12050-0 DELL PB $5.99

The End of the Pier
0-345-37657-9 BALLANTINE PB $5.99

The Five Bells and Bladebone
0-440-20133-0 DELL PB $5.99

Help the Poor Struggler
0-440-13584-2 DELL PB $5.99

The Horse You Came in On
0-345-38755-4 BALLANTINE PB $6.99

Hotel Paradise
0-679-44187-5 KNOPF $24.00

I Am the Only Running Footman
0-440-13924-4 DELL PB $5.99

Jerusalem Inn
0-440-14181-8 DELL PB $5.99

The Man with a Load of Mischief
0-440-15327-1 DELL PB $5.99

The Old Fox Deceiv'd
0-440-16747-7 DELL PB $5.99

The Old Silent
0-440-20492-5 DELL PB $5.99

Rainbow's End
0-345-39426-7 BALLANTINE PB $6.99

P.D. **James**

These are dense, implacably serious whodunits from a "writer who is not going to shirk anything"—H.R.F. Keating

The Black Tower
0-446-31502-8 WARNER PB $5.99

Death of an Expert Witness
0-446-31472-2 WARNER PB $5.99

Devices and Desires
0-446-35975-0 WARNER PB $6.50

Original Sin
0-446-60234-5 WARNER PB $6.99

P.D. James

Shroud for a Nightingale
0-446-31303-3 WARNER PB $5.99

The Skull Beneath the Skin
0-446-35372-8 WARNER PB $5.99

A Taste for Death
James's most ambitious book—and one of her best

0-446-32352-7 WARNER PB $5.99

Unnatural Causes
0-446-31219-3 WARNER PB $5.99

An Unsuitable Job for a Woman
Amateur sleuthing at Oxford. "Superb, with clear echoes of both Dorothy Sayers and Charles Dickens"—Robin Winks

0-446-31517-6 WARNER PB $5.99

Nicholas **Meyer**, editor

The Canary Trainer: From the Memoirs of John H. Watson, M.D.
From the author of the sensational *The Seven-Per-Cent Solution* comes a "recently discovered" manuscript detailing the great detective's adventures while he was employed as a violinist in the Paris Opera

0-393-31241-0 NORTON PB $10.00

John **Mortimer**

Rumpole and the Angel of Death

Six new stories feature the "barrister [who's] as much detective as Sherlock Holmes or Hercule Poirot" (*Boston Sunday Globe*), immortalized on PBS as "Rumpole of the Bailey." From animal rights to the European court of human rights, these stories will delight old fans and convert new ones

0-670-86451-X VIKING $22.95

Rumpole for the Defence

0-14-025013-1 VIKING PB $9.95

Rumpole of the Bailey

0-14-025012-3 VIKING PB $9.95

The Trials of Rumpole

0-14-024697-5 VIKING PB $9.95

Rumpole on Trial

0-14-017510-5 PENGUIN PB $10.00

Patricia **Moyes**

Who Is Simon Warwick?

Who, that is, should inherit a dead millionaire's estate? Old-fashioned sleuthing with a few very modern wrinkles

0-8050-0719-9 HOLT PB $5.95

Ellis **Peters**

Mystery meets sinewy costume drama; the detections of a Benedictine monk and herbalist in 12th-century Shrewsbury

Monk's Hood

0-446-40300-8 MYSTERIOUS PB $5.99

The Summer of the Danes

The 12th-century monk, detective Brother Cadfael, pitted against an army of Danish mercenaries intervening in a Welsh political conflict. "Enchanting…Medieval England comes marvelously alive"—*Washington Post*

0-446-40018-1 MYSTERIOUS PB $5.99

Traditional Mysteries, American-Style

George **Baxt**

The Bette Davis Murder Case

0-312-10939-3 ST. MARTIN'S $18.95

The Greta Garbo Murder Case

0-312-06988-X ST. MARTIN'S $17.95

The Humphrey Bogart Murder Case

0-312-11828-7 ST. MARTIN'S $18.95

The Mae West Murder Case

0-312-09864-2 ST. MARTIN'S $17.95

A Queer Kind of Love

Eccentric, satiric, nearly surreal; murder in New York's underground gay/black subculture, c. 1966

0-312-13152-6 ST. MARTIN'S PB $8.95

K.K. **Beck**

Beck's period mysteries set in the roaring '20s abound in sparkle and wit.

Amateur Night

0-446-40145-5 MYSTERIOUS PB $5.50

The Body in the Cornflakes

0-8041-1175-8 IVY PB $4.99

Cold Smoked

0-446-40351-2 MYSTERIOUS PB $5.99

Death in a Deck Chair

0-8027-5601-8 WALKER $12.95

Electric City

0-446-40350-4 MYSTERIOUS PB $5.50

Rick **Boyer**

Billingsgate Shoal

Edgar-winning detection and action at sea, featuring a Massachusetts oral surgeon in midlife crisis

0-8041-0551-0 IVY PB $4.99

Pirate Trade

0-8041-0612-6 IVY PB $4.99

Yellow Bird

0-8041-1036-0 IVY PB $4.99

Lilian Jackson **Braun**

Reporter Jim Qwilleran solves crimes with the aid of his Siamese cats, Koko and Yum Yum.

The Cat Who Ate Danish Modern

0-515-08712-2 JOVE PB $5.99

The Cat Who Could Read Backwards

0-515-09017-4 JOVE PB $5.99

The Cat Who Knew a Cardinal

0-515-10786-7 JOVE PB $5.99

The Cat Who Moved a Mountain

0-515-10950-9 JOVE PB $5.99

The Cat Who Played Brahms

0-515-09050-6 JOVE PB $5.99

The Cat Who Played Post Office

0-515-09320-3 JOVE PB $5.99

The Cat Who Saw Red

0-515-09016-6 JOVE PB $5.99

The Cat Who Turned On and Off

0-515-08794-7 JOVE PB $5.99

Edna **Buchanan**

Act of Betrayal

When an outspoken TV commentator is blown up in his car, Buchanan's intrepid reporter Britt Montero enters a Miami underworld of expatriate Cubans, missing children, and forces as destructive as the hurricane that is bearing down on the Florida coast. "I doubt if anyone is doing it any better—in fiction or nonfiction" —*Washington Post Book World*

0-7868-6098-7 HYPERION $21.95

Amanda **Cross**

These campus mysteries are for those who care about Auden, Freud, sex roles, and cultivated conversation.

Death in a Tenured Position

0-345-34041-8 BALLANTINE PB $5.99

In the Last Analysis

0-380-54510-1 AVON PB $4.99

Poetic Justice

0-380-44222-1 AVON PB $4.99

Sweet Death, Kind Death

9-995-55948-X BALLANTINE PB $5.99

Stephen **Dobyns**

Saratoga Fleshpot

0-393-03805-X NORTON $21.00
0-14-025535-4 PENGUIN PB $5.95

Saratoga Trifecta

A compendium of Dobyns's racetrack mysteries, including *Saratoga Longshot, Saratoga Swimmer,* and *Saratoga Headhunter*

0-14-025196-0 PENGUIN PB $14.95

Kinky **Friedman**

Armadillos & Old Lace

0-553-57447-7 BDD PB $5.50

Elvis, Jesus, & Coca-Cola

"Elvis and Jesus freaks alert: here's the mystery you've been waiting for"—*Kirkus Reviews*

0-553-56891-4 BDD PB $5.50

God Bless John Wayne

From Miami to Manhattan and ending in the posh New York suburb of Chappaqua. "For a guy who isn't me, the Kinkster can really write" —Robert Parker

See also **MOVIE STARS** under **FILM** in **PERFORMING ARTS AND MEDIA**

0-684-81051-4 SIMON & SCHUSTER $22.00
0-553-57633-X BDD PB $5.50

The Love Song of J. Edgar Hoover

0-684-80377-1 SIMON & SCHUSTER $23.00

Susan **Isaacs**

Compromising Positions

Who killed the lecherous Long Island periodontist? A suburban housewife turns sleuth

0-515-09302-5 JOVE PB $6.99

Magic Hour

A movie mogul is slain at poolside in the Hamptons while talking into his portable phone: a witty mystery romp through a Long Island summer of "power softball games, power clambakes, power naps" by the author of *Almost Paradise* and *Compromising Positions*

0-06-109948-1 HARPERCOLLINS PB $6.99

Jonathan **Kellerman**

Bad Love

0-553-56870-1 BDD PB $6.50

Blood Test

0-553-56963-5 BDD PB $6.99

The Clinic

0-553-08922-6 BDD $25.00

Devil's Waltz

0-553-56352-1 BDD PB $6.50

Self-Defense

0-553-57220-2 BDD PB $6.99

The Web

0-553-08921-8 BDD $23.95
0-553-57227-X BDD PB $6.99
0-553-84006-1 BDD PB $6.99

Jonathan **Kellerman**

When the Bough Breaks
Grim findings by a California child psychologist
0-553-56961-9 BDD PB $6.50

Harry **Kemelman**

The sociology of Jewish-American religious life in the suburbs, as mirrored in the subdued detection of Rabbi David Small.

Conversations with Rabbi Small
0-449-24527-6 FAWCETT PB $5.99

The Day the Rabbi Resigned
0-449-21908-9 CREST PB $5.99

Friday the Rabbi Slept Late
0-449-21180-0 FAWCETT PB $4.99

Monday the Rabbi Took Off
0-449-21001-4 FAWCETT PB $4.95

One Fine Day the Rabbi Bought a Cross
0-449-20687-4 CREST PB $5.99

Saturday the Rabbi Went Hungry
0-449-21392-7 FAWCETT PB $4.95

Someday the Rabbi Will Leave
0-449-20945-8 FAWCETT PB $5.99

Sunday the Rabbi Stayed Home
0-449-21000-6 FAWCETT PB $4.95

That Day the Rabbi Left Town
0-449-91002-4 FAWCETT $22.00

Thursday the Rabbi Walked Out
0-449-21157-6 FAWCETT PB $4.99

Tuesday the Rabbi Saw Red
0-449-21321-8 FAWCETT PB $4.95

Wednesday the Rabbi Got Wet
0-449-21328-5 FAWCETT PB $5.99

Jane **Langton**

Divine Inspiration
0-14-017376-5 PENGUIN PB $5.95

Emily Dickinson Is Dead
Murder at Amherst, with literary motives and Yankee charm
0-14-007771-5 VIKING PB $5.95

God in Concord
0-14-016594-0 PENGUIN PB $5.95

The Shortest Day: Murder at the Revels
0-14-017377-3 PENGUIN PB $5.95

Gregory **McDonald**

Fletch Reflected
0-515-11676-9 JOVE PB $5.99

Barbara **Michaels**

The reigning queen of romantic suspense and in 1986 named Grandmaster in the first Anthony awards, Michaels also writes bestselling mysteries as Elizabeth Peters.

House of Many Shadows
0-425-15189-1 BERKLEY PB $6.50

Houses of Stone
0-425-14306-6 BERKLEY PB $6.99

Search the Shadows
0-425-11183-0 BERKLEY PB $6.50

Shattered Silk
"Superior Michaels! Like the antique gowns its heroine collects, *Shattered Silk* glitters"
—Kirkus Reviews
0-06-101008-1 HARPERCOLLINS PB $5.99

Smoke and Mirrors
0-425-11911-4 BERKLEY PB $6.99

Vanish with the Rose
0-425-13898-4 BERKLEY PB $6.99

Witch
0-425-11831-2 BERKLEY PB $6.99

Elizabeth **Peters**

Peters's spunky, outspoken heroines—Victorian Egyptologist Amelia Peabody and the contemporary art historian Vicki Bliss and librarian Jacqueline Kirby—are especially popular with women readers.

The Deeds of the Disturber
0-446-35333-7 MYSTERIOUS PB $5.99

Devil-May-Care
0-8125-0789-4 TOR PB $4.50

Lion in the Valley
"To our knowledge, Jane Austen never attempted a mystery novel. If she had, it might have been something not unlike the fiction Elizabeth Peters serves up"
—Cleveland Plain Dealer
0-8125-1242-1 TOR PB $4.99

The Seventh Sinner
0-445-40778-6 MYSTERIOUS PB $5.50

Trojan Gold
0-8125-2357-1 TOR PB $5.99

Sandra **Scoppettone**

A Creative Kind of Killer
0-7867-0229-X CARROLL & GRAF PB $4.50

Donato & Daughter
0-7867-0284-2 CARROLL & GRAF PB $6.95

I'll Be Leaving You Always
0-345-38269-2 LITTLE, BROWN PB $4.99

Let's Face the Music and Die
0-316-77664-5 LITTLE, BROWN $21.95

My Sweet Untraceable You
A new addition to the ground-breaking Lauren Laurano mystery series about a lesbian detective, in which Laurano uses all her New York City savvy to crack a 30-year-old small-town murder case.
0-345-39162-4 DEL RAY PB $5.99

Razzamatazz
0-7867-0230-3 CARROLL & GRAF PB $5.95

Some Unknown Person
0-7867-0285-0 CARROLL & GRAF PB $5.95

Crimes and Capers

Nowadays lawbreakers of all kinds can be heroes; many of them, unlike Rico in *Little Caesar*, are even allowed to get away with murder. And while some treatments of outlaw activity reach for pathos or tragedy, more often it is irreverent comedy—light (Donald Westlake), dark (Richard Condon), and darker (Elmore Leonard)—that energizes these sharp-edged excursions into a world of matter-of-fact crime.

Lawrence **Block**

The Burglar Who Liked to Quote Kipling
Burglar as likable, light-hearted hero in peril
0-525-94159-2 DUTTON $22.95

The Burglar Who Thought He Was Bogart
0-451-18634-6 ONYX PB $6.99

James Lee **Burke**

Burning Angel
0-7838-1492-5 GK HALL $24.95
0-7868-6082-0 HYPERION $22.95
0-7868-8904-7 HYPERION PB $6.99

Jim **Cirni**

The Big Squeeze
1-56947-058-8 SOHO PB $12.00

Jonathan **Gash**

The Grace in Older Women
0-14-024662-2 PENGUIN PB $5.95

The Grail Tree
0-14-023015-7 SELECT PENGUIN PB $5.95

Jade Woman
0-14-012280-X PENGUIN PB $5.95

The Judas Pair
0-14-012688-0 SELECT PENGUIN PB $5.95

Paid and Loving Eyes
0-14-023557-4 PENGUIN PB $5.95

The Possessions of a Lady
0-670-86933-3 VIKING $21.95

The Sin Within Her Smile
0-14-023839-5 PENGUIN PB $5.95

The Tartan Sell
0-14-014596-6 SELECT PENGUIN PB $5.95

The Vatican Rip
A raffish antique dealer out to steal a Chippendale table in Rome
0-14-006431-1 VIKING PB $5.95

The Very Last Gambado
0-14-014738-1 PENGUIN PB $5.95

Carl **Hiaasen**

Stormy Weather
In the wake of a ferocious hurricane, southern Florida fills with a collection of con artists that only Hiassen, with his years of experience at *The Miami Herald*, could conceive. As the cons' various scams become intertwined, their veneers

are stripped away to reveal among the flotsam of crooks and corruption some surprisingly honest criminals and some shockingly criminal citizens
0-679-41982-9 KNOPF $24.00

Strip Tease

The veteran *Miami Herald* reporter sends up his home state in a comic tale of sleaze and suspense: this time about a drunken congressman who frequents a Fort Lauderdale strip joint. When blackmailers try to profit from his lowlife tastes, the powerful sugar industry—which owns the corrupt congressman in the first place—comes murderously to his defense
0-679-41981-0 KNOPF $21.00
0-446-60066-0 WARNER PB $6.50

George V. **Higgins**

Sandra Nichols Found Dead

Trademark suspense, plot, and dialogue make this new Jerry Kennedy courtroom novel vintage Higgins. "Higgins has created a genre of his own, in which people are so real that it doesn't matter what they're doing or how they go about doing it; just being in their company is pleasure enough"—*NY Times Book Review*
0-8050-3747-0 HOLT $23.00

Elmore **Leonard**

Leonard's heroes encompass a wide social spectrum: they have included cops, robbers, ex-cons, photographers, and even a stigmatic candidate for sainthood (Touch). Leonard has a remarkable ear for street talk and a gift for ferocious pacing. Asked to explain his books' appeal, he is said to have replied: "I leave out the parts that people skip."

52 Pick-Up

An adulterous husband gets more than he bargained for when his mistress is murdered by blackmailing thugs
0-380-65490-3 AVON PB $4.99

Cat Chaser

9-995-19203-9 AVON PB $4.99

City Primeval: High Noon in Detroit

0-380-56952-3 AVON PB $4.99

Freaky Deaky

0-446-35039-7 WARNER PB $5.95

Get Shorty

Elmore Leonard goes Hollywood. Drawing on his many years of experience in the movie business, the master of the picaresque crime story spins one of his most raucous and entertaining yarns to date. The basis for the popular motion picture starring John Travolta
0-385-31567-8 BANTAM PB $8.95

Glitz

0-446-34343-9 WARNER PB $6.99

Killshot

0-446-35041-9 WARNER PB $5.95

Maximum Bob

A bigoted judge comes under lethal attack in Palm Beach County, Florida, and a young female probation officer finds herself in a threatening situation. *Newsweek* has called Elmore Leonard "the best American writer of crime fiction alive"
0-440-21218-9 DELL PB $6.50

Elmore Leonard (photo by Joan Leonard)

Mr. Majestyk

A melon farmer fights it out with labor racketeers
0-445-40228-8 POPULAR LIBRARY PB $5.99

Out of Sight

0-385-30848-5 DELACORTE $22.95

Pronto

Just as he's about to retire, Miami bookie Harry Arno's past catches up with him: soon he's caught between the wiseguys and the Feds. "Elmore Leonard grabs you and doesn't let go"—*LA Times Book Review*
0-440-21443-2 DELL PB $6.50

Riding the Rap

"America's funniest lowlife novelist" —*The Boston Globe*
0-385-30847-7 DELACORTE $22.95
0-440-21441-6 DELL PB $6.50

Rum Punch

Leonard's remarkable timing, sense of plotting, characterization, and dialogue are at their peak here. "Leonard's control of [his] complex scenario and its brilliantly realized actors is breathtaking"—*Kirkus Reviews*
0-440-21415-7 DELL PB $6.50

Stick

The hapless hero of *Swag* is released from prison only to find himself knee-deep in Miami corruption: one of Leonard's best
0-380-67652-4 AVON PB $5.99

Swag

Armed robbery for fun and profit
0-440-18424-X DELL PB $5.99

The Switch

Lovable thugs kidnap a rich man's wife
0-440-20831-9 DELL PB $6.50

Iain **Pears**

The Raphael Affair

Forgery, fraud, and murder create a dangerous pattern in this tightly plotted thriller featuring General Bottando of the Italian National Art Theft Squad. Art historian Iain Pears sets his highly original novel against the glamorous background of the international art world
0-15-178912-6 HARCOURT BRACE $18.95

T.R. **Pearson**

Cry Me a River

Firmly anchored as a murder mystery with a fallen cop and a wayward woman as its focus, Pearson's sixth novel is first and foremost the portrait of a contemporary small Southern town. A highly original writer with an engaging colloquial voice all his own, "Pearson writes sentences like a man peeling an apple in a single stroke"—*LA Times*

See also **SINCE 1945** under **20TH-CENTURY AMERICAN FICTION** in **LITERATURE OF THE AMERICAS**

0-8050-3187-1 OWLET PB $12.00

Thomas **Perry**

The Butcher's Boy

Hit man on a killing spree, chased by a female Treasury agent
1-56849-615-X BUCCANEER $24.95

The Police Procedural: USA

In the '60s and '70s, the American cop novel got rougher, deeper, and much more popular. While some writers continued to see policemen as reassuring authority figures, others—like Joseph Wambaugh and Charles Willeford—gave us burnouts, flakes, alcoholics, and sadists, as well as cops with more manageable problems.

Michael **Connelly**

The Black Echo

An astonishing debut, Connelly's first novel follows Detective Hieronymus "Harry" Bosch—loner, nighthawk, 'Nam vet—as he tracks the murderer of a former comrade-in-arms
0-312-95048-9 ST. MARTIN'S PB $5.99

The Black Ice

0-312-95281-3 ST. MARTIN'S PB $6.99

The Concrete Blonde

0-312-95500-6 ST. MARTIN'S PB $5.99

The Last Coyote

0-312-95845-5 ST. MARTIN'S PB $6.99

The Poet

0-446-60261-2 WARNER PB $4.99

Trunk Music

0-316-15244-7 LITTLE, BROWN $23.95

K.C. **Constantine**

Always a Body to Trade

0-87923-952-2 GODINE PB $5.95

The Man Who Liked Slow Tomatoes

0-87923-953-0 GODINE PB $5.95

Patricia D. **Cornwell**

All that Remains
9995644010 AVON PB $6.50

All that Remains
0-380-71833-2 AVON PB $6.99

Body of Evidence
0-380-71701-8 AVON PB $6.99

Cause of Death
0-399-14146-4 PUTNAM $25.95
0-7838-1793-2 GK HALL PB $20.00

Cruel and Unusual
"No one does authenticity better than Cornwell"'—*Philadelphia Inquirer*
0-684-19530-5 SCRIBNERS $21.00
0-380-71834-0 AVON PB $6.99

From Potter's Field
0-425-15409-2 BERKLEY PB $6.99

Postmortem
0-380-71021-8 AVON PB $6.99

Thomas **Harris**

Red Dragon
The most chilling treatment yet of a police manhunt for a psychopathic serial killer
0-440-20615-4 DELL PB $6.50

The Silence of the Lambs
The search for yet another serial killer, told with flair. The basis for the Academy Award-winning film starring Anthony Hopkins and Jodie Foster
0-312-92458-5 ST. MARTIN'S PB $6.99

Tony **Hillerman**

Haunting, lyrical investigation by Navajo reservation policemen—with plots that turn on questions of cultural identity and tribal beliefs.

Coyote Waits
"The rewards in Mr. Hillerman's detective-Western hybrid include ample amounts of regional description (Albuquerque, northern New Mexico, and the Navajo reservation), of Indian myth and of villainy. And in this book, the author continues to prove himself one of the nation's most convincing and authentic interpreters of Navajo culture, as well as one of our best and most innovative modern mystery writers"
—Robert F. Gish, *NY Times Book Review*
0-06-109932-5 HARPERCOLLINS PB $6.99

Finding Moon
0-06-109261-4 HARPERCOLLINS PB $6.99
0-7862-0575-X THORNDIKE PB $20.00

People of Darkness
0-06-109915-5 HARPERCOLLINS PB $5.99

Sacred Clowns
Edgar Award-winning Hillerman reprises his popular characters Jim Chee and Joe Leaphorn in a mystery that encompasses the grisly deaths of a Pueblo tribal official and a schoolteacher, and a stolen piece of Native American history. "One of the finest and most original craftsmen at work in the genre today"—*Boston Globe*
0-06-109260-6 HARPERCOLLINS PB $6.99

Skinwalkers
0-06-100017-5 HARPERCOLLINS PB $5.99

Talking God
0-06-109918-X HARPERCOLLINS PB $5.99

Lia **Matera**

Last Chants: A Willa Jansson Mystery
Edgar nominee Matera (*Prior Convictions*) reprises her disenchanted lawyer-sleuth Lia Jannson in a thrilling murder mystery that includes mountain cabins, Kwakiutl shamans, and computer designers. "Surely the wittiest of women sleuths"—*NY Times Book Review*
0-684-81085-9 SIMON & SCHUSTER $21.00

Ridley **Pearson**

No Evidence
Named by *Entertainment Weekly* "the thinking person's Robert Ludlum," Pearson offers a forensic thriller in which an identical rare chemical has shown up in a number of Connecticut murders, and Joe Dartelli, a genius in the field of forensic medicine, goes after the killer. Sensational suspense
0-7868-6172-X HYPERION $22.95

Lawrence **Sanders**

The First Deadly Sin
The Big Daddy of the cops vs. psycho genre
1-56849-330-4 BUCCANEER $29.95
0-425-10427-3 BERKLEY PB $6.99

The Loves of Harry Dancer
0-425-12785-0 BERKLEY PB $5.99

McNally's Luck
9-995-60801-4 BERKLEY PB $6.50

McNally's Trial
0-425-14755-X BERKLEY PB $6.99

The Pleasures of Helen
0-425-10168-1 BERKLEY PB $6.99

The Seduction of Peter S
0-425-12462-2 BERKLEY PB $6.99

The Seventh Commandment
9-995-46922-7 BERKLEY PB $6.99

Joseph **Wambaugh**

The Black Marble
A crime novel involving dogs and dog owners
0-440-10644-3 DELL PB $6.50

The Blue Knight
0-440-10607-9 DELL PB $6.50

The Choirboys
See also **THE '70S** under **THE GREAT FICTION BESTSELLERS 1930-1995**
0-440-11188-9 DELL PB $6.50

The Delta Star
The think-tank world of Nobel Prize chemistry intersects with the sleazy underworld of a murdered streetwalker
0-553-27386-8 BDD PB $6.50

Finnegan's Week
"A master storyteller"—*Entertainment Weekly*
0-553-56440-4 BDD PB $6.50

Floaters
0-553-10351-2 BDD $22.95

The Glitter Dome
Four sets of police partners amid the glamour and grime of Hollywood
See also **THE '80S** under **THE GREAT FICTION BESTSELLERS 1930-1995**
0-553-27259-4 BDD PB $6.50

Lines and Shadows
"Ten San Diego police officers assigned to patrol the cactus-filled, snake-infested canyons along the Mexican border"—*Kirkus Reviews*
0-553-27148-2 BDD PB $5.99

The New Centurions
Three new cops on the Los Angeles beat
0-440-16417-6 DELL PB $6.99

The Secrets of Harry Bright
A detective investigates the murder of a Palm Springs teenager and the meaning of his own son's death
0-553-27430-9 BDD PB $6.50

Donald E. **Westlake**

Baby, Would I Lie?
0-446-40342-3 MYSTERIOUS PB $5.99

Smoke
See also **SINCE 1945** under **20TH-CENTURY AMERICAN FICTION** in **LITERATURE OF THE AMERICAS**
0-89296-534-7 MYSTERIOUS $21.95
0-446-40344-X WARNER PB $6.50

What's the Worst that Could Happen
0-89296-586-X MYSTERIOUS $22.00

Stuart **Woods**

Chiefs
Three generations of police chiefs in a small Georgia town, all after the same sex-driven killer
0-380-70347-5 AVON PB $6.50

Dirt
0-06-017666-0 HARPERCOLLINS $24.00

The Police Procedural: International

Pieke **Bierman**

Violetta
Rough doings in Germany. "Pieke Biermann has an apocalyptic imagination"—Sara Peretsky
1-85242-289-0 SERPENT'S TAIL PB $13.99

Nicolas **Freeling**

Inspector Van der Valk—the Maigret of Amsterdam—offers social commentary as well as detection. "[Freeling] has moved almost continuously toward the creation of character studies which are also crime stories."
—Julian Symons

The King of the Rainy Country
9-997-51263-4 HARPERCOLLINS $10.00

The Seacoast of Bohemia
From the winner of an Edgar award, a Gold Dagger, and the celebrated French *Grand Prix de Roman*, a savage kidnapping in Germany sets

off a brutal trail of suspense that has roots in the Third Reich
0-89296-555-X MYSTERIOUS $18.95
0-446-40371-7 WARNER PB $5.99

You Who Know
0-446-40370-9 MYSTERIOUS PB $5.50

Bartholomew **Gill**

McGarr and the Method of Descartes
Dublin-based police work, with the IRA and other political pressures always shadowing the proceedings
0-670-46432-5 VIKING $14.95

Reginald **Hill**

With each novel about the Yorkshire policemen Dalziel and Pascoe, Hill reaffirms his standing as one of today's great crime novelists. Blending artful, Christie-like plotting with powerful, often perverse character studies, he raises the police procedural to new levels of density and social detail.

Asking for the Moon
0-88150-382-7 COUNTRYMAN $21.00

Blood Sympathy
0-373-26210-8 HARLQ PB $4.99

Bones and Silence
"Hill's strongest novel to date"
— *Publishers Weekly*
0-440-20935-8 DELL PB $4.99

Exit Lines
0-451-16166-1 SIGNET PB $4.99

Pictures of Perfection
0-385-31270-9 DELACORTE $19.95
0-440-21800-4 DELL PB $4.99

Recalled to Life
0-440-21573-0 DELL PB $4.99

Ruling Passion
0-440-16889-9 DELL PB $5.50

The Wood Beyond
0-385-31271-7 BDD $21.95

Seicho **Matsumoto**

Inspector Imanishi Investigates
Seicho Matsumoto, author of the classic *Points and Lines*, is Japan's best-known writer of crime fiction. His police procedurals offer a gritty and unsensational picture of the underside of modern Japanese life. This 1961 novel, one of his most popular, begins with the discovery of a corpse at Tokyo's Kamata Station and ends up taking Imanishi into some of the remotest corners of Japan
TRANSLATED BY BETH CARY
0-939149-28-1 SOHO $18.95

Maj **Sjowall** & Per **Wahloo**

Provocative police work in Stockholm—from the husband/wife team whose declared intent is to "…use the crime novel as a scalpel cutting open the belly of an ideologically pauperized and morally debatable so-called welfare state of the bourgeois type."

The Laughing Policeman
0-679-74223-9 VINTAGE PB $10.00

The Locked Room
"The Wahloos' best—their densest in person and place, their most penetrating in sociology and psychology, their most complex in plot and resolution"—Judith Crist
0-679-74222-0 VINTAGE PB $11.00

The Man on the Balcony: The Story of a Crime
0-679-74596-3 VINTAGE PB $9.00

The Man Who Went Up in Smoke
0-679-74597-1 VINTAGE PB $9.00

Roseanna
0-679-74598-X VINTAGE PB $9.00

Martin Cruz **Smith**

Gorky Park
The best of several attempts to write a Moscow police procedural
0-345-29834-9 BALLANTINE PB $5.99

Paco Ignacio **Taibo II**

Life Itself
TRANSLATED BY BETH HENSON
0-89296-518-5 MYSTERIOUS $18.95
0-446-40331-8 WARNER PB $5.99

Trevanian

The Eiger Sanction
Wicked satire, nasty violence, and fine climbing action
0-343-31737-8 BALLANTINE PB $5.99

The Main
A broken-down cop in a tough section of Montreal
0-515-09272-X JOVE PB $5.99

Shibumi
0-345-31180-9 BALLANTINE PB $6.99

Janwillem **van de Wetering**

A wise old police chief, a gruff middle-aged detective, a young sergeant into Zen and music: quirky legwork in Amsterdam.

The Corpse in the Dike
1-56947-049-9 SOHO PB $11.00

Death of a Hawker
1-56947-079-0 SOHO PB $11.00

The Hollow-Eyed Angel
1-56947-056-1 SOHO $22.00

The Japanese Corpse
1-56947-057-X SOHO PB $12.00

Just a Corpse at Twilight
"The many fans of the series should find enjoyment in *Just a Corpse at Twilight*, as should those readers who prefer their fictional crimes unorthodox, cerebral and slightly outrageous"
—Bill Pronzini, *NY Times Book Review*
1-56947-016-2 SOHO $20.00
1-56947-075-8 SOHO PB $11.00

The Maine Massacre
1-56947-064-2 SOHO $42.00

Outsider in Amsterdam
1-56947-017-0 SOHO PB $11.00

Tumbleweed
1-56947-018-9 SOHO PB $10.00

Robert **Van Gulik**

Shrewd tales involving Chinese administration and criminal law, as dispensed by Judge Dee, a magistrate of the 7th-century T'ang dynasty

The Chinese Bell Murders
0-226-84862-0 CHICAGO PB $8.95

The Chinese Nail Murders
0-226-84863-9 CHICAGO PB $7.95

The Emperor's Pearl
0-226-84872-8 CHICAGO PB $6.95

The Haunted Monastery & the Chinese Maze Murders
0-486-23502-5 DOVER PB $8.95

Judge Dee at Work: Eight Chinese Detective Stories
0-226-84866-3 CHICAGO PB $6.95

The Lacquer Screen
0-226-84867-1 CHICAGO PB $6.95

The Monkey and the Tiger
0-226-84869-8 CHICAGO PB $6.95

Murder in Canton
0-226-84874-4 CHICAGO PB $6.95

Necklace and Calabash
0-226-84870-1 CHICAGO PB $6.95

The Phantom of the Temple
0-226-84877-9 CHICAGO PB $8.95

Poets and Murder
0-226-84876-0 CHICAGO PB $7.95

The Red Pavilion
0-226-84873-6 CHICAGO PB $6.95

The Willow Pattern
0-226-84875-2 CHICAGO PB $5.95

Psychological Suspense

"The violence that lives behind the bland faces most of us present to the world"—that, in Julian Symons's words, continues to be the primary theme of psychological crime fiction. The personalities of both villains and victims are subjected to intense, often ironic scrutiny, and society's presumptions about guilt and innocence, right and wrong, are frequently challenged.

Mary Higgins **Clark**

Clark's fast-paced suspense dramas have made her one of the highest-paid mystery writers in the world.

All Around the Town
From the bestselling "Queen of Suspense." A college professor is found murdered, a young student is suspected, and the tale that follows is Clark at her most riveting
1-56849-264-2 BUCCANEER $32.95
0-671-79348-9 POCKET PB $6.99

Mary Higgins **Clark**

The Cradle Will Fall
0-671-74119-5 POCKET PB $7.50

I'll Be Seeing You
Murder, in-vitro pregnancy, dopplegangers, and deliciously deceptive and dastardly deeds move this latest suspense novel by the best selling phenomenon
0-671-88858-7 POCKET PB $7.50

Silent Night
Christmas Eve suspense, with a terrifying premise: while watching a street musician near Rockefeller Center's Christmas tree, a boy sees a strange woman steal his mother's wallet, which contains not just money but irreplaceable family mementos. Without telling his mother, he follows the thief onto the subway and into a journey that will change his life, as well as his mother's and the thief's, forever
0-684-81545-1 SIMON & SCHUSTER $16.00

A Stranger Is Watching
1-56849-071-2 BUCCANEER $25.95

Where Are the Children?
Inspired by the notorious Alice Crimmins child-murder case
0-671-74118-7 POCKET PB $6.99

Peter **Dickinson**

King and Joker
A brilliantly elaborate, ultimately disturbing puzzle involving an alternate British Royal Family
0-446-40309-1 MYSTERIOUS PB $4.99

Play Dead
0-446-40112-9 WARNER PB $4.99

The Yellow Room Conspiracy
0-446-40373-3 MYSTERIOUS PB $5.99

Robert **Ferrigno**

Dead Silent
0-399-14148-0 PUTNAM $24.95

Celia **Fremlin**

The Hours Before Dawn
The domestic terrors of a new mother. "[Fremlin's] great gift is to see horror in the ordinary"—William Weaver
0-89733-101-X ACADEMY CHICAGO PB $5.95

George Dawes **Green**

The Juror
A remorselessly terrifying drama in which a single mother, serving as a juror on a Mafia trial, is stalked, seduced, and threatened—a good plot that in Green's sure hands becomes a major novel
0-446-60269-8 WARNER PB $6.99

Lynn S. **Hightower**

Eyeshot
0-06-017649-0 HARPERCOLLINS $23.00

Flashpoint
0-06-109456-0 HARPERCOLLINS PB $5.99

Andrew **Klavan**

The Animal Hour
A thickly woven, high-pressure follow-up to Klavan's last, *Don't Say a Word*, described by *Kirkus Reviews* as "worthy of Hitchcock at his best." Here, unrelated lives tangle on a Halloween day in New York in a harrowing rollercoaster ride of horror and suspense. "Maneuvering the plot of his latest urban thriller with the irresistible skill of a three-card monte expert, Klavan leaves his mesmerized readers the winners"—*Publishers Weekly*
0-671-74011-3 POCKET PB $5.50

Corruption
When a local journalist uncovers the secret past of the town's sheriff, passions and ambitions that lie below the community's placid surface are uncovered and local innocence is shattered forever. "If you like nerve-jangling suspense, Klavan is as good as they get"—Tony Hillerman
0-312-95681-9 ST. MARTIN'S PB $6.50

Don't Say a Word
"Relentless pacing and tersely graphic prose propel [the] story from kidnap to violent climax"—Albert Mobilio, *VLS*
0-671-74009-1 POCKET PB $5.99

True Crime
Superb characterization, exquisite suspense, and warm humor from the two-time Edgar-winner
0-517-70213-4 CROWN $21.00

Jack **O'Connell**

The Skin Palace
A suspense novel set in the underworld of the pornography trade
0-89296-547-9 MYSTERIOUS $21.95
0-446-40357-1 WARNER PB $5.99

Wireless
"A wildly colored narrative collage" —*Publishers Weekly*
0-446-40356-3 MYSTERIOUS PB $5.99

T. Jefferson **Parker**

The Triggerman's Dance
0-7868-6142-8 HYPERION $21.95

Derek **Raymond**

State of Denmark
1-85242-315-3 SERPENT'S TAIL PB $12.99

Ruth **Rendell**

"Ruth Rendell is the best mystery writer in the English-speaking world"—Time. *"Rendell tells her story with such elegance and restraint, with such a literate voice and an insightful mind, that her book transcends the mystery genre and achieves something almost sublime."*—LA Times

The Best Man to Die
0-345-34530-4 BALLANTINE PB $5.99

Blood Lines: Long and Short Stories
Nine new stories from the master. "Ruth Rendell is, unequivocally, the most brilliant mystery novelist of our time. Her stories are a lesson in a human nature as capable of the most exotic love as it is of the cruelest murder. She does not avert her gaze. Once again, she magnificently triumphs in a style that is uniquely hers and mesmerizing"—Patricia Cornwell
0-517-70323-8 CROWN $23.00

The Crocodile Bird
Obsessive love between mother and daughter triggers a series of mysterious deaths in a remote English manor
0-517-59576-1 CROWN $20.00

Death Notes
0-345-34198-8 BALLANTINE PB $5.99

From Doon with Death
0-345-34817-6 BALLANTINE PB $4.95

A Guilty Thing Surprised
0-345-34811-7 BALLANTINE PB $5.99

The Keys to the Street
0-517-70685-7 CROWN $24.00

Ruth Rendell (photo by Sally Soames)

Kissing the Gunner's Daughter
Chief Inspector Reginal Wexford returns to solve the murder of anthropologist and author Davina Flory and her family in "a superbly characterized, deftly plotted puzzler that explores the dark side of family life. This is among the very best from the accomplished, prolific author of *The Veiled One* and *The Bridesmaid*"—*Kirkus Reviews*
0-446-40334-2 MYSTERIOUS PB $5.50

Master of the Moor
The horrifying secret behind a series of killings
0-345-34147-3 BALLANTINE PB $5.95

Simisola
In the 16th Inspector Wexford novel, Rendell once again plumbs the emotional depths of the mystery genre with an exploration of racism, sexual violence, and urban ills. Here, as always, Rendell reads with aching suspense
0-517-70073-5 CROWN $23.00
0-440-22202-8 DELL PB $5.99
0-7838-1588-3 GK HALL PB $22.00

It was always their wives, Wexford thought. They projected their emotions on to their wives. My wife is rather anxious about it. It's bothering my wife. I'm taking this step because, frankly, the whole thing is affecting my wife's health. As strong men themselves, *macho* men, they would like you to believe they were prey to no fears, no anxieties, and to no desires either, no longings, no passions, no needs.

SIMISOLA

Sins of the Fathers
0-345-34253-4 BALLANTINE PB $5.99

The Veiled One
0-345-35994-1 BALLANTINE PB $5.99

Barbara **Vine**

The Brimstone Wedding
"The kind of book that makes you wish Hitchcock were still around to film it"
—*Washington Post Book World*
0-517-70339-4 HARMONY $24.00

A Dark-Adapted Eye
"It's no secret that Barbara Vine is the distinguished crime writer Ruth Rendell and in *A Dark-Adapted Eye* we have Ms. Rendell at the height of her powers…combines excitement and psychological subtlety"—P.D. James
0-452-27064-2 PLUME PB $6.95

Scott **Smith**

A Simple Plan
When three friends find a million dollars and decide to keep it, they're led into a world of murder and horror. "An eerily flat confessional whose horror is only deepened by its flashes of tenderness. Think of a backwater James M. Cain, or a contemporary midwestern *Unforgiven*—and don't think about getting any sleep tonight"—*Kirkus Reviews*
0-312-95271-6 ST. MARTIN'S PB $5.99

Rafael **Yglesias**

Dr. Neruda's Cure for Evil
0-446-52005-5 WARNER $24.95

Legal Thrillers

John **Grisham**

Grisham is the most prominent legal thriller writer in America as reflected in his legions of fans and the number of his books that top the sales charts. The numerous motion pictures spawned by his novels have become a genre in their own right and many of his recent books read as if he is scripting the next film adaptation in advance.

The Chamber
0-440-22060-2 BDD PB $7.50

The Client
A young boy who witnesses a mob hit is protected by a lawyer
0-385-42471-X DOUBLEDAY $23.50
0-440-21352-5 DELL PB $6.99

The Firm
Grisham's first, and most effective, book tells the story of Mitch McDeere, a young Harvard law grad who is recruited by a small, Southern firm and given the deal of a lifetime—a deal he soon finds out is too good to be true
0-440-21145-X DELL PB $7.50

The Pelican Brief
0-440-21404-1 DELL PB $6.99

The Rainmaker
A courtroom drama of legal intrigue and corporate greed
0-385-42473-6 DOUBLEDAY $25.95
0-440-22165-X BDD PB $7.99

The Runaway Jury
0-385-47294-3 DOUBLEDAY $26.95

A Time to Kill
0-440-21172-7 DELL PB $6.99

Richard North **Patterson**

The Final Judgment
The Edgar Award-winning trial lawyer offers a new novel of murder and courtroom suspense. When a recent presidential nominee to the Court of Appeals is summoned home to defend a niece against a murder charge, she finds herself engulfed by her past and confronting the fears that have motivated her adult life. A perceptive and involving story
0-679-42989-1 KNOPF $25.00
0-7838-1581-6 GK HALL PB $25.00

Scott **Turow**

The Burden of Proof
A criminal lawyer (the protagonist of Turow's previous bestseller *Presumed Innocent*) embarks on a troubled voyage of self-discovery when his wife commits suicide
0-374-11734-9 FS&G $22.95
0-446-36058-9 WARNER PB $6.99

The Laws of Our Fathers
0-374-18423-2 FS&G $26.95

Pleading Guilty
From the bestselling author of *Presumed Innocent* and *The Burden of Proof* comes a story of missing millions and disappeared lawyers
0-374-23457-4 FS&G $24.00
0-446-36550-5 WARNER PB $6.99

Presumed Innocent
See also THE '80S under THE GREAT FICTION BESTSELLERS 1930–1995
0-374-23713-1 FS&G $22.95
0-446-35986-6 WARNER PB $6.99

Scott Turow

Odd Ones Out: Experiments and Mixed Genres

Caleb **Carr**

The Alienist
1896. The mutilated body of a young male prostitute is found in the East River. New York journalist Moor and his friend Kreizler, a pioneer in the new field of psychology, set out on a revolutionary attempt to identify a vicious serial killer by building a psychological profile. Their quest takes them through a brilliant historical re-creation of turn-of-the-century New York and deep inside a twisted, tortured mind
See also THE '90S under THE GREAT FICTION BESTSELLERS 1930–1995
See also NEW WRITERS OF THE '90S under 20TH-CENTURY AMERICAN FICTION
0-553-57299-7 BDD PB $7.50
0-679-41779-6 RANDOM HOUSE $22.00

Mark Frost (photo by Joey House)

Mark **Frost**

The List of 7
The co-creator of *Twin Peaks* has written a spectacular thriller involving Arthur Conan Doyle, a dangerous group of elite Satanists, and one Jack Sparks, the real-life special agent to Queen Victoria who inspired the creation of Sherlock Holmes
0-380-72019-1 AVON PB $5.99

Joan **Hess**

Busy Bodies
0-451-40560-9 ONYX PB $5.50

Death by the Light of the Moon
0-345-37838-5 BALLANTINE PB $4.99

Madness in Maggody
0-451-40299-5 ONYX PB $5.50

Maggody in Manhattan
"A side-splitting romp…both…spoof of the unrealistic amateur-sleuth story and the pretentious culinary-mystery genre"
—*NY Times Book Review*
0-451-40376-2 ONYX PB $5.50

Martians in Maggody
0-451-40592-7 ONYX PB $5.50

Joan **Hess**

Miracles in Maggody

0-451-40656-7 ONYX PB $5.99

O Little Town of Maggody

0-451-40457-2 ONYX PB $4.50

Tickled to Death

0-451-40550-1 ONYX PB $4.99

William **Hjortsberg**

Nevermore

0-87113-579-5 ATLANTIC MONTHLY $21.00

Peter **Hoeg**

Smilla's Sense of Snow

Expert writing and intricate plotting make this tale of a remarkable woman's search for the killer of a small boy so compelling. An international bestseller

See also **DANISH LITERATURE** under **SCANDINAVIAN LITERATURE** in **LITERATURE OF EUROPE, AFRICA, AND ASIA**

0-374-26644-1 FS&G $21.00

Susan **Isaacs**

After All These Years

A suburban housewife must solve her ex-husband's murder, or face a jury. Another winner by the author of *Compromising Positions*. "Broad humor, ebulliently proffered" —*Kirkus Reviews*

0-06-109179-0 HARPERCOLLINS PB $6.99

Philip **Kerr**

Berlin Noir: March Violets, The Pale Criminal, A German Requiem

A German private eye in the Hitler era and after. "Blends high-powered story-telling with a surprisingly rich piece of historical re-creation"— *Independent*

0-14-023170-6 PENGUIN PB $13.95

A Philosophical Investigation

Serial killings and Wittgenstein's philosophy of language are among the elements of this futuristic thriller

0-452-27140-1 PLUME PB $10.95

Phillip M. **Margolin**

Gone, But Not Forgotten

From a criminal defense lawyer specializing in murder cases, a thriller calculated to take up where *Presumed Innocent* left off

0-553-56903-1 BDD PB $6.99

Paule **Marshall**

Daughters

When Marshall writes about those she truly loves, she cannot be resisted. She brings…an instinctive understanding, a generosity, and a free humor that combine to form a style remarkable for its courage, color and its natural control"—*New Yorker*

0-452-26912-1 PLUME PB $12.95

Donald E. **Westlake**

Humans

A fast-paced confection of a mystery concerning the end of the world, starring angels, demons, God, a Russian gag-writer, a Nairobi prostitute, a Chinese dissident, and a career criminal from Omaha. Westlake has been called "the Mel Brooks of Mayhem," "the Noel Coward of Crime," and even "the Neil Simon of the crime novel," and his 1991 screenplay for *The Grifters* was nominated for an Academy Award as well as an Edgar

0-446-40094-7 MYSTERIOUS PB $5.99

About Crime Fiction

General Studies

Michael L. **Cook**

Mystery, Detective, and Espionage Fiction: A Checklist of Fiction in U.S. Pulp Magazines

0-8240-7539-0 GARLAND $117.00

Nicolas **Freeling**

Criminal Convictions: Errant Essays on Perpetrators of Literary License

From the world-class detective fiction writer comes this glorious volume of essays on the genre he knows best. Peppered with fiesty expostulations, often delightfully personal, this collection examines the work of Arthur Conan Doyle, Dorothy Sayers, and Georges Simenon, as well as less likely candidates: Dickens, Kipling, Stendhal, and Conrad. Loquacious and at times opinionated, this collection should not be missed

0-87923-973-5 GODINE $22.95

Howard **Haycraft**

Murder for Pleasure: The Life and Times of the Detective Story

Shrewd summing up, as of the early '40s, from the dean of American mystery-watchers. Limited in scope (no thrillers), but still persuasive and flavorsome

0-88184-071-8 CARROLL & GRAF PB $10.95

Howard **Haycraft**, editor

The Art of the Mystery Story

The definitive collection of critical essays, circa 1946—from Edmund Wilson's "Who Cares Who Killed Roger Ackroyd?" to more positive reflections by Sayers, Queen, Anthony Boucher, James Sandoe, and others

0-88184-878-6 CARROLL & GRAF PB $15.95

John T. **Irwin**

The Mystery to a Solution: Poe, Borges, and the Analytic Detective Story

0-8018-4650-1 JOHNS HOPKINS $49.95

H.R.F. **Keating**

Crime and Mystery: The 100 Best Books

The choices range from obvious to idiosyncratic to perverse. The mini-essays of appreciation meander. Nonetheless: charming enthusiasms

0-88184-441-1 CARROLL & GRAF PB $8.95

Kathleen Gregory **Klein**

The Woman Detective: Gender & Genre

0-252-06463-1 ILLINOIS PB $14.95

David **Lehman**

The Perfect Murder: A Study in Detection

A wide-ranging, intellectually lively look at the methods and effects of crime fiction. With a poet's eye, Lehman looks at the structural games played by such writers as Agatha Christie, John Dickson Carr, and Ross Macdonald

0-02-919770-8 FREE PRESS $24.95

Susan **Oleksiw**

A Reader's Guide to the Classic British Mystery

0-89296-968-7 MYSTERIOUS PB $19.95

Lee **Server**

Danger Is My Business: An Illustrated History of the Fabulous Pulp Magazines, 1896-1953

0-8118-0112-8 CHRONICLE PB $17.95

Over My Dead Body: The Sensational Age of the American Paperback, 1945-1955

0-8118-0646-4 CHRONICLE $29.95
0-8118-0550-6 CHRONICLE PB $16.95

Julian **Symons**

Bloody Murder: From the Detective Story to the Crime Novel

0-89296-496-0 MYSTERIOUS $21.95

Ralph **Willett**

The Naked City: Urban Crime Fiction in the USA

0-7190-4301-8 MANCHESTER PB $17.95

Studies of Individual Writers

Eric **Ambler**

Here Lies: An Autobiography

0-89296-940-7 MYSTERIOUS PB $8.95

Janet A. **Smith**

John Buchan: A Biography

0-19-281866-X OXFORD PB $8.95

Frank **MacShane**, editor

Selected Letters of Raymond Chandler

See also **THE 20TH CENTURY** under **STUDIES OF INDIVIDUAL AUTHORS (ALPHABETICAL BY SUBJECT)** under **AMERICAN LITERATURE: ANTHOLOGIES AND CRITICAL STUDIES** in **LITERATURE OF THE AMERICAS**

0-231-05080-1 COLUMBIA $49.50

Marvin **Kaye**, editor

The Game Is Afoot: Parodies, Pastiches and Ponderings of Sherlock Holmes

0-312-11797-3 ST. MARTIN'S PB $13.95

Julian **Symons**

Conan Doyle: Portrait of an Artist

0-89296-926-1 MYSTERIOUS PB $9.95

Charles **Viney**

Sherlock Holmes in London: A Photographic Record of Conan Doyle's Stories

0-8317-1889-7 SMITHMARK $12.98

Michael **Hardwick**

The Complete Guide to Sherlock Holmes

0-312-07248-1 ST. MARTIN'S PB $11.95

James **Ellroy**

My Dark Places

0-679-44185-9 KNOPF $25.00
0-679-76205-1 RANDOM HOUSE PB $10.00

Ross **Macdonald**

The bleak, past-haunted investigations of Lew Archer take him through a corrupted Southern California full of confused adolescents, hints of incest, family secrets.

Inward Journey

Includes tributes to Macdonald by Gilbert Sorrentino, John D. MacDonald, and others

EDITED BY RALPH B. SIPPER

0-89296-902-4 MYSTERIOUS PB $8.95

John **Mortimer**

Murderers and Other Friends: Another Part of Life

The memoirs of the British barrister/writer. "This book is to be savoured, like a glass of Rumpole's favorite claret..." —*The Philadelphia Enquirer*

0-14-024800-5 PENGUIN PB $11.95

Barbara **Reynolds**, editor

The Letters of Dorothy Sayers, 1899-1936: The Making of a Detective Novelist

0-312-14001-0 ST. MARTIN'S $26.95

Patrick **Marnham**

The Man Who Wasn't Maigret: A Portrait of Georges Simenon

0-15-600059-8 HARVEST PB $14.95

Robert **Polito**

Savage Art: A Biography of Jim Thompson

An impressive full-scale biography that situates the author of *The Killer Inside Me* in the historical currents of modern American literature

0-394-58407-4 KNOPF $30.00

Spy Fiction

The Early Spy Novel

James Fenimore Cooper's *The Spy* (1821)—which followed a double agent through the Revolutionary War—is generally acknowledged to be the first espionage novel. Nearly a century later, Joseph Conrad's *The Secret Agent* (1907) and *Under Western Eyes* (1911) explored the tormented souls of double-crossed, double-crossing agents. But while these writers foreshadow the serious and ambivalent nature of mid-20th-century espionage fiction, the spy novel as popular genre begins, somewhat ignominiously, with turn-of-the-century thriller writers such as William Le Queux, whose fiercely patriotic, stylistically crude novels set the genre's tone for decades.

John **Buchan**

Four Adventures of Richard Hannay

Including *The 39 Steps, Greenmantle, Mr. Standfast*, and *The Three Hostages*. Clear-cut enemies (usually German), high romanticism, and a patriotic hero in scenic, adventurous action

0-87923-871-2 GODINE PB $19.95

Greenmantle

0-19-282953-X OXFORD PB $7.95

Huntingtower

0-19-283229-8 OXFORD PB $10.01

Prester John

0-19-282936-X OXFORD PB $8.95

The Thirty-Nine Steps

0-14-001130-7 PENGUIN PB $6.95

The Three Hostages

0-19-282419-8 OXFORD $42.00

Erskine **Childers**

The Riddle of the Sands

"Not only a good spy story but also one of the finest tales about small sailing-craft ever written"—Eric Ambler

INTRODUCTION BY GEOFFREY HOUSEHOLD

0-14-000905-1 VIKING PB $7.95

Manning **Coles**

All that Glitters

0-88184-338-5 CARROLL & GRAF PB $3.95

E. Phillips **Oppenheim**

The Great Impersonation

An aristocrat in disgrace redeems himself by one-upping German spies in East Africa

0-486-23607-2 DOVER PB $5.95

Sax **Rohmer**

Fu Manchu

The yellow peril strikes again

0-8065-0899-X LYLE STUART PB $6.95

Edgar **Wallace**

The Four Just Men

Wallace's novel of international terrorism, published at the dawn of the twentieth century, is amazingly prescient for all its melodramatic trappings

0-19-282388-4 OXFORD PB $7.95

Modern Spy Novel

The cheery complacency of the pre-1930s thriller—like that of the cozy Golden Age whodunit—was profoundly challenged between the wars by darker, more skeptical attitudes. The absolute rightness of British and American national interests could no longer be assumed. The enemy—once so clearly identifiable—became a shifting, fuzzy target, and agents were revealed to have divided loyalties, ambivalent politics, and a perhaps healthy streak of every-man-for-himself ruthlessness.

Eric **Ambler**

"Ambler was fascinated by European cities, and his hunts take place against convincing backgrounds in Istanbul, Sofia, Belgrade, Milan. He was interested also in the problems of frontiers and passports, so that the difficulty of moving from one country to another plays a large part in the stories. And he showed from the beginning a high skill, which became master, in the construction of plot."
—Julian Symons

Background to Danger

Mussolini's fascist Italy is the backdrop here

0-88184-611-2 CARROLL & GRAF PB $3.95

Epitaph for a Spy

A young teacher—once Hungarian, once Yugoslav, now stateless—becomes entangled in espionage in a Europe (circa 1937) where Communism often looks better than social democracy

0-88184-716-X CARROLL & GRAF PB $3.95

The Light of Day

Late, supremely cynical Ambler: the harrowing ordeal of a seedy con man in Turkey, forced to smuggle weapons and spy for the local police

0-88184-836-0 CARROLL & GRAF PB $3.95

Passage of Arms

0-88184-837-9 CARROLL & GRAF PB $3.95

The Schirmer Inheritance

0-88184-767-4 CARROLL & GRAF PB $3.95

Agatha **Christie**

N or M?

Light-hearted espionage with Tommy and Tuppence Beres Ford

0-425-09845-1 BERKLEY PB $4.99

Manning **Coles**

Toast to Tomorrow

Tommy Hambledon, language expert and British agent, undercover in World War I Germany: part old-style derring-do, part understated realism

0-918172-15-2
IND PUB GROUP PB $5.95

Ian **Fleming**

Casino Royale
1-56849-655-9 BUCCANEER $24.95

Diamonds Are Forever
1-56731-050-8 AMEREON $19.95

From Russia with Love
0-7927-1268-4 CHIVERS PB $15.95

The Man with the Golden Gun
See also **THE '60S** under **THE GREAT FICTION BESTSELLERS 1930–1995**
0-451-15855-5 SIGNET PB $4.50

Ian Fleming

Octopussy
0-451-15624-2 SIGNET PB $4.50

Graham **Greene**

The Confidential Agent
An anti-Fascist emissary in London encounters a nightmare world of betrayal and murder
See also **THE EARLY 20TH CENTURY** under **20TH-CENTURY BRITISH AND IRISH FICTION** in **LITERATURE OF THE BRITISH ISLES**
0-14-018538-0 VIKING PB $7.95

The Ministry of Fear
A thriller about a network of Nazi spies in wartime London
0-14-018536-4 VIKING PB $9.95

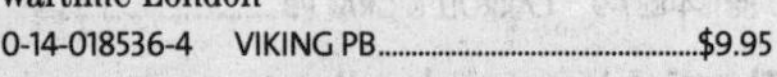

Graham Greene

Our Man in Havana
An ironic touch alleviates the tragic consequences of a vacuum salesman's unwitting involvement in spy games between great powers
0-14-018493-7 PENGUIN PB $10.95

Geoffrey **Household**

Rogue Male
A British sportsman sets out to assassinate Europe's foulest tyrant (circa 1939) and ends up as target and fugitive: the quintessential hunted-man adventure
0-89190-435-2 AMEREON $18.95

Helen **MacInnes**

Above Suspicion
Perilous honeymoon: an Oxford professor and his bride are enlisted to track down a missing agent in pre-World War II Germany
0-15-102707-2 HARCOURT BRACE $24.95

The Double Image
See also **THE '60S** under **THE GREAT FICTION BESTSELLERS 1930–1995**
0-89190-105-1 AMEREON $22.95

Ride a Pale Horse
0-449-20726-9 FAWCETT PB $5.99

Contemporary Spy Fiction

Loyalty to one's country—which may be in the wrong hands—is no longer a given in espionage fiction. Loyalty to oneself or one's friend or some higher principle might be a worthier priority. This is the central dilemma of the contemporary spy novel, especially as exemplified by the work of John le Carré, the genre's chief practitioner.

William F. **Buckley**, Jr.

High Jinks
0-440-13957-0 DELL PB $4.50

Len **Deighton**

Berlin Game
0-345-31498-0 BALLANTINE PB $5.95

Charity
0-06-018728-X HARPERCOLLINS $25.00

City of Gold
A riveting spy drama set in 1942. Rommel's army is approaching Cairo and it becomes clear someone is leaking British secrets to them. "Unrelenting tension"—*Publisher Weekly*
0-06-109041-7 HARPERCOLLINS PB $5.99

Faith
0-06-109419-6 HARPERCOLLINS PB $6.99

The Ipcress File
The first adventure of rebellious secret agent Harry Palmer
0-06-100816-8 HARPERCOLLINS PB $5.50

London Match
0-345-33268-7 BALLANTINE PB $5.95

Spy Hook
0-345-36520-8 BALLANTINE PB $5.99

Spy Line
0-345-37006-6 BALLANTINE PB $5.99

Spy Story
0-345-31569-3 BALLANTINE PB $4.95
0-06-100265-8 HARPERCOLLINS PB $5.50

Violent Ward
"If America is a lunatic asylum then California is the Violent Ward." "This novel respects the reader's intelligence and almost begs for a reading just to savor how skillfully Deighton has woven everything together"—*Publishers Weekly*
0-7927-2023-7 CHIVERS NORTH AMERICA $19.95
0-06-109195-2 HARPERCOLLINS PB $6.50

Ken **Follett**

The 3rd Twin
See also **THE MIDDLE GENERATION** under **20TH-CENTURY BRITISH AND IRISH FICTION** in **LITERATURE OF THE BRITISH ISLES**
0-517-70296-7 CROWN $25.95

The Big Needle
0-8217-4516-6 ZEBRA PB $3.99

A Dangerous Fortune
The master storyteller of *Eye of the Needle, The Key to Rebecca,* and *The Pillars of the Earth* makes another departure into the world of Victorian England to tell the tale of a merchant banking family torn apart by greed, lust, and a passion for power
See also **THE '90S** under **THE GREAT FICTION BESTSELLERS 1930–1995**
0-440-21749-0 DELL PB $6.99

A Place Called Freedom
See also **THE MIDDLE GENERATION** under **20TH-CENTURY BRITISH AND IRISH FICTION** in **LITERATURE OF THE BRITISH ISLES**
0-517-70176-6 CROWN $25.00
0-449-22515-1 CREST PB $6.99

Frederick **Forsyth**

The Day of the Jackal
Forsyth's first novel, about a plot to kill De Gaulle, remains in many ways his most compelling
0-553-26630-6 BDD PB $6.99

The Devil's Alternative
0-553-26490-7 BDD PB $6.99

The Dogs of War
The inner workings of an African coup engineered by an English magnate
0-553-26846-5 BDD PB $6.99

The Fourth Protocol
A lethal Soviet agent on the loose in England. Documentary-style espionage in convincing detail
0-553-25113-9 BDD PB $6.99

The Negotiator
0-553-28393-6 BDD PB $6.99

The Odessa File
A journalist on the trail of Nazi war criminals
0-553-27198-9 BDD PB $6.99

Sam **Greenlee**

The Spook Who Sat by the Door
An eerie tale of a black man infiltrating a CIA-type organization
1-88308-001-0 KAYODE PB $6.95

Adam **Hall**

The Quiller Memorandum

1-56849-396-7 BUCCANEER LIBRARY EDITION........$24.95

James W. **Hall**

Gone Wild

0-385-31231-8 DELACORTE........$21.95
0-440-21781-4 DELL PB........$6.50

Robert **Harris**

Enigma

0-679-42887-9 RANDOM HOUSE........$23.00
0-8041-1548-6 IVY PB........$6.99

Anthony **Hyde**

Formosa Straits

0-679-44039-9 KNOPF........$23.00

Joseph **Koenig**

Brides of Blood

Darius Bakhtiar, Chief of Homicide in Teheran, untangles a plot to arm the Islamic Republic with one of the deadliest biological weapons known to humankind. "This is a sophisticated evocation of another society and culture; an exotic background made palpably sinister through proven thriller techniques"
—*Publishers Weekly*

0-380-72258-5 AVON PB........$5.50

John **le Carré**

The Honourable Schoolboy

The scene shifts to Hong Kong as Smiley continues to trace the elusive trail of KGB spymaster Karla

0-553-27437-6 BDD PB........$6.99

The Looking-Glass War

0-345-37736-2 BALLANTINE PB........$6.99

The Night Manager

With the Cold War over, all the spies have come home to fight terrorists, drug smugglers, and arms dealers. These new villains are even more ruthless than their communist predecessors and driven by greed, not ideology

0-345-38576-4 BALLANTINE PB........$6.99

John le Carré

Our Game

In the wake of the Cold War, a retired British agent gets involved in ethnic warfare in the former Soviet Union

0-345-40000-3 BALLANTINE PB........$6.99

The Russia House

0-394-57789-2 KNOPF........$19.95

The Secret Pilgrim

"A grand summation of all John le Carré's themes. The effects of *The Secret Pilgrim* steal over the reader very gradually. But they leave you finally feeling chilled to the marrow"
—*NY Times*

0-345-37476-2 BALLANTINE PB........$5.99

The Spy Who Came in from the Cold

The novel that established le Carré as the most original of modern espionage writers

0-345-37737-0 BALLANTINE PB........$5.99

The Tailor of Panama

0-679-77413-0 RANDOM HOUSE........$25.00

Tinker, Tailor, Soldier, Spy

The best of the Smiley books is a complex study of betrayal in the heart of British intelligence

0-553-26778-7 BDD PB........$6.99

Robert **Ludlum**

Ludlum's immensely popular novels are non-stop exercises in global paranoia at its most unfettered.

The Bourne Identity

The first in Ludlum's enormously popular series of global chillers about the mysterious assassin Jason Bourne and the international conspiracy known as Medusa

0-553-26011-1 BDD PB........$6.99

The Bourne Supremacy

0-553-26322-6 BDD PB........$6.99

The Chancellor Manuscript

0-553-26094-4 BDD PB........$6.99

The Osterman Weekend

0-553-26430-3 BDD PB........$6.99

The Scarlatti Inheritance

0-553-27146-6 BDD PB........$6.99

William **Safire**

Sleeper Spy

0-679-43447-X RANDOM HOUSE........$24.00

Martin Cruz **Smith**

Red Square

The Party is dead and the ruble is worthless. When a black-market banker goes up in flames with a fortune in dollars and deutsche marks, Inspector Arkady Renko's investigation brings him into conflict with Moscow's rulers

0-345-38473-3 BALLANTINE PB........$5.99

Ross **Thomas**

Briarpatch

0-14-007990-4 PENGUIN PB........$5.95

Chinaman's Chance

0-445-40725-5 MYSTERIOUS PB........$5.99

The Cold War Swap

Comically horrific tangles involving reluctant or expendable spies and semi-innocent bystanders; the novel that introduced the McCorkle and Padillo partnership

0-446-40168-4 MYSTERIOUS PB........$5.99

The Eighth Dwarf

0-445-40754-9 POPULAR LIBRARY PB........$5.99

Missionary Stew

0-14-007413-9 PENGUIN PB........$5.95

Out on the Rim

0-445-40693-3 MYSTERIOUS PB........$5.99

Trevanian

The Eiger Sanction

Wicked satire, nasty violence, and fine climbing action: a CIA assassin's tricky mission

0-345-31737-8 BALLANTINE PB........$5.99

Donald **Westlake**

Kahawa

Idi Amin's Uganda provides the memorable backdrop for this adventurous thriller

0-89296-533-9 MYSTERIOUS........$21.95
0-446-40343-1 WARNER PB........$5.99

About Spy Fiction

John **Atkins**

The British Spy Novel

0-7145-4056-0 RIVERRUN PB........$14.95

Michael **Cox**, editor

The Oxford Book of Spy Stories

0-19-214242-9 OXFORD........$25.00
0-19-283267-0 OXFORD PB........$25.01

Andrew **Lycett**

Ian Fleming: The Man Behind James Bond

1-57036-343-9 TURNER........$24.95

True Crime

People have always been fascinated by real-life stories of murder and other crimes. Like mystery novels, books on true crimes let the reader vicariously enter a world of danger and intrigue made more unsettling by the fact that these crimes are often committed in the familiar landscapes of everyday life.

Classic Criminal Cases

Idanna **Pucci**

The Trials of Maria Barbella

1-56858-061-4 FOUR WALLS........$22.00
0-679-77604-4 VINTAGE........$12.00

Angus **McLaren**
A Prescription for Murder: The Victorian Serial Killings of Dr. Thomas Neill Cream
0-226-56068-6 CHICAGO PB..........$12.95

E.R. **Milner**
The Lives and Times of Bonnie and Clyde
0-8093-1977-2 SOUTHERN ILLINOIS..........$24.95

Arnold R. **Brown**
Lizzie Borden: The Legend, the Truth, the Final Chapter
0-440-21315-0 DELL PB..........$5.99

Robert A. **Flynn**
Lizzie Borden and the Mysterious Axe
0-9614811-4-5 KINPH PB..........$10.00

David **Kent**
Forty Whacks: New Evidence in the Life and Legend of Lizzie Borden
0-89909-351-5 YANKEE BOOKS..........$19.95

David **Kent**, editor
The Lizzie Borden Sourcebook
0-8283-1950-2 BRANDEN..........$29.95

George **Cooper**
Lost Love: A True Story of Passion, Murder and Justice in Old New York
Sensational murder trial in New York after the Civil War. "History at its best—dramatic, riveting and heart-rending"—Doris Kearns Goodwin
See also **CRIME AND PUNISHMENT** under **TOPICS IN AMERICAN STUDIES** in **HISTORY OF THE AMERICAS**
See also **THE GILDED AGE AND THE PROGRESSIVE ERA** under **US HISTORY, 1877–1945** in **HISTORY OF THE AMERICAS**
0-679-75699-X VINTAGE PB..........$12.00

Michael **Wallis**
Pretty Boy: The Life and Times of Charles Arthur Floyd
The Oklahoma outlaw whose legend depicted him as a "modern-day Robin Hood"
0-312-07071-3 ST. MARTIN'S..........$24.95

Paul **Begg**
Jack the Ripper A to Z
0-7472-5522-9 TRAFALGAR SQUARE PB..........$15.99

Stephen **Knight**
Jack the Ripper: The Final Solution
Knight theorizes that the Ripper killings were the culmination of a top-level cover-up by the English government
0-89733-209-1 ACADEMY CHICAGO PB..........$9.00

Philip **Sugden**
The Complete History of Jack the Ripper
0-7867-0276-1 CARROLL & GRAF PB..........$14.95

James **Maybrick**
The Diary of Jack the Ripper: The Chilling Confessions of James Maybrick
0-671-52099-7 POCKET PB..........$5.99

P.D. **James** & T.A. **Critchley**
The Maul and the Pear Tree
The story of the Ratcliffe Highway murders, a series of crimes that shocked London in the early 19th century
0-445-40562-7 MYSTERIOUS PB..........$5.99

Jeffrey Mousaieff **Masson**
Lost Prince: The Unsolved Mystery of Kaspar Hauser
A controversial treatment of the famous case of the sensorily-deprived foundling whom some believed to be of royal descent
0-684-82296-2 FREE PRESS..........$23.00

Noel **Behn**
Lindbergh: The Crime
The Lindberg kidnapping caused international shock and fascination. Now, more than six decades after the fact, doubt still lingers over the conviction and execution of Richard Bruno Hauptman. This true crime thriller weaves together the disparate threads of evidence to reach its provocative and highly plausible conclusion
0-451-40589-7 ONYX PB..........$5.99

Mary **Phagan**
The Murder of Little Mary Phagan
Another investigation of the Mary Phagan case, by a descendant of the victim's family
0-88282-039-7 NEW HORIZON..........$21.95

Gerald **Tomlinson**
Murdered in Jersey
The Hall-Mills murders and other famous crimes committed in New Jersey
0-8135-2078-9 RUTGERS PB..........$14.95

Modern Criminal Cases

David **Abrahamsen**
Confessions of Son of Sam
The story of David Berkowitz, who terrorized New York as the "Son of Sam" with a series of killings in the '70s
0-231-05760-1 COLUMBIA..........$39.50

Susan Crain **Bakos**
Appointment for Murder
The story of a respectable St. Louis dentist who murdered seven people over a 20-year period
1-55817-552-0 PINNACLE PB..........$4.95

John **Berendt**
Midnight in the Garden of Good and Evil
A story of murder in a brilliantly rendered Savannah
0-679-42922-0 RANDOM HOUSE..........$25.00

Edna **Buchanan**
The Corpse Had a Familiar Face: Covering Miami, America's Hottest Beat
From the legendary *Miami Herald* crime reporter—one of the first women ever to cover the police beat—who has seen "over five thousand corpses"
0-425-12994-2 DIAMOND PB..........$5.99

Never Let Them See You Cry: More Tales of Murder and Mayhem in Miami
Ace crime-reporter Buchanan is legendary for being first on the scene, and her dispatches set the standard for true-crime writing. Miami's lurid events make fertile material: a flamboyant millionaire gunned down in broad daylight, a corpse that walks, a three-year-old witness, and even a stray duck come to life (or death) in the pages of Buchanan's latest work
See also **THE PRACTITIONERS: A SAMPLER** under **JOURNALISM** in **PERFORMING ARTS AND MEDIA**
0-425-13824-0 BERKLEY PB..........$5.99

William J. **Buchanan**
Execution Eve
For the brutal, much-publicized double-murder of golf superstar Marion Miley and her mother, three men were sentenced to death in Kentucky State Prison. But the warden responsible for overseeing the execution (Buchanan's father) had agonizing doubts about their guilt. His unorthodox way of determining the truth of the case was to have profound effects on him and on capital punishment in America. "Buchanan is expert in mining uncommon ore in a commonplace world....Here is a genuine master at work"—Tony Hillerman
0-88282-121-0 NEW HORIZON..........$22.95

Vincent **Bugliosi**
Outrage: The Five Reasons Why O.J. Simpson Got Away with Murder
0-393-04050-X NORTON..........$25.00

Vincent **Bugliosi** & Curt **Gentry**
Helter Skelter
A harrowing account of the Manson family's 1969 murder spree
0-553-27829-0 BDD PB..........$6.99

Fox **Butterfield**
All God's Children: The Bosket Family and the American Tradition of Violence
See also **CRITICAL COMMENTARY ON AMERICAN CULTURE** under **TOPICS IN MODERN SOCIOLOGY** under **SOCIOLOGY** in **SOCIAL STUDIES**
0-394-58286-1 KNOPF..........$27.50

Teresa **Carpenter**
Missing Beauty: A Story of Murder and Obsession
A fascinating account of a distinguished professor's obsession with a prostitute
0-8217-2755-9 ZEBRA PB..........$4.95

Truman **Capote**

In Cold Blood

The original "nonfiction novel," first published in 1966, chronicling the murder of a Kansas family by two drifters

See also **REPORTING** under **20TH-CENTURY AMERICAN ESSAYS AND JOURNALISM** in **LITERATURE OF THE AMERICAS**

See also **SINCE 1945** under **20TH-CENTURY AMERICAN FICTION** in **LITERATURE OF THE AMERICAS**

0-679-60023-X MODERN LIBRARY $15.50
0-679-74558-0 VINTAGE PB $12.00

Joyce **Eggington**

From Cradle to Grave: The Short Lives and Strange Deaths of Marybeth Tinning's Nine Children

The chilling story of the mysterious deaths of Tinning's 9 children, undetected until she was arrested for the murder of her 9th and last child

0-515-10301-2 JOVE PB $6.99

Mikal **Gilmore**

Shot in the Heart

"This is a murder story told from inside the house where murder is born." So writes Mikal Gilmore in this powerfully honest book about the circumstances and upbringing that made the murderous psychopathology of his brother Gary almost a fait accompli. The miracle, one feels after reading this book, is that Mikal was able to resist the same path

0-385-47800-3 ANCHOR PB $14.95

> I have a story to tell. It is a story of murders: Murders of the flesh, and of the spirit; murders born of heartbreak, of hatred, of retribution. It is the story of where those murders begin, of how they take form and enter our actions, how they transform our lives, how their legacies spill into the world and the history around us. And it is a story of how the claims of violence and murder end—if, indeed, they ever end.
>
> SHOT IN THE HEART

Jean **Harris**

Stranger in Two Worlds

The convicted murderess tells her own story—a story which brings her guilt into question

0-8217-4313-9 ZEBRA PB $4.99

They Always Call Us Ladies: Stories from Prison

Written from Harris's years spent doing time

0-8217-4314-7 ZEBRA PB $4.99

Norman **Mailer**

The Executioner's Song

Really two books: the first about the brutal life and death of convicted killer Gary Gilmore, the second about the media's no less savage fight for the story rights. "Not since *The Grapes of Wrath* has there been an American book that so discovered the voices in our culture" —*Philadelphia Inquirer*

See also **SINCE 1945** under **20TH-CENTURY AMERICAN FICTION** in **LITERATURE OF THE AMERICAS**

0-679-42471-7 MODERN LIBRARY $21.00

Joe **McGinnis**

Fatal Vision

The story of Dr. Jeffrey MacDonald, the former Green Beret accused of killing his pregnant wife and two children, a crime he still denies committing

0-451-16566-7 NEW AMERICAN LIBRARY PB $6.99

Blind Faith

How a New Jersey businessman plotted to murder his wife. "A harrowing portrait of the American dream misunderstood to the point of perversion"—*Washington Post*

0-451-16218-8 NEW AMERICAN LIBRARY PB $5.99
0-451-16806-2 READER'S CATALOG PB $5.99

Ron **Soble** & John **Johnson**

Blood Brothers: The Inside Story of the Menendez Murders

0-451-40547-1 SIGNET PB $4.99

Randall **Sullivan**

The Price of Experience: Power, Money, Image and Murder in Los Angeles

The account of Joe Hunt's Billionaire Boys Club, where murder and manipulation mixed with business resulted in five murder charges and Hunt's life sentence without parole in Folsom Prison

0-87113-512-4 ATLANTIC MONTHLY $27.50

Joseph **Wambaugh**

Echoes in the Darkness

A reconstruction of the 1979 murder of a Pennsylvania schoolteacher, a bizarre crime involving other faculty members at the slain woman's high school

0-553-26932-1 BDD PB $6.50

Alec **Wilkinson**

A Violent Act

The story of Mike Wayne Jackson, who killed his probation officer in September 1986 and went on a rampage, killing two more people on the way. Treating the killer with compassion and examining all details with interest, Wilkinson helps to demystify a subject that troubles us all—American violence. "His god is in the details. He lays them out with impeccable clarity and timing"—*Entertainment Weekly*

0-679-74982-9 VINTAGE PB $11.00

Organized Crime

Laurence **Bergreen**

Capone: The Man and the Era

0-684-82447-7 TOUCHSTONE PB $16.00

Ralph **Blumenthal**

Last Days of the Sicilians: The New FBI at War with the Mafia

Recent attempts to crack down on the mob

0-671-68277-6 POCKET PB $5.99

Willie **Fopiano**

The Godson: My Life in the Mafia

In the suspenseful and brutal tradition of *Wiseguys*, this true-crime autobiography traces the career path and criminal exploits of a young mobster from street thug to millionaire criminal. Includes sections on Meyer Lansky, the Brinks Robbery, Joseph Kennedy, the Boston Strangler, and more. "Fast action in a moral vacuum: frightening and compelling"—*Kirkus Reviews*

0-312-09748-4 ST. MARTIN'S $20.95
0-312-95323-2 ST. MARTIN'S PB $4.99

Norman **Lewis**

Honoured Society: The Sicilian Mafia Observed

The Sicilian roots of the Mafia

0-907871-80-1 HIPPOCRENE PB $14.95

Nicholas **Pileggi**

Casino

Wiseguys go to Las Vegas and come to bad ends: the source for Scorsese's movie

0-571-17992-4 FABER PB $12.95

Carl **Sifakis**

The Mafia Encyclopedia

More than 400 entries covering everything known about the Mafia

0-8160-1172-9 FACTS ON FILE $40.00
0-8160-1856-1 FACTS ON FILE PB $19.95

Gay **Talese**

Honor Thy Father

Acclaimed portrayal of the Bonanno mafia dynasty

See also **REPORTING** under **20TH-CENTURY AMERICAN ESSAYS AND JOURNALISM** in **LITERATURE OF THE AMERICAS**

0-8041-1058-1 IVY PB $5.99

Gay Talese

The Police

Carsten **Stroud**

Deadly Force: In the Streets With the U.S. Marshals

0-553-09994-9 BDD $23.95

Joseph **Wambaugh**

The Onion Field

A gripping account of the aftermath of a cop killing

0-440-17350-7 DELL PB $6.50

Cyril **Wecht** & others

Cause of Death: The Final Diagnosis

Here one of America's leading forensic pathologists looks at the deaths that continue to fascinate the public: JFK, RFK, Elvis Presley, Mary Jo Kopechne, and others. Demonstrates that Elvis could not have died of a heart attack, and offers proof that Sirhan Sirhan could not have shot RFK. Persuasive scientific rebuttals to official reports provide compelling true crime, medical, and legal reading

0-451-18141-7 ONYX PB $5.99

General Reference

Mike **Ashley**, editor
The Mammoth Book of Historical Detectives
0-7867-0214-1 CARROLL & GRAF PB........................$9.95

Thomas H. **Flaherty**
Unsolved Crimes
0-7835-0012-2 TIME BOOKS........................$14.95

Carl **Sifakis**
The Encyclopedia of American Crime
Comprehensive listings on crime in the United States throughout its history
0-8317-2767-5 SMITHMARK........................$19.98

Espionage

For related reading, see AMERICAN POLITICS AND FOREIGN POLICY in HISTORY OF THE AMERICAS

For related reading, see THE SECOND WORLD WAR in WORLD HISTORY AND CURRENT AFFAIRS

Overviews

Philip **Knightley**
The Second Oldest Profession: Spies and Spying in the 20th Century
A history and critique of modern espionage, in which such famous spies as Mata Hari and Kim Philby are examined
0-393-02386-9 NORTON........................$19.95

Espionage Tales

James **Adams**
Sellout: Aldrich Ames and the Corruption of the CIA
See also **THE CIA, FBI, AND ESPIONAGE** under **AMERICAN POLITICS AND FOREIGN POLICY** in **HISTORY OF THE AMERICAS**
0-670-86236-3 VIKING........................$23.95

Christopher **Andrew** & Oleg **Gordievsky**
KGB: The Inside Story
A KGB defector teams up with the author of *Her Majesty's Secret Service* to provide an exhaustive picture of the agency's inner workings
0-06-092109-9 HARPERPERENNIAL PB........................$20.00

Wolf **Blitzer**
Territory of Lies: The Rise, Fall and Betrayal of Jonathan J. Pollard
An account of how Pollard spied on the U.S. for Israel, and how he was caught
0-06-100024-8 HARPERCOLLINS PB........................$4.95

Ian **Black** & Benny **Morris**
Israel's Secret Wars: A History of Israel's Intelligence Services
A full-scale, documented history of Israeli intelligence, with detailed treatment of the Suez crisis, the Entebbe raid, the Iran/Contra affair, and the Intifada
0-8021-3286-3 GROVE PB........................$16.95

Tom **Bower**
The Perfect English Spy: The Unknown Man in Charge During the Most Tumultuous, Scandal-Ridden Era in Espionage History
See also **BRITAIN SINCE 1945** under **GREAT BRITAIN AND IRELAND** in **WORLD HISTORY AND CURRENT AFFAIRS**
0-312-13584-X ST. MARTIN'S........................$26.95

Leslie **Colitt**
Spymaster: The Real-Life "Karla," His Moles, and the East German Police
See also **GERMANY SINCE 1945** under **EUROPE SINCE 1945** in **WORLD HISTORY AND CURRENT AFFAIRS**
0-201-40738-8 ADDISON-WESLEY........................$23.00

William R. **Corson** & Robert T. **Crowley**
THE NEW KGB: Engine of Soviet Power
Two former senior intelligence officers share the insights gained from 68 years of combined experience
0-688-04183-3 MORROW........................$19.95

Brian **Freemantle**
KGB
Foreign espionage activities and intelligence operations of the Russian security police
0-03-071059-6 HOLT PB........................$2.98

H. Keith **Melton**
The Ultimate Spy Book
0-7894-0443-5 DORLING KINDERSLEY........................$29.95

David **Morehouse**
Psychic Warrior: Inside the CIA's Stargate Program: The True Story of a Soldier's Espionage and Awakening
0-312-14708-2 ST. MARTIN'S........................$23.95

Verne W. **Newton**
The Cambridge Spies: The American Cover-Up of the Maclean, Philby, Burgess Scandal
A look at the American side of the famous British spy scandal, focusing on the period when Maclean, Philby, and Burgess were active at the British embassy in Washington, D.C., and revealing the extent of the damage done by their activities
0-8191-8059-9 MADISON........................$24.95

Anthony Cave **Brown**
Treason in the Blood: H. St. John Philby, Kim Philby, and the Spy Case of the Century
Uniquely effective, this dual biography of Kim Philby—considered by the CIA to be "the most remarkable spy of our generation" and by the KGB "one of the most important men of the century"—and his father provides unmatched insight into the anatomy of treachery. With sources from America, Britain, Switzerland, France, and Moscow as well as new photographs and KGB memoranda, this is an enormously compelling view of one of the century's most fascinating figures
0-395-63119-X HOUGHTON MIFFLIN........................$29.95

Norman **Polmar** & Thomas B. **Allen**
Spy Book: The Encyclopedia of Espionage
0-679-42514-4 RANDOM HOUSE........................$30.00

Douglas **Porch**
The French Secret Service: From the Dreyfus Affair to the Gulf War
See also **RECENT HISTORY AND CURRENT AFFAIRS** under **FRANCE SINCE 1945** under **EUROPE SINCE 1945** in **WORLD HISTORY AND CURRENT AFFAIRS**
0-374-15853-3 FS&G........................$32.50

Gordon W. **Prange** & D.M. **Goldstein**
Target Tokyo: The Story of the Sorge Spy Ring
A look at Soviet spy Richard Sorge, who was tried and hanged by the Japanese in 1941
See also **SPIES AND CODE-BREAKERS** under **THE SECOND WORLD WAR** in **WORLD HISTORY AND CURRENT AFFAIRS**
0-07-050677-9 MCGRAW HILL........................$24.95

Countess Aline **Romanones**
The Spy Wore Red: My Adventures as an Undercover Agent in World War II
Memoirs of an American model who, in 1943, infiltrated the upper levels of Spanish society in order to uncover high-society intelligence links to Hitler
0-515-10653-4 CHARTER PB........................$5.99

Science Fiction and Fantasy

Although Mary Shelley's *Frankenstein* was published in 1818, science fiction's full-scale development has occurred largely within a lifetime; indeed, some of the pioneers of the field remain active within it. But if science fiction's history has been brief, it has also been remarkably varied. In part this is because science fiction, like a volatile chemical, combines readily with other genres. Mysteries, detective stories, romances, adventures, experimental writing: the genre encompasses all of these. Science fiction has also become more complex and demanding as it has evolved. The technological and sociological concepts on which so much SF is based have grown increasingly complex, and SF writers these days tend to be more sophisticated stylists. The best of the current lot is a far cry from the simple-minded space operas of the pulp magazines.

A word on series, with which science fiction and fantasy are riddled. There are series built around charismatic characters and series devoted to worlds and futures in which any number of plots can be set. There has been a tendency toward ever-lengthier works, with an increasing number of trilogies and tetralogies that are really single works published in multiple volumes. In the lists below, these various multiplicities have been handled on a case-by-case basis. Generally, if the initial volume is complete in itself, sequels are noted without being specifically named.

Early Science Fiction

Edwin A. **Abbott**

Flatland

A two-dimensional world

See also ADVANCED GEOMETRY under GEOMETRY under MATHEMATICS in SCIENCE

0-06-463573-2 BARNES & NOBLE PB $11.00
0-14-007615-8 PENGUIN PB $6.95
0-691-02525-8 PRINCETON PB $8.95

Alexander **Bogdanov**

Red Star: The First Bolshevik Utopia

0-253-20317-1 INDIANA PB $13.95

Edgar Rice **Burroughs**

A Princess of Mars

The first of a series of classic adventures on the red planet of Barsoom

0-345-33138-9 BALLANTINE PB $4.99

Tanar of Pellucidar

0-345-36670-0 DEL RAY PB $3.95

Karel **Capek**

Capek was a major playwright, novelist, and essayist, the leading Czech writer of the post-World War I period. In his play R.U.R. *hee coined the word "robot"; the satirical science-fiction novel* War with the Newts *was a remarkable blend of political and ecological vision. His works also include travel books, essays on gardening, and philosophical mystery stories. "Fifty years after his death, Capek's work has lost nothing of its freshness and luster … He is as great a delight to read today as he ever was."*—NY Times Book Review

War with the Newts

An intelligent species of newt threatens humanity with extinction, in Capek's most successful work of science fiction, filled with inventive satirical digressions

See also CZECH LITERATURE under EASTERN EUROPEAN LITERATURE in LITERATURE OF EUROPE, AFRICA, AND ASIA

0-945774-10-9 AMS PB $11.95

Arthur Conan **Doyle**

The Best Science Fiction of Arthur Conan Doyle

EDITED BY CHARLES G. WAUGH & MARTIN H. GREENBERG

0-8093-1046-5 SOUTHERN ILLINOIS $19.95

Arthur Conan Doyle

The Lost World

The scientist-hero Professor Challenger discovers a realm of living dinosaurs

See also 19TH-CENTURY FICTION under THE 19TH CENTURY in LITERATURE OF THE BRITISH ISLES

0-19-283186-0 OXFORD PB $7.95

William Hope **Hodgson**

The House on the Borderland

0-7867-0282-6 CARROLL & GRAF PB $4.95

C.S. **Lewis**

Lewis's space trilogy, with its peculiar mix of theology and science, is unique in science fiction.

Out of the Silent Planet

See also THE EARLY 20TH CENTURY under 20TH-CENTURY BRITISH AND IRISH FICTION in LITERATURE OF THE BRITISH ISLES

0-684-83364-6 SCRIBNERS $22.00

Perelandra

0-02-570845-7 MACMILLAN $40.00
0-684-83365-4 SCRIBNERS $22.00

That Hideous Strength

0-02-086960-6 COLLIER PB $5.95

Mary Wollstonecraft **Shelley**

Frankenstein

Those who know the story only from the film versions will be amazed by the depth and sophistication of the novel

EDITED BY MAURICE HINDLE

0-679-40999-8 EVERYMAN'S $15.00
0-553-21247-8 BDD PB $2.95
0-14-043362-7 PENGUIN PB $6.95

It was on a dreary night of November, that I beheld the accomplishment of my toils. With an anxiety that almost amounted to agony, I collected the instruments of life around me, that I might infuse a spark of being into the lifeless thing that lay at my feet. It was already one in the morning; the rain pattered dismally against the panes, and my candle was nearly burnt out, when, by the glimmer of the half-extinguished light, I saw the dull yellow eye of the creature open; it breathed hard, and a convulsive motion agitated its limbs.

FRANKENSTEIN

The Last Man

An odd, variegated account of a worldwide plague

0-8032-5182-3 NEBRASKA PB $5.95

Olaf **Stapledon**

Far Future Calling

1-88041-806-1 GRANT $12.00

Last and First Men & Star Maker

A staggering "future history" of mankind through the next two billion years and 18 species

0-486-21962-3 DOVER PB $9.95

Odd John & Sirius: Two Science Fiction Novels

0-486-21133-9 DOVER PB $8.95

An Olaf Stapledon Reader

EDITED BY ROBERT CROSSLEY

0-8156-0430-0 SYRACUSE PB $10.01

Robert Louis **Stevenson**

Dr. Jekyll and Mr. Hyde & Weir of Hermiston

Stevenson's great fantasy on the moral aspects of scientific progress. Also included is *Weir of Hermiston* his final, unfinished novel of Scotland

0-19-281740-X OXFORD PB $4.95

The Strange Case of Dr. Jekyll and Mr. Hyde

An elegant new edition of the classic statement of the dual identity theme

ILLUSTRATED BY BARRY MOSER

INTRODUCTION BY JOYCE CAROL OATES

0-89968-552-8 BUCCANEER $16.95
0-8032-4212-3 NEBRASKA $25.00

Robert Louis Stevenson

Jules **Verne**

Verne was a varied and profound writer whose obsession with scientific, geographical, and political information combines with a capacity for broad and potent—and often unconscious—symbolism.

Around the World in Eighty Days

0-19-283093-7 OXFORD PB $8.95

From the Earth to the Moon

0-553-21420-9 BDD PB $4.95

A Journey to the Center of the Earth

Verne's first great popular success describes a geological descent that takes on dreamlike fascination

See also **YOUNG ADULT FICTION** in **BOOKS FOR YOUNG READERS**

See also **THE LATER 19TH CENTURY: SYMBOLISM, NATURALISM, AND ROOTS OF MODERNISM** under **FRENCH LITERATURE TO 1900** in **LITERATURE OF EUROPE, AFRICA, AND ASIA**

0-8049-0060-4 AIRMONT PB $3.50
0-19-585460-8 OXFORD PB $4.95

Jules Verne: Five Complete Novels

Includes *Twenty Thousand Leagues Under the Sea* and *Journey to the Center of the Earth*

0-517-12250-2 GRAMERCY $12.99

The Mysterious Island

Captain Nemo's last stand

0-451-52491-8 NEW AMERICAN LIBRARY PB $5.95

Twenty Thousand Leagues Under the Sea

Notable for the powerful archetypal figure of Captain Nemo

9-99-267965-4 GLOBE FEARON PB $10.06
0-19-585469-1 OXFORD PB $5.25

H.G. **Wells**

Best Science Fiction Stories

0-486-21531-8 DOVER PB $7.95

The Conquest of Time

0-87975-920-8 PROMETHEUS PB $7.95

The First Men in the Moon

0-19-282828-2 OXFORD PB $6.95

Food of the Gods

0-8488-1216-6 AMEREON $18.95

The Island of Dr. Moreau

0-679-60230-5 MODERN LIBRARY $14.50

Seven Science Fiction Novels of H.G. Wells

A comprehensive edition of Wells's greatest speculative works. Includes *The First Men in the Moon, The Island of Dr. Moreau, The War of the Worlds, The Invisible Man, The Time Machine, The Food of the Gods,* and *In the Days of the Comet*

See also **YOUNG ADULT FICTION** in **BOOKS FOR YOUNG READERS**

0-486-20264-X DOVER $29.95

Three Prophetic Science-Fiction Novels of H.G. Wells

Includes *When the Sleeper Wakes, A Story of the Days to Come,* and *The Time Machine*

0-486-20605-X DOVER PB $9.95

The Time Machine

0-460-87735-6 EVERYMAN'S PB $3.95

The War of the Worlds

See also **THE EARLY 20TH CENTURY** under **20TH-CENTURY BRITISH AND IRISH FICTION** in **LITERATURE OF THE BRITISH ISLES**

AFTERWORD BY ISAAC ASIMOV

0-451-52276-1 NEW AMERICAN LIBRARY PB $4.95

The War of the Worlds

0-19-282826-6 OXFORD PB $6.95

When the Sleeper Wakes

0-460-87499-3 EVERYMAN'S PB $7.95

Evgeny **Zamyatin**

Evgeny Zamyatin (1884-1937) was the moving spirit behind the Serapion Brothers, a literary group and movement formed in 1921 whose initial aim was to reject the spirit of philistinism in the Proletkult school, and interpret the Russian Revolution in an individual way

We

See also **FICTION AND OTHER PROSE** under **EARLY 20TH CENTURY** under **RUSSIAN LITERATURE** in **LITERATURE OF EUROPE, AFRICA, AND ASIA**

TRANSLATED BY CLARENCE BROWN

0-14-018585-2 PENGUIN PB $10.95

The Golden Age

The period around 1950 was the so-called Golden Age, when the genre was still confined to magazines but was beginning to outgrow the mad scientists and bug-eyed monsters of the pulps. The editor John W. Campbell attracted a stable of brilliant young writers to his magazine *Astounding*, and for the first time the action-adventure and cosmic space operas of American SF were combined with the intelligent extrapolation typical of English writers like Wells and Stapledon. The primary idea, however, was to create worlds and futures founded on a broader base than speculative inventions.

Paul **Anderson**

Brain Wave

The intelligence of mankind and other mammals increases suddenly

0-89968-327-4 LIGHTYEAR $18.95

Isaac **Asimov**

The Caves of Steel

0-553-29340-0 SPECTRA PB $5.99

The Currents of Space

0-553-29341-9 SPECTRA PB $5.99

Foundation

The first installment of Asimov's five-part epic of a galactic empire

0-553-29335-4 BDD PB $6.50

Foundation and Empire

0-345-33628-3 BALLANTINE PB $5.95

Gold: The Final Science Fiction Collection

0-06-105409-7 HARPERCOLLINS PB $5.99

I, Robot

0-553-29438-5 BDD PB $5.99

Magic: The Final Fantasy Collection

0-06-105205-1 HARPER PRISM $22.00
0-06-105412-7 HARPERCOLLINS PB $5.99

Prelude to Foundation

A "prequel" to the Foundation cycle

0-553-27839-8 SPECTRA PB $5.99

Robot Dreams

0-441-73154-6 ACE PB $5.99

Robot Visions

0-451-45064-7 NEW AMERICAN LIBRARY PB $6.99

Second Foundation

0-345-33629-1 BALLANTINE PB $5.95

Isaac **Asimov** & Robert **Silverberg**

Nightfall

0-553-29099-1 BDD PB $5.99

The Positronic Man

0-553-56121-9 BDD PB $5.99

The Ugly Little Boy

Two celebrated science fiction writers have expanded on Asimov's classic story of a Neanderthal boy taken out of his time and brought into a future world. "This is a collaborative effort that surpasses the original…a fresh and satisfying version, primarily because the characters have been made richer…and the history of the Neanderthal tribe more fully given"—*Publishers Weekly*

0-553-56122-7 BDD PB $5.99

Janet **Asimov** & Isaac **Asimov**

Norby and the Court Jester

0-441-00341-9 ACE PB $5.50

Alfred **Bester**

The Demolished Man

An unscrupulous businessman uses future technology for criminal ends

0-679-76781-9 VINTAGE PB $11.00

The Stars My Destination

A stunning precursor to much modern SF

0-89968-328-2 LIGHTYEAR $18.95
0-679-76780-0 VINTAGE PB $11.00

Ray **Bradbury**

Bradbury's early novels and stories were key works in the evolution of science fiction.

Fahrenheit 451

0-345-34296-8 BALLANTINE PB $5.99

The Illustrated Man

0-553-25483-9 BDD PB $4.99

The Martian Chronicles

0-553-27822-3 BDD PB $5.50

The October Country

Contains most of the stories from his first, very good, very rare collection, *Dark Carnival*

0-345-32448-X BALLANTINE PB $5.99

Something Wicked this Way Comes

0-553-28032-5 BDD PB $5.50

The Stories of Ray Bradbury
0-394-51335-5 KNOPF $40.00

Arthur C. **Clarke**
There is no greater master of fiction based on highly complex scientific theories than Clarke. The theoretical basis of his stories is always clear but never gets in the way of his plots.

2001: A Space Odyssey
Clarke's visionary work provided the basis for Stanley Kubrick's film
0-451-45273-9 NEW AMERICAN LIBRARY PB $5.95

2010: Odyssey Two
0-345-30306-7 BALLANTINE PB $5.95

2061: Odyssey Three
0-345-35879-1 BALLANTINE PB $5.95

Cradle
0-446-35601-8 WARNER PB $5.99

Garden of Rama
0-553-29817-8 BDD PB $6.50

The Hammer of God
0-553-56871-X BDD PB $5.99

Rama Revealed
0-553-56947-3 BDD PB $6.50

Rendezvous with Rama
A guided tour of a gigantic alien ship on a flythrough of our system
0-89968-449-1 LIGHTYEAR $26.95
0-553-28789-3 BDD PB $5.99

The Songs of Distant Earth
A gentle portrait of a human colony on a distant world
0-345-32240-1 BALLANTINE PB $5.95

Jack **Finney**

Invasion of the Body Snatchers
Finney's paranoid vision of extraterrestrial takeover has been filmed three times
0-671-68211-3 FIRESIDE PB $8.95

Robert **Heinlein**

The Star Beast
0-345-35059-6 BALLANTINE PB $5.99

Robert A. **Heinlein**

The Cat Who Walks Through Walls: A Comedy of Manners
0-441-09499-6 BERKLEY PB $6.99

Citizen of the Galaxy
Published as a juvenile, but among his best
0-345-34244-5 BALLANTINE PB $5.99

The Door into Summer
0-345-33012-9 BALLANTINE PB $5.99

Glory Road
An amusing sci-fi takeoff on epic fantasy
0-671-72167-4 BAEN PB $10.00

The Green Hills of Earth
0-88411-881-9 AMEREON $19.95

The Moon Is a Harsh Mistress
Revolt in a lunar colony
0-312-86176-1 TOR $23.95

The Notebooks of Lazarus Long
0-87654-473-1 POMEGRANATE PB $15.95

The Puppet Masters
0-345-33014-5 DEL RAY PB $5.99

Stranger in a Strange Land
For the first time, the unabridged text of one of the most influential science fiction novels ever written
0-441-79034-8 ACE PB $6.99

To Sail Beyond the Sunset
0-441-74860-0 ACE PB $6.99

Tramp Royale
0-441-00409-1 ACE PB $15.00

Walter M. **Miller**, Jr.

A Canticle for Leibowitz
Hugo winner: a widely read dystopia of a postnuclear world
0-553-27381-7 BDD PB $5.99

James **Schmitz**

The Witches of Karres
0-89968-361-4 LIGHTYEAR $18.95

Clifford **Simak**

All Flesh Is Grass
0-7867-0045-9 CARROLL & GRAF PB $4.95

Cemetery World
0-88184-985-5 CARROLL & GRAF PB $3.50

The Goblin Reservation
0-88184-897-2 CARROLL & GRAF PB $3.95

Ring Around the Sun
0-88184-852-2 CARROLL & GRAF PB $3.95

Way Station
0-02-024871-7 COLLIER PB $9.00

Theodore **Sturgeon**

The Dreaming Jewels
Sturgeon was a preeminent stylist among '50s science fiction writers
0-88184-351-2 CARROLL & GRAF PB $3.95

The Golden Helix
0-88184-450-0 CARROLL & GRAF PB $3.95

More than Human
A mutant humanity—a "gestalt" personality of multiple individuals
0-88184-918-9 CARROLL & GRAF PB $3.95

The Ultimate Egoist: The Complete Stories
EDITED BY PAUL WILLIAMS
1-55643-182-1 NORTH ATLANTIC $25.00

A.E. **Van Vogt**

Slan
A totalitarian future where telepaths are persecuted
0-89190-454-9 AMEREON $18.95

John **Wyndham**

The Chrysalids
Mutant telepaths on the run in a post-nuclear world governed by contending tribes
0-7867-0041-6 CARROLL & GRAF PB $3.95

Day of the Triffids
Intelligent plants invade Earth, in a novel in the spirit of Wells
0-88184-989-8 CARROLL & GRAF PB $3.95

The Midwich Cuckoos
Women of an English village are impregnated by aliens: the basis for the movie *Village of the Damned*
0-89968-387-8 LIGHTYEAR $18.95

Contemporary Science Fiction

Most of the science fiction being read today was written in the last 20 years. During the '60s the genre grew phenomenally in quality, quantity, and popularity, and the results have been extraordinarily diverse. The various "streams" of contemporary SF range from the society-building of Ursula K. Le Guin through the hallucinatory dreams of Philip K. Dick to the high-tech extrapolations of Larry Niven—not to mention those who, like the polymath Samuel R. Delany, combine all these tendencies.

The traditional vein of SF—the story based on hard science, usually revolving around the solution of a scientific puzzle—has become steadily more complex. Sociology as the basis for extrapolation, as with Ursula K. Le Guin's landmark novel *The Left Hand of Darkness*, is used to create future human societies with changed cultures and genetics. The "cyberpunk" of SF's youngest writers offers a pessimistic view of science and technology, with futures characterized by direct input into and manipulation of the human mind through electronics and computers.

Twenty-five years ago the idea of science fiction with literary merit would have met with derision. Writers and readers had traditionally valued concept over style; if the ideas were good, minimal skill in presenting them was acceptable. Despite its increased complexity, the level of writing in the genre has risen astonishingly, and many of its practitioners have achieved wide critical recognition.

Douglas **Adams**

Hitchhiker's Guide to the Galaxy
See also **YOUNG ADULT FICTION** in **BOOKS FOR YOUNG READERS**
0-345-39180-2 BALLANTINE PB $6.99

The Illustrated Hitchhiker's Guide to the Galaxy
The perennially attractive cult classic, now illustrated with state-of-the-art digital graphics that do not alter the original ascii set, that is, the text
0-517-59924-4 HARMONY $42.00

Life, the Universe and Everything
0-345-39182-9 BALLANTINE PB $6.99

The Long Dark Tea-Time of the Soul
0-671-74251-5 POCKET PB $5.99

Mostly Harmless
Douglas Adams is "irresistable!"—Boston Globe. "Wacky, loony and zany!"—Los Angeles Herald
0-517-57740-2 HARMONY $20.00

Douglas **Adams**

The Restaurant at the End of the Universe
0-345-39181-0 BALLANTINE PB $6.99

The Salmon of Doubt: A Dirk Gently Novel
0-517-57743-7 HARMONY $23.00

Brian **Aldiss**

Common Clay: 20-Odd Stories
0-312-13948-9 ST. MARTIN'S $24.95

Last Orders
0-88184-617-1 CARROLL & GRAF PB $3.95

A Tupolev Too Far: And Other Stories
0-312-10565-7 ST. MARTIN'S $18.95

Poul **Anderson**

All One Universe
0-312-85873-6 TOR $22.95

The Boat of a Million Years
0-8125-3135-3 TOR PB $5.99

The Day of Their Return
0-8125-2309-1 TOR PB $4.99

Flandry: Defender of the Terran Empire
0-671-72149-6 BAEN PB $4.99

Harvest of Stars
0-8125-1946-9 TOR PB $5.99

Harvest the Fire
0-312-85943-0 TOR $19.95

Operation Chaos
0-671-72102-X BAEN PB $3.99

Orion Shall Rise
0-671-72090-2 BAEN PB $4.99

The Stars Are Also Fire
0-8125-3022-5 TOR PB $5.99

Three Hearts and Three Lions
See also **FANTASY**
0-671-72186-0 BAEN PB $4.99

The Time Patrol
0-312-85636-9 TOR PB $14.95

The Winter of the World
0-8125-2311-3 TOR PB $4.99

Poul **Anderson** & Karen **Anderson**

The King of Ys
0-671-87729-1 BAEN PB $15.00

Piers **Anthony**

Balook
0-441-00398-2 ACE PB $5.99

Chaos Mode
0-441-00132-7 ACE PB $5.99

Mercycle
0-441-52562-8 ACE PB $5.99

Vale of the Vole
9-995-68728-3 AVON PB $5.50

Robert **Asprin** & Linda **Evans**

Time Scout
0-671-87698-8 BAEN PB $5.99

Wagers of Sin
0-671-87730-5 BAEN PB $5.99

J.G. **Ballard**

The Atrocity Exhibition
See also **THE MIDDLE GENERATION** under **20TH-CENTURY BRITISH AND IRISH FICTION** in **LITERATURE OF THE BRITISH ISLES**
0-940642-18-2 V/SEARCH PB $13.99

The Drowned World
The end of civilization, along lines suggested by the title
0-88184-324-5 CARROLL & GRAF PB $3.95

Rushing to Paradise
0-312-13415-0 PICADOR PB $12.00

The Terminal Reach
0-88184-370-9 CARROLL & GRAF PB $3.50

Vermilion Sands
0-88184-422-5 CARROLL & GRAF PB $3.95

Peter S. **Beagle**

A Fine and Private Place
0-451-45096-5 NEW AMERICAN LIBRARY PB $9.00

The Innkeeper's Song
0-451-45414-6 NEW AMERICAN LIBRARY PB $11.95

The Unicorn Sonata
1-57036-288-2 TURNER $16.95

Greg **Bear**

Blood Music
0-441-00348-6 ACE PB $13.95

EON
Piles outrageous concept on outrageous concept until it reaches epic proportions
0-8125-2047-5 TOR PB $6.99

Eternity
0-446-60188-8 WARNER PB $5.99

Legacy
0-8125-2481-0 TOR PB $6.99

Moving Mars
0-8125-2480-2 TOR PB $5.99

Queen of Angels
0-446-36130-5 WARNER PB $5.99

Songs of Earth and Power
0-8125-3603-7 TOR PB $6.99

Gregory **Benford**

Benford devotes much narrative space to the laboratory and those who work in it.

Against Infinity
0-671-46491-4 SIMON & SCHUSTER $25.00

Artifact
Two antimatter black holes are loose in the earth's interior
0-312-93048-8 TOR $16.95

Foundations' Fear
0-06-105243-4 HARPER PRISM $23.00

Sailing Bright Eternity
0-553-57332-2 BDD PB $5.99

Timescape
A novel built around a complex theory of time travel involving the behavior of tachyons. The theoretical physics presents a considerable challenge to the reader
0-553-29709-0 SPECTRA PB $5.99

Gregory **Benford** & William **Rotsler**

Shiva Descending
0-8125-1690-7 TOR PB $5.99

David **Brin**

Brin writes novels as speedy and cosmic as the old pulp space operas, but with a modern sensibility and a good deal more content.

Brightness Reef
0-553-57330-6 BDD PB $6.50

Earth
An epic novel of ecological crisis and global conspiracy, by one of today's most conceptually original science fiction writers. "An outstandingly satisfying novel … Brin's exciting prose style will probably make this a Hugo nominee"—*Publishers Weekly*
0-553-29024-X SPECTRA PB $5.99

Glory Season
0-553-56767-5 BDD PB $6.50

Infinity's Shore
0-553-10173-0 SPECTRA $23.95

Otherness: Collected Stories by a Modern Master of Science Fiction
0-553-29528-4 SPECTRA PB $5.99

The Postman
A sensitive study of the revival of civilization after a nuclear war
0-553-27874-6 BDD PB $5.99

The Practice Effect
0-553-26981-X BDD PB $5.99

The River of Time
0-553-26281-5 BDD PB $5.99

Startide Rising
0-553-27418-X SPECTRA PB $5.99

Sundiver
0-553-26982-8 BDD PB $5.99

The Uplift War
Related to *Startide Rising*, although not a sequel
0-553-27971-8 BDD PB $5.99

John **Brunner**

Stand on Zanzibar
A Hugo winner
0-345-34787-0 BALLANTINE PB $5.99

Octavia E. **Butler**
"What [William] Gibson does for young, disaffected persons of high tech and low life, Octavia E. Butler does for people of color. She gives us a future."—Vibe

Adulthood Rites
0-445-20903-8 QUEST PB $5.99

Bloodchild: Novellas and Stories
To say that Butler, a Hugo and Nebula Award winner, is the inventor of a genre—African-American-feminist science fiction—might imply that her stories are ideological excercises. Instead they are riveting prose dramas that bring universal experiences to life

See also **SINCE 1945** under **20TH-CENTURY AMERICAN FICTION** in **LITERATURE OF THE AMERICAS**

1-56858-055-X FOUR WALLS $18.00
1-88836-336-3 SEVEN STORIES PB $10.00

Bloodchild is my pregnant man story. I've always wanted to explore what it might be like for a man to be put into that most unlikely of all positions. Could I write a story in which a man chose to become pregnant *not* through some sort of misplaced competitiveness to prove that a man could do anything a woman could do, not because he was forced to, not even out of curiosity? I wanted to see whether I could write a dramatic story of a man becoming pregnant as an act of love—choosing pregnancy in spite of as well as because of surrounding difficulties.
BLOODCHILD: NOVELLAS AND STORIES

Dawn
0-445-20779-5 POPULAR LIBRARY PB $5.99

Kindred
INTRODUCTION BY ROBERT CROSSLEY
0-8070-8305-4 BEACON PB $12.95

Mind of My Mind
0-446-36188-7 QUEST PB $5.99

Parable of the Sower
A young woman suffers from a hereditary trait that causes her to feel others' pain as well as her own, and is pursued by bands of drug addicted arsonists and marauders. "Butler is among the best contemporary SF writers…Her prose is lean and literate, her ideas expansive and elegant"—*The Houston Post*
0-941423-99-9 FOUR WALLS $19.95
1-88836-325-8 SEVEN STORIES $19.95
0-446-60197-7 WARNER PB $5.99

Patternmaster
0-446-36281-6 WARNER PB $5.50

Wild Seed
0-445-20537-7 QUEST PB $5.99

Orson Scott **Card**

Alvin Journeyman
0-8125-0923-4 TOR PB $6.99

The Call of the Earth
0-8125-3261-9 TOR PB $6.99

Children of the Mind
0-312-85395-5 TOR $23.95

Earthborn
0-8125-3298-8 TOR PB $6.99

Earthfall
0-8125-3296-1 FORGE PB $6.99

Ender's Game
0-8125-5070-6 TOR PB $5.99

Lost Boys
The award-winning science fiction writer here blends the natural and the supernatural in a tale of a family's search for their missing son. "Once again, Card writes superbly about children…Affecting, genuine, poignant, uplifting: a limpid, beautifully orchestrated new venture"—*Kirkus Reviews*
0-06-109131-6 HARPERCOLLINS PB $5.99

The Memory of Earth
0-8125-3259-7 TOR PB $5.99

Pastwatch
0-8125-0864-5 TOR PB $6.99

Pastwatch: The Redemption of Christopher Columbus
0-312-85058-1 TOR $23.95

Songmaster
0-8125-2486-1 TOR PB $6.99

Speaker for the Dead
0-8125-5075-7 TOR PB $5.99

Treasure Box: A Novel
0-06-017654-7 HARPERCOLLINS $24.00

The Worthing Saga
0-8125-3331-3 TOR PB $5.99

Xenocide
0-312-86187-7 TOR PB $13.95

Orson Scott **Card** & Kathryn H. **Kidd**

Lovelock
0-8125-1805-5 TOR PB $5.99

Jack L. **Chalker**

Changewinds
9-996-46331-1 BEANP PB $12.00

The Cybernetic Walrus
0-345-38847-X DEL RAY PB $5.99

Echoes of the Well of Souls
0-345-38686-8 DEL RAY PB $5.99

Exiles at the Well of Souls
0-345-32437-4 BALLANTINE PB $5.99

Horrors of the Dancing Gods
0-345-37692-7 DEL RAY PB $5.99

A Jungle of Stars
0-345-34190-2 DEL RAY PB $4.99

The March Hare Network
0-345-38848-8 DEL RAY PB $5.99

Quest for the Well of Souls
0-345-32450-1 BALLANTINE PB $5.99

Wonderland Gambit
0-345-38691-4 DEL RAY PB $11.00

C.J. **Cherryh**

Cuckoo's Egg
A human raised by aliens
0-88677-371-7 DAW PB $4.99

Invader
0-88677-638-4 DAW $19.95
0-88677-687-2 DAW PB $5.99

Hal **Clement**
Clement was the main exponent of the high-tech vein back in the '40s and has successfully extended his work along those lines.

Fossil: Isaac's Universe
0-88677-573-6 DAW PB $4.99

Mission of Gravity
0-89968-336-3 LIGHTYEAR $18.95

Ellen **Datlow**, editor

Alien Sex
Sci-fi's most outrageous authors consider the impact of extra-terrestrials on Earth's dating scene. This is sizzling short fiction from the masters of the genre
9-995-76993-X NEW AMERICAN LIBRARY PB $4.99

Samuel R. **Delany**

The Mad Man
1-56333-193-4 MASQUERADE $23.95
1-56333-408-9 MASQUERADE PB $8.99

Philip K. **Dick**
Dick's hip, hallucinogenic novels have achieved cult status since his death in 1982. From Paris to Tokyo, Philip K. Dick is increasingly regarded as the most significant modern writer of science fiction, a prolific and boldly experimental artist who transcended genre clichés.

Blade Runner
Source of the Ridley Scott film, originally published as *Do Androids Dream of Electric Sheep?*
0-345-35047-2 BALLANTINE PB $5.99

The Collected Stories of Philip K. Dick

Volume 1
The Short Happy Life of the Brown Oxford
0-8065-1153-2 CITADEL PB $12.95

Volume 2
We Can Remember It for You Wholesale
0-8065-2091-2 CITADEL PB $12.95

Volume 3
Second Variety
0-8065-1226-1 CITADEL PB $12.95

Volume 4
The Minority Report
0-8065-1276-8 CITADEL PB $12.95

Volume 5
The Eye of the Sibyl
0-8065-1328-4 CITADEL PB $12.95

Divine Invasion
0-679-73445-7 VINTAGE PB $11.00

Do Androids Dream of Electric Sheep?
0-345-40447-5 DEL RAY PB $11.00

Philip K. **Dick**

Eye in the Sky
0-02-031591-0 COLLIER PB $9.00

Galactic Pot-Healer
0-679-75297-8 VINTAGE PB $10.00

Game Players of Titan
0-679-74065-1 VINTAGE PB $11.00

The Man in the High Castle
A Hugo winner
0-679-74067-8 VINTAGE PB $12.00

Martian Time-Slip
0-679-76167-5 VINTAGE PB $10.00

A Maze of Death
0-679-75298-6 VINTAGE PB $10.00

Scanner Darkly
0-679-73665-4 VINTAGE PB $11.00

Time Out of Joint
0-88184-352-0 CARROLL & GRAF PB $4.95

The Transmigration of Timothy Archer
The last of the trilogy, based on the strange career of Bishop James Pike
0-679-73444-9 VINTAGE PB $12.00

Valis
The first volume in Dick's final trilogy
0-679-73446-5 VINTAGE PB $11.00

We Can Build You
0-679-75296-X VINTAGE PB $11.00

Paul **DiFilippo**

The Steampunk Trilogy: Victoria, Hottentots, Walt and Emily
1-56858-028-2 FOUR WALLS $20.00

Thomas M. **Disch**

Camp Concentration
0-88184-386-5 CARROLL & GRAF PB $3.95

Stephen R. **Donaldson**

Chaos and Order: The Gap into Madness
0-553-57253-9 SPECTRA PB $5.99

A Dark and Hungry God Arises: The Gap into Power
0-553-56260-6 SPECTRA PB $5.99

This Day All Gods Die: The Gap into Ruin
0-553-07180-7 BDD $22.95

Mary **Gentle**

Golden Witchbreed
Adventures of a human envoy to a complex alien culture
0-451-45016-7 NEW AMERICAN LIBRARY PB $4.95

David **Gerrold**

The Man Who Folded Himself
A man's relationships with himself at different points in time
0-88411-191-1 AMEREON $17.95

A Matter for Men
0-553-27782-0 BDD PB $5.99

William **Gibson**

"Gibson distills a technopunk sensibility with a kick of white lightning and the clarity of white light."—Village Voice

Burning Chrome
See also **SINCE 1945** under **20TH-CENTURY AMERICAN FICTION** in **LITERATURE OF THE AMERICAS**
0-441-08934-8 ACE PB $5.50

Count Zero
0-441-11773-2 ACE PB $5.99

Idoru
0-399-14130-8 PUTNAM $24.95

Johnny Mnemonic
0-441-00234-X ACE PB $12.00

Mona Lisa Overdrive
0-553-28174-7 BDD PB $5.99

Neuromancer
A Hugo and Nebula winner. "State of the art" —*Washington Post*
0-441-56959-5 ACE PB $6.50

Virtual Light
It's 2005, and in California the obscenely rich and the horribly poor live side by side in a grim dystopia. When a messenger steals a pair of "virtual light" glasses that stores secret data, a virtual reality hacker sets off to recover them—only to find that right and wrong are never simple in this surreal world. Gibson is "a genuine cultural phenomenon …one of science fiction's chief visionaries"—*Publishers Weekly*
0-553-56606-7 SPECTRA PB $6.50

William **Gibson** & Bruce **Sterling**

The Difference Engine
0-553-29461-X SPECTRA PB $5.99

Barry **Gifford**

Baby Cat-Face
0-15-100183-9 HARCOURT BRACE $20.00

Simon R. **Green**

Blue Moon Rising
0-451-45095-7 NEW AMERICAN LIBRARY PB $5.50

Deathstalker
0-451-45435-9 NEW AMERICAN LIBRARY PB $5.99

Deathstalker Rebellion
0-451-45552-5 NEW AMERICAN LIBRARY PB $5.99

Shadows Fall
0-451-45363-8 NEW AMERICAN LIBRARY PB $5.99

Joe **Haldeman**

The Forever War
0-380-70821-3 AVON PB $4.99

Frank **Herbert**

Dune
The first volume of an enormously successful series about an interstellar empire
0-441-17271-7 ACE PB $6.99

Dune Messiah
0-441-17269-5 ACE PB $6.50

God Emperor of Dune
See also **THE '80S** under **THE GREAT FICTION BESTSELLERS 1930-1995**
0-441-29467-7 ACE PB $6.99

Frank Herbert (photo by Andrew Unangst)

Dean **Koontz** & Robert **Silverberg**

Santa's Twin
0-06-105355-4 HARPER PRISM $20.00

Keith **Laumer**

The Unconquerable
0-671-87629-5 BAEN PB $5.99

Keith **Laumer** & David **Weber**

The Triumphant
0-671-87683-X POCKET PB $5.99

Ursula K. **Le Guin**

With 15 novels, 60 short stories, poetry, children's books, criticism, and screenplays to her name—as well as a National Book Award—Le Guin is the preeminent science fiction writer in America, as well as a major literary voice transcending genre classifications.

Buffalo Gals, Won't You Come Out Tonight?
0-87654-071-X POMEGRANATE $16.95

The Compass Rose
0-06-105607-3 HARPERCOLLINS PB $4.99

The Dispossessed
A complex study of political conflict in the future
0-06-100137-6 HARPERCOLLINS PB $4.50

A Fisherman of the Inland Sea: Science Fiction Stories
0-06-105200-0 HARPER PRISM $19.99
0-06-105491-7 HARPERCOLLINS PB $4.99

Four Ways to Forgiveness
Four interlinked novellas from the only science fiction writer ever to win the National Book Award. Creating a nightmare world of slaves and owners, Le Guin studies the surprising and delicate forms that freedom can take: love, learning, compassion, courage
0-06-105234-5 HARPER PRISM $20.00
0-06-105401-1 HARPER PRISM PB $5.99

The Lathe of Heaven
0-380-01320-7 AVON PB $5.50

The Left Hand of Darkness
In this Hugo and Nebula winner, Le Guin hypothesizes a hermaphroditic society and says some pertinent things about sexism along the way
0-8027-1302-5 WALKER $27.50

Searoad: Chronicles of Klatsand
0-06-105400-3 HARPERCOLLINS PB $4.99

Tehanu: The Last Book of Earthsea
This is billed as the last volume of Le Guin's long-running Earthsea fantasy, although *The New Yorker* notes: "Le Guin has always challenged assumptions about sex and politics in her science fiction, but her fantasy has followed more closely the conventions of Tolkien and Lewis. Here, however, like her heroine, the author reexamines the tenets of her world … It seems unthinkable that LeGuin would now abandon this world so newly rich with possibility"
0-553-28873-3 SPECTRA PB $5.99

Unlocking the Air and Other Stories
"Lyric and luminous.…A major imaginative vision"—*NY Times Book Review*. "Le Guin fashions ideas like a goldsmith; intricate, involved, and confident"—*Chicago Daily News*
0-06-017260-6 HARPERCOLLINS $22.00

Worlds of Exile and Illusion
0-312-86211-3 ST. MARTIN'S PB $14.95

Ursula K. **Le Guin** & Brian **Attebury**, editors

The Norton Book of Science Fiction
0-393-03546-8 NORTON $27.50

Gentry **Lee**

Bright Messengers
0-553-57329-2 BDD PB $6.50

Stanislaw **Lem**

The prolific Lem is an internationally renowned writer of science fiction with a strong philosophical dimension.

The Cyberiad: Fables for the Cybernetic Age
Robots roam the cosmos creating beasts and machines
See also POLISH LITERATURE under EASTERN EUROPEAN LITERATURE in LITERATURE OF EUROPE, AFRICA, AND ASIA
TRANSLATED BY MICHAEL KENDAL
0-15-623550-1 HARCOURT BRACE PB $9.00

Eden
TRANSLATED BY MARC E. HEINE
0-15-627806-5 HARCOURT BRACE PB $12.00

Solaris
A Polish masterpiece: planet as intelligent organism
0-15-683750-1 HARCOURT BRACE PB $9.00

Julian **May**

May's four-volume "Saga of Pleistocene Exile" incorporates time travel, space travel, alien cultures, telepathy, psi powers, and the birth of the Mediterranean in a grand potpourri of SF themes.

The Adversary
0-345-35244-0 DEL RAY PB $5.99
0-345-31422-0 DEL RAY PB $4.95

The Golden Torc
0-345-32419-6 BALLANTINE PB $5.99

The Many-Colored Land
0-345-32444-7 BALLANTINE PB $5.99

The Nonborn King
0-345-34749-8 BALLANTINE PB $5.95

Anne **McCaffrey**

The Crystal Singer Trilogy
0-345-40292-8 DEL RAY PB $16.00

Dragonflight
The first of a series involving benign aliens
0-345-33546-5 BALLANTINE PB $5.95

Robyn **Miller** & Rand **Miller**

MYST: The Book of Atrus
0-7868-6159-2 HYPERION $22.95
0-7868-8188-7 WARNER PB $5.99

Naomi **Mitchison**

Solution Three
AFTERWORD BY SUSAN M. SQUIER
1-55861-096-0 FEMINIST PRESS $10.95

Larry **Niven**

Crashlander
0-345-38168-8 DEL RAY PB $4.99

Flatlander
0-345-39480-1 DEL RAY PB $5.99

The Integral Trees
Posits a colony of gigantic trees that exist in deep space, creating an environment in which other living things can exist: a world without a world, as it were
0-345-32065-4 BALLANTINE PB $5.99

The Man-Kzin Wars I
0-671-72076-7 BAEN PB $5.99

The Man-Kzin Wars II
0-671-72036-8 BAEN PB $5.99

Man-Kzin Wars III
0-671-72008-2 BAEN PB $5.99

Man-Kzin Wars IV
0-671-87607-4 BAEN PB $5.99

Man-Kzin Wars V
0-671-87670-8 BAEN PB $5.99

The Mote in God's Eye
Warfare with an alien race
0-671-74192-6 POCKET PB $5.99

Neutron Star
0-345-33694-1 BALLANTINE PB $5.99

Ringworld
0-345-33392-6 BALLANTINE PB $5.99

The Ringworld Throne
0-345-35861-9 BALLANTINE $23.00

Three Books of Known Space
0-345-40448-3 DEL RAY PB $12.95

Larry **Niven** & Jerry **Pournelle**

Niven has a flair for outrageous ideas neatly supported by science.

Footfall
Invading aliens launch an asteroid at Earth
0-345-32344-0 DEL RAY PB $6.99

Larry **Niven** & others

Beowulf's Children
0-8125-2496-9 TOR PB $6.99

Jeff **Noon**

Automated Alice
See also LATE ARRIVALS in LITERATURE OF THE BRITISH ISLES
0-517-70490-0 CROWN $21.00

Pollen
0-517-59990-2 CROWN $23.00

Vurt
Drug of the future is a hallucination-inducing feather in the cyberpunk fantasia
0-312-14144-0 ST. MARTIN'S PB $13.95

George **Orwell**

1984
Orwell's bleak 1948 vision of a totalitarian England under Big Brother
See also CLASSICS under POLITICAL THOUGHT in SOCIAL STUDIES
See also THE EARLY 20TH CENTURY under 20TH-CENTURY BRITISH AND IRISH FICTION in LITERATURE OF THE BRITISH ISLES
84-233-0983-5 DESTINO PB $15.50
0-452-26293-3 NEW AMERICAN LIBRARY PB $11.95
0-451-52493-4 NEW AMERICAN LIBRARY PB $4.95

Frederik **Pohl**

Gateway
A Nebula winner
0-345-34690-4 BALLANTINE PB $5.99

Jerry **Pournelle**

Janissaries
Future mercenaries
0-671-87709-7 BAEN PB $5.99

Joanna **Russ**

The Female Man
0-8070-6313-4 FS&G PB $11.00

Robert **Silverberg**

The Face of the Waters
0-553-29907-7 SPECTRA PB $5.99

Letters from Atlantis
0-446-36286-7 QUEST PB $4.99

Lord Valentine's Castle
0-06-105487-9 HARPERCOLLINS PB $5.99

Majipoor Chronicles
0-06-105485-2 HARPERCOLLINS PB $5.99

New Springtime
0-446-36172-0 WARNER PB $4.95

Sorcerers of Majipoor
0-06-105254-X HARPER PRISM $23.00

Starborne
0-553-10264-8 SPECTRA $22.95

Robert **Silverberg**
To the Land of the Living
0-445-20844-9 QUEST PB $4.95

Alison **Sinclair**
Legacies
0-06-105699-5 HARPER PRISM PB $5.50

Bruce **Sterling**, editor
Mirrorshades: The Cyberpunk Anthology
0-441-53382-5 ACE PB $5.50

James **Tiptree**, Jr.
Brightness Falls from the Air
A weekend house-party murder mystery on another planet
0-312-85407-2 ST. MARTIN'S PB $9.95

John **Varley**
Millennium
0-441-53183-0 ACE PB $4.99

Gene **Wolfe**
Lake of the Long Sun
0-312-85494-3 TOR $22.95
0-8125-5068-4 TOR PB $5.99

Fantasy

Fantasy encompasses allegory, surrealism, erotica, fairy tales, science fiction, and almost anything else its creators can dream up. One flourishing subgenre—variously characterized as "pure fantasy," "sword and sorcery," and "high fantasy"—owes much to J.R.R. Tolkien's Middle Earth chronicles, with their elaborately detailed, adult-oriented depiction of a world of working magic and mythical creatures.

Poul **Anderson**
Three Hearts and Three Lions
See also **CONTEMPORARY SCIENCE FICTION**
0-671-72186-0 BAEN PB $4.99

Piers **Anthony**
Demons Don't Dream
0-8125-3483-2 TOR PB $5.99

For Love of Evil
0-380-75285-9 AVON PB $5.99

Geis of the Gargoyle
0-8125-3485-9 TOR PB $5.99

Isle of View
0-380-75947-0 AVON PB $5.50

Isle of Woman
0-312-85564-8 TOR $23.95

Letters to Jenny
0-8125-2282-6 TOR PB $4.99

Night Mare
0-345-35493-1 BALLANTINE PB $5.95

Ogre, Ogre
0-345-35492-3 BALLANTINE PB $5.95

Roc and a Hard Place
0-8125-3486-7 TOR PB $5.99

Shame of Man
0-8125-5091-9 FORGE PB $5.99

Tales from the Great Turtle
0-8125-3490-5 FORGE PB $5.99

Yon Ill Wind
0-312-86227-X TOR $23.95

Piers **Anthony** & Robert **Kornwise**
Through the Ice
0-671-72113-5 BAEN PB $5.99

Robert **Asprin**
Another Fine Myth
0-441-02362-2 ACE PB $4.99

Myth Conceptions
0-441-55521-7 ACE PB $5.50

Phule's Paradise
0-441-66253-6 ACE PB $5.50

Sweet Myth-Tery of Life
0-441-00194-7 ACE PB $5.50

Robert L. **Asprin**
M.Y.T.H. Inc. in Action
0-441-55282-X ACE PB $5.50

Peter S. **Beagle**
The Last Unicorn
Odd, fey odyssey of the last of the species
0-451-45052-3 NEW AMERICAN LIBRARY PB $9.95

Marion Zimmer **Bradley**
Adept at every form of light entertainment from science fiction to fantasy romance, Bradley turns to the ancient myths of the fall of Troy and the legends of Arthurian Britain.

The Bloody Sun: A Novel of Darkover
0-88677-603-1 DAW PB $4.99

Exile's Song: A Novel of Darkover
0-88677-705-4 DAW $21.95

The Firebrand
See also **HISTORICAL AND ROMANTIC FICTION**
0-671-74406-2 POCKET PB $6.99

The Forest House
Returning to the territory of her bestselling *The Mists of Avalon,* Bradley delivers a brilliant historical fantasy. Eilan, the future high priestess of the Druids, must choose between her religious calling and her love for a Roman soldier who is occupying her land and destroying its ancient ways. Myth, magic, romance, and history in a uniquely compelling historical fiction
0-451-45424-3 NEW AMERICAN LIBRARY PB $14.95

Free Amazons of Darkover
0-88677-430-6 DAW PB $3.95

Ghostlight
0-312-86218-0 TOR PB $13.95

Glenraven
0-671-87738-0 BAEN $23.00

The Heirs of Hammerfell
0-88677-451-9 DAW PB $4.99

The Heritage of Hastur
0-88677-413-6 DAW PB $4.99

The Inheritor
0-312-86293-8 TOR $25.01

The Keeper's Price
0-88677-236-2 DAW PB $3.99

Lady of the Trillium
0-553-57263-6 SPECTRA PB $5.99

Leroni of Darkover
0-88677-494-2 DAW PB $4.99

The Mists of Avalon
The Arthurian saga from the viewpoint of the women in the legends
0-345-35049-9 DEL RAY PB $14.00

The Other Side of the Mirror
0-88677-185-4 DAW PB $4.50

Rediscovery : A Novel of Darkover
0-88677-529-9 NEW AMERICAN LIBRARY PB $4.99

Sharra's Exile
0-88677-309-1 DAW PB $4.99

Snows of Darkover
0-88677-601-5 DAW PB $4.99

Star of Danger
0-88677-607-4 DAW PB $4.99

The Winds of Darkover & The Planet Savers
0-88677-630-9 DAW PB $4.99

Witchlight
0-312-86104-4 ST. MARTIN'S $23.95

The World Wreckers
0-88677-629-5 DAW PB $4.99

Terry **Brooks**
The Black Unicorn
0-345-33528-7 BALLANTINE PB $6.99

The Druid of Shannara
0-345-37559-9 DEL RAY PB $6.99

The Elf Queen of Shannara
0-345-37558-0 DEL RAY PB $6.99

Elfstones of Shannara
0-345-90956-9 DEL RAY PB $7.99

First King of Shannara
0-345-39652-9 DEL RAY $23.50

The Scions of Shannara
0-345-37074-0 DEL RAY PB $6.99

Sword of Shannara
0-345-31425-5 BALLANTINE PB $6.99

The Talismans of Shannara
0-345-38674-4 DEL RAY PB $6.99

The Tangle Box
0-345-38700-7 BALLANTINE PB $6.99

The Wishsong of Shannara
0-345-35636-5 BALLANTINE PB $6.99

Witches' Brew
0-345-38702-3 DEL RAY PB $6.99

Edgar Rice **Burroughs**

Tarzan of the Apes
0-14-018464-3 PENGUIN PB $8.95

C.J. **Cherryh**

The Dreamstone
An evocation of the fairy folk of Ireland

0-88677-013-0 DAW PB $2.95

Nicholas **Christopher**

Nicholas Christopher was born in New York City in 1951 and is a graduate of Harvard College. He received a Guggenheim Fellowship for 1993-94 and currently lives in New York City, where he teaches seminars and classes at a variety of arts organizations and universities.

Veronica
"Christopher has conjured a magical Borgesian realm where the vectors of history align and synchronism reigns, where the hard-boiled detective novel meets *The Tibetan Book of the Dead* and the English School of Night, where time is a door continually opening and closing"—Edward Hirsch

0-385-31471-X BDD $22.95

Louise **Cooper**

Aisling
0-8125-0808-4 TOR PB $4.99

Avatar
0-8125-0802-5 TOR PB $4.99

Inferno
0-8125-0246-9 TOR PB $3.95

Revenant
0-8125-0807-6 TOR PB $4.99

Star Ascendant
0-8125-5175-3 TOR PB $6.99

Troika
0-8125-0799-1 TOR PB $4.50

L. Sprague **De Camp** & Fletcher **Pratt**

The Compleat Enchanter
Adventures in alternate worlds based on *The Faerie Queen*, Norse mythology, and other sources

0-671-69809-5 BAEN PB $5.99

Tom **Deitz**

Above the Lower Sky
0-380-77483-6 AVON PB $5.99

The Demons in the Green
0-380-78271-5 AVON PB $5.99

Dreamseeker's Road
0-380-77484-4 AVON PB $5.99

Fireshaper's Doom
0-380-75329-4 AVON PB $3.95

Ghostcountry's Wrath
0-380-76838-0 AVON PB $5.50

Windmaster's Bane
0-380-75029-5 AVON PB $4.99

David **Eddings**

Pawn of Prophecy
First of "The Belgariad," a series of five novels

0-345-33551-1 BALLANTINE PB $6.99

Jack **Finney**

Time and Again
Wonderfully researched time travel back to New York City in 1880

See also **SUPERNATURAL FANTASY AND HORROR**

0-684-80117-5 SIMON & SCHUSTER $25.00
0-684-80105-1 SCRIBNERS PB $12.00

From Time to Time
The sequal to *Time and Again*

See also **SINCE 1945** under **20TH-CENTURY AMERICAN FICTION** in **LITERATURE OF THE AMERICAS**

0-684-81844-2 SCRIBNERS PB $12.00

Barbara **Hambly**

The Time of the Dark
0-345-31965-6 BALLANTINE PB $5.99

Diana W. **Jones**

Howl's Moving Castle
9-992-03742-3 MORROW LIBRARY EDITION $5.00

Guy G. **Kay**

The Summer Tree
The first of a series

0-451-45138-4 NEW AMERICAN LIBRARY PB $5.99

Richard **Knaak**

The Legend of Huma
0-88038-548-0 RANDOM HOUSE PB $5.99

Richard A. **Knaak**

The Crystal Dragon
0-446-36432-0 QUEST PB $4.99

The Dragon Crown
0-446-36464-9 QUEST PB $5.50

Dutchman
0-446-60151-9 WARNER PB $5.99

Frostwing
0-446-60149-7 WARNER PB $5.99

The Janus Mask
0-446-60150-0 WARNER PB $5.99

King of the Grey
0-446-36463-0 QUEST PB $5.50

Katherine **Kurtz**

The Adept
0-441-00343-5 ACE PB $5.99

The Bastard Prince
0-345-39177-2 DEL RAY PB $5.99

Death of an Adept
0-441-00367-2 ACE $21.95

Deryni Rising
The first of an ongoing series

0-345-34763-3 BALLANTINE PB $5.99

The Lodge of the Lynx
0-441-00344-3 ACE PB $5.99

Tales of the Knights of Templar
0-446-60138-1 WARNER PB $5.50

Keith **Laumer**

The Compleat Bolo
0-671-69879-6 BAEN PB $4.99

Stephen R. **Lawhead**

Arthur
0-310-20507-7 ZONDERVAN PB $13.00

Byzantium
0-06-017604-0 ZONDERVAN $24.00

Dream Thief
0-310-20552-2 ZONDERVAN PB $11.00

Endless Knot
0-380-71648-8 AVON PB $5.99

The Paradise War
0-380-71646-1 AVON PB $5.99

Pendragon
0-380-71757-3 AVON PB $5.99

Taliesin
0-380-70613-X AVON PB $6.50

Patricia A. **McKillip**

McKillip's "Riddle-Master" novels are on a smaller scale than many works in the genre: they might be described as "chamber fantasies."

Harpist in the Wind
0-345-32440-4 BALLANTINE PB $5.99

Heir of Sea and Fire
0-345-35184-3 BALLANTINE PB $5.99

Michael **Moorcock**

The Bane of the Black Sword
0-441-04885-4 ACE PB $4.99

Blood: A Southern Fantasy
0-380-78078-X AVON PB $12.00
0-88677-410-1 DAW PB $4.50

Elric of Melnibone
The first of a complex series

0-441-20398-1 ACE PB $4.99

The Sailor on the Seas of Fate
0-441-74863-5 BERKLEY PB $4.99

Stormbringer
0-441-78754-1 ACE PB $4.99

The Vanishing Tower
0-441-86039-7 BERKLEY PB $4.99

The Weird of the White Wolf
0-441-88805-4 ACE PB $4.99

Andre **Norton**

Golden Trillium
0-553-56095-6 SPECTRA PB $5.99

The Hands of Lyr
0-380-77097-0 AVON PB $5.50

Andre **Norton**

Mirror of Destiny

0-380-77976-5 AVON PB $5.99

The Warding of Witch World

0-446-51991-X WARNER $22.95

Andre **Norton** & Mercedes **Lackey**

Elvenblood

0-8125-6319-0 TOR PB $5.99

Andre **Norton** & Susan **Shwartz**

Empire of the Eagle

0-8125-1393-2 TOR PB $5.99

Mervyn **Peake**

The Gormenghast Trilogy

An extraordinary mix of the Gothic and the Dickensian

See also **THE MIDDLE GENERATION** under **20TH-CENTURY BRITISH AND IRISH FICTION** in **LITERATURE OF THE BRITISH ISLES**

INTRODUCTION BY ANTHONY BURGESS

0-87951-628-3 OVERLOOK PB $23.95

Terry **Pratchett**

Feet of Clay: A Novel of Discworld

0-06-105250-7 HARPER PRISM $20.00

Lords and Ladies: A Novel of Discworld

0-06-105692-8 HARPERCOLLINS PB $5.99

Wyrd Sisters

0-451-45012-4 NEW AMERICAN LIBRARY PB $5.99

Tom **Shippey**, editor

The Oxford Book of Fantasy Stories

Trolls, werewolves, spells, and sorcerers: from H.P Lovecraft to Angela Carter, Shippey's selection is an invaluable introduction and an unparalleled overview of a compelling and popular literary form. "Offers insights into the breadth of the field, its historical development, and its many beauties"—*Publishers Weekly*

0-19-214216-X OXFORD $30.00

0-19-282398-1 OXFORD PB $14.95

Nancy **Springer**

Fair Peril

0-380-78413-0 AVON PB $12.00

Larque on the Wing

0-380-97234-4 AVON PB $10.00

Rosemary **Sutcliff**

Sword at Sunset

Virtuoso transformation of the legend of Arthur into the historical reality of a Roman-trained Briton trying to save the remnants of Mediterranean civilization from the northern barbarians

See also **HISTORICAL AND ROMANTIC FICTION**

0-8125-8852-5 TOR PB $4.50

J.R.R. **Tolkien**

The Fellowship of the Ring

The first of *The Lord of The Rings* trilogy, which includes *The Two Towers* and *The Return of the King*

0-345-33970-3 BALLANTINE PB $5.99

The Hobbit

Prelude to *The Lord of the Rings*

0-345-33968-1 BALLANTINE PB $5.99

The Lays of Beleriand

0-345-38818-6 DEL RAY PB $5.99

The Lost Road and Other Writings

0-345-40685-0 DEL RAY PB $6.99

Morgoth's Ring

EDITED BY CHRISTOPHER TOLKIEN

0-395-68092-1 TICKNOR & FIELDS $29.95

J. R. R. Tolkien

The Peoples of Middle-Earth

EDITED BY CHRISTOPHER TOLKIEN

0-395-82760-4 HOUGHTON MIFFLIN $27.95

The Return of the King

0-345-33973-8 BALLANTINE PB $5.99

The Two Towers

0-345-33971-1 BALLANTINE PB $5.99

The War of the Jewels

EDITED BY CHRISTOPHER TOLKIEN

0-395-71041-3 HOUGHTON MIFFLIN $27.95

T.H. **White**

The Once and Future King

This retelling of King Arthur was the basis for *Camelo,* and contains fascinating information about living in the Middle Ages

See also **YOUNG ADULT FICTION** in **BOOKS FOR YOUNG READERS**

See also **BRITISH AND CELTIC** under **EUROPEAN MYTHOLOGY** under **MYTHOLOGY AND FOLKLORE** in **RELIGION, SPIRITUALITY, AND PHILOSOPHY**

0-441-62740-4 ACE PB $6.99

Roger **Zelazny**

Nine Princes in Amber

First of the "Amber" series

0-380-01430-0 AVON PB $4.99

Supernatural Fantasy and Horror

Clive **Barker**

The Books of Blood

Stories by a writer praised for the originality of his horrific visions

0-425-08389-6 BERKLEY PB $5.99

Weaveworld

Barker's first novel

0-671-70418-4 POCKET PB $6.99

Algernon **Blackwood**

Best Ghost Stories of Algernon Blackwood

The best of Blackwood's classic tales, such as *The Willows,* can still frighten

0-486-22977-7 DOVER PB $8.95

Jack **Finney**

Time and Again

Wonderfully researched time travel back to New York City in 1880

See also **FANTASY**

See also **SINCE 1945**

0-684-80117-5 SIMON & SCHUSTER $25.00

0-684-80105-1 SCRIBNERS PB $12.00

M.R. **James**

Ghost Stories of an Antiquary

Contains such classics as *Casting the Runes,* by the master of the traditional English ghost story

0-486-22758-8 DOVER PB $4.95

Stephen **King**

The Bachman Books: Four Early Novels

0-452-27775-2 PLUME PB $15.95

Carrie

King's first novel, about a telepathic girl tormented by her high school classmates, has entered American mythology

0-385-08695-4 DOUBLEDAY $25.00

0-451-15744-3 NEW AMERICAN LIBRARY PB $6.99

Christine

0-670-22026-4 VIKING $27.95

0-451-16044-4 NEW AMERICAN LIBRARY PB $6.99

Cujo

0-670-45193-2 VIKING $27.95

0-451-16135-1 NEW AMERICAN LIBRARY PB $6.99

The Dark Half

0-670-82982-X VIKING $27.95

0-451-16731-7 SIGNET PB $6.99

The Dead Zone

An ingenious novel of clairvoyance and political anxiety: an unwilling prophet is driven to become an assassin

0-451-15575-0 NEW AMERICAN LIBRARY PB $6.99

Desperation

0-670-86836-1 VIKING $27.95

Desperation/The Regulators

0-670-77605-X VIKING $52.90

Dolores Claiborne

King's explosive story of murder and mother love is told in the fierce, ornery, compelling voice of a Maine woman accused of killing her senile employer

0-670-84452-7 VIKING $23.50
0-451-17709-6 SIGNET PB $6.99

Stephen King

Firestarter

0-670-31541-9 VIKING $29.95
0-451-16780-5 NEW AMERICAN LIBRARY PB $6.99

Gerald's Game

When a round of "Gerald's game" leaves Gerald dead and his wife handcuffed to a bed, the stage is set for King to go to work. "One of the best-written stories King has ever published" —*Kirkus Reviews*

0-8317-2752-7 SMITHMARK $6.98

The Green Mile

0-451-19057-2 NEW AMERICAN LIBRARY PB $3.99

Insomnia

Insomnia explores the nighttime hallucinations of Ralph Roberts following the death of his wife. Thing is, can they be hallucinations when his neighbor shares them? Another irresistible visit to a small town in Maine, guided by the sure and practiced hand of the horrormeister himself

0-670-85503-0 VIKING $27.95
0-451-18496-3 SIGNET PB $7.50

It

0-451-16951-4 NEW AMERICAN LIBRARY PB $6.99

Misery

A fan's revenge on an uncooperative novelist

0-670-81364-8 VIKING $25.00
0-451-16952-2 NEW AMERICAN LIBRARY PB $6.99

Needful Things

A huge cast and multiple story lines are entwined in a terror-filled soap opera that, this time, ends in true holocaust

0-8317-7841-5 SMITHMARK $7.98
0-670-83953-1 VIKING $24.95
0-451-17281-7 SIGNET PB $6.99

Night Shift

0-385-12991-2 DOUBLEDAY $25.00
0-451-17011-3 SIGNET PB $6.99

Nightmares & Dreamscapes

Terror and suspense abound in this collection of 23 previously uncollected stories

0-670-85108-6 VIKING $27.50

Pet Sematary

0-385-18244-9 DOUBLEDAY $25.00
9-995-20865-2 NEW AMERICAN LIBRARY PB $6.99

Rose Madder

A woman, pursued by her unbalanced husband, flees a miserable existence, to start a new life

0-670-85869-2 VIKING $25.95
0-451-18636-2 SIGNET PB $7.50

Salem's Lot

0-385-00751-5 DOUBLEDAY $25.00
0-451-16808-9 NEW AMERICAN LIBRARY PB $6.99

The Shining

0-385-12167-9 DOUBLEDAY $25.00
0-451-16091-6 NEW AMERICAN LIBRARY PB $6.99

The Stand

Stephen King's epic novel of apocalypse and its aftermath, considered by many to be his masterpiece; this version restores hundreds of pages deleted from the first edition

0-385-19957-0 DOUBLEDAY $34.95

The Tommyknockers

0-451-15660-9 NEW AMERICAN LIBRARY PB $6.99

T.E. **Klein**

The Ceremonies

0-670-20982-1 VIKING $16.95

Dean **Koontz**

3 Complete Novels: The House of Thunder, Shadowfires, Midnight

0-399-14125-1 PUTNAM $12.98

Dark Rivers of the Heart

A man and a woman meet in a bar; the woman is being hunted by a clandestine intelligence agency; the man is mistaken as her partner, and the chase generates the kind of suspense of which Koontz is a master

0-679-42524-1 KNOPF $24.00
0-345-39657-X BALLANTINE PB $7.99

The Eyes of Darkness

0-425-15397-5 BERKLEY PB $7.50

Intensity

0-679-42525-X KNOPF $25.00
0-345-38436-9 BALLANTINE PB $7.99

Lightning

0-425-11580-1 BERKLEY PB $7.50

Phantoms

0-425-10145-2 BERKLEY PB $7.50

The Servants of Twilight

0-425-12125-9 BERKLEY PB $7.50

Strange Highways

0-446-60339-2 WARNER PB $6.99

Strangers

0-425-11992-0 BERKLEY PB $7.50

Tick Tock: A Novel

0-345-38430-X BALLANTINE PB $7.99

Twilight Eyes

0-425-10065-0 BERKLEY PB $6.99

The Vision

0-425-09860-5 BERKLEY PB $7.50

The Voice of the Night

0-425-12816-4 BERKLEY PB $7.50

Watchers

0-425-10746-9 BERKLEY PB $7.50

Joseph Sheridan **Le Fanu**

"He took great pleasure in ghost stories, and was fascinated by hints of the supernatural…He was a writer of remarkable power in creating suspense, at his best a master of plot, and the creator of some of the most satisfying villains in Victorian literature."—Julian Symons

Best Ghost Stories

Includes "Carmilla" (one of the best—and most erotic—of vampire stories) and the brief shocker "Green Tea," among others

See also **19TH-CENTURY FICTION** under **THE 19TH CENTURY** in **LITERATURE OF THE BRITISH ISLES**

EDITED BY E.F. BLEILER

0-486-20415-4 DOVER PB $8.95

Ghost Stories & Mysteries

EDITED WITH AN INTRODUCTION BY E.F. BLEILER

0-486-20715-3 DOVER PB $8.95

In a Glass Darkly

Le Fanu's most famous collection of supernatural tales

0-86299-379-2 ALAN SUTTON PB $6.00

Fritz **Leiber**

Conjure Wife/Our Lady of Darkness

This famous novel of witchcraft on campus has been filmed many times

0-8125-1296-0 TOR PB $4.99

H.P. **Lovecraft**

Lovecraft's stories are still quite hair-raising, despite, or perhaps because of, their unrestrained purple prose.

At the Mountains of Madness & Other Tales of Terror

0-345-32945-7 BALLANTINE PB $5.99

The Best of H.P. Lovecraft

0-345-35080-4 DEL RAY PB $10.00

The Case of Charles Dexter Ward

Necromancy in New England: one of Lovecraft's most coherent and frightening works

0-345-35490-7 BALLANTINE PB $5.99

The Doom that Came to Sarnath

0-345-33105-2 BALLANTINE PB $5.99

The Dream Cycle of H.P. Lovecraft: Dreams of Terror and Death

0-345-38421-0 DEL RAY PB $10.00

H.P. **Lovecraft**

The Dream-Quest of Unknown Kadath

0-345-33779-4 BALLANTINE PB $5.99

The Horror in the Museum

0-7867-0387-3 CARROLL & GRAF $4.95

The Lurking Fear & Other Stories

0-345-32604-0 BALLANTINE PB $5.99

The Watchers Out of Time

0-88184-769-0 CARROLL & GRAF PB $4.95

Alison **Lurie**

Women and Ghosts

0-385-47392-3 DOUBLEDAY $21.00
0-380-72501-0 AVON PB $9.00

Alison Lurie

Anne **Rice**

The chronicler of the millenia-old society and the personal lives of vampires can also focus her baroque sensibility on the castrati of the Venetian opera or the mores of decadent New Orleans families.

Lasher

The story of Rowan Mayfair—queen of the Coven—and her flight, with their child, from her onetime lover, the demon Lasher. Rice's fictional universe encompasses the globe and moves through time in this story of the human and the demonic, of occult fears and passions

0-679-41295-6 KNOPF $25.00
0-345-37764-8 BALLANTINE PB $14.00

Memnoch the Devil

0-345-38940-9 BALLANTINE PB $14.00

The Queen of the Damned

The third of Rice's bestselling vampire chronicles

See also THE '80S under THE GREAT FICTION BESTSELLERS 1930–1995

0-345-35152-5 BALLANTINE PB $6.99

The Tale of the Body Thief

The Vampire Lestat wants to commit suicide, but he has lent his body to a con man who won't give it back. More dark, delicious fun from the incurable queen of macabre. "Her most inspired pages ever"—*Kirkus Reviews*

0-679-40528-3 KNOPF $24.00
0-517-11710-X RANDOM HOUSE $6.99
0-345-38475-X BALLANTINE PB $6.99

Anne Rice (credit: ©Victoria Rouse)

Taltos

0-679-42573-X KNOPF $25.00
0-345-40431-9 BALLANTINE PB $6.99

Dan **Simmons**

Lovedeath

"I am in awe of Dan Simmons," said Stephen King after reading this World Fantasy Award winner's formidable fiction. "Writing of an unhackneyed freshness seldom found among the kings and queens of gore…Enduring stuff" —*Kirkus Reviews*.
"Dan Simmons is brilliant"—Dean Koontz

0-446-60077-6 WARNER PB $5.99

Bram **Stoker**

Dracula

The definitive literary incarnation of the undead
EDITED BY A.N. WILSON

0-19-281598-9 OXFORD PB $4.95

Dracula

0-89375-782-9 TROLL PB $2.95

The Jewel of Seven Stars

0-19-283219-0 OXFORD PB $8.95

Midnight Tales

Twelve Victorian stories about the gruesome, the macabre, and the strange
EDITED BY PETER HAINING

0-7206-0971-2 DUFOUR PB $22.95

Peter **Straub**

Floating Dragon

0-425-09725-0 BERKLEY PB $6.99

Ghost Story

0-671-68563-5 POCKET PB $6.99

The Hellfire Club

0-679-40137-7 RANDOM HOUSE $25.95

Koko

0-451-16214-5 SIGNET PB $6.99

Shadowland

0-425-09726-9 BERKLEY PB $6.99

The Throat

0-451-17918-8 SIGNET PB $6.99

Peter **Straub**, editor

Peter Straub's Ghosts

0-671-88599-5 POCKET PB $5.99

James **Tiptree**, Jr.

Tales of the Quintana Roo

ILLUSTRATED BY GLENNRAY TUTOR

0-87054-152-8 ARKHAM $11.95

Dennis **Wheatley**

The Devil Rides Out

0-7493-2491-0 R.B.H.P. PB $6.99

The Haunting of Toby Jugg

0-7493-2496-1 R.B.H.P. PB $6.99

Strange Conflict

0-7493-2486-4 R.B.H.P. PB $6.99

Dennis **Wheatly**

The Ka of Gifford Hillary

0-7493-2402-3 R.B.H.P. PB $6.99

Anthologies

Jack **Adrian**, editor

Strange Tales from the Strand

0-19-212305-X OXFORD $22.95
0-19-282997-1 OXFORD PB $13.95

Nina **Auerbach** & U.C. **Knoepflmacher**, editors

Forbidden Journeys: Fairy Tales and Fantasies by Victorian Women Writers

0-226-03203-5 CHICAGO $31.95
0-226-03204-3 CHICAGO PB $11.95

Chris **Baldick**, editor

The Oxford Book of Gothic Tales

This collection of horror, suspense, and moody doom includes works by Edgar Allan Poe, Thomas Hardy, William Faulkner, Arthur Conan Doyle, as well as Joyce Carol Oates, Jorge Luis Borges, Isak Dinesen, and Isabelle Allende. "A sumptuous spread of eeriness, horror, and decay"—*The Sunday Times* [London]

0-19-283117-8 OXFORD PB $14.95

Everett F. **Bleiler**, editor

Five Victorian Ghost Novels

Includes Riddell's *The Uninhabited House,* Meinhold's *The Amber Witch,* Edwards's *Monsieur Maurice,* Lee's *The Phantom Laper,* and Beale's *The Ghost of Guir House*

0-486-22558-5 DOVER PB $8.95

Michael A. **Cox** & R.A. **Gilbert**, editors

The Oxford Book of English Ghost Stories

0-19-282666-2 OXFORD PB $13.95

Victorian Ghost Stories: An Oxford Anthology

The late 19th and early 20th centuries were the heyday of the English supernatural tale, and this collection offers a trove of chilling classics from Robert Louis Stevenson, Rudyard Kipling, Arthur Conan Doyle, Henry James, M.R. James, J.S. LeFanu, and other masters of the genre, including many hitherto neglected women writers such as Mrs. Henry Wood, Amelia B. Edwards, Charlotte Riddell, and Mrs. Craik

0-19-214202-X OXFORD $30.00

Richard **Dalby**, editor

Victorian Ghost Stories

0-88184-473-X CARROLL & GRAF $18.95

Italo **Calvino**, editor

Fantastical Tales

The late modern Italian master (*Invisible Cities, If on a Winter's Night a Traveler*) counts these tales among the most significant products of the 19th-century. Includes work by Balzac, Walter Scott, Gogol, Hawthorne, and others, whose supernatural fictions, Calvino says, speak to us "like the rebellion of the unconscious." "Calvino possesses the power of seeing into the deepest recesses of human minds and then bringing their dreams to life"—Salman Rushdie

See also FICTION ANTHOLOGIES under WORLD LITERATURE: WORLD LITERATURE SURVEYS AND ANTHOLOGIES in LITERATURE OF EUROPE, AFRICA, AND ASIA

0-679-41526-2 PANTHEON $25.00

Italo Calvino

Larry **Dark**, editor

The Literary Ghost: Great Contemporary Ghost Stories

This anthology displays a range of unconventional approaches to the traditional ghost story. Among the writers included are Anne Sexton, Isaac Bashevis Singer, V.S. Pritchett, M.F.K. Fisher, Donald Barthelme, and Fay Weldon

0-87113-474-8 ATLANTIC MONTHLY $21.95

Christopher **Frayling**

Vampyres: Lord Byron to Count Dracula

An anthology of fiction and nonfiction, containing stories by Byron, Dumas, Tolstoy, and others, creating a "psychoanalysis of Count Dracula." "Definitive"
—*Times Educational Supplement* [London]

0-571-16792-6 FABER PB $14.95

Joan C. **Kessler**, editor

Demons of the Night: Tales of the Fantastic, Madness, and the Supernatural from 19th-Century France

See also THE 19TH CENTURY: ROMANTICISM AND REALISM under FRENCH LITERATURE TO 1900 in LITERATURE OF EUROPE, AFRICA, AND ASIA

0-226-43207-6 CHICAGO $45.00
0-226-43208-4 CHICAGO PB $14.95

Brad **Leithauser**, editor

The Norton Book of Ghost Stories

0-393-03564-6 NORTON $25.00

Alison **Lurie**, editor

The Oxford Book of Modern Fairy Tales

See also FICTION under BOOKS FOR EIGHTS, NINES, AND UP in BOOKS FOR YOUNG READERS

0-19-214218-6 OXFORD $30.00
0-19-282385-X OXFORD PB $14.95

Bradford **Morrow** & Patrick **McGrath**, editors

The New Gothic: A Collection of Contemporary Gothic Fiction

From the grotesquely nightmarish to the quietly unhinging, *The New Gothic* presents an array of outstanding contemporary writers exploring the dark corners of life

0-679-73075-3 VINTAGE PB $13.00

Alan **Ryan**, editor

The Penguin Book of Vampire Stories

0-14-012445-4 PENGUIN PB $13.95

Pamela **Sargent**, editor

Nebula Awards 30: SFWA's Choices for the Best Science Fiction and Fantasy of the Year

The 11th consecutive year of the Nebula Awards offers both the connoisseur and the dabbler a generous sampling of the best in sci-fi: stories, poetry, and essays that will not be found in any other anthology. Ben Bova, Maureen F. McHugh, Mary N. Malzberg, and Ursula K. Le Guin are a few of the stellar contributors. "An indispensable representation of the genre's best recent writing and a reliable indicator of its leading edge"—*Booklist*

0-15-100113-8 HARCOURT BRACE $25.00
0-15-600097-0 HARVEST PB $13.00

Women of Wonder: The Classic Years: Science Fiction by Women from the 1940s to the 1970s

0-15-600031-8 HARVEST PB $15.00
0-15-600033-4 HARVEST PB $15.00

Phyllis Cerf **Wagner** & Herbert **Wise**, editors

Great Tales of Terror and the Supernatural

A classic anthology covering many of the best-known stories in this field, including Oliver Onions's great *The Beckoning Fair One*; excellent as a starting point

0-679-60128-7 MODERN LIBRARY $22.00

History and Criticism

Brian W. **Aldiss**

The Detached Retina: Aspects of Sci-Fi and Fantasy

0-8156-0370-3 SYRACUSE PB $16.95

Sharona **Ben-Tov**

The Artificial Paradise: Science Fiction and American Reality

0-472-10580-9 MICHIGAN $29.95

Damien **Broderick**

Reading by Starlight: Postmodern Science Fiction

0-415-09789-4 ROUTLEDGE PB $16.95

John **Clute**

Science Fiction: The Illustrated Encyclopedia

0-7894-0185-1 DORLING KINDERSLEY $39.95

Samuel R. **Delany**

Neveryona, or the Tale of Signs & Cities: Some Informal Remarks Towards the Molecular Calculus, Part Four

0-8195-6271-8 WESLEYAN PB $14.95

Silent Interviews: On Language, Race, Sex, Science Fiction, and Some Comics

0-8195-5276-3 WESLEYAN $45.00
0-8195-6280-7 WESLEYAN PB $17.95

Tales of Neveryon

0-8195-6270-X WESLEYAN PB $13.95

Walter **Kendrick**

The Thrill of Fear: 250 Years of Scary Entertainment

A wide-ranging, witty, and imaginative survey of the function of terror in popular art, and its varied manifestations from Mrs. Radcliffe's *The Romance of the Forest* to E.C. horror comics and Edward Wood, Jr.'s *Orgy of the Dead*

0-8021-3246-4 GROVE PB $12.95

Stephen **King**

Danse Macabre

A jaunt through horror fiction and films

0-425-10433-8 BERKLEY PB $7.50

Stanislaw **Lem**

The prolific Lem is an internationally renowned writer of science fiction with a strong philosophical dimension.

Microworlds: Writings on Science Fiction and Fantasy

0-15-659443-9 HARCOURT BRACE PB $6.95

H.P. **Lovecraft**

Supernatural Horror in Literature

An idiosyncratic survey of the supernatural up to the '20s

0-486-20105-8 DOVER PB $5.95

Alexei **Panshin**

Heinlein in Dimension

Heinlein's writing career through 1969

INTRODUCTION BY JAMES BLISH

0-911682-01-5 ADVENT $14.00
0-911682-12-0 ADVENT PB $7.00

Michael **Riley**

Conversations with Anne Rice

0-345-39636-7 FAWCETT PB $12.00

Larry **McCaffery**

Across the Wounded Galaxies: Interviews with Contemporary American Science Fiction Writers

An engrossing series of conversations with the most innovative voices in science fiction today, including William Gibson, Bruce Sterling, Thomas Disch, Octavia Butler, Ursula K. Le Guin, Samuel Delany, and Joanna Russ

0-252-01692-0 ILLINOIS $29.95
0-252-06140-3 ILLINOIS PB $12.95

For us the apocalypse movie or document is a vehicle of psychic fulfillment in that its promise enables us to avoid confronting the complexities of our postindustrial existence. Everything is simplified when you've got to kill your neighbor for gasoline or a can of dogfood, plus you get to wear nifty black leather clothes and drive around real fast. High speed and hallucinogenic drugs—the two twentieth-century pleasures. I regard that as essentially morbid and decadent in the classic sense of indicating the collapse of the set of values. So I feel it's a moral and ideological necessity for SF writers to develop a portrait of a future we might actually be living.—Bruce Sterling
ACROSS THE WOUNDED GALAXIES: INTERVIEWS WITH CONTEMPORARY AMERICAN SCIENCE FICTION WRITERS

Donald H. **Tuck**

Encyclopedia of Science Fiction and Fantasy

A three-volume set

0-911682-27-9 ADVENT $95.00

Westerns

Classic Western Writers

Elliot **Arnold**

Blood Brother

0-8032-5901-8 NEBRASKA PB $13.95

Mary **Austin**

A Mary Austin Reader

0-8165-1620-0 ARIZONA PB $17.95

Thomas **Berger**

Little Big Man

An 111-year-old man who has seen the worlds of both the white man and the Cheyenne Indian. "The sort of book that many a writer writes in his sleep but hasn't the courage to wake up and put down on paper"—Henry Miller

0-385-29829-3 DELACORTE PB $12.95

Max **Brand**

The Bells of San Carlos and Other Stories

0-8032-1266-6 NEBRASKA $25.00

Bull Hunter

0-8439-4047-6 LEISURE PB $4.50

Bull Hunter's Romance

0-8439-4057-3 LEISURE PB $4.50

Destry Rides Again

0-86025-192-6 AEONIAN $21.95

Donnegan

0-8439-4086-7 LEISURE PB $4.50

Farewell, Thunder Moon

0-8032-1267-4 NEBRASKA $20.00

The Legend of Thunder Moon

0-8032-1269-0 NEBRASKA $25.00

The Outlaw Tamer

0-8439-4076-X LEISURE PB $4.50

Pride of Tyson

0-8439-4113-8 LEISURE PB $4.50

Red Wind and Thunder Moon

0-8032-1268-2 NEBRASKA $25.00

Thunder Moon and the Sky People

0-8032-1264-X NEBRASKA $25.00

Benjamin **Capps**

The Brothers of Uterica

0-87074-258-2 TEXAS A & M PB $10.95

Sam Chance

0-87074-250-7 SMU $22.50
0-87074-251-5 SMU PB $10.95

The Trail to Ogallala

0-87565-012-0 TEXAS CHRISTIAN $16.95
0-87565-013-9 TEXAS CHRISTIAN PB $9.95

The Warren Wagontrain Raid: The First Complete Account of an Historic Indian Attack

0-87074-295-7 SMU PB $12.95

Walter Van Tilburg **Clark**

The Ox-Bow Incident

The famous novel of a lynching

See also **SINCE 1945** under **20TH-CENTURY AMERICAN FICTION** in **LITERATURE OF THE AMERICAS**

0-88411-135-0 AMEREON $22.95
0-451-52525-6 NEW AMERICAN LIBRARY PB $4.95

Zane **Grey**

The Desert of Wheat

0-671-52643-X POCKET PB $4.99

The Last Trail: A Story of Early Days in the Ohio Valley

0-8032-7063-1 NEBRASKA PB $12.00

The Man of the Forests

0-8032-7062-3 NEBRASKA PB $15.00

The Rainbow Trail

0-671-52666-9 POCKET PB $4.99

Riders of the Purple Sage

0-06-100469-3 HARPERCOLLINS PB $3.99
0-14-018440-6 PENGUIN PB $9.95

Roping Lions in the Grand Canyon

0-8125-6353-0 TOR PB $4.99

Stranger from the Tonto

0-06-100174-0 HARPERCOLLINS PB $3.99

The Spirit of the Border: A Romance of the Early Settlers in the Ohio Valley

0-8032-7061-5 NEBRASKA PB $12.00

The Thundering Herd: The Authorized Edition

0-8032-7065-8 NEBRASKA PB $16.00

Western Union

0-06-100222-4 HARPERCOLLINS PB $3.99

A.B. **Guthrie**

The Big Sky

One of the most famous Westerns ever written, a novel of early exploration on the Missouri

INTRODUCTION BY WALLACE STEGNER

0-553-26683-7 BDD PB $5.99
0-395-61153-9 HOUGHTON MIFFLIN PB $12.95

The Way West

Dick Summers guides a group of settlers along the difficult Oregon Trail. "With sure skill, with absolute command of every detail of equipment, custom, speech and thought, with artful simplicity and eloquent feeling, Mr. Guthrie has written a stirring and a tenderly moving book" —*NY Times*

0-395-65662-1 HOUGHTON MIFFLIN PB $11.95

Ernest **Haycox**

Canyon Passage

1-55817-651-9 PINNACLE PB $3.50

Elmer **Kelton**

The Day the Cowboys Quit

0-87565-054-6 TEXAS A & M PB $10.95

The Good Old Boys

0-912646-96-9 TEXAS CHRISTIAN $19.95
0-912646-97-7 TEXAS A & M PB $12.95

The Time It Never Rained

0-912646-91-8 TEXAS CHRISTIAN $16.95
0-912646-89-6 TEXAS A & M PB $9.95

The Wolf and the Buffalo

0-87565-058-9 TEXAS CHRISTIAN $17.95
0-87565-059-7 TEXAS A & M PB $12.95

Louis **L'Amour**

L'Amour was a legendary figure among Western writers, enduringly popular and tremendously prolific. The following are only a few of his many novels.

The Burning Hills

0-553-28210-7 BDD PB $3.99

Down the Long Hills

0-553-28081-3 BDD PB $3.99

Dutcham's Flat

0-553-28111-9 BDD PB $3.99

The Haunted Mesa

Supernatural elements play a part in this story about the Anasazi of the prehistoric Southwest

See also **THE '80S** under **THE GREAT FICTION BESTSELLERS 1930–1995**

0-553-27022-2 BDD PB $5.50

High Lonesome

0-553-25972-5 BDD PB $3.99

Jubal Sackett
0-553-27739-1 BDD PB $5.50

Last Stand at Papago Wells
0-553-25807-9 BDD PB $3.99

Lonigan
0-553-27536-4 BDD PB $3.99

The Tall Stranger
0-553-28102-X BDD PB $3.99

Valley of the Sun: Frontier Stories
0-553-09962-0 BDD $19.95
0-7862-0587-3 THORNDIKE $21.95

Frederick **Manfred**

Conquering Horse
0-451-08739-9 SIGNET PB $4.50

The Frederick Manfred Reader
0-930100-67-0 HOLY COW PB $21.95

Lord Grizzly
"Held me spellbound from beginning to end. I have never in a lifetime of reading about our West met with anything like it"
—William Carlos Williams
0-451-18413-0 SIGNET PB $4.50

Wayne D. **Overholser**

The Best Western Stories of Wayne D. Overholser
EDITED BY BILL PRONZINI & MARTIN H. GREENBERG
0-8040-0913-9 SWALLOW PB $12.95

Lewis B. **Patten**

The Best Western Stories of Lewis B. Patten
EDITED BY BILL PRONZINI & MARTIN H. GREENBERG
0-8040-0925-2 OHIO PB $12.95

Charles **Portis**

True Grit
0-19-581554-8 OXFORD PB $5.25

Eugene Manlove **Rhodes**

The Best Novels and Stories of Eugene Manlove Rhodes
EDITED BY FRANK V. DEARING
0-8032-8928-6 NEBRASKA PB $14.95

Conrad **Richter**

The Light in the Forest
1-56849-064-X BUCCANEER $21.95

The Sea of Grass
0-8214-1026-1 OHIO PB $9.95

The Trees
0-8214-0978-6 OHIO PB $12.95

Jack **Schaefer**

Conversations with a Pocket Gopher and Other Outspoken Neighbors
0-88496-348-9 CAPRA PB $8.95

Helen Cody **Wetmore** & Zane **Grey**

Last of the Great Scouts
0-8125-6354-9 TOR PB $4.99

Owen **Wister**

The Virginian
0-14-039065-0 PENGUIN PB $10.95

It was now the Virginian's turn to bet, or leave the game, and he did not speak at once. Therefore Trampas spoke. "Your bet, you son-of-a-." The Virginian's pistol came out, and his hand lay on the table, holding it unaimed. And with a voice as gentle as ever, the voice that sounded almost like a caress, but drawling a very little more than usual, so that there was almost a space between each word, he issued his orders to the man Trampas:—"When you call me that, *smile!*"

THE VIRGINIAN

James C. **Work**, editor

Gunfight: Thirteen Western Stories
0-8032-4780-X NEBRASKA $25.00

Contemporaries

Bill **Barich**

Hard to Be Good
A collection of seven short stories. "Bill Barich is a true voice of the New West"
— Harold Brodkey
0-374-16812-1 FS&G $15.95

Baxter **Black**

Hey, Cowboy, Wanna Get Lucky?
NPR commentator and nationally known cowboy poet, Black delivers the escapades of two cowboys called Lick and Cody. Against the background of the rodeo circuit, they encounter sex, violence, intrigue, and still find time for the occasional philosophical ruminations. "It could make a dead man sit up and laugh!"
—*Washington Post Book World*
0-14-025093-X PENGUIN PB $9.95

James Carlos **Blake**

The Pistoleer: A Novel
0-425-15412-2 BERKLEY PB $5.99

Frank **Bonham**

One Ride Too Many and Twelve Other Action-Packed Stories of the Wild West
1-56980-034-0 BARRICADE PB $12.00

Dan **Cushman**

Rusty Irons
0-8027-4031-6 WALKER $12.95

Ed **Gorman**

Gunslinger and Nine Other Action-Packed Stories of the Wild West
1-56980-036-7 BARRICADE PB $12.00

Martin H. **Greenberg**, editor

Great Stories of the American West
1-55611-481-8 FINE $22.95

Ryerson **Johnson** & others

Torture Trek: And Eleven Other Action-Packed Stories of the Wild West
1-56980-033-2 BARRICADE PB $12.00

Larry **McMurtry**

Anything for Billy
McMurtry takes on Billy the Kid
0-671-74605-7 POCKET PB $5.99

Larry McMurtry (photo by Lee Marmon)

Buffalo Girls
McMurtry follows up his earlier evocations of the Old West, *Lonesome Dove* and *Anything for Billy,* with a fictional recreation of the extraordinary life of Calamity Jane

See also **SINCE 1945** under **20TH-CENTURY AMERICAN FICTION** in **LITERATURE OF THE AMERICAS**

0-671-53615-X POCKET PB $6.99

Dead Man's Walk
The prequel to *Lonesome Dove* concerns the legendary story of the Texas Republic, the Indian Wars, and the Texas Rangers' glory days
0-684-80753-X SIMON & SCHUSTER $26.00
0-671-00116-7 POCKET PB $6.99

Lonesome Dove
A long and constantly absorbing western saga, full of humor and incident
0-671-50420-7 SIMON & SCHUSTER $24.95
0-671-68390-X POCKET PB $7.99
0-671-79589-9 POCKET PB $6.99

Texasville
0-671-73517-9 POCKET PB $6.99

Zeke and Ned
0-684-81152-9 SIMON & SCHUSTER $25.00

Les **Savage**, Jr.

Six-Gun Bride of the Teton Bunch and Seven Other Action-Packed Stories of the Wild West
1-56980-035-9 BARRICADE PB $12.00

Historical and Romantic Fiction

Jean M. **Auel**
The timeless realities of love and war in the story of a primitive tribe's struggle for survival in the Ice Age.

The Clan of the Cave Bear
0-517-54202-1 CROWN $19.95
0-553-25042-6 BDD PB $7.50

The Mammoth Hunters
0-553-28094-5 BDD PB $6.99

The Valley of Horses
0-517-54489-X CROWN $19.95
0-553-25053-1 BDD PB $6.99

Barbara Taylor **Bradford**

Dangerous to Know
0-06-109208-8 HARPERCOLLINS PB $6.99

Her Own Rules
0-06-017721-7 HARPERCOLLINS $24.00

Love in Another Town
0-06-109209-6 HARPERCOLLINS PB $5.99

A Secret Affair
0-06-018650-X HARPERCOLLINS $16.00

Marion Zimmer **Bradley**
Adept at every form of light entertainment from science fiction to fantasy romance, Bradley turns to the ancient myths of the fall of Troy and the legends of Arthurian Britain.

The Firebrand
See also **FANTASY** under **SCIENCE FICTION AND FANTASY**
0-671-74406-2 POCKET PB $6.99

Marion Zimmer Bradley's Darkover
0-88677-593-0 NEW AMERICAN LIBRARY PB $4.99

The Mists of Avalon
The Arthurian saga from the viewpoint of the women in the legends
See also **FANTASY** under **SCIENCE FICTION AND FANTASY**
0-345-35049-9 DEL RAY PB $14.00

Taylor **Caldwell**
These love stories do not all have a historical setting, but they explore the larger world of politics and business and are filled with sharp psychological observation.

The Balance Wheel
0-88411-153-9 AMEREON $29.95

The Child from the Sea
1-56849-488-2 BUCCANEER $39.95

The Devil's Advocate
0-88411-163-6 AMEREON $24.95

Dialogues with the Devil
0-89190-279-1 AMEREON $20.95

The Eagles Gather
0-88411-165-2 AMEREON $28.95

The Earth Is the Lord's
0-88411-154-7 AMEREON $30.95

Melissa
0-88411-159-8 AMEREON $25.95

Testimony of Two Men
See also **THE '70S** under **THE GREAT FICTION BESTSELLERS 1930-1995**
0-449-20572-X FAWCETT PB $5.95

This Side of Innocence
0-88411-164-4 AMEREON $29.95

The Turnbulls
0-88411-155-5 AMEREON $29.95

Wicked Angel
0-88411-167-9 AMEREON $17.95

James **Clavell**
East and West clash in settings ranging from the Tokugawa expulsion of Westerners in the 17th century to Japanese expansionism and Iranian revolution in the 20th.

The Children's Story
0-440-20468-2 DELL PB $4.99

Gai-Jin: A Novel of Japan
0-440-21680-X DELL PB $7.99

King Rat
0-440-14546-5 DELL PB $6.99

Noble House
0-440-16484-2 DELL PB $6.99

Shogun
0-440-17800-2 DELL PB $6.99

Eleanor **Cooney** & David **Altieri**

The Court of the Lion: A Novel of the Tang Dynasty
0-380-70985-6 AVON PB $6.50

Janet **Dailey**

The Rivals
0-449-14613-8 FAWCETT PB $6.99

Dorothy **Dunnett**

Checkmate
0-89966-319-2 BUCCANEER $39.95
0-8488-1292-1 AMEREON PB $32.95

The Disorderly Knights
0-89966-295-1 BUCCANEER $36.95

The Game of Kings
0-89977-318-4 BUCCANEER $37.95

Pawn in Frankincense
0-89966-321-4 BUCCANEER $36.95

Queens Play
0-89966-320-6BUCCANEER $33.95

The Ringed Castle
0-89966-322-2 BUCCANEER $37.95

To Lie with Lions
0-394-58629-8 KNOPF $27.00

The Unicorn Hunt
0-394-58628-X KNOPF $25.00

Thomas **Flanagan**
Historical expertise went into the creation of these stories of the French invasion of Ireland in the 18th century (The Year of the French), *and the long and savage political struggles of the 19th century from the Act of Union to Parnell* (The Tenants of Time).

The End of the Hunt
See also **THE MIDDLE GENERATION** under **20TH-CENTURY BRITISH AND IRISH FICTION** in **LITERATURE OF THE BRITISH ISLES**
0-446-36046-5 WARNER PB $6.99

The Tenants of Time
0-446-35342-6 WARNER PB $6.99

The Year of the French
In 1798 French troops aid an Irish rebellion against the British. "The only great historical novel in English"—*St. Louis Post-Dispatch*
0-8050-1020-3 HOLT PB $14.95

C.S. **Forester**
The Napoleonic Wars were a duel between a tiger and a shark. France dominated the Continent, but Hornblower's exciting shipboard adventures show why Britain ruled the waves.

Admiral Hornblower in the West Indies
0-316-28941-8 LITTLE, BROWN PB $12.95

The Adventures of John Wetherell
0-7181-3844-9 JOSEPH PB $11.95

The African Queen
0-8161-7459-8 GK HALL $19.95

Beat to Quarters
0-316-28932-9 LITTLE, BROWN PB $12.95

Commodore Hornblower
0-316-28938-8 LITTLE, BROWN PB $14.95

Hornblower and the Atropos
0-316-28929-9 LITTLE, BROWN PB $14.95

Hornblower and the Hotspur
0-316-28928-0 LITTLE, BROWN PB $14.95

The Hornblower Companion
1-56849-050-X BUCCANEER $29.95

Hornblower During the Crisis
0-316-28944-2 LITTLE, BROWN PB $11.95

Lord Hornblower
0-316-28943-4 LITTLE, BROWN PB $14.95

Mr. Midshipman Hornblower
0-316-28912-4 LITTLE, BROWN PB $13.95

Ship of the Line
0-316-28936-1 LITTLE, BROWN PB $12.95

George MacDonald **Fraser**
The Flashman novels are a rollicking series of historical adventures set in the 19th century.

The Candlemass Road
0-00-271362-4 HARPERCOLLINS $20.00

Flashman & the Angel of the Lord: From the Flashman Papers, 1858-59
0-679-44172-7 KNOPF $24.00

Flashman and the Dragon
0-452-26191-0 NEW AMERICAN LIBRARY PB $10.95

Mr. American
0-00-271235-0 HPCL P PB $16.00

The Pyrates
0-00-271401-9 HARPERCOLLINS PB $14.00

Julien **Green**

This French-American novelist explores the theme of anguish issuing from the conflict between spirit and flesh.

The Distant Lands
Exploring a landscape reminiscent of *Gone with the Wind,* Julian Green's 906-page novel, originally a huge success in Europe, focuses on the destructive passions of a young Englishwoman who becomes involved with the plantation culture of the old American South

See also **FICTION** under **MODERN FRENCH LITERATURE** in **LITERATURE OF EUROPE, AFRICA, AND ASIA**

TRANSLATED BY BARBARA BEAUMONT

0-7145-2909-5 MARION BOYARS $24.95

Hella **Haasse**

In a Dark Wood Wandering
The larger-than-life characters in this historical novel of the Hundred Years' War include Charles VI, Louis of Orleans, Richard II, and Henry V. "The great colorful pageant of events here unfolded... [is] described with scholarship and admirable lucidity. The characters really come to life"—*TLS*

See also **THE '90S** under **THE GREAT FICTION BESTSELLERS 1930-1995**

See also **DUTCH LITERATURE**

TRANSLATED BY LEWIS KAPLAN & ANITA MILLER

0-89733-336-5 ACADEMY CHICAGO $22.95

The Scarlet City
The author of *In a Dark Wood Wandering* brings to life the world of the Borgias, Machiavelli, Michelangelo, and Aretino, the strange mix of the savage and the civilized that marked the 16th century in Italy

See also **DUTCH LITERATURE** in **LITERATURE OF EUROPE, AFRICA, AND ASIA**

TRANSLATED BY ANITA MILLER

0-89733-349-7 ACADEMY CHICAGO $22.95

Threshold of Fir: A Novel of Fifth Century Rome
0-89733-390-X ACADEMY CHICAGO $19.95

Georgette **Heyer**

In these lively and witty romances of the Regency period, feisty country ladies overcome their town rivals and bring to heel the brightest beau.

April Lady
0-06-100242-9 HARPERCOLLINS PB $3.99

Bath Tangle
0-06-100204-6 HARPERCOLLINS PB $4.50

The Grand Sophy
0-8488-0814-2 AMEREON $23.95

The Masqueraders
0-89190-782-3 AMEREON $20.95

These Old Shades
0-8488-0816-9 AMEREON $24.95

1-56723-058-X YESTERMORROW $24.95

The Toll Gate
0-06-100219-4 HARPERCOLLINS PB $3.99

Victoria **Holt**

The historical settings of Holt's romances range from Elizabethan times to the fall of Marie Antoinette and to the Gothic aspects of Victorian England.

The Curse of the Kings
0-449-20951-2 CREST PB $5.99

The Demon Lover
0-449-20098-1 CREST PB $5.99

The India Fan
0-449-21697-7 CREST PB $5.99

The Landower Legacy
0-449-20727-7 FAWCETT PB $5.99

Legend of the Seventh Virgin
0-449-21123-1 CREST PB $5.99

Lord of the Far Island
0-449-21183-5 FAWCETT PB $5.99

The Mask of the Enchantress
0-449-21084-7 FAWCETT PB $5.99

Mistress of Mellyn
0-449-23924-1 FAWCETT PB $5.99

The Road to Paradise Island
0-449-20888-5 CREST PB $5.99

Secret for a Nightingale
0-449-21296-3 FAWCETT PB $5.95

The Secret Woman
0-449-20878-8 FAWCETT PB $5.99

The Shadow of the Lynx
0-449-20231-3 CREST PB $5.99

Silk Vendetta
0-449-21548-2 FAWCETT PB $5.95

The Spring of the Tiger
0-449-20845-1 FAWCETT PB $5.99

The Time of the Hunter's Moon
0-449-20511-8 FAWCETT PB $5.99

Susan **Howatch**

Victorian family sagas unfold in the gloomy, haunted atmosphere of ancient houses in the west of England.

Absolute Truths
0-449-22555-0 CREST PB $6.50

Cashelmara
0-449-20623-8 FAWCETT PB $5.99

Mystical Paths
0-449-22122-9 CREST PB $5.99

Penmarric
0-449-20622-X FAWCETT PB $6.99

Scandalous Risks
0-449-21982-8 FAWCETT PB $5.99

The Wheel of Fortune
0-449-20624-6 FAWCETT PB $6.99

John **Jakes**

The Americans
See also **THE '80S** under **THE GREAT FICTION BESTSELLERS 1930-1995**

0-515-09133-2 JOVE PB $6.50

The Bastard
See also **THE '70S** under **THE GREAT FICTION BESTSELLERS 1930-1995**

0-515-09927-9 JOVE PB $7.50

The Furies
0-515-09157-X JOVE PB $7.50

Heaven and Hell
0-440-20170-5 DELL PB $6.99

The Lawless
0-515-09158-8 JOVE PB $7.50

Love and War
0-15-154496-4 HARCOURT BRACE $19.95

0-440-15016-7 DELL PB $7.50

North and South
0-440-16205-X DELL PB $6.99

The Rebels
0-515-09206-1 JOVE PB $7.50

The Seekers
0-515-09038-7 JOVE PB $6.99

The Titans
0-515-09928-7 JOVE PB $6.99

The Warriors
0-515-09209-6 JOVE PB $7.50

John **Jakes**, editor

New Trails: Twenty-Three Original Stories of the West from Western Writers of America
0-553-57316-0 BDD PB $5.99

Gary **Jennings**

Azteca
84-08-01207-X PLANETA $12.95

El Viajero
84-08-01229-0 PLANETA $15.55

Halcon
84-08-01257-6 PLANETA $17.05

The Journeyer
Marco Polo tells of his encounters in his travels across Asia

0-380-69609-6 AVON PB $6.99

Lentejuelas
84-320-4056-8 PLANETA PB $33.05

Raptor
0-553-56282-7 BDD PB $6.99

Karleen **Koen**

Now Face to Face
0-394-56929-6 RANDOM HOUSE $27.50

Through a Glass Darkly
A romance tale of early Hanoverian England and the defeated and decadent France of the Regency

0-380-70416-1 AVON PB $6.99

Norah **Lofts**

The House at Old Vine

0-89190-226-0 AMEREON $25.95
0-89244-049-X QUEEN'S HOUSE $24.95

Amin **Maalouf**

Leo Africanus

Exiled with other Jews and Muslims by the Spanish conquest of Granada, Leo's wanderings over North Africa and Asia gain him a position as papal geographer
1-56131-022-0 NEW AMSTERDAM PB $14.95

John **Masters**

British India is the setting for these tales of adventure and adultery in the closely woven social worlds of native and sahib.

Bhowani Junction

0-88184-310-5 CARROLL & GRAF PB $4.50

Colleen **McCullough**

The Ladies of Missalonghi

See also **AUSTRALIAN LITERATURE** in **LITERATURE OF EUROPE, AFRICA, AND ASIA**
0-380-70458-7 AVON PB $4.99

Patrick **O'Brian**

The Golden Ocean

See also **PATRICK O'BRIAN'S AUBREY/MATURIN NOVELS** under **20TH-CENTURY BRITISH AND IRISH FICTION** in **LITERATURE OF THE BRITISH ISLES**
0-393-03630-8 NORTON $22.50
0-393-31537-1 NORTON PB $12.00

The Unknown Shore

This reissue of O'Brian's second novel, the immediate precursor to the Aubrey/Maturin series, follows the fates of the *Wager*, a ship that was parted from Commodore Anson's fateful circumnavigation in 1740 and was shipwrecked on the coast of Chile
0-393-03859-9 NORTON $23.00
0-393-31538-X NORTON PB $12.00

Jean **Plaidy**

Under her pseudonym, Victoria Holt shows the same command of historical periods, from the great Franco-British House of Plantagenet to the tragic Henrietta Maria, wife of the executed Charles I.

The Shadow of the Pomegranate

0-399-13967-2 PUTNAM $22.95

William's Wife

0-449-22284-5 CREST PB $5.99

Jean **Plaidy** & Eleanor **Hibbert**

The King's Secret Matter

0-399-14111-1 PUTNAM $22.95

Belva **Plain**

Family life of 19th-and early 20th-century America in the Caribbean plantations, the Civil War in New Orleans, and the Lower East Side of New York.

Crescent City

0-440-11549-3 DELL PB $6.99

Eden Burning

0-440-12135-3 DELL PB $6.99

The Golden Cup

0-440-13091-3 DELL PB $6.99

Evergreen

See also **THE '70S** under **THE GREAT FICTION BESTSELLERS 1930-1995**
0-440-13278-9 DELL PB $6.99

Promises

0-7838-1841-6 GK HALL PB $10.00

Random Winds

See also **THE '80S** under **THE GREAT FICTION BESTSELLERS 1930-1995**
0-440-17562-3 DELL PB $6.99

Mary **Renault**

Renault uses her wide knowledge of the ancient world, from the historical reality to the great Athenian myths, to depict daily life during the war with Sparta and the conquests of Alexander.

The Bull from the Sea

See also **THE EARLY 20TH CENTURY** under **20TH-CENTURY BRITISH AND IRISH FICTION** in **LITERATURE OF THE BRITISH ISLES**
0-394-71504-7 RANDOM HOUSE PB $8.00

Fire from Heaven

0-394-72291-4 RANDOM HOUSE PB $10.00

The King Must Die

Fascinating story set in the Minoan period as Theseus, mythical king of Athens, saves the city from its annual tribute of young men and maidens for sacrifice to the Minotaur
0-394-75104-3 VINTAGE PB $11.00

The Last of the Wine

A young Athenian actor tells of his troupe's exciting travels through Greece during the Peloponnesian War
0-394-71653-1 RANDOM HOUSE PB $8.95

The Persian Boy

A first-person account by a beautiful young captive of the Macedonian army who becomes the catamite of the conqueror Alexander
0-394-75101-9 VINTAGE PB $13.00

Anne **Rice**

Cry to Heaven

0-394-52351-2 KNOPF $25.00
0-345-37370-7 BALLANTINE PB $12.00

The Feast of All Saints

0-345-33453-1 BALLANTINE PB $6.99

Interview with the Vampire

A compulsively readable biography of a long-lived drinker of blood
0-345-33766-2 BALLANTINE PB $6.99

The Mummy: Or Ramses the Damned

0-345-36000-1 BALLANTINE PB $14.00

The Vampire Lestat

The sequel to *Interview*
0-394-53443-3 KNOPF $25.00
0-345-31386-0 BALLANTINE PB $6.99

Alexandra **Ripley**

Charleston

0-446-36000-7 WARNER PB $6.50

From Fields of Gold

0-446-60249-3 WARNER P PB $6.50

A Love Divine

0-446-51691-0 WARNER $25.00

New Orleans Legacy

0-446-34210-6 WARNER PB $6.50

Scarlett

The long-delayed sequel to *Gone with the Wind*
0-446-36325-1 WARNER PB $6.99

The Time Returns

0-446-60258-2 WARN P PB $6.50

Edward **Rutherford**

London

0-517-59181-2 RANDOM HOUSE $25.00

Sarum

A brilliant tapestry of English history, tracing the continuity of five Salisbury families from the building of Stonehenge to colonial preeminence in the 19th century
0-8041-0298-8 IVY PB $6.99

Erich **Segal**

Love Story

0-553-27528-3 BDD PB $5.99

Jeff **Shaara**

Gods and Generals

0-345-40492-0 BALLANTINE $25.00

Michael **Shaara**

The Broken Place

0-671-89865-5 POCKET PB $5.99

For Love of the Game: A Novel

0-7867-0114-5 CARROLL & GRAF PB $8.95

The Killer Angels: A Novel About the Four Days at Gettysburg

The detailed story of the battle seen through the dispatches of Robert E. Lee and his lieutenant
0-679-42541-1 RANDOM HOUSE $21.00
0-345-34810-9 BALLANTINE PB $5.99

The Noah Conspiracy

0-671-89866-3 POCKET PB $5.99

Jane **Smiley**

The Greenlanders

Calls up the barren, violent, heroic world of 14th-century Norsemen through the eyes of a Greenland maiden fascinated by a warrior who has learned courtly manners in the south
See also **SINCE 1945** under **20TH-CENTURY AMERICAN FICTION** in **LITERATURE OF THE AMERICAS**
0-8041-0453-0 IVY PB $6.99

Mary **Stewart**

Stewart specializes in historical legends, among them a retelling of the Arthurian myth from the point of view of Merlin the enchanter.

The Crystal Cave

0-449-20644-0 FAWCETT PB $5.99

The Hollow Hills

0-449-20645-9 FAWCETT PB $5.95

Mary Stewart's Merlin Trilogy

Includes *The Crystal Cave, The Hollow Hills,* and *The Last Enchantment*
0-688-00347-8 MORROW $19.95

The Prince and the Pilgrim
0-688-14538-8 MORROW $23.00

The Stormy Petrel
0-449-22085-0 CREST PB $5.99

The Wicked Day
A new installment of the Merlin cycle
0-449-20519-3 FAWCETT PB $5.95

Irving **Stone**
In these fictional biographies of famous men and women of the past, historical events and personalities receive colorful treatment.

The Agony and the Ecstasy
A life of Michelangelo Buonarroti with a fine portrait of Pope Julius II
See also **THE '60S** under **THE GREAT FICTION BESTSELLERS 1930-1995**
0-451-17135-7 NEW AMERICAN LIBRARY PB $6.99

Depths of Glory: A Biographical Novel of Camille Pissarro
0-452-27501-6 PLUME PB $14.95

Lust for Life
A fictionalized biography of Van Gogh
1-56849-480-7 BUCCANEER $29.95
0-452-26249-6 NEW AMERICAN LIBRARY PB $13.95

The President's Lady
A novel about the wife of Andrew Jackson
1-55853-431-8 RUTLEDGE HILL PB $12.95

Rosemary **Sutcliff**

Sword at Sunset
Virtuoso transformation of the legend of Arthur into the historical reality of a Roman-trained Briton trying to save the remnants of Mediterranean civilization from the northern barbarians
See also **FANTASY** under **SCIENCE FICTION AND FANTASY**
0-8125-8852-5 TOR PB $4.50

Angela **Thirkell**

Ankle Deep
1-55921-158-X MOYER BELL PB $12.95

August Folly
0-7867-0272-9 CARROLL & GRAF PB $11.95

Before Lunch
0-88184-397-0 CARROLL & GRAF PB $5.95

The Brandons
0-88184-361-X CARROLL & GRAF PB $4.95

The Brandons: A Barsetshire Novel
0-7867-0362-8 CARROLL & GRAF PB $12.95

Cheerfulness Breaks In
0-7867-0318-0 CARROLL & GRAF PB $11.95

The Demon in the House
1-55921-159-8 MOYER BELL PB $12.95

Growing Up
1-55921-149-0 MOYER BELL PB $11.95

The Headmistress
1-55921-150-4 MOYER BELL PB $12.95

High Rising
0-88184-463-2 CARROLL & GRAF PB $5.95

Marling Hall: A Barsetshire Novel
0-7867-0273-7 CARROLL & GRAF PB $11.95

Miss Bunting
1-55921-174-1 MOYER BELL PB $12.95

Northbridge Rectory: A Barsetshire Novel
0-7867-0380-6 CARROLL & GRAF PB $12.95

O, These Men, These Men
1-55921-173-3 MOYER BELL PB $12.95

Pomfret Towers
0-88184-276-1 CARROLL & GRAF PB $4.95

Wild Strawberries
0-88184-555-8 CARROLL & GRAF PB $4.95

Gore **Vidal**
Vidal's novels include witty and iconoclastic fictional rewritings of American history, and an imaginary autobiography of the emperor who tried to save Rome from Christianity.

Burr
One of the best of Vidal's historical novels, about the man who shot Alexander Hamilton
See also **SINCE 1945** under **20TH-CENTURY AMERICAN FICTION** in **LITERATURE OF THE AMERICAS**
0-345-33921-5 BALLANTINE PB $6.99

Aaron Burr

Creation
A fictional tour of the ancient world
9-993-93197-7 BALLANTINE PB $6.99

Empire
An epic of America in the Gilded Age. "In writing about how the US became an empire, Vidal gives us a rich and dazzling novel filled with more of the social observations, behavioral insights, political arguments, and personal quirks that have made him our most public of writers"
— Webster Schott, *Cleveland Plain Dealer*
0-394-56123-6 RANDOM HOUSE $2.98
0-345-35472-9 BALLANTINE PB $6.99

Lincoln
"The portrait is reasoned, judicious, straightforward and utterly convincing"
—Joyce Carol Oates, *NY Times*
0-679-60048-5 MODERN LIBRARY $19.00

Washington, D.C.
Set in the late Depression, this skillful historical novel traces the parallel fives of a senator and a newspaper publisher joined by a startling marriage between the former's protégé and the latter's daughter
0-345-34236-4 BALLANTINE PB $5.99

The Great Fiction Bestsellers 1930-1995

The '30s

Pearl S. **Buck**

The Good Earth
See also **FROM THE TURN OF THE CENTURY TO WORLD WAR II** under **20TH-CENTURY AMERICAN FICTION** in **LITERATURE OF THE AMERICAS**
0-89966-299-4 BUCCANEER $27.95

Lloyd C. **Douglas**

The Magnificent Obsession
0-395-07634-X HOUGHTON MIFFLIN $27.50

Daphne **Du Maurier**

Rebecca
The famous Gothic novel of an aristocrat's ingenuous second wife struggling against the malevolent influence of her dead predecessor
See also **ENGLAND** under **RISE OF THE MODERN CRIME NOVEL** under **CRIME FICTION**
See also **THE EARLY 20TH CENTURY** under **20TH-CENTURY BRITISH AND IRISH FICTION**
0-385-04380-5 DOUBLEDAY $20.00
0-380-77855-6 AVON PB $6.50

Walter D. **Edmonds**

Drums Along the Mohawk
0-89966-291-9 BUCCANEER $29.95

Hans **Fallada**

Little Man, What Now?
TRANSLATED BY ERIC SUTTON
0-89733-086-2 ACADEMY CHICAGO PB $14.95

Edna **Ferber**

Cimarron
0-88411-548-8 AMEREON $26.95
0-89968-279-0 BUCCANEER $29.95

Ellen **Glasgow**

The Sheltered Life
0-8139-1514-7 VIRGINIA PB $12.95

Vein of Iron
0-15-193497-5 HARCOURT BRACE PB $7.95

James **Hilton**

Goodbye, Mr. Chips
0-553-27321-3 BDD PB $3.99

Lost Horizon
0-89966-450-4 BUCCANEER $28.95

Jim **Lehrer**

The Last Debate

0-679-44159-X RANDOM HOUSE $23.00

Margaret **Mitchell**

Gone with the Wind

"A remarkable book, a spectacular book, a book that will not be forgotten"—*Chicago Tribune*

0-446-36538-6 WARNER PB $6.99

Marjorie Kinnan **Rawlings**

The Yearling

The enduringly popular novel of a boy and his pet deer; winner of the 1938 Pulitzer Prize

0-02-044931-3 ALADDIN PB $5.95

Mary Roberts **Rinehart**

The Door

0-8217-3526-8 ZEBRA PB $3.95

Franz **Werfel**

The Forty Days of Musa Dagh

0-88184-668-6 CARROLL & GRAF PB $13.95

The '40s

Lloyd C. **Douglas**

The Robe

FOREWORD BY ANDREW GREELEY

0-395-07635-8 HOUGHTON MIFFLIN $24.95

0-395-40799-0 HOUGHTON MIFFLIN PB $14.95

John **Hersey**

A Bell for Adano

American GIs in an Italian town liberated from the Nazis

See also **SINCE 1945** under **20TH-CENTURY AMERICAN FICTION** in **LITERATURE OF THE AMERICAS**

0-394-75695-9 RANDOM HOUSE PB $13.00

John Hersey

Richard **Llewellyn**

How Green Was My Valley

0-02-022372-2 COLLIER PB $10.00

John P. **Marquand**

H.M. Pulham, Esq.

0-89733-231-8 ACADEMY CHICAGO PB $11.00

Point of No Return

An apparently successful banker reevaluates his life after returning to his hometown in Massachusetts

0-89733-174-5 ACADEMY CHICAGO PB $12.00

Wickford Point

0-8446-2666-X SMITH $14.50

Ayn **Rand**

The Fountainhead

The meteoric rise of a callous young architect (modeled on Frank Lloyd Wright) to the peaks of power; influential in its day

0-02-600910-2 BOBBS-MERRILL $40.00

0-451-17512-3 SIGNET PB $7.99

Betty **Smith**

A Tree Grows in Brooklyn

0-06-080126-3 HARPERCOLLINS PB $7.00

Lillian E. **Smith**

Strange Fruit

0-15-685636-0 HARCOURT BRACE PB $11.95

Franz **Werfel**

The Song of Bernadette

0-312-03429-6 ST. MARTIN'S PB $13.95

The '50s

Eugene **Burdick** & William J. **Lederer**

The Ugly American

0-449-21526-1 FAWCETT PB $5.95

0-393-00305-1 NORTON PB $10.95

Patrick **Dennis**

Auntie Mame

0-345-37650-1 BALLANTINE PB $5.99

Allen **Drury**

Advise and Consent

1-56849-060-7 BUCCANEER $45.95

Edna **Ferber**

Giant

0-89966-806-2BUCCANEER $31.95

Ice Palace

0-89968-278-2 LIGHTYEAR $29.95

John **Hersey**

The Wall

The famous novel of life in the Warsaw ghetto during World War II

See also **HOLOCAUST FICTION** under **ART AND LITERATURE** under **THE HOLOCAUST** in **WORLD HISTORY AND CURRENT AFFAIRS**

0-394-75696-7 VINTAGE PB $14.00

James **Jones**

From Here to Eternity

A naval base in Hawaii in the days preceding Pearl Harbor

0-440-32770-9 DELL PB $6.99

MacKinley **Kantor**

Andersonville

0-452-26956-3 PLUME PB $15.95

James A. **Michener**

Hawaii

0-394-42797-1 RANDOM HOUSE $45.00

0-449-21335-8 FAWCETT PB $6.99

Return to Paradise

0-449-20650-5 CREST PB $5.99

Edwin **O'Connor**

The Last Hurrah

The decline of an Irish-American political boss

0-316-62659-7 LITTLE, BROWN PB $12.95

John **O'Hara**

From the Terrace

O'Hara's attempt at an epic of American life in the first half of the century. "A tremendous story about love, money, and war"—*NY Times*

See also **FROM THE TURN OF THE CENTURY TO WORLD WAR II** under **20TH-CENTURY AMERICAN FICTION** in **LITERATURE OF THE AMERICAS**

0-88184-971-5 CARROLL & GRAF PB $7.95

John O'Hara

Ten North Frederick

0-88184-173-0 CARROLL & GRAF PB $4.50

Ayn **Rand**

Atlas Shrugged

0-525-93418-9 DUTTON $39.95

0-451-17192-6 SIGNET PB $7.99

Annemarie **Selinko**

Desiree

1-56849-548-X BUCCANEER $27.95

Nevil **Shute**

On the Beach

A suspenseful, apocalyptic novel in which Australia becomes the last haven in a world devastated by nuclear holocaust

See also **AUSTRALIAN LITERATURE** in **LITERATURE OF EUROPE, AFRICA, AND ASIA**

0-89968-365-7 LIGHTYEAR $18.95

0-345-31148-5 BALLANTINE PB $5.99

Boris **Pasternak**

Doctor Zhivago

Pasternak's lyrical novel of the Russian Revolution and Civil War won him the Nobel Prize in 1958, but he relinquished the award under government pressure

See also **FICTION AND OTHER PROSE** under **EARLY 20TH CENTURY** under **RUSSIAN LITERATURE** in **LITERATURE OF EUROPE, AFRICA, AND ASIA**

0-679-40759-6 EVERYMAN'S........$20.00
0-345-34100-7 BALLANTINE PB........$5.95

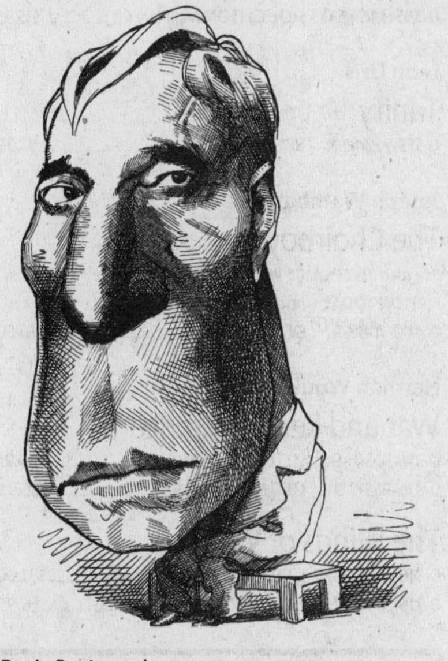

Boris Pasternak

Robert **Traver**

Anatomy of a Murder

0-312-03356-7 ST. MARTIN'S PB........$11.95

Leon **Uris**

Battle Cry

0-553-25983-0 BDD PB........$6.99

Exodus

0-553-25847-8 BDD PB........$6.99

Herman **Wouk**

The Caine Mutiny

0-316-95510-8 LITTLE, BROWN PB........$15.95

Marjorie Morningstar

0-316-95513-2 LITTLE, BROWN PB........$14.95

The '60s

Michael **Crichton**

The Andromeda Strain

0-394-41525-6 KNOPF........$25.00
0-345-37848-2 BALLANTINE PB........$6.99

Giuseppe **di Lampedusa**

The Leopard

The decline of the Sicilian aristocracy traced in a classic novel that is both an indictment and a lament

See also **FICTION** under **THE 20TH CENTURY** under **ITALIAN LITERATURE** in **LITERATURE OF EUROPE, AFRICA, AND ASIA**

TRANSLATED BY ARCHIBALD COLQUHOUN

0-679-40757-X EVERYMAN'S........$16.50
0-679-73121-0 PANTHEON PB........$12.00

Ian **Fleming**

The Man with the Golden Gun

See also **MODERN SPY NOVEL** under **SPY FICTION**

0-451-15855-5 SIGNET PB........$4.50

Arthur **Hailey**

Airport

1-56849-562-5 BUCCANEER........$27.95

Harper **Lee**

To Kill a Mockingbird

A vivid autobiographical account of growing up in the South

0-446-31078-6 WARNER PB........$4.99

Helen **MacInnes**

The Double Image

See also **MODERN SPY NOVEL** under **SPY FICTION**

0-89190-105-1 AMEREON........$22.95

Mary **McCarthy**

The Group

Eight Vassar girls of the class of 1933

See also **SINCE 1945** under **20TH-CENTURY AMERICAN FICTION** in **LITERATURE OF THE AMERICAS**

0-15-137281-0 HARCOURT BRACE........$15.95
0-15-637208-8 HARCOURT BRACE PB........$11.00

Richard **McKenna**

The Sand Pebbles

0-87021-592-2 NAVAL INSTITUTE........$32.95

James A. **Michener**

Caravans

0-449-21380-3 FAWCETT PB........$6.95

The Source

0-449-21147-9 FAWCETT PB........$6.99

Katherine Anne **Porter**

Ship of Fools

An intensely wrought portrait of a group of misfits

See also **FROM THE TURN OF THE CENTURY TO WORLD WAR II** under **20TH-CENTURY AMERICAN FICTION** in **LITERATURE OF THE AMERICAS**

0-316-71390-2 LITTLE, BROWN PB........$13.95

Mario **Puzo**

Fools Die

0-451-16019-3 SIGNET PB........$6.99

The Godfather

The Mafia, romantic-epic style

0-451-16771-6 SIGNET PB........$6.99

Mario Puzo

Harold **Robbins**

The Adventurers

0-671-87482-9 POCKET PB........$6.99

The Inheritors

0-671-87489-6 POCKET PB........$6.99
0-671-54761-5 POCKET PB........$5.99

Terry **Southern** & Mason **Hoffenberg**

Candy

A pornographic comedy that helped break publishing barriers in the '60s

0-8021-3429-7 GROVE PB........$12.00

Irving **Stone**

The Agony and the Ecstasy

A life of Michelangelo Buonarroti with a fine portrait of Pope Julius II

See also **HISTORICAL AND ROMANTIC FICTION**

0-451-17135-7 NEW AMERICAN LIBRARY PB........$6.99

Leon **Uris**

Mila 18

Leon Uris's fictional account of a family trapped in the horrors of the Warsaw Ghetto.

See also **HOLOCAUST FICTION** under **ART AND LITERATURE** under **THE HOLOCAUST** in **WORLD HISTORY AND CURRENT AFFAIRS**

0-553-24160-5 BDD PB........$7.99

Gore **Vidal**

Myra Breckinridge & Myron

Vidal's comic sendup of sexual mores

0-394-55376-4 RANDOM HOUSE........$19.95

Herman **Wouk**

Don't Stop the Carnival

0-316-95512-4 LITTLE, BROWN PB........$15.95

The '70s

Richard **Adams**

Watership Down

The quest of a band of Berkshire rabbits for a new home has allegorical overtones but treats the conditions of wildlife with astonishing fidelity. "His true achievement lies in the altogether enchanting civilization he has created"—Peter S. Prescott

See also **YOUNG ADULT FICTION** in **BOOKS FOR YOUNG READERS**

See also **THE MIDDLE GENERATION** under **20TH-CENTURY BRITISH AND IRISH FICTION** in **LITERATURE OF THE BRITISH ISLES**

0-02-700030-3 MACMILLAN........$40.00
0-380-00293-0 AVON PB........$5.99

Richard **Bach**

"Bach has a passion and a pen and he puts the two together with warmth and skill"
—Saturday Evening Post

Illusions: The Adventure of a Reluctant Messiah

See also **WESTERN** under **20TH-CENTURY SPIRITUAL LEADERS** under **SPIRITUALITY** in **RELIGION, SPIRITUALITY, AND PHILOSOPHY**

0-385-28501-9 DOUBLEDAY........$18.95
0-440-20488-7 DELL PB........$5.99

Jonathan Livingston Seagull

0-380-01286-3 AVON PB........$5.50

Richard **Bach**

There's No Such Place as Far Away

ILLUSTRATED BY RON WEGEN

0-385-30211-8 DELACORTE $18.95

0-385-29038-1 DELACORTE $17.95

Taylor **Caldwell**

These love stories do not all have a historical setting, but they explore the larger world of politics and business and are filled with sharp psychological observation.

Testimony of Two Men

0-449-20572-X FAWCETT PB $5.95

This Side of Innocence

See also HISTORICAL AND ROMANTIC FICTION

0-88411-164-4 AMEREON $29.95

James **Clavell**

Noble House

0-440-16484-2 DELL PB $6.99

Shogun

0-440-17800-2 DELL PB $6.99

Robin **Cook**

Coma

0-451-15953-5 SIGNET PB $5.99

Margaret **Craven**

I Heard the Owl Call My Name

See also YOUNG ADULT FICTION in BOOKS FOR YOUNG READERS

0-440-34369-0 LAUREL LEAF PB $4.99

Ken **Follett**

Triple

0-451-16354-0 NEW AMERICAN LIBRARY PB $5.99

Alex **Haley**

Roots

READERS

See also CLASSIC AUTOBIOGRAPHIES under BLACK VOICES, BLACK LIVES under AFRICAN-AMERICAN STUDIES in HISTORY OF THE AMERICAS

0-385-03787-2 DOUBLEDAY $25.00

0-440-17464-3 DELL PB $6.99

Jack **Higgins**

The Eagle Has Landed

0-671-72773-7 POCKET PB $6.50

Storm Warning

0-671-74629-4 POCKET PB $6.50

John **Jakes**

The Bastard

0-515-09927-9 JOVE PB $7.50

The Lawless

0-515-09158-8 JOVE PB $7.50

The Warriors

0-515-09209-6 JOVE PB $7.50

Erica **Jong**

Fear of Flying

0-451-18556-0 SIGNET PB $5.99

Judith **Krantz**

Scruples

0-553-56111-1 BDD PB $6.99

Robert **Ludlum**

The Holcroft Covenant

0-553-26019-7 BDD PB $6.99

The Matarese Circle

0-553-25899-0 BDD PB $7.50

The Matlock Paper

0-553-27960-2 BDD PB $6.99

The Rhinemann Exchange

0-553-28063-5 BDD PB $6.99

John D. **MacDonald**

Condominium

0-449-20737-4 FAWCETT PB $5.99

Colleen **McCullough**

The Thorn Birds

See also AUSTRALIAN LITERATURE in LITERATURE OF EUROPE, AFRICA, AND ASIA

0-380-01817-9 AVON PB $6.99

James A. **Michener**

Centennial

0-449-21419-2 FAWCETT PB $6.99

Chesapeake

0-394-50079-2 RANDOM HOUSE $45.00

0-449-21158-4 FAWCETT PB $6.99

The Drifters

0-449-21353-6 FAWCETT PB $6.99

Belva **Plain**

Evergreen

0-440-13278-9 DELL PB $6.99

Harold **Robbins**

The Betsy

1-56849-641-9 BUCCANEER $29.95

Dreams Die First

0-671-87487-X POCKET PB $6.99

Memories of Another Day

9995404206 POCKET PB $6.99

0-671-87491-8 POCKET PB $5.99

The Pirate

0-671-87493-4 POCKET PB $6.99

Judith **Rossner**

Looking for Mr. Goodbar

A young schoolteacher flirts with danger while cruising New York's singles bars

0-671-73575-6 POCKET PB $5.95

Erich **Segal**

Love Story

0-553-27528-3 BDD PB $5.99

Oliver's Story

0-553-27529-1 BDD PB $5.99

Sidney **Sheldon**

Bloodline

0-446-35744-8 WARNER PB $6.99

A Stranger in the Mirror

0-446-35657-3 WARNER PB $6.99

Danielle **Steel**

The Promise

0-440-17079-6 DELL PB $5.99

Mary **Stewart**

The Last Enchantment

0-449-20646-7 FAWCETT PB $5.95

J.R.R. **Tolkien**

The Silmarillion

0-345-32581-8 BALLANTINE PB $5.95

0-395-34646-0 HOUGHTON MIFFLIN PB $15.95

Leon **Uris**

Trinity

0-553-25846-X BDD PB $7.99

Joseph **Wambaugh**

The Choirboys

See also THE POLICE PROCEDURAL: USA under CRIME FICTION TODAY under CRIME FICTION

0-440-11188-9 DELL PB $6.50

Herman **Wouk**

War and Remembrance

0-316-95501-9 LITTLE, BROWN $29.95

0-316-95515-9 LITTLE, BROWN PB $6.99

The Winds of War

0-316-95500-0 LITTLE, BROWN $35.00

0-316-95516-7 LITTLE, BROWN PB $6.99

The '80s

V.C. **Andrews**

Flowers in the Attic

0-671-72941-1 POCKET PB $6.99

Garden of Shadows

0-671-72942-X POCKET PB $6.50

Heaven

0-671-72944-6 POCKET PB $6.99

If There Be Thorns

0-671-72945-4 POCKET PB $6.50

My Sweet Audrina

0-671-72946-2 POCKET PB $6.50

Petals on the Wind

0-671-72947-0 POCKET PB $6.50

Seeds of Yesterday

0-671-72948-9 POCKET PB $6.50

Jeffrey **Archer**

Kane and Abel

0-06-100712-9 HARPERCOLLINS PB $6.99

A Matter of Honor

0-06-100713-7 HARPERCOLLINS PB $6.50

The Prodigal Daughter

0-06-100714-5 HARPERCOLLINS PB $6.99

Isaac **Asimov**

The Robots of Dawn

0-345-31571-5 BALLANTINE PB $5.95

Richard **Bach**
One
0-440-20562-X DELL PB $6.50

Sybille **Bedford**
A Legacy
"A book of entirely delicious quality. Two families, vastly dissimilar, the one Jewish inartistic millionaires, the other slightly decadent Catholic aristocrats, become joined in marriage. Everything is new, cool, witty, elegant, and some scenes are uproariously funny"
—Evelyn Waugh

See also **THE EARLY 20TH CENTURY** under **20TH-CENTURY BRITISH AND IRISH FICTION** in **LITERATURE OF THE BRITISH ISLES**

0-912946-26-1 NORTON PB $8.50

Barbara Taylor **Bradford**
Act of Will
0-06-100811-7 HARPERCOLLINS PB $6.50

A Woman of Substance
0-06-100807-9 HARPERCOLLINS PB $6.50

Tom **Clancy**
The Cardinal of the Kremlin
0-425-11684-0 BERKLEY PB $7.50

The Hunt for Red October
0-87021-285-0 NAVAL INSTITUTE $24.95
0-425-13351-6 BERKLEY PB $7.50

Patriot Games
0-425-13435-0 BERKLEY PB $5.99

Red Storm Rising
0-425-10107-X BERKLEY PB $6.99

Mary Higgins **Clark**
Weep No More, My Lady
0-440-20098-9 DELL PB $6.99

Jackie **Collins**
Hollywood Husbands
0-671-72451-7 POCKET PB $6.50

Hollywood Wives
0-671-70459-1 POCKET PB $6.99

Lucky
0-671-52496-8 POCKET PB $4.95

Shirley **Conran**
Lace
0-671-73745-7 POCKET PB $5.99

Pat **Conroy**
The Prince of Tides
0-395-35300-9 HOUGHTON MIFFLIN $25.00
0-553-26888-0 BDD PB $6.99

Robin **Cook**
Brain
0-451-15797-4 SIGNET PB $5.99

Sphinx
0-451-15949-7 NEW AMERICAN LIBRARY PB $5.99

Stephen **Coonts**
Final Flight
0-440-20447-X DELL PB $6.99

Clive **Cussler**
Cyclops
0-671-70464-8 POCKET PB $6.99

Treasure
0-671-70465-6 POCKET PB $6.99

Stephen R. **Donaldson**
The White Gold Wielder
0-345-34870-2 BALLANTINE PB $6.99

Dominick **Dunne**
The Two Mrs. Grenvilles
0-553-25891-5 BDD PB $6.99

Ken **Follett**
The Key to Rebecca
0-451-16349-4 NEW AMERICAN LIBRARY PB $5.99

Lie Down with Lions
0-451-18292-8 NEW AMERICAN LIBRARY PB $5.99

The Man from St. Petersburg
0-451-16351-6 NEW AMERICAN LIBRARY PB $5.99

Donald F. **Glut**
The Empire Strikes Back
0-345-32022-0 BALLANTINE PB $5.99

Arthur **Hailey**
Strong Medicine
0-440-18366-9 DELL PB $5.99

Shirley **Hazzard**
The Transit of Venus
0-14-010747-9 PENGUIN PB $11.95

Frank **Herbert**
God Emperor of Dune
See also **CONTEMPORARY SCIENCE FICTION** under **SCIENCE FICTION AND FANTASY**

0-441-29467-7 ACE PB $6.99

Garrison **Keillor**
Lake Wobegon Days
See also **HUMOR WRITERS** under **HUMOR**

0-14-013161-2 PENGUIN PB $11.95

Garrison Keillor

Leaving Home: A Collection of Lake Wobegon Stories
0-14-013160-4 PENGUIN PB $11.95

John **Jakes**
The Americans
See also **HISTORICAL AND ROMANTIC FICTION**

0-515-09133-2 JOVE PB $6.50

Heaven and Hell
0-440-20170-5 DELL PB $6.99

Love and War
0-15-154496-4 HARCOURT BRACE $19.95
0-440-15016-7 DELL PB $7.50

North and South
0-440-16205-X DELL PB $6.99

Stephen **King** & Peter **Straub**
The Talisman
0-425-10533-4 BERKLEY PB $7.50

William **Kotzwinkle**
E.T.: The Extra Terrestrial Storybook
0-425-11559-3 BERKLEY PB $3.95

Judith **Krantz**
I'll Take Manhattan
0-553-26407-9 BDD PB $6.99

Mistral's Daughter
0-553-25917-2 BDD PB $6.99

Princess Daisy
0-553-25609-2 BDD PB $6.99

Till We Meet Again
0-553-28014-7 BDD PB $6.99

Louis **L'Amour**
The Haunted Mesa
Supernatural elements play a part in this story about the Anasazi of the prehistoric Southwest

See also **CLASSIC WESTERN WRITERS** under **WESTERNS**

0-553-27022-2 BDD PB $5.50

Jubal Sackett
0-553-27739-1 BDD PB $5.50

Last of the Breed
0-553-28042-2 BDD PB $5.50

The Lonesome Gods
0-553-27518-6 BDD PB $5.50

The Walking Drum
0-553-28040-6 BDD PB $5.50

Anne **McCaffey**
Moreta: Dragonlady of Pern
0-345-29873-X DEL RAY PB $5.95

Colleen **McCullough**
An Indecent Obsession
A psychiatric hospital is the setting for an odd mixture of romance, violence, and paranoia

See also **AUSTRALIAN LITERATURE** in **LITERATURE OF EUROPE, AFRICA, AND ASIA**

0-380-60376-4 AVON PB $6.99

Robert **Ludlum**

The Aquitaine Progression
0-553-26256-4 BDD PB $6.99

The Icarus Agenda
0-553-27800-2 BDD PB $6.99

Robert Ludlum (credit: ©Michelle Ryder)

The Parsifal Mosaic
0-553-25270-4 BDD PB $6.99

The Road to Gandolfo
0-553-27109-1 BDD PB $6.99

John D. **MacDonald**

Free Fall in Crimson
0-449-22482-1 FAWCETT PB $5.99
0-449-13253-6 FAWCETT PB $4.95

James A. **Michener**

Alaska
0-449-21726-4 CREST PB $6.99

The Covenant
0-449-21420-6 FAWCETT PB $6.95

Poland
0-449-20587-8 FAWCETT PB $6.99

Space
0-449-20379-4 FAWCETT PB $6.99

Belva **Plain**

Random Winds
See also **HISTORICAL AND ROMANTIC FICTION**
0-440-17562-3 DELL PB $6.99

Anne **Rice**

The Queen of the Damned
The third of Rice's bestselling vampire chronicles
See also **SUPERNATURAL FANTASY AND HORROR** under **SCIENCE FICTION AND FANTASY**
0-345-35152-5 BALLANTINE PB $6.99

Harold **Robbins**

Descent from Xanadu
0-671-87485-3 POCKET PB $6.99
0-671-73554-3 POCKET PB $5.99

Goodbye, Janette
0-671-87488-8 POCKET PB $5.99

Spellbinder
0-671-65752-6 POCKET PB $5.99

Rosemary **Rogers**

Lost Love, Last Love
0-380-75515-7 AVON PB $5.99

Surrender to Love
0-380-80630-4 AVON PB $5.99

Judith **Rossner**

August
A woman's relationship with her therapist
0-446-35224-1 WARNER PB $6.99

Carl **Sagan**

Contact
0-671-70180-0 POCKET PB $6.50

Lawrence **Sanders**

The Eighth Commandment
0-425-10005-7 BERKLEY PB $6.50

The Tenth Commandment
0-425-10431-1 BERKLEY PB $6.99

The Third Deadly Sin
0-425-10429-X BERKLEY PB $6.99

Helen H. **Santmyer**

...and Ladies of the Club
0-425-10243-2 BERKLEY PB $8.99

Sidney **Sheldon**

If Tomorrow Comes
0-688-04217-1 MORROW $22.95
0-446-35742-1 WARNER PB $6.99

Master of the Game
0-446-35545-3 WARNER PB $6.99

Rage of Angels
0-688-03687-2 MORROW $18.95
0-446-35661-1 WARNER PB $6.99

The Sands of Time
0-446-35683-2 WARNER PB $6.99

Windmills of the Gods
0-446-35010-9 WARNER PB $6.99

Danielle **Steel**

Changes
0-440-11181-1 DELL PB $5.99

Crossings
0-440-11585-X DELL PB $5.99

Family Album
0-440-12434-4 DELL PB $5.99

Fine Things
0-385-29527-8 DOUBLEDAY $18.95
0-440-20056-3 DELL PB $5.99

Full Circle
0-440-12689-4 DELL PB $5.99

Kaleidoscope
0-385-29594-4 DELACORTE $18.95
0-440-20192-6 DELL PB $5.99

A Perfect Stranger
0-440-16872-4 DELL PB $5.99

Remembrance
0-385-28843-3 DELACORTE $24.95
0-440-17370-1 DELL PB $6.50

The Ring
0-385-28872-7 DELACORTE $23.00
0-440-17392-2 DELL PB $6.50

Secrets
0-440-17648-4 DELL PB $6.50

Thurston House
0-440-18532-7 DELL PB $6.50

Wanderlust
0-385-29463-8 DELACORTE $17.95
0-440-19361-3 DELL PB $5.99

Zoya
0-385-29649-5 DELACORTE $19.95
0-440-20385-6 DELL PB $6.50

Trevanian

Shibumi
0-345-31180-9 BALLANTINE PB $6.99

Scott **Turow**

Presumed Innocent
See also **LEGAL THRILLERS** under **CRIME FICTION TODAY** under **CRIME FICTION**
0-374-23713-1 FS&G $22.95
0-446-35986-6 WARNER PB $6.99

Leon **Uris**

The Haj
0-553-24864-2 BDD PB $7.99

Joseph **Wambaugh**

The Glitter Dome
Four sets of police partners amid the glamor and grime of Hollywood
See also **THE POLICE PROCEDURAL: USA** under **CRIME FICTION TODAY** under **CRIME FICTION**
0-553-27259-4 BDD PB $6.50

Tom **Wolfe**

The Bonfire of the Vanities
0-374-11534-6 FS&G $19.95
0-553-27597-6 BDD PB $6.99

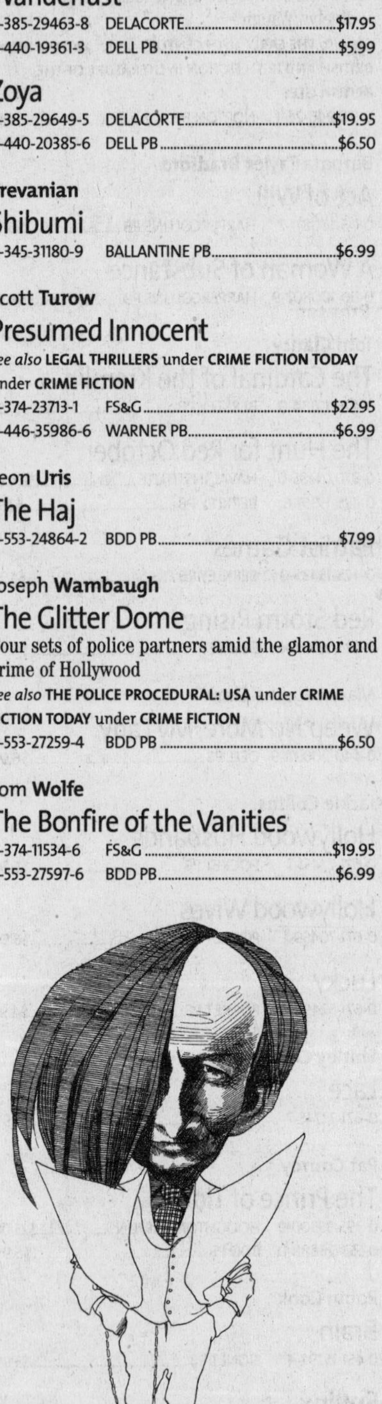

Tom Wolfe

Kathleen E. **Woodiwiss**

Come Love a Stranger

0-380-89936-1 AVON PB $5.99

A Rose in Winter

0-380-84400-1 AVON PB $6.50

The '90s

Cleveland **Amory**

The Cat Who Came for Christmas

On the *New York Times* bestseller list for eight straight years

0-14-025273-8 PENGUIN PB $9.95

Anonymous

Primary Colors: A Novel of Politics

The phenomenal bestseller written by "Anonymous." However, the author has been revealed to be columnist Joe Klein

0-679-44859-4 RANDOM HOUSE $24.00

Po **Bronson**

Bombardiers

"Hilarious, mad-as-hell entertainment that bites like an alligator...filled with the most memorable cast of loonies and sharpies since *One Flew Over the Cuckoo's Nest*"—*New York Daily News*

0-14-025450-1 PENGUIN PB $11.95

Caleb **Carr**

The Alienist

See also **ODD ONES OUT: EXPERIMENTS AND MIXED GENRES** under **CRIME FICTION TODAY** under **CRIME FICTION**

See also **NEW WRITERS OF THE '90S** under **20TH-CENTURY AMERICAN FICTION**

0-553-57299-7 BDD PB $7.50

Michael **Crichton**

Rising Sun

Controversial, high-tech murder mystery set in the arena of Japanese-American relations

0-394-58942-4 KNOPF $22.00

Dominick **Dunne**

A Season in Purgatory

After 20 years of covering up the peccadilloes of his wealthy, politically charismatic chum, Harrison Burns is forced to be exposed. A story of Kennedyesque privilege and power by the author of *An Inconvenient Woman* who knows this territory like few others

See also **SINCE 1945** under **20TH-CENTURY AMERICAN FICTION** in **LITERATURE OF THE AMERICAS**

0-517-58386-0 CROWN $22.00
0-679-42539-X RANDOM HOUSE $24.00
0-553-29076-2 BDD PB $6.99

Carrie **Fisher**

Delusions of Grandma

"*New York Times* best selling author Carrie Fisher is back with a novel about motherhood and modern-day families that is funny and touching"—Richard Rayner, *Harper's Bazaar*

0-671-73227-7 SIMON & SCHUSTER $22.00
0-671-73862-3 POCKET PB $5.99

Ken **Follett**

A Dangerous Fortune

The master storyteller of *Eye of the Needle, The Key to Rebecca,* and *The Pillars of the Earth* makes another departure into the world of Victorian England to tell the tale of a merchant banking family torn apart by greed, lust, and a passion for power

See also **CONTEMPORARY SPY FICTION** under **SPY FICTION**

0-440-21749-0 DELL PB $6.99

Hella **Haasse**

In a Dark Wood Wandering

The larger-than-life characters in this historical novel of the Hundred Years' War include Charles VI, Louis of Orleans, Richard II, and Henry V. "The great colorful pageant of events here unfolded... [is] described with scholarship and admirable lucidity. The characters really come to life"—*TLS*

See also **HISTORICAL AND ROMANTIC FICTION**

See also **DUTCH LITERATURE**

TRANSLATED BY LEWIS KAPLAN & ANITA MILLER

0-89733-336-5 ACADEMY CHICAGO $22.95

Terry **McMillan**

Disappearing Acts

The touching and often funny story of an educated black woman who falls in love with a construction worker

0-670-82461-5 VIKING $24.95

How Stella Got Her Groove Back

0-670-86990-2 VIKING $23.95

Mama

A tough, feisty heroine who'll do anything to keep her family together

0-671-74523-9 WASHINGTON SQUARE PB $14.00

Terry McMillian

Waiting to Exhale

This story of four black professional women and their search for a mature male has received enormous critical acclaim. *Waiting to Exhale* is "thought-provoking, thoroughly entertaining, and very, very comforting" —*NY Times Book Review*

0-670-83980-9 VIKING $22.95

James A. **Michener**

Caribbean

0-449-21749-3 CREST PB $6.99

Mario **Puzo**

The Last Don

0-679-45270-2 RANDOM HOUSE $24.00
0-679-75900-X RANDOM HOUSE PB $25.95

Martin Cruz **Smith**

Rose

The author of Gorky Park returns with a rich and intricate novel set in the coal country of Lancashire. Richly detailed and compelling, Rose promises to be Cruz's most accomplished and fascinating work of fiction to date

0-679-42661-2 RANDOM HOUSE $25.00
0-679-75878-X RANDOM HOUSE PB $25.00

Leon **Uris**

Redemption

Continuing in the same vein as his *Trinity,* Uris again takes us to Ireland at the turn of the century

0-06-018333-0 HARPERCOLLINS $25.00
0-06-109174-X HARPERCOLLINS PB $7.99

Robert James **Waller**

Puerto Vallarta Squeeze

0-446-51747-X WARNER $18.95

Comics

A circulation war between Joseph Pulitzer's *New York World* and William Randolph Hearst's *Journal* led to the birth of the color comic strip. After the *World* added color to *The Yellow Kid*, Hearst countered with his own color comics weekly, billed as "eight pages of polychromatic effulgence that make the rainbow look like a lead pipe." By 1900, cartoonists had established the now-familiar conventions of separate panels, sequential narrative, and dialogue in balloons.

The first successful daily black-and-white strip series began in 1907. Subsequent decades saw the emergence of an incredible variety of strips which have proven to be some of the most enduring and influential creations of American culture: *Little Nemo in Slumberland, Krazy Kat, Little Orphan Annie, Dick Tracy, Popeye, Flash Gordon, Li'l Abner, Prince Valiant, Terry and the Pirates,* among many others.

Comics expanded further in the '30s with the creation of the comic book, which in short order became the most notorious of American literary forms as superhero adventures gave way to the crime and horror extravaganzas of the '50s and, a decade later, to the delirious excesses of *Zap!* and other underground comics. By then comics were an international phenomenon, mutating into dramatically different forms and levels of seriousness in Europe, Asia, and Latin America. Today's "graphic novels" and "graphic albums" explore a constantly expanding range of genres, with a generous dose of the futuristic, the erotic, and the anarchically comic. A work like Art Spiegelman's *Maus*, in which the Holocaust experiences of Spiegelman's father are transmuted into an archetypal drama of stylized cats and mice, testifies to the continuing evolution of the medium.

General Studies and Reference

Martin **Barker**

A Haunt of Fears: The Strange History of the British Horror Comics Campaign

The early '50s crusade which led to Britain's Harmful Publications Act

0-87805-593-2 MISSISSIPPI $35.00
0-87805-594-0 MISSISSIPPI PB $15.95

Will **Eisner**

Graphic Storytelling

0-9614728-2-0 POORE PB $24.95

Robert C. **Harvey**

The Art of the Comic Book

0-87805-758-7 MISSISSIPPI PB $19.95

Martin **Sheridan**

Classic Comics and Their Creators

An early account, first published in 1942

0-911160-59-0 POST-ERA PB $14.95

Joseph **Witek**

Comic Books as History: The Narrative Art of Jack Jackson, Art Spiegelman, and Harvey Pekar

0-87805-406-5 MISSISSIPPI PB $15.95

Comic Strips

Milton **Caniff**

The Complete Dickie Dare

Caniff's first comic strip, featuring the exploits of Dickie Dare, Dan Flynn, and Kim Sheridan

0-930193-21-0 FANTAGRAPHICS PB $12.95

In Formosa's Dire Straits: A Steve Canyon Adventure

0-87816-044-2 KITCHEN SINK PB $11.95

Terry and the Pirates

Some volumes not listed here may be out of print. Please call with requests

Volume 3
Dragon Lady's Revenge

0-918348-26-9 N.B.M. PB $6.95

Volume 5
Shanghaied

0-918348-35-8 N.B.M. PB $5.95

Volume 6
The Warlord Klans

0-918348-37-4 N.B.M. PB $6.95

Volume 7
The Hunter

0-918348-42-0 N.B.M. PB $6.95

Volume 8
The Baron

0-918348-24-2 N.B.M. PB $6.95

Volume 9
Feminine Venom

0-918348-40-4 N.B.M. PB $6.95

Volume 10
Network of Intrigue

0-918348-60-9 N.B.M. PB $6.95

Volume 11
Gal Got Our Pal

0-918348-63-3 N.B.M. PB $6.95

Volume 17
Training with Flip Corkin 1943

0-918348-91-9 N.B.M. PB $6.95

Volume 19
Joker Among Aces, 1943-44

1-56163-008-X N.B.M. PB $3.50

Volume 20

1-56163-013-6 N.B.M. PB $6.95

Al **Capp**

Li'l Abner: Dailies

The first in a reprint series devoted to the chronicles of Dogpatch

0-87816-037-X KITCHEN SINK PB $16.95

Condo & Paper

The Outbursts of Everett True

Everett True, a portly man with a short fuse, has been described as a "living protest against the incarnate irritants that are with us always." This collection first appeared in 1907

0-911572-30-9 VESTAL PB $4.95

Lyonel **Feininger**

The Kin-Der-Kids: All 31 Strips in Full Color

The Bauhaus painter's contribution to comic strips, which first appeared in the *Chicago Sunday Tribune* in 1906

0-486-23918-7 DOVER PB $7.95

Lyonel Feininger

Hal **Foster**

Prince Valiant
Volume 29
Monastery of Demons

0-930193-08-3 FANTAGRAPHICS PB $14.95

Volume 30
Arn, Son of Valiant

0-930193-22-9 FANTAGRAPHICS PB $9.95

Volume 31
A Joust for Aleta

0-930193-37-7 FANTAGRAPHICS PB $9.95

Prince Valiant: The Sun Goddess

The controversy rages on: Columbus discovered America. Leif Erickson discovered America. Irish monks discovered America. But comic strip devotees have known since 1947 that Prince Valiant discovered America, in company with his golden-tressed Princess Aleta

1-56097-059-6 FANTAGRAPHICS PB $16.95

Chester **Gould**

Dick Tracy: America's Most Famous Detective

EDITED BY BILL CROUCH, JR.

0-8065-1059-5 CITADEL PB $14.95

Harold **Gray**

The Complete Little Orphan Annie

Volume 1 is currently out of print

Volume 2: 1932

0-930193-60-1 FANTAGRAPHICS PB $14.95

Volume 3: 1933

1-56097-039-1 FANTAGRAPHICS PB $16.95

R. C. **Harvey**

Cartoons of the Roaring Twenties

9-99188-692-3 FANTAGRAPHICS PB $8.95

George **Herriman**

Krazy and Ignatz: Pilgrims on the Road to Nowhere: Komplete Kat Komics

1-56060-024-1 TURTLE ISLAND PB $9.95

Jack **Jackson**

God's Bosom and Other Stories: The Historical Strips of Jack Jackson

1-56097-171-1 FANTAGRAPHICS PB $14.95

Walt **Kelly**

Pogo

1-56097-126-6 FANTAGRAPHICS PB $9.95
1-56097-190-8 FANTAGRAPHICS PB $9.95

Pogo Files for Pogophiles

A retrospective on 50 years of Walt Kelly's classic comic strip

0-945185-04-9 SPRIW $35.00

Hank **Ketcham**

Dennis the Menace: His First 40 Years

Ketcham himself has selected for this book almost 900 of his strips, given them wisecracking

commentary, and tells some of his own tales as cartoon artist with a reading public of 100 million
1-55859-157-5 ABBEVILLE PB $15.95

Joseph Moncure **March**
The Wild Party: The Lost Classic
Spiegelman's brilliant tribute to illustrations of the '20s brings new life to March's celebrated doggerel epic of Hollywood decadence. As Spiegelman notes: "Maybe it's March's perfectly pitched tone of bewildered innocence curdled into worldly cynicism that resonates so well in our nineties"
ILLUSTRATED BY ART SPIEGELMAN
0-679-42450-4 PANTHEON $22.00

Winsor **McCay**
The Complete Little Nemo in Slumberland
All six volumes of this series are in print; however they are often difficult to obtain
EDITED WITH AN INTRODUCTION BY RICHARD MARSHALL
0-930193-63-6 FANTAGRAPHICS $35.00

Day Dreams and Nightmares: Black and White Art of Winsor McCay
0-930193-56-3 FANTAGRAPHICS PB $19.95

Dreams of the Rarebit Fiend
The surreal effects of eating Welsh rarebit, documented with McCay's usual precision and splendor in a run of strips first collected in 1905
0-486-21347-1 DOVER PB $4.95

Little Nemo in the Palace of Ice
Full-color reproductions of some of the best episodes from *Little Nemo in Slumberland*
0-486-23234-4 DOVER PB $8.95

Patrick **McDonnell**
Krazy Kat: The Art of George Herriman
"From the appearance of *Krazy Kat* before the First World War, it's been widely recognized that Herriman had achieved something not only entrancing on its own terms but also uncannily modern, bearing deep affinities to the spirit and form of crucial styles in vanguard art"
—Adam Gopnik, *NY Review of Books*
INTRODUCTION BY GILBERT SELDES
0-8109-2313-0 ABRAMS PB $14.95

Richard F. **Outcault**
Buster Brown
Fifteen episodes from the turn-of-the-century strip, reproduced in the original full colors
0-88355-661-8 HYPERION $16.50

Alex **Raymond**
Flash Gordon: Volume 1 —Mongo, the Planet of Doom
Sunday color episodes of the greatest of space adventures, originally published in 1934 and 1935. Raymond's storytelling verve reigns supreme
0-87816-162-7 KITCHEN SINK PB $21.95

Brian **Walker**
The Best of Ernie Bushmiller's Nancy
A wonderful compilation of one of the most popular and most imaginative comic strips ever
0-8050-0925-6 HOLT PB $10.95

Alex **Raymond** & others
Secret Agent X-9
Not the best of Hammett, and a far cry from his usual hardboiled heroes, but Alex Raymond's artwork is outstanding as always
0-93033-005-6 INTL POLYGONICS PB $9.95

E.C. **Segar**
The Complete Segar Popeye: Volume 1
The most popular and enduring comic strip character ever created, presented in oversized format. While many of the volumes in this 11-part series are currently out of print, others, still in print, may be difficult to find. Please call for information on individual volumes
0-930193-00-8 FANTAGRAPHICS PB $12.95

Art Spiegelman's Favorites

Bill **Blackbeard**, editor
The Comic Strip Century: Celebrating 100 Years of an American Art Form
An Anthology from the *Yellow Kid* through *Calvin and Hobbes* that expands and perfectly complements the editor's previous seminal anthology—*The Smithsonian Book of Comic Strips*
0-87816-355-7 KITCHEN SINK $79.95

Chester **Brown**
I Never Liked You: A Comic Book
0-9696701-6-8 DRAWN PB $12.95

Playboy
Haunting and memorable
0-9696701-1-7 DRAWN PB $12.95

Bob **Callahan**, editor
The New Comix
A perfect introduction, well-selected, of the new comics. As I blurbed it: "the best one-stop shop for what's been happening in 21st century lit"
0-02-009361-6 COLLIER PB $19.95

Howard **Cruse**
Stuck Rubber Baby
One of the very few graphic novels that is not just a euphemistically re-named long comic book, but an autobiographically-rooted, gay coming-of-age story that really has the texture of a novel in its structure and detailed observation
1-56389-216-2 WARNER $24.95

Lyonel **Feininger** & Bill **Blackbeard**
The Comic Strip Art of Lyonel Feininger
The complete comics output of Sunday pages by the Bauhaus painter who is every bit as inventive a fantasist in his own way as Winsor McCay
0-87816-294-1 KITCHEN SINK PB $16.95

Scott **McCloud**
Understanding Comics
Cleverly disguised as an easy to read comic book. McCloud deconstructs the secret language of comics and builds an aesthetic base for critical understanding. A must-have item
0-87816-244-5 KITCHEN SINK $27.95

Steven **Heller** & Seymour **Chwast**
Jackets Required: An Illustrated History of Book Jacket Design, 1920-1950
A graphic feast for graphic artists, students of design, and cultural historians
See also **BOOKBINDING AND PAPER CRAFTS** under **CRAFTS** in **ARCHITECTURE, DESIGN, AND HOMES**
0-8118-0396-1 CHRONICLE PB $19.95

David **Kunzle**
The History of the Comic Strip: The Nineteenth Century
An overwhelming work of scholarship, lavishly illustrated, that unearths the "pre-history" of comics from Cruikshank through Topffer, Busch and Doré. The first volume (out-of-print), *The Early Comic Strip,* and this are landmark works in understanding the development of 20th-century visual media
0-520-05775-9 CALIFORNIA $135.00

Joe **Sacco**
Palestine: A Nation Occupied
First-person jounalism in comix format. Sacco is partisan, though fair and complex, in reporting on several months, of travel and interviews in Israel and the West Bank. He's a cartoonist with a flair for eye-popping page layouts
1-150-97150-9 FANTAGRAPHICS PB $14.95

Comics of the 1950s and '60s

Carl **Barks**
Uncle Scrooge McDuck: His Life and Times
A sumptuous anthology, beautifully colored, filled with masterpieces by the legendary "good duck artist"
EDITED BY EDWARD SUMMER
INTRODUCTION BY GEORGE LUCAS
0-89087-511-1 CELESTIAL ARTS $59.95

Les **Daniels**
Marvel: Five Fabulous Decades of the World's Greatest Comics
A lavishly illustrated chronicle of the thriving workshop where *The Incredible Hulk, The Avengers, Spider-Man,* and countless other icons of America's fantasy life were hatched. "Simply marvelous"
—*Atlanta Journal-Constitution*
0-8109-3821-9 ABRAMS $49.50
0-8109-2566-4 ABRAMS PB $24.95

Dick **DeBartolo**
Good Days at Mad: A Hysterical Tour Behind the Scenes at Mad Magazine
From the birth of the magazine and its instant success in 1952 through its struggles with censorship and the in-office shenanigans of those immortal artists, Al Jaffee, Jack Davis, and Don Martin, this is the real story
1-56025-077-1 THUNDER'S MOUTH $29.95

The Editors and Contributors of MAD Magazine

Mad About the Sixties: The Best of the Decade

No longer just for the baby boomers who grew up with it, *MAD Magazine* has been discovered by a whole new generation. This retrospective showcases the magazine's best from the era of Tiny Tim and Timothy Leary—annotated for those too young to get the period references. Parodies include "Star Blecch" and "The Phewgitive," a *West Side Story* with Khrushchev and Castro dancing in the streets, and a brilliant satire of the—then—new administration, "A Day with JFK"

0-316-33418-9 LITTLE, BROWN PB $19.95

Will **Eisner**

The Outer Space Spirit

The Spirit's 1952 finale

INTRODUCTIONS BY PETE HAMILL & CATHERINE YRONWODE

0-87816-007-8 KITCHEN SINK $15.95
0-87816-012-4 KITCHEN SINK PB $9.95

Mark J. **Estren**

The History of Underground Comics

This much-requested book is now back in print—a superbly (and often explicitly) detailed look at Crumb, Deitch, Shelton, and all the other mad geniuses of underground comics

0-914171-64-X RONIN PB $19.95

Harvey **Kurtzman**

Harvey Kurtzman's Jungle Book

A 1958 classic written and drawn by the creator of *Mad*, including such indelible parodies as "The Organization Man in the Grey Flannel Executive Suite" and the *Peter Gunn*-derived "Thelonious Violence." "Highly recommended for a taste of Kurtzman on his own and at his sharpest"—*Village Voice*

0-87816-033-7 KITCHEN SINK PB $14.95

Maria **Reidelbach**

Completely Mad: A History of the Comic Book and Magazine

An intelligent, well-designed popular history, profusely illustrated, of the magazine that shaped a generation

0-316-73891-3 LITTLE, BROWN PB $24.95

Dick **Voll**, editor

Wolvertoons: The Art of Basil Wolverton

Wolverton's grotesque drawings, appearing in *Mad* and elsewhere, represented the outer limits of comics art in the '50s. Wolverton was a major influence on the underground artists who followed

INTRODUCTION BY GAHAN WILSON

1-56097-022-7 FANTAGRAPHICS PB $19.95

New Yorker Anthologies

The New Yorker

The New Yorker Book of Cat Cartoons

0-394-58795-2 KNOPF $20.00

Charles **Addams**

The World of Charles Addams

A celebration of the macabre genius who contributed more than 1,300 cartoons and covers to *The New Yorker;* 300 of the best of them are reproduced here

0-394-58822-3 KNOPF $35.00

The New Yorker Book of Doctor and Psychiatrist Cartoons

0-679-76573-5 KNOPF PB $10.00

The New Yorker Book of Dog Cartoons

Dogs in an endless variety of incarnations—drawn from 65 years of *The New Yorker*—by Charles Addams, George Booth, Roz Chast, Edward Koren, Edward Sorel, Saul Steinberg, and James Thurber

See also **DOG STORIES AND HUMOR** under **DOGS** under **PETS** in **FOOD, TRAVEL, AND LEISURE**

0-679-41680-3 KNOPF $20.00
0-679-76542-5 KNOPF PB $9.00

The New Yorker Book of Lawyer Cartoons

0-679-43068-7 KNOPF $20.00
0-679-76574-3 KNOPF PB $10.00

Contemporary Comic Strip Artists and Cartoonists

Max **Andersson**

Pixy

Sweden's hot new cartoonist has created a world of safe-sex suits, buildings, drunken fetuses with bazookas, money that shits on you, and recyclable bodies

1-56097-131-2 FANTAGRAPHICS PB $11.95

Berke **Breathed**

Bloom County Babylon: Five Years of Bask Naughtiness

0-316-10309-8 LITTLE, BROWN PB $13.95

Goodnight Opus

This full-color illustrated book takes everyone's (or mostly everyone's) favorite penguin to an adventure where the imagination—even an unusually active one—hits its limit

0-316-10853-7 LITTLE, BROWN $14.95
0-316-10599-6 LITTLE, BROWN PB $5.95

John **Callahan**

Do What He Says! He's Crazy!

"There are two basic reasons I like Callahan's [cartoons] so much" writes Gary Larson (*The Far Side*): "First, I think [he's] plain funny, and second, he makes my own work look normal." Political correctness, codependency, and Dan Quayle are just a few of the targets in Callahan's look at America in the '90s. "The freshest young cartoonist of our time"—*The Miami Herald*

0-688-11815-1 QUILL PB $8.00

Roz **Chast**

Mondo Boxo

0-06-015824-7 HARPERCOLLINS $49.50

Dan **Clowes**

Lout Rampage

This collection of stories from early issues of *Eightball* and various other sources gets an extra shot in the arm with six stories now printed in full color

1-56097-070-7 FANTAGRAPHICS PB $14.95

The Official Lloyd Llewellyn Collection

Ninty-six pages of astro beatniks, babes, LSD, monsters, chicks, bad rock'n'roll, strippers, sex-crazed aliens, communist cuties, wet cigarettes, and more

0-930193-90-3 FANTAGRAPHICS PB $10.95

Like a Velvet Glove Cast in Iron

Clowes's epic exploration of the seamy underbelly of America makes *Twin Peaks* look like *Captain Kangaroo*

1-56097-116-9 FANTAGRAPHICS PB $16.95

Joe **Coleman**

Cosmic Retribution: The Infernal Art of Joe Coleman

Legendary performance artist–painter Joe Coleman has outraged audiences for over a decade. This may be his greatest outrage yet

0-922915-06-7 FANTAGRAPHICS PB $22.95

Howard **Cruse**

Dancin' Nekkid with the Angels

Comic strips from the creator of Wendel

See also **HUMOR** under **GAY, LESBIAN, AND BISEXUAL STUDIES** in **SOCIAL STUDIES**

0-312-01104-0 ST. MARTIN'S PB $9.95

Jim **Davis**

The Garfield Treasury

0-345-32106-5 BALLANTINE PB $11.95

The Second Garfield Treasury

9-995-14780-7 STOHS $15.25

The Fourth Garfield Treasury

0-345-34726-9 BALLANTINE PB $10.95

The Fifth Garfield Treasury

0-345-36268-3 BALLANTINE PB $12.00

The Sixth Garfield Treasury

0-345-37367-7 BALLANTINE PB $10.95

The Seventh Garfield Treasury

0-345-38427-X BALLANTINE PB $10.95

The Eighth Garfield Treasury

0-345-39778-9 BALLANTINE PB $12.00

Kim **Deitch**

Beyond the Pale

Deitch's best work from the '70s and '80s is featured in this mammoth collection

0-930193-83-0 FANTAGRAPHICS PB $14.95

A Shroud for Waldo

1-56097-081-2 FANTAGRAPHICS PB $7.95

Michael **Dougan**

East Texas: Tales from Behind the Pine Curtain

"Michael Dougan's *East Texas* whomps you on the behind and makes your eyeballs bug straight out of your head"—Lynda Barry

0-941104-25-7 REAL COMET PB $7.95

Drew **Friedman** & Josh **Friedman**

Any Similarity to Persons Living or Dead Is Purely Coincidental

Born-again black humor from the caustic chroniclers of celebrity geeksville

0-930193-27-X FANTAGRAPHICS PB $12.95

George **Gately**

Heathcliff

0-8125-6814-1 TOR PB $2.50

Edward **Gorey**

Amphigorey

The oblique and macabre black humor of the contemporary American artist

See also **BOOK ILLUSTRATION** under **ILLUSTRATION AND POPULAR GRAPHICS** in **ART**

0-399-50433-8 PERIGEE PB $16.00

Amphigorey Too

0-399-50420-6 PERIGEE PB $16.00

Bill **Griffith**

Zippy: Nation of Pinheads

0-86719-365-4 LAST GASP PB $5.95

Zippy Stories

0-86719-325-5 LAST GASP PB $14.95

Zippy's House of Fun: 54 Months of Sundays

A handsome collection of Zippy Sunday strips in full color. Unquestionably of the quirkiest and most intelligent strips to actually and improbably appear in daily newspapers!

1-56097-162-2 FANTAGRAPHICS $39.95

Matt **Groening**

"Matt Groening is the rambunctious, unpredictable, taboo-defying alternative cartoonist who makes Gary Trudeau's Doonesbury seem, by comparison, reminiscent of Mary Worth."—LA Times

Akbar and Jeff's Guide to Life

This new collection of cartoons by the creator of *Love is Hell, Work Is Hell,* and *Childhood Is Hell* confirms Matt Groening as one of the most distinctive comic talents of recent years, unmatched for deadpan absurdity and disturbingly sharp insights

0-679-72680-2 PANTHEON PB $7.95

Cartooning with the Simpsons

Learn to draw America's favorite cartoon family, with instructions by the characters themselves. Includes such useful tips as how high to make Marge Simpson's hair while teaching basic drawing techniques

0-06-096874-5 HARPERPERENNIAL PB $12.00

Childhood Is Hell

0-679-72055-3 PANTHEON PB $7.95

Matt Groening (photo courtesy of Pantheon Books)

School Is Hell

0-394-75091-8 PANTHEON PB $7.95

Work Is Hell

0-394-74864-6 RANDOM HOUSE PB $7.95

Robert C. **Harvey**

The Art of the Funnies: An Aesthetic History

0-87805-612-2 MISSISSIPPI $42.50

Nicole **Hollander**

Never Tell Your Mother this Dream

"Please send me more feminists like the saucy Nicole Hollander, creator of the fiftyish, wisecracking, chain-smoking, beer-swilling Sylvia"—Mordecai Richler, *NY Times*

0-312-56480-5 ST. MARTIN'S PB $4.95

The Whole Enchilada: A Spicy Collection of Sylvia

0-312-87757-9 ST. MARTIN'S PB $11.95

Kaz

Buzzbomb

Frenetic and explosive work by a cartoonist who has appeared in *Weirdo* and *Raw*

0-930193-57-1 FANTAGRAPHICS PB $9.95

B. **Kliban**

Cat

1-56305-284-9 WORKMAN PB $7.95

Never Eat Anything Bigger than Your Head & Other Drawings

0-911104-67-4 WORKMAN PB $5.95

Russell **Myers**

Broom Hilda: The Backward Heimlich

0-686-87085-9 FAWCETT PB $1.95

Jean-Jacques **Sempe**

The Musicians

Sixteen color and 49 black-and-white illustrations by the *New York* cover artist

0-89480-099-X WORKMAN $14.95

Garry B. **Trudeau**

I'd Go with the Helmet, Ray

The Trudeau team confronts the Gulf crisis: a much-needed satiric footnote to recent history

0-8362-1870-1 ANDREWS & MCMEEL PB $6.95

Doonesbury Deluxe: Selected Glances Askance

0-8050-0596-X HOLT PB $16.95

The Peoples Doonesbury: Notes from Underfoot

0-8050-1074-2 HOLT PB $18.95

Welcome to Club Scud!

This volume contains some of the best reporting on the Gulf War, a no-holds-barred indictment of Kitty Kelley's Nancy Reagan biography, and a sardonic view of Malibu-style group therapy

0-679-40641-7 PANTHEON $18.00

0-8362-1882-5 ANDREWS & MCMEEL PB $6.95

Peter **Van Straaten**

This Literary Life

A Dutch cartoonist's wry, sometimes painfully funny vignettes of the writer's life—and the agent's, the publisher's, and the bookseller's

0-918273-92-7 COFFEE HOUSE PB $7.50

Bill **Watterson**

Calvin and Hobbes

0-8362-2088-9 ANDREWS & MCMEEL PB $9.95

The Essential Calvin and Hobbes

0-8362-1805-1 ANDREWS & MCMEEL PB $12.95

Political Cartoonists

Herbert **Block**

Herblock: A Cartoonist's Life

For more than 50 years Block's work at *The Washington Post* has been *the* definition of that concise and devastating form known as the political cartoon. A trenchant critic of McCarthyism (a term he invented), Nixon, Bush, et al., Block regales us with the fascinating story of his life and the powerful people he's known, peppered with 200 of his favorite cartoons. "Herblock is the only genius who proves it every day"—Bob Woodward

0-02-511895-1 MACMILLAN $24.00

Charles **Brooks**, editor

Best Editorial Cartoons of the Year: 1992 Edition

0-88289-910-4 PELICAN PB $14.95

Best Editorial Cartoons of the Year: 1993 Edition

0-88289-968-6PELICAN PB $14.95

Best Editorial Cartoons of the Year: 1994 Edition

1-56554-011-5 PELICAN PB $14.95

Best Editorial Cartoons of the Year: 1995 Edition

1-56554-117-0 PELICAN PB $14.95

Best Editorial Cartoons of the Year: 1996 Edition

1-56554-201-0 PELICAN PB $14.95

George **Fisher**

The Best of Fisher: 28 Years of Editorial Cartoons from Faubus to Clinton

Native Arkansan Fisher has been drawing cartoons about his home state since the time of Governor Faubus. With one of his own now in the White House, he continues to publish cartoons in newspapers—many about Arkansas, all about the American way of punditry

1-55728-268-4 ARKANSAS $24.95
1-55728-269-2 ARKANSAS PB $14.95

Joe **Sacco**

Palestine: Book II: In the Gaza Strip

1-56097-300-5 FANTAGRAPHICS PB $16.95

War Junkie

Collected from Joe Sacco's *Yahoo, War Junkie* reprints issues #2-5, including "In the Company of Lonir," "When Good Bombs Happen to Bad People," "A Disgusting Experience," and "How I Loved the War," Sacco's sardonic take on the Gulf War and the media frenzy

1-56097-170-3 FANTAGRAPHICS PB $14.95

Zbynek **Zeman**

Heckling Hitler: Caricatures of the Third Reich

A study of anti-Nazi cartoons, with profiles of the artists and numerous illustrations

See also **HITLER: STUDIES IN TYRANNY** under **20TH-CENTURY EUROPE TO THE SECOND WORLD WAR** in **WORLD HISTORY AND CURRENT AFFAIRS**

0-87451-403-7 NEW ENGLAND PB $19.95

American Comic Books

Vaughn **Bode**

The Bode Sketchbook Diaries

1-56097-053-7 FANTAGRAPHICS PB $10.95

John **Byrne** & Dick **Giordano**

Superman: The Man of Steel

New adventures of a Superman revamped in the '80s

1-56389-067-4 DC COMICS PB $3.95

Graham S. **Chaffee**

Big Wheels

9-99469-279-8 FANTAGRAPHICS PB $6.95

Robert **Crumb**

The Complete Crumb Comics

Volume 1
Early Years of Bitter Struggle

Early strips and drawings by the emperor of underground comics. "Makes me proud to be an American"—Kurt Vonnegut, Jr.

0-93019-342-4 FANTAGRAPHICS PB $19.95

Volume 2
More Early Years of Bitter Struggle

Includes Crumb's letters and a biographical article from childhood friend Marty Pahls

0-930193-62-8 FANTAGRAPHICS PB $19.95

Volume 3
Starring Fritz the Cat

Includes rare art, "Fritz Bugs Out," and more of Pahls's article, which began in the previous volume

0-930193-79-2 FANTAGRAPHICS PB $19.95

Volume 4
Mister Sixties

This volume reprints *Zap* #0 and #1 (the comics that defined the underground look). Includes photos and an introduction by the author

0-930193-80-6 FANTAGRAPHICS $39.95

Volume 5
Happy Hippy Comix

Includes early "Mr. Natural" and "Angelfood McSpade" stories. Rarities include alternate covers to "Cheap Thrills" and *Zap* #3

0-930193-91-1 FANTAGRAPHICS $39.95
0-930193-92-X FANTAGRAPHICS PB $18.95

Volume 6
On the Crest of a Wave

Features comics and illustrations from 1969 and 1970, including the controversial X-rated teenage-incest story "Joe Blow"

1-56097-056-1 FANTAGRAPHICS PB $18.95

Volume 7
Hot 'n' Heavy

Early work from the '70s, including underground sex comics, album covers, and greeting cards

1-56097-061-8 FANTAGRAPHICS PB $16.95

Volume 8
Death of Fritz the Cat

Includes the "Whiteman Meets Bigfoot" story, as well as the complete *Mr. Natural* #2

1-56097-076-6 FANTAGRAPHICS PB $16.95

Volume 9
R. Crumb vs. The Sisterhood

Read the title story and discover for yourself whether Crumb is a misogynist or not. Also includes illustrations from the cookbook *Eat It* and photos of Crumb with the Cheap Suit Serenaders

1-56097-107-X FANTAGRAPHICS PB $18.95

Volume 10
Crumb Advocates Violent Overthrow

Includes the first book-length "Dirty Laundry," co-created by Aline Kominsky-Crumb

INTRODUCTION BY JESSE CRUMB

1-56097-137-1 FANTAGRAPHICS PB $16.95

Volume 11
Mr. Natural Committed to a Mental Institution

Features the forty-page Mr. Natural epic from *The Village Voice*

1-56097-172-X FANTAGRAPHICS PB $18.95

Matt **Feazell**

Cynicalman: The Paperback

Collects Stupid Boy, the Amazing Cynicalman, Cutegirl, and other stick-figure characters; a glimpse into the unpredictable world of small-press minicomics

0-917976-75-4 THUNDER BAAS PB $7.95

Ron **Goulart**

The Great Comic Book Artists

0-312-34557-7 ST. MARTIN'S PB $12.95

Gilbert **Hernandez**

The Collected Birdland

Libidinous fun

1-56097-200-9 FANTAGRAPHICS PB $12.95

Poison River: Love and Rockets Collection

1-56097-151-7 FANTAGRAPHICS PB $16.95

The Reticent Heart

Eight "Heartbreak Soup" and "Errata Stigmata" stories from *Love and Rockets.* "Mixes Al Capp's blunt carnality with Preston Sturges's compulsive complexities"—*Village Voice*

0-930193-65-2 FANTAGRAPHICS PB $10.95

Jaime **Hernandez**

The Lost Women & Others Stories

"Mechanics" and "Locas" stories reprinted from the popular comic *Love and Rockets.* "No one has ever caught the punk milieu as well as Jaime Hernandez"—*Louisville Times Scene*

0-930193-66-0 FANTAGRAPHICS PB $10.95

Wig Wam Bam

1-56097-121-5 FANTAGRAPHICS PB $14.95

Los Brothers Hernandez

Love and Rockets X: Complete Series

1-5609-7101-0 FANTAGRAPHICS PB $11.95

Burne **Hogarth**

The Arcane Eye of Hogarth

1-56097-087-1 FANTAGRAPHICS PB $19.95

Harvey **Kurtzman** & Will **Elder**

Goodman Beaver

Kurtzman's Candide-like hero encounters Superman, Tarzan, and other media figures in these reprints from the '60s magazine *Help!*

0-87816-008-6 KITCHEN SINK PB $9.95

Dave **Stevens**

The Rocketeer

Action and adventure in '30s Los Angeles

1-56971-092-9 DARK HORSE COMICS PB $10.00

Erick **Wujcik** & others

Teenage Mutant Ninja Turtles & Others Strangeness

0-916211-14-2 PALLADIUM PB $11.95

American Graphic Novels

Kyle **Baker**

The Cowboy Wally Show

A show-biz satire tracing the career of "legendary film star" Cowboy Wally

1-56924-834-6 MARLOWE PB $14.95

Howard **Cruse**

Early Barefoot

1-56097-052-9 FANTAGRAPHICS PB $11.95

Eric **Drooker**

FLOOD!: A Novel in Pictures

The tale of a day-dreaming, struggling artist, set amid the hard daily life of Manhattan's Lower East Side, *FLOOD!* bridges the gap between fine art graphics and popular comics. "Drooker can draw like a demon"—*Village Voice*

0-941423-79-4 FOUR WALLS PB....................$15.95

Will **Eisner**

The Building

The interconnections between four individuals involved with a city building under demolition. "A brilliant, graceful graphic novel by the master. It brought tears to my cynical eyes" —Max Allan Collins, *Comic Buyer's Guide*

0-87816-025-6 KITCHEN SINK PB....................$12.95

A Contract with God

The lives of tenants at 55 Dropsie Avenue in the Bronx during the '30s

0-87816-018-3 KITCHEN SINK PB....................$11.95

Dropsie Avenue: The Neighborhood

0-87816-348-4 KITCHEN SINK PB....................$15.95

Will Eisner Reader: Seven Graphic Stories by a Comic Master

0-87816-129-5 KITCHEN SINK PB....................$9.95

The Will Eisner Sketchbook

0-87816-400-6 KITCHEN SINK....................$39.95
0-87816-399-9 KITCHEN SINK PB....................$17.95

Bob **Foster**

The Evolution and History of Moosekind

A legitimate history of the world in cartoon form—except all the players have been replaced by moose, with moose-punning names

0-930193-96-2 FANTAGRAPHICS PB....................$6.95

Rick **Geary**

At Home with Rick Geary

Strange humor from *National Lampoon* and elsewhere. "At once an education, a compendium of magic, and a lot of laughs"—Alan Moore

0-930193-14-8 FANTAGRAPHICS PB....................$9.95

A Treasury of Victorian Murder

Graphic novellas of murders researched from 19th-century British newspapers

0-918348-41-2 N.B.M. PB....................$6.95

Larry **Gonick**

The Cartoon History of the Universe: Volumes 1-7

A funny but deep-down serious pictorial account of what happened between the Big Bang and Alexander the Great. "Obviously one of the great books of all time"—Terry Jones

0-385-26520-4 DOUBLEDAY PB....................$17.50

The Cartoon History of the Universe II, Volumes 8-13: From the Springtime of China to the Fall of Rome

"An ideal Christmas or Chanukah gift…The kids will love it, once you stop reading and hand it over…This truly fun book covers thirteen billion years of history and explains and illustrates the major achievements of modern civilization…I was totally fascinated and I'm sure you will be, too"—Ann Landers

0-385-42093-5 MAIN STREET PB....................$15.95

Paul **Karasik** & David **Mazzucchelli**

Neon Lit: Paul Auster's City of Glass

First of a series of "Neon Lit" adaptations of post-modern crime novels made into comics form. This adaptation of the first part of Auster's "New York Trilogy" is a model of how flexible the comix medium can be, even to adapting a novel as relentlessly non-visual as Auster's

0-380-77108-X AVON PB....................$12.50

Peter **Kuper**

New York, New York

Twelve tales of angst in the Big Apple. "It is Peter Kuper's bent to find the personality lurking within the inanimate and pull it to the surface in all its ironic glory"—*Print Magazine*

0-930193-54-7 FANTAGRAPHICS PB....................$9.95

Stripped

This unauthorized autobiography collects the best pieces from *Bleeding Heart and Wild Life* plus eight new pages

1-56097-177-0 FANTAGRAPHICS PB....................$9.95

Terry **Laban**

International Bob

1-56097-135-5 FANTAGRAPHICS PB....................$9.95

Love's Not a Three Dollar Fare

This new collection compiles all the "Danny and Suzy" tales from *Unsupervised Existence,* including the hard-to-find minicomics stories and the classic birthday-blues story "Twenty-Six"

1-56097-165-7 FANTAGRAPHICS PB....................$14.95

Solano **Lopez**

Ana

Internationally renowned Argentinean cartoonist Lopez collaborated with his son on the story of a young woman caught in the grip of a fascist police state. The imagery is often brutal, but never exploitive

1-56097-066-9 FANTAGRAPHICS PB....................$12.95

David Zane **Mairowitz** & Robert **Crumb**

Introducing Kafka

This comics adaptation of Kafka stories and gloss on Kafka's life by a contemporary comix master may be best read as literary criticism rather than as an introduction, but it is a virtuoso performance by Crumb

1-87416-609-9 TOTEM PB....................$9.95

Frank **Miller**

Batman: The Dark Knight Returns

An aged Batman combats '80s-style street crime

0-446-38505-0 WARNER PB....................$13.95

Ronin

A dishonored 13th-century samurai resurrected in 21st-century New York: a graphic triumph, with a remarkable contribution by colorist Lynn Varley

0-930289-21-8 WARNER PB....................$14.95

Frank **Miller** & David **Mazzucchelli**

Batman: Year One

0-446-38923-4 WARNER PB....................$10.95

Steve **Moncuse**

Fish Police

An underwater fantasy which Harlan Ellison has called "a mystery and a comedy and a wonky look at a world where what is ain't really what it's supposed to be"

0-446-38739-8 WARNER PB....................$8.95

Pepe **Moreno**

Zeppelin

Fantastic visions of warfare

0-87416-021-9 CATALAN PB....................$10.95

Harvey **Pekar** & Joyce **Brabner**

Our Cancer Year

Here he and his wife narrate Pekar's encounter with cancer in the year of the Persian Gulf War—a mortal struggle against the backdrop of a militaristic absurdity

ILLUSTRATIONS BY FRANK STACK

1-56858-011-8 FOUR WALLS PB....................$17.95

Art **Spiegelman**

Maus: A Survivor's Tale

When Art Spiegelman undertook an epic account of the Holocaust and its impact on the American son of an Auschwitz survivor in the form of a comic book featuring mice, cats, and other emblematic animals, few could have foreseen the masterpiece that resulted. Available in separate volumes or as a set, in both paperback and hardcover. "The most affecting and successful narrative ever done about the Holocaust" —*Wall Street Journal*

Volume 1
My Father Bleeds History

See also **HOLOCAUST FICTION** under **ART AND LITERATURE** under **THE HOLOCAUST** in **WORLD HISTORY AND CURRENT AFFAIRS**

0-394-54155-3 PANTHEON....................$22.00
0-394-74723-2 PANTHEON PB....................$14.00

Volume 2
And Here My Troubles Began

0-394-55655-0 PANTHEON....................$22.00
0-679-72977-1 PANTHEON PB....................$14.00

Boxed set of both volumes

0-679-41038-4 PANTHEON....................$44.00
0-679-74840-7 PANTHEON PB....................$28.00

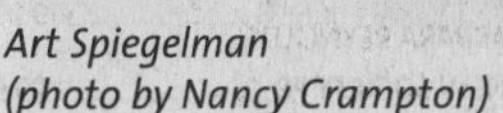

Art Spiegelman (photo by Nancy Crampton)

Stan **Sakai**

Usagi Yojimbo: Book One

The adventures of a samurai rabbit

0-930193-35-0 FANTAGRAPHICS PB........$12.95

Ralph **Steadman**

America

The artist who added his savage visions to Hunter S. Thompson's classic treatises on Las Vegas, the Hell's Angels, and Nixon's presidential campaign serves up a helping of graphic vitriol.

0-930193-78-4 FANTAGRAPHICS PB........$14.95

Carol **Tyler**

The Job Thing

1-56097-111-8 FANTAGRAPHICS PB........$7.95

Jim **Woodring**

The Book of Jim

1-56097-091-X FANTAGRAPHICS PB........$17.95

Japanese Comics

"These are the legendary *manga,* the picture books that account for more than a fourth of Japan's publishing and that may yet make literature obsolete. Open one at random and you might find anything—a sleek extraterrestrial landscape, an illustrated treatise on golf or fishing, an episode of torture, an elaborate reconstruction of 16th-century court life or 20th-century gang warfare, a sexy or caricatural romp among high school students—all rendered in a black-and-white so richly varied it makes color beside the point."—*Village Voice*

The world of Japanese comics is only beginning to make its impact felt in America, but the following titles offer some hint of its riches and oddities.

Shotaro **Ishinomori**

Japan, Inc.: Introduction to Japanese Economics

A full-scale comic book version of a textbook on the Japanese economy, with a melodramatic plot to speed things along

See also **ECONOMICS AND BUSINESS** under **JAPAN** in **WORLD HISTORY AND CURRENT AFFAIRS**

INTRODUCTION BY PETER DUUS

0-520-06289-2 CALIFORNIA PB........$15.95

Keiji **Nakazawa**

Barefoot Gen: A Cartoon Story of Hiroshima

Nakazawa was a child in Hiroshima when the bomb fell, and in the dense and realistic *Barefoot Gen* he recounts his life up to and including that day

See also **THE ATOMIC BOMB** under **FROM THE MEIJI RESTORATION TO THE END OF THE EMPIRE: 1868–1945** under **JAPAN** in **WORLD HISTORY AND CURRENT AFFAIRS**

0-86571-095-3 NEW SOCIETY PB........$12.95

Barefoot Gen: The Day After

A continuation of Nakazawa's autobiographical life-work

FOREWORD BY BARBARA REYNOLDS

0-86571-123-2 NEW SOCIETY PB........$9.95

Frederik **Schodt**

Manga! Manga!: The World of Japanese Comics

A superbly researched and elegantly written history of Japanese comics, including 96 pages of complete translated stories. "Definitive…An unlikely fusion of scholarship, enthusiasm, and wit"—*Village Voice*

See also **CONTEMPORARY SOCIETY AND CULTURE** under **JAPAN** in **WORLD HISTORY AND CURRENT AFFAIRS**

0-87011-752-1 KODANSHA PB........$22.00

Yoshihiro **Tatsuiti**

Good-Bye & Other Stories

Life in postwar Japan, rendered with unusual realism

0-87416-056-1 CATALAN PB........$10.95

European Comics

Enki **Bilal**

Gods in Chaos

Aliens in Paris in the year 2023

0-87416-049-9 CATALAN PB........$12.95

Pierre **Christin** & Enki **Bilal**

The Hunting Party

A striking new work by two European masters of the graphic novel: a hunting party undertaken by a group of old-line Communist leaders in Eastern Europe becomes a study in corruption and decay

0-87416-053-7 CATALAN PB........$14.95

Guido **Crepax**

Anita

1-56163-044-6 N.B.M. PB........$11.95

Anita Live

1-56163-031-4 N.B.M. PB........$11.95

Emmanuelle

0-918348-87-0 N.B.M. PB........$11.95

Emmanuelle Three: Anti-Virgin

1-56163-057-8 N.B.M. PB........$11.95

The Man from Harlem

Crime and jazz in New York during the bebop era

0-87416-040-5 CATALAN PB........$10.95

Venus in Furs

Another uninhibited sexual fantasia from an Italian artist noted for the swirling energy of his graphics

0-87416-091-X CATALAN PB........$11.95

Jean-Pierre **Dionnet** & Enki **Bilal**

Exterminator Seventeen

0-87416-024-3 CATALAN PB........$11.95

Jean-Claude **Forest** & Paul **Gillon**

Lost in Time: Labyrinths

A 20th-century couple revived in 3000 AD, from the creator of *Barbarella*

0-918348-18-8 N.B.M........$8.95

Vittorio **Giardino**

Cases from the Files of Sam Pezzo, P.I.

A detective adventure in a contemporary setting

0-87416-057-X CATALAN PB........$8.95

Orient Gateway

An Istanbul thriller featuring the hero of *Hungarian Rhapsody*

0-87416-041-3 CATALAN PB........$12.95

Loustal & Paringaux

Barney and the Blue Note

Downbeat lives and loves in the jazz world, captured in panels of somber beauty

90-72118-12-X FANTAGRAPHICS PB........$14.95

Lorenzo **Mattotti**

Fires

Ecological expressionism as naval officer Lieutenant Absinthe, entranced by a magical island, deserts his ship to save this paradise from destruction

0-87416-048-0 CATALAN PB........$12.95

Nazario

Anarcoma

The gay scene in Barcelona, featuring "streetwise transvestite and self-styled detective" Anarcoma

0-87416-000-6 CATALAN........$9.95

Hugo **Pratt**

Corto Maltese in Africa

World War I-era adventures by a popular European comics artist

0-918348-38-2 N.B.M. PB........$8.95

Roberto **Raviola**

The Specialist: Full Moon in Dendera

Terrorists and multinationals battle it out in the Middle East

0-87416-044-8 CATALAN PB........$8.95

Marti **Riera**

The Cabbie

Barcelona artist Marti spent three years recapturing the style of Chester Gould's *Dick Tracy* in his own story about a cabdriver, a "prototypical solitary individual, out of touch and helpless in a predatory and hostile world that doesn't have time for people who can't keep up with the twentieth century"

INTRODUCTION BY ART SPIEGELMAN

0-87416-042-1 CATALAN PB........$10.95

Carlos **Sampayo** & José **Muñoz**

Joe's Bar

Expressionistic drawings by Muñoz illustrate Sampayo's short stories centered on a New York City bar

INTRODUCTIONS BY ART SPIEGELMAN

0-87416-046-4 CATALAN PB........$10.95

Carlos **Sampayo** & F. **Solano-López**

Evaristo: Deep City

Violent tales of a Buenos Aires police commissioner in the late '50s and early '60s

0-87416-034-0 CATALAN PB........$10.95

Schuiten & Peeters

The Great Walls of Samaris

The Belgian artist Schuiten illustrates a haunting tale of the mysterious city Samaris in this large-format graphic novel, first serialized in *Heavy Metal*

0-918348-36-6 N.B.M. PB........$9.95

Matthias **Schultheiss**

Bell's Theorem

Eerie science fiction from a West German writer-artist, about a dead scientist's mind resurfacing in an escaped convict

0-87416-037-5 CATALAN PB $10.95

Stefano **Tamburini** & Gaetano **Liberatore**

Ranxerox in New York

INTRODUCTION BY RICHARD CORBEN

0-87416-027-8 CATALAN PB $10.95

Tintin

Hergé

Tintin is a boy who has sensational adventures in the company of a little white dog and an odd character known as the Captain. Kids still like these unusual cartoon adventure classics.

The Black Island

0-316-35835-5 LITTLE, BROWN PB $8.95

The Calculus Affair

0-316-35847-9 LITTLE, BROWN PB $8.95

The Castafiore Emerald

0-316-35842-8 LITTLE, BROWN PB $8.95

Cigars of the Pharoah

0-316-35836-3 LITTLE, BROWN PB $8.95

The Crab with the Golden Claws

0-316-35833-9 LITTLE, BROWN PB $8.95

King Ottokar's Sceptre

0-316-35831-2 LITTLE, BROWN PB $8.95

Prisoners of the Sun

0-316-35843-6 LITTLE, BROWN PB $8.95

Red Rackham's Treasure

0-316-35834-7 LITTLE, BROWN PB $8.95

The Secret of the Unicorn

0-316-35832-0 LITTLE, BROWN PB $8.95

The Seven Crystal Balls

0-316-35840-1 LITTLE, BROWN PB $8.95

The Shooting Star

0-316-35851-7 LITTLE, BROWN PB $8.95

Tintin and the Picaros

0-316-35849-5 LITTLE, BROWN PB $8.95

Tintin in America

0-316-35852-5 LITTLE, BROWN PB $8.95

Tintin in Tibet

0-316-35839-8 LITTLE, BROWN PB $8.95

Benoit **Peeters**

Tintin and the World of Hergé: An Illustrated History

Hergé's comic creation has been praised by everyone from Charles De Gaulle to Warhol. His life and the evolution of his influential meticulous-yet-simple style are examined via a large collection of sketches, cover reproductions, and letters

0-316-69752-4 JOY STREET $45.00

Other Comics

Nick **Bantock**

Griffin & Sabine

0-87701-788-3 CHRONICLE $17.95

Sabine's Notebook

0-8118-0180-2 CHRONICLE $17.95

The Golden Mean

The conclusion of the unusual correspondence of Griffin and Sabine will satisfy the fans who made the first volume a bestseller, hailed as "a gorgeous book that deserves to be a classic" —*The Boston Globe*

0-8118-0298-1 CHRONICLE $17.95

The Griffin & Sabine Trilogy: Boxed Set

"This fantastical and peerless tale…is a must-have"—*Publishers Weekly*

0-8118-0696-0 CHRONICLE $49.95

Tsai **Chih Chung**

Zhuangzi Speaks: The Music of Nature

This Chinese comic book bestseller illustrates the parables of the Taoist text *Zhuangzi.* While this text is both profound and humorous, so are the author's characters, whose enactments of the core tenets of the *Zhuangzi* make accessible that which is largely cryptic

TRANSLATED BY BRIAN BRUYA

0-691-05694-3 PRINCETON $24.95

0-691-00882-5 PRINCETON PB $13.95

Humor

Regina **Barreca**, editor

The Penguin Book of Women's Humor

Called by *Ms.* magazine the "feminist humor maven," the author of the celebrated *They Used to Call Me Snow White…But I Drifted* has compiled the ultimate anthology of women's humor. From the 1700s to the 1900s, to politics, fate and frustrations, selections include Anita Loos, Mae West, Lily Tomlin, Ntozake Shange, Jane Austen, Emily Dickinson, Dorothy Parker, and Cynthia Heimel

See also **HUMOR** under **ARTS AND LETTERS** under **WOMEN'S STUDIES** in **SOCIAL STUDIES**

0-14-017294-7 PENGUIN PB $15.95

Erma **Bombeck**

All I Know About Animal Behavior I Learned in Loehmann's Dressing Room

There's not anything actually to say about this new book from *The New York Times* bestselling American humorist, except to point out that it's riotously funny, cutting-edge, and filled with warmth

0-06-017788-8 HARPERCOLLINS $22.00

Fran **Lebowitz**

The Fran Lebowitz Reader

A selection of biting social commentary from the wry observer of New York City life

0-679-76180-2 VINTAGE PB $13.00

David **Letterman**

David Letterman's Second Book of Top Ten Lists from the Late Show with David Letterman

0-553-10243-5 BDD $16.00

Humor Writers

Woody **Allen**

Getting Even

0-394-72640-5 RANDOM HOUSE PB $8.00

Woody Allen

Side Effects

0-345-34335-2 BALLANTINE PB $5.99

Without Feathers

0-345-33697-6 BALLANTINE PB $5.99

Dave **Barry**

Dave Barry in Cyberspace

0-517-59575-3 CROWN $21.00

Dave Barry Is Not Making This Up

A collection of greatest hits from Barry's syndicated column, where an exploration of answering machine capabilities reaches epic proportions and getting the real scoop on UFO sightings becomes a high priority

CARTOONS BY JEFF MACNELLY

0-449-90973-5 FAWCETT PB $10.00

Dave Barry's Guide to Guys: A User's Manual

Dave Barry's *Baedeker* to the animal

0-679-40486-4 RANDOM HOUSE $21.00

Dave Barry Talks Back

A bestselling, biting, and hilarious collection of short pieces from "the funniest man in America"—*NY Times Book Review*

0-517-58868-4 CROWN PB $10.00

Today, in our continuing series on How Guys Think, we explore the question: How come guys care so much about sports?

This is a tough one, because caring about sports is, let's face it, silly. I mean, suppose you have a friend who, for no apparent reason, suddenly becomes obsessed with the Amtrak Corporation. He babbles about Amtrak constantly, citing obscure railroad statistics from 1978; he puts Amtrak bumper stickers on his car; and when something bad happens to Amtrak, such as a train crashes and investigators find that the engineer was drinking and wearing a bunny suit, your friend becomes depressed for weeks. You'd think he was crazy, right? "Bob," you'd say to him, as a loving and caring friend, "you're a moron. The Amtrak Corporation has *nothing to do with you.*"

But if Bob is behaving exactly the same deranged way about, say, the Pittsburgh Penguins, it's considered normal guy behavior.

DAVE BARRY TALKS BACK

Dave Barry's Bad Habits: A 100% Fact-Free Book

Sagacious advice on how to cope with the monumental problems of life from the habit-forming, Pulitzer Prize-winning columnist, called "the funniest man in America" by *NY Times.* Dave Barry is nothing less than the smart-aleck Peter Pan of American letters" —*The Seattle Times*

0-8050-2964-8 HOLT PB $8.95

Dave Barry's Gift Guide to End All Gift Guides

Why go for the run of the mill when, guided by the inimitable Barry, you can offer the perfect present every time? A lifelike replica of a full pound of human fat; a pair of elephant print Republican pants, or partially digested rodent bones from an owl are *really and truly* yours for the ordering with the help of this invaluable and utterly hilarious offering from one of our country's funniest writers

0-517-79952-9 CROWN $15.00

Robert **Benchley**

The Benchley Roundup: Selection by Nathaniel Benchley of His Favorites

ILLUSTRATED BY GLUYAS WILLIAMS

0-226-04218-9 CHICAGO PB $17.95

Will **Cuppy**

The Decline and Fall of Practically Everybody

ILLUSTRATED BY WILLIAM STEIG

0-87923-514-4 GODINE PB $12.95

Ellen **DeGeneres**

My Point...and I Do Have One

0-553-09955-8 BDD $19.95

Who am I? How did I get to be me? If I wasn't me, who would I be? How can you mend a broken heart? These are all good questions. Well, almost all good questions—I'm pretty sure the last on is just a Bee Gees song. Anyway, what I'm trying to say is who I am now is what I was then, plus all the stuff in between, minus a few years during the seventies.

MY POINT...AND I DO HAVE ONE

Al **Franken**

Rush Limbaugh Is a Big Fat Idiot and Other Observations

0-385-31474-4 DELACORTE $21.95

Ian **Frazier**

Coyote v. Acme

The author of *Dating Your Mom*, *Family*, and *Great Plains* offers a hilarious new collection of essays in a style that has been compared with Perelman, Benchley, and Woody Allen. Starting with the opening statement of the lawyer representing Wile E. Coyote in a product-liability suit against the Acme Company, Frazier's new collection goes on to the golfing career of Bob Hope, a graduation speech by a Satanist college president, and theories of revolutionary stand-up comedy from Stalin. "Ian Frazier is the funniest writer alive"—Veronica Geng

0-374-13033-7 FS&G $17.00

Dating Your Mom

"Not since Woody Allen's several collections of short stories has there been so delightfully distorted a worldview as the one that permeates this little book"—*The Baltimore Sun*

0-374-52482-3 NOONDAY PB $9.00

Robert **Fulghum**

All I Really Need to Know I Learned in Kindergarten

Also available, Fulghum's other easygoing meditations on the vicissitudes of life:

0 394571029 RANDOM HOUSE $18.95
0-449-90857-7 FAWCETT PB $10.00
0-8041-0526-X IVY PB $5.99

Paul **Fussell**

Bad: The Dumbing of America

A satirical guide to everything loathsome, pretentious, and fraudulent about contemporary American culture, from advertisements for banks to the muzak played while one is put on hold. Witty and savage, as might be expected from the author of *Wartime, Class,* and *Thank God for the Atom Bomb*

0-671-67652-0 TOUCHSTONE PB $19.00

Cynthia **Heimel**

If You Leave Me Can I Come Too?

Heimel is at the peak of her form in this new collection of essays

See also HUMOR under ARTS AND LETTERS under WOMEN'S STUDIES in SOCIAL STUDIES

0-87113-603-1 GROVE $20.00

Sex Tips for Girls

A New York City humor columnist gives advice on "The Great Boyfriend Crunch," "Lingerie Dos and Don'ts," and "How to Cure a Broken Heart." Hilarious

See also COURTSHIP AND DATING under COURTSHIP, LOVE, SEX, AND MARRIAGE in LIFESTYLES AND PRACTICAL ADVICE

See also ADVICE AND CONSENT under CUTTING EDGE

0-671-47725-0 SIMON & SCHUSTER PB $9.00

When the Phone Doesn't Ring, It'll Be Me!

Caustic, wicked, and true, Heimel offers new and ever more bitterly hilarious observations on the war between the sexes. From nature and dogs to shopping and living, "Heimel gets funnier, meaner, and possibly even smarter, every time around"—*NY Times Book Review*

0-87113-634-1 GROVE PB $11.00

Garrison **Keillor**

Cat, You Better Come Home

The adventures of Puff, the cat who runs away to seek her fortune

ILLUSTRATED BY STEVE JOHNSON & LOU FANCHER

0-670-85112-4 VIKING $15.99

Happy to Be Here: Even More Stories and Comic Pieces

0-14-006482-6 PENGUIN PB $8.95

Lake Wobegon Days

See also THE '80s under THE GREAT FICTION BESTSELLERS 1930-1995

0-14-013161-2 PENGUIN PB $11.95

Leaving Home: A Collection of Lake Wobegon Stories

0-14-013160-4 PENGUIN PB $11.95

WLT: A Radio Romance

If ever a book was meant to be read aloud, this is it. Keillor narrates his own work, a history of a fictional Minneapolis radio station. Four cassettes

See also BIOGRAPHIES AND MEMOIRS under RADIO in PERFORMING ARTS AND MEDIA

0-14-010380-5 PENGUIN PB $11.00

Merrill **Markoe**

How to Be Hap-Hap-Happy Like Me

The writer behind the original David Letterman show follows the how-to-be-happy suggestions of every inspiring publication, spiritual guide, and self-help guru she can find. Only her interpretation of the advice is perhaps not quite what the inspirational authors intended: "Take the time to improve your knowledge of history" leads her to a restaurant called "Medieval Times"; "enroll in a class or lecture that interests you" inspires her to a continuing-education course in becoming a dominatrix

0-670-85332-1 VIKING $18.95

What the Dogs Have Taught Me: And Other Amazing Things I've Learned

Essays from *New York Woman* magazine features her inimitable views on those two central relationships for a woman: with her man and with her dog. Includes a full day sharing dogs' "hopes, their dreams, their squeaking vinyl lamb chops and their drinking space at the toilet"

0-14-016682-3 PENGUIN PB $10.00

Don **Marquis**

Archy & Mehitabel

Began as a column for *The New York Sun* in 1916, Archy, literary cockroach who types out *vers libre* by banging his head against the keys (but can't reach the shift key), and Mehitabel, the sultry cat reincarnated from Cleopatra, have since gained a worldwide following

See also **THE MODERNIST GENERATIONS** under **20TH-CENTURY AMERICAN POETRY** in **LITERATURE OF THE AMERICAS**

0-385-09478-7 ANCHOR PB $8.95

Archyology: The Long Lost Tales of Archy and Mehitabel

Now, rescued from a trunk where they have been stored since Marquis's death, dozens of original Archy missives have been resuscitated. "Archy's profound musings on love, politics, and much, much more are perfectly illustrated by Edward Frascino's witty and beautiful drawings" —Roz Chast

WITH ORIGINAL ILLUSTRATIONS BY ED FRASCINO

0-87451-745-1 NEW ENGLAND $14.95

Groucho **Marx**

Groucho Marx and Other Short Stories and Tall Tales: Selected Writings of Groucho Marx

Groucho lives! In this collection one third (or is that one quarter) of the comic team speaks out on everything from the Great Depression and vaudeville to World War II and the Sexual Revolution. Culled from the irreverent comic's articles in publications such as *The New York Times, The Saturday Evening Post*, and *Variety*, this collection is Groucho as you've never seen him

0-571-19820-1 FABER $21.95

Groucho Marx

Peter **Mayle**

Acquired Tastes

From the upkeep involved in maintaining a mistress to proper limousine etiquette, this volume covers both the peculiar tastes and fascinating foibles of the leisure class. "Voluptuous reading for the sybarite in all of us"—Stephen Birmingham

0-553-37183-5 BANTAM PB $10.95

Patrick F. **McManus**

How I Got This Way

"Everybody should read Patrick McManus" —*NY Times Book Review*

0-8050-3482-X HOLT PB $8.95

Never Cry "Arp!"

Better than anyone, McManus has always understood that the outdoor life offers unprecedented opportunities for mishaps and strange characters. From Crazy Eddie Muldoon to Rancid Crabtree, the strange and hilarious world of Patrick F. McManus grows ever stranger with each story here collected. "Everybody should read Patrick McManus"—*NY Times*

0-8050-4662-3 HOLT $15.95

Michael **Moore**

Downsize This!: Random Threats from an Unarmed American

Seriously funny musings. "Michael Moore is a hybrid of two Ralphs—Kramden and Nader—and he is blessed with brilliant comic timing" —*Time*

See also **LIBERALS AND THE LEFT** under **CURRENT POLITICAL THOUGHT AND ISSUES** under **AMERICAN POLITICS AND FOREIGN POLICY** in **HISTORY OF THE AMERICAS**

0-517-70739-X CROWN $21.00

Ogden **Nash**

I Wouldn't Have Missed It: Selected Poems of Ogden Nash

INTRODUCTION BY ARCHIBALD MACLEISH

0-316-59830-5 LITTLE, BROWN $29.95

P.J. **O'Rourke**

Age and Guile Beat Youth, Innocence, and a Bad Haircut: 25 Years of P.J. O'Rourke

The chronicler of midlife conservatism traces his evolution from his '70s radicalism to his present-day Republicanism—or at least his passage from long hair, striped shirt, and a cigarette to short hair, polka-dot tie, and big cigar

0-87113-609-0 ATLANTIC MONTHLY $29.95
0-87113-653-8 ATLANTIC MONTHLY PB $12.00

All the Trouble in the World

The bestselling author of *Parliament of Whores* and *Give War a Chance* weighs in this year with his conservative take on overpopulation (a comparison of Bangladesh and Fremont, CA), multiculturalism, ecology ("If the outdoors is so swell, how come the homeless aren't more fond of it?"), and, as always, political correctness in all its errant and evil guises

0-87113-611-2 GROVE PB $12.00

The Bachelor Home Companion: A Practical Guide to Keeping House Like a Pig

Political satirist O'Rourke is still calling 'em as he sees 'em—this time on the politics of bachelor housekeeping. His attitudes on cooking, grocery shopping, yard-work, and the like won't necessarily help keep a bachelor's affairs in order; it may, in fact, make them become even more stubbornly proud of their messes. As O'Rourke says: "This is a book about cooking, cleaning, and housekeeping for people who don't know how to do those things and aren't about to learn"

0-87113-489-6 ATLANTIC MONTHLY $16.00

Give War a Chance

By the nonconformist author *The Parliament of Whores*, O'Rourke's new book casts a cold eye on such topics as freedom, the '60s, drug testing and the Gulf War. "Rare is the writer who can make his readers laugh out loud in the privacy of their living rooms, much less in the middle of a crowded railroad car. P.J. O'Rourke is one of these fortunate souls"—*NY Times Book Review*

0-87113-520-5 ATLANTIC MONTHLY $20.95
0-679-74201-8 VINTAGE PB $12.00

Dorothy **Parker**

The Portable Dorothy Parker

Stories, poems, and criticism

See also **FROM THE TURN OF THE CENTURY TO WORLD WAR II** under **20TH-CENTURY AMERICAN FICTION** in **LITERATURE OF THE AMERICAS**

0-14-015074-9 VIKING PB $13.95

By the time you swear you are his,
Shivering and sighing,
And he swears his passion is
Infinite, undying—
Lady, make a note of this:
One of you is lying.

THE PORTABLE DOROTHY PARKER

Paul **Reiser**

Couplehood

Following in the tradition of *SeinLanguage*, number two in the books-by-comics trend, this time by the infinitely agreeable star of *Mad About You*

0-553-57313-6 BDD PB $5.99

Damon **Runyon**

Guys and Dolls: The Stories of Damon Runyon

"It is the language, of course, that keeps Runyon's tall tales of Broadway con men and sporting ladies so vibrant and appealing. Every page drawls with that nasal slangy cool-guy voice"—*Washington Post Book World*

0-670-84868-9 PENGUIN PB $27.50

Will **Self**

The Quantity Theory of Insanity

"If a manic J.G. Ballard and a depressed David Lodge got together, they might produce something like *The Quantity Theory of Insanity*. But Will Self's world is all his own; it is both exotic and institutionalized, full of dread and dowdiness and entirely unsuspected comedy"—Martin Amis

See also **NEW WRITERS OF THE 90S** under **20TH-CENTURY BRITISH AND IRISH FICTION** in **LITERATURE OF THE BRITISH ISLES**

0-87113-585-X GROVE $21.00
0-679-75094-0 VINTAGE PB $12.00

Danny **Shanahan**

Buckledown the Workhound

A regular contributor to *The New Yorker*, Shanahan has created this delightful hound who cannot seem to find tail-wagging joy in his high-powered position at Pawprint Industries. Tired of the dog-eat-dog world of big business, he leaves, at first skeptically, for a simplier life of stick-fetching and squirrel chasing on a rural farm

0-316-78276-9 LITTLE, BROWN $14.95

Garry **Shandling**

The Autobiography of Larry Sanders

Here is the uproarious and outrageous autobiography of the neurotic, paranoid, madcap talk-show host, Larry Sanders, portrayed so brilliantly by Garry Shandling. Like the show, it is a hilarious blend of fact, fiction, and caricature

0-684-00107-1 SIMON & SCHUSTER........$21.00

Robin **Skynner** & John **Cleese**

Life and How to Survive It

Skynner, a psychiatrist and family therapist, and Cleese, the starring actor and creator of *Monty Python's Flying Circus*, combine forces to understand what makes people, schools, businesses, and societies tick. Their answers reveal universal principles of living and changing in the modern world. "It is a mind-stretching privilege to listen in on the conversation between these two gifted observers of the life scene. Their exchanges are literate, wise, playfully humorous, disturbing, and brilliant"—James L. Framo, Ph.D.

WITH CARTOONS BY BUD HANDELSMAN

0-393-03742-8 NORTON........$25.00

James **Thurber**

James Thurber: Writings and Drawings

The most comprehensive collection of the works of this American humorist available. Includes over 100 pieces and nearly 500 cartoons and drawings. "A comic continent unto itself" —Roy Blount, Jr.

1-88301-122-1 LIBRARY OF AMERICA........$35.00

My Life and Hard Times

0-06-091642-7 HARPERCOLLINS PB........$10.00

People Have More Fun than Anybody: A Centennial Celebration

A centennial edition of previously uncollected cartoons, stories, essays, and drawings by the great Thurber. "Even the skeptical will find most of these samples to be vintage Thurber" —*Chicago Tribune*

EDITED BY MICHEL J. ROSEN

0-15-100094-8 HARCOURT BRACE........$22.95
0-15-600235-3 HARVEST PB........$15.00

A Thurber Carnival

0-06-090445-3 HARPERCOLLINS PB........$13.00

Thurber on Crime

Thurber gives a whimsical spin to murder and other crimes in this collection of stories, articles, and drawings including "The Catbird Seat" and "Mr. Preble Gets Rid of His Wife"

0-89296-450-2 MYSTERIOUS........$18.95

James **Thurber** & E.B. **White**

Is Sex Necessary?: Or, Why You Feel the Way You Do

0-06-091102-6 HARPERCOLLINS PB........$12.00

Calvin **Trillin**

Deadline Poet: Or, My Life as a Doggerelist

"The news presents a motley little band/That I observe, tomato in my hand." Trillin's take on recent America, in rhyme

0-374-13552-5 FS&G........$18.00

Too Soon to Tell

"Timelessly enjoyable…as easy to enjoy as a glass of iced tea after a long day" —Washington Post

0-374-27846-6 FS&G........$18.00
0-446-67230-0 WARNER PB........$11.99

Travels with Alice

The author's travels with his wife and children, from Tuscany to Guadeloupe

0-380-71209-1 AVON PB........$9.00

The Tummy Trilogy

New Yorker staff writer, poet, memoirist, and our country's "funniest food writer," described by Craig Claiborne as "the Walt Whitman of American eats," offers his three hilarious classics of unabashed eating under one cover: *American Fried, Alice, Let's Eat,* and *Third Helpings.*

0-374-27950-0 NOONDAY........$25.00
0-374-52417-3 NOONDAY PB........$12.00

P.G. **Wodehouse**

Carry On, Jeeves

0-14-001174-9 VIKING PB........$8.95

The Code of the Woosters

0-394-72028-8 VINTAGE PB........$8.00

P.G. Wodehouse

How Right You Are, Jeeves

0-06-096499-5HARPERCOLLINS PB........$11.00

The Inimitable Jeeves

0-14-000933-7 VIKING PB........$8.95

Jeeves and the Feudal Spirit

An opportunity to make your commute in the company of one of the greatest minds of the 20th century—Wodehouse's inimitable butler Jeeves

0-06-096500-2HARPERCOLLINS PB........$10.00

Jeeves and the Tie that Binds

0-06-097283-1 HARPERCOLLINS PB........$10.00

Jeeves in the Morning

0-06-097282-3 HARPERCOLLINS PB........$11.00

Life at Blandings, Something Fresh & Summer Lightning

0-14-005903-2 PENGUIN PB........$14.95

Life with Jeeves, Right Ho, Jeeves & The Inimitable Jeeves

0-14-005902-4 VIKING PB........$14.95

The Most of P.G. Wodehouse

0-671-20349-5 SIMON & SCHUSTER PB........$12.95

Plum's Peaches

1-55882-100-7 INTL POLYGONICS........$21.95
1-55882-129-5 INTL POLYGONICS PB........$12.95

The Return of Jeeves

0-06-096502-9HARPER PERENNIAL PB........$11.00

Right Ho, Jeeves

0-14-000934-5 VIKING PB........$8.95

Summer Lightning

0-14-000995-7 VIKING PB........$8.95

Thank You, Jeeves

0-89190-294-5 AEONIAN........$21.95

Uneasy Money

"Wodehouse was a master of the language, he created an idyllic world, the perfect English pastoral, he was the cleverest plotter in the business and side-splittingly funny"— Susan Hill

0-14-001273-7 PENGUIN PB........$6.00

"A woman has the right to expect the man she is about to marry to regard their troth as a sacred obligation that shall keep him as pure as a young knight who has dedicated himself to the quest of the Holy Grail. And I find you in a public restaurant dancing with a creature with yellow hair, upsetting waiters, and staggering about with pats of butter all over you."

Here, a sense of injustice stung Lord Dawlish. It was true that after his regrettable collision with Heinrich, the waiter, he had discovered butter upon his person, but it was only one pat. Claire had spoken as if he had been festooned with butter.

UNEASY MONEY

Very Good, Jeeves

0-14-001173-0 VIKING PB........$8.95

P.G. **Wodehouse** & D.R. **Bensen**, editor

Wodehouse Is the Best Medicine

Eleven classic stories from the inimitable master focus on the therapeutic: Jeeves's hangover remedy, Bobbie Wickham's treatment for nervousness, how to quit smoking. Few thematic volumes of Wodehouse—as he is so often collected—succeed this well in grasping the familiar best of Wodehouse's generous humor

FOREWORD BY LENDON H. SMITH, M.D.

1-55882-026-4 INTL POLYGONICS PB........$12.95

Visual Humor, Novelty Items, and Joke Books

Henry **Beard**

Mulligan's Laws

What Murphy's Laws are to life, Mulligan's are to that more serious pursuit, golf. Beard, one of the founders of *The National Lampoon,* presents this brilliantly edited compilation of Mulligan's wisdom, just in time for the 200th anniversary of the legendary duffer's birth. Included are such insightful tidbits as: "The score a player reports should always be regarded as his opening offer"

0-385-46999-3 DOUBLEDAY $14.95

Henry **Beard** & Christopher **Cerf**

The Official Politically Correct Dictionary and Handbook

A riotously funny guide to the jargon of "political correctness." Includes 14 ways to say "you're fired," and an extensive list of phrases that will guard against verbal *faux pas* in company of any ideological persuasion

0-679-74113-5 VILLARD PB $10.00

Jess **Borgeson** & others

The Compleat Works of Wllm Shspre (abridged)

The companion guide to the play that created a sensation in London and the US by condensing all the Bard's 37 plays and every sonnet into two madcap hours. Features not only the complete plays and sonnets, but 11 hopelessly pretentious prefaces, a multitude of endlessly stupid and inaccurate footnotes, and more. "So Forsooth! Get thee to the RSC's delightfully fractured complete works"—*LA Herald*

1-55783-157-2 APPLAUSE THEATRE PB $8.95

Benjamin **Darling**

Tips for Teens

All the major issues of adolescence are covered in this illustrated handbook to making it through successfully. From planning parties and the dos and don'ts of dating to making Jell-O molds and the rules of petting, this is perfect for the baby-booming nostalgic set and anyone wanting to return to or discover "the good old days"

0-8118-0520-4 CHRONICLE $9.95

Brian R. **Duffy**

The Poor Boy's Guide to Marrying a Rich Girl

0-14-009721-X PENGUIN PB $6.95

Jack **Handey**

Deeper Thoughts: All New, All Crispy

A regular feature on *Saturday Night Live,* Jack Handey's *Deep Thoughts* have brought merriment, laughter, and befuddlement—if not actual solace—to millions. Pearls of platitudinous wisdom such as "The face of a child can say it all, especially the mouth part of the face" will entertain those who "get it" and educate those who don't

1-56282-840-1 HYPERION PB $7.95

Penn **Jillette** & Teller **Jillette**

Penn & Teller's How to Play with Your Food

As in their previous how-to book of stylish warped legerdemain, *Cruel Tricks for Dear Friends,* Penn & Teller here coach you on how to be a complete, obnoxious and vile outrage. Easy-to-learn, sure-to-impress tricks included psychic spoon-bending, fruit bouncing, and terrorist fortune cookies. No doubt a winner of a gift

0-679-74311-1 VILLARD PB $20.00

Sean **Kelly** & Rosemary **Rogers**

Saints Preserve Us: Everything You Need to Know About Every Saint You'll Ever Need

We already know who is the patron saint of travel, but who are the saints of hemorrhoids or dog bites, and where are they when we really need them? This comprehensive, cross-referenced guide will tell you who in heaven to invoke for your every triumph and calamity

0-679-41629-3 RANDOM HOUSE PB $10.00

Tony **Kornheiser**

Pumping Irony: Working Out the Angst of a Lifetime

A collection of his funniest work by the syndicated *Washington Post* humorist whom *The Washingtonian* rated as the best columnist, better than Dave Barry, Art Buchwald, and George Will. From comments on the obligation to put on a swimming suit ("I look like a cantaloupe with back hair") to home appliances (a friend stands in front of the refrigerator "with the door open and the light on so often that he has come to think of it as a small den"), this book is a veritable treasure

0-8129-2474-6 TIME BOOKS $20.00
0-8129-2831-8 TIME BOOKS PB $12.00

Leslie **Nielsen** & Henry **Beard**

Leslie Nielsen's Stupid Little Golf Book

Who is better to parody *Harry Penick's Little Red Book,* the bestselling sports book of all time, than the Arnold Palmer of Bad Golf himself?

0-385-47598-5 DOUBLEDAY $17.50

Tom **Parker**

Rules of Thumb

0-395-34642-8 HOUGHTON MIFFLIN PB $9.95

E.O. **Parrott**, editor

How to Become Ridiculously Well-Read in One Evening: A Collection of Literary Encapsulations

0-14-007451-1 PENGUIN PB $7.00

Patti **Putnicki**

101 Things Not to Say During Sex

On each page, two poignant, desperate, and insensitive pairs of eyes in the dark utter unromantic words to each other

0-446-15590-X WARNER PB $6.99

Victoria **Roberts**

Cattitudes

New Yorker cartoonist captures the eccentric soul of the cat in this collection of her superbly detailed, fanciful drawings. Gossiping cats at the beauty salon, cats in therapy, the inner circle of artist cats. These original drawings tell everything about felines and almost everything about their owners, too

0-679-42361-3 VILLARD $15.00

Dr. **Seuss**

Oh, the Places You'll Go!

Dr. Seuss's book for adults has been *two years* on the *The New York Times* bestseller list. "A joyful song to life"—*Denver Post*

0-679-80527-3 RANDOM HOUSE $16.00

Neil **Steinberg**

Complete and Utter Failure

It's out there waiting for each and every one of us—rank failure—so don't run *from* it, run *to* it. Steinberg joyfully recounts some of the dumber attempts to scale Mount Everest, the thought behind such immortal product flops as Baby Jesus dolls and Reddi-Bacon

0-385-47291-9 DOUBLEDAY $17.50
0-385-47970-0 MAIN STREET PB $9.95

Linda **Sunshine**

Dating Iron John and Other Pleasures: A Woman's Survival Guide for the '90s

Included are such chapters as "How to Satisfy a Woman 30% of the Time," "Carol Warmus and Amy Fisher Reveal Everything You Didn't Want to Know about Dating a Married Man," and "Sexual Harassment: Dating Tactics for the '90s?"

1-55972-175-8 BIRCH LANE PB $16.95

Cutting Edge

This section is an attempt to provide a showcase of all the literature you either did not know existed, or were aware of and could not find. A museum of subversive artifacts, or, more appropriately, the hall of mirrors in the circus funhouse where you can see a reflection of youself you did not expect.

Writing from the Edge

Anyone can stop in the local bookstore and pick up *Tropic of Cancer,* or even find some perverse kinship in Aldous Huxley's *Doors of Perception.* But when was the last time you found yourself paging through a graphic anthology of biographical synopses of Dostoevsky panicked over a roulette wheel; Harry Houdini starting a brawl at a seance; or Franz Kafka looking over a snail's shoulder as it writes in his journal? There are always stories of someone going further. These are some of the best.

Georges **Bataille**

"One of the most original and unsettling of those thinkers who, in the wake of Sade and Nietzsche, have confronted the possibility of thought in a world that has lost its myth of transcendence"
—*Peter Brooks,* NY Times Book Review

Erotism: Death and Sensuality
Originally published in 1957, updated by City Lights in 1986, this book provides Bataille's perspective on sacrifice, language, taboos, cruelty, and "mystical ecstasy." Positing eroticism as a "psychological quest not alien to death," Bataille plums the theories of figures ranging from Emily Brontë to the Marquis de Sade. How can you put a book down that begins: "Eroticism, it may be said, is assenting to life up to the point of death?"
See also **ESSAYS: PERSONAL, LITERARY, PHILOSOPHICAL** under **MODERN FRENCH LITERATURE** in **LITERATURE OF EUROPE, AFRICA, AND ASIA**
TRANSLATED BY MARY DALWOOD
0-87286-190-2 CITY LIGHTS PB........$14.95

Story of the Eye
The centerpiece of the Surrealist movement's erotic literature, *Eye* was published in 1928 anonymously and follows the sexual awakening of a young man as he quickly discovers that only those acts which can be described as "dirty" are worthy of his attention. Fortunately, he finds Simone, a woman who shares his appetites and knocks down more boundaries than the young man knew existed. Shocking even by '90s standards
See also **FICTION** under **MODERN FRENCH LITERATURE** in **LITERATURE OF EUROPE, AFRICA, AND ASIA**
See also **EROTICA** under **COURTSHIP, LOVE, SEX, AND MARRIAGE** in **LIFESTYLES AND PRACTICAL ADVICE**
0-87286-209-7 CITY LIGHTS PB........$7.95

Jan Harold **Brunvand** & others
The Big Book of Urban Legends
Another in this series of cartoon strips. This one covers all the stories told by the guy who heard it from the guy who swore he knows the person this happened to
1-56389-165-4 WARNER PB........$12.95

Carl A. **Posey** & others
The Big Book of Weirdos
A unique presentation of short summaries of historical figures and their most infamous actions. Depicted in comic strip format by different artists with varying drawing styles. This is a must for anyone with a short attention span who wanted to know exactly why William Burroughs shot his wife or why "sadism" originated with the experiments of Marquis de Sade
1-56389-180-8 DC COMICS PB........$12.95

Marquis **De Sade**
Philosophy in the Boudoir
Sade provided the groundwork for the delineation of human possibility in an erotic framework. Beautiful and daring, this book provides an excellent introduction to the works of Sade
1-87159-209-7 SUBTERRANEAN PB........$12.95

Photography

A singularly limitless art form, photography encourages the voyeur in all of us to visit bedrooms, backrooms, and the basements of human desire. Sometimes beautiful, sometimes grotesque, these photos are stories in and of themselves with no clear resolution, leaving the viewer free to draw his or her own conclusions.

Jeanette **Jones**
A Walk on the Wild Side
A collection of transsexuals, cross-dressers, and drag artists captured by a London photographer
1-56980-054-5 BARRICADE........$30.00

Richard **Kern**
New York Girls
1-900106-10-8 D.A.P. PB........$29.95

Doris **Kloster**
Doris Kloster
3-8228-8875-3 TASCHEN........$29.99

Eric **Kroll**
Eric Kroll's Fetish Girls
A photography book that depicts just about every fetish scenario imaginable. Very creative
3-8228-8916-4 TASCHEN PB........$24.99

Re/Search

A series covering different subjects from female performance artists with axes, to Bob Flanagan, perhaps the only man ever to drive nails through his scrotum. Re/Search provides a forum for people and subjects that would otherwise remain voiceless.

Bob **Flanagan**
Re/Search Bob Flanagan, Super-Masochist
0-940642-25-5 RE/SEARCH PB........$14.99

Octave **Mirbeau**
The Torture Garden
"The most sickening work of art of the nineteenth century" is back in print thanks to the fearless geniuses at Re/Search. Originally published in 1899, this story was far ahead of its time. A bourgeois Frenchman submits to the wiles of an Englishwoman who leads him to a garden in China where all his dreams and nightmares of degradation are realized. Wow. Text with accompanying photos
See also **THE LATER 19TH CENTURY: SYMBOLISM, NATURALISM, AND ROOTS OF MODERNISM** under **FRENCH LITERATURE TO 1900** in **LITERATURE OF EUROPE, AFRICA, AND ASIA**
0-9651042-6-5 RE/SEARCH PB........$13.99

RE/Search
Incredibly Strange Films
In-depth interviews with Herschell Gordon Lewis, Doris Wishman, Larry Cohen, and other critically ghettoized masters of "B" movie horror and gore. "This book is a must for anyone truly interested in the history of the cinema. It shows the fallacy of most so-called 'complete' histories of film. Fun and incredibly strange"—*Film Folio*
See also **GENRES AND THEMES** under **FILM** in **PERFORMING ARTS AND MEDIA**
0-940642-09-3 RE/SEARCH PB........$17.99

Paul **Spinrad**
The Re/Search Guide to Bodily Fluids
0-940642-28-X RE/SEARCH PB........$15.99

V. **Vale**, editor
Industrial Culture Handbook
0-940642-07-7 RE/SEARCH PB........$13.99

Modern Primitives: An Investigation of Contemporary Adornment & Ritual
0-940642-14-X RE/SEARCH PB........$17.99

Film

These books and guides provide information denied to many of us in the mainsteam environment. Film theory, essays on censorship and free expression, reviews, sex and violence, as well as the artists who have plumbed the underground and why. They for anyone who prefers to make informed decisions about what constitutes art.

David **Kerekes**
Sex, Murder, Art: Films of Jorg Buttgereit
0-9523288-2-8 A.K. PRESS DISTRIBUTION PB........$19.95

David **Lynch**
Images
A photologue of images taken from and inspired by the maverick of the small-town nightmare
0-7868-6060-X HYPERION........$40.00

Maitland **McDonagh**
The Fifty Most Erotic Films of All Time: From Pandora's Box to Basic Instinct
0-8065-1697-6 CITADEL PB........$19.95

Videohound's Complete Guide to Cult Flicks and Trash Pics
0-7876-0616-2 VISIBLE INK PB........$16.95

Michael **Weldon**
The Psychotronic Video Guide to Film
Endorsed by John Waters. Replete with all the stills and film posters you never seem to see at the local Blockbuster
0-312-13149-6 ST. MARTIN'S PB........$29.95

Body Modification

This grouping charts the progress of marks on, or alterations to the body through history. With origins in primitive cultures, the practice of body modification has become a socially accepted phenomenon with a variety of meanings. Among these listings are photography collections of body art, sociological treatises on the symbolism of the act, and comparisons between the body art of diverse cultures.

Michelle **Delio**
Tattoo: The Exotic Art of Skin Decoration
Nice section on celebrity tattoos (featuring Cher's butterfly tattoo)
0-312-10148-1 ST. MARTIN'S PB........$14.95

Frances E. **Mascia-Lees** &
Patricia **Sharpe**, editor

Tattoo, Torture, Mutilation, and Adornment: The Denaturalization of the Body in Culture and Text

0-7914-1065-X SUNY $59.50

Samuel M. **Steward**

Bad Boys and Tough Tattoos: A Social History of the Tattoo with Gangs, Sailors, and Street-Corner Punks

1-56024-023-7 HAWORTH $29.95
0-918393-76-0 HARRP PB $10.95

Daniel **Wojcik**

Punk and Neo-Tribal Body Art

See also **FASHION AND COSTUME** in **ARCHITECTURE, DESIGN, AND HOMES**

0-87805-735-8 MISSISSIPPI $29.95
0-87805-736-6 MISSISSIPPI PB $15.95

Chris **Wroblewski**

Skin Shows

0-86369-272-9 CAROL PB $19.95

Skin Shows II

0-86369-517-5 CAROL PB $19.95

Skin Shows III

0-86369-677-5 CAROL PB $19.95

Skin Shows IV

0-86369-948-0 VRGNB PB $21.95

Katharine **Young**, editor

Bodylore

Sociology and anthropology of various cultures and their traditional rituals and folklore told through body art

0-87049-890-8 TENNESSEE PB $18.00

Love Potions and Toys

What is fact and what is lore? Is there a difference? Who had the first penile enlargement surgery? Is kiwi fruit a mystical magic myth or a genuine biological hormone enhancer? Which is the best vibrator to use in the car? Do you need an adaptor for it if you travel in Europe? There is more practical wisdom in these books than seems possible.

Hoag **Levins**

American Sex Machines: The Hidden History of Sex at the U.S. Patent Office

Everything you didn't want to know about penile implants and the history of the dildo. includes diagrams and historical documents pertaining to every sex device patented in the U.S.

1-55850-534-2 ADAMS PB $9.95

Richard Alan **Miller**

The Magical and Ritual Use of Aphrodisiacs

A chemist's eye view of the "foods of love"

0-89281-402-0 INNER TRADITIONS PB $10.95

Anne **Semans** & Cathy **Winks**

The Good Vibrations Guide to Sex: How to Have Safe, Fun Sex in the '90s

Helpful tips and diagrams for the use of a "woman's (or man's) best friend" by the owners of the store of the same name

0-939416-83-2 CLEIS $29.95
0-939416-84-0 CLEIS PB $16.95

Cynthia Mervis, M.D. **Watson**

Love Potions: A Guide to Aphrodisiacs and Sexual Pleasures

A guide to all the chemicals, internal and external, that could affect your sex drive. Decidedly academic, it tells you what you want to know about the legendary "love potions"

0-87477-724-0 TARCHER PB $10.95

Harry E. **Wedeck**

A Dictionary of Aphrodisiacs

A historical pedia of lovers' timeless search for the "ultimate sex stimulus"

0-87131-675-7 EVANS PB $9.95

Fetishes

Gloria G. **Brame** & others

Different Loving: A Complete Exploration of the World of Sexual Dominance and Submission

Contains more than the title suggests. Starts with the question "What is normal?," then assaults your preconceived notions. Eye-opening and comprehensive

0-679-76956-0 VILLARD PB $18.00

Mistress **Jacqueline**

Whips and Kisses: Parting the Leather Curtain

0-87975-656-X PROMETHEUS $25.95

Brenda **Love**

The Encyclopedia of Unusual Sex Practices

Exactly what the title says. Alphabetical listings in dictionary format, accompanied by drawings and photographs. Very user-friendly

0-942637-64-X BARRICADE $29.95

Valerie **Steele**

Fetish: Fashion, Sex, and Power

From leather to fishnets, taking control with your wardrobe

See also **THE PSYCHOLOGY OF CLOTHES** under **FASHION AND COSTUME** in **ARCHITECTURE, DESIGN, AND HOMES**

0-19-509044-6 OXFORD $35.00

Thomas S. **Weinberg**, editor

S&M: Studies in Dominance & Submission

A sociologist and his friends provide research on everything from the straight and gay and lesbian S&M scenes to S&M organizations to "unusual body modifications, including piercing, branding, and burning!"

0-87975-978-X PROMETHEUS PB $16.95

The Industry of Sex

Lisa **Carver**

Rollerderby: The Book

Filled with photographs

0-922915-38-5 FERAL HOUSE PB $14.95

Frederique **Delacoste** & Priscilla **Alexander**

Sex Work: Writings by Women in the Sex Industry

A genuine and candid look behind the curtains and into the hotel rooms and massage parlors where these women do their work. Printed in short story, essay, and poetry format, but always real

0-939416-11-5 CLEIS PB $16.95

Karen **Essex** & James L. **Swanson**

Bettie Page: The Life of a Pin-Up Legend

Bettie Page became the ultimate pin-up girl, breaking taboos and providing a model for future divas. Her image graced movie posters, porno magazines, and as she registered "more magazine appearances than Marilyn Monroe and Cindy Crawford combined" before fading into inexplicable obscurity

1-88164-962-8 GENERAL PUBLISHING $40.00

Wendy **McElroy**

XXX: A Women's Right to Pornography

0-312-13626-9 ST. MARTIN'S $21.95

Sylvia **Plachy** & James **Ridgeway**

Red Light: Inside the Sex Industry

Text accompanied by photos, covering pornography, prostitution, and other related sex markets

See also **HISTORY OF SEXUALITY** under **TOPICS IN AMERICAN STUDIES** in **HISTORY OF THE AMERICAS**

1-57687-000-6 D.A.P. $39.95

Dr. Robert J. **Stoller**

Porn: Myths for the Twentieth Century

A scholarly work

0-300-05092-5 YALE $35.00
0-300-05755-5 YALE PB $15.00

Bunny **Yeager**, editor

Bunny's Honeys

In 1953, she was declared the "most beautiful photographer in the world." After establishing herself as a versatile model, she shifted behind the camera and proceeded to capture "every man's dreams in pictures"

3-8228-9329-3 TASCHEN $24.99

Advice and Consent

These books allow us to see ourselves as "normal" by proving that no one is. Cynthia Heimel gives us permission and a healthy nudge to laugh at ourselves by being observant of our common inexplicable behavior. Nancy Friday asks what our darkest fear or most shameful desire is, then produces testimony from three hundred other people who think the same way we do. "I don't like crackers in my soup, but if you told me I could become multiorgasmic by eating my chicken noodle with some crushed up Ritz, I'd certainly give it a try."—Jay Fernandez

Nancy **Friday**

Men in Love, Male Sexual Fantasies: The Triumph of Love over Rage

Men from the ages of 14 to 60 discuss their sexual fantasies. The author's intent is to encourage awareness and acceptance of erotic pleasures

See also **SEX** under **COURTSHIP, LOVE, SEX, AND MARRIAGE** in **LIFESTYLES AND PRACTICAL ADVICE**

0-440-15903-2 DELL PB $6.99

Women on Top: How Real Life Has Changed Women's Sexual Fantasies

This woman provides enough "real people's" fantasies to keep readers awake at night. All night

0-671-64845-4 POCKET PB $6.99

Naura **Hayden**

How to Satisfy a Woman Every Time...and Have Her Beg for More!

Impossible? Hayden thinks not

0-942104-01-3 DUTTON $15.95

Cynthia **Heimel**

Sex Tips for Girls

A New York City humor columnist gives advice on "The Great Boyfriend Crunch," "Lingerie Dos and Don'ts," and "How to Cure a Broken Heart." Hilarious

See also **HUMOR** under **ARTS AND LETTERS** under **WOMEN'S STUDIES**

0-671-47725-0 SIMON & SCHUSTER PB $9.00

Michael **Watts**

Lovescript: What Handwriting Reveals About Love and Romance

The moral here? Always get a writing sample before making any sort of commitment. If you get a love note from your man with too many smudgy or jagged letters, he could have violent tendencies. If you receive a poem d'amour from your new love interest in which the "G"'s have oversize loops or a felt-tip pen is used, she may be "sex-crazed." Apparently, it's all in the fingers

0-312-14118-1 ST. MARTIN'S PB $10.95

Culture on the Edge

These books explore every subject considered outside the mainstream: sexuality theory, cross-dressing, sociology, pornography, drug use, physical deformity, performance art, satanism, postmodernist cyber-immersion. Where do you want to go today? Where have you been? This might be a good place to start.

Blanche **Barton**

Secret Life of a Satanist: The Authorized Biography of Anton Lavey

Tracks the life of the man who formed the Church of Satan in 1966

0-922915-12-1 FERAL HOUSE PB $12.95

Leslie **Fiedler**

Freaks: Myths and Images of the Secret Self

A social critic uses history, biology, psychology, literature, and pop culture to analyze our fascinations with and reactions to society's "freaks"

0-385-47013-4 ANCHOR PB $14.00

Marjorie **Garber**

Vice Versa: Bisexuality and the Eroticism of Everyday Life

Harvard English professor (*Vested Interests: Cross-Dressing and Cultural Anxiety*) posits that bisexuality is a continuum, not a "third" category or a period of confusion. She analyzes the lives of dozens of celebrities as well as bisexual themes in books and movies

See also **SEX AND SEXUALITY** under **GAY, LESBIAN, AND BISEXUAL STUDIES** in **SOCIAL STUDIES**

0-684-80308-9 SIMON & SCHUSTER $30.00
0-684-82412-4 SIMON & SCHUSTER PB $16.00

Marjorie B. **Garber**

Vested Interests: Cross-Dressing & Cultural Anxiety

0-06-097524-5 HARPERPERENNIAL PB $20.00

Laura **Kipnis**

Bound and Gagged: Pornography and the Politics of Fantasy in America

Five essays by a "lively and engaging writer who argues, often convincingly, that we would be better off simply thinking of pornography as just another form of science fiction"
—*Publishers Weekly*

See also **PORNOGRAPHY** under **FEMINIST THEORY** under **WOMEN'S STUDIES** in **SOCIAL STUDIES**

0-8021-1584-5 GROVE $22.00

Timothy **Leary**

Chaos and Cyberculture

Leary and friends approach the boundaries of '90s computer culture and then give it a cerebral kick in the head. William Gibson, William S. Burroughs, David Byrne, and special guests assist Leary in his encouragement of independent thinking and punching holes in society's barriers

See also **THE CYBERNETIC SOCIETY** under **THE COMPUTER REVOLUTION** in **SCIENCE**

0-914171-77-1 RONIN PB $19.95

John **Miller** & Randall **Koral**, editors

White Rabbit: A Psychedelic Reader

Miles Davis, Oscar Wilde, Gauguin, Leary, Huxley, Freud, Philip K. Dick, and more recount their stories of drug experimentation and its effects

0-8118-0666-9 CHRONICLE PB $13.95

Jim **Rose** & Melissa **Rossi**

Freak Like Me: Inside the Jim Rose Circus Sideshow

There is no one more qualified than Jim Rose of the Jim Rose Circus Sideshow featured at the Lollapalooza festival. Hey, the guy washes his face with *broken glass*

0-440-50744-8 DELL PB $13.95

Part 10

Art

Vincent van Gogh

Asian Art

1800 BC

1751–1111 BC: Shang, China
Tao Tieh monster mask from ritual food vessel (*ting*). This image recurs in more or less abstract form on ritual vessels for many centuries.

1205

900 BC

481–221 BC: Late Zhou, China
A bronze mirror was often buried with the dead, in some cases suspended over the body with the polished side down to represent the sun. This mirror features an early appearance of what was to become the omnipresent symbol of imperial power in Chinese art: the dragon.

1204

AD 1

1c: Mauryan, India
The solid, domed stupa is the prototypical Buddhist monument. Dated to the first century AD, the stupa at Sanchi, India, with its four gates decorated in low relief, is a masterpiece of early Indian art.

1203

320–550: Gupta, India
"With the Gupta period, a long evolution, both formal and iconographic, came to fruition in some of the greatest sculptures ever produced anywhere in the world."
—J.C. Harle

1203

AD 500

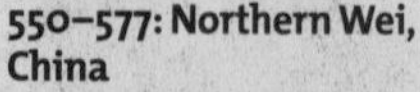

550–577: Northern Wei, China
As Buddhist sculpture becomes more Sinified, the lines of the body are increasingly obscured by drapery and jewels. In the periods of strongest Indian influence—the early Northern Wei (450–500) and early T'ang (618–750)—sculpture is far more sensuous, and figures are disrobed.

1204

618–909: T'ang, China
"In a T'ang vessel, neck, body and foot are clearly differentiated, but in many Song wares the parts are so smoothly connected that it is hard to know where the neck commences, the body leaves off and the foot begins."
—Sherman E. Lee
The History of Far Eastern Art

1202

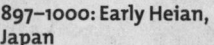

9c: Chola, India
Bronze casting in India dates back to its earliest history, but the most beautiful work was produced under the Southern Chola dynasty. Southern India escaped the ravages of Muslim invasion, and many of these pieces are still in their original temple locations.

1203

897–1000: Early Heian, Japan
Early Heian Buddhist wood sculpture is one of "the most difficult sculptural styles in the world, confronting modern art historians with the familiar problem of unintelligibility in relation to art. It is produced in the service of faith and strictly related to faith." (Sherman E. Lee)

1206

AD 1000

1000–1100: Mid-Koryo, Korea
Koryo celadons (porcelaneous stoneware) were admired for their kingfisher color—in the words of one Chinese Song commentator, they are "first beneath Heaven."

1202

AD 1200

16c: Tokugawa, Japan

The Tokugawa craftsman became an artist in his own right. Kutani ware is known for its striking pictorial design. This example shows a bird's-eye view of a rice field.

1206

1600: Persia
Habib Allah' s illustration to Attar's famous 12c mystical poem *Conference of the Birds* shows the delicacy of line that distinguishes the art of the great Persian miniaturists.

1202

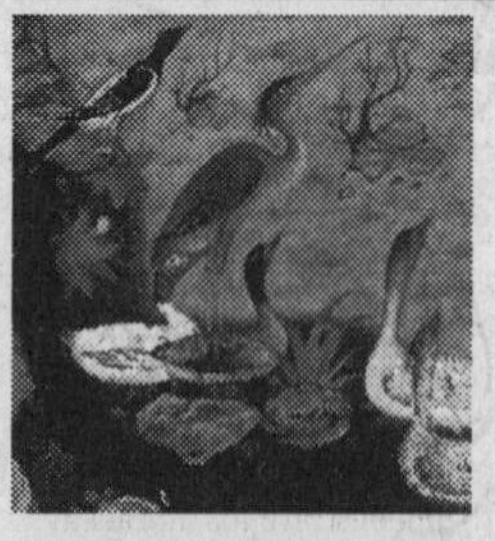

AD 1600

1605–1627: Mughal, India
Shah Jahangir was impressed by how illness had wasted the debauched courtier Inayat Khan, and called for an artist to paint him on his deathbed. Mughal miniatures are known for their worldly spirit and attention to the detail of daily existence.

1203

c. 1785: Kangra, India
The Kangra painters of the northern hills brought a light palette and an elegantly fluent sense of line to the depiction of scenes of love and dalliance.

1203

AD 1800

The Divine Image

1 Sumer
Big eyes; hair brushed flat and symmetrically arranged (not a sociable do, but a helmet); flat, angular, forward face—this Sumerian goddess looks right through us. The image, we are to understand, sees more truly than we, the observers, ever can.
1144

2 Kukailimoku
This Hawaiian image of the war god is made of feathers over wickerwork, with pearl shells and dog teeth. The bared teeth, flared nostrils, and overall bristling energy of the war god are based on common human and animal ways of displaying anger.
1129

3 A'a
This rare wooden Polynesian statue, one of the few to survive the arrival of Christian missionaries in the South Pacific, depicts A'a, the ancestor figure of the ruling clan on the island of Rurutu. The god's features are composed of the bodies of his numerous lineal descendants.
1200

4 Shri Lakshmi
Greek sculpture is famous for its concern with the muscular and skeletal substructure of the human figure; Indian sculpture sees the body as a sensuous surface. In this South Indian image, the wasp-waisted Goddess Lakshmi might as well be boneless, and yet her swelling limbs are taut with supple life.
1203

5 Gu
To the peoples of West Africa, iron was a sacred and precious substance, given by the gods and ritually worked. This image of Gu, recognized by the Fon tribe as the god of iron and war, would have been admired as much for its precious material as for its astonishing sculptural character.
1199

6 Greta Garbo
In Cecil Beaton's famous photograph, Garbo's wide, staring eyes and masklike features give her the aspect of a stern, archaic goddess.
1215

7 Siva
Islamic invaders, whose iconoclasm destroyed much of Northern India's Hindu artistic legacy, never quite penetrated to the southern limits of the subcontinent. This 1c AD lingam with the Hindu deity Siva, shiny from applications of clarified butter, is still venerated today.
1203

8 Venus
Canova's portrait of Pauline Borghese, sister to Napoleon, as Venus, combines sensual charm and immediacy with an air of divinely decorous reserve. The sculpture is a masterpiece of social compliment.
1161

9 Jesus
Jesus's flesh is green with decay even as it runs with blood; his arms are wrenched from their sockets; his fingers are locked forever in the throes of death. In the crucifixion panel of the Isenheim altarpiece, the early-16c German painter Grünewald was determined that the individual viewer should practically feel how his Savior suffered upon the cross.
1155

10 Vespasian
Like the other Roman emperors, he was formally deified by the Senate. His portraits, however, continued to reflect an old republican realism, in which the subject's willingness to be depicted warts and all helped to demonstrate his moral superiority.
1146

11 Mercury
The late 16c virtuoso Giambologna shows Mercury lifted into the air on a puff of the south wind. The artist was perhaps even more eager to show that he could pull off the apparently impossible—making a perfectly weightless sculpture.
1152

Pictorial Styles

AD 1

1c: Zeuxis and Apelles
Mural painting was an important and much admired art in antiquity, and such masters as Zeuxis and Apelles remain legendary. Their work and that of their contemporaries has all been lost, however, and we can only guess at its nature from the more or less free copies with which wealthy Romans often decorated their houses.
1146

AD 500

13c: Villard de Honnecourt
The itinerant architect Villard de Honnecourt noted beside this drawing of a lion that it was done from life—life rationalized, however, in the spirit of the perfect circle. Such a combination of observation and analysis is characteristic of Gothic art.
1148

15c: Flemish painters
Christian light-mysticism, an eye for detail born of the business of illuminating books, and the new, highly versatile medium of oil paint all helped to give an illusionistic precision and polish to the work of the Flemish painters of the early 1400s.
1155

AD 1500

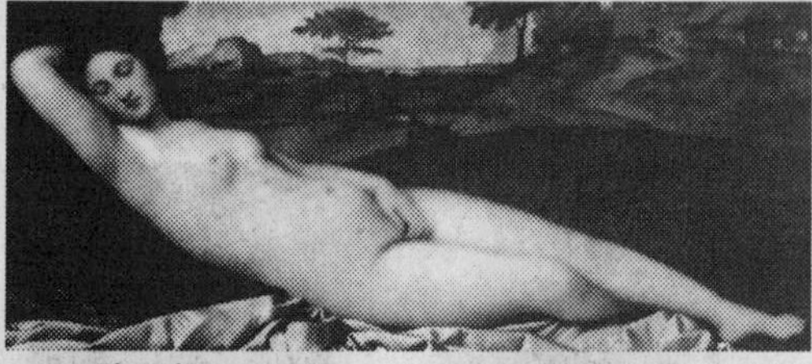

1500: Giorgione
Like other Venetian painters of the High Renaissance, he excelled in the depiction of shine, texture, and shadow, dwelling lovingly in his work on such things as metal, fabric, flesh, and hair. Florentine rivals dismissed Venetian achievements as merely coloristic.
1153

1500: Raphael
Raphael's apparently effortless ability to join grace and grandeur, elegance and expressiveness, has made his work the exemplary manifestation of High Renaissance decorum.
1154

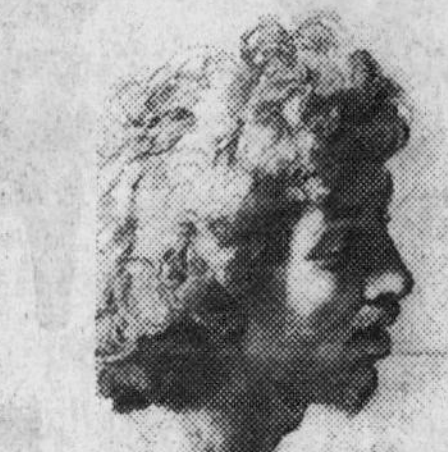

AD 1550

1540: Pontormo
He transformed Michelangelo's muscular giants into attenuated, elongated beings that are not so much spiritualized as introverted.
1154

AD 1600

1600: Caravaggio
The harshly realistic appearance of Caravaggio's work was achieved, paradoxically, by his manipulation of entirely artificial effects such as theatrical spotlighting.
1156

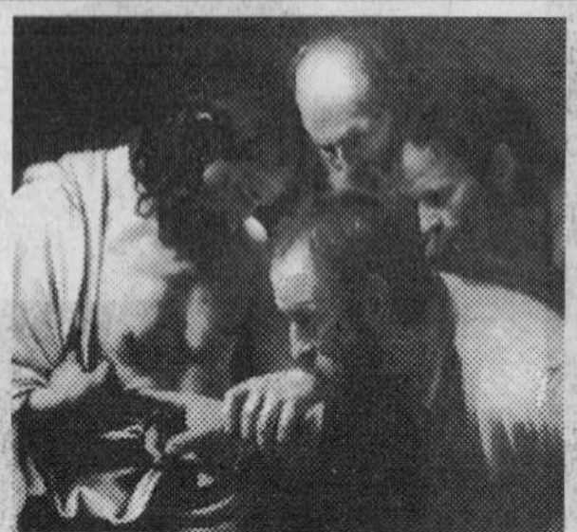

AD 1650

1650: Rembrandt
He found in etching a medium that allowed him to work and rework his image freely, until the picture became as much a record of its making as a depiction of its subject.
1159

1650: Poussin
Like Caravaggio, was a master of paradox. He developed a classical style so severe as to seem awkward, making paintings that would prompt reflection, more than please or impress.
1156

AD 1700

AD 1750

AD 1800

19c: Gericault & Ingres
French art of the first part of the 19c was divided between romantic artists like Gericault and academic classicists like Ingres. Their very different work shares the specificity of the French realist novelists.
1163

1826: Nièpce
Artists and critics have fretted that the apparent "truth to nature" of photography would limit the appeal of painting or even render it superfluous as an art. No need to worry: photographs record time instead of space; they don't show things as they are, but as they were.
1213

Art History: General Studies

General

Laurie Schneider **Adams**

A History of Western Art

0-8109-3425-6 ABRAMS $55.00
0-697-13182-3 BROWN & BENCHMARK PB $37.50

André **Chastel**

French Art: Prehistory to the Middle Ages

2-08-013617-8 ABBEVILLE $75.00
2-08-013566-X ABBEVILLE $75.00

French Art: the Ancient Regime

2-08-013617-8 ABBEVILLE $75.00

Horst **de la Croix** & Richard **Tansey**

Gardner's Art Through the Ages

An excellent two-volume survey, on a par with Janson's *History of Art*; particularly useful for its inclusion of non-Western art. Hardcover edition includes both volumes

0-15-503763-3 HARCOURT BRACE $55.86

Sally **Fisher**

The Square Halo and Other Mysteries of Western Art: Images and the Stories that Inspired Them

0-8109-4463-4 ABRAMS $29.95

David **Frankel**

Masterpieces: The Best-Loved Painting from America's Museums

0-684-80197-3 SIMON & SCHUSTER $35.00

E.H. **Gombrich**

The Story of Art

Gombrich's unparalleled single-volume history of art has been a world bestseller for four decades. It is cherished for the author's wisdom and erudition, but above all for his deep and deeply communicated love of his subject. This complete redesign includes color illustrations throughout, gatefolds, and an updated and revised text with a number of new artists and redrawn maps and charts

0-7148-3247-2 PHAIDON PB $29.95

Grace Cohen **Grossman**

Jewish Art

Three thousand years of Jewish artistic expression are captured here, from an 8th century BC vase found in King Solomon's Temple to works by Marc Chagall and Larry Rivers. Featuring objects collected from around the world—India, Yemen, Russia, Israel, and elsewhere—and including views of the world's most beautiful synagogues, this volume is a testimonial to the vibrant life of Jewish visual arts

0-88363-695-6 LEVIN $75.00

Frederick **Hartt**

Art: A History of Painting, Sculpture and Architecture

A sweeping history, recommended for the quality and scope of its reproductions. This most recent edition includes Far Eastern art

0-8109-1921-4 ABRAMS $60.00

Arnold **Hauser**

Social History of Art

Volume 1

Prehistoric Times, Ancient Oriental Urban Cultures, Greece and Rome, the Middle Ages

0-39470-114-3 RANDOMHOUSE PB $14.00

Volume 2

Renaissance to Baroque Ages

0-39470-115-3 RANDOMHOUSE PB $14.00

Volume 3

Rococo, Classicism, and Romanticism

0-39470-116-X RANDOMHOUSE PB $12.95

Volume 4

Naturalism of the Film Age

0-39470-117-8 RANDOMHOUSE PB $12.95

Nancy G. **Heller**

Women Artists: An Illustrated History

1-55859-211-3 ABBEVILLE PB $35.00

Elizabeth **Holt**

A Documentary History of Art

A comprehensive documentary history

Volume 1

The Middle Ages and the Renaissance

0-691-00333-5 PRINCETON PB $19.95

Volume 2

Michelangelo and the Mannerists, the Baroque and the 18th Century

0-691-00344-0 PRINCETON PB $18.95

Hugh **Honour** & John **Fleming**

The Visual Arts: A History

The best historical survey of the visual arts

0-8109-3928-2 ABRAMS $65.00

H.W. **Janson**

The History of Art

The standard reference book; a solid, judicious, and complete guide; well illustrated

0-8109-3421-3 ABRAMS $60.00
0-13-158411-1 PRENTICE HALL PB $44.00

H.W. **Janson** & Anthony F. **Janson**

The History of Art for Young People

0-8109-3405-1 ABRAMS $35.00

Edward **Lucie-Smith**

Art and Civilization

0-8109-1924-9 ABRAMS $60.00

Kathleen **Krull**

Lives of the Artists: Masterpieces, Messes (and What the Neighbors Thought)

ILLUSTRATED BY KATHRYN HEWITT

0-15-200103-4 HARCOURT BRACE $19.00

James Smith **Pierce**

From Abacus to Zeus: A Handbook of Art History

Provides basic definitions

0-13-324914-X PRENTICE HALL PB $16.16

Herbert **Read**

The Meaning of Art

A popular introduction to understanding and appreciating art, with an illustrated historical survey

0-571-09658-1 FABER PB $12.95

Walter **Robinson**

Instant Art History: From Cave Art to Pop Art

0-449-90698-1 FAWCETT PB $10.00

Larry **Silver**

Art in History

0-13-052333-X PRENTICE HALL PB $58.85

Marilyn **Stokstad** & others

Art History

A completely new world survey of the history of art in its many cultural contexts, complete with maps, time-lines, drawings, diagrams, architectural plans, cutaways, and special illustrated sections on techniques

0-8109-1960-5 ABRAMS $60.00

Joshua **Taylor**

Learning to Look: A Handbook for the Visual Arts

A useful introduction to formal analysis

0-226-79154-8 CHICAGO PB $9.95

David G. **Wilkins** & Bernard **Schultz**

Art Past/Art Present

KATHERYN M. LINDUFF

0-8109-1937-0 ABRAMS $49.50

The Pelican History of Art

The Pelican History of Art books are the standard scholarly accounts in English.

John **Beckwith**

Early Christian and Byzantine Art

An accomplished survey of the dissemination of Christian ideals and art throughout the East; with extensive illustrations

See also EARLY CHRISTIAN AND BYZANTINE under EUROPEAN ART: BYZANTINE AND MEDIEVAL

0-300-05295-2 YALE $50.00
0-300-05296-0 YALE PB $25.00

Sheila S. **Blair** & Jonathan M. **Bloom**
The Art and Architecture of Islam
"A volume that will stand the test of time and that I, and anyone interested in Islamic art, will refer to again and again"—Hugh Kennedy, *American Historical Review*
See also **GENERAL STUDIES** under **ISLAMIC ART AND ARCHITECTURE**
See also **COMMUNITY AND SOCIETY** under **THE MEDIEVAL MIDDLE EASTERN WORLD** under **THE ISLAMIC WORLD TO WORLD WAR I**
0-300-05888-8 YALE........$70.00

Anthony **Blunt**
Art and Architecture in France, 1500-1700
A good introduction, written by the authority on Poussin; stresses the Italian influence on the development of early French art
See also **FRANCE** under **BAROQUE AND ROCOCO** under **EUROPEAN ARCHITECTURE TO 1900** in **ARCHITECTURE, DESIGN, AND HOMES**
See also **BAROQUE AND ROCOCO IN FRANCE** under **EUROPEAN ART: BAROQUE AND ROCOCO**
0-300-05314-2 YALE PB........$25.00

Axel **Boethius**
Etruscan and Early Roman Architecture
From 1400 BC to the Hellenized buildings of Pompeii and Herculaneum
See also **GREEK AND ROMAN** under **EUROPEAN ARCHITECTURE TO 1900** in **ARCHITECTURE, DESIGN, AND HOMES**
See also **THE ETRUSCANS AND EARLY ROME** under **FROM ANTIQUITY TO FEUDALISM** under **ANCIENT ROME** in **WORLD HISTORY AND CURRENT AFFAIRS**
0-300-05290-1 YALE PB........$25.00

Otto J. **Brendel**
Etruscan Art
Centered in the life of the family and a continuing life in the tomb, Etruscan art is private, aristocratic, and luxurious. Brendel's book is the first important study of Etruscan sculpture, wall-painting, metalware, ceramics, and jewelry, which, though influenced by Greek artforms, were profoundly original. "Time has not detracted from Otto Brendel's remarkable ability to make his readers look and think" —*NY Review of Books*
0-300-06446-2 YALE PB........$27.50

C.R. **Dodwell**
The Pictorial Arts of the West, 800-1200
Illustrated with 75 color and 325 black-and-white plates, this comprehensive guide illuminates a fascinating period of medieval art history
0-300-05348-7 YALE........$65.00
0-300-06493-4 YALE PB........$35.00

Henri **Frankfort**
The Art and Architecture of the Ancient Orient
A classic survey of Mesopotamian, Syrian, Anatolian, and Persian art and architecture, by a distinguished art historian
See also **THE ANCIENT NEAR EAST** under **ART OF EGYPT AND THE ANCIENT NEAR EAST**
0-300-05331-2 YALE PB........$25.00

Richard **Ettinghausen** & Oleg **Grabar**
The Art and Architecture of Islam: 650-1250
0-300-05330-4 YALE PB........$25.00

S.J. **Freedberg**
Painting in Italy: 1500-1600, 3rd Ed.
A revised edition of the classic work, with color illustrations, updated text, and a new bibliography
See also **ITALY** under **EUROPEAN ART: THE RENAISSANCE**
0-300-05586-2 YALE........$65.00
0-300-05587-0 YALE PB........$28.50

George Heard **Hamilton**
The Art and Architecture of Russia
The latest edition of the standard account of the subject
0-300-05326-6 YALE........$50.00
0-300-05327-4 YALE PB........$25.00

Painting and Sculpture in Europe, 1880-1940
See also **GENERAL** under **20TH-CENTURY ART**
0-300-05648-6 YALE........$60.00
0-300-05649-4 YALE PB........$27.50

J.C. **Harle**
Art and Architecture of the Indian Subcontinent
A thoroughgoing and enormously erudite survey of Indian art, replete with information on intellectual, cultural, and social life
See also **THE INDIAN SUBCONTINENT** in **WORLD HISTORY AND CURRENT AFFAIRS**
See also **INDIA** under **EAST ASIAN ART**
0-300-05329-0 YALE PB........$26.50

Ludwig H. **Heydenreich** & Paul **Davies**
Architecture in Italy, 1400-1500
0-300-06467-5 YALE PB........$27.50

Sinclair **Hood**
The Arts in Prehistoric Greece
An amply illustrated introduction to pottery and figurines of the Bronze Age
See also **GREECE** under **ART OF THE CLASSICAL WORLD**
0-300-05287-1 YALE PB........$25.00

Richard **Krautheimer**
Medieval Early Christian and Byzantine Architecture
0-300-05294-4 YALE PB........$26.50

George **Kubler**
The Art and Architecture of Ancient America: The Mexican, Maya, and Andean Peoples
See also **MEXICO AND CENTRAL AMERICA** under **NATIVE AMERICAN ARTS**
0-300-05325-8 YALE PB........$26.50

Peter **Lasko**
Ars Sacra, 800-1200
A beautiful book that traces the development of the so-called "minor arts"—such as bronze doors, gold, ivory, and jeweled book covers, and reliquary caskets—and the major role they played alongside other pictorial arts and sculpture of the period
See also **CRAFTS** under **MEDIEVAL ART: 600-1400** under **EUROPEAN ART: BYZANTINE AND MEDIEVAL**
0-300-06048-3 YALE........$65.00

Michael **Levey**
Painting and Sculpture in France, 1700-1789
See also **BAROQUE AND ROCOCO IN FRANCE** under **EUROPEAN ART: BAROQUE AND ROCOCO**
0-300-06494-2 YALE PB........$30.00

Wolfgang **Lotz** & Deborah **Howard**
Architecture in Italy, 1500-1600
See also **ITALY** under **EUROPEAN ART: THE RENAISSANCE**
0-300-06469-1 YALE PB........$27.50

Fritz **Novotny**
Painting and Sculpture in Europe, 1780-1880
See also **EUROPEAN ART: 1750-1900**
0-300-05321-5 YALE PB........$25.00

R. **Paine** & Alexander **Soper**
The Art and Architecture of Japan
Good on painting and architecture, but decorative arts are omitted
See also **JAPAN** under **EAST ASIAN ART**
0-300-05333-9 YALE PB........$26.50

Jakob **Rosenberg**
Dutch Art and Architecture: 1600-1800
Primarily concerned with the 17th century and Rembrandt, Hals, and Vermeer; with numerous black-and-white illustrations
See also **FLANDERS AND THE NETHERLANDS: 1600-1800** under **EUROPEAN ART: BAROQUE AND ROCOCO**
0-300-05312-6 YALE PB........$26.50

N.K. **Sanders**
Prehistoric Art in Europe
See also **PREHISTORIC ART**
0-300-05286-3 YALE PB........$26.50

Laurence **Sickman** & Alexander **Soper**
Art and Architecture in China
A good survey of architecture, sculpture, and painting, leaving out crafts and decorative arts
See also **CHINA** under **EAST ASIAN ART**
0-300-05334-7 YALE PB........$26.50

Seymour **Slive**
Dutch Painting, 1600-1800
This lavishly illustrated book, a standard in its field, is a new updated version of the classic *Dutch Art and Architecture: 1600-1800*. Slive has rewritten and expanded the original text, taking into account recent scholarship. The book is an in-depth exploration of the Dutch Masters, including Hals, Rembrandt, Vermeer, and Ruisdael
See also **FLANDERS AND THE NETHERLANDS: 1600-1800** under **EUROPEAN ART: BAROQUE AND ROCOCO**
0-300-06418-7 YALE........$60.00

Donald **Strong**
Roman Art
See also **ROME AND THE ETRUSCANS** under **ART OF THE CLASSICAL WORLD**
0-300-05293-6 YALE PB........$25.00

John Newenham **Summerson**

Architecture in Britain, 1530-1830

0-300-05886-1 YALE PB $26.50

J.B. **Ward-Perkins**

Roman Imperial Architecture

The Hellenistic tradition revolutionized by the Roman invention of concrete. Fully illustrated

See also **ARTS** under **TOPICS IN ROMAN HISTORY** under **ANCIENT ROME** in **WORLD HISTORY AND CURRENT AFFAIRS**

0-300-05292-8 YALE PB $26.50

Ellis **Waterhouse**

Painting in Britain, 1530-1790

0-300-05833-0 YALE PB $25.00

Margaret **Whinney**

Sculpture in Britain, 1530-1830

See also **18TH-CENTURY ENGLAND** under **EUROPEAN ART: BAROQUE AND ROCOCO**

0-300-05318-5 YALE PB $26.50

John **White**

Art and Architecture in Italy, 1250-1400

A new edition, with color reproductions and an updated bibliography

See also **THE RISE OF ITALIAN PAINTING** under **MEDIEVAL ART: 600-1400** under **EUROPEAN ART: BYZANTINE AND MEDIEVAL**

0-300-05584-6 YALE $60.00
0-300-05585-4 YALE PB $27.50

Rudolf **Wittkower**

Art and Architecture in Italy, 1600-1750

A first-rate survey; composed by a master scholar of Italian painting, sculpture, and architecture

See also **THE BAROQUE IN ITALY** under **EUROPEAN ART: BAROQUE AND ROCOCO**

See also **ITALY** under **BAROQUE AND ROCOCO** under **EUROPEAN ARCHITECTURE TO 1900**

0-300-05306-1 YALE $60.00
0-300-05308-8 YALE PB $27.50

Thames & Hudson World of Art

The *World of Art* series offers well-illustrated and informative books on a wide range of artists and artistic traditions and styles at very reasonable prices. The series also includes a number of handy and reliable works of reference.

Cyril **Aldred**

Egyptian Art

Three thousand years of architecture, painting, and sculpture, and their political and social setting

See also **EGYPT** under **ART OF EGYPT AND THE ANCIENT NEAR EAST**

0-500-20180-3 THAMES & HUDSON PB $14.95

David **Anfam**

Abstract Expressionism

See also **THE NEW YORK SCHOOL AND THE 50S** under **POSTWAR AMERICAN ART** under **ART SINCE 1945**

0-500-20243-5 THAMES & HUDSON PB $14.95

Bruce **Arnold**

Irish Art: A Concise History

0-500-20148-X THAMES & HUDSON PB $11.95

John **Russell**

Francis Bacon

See also **POSTWAR EUROPEAN ART** under **ART SINCE 1945**

0-500-20271-0 THAMES & HUDSON PB $12.95

Germain **Bazin**

Baroque and Rococo

The stylistic currents in the arts of western Europe, from 1600 through 1760. A fast-faced illustrated survey by the Louvre

See also **EUROPEAN ART: BAROQUE AND ROCOCO**

0-500-20018-1 THAMES & HUDSON PB $14.95

John **Beckwith**

Early Medieval Art: Carolingian, Ottonian, Romanesque

A concise, authoritative survey of the architecture, painting, sculpture, illuminations, and ivories of the three great periods of early medieval art

See also **EARLY MEDIEVAL** under **MEDIEVAL ART: 600-1400** under **EUROPEAN ART: BYZANTINE AND MEDIEVAL**

0-500-20019-X THAMES & HUDSON PB $14.95

John **Boardman**

Athenian Red Figure Vases: The Classical Period, A Handbook

See also **GREECE** under **ART OF THE CLASSICAL WORLD**

0-500-20244-3 THAMES & HUDSON PB $11.95

Greek Art

A fluent and engaging introduction by the pre-eminent authority in the field

0-500-20292-3 THAMES & HUDSON PB $16.95

Greek Sculpture: The Late Classical Period and Sculpture in Colonies and Overseas

0-500-20285-0 THAMES & HUDSON PB $14.95

Alan **Bowness**

Modern European Art

See also **GENERAL** under **20TH-CENTURY ART**

0-500-20205-2 THAMES & HUDSON PB $14.95

Wally **Caruana**

Aboriginal Art

See also **ART OF OCEANIA, AUSTRALIA, AND NEW ZEALAND**

0-500-20264-8 THAMES & HUDSON PB $14.95

Richard **Verdi**

Cézanne

See also **IMPRESSIONISM: INDIVIDUAL ARTISTS** under **FRANCE** under **EUROPEAN ART: 1750-1900**

0-500-20258-3 THAMES & HUDSON PB $12.95

Whitney **Chadwick**

Women, Art and Society

In this extensively revised edition of her brilliant study, Chadwick utilizes new research and a critical feminist perspective to identify the aesthetics and ideologies that have shaped ten centuries of women's relationships to the visual arts and their histories

0-500-20293-1 THAMES & HUDSON PB $16.95

Elizabeth **Cumming**

Arts and Crafts Movement

0-500-20248-6 THAMES & HUDSON PB $14.95

Dawn **Ades**

Dalì

See also **DADA AND SURREALISM** under **20TH-CENTURY ART**

0-500-20280-X THAMES & HUDSON PB $14.95

Bernard **Denvir**

Post-Impressionism

See also **POSTIMPRESSIONISM** under **FRANCE** under **EUROPEAN ART: 1750-1900**

0-500-20255-9 THAMES & HUDSON PB $12.95

Bernard **Denvir**, editor

The Thames and Hudson Encyclopedia of Impressionism

See also **IMPRESSIONISM: GENERAL STUDIES** under **FRANCE** under **EUROPEAN ART: 1750-1900**

0-500-20239-7 THAMES & HUDSON PB $11.95

Alastair **Duncan**

Art Deco

0-500-20230-3 THAMES & HUDSON PB $14.95

Art Nouveau

0-500-20273-7 THAMES & HUDSON PB $14.95

Christian F. **Feest**

Native Arts of North America

See also **NORTH AMERICA** under **NATIVE AMERICAN ARTS**

0-500-20262-1 THAMES & HUDSON PB $14.95

Robert E. **Fisher**

Buddhist Art and Architecture

0-500-20265-6 THAMES & HUDSON PB $14.95

Kenneth **Frampton**

Modern Architecture: A Critical History

Amazing that there could be so much, and of such importance, in this compact treatment; a "survey," but as imaginative as it is scholarly—and thorough

See also **HISTORY** under **20TH-CENTURY ARCHITECTURE** in **ARCHITECTURE, DESIGN, AND HOMES**

0-500-20257-5 THAMES & HUDSON PB $14.95

Peter **Fuller**

Henry Moore

See also **POSTWAR EUROPEAN ART** under **ART SINCE 1945**

0-500-20231-1 THAMES & HUDSON PB $11.95

Marco **Livingstone**

David Hockney

0-500-20291-5 THAMES & HUDSON PB $14.95

Frank **Whitford**

Klimt

See also **EXPRESSIONISM OUTSIDE OF GERMANY** under **EXPRESSIONISM AND THE BLUE RIDER** under **20TH-CENTURY ART**

0-500-20246-X THAMES & HUDSON PB $14.95

Lloyd **Laing** & Jennifer **Laing**

Art of the Celts

0-500-20256-7 THAMES & HUDSON PB $14.95

Michael **Levey**
From Giotto to Cézanne: A Concise History of Painting
A compact historical survey focusing on technical developments
0-500-20024-6 THAMES & HUDSON PB $14.95

Homan **Potterman**
The National Gallery, London
See also **MUSEUMS AND COLLECTIONS**
0-500-20161-7 THAMES & HUDSON PB $11.95

Edward **Lucie-Smith**
Latin American Art of the 20th Century
See also **ART OF LATIN AMERICA** under **20TH-CENTURY ART**
0-500-20260-5 THAMES & HUDSON PB $14.95

Movements in Art Since 1945
See also **ART SINCE 1945**
0-500-20282-6 THAMES & HUDSON PB $14.95

Alan **Krell**
Manet and the Painters of Contemporary Life
See also **IMPRESSIONISM: INDIVIDUAL ARTISTS** under **FRANCE** under **EUROPEAN ART: 1750-1900**
0-500-20289-3 THAMES & HUDSON PB $14.95

Carol **Mann**
Modigliani
See also **OTHER ARTISTS IN PARIS** under **20TH-CENTURY ART**
0-500-20176-5 NORTON PB $14.95

Andrew **Martindale**
Gothic Art
A sensible and manageable introduction
See also **GOTHIC** under **MEDIEVAL ART: 600-1400** under **EUROPEAN ART: BYZANTINE AND MEDIEVAL**
0-500-20058-0 THAMES & HUDSON PB $14.95

Linda **Murray**
Michelangelo
See also **INDIVIDUAL ARTISTS** under **ITALY** under **EUROPEAN ART: THE RENAISSANCE**
0-500-20174-9 THAMES & HUDSON PB $14.95

Mary Ellen **Miller**
The Art of Mesoamerica: From Olmec to Aztec
See also **MEXICO AND CENTRAL AMERICA** under **NATIVE AMERICAN ARTS**
0-500-20290-7 THAMES & HUDSON PB $14.95

Anna **Moszynska**
Abstract Art
0-500-20237-0 THAMES & HUDSON PB $14.95

Roberta J.M. **Olson**
Italian Renaissance Sculpture
See also **ITALY** under **EUROPEAN ART: THE RENAISSANCE**
0-500-20253-2 THAMES & HUDSON PB $14.95

Richard J. **Powell**
Black Art and Culture in the 20th Century
A brilliant new study of the philosophical and social forces that have shaped a black presence in 20th-century art and culture. Topics include the emergence of the "New Negro" in Jazz-Age America and France, the use of black folk imagery in post-Depression art, and the ideological tug-of-war between racial pride and cultural assimilation
0-500-18195-0 THAMES & HUDSON $29.95

Philip S. **Rawson**
The Art of Southeast Asia: Cambodia, Vietnam, Thailand, Laos, Burma, Java, and Bali
See also **SOUTHEAST ASIA** under **EAST ASIAN ART**
0-500-20060-2 THAMES & HUDSON PB $14.95

Herbert **Read**
A Concise History of Modern Painting
0-500-20141-2 THAMES & HUDSON PB $14.95

Herbert **Read**, editor
The Thames and Hudson Dictionary of Art and Artists
0-500-20274-5 THAMES & HUDSON PB $14.95

Colin **Rhodes**
Primitivism and Modern Art
A groundbreaking book that draws on a wide range of material, from high art to popular entertainment, to assess the important role played by tribal art in the history of modern art in the West
See also **SPECIAL TOPICS** under **GENERAL** under **20TH-CENTURY ART**
0-500-20276-1 THAMES & HUDSON PB $14.95

Bernard **Champigneulle**
Rodin
A reappraisal of Rodin's significance as an innovator in sculpture combined with a revealing account of his personality and troubled private life
See also **FRENCH SCULPTORS** under **FRANCE** under **EUROPEAN ART: 1750-1900**
0-500-20061-0 THAMES & HUDSON PB $14.95

Frank **Whitford**
Egon Schiele
See also **EXPRESSIONISM OUTSIDE OF GERMANY** under **EXPRESSIONISM AND THE BLUE RIDER** under **20TH-CENTURY ART**
0-500-18183-7 THAMES & HUDSON $19.95
0-500-20183-8 THAMES & HUDSON PB $14.95

Nikos **Stangos**
Concepts of Modern Art
An invaluable collection of essays
0064-30104 HARPER & ROW PB $12.95
0-500-20268-0 THAMES & HUDSON PB $14.95

Rebecca **Stone-Miller**
Art of the Andes: From Chavin to Inca
See also **MEXICO AND CENTRAL AMERICA** under **NATIVE AMERICAN ARTS**
0-500-20286-9 THAMES & HUDSON PB $14.95

Robert **Tavernor**
Palladio and Palladianism
0-500-20242-7 THAMES & HUDSON PB $12.95

Nicholas **Thomas**
Oceanic Art
See also **ART OF OCEANIA, AUSTRALIA, AND NEW ZEALAND**
0-500-20281-8 THAMES & HUDSON PB $14.95

Bernard **Denvir**
Toulouse-Lautrec
See also **POSTIMPRESSIONISM** under **FRANCE** under **EUROPEAN ART: 1750-1900**
0-500-20250-8 THAMES & HUDSON PB $12.95

Julian **Treuherz**
Victorian Painting
0-500-20263-X THAMES & HUDSON PB $12.95

William **Vaughan**
Romanticism and Art
See also **EUROPEAN ART: 1750-1900**
0-500-20275-3 THAMES & HUDSON PB $14.95

Roald **Nasgaard**
National Gallery of Art, Washington
See also **MUSEUMS AND COLLECTIONS**
0-500-20251-6 THAMES & HUDSON PB $14.95

Mortimer **Wheeler**
Roman Art and Architecture
A survey of architecture, town planning, sculpture and painting, silver, glass, pottery, and other achievements
See also **ARTS** under **TOPICS IN ROMAN HISTORY** under **ANCIENT ROME** in **WORLD HISTORY AND CURRENT AFFAIRS**
0-500-20021-1 THAMES & HUDSON PB $14.95

Sarah **Whitfield**
Fauvism
The first book in many years to offer a critical reappraisal of the movements' artists, their work, their relationships with each other, and the critical and commercial response to their work which was initially met with hostility but which paved the way for Cubism
See also **MATISSE AND FAUVISM** under **20TH-CENTURY ART**
0-500-20227-3 THAMES & HUDSON PB $14.95

Frank **Willett**
African Art: An Introduction
See also **GENERAL STUDIES** under **ARTS OF AFRICA**
0-500-20267-2 THAMES & HUDSON PB $14.95

Reference

Robert **Atkins**
Artspeak: A Guide to Contemporary Ideas, Movements, and Buzzwords
1-55859-010-2 ABBEVILLE PB $15.95

Artspoke: A Guide to Modern Ideas, Movements, and Buzzwords, 1848-1944
See also **SPECIAL TOPICS** under **GENERAL** under **20TH-CENTURY ART**
1-55859-388-8 ABBEVILLE PB $17.95

An A-Z of Artists
The Art Book
An innovative and fun guide to 500 great painters and sculptors from medieval to modern times, each illustrated by a full-color plate and accompanied by an informative text. Entries are cross-referenced, and exhaustive glossaries of technical terms and historic movements are provided, making this not only a feast for the eye but an invaluable reference as well
0-7148-2984-6 PHAIDON $39.95

Dawson **Carr** & Mark **Leonard**
Looking at Paintings: A Guide to Technical Terms
0-89236-213-8 OXFORD PB $11.95

Ian **Chilvers**, editor
The Oxford Dictionary of Art
From Byzantine to Junk Art and beyond, with over 3000 entries on artists, schools, periods, techniques, critical terms, museums, and art historians
0-19-866133-9 OXFORD $49.95

Getty Art History Information Program
Art and Architecture Thesaurus
0-19-508884-0 GETTY MUSEUM $375.00

Paul **Goldman**
Looking at Prints, Drawings, and Watercolours: A Guide to Technical Terms
0-89236-148-4 GETTY MUSEUM PB $11.95

Sir Lawrence **Gowing**, editor
A Biographical Dictionary of Artists
With 1,340 illustrated articles, this biographical dictionary offers an unparalleled guide to the visual arts. Containing authoritative articles on artists Western and non-Western alike, and illustrated in color throughout, this is a vital and useful addition to any bookshelf
0-8160-3252-1 FACTS ON FILE $50.00

James **Hall**
Dictionary of Subjects and Symbols in Art
INTRODUCTION BY KENNETH CLARK
0-06-430100-1 ICON PB $16.00

Edward **Lucie-Smith**
The Thames and Hudson Dictionary of Art Terms
0-500-20222-2 THAMES & HUDSON PB $14.95

Peter **Murray** & Linda **Murray**
The Penguin Dictionary of Art and Artists
The last seven centuries, with short biographies and explication of terms. "A vast amount of information, carefully detailed, abreast of current thought and scholarship and easy to read"—*TLS*
0-14-051133-4 VIKING PB $8.95

Harold **Osborne**
The Oxford Companion to Art
An excellent companion guide and a widely valued handbook
0-19-866107-X OXFORD $55.00

Sandro **Sproccati**
A Guide to Art: A Handy Reference to Artists, Their Works, and Artistic Movements from the Fourteenth Century to the Present Day
0-8109-3366-7 ABRAMS $29.95

Anabel **Thomas**
Illustrated Dictionary of Narrative Painting
0-7195-5290-7 MURRAY PB $24.95

Jane **Turner**, editor
The Dictionary of Art
"This result of 14 years of work and a $50 million investment includes 34 volumes, weighs 187 pounds and occupies 5 feet 8 inches of bookshelf space. Inside its pages are 26.3 million words and 15,000 illustrations. Indeed, with 45,000 articles written by 6,800 contributors from all over the world, the dictionary can probably justify its claim to be the largest international collaboration in the history of art publishing"—*NY Times*
1-88444-600-0 GROVE $8,000.00

Philip **Yenawine**
Key Art Terms for Beginners
Yenawine presents the key terms that will help beginning art enthusiasts
0-8109-1225-2 ABRAMS $24.95

Themes, Techniques, and Genres

Josef **Albers**
Interaction of Color
0-300-01846-0 YALE PB $10.00

Colin B. **Bailey** & Carrie A. **Hamilton**
The Loves of the Gods: Mythological Painting from Watteau to David
0-8478-1521-8 RIZZOLI $75.00

Monica **Bohm-Duchen**
The Nude
1-85759-004-X SCALA $9.95

George Brant **Bridgman**
The Book of a Hundred Hands
0-486-22709-X DOVER PB $5.95

Constructive Anatomy
0-486-21104-5 DOVER PB $5.95

Richard **Brilliant**
Portraiture
A lively discussion of the genre from one of the most intelligent art historians at work today
0-674-69176-8 HARVARD PB $19.50

Norman **Bryson**
Looking at the Overlooked: Four Essays on Still Life Painting
0-674-53906-0 HARVARD PB $19.95

Kenneth **Clark**
The Nude: A Study in Ideal Form
0-691-09792-5 PRINCETON $95.00
0-691-01788-3 PRINCETON PB $24.95

Rex Vicat **Cole**
Perspective for Artists: The Practice and Theory of Perspective as Applied to Pictures with a Section Dealing with its Application to Architecture
0-486-22487-2 DOVER PB $6.95

Luigina **De Grandis**
Theory and Use of Color
0-13-914441-2 PRENTICE HALL PB $25.95

L. M. **Delaisse**
Illuminated Manuscripts
A lavishly illustrated history
0-7078-0070-6 RIZZOLI $120.00

Penelope Reed **Doob**
Idea of the Labyrinth: From Classical Antiquity to the Middle Ages
0-8014-2393-7 CORNELL $45.00
0-8014-8000-0 CORNELL PB $16.95

Wilhelm **Ellenberger**
An Atlas of Animal Anatomy for Artists
0-486-20082-5 DOVER PB $9.95

Gary **Faigin**
The Artist's Complete Guide to Facial Expression
0-8230-1628-5 WATSON-GUPTILL $35.00

Edmond J. **Farris**
Art Students' Anatomy
0-486-20744-7 DOVER PB $5.95

Alan J. **Grieco**
The Meal
1-85759-002-3 SCALA $9.95

Egbert **Haverkamp-Begemann**
Creative Copies: Interpretative Drawings from Michelangelo to Picasso
0-85667-350-1 SOTHEBY PARKE BERNET $55.00

Michael **Levey**
The Painter Depicted: Painters as a Subject in Painting
Engaging thoughts on the historical development of the artist's self-representation
0-500-55013-1 THAMES & HUDSON $10.95

Martin **Kemp**
The Science of Art: Optical Themes in Western Art from Brunelleschi to Seurat
"…Kemp's book not only offers new ways of understanding the history of science and the history of art, but it also raises a host of historical and historigraphical questions" —Geoffrey Cantor
0-300-05241-3 YALE PB $35.00

Edward **Lucie-Smith**
Sexuality in Western Art
0-500-20252-4 THAMES & HUDSON PB $14.95

Ralph **Mayer** & Steven **Sheehan**
The Artist's Handbook of Materials and Techniques
0-670-83701-6 VIKING $45.00

W.J.T. **Mitchell**
Landscape and Power
Landscape and Power goes beyond an approach to landscape as a genre. It shows how landscape has functioned as a cultural practice throughout history, from an imperialist endeavour to an emotional reflection of modern national identity
0-226-53206-2 CHICAGO $42.50
0-226-53207-0 CHICAGO PB $13.95

National Gallery of Australia, editor
Don't Leave Me this Way: Art in the Age of Aids
This anthology combines essays, poems, and paintings to explore and document the influence of the AIDS epidemic on art. Contributors include Edmund White, Keith Haring, Cindy Sherman, and Andres Serrano
See also **THE CONTEMPORARY SCENE** under **ART SINCE 1945**
0-500-97420-9 NORTON PB $19.95

Erwin **Panofsky**
Tomb Sculpture: Four Lectures on Its Changing Aspects from Ancient Egypt to Bernini
0-8109-3870-7 ABRAMS $75.00

John **Pope-Hennessy**
The Portrait in the Renaissance
Stimulating and colorful essays by the eminent art historian; with exemplary illustrations
See also **ITALY** under **EUROPEAN ART: THE RENAISSANCE**
0-691-09795-X PRINCETON $95.00

John Pope-Hennessy

Madeleine **Pinault**
The Painter as Naturalist: From Durer to Redoute
2-08-013516-3 ABBEVILLE $39.98

Lionello **Puppi**
Torment in Art: Pain, Violence, and Martyrdom
0-8478-1406-8 RIZZOLI $75.00

Monona **Rossol**
The Artist's Complete Health & Safety Guide
1-88055-918-8 ALLWORTH PB $19.95

Norbert **Schneider**
The Art of the Portrait
A history of 250 years of portraiture through a close look at 50 major works since the Renaissance
3-8228-9651-9 TASCHEN $25.01

Marc **Shell**
Art & Money
0-226-75213-5 CHICAGO $35.00

Ray **Smith**
The Artist's Handbook
Techniques include etching, scratchboard, and painting
See also **BOOKS FOR YOUNG READERS**
0-394-55585-6 KNOPF $40.00

Ruth **Westheimer**
Art of Arousal
The most famous sex therapist in history takes a step into high culture, but there's only one thing on her mind. A collection of 120 artworks across history which document the full range of erotic relationships, from shy flirtation to blissful exhaustion
1-55859-330-6 ABBEVILLE $35.00

Rudolf **Wittkower** & Margot **Wittkower**
Born Under Saturn: The Character and Conduct of Artists
A historical overview of the phenomenon of the mad and melancholic artist
0-393-00474-0 NORTON PB $13.95

Jeremy **Wood**
The Nativity
1-85759-005-8 SCALA $9.95

Drawings

George Brant **Bridgman**
Bridgman's Life Drawing
0-486-22710-3 DOVER PB $5.95

Paul **Cummings**, editor
Twentieth-Century Drawings: Selections from the Whitney Museum of American Art
0-486-24143-2 DOVER PB $8.95

Betty **Edwards**
Drawing on the Right Side of the Brain: A Course in Enhancing Creativity and Artistic Confidence
See also **CREATIVITY** under **SPECIAL TOPICS IN PSYCHOLOGY** under **PSYCHOLOGY** in **SOCIAL STUDIES**
0-87477-513-2 TARCHER PB $14.95

Kimon **Nicolaides**
The Natural Way to Draw: A Working Plan for Art Study
0-395-53007-5 HOUGHTON MIFFLIN PB $11.95

Philip **Rawson**
Drawing
0-8122-1251-7 PENNSYLVANIA PB $20.95

John **Ruskin**
The Elements of Drawing
INTRODUCTION BY LAWRENCE CAMPBELL
1-87156-933-8 NEW AMSTERDAM PB $24.95

James **Spero**
Old Master Landscape Drawings
Includes 45 works
0-486-26947-7 DOVER PB $3.95

Old Master Life Drawings
Forty-four plates
0-486-25233-7 DOVER PB $4.95

Old Master Portrait Drawings
0-486-26364-9 DOVER PB $3.95

Anthony **Toney**
150 Masterpieces of Drawing
0-486-21032-4 DOVER PB $9.95

Universe Editors
Artists' Sketchbooks
1-55550-683-6 UNIVERSE $9.95

Painting

"Painting is a science, and should be pursued as an inquiry into the laws of nature. Why, then, may not landscape painting be considered a branch of natural philosophy, of which pictures are but the experiments?"—John Constable

Bill **Creevy**
The Oil Painting Book: Materials and Techniques for Today's Artist
0-8230-3273-6 WATSON-GUPTILL $35.00

David **Curtis**
A Personal View: The Landscape in Watercolor
0-7153-0287-6 DAVID & CHARLES $27.95

Walter **Koschatzky**
The Art of Watercolor
Analyzes and explains its technique, history, and significance; abundantly illustrated
0-89835-265-7 ABARIS $59.50

Gregg **Kreutz**

Problem Solving for Oil Painters

0-8230-4408-4 WATSON-GUPTILL $24.95

Arthur Pillans **Laurie**

Painter's Methods and Materials

0-486-21868-6 DOVER PB $8.95

Patricia **Monahan** & Jenny **Rodwell**

The Oil Painter's Handbook

0-289-80137-0 STERLING $24.95

The Watercolor Painter's Handbook

0-289-80136-2 STERLING $29.95

Graham **Reynolds**

Water Colors: A Concise History

0-500-20109-9 THAMES & HUDSON PB $12.95

Joseph **Sheppard**

How to Paint Like the Old Masters

0-8230-2671-X WATSON-GUPTILL PB $22.50

Daniel **Thompson**

The Materials Techniques of Medieval Painting

Manuscripts, laboratory analyses, and information gleaned from medieval sources

See also **CRAFTS** under **MEDIEVAL ART: 600–1400** under **EUROPEAN ART: BYZANTINE AND MEDIEVAL**

FOREWORD BY BERNARD BERENSON

0-486-20327-1 DOVER PB $6.95

Prints

Riva **Castelman**

Prints of the Twentieth Century

A survey of this important medium

See also **GENERAL** under **20TH-CENTURY ART**

0-500-20228-1 THAMES & HUDSON PB $11.95

Bamber **Gascoigne**

How to Identify Prints

0-500-23454-X THAMES & HUDSON $50.00

Robert Beverly **Hale** & Terence **Coyle**

Albinus on Anatomy

Includes eighty original Albinus plates

0-486-25836-X DOVER PB $12.95

Linda C. **Hults**

The Print in the Western World

Abundantly illustrated and with a full glossary

0-299-13700-7 WISCONSIN $65.00

Ruth **Leaf**

Etching, Engraving and Other Intaglio Printmaking Techniques

0-486-24721-X DOVER PB $11.95

A. Hyatt **Mayor**

Prints and People: A Social History of Printed Pictures

A classic study

0-691-00326-2 PRINCETON PB $35.00

Ernest S. **Lumsden**

The Art of Etching

0-486-20049-3 DOVER PB $7.95

Innis **Shoemaker** & Elizabeth **Brown**

The Engravings of Marcantonio Raimondi

A good introduction to Raphael's engraver and the first master of the reproductive print

0-913689-04-1 SPENCER MUSEUM PB $18.50

Susan **Tallmann**

The Contemporary Print: Pre-Pop to Postmodern

The medium of printmaking has become crucial to the work of many contemporary artists. This formidable survey of recent works, illustrated with 330 plates, 160 in color, is essential for anyone concerned with the art of our time

See also **ART SINCE 1945**

0-500-23684-4 THAMES & HUDSON $50.00

Sculpture

Oliver **Andrews**

Living Materials: A Sculptor's Handbook

0-520-06452-6 CALIFORNIA PB $29.95

Edouard **Lanteri**

Modelling and Sculpting Animals

0-486-25007-5 DOVER PB $8.95

Modelling and Sculpting the Human Figure

0-486-25006-7 DOVER PB $10.95

John **Mack**, editor

Masks and the Art of Expression

0-8109-3641-0 ABRAMS $45.00

Jack **Rich**

The Materials and Methods of Sculpture

0-486-25742-8 DOVER PB $12.95

Museums and Collections

Giovanna Nepi **Scire**

Treasures of Venetian Painting: The Galleria dell'Accademia

Masterpieces from the famous Venetian museum, many newly restored, for the first time in an oversize, full-color book. The 220 illustrations include Giorgione's mysterious *The Tempest;* Titian's *Presentation in the Temple* and *The Deposition of Christ,* and numerous others by Gentile Bellini, Tintoretto, and Veronese

0-86565-127-2 VENDOME $65.00

Barnes Foundation

Great French Paintings from the Barnes Foundation

This affordable paperback brings the French masterpieces of the wondrous Barnes Foundation to those who missed the collection's last tour. Over 100 landmark canvases of European painting, reproduced in full color, unite works by Manet, Renoir, Monet, Cezanne, Van Gogh, Gauguin, and virtually every other major Impressionist, Post-Impressionist, and Early Modern French painter. Enriched by insightful and readable scholarly commentary

0-679-76221-3 KNOPF PB $40.00

Great French Paintings from the Barnes Foundation: Impressionist, Post-Impressionist, and Early Modern

Controversy has surrounded the Barnes collection for decades. Here are some of the greatest works of Manet, Renoir, Cezanne, Gauguin, Seurat, Toulouse-Lautrec, Picasso, and more in full color for the first time ever. Includes text and essays from eminent French and American scholars and curators

0-679-40963-7 KNOPF $65.00

Christian **Geelhaar**

The Museum of Fine Arts, Basel: 250 Master Paintings

0-8109-3133-8 ABRAMS $75.00

Theodore **Stebbins** & Peter **Sutton**

Masterpieces from the Museum of Fine Arts, Boston

0-8109-1424-7 ABRAMS $49.50

Thomas **Krens** & others

Art of this Century: The Guggenheim Collection

0-89207-072-2 GUGGENHEIM $60.00

Enez **Whipple**

Guild Hall of East Hampton, An Adventure in the Arts: The First 60 Years

0-8109-3384-5 ABRAMS $45.00

Marjorie B. **Cohn** & Ivan **Gaskell**

Harvard's Art Museums: 100 Years of Collecting

An illustrated history of one hundred years of scholarship and acquisition by Harvard's great museums, the Fogg, the Busch-Reisinger, and the Arthur M. Sackler

0-8109-3427-2 ABRAMS $60.00

Alice Cooney **Frelinghuysen** & others

Splendid Legacy: The Havemeyer Collection

0-8109-6426-0 METROPOLITAN MUSEUM $85.00

Colin **Eisler**

Paintings in the Hermitage

Begun with the ambitious acquisitions of Catherine the Great of Russia, the Hermitage museum remains one of the most impressive collections of art. This survey includes over 750 full-color reproductions of masterpieces by Ingres, Rembrandt, Rubens, Van Dyck, Van Gogh, Gauguin, and many others

1-55670-419-4 STEWART, TABORI $59.95

Mikhail B. **Piotrovsky**
Great Art Treasures of the Hermitage Museum, St. Petersburg
0-8109-3428-0 ABRAMS $195.00

Raymond **Keaveney** & others
National Gallery of Ireland
1-87024-858-9 SCALA $25.00
0-903162-05-9 OLYMPIC PB $9.95

Hilliard T. **Goldfarb**
The Isabella Stewart Gardner Museum: A Companion Guide and History
One of the preeminent art collections in the United States, the Isabella Stewart Gardner Museum is the home of some 2,500 treasures, covering many periods of art, from ancient Chinese sculpture to paintings by Titian and Matisse. This beautiful book, illustrated with over 100 colorplates, is an in-depth study of the collection, collector, and her museum, one of America's best
0-300-06341-5 YALE PB $20.00

Martin **Weyl**
The Israel Museum
This catalog of the rich and unusual Israel Museum is organized into three parts: biblical archaeology, Jewish ethnography, and art collection. From the Dead Sea Scrolls to the Naguchi-designed Billy Rose Sculpture Garden, the remarkable collection of Old Masters to the remarkable Biblical archaeology, this magnificently photographed volume provides a unique introduction to one of the world's most exceptional museums
0-86565-960-5 VENDOME $65.00

Marilyn **Perry** & others
A Gift to America: Masterpieces of European Painting from the Samuel H. Kress Collection
0-8109-3383-7 ABRAMS $49.50

Walter **Liedtke** & others
Masterworks from the Musée des Beaux-Arts, Lille
0-8109-6417-1 METROPOLITAN MUSEUM $60.00

Michel **Laclotte**
The National Gallery Companion Guide
A guide to one of London's great museums
0-300-06133-1 YALE PB $20.00

Homan **Potterman**
The National Gallery, London
See also **THAMES & HUDSON WORLD OF ART**
0-500-20161-7 THAMES & HUDSON PB $11.95

Michael **Wilson**
The National Gallery
London's painting treasures
0-935748-57-1 SCALA PB $14.95

Sir Lawrence **Gowing**
Paintings in the Louvre
An extensive, sumptuously illustrated volume. "Gowing is a perfect guide. With a painter's confidence he goes right for the essence of a picture, and he has the language to capture it, strong, fluent and vivid"—John Walsh
1-55670-007-5 STEWART, TABORI $59.95

Michel **Laclotte**
Treasures of the Louvre
0-89660-037-8 ABBEVILLE $29.98

Senior Curators
The Mauritshuis
1-85759-031-7 SOTHEBY'S $29.95

Walter **Hopps**, editor
The Menil Collection: A Selection from the Paleolithic to the Modern Era
0-8109-1440-9 ABRAMS $49.50

Katharine **Baetjer**
European Paintings in the Metropolitan Museum of Art by Artists Born Before 1865: A Summary Catalogue
0-8109-6431-7 METROPOLITAN MUSEUM $95.00

Joy **Richardson**
Inside the Museum: A Children's Guide to the Metropolitan Museum of Art
0-8109-2561-3 ABRAMS PB $12.95

Erich **Steingraber**
The Alte Pinakothek, Munich
0-85667-222-X SCALA $25.00

Françoise **Cachin**
Treasures of the Musée d'Orsay
0-89660-054-8 ARTABRAS $24.98

Michel **Laclotte**
Paintings at the Musée d'Orsay
Paris's superb new museum devoted to 19th-century art
0-935748-72-5 SCALA $29.95

Robert **Rosenblum**
Paintings in the Musée d'Orsay
More than 820 full-color reproductions—including over 250 central Impressionist works—catalog the paintings of France's inimitable Musée d'Orsay. "Will more than suffice to bedazzle the eye"—*NY Times*. "A joy to read"—*Library Journal*
FOREWORD BY FRANCOISE CACHIN, DIRECTOR OF THE MUSEUMS OF FRANCE
1-55670-099-7 STEWART, TABORI $59.95

John **Elderfield**, editor
The Museum of Modern Art at Mid-Century
0-8109-6133-4 MOMA PB $19.95

H. Richard **West** & others
Treasures of the National Museum of the American Indian
0-7892-0105-4 ABBEVILLE PB $11.95

John **Plummer**, editor
In August Company: The Collections of the Pierpont Morgan Library
0-8109-3863-4 ABRAMS $49.50

Santiago Alcolea **Blanch**
The Prado
0-8109-8147-5 ABRADALE $39.98

Jose Rogelio **Buendia**
Paintings of the Prado
Four hundred paintings from one of the world's great collections of European art, lavishly reproduced, make this book a virtual tour of the Prado. Velazquez, Juan Gris, Raphael, Titian, Durer, Boticelli, Poussin, Watteau are just a sampling of the paintings showcased, explicated, and studied in this beautiful volume
0-8212-2235-X BULFINCH $125.00

Felipe Vicente Garin **Llombart**
Treasures of the Prado
1-55859-558-9 ABBEVILLE PB $11.95

Alfonso Perez **Sanchez**
The Prado
0-935748-75-X SCALA $29.95

Brenda **Richardson**
Dr. Claribel and Miss Etta: The Cone Collection of the Baltimore Museum of Art
0-912298-58-8 BALTIMORE MUSEUM PB $29.95

Emile **Meijer**
The Treasures of the Rijksmuseum
0-935748-63-6 SCALA $15.95

Marc **Simpson**
The Rockefeller Collection of American Art at the Fine Arts Museum of San Francisco
0-8109-3774-3 SAN FRANCISCO MUSEUM $50.00

James **Conaway**
The Smithsonian: 150 Years of Adventure, Discovery, and Delight
Giant pandas, the Hope Diamond, the Spirit of St. Louis: since 1846, the Smithsonian Institution has housed a staggering variety of national treasures. On the occasion of its sesquicentennial, this entertaining and authoritative account of the great American institution brings its century and a half of history to life with hundreds of photographs, paintings, anecdotes, and profiles
See also **CULTURAL AND SOCIAL HISTORY** under **TOPICS IN AMERICAN STUDIES** in **HISTORY OF THE AMERICAS**
0-679-44175-1 KNOPF $60.00

Cynthia R. **Field** & E. **Stamm**
The Castle: An Illustrated History of the Smithsonian Building
HEATHER P. EWING
1-56098-287-X SMITHSONIAN PB....$16.95

Robert **Upstone**
Treasures of British Art: Tate Gallery
1-55859-772-7 ABBEVILLE PB....$11.95

Vivian Endicott **Barnett** & Fred **Licht**
The Thannhauser Collection
PAUL TUCKER
0-89207-074-9 GUGGENHEIM....$40.00

Cara **Denison**
Drawings from the Collection of Mr. and Mrs. Eugene Victor Thaw
One of the finest contemporary collections, old masters to moderns
0-87598-082-1 PIERPONT MORGANPB....$29.95

Luciano **Berti** & Anna Maria Petrioli **Tofani**
The Uffizi
1-87024-881-3 SCALA....$35.00

Giovanni **Morrello,** editor
Vatican Treasures: 2,000 Years of Art and Culture in the Vatican and Italy
1-55859-298-9 ELECTA....$55.00

Victoria and Albert Museum Curators
The Victoria and Albert Museum
1-87024-867-8 SCALA....$30.00

William **Agee**
Walker Art Center: Painting and Sculpture from the Collection
0-8478-1267-7 RIZZOLI....$85.00

Rainer **Budde** & senior curators
Wallraf-Richartz Museum, Cologne
1-87024-876-7 SCALA....$29.95

Christopher **Baker** & Tom **Henry**
The National Gallery Complete Illustrated Catalogue
This volume, lavishly illustrated with 2,200 illustrations, most in color, explores the National Gallery's collection of European painting, one of the richest and most comprehensive in the world. The book is an essential reference work for scholars, teachers, students, or anyone else interested in the field
0-300-06362-8 YALE....$150.00

Roald **Nasgaard**
National Gallery of Art, Washington
See also **THAMES & HUDSON WORLD OF ART**
0-500-20251-6 THAMES & HUDSON PB....$14.95

John **Walker**
The National Gallery of Art, Washington
0-8109-1370-4 ABRAMS....$75.00

Collectors and Dealers

Peter **Gay**
Sigmund Freud and Art: His Personal Collection of Antiquities
0-8109-2551-6 ABRAMS PB....$24.95

Francis **Haskell**
Patrons and Painters: A Study in the Relations Between Italian Art and Society in the Age of the Baroque
A social history of art
See also **THE BAROQUE IN ITALY** under **EUROPEAN ART: BAROQUE AND ROCOCO**
0-300-02537-8 YALE....$70.00
0-300-02540-8 YALE PB....$25.00

Dan **Hofstadter**
Goldberg's Angel
Seeking to uncover the truth behind a Midwestern art dealer's attempted purchase of a Byzantine mosaic—and her subsequent court battle with the Republic of Cyprus—Hofstadter (writing for *The New Yorker*) descended into an unbelievable underworld of smugglers, thieves, tomb-robbers, and art collectors. "As full of intrigue, shady characters, and exotic hotel lobbies as the latest spy thriller. But this is a true story....With sensual prose and keen psychological portraits, [Hofstadter] presents an incredible look at a labyrinthine world"
—Kirkus Reviews
0-374-10507-3 FS&G....$22.00

Thomas **Hoving**
False Impressions: The Hunt for Big Time Art Fakes
The former director of the Metropolitan Museum's witty and wicked book tells the story of the art world's biggest, best, and most embarrassing forgeries. Duplicitous criminals, hapless dupes, imaginative scam-artists, and talented truth-seekers people these stories from a little-known, mysterious world
0-684-81134-0 SIMON & SCHUSTER....$26.00

Making the Mummies Dance: Inside the Metropolitan
0-671-88075-6 TOUCHSTONE PB....$13.00

David **Howarth**
Lord Arundel and His Circle
0-300-03469-5 YALE....$55.00

Gervase **Jackson-Stops**, editor
The Treasure Houses of Britain: 500 Years of Private Patronage and Art Collecting
The contents of the great English country houses, amassed on grand tours through Europe and selected for the exhibition held at the National Gallery in Washington
See also **BRITISH AND IRISH FURNITURE** under **FURNITURE** under **EUROPEAN DECORATIVE ARTS** in **ARCHITECTURE, DESIGN, AND HOMES**
0-300-03533-0 YALE....$42.00

John **McPhee**
The Ransom of Russian Art
The amazing McPhee's 23rd book documents Norton Dodge's clandestine tour in the '60s and '70s through the world of underground Russian artists. Smuggling their officially forbidden work out of the country, he assembled the world's largest collection of this threatened artwork and donated it to Rutgers University. McPhee takes us on a chilling, suspenseful, and enormously readable tour of Dodge's adventure
0-374-24682-3 FS&G....$20.00
0-374-52450-5 NOONDAY PB....$10.00

Marjorie **Phillips**
Duncan Phillips and His Collection
0-393-01608-0 NORTON....$35.00
0-393-30041-2 NORTON PB....$18.95

Ernest **Samuels**
Bernard Berenson
Volume 1
The Making of a Connoisseur
A recent biography covering his latter five decades. "Makes for even better reading than one might anticipate, for at the center of it all, beyond our greatest art critic, is art itself"
—NY Times
0-674-06775-4 HARVARD....$27.50
0-674-06777-0 HARVARD PB....$14.95

Volume 2
The Making of a Legend
0-674-06779-7 HARVARD....$33.00

Charles **Smith**
Auctions: The Social Construction of Value
A guide to the economic and social dynamics of price, value, and auction prices
0-02-929530-0 FREE PRESS....$29.95
0-520-07201-4 CALIFORNIA PB....$12.95

Peter **Thornton** & Helen **Dorey**
Sir John Soane: The Architect as Collector
0-8109-3827-8 ABRAMS....$39.95

Francis **Taylor**
Pierpont Morgan as Collector and Patron: 1837-1913
0-87598-033-3 PIERPONT MORGANPB....$4.00

John **Walker**
The Armand Hammer Collection: Five Centuries of Masterpieces
0-8109-1069-1 ABRAMS....$85.00

Fran **Weitzenhoffer**
The Havemeyers: Impressionism Comes to America
A fascinating account of the Havemeyers' superb collection, now at the Metropolitan Museum. Filled with anecdotes about Mary Cassatt and the prominent art dealers of the time, well-illustrated with photographs and works of art
0-8109-1096-9 ABRAMS....$39.95
0-8109-2523-0 ABRAMS PB....$24.95

David **Wilson**

The Forgotten Collector: Augustus Wollaston Franks of the British Museum

The lively story of the Keeper of British and Medieval Antiquities and Ethnography who acquired some of the museum's greatest treasures during the 19th century

0-500-55016-6 THAMES & HUDSON $12.95

Artists on Art

Max **Beckmann**

Self-Portrait in Words: Collected Writings and Statements, 1903-1950

See also **GERMAN EXPRESSIONISM** under **EXPRESSIONISM AND THE BLUE RIDER** under **20TH-CENTURY ART**

EDITED AND TRANSLATED BY BARBARA COPELAND BUENGER

0-226-04135-2 CHICAGO $34.95
0-226-04136-0 CHICAGO PB $42.00

Thomas Hart **Benton**

An Artist in America

The artist's own story, with a foreword by Matthew Baigell

0-8262-0399-X MISSOURI PB $24.95

Benjamin H.D. **Buchloh**, editor

Broodthaers: Writings, Interviews, Photographs

See also **POSTWAR EUROPEAN ART** under **ART SINCE 1945**

0-262-02281-8 MIT $30.00
0-262-52135-0 MIT PB $12.50

Michelangelo **Buonarotti**

Life, Letters and Poetry

An anthology of sonnets and other writings, with a contemporary biography

See also **ARTISTS** under **THE RENAISSANCE** under **ITALIAN LITERATURE** in **LITERATURE OF EUROPE, AFRICA, AND ASIA**

EDITED BY GEORGE BULL

0-19-281603-9 OXFORD PB $8.95

Paul **Cézanne**

Letters

See also **IMPRESSIONISM: INDIVIDUAL ARTISTS** under **FRANCE** under **EUROPEAN ART: 1750-1900**

EDITED BY JOHN REWALD

0-306-80630-4 DA CAPO PB $15.95

C.R. **Leslie**

Memoirs of the Life of John Constable: Composed Chiefly of His Letters

See also **ENGLAND** under **EUROPEAN ART: 1750-1900**

0-7148-3360-6 PHAIDON PB $14.95

Joseph **Cornell**

Joseph Cornell's Theater of the Mind: Selected Diaries, Letters, and Files

EDITED BY MARY ANN CAWS

0-500-01544-9 THAMES & HUDSON $35.00

Salvador **Dali**

Diary of a Genius

See also **DADA AND SURREALISM** under **20TH-CENTURY ART**

1-87159-226-7 SUBTERRANEAN $13.95

Giorgio **de Chirico**

The Memoirs of Giorgio de Chirico

0-306-80568-5 DA CAPO PB $13.95

Elaine **de Kooning**

Elaine de Kooning: The Spirit of Abstract Expressionism: Selected Writings

Twenty-eight essays by a major member of the New York School, who was also an incisive and influential critic. Provides rare insight into Abstract Expressionism while revealing the scope of Elaine de Kooning's vigorous mind. "De Kooning's irreverent contemporary portraits restore the human scale…Perhaps only an artist could write about other artists with such genuine curiosity and open-mindedness" —*Kirkus Reviews*

See also **THE NEW YORK SCHOOL AND THE 50S** under **POSTWAR AMERICAN ART** under **ART SINCE 1945**

0-8076-1337-1 BRAZILLER $23.50

Willem **de Kooning**

Collected Writings of Willem de Kooning

0-937815-13-6 HANUMAN PB $5.95

Eugene **Delacroix**

The Journal of Eugene Delacroix

The musings of one of the most intelligent and, most likely, the most literate, painter ever

See also **FROM THE REVOLUTION TO IMPRESSIONISM** under **FRANCE** under **EUROPEAN ART: 1750-1900**

TRANSLATED BY WALTER PACH

0-7148-3359-2 PHAIDON PB $14.95

Marcel **Duchamp**

Writings

EDITED BY MICHEL SANOUILLET AND ELMER PETERSON

0-306-80341-0 DA CAPO PB $12.95

Pierre **Cabanne**

Dialogues with Marcel Duchamp

"These conversations are more than mere interviews. They are Marcel Duchamp's summing up, and constitute as vivid a self-portrait as we posses of a major twentieth-century artist, thanks to Duchamp's intelligence, scrupulousness, and disdain for the petty" —Robert Motherwell

0-306-80303-8 DA CAPO PB $9.95

Paul **Gauguin**

Noa Noa: The Tahiti Journal of Paul Gauguin

A marvelous publication—handsomely produced, exquisitely illustrated—of Gauguin's written diary and the woodblock prints and sketches the author made to accompany the text. A true delight

See also **POSTIMPRESSIONISM** under **FRANCE** under **EUROPEAN ART: 1750-1900**

INTRODUCTION BY SOMERSET MAUGHAM

0-8118-0366-X CHRONICLE $17.95
0-486-24859-3 DOVER PB $3.95

Robert **Goldwater** & Marco **Treves**, editors

Artists on Art: From the 14th to the 20th Century

0-394-70900-4 RANDOM HOUSE PB $18.00

Marsden **Hartley** & Susan Elizabeth **Ryan**

Somehow a Past: The Autobiography of Marsden Hartley

See also **AMERICAN ART BEFORE THE 1940S** under **20TH-CENTURY ART**

0-262-08251-9 MIT $25.00

Wassily **Kandinsky**

Concerning the Spiritual in Art

Kandinsky's primary statement of his philosophy of art

See also **EXPRESSIONISM OUTSIDE OF GERMANY** under **EXPRESSIONISM AND THE BLUE RIDER** under **20TH-CENTURY ART**

0-486-23411-8 DOVER PB $3.95

Paul **Klee**

The Diaries of Paul Klee

See also **GERMAN EXPRESSIONISM** under **EXPRESSIONISM AND THE BLUE RIDER** under **20TH-CENTURY ART**

EDITED BY FELIX KLEE

0-520-00653-4 CALIFORNIA PB $15.95

Paul Klee on Modern Art

A collection of his writing

0-571-06682-8 FABER PB $10.95

Paul Klee

Leonardo **da Vinci**

The Notebooks of Leonardo Da Vinci

A one-volume selection from Leonardo's voluminous journals

See also **ARTISTS** under **THE RENAISSANCE** under **ITALIAN LITERATURE** in **LITERATURE OF EUROPE, AFRICA, AND ASIA**

EDITED BY IRMA RICHTER

0-19-281538-5 OXFORD PB $6.95

Jack **Flam**

Matisse on Art

The first collection of Matisse's major writings, including transcriptions of interviews and broadcasts

See also **MATISSE AND FAUVISM** under **20TH-CENTURY ART**

0-520-20032-2 CALIFORNIA PB $15.00

Piet **Mondrian**

The New Art—The New Life: The Collected Writings of Piet Mondrian

See also **MONDRIAN AND DE STIJL** under **20TH-CENTURY ART**

EDITED BY HARRY HOLTZMAN AND MARTIN S. JAMES

0-306-80508-1 DA CAPO PB $24.95

Natural Reality and Abstract Reality: An Essay in Trialogue Form

0-8076-1371-1 BRAZILLER $25.00

0-8076-1372-X BRAZILLER PB $14.95

Robert **Motherwell**, editor

The Dada Painters and Poets

An anthology compiled by the Dada painters and poets themselves in the 1940s, which became a classic of counterculture in 20th-century art and had a tremendous influence on the New York school of poets. Allen Ginsberg attributes the existence of "Howl" to reading this book

See also **DADA AND SURREALISM** under **20TH-CENTURY ART**

0-674-18500-5 BELKNAP PB $24.95

Barnett **Newman**

Barnett Newman: Selected Writings and Interviews

See also **THE NEW YORK SCHOOL AND THE 50S** under **POSTWAR AMERICAN ART** under **ART SINCE 1945**

EDITED BY JOHN P. O'NEILL

0-520-07817-9 CALIFORNIA PB $16.00

Dore **Ashton**, editor

Picasso on Art: A Selection of Views

See also **PABLO PICASSO** under **CUBISM** under **20TH-CENTURY ART**

0-306-80330-5 DA CAPO PB $11.95

Fairfield **Porter**

Art in its Own Terms

EDITED WITH AN INTRODUCTION BY RACKSTRAW DOWNES

0-944072-31-3 ZOLAND PB $10.95

Odilon **Redon**

To Myself: Notes on Life, Art and Artists

The journals of the French Symbolist painter noted for his delicate, mysterious watercolors

0-8076-1146-8 BRAZILLER PB $14.95

Ad **Reinhardt**

Art-as-Art: The Selected Writings of Ad Reinhardt

See also **THE NEW YORK SCHOOL AND THE 50S** under **POSTWAR AMERICAN ART** under **ART SINCE 1945**

EDITED BY BARBARA ROSE

0-520-07670-2 CALIFORNIA PB $14.00

Sir Joshua **Reynolds**

Discourses on Art

The 18th-century artist's view of the relation of genius to the classical rules presented in its original form to the Royal Academy

See also **18TH-CENTURY ENGLAND** under **EUROPEAN ART: BAROQUE AND ROCOCO**

0-300-02775-3 YALE PB $23.00

Gerhard **Richter** & Peter **Gidal**

Painting in the Nineties

See also **THE CONTEMPORARY SCENE** under **ART SINCE 1945**

0-947564-60-8 D.A.P. $45.00

Richard **Serra**

Writings/Interviews

The powerful and sometimes controversial sculptures of Richard Serra have had a tremendous impact on contemporary art. This book goes right to the source for explanations and insights

See also **MINIMALISM AND CONCEPTUALISM** under **POSTWAR AMERICAN ART** under **ART SINCE 1945**

0-226-74880-4 CHICAGO PB $17.95

Ben **Shahn**

The Shape of Content

0-674-80570-4 HARVARD PB $7.95

Robert **Smithson**

Robert Smithson: The Collected Writings

See also **POP ART** under **POSTWAR AMERICAN ART** under **ART SINCE 1945**

EDITED BY JACK FLAM

0-520-20385-2 CALIFORNIA PB $24.95

Frank **Stella**

Working Space

The text of Stella's Charles Eliot Norton lectures

See also **THE BAROQUE IN ITALY** under **EUROPEAN ART: BAROQUE AND ROCOCO**

See also **AMERICAN ART OF THE 1960S AND '70S** under **POSTWAR AMERICAN ART** under **ART SINCE 1945**

0-674-95960-4 HARVARD $49.95

0-674-95961-2 HARVARD PB $22.95

Anne **Truitt**

Daybook: The Journal of an Artist

"A remarkable record of a woman's reconciliation of art, motherhood, memories of childhood, and present-day demands"—Anne Morrow Lindbergh

0-14-006963-1 VIKING PB $12.95

Prospect: The Journal of an Artist

Intensely personal and intimate, *Prospect* is resonant with wisdom. A stunning and graceful writer, Truitt offers prose, as May Sarton said, "illuminating and nourishing, to read and reread"

0-684-81835-3 SCRIBNERS $22.00

Anne Truitt (credit: John Dolan)

Vincent **van Gogh**

The Letters of Vincent van Gogh

See also **POSTIMPRESSIONISM** under **FRANCE** under **EUROPEAN ART: 1750-1900**

EDITED BY RONALD DE LEEUW

TRANSLATED BY ARNOLD POMERANS

0-7139-9135-6 PENGUIN $32.95

0-689-70167-5 ATHENEUM PB $10.95

Andy **Warhol**

The Philosophy of Andy Warhol: From A to B and Back

The muteness of Warhol's art was surpassed only by the chattiness of his public persona

See also **POP ART** under **POSTWAR AMERICAN ART** under **ART SINCE 1945**

0-15-671720-4 HARCOURT BRACE PB $13.00

> What's great about this country is that America started the tradition where the richest consumers buy essentially the same things as the poorest. You can be watching TV and see Coca-Cola, and you can know that the president drinks Coke, Liz Taylor drinks Coke and, just think, you can drink Coke too. A Coke is a Coke, and no amount of money can get you a better Coke than the one the bum on the corner is drinking. All the Cokes are the same and all the Cokes are good. Liz Taylor knows it, the president knows it, the bum knows it, and you know it.
>
> **THE PHILOSOPHY OF ANDY WARHOL: FROM A TO B AND BACK**

James **Whistler**

The Gentle Art of Making Enemies

A witty memoir by the expatriate American painter, dandy, and exponent of art for art's sake

See also **AMERICAN ARTISTS ABROAD** under **THE 19TH CENTURY** under **AMERICAN ART**

0-486-21875-9 DOVER PB $8.95

Critics and Writers on Art

Guillaume **Apollinaire**

This tirelessly inquisitive intellectual was not only involved with Cubism and Futurism but is also credited with coining the terms "Orphism" and "Surrealism."

Apollinaire on Art: Essays and Reviews, 1902-1918

The poet and art critic who introduced Picasso to Braque

See also **CUBISM** under **20TH-CENTURY ART**

0-306-80312-7 DA CAPO PB $13.95

John **Ashbery**

Ashbery's adoption by the critical establishment seems to have surprised even himself. He continues to work in the same absolutely individual voice whose echoes are everywhere in contemporary American poetry.

Reported Sightings: Art Chronicles, 1957-1987

See also **THEORY AND CRITICISM** under **ART SINCE 1945**

EDITED BY DAVID BERGMAN

0-674-76225-8 KNOPF PB $16.95

William **Corbett**
Philip Guston's Late Work: A Memoir
See also **THE NEW YORK SCHOOL AND THE 50S** under **POSTWAR AMERICAN ART** under **ART SINCE 1945**
0-944072-43-7 ZOLAND $17.50

Denis **Diderot**
Diderot on Art
Volume I
Salon of 1765 and Notes on Painting
EDITED AND TRANSLATED BY JOHN GOODMAN
0-300-06248-6 YALE $40.00
0-300-06251-6 YALE PB $18.00
Volume II
Salon of 1767
0-300-06252-4 YALE PB $20.00
Two Volume Set
0-300-06225-0 YALE $85.00

Jules **de Goncourt** & Edmond **de Goncourt**
French Eighteenth-Century Painters
See also **BAROQUE AND ROCOCO IN FRANCE** under **EUROPEAN ART: BAROQUE AND ROCOCO**
0-7148-3362-2 PHAIDON PB $14.95

Daniel **Halpern**, editor
Writers on Artists
Proust on Chardin, Sartre on Tintoretto, Huxley on El Greco, Hemingway on Miro, and more
0-86547-340-4 FS&G PB $15.95

Raymond **Mortimer**, editor
Bernard Berenson: The Passionate Sightseer
Berenson was renowned as the world's foremost authority on Italian painting. This book gathers selections from his later diaries
0-500-27457-6 THAMES & HUDSON PB $14.95

Bernard Berenson

John **Hollander**
The Gazer's Spirit: Poems Speaking to Silent Works of Art
Hollander's critical commentaries accompany an anthology of poems about works of art
See also **POETRY ANTHOLOGIES** under **WORLD LITERATURE: WORLD LITERATURE SURVEYS AND ANTHOLOGIES** in **LITERATURE OF EUROPE, AFRICA, AND ASIA**
0-226-34949-7 CHICAGO $39.95

Ezra **Pound**
Gaudier-Brzeska: A Memoir
See also **VORTICISM** under **20TH-CENTURY ART**
0-8112-0527-4 NEW DIRECTIONS PB $7.95

Rainer Maria **Rilke**
Letters on Cézanne
See also **POETRY** under **MODERN GERMAN LITERATURE: TO 1945** under **GERMAN LITERATURE** in **LITERATURE OF EUROPE, AFRICA, AND ASIA**
TRANSLATED BY JOEL AGEE
0-88064-022-7 FROMM PB $14.95

John **Ruskin**
"He was one of those rare men who think with their hearts, and so he thought and said not only what he himself had seen and felt, but what everyone will think and say in the future."—Leo Tolstoy
The Art Criticism of John Ruskin
0-306-80310-0 DA CAPO PB $12.95
The Lamp of Beauty: Writings on Art
See also **19TH-CENTURY PROSE** under **THE 19TH CENTURY** in **LITERATURE OF THE BRITISH ISLES**
0-7148-3358-4 PHAIDON PB $14.95
Lectures on Art
1-88055-954-4 ALLWORTH PB $18.95
Selected Writings
Includes selections from *Modern Painters, The Stones of Venice, The Seven Lamps of Architecture,* and *Praeterita*
See also **19TH-CENTURY PROSE** under **THE 19TH CENTURY** in **LITERATURE OF THE BRITISH ISLES**
See also **THE PRE-RAPHAELITES** under **ENGLAND** under **EUROPEAN ART: 1750-1900**
EDITED BY PHILIP DAVIS
0-460-87460-8 EVERYMAN'S PB $8.50

Mark **Strand**
Hopper
0-88001-343-5 ECCO $21.00

Jeanette **Winterson**
Art Objects: Essays on Ecstasy and Effrontery
Ten interlocking essays from "one of our most important writers in English" (*Washington Post*) center on the importance of the arts in our lives. From pieces on modernism, painting, autobiography, and the future of fiction to intimate reflections on her own work and books, *Art Objects* shows Winterson, again, as "a brilliant and deeply feeling artist at work" *—San Francisco Chronicle*
See also **20TH-CENTURY BRITISH ESSAYS AND OTHER PROSE** in **LITERATURE OF THE BRITISH ISLES**
0-679-44644-3 KNOPF $21.00
0-679-76820-3 VINTAGE $11.00

Theory

"I have generally found that persons who had studied painting least were the best judge of it."—William Hogarth

Kathleen **Adler**, editor & Marcia **Pointon**
The Body Imaged: The Human Form and Visual Culture Since the Renaissance
0-521-41536-5 CAMBRIDGE $69.95
0-521-44768-2 CAMBRIDGE PB $19.95

Rudolf **Arnheim**
Art and Visual Perception: A Psychology of the Creative Eye
Influenced by Gestalt psychology, Arnheim finds the relation of artistic form and perception in the operation of an ordering intelligence
See also **ART AND PERCEPTION** under **SPECIAL TOPICS IN PSYCHOLOGY** under **PSYCHOLOGY** in **SOCIAL STUDIES**
0-520-02613-6 CALIFORNIA PB $17.95
Parables of Sun Light: Observations on Psychology, the Arts, and the Rest
0-520-06516-6 CALIFORNIA PB $27.50
The Split and the Structure: Twenty-Eight Essays
0-520-20477-8 CALIFORNIA $40.00
0-520-20478-6 CALIFORNIA PB $14.95

Mosche **Barasch**
Theory of Art from Plato to Winckelmann
A thorough analysis and reassessment of major trends in European art theory
0-8147-1060-3 NYU $55.00
0-8147-1061-1 NYU PB $18.50

Michael **Baxandall**
Patterns of Intention: On the Historical Explanation of Pictures
A brilliant art history book, concerning such topics as the technique of Chardin, the aesthetics of the Bridge at Firth, and Picasso's artistic and social options as a young man
0-300-03465-2 YALE $25.00
0-300-03763-5 YALE PB $16.00
Shadows and Enlightenment
An eminent art historian draws on contemporary cognitive science and 18th-century theories of visual perception to discuss the history of shadows in painting and the visual knowledge they can offer
0-300-05979-5 YALE $30.00

Hans **Belting**
The End of the History of Art
A famous scholar discusses the limits of his field
TRANSLATED BY CHRISTOPHER S. WOOD
0-226-04223-5 CHICAGO PB $13.95

Likeness and Presence: A History of the Image Before the Era of Art

A major scholar's magnus opus—a study of how works of art changed from being religious to aesthetic objects

See also **GENERAL STUDIES: MEDIEVAL ART** under **MEDIEVAL ART: 600-1400** under **EUROPEAN ART: BYZANTINE AND MEDIEVAL**

0-226-04214-6 CHICAGO $65.00
0-226-04215-4 CHICAGO PB $39.95

John **Berger**

A celebrated Marxist art critic, John Berger is also a novelist, screenwriter, and painter.

About Looking

Essays across ten years, most of which first appeared in *New Society*, focusing on the search for meaning within and behind what is looked at. Includes discussions of Millet, Courbet, Turner, Magritte, and Francis Bacon

0-8446-6635-1 SMITH $21.75
0-679-73655-7 VINTAGE PB $12.00

The Sense of Sight

A wide-ranging collection of essays spanning three decades. Includes the classic "Moment of Cubism"

See also **20TH-CENTURY BRITISH ESSAYS AND OTHER PROSE** in **LITERATURE OF THE BRITISH ISLES**

0-8446-6612-2 SMITH $22.30
0-679-73722-7 VINTAGE PB $14.00

Ways of Seeing

An essay on the ideological and technological conditioning of our ways of seeing both art and the world, based on the acclaimed BBC series

0-8446-6175-9 SMITH $21.25
0-14-013515-4 VIKING PB $10.95

Albert **Boime**

Art in an Age of Revolution, 1750-1800

This is the first volume in a social history of art in the tradition of Arnold Hauser

0-226-06334-8 CHICAGO PB $24.00

Anita **Brookner**

The Genius of the Future: Essays in French Art Criticism

By the noted British art historian and novelist

0-8014-9540-7 CORNELL PB $15.95

Norman **Bryson**

Vision and Painting: The Logic of the Gaze

The first comprehensive treatment of art history from a structuralist viewpoint

0-300-02855-5 YALE $42.50
0-300-03583-7 YALE PB $15.00

Norman **Bryson**, editor

Calligram: Essays in New Art History from France Featuring Pieces by Barthes, Baudrillard, Foucault, Kristeva, Marin, and Others

0-521-35046-8 CAMBRIDGE $70.00
0-521-35927-9 CAMBRIDGE PB $19.95

Whitney **Chadwick**

Women, Art and Society

In this extensively revised edition of her brilliant study, Chadwick utilizes new research and a critical feminist perspective to identify the aesthetics and ideologies that have shaped ten centuries of women's relationships to the visual arts and their histories

See also **THAMES & HUDSON WORLD OF ART**

0-500-20293-1 THAMES & HUDSON PB $16.95

Kenneth **Clark**

What Is a Masterpiece?

A compelling approach, with reference to works of the 15th to 17th centuries

0-500-27206-9 THAMES & HUDSON PB $7.95

Hubert **Damisch**

The Judgment of Paris

TRANSLATED BY JOHN GOODMAN

0-226-13510-1 CHICAGO $55.00
0-226-13512-8 CHICAGO PB $19.95

Neil H. **Donahue**, editor

Invisible Cathedrals: The Expressionist Art History of Wilhelm Worringer

The first book devoted to the important art critic who helped to engender German Expressionism

0-271-01306-0 PENN STATE $45.00

Carol **Duncan**

The Aesthetics of Power: Essays in the Critical History of Art

0-521-42044-X CAMBRIDGE $60.00
0-521-42187-X CAMBRIDGE PB $18.95

James **Elkins**

The Object Stares Back: On the Nature of Seeing

Appealing essays about the phenomenology of vision

0-684-80095-0 SIMON & SCHUSTER $24.00

Our Beautiful, Dry and Distant Texts: On the History of Art as Writing

0-271-01630-2 PENN STATE $42.01

Henri **Focillon**

The Life of Forms in Art

A beautifully written excursus on the nature of stylistic transformation. A classic

0-942299-57-4 ZONE PB $14.95

David **Freedberg**

The Power of Images: Studies in the History and Theory of Response

A wide-ranging book about the extra-esthetic factors that inform our response to images. Fascinating illustrations

0-226-26146-8 CHICAGO PB $22.95

Roger **Fry**

A Roger Fry Reader

Fry, a member of the Bloomsbury group, was the most influential and eloquent English supporter of modern art

EDITED AND WITH ITRODUCTORY ESSAYS BY CHRISTOPHER REED

0-226-26642-7 CHICAGO PB $19.95

John **Gage**

Color and Culture: Practice and Meaning from Antiquity to Abstraction

A major examination of what has always been one of the most controversial and stimulating issues in art and art theory

0-8212-2043-8 BULFINCH $65.00

Mary Matthews **Gedo**

Looking at Art from the Inside Out: The Psycho-iconographic Approach to Modern Art

0-521-43407-6 CAMBRIDGE $70.00
0-521-43567-6 CAMBRIDGE PB $18.95

Richard **Woodfield**, editor

The Essential Gombrich

An accessible and wide-ranging selection of Gombrich's writing, ranging from the nature of representation and the psychology of perception to problems of symbolism and meaning in art. A splendid introduction to the work of a great humanist

0-7148-3487-4 PHAIDON PB $29.95

E.H. **Gombrich**

Art & Illusion: A Study in the Psychology of Pictorial Presentation

A classic examination of the ideal of representation in Western art and the means used to achieve it; profusely and brilliantly illustrated

See also **ART AND PERCEPTION** under **SPECIAL TOPICS IN PSYCHOLOGY** under **PSYCHOLOGY** in **SOCIAL STUDIES**

0-691-09785-2 PRINCETON $80.00
0-691-01750-6 PRINCETON PB $29.95

Ideals and Idols: Essays on Values in History and in Art

0-7148-3127-1 PHAIDON PB $22.95

The Image & the Eye: Further Studies in the Psychology of Pictorial Representation

0-7148-3243-X PHAIDON PB $22.95

Reflections on the History of Art: Views and Reviews

0-520-06189-6 CALIFORNIA $40.00

The Sense of Order: A Study in the Psychology of Decorative Arts

A psychological explanation of ornamental form

See also **ART AND PERCEPTION** under **SPECIAL TOPICS IN PSYCHOLOGY** under **PSYCHOLOGY** in **SOCIAL STUDIES**

0-7148-2259-0 PHAIDON $24.95

E.H. **Gombrich**

Shadows: The Depiction of Cast Shadows in Western Art

0-300-06357-1 YALE $12.50

Topics of Our Time: Twentieth-Century Issues in Learning and in Art

0-520-07516-1 CALIFORNIA $45.00

E.H. **Gombrich** & others

Art, Perception, and Reality

0-8018-1552-5 JOHNS HOPKINS PB $14.95

Michael **Hall**

The Artist Outsider: Creativity and The Boundaries of Culture

1-56098-334-5 SMITHSONIAN $62.00
1-56098-335-3 SMITHSONIAN PB $29.95

Francis **Haskell**

History and Its Images: Art and Interpretation of the Past

How history, one literary branch of the humanist tradition, regarded the visual arts between the 15th and early 20th centuries

See also **NEW DIRECTIONS** under **HISTORIOGRAPHY** in **WORLD HISTORY AND CURRENT AFFAIRS**

0-300-05540-4 YALE $50.00

Anne **Hollander**

Moving Pictures

The traditions of Western art in which paintings, prints, and movies depict moments of human life. The relation between originals and prints, between high art and popular culture

0-674-58828-2 HARVARD PB $18.95

Elizabeth G. **Holt**

The Triumph of Art for the Public, 1785-1848

This well-selected and organized anthology of writings from journals and catalogues offers a fascinating synoptic overview of the emerging role of exhibitions and critics in Europe that prefigures many of our cultural concerns today

0-691-00349-1 PRINCETON PB $19.95

The Art of All Nations: 1850-1873: The Emerging Role of Exhibitions and Critics

0-691-03996-8 PRINCETON $80.00

Barbara **Kruger**

Remote Control: Power, Cultures, and the World of Appearances

0-262-11177-2 MIT $22.50
0-262-61106-6 MIT PB $10.95

George **Kubler**

Shape of Time: Remarks on the History of Things

A concise and highly sitmulating account of the nature of stylistic change

See also **THE CONTEMPORARY SCENE** under **ART SINCE 1945**

0-300-00144-4 YALE PB $11.00

Irving **Lavin**

Past-Present: Essays on Historicism in Art from Donatello to Picasso

Collects the essays of a distinguished and unusually wide-ranging scholar

0-520-06816-5 CALIFORNIA $65.00

Gotthold **Lessing**

Laocoon: An Essay on the Limits of Painting and Poetry

An enormously influential 18th-century essay about the fundamental difference between poetry and the plastic arts

See also **ENLIGHTENMENT, STURM UND DRANG, AND CLASSICISM** under **GERMAN LITERATURE** in **LITERATURE OF EUROPE, AFRICA, AND ASIA**

TRANSLATED BY EDWARD MCCORMICK

0-8018-3139-3 JOHNS HOPKINS PB $14.95

Louis **Marin**

To Destroy Painting

A study of Caravaggio and Poussin which draws on semiotics and psychoanalysis

See also **THE BAROQUE IN ITALY** under **EUROPEAN ART: BAROQUE AND ROCOCO**

TRANSLATED BY METTE HJORT

0-226-50534-0 CHICAGO $39.95
0-226-50535-9 CHICAGO PB $15.95

Paul **Mattick**, Jr.

Eighteenth-Century Aesthetics and the Reconstruction of Art

0-521-43106-9 CAMBRIDGE $55.00

Vernon Hyde **Minor**

Art History's History

A basic historiographic introduction

0-8109-1944-3 ABRAMS $29.95
0-13-194606-4 PRENTICE HALL PB $24.14

W. J. T. **Mitchell**

The Language of Images

0-226-53215-1 CHICAGO PB $17.95

Iconology: Image, Text, Ideology

A new look at the old practice of "reading" pictures

0-226-53229-1 CHICAGO PB $9.95

Picture Theory

This award-winning book is an exploration of recent theories of pictorial representation. In it, Mitchell eloquently explains the social, political, and emotional impact of images

0-226-53232-1 CHICAGO PB $17.95

Keith P. **Moxey** & others, editors

Visual Culture: Images of Interpretation

A useful collection of essays discussing the currently hot topic of "visual culture"

0-8195-6267-X WESLEYAN PB $21.00

Linda **Nochlin**

Women, Art, and Power: and Other Essays

See also **ART AND PHOTOGRAPHY** under **ARTS AND LETTERS** under **WOMEN'S STUDIES** in **SOCIAL STUDIES**

0-06-430183-4 ICON PB $14.00

Erwin **Panofsky**

Meaning in the Visual Arts

The best introduction to the thoughtful master of iconological interpretation

0-226-64551-7 CHICAGO PB $18.95

Perspective as Symbolic Form

This classic study by an eminent art historian asserts that Renaissance perspective is conventional, not natural

See also **PERSPECTIVE** under **ITALY** under **EUROPEAN ART: THE RENAISSANCE**

0-942299-52-3 MIT $24.95

Renaissance and Renascences in Western Art

Was there a Renaissance and, if so, how did it differ from medieval revivals also called renaissances?

0-06-430026-9 ICON PB $21.00

Studies in Iconology: Humanistic Themes in the Art of the Renaissance

A classic of art historical analysis that includes a fine essay on Michelangelo's relation to Neoplatonism

0-8446-6619-X SMITH $30.80

Three Essays on Style

0-262-16151-6 MIT $30.00

Michael Ann **Holly**

Panofsky and the Foundations of Art History

Provides useful summaries of early, untranslated German essays by the great iconographer

0-8014-9896-1 CORNELL PB $13.95

Erwin **Panofsky** & Dora **Panofsky**

Pandora's Box: The Changing Aspects of a Mythical Symbol

Examines the transformations of a motif through time

0-691-01824-3 PRINCETON PB $15.95

Michael **Podro**

The Critical Historians of Art

Philosophy's impact on German art historiography is the subject of this useful overview of figures that range from Semper to Panofsky

0-300-02862-8 YALE $45.00
0-300-03223-4 YALE PB $13.00

Griselda **Pollock**

Vision and Difference: Femininity, Feminism, and the Histories of Art

An influential effort to articulate a theory of feminist art history

See also **ART AND PHOTOGRAPHY** under **ARTS AND LETTERS** under **WOMEN'S STUDIES** in **SOCIAL STUDIES**

0-415-00722-4 METHUEN PB $16.95

Alex **Potts**

Flesh and the Ideal: Winckelmann and the Origins of Art History

An intellectual biography of one of the most important figures ever to have written about art, considered by many to be the father of modern art history

0-300-05813-6 YALE $32.00

Alois **Riegl**

Problems of Style: Foundations for a History of Ornament

An early work in which Riegl provides a stylistic analysis of the genesis of such ornamental motifs as the acanthus leaf

0-691-04087-7 PRINCETON $55.00

Margaret **Iversen**

Alois Riegl: Art History and Theory

0-262-09030-9 MIT $37.50

Margaret **Olin**

Forms of Representation in Alois Riegl's Theory of Art

The mind that discovered, in 1901, in the supposed decline of Roman art, a matter of great modernist interest was more complex than some busy moderns now would prefer. Thorough, solid, and very well illustrated

0-271-00777-X PENN STATE $42.50

Mark W. **Roskill**

The Interpretation of Pictures

Given the inherently ambiguous nature of meaning, and other situations encountered, interpretation is intrinsic—not extrinsic—to art history. Lucid case studies of paintings whose problematic natures lend themselves to Roskill's argument

0-87023-661-X MASSACHUSETTS PB $13.95

Meyer **Schapiro**

Selected Papers of Meyer Schapiro

Volume 1
Romanesque Art

See also **ROMANESQUE** under **MEDIEVAL ART: 600-1400** under **EUROPEAN ART: BYZANTINE AND MEDIEVAL**

0-8076-1294-4 BRAZILLER PB $19.95

Volume 2
Modern Art

Selected essays by the art historian, whose profound cultural approach to the art object set the standard for the field. Includes *The Apples of Cezanne* and *The Nature of Abstract Art*

See also **THEORY AND CRITICISM** under **GENERAL** under **20TH-CENTURY ART**

0-8076-1034-8 BRAZILLER PB $23.00

Volume 3
Late Antique, Early Christian, and Medieval Art

See also **EARLY CHRISTIAN AND BYZANTINE** under **EUROPEAN ART: BYZANTINE AND MEDIEVAL**

0-8076-1295-2 BRAZILLER PB $19.95

Volume 4
Theory and Philosophy of Art: Style, Artist and Society

0-8076-1356-8 BRAZILLER $27.50

Jean Louis **Schefer**

The Enigmatic Body: Essays on The Arts by Jean Louis Schefer

0-521-37204-6 CAMBRIDGE $49.95

Gert **Schiff**, editor

German Essays on Art History

An anthology of work from Winckelmann to Panofsky

0-8264-0308-5 CONTINUUM $27.50

Cyril Stanley **Smith**

A Search for Structure: Selected Essays on Science, Art and History

This is not some superficial crypto-formalism of blown-up nature details looking like Jackson Pollocks, but cross-disciplinary thought on the highest level. Remarkable discussions of early Chinese bronzes by this metallurgist who also knows and loves ancient Chinese art

0-262-69082-9 MIT PB $19.95

Ellen Handler **Spitz**

Art and Psyche: A Study in Psychoanalysis and Aesthetics

0-300-04620-0 YALE PB $15.00

Image and Insight: Essays in Psychoanalysis and the Arts

0-231-07297-X COLUMBIA PB $16.50

Museums of the Mind: Magritte's Labyrinth and Other Essays in the Arts

0-300-06029-7 YALE $32.50

Mark C. **Taylor**

Disfiguring: Art, Architecture, Religion

0-226-79133-5 CHICAGO PB $29.95

Edgar **Wind**

Art and Anarchy

Stimulating lectures that range far and wide, from one of the most inventive of iconologists

0-8101-0662-0 NORTHWESTERN PB $14.95

The Eloquence of Symbols: Studies in Humanist Art

0-19-817222-2 CLARENDON PB $42.00

Rudolf **Wittkower**

Allegory and the Migration of Symbols

Essays on specialized and often uniquely interesting themes, especially antique survivals and revivals in Renaissance and later art and architecture

0-500-27470-3 THAMES & HUDSON PB $14.95

Janet **Wolff**

Aesthetics and the Sociology of Art

0-472-06499-1 MICHIGAN PB $14.95

The Social Production of Art

An introduction to the sociology of art

0-8147-9270-7 NYU PB $17.50

Heinrich **Wolfflin**

Classic Art: An Introduction to the Italian Renaissance

An early study in which the method of appraising individual works by formal analysis is established

0-7148-2974-9 PHAIDON PB $19.95

Principles of Art History: The Problem of the Development of Style in Later Art

In what is probably the most influential work of art history ever written, Wolfflin pioneered the method of comparing and contrasting artworks which dominates classroom surveys of art history to this day

0-486-20276-3 DOVER PB $7.95

Renaissance and Baroque

A study of independent development in architecture from its maturity during the High Renaissance to its decline in the second half of the 16th century

See also **ITALIAN RENAISSANCE** under **EUROPEAN ARCHITECTURE TO 1900** in **ARCHITECTURE, DESIGN, AND HOMES**

0-8014-9046-4 CORNELL PB $16.95

Sense of Form in Art

0-8284-0153-5 CHELSEA PB $7.50

0-521-29706-0 CAMBRIDGE PB $10.95

Prehistoric Art

E.J.W. **Barber**

Prehistoric Textiles: The Development of Cloth in the Neolithic and Bronze Ages

0-691-03597-0 PRINCETON $90.00

0-691-00224-X PRINCETON PB $35.00

Aubrey **Burl**

From Carnac to Callanish: The Prehistoric Stone Rows of Britain, Ireland, and Brittany

The first comprehensive book to discuss the rows of stones that were the focus of rituals in Britain, Ireland, and Brittany for over two thousand years, complete with distribution maps, plans, diagrams, and photographs

See also **PREHISTORIC MONUMENTS** under **EUROPEAN ARCHITECTURE TO 1900** in **ARCHITECTURE, DESIGN, AND HOMES**

0-300-05575-7 YALE $52.00

Jean-Marie **Chauvet** & others

Dawn of Art: The Chauvet Cave: The Oldest Known Paintings in the World

0-8109-3232-6 ABRAMS $39.95

N.K. **Sandars**

Prehistoric Art in Europe

See also **THE PELICAN HISTORY OF ART** under **ART HISTORY: GENERAL STUDIES**

0-14-056130-7 PENGUIN PB $26.50

Art of Egypt and the Ancient Near East

Egypt

"Egyptian civilization has long been regarded as the most rigid and conservative ever. Plato said that Egyptian art had not changed in 10,000 years...The basic pattern of Egyptian institutions, beliefs, and artistic ideas was formed during the first few centuries of that vast span of years and kept reasserting itself until the very end...Egyptian art alternates between conservatism and innovation, but is never static. Some of its great achievements had a decisive influence on Greek and Roman art, and thus we can still feel ourselves linked to the Egypt of 5000 years ago by a continuous, living tradition."—H.W. Janson, *The History of Art*

Cyril **Aldred**

Egyptian Art

Three thousand years of architecture, painting, and sculpture, and their political and social setting

See also **THAMES & HUDSON WORLD OF ART** under **ART HISTORY: GENERAL STUDIES**

See also **THAMES & HUDSON WORLD OF ART** under **ART HISTORY: GENERAL STUDIES**

0-500-20180-3 THAMES & HUDSON PB $14.95

Euphrosyne **Doxiadis**

The Mysterious Fayum Portraits: Faces from Ancient Egypt

During the first three centuries AD, in the Fayum district of Roman Egypt, a large majority of the dead were embalmed and their portraits were painted by skilled artists and placed over the mummified bodies. The resulting paintings, known today as the Fayum portraits, make up the most outstanding and revealing body of portraiture to survive from antiquity

FOREWORD BY DOROTHY J. THOMPSON

0-8109-3331-4 ABRAMS $75.00

Francoise **Dunand** & Roger **Lichtenberg**

Mummies: A Voyage Through Eternity

TRANSLATED BY RUTH SHARMAN

0-8109-2886-8 ABRAMS PB $12.95

Richard **Fazzini**

Ancient Egyptian Art: The Brooklyn Museum

Sculpture, relief, funerary articles, and accessories from one of the world's finest collections. Well illustrated

0-500-23547-3 THAMES & HUDSON $45.00

Christopher **Frayling**

The Face of Tutankhamun

Why does King Tut fascinate us so? Released in time for the 70th anniversary of the opening of Tut's tomb, this anthology begins with the story of the 1912 excavation, then explains why our culture is so enthralled by Egyptian artifacts

0-571-16845-0 FABER PB $18.95

I suppose most excavators would confess to a feeling of awe—embarrassment almost—when they break into a chamber closed and sealed by pious hands so many centuries ago. For the moment, time as a factor in human life has lost its meaning. Three thousand, four thousand years maybe, have passed and gone since human feet last trod the floor on which you stand, and yet, as you note the signs of recent life around you—the half-filled bowl of mortar for the door, the blackened lamp, the finger-mark upon the freshly painted surface, the farewell garland dropped upon the threshold—you feel it might have been but yesterday. The very air you breathe, unchanged throughout the centuries, you share with those who laid the mummy to its rest. Time is annihilated by little intimate details such as these, and you feel an intruder.
THE FACE OF TUTANKHAMUN

Patrick F. **Houlihan**

Animal World of the Pharaohs

A lavishly illustrated and comprehensive treatment of the hugely important relationship between people and animals in ancient Egypt, based on paintings and reliefs on tomb walls, drawings on papyri, and in stone, clay, and wooden sculptures, as well as evidence from ancient texts, mummified animals, food offerings, and bones recovered from settlement sites

0-500-01731-X THAMES & HUDSON $39.95

T.G. **James** & W.V. **Davies**

Egyptian Sculpture

0-674-24161-4 HARVARD PB $9.95

Bernadette **Letellier** & Lawrence M. **Berman**

Pharoahs: Treasures of Egyptian Art from the Louvre

A fascinating tour of the best-known Egyptian galleries in the world, those of the Louvre. Ranging from tiny statuettes to over-lifesize statues, beautiful illustrations and a learned text provide a virtual primer to the study of Egyptian art

0-19-521235-5 OXFORD PB $19.95

Stephen **Quirke** & Jeffrey **Spencer**, editors

The British Museum Book of Ancient Egypt

A visual and textual guide to every aspect of the culture, from prehistoric times to the years of late Roman antiquity, taking account of recent discoveries and utilizing the British Museum's vast collections to illustrate social and economic life, religious beliefs, funerary practices, and technical achievements

0-500-27902-0 THAMES & HUDSON PB $24.95

Nicholas **Reeves** & John H. **Taylor**

Howard Carter Before Tutankhamen

0-8109-3186-9 ABRAMS $29.95

Nicholas **Reeves** & Richard H. **Wilkinson**

The Complete Valley of the Kings: Tombs and Treasures of Ancient Egypt's Royal Burial Site

The definitive account of all the tombs in the famous valley, including the recently discovered tomb complex of Rameses the Great's many sons, complete with computer-generated perspectives, detailed site plans and maps, timelines, histories, and the stories of the explorers, from Greek and Roman times to Howard Carter and the present day

0-500-05080-5 THAMES & HUDSON $29.95

W. Stevenson **Smith**

The Art and Architecture of Ancient Egypt

0-300-05328-2 YALE PB $26.50

The Ancient Near East

Dominique **Collon**

First Impressions: Cylinder Seals in the Ancient Near East

The new standard introductions to cylinder seals and sealing practices in ancient western Asia by a research curator in the British Museum, house of one of the largest collections of these devises in the world. This study is a key to the understanding of the art and culture of the time

0-226-11389-2 CHICAGO PB $21.95

Susan **Downey**

Mesopotamian Religious Architecture: Alexander Through the Parthians

How invading powers modified indigenous art

0-691-03589-X PRINCETON $68.00

Henri **Frankfort**

The Art and Architecture of the Ancient Orient

A classic survey of Mesopotamian, Syrian, Anatolian, and Persian art and architecture, by a distinguished art historian

0-300-05331-2 YALE PB $25.00

Prudence O. **Harper**

The Royal City of Susa: Ancient Near Eastern Treasures in the Louvre

0-8109-6422-8 METROPOLITAN MUSEUM $60.00

Gwendolyn **Leick**

A Dictionary of Ancient Near Eastern Architecture

0-415-00240-0 ROUTLEDGE $65.00

Seton **Lloyd** & Hans **Muller**

Ancient Architecture: Mesopotamia, Egypt, Crete

0-8478-0692-8 RIZZOLI PB $29.95

Julian **Reade**

Assyrian Sculpture

Wall reliefs and three-dimensional sculpture

0-674-05016-9 HARVARD PB $12.50

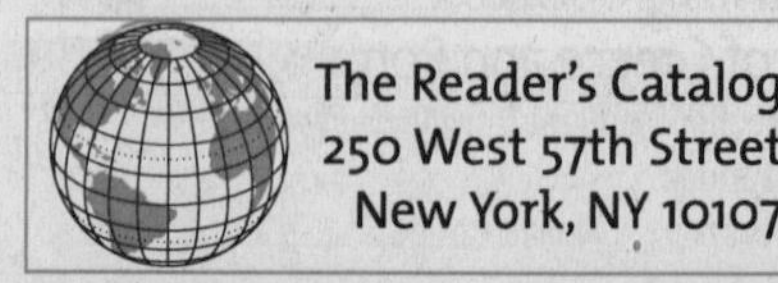

Art of the Classical World

John **Boardman**

The Diffusion of Classical Art in Antiquity

This book "explores the record of Greek art as a *foreign* art introduced to peoples who may have had strong artistic traditions of their own" —John Boardman

0-691-03680-2 PRINCETON $52.50

John **Boardman**, editor

The Oxford History of Classical Art

0-19-814386-9 OXFORD $55.00

Peter J. **Holliday**, editor

Narrative and Event in Ancient Art

0-521-43013-5 CAMBRIDGE $75.00

Carol C. **Mattusch**

Classical Bronzes: The Art and Craft of Greek and Roman Statuary

0-8014-3182-4 CORNELL $45.00

Stuart **Piggott**

Antiquity Depicted: Aspects of Archaeological Illustration

Records the changing perceptions of antiquity and its artifacts

0-500-55010-7 NORTON $9.95

Jeffrey **Spier**

Ancient Gems and Finger Rings: Catalogue of the Collections, the J. Paul Getty Museum

0-89236-215-4 GETTY MUSEUM $65.00

Cornelius **Vermeule**

Greek and Roman Sculpture in America: Masterpieces in Public Collections in the United States and Canada

From prehistoric Cycladic marble statuettes to late Roman portraits and sarcophagi. Splendid photographs

0-520-04324-3 CALIFORNIA $70.00
0-520-04451-7 CALIFORNIA PB $30.00

Susan **Woodford**

Art of Greece and Rome

An excellent general introduction with fine illustrations

0-521-29873-3 CAMBRIDGE PB $12.95

Greece

Martin **Bernal**

Black Athena: The Afroasiatic Roots of Ancient Civilization

These books put forth the claim that Greece was invaded, conquered, and civilized by Egyptians about 1800 BCE. "The political purpose of *Black Athena* is, of course, to lessen European cultural arrogance"—Martin Bernal

Volume 1 The Fabrication of Ancient Greece, 1785-1985

See also **GREEK INFLUENCE** under **TOPICS IN ANCIENT GREEK HISTORY** under **ANCIENT GREECE** in **WORLD HISTORY AND CURRENT AFFAIRS**

0-8135-1276-X RUTGERS $60.00
0-8135-1277-8 RUTGERS PB $16.95

Volume 2 The Archaeological and Documentary Evidence

0-8135-1584-X RUTGERS PB $19.95

P.P. **Betancourt**

The History of Minoan Pottery

Considers a wide range of indigenous styles; with fine reproductions

0-691-03579-2 PRINCETON $85.00

John **Boardman**

Athenian Black-Figure Vases

"Comprehensive and concise yet never offers less than adequate discussion in crisp, lucid prose" —*TLS*

0-500-20138-2 THAMES & HUDSON PB $12.95

Athenian Red-Figure Vases: The Archaic Period

The painters, styles, and development of the vases decorated using the technique invented in Athens in the 6th century BC

0-500-20143-9 THAMES & HUDSON PB $14.95

Athenian Red-Figure Vases: The Classical Period

See also **THAMES & HUDSON WORLD OF ART** under **ART HISTORY: GENERAL STUDIES**

0-500-20244-3 THAMES & HUDSON PB $11.95

Greek Art

A fluent and engaging introduction by the pre-eminent authority in the field

0-500-20292-3 THAMES & HUDSON PB $16.95

Greek Sculpture: The Archaic Period

An informative handbook to works of the 8th-6th centuries BC, reviewing their public function and artistic development

See also **ARTS** under **TOPICS IN ANCIENT GREEK HISTORY** under **ANCIENT GREECE** in **WORLD HISTORY AND CURRENT AFFAIRS**

0-500-20198-6 THAMES & HUDSON PB $14.95

Greek Sculpture: The Late Classical Period and Sculpture in Colonies and Overseas

See also **THAMES & HUDSON WORLD OF ART** under **ART HISTORY: GENERAL STUDIES**

0-500-20285-0 THAMES & HUDSON PB $14.95

Diana **Bruitron-Oliver**

The Greek Miracle: Classical Sculpture from the Dawn of Democracy, 5th Century B.C.

Divided by 2,000 years, yet linked by a system of government as enduring as the concept of beauty, the modern world meets the ancient in this extraordinary offering. Among the well-known pieces selected are *Kritios Boy, Contemplative Athena Calvary* from the Parthenon Frieze, and *Nike Unbinding Her Sandal,* all depicted from a variety of views

0-8109-3371-3 NATIONAL GALLERY OF ART $49.50

Pat **Getz-Preziosi**

Early Cycladic Sculpture: An Introduction

0-89236-220-0 GETTY MUSEUM PB $27.50

Reynold **Higgins**

Minoan and Mycenaean Art

An illustrated introduction to the statuary, architecture, painting, pottery, and jewelry of the rich Bronze Age culture

0-19-520256-2 OXFORD $19.95

Sinclair **Hood**

The Arts in Prehistoric Greece

An amply illustrated introduction to pottery and figurines of the Bronze Age

See also **THE PELICAN HISTORY OF ART** under **ART HISTORY: GENERAL STUDIES**

0-300-05287-1 YALE PB $25.00

Mary R. **Lefkowitz**

Not Out of Africa: How Afrocentrism Became an Excuse to Teach Myth as History

A critical response to Bernal's *Black Athena*

See also **NEW DIRECTIONS** under **HISTORIOGRAPHY** in **WORLD HISTORY AND CURRENT AFFAIRS**
See also **GREEK INFLUENCE** under **TOPICS IN ANCIENT GREEK HISTORY** under **ANCIENT GREECE** in **WORLD HISTORY AND CURRENT AFFAIRS**

0-465-09837-1 BASIC $24.00

Mary R. **Lefkowitz** & Guy MacLean **Rogers**, editors

Black Athena Revisited

0-8078-2246-9 NORTH CAROLINA $55.00
0-8078-4555-8 NORTH CAROLINA PB $19.95

Susan B. **Matheson**

Polygnotos and Vase Painting in Classical Athens

0-299-13870-4 WISCONSIN $60.00

John Griffiths **Pedley**

Greek Art and Archaeology

0-8109-3369-1 ABRAMS $55.00

Jerome **Pollitt**

Art in the Hellenistic Age

An interpretative history of Greek art from the era of Alexander the Great in 323 BC to the end of the 1st century BC

0-521-27672-1 CAMBRIDGE PB $36.95

Colin **Renfrew**

The Cycladic Spirit: Masterpieces from the Nicholas P. Goulandris Collection

Renfrew combines archaeology and art history to create a compelling survey of the vanished civilization that produced some of the earliest marble sculptures known. Cycladic art achieved an abstraction and simplicity unequaled until the advent of Brancusi and Modigliani. Executed between 2700 and 2400 B.C. in the Cycladic islands of Greece, the works include some of the first life-size figures in the history of art

0-8109-3169-9 ABRAMS $49.50

Gisela **Richter**

The Portraits of the Greeks

The gradual evolution from a generalized to an individual likeness

0-8014-1683-3 CORNELL $49.95

Martin **Robertson**

A Shorter History of Greek Art

A well-illustrated chronological treatment from prehistory through the Hellenistic period

0-521-23629-0 CAMBRIDGE $80.00
0-521-28084-2 CAMBRIDGE PB $33.95

Nigel **Spivey**

Understanding Greek Sculpture: Ancient Meanings, Modern Readings

An eloquent examination of the social production of Greek sculpture and the contexts in which it was displayed—brightly painted, massed together, and elevated on pediments and friezes—that will transform the way we look at Greek sculpture.

0-500-27876-8 THAMES & HUDSON PB $24.95

Andrew **Stewart**

Greek Sculpture: An Exploration

A stimulating account of large-scale Greek sculpture from the Dark Ages to Augustus (c. 1200-30 BC) that places each monument in its social and political context. With over 900 illustrations. "Stewart's book will surely remain the definitive handbook on Greek sculpture for many years"—Richard Brilliant, *History*

0-300-04072-5 YALE $135.00
0-300-05208-1 YALE PB $55.00

Cornelius **Vermeule**

Greek Art: Socrates to Sulla, from the Peloponnesian Wars to the Rise of Julius Caesar

0-87846-111-6 MUSEUM OF FINE ARTS PB $50.00

Dyfri **Williams** & Jack **Ogden**

Greek Gold: Jewelry of the Classical World

See also **JEWELRY** under **ACCESSORIES** under **FASHION AND COSTUME** in **ARCHITECTURE, DESIGN, AND HOMES**

0-8109-3388-8 ABRAMS $45.00

Rome and the Etruscans

Otto J. **Brendel**

Etruscan Art

Centered in the life of the family and a continuing life in the tomb, Etruscan art is private, aristocratic, and luxurious. Brendel's book is the first important study of Etruscan sculpture, wall-painting, metalware, ceramics, and jewelry, which, though influenced by Greek artforms, were profoundly original.

See also **THE PELICAN HISTORY OF ART** under **ART HISTORY: GENERAL STUDIES**

See also **THE ETRUSCANS AND EARLY ROME** under **FROM ANTIQUITY TO FEUDALISM** under **ANCIENT ROME**

0-300-06446-2 YALE PB $27.50

Jas **Elsner**

Art and The Roman Viewer

0-521-45354-2 CAMBRIDGE $60.00

George **Hanfmann**

Roman Art: A Modern Survey of the Art of Ancient Rome

A rich introduction by a leading scholar, covering major works of architecture and statuary

0-393-09222-4 NORTON PB $14.95

Sybille **Haynes**

Etruscan Bronzes

Solid historical and stylistic background accompanied by fine reproductions

0-85667-195-9 SOTHEBY PARKE BERNET $160.00

Martin **Henig**, editor

A Handbook of Roman Art

0-8014-1539-X CORNELL $59.95
0-8014-9242-4 CORNELL PB $25.95

Diana E.F. **Kleiner**

Roman Sculpture

0-300-05948-5 YALE PB $32.50

Claude **Moatti**

The Search for Ancient Rome

TRANSLATED BY ANTHONY ZIELONKA

0811092839 ABRAMS PB $12.95

Donald **Strong**

Roman Art

See also **THE PELICAN HISTORY OF ART** under **ART HISTORY: GENERAL STUDIES**

0-300-05293-6 PENGUIN PB $25.00

Mortimer **Wheeler**

Roman Art and Architecture

A survey of architecture, town planning, sculpture and painting, silver, glass, pottery, and other achievements

See also **ARTS** under **TOPICS IN ROMAN HISTORY** under **ANCIENT ROME**

0-500-20021-1 THAMES & HUDSON PB $14.95

Paul **Zanker**

The Power of Images in the Age of Augustus

An excellent book about the ideological manipulation of art in the nascent Roman Empire

0-472-08124-1 MICHIGAN PB $21.95

European Art: Byzantine and Medieval

Early Christian and Byzantine

John **Beckwith**

Early Christian and Byzantine Art

An accomplished survey of the dissemination of Christian ideals and art throughout the East; with extensive illustrations

See also **THE PELICAN HISTORY OF ART** under **ART HISTORY: GENERAL STUDIES**

0-300-05295-2 YALE $50.00
0-300-05296-0 YALE PB $25.00

Kathleen **Corrigan**

Visual Polemics in Ninth-Century Byzantine Psalters

0-521-40050-3 CAMBRIDGE $105.00

David Talbot **Rice**

Art of the Byzantine Era

Emphasizes stylistic developments throughout the Byzantine Empire, including the early Christian centers in Italy and the East; amply illustrated

0-500-20004-1 THAMES & HUDSON PB $14.95

Lyn **Rodley**

Byzantine Art and Architecture

0-521-35724-1 CAMBRIDGE PB $29.95

Meyer **Schapiro**

Selected Papers of Meyer Schapiro Volume III Late Antique, Early Christian, and Medieval Art

See also **THEORY** under **ART HISTORY: GENERAL STUDIES**

0-8076-1295-2 BRAZILLER PB $19.95

Otto von **Simson**

Sacred Fortress: Byzantine Art and Statecraft in Ravenna

0-691-00276-2 PRINCETON PB $16.95

Medieval Art: 600-1400

General Studies: Medieval Art

Jonathan J.G. **Alexander**

Medieval Illuminators and Their Methods of Work

A survey of European manuscript illumination from the fourth to the 16th centuries that discusses the social and historical contexts of the artists' lives, their methods of work, and the range and nature of their visual sources

0-300-05689-3 YALE $60.00
0-300-06073-4 YALE PB $27.50

Hans **Belting**

Likeness and Presence: A History of the Image Before the Era of Art

A major scholar's magnus opus—a study of how works of art changed from being religious to aesthetic objects

See also **THEORY** under **ART HISTORY: GENERAL STUDIES**

0-226-04214-6 CHICAGO $65.00
0-226-04215-4 CHICAGO PB $39.95

Janetta Rebold **Benton**

The Medieval Menagerie: Animals in the Art of the Middle Ages

1-55859-133-8 ABBEVILLE $29.95

Robert **Calkins**

Illuminated Books of the Middle Ages

Focuses on the nature, use, and structure of medieval liturgical books, with excellent color reproductions

0-8014-1506-3 CORNELL $69.50

Monuments of Medieval Art

A sweeping guide to the major art forms and stylistic developments, emphasizing the significance of works within their historical context

0-8014-9306-4 CORNELL PB $16.95

Caecilia **Davis-Weyer**, editor

Early Medieval Art, 300-1150 AD: Sources and Documents

An informative guide, ranging from theological tracts to painters' instructions

0-8020-6628-3 TORONTO PB $12.95

Jerrilynn D. **Dodds** & others

The Art of Medieval Spain AD, 500-1200

0-8109-6433-3 METROPOLITAN MUSEUM $75.00

Mireille **Mentre**

The Illuminated Manuscripts of Medieval Spain

As the end of the first millennium drew near and many expected the end of the world, the beleaguered Christian communities of Spain, still dominated by Islam, experienced a profound spiritual crisis. To make sense of their predicament, they turned to the Revelation of St. John the Divine and its commentaries regarding a vision of the apocalypse. This book takes us on a visual and theological tour through the twenty or so manuscripts that survive, all illuminated in a bizarre and colorful style known as Mozarabic—a combination of Carolingian, Islamic, Byzantine, and Visigothic styles

0-500-01732-8 THAMES & HUDSON $75.00

Whitney **Stoddard**

Art and Architecture in Medieval France

Recommended for its historic overviews and attempts to relate artistic production to the political realities of the time. Best on the Gothic period

See also **GOTHIC AND ROMANESQUE** under **EUROPEAN ARCHITECTURE TO 1900** in **ARCHITECTURE, DESIGN, AND HOMES**

0-06-430022-6 ICON PB $24.00

Marilyn **Stokstad**

Medieval Art

A recent study notable for covering a broad geographical range of artistic production, placing works within their social and aesthetic context. With maps, chronological table, and a glossary

See also **THE MEDIEVAL AESTHETIC** under **MEDIEVAL AND RENAISSANCE EUROPE** in **WORLD HISTORY AND CURRENT AFFAIRS**

0-06-430132-X ICON PB $30.00

Early Medieval

Janet **Backhouse**

The Lindisfarne Gospels

A vivid discussion of production, techniques, text, and script, as well as earlier and contemporary works of art, with comprehensive illustrations

0-7148-2461-5 PHAIDON PB $14.95

John **Beckwith**

Early Medieval Art: Carolingian, Ottonian, Romanesque

A concise, authoritative survey of the architecture, painting, sculpture, illuminations, and ivories of the three great periods of early medieval art

See also **THAMES & HUDSON WORLD OF ART** under **ART HISTORY: GENERAL STUDIES**

0-500-20019-X THAMES & HUDSON PB $14.95

Wolfgang **Grape**

The Bayeux Tapestry

The monument of medieval textile art—over 75 yards long—is brought to life in a lively text that has the immediacy of a historical novel. Profusely illustrated

3-7913-1365-7 TE NEUS PB $29.95

Francoise **Henry**, editor

The Book of Kells

A lavish book, with 126 color and 70 black-and-white plates

0-394-49475-X KNOPF $124.50

Ernst **Kitzinger**

Early Medieval Art

A classic, based on the British Museum collections

0-253-20065-2 INDIANA PB $12.95

Luther **Link**

The Devil: The Archfiend in Art from the Sixth to the Seventh Century

0-8109-3226-1 ABRAMS $29.95

Florentine **Mutherich** & J.E. **Gaehde**

Carolingian Painting

A fine introduction to the major manuscripts of the period, with individual commentary on the plates

0-8076-0851-3 BRAZILLER $19.95
0-8076-0852-1 BRAZILLER PB $11.95

David **Wilson** & Ole **Klindt-Jensen**

Viking Art

A scholarly study, with black-and-white illustrations

0-8166-0974-8 MINNESOTA $29.50

Romanesque

M.F. **Hearn**

Romanesque Sculpture: The Revival of Monumental Stone Sculpture in the 11th and 12th Centuries

The only existing survey, with a core bibliography

0-8014-9304-8 CORNELL PB $27.95

Marcia **Kupfer**

Romanesque Wall Painting in Central France: The Politics of Narrative

An interpretation of the social and political roles of the monumental wall paintings that once embellished countless rural churches in France during the 11th and 12th centuries

0-300-05720-2 YALE $60.00

Elizabeth **Parker** & Charles T. **Little**

The Cloisters Cross: Its Art and Meaning

0-8109-6434-1 METROPOLITAN MUSEUM $60.00

Andreas **Petzold**

Romanesque Art

0-8109-2744-6 ABRAMS PB $16.95

Meyer **Schapiro**

Selected Papers of Meyer Schapiro Volume I Romanesque Art

See also **THEORY** under **ART HISTORY: GENERAL STUDIES**

0-8076-1294-4 BRAZILLER PB $19.95

Hanns **Swarzenski**

Monuments of Romanesque Art: The Art of Church Treasures

Excellent illustrations of ivory, gold, bronze, enamel, and manuscript painting in northwestern Europe from 800-1200, with a brief introduction

0-226-78605-6 CHICAGO $40.00
0-226-78606-4 CHICAGO PB $10.95

John **Williams** & Barbara A. **Shailor**

A Spanish Apocalypse: The Morgan Beatus Manuscript

"When Fernand Leger was here in New York in the year 1934, he asked what single piece of art he should see if he had only enough time for that. I responded without hesitation—The Morgan Beatus."

0-8076-1262-6 BRAZILLER $175.00

Gothic

Henry **Adams**

Mont Saint-Michel and Chartres

A study of the medieval imagination through the religion, art, and architecture of the 12th century. "From beginning to end, it reads as from a man in the fresh morning of life, with a frolic power unusual to historic literature" —William James

See also **THE MEDIEVAL AESTHETIC** under **MEDIEVAL AND RENAISSANCE EUROPE** in **WORLD HISTORY AND CURRENT AFFAIRS**

INTRODUCTION BY RAYMOND CARNEY

0-14-039054-5 PENGUIN PB $11.95

Henry Adams

Michael **Camille**

Gothic Art: Glorious Visions

0-8109-2701-2 ABRAMS PB $16.95

The Gothic Idol: Ideology and Image-Making in Medieval Art

0-521-42430-5 CAMBRIDGE PB $34.95

Master of Death: The Lifeless Art of Pierre Remiet, Illuminator

0-300-06457-8 YALE $40.00

Adolfo Salvatore **Cavallo**

Medieval Tapestries in the Metropolitan Museum of Art

0-8109-6420-1 METROPOLITAN MUSEUM $50.00

Alain **Erlande-Brandenburg**

Gothic Art

0-8109-0631-7 ABRAMS $175.00

Theresa **Frisch**, editor

Gothic Art, 1140-c.1450: Sources and Documents

The companion volume to Davis-Weyer, recently revised

0-8020-6679-8 TORONTO PB $8.95

Dillian **Gordon**

Making & Meaning: The Wilton Diptych

A complete account of the artist's first stay in Rome from 1496 to 1501, a crucial period in his career when he created the celebrated *Bacchus* and *Pietá* sculptures

0-300-06150-1 YALE PB $15.00

Emile **Mâle**

Religious Art in France: A Study of Medieval Iconography and Its Sources

Volume 2: The 13th Century

0-691-09913-8 PRINCETON $125.00

Volume 3: The Late Middle Ages

0-691-09914-6 PRINCETON $99.50

The Gothic Image

0-064-30032-3 ICON $21.00

Religious Art from the 12th to 18th Century

0-691-00347-5 PRINCETON PB $18.75

Andrew **Martindale**

Gothic Art

A sensible and manageable introduction

See also **THAMES & HUDSON WORLD OF ART** under **ART HISTORY: GENERAL STUDIES**

0-500-20058-0 THAMES & HUDSON PB $14.95

Millard **Meiss**

French Paintings in the Time of Jean de Berry: The Limbourgs and Their Contemporaries

Manuscript production of 14th and 15th-century France studied in its intellectual context, with stunning reproductions. A two-volume set

0-8076-0734-7 BRAZILLER $110.00

Millard **Meiss**, editor

The Rohan Master

0-8076-0690-1 BRAZILLER $100.00

The Très Riches Heures of Jean, Duc de Berry

0-8076-0512-3 BRAZILLER $100.00

0-8076-1220-0 BRAZILLER PB $24.95

Lucy **Sandler**

Gothic Manuscripts

An introductory essay with copious reproductions

0-19-921037-3 OXFORD $130.00

John W. **Steyaert**

Late Gothic Sculpture: The Burgundian Netherlands

0-8109-3577-5 ABRAMS $60.00

Marcel **Thomas**

The Golden Age: Manuscript Painting at the Time of Jean, Duke of Berry

0-8076-0923-4 BRAZILLER $24.95

0-8076-0924-2 BRAZILLER PB $12.95

Paul **Williamson**

Gothic Sculpture, 1140-1300

This book is the first to examine the development of Gothic sculpture throughout Europe. Written by the curator of sculpture at London's Victoria and Albert Museum, the volume is lavishly illustrated with 125 color and 261 black-and-white plates

0-300-06338-5 YALE $65.00

Crafts

Marian **Campbell**

An Introduction to Medieval Enamels

Enamels and goldsmith work from the Victoria and Albert Museum, from the Celtic period to the 15th century, with a concise discussion of history and technique

0-88045-021-5 STEMMER $14.95

Peter **Lasko**

Ars Sacra, 800-1200

A beautiful book that traces the development of the so-called "minor arts"—such as bronze doors, gold, ivory, and jeweled book covers, and reliquary caskets—and the major role they played alongside other pictorial arts and sculpture of the period

See also **THE PELICAN HISTORY OF ART** under **ART HISTORY: GENERAL STUDIES**

0-300-06048-3 YALE $65.00

Theophilus

On Divers Arts: The Foremost Medieval Treatise on Painting, Glassmaking, and Metalwork

A unique discourse, mostly technical, with a brief commentary on the role of the medieval artist, probably written during the first half of the 12th century by a German author

TRANSLATED BY JOHN HAWTHORNE & CYRIL SMITH

0-486-23784-2 DOVER PB $8.95

Daniel **Thompson**

The Materials Techniques of Medieval Painting

Manuscripts, laboratory analyses, and information gleaned from medieval sources

See also **PAINTING** under **THEMES, TECHNIQUES, AND GENRES** under **ART HISTORY: GENERAL STUDIES**

FOREWORD BY BERNARD BERENSON

0-486-20327-1 DOVER PB $6.95

Paul **Williamson**

Introduction to Medieval Ivory Carvings

A solid reference work based primarily on the collection of the Victoria and Albert Museum, with numerous color reproductions

0-88045-006-1 STEMMER $14.95

The Rise of Italian Painting

Michael **Baxandall**

Giotto and the Orators: Humanist Observers of Painting in Italy and the Discovery of Pictorial Composition, 1350-1450

A classic study of the intersection between literary and visual culture in the early Renaissance

0-19-817387-3 CLARENDON PB $29.95

David **Bomford** & others

Italian Painting Before 1400: Art in the Making

0-300-06144-7 YALE PB $30.00

Martin **Davies**

The Earlier Italian Schools

0-300-06139-0 YALE PB $28.00

The Early Italian Schools Before 1400

0-300-06138-2 YALE PB $30.00

Paul **Hills**

The Light of Early Renaissance Painting

0-300-04698-7 YALE PB $18.00

Laurence B. **Kanter** & others

Painting and Illumination in Early Renaissance Florence, 1300-1450

0-87099-725-4 METROPOLITAN MUSEUM $60.00

Marilyn Aronberg **Lavin**

The Place of Narrative: Mural Decoration in Italian Churches, 431-1600

0-226-46960-3 CHICAGO PB $49.95

Millard **Meiss**

Painting in Florence and Siena After the Black Death: The Arts, Religion and Society in the Mid-14th Century

0-691-00312-2 PRINCETON PB $19.95

Millard **Meiss**, editor

The Visconti Hours

0-8076-0651-0 BRAZILLER $100.00

Diana **Norman**, editor

Siena, Florence, and Padua: Art, Society, and Religion, 1280-1400

Volume I
Interpretive Essays

A comprehensive examination of the artistic legacy of these three major centers during the 14th century that locates the various works of art produced there within a social, religious, and cultural context

0-300-06124-2 YALE $55.00
0-300-06125-0 YALE PB $27.50

Volume II
Case Studies

0-300-06126-9 YALE $55.00
0-300-06127-7 YALE PB $27.50

John **White**

Art and Architecture in Italy, 1250-1400

A new edition, with color reproductions and an updated bibliography

See also **THE PELICAN HISTORY OF ART** under **ART HISTORY: GENERAL STUDIES**

0-300-05584-6 YALE $60.00
0-300-05585-4 YALE PB $27.50

Italian Artists

"Giotto obscured the fame of Cimabue, as a great light outshines a lesser. Although Cimabue may well be considered the first to have restored the art of painting, Giotto threw open the gates and showed the path to that perfection."
—Giorgio Vasari

Cecilia **Jannella**

Duccio di Buoninsegna

1-87835-118-4 RIVERSIDE PB $12.99

Andrew **Ladis**

Taddeo Gaddi: A Critical Reappraisal and Catalogue Raisonné

Mostly black-and-white illustrations of the work of Giotto's pupil

0-8262-0382-5 MISSOURI $70.00

Bruce **Cole**

Giotto: The Scrovegni Chapel, Padua

0-8076-1310-X BRAZILLER $25.00

Francesca Flores **d'Arcais**

Giotto

1-55859-774-3 ABBEVILLE $95.00

Jacqueline & Maurice **Guillaud**

Giotto: The Architecture of Color and Form

An oversize book with beautiful reproductions that capture the texture of the frescoes

0-517-56702-4 CLARKSON POTTER $100.00

Paul **Joannides**

Masaccio and Masolino: A Complete Catalogue

0-8109-3636-4 ABRAMS $195.00

Perri Lee **Roberts**

Masolino da Panicale

0-19-817509-4 CLARENDON $115.00

European Art: The Renaissance

Jill **Dunkerton** & others

Giotto to Durer: Early Renaissance Painting in the National Gallery

A detailed examination of some of the finest and best-known paintings in the National Gallery, London—including works by Duccio, Van Eyck, Bellini, Raphael, and Leonardo—that offers a stimulating discussion of how and why they were made

0-300-05070-4 YALE $65.00
0-300-05082-8 YALE PB $32.50

Claire **Farago**, editor

Reframing the Renaissance: Visual Culture in Europe and Latin America, 1450-1650

See also **STYLE AND FASHION** under **EARLY MODERN EUROPE** in **WORLD HISTORY AND CURRENT AFFAIRS**

0-300-06295-8 YALE $45.00

Bertrand **Jestaz**

Art of the Renaissance

TRANSLATED BY I. MARK PARIS

0-8109-1948-6 ABRAMS $175.00

David **Landau** & Peter W. **Parshall**

The Renaissance Print, 1470-1550

The fullest account ever written of the ways in which Renaissance prints were produced, distributed, and acquired

0-300-05739-3 YALE $70.00

Jay A. **Levenson**, editor

Circa 1492: Art in the Age of Exploration

The catalog for a major exhibit devoted to the extraordinary art of the Age of Exploration, not only in Europe but in the Far East and the Americas. A team of art historians, historians, and anthropologists examines the cultural interrelationships of an era of unprecedented flux. Includes 500 color plates and 75 black-and-white illustrations

INTRODUCTION BY DANIEL J. BOORSTIN

0-300-05167-0 YALE $30.00

Martin **Warnke**

The Court Artist: On the Ancestry of the Modern Artist

TRANSLATED BY DAVID MCLINTOCK

0-521-36375-6 CAMBRIDGE $59.95

Italy

"The achievements of the early Renaissance in Italy transformed in a single century not only the visual arts but the nature and purpose of art itself and the social position of the artist more radically than they had been changed in the preceding 1000 years...The great innovators of central Italy—then, a generation later, those of northern Italy—produced a new art able to represent credibly anything the eye could see, approximating reality in form, space, and color. They infused these optical impressions of the visible world with a sense of inner structure that derived from their own researches in the sphere of proportional, perspective, and anatomical theory, perhaps even more than from their study of antiquity. On this balance between sight and structure depends the beauty of early Renaissance art."—Frederick Hartt, *Art: A History of Painting, Sculpture, Architecture*

Bernard **Berenson**

Italian Painters of the Renaissance

Essays by the great early critic and connoisseur on the regional schools; abundantly illustrated

1-88314-505-8 URSUS $35.00

Fernand **Braudel**

Out of Italy: 1450-1650

2-08-013500-7 ABBEVILLE $50.00

André **Chastel**

A Chronicle of Italian Renaissance Painting

An engaging collection of original documents with striking reproductions, 60 color, 140 black-and-white; perhaps the finest handbook

0-8014-1524-1 CORNELL $125.00

Alison **Cole**

Virtue and Magnificence: Art of The Italian Renaissance Courts

0-8109-2733-0 ABRAMS PB $16.95

Bruce **Cole**

The Renaissance Artist at Work

His methods, materials, studio practice, and social status

0-06-430129-X ICON PB $16.00

S.J. **Freedberg**

Painting in Italy: 1500-1600

A revised edition of the classic work, with color illustrations, updated text, and a new bibliography

See also THE PELICAN HISTORY OF ART under ART HISTORY: GENERAL STUDIES

0-300-05586-2 YALE $65.00
0-300-05587-0 YALE PB $28.50

Anthony **Grafton**, editor

Rome Reborn: The Vatican Library and Renaissance Culture

A profusely illustrated introduction to the history of the Vatican library and its development during the Renaissance as the richest collection of Western manuscripts and early printed books in the world

0-300-05442-4 YALE $65.00

J.R. **Hale**, editor

A Concise Encyclopedia of the Italian Renaissance

A sturdy and exhaustive illustrated reference book for the general reader

See also RENAISSANCE ITALY AND THE COMING OF HUMANISM under MEDIEVAL AND RENAISSANCE EUROPE in WORLD HISTORY AND CURRENT AFFAIRS

0-500-23333-0 NORTON $19.95
0-500-20191-9 THAMES & HUDSON PB $14.95

Frederick **Hartt** & David G. **Wilkins**

History of Italian Renaissance Art

0-8109-3417-5 ABRAMS $60.00

George L. **Hersey**

High Renaissance Art in St. Peter's and the Vatican

0-226-32782-5 CHICAGO PB $24.95

Bram **Kempers**

Painting, Power and Patronage: The Rise of the Professional Artist in the Italian Renaissance

TRANSLATED BY BEVERLEY JACKSON

0-14-012488-8 PENGUIN PB $14.95

Rosa **Letts**

The Renaissance

Accessible, informative, lively, and well-illustrated

0-521-23394-1 CAMBRIDGE $24.95
0-521-29957-8 CAMBRIDGE PB $12.95

Wolfgang **Lotz** & Deborah **Howard**

Architecture in Italy, 1500-1600

See also THE PELICAN HISTORY OF ART under ART HISTORY: GENERAL STUDIES

0-300-06469-1 YALE PB $27.50

Peter **Murray** & Linda **Murray**

The Art of the Renaissance

The Renaissance as an international phenomenon; the works of Piero della Francesca, Van Eyck, Mantegna, Bellini, and Durer figure prominent

0-500-20008-4 THAMES & HUDSON PB $14.95

Roberta J.M. **Olson**

Italian Renaissance Sculpture

0-500-20253-2 THAMES & HUDSON PB $14.95

John **Pope-Hennessy**

The Portrait in the Renaissance

Stimulating and colorful essays by the eminent art historian; with exemplary illustrations

See also THEMES, TECHNIQUES, AND GENRES under ART HISTORY: GENERAL STUDIES

0-691-09795-X PRINCETON $95.00
0-691-01825-1 PRINCETON PB $35.00

Theory and Criticism

Michael **Baxandall**

Painting and Experience in 15th Century Italy

Pictorial style as an aspect of social history; an excellent introduction to pictorial language, with numerous illustrations

0-19-881329-5 OXFORD PB $12.95

Anthony **Blunt**, editor

Artistic Theory in Italy, 1450-1600

A clear account of the various theories of art that arose in the Renaissance

0-19-881050-4 OXFORD PB $19.95

Bruce **Cole**

Italian Art, 1250-1550: The Relation of Art to Life and Society

Copiously illustrated in black and white

0-06-430162-1 ICON PB $30.00

Charles **Dempsey**

The Portrayal of Love: Botticelli's Primavera and Humanist Culture at the Time of Lorenzo the Magnificent

A fine essay in intellectual history and a new interpretation of one of the world's most famous paintings from a distinguished scholar

0-691-03207-6 PRINCETON $45.00

E.H. **Gombrich**

Studies in the Art of the Renaissance

Volume 1
Norm and Form

Brilliant essays questioning problems of style, patronage, and taste; with fine illustrations

0-7148-2380-5 PHAIDON PB $22.95

Volume 2
Symbolic Images

0-7148-2381-3 PHAIDON PB $22.95

Volume 3
The Heritage of Apelles

0-7148-2011-3 PHAIDON PB $22.95

Volume 4
New Light on Old Masters

0-226-30219-9 CHICAGO $45.00
0-226-30220-2 CHICAGO PB $21.00

Marcia B. **Hall**

Color and Meaning: Practice and Theory in Renaissance Painting

0-521-39222-5 CAMBRIDGE $70.00

Walter **Pater**

The Renaissance

A touchstone of aestheticism

See also 19TH-CENTURY PROSE under THE 19TH CENTURY in LITERATURE OF THE BRITISH ISLES

EDITED BY ADAM PHILIPS

0-19-281737-X OXFORD PB $6.95

The Renaissance: Studies in Art and Poetry

A scholarly edition

EDITED BY DONALD H. HILL

0-520-03664-6 CALIFORNIA PB $16.95

Patricia Lee **Rubin**

Giorgio Vasari: Art and History

A fresh look at Vasari's *Lives of the Painter, Sculptors, and Architects*, a key text for the study of Italian Renaissance art, that views it as a product of the conventions and convictions of the historical writing of the time

0-300-04909-9 YALE $45.00

John **Shearman**

Only Connect...: Art and the Spectator in the Italian Renaissance

Fine interpretations of a number of Renaissance art works and monuments, including Donatello's *David* and Raphael's Chigi chapel

0-691-01917-7 PRINCETON PB $24.95

Leo **Steinberg**

The Sexuality of Christ in Renaissance Art and in Modern Oblivion

Steinberg argues that there was a theological significance to Renaissance depictions of Jesus' phallus, erect and otherwise, that modern scholarship has repressed

See also MIDDLE AGES AND RENAISSANCE under HISTORY under CHRISTIANITY in RELIGION, SPIRITUALITY, AND PHILOSOPHY

0-226-77186-5 CHICAGO $85.00
0-226-77187-3 CHICAGO PB $29.95

Edgar, **Wind**

Pagan Mysteries in the Renaissance

Includes a classic iconographical interpretation of Botticelli's *Primavera*

0-393-00475-9 NORTON PB $13.95

Contemporary Sources

Leon Battista **Alberti**

Leone Battista Alberti on Painting

EDITED AND TRANSLATED BY JOHN R. SPENCER

0-300-00001-4 YALE PB $11.00

Benvenuto **Cellini**

The Autobiography of Benvenuto Cellini

A vivid picture of the Renaissance sculptor and metalsmith, and an unforgettable evocation of high life and low life in 16th-century Italy

See also **ARTISTS** under **THE RENAISSANCE** under **ITALIAN LITERATURE** in **LITERATURE OF EUROPE, AFRICA, AND ASIA**

EDITED BY GEORGE BULL

0-14-044049-6 PENGUIN PB $9.95

Cennino **Cennini**

The Craftsman's Handbook

A valuable source, written by a Florentine painter around 1390; central to understanding the theory and practice of art at that time

TRANSLATED BY D.V. THOMPSON

0-486-20054-X DOVER PB $6.95

Charles **O'Malley** & J.B. **Saunders**, translators

Leonardo on the Human Body

Excerpts from Leonardo's writings, with fine reproductions of graphic and painted works

0-486-24483-0 DOVER PB $18.95

Michelangelo **Buonarotti**

The Poetry of Michelangelo: An Annotated Translation

The best available translation

TRANSLATED BY JAMES M. SASLOW

0-300-04960-9 YALE $55.00
0300055090 YALE PB $20.00

Carlo **Ridolfi**

Life of Tintoretto, and of His Children Domenico and Marietta

See also **THEORY AND CRITICISM**

0-271-00369-3 PENN STATE $28.50

The Life of Titian

EDITED BY JULIA CONAWAY BONDANELLA AND OTHERS

0-271-01547-0 PENN STATE $40.00
0-271-01627-2 PENN STATE PB $19.95

Giorgio **Vasari**

Perhaps the most entertaining work of art history ever written. This generous selection includes an appendix correcting some of Vasari's attributions and biographical data. Impresario and Michelangelo-idolater, Vasari writes candidly and engagingly

Lives of the Artists

0-19-281754-X OXFORD PB $11.95

Volume 1

0-14-044500-5 PENGUIN PB $10.95

Volume 2

See also **ARTISTS** under **THE RENAISSANCE** under **ITALIAN LITERATURE** in **LITERATURE OF EUROPE, AFRICA, AND ASIA**

See also **RENAISSANCE CLASSICS** under **RENAISSANCE ITALY AND THE COMING OF HUMANISM** under **MEDIEVAL AND RENAISSANCE EUROPE** in **WORLD HISTORY AND CURRENT AFFAIRS**

0-14-044460-2 PENGUIN PB $11.95

Lives of the Painters, Sculptors, and Architects

A complete edition

See also **ARTISTS** under **THE RENAISSANCE** under **ITALIAN LITERATURE** in **LITERATURE OF EUROPE, AFRICA, AND ASIA**

TRANSLATED BY GASTON DE VERE

0-679-45101-3 KNOPF $60.00

On Technique

Selected passages from *Lives of the Artists*

EDITED BY BALDWIN B. BROWN

0-486-20717-X DOVER PB $11.95

Perspective

Hubert **Damisch**

The Origin of Perspective

A structuralist analysis

TRANSLATED BY JOHN GOODMAN

0-262-54077-0 MIT PB $25.00

James **Elkins**

The Poetics of Perspective

0-8014-8379-4 CORNELL PB $16.95

Michael **Kubovy**

The Psychology of Perspective and Renaissance Art

"A unique study, applying for the first time the special skills of a trained perceptual psychologist to the historical facts of Renaissance art"—Samuel Edgerton

0-521-36849-9 CAMBRIDGE PB $22.95

Erwin **Panofsky**

Perspective as Symbolic Form

The assertion that Renaissance perspective is conventional, not natural, is the argument of this classic study by an eminent art historian

See also **THEORY** under **ART HISTORY: GENERAL STUDIES**

0-942299-52-3 MIT $24.95

Venice and the North

Patricia Fortini **Brown**

Venetian Narrative Painting in the Age of Carpaccio

Paintings for government council chambers and religious fraternities in relation to each other and to social context; beautiful reproductions

0-300-04025-3 YALE $65.00
0-300-04743-6 YALE PB $30.00

Michael **Dummett**

The Visconti-Sforza Tarot Cards

A fine example of court art, beautifully reproduced. One of three extant packs of cards devised in 15th-century Italy

0-8076-1141-7 BRAZILLER PB $15.95

Peter **Humfrey**

The Altarpiece in Renaissance Venice

The painting and carving of altarpieces was one of the most important tasks of the Renaissance artist. This book reconstructs the original physical and liturgical contexts of several great Venetian altarpieces and analyses the ways in which artists met the challenges posed by specific commissions

0-300-05358-4 YALE $70.00

Painting in Renaissance Venice

A comprehensive introduction to painting in Venice from Bellini to Titian to Tintoretto, set against the background of the political, social, and religious aspects of the Renaissance

0-300-06247-8 YALE $35.00

Norbert **Huse** & Wolfgang **Wolters**

The Art of Renaissance Venice: Architecture, Sculpture, and Painting, 1460-1590

This book, complete with over 330 illustrations, is the first modern single-volume survey of all three major arts of the Venetian Renaissance. The book achieves a sense of that which is distinctly Venetian

0-226-36109-8 CHICAGO PB $34.95

George **Keyes** & others, editors

Treasures of Venice: Paintings from the Museum of Fine Arts, Budapest

0-8109-3880-4 ABRAMS $49.50

John **Steer**

Venetian Painting: A Concise History

A broad study concentrating on Renaissance works

0-500-20101-3 THAMES & HUDSON PB $14.95

Hans **Tietze** & Erica **Tietze-Conrat**

The Drawings of the Venetian Painters in the 15th and 16th Centuries

0-87817-254-8 HACKER $60.00

Johannes **Wilde**

Venetian Art from Bellini to Titian

"The most intelligent, well-informed, careful, and suggestive introduction to Venetian High Renaissance painting"—*Burlington*

0-19-817331-8 OXFORD PB $38.00

Central Italy: Florence and Rome

Glenn **Andres**

The Art of Florence

0-89659-402-5 ABBEVILLE $385.00

Frederick **Antal**

Florentine Painting and Its Social Background

Major stylistic developments as related to changing economic and social structures, with numerous black-and-white illustrations

0-403-07218-2 SOMERSET $125.00

Sydney **Freedberg**

Painting of the High Renaissance in Rome and Florence

A comprehensive two-volume survey recently reissued

0-87817-301-3 HACKER $120.00

Michael **Hirst** & Carlo **Pietrongeli**

The Sistine Chapel: A Glorious Restoration

0-8109-3840-5 ABRAMS $75.00

Andrew **Ladis**

The Brancacci Chapel, Florence

0-8076-1311-8 BRAZILLER $25.00

Michael **Levey**

Florence: A Portrait

"An appreciation of a large number of Florentine works of art…blended with a very general account of Florentine history. [The text is] lucid, well informed and wide ranging"
—*NY Review of Books*

See also **RENAISSANCE CITIES** under **RENAISSANCE ITALY AND THE COMING OF HUMANISM** under **MEDIEVAL AND RENAISSANCE EUROPE** in **WORLD HISTORY AND CURRENT AFFAIRS**

0-674-30657-0 HARVARD $35.00

Loren W. **Partridge**

The Art of Renaissance Rome: 1400-1600

Filled with illustrations of churches, palaces, villas, frescoes, fountains, and sculptures, this inspiring book rediscovers this extraordinary and ancient city with new outlook. The author, Loren Partridge, is a professor of Art History at Berkeley

0-8109-2718-7 ABRAMS PB $16.95

Fiamma **Domestici**

Della Robbia: A Family of Artists

An examination of the first family of majolica and their influence on the ceramic arts

See also **INDIVIDUAL ARTISTS**

1-87835-145-1 RIVERSIDE PB $12.99

Individual Artists

"While he was in Andrea Verrocchio's shop, that master was engaged on a picture of Saint John Baptizing Jesus Christ. Leonardo painted an angel holding some vestments, and, although he was then but a youth, the angel was the best part of the picture. This caused Verrocchio never to touch color again, so much was he chagrined to be outdone by a mere child."—Giorgio Vasari

John R. **Spencer**

Andrea del Castagno and His Patrons

0-8223-1150-X DUKE $39.95

William **Hood**

Fra Angelico at San Marco

An analysis of the newly cleaned frescos set against the background of 15th-century Florentine artistic, political, cultural, and religious history, including the ideals, daily rituals, and pictorial traditions of the Dominican order

0-300-05734-2 YALE $65.00

Paolo **Morachiello**

Fra Angelico: The San Marco Frescoes

Fra Angelico's frescos in the tiny whitewashed cells of the Dominican convent of San Marco are renowned for their deep spirituality and exhilarating beauty. This book is an unprecedented record of the complete series in its newly cleaned and restored state

0-500-23729-8 THAMES & HUDSON $100.00

Achille Bonito **Oliva**

Arcimboldo

A study of the 16th-century Milanese painter, in a deluxe edition

INTRODUCTORY ESSAY BY ROLAND BARTHES

0-8478-5309-8 RIZZOLI $150.00

Roger **Fry**

Giovanni Bellini

1-88314-503-1 URSUS $19.95

Rona **Goffen**

Giovanni Bellini

A comprehensive recent study of the artist

0-300-04334-1 YALE $70.00

Mariolina **Olivair**

Giovanni Bellini

1-87835-109-5 RIVERSIDE PB $12.99

Colin **Eisler**

The Genius of Jacopo Bellini: The Complete Paintings and Drawings

This book, whose reproductions are of the finest quality, presents the complete work of the best-known artist of early Renaissance Venice—father of Giovanni and Gentile Bellini, father-in-law of Mantegna. The drawings from the Louvre and the British Museum are arranged innovatively by subject matter. The appendices include a catalogue raisonné of the paintings

0-8109-0727-5 ABRAMS $195.00

Sandro **Botticelli**

Drawings

0-486-24248-X DOVER PB $3.95

Barbara **Deimling**

Botticelli

A basic introduction

3-8228-9313-7 TASCHEN $9.99

Bruno **Santi**

Botticelli

1-87835-117-6 RIVERSIDE PB $12.99

Vittorio **Sgarbi**

Carpaccio

0-7892-0000-7 ABBEVILLE $95.00

Lucia **Schianchi**

Correggio

1-87835-146-X RIVERSIDE PB $12.99

Giovanna G. **Bertela**

Donatello

1-87835-119-2 RIVERSIDE PB $12.99

Ronald **Lightbown**

Donatello and Michelozzo: An Artistic Partnership and Its Patrons in the Early Renaissance

A two-volume set

0-19-921024-1 GORDON & BREACH $85.00

Donatello

Joachim **Poeschke**

Donatello and His World: Italian Renaissance Sculpture

0-8109-3211-3 ABRAMS $95.00

John **Pope-Hennessy**

The Piero della Francesca Trail

0-500-27703-6 THAMES & HUDSON PB $10.95

Keith **Christansen**

Gentile Da Fabriano

The early 15th-century painter from Venice who also worked in Rome and Florence; fine reproductions

0-8014-1360-5 CORNELL $95.00

Richard **Krautheimer** &
Trude **Krautheimer-Hess**

Lorenzo Ghiberti

The standard monograph on the Florentine master of bronze reliefwork

0-691-00336-X PRINCETON PB $39.50

Emma **Micheletti**

Domenico Ghirlandaio

1-87835-108-7 RIVERSIDE PB $12.99

Mauro **Lucco**

Giorgione

88-435-5189-2 ART BOOKS INTERNATIONAL $56.50

Salvatore **Settis**

Giorgione's Tempest: Interpreting the Hidden Subject

Settis offers a surprising and plausible new interpretation of Giorgione's mysterious painting, along with an overview of past critics' various accounts

EDITED BY ELLEN BIANCHINI

0-226-74893-6 CHICAGO $35.95

Cristina Acidini **Luchinat**

Benozzo Gozzoli

1-87835-147-8 RIVERSIDE PB $12.99

Kenneth **Clark**

Leonardo da Vinci

A classic, recently reissued

INTRODUCTION BY MARTIN KEMP

0-14-016982-2 PENGUIN PB $19.95

Leonardo **da Vinci**

Drawings

Sixty plates

0-486-23951-9 DOVER PB $4.95

Jean-Claude **Frere**

Leonardo

With 150 full color illustrations, this stunning volume reveals Leonardo as a painter, engineer, inventor, mathematician, architect, and Renaissance genius richly alive in the many complex facets of his imagination. A delightful book to own and a splendid gift

2-87939-036-2 STEWART, TABORI PB $24.95

Bruno **Santi**

Leonardo da Vinci

1-87835-110-9 RIVERSIDE PB $12.99

Richard **Turner**

Inventing Leonardo

0-679-41551-3 KNOPF $27.50

Leonardo da Vinci

Jack **Wasserman**

Leonardo da Vinci

Laudable reproductions of all the major works in color, incorporated in a written survey of Leonardo's life and career

0-8109-1285-6 ABRAMS $22.95

Jeffrey **Ruda**

Fra Filippo Lippi

Life and work with a complete catalogue

0-8109-3568-6 ABRAMS $195.00

Ettore **Camesasca**

Mantegna

1-87835-116-8 RIVERSIDE PB $12.99

Suzanne **Boorsch** & others

Andrea Mantegna

0-8109-6415-5 METROPOLITAN MUSEUM $85.00

Michele **Cordaro**

Mantegna: La Camera Degli Sposi

1-55859-581-3 ELECTA $90.00

John T. **Spike**

Masaccio

0-7892-0090-2 ABBEVILLE $95.00

Giulio Carol **Argan** & Bruno **Contardi**

Michelangelo Architect

A profusely illustrated volume that offers new insights into Michelangelo's architectural projects. Designs, plans, contracts, correspondence, and extracts from the artist's "poetry-diary" reveal that architecture was an integral part of his intellectual and artistic development

See also **INDIVIDUAL ARCHITECTS** under **ITALIAN RENAISSANCE** under **EUROPEAN ARCHITECTURE TO 1900** in **ARCHITECTURE, DESIGN, AND HOMES**

0-8109-3638-0 ABRAMS $125.00

Paul **Barolsky**

The Faun in the Garden: Michelangelo and the Poetic Origins of Italian Renaissance Art

0-271-01303-6 PENN STATE $28.95

Charles **de Tolnay**

Michelangelo: Sculptor, Painter, Architect

A one-volume condensation of the six-part survey of Michelangelo's artistic output; essential reading, well-illustrated

0-691-03876-7 PRINCETON $110.00

Michelangelo: The Sistine Ceiling

0-691-03856-2 PRINCETON $135.00

John **Gere**

Drawings by Michelangelo from the British Museum

0-87598-068-6 PIERPONT MORGANPB $29.95

Ludwig **Goldscheider**

Michelangelo: Paintings, Sculpture, Architecture

First published in 1953, Goldscheider's classic is now available in a beautiful and affordable paperback. Contains fine reproductions of all Michelangelo's work excluding his drawings, with a survey of leading scholars of the artist and extensive commentary and bibliography

0-7148-3296-0 PHAIDON PB $29.95

Howard **Hibbard**

Michelangelo

An excellent introduction to all areas of Michelangelo's career, with extensive illustrations

0-06-430148-6 ICON PB $22.95

Michelangelo

Michael **Hirst** & Jill **Dunkerton**

The Young Michelangelo: Making and Meaning, The Artist in Rome, 1496-1501

0-300-06135-8 YALE $30.00

Richard **McLanathan**

Michelangelo

0-8109-3634-8 ABRAMS $19.95

Linda **Murray**

Michelangelo

0-500-20174-9 THAMES & HUDSON PB $14.95

Michelangelo Buonarroti

Life Drawings

0-486-23876-8 DOVER PB $4.95

Carlo **Bertelli**

Piero della Francesca

0-300-05703-2 YALE $65.00

Marilyn Aronberg **Lavin**

Piero della Francesca

0-8109-3210-5 ABRAMS $22.95
0-8076-1317-7 BRAZILLER $25.00

Ronald **Lightbrown**

Piero Della Francesca

1-55859-168-0 ABBEVILLE $95.00

Sharon **Fermor**

Piero di Rosimo: Fiction, Invention and Fantasia

0-94846-236-1 REAKTION $55.00

John **Pope-Hennessy**

Donatello

1-55859-645-3 ABBEVILLE $95.00

James **Beck**
Raphael
A beautifully illustrated study
0-8109-3777-8 ABRAMS $22.95

Raphael: The Stanze della Segnatora
0-8076-1314-2 BRAZILLER $25.00

Thomas **Connolly**
Mourning into Joy: Music, Raphael, and Saint Cecilia
A major new interpretation of Raphael's art, based on a history of the cult of St. Cecilia, patron saint of music, and its iconography, from its beginnings in Christian antiquity to the Renaissance
0-300-05901-9 YALE $35.00

J. A. **Gere**
Drawings by Raphael and His Circle
An exhibition catalog of drawings from British and American collections
0-87598-083-X PIERPONT MORGAN PB $24.95

Richard **Jones** & Nicholas **Penny**
Raphael
An excellent survey of the artist's career
0-300-04052-0 YALE PB $27.50

Raphael in the Apartments of Julius II and Leo X
1-55859-875-8 ELECTA $130.00

Bruno **Santi**
Raphael
1-87835-115-X RIVERSIDE PB $12.99

Fiamma **Domestici**
Della Robbia: A Family of Artists
An examination of the first family of majolica and their influence on the ceramic arts
See also **PORCELAIN AND POTTERY** under **EUROPEAN DECORATIVE ARTS** in **ARCHITECTURE, DESIGN, AND HOMES**
See also **CENTRAL ITALY: FLORENCE AND ROME**
1-87835-145-1 RIVERSIDE PB $12.99

Antonio **Paolucci**
Luca Signorelli
1-87835-112-5 RIVERSIDE PB $12.99

Jonathan B. **Riess**
Luca Signorelli: The San Brizio Chapel, Orvieto
0-8076-1312-6 BRAZILLER $25.00

Katya Berger **Andreadakis** & John **Berger**
Titian: Nymph and Shepherd
An intriguing illustrated presentation of the major concerns of art and art history presented as a series of letters between art critic Berger and his daughter Katya, who claims to have met Titian's ghost at an exhibition of the master's work. Berger accepts her encounter at face value and provides historical background to the old painter's remarks as the three of them discuss painting, bodies, animals, Greece, being a woman today, and the enigma of existence and daily life
3-7913-1672-9 PRESTEL $25.00

Filippo **Bedrocco**
Titian
1-87835-114-1 RIVERSIDE PB $12.99

G. **Benzoni** & others
Titian: Prince of Painters
3-7913-1102-6 PRESTEL $85.00

Titian

Carlo **Ridolfi**
The Life of Titian
See also **CONTEMPORARY SOURCES**
EDITED BY JULIA CONAWAY BONDANELLA AND OTHERS
0-271-01547-0 PENN STATE $40.00
0-271-01627-2 PENN STATE PB $19.95

Harold **Wethey**
Titian and His Drawing: With Reference to Giorgione and Some Close Contemporaries
A comprehensive, finely illustrated account
0-691-04040-0 PRINCETON $145.00

Franco **Borsi** & Stefano **Borsi**
Paolo Uccello
0-8109-3919-3 ABRAMS $95.00

Loretta **Dolcini**, editor
Verrocchio's Christ and St. Thomas: A Masterpiece of Sculpture from Renaissance Florence
0-8109-6429-5 METROPOLITAN MUSEUM $49.50

Mannerism

Mario **Scalini**
Benvenuto Cellini
1-87835-150-8 RIVERSIDE PB $12.99

André **Chastel**
The Sack of Rome, 1527
Vivid account of the cultural repercussions of a moment, including the spread of the mannerist style; informatively illustrated
0-691-09947-2 PRINCETON $70.00

Walter **Friedlaender**
Mannerism and Anti-Mannerism in Italian Painting
An important essay on the style of Pontormo, Rosso, and Parmigianino and the reaction it generated, with 50 black-and-white illustrations
0-231-08388-2 COLUMBIA PB $13.00

Charles **Avery**
Giambologna: The Complete Sculpture
0-7148-2953-6 PHAIDON PB $35.00

Mary Weitzel **Gibbons**
Giambologna: Narrator of the Catholic Reformation
0-520-08213-3 CALIFORNIA $50.00

Cecil **Gould**
Parmigianino
1-55859-892-8 ABBEVILLE $90.00

E. **Letta**
Pontormo, Rosso Fiorentino
1-87835-148-6 RIVERSIDE PB $12.99

Salvatore S. **Nigro**
Pontormo: Paintings and Frescoes
0-8109-3727-1 ABRAMS $75.00

David **Franklin**
Rosso in Italy: The Italian Career of Rosso Fiorentino
An account of the life and work of a crucial figure among the mannerists, illustrated with some of the most powerful works of the Renaissance
0-300-05893-4 YALE $60.00

John **Shearman**
Mannerism
Considers a wide variety of works and elucidates the genesis and significance of the term "mannerism"; numerous illustrations
0-14-020808-9 VIKING PB $10.00

Northern Europe

Michael **Baxandall**
The Limewood Sculptors of Renaissance Germany, 1475-1525
A critically acclaimed cultural study of three generations of sculptors
0-300-02423-1 YALE $75.00
0-300-02829-6 YALE PB $27.00

Thomas **DaCosta Kaufmann**
The School of Prague: Painting at the Court of Rudolph II
Mannerism under Rudolf II, its sources and influence on later Dutch developments; numerous reproductions
0-226-42727-7 CHICAGO $54.00

Martin **Davies**
The Early Netherlandish School
0-300-06184-6 YALE PB $22.50

Colin **Eisler**

Early Netherlandish Painting

Masterpieces from the Thysser-Bornemisza Collection, including works by Petrus Christus, Hans Memling, and Rogier van der Weyden, beautifully illustrated

0-85667-353-6 SOTHEBY PARKE BERNET $145.00

Eugene **Fromentin**

The Masters of Past Time: Dutch and Flemish Painting from Van Eyck to Rembrandt

Interesting and opinionated critical survey by a 19th-century painter

0-7148-3361-4 PHAIDON PB $14.95

Walter S. **Gibson**

Mirror of the Earth: The World Landscape in 16th-Century Flemish Painting

0-691-04054-0 PRINCETON $72.50

John **Hand** & others

The Age of Bruegel: Netherlandish Art of the 16th Century

A lavishly illustrated catalog assembled by four renowned scholars

0-521-34196-5 CAMBRIDGE $100.00

Joseph Leo **Koerner**

The Moment of Self-Portraiture in German Renaissance Art

An important, if somewhat self-consciously monumental, study

0-226-44999-8 CHICAGO PB $34.95

James **Marrow**

The Golden Age of Dutch Manuscript Painting

0-8076-1227-8 BRAZILLER $65.00

Keith **Moxey**

Peasants, Warriors and Wives: Popular Imagery in the Reformation

An exercise in the social history of art

0-226-54391-9 CHICAGO $35.95

Maurits **Smeyers** & Jan **Van Der Stock**, editors

Flemish Illuminated Manuscripts, 1475-1550

At a time when printed books, woodcuts, and copper engravings were gaining in popularity, many still coveted hand-painted illuminated manuscripts. This lavish volume documents a period when Flemish miniature painting flourished as never before, with masterful effects of light and shadow offering a new realism, and margins sprinkled with trompe l'oeil flowers and insects

0-8109-6318-3 ABRAMS $60.00

James **Snyder**

Northern Renaissance Art: Painting, Sculpture, and the Graphic Arts from 1350 to 1575

A strong survey of major, and some minor, developments, with excellent reproductions

0-13-623596-4 PRENTICE HALL $64.00

Roy **Strong**

The Cult of Elizabeth: Elizabethan Portraiture and Pageantry

With 94 black-and-white photos and four color plates

See also **THE REFORMATION THROUGH THE REIGN OF ELIZABETH I** under **THE TUDORS: 1485-1603** under **GREAT BRITAIN AND IRELAND** in **WORLD HISTORY AND CURRENT AFFAIRS**

0-520-05840-2 CALIFORNIA $55.00
0-520-05841-0 CALIFORNIA PB $18.95

Individual Artists

Christopher S. **Wood**

Albrecht Altdorfer and the Origins of Landscape

0-226-90601-9 CHICAGO $65.00

Walter **Gibson**

Bosch

A compact survey emphasizing the iconography, literary sources, and cultural significance of the visionary Flemish painter. "Probably the best straightforward account of Bosch and his works we shall have for some time"—*TLS*

0-500-20134-X THAMES & HUDSON PB $14.95

Jacqueline **Guillaud** & Maurice **Guillaud**

Bosch: The Garden of Earthly Delights

Another beautiful volume from the Guillauds, printed on onionskin, with hundreds of details of Bosch's great work

0-517-57230-3 CLARKSON POTTER $100.00

Carl **Linfert**

Bosch

A beautifully illustrated account of Bosch's work, stressing visual impact rather than iconographic interpretation

0-8109-0043-2 ABRAMS $22.95

Walter **Gibson**

Bruegel

A compact and well illustrated critical introduction and biography of the Flemish master cherished for his charming and enigmatic peasant paintings

0-500-18159-4 NORTON $19.95

Arthur **Klein**, editor

The Graphic Worlds of Pieter Bruegel: 64 Engravings and a Woodcut

0-486-21132-0 DOVER PB $13.95

Willi **Kurth**

The Complete Woodcuts of Albrecht Durer

0-486-21097-9 DOVER PB $12.95

Erwin **Panofsky**

The Life and Art of Albrecht Durer

"Here is the life, the times, the works of that extraordinary artist whose genius bridged the difficult transition from medieval to Renaissance, effected a union between Mediterranean and northern concepts, and met the challenge of new processes with a magnificence that has never been equaled" —*Kenyon Review*

0-691-00303-3 PRINCETON PB $35.00

Walter **Strauss**, editor

The Complete Engravings, Etchings and Drypoints of Albrecht Durer

0-486-22851-7 DOVER PB $13.95

P. **Strieder**

Albrecht Durer: Drawings, Prints, and Paintings

0-89835-057-3 ABARIS $95.00

Heinrich **Wölfflin**

Drawings of Durer

0-486-22352-3 DOVER PB $10.95

Linda **Seidel**

Jan Van Eyck's Arnolfini Portrait: Stories of an Icon

0-521-43125-5 CAMBRIDGE $65.00

W. L. **Gundersheimer**, editor

The Dance of Death: 41 Woodcuts by Hans Holbein the Younger

A complete facsimile of the 1538 French edition

0-486-22804-5 DOVER PB $6.95

Hans **Holbein**

Holbein Portrait Drawings: 44 Plates

0-486-24937-9 DOVER PB $4.95

Ellen **Jacobowitz** & Stephanie **Stepanek**

Prints of Lucas Van Leyden and His Contemporaries

0-691-03853-8 PRINCETON $95.00

Elise Lawton **Smith** & Lucas **Van Leyden**

The Paintings of Lucas Van Leyden: A New Appraisal, With Catalogue Raisonné

0-8262-0824-X MISSOURI $59.95

Dirk **De Vos**

Hans Memling: The Complete Oeuvre

0-8109-3649-6 ABRAMS $145.00

Maryan **Ainsworth**

Petrus Christus: Renaissance Master of Bruges

0-8109-6482-1 METROPOLITAN MUSEUM $60.00

European Art: Baroque and Rococo

Germain **Bazin**

Baroque and Rococo

The stylistic currents in the arts of western Europe, from 1600 through 1760. A fast-faced illustrated survey by the Louvre

See also THAMES & HUDSON WORLD OF ART under ART HISTORY: GENERAL STUDIES

0-500-20018-1 THAMES & HUDSON PB $14.95

Julius **Held** & Donald **Posner**

17th and 18th-Century Art: Baroque Painting, Sculpture and Architecture

A deft, thorough survey with over 1000 illustrations in color and black-and-white, by two major scholars, covering the art of Italy, France, Spain, and the Netherlands

0-13-807339-2 PRENTICE HALL $60.95

Michael **Levey**

The Seventeenth and Eighteenth Century Italian Schools

0-300-06142-0 YALE PB $25.00

The Baroque in Italy

Jennifer **Montagu**

Alessandro Algardi

A definitive monograph on the work of Bernini's chief competitor

0-300-03173-4 YALE $130.00

Charles **Scribner**

Gianlorenzo Bernini

0-8109-3111-7 ABRAMS $22.95

Bernini

Giovanni **Careri**

Bernini: Flights of Love, The Art of Devotion

TRANSLATED BY LINDA LAPPIN

0-226-09272-0 CHICAGO $39.95
0-226-09273-9 CHICAGO PB $16.95

Howard **Hibbard**

Bernini

An excellent introduction to Bernini's extraordinary fusion of sculpture and architecture

See also ITALY under BAROQUE AND ROCOCO under EUROPEAN ARCHITECTURE TO 1900 in ARCHITECTURE, DESIGN, AND HOMES

0-14-020701-5 PENGUIN PB $12.00

John **Gash**

Caravaggio

0-8478-5762-X RIZZOLI PB $7.95

Howard **Hibbard**

Caravaggio

A psychological reading of his life and work; a lucid and well-composed study

0-06-430128-1 ICON PB $30.00

Alfred **Moir**

Caravaggio

Individual entries on 45 color plates, as well as a biographical essay

0-8109-0757-7 ABRAMS $45.00

Charles **Dempsey**

Annibale Carracci: The Farnese Gallery, Rome

0-8076-1316-9 BRAZILLER $25.00

Peitro **da Cortona**

The Anatomical Plates of Pietro da Cortona

0-486-25081-4 DOVER PB $7.95

John **Spike**

Giuseppe Maria Crespi and the Emergence of Genre Painting in Italy

The works by the most innovative Bolognese painter of the first half of the 18th century and his contemporaries, elegantly displayed in this fine exhibition catalog; 50 full-page color plates

0-295-96529-0 WASHINGTON PB $24.95

Sydney **Freedberg**

Circa 1600: A Revolution of Style in Painting

An accessible account of the shift in style from mannerism to baroque, notable for its sustained attention to individual works and the careers of Annibale Carracci, Caravaggio, and Ludovico Carracci

0-674-13156-8 BELKNAP PB $23.50

Mary **Garrard**

Artemisia Gentileschi: The Female Hero in Italian Baroque Art

Perhaps the most important woman artist before the modern period, discussed in the first full-length study. Much is made of her unique representations of the female hero—Susanna, Judith, Lucretia, Cleopatra

See also ART AND PHOTOGRAPHY under ARTS AND LETTERS under WOMEN'S STUDIES in SOCIAL STUDIES

0-691-04050-8 PRINCETON $110.00

Michael **Russell** & Francis **Helston**

Guercino in Britain: Paintings from British Collections

0-947645-98-5 NATIONAL GALLERY PB $14.95

David M. **Stone**

Guercino, Master Draftsman: Works from North American Collections

88-7779-263-9 FOGG $45.00

Francis **Haskell**

Patrons and Painters: A Study in the Relations Between Italian Art and Society in the Age of the Baroque

A social history of art

See also COLLECTORS AND DEALERS under ART HISTORY: GENERAL STUDIES

0-300-02537-8 YALE $70.00
0-300-02540-8 YALE PB $25.00

Christopher M.S. **Johns**

Papal Art and Cultural Politics: Rome in the Age of Clement XI

0-521-41639-6 CAMBRIDGE $80.00

Margaretha Rossholm **Lagerlof**

Ideal Landscape: Annibale Carracci, Nicolas Poussin and Claude Lorrain

0-300-04763-0 YALE $50.00

Louis **Marin**

To Destroy Painting

A study of Caravaggio and Poussin which draws on semiotics and psychoanalysis

See also THEORY under ART HISTORY: GENERAL STUDIES

TRANSLATED BY METTE HJORT

0-226-50534-0 CHICAGO $39.95
0-226-50535-9 CHICAGO PB $15.95

Jennifer **Montagu**

Gold, Silver and Bronze: Metal Sculpture of the Roman Baroque

0-691-02736-6 PRINCETON $59.50

Roman Baroque Sculpture

A look at the physical, social, economic, and industrial world of the great sculptors of the Roman baroque. "A rich and witty book, food for thought in more ways than one. In it baroque sculptors appear less as master theologians and more as real men trying to make both a living and art in a complicated world"
—Joseph Connors, *NY Review of Books*

0-300-04392-9 YALE $50.00
0-300-05366-5 YALE PB $30.00

Anthony **Colantuono**

Guido Reni's Abduction of Helen: The Politics and Rhetoric of Painting in Seventeenth-Century Europe

0-521-56397-6 CAMBRIDGE $25.01

Carlo C. **Malvasia**

The Life of Guido Reni

0-271-00264-6 PENN STATE $28.50

Nicola **Spinosa**

Jusepe De Ribera: 1591-1652

Known for the stunning and uncompromising realism of his work, Ribera influenced such artists as Velazquez and Manet. The complete catalog to a recent comprehensive exhibition includes 100 full-color illustrations

0-8109-6416-3 ABRAMS $60.00

Jonathan **Scott**

Salvator Rosa: His Life and Times

0-300-06416-0 YALE $60.00

Elizabeth **Cropper**

Pietro Testa, 1612-1650: Prints & Drawings

0-8122-7960-3 PENNSYLVANIA $49.95

Hermann **Voss**

Baroque Painting in Rome

Volume I
Caravaggio, Carracci, Domenichino and Their Followers, 1585-1640

1-55660-187-5 ALAN WOFSY FINE ARTS $125.00

Volume II
The High and Late Baroque, Rococo and Early Neoclassicism, 1620-1790

1-55660-258-8 ALAN WOFSY FINE ARTS $125.00

Rudolf **Wittkower**

Art and Architecture in Italy, 1600-1750

A first-rate survey; composed by a master scholar of Italian painting, sculpture, and architecture

See also **THE PELICAN HISTORY OF ART** under **ART HISTORY: GENERAL STUDIES**

0-300-05306-1 YALE $60.00
0-300-05308-8 YALE PB $27.50

Italian Rococo

Filippo **Pedrocco**

Canaletto and the Venetian Vedutisti

1-87835-149-4 RIVERSIDE PB $12.99

Terisio **Piganati**

Canaletto: Drawings

0-271-00105-4 PENN STATE $125.00

Antonio **Canaletto**

Drawings

Includes 47 works

0-486-26647-8 DOVER PB $3.95

Michael **Levey**

Painting in Eighteenth-Century Venice

An introduction to 18th-century Venetian painting—portraits, genre paintings, landscapes, history paintings, and religious works—and to the society, patronage, and intellectual climate of the period

0-300-06057-2 YALE PB $20.00

George **Knox**

Giambattista Piazzetta, 1682-1754

0-19-817393-8 OXFORD $150.00

Andrew **Robison**, editor

The Glory of Venice: Art in the Eighteenth Century

A sumptuous examination of the whole range of the arts in Venice, including paintings, pastels and gouaches, drawings, watercolors, prints, books, sculpture, and monumental furniture, by a group of leading scholars

0-300-06185-4 YALE $60.00

Giovanni Battista **Tiepolo**

Drawings

Forty-four plates

0-486-25366-X DOVER PB $3.95

Svetlana **Alpers** & Michael **Baxandall**

Tiepolo and the Pictorial Intelligence

A discussion of the peculiarities of the medium of painting, by way of an analysis of Tiepolo's distinctive modes of representation. Both art criticism and a practical polemic, it includes a list of Tiepolo paintings that can still be seen in the places for which he painted them

0-300-05978-7 YALE $55.00
0-300-06817-4 YALE PB $27.50

Michael **Levey**

Giambattista Tiepolo: His Life and Art

The career of the 18th-century Venetian painter and decorative artist. "As an aid to seeing and enjoying Tiepolo this book will surely become a classic"—Deborah Howard, *Art History*

0-300-06046-7 YALE PB $30.00

Baroque and Rococo in France

Anthony **Blunt**

Art and Architecture in France, 1500-1700

A good introduction, written by the authority on Poussin; stresses the Italian influence on the development of early French art

See also **FRANCE** under **BAROQUE AND ROCOCO** under **EUROPEAN ARCHITECTURE TO 1900** in **ARCHITECTURE, DESIGN, AND HOMES**

See also **THE PELICAN HISTORY OF ART** under **ART HISTORY: GENERAL STUDIES**

0-300-05314-2 YALE PB $25.00

Philip **Conisbee**

Chardin

An agile discussion, taking both contemporary painting and the development of art criticism as a literary genre into account; with excellent reproductions

0-8387-5091-5 BUCKNELL $75.00

Chardin

Marianne **Roland Michel**

Chardin

A beautiful book that brings to light a wealth of new material on this seminal figure in French still-life painting, including paintings newly discovered within the last decade

0-8109-4041-8 ABRAMS $125.00

Pierre **Rosenberg**

Chardin

Exhibition catalog by the Louvre curator; works discussed chronologically and represented by many fine reproductions, including superb details

0-8478-1350-9 RIZZOLI PB $25.00

Claude Lorrain

Claude Lorrain: The Paintings—The Catalogue Raisonné

0-87817-244-0 HACKER $100.00

Jules **de Goncourt** & Edmond **de Goncourt**

French Eighteenth-Century Painters

See also **CRITICS AND WRITERS ON ART** under **ART HISTORY: GENERAL STUDIES**

0-7148-3362-2 PHAIDON PB $14.95

Jean Montague **Massengale**

Fragonard

0-8109-3313-6 ABRAMS $22.95

Michael **Fried**

Absorption and Theatricality: Painting and the Beholder in the Age of Diderot

An original interpretation of the evolution of painting in France from the mid-18th century; paintings are viewed in the light of the art criticism of the time

0-226-26213-8 CHICAGO PB $17.95

Pierre **Rosenberg** & Jacques **Thuillier**

Laurent de La Hyre

0-8478-5530-9 RIZZOLI $75.00

Philip **Conisbee**, editor

Georges de la Tour and His World

0-300-06948-0 YALE $50.00

Jacques **Thuillier**

Georges de la Tour

2-08-013524-4 ABBEVILLE $90.00

Michel **Gareau** & Lydia **Beauvais**

Charles le Brun: First Painter to King Louis XIV

0-8109-3567-8 ABRAMS $85.00

Jennifer **Montagu**

The Expression of the Passions: The Origin and Influence of Charles le Brun's "Conference sur L'Expression Generale et Particulière"

In 1688 Charles Le Brun, a French academician, delivered a lecture on facial expression that was so popular it was published in 63 separate editions and influenced artists throughout Europe for over a century. This book reconstructs the text and its accompanying images and explores the context in which the treatise was conceived, received, and finally rejected

0-300-05891-8 YALE $50.00

Michael **Levey**

Painting and Sculpture in France, 1700-1789

A brilliant survey of the vast outpouring of creative activity and inspired patronage that marked the last years of France's *ancien régime*

See also **THE PELICAN HISTORY OF ART** under **ART HISTORY: GENERAL STUDIES**

0-300-06494-2 YALE PB $30.00
0-300-05344-4 YALE $60.00

Rococo to Revolution: Major Trends in 18th-Century Painting

Stylistic developments from Watteau's roots in the rococo to the revolutionary ideals of David, Gros, and Goya

0-500-20050-5 THAMES & HUDSON PB $14.95

Louis **Marin**

Portrait of the King

The image and symbols of royalty from an historian and semiotician

See also **EARLY MODERN FRANCE** under **EARLY MODERN EUROPE** in **WORLD HISTORY AND CURRENT AFFAIRS**

TRANSLATED BY MARTHA M. HOULE

0-8166-1603-5 MINNESOTA $39.95

Andrew **McClellan**

Inventing the Louvre: Art, Politics, and the Origins of the Modern in 18th-Century Paris

0-521-45065-9 CAMBRIDGE $65.00

Alain **Merot**

French Painting in the Seventeenth Century

Merot explores this diverse and fruitful period of French art. Approximately 200 color plates and 150 black-and-white illustrations of works by Poussin, La Tour, and Vouet, among many others

0-300-06550-7 YALE $65.00

Pinkney L. **Near**

Three Masters of Landscape: Fragonard, Robert, and Boucher

0-917046-11-0 VIRGINIA MUSEUM PB $3.95

Hal **Opperman**

Jean Baptiste Oudry, 1686-1755

One of the greatest French painters of hunting, animal, and still-life subjects, particularly those with game

0-912804-11-4 WASHINGTON $50.00

Anthony **Blunt**

Poussin

Though somewhat outdated, this major scholarly monograph by a scrupulous art historian is still the most comprehensive account of Poussin's career and work

1-87342-964-9 BOYDELL & BREWER PB $45.00

Martin **Clayton**

Poussin: Works on Paper

0-500-23700-X THAMES & HUDSON $65.00

Nicolas Poussin

Elizabeth **Cropper** & Charles **Dempsey**

Nicolas Poussin: Friendship and the Love of Painting

A look at the painter's friends and possibly intellectual contacts in Rome by two scholars who have long been involved with his work

0-691-04449-X PRINCETON $95.00

Richard **Verdi**

Nicolas Poussin, 1594-1665

The catalogue to the great 1995 retrospective

0-302-00647-8 ZWEMMER $70.00

Donald **Posner**

Watteau

An interpretive study, covering the "Flemish Watteau" of early genre pieces through his theatrical productions and later *fetes galantes* paintings; beautiful reproductions

0-8014-1571-3 CORNELL $90.00

Humphrey **Wine**

Watteau

1-85759-000-7 SCALA $9.95

The Baroque in Spain

Jonathan **Brown** & John **Elliot**

A Palace for a King: The Buon Retiro and the Court of Philip IV

This baroque palace outside Madrid originally housed a collection of over 800 paintings, commissioned from the likes of Velazquez, Zurbaran, Rubens, Poussin, and Claude Lorrain. Art historian and historian collaborate to portray the political and cultural life of the Spanish court

0-300-03621-3 YALE PB $27.50

Jay **Levenson**, editor

The Age of the Baroque in Portugal

The first major work in English devoted to the 18th-century golden age for the visual arts in Portugal, a time when the discovery of fabulous deposits of gold, diamonds, and emeralds in Brazil made Portugal's court the wealthiest in Europe

0-300-05841-1 NATIONAL GALLERY OF ART $65.00

Suzanne L. **Stratton**

The Immaculate Conception in Spanish Art

0-521-41437-7 CAMBRIDGE $60.00

Jonathan **Brown**

Diego de Velazquez: Painter and Courtier

Velazquez the courtier, official of the royal household of Philip IV, in conflict with Velazquez the artist searching for a new approach to the art of painting. A stunning book by the leading English authority

0-300-03466-0 YALE $75.00
0-300-03894-1 YALE PB $35.00

Steven N. **Orso**

Velazquez, Los Borrachos, and Painting at the Court of Philip IV

0-521-44452-7 CAMBRIDGE $75.00

Maurice **Serullaz**

Velazquez

A suggestive essay on Velazquez' complex realism, comments on his drawings, and superlative annotated illustrations individually discussed

0-8109-1712-2 ABRAMS $22.95

Jonathan **Brown**

Francisco de Zurbaran

0-8109-3962-2 ABRAMS $22.95

Diego de Velazquez

Flanders and the Netherlands: 1600-1800

Svetlana **Alpers**

The Art of Describing: Dutch Art in the 17th Century

A highly original counterstatement to the view that Dutch imagery is saturated with symbolic meaning; a description of visual culture within which the art of describing, as opposed to the Italian art of narrative, was produced

0-226-01512-2 CHICAGO $51.00
0-226-01513-0 CHICAGO PB $24.95

Christopher **Brown**

The Paintings of Carel Fabritius: Complete Edition with a Catalogue Raisonné

A complete catalog, with a study of the short life and experimental work of perhaps the finest of Rembrandt's pupils and the supposed master of Vermeer

0-8014-1394-X CORNELL $97.50

Zirka **Filipczak**

Picturing Art in Antwerp, 1550-1700

A recent study of art depicting art, with Dutch concepts of self-representation

0-691-04047-8 PRINCETON $73.00

Wayne E. **Franits**

Paragons of Virtue: Women and Domesticity in Seventeenth-Century Dutch Art

0-521-49875-9 CAMBRIDGE PB $24.95

R.H. **Fuchs**

Dutch Painting

A fast-paced survey to the 20th century

0-500-18168-3 THAMES & HUDSON $19.95
0-500-20167-6 NORTON PB $14.95

Bob **Haak**

The Golden Age: Dutch Painters of the 17th Century

An excellent survey placing art within its historic and political context; over 1000 illustrations, many unconventional, discussed individually in great detail

1-55670-484-4 STEWART, TABORI $85.00

Seymour **Slive**

Frans Hals

The definitive volume on the master. "…one of the finest works of scholarship and connoisseurship we have been given in some time… Taste and intelligence of this kind…is…to be applauded"
—Hilton Kramer, *Journal of Art*

3-7913-1032-1 PRESTEL $90.00

Madlyn **Kahr**

Dutch Painting in the 17th Century

A straightforward survey of its most prominent developments

0-06-430219-9 HARPERCOLLINS PB $27.50

James A. **Welu** & Pieter **Biesboer**, editors

Judith Leyster: A Dutch Master and Her World

Judith Leyster (1609-1660) was the most famous woman painter of the Dutch golden age. This book gives new insights into her life and art and discusses the social and economic factors that affected Leyster and other working women in the 17th century

0-300-05564-1 YALE $65.00

Svetlana **Alpers**

Rembrandt's Enterprise: The Studio and the Market

A groundbreaking reading of Rembrandt's relation to his materials, market, and studio

0-226-01514-9 CHICAGO $35.95
0-226-01518-1 CHICAGO PB $19.95

Mieke **Bal**

Reading Rembrandt: Beyond the Word Image Opposition

Not so readable

0-521-46664-4 CAMBRIDGE PB $34.95

David **Bomford** & others

Rembrandt: Art in the Making

0-300-06145-5 YALE PB $30.00

Pascal **Bonafoux**

Rembrandt: Master of the Portrait

0-8109-2813-2 ABRAMS PB $12.95

Jacqueline **Guillaud** & Maurice **Guillaud**

Rembrandt: The Human Form and Spirit

A highly innovative production; meditative texts accompany an abundance of stunning reproductions of works in all media; a visual feast

0-517-56341-X WELLFLEET $39.98

Rembrandt

Ludwig **Munz** & Bob **Haak**

Rembrandt

Recommended for its illustrations, which are accompanied by an introductory text

0-8109-1594-4 ABRAMS $22.95

Gary **Schwartz**

Rembrandt: Complete Etchings

1-55521-188-7 BOOK SALES $24.98

Rembrandt

0-81093-760-3 ABRAMS $19.95

Rembrandt: His Life, His Paintings

A controversial attempt to reconstruct the web of patronage and social affiliations within which Rembrandt worked and, according to Schwartz, failed; close consideration of Rembrandt's character with comprehensive illustration of works

0-67080-876-8 BOOK SALES $25.98

Rembrandt Van Rijn

Bible Drawings

Sixty plates

0-486-23878-4 DOVER PB $3.95

Drawings

0-486-21485-0 DOVER PB $17.95

Landscape Drawings

0-486-24160-2 DOVER PB $3.95

Jakob **Rosenberg**

Dutch Art and Architecture: 1600-1800

Primarily concerned with the 17th century and Rembrandt, Hals, and Vermeer; with numerous black-and-white illustrations

See also **THE PELICAN HISTORY OF ART** under **ART HISTORY: GENERAL STUDIES**

0-300-05312-6 PENGUIN PB $26.50

John **Rowlands**

Hercules Segers

A nicely bound introduction to the work of the greatest experimental etcher of the 17th century, with numerous color reproductions of both his prints and paintings

0-8076-0909-9 BRAZILLER $30.00

Peter Paul **Rubens**

Drawings

Forty-four plates

0-486-25963-3 DOVER PB $4.95

Svetlana **Alpers**

The Making of Rubens

Finding in Rubens's art and life an identifiably modern predicament, Alpers addresses the problems of the relationship between art and national consciousness, art and consumption, and the nature of creativity itself

0-300-06010-6 YALE $35.00
0-300-06744-5 YALE PB $20.00

Peter Paul Rubens

Julius **Held**

The Oil Sketches of Peter Paul Rubens: A Critical Catalogue

A colossal two-volume work defining one of the most exciting aspects of Rubens's artistic production. Exquisite illustrations of these complete preliminary works

0-691-03929-1 PRINCETON $197.50

Richard **McLanathan**

Peter Paul Rubens

0-8109-3780-8 ABRAMS $19.95

Felice **Stampfle**

Rubens and Rembrandt in Their Century

Superb collection of Flemish and Dutch drawings of the 17th century from the Pierpont Morgan Library

0-87598-069-4 PIERPONT MORGANPB $13.95

Martin **Warnke**

Peter Paul Rubens: Life and Work

A modest and essential introduction to the master of the baroque

0-8120-2101-0 BARRONS PB $6.95

Christopher **White**

Peter Paul Rubens: Man and Artist

Scintillating visual and textual presentation of Rubens's career within the international context of the baroque period—a sumptuous volume

0-300-03778-3 YALE $75.00

Simon **Schama**

The Embarrassment of Riches: An Interpretation of Dutch Culture in the Golden Age

A generous illustrated analysis, of interest to students both of art history and social history. "With wit and intense curiosity [Schama] teases out the meaning of every aspect of Dutch 17th-century life, from its ideas about sea monsters to its obsessions with hygiene"—Robert Hughes

See also **THE NETHERLANDS** under **EARLY MODERN EUROPE** in **WORLD HISTORY AND CURRENT AFFAIRS**

0-394-51075-5 KNOPF $39.95

Seymour **Slive**

Dutch Painting, 1600-1800

This lavishly illustrated book, a standard in its field, is a new updated version of the classic *Dutch Art and Architecture: 1600-1800*. Slive has rewritten and expanded the original text, taking into acount recent scholarship. The book is an in-depth exploration of the Dutch Masters, including Hals, Rembrandt, Vermeer, and Ruisdael

See also **THE PELICAN HISTORY OF ART** under **ART HISTORY: GENERAL STUDIES**

0-300-06418-7 YALE $60.00

Wolfgang **Stechow**

Dutch Landscape Painting of the 17th Century

A comprehensive introduction organized by types: Panoramas, Rivers and Canals, The Sea, The Town, and so on. With nearly 400 illustrations

0-87817-268-8 HACKER $60.00
0-8014-9228-9 CORNELL PB $19.95

Peter **Sutton** & others

Masters of 17th-Century Dutch Landscape Painting

A recent exhibition catalog, sumptuously illustrated

0-87846-282-1 MUSEUM OF FINE ARTS PB $24.95

Paul **Taylor**

Dutch Flower Painting, 1600-1720

During the great tulip speculation of 1630 the most desirable tulip bulbs were auctioned for more than the price of a house. This book documents the flower paintings that were purchased by Dutch families as substitutes for the real thing

0-300-05390-8 YALE $45.00

Christopher **Brown**

Van Dyck

An impressive art book, filled with handsome reproductions. Brown maintains that Van Dyck's precociousness, religiosity, and love of court life had a significant influence on the type of pictures he painted and the way he painted them

0-8014-1537-3 CORNELL $55.00

Alfred **Moir**

Anthony Van Dyck

0-8109-3917-7 ABRAMS $22.95

John **Nash**

Vermeer

1-87024-862-7 SCALA $25.00

Edward **Snow**

A Study of Vermeer

0-520-07130-1 CALIFORNIA $45.00
0-520-07132-8 CALIFORNIA PB $25.00

Arthur K. **Wheelock**, Jr.

Vermeer

Beautiful reproductions of all of Vermeer's art accompanied by an essay on Vermeer's life and work by the National Gallery curator

0-8109-1737-8 ABRAMS $22.95

Vermeer and the Art of Painting

With 100 illustrations, Wheelock examines the creative process and technical means by which Vermeer achieved his luminous colors and gradations of reflected light

0-300-06239-7 YALE $45.00

Arthur K. **Wheelock**, Jr., editor

Johannes Vermeer

0-300-06558-2 YALE $45.00

John **Walsh** & Cynthia **Schneider**

A Mirror of Nature: Dutch Paintings from the Collection of Mr. and Mrs. Edward William Carter

A superb collection of cabinet-size Dutch landscape, seascape, still-life, and flower paintings of the highest quality, with many color plates

1-55859-445-0 CROSS RIVER $45.00
0-87587-103-8 L.A. COUNTY MUSEUM PB $19.95

18th-Century England

John **Barrell**

The Political Theory of Painting from Reynolds to Hazlitt

A discussion of how British artists and writers of the late 18th century, including Sir Joshua Reynolds, William Blake, and James Barry, wrestled with the function of painting in a commercial society. "I have learned as much from this book as from any work of art history I know"—Thomas Crow, *London Review of Books*

0-300-06355-5 YALE PB $20.00

John **Hayes**

Drawings of Thomas Gainsborough

A two-volume complete catalog, for general reader and student alike

0-300-01425-2 YALE $125.00

Nicola **Kalinsky** & Thomas **Gainsborough**

Gainsborough

0-7148-3178-6 PHAIDON PB $14.95

David **Bindman**

Hogarth

A lucid and amply illustrated introduction

0-500-18182-9 THAMES & HUDSON $19.95
0-500-20182-X THAMES & HUDSON PB $14.95

Sean **Shesgreen**, editor
The Engravings of Hogarth
The medium through which Hogarth spread his fame as a social satirist
0-486-22479-1 DOVER PB........$19.95

Hogarth

David **Howarth**, editor
Art and Patronage in the Caroline Courts
0-521-43185-9 CAMBRIDGE........$75.00

Lawrence **Gowing**
The Originality of Thomas Jones
0-500-55017-4 THAMES & HUDSON........$12.95

Marcia **Pointon**
Hanging the Head: Portraiture and Social Formation in Eighteenth-Century England
A stimulating demonstration of how portraiture in 18th-century England provided mechanisms both for constructing and accessing a national past and for controlling a present that appeared increasingly unruly
0-300-05738-5 YALE........$70.00

Martin Joseph **Postle**
Sir Joshua Reynolds: The Subject Pictures
0-521-42066-0 CAMBRIDGE........$75.00

Sir Joshua **Reynolds**
Discourses on Art
The 18th-century artist's view of the relation of genius to the classical rules presented in its original form to the Royal Academy
See also **ARTISTS ON ART** under **ART HISTORY: GENERAL STUDIES**
0-300-02775-3 YALE PB........$23.00

David H. **Solkin**
Painting for Money: The Visual Arts and the Public Sphere in Eighteenth-Century England
A discussion of how major developments in English painting went hand in hand with rapid economic expansion and how the rise of the first public spaces for the display of art radically transformed pictorial theory and practice
0-300-05741-5 YALE........$55.00
0-300-06720-8 YALE PB........$30.00

Judy **Egerton**
George Stubbs, 1724-1806
1-85437-187-8 TATE GALLERY........$60.00

Margaret **Whinney**
Sculpture in Britain, 1530-1830
See also **THE PELICAN HISTORY OF ART** under **ART HISTORY: GENERAL STUDIES**
0-300-05318-5 PENGUIN PB........$26.50

Edgar **Wind**
Hume and the Heroic Portrait: Studies in Eighteenth-Century Imagery
0-19-817371-7 OXFORD........$80.00

European Art: 1750-1900

G.C. **Argan** & others
Antonio Canova
0-941419-72-X MARSILIO........$65.00

Rudolph **Binion**
Love Beyond Death: The Anatomy of a Myth in the Arts
From Keats to Whitman, Zola to Flaubert, this heavily illustrated book explores the eroticization of death in the art of the 19th century, and shows how this obsession made its way into current popular culture. Eighty black-and-white illustrations
0-8147-1189-8 NYU........$40.00

Jonathan **Crary**
Techniques of the Observer: On Vision and Modernity in the Nineteenth Century
A much-acclaimed account of a supposed paradigm shift in the conception of vision
0-262-53107-0 MIT PB........$14.95

Henri **Dorra**, editor
Symbolist Art Theories: A Critical Anthology
0-520-07768-7 CALIFORNIA PB........$15.95

Hugh **Honour**
Romanticism
Lavishly illustrated and a good introduction
0-06-430089-7 ICON PB........$17.00

H.W. **Janson**
Nineteenth-Century Sculpture
A comprehensive survey with striking photography
0-8109-1369-0 ABRAMS........$60.00

Linda **Nochlin**
Realism
A pioneering work which defines the mid-century movement throughout Europe
0-14-013222-8 VIKING PB........$12.00

Fritz **Novotny**
Painting and Sculpture in Europe, 1780-1880
See also **THE PELICAN HISTORY OF ART** under **ART HISTORY: GENERAL STUDIES**
0-300-05321-5 YALE PB........$25.00

Maureen **O'Brien**
In Support of Liberty: European Paintings at the 1883 Pedestal Fund Art Loan Exhibition
Re-creation of an influential exhibition held in New York in 1883 to raise money for the pedestal of the Statue of Liberty; includes works by Corot, Courbet, Tissot, and others
0-943526-14-0 PARRISH PB........$25.00

Robert **Rosenblum**
The Romantic Child: From Runge to Sendak
Painting as a mirror of the changing attitudes toward children in the Romantic era
0-500-55020-4 THAMES & HUDSON........$12.95

Transformations in Late 18th-Century Art
Four essays on the background and influence of late-18th-century styles in architecture and painting
0-691-03846-5 PRINCETON........$58.00
0-691-00302-5 PRINCETON PB........$19.95

Robert **Rosenblum** & H.W. **Janson**
Nineteenth-Century Art
The most up-to-date general survey; a massive volume describing the major movements from 1776 to 1900 and their connection with historical events; considers art outside Paris as well. Plenty of illustrations
0-13-622621-3 PRENTICE HALL........$64.00

William **Vaughan**
Romantic Art
A concise and well-illustrated handbook presenting Blake, Friedrich, Goya, and Turner among other artists who, in the late 18th and early 19th centuries, developed an intensely emotional or visionary approach to art
0-500-18160-8 NORTON........$19.95
0-500-20157-9 THAMES & HUDSON PB........$12.95

Romanticism and Art
See also **THAMES & HUDSON WORLD OF ART** under **ART HISTORY: GENERAL STUDIES**
0-500-20275-3 THAMES & HUDSON PB........$14.95

Goya

"[Goya's] importance for the Neo-Baroque Romantic painters of France is well attested by the greatest of them all, Eugene Delacroix, who said that the ideal style would be a combination of Michelangelo's art with Goya's."
—H.W. Janson, *The History of Art*

Jeannine **Baticle**
Goya: Painter of Terrible Splendor
TRANSLATED BY ALEXANDRA CAMPBELL
0-8109-2818-3 ABRAMS PB........$12.95

Ann **Walron**

Francisco Goya

0-8109-3368-3 ABRAMS $19.95

Juliet **Wilson-Bareau**

Goya: Fantasy and Invention

A survey of the small-scale works produced by Goya throughout his career, including his celebrated small portraits, tragicomic paintings of witchcraft and violence, and all the surviving sketches for his tapestry cartoons and major altarpieces

0-300-05863-2 YALE $60.00

Francisco **Goya**

Disasters of War

0-486-21872-4 DOVER PB $8.95

Drawings

Forty-four plates

0-486-25062-8 DOVER PB $4.95

Los Caprichos

0-486-22384-1 DOVER PB $7.95

Perez **Sanchez**

Goya and the Spirit of the Enlightenment

This well-illustrated catalogue to a large and influential traveling exhibition examines the social and political context of Goya's work

0-87846-299-6 BOOK SALES $39.98

Janis **Tomlinson**

Francisco Goya y Lucientes, 1746-1828

0-7148-2912-9 PHAIDON $69.95

Goya in the Twilight of Enlightenment

0-300-05462-9 YALE $50.00

Graphic Evolution: The Print Series of Francisco Goya

0-231-06865-4 COLUMBIA PB $15.00

Germany

Keith **Andrews**

The Nazarenes: A Brotherhood of German Painters in Rome

A study of the early 19th-century movement led by Overbeck and Pforr intended to regenerate German religious art according to late medieval and Renaissance ideals and practice

0-87817-306-4 HACKER $50.00

Keith **Hartley** & Henry Meyric **Hughs,** editors

The Romantic Spirit in German Art: 1790-1990

A group of leading scholars assess the continued importance of the Romantic movement in modern and contemporary German art

0-500-23693-3 THAMES & HUDSON $75.00

Joseph Leo **Koerner**

Caspar David Friedrich and the Subject of Landscape

0-300-06547-7 YALE PB $25.00

Jens Christian **Jensen**

Caspar David Friedrich

An indispensable introduction to the haunting work of the greatest German Romantic artist; brief and lucid

0-8120-2102-9 BARRONS PB $6.95

Sabine **Rewald,** editor

The Romantic Vision of Caspar David Friedrich: Paintings and Drawings from the USSR

A fresh look at some little-known works by the quintessential painter of Romanticism, published in conjunction with New York's Metropolitan Museum of Art

ESSAYS BY ROBERT ROSENBLUM & BORIS ASVARISHCH

0-8109-6402-3 METROPOLITAN MUSEUM PB $22.50

Wieland **Schmie**

Caspar David Friedrich

The catalog from the 1995 exhibition

0-8109-3327-6 ABRAMS $22.95

William **Vaughan**

German Romantic Painting

An account of the role played by painting in Germany in the great cultural revival commonly known as the Romantic Movement, with fresh interpretations of the lives and work of such artists as Friedrich, Runge, Menzel, and the Nazarenes. "By far the most important synthesis of art in Germany in the nineteenth century to appear outside Germany"
—Jon Whiteley, *Art History*

0-300-06047-5 YALE PB $24.00

France

Janis **Bergman-Carton**

The Woman of Ideas in French Art, 1830-1848

A study of visual representations of the "woman of ideas" during a period that marked the first era of revitalized female literary and political activity after the Revolution

0-300-05380-0 YALE $30.00

Kermit S. **Champa**

The Rise of Landscape Painting in France: Corot to Monet

0-8109-2520-6 ABRAMS $29.95

Thomas **Crow**

Emulation: Making Artists for Revolutionary France

The world of French art from David's *Oath of the Horatii* (1785) to Gericault's *Raft of the Medusa* (1819)

0-300-06093-9 YALE $45.00

Painters and Public Life in 18th-Century Paris

A groundbreaking study of the French Academy state patronage, and the public, focusing on David, Greuze, Watteau, and others

0-300-03764-3 YALE PB $26.00

Daniel J. **Sherman**

Worthy Monuments: Art Museums and the Politics of Culture in Nineteenth-Century France

0-674-96230-3 HARVARD $38.50

Harrison C. **White** & Cynthia A. **White**

Canvases and Careers: Institutional Change in the French Painting World

An excellent study of patronage in French art, this book explores the evolution of artistic careers, from the world of the Royal Academy to the fascinating networks of patronage established by the Impressionists

0-226-89487-8 CHICAGO PB $13.95

Richard **Wrigley**

The Origins of French Art Criticism: From the Ancien Regime to the Restoration

0-19-817409-8 CLARENDON PB $32.50

From the Revolution to Impressionism

Susan L. **Siegfried**

The Art of Louis-Leopold Boilly: Modern Life in Napoleonic France

0-300-06332-6 YALE $55.00

Philip **Conisbee** & others

In the Light of Italy: Corot and Early Open-Air Painting

0-300-06794-1 NATIONAL GALLERY OF ART $50.00

Madeleine **Hours**

Corot

A general essay on the master of classically serene lyricism, with commentary on numerous color plates; many drawings and etchings reproduced

0-8109-0796-8 ABRAMS $22.95

Michael **Pantazzi** & others

Corot

0-8109-6501-1 ABRAMS $75.00

Gerard De **Wallens** & Vincent **Pomarede**

Corot: Extraordinary Landscapes

Designed to coincide with a major international Corot exhibition marking the 200th anniversary of the artist's birth, this magnificently illustrated book is filled with vivid descriptions of this renowned French landscape painter's life and art

0-8109-6327-2 ABRAMS PB $12.95

Sarah **Faunce**

Courbet

0-8109-3182-6 ABRAMS $22.95

Michael **Fried**

Courbet's Realism

0-226-26215-4 CHICAGO PB $25.95

Colta **Ives** & Margaret **Stuffmann**

Daumier Drawings

MARTIN SONNABEND

0-8109-6423-6 METROPOLITAN MUSEUM $65.00

Honoré Daumier

Charles **Ramus**, editor

Daumier: 120 Great Lithographs

A good selection of Daumier's incomparable satire and social observation

0-486-23512-2 DOVER PB $10.95

Luc **de Nanteuil**

David

A commendable essay on the career of the versatile neoclassical artist followed by individually discussed color reproductions

0-8109-0833-6 ABRAMS $49.50

Brahim **Alaoui**, editor

Delacroix in Morocco

2-08-013572-4 ABBEVILLE $55.00

Eugene Delacroix

Eugene **Delacroix**

The Journal of Eugene Delacroix

The musings of one of the most intelligent and, most likely, the most literate, painter ever

See also ARTISTS ON ART under ART HISTORY: GENERAL STUDIES

TRANSLATED BY WALTER PACH

0-7148-3359-2 PHAIDON PB $14.95

Lee **Johnson**

Delacroix Pastels

A unique gathering of all the extant pastels of Delacroix, housed in collections that range from Los Angeles to Cairo, and rarely exhibited due to their fragility. Published here in full color, these works are delightful in their own right as well as providing enormous insight into the inventiveness of the artist. Johnson, a preeminent Delacroix scholar and curator, provides a readable introduction and commentary

0-8076-1395-9 BRAZILLER $75.00

Walter **Friedlaender**

David to Delacroix

Traces the fundamental tension underlying 19th-century French painting, the opposing currents of classicism and neobaroque; an elegant and widely acclaimed study

0-674-19401-2 HARVARD PB $14.95

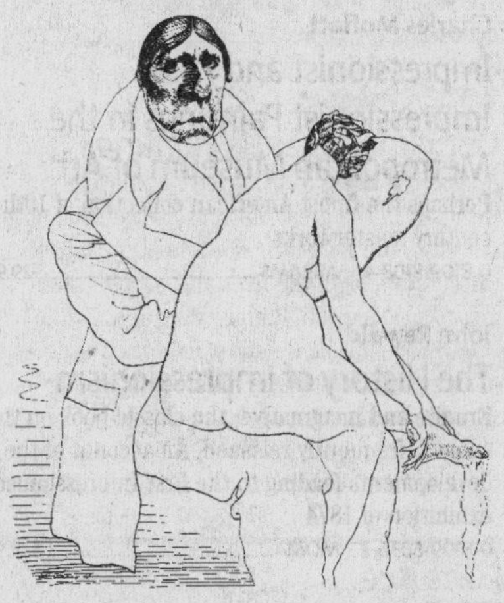

Jean Auguste-Dominique Ingres

Carol **Ockman**

Ingres's Eroticized Bodies

The first full-length feminist and sociohistorical study of Ingre's art, tracing the shift in late 18th-century French art from neoclassical representations of the heroic male, to the sensualized, homoerotic male nude, to the 19th-century emphasis on the female nude

0-300-05961-2 YALE $40.00

Robert **Rosenblum**

Ingres

Introductory essay on Ingres's career and wide diversity of styles followed by individually discussed full color plates

0-8109-0195-1 ABRAMS $49.50

Georges **Vigne**

Ingres

One of the most important and influential artists of the 19th century, French painter Jean Auguste-Dominique Ingres (1780-1867) is brought to life in this sumptuous volume. More than 200 colorplates and a glowing text written by Georges Vigne, curator of the Ingres Museum in Montauban, France, make this book a must for all enthusiasts of great painting

0-7892-0060-0 ABBEVILLE $95.00

Jean-Auguste **Ingres**

Portrait Drawings

Includes 44 works

0-486-27621-X DOVER PB $3.95

John **Elderfield**

The Language of the Body: Drawings by Pierre-Paul Prud'hon

Best known as a painter of mythological and allegorical scenes, French artist Pierre-Paul Prud'hon (1758-1823) also created exquisite chalk studies of nudes called *academies*. This volume is the first comprehesive study of these drawings with a text by John Elderfield, Chief Curator at the Museum of Modern Art, New York City

0-8109-3585-6 ABRAMS $75.00

Aimee Brown **Price**

Pierre Puvis de Chavannes

0-8478-1826-8 RIZZOLI $60.00

Mary D. **Sheriff**

The Exceptional Woman: Elisabeth Vigée-Lebrun and the Cultural Politics of Art

0-226-75275-5 CHICAGO $40.00

Impressionism: General Studies

"Green, violet, flowing pink. In lively, proliferating brushstrokes, light trembling foliage, zigzag reflections on the water, the wakes of fishing boats and yawls. A heightening of colors, almost of the very odors, in the sap-filled orchards. Couples dancing, the close of a meal, streets decked with flags, boulevards swarming with carriages and pedestrians, ballerinas in the glare of theater spotlights, Sunday promenades on the islands of the Seine—such are the themes of Impressionism."
—Pierre Courthion, *Impressionism*

Norma **Broude**

Impressionism: A Feminist Reading: Gendering of Art, Science, Nature in the 19th Century

0-8478-1397-5 RIZZOLI $40.00

T.J. **Clark**

The Painting of Modern Life: Paris in the Art of Manet and His Followers

An acclaimed Marxist scholar imaginatively reconstructs the relation of form to content as conveyed in the works and aesthetics of this "bourgeois style"; with numerous illustrations

0-691-00275-4 PRINCETON PB $22.95

Florence **Coman**

Treasures of Impressionism and Post-Impressionism: National Gallery of Art

1-55859-561-9 ABBEVILLE PB $11.95

Pierre **Courthion**

Impressionism

A great compendium of pictures and an introductory critical text; painters from Turner and Corot to the post-Impressionist period are represented

0-8109-2067-0 ABRAMS PB $14.95

Bernard **Denvir**

The Chronicle of Impressionism: A Timeline History of Impressionist Art

A richly detailed sourcebook captures the cultural and political atmosphere in which Impressionism flourished. Chronicles the major exhibitions, the intense rivalries in the movement, and the enduring lives of the great Impressionist paintings, right up to their coveted place in present-day collections and auctions

0-8212-2042-X BULFINCH $40.00

Bernard **Denvir**, editor

The Thames and Hudson Encyclopedia of Impressionism

See also **THAMES & HUDSON WORLD OF ART** under **ART HISTORY: GENERAL STUDIES**

0-500-20239-7 THAMES & HUDSON PB $11.95

Denis **Farr** & John **House**

Impressionist and Post-Impressionist Masterpieces from the Courtauld Collection

A recent catalog; beautiful reproductions from a spectacular collection. Contains revealing technical analyses

0-300-03891-7 YALE PB $22.00

Frank **Getlein**

25 Impressionist Masterpieces

0-8109-2607-5 ABRAMS PB $14.95

Robert **Herbert**

Impressionism: Art, Leisure and Parisian Society

By one of the leading scholars of Impressionism. The actual context of the movement brilliantly reconstructed, with emphasis on society's relation to artistic practices; handsomely illustrated

0-300-04262-0 YALE $65.00

John **House** & others

Impressionism for England: Samuel Courtauld as Patron and Collector

The story of British industrialist Samuel Courtauld's patronage and collection of French Impressionist and post-Impressionist paintings

0-300-06128-5 YALE $50.00

Diane **Kelder**

The Great Book of French Impressionism

1-55859-336-5 ABBEVILLE PB $11.95

Albert **Kostenevich**

Hidden Treasures Revealed: Impressionist Masterpieces from the Hermitage Museum

0-8109-3432-9 ABRAMS $49.50

Edward **Lucie-Smith**

Impressionist Women

0-89660-039-4 ARTABRAS $19.98

Kenneth **McConkey** & Anna Greutzner **Robins**

Impressionism in Britain

A beautiful book that describes the activities of French Impressionists on their visits to Britain, considers the dissemination of their work through British collectors and dealers, and explores the response to the style by British and Irish artists

0-300-06334-2 YALE $50.00

Charles **Moffett**

Impressionist and Post-Impressionist Paintings in the Metropolitan Museum of Art

Perhaps the finest American collection of 19th-century masterworks

0-8109-8108-4 ABRAMS $29.98

John **Rewald**

The History of Impressionism

Erudite and imaginative; the classic book on the subject, frequently reissued. An account of the developments leading to the first Impressionist exhibition of 1874

0-8109-6036-2 MOMA $29.95

Eric **Shanes**

Impressionist London

1-55859-567-8 ABBEVILLE $40.00

Paul **Smith**

Impressionism: Beneath the Surface

0-8109-2715-2 ABRAMS PB $16.95

Michael **Wilson**

The Impressionists

A beautiful volume that illustrates and explains the Impressionist circle, from its inception in 1861 to its final group exhibition in 1886. With over 180 illustrations, this is an affordable yet exhaustive catalog of a powerful artistic movement

0-7148-2661-8 PHAIDON PB $19.95

Impressionism: Individual Artists

Anne **Distel** & others

Gustave Caillebotte

Offers a glimpse of life in late-19th-century Paris seen through the eyes of a great painter

0-7892-0041-4 ABBEVILLE $65.00
0-86559-129-6 ABBEVILLE $14.95

Kirk **Varnedoe**

Gustave Caillebotte

The catalog to the exhibition that revived the reputation of this exciting pivotal figure of the Impressionist movement; beautifully illustrated

0-300-03722-8 YALE $47.50

Richard **Kendall**, editor

Cézanne by Himself

Cezanne as he presented himself, through his own writings, conversations, drawings, watercolors, and paintings

0-8212-1709-7 BOOK SALES $36.98

Erle **Loran**

Cézanne's Composition

"An understanding of Cézanne's art more essential than any other I have seen in print" —Clement Greenberg

0-520-00768-9 CALIFORNIA $45.00

Pavel **MacHotka**

Cézanne: Landscape into Art

0-300-06701-1 YALE $45.00

John **Rewald**

Cézanne: A Biography

The newest edition of the classic monograph providing a detailed account of Cézanne's great friendship with the critic and writer Emile Zola; complemented by sumptuous color reproductions

0-8109-0775-5 ABRAMS $75.00

William **Rubin**

Cézanne: The Late Work

Catalog of the blockbuster exhibition, with essays by such art historians as Theodore Reff, John Rewald, and William Rubin

0-87070-278-5 NY GRAPHIC $55.00

> "Without knowing it, Cézanne, the timid little conventional man sheltering behind his wife and sister and the Jesuit father, was a pure revolutionary. When he said to his models: 'Be an apple! Be an apple!' he was uttering the foreword to the fall not only of Jesuits and the Christian idealists altogether, but to the collapse of our whole way of consciousness, and the substitution of another way."—D.H. Lawrence, *Phoenix I*

Meyer **Schapiro**

Cézanne

Penetrating psychologizing interpretation of the modern master of color as form; numerous fine reproductions

0-8109-0052-1 ABRAMS $49.50

E. **Schmitt**

Cézanne in Provence

An illustrated survey of the artist's lifelong involvement with the landscape of Provence

3-7913-1451-3 PRESTEL $25.00

Richard **Shiff**

Cézanne and the End of Impressionism

"Shiff's essay has proved to be the most stimulating reevaluation of Impressionism of the last two decades"—Robert Herbert

0-226-75306-9 CHICAGO PB $25.00

Paul Cézanne

0-8478-1755-5 RIZZOLI PB $7.95

Richard **Verdi**

Cézanne

See also **THAMES & HUDSON WORLD OF ART** under **ART HISTORY: GENERAL STUDIES**

0-500-20258-3 THAMES & HUDSON PB $12.95

Paul **Cézanne**

Letters

See also **ARTISTS ON ART** under **ART HISTORY: GENERAL STUDIES**

EDITED BY JOHN REWALD

0-306-80630-4 DA CAPO PB $15.95

Gotz **Adriani**

Cézanne Paintings

0-8109-4026-4 ABRAMS $85.00

Françoise **Cachin** & others

Cézanne

The catalogue to the great 1996 retrospective of the artist's work

0-8109-4039-6 ABRAMS $75.00
0-87633-101-0 MUSEUM GUIDE $42.00

Philip **Callow**

Lost Earth: A Life of Cézanne

"His prose is clear and easy and elegant, his observation sharp but kind and never superficial"—V.S. Naipaul

1-56663-084-3 DEE $30.00

Sidney **Geist**

Interpreting Cézanne

0-674-45955-5 HARVARD $49.50

Lawrence **Gowing**

Paul Cézanne: The Basel Sketchbooks

0-8109-6018-4 MOMA $45.00

Michel **Hoog**

Cézanne: Father of 20th-Century Art

TRANSLATED BY ROSEMARY STONEHEWER

0-8109-2879-5 ABRAMS PB $12.95

Karen **Wilkin**

Paul Cézanne

0-7892-0124-0 ABBEVILLE PB $11.95

Edgar **Degas**

Drawings

0-486-21233-5 DOVER PB $8.95

Jean Sutherland **Boggs**

Degas

A lavish catalog for the recent retrospective exhibition, which includes essays by eminent experts, over 280 color and 440 black & white illustrations

0-8109-6324-8 ABRAMS $19.95

Robert **Gordon** & Andrew **Forge**

Degas

An impressive volume, organized by subject—theater, horses and riders, portraits, dancers, bathers—and magnificently illustrated

0-8109-1142-6 ABRAMS $34.98

Anthea **Callen**

The Spectacular Body: Science, Method, and Meaning in the Work of Degas

An exploration of the ways in which the human body was visualized by artists in late 19th-century Paris, focusing on the work of Degas and discussing issues of gender, sexuality, and visual representation

0-300-05443-2 YALE $50.00

Edgar Degas

Richard **Kendall**

Degas Landscapes

The first comprehensive treatment of Degas's challenging and varied landscapes, their place in his evolving view of art, and their relationship to his better-known subjects

0-300-05837-3 YALE $60.00

Eunice **Lipton**

Looking into Degas: Uneasy Images of Women and Modern Life

An important and nuanced essay dealing with issues of class, sex, and work which resonate in the paintings of Degas

0-520-05604-3 CALIFORNIA $55.00
0-520-06340-6 CALIFORNIA PB $17.00

Henri **Loyrette**

Degas: The Man and His Art

0-8109-2897-3 ABRAMS PB $12.95

Susan E. **Meyer**

Edgar Degas

0-8109-3220-2 ABRAMS $19.95

Theodore **Reff**

Degas: The Artist's Mind

The foremost Degas scholar explores the psychology of creativity

0-674-19543-4 BELKNAP PB $22.50

Denys **Sutton**

Edgar Degas: Life and Work

Elegant presentation, textual and visual, of the times and career of Degas; by the editor of *Apollo*

0-89660-024-6 ARTABRAS $39.98

Richard **Thomson**

Edgar Degas: Waiting

0-89236-323-1 OXFORD PB $15.95

Richard **Kendall**

Degas: Beyond Impressionism

The exhibition catalog

0-300-06979-0 YALE $50.00

Michael **Fried**

Manet's Modernism

0-226-26216-2 CHICAGO $50.00

Francoise **Cachin**

Manet: The Influence of the Modern

0-8109-2892-2 ABRAMS PB $12.95

Pierre **Courthion**

Manet

Introductory text accompanying lavish color plates

0-8109-1318-6 ABRAMS $22.95

Hajo **Duchting**

Edouard Manet: Images of Parisian Life

A finely illustrated book that provides a new and refreshing perspective to the work of the artist whose technique scandalized so many of his contemporaries

3-7913-1452-1 PRESTEL $25.00

Edouard Manet

Alan **Krell**

Manet and the Painters of Contemporary Life

See also **THAMES & HUDSON WORLD OF ART** under **ART HISTORY: GENERAL STUDIES**

0-500-20289-3 THAMES & HUDSON PB $14.95

Robert **Gordon** & Andrew **Forge**

Monet

Thematic organization covering his entire career; with stunning reproductions. "Monet is only an eye—but heavens what an eye!" —Paul Cézanne

0-8109-8091-6 ABRADALE $34.98

Robert L. **Herbert**

Monet on the Normandy Coast: Tourism and Painting, 1867-1886

A magnificently illustrated discussion of how Monet's seascapes of resort areas on the Normandy coast reflect a dialogue between the modern city and pre-modern nature that underlay the rise of tourism

0-300-05973-6 YALE $55.00

John **House**

Monet: Nature into Art

Traces the production of Monet's paintings, with illustrated discussions of light, color, form and the limits of naturalism

0-300-03785-6 YALE $65.00
0-300-04361-9 YALE PB $24.95

Stephan **Koja**

Claude Monet

A color survey of the artist's work, including many rarely seen works from European, American, and Japanese collections

3-7913-1671-0 PRESTEL $65.00

Steven Z. **Levine**

Monet, Narcissus, and Self-Reflection: The Modernist Myth of The Self

0-226-47543-3 CHICAGO $70.00
0-226-47544-1 CHICAGO PB $29.95

Sylvie **Patin**

Monet: The Ultimate Impressionist

0-8109-2883-3 ABRAMS PB $12.95

Karin **Sagner-Duchting**

Monet at Giverny

A beautifully illustrated survey of the works inspired by the area's romantic garden landscapes

3-7913-1384-3 PRESTEL $25.00

William **Seitz**

Monet

Sensitive formal readings of nearly 50 major works, reproduced in color

0-8109-1341-0 ABRAMS $22.95

Virginia **Spate**

Claude Monet: Life and Work

Based on his surviving 3,000 letters and contemporary documentary material, this is "An extraordinary book…a new, original study of the work and times of Claude Monet…a major contribution, it will replace all previous studies"—Linda Nochlin, Professor of Art History, Yale University. 300 illustrations, 135 in color

0-8478-1571-4 RIZZOLI $75.00

Charles F. **Stuckey**

Claude Monet: 1840-1926

The comprehensive catalog to the July 1995 Monet exhibition at the Art Institute of Chicago presents, in full color, 130 of the artist's works drawn front collcctions worldwide

0-500-09246-X THAMES & HUDSON $50.00
0-500-27904-7 THAMES & HUDSON PB $29.95

Paul **Tucker**

Claude Monet

0-300-06298-2 YALE $40.00

Monet at Argenteuil, 1871-1877

Monet's Parisian leisure subjects considered in relation to the spread of industrialization

0-300-02577-7 YALE $45.00
0-300-03206-4 YALE PB $22.50

Monet in the '90s

0-300-04659-6 YALE $55.00
0-300-04913-7 YALE PB $32.00

Paul **Tucker** & Elizabeth **Murray**

Monet: Late Paintings of Giverny from the Musée Marmottan

LYNN FEDERLE ORR

0-8109-2610-5 ABRAMS PB $14.95

Daniel **Wildenstein**

Monet's Years at Giverny: Beyond Impressionism

The consummate achievements of Monet's later period, including *Waterlilies*

0-8109-1336-4 ABRAMS $29.95
0-8109-2183-9 ABRAMS PB $16.95

Anne **Higonnet**

Berthe Morisot's Images of Women

Morisot has recently taken her place alongside Cassat and Renoir as one of the founders of Impressionism. Skillfully combining social history, art criticism, and psychological insights, the author shows how the artist's attempts to represent the experience of daily life led her to rethink the role of women in 19th-century society. Especially moving are Morisot's female nudes, and her pictorial exploration of the mother-daughter relationship. Twelve color illustrations, 111 halftones.

0-674-06798-3 HARVARD $49.95

Christopher **Lloyd**

Pissarro

Exquisite reproductions accompanied by basic introductory text

0-7148-2729-0 PHAIDON PB $14.95

Joachim **Pissarro**

Camille Pissarro

An engaging look at the oldest Impressionist that reveals a ceaselessly experimental and innovative painter, not at all the follower that some art historians have portrayed. 205 color and 149 black-and-white images with commentary by the artist's great-grandson, a graduate of the Sorbonne and a noted expert on Pissarro's life and work

0-8109-3724-7 ABRAMS $75.00

Camille Pissarro

Richard R. **Brettell**

The Impressionist and the City: Pissarro's Series Paintings

0-300-05350-9 YALE $55.00

Pissarro and Pontoise

0-300-04336-8 YALE $55.00

Steven **Kern**

A Passion for Renoir: Sterling and Francine Clark Collect, 1916-1951

This is the first study published on Robert Sterling Clark's renowned Renoir collection, assembled between 1916 and 1951. It includes insightful and informative essays by a group of distinguised art historians along with 33 splendid full-page color plates

0-8109-3746-8 ABRAMS $35.00

Walter **Pach**

Renoir

A good visual introduction with basic critical text, recommended for its excellent reproductions

0-8109-1593-6 ABRAMS $22.95

Alfred Sisley

0-300-05244-8 YALE $35.00

Post-Impressionism

Charles **Chadwick**

Symbolism

The earliest scholarly attempt to come to terms with a central tendency in early modern art

0-06-430095-1 ICON PB $33.75

Herschel **Chipp**, editor

Theories of Modern Art: A Source Book by Artists and Critics

A rich selection of letters, manifestoes, reviews, interviews, and other writings related to the study of modern art, from Cézanne to the mid-20th century

See also **GENERAL** under **20TH-CENTURY ART**

0-520-05256-0 CALIFORNIA PB $17.95

Bernard **Denvir**

Post-Impressionism

See also **THAMES & HUDSON WORLD OF ART** under **ART HISTORY: GENERAL STUDIES**

0-500-20255-9 THAMES & HUDSON PB $12.95

Françoise **Cachin**

Gauguin: The Quest for Paradise

0-8109-2800-0 ABRAMS PB........$12.95

Paul **Gauguin**

Noa Noa: The Tahiti Journal of Paul Gauguin

A marvelous publication—handsomely produced, exquisitely illustrated—of Gauguin's written diary and the woodblock prints and sketches the author made to accompany the text. A true delight

See also **ARTISTS ON ART** under **ART HISTORY: GENERAL STUDIES**

INTRODUCTION BY SOMERSET MAUGHAM

0-8118-0366-X CHRONICLE........$17.95

0-486-24859-3 DOVER PB........$3.95

Robert **Goldwater**

Gauguin

A classic study, with commendable reproductions

0-8109-0983-9 ABRAMS........$22.95

Eckhard **Hollmann**

Paul Gauguin: Noa Noa Images from the South Seas

A lavishly illustrated assessment of the artist's Tahitian period paintings, his living conditions, and his writings that casts fresh light on the French painter's self-dramatizing role as artistic rebel and outsider

3-7913-1673-7 PRESTEL........$25.00

Belinda **Thomson**

Gauguin

A handy critical introduction, with numerous illustrations

0-500-20220-6 THAMES & HUDSON PB........$11.95

Howard **Greenfeld**

Paul Gauguin

0-8109-3376-4 ABRAMS........$19.95

Jane **Kinsman** & others

Paris in the 1890s

Based on works from both the Musée d'Orsay and the National Gallery of Australia, this book surveys what emerged from, or was drawn to Paris as a center of artistic, cultural, and intellectual life at the close of the last century

0-500-97440-3 THAMES & HUDSON PB........$24.95

Sven **Loevgren**

The Genesis of Modernism: Seurat, Gauguin, Van Gogh, and French Symbolism in the 1880s

A well-informed account of the early avant-garde movement in its broader artistic context

0-87817-280-7 HACKER........$40.00

Patricia **Mainardi**

The End of the Salon: Art and State in the Early Third Republic

0-521-46921-X CAMBRIDGE PB........$19.95

Pierre-Louis **Mathieu**

The Symbolist Generation

0-8478-1218-9 RIZZOLI........$50.00

John **Milner**

The Studios of Paris: The Capital of Art in the Late Nineteenth Century

The art world of the grand boulevards—Saint Germain, St. Michel, Montparnasse—the Latin Quarter, the Ecole des Beaux Arts. "A wonderfully evocative history of the quasi-official art industry in Paris during the years of its full flowering"—*New Yorker*

0-300-04749-5 YALE PB........$28.00

Paul Gauguin

Stephen F. **Eisenman**

The Temptation of Saint Redon: Biography, Ideology, and Style in the Noirs of Odilon Redon

0-226-19548-1 CHICAGO........$60.00

Odilon **Redon**

To Myself: Notes on Life, Art and Artists

The journals of the French Symbolist painter noted for his delicate, mysterious watercolors

See also **ARTISTS ON ART** under **ART HISTORY: GENERAL STUDIES**

0-8076-1146-8 BRAZILLER PB........$14.95

John **Rewald**

Post-Impressionism: From Van Gogh to Gauguin

Companion volume to his renowned *History of Impressionism* and a classic in its own right; covers the period from 1886 to Cézanne's death

0-87070-532-6 NY GRAPHIC........$60.00

Studies in Post-Impressionism

A collection of important and ambitious essays

0-8109-1632-0 ABRAMS........$39.95

Robert **Herbert**

Seurat: 1859-1891

The companion volume to the overwhelmingly successful Metropolitan Museum of Art show on the career of pointillism's founder. A compelling examination of the artist's brief life, embodying a generation's thoughts and scholarship on his work. Includes 325 illustrations, 240 in color

0-8109-6410-4 ABRAMS........$70.00

John **Rewald**

Seurat: A Biography

Long out of print, Rewald's classic biography of the pointillist master who died at 31 has now been reissued in an edition featuring 118 full-color reproductions of Seurat's major works

0-8109-8124-6 ABRAMS........$34.98

John **Russell**

Seurat

An engaging critical introduction, with numerous illustrations, by the *New York Times* art critic

0-500-20032-7 THAMES & HUDSON PB........$14.95

Russell **Ash**

James Tissot

Tissot used a bright impressionist palette to depict scenes of social life

0-8109-3864-2 ABRAMS........$29.95

Michael **Wentworth**

James Tissot

A scholarly consideration of his career and influences

0-912964-07-3 MINNEAPOLIS INSTITUTE PB........$20.00

Gotz **Adriani**

Toulouse-Lautrec

A well-illustrated study of the great painter of bohemian Paris

0-500-09188-9 THAMES & HUDSON........$60.00

Douglas **Cooper**

Toulouse-Lautrec

A lucid and well-illustrated introduction, with many individually discussed color plates

0-8109-1678-9 ABRAMS........$22.95

Bernard **Denvir**

Toulouse-Lautrec

See also **THAMES & HUDSON WORLD OF ART** under **ART HISTORY: GENERAL STUDIES**

0-500-20250-8 THAMES & HUDSON PB........$12.95

Claire **Frechhes** & Jose **Frechhes**

Toulouse-Lautrec: Scenes of the Night

0-8109-2863-9 ABRAMS PB........$12.95

Julia **Frey**

Toulouse-Lautrec: A Life

0-670-80844-X VIKING........$34.95

Patrick **O'Connor**

Nightlife of Paris: The Art of Toulouse-Lautrec

A history of steamy, haunting *fin-de-siécle* Paris and its chief chronicler, post-Impressionist Henri de Toulouse-Lautrec. Here are rare photographs of the artist and the circuses, theaters, brothels, and dance halls that inspired him, as well as 32 full-color reproductions of his paintings, drawings, and lithographs. Contemporary documents and selections from Toulouse-Lautrec's correspondence augment the text

0-87663-622-9 UNIVERSE........$25.95

Wolfgang **Wittrock**

Toulouse-Lautrec: The Complete Prints

0-85667-192-4 SOTHEBY PARKE BERNET
2 VOLUME BOXED SET $295.00

Henri de Toulouse-Lautrec

Sasha M. **Newman** & others

Felix Vallotton

0-89467-057-3 ARTHUR SCHWARTZ PB $36.00

Vincent **van Gogh**

Drawings

0-486-25485-2 DOVER PB $4.95

W.H. **Auden**, editor

Van Gogh: A Self-Portrait, Letters Revealing His Life as a Painter

1-56924-862-1 MARLOWE PB $12.00

Pascal **Bonafoux**

Van Gogh: The Passionate Eye

0-8109-2828-0 ABRAMS PB $12.95

Alfred **Nemeczek**

Van Gogh in Arles

On his first visit to this region of Provence, Van Gogh was stunned by its color, light, and landscape. He returned later and remained there until his death

3-7913-1484-X TE NEUS $25.00

Meyer **Schapiro**

Van Gogh

A classic and informative study of the man, his work, and troubled life; many fine color reproductions

0-8109-0524-8 ABRAMS $22.95

Vincent **van Gogh**

The Letters of Vincent van Gogh

See also **ARTISTS ON ART** under **ART HISTORY: GENERAL**

STUDIES
EDITED BY RONALD DE LEEUW
TRANSLATED BY ARNOLD POMERANS
0-7139-9135-6 PENGUIN $32.95
0-689-70167-5 ATHENEUM PB $10.95

Gloria Lynn **Groom**

Edouard Vuillard: Painter-Decorator, Patrons and Projects, 1892-1912

Vuillard is known primarily for his intimate easel paintings that capture the charm and mystery of everyday life, but he was also commissioned to create a number of large-scale canvases, panels, and screens to decorate the homes of his patrons. This book is a lavishly illustrated survey of this little-known but important aspect of his oeuvre

0-300-05555-2 YALE $60.00

Stuart **Preston**

Vuillard

0-8109-1706-8 ABRAMS $22.95

French Sculptors

Anne **Wagner**

Jean-Baptiste Carpeaux: Sculptor of the Second Empire

An accomplished study of the principal French sculptor of his day whose work, questioned at the time on moral grounds, was an important precedent for Rodin

0-300-03605-1 YALE $60.00
0-300-04751-7 YALE PB $35.00

Anne **Delbee**

Camille Claudel: Une Femme

TRANSLATED BY CAROL COSMAN
1-56279-094-3 MERCURY HOUSE PB $16.95

Sam **Hunter**

Lachaise

1-55859-562-7 CROSS RIVER $45.00

Bertrand **Lorquin**

Maillol

0-500-97417-9 THAMES & HUDSON $40.00

Aristide **Maillol**

Maillol Nudes: 35 Lithographs

0-486-24000-2 DOVER PB $4.95

Ruth **Butler**

Rodin: The Shape of Genius

The definitive biography, lavishly illustrated with more than 200 archival photographs and incorporating many previously inaccessible letters. "Marvelous. Based on much new archival material and original thought, this book is the best analysis of Rodin as a person, his relationships with women, and the contexts within which he made his most important art" —Albert Elsen, author of *Rodin's "Thinker" and the Dilemmas of Modern Public Sculpture*

0-300-06498-5 YALE PB $20.00

Bernard **Champigneulle**

Rodin

A reappraisal of Rodin's significance as an innovator in sculpture combined with a revealing account of his personality and troubled private life

See also **THAMES & HUDSON WORLD OF ART** under **ART HISTORY: GENERAL STUDIES**

0-500-20061-0 THAMES & HUDSON PB $14.95

Gen. J.A. **Eisenwerth Schmoll**

Auguste Rodin and Camille Claudel

An examination of the interplay of passion, self-destruction, and aesthetic experimentation that characterized one of the most artistically productive yet ultimately tragic artist-model love affairs

3-7913-1382-7 PRESTEL $25.00

Claudine **Mitchell**

Rodin

A new and comprehensive study that examines the dynamics of Rodin's formidable success though a visual analysis of the major works, a discussion of the late drawings, and the impact the artist's work had upon the intellectual avant-garde of late 19th-century France

0-500-20296-6 THAMES & HUDSON PB $14.95

Auguste Rodin

Hélène **Pinet**

Rodin: The Hands of Genius

0-8109-2888-4 ABRAMS PB $12.95

Auguste **Rodin**

Auguste Rodin: Erotic Watercolors

Rodin's series of erotic female nudes, produced during the final two decades of the artist's life, were considered so scandalous by his contemporaries that they could not be shown. Here, 107 watercolors are collected for the first time, intimate masterpieces that have long exerted a crucial influence on avant-garde art in the 20th century

INTRODUCTION BY ANNE-MARIE BONNET
1-55670-428-3 STEWART, TABORI $85.00

England

William **Blake**

William Blake

Ninety-two studies

0-486-22303-5 DOVER PB $10.95

Martin **Butlin** & Evelyn **Joll**

The Paintings of William Blake

An extraordinary effort at coordinating the complete works; two volumes, one of text, the second of black-and-white plates

0-300-03276-5 YALE $300.00

THE WILLIAM BLAKE TRUST FACSIMILE EDITIONS OF THE ILLUMINATED POEMS ARE LISTED *under* LITERATURE OF THE BRITISH ISLES

Robert N. **Essick**

William Blake at the Huntington

0-8109-2589-3 ABRAMS PB $29.95

Kathleen **Raine**

William Blake

A brief but informative introduction; the visionary artist viewed in the context of the Greek revival

See also **THE 19TH CENTURY** under **STUDIES OF INDIVIDUAL AUTHORS** under **ANTHOLOGIES AND STUDIES** in **LITERATURE OF THE BRITISH ISLES**

0-500-20107-2 THAMES & HUDSON PB $14.95

Christine **Alexander** & Janne **Sellars**

The Art of the Brontës

0-521-43841-1 CAMBRIDGE PB $34.95

C.R. **Leslie**

Memoirs of the Life of John Constable: Composed Chiefly of His Letters

See also **ARTISTS ON ART** under **ART HISTORY: GENERAL STUDIES**

0-7148-3360-6 PHAIDON PB $14.95

Leslie **Parris** & Ian-Fleming **Williams**

Constable

1-85437-072-3 TATE GALLERY PB $20.00

Graham **Reynolds**

The Earlier Paintings and Drawings of John Constable

This two-volume set (one volume of text, one of plates) features reproductions and descriptions of 1370 paintings and drawings in chronological order, by renown Constable scholar, Graham Reynolds

0-300-06337-7 YALE $175.00

Michael **Rosenthal**

Constable: The Painter and His Landscape

Historical commentary on Constable's East Anglia, where he painted and drew throughout his career; very fine color reproductions

0-300-03014-2 YALE $50.00

0-300-03753-8 YALE PB $30.00

Stephen **Deuchar**

Sporting Art in 18th Century England: A Social and Political History

A distinctive genre which became popular in the early 18th century through such artists as George Stubbs

0-300-04116-0 YALE $50.00

Dennis **Farr**

English Art, 1870-1940

0-19-817208-7 OXFORD $65.00

Andrew **Hemmingway**

Landscape Imagery and Urban Culture in Early Nineteenth-Century Britain

0-521-39118-0 CAMBRIDGE $99.95

Christopher **Newall**

Frederic, Lord Leighton: Eminent Victorian Artist

Lavishly illustrated, this catalogue on Frederic Leighton, the eminent Victorian sculptor and painter, will accompany a retrospective exhibition of his work at the Royal Academy in London. Along with reproductions of his famous figure paintings, the volume includes landscapes, portraits, and a series of insightful essays on his life

0-8109-3578-3 ABRAMS $49.50

Graham **Reynolds**

English Watercolors

From Turner, Bonnington, and Blake to Edward Lear and Wyndham Lewis

0-941533-43-3 NEW AMSTERDAM $35.00

Michael **Rosenthal**

British Landscape Painting

0-8014-1489-X CORNELL $45.00

Peter **Jackson**

George Scharf's London: Sketches and Watercolours of a Changing City, 1820-50

Working in pencil sketches, lithographs, and watercolors, Scharf captured the vitality of everyday life, from hawkers and musicians to the new London Zoo. With 187 black-and-white plates

0-7195-4379-7 MURRAY $34.95

Sam **Smiles**

The Image of Antiquity: Ancient Britain and the Romantic Imagination

Illustrated with images from a wide range of sources, this interdisciplinary study argues that the ancient Britain of the romantic imagination was variously seen as a noble epoch of patriotic wisdom and as a period of savagery and barbarism

0-300-05814-4 YALE $37.00

Julian **Treuherz**

Victorian Painting

See also **THAMES & HUDSON WORLD OF ART** under **ART HISTORY: GENERAL STUDIES**

0-500-20263-X THAMES & HUDSON PB $12.95

John **Gage**

J.M.W. Turner: A Wonderful Range of Mind

An up-to-date, general study of the great English Romantic landscape painter, with splendid reproductions throughout

0-300-03779-1 YALE $50.00

0-300-04695-2 YALE PB $29.95

David **Hill**

Turner on the Thames

Turner's lifelong association with the Thames was a favorite source of inspiration for his paintings, watercolors, and sketches. This beautiful book retraces Turner's journeys along the river during 1805 and analyses the influence of his Thames experience on the rest of his career

0-300-05389-4 YALE $55.00

Robert **Kenner**

J.M.W. Turner

0-8109-3868-5 ABRAMS $19.95

John **Walker**

Turner

A discussion of his life and fortunes; nearly 50 fine color plates with individual commentary

0-8109-1679-7 ABRAMS $22.95

Andrew **Wilton**

J.M.W. Turner: France, Italy, Switzerland, Germany

Fine assemblage of the watercolors produced during Turner's frequent European travels

0-89009-905-7 BOOK SALES $39.98

Turner and the Sublime

Exhibition catalog demonstrating Turner's relation to the predominant philosophical concept of the 18th century; excellent reproductions of many major works

0-226-06189-2 CHICAGO PB $21.95

The Pre-Raphaelites

"It was only one kind of Pre-Raphaelite painting that was so admired in the nineties, whereas ultimately it is the sheer variety of the work produced that impresses. Holman Hunt's symbolic realism, Millais' Tennysonian mood-painting, the colour symbolism and cult of feminine beauty in Rossetti, Burne-Jones' musical and romantic dreams, the modern-life allegories of Maddox Brown, indeed the modern moral subjects of them all."—Alan Bowness

Russell **Ash**

Sir Edward Burne-Jones

0-8109-3126-5 ABRAMS $29.95

Edward **Burne-Jones**
Pre-Raphaelite Drawings
Forty-six plates
0-486-24113-0 DOVER PB $4.95

William Morris

Susan P. **Casteras** & others
John Ruskin and the Victorian Eye
0-8109-3766-2 ABRAMS $45.00

Timothy **Hilton**
The Pre-Raphaelites
A thorough introduction which describes the many aspects of this Romantic, medievalizing movement and its varied responses to Victorian society; Millais, Rossetti, Brown, and Burne-Jones predominate
0-500-20102-1 THAMES & HUDSON PB $14.95

Debra N. **Mancoff**
The Return of King Arthur: The Legend Through Victorian Eyes
See also **THE 19TH CENTURY** under **SPECIALIZED STUDIES** under **ANTHOLOGIES AND STUDIES** in **LITERATURE OF THE BRITISH ISLES**
0-8109-3782-4 ABRAMS $35.00

Paul Hayes **Tucker** & J.N.P. **Watson**
Millais: Three Generations in Nature, Art and Sport
0-948253-28-2 SPORTSMANS $45.00

Fiona **MacCarthy**
William Morris
An excellent recent biography
See also **THE 19TH CENTURY** under **STUDIES OF INDIVIDUAL AUTHORS** under **ANTHOLOGIES AND STUDIES** in **LITERATURE OF THE BRITISH ISLES**
0-394-58531-3 KNOPF $45.00

Linda **Parry**, editor
William Morris
This major volume includes essays by distinguished scholars, curators, and experts on William Morris, one the most influential designers of the 19th century. Abundantly illustrated, the book's lavish reproductions include objects, stained glass, furniture, and tapestries created by Morris and his firm
See also **ARTS AND CRAFTS** under **DECORATIVE MOVEMENTS** under **INTERIOR DECORATION** in **ARCHITECTURE, DESIGN, AND HOMES**
0-8109-4282-8 ABRAMS $49.50

Russell **Ash**
Dante Gabriel Rossetti
0-8109-3784-0 ABRAMS $29.95

John **Ruskin**
The Laws of Fesole: A Familiar Treatise on the Elementary Principles and Practice of Drawing
1-88055-944-7 ALLWORTH PB $18.95

Selected Writings
Includes selections from *Modern Painters, The Stones of Venice, The Seven Lamps of Architecture,* and *Praeterita*
See also **CRITICS AND WRITERS ON ART** under **ART HISTORY: GENERAL STUDIES**
See also **19TH-CENTURY PROSE** under **THE 19TH CENTURY**
EDITED BY PHILIP DAVIS
0-460-87460-8 EVERYMAN'S PB $8.50

Northern Europe

Sharon **Hirsh**
Ferdinand Hodler
An engaging and beautifully presented study of the foremost Swiss symbolist landscape painter
0-8076-1033-X BRAZILLER $50.00

Arne **Eggum** & others
Edvard Munch: The Frieze of Life
0-8109-3630-5 ABRAMS $45.00

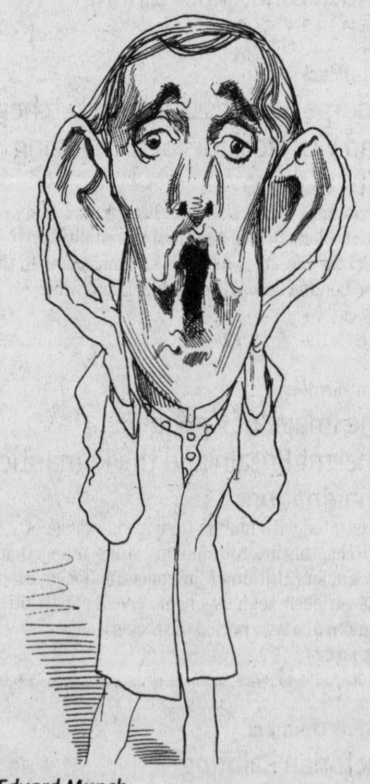
Edvard Munch

J.P. **Hodin**
Edvard Munch
A widely acclaimed critical study of the great Norwegian artist by a celebrated scholar of expressionism; well illustrated
0-500-20122-6 THAMES & HUDSON PB $14.95

Xavier **Tricot**
James Ensor: Catalog Raisonné of the Paintings
0-85667-429-X WILSON
2 VOLUME BOXED SET $350.00

Kirk **Varnedoe**
Northern Light: Realism, and Symbolism in Scandinavian Painting, 1880-1910
A full presentation of the often overlooked early modernist paintings of the North; many beautifully reproduced pictures
0-300-04146-2 YALE $60.00

American Art

General Studies

"When the United States of America came into being, the leaders and citizens of the young republic faced a formidable identity crisis...Creative minds were confronted with the challenge of recording, indeed creating, an accurate 'American' image. This challenge was complicated by the fact that in the young United States, the fine arts of painting and sculpture were regarded with some suspicion and not a little skepticism. To a people engaged daily in the struggle to tame a seemingly endless wilderness, with its attendant physical and psychological hazards, the arts of painting and sculpture were superfluous luxuries."
—Elizabeth Milroy, in *A Proud Heritage: Two Centuries of American Art*

William **Ayres**
Picturing History: American Painting, 1770-1930
0-8478-1745-8 FRAUNCES TAVERN MUSEUM $60.00

Romare **Bearden** & Harry **Henderson**
A History of African-American Artists: From 1792 to the Present
Bearden worked on this monumental book right up to his death in 1988, and fortunately for us the writer Henderson has devoted himself to its completion. Tracing the unique development of African-American art from the enigmatic 18th-century portrait painter Joshua Johnston, the authors provide a context with which to view these important artists in terms of American—and world—art history. A long-overdue, vitally important history
0-394-57016-2 PANTHEON $65.00

Milton **Brown**

American Art: Painting, Sculpture, Architecture, Decorative Arts, Photography

0-8109-0658-9 ABRAMS $60.00

Wayne **Craven**

American Art: History and Culture

0-8109-1942-7 ABRAMS $60.00
0-697-16763-1 BROWN & BENCHMARK PB $55.83

Sculpture in America

0-87413-225-8 ASSOCIATED UNIVERSITIES $60.00

E. McSherry **Fowble**

Two Centuries of Prints in America, 1680-1890: A Selective Catalogue of the Winterthur Collection

Focuses primarily on prints of historical importance, including views

0-8139-1124-9 VIRGINIA $69.50

Thomas W. **Gaehtgens** & Heinz **Ickstat**, editors

American Icons: Transatlantic Perspectives on Eighteenth and Nineteenth-Century American Art

The 12 essays in this volume, supplemented by a profusion of illustrations, explore the concept of an American artistic consciousness. The book is a thorough examination of the complex relationships between American and European art, and explains the evolution of a distinctly American point of view

0-89236-247-2 GETTY CENTER PB $29.95

William **Kloss** & others

Art in the White House: A Nation's Pride

0-8109-3965-7 ABRAMS $60.00

Edward **Lucie-Smith**

American Realism

The school of American Realism has been almost ignored since 1945, when the art history world turned its attention to abstract painting and sculpture. Yet its enduring tradition has enriched our national art and our cultural history. Beginning with the Revolutionary War, and moving through American Impressionism and Urban Realism to today's Postmodern Realism, this is a magnificent homage to American art. 250 illustrations, bibliography notes, and index

0-8109-1941-9 ABRAMS $49.50

John **McCoubrey**, editor

American Art, 1700-1960: Sources and Documents

Includes many letters, reviews, and other documentary material

0-13-024521-6 PRENTICE HALL PB $42.00

Daniel **Mendelowitz**

A History of American Art

A scholarly narrative history

0-03-089475-1 HOLT RINEHART & WINSTON PB $55.53

Barbara B. **Millhouse**

American Originals: Selections from Reynolds House, Museum of American Art

1-55859-067-6 ABBEVILLE $45.00

Donald Martin **Reynolds**

Masters of American Sculpture: The Figurative Tradition

1-55859-276-8 ABBEVILLE $67.50

Irene S. **Sweetkind**, editor

Master Paintings from the Butler Institute of American Art

0-8109-3643-7 ABRAMS $60.00

Painting

Watercolors

Annette **Blaugrund** &
Theodore E. **Stebbins**, Jr., editors

John James Audubon: The Watercolors for the Birds of America

Audubon's watercolors are reproduced here in lush full color. Published in conjunction with the first traveling exhibition of Audubon's paintings since the New York Historical Society acquired them in 1863, the catalog sacrifices none of the breath-taking accuracy and versimilitude of the originals, and gives one the sense of holding the birds in one's hand

0-679-42059-2 VILLARD $75.00

John James Audubon

Roger Tory **Peterson** &
Virginia Marie **Peterson**

Audubon's Birds of America

See also **BIRDS** under **ANIMALS** under **NATURE STUDY** in **SCIENCE**

1-55859-128-1 ABBEVILLE $250.00
1-55859-225-3 ABBEVILLE PB $11.95

Helen **Cooper**

Winslow Homer Watercolors

Homer painted over 600 watercolors of New England, Canada, the Bahamas, Key West, the Adirondacks, and England. His bold brushwork and colors greatly influenced later American watercolor artists

See also **THE 19TH CENTURY**

0-300-03997-2 YALE PB $24.95

Genre Painting

Frederick **Brandt**

American Marine Painting

0-917046-01-3 VIRGINIA MUSEUM PB $6.50

Wayne **Craven**

Down Garden Paths: The Floral Environment in American Art

0-8386-3214-9 FAIRLEIGH DICKINSON $35.00

William **Gerdts** & Bruce **Weber**

In Nature's Ways: American Landscape Painting of the Late 19th Century

0-943411-16-5 NORTON GALLERY PB $23.00

John **Wilmerding**

American Marine Painting

The history of American marine painting from the colonial period to the present

0-8109-1861-7 ABRAMS $45.00

Folk Art

John **Beardsley**

Gardens of Revelation: Environments of Visionary Artists

1-55859-360-8 ABBEVILLE $60.00

Deborah **Chotner** & others

American Native Paintings

0-521-44301-6 NATIONAL GALLERY OF ART $170.00

Howard **Finster** & Tom **Patterson**

Howard Finster, Stranger from Another World

0-89659-902-7 ABBEVILLE $45.00

Henry **Glassie**

The Spirit of Folk Art

Perhaps the most thought-provoking book on the subject

See also **FOLK ART AND AMERICANA** under **GENERAL** under **AMERICAN DECORATIVE ARTS** in **ARCHITECTURE, DESIGN, AND HOMES**

0-8109-2438-2 ABRAMS PB $29.95

Nina **Hellman** & Norman **Brouwer**

A Mariner's Fancy: A Whaleman's Art of Scrimshaw

0-295-97212-2 WASHINGTON PB $22.50

Robert **Hobbs**
Earl Cunningham: Painting an American Eden
0-8109-3189-3 ABRAMS $39.95

William C., Jr **Ketchum**
Grandma Moses: An American Original
0-8317-8085-1 SMITHMARK $10.98

Jean **Lipman** & Elizabeth **Warren**
Young America: A Folk-Art History
An excellent survey by the president or the American Museum of Folk Art, essential for collectors, students, and amateurs
0-933920-75-X HUDSON HILLS $29.98

Roger **Manley**
Signs and Wonders: Outsider Art Inside North Carolina
0-88259-957-7 NORTH CAROLINA PB $19.95

Chuck **Rosenak** & Jan **Rosenak**
Museum of American Folk Art Encyclopedia of Twentieth-Century American Folk Art and Artists
1-55859-041-2 ABBEVILLE $75.00

Steve **Siporin**
American Folk Masters: The National Heritage Fellows
0-8109-1917-6 ABRAMS $49.50

John Michael **Vlach**
Plain Painters: Making Sense of American Folk Art
Comparative studies of folk knowledge and culture
0-87474-926-3 SMITHSONIAN PB $45.00

Early American Art

Emily Ballew **Neff** & William L. **Pressly**
John Singleton Copley in England
0-89090-070-1 MUSEUM OF FINE ARTS $50.00

Carrie **Rebora** & others
John Singleton Copley in America
0-8109-6492-9 METROPOLITAN MUSEUM $75.00

James Thomas **Flexner**
America's Old Masters
Biographies of Benjamin West, John Singleton Copley, Charles Wilson Peale, and Gilbert Stuart
0-486-27957-X DOVER PB $12.95

Eleanore **Mather** & Dorothy **Miller**
Edward Hicks: His Peaceable Kingdoms and Other Paintings
The Quaker artist painted more than 50 versions of his *Peaceable Kingdom,* a biblically inspired work that is regarded as a masterpiece of American naive painting
0-87413-208-8 DELAWARE $40.00

A History of American Painting
The development of painting in colonial America, from the time of the earliest settlements to the American Revolution

Volume 1
First Flowers of Our Wilderness—American Painting, The Colonial Period
0-486-25707-X DOVER PB $8.95

Volume 2
The Light of Distant Skies—1760-1835
0-486-22179-2 DOVER PB $8.95

Lillian **Miller** & Sidney **Hart**, editors
The Selected Papers of Charles Wilson Peale and His Family: Charles Wilson Peale; Artist in Revolutionary America, 1735-1791
Peale was a soldier, inventor, painter of more than 1000 pictures, student of natural history, and founder of one of the first museums in America
0-300-02576-9 YALE $75.00

Nicolai **Cikovsky**, Jr.
Raphael Peale Still Lifes
0-8109-1474-3 NATIONAL GALLERY OF ART $30.00

Helmut **von Erffa** & Allen **Staley**
The Paintings of Benjamin West
Painter of historical subjects and portraits, West moved to England in 1763 and received royal patronage, becoming president of the Royal Academy
0-300-03355-9 YALE $95.00

The 19th Century

Linda **Farber** & Nancy K. **Anderson**
Albert Bierstadt: Art and Enterprise
The epic scale and painstaking elaboration of Bierstadt's canvases of Yosemite Valley and the Rocky Mountains were matched by his energetic promotion of his art. 90 color illustrations
1-55595-059-0 HUDSON HILLS $75.00

Abraham A. **Davidson**
Ralph Albert Blakelock
0-271-01504-7 PENN STATE $65.00

Andres **Cosentino** & Henry **Glassie**
The Capital Image: Painters in Washington, 1800-1915
0-87474-338-9 SMITHSONIAN $45.00

Lloyd **Goodrich**
Thomas Eakins
A biography of the great realist artist, and a study of his work in all media
0-674-88490-6 HARVARD $90.00

William Innes **Homer**
Thomas Eakins: His Life and Art
A much needed re-evaluation of a giant of 19th-century American art. This study of Eakins's career, based on newly discovered primary sources, knocks off the artist's halo without diminishing the brilliance or the importance of his work. 240 illustrations, 100 in full color
1-55859-281-4 ABBEVILLE $95.00

Elizabeth **Johns**
Thomas Eakins: The Heroism of Modern Life
A detailed account of his work as a portraits, centering on five major paintings
0-691-00288-6 PRINCETON PB $35.00

Christopher **Finch**
Nineteenth-Century Watercolors
See also **WATERCOLORS** under **PAINTING**
1-55859-019-6 ABBEVILLE $95.00

Harold **Holzer** & Mark E. **Neely**, Jr.
Mine Eyes Have Seen the Glory: The Civil War in Art
Little attention has been paid to the rich art of the Civil War. This book corrects that. Holzer *(Lincoln on Democracy* with Mario Cuomo) and Pulitzer Prize-winning historian Neely *(The Fate of Liberty)* select the best and the rarest Civil War art, including heroic portraits of military leaders and grisly combat tableaux that ironically juxtapose America's grand view of itself and the reality of its bloody ordeal
0-517-58448-4 ORION $60.00

Winslow **Homer**
Winslow Homer Illustrations: 41 Wood Engravings After Drawings by the Artist
0-486-24392-3 DOVER PB $3.95

Nicolai **Cikovsky**, Jr. & Franklin **Kelly**
Winslow Homer
More than 200 paintings and works on paper are reproduced in this lavish book which serves as the catalogue for a large touring retrospective of Homer's works at the National Gallery in 1995
0-300-06555-8 NATIONAL GALLERY OF ART $60.00
0-89468-132-X NATIONAL GALLERY OF ART PB $30.00

Helen **Cooper**
Winslow Homer Watercolors
Homer painted over 600 watercolors of New England, Canada, the Bahamas, Key West, the Adirondacks and England. His bold brushwork and colors greatly influenced later American watercolor artists
See also **WATERCOLORS** under **PAINTING**
0-300-03997-2 YALE PB $24.95

David **Tatham**
Winslow Homer in the Adirondacks
0-8156-0343-6 SYRACUSE $45.00

Peter H. **Wood** & Karen C.C. **Dalton**
Winslow Homer's Images of Blacks
0-292-79047-3 MENIL PB $22.95

John **Wilmerding**, editor

Paintings by Fitz Hugh Lane

0-8109-1272-4 ABRAMS....$49.50
0-8109-2525-7 ABRAMS PB....$19.95

David M. **Lubin**

Picturing a Nation: Art and Social Change in Nineteenth-Century America

An examination of the work of six artists—John Vanderlyn, George Caleb Bingham, Robert Duncanson, Lilly Martin Spencer, Seymour Guy, and William Harnett—that discusses how their paintings at once embraced and, paradoxically, resisted dominant social values. "This richly-nuanced book is destined to become one of the landmarks of American art history"—Albert Boime, University of California, Los Angeles

0-300-05732-6 YALE....$50.00
0-300-06637-6 YALE PB....$30.00

Russell **Lynes**

The Art Makers: An Informal History of Painting, Sculpture, and Architecture in 19th Century America

Deals with collecting, art patronage, and the relations of the artists with the public

0-486-24239-0 DOVER PB....$10.95

David C. **Miller**

American Iconology: New Approaches to Nineteenth-Century Art and Literature

0-300-05478-5 YALE....$42.50

Barbara **Novak**

American Painting of the Nineteenth Century: Realism, Idealism and the American Experience

0-06-430099-4 ICON PB....$31.05

Nature and Culture: American Landscape and Painting, 1825-1875

0-19-502935-6 OXFORD PB....$27.50

Nineteenth-Century American Painting: The Thyssen-Bornemisza Collection

0-89660-026-2 ARTABRAS....$39.98

William Innes **Homer** & Lloyd **Goodrich**

Albert Pinkham Ryder: Painter of Dreams

A magnificent presentation of the work of one of America's great visionary painters. Lloyd Goodrich writes: "His art is literally a dream world...In his mind reality went through a long process of distillation, emerging as something purely subjective." The text provides the most detailed biography of Ryder to date, and the many reproductions offer an uparalleled vista of Ryder's imaginative world

0-8109-1599-5 ABRAMS....$49.50

Hudson River School

Gerald L. **Carr**

Frederick Edwin Church: Catalogue Raisonné of Works of Art at Olana State Historical Site

0-521-38540-7 CAMBRIDGE....$350.00

Frederik Edwin Church

Franklin **Kelly**

Frederik Edwin Church

The most detailed presentation to date of the life and work of a major figure in American art. Church's epic canvases epitomized many of the central concerns of 19th-century culture. An accompanying essay by Stephen Jay Gould examines the importance of science in Church's work, while James Anthony Ryan gives a detailed analysis of the designs for the painter's home at Olana on the Hudson

0-87474-458-X NATIONAL GALLERY OF ART....$52.00

Matthew **Baigell**

Thomas Cole

Cole is often considered the ablest of the early American landscape painters. One of the founders of the Hudson River School, he was immensely popular and influential in his lifetime

0-8230-0648-4 WATSON-GUPTILL PB....$16.95

Franklin **Kelly**

Thomas Cole's Paintings of Eden

0-88360-083-8 AMON CARTER MUSEUM PB....$17.95

Kenneth **Maddox**

The Unprejudiced Eye: The Drawings of Jasper Cropsey

0-943651-07-7 HUDSON RIVER MUSEUM PB....$10.00

American Artists Abroad

"I have seen, and heard, much of Cockney impudence before now; but never expected to hear a coxcomb ask 200 guineas for flinging a pot of paint in the public's face."
—John Ruskin, on Whistler

Adelyn **Breeskin**

Mary Cassatt: A Catalogue Raisonné of the Graphic Work

1-55660-284-7 ALAN WOFSY FINE ARTS....$135.00

Frank **Getlein**

Mary Cassatt: Paintings and Prints

0-89659-155-7 ABBEVILLE PB....$16.95

Suzanne **Lindsay**

Mary Cassatt and Philadelphia

0-87633-061-8 PHILADELPHIA MUSEUM PB....$14.95

Nancy **Mathews**

Mary Cassatt

0-8109-0793-3 ABRAMS....$45.00

Nancy Mowell **Mathews** & Barbara Stern **Shapiro**

Mary Cassatt: The Color Prints

0-8109-1049-7 ABRAMS....$39.95
0-8109-2524-9 ABRAMS PB....$24.95

Barbara **Novak**

Dreams and Shadows: Thomas H. Hotchkiss in Nineteenth-Century Italy

0-87663-778-0 UNIVERSE PB....$27.50

Margaretta **Lovell**

Venice: The American View, 1860-1920

0-88401-044-9 WASHINGTON PB....$19.95

John Singer **Sargent**

Portrait Drawings

Forty-two works

0-486-24524-1 DOVER PB....$4.95

Trevor **Fairbrother**

John Singer Sargent

0-8109-3833-2 ABRAMS....$45.00

John Singer Sargent

Theodore E. **Stebbins**, Jr. & others
The Lure of Italy: American Artists and the Italian Experience, 1760-1914
0-8109-3561-9 ABRAMS $65.00

Leslie **Furth**
Augustus Vincent Tack: Landscape of the Spirit
0-943044-19-7 PHILLIPS COLLECTION PB $29.95

Regina **Soria**
Elihu Vedder
0-8386-6906-9 FAIRLEIGH DICKINSON $60.00

James McNeill **Whistler**
The Gentle Art of Making Enemies
A witty memoir by the expatriate American painter, dandy, and exponent of art for art's sake
See also ARTISTS ON ART under ART HISTORY: GENERAL STUDIES
0-486-21875-9 DOVER PB $8.95

Whistler on Art: Selected Letters and Writings, 1849-1903
EDITED BY NIGEL THORP
1-85754-094-8 CARCANET PB $10.01

Avis **Berman**
James McNeill Whistler
0-8109-3968-1 ABRAMS $19.95

Pierre **Cabanne** & Carol **Taylor**
Whistler
0-517-88411-9 CROWN PB $12.00

Richard **Dorment** & others
James McNeill Whistler
This catalog of the largest Whistler exhibition since 1903 is the first appreciation ever of the artist's full range and extraordinary variety. Three hundred illustrations, 205 in full color
0-8109-3976-2 ABRAMS $85.00

Margaret F. **MacDonald**
James McNeill Whistler: Watercolors, Pastels, and Drawings, A Catalogue Raisonné
A complete catalogue of over 1,700 works by the artist whose prodigious output and personal eccentricities won him wide recognition
0-300-05987-6 YALE $145.00

Edgar **Munhall**
Whistler and Montesquiou: The Butterfly and the Bat
2-08-013577-5 ABBEVILLE $45.00

John **Waker**
Whistler
0-8109-1786-6 ABRAMS $39.95

Andrew **Young**
The Paintings of James McNeill Whistler
A two-volume catalog of his oil paintings
0-300-02384-7 YALE $250.00

James McNeill Whistler

American Impressionism

Barbara Dayer **Gallati**
William Merritt Chase
0-8109-4029-9 ABRAMS $45.00

Susan A. **Hobbs**
The Art of Thomas Wilmer Dewing: Beauty Reconfigured
WITH AN ESSAY BY BARBARA DAYER GALLATI
1-56098-623-9 SMITHSONIAN PB $29.95

William H. **Gerdts**
American Impressionism
A beautifully illustrated study by the eminent art historian
0-7892-0074-0 ABBEVILLE $80.00

Impressionist New York
1-55859-328-4 ABBEVILLE $40.00

Meredith **Martindale** & others
Lilla Cabot Perry: An American Impressionist
0-7892-0045-7 NATIONAL MUSEUM OF WOMEN IN THE ARTS PB $29.95

George **Szabo**, editor
Maurice Prendergast: The Large Boston Public Garden Sketchbook
0-8076-1184-0 BRAZILLER $60.00

Richard J. **Wattenmaker**
Maurice Prendergast
0-8109-3726-3 ABRAMS $39.95

Richard **Boyle**
John Twachtman
One of the most noted American impressionists, both as a painter and etcher
0-8230-2568-3 WATSON-GUPTILL PB $16.95

Twachtman in Gloucester: His Last Years, 1900-1902
0-87663-526-5 UNIVERSE PB $12.95

H. Barbara **Weinberg** & others
American Impressionism and Realism: Painting of Modern Life, 1885-1915
0-8109-6437-6 METROPOLITAN MUSEUM $75.00
0-87099-701-7 METROPOLITAN MUSEUM PB $45.00

Sculptors

Frederick **Voss**
John Frazee, 1790-1852: Sculptor
Frazee was one of the earliest American sculptors. Without formal training, he became well-known for his marble portrait busts of prominent Americans of the period 1825-1835
0-934552-46-0 BOSTON ATHENEUM PB $10.00

Michael **Richman**
Daniel Chester French: An American Sculptor
The sculptor best known for the Lincoln Memorial
0-89133-048-8 NATIONAL TRUST PB $14.95

John **Dryfhout**
The Work of Augustus Saint-Gaudens
Survey of the work of this prolific sculptor whose career lasted from 1867 to 1907
0-87451-287-5 NEW ENGLAND $29.95

Burke **Wilkinson**
Uncommon Clay: The Life and Works of Augustus Saint-Gaudens
The career of the Irish-born, French-trained American sculptor noted for his portraiture in marble and bronze and his civic monuments
0-15-192749-9 HARCOURT BRACE $9.98

Rick **Stewart**
Charles M. Russell, Sculptor
0-8109-3772-7 ABRAMS $95.00

Regional Art

Alan **Axelrod**
Art of the Golden West
1-55859-103-6 ABBEVILLE $49.98

Bodmer & others
The North American Indian Portfolios
1-55859-601-1 ABBEVILLE PB $11.95

Karl **Bodmer**
Karl Bodmer's America
Collected works of the artist's visits to the American frontier in 1832-43. Watercolors and sketches of such subjects as Prime Minister Maximillian's expedition up the Missouri River
0-8032-1185-6 NEBRASKA $100.00

Sarah E. **Boehme**
Rendezvous to Roundup: The First 100 Years of Art in Wyoming
0-931618-30-4 BUFFALO BILL PB $16.95

Catherine **Campbell** & Marcia **Blaine**
New Hampshire Scenery: A Dictionary of 19th-Century Artists of New Hampshire Mountain Landscapes
0-914659-12-X PHOENIX $25.00

Brian W. **Dippie**, editor
Charles M. Russell, Word Painter: Letters, 1887-1926
0-8109-3764-6 AMON CARTER MUSEUM $95.00

William H. **Gerdts**
Art Across America: Two Centuries of Regional Painting
Volume I
The East and the Mid-Atlantic
0-7892-0061-9 ABBEVILLE $95.00
Volume II
The South and the Midwest
0-7892-0062-7 ABBEVILLE $95.00
Volume III
The Plains States and the West
0-7892-0063-5 ABBEVILLE $95.00

William **Goetzmann**
The West of the Imagination
Early 19th-century interpreters of the West
0-393-30565-1 NORTON PB $17.95

Peter H. **Hassrick**
Treasures of the Old West: Paintings and Sculpture from the Thomas Gilcrease Institute of American History and Art
0-8109-8133-5 ABRADALE $17.98

Joni Louise **Kinsey**
Thomas Moran and the Surveying of the American West
1-56098-170-9 SMITHSONIAN PB $34.95

Alexander **Nemerov**
Frederic Remington and Turn-of-the-Century America
0-300-05566-8 YALE $40.00

Walton **Rawls**
The Great Book of Currier and Ives' America
1-55859-229-6 ABBEVILLE PB $11.95

Michael **Shapiro** & Peter **Hassrick**
Frederic Remington: The Masterworks
0-8109-8104-1 ABRADALE $19.98

Patricia **Trenton**
Independent Spirits: Women Painters of the American West, 1890-1945
0-520-20203-1 CALIFORNIA PB $29.95

Alvia J. **Wardlaw**
The Art of John Biggers: View from the Upper Room
0-8109-1956-7 ABRAMS $35.00

Robert **Workman**
The Eden of America: Rhode Island Landscapes, 1820-1920
0-911517-10-3 RISD PB $18.95

20th-Century Art

The advent of modern art did not altogether coincide with the advent of the 20th century, but it was in this century that the concept of modern art spread beyond France to become an international phenomenon. As Harold Rosenberg pointed out many years ago, one of the most notable aspects of modern art has been the way it made movements more significant than regional traditions: "Instead of 'the Venetians' or 'the Flemish school,' our era presents practitioners of 'esthetic *isms*'....In our era it is art movements that make possible continuity of style, that stimulate interchange of ideas and perceptions among artists, that provide new points of departure for individual invention."

General

Bruce **Altshuler**
The Avant-Garde in Exhibition: New Art in the 20th Century
0-8109-3637-2 ABRAMS $49.50

H.H. **Arnason**
History of Modern Art: Painting, Sculpture, Architecture Photography
A thorough, academic survey organized according to the great movements of modern art
0-8109-1097-7 ABRAMS $60.00

Alan **Bowness**
Modern European Art
See also **THAMES & HUDSON WORLD OF ART** under **ART HISTORY: GENERAL STUDIES**
0-500-20205-2 THAMES & HUDSON PB $14.95

Riva **Castelman**
Prints of the Twentieth Century
A survey of this important medium
See also **PRINTS** under **THEMES, TECHNIQUES, AND GENRES** under **ART HISTORY: GENERAL STUDIES**
0-500-20228-1 THAMES & HUDSON PB $11.95

Herschel **Chipp**, editor
Theories of Modern Art: A Source Book by Artists and Critics
A rich selection of letters, manifestoes, reviews, interviews, and other writings related to the study of modern art, from Cézanne to the mid-20th century
See also **POSTIMPRESSIONISM** under **FRANCE** under **EUROPEAN ART: 1750-1900**
0-520-05256-0 CALIFORNIA PB $17.95

Albert **Elsen**
Origins of Modern Sculpture: Pioneers and Premises
An excellent introduction
0-8076-0737-1 BRAZILLER PB $17.95

Christopher **Finch**
Twentieth-Century Watercolors
0-89659-811-X ABBEVILLE $95.00

John **Golding**
Visions of the Modern
Well known for his seminal history of Cubism, one of the most outstanding art historians of our time covers the vast range of 20th-century art, from Matisse and Cubism, Dada and Surrealism, to the energetic abstractions of the postwar American scene. An admired painter himself, Golding imbues these essays with a uniquely informed eye
0-520-08791-7 CALIFORNIA $40.00
0-520-08792-5 CALIFORNIA PB $18.00

George Heard **Hamilton**
Painting and Sculpture in Europe: 1880-1940
See also **THE PELICAN HISTORY OF ART** under **ART HISTORY: GENERAL STUDIES**
0-300-05648-6 YALE $60.00
0-300-05649-4 YALE PB $27.50

A.M. **Hammacher**
Modern Sculpture: Tradition and Innovation (Enlarged Edition)
This catalogue of the major exhibition at the Guggenheim Museum is the first complete examination of the entire range of abstraction in the 20th century, from Kandinsky, Malevich and Mondrian to Jackson Pollock, Yves Klein, Agnes Martin, and Eva Hesse
0810908908 ABRAMS $75.00

Sam **Hunter** & John **Jacobus**
Modern Art: Painting, Sculpture, Architecture
0-8109-3609-7 ABRAMS $60.00

Herbert **Read**
A Concise History of Modern Painting
See also **THAMES & HUDSON WORLD OF ART** under **ART HISTORY: GENERAL STUDIES**
0-500-20141-2 THAMES & HUDSON PB $14.95

Nikos **Stangos**
Concepts of Modern Art
An invaluable collection of essays
See also **THAMES & HUDSON WORLD OF ART** under **ART HISTORY: GENERAL STUDIES**
0-500-20268-0 THAMES & HUDSON PB $14.95

Peter **Vergo**
Twentieth-Century German Painting: The Thyssen-Bornemisza Collection
0-85667-397-8 SOTHEBY PARKE BERNET $95.00

Theory and Criticism

Yves-Alain **Bois**

Painting as a Model

Essays in a formalist vein on Mondrian, Barnett Newman, and others

0-262-52180-6 MIT PB........$22.50

Matei **Calinescu**

Five Faces of Modernity: Modernism, Avant-Garde, Decadence, Kitsch, Postmodernism

Instead of a smooth postmodern read, this is a critically responsible and amazingly extensive critical survey of important themes with crucial quotations and full apparatus criticus

0-8223-0726-X DUKE........$42.50
0-8223-0767-7 DUKE PB........$19.95

Mark A. **Cheetham**

The Rhetoric of Purity: Essentialist Theory and the Advent of Abstract Painting

0-521-47759-X CAMBRIDGE PB........$18.95

Jonathan **Fineberg**

Art Since 1940: Strategies of Being

Fineberg presents a survey of art from 1940 to the present that concentrates on the artists' lives and their personal responses to the conflict and chaos of the past six decades

0-8109-1951-6 ABRAMS........$60.00

Hal **Foster**

Compulsive Beauty

A theoretical reconsideration of surrealism

0-262-06160-0 MIT........$35.00

Charles **Harrison**

Primitivism, Cubism, Abstraction

A survey of art from the first two decades of the 20th century, beginning with the evocation of the primitive by rural artists' colonies in France and Germany, and ending with a discussion of the semiotics of Cubism and the rise of abstraction. A key theme is an investigation of the relationship between representation, ideology, and social and cultural values

0-300-05515-3 YALE........$55.00
0-300-05516-1 YALE PB........$27.50

Rosalind **Krauss**

Grids: Format and Image in Twentieth-Century Art

0-938608-13-4 PACE GALLERY PB........$20.00

The Optical Unconscious

Krauss uses colloquy, narrative, and fiction to challenge the principles upon which modernist standard-bearers base their aesthetic. This presents a very different account of modernism, including the story of a small, disparate group of artists who gave rise to an unruly, disruptive force that has haunted the field from the '20s to today. Included are 118 illustrations

0-262-11173-X MIT........$27.50

The Originality of the Avant-Garde and Other Modernist Myths

0-262-61046-9 MIT PB........$17.50

Passages in Modern Sculpture

A brilliant collection of critical essays

0-262-61033-7 MIT PB........$17.50

Linda **Nochlin**

The Body in Pieces: The Fragment as a Metaphor of Modernity

0-500-55027-1 THAMES & HUDSON........$14.95

Meyer **Schapiro**

Selected Papers of Meyer Schapiro Volume II Modern Art

Selected essays by the erudite art historian, whose profound cultural approach to the art object has set the standard for the field. Includes the celebrated *The Apples of Cézanne* and *The Nature of Abstract Art*

See also **THEORY** under **ART HISTORY: GENERAL STUDIES**

0-8076-1034-8 BRAZILLER PB........$23.00

Leo **Stein**

Appreciations: Painting, Poetry and Prose

0-8032-9236-8 NEBRASKA PB........$10.00

Leo **Steinberg**

Criteria: Confrontations with 20th-Century Art

0-19-501846-X OXFORD PB........$29.95

Kirk **Varnedoe**

A Fine Disregard: What Makes Modern Art Modern

0-8109-2574-5 ABRAMS PB........$22.50

Special Topics

Robert **Atkins**

Artspoke: A Guide to Modern Ideas, Movements, and Buzzwords, 1848-1944

1-55859-388-8 ABBEVILLE PB........$17.95

Barbara **Braun**

Pre-Columbian Art and the Post-Columbian World: Ancient American Sources of Modern Art

0-8109-3723-9 ABRAMS........$75.00

Richard **Cork**

A Bitter Truth: The Avant-Garde, Art, and the Great War

The first world war had an immensely powerful effect on the artists who participated in it. This book is the first to bring together the full international array of images spawned by the Great War. It shows how avant-garde painters, sculptors, and printmakers challenged the propaganda of recruitment by producing art that reflected the degradation of the trenches

See also **THE GREAT WAR** under **WORLD WAR I** under **20TH-CENTURY EUROPE TO THE SECOND WORLD WAR** in **WORLD HISTORY AND CURRENT AFFAIRS**

0-300-05704-0 YALE........$60.00

Robert **Goldwater**

Primitivism in Modern Art

0-674-70490-8 BELKNAP PB........$17.95

Billy **Kluver** & Julie **Martin**

Kiki's Paris: Artists and Lovers, 1900-1930

0-8109-2591-5 ABRAMS PB........$19.95

Alexander **Liberman**

The Artist in His Studio: The Heroes of Modern Art

A revised edition of this collection of photographs and commentary on the studios of the pioneers of modern art in France. Includes conversations with such artists as Matisse, Braque, Giacometti, and Balthus

0-394-56567-3 RANDOM HOUSE........$50.00

Anna **Moszynska**

Abstract Art

0-500-20237-0 THAMES & HUDSON PB........$14.95

National Gallery of Australia

Virtual Reality

0-500-97419-5 THAMES & HUDSON PB........$19.95

Richard J. **Powell**

Black Art and Culture in the 20th Century

A brilliant new study of the philosophical and social forces that have shaped a black presence in 20th century art and culture. Topics include the emergence of the "New Negro" in Jazz-Age America and France, the use of black folk imagery in post-Depression art, and the ideological tug-of-war between racial pride and cultural assimilation

0-500-18195-0 THAMES & HUDSON........$29.95

Marie Carmen **Ramirez**, editor

El Taller Torres Garcia

0-292-78121-0 TEXAS........$50.00
0-292-78122-9 TEXAS PB........$29.95

Colin **Rhodes**

Primitivism and Modern Art

A groundbreaking book that draws on a wide range of material, from high art to popular entertainment, to assess the important role played by tribal art in the history of modern art in the West

0-500-20276-1 THAMES & HUDSON PB........$14.95

Mark **Rosenthal**

Abstraction in the Twentieth Century: Total Risk, Freedom, Discipline

0-8109-6890-8 ABRAMS........$75.00

William **Rubin**, editor

Primitivism in Twentieth Century Art: Affinity of the Tribal and the Modern

0-87070-518-0 MOMA $100.00

The Subject Is Women: The Art Institute of Chicago

Opens to 7 x 8. Contains 52 color illustrations by Modigliani, Picasso, Degas, Renoir, Monet, and more

1-55550-345-4 UNIVERSE $11.95

Maurice **Tuchman** & others

The Spiritual in Art: Abstract Painting, 1980-1985

1-55859-469-8 ABBEVILLE PB $45.00

Kirk **Varnedoe** & Adam **Gopnik**

High & Low: Modern Art and Popular Culture

0-8109-6002-8 MOMA $60.00

Diane **Waldman**

Collage, Assemblage, and the Found Object

0-8109-3183-4 ABRAMS $85.00

Jeffrey S. **Weiss**

The Popular Culture of Modern Art: Picasso, Duchamp, and Avant-Gardism, 1909-1917

A cultural history of the deeply ambiguous relationship between modern art and popular culture, focusing on the work of Picasso and Duchamp in the first two decades of the century

See also Ideas, Culture, and Society under 19th-Century Europe in World History and Current Affairs

0-300-05895-0 YALE $47.50

American Art

Milton **Brown**

American Painting from the Armory Show to the Depression

0-691-00301-7 PRINCETON PB $24.95

Ilene Susan **Fort**

The Figure in American Sculpture: A Question of Modernity

0-295-97437-0 WASHINGTON $60.00

Sam **Hunter** & John **Jacobus**

American Art of the Twentieth Century: Painting, Sculpture, and Architecture

The standard academic survey

0-8109-0135-8 ABRAMS $60.00

Barbara **Rose**

American Painting: The Twentieth Century

The standard history

0-8478-0716-9 RIZZOLI PB $25.00

Cubism

Cubism was a radical attempt by artists to create a new visual vocabulary which would give form to space. They broke with the tradition of treating space as merely a void, and instead endeavored to describe it as an alternately forceful and malleable substance. Pioneered by Picasso, Braque, and Gris in the early years of the 20th century, Cubism was based on precepts of Cézanne, who saw in nature endless permutations of the sphere, cone, and cube—hence the name. The movement was equally inspired by the sharp angularity and direct emotionalism of African art forms. Picasso, whose 1906 Les Demoiselles d'Avignon is widely regarded as the seminal work in the movement, shows figures, objects, and ground integrated into a single, dynamically fractured space. He subsequently experimented with fractured spaces in a series of landscapes, portraits, and still-lifes, now referred to as Analytical Cubism. Later, in works often grouped together under the term Synthetic Cubism, Picasso and other artists used a collage technique to convey, in each of their images, shifting planes and multiple perspectives. Not long after World War I, Cubism had countless followers and the movement began to seem more and more formulaic and academic. By then, Picasso and others had already largely abandoned it.

Guillaume **Apollinaire**

This tirelessly inquisitive intellectual was not only involved with Cubism and Futurism but is also credited with coining the terms "Orphism" and "Surrealism."

Apollinaire on Art: Essays and Reviews, 1902-1918

The poet and art critic who introduced Picasso to Braque

See also Artists on Art under Art History: General Studies

0-306-80312-7 DA CAPO PB $13.95

Alfred H. **Barr**, Jr.

Cubism and Abstract Art

The catalog from a historically important exhibition organized by the first director of the Museum of Modern Art

0-674-17935-8 BELKNAP PB $24.95

John **Golding**

Cubism: A History and Analysis, 1907-1914

The standard scholarly account of the development of cubism

0-674-17929-3 HARVARD $45.00
0-674-17930-7 HARVARD PB $23.50

Chris **Green**

Cubism and Its Enemies: Modern Movements and Reaction in French Art, 1916-1928

0-300-03468-7 YALE $40.00

Christine **Poggi**

In Defiance of Painting: Cubism, Futurism, and the Invention of Collage

"This book will become the standard reference on the topic of collage and marks a key moment in the evolution of Cubist criticism. Every student of twentieth-century art should read it"—Yve-Alain Bois, Harvard University

0-300-05109-3 YALE $55.00

William **Rubin**

Picasso and Braque: Pioneering Cubism

Decidedly a genuine contribution to the scholarship, Rubin's week-by-week chronicle of the formation of Cubism simultaneously reveals the individuality of these artists' contribution to this most radical visual style and their symbiotic interchange. An entailed historical study of visual signs

0-87070-675-6 MOMA $60.00
0-87070-676-4 ABRAMS PB $30.00

Lynn **Zelevansky**, editor

Picasso and Braque: A Symposium

0-8109-6115-6 MOMA $49.50
0-8109-6117-2 MOMA PB $19.95

Pablo Picasso

John **Berger**

The Success and Failure of Picasso

A bracing antidote to the flattering tone of much writing about Picasso

0-679-73725-1 VINTAGE PB $13.00

Marie-Laure **Bernadac** & Paule **du Bouchet**

Picasso: Master of the New Idea

0-8109-2802-7 ABRAMS PB $12.95

Rosamond **Bernier**

Matisse, Picasso, Miro: As I Knew Them

As editor of the French art monthly L'Oeil, Bernier was confidante to three of the most important artists of the Century. Here she vividly shares these memories with us along with the many penetrating observations on life and art that they inspired. 350 reproductions and photographs. "Enchanting reminiscences, rich in anecdote and insight"—Publishers Weekly

See also Matisse and Fauvism

0-679-74941-1 KNOPF PB $35.00

Aldo **Crommelynck** & others

Picasso: Inside the Image

0-500-09251-6 THAMES & HUDSON $27.50

Pablo Picasso

José Maria **Faerna**, editor

Picasso

0-8109-4690-4 ABRAMS $11.98

Judi **Freeman**

Picasso and the Weeping Women: The Years of Marie-Thérèse Walter and Dora Maar

Catalogue of an exhibition organized around the ever-popular theme of Picasso's mysogyny

0-8478-1800-4 RIZZOLI $50.00

Susan Grace **Galassi**

Picasso's Variations on the Masters: Confrontations with the Past

This innovative book on Pablo Picasso, one of the great artists of the 20th century, illustrates a lesser-known body of work inspired by earlier masters like Manet, Delacroix, and Velasquez. Susan Galassi, its author, is an associate curator and the Frick Collection and a specialist on Picasso

0-8109-3741-7 ABRAMS $39.95

Klaus **Gallwitz**

Picasso: The Heroic Years

0-89659-531-5 ABBEVILLE $75.00

Mary **Gedo**

Picasso: Art as Autobiography

0-226-28483-2 CHICAGO PB $24.00

Françoise **Gilot**

Life with Picasso

0-385-26186-1 ANCHOR PB $8.95

Karen L. **Kleinfelder**

The Artist, His Model, Her Image, His Gaze: Picasso's Pursuit of the Model

In certain ways, Picasso reiterated the traditional relationship between artist and model. This book, however, examines the possibility that Picasso's approach to the artist-model theme was more subversive than anyone suspected

0-226-43983-6 CHICAGO $55.00

James **Lord**

Picasso and Dora: A Personal Memoir

"Astonishing…a wickedly perceptive and daring book"—*NY Times Book Review*

0-88064-162-2 FROMM PB $16.95

Norman **Mailer**

Portrait of Picasso as a Young Man

One of America's most famous writers attempts to portray one of the century's most brilliant artists. Mailer concentrates on the seven-year period when Picasso lived with the extraordinary Fernande Olivier, creating his most revolutionary works (*Les Demoiselles d'Avignon*) and redefining Cubism

0-87113-608-2 ATLANTIC MONTHLY $35.00
0-446-67266-1 WARNER PB $19.99

Maria Theresa **Ocana**

Picasso: Landscapes, 1890-1912

Picasso's landscapes, many rarely exhibited and which have never been published together, will delight fans. Drawn from museums and private collections around the world, these landscapes show a Picasso interpreting the vistas of his native Spain in pre-Cubist style. Delightful on their own and revelatory of the artist's childhood influences and developments

0-8212-2239-2 BULFINCH $75.00

Fernande **Olivier**

In Love with Picasso: A Memoir

The intimate memoirs of Picasso's first love, his mistress from 1904-1912, and the muse and model for some of his greatest works. First published in France in 1988, Olivier's remembrances give an unusually lively picture of Paris at the dawn of the century, peopled with the likes of Max Jacob, Apollinaire, Gertrude Stein, and Alice B. Toklas

COMMENTARY BY JOHN RICHARDSON

0-679-43694-4 RANDOM HOUSE $30.00

Roland **Penrose**

Picasso: His Life and Work

0-520-04207-7 CALIFORNIA PB $16.95

Pablo **Picasso**

The Artist and His Model

Includes 180 drawings

0-486-27877-8 DOVER PB $12.95

Line Drawings and Prints

0-486-24196-3 DOVER PB $3.95

Picasso's Vollard Suite

One hundred superb etchings commissioned by the great art critic and dealer Ambroise Vollard from 1930 to 1937

INTRODUCTION BY HANS BOLLINGER

0-500-27100-3 THAMES & HUDSON PB $14.95

Dore **Ashton**, editor

Picasso on Art: A Selection of Views

0-306-80330-5 DA CAPO PB $11.95

Gerard **Regnier**

Treasures of The Musée Picasso

1-55859-836-7 ABBEVILLÉ PB $11.95

John **Richardson**

A Life of Picasso: 1881-1906

The first volume of a long-awaited biography. Richardson's book has already been widely praised as the best treatment of Picasso to date. "There have been hundreds of books about Picasso but no really satisfactory biography until now"—Robert Hughes, *Time*

WITH THE COLLABORATION OF MARILYN MCCULLY

0-679-76421-6 RANDOM HOUSE PB $30.00

A Life of Picasso: 1907-1917

"A triumph of the biographer's art and one of the most illuminating studies yet written about a major figure of the modern movement"
—Hilton Kramer

0-394-55918-5 RANDOM HOUSE $55.00

William **Rubin**, editor

Picasso and Portraiture: Representation and Transformation

0-8109-6160-1 MOMA $75.00
0-87070-142-8 MOMA PB $35.00

William **Rubin** & others

Les Demoiselles d'Avignon

0-8109-6125-3 MOMA $40.00

Werner **Spies**

Picasso's World of Children

A survey of Picasso's depiction of children, including his own, ranging from works which evoke a tradition of the charm associated with childhood to images which break entirely with conventional notions of the well-protected seclusion of a child's world

3-7913-1375-4 TE NEUS $25.00

Other Cubists

Picasso was not alone in creating Cubism. It resulted from an intense period of collaboration with Georges Braque, during which, as Picasso put it, "it was as if we were husband and wife." The movement soon attracted many adherents, including Juan Gris, in whose hands Cubism took a somewhat didactic turn. Strong personalities like Robert and Sonia Delaunay and Fernand Léger were greatly influenced by Cubism without ever falling fully under its spell.

Georges **Braque**

Illustrated Notebooks, 1917-1955

0-486-20232-1 DOVER PB $6.95

Karen **Wilkin**

Georges Braque

0-89659-944-2 ABBEVILLE $32.95
0-89659-947-7 ABBEVILLE PB $22.95

Christopher **Green** & others

Juan Gris

"Academic" but well written and researched, with winningly beautiful illustrations

0-300-05374-6 YALE $60.00

Mark **Rosenthal**

Juan Gris

0-89659-401-7 ABBEVILLE PB $35.00

Jose Maria **Faerna**, editor

Léger

TRANSLATED BY ALBERTO CUROTTO

0-8109-4688-2 ABRAMS $11.98

Dorothy **Kosinski**, editor

Fernand Léger, 1911-1924: The Rhythm of Modern Life

3-7913-1372-X TE NEUS $75.00

Gladys **Fabre**

Léger and the Modern Spirit: An Avant-Garde Alternative to Non-Objective Art

0-295-96072-8 WASHINGTON PB $35.00

Alan G. **Wilkinson**

The Sculpture of Jacques Lipchitz: A Catalogue Raisonné—The Paris Years

A catalogue raisonné of all of the artist's works created between his arrival in Paris in 1909 up to his arrival in New York in 1941

0-500-09262-1 THAMES & HUDSON PB $60.00

Matisse and Fauvism

Rosamond **Bernier**

Matisse, Picasso, Miró: As I Knew Them

As editor of the French art monthly *L'Oeil*, Bernier was confidante to three of the most important artists of the Century. Here she vividly shares these memories with us along with the many penetrating observations on life and art that they inspired. 350 reproductions and photographs. "Enchanting reminiscences, rich in anecdote and insight"—*Publishers Weekly*

See also **PABLO PICASSO** under **CUBISM**

0-679-74941-1 KNOPF PB $35.00

Pierre **Bonnard** & Henri **Matisse**

Bonnard/Matisse: Letters Between Friends 1925-1946

TRANSLATED BY RICHARD HOWARD

0-8109-2533-8 ABRAMS PB $19.95

Alfred **Werner**

Dufy

0-8109-0848-4 ABRAMS $22.95

Fauve Birds, Butterflies, and Flowers

0-8109-2976-7 ABRAMS PB $14.95

James D. **Herbert**

Fauve Painting: The Making of Cultural Politics

0-300-05068-2 YALE $50.00

Jack **Cowart** & others

Matisse in Morocco

0-8109-2527-3 ABRAMS PB $24.95

John **Elderfield**

Henri Matisse: A Retrospective

The complete illustrated catalog to the show at MoMA, the largest and most comprehensive Matisse exhibition ever assembled. In his exciting introductory essay, the author, curator of the exhibit, interprets the importance of Matisse's work not only to modern art but to modern sensibility as a whole. 400 works, 320 in full color. "Elderfield brilliantly deconstructs Matisse's pictorial language"

—*Publishers Weekly*

0-8109-6116-4 MOMA $75.00

Jose Maria **Faerna**, editor

Matisse

0-8109-4685-8 ABRAMS $11.98

Jack **Flam**, editor

Matisse: A Retrospective

0-88363-073-7 OUTLET $75.00

Henri Matisse

Xavier **Girard**

Matisse: The Wonder of Color

TRANSLATED BY I. MARK PARIS

0-8109-2820-5 ABRAMS PB $12.95

Hayden **Herrera**

Matisse: A Portrait of the Man and His Art

Vivid and entertaining, this brief critical biography examines the paradox of Matisse's tumultuous emotional life, and the "art of balance, of purity and serenity" he mastered. Abundantly illustrated in both color and black and white, this book offers a vital perspective on one of the century's greatest artists—his love of color, his often tumultuous relationship with his wife, his unshakable belief in himself, and his passion for his art

0-15-158183-5 HARCOURT BRACE $29.95

Albert **Kostenvich** & Natalya **Semenova**

Collecting Matisse

2-08-013541-4 ABBEVILLE $60.00

William **Lieberman**

Matisse: Fifty Years of His Graphic Art

0-8076-0037-7 BRAZILLER $30.00

0-8076-1022-4 BRAZILLER PB $12.95

Henri **Matisse**

Drawings: Themes and Variations

0-486-28520-0 DOVER PB $12.95

Jazz

An exceptionally low-priced and beautiful edition of Matisse's classic work, containing all the writings and bold color stencils of the original. Matisse addresses here the themes that pervade his work: circuses, the theater, artistic dedication. Includes handwritten autobiographical notes by the master painter. "Matisse has taught the eye to hear" —Riva Castleman. "[A] classic of our century"—John Russell

INTRODUCTION BY RIVA CASTLEMAN

0-8076-1291-X BRAZILLER $11.95

0-8076-1131-X BRAZILLER PB $29.50

Line Drawings and Prints

Fifty plates

0-486-23877-6 DOVER PB $3.95

Portrait Drawings

Includes 45 drawings

0-486-26438-6 DOVER PB $4.95

Jack **Flam**

Matisse on Art

The first collection of Matisse's major writings, including transcriptions of interviews and broadcasts

0-520-20032-2 CALIFORNIA PB $15.00

Hayden **Herrera**

Matisse

0151581830 HARCOURT BRACE $29.95

Nicholas **Watkins**

Matisse

0-7148-2709-6 PHAIDON PB $14.95

Sarah **Whitfield**

Fauvism

The first book in many years to offer a critical reappraisal of the movements' artists, their work, their relationships with each other, and the critical and commercial response to their work which was initially met with hostility but which paved the way for Cubism

0-500-20227-3 THAMES & HUDSON PB $14.95

Other Artists in Paris

Stanislas Klossowski De **Rola**

Balthus

This book is a comprehensive overview of Balthus's oeuvre by his eldest son, offering new insights into this intensely private and controversial artist's life

0-8109-3134-6 ABRAMS $45.00

Andre **Fermigier**

Pierre Bonnard

Adapted from the recent retrospective exhibition held in Paris; an important contribution with numerous fine reproductions of Bonnard's sensuous, radiant works

0-8109-0732-1 ABRAMS $22.95

Anna C. **Chave**

Constantin Brancusi: Shifting the Bases of Art

While challenging traditional views of Brancusi as a lone visionary of pure form, Chave (*Mark Rothko: Subjects in Abstraction*) is able to demonstrate the prescient sexual content of the artist's work, and its relationship to the changing status of the handmade object in the age of mass production

0-300-05526-9 YALE $55.00

Constantin Brancusi

Eric **Shames**

Constantin Brancusi

0-89659-924-8 ABBEVILLE $32.95

Radu **Varia**

Brancusi

0-7893-0021-4 UNIVERSE PB $45.00

Marc **Chagall**

Drawings for the Bible

0-486-28575-8 DOVER PB $13.95

Marc Chagall: Daphnis and Chloe

Inspired by a journey to Greece, the artist created a series of lithographs that brought new life to this ancient Greek love story

3-7913-1373-8 TE NEUS $25.00

My Life

0-306-80571-5 DA CAPO PB $13.95

Andrew **Kagan**

Marc Chagall

0-89659-932-9 ABBEVILLE $32.95
0-89659-935-3 ABBEVILLE PB $22.95

Jacob **Baal-Teshuva**, editor

Chagall: A Retrospective

Critic, curator, and longtime friend of Chagall, Baal-Teshuva has edited a stunning retrospective collection of and commentary on Chagall's personal and artistic development. Over 240 reproductions of the artist's great work interweave seamlessly with over 100 incisive commentaries that range from Chagall's memoirs to interviews, letters, and writings by Breton, Appollinaire, Aragon, and others

0-88363-495-3 LEVIN $75.00

Stanley **Baron**

Sonia Delaunay: The Life of an Artist

Artist and textile and fashion designer, Delaunay played a central role in the Parisian avant-garde of the early 20th century—a role that, overshadowed by her more famous husband, has never been fully appreciated

0-8109-3222-9 ABRAMS $39.95

Carol **Mann**

Modigliani

See also **THAMES & HUDSON WORLD OF ART** under **ART HISTORY: GENERAL STUDIES**

0-500-20176-5 NORTON PB $14.95

Noel **Alexandre**

The Unknown Modigliani: Drawings from the Collection of Paul Alexandre

The 450 drawings in this volume were purchased by the French physician Alexandre, who was the artist's closest friend, doctor, and only patron when Modigliani arrived in Paris in 1906

0-8109-3642-9 ABRAMS $95.00

Anette **Kruszynski**

Amedeo Modigliani

A color survey of the artist's lifelong involvement with portraiture and the human figure, from the penetrating early psychological studies to his mature depictions of nudes as feminine icons

3-7913-1674-5 PRESTEL $25.00

Christian **Parisot**

Modigliani

Over 230 illustrations document Modigliani in drawings, paintings, and sculptures, from the sensual nudes to the poetic portraits. The text presents the artist with copious biographical details, and showcases the art work with critical interpretations. A refreshing analysis of the style, genius, and legend of Modigliani

2-87939-005-2 STEWART, TABORI PB $24.95

Alfred **Werner**

Modigliani

0-8109-1416-6 ABRAMS $22.95

Expressionism and the Blue Rider

Expressionism is less a well-defined approach to picture-making on the order of Impressionism or Cubism than a recurrent attitude to art, like classicism or romanticism. When we speak more specifically of German Expressionist art of the early 20th century, we are speaking primarily of two groups: on the one hand *Die Brücke* (The Bridge), including Ernst Ludwig Kirchner, Emil Nolde, and Max Pechstein, who exhibited together in Dresden between 1905 and 1913; and on the other the group associated with the Munich periodical *Der Blaue Reiter* (The Blue Rider), whose single issue (published in 1912) was edited by Franz Marc and Wassily Kandinsky. Other artists associated with the Blue Rider included Paul Klee and August Macke. In general, the Blue Rider artists were more involved with abstraction than those of *Die Brücke*, and they later provided the core of the painting faculty at the Bauhaus.

After World War I there was a reaction within Expressionism against the excessive "inwardness" of older artists in the movement. The narrative, often bitterly satirical works of artists such as Otto Dix and Georg Grosz seemed to herald a "new objectivity" (*Neue Sachlichkeit*)—although the most important of these artists, Max Beckmann, far from embodying objectivity, may be seen as the third great mythographer of modern painting after Picasso and Matisse.

Wolf-Dieter **Dube**

The Expressionists

0-500-20123-4 THAMES & HUDSON PB $14.95

Paul **Raabe**, editor

The Era of German Expressionism

An important documentary sourcebook

0-87951-233-4 OVERLOOK PB $16.95

Peter **Selz**

German Expressionist Painting

The classic survey of the period

0-520-02515-6 CALIFORNIA PB $19.95

Kirk **Varnedoe**

Vienna 1900: Art, Architecture, and Design

0-87070-618-7 MOMA $50.00
0-8109-6106-7 MOMA PB $34.95

Peter **Vergo**

Art in Vienna, 1898-1918: Klimt, Kokoschka, Schiele, and Their Contemporaries

0-7148-2967-6 PHAIDON PB $29.95

Annette **Vezin** & Luc **Vezin**

Kandinsky and Der Blaue Reiter

2-87939-043-5 STEWART, TABORI PB $24.95

John **Willett**

Art and Politics in the Weimar Period: The New Sobriety, 1917-1933

From the German typographic revolution to the Brecht-Weill partnership. "An original and challenging book, thoroughly researched and aptly illustrated"—*Times* (London)

See also **PORTRAITS OF WEIMAR** under **THE THIRD REICH** under **20TH-CENTURY EUROPE TO THE SECOND WORLD WAR** in **WORLD HISTORY AND CURRENT AFFAIRS**

0-306-80724-6 DA CAPO PB $17.95

Armin **Zweite**

The Blue Rider in the Lenbachhaus, Munich

A major survey of the movement, with commentaries, biographies, and full-color illustrations

3-7913-0850-5 PRESTEL........$65.00

German Expressionism

Peter **Selz**

Max Beckmann

1-55859-889-8 ABBEVILLE........$35.00

Max **Beckmann**

Self-Portrait in Words: Collected Writings and Statements, 1903-1950

EDITED AND TRANSLATED BY BARBARA COPELAND BUENGER

0-226-04135-2 CHICAGO........$34.95

0-226-04136-0 CHICAGO PB........$24.00

Stephen **Lackner**

Max Beckmann: Memories of a Friendship

0-517-55000-8 CROWN........$14.95

Fritz **Loffler**

Otto Dix: Life and Work

0-8419-0578-9 HOLMES & MEIER........$95.00

Hans **Hess**

George Grosz

0-300-03408-3 YALE........$22.00

Peter **Pachnicke** & Klaus **Honnef**, editors

John Heartfield

0-8109-3413-2 ABRAMS........$95.00

Maria **Jawlensky** & others

Alexej Jawlensky: Catalogue Raisonné of The Oil Paintings

Volume I

1890-1914

0-85667-398-6 SOTHEBY PARKE BERNET........$395.00

Volume II

1914-1933

0-85667-406-0 SOTHEBY PARKE BERNET........$395.00

Volume III

1934-1937

0-85667-420-6 SOTHEBY PARKE BERNET........$395.00

Will **Grohmann**

Klee

0-8109-1208-2 ABRAMS........$22.95

Paul **Klee**

The Diaries of Paul Klee

See also **ARTISTS ON ART** under **ART HISTORY: GENERAL STUDIES**

EDITED BY FELIX KLEE

0-520-00653-4 CALIFORNIA PB........$15.95

Drawings

0-486-24241-2 DOVER PB........$3.95

Paul Klee on Modern Art

A collection of his writing

0-571-06682-8 FABER PB........$10.95

Paul Klee

Käthe **Kollwitz**

Prints and Drawings

0-486-22177-6 DOVER PB........$11.95

Sergiusz **Michalski**

New Objectivity

A major survey of the artists of the Neue Sachlichkeit (the "New Objectivity"), a movement in the early 1920s that replaced the emotionalism and extravagant manifestos of Expressionism with a cooler and more sober perspective that looked at everyday life outside the house, in the streets, and in the gutter

3-8228-9650-0 TASCHEN........$25.01

Martin **Urban**

Emil Nolde: Catalogue Raisonné of the Oil Painting

Volume I

1895-1914

0-85667-320-X SOTHEBY PARKE BERNET........$270.00

Volume II

1915-1951

0-85667-377-3 SOTHEBY PARKE BERNET........$270.00

Expressionism Outside of Germany

Expressionism was not limited to German-speaking countries. In Paris some of the fauves came close; Rouault in particular is often referred to as an Expressionist. The fantastic paintings of Marc Chagall are closely related, and the impulse reached a particularly intense pitch in the work of Chaim Soutine.

Magdalena **Dabrowski**

Vasily Kandinsky Compositions

0-8109-6142-3 ABRAMS........$45.00

Jelena **Hahl-Koch**

Kandinsky

0-8478-1404-1 RIZZOLI........$150.00

Annegret **Hoberg**

Wassily Kandinsky & Gabriele Munter

"The story of their life together. . . is told in letters (some of which are published here for the first time), in diary extracts and memoirs, and in superb reproductions of their finest paintings and sketches"

—Antique Dealer and Collector's Guide

3-7913-1374-6 TE NEUS........$25.00

Vivian Endicott **Barnett**

Kandinsky Watercolors: Catalogue Raisonné

Volume I

1900-1921

0-8014-2690-1 CORNELL........$275.00

Volume II

1922-1944

0-8014-2927-7 CORNELL........$275.00

Wassily **Kandinsky**

Complete Writings on Art

EDITED BY KENNETH CLEMENT LINDSAY AND PETER VERGO

0-306-80570-7 DA CAPO PB........$24.95

Concerning the Spiritual in Art

Kandinsky's primary statement of his philosophy of art

0-486-23411-8 DOVER PB........$3.95

Wassily Kandinsky

Peg **Weiss**

Kandinsky and Old Russia: The Artist as Ethnographer and Shaman

Kandinsky, whom many consider the father of abstract painting, was also a trained ethnographer. This book provides an entirely new interpretation of his art by examining for the first time how his commitment to his ethnic Russian heritage influenced his entire work

0-300-05647-8 YALE........$50.00

Kandinsky in Munich: 1896-1914

0-89207-030-7 GUGGENHEIM PB........$19.50

Gustav **Klimt**
One Hundred Drawings
0-486-22446-5 DOVER PB $8.95

Angelica **Baumer**
Gustav Klimt Women
0-8478-1378-9 RIZZOLI PB $35.00

Christian M. **Nebehay**
Gustav Klimt: From Drawing to Painting
0-8109-3510-4 ABRAMS $75.00

Susanna **Partsch**
Gustav Klimt: Painter of Woman
A sumptuously illustrated collection of Klimt's most important paintings that emphasizes the impact of fashion designer Emilie Flöge's work
3-7913-1428-9 PRESTEL $25.00

Frank **Whitford**
Gustav Klimt
0-517-10291-9 CRESCENT $15.99

Klimt
0-500-20246-X THAMES & HUDSON PB $14.95

Richard **Calvocoressi**
Oskar Kokoschka
0-89207-059-5 GUGGENHEIM PB $25.00

Alice **Strobl** & Alfred **Weidinger**
Oskar Kokoschka: Works on Paper: The Early Years, 1897-1917
0-8109-6879-7 ABRAMS $45.00

Egon **Schiele**
Drawings
Includes 44 works
0-486-28150-7 DOVER PB $4.95

Alessandra **Comini**
Egon Schiele
0-8076-0820-3 BRAZILLER PB $19.95

Nudes: Egon Schiele
0-8478-1841-1 RIZZOLI $25.00

Jane **Kallir**
Egon Schiele
0-8109-3845-6 ABRAMS $45.00
0-8109-2662-8 ABRAMS PB $19.95

Klaus Albrecht **Schroder**
Egon Schiele: Eros and Passion
An appraisal of the uncompromisingly sensual paintings that led to the artist's imprisonment on charges of pornography in 1912
3-7913-1383-5 PRESTEL $25.00

Klaus Albrecht **Schroder** &
Harald **Szeemann**, editor
Egon Schiele and His Contemporaries: Austrian Painting and Drawing from 1900 to 1930
"An extensive and beautifully illustrated survey of the art produced in Austria during a unique era"—*Austrian Information*
3-7913-0921-8 PRESTEL $65.00

Frank **Whitford**
Egon Schiele
See also **THAMES & HUDSON WORLD OF ART** under **ART HISTORY: GENERAL STUDIES**
0-500-18183-7 NORTON $19.95
0-500-20183-8 THAMES & HUDSON PB $14.95

Simon **Wilson**
Egon Schiele
A major figure in modern art worked during the dawn of the Freudian era, the Austrian painter is just now beginning to receive his due. This affordable volume documents the themes of Schiele's brief career, and introduces his central role in the development of Expressionism
0-7148-2927-7 PHAIDON PB $14.99

Futurism

Futurism, invented by a well-to-do *littérateur* named F.T. Marinetti, was probably the first important art movement in which publicity came first and art followed. Futurism's romanticizing of speed, dynamism, and the machine could only have arisen in a less developed part of Europe such as Italy, but it did temporarily attract most of the ambitious Italian painters of the prewar years: Giacomo Balla, Umberto Boccioni, Carlo Carrà, and Gino Severini.

F. T. **Marinetti**
Let's Murder the Moonshine: Selected Writings
See also **ESSAYS, MEMOIRS, AND OTHER PROSE** under **THE 20TH CENTURY** under **ITALIAN LITERATURE** in **LITERATURE OF EUROPE, AFRICA, AND ASIA**
EDITED BY R.W. FLINT
1-55713-101-5 SUN & MOON PB $13.95

Caroline **Tisdall** & Angelo **Bozollo**
Futurism
0-500-18162-4 THAMES & HUDSON $19.95

Vorticism

Strong affinities with Futurism were shown by the English movement known as Vorticism, whose proponents included Wyndham Lewis, Jacob Epstein, Henri Gaudier-Brzeska, and (for a time) David Bomberg. These artists were close to the poet Ezra Pound.

Richard **Cork**
David Bomberg
0-300-03827-5 YALE $100.00
0-300-04194-2 YALE PB $42.00

Ezra **Pound**
Gaudier-Brzeska: A Memoir
See also **CRITICS AND WRITERS ON ART** under **ART HISTORY: GENERAL STUDIES**
0-8112-0527-4 NEW DIRECTIONS PB $7.95

Evelyn **Silber**
Gaudier-Brzeska
The first major study of the life and work of the artist who was killed in the trenches in 1915, incorporating a catalogue raisonné of his sculpture. A pioneering direct carver, he was a protegé of Ezra Pound, a member of the London circle that included Wyndham Lewis, Jacob Epstein, and Roger Fry, and an acknowledged influence on Henry Moore and Barbara Hepworth
0-500-09261-3 THAMES & HUDSON $65.00

Tom **Normand**
Wyndham Lewis, The Artist: Holding the Mirror Up to Politics
0-521-41054-1 CAMBRIDGE $79.95

Russian Futurism and Constructivism

Russian artists of the early 20th century were attuned to new developments in Paris as well as to Italian Futurism, and at the same time were tremendously interested in Russia's icon and folk art traditions, with their innocence of Western naturalism. The result was an artistic ferment from which two primary trends stand out: the purely non-objective tendency which Kasimir Malevich called Suprematism, and the utilitarian, antiesthetic direction championed by Vladimir Tatlin and El Lissitsky, which by 1920 was known as Constructivism.

Barbara **Rose**
Magdalena Abakanowicz
0-8109-1947-8 ABRAMS $49.50

Susan **Compton**
Russian Avant-Garde Books, 1917-34
See also **TYPOGRAPHY** under **ILLUSTRATION AND POPULAR GRAPHICS**
0-262-03201-5 MIT $29.95

Catherine **Cooke** & others
The Russian and Soviet Avant-Garde, 1915-1932
0-8109-6868-1 GUGGENHEIM $85.00

Alla **Efimova** & Lev **Manovich**, editors & translators
Tekstura: Russian Essays on Visual Culture
The West is fascinated with the Russian avant-garde. But how do the Russians view their own cultural and artistic experiences? This translation of 13 essays by Russian authors, most produced within the last 20 years, is an excellent way to find out
0-226-95123-5 CHICAGO $34.95
0-226-95124-3 CHICAGO PB $13.95

Serge **Fauchereau**
Malevich
0-8478-1738-5 RIZZOLI $27.50

Gerald **Janecek**
The Look of Russian Literature: Avant-Garde Visual Experiments, 1900-1930
An important study in the Slavic formation of modern aesthetics, this book "…raises—and skillfully addresses—one of the most intriguing methodological questions in current literary theory: namely, the complex interplay between verbal and visual features in experimental texts…"—F. W. Galan
0-691-06604-3 PRINCETON $60.00
0-691-01457-4 PRINCETON PB $18.95

Sophie **Lissitzky-Kuppers**
El Lissitzky: Life, Letters, Texts
0-500-23090-0 THAMES & HUDSON $70.00

Charlotte **Douglas**
Malevich
0-8109-3645-3 ABRAMS $22.95

Aleksandr M. **Rodchenko** & Varvara F. **Stepanova**
The Future Is Our Only Goal
EDITED BY PETER NOEVER
3-7913-1134-4 PRESTEL $65.00

Mondrian and De Stijl

"In the future," wrote the Dutch painter Piet Mondrian, "the tangible embodiment of pictorial values will supplant art. Then we shall no longer need painting, for we shall be in the midst of realized art." Mondrian, along with Theo van Doesburg, edited an influential review called *De Stijl*, whose name became attached to their work, which is also known as neo-Plasticism. Their work is notable for its rather Calvinist sobriety and restraint; they restricted their palette to the primary colors red, yellow, and blue, along with black, white, and gray, structured by straight lines and right angles. Their adherence to doctrine was so strict that the two artists fell out in a dispute over the admissibility of diagonals in painting.

Carel **Blotkamp**
Mondrian: The Art of Destruction
0-8109-3646-1 ABRAMS $49.50

Serge **Fauchereau**
Mondrian
0-8478-1832-2 RIZZOLI $27.50

Hans **Jaffe**
Mondrian
0-8109-1413-1 ABRAMS $22.95

Joop **Joosten** & Angelica Zander **Rudenstine**
Piet Mondrian, 1872-1944
0-8212-2164-7 BULFINCH $75.00

John **Miller**
Mondrian
1-55859-400-0 PHAIDON PB $50.00

Piet **Mondrian**
The New Art—The New Life: The Collected Writings of Piet Mondrian
EDITED BY HARRY HOLTZMAN AND MARTIN S. JAMES
0-306-80508-1 DA CAPO PB $24.95

Natural Reality and Abstract Reality: An Essay in Trialogue Form
0-8076-1371-1 BRAZILLER $25.00
0-8076-1372-X BRAZILLER PB $14.95

Meyer **Schapiro**
Mondrian: On the Humanity of Abstract Painting
0-8076-1370-3 BRAZILLER PB $12.50

Paul **Overy**
De Stijl
0-500-20240-0 THAMES & HUDSON PB $12.95

The Bauhaus and Related Constructivism

Another group, more didactic and experimental, centered around the Bauhaus, the school founded in Weimar by architect Walter Gropius. Among the artists who taught there were Oskar Schlemmer, Lyonel Feininger, and László Moholy-Nagy, as well as some earlier associated with Expressionism, like Kandinsky and Klee. A number of the Russian vanguardists arrived after 1922, as the climate for modern art grew chilly at home.

Nicholas **Weber**
Josef Albers: A Retrospective
0-8109-1876-5 ABRAMS $65.00

Krisztina **Passuth**
Moholy-Nagy
See also **PHOTOGRAPHERS** under **PHOTOGRAPHY**
0-500-27449-5 THAMES & HUDSON PB $24.95

George **Rickey**
Constructivism: Origins and Evolution, Revised Edition
0-8076-1381-9 BRAZILLER PB $25.00

Margit **Rowell**
The Planar Dimension: Europe, 1912-1932
An essential study of international Constructivist sculpture
0-295-96290-9 WASHINGTON PB $14.95

Sigrid Wortmann **Weltge**
Women's Work: Textile Art from the Bauhaus
This book focuses on the little-acknowledged work of the predominantly female Bauhaus Weaving Workshop. Talented craftswomen developed ingenious, innovative ways of designing beautiful textiles for mass production. Rare illustrations, archival photographs, and in-depth interviews celebrate the legacy that lives on in fabrics still being produced today
See also **FLOOR COVERINGS, TEXTILES, AND WALLPAPER** under **EUROPEAN DECORATIVE ARTS** in **ARCHITECTURE, DESIGN, AND HOMES**
0-8118-0466-6 CHRONICLE $40.00

Dada and Surrealism

While Fauvism, Cubism, and even Expressionism can all be seen as modes of pictorial organization, Dada (as André Breton said) "is a state of mind." The artists who gathered under the banner of Dada came through the years of the Great War with a combination of deadpan nihilism and desperate playfulness that gave their work a new disruptive power—the power of antiart. The movement was international, with manifestations in Zurich, Berlin, Paris, and even New York.

David **Batchelor** & others
Realism, Rationalism, Surrealism: Art Between the Wars
A discussion of how Dada, Surrealism, and abstraction are related to the ethos of postwar reconstruction and questions of sexuality and gender posed by Freudian theory
0-300-05519-6 YALE PB $27.00

Margaret **Cohen**
Profane Illumination: Walter Benjamin and the Paris of Surrealist Revolution
Cohen's encounter with Walter Benjamin, one of the seminal cultural and literary critics of the century, has produced this incisive new reading of the Surrealists, their lives and work. Benjamin's challenge to Marxism is explored in dialogue with André Breton's surrealist interpretation of psychoanalysis and Marxist theory, and this compelling exchange is shown as shaping intellectual theory in postwar Europe and beyond
0-520-08023-8 CALIFORNIA $35.00

André **Breton**
Manifestoes of Surrealism
See also **ESSAYS: PERSONAL, LITERARY, PHILOSOPHICAL** under **MODERN FRENCH LITERATURE** in **LITERATURE OF EUROPE, AFRICA, AND ASIA**
TRANSLATED BY RICHARD SEAVER & HELEN R. LANE
0-472-06182-8 MICHIGAN PB $15.95

Dawn **Ades**
Dalì
See also **THAMES & HUDSON WORLD OF ART** under **ART HISTORY: GENERAL STUDIES**
0-500-20280-X THAMES & HUDSON PB $14.95

Salvador **Dalì**
Diary of a Genius
1-87159-226-7 SUBTERRANEAN $13.95

Salvador **Dalì** & Philippe **Halsman**
Dalì's Mustache
Dalì, the master of Surrealism, and Halsman, portrait photographer, were friends and collaborators for over 30 years. This photographic interview reveals the wit, absurdity, and profundity for which Dalì is famous while the inspired images of his mustache display Halsman's inventiveness and skill
2-08-013560-0 ABBEVILLE $12.00

Robert **Descharnes**
Dalì: The Work, the Man
Over 1000 illustrations
0-8109-8131-9 ABRADALE $24.98

Hayward Gallery
Salvador Dalì: The Early Years
The first book to explore in depth the development of Dalì's early work up to about 1930, and a highly original reassessment of his artistic complexity and importance as an innovator
0-500-23689-5 THAMES & HUDSON $50.00

Jose Maria **Faerna**, editor
Dalì
0-8109-4679-3 ABRAMS $11.98

Giorgio **de Chirico**
The Memoirs of Giorgio de Chirico
0-306-80568-5 DA CAPO PB $13.95

Marc **Rombaut**
Paul Delvaux
0-8478-1201-4 RIZZOLI $27.50

Thierry **de Duve**
Pictorial Nominalism: On Marcel Duchamp's Passage from Painting to the Readymade
0-8166-1565-9 MINNESOTA PB $15.95

Thierry **de Duve**, editor
The Definitively Unfinished Marcel Duchamp
0-262-54072-X MIT PB $30.00

Marcel **Duchamp**
Writings
See also **ARTISTS ON ART** under **ART HISTORY: GENERAL STUDIES**
EDITED BY MICHEL SANOUILLET AND ELMER PETERSON
0-306-80341-0 DA CAPO PB $12.95

Pierre **Cabanne**
Dialogues with Marcel Duchamp
"These conversations are more than mere interviews. They are Marcel Duchamp's summing up, and constitute as vivid a self-portrait as we posses of a major twentieth-century artist, thanks to Duchamp's intelligence, scrupulousness, and disdain for the petty"—Robert Motherwell
See also **ARTISTS ON ART** under **ART HISTORY: GENERAL STUDIES**
0-306-80303-8 DA CAPO PB $9.95

Pontus **Helten**, editor
Marcel Duchamp: Work and Life
0-262-08225-X MIT $75.00

William **Canfield**
Max Ernst: Dada and the Dawn of Surrealism
A compelling account of Ernst's life from 1912-1927; and the vibrant social and political milieu, as well Ernst's relationships with Picasso, Klee, and de Chirico
3-7913-1260-X PRESTEL $70.00

Werner **Spies**, editor
Max Ernst: A Retrospective
The most complete survey of the surrealist painter's work ever published, on the occasion of the 1991 centenary exhibit at the Tate Gallery. 250 color and 190 black-and-white illustrations
3-7913-1621-4 PRESTEL PB $29.95

Suzi **Gablik**
Magritte
0-500-20199-4 THAMES & HUDSON PB $14.95

Pere **Gimferrer**
Magritte
0-8478-0809-2 RIZZOLI $27.50

Michel **Foucault**
This Is Not a Pipe: Illustrations and Letters by René Magritte
Explores the nuances and ambiguities of Magritte's visual critique of language
TRANSLATED BY JAMES HARKNESS
ILLUSTRATED BY RENÉ MAGRITTE
0-520-04916-0 CALIFORNIA PB $12.95

A.M. **Hammacher**
Magritte
0-8109-8137-8 ABRADALE $19.98

David **Sylvester**
Magritte: The Silence of the World
Magritte's powerful surrealist work has had a seminal influence on art and mass culture. Three hundred illustrations, 220 in full color. "Sylvester succeeds in making us see exactly what Magritte meant when he wrote of his 'determination to make the most familiar objects yell' "
—Richard Dorment, *NY Review of Books*
0-8109-3626-7 ABRAMS $75.00

David **Sylvester** & others, editors
René Magritte Catalogue Raisonné
Volume I
Oil Paintings 1916-1930
0-85667-423-0 SOTHEBY PARKE BERNET $180.00
Volume II
Oil Paintings and Objects 1931-1948
0-85667-424-9 RIZZOLI $180.00

Dawn **Ades**
André Masson
0-8478-1799-7 RIZZOLI $27.50

J.H. **Matthews**
Eight Painters: The Surrealist Context
0-8156-2302-X SYRACUSE PB $18.95

Barbara **Catoir**
Miró on Mallorca
A survey of the artist's works inspired by the optimistic and carefree atmosphere of this Mediterranean island
3-7913-1483-1 PEGAS $25.00

Jacques **Dupin**
Miró
0-8109-3632-1 ABRAMS $95.00

Rudi **Fuchs** & others
Joan Miró, 1893-1993
0-8212-2024-1 BULFINCH $85.00

Carolyn **Lanchner**
Joan Miró
Miró's early association with Surrealism produced a universe of painting, formally innovative and enormously playful. This beautiful volume, published to accompany the centennial retrospective at the Museum of Modern Art (October 1993-January 1994), covers the painter's entire career
0-8109-6123-7 MOMA $75.00

Margit **Rowell**, editor
Joan Miró: Selected Writings and Interviews
0-8057-9956-7 TWAYNE $36.00
0-306-80485-9 DA CAPO PB $14.95

Joan **Miró**
Joan Miró: A Retrospective
0-8109-6162-8 GUGGENHEIM PB $29.50

Miró: A Toute Epreuve
Taking over ten years to create, *A Toute Epreuve (Ready for Anything)* perfectly combines Miró's entrancing amorphous forms with Eluard's poetry, inviting the reader to skip from text to imagery almost interchangeably. "One of the most triumphant feats of book illustration in our century"—James Thrall Soby
See also **BOOK ILLUSTRATION** under **ILLUSTRATION AND POPULAR GRAPHICS**
POEMS BY PAUL ELUARD
0-8076-1330-4 BRAZILLER PB $29.50

Roland **Penrose**
Miró
0-500-20099-8 THAMES & HUDSON PB $14.95

Robert **Motherwell**, editor
The Dada Painters and Poets
An anthology compiled by the Dada painters and poets themselves in the 1940s, that became a classic of counterculture in 20th-century art and had a tremendous influence on the New York school of poets. Allen Ginsberg attributes the existence of "Howl" to reading this book
See also **ARTISTS ON ART** under **ART HISTORY: GENERAL STUDIES**
0-674-18500-5 BELKNAP PB $24.95

Francis M. **Naumann**
New York Dada, 1915-23
0-8109-3676-3 ABRAMS $60.00

Neil **Baldwin**
Man Ray: American Artist
A new biography
0-306-80423-9 DA CAPO PB $16.95

Merry **Foresta** & others
Perpetual Motif: The Art of Man Ray
0-89659-870-5 ABBEVILLE $65.00

Dorothea **Dietrich**
The Collages of Kurt Schwitters: Tradition and Innovation
0-521-41936-0 CAMBRIDGE $70.00
0-521-49891-0 CAMBRIDGE PB $24.95

Jean Christophe **Bailly** & Richard **Howard**, translator
Dorothea Tanning
A sumptuous and original overview of a unique figure in American art, the American wife of Max Ernst, whose work and life spanned the world of Surrealism in Paris and continue today in New York. "[Tanning] is heir to the surrealist magic, the keeper of its uncompromising flame. Still urgently in pursuit of the marvelous, she comes up with pictures that are so purely fantasy that they can be read as allegorical

personifications of the unconscious itself"
—Donald Kuspit
INTRODUCTION BY JOHN RUSSELL AND AN AFTERWORD BY DOROTHEA TANNING
0-8076-1402-5 BRAZILLER $75.00

Dorothea **Tanning**
Birthday
A luminous memoir of the artist's marriage to Max Ernst
0-932499-15-5 LAPIS $19.95
0-932499-16-3 LAPIS PB $12.95

Dickran **Tashjian**
A Boatload of Madmen: Surrealism and the American Avant-Garde, 1920-1950
An insightful cultural history of what America made of the Surrealism and what Surrealists such as Dalí and Man Ray made of America. "Christopher Columbus should have set out to discover America with a boatload of madmen"
—André Breton
0-500-23687-9 THAMES & HUDSON $29.95

Art in England

Jane **Hill**
The Art of Dora Carrington
A major study of the artist's achievements, discussed in terms of her personal relationships with her Bloomsbury friends, favorite places, and current events and trends
0-500-27857-1 THAMES & HUDSON PB $15.95

Dora Carrington

Diane Filby **Gillespie**
The Sister's Arts: The Writing and Painting of Virginia Woolf and Vanessa Bell
0-815-62529-2 SYRACUSE $17.95

Charles **Harrison**
English Art and Modernism, 1900-1939
A detailed history of modern art in early 20th-century England and of the development of the concept of modernism among English artists, critics, and theorists
0-300-05986-8 YALE PB $27.50

David **Jenkins**
Barbara Hepworth
0-905005-83-X WASHINGTON PB $10.00

Jeremy **Lewison**
Ben Nicholson
0-8478-1395-9 RIZZOLI $27.50
1-85437-130-4 TATE GALLERY PB $60.00

Wendy **Baron** & Richard **Stone**
Sickert: Paintings
0-300-05373-8 YALE $65.00

Keith **Bell**
Stanley Spencer: A Complete Catalogue of the Paintings
0-8109-3836-7 ABRAMS $175.00

American Art Before the 1940s

American art remained relatively provincial up until the 1940s. In the early 20th century two New York-based groups challenged the derivative academic tradition. One centered around Robert Henri, whose socially oriented naturalism led to the nickname the Ashcan School. More radical and cosmopolitan in outlook were the artists who showed at the 291 Gallery run by photographer Alfred Stieglitz: Arthur Dove, Marsden Hartley, John Marin, and (later) Georgia O'Keefe among them. A group of "synchronists," including Morgan Russell and Stanton McDonald-Wright, practiced an art of color relations comparable to that of the Delaunays in Paris. Among the sculptors active in New York were Gaston Lachaise and Elie Nadelman.

Robert **Hobbs**
Milton Avery
0-933920-95-4 HUDSON HILLS $85.00

Michael **Quick** & others
The Paintings of George Bellows
0-88360-068-4 AMON CARTER MUSEUM PB $29.95

Helen **Yglesias**
Isabel Bishop
9-99307-908-1 HACKER $29.95

John **Baur**
The Inlander: Life and Work of Charles Burchfield, 1893-1967
0-87413-186-3 DELAWARE $50.00

Lincoln **Kirstein**
Paul Cadmus
0-915829-65-7 TALMAN $45.00
0-87654-941-5 POMEGRANATE PB $30.00

Mary Schmidt **Campbell**
Harlem Renaissance: Art of Black America
0-8109-8128-9 ABRADALE $14.98

Deborah **Solomon**
Utopia Parkway: The Life and Work of Joseph Cornell
Diffident, childlike, learned, obsessive, Cornell lived most of his life with his mother and invalid brother on Utopia Parkway in Flushing, New York, magically assembling clippings and odds and ends in little shadow boxes. This first biography draws on 40 years of his diaries and documents his little-known relationships with such artists and writers as Duchamp, Ernst, Warhol, Yoko Ono, Susan Sontag, and Marianne Moore
0-374-18012-1 FS&G $27.50

Karen **Wilkin** & Lewis C. **Kachur**
The Drawings of Stuart Davis: The Amazing Continuity
One of the premier American modernists, Davis and his work are explored in detail by eminent scholars who draw heavily on the artist's own unpublished writings as well as on little-known works. Examined for the first time is Davis's approach to his work as black-and-white "configurations" upon which "color-space compositions" were added in the final phase of completion. Included are 110 illustrations, 40 in full-color plates
0-8109-3215-6 ABRAMS $45.00

Sasha **Newman**
Arthur Dove and Duncan Phillips: Artist and Patron
0-8076-1019-4 BRAZILLER $35.00

William H. **Gerdts**
William Glackens
Glackens was a member of the Ashcan School
ESSAY BY JORGE H. SANTIS
1-55859-868-5 ABBEVILLE $85.00

Marsden **Hartley** & Susan Elizabeth **Ryan**
Somehow a Past: The Autobiography of Marsden Hartley
See also **ARTISTS ON ART** under **ART HISTORY: GENERAL STUDIES**
0-262-08251-9 MIT $25.00

Bruce **Robertson**
Marsden Hartley
0-8109-3416-7 ABRAMS $45.00

Gail **Scott**
Marsden Hartley
99912-967-2-7 HACKER $39.95

Robert **Henri**
The Art Spirit
Henri's writings show why he was such an inspiring teacher, and the center of the Ashcan School
0-06-430138-9 ICON PB $10.00

William **Homer**
Robert Henri and His Circle
0-87817-326-9 HACKER $50.00

Darrel **Sewell**

Henry Ossawa Tanner

A thorough presentation of the career of the African-American painter (1859-1937) who specialized in Biblical and genre scenes, and who spent the latter part of his life in Paris. Includes 150 examples of Tanner's work, 97 of them in color

0-8478-1346-0 PHILADELPHIA MUSEUM $50.00

Edward **Hopper**

Drawings

Forty-four works from the permanent collection of the Whitney Museum of American Art in New York City

0-486-25854-8 DOVER PB $4.95

Lloyd **Goodrich**

Edward Hopper

0-317-30949-8 ABRAMS $39.95

Edward Hopper

Gail **Levin**

Edward Hopper: The Art and the Artist

From the authority on Hopper and 20th-century art, a biography that goes behind the powerful images of alienated men and women to reveal the complexity of this great American artist. Based on Jo Hopper's record of her tempestuous 43-year marriage to the artist, Levin gives us a provocative chronicle of Hopper's development and career, one that will take its place in the canon of artists' biographies

0-394-54664-4 KNOPF $40.00
0-393-31577-0 NORTON PB $35.00

Wieland **Schmied**

Edward Hopper: Portraits of America

An excellent introduction to the work of the artist who created some of the most popular icons of 20th-century American art

3-7913-1485-8 PEGAS $25.00

Richard **Powell**

Homecoming: The Art and Life of William H. Johnson

INTRODUCTION BY MARTIN PURYEAR

0-8478-1421-1 RIZZOLI $45.00
0-393-31127-9 NORTON PB $32.50

Philip **Adams**

Walt Kuhn, Painter: His Life and Work

0-8142-0258-6 OHIO STATE $83.50

Gail **Levin**

Synchronism and American Color Abstraction, 1910-1925

0-8076-0882-3 BRAZILLER $22.50

Robert **Frankel**, editor

Jack Levine

0-8478-0977-3 RIZZOLI $14.98

MacKinley **Helm**

John Marin

0-306-71489-2 DA CAPO $46.00

Marilyn **Cohen**

Reginald Marsh's New York: Paintings, Drawings, Prints and Photographs

0-486-24594-2 DOVER PB $9.95

Lincoln **Kirstein**

Elie Nadelman

0-87130-034-6 EAKINS $125.00

Lincoln **Kirstein**, editor

Elie Nadelman Drawings

0-87817-045-6 HACKER $25.00

Linda **Nochlin** & others

Florine Stettheimer: Manhattan Fantastica

Paintings by an eccentric socialite and friend of Marcel Duchamp whose work has recently attracted new attention

0-8109-6815-0 WHITNEY MUSEUM PB $39.95

Charles C. **Eldredge**

Georgia O'Keeffe: American and Modern

A magnificent book that focuses on the quintessential American qualities of O'Keeffe's art and her idiosyncratic life

0-300-05576-5 YALE $55.00

Georgia **O'Keefe**

Georgia O'Keefe

Her paintings with her writings

0-670-33710-2 VIKING $75.00
0-913697-08-7 WILLIAMS COLLEGE PB $13.95

Sarah Whitaker **Peters**

Becoming O'Keefe: The Early Years

0-89659-907-8 ABBEVILLE $39.95
1-55859-362-4 ABBEVILLE PB $19.95

Roxana **Robinson**

Georgia O'Keefe: A Life

0-06-015965-0 HARPERCOLLINS PB $25.00

Myron **Wood**

O'Keefe at Abiquiu

Wood's lyrical black-and-white images of O'Keefe join together with Patten's reminiscences of working for her to give new insight into the artist's later years

TEXT BY CHRISTINE TAYLOR PATTEN

0-8109-3680-1 ABRAMS $35.00

Bernard **Perlman**

Painters of the Ashcan School: The Immortal Eight

Interviews of such Ashcan artists as Maurice Prendergast and John Sloan, who worked from the 1870s to the end of World War I, under the leadership of Robert Henri

0-486-25747-9 DOVER PB $12.95

The Phillips Collection

Americans in Paris: Man Ray, Gerald Murphy, Stuart Davis, Alexander Calder

1-88717-813-9 COUNTERPOINT $50.00

Honor **Moore**

The White Blackbird: A Granddaughter's Life of the Painter Margarett Sargent

An icon of avant-garde art in the '20s, Sargent defied the Boston Brahmin strictures of her birth to become a major artist of her day, then abandoned her brushes for retirement at 40. Here, her granddaughter, the poet and playwright Honor Moore, documents a life of genius, alcoholism, and stubborn struggle for creative freedom against long odds, at the same time telling the story of the birth of modern art in America

See also **MEMOIRS AND JOURNALS** under **20TH-CENTURY AMERICAN ESSAYS AND JOURNALISM** in **LITERATURE OF THE AMERICAS**

0-670-80563-7 VIKING $29.95

Raphael **Soyer**

Raphael Soyer: Life Drawings and Portraits

0-486-25100-4 DOVER PB $3.95

Gail **Stavitsky** & others

Precisionism in America 1915-1941: Reordering Reality

0-8109-3734-4 ABRAMS $39.95

Barbara **Haskell**

Joseph Stella

0-8109-6813-4 WHITNEY MUSEUM $60.00

Irma B. **Jaffe**

Joseph Stella's Symbolism

1-56640-980-2 POMEGRANATE $24.95

Nicholas Fox **Weber**

Patron Saints: Five Rebels Who Opened America to a New Art, 1928-1943

0-300-06448-9 YALE PB $20.00

Jonathan **Weinberg**

Speaking for Vice: Homosexuality in the Art of Charles Demuth, Marsden Hartley, and the First American Avant-Garde

A provocative exploration of the representation of male homosexuality in American art in the first half of the 20th century, focusing on sexual codes and references in the work of Charles Demuth and Marsden Hartley

0-300-05361-4 YALE $45.00
0-300-06254-0 YALE PB $22.50

James **Dennis**

Grant Wood: A Study in American Art and Culture

0-8262-0616-6 MISSOURI $55.00

Art of Latin America

Dawn **Ades**, editor

Art in Latin America

The first continuous narrative history of Latin American art from the years of the independence movements of the 1820s through the present, exploring both the indigenous roots and the colonial and post-colonial experiences of each country. "The best compendium of the arts of Latin America that has yet appeared" —Edward P. Lawson, *The Washington Post Book World*

0300045563 YALE $65.00
0-300-04561-1 YALE PB $35.00

Diana **Fane**, editor

Converging Cultures: Art and Identity in Spanish America

0-8109-4030-2 ABRAMS $65.00

Shifra M. **Goldman**

Dimensions of The Americas: Art and Social Change in Latin America and the United States

Long-needed in the field of art history, this book is an overview of the social history of Latin American and Latino art. Written in a straight-forward style, the book is accessible to specialists, students as well as general audiences

0-226-30123-0 CHICAGO $80.00
0-226-30124-9 CHICAGO PB $29.95

MacKinley **Helm**

Mexican Painters: Rivera, Orozco, Siqueiros, and Other Artists of the Social Realist School

0-486-26028-3 DOVER PB $11.95

Hayden **Herrera**

Frida: A Biography of Frida Kahlo

0-06-091127-1 HARPERPERENNIAL PB $22.00

Frida Kahlo: The Paintings

Kahlo's biographer has compiled a beautifully produced volume of her paintings, containing 75 full-color and 125 black-and-white illustrations

0-06-092319-9 HARPERPERENNIAL PB $25.00

Frida **Kahlo**

The Diary of Frida Kahlo: An Intimate Self-Portrait

The artistic diary of the Mexican artist whose work mingled Surrealism, folk art, and autobiography in an inimitably haunting style. This never-before published diary provides an intimate view not only into her celebrated technique, but also into her life: her stormy relationship with Diego Rivera, her friendships with Leon Trotsky and Isamu Noguchi. With an introduction by Carlos Fuentes

ESSAYS AND COMMENTARY BY SARAH M. LOWE

0-8109-3221-0 ABRAMS $39.95

Raquel **Tibol**

Frida Kahlo: An Open Life

The author, one of Mexico's most respected art historians, was a close friend of Kahlo and Rivera, and as such is able to combine personal recollection with scholarship in this eclectic biography of one of the most idolized female artists of our time

See also **ART AND PHOTOGRAPHY** under **ARTS AND LETTERS** under **WOMEN'S STUDIES** in **SOCIAL STUDIES**

TRANSLATED BY ELINOR RANDALL

0-8263-1418-X NEW MEXICO $19.95

Martha **Zamora**

Frida Kahlo: The Brush of Anguish

Chronicles the life of the Mexican artists including 75 of her greatest works, historical photographs, and a descriptive essay

0-87701-746-8 CHRONICLE $35.00

Giulio **Blanc**

Wilfredo Lam & His Contemporaries

0-942949-08-0 STUDIO MUSEUM PB $34.95

Edward **Lucie-Smith**

Latin American Art of the 20th Century

See also **THAMES & HUDSON WORLD OF ART** under **ART HISTORY: GENERAL STUDIES**

0-500-20260-5 THAMES & HUDSON PB $14.95

Lika **Mutal** & Dena **Merriam**

Lika Mutal

The work of the major Peruvian artist who brings to her stone sculptures the sensibilities of three cultures—the spirituality of Andean civilization, the rich artistic traditions of her native Holland, and the dynamic vitality of New York City, where she lives part time

0-8109-6320-5 ABRAMS $85.00

James **Oles**

South of the Border: Mexico in the American Imagination, 1914-1947

1-56098-294-2 SMITHSONIAN $75.00
1-56098-295-0 SMITHSONIAN PB $29.95

Alma **Reed**

Jose Clemente Orozco

0-87817-204-1 HACKER $50.00

Octavio **Paz**

Mexico's great modern poet has explored the same themes over many decades, fusing autobiography and metaphysical speculation, eroticism and politics, vibrant imagery and formal experimentation.

Essays on Mexican Art

Paz lyrically compares the work of a remote Mexican villager to the sarcophagi portraits of the Egyptian Fayum and demonstrates how the Mexican muralists Rivera, Siqueiros, and Orozco were influenced by European Cubism, Fauvism, and Expressionism and how in turn they influenced American painters. Written between 1960 and 1986, these wonderful discussions of Mexican artists and their works are illustrated with 16 color plates

TRANSLATED BY HELEN LANE

0-15-129063-6 HARCOURT BRACE $22.95

Ramon **Favela**

Diego Rivera: A Retrospective

0-393-02275-7 NORTON $100.00

Philip **Stein**

Siqueiros: His Life and Works

0-7178-0706-1
INTERNATIONAL PUBLICATIONS PB $29.95

Jose **Corredor-Matheos**

Tamayo

0-8478-0855-6 RIZZOLI $24.95

Art Since 1945

Kate **Linker** & others

Individuals: A Selected History of Contemporary Art, 1945-1986

0-89659-676-1 ABBEVILLE $65.00

Edward **Lucie-Smith**

Movements in Art Since 1945

See also **THAMES & HUDSON WORLD OF ART** under **ART HISTORY: GENERAL STUDIES**

0-500-20282-6 THAMES & HUDSON PB $14.95

Susan **Tallmann**

The Contemporary Print: Pre-Pop to Postmodern

The medium of printmaking has become crucial to the work of many contemporay artists. This formidable survey of recent works, illustrated with 330 plates, 160 in color, is essential for anyone concerned with the art of our time

See also **PRINTS** under **THEMES, TECHNIQUES, AND GENRES** under **ART HISTORY: GENERAL STUDIES**

0-500-23684-4 THAMES & HUDSON $50.00

Daniel **Wheeler**

Art Since the Mid-Century

0-86565-083-7 VENDOME $50.00

Paul **Wood** & others

Modernism in Dispute: Art Since the Forties

A discussion of how American art evolved from the social realism of the 1930s to a predominantly abstract art after the war and how this change was related to America's growing economic and political dominance. The authors then review the challenges to modernism posed by Minimal art, Land art, Conceptual art, and current debates about Postmodernism

0-300-05521-8 YALE $50.00
0-300-05522-6 YALE PB $27.50

Postwar American Art

Diane **Apostolos-Cappaona** & Bruce **Altshuler**

Isamu Noguchi: Essays and Conversations

0-8109-3667-4 ABRAMS $34.95

Gail **Gelburd** & Thelma **Golden**

Romare Bearden in Black and White

This is the first book devoted to the photomontages of Romare Bearden, one of the most prominent African-American artists of the 20th century. The volume includes two critical essays, an interview, the artist's poems, along with all 25 works stunningly reproduced in color

See also PHOTOGRAPHERS under PHOTOGRAPHY

0-8109-6823-1 ABRAMS PB $19.95

Lowery Stokes **Sims**

Romare Bearden

0-8478-1581-1 RIZZOLI PB $7.95

Elizabeth **Bishop**

Exchanging Hats: Thirty-Nine Paintings

The paintings of the American poet

EDITED BY WILLIAM BENTON

0-374-15090-7 FS&G $25.01

Marie-Laure **Bernadac**

Louise Bourgeois

2-08-013600-3 ABBEVILLE $35.00

Charlotta **Kotík** & others

Louise Bourgeois: The Locus of Memory, Works, 1982-1993

0-8109-3127-3 ABRAMS $49.50

Louise **Weiermair**, editor

Louise Bourgeois

3-905514-84-2 D.A.P. $45.00

Guy **Davenport**

The Balance of Quinces: The Paintings and Drawings of Guy Davenport

The artwork of the essayist, short-story writer and translator

COMMENTARY BY ERIC ANDERSON REECE

0-8112-1336-6 NEW DIRECTIONS $25.00

Deborah **Wye** & Carol **Smith**

The Prints of Louise Bourgeois

0-8109-6141-5 MOMA $85.00

John **Elderfield**

The Drawings of Richard Diebenkorn

0-87070-304-8 MOMA PB $30.00

Martin **Friedman** & others

Visions of America: Landscape as Metaphor in the Late Twentieth Century

0-8109-3925-8 DENVER MUSEUM $60.00

Donald **Kuspit**

Leon Golub: Existential-Activist Painter

0-8135-1102-X RUTGERS $50.00
0-8135-1124-0 RUTGERS PB $15.00

Patricia **Hills**

Alice Neel

0-8109-1358-5 ABRAMS $49.50

Bruce **Altshuler**

Noguchi

1-55859-755-7 ABBEVILLE PB $24.95

David S. **Rubin**

It's Only Rock and Roll: Rock and Roll Currents in Contemporary Art

An entertaining discussion of the influence of rock and roll on contemporary art, from the work of Ray Johnson, Andy Warhol, and Richard Hamilton in the late '50s, to more recent work by Warhol, Grooms, Cleveland, Koons, and Mapplethorpe

3-7913-1627-3 PRESTEL PB $29.95

William C. **Seitz**

Art in the Age of Aquarius, 1955-1970

0-87474-868-2 SMITHSONIAN $52.00

Thames & Hudson

Art in Chicago, 1945-1995

A cultural, social, and political history of the painting, sculpture, drawing, and media arts (film, video, performance) by 150 artists who either have always lived and worked in Chicago or have created significant bodies of work there, including Harry Callahan, Phyllis Bramson, Leon Golub, Richard Hunt, Laszlo Moholy-Nagy, Jim Nutt, Ed Paschke, Martin Puryear, Aaron Siskind, Buzz Spector, Tony Tasset, and H.C. Westermann

0-500-23728-X THAMES & HUDSON PB $60.00

Andrew **Wyeth**

Andrew Wyeth: Autobiography

Thomas Hoving has gathered over six decades of Wyeth's tempera, drybrush, and watercolor paintings to provide a comprehensive view of his work

INTRODUCTION BY THOMAS HOVING

0-8212-2159-0 BULFINCH $50.00

Andrew Wyeth

The New York School and the '50s

The origins of the "New York School" of Abstract Expressionism in the '40s are difficult to disentangle. The most evident influences were Surrealist interests in gestural automatism and archetypal subject matter, and a concern for a synthetic treatment of pictorial space derived from Cubism and Matisse. There were two distinct tendencies within the New York School. One reached out to the sublime through large simplified shapes or fields of color and minimal articulations of the unity and flatness of the canvas itself. Clement Greenberg called this approach—exemplified by Barnett Newman, Mark Rothko, Clyfford Still, and Robert Motherwell— "American-type painting." The other broad tendency was what Harold Rosenberg christened "Action Painting": direct painterly gesture channeled fragmentary pictorial impulses into suggestions of sensual volume, activating the canvas as an overall space ("an arena in which to act," in Rosenberg's words). The painters closer to this second approach included Willem de Kooning, Jackson Pollock, Lee Krasner, and Franz Kline. They inspired a "Second Generation" of abstract expressionists, among them Norman Bluhm and Joan Mitchell, just as the "American-type" painters inspired a school of "color-field" painters such as Helen Frankenthaler and Morris Louis, as well as practitioners of a more geometrically oriented, "hard-edge" or "post-painterly" abstraction, such as Ellsworth Kelly.

Abstract Expressionism can best be approached through the writings of its most eloquent champions, Clement Greenberg and Harold Rosenberg.

David **Anfam**

Abstract Expressionism

See also THAMES & HUDSON WORLD OF ART under ART HISTORY: GENERAL STUDIES

0-500-20243-5 THAMES & HUDSON PB $14.95

Dore **Ashton**

The New York School: A Cultural Reckoning

A fine introduction to the cultural milieu of abstract expressionism

0-520-08107-2 CALIFORNIA $40.00
0-520-08106-4 CALIFORNIA PB $16.95

Elaine **de Kooning**

Elaine de Kooning: The Spirit of Abstract Expressionism: Selected Writings

Twenty-eight essays by a major member of the New York School, who was also an incisive and influential critic. Provides rare insight into Abstract Expressionism while revealing the scope of Elaine de Kooning's vigorous mind. "De Kooning's irreverent contemporary portraits restore the human scale…Perhaps only an artist could write about other artists with such genuine curiosity and open-mindedness"
—*Kirkus Reviews*

See also **ARTISTS ON ART** under **ART HISTORY: GENERAL STUDIES**

0-8076-1337-1 BRAZILLER $23.50

Willem **de Kooning**

Collected Writings of Willem de Kooning

0-937815-13-6 HANUMAN PB $5.95

Willem de Kooning: The Late Paintings, the 1980s

De Kooning's later paintings represent some of the most fluid and sensual works of the 20th century. Luminous and exotic, the bold colors and sure strokes are stunning demonstrations of the artist's daring and virtuosity. "The late pictures, tightly drawn with a fine brush, are erotic in an allusive, Matissean way"
—Adam Gopnick, *New Yorker*

ESSAYS BY GARY GARRELS AND ROBERT STORR

0-935640-49-5 D.A.P. $50.00
0-935640-47-9 WALKER ART CENTER PB $29.95

Harry **Gaugh**

Willem de Kooning

1-55859-248-2 ABBEVILLE PB $22.95

David **Sylvester** & others

Willem de Kooning: Paintings

Eighty of de Kooning's most important and energetic paintings, including the famous *Woman* series, the seminal black-and-white abstractions from the '40s, and the lush landscapes, are collected in this sumptuous catalog for a major retrospective of the artist's work at the National Gallery of Art in Washington, at the Met in New York, and at the Tate Gallery in London

0-300-06011-4 YALE $60.00

Sally **Yard**

Willem de Kooning

0-8478-1884-5 RIZZOLI $27.50

Ruth E. **Fine**

Helen Frankenthaler: Prints

0-8109-2536-2 ABRAMS PB $35.00

Michael **Auping**

Arshile Gorky: The Breakthrough Years

0-8478-1875-6 RIZZOLI $45.00

Melvin P. **Lader**

Arshile Gorky

1-55859-249-0 ABBEVILLE PB $22.95

Serge **Guilbaut**

How New York Stole the Idea of Modern Art: Abstract Expressionism, Freedom, and the Cold War

Argues that the creation of the New York School served an ideological purpose in Cold War America

0-226-31038-8 CHICAGO PB $22.50

William **Corbett**

Philip Guston's Late Work: A Memoir

0-944072-43-7 ZOLAND $17.50

Robert **Storr**

Philip Guston

0-89659-656-7 ABBEVILLE PB $22.95

Irving **Sandler**

Al Held

0-933920-38-5 HUDSON HILLS $75.00
0-944680-17-8 ROBERT MILLER GALLERY PB $10.00

Cynthia **Goodman**

Hans Hoffmann

1-55859-251-2 ABBEVILLE PB $22.95

Michael **Auping** & others

Jess: A Grand Collage, 1951-1993

0-914-78285-1 BUFFALO $45.00

Richard **Axsom** & Phylis **Floyd**

The Prints of Ellsworth Kelly: A Catalogue Raisonné, 1949-1985

0-933920-84-9 HUDSON HILLS $50.00
0-933920-86-5 HUDSON HILLS PB $35.00

Harry F. **Gaugh**

Franz Kline

1-55859-770-0 ABBEVILLE $55.00

Susan **Landauer**

The San Francisco School of Abstract Espressionism

INTRODUCTION BY DORE ASHTON

0-520-08611-2 CALIFORNIA PB $34.95

Michael **Leja**

Reframing Abstract Expressionism: Subjectivity and Painting in the 1940's

An original and wide-ranging argument that the abstract painters of the New York School, in their search for the "primitive" and unconscious elements of the self, are aligned with many contemporary essayists, Hollywood filmmakers, journalists, and popular philosophers who also sought to reformulate concepts of individual identity

0-300-04461-5 YALE $55.00

Diane **Upright**

Morris Louis: The Complete Paintings

0-8109-1280-5 ABRAMS $135.00

Lisa Mintz **Messinger**

Abstract Expressionism: Works on Paper—Selections from the Metropolitan Museum of Art

0-8109-6424-4 METROPOLITAN MUSEUM $45.00

H.H. **Arnason** & Barbaralee **Diamonstein**

Robert Motherwell

0-8109-1333-X ABRAMS $90.00

Barnett **Newman**

Barnett Newman: Selected Writings and Interviews

EDITED BY JOHN P. O'NEILL

0-520-07817-9 CALIFORNIA PB $16.00

Elizabeth **Frank**

Jackson Pollock

0-89659-384-3 ABBEVILLE PB $22.95

Ellen G. **Landau**

Jackson Pollock

0-8109-3702-6 ABRAMS $75.00

Carter **Ratcliff**

The Fate of a Gesture: Jackson Pollock and Postwar American Art

The quintessential American artist, Pollock redefined painting in his revolutionary gesture of flinging colors onto canvas. Here, Carter Ratcliff tells the story of postwar American art through the analytic figure of Pollock's gesture, starting in the '40s with the triumph of Abstract Expressionism and continuing through the stars of the go-go '80s

0-374-22331-9 OCTAGON $30.00

Jeffrey **Potter**

To a Violent Grave: An Oral Biography of Jackson Pollock

0-916366-47-2 PUSHCART PB $15.00

Fairfield **Porter**

Art in Its Own Terms

See also **ARTISTS ON ART** under **ART HISTORY: GENERAL STUDIES**

EDITED WITH AN INTRODUCTION BY RACKSTRAW DOWNES

0-944072-31-3 ZOLAND PB $10.95

Ad **Reinhardt**

Art-as-Art: The Selected Writings of Ad Reinhardt

See also **ARTISTS ON ART** under **ART HISTORY: GENERAL STUDIES**

EDITED BY BARBARA ROSE

0-520-07670-2 CALIFORNIA PB $14.00

Yves-Alain **Bois**

Ad Reinhardt

0-8478-1336-3 RIZZOLI $45.00

Dore **Ashton**

About Rothko

0-19-503348-5 OXFORD $35.00

0-306-80704-1 DA CAPO PB $18.95

James E.B. **Breslin**

Mark Rothko

0-226-07405-6 CHICAGO $39.95

Bonnie **Clearwater**

Mark Rothko: Works on Paper

INTRODUCTION BY DORE ASHTON

0-933920-54-7 HUDSON HILLS PB $25.00

Irving **Sandler**

The Triumph of American Painting: A History of Abstract Expressionism

0-06-430075-7 ICON PB $25.00

Stanley **Marcus**

David Smith: The Sculptor and Work

0-8014-1510-1 CORNELL $39.95

David Smith

Karen **Wilkin**

David Smith

1-55859-256-3 ABBEVILLE PB $22.95

Pop Art

Pop art covers an extremely diverse group: Roy Lichtenstein, Claes Oldenburg, James Rosenquist, and Andy Warhol, and perhaps also Jim Dine and Red Grooms. Their work was united by its appropriation of techniques and images from comic strips, billboards, commercial packaging, and newspaper photography. On the West Coast there were a number of artists (Jess, Wayne Thiebaud, Edward Ruscha), working independently of the New York pop artists, whose work paralleled and even anticipated theirs.

Jean E. **Feinberg**

Jim Dine

1-55859-751-4 ABBEVILLE $35.00

1-55859-692-5 ABBEVILLE PB $24.95

Marco **Livingstone**

Jim Dine: Flowers and Plants

0-8109-3214-8 ABRAMS $49.50

Bob **Adelman**

The Art of Roy Lichtenstein: Mural with Blue Brush-Stroke

An inventive detailing of Lichtenstein's creative process—including each step of the making of *Mural with Blue Brush-Stroke.* A unique representation

1-55970-251-6 ARCADE PB $19.95

Lawrence **Alloway**

Roy Lichtenstein

0-89659-331-2 ABBEVILLE PB $22.95

Mary Lee **Corlett**

The Prints of Roy Lichtenstein: A Catalogue Raisonné, 1948-1993

A comprehensive volume of the Pop Art master's prints, beautifully reproduced and bound. Ruth E. Fine's introduction places Lichtenstein's innovative and humorous work in context, showing his enduring influence and technical accomplishment. A handsome volume

1-55595-105-8 HUDSON HILLS $95.00

Constance **Glenn** & Jack **Glenn**, editors

Roy Lichtenstein: Landscape Sketches, 1984-1985

0-8109-1264-3 ABRAMS $29.98

Diane **Waldman**

Roy Lichtenstein

0-8478-1666-4 RIZZOLI PB $7.95

Lucy **Lippard**

Pop Art

A classic international survey

0-500-20052-1 THAMES & HUDSON PB $14.95

Marco **Livingstone**

Pop Art: An International Perspective

0-8478-1476-9 RIZZOLI PB $35.00

Claes Oldenburg: Multiples in Retrospect, 1964-1990

0-8478-1335-5 RIZZOLI $65.00

Susan P. **Casteras** & others

Large Scale Projects: Claes Oldenburg and Coosje van Bruggen

1-88525-404-0 MONACELLI $95.00

Germano **Celant** & others

Claes Oldenburg: An Anthology

0-8109-6887-8 GUGGENHEIM $75.00

Claes Oldenburg

Susan **Brundage**, editor

James Rosenquist: The Big Paintings, 30 Years with Leo Castelli

0-8478-1845-4 RIZZOLI $50.00

Cosntance W. **Glenn**

James Rosenquist: Time Dust, Complete Graphics, 1962-1992

0-8478-1709-1 RIZZOLI $50.00

Yves-Alain **Bois**

Ed Ruscha: Romance with Liquids

0-8478-1730-X GAGOSIAN GALLERY PB $30.00

David **Bourdon**

Warhol

0-8109-1761-0 ABRAMS $49.50

0-8109-2634-2 ABRAMS PB $24.95

Arthur **Danto** & others

The Andy Warhol Museum

1-88161-634-7 CARNEGIE MUSEUM $40.00

Andy Warhol

Thomas **Kellein**, editor

Andy Warhol: Abstracts

3-7913-1328-2 TE NEUS PB $24.95

Linda **Nochlin**
Andy Warhol Nudes
0-87951-647-X OVERLOOK PB $45.00

Carter **Ratcliff**
Andy Warhol
1-55859-257-1 ABBEVILLE PB $22.95

Andy **Warhol**
The Andy Warhol Diaries
EDITED BY PAT HACKETT
0-446-39138-7 WARNER PB $19.95

The Philosophy of Andy Warhol: From A to B and Back
The muteness of Warhol's art was surpassed only by the chattiness of his public persona
0-15-671720-4 HARCOURT BRACE PB $13.00

> What's great about this country is that America started the tradition where the richest consumers buy essentially the same things as the poorest. You can be watching TV and see Coca-Cola, and you can know that the president drinks Coke, Liz Taylor drinks Coke and, just think, you can drink Coke too. A Coke is a Coke, and no amount of money can get you a better Coke than the one the bum on the corner is drinking. All the Cokes are the same and all the Cokes are good. Liz Taylor knows it, the president knows it, the bum knows it, and you know it.
> THE PHILOSOPHY OF ANDY WARHOL: FROM A TO B AND BACK

Andy **Warhol** & Pat **Hackett**
Popism: The Warhol Sixties
0-15-672960-1 HARCOURT BRACE PB $13.00

Sam **Hunter**
Tom Wesselmann
0-8478-1831-4 RIZZOLI $27.50

Minimalism and Conceptualism

Pop art's studious brother was Minimalism. If the former developed the literalness of the image, the objects of Donald Judd, Robert Morris, and, somewhat later, Eva Hesse and Richard Serra explored the literalness of forms and materials. The early paintings of Frank Stella were less extreme but perhaps more inventive cousins.

After minimalism's radical synthesis of the reductive and anti-aesthetic tendencies in modern art, it was only a short step to conceptual art and such related trends as process art and earthworks, which dematerialized the art object or subordinated the work's materiality to the information processed through it, as in the work of Hans Haacke, Bruce Nauman, and Robert Smithson.

Gregory **Battcock**, editor
Minimal Art: A Critical Anthology
0-520-20147-7 CALIFORNIA PB $17.00

David **Bourdon**
Christo: Surrounded Islands, 1980-83
0-8109-0790-9 ABRAMS $95.00

Thomas **Kellein** & Jon **Hendriks**
Fluxus
Fluxus is an art movement that defies most appempts at further classification. A vivid form of anti-art, Fluxus is represented in this book by 145 illustrations and a lucid text that explains the group's peculiar ideology as expressed in art, poetry, and drama
0-500-97422-5 THAMES & HUDSON PB $19.95

Dan **Graham**
Rock My Religion: Writings and Projects, 1965-1990
Graham's artwork and installations have been widely exhibited around the world, and his writing has appeared in *Artforum* and numerous other publications. His iconoclastic disregard for the divisions between "high" and "low" culture makes this original and compelling collection a piece of conceptual art in its own right
0-262-07147-9 MIT $37.50

Chris **Bruce** & others
Eva Hesse Sculpture
0-943221-14-5 TIMKEN PB $45.00

Helen A. **Cooper** & Maurice **Berger**
Eva Hesse: A Retrospective
0-89467-059-X SCHWR PB $40.00

Lucy **Lippard**
Eva Hesse
0-306-80484-0 DA CAPO PB $18.95

Renate **Petzinger** & Hanne **Dannenberger**
Donald Judd: Spaces
3-89322-618-4 D.A.P. $45.00

Klaus **Kertess**
Brice Marden: Paintings and Drawings
0-8109-3627-5 ABRAMS $95.00

Jack **Reynolds** & Andrea **Miller Keller**
Sol LeWitt: Twenty-Five Years of Wall Drawings, 1968-1993
1-879-88634-0 ADDISON PB $29.95

Brice **Marden**
Brice Marden: Paintings and Drawings
Recent paintings and drawings, beautifully reproduced and documented, published here as the hardcover catalog of the October 1995 Brice Marden exhibition at the Matthew Marks Gallery. "I think of Marden's paintings as rigorous attempts to bring into physical and visual proximity the essences…of physical place and insubstantial image, and the yearning that informs all great painting"—John Yau
1-88014-611-8 D.A.P. $35.00

Robert **Morris**
Continuous Project Altered Daily: The Writings of Robert Morris
0-262-63163-6 MIT PB $25.00

Richard **Serra**
Richard Serra: Intersection
3-928762-52-4 D.A.P. $60.00

Richard Serra: La Mormaire
3-928762-54-0 D.A.P. $70.00

Writings/Interviews
The powerful and sometimes controversial sculptures of Richard Serra have had a tremendous impact on contemporary art. This book goes right to the source for explanations and insights
See also **ARTISTS ON ART** under **ART HISTORY: GENERAL STUDIES**
0-226-74880-4 CHICAGO PB $17.95

Robert **Smithson**
Robert Smithson: The Collected Writings
See also **ARTISTS ON ART** under **ART HISTORY: GENERAL STUDIES**
EDITED BY JACK FLAM
0-520-20385-2 CALIFORNIA PB $24.95

Craig E. **Adcock**
James Turrell: The Art of Light and Space
Not merely a monograph, this thoughtful book considers the art of perception without scientific bias
0-520-06728-2 CALIFORNIA $90.00

American Art of the '60s and '70s

While some artists were refining the breakthroughs of their Abstract Expressionist predecessors, others, including Jasper Johns, Robert Rauschenberg, and Cy Twombly, were challenging their dominance with a new literalism inspired by Dada as well as by the most improvisational and antiformal tendencies within Abstract Expressionism itself. Another challenge, although with less immediate impact, came from painters who maintained the European figurative tradition.

John **Hollander**
William Bailey
0-8478-1345-2 RIZZOLI $50.00

Judy **Chicago**
The Dinner Party
See also **ART AND PHOTOGRAPHY** under **ARTS AND LETTERS** under **WOMEN'S STUDIES** in **SOCIAL STUDIES**
0-670-85957-5 VIKING $45.00
0-14-024437-9 VIKING PB $24.95

Thomas E. **Crow**
The Rise of the Sixties: American and European Art in the Era of Dissent
In this compelling account of the 1960s, acclaimed critic Thomas Crow rediscovers a period of political upheaval and cultural experimentation with a fresh and penetrating analysis of the visual arts in America and Europe
0-8109-2731-4 ABRAMS PB $16.95

John **Guare**

Chuck Close: Life and Work, 1988-1995

Chuck Close, one of America's most respected artists, has overcome paralysis to produce amazing, monumental portraits of family, friends, and fellow artists. This beautifully illustrated book is a up-close and personal study of his astonishing achievement

0-500-09253-2 THAMES & HUDSON $35.00

Lisa **Lyons** & Robert **Storr**

Chuck Close

0-8478-0808-4 RIZZOLI $45.00

John **Elderfield**, editor

American Art of the 1960s

0-8109-6099-0 MOMA $40.00

Robert **Doty**, editor

Jane Freilicher: Paintings

0-8008-4302-9 TAPLINGER PB $19.95

Riva **Castleman**

Jasper Johns: A Print Retrospective

0-87070-401-X MOMA PB $24.95

Michael **Crichton**

Jasper Johns

0-8109-3515-5 ABRAMS $60.00

Richard **Francis**

Jasper Johns

1-55859-252-0 ABBEVILLE PB $22.95

Jasper Johns

Christel **Hollevoet** & Kirk **Varnedoe**, editor

Jasper Johns: Interviews and Writings

This book represents artist Jasper Johns from the late 1950s to the present, with a comprehensive selection his writings and interviews. Among the illustrations are selected pages from the artist's previously unpublished sketchbook

0-8109-6166-0 ABRAMS PB $24.95

Jasper **Johns**

35 Years, Leo Castelli

A knowing retrospective of not only an artist's work, but a historic career and an enduring friendship

0-8109-3508-2 ABRAMS $35.00

Jill **Johnston**

Jasper Johns: Privileged Information

In a remarkable fusion of criticism, biography, and interview, Johnston uses a recurring image in the artist's paintings to unlock an autobiographical core in the work of one of the most self-effacing of contemporary artists. The result charts the subtle interplay between Johns's artistic, personal, and public identities

0-500-01736-0 THAMES & HUDSON $27.50

Fred **Orton**

Figuring Jasper Johns

0-674-30117-X HARVARD $41.50

Kirk **Varnedoe** & Roberta **Bernstein**

Jasper Johns: A Retrospective

This most comprehenisve and authoritative book on Jasper Johns, one of America's most influential artists, accompanies a major 1996 retrospective exhibition of his work at the Museum of Modern Art. This lavish volume includes 240 reproductions of his painting and critical essays by leading scholars in the field

0-8109-6165-2 ABRAMS $65.00

Barbara **Haskell**

Agnes Martin

0-8109-6817-7 ABRAMS PB $35.00

Robert Saltonstall **Mattison**

Masterworks: Jasper Johns, Ellsworth Kelly, Roy Lichtenstein, Robert Rauschenberg and Frank Stella in the Jane Meyerhoff Collection

One of the finest collections of contemporary American art, Meyerhoff's Fitzhugh Farm in Maryland, is brought to us in this collection of works by Johns, Kelly, Lichtenstein, Rauschenberg, and Stella. Full-color reproductions are complemented by essays analyzing the works of each artist

1-55595-081-7 HUDSON HILLS $50.00

Susan **Brundage**

Bruce Nauman: 25 Years

0-8478-1817-9 RIZZOLI PB $29.95

Coosje **van Bruggen**

Bruce Nauman

0-8478-0883-1 RIZZOLI $50.00

Toni **Stooss** & Thomas **Kellein**, editors

Nam June Paik: Video Time—Video Space

0-8109-3729-8 ABRAMS $49.50

Rosalind **Krauss**

Beverly Pepper: Sculpture in Place

0-89659-667-2 ABBEVILLE $59.95

William **Rubin**

Frank Stella: 1970-1987

0-8109-6074-5 MOMA $45.00
0-8109-6107-5 ABRAMS PB $29.95

Frank **Stella**

Working Space

The text of Stella's Charles Eliot Norton lectures

See also **ARTISTS ON ART** under **ART HISTORY: GENERAL STUDIES**

0-674-95960-4 HARVARD $49.95
0-674-95961-2 HARVARD PB $22.95

Sidney **Guberman**

Frank Stella: An Illustrated Biography

Guberman, a friend and colleague of Stella's for 40 years, presents an intimate portrait of the artist. Exploring sources as diverse as Jasper Johns, Jean Arp, and Henri Matisse, investigating the technical complexity of Stella's work, offering personal insights into the artist's life, and illustrating the whole with splendid illustrations, Guberman presents an extraordinary overview of the seminal figure in postwar American art

FOREWORD BY RICHARD MEIER

0-8478-1843-8 RIZZOLI $75.00

Kirk **Varnedoe**

Cy Twombly: A Retrospective

0-8109-6129-6 MOMA $55.00

Postwar European Art

While numerous European artists emigrated to the United States during World War II, and invigorated the art scene there, many artists stayed on. In England, artists including Moore, Sutherland, and Nash documented the war as Official War Artists. Immediately after the war, Francis Bacon's anguished figures reflected the horror and sorrow of the period. On the continent, Picasso and Matisse continued to produce important works during and after the war. Other artists who survived the war, including Miro, Giacometti, and Dubuffet, prospered in the years that followed. Eventually, as Europe rebuilt, a new avant-garde emerged. Artistic trends of Europe's postwar years were marked by Existentialist writers and Tachiste painters—artists whose informal abstractions and often passionate gesturalism paralleled the Abstract Expressionist movement in the United States. Major contributions to the new European avant-garde were made by the Spaniard Tapies, France's Yves Klein and Arman, Appel in Holland, and Tinguely in Switzerland. In Germany, performance artist, sculptor, and graphic artist Josef Beuys, who was influenced by Marxist theory, inspired several generations of artists around the world.

Michael **Anthonioz**

Verve: The Ultimate Review of Art and Literature

The influential magazine from the 1940s and '50s, whose contributors included Matisse, Picasso, Chagall, Braque, Sartre, Joyce, and Cartier-Bresson

0-8109-1743-2 ABRAMS $95.00

Donald **Kuspit**
Karel Appel Sculpture: A Catalogue Raisonné
0-8109-1945-1 ABRAMS $60.00

Duncan **Thompson**
Arikha
Struck by "a violent hunger of the eye" after seeing the great Caravaggio exhibition of 1965, Avigdor Arikha abruptly stopped painting and turned his attention to drawing from life. When he returned to painting in 1973, he produced the intensely observed series of portraits (Samuel Beckett and Cartier-Bresson), nudes, and still-lifes for which he is known
0-7148-3010-0 PHAIDON $55.00
0-7148-3521-8 PHAIDON PB $35.00

Donald **Kuspit**
Arman: Monochrome Accumulations, 1986-1989
91-7970-951-6 ABBEVILLE $40.00

Jan **van der Marck**
Arman
0-89659-423-8 ABBEVILLE $69.95

Hugh **Davies** & Sally **Yard**
Francis Bacon
1-55859-245-8 ABBEVILLE PB $22.95

José Maria **Faerna**, editor
Bacon
0-8109-4675-0 ABRAMS $11.98

Lawrence **Gowing** & Sam **Hunter**
Francis Bacon
0-500-09200-1 THAMES & HUDSON $50.00

John **Russell**
Francis Bacon
0-500-18170-5 THAMES & HUDSON $19.95
0-500-20169-2 THAMES & HUDSON PB $12.95

Francis Bacon
See also THAMES & HUDSON WORLD OF ART under ART HISTORY: GENERAL STUDIES
0-500-20271-0 THAMES & HUDSON PB $12.95

David **Sylvester**
The Brutality of Fact: Interviews with Francis Bacon
A rounded view of this complex artist
0-500-27196-8 THAMES & HUDSON PB $14.95

Benjamin H.D. **Buchloh**, editor
Broodthaers: Writings, Interviews, Photographs
See also ARTISTS ON ART under ART HISTORY: GENERAL STUDIES
0-262-02281-8 MIT $30.00
0-262-52135-0 MIT PB $12.50

Nancy **Condee**, editor
Soviet Hieroglyphics: Visual Culture in Late 20th-Century Russia
0-253-20945-5 INDIANA PB $12.95

Germano **Celant**
Tony Cragg
The first comprehensive survey of the work of the British sculptor who considers himself to be a combination of artist and scientist, chemist and alchemist, believer and skeptic, and who has had an immense influence on a whole generation of post-formalist sculptors
0-500-23723-9 THAMES & HUDSON PB $65.00

James T. **Demetrion**
Jean Dubuffet, 1943-1963
1-56098-298-5 SMITHSONIAN $60.00
1-56098-299-3 SMITHSONIAN PB $29.95

Jean **Dubuffet**
Asphyxiating Culture & Other Writings
0-941423-09-3 FOUR WALLS $17.95

Lucien **Freud** & Bruce **Bernard**
Lucian Freud
A comprehensive career overview of the painter Lucian Freud, renowned for his portraits and his massive nudes. Along with a text by his long-time friend Bruce Bernard and photographs of Freud at work, the book contains over 300 reproductions of the artist's paintings, drawings, and etchings, some of which have never been published before
0-679-45254-0 RANDOM HOUSE $175.00

Nicholas **Penny** & Robert **Johnson**
Lucian Freud: Works on Paper
0-500-09185-4 NORTON $40.00

James **Lord**
A Giacometti Portrait
The best introduction to Giacometti: an account of sitting for a portrait by the master
0-374-51573-5 FS&G PB $9.00

Angel **Schneider**, editor
Alberto Giacometti: Sculpture, Paintings, Drawings
0-379-131371-1 TE NEUS $60.00

David **Sylvester**
Looking at Giacometti
0-805-04210-5 HOLT $27.50

John **Hutchinson** & others
Antony Gormley
0-7148-3383-5 PHAIDON PB $29.95

Peter **Clothier**
David Hockney
1-55859-642-9 ABBEVILLE $35.00
0-7892-0036-8 ABBEVILLE PB $24.95

David **Hockney**
That's the Way I See It
Hockney's book continues where he left off with his acclaimed 1976 work *David Hockney by David Hockney* (it is now out of print). It covers 1969 to the present, and contains over 300 reproductions of his work, the majority of which have never before been published in book form
0-8118-0506-9 CHRONICLE $35.00

David Hockney

David **Hockney** & Stephen **Spender**
Hockney's Alphabet
David Hockney has created a special full-color alphabet book, embellished with contributions from an array of writers including Norman Mailer, Seamus Heaney, Doris Lessing, Susan Sontag, John Updike, Julian Barnes, and many others. Proceeds will be donated to the AIDS Crisis Trust
EDITED WITH A PREFACE AND POEM BY STEPHEN SPENDER
0-679-41066-X RANDOM HOUSE $35.00

Marco **Livingstone**
David Hockney
0-500-20291-5 THAMES & HUDSON PB $14.95

Kenneth **Silver**
David Hockney
0-8478-1820-9 RIZZOLI PB $7.95

Andrew **Graham-Dixon**
Howard Hodgkin
0-8109-3418-3 ABRAMS $49.50

Richard **Morphet**, editor
R.B. Kitaj: A Retrospective
A complete examination of the 35 years of Kitaj's work that combines an exploration of his Jewish identity with a powerful response to the human condition. 195 illustrations, 115 in full color
0-8478-1846-2 RIZZOLI $60.00

Institute for the Arts Curators
Yves Klein, 1928 to 1962: A Retrospective
0-914412-27-2 MENIL $45.00

Paul **Moorhouse**, editor
Leon Kossoff
The work of one of the most important British artists of the postwar period, whose main preoccupations have been the changing face of London's urban landscape, portraits, and the human figure
0-500-09264-8 THAMES & HUDSON $45.00

Donald **Kuspit** & others

New Russian Art: Paintings from the Christian Keesee Collection

PHOTOGRAPHS BY JON BURRIS

1-55670-435-6 STEWART, TABORI $55.00

Jean-Clarence **Lambert**

Cobra

The Cobra group (for Copenhagen, Brussels, Amsterdam) followed Dubuffet in accepting the art of children, primitives, and the insane as clues to the direct expression of personal fantasy. The group included Pierre Alechinsky, Karel Appel, and Asger Jorn

0-89659-416-5 ABBEVILLE $125.00

Sam **Hunter**

Marino Marini: The Sculpture

0-8109-3629-1 ABRAMS $75.00

Peter **Fuller**

Henry Moore

See also **THAMES & HUDSON WORLD OF ART** under **ART HISTORY: GENERAL STUDIES**

0-500-20231-1 THAMES & HUDSON PB $11.95

Henry **Moore** & Claude **Allemand-Cosneau**, editor

Henry Moore: From the Inside Out Plasters, Carvings and Drawings

An analysis of Moore's work in the context of 20th-century sculpture, complete with personal background information and statements by the artist as well as illustrations of the artist's working methods and the stages in the creation of a work

3-7913-1666-4 PRESTEL $65.00

John **Berger**

A celebrated Marxist art critic, John Berger is also a novelist, screenwriter, and painter.

Art and Revolution: Ernst Neizvestny and the Role of the Artist in the USSR

A provocative study of a Russian sculptor whose work Berger knows only through photographs. The author has written: "By taking and considering in depth a particular example, it throws light on the character of Russian art, the situation of the visual artist today in the USSR, the meaning of politically revolutionary art and some of the future consequences of revolutionary consciousness"

0-394-41562-0 RANDOM HOUSE PB $14.00

Ronald **Alley**

Graham Sutherland

0-905005-48-1 HARPERCOLLINS $14.95

Roger **Berthoud**

Graham Sutherland: A Biography

0-571-11882-8 OLYMPIC $15.98

Anna **Agusti**

Tapies: The Complete Works, 1976-1981

0-8478-1829-2 RIZZOLI $275.00

Michael **Compton** & Marco **Livingstone**

Tilson

A major monograph on the celebrated artist who was originally associated with the British Pop movement

0-500-97410-1 NORTON $45.00

Carter **Ratcliff**

Bernar Venet

1-55859-699-2 CROSS RIVER $60.00

Heidi E. **Violand-Hobi**

Jean Tinguely: Life and Work

3-791-31430-0 PRESTEL $55.00

The Contemporary Scene

The '80s art boom saw a return to figuration and the traditional mediums of painting and sculpture. Neo-Expressionism was all the rage, with works by Schnabel, Clemente, Salle, Rothenberg, Haring, and Basquiat in the American limelight. In Europe, Kiefer, Polke, and Baselitz presided over the scene. The collapse of the art market in late 1989 ushered in a more insulated, selective art world, but the scene was no less energetic. The early '90s was marked by a renewed interest in abstraction and conceptual art. Artists once again experimented with video, computer art, performance, and installation art. Emerging artists such as Matthew Barney, Lorna Simpson, and Ellen Gallagher brought excitement to the art world in the United States, and abroad, talents such as Damien Hirst, Rachel Whiteread, and Mariko Mori gained notoriety for producing new images and artforms.

Kate **Linker**

Vito Acconci

0-8478-1645-1 RIZZOLI $50.00

Shusaku **Arakawa** & Madeline **Gins**

Arakawa: The Mechanism of Meaning

The writings of an artist who with great wit presses painting into the service of conceptualism

0-89659-809-8 ABBEVILLE $49.95

Dore **Ashton** & Terence **La Noue**

Terence La Noue

1-55595-052-3 HUDSON HILLS $75.00

San Jose Museum of Art

Compassion and Protest: Recent Social and Political Art from the Eli Broad Family Foundation

1-55859-301-2 ABBEVILLE $24.95

Deborah **Eisenberg**

Air:24 Hours: Jennifer Bartlett

0-8109-3128-1 ABRAMS $49.50

Marge **Goldwater**

Jennifer Bartlett

0-89659-519-6 ABBEVILLE PB $65.00

John **Russell**

Jennifer Bartlett: In the Garden

0-8109-0709-7 ABRAMS $49.50

Roberta **Smith**

Jennifer Bartlett: Rhapsody

0-8109-1577-4 ABRAMS $49.50

Richard **Marshall**

Jean-Michel Basquiat

An unprecedented survey of Basquiat's short and brilliant career, from his graffiti-inspired beginnings in the company of Keith Haring and Kenny Scharf to his death at 28 in 1988

See also **ARTISTS AND LITERARY FIGURES** under **BLACK VOICES, BLACK LIVES** under **AFRICAN-AMERICAN STUDIES** in **HISTORY OF THE AMERICAS**

0-8109-6814-2 ABRAMS PB $35.00

John **Beardsley**

Earthworks and Beyond: Contemporary Art in the Landscape

0-89659-963-9 ABBEVILLE PB $29.95

A Landscape for Modern Art: Storm King Art Center

0-89659-587-0 ABBEVILLE $59.95

Lisa **Dennison** & others

Ross Bleckner

0-8109-6880-0 ABRAMS $85.00

Lynn **Gumpert**

Christian Boltanski

2-08-013559-7 ABBEVILLE $24.95

Robert A. **Sobieszek**

Ports of Entry: William S. Burroughs and the Arts

Here, the L.A. County Museum of Art's curator of photography offers illustrations and commentary of Burrough's collages, photomontages, sculptural assemblages, and text/image work, placing them in the context of his peers and collaborators, Keith Haring, Robert Rauschenberg, Brion Gysin, and Philip Taafe

0-500-97435-7 THAMES & HUDSON PB $24.95

Henry **Chalfant** & James **Prigoff**

Spraycan Art

0-500-27469-X THAMES & HUDSON PB $14.95

Francesco **Clemente**

Francesco Clemente: Evening Raga and Paradiso

INTRODUCTION BY FRANCESCO CLEMENTE, ALLEN GINSBERG, & PETER ORLOVSKY

0-8478-1671-0 RIZZOLI PB $35.00

Sue **Coe**

Dead Meat

WITH AN ESSAY BY ALEXANDER COCKBURN

1-56858-050-9 FOUR WALLS $40.00

1-56858-041-X FOUR WALLS PB $22.00

Contemporary Women Artists

1-55859-376-4 ABBEVILLE $9.95

Martha **Cooper** & Henry **Chalfant**

Subway Art

0-8050-0678-8 HOLT PB $17.95

Michael **Desmond** & Kate **Davidson**

Islands: Installations from Australia, Asia, Europe and America

An international survey of some of the best mixed-media installations of the last decade

0-500-97441-1 THAMES & HUDSON PB $17.95

Mark **Di Suvero** & Irving **Sandler**

Mark Di Suvero at Storm King Art Center

The only full-length study in English of the artist's work, designed to accompany a two-year exhibition of fourteen of his soaring, space-defining sculptures at Storm King Art Center, a 400-acre sculpture park 55 miles north of Manhattan in the Hudson River Valley

0-8109-3218-0 ABRAMS $45.00

Amiri **Baraka** & others

Thorton Dial: Image of the Tiger

0-8109-3217-2 ABRAMS $45.00

Rudi **Fuchs**

Jan Dibbets: Interior Light

0-8478-1429-7 RIZZOLI $75.00

Thierry de **Duve** & others

Jeff Wall

0-7148-3349-5 PHAIDON PB $29.95

Ruth E. **Fine**

Gemini G.E.L.: Art and Collaboration

0-89659-506-4 ABBEVILLE $95.00

Audrey **Flack**

Audrey Flack on Painting

0-8109-2235-5 ABRAMS PB $14.95

Thelma **Golden**

Black Male: Representations of Masculinity in Contemporary American Art

0-8109-6816-9 WHITNEY MUSEUM PB $29.95

Terry **Friedman** & Andy **Goldsworthy**, editors

Hand to Earth: Andy Goldsworthy Sculptures, 1976-1990

0-8109-3420-5 ABRAMS $49.50

Robert L. **Hall**

Gathered Visions: Selected Works by American Women Artists

1-56098-106-7 SMITHSONIAN PB $15.95

Barry **Blinderman** & others

Keith Haring: Future Primeval

3-7913-1234-0 PRESTEL PB $35.00

John **Gruen**

Keith Haring: The Authorized Biography

Haring, whose career began in the urban subways and streets, went from being arrested for defacing public property to receiving commissions from the City of New York to create outdoor murals. Gruen offers the definitive work on the life, times, and untimely death of the young artist who blurred the lines between graffiti and art

0-88682-664-0 CREATIVE EDUCATION $25.00

Keith **Haring**

Keith Haring: Journals

Haring's journals not only tell the story of his friendships with Warhol, Leary, and Burroughs, but also illuminate the development of his work from early subway chalk sketches to international exhibitions, showing his deliberate, self-conscious, and extraordinarily successful effort to expand the boundaries of art

See also **MEMOIRS AND JOURNALS** under **20TH-CENTURY AMERICAN ESSAYS AND JOURNALISM** in **LITERATURE OF THE AMERICAS**

INTRODUCTION BY DAVID HOCKNEY

0-670-84774-7 VIKING $27.95

Damien **Hirst** & others

I Want to Spend the Rest of My Life Everywhere, with Everyone, One to One, Always, Forever, Now

1-8852-5438-5 MONACELLI $65.00

Damien **Hirst** & others

Jenny Holzer

0-89207-092-7 GUGGENHEIM $45.00

Diane **Waldman** & Jenny **Holzer**

Jenny Holzer

This revised and expanded edition of Abrams's 1989 retrospective book on Jenny Holzer, an artist who has been at the forefront of the American art scene since the early 80s, has been brought up to date. Spanning her entire career, the volume includes additional texts, all the artist's writings, and new color reproductions of her latest works

0-8109-6892-4 ABRAMS $45.00

Roger **Wollen**

Derek Jarman—A Portrait: Artist, Filmmaker, Designer

Specially commissioned essays explore the artistic, personal, and political motivations behind the filmmaker's paintings, sculptures, garden designs, and stage sets from all periods of his career

0-500-01723-9 THAMES & HUDSON PB $24.95

Ilya **Kabakov**

The Fly with the Wings

0-8109-2535-4 ABRAMS PB $85.00

The Red Wagon

0-8109-2539-7 ABRAMS PB $65.00
3-89322-561-7 D.A.P. PB $14.95

We Are Leaving Here Forever

0-8109-2541-9 ABRAMS PB $95.00

Amei **Wallach** & Ilya **Kabakov**

Ilya Kabakov: The Man Who Never Threw Anything Away

This monograph is the first and most comprehensive treatment in English on Ilya Kabakov, the most influential artist to emerge from the former Soviet Union, who is known as the "Father of Moscow Conceptualism"

0-8109-3525-2 ABRAMS $65.00

Elisabeth **Sussman** & others

Mike Kelley

0-8109-6812-6 ABRAMS PB $39.95

Sarah **Kent**

Shark-Infested Waters: The Saatchi Collection of British Art in the '90s

0-302-00648-6 SOTHEBY PB $40.00

Mark **Rosenthal**

Anselm Kiefer

3-7913-0847-5 TE NEUS PB $55.00

Robert **Rosenblum** & David **Sylvester**

Jeff Koons: Celebration

Famous for his provocative sculptures and highly controversial photographs, Jeff Koons's latest series is splendidly reproduced in this book. These new works include a monumental 10 1/2-foot-high dog, a giant diamond, and his first paintings

0-8109-6893-2 ABRAMS $75.00

Howard **Fox** & others

Robert Longo

0-8478-1105-0 RIZZOLI PB $29.95

Edward **Lucie-Smith**

Race, Sex, and Gender: Issues in Contemporary Art

0-8109-3767-0 ABRAMS $45.00

John **Maizels**

Raw Creation: Outsider Art and Beyond

WITH AN INDRODUCTION BY ROGER CARDINAL

0-7148-3149-2 PHAIDON $69.95

Louis K. **Meisel**

Photorealism Since 1980

0-8109-3720-4 ABRAMS $95.00

Germano **Celant**

Mario Merz

0-8478-1213-8 RIZZOLI PB $40.00

Victor Nieto **Alcaide**

Lucio Munoz

0-8478-1361-4 RIZZOLI $150.00

Sue **Grazel** & Kathy **Halbreich**, editors

Elizabeth Murray: Paintings and Drawings

0-8109-1423-9 ABRAMS $49.50

National Gallery of Australia, editor
Don't Leave Me This Way: Art in the Age of AIDS
This anthology combines essays, poems, and paintings to explore and document the influence of the AIDS epidemic on art. Contributors include Edmund White, Keith Haring, Cindy Sherman, and Andres Serrano
See also **THEMES, TECHNIQUES, AND GENRES** under **ART HISTORY: GENERAL STUDIES**
0-500-97420-9 NORTON PB $19.95

Andreas **Papadakis** & Claire **Farrow**
New Art: An International Perspective
0-8478-1282-0 RIZZOLI $75.00

John **Yau**
A.R. Penck
0-8109-3725-5 ABRAMS $49.50

Tom **Phillips**
A Humument
0-500-97339-3 THAMES & HUDSON PB $19.95

Thomas **McEvilley** & Judith **Nosbitt**
Join the Dots
1-8543-7153-3 TATE PB $30.00

Gerhard **Richter** & Peter **Gidal**
Painting in the Nineties
See also **ARTISTS ON ART** under **ART HISTORY: GENERAL STUDIES**
0-947564-60-8 D.A.P. $45.00

Randy **Rosen** & others
Making Their Mark: Women Artists Move into the Mainstream
1-55859-161-3 ABBEVILLE PB $29.95

Paul **Schimmel** & Dan **Cameron**
Objectives: The New Sculpture
0-8478-1207-3 RIZZOLI $45.00

Rosalind **Krauss**
Cindy Sherman, 1975-1993
0-8478-1756-3 RIZZOLI $60.00

Whitney Museum of American Art
Alexis Smith
0-8478-1446-7 RIZZOLI $50.00

Kristine **Stiles** & Peter **Selz**, editors
Theories and Documents of Contemporary Art: A Sourcebook of Artists' Writings
0-520-20253-8 CALIFORNIA PB $29.95

Wyatt **MacGaffey** & Michael D. **Harris**
Astonishment and Power: Kongo Minkisi: The Art of Renée Stout
1-56098-274-8 SMITHSONIAN PB $34.95

Brian **Wallis**, editor
Blasted Allegories: An Anthology of Artists' Writings
Contributions by Anderson, Nauman, Salle, Smithson, and 40 more
0-262-23128-X MIT $32.50
0-262-73086-3 MIT PB $23.00

Martin **Kunz**, editor
William Wegman: Paintings, Drawings, Photographs, Videotapes
The first complete retrospective of his work in four media
0-8109-2463-3 ABRAMS PB $24.95

Elizabeth **Sussman**
The 1993 Biennial Exhibition: Whitney Museum of American Art
The work of 77 artists explore the social, political, and cultural issues recurrent in the art of the '90s. This catalog of the always-controversial exhibition includes painting, sculpture, video installations, films, biographies, and bibliography
0-8109-2545-1 WHITNEY MUSEUM PB $39.95

Klaus **Kertess**
1995 Biennial Exhibition, Whitney Museum of American Art
0-8109-6818-5 WHITNEY MUSEUM PB $39.95

Lynn **Zelevansky**
Sense and Sensibility: Woman Artists and Minimalism in the Nineties
0-8109-6131-8 MOMA PB $16.95

Lori **Zippay** & others
Artists' Video
More than 200 black-and-white illustrations
1-55859-357-8 ABBEVILLE $59.95

Theory and Criticism

John **Ashbery**
Reported Sightings: Art Chronicles, 1957-1987
See also **CRITICS AND WRITERS ON ART** under **ART HISTORY: GENERAL STUDIES**
EDITED BY DAVID BERGMAN
0-674-76225-8 KNOPF PB $16.95

Norma **Broude** & Mary D. **Garrard**
The Power of Feminist Art: The American Movement of the 1970s, History and Impact
0-8109-3732-8 ABRAMS $49.50
0-8109-2659-8 ABRAMS PB $24.95

Douglas **Crimp**
On the Museum's Ruins
0-262-03209-0 MIT $37.50
0-262-53126-7 MIT PB $16.95

Thierry de **Duve**
Clement Greenberg Between the Lines
Includes a previously unpublished debate with Clement Greenberg
TRANSLATED BY BRIAN HOLMES
2-906571-53-9 D.A.P. PB $32.95

Kant After Duchamp
0-262-04151-0 MIT $39.95

Hal **Foster**
Recodings: Art, Spectacle, Cultural Politics
0-941920-04-6 BAY PB $11.95

Hal **Foster**, editor
The Anti-Aesthetic: Essays on Postmodern Culture
0-941920-01-1 BAY PB $9.95

Suzi **Gablik**
Conversations Before the End of Time
In this book, artist and critic Suzi Gablik addresses complex aesthetic issues in the form of interviews with some of the art world's most influential thinkers. The book is a must for anyone seriously concerned about the future of art and culture
0-500-01673-9 THAMES & HUDSON $24.95
0-500-27838-5 THAMES & HUDSON PB $14.95

Has Modernism Failed?
0-500-27385-5 NORTON PB $15.95

The Reenchantment of Art
0-500-27689-7 THAMES & HUDSON PB $15.95

Jeremy **Gilbert-Rolfe**
Beyond Piety: Critical Essays on the Visual Arts, 1986-1993
0-521-46055-7 CAMBRIDGE $80.00
0-521-46611-3 CAMBRIDGE PB $29.95

Clement **Greenberg**
Art and Culture: Critical Essays
0-8070-6681-8 FS&G PB $16.00

The Collected Essays and Criticism
Two new volumes of Greenberg's art criticism bring into focus his position as the red-hot center of post-1940 modern art. Stern, unapologetic, rigorous, Greenberg could make or break reputations. Included are critical exchanges between Greenberg and artists, remarkably demonstrating the principled passion surrounding the emergence of new challenges in modern art

Volume 1
Perceptions and Judgments, 1939-1944
022630621 CHICAGO PB $14.95

Volume 2
Arrogant Purpose, 1945-1949
0-226-30622-4 CHICAGO PB $16.95

Volume 3
Affirmations and Refusals, 1950-1956
0 226306194 CHICAGO $29.95

Serge **Guilbaut**, editor
Reconstructing Modernism: Art in New York, Paris, and Montreal, 1945-1964
Includes the two of the most outstanding recent scholarly essays on postwar art: T.J. Clark on "Jackson Pollock's Abstraction" and Thierry De Duve on "The Monochrome and the Blank Canvas"
0-262-07120-7 MIT $35.00
0-262-57092-0 MIT PB $20.00

Dave Hickey

The Invisible Dragon: Four Essays on Beauty

Hickey is a recent recipient of the College Art Association's Mather Award, which is presented for the year's most distinguished contribution to art criticism

0-9637264-0-4 D.A.P. PB $12.95

bell hooks

Art on My Mind: Visual Politics

1-56584-263-4 NEW PRESS PB $15.00

Robert Hughes

Nothing If Not Critical

A rich and lengthy gathering of the recent art criticism of one of the foremost commentators on the contemporary are scene. "Hughes's emphasis on social and political contexts and on artistic content balances the storehouse of provocative opinion he dispenses, which becomes increasingly caustic as he taxes his eye on the end of the 20th century" —Publishers Weekly

0-14-016524-X PENGUIN PB $15.95

Late-modernist art teaching (especially in America) has increasingly succumbed to the fiction that the values of the so-called academy—meaning, in essence, the transmission of disciplined skills based on drawing from the live model and the natural motif—were hostile to "creativity." This fiction enabled Americans to ignore the inconvenient fact that virtually all artists who created and extended the modernist enterprise between 1890 and 1950, Beckman to no less than Picasso, Miro and de Kooning as well as Degas or Matisse, were formed by the atelier system and could no more have done without the particular skills it inculcated than an aircraft can fly without an airstrip.
NOTHING IF NOT CRITICAL

Robert Hughes

Hilton Kramer

The Revenge of the Philistines: Art and Culture, 1972-1984

0-02-918470-3 FREE PRESS $35.00

Donald Kuspit

Signs of Psyche in Modern and Postmodern Art

0-521-44611-2 CAMBRIDGE PB $25.95

Joseph Masheck

Modernities: Art-Matters in the Present

"...a provocative collection of essays, this is art criticism informed by an erudite history and art history informed by the sensitivities of the practical critic. He speculates with the greatest inventiveness, but only after having brought the art object into plain view...and arguing with a daunting intellectual authority"—Richard Shiff

0-271-00808-3 PENN STATE $35.00

Thomas McEvilley

Art & Otherness: Crisis in Cultural Identity

A notable and highly influential collection of essays on problems in contemporary art

0-929701-21-6 MCPHERSON $20.00

Art and Discontent: Theory at the Millennium

0-929701-13-5 MCPHERSON $20.00
0-929701-31-3 MCPHERSON PB $12.00

The Exile's Return: Toward a Redefinition of Painting for the Post-Modern Era

0-521-41672-8 CAMBRIDGE $70.00
0-521-45615-0 CAMBRIDGE PB $20.95

W.J.T. Mitchell, editor

Art and the Public Sphere

In the age of publicity, public art has taken on new meanings and dimensions. This book explores the social, political, and aesthetic dynamics of contemporary public art

0-226-53210-0 CHICAGO $41.95
0-226-53211-9 CHICAGO PB $19.95

Brian O'Doherty

Inside the White Cube

0-932499-14-7 LAPIS $25.95
0-932499-05-8 LAPIS PB $15.95

Harold Rosenberg

The Anxious Object

Spirited classics which, though too often nodded to (or, in two or three cases, hissed at), are too seldom read and sometimes even allowed to go out of print

0-226-72682-7 CHICAGO PB $19.95

The De-Definition of Art

0-226-72673-8 CHICAGO PB $17.95

W. Jackson Rushing

Native American Art and the New York Avant-Garde: A History of Cultural Primitivism

0-292-75547-3 TEXAS $39.95

Hans-Ulrich Obrist & others

Gerard Richter: 100 Paintings

3-893-22854-3 DAP $35.00

David Salle

Richard Pandiscio and Others

0-847-81781-4 RIZZOLI $75.00

Peter Schjeldahl

The 7 Days Art Columns, 1988-1990

The short-lived Manhattan weekly 7 Days did at least provide an opportunity for critic Schieldahl to contribute these nimble, off-the-cuff sketches of the New York art world

0-935724-41-9 FIGURES PB $12.50

The Courbet show is right on time for us, but then, when wouldn't it be? We are always in the mood, whether we know it or not, for a brash, authentic arriver who is wild for our approval and, cheerfully absorbing all sorts of abuse, keeps on coming. Gustave Courbet was like that in mid-19th-century Paris—a swaggering fanatic importuning the public with paintings that Edgar Degas said made him feel he was being nozeled by the wet nose of a calf—and Courbet is the same today in Brooklyn, which is a good place for him. He is to great art what a "dem"-and-"dose" accent is to American speech, and in Brooklyn, as in all else, he is off-center in a way that makes the center feel colorless and effete.
THE 7 DAYS ART COLUMNS, 1988-1990

Alex Seago

Burning the Box of Beautiful Things: The Development of a Postmodern Sensibility

0-19-817221-4 OXFORD $55.00
0-19-817405-5 OXFORD PB $29.95

Tom Wolfe

The Painted Word

A caustic essay on modern art

See also REPORTING under 20TH-CENTURY AMERICAN ESSAYS AND JOURNALISM in LITERATURE OF THE AMERICAS

0-374-22878-7 FS&G $18.95
0-553-27379-5 BDD PB $5.99

The Art World

Art dealers and collectors have even more impact than critics on the state of art.

Brian **Allen**, editor

Towards a Modern Art World

An attempt to explain the marginal position of British modern art in art history by examining the development of the London art world—its institutions and individual artists—over the past two centuries

0-300-06380-6 YALE........$40.00

Guerrilla **Girls**

Confessions of the Guerrilla Girls: By the Guerrilla Girls Themselves, Whoever They Are

Combines the famous display—by the anonymous group who wear gorilla masks—of their ads, posters, and letter-writing campaigns that focus on the exclusion of women artists in museums and galleries

See also **ART AND PHOTOGRAPHY** under **ARTS AND LETTERS** under **WOMEN'S STUDIES** in **SOCIAL STUDIES**

INTRODUCTION BY WHITNEY CHADWICK

0-06-095088-9 HARPERPERENNIAL PB........$18.00

Alice Goldfarb **Marquis**

Art Lessons: Learning from the Rise and Fall of Public Arts Funding

"A revolutionary blueprint for democratizing public support for the arts"—*Publishers Weekly*

See also **CULTURAL AND SOCIAL HISTORY** under **TOPICS IN AMERICAN STUDIES** in **HISTORY OF THE AMERICAS**

0-465-00438-5 BASIC PB........$16.00

Philosophy and Art

Theodor W. **Adorno** & others

Aesthetic Theory

0-8166-1799-6 MINNESOTA........$39.95

Roland **Barthes**

The Responsibility of Forms

Barthes's essays on Cy Twombly are among the best on any contemporary artist

See also **ROLAND BARTHES** under **CRITICAL TEXTS** under **SEMIOTICS AND STRUCTURALISM AND AFTER** under **LITERARY THEORY** in **LITERATURE OF EUROPE, AFRICA, AND ASIA**

TRANSLATED BY RICHARD HOWARD

0-8090-8075-3 HILL & WANG........$22.95

Peter **Brunette** & David **Wills**, editors

Deconstruction and the Visual Arts: Art, Media, Architecture

0-521-44271-0 CAMBRIDGE........$65.00

0-521-44781-X CAMBRIDGE PB........$20.95

Peter **Burger**

Theory of the Avant-Garde

Two of the most salient aspects of modern "primitive" past and its concern with advancing into the future

0-8166-1067-3 MINNESOTA........$25.00

0-8166-1068-1 MINNESOTA PB........$13.95

David **Carrier**

The Aesthete in the City: The Philosophy and Practice of American Abstract Painting in the 1980s

0-271-00943-8 PENN STATE........$45.00

Artwriting

0-87023-561-3 MASSACHUSETTS........$25.00

0-87023-562-1 MASSACHUSETTS PB........$13.95

High Art: Charles Baudelaire and the Origins of Modernist Painting

0-271-01527-6 PENN STATE........$39.50

Principles of Art History Writing

0-271-00945-4 PENN STATE PB........$16.95

Arthur C. **Danto**

The Transfiguration of the Commonplace: A Philosophy of Art

A philosopher's mind comes to grip with a fascinating aesthetic situation, the identity of found things and artifacts mimicking them

See also **OTHER 20TH-CENTURY PHILOSOPHERS** under **PHILOSOPHY** in **RELIGION, SPIRITUALITY, AND PHILOSOPHY**

0-674-90346-3 HARVARD PB........$12.95

After the End of Art: Contemporary Art and the Pale of History

To be published February 1997

0-691-01173-7 PRINCETON........$24.95

Encounters & Reflections: Art in the Historical Present

To be published February 1997

0-520-20846-3 CALIFORNIA........$42.00

The Philosophical Disenfranchisement of Art

0-231-06364-4 COLUMBIA........$39.50

0-231-06365-2 COLUMBIA PB........$16.00

Jacques **Derrida**

The Truth of Painting

"Calling into question every certain conclusion, Derrida exposes the impossibility of all final solutions"—*NY Times*

See also **JACQUES DERRIDA** under **POSTSTRUCTURALISM** under **LITERARY THEORY** in **LITERATURE OF EUROPE, AFRICA, AND ASIA**

0-226-14324-4 CHICAGO PB........$23.95

0-226-14323-6 CHICAGO PB........$49.95

George **Dickie** & others

Aesthetics: A Critical Anthology

See also **READINGS IN PHILOSOPHY: ANTHOLOGIES ON SPECIAL TOPICS** under **PHILOSOPHY** in **RELIGION, SPIRITUALITY, AND PHILOSOPHY**

0-312-00309-9 ST. MARTIN'S........$55.98

Denis **Dutton**, editor

The Forger's Art: Forgery and the Philosophy of Art

0-520-05619-1 CALIFORNIA PB........$15.00

Nelson **Goodman**

The Languages of Art

An acclaimed analytic philosophy of art in which the author argues (among other things) that perspective construction is conventional rather than real

0-915144-34-4 HACKETT PB........$12.95

Karsten **Harries**

Meaning of Modern Art: A Philosophical Interpretation

0-8101-0593-4 NORTHWESTERN PB........$15.95

Renato **Poggioli**

The Theory of the Avant-Garde

0-674-88216-4 BELKNAP PB........$15.95

Richard **Wollheim**

Art and Its Objects

An acclaimed work examining the representational properties of art from the point of view of aesthetics

See also **OTHER 20TH-CENTURY PHILOSOPHERS** under **PHILOSOPHY** in **RELIGION, SPIRITUALITY, AND PHILOSOPHY**

See also **THEORY** under **ART HISTORY: GENERAL STUDIES**

See also **ARTISTS ON ART** under **ART HISTORY: GENERAL STUDIES**

0-521-43778-4 CAMBRIDGE PB........$11.95

Painting as an Art

An important contribution to our understanding of how pictures are made; well illustrated

See also **OTHER 20TH-CENTURY PHILOSOPHERS** under **PHILOSOPHY** in **RELIGION, SPIRITUALITY, AND PHILOSOPHY**

0-691-09964-2 PRINCETON........$85.00

0-691-01892-8 PRINCETON PB........$35.00

Arts of Africa

The art of the peoples of sub-Saharan Africa was never a realm apart but an integral aspect of their lives, whether serving religious or secular purposes, tribal or royal institutions. In spite of the interest in "primitive" art that accompanied the modernist movement in the West early in the 20th century, the true scale of achievement of African art has begun to emerge only recently. Archaeologists and art historians have had to overcome the general absence of written records and the tendency of wood objects to decay quickly in the African climate. Today research has revealed much about the significance and history of not only sculpture and masks, the most renowned African arts, but also other forms such as pottery, jewelry, architecture, rock paintings and engravings, costumes, and body art.

General Studies

William **Bascom**

African Art in Cultural Perspective: An Introduction

See also **RELIGION AND CULTURE** under **AFRICA** in **WORLD HISTORY AND CURRENT AFFAIRS**

0-393-09375-1 NORTON PB........$9.95

Ezio **Bassani** & William **Fagg**

Africa and the Renaissance: Art in Ivory

African ivories reached Europe as early as the 15th century, and led to relationships between European patrons and African artists. This fascinating study surveys the remarkable saltcellars, horns, spoons, and other objects

decorated in a fusion of African and European motifs, and considers the deeper implications of this early cultural link between the two continents. 102 full-color and 404 black-and-white illustrations
0-945802-00-5 MUSEUM FOR AFRICAN ART $60.00
3-7913-0880-7 PRESTEL $85.00

The creation of the Afro-Portuguese ivories is a unique event in the history of African art. In no other period of the intercultural relationship between Europe and Africa has artistic creation been so fruitful…Not long after this period, the slave trade and the Industrial Revolution radically transformed the relationship between Europeans and Africans. The slave trade could only exist if Africans could be redefined as inferior beings…The later unequal, and often brutal, encounters contrasted with the reasonably benign relationship between the two cultures during the Renaissance.
AFRICA AND THE RENAISSANCE: ART IN IVORY

Suzanne Preston **Blier**
African Vodun: Art, Psychology, and Power
The art of Vodoo was created for psychological effect, and in this book Blier discusses it's meaning and method. This book is a must for all enthusiasts of African, African-American, and Caribbean art
0-226-05858-1 CHICAGO $50.00
0-226-05860-3 CHICAGO PB $34.95

Sandro **Bocola**, editor
African Seats
A beautifully illustrated survey of the creativity and aesthetic intensity of African seating traditions
3-7913-1426-2 PRESTEL $60.00

Herbert M. **Cole**
Icons: Ideals and Power in the Art of Africa
An examination of some of the leading figurative motifs of African art: the couple, the woman and child, the male hunter, the rider, the stranger. Published in conjunction with a major exhibit, *Icons* features over 200 examples of African art in a tremendous variety of media, from ivory and terracotta to contemporary commercial signs
0-87474-320-6 SMITHSONIAN PB $45.00

Annie E. **Coombes**
Reinventing Africa: Museums, Material Culture, and Popular Imagination in Late Victorian and Edwardian England
British colonial expansion between 1890 and 1918 led to the removal of many African artifacts to Britain. This book analyzes the racial stereotyping and justifications for imperial expansion that were implicit in the way these objects were collected, displayed, and publicized
0-300-05972-8 YALE $50.00

Arthur C. **Danto**, editor
Art/Artifact: African Art in Anthropology Collections
Essays by noted scholars discuss changing definitions of art vs. artifact and how viewers look at objects from cultures with differing classification systems
3-7913-0865-3 PRESTEL $70.00

Werner **Gillon**
A Short History of African Art
An excellent introduction to African art, beginning with prehistoric rock paintings and proceeding by region and historical period to take in the major achievements most African cultures; fully illustrated with black-and-white photographs
0-14-022508-0 PENGUIN PB $17.50

Jean **Kennedy**
New Currents, Ancient Rivers: Contemporary African Artists in a Generation of Change
1-56098-037-0 SMITHSONIAN $49.95

Jacques **Kerchache** & others
Art of Africa
Long thought to be only of "ethnographic" interest, the beauty, complexity, and enormous power of African art is now gaining wide appreciation. Here, in a new resource for collectors and a fine introduction for others, is the most important survey in 20 years of the art of the African continent south of the Sahara. It contains 1,100 illustrations, discusses over 100 African artistic traditions, and includes an essay by philosopher Lucien Stephan that offers the Western reader an introductory framework to art in general and African art in particular
0-8109-0628-7 ABRAMS $195.00

David **Koloane** & others
Seven Stories About Modern Art in Africa
2-08-013599-6 ABBEVILLE $55.00

Jean **Laude**
The Arts of Black Africa
0-520-02358-7 CALIFORNIA PB $15.95

André **Magnin** & Jacques **Soulillou**, editors
Contemporary Art of Africa
0-8109-4032-9 ABRAMS $60.00

Marshall W. **Mount**
African Art: The Years Since 1920
0-306-80373-9 DA CAPO PB $16.95

Mary H. **Nooter**
Secrecy: African Art that Conceals and Reveals
An exploration of the themes of secrecy and privileged access to information found in a variety of ritual art forms
3-7913-1230-8 PRESTEL $70.00

David W. **Penney** & others
African Masterworks in the Detroit Institute of Arts
ESSAYS BY MICHAEL KAN AND ROY SIEBER
1-56098-602-6 SMITHSONIAN PB $34.95

Allen F. **Roberts**
Animals in African Art: From the Familiar to the Marvelous
A beautifully illustrated discussion of animal symbolism in the contexts of leadership, healing, divination, and rites of passage
3-7913-1455-6 PRESTEL $65.00

Werner **Schmalenbach**
African Art: The Barbier-Mueller Collection
A large, handsomely and profusely illustrated book that encompasses art from all major black African cultures, with accompanying text by leading scholars
3-7913-0849-1 PRESTEL $70.00

Theirry **Secretan**
Going into Darkness: Fantastic Coffins from Africa
0-500-27839-3 THAMES & HUDSON PB $24.95

Ladislas **Segy**
Masks of Black Africa
A popular book, revised since its publication in 1952 under the title *African Sculpture Speaks*
0-486-23181-X DOVER PB $13.95

Roy **Sieber** & Roslyn Adele **Walker**
African Art in the Cycle of Life
The catalog of the National Museum of African Art
0-87474-821-6 SMITHSONIAN PB $29.95

Te Neus
Africa: The Art of a Continent
Vivid images of some of the continent's finest objects are accompanied by commentaries by more than 100 scholars in a variety of fields
3-7913-1603-6 TE NEUS $85.00

Carol **Thompson**
African Art Portfolio: An Illustrated Introduction, Masterpieces from the Eleventh to the Twentieth Centuries
By dividing its subject into four main themes—masks, ancestors, nations, and individual artists—this superb portfolio provides a firm context with which to approach nine centuries of African art. Taken from the acclaimed exhibits of the Center for African Art in New York, these unbound, full-color images cover the entire range of styles and materials, from abstract to naturalist, wood to ivory and gold
1-56584-112-3 NEW PRESS PB $17.95

Robert F. **Thompson**
Face of the Gods: Art and Altars of Africa and the African Americas
"Visually and emotionally stirring. . . documents a wide assortment of. . . connections between African and African American religious art"
—*NY Times*
3-7913-1281-2 TE NEUS $85.00

Robert Farris **Thompson**
Flash of the Spirit: African and Afro-American Art and Philosophy
One of the most provocative scholars on the continuity of African art and ritual in the New World
See also **RELIGION AND CULTURE** under **AFRICA** in **WORLD HISTORY AND CURRENT AFFAIRS**
0-394-72369-4 RANDOM HOUSE PB $13.00

Susan **Vogel**

Africa Explores: 20th Century African Art

"Encyclopedic in scope,...*Africa Explores* is the most important publication on modern African art to date. It will long serve as a reference for scholars and as an approachable survey for novices"—*Library Journal*

3-7913-1143-3 PRESTEL $70.00

Allen **Wardwell**

African Sculpture: From the University Museum, University of Pennsylvania

08763300677 PENN STATE PB $14.95

Frank **Willett**

African Art: An Introduction

See also **THAMES & HUDSON WORLD OF ART** under **ART HISTORY: GENERAL STUDIES**

0-500-20267-2 THAMES & HUDSON PB $14.95

Regional Studies

Emmanuel **Asihene**

Understanding the Traditional Art of Ghana

0-8386-2130-9 ASSOCIATED UNIVERSITIES $29.50

Anne-Marie **Bouttiaux** & Anne-Marie **Ndlaye**

Senegal Behind Glass: Images of Religious and Daily Life

A comprehensive selection of the finest examples of glass painting from Senegal that documents the artistry and huge popularity of this art, form which is of major significance in contemporary Africa

3-7913-1424-6 PRESTEL $60.00

Rene **Bravmann**

Islam and Tribal Art in West Africa

0-521-29791-5 CAMBRIDGE PB $23.95

Sarah C. **Brett-Smith**

The Making of Bamana Sculpture: Creativity and Gender

0-521-44484-5 CAMBRIDGE $95.00

Herbert **Cole** & Chike **Amaka**

Ibo Arts: Community & Cosmos

FOREWORD BY CHINUA ACHEBE

0-930741-07-2 CALIFORNIA MUSEUM $35.00

0-930741-01-3 CALIFORNIA MUSEUM PB $25.00

Philip **Dark**

An Illustrated Catalogue of Benin Art

0-8161-0382-8 GK HALL $75.00

Henry **Drewal** & Jon **Pemberton**, III

Yoruba: Nine Centuries of African Art and Thought

A magnificent survey of Yoruba art and culture, from the Yoruba kingdoms of the 9th century to today. With 350 photographs, including 150 in full color

PHOTOGRAPHS BY JERRY L. THOMPSON

0-8109-1794-7 ABRAMS $65.00

0-945802-04-8 MUSEUM FOR AFRICAN ART PB $38.00

Armand **Duchateau**

Benin: Royal Art of Africa

The kingdom of Benin's classical age produced some of the Africa's most spectacular art. Working in brass, ivory, elephant tusks, and other forms, the court artists were without peer. This volume selects and reproduces in full color over 100 works from the Museum füer Vöelkerkunde in Vienna, and presents them in conjunction with essays on creation myths, ritual, and cosmology

3-7913-1368-1 PRESTEL $50.00

0-89090-058-2 MUSEUM OF FINE ARTS PB $35.00

Kate **Ezra**

Art of the Dogon: Selections from the Lester Wunderman Collection

Black-and-white photographs of the elegant wood sculpture, masks, and craftwork of the Dogon region of Mali, with detailed text

0-8109-2428-5 ABRAMS PB $12.95

Royal Art of Benin: The Perls Collection

0-8109-6414-7 ABRAMS $60.00

Timothy F. **Garrard**

Gold of Africa: Jewellery and Ornaments from Ghana, Côte d' Ivoire, Mali and Senegal

The first thorough study of West African gold work, including headdresses, jewelry, and items of royal regalia, lavishly illustrated

3-7913-0914-5 PRESTEL $70.00

Marilyn **Heldman** & others

African Zion: The Sacred Art of Ethiopia

A handsome survey of the art of highland Christian Ethiopia—icons, metalwork, gold coins, and illuminated manuscripts—from the fourth through the 18th centuries, with an emphasis on the political, social, economic, and religious history of the region

0-300-06714-3 YALE PB $30.00

Patrick R. **McNaughton**

The Mande Blacksmiths: Knowledge, Power and Art in West Africa

0-253-20798-3 INDIANA PB $15.95

Jean **Morris** & Eleanor **Preston-Whyte**

Speaking with Beads: Zulu Arts from Southern Africa

A profusely illustrated analysis of the symbolic language of Zulu beads, which may convey coded love messages, the origins of their makers, or information about ethnic identity and religion

0-500-27757-5 THAMES & HUDSON PB $19.95

Enid **Schildkrout** & Curtis **Keim**

African Reflections: Art from Northeastern Zaire

More than 100 new color photographs illustrate this study of Mangbetu art, an aesthetic tradition encompassing both elaborate geometric design and representational sculpture

0-295-96961-X AMERICAN MUSEUM $50.00

Ivor **Powell**

Ndebele: A People & Their Art

0-7892-0073-2 CROSS RIVER $40.00

Mary Nooter **Roberts**
& Allen F **Roberts**, editors

Memory: Luba Art—The Making of History

A profusely illustrated cultural history of the varying ways in which art was used to memorize the complex structure of sovereignty in the Luban empire. Included is an analysis of lukasa, intricate bead and shell-covered "memory boards" used by this Bantu-speaking people to record their history

3-7913-1677-X PRESTEL $75.00

Art of Oceania, Australia, and New Zealand

Terence **Barrow**

An Illustrated Guide to Maori Art

A survey of the Maori art of New Zealand from the time of Captain Cook's landing in 1769 until 1900; illustrated with old drawings and photographs, and objects in contemporary collections

0-8248-0979-3 HAWAII PB $15.95

Tim **Bonyhady**

Images in Opposition: Australian Landscape Painting, 1801-1890

0-19-553259-7 OXFORD PB $35.00

Wally **Caruana**

Aboriginal Art

See also **THAMES & HUDSON WORLD OF ART** under **ART HISTORY: GENERAL STUDIES**

0-500-20264-8 THAMES & HUDSON PB $14.95

Jo-Anne Birnie **Danzker**

Dreamings = Tjukurrpa: Aboriginal Art of the Western Desert

Noted scholars discuss sociocultural aspects of the acrylics painted by Aborigines of Australia's Western Desert

3-7913-1427-0 PRESTEL $55.00

Suzanne **Greub**

Art of Northwest New Guinea

0-8478-1295-2 RIZZOLI $50.00

Joan **Kerr**, editor

Dictionary of Australian Artists, Sketchers, Photographers and Engravers to 1870

0-19-553290-2 OXFORD $225.00

Caterine **Orliac** & Michael **Orliac**

Easter Island: Mystery of the Stone Giants

0-8109-2834-5 ABRAMS PB $12.95

Roger **Neich**

Painted Histories: The Development of Maori Figurative Painting

1-86940-087-9 AUCKLAND $55.00

Barry **Pearce** & Wendy **Whiteley**

Brett Whiteley: Art and Life

One of Australia's most important contemporary artists, Brett Whiteley died in 1992 at age 53. This beautifully illustrated volume examines some 200 paintings, sculptures, drawings, and ceramics, many of which feature Whiteley's signature landscapes and nudes

0-500-09252-4 THAMES & HUDSON $45.00

Andrew **Sayers**

Aboriginal Artists of the Nineteenth Century

0-19-553392-5 OXFORD $75.00

Nicholas **Thomas**

Oceanic Art

See also **THAMES & HUDSON WORLD OF ART** under **ART HISTORY: GENERAL STUDIES**

0-500-20281-8 THAMES & HUDSON PB $14.95

Nancy D.H. **Underhill**

Making Australian Art, 1916-1946: Sidney Ure Smith, Patron and Publisher

0-19-553237-6 OXFORD $45.00

Islamic Art and Architecture

"Anyone who visits an ancient Islamic building or a museum exhibition of Islamic art, or who takes a university course in the subject, readily observes the unified decorative schemes, interest in geometry, paucity of figural imagery, and extensive use of color that characterize the family of artistic traditions we call Islamic art. With a little more study one can see that these characteristics develop over the centuries in all the stylistic branches of Islamic art alike, though in disparate ways."
—Terry Allen, *Five Essays on Islamic Art*

General Studies

Terry **Allen**

Five Essays on Islamic Art

0-944940-00-5 SOLIPSIST PB $35.00

Sheila S. **Blair** & Jonathan M. **Bloom**

The Art and Architecture of Islam

"A volume that will stand the test of time and that I, and anyone interested in Islamic art, will refer to again and again"—Hugh Kennedy, *American Historical Review*

See also **THE PELICAN HISTORY OF ART** under **ART HISTORY: GENERAL STUDIES**

See also **COMMUNITY AND SOCIETY** under **THE MEDIEVAL MIDDLE EASTERN WORLD** under **THE ISLAMIC WORLD TO WORLD WAR I**

0-300-05888-8 YALE $70.00

Images of Paradise in Islamic Art

A wide-ranging evaluation of Islamic conceptions of paradise in a lavishly illustrated catalog: a companion to the exhibit organized by the Hood Museum

0-292-76527-4 HOOD MUSEUM $29.95
0-292-76528-2 TEXAS PB $19.95

Keith **Critchlow**

Islamic Patterns: An Analytical and Cosmological Approach

The cosmological symbolism of typical Islamic art forms

0-500-27071-6 NORTON PB $19.95

Jerrilyn D. **Dodds**

Al-Andalus: The Islamic Arts of Spain

0-8109-6413-9 METROPOLITAN MUSEUM $75.00

Oleg **Grabar**

The Formation of Islamic Art

Seven related essays on the development of the forms of Islamic art and of Islamic attitudes toward it, illustrated with black-and-white photographs and architectural diagrams

0-300-04046-6 YALE PB $20.00

Ernst J. **Grube**, editor

Islamic Art

0-19-921501-4 OXFORD $175.00
0-19-921502-2 OXFORD PB $65.00

Marilyn **Jenkins**

Islamic Art in the Kuwait National Museum: The Al-Sabah Collection

Fine color reproductions of manuscripts, bowls, vases, coins, jewelry, and other objects in the Kuwait collection

0-85667-174-6 SOTHEBY PARKE BERNET $30.00

Ann **Parker** & Avon **Neal**

Hajj Paintings: Folk Art of the Great Pilgrimage

FOREWORD BY ROBERT A. FERNEA

1-56098-546-1 SMITHSONIAN $50.00

David Talbot **Rice**

Islamic Art

Well-chosen illustrations and clear, concise prose make this an ideal introductory guide to the whole range of Islamic art: architecture, mosaics, woodwork, carpets and textiles, miniatures, metalwork, and ceramics

0-500-20150-1 THAMES & HUDSON PB $14.95

Islamic Painting

A brief, clear, well-illustrated historical survey of all major areas and schools

0-85224-112-7 COLUMBIA $20.00

B.W. **Robinson**

Islamic Art in the Keir Collection

Paintings, ceramics, metalwork, and textiles

0-571-13753-9 FABER $150.00

Stephen **Vernoit**

Occidentalism: Islamic Art in the 19th Century

0-19-727620-2 OXFORD $245.00

Islamic Architecture

Martin **Frishman** & Hasan-Uddin **Khan**

The Mosque

Sixteen eminent scholars trace the history, regional diversity, and decorative development of the mosque as a building type from the time of Muhammad to the present day

0-500-34133-8 THAMES & HUDSON $50.00

Robert **Hillenbrand**

Islamic Architecture: Style, Function and Form

0-231-10132-5 COLUMBIA $60.00

John **Hoag**

Islamic Architecture

A comprehensive, richly illustrated guide to Islamic architecture from Spain to India, emphasizing historical context and showing the unity underlying the diversity

0-8478-0796-7 RIZZOLI PB $29.95

Julian **Raby** & Jeremy **Johns**

Bayt-al-Maqdis: 'Abd al-Malik's Jerusalem

0-19-728017-X OXFORD $65.00

Islamic Decorative Arts

James **Allen**

Metalwork of the Islamic World: The Aron Collection

0-85667-327-7 SOTHEBY PARKE BERNET $95.00

Nurhan **Atasoy** & Lulian **Raby**

Iznik: The Pottery of Ottoman Turkey

The definite account of the great ceramic center whose stylistic phases reflect the major changes in Ottoman taste from the late 15th to the 17th century

See also **POTTERY AND PORCELAIN** under **AFRICAN AND ASIAN DECORATIVE ARTS** in **ARCHITECTURE, DESIGN, AND HOMES**

0-500-97374-1 THAMES & HUDSON $100.00

Esin **Atil**

Islamic Metalwork at the Freer Gallery of Art

9997394305
GOVERNMENT PRINTING OFFICE $17.50

Renaissance of Islam: Art of the Mamluks

Exhibition catalog devoted to decorative book illuminations and crafts that flourished under the Mamluk sultans of Egypt from the 13th to the 15th century; color reproductions

0-87474-214-5 SMITHSONIAN $55.00

François **Déroche**

The Abbasid Tradition: Qur'ans of The 8th to 10th Centuries AD

0-19-727600-8 OXFORD $275.00

Ernst J. **Grube**

Cobalt and Lustre: The First Centuries of Islamic Pottery

See also **POTTERY AND PORCELAIN** under **AFRICAN AND ASIAN DECORATIVE ARTS** in **ARCHITECTURE, DESIGN, AND HOMES**

0-19-727607-5 OXFORD $295.00

David **James**

After Timur: Qur'ans of the 15th and 16th Centuries AD

0-19-727602-4 OXFORD $275.00

The Master Scribes: Qur'ans of the 11th to 14th Centuries AD

0-19-727601-6 OXFORD $275.00

Trudy S. **Kawami**

Ancient Iranian Ceramics: From The Arthur M. Sackler Collection

0-8109-1913-3 ABRAMS $65.00

Nasser D. **Khalili** & B.W. **Robinson**

Lacquer of the Islamic Lands

Volume 1

0-19-727619-9 OXFORD $245.00

Volume 2

0-19-727626-1 OXFORD $245.00

Abdelkebir **Khatibi** & Mohammed **Sijelmassi**

The Splendor of Islamic Calligraphy

0-500-01675-5 THAMES & HUDSON $65.00

Glenn **Lowry** & Susan **Nemazee**

A Jeweler's Eye: Islamic Arts of the Book from the Vever Collection

Selections from a remarkable collection recently recovered after its disappearance during World War II

0-295-96677-7 WASHINGTON PB $26.95

Helen **Philon**

Early Islamic Ceramics: Catalogue of Islamic Art in the Benaki Museum

A catalog with black-and-white photographs and several color plates of ceramics in the collection of the Benaki Museum in Athens

0-85667-098-7 SOTHEBY PARKE BERNET $120.00

Annemarie **Schimmel**

Calligraphy and Islamic Culture

An Islamic writer defined calligraphy as "the language of the hand, the idiom of the mind, the ambassador of intellect, and the trustee of thought." Schimmel draws on her deep scholarly knowledge of Islamic religious traditions to explore the full significance of the art of writing

0-8147-7896-8 NYU PB $30.00

Robert **Skelton**

Gems and Jewels of Mughal India

0-19-727616-4 OXFORD $245.00

Rachel **Ward**

Islamic Metalwork

A concise illustrated treatment of the diversity of materials, techniques, motifs, and diverse local styles of this important craft, from the seventh through the 15th centuries

See also **GENERAL** under **AFRICAN AND ASIAN DECORATIVE ARTS** in **ARCHITECTURE, DESIGN, AND HOMES**

0-500-27731-1 THAMES & HUDSON PB $15.95

Marian **Wenzel**

Ornament and Amulet: Rings of The Islamic Lands

0-19-727614-8 OXFORD $245.00

Persian Art

Esin **Atil**

Brush of the Masters: Drawings from Iran and India

0-934686-29-7 FREED-HARDEMAN PB $20.00

Sheila R. **Canby**

Persian Painting

A lucid account of the development of Persian painting from around 1300 to 1900

0-500-27730-3 THAMES & HUDSON PB $15.95

Thomas W. **Lentz** & Glenn D. **Lowry**

Timur and the Princely Vision: Persian Art and Culture in the Fifteenth Century

0-87474-706-6 SMITHSONIAN $79.95

Arthur **Pope**

Persian Architecture

A survey by one of the leading authorities on Persian art

4-89360-027-3 TUTTLE $12.50

Marianna **Simpson**

Arab and Persian Painting in the Fogg Art Museum

Black-and-white plates of miniature paintings, book illustrations, and drawings from the 13th to the 19th centuries, with accompanying text

0-916724-10-7 HARVARD PB $9.95

Abolala **Soudavar**

Art of the Persian Courts

0-8478-1660-5 RIZZOLI $75.00

Mojdeh **Stephenson**

Persian Miniature Designs

0-88045-033-9 STEMMER PB $5.95

East Asian Art

Since the Bronze Age, East Asia has been periodically united and divided by cultural developments. For centuries India and the Himalayas, Southeast and Central Asia, China, Korea, and Japan were bound by the spell of evangelical Buddhism, producing an extraordinary and long-lived international style of figural art. After the 15th century each region found its own identity, yet the various East Asian cultures retained profound and durable affinities.

Western contacts with East Asia go back to the Bronze Age. But the sporadic trade connections, based on such commodities as silk, ivory, precious metals, and porcelain, forged only fragile links between the Orient and the West. Although Western curiosity about East Asia was stimulated by the travels of Marco Polo in the 13th century and the Jesuit missionary efforts that began in the 17th century, the modern Western interest in and knowledge of East Asian art and culture dates from the Age of Enlightenment.

By the late 19th century a measured, scientific study of East Asia had developed. The literature available on 20th-century Asian art can be divided into three groups: a small body of semi-popular pre-World War II writing based on limited materials; a very small number of postwar popularizations; and a large number of postwar specialized studies.

East Asia: General Works

Sherman **Lee**

A History of Far Eastern Art

An excellent book for a broad audience, stressing regional Buddhist art and the interplay of Chinese and Japanese art

0-8109-3414-0 ABRAMS $60.00

T.S. **Maxwell**, editor

Eastern Approaches: Essays on Asian Art and Architecture

0-19-562925-6 OXFORD $35.00

Elinor **Pearlstein** & others

Asian Art in the Art Institute of Chicago

0-8109-1916-8 ART INSTITUTE OF CHICAGO $35.00
0-86559-095-8 ART INSTITUTE OF CHICAGO PB ... $24.95

India

Ananda **Coomaraswamy**

Essays in Early Indian Architecture

EDITED BY MICHAEL W. MEISTER

0-19-563094-7 OXFORD $29.95

History of Indian and Indonesian Art

An important work, first published in 1928

0-486-25005-9 DOVER PB $11.95

Roy **Craven**

Indian Art: A Concise History

A good introduction to Indian art

0-500-20146-3 THAMES & HUDSON PB $14.95

Hermann **Goetz**

Rajput Art and Architecture

3-515-02982-6 CORONET PB $48.50

Tapati **Guha-Thakurta**
The Making of a New "Indian" Art: Artists, Aesthetics and Nationalism in Bengal, c. 1850-1920
0-521-39247-0 CAMBRIDGE $85.00

J.C. **Harle**
Art and Architecture of the Indian Subcontinent
A thoroughgoing and enormously erudite survey of Indian art, replete with information on intellectual, cultural, and social life
See also THE PELICAN HISTORY OF ART under ART HISTORY: GENERAL STUDIES
See also THE INDIAN SUBCONTINENT
0-300-05329-0 PENGUIN PB $26.50

Susan **Huntington** & John **Huntington**
The Art of Ancient India: Buddhist, Hindu, Jain
A more extensive text than Harle, more copiously but less effectively illustrated
0-8348-0183-3 WEATHERHILL $80.00

Stella **Kramrisch**
Hindu Temple
One of the greatest historical stylists, Kramrisch writes about Indian art and architecture in ways that are at once exact and evocative
81-208-0224-1 SOUTH ASIA $88.00

Thomas **Lawton** & Lina **Merrill**
Freer: A Legacy of Art
0-8109-3315-2 ABRAMS $49.50

Barbara Stoler **Miller**
The Powers of Art: Patronage in Indian Culture
See also CRITICAL STUDIES under LITERATURES OF INDIA in LITERATURE OF EUROPE, AFRICA, AND ASIA
0-19-562842-X OXFORD $16.95

Alistair **Shearer**
The Hindu Image
0-500-81043-5 THAMES & HUDSON PB $15.95

Calambur **Sivaramamurti**
The Art of India
0-8109-0630-9 ABRAMS $175.00

Stuart Cary **Welch**
India: Art and Culture, 1300-1900
Indian painting and decorative arts represented by the great Harvard art historian in a lavish exhibition catalog
3-7913-1253-7 PRESTEL $85.00

Indian Philosophies of Art

Ananda **Coomaraswamy**
The Dance of Siva: Essays on Indian Art and Culture
A compelling elucidation of the image of Siva, one of the most creative and complex images in the Hindu cosmology
0-486-24817-8 DOVER PB $7.95

Ranjan K. **Ghosh**
Concepts and Presuppositions in Aesthetics
81-202-0171-X SOUTH ASIA $12.00

Stella **Kramrisch**
The Presence of Siva
PHOTOGRAPHS BY PRAFUL C. PATEL
0-691-01930-4 PRINCETON PB $19.95

Heinrich **Zimmer**
Artistic Form and Yoga in the Sacred Images of India
A famous essay written in 1926, with Jungian touches
0-691-07289-2 PRINCETON $45.00

Sculpture

Carmel **Berkson**
Elephanta: The Cave of Shiva
A good, brief study of one of the great cave temples in India, presenting the monumental 7th-century images on the island of Elephanta
0-691-00371-8 PRINCETON PB $22.95

Pramod **Chandra**
The Sculpture of India: 3000 BC-1300 AD
A concise, knowledgeable introduction, backed by a superb selection of sculptures
0-674-79590-3 HARVARD $75.00

Josef **James**, editor
Contemporary Indian Sculpture: The Madras Metaphor
0-19-563453-5 OXFORD $49.95

R. **Nagaswamy**
Masterpieces of Early South Indian Bronzes
An informative presentation of one of the greatest Indian sculptural achievements
0-940500-90-6 ASIA BOOK CORP PB $52.95

Painting

Indian painting can be divided roughly into three major traditions: early wall painting in caves, temples, and palaces; medieval manuscript painting and illuminations; and miniature painting, characterized by brilliant colors and decorative effects, of the Mughal and native Rajput courts.

Milo Cleveland **Beach**
Mughal and Rajput Painting
0-521-40027-9 CAMBRIDGE $89.95

Carmel **Berkson**
Ellora: Concept and Style
81-7017-277-2 SOUTH ASIA $98.00

W.H. **Mcleaod**
Popular Sikh Art
0-19-562791-1 OXFORD $24.95

Pratapaditya **Pal**
Indian Painting
0-8109-3465-5 L.A. COUNTY MUSEUM $65.00

J.M. **Rogers**
Mughal Miniatures
Focusing on the great flowering of miniature painting under the emperors Akhbar, Jahangir, and Shah Jahan, this book offers a concise survey of the paintings, painters, and royal patrons of Mughal India
0-500-27732-X THAMES & HUDSON PB $15.95

Andrew **Topsfield**
An Introduction to Indian Court Painting
0-88045-041-X STEMMER $14.95

Som Prakash **Verma**
Mughal Painters and Their Work: A Biographical Survey and Comprehensive Catalogue
0-19-562316-9 OXFORD $55.00

Stuart Cary **Welch**
The Emperors' Album: Images of Mughal India
0-8109-0886-7 ABRAMS $65.00

Southeast Asia

Albert **Le Bonheur**
Of Gods, Kings, and Men: Bas-Reliefs of Angkor Wat and Bayon
PHOTOGRAPHS BY JAROSLAV PONCAR
0-906026-37-7 WEATHERHILL PB $39.95

Eleanor **Mannikka**
Angkor Wat: Time, Space, and Kingship
0-8248-1720-6 HAWAII $55.00

Asian Art Museum of San Francisco
Thai Ceramics: The James & Ellen Connell Collection
See also POTTERY AND PORCELAIN under AFRICAN AND ASIAN DECORATIVE ARTS in ARCHITECTURE, DESIGN, AND HOMES
967-65-3043-3 OXFORD PB $75.00

Jean Paul **Barbier** & Douglas **Newton**, editor
Islands and Ancestors: Indigenous Styles of Southeast Asia
A richly illustrated survey of artistic traditions, including art from Vietnam, Sumatra, and Borneo
3-7913-0899-8 PRESTEL $80.00

Wolfgang **Felten** & Martin **Lerner**
Thai and Cambodian Sculpture: From the 6th to the 14th Centuries
0-85667-361-7 SOTHEBY PARKE BERNET $150.00

Joseph **Fischer**
The Folk Art of Java
967-65-3041-7 OXFORD $65.00

Jan **Fontein**
The Sculpture of Indonesia
0-8109-3817-0 ABRAMS $65.00
0-8109-2503-6 ABRAMS PB $29.95

Sylvia **Fraser-Lu**
Burmese Crafts of Indonesia
0-19-588608-9 OXFORD $150.00

John **Gillow**
The Traditional Architecture of Indonesia
0-500-34132-X THAMES & HUDSON $45.00

Traditional Indonesian Textiles
See also **TEXTILES** under **AFRICAN AND ASIAN DECORATIVE ARTS** in **ARCHITECTURE, DESIGN, AND HOMES**
0-500-23641-0 THAMES & HUDSON $40.00
0-500-27820-2 THAMES & HUDSON PB $22.50

Sandra A. **Niessen**
Batak Cloth and Clothing: A Dynamic Indonesian Tradition
An examination of the textile printing method using hot wax and cool vegetable dye that has been utilized in Indonesia for over 1,000 years
See also **TEXTILES** under **AFRICAN AND ASIAN DECORATIVE ARTS** in **ARCHITECTURE, DESIGN, AND HOMES**
967-65-3040-9 OXFORD $49.95

Apinan **Poshyananda**
Modern Art in Thailand in the Nineteenth and Twentieth Centuries
0-19-588562-7 OXFORD $110.00

Philip S. **Rawson**
The Art of Southeast Asia: Cambodia, Vietnam, Thailand, Laos, Burma, Java, and Bali
See also **THAMES & HUDSON WORLD OF ART** under **ART HISTORY: GENERAL STUDIES**
0-500-20060-2 THAMES & HUDSON PB $14.95

Dick **Richards**
South-East Asian Ceramics: Thai, Khmer, and Vietnamese, from the Collection of the Art Gallery of South Australia, Adelaide
967-65-3075-1 OXFORD $95.00

Pamela York **Taylor**
Beasts, Birds, and Blossoms in Thai Art
967-65-3051-4 OXFORD $55.00

Astri **Wright**
Soul, Spirit, and Mountain: Preoccupations of Contemporary Indonesian Painters
967-65-3042-5 OXFORD $105.00

The Himalayas

Roger **Goepper** & others
Alchi: Ladakh's Hidden Buddhist Sanctuary—The Sumtsek
A lavish photographic survey of the magnificent painting and sculpture of Alchi, an 800-year-old Buddhist temple complex that remains spectacularly preserved in a remote part of Ladakh. "Preserved as it is, Alchi is a fantastic survival from the past, and as such, truly one of the wonders of the Buddhist world"—David Snellgrove, author of *A Cultural History of Tibet and Indo-Tibetan Buddhism*
1-57062-240-X SHAMBHALA $150.00

Yuri **Parfionovitch** & others, editors
Tibetan Medical Paintings: Illustrations to the Blue Beryl Treatise of Sangye Gyamtso (1653-1705)
0-8109-3861-8 ABRAMS $195.00

Pratapaditya **Pat**
Art of Nepal: A Catalogue of the Los Angeles County Museum of Art Collection
The most useful single volume on the subject, it includes painting, sculpture, manuscripts, and liturgical objects
0-520-05407-5 CALIFORNIA PB $40.00

Marilyn M. **Rhis** & Robert F. **Thurman**
Wisdom and Compassion: The Sacred Art of Tibet
A thorough examination of religious paintings and objects from the "roof of the world"
0-8109-3957-6 ABRAMS $75.00

Jane Casey **Singer**
Gold Jewelry from Tibet and Nepal
This splendidly illustrated book describes the ways in which jewelry has been used and appreciated in the Himalayas. More than mere ornament, jewelry reflected not only the owner's personal wealth but also the wearer's social and political status, as well as the embodiment of ancient Hindu and Buddhist values
See also **JEWELRY** under **ACCESSORIES** under **FASHION AND COSTUME** in **ARCHITECTURE, DESIGN, AND HOMES**
0-500-97442-X THAMES & HUDSON $35.00

Mary **Slusser**
Nepal Mandala
A first-hand account in two volumes by a leading scholar of Nepal and the Nepalese, emphasizing the context of the mandala
0-691-03128-2 PRINCETON $165.00
0069-1031282 PRINCETON $165.00

Mongolia and Central Asia

Morris **Rossabi** & others
Mongolia: The Legacy of Chinggis Khan
0-500-23705-0 THAMES & HUDSON $60.00

Janet **Harvey**
Traditional Textiles of Central Asia
A spectacularly illustrated survey of the decorative motifs, materials, dyes, and looms, the types of objects made, and their diverse regional and tribal variations
0-500-27875-X THAMES & HUDSON PB $24.95

China

Caroline **Blunden** & Mark **Elvin**
A Cultural Atlas of China
A socio-anthropological compendium useful as background to the study of art
See also **REFERENCE** under **GENERAL HISTORIES** under **CHINA** in **WORLD HISTORY AND CURRENT AFFAIRS**
0-87196-132-6 FACTS ON FILE $45.00

Wen C. **Fong** & James C. Y. **Watt**
Possessing the Past: Treasures from the National Palace Museum, Taipei
An illustrated history of some of the great monuments of Chinese culture, from the Neolithic period through the 18th century, based on the holdings of the National Palace Museum, Taipei, the core of which was collected by the Emperor Ch'ien-lung, who ruled from 1736 to 1795
0-8109-6494-5 ABRAMS $85.00

Scott **Minick** & Jiao **Ping**
Arts and Crafts of China
An excellent introduction to the cultural history of the crafts of China, including textiles, jewelry, lacquer, ceramics, bamboo, wood, and paper, beautifully photographed and complete with advice on collecting
0-500-27896-2 THAMES & HUDSON PB $19.95

Jessica **Rawson**, editor
The British Museum Book of Chinese Art
One of the best introductory overviews of Chinese art, based on the extensive holdings of the British Museum
0-500-27903-9 THAMES & HUDSON PB $24.95

Laurence **Sickman** & Alexander **Soper**
Art and Architecture in China
A good survey of architecture, sculpture, and painting, leaving out crafts and decorative arts
See also **THE PELICAN HISTORY OF ART** under **ART HISTORY: GENERAL STUDIES**
0-300-05334-7 YALE PB $26.50

Michael **Sullivan**
The Arts of China
A balanced and knowledgeable presentation, extending to the early 20th century
0-520-04918-7 CALIFORNIA PB $30.00

Mary **Tregear**
Chinese Art
An up-to-date survey that is a model of compression
0-19-520189-2 NORTON $19.95
0-500-20178-1 THAMES & HUDSON PB $14.95

Mary **Tregear** & Shelagh **Vainker**

Art Treasures in China

0-8109-1949-4 ABRAMS $95.00

William **Watson**, editor

Chinese Ivories: From the Shang to the Ch'ing

0-903421-22-4 BRITISH MUSEUM $50.00
0-85667-191-6 SOTHEBY PARKE BERNET $50.00

Neolithic, Bronze, and Iron Ages

Kwang-Chih **Chang**

The Archaeology of Ancient China

The single most authoritative work on prehistoric, neolithic, and Bronze Age China. Well-illustrated, with a model scholarly text. Written in 1948, before the extraordinary recent archaeological discoveries in China, it serves as a guide to understanding them

0-300-03782-1 YALE $65.00
0-300-03784-8 YALE PB $27.50

William **Watson**

The Arts of China to A.D.900

0-300-05989-2 YALE $65.00

Painting

James **Cahill**

The Compelling Image

0-674-15281-6 BELKNAP PB $28.00

The Lyric Journey: Poetic Painting in China and Japan

0-674-53970-2 HARVARD $45.00

New Dimensions in Chinese Ink Painting: Works from the Collection of John and Alice Z. Berninghausen

0-9625262-3-1 WASHINGTON PB $16.95

The Painter's Practice: How Artists Lived and Worked in Traditional China

0-231-08181-2 COLUMBIA PB $25.00

Three Alternative Histories of Chinese Painting

0-913689-28-9 SPENCER MUSEUM $12.00

James **Cahill** & others, editors

Artists and Patrons: Some Social and Economic Aspects of Chinese Painting

0-295-97148-7 WASHINGTON PB $24.95

Jerome **Silbergeld**

Chinese Painting Style: Media, Methods, and Principles of Form

A serious, succinct, and clear work

0-295-95921-5 WASHINGTON PB $20.00

Robert **Van Gulik**

Chinese Pictorial Art as Viewed by the Connoisseur

A gold mine of information on mountings, how to paint, collectors' tales, fakes, and more—for the general reader

0-87817-264-5 HACKER $95.00

Chinese Theories of Art

Susan **Bush**

Chinese Literati on Painting: Su Shih, 1037-1101, to Tung Ch'i-Ch'ang, 1555-1636

Translations of ancient Chinese sources from the Sung through Ming dynasties

0-674-12425-1 HARVARD PB $9.50

Li **Zehou**

The Path of Beauty: A Study of Chinese Aesthetics

TRANSLATED BY GONG LIZENG

0-19-586526-X OXFORD PB $22.00

Specialized Painting Studies

Wu **Hung**

The Double Screen: Medium and Representation in Chinese Painting

0-226-36073-3 CHICAGO $45.00
0-226-36074-1 CHICAGO PB $24.95

Julia K. **Murray**

Ma Hezhi and the Illustration of The Book of Odes

0-521-41787-2 CAMBRIDGE $105.00

Parting at the Shore: Chinese Painting of the Early and Middle Ming Dynasty, 1368-1580

0-8348-0128-0 WEATHERHILL $37.50

Michael **Sullivan**

The Three Perfections: Chinese Painting, Poetry and Calligraphy

An impeccable distillation of decades of study and viewing with Chinese attitudes always in mind. Well-illustrated in black and white

0-8076-0997-8 BRAZILLER PB $11.95

Richard **Vinograd**

Boundaries of the Self: Chinese Portraits, 1600-1900

0-521-38548-2 CAMBRIDGE $110.00

Calligraphy

Some understanding of calligraphy will aid the study of painting, for in Chinese thought and practice the two are inseparable.

Leon Long-yien **Chang** & Peter **Miller**

Four Thousand Years of Chinese Calligraphy

An appreciation of the aesthetic values underlying Chinese calligraphy and an authoritative guide to its history. Includes more than 300 illustrations, tracing the arts development back some 4,000 years

0-226-10111-8 CHICAGO $55.00

Edoardo **Fazzioli**

Chinese Calligraphy: From Pictograph to Ideogram

The history of 214 essential Chinese/Japanese characters

0-89659-774-1 ABBEVILLE $29.95

Shigemi **Komatsu**, editor

Chinese and Japanese Calligraphy: Masterpieces from 2000 Years

A survey of more than 2,000 years of calligraphic accomplishment, selected from the Heinz Gotze collection. One hundred eighty-one full-color and 28 black-and-white illustrations

3-7913-1026-7 PRESTEL $85.00

Chiang **Yee**

Chinese Calligraphy: An Introduction to Its Aesthetic and Technique

An easy-to-follow introduction, organized by subject and typology

See also **CALLIGRAPHY** under **ILLUSTRATION AND POPULAR GRAPHICS**

0-674-12226-7 HARVARD PB $16.95

20th-Century Artists

C. C. Wang: Landscape Paintings

Works by the pioneer of modern ink painting

INTRODUCTION BY JAMES CAHILL

0-295-96471-5 WASHINGTON $40.00

Haus der Kulturen der Welt, Berlin

China Avant-Garde: Counter-Currents in Art and Culture

0-19-586423-9 OXFORD $75.00

Gardens

Ji **Cheng**

The Craft of Gardens

Published in 1631, this is the earliest manual of Chinese landscape gardening. Includes building design

INTRODUCTION BY MAGGIE KESWICK
TRANSLATED BY ALISON HARDIE

0-300-04182-9 YALE $40.00

Maggie **Keswick**

The Chinese Garden

A persuasive and interesting book, with a section on garden architecture

See also **CHINESE GARDENS** under **GARDEN HISTORY** under **THE OUTDOORS** in **FOOD, TRAVEL, AND LEISURE**

0-312-13382-0 ST. MARTIN'S $50.00

Korea

The understanding of Korean art has been plagued from the beginning of this century: first by Japanese hegemony until World War II, then by the Korean War. There are few available publications on the wonders of Korean art and the importance of its influence as transmitter and catalyst between China and Japan.

Keith **Pratt**
Korean Painting
0-19-585885-9 OXFORD $16.95

Japan

Since 1945, the "Japanese miracle" has been accompanied by an explosion of books on all aspects of Japanese art.

Vadime **Elisseeff** & Danielle **Elisseeff**
Art of Japan
TRANSLATED BY I. MARK PARIS
0-8109-0642-2 ABRAMS $175.00

Masoa **Ishizawa** & Ichimatsu **Tanaka**
The Heritage of Japanese Art
A good if brief overview
0-87011-481-6 KODANSHA $80.00

Penelope **Mason**
History of Japanese Art
Art historian Mason traces Japanese art from the prehistoric age through the mid-20th century. Developing a cohesive theory of a country's art alongside its social and religious traditions, Mason stops along the way to isolate certain works in detail: a 7th-century temple, a 12th-century *Tale of Genji* scroll, a 19th-century tea vessel. Also includes a glossary and an illustrated guide to the literature of Japanese art and Culture
0-8109-1085-3 ABRAMS $60.00
0-13-016395-3 PRENTICE HALL $49.95

R. **Paine** & Alexander **Soper**
The Art and Architecture of Japan
Good on painting and architecture, but decorative arts are omitted
See also THE PELICAN HISTORY OF ART under ART HISTORY: GENERAL STUDIES
0-300-05333-9 PENGUIN PB $26.50

Laurence P. **Roberts**
A Dictionary of Japanese Artists: Painting, Sculpture, Ceramics, Prints, Lacquer
A reference work for names, alternative names, and brief biographies—indispensable for Westerners
0-8348-0235-X WEATHERHILL PB $32.50

Joan **Stanley-Baker**
Japanese Art
A survey of painting, calligraphy, decorative arts, and architecture, from the prehistoric period to the present, addressed to novice and connoisseur alike
0-500-20192-7 THAMES & HUDSON PB $14.95

Langdon **Warner**
The Enduring Art of Japan
A distillation of Warner's sympathy for Japanese art, particularly fine on sculpture and folk art
0-8021-3132-8 GROVE PB $9.95

Painting

Stephen **Addiss**
The Art of Zen: Painting and Calligraphy by Japanese Monks, 1600-1925
0-8109-1886-2 ABRAMS $49.50

Elizabeth **de Sabato Swinton**
The Women of the Pleasure Quarter: Japanese Paintings and Prints of the Floating World
1-55595-115-5 HUDSON HILLS $65.00

Miyeko **Murase**
Masterpieces of Japanese Screen Painting
This magnificent example of the book-making art features over 37 screen paintings and provides an overview of formats, techniques, and subjects from the 14th to the 19th centuries. Includes 120 pages of color, and 13 "gatefold" pages which extend over four feet wide
0-8076-1230-8 BRAZILLER $150.00

Andrew J. **Pekarik**, commentator
The 36 Immortal Women Poets
An anthology of work by a group of poets and prose writers of the imperial court of Japan from the 9th to the 13th centuries. An "imaginary portrait" of each poet in elegant court dress by 18th-century painter Chobunsai Eishi is accompanied by one of her most famous poems. This is a reproduction of an album originally produced by Eishi, one of many such made to be circulated at court as instructional guides for young poets. Includes original translations of all poems cited, and notes on their calligraphy, translations, and pronunciation
0-8076-1256-1 BRAZILLER $45.00
0-8076-1257-X BRAZILLER PB $24.95

Yoshiaki **Shimizu** & John **Rosenfield**
Masters of Japanese Calligraphy: 8th-19th Century
An exhibition based on American collections, a sound introduction to the subject
0-913720-57-7 FREDERICK BELL $75.00

Woodblock Prints

The prints of Ukiyo-e, pictures of the "floating world," introduced great Japanese art to the West. There is an extensive Western literature available, as hanga are the most popular of the art forms outside of Japan.

Cynthea **Bogel** & Israel **Goldman**
Hiroshige: Birds and Flowers
0-8076-1199-9 BRAZILLER $75.00

Henry D. **Smith, II**
Hiroshige: 100 Famous Views of Edo
0-8076-1143-3 BRAZILLER $85.00

James **Michener**, editor
Hokusai Sketchbooks: Selections from the Manga
0-8048-0252-1 TUTTLE $65.00

Peter **Morse**
Hokusai: 100 Poets
0-8076-1213-8 BRAZILLER $80.00

Hokusai: 100 Views of Mount Fuji
0-8076-1195-6 BRAZILLER $35.00

Tuttle Publications
Hokusai's Views of Mount Fuji
Twenty-four prints in miniature, with poems by Easley Stephen Jones
0-8048-0253-X TUTTLE $19.95

Ito **Jakuchu**
On a River Boating Journey
0-8076-1229-4 BRAZILLER $45.00

James T. **Ulak**
Japanese Prints
1-55859-803-0 ABBEVILLE PB $11.95

The Tea Ceremony

Alongside *Ukiyo-e* woodblock prints, the tea ceremony *Chanoyu* is Japan's most famous artistic contribution. It is also the most complete and successful means of aesthetic education ever seen, encompassing architecture, ceramics, painting, calligraphy, metalwork, flower arrangement, and garden design.

Kakuzo **Okakura**
The Book of Tea
In this brief but famous work, Okakura claims that Japan cannot be understood without study of the tea ceremony
0-8048-0069-3 TUTTLE $16.95
4-7700-1542-9 KODANSHA PB $9.00

Paul **Varley** & Kumakura **Isao**, editors
Tea in Japan: Essays on the History of Chanoyu
An anthology of ten essays by distinguished Japanese and American scholars, comprising the first major history in English of *chanoyu*, the tea ceremony which is at once a social, religious, and aesthetic phenomenon. The tea ceremony occupies a crucial place in Japanese culture, encompassing the arts of architecture, garden design, ceramics, lacquerware, painting, and calligraphy. This illustrated collection explores the subtleties of *chanoyu* in remarkable and fascinating detail
0-8248-1218-2 HAWAII $25.00

Gardens

David **Engel**

Japanese Gardens for Today: A Practical Handbook

This book has a practical emphasis that recommends it to active gardeners

See also **JAPANESE GARDENS** under **GARDEN HISTORY** under **THE OUTDOORS** in **FOOD, TRAVEL, AND LEISURE**

0-8048-0301-3 TUTTLE $49.95

The Weatherhill Series

Literature about Japanese art that has been particularly encouraged by Weatherhill/Heibonsha. It can be recommended for all readers.

Tsugiyoshi **Doi**

Momoyama Decorative Painting

0-8348-1024-7 WEATHERHILL $20.00

Toshio **Fukuyama**

Heian Temples: Byodo-In and Chuson-Ji

0-8348-1023-9 WEATHERHILL $20.00

Teiji **Itoh**

Traditional Domestic Architecture of Japan

0-8348-1004-2 WEATHERHILL $20.00

Takeshi **Kobayashi**

Nara Buddhist Art: Todai-Ji

0-8348-1021-2 WEATHERHILL $20.00

Seiichi **Mizuno**

Asuka Buddhist Art: Horyu-Ji

0-8348-1020-4 WEATHERHILL $20.00

Hisashi **Mori**

Sculpture of the Kamakura Period

0-8348-1017-4 WEATHERHILL $20.00

Yujiro **Nakata**

The Art of Japanese Calligraphy

0-8348-1013-1 WEATHERHILL $20.00

Yuzo **Yamane**

Momoyama Genre Painting

0-8348-1012-3 WEATHERHILL $20.00

East and West

The Impressionists' use of Japanese prints is well known. The rest of the story of the mutual influence of East and West since the 19th century is still obscure to Westerners. Judgments of modern Chinese or Japanese work in Western styles or in the native manner remain wavering and uncertain.

Michiaki **Kawakita**

Modern Currents in Japanese Art

0-8348-1028-X WEATHERHILL $20.00

Michael **Sullivan**

The Meeting of Eastern and Western Art

Four centuries of interaction between the artists of China and Japan and the artists of Western Europe

0-520-05902-6 CALIFORNIA $69.95

Shuji **Takashina** & J.T. **Rimer**

Paris in Japan: The Japanese Encounter with European Painting

The most recent publication in the field of modern Japanese art

0-295-96700-5 WASHINGTON PB $30.00

Native American Arts

North America

Jerry J. **Brody**

The Anasazi

0-8478-1208-1 RIZZOLI $75.00

Steven **Brown**

The Spirit Within: The John H. Hauberg Collection of Northwest Coast Native Art

0-8478-1847-0 RIZZOLI $75.00

Brian M. **Fagan**

Ancient North America: The Archaeology of a Continent

Traces the entire course of native American history from the first appearance of humans in the New World 14,000 years ago to the cataclysmic aftermath of European settlement. "A heroic effort to synopsize the occupational history of the United States and Canada…An excellent introductory text"
—*American Antiquity*

See also **GENERAL WORKS** under **NATIVE AMERICAN CULTURES: NORTH AMERICA** in **HISTORY OF THE AMERICAS**

0-500-05075-9 THAMES & HUDSON $45.00
0-500-27606-4 THAMES & HUDSON PB $34.95

Diana **Fane**

Objects of Myth and Memory: American Indian Art at the Brooklyn Museum

Between the beginning of the century and 1912, Stewart Culin amassed more than 9,000 Native American artifacts as founding curator of ethnology at the Brooklyn Museum. The self-taught ethnologist and indefatigable collector kept exhaustive documentation and vivid expedition reports, which the authors have drawn upon to create a precise, richly detailed historical and social context for these masterworks of American Indian art

0-295-97023-5 WASHINGTON $60.00
0-87273-122-7 WASHINGTON PB $35.00

Christian F. **Feest**

Native Arts of North America

A well-ordered overview of the art of 1000 tribes, from Seminole appliqué work of the 1890s to an Arapaho Ghost Dance

See also **THAMES & HUDSON WORLD OF ART** under **ART HISTORY: GENERAL STUDIES**

0-500-20262-1 THAMES & HUDSON PB $14.95

Jill **Furst** & Peter **Furst**

North American Indian Art

0-8478-0572-7 RIZZOLI PB $35.00

Robert **Inverarity**

Art of the Northwest Coast Indians

0-520-00595-3 CALIFORNIA PB $16.95

Harmer **Johnson** & others

Guide to the Arts of the Americas

0-8478-1597-8 RIZZOLI $60.00

Carol **Karasik** & Jeffrey Jay **Foxx**

The Turquoise Trail: Native American Jewelry and Culture of The Southwest

0-8109-3869-3 ABRAMS $49.50

Claude **Lévi-Strauss**

The Way of the Masks

"A fine study of the connections between verbal and plastic objects, it teaches much about Northwest Coast Indian culture, and it applies elegantly structuralist perceptions to carved and painted works of art"
—*Journal of American Folklore*

TRANSLATED BY SYLVIA MODELSKI

0-295-96636-X WASHINGTON PB $18.95

Claude Lévi-Strauss

Diana **Nemiroff**, editor

Land, Spirit, Power: First Nations at The National Gallery of Canada

This fully illustrated volume is a study of the works of 18 Native American artists. The book offers insights into questions of cultural identity and the struggles of Native Americans to establish and preserve their own identity in the midst of oppression and alienation

0-88884-650-9 NAT'L GALLERY CANADA PB $39.95

David **Penney**

Art of the American Indian Frontier: A Portfolio

Penney, curator of Native American Art at the Detroit Institute of Art, documents the extraordinary body of Native American art from the North American woodlands and plains

See also **EARLY PAINTINGS AND PHOTOGRAPHS** under **NATIVE AMERICAN CULTURES: NORTH AMERICA** in **HISTORY OF THE AMERICAS**

0-295-97318-8 DETROIT INSTITUTE PB $39.95
1-56584-251-0 NEW PRESS PB $18.95

Dorothy Jean **Ray**

A Legacy of Arctic Art

See also **NORTHERN CANADIAN AND ARCTIC PEOPLES** under **REGIONAL AND TRIBAL STUDIES** under **NATIVE AMERICAN CULTURES: NORTH AMERICA** in **HISTORY OF THE AMERICAS**

0-295-97507-5 WASHINGTON $40.00
0-295-97518-0 WASHINGTON PB $24.95

Harold **Seidelman**

The Inuit Imagination: Arctic Myth and Sculpture

The first book to present contemporary Inuit sculpture in the context of traditional stories, songs, and oral histories

0-500-01603-8 THAMES & HUDSON $45.00

Richard F. **Townsend**, editor

The Ancient Americas: Art from Sacred Landscapes

"A breathtaking excursion into the imagination and intellect of Amerindian civilization. . . . explores the common threads in fourteen cultures"—*Publishers Weekly*

3-7913-1188-3 TE NEUS $70.00

Andrew **Whiteford**

North American Indian Arts

A handy pocket guide to Indian arts and crafts

0-307-24032-0 GOLDEN PB $6.00

Mexico, Central, and South America

Elizabeth P. **Benson**, editor

Olmec Art of Ancient Mexico

0-8109-6328-0 ABRAMS $80.00

Kathleen **Berrin** & Esther **Pasztory**, editors

Teotihuacan: Art from the City of the Gods

The work of more than a dozen scholars over two decades is brought together for the first time to examine every aspect of the great city's culture, from its role as an urban center, its religion and little-known writing system to its spectacular architecture and art—wall paintings, vessels, figurines, incense burners, masks, and jewelry

0-500-27767-2 THAMES & HUDSON PB $24.95

Barbara **Braun**, editor

Arts of the Amazon

The entire range of Amazonian art, from the sacred to the utilitarian, is photographed and described

TEXT BY PETER ROE

0-500-27824-5 THAMES & HUDSON PB $19.95

Michael D. **Coe**

Breaking the Maya Code

A lively, informative account of how Maya hieroglyphic writing was finally decipered by a distinguished Mayanist

0-500-27721-4 THAMES & HUDSON PB $14.95

Clemency Chase **Coggins** & Orrin C. **Shane III**, editors

Cenote of Sacrifice: Maya Treasures from the Sacred Well at Chichen Itza

More than 300 artifacts; illustrated in black and white, some in color

0-292-71097-6 TEXAS $40.00
0-292-71098-4 TEXAS PB $27.50

Serge **Gruzinski**

The Aztecs: Rise and Fall of an Empire

0-8109-2821-3 ABRAMS PB $12.95

Painting the Conquest: The Mexican Indians and the European Renaissance

2-08-013521-X ABBEVILLE $60.00

Thor **Heyerdahl** & others

Pyramids of Tucume: The Quest for Peru's Forgotten City

Famed explorer and anthropologist Thor Heyerdahl has in recent years focused his attention on the lost cities of ancient Peru. This book is a lavishly illustrated account of his discoveries at the site of the mysterious pyramids in the northern part of the country

0-500-05076-7 THAMES & HUDSON $29.95

George **Kubler**

The Art and Architecture of Ancient America: The Mexican, Maya, and Andean Peoples

See also **THE PELICAN HISTORY OF ART** under **ART HISTORY: GENERAL STUDIES**

0-300-05325-8 PENGUIN PB $26.50

Arthur **Miller**

The Mural Painting of Teotihuacan

Nearly 400 illustrations; presents virtually all the recorded murals from the classic pre-Aztec site north of Mexico City

0-88402-049-5 DUMBARTON OAKS $35.00

Mary Ellen **Miller**

The Art of Mesoamerica: From Olmec to Aztec

See also **THAMES & HUDSON WORLD OF ART** under **ART HISTORY: GENERAL STUDIES**

0-500-20290-7 THAMES & HUDSON PB $14.95

Eduardo Matos **Moctezuma**

The Great Temple of the Aztecs: Treasures of Tenochtitlan

The definitive account of the 1978 rediscovery of the Great Temple and the most spectacular series of excavations ever conducted in Mexico. Six building phases were uncovered which contained literally thousands of ritual deposits such as jaguar skeletons, jade masks, obsidian knives, stone sculptures, and effigy vessels. Fully illustrated and with extensive quotations from contemporary Spanish sources

0-500-27752-4 THAMES & HUDSON PB $19.95

Teotihuacan: The City of the Gods

0-8478-1198-0 RIZZOLI $75.00

Michael E. **Moseley**

The Incas and Their Ancestors

0-500-27723-0 THAMES & HUDSON PB $19.95

Zelia **Nuttall**, editor

The Codex Nuttall: A Picture Manuscript from Ancient Mexico

Color hand-painted facsimile of a Mixtec picture book; the only pre-Columbian codex in an easily affordable edition

0-486-23168-2 DOVER PB $12.95

Esther **Pasztory**

Aztec Art

0-8109-0687-2 ABRAMS $49.50

Tatiana **Proskouriakoff**

An Album of Maya Architecture

Monochrome paintings by an artist-scholar that show the ancient cities as they might have looked in their prime

0-8061-1351-0 OKLAHOMA PB $18.95

Jean-Pierre **Protzen**

Inca Architecture and Construction at Ollantaytambo

0-19-507069-0 OXFORD $79.00

Dorie **Reents-Budet**

Painting the Maya Universe: Royal Ceramics of the Classic Period

A catalog and interpretation of the finest exhibition of the great Maya ceramics

0-8223-1438-X DUKE PB $39.95

Linda **Schele** & Mary **Miller**

The Blood of Kings: Dynasty and Ritual in Maya Art

See also **THE MAYA** under **NATIVE AMERICAN CULTURES: CENTRAL AND SOUTH AMERICA** in **HISTORY OF THE AMERICAS**

0-8076-1159-X BRAZILLER $50.00
0-8076-1278-2 BRAZILLER PB $29.95

Rebecca **Stone-Miller**

Art of the Andes: From Chavin to Inca

See also **THAMES & HUDSON WORLD OF ART** under **ART HISTORY: GENERAL STUDIES**

0-500-20286-9 THAMES & HUDSON PB $14.95

To Weave for the Sun: Ancient Andean Textiles

The catalogue of the collection of ancient and colonial Andean textiles in the Museum of Fine Arts, Boston, this book presents a chronological overview of the astonishing accomplishments of the weaver as artist from 500 B.C. to the 19th century

See also **TEXTILES AND WALLPAPER** under **FURNISHINGS** under **AMERICAN DECORATIVE ARTS** in **ARCHITECTURE, DESIGN, AND HOMES**

0-500-27793-1 THAMES & HUDSON PB $34.95

Richard **Townsend**
The Aztecs
0-500-27720-6 THAMES & HUDSON PB $15.95

Illustration and Popular Graphics

Posters

Dawn **Ades**
The 20th Century Poster
0-89659-433-5 ABBEVILLE PB $55.00

Alan **Adler**, editor
Science-Fiction and Horror Movie Posters in Full Color
0-486-23452-5 DOVER PB $10.95

John **Barnicoat**
Posters: A Concise History
The origins of the poster in the murals, folk art, and book illustration of the second half of the 19th century
0-500-20118-8 THAMES & HUDSON PB $14.95

Mary **Black**
American Advertising Posters of the 19th Century
0-486-23356-1 DOVER PB $16.95

Mildred **Constantine** & Alan **Fern**
Revolutionary Soviet Film Posters
0-8018-1760-9 JOHNS HOPKINS PB $16.95

Joseph **Czestochowski**, editor
Contemporary Polish Posters in Full Color
0-486-23780-X DOVER PB $7.95

Joseph **Darracott**, editor
The First World War in Posters
0-486-22979-3 DOVER PB $11.95

Chistopher **DeNoon**
Posters of the WPA
0-295-96543-6 WASHINGTON $39.95

Charles **Fox**
American Circus Posters in Full Color
0-486-23693-5 DOVER PB $10.95

Paul **Grushkin**
The Art of Rock: Posters from Presley to Punk
See also **VISUAL BOOKS** under **ROCK** in **PERFORMING ARTS AND MEDIA**
1-55859-606-2 ABBEVILLE PB $11.95

Roger **Sainton**
Art Nouveau Posters and Graphics
0-312-05274-X ST. MARTIN'S PB $9.95

Stephen **Rebello** & Richard **Allen**
Reel Art: Great Posters from the Golden Age of the Silver Screen
1-55859-403-5 ABBEVILLE PB $11.95

Markku **Salmi**, editor
National Film Archive Catalogue of Stills, Posters and Designs
0-85170-129-9 BRITISH FILM INST PB $33.95

Rex **Schneider** & Christopher **Buchman**
Movie Posters of the Silent Film Era
0-916144-61-5 STEMMER PB $5.95

Maurice **Sendak**, editor
The Maxfield Parrish Poster Book
0-517-51402-8 CROWN PB $15.00

Illustration

Shelley **Armitage**
John Held Jr., Illustrator of the Jazz Age
A full-length study of the illustrator who immortalized the flapper girls of the 1920s
0-8156-0238-3 SYRACUSE PB $24.95

James **Duff**, editor
An American Vision: Three Generation of Wyeth Art—N.C. Wyeth, Andrew Wyeth, James Wyeth
0-8212-1656-2 BULFINCH PB $29.95

Erté
New Erté Graphics in Full Color
0-486-24645-0 DOVER PB $8.95

Bruno **Ernest**
M.C. Escher: 29 Master Prints
0-8109-2268-1 ABRAMS PB $16.95

M.C. **Escher**
M.C. Escher: His Life and Complete Graphic Work
0-8109-8113-0 ABRAMS $29.98

Charles **Gibson**
The Gibson Girl and Her America
The work of the illustrator who created the turn-of-the-century ideal of feminine beauty
0-486-21986-0 DOVER PB $7.95

Steven **Heller** & Louise **Fili**
Cover Story: The Golden Age of Magazine Covers, 1900-1950
0-8118-0816-5 CHRONICLE PB $18.95

Rockwell **Kent**
It's Me, O Lord: The Autobiography of Rockwell Kent
The story of a major American illustrator of the 1920s and '30s
0-306-77412-7 DA CAPO $98.00

Lee **Lorenz**
The Art of The New Yorker: 1925-1995
Lorenz, *The New Yorker's* art editor for more than two decades, shows the evolution of its distinctive look. With beautifully produced pictures and a narrative filled with anecdotes of life at *The New Yorker*, Lorenz enlivens the history of the American magazine that defined an esthetic. With work by Thurber, Steinberg, Steig, Addams, Booth, Sorel, and others
0-679-43679-0 KNOPF $40.00

Coy **Ludwig**
Maxfield Parrish
One of the most successful and original illustrators of the early 20th century
0-88740-527-4 SCHIFFER $39.95

The New Yorker
The Complete Book of Covers from the New Yorker, 1925-1989
INTRODUCTION BY JOHN UPDIKE
0-394-57841-4 KNOPF $75.00

Christopher **Finch**
Norman Rockwell: 332 Magazine Covers
The dean of magazine illustrators in compact form, with a special emphasis on his work for *The Saturday Evening Post*
1-55859-224-5 ABBEVILLE PB $11.95

Norman Rockwell's America
0-8109-8071-1 ABRADALE $24.98

Norman **Rockwell**
Norman Rockwell: A 60-Year Retrospective
1-56799-209-9 FRIEDMAN/FAIRFAX PB $12.95

Norman **Rockwell** & Tom **Rockwell**
Norman Rockwell: My Adventures as an Illustrator
0-8109-2596-6 ABRAMS PB $19.95

Saul **Steinberg**
The Discovery of America
Saul Steinberg's brilliant drawings—seen in *The New Yorker* and in numerous exhibitions—have been widely admired. Here are the famous map of America from a New Yorker's perspective: the giant duck, and the cowboys and cowgirls together with equally witty, less well-known works, all in full color. "Saul Steinberg is a frontiersman of genres, an artist who cannot be confined to a category"—Harold Rosenberg, author of *Saul Steinberg*
0-679-40278-0 KNOPF $50.00

Rebecca **Zurier**
Art for the Masses, 1911-1917: A Radical Magazine and Its Artists
0-87722-670-9 TEMPLE PB $19.95

Book Illustration

Richard **Wilbur**, editor

A Bestiary: Illustrated by Alexander Calder

This marvelous anthology of classic poetry, essays, plays, fiction, and diaries borrows from Job (on the Horse), Mark Twain (the Ass), Jean de la Fontaine (the Grasshopper), and a host of other authors, perfectly matched with Calder's whimsical, wry line drawings. First published in 1955, this reissue introduces a true classic to a new generation

0-679-42875-5 PANTHEON $25.00

Trinkett **Clark** & H. Nichols **Clark**

Myth, Magic, and Mystery: 100 Years of American Children's Book Illustration

1-57098-079-9 ROBERTS RINEHART PB $29.95

Leonard **de Vries**

A Treasury of Illustrated Children's Books: Early Nineteenth-Century Classics from the Osborne Collection

0-89659-939-6 ABBEVILLE $75.00

Gustave **Doré**

Doré Bible Illustrations

0-486-23004-X DOVER PB $11.95

Doré's Illustrations for Dante's Divine Comedy

0-486-23231-X DOVER PB $8.95

Doré's Illustrations for Don Quixote: A Selection of 190 Illustrations by Gustave Doré

0-486-24300-1 DOVER PB $9.95

Theodor **Geisel**

The Secret Art of Dr. Seuss

A treasure trove of privately held paintings reveals a Dr. Seuss more wildly imaginative and fantastical than even his brilliantly imaginative children's books suggest. Recognizable in their humor, filled with a sophistication not often seen in his children's books, these pictures bring a complex and subtle view of Dr. Seuss to his many readers, a view heightened and explicated by Maurice Sendak's fine introduction

FOREWORD BY AUDREY GEISEL

INTRODUCTION BY MAURICE SENDAK

0-679-43448-8 RANDOM HOUSE $30.00

Clifford **Ross** & Karen **Wilkin**

The World of Edward Gorey

This is the first major book on the American artist and writer Edward Gorey, famous for his dark humor, hand-letterd texts, and pen-and-ink drawings that center on the Edwardian World. A comprehensive interview and extensive texts with numerous illustrations describe this fascinating man's career

0-8109-3988-6 ABRAMS $29.95

Edward **Gorey**

Amphigorey

The oblique and macabre black humor of the contemporary American artist

See also **CONTEMPORARY COMIC STRIP ARTISTS AND CARTOONISTS** under **COMICS** in **POPULAR READING**

0-399-50433-8 PERIGEE PB $16.00

Amphigorey Too

0-399-50420-6 PERIGEE PB $16.00

Amphigorey Also

Gorey at his best. Macabre and drolly wicked, this is required reading for fans new and old. Featuring the same style of pen-and-ink drawings and humor that made *Amphigorey* and *Amphigorey Too* instant classics

0-15-106443-1 HARCOURT BRACE $29.95

0-15-605672-0 HARCOURT BRACE PB $14.95

Michael **Hancher**

The Tenniel Illustrations to the Alice Books

0-8142-0408-2 OHIO STATE PB $49.50

Edward **Hodnett**

Francis Barlow: First Master of English Book Illustration

0-520-03409-0 CALIFORNIA $70.00

Audrey **Isselbacher**

Iliazd and the Illustrated Book

A dynamic figure of the modern movement who designed and produced innovative illustrated books

0-87070-396-X MOMA PB $12.95

Wendell **Minor** &
Florence Friedman **Minor**, editors

Wendell Minor: Art for the Written Word: Twenty-Five Years of Book Cover Art

"I write for a thousand pages and Wendell shows me what I mean in a single image"—Pat Conroy

0-15-600212-4 HARVEST PB $30.00

Joan **Miro**

Miro: A Toute Epreuve

A Toute Epreuve (Ready for Anything) perfectly combines Miro's entrancing amorphous forms with Eluard's poetry, inviting the reader to skip from text to imagery almost interchangeably. "One of the most triumphant feats of book illustration in our century"—James Thrall Soby

See also **DADA AND SURREALISM** under **20TH-CENTURY ART**

POEMS BY PAUL ELUARD

0-8076-1330-4 BRAZILLER PB $29.50

Michael **Olmert**

The Smithsonian Book of Books

An unusually handsome art book with a comprehensive description of the development of bookmaking—from tablets, papyrus, and scrolls to the great works of civilization. It celebrates every aspect of books and bookmaking, examining the exquisite creations of the Chinese Diamond Sutra to a portable Shakespeare built in the form of a temple with 311 color and 27 black-and-white illustrations

0-89599-030-X SMITHSONIAN $50.00

Maurice **Sendak**

Caldecott and Co.: Notes on Books and Pictures

0-374-52218-9 NOONDAY PB $8.95

Judith **Taylor**

Beatrix Potter, 1866-1943: The Artist and Her World

Companion to the Pierpont Morgan Library exhibition

0-723-23561-9 WARNER PB $22.95

Gerald **Ward**

The American Illustrated Book in the 19th Century

0-912724-17-X VIRGINIA $35.00

Nicholas Fox **Weber**

The Art of Babar: The Work of Jean and Laurent de Brunhoff

For every grown-up who loved the adventures of Babar the elephant, this book will bring back the fondest memories. An intriguing look at the story behind Babar and Celeste and their creators is illustrated with previously unpublished original watercolors, which demonstrate the charm and skill of the Brunhoffs' work

0-88365-808-9 ABRAMS $17.98

Jean de Brunhoff

Caricatures

Jean **Cocteau**

Drawings

The elegant line drawings of the versatile French writer

0-486-20781-1 DOVER PB $7.95

David **Duncan** & Mort **Drucker**

Familiar Faces: The Art of Mort Drucker

0-941613-03-8 STABUR $34.95

0-941613-02-X STABUR PB $12.95

Aline **Fruhauf**
Making Faces: Memoirs of a Caricaturist
Drawings of celebrities from the worlds of theater, music, and fashion, from Maurice Ravel to Lilian Gish
0-932020-46-1 SEVEN LOCKS $19.95
0-936784-85-7 DANIEL PB $10.95

Heinrich **Kley**
Drawings of Heinrich Kley
The whimsical, surreal comic fantasies of the 19th-century German artist
EDITED BY DONALD WEEKS
0-486-20024-8 DOVER PB $8.95

Richard **Vogler**
Graphic Works of George Cruickshank
Political and social cartoons, 1814-1877
0-486-23438-X DOVER PB $12.95

Dan **Wasserman**
Paper Cuts: The American Political Scene from Bush to Newt
From the wane of Reagan to the rise of Gingrich, the celebrated *Boston Globe* political cartoonist delivers his own version of the last eight years of American history
FOREWORD BY JIM HIGHTOWER
1-56663-092-4 DEE PB $14.95

Advertising Art

Miles **Beller** & Jerry **Liebowitz**
Hey Skinny
0-8118-0828-9 CHRONICLE PB $10.95

Clarence **Hornung** & Fridolf **Johnson**
200 Years of American Graphic Art
A survey of the printing and advertising arts since the colonial period
0-8076-0791-6 BRAZILLER $25.00

Philip **Lemme**
American Streamline: A Handbook of Neon Advertising Design
0-911380-80-9 ST. PUBLICATIONS PB $12.95

Karal Ann **Marling**
As Seen on TV: The Visual Culture of Everyday Life in the 1950s
0-674-04883-0 HARVARD PB $14.95

Theodore **Menten**
Advertising Art in the Art Deco Style
0-486-23164-X DOVER PB $9.95

Commercial Design

Donald **Bush**
The Streamlined Decade: Design in the 1930s
0-8076-0793-2 BRAZILLER PB $17.95

Jocelyn **de Nobelt**, editor
Industrial Design: Reflection of a Century
Design landmarks like the Gillette razor, the Greyhound bus, and the Macintosh computer have radically changed our visual landscape. This comprehensive survey offers a fascinating look at how these and many other innovative designs overcome the resistance of tradition. Includes biographies of the artists and designers
2-08-013539-2 ABBEVILLE $65.00

Barbara **Radice**, editor
Terrazzo
0-8478-5520-1 RIZZOLI PB $25.00

Paul **Rand**
Design, Form, and Chaos
One of the world's leading graphic designers explains contemporary practice and the processes that foster good design. "A classic" —Steven Heller
0-300-05553-6 YALE $45.00

Ellen **Stern**
The Very Best from Hallmark: Greetings Cards Through the Years
0-8109-1745-9 ABRAMS $17.98

Graphic Design

Sharne **Algotsson** & Denys **Davis**
The Spirit of African Design
The first illustrated guide to the culturally diverse patterns, styles, and traditions available to decorators interested in African-inspired designs, complete with a list of sources and insightful cultural and historical information
0-517-59916-3 CLARKSON POTTER $35.00

Elizabeth **Armstrong**
Tyler Graphics: The Extended Image
The multifaceted art created at the Tyler workshop
0-89659-750-4 ABBEVILLE $55.00

Amy E. **Arntson**
Graphic Design Basics
0-03-055483-7 H.B.J. PB $47.88

Mildred **Friedman**
Graphic Design in America: A Visual Language History
0-8109-1036-5 ABRAMS $49.50

Steven **Heller** & Seymour **Chwast**
Graphic Style: From Victorian to Post-Modern
0-8109-1033-0 ABRAMS PB $49.50

Steven **Heller** & Louise **Fili**
Dutch Moderne: Graphic Design from De Stijl to Deco
0-8118-0303-1 CHRONICLE PB $16.95

Italian Art Deco: Graphic Design Between the Wars
0-8118-0287-6 CHRONICLE PB $16.95

Philip **Meggs**
A History of Graphic Design
From cave pictographs to the most modern designs
0-442-31895-2 VAN NOSTRAND REINHOLD $54.95

Gregory **Mirow**
A Treasury of Design for Artists and Craftsmen
0-486-22002-8 DOVER PB $7.95

Bradbury **Thompson**
The Art of Graphic Design
The work of one of the most important 20th-century graphic designers. Designs for magazines, stamps, and limited-edition books are included in this book elegantly designed by Thompson
0-300-04301-5 YALE $80.00

Graphics: East Asia

Joseph **D'Addetta**
Traditional Japanese Design Motifs
0-486-24629-9 DOVER PB $7.95

A Treasury of Chinese Design Motifs
0-486-24167-X DOVER PB $6.95

James **Fraser** & others
Japanese Modern: Graphic Design Between the Wars
0-8118-0509-3 CHRONICLE PB $16.95

Clarence **Hornung**, editor
Traditional Japanese Stencil Designs
0-486-24791-0 DOVER PB $8.95

Owen **Jones**
Chinese Design and Pattern in Full Color
0-486-24204-8 DOVER PB $7.95

Trademarks and Logos

Eric **Baker** & Tyler **Blik**
Trademarks of the '20s and '30s: A Nostalgic Portfolio of American Trademark Designs
0-87701-360-8 CHRONICLE PB $14.95

Trademarks of the '40s and '50s
0-87701-485-X CHRONICLE PB $14.95

Hayward **Cirker** & Blanche **Cirker**
Monograms and Alphabetic Devices
0-486-22330-2 DOVER PB $10.95

Hal **Morgan**
Symbols of America
The history, folklore, and mystique of the most popular American trademarks and the products they represent
0-14-008077-5 PENGUIN PB $22.50

Package Design

Thomas **Hine**
The Total Package
0-316-36480-0 LITTLE, BROWN $25.95

Hideyuki **Oka**
How to Wrap Five More Eggs: Traditional Japanese Packaging
0-8348-0108-6 WEATHERHILL $39.95

Typography

Kathryn **Atkins**
Masters of the Italic Letter: Twenty Exemplars from the 16th Century
0-87923-594-2 GODINE $45.00

Lewis **Blackwell**
Twentieth-Century Type
0-8478-1596-X RIZZOLI $60.00

Sebastian **Carter**
Twentieth-Century Type Designers
0-393-70199-9 NORTON $35.00

Susan **Compton**
Russian Avant-Garde Books, 1917-34
See also **RUSSIAN FUTURISM AND CONSTRUCTIVISM** under **20TH-CENTURY ART**
0-262-03201-5 MIT $29.95

Johanna **Drucker**
The Visible Word: Experimental Typography and Modern Art, 1909-1923
0-226-16501-9 CHICAGO $35.00
0-226-16502-7 CHICAGO PB $15.95

Eric **Gill**
An Essay on Typography
0-87923-762-7 GODINE $19.95
0-87923-950-6 GODINE PB $9.95

Alexander **Lawson**
Anatomy of a Typeface
A study and classification of typefaces, written for the layman. Over 200 illustrations
0-87923-332-X GODINE $40.00
0-87923-333-8 GODINE PB $24.95

Ruari **McLean**
The Thames and Hudson Manual of Typography
0-500-68022-1 THAMES & HUDSON PB $15.95

Armando **Petrucci**
Public Lettering: Script, Power, and Culture
This book is a fascinating study of inscriptions, from etched tombstones to graffiti. Covering a broad historical range, from ancient times to the present, Petrucci illuminates the social function of graphic design
TRANSLATED BY LINDA LAPPIN
0-226-66386-8 CHICAGO $37.50

Walter **Tracy**
Letters of Credit: A View of Type Design
0-87923-636-1 GODINE $27.50

Jan **Tschichold**
The New Typography
"Probably the most important work on typography and graphic design in the 20th century"—Carl Zahn
0-520-07146-8 CALIFORNIA $40.00

Calligraphy

Albertine **Gaur**
A History of Calligraphy
1-55859-870-7 CROSS RIVER $35.00

Tom **Gourdie**
Basic Calligraphic Hands
0-8008-0667-0 TAPLINGER PB $5.95

Peter **Jensen**
Masterpieces of Calligraphy: 261 Examples
0-486-24100-9 DOVER PB $10.95

Edward **Johnston**
Lessons in Formal Writing
Out of print or previously unpublished material by Edward Johnston
0-8008-4642-7 TAPLINGER PB $19.95

Charles **Pearce**
The Anatomy of Letters
Useful manual for beginning and more advanced students
0-8008-0199-7 TAPLINGER PB $11.95

Rosemary **Sassoon**
The Practical Guide to Calligraphy
0-500-27251-4 THAMES & HUDSON PB $10.95

Margaret **Shepherd**
Learning Calligraphy: A Book of Lettering Design and History
0-02-015550-6 MACMILLAN PB $15.00

Jacqueline **Svaren**
Written Letters: 33 Alphabets for Calligraphers
A classic in handy format, 33 alphabets with clear stroke sequence
0-8008-8735-2 TAPLINGER PB $16.95

Jan **Tschichold**
A Treasury of Calligraphy: 219 Great Examples, 1522-1840
0-486-24700-7 DOVER PB $11.95

Chiang **Yee**
Chinese Calligraphy: An Introduction to Its Aesthetic and Technique
Some understanding of calligraphy will aid the study of painting, for in Chinese thought and practice the two are inseparable.
An easy-to-follow introduction, organized by subject and typology
See also **CALLIGRAPHY** under **CHINA** under **EAST ASIAN ART**
0-674-12226-7 HARVARD PB $16.95

Modern Calligraphy

Heather **Child**
The Calligrapher's Handbook
A book of articles, considered one of the outstanding works on contemporary calligraphy
0-8008-1198-4 TAPLINGER PB $15.95

Margaret **Shepherd**
Modern Calligraphy Made Easy
Instructions and workbook for the Fundamental Alphabet
0-399-51450-3 PERIGEE PB $8.95

Other

Jorge **Enciso**
Design Motifs of Ancient Mexico
Silhouette designs from ancient clay stamps
0-486-20084-1 DOVER PB $6.95

Geoffrey **Williams**
African Designs from Traditional Sources
Designs from the Ashanti, Bashongo, Baule, Mangbetu, Mariba, Masai, Ndebele, Toma, and Zulu nations
0-486-22752-9 DOVER PB $7.95

Photography

In 1839 the painter and inventor L.J.M. Daguerre revealed his discovery of a photographic process (soon to be known as the daguerreotype) to the French Academy. When word reached the public, the academic painter Paul Delaroche memorably proclaimed: "From today, painting is dead!" Meanwhile, across the Channel, the scientist and scholar W.H. Fox

Talbot was perfecting his own process (the calotype), which was to have a far greater influence on the future of photography: whereas Daguerre's technique made a single shining image on a metal plate, Talbot's process used a paper negative to produce any number of prints. Delaroche was not exactly right about the future of painting, but the new inventions have enormously changed both the history of art and the history of publishing.

Histories and General Works

Robert **Adams**

Why People Photograph

Selected essays and reviews on, among others, Paul Strand, Laura Gilpin, Eugene Atget, and Susan Meisalas

0-89381-603-5 APERTURE PB $12.95

Gordon **Baldwin**

Looking at Photographs: A Guide to Technical Terms

0-89236-192-1 GETTY MUSEUM PB $11.95

Roland **Barthes**

Camera Lucida: Reflections on Photography

In a book both highly personal and speculative, Barthes explores in depth the various ways in which the viewer perceives a photographed image. The second half is a meditation on a photograph of the author's mother

See also **ROLAND BARTHES** under **CRITICAL TEXTS** under **SEMIOTICS AND STRUCTURALISM AND AFTER** under **LITERARY THEORY** in **LITERATURE OF EUROPE, AFRICA, AND ASIA**

TRANSLATED BY RICHARD HOWARD

0-374-52134-4 HILL & WANG PB $9.95

Agnes St. Cyr **De Gouvion**

Twentieth-Century French Photography

0-8478-0943-9 RIZZOLI $35.00

Timothy **Druckrey**, editor

Iterations: The New Image

0-262-04143-X INTERNATIONAL CENTER OF PHOTOGRAPHY $42.50

Sally **Eauclaire**

American Independents: 18 Color Photographers

The work of a diverse group of emerging photographers

0-89659-666-4 ABBEVILLE $29.98

Okwui **Enwezor** & others

In/Sight: African Photographers, 1940 to the Present

The catalogue for the exhibition on African photographers at the Guggenheim museum, this volume beautifully presents the work of 30 photographers from all different regions in Africa

0-8109-6895-9 ABRAMS $49.50

David **Finn**

How to Look at Photographs: Reflections on the Art of Seeing

0-8109-2553-2 ABRAMS PB $14.95

Vicki **Goldberg**

Photography in Print

0-8263-1091-5 NEW MEXICO PB $18.95

The Power of Photography: How Photographs Changed Our Lives

1-55859-467-1 ABBEVILLE PB $27.50

Doug **Hall** & Sally Jo **Fifer**

Illuminating Video: An Essential Guide to Video Art

This book provides a much-needed overview of an increasingly important area of art

0-89381-389-3 APERTURE $45.00

Maria Morris **Hambourg**

The New Vision: Photography Between The World Wars—The Ford Motor Company Collection at the Metropolitan Museum of Art

0-8109-6428-7 METROPOLITAN MUSEUM PB $45.00

Maria Morris **Hambourg** & others

The Gilman Collection of Photography

0-8109-6427-9 METROPOLITAN MUSEUM $75.00

Andre **Jammes** & Eugenia P. **Janis**

The Art of French Calotype: With a Critical Dictionary of Photographers, 1845-1870

A beautiful book dealing with some of the most exquisite of all early photographs

0-691-04002-8 PRINCETON $135.00

Lászlo **Moholy-Nagy**

Painting, Photography, Film

One of the first great theoretical treatises of the 20th century, by the Bauhaus master

0-317-56521-4 MIT PB $11.95

Beaumont **Newhall**

The History of Photography: From 1839 to the Present Day

The revised fifth edition of the first history of photography for the general reader, an authoritative work emphasizing photography as an art

0-87070-381-1 LITTLE, BROWN PB $32.50

Beaumont **Newhall**, editor

Photography: Essays and Images—Illustrated Readings in the History of Photography

This anthology of source materials is the companion volume to Newhall's *History*. Classic texts by photographers and critics are illustrated by great images

0-87070-385-4 NY GRAPHIC PB $16.95

Diane Vogt **O'Connor**

Guide to Photographic Collections at the Smithsonian Institution

1-56098-188-1 SMITHSONIAN PB $49.95

John **Pultz**

The Body and the Lens: Photography from 1839 to the Present

0-8109-2703-9 ABRAMS PB $16.95

Eugene **Richards**

Americans We

Richards draws on his wide-ranging view of America from his career as a VISTA volunteer and civil rights activist—honored by the Klu Klux Klan with a severe bearing. He shows us the many, many faces of our country, from gang members to sewer workers, depicted through his vivid, idiosyncratic lens

0-89381-594-2 APERTURE $40.00

Malcolm **Rogers**, editor

Camera Portraits: Photographs from the National Portrait Gallery, London, 1839-1989

A magnificent collection of beautifully reproduced photographic portraits ranging from Dickens and Carlyle to the Beatles and David Hockney. The photographers include Julia Margaret Cameron, Lewis Carroll, Edward Steichen, Man Ray, and Richard Avedon

0-19-520859-5 SMITHSONIAN PB $35.00

Naomi **Rosenblum**

A History of Women Photographers

Long overdue, this lovely volume opens our eyes to the essential contribution by women to the photography of portraiture, documentation, photojournalism, and personal expression. 270 illustrations explore the work of Anna Atkins, Tina Modotti, Margaret Bourke-White, Cindy Sherman, and many other great photographic stylists

1-55859-761-1 ABBEVILLE $60.00

A World History of Photography

An updated and revised version of the standard history, which includes more than 800 photographs, historical to contemporary, from Europe and America to the Far East, and a scholarly yet accessible text

1-55859-054-4 ABBEVILLE $65.00

Martha A. **Sandweiss**, editor

Photography in Nineteenth-Century America

Six essays and nearly 250 photographs document the impact of photography on American culture in the last century. Photographic portraits enhanced the way Americans viewed celebrity, daguerrotypes influenced our literature, the new images explained the opening of the West, and, during the Civil War, the medium not only irrevocably changed how we thought about battle, but also forever altered the way we waged it

0-8109-3659-3 ABRAMS $60.00

Larry J. **Schaaf**

Out of the Shadows: Herschel, Talbot, and the Invention of Photography

Chronicles the first stages of photography's development, focusing on John Herschel and Henry Fox Talbot's letters and diaries, shedding light on questions that have troubled other writers: why did Talbot keep his invention secret? Why did Herschel work so hard to develop the process yet take so few pictures? Enhanced by more than 100 color and duotone reproductions of early photos

0-300-05705-9 YALE $60.00

Grace **Seiberling** & Carolyn **Bloore**

Amateurs, Photography, and the Mid-Victorian Imagination

An intriguing combination of social history, technical explanation, and pictorial interpretation

0-226-74498-1 CHICAGO $47.95

Susan **Sontag**

On Photography

0-385-26706-1 ANCHOR PB $10.95

John **Szarkowski**

Looking at Photographs: 100 Pictures from the Collection of the Museum of Modern Art

Short discussions of these splendid photographs illustrate different aspects of the medium and teach as much about seeing as about photography

0-87070-514-8 MOMA $40.00

Photography Until Now

A rich and idiosyncratic tour of the photographic medium, published in conjunction with a major exhibit, by one of its most persuasive advocates, organized around advances in photographic processes. The selection of images is provocative and intriguing

0-87070-574-1 LITTLE, BROWN PB $40.00

W.H. Fox **Talbot**

Pencil of Nature

0-306-71135-4 DA CAPO $110.00

Alan **Trachtenberg**

Classic Essays on Photography

0-918172-08-X IND PUBLISHERS GROUP PB $10.95

Photographers

Berenice **Abbott**

New York in the Thirties

A coolly modern appraisal of the city as it was then. Abbott photographed both commercial old structures and explored the new skyscrapers rising above them in these striking views

0-486-22967-X DOVER PB $11.95

Harry M. **Callahan**

Ansel Adams in Color

Although Adams began experimenting with color soon after Kodachrome was invented in the '30s, for complex reasons of his own the master American landscape photographer did not allow those pictures to be shown. Near his death, however, he had a change of heart. These 50 spectacular photographs, suffused with the subtleties that are the hallmarks of his famous black-and-white pictures, reveal a new and fascinating dimension to Adams's unique oeuvre

0-8212-1980-4 LITTLE, BROWN $60.00

Ansel **Adams**

Ansel Adams: Classic Images

A selection of great photographs by America's best-loved photographic artist

INTRODUCTION BY JOHN SZARKOWSKI

0-8212-1629-5 NEW YORK GRAPHIC SOCIETY $40.00

Ansel Adams's National Parks

1-55859-817-0 ABBEVILLE PB $11.95

Yosemite

INTRODUCTION BY MICHAEL L. FISCHER

0-8212-2196-5 LITTLE, BROWN PB $18.95

The Portfolios of Ansel Adams

INTRODUCTION BY JOHN SZARKOWSKI

0-8212-0723-7 LITTLE, BROWN $40.00

0-316-71395-3 NY GRAPHIC PB $35.00

Ansel **Adams** & Mary S. **Alinder**

Ansel Adams: An Autobiography

Adams tells of his early training as a concert pianist and of his decision to dedicate his life to photography; with plenty of illustrations

0-8212-1596-5 NEW YORK GRAPHIC SOCIETY $65.00

0-8212-2241-4 LITTLE, BROWN PB $13.95

Jonathan **Spaulding**

Ansel Adams and the American Landscape: A Biography

0-520-08992-8 CALIFORNIA $34.95

Robert **Adams**

Listening to the River: Seasons in the American West

Robert Adams presents a tour of the American West that challenges our very concept of "progress." William Stafford (National Book Award for *Traveling Through the Dark*) accompanies the images with his meditative poetry

0-89381-565-9 APERTURE $45.00

Los Angeles Spring

Glimpses of spring in seasonless, artificial Los Angeles seen with an eye for the occasional felicitous beauty of urban sprawl

0-89381-220-X APERTURE $30.00

0-8212-2105-1 LITTLE, BROWN PB $9.95

Diane Arbus

Diane **Arbus**

Untitled

The images in this third volume of Arbus's work were taken largely at residences for the mentally retarded between 1969 and 1971. Mostly unpublished until now, these photographs, the apotheosis of Arbus's unflinching regard for reality, may well be her most courageous, graceful, and transcendent work

0-89381-623-X APERTURE $50.00

Diane Arbus

This picture book summarizes Arbus's work and contains all her most famous and disturbing images, including her photographs of nudists and freaks

0-912334-40-1 APERTURE $40.00

0-912334-41-X APERTURE PB $29.95

Eve **Arnold**

In Retrospect

0-394-57850-3 KNOPF $50.00

Eugene **Atget**

The Work of Atget Volume 4 Modern Times

This is the only volume of Atget's work currently in print

0-316-95418-7 MOMA $45.00

Molly **Nesbit**

Atget's Seven Albums

Atget produced seven albums of photographs of Paris at the height of the Belle Epoque, prototypes for books that were never produced. Nesbit presents these albums in full as Atget planned them; her text explores the politics of Atget's search for a new vision of popular life and mass culture. A new kind of social and photographic history. "Brilliantly researched and argued..."—Rosalind Krauss

0-300-03580-2 YALE $60.00

Richard **Avedon**

An Autobiography

A definitive retrospective by one of the world's most well-known photographers. Includes his most famous images: Marilyn Monroe, Charlie Chaplin, the Warhol factory; and many previously unpublished photographs arranged in innovative juxtapositions, driven, as Avedon claims, "by their own eccentric logic"

0-679-40921-1 RANDOM HOUSE $100.00

Evidence: 1944-1994

With a biographical essay from *New Yorker* art critic Adam Gopnik; a critical overview of Avedon's controversial career from Jane Livingston, author of the award-winning *The New York School*; and over 100 photographs

0-679-40922-X RANDOM HOUSE $65.00

In the American West: Photographs, 1979-1984

A chillingly elegant and idiosyncratic documentation of the striking faces of an unlikely cross-section of Americans

0-8109-1105-1 ABRAMS PB $49.50

Richard Avedon

Malcolm **Danial**

The Photographs of Édouard Baldus

0-8109-6487-2 MOMA $65.00

Gail **Gelburd** & Thelma **Golden**

Romare Bearden in Black and White

This is the first book devoted to the photomontages of Romare Bearden, one of the most prominent African-American artists of the 20th century. The volume includes two critical essays, an interview, and the artist's poems, along with all 25 works stunningly reproduced in color

See also **POSTWAR AMERICAN ART** under **ART SINCE 1945**

0-8109-6823-1 ABRAMS PB $19.95

Philippe **Garner** & David Alan **Mellor**

Cecil Beaton: Photographs, 1920-1970

Beaton's photographs have achieved immortality for the way they, as Truman Capote put it, "documented and illuminated the exact attitude of the moment." This collection of 50 years of Beaton's work includes Queen Elizabeth, Edith Sitwell, Marlene Dietrich, Picasso, Cocteau, Gary Cooper, Colette, Dali, Marilyn Monroe, Mick Jagger, and illustrates his inimitable blend of wit, invention, and high style

1-55670-433-X STEWART, TABORI $85.00

Hugo **Vickers**

Cecil Beaton: A Biography

1-55611-021-9 FINE PB $12.95

Andrew **Billen**

Jane Bown, Observer

Portraits by the photographer who worked for England's *Observer* for 45 years, including photos of Samuel Beckett, Mick Jagger, John Gielgud, Boy George, Archbishop Tutu, and Woody Allen

0-500-27891-1 THAMES & HUDSON PB $19.95

Karl **Blossfeldt**

Art Forms in the Plant World

Translation and reprint of one of the classic books of the 1920s with close-up botanical studies of common and exotic plants which look like abstract compositions

0-486-24990-5 DOVER PB $9.95

Erskine **Caldwell** & Margaret **Bourke-White**

Say, Is This the U.S.A.?

Reprint of one of the pioneering books of documentary photography of the 1930s

0-306-77434-8 DA CAPO $40.50

Bill **Brandt**

Bill Brandt: Portraits

Brandt's intensity behind the camera resulted in probing portraits that tell as much about what's inside their subjects as outside them

INTRODUCTION BY ALAN ROSS

0-8161-0616-9 GK HALL $90.00

Mark **Haworth-Booth** & David **Mellor**

Bill Brandt: Behind the Camera

0-89381-191-2 APERTURE PB $17.50

Brassai

Henry Miller: The Paris Years

Brassai, a lifetime friend, documents Miller's Paris life in photographs and essays

See also **THE 20TH CENTURY** under **STUDIES OF INDIVIDUAL AUTHORS (ALPHABETICAL BY SUBJECT)** under **AMERICAN LITERATURE: ANTHOLOGIES AND CRITICAL STUDIES** in **LITERATURE OF THE AMERICAS**

1-55970-287-7 ARCADE $23.95

Rudy **Burckhardt** & Simon **Pettet**

Talking Pictures: The Photographs of Rudy Burckhardt

0-944072-42-9 ZOLAND PB $26.95

Keith F. **Davis**

Harry Callahan: New Color Photographs

Rich color views of many places from one of the masters of modern photography whose early work was principally in black and white

0-8263-1196-2 HALLMARK $19.95

Sarah **Greenough**, editor

Harry Callahan

The work of the preeminent formalist American photographer is captured in its full scope in this companion to the National Gallery of Art retrospective

TEXT BY SARAH GREENOUGH

0-8212-2313-5 BULFINCH $50.00

Paul **Caponigro**

Masterworks from Forty Years: Photographs by Paul Caponigro

0-9616515-5-5 PHOTOGRAPHY WEST $50.00

Helmut **Gernsheim**

Lewis Carroll: Photographer

0-486-22327-2 DOVER PB $8.95

Henri **Cartier-Bresson**

America in Passing

Ninety-nine duotone photographs of America between the '30s and the '80s. This is a record of an extraordinary vision of America, rural and urban, rich and poor, all informed by a fascination with this country

INTRODUCTION BY GILLES MORA

0-8212-2332-1 BULFINCH PB $34.00

Henri Cartier-Bresson

"For me, the camera is a sketchbook, an instrument of intuition and spontaneity…To take photographs is to hold one's breath while all faculties converge in the face of fleeing reality"—Henri Cartier-Bresson

0-89381-281-1 APERTURE $22.95
0-89381-265-X APERTURE PB $15.95

Henri Cartier-Bresson: Photographer

The definitive volume of the legendary photographer's work includes images produced in the '80s and never before published, and also brings many less well-known images to the fore. Enhanced by a concise biography and bibliography as well as a note by the photographer

0-8212-1986-3 BULFINCH $125.00

Henri Cartier-Bresson's Paris

Poplars in the rain; a flock of jubilant schoolboys; a sunbather by the Seine. 144 perfectly composed, evocative images of the fabulous City of Light captured in Cartier-Bresson's characteristic "decisive moment." Texts by André Pieyre de Mandiargues and Vera Feyder

0-8212-2064-0 BULFINCH $60.00

Henri Cartier-Bresson in India

FORWARD BY MULK RAJ ANAND

0-500-27712-5 THAMES & HUDSON PB $24.95

L'Art Sans Art

Classic and never-before-published photographs from the great Cartier-Bresson, collected under the photographer's supervision and remarked on by Jean-Pierre Montier, provide a startling and comprehensive view of perhaps the world's greatest photographer's lifetime work

EDITED BY JEAN-PIERRE MONTIER

0-8212-2285-6 BULFINCH $75.00

Mexican Notebooks

WITH TEXT BY CARLOS FUENTES

0-500-54199-X THAMES & HUDSON $29.95

Peter **Galassi**

Henri Cartier-Bresson: The Early Work

The first book to place Cartier-Bresson's photographs of fleeting instants in their historical context. Galassi considers his training as a painter as well as the evolution of his photographic style

0-8109-6092-3 ABRAMS PB $24.95

Mario **Vargas Losa** & others

Martin Chambi: Photographs, 1920-1950

1-56098-244-6 SMITHSONIAN PB $39.95

Alvin Langdon **Coburn**

Alvin Langdon Coburn, Photographer: An Autobiography

Coburn was one of the great pictorialist photographers of the Stieglitz circle at the beginning of this century. He left Boston to settle in London, where he produced remarkable portraits of famous figures, and—in 1917—some of the first deliberately abstract photographs

EDITED BY HELMUT GERNSHEIM & ALISON GERNSHEIM

0-486-23685-4 DOVER PB $8.95

Mike **Weaver**

Alvin Langdon Coburn: Symbolist Photographer

A probing interpretation of the symbolic meanings deliberately encoded in Coburn's photographs, this study provides a new vision of his work and thought

0-89381-240-4 APERTURE $25.00
0-89381-246-3 APERTURE PB $19.95

Lynne **Cohen**

Occupied Territory

Cohen's deadpan photographs of vernacular interiors are at once disturbing and fascinating. Her lucid views of schools, offices, factories, labs, and police training centers are an unparalleled cumulative portrait of North American society

EDITED BY WILLIAM A. EWING
INTRODUCTION BY DAVID BYRNE
0-89381-313-3 APERTURE $25.00

Imogen **Cunningham**

Imogen Cunningham: Flora

Cunningham photographed plant life throughout her long career, exploring the sensual with a rigorous formal aesthetic. Presented by her long-time curator and cataloguer, this carefully annotated and introduced collection of Cunningham's botanical work is a splendid edition for photography fans and flower lovers alike

TEXT BY RICHARD LORENZ
0-8212-2221-X BULFINCH $45.00

Bruce **Davidson**

Central Park

Known for his explorations of urban terrain, Magnum photographer Bruce Davidson explores a democratic haven of natural beauty and ecological secrets: New York City's Central Park. In the park Davidson discovers a microcosm of a complex city—a roller-blader, a newborn bird, a man seeking refuge. "Bruce Davidson is an artist who uses a camera. He is a master of composition"—*The New Republic*

0-89381-625-6 APERTURE $40.00

Patrick **Demarchelier**

Patrick Demarchelier: Photographs

One of the most sought-after fashion photographers working today, Demarchelier presents his first large-format collection. Starting with African landscapes, he moves on to provocative nudes and portraits of Paul Newman, Warren Beatty, Meg Ryan, and many others. From there he goes on to fashion supermodels Cindy Crawford, Naomi Campbell, Claudia Schiffer. "One of fashion photography's most important creators"—*American Photo*

0-8212-2169-8 BULFINCH $65.00

Peter **Hamilton**

Robert Doisneau: A Photographer's Life

Comprising 500 duotone and 20 color plates, this definitive volume explores the life and work of a photographer whose images capture the mood and character of Paris in the early modern era

0-7892-0020-1 ABBEVILLE $75.00
1-85043-565-0 I.B. TAURIS PB $19.95

Alfred **Eisenstaedt**

Eisenstaedt: Martha's Vineyard

TEXT BY POLLY BURROUGHS
0-8487-0739-7 OXMOOR $35.00

James Agee

James **Agee** & Walker **Evans**

Let Us Now Praise Famous Men

The 1941 classic about cotton-farming tenantry among white sharecroppers, told through Agee's poetic prose and Evans's stark photographs

See also **REPORTING** under **20TH-CENTURY AMERICAN ESSAYS AND JOURNALISM** in **LITERATURE OF THE AMERICAS**

0-395-48897-4 HOUGHTON MIFFLIN PB $16.95
0-395-48901-6 HOUGHTON MIFFLIN $29.95

Gilles **Mora**

Walker Evans: Havana, 1933

Without Evans there would be no school of stark, unrepentant American portraiture. He was the Edward Hopper of American photographers, one of our greatest, and in this timeless book the entire breadth of his unparalleled career is covered

0-8109-3259-8 ABRAMS $65.00
0-394-57493-1 PANTHEON PB $35.00

Michael **Brix** & Birgit **Mayer**, editors

Walker Evans—America

0-8478-1344-4 RIZZOLI $60.00

Walker **Evans**

American Photographs

A re-creation of one of the great classics of photographic publishing from the 1930s. Especially notable are Evans's sequencing of images and his insistence that each image be respected on its own terms within the book. The subjects range from Depression-ravaged cities to architectural splendors

0-87070-238-6 MOMA PB $19.95

Walker Evans: Photographs for the Farm Security Administration, 1935-1938

Many of Evans's most important photographs of the '30s were made in the service of the government's Farm Security Administration, which sought to document the hardships of the Depression and the effects of the aid provided by Roosevelt's New Deal

INTRODUCTION BY JERALD C. MADDOX
0-306-70099-9 DA CAPO $39.50

Lloyd **Fonvielle**

Walker Evans

0-89381-551-9 APERTURE $22.95

Andreas **Feininger**

Feininger's Chicago: 1941

0-486-23991-8 DOVER PB $8.95

Industrial America, 1940-1960: 176 Photographs

0-486-24198-X DOVER PB $11.95

Nature and Art: A Photographic Exploration

0-8446-6145-7 SMITH $17.00

Nature Close Up: A Fantastic Journey into Reality

0-486-24102-5 DOVER PB $12.95

New York in the Forties

A close look at the urban texture of New York that finds beauty in the patterns and geometry of modernity

0-486-23585-8 DOVER PB $12.95

Roger **Fenton**

Roger Fenton

0-89381-270-6 APERTURE $22.95
0-89381-271-4 APERTURE PB $15.95

Robert **Frank**

Lines of My Hand

A new, long-awaited book from the now-reclusive photographer, revealing a more contemplative style than his groundbreaking earlier work

0-394-55255-5 PANTHEON $45.50

The Americans

First published in Paris, then released in this country where it became an underground sensation and finally a classic, this book was the visual bible for the beat generation. The gritty scenes of American cities and roadsides told a story of alienation, segregation, and unexpected beauty, all seen through the eyes of a disaffected European photographer

1-88161-612-6 RANDOM HOUSE PB $32.50

Lee **Friedlander**

Maria

1-56098-207-1 SMITHSONIAN PB $15.95

Nudes

Friedlander's images rival the classic nudes of Bill Brandt and Edward Weston. Reproduced in tri-tone, the 84 plates in this book represent his 15-year odyssey of examination into the realms of Western art and the theme of the female nude

0-224-03217-8 CAPE PB $35.00

Lee Friedlander: Portraits

Offbeat but revealing portraits by a photographer best known for his depictions of the "new social landscape" of parking lots, suburbs, and telephone wires

FORWARD BY R.B. KITAJ
0-316-51252-4 NEW YORK GRAPHIC SOCIETY $60.00

Alexander **Gardner**

Gardner's Photographic Sketch Book of the Civil War

Unlike 20th-century journalists, Gardner and his team of photographers were not able to document actual battles. These pictures show the bodies left on the field after the battle, the buildings destroyed, the fields burned and scarred

0-486-22731-6 DOVER PB $9.95

Allen **Ginsberg**

Photographs

Few know that the trailblazing Beat poet has been a passionate photographer for 40 years. This collection of such closely observed friends as William Burroughs, Jack Kerouac, and Neal Cassady is both a work of art and a singular visual document of American cultural history. Ginberg's reminiscences accompany each photo, creating a personal album of an amazing life

0-942642-42-2 TWELVETREES $55.00

Snapshot Poetics: Allen Ginsberg's Photographic Memoir of the Beat Era

A unique opportunity to experience some of the Beat generation's brightest lights from the perspective of one of the movement's most celebrated personalities. Candid, sometimes bizarre images of, among others, Norman Mailer, Lou Reed, and Kathy Acker accompany Ginsberg's quirky captions

0-8118-0372-4 CHRONICLE PB $12.95

Jim **Goldberg**

Rich and Poor

Goldberg photographed people at economic extremes and then invited his subjects to write their thoughts in the margins of the portraits. An often hilarious exposé of raw inequality

0-394-54426-9 RANDOM HOUSE $35.00

Nan **Goldin** & Nobuyoshi **Araki**

Tokyo Love

Goldin continues her extraordinary documentation of life on the margins of consumeristic society by documenting young lovers living on the fringe of Tokyo's bars and clubs: transvestites, gays, and fetishists. Araki, Goldin's collaborator in this singular document, pursued more chaste but equally revelatory portraits of teenage girls on the edge of sexual fashions. Together they have created a portrait of life that will not be ignored

1-88161-657-6 D.A.P. PB $45.00

Nan **Goldin**

The Ballad of Sexual Dependency

Goldin's pictures of nightclubs and Lower East Side apartments are as saturated with acid color is they are with brittle emotion. Like reports from the front, these pictures chronicle the momentary vicissitudes of a struggle

0-89381-339-7 APERTURE PB $27.50

Constance **Sullivan** & Susan **Weiley**, editors

Pure Invention: Photographs by Jan Groover

1-56098-005-2 SMITHSONIAN PB $15.95

Lewis W. **Hine**

Men At Work

0-486-23475-4 DOVER PB $6.95

Daile **Kaplan**, editor

Photo Story: Selected Letters and Photographs of Lewis W. Hine

FOREWORD BY BERENICE ABBOTT

1-56098-169-5 SMITHSONIAN $34.95

Maud **Lavin**

Cut with the Kitchen Knife: The Weimar Photomontages of Hanna Höch

An investigation of the ambiguous, multilayered social construction of women in Weimar Germany, based on the powerful work of one of the most innovative practitioners of photomontage in the Berlin Dada group

0-300-04766-5 YALE $47.50

0-300-06164-1 YALE PB $25.00

George **Hurrell**

Hurrell Hollywood: Photographs, 1928-1990

Hurrell's camera captured every major figure of Hollywood's Golden Age, from Garbo and Harlow to Gable and Tracy. One hundred forty full- and double-page duotone reproductions of Hollywood's reigning stars—the most lavish collection of Hurrel's work yet assembled. "Just as Velazquez glorified the court of Philip IV…Hurrell immortalized Hollywood's Golden Age"—*Vanity Fair*

0-312-08220-7 ST. MARTIN'S $69.95

The Portfolios of George Hurrell

This lavishly produced volume features 30 large-format portraits of legendary figures from the Golden Age of the movie star. Jean Harlow, Marlene Dietrich, and Humphrey Bogart are some of the iconic figures alluringly captured by Hurrell's trademark style that became the visual definition of Hollywood glamour in the '30s and '40s

0-9630570-0-6 GRAYSTONE $50.00

Constance **Sullivan** & Susan **Weiley**, editors

Travels in the American West: Photographs by Len Jenshel

1-56098-148-2 SMITHSONIAN PB $15.95

Yousuf **Karsh**

Karsh: A 50-Year Retrospective

Portraitist rather than art photographer, Karsh's subjects have included a staggering number of celebrities, heads of state, artists, beauties, and personalities

0-8212-1906-5 BULFINCH $50.00

Carole **Kismaric**

Andre Kertesz

0-89381-362-1 APERTURE $22.95

0-89381-363-X APERTURE PB $15.95

William **Klein**

In and Out of Fashion

Photographer and filmmaker Klein climbed the heights of the fashion world in Paris and New York, working for *Vogue* for over a decade. This book draws from his long career of original iconography, in film stills, black-and-white, and color work that illustrate and catalog the innovations—open flash, wide angle lens—of Klein's historic contribution to fashion and to photography

0-679-43424-0 RANDOM HOUSE $65.00

Dorothea **Lange**

American Photographs

Essays by Sandra S. Phillips, John Szarkowski, and Therese Than Heyman underscore the degree to which Dorothea Lange's unforgettable portraits of migrant families in the '30s are etched in our consciousness as American classics. Lange's documentation of the wartime relocation of Japanese Americans and the moral and aesthetic starkness of her images had a profound influence on documentary photography

0-8118-0725-8 CHRONICLE PB $24.95

Dorothea Lange: Photographs of a Lifetime

With a biographical essay by Robert Coles, the author of *The Spiritual Life of Children*, this collection of Lange's work is the most complete collection ever published. "Many of the pictures here have become classics, not only of photography but of the history of America" —*NY Times*

0-89381-657-4 APERTURE $50.00

Christopher **Cox**

Dorothea Lange

A volume in the *Masters of Photography* series

0-89381-283-8 APERTURE PB $15.95

Keith F. **Davis**

The Photographs of Dorothea Lange

The catalogue to the wonderful exhibit at the Metropolitan Museum of Art

0-8109-6496-1 METROPOLITAN MUSEUM $39.95

Eugene P. **Janis**

The Photography of Gustave Le Gray

Technical innovator and magnificent artist, Le Gray was perhaps the greatest of the French painter-photographers who moved in the Barbizon School circle of the 1850s

0-226-39210-4 CHICAGO $120.00

Annie **Leibovitz**

Dancers

1-56098-208-X SMITHSONIAN PB $15.95

Helen **Levitt**

In the Street: Chalk Drawings and Messages, New York City, 1938-1948

Levitt's humorous and compassionate photographs of people, particularly children, in urban streets are testaments to the vitality of the human spirit

INTRODUCTION BY ROBERT COLES

0-8223-0771-5 DUKE PB $24.50

Alexander **Liberman**

Then: Photographs, 1924-1994

Art director of *Vogue*, editorial director of Conde Nast, painter, sculptor, and photographer, the *eminence grise*of Condé Nast here offers portraits from his life

0-679-44524-2 RANDOM HOUSE $65.00

George **Platt Lynes**

Portraits, 1929-1954

One of the world's consummate portrait takers before his untimely death in 1955, Lynes is famous for his penetrating, intensely human sittings with Colette, Igor Stravinsky, André Gide, and Gertrude Stein, among many others. A beautifully produced, casebound volume with 100 11-by-14 sheet-fed gravures

0-944092-27-6 TWIN PALMS $65.00

Sally **Mann**

Immediate Family

Her work, says Mann, "is about everybody's fears, as well as their memories." Contains 65 of Mann's most memorable images of her children, with an essay by celebrated author Reynolds Price

0-89381-523-3 APERTURE PB $24.95

Still Time

"The world of childhood that Ms. Mann presents in her pictures is both luminous and scary, rife with magic and ritual and suffused with complex, half recognized emotions"—*NY Times*

0-89381-593-4 APERTURE PB $29.95

Robert **Mapplethorpe**

Altars

AFTERWORD BY EDMUND WHITE

0-679-42721-X RANDOM HOUSE $100.00

Mapplethorpe

Nearly 300 duotone images track the full course of Mapplethorpe's career, from his early Polaroids to his last sepulchral self-portraits. The introduction by Arthur C. Danto received the 9th Annual Infinity Prize for Writing on Photography from the International Center of Photography

0-679-40804-5 RANDOM HOUSE $125.00

Arthur C. **Danto**

Playing with the Edge: The Photographic Achievement of Robert Mapplethorpe

The art critic for *The Nation* provides a sympathetic account of Mapplethorpe's career and aesthetics. While addressing the public dimension of Mapplethorpe's career—the pornographic brandings and the legal and censorship issues—Danto refuses to reduce Mapplethorpe to these sensational dimensions, insisting on returning to him as an artist and arguing convincingly for his enduring position in the history of art

0-520-20051-9 CALIFORNIA $24.95

Jack **Fritscher**

Mapplethorpe: Assault with a Deadly Camera

Mapplethorpe radicalized gay aesthetics during the '70s and '80s and seriously affected the mainstream. Fritscher probes into Mapplethorpe's personality and influence, from his job as a bookstore clerk with Patti Smith to his ascension as an internationally recognized figure. A raw, explicit, and analytic biography

0-8038-9362-0 HASTINGS $24.95

Patricia **Morrisroe**

Mapplethorpe

0-394-57650-0 RANDOM HOUSE $27.50

Mary Ellen **Mark**

The Photo Essay

1-56098-003-6 SMITHSONIAN PB $15.95

Marianne **Fulton**

Mary Ellen Mark: 25 Years

Mark, a leading documentary photographer, explores the worlds of the disenfranchised in sobering images of great dignity. Her award-winning photographs of the brothels of Falkland Road, Mother Theresa's hospices for the dying, and the lives of autistic children are here combined with a largely unpublished body of work on the circus in India

0-8212-1838-7 BULFINCH PB $35.00

Joel **Meyerowitz**

Cape Light: Color Photographs

One of the most enduringly popular of all photography books. Meyerowitz concentrates on the subtle action of the light of Cape Cod on local architecture and sand

0-87846-131-0 BULFINCH PB $29.95

Duane **Michaels**

ALBUM: The Portraits of Duane Michaels, 1958-1988

Andy Warhol, Jasper Johns, and Robert Rauschenberg are some of the portraits shot by Michaels for magazines, collected here

0-942642-31-7 TWELVETREES $55.00

Ken **Miller**

Open All Night

Hyper-real and brutally skilled, Miller's works are in the permanent collection of the museums of Modern Art in New York and San Francisco, the Fogg Art Museum, and the Brooklyn Museum of Art. Here, he presents his first collection of American images: a world of skinheads, electroshock patients, addicts, and prostitutes. These pictures, in concert with William T. Vollmann's text, document a peculiar American reality. "Ken Miller's pictures are relentlessly, mercilessly, bitterly true. The choices and accidental destinies depicted here are all real, as clearly seen and described as anything in the history of the medium"—Jock Sturges

TEXT BY WILLIAM T. VOLLMANN

0-87951-571-6 OVERLOOK $40.00

Sarah M. **Lowe**

Tina Modotti: Photographs

0-8109-4280-1 ABRAMS $45.00

Margaret **Hooks**

Tina Modotti: Photographer and Revolutionary

Incorporating interviews with Modotti's contemporaries with her images of Mexican peasants, revolutionaries, and workers, this is a magnificent documentation of her beginnings in Italy, her Hollywood life in the '20s, and her relationships with Edward Weston, Frida Kahlo, Pablo Neruda, and John Dos Passos. Hooks revives the extraordinary political and artistic life of an iconoclastic woman

0-04-440925-7 HARPERCOLLINS PB $22.00

Lászlo **Moholy-Nagy**

Moholy-Nagy

EDITED BY RICHARD KOSTELANETZ

0-932360-11-4 DA CAPO $50.00

0-306-80455-7 DA CAPO PB $15.95

Krisztina **Passuth**

Moholy-Nagy

See also THE BAUHAUS AND RELATED CONSTRUCTIVISM under 20TH-CENTURY ART

0-500-27449-5 THAMES & HUDSON PB $24.95

Maria **Morris Hambourg**

Nadar: The Metropolitan Museum of Art

Writer, journalist, bohemian, utopian, balloonist, photographer: Nadar seemed to invent himself over and over again through all the possibilities of the 19th century. This catalog of a Metropolitan Museum exhibition captures Nadar in his most famous role as portrait photographer of the great men and women of his time: Dumas, Baudelaire, Sarah Bernhardt, Berlioz, George Sand, Delacroix, and more

0-8109-6489-9 ABRAMS $65.00

Nadar

Eadward **Muybridge**

Animals in Motion

This classic, groundbreaking collection of animal stop-motion photos forever settled the ancient question of whether or not horses ever simultaneously have all four feet off the ground during the course of a natural stride in any gait. Includes 4000 high speed shots of 34 different animals and birds, most against ruled backgrounds

EDITED BY LEWIS S. BROWN

0-486-20203-8 DOVER $29.95

Muybridge's Complete Human and Animal Locomotion: All 781 Plates

Muybridge's use of the camera to analyze the rhythms of motion in man and beast resulted in these photographic sequences. The product of scientific study, they have been widely used by artists

Volume 1

0-486-23792-3 DOVER $75.00

Volume 2
0-486-23793-1 DOVER $60.00

Volume 3
0-486-23794-X DOVER $75.00

Peter **Galassi**

Nicholas Nixon: Pictures of People
A wide range of quietly compelling, empathetic photographs of strangers and family, the aged and the dying (AIDS patients), as well as the buoyantly healthy

0-8109-6056-7 MOMA $45.00

Miles **Barth**, editor

Intimate Visions: The Photographs of Dorothy Norman
A comprehensive look at the artistic career of one of the most influential artistic personalities of her time. This collection explores the development of Norman's work, highlighting her sensitive portraits of some of the 20th century's most influential writers, artists, and political figures .

0-8118-0399-6 CHRONICLE $27.50
0-8118-0364-3 CHRONICLE PB $17.95

Martin **Harrison**

Norman Parkinson: Photographs 1935-1989
0-8478-1825-X RIZZOLI $65.00

Irving **Penn**

Passage
This retrospective selection of 468 black-and-white and color plates was designed by Penn himself using an innovative printing technique. The accompanying text illuminates his portraits of the famous, ethnographical portraits of tribesmen, *Vogue* fashion photos, advertising work, still lifes, and his own drawings

INTRODUCTION BY ALEXANDER LIBERMAN

0-679-40491-0 KNOPF $100.00

Jed **Perl**

Man Ray
A volume in the *Masters of Photography* series

0-89381-307-9 APERTURE PB $15.95

Man **Ray**

Photographs by Man Ray: 1920-1934
Man Ray's most striking photographs, including many of his abstract "rayographs" or photograms (cameraless photographs)

0-486-23842-3 DOVER PB $11.95

Donald **Kuspit**

Albert Renger-Patzsch: Joy Before the Object
0-89236-273-1 OXFORD $40.00

Leni **Riefenstahl**

The Last of the Nuba
Between 1962 and 1969 the acclaimed film director—director of the Nazi classics *Triumph of the Will* and *Olympia*—lived among the mysterious African tribes of the Nuba, learning their language, photographing their way of life

0-312-13642-0 ST. MARTIN'S $40.00

Jacob **Riis**

How the Other Half Lives: Studies Among the Tenements of New York
A landmark study in investigative photojournalism, Riis's book first appeared nearly 100 years ago. He photographed with the (then new) flash technique inside tenements in the most sordid and dangerous districts of New York

EDITED BY SAM B. WARNER, JR.
INTRODUCTION BY C.A. MADISON

0-486-22012-5 DOVER PB $10.95

Andres **Serrano**

Body and Soul
This volume captures Serrano's genius for exposing naked coldness and the horror of body and soul in unforgettable works of art

TEXT BY BELL HOOKS

1-88348-911-3 TAKARAJIMA $50.00

Mark **Haworth-Booth**

Camille Silvy: River Scene
0-89236-205-7 GETTY MUSEUM PB $15.95

W. Eugene **Smith**

W. Eugene Smith
A volume in the Pantheon Photo Library

9-994-14065-5 CREATIVE PHOTOGRAPHY PB $15.00

Phil **Stern**

Phil Stern's Hollywood: Photographs, 1940-1979
From a pregnant Marilyn Monroe walking on a backlot at 20th Century-Fox to a serious Groucho Marx, this selection from Stern's four decades as the Hollywood chronicler for *Life* offers a fresh, startling look at Hollywood in the act of being itself

0-394-58110-5 KNOPF $40.00

Sue D. **Lowe**

Stieglitz: A Memoir-Biography
Stieglitz's life with his family, his second wife Georgia O'Keeffe, and a wide circle of artistic and literary friends make a good story in itself, and an invaluable aid to understanding how modern art rose in America

0-374-26990-4 FS&G $25.50

Dorothy **Norman**

Alfred Stieglitz: An American Seer
0-89381-429-6 APERTURE $29.95
0-89381-425-3 APERTURE PB $16.95

Alfred **Stieglitz**

Alfred Stieglitz
EDITED BY DOROTHY NORMAN

0-89381-308-7 APERTURE $22.95
0-89381-309-5 APERTURE PB $15.95

Alfred Stieglitz at Lake George
In the '20s and '30s, after a decade of intense public life, Stieglitz began taking photographs of his world at Lake George in the New York Adirondacks. The landscape, the architecture, and the intimate life he led with his family and friends make up this radical and private body of work

EDITED BY JOHN SZARKOWSKI

0-8109-6149-0 ABRAMS $35.00
0-87070-139-8 MOMA PB $19.95

Paul **Strand**

Paul Strand
Strand's unique position as an apostle of modernism and social change is reflected in his austere studies and portraits of peasants and working-class people

0-89381-077-0 APERTURE $22.95
0-89381-259-5 APERTURE PB $15.95

Calvin **Tomkins**

Paul Strand: Sixty Years of Photographs
0-912334-81-9 APERTURE PB $35.00

Jock **Sturges**

The Last Day of Summer
Sturges captured the summer moods of friends and children in 60 extraordinarily poignant portraits. Includes many photos taken by the FBI in the notorious child pornography seizure of 1990, returned to the artist after no charges were brought Essay by Jayne Anne Phillips

0-89381-494-6 APERTURE $45.00
0-89381-538-1 APERTURE PB $24.95

Radiant Identities
"Sturge's people are grave, well-formed, and poetic. Best to think of his world as an inviting fiction: one photographer's Eden, where a little knowledge doesn't get you expelled from the garden"—*People*

INTRODUCTION BY ELIZABETH BEVERLY, AFTERWORD BY A.D. COLEMAN

0-89381-649-3 APERTURE PB $24.95
0-89381-595-0 APERTURE $40.00

Anna **Farova**

Josef Sudek: Poet of Prague—A Photographer's Life
A biography of the great Czech photographer, with 160 duotone reproductions of his work

0-89381-386-9 APERTURE $45.00

Jerry N. **Uelsmann**

Uelsmann: Process and Perception
Uelsmann's pop surrealism has long been underestimated in term of both his extraordinary technical virtuosity and his complex dream imagery. This book analyzes his methods and goals

0-8130-0830-1 FLORIDA PB $24.95

Ann **Vachon**, editor

Poland, 1946: The Photographs and Letters of John Vachon
INTRODUCTION BY BRIAN MOORE

1-56098-540-2 SMITHSONIAN $39.95

Bruce **Weber**

Hotel Room with a View
1-56098-147-4 SMITHSONIAN PB $15.95

Weegee

Naked City
A startlingly rough and intimate portrait of New York and its people, rich and poor, honest and criminal. In the 1940s these pictures fascinated because of their immediacy and then-shocking content

0-306-80241-4 DA CAPO PB $13.95

Weegee

Weegee's People

0-306-80242-2 DA CAPO PB $13.95

Gilles **Mora**, editor

Edward Weston: Forms of Passion

The classic body of Weston's black-and-white photographs, concentrating on natural forms: the nude female, seashells, plants, and vegetables, from "the founding father of American photography"—Beaumont Newhall

0-8109-3979-7 ABRAMS $65.00

Nancy **Newhall**

Edward Weston: The Flame of Recognition

A reissue of Weston's classic monograph, which brings together a careful selection of his photographs with excerpts from the artist's letters and diaries. "His kind of photography opened up wonderful worlds of seeing and doing"—Ansel Adams

0-89381-533-0 APERTURE PB $24.95

Edward **Weston**

Edward Weston Portraits

A volume of intimate and revealing portraits taken between 1917 and 1948, documenting the famous and the fascinating figures of the photographer's life: Diego Rivera, Frida Kahlo, Tina Modotti, James Cagney, D.H. Lawrence, e.e. cummings, and others. "Weston understood thoughts and concepts which dwell on simple mystical levels. His work—direct and honest as it is—leaped from a deep intuition and belief in the forces beyond the apparent and factual"—Ansel Adams

0-89381-605-1 APERTURE $40.00

Ben **Maddow**

Edward Weston: His Life and Photographs

PREFACE BY COLE WESTON

0-89381-369-9 APERTURE PB $16.95

Edward **Weston**

Edward Weston

A volume in the *Masters of Photography* series

EDITED BY R.H. CRAVENS

0-89381-305-2 APERTURE PB $15.95

Deborah **Willis-Braithwaite**

Vanderzee, Photographer: 1886-1983

0-8109-3923-1 ABRAMS $45.00

John **Szarkowski**

Winogrand: Figments from the Real World

This book is a full tribute to Gary Winogrand, whose recent death ended a career that began in the 1950s: street photography, series of animals, rodeos, airports, women, and other repeated everyday motifs

0-8109-6088-5 ABRAMS PB $19.95

Emile **Zola** & Francois **Massin**

Zola: Photographer

A look at turn-of-the-century Paris, the Universal Exposition of 1900, and Zola's daily life and family through the novelist's own lens

TRANSLATED BY LILIAN EMERY TUCK

0-8371-9820-8 GREENWOOD $49.75

Photojournalism and Historical Documentary

Peter **Bellamy**

The Artist Project: Portraits of the Real Art World

1-55859-563-5 IN PRESS $45.00

Leah **Bendavid-Val**

National Geographic: The Photographs

A retrospective of the *National Geographic*'s far-ranging, always artful cameras. The Land, Underwater, Science, The United States, and The World compose the five parts of this august institution's documentary and photojournalistic mission

0-87044-986-9 NATIONAL GEOGRAPHIC $50.00

Ian **Berry**

Living Apart: South Africa Under Apartheid

From the Sharpeville Massacre to the first free elections in South Africa, Magnum photographer Ian Barry memorialized the birth, growth, and dismantlement of the doctrine of "living apart," Apartheid. Now that it is legislatively over, his unique photographic documentation shows its effects cannot be easily or quickly forgotten

0-7148-3523-4 PHAIDON $69.95

Michael L. **Carlebach**

The Origin of Photojournalism in America

1-56098-159-8 SMITHSONIAN PB $29.95

Seiichi **Furuya**

Memoires, 1995

1-88161-654-1 D.A.P. $35.00

Carole **Gallagher**

American Ground Zero: The Secret Nuclear War

An extraordinary product of one photojournalist's ten-year commitment to documenting the experiences of people whose lives were crossed by the nuclear fallout from government testing in Nevada in the '50s and early '60s. This collection of photographs and interviews penetrates the dual challenges of official secrecy and anonymity in order to create a striking portrait of the undecorated casualties in an undeclared war

0-262-07146-0 MIT $60.00
0-679-75432-6 RANDOM HOUSE PB $30.00

Irving **Haberman** & Miles **Barth**

Eyes on an Era: Four Decades of Photojournalism by Irving Haberman

COMMENTARY BY WALTER CRONKITE

0-8478-1867-5 RIZZOLI $40.00

Carolyn **Jones**

Living Proof: Courage in the Face of AIDS

1-55859-713-1 ABBEVILLE $19.95

David Hume **Kennerly**

Photo Op

Images from the last 30 years of American history: student protests against the war in Vietnam, RFK's assassination, Nixon's election, Watergate, and the crumbling of the Soviet Union. A vital record of events that shaped our times

INTRODUCTION BY JEFF MACNELLY

0-292-74323-8 TEXAS $29.95

Susan **Kismaric**

American Politicians: Photographs from 1843 to 1993

Superb collection showing how photography has pictured and helped to transform American politics, published in conjunction with a Museum of Modern Art exhibit

See also **POLITICAL HISTORY** under **AMERICAN POLITICS AND FOREIGN POLICY** in **HISTORY OF THE AMERICAS**

0-8109-6135-0 MOMA $39.95

Jay **Maisel**

On Assignment

1-56098-002-8 SMITHSONIAN PB $15.95

William **Manchester**

In Our Time: The World as Seen by Magnum Photographers

Magnum is an extraordinary consortium of photojournalists, founded in 1947 and still active. Our vision of current events and world history is often filtered through the eyes of Magnum's elite corps of press photographers

0-393-02767-8 NORTON $65.00
0-393-31129-5 NORTON PB $39.95

Don **McCullin**

Sleeping with Ghosts: A Life's Work in Photography

One of the most brilliant photojournalists of our time presents war images from Israel and Iraq to Vietnam and Cambodia, as well as unemployed miners, the down-and-out in London's East End, and the homeless in Bradford. 200 of his best photographs

0-89381-659-0 APERTURE $45.00

Carl **Mydans** & **Kunhardt, Jr., Philip B.**

Carl Mydans, Photojournalist

0-8109-1323-2 ABRAMS $39.95

James **Nachtwey**

A World at War: Photographs, 1981-88

Pictures of war in Northern Ireland, Nicaragua, El Salvador, Guatemala, Lebanon, the West Bank and Sinai, Sub-Saharan Africa, the Philippines, Korea, Sri Lanka, and Afghanistan

INTRODUCTION BY ROBERT STONE

0-8128-8057-9 STEIN & DAY PB $3.95

Tim **Page**

Mid-Term Report

Since his spectacular exploration of Indochina and Vietman during the war, Page has brought his insight and compassion to other war zones, both actual and metaphoric. From mid-career he looks back over his oeuvre

0-500-27795-8 THAMES & HUDSON PB $29.95

Tim Page's Nam
"Brutal, vivid, weirdly beautiful pictures"
—*Atlantic Monthly*
INTRODUCTION BY WILLIAM SHAWCROSS
0-500-27280-8 THAMES & HUDSON PB $19.95

Mark **Riboud**
Angkor: The Serenity of Buddhism
The ancient Cambodian city of Angkor, with its magnificent temples and sculpture is one of the artistic and architectural wonders of the world. Riboud offers an inspired vision of this timeless place, where Buddhist monks and pilgrims continue to worship at the temples
0-500-54182-5 THAMES & HUDSON $65.00

Mark Riboud: Photographs at Home and Abroad
One of the most artistic of the roving photojournalists, his pictures bring a unique vision to exotic locations
0-8109-1566-9 ABRAMS $45.00

Eugene **Richards** & Christiane **Bird**
Below the Line: Living Poor in America
An impassioned look at the reality of life for the poor, homeless, and sometimes hopeless people of this wealthy nation. Fine photography movingly deployed to tell a painful story
0-89043-061-6 CONSUMER REPORTS PB $20.00

Thomas **Roma**
Found in Brooklyn
"Only the dead," wrote Thomas Wolfe in his famous short story, "know Brooklyn." 20 years of Roma's work capture the forlorn, the amusing, the stunning, and the surreal of this mad and beautiful borough
INTRODUCTION BY ROBERT COLES
0-393-31430-8 NORTON PB $18.95

Sebastiao **Salgado**
An Uncertain Grace
From the Andes to Ethiopia to Chad and Mali, the struggle to survive is captured in shocking and memorable images. 129 duotones. "Some of the most compelling photojournalism that has been made"—*NY Times*
INTRODUCTION BY EDUARDO GALEANO
0-89381-421-0 APERTURE $60.00
0-89381-460-1 APERTURE PB $39.95

Special Topics

Mikkel **Aaland** & Rudolph **Burger**
Digital Photography
This comprehensive guide brings readers up to date on the latest technology and techniques of digital photography. Included are a survey of currently available hardware and software, as well as a section on the ethical questions of computerized image manipulation
0-679-74260-3 RANDOM HOUSE PB $20.00

Dawn **Ades**
Photomontage
0-500-20208-7 THAMES & HUDSON PB $14.95

Aperture
The Body in Question
A special issue of *Aperture* devoted to the issues raised by AIDS, censorship, pornography, abortion, and domestic violence in the combative atmosphere of the '90s. Karen Finley, David Wojnarowicz, Donna Ferrato, Peter Greenaway, Allen Ginsberg, and others look at sex roles and sexual identity today. With 36 four-color and 48 black-and-white photographs
0-89381-464-4 APERTURE PB $19.95

Ruth **Bernhard**
The Eternal Body: A Collection of Fifty Nudes
Half a century of Bernhard's reserved, sensual, and ethereal female nudes collected in 50 beautifully produced duotones. An insightful text enhances our understanding of a preeminent American photographer. "Outstanding...the greatest photographer of the nude"—Ansel Adams
0-8118-0826-2 CHRONICLE $60.00
0-8118-0801-7 CHRONICLE PB $29.95

Paul **Bowles** & Barry **Brukoff**
Morocco
Brukoff's accomplished imagery captures, in 80 full-color photographs, the look and feel of North African light, the brilliant colors of Arab mosaics, the bustle of native markets, and the serenity of a desert oasis. Seven long-unavailable essays by Bowles accompany the stunning photos
0-8109-3631-3 ABRAMS $49.50

Lois **Conner**
Panoramas from the Far East
1-56098-331-0 SMITHSONIAN PB $15.95

Jed **Devine** & Jim **Dinsmore**
Friendship
"Writing and photography are as polar as opposite seasons, but, as complements, each can provide something that the other cannot. Like fishermen, we worked the same water but set our own traps. This is our haul." So writes photographer Devine of his collaboration with writer Dinsmore in creating this stunning work. 64 palladium prints, a process in which Devine is an acknowledged master, comprise this meditative, inspiring homage to the authors' friendship, and to the luminous island of Friendship, Maine
0-88448-137-9 TILBURY PB $40.00

Diana **Edkins**, editor
Animal Attractions
One hundred photographs by contemporary artists explore the relationship between people and animals. Includes photographs and essays by Wegman, Mapplethorpe, and others
0-8109-1959-1 ABRAMS $29.95

Elizabeth **Edwards**, editor
Anthropology and Photography, 1860-1920
A fascinating political, historical, and theoretical study of the role of photography in anthropology, focusing on British still photography from the height of the colonial era
0-300-05944-2 YALE PB $22.50

Viviane **Esders**, editor
Our Mothers: Portraits by 72 Women Photographers
Portraits of their mothers and themselves by, among others, Annie Leibovitz, Mary Ellen Mark, Inge Morath, Elizabeth Lennard, and Gisele Freund. "An absolutely mesmerizing work—touching, profound, evocative of a whole raft of ambivalent feelings, a loving tribute to mothers everywhere"—Barbara Morrow
FOREWORD BY KATHY RYAN
1-55670-442-9 STEWART, TABORI $29.95

William A. **Ewing**
The Fugitive Gesture: Masterpieces of Dance Photography
Ewing's tribute to the demanding photographic genre that captures the most ephemeral of the arts. Over 200 duotone images by Beaton, Steichen, Horst, Man Ray, and more, capture ballet, waltz, tango, tap, by figures such as Nijinsky, Astaire, Fonteyn. "An absolute delight...full of inspiration...Anyone interested in people and movement will find this book invaluable"—*Image*
0-500-27806-7 THAMES & HUDSON PB $29.95

William A. **Ewing**, editor
The Body
From medicine to fashion, the camera's eye returns again and again to the human body. Compiles the best images from Horst, Lartigue, Stieglitz, Sally Mann, Mapplethorpe, Man Ray, Leni Riefenstahl, Herb Ritts, and more. Gloriously printed duotone and full-color reproductions
0-8118-0762-2 CHRONICLE PB $29.95

Ronnie **Farley**
Women of the Native Struggle: Portraits and Testimony of Native American Women
These poignant portraits acquaint us with a range of Native America women, some on the reservation, some in the cities, each dealing with her rich and tragic legacy. With commentary by the women themselves to complement the vivid images
0-517-88113-6 ORION PB $22.00

Herb **Ritts**
Duo: Herb Ritts Photographs Bob Paris & Rod Jackson
These intimate compositions combine Ritts's now classic "clean" pictures with the quietly homoerotic depictions of two lovers. A splendid casebound volume. All royalties will be donated by the author to the American Foundation for AIDS Research
0-944092-17-9 TWIN PALMS $45.00

Paula Richardson **Fleming** & Judith **Luskey**
The North American Indians
Fascinating historical documents and portraits of Native Americans
0-06-015549-3 HARPER & ROW $34.50

Paula Richardson **Fleming** &
Judith Lynn **Luskey**

Grand Endeavors of American Indian Photography

1-56098-297-7 SMITHSONIAN $42.50

Willy **George**

In the Warsaw Ghetto: Summer, 1941

George, a photographer in the German Army, shot four rolls of film in the Warsaw ghetto one summer day in 1941. Published on the 50th anniversary of the uprising, this compilation provides a clear-eyed and chilling record of the end of one of the greatest Jewish communities in history

FOREWORD BY ELIE WIESEL
0-89381-526-8 APERTURE $40.00

Dennis **Hopper**

Out of the Sixties

Recognized by *The New York Times Book Review* as one of the year's best books, these surprising photographs by the deviant Hollywood hipster portray some of the greatest players of the '60s in all their brilliant, stoned-out splendor

0-942642-25-2 TWELVETREES $45.00

Britta **Jaschinski**

Zoo

An exquisite, thought-provoking exploration of the zoo, as an institution, as an exhibition, and as a habitat for shadowy, enigmatic, and utterly foreign life forms. The 1995 Agfa and Bilderberg Young Photojournalist of the Year competition runner-up presents a series of stark images that pose fundamental questions about the zoo and our relationship to its denizens

0-7148-3472-6 PHAIDON $19.95

Susan **Jonas** & Marilyn **Nissenson**

Going, Going, Gone: Vanishing Americana

Poignant photographic essays that eulogize more than 70 seemingly "eternal" American institutions headed for extinction. From paper dolls to automats, carbon copies to the milkman, *Going, Going, Gone* reminds us of the constant loss and change of our daily lives

0-8118-0292-2 CHRONICLE PB $18.95

Marla Hamburg **Kennedy**

Kissing: Photographs and Essays on the Wonderful Act of Kissing

See also **LOVE AND ROMANCE** under **COURTSHIP, LOVE, SEX, AND MARRIAGE** in **LIFESTYLES AND PRACTICAL ADVICE**

0-9630570-4-9 D.A.P. $16.95

Brian **Lanker**

I Dream a World: Portraits of Black Women Who Changed America

"Control yourself, because the Holy Spirit will use you up in one performance," says gospel singer Willie Mae Ford Smith as she faces the camera in a white-feathered hat. This deeply moving collection of portraits of 76 African-American women, vital but historically neglected catalysts of the civil rights movement all, has sold more than 330,000 copies since 1989

1-55670-063-6 STEWART, TABORI $40.00
1-55670-092-X STEWART, TABORI PB $24.95

Victoria **Lautman**

The New Tattoo

1-55859-785-9 ABBEVILLE $35.00

Michael **Lesy**

Wisconsin Death Trip

"Michael Lesy's grim collection of American Gothic uses old glass-plate negatives to clobber an old myth: the idyll of 'pioneers' escaping the city's evils to reap happiness on the open prairies….Lesy's reading of rural decay is history with a wrench"—*Newsweek*

See also **AMERICA MOVES WEST** under **AMERICAN REGIONAL HISTORY: THE WEST AND THE SOUTH** in **HISTORY OF THE AMERICAS**

0-385-41215-0 ANCHOR PB $19.95

Joseph S. **Levine**

The Coral Reef at Night

"No experience on land can prepare you for the sensation of night diving in a tropical sea," says author and filmmaker Levine. This wondrous book brings you as close to that experience as you can get without actually taking the plunge

0-8109-3190-7 ABRAMS $39.95

Lucy R. **Lippard**, editor

Partial Recall: Photographs of Native North Americans

Twelve Native American artists and writers discuss the role of images in the historical relationships between natives and non-natives

1-56584-016-X NEW PRESS $35.00
1-56584-041-0 NEW PRESS PB $19.95

Jane **Livingston**

The New York School: Photographs, 1936-1963

The *New York School* includes artists Diane Arbus, Richard Avedon, Robert Frank, and Weegee, who worked in New York in the '30s to the late '50s, and whose aesthetic values were identified with film noir

1-55670-239-6 STEWART, TABORI $75.00

Gina **Lollobrigida**

The Wonder of Innocence

Lollobrigida introduced by Mother Teresa. This sixth work of the acclaimed actress and accomplished photographer creates a fantasy world of children and animals, where a boy climbs an ostrich's neck and a girl dances on a seal

FOREWORD BY MOTHER TERESA OF CALCUTTA
0-8109-3573-2 ABRAMS $29.95

Jacques **Lowe**

JFK Remembered: An Intimate Portrait by His Personal Photographer

198 photographs, both classic and previously unpublished, by the photographer who enjoyed unprecedented access to the president, at work in the White House or at play with his family

FOREWORD BY ARTHUR SCHLESINGER, JR.
0-679-42399-0 RANDOM HOUSE $37.50

Peter **Mayle**

Provence

The best-selling author of *A Year in Provence* and *Toujours Provence* goes out of his way to consolidate his monopoly on that charmed corner of France in partnership with the celebrated aerial photographer Jason Hawkes.

PHOTOGRAPHS BY JASON HAWKES
0-684-19664-6 MACMILLAN $14.00

Linda **McCartney**

Linda Mccartney's Sixties: Portrait of an Era

This bestselling album, now available in paperback, gives any fan of rock a unique insider's perspective. Famous rock legends like Jagger, Hendrix, the Grateful Dead, and, not surprisingly, the Beatles, are captured with unique intimacy

See also **REFERENCE** under **ROCK** in **PERFORMING ARTS AND MEDIA**

INTRODUCTION BY PAUL MCCARTNEY
0-8212-2056-X BULFINCH PB $19.95

The Beatles

Ken **Miller**

The Hamptons: Long Island's East End

This full-color photographic record captures the enormous variety of architectural, historic, and geographic settings that have made the east end of New York's Long Island so enticing for centuries

0-8478-1694-X RIZZOLI $45.00

Courtney **Milne**

Sacred Places in North America: A Journey of the Spirit

Milne, the celebrated nature photographer from Canada, captures over 50 sacred places throughout North America

1-55670-414-3 STEWART, TABORI $27.50

Barbara **Norfleet**

Looking at Death

A shocking and thought-provoking book of 107 duotone photographs—striking images of death and dying in war, medicine, social violence, collected (and with text by) Norfleet, a photographer, historian, and Harvard lecturer. Humor, pathos, art, and artifice are reflected in these controversial pages

0-87923-964-6 GODINE $40.00
0-87923-965-4 GODINE PB $25.00

Tillie **Olsen** & others

Mothers & Daughters: That Special Quality, an Exploration in Photographs

The work of some 75 contemporary photographers is brought together with an insightful text by Estelle Jussim and a poetic essay by Tillie Olsen to create this "moving tribute to the emotional, cultural, and intellectual resources of women"—*USA Today*. Includes work by Bruce Davidson, Eudora Welty, Danny Lyon, and Nan Goldin

See also **MOTHERHOOD** under **THE FEMALE EXPERIENCE** under **WOMEN'S STUDIES** in **SOCIAL STUDIES**

0-89381-379-6 APERTURE PB $24.95

Nissan **Perez**

Focus East: Early Photography in the Near East, 1839-1885

This is a comprehensive survey of the practice of photography by many individuals in the Middle East. Scientists, travelers, artists, and antiquarians all took up cameras to record the people, objects, and scenery of the Holy Land

0-8109-0924-3 ABRADALE $12.98

Jane M. **Rabb**, editor

Literature and Photography: Interactions, 1840-1990

0-8263-1663-8 NEW MEXICO PB $39.95

Cervin **Robinson** & Joel **Herschman**

Architecture Transformed: A History of the Photography of Buildings from 1839 to the Present

Essays and reproductions representing the history of architectural photography from the earliest days to the present. A remarkable range of images

0-262-68064-5 MIT PB $35.00

The Rolling Stone Editors

Rolling Stone Images of Rock & Roll

0-316-75468-4 LITTLE, BROWN $50.00

Steven **Rothfeld**

French Dreams

Ninety hauntingly beautiful photographs: landscapes, portraits, still lives, and vignettes that bring to life a country and its people in fascinating detail

1-56305-469-8 WORKMAN $19.95

Robert A. **Sobieszek**

The Camera I: Great Photographic Self-Portraits

The self-portrait has long provided a means for artists of every kind to test and to illustrate their powers. This collection unites photographic self-portraits from André Kertesz, Cecil Beaton, Irving Penn, Cindy Sherman, Henri Cartier-Bresson, Walker Evans, Nancy Burson, and many others

0-8109-3197-4 ABRAMS $49.50

Peter **Stackpole**

Life in Hollywood: 1936-1952

One of *Life* magazine's original four photographers, Stackpole gave us a Hollywood in love with itself and the movies. From a classic shot of Errol Flynn high on the mast of his yacht to a young Orson Welles writing while Rita Hayworth suns herself—the photographs of Peter Stackpole captured the glamour and wit of a dazzling era

0-944439-18-7 CLARK CITY $50.00

Edward **Steichen**

The Family of Man

The photographic bestseller of all time, this book began as an exhibition at the Museum of Modern Art just after World War II

0-8109-6169-5 ABRAMS PB $19.95

Alfred **Stieglitz**

Camera Work: A Pictorial Guide

Camera Work was Stieglitz's deluxe magazine of photography, promoting an artistic revolution in photography and establishing that medium as a fine art. This volume reprints every photograph published in the magazine, including works by Steichen, Strand, White, Kasebier, Stieglitz himself, and many others

EDITED BY MARIANNE F. MARGOLIS

0-486-23591-2 DOVER PB $14.95

John **Thomson**

China and Its People in Early Photographs

A picturesque excursion in 19th-century photographic sociology in China

FOREWORD BY JANET LEHR

0-486-24393-1 DOVER PB $13.95

Alan **Trachtenberg**

Reading American Photographs: Images as History from Mathew Brady to Walker Evans

The role of photographers in shaping the American perception of the past

See also **CULTURAL AND SOCIAL HISTORY** under **TOPICS IN AMERICAN STUDIES** in **HISTORY OF THE AMERICAS**

0-374-52249-9 HILL & WANG PB $16.00

Vogue Editors

On the Edge: Images from 100 Years of Vogue

Irving Penn, Richard Avedon, Herb Ritts, and Toni Frisell are just a few of the photographers. Cocteau, Marlene Dietrich, Henri Matisse, and Marilyn Monroe are only some of the subjects. And Suzy Parker, Twiggy, Cindy Crawford, and Linda Evangelista are a sampling of the models

0-679-41161-5 RANDOM HOUSE $50.00

William **Webb**

Henry and Friends: The California Years, 1946-1977

A collection of striking black-and-white images of Henry Miller and the members of his Big Sur circle—painters Ephraim Doner, Emil White, and Varda, photographers Wynn Bullock and Brassai, and countless others

0-88496-343-8 CAPRA PB $18.95

Michael S. **Yamasita**

Mekong: A Journey on the Mother of Waters

"It has been my dream to follow the 2,600 miles of the Mekong River. Yamashita has not only lived that dream, he has photographed it beautifully…it's a great one"—Ted Koppel

1-88348-909-1 TAKARAJIMA $39.95

Processes and Techniques

Ansel **Adams**

Examples: The Making of 40 Photographs

A behind-the-scenes look at what went into the making of 40 of Adams's photographs. His legendary previsualization, zone system, and printing technique all combine to produce these celebrated images

0-8212-1750-X BULFINCH PB $27.50

Photography

Book 1
The Camera

0-8212-2184-1 LITTLE, BROWN PB $21.95

Book 2
The Negative

0-8212-2186-8 LITTLE, BROWN PB $21.95

Book 3
The Print

0-8212-2187-6 LITTLE, BROWN PB $21.95

William **Crawford**

The Keepers of Light: A History and Working Guide to Photographic Processes

A detailed study of early and unusual photographic processes, including do-it-yourself recipes. Of interest both to practitioners and more casual readers

0-87100-158-6 MORGAN PB $35.00

Minor **White**

New Zone System Manual: Previsualization, Exposure, Development, Printing

0-87100-195-0 MORGAN PB $30.00

Art **Wolfe** & Martha **Hill**

The Art of Nature Photography

Premier nature photographer Wolfe and top photographic editor Martha Hill reveal, with 250 color photographs (and side-by-side comparisons), what makes the best photographs so captivating. Learn how to make ordinary photographs better, and to see like a professional while shooting and while editing the results

0-517-88034-2 CROWN PB $27.50

Part 11

Architecture & Design

Louis Sullivan

Private Comforts

1700 BC: The Minoan Queen's Bathtub
The earliest known. Daedalus, builder of mazes, first aeronaut, and father of architecture, designed the palace of Knossos with plumbing unrivaled until the rise of Rome.
18

1500BC

1350 BC: Limestone Toilet Seat, Egypt
15

500BC

500 BC: Upholstered Chairs
Of unprecedented elegance and comfort, they are widespread in the Greek world.
1228

100 BC: Roman Aqueducts
The completion of the Pont du Garde near Nîmes heralds a golden age of public works and health. Public baths abound (some serving as many as 3,000 bathers at once), and sewers are built that will flow for centuries to come. Hot and cold running water is common in the homes of the well-to-do; some houses in Pompeii have as many as 30 taps.
1228

AD1

455: The Vandals Sack Rome
The introduction of an age not only dark but also poorly furnished and worse plumbed. The chair is forgotten, save for stiff-backed formal seats reserved for important persons; people sit on stools and hard benches, and a total ignorance of attached upholstery settles over Europe. Aqueducts and sewers crumble, water is filthy, baths rare, and epidemics are the rule. "The taps were turned off all over Europe; they would not be turned on again for nearly a thousand years." (Charles Wright)
30

AD500

13c: Crusaders
They rediscover the delights of bathing and carry home a public bath culture (hence, the "Turkish bath"). Guests and hosts, men and women, mingle un-selfconsciously, nude but for headdress and jewelry, to feast, flirt, and listen to music.
35

1500: Leonardo da Vinci
Proposes a system to premix hot and cold bathwater for Isabella of Aragon, and a network of flushing, ventilated toilets (with self-raising counterweighted toilet seats) for Francis I.
1231

AD1500

16c: Europe Gets Dirty Again
The public bath degenerates into a brothel and is banned across Europe; a reputation for immorality will taint its various names—bordello, *bagnio*, stew—for centuries.
44

1596: Sir John Harrington
Publishes a design for the first flushing, valved water closet (dubbed "Ajax"), with instructions—and a comic verse on the moral theology of praying while sitting on it.
88

AD1600

1665: Elegant, But...
Escaping the plague, Charles II and his court spend the summer in Oxford. Their host, a scholar at the university, describes them: "Though they were neat and gay in their apparell, yet they were very nasty and beastly, leaving at their departure their excrements in every corner, in chimneys, studies, colehouses, cellers. Rude, rough, whoremongers; vaine, empty, careless." (Charles Wright).
88

AD1700

1750s: Versailles
Under Louis XV the chair returns to its ancient glories of comfort and style; the good news spreads across Europe.
1254

1850s: The Revival of the Bath
At first for health, and ever more for pleasure, Europeans take advantage of new access to clean and reliable central water supplies and sewers. Architects design larger and more elaborate rooms specifically for bathing. The English, of course, claim to prefer a bracingly cold bath.
1228

AD1850

1870s: America
Architects bring the previously scattered bath, shaving table, and toilet together into one room.
1264

1879: Wasson and Harris
Patent the pedal shower, in which a continuous treading motion recirculates a fixed water supply.
7

AD1900

1950s: America's Postwar Building Boom
For the first time, large numbers of people are prosperous enough to live in houses that incorporate the fruit of several millennia of experiment. The bathroom achieves its final form: a machine for keeping "clean and decent."
1238

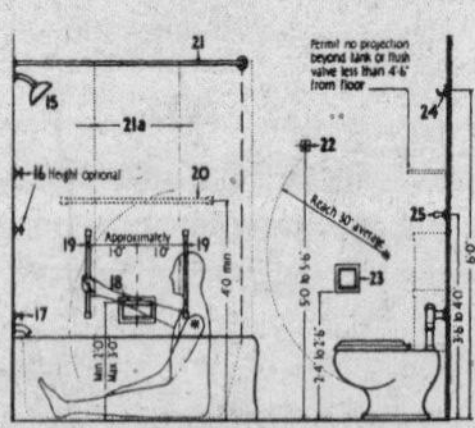

AD1950

Temples, Malta (c. 3000-2000 BC)
The earliest known free-standing stone buildings employ the same basic post and lintel construction as the great Egyptian and Greek temples.
1229

Southwell Minster, England (c. 1290)
John Ruskin thought that the heart and soul of Gothic architecture lay in its anonymous stonecarvers' beautiful, seemingly almost improvisational mastery of detail.
1229

La Rotonda, Veneto, Italy (1560)
Andrea Palladio, the architect of La Rotonda, said its site is "one of the most agreeable and delightful that may be found, on a hillock with gentle approaches and surrounded by other charming hills, all cultivated, that give the effect of a huge theater."
1231

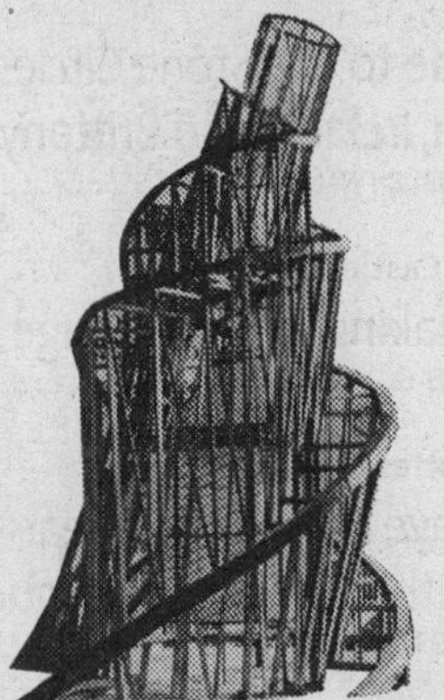

Monument to the Third International (1919–1920)
Resembling both a cannon and a ziggurat, Tatlin's unbuilt revolutionary monument was planned as a double skew spiral of open steel girders containing several vast revolving halls and rising a third of a mile.
1243

Pantheon, Rome (130)
Cement, the arch, and the dome were Roman innovations that made possible the great interior spaces of Western architecture.
1146

San Ivo, Rome (1650)
Bernini declared that his rival Borromini had come to destroy true architecture, but meticulous craftsmanship and visionary mathematics undergird the astonishing, convulsive energy with which this great baroque architect invested classical forms.
1231

Memorial to the Missing of the Somme (1927–1932)
Sir Edwin Lutyens's strangely disproportionate and precariously balanced triumphal arch presides over one of the First World War's vast graveyards.
1234

Kandariya Mahadeva Temple, Khajuraho, India (c. 1000)
Hindu temples repeat structural forms to textural effect, giving them a presence that is both sculptural and organic.
1202

Kalyan Minaret, Bukhara, Turkestan (1127)
In buildings like the Kalyan minaret, the most famous in the Islamic world in its day, brick is laid out in elaborate patterns derived from wickerwork. The building's basic structural component serves simultaneously as its decoration, and a traditional architectural antithesis is overcome. The result is building of almost apparitional lightness and grace.
1201

Design for a Column House (1789)

Etienne-Louis Boullée, a visionary of the revolutionary enlightenment, fought to purify architecture of classical precedents, but his work is also marked by a melancholy consciousness of the historical—hence mortal—character of all style. Every building is a ruin in the making.
1233

Robert Frank: Gas Station (1956)
Don't look back.
1216

European Architecture to 1900

General Works

Rudolf **Arnheim**

Dynamics of Architectural Form

The principles of Gestalt psychology as they apply to the perception of three-dimensional objects and buildings; by the author of *Art and Visual Perception*

0-520-03551-8 CALIFORNIA PB $15.95

Sophia **Behling** & Stefan **Behling**

Sol Power: The Evolution of Solar Architecture

A visual chronicle of the various ways in which buildings have been designed throughout the ages to make maximum use of the power of the sun, together with a biting criticism of certain modern trends and an outline of the positive and exciting ways in which contemporary architecture can lead to energy-conscious buildings

3-7913-1670-2 PRESTEL $65.00

Francis D.K **Ching**

A Visual Dictionary of Architecture

This author is well known to all students in the field; this dictionary brings his explicit rendering and textual clarity to a wider audience

0-442-00904-6
VAN NOSTRAND REINHOLD $42.95

John **Fleming**, editor

The Penguin Dictionary of Architecture: Fourth Edition

0-14-051241-1 PENGUIN PB $13.95

Banister **Fletcher**

Sir Banister Fletcher's History of Architecture

Revised, expanded edition of the encyclopedic single-volume work. An invaluable reference

0-408-01587-X
BUTTERWORTH ARCHITECTURE $110.00

Spiro **Kostof**

A History of Architecture: Settings and Rituals

An eccentric presentation in terms of styles, literature, and social concerns

0-19-503472-4 OXFORD $65.00
0-19-503473-2 OXFORD PB $38.00

John **Onians**

Bearers of Meaning: The Classical Orders in Antiquity, the Middle Ages, and the Renaissance

The specific cultural messages borne by the orders, with emphasis on their impact on the urban viewer

0-691-04043-5 PRINCETON $89.50
0-691-00219-3 PRINCETON PB $29.95

David **Macauley**
Large format books with line drawings illustrating the fascinating design of these ancient buildings.

Cathedral: The Story of Its Construction

0-395-17513-5 HOUGHTON MIFFLIN $16.95
0-395-31668-5 HOUGHTON MIFFLIN PB $7.95

City: A Story of Roman Planning and Construction

0-395-19492-X HOUGHTON MIFFLIN $16.95
0-395-34922-2 HOUGHTON MIFFLIN PB $7.95

Pyramid

0-395-21407-6 HOUGHTON MIFFLIN $16.95
0-395-32121-2 HOUGHTON MIFFLIN PB $7.95

Nikolaus **Pevsner**

A History of Building Types

Focuses on the 19th century, from the most ceremonial buildings to the most utilitarian

0-691-09904-9 PRINCETON $95.00

An Outline of European Architecture

A classic

0-14-013524-3 PENGUIN PB $22.95

Steen Eiler **Rasmussen**

Experiencing Architecture

A reliable introduction to the idioms of architecture

0-262-68002-5 MIT PB $10.95

Witold **Rybczinski**

Home: A Short History of an Idea

The idea of "the home," the concept of comfort, the effects of invention, and how social and cultural changes influence styles of decoration and furnishing. "Serious, historically minded, and exquisitely readable"—*New Yorker*

0-14-010231-0 PENGUIN PB $12.95

The Most Beautiful House in the World

An elegant discussion of what architects do and how we experience space

0-14-010566-2 VIKING PB $8.95

Joseph **Rykwert**

The Dancing Column: On Orders of Architecture

0-262-18170-3 MIT $75.00

Mario **Salvadori**

Why Buildings Stand Up: The Strength of Architecture

0-393-30676-3 NORTON PB $11.95

John **Summerson**

The Classical Language of Architecture

Classical idioms from the ancients through the moderns

0-262-69012-8 MIT PB $6.95

Roger **Scruton**

The Aesthetics of Architecture

An inquiry into the concept of beauty by the well-known British philosopher

0-691-00322-X PRINCETON PB $18.95

Roger Scruton

David **Watkin**

A History of Western Architecture

An extensively illustrated survey by a distinguished historian

0-500-34100-1 NORTON PB $45.00

Prehistoric Monuments

Aubrey **Burl**

From Carnac to Callanish: The Prehistoric Stone Rows of Britain, Ireland, and Brittany

The first comprehensive book to discuss the rows of stones that were the focus of rituals in Britain, Ireland, and Brittany for over two thousand years, complete with distribution maps, plans, diagrams, and photographs

See also **ART**

0-300-05575-7 YALE $52.00

A Guide to The Stone Circles of Britain, Ireland, and Brittany

0-300-06331-8 YALE PB $14.00

Rodney **Castleden**

The Making of Stonehenge

0-415-08513-6 ROUTLEDGE $39.95

Jean **Clottes** & Jean **Courtin**

The Cave Beneath the Sea: Paleolithic Images at Cosquer

0-8109-4033-7 ABRAMS $60.00

Ann **MacSween** & Mick **Sharp**

Prehistoric Scotland

An evocative description, with profuse illustrations, of over 100 prehistoric sites in Scotland, from the neolithic through the Bronze and Iron Ages

0-941533-87-5 NEW AMSTERDAM $30.00

N.K. **Sandars**
Prehistoric Art in Europe
See also **THE PELICAN HISTORY OF ART** under **ART HISTORY: GENERAL STUDIES** in **ART**
0-14-056130-7 PENGUIN PB $26.50

Greek and Roman

"Practically every town of decent size in the Western world has its quota of Doric, Ionic and Corinthian. And some of the great modern buildings, from the Pantheon in Paris, to the Capitol in Washington, to the Imperial Palace in Tokyo, across Southeast Asian countries that have practically nothing to do with classical civilization and back around the world to the government structures of Leningrad, Warsaw, and Brussels, are monumental essays in the use of the orders. Greco-Roman classicism was not only the architecture of the Greeks and the Romans and of their empires, it was also the architecture, mutatis mutandis, of Romanesque Europe and of Byzantium, of the Renaissance and the Baroque, of Neoclassicism, the Baroque Revival, the Beaux Arts, and fascism; and it is even, in a peculiar but strong way, a contributor to postmodernism."—George Hersey, *The Lost Meaning of Classical Architecture*

Axel **Boethius**
Etruscan and Early Roman Architecture
From 1400 BC to the Hellenized buildings of Pompeii and Herculaneum
See also **THE ETRUSCANS AND EARLY ROME** under **FROM ANTIQUITY TO FEUDALISM** under **ANCIENT ROME** in **WORLD HISTORY AND CURRENT AFFAIRS**
0-300-05290-1 PENGUIN PB $25.00

George **Hersey**
The Lost Meaning of Classical Architecture: Speculations on Ornament from Vitruvius to Venturi
A metaphorical interpretation of the classical orders
0-262-58089-6 MIT PB $13.95

Cyril **Mango**
Byzantine Architecture
An informative account, from the early basilicas of the 4th century through the diffusion of the style in 12th-century Europe
0-8478-0615-4 RIZZOLI PB $29.95

Marcus Vitruvius **Pollio**
The Ten Books of Architecture
The classic text by the Roman architect and engineer, rediscovered and illustrated during the Renaissance, describes the classical principles of symmetry, harmony, and proportion
0-486-20645-9 DOVER PB $8.95

L. **Richardson**, Jr
Pompeii: An Architectural History
Comprehensive, up-to-date, and beautifully illustrated
0-8018-3533-X JOHNS HOPKINS $65.00

Donald **Robertson**
Greek and Roman Architecture
A handbook to the progressive achievements of the ancient world
0-521-09452-6 CAMBRIDGE PB $33.95

Vincent Joseph **Scully**
The Earth, the Temple, and the Gods: Greek Sacred
An eloquent book that examines the Greek temples' relation to the landscape
0-300-02397-9 YALE PB $23.00

Susan **Woodford**
The Parthenon
A lucid and scholarly introduction to the monument and its elaborate sculptural program
See also **ARTS** under **TOPICS IN ANCIENT GREEK HISTORY** under **ANCIENT GREECE** in **WORLD HISTORY AND CURRENT AFFAIRS**
0-521-22629-5 CAMBRIDGE PB $9.95

Gothic and Romanesque

"The spire is the simplest part of the romanesque or gothic architecture, and needs least study in order to be felt. It is a bit of sentiment almost pure of practical purpose. It tells the whole of its story at a glance, and its story is the best that architecture had to tell, for it typified the aspirations of man at the moment when man's aspirations were highest. Yet nine persons out of ten—perhaps 99 in 100—who come within sight of the two spires of Chartres will think it a jest if they are told that the smaller of the two, the simpler, the one that impresses the least, is the one which they are expected to recognize as the most perfect piece of architecture in the world."
—Henry Adams, *Mont St. Michael and Chartres*

Henry **Adams**
Mont-Saint Michael and Chartres: A Study of 13th-Century Unity
0-691-00335-1 PRINCETON PB $17.95

Jean **Bony**
French Gothic Architecture of the 12th and 13th Centuries
An excellent introduction: effective photography and numerous plans
0-520-05586-1 CALIFORNIA PB $52.50

Robert **Branner**
Burgundian Gothic Architecture
A detailed study of this important region
0-302-02751-3 RIZZOLI PB $39.95

Gothic Architecture
An authoritative account of its genesis and culminating achievements, primarily in France
0-8076-0332-5 BRAZILLER PB $10.95

St. Louis and the Court Style in Gothic Architecture
The high point of Gothic architecture in mid-13th-century Paris, and its influence throughout Europe
0-302-02753-X SOTHEBY PARKE BERNET PB $39.95

Wolfgang **Braunfelds**
Monasteries of Western Europe: The Architecture of the Orders
A major investigation of the relation of architectural style to liturgy and ritual
See also **THE MEDIEVAL AESTHETIC** under **MEDIEVAL AND RENAISSANCE EUROPE** in **WORLD HISTORY AND CURRENT AFFAIRS**
0-500-27201-8 THAMES & HUDSON PB $34.95

Caroline Astrid **Bruzelius**
The 13th-Century Church At St. Denis
The structure, chronology, and influence of the 13th-century rebuilding of the great abbey church of St. Denis
0-300-03190-4 YALE $35.00

Sumner McKnight **Crosby**
The Royal Abbey of St. Denis: From Its Beginnings to the Death of Suger, 475-1151
0-300-03143-2 YALE $75.00

Erwin **Panofsky** &
Gerda **Panofsky-Soergel**, editors
Suger, Abbot of St. Denis: Abbot Suger on the Abbey Church of St. Denis and Its Art Treasures
An invaluable anthology of archaeological, historical, and artistic documents
0-691-00314-9 PRINCETON PB $18.95

Georges **Duby**
The Age of the Cathedrals: Art and Society, 980-1240
A survey of medieval mentalities as reflected in the architecture of the monastery, the cathedral, and the palace
0-226-16770-4 CHICAGO PB $17.95

Alain **Erlande-Branenberg**
Cathedrals and Castles: Building in The Middle Ages
TRANSLATED BY ROSEMARY STONEHEWER
0-8109-2812-4 ABRAMS PB $12.95

Louis **Grodecki**
Gothic Architecture
A well-illustrated volume tracing its 400-year dominance in Europe; with tables and bibliography
0-8478-0473-9 RIZZOLI PB $29.95

Hans Erich **Kubach**
Romanesque Architecture
A well-illustrated survey
0-8478-0920-X RIZZOLI PB $29.95

Erwin **Panofsky**
Gothic Architecture and Scholasticism: An Inquiry into the Analogy of the Arts, Philosophy, and Religion in the Middle Ages
How architectural style and structure replicated scholastic definitions of the order and form of thought
See also **THE MEDIEVAL AESTHETIC** under **MEDIEVAL AND RENAISSANCE EUROPE** in **WORLD HISTORY AND CURRENT AFFAIRS**
0-452-00995-2 NEW AMERICAN LIBRARY PB $12.95

Whitney **Stoddard**

Art and Architecture in Medieval France

Recommended for its historic overviews and attempts to relate artistic production to the political realities of the time. Best on the Gothic period

See also MEDIEVAL ART: 600–1400 under EUROPEAN ART: BYZANTINE AND MEDIEVAL in ART

0-06-430022-6 ICON PB $24.00

The Gothic Cathedral

Robert **Branner**

Chartres Cathedral

A thorough introduction to the great cathedral, with critical essays and illustrations

0-393-09851-6 NORTON PB $8.95

Jean **Gimpel**

The Cathedral Builders

A vivid, illustrated account of the construction of Gothic cathedrals emphasizing technical, political, and aesthetic considerations

0-06-091158-1 HARPERPERENNIAL PB $13.00

Stephen **Murray**

Beauvais Cathedral: Architecture of Transcendence

0-691-04236-5 PRINCETON $65.00

Notre-Dame Cathedral of Amiens: The Power of Change

0-521-49735-3 CAMBRIDGE $95.00

Otto von **Simson**

The Gothic Cathedral

A convincing thesis—that Gothic cathedrals must be understood in terms of the religious experience of the High Middle Ages

0-691-01867-7 PRINCETON PB $15.95

Edwin **Smith** & Olive **Cook**

English Cathedrals

A visual and social history

0-906969-62-X NEW AMSTERDAM $40.00

Christopher **Wilson**

The Gothic Cathedral

0-500-34105-2 THAMES & HUDSON PB $39.95

Italian Renaissance

Giulio **Argan**

The Renaissance City

0-8076-0521-2 BRAZILLER PB $9.95

Jacob **Burckhardt**

The Architecture of the Italian Renaissance

Impressive for its methodology and cohesive theory of a social and typological history of architecture

0-226-08049-8 CHICAGO PB $29.95

David **Coffin**

The Villa in the Life of Renaissance Rome

The change in function of the country residence from a productive farm to a center of pleasurable relaxation

See also RENAISSANCE CITIES under RENAISSANCE ITALY AND THE COMING OF HUMANISM under MEDIEVAL AND RENAISSANCE EUROPE in WORLD HISTORY AND CURRENT AFFAIRS

0-691-00279-7 PRINCETON PB $26.95

Tracey E. **Cooper**

Renaissance

A handbook of Renaissance arts, style, and architecture, as they spread from Italy to French Chateaux, German town halls, and English country houses

0-7892-0023-6 ABBEVILLE $12.95

Michele **Furnari**

Formal Design in Renaissance Architecture: From Brunelleschi to Palladio

A formal analyses of 100 of the most important buildings of the Italian Renaissance, including plans, sections, elevations, perspectives, and axonometrics

0-8478-1890-X RIZZOLI $50.00
0-8478-1860-8 RIZZOLI PB $30.00

Peter **Murray**

The Architecture of the Italian Renaissance

A good introduction

0-8052-0807-0 SCHOCKEN PB $16.00

Geoffrey **Scott**

The Architecture of Humanism: A Study in the History of Taste

An aesthetic theory of the Renaissance style, beautifully written

0-8446-1399-1 SMITH $14.50

Rudolf **Wittkower**

Architectural Principles in the Age of Humanism

Through a study of the theory and practice of Alberti and Palladio, this work proves that the forms of Renaissance architecture were charged with the symbolic values of contemporary humanism

0-312-02082-1 ST. MARTIN'S $35.00
0-393-00599-2 NORTON PB $9.95

Heinrich **Wölfflin**

Renaissance and Baroque

A study of independent development in architecture from its maturity during the High Renaissance to its decline in the second half of the 16th century

See also THEORY AND CRITICISM under ART HISTORY: GENERAL STUDIES in ART

0-8014-9046-4 CORNELL PB $16.95

Contemporary Sources

Leon Battista **Alberti**

On the Art of Building in Ten Books

A new English translation, richly annotated and illustrated with prints from the 1550 Italian edition

0-262-51060-X MIT PB $25.00

The Ten Books of Architecture

Reprint of the 1755 English edition of the original *De Re Aedificatoria*. The first modern work on architecture

0-486-25239-6 DOVER PB $14.95

Andrea **Palladio**

The Four Books of Architecture

Reprint of the 1738 English edition based on the original 1570 Venetian edition. Discusses the orders, building techniques, public and private buildings, Roman temples, and includes Palladio's own inventions

0-486-21308-0 DOVER PB $14.95

Sebastiano **Serlio**

The Five Books of Architecture

Incorporating extensive illustrations on geometry and perspective, the orders, building types, and planning, this treatise influenced Europe throughout the Renaissance

0-486-24349-4 DOVER PB $17.95

Architects

Giulio Carol **Argan** & others

Michelangelo Architect

A profusely illustrated volume that offers new insights into Michelangelo's architectural projects. Designs, plans, contracts, correspondence, and extracts from the artist's "poetry-diary" reveal that architecture was an integral part of his intellectual and artistic development

See also INDIVIDUAL ARTISTS under ITALY under EUROPEAN ART: THE RENAISSANCE in ART

0-8109-3638-0 ABRAMS $125.00

Alexander **Liberman**, photographer

Campidoglio: Michelangelo's Roman Capital

Photographs by the inimitable Liberman and text by Nobel Prize-winner Joseph Brodsky document and illustrate one of the Renaissance's great architectural triumphs. The Roman Capital, reconstructed by Michelangelo in the 16th century, is a key not only to antiquity but to the conception of public space in the Renaissance. A unique testament to the power of sculpture in a dramatic setting. Liberman's beautiful color pictures are not to be missed

0-679-43052-0 RANDOM HOUSE $75.00

James **Ackerman**

The Architecture of Michelangelo

A definitive study, with extensive bibliography

0-226-00240-3 CHICAGO PB $23.95

Bruce **Boucher**

Andrea Palladio: The Architect in His Time

An insightful study of the architect's life and work, with newly commissioned photography, set against the backdrop of the events and personalities of his time and richly illustrated with period drawings

1-55859-381-0 ABBEVILLE $95.00

Joseph **Farber** & others

Palladio's Architecture and Its Influence: A Photographic Guide

0-486-23922-5 DOVER PB $9.95

Palladio

A classic introduction to his theory and works

0-14-013500-6 VIKING PB $12.95

Caroline **Constant**

The Palladio Guide

A succinct guide to all the major edifices

1-87827-185-7 PRINCETON ARCHITECTURAL PB .. $19.95

Vincent **Scully**

The Villas of Palladio

A photographic documentation

0-8212-1898-0 BULFINCH PB $35.00

Christoph L. **Frommel** & others, editors

The Architectural Drawings of Antonio da Sangallo the Younger and His Circle

Drawings from the archive of one of the most productive architectural teams in early modern Europe

0-262-06155-4 MIT $95.00

Deborah **Howard**

Jacopo Sansovino: Architecture and Patronage in Renaissance Venice

Arriving in Venice in 1527, Sansovino introduced the Roman High Renaissance style. His important commissions are perceptively studied and presented

0-300-03890-9 YALE PB $19.00

Paolo **Galluzzi**, editor

Leonardo da Vinci: Engineer and Architect

Includes a large selection of drawings, models, and reconstructions

2891920848 MCCLELLAND & STEWART $49.95

Leonardo da Vinci

English Renaissance

James **Lees-Milne**

The Age of Inigo Jones

0-403-03878-2 SOMERSET $39.00

John **Summerson**

Architecture in Britain, 1530-1830

Introduced into England during the reign of Henry VIII, classical architecture flourished for over 300 years

0-14-056103-X PENGUIN PB $26.50

Simon **Thurley**

The Royal Palaces of Tudor England

An intriguing look at English architecture and life at court, from the two-room lodging of the Plantagenets, to the 60 houses of Henry VIII

0-300-05420-3 YALE $55.00

Rudolf **Wittkower**

Palladio and English Palladianism

A collection of essays on Inigo Jones and the adoption of Renaissance architecture in Britain

0-500-27296-4 THAMES & HUDSON PB $18.95

Country Houses

James **Crathorne**

Cliveden: The English Country Home of the American Astors

A new history of the great English country house and its magnificent contents

1-85585-223-3 TRAFALGAR SQUARE $55.00

Mark **Girouard**

Life in the English Country House

Designed for pleasure as well as status, country houses have created the habits, diversions, and obligations of the English upper classes

See also **ENGLISH DECORATION** under **INTERIOR DECORATION**

0-300-02273-5 YALE $55.00

0-300-05870-5 YALE PB $27.50

Robert Smythson and the Elizabethan Country House

The country house is used to discuss the history and ideals of Elizabethan and Jacobean architecture. Richly illustrated

0-300-02389-8 YALE PB $25.00

Baroque and Rococo

Italy

Paul Freart **de Chantelou**

Diary of the Cavaliere: Bernini's Visit to France in 1665

The 66-year-old Bernini arrived in Paris commissioned to redesign the Louvre. Chantelou, assigned by the king to attend him, kept a dary of the visit

See also **LOUIS XIV AND THE ANCIEN REGIME** under **EARLY MODERN FRANCE** under **EARLY MODERN EUROPE** in **WORLD HISTORY AND CURRENT AFFAIRS**

0-691-04028-1 PRINCETON $54.50

Howard **Hibbard**

Bernini

An excellent introduction to Bernini's extraordinary fusion of sculpture and architecture

See also **THE BAROQUE IN ITALY** under **EUROPEAN ART: BAROQUE AND ROCOCO** in **ART**

0-14-020701-5 PENGUIN PB $12.00

Tod A. **Marder**

Bernini's Scala Regia at the Vatican Palace

0-521-43198-0 CAMBRIDGE $25.00

Anthony **Blunt**

Borromini

An excellent overview of the world of the most innovative of Italian baroque architects

0-674-07926-4 HARVARD PB $17.95

Richard **Krautheimer**

The Rome of Alexander VII, 1655-1667

The New Rome as envisioned by Alexander and his architect Bernini

0-691-00277-0 PRINCETON PB $16.95

Cavaliere Bernini

Harold Alan **Meek**

Guarino Guarini and His Architecture

Poised between rationalism and mysticism, the principles and buildings of this 17th-century priest, architect, and theologian epitomize a turning point in the history of architecture

0-300-03989-1 YALE $65.00

0-300-04748-7 YALE PB $30.00

John **Varriano**

Italian Baroque and Rococo Architecture

A general survey incorporating recent research and illustrated with period views, plans, and details

0-19-503548-8 OXFORD PB $28.00

Rudolf **Wittkower**

Art and Architecture in Italy, 1600-1750

A first-rate survey; composed by a master scholar of Italian painting, sculpture, and architecture

See also **THE PELICAN HISTORY OF ART** under **ART HISTORY: GENERAL STUDIES** in **ART**

0-300-05306-1 YALE $60.00
0-300-05308-8 YALE PB $27.50

France

Hilary **Ballon**

The Paris of Henri IV: Architecture and Urbanism

An original account of the crucial period between 1605 and 1610 when Paris was transformed from a medieval city decimated by war and neglect into a modern capital by a building program unmatched in France for more than two centuries

0-262-52197-0 MIT PB $20.00

Robert **Berger**

In the Garden of the Sun King: Studies in the Park of Versailles Under Louis XIV

It is the garden at Versailles, more than the grandeur of its exteriors or the virtuosity of its interiors, that reveals the complex mythology of the French monarchy

0-88402-141-6 DUMBARTON OAKS $35.00

Louis XIV

Anthony **Blunt**

Art and Architecture in France, 1500-1700

A good introduction, written by the authority on Poussin; stresses the Italian influence on the development of early French art

0-300-05314-2 PENGUIN PB $25.00

Francois Mansart and the Origin of French Architecture

The architect who perfected the French tradition, and whose work showed little influence from abroad

1-87859-212-2 NATIVE AMERICAN BOOKS $59.00

Genevieve **Bresc**

The Louvre: An Architectural History

A lavish visual history of the evolution of the great urban complex

0-86565-963-X VENDOME $75.00

Rosalys **Coope**

Salomon De Brosse & the Development of the Classical Style in French Architecture from 1565 to 1630

A coherent conception of classicism in which the use of the orders produced the first examples of an essentially French character

0-271-00140-2 PENN STATE $60.00

Michael **Dennis**

Court and Garden: From the French Hotel to the City of Modern Architecture

A detailed, illustrated history of the aristocratic town house developed in Paris between 1500 and 1790

0-262-54051-7 MIT PB $30.00

Jean **Dethier**, editor

Chateaux Bordeaux: Wine, Architecture, and Civilization

Richly illustrated survey of the great wine chateaux

INTRODUCTION BY HUGH JOHNSON

1-55859-494-9 CROSS RIVER $45.00

Philippe **Seydoux**

Chateaux of the Val de Loire

An invaluable photographic reference book for the cultural tourist, giving unparalleled coverage to over 300 great chateaux

0-86565-134-5 VENDOME $50.00

Spain

George **Kubler**

Building the Escorial

A chronicle of Philip II's grandiose monastery and palace, built to commemorate victory over the French

0-691-03975-5 PRINCETON $70.00

Earl **Rosenthal**

The Palace of Charles V in Granada

A masterful interpretation of imperial iconography

0-691-04034-6 PRINCETON $95.00

England

Kerry **Downes**

Vanbrugh

A study of the architect's monumental projects

0-302-02769-6 RIZZOLI $125.00

Vaughan **Hart**

St. Paul's Cathedral, London 1675-1710 Architect: Christopher Wren

0-7148-2998-6 PHAIDON PB $29.95

James **Milne**

English Country Houses: Baroque, 1685-1715

1-85149-043-4 ANTIQUE COLLECTORS $59.50

Marcus **Whiffen**

Thomas Archer: Architect of the English Baroque

For his free use of curves and his imitation of Bernini and Borromini, Archer has been called the most baroque of English architects

0-912158-23-9 HENNESSEY $12.95

Giles **Worsley**

Classical Architecture in Britain

A comprehensive reassessment of British architecture in the 17th and 18th centuries and an analysis of its influence on building in Europe and America

0-300-05896-9 YALE $55.00

Northern Europe

Jorge **Guillermo**

Dutch Houses and Castles

A richly illustrated introduction to the glories of Dutch domestic architecture and interiors, both public and private

See also **OTHER DECORATIVE STYLES** under **INTERIOR DECORATION**

0-935748-94-6 SCALA $55.00

Samuel John **Klingensmith** & others, editors

The Utility of Splendor: Ceremony, Social Life, and Architecture at the Court of Bavaria, 1600-1800

0-226-44330-2 CHICAGO $47.50

Wolfgang **Kraus** & Peter **Müller**

Palaces of Vienna

Interiors decorated by grandees of unparalleled wealth, many of them inaccessible to the public and published for the first time

0-86565-132-9 VENDOME $60.00

Jiri **Pesek** & Zdenek **Hojda**

The Palaces of Prague

A lavish presentation of the glittering palaces that give witness to three Golden Ages of the Bohemian—the 14th-century Flamboyant Gothic of Charles IV, the 16th-century Renaissance of Rudolph II, and the grandiose elaboration of the mid-17th-century Counter-Reformation

0-86565-958-3 VENDOME $65.00

18th and 19th Centuries

James **Cracraft**

The Petrine Revolution in Russian Architecture

Recounts how modern architectural standards supplanted traditional norms following the massive infusion of foreign expertise initiated by Peter the Great

0-226-11664-6 CHICAGO $45.00

Peter the Great

Henry Russell **Hitchcock**

Architecture: The 19th and 20th Centuries

A comprehensive chronology of buildings and standards of taste from 1800 through Le Corbusier's pilgrimage chapel at Ronchamp

0-300-05320-7 YALE PB $28.50

Emile **Kaufmann**

Architecture in the Age of Reason: Baroque and Post-Baroque Architecture in England, Italy and France

A pioneering study of architecture's cultural and philosophical links to the Enlightenment

0-486-21928-3 DOVER PB $8.95

Lionel **Lambourne**

The Aesthetic Movement

0-7148-3000-3 PHAIDON $59.95

John **Summerson**

The Architecture of the Eighteenth Century

An elegant and amply illustrated account of the period of "class perfection" by England's leading architectural historian

0-500-20202-8 THAMES & HUDSON PB $14.95

David **Watkin**

The Rise of Architectural History

A survey of architectural theory and criticism as it emerged simultaneously in English literature on taste, in French treatises, and in works by the German founders of the history of art

0-89860-040-5 EASTVIEW EDITIONS $18.00

Italy

G.B. **Piranesi** & Herschel **Levit**

Views of Rome: Then and Now

0-486-23339-1 DOVER PB $14.95

John **Wilton-Ely**

Piranesi as Architect and Designer

The first book to examine the actual architectural and design activities of the artist best known for his visionary prints of architectural fantasies

0-300-05382-7 YALE $45.00

England, Scotland, Ireland, and Wales

Hugh **Cantlie**

Ancestral Castles of Scotland

A history of Scottish castles, from the large and famous to smaller family homes, which links each structure with great events in Scottish history

1-85585-118-0 TRAFALGAR SQUARE PB $19.95

Wendy **Kaplan**, editor

Charles Rennie Mackintosh

1-55859-791-3 ABBEVILLE $60.00

Hugh **Montgomery-Massingberd**

Great Houses of England and Wales

An architectural and social history of what Evelyn Waugh called "Britain's chief national artistic achievement," full of memorable characters, anecdotes, and insights and complete with photographs of landscapes, gardens and interiors

0-8478-1824-1 RIZZOLI $75.00

Stefan **Muthesius**

The English Terraced House

A survey of townhouse types throughout London and western England

0-300-02871-7 YALE $50.00
0-300-03176-9 YALE PB $25.00

John **Nash**

Views of the Royal Pavillion

The complete aquatints from 1827 of the fanciful structure in Brighton

COMMENTARY BY GERVASE JACKSON-STOPS
FOREWORD BY HRH THE PRINCE OF WALES

1-55859-340-3 ABBEVILLE $19.98

Neoclassicism

John **Lowrey**, editor

Robert Adam

0-7486-0462-6 EDINBURGH PB $25.00

Robert **Adam**

The Works in Architecture of Robert and James Adam

0-404-17233-4 AMS $135.00

John **Harris**

Sir William Chambers

Chambers differed from other 18th-century architects in the range and depth of his interests and scholarship, epitomized in his treatise on civil architecture of 1759

0-300-06940-5 YALE $55.00

Peter **Leach**

James Paine

A leading exponent of English Palladianism

0-302-00602-8 SOTHEBY PARKE BERNET $95.00

John **Summerson**

John Soane

Essays that identify the principal features of Soane's architecture and set his work in historical context. Richly illustrated with original watercolors and plans

0-312-44462-1 ST. MARTIN'S $45.00
0-312-44461-3 ST. MARTIN'S PB $30.00

Diane **Stillman**

English Neo-classical Architecture

A massive, two-volume survey, beautifully illustrated and produced

0-302-00601-X ZWEMMER $295.00

David **Watkin**

Athenian Stuart: Pioneer of the Greek Revival

The architect who first published full measurements of the buildings of Athens, thus introducing the Greek Revival into England

0-04-720027-8 UNWIN HYMAN PB $9.95

Gothic Revival

Kenneth **Clark**

The Gothic Revival: An Essay in the History of Taste

0-7195-5454-3 MURRAY PB $24.95

Charles **Eastlake**

History of the Gothic Revival

Reprint of the first scholarly study of its social, stylistic, and iconographic characteristics

0-89257-035-0 AMERICAN LIFE PB $10.00

James **Massey** & Shirley **Maxwell**

Gothic Revival

A concise handbook to the movement's key figures and accomplishments, with a timeline and a list of landmark and preservation societies

1-55859-823-5 ABBEVILLE $12.95

Michael **McCarthy**

The Origins of the Gothic Revival

Focuses on Horace Walpole, his contemporaries, and two major principles of the Gothic revival: fidelity to historical precedents, and the use of irregularity or lack of symmetry in planning

0-300-03723-6 YALE $47.50

John **Ruskin**

The Seven Lamps of Architecture

See also 19TH-CENTURY PROSE under THE 19TH CENTURY in LITERATURE OF THE BRITISH ISLES

0-374-50188-2 FS&G PB $8.95

Michael **Brooks**

John Ruskin and Victorian Architecture

The influence of early 19th-century architecture on Ruskin, and Ruskin's influence in England and America

0-8135-1205-0 RUTGERS $40.00

Queen Anne and Victorian

Mark **Girouard**

Sweetness and Light: The Queen Anne Movement, 1860-1900

A lively account of this transitional style and its important contributions to English country house design

0-300-03068-1 YALE PB $27.50

The Victorian Country House

The social and architectural concerns of country life

0-300-03472-5 YALE PB $30.00

0-300-02390-1 YALE $50.00

Henry Russell **Hitchcock**

Early Victorian Architecture in Great Britain

0-306-80036-5 DA CAPO PB $7.95

Nikolaus **Pevsner**

Studies in Art, Architecture and Design: Victorian and After

Explores the intricacies of Victorian eclecticism and its vision of the past and the future

0-691-03998-4 PRINCETON PB $59.50

John **Summerson**

The Architecture of Victorian London

Although lacking a general plan, the rebuilding of London during the 19th century involved almost every section of the city

0-8139-0592-3 VIRGINIA $14.95

Victorian and Edwardian Architects

Richard A. **Fellows**

Sir Reginald Blomfield: An Edwardian Architect

Blomfield advocated a tradition of restrained, un-self-conscious classicism in his work and writings

0-302-00590-0 SOTHEBY PARKE BERNET PB $29.95

Christopher **Hussey**

The Life of Sir Edwin Lutyens

0-907462-59-6 APOLLO $69.50

Frank **Jackson**

Sir Raymond Unwin: Architect, Planner and Visionary

Unwin's failure to reconcile medieval nostalgia with bureaucratic control set the stage for later English town planning

0-302-00591-9 SOTHEBY PARKE BERNET PB $29.95

Arts and Crafts

William **Lethaby**

Architecture, Mysticism, and Myth

An evocative account of the importance of mythology for this thinker, teacher, architect, and promoter of the first architectural workshop to gain official recognition in Britain

1-87361-605-8 SOLOS PB $12.95

France

Barry **Bergdoll**

Leon Vaudoyer: Historicism in the Age of Industry

0-262-02380-6 MIT $65.00

Allan **Braham**

The Architecture of the French Enlightenment

The major developments in architectural thought and practice of the period

0-520-06739-8 CALIFORNIA PB $34.95

J.C. **Lemagny** & Dominique De **Menil**

Visionary Architects: Boullée, Ledoux, Lequeu

Seminal figures behind the late 18th-century reaction to the excesses of the Baroque and Rococo

0-914412-21-3 MENIL PB $27.95

Christopher **Tadgell**

Ange Jacques Gabriel

France's finest 18th-century architect brought the French classical tradition to its ultimate achievement

0-302-02781-5 RIZZOLI $125.00

E.E. **Viollet-le-Duc**

Lectures on Architecture

Volume 1

Major documents of 19th-century architectural literature

0-486-25520-4 DOVER PB $13.95

Volume 2

0-486-25521-2 DOVER PB $13.95

Germany

Barry **Bergdoll**

Karl Friedrich Schinkel: An Architecture for Prussia

PHOTOGRAPHS BY ERICH LESSING

0-8478-1527-7 RIZZOLI $55.00

John **Zukowsky**, editor

Karl Friedrich Schinkel 1781-1841: The Drama of Architecture

3-8030-2822-1 D.A.P. $70.00

Wolfgang **Herrmann**

Gottfried Semper: In Search of Architecture

First English monograph on one of the leading 19th-century architectural theorists, the most admired architect in Germany of the generation after Schinkel

0-262-08144-X MIT $52.50

David **Watkin** & Tilman **Mellinghoff**

German Architecture and the Classical Ideal

Extensively illustrated account of classicism's impact on palaces, houses, public buildings, and on urban planning throughout the 18th and 19th centuries

0-262-23125-5 MIT $65.00

Traditional Architecture of Asia, Africa, and the Middle East

Viacheslav I. **Atroshenko** & Milton **Grundy**

Mediterranean Vernacular

200 color photographs illuminate the exceptional architectural traditions of the sunny villages of Italy, Spain, Greece, Morocco, and Tunisia. The text elucidates the history and the influence of Mediterranean buildings on modern design

0-8478-1386-X RIZZOLI $45.00

Susan **Denyer**

African Traditional Architecture

0-8419-0287-9 HOLMES & MEIER $48.00

Teiji **Itoh**

The Elegant Japanese House: Traditional Sukiya Architecture

A beautiful book on what is considered the culmination of traditional Japanese domestic architecture

0-8348-1500-1 WEATHERHILL $150.00

Chuji **Kawashima**

Minka: Traditional Houses of Rural Japan

A throughly illustrated account of the structure, material, and building techniques of Japan's pre-modern rural dwellings

0-87011-721-1 KODANSHA $100.00

Ronald G. **Knapp**

China's Vernacular Architecture: House Form and Culture

0-8248-1204-2 HAWAII $38.00

Edward **Morse**

Japanese Homes and Their Surroundings

The most authoritative description of Japanese domestic architecture, first published in 1886

0-8048-0998-4 TUTTLE PB $16.95

Kenizé **Mourad** & Jérôme **Darblay**

Living in Istanbul

Istanbul is a city where the quarters remain divided by what the Byzantine historian Procopius called a "garland of waters." Visually we enter private homes, delicate wooden *yalis* and magnificent palaces on the shore of the Bosporus, visit the Egyptian market, watch the craftsmen in the *hans* create kilims, carpets, painted tiles, and end up in the bustling center of this timeless cosmopolis

2-08-013563-5 ABBEVILLE $45.00

María Sáenz **Quesada**

Estancias: The Great Houses and Ranches of Argentina

Color survey of rural Argentine elegance

1-55859-270-9 ABBEVILLE $65.00

American Architecture to 1900

This section includes premodern American architecture, with later developments to be found under 20th-Century Architecture. The division is not strict since many architects included here in American Architecture clearly belong to 20th-Century Architecture as well.

General Works

Wayne **Andrews**

Architecture, Ambition, and the Americans

A social history of American architecture

0-02-900750-X FREE PRESS PB $14.95

Architect's Emergency Committee

Great Georgian Houses of America

Volume 1

A large-format pictorial reference with black-and-white plates

0-486-22491-0 DOVER PB $15.95

Volume 2

0-486-22492-9 DOVER PB $14.95

Catherine **Beecher** & Harriet Beecher **Stowe**

The American Woman's Home

A 19th-century work on the relation of women's social status to architectural design

0-917482-04-2 STOWE-DAY PB $12.95

David **Handin**

American Architecture: A Critical History

Covers the main developments from the colonial style through modernism

0-500-20200-1 THAMES & HUDSON PB $12.95

Clay **Lancaster**

The American Bungalow, 1880-1930

A thorough study of the widespread architectural style

0-486-28678-9 DOVER PB $17.95

Lewis **Mumford**

"Mumford is one of the most sensitive critics of the world we see about us; he has been one of the most energetic, sincere, and completely devoted apologists of modern architecture in both the US and Great Britain; a 20th-century Ruskin, he has educated a whole generation to the understanding of his enthusiasm and the appreciation of his prejudice."—Colin Rowe

The Brown Decades: A Study of the Arts in America, 1865-1895

See also **HISTORY, POLITICS, AND SOCIETY** under **20TH-CENTURY AMERICAN ESSAYS AND JOURNALISM** in **LITERATURE OF THE AMERICAS**

0-486-20200-3 DOVER PB $6.95

Lewis Mumford

Roots of Contemporary American Architecture

Thirty-seven essays dealing with the mid-19th century onwards and representing the chief critical traditions in today's architecture

0-486-22072-9 DOVER PB $11.95

Sticks and Stones

Investigates the evolution of architectural style in the US and reveals its relationship to broader cultural trends

0-486-20202-X DOVER PB $5.95

Peter **Nabokov** & Robert **Easton**

Native American Architecture

Rich and fully illustrated, with detailed chapters on the wigwam, longhouse, chickee, earthlodge, tipi, pit house, iglu, tent, plank house, hogan, ki, and ramada

0-19-503781-2 OXFORD $65.00
0-19-506665-0 OXFORD PB $29.95

William **Pierson**, Jr. & William **Jordy**

American Buildings and Their Architects

Volume 1

The Colonial and Neo-Classical Styles

The most comprehensive survey available, regularly updated. Volumes two and three are currently out of print

0-19-504216-6 OXFORD PB $19.95

Volume 4

Progressive and Academic Ideals at the Turn of the 20th Century

0-19-504218-2 OXFORD PB $19.95

Volume 5

The Impact of European Modernism in the Mid-20th Century

0-19-504219-0 OXFORD PB $19.95

Henry Hope **Reed**

Golden City

The controversy between the "modern" and the "classical" tradition with an eloquent denunciation of the former

0-393-00547-X NORTON PB $4.95

William **Seale**

The President's House: A History

"Before I end my letter, I pray Heaven to bestow the best of Blessings on this House and all that shall hereafter inhabit it. May none but honest and wise Men ever rule under this roof"
—John Adams, on his second evening in the damp, unfinished rooms of the White House

0-8109-1490-5 ABRAMS $39.95

G.E. Kidder **Smith**

Source Book of American Architecture

An unprecedented masterwork, surveying 500 of America's most distinguished buildings, spanning over a thousand years of architectural development

1-56898-024-8 PRINCETON ARCHITECTURAL $50.00
1-56898-025-6 PRINCETON ARCHITECTURAL PB $34.95

Paul Venable **Turner**

Campus: An American Planning Tradition

From Jefferson's University of Virginia through the modern age, the university campus has witnessed a long tradition of experimentation in design

0-262-70032-8 MIT PB $25.00

William **Ware**

The American Vignola: A Guide to the Making of Classical Architecture

Reprint of the highly influential treatise containing measured drawings of the classical orders. First published in 1902

0-486-28310-0 DOVER PB $8.95

Marcus **Whiffen**

American Architecture Since 1780: A Guide to the Styles

A useful reference work

0-262-23034-8 MIT $30.00
0-262-73097-9 MIT PB $16.50

Marcus **Whiffen** & Frederick **Koeper**

American Architecture

Volume 1

1607-1860

A valuable overview

0-262-73069-3 MIT PB $20.00

Volume 2

1860-1976

0-262-73070-7 MIT PB $20.00

Premodern Architectural Styles

Colonial

Roger G. **Kennedy** & David **Larkin**

Mission: The History and Architecture of the Missions of North America

0-395-63416-4 HOUGHTON MIFFLIN $45.00

Rexford **Newcomb**

Spanish-Colonial Architecture in the United States

0-486-26263-4 DOVER PB $12.95

Allen **Noble**

Wood, Brick and Stone: The North American Landscape

Volume 1: Houses

An excellent account of early vernacular architecture

0-87023-411-0 MASSACHUSETTS $35.00

0-87023-410-2 MASSACHUSETTS PB $18.95

Volume 2: Barns and Farm Structures

0-87023-518-4 MASSACHUSETTS $18.95

Greek Revival

Robert Kent **Sutton**

Americans Interpret the Parthenon: The Progression of Greek Revival Architecture from the East Coast to Oregon, 1800-1860

0-87081-259-9 COLORADO $35.00

American Renaissance and Victorian

Edmund **Gillon** & Clay **Lancaster**

Victorian Houses: A Treasury of Lesser-Known Examples

Over 100 photographs and individual commentaries

0-486-22966-1 DOVER PB $9.95

Arnold **Lewis** & Kate **Morgan**

American Victorian Architecture

Essential documents and monuments reproduced and briefly discussed

0-486-23177-1 DOVER PB $12.95

Vincent **Scully**

The Shingle Style and the Stick Style: Architectural Theory and Design from Richardson to the Origins of Wright

The definitive study of the complex inspirations and cultural influences fused in the wooden suburban and resort buildings of the 1870s and 1880s

0-300-01519-4 YALE PB $22.00

Regional Architecture

Henry Russell **Hitchcock**

Rhode Island Architecture

Rhode Island has some of the finest examples of pre-modern American architecture

0-306-71037-4 DA CAPO $42.50

Lisa **Mahar-Keplinger**

Grain Elevators

"Anyone who's ever seen the immense grain elevators scattered like cathedrals across the American landscape will be enchanted with this beautifully designed and illustrated book"
—*Travel Books Worldwide*

1-87827-135-0 PRINCETON ARCHITECTURAL PB .. $19.95

Hermann Valentin **von Holst**

Country and Suburban Homes of the Prairie School Period

A reprint of the 1913 edition of one of American architecture's finest primary sources of residential design. Over 400 photographs and finely rendered plans

0-486-24373-7 DOVER PB $9.95

American Cities

"The architects of this land and generation are now brought face to face with something new under the sun—namely that evolution and integration of social conditions, that special grouping of them, that results in a demand for the erection of tall office buildings... Problem: How shall we impart to this sterile pile, this crude, harsh, brutal agglomeration, this stark, staring exclamation of eternal strife, the graciousness of those higher forms of sensibility and culture that rest on the lower and fiercer passions? How shall we proclaim from the dizzy height of this strange, weird modern housetop the peaceful evangel of sentiment, of beauty, the cult of a higher life?"—Louis Sullivan, 1896

Stanley **Appelbaum**

The Chicago World's Fair of 1893: A Photographic Record

A brief overview of the fair's plans and concepts, with a discussion of the personalities, rivalries and controversy surrounding its Beaux-Arts architecture

0-486-23990-X DOVER PB $9.95

Ira **Bach**

Chicago's Famous Buildings: A Photographic Guide to the City's Architectural Landmarks and Other Notable Buildings

0-226-74061-7 CHICAGO $27.50

0-226-74062-5 CHICAGO PB $10.95

Reyner **Banham**

Los Angeles

In this entertaining book, Banham sets the works of designers as diverse as Frank Lloyd Wright, Charles Eames, Richard Neutra, and Watts Towers constructor Simon Rodia in their geographical and man-made contexts

0-14-021178-0 PENGUIN PB $10.00

Carl **Condit**

The Chicago School of Architecture: A History of Commercial and Public Building in the Chicago Area, 1875-1925

A thoroughly illustrated work, from William Le Baron's early functional innovations to their imaginative development by Louis Sullivan and Frank Lloyd Wright

0-226-11455-4 CHICAGO PB $28.50

Phyllis **Lambert** & Alan **Stewart**, editors

Opening the Gates of Eighteenth-Century Montreal

0-262-62086-3 MIT PB $15.95

George A. **Larson** & Jay **Pridmore**

Chicago Architecture and Design

Chicago became a center for creative trends and new technologies in the aftermath of the Great Fire of 1871. This book handsomely documents the influential structures that resulted and is the first major examination of the city's finest buildings to fully explore their interior spaces

0-8109-3192-3 ABRAMS $49.50

Patrick **McGrew** & Robert **Julian**

Landmarks of Los Angeles

A complete guide to over 500 officially protected sites and a richly rewarding architectural and social history of Los Angeles since its days as a missionary outpost

0-8109-3572-4 ABRAMS $49.50

Susan **Southworth** & Michael **Southworth**

Aia Guide to Boston

0-87106-188-0 GLOBE PEQUOT PB $19.95

Larry **Viskochil**

Chicago At the Turn of the Century in Photographs

Historic views from the collections of the Chicago Historical Society

0-486-24656-6 DOVER PB $12.95

Carol **Willis**

Form Follows Finance: Skyscrapers and Skylines in New York and Chicago

Beautifully written and richly illustrated, this brilliant study expands architectural history, taking us behind facades and explaining downtown areas in three dimensions of form, space, and money"—Kenneth Jackson, editor, *The Encyclopedia of New York City*

1-56898-070-1 PRINCETON ARCHITECTURAL........$35.00
1-56898-044-2 PRINCETON ARCHITECTURAL PB..$22.50

John **Zukowsky**, editor

Chicago Architecture, 1872-1922: Birth of a Metropolis

Catalog of an important recent exhibition highlighting the city's achievements during the classical revival in modernism

3-7913-0837-8 PRESTEL........$70.00

New York City

Andrew **Alpern**

New York's Fabulous Luxury Apartments

Over 100 floor plans and black-and-white photographs splendidly reveal the architectural and decorative details of life at the top

0-486-25318-X DOVER PB........$7.95

Stanley **Appelbaum**

The New York World's Fair, 1939-1940

A history of the people and principles involved

0-486-23494-0 DOVER PB........$9.95

Daniel **Badger**

Badger's Illustrated Catalogue of Cast-Iron Architecture

A reprint of the 1865 catalog. In many ways, cast-iron buildings represented the beginning of mass-production and foreshadowed the modern steel-frame skyscraper

0-486-24223-4 DOVER PB........$10.95

Barbaralee **Diamonstein**

The Landmarks of New York II

A revised, updated, and expanded edition of the author's acclaimed *Landmarks of New York*, documenting more than 936 landmarks in five boroughs. "Much more than just an encyclopedia—the book is a pleasure to read, for here one can indulge oneself in the very best of New York"—Paul Goldberger, *NY Times*

0-8109-3569-4 ABRAMS........$49.50

Margot **Gayle** & Edmund **Gillon**

Cast-Iron Architecture in New York

A pictorial anthology of commercial structures typical of mid-19th-century New York

0-486-22980-7 DOVER PB........$6.00

Sarah Bradford **Landau** & Carl W. **Condit**

The Rise of the New York Skyscaper, 1865-1913

0-300-06444-6 YALE........$50.00

Edmund **Gillon** & Henry Hope **Reed**

Beaux-Arts Architecture in New York: A Photographic Guide

A panoramic view of visual and documentary importance

0-486-25698-7 DOVER PB........$9.95

Donald **MacKay**

The Building of Manhattan: How Manhattan Was Built Overground and Underground, from the Dutch Settlers to the Skyscrapers

A compelling, illustrated account

0-06-091603-6 HARPERCOLLINS PB........$18.00

Henry Hope **Reed**

The New York Public Library: Its Architecture and Decoration

A lavish and detailed exploration of New York's great Beaux-Arts landmark

0-393-30336-5 NORTON PB........$16.95

Elliot **Willensky** & Norval **White**

Aia Guide to New York City

Exuberant and opinionated, this recently revised classic is both an encyclopedia of the city's architecture and a high-spirited guide to its multifaceted 350-year history

0-15-603600-2 HARCOURT BRACE PB........$24.00

G. **Wolfe**

New York: A Guide to the Metropolis

Walking tour of architecture and history

0-07-071397-9 MCGRAW HILL PB........$19.95

John **Yang**

Over the Door: The Ornamental Stonework of New York

An intensive photographic study of the ornamental sandstone reliefs on New York City brownstones and tenements of the late 19th century

1-56898-057-4 PRINCETON ARCHITECTURAL........$34.95

Summer Places and Country Houses

Arnold **Lewis**

American Country Houses of the Gilded Age

A reprint of George Sheldon's 1886 *Artistic County Seats* describing 93 houses of New England and the middle Atlantic states

0-486-24301-X DOVER PB........$10.95

Individual Architects

Douglass **Shand-Tucci**

Boston Bohemia, 1881-1900: Ralph Adams Cram, Life and Literature

1-55849-061-2 MASSACHUSETTS PB........$19.95

Thomas **Hines**

Burnham of Chicago: Architect and Planner

A skilled administrator who, with his versatile partner Root, had an important share in the evolution of the Chicago school

0-226-34171-2 CHICAGO PB........$19.95

James **O'Gorman**

The Architecture of Frank Furness

A catalog of the works of the renowned Philadelphia architect who was Sullivan's first employer

0-8122-7957-3 PENNSYLVANIA........$59.95

Polly Wynn **Allen**

Building Domestic Liberty: Charlotte Perkin Gilman's Architectural Feminism

A study of the outspoken late 19th-century proponent of the "kitchen-less house," for whom home-sweet-home was a bogus morality for not-so-sweet housekeeping

0-87023-627-X MASSACHUSETTS........$27.50
0-87023-628-8 MASSACHUSETTS PB........$15.95

Suzanne **Stein**, editor

The Architecture of Richard Morris Hunt

A collection of essays with numerous illustrations

0-226-77168-7 CHICAGO........$48.00
0-226-77169-5 CHICAGO PB........$23.95

William Howard **Adams**

Jefferson's Monticello

A history of the house and its illustrious owner/designer

0-89659-950-7 ABBEVILLE PB........$35.00

Thomas Jefferson

Jack **McLaughlin**

Jefferson and Monticello: The Biography of a Builder

National Book Award nominee (1988)

See also **BIOGRAPHY** under **US HISTORY TO THE CIVIL WAR** in **HISTORY OF THE AMERICAS**

0-8050-1463-2 HOLT PB........$14.95

Susan R. **Stein**

The World of Thomas Jefferson at Monticello

A comprehensive presentation of the wonderful objects and furniture with which Jefferson furnished his home

See also **REVOLUTIONARY LIVES** under **THE REVOLUTIONARY WAR** under **US HISTORY TO THE CIVIL WAR** in **HISTORY OF THE AMERICAS**

0-8109-3967-3 ABRAMS $65.00

Frederick **Nichols** & others

Thomas Jefferson, Landscape Architect

A short catalog, focusing on Monticello, that highlights Jefferson's anti-urban vision

0-8139-0899-X VIRGINIA PB $8.95

Henry Russell **Hitchcock**

The Architecture of H.H. Richardson and His Times

Hitchcock was the first to regard Richardson as a pioneer of modern architecture, a man who "created out of a confusion which was actually worse than a mere void the beginning of a new architecture"—Lewis Mumford

0-262-58005-5 MIT PB $14.95

Jeffrey Karl **Ochsner**

H.H. Richardson: Complete Architectural Works

His entire output, represented in plans, drawings, photographs, and description

0-262-65015-0 MIT PB $42.50

James O'Gorman

H.H. Richardson: Architectural Forms for an American Society

Based on new biographical material, the author contends that Richardson consciously sought to reflect changing social mores of 19th-century America in his architecture of "big stones"

0-226-62069-7 CHICAGO $29.95

Mariana Griswold **Van Rensselaer**

Henry Hobson Richardson and His Works

An unabridged republication of the first monograph on Richardson, published in 1888

0-8446-4801-9 SMITH $16.50

Donald **Hofmann**

The Architecture of John Wellborn Root

One of the principal figures of the Chicago school

0-226-34793-1 CHICAGO PB $16.95

Mark Alan **Hewitt**

The Architecture of Mott B. Schmidt

The first book on the master architect who designed Gracie Mansion and New York townhouses for the Vanderbilts, Astors, and Morgans. A large and lavish book that presents a scrapbook of New York at the height of its cosmopolitan grandeur

0-8478-1399-1 RIZZOLI $50.00

Charles **Baldwin**

Stanford White

A pupil of Richardson, and later a partner of McKim Mead & White

0-306-80031-4 DA CAPO PB $6.95

Suzannah **Lessard**

The Architect of Desire: Beauty and Danger in the Stanford White Family

0-385-31445-0 BDD $24.95

20th-Century Architecture

History

Reyner **Banham**

A Concrete Atlantis: U.S. Industrial Building and European Modern Architecture

Proposes that the European fascination with technology found its visual sources in the United States, as evidenced by the early writings of Le Corbusier and Gropius

0-262-02244-3 MIT $37.50

Hilda **Becher** & Bernd **Becher**

Industrial Facades

Stark photographs

0-262-02388-1 MIT $75.00

Peter **Blake**

The Master Builders: Le Corbusier, Mies Van Der Rohe, and Frank Lloyd Wright

"If one could have only one book on the general subject, since it illuminates the whole field by attention to the key forces, this would be it" —*Nation*

0-393-31504-5 NORTON PB $15.95

Jean Louis **Cohen**

Scenes of the World to Come: European Architecture and the American Challenge 1893-1960

Visions of America by Europe's foremost modern architects, and the subsequent influence that New World design came to have on the urban landscape of Europe today

2-08-013576-7 ABBEVILLE PB $50.00

Ulrich **Conrads**, editor

Programs and Manifestoes on 20th Century Architecture

Important for understanding modern architecture in its cultural context

0-262-53030-9 MIT PB $13.00

William **Curtis**

Modern Architecture Since 1900

0-13-586694-4 PRENTICE HALL PB $61.18

Occasionally a single artist emerges who so profoundly reorganizes the basic assumptions of a period that he deserves to be considered in isolation…In the formation of modern architecture two figures of this imaginative and intellectual caliber obviously stand out: Le Corbusier and Frank Lloyd Wright.

MODERN ARCHITECTURE SINCE 1900

George **Dudley**

Workshop for Peace: Designing the United Nations Headquarters

0-262-04137-5 MIT $67.50

Edward R. **Ford**

Details of Modern Architecture

0-262-06121-X MIT $75.00

0-262-06185-6 MIT $75.00

Kenneth **Frampton**

Modern Architecture: A Critical History

Amazing that there could be so much, and of such importance, in this compact treatment; a 'survey,' but as imaginative as it is scholarly—and thorough

See also **THAMES & HUDSON WORLD OF ART** under **ART HISTORY: GENERAL STUDIES** in **ART**

0-500-20257-5 THAMES & HUDSON PB $14.95

Kenneth **Frampton** & David **Larkin**, editor

American Masterworks: The Twentieth-Century House

This collection presents some of the masterpieces of modern residential architecture, featuring houses by Saarinen, Wright, Gropius, Johnson, Kahn, and others. Not only seminal influences on American living, but also actual residences that practically incorporate their innovative elements into real life. Frampton's collection of photos and explanations is an essential primer in 20th-century architectural design

PHOTOGRAPHY BY MICHAEL FREEMAN AND PAUL ROUCHELEAU

0-8478-1894-2 RIZZOLI $65.00

Gustavo G. **Galfetti**

Domestic Retreats

A survey of small-scale 20th-century houses built in what might be classified as minimal style—the simple material expression of the basic human need for shelter. Text in English and Spanish

84-252-1651-6 WATSON-GUPTILL PB $45.00

Siegfried **Giedion**

Mechanization Takes Command

Documents the mechanization of the household from the Middle Ages to the modern period, focusing on the latter

0-393-00489-9 NORTON PB $16.95

Space, Time and Architecture: The Growth of a New Tradition

Though its point of view is now challenged, this is still an important interpretation of the history of the modern movement

0-674-83040-7 HARVARD $49.95

Ada Louise **Huxtable**

The Tall Building Artistically Reconsidered: The Search for a Skyscraper Style

0-520-06195-0 CALIFORNIA PB $15.95

Esther **McCoy**

Vienna to Los Angeles: Two Journeys

Traces the careers of Neutra and Schindler from their early training in Vienna to the erection of their white stucco houses in southern California

0-931228-01-8 ARTS & ARCHITECTURE $19.50
0-931228-02-6 ARTS & ARCHITECTURE PB $11.95

Dietrich **Neumann**, editor

Film Architecture: From Metropolis to Blade Runner

Through detailed case studies of set designs that range from *The Cabinet of Dr. Caligari* to *Batman*, scholars of film and architecture discuss the symbiotic relationship between the two creative forms and theorize its importance in defining both imaginary worlds and contemporary urban realities

3-7913-1605-2 PRESTEL $65.00

John **Peter**

The Oral History of Modern Architecture: Interviews with the Greatest Architects of the 20th Century

The story of the modern movement in the words of the people who created it: 40 years' worth of interviews with 60 of the world's most prominent architects and engineers, accompanied by photographs, models, plans, and sketches. Includes a compact disc of 16 modern masters speaking about their work

0-8109-3669-0 ABRAMS $75.00

Nikolaus **Pevsner**

Sources of Modern Architecture and Design

A brief and well-illustrated survey

0-500-20072-6 THAMES & HUDSON PB $14.95

Edward **Relph**

The Modern Urban Landscape: 1880 to the Present

0-8018-3559-3 JOHNS HOPKINS $40.00
0-8018-3560-7 JOHNS HOPKINS PB $15.95

Bernard **Rudovsky**

Architecture Without Architects: A Short Introduction to Non-Pedigreed Architecture

This highly visual presentation of traditional vernacular architectures of the world has had great influence

0-8263-1004-4 NEW MEXICO PB $17.95

Vincent **Scully**

Modern Architecture

A penetrating and classic study by the eminent Yale professor

0-8076-0334-1 BRAZILLER PB $14.95

Terry **Smith**

Making The Modern: Industry, Art, and Design in America

0-226-76347-1 CHICAGO PB $34.95

Petr **Wittlich**

Prague: Fin de Siécle (1890-1914)

A beautifully illustrated and penetrating analysis of the social and political turmoil of the 1890s, linking trends in art and literature to developments in architecture and design

0-685-57515-2 ABBEVILLE $75.00

20th-Century Individual Architects

Malcolm **Quantrill**

Alvar Aalto: A Critical Study

One of the best available books on Aalto, offering new interpretations of the master whose legacy will only increase in stature as the years unfold

0-941533-35-2 NEW AMSTERDAM PB $30.00

Mardges **Bacon**

Ernest Flagg: Beaux-Arts Architect and Urban Reformer

Architect of the famous Singer building, Flagg's diverse work includes the Corcoran Gallery and much low-cost housing

0-262-02222-2 MIT $45.00

George **Collins** & others

The Designs and Drawings of Antonio Gaudi

His flamboyant and extravagant designs are fully reflected in this comprehensively illustrated catalog

0-691-03985-2 PRINCETON $190.00

Xavier **Güell**

Antonio Gaudi

The Catalan synthesizer of Gothic, Moorish, and Art Nouveau influences

84-252-1445-9 GILI PB $18.95

Edward **Sekler**

Josef Hoffmann: The Architectural Work

The large-format catalogue raisonné of a leading member of the Secession movement and the Wiener Werkstattë, with superb color reproductions

0-691-06572-1 PRINCETON $195.00

Michael **Brawne**

Kimbell Art Museum: Louis I. Kahn

0-7148-2745-2 PHAIDON PB $29.95

David B. **Brownlee** & others

Louis I. Kahn: In the Realm of Architecture

The first major study on one of the greatest architects and teachers of the century. "Lavish, well conceived…authoritative in scholarship…clearly written so that the general public as well as scholars will learn from it"
—*NY Times Book Review*

0-8478-1330-4 RIZZOLI PB $42.50

James **Steele**

Salk Institute: Louis I. Kahn

0-7148-2914-5 PHAIDON PB $29.95

Adolf **Loos**

Adolf Loos: Theory and Words

A richly illustrated definitive study on the work of one of the first true modernists, who argued vociferously against superfluous decoration in architecture

PREFACE BY ALDO ROSSI

0-948835-16-8 D.A.P. PB $39.95

Panayotis **Tournikiotis**

Adolf Loos

"An exemplary overview of the enigmatic Austrian modernist"
—Michael Webb, L.A. architect

1-87827-180-6 PRINCETON ARCHITECTURAL $24.95

Donald **Curl**

Mizner's Florida: American Resort Architecture

Picturesque and theatrical buildings from the originator of the Spanish revival in Florida

0-262-53068-6 MIT PB $16.00

Sara Holmes **Boutelle**

Julia Morgan, Architect

Designer and builder of more than 700 structures including Hearst Castle, Morgan was one of America's most accomplished 20th-century architects. This handsome volume documents her life and work with letters, sketches, blueprints, and striking photographs

0-7892-0019-8 ABBEVILLE PB $35.00

Paul **Spreiregen**

The Architecture of William Morgan

The innovative architect who used earth as an architectural element to link building and site

0-292-79023-6 TEXAS $60.00

Manfred **Sack** & Richard **Neutra**

Richard Neutra

A new volume documenting the modern master's most significant works, including his town planning projects, and furniture designs, some which are published here for the first time

1-87405-620-X ARTEMIS PB $24.95

David **Underwood**

Oscar Niemeyer and the Architecture of Brazil

A penetrating analysis of the work of the man who designed all of the major buildings of Brasilia and left his mark on the contemporary design of an entire nation

0-8478-1686-9 RIZZOLI $60.00
0-8478-1687-7 RIZZOLI PB $35.00

M. **Küper** & others

Gerrit Rietveld: The Complete Works

The famed architect and designer's complete projects and designs

1-87827-178-4 PRINCETON ARCHITECTURAL $75.00

Steven **Ruttenbaum**

Mansions in the Clouds: The Skyscraper Palazzi of Emery Roth

The first monograph on the life and work of Roth, architect of many of New York's outstanding skyscrapers of the '20s and '30s as well as numerous luxury apartment buildings

0-917439-09-0 BALSAM $40.00

Francesco Dal **Co** & others, editors

Carlo Scarpa: The Complete Works

A comprehensive documentation of both the completed and unrealized projects of the architect and designer who died in 1978, with an in-depth interview and essays by Bruno Zevi, Arata Isozaki, Vincent Scully, and others

0-8478-0591-3 RIZZOLI PB $39.95

Christoph **Bürkle**

Hans Scharoun

The work of the German architect and intellectual opponent of Le Corbusier who was one of the leaders of the Expressionist or Organic movement—a powerful alternative to the rationalist International Style

1-87405-680-3 ARTEMIS PB $24.95

Stephen **White**

Building in the Garden: The Architecture of Joseph Allen Stein in India and California

0-19-563223-0 OXFORD PB $15.95

Louis **Sullivan**

Kindergarten Chats and Other Writings

In which Sullivan's theories about architecture, art, education, and life in general are presented in the classical form of dialogues or "chats" between an architect and a novice

See also LITERATURE under 20TH-CENTURY AMERICAN ESSAYS AND JOURNALISM in LITERATURE OF THE AMERICAS

0-486-23812-1 DOVER PB $7.95

Hugh **Morrison**

Louis Sullivan: Prophet of Modern Architecture

The first monograph, responsible for the genesis of the Sullivan legend, and still the standard biography

0-393-00116-4 NORTON PB $8.95

Louis **Sullivan**

Autobiography of an Idea

Written in Sullivan's later years, these provocative recollections reveal the growth of the organic theory of architecture

0-486-20281-X DOVER PB $9.95

Robert **Twombly**

Louis Sullivan: His Life and Work

A historian's biography that considers the social, economic, and aesthetic background of the father of the American skyscraper

0-226-82006-8 CHICAGO PB $19.95

Hans **Frei**

Louis Henry Sullivan

A chronological account of the major works of the seminal figure in the history of American architecture, including many photographs taken at the time of their completion

1-87405-615-3 ARTEMIS PB $24.95

Randolph **Carter** & others

Joseph Urban: Architecture, Theatre, Opera, Film

Masterful coverage of the visionary architect and designer

0-89659-912-4 ABBEVILLE $55.00

Frank Lloyd Wright

Frank Lloyd **Wright**

The Collected Writings of Frank Lloyd Wright

"Among the most ambitious American architectural projects ever undertaken"
—*Chicago Tribune*

Volume 1: 1894-1931

0-8478-1547-1 RIZZOLI PB $40.00

Volume 2: 1931-1932

0-8478-1549-8 RIZZOLI PB $40.00

Volume 3: 1931-1939

0-8478-1699-0 RIZZOLI $60.00
0-8478-1700-8 RIZZOLI PB $40.00

Volume 4: 1929-1949

0-8478-1804-7 RIZZOLI PB $40.00

Volume 5: 1949-1959

0-8478-1854-3 RIZZOLI $60.00
B08478185 RIZZOLI PB $40.00

H. Allen **Brooks**

The Prairie School: Frank Lloyd Wright and His Midwest Contemporaries

The definitive study of the Prairie School

See also INDIVIDUAL ARCHITECTS under AMERICAN ARCHITECTURE TO 1900

0-393-31439-1 NORTON PB $22.50

Joseph **Connors**

The Robie House of Frank Lloyd Wright

0-226-11542-9 CHICAGO PB $16.95

Thomas A. **Heinz**

Frank Lloyd Wright: Glass Art

1-85490-296-2 ACADEMY $90.00
1-85490-295-4 ST. MARTIN'S $85.00

Henry Russell **Hitchcock**

In the Nature of Materials: The Buildings of Frank Lloyd Wright, 1887-1941

The best introduction to the life and work of Wright; reprint of the 1942 edition

0-306-71283-0 DA CAPO $46.00
0-306-80019-5 DA CAPO PB $18.95

Neil **Levine**

The Architecture of Frank Lloyd Wright

0-691-03371-4 PRINCETON $85.00

Edgar **Kaufmann**, Jr., editor

Fallingwater: A Frank Lloyd Wright Country House

A lavish monograph on Wright's great work, with over 200 illustrations, measured plans, and elevations

0-89659-662-1 ABBEVILLE $55.00

Grant **Manson**

Frank Lloyd Wright to 1910: The First Golden Age

A companion to Hitchcock's book and a classic in its own right

0-442-26130-6 VAN NOSTRAND REINHOLD PB $33.95

Terence **Riley**, editor

Frank Lloyd Wright: Architect

Essays by Anthony Alofsin, William Cronon, Kenneth Frampton, Terence Riley, and Gwendolyn Wright

0-8109-6122-9 MOMA $60.00

Arlene **Sanderson**, editor

Wright Sites: A Guide to Frank Lloyd Wright Public Places

See also MUSEUMS AND ART under SPECIALIZED GUIDES under TRAVEL GUIDES in FOOD, TRAVEL, AND LEISURE

1-56898-041-8 PRINCETON ARCHITECTURAL PB $12.95

Meryle **Secrest**

Frank Lloyd Wright: A Biography

A far-ranging and highly readable biography of the contradictory and brilliant architect. 121 photos. "Secrest…does a superb job in telling the human side of Wright's story…Definitive"
—*Kirkus Reviews*

0-394-56436-7 KNOPF $30.00

Kathryn **Smith**

Frank Lloyd Wright: Hollyhock House and Olive Hill: Buildings and Projects for Aline Barnsdall

A comprehensive documentation, the project of ten years research, of one of Wright's largest commissions: an entire theater community in Hollywood on a 36-acre estate

0-8478-1540-4 RIZZOLI $45.00

William Allin **Storrer**

The Architecture of Frank Lloyd Wright: A Complete Catalog

The most complete guide available, containing 437 entries with photographs, locations, descriptions, and maps

0-262-69080-2 MIT PB $19.95

The Frank Lloyd Wright Companion

0-226-77624-7 CHICAGO $85.00

Robert **Twombly**

Frank Lloyd Wright: His Life and His Architecture

The definitive biography

0-471-85797-1 WILEY PB $32.95

Frank Lloyd **Wright**

Drawings, Plans of Frank Lloyd Wright: The Early Period, 1893-1909

A reprint of the famous Wasmuth edition, with numerous photographs and original views

0-486-24457-1 DOVER PB..........$11.95

Scot **Zimmerman**, Photographer

Details of Frank Lloyd Wright: The California Work, 1909-1974

Wright lavished attention on the smallest details of his buildings. The 175 color photographs and the thoughtful, readable text that accompany this look at such elements of his work as decoration and lighting make it an outstanding introduction to the work of America's foremost architect

0-8118-0082-2 CHRONICLE..........$35.00

Ludvig Mies Van Der Rohe

Detlef **Mertins**, editor

The Presence of Mies

An interdisciplinary collection of critical essays that reconsider the work of the modern master Mies Van Der Rohe

1-56898-013-2 PRINCETON ARCHITECTURAL PB..$19.95

Franz **Schulze**

Mies Van Der Rohe: A Critical Biography

An acclaimed biography with detailed analysis of his relations with Behrens, Johnson, and Wright. Includes many previously unpublished photos

0-226-74060-9 CHICAGO PB..........$24.95

Le Corbusier

Le Corbusier

The Decorative Art of Today

0-262-62055-3 MIT PB..........$13.95

Towards a New Architecture

A major work that presents the philosophical, cultural, and visual concerns of the avant-garde and shows how they inform modern design

0-486-25023-7 DOVER PB..........$9.95

William **Curtis**

Le Corbusier: Ideas and Forms

Based on new archival material and focusing on the formative years, architectural ideals, and social realities

0-7148-2790-8 PHAIDON PB..........$29.95

Jacques **Guiton**

The Ideas of Le Corbusier: On Architecture and Urban Planning

Le Corbusier promoted his ideas in lectures and speeches, illustrated with his drawings; such material is here reassembled

0-8076-1005-4 BRAZILLER PB..........$11.95

Jean **Jenger**

Le Corbusier: Architect, Painter, Poet

This in-depth study on Le Corbusier examines the life and art of one of the most prominent figures in the history of architecture. Prepared in cooperation with the Corbusier Foundation, the book provides excerpts from his writings and 182 splendid illustrations

0-8109-2880-9 ABRAMS PB..........$12.95

Charles **Jencks**

Le Corbusier and the Tragic View of Architecture

An eccentric study by a theorist of postmodernism who traces the crisis of modern architecture to Le Corbusier's later ideas

0-674-51860-8 HARVARD..........$25.00
0-674-51861-6 HARVARD PB..........$14.95

Le Corbusier

Theory and Criticism

Diana I. **Agrest**

Architecture from Without

0-262-51067-7 MIT PB..........$16.50

Gaston **Bachelard**

The Poetics of Space

Reveries by the French philospher/poet. A perennial favorite

FOREWORD BY ETIENNE GILSON

0-8070-6439-4 BEACON PB..........$14.00

Georges **Bataille**

Against Architecture: The Writings of Georges Bataille

EDITED BY DENIS HOLLIER

0-262-08186-5 MIT..........$19.95

Kent **Bloomer** & Charles **Moore**

Body, Memory and Architecture

Essays on context and memory in the experience of architecture

0-300-02142-9 YALE PB..........$19.00

Stewart **Brand**

How Buildings Learn

From the creator of *The Whole Earth Catalog*. "A stunning exploration of the design of design... *How Buildings Learn* will irrevocably alter your sense of place, space, and the artifacts that shape them."—Michael Shrage, *Wired*
"A classic and probably a work of genius"
—Jane Jacobs

0-14-013996-6 PENGUIN PB..........$20.00

Santiago **Calatrava**

High Rises

An anthology of essays on a wide variety of issues associated with high- rise construction, extensively illustrated

3-7757-0476-0 D.A.P...........$40.00

D. **Coleman** & others, editors

Architecture and Feminism

A collection of articles that address the relationship between feminism and architecture as critiques of modern Western theoretical conventions and impulses toward social reform

1-56898-043-4 PRINCETON ARCHITECTURAL PB..$19.95

Alan **Colquhoun**

Essays in Architectural Criticism: Modern Architecture and Historical Change

Focuses on much-debated buildings and concepts

0-262-53063-5 MIT PB..........$18.95

Modernity and the Classical Tradition: Architectural Essays, 1980-1987

The prominent theoretical concepts—classicism, romanticism, historicism, and rationalism—as they have developed with the changing meaning of history

0-262-03138-8 MIT..........$37.50
0-262-53101-1 MIT PB..........$17.50

Cynthia **Davidson**, editor

Anyone

0-8478-5592-9 RIZZOLI PB..........$45.00

Anywhere

0-8478-1617-6 RIZZOLI PB..........$45.00

Jacques **Derrida** & others

Chora L. Works

1-88525-440-7 MONACELLI PB..........$40.00

Gregory K. **Dreicer**, editor

Between Fences

Looked over but often overlooked, fences have played an essential role in American architecture since colonial times. Lavishly illustrated, this anthology assembles a distinguished group of architects, theorists, and historians who address this fundamental aspect of our built environment

1-56898-080-9 PRINCETON ARCHITECTURAL PB...$17.95

Robin **Evans**

The Projective Cast: Architecture and Its Three Geometries

0-262-05049-8 MIT..........$52.50

Nan **Ellin**, editor

Architecture of Fear

A critical anthology that examines the ways in which the contemporary landscape is shaped by our society's preoccupation with fear, as seen in home design, security systems, gated communities, zoning regulations, and cyberspace

1-56898-086-8 PRINCETON ARCHITECTURAL........$29.95
1-56898-082-5 PRINCETON ARCHITECTURAL PB..$19.95

D. **Fausch** & others, editors

Architecture: In Fashion

Critical essays that explore the complicity between architecture and fashion

1-87827-199-7 PRINCETON ARCHITECTURAL PB..$18.95

Diane **Ghirardo**, editor

Out of Site: A Social Criticism of Architecture

A provocative collection of essays that calls into question the ways in which contemporary architecture engages a broad spectrum of social and political issues

0-941920-19-4 BAY PB........$16.95

Robert **Harbison**

The Built, the Unbuilt and the Unbuildable: In Pursuit of Architectural Meaning

0-262-08204-7 MIT........$32.50
0-262-58122-1 MIT PB........$12.95

K. Michael **Hays**

Modernism and The Posthumanist Subject: The Architecture of Hammes Meyer and Ludwig Hilberseimer

0-262-58141-8 MIT PB........$16.95

K. Michael **Hays**, editor

Hejduk's Chronotope

Essays that examine today's tendency toward theoretical production, as exemplified by John Hejduk, known for his non-practical projects

1-56898-078-7 PRINCETON ARCHITECTURAL PB..$19.95

Bill **Hubbard**, Jr.

A Theory for Practice: Architecture in Three Discourses

0-262-08235-7 MIT........$24.50

David **Kolb**

Postmodern Sophistications: Philosophy, Architecture, and Tradition

In this book, Professor Kolb discusses postmodern styles in architecture and shows its evolution from the context of philosophical ideas of modernism

0-226-45028-7 CHICAGO PB........$15.95

Joseph **Masheck**

Building-Art: Modern Architecture Under Cultural Construction

0-521-44013-0 CAMBRIDGE........$60.00
0-521-44785-2 CAMBRIDGE PB........$20.95

C. Thomas **Mitchell**

Redefining Designing: From Form to Experience

A very insightful exploration of what's wrong with the current design methodologies, together with a few examples of what's right

0-442-00987-9 VAN NOSTRAND REINHOLD PB.....$37.95

Mohesn **Mostafavi** & David **Leatherbarrow**

On Weathering: The Life of Buildings in Time

0-262-13291-5 MIT........$31.50
0-262-63144-X MIT PB........$14.95

Gülsüm Baydar **Nalbantoglu** & Wong Chong **Thai**, editors

Postcolonial Space(s)

Eight essays that explore a new language for rethinking contemporary architecture and urban conditions in the postcolonial world

1-56898-075-2 PRINCETON ARCHITECTURAL PB..$19.95

Kate **Nesbitt**, editor

Theorizing a New Agenda for Architecture: An Anthology of Architectural Theory 1965-1995

Fifty-one complete essays from the last 30 years of architectural theory, with a critical introduction to each essay, a bibliography, and notes on the contributors

1-56898-053-1 PRINCETON ARCHITECTURAL........$50.00
1-56898-054-X PRINCETON ARCHITECTURAL PB.$34.95

Joan **Ockman**

Architecture Culture 1943-1968: A Documentary Anthology

A collection of 74 of the most important primary documents on the evolution of modern architecture, with critical commentary. Includes writings by such eminent figures as Asalto, Buckminster Fuller, Hitchcock, Johnson, Kahn, Le Corbusier, Van Der Rohe, Rossi, Venturi, and Frank Lloyd Wright

0-8478-1511-0 RIZZOLI........$50.00

Albert **Pope**

Ladders

An examination of the forces—including demographic upheavals, market expansions, and technological developments—that have transformed the American landscape since World War II and resulted in the proliferation of vast parking lots, zones of urban blight, corporate plazas, expressways, and suburban lawns

1-88523-201-2 PRINCETON ARCHITECTURAL PB...$17.95

Joel **Sanders**, editor

Stud: Architectures of Masculinity

An interdisciplinary exploration of the active role played by architecture in the construction of male identity. Architects, artists, and theorists investigate how sexuality is constructed through material organization of objects and human subjects in actual space

1-56898-076-0 PRINCETON ARCHITECTURAL PB..$19.95

Alison **Smithson**

Team 10 Meetings 1953-1981

0-8478-1311-8 RIZZOLI PB........$29.95

William S. **Saunders**, editor

Reflection on Architectural Practices in the Nineties

A collection of essays by architects, historians, and theorists who speculate on future paths for both education and practice

1-56898-056-6 PRINCETON ARCHITECTURAL PB..$18.95

Daphne **Spain**

Gendered Spaces

This is one of the first books to apply feminist theory to building designs

0-8078-4357-1 NORTH CAROLINA PB........$17.95

John **Templer**

The Staircase: History and Theories

0-262-70056-5 MIT PB........$16.95
0-262-70055-7 MIT PB........$14.95

Craig **Whitaker**

Architecture and the American Dream

An award-winning architect and city planner reflects on ways in which cultural ideals such as freedom, progress, mobility and individual liberty are expressed in America's architectural eclecticism

0-517-70378-5 CLARKSON POTTER........$40.00

Ken **Yeang**

Designing with Nature: The Ecological Basis for Architectural Design

0-07-072317-6 MCGRAW HILL........$34.95

France

"If we eliminate from our hearts and minds all dead concepts in regard to the houses, and look at the question from a critical and objective point of view, we shall arrive at the 'House-Machine,' the mass-production house, healthy (and morally so too) and beautiful in the same way that the working tools and instruments which accompany our existence are beautiful."
—Le Corbusier, *Towards a New Architecture*

Meredith L. **Clausen**

Frantz Jourdain and the Samaritaine: Art Nouveau Theory and Criticism

90-04-07879-7 E.J. BRILL........$99.50

Norma **Evenson**

Paris: A Century of Change, Eighteen Seventy-Eight to Nineteen Seventy-Eight

0-300-02667-6 YALE PB........$30.00

Maurice **Rheims**

Hector Guimard

The first complete visual overview of the premier Art Nouveau architect, by the noted art critic

0-8109-0973-1 ABRAMS........$65.00

Ian **Scargill**
Urban France
0-312-83449-7 ST. MARTIN'S $24.95

Germany and Austria

Herbert **Bayer**, editor
Bauhaus: 1919-1928
Reprint of the catalog for the famous 1938 Museum of Modern Art exhibition, which introduced the central emigrating figures of the Bauhaus—Gropius, Bayer, Albers, Moholy-Nagy, and others—to the American public
0-8109-6013-3 MOMA PB $16.95

Joan **Campbell**
The German Werkbund
The German institution that pursued modern design in all its manifestations, from industrial plant to social housing
0-691-05250-6 PRINCETON $55.00

Walter **Gropius**
New Architecture and the Bauhaus
The international aims of the Bauhaus
0-262-57006-8 MIT PB $9.00

Frank **Whitford**
Bauhaus
An introduction tracing the ideas behind the Bauhaus, its teaching methods, and its innovative artists
0-500-20193-5 THAMES & HUDSON PB $14.95

Hans **Wingler**
Bauhaus: Weimar, Dessau, Berlin, Chicago
The standard comprehensive treatment
0-262-23033-X MIT $195.00
0-262-73047-2 MIT PB $42.50

Vittorio Magnago **Lampugnani**
Modern Architecture in Germany from 1900 to 1950
A comprehensive survey of the movement known as "Neue Sachlichkeit"
3-7757-0452-3 D.A.P. $85.00

Barbara **Lane**
Architecture and Politics in Germany, 1918-1945
Illuminates the complex interplay of art and culture in the Weimar and Nazi periods
0-674-04350-2 HARVARD $18.50
0-674-04370-7 HARVARD PB $16.50

Iain Boyd **Whyte**, editor
The Crystal Chain Letters: Architectural Fantasies by Bruno Taut and His Circle
The Crystal Chain was a utopian correspondence, initiated by Taut in 1919, in which a small group of like-minded architects and artists exchanged ideas on the architecture of the future
0-262-23121-2 MIT $42.50

Italy

Richard **Etlin**
Modernism in Italian Architecture, 1890-1940
A sweeping, generously illustrated study; Etlin explores the changing idea of modernism in Italian architecture over five crucial decades
0-262-05038-2 MIT $70.00

Vittorio **Gregotti**
New Directions in Italian Architecture
0-8076-0480-1 BRAZILLER $7.95

Thomas L. **Schumacher**
The Danteum: Architecture, Poetics, and Politics Under Italian Fascism
Mussolini's unbuilt 1938 commission for a monument to Dante, designed in the Italian rationalist style
1-87827-182-2 PRINCETON ARCHITECTURAL PB $17.95

Manfredo **Tafuri**
History of Italian Architecture, 1944-1985
Critic/historian Tafuri surveys the rich but fragmented recent history of Italy's architecture
0-262-70043-3 MIT PB $15.95

The Netherlands and Belgium

Brigitte **Tietzel** & others
Made in Holland: Design in the Netherlands
A survey of the last 20 years of Dutch design, from interior and industrial design to graphics and jewelry, with essays by leading scholars, designers, and critics
3-8030-3061-7 D.A.P. $40.00

Russia

William Craft **Brumfield**
Lost Russia: Photographing the Ruins of Russian Architecture
0-8223-1568-8 DUKE PB $27.95

The Origins of Modernism in Russian Architecture
0-520-06929-3 CALIFORNIA $75.00

Reshaping Russian Architecture: Western Technology, Utopian Dreams
0-521-39418-X CAMBRIDGE $70.00

Catherine **Cooke**
Russian Avant-Garde: Theories of Art, Architecture and the City
0-312-69612-4 ST. MARTIN'S PB $19.95

Andreas C. **Papadakis** & others
The Avant-Garde: Russian Architecture in the Twenties
0-312-06793-3 ST. MARTIN'S PB $19.95

Russian Constructivism

Hatje, editors
Konstruktivistische Internationale 1922-1927
A comprehensive survey of international constructivist design and architecture in the '20s, with numerous reproductions of plans, drawings, prototypes, and finished projects by such artists as El Lissitzky, Laszlo Moholy-Nagy, Theo van Doesburg, and Kurt Schwitters
3-7757-0376-4 D.A.P. $85.00

Soviet Architecture Avantgarde 1924-1937
A critical analysis of the development of Soviet architecture from Lenin's death to the beginning of World War II
3-7757-0425-6 D.A.P. $75.00

Anatole **Kopp**
Constructivist Architecture in the U.S.S.R.
The constructivists attempted to evolve a training guide for their new concept of the "artist-constructor" following the 1917 revolution
0-312-16599-4 ST. MARTIN'S $45.00

Frederick **Starr**
Melnikov: Solo Architect in a Mass Society
In his imaginative use of materials and techniques, Melnikov achieved a formalism in which traditional and vernacular elements are transformed in relation to contemporary social programs
0-691-00331-9 PRINCETON PB $27.95

Asia

Yoshinobu **Ashihara**
The Hidden Order: Tokyo Through the Twentieth Century
Using architecture as a metaphor for culture, Japanese architect Ashihara offers an insider's look at the apparent chaos that is Tokyo today
See also **CITIES AND CITY PLANNING**
0-87011-912-5 KODANSHA $17.95
4-7700-1664-6 KODANSHA PB $9.00

Botond **Bognar**
The Japan Guide
See also **MUSEUMS AND ART** under **SPECIALIZED GUIDES** under **TRAVEL GUIDES** in **FOOD, TRAVEL, AND LEISURE**
1-87827-133-4 PRINCETON ARCHITECTURAL PB $24.95

Togo Murano: Master Architect of Japan
0-8478-1887-X RIZZOLI $45.00

Kisho **Kurokawa**

New Wave Japanese Architecture

1-85490-153-2 ST. MARTIN'S $80.00

David **Stewart**

The Making of a Modern Japanese Architecture: 1868 to the Present

From Victorianism to postmodernism, Stewart follows the intraction of tradition and innovation in modern and contemporary Japanese architecture and urban planning

0-87011-844-7 KODANSHA $60.00

Spain and Portugal

Antonio **Armesto** & Joaquim **Padro**

Atlantic Houses: Galicia and Northern Portugal

A rich selection of houses in often spectacular settings, by some of Spain's and Portugal's leading architects. Text in English and Spanish

84-252-1666-4 WHITNEY LIBRARY OF DESIGN PB ... $50.00

Martí **Lucena** & Salvador **Roig**

Mediterranean Houses: Balearic Islands

The interiors and exteriors of 23 extraordinary residences on Ibiza, Mallorca, and Menorca, including Francisco de la Guardia's Polanski house and Jørn Utzon's self-designed house

84-252-1441-6 GILI $49.95

Ignasi de Solá-Morales **Rubio** & Anton Gonzalez **Capitel**

Contemporary Spanish Architecture: An Eclectic Panorama

The evolution of Spanish architecture over the past three decades

See also **CONTEMPORARY ARCHITECTURE**

0-8478-0708-8 RIZZOLI PB $27.50

Pauline **Saliga** & Martha **Thorne**

Building in a New Spain: Contemporary Spanish Architecture

A survey of the state of Spanish architecture since the death of Franco

84-252-1577-3 ARTEMIS $45.00

Ignasi de **Solá-Morales**

Fin de Siècle Architecture in Barcelona

Moving beyond the analysis of a handful of famous buildings, this book considers the cultural history of the entire creative movement and its relationship to developments in other European cities of the time

84-252-1564-1 GILI $69.95

Contemporary Architecture

Jonathan **Hale**

The Old Way of Seeing: How Architecture Lost Its Magic—And How to Get It Back

"An eloquent plea for a new way of thinking about architecture"—Betty Edwards, *Drawing on the Right Side of the Brain*

0-395-74010-X DORLING KINDERSLEY PB $14.95

Heinrich **Klotz**, editor

New York Architecture: 1970-1990

0-8478-1138-7 RIZZOLI $75.00

Bill **Lacy** & Susan **deMenil**

Angels and Franciscans

An overview of the most exciting contemporary architects working in Los Angeles and San Francisco, including Frank Gehry, Thom Mayne, Eric Owen Moss, Mark Mack, and Stanley Saitowitz

0-8478-1630-3 RIZZOLI PB $29.95

Ignasi de Solá-Morales **Rubio** & Anton Gonzalez **Capitel**

Contemporary Spanish Architecture: An Eclectic Panorama

The evolution of Spanish architecture over the past three decades

See also **SPAIN AND PORTUGAL** under **20TH-CENTURY ARCHITECTURE**

0-8478-0708-8 RIZZOLI PB $27.50

Alexander **Tzonis** & Liane **Lefaivre**

Architecture in Europe Since 1968: Memory and Invention

The first comprehensive survey of the compelling, contrasting, and often pioneering work produced in Europe during the last 25 years

0-8478-1624-9 RIZZOLI $60.00

Alexander **Tzonis** & others

Architecture in North America Since 1960

The first comprehensive study of recent North American architecture, from the glass and steel sleekness of the International Style to the lighthearted flourishes of postmodernism, covering everything from skyscrapers to technology parks, and theaters, houses, museums, and sports facilities

0-8212-2228-7 BULFINCH $65.00

Paul **Virilio**

Bunker Archaeology

1-56898-015-9 PRINCETON ARCHITECTURAL PB . $34.95

Postmodernism

Diane **Ghirardo**

Architecture After Modernism

An eloquent examination of the widely divergent paths taken by architecture and its theories in the last quarter century, set in their political and social contexts. Topics include such "megaprojects" as the rise of the Disney empire, residential projects in Berlin, and London's Docklands, as well as the work of women architects and lesser-known designers

0-500-20294-X THAMES & HUDSON PB $14.95

Sir Denys **Lasdun**

Architecture in an Age of Scepticism: A Practitioner's Anthology

Lasdun questions the basic assumptions of his previous theory and moves toward an idiosyncratic response to current theory

0-19-520445-X OXFORD $50.00

Paolo **Portoghesi**

Postmodern: The Architecture of the Post-Industrial Society

Inspired by the *Strada Novissima* at the 1980 Venice Biennale, an architect/critic explores recent developments

0-8478-0472-0 RIZZOLI PB $35.00

Aldo **Rossi**

The Architecture of the City

Questions the functionalist tenets of the modern movement, thereby setting the stage for the rediscovery of history as an architectural vocabulary and tool

0-262-68043-2 MIT PB $16.95

Deyan **Sudjic**

The Architecture of Richard Rogers

The first comprehensive examination of the work of the acclaimed British architect

0-8109-1954-0 ABRAMS $45.00

Robert **Venturi**

Complexity and Contradiction in Architecture

The manifesto that marked the theoretical origin of many postmodernist ideas

INTRODUCTION BY VINCENT SCULLY

0-8109-6023-0 MOMA PB $12.95

Iconography and Electronics Upon a Generic Architecture

0-262-22051-2 MIT $40.00

Learning from Las Vegas: The Forgotten Symbolism of Architectural Form

The aesthetic messages conveyed by everyday visual reality

0-262-72006-X MIT PB $15.95

Mother's House: The Evolution of Vanna Venturi's House in Chestnut Hill

A monograph on the house that Venturi designed for his mother in the '60s that became one of the most architecturally influential residences of the second half of the 20th century

0-8478-1141-7 RIZZOLI $39.95
0-8478-1142-5 RIZZOLI PB $22.50

Individual Architects

Diana **Agrest** & others

Agrest and Gandelsonas: Works

Over 40 projects for urban buildings, residential designs, interiors, and theoretical works by the firm whose designs are sleek, sophisticated, and witty

1-87827-190-3 PRINCETON ARCHITECTURAL PB. $40.00

Peter **Buchanan**

Emilio Ambasz, Inventions: Reality of the Ideal

Ambasz's recent landscape and architectural projects, plus industrial, exhibition, and graphic designs and his new designs for computers, toothbrushes, pens, watches, and luggage

0-8478-1608-7 RIZZOLI PB $40.00

Peter **Blake**

Edward Larrabee Barnes, Architect

A major monograph covering the full range of Barnes's practice, from the modernism of the postwar years to his more recent designs for offices, museums, and houses

0-8478-1822-5 RIZZOLI PB $35.00

Luis **Barragán**

Barragán: The Complete Works

Every project by the creative architect who transformed the Mexican building tradition into an abstract architectural language of light and color

1-56898-085-X PRINCETON ARCHITECTURAL $60.00

Brian Brace **Taylor**

Geoffrey Bawa

A comprehensive survey of the architect's highly personal work whose influence now extends far beyond the boundaries of his native Sri Lanka. "Bawa is an outstanding architect. . .one of his achievements is to have created a style related to the surviving peasant vernacular but suited to the larger scale of contemporary building programs"—*Architectural Review*

0-500-27858-X THAMES & HUDSON PB $39.95

Warren **James**, editor

Ricardo Bofill, Taller De Arquitectura: Buildings and Projects, 1960-1985

A catalogue raisonné and monograph on the work of this important Spanish architect and his multidisciplinary team. Featured are Kafka's Castle, Xanadu, Walden-7, and many other projects

0-8478-0739-8 RIZZOLI $60.00

Francesco **Dal Co**

Mario Botta: Architecture, 1960-1985

Botta's buildings and projects, including his earliest works, with superb illustrations

0-8478-0839-4 RIZZOLI PB $39.95

Emilio **Pizzi**, editor

Mario Botta: The Complete Works

Documenting over 90 buildings and projects, this volume covers the first 25 years of the career of one of the great architects of the 20th century

1-87405-660-9 ARTEMIS $74.95

Carol Herselle **Krinsky**

Gordon Bunshaft of Skidmore, Owings and Merrill

For many years an executive partner of SOM, Bunshaft is best known for Lever House in Manhattan

0-262-11130-6 MIT $65.00

Sebastiano **Brandolini** & others

Jo Coenen

A chronological survey of the recent work of the Dutch architect who has worked with Luigi Snozzi, James Stirling, Aldo van Eyck, and Theo Bosch

84-252-1674-5 WATSON-GUPTILL PB $29.95

Kenneth **Frampton**

Santiago Calatrava: Bridges

A complete survey of the bridge designs by one of the most innovative architect/engineers working in Europe today

1-87405-675-7 ARTEMIS $95.00

Sutherland **Lyall**

Santiago Calatrava: Dynamic Equilibrium

Recent projects by the leading Spanish architect known for his innovative use of materials and technology

1-87405-605-6 ARTEMIS PB $29.95

Peter **Buchanan**

Varquez Consuegra

The Seville architect's fresh and exciting designs since 1975. Text in English and Spanish

84-252-1554-4 GILI PB $28.95

Peter **Eisenman**

Re: Working Eisenman

1-85490-112-5 ACADEMY $70.00

Peter **Eisenman** & Frank **Gehry**

Peter Eisenman and Frank Gehry

0-8478-1479-3 RIZZOLI PB $25.00

Alan **Balfour** & others

Cities of Artificial Excavation: The Work of Peter Eisenman, 1979-1988

0-8478-1761-X RIZZOLI PB $35.00

David **Turnbull**

Tony Felton

The work of the English architect whose projects extend beyond building to photography, performance, writing, and exhibition designs. Text in English and Spanish

84-252-1655-9 GILI PB $29.95

Joseph **Giovanni** & others

Frederick Fisher, Architect

The work of the southern California architect who emphasizes the perception of space, light, and natural materials in his designs for museums and studios for artists, photographers, and filmmakers

0-8478-1864-0 RIZZOLI $60.00
0-8478-1865-9 RIZZOLI PB $40.00

Charles **Jencks** & others, editors

Frank Gehry: Individual Imagination and Cultural Conservationism

1-85490-408-6 ACADEMY PB $30.00

Janet **Abrams**

Michael Graves: Buildings and Projects, 1990-1994

Recent work by the renowned and influential American architect, whose extensive oeuvre includes the Swan and Dolphin hotels at Disney World, the San Juan Capistrano Library in California, and a highly successful line of furniture, furnishings, and artifacts

0-8478-1901-9 RIZZOLI $65.00
0-8478-1902-7 RIZZOLI PB $40.00

Peter **Adam**

Eileen Gray, Architect/ Designer: A Biography

0-8109-0996-0 ABRAMS $39.95

James **Steele**

Schnabel House: Frank Gehry

0-7148-2749-5 PHAIDON PB $29.95

Peter **Eisenman**

Gwathmey Siegel: Buildings and Projects 1984-1992

The work of the popular and distinguished firm, ranging from the addition to Frank Lloyd Wright's Guggenheim Museum, to corporate skyscrapers, showrooms, offices, and houses for David Geffen, Faye Dunaway, and Oprah Winfrey

0-8478-1675-3 RIZZOLI $60.00
0-8478-1676-1 RIZZOLI PB $40.00

Ron **Herron** & others

Herron Notebooks: Buildings in Japan

London-based Archigram member Ron Herron's designs for three small projects in Japan—a canopy for Kosugi Railway Station, and a bus shelter and "tower of wind at water" at Daimon, all produced under very tight deadlines. Provides real insight into the way buildings actually get made

1-87405-690-0 ARTEMIS PB $39.95

Wilfried **Wang**

Herzog & de Meuron

Recent work by the innovative Swiss team who use inexpensive materials such as sheet metal and plywood to create surprising yet sensual forms. Text in English and German

1-87405-635-8 ARTEMIS PB $24.95

Kurt W. **Forster**

Hodgetts + Fung: Scenarios and Spaces

A provocatively designed volume documenting the firm's brightly colored, eclectic structures that celebrate the theatricality of the visual, media-oriented culture of southern California

0-8478-1812-8 RIZZOLI $60.00
0-8478-1813-6 RIZZOLI PB $40.00

Frank **Gehry**
Franklin D. Israel: Buildings and Projects
An important young architect working in the tradition of California modernism
0-8478-1539-0 RIZZOLI PB $35.00

Lisbet **Jorgensen** & others
Arne Jacobsen
A comprehensive monograph on work of the architect/designer who created the world famous Egg Armchair
84-85424-27-1 GILI $60.00

Nory **Miller**
Helmut Jahn
The commercial buildings of the Chicago-based architect have made him a celebrity in the world of real estate development
0-8478-0561-1 RIZZOLI $60.00

Philip **Johnson** & Hilary **Lewis**
Philip Johnson: The Architect in His Own Words
0-8478-1823-3 RIZZOLI $50.00

Jeffrey **Kipnis**
Philip Johnson Recent Work
1-85490-284-9 ACADEMY PB $38.00

Carlton **Knight III** & others, editors
Philip Johnson-John Burgee: Architecture, 1979-1985
Focuses on 25 major projects, predominantly high-rise buildings and cultural centers
0-8478-0658-8 RIZZOLI $50.00

Franz **Schulze**
Philip Johnson: Life and Work
0-226-74058-7 CHICAGO PB $16.95

David **Whitney** & Jeffrey **Kipnis**, editors
Philip Johnson: The Glass House
0-679-42373-7 PANTHEON $35.00

Robert **Bruegmann**
Ralph Johnson of Perkins & Will: Buildings and Projects
The first monograph on the architect who revitalized the venerable Chicago firm and who has been widely acclaimed for developing contemporary forms that reflect the influence of European high modernism
0-8478-1862-4 RIZZOLI $60.00
0-8478-1863-2 RIZZOLI PB $40.00

Rem **Koolhaas**
Delirious New York: A Retroactive Manifesto for Manhattan
1-88525-400-8 MONACELLI PB $35.00

S,M,L,XL
EDITED BY BRUCE MAU
1-88525-401-6 MONACELLI $75.00

Conversations with Students
Texts collected from a recent series of seminars run by Koolhaas at Rice University, plus an essay by the architect on the urban and architectural implications of several large-scale projects
1-88523-202-0 PRINCETON ARCHITECTURAL PB .. $14.95

Jaques **Lucan**, editor
Rem Koolhaas/OMA
Essays and designs by the renowned architect. "Read Koolhaas's essays, which are among the most accurate descriptions going on contemporary architecture. Enjoy his opposition to illusory utopia, bogus wholeness, and dreams of salvation through architecture"
—Rowan Moore, *Blueprint*
1-87827-155-5 PRINCETON ARCHITECTURAL PB . $29.95

Rob **Krier**
Architectural Compositions
A theoretical and visual analysis illustrating the creative process that informs Krier's practice and teaching
0-8478-0965-X RIZZOLI $65.00

M.A. **Baldellou** & others
J. Manuel Gallego
The Spanish architect's work, from 1967 to 1991. Text in English and Spanish
84-252-1537-4 GILI PB $28.95

Dietmar **Steiner**
José Luis Mateo
Works by the respected theorist, whose reputation now extends to practice as well. Text in English and Spanish
84-252-1581-1 GILI PB $28.95

Richard **Meier**
Richard Meier: Architect
08478-0496-8 RIZZOLI PB $60.00

Kevin P. **Keim**
An Architectural Life: Memoirs and Memories of Charles W. Moore
0-8212-2167-1 LITTLE, BROWN $50.00

Eugene **Johnson**
Charles Moore: Buildings and Projects, 1949-1986
A well-illustrated survey of an important American architect and his witty, whimsical buildings
0-8478-0759-2 RIZZOLI PB $35.00

Eric Owen **Moss**
Eric Owen Moss: Buildings and Projects
A lavishly illustrated presentation of 27 buildings that showcase Moss's unique ability to combine glass, wallboard, and trusswork
FOREWORD BY PHILIP JOHNSON
0-8478-1909-4 RIZZOLI $60.00
0-8478-1910-8 RIZZOLI PB $40.00

Michael T. **Cannell**
I.M. Pei: Mandarin of Modernism
The first biography of the architect whose vision and political skill have shaped the international architectural landscape. Cannell reveals the history and personality behind the enigmatic master of monumental modernism, covering his mandarin upbringing in Shanghai, his studies under Gropius and his handling of such clients as Jackie Kennedy, Ross Perot, and Francois Mitterand
0-517-79972-3 CLARKSON POTTER $35.00

Jean-Francois **Pinchon**, editor
Rob Mallet-Stevens: Architecture, Furniture, Interior Design
The first book in English on the career of this controversial architect of the modern movement, who along with Le Corbusier was one of the most influential figures between the wars. His most important projects and their impact are discussed, as well as the influence of Josef Hoffman, and the architect's fascination with the Secessionist style.
0-262-16116-8 MIT $35.00

Antoine **Predock**
Architectural Journeys
Reproductions of sketches in pastel, ink, watercolor, collage, and clay that document the travels and working methods of the architect renowned for his eclectic work in the American Southwest
0-8478-1904-3 RIZZOLI $35.00

Brad **Collins** & others
Antoine Predock, Architect
The first chronicle of Predock's acclaimed projects that interpret the spirit of their settings, from the American Southwest to France, Spain, and Morocco
0-8478-1698-2 RIZZOLI PB $35.00

Hani **Rashid** & others
Asymptote: Architecture at the Interval
A comprehensive treatment of the New York firm whose work questions traditional understanding of space, form, and representation through an exploration of media, information networks, virtual reality, and cyberspace
0-8478-1861-6 RIZZOLI PB $30.00

Aldo **Rossi**
A Scientific Autobiography
A charming presentation of the architect's repertoire
0-262-68041-6 MIT PB $13.95

Morris **Adjmi**, editor
Aldo Rossi, Architecture 1981-1991
The 1990 Pritzker Prize winner's designs for Il Palazzo Hotel, Fukuoka, the German History Museum, Berlin, the San Carlo alla Barona Church in Milan, and many others
1-87827-115-6 PRINCETON ARCHITECTURAL $60.00

Barbara **Radice**
Ettore Sottsass: A Critical Biography
A sensitive account of the life and working methods of the celebrated architect and designer, noted for his products for Olivetti and his highly colorful Memphis furniture
0-8478-1681-8 RIZZOLI $50.00

Robert A.M. **Stern**
Robert A.M. Stern: Buildings and Projects 1987-1992
"Stern is a notable exponent of stylistic freedom in architecture…his response is to reestablish historical continuity with traditional forms. A lavish book for large architectural collections"
—*Library Journal*
INTRODUCTION BY VINCENT SCULLY
0-8478-1619-2 RIZZOLI PB $40.00

Peter **Arnell** & others, editors

James Stirling: Buildings and Projects

Includes virtually every project by this internationally acclaimed architect, with 1,000 illustrations

0-8478-0449-6 RIZZOLI PB $35.00

Paolo **Polledri**

Shin Takamatsu, Architect

Exhibition catalog for the San Francisco Museum of Modern Art exhibition of the work of one of the fastest rising new stars of Japanese architecture, whose international renown is based on a vast repertoire of built works

0-8478-1746-6 RIZZOLI PB $29.95

Kenneth **Frampton** & others

Harry Wolf

Twenty years of the work of the Los Angeles-based architect, noted for his orderly geometric designs. Text in English and Spanish

84-252-1580-3 GILI PB $28.95

Rizzoli New Architecture Series

Botond **Bognar**

The New Japanese Architecture

0-8478-1225-1 RIZZOLI $35.00

Frank **Dimster**

The New Austrian Architecture

0-8478-1757-1 RIZZOLI $50.00

0-8478-1758-X RIZZOLI PB $35.00

Gerhard G. **Feldmeyer**

The New German Architecture

0-8478-1672-9 RIZZOLI $50.00

0-8478-1673-7 RIZZOLI PB $35.00

Wojciech **Lesnikowski**

The New French Architecture

0-8478-1224-3 RIZZOLI $35.00

Anatxu **Zabalbeascoa**

The New Spanish Architecture

0-8478-1532-3 RIZZOLI $50.00

0-8478-1533-1 RIZZOLI PB $35.00

Cities and City Planning

Yoshinobu **Ashihara**

The Hidden Order: Tokyo Through the Twentieth Century

Using architecture as a metaphor for culture, Japanese architect Ashihara offers an insider's look at the apparent chaos that is Tokyo today

See also **ASIA** under **20TH-CENTURY ARCHITECTURE**

0-87011-912-5 KODANSHA $17.95

4-7700-1664-6 KODANSHA PB $9.00

Reyner **Banham**

Los Angeles

In this entertaining book, Banham sets the works of designers as diverse as Frank Lloyd Wright, Charles Eames, Richard Neutra, and Watts Towers constructor Simon Rodia in their geographical and man-made contexts

0-14-021178-0 PENGUIN PB $10.00

Leonardo **Benevolo**

The European City

A cultural and intellectual history of urban life from the early Middle Ages to the present

0-631-17302-1 BLACKWELL $49.95

0-631-19893-8 BLACKWELL PB $21.95

A. **Breen**

Waterfronts: Cities Reclaim Their Edge

0-07-068458-8 MCGRAW HILL $49.95

George **Collins** & Christian Crasemann **Collins**

Camillo Sitte: The Birth of Modern City Planning

Originally published in 1889, Sitte's work revolutionized urban planning and ushered the discipline into the 20th century; with original drawings and plates

0-8478-0556-5 RIZZOLI PB $29.95

Le **Corbusier**

The City of Tomorrow

A provocative essay, written in 1929, advocating a rationalized environment in which traditional urban features would become obsolete

0-486-25332-5 DOVER PB $10.95

Richard **Dattner**

Civil Architecture: The New Public Infrastructure

An illustrated guide to the planning and design of public architecture, with case studies of successful recent projects

0-07-015665-4 MCGRAW HILL $46.95

Nan **Ellin**

Postmodern Urbanism

Although architecture has figured centrally in discussion of postmodernism, urban design has been largely overlooked. Combining insights from anthropology, history, political economy, and literary criticism, this book fills a void by presenting a lucid account of what postmodernism means for designers of large-scale environments and those who inhabit them

1-55786-363-6 BLACKWELL PB $19.95

Tony **Garnier**

La Cité Industrielle

An influential book showing Garnier's plans for a utopian community of 35,000, including buildings for industry, housing, and government

0-910413-47-9 PRINCETON ARCHITECTURAL $60.00

Dolores **Hayden**

The Power of Place: Urban Landscapes as Public History

0-262-08237-3 MIT $32.50

Thomas **Herzog**, editor

Solar Energy in Architecture and Urban Planning

A visual and textual documentation of sixty of the finest recently completed and future building projects from across Europe that utilize and harness the power of the sun

3-7913-1652-4 PRESTEL $65.00

Jane **Jacobs**

The Death and Life of Great American Cities

An attack on the principles and aims that have shaped modern orthodox city planning and rebuilding. "This is one of the most remarkable books ever written about the city"
—William Whyte

See also **URBAN ECONOMICS** under **SPECIAL TOPICS** under **ECONOMICS** in **SOCIAL STUDIES**

0-679-60047-7 MODERN LIBRARY $17.50

0-679-74195-X VINTAGE PB $13.00

The Economy of Cities

"This book is radiant with ideas about what makes cities rich or poor, how cities grow, and how city growth affects national economies"
—*New Yorker*

See also **HISTORY, POLITICS, AND SOCIETY** under **20TH-CENTURY AMERICAN ESSAYS AND JOURNALISM** in **LITERATURE OF THE AMERICAS**

0-394-70584-X RANDOM HOUSE PB $10.00

Edge of Empire: Post Colonialism and the City

See also **URBAN AMERICA** under **AMERICAN PEOPLE AND PLACES** in **HISTORY OF THE AMERICAS**

0-415-12007-1 ROUTLEDGE PB $19.95

P. **Katz**

The New Urbanism: Toward an Architectural Community

New urban design strategies

0-07-033889-2 MCGRAW HILL $49.95

Naomi **Miller** & Keith **Morgan**

Boston Architecture: 1975-1990

An excellent introduction to the buildings and developments that radically transformed Boston's skyline between 1975 and 1990, and the ways in which historic structures have been creatively preserved or reused to meet contemporary needs

3-7913-1679-6 PRESTEL PB $29.95

Bill **Risebero**

Fantastic Form: Architecture and Planning Today

A critical look at theory, practice, and social policy in the wake of current trends in art, education, philosophy, and literary theory

1-56131-057-3 NEW AMSTERDAM $30.00

J. **Simmonds**

Garden Cities 21: Creating a Livable Urban Environment

0-07-057620-3 HARVARD BUSINESS $42.00

Martha **Rosler**

If You Lived Here...The City in Art, Theory, and Social Activism

An extraordinary project documenting the current crisis of the American city through a critique of urban housing policies. It offers solutions and hope in portraying how artists and activists have fought against government neglect, shortsighted policy, and unfettered real estate speculation

0-941920-18-6 BAY PB $16.95

James **Steele**

Sustainable architecture

A groundbreaking book that outlines why 20th-century building technology has been so environmentally destructive, together with a problem-solving strategy for refining the post-industrial role of urban architecture

0-07-060949-7 MCGRAW HILL $49.95

Anthony **Sutcliffe**

Paris: An Architectural History

0-300-06886-7 YALE PB $25.00

Raymond **Unwin**

Town Planning in Practice: An Introduction to the Art of Designing Cities and Suburbs

First published in 1909, this book is an excellent compendium of images and theories on urban design. Unwin was perhaps the greatest figure of the Garden City movement, which had a tremendous impact on planning in Europe and the United States

1-56898-004-3 PRINCETON ARCHITECTURAL $75.00

Sophie **Watson** & Katherine **Gibson**, editors

Postmodern Cities and Spaces

An anthology of recent theory

0-631-19404-5 BLACKWELL PB $22.95

William H. **White**

City: Rediscovering Its Center

0-385-26209-4 ANCHOR PB $19.95

Sharon **Zulkin**

The Cultures of Cities

Tracing the connections between real estate development, popular expression, and elite visions of the arts, this book argues that cultures are constantly negotiated in a city's central spaces

1-55786-436-5 BLACKWELL $49.95

1-55786-437-3 BLACKWELL PB $21.95

Landscape Architecture and Garden Design

General

Mark **Girouard**

Town and Country

A beautifully illustrated history of society and architecture, from the evolution of an 18th-century English seaside resort to changing attitudes toward landscape among 20th-century English and American architects. Witty and entertaining

0-300-05185-9 YALE $50.00

Charles W. **Moore**

Water and Architecture

Renowned architect Charles Moore collaborates with photographer Jane Lidz to celebrate the magic relationship of water and architecture throughout the world. Through structures and sites ranging from classical to postmodern, they address the symbolism and use of water, environmental issues, and basic design principles in a wide range of architectural contexts

0-8109-3975-4 ABRAMS $60.00

Monique **Mosser** & Georges **Eyssot**, editors

The Architecture of Western Gardens: A Design History from the Renaissance to the Present Day

A sumptuous international survey of garden design since the Renaissance, with 70 essays commissioned especially for this book and over 650 illustrations, including meticulous ground plans, drawings, reconstructions, paintings, and photographs

0-262-13264-8 MIT $135.00

George **Plumptre**

Great Gardens, Great Designers

A comprehensive history of garden design from the late 19th century to the present day

0-7063-7203-4 WARD LOCK $35.00

Gabrielle van **Zuylen**

Paradise on Earth: The Gardens of Western Europe

A history of Western gardens from their source in Mesopotamia, through the influence of Islam, and the cloister gardens of the Middle Ages, to the labyrinths of Renaissance princes and the urban gardens of today. Includes a glossary and a list of great European gardens

0-8109-2851-5 ABRAMS PB $12.95

European

Patrick **Bowe**

Gardens in Central Europe

An exploration of the great variety that has developed under the varied cultural influences of Central Europe, with much information on climate, flora, architects, and patrons

0-85667-399-4 ANTIQUE COLLECTORS $49.50

Bernd H. **Dams** & Andrew **Zega**

Pleasure Pavillions and Follies in the Gardens of the Ancien Régime

A major contribution to our knowledge of the imaginative garden follies built for the pleasure of the pre-Revolutionary Bourbon kings. The authors' watercolor renderings reconstruct these magnificent structures, and their text brings the vanished world that created them vividly to life

See also **FRENCH GARDENS** under **GARDEN HISTORY** under **THE OUTDOORS** in **FOOD, TRAVEL, AND LEISURE**

2-08-013561-9 ABBEVILLE $50.00

Denise Le **Dantec** & Jean-Pierre Le **Dentec**

Reading the French Garden

Combining discursive accounts with fictional vignettes, the authors skillfully integrate the history of French gardens with a modern history of ideas

TRANSLATED BY JESSICA LEVINE

0-262-62087-1 MIT PB $13.95

John Dixon **Hunt**

William Kent: Landscape Garden Designer

The first book devoted to William Kent, precursor of Capability Brown and the most important contributor to the English landscape garden; includes a catalogue raisonné of 115 designs, individually illustrated

0-302-00600-1 SOTHEBY PARKE BERNET $60.00

John Dixon **Hunt** & Peter **Willis**, editors

The Genius of the Place: The English Landscape Garden, 1620-1820

For 200 years, landscape gardens reflected the same changes in attitude about nature, liberty, and order as did literature and painting

0-262-58092-6 MIT PB $22.00

Louisa **Jones**

Gardens in Provence

A tour through the enchanting unknown private gardens of Provence, hidden behind high walls that surround both modest cottages and imposing chateaux

2-08-013523-6 ABBEVILLE $50.00

Gardens of the French Riviera

Private terraces and secluded enclaves form one of the world's most spectacular settings for landscape design, many never before photographed

2-08-013555-4 ABBEVILLE $50.00

Pierre André **Lablaude**

The Gardens of Versailles

A history of the evolution of taste, art, and philosophy, as seen through the development of the grounds around the famous palace, from the hunting park of Louis XIII to the grand schemes of Le Nôtre for Louis XIV

0-302-00659-1 SOTHEBY'S $40.00

Stephane **Pincas**

Versailles: The History of the Gardens and Their Sculpture

A complete visual tour of the gardens, including every statue, fountain, and grove, complete with a note of its origin and unique place within the garden as a whole, plus extracts from hundreds of contemporary documents

0-500-01701-8 THAMES & HUDSON PB $75.00

Vincent **Scully**

French Royal Gardens: The Designs of André Le Nôtre

The influential work of the director of gardening under Louis XIII and Louis XIV, whose work exudes a sense of immortality and power—an image of nature perfectly controlled by man

0-8478-1602-8 RIZZOLI $40.00

Louis XIV

John C. **Shepherd** & Geoffrey A. **Jellicoe**

Italian Gardens of the Renaissance

Reprint of a classic volume that traces the development of Italian garden design from the work of Michelozzi, Bramante, and Rossellino, to that of Palladio and Scamozzi, through the Baroque to the abandonment of Renaissance ideals in the 18th century

1-85490-372-1 ST. MARTIN'S PB....$45.00

Marie-Francoiose **Valery**

Gardens in Normandy

From Monet's garden at Giverny to the Bois de Moutiers at Varengeville, a breathtaking tour from the gardens in the fertile Seine valley to the cliffs over the English Channel

See also **FRENCH GARDENS** under **GARDEN HISTORY** under **THE OUTDOORS** in **FOOD, TRAVEL, AND LEISURE**

PHOTOGRAPHY BY VINCENT MOTTE & CHRISTIAN SARRAMON

2-08-013579-1 ABBEVILLE....$50.00

Allen **Weiss**

Mirrors of Infinity: The French Formal Garden and 17th-Century Metaphysics

Unanimously acclaimed for its remarkable ability to combine philosophical insights and social history with analyses of 17th-century French gardens such as Vaux-le-Vicomte, Chantilly, and Versailles

1-56898-050-7 PRINCETON ARCHITECTURAL PB ..$14.95

American

Diana **Balmori**

Beatrix Farrand's American Landscapes: Her Gardens and Campuses

The designer of Dumbarton Oaks and many other important private gardens and public sites

See also **AMERICAN GARDENS** under **GARDEN HISTORY** under **THE OUTDOORS** in **FOOD, TRAVEL, AND LEISURE**

0-89831-003-2 TIMBER PB....$24.95

Charles **Beveridge** & David **Larkin**, editor

Frederick Law Olmstead: Designing the American Landscape

A sumptuous presentation of Olmstead's remarkable 40-year career that included the design of New York's Central Park and the US Capitol grounds, together with an engaging social history of his work as an administrator, social reformer, and community activist

PHOTOGRAPHY BY PAUL ROCHELEAU

0-8478-1842-X RIZZOLI....$70.00

Elizabeth Barlow **Rogers**

Rebuilding Central Park: A Management and Restoration Plan

The master design and management plan for America's first large-scale-public space, with a history of Olmsted's design

0-262-18127-4 MIT....$37.50

David C. **Streatfield**

California Gardens: Creating a New Eden

Lush photographs and an authoritative text capture the history of the California garden and its worldwide influence

1-55859-453-1 ABBEVILLE....$55.00

Asian and African

John **Brookes**

Gardens of Paradise: The History and Design of the Great Islamic Gardens

One of England's foremost landscape designers traces the spread of the Islamic image of a garden paradise through India, Persia, Turkey, Egypt, Sicily, North Africa, and Muslim Spain

See also **ISLAMIC ART AND ARCHITECTURE** in **ART**

See also **ISLAMIC GARDENS** under **GARDEN HISTORY** under **THE OUTDOORS** in **FOOD, TRAVEL, AND LEISURE**

0-941533-07-7 NEW AMSTERDAM....$36.00

David H. **Engel**

A Thousand Mountains, A Million Hills: Creating the Rock Work of Japanese Gardens

The history and philosophy of rocks in Japanese gardens, with detailed advice on how to create designs and tips on selection, composition, and setting

0-87040-969-7 JAPAN PUBLICATIONS....$29.00

Muchio **Fujioka**

Japanese Residences and Gardens: A Tradition of Integration

Using the homes of the Japanese aristocracy and military shoguns as examples, this book documents the intimate relationship between architecture and gardens

4-7700-1977-7 KODANSHA....$28.00

Interior Decoration

"Whenever I pass through a city, I never fail to visit whatever illustrious furnished houses are open to outsiders. Galleries, churches, famous views, landscapes made immortal by the poets, yes, all of these find me far from indifferent; but for houses I have a special weakness. It's not only that I find myself more in touch with the past: the very arrangement of the furnishings acts on me like a spell. The odor of the furniture, of the wax on the floors, of the ancient rooms is as pleasing to me—or even more pleasing— than the scent of meadows in spring."—Mario Praz, *An Illustrated History of Interior Decoration*

General Histories

Tania **Bayard**

A Medieval Home Companion: Housekeeping in the 14th Century

Bayard has translated portions of a handbook written in 1394 by an elderly French burgher for presentation to his bride, aged 15. The author's attention to the details of moral and household arts makes the work an intriguing read, as he describes the proper way to manage servants, cure toothaches, remove stains from clothing, plant gardens, select cheeses, and plan banquets

0-06-016654-1 HARPERPERENNIAL PB....$19.95

Charlotte **Gere** & Michael **Whiteway**

Nineteenth-Century Design

A new appraisal of 19th-century design that considers the period as a whole—from Gothic Revival to Art Nouveau—and includes all of the design arts, such as glass, metalwork, ceramics, textiles, jewelry, and furniture

0-8109-3672-0 ABRAMS....$95.00

Kathleen **Mahoney**

Gothic Style: Architecture and Interiors from the Eighteenth Century to the Present

A visual survey of the expression of the style in Britain and America together with a social history that conveys the romantic spirit with which tastemakers, architects, and designers have attempted to capture the medieval past

0-8109-3381-0 ABRAMS....$60.00

James **Parker**, editor

Period Rooms in the Metropolitan Museum of Art

This book contains magnificent examples of interior design throughout the ages, on view in the period rooms of the Metropolitan Museum, New York. Thirty-five installations are sumptuously reproduced here along with informative and fascinating narrative descriptions

0-8109-3744-1 METROPOLITAN MUSEUM PB....$60.00

Peter **Thornton**

Seventeenth Century Interior Decoration in England, France, and Holland

0-300-02776-1 YALE PB $32.00

Anatxu **Zabalbeascoa**

The House of the Architect

An exclusive look inside the houses of 30 of the world's best-known architects, from Peter Eisenman in New York, Gae Aulenti in Milan, and Frank Gehry in Los Angeles, to Arata Isozaki in Tokyo

0-8478-1873-X RIZZOLI $50.00

American Decoration

"Rooms may be decorated in two ways: by a superficial application of ornament totally independent of structure, or by means of architectural features which are part of the organism of every house, inside as well as out."
—Edith Wharton, *The Decoration of Houses*

Jennifer **Ash**

Private Palm Beach

A survey of Palm Beach's elegant formal mansions

1-55859-269-5 ABBEVILLE $45.00

Joseph **Bryon**

Photographs of New York Interiors At the Turn of the Century

Includes the Astor and other famous residences

0-486-24863-1 DOVER PB $12.95

Wendy A. **Cooper**

Classical Taste in America, 1800-1840

A revealing study of the impact of classicism in the early American republic

INTRODUCTION BY RICHARD L. BUSHMAN

1-55859-385-3 ABBEVILLE $65.00

Mary **Emmerling**, editor

Mary Emmerling's American Country South

PHOTOGRAPHS BY LANGDON CLAY

0-517-56175-1 CLARKSON POTTER $40.00

Wendell **Garrett**

Classic America: The Federal Style & Beyond

A glorious look at the domestic architecture and design of the early United States

See also **PERIOD FURNITURE** under **FURNISHINGS** under **AMERICAN DECORATIVE ARTS**

0-7893-0024-9 UNIVERSE PB $25.00

Charlotte **Gere**

Nineteenth-Century Decoration: The Art of the Interior

0-8109-1382-8 ABRAMS $95.00

Robin **Guild**

The Victorian House Book

0-8478-1095-X RIZZOLI $50.00

Chippy **Irvine**

Private New York: Remarkable Residences

A look inside some of the most beautiful New York residences

1-55859-106-0 ABBEVILLE $50.00

Dan **Klein**

Decorative Art, 1880-1990: Arts and Crafts, Art Nouveau, Art Deco, Postwar

Glass, furniture, textiles, bronzes, jewelry

0-7148-8025-6 PHAIDON $50.00

David **Larkin**

Colonial: Design and the New World

Interiors and furniture

1-55670-043-1 WORKMAN $29.99

Deborah **Turbeville** & Louis **Auchincloss**

Newport Remembered: A Photographic Portrait of a Gilded Past

A renowned photographer and a distinguished writer collaborate to present a unique vision of the gardens and interiors of Newport's glorious mansions of the gilded age

0-8109-3673-9 ABRAMS $60.00

Edith **Wharton** & Ogden **Codman**

The Decoration of Houses

In this first American book on interior decoration, Mrs. Wharton explained her preference for French taste over the more prevalent ornate Victorian style

0-393-00840-1 NORTON PB $15.95

Edith Wharton

English Decoration

"It is in the country that the Englishman gives scope to his natural feelings…He manages to collect around him all the conveniences and elegances of polite life and to banish its restraints. His country seat abounds with every requisite, either for studious retirement, tasteful gratification, or rural exercise. Books, paintings, music, horses, dogs, and sporting implements of all kinds are at hand."
—Washington Irving, *Sketch Book*

Geoffrey **Beard**

Craftsmen and Interior Decoration in England, 1660-1820

A dictionary with over 700 names and 6,000 entries

0-8419-0703-X HOLMES & MEIER $125.00

Nina **Campbell**

The Art of Decoration

A colorful survey of ten residential projects by the award-winning decorator most closely associated with the classic English country look

0-517-70466-8 CLARKSON POTTER $40.00

Jeremy **Cooper**

Victoria and Edwardian Decor: From the Gothic Revival to Art Nouveau

A comprehensive history, with 680 illustrations

0-89659-768-7 ABBEVILLE $60.00

Alan **Gore** & Ann **Gore**

The History of English Interiors

A broad overview of the sequence and main characteristics of each style and period, from the 11th century to the present day

0-7148-3468-8 PHAIDON PB $29.95

Constance M. **Greiff**

Early Victorian

A comprehensive handbook to designers, furnishings, and key building types, including Second Empire and Egyptian revival, with a timeline and information about landmark and preservation societies

0-7892-0011-2 ABBEVILLE $12.95

Thomas **Hope**

Regency Furniture and Interior Decoration

Facsimile of the book that announced the Regency style

See also **BRITISH AND IRISH FURNITURE** under **FURNITURE** under **EUROPEAN DECORATIVE ARTS**

0-486-21710-8 DOVER PB $9.95

Christopher **Hussey**

English Country Houses: Early, Middle, and Later Georgian Houses

0-907462-68-5 ANTIQUE COLLECTORS PB $145.00

Gervase **Jackson-Stops** & James **Pipkin**

The English Country House: A Grand Tour

Architectural and decorative details in furniture, silver, carpets, clocks, and woodwork

0-8212-1598-1 NY GRAPHIC $29.45

Chester **Jones**

Colefax and Fowler: The Best in English Interior Decoration

A stunningly illustrated account of the preeminent British design firm, which developed the traits of English Country style: faded chintz, fringed curtains, comfortable upholstered furniture, and beautiful antiques. Lovely photographs of rooms designed by Colefax and Fowler, of wallpaper and other decorative elements which exemplify their work

0-8212-1746-1 BULFINCH $40.00

John **Morely**

Regency Design 1790-1840: Gardens, Buildings, Interiors, Furniture

The most ambitious survey of the period ever undertaken, lavishly illustrated with prints, watercolors, paintings, plans, and photographs of extant buildings and gardens

See also **GENERAL** under **EUROPEAN DECORATIVE ARTS**

0-8109-3768-9 ABRAMS $150.00

Steven **Parissen**

The Georgian House in Britain and America

Written with the owner or would-be owner of a house in mind, this book enables the preservationist, historian, architect, carpenter, and decorator to understand the craftsmanship and context of the Georgian house

FOREWORD BY HER MAJESTY QUEEN ELIZABETH THE QUEEN MOTHER

0-8478-1911-6 RIZZOLI $60.00

John **Pym**

Merchant Ivory's English Landscape: Rooms, Views, and Anglo-Saxon Attitudes

A detailed account of four classic Merchant Ivory films—*A Room with a View*, *Maurice*, *Howard's End* and *The Remains of the Day*—which takes readers behind the scenes to reveal how locations were chosen and decorations researched. Complete with travel directions, opening hours, and descriptions of nearby places of interest

FOREWORD BY JAMES IVORY

0-8109-4275-5 ABRAMS $35.00

Pat **Ross**

Formal Country

PHOTOGRAPHS BY DAVID PHELPS

0-670-82574-3 VIKING $40.00

Caroline **Seebohm**

English Country: Living in England's Private Houses

A guided tour of stately homes as lived-in houses, with separate chapters on the decorative elements

PHOTOGRAPHS BY CHRISTOPHER SIMON SYKES

0-517-56060-7 CLARKSON POTTER $45.00

0-517-88459-3 CLARKSON POTTER PB $12.00

Scottish, Irish, and Welsh

Leslie **Astaire** & Roddy **Martine**

At Home in Scotland

Richly illustrated survey of great houses, castles, and country estates

0-89659-767-9 ABBEVILLE $45.00

French Decoration

"I have often said to myself that if I were not a man of letters, if I had not got money, my chosen profession would have been to invent interiors for rich people. I should have loved being allowed to have my own way by some banker who would have given me *carte blanche* to work out the decoration and furniture of a palace with just four bare walls, using what I could find from dealers, artists, modern industry, and in my own head."—Edmond de Goncourt

Linda **Dannenberg** & others

Pierre Deux's Paris Country: A Style and Source Book of the Ile-de-France

The internationally acclaimed designers of Pierre Deux turn to Paris and its environs for decoration ideas, further exploring the aesthetic of French Country decor

0-517-56436-X CLARKSON POTTER $45.00

Madeleine **Deschamps**

Empire

An opulent and authoritative survey of the French Empire style and its impact throughout Europe and America

1-55859-032-3 ABBEVILLE $85.00

Traditional Houses of Rural France

Stunning images of vernacular architectural style from Normandy, Brittany, Burgundy, Dordogne, Pays-Basque, and Provence illustrate this breathtaking visual tour of the French countryside. 150 color illustrations

1-55859-222-9 ABBEVILLE $27.50

Lisa **Lovatt-Smith**

Paris Interiors

A comprehensively illustrated private view of Parisian residences, with a trilingual text in English, French, and German

3-8228-8932-6 TASCHEN $39.99

Christiane de **Nicolay-Mazery** & Jean-Bernard **Naudin**

The French Chateau

A visually rich account of the privileged lives that continue to flourish in the grand historic houses of France

0-500-23631-3 THAMES & HUDSON $45.00

John **Whitehead**

The French Interior in the 18th Century

A glorious presentation of the highly influential, elegant, and sophisticated styles of one of the greatest periods in French decorative art, with superb illustrations of many previously unphotographed interiors

0-525-93444-8 STUDIO $50.00

Other Decorative Styles

JoAnn **Barwick**

Scandinavian Country

A look at the fresh, light-filled interiors of a wide variety of exceptional residences in Sweden, Norway, Denmark, and Finland

0-517-88460-7 CLARKSON POTTER PB $12.00

Jeffrey **Becom**

Mediterranean Color

Sumptuous color illustrations of the vernacular architecture of southern Europe

FOREWORD BY PAUL GOLDBERGER

0-89659-925-6 ABBEVILLE $45.00

Marcus **Binney**

Country Manors of Portugal: A Passage Through Seven Centuries

A colorful and revealing portrait of Portugal's little-known country manors, ranging from austere medieval tower houses through elegant Renaissance mansions to sumptuous Baroque interiors

0-935748-74-1 SCALA $55.00

Carlo **Cresti** & Massimo **Listri**

Villas of Tuscany

A private view of the architecture, interiors, gardens, and family histories of Tuscany's great villas

0-86565-144-2 VENDOME $85.00

Cesare M. **Cunaccia** & Mark E. **Smith**

Venice: Hidden Splendors

A survey of Venetian interior design, from churches, palaces and cathedrals, to cafes, hotels, and libraries, from the 11th century to the present day, including the work of Bellini, Tintoretto, Tiepolo, Titian, and Veronese

2-08-013573-2 ABBEVILLE $35.00

Paul **Duncan**

Traditional Houses of Rural Italy

The vernacular architecture of six northern regions, from the fortified hill towns of Umbria to the elegant classical structures of the Veneto, lavishly illustrated in color

1-55859-637-2 ABBEVILLE $27.50

Elizabeth **Gaynor** & K. **Haavistio**

Russian Houses

A look at Russia's rich and varied residences, from modest wooden peasant cottages to the opulence of imperial summer palaces and elegant town houses

3-8228-9049-9 TASCHEN $29.99

Elizabeth **Gaynor**

Finland: Living Design

A lavish exploration of the relationships between folk and modern, and the manmade and the natural, in the great range of Finnish furniture, glass, textile, crafts, and ceramics used in the interiors of houses, cottages, and even saunas

0-8478-1885-3 RIZZOLI PB $29.95

Myron **Goldfinger**

Villages in the Sun: Mediterranean Community Architecture

An exceptional pictorial record of the glorious Mediterranean villages of Greece, Italy, Spain, Morocco, and Tunisia, newly re-issued with all color photography

FOREWORD BY LOUIS I. KAHN

0-8478-1528-5 RIZZOLI $50.00

0-8478-1529-3 RIZZOLI PB $35.00

Jorge **Guillermo**

Dutch Houses and Castles

A richly illustrated introduction to the glories of Dutch domestic architecture and interiors, both public and private

See also **NORTHERN EUROPE** under **BAROQUE AND ROCOCO** under **EUROPEAN ARCHITECTURE TO 1900**

0-935748-94-6 SCALA $55.00

Kathryn B. **Hiesinger** & Felice **Fischer**

Japanese Design: A Survey Since 1950

0-8109-3509-0 ABRAMS....$60.00

Elisabeth **Holte**

Living in Norway

A colorful tour of traditional Norwegian interior design motifs

2-08-013545-7 ABBEVILLE....$45.00

Miranda **Innes**

Ethnic Style: From Mexico to the Mediterranean

A collection of lively homes and interiors that reveal a sense of heritage and roots

1-55859-368-3 ABBEVILLE....$35.00

Juan José **Jungquera y Matos**

Spanish Splendor: Palaces, Castles, and Country Houses

A landmark volume on Spain's grand and historic private residences, including detailed information about each property's owners, architects, decorators, and landscapers, with brilliant photographs

0-8478-1497-1 RIZZOLI....$125.00

Wolfgang **Kraus** & Peter **Müller**

Palaces of Vienna

Interiors decorated by grandees of unparalleled wealth, many of them inaccessible to the public and published for the first time

0-86565-132-9 VENDOME....$60.00

Bill **Laws**

The Perfect Country Cottage

The idyllic beauty of simple country design, with 175 full-color illustrations

1-55859-784-0 ABBEVILLE....$30.00

Suzi **Moore**

Under the Sun: Desert Style and Architecture

A tour of desert architecture and interiors, from North Africa and Spain to Mexico and the American Southwest, filled with innovative and ecologically sound ideas

0-8212-2226-0 BULFINCH....$45.00

Catherine **Sabino**

Italian Country

0-517-56017-8 CLARKSON POTTER....$45.00
0-517-88401-1 CLARKSON POTTER PB....$12.00

Suzanne **Slesin**

Greek Style

From fishermen's houses to holiday villas

0-517-56874-8 CLARKSON POTTER....$40.00

Suzanne **Slesin** & others

Mittel Europa

A wonderful variety of interiors, from the small villages of the Danube, to the great cities of Vienna, Prague, Budapest, and Trieste, from Baroque opulence and simple country dwellings, to 19th-century solidity and revolutionary 20th-century design

0-517-58803-X CLARKSON POTTER....$50.00
0-500-01630-5 THAMES & HUDSON PB....$29.95

Spanish Style

Over 700 illustrations capture the unique blend of Moorish and Western European influences that have produced an exceptionally rich heritage of architectural and interior design

0-517-57438-1 CLARKSON POTTER....$45.00

Anne de **Stoop**

Living in Portugal

A lively portrait, in superb photos and text, of Portugal's rich architectural heritage, from the Baroque opulence of Lisbon to the bright colors and sparkling whitewash of the Alentejo

2-08-013567-8 ABBEVILLE....$50.00

Marketa **Theinhardt** & Pascal **Varejka**

Prague: Hidden Splendors

A superbly illustrated visit inside 500 years of interiors, from the Gothic halls of the Holy Roman Emperors to Mucha's Art Nouveau residences

2-08-013554-6 ABBEVILLE....$35.00

William **Warren**

Thai Style

Humble and lavish houses, traditional Siamese motifs, Chinese- and Indian-influenced styles, and modern adaptations

0-8478-1043-7 RIZZOLI....$45.00

Angus **Wilkie**

Biedermeier

A survey of the popular 19th-century style, lavishly illustrated. A special collector's edition bound in Biedermeier fabric

See also **OTHER EUROPEAN FURNITURE** under **FURNITURE** under **EUROPEAN DECORATIVE ARTS**

0-89659-749-0 ABBEVILLE....$75.00

Alvise **Zorzi**

Venetian Palaces

A luxurious tour of the greatest Venetian houses from the Doge's Palace to the Palazzo Grazzi and St. Mark's Library

0-8478-1200-6 RIZZOLI....$95.00

Decorative Movements

Arts and Crafts

"The teachings of Philip Webb, William Morris and Charles Eastlake which had inspired the Arts and Crafts Movement in England were heeded in America with enthusiasm by Gustav Stickley in the 1890s. He evolved an extreme variant of the honest Arts and Crafts manner, the so-called 'Craftsman' style."
—Peter Thornton, *Authentic Decor*

James **Massey** & Shirley **Maxwell**

Arts & Crafts

A compact guide to the movement's key styles, from Morris fabrics and wallpapers, to Stickley chairs and Mission tables, complete with a timeline and list of landmark and preservation societies

0-7892-0010-4 ABBEVILLE....$12.95

Linda **Parry**, editor

William Morris

This major volume includes essays by distinguished scholars, curators and experts on William Morris, one the most influential designers of the 19th century. Abundantly illustrated, the book's lavish reproductions include objects, stained glass, furniture and tapestries created by Morris and his firm

See also **THE PRE-RAPHAELITES** under **ENGLAND** under **EUROPEAN ART: 1750-1900** in **ART**

0-8109-4282-8 ABRAMS....$49.50

William Morris

Kenneth R. **Trapp** & others

The Arts and Crafts Movement in California: Living the Good Life

A fully illustrated treatment of the movement in California

1-55859-393-4 ABBEVILLE....$55.00

Art Nouveau

"There has been much laughing at *Art Nouveau*, but no one can deny that, after the last gasp of Neoclassicism in the chaotic eclecticism of the 19th century, this style offered the first kind of decoration with a well-defined personality...The furniture, which in the classic style had been independent cubes and parallelepipeds, was not reabsorbed into the walls, camouflaged, melting into the general decoration of which they became fixed parts."—Mario Praz, *An Illustrated History of Interior Decoration*

Constance M. **Greiff**

Art Nouveau

A handbook to the "art of the new" style as it developed throughout Europe and the United States

0-7892-0024-4 ABBEVILLE....$12.95

Gabriel **Weisberg**

Art Nouveau Bing: Paris Style, 1900

Superb reproductions of works designed and made by Siegfried Bing, art dealer and dynamic figure in the decorative arts in Paris

99914-82-78-4 JOSLYN MUSEUM PB....$25.00

Siegfried **Wichmann**

Jugendstil Art Nouveau

Floral and functional forms of the German and Austrian version of Art Nouveau: a study of its origins, development, and international connections, focusing on the works of Hoffmann, Thonet, and others

0-8212-1607-4 BOOK SALES........$29.98

Elizabeth **Wilhide**

The Mackintosh Style

A look at Macintosh's life and work and how his still-vigorous ideas can be freshly reinterpreted today

0-8118-1032-1 CHRONICLE........$29.95

Art Deco

Victor **Arwas**

Art Deco

"This must be the most lavish book on Art Deco ever published. It may even be the last word on the movement"—*Artforum*

0-8109-1926-5 ABRAMS........$75.00

Patricia **Bayer**

Art Deco Architecture: Design, Decoration, and Detail from the Twenties and Thirties

The first international survey of the style, incorporating architects' drawings, archival pictures, and new photography

0-8109-1923-0 ABRAMS........$65.00

Alastair **Duncan**

American Art Deco

0-8109-1850-1 ABRAMS........$65.00

Kathryn **Hiesinger** & George **Marcus**

Landmarks of Twentieth-Century Design: An Illustrated Handbook

Highpoints and major monuments of modern design, with 400 illustrations

1-55859-279-2 ABBEVILLE........$55.00
0-7892-0008-2 ABBEVILLE PB........$29.95

Klaus-Jurgen **Sembach**

Style 1930

0-87663-865-5 ST. MARTIN'S PB........$14.95

Richard **Striner**

Art Deco

A comprehensive handbook to Art Deco architecture and style

1-55859-824-3 ABBEVILLE........$12.95

Modern and Contemporary Design

Andrea **Branzi**

The Hot House: Italian New Wave Design

0-262-02211-7 MIT........$32.50

Carla **Breeze**

New Modern

"New Modern" is a term used to describe the style of a generation of designers comfortable with the past yet enthusiastic about mass-produced elements and popular culture. The book provides examples of recent designs that use period styles and details, recycling, and both industrial and traditional materials

0-86636-327-0 PBC........$47.50

Andrea **DiNoto**

Art Plastic

The history of plastic and plastic objects

0-89659-437-8 ABBEVILLE........$55.00

Carol Soucek **King**

Designing with Glass

Visual tips for the creative use of today's new repertoire of glass products, as shown in over 100 houses around the world

0-86636-330-0 PBC........$42.50

Designing with Tile, Stone & Brick: The Creative Touch

Basic design materials, as used by acclaimed international interior designers and architects in contemporary residences

0-86636-328-9 PBC........$42.50

Designing with Wood: The Creative Touch

Color photographs explore the use of wood in contemporary interiors in a variety of styles

0-86636-329-7 PBC........$42.50
0-86636-427-7 PBC PB........$10.00

European Decorative Arts

General

Elizabeth **Gaynor**

Scandinavia Living Design

1-55670-364-3 STEWART, TABORI PB........$27.50

Lesley **Hoskins**, editor

The Papered Wall: History, Pattern, Technique

0-8109-3730-1 ABRAMS........$49.50

Owen **Jones**

The Grammar of Ornament: All 100 Color Plates from the Folio Edition of the Great Victorian Sourcebook of Historic Design

A reference book on style, first published in 1856. Includes Oriental, primitive, classical, medieval, and Renaissance design

0-486-25463-1 DOVER PB........$16.95

John **Morely**

Regency Design 1790-1840: Gardens, Buildings, Interiors, Furniture

The most ambitious survey of the period ever undertaken, lavishly illustrated with prints, watercolors, paintings, plans, and photographs of extant buildings and gardens

See also **ENGLISH DECORATION** under **INTERIOR DECORATION**

0-8109-3768-9 ABRAMS........$150.00

Nikolaus **Pevsner**

Pioneers of Modern Design

From William Morris to Walter Gropius, this is the first account of the development of the modern movement in design

0-14-055211-1 PENGUIN PB........$11.00
0-14-013714-9 VIKING PB........$13.95

Nancy J. **Troy**

Modernism and the Decorative Arts in France: Art Nouveau to Le Corbusier

0-300-04554-9 YALE........$42.50

Furniture

Charles **Boyce**

Dictionary of Furniture

The most comprehensive one-volume dictionary of furniture terminology, style, manufacture, and makers in all countries

0-8050-0752-0 HOLT PB........$22.50

Florence **de Dampierre**

The Best of Painted Furniture

Furniture from all periods; well-illustrated

0-8478-0804-1 RIZZOLI........$40.00
0-8478-1886-1 RIZZOLI PB........$34.95

Marian **Page**

Furniture Designed by Architects

The work of 26 prominent architects, from Kent and Adams to William Morris and Charles Eames

0-8230-7181-2 WATSON-GUPTILL PB........$24.95

Christopher **Payne**, editor

Sotheby's Concise Encyclopedia of Furniture

See also **FURNISHINGS** under **AMERICAN DECORATIVE ARTS**

1-85029-649-9 ANTIQUE COLLECTORS PB........$24.95

British and Irish Furniture

"Chippendale chairs imparted a lesson of sanity and balance. There was no attempt to conceal the practical purpose of the piece, asserted by its simple solid, straight legs. But on the back of the chair, delicately varied in Rococo or Gothic or exotic motifs and crowned with Cupid's bow, the decorative imagination was expressed."
—Mario Praz, *An Illustrated History of Interior Decoration*

J. Andrews
Price Guide to British Antique Furniture
0-907462-79-0 ANTIQUE COLLECTORS $59.50

Price Guide to Victorian, Edwardian and 1920s Furniture
0-902028-89-8 ANTIQUE COLLECTORS $59.50

Annette **Carruthers** & others
Good Citizens Furniture: The Arts and Crafts Collection at Cheltenham
0-85331-650-3 HUMANITIES PB $35.00

Clive D. **Edeards**
Victorian Furniture: Technology and Design
0-7190-3783-2 MANCHESTER PB $22.95

Christopher **Gilbert** & Tessa **Murdoch**
John Channon and Brass-Inlaid Furniture 1730-1760
0-300-05812-8 YALE $50.00

Nathaniel **Harris**
Chippendale
Thomas Chippendale, 1718-1779, was an English cabinetmaker so widely followed that much 18th-cent. English furniture is grouped under his name, though few pieces can be reliably traced to his workshop. His work was eclectic; to the Queen Anne and Georgian styles he added Chinese, Gothic, and rococo motifs
1-55521-390-1 BOOK SALES $14.98

George **Hepplewhite**
The Cabinet-Maker and Upholsterer's Guide
A 1794 manual
0-486-22183-0 DOVER PB $9.95

F. Lewis **Hinckley**
Hepplewhite, Sheraton and Regency Furniture
The styles which were popular during the regency of George IV (1811-1830), and the cabinetmakers who practiced them
0-8147-3446-4 NYU $70.00

Queen Anne and Georgian Looking Glasses: Old English and Early American
0-8147-3447-2 NYU $65.00

Gervase **Jackson-Stops**, editor
The Treasure Houses of Britain: 500 Years of Private Patronage and Art Collecting
The contents of the great English country houses, amassed on grand tours through Europe and selected for the exhibition held at the National Gallery in Washington
See also **COLLECTORS AND DEALERS** under **ART HISTORY: GENERAL STUDIES** in **ART**
0-300-03533-0 YALE $42.00

Thomas **Hope**
Regency Furniture and Interior Decoration
Facsimile of the book that announced the Regency style
See also **ENGLISH DECORATION** under **INTERIOR DECORATION**
0-486-21710-8 DOVER PB $9.95

Claudia **Kinmonth**
Irish Country Furniture, 1700-1950
The first study of Ireland's vernacular furniture, this thought-provoking book is well illustrated both with Kinmont's gorgeous color and a variety of vintage black-and-white photos. "A wonderful, inspiring book"—*World of Interiors*
0-300-06396-2 YALE PB $30.00

David **Linley**
Classical Furniture
Viscount Linley, himself a cabinetmaker of some repute, here discusses furniture
0-8109-3188-5 ABRAMS $60.00

Norman **Vandal**
Queen Anne Furniture: History, Design, and Construction
0-942391-07-1 TAUNTON $39.95

French Furniture

"Under Louis XIV came that sharp distinction between court furniture and bourgeois furniture which lasted up until the Neoclassical period: the bourgeois credenza, used to display handsome pottery, corresponded to the patrician cabinet, used for keeping precious objects." —Mario Praz, *An Illustrated History of Interior Decoration*

Leora **Auslander**
Taste and Power: Furnishing Modern France
Louis XIV, Regency, Rococo, Neoclassical, Empire, art nouveau: the changing meaning of furniture from the mid-17th century to World War I. A rich book about many things
See also **STYLE AND FASHION** under **EARLY MODERN EUROPE** in **WORLD HISTORY AND CURRENT AFFAIRS**
0-520-08894-8 CALIFORNIA $40.00

Yvonne **Brunhammer**
L'Art de Vivre: Decorative Arts and Design in France, 1789-1989
The finest in French furniture, tableware, clothes, jewelry, and design
0-86565-976-1 VENDOME $60.00

William **Rieder**
France, 1700-1800
A small but thorough guide to the decorative arts
0-87633-052-9 PHILADELPHIA MUSEUM PB $3.50

Jeanne **Siegel**
How to Speak Furniture with an Antique French Accent
1-56625-003-X BONUS PB $14.95

Other European Furniture

Antoine **Cheneviere**
The Golden Age of Russian Furniture, 1780-1850
Extravagant wood furniture, decorated with metals, porcelain, and precious stones. Includes objects from the collections of Catherine the Great
0-86565-099-3 VENDOME $75.00

George **Himmelheber**
Biedermeier, 1815-1835: Architecture, Painting, Sculpture, Decorative Art, Fashion
Named for the pseudonym of a group of German poets, Biedermeier was a movement which made high style comfortable and affordable
See also **GERMAN CULTURAL STUDIES** under **GERMANY** under **19TH-CENTURY EUROPE** in **WORLD HISTORY AND CURRENT AFFAIRS**
3-7913-1023-2 PRESTEL $75.00
3-7913-1620-6 PRESTEL PB $29.95

Gabriel P. **Weisberg**
Stile Floreale: The Cult of Nature in Italian Design
0-295-96671-8 WASHINGTON $45.00
0-295-96670-X WASHINGTON PB $24.95

Angus **Wilkie**
Biedermeier
A survey of the popular 19th-century style, lavishly illustrated. A special collector's edition bound in Biedermeier fabric
See also **OTHER DECORATIVE STYLES** under **INTERIOR DECORATION**
0-89659-749-0 ABBEVILLE $75.00

Modern Furniture

Arthur **Danto**
397 Chairs
A diverse selection of chairs made in the '70s and '80s included in an exhibition at the Architectural League
0-8109-1698-3 ABRAMS $34.95

Renato **de Fusco**
Le Corbusier, Designer: Furniture, 1929
An illustrated study
0-8120-5148-3 BARRONS $24.95

Christopher **Wilk**
Marcel Breuer: Furniture and Interior Design
0-87070-264-5 MOMA $22.50

Porcelain and Pottery

"The most beautiful vessels and plates of porcelain that one can describe are made here [in China]...And at a great scale, so great that for one Venetian groat you would actually have three bowls so beautiful that none would know how to devise them better."—Marco Polo

For related reading, see EAST ASIAN ART in ART

John A. **Bartlett**
British Ceramic Art 1870-1940
An illustrated tour of the world of clay in modern Britain
0-88740-456-1 SCHIFFER $69.95

David **Battie**
David Battie's Guide to Understanding 19th & 20th Century British Porcelain
1-85149-123-6 SOTHEBY'S $59.50

Victoria **Bergesen**
Encyclopaedia of British Art Pottery 1870-1920
0-7126-3822-9 BARRIE & JENKINS $100.00

Peter **Bradshaw**
18th Century English Porcelain Figures
0-902028-83-9 ANTIQUE COLLECTORS $49.50

A.W. **Coysh** & R.K. **Henrywood**
The Dictionary of Blue and White Pottery
0-907462-06-5 ANTIQUE COLLECTORS $79.50

Geoffrey **de Bellaigue**
The Louis XVI Service: The Sevres Porcelain in the Collection of Her Majesty the Queen
A sumptuous book describing the service made for Marie Antoinette's personal use at Versailles
0-521-26637-8 CAMBRIDGE $259.95

Richard K. **Degenhardt**
Belleek: The Complete Collector's Guide and Illustrated Reference
The second edition of this most thorough of guides to the famed Irish china
0-87069-698-X WALLACE-HOMESTEAD $60.00

Fiamma **Domestici**
Della Robbia: A Family of Artists
An examination of the first family of majolica and their influence on the ceramic arts
See also **VENICE AND THE NORTH** under **ITALY** under **EUROPEAN ART: THE RENAISSANCE** in **ART**
1-87835-145-1 RIVERSIDE PB $12.99

Michael **Doulton** & Vinny **Lee**
Discovering Royal Doulton
1-85310-343-8 VOYAGEUR $37.95

S.W. **Fisher**
English Pottery and Porcelain Marks: Including Scottish and Irish Marks
0-572-00711-6 FOULSHAM PB $7.99

Geoffrey **Godden**
British Porcelain: An Illustrated Guide
0-214-66851-7 BARRIE & JENKINS $100.00

English China
0-09-158300-4 DAVID & CHARLES $75.00

Geoffrey A. **Godden** & Michael **Gibson**
Collecting Lustreware
0-7126-4682-5 BARRIE & JENKINS $150.00

David **Howard**
Chinese Armorial Porcelain
By the leading expert in Chinese export porcelain
0-571-09811-8 FABER $225.00

Joan **Jones**
Minton the First Two Hundred Years of Design and Production
1-85310-283-0 ANTIQUE COLLECTORS $140.00

Marion **Langham**
Belleek Irish Porcelain: An Illustrated Guide to over Two Thousand Pieces
1-87094-877-7 QUILL $79.95

John & Griselda **Lewis**
Pratt Ware: English and Scottish Relief Decorated and Underglaze Coloured Earthenware 1780-1840
0-907462-56-1 ANTIQUE COLLECTORS $89.50

Joan **Liebowitz**
Yellow Ware
An illustrated guide to this type of pottery
0-88740-508-8 SCHIFFER PB $19.95

Mitchell W. **Marken**
Pottery from Spanish Shipwrecks 1500-1800
0-8130-1268-6 FLORIDA $49.95

Peter **Meister** & Horst **Reber**
European Porcelain of the 18th Century
0-8014-1443-1 CORNELL $99.50

Waltraud **Neuwirth**
Wiener Werkstatte Keramik: Original Ceramics, 1920-1931
3-900282-17-X SEVEN HILLS $79.00

Ann Marie **O'Neill**
Quimper Pottery
An illustrated guide to this French ware, produced in the city of Quimper near the Bay of Biscay
0-88740-650-5 SCHIFFER PB $16.95

Herbert **Schiffer** & others
Chinese Export Porcelain: Standard Patterns and Forms, 1780-1880
0-916838-01-3 SCHIFFER $37.50

Jeffrey B. **Snyder** & Leslie **Bockol**
Majolica: American & European Wares
0-88740-561-4 SCHIFFER PB $29.95

Gunther **Sterba**
Meissen Domestic Porcelain
0-7126-5047-4 BARRIE & JENKINS $100.00

Francis **Watson** & Gillian **Watson**
Mounted Oriental Porcelain in the J. Paul Getty Museum
0-89236-034-8 GETTY MUSEUM $49.95
0-295-96537-1 INTERNATIONAL EXHIBITIONS FOUNDATION PB $14.95

Glass

David **Battie** & Simon **Cottle**, editors
Sotheby's Concise Encyclopedia of Glass
An asset to any collector, this is a history of glassware from its inception to the present day. The book includes sections on Roman glass, Murano, paperweights, and 18th-century drinking glasses, and is illustrated with 300 color photographs and line drawings. Battie and Cottle have produced a volume which is as vibrant as it is informative
1-85029-654-5 ANTIQUE COLLECTORS PB $24.95

Vivienne **Becker** & John Bigelow **Taylor**
Swarovski: The Magic of Crystal
0-8109-4454-5 ABRAMS $39.95

R.J. **Charleston**
English Glass and the Glass Used in England, Circa 400-1940
0-04-748003-3 UNWIN HYMAN $40.00

Marianne **Stern** & Birgit **Schlick-Nolte**
Early Glass of the Ancient World
3-7757-0503-1 DISTRIBUTED ART PUB $80.00

Silver

Carl **Hernmarck**
The Art of the European Silversmith, 1430-1830
Two lavishly illustrated volumes
0-85667-034-0 SOTHEBY PARKE BERNET $195.00

Harold **Newman**
An Illustrated Dictionary of Silverware
British and American silverware, its decoration, makers, techniques, and styles. From 1500 to the present, with over 2300 entries
See also **SILVER AND PEWTER** under **FURNISHINGS** under **AMERICAN DECORATIVE ARTS**
0-500-23456-6 THAMES & HUDSON $39.95

Seymour **Wyler**
The Book of Old Silver: English, American, Foreign
This is the most comprehensive guide to hallmarks ever published, and even includes Sheffield plate marks. Here is advice on detecting frauds, a history of the world's great silversmiths, and a survey of the craft as practiced from Dublin to Calcutta, all in one volume
0-517-00089-X CROWN $28.00

Objets de Vertu and Objets d'Art

"It is perhaps not uninstructive to note that we have no English word to describe the class of household ornaments which French speech has provided with at least three designations, each indicating a delicate and almost imperceptible gradation of quality. In place of *bric-à-brac*, *bibelots*, *objets d'art*, we have only knickknacks."
—Edith Wharton, *The Decoration of Houses*

Abrams **Editors**
Lacquer: An International History and Illustrated Survey
From the sophisticated wares of 16th-century China and 17th-century Japan to its European and American adaptations
0-8109-1279-1 ABRAMS $75.00

Geza **von Habsburg**
Fabergé
The extensive catalogue of the 1987 Munich exhibition
0-8109-3320-9 ABRAMS $65.00

Rugs and Carpets

Enza **Milanesi**
The Bulfinch Guide to Carpets: How to Identify, Classify, and Evaluate Antique Carpets and Rugs
0-8212-2057-8 BULFINCH $19.95

Floor Coverings, Textiles, and Wallpaper

Murray **Douglas** & Chippy **Irvine**
Brunschwig & Fils Style
A lavish book celebrating the centennial of one of the most renowned textile houses in the world. Hundreds of color photos will inspire even the professional decorator
0-8212-2041-1 BULFINCH $45.00

French Provincial: 18th-Century Textile Designs
0-8109-2964-3 ABRAMS PB $14.95

Jennifer **Harris**, editor
Textiles: 5,000 Years, An International History and Illustrated Survey
See also **TEXTILES** under **AFRICAN AND ASIAN DECORATIVE ARTS**
0-8109-3875-8 ABRAMS $75.00

Donald **King** & Santina **Levey**
The Victoria & Albert Museum's Textile Collection : Embroidery in Britain from 1200 to 1750
1-55859-652-6 ABBEVILLE PB $24.95

Catherine **McDermott**, editor
English Eccentrics: The Textile Designs of Helen Littman
0-7148-2915-3 PHAIDON PB $19.95

Mary **Schoeser** & Kathleen **Dejardin**
French Textiles: From 1760 to the Present
1-85669-006-7 TRAFALGAR SQUARE $75.00

Christa C. Mayer **Thurman**
Textiles in The Art Institute of Chicago
0-8109-3856-1 ART INSTITUTE OF CHICAGO $35.00

The Victoria & Albert Museum
Novelty Fabrics, Designs For Shawls, Japanese Stencils, Thirties Floral Fabrics
Fabrics depicting Felix the Cat, cashmere shawls, Japanese patterns, and floral designs are beautifully reproduced in this set of small-sized books
0-8109-1741-6 ABRAMS $11.95

The Victoria & Albert Museum's Textile Collection: British Textiles from 1900-1937
1-55859-436-1 ABBEVILLE PB $24.95

Angela **Volker** & Ruperta **Pichler**
Textiles of the Wiener Werkstatte, 1910-1932
0-8478-1764-4 RIZZOLI $65.00

Sigrid Wortmann **Weltge**
Women's Work: Textile Art from the Bauhaus
This book focuses on the little acknowledged work of the predominantly female Bauhaus Weaving Workshop. Talented craftswomen developed ingenious, innovative ways of designing beautiful textiles for mass production. Rare illustrations, archival photographs, and in-depth interviews celebrate the legacy that lives on in fabrics still being produced today
See also **THE BAUHAUS AND RELATED CONSTRUCTIVISM** under **20TH-CENTURY ART** in **ART**
0-8118-0466-6 CHRONICLE $40.00

American Decorative Arts

General

Alastair **Duncan**
Masterworks of Louis Comfort Tiffany
0-8109-8118-1 ABRADALE $19.98

Steven **Heller** & Louise **Fili**
Streamline: American Art Deco Graphic Design
0-8118-0662-6 CHRONICLE PB $16.95

Pat **Kirkham**
Charles and Ray Eames: Designers of the 20th Century
See also **AMERICAN DECORATION** under **INTERIOR DECORATION**
0-262-11199-3 MIT $55.00

Philip **Kopper**
Colonial Williamsburg
See also **EARLY AMERICAN FURNITURE** under **FURNISHINGS**
0-8109-0787-9 ABRAMS $60.00

Susan Grant **Lewin**
Formica and Design: From the Counter Top to High Art
0-8478-1334-7 RIZZOLI $50.00

Gillian **Naylor**
The Encyclopedia of Arts and Crafts: The International Arts Movement, 1850-1920
0-525-24804-8 PENGUIN $14.98

Eva **Weber**
American Art Deco
0-517-06712-9 CRESCENT $16.99

Gillian **Wilson**
Selections from the Decorative Arts in the J. Paul Getty Museum
0-89236-050-X GETTY MUSEUM PB $29.95
0-89236-037-2 GETTY MUSEUM PB $39.95

Shaker Arts

Beverley **Gordon**
Shaker Textile Arts
0-87451-242-5 NEW ENGLAND PB $19.95

John **Kassay**
The Book of Shaker Furniture
0-87023-275-4 MASSACHUSETTS $60.00

David **Larkin**
The Essential Book of Shaker: Discovering the Design, Function, and Form
Larkin's informative text is illustrated by color photos of Shaker interior and exterior detail. Discusses the origins, forms, and elements that combine to create Shaker style. From the author of *Wooden Ship*
0-7893-0007-9 UNIVERSE $17.95

Robert F. W. **Meader**
Illustrated Guide to Shaker Furniture
An authoritative guide, describing the distinguishing marks and details such as finials,

caning, and decals. 175 photos showing 267 individual pieces
0-486-22819-3 DOVER PB $9.95

Charles **Muller** & Timothy **Rieman**
The Shaker Chair
A thorough study of its style and production
0-87023-795-0 MASSACHUSETTS PB $26.95

Timothy D. **Rieman** & Jean M. **Burks**
The Complete Book of Shaker Furniture
The most extensive survey of Shaker furniture to date examines its 130-year history (not just the classic period 1820-1850); organized by community of origin, with 162 illustrations and 300 photographs
0-8109-3841-3 ABRAMS $75.00

June **Sprigg**
Inner Light: The Shaker Legacy
0-917788-57-5 GNOMON PB $24.95

Shaker Design
Exhibition catalog from the Whitney Museum
0-393-30544-9 NORTON PB $39.95

Folk Art and Americana

Jay **Cantor**
Winterthur
The first serious private collection of Americana, now an important museum
0-8109-1785-8 ABRAMS $60.00

Mary Randolph **Carter**
American Junk
An inspirational book for anyone who's ever been tempted by junk shops or garage sales. Carter describes how to care for and decorate with Fiestaware, Western junk, paint-by-number pictures, camp crafts, and more
0-670-84400-4 STUDIO $32.95

Mary **Emmerling** & Richard **Trask**
Collecting American Country: How to Select, Maintain and Display Country Pieces
0-517-54957-3 CROWN $45.00

Tobin **Fraley**
The Carousel Animal
This handsome book by one of the country's premier carousel animal restorers is breathtaking. Color photos and informative text on the chariots, rabbits, geese, mermen, zebras, and of course, horses that make merry-go-rounds so memorable
See also **CRAFTS**
0-87701-454-X CHRONICLE PB $16.95

Frederick **Fried**
A Pictorial History of the Carousel
A large-format book on carousel animals, their history, and the artisans and factories that made them
0-911572-29-5 VESTAL $34.95

Henry **Glassie**
The Spirit of Folk Art
Perhaps the most thought-provoking book on the subject
See also **FOLK ART** under **AMERICAN ART** in **ART**
0-8109-2438-2 ABRAMS PB $29.95

Steve **Miller**
The Art of the Weathervane
0-88740-005-1 SCHIFFER $35.00

Jacquelyn **Oak**
Sotheby's Guide to American Folk Art
Tells the collector where to find and how to buy everything from weathervanes and whirlygigs, textiles, paintings, furniture, and more. Includes information on judging rarity, evaluating quality, and caring for and protecting folk art of all varieties
0-671-89950-3 FIRESIDE PB $16.00

Rebecca **Sawyer-Fay**
Living With Folk Art
0-688-11666-3 HEARST $25.00

Crafts

Louis D. **Rubin**, Jr.
Small Craft Advisory: A Book About the Building of a Boat
In the tradition of Mark Twain and Herman Melville, Rubin explores humankind's long-time passion for boats through his own often hilarious memoirs of boating adventures. *Small Craft Advisory* will prove delightful for landlubbers and sailors alike
0-87113-533-7 ATLANTIC MONTHLY PB $12.00

Peter H. **Spectre** & David **Larkin**
Wooden Ship: The Art, History, and Revival of Wooden Boatbuilding
A splendid illustrated guide to traditional boatbuilding, by America's leading authority on wooden boats in collaboration with an eminent book designer. Includes 200 color photographs
0-395-56692-4 HOUGHTON MIFFLIN $50.00

Constance **Stapleton**
Crafts of America: A Guide to the Finest Traditional Crafts Made in the United States
How they are made, who makes them, and where to buy them
0-060-96079-5 HARPER & ROW $39.95

Carol **Sterbenz**
American Country Folk Crafts: 50 Country Craft Projects For Decorating Your Home
Includes instructions for quilts, hooked rugs, stuffed animals, and cigar Indians. An attractive gift book
0-8109-1857-9 ABRAMS $29.95

Decoys

Adele **Earnest**
The Art of the Decoy: American Bird Carvings
0-916838-58-7 SCHIFFER PB $19.95

Henry A. **Fleckenstein**
Decoys of the Mid-Atlantic Region
0-88740-174-0 SCHIFFER PB $19.95

Southern Decoys, of Virginia and the Carolinas
0-916838-86-2 SCHIFFER $39.50

Shore Bird Decoys
0-916838-32-3 SCHIFFER $35.00

Linda **Kangas** & Gene **Kangas**
Collector's Guide to Decoys
0-87069-580-0 WALLACE-HOMESTEAD PB $17.95

Quilts

Roderick **Kiracofe**
The American Quilt: A History of Cloth and Comfort 1750-1950
More than just decorative or functional household items, American quilts are a true folk art that tell the story of the people who created them and the times they lived in. This wonderfully researched book, featuring over 250 full-color illustrations, places quilts and the women who created them in their historical and cultural context, while imparting practical guidelines for dating, evaluating and caring for quilts
PHOTOGRAPHS BY SHARON RISEDORPH
0-517-57535-3 CLARKSON POTTER $60.00

Elizabeth V. **Warren** & Sharon L. **Eisenstat**
Glorious American Quilts: The Quilt Collection of the Museum of American Folk Art
0-670-86913-9 STUDIO $34.95

Furnishings

Jeremy **Adamson**
American Wicker: Woven Furniture from 1850 to 1930
0-8478-1670-2 RIZZOLI $45.00

Luke **Beckerdite**, editor
American Furniture 1996
0-87451-793-1 NEW ENGLAND PB $49.95

Ethel **Bjerkoe**
Cabinetmakers of America
0-916838-00-5 APOLLO $22.50

Joseph **Butler**

Field Guide to American Antique Furniture: A Unique Visual System For Identifying the Style of Virtually Any Piece of American Antique Furniture

Clearly illustrates the subtle differences between virtually all styles of furniture crafted in the United States, from 17th-century pieces to examples of the Arts & Crafts style. 1700 drawings

0-8050-0124-7 HOLT PB $19.95

Edward S. **Cooks**

New American Furniture: The Second Generation of Studio Furnituremakers

0-87846-315-1 MUSEUM OF FINE ARTS PB $18.95

Eileen **Dubrow** & Richard **Dubrow**

American Furniture of the Nineteenth Century: 1840-1880

0-916838-68-4 SCHIFFER $30.00

Richard **Dubrow** & Eileen **Dubrow**

Furniture Made in America, 1875-1905

0-88740-695-5 SCHIFFER PB $24.95

William **Elder** & Jayne **Stokes**

American Furniture, 1680-1880: From the Collection of the Baltimore Museum

0-912298-62-6 BALTIMORE MUSEUM PB $20.00

Don **Fredgant**

American Manufactured Furniture: A Complete Guide to Furniture Produced in the 1920s

0-88740-770-6 SCHIFFER PB $37.50

Emyl **Jenkins**

Emyl Jenkins' Appraisal Book: Identifying, Understanding, and Valuing Your Treasures

An indispensable guide to just about anything to do with antique furniture, from making a photo inventory to holding a garage sale or settling an estate. "It's a jungle out there in personal property land… [This] is just the sharp edge that may help you cut your way out of it" —Samuel Pennington, *Maine Antiques Digest*

0-517-88434-8 CROWN PB $15.00

Emyl Jenkins' Reproduction Furniture: Antiques for the Next Generation

"Emyl shows us why Nineteenth and early Twentieth Century reproductions soon will be valued the same way we now prize our Eighteenth Century antiques"—Mario Buatta, Interior Designer

0-517-58527-8 CROWN $25.00

Myrna **Kaye**

Fake, Fraud Or Genuine: Identifying Authentic American Antique

Examines American furniture of the last three centuries, with intriguing stories of some spectacular frauds. "This book is to be studied thoroughly, until you have memorized every morsel"—*Antique Monthly*

0-8212-1825-5 BULFINCH PB $29.95

William C. **Ketchum**, Jr.

American Cabinetmakers: Marked American Furniture, 1640-1940

Catalogs and illustrates all known American wood furniture pieces marked by the signatures, brands, or labels of their makers. Documents over 1,600 artisans

0-517-59562-1 CROWN $45.00

Milo M. **Naeve**

Identifying American Furniture: A Pictorial Guide to Styles and Terms, Colonial to Contemporary

0-910050-96-1 ALTMR PB $15.00

Patricia **Petraglia**

American Antique Furniture: Styles and Origins, 1640-1840

0-8317-0290-7 SMITHMARK $14.98

Sotheby's Guide to American Furniture

An authoritative and fully illustrated field guide to every style of American furniture, from Pilgrim to Design Reform. Includes a list of locations, open to the public, where can one see the best examples of each

0-684-80681-9 FIRESIDE PB $18.00

Albert **Sack**

The New Fine Points of Furniture: Early American, Good, Better, Best, Superior, Masterpiece

An expansion on Sack's ground-breaking "good, better, best" rating system for American furniture pieces, evaluating all new material. Compares similar pieces to highlight what makes the difference between a "good" piece and a masterpiece. 650 color photos

0-517-58820-X CROWN $50.00

Jeanne **Siegel**

How to Speak Furniture With an Antique American Accent: Buying, Selling, and Appraisal Tips Plus Price Guides

0929287368 BONUS PB $12.95

Bernice **Steinbaum**

The Rocker: An American Design Tradition

0-8478-1587-0 RIZZOLI $40.00

Robert **Swedberg** & Harriet **Swedberg**

American Oak Furniture Styles and Prices

A brief study

0-87069-475-8 WALLACE-HOMESTEAD PB $16.95

Gerald W.R. **Ward**

American Case Furniture in the Mabel Brady Garvan and Other Collections At Yale University

"Illustrates and documents 233 chests, boxes, desks, sideboards, cupboards, cellarettes, pianos, and even a radio, made between 1650 and 1935"—*Maine Antique Digest*

0-300-03357-5 YALE $60.00

Early American Furniture

John A. **Fleming**

The Painted Furniture of French Canada: 1700-1840

0-921820-85-2 CAMDEN $34.95

Russell **Kettell**

Pine Furniture of Early New England

Every aspect and type of Colonial pine furniture. A guide for collectors, with more than 200 examples

0-486-20145-7 DOVER PB $19.95

Philip **Kopper**

Colonial Williamsburg

0-8109-0787-9 ABRAMS $60.00

Charles **Santore**

The Windsor Style in America: A Continuing Study of the History and Regional Characteristics of the Most Popular Furniture Form of 18th Century America, 1730-1840

The definitive study, with 275 illustrations and original drawings

1-56138-057-1 RUNNING PRESS $60.00

Mary Dodds **Schlick**

Columbia River Basketry: Gift of the Ancestors, Gift of the Earth

0-295-97249-1 WASHINGTON $60.00

0-295-97289-0 WASHINGTON PB $35.00

Period Furniture

George **Stickley**

Stickley Craftsman Furniture Catalogs

Reprints of two 1910 mission furniture catalogs

0-486-23838-5 DOVER PB $9.95

el **Donbar**
Federal Furniture
A solid overview of this American style
0-8446-6445-6 SMITH $25.25

Eileen **Dubrow**
Furniture Made in America, 1875-1985
0-916838-66-8 SCHIFFER PB $19.95

Eileen **Dubrow** & Richard **Dubrow**
American Furniture of the 19th Century, 1840-80
0-686-47035-4 SCHIFFER $30.00

Wendell **Garrett**
Classic America: The Federal Style & Beyond
A glorious look at the domestic architecture and design of the early United States
See also **AMERICAN DECORATION** under **INTERIOR DECORATION**
0-7893-0024-9 UNIVERSE PB $25.00

L. **Stickley** & J.G. **Stickley**
Early L. & J.G. Stickley Furniture: From Onondaga Shops to Handcraft
A comprehensive look at the designs of two of Gustav Stickley's brothers, who founded their own Arts & Crafts Workshop. 260 illustrations
0-486-26926-4 DOVER PB $9.95

Christopher **Wills**
Thonet Bentwood and Other Furniture: The 1904 Illustrated Catalogue and Supplements
One of the firm's rarest catalogs; an invaluable guide for identifying and authenticating vintage Thonet bentwood. Line drawings with descriptions
See also **MODERN FURNITURE**
0-486-24024-X DOVER PB $14.95

Regional and Rustic Furniture

Elmo **Baca**
Rio Grande High Style: Furniture Craftsmen
0-87905-621-5 GIBBS SMITH $39.95

Richard C.R. **Barder**
Georgian Bracket Clocks, 1714-1830
1-85149-158-9 ANTIQUE COLLECTORS $89.50

Marilyn Conover **Barker**
The Legacy of Mormon Furniture
Brigham Young, a trained cabinet maker in his own right, commissioned countless pieces of furniture from Mormon craftsmen, many of them Europeans who had converted to his faith. The richly detailed style that arose amongst the L.D.S. settlements combines elements of Empire and Scandinavian design in a truly distinctive manner
0-87905-632-0 GIBBS SMITH $29.95

Isabella **de Lisle Selby**
Wrist Watches: The Collector's Guide to Selecting, Acquiring, and Enjoying New and Vintage Wrist Watches
1-56138-431-3 COURAGE $9.98

Elizabeth Clair **Flood**
Cowboy High Style: Thomas Molesworth to the New West
An intriguing examination of Cody, Wyoming, "cowboy" furniture designer Thomas Molesworth, and the contemporary renaissance of the rustic style he originated
0-87905-672-X GIBBS SMITH PB $24.95

Brock W. **Jobe**
Portsmouth Furniture: Masterworks from the New Hampshire Seacoast
0-87451-608-0 NEW ENGLAND PB $45.00

Ralph R. **Kylloe**
Rustic Furniture Makers
This volume takes a look at the wild elegance of 15 artisans' work. 140 color photos
0-87905-680-0 GIBBS SMITH $29.95

Rustic Traditions
0-87905-670-3 GIBBS SMITH PB $24.95

Brian **Loomes**
Painted Dial Clocks
1-85149-183-X ANTIQUE COLLECTORS $59.50

Derek **Roberts**
Carriage and Other Traveling Clocks
0-88740-454-5 SCHIFFER $99.95

Robert **Swedberg** & Harriett **Swedberg**
American Clocks and Clockmakers
A concise and informative look at 350 clocks available to the collector, including pricing guidelines and tips on smart buying practices, plus a considered horological history of the United States
0-87069-525-8 WALLACE-HOMESTEAD PB $16.95

Ly D. **Tran**
Longcase Clocks and Standing Regulators: Machine Made Clocks
0-930163-60-5 ARLINGTON $69.50

Modern Furniture

Mel **Byars**
The Chairs of Frank Lloyd Wright: Seven Decades of Design
0-471-14372-3 PRESERVATION $39.95

Cara **Greenberg**
Mid-Century Modern: Furniture of the 1950s
PHOTOGRAPHS BY TIM STREET-PORTER
0-517-88475-5 HARMONY PB $22.50

Clive D. **Edwards**
Twentieth-Century Furniture: Materials, Manufacture and Markets
0-7190-4066-3 MANCHESTER $69.95
0-7190-4067-1 MANCHESTER PB $19.95

Steven **Rouland** & Roger W. **Rouland**
Heywood-Wakefield Modern Furniture
0-89145-624-4 COLLECTOR PB $18.95

Ghenete **Zelleke** & others
Against the Grain: Bentwood Furniture from the Collection of Fern and Manfred Steinfeld
0-86559-113-X ART INSTITUTE OF CHICAGO $29.95

Glass

Bill **Edwards**
Standard Encyclopedia of Carnival Glass
Over 1000 pieces of glass in full iridescent color. American, English, and Australian examples are all featured in this definitive guide
0-89145-689-9 COLLECTOR $24.95
0-89145-187-0 COLLECTOR $24.95

Gene **Florence**
Collectible Glassware from the '40s, '50s, '60s: An Illustrated Value Guide
As Depression glass becomes more and more popular among collectors, much attention has begun to focus on the glassware of the following decades. Should become the standard reference in this field.
0-89145-662-7 COLLECTOR $19.95

The Collector's Encyclopedia of Depression Glass
This is the 11th edition of the best-selling book on glassware in America. Lavishly illustrated in color, it details everything from "A to W," Adam to Windsor, and even describes how to spot reproductions
0-89145-554-X COLLECTOR $19.95

Mollie Helen **McCain**
Collector's Encyclopedia of Pattern Glass
0-89145-211-7 COLLECTOR PB $12.95

Albert **Revi**
Nineteenth Century Glass
0-916838-43-9 SCHIFFER $29.50

John **Shuman**
The Collector's Encyclopedia of American Art Glass
0-89145-355-5 COLLECTOR $29.95

Martha **Swan**
American Cut and Engraved Glass of the Brilliant Period
The special vocabulary used to describe motifs and designs, how to judge the age of pieces, and how to assess the value of signatures from the period 1876-1916
0-87069-713-7 WALLACE-HOMESTEAD $45.00

Pottery and Porcelain

Tile

Ronald L. **Rindge**
Ceramic Art of the Malibu Potteries 1926-1932
The Malibu Potteries made brightly colored, patterned art tile in the Spanish tradition which was used to decorate many California houses, including the ranch of "The Cisco Kid"
0-295-97372-2 WASHINGTON PB $35.00

Roslyn **Siegel**
Country Floors Decorating With Tiles
Advice from the premier tile retailer in America, gorgeously illustrated
1-56799-150-5 FRIEDMAN/FAIRFAX PB $15.95

Ceramics

Warren F. **Broderick** & William **Bouck**
Pottery Works: Potteries of New York State's Capital District and Upper Hudson Region
0-8386-3538-5 FAIRLEIGH DICKINSON $59.50

Garth **Clark** & others
The Mad Potter of Biloxi: The Art and Life of George Ohr
0-89659-927-2 ABBEVILLE $85.00

Alice Cooney **Frelinghuysen**
American Art Pottery: Selections from the Charles Hosmer Morse Museum of American Art
1-88069-904-4 ORLANDO MUSEUM OF ART PB $35.00

American Porcelain, 1770-1920
Published to coincide with an exhibition at the Metropolitan Museum of Art, this book includes outstanding illustrations and a detailed history of stylistic development
0-8109-1887-0 METROPOLITAN MUSEUM $60.00

Mary Frank **Gaston**
Collector's Encyclopedia of Flow Blue China
0-89145-580-9 COLLECTOR $24.95

Lucile **Henzke**
Art Pottery of America
A revised edition
0-7643-0159-4 SCHIFFER $45.00

Bob **Huxford** & Sharon **Huxford**
The Collector's Encyclopedia of Fiesta: With Harlequin and Riviera
0-89145-449-7 COLLECTOR $19.95

Ralph **Kovel** & Terry **Kovel**
Kovels' American Art Pottery: The Collector's Guide to Makers, Marks, and Factory Histories
0-517-58012-8 CROWN $60.00

Jim **Mangus** & Bev **Mangus**
Shawnee Pottery: An Identification & Value Guide
0-89145-574-4 COLLECTOR $24.95

Bill **Mercer**
Singing the Clay: Pueblo Pottery of the Southwest, Yesterday and Today
0-931537-18-5 CINCINNATI ART MUSEUM PB $12.50

Betty **Newbound** & Bill **Newbound**
Blue Ridge Dinnerware: Southern Potteries Incorporated: An Illustrated Value Guide
0-89145-391-1 COLLECTOR PB $14.95

Alex **Patterson**
Hopi Pottery Symbols
1-55566-120-3 JOHNSON PB $17.95

Mitch **Tuchman**
Bauer: Classic American Pottery
The J.A. Bauer Pottery company (1885-1962) originated the idea of colored pottery for the dinner table. 86 color photos chronicle the history of this remarkable company's wares
0-8118-0901-3 CHRONICLE $18.95

Silver and Pewter

John **Adair**
The Navajo and Pueblo Silversmiths
0-8061-2215-3 OKLAHOMA PB $13.95

Charles **Carpenter**
Gorham Silver, 1831-1981
1-55660-244-8 ALAN WOFSY FINE ARTS $135.00

Tiffany Silver
1-55660-243-X ALAN WOFSY FINE ARTS $125.00

M. **Dolan**
American Sterling Silver Flatware 1830s-1990s: A Collector's Identification and Value Guide
0-89689-095-3 BOOKS AMERICANA PB $22.95

Stephen **Ensko**
American Silversmiths and Their Marks
The definitive directory for serious collectors. Over 3000 goldsmiths and silversmiths working from 1650 to 1850 are listed with biographical details, location of shops, and maps of smithing centers
0-87923-778-3 GODINE $65.00
0-486-24428-8 DOVER PB $8.95

George S. **Gibb**
Whitesmiths of Taunton: A History of Reed and Barton, 1824-1943
0-405-08071-9 AYER $51.95

John A. **Hyman**
Silver at Williamsburg: Drinking Vessels
0-87935-125-X
COLONIAL WILLIAMSBURG FOUNDATION PB $19.95

Henry J. **Kauffman**
The American Pewterer: His Techniques & His Products
1-87933-553-0 ASTRAGAL PB $22.95

Harold **Newman**
An Illustrated Dictionary of Silverware
British and American silverware, its decoration, makers, techniques, and styles. From 1500 to the present, with over 2300 entries
See also **SILVER** under **EUROPEAN DECORATIVE ARTS**
0-500-23456-6 THAMES & HUDSON $39.95

Richard **Osterberg**
Sterling Silver Flatware for Dining Elegance: With Price Guide
0-88740-630-0 SCHIFFER $39.95

Dorothy T. **Rainwater**
Encyclopedia of American Silver Manufacturers
0-88740-046-9 SCHIFFER PB $19.95

Dorothy T. **Rainwater** & Ivan H. **Rainwater**
American Silverplate
0-88740-128-7 SCHIFFER $37.50

Textiles and Wallpaper

Gideon **Bosker** & others
Fabulous Fabrics of the '50s: And Other Terrific Textiles of the '20s, '30s, and '40s
0-87701-811-1 CHRONICLE PB $16.95

Katharine W. **Fernstrom** & Anita E. **Jones**
Northern Lights: Inuit Textile Art from the Canadian Arctic
0-912298-66-9 BALTIMORE MUSEUM PB $14.95

Nora **Fisher**
Rio Grande Textiles
0-89013-266-6 MUSEUM OF NEW MEXICO PB $29.95

Richard C. **Nylander**
Wallpapers for Historic Buildings: A Guide to Selecting Reproduction Wallpapers
0-471-14431-2 PRESERVATION PB $19.95

Ronald **Rees**
Interior Landscapes: Gardens and the Domestic Environment
An examination of the mural
0-8018-4467-3 JOHNS HOPKINS $35.00

Margot Blum **Schevill** & Christopher H. **Lutz**
Maya Textiles of Guatemala: The Gustavus A. Eisen Collection, 1902 at the Hearst Museum of Anthropology
0-292-75143-5 TEXAS $65.00
0-292-77665-9 TEXAS PB $29.95

Rebecca **Stone-Miller**
To Weave for The Sun: Ancient Andean Textiles
The catalogue of the collection of ancient and colonial Andean textiles in the Museum of Fine Arts, Boston, this book presents a chronological overview of the astonishing accomplishments of the weaver as artist from 500 B.C. to the 19th century
See also **MEXICO AND CENTRAL AMERICA** under **NATIVE AMERICAN ARTS** in **ART**
0-500-27793-1 THAMES & HUDSON PB $34.95

Rugs, Carpets, and Blankets

Tyrone **Campbell** & others
Navajo Pictorial Weaving, 1880-1950
0-8263-1617-4 NEW MEXICO PB $29.95

Don **Dedera**
Navajo Rugs: How to Find, Evaluate, Buy, and Care for Them
0-87358-635-2 NORTHLAND PB $14.95

Bill **Harmsen**
Patterns and Sources of Navajo Weaving
0-9601322-2-8 HARMS PB $14.95

Joel **Kopp** & Kate **Kopp**
American Hooked and Sewn Rugs: Folk Art Underfoot
0-8263-1616-6 NEW MEXICO PB $29.95

Marian E. **Rodee**
One Hundred Years of Navajo Rugs
0-8263-1576-3 NEW MEXICO PB $29.95

African and Asian Decorative Arts

Soetsu **Yanagi**
The Unknown Craftsman: A Japanese Insight into Beauty
0-87011-948-6 KODANSHA PB $32.00

General

Henry **Glassie**
Turkish Traditional Art Today
A gorgeously illustrated compendium on Anatolian decorative arts, by a master in the field
0-253-32555-2 INDIANA $89.95

Thomas F. **Judge**
Edo Craftsmen: Master Artisans of Old Tokyo
PHOTOGRAPHS BY TOMITA, HIROYUKI
0-8348-0280-5 WEATHERHILL $34.95

Rachel **Ward**
Islamic Metalwork
A concise illustrated treatment of the diversity of materials, techniques, motifs, and diverse local styles of this important craft, from the seventh through the fifteenth centuries
See also **ISLAMIC DECORATIVE ARTS** under **ISLAMIC ART AND ARCHITECTURE** in **ART**
0-500-27731-1 THAMES & HUDSON PB $15.95

William **Warren** & Luca Invernizzi **Tettoni**
Arts and Crafts of Thailand
0-8118-1026-7 CHRONICLE $35.00

Herbert **Ypma**
India Modern: Traditional and Contemporary Design
The first photographic examination of contemporary Indian architecture, design, and craft. Without ignoring India's rich classical heritage, Ypma elucidates the dramatic aesthetics of a design rooted in tradition but teeming with modernity
0-7148-3185-9 PHAIDON $49.95

Lacquerware

Derek **Clifford**
Chinese Carved Lacquer
1-87007-620-6 ANTIQUE COLLECTORS $59.50

Michael **Knight**
East Asian Lacquers in the Collection of the Seattle Art Museum
0-932216-42-0 SEATTLE ART MUSEUM PB $4.95

Pierre-F. **Schneeberger**
Japanese Lacquer
0-7103-0396-3 COLUMBIA $374.00

James C. Y. **Watt** & Barbara Brennan **Ford**
East Asian Lacquer: The Florence and Herbert Irving Collection
0-8109-6406-6 METROPOLITAN MUSEUM $65.00

Tile

Stefano **Carboni** & Tomoko **Masuya**
Persian Tiles
0-8109-6469-4 METROPOLITAN MUSEUM PB $5.95

Hans Van **Lemmen**
Tiles: A Collector's Guide
0-285-62957-3 INTL SPECIALIZED $14.95

Venetia **Porter**
Islamic Tiles
1-56656-191-4 INTERLINK PB $16.95

Pottery and Porcelain

Asian Art Museum of San Francisco
Thai Ceramics: The James & Ellen Connell Collection
See also **SOUTHEAST ASIA** under **EAST ASIAN ART** in **ART**
967-65-3043-3 OXFORD PB $75.00

Nurhan **Atasoy** & Lulian **Raby**
Iznik: The Pottery of Ottoman Turkey
The definite account of the great ceramic center whose stylistic phases reflect the major changes in Ottoman taste from the late 15th to the 17th century
See also **ISLAMIC DECORATIVE ARTS** under **ISLAMIC ART AND ARCHITECTURE** in **ART**
0-500-97374-1 THAMES & HUDSON $100.00

Gerald **Davison**
The Handbook of Marks on Chinese Ceramics
0-906610-20-6 ANTIQUE COLLECTORS $60.00

John Quentin **Feller**
Chinese Export Porcelain in the 19th Century: The Canton Famille Rose Porcelains
0-87577-069-X PEABODY ESSEX MUSEUM PB $15.00

Ernst J. **Grube**
Cobalt and Lustre: The First Centuries of Islamic Pottery
0-19-727607-5 OXFORD $295.00

Hiromu **Honda** & Noriki **Shimazu**
Vietnamese and Chinese Ceramics Used in the Japanese Tea Ceremony
0-19-588607-0 OXFORD $85.00

David S. **Howard**

The Choice of the Private Trader: The Private Market in Chinese Export Porcelain Illustrated in the Hodroff

0-302-00642-7 SOTHEBY'S $80.00

Douglas Moore **Kenrick**

Jomon of Japan: The World's Oldest Pottery

0-7103-0475-7 KEGAN & PAUL $144.50

Frances **Klapthor**

Chinese Ceramics: From the Collection of the Baltimore Museum of Art

A magnificent collection of Chinese pottery and porcelain

0-912298-65-0 BALTIMORE MUSEUM PB $14.95

Duncan **MacIntosh**

Chinese Blue and White Porcelain

1-85149-210-0 SOTHEBY'S $59.50

Jean McClure **Mudge**

Chinese Export Porcelain for the American Trade, 1785-1835

0-87413-166-9 DELAWARE $55.00

Charles K. **Wilkinson**

Nishapur: Pottery of the Early Islamic Period

0-8109-6465-1 METROPOLITAN MUSEUM $45.00

Textiles

Peter **Adler** & Nicholas **Barnard**

African Majesty: The Textile Art of the Ashanti and Ewe

0-500-27844-X THAMES & HUDSON PB $29.95

Asafo!: African Flags of the Fante

0-500-27684-6 THAMES & HUDSON PB $19.95

Nicholas **Barnard**

Living With Decorative Textiles: Tribal Art from Africa, Asia and the Americas

0-500-27821-0 THAMES & HUDSON PB $24.95

Joyce **Burnard**

Chintz and Cotton: India's Textile Gift to the World

0-86417-597-3 KANGAROO $24.95

Sukla **Das**

Fabric Art: Heritage of India

81-7017-264-0 SOUTH ASIA $98.50

John **Gillow**

Traditional Indonesian Textiles

See also **SOUTHEAST ASIA** under **EAST ASIAN ART** in **ART**

0-500-23641-0 THAMES & HUDSON $40.00
0-500-27820-2 THAMES & HUDSON PB $22.50

Jennifer **Harris**, editor

Textiles: 5,000 Years, An International History and Illustrated Survey

See also **FLOOR COVERINGS, TEXTILES, AND WALLPAPER** under **EUROPEAN DECORATIVE ARTS**

0-8109-3875-8 ABRAMS $75.00

Kokyo **Hatanaka**

Textile Arts of India

0-8118-1084-4 CHRONICLE $60.00

Sandra A. **Niessen**

Batik Cloth and Clothing: A Dynamic Indonesian Tradition

An examination of the textile printing method using hot wax and cool vegetable dye that has been utilized in Indonesia for over 1,000 years

See also **SOUTHEAST ASIA** under **EAST ASIAN ART** in **ART**

967-65-3040-9 OXFORD $49.95

Rugs and Carpets

Lee **Allane**

Chinese Rugs: A Buyer's Guide

What you need to know when in the market for a Chinese rug

0-500-01541-4 THAMES & HUDSON $24.95
0-500-27701-X THAMES & HUDSON PB $15.95

Jeff W. **Boucher**

Baluchi Woven Treasures

An intensive guide to the rustic rugs of the nomadic Persians known as Baluch, now mostly associated with Afghan and Pakistani designs

1-85669-079-2 ANTIQUE COLLECTORS $50.00

P.R.J. **Ford**

Oriental Carpet Design: A Guide to Traditional Motifs, Patterns and Symbols

This in-depth examination of rug motifs and patterns is fully illustrated

0-500-27664-1 THAMES & HUDSON PB $34.95

Leonard **Harrow**

The Fabric of Paradise

In Persian, the words paradise, garden, and rug are all related

0-905906-67-5 INTERLINK $39.95

Leonard M. **Helfgott**

Ties That Bind: A Social History of the Iranian Carpet

1-56098-269-1 SMITHSONIAN $39.00
1-56098-726-X SMITHSONIAN PB $19.95

Jenny **Housego**

Tribal Rugs: An Introduction to the Weaving of the Tribes of Iran

The deep, rich colors and rugged patterns of these rugs have made them popular with today's collector

1-56656-218-X INTERLINK PB $19.95

Alastair **Hull** & Nicholas **Barnard**

Living With Kilims

0-500-27822-9 THAMES & HUDSON PB $24.95

Alastair **Hull** & Jose **Luczyc-Wyhowska**

Kilim: The Complete Guide: History, Pattern, Technique, Identification

What eveyone should know about these woven Turkish rugs and textiles prized for their geometric designs in rich, brilliant hues

0-8118-0359-7 CHRONICLE $75.00

Aram K. **Jerrehian**, Jr.

Oriental Rug Primer: Buying and Understanding New Oriental Rugs

Covers each country, with a comprehensive glossary

0-89471-077-X RUNNING PRESS PB $14.95

Louise **MacKie** & Jon **Thompson**, editor

Turkmen: Tribal Carpets and Traditions

0-295-96595-9 WASHINGTON $75.00

R.D. **Parsons**

Oriental Rugs: The Rugs of Afghanistan

Covers the entire history of Afghani rugs, including the newer war textiles, sometimes called "Helicopter Baluchis," now being collected worldwide

1-85149-144-9 ANTIQUE COLLECTORS $59.50

Essie **Sakhai**

Oriental Carpets: A Buyer's Guide

An illustrated introduction to the world of the oriental rug

1-55921-146-6 MOYER BELL PB $16.95

Jon **Thompson**

Oriental Carpets: From the Tents, Cottages and Workshops of Asia

Originally titled carpet magic, this is the best introductory volume to orientals on the market today. Shows rugs as they were used by their makers, with articulate explanations of the craft

0-525-48426-4 DUTTON PB $24.95

Furniture

Ruan **Changjiang**

Illustrated Chinese Furniture Through the Ages

9576380898 ORIENTAL BOOK STORE PB $22.00

Sandra Lok Fu **Chin**

Classical Chinese Wood Furniture

1-87774-202-3
SAN FRANCISCO CRAFT & FOLK ART PB $12.00

Kazuko **Koizumi**

Traditional Japanese Furniture: A Definitive Guide

0-87011-722-X KODANSHA $85.00

Wang **Shixiang**

Classic Chinese Furniture

1-87852-902-1 ARTMI $110.00

The Home

Buying A House

George **Hoffman**

How to Inspect a House: Exactly What to Look for Before You Buy

A guide for home buyers on how to save money in professional fees

0-201-57708-9 ADDISON-WESLEY PB $9.95

Robert **Irwin**

Making Mortgages Work for You

A guide to all types of mortgage financing, with useful payment tables

See also **BUYING A HOME** under **REAL ESTATE** under **INVESTING, TAXES, AND BUSINESS ADVICE** in **BUSINESS AND REFERENCE**

0-07-032129-9 MCGRAW HILL $24.95
0-07-032128-0 MCGRAW HILL PB $14.95

Robert **Irwin**, editor

The McGraw-Hill Real Estate Handbook

By the author of many successful real estate books

0-07-032056-X MCGRAW HILL $69.50

Building A House

As construction becomes increasingly expensive, many people are relying on their own skills to build or enlarge their home. These books, for novice and experienced builder alike, have all been selected for their easy-to-follow, well-diagrammed instructions.

Tracy **Kidder**

House

A popular account of a family building their first home: struggles with builders and contractors, daily frustrations, and ultimate satisfaction

0-380-71114-1 AVON PB $12.00

Richard **Manning**

A Good House: Building a Life on the Land

"A practical, philosophical, conscientious, and richly generous version of what it takes to put together a thoughtful house, a thoughtful life"
—Louise Erdrich

0-14-023407-1 PENGUIN PB $12.95

Reader's Digest

New Complete Do-It-Yourself Manual

An updated edition of the indispensable handbook to home building and home repair that has sold over 7 million copies. Includes over 4,000 illustrations and photographs

0-89577-378-3 READERS DIGEST $30.00

Design and Construction

Norm **Abram**

Measure Twice, Cut Once: Lessons from a Master Carpenter

The master carpenter of "This Old House" presents a lifetime of woodwork experience in 60 short, simple lessons: a firm basis of good habits for the beginning carpenter, a valuable checklist of essentials for the experts. From the best kind of carpenter's pencil to how to drill exploratory holes without damaging plumbing or wiring, Abrams offers tricks of the trade to benefit any home improvement

0-316-00494-4 LITTLE, BROWN $17.95

Norm Abram's New House: America's Favorite Carpenter and His Wife, Laura, Build Their Dream Home

Abram, the host of "This Old House," takes us through the four years he spent, with his wife, building their home in rural Massachusetts

0-316-00487-1 LITTLE, BROWN $22.95

Lupe **DiDonno** & Phyllis **Sperling**

How to Design and Build Your Own House

Illustrated with line drawings, this book concentrates on design, planning, and selection of the best materials and tools

0-394-75200-7 KNOPF PB $25.00

Elizabeth **Hilliard**

Designing with Tiles

Beginning with commentary on the history, origins, and influences of tiles and ending with a wealth of innovative, traditional, and practical ideas for the modern home, this is *the* complete sourcebook on tiles. Also includes sections on installation, maintenance, and repair. Fully illustrated

1-55859-639-9 PAVILION $39.95

John **Pile**

Interior Design

A wealth of detail and practical information on the basic issues in residential and commercial design. "Its 540 pages and 700 pictures alone make [it] a tome. But, for many amateurs and students of design, the comprehensiveness and insight of the text make it a kind of bible"
—*NY Times*

0-8109-1121-3 ABRAMS $55.00
0-13-469248-9 PRENTICE HALL PB $58.95

Reader's Digest

The Family Handyman Decks, Patios, and Porches: Plans, Projects, and Instructions for Expanding Your Home

An illustrated, easy-to-use guide

0-89577-852-1 READER'S DIGEST PB $19.95

S.C. **Reznikoff**

Interior Graphic and Design Standards

0-8230-7298-3 WHITNEY LIBRARY OF DESIGN $95.00

Robert **Roskind**

Building Your Own House: The First Part from Foundations to Framing

An award-winning guidebook, well illustrated with diagrams, drawings, and photographs

0-89815-110-4 TEN SPEED PB $21.95

Louis **Sagar**

Zona Home: Essential Designs for Living

This more relaxed approach to design covers a myriad of considerations and approaches, with an offering of 240 lavish photos for illustration

0-06-270169-X HARPER & ROW $50.00

Richard M. **Scutella**

How to Plan, Contract and Build Your Own House

0-8306-3584-X TAB PB $19.95

Sunset

Making the Most of Your Own Backyard

A primer for designing and building outdoors, with special emphasis on playing, gardening and eating. All phases of projects are included here, as well as photos and drawings that serve to help analyze the space and illustrate the possibilities

0-376-03078-X SUNSET PB $24.95

Eva **Wong**

Feng-Shui: The Ancient Art of Harmonious Living for Modern Times

How to apply the ancient Chinese concepts in contemporary design

1-57062-100-4 SHAMBHALA PB $22.00

May **Woods** & Arete **Warren**

Glass Houses

A history of the glass house from the Romans to today, with lavish illustrations of unusual houses, conservatories, and greenhouses

1-85410-113-7 LONDON BRIDGE PB $24.95

Frank Lloyd **Wright** & William Herman **Winslow**

The House Beautiful

0-87654-597-5 POMEGRANATE $29.95

Renovation

Joanna **Krotz**

Metropolitan Home Renovation Style

Includes ideas for brownstones, lofts, condominiums, ranches, and Victorian houses

0-394-75819-6 RANDOM HOUSE PB $25.00

Martin **Miller** & Judith **Miller**

Periods Details: A Sourcebook For House Restoration

A useful source; attractively illustrated

FOREWORD BY MARIO BUATTA

0-517-88013-X CROWN PB $22.00

Penny **Radford**

Designer's Guide to Surface Finishes

How to renovate walls, floors, ceilings, windows, and trim. A well-organized and attractive book on types of finishes, preparation, and application

0-8230-1311-1 WHITNEY LIBRARY OF DESIGN PB....$24.95

Reader's Digest

Home Improvement Manual

A thorough guide to renovating, modernizing, and adding space to a house. Includes American house styles, building codes, estimated costs, and projects for interior and exterior improvements. An essential one-volume reference

0-89577-410-0 READER'S DIGEST....$30.00

Reader's Digest

The Family Handyman Updating Your Home: Easy Ways to Make Your Home Look and Work Better

Small renovation projects with step-by-step instructions

0-89577-851-3 READER'S DIGEST PB....$19.95

Bob **Vila**

This Old House: Restoring Rehabilitating and Renovating

0-316-17702-4 LITTLE, BROWN PB....$24.95

Bathrooms

"The idea of locating the water closet and bathtub together in a single room, for the common use of all the family, was an American one…By the turn of the [19th] century the compact three-fixture bathroom, with the tub placed across the end of the room and the water closet and sink side by side, was commonplace. This was not the case in Europe."—Witold Rybczinski, *Home: A Short History of an Idea*

Diane **Berger**

The Bathroom

Equipment and decorating advice with photos by Fritz von der Schulenburg

0-7892-0086-4 ABBEVILLE....$29.95

Wanda P. **Jankowski**

Kitchens & Baths: Designs For Living

It is challenging to design a kitchen or bathroom that is both aesthetically pleasing and utilitarian—important factors in that these rooms are often paramount in the resale of a house. This beautiful book showcases outstanding kitchen and bath designs by some of today's leading designers, with chapters on remodeling, small spaces, and renovation. Includes over 250 full-color photographs

0-86636-148-0 PBC....$55.00

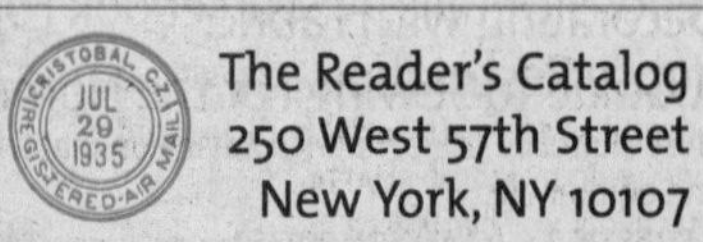

The Reader's Catalog
250 West 57th Street
New York, NY 10107

Kitchens

Terence **Conran**

Terence Conran's Kitchen Book

The man behind the *Habitat* and *Conran's* stores, brings his expertise into your home. Traditional or high-tech and everything in between, this sourcebook includes all that you need to know when installing or renovating a kitchen. Sections include advice on floorplans, decoration, appliances

0-87951-513-9 OVERLOOK....$45.00
0-87951-623-2 PENGUIN PB....$28.95

Deborah **Krasner**

Kitchens For Cooks: Planning Your Perfect Kitchen

Krasner, a celebrated food journalist, offers architect-drawn floor plans and diagrams, based on professional kitchens, to replace the outdated "work triangle" kitchen with a four-zone model much more suited to today's culinary habits. Resourceful, extensively researched, and adaptable, this is the essential book for any new kitchen

PHOTOGRAPHS BY WILLIAM STITES

0-14-024811-0 STUDIO PB....$17.95

Angela **Phelan**

Kitchens: Designs for Living

An offering of designs to match a wide range of lifestyles

1-56799-295-1 METRO....$24.98

Carpentry

Norm **Abram**

The New Yankee Workshop

Thirteen handsome and useful projects from the master carpenter, star of the PBS television series

See also **WOODWORK AND FURNITURE MAKING** under **CRAFTS**

0-316-00454-5 LITTLE, BROWN PB....$19.95

Nick **Engler**

The Workshop Companion: Workbenches and Shop Furniture

The one guide you'll need in designing and building your own home woodworking shop. Includes the pros and cons of each design that will help you identify your needs and preferences. From the very small to the most spacious shop, this covers it all

0-87596-680-2 RODALE....$19.95
0-87596-581-4 RODALE....$19.95

Gaspar **Lewis**

Carpentry

A master carpenter's comprehensive guide to the craft, with over 900 illustrations. Includes sections on tools, materials, rough carpentry, exterior finishing, furniture

0-8095-7600-7 BORGO....$47.00

Herbert **Schiffer** & Nancy **Schiffer**

Woods We Live With

A wonderful book identifying and describing the properties of different woods, with actual wood samples. Extremely useful for carpenters and for anyone repairing wood surfaces

0-916838-10-2 SCHIFFER....$24.95

Cabinets and Storage

Samuel A. **Humphrey**

Thomas Elfe: Cabinetmaker

A detailed study of the life and work of a renowned 18th-century cabinetmaker, based in Charleston, South Carolina. The author, a naval engineer and amateur cabinetmaker, tracked down Elfe's pieces in homes and museums, prepared measured drawings, and consulted archival records in order to complete this compelling history

0-941711-15-3 WYRICK PB....$24.95

Henry **Lapp**

A Craftsman's Handbook

Lapp, a 19th-century Amish cabinetmaker and folk artist who was born deaf, sold his furniture and household designs by rendering them in watercolors and showing his sketches around Philadelphia. Long out of print, these works were originally offered in book form by the Philadelphia Museum of Art, which added text and captions. Lapp's designs, shown in 47 color plates, are functional and handsome, and the collection includes his plans for mousetraps, eggbeaters, and ladders as well as fine furniture

1-56148-014-2 GOOD BOOKS PB....$15.95

Byron **Maguire**

Cabinetmaking: From Design to Finish

0-934041-62-8 CRAFTSMAN PB....$22.00

Maxine **Ordesky**

Maxine Ordesky's Complete Home Organizer: A Guide to Functional Storage Space For All the Rooms in Your Home

Ordesky, a professional organizing consultant since 1975, shows that "organized and well used space is enough space." This ingenious book gives us detailed, step-by-step instructions on how to minimize clutter and maximize accessibility in every room in the house. Includes 150 color illustrations and helpful drawings

0-8021-3340-1 GROVE PB....$22.00

Floors

Time-Life Books

Floors and Stairways

0-8094-2394-4 TIME BOOKS....$11.95

Interior Decorating

Rachel **Ashwell** & Glynis **Costin**

Shabby Chic

How to decorate in the unique style of Ashwell the "Shabby Chic" stores owner

0-06-098204-7 HARPERCOLLINS....$30.00

Mary Ellisor **Emmerling**

Mary Emmerling's American Country Cottages

Emmerling and photographer Joshua Green ventured across America to document the warmth and magic of cottage living. They found great decorating ideas and housekeeping solutions for informal living in cozy spaces

0-517-58365-8 CLARK $25.00

Melanie **Fleishmann**

In the Neoclassic Style: Empire, Biedermeier and the Contemporary Home

Help with decorating in the Empire style or introducing neoclassical elements into existing decoration. With photographs by Mick Hales

0-500-27905-5 THAMES & HUDSON PB $24.95

Carol Cooper **Garey** &
the editors of **House Beautiful**

House Beautiful Decorating Style

A sourcebook for a vast array of design questions, from storage to window treatments, slipcovers to original details. This is a timeless and graceful handbook of style that emphasizes creativity rather than one's checkbook. Includes 250 color photographs from outstanding design photographers

0-688-09734-0 HEARST $30.00

Mary **Gilliatt**

Decorating Book

A complete and useful problem-solving book

0-394-75243-0 PANTHEON PB $35.00

Mary Gilliatt's New Guide to Decorating

Each step of the process, from planning to selecting fabrics and furnishings

0-316-31385-8 LITTLE, BROWN $40.00

Linda **Gray** & Jocasta **Innes**

The Complete Book of Decorating Techniques

Such decorative techniques as dragging, stencilling, trompe-l'oeil, and marbleizing

0-316-32757-3 LITTLE, BROWN PB $19.95

Tricia **Guild**

Tricia Guild on Color

A richly inspiring book of interior design solutions with color, by the founder of The Designers Guild in London. Invaluable in its clear, accessible, step-by-step tutorial in the theory and use of color, light, scale, and proportion to bring new life to a decorative scheme

0-8478-1643-5 RIZZOLI PB $37.50

David **Halle**

Inside Culture: Art and Class in the American Home

This fascinating study seeks to connect the art in private homes to social, racial, and cultural influences and tastes. Inventories of artwork in a range of homes and interviews with the families, from the urban affluent to suburban to inner city, provide provocative and insightful commentary on the meaning consumers attach to their collections

0-226-31367-0 CHICAGO $29.95
0-226-31368-9 CHICAGO PB $14.95

Horst P. **Horst**

Horst: Interiors

The best of 40 years of unmatched interior design photos by the legendary photographer. Included among the 200 photos are the residences of the Duke and Duchess of Windsor, Oscar de La Renta, and Paloma Picasso. Text and interviews by noted design author Barbara Plumb

0-8212-2046-2 BULFINCH $75.00

Jocasta **Innes** & Stewart **Walton**

Simply American

0-517-58710-6 RANDOM HOUSE PB $15.00

Simply Mexican

0-517-58707-6 RANDOM HOUSE PB $15.00

Julie V. **Iovine**

Chic Simple: Home

An illustrated guide to tasteful style that brings practical, up-to-the-moment concepts home. The perfect gift idea

0-679-42167-X KNOPF $30.00

Chris Casson **Madden**

Rooms with a View: Two Decades of Outstanding American Interior Design

For two decades the Kips Bay Decorator Show House has been the premier forum for trendsetting interior design. This stunning book, complete with over 275 lavish photographs, presents the best of these designs, covering a variety of interior decorating styles

0-86636-190-1 PBC $45.00

Martin **Miller** & Judith **Miller**

Period Details: A Sourcebook For House Restoration

0518-8013X CROWN PB $20.00

Julia Hamilton **Thomason**

Creative Ideas For Decorating

Decorating for comfort and style; imaginative ideas and simple instructions for projects

0-7924-4898-7 OXMOOR $14.98

Carolyn **Warrender**

Color Style: How to Identify the Colors that are Right for You

An explanation of how to use color as an expression of individuality in the home, by British designer Warrender

0-7892-0255-7 ABBEVILLE $24.95

Furniture

James **Brumbaugh**

Wood Furniture: Finishing, Refinishing, Repairing

A good, reliable guide

0-02-517871-7 AUDEL $30.00

George **Grotz**

The Furniture Doctor

Best-selling book for amateurs and professionals, covering all manner of repairs and restoration

0-385-26670-7 DOUBLEDAY PB $14.95

Daniel **Mack**

The Rustic Furniture Companion: Traditions, Techniques, and Inspirations

Projects and techniques to revive furniture

0-937274-97-6 LARK BOOKS $26.95

Wallace **Nutting**

Furniture Treasury Volumes 1 & 2

The essential reference book on furniture of all types

0-02-590980-0 MACMILLAN $75.00

David **Stiles** & Jeanie **Stiles**

Kids' Furniture You Can Build

You *can* build them, and you'll *want* to the moment you see their prices in stores. From built-in beds to toy-storage wagons, this book takes you from the elementary points to the finished product, with a primer on electric tools, tricks of the trade, and facts about hardware

1-88152-749-2 CHAPTERS PB $17.95

Upholstery

"Originally, the upholsterer had been concerned solely with textiles and upholstery coverings, but, being a tradesman and recognizing a business opportunity, he had enlarged his service to include coordination of all interior furnishings and set himself up, according to a 1747 British trade paper, 'as a connoisseur in every article that belongs to a house'...By the time that architects realized that they had lost control of the interior arrangement of the house, it was too late. Upholsterers, or interior decorators as they were later called, came increasingly to dominate domestic comfort."
—Witold Rybczinski, *Home: A Short History of an Idea*

James **Brumbaugh**

Upholstering

A good, technical guide for laymen and apprentices; each step in the process is clearly explained

0-02-517862-8 AUDEL $30.00

W.L. **Gheen**

Upholstery Techniques Illustrated

0-8306-0402-2 TAB PB $17.95

Peter **Nesovich**

Reupholstering At Home: A Do-It-Yourself Manual For Turning Old Furniture Into New Showpieces

0-88740-376-X SCHIFFER PB $14.95

Fabric

Donna **Lang** & Lucretia **Robertson**

Decorating with Fabric: A Guide to Sewing For the Home

More than 200 projects; with advice on materials and equipment

0-517-55278-7 CLARKSON POTTER $19.95

Melanie **Paine**

Fabric Magic

How to use everyday fabrics in imaginative ways. Includes chapters on window treatments, coverings, bedding, what material to buy, and what styles to choose

0-679-72598-9 PANTHEON PB....$24.00

Sue **Peverill**

The Fabric Decorator: Painting, Printing, and Dyeing Fabrics For the Home

0-316-70390-7 LITTLE, BROWN....$29.95

Paint and Wallpaper

Jocasta **Innes**

Decorating with Paint

"Explores overall wall finishes in greater depth and also explains how to marbleize woodwork, apply stencils and mix your own paints"
—*House Beautiful*

0-517-57229-X HARMONY PB....$21.00

The New Decorator's Handbook: Decorative Paint Techniques for Every Room

Innes, whose bestselling *Paint Magic* introduced nearly 200,000 people to her decorating genius, offers realistic, inexpensive, and creative ways to use lighting, color, and texture in decorating the home. From woodwork and floors to walls and furniture, this compendium of decorating techniques includes lists, charts, and quick-reference graphics

0-06-270143-6 HARPERCOLLINS....$23.00

Isabel **O'Neil**

The Art of the Painted Finish For Furniture and Decoration

The most complete guide, combining old methods with modern materials and tools. Sections on antiquing, lacquering, and gilding by an expert on decorative paint

0-688-06070-6 MORROW PB....$17.95

Gregg **Sandreuter**

Complete Painter's Handbook: How to Paint Your House—Inside and Out—the Right Way

For the novice painter: advice for the entire process, from selecting tools to cleaning up

0-87857-756-4 RODALE PB....$14.95

Time-Life Books

Paint and Wallpaper

0-8094-2354-5 TIME BOOKS....$11.95

Stenciling

JoAnne **Day**

The Complete Book of Stencilcraft

0-486-25372-4 DOVER PB....$10.95

Framing and Hanging Pictures

Pete **Bingham**

Picture Framing: A Practical Guide to All Aspects of the Art and the Craft

0-8117-1175-7 STACKPOLE....$29.95

Caroline **Clifton-Mogg**

Displaying Pictures and Photographs

0-517-56628-1 CROWN....$24.95

Max **Hyder**

Matting, Mounting and Framing Art

0-8230-3027-X WATSON-GUPTILL....$29.95

Hal **Rogers** & Ed **Reinhart**

How to Make Your Own Picture Frames

0-8230-2452-0 WATSON-GUPTILL PB....$14.95

Home Repair

Beverly **Dejulio**

Handyma'am

Discovery Channel's "Easy Does It" co-host wrote this step-by-step geared for women

9-99-646324-9 HARPERCOLLINS....$23.00

Everyday Home Repairs

0-8118-0594-8 CHRONICLE PB....$9.95

Household Emergencies

0-8118-0580-8 CHRONICLE PB....$9.95

Reader's Digest

Fix-It-Yourself Manual

0-89577-040-7 READER'S DIGEST....$26.00

The Family Handyman Easy Repairs: 60 Simple Solutions to the Most Common Problems in Your Home

Step-by-step instructions, helpful hints, buying guides, supplier lists, and first-rate illustrations make this the most uncommonly useful guide to most of the common house problems you will ever encounter

0-89577-624-3 READER'S DIGEST....$19.95

Reader's Digest Book of Skills and Tools

Step-by-step, illustrated instructions make this the perfect beginner handyperson's guide. Also included is a complete list of the most widely used as well as obscure tools and hardware employed in wood, metal, masonry, painting, and other common do-it-yourself projects

0-89577-469-0 READER'S DIGEST....$30.00

Time-Life Books

How Things Work in Your Home: And What to Do When They Don't

0-8050-0126-3 HOLT PB....$19.95

Electrical, Plumbing, and Heating

Sydney **Cooper** & Anne **Beller**

Home Security

0-89043-312-7 CONSUMER REPORTS....$24.95

Fix Your Plumbing

0-8118-0599-9 CHRONICLE PB....$9.95

Time-Life Books

Heating and Cooling

A well-organized, illustrated walk through home heating and cooling projects

0-7835-3897-9 TIME BOOKS PB....$18.95

Basic Wiring

0-8094-7362-3 TIME BOOKS....$15.93

Heating and Cooling

0-8094-2378-2 TIME BOOKS....$15.93

Kitchen and Bathroom Plumbing

0-8094-6208-7 TIME BOOKS....$15.95

Household Appliances and Tools

"The much needed carpet sweeper made its appearance in the 1860s…One model required the user to push the handle up and down like a pogo stick, another had long handles which were pumped sideways, like an enormous pair of shears. The most bizarre vacuum cleaner consisted of two bellows which the hapless maid was to wear as shoes, and which caused the nozzle to suck air as she walked around the room."—Witold Rybczinski, *Home: A Short History of an Idea*

Consumer Reports

Consumer Reports Buying Guide Issue 1997

The ideal reference for household appliances, tools of any type, electronic equipment, cars, and a host of other products

0-89043-851-X CONSUMER REPORTS PB....$8.99

Time-Life Books

Major Appliances

Chapters on tools, refrigerators, electric ranges, dishwashers, washers, and dryers

0-8094-6204-4 TIME BOOKS....$15.95

Household Hints

Jeff **Campbell**

The Clean Team: Speed Cleaning

A humorous collection of shortcuts by the owner of a cleaning service

0-440-58015-3 DELL PB....$6.99

Patricia **Coen** & Bryan **Milford**

Closets: Designing and Organizing the Personalized Closet

How to reorganize your closet and wardrobe

0-8021-3228-6 GROVE PB....$16.00

Efficient Housecleaning
0-8118-0625-1 CHRONICLE PB....................$9.95

Mary Kerney **Levenstein** & Cordelia Frances **Biddle**
Caring For Your Cherished Possessions
0-517-88226-4 CROWN PB....................$12.00

Candace **Ord Manroe**
Storage Made Easy: Great Ideas for Organizing Every Room of Your Home
0-89577-820-3 READER'S DIGEST....................$25.00

Mary Ellen **Pinkham**
Mary Ellen's Best of Helpful Hints
0-446-38121-7 WARNER PB....................$7.99

Reader's Digest
How to Do Just About Anything
A guide to over 1200 small practical problems, arranged alphabetically. Practical advice on such topics as plumbing, gardening, and first aid
0-89577-218-3 READER'S DIGEST....................$30.00

Deniece **Schofield**
Deniece Schofield's Kitchen Organization Tips and Secrets
1-55870-423-X F&W PUBLICATIONS PB....................$12.99

Don **Vandervort**
Home Magazine's How Your House Works
0-345-38178-5 BALLANTINE....................$23.00

John **Warde**
The New York Times Season-By-Season Guide to Home Maintenance
This book, based on Warde's homecare column, gives straightforward, thorough instructions for completing 100 maintenance projects. The topics, organized by season, form a well-rounded owner's manual for either the house or apartment dweller
0-8129-1882-7 TIME BOOKS....................$28.00

Joanna **Wissinger**
The Home Management Desk Reference
Decorating, organizing, cleaning, cooking, storage, pets, gardening, and more are covered
0-06-270103-7 HARPERCOLLINS....................$25.00

Home Entertaining

Martha **Stewart**
Holidays: The Best of Martha Stewart Living
Collected from her popular magazine, here are hundreds of great ideas that cover Thanksgiving through the New Year. Table settings, party recipes and planned meals, entertainment ideas, decorations, gifts and wrappings, and more
0-517-88271-X RANDOM HOUSE PB....................$20.00

Etiquette

Letitia **Baldrige**
The Amy Vanderbilt Complete Book of Etiquette
A classic, now updated by a public relations specialist
0-385-14238-2 DOUBLEDAY....................$27.50

Letitia Baldrige's Complete Guide to the New Manners: Plus the Time-Honored Ones That Everyone Needs to Know
0-89256-320-6 SCRIBNERS....................$27.50

Sarah **Kortun**
The Hatless Man: An Anthology of Odd and Forgotten Manners
ILLUSTRATED BY RONALD SEARLE
0-670-86497-8 VIKING....................$29.95

Judith **Martin**
Miss Manners Basic Training: Communication
0-517-70673-3 CROWN....................$14.00

Miss Manners Guide for the Turn of the Millennium
ILLUSTRATED BY GLORIA KAMEN
0-671-72228-X FIRESIDE PB....................$17.00

Elizabeth L. **Post**
Emily Post's Etiquette
The 21st edition brought up to date by a descendant of Emily Post
0-06-270047-2 HARPERCOLLINS....................$28.00

Entertaining

Trish **Foley**
Having Tea: Recipes and Table Settings
Tips on tea drinking, and presentation
0-517-56007-0 CLARKSON POTTER....................$21.00

Barbara **Ohrbach**
The Scented Room: Cherchez's Book of Dried Flowers, Fragrance, and Potpourri
Recipes for a sweet-smelling house, with attractive photographs
0-517-56081-X CLARKSON POTTER....................$18.00

Martha **Stewart**
Weddings
Lavish photographs and detailed instructions for more than 40 weddings, including such elements as music, flower arrangements, table decorations, and menus
See also **WEDDINGS** under **COURTSHIP, LOVE, SEX, AND MARRIAGE** in **LIFESTYLES AND PRACTICAL ADVICE**
0-517-55675-8 CLARKSON POTTER....................$70.00

Roger **Verge**
Roger Verge's Entertaining in the French Style
A beautiful book, with advice for presenting a French meal
See also **ENTERTAINING** under **FOOD** in **FOOD, TRAVEL, AND LEISURE**
0-941434-90-7 STEWART, TABORI....................$60.00

Peri **Wolfman** & Charles **Gold**
The Perfect Setting
0-8109-1482-4 ABRAMS....................$45.00

Flower Arranging

Penny **Black**
The Book of Pressed Flowers
Pressing, drying, and arranging flowers. This attractive book includes chapters on making pictures and samplers with pressed flowers and leaves
0-671-66071-3 SIMON & SCHUSTER....................$22.00

Susan **Condor**
Dried Flowers: Drying and Arranging
Easy-to-follow instructions for making 86 varieties of dried flowers, with new and unusual designs for arranging them
0-87923-719-8 GODINE....................$20.00

Anne **Hamilton** & Kathleen **White**
Silk Flowers
A step-by-step guide to making silk roses, chrysanthemums, and other flowers, with instructions for floral arrangements and bouquets
0-87923-765-1 GODINE....................$22.50

Malcolm **Hillier**
Decorating with Dried Flowers
0-517-56923-X CROWN....................$23.00

Malcolm **Hillier** & Colin **Hilton**
The Complete Book of Dried Flowers
0-671-61939-X SIMON & SCHUSTER....................$27.50

Crafts

Clois **Kicklighter** & Ronald **Baird**
Crafts: Illustrated Designs and Techniques
Basic instructions in 39 different crafts from basketry to woodcraft, with 400 projects
0-87006-592-0 GOODHEART-WILCOX....................$30.60

Reader's Digest
Crafts and Hobbies
An excellent collection of advice for making everything from baskets to mosaics
0-89577-063-6 READER'S DIGEST....................$24.95

Needlework

Tatting is the art of creating delicate handmade lace by looping and knotting a single thread.

Judy **Brittain**
Needlecraft
Step-by-step instructions and practical tips for practitioners of embroidery, needlepoint, patchwork, quilting, appliqué, knitting, and crochet. Comprehensive and extensively illustrated
0-89577-350-3 READER'S DIGEST PB........................$16.00

Judy **Heim**
The Needlecrafter's Computer Companion
Hundreds of tips on using your computer for a variety of needlecrafts, from using photos to generate charts to putting your craft business on the Internet. Includes 2 IBM PC disks containing popular DOS and Windows software. Macintosh version also available
1-88641-101-8 NO STARCH PRESS PB........................$34.95

Judith Baker **Montano**
Elegant Stitches: An Illustrated Stitch Guide and Source Book of Inspiration
Illustrates 117 embroidery stitches and includes instructions for silk ribbon work, punch needle embroidery, and 130 crazy quilt combination stitches
0-914881-85-X C & T........................$24.95

Elgiva **Nicholls**
Tatting: Technique and History
A good illustrated guide for beginners and more advanced tatters
0-486-24612-4 DOVER PB........................$5.95

Anne **Orr**
Anne Orr's Classic Tatting Patterns
Ninety patterns for doilies, edgings, and more
0-486-24897-6 DOVER PB........................$3.50

Reader's Digest
Complete Guide to Needlework
Well-organized, practical coverage of the subject: embroidery, needlepoint, knitting macramé, lacework, rug-making, and more
0-89577-059-8 READER'S DIGEST........................$28.00

Rita **Weiss**
Traditional Tatting Patterns
Doilies, edgings, collars, and other items
0-486-25066-0 DOVER PB........................$3.95

Crewel Embroidery

Gail **Bett** & others
Embroidery from a Country Barn: 28 Stitching Ideas Combining Crewel Work, Appliqué and Quilting
1-86373-619-0 ALLEN & UNWIN........................$24.95

Frances M. **Bradbury**
Early American Crewel Design
0-88045-092-4 STEMMER PB........................$5.95

English Crewel Designs: 16th to 18th Centuries
0-88045-015-0 STEMMER PB........................$5.95

Embroidery

These books include general technique guides and design anthologies.

Pauline **Brown**
The Encyclopedia of Embroidery Techniques
A visual directory of major embroidery styles, from Kloster blocks to chessboard filling
0-14-023771-2 STUDIO PB........................$19.95

Karen **Elder** & Pam **Krauss**
Embroidery
A project book handsomely illustrated with color drawings and photos. Suitable for all abilities of needleworkers, from the novice to the most advanced
0-517-88469-0 CLARKSON POTTER PB........................$16.00

Marion **Nichols**
Encyclopedia of Embroidery Stitches Including Crewel
One hundred seventy-eight clearly explained stitches
0-486-22929-7 DOVER PB........................$9.95

Barbara Lee **Smith**
Celebrating the Stitch: Contemporary Embroidery of North America
A look at the thriving culture of modern needlework, profiling the work of 100 hand and machine embroiderers
0-942391-39-X TAUNTON........................$34.95

Mary **Thomas**
Mary Thomas' Embroidery Book
0-486-24530-6 DOVER PB........................$7.95

Lace Making

Claire **Burkhard**
Fifty New Bobbin Lace Patterns
0-7134-6985-4 BATSFORD........................$39.95

Bridget M. **Cook**
Russian Lace Making
0-7134-6101-2 BATSFORD........................$39.95

Birgitta **Fuhrmann**
Bobbin Lace: An Illustrated Guide to Traditional and Contemporary Techniques
Clear instructions for making every type of bobbin lace—including history, tools, and patterns
0-486-24902-6 DOVER PB........................$9.95

Mrs. F. Nevill **Jackson**
Old Handmade Lace: With a Dictionary of Lace
Well-illustrated study of lace making from ancient Egypt to the late 19th century
0-486-25309-0 DOVER PB........................$10.95

Elizabeth **Minkoff** & Margaret **Marriage**
Pillow or Bobbin Lace: Technique, Patterns, History
This 1907 classic includes a survey of lace in Europe, necessary materials, and basic techniques, along with 50 designs
0-8446-6327-1 SMITH........................$16.00

Patricia **Read** & Lucy **Kincaid**
Milanese Lace: An Introduction
0-7134-5707-4 BATSFORD........................$39.95

Elisa **Ricci**
Italian Lace Designs: 243 Classic Examples
0-486-27588-4 DOVER PB........................$7.95

Doris **Southard**
Lessons in Bobbin Lacemaking
0-486-27122-6 DOVER PB........................$12.95

Elizabeth **Wade**
Torchon Lacemaking: Manual of Techniques
1-85223-979-4 CROWOOD PB........................$29.95

Needlepoint

Jennifer **Berman** & Carole **Lazarus**
Glorafilia: The Miniature Needlepoint Collection
Small, easy-to-make, yet beautiful projects, from pincushions to bookmarks and more
0-517-79986-3 CROWN........................$22.50

Kaffe **Fassett**
Glorious Needlepoint
Unusual designs for pillows, screens, rugs, and clothes
0-517-59198-7 CLARKSON POTTER PB........................$22.00

Julia **Hickman**
Decorative Needlepoint: Tapestry and Beadwork
A superb collection of fine needlepoint projects, incorporating the crafts of tapestry and beadwork. Beautifully illustrated in color
0-89577-591-3 READER'S DIGEST........................$28.00

Carole **Lazarus** & Jennifer **Berman**
Glorafilia: The Ultimate Needlepoint Collection
0-8212-2330-5 BULFINCH........................$29.95

Alice **Starmore**
Celtic Needlepoint
An impressive collection of 18 charted designs based on traditional Celtic patterns and motifs
1-57076-006-3 TRAFALGAR SQUARE........................$29.95

Beth **Russell** & Jane **Cavolina**, editor

Beth Russell's William Morris Needlepoint

Twenty-two projects based on Morris' Arts and Crafts designs. Lavishly illustrated

0-517-70166-9 CROWN $30.00

Erica **Wilson**

Erica Wilson's Needlepoint: Adapted from Objects in the Collections of The Metropolitan Museum of Art

Seventeen needlepoint projects based on works housed in the Metropolitan Museum of Art, including blue and white porcelain, French textiles, and Tiffany windows. Gorgeously illustrated with color photos of both the finished projects and the artworks on which they are based

See also **CRAFTS** under **AMERICAN DECORATIVE ARTS**

PHOTOGRAPHS BY RANDY O'ROURKE

0-8109-3980-0 ABRAMS $29.95

Samplers

Jane **Alford** & others

Flowers in Cross Stitch

Over 80 charted designs, suitable for all ability levels. "Great ideas for finishing your work—with everything from samplers to shelf borders"—*Cross Stitcher*

1-57215-198-6 WORLD PUBNS $15.99

Patrice **Boerens**

One Hour Cross Stitch

Full-color volume of 170 fast and easy projects, all of which can be completed in an hour or less—even by the beginner

0-8487-1097-5 OXMOOR $24.95

Two-Hour Cross-Stitch: 515 Fabulous Designs

Over 500 small-scale projects for decorating sachets, ornaments, magnets, and more. Color photos and easy-to-follow instructions

0-8069-0952-8 STERLING $24.95

Melinda **Coss**

The Cross-Stitch Garden

70 original designs inspired by natural settings, from terraces to formal gardens. Color photos and charts

0-696-20456-8 MEREDITH $24.95

Julie S. **Hasler**

Julie Hasler's Cross Stitch Designs

Contains 200 charted designs for borders, samplers, alphabets, and more

0-312-13419-3 ST. MARTIN'S PB $16.95

Jane **Kendon**

Cross-Stitch Samplers

0-312-17681-3 ST. MARTIN'S PB $9.95

Gloria **Nicol** & others

Cross-Stitch

Color photos of each project, from sprightly laundry bags for kids to elegant monogrammed pillowcases for grownups

0-517-88470-4 CLARKSON POTTER PB $16.00

Laurie Pate **Sewell**, editor

Vanessa-Ann's Victorian Cross-Stitch

Projects that capture the color and charm of a bygone era. Includes extensive instructions for completing everything from a Christmas stocking to a pleated velvet pillow

0-8487-1425-3 OXMOOR PB $14.95

Eleanor **Van Zandt**

Reader's Digest Complete Book of Cross Stitch and Counted Thread Techniques

Twenty-five projects, including step-by-step instruction for simple cross stitch, blackwork, pattern darning, pulled work, drawn thread work, and more

0-89577-621-9 READER'S DIGEST $25.00

Vanessa-Ann Collection

Storybook Cross-Stitch

Nursery rhymes, fairy tales, and fables charmingly rendered in 25 cross-stitch projects

0-696-20436-3 MEREDITH PB $19.95

Sewing

Leila **Aitken**

Dressmaking: A Step-By-Step Course

Advice for the novice on everything from pattern choice and appropriate fabrics to stitching and finishing apparel

0-8069-0628-6 STERLING PB $14.95

Maxine **Henry**

The A-Z of the Sewing Machine

This book tells you how to get the most out of that old Singer, describing how to use your machine to produce braids, cords, cutwork, lace, smocking and more

0-7134-7324-X BATSFORD PB $19.95

Linda **Lee** & Kit **Schlich**

Vogue & Butterick's Designer Sewing Techniques

Companion volume to the PBS television series "Sewing Today." Includes tips from Donna Karan, Todd Oldham, and Bill Blass, among others

0-671-88878-1 FIRESIDE PB $17.00

Carol **Parks** & Kay Holmes **Stafford**

Sewing the New Classics: Clothes With Easy Style

Ten basic patterns from which to create a timeless casual wardrobe. Scaled patterns and comprehensive instructions

0-8069-3194-9 LARK BOOKS PB $14.95

Reader's Digest

Complete Guide to Sewing

Well-organized and clearly presented

0-89577-026-1 RANDOM HOUSE $28.00

Singer Sewing

More Sewing For the Home

0-86573-236-1 DE COSSE PB $16.95

Sewing Essentials

0-86573-202-7 DE COSSE PB $16.95

Sewing For the Home

0-86573-204-3 DE COSSE PB $16.95

Timesaving Sewing

0-86573-216-7 DE COSSE PB $16.95

Claire B. **Shaeffer**

Couture Sewing Techniques

Covering everything from hand-stitching to the embellishment of evening wear, this valuable compendium of advanced techniques is a must for the advanced sewer

0-942391-88-8 TAUNTON $39.95

Sue **Thompson**

The Essentials of Sewing

A complete guide to the techniques of sewing for the novice, extensively illustrated. Includes instructions for a number of home decor and apparel projects

0-517-88467-4 CLARKSON POTTER PB $16.00

Sandra Betzina **Webster**

Fearless Sewing: Power Sewing for Beginners

Needle-and-thread-phobic no more! Everything the beginner needs to know to start producing beautiful clothing at home

1-88063-015-X PRACTICALITY PB $7.95

More Power Sewing: Masters Techniques for the 21st Century

This is the ideal volume for the advanced sewer who wants more knowledge of professional techniques. Includes tips on inner structure, pattern refinements, and finishing techniques

1-88063-014-1 POWER SEWING $29.95

Smocking

Jenny **Bradford**

Original Designs for Smocking

1-86351-087-7 MILNER PB $12.95

Dianne **Durand**

Smocking: Techniques, Projects and Designs

Complete instructions from a leading smocking designer

0-486-23788-5 DOVER PB $3.95

Ellen D. **McCarn**

Picture Smocking With Ellen McCarn

0-9618066-2-1 MCCARN PB $12.00

Fiona J. **Roediger**

Smocking Ideas

0-86417-508-6 SEVEN HILLS PB $12.95

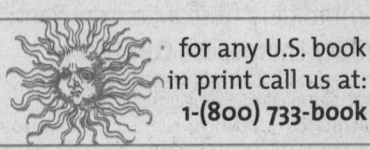

Knitting and Crocheting

Erica **Wilson**

For the Baby: Smocks and Sweaters, Samplers, Nursery Accessories, Cuddlies, and Toys to Knit, Crochet

Beautifully detailed clothing, toys, and accessories for infants and children, from Babar sweaters to Battenburg lace christening dresses. Color photos

0-316-94482-3 LITTLE, BROWN $19.95

General Knitting

Debbie **Bliss**

Baby Knits: 32 Original Designs for 0-3 Year Olds

Charming designs for many baby sweaters and accessories. Beautifully illustrated with color photos

0-312-02061-9 ST. MARTIN'S PB $18.95

New Baby Knits: More Than 30 Patterns for 0-3 Year Olds

More great baby and toddler apparel from the author of *Baby Knits*. This is a wonderful gift for the expectant mother who knits, and a great idea source for baby gifts

0-312-07397-6 ST. MARTIN'S PB $16.95

Toy Knits: More Than 30 Irresistible and Easy-To-Knit Patterns

Thirty easy-to-make knitted toys, from pigs and sailor bears to sheep and kangaroos. Instructions and photos for each toy

0-312-11901-1 ST. MARTIN'S PB $18.95

Maggie **Righetti**

Knitting in Plain English

An outstanding compendium of easy-to-understand directions and illustrations that is an essential addition to any knitter's library.

0-312-45853-3 ST. MARTIN'S PB $14.95

Nola **Theiss** & Chris **Rankin**

Floral Knits: More Than 40 Beautiful Timeless Sweaters to Make

Over 40 cardigans and pullovers in a variety of floral patterns. Includes instructions for embellishing "store-bought" sweaters

0-8069-8367-1 LARK BOOKS PB $14.95

Mary **Thomas**

Mary Thomas' Book of Knitting Patterns

A classic (1943), with patterns ranging from elementary to complex

0-486-22818-5 DOVER PB $7.95

Mary Thomas' Knitting Book

Everything from winding yarn and the basic stitches to making garments and blocking

0-486-22817-7 DOVER PB $6.95

Vogue Knitting Magazine

Vogue Knitting: The Ultimate Knitting Book

0-394-58157-1 PANTHEON $34.95

Elizabeth **Zimmerman**

Knitting Without Tears

A best-selling guide for beginners

0-684-13505-1 MACMILLAN PB $15.00

Knitting Techniques and Styles

Debbie **Bliss**

Classic Knits for Kids: Thirty Traditional Aran and Guernsey Designs for 0-6 Years

Gorgeous traditional Aran and Guernsey designs for newborns to six year olds. Includes instructions for coordinated accessories for many of the sweaters

0-943955-88-2 TRAFALGAR SQUARE $19.95

Catherine **Cartwright-Jones** & Roy **Jones**

The Tap Dancing Lizard: 337 Fanciful Charts for the Adventurous Knitter

Cats, dogs, reptiles, and mythical beasts graphed at the correct proportion for the knitter. A charming collection

0-934026-78-5 INTERWEAVE PB $18.95

Sarah **Don**

A Practical Handbook of Traditional Designs: Fair Isle Knitting

An inspirational collection of pattern samples from the Shetland Islands for knitting with two or more colors. Includes photos of completed sweaters

0-312-27960-4 ST. MARTIN'S PB $9.95

Kaffe **Fassett**

Kaffe's Classic: 25 Favorite Knitting Patterns for Sweaters, Jackets, Vests and More

A riot of sumptuous colors and textures, Fassett's designs will inspire even the non-knitter to pick up the needles. His work has been exhibited at the Victoria and Albert Museum, London

0-316-27503-4 LITTLE, BROWN $29.95

Shelagh **Hollingworth**

The Complete Book of Traditional Aran Knitting

0-312-15635-9 ST. MARTIN'S PB $14.95

Knitting Around the World from Threads

Aran, Swedish, Japanese, and Fair Isle techniques extensively documented and fully illustrated. A wealth of information for knitters of all abilities

1-56158-026-0 TAUNTON PB $15.95

Linda **Ligon**

Homespun, Handknit: Caps, Socks, Mittens and Gloves

Handy small projects

0-934026-26-2 INTERWEAVE PB $15.00

Debra **Mountford**, editor

The Harmony Guide to Aran and Fair Isle Knitting

A comprehensive sourcebook for two of the most beloved knitting styles. Features almost 400 stitches. "Offers… a great deal of visual pleasure" —*NY Times Book Review*

0-517-88405-4 CROWN PB $17.00

James **Norbury**

Traditional Knitting Patterns from Scandinavia the British Isles, France, Italy and Other European Countries

Hundreds of patterns, including an especially good selection of fisherman's sweaters

0-486-21013-8 DOVER PB $7.95

Alice **Starmore**

Alice Starmore's Book of Fair Isle Knitting

Includes a 17-page library of charted Fair Isle patterns, and instructions for more than 14 of the author's original designs. "Augments all the existing Fair Isle books and rises to the top of the heap"—*Knitter's Magazine*

0-918804-97-3 TAUNTON $34.95

Crochet

Wanda **Bonando**

Stitches, Patterns and Projects For Crocheting

A good reference book, in a practical size. The stitches are clearly illustrated by color photographs

0-06-091096-8 HARPERCOLLINS PB $4.98

Anne Van Wagner **Childs**

Crochet Collection

Chock-full of projects and ideas, including snowflake Christmas ornaments, lacy lampshade covers, and ice cream cone pins

0-942237-55-2 LEISURE PB $14.95

Anne Van Wagner **Childs**, editor

At Home With Crochet

Clothing, home accessories, and gifts highlight this volume of creative projects. Many are quite ingenious, including a bathmat stitched from plastic bags

0-942237-59-5 LEISURE PB $14.95

Anne **Orr**

Crochet Designs of Anne Orr

0-486-23621-8 DOVER PB $3.50

Chris **Rankin**

The Filet Crochet Book

This book of patterns for "country lace" will enable even a beginner to master the art. All 100 projects depicted in color

0-8069-5823-5 LARK BOOKS PB $16.95

Dorling-Kindersley **Staff**

Pattern Library: Crochet

A small book, one of a very handy series, with patterns presented in color photographs

0-345-32711-X BALLANTINE PB $8.00

Mary Carolyn **Waldrep**, editor

The Crocheter's Treasure Chest: 80 Classic Patterns for Tablecloths, Bedspreads, Doilies and Edgings

Includes classic patterns for over 80 projects: elegant tablecloths, doilies, and edgings galore

0-486-25833-5 DOVER PB $5.95

Afghans

Nancy J. **Fitzpatrick**, editor

Vanna's Afghans A to Z: 52 Crochet Favorites

Yes, the lovely spokesmodel for "Wheel of Fortune" is a crocheter in her spare time. This volume includes instructions for completing 52 afghans, two for each letter of the alphabet. After all, "you know how I love letters," says Vanna

0-8487-1476-8 OXMOOR PB $14.95

Anne **Orr**

Anne Orr's Afghans to Crochet and Knit

0-486-25440-2 DOVER PB $3.50

Rita **Weiss**

Crocheting Afghans

0-486-23883-0 DOVER PB $2.95

Old-Fashioned Afghans to Knit and Crochet

Patterns from the '40s and '50s, from simple to intricate

0-486-25054-7 DOVER PB $3.50

Quilting

Janet Carija **Brandt**

Wow! Wool-On-Wool Folk Art Quilts

Nine fast-and-easy wool quilt projects, with in-depth instructions on working with woolen fabrics

1-56477-117-2 THAT PATCHWORK PLACE PB $19.95

Mary Clare **Clark**

Story Quilts and How to Make Them

A handsome volume that details twelve charming panel quilt projects based on classic designs. Illustrated with photos, watercolors, and drawings

0-8069-1316-9 STERLING $27.95

Jenni **Dobson**

Beautiful Quilts: Art Deco: Making Classic Quilts and Modern Variations

Thirty-two quilts based on traditional deco patterns, suitable for all ability levels. Detailed watercolor illustrations and extensive tips, instructions, and shortcuts

0-8069-1326-6 STERLING $24.95

Marge **Edie**

Bargello Quilts

Eye-catching contemporary quilt designs inspired by a traditional needlepoint stitch. Appropriate for all ability levels

1-56477-067-2 THAT PATCHWORK PLACE PB $19.95

Dolores **Hinson**

Quilting Manual

Both a how-to manual and a collector's guide; with over 400 illustrations

0-486-23924-1 DOVER PB $5.95

Barbara T. **Lister**

Quilting Bees: Swarms of Ideas and Projects for Friends

Historically, quiltmaking has been a communal effort. Here's everything you need to know to start a "bee" and keep it buzzing, with lots of group projects, a gallery of finished quilts in color, and more

1-88097-208-5 THAT PATCHWORK PLACE PB $19.95

Ruth B. **McDowell**

Symmetry: A Design System for Quiltmakers

A guide to developing original designs, using a series of seventeen symmetrical patterns. Includes templates, color photos, yardage charts, and in-depth instructions

0-914881-78-7 C & T PB $21.95

Judith **Montano**

Crazy Quilt Odyssey: Adventures in Victorian Needlework

Contains 17 new projects rendered in centimeters and inches, including sections on punch needle and ribbon embroidery, from the author of the best-selling *Crazy Quilt Book*

0-914881-41-8 C & T PB $21.95

Nihon Vogue Staff

Sashiko: Traditional Japanese Quilt Designs

A single-stitch technique traditionally used to make winter clothing in Japan. A beautiful little book sure to inspire Western quiltmakers to new heights of creativity

0-87040-769-4 JAPAN PUBLICATIONS PB $11.95

Kumiko **Sudo**

East Quilts West

The traditional quilt block is given a fresh, cross-cultural treatment by artist and fashion designer Sudo. One of the most eye-catching quilt books on the market, with gorgeous color photos throughout

0-913327-47-6 QUILT DIGEST PB $21.95

East Quilts West II

More killer quilts from Kumiko Sudo, whose works are internationally renowned. Lavishly illustrated in color, this volume makes an outstanding gift for the textile enthusiast

0-8442-2643-2 N.T.C. PB $21.95

Jane **Townswick**

Quiltmaking Tips and Techniques

Over 1,000 ingenious tips and techniques from 60 outstanding quilters and the editors of *Quilter's Newsletter Magazine*, one of which is how to use skateboarder's tape to facilitate the quiltmaking process

0-87596-588-1 RODALE $27.95

Patchwork

Nedda **Anders**

Appliqué Old and New, Including Patchwork and Embroidery

An excellent book that includes antique and new examples, materials, quilts, and projects for children

0-486-23246-8 DOVER PB $4.95

Arlene **Dettore**

Victorian Patchwork & Quilting

Contemporary designs based on Victorian quilts, incorporating embroidery, beadwork, and more into great-looking projects

0-696-20433-9 MEREDITH PB $19.95

Dixie **Haywood**

Crazy Quilt Patchwork: A Modern Approach with 19 Projects

Design-as-you-go method

0-486-25042-3 DOVER PB $6.95

Judy **Martin**

Patchwork: Easy Lessons For Quilt Design and Construction

0-486-27844-1 DOVER PB $9.95

Ruby **McKim**

One Hundred and One Patchwork Patterns

Modern and traditional designs; includes quilt folklore

0-8446-1711-3 SMITH $16.05

0-486-20773-0 DOVER PB $5.95

Sylvia **Miller**, editor

Better Homes and Gardens 501 Quilt Blocks: A Treasury of Patterns for Patchwork & Appliqué

An amazing variety of blocks, plus 40 projects in which to use them

0-696-01997-3 BETTER HOMES & GARDENS $29.95

0-696-20480-0 BETTER HOMES & GARDENS PB $19.95

Hooking and Rag Rugs

Alice **Beatty** & Mary **Sargent**

Basic Rug Hooking

0-8117-2306-2 STACKPOLE PB $18.95

Thom **Boswell**, editor

Celebration of Hand Hooked Rugs V

9995254018 RUGHOOK PB $16.95

Thom **Boswell**, editor
The Rug Hook Book: Techniques, Projects and Patterns for This Easy, Traditional Craft
0-8069-8359-0 LARK BOOKS PB $16.95

Peter **Collingwood**
Rug Weaving Techniques: Beyond the Basics
0-934026-62-9 INTERWEAVE $29.95

Gloria **Crouse**
Hooking Rugs
6-301-91902-5 TAUNTON VIDEOTAPES $24.99

Ann **Davies**
Rag Rugs: How to Use Ancient and Modern Rug-Making Techniques to Create Rugs, Wall Hangings, Even Jewelry
0-8050-2812-9 OWLET PB $14.95

Pat **Hornafius**
Victorian Cottage Rugs: How to Hook 16 Traditional Patterns
0-8117-2593-6 STACKPOLE PB $24.95

Janet **Meany** & Paula **Pfaff**
Rag Rug Handbook
1-88301-028-4 INTERWEAVE $19.95

Jessie **Turbayne**
The Hooker's Art: Evolving Designs in Hooked Rugs
0-88740-459-6 SCHIFFER $49.95

Weaving

Mary **Black**
The Key to Weaving
The classic handbook for beginners, updated
0-02-511170-1 MACMILLAN $49.95

Rachel **Brown**
The Weaving, Spinning and Dyeing Book
Complete and specific; highly recommended
0-394-71595-0 KNOPF PB $40.00

Candace **Crockett**
Card Weaving
A boxed set of sixteen cards and book allows anyone to engage in this ancient art form
0-934026-61-0 INTERWEAVE PB $21.95

Ann **Hecht**
The Art of the Loom: Weaving Spinning and Dyeing Across the World
0-8478-1147-6 RIZZOLI $35.00

G.H. **Oelsner**
A Handbook of Weaves
A comprehensive guide, with clear text and more than 1800 diagrams
0-486-23169-0 DOVER PB $10.95

Iona **Plath**
The Handweaver's Pattern Book
Over 120 designs for curtains, upholstery, place mats, and other items
0-8446-5909-6 SMITH $16.80

Else **Regensteiner**
The Art of Weaving
Covers looms, weaves, patterns, and designs
0-88740-079-5 SCHIFFER PB $19.95

Carol **Strickler**, editor
A Weaver's Book of 8-Shaft Patterns: From the Friends of Handwoven
0-934026-67-X INTERWEAVE $36.95

Blair **Tate**
The Warp: A Weaving Reference
0-937274-33-X LARK BOOKS PB $14.95

Dyeing

Nancy **Belfer**
Batik and Tie Dye Techniques
A comprehensive and copiously illustrated sourcebook which examines the history and evolution of these dyeing processes
0-486-27131-5 DOVER PB $8.95

Elijah **Bemiss**
The Dyer's Companion
0-486-20601-7 DOVER PB $7.95

Jenny **Dean**
The Craft of Natural Dyeing
Yellow from goldenrod, pale green from birch leaves, and more. Dean examines techniques for natural home dyeing with simple equipment
0-85532-744-8 ARTHUR SCHWARTZ PB $16.95

Noel **Dyrenforth**
The Technique of Batik
0-7134-0407-8 BATSFORD $55.00

Francis J. **Kafka**
Batik Tie Dyeing, Stenciling, Silk Screen, Block Printing: The Hand Decoration of Fabrics
A well-known introduction to fabric design, first published in 1959. Includes 350 illustrations and clear instructions for each technique
0-486-21401-X DOVER PB $7.95

Melanie **Williams**
Fabric Painting: Get Started in a New Craft With Easy-To-Follow Projects for Beginners
0-7858-0061-1 BOOK SALES $8.98

Basket Making

Olivia Elton **Barratt**
Basket Making: How to Use Classic Basket-Making Techniques With Modern Materials to Create 10 Unusual Baskets
0-8050-2617-7 OWLET PB $14.95

Frederick **Christopher**
Basketry
0-486-20677-7 DOVER PB $3.95

Liz **Doyle**
Raffia Hats and Baskets
0-86417-457-8 UNICORN PB $14.95

Maryanne **Gillooly**, editor
Natural Baskets: Create over 20 Unique Baskets With Materials Gathered in Gardens, Fields, and Woods
0-88266-793-9 STOREY PB $16.95

Carol **Hart** & Dan **Hart**
Natural Basketry
Eight well-diagrammed projects for wicker and twined baskets
0-8230-3155-1 WATSON-GUPTILL PB $14.95

Virginia **Harvey**
The Techniques of Basketry
0-295-96415-4 WASHINGTON PB $14.95

Pat **Laughridge**
Let's Weave Color Into Baskets
A well-presented slim book of attractive designs
0-88740-056-6 SCHIFFER PB $12.95

Barbara **Maynard**
Modern Basketry Techniques
0-7134-6160-8 BATSFORD PB $29.95

Helen **Richardson**, editor
Fibre Basketry: Homegrown and Handmade
0-86417-265-6 KANGAROO $39.95

Lyn **Siler**
The Basket Book
Over 30 basketweaving projects using a variety of techniques and materials. Step-by-step instructions and watercolor illustrations
0-8069-6830-3 LARK BOOKS PB $12.95

Susie **Vaughan**
Handmade Baskets: From Nature's Colourful Materials
0-85532-755-3 SEARCH PB $16.95

Bernard **Verdet-Fierz** & Regula **Verdet-Fierz**
Willow Basketry
0-934026-88-2 INTERWEAVE $21.95

Bookbinding and Paper Crafts

Manly **Banister**
The Craft of Bookbinding
0-486-27852-2 DOVER PB........$7.95

John Paul **Barrett**
How to Make a Book: An Illustrated Guide to Making Books by Hand
0-9619629-3-3 GAFFP........$17.50

Betty **Christy**
Easy to Cut Silhouette Designs
0-486-25061-X DOVER PB........$4.95

Sophie **Dawson**
A Hand Papermaker's Sourcebook
The essential reference for all papermakers, professionals and amateurs alike. Lists supply sources, kits, workshops, magazines, and videos as well as a variety of equipment for the craft
1-55821-389-9 LYONS & BURFORD PB........$26.95

Edith **Diehl**
Bookbinding: Its Background and Technique
A fat volume by the eminent bookbinder; an historical survey and practical guide
0-486-24020-7 DOVER PB........$16.95

Flora **Fennimore**
The Art of the Handmade Book: Designing, Decorating, and Binding One-Of-A-Kind Books
1-55652-146-4 CHICAGO REVIEW PB........$11.95

Steven **Heller** & Seymour **Chwast**
Jackets Required: An Illustrated History of Book Jacket Design, 1920-1950
A graphic feast for graphic artists, students of design and cultural historians
See also **ART SPIEGELMAN'S FAVORITES** under **COMIC STRIPS** under **COMICS** in **POPULAR READING**
0-8118-0396-1 CHRONICLE PB........$19.95

Julian **Horsey** & Chris **Knowles**
The Paper Shoe Book: Step-By-Step Instructions on How to Make Paper Shoes and Everything You Need to Make Your First Pair
If you own this book, you can make a custom pair of shoes out of it. The cover turns into soles, the pages uppers and treads, and the velcro tabs into fasteners
0-517-88439-9 CLARKSON POTTER PB........$20.00

Dard **Hunter**
Papermaking: The History and Technique of an Ancient Craft
From the origins of paper in Asia to its introduction to Europe and the Americas. Covers watermarking, hand molds, maceration techniques and more. 320 illustrations
0-486-23619-6 DOVER PB........$13.95

Paul **Jackson**
Encyclopedia of Origami and Papercraft
Incudes a variety of projects using paper sculpture, crumpling, modelling, and more. Examples of each craft by paper artisans from around the world
1-56138-063-6 RUNNING PRESS........$24.95

Arthur **Johnson**
Thames & Hudson Manual of Bookbinding
0-500-68011-6 THAMES & HUDSON PB........$15.95

Francis **Kafka**
How to Clothbind a Paperback Book: A Step-By-Step Guide For Beginners
0-486-23837-7 DOVER PB........$2.95

Shereen **Laplantz**
Cover to Cover: Creative Techniques for Making Beautiful Books, Journals & Albums
0-937274-81-X LARK BOOKS........$24.95

Simon **Larbalestier**
The Art and Craft of Collage
0-8118-0806-8 CHRONICLE PB........$17.95

Arthur **Lewis**
Basic Bookbinding
0-486-20169-4 DOVER PB........$4.95

Marianne **Saddington**
Making Your Own Paper
A thorough introduction to papermaking, paper crafts, and paper art. Clear instructions and extensive illustrations on everything from making paper from plants to the construction of Japanese foldbooks
0-88266-784-X STOREY PB........$18.95

Faith **Shannon**
The Art and Craft of Paper
Produced in association with the Florentine marbling firm Il Papiro, this stunningly illustrated volume explores the methods used to create boxes, trays, books, bowls, and more from paper
0-8118-0788-6 CHRONICLE PB........$18.95

Gillian **Souter**
Papercrafts: 50 Extraordinary Gifts and Projects, Step-By-Step
Includes instructions for papermaking, pâpier-mâché, and découpage as well as a plethora of items made from paper, such as mâché and toy theaters
0-517-88484-4 CROWN PB........$18.00

Aldren **Watson**
Hand Bookbinding: A Manual of Instruction
0-486-29157-X DOVER PB........$8.95

Thay **Yang**
Exquisite Interceptors: Easy to Fold Airplanes from One Sheet of Paper
1-87938-427-2 CYPRESS HOUSE PB........$9.99

Marbling

Anne **Chambers**
Marbling on Fabric
0-85532-788-X ARTHUR SCHWARTZ PB........$12.95

The Practical Guide to Marbling Paper
An attractive book that can be used by beginners
0-500-27421-5 THAMES & HUDSON PB........$14.95

Gabriele **Grunebaum**
How to Marbleize Paper
0-486-24651-5 DOVER PB........$2.95

Einen **Miura**
The Art of Marbled Paper: Marbled Patterns and How to Make Them
Miura traces the history of paper marbling, drawing from her unrivaled collection of over 5,000 examples of the craft. This is a comprehensive source of both inspiration and step-by-step instruction. Includes 125 full-color illustrations, with additional black-and-white photography and diagrams throughout
4-7700-1548-8 KODANSHA........$45.00

Patty **Schleicher** & Mimi **Schleicher**
Marbled Designs: A Complete Guide to Fifty-Five Elegant Patterns
0-937274-69-0 LARK BOOKS........$24.95

Carol **Taylor** & others
Marbling Paper & Fabric
0-8069-8323-X LARK BOOKS PB........$12.95

Découpage

Holly **Boswell**
The Découpage Book: More Than 60 Decorative Projects Using Simple Techniques
Includes 60 projects, incorporating techniques from the elevated "vue d'optique" to the filled and embossed "repoussé." For the advanced paper crafter
0-8069-0610-3 LARK BOOKS........$27.95
0-8069-0611-1 LARK BOOKS PB........$14.95

Vivienne **Garforth**
Découpage With Scrapbook Pictures
0-86417-524-8 SEVEN HILLS PB........$12.95

Edmund **Gillon**

Picture Sourcebook For Collage and Découpage

0-486-23095-3 DOVER PB $9.95

Kaye **Healy**

Country Crafts Découpage

0-517-08798-7 CRESCENT $5.99

Joanna **Jones**

Découpage: A Practical Step-By-Step Guide

Describes how to transform furniture, glassware, and boxes with the application of paper cutouts. Includes 15 basic projects

1-56799-152-1 FRIEDMAN/FAIRFAX PB $8.95

Val **Lade**

18th Century Découpage: The Definitive Guide

1-86351-133-4 MILNER $19.95

Hiram **Manning**

Manning on Découpage

Authoritative book by an expert; includes 18th-century techniques. The patterns are lovely

0-486-24028-2 DOVER PB $9.95

Juliet **Moxley**

Découpage: How to Cut, Glue, and Varnish to Make Decorative Découpage Objects from Ordinary Household Items

0-8050-2813-7 OWLET PB $14.95

Judy **Newman**

Paper Tole: Three Dimensional Découpage

1-86351-144-X MILNER PB $12.95

Eleanor **Rawlings**

Découpage: The Big Picture Sourcebook

0-486-23182-8 DOVER PB $10.95

Nerida **Singleton**

Nerida Singleton's Découpage Project Kit Book: With Images, Papers and Projects

1-86351-149-0 MILNER PB $14.95

Origami

Isamu **Asahi**

Origami Monsters

0-8048-1867-3 TUTTLE PB $8.95

Steve **Biddle** & Megumi **Biddle**

Origami Safari

Includes two dozen sheets of origami paper

0-688-13570-6 TUPELO PB $8.95

Masahiro **Chatani** & Keiko **Nakazawa**

Great American Buildings: Origami Cutouts of Everybody's Favorite Landmarks

4-7700-1538-0 KODANSHA PB $15.95

Pop-Up Geometric Origami

0-87040-943-3 JAPAN PUBLICATIONS PB $13.95

Isao **Honda**

The World of Origami

0-87040-383-4 JAPAN PUBLICATIONS PB $24.00

Eric **Kenneway**

Complete Origami

One hundred projects for all levels of skill

0-312-00898-8 ST. MARTIN'S PB $15.95

Yoshihide **Momotani**

Trick Origami

0-87040-929-8 KODANSHA PB $15.00

John **Montroll**

Birds in Origami

0-486-28341-0 DOVER PB $2.95

North American Animals in Origami

0-486-28667-3 DOVER PB $9.95

Campbell **Morris**

Fold Your Own Dinosaurs

ILLUSTRATED BY PAUL JACKSON

0-399-51794-4 PERIGEE PB $7.95

Eiji **Nakamura**

Quick and Easy Flying Origami

Includes a 60-page book and 3 packs of origami paper. The birds, planes, and more described herein really fly

0-87040-925-5 JAPAN PUBLICATIONS PB $17.00

Robert **Neale** & Thomas **Hull**

Origami, Plain and Simple

Black-and-white images detail the construction of 30 models, including sea serpents, striking cobras, and somersaulting frogs

0-312-10516-9 ST. MARTIN'S PB $10.95

K. **Needham**

The Usborne Book of Origami

A wonderful kit for the origami novice, with the clear, concise text for which Usborne is widely known. Contains everything needed to venture into many facets of this paper craft

0-88110-657-7 E.D.C. PB $12.95

Jon **Tremaine**

The Step by Step Art of Origami

A book of fun projects, from boxes and baskets to floral bouquets and flamingoes. Hexaflexagons, too!

1-55110-243-9 GRAPHIC ARTS PB $12.95

Makoto **Yamaguchi**

Kusudama: Ball Origami

0-87040-863-1 JAPAN PUBLICATIONS PB $13.00

Pâpier-Mâché

Juliet **Bawden**

The Art and Craft of Pâpier-Mâché

Examines the history of and contemporary applications for pâpier-mâché. 125 color photos and 100 color diagrams allow anyone to complete dozens of projects

PHOTOGRAPHS BY PETER MARSHALL

0-8118-0805-X CHRONICLE PB $17.95

Dawn **Cusick**

Paper & Fabric Mâché: 100 Imaginative & Ingenious Projects to Make

100 projects, from rhino and elephant heads to candelabras and dog beds. Color photos

0-8069-0608-1 LARK BOOKS $27.95

0-8069-0609-X LARK BOOKS PB $14.95

Susanne **Haines**

Rediscovering Pâpier Mâché: How to Adapt the Art of Papier Mache to Make Vivid, Modern Objects

Twelve inspirational projects, including a potted tulip, a footed bowl, and an articulated doll—all gorgeously colored and decorated

0-8050-2618-5 OWLET PB $15.95

Miranda **Innes**

Pâpier-Mâché

An eye-catching book of innovative projects, incorporating metallic powders, colored pulp, wallpaper paste, balloons, strings, and more. Lavishly illustrated

0-7894-0335-8 DORLING KINDERSLEY $19.95

Sheila **McGraw**

Pâpier-Mâché for Kids

0-920668-93-3 FIREFLY PB $9.95

Pâpier-Mâché Today

An extensive foray into the medium, this book examines everything from paste recipes to surface textures and the incorporation of découpage

0-920668-85-2 FIREFLY PB $19.95

Beads and Beading

Ann **Benson**

Ann Benson's Beadwear: Making Beaded Accessories and Adornments

Techniques for beading sweaters, hats, belts and more with bugle and seed beads, plus pearls, crystals, and semi-precious stones

0-8069-0812-2 STERLING $27.95

Beadwork Basics

Noted bead artist Benson outlines 29 projects, including a mille fleur bracelet, a Marilyn Monroe pin, and a sunset rose clutch-purse

0-8069-0877-7 STERLING $27.95

Lois Sherr **Dubin**

The History of Beads: From 30,000 BC to the Present

An unusual book on the history of beads as a medium of trade, talismans, and adornment. Beautiful color illustrations

See also **JEWELRY** under **ACCESSORIES** under **FASHION AND COSTUME**

0-8109-0736-4 ABRAMS $75.00
0-8109-2617-2 ABRAMS PB $19.95

Peter **Francis**, Jr.

Beads of the World: A Collector's Guide With Price Reference

The first bead price guide ever published, with extensive notes on the history of this oldest artform. Extensively illustrated in color

0-88740-559-2 SCHIFFER PB $19.95

Linda Fry **Kenzle**

The Irresistible Bead: Designing and Creating Exquisite Beadwork Jewelry

A how-to

0-8019-8843-8 CHILTON PB $19.95

Alexandra **Kidd**

Beautiful Beads: How to Create Beautiful, Original Gifts and Jewelry for Every Occasion

Instructions for over 50 bead projects, from jewelry to evening bags and apparel, even household items like pitcher covers and lampshades

0-8019-8629-X CHILTON PB $19.95

Eliza **McClelland**

Traditional Beadwork

Twenty projects utilizing beadwork on canvas, with photos of the finished works and the pieces that provided the design inspiration, including a Japanese makeup box and a glasses case of Aboriginal pattern

1-85470-198-3 TRAFALGAR SQUARE $29.95

Maureen **Murray**

All About Beads: A Guide to Beads and Bead Jewellery Making

Illustrated, step-by-step instructions for 15 bead jewelry projects, from a peacock bead fringe and earrings to a square knot and glass bead collar

0-7134-7863-2 TRAFALGAR SQUARE $29.95

Ruth **Poris**

Advanced Beadwork

A clear and comprehensive guide to such techniques as metalwork, soldering, loom weaving, knitting, and crochet incorporating beads

0-9616422-0-3 GOLDEN HANDS PB $14.99

Debbie **Siniska**

Decorative Beadwork

Twelve projects, from fruit napkin rings to a "Moonshower" hat and a beaded curtain. Well illustrated

0-8050-3894-9 HOLT PB $16.95

Stefany **Tomalin**

Bead Jewelry Workstation

A book and beginning beader's supply kit in one, including beads, a handy worktray and information on threading and beadmaking, as well as a suppliers list

0-8431-3760-6 PRICE, STERN, & SLOAN $21.95

Glass

Barry **Bier**

The Art of Stained Glass Made Easy

Sixty designs with templates for house numbers, picture frames, wall clocks, and more. Step-by-step instructions for each project

1-85368-226-8 STERLING PB $14.95

Robert **Capp** & Robert **Bush**

Glass Etching: 46 Patterns with Complete Instructions

0-486-24578-0 DOVER PB $5.95

Connie Clough **Eaton**

Tiffany-Style Stained Glass Lampshades

Includes full-size templates on sturdy paper stock for 11 different lampshades. Patterns for the traditional dragonfly, magnolia, poppy, wisteria, and other designs

0-486-27589-2 DOVER PB $6.95

William **Fraser**

Picture in Glass

0-86417-392-X KANGAROO PB $8.95

Anita **Isenberg** & Stewart **Isenberg**

How to Work in Stained Glass

0-8019-7355-4 CHILTON PB $19.95

James **McDonell**

Stained Glass Craft Made Simple: Step-By-Step Instructions Using the Modern Copper Foil Method

0-486-24963-8 DOVER PB $3.95

Terrance **Plowright**

Stained Glass: Inspirations and Designs

Includes color plates of the author's work, and 32 patterns for use at home. Clear instructions for creating original designs as well

0-86417-495-0 SEVEN HILLS $24.95

Kay Bain **Weiner**

Stained Glass: A Guide to Today's Tiffany Copper Foil Technique

This stained glass method is ideal for two- or three-dimensional glass applications. Includes 250 illustrations and 16 pages of patterns

0-8230-4913-2 WATSON-GUPTILL PB $24.95

Tole Painting

Lola **Ades**

Tole Painting

1-56010-022-2 FOSTER PB $5.50

Kate **Coombe**

Folk Art and Tole Painting: New Designs for Decorative Paintwork

1-86351-057-5 STERLING PB $12.95

The Painted Garden: Designs for Folk Art and Tole Painting

1-86351-082-6 STERLING PB $12.95

Lyn **Zuhlke** & Cathy **Skinner**

How to Tole Paint If You Know You Can't: A Step-By-Step Guide

0-933491-34-4 HOT OFF THE PRESS PB $5.95

Pottery

Tony **Birks**

The Complete Potter's Companion

A revised and updated edition including 440 color photos. "His prose, like a good pot, has beauty of form, and is a delight to read" — *Raleigh News and Observer*

0-8212-2014-4 BULFINCH PB $24.95

Steve **Branfman**

Raku: A Practical Approach

0-8019-8023-2 CHILTON PB $26.95

Sandra L. **Brown**

Creative Effects in Porcelain and Ceramics

New ideas for the porcelain and ceramic artist, with eight heavily illustrated lessons to help you master advanced overglaze techniques

0-86417-635-X KANGAROO $24.95

Frank **Giorgini**

Handmade Tiles: Designing, Making, Decorating

Includes detailed instructions on how to design and fabricate flat and relief tiles, create mosaics, and install finished tiles. Inspires as well as instructs

0-937274-76-3 LARK BOOKS $24.95

Frank **Hamer** & Janet **Hamer**

The Potter's Dictionary of Materials and Techniques

A comprehensive reference for potters at all levels, well illustrated

0-8122-3112-0 PENNSYLVANIA $49.95

David **Hamilton**

The Thames & Hudson Manual of Stoneware and Porcelain

0-500-68024-8 THAMES & HUDSON PB $12.95

Janet **Mansfield**

Salt-Glaze Ceramics: An International Perspective

0-8019-8344-4 CHILTON $39.95

Glenn **Nelson**

Ceramics: A Potter's Handbook

A successful basic manual covering techniques, material, history, and vocabulary

0-03-063227-7 HOLT RINEHART & WINSTON PB ..$43.23

Susan **Peterson**

Shoji Hamada: A Potter's Way & Work

This biography of Hamada, a ceramist designated a national treasure by the Japanese government in 1955, is also an in-depth examination of his technique and processes

0-8348-0345-3 WEATHERHILL PB....................$22.95

Charlotte F. **Speight** & John **Toki**

Hands in Clay: An Introduction to Ceramics

An in-depth text, now in its third edition, that examines every aspect of working with clay. Includes a color chart showing test results of clay, glaze, and slip formulas keyed to the appendices.

1-55934-312-5 MAYFIELD PB....................$39.95

Richard L. **Wilson**

Inside Japanese Ceramics: A Primer of Materials, Techniques, and Traditions

A practical, hands-on manual for reproducing the techniques and styles of the Japanese ceramic tradition. Covers tools, materials, and procedures

0-8348-0346-1 WEATHERHILL....................$32.95

Elsbeth S. **Woody**

Handbuilding Ceramic Forms

Woody describes basic handbuilding processes, then examines the techniques of 10 contemporary ceramists. One sample of each artist's work appears in color

0-374-51449-6 FS&G PB $25.00

Pottery on the Wheel

A clear exposition for the novice of how to throw basic pottery forms using a wheel, with chapters on more advanced techniques

0-374-51234-5 FS&G PB....................$23.00

Woodwork and Furniture Making

Norm **Abram**

Classics from the New Yankee Workshop

How to build a rocking horse, Adirondack chair, butler's table, and more. "What Julia Child is to the culinary crowd, Norm Abram is to the hammering masses"—*Chicago Tribune*

0-316-00455-3 LITTLE, BROWN PB....................$21.95

The New Yankee Workshop

Thirteen handsome and useful projects from the master carpenter, star of the PBS television series

See also **CARPENTRY** under **BUILDING A HOUSE** under **THE HOME**

0-316-00454-5 LITTLE, BROWN PB....................$19.95

John **Feirer** & Gilbert **Hutchings**

Advanced Woodwork and Furniture Making

0-02-662110-X BENNET & MCKNIGHT....................$40.95
0-02-662120-7 BENNET & MCKNIGHT PB....................$7.96

Ron **Fuller** & Cathy **Meeus**

The Art and Craft of Wooden Toys

Details how to make 19 toys, from a crankable lion and tamer to a pecking hen and egg-laying puffin. Beautifully illustrated in color

1-56138-535-2 RUNNING PRESS $24.95

Don **Geary**

How to Sharpen Every Blade in Your Woodshop

Describes how to make easy jigs for sharpening, and includes hints on edge-protecting storage for all your blades

1-55870-342-X BETTERWAY PB....................$17.99

Kingsley H. **Hammett**

Crafting New Mexican Furniture: A Handbook to Design, Plans, and Techniques

From bookshelves to beds, cabinets to chairs, this volume showcases the popular Southwestern style in a variety of handsome projects

1-87861-033-3 RED CRANE PB $19.95

Hands On Magazine

Woodworking Projects II

For beginners and advanced craftsmen, instructions for home decoration and furnishing, as well as smaller projects

0-87857-616-9 RODALE PB....................$9.95

Jack **Hill**

Country Woodworker: How to Make Rustic Furniture, Utensils, and Decorations

A lavishly illustrated volume with instructions and templates for 18 projects, including a hooded cradle, traditional whirligigs, and a five-board bench

0-8118-1086-0 CHRONICLE $29.95

William H. **Hylton**

Country Pine: Furniture You Can Make With the Table Saw and Router

Detailed instructions for dozens of century-old pine designs, from a Quebec Bonnet Cupboard to dry sinks and candle boxes. Hints on techniques as well as step-by-step information on building each piece

0-87596-650-0 RODALE $27.95

Albert **Jackson** & David **Day**

Care & Repair of Furniture

1-56158-096-1 TAUNTON....................$27.95

The Complete Manual of Woodworking

An ideal book for practitioners of one of the most popular hobbies, invaluable for the novice as well as the skilled expert. It includes over 3,000 illustrations on every aspect of the craft—its history, principles of design, materials, tools, and techniques

0-394-56488-X KNOPF....................$40.00

Good Wood Handbook

A handy little volume for everyone from the home handyperson to the professional cabinetmaker. Pocket-sized so you can bring it with you to the lumberyard

1-55870-427-2 BETTERWAY $19.99

Bruce **Johnson**

The Weekend Refinisher: How to Make the Most of Your Furniture : A Step-By-Step Guide

Country Living antiques columnist Johnson reveals the tricks of the trade with charts, tables, and easy-to-follow illustrated instructions

0-345-35866-X BALLANTINE PB $12.00

Bernard **Jones**

The Complete Woodworker

0-89815-034-5 TEN SPEED PB....................$16.95

The Practical Woodworker

0-89815-111-2 TEN SPEED PB....................$16.95
0-89815-106-6 TEN SPEED PB....................$9.95

Edwin **Monk**

How to Build Wooden Boats: With 16 Small-Boat Designs

16 small boat designs, from dinghies to hydroplanes and keel sloops, for the amateur. Revised from the 1934 edition

0-486-27313-X DOVER PB $7.95

Thomas **Moser**

Measured Shop Drawings For American Furniture

Designs and techniques, with illustrations

0-8069-6792-7 STERLING PB....................$19.95

John A. **Nelson**

52 Toys and Puzzles for the Weekend Woodworker

How to make great projects like a tractor-trailer to hold crayons, a '40s cargo ship, a rocking horse, and a number of pull toys for toddlers

0-8069-0644-8 STERLING PB....................$14.95

Pierre **Ramond**

Marquetry

Ramond, professor of marquetry (also known as inlay) at l'Ecole Boulle in Paris, is the world's foremost teacher and practitioner of this delicate art. Dozens of color plates, plus information on tools, techniques, the history of the craft, and more

0-942391-19-5 TAUNTON $75.00

Abby **Ruoff**

Making Twig Furniture & Household Things

Describes how to identify twigs and branches, use simple tools, and work with appropriate materials to craft 48 projects. Revised edition (13 new pieces included)

0-88179-120-2 HARTLEY & MARKS PB $21.95

Verna **Salomonsky**

Masterpieces of Furniture in Photographs and Measured Drawings

0-486-21381-1 DOVER PB $10.95

Harry **Smith**

The Art of Making Furniture in Miniature

0-89024-159-7 KALMBACK PB $29.95

Patrick **Spielman** & James **Reidle**

Victorian Gingerbread: Patterns & Techniques

Full-size patterns for brackets, corbels, running trim, gable ornaments, trellises, and more. Thoroughly illustrated

0-8069-7452-4 STERLING PB $14.95

Sunset Books

Basic Woodworking

Shows everything from how to use a table saw to how to apply lacquer, in the distinctively clear style *Sunset* has become known for

0-376-01585-3 SUNSET PB $9.99

Stephen **Taylor**

Building Thoreau's Cabin: A Modern Guide

Like Thoreau, Taylor undertook to construct a simple one-room retreat at low cost and with the simplest materials. He provides a step-by-step guide, with photographs illustrating every step of the process

PHOTOGRAPHS BY KEN ROBBINS

0-916366-17-0 NORTON PB $20.00

Bob **Vila**

Bob Vila's Workshop: The Ultimate Illustrated Handbook for the Home Workshop

Everything you need to know to set up a woodworking shop

0-688-11736-8 MORROW $29.95

John D. **Wagner**

Building Adirondack Furniture: The Art, the History, and the How-To

A complete and practical sourcebook, the designs of which are based on traditional turn-of-the-century furniture from Upstate New York

0-913589-87-X WILLIAMSON PB $12.95

Woodcarving

Philip R. **Eck**

Custom Gunstock Carving

0-8117-0348-7 STACKPOLE $34.95

Antony **Denning**

The Art and Craft of Woodcarving: A Complete Course, With Twelve Original Projects

1-56138-408-9 RUNNING PRESS $24.95

Fine Woodworking Magazine

Carving

0-918804-52-3 TAUNTON PB $9.95

Paul **Hasluck**

Manual of Traditional Wood Carving

A thorough and interesting book on traditional woodcarving, with sections on tools, styles, ornamentation; helpful drawings and photographs

0-486-23489-4 DOVER PB $11.95

Anthony **Hillman**

Carving Birds of Prey: With Patterns and Instructions for 12 Projects

0-486-27305-9 DOVER PB $6.95

Carving Traditional Fish Decoys: With Patterns and Instructions for 17 Projects

0-486-27500-0 DOVER PB $7.95

H. Leroy **Marlow**

Classic Carousel Carving: From 1/8 Scale to Full-Size: The Dentzel Patterns

0-8069-8252-7 STERLING PB $19.95

Ian **Norbury**

Fundamentals of Figure Carving

0-941936-26-0 LINDEN $31.95

Reg **Parsons**

Woodcarving: A Manual of Techniques

1-85223-770-8 CROWOOD PB $24.95

Harley **Refsal**

Woodcarving in the Scandinavian Style

0-8069-8633-6 STERLING PB $14.95

E. J. **Tangerman**

Carving Animals in Wood

0-486-28413-1 DOVER PB $6.95

1001 Designs for Whittling and Woodcarving

0-486-28362-3 DOVER PB $13.95

Tom **Wolfe**

Carving Canes & Walking Sticks With Tom Wolfe

0-88740-587-8 SCHIFFER PB $12.95

Miscellaneous Crafts

Fern-Rae **Abraham**

Tin Craft: A Work Book

9-994-75115-8 SUNSTONE PB $5.95

Edward A. **Baldwin**

PVC Furniture

0-8306-4076-2 TAB PB $12.95

Laurie **Carlson**

Ecoart!: Earth-Friendly Art and Craft Experiences for 3-To 9-Year-Olds (Kids Can Series, No 9)

0-913589-68-3 WILLIAMSON PB $12.95

Diana **Cross**

Craft from Recycled Materials

1-86351-083-4 MILNER PB $12.95

Jodie **Davis**

Easy-To-Make Scrap Crafts

0-913589-75-6 WILLIAMSON PB $13.95

Gwen **Diehn** & Terry **Krautwurst**

Kid Style Nature Crafts: 50 Terrific Things to Make With Nature's Materials

0-8069-0996-X LARK BOOKS $21.95

Brigitte **Eckardt**

Pressed Flower Art

1-86351-129-6 MILNER $17.95

Camilla **Gryski**

Lanyard: Having Fun With Plastic Lace

0-688-13325-8 MORROW $14.93

Lesley **Harle** & Simon **Willis**

Painting Ceramics: How to Paint and Stencil Already-Made Ceramics Pieces-12 Projects

0-8050-2383-6 OWLET PB $14.95

Christine **Harris**

French Knot Pictures

1-86351-112-1 DAVID & CHARLES $17.95

Ceci **Johnson**

Quick and Easy Ways With Ribbon: Techniques for Woven-Edge Ribbon-Ideas and Projects for Clothing

0-8019-8498-X CHILTON PB $14.95

Jenni **Kirkham**

The Wedding Craft Book

0-86417-581-7 KANGA PB $19.95

Deborah **Kneen**

Deborah Kneen's Handpainted Heirlooms

1-86351-123-7 MILNER PB $17.95

North Light **Staff**
Paint Craft
0-89134-650-3 NORTH LIGHT PB $16.95

Rose **Verney**
The Appliqué Book: A Guide to the Art and Craft of Appliqué
0-679-73280-2 KNOPF PB $19.95

The Business of Crafts

Edwin M. **Field** & Selma G. **Field**
Promoting and Marketing Your Crafts
0-02-537742-6 AUDEL PB $20.00

William G. **Hynes**
Start and Run a Profitable Craft Business: A Step-By-Step Business Plan
0-88908-760-1 SELF COUNSEL PRESS PB $12.95

Dan **Ramsey**
The Woodworker's Guide to Pricing Your Work
The author explains how to calculate the value of your materials, craftsmanship, and time when selling your work. Includes advice on negotiating and marketing
1-55870-372-1 BETTERWAY PB $18.99

Collectibles

"The collector not only transports himself, as in a dream, to a distant or past world, but also to a better world, in which men are not provided with the things they need any more than in the everyday world, but things themselves are freed from the servitude of having to be useful."
—Mario Praz, *An Illustrated History of Interior Decoration*

Roger **Fischer**
Tippecanoe and Trinkets Too: The Material Culture of American Presidential Campaigns, 1828-1984
0-252-00960-6 ILLINOIS $34.95

Ralph **Kovel** & Terry **Kovel**
Kovel's Know Your Collectibles
The bestselling guide to evaluating, buying, and caring for collectibles by two of America's foremost experts
0-517-58840-4 CROWN PB $16.00

Derek **Roberts**
Continental and American Skeleton Clocks
0-88740-182-1 SCHIFFER $79.95

Coins

Michael **Bates** & Elizabeth **Savage**
Dinars and Dirhams, Coins of The Islamic Lands: The Early Period
0-19-727617-2 OXFORD $245.00

Walter **Breen**
Walter Breen's Complete Encyclopedia of U.S. and Colonial Coins
The definitive reference book, with more than 4000 illustrations
0-385-14207-2 DOUBLEDAY $100.00

Coin World
Coin World Almanac
More than 500,000 historical and recent facts and figures for collectors and investors, from the most authoritative American numismatic publication. This 5th edition includes current issues, trends, and record prices
0-88687-462-9 PHAROS $29.95
0-944945-07-4 AMOS PB $15.95

Dolls and Dollhouses

BillyBoy
Barbie: Her Life and Times
Barbie dressed by the great couturiers, as well as the evolution of Barbie
0-517-59063-8 CROWN PB $22.00

Catherine **Christopher**
Complete Book of Doll Making and Collecting
0-8446-0058-X SMITH $20.05
0-486-22066-4 DOVER PB $7.95

Maps

Lloyd **Brown**
The Story of Maps
The standard history of cartography, from earliest times to the present
0-486-23873-3 DOVER PB $11.95

Movie and TV Memorabilia

Anthony **Slide** & John **Hegenberger**
A Collector's Guide to Movie Memorabilia
0-87069-377-8 WALLACE-HOMESTEAD PB $16.95

Music

L.R. **Docks**
American Premium Record Guide: 78s, 45s, 1915-1965
0-89689-088-0 BOOKS AMERICANA PB $22.95

David **Bowers**
Encyclopedia of Automatic Musical Instruments
An extensive book (1000 pages) on music boxes, player pianos, and organs, and all variations of automatic music machines
0-911572-08-2 VESTAL $74.95

Rare Books

John **Carter**
ABC For Book Collectors
An essential reference, with over 450 entries on the vocabulary and conventions of book collecting
0-394-41403-9 KNOPF $25.00

G. **Uden**
Understanding Book Collecting
For the novice and experienced collector: first editions, the condition of books, and other technical aspects, written with great enthusiasm
0-907462-13-8 ANTIQUE COLLECTORS $29.50

Sports Memorabilia

John **Oman** & Morton **Oman**
Encyclopedia of Golf Collectibles
0-89689-050-3 BOOKS AMERICANA PB $14.95

Stamps

Herman **Herst**
Fun and Profit in Stamp Collecting
0-940403-05-6 LINN'S STAMP PB $7.95

James **MacKay**
The Guinness Book of Stamp Facts and Feats
Facts and trivia by a noted stamp author
0-85112-351-1 STERLING PB $19.95

Toys and Games

Linda **Baker**
Modern Toys, 1930-1980
0-89145-277-X COLLECTOR $19.95

Lee **Dennis**
Warman's Antique American Games, 1840-1940
0-87069-630-0 WARMAN PB $17.95

Everett **Grist**
Antique and Collectible Marbles
0-89145-357-1 COLLECTOR PB $9.95

Margaret **Mandel**
Teddy Bears and Steiff Animals
0-89145-356-3 COLLECTOR PB $19.95
0-89145-267-2 COLLECTOR PB $9.95

Henry **Wiencek**
The World of Lego Toys
0-8109-2362-9 ABRAMS PB $19.95

Other

Mary **Benjamin**
Autographs: A Key to Collecting
Emphasizes autographs of prominent American presidents and statesmen
0-486-25035-0 DOVER PB $10.95

Theodore **Hake**
Political Buttons
Volume 1
1789-1916
0-918708-03-6 HAKE'S AMERICANA PB $30.00
Volume 2
1920-1976
0-918708-01-X HAKE'S AMERICANA PB $30.00

Lou **McCulloch**
Card Photographs: A Guide to Their History and Value
0-916838-56-0 SCHIFFER $30.00

Cyril **Permutt**
Collecting Old Cameras
0-306-70855-8 DA CAPO $34.00

Hugh **Tait**
Clocks and Watches
0-674-13570-9 HARVARD PB $9.95

Bernard **Watney** & Homer **Babbidge**
Corkscrews For Collectors
Whimsical and sophisticated designs for corkscrews
See also **COMMENTARIES** under **WINE AND BEVERAGES** in **FOOD, TRAVEL, AND LEISURE**
0-85667-113-4 SOTHEBY PARKE BERNET $39.95

Fashion and Costume

Books on fashion and costume can be divided into histories, picture and photography books, social commentary, biographies, and practical guides. The strength of each area is determined by our current preoccupations. Fashion is perhaps the most capricious business in America, and this trend is reflected in its literature.

Charlotte **Calasibetta**
Essential Terms of Fashion: A Collection of Definitions
Both books are useful for those in the fashion profession
0-87005-519-4 FAIRCHILD PB $27.00

Fairchild's Dictionary of Fashion
0-87005-635-2 FAIRCHILD $60.00

Alfred **D'Ortenzio**
Fashion Sketching: Drawing the Fashion Figure
A basic guide for the beginner, essentials of drawing the fashion figure
0-8273-7650-2 DELMR PB $37.95

Catherine **Houck**
The Fashion Encyclopedia: An Essential Guide to Everything You Need to Know About Clothes
0-312-28401-2 ST. MARTIN'S PB $14.95

Richard **Martin**, editor
St. James Fashion Encyclopedia: A Survey of Style from 1945 to the Present
From the director of the Fashion Institute at the Metropolitan Museum
0-7876-1036-4 VISIBLE INK $29.95

Georgina **O'Hara**
The Encyclopedia of Fashion
INTRODUCTION BY CARRIE DONOVAN
0-8109-0882-4 ABRAMS $34.95

The Psychology of Clothes

Juliet **Ash** & Elizabeth **Wilson**, editors
Chic Thrills: A Fashion Reader
0-520-08339-3 CALIFORNIA PB $17.00

Malcolm **Barnard**
Fashion As Communication
What you're really saying when you wear red. Learn to make use of fashion statements
0-415-11158-7 ROUTLEDGE PB $17.95

Ann **Hollander**
Seeing Through Clothes
A classic analysis of the function of clothes
0-520-08231-1 CALIFORNIA PB $19.95

Aileen **Ribeiro**
Dress and Morality
A provocative account of the role of dress from ancient Greece to the present
0-8419-1091-X HOLMES & MEIER $44.50

Valerie **Steele**
Fetish: Fashion, Sex, and Power
From leather to fishnets, taking control with your wardrobe
See also **FETISHES** under **CUTTING EDGE** in **POPULAR READING**
0-19-509044-6 OXFORD $35.00

Elizabeth **Wilson**
Adorned in Dreams: Fashion and Modernity
Argues that fashion should not be regarded merely as an illustration of the oppression of women but should be explored for its many cultural and political meanings
0-520-06212-4 CALIFORNIA PB $14.95

History of Fashion

Ariel Books
Fashion: Bustles to Bikinis
A history of underwear and intimate apparel
0-8362-0996-6 ANDREWS & MCMEEL $3.95

Jane **Ashelford**
The Art of Dress: Clothes and Society, 1500-1914
From royal court to courtroom to ballroom, the fashion of four centuries of society
PHOTOGRAPHS BY ANDREAS VON EINSIEDEL
0-8109-6317-5 ABRAMS $49.50

Martin **Battersby**
Art Deco Fashion: French Designers, 1908 to 1925
0-312-05181-6 ST. MARTIN'S PB $10.95

Stella **Blum**
Victorian Fashions and Costumes from Harper's Bazaar, 1898-1967
Fashion plates selected by an eminent authority and former curator of the Metropolitan Museum's Costume Institute
0-486-22990-4 DOVER PB $14.95

Stella **Blum**, editor
Ackermann's Costume Plates: Women's Fashions in England, 1818-1828
0-486-23690-0 DOVER PB $8.95
Eighteenth Century French Fashion Plates: 64 Engravings from the Galerie Des Modes, 1778-1787
0-486-24331-1 DOVER PB $13.95
Paris Fashions of the 1890s: A Picture Source Book with 450 Designs
Including 24 in Full Color
0-486-24534-9 DOVER PB $9.95

Anne **Buck**
Dress in 18th Century England
A vivid picture of those who made, wore, and admired clothes in 18th-century England
0-8419-0517-7 HOLMES & MEIER $49.50

Deirdre **Clancy**
Costume Since 1945: Couture, Street Style, and Anti-Fashion
0-89676-146-0 DRAMA PUBLISHERS $25.00

Madeleine **Ginsburg**
400 Years of Fashion
Mannequins model fashions from the Victoria & Albert Museum collections
0-00-217189-9 FABER PB $14.95

Anne **Hollander**

Sex and Suits

The art critic and author (*Moving Pictures*) brings her piercing eye to bear on the history of women's clothing from the late Middle Ages to the present. "This iconoclastic, continually stimulating essay argues that women's clothes, even after 1800, slavishly echoed ancient, traditional sartorial custom; modernizing women's clothing has meant copying men's garments, directly or indirectly"
—*Publishers Weekly*

See also **STYLE AND FASHION** under **EARLY MODERN EUROPE** in **WORLD HISTORY AND CURRENT AFFAIRS**

1-56836-101-7 KODANSHA PB....................$13.00

Valerie R. **Hotchkiss**

Clothes Make the Man: Female Cross Dressing in Medieval Europe

0-8153-2369-7 GARLAND....................$30.00

Lesley **Jackson**

The New Look: Design in the Fifties

The New Look introduced by Christian Dior in 1947 was only the beginning of a series of trends in fashion, design, and interior decoration—trends that helped define the '50s and that are being enthusiastically rediscovered today. 240 illustrations, 90 in color

0-500-27644-7 THAMES & HUDSON PB....................$24.95

Dodie **Kazanjian**

Icons: The Absolutes of Style

0-312-13518-1 ST. MARTIN'S....................$22.95

Ellie **Laubner**

Fashions of the Roaring '20s

From flappers to charleston dresses, the most elegant period of this century

0-7643-0017-2 SCHIFFER PB....................$29.95

James **Laver**

Costume and Fashion

An excellent concise history

0-500-20190-0 THAMES & HUDSON PB....................$14.95

Alice **Mackrell**

Coco Chanel

The celebrated Parisian couturier, Coco Chanel (1883-1971), was by the '20s one of the most influential figures in the history of fashion design

0-8419-1301-3 HOLMES & MEIER PB....................$25.95

Caroline Rennolds **Milbank**

New York Fashion: The Evolution of American Style

An entertaining and informative history of American fashion, beautifully illustrated with over 300 plates. Milbank, the author of *Couture*, describes the trends of each period from the beginning of the 19th century to the present, how events have influenced clothing styles, the characteristics of the uniquely American way of dress, and the international emergence of American fashion. Each chapter includes details on the prominent designers of the time

0-8109-2647-4 ABRAMS PB....................$29.95

Josephine **Paterek**

Encyclopedia of American Indian Costume

0-393-31382-4 NORTON PB....................$19.95

John **Peacock**

The Chronicle of Western Fashion: From Ancient Times to the Present Day

More than 1,000 illustrations trace the development of fashion from ancient Egypt to contemporary Paris

0-8109-3953-3 ABRAMS....................$35.00

Philippe **Perrot**

The Bourgeoisie Inside Out: A History of Clothing in the Nineteenth Century

0-691-00081-6 PRINCETON PB....................$15.95

Auguste **Racinet**

The Historical Encyclopedia of Fashion

A recent edition of this classic history, illustrated with 2000 lithographs

0-8160-1976-2 FACTS ON FILE....................$45.00

Lynn **Schnurnberger**

Let There Be Clothes: 40,000 Years of Fashion from Cro-Magnon to Lacroix

A witty romp through the history of fashion, including fads and trivia

0-89480-833-8 WORKMAN PB....................$19.95

Joan **Severa**

Dressed for the Photographer: Ordinary Americans and Fashion, 1840-1900

FOREWORD BY CLAUDIA BRUSH KIDWELL, WITH NANCY REXFORD

0-87338-512-8 KENT STATE....................$60.00

Marie **Simon**

Fashion in Art: The Second Empire and Impressionism

0-302-00658-3 ZWEMMER....................$50.00

Charles **Spencer**

Erté

Biography of the fashion illustrator and costume designer

0-517-54391-5 CROWN PB....................$16.95

Fequiere **Vilsaint** & Maude **Heurtelou**

African Fashion: Illustrations

1-88183-945-1 EDVIS PB....................$5.99

Diana **Vreeland**

D.V.

The eccentric views and sayings of the redoubtable and tremendously infuential *Vogue* editor

EDITED BY GEORGE PLIMPTON & CHRISTOPHER HEMPHILL

0-394-50341-4 KNOPF....................$15.95

Verity **Wilson** & Ian **Thomas**

Chinese Dress

Ancient Asian fashion explained

0-8348-0368-2 WEATHERHILL PB....................$42.00

Haute Couture

Francois **Baudot**

Coco Chanel

The mother of modern sportswear, perfume, and cosmetics

0-7893-0064-8 VENDOME....................$18.95

Marie-France **Pocha**

Dior

Post WWII genius and originator of the New Look is explored in depth

0-7893-0065-6 VENDOME....................$18.95

Marie France **Pochna**

Christian Dior: The Man Who Made the World Look New

TRANSLATED BY JOANNA SAVILL

1-55970-340-7 ARCADE....................$25.95

Pierre **Berge**

Yves Saint Laurent

The most famous fashion colorist is documented briefly and succinctly

0-7893-0067-2 VENDOME....................$18.95

Alice **Rawsthorn**

Yves Saint Laurent: A Biography

0-385-47645-0 BDD....................$27.50

Guillermo **de Osma**

Mariano Fortuny: His Life and Work

The designer best known for his use of pleated fabric

0-8478-0641-3 RIZZOLI PB....................$35.00

Bernadine **Morris**

Valentino

Italy's most celebrated couturier—bravo

0-7893-0066-4 VENDOME....................$18.95

Victor **Skrebneski** & Laura **Jacobs**

The Art of Haute Couture

Haute couture, the finest fashion, examined and explored. Fabulous photographs

0-7892-0022-8 ABBEVILLE....................$75.00

Palmer **White**

Elsa Schiaparelli: Empress of Paris Fashion

"Empress" says it all—the '30s diva of fashion

1-85410-358-X AURUM PB....................$24.95

International Contemporary Fashion

Richard **de Combray**

Armani

The work of the Italian sportswear king

0-8478-5418-3 RIZZOLI....................$150.00

Brenda **Cullerton**
Geoffrey Beene: The Anatomy of His Work
The Frank Lloyd Wright of fashion—absolute modernism
0-8109-3141-9 ABRAMS $49.50

Marian **Fowler**
The Way She Looks Tonight: Five Women of Style
A guided tour of the wardrobes of five fabulous women
0-312-14757-0 ST. MARTIN'S $24.95

Patrick **Mauries**
Christian Lacroix: The Diary of a Collection
More is *more*. Fashion opulence from France's frou-frou designer extrodinaire
0-684-83259-3 SIMON & SCHUSTER $50.00

Arnold **Scaasi** & others
Scaasi: A Cut Above
America's only true couturier. Designer to Nancy Reagan and others
0-8478-1987-6 RIZZOLI $55.00

Francesco **Scavullo**
Scavullo Women
The beauty secrets of the photographer's celebrity subjects
0-06-014838-1 HARPERCOLLINS $24.95

Fred **Vermorel**
Vivienne Westwood: Fashion, Perversity and the Sixties Laid Bare
The bad girl of the '60s and '70s is still pumping out sex, style, and decadence
0-87951-691-7 OVERLOOK $23.95

Special Fashions

Tyler **Beard**
The Cowboy Boot Book
A knockout overview of a particularly American folk art form. Here are boots sporting inlays of everything from oil derricks to diamonds, family crests to Absolut vodka bottles
0-87905-471-9 GIBBS SMITH PB $17.95

Ida **Panicelli**
Fellini: Costumes and Fashion
Italy's film god explores the costumes of his work
88-86158-82-3 DISTRIBUTED ART PB $35.00

Barbara **Radice**
Jewelry by Architects
Jewelry by some of the best known postmodern architects, with interviews explaining their designs
0-8478-0798-3 RIZZOLI $35.00

Dyer **Spark**
Fit to Be Tied
Vintage neckties
0-89659-756-3 ABBEVILLE $27.50

Thomas **Steele**
The Hawaiian Shirt: Its Art and History
1-55-5859418-3 ABBEVILLE PB $13.95

Accessories

Andrew **Baseman**
The Scarf
Couture scarves, gaily printed bandanas, humorous souvenir scarves, extravagant shawls—and ideas for tying and wearing them
0-8317-7202-6 STEWART, TABORI $7.98

Kate **de Castelbajac** & others
The Face of the Century: 100 Years of Makeup and Style
From Max Factor to RuPaul, an authoritative history of cosmetics
0-8478-1895-0 RIZZOLI $50.00

Diana **Epstein** & Millicent **Safro**
Buttons
A lavish presentation of over 1,000 unexpectedly rare, intricate, whimsical and astonishing buttons, put together by the proprietors of the ultra-fashionable Manhattan boutique Tender Buttons. Includes 208 pictures. Photography by John Parnell
PREFACE BY TOM WOLFE
0-8109-3113-3 ABRAMS $49.50

Christina **Probert**
Sportswear in Vogue Since 1910
0-89659-499-8 ABBEVILLE PB $12.95

Mary **Trasko**
Heavenly Soles: Extraordinary Twentieth-Century Shoes
9-993-09986-4 SHOE TRADES PB $25.00

Jewelry

Joanne Dubbs **Ball** & Dorothy Hehl **Torem**
Masterpieces of Costume Jewelry
Includes value guide
0-88740-900-8 SCHIFFER $49.95

Kevin K. **Casey**
Jewelry: Customs, Costumes, and Cultures
An anthropological journey into jewelry
0-86625-597-4 ROURKE $42.00

Franco **Cologni** & Eric **Nussbaum**
Platinum by Cartier: Triumphs of the Jewelers' Art
Opulent and expensive, the finest of all jewelry presented by the couturier himself
0-8109-3738-7 ABRAMS $85.00

Meryl **Doney**
Jewelry
0-531-14406-2 FRANKLIN WATTS $18.00

Helen Williams **Drutt** & others
Jewelry of Our Time: Art, Ornament and Obsession
0-8478-1914-0 RIZZOLI $55.00

Lois Sherr **Dubin**
The History of Beads: From 30,000 BC to the Present
An unusual book on the history of beads as a medium of trade, talismans, and adornment. Beautiful color illustrations
See also **BEADS AND BEADING** under **CRAFTS**
0-8109-0736-4 ABRAMS $75.00
0-8109-2617-2 ABRAMS PB $19.95

Martha Gandy **Fales**
Jewelry in America: 1600-1900
An authoritative guide
1-85149-223-2 ANTIQUE COLLECTORS $69.50

Tony **Grasso**
Bakelite Jewelry
Trendy and fabulous, Bakelite was plastic jewelry popular in the '30s and '40s
0-7858-0276-2 BOOK SALES $12.98

Toni **Greenbaum**
Messengers of Modernism: American Studio Jewelry, 1940-1960
2-08-013593-7 ABBEVILLE $37.50

Lois Essary **Jacka**
Navajo Jewelry: A Legacy of Silver and Stone
0-87358-609-3 NORTHLAND PB $14.95

David **Lancaster**
Art Nouveau Jewelry
Part of the Christie's Collectibles series
0-8212-2270-8 BULFINCH $12.95

Jan **Lindenberger**
Clothing & Accessories from the '40s, '50s & '60s: A Handbook and Price Guide
A guide to collecting
0-7643-0023-7 SCHIFFER PB $16.95

John **Mack**
Ethnic Jewelry
Noncommercial jewelry from around the world
0-8109-0891-3 ABRAMS $49.50

Hans **Nadelhoffer**
Cartier: Jewelers Extraordinary
The great designers of art deco jewelry
0-8109-0770-4 ABRAMS $65.00

Gilles **Neret**
Boucheron: Four Generations of a World Renowned Jeweller
A beautiful book on one of the most daring of the grand French jewelers
0-8478-0987-0 RIZZOLI $85.00

Clare **Phillips**

Jewelry: From Antiquity to the Present

A complete guide. Small but informative

See also **THAMES & HUDSON WORLD OF ART** under **ART HISTORY: GENERAL STUDIES** in **ART**

0-500-20287-7 THAMES & HUDSON PB $14.95

Boo **Poulin**

The Art of Jewelry Design

1-56496-192-3 ROCKP PB $29.99

Penny **Proddow** & others

Hollywood Jewels: Movies, Jewelry, Stars

Hooray for Hollywood. A tour de force of glitz and glamour in tinseltown

0-8109-8145-9 ABRADALE $22.98

Nancy **Schiffer** & Tim **Scott**

The Best of Costume Jewelry

0-7643-0001-6 SCHIFFER PB $29.95

Jane Casey **Singer**

Gold Jewelry from Tibet and Nepal

This splendidly illustrated book describes the ways in which jewelry has been used and appreciated in the Himalayas. More than mere ornament, jewelry reflected not only the owner's personal wealth but also the wearer's social and political status, as well as the embodiment of ancient Hindu and Buddhist values

See also **THE HIMALAYAS** under **EAST ASIAN ART** in **ART**

0-500-97442-X THAMES & HUDSON $35.00

Willaim A. **Turnbaugh**

Indian Jewelry of the American Southwest

0-88740-905-9 SCHIFFER PB $12.95

Ralph **Turner**

Jewelry in Europe and America: New Times, New Thinking

0-500-27879-2 THAMES & HUDSON PB $24.95

Oppi **Untracht**

Traditional Jewelry of India

0-8109-3886-3 ABRAMS $25.00

Geza **von Habsburg**

Fabergé in America

The comprehensive catalogue of the exhibition of works in American collections by the Russian goldsmith and jeweler that recently toured the United States. More than an assembly of spectacularly sumptuous objects, the book places the social history of American collecting against the backdrop of America's ongoing fascination with imperial Russia

0-500-01699-2 THAMES & HUDSON $50.00

Dyfri **Williams** & Jack **Ogden**

Greek Gold: Jewelry of The Classical World

See also **GREECE** under **ART OF THE CLASSICAL WORLD** in **ART**

0-8109-3388-8 ABRAMS $45.00

Menswear

Bruce **Boyer**

Elegance: A Guide to Quality In Menswear

A *Town & Country* writer's advice on stylish dress

0-393-30438-8 NORTON PB $9.95

Diana **de Marly**

Fashion For Men: An Illustrated History

How men's styles and the masculine ideal have varied through the centuries

0-8419-1240-8 HOLMES & MEIER PB $27.95

John **Peacock**

Men's Fashion: The Complete Sourcebook

The last word on men's fashion

0-500-01725-5 THAMES & HUDSON $29.95

The Fashion Business

"The fashion industry is no more able to preserve a style that men and women have decided to abandon than to introduce one they do not choose to accept. In America, for instance, huge advertising budgets and the wholehearted cooperation of magazines such as *Vogue* and *Esquire* have not been able to save the hat, which for centuries was an essential part of everyone's outdoor (and often of their indoor) costume. It survives now mainly as a utilitarian protection against weather, as part of ritual dress (at formal weddings, for example) or as a sign of age or individual eccentricity."
—Alison Lurie, *The Language of Clothes*

Beauty Salons & Fashion Boutiques: Including Shoe Stores & Jewelry Stores

4-7858-0030-5 BOOKS NIPPAN $59.95

Nicholas **Drake**

Fashion Illustration Today

More than 20 fashion illustrators from Paris, Milan, New York, and London

0-500-27486-X THAMES & HUDSON PB $22.50

Jeannette A. **Jarnow** & Ketty G. **Dickerson**

Inside the Fashion Business

An insider's guide to the cut-throat industry

0-13-238148-6 PRENTICE HALL $25.00

Ann **Stegemeyer**

Who's Who in Fashion

0-87005-574-7 FAIRCHILD PB $33.00

How to Dress

Natasha **Esch** & C. L. **Walker**

The Wilhelmina Guide to Modeling

The "how to" book for the beautiful, from the premier New York City modeling agency

0-684-81491-9 FIRESIDE PB $14.00

Paula **Begoun**

Blue Eyeshadow Should Absolutely Be Illegal: The Definitive Guide to Skin Care and Makeup Application

Flattering, fast, and inexpensive cosmetic application for the '90s based on a $10 skincare routine. Includes answers to the 50 most commonly asked makeup questions, updated information on Retin-A, and discussions of industry fads and marketing, skin-care product ingredients, and false advertising claims. "Simply the most unique, one-of-a-kind book on makeup and skincare I've ever seen"
—Oprah Winfrey

1-87798-804-9 BEGINNING PRESS PB $12.95

Theodora **Faiola** & Jo **Pullen**

McGraw-Hill Guide to Clothing

0-07-019855-1 MCGRAW HILL $40.50

Rita **Farro**

Life Is Not a Dress Size: Rita Farro's Guide to Attitude, Style, and a New You

Plus size women speak out and look beautiful

0-8019-8758-X CHILTON PB $16.95

Elsa **Klensch** & Beryl **Meyer**

Style With Elsa Klensch: Developing the Real You

CNN's fashion guru guides everyone from the fashion neophyte to the aficionado

0-312-06960-X ST. MARTIN'S $24.95

John **Molloy**

The Woman's Dress For Success Book

Tips on how to get promoted: one way is to wear a gray suit and demure blouse

0-446-38586-7 WARNER PB $11.99

New Women's Dress for Success: The Classic Primer Updated and Revised for Today's Office

0-446-67223-8 WARNER PB $12.99

Norio **Yamanaka**

The Book of Kimono

A practical guide on how to select, wear, and take care of the kimono

0-87011-785-8 KODANSHA PB $25.00

Costume

Alicia **Finkel**

Romantic Stages: Set and Costume Design in Victorian England

0-7864-0234-2 MCFARLAND $38.50

Carl **Kohler**

History of Costume

Detailed illustrated history, up to 1870

0-486-21030-8 DOVER PB $9.95

Michael **Mullin**

Design by Motley

England's renowned theatrical design school displays its finest work

0-87413-569-9 DELAWARE $55.00

Shirley Miles **O'Donnoll**

American Costume, 1915-1970: A Source Book For the Stage Costume

0-253-20543-3 INDIANA PB $19.95

Susan **Train**

Theatre De La Mode

Figurines in theatrical decors by Cocteau, Christian Berard, and others recreate the exhibit which marked the resurrection of French haute couture after World War 11

0-8478-1340-1 RIZZOLI $45.00

R. Turner **Wilcox**

The Mode in Costume

Illustrated with drawings; includes an amusing section on women's hairdresses

0-684-13913-8 MACMILLAN PB $18.00

Part 12

Performing Arts & Media

Billie Holiday

Pop Quiz: Name That Star!

1 SEPTEMBER 14, 1927
DANCE DIVA
DEAD IN ITALY
STRANGE LAST DANCE!!
1319

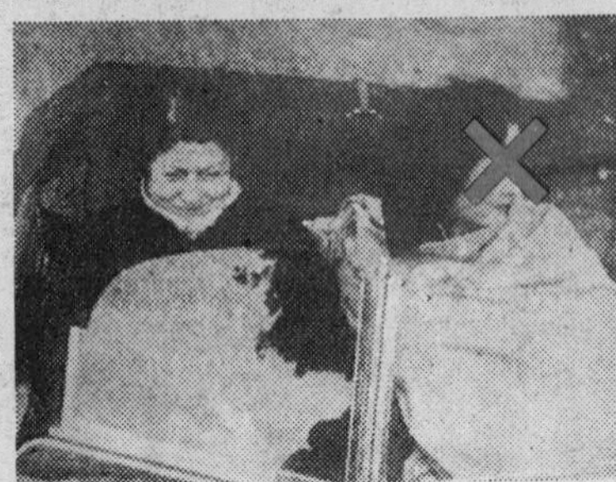

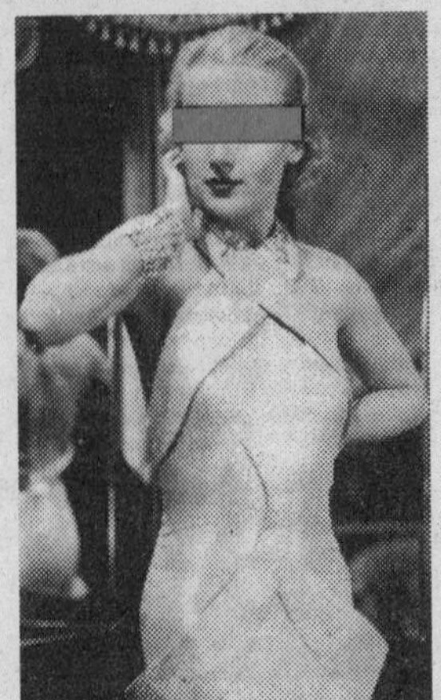

2 JANUARY 16, 1942
SCREEN STAR **KILLED**
IN NEVADA **AIR CRASH** AFTER
WRAPPING *LAST MOVIE!!*
1332

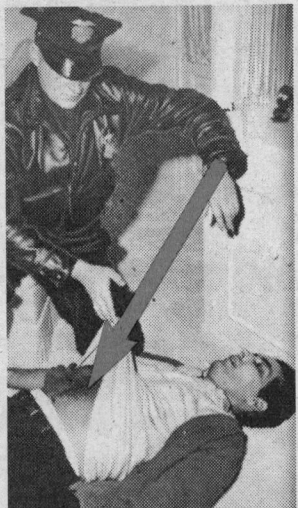

3 FEBRUARY 2, 1959
AIR CRASH IN IOWA
ALL DEAD!!
LONE MUSICIAN
TAKES BUS INSTEAD—
AND SURVIVES!!
1312

4 JUNE 29, 1967
SCREEN IDOL
DECAPITATED
IN LOUISIANA WRECK!!
1332

5 OCTOBER 4, 1970
ROCK STAR
DEAD IN BED!!
EX-FRIEND PROCLAIMS:
"THE BITCH BEAT ME!"
1312

6 APRIL 4, 1958
DAUGHTER OF **STAR**
MURDERS MOTHER'S LOVER
WITH A *KITCHEN KNIFE!!*
1332

7 DECEMBER 19, 1985
FAN SHOT!! ASKED WRONG
COUNTRY MUSIC STAR:
"HAVE YOU EVER TRIED SQUIRREL MEAT?"
1301

8 OCTOBER 11, 1978
CHELSEA GIRL DEAD
IN *VICIOUS STABBING!!*
1350

9 JUNE 13, 1989
DEAD IN AMSTERDAM:
"GABRIEL" PLUNGES
FROM *HOTEL WINDOW!!*
1304

10 OCTOBER 23, 1983
TV ANCHORWOMAN
DROWNED IN FREAK
AUTO ACCIDENT!!
1350

11 January 1, 1997
REBEL WITHOUT A CAUSE **STAR**
STILL ALIVE AND WELL!!
1366

1 Isadora Duncan; driving at top speed in a sports car, her long scarf caught in the back axle and broke her neck.
2 Carole Lombard; *To Be or Not to Be*
3 The Big Bopper, Richie Valens, Buddy Holly, and Roger Peterson, the pilot; Waylon Jennings, who decided at the last moment not to get on the plane
4 Jayne Mansfield
5 Janis Joplin, dead of a heroin overdose at the Landmark Hotel in Los Angeles; Jim Morrison (who would be dead in nine months and a day)
6 Lana Turner; Johnny Stompanato
7 Johnny Paycheck
8 Nancy Spungen: stabbed to death in the Chelsea Hotel by her boyfriend, Sid Vicious, bassist for the Sex Pistols
9 Chet Baker, jazz trumpeter
10 Jessica Savitch
11 Dennis Hopper

Iago
I am your own forever.
—William Shakespeare
Othello
792

Dido
No, faithless man, thy course pursue,
I'm now resolv'd as well as you.
No repentence shall reclaim
The injur'd Dido's slighted flame,
For 'tis enough, whate'er you now decree,
That you had once a thought of leaving me.
—Nahum Tate
Dido and Aeneas
1296

Kinde Are Her Answeres
But her performance keeps no day,
Breaks time, as dancers
From their own Musike when they stray:
All her free favors
And smooth words wing my hopes in vaine.
O did ever voice so sweet but only fain?
Can true love yeeld such delay,
Converting joy to pain?
—Thomas Campion
The Third Book of Ayres
1289

My Dear Lady!
This is the catalogue of the women my master has loved. In Italy, six hundred and forty; in Germany, two hundred and thirty-one; a hundred in France; ninety-one in Turkey—but in Spain there are already a thousand and three. Among them are country girls, ladies from the city, chambermaids, princesses, and women of every class, every figure, every age! He never thinks of whether she's rich, ugly or beautiful—as long as she wears a skirt, you know very well what he does!
—Lorenzo da Ponte
Don Giovanni
1298

Songs of Love and Grief
A young man loves a maiden,
Who chose another instead;
That other loves another
And led her to altar and bed.

The maiden in her anger
Weds the first likely lad
That happened to come across her;
The young man's lot is sad.

It is a time-worn story,
And yet it is ever new;
And when it happens to someone
It breaks his heart in two.
—Heinrich Heine
1291

The Merry Widow
When you marry you will live, quite in the modern style;
And freedom you will take and give–that is the modern style!
And if your husband goes astray,
Then I shall only smile.
Return his lead when you're to play–
Quite in the modern style.
—Franz Lehár
1297

Venus, Mars, and Vulcan by Enea Vico (after Parmigianino)

Make Me a Pallet
Make me a pallet on your floor
Make me a pallet on your floor
Just make me a pallet
Baby, down upon your floor
When your main girl come
I swear, she will never know.
—Ma Yancey
"Make Me a Pallet on the Floor"
1302

Don't Explain
Skip that lipstick
Don't explain
—Billie Holiday
1309

Do Nothing Till You Hear from Me
True I've been seen with somebody new,
But does that mean I'm untrue?
—Bob Russell
1308

Pardon Me
I warned him not to try and take her from me
He laughed and said, "If I can you know I will"
So tonight when they get home, I'll be waiting
Pardon me, I've got someone to kill.
—Johnny Paycheck
1301

Soap
In 1974, nurse Augusta McLeod killed Dr. Phil Brewer with a paperweight because she feared he would tell Diana Taylor that she was pregnant with Diana's husband Peter's child. To silence Phil, Augusta hit him over the head and, after finally confessing months later, went to jail—where she gave birth to her baby.
—*"General Hospital": The Complete Scrapbook*
1353

A Confession
Priest: What sins have you to confess?
Loretta: Twice I took the name of the Lord in vain, once I slept with the brother of my fiancé, and once I bounced a check at the liquor store—but that was really an accident.
Priest: Then it's not a sin. But what was that second thing you said, Loretta?
—*Moonstruck*
1330

Western Classical Music

Reference

Christine **Ammer**

Harper Collins Dictionary of Music

"Sufficiently comprehensive for amateurs and laymen"—*Saturday Review*

0-06-181020-7 HARPERCOLLINS PB $14.00

Denis **Arnold**, editor

The New Oxford Companion to Music

0-19-311316-3 OXFORD $135.00

Harold **Barlow** & Sam **Morgenstern**

A Dictionary of Musical Themes

An ideal reference guide to 10,000 themes by composers ranging from Adolphe Adam to Efrem Zimbalist

0-7812-9266-2 REPRINT SERVICES................$109.00

Jonathan **Buckley**, editor

The Rough Guide to Classical Music on CD

Informal, serious, and forthright, this guide takes an unusually effective multi-levelled approach to classical music, providing first the context of the composers, then the works themselves as well as the best recordings on CD—including budget and mid-price options, and historic and contemporary recordings. This A-Z of composers includes all the regulars, but also a number of unjustly neglected subjects, and in particular, women composers. Illustrated throughout

1-85828-113-X ROUGH GUIDES PB $19.95

Ron Van **der Meer** & Michael **Berkeley**

The Music Pack

From the creators of *The Art Pack*—an innovative, ingenious pop-up tour through the world of art—comes *The Music Pack.* 3D models of instruments you can remove and "play," instructive and imaginative pop-ups (including an entire orchestra), and a 75-minute CD take you through the world of music

0-679-43098-9 KNOPF $50.00

Edward **Downes**

The Guide to Symphonic Music

0-8027-7177-7 WALKER PB $29.95

New York Philharmonic Guide to the Symphony

0-8027-0540-5 WALKER $65.00

Phil G. **Goulding**

Classical Music: The 50 Greatest Composers and Their 1,000 Greatest Works

Bach to Beethoven, *Bolero* to *La Boheme*, this is a one-volume classical music education, witty and winning. "One terrific music appreciation book…easy to use…well-chosen recordings…surprisingly detailed and concisely presented"–*Arizona Daily Star*

0-449-91042-3 BALLANTINE PB........................$15.00

Craig **Heller**

From Metal to Mozart: Rock and Roll Guide to Classical Music

0-8118-0576-X CHRONICLE PB $9.95

Arthur **Jacobs**

The Penguin Dictionary of Music

0-14-051159-8 PENGUIN PB $12.95

Michael **Kennedy**

Oxford Dictionary of Music

0-19-311333-3 OXFORD $49.95

Norman **Lebrecht**

The Book of Musical Anecdotes

Seven hundred eighty-six tales about composers, performers, and their art. For example: "Donizetti, when asked which of his own operas he thought the best, replied, 'How can I say which? A father always has a preference for a crippled child, and I have so many'"

0-02-918710-9 FREE PRESS $27.95

Ivan **March** & others

The Complete Penguin Guide to Compact Discs and Cassettes: The Guide to Excellence in Recorded Classical Music

Designed to help buyers make smart choices about the overwhelming quantity of classical music now available. This guide lists the most important recent releases on CD and cassette, and offers advice on how to obtain best value for the money. It points out recordings that are unique or valuable, great "best of" collections and live performances, and also guides readers to the best of the older releases. "The authors' scope and zeal are stunning, their standards of judgement and accuracy high"
—*Sunday Times* [London]

0-14-046918-4 PENGUIN PB.............................$23.50

Brian **Morton**, editor

The Blackwell Guide to Recorded Contemporary Music

Studies the 150 most important musical works since 1939, setting each in the context of its specific period and considering the developments of musical genres and instrumental groupings. From this groundwork, it moves on to discographical information, suggestions for further listening and reading, and much more, making it one of the most authentic and authoritative educations in contemporary music available

0-631-18881-9 BLACKWELL $49.95
0-631-20138-6 BLACKWELL PB.........................$22.95

Don M. **Randel**, editor

The New Harvard Dictionary of Music

"Drawing on the latest musical research and buttressed by a large group of advisers and readers, Professor Randel has provided concise, accurate, and literate entries pertaining to the entire field of music"— Philip Gossett, University of Chicago

See also **SPECIALIZED DICTIONARIES** under **REFERENCE** in **BUSINESS AND REFERENCE**

0-674-61525-5 BELKNAP $39.95

Stanley **Sadie**, editor

The New Grove Dictionary of Musical Instruments

From "A"—an obsolete Korean barrel drum—to "Zye-zye"—the iron ankle rattle of the Angas people of Nigeria—this three-volume reference work does for instruments what its larger relative did for all of musical life and history

0-943818-05-2 GROVE $550.00

Nicholas **Slonimsky**

Music Since 1900

See also **20TH-CENTURY MUSIC**

0-02-872418-6 SCHIRMER $125.00

Nicolas **Slonimsky**, editor

Baker's Biographical Dictionary of Musicians

This is a sparkling, scrupulous account of musicians' lives and works, both familiar and exotic, spiced with Nicolas Slonimsky's personal style

0-02-871225-0 MACMILLAN PB $20.00

Music History

Gerald **Abraham**

Concise Oxford History of Music

The abridged version for readers on all levels

0-19-284010-X OXFORD PB $25.00

Donald **Grout** & Donald **Jay**

A History of Western Music

An introductory course in musical history, written with judgment and care

0-393-95627-X NORTON $47.95

Oxford University Press

New Oxford History of Music

Volume 1: Ancient and Oriental Music

An encyclopedic, integrated survey, detailed and invaluable for both scholars and general readers

0-19-316301-2 OXFORD $95.00

Volume 2: Early Middle Ages to 1300

0-19-31632-92 OXFORD..................................$105.00

Volume 3: Ars Nova and the Renaissance

0-19-316303-9 OXFORD $95.00

Volume 4: The Age of Humanism

0-19-316304-7 OXFORD $95.00

Volume 5: Opera and Church Music, 1630-1750

0-19-316305-5 OXFORD $95.00

Volume 7: Age of Enlightenment, 1745-1790

0-19-316307-1 OXFORD $95.00

Volume 8:
The Age of Beethoven, 1790-1830
0-19-316308-X OXFORD $95.00

Volume 9: Romanticism
0-19-316309-8 OXFORD $110.00

Volume 10:
The Modern Age, 1890-1960
0-19-316310-1 OXFORD $95.00

Claude V. **Palisca**, editor
Norton Anthology of Western Music: Ancient to Baroque
0-393-96906-1 NORTON PB $29.95

The Norton Anthology of Western Music: Classic to Modern
0-393-96907-X NORTON PB $29.95

Oliver **Strunk**, editor
Source Readings in Music History
A five-volume series
0-393-09742-0 NORTON $24.95

Middle Ages and Renaissance

Friedrich **Blume**
Renaissance and Baroque Music: A Comprehensive Survey
0-393-09710-2 NORTON PB $9.95

Giulio **Cattin**
Music of the Middle Ages
Volume 1
Devoted to the vast repertory of monophonic music that forms the basis of Europe's musical tradition
0-521-28489-9 CAMBRIDGE PB $19.95

Robert **Donington**
The Interpretation of Early Music
The issues involved in performing early music, from the meaning of notation to the choice of instrumentation, are many and complex
0-393-02827-5 NORTON $50.00

Iain **Fenlon**
Music, Print and Culture in Early Sixteenth-Century Italy
0-7123-0412-6 BRITISH LIBRARY PB $32.00

Harry **Haskell**
The Early Music Revival: A History
"A fine companion to the music and musicians it celebrates"—John Rockwell, *NY Times*
0-486-29162-6 DOVER PB $10.95

Richard **Hoppin**
Medieval Music
Ranges from the earliest chants of the Roman church to polyphony in the beginning of the 15th century
0-393-09090-6 NORTON $33.95

Nicholas **Kenyon**, editor
Authenticity and Early Music
0-19-816153-0 OXFORD PB $22.00

Leo **Schrade**
Monteverdi, Creator of Modern Music
0-306-79565-5 DA CAPO $49.00

Graham **Strahle**
An Early Music Dictionary: Musical Terms from British Sources, 1500-1740
0-521-41688-4 CAMBRIDGE $95.00

Baroque

Nicholas **Anderson**
Baroque Music: From Monteverdi to Handel
0-500-01606-2 THAMES & HUDSON $29.95

Malcolm **Boyd**
Bach
See also **CAMBRIDGE GUIDES** under **HANDBOOKS AND GUIDES** under **OPERA**
0-521-38713-2 CAMBRIDGE PB $10.95

Hans **David** & Arthur **Mendel**, editors
The Bach Reader
This classic text reprints documents of the period, accounts by contemporaries, the first published biography by Forkel, and an account of the Bach revival in the mid-19th century
0-393-00259-4 NORTON PB $14.95

Archibald T. **Davison**
Bach and Handel: The Consummation of the Baroque in Music
0-306-76258-7 DA CAPO $21.50

Anthony **Newman**
Bach and the Baroque: European Source Materials from the Baroque and Early Classical Periods
0-945193-64-5 PENDN $48.00

Philip **Spitta** & Johann Sebastian **Bach**, bio
Johann Sebastian Bach: His Work and Influence
Volume 1
This survey of Bach's music and life was the first "modern" study of the composer, its two volumes dating from 1873 and 1880. Spitta not only used modern techniques of scholarship, but sensitively attended to the symbolism and spirit of the music, helping to lay the groundwork for the Bach revival
0-486-22278-0 DOVER $18.75

Volume 2
0-486-22279-9 DOVER $18.75

Karl **Geiringer** & Irene **Geiringer**
Johann Sebastian Bach: The Culmination of an Era
0-19-500554-6 OXFORD $39.95

Johann Sebastian Bach

George Friedric **Handel**
Messiah: The Wordbook For the Oratorio (an Audio Cassette and Book Package)
Produced to mark the 250th anniversary of the premiere performance of *The Messiah*, Handel's baroque masterpiece. Perfect for singing along with at home or in church, this book contains the lyrics, an introduction by conductor Christopher Hogwood, and watercolor illustrations
PAINTINGS BY BARRY MOSER
0-486-26067-4 DOVER PB $12.95

Ralph **Kirkpatrick**
Domenico Scarlatti
A biography and musicological study of the baroque composer that reintroduced him to our era, by one of the premier harpsichordists of the 20th century
0-691-02708-0 PRINCETON PB $24.95

Joshua **Rifkin**
The New Grove North European Baroque Masters
0-393-30099-4 NORTON PB $9.95

Classical

The classical composers—Haydn, Mozart, Beethoven, and Schubert—remain at the heart of Western musical culture, while other tastes vary according to fashion. "I do not want to turn Haydn, Mozart, and Beethoven into Hegelians," Charles Rosen writes in his book *The Classical Style: Haydn, Mozart, Beethoven*, "but the simplest way to summarize classical form is as the symmetrical resolution of opposing forces. If this seems so broad as to be a definition of artistic form in general, that is because the classical style has largely become the standard by which we judge the rest of music—hence its name."

Phillipe A. **Autexier**
Beethoven: The Composer as Hero
0-8109-2832-9 ABRAMS PB $12.95

George **Grove**
Beethoven and His Nine Symphonies
0-486-20334-4 DOVER PB $8.95

Michael **Hamburger**, editor & translator

Beethoven: Letters, Journals and Conversations

"A portrait of Beethoven that has the fascination of a documentary film"—*New Yorker*

0-500-27324-3 THAMES & HUDSON PB..........$14.95

Joseph **Kerman**

The Beethoven Quartets

0-393-00909-2NORTON PB..............................$14.95

William **Kinderman**

Beethoven

0-520-08796-8 CALIFORNIA..........................$35.00

Maynard **Solomon**

Beethoven

This fine example of psychoanalytic biography, by a preeminent—and nonacademic—Beethoven scholar, discerns the psychological themes of the life and connects them with the stylistic transformations of the music

0-02-872240-X MACMILLAN PB.....................$16.00

Oscar **Sonneck**, editor

Beethoven: Impressions by Contemporaries

0-486-21770-1 DOVER PB...........................$7.95

Robert **Winter** & Robert **Martin**, editors

The Beethoven Quartet Companion

This authoritative study guides us through these personal and often enigmatic works, helpful even to seasoned concertgoers. This collection offers a selection of essays (among contributors are Joseph Kerman and Leon Botstein) that reveals the identity of the quartets' audiences, how they originally were written, what socio-economic standards affected their reception, and what sorts of interpretive decisions are made by performers today

0-520-08211-7 CALIFORNIA............................$35.00

Friedrich **Blume**

Classic and Romantic Music

The concepts of "classic" and "romantic" in their historical contexts and the range of interpretations they have undergone

0-393-09868-0NORTON PB.............................$8.95

Franz Joseph Haydn

Hans **Keller**

The Great Haydn Quartets

0-8076-1167-0 BRAZILLER $22.50

Jens **Larsen** & Georg **Feder**

The New Grove Haydn

Haydn's life and development, and an authoritative listing of his output by two leading scholars

0-393-01681-1 NORTON PB............................$25.00

Daniel **Heartz**

Haydn, Mozart and the Viennese School: 1740-1780

0-393-03712-6 NORTON..................................$65.00

Alfred **Einstein**

Mozart: His Character, His Work

Einstein provides a model for writing about music. He is scholarly, well informed, and precise, but also a critic of grace and worldly insight

0-19-500732-8 OXFORD PB.............................$15.95

H. C. **Robbins-Landon** & Donald **Mitchell**, editors

A Mozart Companion

0-393-00499-6 NORTON PB $12.95

H. C. **Robbins-Landon**

Mozart: The Golden Years

0-02-872025-3 SCHIRMER..............................$29.95

The Mozart Compendium

A pair of handy reference guides to mark the bicentenary of Mozart's death

0-02-871321-4 SCHIRMER..............................$34.95

Paul **Lang**, editor

The Creative World of Mozart

0-393-00218-7 NORTON PB...............................$9.95

Robert **Marshall**

Mozart Speaks: Views on Music, Musicians, and the World

An illuminating selection from Mozart's correspondence with friends, family, and patrons—revealing his thoughts on everything from the nature of his musical genius to his enjoyment of billiards. An intimate and compelling self-portrait

0-02-871356-7 SCHIRMER PB..........................$20.00

You see that my intentions are good—only what one cannot do one cannot! I am really unable to scribble off inferior Stuff.—*Mozart to his father*

MOZART SPEAKS: VIEWS ON MUSIC, MUSICIANS, AND THE WORLD

Stanley **Sadie**

The New Grove Mozart

0-393-30084-6 NORTON PB $12.95

Maynard **Solomon**

Mozart

The award-winning author of *Beethoven* who, according to *Music & Letters* is "the leading musicologist-biographer of our time," solves some of the central mysteries of Mozart's life. He uncovers a long-overlooked love affair, answers Mozart's famous "Zoroastrian Riddles" for the first time, and explodes the myth of the composer as "eternal child." The first full-scale biography of Mozart in 40 years

0-06-019046-9HARPERCOLLINS $35.00

Neal **Zaslaw** & William **Cowdery**, editors

The Compleat Mozart: A Guide to the Musical Works of Wolfgang Amadeus Mozart

0-393-02886-0NORTON..................................$35.00

Wolfgang A. Mozart

Charles **Rosen**

The Classical Style: Haydn, Mozart, Beethoven

"The word 'masterpiece' should be used rarely if at all," wrote George Steiner, "but it applies to Charles Rosen's *The Classical Style.*" This 1971 book is recognized as the most important and influential work of music criticism in our time. Even the layman will come away ready to hear musical tensions, symmetries, and dramas in new ways

0-393-04020-8NORTON.................................$35.00

0-393-00653-0 NORTON PB $16.95

Maurice **Brown** & Eric **Sams**

The New Grove Schubert

0-393-01683-8 NORTON...............................$25.00

Romantic

The word "romanticism" has become as commonplace in musicological description as the word "classical." The personal, the imagistic, the overtly expressive, the impassioned: these are our associations with romantic music. But the transformation is more central—not just a matter of heart in place of head, but a new function for both. As Claude Levi-Strauss once suggested, this is the music that has taken over the function of myth in our culture, giving us gods, detailing our origins, and telling tales of our desires and fates.

Hector **Berlioz**

Memoirs

Berlioz wrote music as if it were programmatic literature; he was also one of music's first men of letters. His description of coming of musical age in France when romanticism was young makes for an unsurpassed musical autobiography, a counterpart to the musical autobiographies penned in his scores

0-486-21563-6 DOVER PB..............................$12.95

Jacques **Barzun**

Berlioz and His Century: An Introduction to the Age of Romanticism

"In order to understand the nineteenth century, it is essential to understand Berlioz, and in order to understand Berlioz, it is essential to read Professor Barzun"—W.H. Auden

0-226-03861-0 CHICAGO PB $16.95

Julian **Rushton**

The Musical Language of Berlioz

This learned treatment of Berlioz's music envisions him outside the mainstream of the musical tradition, owing little to others and leaving few heirs

0-521-24279-7 CAMBRIDGE $59.50

Karl **Geiringer**

Brahms: His Life and Work

0-306-80223-6 DA CAPO PB $13.95

Jean-Jacques **Eigeldinger**

Chopin: Pianist and Teacher as Seen by His Pupils

0-521-36709-3 CAMBRIDGE PB $24.95

James **Huneker**

Chopin: The Man and His Music

This turn-of-the-century American critic wrote about music as if it were a sort of rich confection for the soul

0-486-21687-X DOVER PB $6.95

Alfred **Einstein**

Music in the Romantic Era

0-393-09733-1 NORTON $24.95

J.M. **Nectou**

Gabriel Fauré: His Life Through His Letters

0-7145-2768-8 MARION BOYARS $40.00

Ernst **Burger**

Franz Liszt: A Chronicle of His Life in Pictures and Documents

0-691-09133-1 PRINCETON $83.50

Alan **Walker**

Franz Liszt: The Weimar Years, 1848-1861

0-8014-9721-3 CORNELL PB $19.95

Franz Liszt

Franz Liszt: The Virtuoso Years, 1811-1847

0-8014-9421-4 CORNELL PB $22.50

Derek **Watson**

Liszt

0-02-872705-3 SCHIRMER $24.95

Rey **Longyear**

Nineteenth-Century Romanticism in Music

0-13-622697-3 PRENTICE HALL PB $35.80

Norman **Lebrecht**, editor

Mahler Remembered

Anecdotes about a composer whose time has, as he himself predicted, finally come

0-393-02572-1 NORTON $25.00

Gustav Mahler

Donald **Mitchell**

Gustav Mahler: The Early Years

0-520-05578-0 CALIFORNIA $55.00
0-520-04141-0 CALIFORNIA $50.00

Leon **Plantinga**

Romantic Music: A History of Musical Style

0-393-95196-0 NORTON $32.95

Charles **Rosen**

The Romantic Generation

0-674-77933-9 HARVARD $39.95

Nancy **Reich**

Clara Schumann: The Artist and the Woman

0-8014-9388-9 CORNELL PB $16.95

Gerd **Nauhaus**, editor

Marriage Diaries of Robert and Clara Schumann: From Their Wedding Day Through the Russian Trip

TRANSLATED BY PETER OSTWALD

1-55553-171-7 NORTHEASTERN $35.00

Peter **Ostwald**

Schumann: The Inner Voices of a Musical Genius

1-55553-014-1 NORTHEASTERN PB $15.95

Eric **Sams**

The Songs of Robert Schumann

INTRODUCTION BY GERALD MOORE

0-253-20809-2 INDIANA PB $15.95

Robert Schumann

Burnett D. **James**

The Music of Jean Sibelius

A musical study of the "voice of the north," who combined the late-romantic appetite for nationalistic music with Nordic detachment and foreboding

0-8386-3070-7 FAIRLEIGH DICKINSON $29.50

Egon **Gartenberg**

Johann Strauss: The End of an Era

0-271-01131-9 PENN STATE $40.00

John **Warrack**

The New Grove Early Romantic Masters, II: Weber, Berlioz, and Mendelssohn

0-393-30096-X NORTON PB $9.95

John **Warrack**, editor

Carl Maria Von Weber: Writings on Music

0-521-29121-6 CAMBRIDGE PB $29.95

Russian Music

David **Brown**

Tchaikovsky: The Crisis Years, 1874-1878

0-393-03099-7 NORTON $40.00

Rostislav **Dubinsky**

Stormy Applause: Making Music in a Worker's State

"Well written and colloquial, it evokes the core of the life of a Soviet musician from the death of Stalin to the time of Mr. Dubinsky's departure from the Soviet Union"—Isaac Stern

1-55553-119-9 NORTHEASTERN PB $15.95

Roy **Blokker** & Robert **Dearling**

The Music of Dmitri Shostakovich, the Symphonies

0-8386-1948-7 ASSOCIATED UNIVERSITIES $29.50

Dmitri **Shostakovich**

Testimony: The Memoirs of Dmitri Shostakovich

The composer's bitter, ironic, and scathing memoirs

0-87910-021-4 PROSCENIUM PB $17.95

Christopher **Norris**

Shostakovich: The Man and His Music

0-7145-2778-5 MARION BOYARS $25.00

Modern French Music

Claude **Debussy**

Letters

"I had dinner with André Gide some time ago," the composer writes in one of his letters. "He's like an old spinster, timid, gracious and polite in the English manner, but he's charming and very swift at coming up with subtle and ingenious ideas. He has a horror of Wagner—a sure sign of a refined intelligence"

0-674-19429-2 HARVARD $32.95

François **Lesure** & Richard **Smith**, editors

Debussy on Music

0-8014-9420-6 CORNELL PB $15.95

Leon **Vallas**

Claude Debussy: His Life and Works

Traces Debussy's rebellious years at the Conservatoire that culminated in his winning of the Prix de Rome, and his absorption in the bohemian life of Paris

0-486-22916-5 DOVER PB $8.95

Claude Debussy

Arbie **Orenstein**

Ravel: Man and Musician

0-486-26633-8 DOVER PB $9.95

Maurice Ravel

Rollo **Myers**

Erik Satie

0-486-21903-8 DOVER PB $5.95

Nancy **Perloff**

Art and the Everyday: Popular Entertainment and the Circle of Erik Satie

0-19-816194-8 CLARENDON $65.00

0-19-816398-3 CLARENDON PB $17.95

20th-Century Music

Richard **Burbank**

Twentieth Century Music

0-87196-464-3 FACTS ON FILE $50.00

Nicholas **Slonimsky**

Music Since 1900

See also **REFERENCE**

0-02-872418-6 SCHIRMER $125.00

20th-Century European Music

Elliott **Antoholetz**

The Music of Bela Bartok: A Study of Tonality and Progression in 20th-Century Music

A detailed analysis of Bartok's unorthodox compositional technique, which resulted in an often bizarre mixture of the folkish, the modernist, and the romantic

0-300-02422-3 YALE $55.00

Mosco **Carner**

Alban Berg: The Man and the Work

0-8419-0841-9 HOLMES & MEIER $49.95

Donald **Harris**, editor

The Berg-Schoenberg Correspondence: Selected Letters

Devotion, authority, innovation, reflection—a complex relationship between disciple and master emerges in this unusual collection

0-393-01919-5 NORTON $35.00

John E. **Bowlt**, editor

The Salon Album of Vera Sudeikin-Stravinsky

0-691-04424-4 PRINCETON $65.00

Paul **Griffiths**

Modern Music: The Avant-Garde Since 1945

Pierre Boulez is quoted at the beginning of this survey: "In 1945 or 1946, nothing was finished, everything was still to be done." Musical fashion raced through radical serialism and academicism, enlarged playfulness to include chance and randomness, made a fetish of technological innovation and electronic sound. Griffiths gives a nonpartisan account of these developments

See also **MUSIC SINCE 1945**

0-8076-1018-6 BRAZILLER PB $12.95

0-500-20164-1 THAMES & HUDSON PB $12.95

Paul **Griffiths** & George **Perle**

The New Grove Second Viennese School

Traces the development of atonality and the careers of its major practitioners—Schoenberg, Webern, and Berg

0-393-01686-2 NORTON $25.00

Leos **Janacek**

Janacek's Uncollected Essays on Music

0-7145-2857-9 MARION BOYARS $35.00

0-7145-2951-6 MARION BOYARS PB $18.95

Margaret **Crosland**

Piaf

This first rather sensational English biography still captures something of the passion, irony, and despair of the French torch-singer's life

See also **OTHER AND GENERAL** under **WORLD MUSIC: OTHER TRADITIONS**

0-88064-069-3 FROMM PB $8.95

Wilfrid **Mellers**

Francis Poulenc

0-19-816338-X OXFORD PB $19.95

Arnold **Schoenberg**

Style and Idea: Selected Writings of Arnold Schoenberg

Among the most important essays about music to be published this century, the sections include Personal Evaluation and Retrospect, Folk Music and Nationalism, Theory and Composition, and Social and Politic Matters

0-520-05294-3 CALIFORNIA PB $15.95

Charles **Rosen**

Arnold Schoenberg

Rosen emphasizes that Schoenberg emerged at a complex moment in music history, at which conservative tonal forms and concepts were combined with avant-garde techniques and revolutionary ambitions

0-226-72643-6 CHICAGO PB $10.95

Carl **Dahlhaus**

Schoenberg and the New Music

This collection of essays on Schoenberg and related subjects, Written as a response to

Theodor Adorno's famous book on "new music," rises above arcane musicological issues
0-521-33783-6 CAMBRIDGE PB $22.95

Arnold Schoenberg

Laszlo **Somfai**
The New Grove Modern Masters: Bartok, Stravinsky, Hindemith
0-393-01693-5 NORTON....................$25.00
0-393-30097-8 NORTON PB....................$9.95

Paul **Horgan**
Encounters with Stravinsky: A Personal Record
0-8195-6215-7 WESLEYAN PB....................$15.95

Igor **Stravinsky**
Expositions and Developments
0-520-04403-7 CALIFORNIA PB....................$10.95

Igor Stravinsky

Memories and Commentaries
0-520-04402-9 CALIFORNIA PB....................$10.95

The Poetics of Music: In the Form of Six Lessons
0-674-67856-7 HARVARD PB....................$10.95

Themes and Conclusions
0-520-04652-8 CALIFORNIA PB....................$10.95

Richard **Taruskin**
Stravinsky and the Russian Traditions: A Biography of the Works Through Maura
0-520-07099-2 CALIFORNIA....................$125.00

David **Drew**
Kurt Weill: A Handbook
The first detailed guide to the works of Kurt Weill by the British scholar who is now writing the definitive biography
0-520-05839-9 CALIFORNIA....................$58.00

Ronald **Sanders**
The Days Grow Short: The Life and Music of Kurt Weill
"Sanders asks readers to join him in taking all of Weill's work seriously—from his 1920s avant-garde orchestral works and *The Threepenny Opera* to the popular but elegant scores for Broadway musicals of the '40s and '50s"
—Booklist
1-87950-506-1 SAMUEL FRENCH PB....................$14.95

Lys **Symonette** & Kim H. **Kowalke**, editors
Speak Low (When You Speak Love): The Letters of Kurt Weill and Lotte Lenya
The written record of a long marriage and creative partnership, more intense than tranquil
0-520-07853-5 CALIFORNIA....................$39.95

20th-Century English Music

Christopher **Palmer**, editor
The Britten Companion
0-521-26121-X CAMBRIDGE....................$54.95

Arnold **Whittall**
The Music of Britten and Tippett: Studies in Themes and Techniques
0-521-23523-5 CAMBRIDGE....................$69.95
0-521-38668-3 CAMBRIDGE PB....................$22.95

Lionel **Carley**
Delius: A Life in Letters, 1862-1908
The British-born composer with German parentage received his musical education in Florida
0-85967-717-6 SCOLAR....................$84.95

Christopher **Palmer**
Delius: Portrait of a Cosmopolitan
0-8419-0274-7 HOLMES & MEIER....................$34.50

Michael **Kennedy**
Portrait of Elgar
"The comments on the music are informed, perceptive and fired by great enthusiasm"
—Classical Music Weekly
0-19-816365-7 OXFORD PB....................$24.95

Jerrold **Moore**
Edward Elgar: A Creative Life
"Shows us Elgar through a large, clear pane, offering a view that is fully and scrupulously lit"—*The Times* [London]
0-19-315447-1 OXFORD....................$105.00

Susana **Walton**
William Walton: Behind the Facade
0-19-282635-2 OXFORD PB....................$7.50

Diana **McVeagh** & Anthony **Payne**
The New Grove Twentieth-Century English Masters: Elgar, Delius, Vaughan-Williams, Tippett, Holst, Walton, and Britten
0-393-02285-4 NORTON....................$25.00
0-393-30351-9 NORTON PB....................$16.95

20th-Century American Music

Meryle **Secrest**
Leonard Bernstein: A Life
Secrest, the accomplished biographer of Frank Lloyd Wright, Kenneth Clark, and others, has written the definitive biography of the American folk hero. From his Hasidic roots and his first piano to his brilliant career as the Pied Piper of the American music scene, here is Bernstein in a most thoughtful portrayal
0-679-40731-6 KNOPF....................$30.00

John **Cage**
Empty Words
Cage's playful, maddening musical escapades have their textual counterpart in these books, containing his poems, koans, diaries, and meditations on his favorite subject (mushrooms). Many selections were composed using "chance" operations; all were composed to shock, unsettle, or inspire. "John Cage is one of those few contemporaries who do important work in more than one art"
—NY Times Book Review
0-8195-6067-7 WESLEYAN PB....................$15.95

M: Writings '67-'72
0-8195-6035-9 WESLEYAN PB....................$18.95

Silence: Lectures and Writings
0-8195-6028-6 WESLEYAN PB....................$19.95

A Year from Monday: New Lectures and Writings
0-8195-6002-2 WESLEYAN PB....................$15.95

Allen **Edwards**
Flawed Words and Stubborn Sounds: A Conversation with Elliott Carter
The important contemporary American composer discusses his style, his career, and the state of American musical life, and offers hints for understanding his difficult music
0-393-02159-9 NORTON....................$7.95

Arthur **Berger**
Aaron Copland
0-306-76266-8 DA CAPO....................$26.00

Aaron **Copland** & Vivian **Perlis**
Copland: 1900 Through 1942
"A valuable, readable, endearing record of his achievement"—*NY Times*
0-312-01149-0 ST. MARTIN'S PB....................$12.95

Charles **Schwartz**
Gershwin: His Life and Music
0-306-80096-9 DA CAPO PB....................$14.95

John Cage

Richard **Kostelanetz**
Conversing with Cage
Witticisms and twists of logic from the avant-garde master of the random and iconoclastic. "I was with de Kooning once in a restaurant," John Cage tells his Variant interviewer, "and he said, 'If I put a frame around these bread crumbs, that isn't art.' And what I'm saying is that it is"
0-87910-100-8 LIMELIGHT PB $16.95

J. Peter **Burkholder**, editor
Charles Ives and his World
0-691-01164-8 PRINCETON $55.00
0-691-01163-X PRINCETON PB $19.95

Vivian **Perlis**
Charles Ives Remembered
One of the dozens of raconteurs recalls: "The *Universe Symphony*, the unfinished one, he didn't intend to finish. He told me that anybody else could add to it if they felt like it…Maybe someday they'll do it [as he envisioned], with orchestras here and there on the hills, and different choruses all around the countryside." This is an extraordinary book of recollections about one of the most storied of all composers
0-306-80576-6 DA CAPO PB $13.95

Jan **Swafford**
Charles Ives: A Life With Music
0-393-03893-9 NORTON $30.00

Charles Ives

H. Wiley **Hitchcock**
Music in the United States: A Historical Introduction
0-13-608407-9 PRENTICE HALL PB $36.80

A. **Oldsstead**
Conversations with Roger Sessions
1-55553-010-9 NORTHEASTERN $35.00

S. Frederick **Starr**
Bamboula!: The Life and Times of Louis Moreau Gottschalk
The life, music travels, romances and untimely death of America's first internationally acclaimed composer. The musical life of New York, New Orleans, Europe and Latin America springs to life in a vibrant, richly informative account of this utterly engaging bon vivant composer-entrepreneur
0-19-507237-5 OXFORD $35.00

John Warthen **Struble**
The History of American Classical Music: MacDowell Through Minimalism
0-8160-2927-X FACTS ON FILE $35.00
0-8160-3493-1 FACTS ON FILE PB $18.95

Virgil **Thomson**
Music with Words: A Composer's View
0-300-04505-0 YALE $25.00

Anthony **Tommasini**
All My Long Life: A Biography of Virgil Thomson
0-393-04006-2 NORTON $30.00

Music Since 1945

Joan **Peyser**
Boulez: Composer, Conductor, Enigma
A psychological portrait that connects Boulez's cool, aloof intellect with the fashions of postwar musical life
0-912483-98-9 PRO AM MUSIC RESOURCES ... $24.95

Carlos **Chavez**
Toward a New Music: Music and Electricity
0-306-70719-5 DA CAPO $34.00

Richard **Dufallo**
Trackings: Composers Speak with Richard Dufallo
0-19-505816-X OXFORD $40.00

Paul **Griffiths**
Modern Music: The Avant-Garde Since 1945
Pierre Boulez is quoted at the beginning of this survey: "In 1945 or 1946, nothing was finished, everything was still to be done." Musical fashion raced through radical serialism and academicism, enlarged playfulness to include chance and randomness, made a fetish of technological innovation and electronic sound. Griffiths gives a nonpartisan account of these developments
See also **20TH-CENTURY EUROPEAN MUSIC**
0-8076-1018-6 BRAZILLER PB $12.95
0-500-20164-1 THAMES & HUDSON PB $12.95

Modern Music and After: Directions Since 1945
0-19-816511-0 OXFORD PB $17.95

Elliott **Schwartz** & Barney **Childs**, editors
Contemporary Composers on Contemporary Music
Published in 1967
0-306-77587-5 DA CAPO $52.00

Karl H. **Worner**
Stockhausen: His Life and Work
0-520-03272-1 CALIFORNIA PB $10.95

Critical Essays

Theodor **Adorno**
Quasi Una Fantasia: Essays on Modern Music
Adorno composed as a young man and devoted much of his philosophical energy to formulating a critical aesthetic of music
See also **OTHER 20TH-CENTURY PHILOSOPHERS** under **PHILOSOPHY** in **RELIGION, SPIRITUALITY, AND PHILOSOPHY**
TRANSLATED BY RODNEY LIVINGSTONE
0-86091-613-8 NORTON PB $19.95

Leonard **Bernstein**
The Joy of Music
Probably the most popular, clear, and entertaining explanation of music ever published
0-385-47201-3 ANCHOR PB $14.95

Carl **Dahlhaus**
Aesthetics of Music
This important historian and philosopher asks how music history is interpreted, why music was considered romantic when fine arts were considered realist, and how music changed with the coming of modernity
0-521-28007-9 CAMBRIDGE PB $16.95

Foundations of Music History
0-521-29890-3 CAMBRIDGE PB $16.95

Leonard B. **Meyer**
Emotion and Meaning in Music
"Clears the air of many confused notions… and lays the groundwork for exhaustive study of the basic problem of music theory and aesthetics, the relationship between pattern and meaning"—*Journal of Music Theory*
0-226-52139-7 CHICAGO PB $11.95

Ernest **Newman**
Essays from the World of Music
0-7145-3548-6 RIVERRUN $14.95

Ned **Rorem**
Other Entertainment: A Collection of Pieces
0-684-82249-0 SIMON & SCHUSTER $25.00

Charles **Rosen**

The Frontiers of Meaning: Three Informal Lectures on Music

What, if anything, does music mean? And how is taking pleasure from music related to understanding it? These are among the questions that the well-known pianist and scholar Charles Rosen explores in these three lucid and insightful essays. The inaugural volume in a new series featuring eminent authorities writing about their respective fields

0-8090-7254-8 HILL & WANG $21.00

Edward **Rothstein**

Emblems of Mind: The Inner Life of Music and Mathematics

The music critic for *The New York Times* probes the mysteries of musical form in relation to mathematics

See also **CULTURAL INTERPRETATIONS** under **PHILOSOPHY OF MATHEMATICS** under **MATHEMATICS** in **SCIENCE**

0-8129-2298-0 TIME BOOKS $25.00

0-380-72747-1 AVON PB $13.00

Musical Forms

Roger **Lax** & Frederick **Smith**

The Great Song Thesaurus

Popular songs from the 16th century to today

0-19-505408-3 OXFORD $85.00

William **Newman**

The Sonata in the Baroque Era

0-393-95275-4 NORTON $18.95

The Sonata in the Classic Era

Newman's works are an encyclopedic survey of the central musical form of our tradition—its revolution and importance

0-393-95286-X NORTON $22.50

Charles **Rosen**

Sonata Forms

"To familiar and unfamiliar music alike Rosen brings not only an uncommonly refined ear and sensibility, but also, again and again, unerring insight into just the features that make the music special and fine"
—Joseph Kerman, *NY Review of Books*

0-393-30219-9 NORTON PB $16.95

Denis **Stevens**, editor

A History of Song

Scholars on song from the Middle Ages to modern Czechoslovakia. "The best yet in English on the subject of the secular art song"
—*Library Journal*

0-393-00536-4 NORTON PB $15.95

Music Theory

Aaron **Copland**

Music and Imagination

"Aaron Copland is a notable contemporary example of the 'initial composer,' the man who can write about music with the same persuasiveness that he writes music itself"
—*Saturday Review*

0-674-58915-7 HARVARD PB $9.95

Aaron Copland

What to Listen For in Music

INTRODUCTION BY WILLIAM SCHUMAN

0-451-62735-0 MENTOR PB $5.99

Joseph **Kerman**

Listen

0-87901-127-0 WORTH $47.95

Maurice **Lieberman**

Ear Training and Sight Seeing

0-393-09519-3 NORTON PB $20.95

Joseph **Machlis**

The Enjoyment of Music

Introduces students and new listeners to musical history and ideas

0-393-99155-5 NORTON $44.95

Walter **Piston**

Harmony

0-393-95480-3 NORTON $41.95

Orchestration

Analysis of orchestration, covering instrumentation of primary and secondary melodies, part writing, chords, and contrapuntal techniques

0-393-09740-4 NORTON $31.95

Felix **Salzer** & Carl **Schachter**

Counterpoint in Composition

0-231-07039-X COLUMBIA PB $27.50

Heinrich **Schenker**

This most influential Viennese scholar (1868-1935) was remarkable for his insights into how we hear music, his discernment of a universal structural line in all tonal music, and his reform of musical analysis.

Counterpoint

0-02-873220-0 SCHIRMER $104.00

Harmony

0-226-73734-9 CHICAGO PB $23.95

Instrumental History and Performers

Keyboard Music

Willi **Apel**

The History of Keyboard Music to 1700

0-253-32795-4 INDIANA $89.95

C.P.E. **Bach**

Essay on the True Art of Playing Keyboard Instruments

This classic 18th-century manual by J.S. Bach's son influenced generations of pianists and remains a guide to the playing of the music of the period

0-393-09716-1 NORTON $29.95

Dieter **Hildebrandt**

Pianoforte: A Social History of the Piano

A history of the single most important instrument in the musical life of the 19th century

INTRODUCTION BY ANTHONY BURGESS

0-8076-1182-4 BRAZILLER $19.95

William **Newman**

The Pianist's Problems

0-306-80269-4DA CAPO PB $12.95

David **Sudnow**

Ways of the Hand

An ethnographer and sociologist gives a "phenomenological account" of his learning to improvise in a jazz style at the keyboard. His epigram is from Heidegger; his accounts are riffs on the miracle of playing

0-674-94833-5 HARVARD $25.00

Konrad **Wolff**

Masters of the Keyboard: Individual Style Elements in the Piano Music of Bach, Haydn, Mozart, Beethoven, and Schubert

0-253-33690-2 INDIANA $35.00

Franz Schubert

Pianists

David **Dubal**
The Art of the Piano: Its Performers, Literature, and Recordings
0-15-600019-9 HARVEST PB $20.00

Tim **Page**, editor
The Glenn Gould Reader
"I'm a Streisand freak and make no bones about it. With the possible exception of Elisabeth Schwarzkopf, no vocalist has brought me greater pleasure or more insight into the interpreter's art." Gould on art: "I feel that art should be given the chance to phase itself out. I think that we must accept the fact that art is not inevitably benign, that it is potentially destructive." Gould on any subject is worth reading
0-679-73135-0 VINTAGE PB $17.00

Linda **Noyle**
Pianists on Playing: Interviews with Twelve Concert Pianists
0-8108-1953-8 SCARECROW $20.00

Artur **Schnabel**
My Life and Music
A memoir by the pianist who set new standards for the performance of Beethoven, Mozart and Schubert
0-486-25571-9 DOVER PB $7.95

Harold **Schoenberg**
The Great Pianists
Schoenberg's learning and scholarship are worn lightly but carefully in this exuberant book about the great virtuosos. Behind the irresistible anecdotes and lore is the *NY Times* critic's impassioned advocacy for the powers of performance and personality
0-671-63837-8 FIRESIDE PB $14.95

The Great Pianists from Mozart to the Present
0-671-28999-3 FIRESIDE PB $14.95

Ronald **Ratcliffe**
Steinway
0-87701-592-9 CHRONICLE $45.00

String Instruments

Alberto **Bachmann**
An Encyclopedia of the Violin
INTRODUCTION BY EUGENE YSAYE
0-306-80004-7 DA CAPO PB $14.95

David **Boyden**
History of Violin Playing: From Its Origins to 1761 and Its Relationship to the Violin and Violin Music
0-19-816183-2 CLARENDON PB $45.00

Yehudi **Menuhin**
The Violin
2-08-013623-2 ABBEVILLE $50.00

Ben C. **Riley**
The History of the Viola
0-9603150-5-5 RILEY PB $24.50

Robin **Stowell**, editor
The Cambridge Companion to the Violin
0-521-39923-8 CAMBRIDGE PB $19.95

String Players

David **Blum**
The Art of Quartet Playing: The Guarneri Quartet in Conversation with David Blum
0-8014-9456-7 CORNELL PB $15.95

David **Blum** & Pablo **Casals**
Casals and the Art of Interpretation
INTRODUCTION BY PAUL TORTELIER
0-520-04032-5 CALIFORNIA PB $15.95

Joseph **Szigeti**
Szigeti on the Violin
0-486-23763-X DOVER PB $6.95

Woodwind, Brass, and Percussion Instruments

Anthony **Baines**
Brass Instruments: Their History and Development
0-486-27574-4 DOVER PB $9.95

James **Blades**
Percussion Instruments and Their History
0-933224-69-9 BOLD STRUMMER $50.00
0-933224-61-3 BOLD STRUMMER PB $40.00

Adam **Carse**
Musical Wind Instruments: A History of the Wind Instruments Used in European Orchestras, from the Later Middle Ages to the Present
0-306-70906-6 DA CAPO $52.00
0-7812-9496-7 REPRINT SERVICES $89.00

Conductors

Carl **Bamberger**, editor
The Conductor's Art
0-231-07128-0 COLUMBIA $59.50

Thomas **Beecham**
A Mingled Chime: An Autobiography
0-306-70791-8 DA CAPO $45.50

Joseph **Horowitz**
Understanding Toscanini: How He Became an American Culture-God and Helped Create a New Audience For Old Music
A controversial account that holds Toscanini and the marketing geniuses who promoted him largely responsible for the decline of musical life
0-8166-1678-7 MINNESOTA PB $15.95

Harvey **Sachs**
Toscanini
A sober and careful biography by an admiring writer
0-306-80137-X DA CAPO PB $8.95

Arturo Toscanini

Opera

Opera Histories

Sam **Abel**
Opera in the Flesh: Sexuality in Operatic Performance
0-8133-2900-0 WESTVIEW $24.00
0-8133-2901-9 WESTVIEW PB $17.95

Patrick **Barbier**
Opera in Paris, 1800-1850: A Lively History
0-931340-83-7 AMADEUS $29.95

Catherine **Clement**
Opera, Or the Undoing of Women
A feminist approach to opera's tragic heroines
0-8166-1655-8 MINNESOTA PB $14.95

Peter **Conrad**
A Song of Love and Death: The Meaning of Opera
A reissue of a celebrated essay on opera's most profound concerns
1-55597-241-1 GRAYWOLF PB $16.00

Edward **Dent**
Foundations of English Opera
0-306-70905-8 DA CAPO $37.50

John **Dizikes**
Opera in America: A Cultural History
An older and more varied story than anyone could have imagined, presented in exuberant detail in this study which won the National Book Critics' Circle Award
0-300-05496-3 YALE $37.50
0-300-06101-3 YALE PB $18.00

Phil G. **Goulding**
Ticket to the Opera: Discovering and Exploring 100 Famous Works, History, Lore, and Singers
0-449-90900-X FAWCETT $25.00

Donald **Grout** & Hermine **Williams**
A Short History of Opera
0-231-06192-7 COLUMBIA $49.50

Joseph **Kerman**
Opera as Drama
Kerman is literate and controversial in a field long dominated by writers who are neither. This is still the most important book of opera criticism written by an American; its most famous line: calling *Tosca* a "shabby little shocker"
0-520-06273-6 CALIFORNIA $40.00

David **Kimbell**
Italian Opera
0-521-46643-1 CAMBRIDGE PB $25.95

Wayne **Koestenbaum**
The Queen's Throat: Opera, Homosexuality, and the Mystery of Desire
The author, a self-proclaimed "opera queen," probes in personal terms the link between opera and gay sexuality
0-679-74985-3 VINTAGE PB $12.00

Paul **Lang**
The Experience of Opera
0-393-00706-5 NORTON PB $12.95

Ethan **Mordden**
Opera Anecdotes
Mordden recounts a famous miscue: "Backstage at *Lohengrin* entrance, Leo Slezak was bemused to see the swan-boat take off just before he got into it; a stagehand had jumped the cue. As the boat glided into the opera without its silver knight, Slezak turned to someone and asked, 'What time's the next swan?'"
0-19-505661-2 OXFORD PB $10.95

Leslie **Orrey**
Opera: A Concise History
0-500-20217-6 THAMES & HUDSON PB $14.95

Roger **Parker**, editor
The Oxford History of Opera
0-19-284028-2 OXFORD PB $15.95

The Oxford Illustrated History of Opera
0-19-816282-0 OXFORD $49.95

John **Rosselli**
Singers of Italian Opera: The History of a Profession
0-521-41683-3 CAMBRIDGE $50.00

Stanley **Sadie**
History of Opera
0-393-02506-3 NORTON $39.95

F. W. **Sternfeld**
The Birth of Opera
0-19-816573-0 CLARENDON PB $19.95

Richard **Traubner**
Operetta: A Theatrical History
0-19-520778-5 OXFORD PB $16.95

Opera Composers and Their Operas

D. Kern **Holoman**
Berlioz
0-674-06778-9 HARVARD $35.00

Hector Berlioz

H. Wiley **Hitchcock**
Marc-Antoine Charpentier
0-19-316411-6 OXFORD PB $32.50

Charles **Hayter**
Gilbert and Sullivan
0-333-40759-8 ST. MARTIN'S PB $11.95

Harold **Orel**
Gilbert and Sullivan: Interviews and Recollections
0-87745-476-0 IOWA PB $14.95

Jonathan **Miller**, editor
Don Giovanni: Myths of Seduction and Betrayal
The figure of Don Juan—particularly as transmuted by Mozart into Don Giovanni—permeates Western culture. Miller has brought together a fascinating group of essays which explore the historical, philosophical, and psychological roots of the legend and the opera. Includes writing by Peter Gay, Marina Warner, Robert Darnton, and Joseph Kerman. "An entertaining and informative book"
—Anthony Burgess
0-8018-4332-4 JOHNS HOPKINS PB $10.95

William **Ashbrook**
The Operas of Puccini
0-19-500394-2 OXFORD $7.95
0-8014-9309-9 CORNELL PB $16.95

Mosco **Carner**
Puccini: A Critical Biography
0-8419-1326-9 HOLMES & MEIER $59.95

Julian **Budden**
The Operas of Verdi
Volume 1
From Oberto to Rigoletto
0-19-520449-2 CLARENDON PB $22.50
Volume 2
From Il Trovatore to La Forza del Destino
0-19-520450-6 CLARENDON PB $22.50
Volume 3
From Don Carlo to Falstaff
0-19-520451-4 CLARENDON PB $22.50

George **Martin**
Verdi at the Golden Gate: Opera and San Francisco in the Gold Rush Years
0-520-08123-4 CALIFORNIA $30.00

Charles **Osborne**
The Complete Operas of Verdi
0-306-80072-1 DA CAPO PB $14.95

Mary Jane **Phillips-Matz**
Verdi: A Biography
0-19-816600-1 OXFORD PB $22.50

William **Weaver**, translator
Seven Verdi Librettos
Includes *Rigoletto, Il Trovatore, La Traviata, Un Ballo in Maschera, Aida, Othello,* and *Falstaff*
0-393-00852-5 NORTON PB $15.95

Richard **Wagner**
My Life
TRANSLATED BY ANDREW GRAY
EDITED BY MARY WHITTALL
0-306-80481-6 DA CAPO PB $18.95

John **Dahlhaus** & Carl **Dahlhaus**
The New Grove Wagner
0-393-30092-7 NORTON PB $14.95

Barry **Millington**
Wagner
0-691-02722-6 PRINCETON PB $14.95

Richard **Wagner**

Judaism in Music & Other Essays

0-8032-9766-1 NEBRASKA PB $15.00

Richard Wagner

Marc A. **Weiner**

Richard Wagner and the Anti-Semitic Imagination

0-8032-4775-3 NEBRASKA $45.00

Ernest **Newman**

Wagner as Man and Artist

0-8446-2653-8 SMITH $14.50

Opera and Drama

0-8032-9765-3 NEBRASKA PB $15.00

"The Art-Work of the Future" and Other Works

TRANSLATED BY WILLIAM ASHTON

0-8032-9752-1 NEBRASKA PB $15.00

Stendhal & Gioacchino Antonio **Rossini**

Barely appreciated in his own lifetime, Stendhal evolved a style combining elegant aphorism and realistic psychological description.

Life of Rossini

TRANSLATED BY RICHARD COE

0-7145-0632-X RIVERRUN PB $13.95

Handbooks and Guides

Sir Denis **Forman**

The Irreverent Guide to Great Opera

Forman, for years the deputy chairman of the Royal Opera House in London, has written an intelligent, humorous, and individual guide to the opera, packaged with a 17-track CD of great operatic highlights. Working directly against the form's reputation as elitist and intimidating, Forman dissects the 83 most popular operas, providing plot summaries, casts of characters, historical context and frank opinions. Fresh, entertaining, and informative

0-679-44553-6 RANDOM HOUSE $40.00

Paul **Griffiths**

Igor Stravinsky: The Rake's Progress

0-521-28199-7 CAMBRIDGE PB $19.95

Paul **Gruber**, editor

The Metropolitan Opera Guide to Recorded Opera

Musicians, critics, and discophiles collaborated on this comprehensive guide to recorded opera. This expansive volume includes versions currently available, notes on the sound quality of each version, reviews, and recommendations

0-393-03444-5 NORTON $35.00

Earl of **Harewood**, editor

The Definitive Kobbe's Opera Book

An essential companion for the lover, giving basic information on composers and performance history, with crystalline summaries of even the most impossibly operatic plots

0-399-13180-9 PUTNAM $40.00

James **Hepokoski**

Giuseppe Verdi: Falstaff

0-521-25885-5 CAMBRIDGE $49.95

0-521-28016-8 CAMBRIDGE PB $19.95

Giuseppe Verdi

Amanda **Holden** & others, editors

The Penguin Opera Guide

This comprehensive paperback opera guide capitalizes on the enormous experience of its team of editors: Holden is a musician, translator, and editor; Kenyon was formerly music critic of *New Yorker* and the *Observer*, and Walsh is a professor of music and author of numerous books on music. Together they marshal the expertise of over 50 international contributors to provide an essential reference to the world of opera

PREFACE BY SIR COLIN DAVIS

0-14-025131-6 PENGUIN PB $19.95

Arthur **Jacobs** & Stanley **Sadie**

The Limelight Book of Opera

0-87910-044-3 LIMELIGHT PB $19.95

Nicholas **John**, editor

Georges Bizet: Carmen

0-7145-3937-6 RIVERRUN PB $9.95

Ian **Kemp**

Hector Berlioz: Les Troyens

0-9522006-7-8 MIT $35.00

M. Owen **Lee**

First Intermissions: Twenty-One Great Operas Explored, Explained, and Brought to Life from the Met

From the experts, a rigorous interpretation and explication of 21 great operas, enriching and readable. From *La Boheme* to *Faust,* this probing collection deepens the appreciation of the emotive and philosophical scope of the form

0-19-509255-4 OXFORD $23.00

0-19-510649-0 OXFORD PB $12.95

Metropolitan Opera

0-8478-5594-5 RIZZOLI $10.95

Harold **Rosenthal** & John **Warrack**, editors

The Concise Oxford Dictionary of Opera

0-19-311321-X OXFORD PB $15.95

Stanley **Sadie**, editor

The New Grove Dictionary of Opera

Four volumes, some 10,000 articles—readable and eloquent—by 1,000 contributors on a wide range of subjects. Extensive bibliographies complete this monumental work

0-935859-92-6 GROVE $850.00

Henry W. **Simon**

100 Great Operas and Their Stories

0-385-05448-3 ANCHOR PB $11.95

Opera Stars

Schuyler G. **Chapin**

Sopranos, Mezzos, Tenors, Bassos, and Other Friends

Pavarotti, Domingo, Sutherland, Tebaldi, and Horne are just a few of the artists profiled in this deft combination of text and photographs that evokes the drama of grand opera. Drawing on his experience as general manager of the Metropolitan Opera, Chapin reveals the rich inner world of the opera

PHOTOGRAPHS AND CAPTIONS BY JAMES-DANIEL RADICHES

0-517-58864-1 CROWN $50.00

George **Jellinek**

Callas: Portrait of a Prima Donna

0-486-25047-4 DOVER PB $9.95

Michael **Scott**

Maria Meneghini Callas

Scott, the only Callas biographer to have seen the great singer perform regularly, draws on a host of newly available sources to throw light on her difficult life. His extensive knowledge of vocal music's history provides a reference for considerations of each of her major performances and recordings. Includes discography, complete list of the diva's performances, and photographs

1-55553-146-6 NORTHEASTERN $29.95

Maria Callas

James **Camner**, editor

The Great Opera Stars in Historic Photographs: 343 Portraits from the 1850s to the 1940s

0-486-23575-0 DOVER PB $14.95

Stars of the Opera, 1950-1985, in Photographs

0-486-25240-X DOVER PB $10.95

Michael **Scott**

The Great Caruso

1-55553-061-3 NORTHEASTERN PB $15.95

Luciano **Pavarotti** & William **Wright**

Pavarotti: My Own Story

0-7838-1585-9 GK HALL PB $25.00

Pavarotti: My World

"I want to tell the people who are interested in me," says Pavarotti in his preface, "about all the fun and excitement I have had. I have tried to explain how I feel about things that are important to me and to pass on whatever wisdom I have gained as an artist and as a human being." Fifteen years after *Pavarotti: My Story* was a *New York Times* bestseller, comes this book documenting Pavarotti's dominance of the world of opera

0-517-70027-1 CROWN $25.00

A woman might write that she loves my singing so much that she would do anything for me in return. Now, "anything" can mean many things. If I telephoned to accept her offer in an improper way, the lady might be horrified. Or she might say that lovemaking was exactly what she had in mind. I don't ever plan to find out what she meant. In this way, it can remain a matter of sweet mystery.

PAVAROTTI: MY WORLD

Cambridge Guides

Thomas **Bauman**

W.A. Mozart: The Abduction from the Seraglio

0-521-31060-1 CAMBRIDGE PB........................$19.95

Lucy **Beckett**

Richard Wagner: Parsifal

0-521-29662-5 CAMBRIDGE PB........................$19.95

Geoffrey Holden **Block**

Ives, Concord Sonata: Piano Sonata No. 2 ("Concord, Mass., 1840-1860

0-521-49821-X CAMBRIDGE PB........................$42.01

Malcolm **Boyd**

Bach

See also **BAROQUE** under **MUSIC HISTORY**

0-521-38713-2 CAMBRIDGE PB........................$10.95

David Lee **Brodbeck**

Brahms, Symphony No. 1

0-521-47959-2 CAMBRIDGE PB........................$25.00

Donald **Burrows**

Handel: Messiah

0-521-37620-3 CAMBRIDGE PB........................$10.95

John **Butt**

Bach: Mass in B Minor

0-521-38716-7 CAMBRIDGE PB........................$10.95

Tim **Carter**

W.A. Mozart: The Marriage of Figaro

0-521-31606-5 CAMBRIDGE PB........................$16.95

Nicholas **Cook**

Beethoven: Symphony Number 9

0-521-39924-6 CAMBRIDGE PB........................$10.95

Mervyn **Cooke**

Britten, War Requiem

0-521-44633-3 CAMBRIDGE PB........................$10.01

David **Cooper**

Bartok, Concerto for Orchestra

0-521-48505-3 CAMBRIDGE PB........................$10.95

William **Drabkin**

Beethoven: Missa Solemnis

0-521-37831-1 CAMBRIDGE PB........................$10.95

Jonathan **Dunsby**

Schoenberg: Pierrot Lunaire

0-521-38715-9 CAMBRIDGE PB........................$11.95

Peter **Franklin**

Mahler: Symphony No. 3

0-521-37947-4 CAMBRIDGE PB........................$10.95

Richard **Greene**

Holst: The Planets

0-521-45633-9 CAMBRIDGE PB........................$10.95

Kenneth **Hamilton**

Liszt: Sonata in B Minor

0-521-46963-5 CAMBRIDGE PB........................$10.95

0-521-46570-2 CAMBRIDGE $29.95

James A. **Hepokoski**

Sibelius: Symphony No. 5

0-521-40958-6 CAMBRIDGE PB........................$10.95

Patricia **Howard**

C.W. von Gluck: Orpheus and Eurydice

0-521-29664-1 CAMBRIDGE PB........................$19.95

Douglas **Jarman**

Alban Berg: Wozzeck

0-521-28481-3 CAMBRIDGE PB........................$19.95

Colin **Lawson**

Mozart, Clarinet Concerto

0-521-47929-0 CAMBRIDGE PB........................$10.95

Nicholas **Marston**

Schumann: Fantasie, Op. 17

0-521-39892-4 CAMBRIDGE PB........................$10.95

Michael **Musgrave**

Brahms, a German Requiem

0-521-40995-0 CAMBRIDGE PB........................$10.95

Roger **Nichols** & Richard **Langham Smith**

Claude Debussy: Pelleas et Melisande

0-521-31446-1 CAMBRIDGE PB........................$19.95

Anthony **Pople**

Berg: Violin Concerto

0-521-39976-9 CAMBRIDGE PB........................$10.95

David **Rosen**

Verdi: Requiem

0-521-39767-7 CAMBRIDGE PB........................$10.95

Julian **Rushton**

Berlioz: Romeo et Juliette

0-521-37767-6 CAMBRIDGE PB........................$10.95

Michael **Russ**

Musorgsky: Pictures at an Exhibition

0-521-38607-1 CAMBRIDGE PB........................$10.95

Jim **Samson**

Chopin: The Four Ballades

0-521-38615-2 CAMBRIDGE PB........................$10.95

Elaine R. **Sisman**

Mozart: The 'Jupiter' Symphony: No. 41 in C Major, K. 551

0-521-40924-1 CAMBRIDGE PB........................$10.95

W. Dean **Sutcliffe**

Haydn, String Quartets, Op. 50

0-521-39995-5 CAMBRIDGE PB........................$10.95

Nicholas **Temperley**

Haydn: The Creation

0-521-37865-6 CAMBRIDGE PB........................$10.95

Simon **Trezise**
Debussy: La Mer
0-521-44656-2 CAMBRIDGE PB........................$10.95

Vivaldi the Four Seasons and Other Concertos Op. 8
0-521-40692-7 CAMBRIDGE PB........................$10.95

Stephen **Walsh**
Stravinsky: Oedipus Rex
0-521-40778-8 CAMBRIDGE PB........................$10.95

John **Whenham**, editor
Claudio Monteverdi: Orfeo
0-521-28477-5 CAMBRIDGE PB........................$19.95

John **Williamson**
Strauss, Also Sprach Zarathustra
0-521-40935-7 CAMBRIDGE PB........................$10.95

Paul **Wingfield**
Janacek: Glagolitic Mass
0-521-38901-1 CAMBRIDGE PB........................$11.95

David **Wyn Jones**
Beethoven, Pastoral Symphony
0-521-45684-3 CAMBRIDGE PB........................$10.95

Susan **Youens**
Schubert: Die Schone Mullerin
0-521-42279-5 CAMBRIDGE PB........................$10.95

American Popular Music

General Surveys

Richard **Crawford**
The American Musical Landscape
0-520-07764-4 CALIFORNIA........................$45.00

Philip **Furia**
The Poets of Tin Pan Alley: A History of America's Great Lyricists
0-19-506408-9 OXFORD........................$27.50

Charles **Hamm**
Yesterdays: Popular Song in America
0-393-30062-5 NORTON PB........................$16.95

William G. **Hyland**
The Song is Ended: Songwriters and American Music, 1900-1950
0-19-508611-2 OXFORD........................$25.00

Peter **Van Der Merwe**
Origins of the Popular Style: The Antecedents of Twentieth-Century Popular Music
See also **MUSIC OF THE AMERICAS** under **WORLD MUSIC: OTHER TRADITIONS**
0-19-816305-3 CLARENDON PB........................$19.95

Alec **Wilder**
American Popular Song: The Great Innovators, 1900-1950
Wilder, himself a fine composer and songwriter, has a sharp mind and a cultivated writing style
0-19-501445-6 OXFORD........................$35.00

Songwriters

Edward **Jablonski**
Harold Arlen: Happy with the Blues
A life of the songwriter from his early days in midwestern vaudeville to the Broadway stage. Known primarily as the musical force behind *The Wizard of Oz*, Arlen maintained a lifelong passion for the blues
0-306-80274-0 DA CAPO PB........................$10.95

Mary Ellen **Barrett**
Irving Berlin: A Daughter's Memoir
Big surprise—his daughter can write, and she's probably more dependable than Lawrence Begreen
See also **MEMOIRS AND JOURNALS** under **20TH-CENTURY AMERICAN ESSAYS AND JOURNALISM** in **LITERATURE OF THE AMERICAS**
0-87910-078-8 LIMELIGHT PB........................$14.95

Laurence **Bergreen**
As Thousands Cheer: The Life of Irving Berlin
0-306-80675-4 DA CAPO PB........................$18.95

Ian **Whitcomb**
Irving Berlin and Ragtime America
0-87910-115-6 LIMELIGHT........................$18.95

Philip **Hoare**
Bitter Sweet: A Biography of Noel Coward
When we think of Noel Coward, we think of effortless sophistication. To the contrary, writes Hoare, this socially adept and scathingly witty artist crafted his life as carefully as he did his plays in his rise from a middle-class suburban childhood to the zenith of urbanity. An extraordinary work revealing the gulf between the image and reality of Coward
See also **THE 20TH CENTURY** under **STUDIES OF INDIVIDUAL AUTHORS** under **ANTHOLOGIES AND STUDIES** in **LITERATURE OF THE BRITISH ISLES**
See also **SELECTED MEMOIRS AND BIOGRAPHIES** under **THEATER**
0-684-80937-0 SIMON & SCHUSTER........................$30.00

Robert **Kimball**, editor
The Complete Lyrics of Ira Gershwin
0-394-55651-8 KNOPF........................$50.00

Frederick **Nolan**
A Poet on Broadway: The Life & Lyrics of Lorenz Hart
0-19-506837-8 OXFORD........................$25.00

Michael **Freedland**
Jerome Kern: A Biography
Along with Berlin and the Gershwins, Kern defined the American musical theater in its formative years. A celebratory and informative overview of his career
0-88186-700-4 PARKWEST PB........................$6.95

Stephen **Citron**
Noel and Cole: The Sophisticates
0-19-508385-7 OXFORD........................$30.00

David **Grafton**
Red, Hot and Rich: An Oral History of Cole Porter
0-8128-3112-8 STEIN & DAY........................$17.95

Cole Porter

Charles **Schwartz**
Cole Porter: A Biography
Comprehensive biography of perhaps the wittiest stylist of the golden age of popular song. Illustrated, with a listing of recordings and state-production history
0-306-80097-7 DA CAPO PB........................$14.95

Desmond **Stone**
Alec Wilder In Spite of Himself: A Life of the Composer
The intensely private life and brilliant creativity of the composer (and historian of popular song) who won more applause from his peers than from the public
0-19-509600-2 OXFORD........................$30.00

Singers

Whitney **Balliett**
American Singers
Profiles of popular singers, by the *New Yorker's* jazz writer
0-19-504610-2 OXFORD........................$27.95

Bing **Crosby** & Pete **Martin**

Call Me Lucky

INTRODUCTION BY GARY GIDDINS

0-306-80504-9 DA CAPO PB $13.95

Gene **Lees**

The Singers and the Song

Lees is a longtime jazz writer and also a lyricist with several songs to his credit. These are his meditations on the performers and the milieu of American non-rock popular singers

0-19-504293-X OXFORD $24.95

Kitty **Kelley**

His Way: The Unauthorized Biography of Frank Sinatra

The controversial and best-selling portrait of a true American icon is full of juicy details, though at times almost too well researched. Glitz aside, it is an important document about a giant of contemporary popular culture

0-553-26515-6 BDD PB $5.99

Ed **O'Brien** & Scott **Sayers**

Sinatra: The Man and His Music—The Recording Artistry of Francis Albert Sinatra, 1939-1992

INTRODUCTION BY BILLY MAY

0-934367-24-8 TEXAS STATE DIRECTORY $39.95

Frank Sinatra

James **Spada**

Streisand: Her Life

From the biographer of Grace Kelly and Peter Lawford, the definitive biography of Barbra Streisand—singer, actress, director, political activist, and star. The result of 30 years of Streisand Watching, Spada takes us from *Funny Girl* to her recent lecture at Harvard University's Kennedy School of Government. Along the way he tells the story of the girl from Brooklyn who became the toast of Broadway, "the last great star" of Hollywood, and one of the most powerful forces in the world of entertainment

0-517-59753-5 CROWN $25.00

Country and Folk Music

General Surveys

Mary A. **Bufwack** & Robert K. **Oermann**

Finding Her Voice: The Illustrated Guide to Women in Country Music

From Patsy Cline to Emmy Lou Harris. With black and white photographs throughout

See also **MUSIC AND THEATER** under **ARTS AND LETTERS** under **WOMEN'S STUDIES** in **SOCIAL STUDIES**

0-8050-4265-2 HOLT PB $18.95

Bill C. **Malone**

Country Music, U.S.A

A well-documented, scholarly history by the foremost authority on country music, covering the entire lifespan of the genre, with bibliography and discography

0-292-71095-X TEXAS $27.95

0-292-71096-8 TEXAS PB $19.95

Bill C. **Malone** & Judith **McCullough**, editors

Stars of Country Music: Uncle Dave Macon to Johnny Rodriguez

Full-length studies of the 23 most important figures from the last 50 years of country music

0-252-00527-9 ILLINOIS $29.95

Neil V. **Rosenberg**

Bluegrass: A History

Charts the growth of bluegrass from its minstrel roots in the early 1990s to the present, with a focus on Bill Monroe, the "Father of Bluegrass"

0-252-00265-2 ILLINOIS PB $29.95

William W. **Savage**

Singing Cowboys and All That Jazz: A Short History of Popular Music in Oklahoma

0-8061-1648-X OKLAHOMA $19.95

Myron **Tassin** & Jerry **Henderson**

Fifty Years At the Grand Ole Opry

A tribute to one of the longest-running and most influential musical radio programs in America, with celebrity and fan photos

FOREWORD BY MINNIE PEARL

0-88289-089-1 PELICAN $9.95

Folk Traditions

The work of John Lomax and, later, his son Alan set a precedent for musicologists and folklorists that continues today. For almost a century they have located, transcribed and researched thousands of cowboy ballads, hymns, spirituals, and blues songs, and regional vocal traditionals from every corner of the United States.

Philip V. **Bohlman**

The Study of Folk Music in the Modern World

0-253-35555-9 INDIANA $35.00

0-253-20464-X INDIANA PB $15.95

Robert S. **Cantwell**

Bluegrass Breakdown: The Making of the Old Southern Sound

A useful introduction to the sources of bluegrass music, its instruments, performers, and subgenres

0-252-01054-X ILLINOIS $24.95

When We Were Good: The Folk Revival

This compelling study traces the fortunes of folk music from 19th-century blackface minstrelsy to its enormously popular revival in the '60s. Along the way it studies the Jewish entertainment and political cultures of New York in the '30s, the wartime crises of the '40s, and the cold-war reactionism of the '50s, whence it blossomed as an instrument of self-discovery, and mouthpiece for political activism, civil rights, and the Beat movement

0-674-95132-8 HARVARD $24.95

Vance **Randolph**

Ozark Folksongs

An abridgment of Randolph's immense collection of music and lyrics from the South and Midwest, not just from the Ozark region

EDITED BY NORM COHEN

0-252-00815-4 ILLINOIS $49.95

0-252-00952-5 ILLINOIS PB $16.95

Art **Rosenbaum** & Margo **Rosenbaum**

Folk Visions and Voices: Traditional Music and Song in North Georgia

A thorough collection of African-American music and lyrics from the Deep South

FOREWORD BY PETE SEEGER

0-8203-0682-7 GEORGIA $29.95

Individual Artists

Elizabeth **Schlappi**

Roy Acuff: The Smoky Mountain Boy

Biography of a quintessential country-and-western singer-songwriter

0-88289-144-8 PELICAN PB $14.95

Johnny **Cash**

Johnny Cash Lyrics 1955-1995

Best known for his vocal stylings, Cash is also a lyricist of power and insight. Another in the "Country Poets" series published by St. Martin's

EDITED BY DON CUSIC

0-312-13099-6 ST. MARTIN'S $18.95

Mark **Bego**
I Fall to Pieces: The Music and the Life of Patsy Cline
The story of Cline's rise from nowhere to Carnegie Hall
1-55850-476-1 ADAMS........$20.00
1-55850-608-X ADAMS PB........$9.95

Margaret **Jones**
Patsy: The Life and Times of Patsy Cline
A haunting, operatic singing style, an addiction to fast living, and a tragic death in 1963 made Cline the first woman superstar of country music. Jones's biography is the fascinating back story of one performer and her continuing inspiration to the current generation of country singers. In a larger sense, this is a history of the roots of country music and how it has grown
0-06-092211-7 HARPERPERENNIAL PB........$13.00

Ellis **Nassour**
Honky Tonk Angel: The Intimate Story of Patsy Cline
0-312-95158-2 ST. MARTIN'S PB........$5.99

Alton **Delmore**
Truth is Stranger Than Publicity
Memoirs of one half of a celebrated country music team whose hits included *Freight Train Boogie* and *Rounder's Blues*
0-915608-15-4
COUNTRY MUSIC FOUNDATION PB........$14.95

John **Bauldie**, editor
Wanted Man: In Search of Bob Dylan
0-8065-1266-0 CITADEL PB........$9.95

Clinton **Heylin**
Bob Dylan: A Life in Stolen Moments Day by Day: 1941-1995
A detailed, diary-like account of Dylan's various tours and recording sessions
0-02-864676-2 SCHIRMER........$25.00

Tim **Riley**
Hard Rain: A Dylan Commentary
0-679-74527-0 VINTAGE PB........$13.00

George **Jones** & Tom **Carter**
I Lived to Tell It All
Hard-living country legend recounts the musical peaks, and personal valleys that have marked his career
0-679-43869-6 VILLARD........$23.00

Woody **Guthrie**
Seeds of Man: An Experience Lived and Dreamed
The life and times of the great chronicler of 1930s dustbowl America
0-8032-7053-4 NEBRASKA PB........$15.00

Bound For Glory
Guthrie's colorful autobiography paints a saga of America from the 1920S to the 1950s
INTRODUCTION BY PETE SEEGER
0-8446-6178-3 SMITH........$22.25
0-452-26445-6 NEW AMERICAN LIBRARY PB...$13.95

Woody Guthrie

Charles **Wolfe** & Kip **Lornell**
The Life and Legend of Leadbelly
Jailed once for murder, twice for assault, the blues/folk artist Leadbelly sang his way out of prison in 1934. With the help of white folklorists John and Alan Lomax, he became as popular and important a practitioner of rural, political folk music as Woody Guthrie. This biography draws upon interviews and new archival material to give a rounded picture of the man
0-06-016862-5 HARPERPERENNIAL PB........$14.50

Ira B. **Nadel**
Various Positions: A Life of Leonard Cohen
A window into the life and art of the Canadian-born songwriter
0-679-44235-9 PANTHEON........$26.00

Willie **Nelson**
Willie Nelson: Lyrics 1957-1994
Nelson is perhaps the most prolific country songwriter in history. Part of the St. Martin's "Country Poets Series"
EDITED BY DON CUSIC
0-312-11917-8 ST. MARTIN'S........$16.95

Hank **Snow**
The Hank Snow Story
0-252-02089-8 ILLINOIS........$29.95

Hank **Williams**
Hank Williams: The Complete Lyrics
Williams set the standard by which all future country and folk songwriters would be measured
0-312-08892-2 ST. MARTIN'S........$12.95

Colin **Escott** & others
Hank Williams: The Biography
A look at the many sides—the luminous songwriting, the bouts with alcohol, the womanizing— of the original country music genius
0-316-24986-6 LITTLE, BROWN........$22.95
0-316-24938-6 LITTLE, BROWN PB........$12.95

Roger M. **Williams**
Sing a Sad Song: The Life of Hank Williams
A dispassionate, sometimes overly grim but powerful look at a short and tragic life
0-252-00861-8 ILLINOIS PB........$12.95

Ruth **Sheldon**
Bob Wills: Hubbin' It
0-915608-18-9 VANDERBILT PB........$12.95

Charles **Townsend**
San Antonio Rose: The Life and Music of Bob Wills
The definitive chronicle of Bob Wills, the creator and most talented exponent of country jazz
0-252-01362-X ILLINOIS PB........$17.95

Reference

Richard **Carlin**
The Big Book of Country Music: A Biographical Encyclopedia
Hardly exhaustive in scope, but a good general guide
0-14-023509-4 PENGUIN PB........$16.95

Patrick **Carr** & Steve **Wasserman**, editors
The Illustrated History of Country Music
0-8129-2455-X TIME BOOKS PB........$25.00

Barry **McCloud** & others
Definitive Country: The Ultimate Encyclopedia of Country Music and Its Performers
A monumental reference source
0-399-51890-8 PERIGEE........$40.00

Fred **Dellar** & others
The Harmony Illustrated Encyclopedia of Country Music
The most thorough and useful overview of the country-and-western music scene
0-517-56503-X CROWN PB........$13.95

Jazz

"What is jazz? If you have to ask, you'll never know."

This famous rejoinder, attributed to both Louis Armstrong and Fats Waller, hasn't stopped legions of writers from trying to define, analyze, criticize, and codify this most democratic and American of musical forms. Jazz resists definition because it is more an attitude toward playing music than a canon of specific techniques or repertoire. The music called jazz has its roots in the cross-pollination that occurred when the musical forms that African slaves brought to America began modifying, and being modified by, the forms they encountered in the New World. Thus, it is primarily a music of encounter and contrast, music of the action of one rhythm on another, one musician's style on another's. It is truly a New World, American, and profoundly democratic music, in that its finest moments occur when a balance is achieved between the individual musician's stylistic demands and the direction of the group.

Surveys of Jazz History

Joachim **Berendt**

The Jazz Book: From Ragtime to Fusion and Beyond with a New American Discography

An excellent survey, updated and translated by Dan Morgenstern, head of the Institute of Jazz Studies at Rutgers University

1-55652-098-0 LAWRENCE HILL PB $16.95

Leonard **Feather**

The Jazz Years: Ear Witness to an Era

0-306-80296-1 DA CAPO PB $12.95

Andre **Francis**

Jazz

A serious study of the major players by an important European critic

0-306-70812-4 DA CAPO $29.00

Nat **Shapiro** & Nat **Hentoff**, editors

Hear Me Talkin' to Ya: The Story of Jazz by the Men Who Made It

This invaluable anecdotal history, told in interview snippets by many of the heroes of early jazz, is the source of many oft-repeated quotes

0-486-21726-4 DOVER PB $9.95

Marshall W. **Stearns**

The Story of Jazz

This standard one-volume history provides a reliable chronology of the music's history and major figures

0-19-501269-0 OXFORD PB $12.95

Martin **Williams**

The Jazz Tradition

The standard by which jazz critique is measured

See also **JAZZ APPRECIATION AND THEORY**

0-19-507816-0 OXFORD PB $13.95

Blues and Gospel

Blues and gospel music represent the profane and the sacred sides of the same coin: both are folk forms. The blues are usually a rhythmic statement of romantic complaint; gospel a rhythmic statement of religious hope or faith. Both idioms had a large influence on the feeling of jazz.

William **Barlow**

"Looking Up at Down": The Emergence of Blues Culture

0-87722-722-5 TEMPLE PB $18.95

Stephen **Calt**

I'd Rather Be the Devil: Skip James and the Blues

0-306-80579-0 DA CAPO PB $14.95

Samuel B. **Charters**

The Country Blues

A groundbreaking although sometimes inaccurate study of the major figures of rural blues by a dedicated early student

0-306-80014-4 DA CAPO PB $12.95

The Legacy of the Blues: Art and Lives of Twelve Great Bluesmen

0-306-80054-3 DA CAPO PB $9.95

Lawrence **Cohn**, editor

Nothing But the Blues

This popular history covers it all—hokum blues, holy blues, white country blues, barrelhouse blues, rhythm and blues, and jugband

INTRODUCTION BY B.B. KING

1-55859-271-7 ABBEVILLE $45.00

Helen Oakley **Dance**

Stormy Monday: The T-Bone Walker Story

A jazz-influenced blues guitarist and singer whose career began in the '40s, Walker influenced many others, notably B.B. King and Chuck Berry

FOREWORD BY B.B. KING

0-8071-1355-7 LSU $24.95

David **Evans**

Big Road Blues: Tradition and Creativity in the Folk Blues

0-306-80300-3 DA CAPO PB $15.95

William **Ferris**

Blues from the Delta

INTRODUCTION BY BILLY TAYLOR

0-306-80327-5 DA CAPO PB $11.95

Laurraine **Goreau**

Just Mahalia, Baby: The Mahalia Jackson Story

0-88289-441-2 PELICAN PB $18.95

Frank John **Hadley**

The Grove Press Guide to the Blues on CD

Largely thanks to the compact disk—and techniques that are improving scratchy records—the blues are hugely popular once again, and more importantly, widely available. *The Grove Press Guide* helps readers evaluate the hundreds of blues recordings, both new and old, being released on CD. A five-point rating system and extensive cross indexing will be useful to both newcomers and initiates

0-8021-3328-2 GROVE PB $14.95

Daphne Duval **Harrison**

Black Pearls: Blues Queens of the 1920s

0-8135-1279-4 RUTGERS PB $13.95

Anthony **Heilbut**

The Gospel Sound: Good News and Bad Times

The definitive study of the world of gospel music

0-87910-034-6 PROSCENIUM PB $14.95

James Weldon **Johnson** & J. Rosamond **Johnson**

The Books of American Negro Spirituals

Early anthology of Spirituals, arranged for voice and piano. With commentary by one of the most important black poets of the early 20th century

0-306-80074-8 DA CAPO PB $15.95

Charles **Keil**

Urban Blues

An important survey of electric blues traditions

0-226-42960-1 CHICAGO PB $11.95

Alan **Lomax**

The Land Where the Blues Began

Lomax, who discovered Leadbelly and many other performers now recognized as giants, has done more than anyone to make the blues and other indigenous American music known. In this book, he sums up his 60-year exploration of the South as he recounts the second long trip he made through the Mississippi Delta when he recorded Big Bill Broonzy, Muddy Waters, and others for the Library of Congress. "Singingly well-written…a *summa musicologia* whose sobering humanity and thoughts about an American voice echo Whitman"—*Kirkus Reviews*

0-679-40424-4 PANTHEON $25.00

0-385-31285-7 DELTA PB $14.95

Kip **Lornell**

Virginia's Blues, Gospel, and Country Records, 1902-1943

0-8131-1658-9 KENTUCKY $27.00

Paul **Oliver**

Blues Off the Record: Thirty Years of Blues

0-306-80321-6 DA CAPO PB $13.95

Screening the Blues

0-306-80344-5 DA CAPO PB $13.95

Robert **Palmer**

Deep Blues

A first-rate study of the blues styles and major performers of the Mississippi delta. Meticulously researched by a leading writer in the field

0-14-006223-8 VIKING PB $12.95

Bernice Johnson **Reagon**, editor

"We'll Understand It Better By and By": Pioneering African American Gospel Composers

Reagon focuses on six of gospel music's pioneer composers, showing the impact of their work on African American church traditions and 20th-century music. She investigates the lives and work of Charles Tindley, Thomas Dorsey, Roberta Martin, and others, and includes 49 complete gospel scores

1-56098-167-9 SMITHSONIAN PB $24.95

Mike **Rowe**

Chicago Blues: The City and the Music

Detailed study of the electric blues tradition of the most important urban blues center

0-306-80145-0 DA CAPO PB $13.95

Robert **Santelli**

The Big Book of Blues: A Biographical Encyclopedia

More than 600 entries detail every aspect and major performer in the most American of music, as well as all its subgenres, from urban blues and blues rock to rhythm-and-blues and Delta blues. Includes biographical information on virtually every performer of note as well as listings of essential listening

0-14-015939-8 PENGUIN PB $16.95

Charles **Sawyer**

The Arrival of B.B. King: The Authorized Biography

The life and work of the major figures in postwar blues

0-306-80169-8 DA CAPO PB $12.95

Ragtime

In vogue around the turn of the century, ragtime was a syncopated music played by solo pianists, brass bands, and other instrumental combinations. It formed the rhythmic basis of the early New Orleans band music that constituted jazz's first flowering.

Edward A. **Berlin**

Ragtime: A Musical and Cultural History

0-520-05219-6 CALIFORNIA PB $12.00

Early Jazz: New Orleans and Beyond

Jazz's early years were a process of sorting out many questions: how ensembles would play together, what a solo instrumentalist's role was, what was appropriate repertoire. Much of the most important experimentation went on in New Orleans, home of jazz's first great soloist, Louis Armstrong, and its first great composer, Jelly Roll Morton. But the sound was heard all over the country and, eventually, the world. Before the 1920s were out, many regions and sensibilities had put their distinctive stamps on the music.

Richard **Hadlock**

Jazz Masters of the Twenties

Informative portraits of major figures of the period

0-306-80328-3 DA CAPO PB $11.95

Thomas J. **Hennessey**

From Jazz to Swing: African-American Jazz Musicians and Their Music, 1890-1935

0-8143-2179-8 WAYNE STATE PB $15.95

Donald M. **Marquis**

In Search of Buddy Bolden: First Man of Jazz

Investigative reportage on a legendary, little-documented New Orleans progenitor of jazz

0-8071-1857-5 LSU PB $11.95

Rick **Kennedy**

Jelly Roll, Bix, and Hoagy: Gennett Studios and the Birth of Recorded Jazz

A solid, entertaining history of Gennett Records, which helped introduce jazz to the world

0-253-33136-6 INDIANA $24.95

Nathan W. **Pearson**, Jr.

Goin' to Kansas City

0-252-01336-0 ILLINOIS $24.95

Frederick **Ramsey** & Charles Edward **Smith**

Jazzmen

Reprint of a 1939 collection of lyrical essays about the people and places of early jazz, especially New Orleans and Chicago. An enjoyable period piece

0-87910-039-7 PROSCENIUM PB $9.95

Al **Rose** & Edmond **Souchon**

New Orleans Jazz: A Family Album

A beautifully illustrated guided tour from earliest times to the present

0-8071-1173-2 LSU PB $19.95

Gunther **Schuller**

Early Jazz: Its Roots and Musical Development

A classic study by a musician and composer trained in European music as well as jazz. Sensitive and scholarly analysis of the music's first flowering

0-19-504043-0 OXFORD PB $14.95

Arnold **Shaw**

The Jazz Age: Popular Music in the 1920s

0-19-503891-6 OXFORD $27.95

Martin **Williams**

Jazz Masters of New Orleans

Portraits of jazz pioneers by a knowledgeable writer

0-306-77541-7 DA CAPO $37.50

Swing and Big Band

Through the 1920s, arrangers and bandleaders such as Fletcher Henderson, Don Redman, and Duke Ellington transferred the formulas worked out in New Orleans ensembles to the standard dance band ensembles. They produced and refined a big-band jazz style that ripened, in the 1930s, into the swing era, a period of unprecedented appreciation of jazz-based music.

Stanley **Dance**

Jazz Era: The Forties

Biographies of major figures of this era

0-306-76191-2 DA CAPO $32.00

Drew **Page**

Drew's Blues: A Sideman's Life with the Big Bands

0-8071-0686-0 LSU $24.95

Gunther **Schuller**

The Swing Era: The Development of Jazz, 1930-1945

For the second volume of his jazz history, Schuller turns to the great swing bands of the height of jazz's popularity. At 900-plus pages, this is once again the most thorough and exhaustive scholarly analysis on the subject. Duke Ellington gets the most detailed treatment, but every important figure from Benny Goodman to Billie Holiday is covered individually

0-19-507140-9 OXFORD PB $17.95

George T. **Simon**

The Big Bands

A study by a former editor of the jazz journal *Metronome*

0-02-872430-5 SCHIRMER PB $23.00

Rex **Stewart**

Jazz Masters of the Thirties

A great trumpet player from the Ellington and Fletcher Henderson bands paints unusual portraits of his contemporaries and peers, in a penetrating, anecdotal style

INTRODUCTION BY MARTIN WILLIAMS

0-306-80159-0 DA CAPO PB $11.95

Bebop and Post-Bop

Sometime around 1940, a number of musicians began experimenting with the musical assumptions under which jazz had been operating for over a decade. In informal sessions, they began working out a new approach, which became known as bebop, stressing fluency of execution, harmonic sophistication, quick reflexes, and mordant wit. Through the 1950s, musicians, many of them half a generation younger than bop's founders, continued to refine and expand the new possibilities introduced by the boppers.

Frank **Bergerot** & Arnaud **Merlin**

The Story of Jazz: Bop and Beyond

0-8109-2876-0 ABRAMS PB $12.95

Leonard **Feather**

Inside Jazz

Originally published during bebop's heyday, this remains an entertaining introduction to the jazz revolution of the late '40s, by a champion of what was then the "new" jazz

0-306-80076-4 DA CAPO PB $9.95

Ted **Gioia**

West Coast Jazz: Modern Jazz in California, 1945-1960

0-19-506310-4 OXFORD $25.00

Ira **Gitler**

Jazz Masters of the Forties

A flavorful survey of the main figures, by a longtime writer and enthusiast

0-306-76126-2 DA CAPO $29.50
0-306-80224-4 DA CAPO PB $12.95

Swing to Bop: An Oral History of the Transition in Jazz in the 1940s
"An era when black musicians tried innovatively to wrest control of their music from white big-band leaders"—Mel Watkins, *American Visions*
See also **THE BLACK AESTHETIC** under **CULTURE** under **AFRICAN-AMERICAN STUDIES** in **HISTORY OF THE AMERICAS**
0-19-505070-3 OXFORD PB $13.95

Joe **Goldberg**
Jazz Masters of the Fifties
This worthy sequel to the Gitler volume includes portraits of Thelonious Monk, Miles Davis, and others
0-306-80197-3 DA CAPO PB..............................$11.95

Thomas **Owens**
Bebop: Its Vocabulary and Its Players
0-19-505287-0 OXFORD $25.00
0-19-510651-2 OXFORD PB..............................$14.95

David H. **Rosenthal**
Hard Bop: Jazz and Black Music 1955-1965
Rosenthal, a poet and translator, writes incisively of neglected aspects of the period
0-19-508556-6 OXFORD PB..............................$10.95

A.B. **Spellman**
Four Lives in the Bebop Business
Four realistic portraits of musicians of the 1950s (some becoming major figures in the 1960s) and their tribulations: Ornette Coleman, Cecil Taylor, Jackie McLean, and Herbie Nichols. Outstanding
See also **STUDIES OF INDIVIDUAL ARTISTS**
0-87910-042-7 PROSCENIUM PB......................$13.95

The '60s and '70s: Fusion and the New Thing

As happened when the swing era ripened, musicians in the late 1950s and early '60s began to feel restive with the vocabulary that had been standard since 1945. Some experimented with totally free- form playing (with no preestablished harmonic or rhythmic basis), some became traditionalists, and some tried to incorporate so-called rock elements into jazz.

Ekkehard **Jost**
Free Jazz
Analysis of the musical approaches of the '60s, including thoughts on John Coltrane, Ornette Coleman, Cecil Taylor, and other avant-garde figures
0-306-80556-1 DA CAPO PB $13.95

John **Litweiler**
The Freedom Principle: Jazz After 1958
First published in 1984, Litweiler's level-headed study is probably the most authoritative single-volume on the "free jazz" movement of the 1960s. Chapters are arranged around pivotal figures like Ornette Coleman, John Coltrane, Sun Ra, Albert Ayler, and Cecil Taylor. Litweiler places "free jazz" within the jazz continuum, yet celebrates its spirit of radical experimentation for breaking up the ossified bebop conventions of the late fifties
0-306-80377-1 DA CAPO PB $13.95

Barry **McRae**
The Jazz Cataclysm
Study of the transitional period that resulted in the free jazz revolution of the 1960s
0-306-76240-4 DA CAPO $29.00

Essays and Reviews

Whitney **Balliett**
American Musicians: 56 Portraits in Jazz
Balliett, for over 30 years a knowledgeable and eloquent contributor to *New Yorker*, at his best brings a fine fiction writer's eye to portraits of musicians, singers, and songwriters
0-19-503758-8 OXFORD $35.00

The Sound of Surprise
0-306-77543-3 DA CAPO $34.00

Amiri **Baraka**
Blues People: Negro Music in White America
Baraka (aka LeRoi Jones) is a prominent black poet and playwright who has written consistently about jazz, championing particularly the "new thing," or avant-garde, players of the '60s. His essays are opinionated and thought-provoking
0-688-18474-X MORROW PB............................$10.00

Amiri Baraka

Robert **Brustein**
Revolution as Theatre: Essays on Radical Style
0-87140-238-6 NORTON PB $1.95

Hayden **Carruth**
Sitting In: Selected Writings on Jazz, Blues, and Related Topics
A distinguished poet's thoughts on the music
0-87745-423-X IOWA PB..................................$13.95

Francis **Davis**
Outcats: Jazz Composers, Instrumentalists, and Singers
This collection of pieces revolves around the recurring theme of alienation and cultural exile among jazz musicians—the anomaly of a brilliant art form unrecognized in its country of origin. Profiled musicians include figures like Lester Young and Bobby Short, but Davis is mostly concerned with the "outcats" on the fringe of media and public recognition, like Herbie Nichols, Borah Bergman, Henry Threadgill, and Cecil Taylor. "[Davis is] a very impressive critic. He doesn't pin fancy phrases on his chest; he gets at what he resounds to and why. You feel you're reading an honest man"—Pauline Kael
0-19-505587-X OXFORD..................................$22.95

Geoff **Dyer**
But Beautiful: A Book About Jazz
Dyer, the British novelist and critic, has assembled an unusually incisive evocation of the jazz world, drawing on photos, anecdotes, and above all his deep love for the music. We see Lester Young fading away in his hotel room, Mingus storming down the streets of New York, and others including Thelonious Monk, Duke Ellington, Ben Webster, and Chet Baker. "There can be few books on jazz written with such tenderness and care."—*TLS*.
0-86547-490-7 NORTH POINT..........................$21.00

Leonard **Feather**
From Satchmo to Miles
Anecdotal collection of essays on major figures
See also **SURVEYS OF JAZZ HISTORY**
0-306-80302-X DA CAPO PB $12.95

Gary **Giddins**
Riding on a Blue Note: Jazz and American Pop
Essays on the nexus of jazz and pop
0-19-502835-X OXFORD $24.95

Ted **Gioia**
The Imperfect Art: Reflections on Jazz and Modern Culture
0-19-505343-5 OXFORD $21.95

Robert **Gottlieb**, editor
Reading Jazz: A Gathering of Autobiography, Reportage, and Criticism from 1917 to 1995
A much anticipated, 1,000-plus page compendium
0-679-44251-0 PANTHEON..............................$40.00

Nat **Hentoff**
The Jazz Life
Combines social criticisms with Hentoff's knowledge of musicians' lives
0-306-80088-8 DA CAPO PB............................$11.95

Listen to the Stories
Hentoff—critic, columnist, and jazz writer for the *Village Voice* and *The Wall Street Journal*—delivers intimate, authoritative, and opinionated discussions of jazz, blues, country, and gospel
0-06-019047-7 HARPERCOLLINS $23.00
0-06-092712-7 HARPERPERENNIAL PB $12.00

Andre **Hodeir**
Toward Jazz
0-306-70810-8 DA CAPO $29.00

Nat **Hentoff**, editor

Jazz: New Perspectives on the History of Jazz by Twelve of the World's Foremost Jazz Critics and Scholars

A useful collection of essays edited by a sensitive and knowledgeable writer

0-306-80002-0 DA CAPO PB $14.95

Orrin **Keepnews**

The View from Within: Jazz Writings, 1948-1987

The articulate and knowledgeable Keepnews, who founded the Riverside and Milestone labels, has been one of the most significant record producers in jazz

0-19-506330-9 OXFORD PB $8.95

Philip **Larkin**

All What Jazz: A Record Diary

Distinguished British poet's collection of highly opinionated reviews from the 1960s

0-374-10340-2 FS&G $19.95

0-374-51908-0 FS&G PB $9.95

Philip Larkin

Wynton **Marsalis**

Marsalis on Music

The most popular and acclaimed jazz musician, composer, and classical trumpet player of his generation, Wynton Marsalis shows himself here in the guise of teacher in the tradition of Leonard Bernstein's Young People's Concerts. With wonderful examples and analogies from sports and elsewhere in a child's world, Marsalis makes so-called "difficult" music vivid and fun. A perfect book for families eager to give children an opening into the appreciation of classical music and jazz

0-393-03909-9 NORTON $25.00

Albert **Murray**

Stomping the Blues

The aesthetics of jazz and the blues, magisterially laid out by a brilliant and erudite critic. "No responsible critic of American culture will be able to approach his task without consulting Mr. Murray's eloquent insights"—Ralph Ellison.

0-306-80362-3 DA CAPO PB $13.95

"Another thing about the honky-tonks was the big risk you were always running just by being anywhere near them. There was no admission fee; but not only were they forever being raided, broken up either by the country sheriff and his deputies or by the city police, there was also no telling when somebody was going to start another knock-down drag-out rumpus, or there would be another cutting scrape, or the bullets would start flying again. Because the music always added up to a good-time atmosphere. But not for everybody. For some, acceleration of the festivities only aggravated their torment, especially when the object of their passion was there having a good time with somebody else"

STOMPING THE BLUES

Robert **Reisner**

The Jazz Titans

Sketches of major jazz musicians

0-306-70866-3 DA CAPO $25.00

Gene **Santoro**

Dancing in Your Head: Jazz, Blues, Rock, and Beyond

Santoro, a young critic for *The Nation,* writes about a broad spectrum without stretching himself too thin: one of our best cultural commentators, here he offers up his liveliest reviews and essays about James Brown, Sun Ra, Nat "King" Cole, Public Enemy, Neil Young and even George Hay, the founder of the Grand Ole Opry

0-19-507887-X OXFORD $27.50

0-19-510123-5 OXFORD PB $11.95

Ben **Sidran**

Black Talk

INTRODUCTION BY ARCHIE SNAPP

0-306-80184-1 DA CAPO PB $10.95

Martin **Williams**

The Jazz Tradition

The standard by which jazz critique is measured

See also **SURVEYS OF JAZZ HISTORY**

0-19-507816-0 OXFORD PB $13.95

Martin **Williams**, editor

Jazz Panorama

A mixed bag of essays and interviews from the short-lived but excellent magazine *The Jazz Review*, ranging from the earliest jazz to the "new thing" of the '60s

0-306-79574-4 DA CAPO $37.50

Valerie **Wilmer**

Jazz People

Verbal and photographic portraits whose subjects include Billy Higgins, Jimmy Heath, Randy Weston, Archie Shepp, and others

0-306-80434-4 DA CAPO PB $11.95

Al **Young**

Things Ain't What They Used to Be: Musical Memoirs

From the tango to the bossa nova, Young recaptures the past through the power of music

See also **MEMOIRS AND JOURNALS** under **20TH-CENTURY AMERICAN ESSAYS AND JOURNALISM** in **LITERATURE OF THE AMERICAS**

0-88739-024-2 CREATIVE ARTS PB $8.95

Jazz Appreciation and Theory

David **Baker**

Jazz Improvisation: A Comprehensive Method For All Musicians

0-89917-397-7 ALFRED PUB CO PB $21.95

Paul **Berliner**

Thinking in Jazz

This 883-page book is by far the most thorough and comprehensive field study ever written on the art, craft, ritual, social protocol, cultural context, and thought processes of jazz improvisation. Berliner's research draws on extensive interviews with musicians and transcriptions of collective improvisations, as well as his own experiences as a jazz trumpeteer. A landmark in jazz scholarship

0-226-04381-9 CHICAGO PB $29.95

Jerry **Coker**

Improvising Jazz

Standard, useful guide to the theory behind jazz improvisation

0-671-62829-1 TOUCHSTONE PB $11.00

Barry **Kernfeld**

What to Listen for in Jazz

0-300-05902-7 YALE $40.00

The Jazz Scene

Richard N. **Albert**, editor

From Blues to Bop: A Collection of Jazz Fiction

0-8071-1616-5 LSU $24.95

Samuel B. **Charters** & Leonard **Kunstadt**

Jazz: A History of the New York Scene

A colorful survey of the New York scene of the 1920s, '30s, and '40s, from contemporary sources

0-306-80225-2 DA CAPO PB $13.95

Bill **Crow**

From Birdland to Broadway: Scenes from a Life in Jazz

Crow, a bass player, was involved in jazz when New York's 52nd Street was a nonstop carnival of immortal music. This memoir of the jazz life describes Crow's career as he watched and sat in with many of the greats over the course of 40 years—Billie Holiday, Lennie Tristano, Stan Getz, Harry Belafonte, Benny Goodman, and others

0-19-506988-9 OXFORD $25.00

Jazz Anecdotes

Learning music, stage fright, life on the road, discrimination, and the importance of a good nickname are among the topics covered in these stories about Duke Ellington, Louis Armstrong, Bessie Smith, Charlie Parker, Dizzy Gillespie, and many others

0-19-505588-8 OXFORD PB $19.95

Sidney **Finkelstein** & Jules **Halfant**

Jazz, A People's Music

0-306-70659-8 DA CAPO $34.00

Ted **Fox**

Showtime At the Apollo

Fascinating history of the major Harlem venue for black performing artists in New York City

See also **RAP, R&B, MOTOWN, AND SOUL** under **ROCK**

0-306-80503-0 DA CAPO PB $13.95

Art **Lange** & Nathaniel **Mackey**, editors

Moment's Notice: Jazz in Poetry and Prose

See also **ANTHOLOGIES** under **20TH-CENTURY AMERICAN POETRY** in **LITERATURE OF THE AMERICAS**

1-56689-001-2 COFFEE HOUSE PB $17.50

Mezz **Mezzrow** & Bernard **Wolfe**

Really the Blues

A famous and influential memoir of the jazz world, originally published in 1946. "Mezzrow's *Really the Blues,* read at counter of Columbia U Bookstore in mid-forties, was for me the first signal into white culture of the underground black, hip culture that preexisted before my own generation"—Allen Ginsberg

See also **STUDIES OF INDIVIDUAL ARTISTS**

0-87910-112-1 CAROL PB $9.95
0-8065-1205-9 CAROL PB $12.95

Francis **Newton**

The Jazz Scene

An English critic's social history of jazz

0-306-70685-7 DA CAPO $40.50

Arnold **Shaw**

Fifty Second Street: Street of Jazz

Entertaining, episodic history of the heyday of New York's block-long entertainment center during the 1930s and '40s, where every musician of interest played at one time or another

0-306-80068-3 DA CAPO PB $12.95

Arthur **Taylor**

Notes and Tones: Musician-To-Musician Interviews

As a trusted fellow musician, the late drummer Arhtur Taylor was able to elicit astonishingly candid statements from the musicians he interviewed between 1968 and 1972. The transcriptions are unfiltered, providing a window on the musical transitions and racial politics of the time. The 29 interviews include the likes of Art Blakey, Betty Carter, Ornette Coleman, and Nina Simone, as well as Taylor's former bandmates like Miles Davis, Sonny Rollins, and Thelonious Monk

0-306-80526-X DA CAPO PB $13.95

Visual Books

William **Claxton**

Jazz

A beautifully produced large-format book of photos by a preeminent photographer

0-8118-1351-7 CHRONICLE PB $22.95

Frank **Driggs** & Harris **Lewine**

Black Beauty, White Heat: A Pictorial History of Classic Jazz, 1920-1950

A lavish, large-format pictorial book; rare photos, record labels, handbills, and more from jazz's "golden age," 1920-1950

0-306-80672-X DA CAPO PB $29.95

Lee **Tanner**, editor

Dizzy: John Birks Gillespie in His Seventy-Fifth Year

The great trumpeter's career in photographs

1-56640-396-0 POMEGRANATE $19.95

Milt **Hinton** & David **Berger**

Bass Line: The Stories and Photographs of Milt Hinton

Brilliant photographs, memorable anecdotes

0-87722-518-4 TEMPLE $44.95

Graham **Marsh**

Blue Note: The Album Cover Art

0-8118-0036-9 CHRONICLE PB $24.95

Graham **Marsh** & Glyn **Callingham**, editors

New York Hot: East Coast Jazz of the '50s & '60s: the Album Cover Art

Just as jazz broke through the boundaries of musical tradition, the album covers that housed the vinyl were in the vanguard of design. This lavish volume of more than 200 covers—including such greats as John Coltrane, Miles Davis, Herbie Mann, and Charlie Mingus—is certain to find an appreciative audience among jazz fans with a graphic eye to match a discriminating ear

0-8118-0416-X CHRONICLE PB $24.95

Valerie **Wilmer**

The Face of Black Music

Work by one of the most prominent jazz photographers of the 1960s

0-306-80039-X DA CAPO PB $13.95

Studies of Individual Artists

Among the artists in this section are four of jazz's all- time greats: Fats Waller, master of stride piano and popular entertainer of the 1930s, who composed such perennially popular songs as "Honeysuckle Rose," "Squeeze Me," and "Ain't Misbehavin'"; Louis Armstrong, who, as well as being one of America's most beloved entertainers, was also the first great jazz soloist, the man who set the rules, as trumpeter and singer, for everyone who came after, regardless of instrument; Charlie Parker, one of the inventors of modern jazz, who redefined the soloist's language and, by extension, the notion of how groups played together; and Duke Ellington, whose career spanned over 50 years, during which he became jazz's most important composer and bandleader. He was a magnetic personality, a unique pianist, and a cultural figure of the highest significance in America.

Whitney **Balliett**

American Musicians: Seventy-One Portraits in Jazz

This collection of biographical essays, written from 1962 to 1986, are for Balliet "a gapped history, a sort of highly personal encyclopedia, a series of close accounts of how a beautiful music grew, flourished, and (perhaps) began the long trek back to its native silence." Balliet has been a jazz critic for the *New Yorker* since 1957. "Whitney Balliet is, without a rival in sight, the most literate and knowledgeable living writer on jazz"—Alistair Cooke

0-19-509538-3 OXFORD $35.00

Louis **Armstrong**

Satchmo: My Life in New Orleans

Full of the sound of Armstrong's voice, characteristic humor, and vitality; covers the period up until he left New Orleans for Chicago

0-306-80276-7 DA CAPO PB $11.95

Swing That Music

0-306-80544-8 DA CAPO PB $12.95

Donald **Bogle** & others

Louis Armstrong: A Cultural Legacy

See also **ATHLETES AND ENTERTAINERS** under **BLACK VOICES, BLACK LIVES** under **AFRICAN-AMERICAN STUDIES** in **HISTORY OF THE AMERICAS**

0-295-97383-8 WASHINGTON PB $29.95

Gary **Giddins**

Satchmo

Pictorial biography of Louis Armstrong, based in large part on previously unexamined writings of Armstrong

0-385-24429-0 ANCHOR PB $15.00

Robert **Goffin**

Horn of Plenty: The Story of Louis Armstrong

A portrait covering Satchmo's career through the mid-1940s

0-306-77430-5 DA CAPO $32.50
0-313-20398-9 GREENWOOD $59.75

Max **Jones** & John **Chilton**

Louis: The Louis Armstrong Story, 1900-1971

The best single volume available about Armstrong

0-306-80324-0 DA CAPO PB $12.95

Hugues **Panassie**

Louis Armstrong

Thin but affectionate biography by a Frenchman who was one of the first jazz critics

0-306-79611-2 DA CAPO $29.00
0-306-80116-7 DA CAPO PB $7.95

Count **Basie** & Albert **Murray**

Good Morning Blues: The Autobiography of Count Basie

Portrait of jazz giant, pianist, bandleader, covering his more than 50-year career in great detail

0-917657-89-6 FINE PB $10.95

Charlie **Barnet** & Stanley **Dance**
Those Swinging Years: The Autobiography of Charlie Barnet
Autobiography of a well-known bandleader and saxophonist of the swing era
FOREWORD BY BILLY MAY
0-306-80492-1 DA CAPO PB $12.95

Reid **Badger**
James Reese Europe: A Life in Ragtime
0-19-506044-X OXFORD $30.00

Sidney **Bechet**
Treat It Gentle: An Autobiography
One of the best jazz autobiographies, lyrical and even poetic in spots, covering the career of the great clarinetist and soprano saxophonist from the beginnings through the early 1950s
FOREWORD BY DESMOND FLOWER
0-306-80086-1 DA CAPO PB $12.95

Graham **Lock** & Nick **White**
Forces in Motion: The Music and Thoughts of Anthony Braxton
Lock, a British journalist, provides a rigorous musical analysis and informal, day-to-day working portrait of one of the most complex and important mavericks in modern improvised music. Braxton emerged from the free jazz movement in Chicago in the 1960s, and is now a professor at Wesleyan
0-306-80342-9 DA CAPO PB $13.95

Bill **Cole**
John Coltrane
0-306-80530-8 DA CAPO PB $13.95

Eric **Nisenson**
Ascension: John Coltrane and His Quest
0-312-09838-3 ST. MARTIN'S $22.95

C.O. **Simpkins**
Coltrane
0-933121-20-2 BLACK CLASSIC PB $14.95

J.C. **Thomas**
Chasin' the Trane
0-306-80043-8 DA CAPO PB $10.95

Miles **Davis** & Quincy **Troupe**
Miles: The Autobiography
A tough, rapid-fire narration of Davis' musical career, from his collaboration with Charlie Parker in the '40s through the famous '50s quartet and the later fusion experiments. A frank and sometimes harsh representation of the rarely shown realities of the jazz scene
See also **ATHLETES AND ENTERTAINERS** under **BLACK VOICES, BLACK LIVES** under **AFRICAN-AMERICAN STUDIES** in **HISTORY OF THE AMERICAS**
0-671-72582-3 TOUCHSTONE PB $12.95

Bill **Cole**
Miles Davis: The Early Years
0-306-80554-5 DA CAPO PB $13.95

Daryl **Long**
Miles Davis for Beginners
0-86316-153-7 WRITERS & READERS PB $9.00

James Lincoln **Collier**
Duke Ellington
A controversial recent biography
0-02-722985-8 SIMON & SCHUSTER $13.95

Stanley **Dance**
The World of Duke Ellington
Portraits of Ellington, his sidemen, and aides-de-camp, illustrated with fine pictures, by a writer who traveled with the band and knew them for decades
FOREWORD BY DUKE ELLINGTON
0-306-80136-1 DA CAPO PB $12.95

Duke **Ellington**
Music Is My Mistress
A uniquely flavored book of reminiscences and anecdotes by the man himself. Loosely structured, but entertaining and liberally illustrated
0-306-80033-0 DA CAPO PB $15.95

Duke Ellington

Mercer **Ellington** & Stanley **Dance**
Duke Ellington in Person
A revealing, candid memoir by Ellington's son, himself a talented composer, arranger, and trumpeter
0-306-80104-3 DA CAPO PB $11.95

John Edward **Hasse**
Beyond Category: The Life and Genius of Duke Ellington
From the Curator of American Music at The Smithsonian Institute comes this comprehensive biography of the man and his music. Compiled from a wealth of source material including recorded interviews, sheet music, letters, and family papers, this is a portrait worthy of Ellington's genius. Includes photos
0-671-70387-0 SIMON & SCHUSTER $25.00
0-306-80614-2 DA CAPO PB $15.95

Ken **Rattenbury**
Duke Ellington
0-300-05507-2 YALE PB $20.00

Mark **Tucker**
Ellington: The Early Years
0-252-01425-1 ILLINOIS $34.95

Mark **Tucker**, editor
The Duke Ellington Reader
A trove, with more surprises than all the conventional Ellington biographies put together. This would make any jazz lover's top ten
See also **ATHLETES AND ENTERTAINERS** under **BLACK VOICES, BLACK LIVES** under **AFRICAN-AMERICAN STUDIES** in **HISTORY OF THE AMERICAS**
0-19-505410-5 OXFORD $30.00

Barry **Ulanov**
Duke Ellington
The first full-length biography of Ellington, by one of the best and brightest critics of the 1940s and '50s, covers the maestro's career to the late '40s
0-306-70727-6 DA CAPO $40.50

Donald L. **Maggin**
Stan Getz: A Life in Jazz
0-688-12315-5 MORROW $25.00

James Lincoln **Collier**
Benny Goodman and the Swing Era
0-19-505278-1 OXFORD $35.00

Ross **Firestone**
Swing, Swing, Swing: The Life and Times of Benny Goodman, Book and CD
Swing was an innovative, socially controversial new form of popular music. Firestone profiles Goodman, the intense, moody man who brought the new music to the limelight, from his boyhood in Chicago's slums to his triumphs as leader of the first integrated jazz band. Establishes Goodman as one of the crucial influences on 20th-century music. "The Goodman story *swings* here....Benny blows—and the angels sing"—*Kirkus Reviews*
0-393-03371-6 NORTON $29.95

Benny **Goodman**
Benny: King of Swing
The clarinetist and bandleader Benny Goodman, called the King of Swing during the 1930s, played a major role as a popularizer of the big-band jazz sound
0-306-80289-9 DA CAPO PB $14.95

John **Chilton**
The Song of the Hawk: The Life and Recordings of Coleman Hawkins
Hawkins has often been called "the father of the tenor saxophone"; his work created a revolution in tone and improvisational style, and he remained at the forefront of jazz musicians throughout his long career. Chilton's book is the first full-length biography
0-472-10212-5 MICHIGAN $32.50
0-472-08201-9 MICHIGAN PB $24.95

Edward A. **Berlin**
Scott Joplin: King of Ragtime
0-19-508739-9 OXFORD $25.00

Susan **Curtis**
Dancing to a Black Man's Tune: A Life of Scott Joplin
0-8262-0949-1 MISSOURI $29.95

Andy **Kirk**

Twenty Years on Wheels: As Told to Amy Lee

0-472-10134-X MICHIGAN $21.95

Mezz **Mezzrow** & Bernard **Wolfe**

Really the Blues

A famous and influential memoir of the jazz world, originally published in 1946. "Mezzrow's *Really the Blues,* read at the counter of Columbia U Bookstore in mid-forties, was for me the first signal into white culture of the underground black, hip culture that preexisted before my own generation"—Allen Ginsberg

See also **THE JAZZ SCENE**

0-87910-112-1 CAROL PB $9.95

0-8065-1205-9 CAROL PB $12.95

George T. **Simon**

Glenn Miller and His Orchestra

The celebrated bandleader of the late 1930s was never a significant force in jazz, but rather an important popularizer

INTRODUCTION BY BING CROSBY

0-306-80129-9 DA CAPO PB $14.95

Charles **Mingus**

Beneath the Underdog

Compelling, turbulent autobiography

0-679-73761-8 VINTAGE PB........................$14.00

Janet **Coleman** & Al **Young**

Mingus/Mingus

Bassist and composer Charles Mingus was very influential in the 1950s and '60s as a bandleader as well. His volatile personality and opinions made him a visible figure to the public at large

0-88739-067-6 CREATIVE ARTS........................$14.95

Brian **Priestley**

Mingus: A Critical Biography

0-306-80217-1 DA CAPO PB $13.95

Gary **Giddins** & Charlie **Parker**

Celebrating Bird: The Triumph of Charlie Parker

A large-format book, lavishly illustrated and with a perceptive text

0-688-05951-1 BEECH TREE PB........................$12.95

Robert G. **Reisner**, editor

Bird: The Legend of Charlie Parker

Illustrated series of interviews with Parker's associates, friends and fans: a multi-faceted picture of a protean genius

0-306-80069-1 DA CAPO PB $13.95

Art **Pepper** & Laurie **Pepper**

Straight Life

The autobiography of the troubled West Coast saxophonist Art Pepper, detailing his sexual and pharmaceutical preoccupations. A fascinating, if sometimes depressing, look into the jazz scene of a certain time and place

0-306-80558-8 DA CAPO PB........................$17.95

Charles **Delaunay**

Django Reinhardt

A biography by an important early French critic of the European Gypsy guitarist who brought a unique, lyrical sensibility to the jazz of the 1930s, and who often recorded with American musicians such as Coleman Hawkins and Rex Stewart

0-306-76057-6 DA CAPO $32.00

Artie **Shaw**

The Trouble with Cinderella

The entertaining colorful autobiography of a much-married, highly individualistic clarinetist and bandleader

1-56474-020-X FITHIAN PRESS PB $12.95

David **Hajdu**

Lush Life: A Biography of Billy Strayhorn

This well-researched biography has already removed the pianist and composer Billy Strayhorn (1915-1967) out from under the shadow of his mentor and long-time collaborator, Duke Ellington. Hajdu reaffirms Strayhorn's as a composer in his own right, and sensitively handles Strayhorn's homosexuality, his "lush life" in Harlem and Paris, and his intimate, symbiotic relationship with Ellington

0-374-19438-6 FS&G........................$27.50

Willie "The Lion" **Smith** & George **Hoefer**

Music on My Mind: The Memoirs of an American Pianist

Autobiography of the legendary pianist, a giant of the stride piano school of the 1920s

FOREWORD BY DUKE ELLINGTON

0-306-70684-9 DA CAPO $37.50

A.B. **Spellman**

Four Lives in the Bebop Business

Four realistic portraits of musicians of the 1950s (some becoming major figures in the 1960s) and their tribulations: Ornette Coleman, Cecil Taylor, Jackie McLean, and Herbie Nichols. Outstanding

See also **BEBOP AND POST-BOP** under **SURVEYS OF JAZZ HISTORY**

0-87910-042-7 PROSCENIUM PB........................$13.95

James **Lester**

Too Marvelous for Words: The Life and Genius of Art Tatum

0-19-508365-2 OXFORD $25.00

Jay D. **Smith** & Len **Guttridge**

Jack Teagarden: The Story of a Jazz Maverick

Teagarden was one of the most important trombonists in early jazz, and a fine singer with extremely natural blues phrasing

0-306-80322-4 DA CAPO PB $9.95

Ed **Kirkeby**

Ain't Misbehavin': The Story of Fats Waller

The master of stride piano, and a popular entertainer in the 1930s, Waller composed such perennially popular songs as "Honeysuckle Rose," "Squeeze Me," and "Ain't Misbehavin' "

0-306-80015-2 DA CAPO PB........................$11.95

Lewis **Porter**, editor

A Lester Young Reader

See also **ATHLETES AND ENTERTAINERS** under **BLACK VOICES, BLACK LIVES** under **AFRICAN-AMERICAN STUDIES** in **HISTORY OF THE AMERICAS**

1-56098-065-6 SMITHSONIAN PB........................$19.95

Frank **Buchmann-Moller**

You Just Fight For Your Life: The Story of Lester Young

The most thorough biography of Prez yet written, full of meticulously documented details about his early years, his career with the Basic band, his grim experiences in the military, and the postwar period

0-275-93265-6 PRAEGER $24.95

I developed my saxophone to play a sound like an alto, make a sound like a tenor, make sound like a bass and everything, and I'm not through with it all yet. That's why they get all trapped up. They say: "Goddam, I never heard Prez play like this!" That's the way I want them. That's "modern," dig? Fuck what you played back in 49. It's what you play today. So that's why they get lost and walked out. Do you play the same thing every day? In my mind, the way I play, I try not to be a repeater pencil, you dig? I'm always loosening spaces, laying out, or something like that. I don't think you'll catch me like that, playing like "Lester Leaps In," or something like that. That's my crip, you know, that type of shit—*Lester Young*

YOU JUST FIGHT FOR YOUR LIFE: THE STORY OF LESTER YOUNG

Luc **Delannoy**

Pres: The Story of Lester Young

1-55728-264-1 ARKANSAS PB $16.00

Singers

Will **Friedwald**

Jazz Singing: America's Great Voices from Bessie Smith to Bebop and Beyond

A fan's notes-but what a fan! and what good notes. Save this book, it is in danger of going out of print

0-306-80712-2 DA CAPO PB $16.95

John **Chilton**

Billie's Blues

Holiday's phrasing and sensibility made her one of the most influential of all jazz singers

0-306-80363-1 DA CAPO PB $13.95

Donald **Clarke**

Wishing on the Moon: The Life and Times of Billie Holiday

A short, tragic life but an enduring musical tradition, Lady Day has long held a particular place in the American mythos. Clarke peers behind the myths to capture Holiday from her childhood on the streets of Baltimore to her years of fame in Harlem. With his vivid recreation of four decades of the jazz world, Clarke permits us a clear and unromantic view of a great American musician

0-670-83771-7 VIKING........................$24.95

Billie **Holiday** & William **Dufty**

Lady Sings the Blues

A raw, powerful autobiography

0-14-006762-0 PENGUIN PB........................$10.95

Anita **O'Day** & George **Eells**

High Times, Hard Times

0-87910-118-0 LIMELIGHT PB........................$15.00

Stuart **Nicholson**

Ella Fitzgerald: A Biography of the First Lady of Jazz

0-306-80642-8 DACAPO PB $14.95

Reference

John **Chilton**

Who's Who of Jazz

Biographical entries; very useful and authoritative

0-306-80243-0 DA CAPO PB $13.95

Richard **Cook** & Brian **Morton**

The Penguin Guide to Jazz on CD

The most thorough and erudite CD buying guide for jazz listeners on the market. Each CD is well-annotated and rated within a one- to five-star ranking system

0-14-051368-X PENGUIN PB $23.95

The Penguin Guide to Jazz on CD, LP & Cassette

The new *Penguin Guide* will help readers answer almost any question about jazz. It offers an encyclopedic cataloging of currently available recordings, a critical assessment of their relation to the artists's other work, a full line-up of musicians appearing on each, accurate label and number details, and an authoritative critical rating

0-14-015364-0 PENGUIN PB $22.50

Leonard **Feather**

The Encyclopedia of Jazz

Important book of biographies, musical examples, and fascinating peripheral material; covers period through 1960

0-306-80214-7 DA CAPO PB $22.95

Leonard **Feather** & Ira **Gitler**

The Encyclopedia of Jazz in the '70s

A further update

INTRODUCTION BY QUINCY JONES

0-306-80290-2 DA CAPO PB $17.95

Max **Harrison** & others

The Essential Jazz Records, Volume One: Ragtime to Swing

Idiosyncratic, exhaustively annotated, opinionated guide by three British critics

0-306-80326-7 DA CAPO PB $14.95

Barry **Kernfeld**, editor

The New Grove Dictionary of Jazz

Performers, jazz terms, styles, festivals, instruments. Previously available only as a two-volume limited edition, now available to everyone in a one-volume, affordable edition. "A must for every serious jazz lover"
—Dizzy Gillespie

0-312-11357-9 ST. MARTIN'S $50.00

Len **Lyons**

The 101 Best Jazz Albums: A History of Jazz on Records

0-688-08720-5 MORROW PB $14.95

Tom **Piazza**

The Guide to Classic Recorded Jazz

0-87745-489-2 IOWA PB $22.95

Frederick Jr. **Ramsey**

A Guide to Long-Play Jazz Records

Interesting mainly to hard-core collectors and researchers, this surveys records from 1948-1953

0-306-70891-4 DA CAPO $37.50

Rock

General Criticism and Consumer Guides

Lester **Bangs**

Psychotic Reactions and Carburetor Dung: An Anthology of Writings by Lester Bangs

The critics' critic, who died in 1982 at age 33, was funny and illuminating

EDITED BY GREIL MARCUS

0-679-72045-6 VINTAGE PB $16.00

Julie **Burchill** & Tony **Parsons**

"The Boy Looked At Johnny": The Obituary of Rock and Roll

"It's either the best expose of rock I've ever read—a cult book?—or it's the biggest con that's ever been published"—*Tribune* (UK). It's all three

INTRODUCTION BY LENNY KAYE

0-571-12992-7 FABER PB $9.95

Simon **Frith**

Sound Effects: Youth, Leisure and the Politics of Rock 'n' Roll

Acclaimed, influential study of rock and roll's cultural and economic impact

0-394-74811-5 RANDOM HOUSE PB $11.54

Clinton **Heylin**, editor

The Penguin Book of Rock and Roll Writing

"A resounding success"— Chicago Sun-Times

0-14-016836-2 PENGUIN PB $14.95

Greil **Marcus**

Mystery Train: Images of America in Rock 'n' Roll Music

A revised edition of what is probably the single most influential work of rock criticism

0-452-26712-9 PLUME PB $14.95

Simon **Reynolds** & Joy **Press**

The Sex Revolts: Gender, Rebellion and Rock 'n Roll

0-674-80273-X HARVARD PB $15.95

History and Profiles

Pamela **Des Barres**

I'm with the Band: Confessions of a Groupie

Charming, funny, and surprisingly likable memoirs of an ex-groupie

0-515-09712-8 JOVE PB $4.99

Gillian G. **Gaar**

She's a Rebel: The History of Women in Rock and Roll

The first history of women in rock, an account that covers everyone from Janis Martin, the female Elvis, to classic pop songwriter Carole King; from punk crooner Siouxie Sioux to the postmodern Cramps. "Smart and lively... Gaar brings feminist savvy to her study, and that itself is a milestone in rock history"
—*Entertainment Weekly*

1-87806-708-7 SEAL PB $16.95

Charlie **Gillett**

The Sound of the City: The Rise of Rock and Roll

0-306-80683-5 DA CAPO PB $16.95

George **Gimarc**

Punk Diary, 1970-1979

0-312-11048-0 ST. MARTIN'S BOOK WITH CD . $21.95

Clinton **Heylin**

From the Velvets to the Voidoids: A Pre-Punk History for a Post-Punk World

0-14-017970-4 PENGUIN PB $14.95

Greil **Marcus**

Ranters and Crowd Pleasers: Punk in Pop Music, 1977-92

0-385-41721-7 ANCHOR PB $14.00

Dave **Marsh**

Louie Louie: The History and Mythology of the World's Most Famous Rock 'n'Roll Song

1-56282-865-7 HYPERION $19.95

0-7868-8028-7 HYPERION PB $12.95

George **Martin** & William **Person**

With a Little Help From My Friends: The Making of Sgt. Pepper

0-316-54783-2 LITTLE, BROWN $22.95

Legs **McNeil** & Gillian **McCain**

Please Kill Me: The Uncensored Oral History of Punk

"...true to its subject, *Please Kill Me* is lurid, insolent, disorderly, funny, sometimes gross, sometimes mean and occasionally touching"
—*NY Times*

0-8021-1588-8 GROVE $25.00

Robert **Palmer**

Rock & Roll: An Unruly History

0-517-70050-6 HARMONY $40.00

Jim **Miller**, editor

The Rolling Stone Illustrated History of Rock & Roll

Heavy on facts, strong on analysis, and amply illustrated, the best historical overview to date charts rock's history in over 80 critical essays

0-679-73728-6 RANDOM HOUSE PB $25.95

Lucy **O'Brien**

She Bop: The Definitive History of Women in Rock, Pop and Soul

0-14-025155-3 PENGUIN PB $14.95

Jeff **Pike**

The Death of Rock 'n' Roll: Untimely Demises, Morbid Preoccupations, and Forecasts of Doom in Rock Music

Explores the death-rock connection, from the poisoning of the great "devil possessed" bluesman Robert Johnson in the '30s, to the asphyxiation of Jimi Hendrix, the murder of Lennon, and the obsessively morbid Elvis sightings that plague the American psyche

0-571-19808-2 FABER PB $14.95

Amy **Raphael**

GRRRLS: Women Rewrite Back

British journalist interviews 14 contemporary female rockers including American groovettes Courtney Love, Liz Phair, Kim Gordon, and Tanya Donnelly

See also **MUSIC AND THEATER** under **ARTS AND LETTERS** under **WOMEN'S STUDIES** in **SOCIAL STUDIES**

0-312-14109-2 ST. MARTIN'S PB $12.95

Timothy W. **Ryback**

Rock Around the Bloc: A History of Rock Music in Eastern Europe and the Soviet Union

0-19-505633-7 OXFORD $25.00

Jon **Savage**

England's Dreaming: Anarchy, Sex Pistols, Punk Rock and Beyond

0-312-08774-8 MORROW PB $17.95

Joe **Smith**

Off the Record: An Oral History of Popular Music

Record company executive and longtime insider Smith presents the history of popular music in a series of anecdotes from Paul McCartney, Bob Dylan, Tony Bennett, Woody Herman, Jerry Lee Lewis, Mick Jagger, Ray Charles, and others

0-446-39090-9 WARNER PB $14.95

Ian **Whitcomb**

After the Ball: Pop Music from Rag to Rock

A '60s rock star's enjoyable examination of pop music in the pre-rock years

0-87910-063-X LIMELIGHT PB $17.95

Timothy **White**

Rock Lives: Profiles & Interviews

0-8050-1861-1 HOLT PB $16.95

Music to My Ears: The Billboard Essays 1992-1996

0-8050-3975-9 HOLT $27.50

Rap, R&B, Motown, and Soul

For related reading, see BLACK VOICES, BLACK LIVES under AFRICAN-AMERICAN STUDIES in HISTORY OF THE AMERICAS

Houston A. **Baker**, Jr.

Black Studies, Rap, and the Academy

See also **ARTISTS AND LITERARY FIGURES** under **BLACK VOICES, BLACK LIVES** under **AFRICAN-AMERICAN STUDIES** in **HISTORY OF THE AMERICAS**

0-226-03520-4 CHICAGO $16.95

David **Bianco**

Heat Wave: The Motown Fact Book

Every Motown lover's dream: complete discographies, illustrated artist and label principal profiles

0-87650-204-4 PIERIAN $55.00

Stanley **Booth**

Rhythm Oil: A Journey Through the Music of the American South

Booth starts out in the Mississippi Delta with an account of Robert Johnson's crossroads run-in with the Devil, and goes on to bluesman John Hurt's funeral. He visits Memphis, a town still in the thrall of the Civil War, where he meditates on the lives and influence of Elvis Presley, B.B. King, Otis Redding, and James Brown. "An indispensable volume for anyone who cares about American Popular music"
—*Chicago Tribune*

0-679-74174-7 VINTAGE PB $12.00

Gerald **Early**

One Nation Under A Groove: Motown and American Culture

0-88001-379-6 ECCO $17.00
0-88001-472-5 ECCO PB $12.00

S.H. **Fernando**

The New Beats: Exploring the Music, Culture, and Attitudes of Hip-Hop

0-385-47119-X ANCHOR PB $14.95

Ted **Fox**

Showtime At the Apollo

Fascinating history of the major Harlem venue for black performing artists in New York City

See also **THE JAZZ SCENE** under **JAZZ**

0-306-80503-0 DA CAPO PB $13.95

Nelson **George**

The Death of Rhythm and Blues

0-452-26697-1 OBELISK PB $11.95

Seduced: The Life and Times of a One-Hit Wonder

0-399-14169-3 PUTNAM $23.95

Where Did Our Love Go?: The Rise and Fall of the Motown Sound

An informative history of the label, which clearly empathizes with those out of the spotlight

0-312-01109-1 ST. MARTIN'S PB $9.95

Berry **Gordy**

To Be Loved: The Music, the Magic, the Memories of Motown—An Autobiography

0-446-51523-X WARNER $22.95
0-446-60236-1 WARNER PB $6.99

Hugh **Gregory**

Soul Music A-Z

0-306-80643-6 DA CAPO PB $17.95

Peter **Guralnick**

Feel Like Going Home: Portraits in Blues and Rock 'n' Roll

0-06-097175-4 HARPERPERENNIAL PB $14.00

Lost Highway: Journeys and Arrivals of American Musicians

0-06-097174-6 HARPERPERENNIAL PB $15.00

Searching for Robert Johnson

0-525-24801-3 OBELISK $15.00

Sweet Soul Music: Rhythm and Blues and the Southern Dream of Freedom

Must reading for every serious rock fan, Guralnick's account of soul music's rise and fall—artistic and economic—is revealing

0-06-096049-3 HARPERPERENNIAL PB $18.00

William Eric **Perkins**, editor

Droppin' Science: Critical Essays on Rap Music and Hip Hop Culture

1-56639-362-0 TEMPLE PB $18.95

Tricia **Rose**

Black Noise: Rap Music and Black Culture in Contemporary America

0-8195-6275-0 WESLEYAN PB $15.95

Michael **Small**

Break It Down: The Inside Story from the New Leaders of Rap

0-8065-1361-6 CITADEL PB $16.95

Eileen **Southern**

The Music of Black Americans: A History

0-393-03843-2 NORTON $35.00

David **Toop**

Rap Attack, No.2: African Rap to Global Hip Hop

1-85242-243-2 SERPENT'S TAIL PB $17.99

Rickey **Vincent**
Funk: The Music, the People, and the Rhythm of the One
0-312-13499-1 ST. MARTIN'S PB $15.95

Jerry **Wexler**
Rhythm and Blues
"A terrific read…Some of the juiciest music history one could hope to find"
—Kirkus Reviews
0-312-11376-5 ST. MARTIN'S PB $14.95

Jerry **Wexler** & David **Ritz**
Rhythm and the Blues: A Life in American Music
"Wexler's account of how he talked his way into the co-ownership of Atlantic records and went on to produce some of the century's great pop music makes for some of the juiciest music history one could hope to find. A superlative read"—*Kirkus Reviews*
0-679-40102-4 KNOPF $25.00

Groups and Individual Artists

Brad **Elliott**
Surf's Up: Beach Boys on Record, 1961-1981
Extensive discography
1-56075-022-7 PIERIAN $39.50
0-87650-118-8 PIERIAN $34.50

Domenic **Priore**
Look! Listen! Vibrate! Smile !
The Beach Boys during the period they made *Smile,* a legendary recording which was never released as originally envisioned, but which gave birth to the band's biggest selling single, "Good Vibrations." This book collects virtually everything that has been published on the subject
0-86719-417-0 LAST GASP $19.95

Timothy **White**
The Nearest Faraway Place: Brian Wilson, the Beach Boys, and the Southern California Experience
0-8050-4702-6 HOLT PB $15.95

Harry **Benson**
The Beatles: In the Beginning
Benson's unique eye and marvelous photographic talent defined the classic images of the fab four
0-87663-642-3 UNIVERSE $24.95

Peter **Brown** & Steven **Gaines**
The Love You Make: An Insider's Story of the Beatles
Sensationalistic, best-selling account by longtime Beatles associate Brown. Filled with hot gossip
0-451-12797-8 NEW AMERICAN LIBRARY PB....$5.99

Harry **Castleman** & Walter **Podrazik**
The Beatles Again
Supplements and updates *All Together Now*
0-87650-089-0 PIERIAN $32.00

Barbara **Fenick**
Collecting the Beatles: An Introduction and Price Guide to the Fab Four Collectibles, Records, and Memorabilia
0-87650-176-5 PIERIAN $34.50

The Beatles

Geoffrey **Giuliano**
The Beatles Album: Thirty Years of Music and Memorabilia
0-14-023777-1 STUDIO PB $18.95

The Lost Beatles Interviews
Giuliano has found a wealth of previously unknown interviews—candid, revealing, and funny—with the Beatles and their contemporaries: Clapton, Ono, Donovan, Ginger Baker, and more
0-525-93818-4 DUTTON $23.95

Bill **Harry**
The Ultimate Beatles Encyclopedia
History, gossip, fact, and myth are all sorted out here in more than 700 pages. This volume includes everything you ever wanted to know about the Fab Four and their music. Over 1,500 entries, 300 photographs, and memorabilia
1-56282-814-2 HYPERION $35.00
0-7868-8071-6 HYPERION PB $19.95

Philip **Norman**
Shout!: The Beatles in Their Generation
An international best-seller
See also **20TH-CENTURY BIOGRAPHY** under **GREAT BRITAIN AND IRELAND** in **WORLD HISTORY AND CURRENT AFFAIRS**
0-684-83067-1 FIRESIDE PB $13.00

Carol D. **Terry**
Here, There and Everywhere: The First International Beatles Bibliography, 1962-1982
0-87650-163-3 PIERIAN $34.50

John **Howell**
David Byrne
1-56025-031-3 THUNDER'S MOUTH PB $11.95

Ray **Charles** & David **Katz**
Brother Ray: Ray Charles' Own Story
An updated edition of the great musician's frank memoirs
0-306-80482-4 DACAPPO $13.95

Christofer **Sanford**
Kurt Cobain
The first full-length biography of the late leader of Nirvana
0-786-70394-6 CARROLL & GRAF PB $13.95

Ray **Davies**
X-Ray: The Unauthorized Autobiography
"An extraordinary 'unauthorized autobiography'…[that] goes straight into the canon of rock'n'roll mythology"—*Esquire*
0-87951-664-X PENGUIN PB $15.95

Bob **Dylan**
Lyrics: 1962-1985
Well-produced collection of Dylan's lyrics
0-394-54278-9 KNOPF $35.00

Boy **George** & Spencer **Bright**
Take it Like a Man: The Autobiography of Boy George
0-06-017368-8 HARPERCOLLINS $25.00
0-283-99217-4 SIDGWICK & JACKSON $42.50

Charles S. **Murray**
Crosstown Traffic: Jimi Hendrix and the Post-War Rock 'n' Roll Revolution
0-312-06324-5 ST. MARTIN'S PB $9.95

John **Goldrosen** & John **Beecher**
Remembering Buddy: The Definitive Biography of Buddy Holly
Thoroughly researched tribute to Holly's brief but influential career, with a wealth of rare photos
0-306-80715-7 DA CAPO PB $18.95

Carol **Terry**
Sequins and Shades: The Michael Jackson Reference Guide
With six indexes, complete US and UK discographies, and bibliographies, the ultimate reference work
0-87650-205-2 PIERIAN $39.50

Laura **Joplin**
Love, Janis
An intimate look at the outrageous rock star who set the tone for a generation of women singers, written with affection and insight by her sister Laura. Using her letters home and personal knowledge of Janis's early days in Texas and San Francisco, Laura Joplin gives us a portrait of her sister as we've never seen her—a troubled yet

determined young woman who was present at the ground-breaking for the new pop culture
0-679-41605-6 VILLARD $22.50

June 6, 1966
Mother & Dad…
With a great deal of trepidation, I bring the news. I'm in San Francisco. Now let me explain—when I got to Austin, I talked to Travis Rivers who gave me a spiel about my singing w/a band out here. Seems Chet Helms, oldfriend, now is Mr. Big in S.F. Owns 3 big working Rock & Roll bands with bizarre names like Captain Beefheart & his Magic Band, Big Brother & the Holding Co. etc. Well, Big Brother et al needs a vocalist. So I called Chet to talk to him about it. He encouraged me to come out—seems the whole city had gone rock & roll (and it has!) and assured me fame & fortune. I told him I was worried about being hung up out here w/no way back & he agreed to furnish me w/ a bus ticket back home if I did just come & try. So I came.
…I'm awfully sorry to be such a disappointment to you….Guess I'll write more when I have more news, until then, address all criticism to the above address. And please believe that you can't possibly want for me to be a winner more than I do.
LOVE, JANIS

John **Lennon**
John Lennon: Drawings, Performances, Films
A vivid documentation of John Lennon as artist, poet, designer, photographer, and performance artist. Lavishly illustrated and containing much material never-before seen, this fascinating book shows that in many ways, Lennon's artistic life did not end, but took off with the breakup of the Beatles
3-89322-734-2 D.A.P. PB $39.95

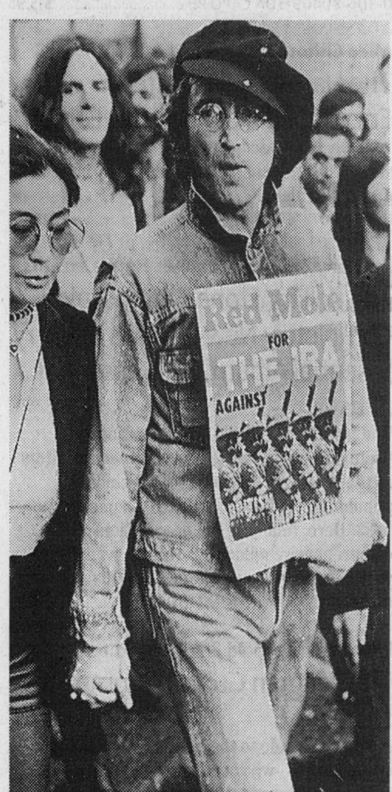

John Lennon
(credit: ©Red Mole/Courtesy of Tariq Ali)

Elizabeth **Thomson** & David **Gutman**, editors
The Lennon Companion: 25 Years of Comment
A collection of 60 essays and articles from a wide range of sources (a few written especially for this collection)
0-02-872595-6 SCHIRMER PB $15.95

Douglas **Thompson**
Madonna Revealed: The Unauthorized Biography
0-8439-3319-4 LEISURE PB $4.99

Paul **Taylor**, editor
Impresario: Malcolm McLaren and the British New Wave
0-262-70035-2 MIT PB $14.95

Jim **Morrison**
The Lords and the New Creatures
Posthumous collection of poetry. He considered himself a serious writer first, then a rock star
0-671-21044-0 SIMON & SCHUSTER PB $9.00

Wilderness: The Lost Writing of Jim Morrison
0-679-72622-5 VINTAGE PB $11.00

Jerry **Hopkins** & Daniel **Sugerman**
No One Here Gets Out Alive
This top-selling, sensational biography of The Doors and the group's late charismatic leader, Jim Morrison, helped fuel their revival and crystallize the myth
0-446-34268-8 WARNER PB $5.95

Marc **Eliot**
Death of a Rebel: A Biography of Phil Ochs
0-531-15111-5 CITADEL PB $18.95

Peter **Guralnick**
Last Train to Memphis: The Rise of Elvis Presley
Never will the epic of Elvis cease to enthrall, from his humble beginnings to his definition of a style of music, to his ascension as an American icon. Guralnick, called "a thinking man's music writer" by the *Boston Globe* and "a national resource" by Nat Hentoff, has produced a graceful, literate, biography "The first volume in two in what is bound to be the definitive biography of the King….A serious, musically literate, and historically attuned biography. An American epic that belongs on every shelf"—*Kirkus Reviews*
See also HISTORY AND PROFILES
0-316-33220-8 LITTLE, BROWN $24.95
0-316-33225-9 LITTLE, BROWN PB $14.95

Jerry **Hopkins**
Elvis: The Final Years
One of the first accounts of the King's last years. Still a good read, despite subsequent new info
0-425-09880-X BERKLEY PB $5.99

Ernst **Jorgensen**
Reconsider Baby: The Definitive Elvis Sessionography, 1954-1977
0-87650-220-6 PIERIAN $28.50

Jerry **Leiber** & Bob **Spitz**
A Hound Dog's Life: Gospel, Half-Truths, Rumors, and Outrageous Lies
A heartfelt and hilarious memoir from the writer and producer who has authored songs for Elvis, Sinatra, Mama Cass, and Cher, and whose *Smokey Joe's Cafe* became a hit Broadway show. Chronicling his remarkable career and telling tales that range from Mob shakedowns to a night-time drag race with James Dean, this extraordinary memoir is a virtual guide to the history of pop music
0-06-017436-6 HARPERCOLLINS $25.00

Greil **Marcus**
Dead Elvis: A Chronicle of a Cultural Obsession
The many levels of Elvis' survival after death, from Graceland to supermarket tabloids to underground comics, charted by the author of *Mystery Train* and *Lipstick Traces*
0-385-41718-7 DOUBLEDAY PB $25.00

Richard **Peabody** & Lucinda **Ebersole**
Mondo Elvis: A Collection of Fiction and Poetry about the King
0-312-10505-3 ST. MARTIN'S PB $12.95

Kevin **Quain**
The Elvis Reader: Texts and Sources on the King of Rock'n'roll
The Director of Toronto's Institute for Elvis Studies has assembled an uncompromising and astute collection of writings on the ultimate pop icon: Elvis the Myth, Elvis the Southerner, Elvis the Metaphysical, Elvis the Sacred and Profane. Includes pieces by W.P. Kinsella, Don DeLillo, Linda Ray Pratt, and Richard Corliss, to name but a few
0-312-06966-9 ST. MARTIN'S PB $13.95

Elvis Presley

Ger J. **Rijff**
Long Lonely Highway: A 1950s Elvis Scrapbook
0-87650-237-0 PIERIAN $28.50

Red **West**

Elvis: What Happened?

Published just weeks before Presley's death in 1977, three ex-employees expose Elvis's drug abuse in this so-called "bodyguard" book

0-345-30635-X BALLANTINE PB........................$4.99

Victor **Bockris**

Transformer: The Lou Reed Story

The biographer of Warhol, Burroughs, and Keith Richards turns his attention to Lou Reed

0-684-80366-6 SIMON & SCHUSTER...............$25.00

Martha **Reeves** & Mark **Bego**

Dancing in the Street: Confessions of a Motown Diva

0-7868-6024-3 HYPERION $22.95

0-7868-8094-5 HYPERION PB $14.95

Stanley **Booth**

The True Adventures of the Rolling Stones

Booth began this in 1969 as an authorized group biography. A personal firsthand account of the Stones during the American tour that culminated in Altamont

0-394-74110-2 RANDOM HOUSE PB................$11.00

A.E. **Hotchner**

Blown Away: The Rolling Stones and the Death of the Sixties

0-685-47237-X SIMON & SCHUSTER...............$21.95

Mick Jagger

Jessica **MacPhail**

Yesterday's Papers: The Rolling Stones in Print, 1964-1984

0-87650-209-5 PIERIAN $39.50

Ronnie **Spector** & Vince **Waldron**

Be My Baby: How I Survived Mascara, Miniskirts, and Madness

Spector writes of her career in the Ronettes and after, and her disastrous marriage to Phil Spector. "Ronnie went through some tough times, but the important thing is she survived, and she's still around to tell the tale… It's an amazing story"—Cher

0-517-57993-6 CROWN.....................................$19.95

Fred **Dannen**

Bruce Springsteen, the Rolling Stone File: The Ultimate Compendium of Interviews, Articles, Facts, and Opinions from the Files of Rolling Stone

0-7868-8153-4 HYPERION PB...........................$12.95

Robert **Hilburn**

Springsteen

A safe, somewhat bland account of the Boss's career. Recommended for those new to Bruce

0-684-18456-7 SCRIBNERS..............................$29.95

Dave **Marsh**

Born to Run: The Bruce Springsteen Story

An informative best-seller, this 1981 revision covers Springsteen's career up to *The River* LP

1-56025-102-6 THUNDER'S MOUTH PB..........$13.95

Sandy **Troy**

Captain Trips: A Biography of Jerry Garcia

"The life and work of the rock legend, from childhood, through the Summer of Love, three marriages, and the legendary career of the Dead. Troy has put together an exhaustive biography of Garcia the man, the musician, the cultural hero, the bon vivant.[His] well-documented profile adds much to our background knowledge of an influential cultural figure"—*Booklist*

1-56025-090-9 THUNDER'S MOUTH PB..........$13.95

Tina **Turner** & Kurt **Loder**

I, Tina

A frank autobiography of the '60s soul star whose dazzling 1983 comeback was a personal and professional triumph

0-380-70097-2 AVON PB...................................$5.99

Ben **Watson**

Frank Zappa: The Negative Dialectics of Poodle Play

Conscientious, sometimes labored explication of the cultural significance of the founder of the Mothers of Invention

0-312-11918-6 ST. MARTIN'S $27.50

0-312-14124-6 ST. MARTIN'S PB $17.95

Dave **Marsh**

Before I Get Old: The Story of The Who

Marsh combines a fan's passion, a critic's insight, and a historian's quest for the facts in this important account of the English group

0-312-07155-8 ST. MARTIN'S PB......................$10.95

Mary **Wilson** & others

Dreamgirl: My Life as a Supreme

Best-selling autobiography of an original Supreme. "Never before has a Motown veteran spoken out as a first-person witness from inside Hitsville"—*NY Times*

0-312-21959-8 ST. MARTIN'S $16.95

Reference

Mark **Bego**

The Rock & Roll Almanac

0-02-860432-6 MACMILLAN PB........................$12.95

David **Bianco**, editor

Who's New Wave in Music: An Illustrated Encyclopedia, 1976-1982

0-87650-173-0 PIERIAN $45.00

Fred **Bronson**

The Billboard Book of Number One Hits: 2nd Edition

The stories behind every single to hit the top of the chart from 1955 to 1987

0-8230-8298-9 BILLBOARD PB $21.95

Robert **Christgau**

Christgau's Record Guide: Rock Albums of the '80s

Christgau's compressed, highly informed style is fully in evidence in these 2,800 capsule reviews

See also **OTHER** under **REFERENCE** in **BUSINESS AND REFERENCE**

0-306-80582-0 DA CAPO PB...............................$17.95

Rock Albums of the '70s: A Critical Guide

"[Christgau] can say in 50 words what others may need 500 to 5,000 words to say… You'll not find a reviewer who so passionately suffers to comprehend the essence of even the most superfluous recordings"—*Newsday*

See also **OTHER** under **REFERENCE** in **BUSINESS AND REFERENCE**

0-306-80409-3 DA CAPO PB $15.95

Mike **Clifford**

The Harmony Illustrated Encyclopedia of Rock: 6th Edition

Lavishly illustrated, featuring Pete Frame's wonderful genealogy charts. Reliable, but with an English slant

0-517-59078-6 HARMONY PB $19.00

Anthony **DeCurtis** & James **Henke**, editors

The Rolling Stone Album Guide: Completely New Reviews of Every Essential Album, Every Essential Artist

The last *Rolling Stone* guide to records—a useful star-rating guide written by contributors to the magazine and covering all kinds of popular music from folk to rap—came out in 1983. Here, finally, is the new edition: a comprehensive guide to currently available CDs, written with personality and authority

0-679-73729-4 RANDOM HOUSE PB $20.00

Edward **Greenfield** & others, editors

The Penguin Guide to Compact Discs 1996

A 512-page guide to the best in music and the spoken word—who conducted whom, which guitarist performed the hot tiff on the B-side, and which classics are now available in new formats

0-14-051367-1 PENGUIN PB.............................$23.95

Michael **Heatley**, editor

The Ultimate Encyclopedia of Rock

The music that has been too loud for 40 years matures into middle age with a comprehensive A to Z encyclopedia. Band bios, artist profiles, historic musical events, behind-the-scenes tales, and rare photos, make this an invaluable sourcebook for music lovers

0-06-271576-3 HARPERCOLLINS PB $40.00

Barry **Lazell**, editor

Movers and Shakers: An A-Z of the People Who Made Rock Happen

0-8230-7609-1 BILLBOARD PB $19.95

Linda **McCartney**

Linda Mccartney's Sixties: Portrait of an Era

This bestselling photo album, now available in paperback, gives any fan of rock a unique insider's perspective. Famous rock legends like Jagger, Hendrix, the Grateful Dead, and, not surprisingly, the Beatles, are captured with unique intimacy

See also **SPECIAL TOPICS** under **PHOTOGRAPHY** in **ART**

INTRODUCTION BY PAUL MCCARTNEY

0-8212-2056-X BULFINCH PB $19.95

The Beatles

Ira **Robbins**, editor

The New Trouser Press Record Guide

Indispensable guide to a wide range of newer genres (hardcore, rap, punk, electronic), edited by the founder of the sadly missed *Trouser Press* magazine

0-02-036361-3 COLLIER PB $20.00

Linda J. **Sandahl**

Rock Films: A Viewer's Guide to Three Decades of Musicals, Concerts, Documentaries and Soundtracks

See also **GENRES AND THEMES** under **FILM**

9990797692 BOOK SALES PB $4.98

0-8160-1576-7 FACTS ON FILE PB $14.95

Joel **Whitburn**

The Billboard Book of Top 40 Albums

0-8230-7534-6 WATSON-GUPTILL PB $19.95

Visual Books

Paul **Grushkin**

The Art of Rock: Posters from Presley to Punk

See also **POSTERS** under **ILLUSTRATION AND POPULAR GRAPHICS** in **ART**

1-55859-606-2 ABBEVILLE PB $11.95

Charles **Hirshberg** & The Editors of *Life Magazine*

Elvis: A Celebration in Pictures

0-446-52020-9 WARNER $22.95

The Music Industry

Fredric **Dannen**

Hit Men: Power Brokers & Fast Money Inside the Music Business

The mechanisms and machinations of the recording industry seen from the inside, with a wickedly cold eye: a brilliant piece of reporting

0-679-73061-3 VINTAGE PB $15.00

Bruce **Haring**

Off The Charts: Ruthless Days and Reckless Nights Inside the Music Industry

1-55972-316-5 BIRCH LANE $19.95

Diane Sward **Rapaport**

How to Make and Sell Your Own Record: 3rd Edition

The best guide of its type available

0-13-402314-5 PRENTICE HALL PB $29.95

World Music: Other Traditions

African Music

Francis **Bebey**

African Music: A People's Art

An authoritative and informative overview of native African musical styles, instruments, and traditions, with an essential pre-Afro-pop discography

TRANSLATED BY JOSEPHINE BENNETT

0-88208-050-4 CHICAGO REVIEW PB $9.95

Wolfgang **Bender**

Sweet Mother: Modern African Music

TRANSLATED BY WOLFGANG FREIS

0-226-04254-5 CHICAGO PB $17.95

Joseph H. **Nketia**

The Music of Africa

0-393-09249-6 NORTON PB $13.95

Paul F. **Berliner**

The Soul of Mbira: Music and Traditions of the Shona People of Zimbabwe: With an Appendix, Building and Playing a Shona Karimba

0-226-04379-7 CHICAGO PB $14.95

John M. **Chernoff**

African Rhythm and African Sensibility: Aesthetics and Social Action in African Musical Idioms

Travelogue and sociological investigation, based on travels in Ghana in the early 1970s

See also **ART** under **SPECIALIZED STUDIES** under **ANTHROPOLOGY** in **SOCIAL STUDIES**

See also **RELIGION AND CULTURE** under **AFRICA** in **WORLD HISTORY AND CURRENT AFFAIRS**

0-226-10345-5 CHICAGO PB $13.95

John **Collins**

Music Makers of West Africa

The explosive development of contemporary African pop styles such as juju, highlife, and Afro-beat over the past two decades

0-89410-075-0 THREE CONTINENTS $20.00

West African Pop Roots

0-87722-916-3 TEMPLE PB $19.95

Graeme **Ewens**

Africa O-Ye!: A Celebration Of African Music

A profusely illustrated survey

0-306-80461-1 DA CAPO $27.95

Ronnie **Graham**

The Da Capo Guide to Contemporary African Music

For both layman and expert, a reliable reference on modern African music, arranged by country, region, and artist, with a good index

See also **RELIGION AND CULTURE** under **AFRICA** in **WORLD HISTORY AND CURRENT AFFAIRS**

0-306-80325-9 DA CAPO PB $13.95

Louis **Sarno**

Song From the Forest: My Life among the Ba-Benjelle Pygmies

The haunting music of the Ba-Benjelle has acquired, ironically in view of their own endangered position, a ubiquitous influence on pop music in recent years

0-395-61331-0 HOUGHTON MIFFLIN $22.95

Christopher Alan **Waterman**

Juju: A Social History and Ethnography of an African Popular Music

The evolution of Nigeria's great popular music form, from the 1930s to its present-day international success through such artists as Sunny Ade and Ebenezer Obey. Waterman's detailed study includes maps, photographs, musical transcriptions, and interviews with musicians

0-226-87465-6 CHICAGO PB $19.95

Music of the Americas

David P. **Appleby**

The Music of Brazil

Discusses—from a decidedly Western perspective—traditional musical forms as they relate to more conventional composers such as Villa-Lobos

0-292-75111-7 TEXAS PB $12.95

Barbara **Browning**

Samba: Resistance in Motion

A longtime student of Brazillian dance, Browning arrives at a theoretical account of samba, capoiera and other dances of the carnival culture through her personal experiences. She suggests that the dancing body speaks, without words, an eloquent political rhetoric of protest

See also **SOCIAL AND FOLK DANCING** under **SPECIAL TOPICS** under **DANCE**

0-253-32867-5 INDIANA $29.95
0-253-20956-0 INDIANA PB $14.95

Stephen **Davis** & Peter **Simon**

Reggae Bloodlines

Precursor to Reggae International and first American attempt to grasp Jamaican music, covering artists from Toots and The Maytals to Bob Marley

0-306-80496-4 DA CAPO PB $16.95

Alma **Guillermoprieto**

Samba

An intimate look at the heart of Brazilian life. The author spent a year training in a village samba school in preparation for Rio's Carnival parade. "Eloquent and persuasive in bringing it all to life"—*New Yorker*

See also **SOUTH AMERICA** under **TRAVEL LITERATURE** in **FOOD, TRAVEL, AND LEISURE**

See also **SOCIAL AND FOLK DANCING** under **SPECIAL TOPICS** under **DANCE**

0-679-73256-X VINTAGE PB $12.00

Donald R. **Hill**

Calypso Calaloo: Early Carnival Music in Trinidad

0-8130-1221-X FLORIDA $49.95
0-8130-1222-8 FLORIDA PB $24.95

John Storm **Roberts**

The Latin Tinge: The Impact of Latin American Music on the United States

Documents 100 years of Caribbean musical traditions and their influence on current Western pop music

0-9614458-1-5 RIVERRUN PB $13.95

Jonathan **Runge**

Rum and Reggae: What's Hot and What's Not in the Caribbean

The unofficial bible for American travelers to the Caribbean, now revised and expanded to include every island in the magic sea. Runge descends into a volcano on St. Vincent's, parties nonstop at the carnival in Tobago, windsurfs off Barbados, and more

See also **CARIBBEAN AND LATIN AMERICA** under **GUIDES TO MEXICO, THE UNITED STATES, AND CANADA** under **TRAVEL GUIDES** in **FOOD, TRAVEL, AND LEISURE**

0-679-74716-8 RANDOM HOUSE PB $17.00
0-312-01509-7 RANDOM HOUSE PB $9.95

Stephen **Stuempfle**

The Steelband Movement: The Forging of a National Art in Trinidad and Tobago

0-8122-3329-8 PENNSYLVANIA $38.95
0-8122-1565-6 PENNSYLVANIA PB $16.95

Peter **Van Der Merwe**

Origins of the Popular Style: The Antecedents of Twentieth-Century Popular Music

Traces the roots of American popular music through European, African, and even Arabic traditions

See also **AMERICAN POPULAR MUSIC**

0-19-816305-3 CLARENDON PB $19.95

Anita M. **Waters**

Race, Class and Political Symbols: Rastafari and Reggae in Jamaican Politics

0-88738-632-6 TRANSACTION PB $19.95

Timothy **White**

Catch a Fire: The Life of Bob Marley, Revised Edition

A straightforward landmark portrait that clearly defines Marley's tremendous influence on US and British music of the 1970s and later

0-8050-1152-8 HOLT PB $13.95

Asian Music

William **Malm**

Six Hidden Views of Japanese Music

Informative studies on the subtle role of music in Japanese society, culture, and mores

0-520-05045-2 CALIFORNIA $47.50

Other and General

Simon **Broughton** & others, editors

The Rough Guide to World Music

Sixty experts composed of broadcasters, journalists, and musicians conduct us through the burgeoning field of world music. Also known as "roots" or local music, the term encompasses any popular music outside the USA: African soukous and highlife, Latin and Caribbean salsa, zouk, and reggae, Indonesian dangdut, Transylvanian gypsy music, Indian ragas, and here in America, Cajun and bluegrass

1-85828-017-6 ROUGH GUIDES PB $22.95

Cesaria Evora is the best-known Cape Verdean artist in Europe, a powerful singer of the potently sentimental morna style of nostalgia-laden ballad… A whiskey-drinking, cigarette-puffing grandmother, married three times, thrice deserted and now scornfully independent, Cesaria Evoria is an unlikely diva. At her age she has little interest in the frills and thrills of stardom: "I wasn't astonished by Europe and I was never that impressed by the speed and grandeur of modern America. I only regret my success has taken so long to achieve."

THE ROUGH GUIDE TO WORLD MUSIC

Elizabeth **May**, editor

Musics of many Cultures: An Introduction

1-520-04778-8 CALIFORNIA PB $24.95

John Storm **Roberts**

Black Music of Two Worlds

A survey by one of the savviest recorders and distributors of world music. "A genuine Baedecker to the music of Africa, South America, and the American Blacks."
— *Publishers Weekly*

0-9614458-0-7 ORIGINAL MUSIC PB $13.95

Dance

Histories

Janet **Adshead-Lansdale** & June **Layson**

Dance History: An Introduction

A provocative collection of essays focused on various problems in dance history

0-415-09030-X ROUTLEDGE PB $19.95

Susan **Au**

Ballet and Modern Dance

0-500-20219-2 THAMES & HUDSON PB $14.95

Selma **Cohen**, editor

Dance as a Theatre Art: Source Readings in Dance History from 1581 to the Present

0-87127-173-7 PRINCETON BOOK CO PB $16.95

Lynne **Emery**

Black Dance: From 1619 to Today

The standard history

0-916622-63-0 PRINCETON BOOK CO PB $19.95

Lincoln **Kirstein**

Dance: A Short History of Classic Theatrical Dancing

A brilliant and unsettling history, from primitive times to America's golden age

0-87127-019-6 PRINCETON BOOK CO PB $17.95

Four Centuries of Ballet: Fifty Masterworks

Encyclopedic. Discusses ballet as art, spectacle, and history. Nearly 500 illustrations, many reproduced here for the first time

0-486-24631-0 DOVER PB $16.95

Allen **Robertson** & Donald **Hutera**

The Dance Handbook

Concise entries on the history of dance and current figures in the different branches of dance

0-8161-1829-9 GK HALL PB $16.95

Paul **Magriel**, editor

Chronicles of the American Dance: From the Shakers to Graham

Fascinating documents from colonial to modern times

0-306-80082-9DA CAPO PB $7.95

Natalia **Roslavleva**

The Era of Russian Ballet

A standard book, spanning the era of Didelot to the 1960s

0-306-79536-1 DA CAPO $43.50

Marcia **Siegel**

The Shapes of Change: Images of American Dance

Analyses of 20th-century choreography for American themes and techniques

See also DANCE THEORY AND CRITICISM

0-520-04212-3 CALIFORNIA PB $14.95

Suzanne **Walther**

The Dance of Death: Kurt Jooss and the Weimar Years

3-7186-5702-3 HARWOOD $57.00

Pre-19th Century

Steven H. **Lonsdale**

Dance and Ritual Play in Greek Religion

0-8018-4594-7 JOHNS HOPKINS $39.95

Maria-Gabriele **Wosien**

Sacred Dance

0-500-81006-0 THAMES & HUDSON PB $14.95

Fabritio **Caroso**

Courtly Dance of the Renaissance: A New Translation and Edition of the Nobilta Di Dame

A well-known manual of aristocratic social dancing, complete with musical scores and guides to dance etiquette, an essay by the translator and annotated scores for the 20th century scholar

EDITED AND TRANSLATED BY JULIE SUTTON

0-486-28619-3 DOVER PB $14.95

Wendy **Hilton**

Dance of Court and Theater: The French Noble Style 1690-1725

A classic

0-916622-09-6 PRINCETON BOOK CO $39.95

Richard **Ralph**

The Life and Works of John Weaver

The first English dance historian

0-87127-139-7 DANCE HORIZONS $125.00

The 19th Century

This was the moment when the ballerina rose onto pointe and the ballet as we know it rose into being. Romantic ballet—ethereal in atmosphere, tragic in theme—dominated the century, as both a positive influence and a springboard for rebellion.

Elizabeth **Aldrich**

From the Ballroom to Hell: Grace and Folly in Nineteenth-Century Dance

Evoking a mostly forgotten social milieu, Aldrich describes with wit and insight the ballroom dance, etiquette, music, and fashion

See also CULTURAL AND SOCIAL HISTORY under TOPICS IN AMERICAN STUDIES in HISTORY OF THE AMERICAS

0-8101-0913-1 NORTHWESTERN PB $19.95

Edwin **Binney**

Glories of the Romantic Ballet

Features 130 prints

0-903102-83-8 PRINCETON BOOK CO PB $23.95

Ivor **Guest**

Victorian Ballet Girl: The Tragic Story of Clara Webster

A 19th-century dancer who died in a theater fire

0-306-76043-6 DA CAPO $29.00

Charles **Heath**

Beauties of the Opera and Ballet

Facsimile of a charming period album telling the plot of the major romantic works. Illustrated with intricate line drawings

0-306-70844-2 DA CAPO $34.00

Ballets

Cyril **Beaumont**

The Ballet Called Giselle

An indispensable handbook with an account of the changes to the choreography of *Giselle* over the century

1-85273-004-8 PRINCETON BOOK CO PB $14.95

Roland **Wiley**

Tchaikovsky's Ballets: Swan Lake, Sleeping Beauty, Nutcracker

Includes extensive and provocative discussions of the music and the Maryinsky Theater productions

0-19-315314-9 CLARENDON PB $75.00

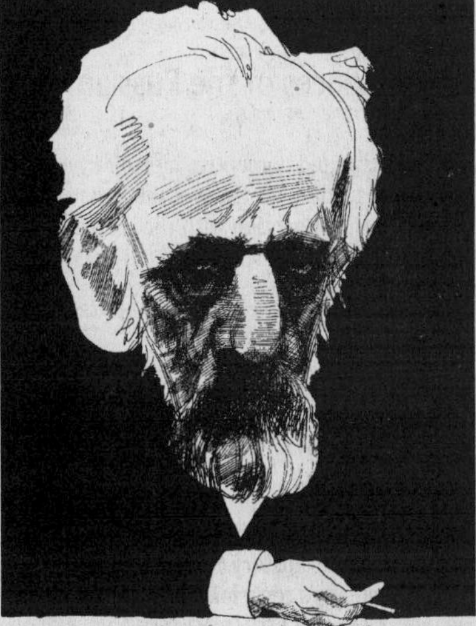

Pyotr Ilyich Tchaikovsky

The 20th Century

Ballet in our time has been dominated by Diaghilev's universally influential Ballets Russes and by George Balanchine. The rise of modern dance in America and Germany was a dramatic reaction by individual rebels to a classical tradition perceived as monolithic.

Joan **Acocella** & Lynn **Garafola**, editors

Andre Levinson on Dance: Writings from Paris in the Twenties

Key essays and reviews from the 1920's

See also DANCE THEORY AND CRITICISM

0-8195-5227-5 WESLEYAN $25.00

Nancy Van Norman **Baer**

Paris Modern: The Swedish Ballet 1920-1925

Celebrates the short-lived upstart ballet company that for a few years challenged Diaghilev's Ballet Russes's domination in Paris. Published in conjunction with the exhibition of the same name

0-88401-081-3 SAN FRANCISCO MUSEUM PB ..$24.95

Michael **Huxley** & Noel **Witts**, editors

The Twentieth-Century Performance Reader

An introduction to all types of performance (dance, drama, music, theater, live art) inviting cross-disciplinary comparisons. Contributions of interest to dance audiences include Doris Humphrey, Sally Banes, Mary Wigman, as well as artists and theorists who have integrated movement and theater, such as Robert Wilson, Peter Brook and Antonin Artaud

See also **DANCE THEORY AND CRITICISM**

0-415-11627-9 ROUTLEDGE........................$69.95
0-415-11628-7 ROUTLEDGE PB....................$22.95

Diaghilev and the Ballets Russes

Alexander **Benois**

Reminiscences of the Russian Ballet

An informative and perceptive memoir by a founder and leading designer of the Ballets Russes, whose connection with the company ended in 1914

0-306-77426-7 DA CAPO........................$52.00

Lynn **Garafola**

Diaghilev's Ballets Russes

0-19-505701-5 OXFORD........................$7.98

Nesta **MacDonald**

Diaghilev Observed

The only Diaghilev history currently in print with the company's repertoire as its focus

0-903102-14-5 PRINCETON BOOK CO............$69.95

Sergei Diaghilev

Deborah Menaker **Rothschild**

Picasso's Parade: From Street to Stage

Jean Cocteau's ballet *Parade* provoked riots when it opened in Paris in 1917. With cubist curtain, decor and costumes by Picasso, music by Erik Satie, and choreography by Leonid Massive, it introduced radical modernism into ballet. Illustrated

0-85667-392-7 SOTHEBY PARKE BERNET.......$90.00

George Balanchine and the New York Ballet

Robert **Garis**

Following Balanchine

A fan's personal history of four decades watching the master's work. Closely observed and deeply caring, which lends weight to sometimes controversial conclusions

See also **BALLET DANCERS AND CHOREOGRAPHERS**

0-300-06178-1 YALE........................$30.00

Lincoln **Kirstein**

Union Jack: The New York City Ballet

A lively souvenir volume, commemorating this 1977 Balanchine ballet

PHOTOGRAPHS BY MARTHA SWOPE

0-87130-047-8 EAKINS PB........................$15.00

Ballet Companies and Schools

Sasha **Anawalt**

The Joffrey Ballet: Robert Joffrey and the Making of an American Dance Company

0-684-19724-3 SCRIBNERS........................$35.00

Jack **Anderson**

The One and Only: The Ballet Russe De Monte Carlo

An account of the company that Leonide Massine co-founded with Sergei Denham

0-903102-65-X PRINCETON BOOK CO............$29.95

Oleg **Briansky**

100 Lessons in Classical Ballet

0-87910-068-0 PROSCENIUM PB....................$18.95

Anthony **Crickmay**

A Portrait of the Royal Ballet

Photographic portraits of each member of the Royal Ballet, along with a brief history of the company by its director

INTRODUCTION BY ANTHONY DOWELL

0-948397-04-7 OMARA........................$36.50

Juri **Slonimsky**

Soviet Ballet

0-306-71897-9 DA CAPO........................$39.50

Agrippina **Vaganova**

Basic Principles of Classical Ballet

A lively discussion of the classic technique that distinguishes Soviet ballet and the Kirov school

0-486-22036-2 DOVER PB........................$4.95

Ballet Dancers and Choreographers

A.H. **Franks**

Svetlana Beriosova: A Biography

0-306-79537-X DA CAPO........................$25.00

Ninette **De Valois**

Come Dance with Me: A Memoir, 1898-1956

0-306-79616-3 DA CAPO........................$29.50

Carol **Easton**

No Intermissions: The Life of Agnes De Mille

See also **MODERN DANCERS, CHOREOGRAPHERS, AND SCHOOLS**

See also **TAP, JAZZ, BROADWAY, AND HOLLYWOOD**

0-316-19970-2 LITTLE, BROWN....................$29.95

Robert **Garis**

Following Balanchine

A fan's personal history of four decades watching the master's work. Closely observed and deeply caring, which lends weight to sometimes controversial conclusions

See also **GEORGE BALANCHINE AND THE NEW YORK BALLET**

0-300-06178-1 YALE........................$30.00

Tamara **Karsavina**

Theatre Street: The Reminiscences of Tamara Karsavina

0-903102-47-1 PRINCETON BOOK CO............$29.95

Gelsey **Kirkland** & Greg **Lawrence**

Dancing on My Grave

A sobering look at the difficult life of a ballerina, with some startling revelations

0-425-13500-4 BERKLEY PB........................$6.50

Lydia **Kyasht**

Romantic Recollections

0-306-77572-7 DA CAPO........................$29.50

Paul **Magriel**, editor

Nijinsky, Pavlova, Duncan: Three Lives in Dance

If you were to buy only one work about 20th-century dancers, you might consider this one. It depicts the three legendary muses of the century of whom there is little or (in Nijinsky's case) no film footage

0-306-80035-7 DA CAPO PB........................$14.95

Romola **Nijinsky**, editor

The Diary of Vaslav Nijinsky

0-520-00945-2 CALIFORNIA PB....................$11.95

Howard **Brown**, editor

Nureyev

"No real Rudi fan will be without this book."
—*Time Out*

See also **DANCE PRINTS, PHOTOGRAPHS, AND FILMS**

0-7148-2966-8 PHAIDON........................$49.95
0-7148-3470-X PHAIDON PB........................$29.95

Peter **Ostwald**

Vaslav Nijinsky: A Leap into Madness

Authoritative

0-8184-0535-X LYLE STUART........................$19.95
0-8065-1681-X CITADEL PB........................$14.95

Mary **Clarke**

Antoinette Sibley

INTRODUCTION BY FREDERICK ASHTON

0-903102-64-1 PRINCETON BOOK CO............$29.95

Otis **Stuart**

Perpetual Motion: The Public and Private Lives of Rudolf Nureyev

The first American biography of the ballet legend who died in 1993 of AIDS

See also **BIOGRAPHIES** under **GAY, LESBIAN, AND BISEXUAL STUDIES** in **SOCIAL STUDIES**

0-671-87539-6 SIMON & SCHUSTER $24.00

0-452-27579-2 PLUME PB..................................$13.95

Elizabeth **Souritz**

Soviet Choreographers in the 1920's

See also **MODERN DANCERS, CHOREOGRAPHERS, AND SCHOOLS**

0-8223-0952-1 DUKE $31.95

Donna **Perlmutter**

Shadowplay: The Life of Antony Tudor

Appropriately for this choreographer of pared down psychological dance dramas, this is a biography with psychological perspective

0-87910-189-X LIMELIGHT PB..........................$18.95

Modern Dance

Jack **Anderson**

The American Dance Festival

0-8223-0683-2 DUKE $34.95

Sally **Banes**

Democracy's Body: Judson Dance Theater, 1962-1964

0-8223-1399-5 DUKE PB...................................$16.95

Greenwich Village 1963: Avant-Garde Performance and the Effervescent Body

Looks at experimental dance a la Yvonne Rainer, in the midst of an avant-garde aesthetic movement

0-8223-1357-X DUKE $49.95

0-8223-1391-X DUKE PB $17.95

Terpsichore in Sneakers: Post-Modern Dance

The definition of "postmodern dance"

0-8195-6160-6 WESLEYAN PB...........................$18.95

Jean **Brown**, editor

The Vision of Modern Dance

Interviews with choreographers

0-916622-12-6 PRINCETON BOOK CO PB.........$14.95

Gay **Cheney**

Basic Concepts in Modern Dance: A Creative Approach

A primer for students and audiences

0-916622-76-2 PRINCETON BOOK CO PB.........$10.95

Selma **Cohen**, editor

The Modern Dance: Seven Statements of Belief

Seven choreographers plan imaginary versions of a dance about the prodigal son

0-8195-6003-0 WESLEYAN PB $15.95

John **Martin** & Jack **Anderson**

The Dance in Theory

First third of Martin's seminal *Introduction to the Dance* which is out of print. An illuminating look at the choreography of modern dance

0-916622-90-8 DANCE HORIZONS PB $12.95

Modern Dancers, Choreographers, and Schools

"I am a thief—and I glory in it—I steal from the present and from the glorious past—and I stand in the dark of the future as a glorying and joyous thief—There are so many wonderful things of the imagination to pilfer—so I stand accused—I am a thief—but with this reservation—I think I know the value of what I steal and I treasure it for all time—not as a possession but as a heritage and as legacy."—Martha Graham, *The Notebooks of Martha Graham*

Alvin **Ailey** & A. Peter **Bailey**

Revelations: The Autobiography of Alvin Ailey

FOREWORD BY LENA HORNE

1-55972-255-X BIRCH LANE.............................$18.95

Jack **Mitchell**

Alvin Ailey American Dance Theater: Jack Mitchell Photographs

See also **DANCE PRINTS, PHOTOGRAPHS, AND FILMS**

0-8362-4508-3 ANDREWS & MCMEEL PB $19.95

Jean-Claude **Baker** & Chris **Baker**

Josephine: The Hungry Heart

Staggering research and high temperament

0-679-40915-7 RANDOM HOUSE.....................$27.50

Isadora **Duncan**

My Life

The first "modern dancer" describes her solitary quest for true expression in movement—"seeking that dance which might be the divine expression of the human spirit through the medium of the body's movement"

0-87140-158-4 NORTON PB..............................$14.00

Ann **Daly**

Done into Dance: Isadora Duncan in America

Why was Isadora's dancing so compelling? A critical study of Duncan's career that reveals her within the social and cultural climate of her time

0-253-32924-8 INDIANA $39.95

0-253-20989-7 INDIANA PB..............................$18.95

Doree **Duncan** & others, editors

Life into Art: Isadora Duncan and Her World

The catalog of the traveling exhibition that will open in Moscow and then come to New York. These stunning photographs and art works show Duncan in all her avatars: Rodin's sketches of the young dancer, Steichen's photograph of the great beauty, and a constructivist portrait by Anenkov of the revolutionary during her final years in Russia. A vivid portrait of the flamboyant artist and feminist whom many believe to be the mother of modern dance

0-393-03507-7 NORTON $40.00

Isadora Duncan

Katherine **Dunham**

Island Possessed

This pioneering dancer, choreographer and anthropologist who first visited Haiti as a graduate student offers vivid personal sketches of the island and its people

See also **HAITI** under **LATIN AMERICA AND THE CARIBBEAN** in **HISTORY OF THE AMERICAS**

0-226-17113-2 CHICAGO PB.............................$11.95

A Touch of Innocence: Memoirs of Childhood

See also **ARTISTS AND LITERARY FIGURES** under **BLACK VOICES, BLACK LIVES** under **AFRICAN-AMERICAN STUDIES** in **HISTORY OF THE AMERICAS**

0-226-17112-4 CHICAGO PB $12.95

Carol **Easton**

No Intermissions: The Life of Agnes De Mille

See also **TAP, JAZZ, BROADWAY, AND HOLLYWOOD** under **SPECIAL TOPICS**

See also **BALLET DANCERS AND CHOREOGRAPHERS**

0-316-19970-2 LITTLE, BROWN........................$29.95

Anna **Halprin**

Moving Toward Life: Five Decades of Transformational Dance

This seminal artist has forged a path away from dance performance as a commercial exchange between audience and performer, working in such forms as improvisational street-theater and dances to heal the earth. "Here, all in one place, are documents of the theory and practice that have made Anna Halprin a magnet for generations of experimental dance. In a field obsessed with surfaces, she plumbs the motive for movement—Elizabeth Zimmer, *Village Voice*

EDITED BY RACHEL KAPLAN

0-8195-5284-4 WESLEYAN $45.00

0-8195-6286-6 WESLEYAN PB..........................$19.95

Merle **Armitage**, editor

Martha Graham: The Early Years

0-306-79504-3 DA CAPO $29.00

Agnes **De Mille** & Martha **Graham**

Martha: The Life and Work of Martha Graham

A twenty-year labor of love

0-679-74176-3 VINTAGE PB..............................$18.00

Martha Graham

Erick **Hawkins**

The Body Is a Clear Place and Other Statements on Dance

Inspiring philosophizing on the art form from the recently deceased choreographer

0-87127-166-4 PRINCETON BOOK CO PB.........$14.95

Deborah **Hay**

Lamb at the Altar: The Story of a Dance

PHOTOGRAPHY BY PHYLLIS HIEDEKER

0-8223-1448-7 DUKE..............................$49.95

0-8223-1439-8 DUKE PB..............................$15.95

Richard **Kostelanetz**, editor

Merce Cunningham: Dancing in Space and Time

A collection of essays by critics Jack Anderson, Arlene Croce, Calvin Tompkins, Edwin Denby and Marcia Siegel; compser John Cage; and dancers Remy Charlip, Kenneth King, James Waring; and by Merce himself. And more

1-55652-152-9 IND PUBLISHERS GROUP PB....$16.95

Merce Cunningham

Doris **Humphrey**

Doris Humphrey: An Artist First

0-87127-201-6 PRINCETON BOOK CO PB.........$18.95

The Art of Making Dances

0-87127-158-3

INDEPENDENT PUBLISHERS GROUP PB...........$14.95

Bill T. **Jones** & Peggy **Gillespie**

Last Night on Earth

If, like Arlene Croce, you never saw the dance of the same title, or if you're a fan of its fabulously charismatic choeographer, this book (part memoir, part meditation, full of photos) is for you

0-679-43926-9 PANTHEON..............................$30.00

Susan A. **Manning**

Ecstasy and the Demon: Feminism and Nationalism in the Dances of Mary Wigman

0-520-08193-5 CALIFORNIA..............................$30.00

Joan **Acocella**

Mark Morris

Follows the outrageous persona of the extradordinarily successful career of the young modern dance choreographer

0-374-52418-1 NOONDAY PB..............................$17.00

0-374-20295-8 FS&G..............................$27.50

Barbara **Pollack** & Charles Humphrey **Woodford**

Dance Is a Moment: A Portrait of Jose Limon in Words and Pictures

A personal chronicle of Limon's making *There is a Time* over thirty-five years ago

0-87127-183-4 PRINCETON BOOK CO PB.........$19.95

Marcia **Siegel**

Days on Earth: The Dance of Doris Humphrey

A provocative and illuminating biography

0-8223-1346-4 DUKE PB..............................$15.95

Elizabeth **Souritz**

Soviet Choreographers in the 1920's

See also **BALLET DANCERS AND CHOREOGRAPHERS**

0-8223-0952-1 DUKE..............................$31.95

Special Topics

Angna **Enters**

On Mime

A summary of wisdom accumulated by one of the celebrated mimes of the 20th century

0-8195-6056-1 WESLEYAN PB..............................$13.95

Terry **Trucco**

The New York Book of Dance

A travel guide to New York as dance capital, describing the downtown dance scene, the big ballet companies, ballroom schools, hip-hop clubs…and where to find them

1-88549-222-7 CITY & CO...............................$17.00

Dance and Anthropology

Eugenio **Barba** & Nicole **Savarese**

A Dictionary of Theatre Anthropology: The Secret Art of the Performer

A sourcebook that discusses both eastern and western theater and dance techniques, focusing on what makes the performance work: balance, opposition, montage, rhythm, etc. Lusciously illustrated, a useful reference for audience, student and practitioner

See also **WORLD DANCE**

TRANSLATED BY RICHARD FOWLER

0-415-05308-0 ROUTLEDGE PB..............................$35.00

Frank M. **Calabria**

Dance of the Sleepwalkers: The Dance Marathon Fad

Tells the colorful and bizarre story of this uniquely American form of amusement, popular in the '20s and '30s, which revealed the underside of the American psyche

0-87972-569-9 BOWLING GREEN..............................$39.95

0-87972-570-2 BOWLING GREEN PB..............................$19.95

Yvonne **Daniel**

Rumba: Dance and Social Change in Contemporary Cuba

An ethnographic report on the rumba and its development from once a lower class recreational dance to a symbol of egalitarianism in post-revolutionary Cuba

See also **CUBA UNDER COMMUNISM** under **CUBA** under **LATIN AMERICA AND THE CARIBBEAN** in **HISTORY OF THE AMERICAS**

0-253-31605-7 INDIANA..............................$29.95

0-253-20948-X INDIANA PB..............................$12.95

Mary McNab **Dart**

Contra Dance Choreography: A Reflection of Social Change

0-8153-1984-3 GARLAND..............................$75.00

Judith **Hanna**

Dance, Sex, and Gender: Signs of Identity, Dominance, Defiance, and Desire

0-226-31551-7 CHICAGO PB..............................$18.95

The Performer-Audience Connection: Emotion to Metaphor in Dance and Society

0-292-76480-4 TEXAS PB..............................$11.95

To Dance Is Human: A Theory of Nonverbal Communication

0-226-31549-5 CHICAGO PB..............................$18.95

Jamake **Highwater**

Dance: Rituals of Experience

0-19-511205-9 OXFORD..............................$19.95

Judith **Jamison** & Howard **Kaplan**

Dancing Spirit: An Autobiography

Alvin Ailey's muse and star dancer Judith Jamison has directed his company since his death. Here is her autobiography. "This is a book about passion

and will, about dance, about black history, about carrying on."—*Washington Post Book World*
0-385-42558-9 ANCHOR PB $14.95

Jacqui **Malone**
Steppin' on the Blues: The Visible Rhythms of African American Dance
A broad social and aesthetic history
0-252-02211-4 ILLINOIS $44.95
0-252-06508-5 ILLINOIS PB $16.95

Barbara **Sellers-Young**
Teaching Personality With Gracefulness: The Transmission of Japanese Cultural Values Through Japanese Dance Theater
0-8191-9014-4 UNIV PRESS OF AMERICA $52.00
0-8191-9015-2 UNIV PRESS OF AMERICA PB...$27.50

Dance and Music

Elizabeth **Sawyer**
Dance with the Music: The World of the Ballet Musician
A discussion of musicality in dancing by a longtime dance accompanist. Enthusiastic about the musical instincts of Antony Tudor, cool on Balanchine
0-521-26502-9 CAMBRIDGE $74.95

Janet Mansfield **Soares**
Louis Horst: Musician in a Dancer's World
Excellent research
0-8223-1226-3 DUKE $32.95

Katherine **Teck**
Ear Training for the Body: A Dancer's Guide to Music
0-87127-192-3 PRINCETON BOOK CO PB.........$19.95

Social and Folk Dancing

Brendan **Breathnach**
Folk Music and Dances of Ireland
0-85342-509-4 IRISH BOOK CENTER PB $13.95

Barbara **Browning**
Samba: Resistance in Motion
A longtime student of Brazillian dance, Browning arrives at a theoretical account of samba, capoiera and other dances of the carnival culture through her personal experiences. She suggests that the dancing body speaks, without words, an eloquent political rhetoric of protest
See also **MUSIC OF THE AMERICAS** under **WORLD MUSIC: OTHER TRADITIONS**
0-253-32867-5 INDIANA $29.95
0-253-20956-0 INDIANA PB $14.95

Simon **Collier** & others
Tango!: The Dance, the Song, the Story
A lively illustrated history of the Argentine form
0-500-01671-2 THAMES & HUDSON..............$40.00

Irene **Castle**
Castles in the Air
Memoirs of the ballroom dancer who, with her husband Vernon, popularized the Castle Walk the Foxtrot, and other social dances
INTRODUCTION BY GINGER ROGERS
0-306-80122-1 DA CAPO PB $6.95

Jim **Dawson**
The Twist: The Story of the Song and Dance that Changed the World
0-571-19852-X FABER PB $14.95

Alma **Guillermoprieto**
Samba
An intimate look at the heart of Brazilian life. The author spent a year training in a village samba school in preparation for Rio's Carnival parade. "Eloquent and persuasive in bringing it all to life"—*New Yorker*
See also **MUSIC OF THE AMERICAS** under **WORLD MUSIC: OTHER TRADITIONS**
See also **SOUTH AMERICA** under **TRAVEL LITERATURE**
0-679-73256-X VINTAGE PB $12.00

Julie **Malnig**
Dancing Till Dawn: A Century of Exhibition Ballroom Dance
"A delightful and much-needed examination of twentieth century American ballroom dance and its relation to other performing arts. Malnig employs a lively, rapid-fire writing style…an important historical and cultural guide."
—*Theatre Journal*
0-8147-5528-3 NYU PB $15.95

Marta E. **Savigliano**
Tango and the Political Economy of Passion
The tango seen in relation to Argentine history, colonialism and 'decolonialization.' "A milestone achievement in dance scholarship"—Susan Leigh Foster, author of *Reading Dancing*
0-8133-1638-3 WESTVIEW PB $24.50

Peggy **Spencer**
Ballroom Dancing: The Imperials Society of Teachers of Dancing
Written with the absolute beginner in mind
0-8442-3908-9 TEACH YOURSELF PB..................$8.95

Richard M. **Stephenson** & Joseph **Iaccarino**
The Complete Book of Ballroom Dancing
0-385-42416-7 BANTAM PB $17.50

Scenic and Costume Design

Toni **Bentley**
Costumes by Karinska
Balanchine said, "There is Shakespeare for literature and Karinska for costume." Former City Ballet dancer Bentley shows us why
0-8109-3516-3 ABRAMS $60.00

Tap, Jazz, Broadway, and Hollywood

Carol **Easton**
No Intermissions: The Life of Agnes De Mille
See also **MODERN DANCERS, CHOREOGRAPHERS, AND SCHOOLS** under **THE 20TH CENTURY**
See also **BALLET DANCERS AND CHOREOGRAPHERS** under **THE 20TH CENTURY**
0-316-19970-2 LITTLE, BROWN $29.95

Rusty E. **Frank**
Tap: The Greatest Tap Dance Stars and Their Stories,1900-1955
Excellent Interviews
0-306-80635-5 DA CAPO PB $19.95

Gus **Giordano**
Jazz Dance Class: Beginning Thru Advanced
See also **BODY SCIENCE, KINESICS, TECHNIQUE, AND PEDAGOGY**
1-85273-040-4 PRINCETON BOOK CO PB.........$19.95

Svetlana McLee **Grody** & Dorothy Daniels **Lister**
Conversations With Choreographers
Well-known Broadway choreographers talk about the creative process
0-435-08697-9 HEINEMANN PB $19.95

Serge **Leslie**
A Dancer's Scrapbook
A memory book about Doris Niles, Broadway dancer of the 1920s and '30s
1-85273-001-3 PRINCETON BOOK CO $34.95

William H. **McNeill**
Keeping Together in Time: Dance and Drill in Human History
See also **BODY SCIENCE, KINESICS, TECHNIQUE, AND PEDAGOGY**
See also **PERSPECTIVES IN HISTORY**
0-674-50229-9 HARVARD $22.00

Marshall **Stearns** & Jean **Stearns**
Jazz Dance: The Story of American Vernacular Dance
The basic history, full of facts
0-306-80553-7 DA CAPO PB $16.95

World Dance

Kariamu Welsh **Asante**, editor
African Dance: An Artistic, Historical and Philosophical Inquiry
0-86543-196-5 AFRICA WORLD $49.95
0-86543-197-3 AFRICA WORLD PB $16.95

Eugenio **Barba** & Nicole **Savarese**

A Dictionary of Theatre Anthropology: The Secret Art of the Performer

A sourcebook that discusses both eastern and western theater and dance techniques, focusing on what makes the performance work: balance, opposition, montage, rhythm, etc. Lusciously illustrated, a useful reference for audience, student and practitioner

See also DANCE AND ANTHROPOLOGY

TRANSLATED BY RICHARD FOWLER

0-415-05308-0 ROUTLEDGE PB $35.00

Wendy **Buonaventura**

Serpent of the Nile: Women and Dance in the Arab World

"A lively and lavishly illustrated excursion into the history of the solo woman's dance…" —*NY Times Book Review*

1-56656-117-5 INTERLINK PB $35.00

Hilary S. **Carty**

Folk Dances of Jamaica: An Insight

1-85273-007-2 DANCE BOOKS PB $17.95

Katherine **Dunham**

Dances of Haiti

FOREWORD BY CLAUDE LEVI-STRAUSS

0-934934-11-8 CALIFORNIA PB $10.50

Michel **Huet**

The Dances of Africa

TEXT BY CLAUDE SAVARY

0-8109-3228-8 ABRAMS $39.95

K. Bharatha **Iyer**

Dance Dramas of India and the East

0-86590-029-9 STOSIUS/ADVENT $45.00

Reginald **Massey**

Dances of India: A General Survey & Dancers' Guide

0-948725-04-4 SOUTH ASIA $30.00

Claus **Schreiner**, editor

Flamenco: Gypsy Dance and Music from Andalusia

An introduction to the history and practice of the dance form created by gypsies in the Andalusian region of Spain. Includes a discography and sources on where to see and study flamenco

1-57467-013-1 AMADEUS PB $14.95

Matteo **Vittucci** & Carola **Goya**

The Language of Spanish Dance

A first-class dictionary

See also DANCE THEORY AND CRITICISM

0-8061-2532-2 OKLAHOMA PB $24.95

Dance Theory and Criticism

Jack **Anderson**

Choreography Observed

Anderson is a poet and dance critic for the *NY Times*

0-87745-172-9 IOWA $35.00

Joan **Acocella** & Lynn **Garafola**, editor

Andre Levinson on Dance: Writings from Paris in the Twenties

Key essays and reviews from the 1920's

See also THE 20TH CENTURY

0-8195-5227-5 WESLEYAN $25.00

Alexander **Bland**

Observer of the Dance: 1958-1982

Alexander Bland is the pen name for English critics Mary Clarke and Clement Crisp

INTRODUCTIONS BY MARGOT FONTEYN & OTHERS

0-903102-91-9 DANCE BOOKS $49.95

Ramsay **Burt**

The Male Dancer: Bodies, Spectacle, Sexualities

This gender study examines the representation of maleness in the works of Bausch, Graham, Nijinsky et al in light of social, political and aesthetic contexts

0-415-08899-2 ROUTLEDGE $49.95

0-415-08900-X ROUTLEDGE PB $16.95

Selma **Cohen**

Next Week, Swan Lake: Reflections on Dance and Dances

A book-length essay on dance aesthetics

0-8195-6110-X WESLEYAN PB $16.95

Roger **Copeland** & Marshall **Cohen**

What Is Dance: Readings in Theory and Criticism

A comprehensive anthology, which addresses the major intellectual and aesthetic issues of dance

0-19-503197-0 OXFORD PB $17.95

Susan Leigh **Foster**

Reading Dancing: Bodies and Subjects in Contemporary Dance

A controversial study of dance texts, influenced by semiotics

0-520-06333-3 CALIFORNIA PB $21.95

Susan Leigh **Foster**, editor

Corporealities: Dancing Knowledge, Culture and Power

The groundbreaking essays collected here attempt to translate movement in all its ephemerality into critical discourse. Dance in view of the "dancing body", as seen in phys-ed class, pageants, festivals, and social and theoretical dances

0-415-12139-6 ROUTLEDGE PB $16.95

Mark **Franko**

Dancing Modernism/Performing Politics

Takes issue with the idea that dance reflects its culture directly, and instead explores the relation of the modern dance aesthetic to politics

0-253-32432-7 INDIANA $29.95

0-253-20947-1 INDIANA PB $12.95

Deborah **Jowitt**

Time and the Dancing Image

Historical essays on the image and role of the dancer in 19th-and 20th-century Western choreography

0-520-06627-8 CALIFORNIA PB $18.95

Michael **Huxley** & Noel **Witts**, editors

The Twentieth-Century Performance Reader

An introduction to all types of performance (dance, drama, music, theater, live art) inviting cross-disciplinary comparisons. Contributions of interest to dance audiences include Doris Humphrey, Sally Banes, Mary Wigman, as well as artists and theorists who have integrated movement and theater, such as Robert Wilson, Peter Brook and Antonin Artaud

See also THE 20TH CENTURY

0-415-11627-9 ROUTLEDGE $69.95

0-415-11628-7 ROUTLEDGE PB $22.95

Lincoln **Kirstein**

Ballet: Bias and Belief

0-87127-133-8 DANCE HORIZONS $39.95

Amy **Koritz**

Gendering Bodies/Performing Art: Dance and Literature in Early Twentieth-Century British Culture

0-472-10616-3 MICHIGAN $37.50

Andre **Levinson**

Ballet Old and New

Levinson was a brilliant, deeply conservative critic, born in Russia, where he witnessed the end of Imperial Ballet. He emigrated to Europe following the Revolution. He is especially interesting for his dislikes, which include the modernist phase of Diaghilev's Ballets Russes, and the style of Isadora Duncan

0-87127-130-3 DANCE HORIZONS PB $15.95

Maxine **Sheets-Johnstone**, editor

Illuminating Dance: Philosophical Explorations

A collection of essays

0-8387-5063-X BUCKNELL $32.50

Marcia **Siegel**

The Shapes of Change: Images of American Dance

Analyses of 20th-century choreography for American themes and techniques

See also HISTORIES

0-520-04212-3 CALIFORNIA PB $14.95

Marcia B. **Siegel**

The Tail of the Dragon: New Dance, 1976-1982

This collection tracks a radical art form and its movement into the mainstream

0-8223-1156-9 DUKE $41.95

0-8223-1166-6 DUKE PB $15.95

Rachel **Vigier**

Gestures of Genius: Women, Dance, and the Body

A history of women in dance from a personalized female perspective, focusing on dance as female ritual, and on societal restrictions on women's movement. Features eleven interviews with diverse and current female dance artists

1-55128-012-4 INBOOK PB $16.95

Dance Prints, Photographs, and Films

Lynne Anne **Blom** & L. Tarin **Chaplin**

The Moment of Movement: Dance Improvisation

Ways to teach and lead improvisation, a mainstay of much current dance training from preschool to college

0-8229-3586-4 PITTSBURGH $29.95
0-8229-5405-2 PITTSBURGH PB $14.95

Howard **Brown**, editor

Nureyev

"No real Rudi fan will be without this book." —*Time Out*

See also BALLET DANCERS AND CHOREOGRAPHERS under THE 20TH CENTURY

0-7148-2966-8 PHAIDON $49.95
0-7148-3470-X PHAIDON PB $29.95

William A. **Ewing** & Lois **Greenfield**

Breaking Bounds: The Dance Photography of Lois Greenfield

0-8118-0232-9 CHRONICLE PB $22.95

Lotte **Jacobi**

Theater and Dance Photographs

Haunting German expressionist-style pictures of German and American modern dancers

INTRODUCTION BY CORNELL CAPE

0-914378-93-7 COUNTRYMAN PB $10.95

Parmenia **Migel**

Great Ballet Prints of the Romantic Era

0-486-24050-9 DOVER PB $9.95

Jack **Mitchell**

Alvin Ailey American Dance Theater: Jack Mitchell Photographs

See also MODERN DANCERS, CHOREOGRAPHERS, AND SCHOOLS under THE 20TH CENTURY

0-8362-4508-3 ANDREWS & MCMEEL PB $19.95

Philip **Trager** & Ralph **Lemon**, editors

Persephone

Remarkable photographs of *Persephone*, as performed by the Ralph Lemon Company, accompany poems based on the myth

WITH POEMS BY RITA DOVE AND EAVAN BOLAND

0-8195-5303-4 WESLEYAN $19.95

Jack **Woody**, editor

George Platt Lynes: Photographs, 1931-1955

Includes the notorious and beautiful nude versions of the "Orpheus and Dark Angel" sequence from Balanchine's *Orpheus*. Contributions by George Balanchine, Lincoln Kirstein, and Glenway Wescott

0-942642-00-7 TWELVETREES $55.00

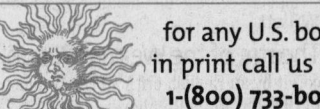

Body Science, Kinesics, Technique, and Pedagogy

Ray **Birdwhistell**

Kinesics and Context: Essays on Body Motion Communication

0-8122-1012-3 PENNSYLVANIA PB $20.95

Moshe **Feldenkrais**

Awareness Through Movement: Health Exercises for Personal Growth

Exercises for renewed health and increased sensory awareness by the inventor of Functional Integration, otherwise known as the Feldenkrais technique

0-06-250322-7 HARPERCOLLINS PB $12.00

Gus **Giordano**

Jazz Dance Class: Beginning Thru Advanced

See also TAP, JAZZ, BROADWAY, AND HOLLYWOOD under SPECIAL TOPICS

1-85273-040-4 PRINCETON BOOK CO PB $19.95

Rudolf **Laban**

Life for Dance: The Autobiography of Rudolf Laban

TRANSLATED BY LISA ULLMAN

0-7121-1648-6 PRINCETON BOOK CO $14.95
0-7121-1231-6 PRINCETON BOOK CO $19.95

Kenneth **Laws** & Cynthia **Harvey**

Physics, Dance, and the Pas De Deux

With stop-action photos. A physicist and a prima-ballerina join forces to explain how classical ballet partnering works

PHOTOGRAPHY BY MARTHA SWOPE

0-02-871326-5 MACMILLAN PB $22.00

Thalia **Mara**

First Steps in Ballet: Basic Exercises At the Barre

An old and reliable book

0-916622-53-3 PRINCETON BOOK CO PB $6.95

Fourth Steps in Ballet: On Your Toes! Basic Pointe Work

0-916622-56-8 PRINCETON BOOK CO PB $6.95

Second Steps in Ballet: Basic Center Exercises

0-916622-54-1 PRINCETON BOOK CO PB $6.95

Third Steps in Ballet: Basic Allegro Steps

0-916622-55-X PRINCETON BOOK CO PB $6.95

William H. **McNeill**

Keeping Together in Time: Dance and Drill in Human History

See also PERSPECTIVES IN HISTORY under THE VARIETIES OF CIVILIZATION in WORLD HISTORY AND CURRENT AFFAIRS

See also TAP, JAZZ, BROADWAY, AND HOLLYWOOD under SPECIAL TOPICS

0-674-50229-9 HARVARD $22.00

Jean **Newlove**

Laban for Actors and Dancers: Putting Laban's Movement Theory into Practice

A practical handbook

0-87830-044-9 THEATRE ARTS PB $16.95

Andrea **Olsen** & Caryn **McHose**

Bodystories: A Guide to Experiential Anatomy

Anatomical, anecdotal, massage information for dancers, teachers, athletes, or anyone interested in the body and how it works. Unique art by prominent contemporary artists provocatively illustrates this uncategorizable book

See also MIND-BODY HEALING under HOLISTIC MEDICINE under HEALTH in LIFESTYLES AND PRACTICAL ADVICE

0-88268-106-0 STATION HILL PB $24.95

Royal Academy of Dancing

Step-By-Step Ballet Class: The Official Illustrated Guide

A legible and useful guide to classical ballet training in the very well codified British (Royal Academy of Dancing) system

0-8092-3499-8 CONTEMPORARY PB $12.95

Rudolf **Steiner**

An Introduction to Eurythmy: Talks Given Before Sixteen Eurythmy Performances

0-88010-042-7 ANTHROPOSOPHIC PB $8.95

Stuart **Wright**

The Dancer's Guide to Injuries of the Lower Extremity: Diagnosis, Treatment, and Care

0-8453-4782-9 CORNWALL $18.95

Being a Dancer

Allegra **Kent**

The Dancer's Body Book

Advice from the former New York City Ballet star

0-688-01539-5 MORROW PB $12.00

Daniel **Nagrin**

How to Dance Forever: Surviving Against the Odds

A guide for those driven to careers as dancers: caring for the body, focusing the mind, and how to find the best jobs to support one's dancing

0-688-07479-0 MORROW PB $14.95

Dance and the Specific Image: Improvisation

Improvisational structures for classes and creative work by a modern dancer and choreographer interested in movement as metaphor

0-8229-3776-X PITTSBURGH $49.95
0-8229-5520-2 PITTSBURGH PB $19.95

Ruth **Solomon** & others

Preventing Dance Injuries: An Interdisciplinary Perspective

0-88314-425-5 AMERICAN ALLIANCE PB $34.00

Reference

George **Balanchine** & Francis **Mason**

101 Stories of the Great Ballets

Contains entries on more than 400 works, with extensive discussion of differences between major productions. Also offers an excellent chronology of ballet, and several essays by and interviews with Balanchine

0-385-03398-2 ANCHOR PB $12.95

Leslie **Getz**

Dancers and Choreographers: A Selected Bibliography

Extensive English language bibliography on ballet and modern dance

1-55921-109-1 MOYER BELL PB $18.95

Gail **Grant**

Technical Manual and Dictionary of Classical Ballet

0-486-21843-0 DOVER PB $4.95

Theater

Although performance is the most evanescent of arts, the institution of theater and some of its literature have endured remarkably. The Rodgers and Hart musical of *The Boys from Syracuse*, for instance, was a culmination of more than 2300 years of stealing and borrowing. It was inspired by *The Comedy of Errors*, which Shakespeare took from Plautus, who in turn adapted it from a Greek model. And the text of Euripides' tragedy *The Bacchae*, that most joyful of pagan plays, has been partially preserved in a medieval version in which the god Dionysus is transformed into the suffering Christ.

For related reading, see SHAKESPEARE in LITERATURE OF THE BRITISH ISLES

For related reading, see 20TH-CENTURY BRITISH AND IRISH DRAMA in LITERATURE OF THE BRITISH ISLES

For related reading, see 20TH-CENTURY AMERICAN DRAMA in LITERATURE OF THE AMERICAS

For related reading, see MODERN EUROPEAN DRAMA in LITERATURE OF EUROPE, AFRICA, AND ASIA

History

Oscar G. **Brockett**

The Theatre: An Introduction

For the serious student, by the most comprehensive and academically sound of contemporary American historians

0-03-021676-1 HOLT RINEHART & WINSTON .. $47.88

Oscar G. **Brockett** & Mark **Pape**

World Drama

0-03-057668-7 HOLT RINEHART & WINSTON PB .. $30.59

Phyllis **Hartnoll**

The Theatre: A Concise History

Provides a good overview with pictures

0-500-20073-4 THAMES & HUDSON PB $14.95

Mary C. **Henderson**

Theater in America: 250 Years of Plays, Players, and Productions

Updated edition

0-8109-3884-7 ABRAMS $60.00

0-8109-1084-5 ABRAMS PB $19.98

A.M. **Nagler**

Source Book in Theatrical History

A classic anthology of writing about the theater by its practitioners

0-486-20515-0 DOVER PB $11.95

Ancient

Aristotle

Aristotle's Poetics

0-393-95216-9 NORTON PB $7.95

John **Jones**

On Aristotle and Greek Tragedy

A difficult but important book about the (mis)interpretation of Aristotle as it affects our understanding of Greek drama

0-8047-1092-9 STANFORD $39.50

0-8047-1093-7 STANFORD PB $14.95

H.D. F. **Kitto**

Greek Tragedy: A Literary Study

Cogent and passionately argued essays about the meaning of drama in the mid-20th century

See also **GREEK TRAGEDY** under **CRITICAL STUDIES** under **ANCIENT GREEK LITERATURE** in **LITERATURE OF EUROPE, AFRICA, AND ASIA**

0-416-68900-0 ROUTLEDGE PB $16.95

Medieval and Elizabethan

Simon **Shepherd**

Marlowe and the Politics of Elizabethan Theatre

0-312-51546-4 ST. MARTIN'S $39.95

Peter **Thomson**

Shakespeare's Theatre

0-415-05148-7 ROUTLEDGE PB $17.95

Britain and Ireland

Peter **Kavanagh**

The Story of the Abbey Theatre

0-915032-29-5 NATIONAL POETRY FOUNDATION $25.00

0-915032-30-9 NATIONAL POETRY FOUNDATION PB $12.95

Catherine **Itzin**

Stages in the Revolution: Political Theatre in Britain Since 1968

This book by a leading British feminist chronicles the second wave of Britain's Angry Generation

0-413-39180-9 METHUEN PB $15.95

George **Rowell** & Anthony **Jackson**

The Repertory Movement: A History of Regional Theatre in Britain

0-521-31919-6 CAMBRIDGE PB $20.95

Europe

Andre **Antoine**

Memories of the Theatre-Libre

Antoine (1858-1943) founded the art-theater movement which spread from Paris to other European cities. One of the fathers of modern theater, he helped establish Ibsen's realistic social dramas

EDITED BY H.D. ALBRIGHT

0-87024-034-X MIAMI $13.95

Bohdan **Drozdowsky**, editor

Twentieth-Century Polish Theatre

More experimental and less realistic than other Eastern European countries, the Polish theater has had a major impact on Western drama

0-7145-3738-1 RIVERRUN $14.95

Pierre L. **Ducharte**

Italian Comedy: The Improvisation, Scenarios, Lives, Attribute, Portraits and Mask of the Illustrious Characters of the Commedia Dell'arte

A reprint of this 1929 account of the *commedia dell'arte*

0-486-21679-9 DOVER PB $16.95

Wallace **Fowlie**

Dionysus in Paris: A Guide to Contemporary French from Valery to Sartre

See also **GENERAL STUDIES** under **CRITICAL STUDIES** under **MODERN FRENCH LITERATURE** in **LITERATURE OF EUROPE, AFRICA, AND ASIA**

0-8446-0096-2 SMITH $11.55

August **Strindberg**

Open Letters to the Intimate Theater

Between 1907 and 1913, Stockholm's Intima Teatern staged some two dozen of Strindberg's chamber plays and changed the course of modern drama

TRANSLATED BY WALTER JOHNSON

0-295-74055-8 WASHINGTON $15.00

John **Willett**

The Theatre of the Weimar Republic

An account by an English critic of the Weimar period (1920-33), from Reinhardt to the

expressionists, from the Bauhaus to Piscator, Brecht, and Kurt Weill
See also **CRITICAL STUDIES** under **GERMAN LITERATURE** in **LITERATURE OF EUROPE, AFRICA, AND ASIA**
0-8419-0759-5 HOLMES & MEIER..................$79.50

Africa

Russell **Vandenbroucke**
Truths the Hand Can Touch: The Theater of Athol Fugard
0-930452-45-3 THEATRE COMM. PB $12.50

Asia

James R. **Brandon**
Theater in Southeast Asia
0-674-87587-7 HARVARD PB $15.00

Komparu **Kunio**
The Noh Theater: Principles and Perspectives
An absolutely thorough, sometimes quite technical description of the many elements involved in a Noh performance
See also **DRAMA** under **CRITICAL STUDIES AND HISTORIES** under **JAPANESE LITERATURE** in **LITERATURE OF EUROPE, AFRICA, AND ASIA**
0-8348-1529-X WEATHERHILL $32.50

Constantine **Tung** & Colin **MacKerras**
Drama in the People's Republic of China
0-88706-389-6 SUNY $57.50
0-88706-390-X SUNY PB....................................$19.95

North America

Gerald **Bordman**
American Theatre: A Chronicle of Comedy and Drama, 1914-1930
0-19-509079-9 OXFORD.....................................$42.00
0-19-509078-0 OXFORD.....................................$49.95

John **Culhane**
The American Circus: An Illustrated History
A splendid tribute to the great mythic arena of popular entertainment
0-8050-1647-3 HOLT PB $19.95

Hallie **Flanagan**
Arena
An important account of the Federal Theatre Project of the 1930s by the woman who ran it
FOREWORD BY JOHN HOUSEMAN
0-405-06726-7 AYER..$28.95

Stanley **Green**
The Great Clowns of Broadway
0-19-503471-6 OXFORD......................................$30.00

Peter **Hay**
Broadway Anecdotes
Great stories from the Great White Way, from tales of Americans first taking to the stage in the colonial era to more recent exploits of Marilyn Monroe, Tennessee Williams, Mae West, Katherine Hepburn. An amusing compilation for every theater lover
0-19-504621-8 OXFORD PB..................................$19.95

Errol **Hill**, editor
The Theatre of Black Americans
See also **DRAMA** under **GENERAL STUDIES: THE 20TH CENTURY** under **AMERICAN LITERATURE: ANTHOLOGIES AND CRITICAL STUDIES** in **LITERATURE OF THE AMERICAS**
0-936839-27-9 APPLAUSE THEATRE PB............$15.95

William **Redfield**
Letters from an Actor
A gossipy and useful account of the famous 1964 Gielgud production of *Hamlet* with Richard Burton on Broadway
0-87910-007-9 PROSCENIUM PB..........................$7.95

Robert C. **Toll**
The Entertainment Machine: American Show Business in the 20th-Century
0-19-503232-2 OXFORD PB..................................$13.95

Contemporary and Avant-Garde

Eileen **Blumenthal**
Joseph Chaikin
0-521-28589-5 CAMBRIDGE PB...........................$21.95

C. **Carr**
On Edge: Performance at the End of the Twentieth Century
0-8195-6269-6 WESLEYAN PB..............................$18.95

Rose Lee **Goldberg**
Performance Art: From Futurism to the Present
Traces the roots of this marriage of art and theater from early in the century to the present
0-8109-2371-8 ABRAMS PB..................................$12.95

The Musical Theater

Gerald **Bordman**
American Musical Comedy: From Adonis to Dreamgirls
Adonis was the first musical comedy (1884) to rack up more than 500 performances on Broadway; Bordman charts almost 100 years in the evolution of this genre
0-19-503104-0 OXFORD......................................$30.00

American Musical Theatre: A Chronicle
"Much more than a source book. It is fun to read"—John S. Wilson, *NY Times*
0-19-507242-1 OXFORD......................................$60.00

American Operetta: From H.M.S. Pinafore to Sweeney Todd
Links the American musical to its European roots and predecessors
0-19-502869-4 OXFORD......................................$30.00

Broadway Musicals—Show by Show
More facts than one is ever likely to need about musicals from *The Black Crook* (1866) to *Les Miz*
0-7935-3083-0 LEONARD PB $16.95

Stanley **Green**
Broadway Musicals of the '30s
A complete list, including discography and film versions; many illustrations
INTRODUCTION BY BROOKS ATKINSON
0-306-80165-5 DA CAPO PB $14.95

Encyclopedia of the Musical Theatre
Contains complete listings of productions and personalities of the British and American musical to the 1970s
0-306-80113-2 DA CAPO PB...............................$16.95

The World of Musical Comedy
A history mainly of Broadway in its golden age
0-306-80207-4 DA CAPO PB $24.50

Foster **Hirsch**
Harold Prince and the American Musical Theater
FOREWORDS BY HAROLD PRINCE & STEPHEN SONDHEIM
0-521-33314-8 CAMBRIDGE..................................$44.95
0-521-33609-0 CAMBRIDGE PB $17.95

Gerald **Mast**
Can't Help Singin': The American Musical on Stage and Screen
This is a posthumously published masterpiece by a writer who knew everything about songs and what they mean to us
0-87951-283-0 OVERLOOK..................................$24.95
0-87951-362-4 OVERLOOK PB............................$15.95

Ethan **Mordden**
Broadway Babies: The People Who Made the American Musical
Brings to life the great personalities who created the Broadway musical, from Florenz Ziegfeld to Harold Prince and Stephen Sondheim; with an extensive discography
0-19-505425-3 OXFORD PB.................................$10.95

Richard **Rodgers**
Musical Stages: An Autobiography
0-306-80634-7 DA CAPO PB $14.95

Rodgers and Hammerstein: A Celebration
0-8065-1469-8 CITADEL PB $19.95

Joanne **Gordon**
Art Isn't Easy: The Theatre of Stephen Sondheim, Updated Edition
0-306-80468-9 DA CAPO PB...............................$16.95

Martin **Gottfried**
Stephen Sondheim
0-8109-3844-8 ABRAMS $49.50

Graig **Zadan**
Sondheim and Co., Revised Edition
0-06-091400-9 DA CAPO PB $17.95

Joseph P. **Swain**
The Broadway Musical: A Critical and Musical Survey
Beyond anecdotes or production histories, a detailed analysis of the music for the most important or representative Broadway musicals
0-19-505434-2 OXFORD $30.00

Selected Memoirs and Biographies

Gene **Fowler**
Good Night, Sweet Prince: The Life and Times of John Barrymore
0-916515-56-7 MERCURY HOUSE PB $12.95

Claire **Bloom**
Leaving a Doll's House: A Memoir
0-316-09980-5 LITTLE, BROWN $23.95

John **Fuegi**
Brecht and Company: Sex, Politics, and the Making of the Modern Drama
A controversial study that depicts Brecht's relations with his (frequently unacknowledged) collaborators in less than flattering terms
See also **STUDIES OF INDIVIDUAL AUTHORS** under **CRITICAL STUDIES** under **GERMAN LITERATURE** in **LITERATURE OF EUROPE, AFRICA, AND ASIA**
0-8021-1529-2 GROVE $32.50

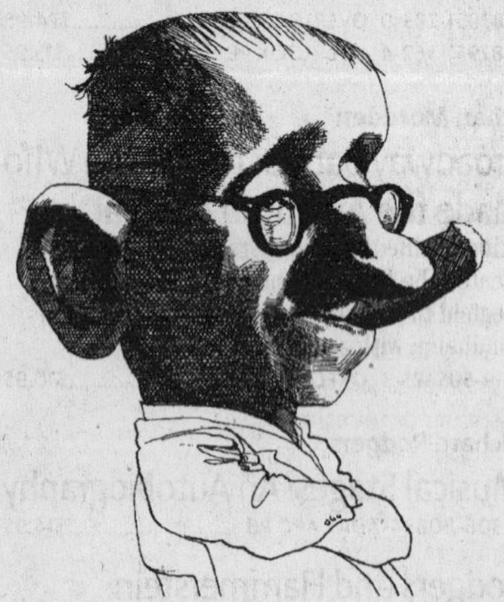

Bertolt Brecht

Lenny **Bruce**
How to Talk Dirty and Influence People: An Autobiography
0-671-75108-5 FIRESIDE PB $11.00

Lenny Bruce

Philip **Hoare**
Bitter Sweet: A Biography of Noel Coward
When we think of Noel Coward, we think of effortless sophistication. To the contrary, writes Hoare, this socially adept and scathingly witty artist crafted his life as carefully as he did his plays in his rise from a middle-class suburban childhood to the zenith of urbanity. An extraordinary work revealing the gulf between the image and reality of Coward
See also **SONGWRITERS** under **AMERICAN POPULAR MUSIC**
See also **THE 20TH CENTURY** under **STUDIES OF INDIVIDUAL AUTHORS** under **ANTHOLOGIES AND STUDIES**
0-684-80937-0 SIMON & SCHUSTER $30.00

Eva Le **Gallienne**
The Mystic in the Theatre: Eleonora Duse
One great actress pays tribute to another
0-8093-0631-X SOUTHERN ILLINOIS PB $12.95

John **Gielgud**
Early Stages
0-916515-57-5 MERCURY HOUSE PB $11.95

Hugh **Fordin**
Getting to Know Him: A Biography of Oscar Hammerstein II
This 1977 biography, based on archives and interviews, is introduced by Stephen Sondheim
0-306-80668-1 DA CAPO PB $15.95

Joseph **Jefferson**
The Autobiography of Joseph Jefferson
This beguiling book (1890) by one of the greatest and best-loved actors of the 19th century is still a landmark in American theatrical writing
EDITED BY ALAN S. DOWNER
0-674-05350-8 HARVARD $27.50

Jerome **Lawrence**
Actor: The Life and Times of Paul Muni
A detailed biography of the Yiddish character actor who conquered Broadway and Hollywood
0-573-69034-0 SAMUEL FRENCH PB $8.95

Donald **Spoto**
Laurence Olivier: A Biography
0-06-109035-2 HARPERCOLLINS PB $5.99

Brenda **Murphy**
Tenessee Williams and Elia Kazan: A Collaboration in the Theatre
0-521-40095-3 CAMBRIDGE $44.95

Jose **Quintero**
If You Don't Dance They Beat You
This 1974 autobiography by the director of the major O'Neill revivals deals with an important period of American theater in the 1950s and '60s
0-312-02222-0 ST. MARTIN'S PB $10.95

Richard **Ziegfeld** & Paulette **Ziegfeld**
The Ziegfeld Touch: The Life and Times of Florenz Ziegfeld, Jr.
A dazzling showman, Flo Ziegfeld was as extravagant in his personal life as in his stage productions. This lavish book chronicles Ziegfeld's life and times, from his gambling and womanizing to the production of such American classics as *Show Boat* and *The Ziegfeld Follies.* The cast of characters includes Fanny Brice, Roy Rogers, W. C. Fields, Jerome Kern, Irving Berlin, and others. 385 illustrations
0-8109-3966-5 ABRAMS $49.50

Dramatic Theory and Criticism

Adolpho **Appia**
The Work of Living Art & Man Is the Measure of All Things
Two seminal works by the French-Swiss artist who revolutionized lighting design at the turn of the century
0-87024-305-5 MIAMI PB $12.95

Antonin **Artaud**
The Theater and Its Double
These major statements of dramatic theory, influenced by Balinese and Mexican Indian culture, focus on restoring myth and mystery to the stage. They deeply influenced the absurdists, and inspired the Theater of Cruelty in the 1960s
See also **ESSAYS: PERSONAL, LITERARY, PHILOSOPHICAL** under **MODERN FRENCH LITERATURE** in **LITERATURE OF EUROPE, AFRICA, AND ASIA**
TRANSLATED BY MARY C. RICHARDS
0-8021-5030-6 GROVE PB $9.95

Antonin Artaud

Bertolt **Brecht**

Brecht on Theatre

Selected writings on epic theater and the alienation effect and how these concepts apply to Brecht's own work

See also **EARLY 20TH CENTURY** under **MODERN EUROPEAN DRAMA** in **LITERATURE OF EUROPE, AFRICA, AND ASIA**

TRANSLATED BY JOHN WILLETT

0-8090-0542-5 HILL & WANG PB $14.00

Peter **Brook**

The Empty Space

"What I treasure most in the book is that it always harks back to the artistic, social, psychological, practical basis of the theater as a concern of cultural significance"—Harold Clurman

0-689-70558-1 SIMON & SCHUSTER PB $9.00

Marvin **Carlson**

Theories of the Theatre: A Historical and Critical Survey from the Greeks to the Present

An overview of the aesthetic and philosophical movements that have shaped (mainly) Western theater

0-8014-8154-6 CORNELL PB $19.95

Martin **Esslin**

An Anatomy of Drama

A straightforward introduction to dramatic analysis and the whole theatrical experience

0-8090-0550-6 FS&G PB $8.95

Friedrich **Nietzsche**

The Birth of Tragedy

Tragedy considered as a synthesis of the turbulent Dionysian and serene Apollonian elements in Greek culture, and Socrates as the embodiment of a perverse rationalism that killed it off

See also **NIETZSCHE** under **PHILOSOPHY** in **RELIGION, SPIRITUALITY, AND PHILOSOPHY**

TRANSLATED BY WALTER KAUFMANN

0-394-70369-3 RANDOM HOUSE PB $9.00

Richard **Schechner**

Between Theater and Anthropology

FOREWORD BY VICTOR TURNER

0-8122-1225-8 PENNSYLVANIA PB $20.95

James **Schevill**

Breakout: In Search of New Theatrical Environments

0-8040-0574-5 OHIO $18.00

J.L. **Styan**

Elements of Drama

A clear introduction, illustrated with example from the works of the great modern dramatists

0-521-09201-9 CAMBRIDGE PB $20.95

Victor **Turner**

From Ritual to Theatre: The Human Seriousness of Play

Essays on comparative symbology, social dramas, dramatic ritual/ritual drama, and more

0-933826-17-6 PAJ PUBLICATIONS PB $14.95

J. Michael **Walton**, editor

Craig on Theatre

0-413-49540-X METHUEN PB $19.95

Essays and Criticism

Eric **Bentley**

The Life of the Drama

1-55783-110-6 APPLAUSE THEATRE PB $12.95

Thinking About the Playwright

Essays and reviews by the distinguished critic

0-8101-0733-3 NORTHWESTERN PB $15.95

Peter **Brook**

The Open Door: Thoughts on Acting and Theatre

Those who have been fortunate enough to see Brook's productions of *Marat Sade* or *Carmen* know that he is one of the finest stage directors at work today. These three essays on how he chooses his plays, what he expects from them, and how he motivates his actors are indispensable to anyone interested in the theater. "Peter Brook is one of the artistic geniuses of our time"—*San Francisco Chronicle*

0-679-42806-2 PANTHEON $21.00

Peter Brook

Robert **Brustein**

The Theatre of Revolt: An Approach to the Modern Drama

Early studies in the modern movement: Ibsen, Strindberg, Chekhov, Shaw, Brecht, Pirandello, O'Neill, and Genet

0-929587-53-7 DEE PB $13.95

Martin **Esslin**

The Theater of the Absurd

The most influential book about the revolution in modern drama wrought by Beckett, Ionesco, Genet, Adamov, and other writers in the 1950s

0-14-013728-9 VIKING PB $13.95

Francis **Fergusson**

The Idea of a Theater: The Art of Drama in Changing Perspective

This influential study, first published in 1949, started a reevaluation of the purpose of theater and the revival of noncommercial theater in America. The ten plays analyzed range from *Oedipus Rex* to *Murder in the Cathedral*

0-691-01288-1 PRINCETON PB $14.95

Ronald **Hayman**

How to Read a Play

A straightforward introduction to dramatic analysis

0-8021-3042-9 GROVE PB $7.95

Walter **Kerr**

Tragedy and Comedy

This 1967 book by the eminent newspaper critic is more readable and insightful than most academic books

INTRODUCTION BY WILLIAM ALFRED

0-306-80249-XDA CAPO PB $9.95

Helene **Keyssar**

Feminist Theatre

0-312-04129-2 ST. MARTIN'S PB $12.95

Jan **Kott**

The Theater of Essence

A stimulating collection of essays ranging from Shakespeare and Ibsen to Japanese theater, Grotowski, and Peter Brook

INTRODUCTION BY MARTIN ESSLIN

0-8101-0665-5 NORTHWESTERN PB $14.95

John **Lahr**

Light Fantastic: Adventures in Theatre

0-385-31546-5 BANTAM DOUBLEDAY DELL $23.95

0-385-31550-3 DOUBLEDAY PB $10.00

Bonnie **Marranca**

Theatrewritings

Includes essays on the avant-garde theater and performance art, and surprisingly fresh insights into Lillian Hellman, Pirandello, and Chekhov

0-933826-67-2 PAJ PUBLICATIONS $19.95

0-933826-68-0 PAJ PUBLICATIONS PB $14.95

John **Peter**

Vladimir's Carrot: Modem Drama and the Modern Imagination

The most recent studies of postwar avant-garde drama by the critic of the *Times* (London)

0-226-66265-9 CHICAGO $24.95

Jan **Kott**

Shakespeare Our Contemporary

This important political interpretation of Shakespeare's plays has influenced Peter Brook and a host of Eastern European directors active in America today

See also **SHAKESPEARE** under **STUDIES OF INDIVIDUAL AUTHORS** under **ANTHOLOGIES AND STUDIES** in **LITERATURE OF THE BRITISH ISLES**

INTRODUCTION BY MARTIN ESSLIN

0-393-00736-7 NORTON PB $13.95

Kenneth **Tynan**

Letters

See also **20TH-CENTURY BRITISH ESSAYS AND OTHER PROSE** in **LITERATURE OF THE BRITISH ISLES**

0-679-42610-8 RANDOM HOUSE $30.00

Profiles

See also **20TH-CENTURY BRITISH ESSAYS AND OTHER PROSE** in **LITERATURE OF THE BRITISH ISLES**

0-679-75639-6 RANDOM HOUSE PB $20.00

The Art and Practice of Theater

Playwriting

George P. **Baker**

Dramatic Technique

The classic book by the father of American playwriting

0-306-80030-6 DA CAPO PB $16.95

Toby **Cole**, editor

Playwrights on Playwriting: The Meaning and Making of Modern Drama

A broad and useful selection

INTRODUCTION BY JOHN GASSNER

0-8090-0529-8 FS&G PB $9.95

Lajos **Egri**

The Art of Dramatic Writing

This compelling book from the 1940s is still a staple of many university courses; some writers have claimed that reading Egri changed their lives

0-671-21332-6 SIMON & SCHUSTER PB $10.95

Directing

Nikolai M. **Gorchakov**

Stanislavsky Directs

This pupil kept notes and diaries between 1924 and 1936, while Stanislavsky lectured and worked on five productions

TRANSLATED BY MIRIAM GOLDINA

0-87910-051-6 PROSCENIUM PB $17.95

Charles **Marowitz**

Prospero's Staff: Acting and Directing in the Contemporary Theater

0-253-34622-3 INDIANA $12.95

Alexander **Tairov**

Notes of a Director

Tairov (1885-1950), one of the great anti-naturalistic directors of the Russian theater; did much of his work in opposition to the party line

0-87024-309-8 MIAMI PB $10.95

Acting

Richard **Boleslavsky**

Acting: The First Six Lessons

A classic that bridges the Russian tradition and the American "Method"

0-87830-000-7 THEATRE ARTS $16.95

Simon **Callow**

Being an Actor

0-312-13433-9 ST. MARTIN'S PB $12.95

Toby **Cole** & Helen K. **Chinoy**, editors

Actors on Acting

A store of historical information and experiences

0-517-54048-7 CROWN PB $14.00

Hume **Cronyn**

A Terrible Liar

Married for nearly half a century to actress Jessica Tandy, Cronyn has worked with such legends as Alfred Hitchcock, Tallulah Bankhead, John Gielgud, and Elia Kazan. "A delight…crammed with entertaining stories about show-biz friends"—*Publishers Weekly*

0-688-10080-5 QUILL PB $23.00

Uta **Hagen** & Haskel **Frankel**

Respect For Acting

An acclaimed book by the distinguished actress

0-02-547390-5 MACMILLAN $18.95

Gordon **Hunt**

How to Audition

0-06-273286-2 HARPERCOLLINS PB $13.50

Robert **Lewis**

Advice to the Players

One of the major exponents of "Method" acting reveals a lifetime of experience

INTRODUCTION BY HAROLD CLURMAN

1-55936-003-8
THEATRE COMMUNICATIONS PB $10.95

Katinka **Matson**

The Working Actor: A Guide to the Profession

0-14-046343-7 PENGUIN PB $12.00

Sanford **Meisner** & Dennis **Longwell**

Sanford Meisner on Acting

A detailed transcription of a great acting teacher's classes and methods

0-394-75059-4 VINTAGE PB $12.00

Sonia **Moore**

The Stanislavski System: The Professional Training of an Actor

INTRODUCTION BY JOSHUA LOGAN

PREFACE BY JOHN GIELGUD

0-14-046660-6 PENGUIN PB $10.95

Frank **Pike** & Thomas G. **Dunn**

Scenes and Monologues from the New American Theather

0-451-62547-1 NEW AMERICAN LIBRARY PB $5.99

Michael **Shurtleff**

Audition: Everything an Actor Needs to Know

INTRODUCTION BY BOB FOSSE

0-553-27295-0 BDD PB $6.50

Constantin **Stanislavksi**

An Actor Prepares

0-87830-983-7 THEATRE ARTS PB $16.95

Building a Character

0-87830-982-9 THEATRE ARTS PB $15.95

Creating a Role

TRANSLATED BY ELIZABETH R. HAPGOOD

EDITED BY HERMINE I. POPPER

0-87830-024-4 THEATRE ARTS $45.00

0-87830-981-0 THEATRE ARTS PB $15.95

Lee **Strasberg**

A Dream of Passion: The Development of the Method

The "Method" from the horse's mouth

0-452-26198-8 NEW AMERICAN LIBRARY PB $10.95

Jack **Temchin**, editor

One on One: Best Monologues for the Nineties (Men & Women)

A demanding workout for the aspiring and accomplished actor alike; a compelling read for the theater lover, *One on One* is the most complete collection of monologues available. From Neil Simon to Elizabeth Swados and Harold Pinter, electrifying moments of dramatic art abound in these splendid volumes

1-55783-152-1 APPLAUSE THEATRE PB $7.95

1-55783-151-3 APPLAUSE THEATRE PB $7.95

Design

Arnold **Aronson**

American Set Design

0-930452-39-9
THEATRE COMMUNICATIONS PB $22.95

Robert Edmond **Jones**

The Dramatic Imagination

One of the few classics about design by the man who dominated American stage design between the wars

0-87830-592-0 THEATRE ARTS PB $13.95

Oren W. **Parker** & Harvey K. **Smith**

Scene Design and Stage Lighting

0-03-028777-4 HOLT $41.23

Harold B. **Segal**

Pinocchio's Progeny: Puppets, Marionettes, Automatons, and Robots in Modernist and Avant-Garde Drama

0-8018-5262-5 JOHNS HOPKINS PB $16.95

Gift and Picture Books

Fred **Fehl**

On Broadway

Fehl's performance photographs from the 1940s and '50s are enhanced by quotes, reminiscences, and anecdotes

0-292-76010-8 TEXAS $29.95

George **Perry**

The Complete Phantom of the Opera

Contains Andrew Lloyd Weber's libretto, much peripheral information, and photos

0-8050-0657-5 HOLT $29.95

Selected Drama Anthologies

Sylvan **Barnet**, editor

Eight Great Comedies

Includes *The Clouds, Mandragola, Twelfth Night, The Miser, The Beggar's Opera, The Importance of Being Earnest, Uncle Vanya,* and *Arms and the Man*

0-452-01170-1 SPORTS ILLUSTRATED $42.00

Ian **Brown** & Mark **Fisher**, editors

Made in Scotland: An Anthology of New Scottish Plays

These prize-winning plays, produced in Scotland, celebrate the tremendous wealth and creativity of Scottish writing for the theatre. The plays in this colleciton are Simon Donald's *The Life of Stuff*; Sue Glover's *Bondagers*; Duncan McLean's *Julie Allardyce*; and *The Cut* by ex-miner Mike Cullen

See also **ANTHOLOGIES** under **20TH-CENTURY BRITISH AND IRISH DRAMA** in **LITERATURE OF THE BRITISH ISLES**

0-413-69180-2 HEINEMANN PB $19.95

John M. **Clum**, editor

Staging Gay Lives: An Anthology of Contemporary Gay Theater

0-8133-2505-6 HARPERCOLLINS PB $24.95

Harold **Clurman**, editor

Nine Plays of the Modern Theater

Includes *Waiting for Godot, The Visit, Tango, The Caucasian Chalk Circle, The Balcony, The Rhinoceros, American Buffalo, The Birthday Party,* and *Rosencrantz and Guildenstern Are Dead*

0-8021-5032-2 GROVE PB $19.95

Harry Justin **Elam** & Robert **Alexander**, editors

Colored Contradictions: An Anthology of Contemporary African-American Plays

0-452-27497-4 PLUME PB $16.95

Kathy A. **Perkins** & Roberta **Uno**, editors

Contemporary Plays by Women of Color: An Anthology

0-415-11377-6 ROUTLEDGE $59.95

Reference

Gerald **Bordman**

The Oxford Companion to American Theatre

An encyclopedia of the major figures, plays, historical trends from colonial times to the present

0-19-507246-4 OXFORD $60.00

Phyllis **Hartnoll**, editor

The Oxford Companion to the Theatre

Despite some shortcomings, this encyclopedia is the most up-to-date reference book about world theater

0-19-211546-4 OXFORD $60.00

Isabelle **Stevenson**

The Tony Award: A Complete Listing of Winners and Nominees with a History of the American Theater Wing

0-435-08658-8 HEINEMANN PB $14.95

Film

When the pioneering filmmaker Louis Lumire abandoned movie production at the turn of the century, he dismissed the medium as being without commercial potential. By the 1920s, movies were established as both the primary form of mass entertainment and, for many visionaries, as "the art of the 20th century."

Three decades ago, film history consisted largely of Griffith, Chaplin, and the Odessa Steps; a close-up was a close-up, montage was montage, and that was about all the theory you needed to get by. Around 1960, new elements emerged in rapid succession: the New Wave, the auteur theory, the pop obsession with Hollywood imagery, the breaching of censorship barriers, and the surfacing of the underground. With the elevation of film studies to full academic stature came an industry devoted to churning out monographs, filmographies, and theoretical treatises—a flood that shows no signs of abating. The trick is to uncover, amid heaps of glorified fan mail, cut-and-paste nostalgia, and dutifully dull scholarship, the smaller pile of books that really prompt a refreshment of vision.

Introductions and General Histories

The movies do not lend themselves to broad overview. Large-scale histories suffer from the fact that there are simply too many movies. Even the best of such surveys tend to rely on convenient generalizations and relentless pigeonholing to tie together their disparate subject matter. The following reasonably up-to-date books do their best with a thankless task.

Richard **Abel**

Silent Film

0-8135-2226-9 RUTGERS PB $20.00

Gilbert **Adair**

Flickers: A History of Cinema in 100 Images

Adair offers witty commentary on images ranging from workers leaving the Lumiere factory in 1897 to Johnny Depp impersonating Ed Wood in 1994

0-571-17309-8 FABER PB $22.95

For heaven's sake, how can Jerry Lewis be Art? Doesn't it smack just a tad of the Fordist (Henry, not John) assembly line when a film looks as new, as indecently streamlined, as a new car or kitchen unit? And yet, exactly as if a Saturday Evening Post cover by Norman Rockwell were to be exhibited in the Prado, where its usurped prominence would take some getting used to, but, once you had got used to it, why yes, yes! it didn't seem at all incongruous beside the El Grecos and the Goyas and the Velasquezes, just so does Mantra-like contemplation of goofy, buck-toothed Jerry and his web of candy-coloured beakers start to prompt untoward stirrings in the cinephile's vitals. At which point another auteurist is born.

FLICKERS: A HISTORY OF CINEMA IN 100 IMAGES

Erik **Barnouw**

Documentary: A History of the Non-Fiction Film

A useful supplement, since most histories focus on fiction film

0-19-507898-5 OXFORD PB $13.95

David **Bordwell** & Kristin **Thompson**

Film Art: An Introduction

A serviceable tour of the film-studies syllabus, incorporating recent critical trends

0-07-006446-6 MCGRAW HILL PB $33.75

Michael C. **Carnes**, editor

Past Imperfect: History According to the Movies

0-8050-3759-4 HOLT $30.00

David A. **Cook**

A History of Narrative Film

A reliable and widely used one-volume text on cinema history

0-393-95553-2 NORTON PB $44.95

Roger **Ebert**, editor

Roger Ebert's Book of Film

Ebert compiles some of the greatest essays ever written on the topic of cinema. An eclectic and engrossing collection featuring the likes of Norman Mailer, Pauline Kael, Quentin Tarantino, and more

0-393-04000-3 NORTON $30.00

James **Monaco**

How to Read a Film

A useful introductory study of the art and technology of film, with an extensive bibliography

0-19-502806-6 OXFORD PB $17.95

David **Shipman**

The Story of Cinema: A Complete Narrative History from the Beginnings to the Present

PREFACE BY INGMAR BERGMAN

0-312-76280-1 ST. MARTIN'S PB $19.95

Robert **Sklar**

Film: An International History of the Medium

A literate and profusely illustrated survey published to celebrate the cinema's centenary

0-13-328014-4 PRENTICE HALL PB $47.00

Emmanuelle **Toulet**

Birth of the Motion Picture

TRANSLATED BY SUSAN EMANUEL

0-8109-2874-4 ABRAMS PB $12.95

National Cinemas

France

Mary Lea **Bandy**
Rediscovering French Film
A series of interesting and unusual essays
0-316-72935-3 NY GRAPHIC PB $15.50

Colin **Crisp**
The Classic French Cinema, 1930-1960
0-253-31550-6 INDIANA..................................$59.95

Lynn A. **Higgins**
New Novel, New Wave, New Politics: Fiction and the Representation of History in Postwar France
0-8032-2377-3 NEBRASKA..............................$40.00

T. Jefferson **Kline**
Screening the Text: Intertextuality in New Wave French Cinema
See also CONTEMPORARY THEORY under FILM THEORY
0-8018-4267-0 JOHNS HOPKINS......................$37.50

Germany

Timothy **Corrigan**
New German Film: The Displaced Image
Critical studies of films by Wenders, Herzog, Syberberg, Schlondorff, Fassbinder, and Kluge
0-253-31439-9 INDIANA $35.00
0-253-20841-6 INDIANA PB.............................$14.95

Marlene Dietrich

Lotte **Eisner**
The Haunted Screen
Eisner was the great chronicler of German expressionism, its roots and its impact
TRANSLATED BY ROGER GREAVES
0-520-02479-6 CALIFORNIA PB $16.95

Thomas **Elsaesser**
New German Cinema: A History
Fassbinder, Herzog, Wenders, Kluge, and many more are reassessed
0-8135-1392-8 RUTGERS PB..............................$14.95

Siegfreid **Kracauer**
From Caligari to Hitler: A Psychological History of the German Film
Kracauer uncovers proto-Nazi elements in the classics of German expressionism
0-691-02505-3 PRINCETON PB..........................$17.95

Great Britain

Charles **Barr**, editor
All Our Yesterdays: 90 Years of British Cinema
An entertaining collection of essays, with many illustrations
0-85170-179-5 BRITISH FILM INST PB.............$29.95

Charles **Barr** & Stephen **Frears**
Typically British: A Short History of the Cinema in Britain
0-85170-503-0 BRITISH FILM INST PB.............$14.95

Marcia **Landy**
British Genres: Cinema and Society, 1930-1960
Well-researched survey of a woefully neglected popular cinema, but rather plodding in its political interpretations
0-691-03176-2 PRINCETON $65.00
0-691-00836-1 PRINCETON PB $24.95

Italy

Peter **Bondanella**
Italian Cinema: From Neorealism to the Present
0-8044-6061-2 CONTINUUM PB $14.95

Angela **Dalle Vacche**
The Body in the Mirror: Shapes of History in Italian Cinema
0-691-00872-8 PRINCETON PB $21.95

Millicent **Marcus**
Italian Film in the Light of Neorealism
0-691-10208-2 PRINCETON PB $24.95

Luca **Palmerini** & Gaetano **Mistretta**
Spaghetti Nightmares: Italian Fantasy-Horrors as Seen Through the Eyes of Their Protagonists
A boon for fans of the gaudily outrageous Italian genre films of the 60's and 70's, featuring interviews with Dario Argento, Lucio Fulci, Mimsy Farmer, Terence Stamp, and many others
0-9634982-7-4 FANTASMA PB $25.95

Federico Fellini

Roger **Witcombe**
The New Italian Cinema
0-19-520381-X OXFORD $30.00

Russia and Eastern Europe

Sergei **Eisenstein**
Selected Works: Writings, 1934-47
See also DIRECTORS
TRANSLATED BY WILLIAM POWELL
EDITED BY RICHARD TAYLOR
0-85170-530-8 BRITISH FILM INST $55.00

Beyond the Stars: The Memoirs of Sergei Eisenstein
The Russian master in his own words
See also DIRECTORS
EDITED BY RICHARD TAYLOR
TRANSLATED BY WILLIAM POWELL
0-85170-460-3 BRITISH FILM INST $75.00

Mira **Liehm** & Antonin **Liehm**
The Most Important Art: Soviet and East European Film After 1945
0-520-03157-1 CALIFORNIA.............................$50.00

Neya **Zorkaya**
The Illustrated History of Soviet Cinema
0-87052-134-9 HIPPOCRENE PB $11.95

Japan

Joseph L. **Anderson** & Donald **Richie**
The Japanese Film: Art and Industry
This recently revised study remains the best survey
FOREWORD BY AKIRA KUROSAWA
0-691-00792-6 PRINCETON PB $24.95

Noel **Burch**

To the Distant Observer: Form and Meaning in Japanese Cinema

An intellectually dense, graphically beautiful book; Burch gives preference to pre-war films, which he considers more original in style

0-520-03605-0 CALIFORNIA $48.00

David **Desser**

Eros Plus Massacre: An Introduction to the Japanese New Wave Cinema

A thematic survey of Japan's New Wave, focusing on the work of such directors as Oshima Shinoda, Imamura, and Yoshida

See also **CONTEMPORARY SOCIETY AND CULTURE** under **JAPAN** in **WORLD HISTORY AND CURRENT AFFAIRS**

0-253-20469-0 INDIANA PB $5.25

Kyoko **Hirano**

Mr. Smith Goes to Tokyo

The impact of the American military occupation on Japanese film: a long overdue account

1-56098-402-3 SMITHSONIAN PB $15.95

Alain **Silver**

The Samurai Film

0-87951-246-6 VIKING PB $12.95

China

Chris **Berry**, editor

Perspectives on Chinese Cinema

0-85170-272-4 BRITISH FILM INST PB $21.95

Nick **Browne**, editor

New Chinese Cinemas: Forms, Identities, Politics

0-521-44409-8 CAMBRIDGE $57.95
0-521-44877-8 CAMBRIDGE PB $17.95

Rey **Chow**

Primitive Passions: Visuality, Sexuality, Ethnography, and Contemporary Chinese Cinema

0-231-07683-5 COLUMBIA PB $16.50

Stefan **Hammond** & Mike **Wilkins**

Sex and Zen and a Bullet in the Head: The Essential Guide to Hong Kong's Mind-Bending Films

0-684-80341-0 FIRESIDE PB $12.00

Other Countries

Roy **Armes**

Third World Film Making and the West

The first fully comprehensive account of film production in Third World countries which, though usually ignored and marginalized in histories of "world cinema," now produce well over half of the world's films

0-520-05690-6 CALIFORNIA PB $21.00

Julianne **Burton**, editor

Cinema and Social Change in Latin America

Twenty interviews with key figures of Latin American cinema, covering three decades and ranging from Argentina to Mexico

See also **SOCIAL THOUGHT, CULTURE, AND AESTHETICS** under **ASPECTS OF LATIN AMERICA** under **LATIN AMERICA AND THE CARIBBEAN** in **HISTORY OF THE AMERICAS**

0-292-72453-5 TEXAS $25.00
0-292-72454-3 TEXAS PB $16.95

Judith **Goldberg**

Laughter Through Tears: The Yiddish Cinema

A retrospective examination of some of the 130 Yiddish films made between 1910 and 1941

0-8386-3074-X FAIRLEIGH DICKINSON $29.50

Virginia **Higginbotham**

Spanish Film Under Franco

0-292-77603-9 TEXAS PB $11.95

Randal **Johnson** & Robert **Stam**, editors

Brazilian Cinema

0-292-70767-3 TEXAS PB $14.95

Brian **McFarlane**

Australian Cinema

0-231-06728-3 COLUMBIA $39.50

Carl J. **Mora**

Mexican Cinema: Reflections of a Society

See also **ASPECTS OF MEXICAN CULTURE** under **MEXICO** under **LATIN AMERICA AND THE CARIBBEAN** in **HISTORY OF THE AMERICAS**

0-520-04304-9 CALIFORNIA PB $14.95

Paulo Antonio **Parangua**, editor

Mexican Cinema

TRANSLATED BY ANA LÓPEZ

0-85170-515-4 BRITISH FILM INST $70.00
0-85170-516-2 BRITISH FILM INST PB $29.95

Eric **Reade**

History and Heartburn: The Saga of Australian Film, 1896-1978

0-8386-3082-0 FAIRLEIGH DICKINSON $60.00

Film in America

Kenneth **Anger**

Hollywood Babylon

The famously scurrilous account of filmland scandals by the director of *Scorpio Rising*

0-440-15325-5 DELL PB $7.50

Hollywood Babylon II

0-452-25721-2 PLUME $18.95

Tino **Balio**

United Artists: The Company Built by the Stars

Carries on Balio's account of the studio from 1951 onward

0-299-11440-6 WISCONSIN $19.95
0-299-06944-3 WISCONSIN PB $14.95

D. W. Griffith

Jeanine **Basinger**

American Cinema: One Hundred Years of Filmmaking

0-8478-1814-4 RIZZOLI $50.00

A Woman's View: How Hollywood Spoke to Women, 1930-1960

Explores a recurrent structure of the Hollywood golden era: a female character was often permitted in the beginning of a movie a certain liberation—whether romantic, sexual, or antisocial—only to be reassuringly returned, by the end, to traditional roles

0-394-56351-4 KNOPF $32.50
0-8195-6291-2 WESLEYAN PB $18.95

Alain **Bergala**

Magnum Cinema: Photographs from 50 Years of Movie-Making

0-7148-3375-4 PHAIDON $69.95

Walter **Bernstein**

Inside Out: A Memoir of the Blacklist

See also **THE MCCARTHY ERA** under **THE TRUMAN AND EISENHOWER YEARS** under **US HISTORY, 1945 TO THE PRESENT** in **HISTORY OF THE AMERICAS**

0-394-58341-8 KNOPF $24.00

Donald **Bogle**

Blacks in American Films and Television

See also **HISTORY OF TELEVISION** under **TELEVISION**

0-8240-8715-1 GARLAND $85.00

David **Bordwell**

The Classical Hollywood Cinema: Film Style and Mode of Production to 1960

The technical norms that conditioned American movies between 1917 and 1960. By far the most comprehensive book of its kind, it typifies current concern for ordinary rather than extraordinary film

0-231-06055-6 COLUMBIA PB $32.50

Herb **Bridges** & Terryl C. **Boodman**

Gone with the Wind: The Definitive Illustrated History of the Book, the Movie, and the Legend

0-671-68451-5 FIRESIDE PB $29.95
0-671-68387-X FIRESIDE PB $17.00

Samuel Goldwyn

Kevin **Brownlow**

Behind the Mask of Innocence

One of the most entertaining of film histories: Brownlow reveals a world of early filmmaking unknown to most viewers, a world which reveled in the exploitation of political scandal and social upheaval

0-520-07626-5 CALIFORNIA PB........................$25.00

The Parade's Gone By...

A beautifully designed book about the glories of silent filmmaking

0-520-03068-0 CALIFORNIA PB........................$25.00

Francis B. **Couvares**, editor

Movie Censorship and American Culture

1-56098-669-7 SMITHSONIAN PB $17.95

Neal **Gabler**

An Empire of Their Own: How the Jews Invented Hollywood

An examination of the careers of Samuel Goldwyn, Louis B. Mayer, and other movie producers, showing how they successfully imposed their fantasies of American life on to the American screen

See also **JEWISH CULTURE** under **JEWISH HISTORY** in **WORLD HISTORY AND CURRENT AFFAIRS**

0-385-26557-3 ANCHOR PB..............................$14.00

Nancy **Griffin** & Kim **Masters**

Hit and Run: How Jon Peters and Peter Guber Took Sony for a Ride in Hollywood

Major bombs, large severance packages

0-684-80931-1 SIMON & SCHUSTER $25.00

Boze **Hadleigh**

Hollywood, Babble On

Ever want to dish with the pros? *Hollywood, Babble On* will put you in the slimelight with such categories as Catty Women on Women, Ex-Husbands and Wives, Lavender Limelight, and Co-stars Wars. An example from Susan Sarandon: "Mel Gibson is somewhere to the right of Attila the Hun. He's beautiful, but only on the outside." A juicy piece of research from the author of *The Lavender Screen* and *Conversations with My Elders*

1-55972-219-3 BIRCH LANE..............................$19.95

Jan Christopher **Horack**, editor

Lovers of Cinema: The First American Film Avant-Garde, 1919-1945

0-299-14680-4 WISCONSIN..............................$49.95

Nicolas **Kent**

Naked Hollywood: Money and Power in the Movies Today

The companion book to the BBC/A&E series, a blistering indictment of the contemporary film industry. The targets of Kent's merciless probe include leading stars, agents, and producers. Among the many voices heard from: Arnold Schwarzenegger, Steven Spielberg, Oliver Stone, Martin Scorsese, John Sayles, Penny Marshall, Mel Brooks, and Ivan Reitman. Includes 150 photos

0-312-07040-3 ST. MARTIN'S PB $22.95

Rod **Lurie**

Once Upon a Time in Hollywood: Movie Making, Con Games, and Murder in Glitter City

0-679-43522-0 PANTHEON $25.00

John **Pierson**

Spike, Mike, Slackers & Dykes: A Guided Tour Across a Decade of American Independent Cinema

A knowing look at the rise of American indies

0-7868-6189-4 HYPERION $22.95

David **Robinson**

From Peep Show to Palace: The Birth of American Film

FOREWORD BY MARTIN SCORSESE

0-231-10338-7 COLUMBIA $29.50

Michael **Rogin**

Blackface, White Noise: Jewish Immigrants in the Hollywood Melting Pot

0-520-20407-7 CALIFORNIA..............................$24.95

Andrew **Sarris**

The American Cinema: Directors and Directions, 1929-1968

Sarris's influential rating of American directors, from the "pantheon" on down, with filmographies up to 1968; a classic statement of the auteurist position

See also **FILM THEORY**

0-306-80728-9 DA CAPO PB..............................$14.95

P. Adams **Sitney**

Visionary Film: The American Avant-Garde 1943-1978

0-19-502486-9 OXFORD PB..............................$16.95

Gore **Vidal**

Screening History

"Our greatest living man of letters" looks at history as it has been represented in movies to show how they have influenced the way we live and what we believe. *Screening History* captures the hold movies have had on the way we view American life and its history. "Gore Vidal remains a vital if enigmatic force on the literary scene… [*Screening History* is] a fresh piece of non-fiction" —*NY Times Book Review*

0-674-79586-5 HARVARD..............................$14.95

As I now move, graciously, I hope, toward the door marked Exit, it occurs to me that the only thing I ever really liked to do was go to the movies. Naturally, Sex and Art always took precedence over the cinema. Unfortunately, neither ever proved to be as dependable as the filtering of present light through that moving strip of celluloid which projects past images and voices onto a screen. Thus, in a seemingly simple process, screening history.

SCREENING HISTORY

Mason **Wiley** & Damien **Bona**

Inside Oscar: The Unofficial History of the Academy Awards

0-345-38177-7 BALLANTINE PB........................$20.00

Michael **Wood**

America in the Movies

"A brilliant romp through the fertile field of Hollywood's vision of America in the 1940's and '50s. With geniality and insight, Michael Wood exposes the tangle of fantasy and reality in the waning days of the studio system"— Leo Braudy

0-231-07099-3 COLUMBIA PB........................$15.50

Robin **Wood**

Hollywood from Vietnam to Reagan

Wood combines formal analysis with an intensely political reading of recent American film

0-231-05777-6 COLUMBIA PB $17.50

Ronald Reagan

Genres and Themes

Jeanine **Basinger**

The World War II Combat Film: Anatomy of a Genre

An analytical study of *The Dirty Dozen, Tora Tora Tora!*, and many others

0-231-05953-1 COLUMBIA PB $18.00

Andrew **Bergman**

We're in the Money

The novelist and director writes sympathetically of Depression-era movies

0-929587-85-5 DEE PB $9.95

Donald **Bogle**

Toms, Coons, Mulattoes, Mammies and Bucks: An Interpretive History of Blacks in American Film

A historical overview of how Hollywood has portrayed blacks

See also **THE BLACK AESTHETIC** under **CULTURE** under **AFRICAN-AMERICAN STUDIES** in **HISTORY OF THE AMERICAS**

0-8264-0416-2 CONTINUUM PB $15.95

Ronald V. **Borst**

Graven Images: The Best of Horror, Fantasy, and Science Fiction Film Art

0-8021-1484-9 GROVE.......................................$19.95

Ian **Cameron**, editor

The Book of Film Noir

Beautifully designed and illustrated, staunchly theory-minded in its approach, this collection of essays deals with a host of neglected classics such as *Fallen Angel, Angelface,* and *The Big Combo*

0-8264-0589-4 CONTINUUM.............................$24.95

Stanley **Cavell**

Contesting Tears: The Hollywood Melodrama of the Unknown Woman

See also **CONTEMPORARY THEORY** under **FILM THEORY**

0-226-09814-1 CHICAGO.................................$36.00

0-226-09816-8 CHICAGO PB.............................$14.95

Pursuits of Happiness: The Hollywood Comedy of Remarriages

0-674-73906-X HARVARD PB............................$13.95

Carol J. **Clover**

Men, Women, and Chainsaws: Gender in the Modern Horror Film

Clover offers original analyses of some of the most critically despised films of recent decades, including *I Spit on Your Grave* and *Friday the 13th*

0-691-04802-9 PRINCETON $50.00

0-691-00620-2 PRINCETON PB $13.95

Pam **Cook** & Philip **Dodd**, editors

Women and Film: A Sight and Sound Reader

1-56639-142-3 TEMPLE...................................$54.95

1-56639-143-1 TEMPLE PB..............................$18.95

Mary Anne **Doane**

The Desire to Desire: The Woman's Film of the 1940s

"Insightful elaboration of the mechanics of the assertion and denial of desire in the four subgenres of the woman's film"—*Film Quarterly*

0-253-20433-X INDIANA PB..............................$14.95

Barry **Gifford**

The Devil Thumbs a Ride & Other Unforgettable Films

0-8021-3078-X GROVE PB...................................$7.95

Ed **Guerrero**

Framing Blackness: The African-American Image in Film

1-56639-126-1 TEMPLE PB..............................$18.95

Phil **Hardy**

These three genre guides are the most informative ever published, with detailed credits and critiques and profuse illustrations

The Western

0-879-51625-9 OVERLOOK..............................$40.00

Science Fiction

0-879-51626-7 OVERLOOK..............................$40.00

Horror

0-879-51624-0 OVERLOOK..............................$40.00

Molly **Haskell**

From Reverence to Rape: The Treatment of Women in the Movies

An excellent study of how film has reflected and reshaped images of women

See also **FILM** under **ARTS AND LETTERS** under **WOMEN'S STUDIES** in **SOCIAL STUDIES**

0-226-31885-0 CHICAGO PB.............................$16.95

Robert **Heide** & John **Gilman**

Box-Office Buckaroos: The Cowboy Hero from the Wild West Show to the Silver Screen

From real to reel: how the working cowpoke was transformed into a romantic hero, first by dime novels, pulp magazines, and Wild West shows, then by film, radio, and television. Illustrated with an amazing gathering of collectibles from pulps and paperbacks to lunchboxes, cut-out dolls, radio premiums, and mood lamps

1-55859-070-6 ABBEVILLE PB.........................$19.95

Robert P. **Kolker**

A Cinema of Loneliness: Penn, Kubrick, Scorsese, Spielberg, Altman

Kolker analyzes selected works by each director with an emphasis on their distinct themes of "American" loneliness

0-19-505390-7 OXFORD PB...............................$17.95

Maitland **McDonagh**

The Fifty Most Erotic Films of All Time: From Pandora's Box to Basic Instinct

See also **FILM** under **CUTTING EDGE** in **POPULAR READING**

0-8065-1697-6 CITADEL PB..............................$19.95

Eddie **Muller** & Daniel **Faris**

Grindhouse: The Forbidden World of "Adults Only" Cinema

Profusely illustrated survey of exploitation movies of the pre-porn era. "The films discussed here—from primeval exploitation fare, like *Mad Youth* and *Slaves in Bondage,* to such choice '60s titles as *Sin in the Suburbs* and the *Orgy at Lil's Place*—are not discussed in standard film histories; until recently their very existence was scarcely acknowledged"—from the foreword by Geoffrey O'Brien

0-879-10197-0 LIMELIGHT PB.........................$20.00

RE/Search

Incredibly Strange Films

In-depth interviews with Herschell Gordon Lewis, Doris Wishman, Larry Cohen, and other critically ghettoized masters of "B" movie horror and gore. "This book is a must for anyone truly interested in the history of the cinema. It shows the fallacy of most so-called 'complete' histories of film. Fun and incredibly strange"—*Film Folio*

See also **RE/SEARCH** under **CUTTING EDGE** in **POPULAR READING**

0-940642-09-3 V/SEARCH PB...........................$17.99

Jonathan **Romney**, editor

Celluloid Jukebox: Popular Music and the Movies Since the '50s

PREFACE BY MARTIN SCORSESE

0-85170-507-3 BRITISH FILM INST PB..............$19.95

Stanley Kubrick

Alan **Rosenthal**, editor

New Challenges For Documentary

0-520-05724-4 CALIFORNIA PB.........................$24.95

Vito **Russo**

The Celluloid Closet: Homosexuality in the Movies

A groundbreaking, provocative study

See also **THEATER AND FILM** under **ARTS AND LETTERS** under **GAY, LESBIAN, AND BISEXUAL STUDIES** in **SOCIAL STUDIES**

0-8095-9107-3 BORGO $35.00

0-06-096132-5 HARPERCOLLINS PB.................$14.00

Linda J. **Sandahl**

Rock Films: A Viewer's Guide to Three Decades of Musicals, Concerts, Documentaries and Soundtracks

See also **REFERENCE** under **ROCK**

9990797692 BOOK SALES PB $4.98

0-8160-1576-7 FACTS ON FILE PB...................$14.95

Paul **Schrader**

Transcendental Style in Film: Ozu, Bresson, Dreyer

Director and screenwriter Schrader's famous study of three directors notable for their formal rigor and spiritual intensity

0-306-80335-6 DA CAPO PB $12.95

David J. **Skal**

Hollywood Gothic

An informative history of the successive incarnations of *Dracula* as novel, stage play, and movie

0-393-30805-7 NORTON PB $15.95

The Monster Show

An ambitious, engaging study of how horror became a crucial element of popular culture

0-393-03419-4 NORTON $25.00

0-14-024002-0 PENGUIN PB $13.95

Vivian **Sobchack**

Screening Space: The American Science Fiction Film

A detailed and subtle survey, with many illustrations. "Her writing style is clear, witty and concise as she shapes new definitions of the SF film"—*Film Bulletin*

0-8044-6886-9 UNGAR PB $17.95

Helen **Taylor**

Scarlett's Women: Gone with the Wind and Its Female Fans

0-8135-1496-7 RUTGERS PB $12.95

Cathal **Tohill** & Pete **Tombs**

Immoral Tales: European Sex & Horror Movies 1956-1984

Accept no substitute: despite its almost indistinguishably sleazy cover art, this is an intelligent and superbly researched exploration of the strange world of European horror/sex/fantasy directors like Jess Franco, Jean Rollin, and Jose Larraz

0-312-13519-X ST. MARTIN'S PB $17.95

BFI Film Classics

These small, elegantly designed books reflect a list of key films in cinema history selected by the British Film Institute. Style and approach vary with each volume, but the standards are generally high, with notable contributions from Salmon Rushdie, Richard Corliss, and J. Hoberman

Melvyn **Bragg**

Seventh Seal

0-85170-391-7 BRITISH FILM INST PB $9.95

Edward **Buscombe**

Stagecoach

0-85170-299-6 BRITISH FILM INST PB $9.95

Richard **Corliss**

Lolita

0-85170-368-2 BRITISH FILM INST PB $9.95

Peter **Cowie**

Annie Hall

0-85170-580-4 BRITISH FILM INST PB $9.95

Taylor **Downing**

Olympia

0-85170-341-0 BRITISH FILM INST PB $9.95

Richard **Dyer**

Brief Encounter

0-85170-362-3 BRITISH FILM INST PB $9.95

Peter **Evans**

Women on the Verge of a Nervous Breakdown

0-85170-540-5 BRITISH FILM INST PB $9.95

Christopher **Frayling**

Things to Come

0-85170-480-8 BRITISH FILM INST PB $9.95

Philip **French** & Kersti **French**

Wild Strawberries

0-85170-481-6 BRITISH FILM INST PB $9.95

Sean **French**

The Terminator

0-85170-553-7 BRITISH FILM INST PB $9.95

Frieda **Grafe**

The Ghost and Mrs. Muir

0-85170-484-0 BRITISH FILM INST PB $9.95

Lee **Hill**

Easy Rider

0-85170-543-X BRITISH FILM INST PB $9.95

J. **Hoberman**

42nd Street

0-85170-355-0 BRITISH FILM INST PB $9.95

Penelope **Houston**

Went the Day Well

0-85170-318-6 BRITISH FILM INST PB $9.95

Nelly **Kaplan**

Napoleon

0-85170-466-2 BRITISH FILM INST PB $9.95

Gerald **Kaufman**

Meet Me in St. Louis

0-85170-501-4 BRITISH FILM INST PB $9.95

Jim **Kitses**

Gun Crazy

0-85170-579-0 BRITISH FILM INST PB $9.95

Marcia **Villarejo** & Amy **Landy**

Queen Christina

0-85170-523-5 BRITISH FILM INST PB $9.95

Simon **Louvish**

It's a Gift

0-85170-472-7 BRITISH FILM INST PB $9.95

Colin **MacArthur**

The Big Heat

0-85170-342-9 BRITISH FILM INST PB $9.95

Dana **Polan**

In a Lonely Place

0-85170-360-7 BRITISH FILM INST PB $9.95

Laura **Mulvey**

Citizen Kane

0-8317-4573-8 GALLERY BOOKS $14.98

0-85170-339-9 BRITISH FILM INST PB $9.95

Sam **Rohdie**

Rocco and his Brothers

0-85170-340-2 BRITISH FILM INST PB $9.95

Jonathan **Rosenbaum**

Greed

0-85170-358-5 BRITISH FILM INST PB $9.95

Salman **Rushdie**

The Wizard of Oz

See also **20TH CENTURY LITERATURE OF THE INDIAN SUBCONTINENT** under **LITERATURES OF INDIA** in **LITERATURE OF EUROPE, AFRICA, AND ASIA**

0-85170-300-3 BRITISH FILM INST PB $9.95

The ten-year-old who watched *The Wizard of Oz* at Bombay's Metro cinema knew very little about foreign parts and even less about growing up. He did, however, know a great deal more about the cinema of the fantastic than any Western child of the same age… Blonde Glinda arriving at Munchkinland in her magic bubble might cause Dorothy to comment on the high speed and oddity of local transport operating in Oz, but to an Indian audience she was arriving exactly as a god should arrive: ex machina, out of her own machine.

THE WIZARD OF OZ

Tom **Ryall**

Blackmail

0-85170-356-9 BRITISH FILM INST PB $9.95

Mark **Sanderson**

Don't Look Now

0-85170-572-3 BRITISH FILM INST PB $9.95

Richard **Schickel**

Double Indemnity

0-85170-298-8 BRITISH FILM INST PB $9.95

Dai **Vaughan**

Odd Man Out

0-85170-493-X BRITISH FILM INST PB $9.95

Marina **Warner**

L'Atalante

0-85170-357-7 BRITISH FILM INST PB $9.95

Peter **Wollen**

Singin' in the Rain

0-85170-351-8 BRITISH FILM INST PB $9.95

Rutgers Film in Print Series

Rutgers University's Film in Print series contributes substantially toward keeping in print great screenplays from the history of cinema. It is particularly heavy on major director's lesser-know works and foreign films, most notably those of South America.

Charles **Affron**, editor

8 1/2: Federico Fellini, Director

0-8135-1210-7 RUTGERS $35.00

0-8135-1211-5 RUTGERS PB $15.00

Peter **Bondanella** & Manuela **Gieri**, editors

La Strada: Federico Fellini, Director

0-8135-1236-0 RUTGERS....$30.00
0-8135-1237-9 RUTGERS PB....$13.00

Peter **Brunette**, editor

Shoot the Piano Player: François Truffault, Director

0-8135-1941-1 RUTGERS....$40.00
0-8135-1942-X RUTGERS PB....$15.00

Seymour **Chatman** & Guido **Fink**, editors

L' Avventura: Michelangelo Antonioni, Director

0-8135-1334-0 RUTGERS....$30.00
0-8135-1335-9 RUTGERS PB....$15.00

Rainer Werner **Fassbinder**

The Marriage of Maria Braun

See also **INDIVIDUAL FILMS** under **SCREENPLAYS**

EDITED BY JOYCE RHEUBAN

0-8135-1129-1 RUTGERS....$30.00
0-8135-1130-5 RUTGERS PB....$16.00

Lucy **Fischer**, editor

Imitation of Life: Douglas Sirk, Director

0-8135-1644-7 RUTGERS....$37.00
0-8135-1645-5 RUTGERS PB....$15.00

Jean-Luc **Godard**

Breathless

See also **INDIVIDUAL FILMS** under **SCREENPLAYS**

EDITED BY DUDLEY ANDREW

0-8135-1252-2 RUTGERS....$30.00
0-8135-1253-0 RUTGERS PB....$15.00

Tomas **Gutierrez** & others

Memories of Underdevelopment and Inconsolable Memories

0-8135-1536-X RUTGERS....$37.00
0-8135-1537-8 RUTGERS PB....$15.00

John **Huston**

The Maltese Falcon

EDITED BY WILLIAM LUHR

0-8135-2236-6 RUTGERS....$48.00
0-8135-2237-4 RUTGERS PB....$16.00

Al **La Valley**, editor

Invasion of the Body Snatchers: Don Siegel, Director

0-8135-1460-6 RUTGERS....$32.00
0-8135-1461-4 RUTGERS PB....$15.00

Robert **Lang**, editor

The Birth of a Nation: D.W. Griffith, Director

0-8135-2026-6 RUTGERS....$42.00
0-8135-2027-4 RUTGERS PB....$15.00

Robert **Lyons**, editor

My Darling Clementine: John Ford, Director

0-8135-1050-3 RUTGERS....$30.00

Kenji **Mizoguchi**

Ugetsu

EDITED BY KEIKO I. MCDONALD

0-8135-1861-X RUTGERS....$37.00
0-8135-1862-8 RUTGERS PB....$15.00

James **Naremore**, editor

North by Northwest: Alfred Hitchcock, Director

0-8135-2006-1 RUTGERS....$40.00
0-8135-2007-X RUTGERS PB....$15.00

Donald **Richie**, editor

Rashomon: Akira Kirosawa, Director

0-8135-1179-8 RUTGERS....$32.00
0-8135-1180-1 RUTGERS PB....$16.00

Eric **Rohmer**

My Night at Maud's

0-8135-1939-X RUTGERS....$40.00

François **Truffaut** & Suzanne **Schiffman**

The Last Metro

EDITED BY MIRELIA AFFRON & E. RUBINSTEIN

0-8135-1065-1 RUTGERS....$25.00
0-8135-1066-X RUTGERS PB....$15.00

Orson **Welles**

Chimes At Midnight

EDITED BY BRIDGET GELLERT LYONS

0-8135-1338-3 RUTGERS....$40.00
0-8135-1339-1 RUTGERS PB....$15.00

Touch of Evil

EDITED BY TERRY COMITO

0-8135-1097-X RUTGERS PB....$15.00

Virginia W. **Wexman**, editor

Letter from an Unknown Woman: Max Ophuls, Director

0-8135-1159-3 RUTGERS....$30.00
0-8135-1160-7 RUTGERS PB....$15.00

Charles **Wolfe**, editor

Meet John Doe: Frank Capra, Director

0-8135-1386-3 RUTGERS....$32.00
0-8135-1387-1 RUTGERS PB....$15.00

Directors

"Making a film means, first of all, to tell a story. That story can be an improbable one, but it should never be banal. It must be dramatic and human. What is drama, after all, but life with the dull bits cut out."—Alfred Hitchcock from Franois Truffaut's *Hitchcock*

Edwin T. **Arnold** & Eugene L. **Miller**

The Films and Career of Robert Aldrich

A biographical and critical study of the director of *Kiss Me Deadly* and *Vera Cruz* written in close collaboration with Aldrich

0-87049-504-6 TENNESSEE....$34.00

Alain **Silver** & James **Ursini**

Whatever Happened to Robert Aldrich?: His Life and His Films

0-87910-185-7 LIMELIGHT....$25.00

Woody **Allen**

Woody Allen on Woody Allen

"It has been said," writes Allen in this collection of anecdotal interviews, "that if I have any one big theme in my movies, it's got to do with the difference between reality and fantasy…I think what it boils down to, really, is that I hate reality. And, yet, unfortunately it's the one place where we can get a good steak dinner." A unique self-portrait of a great American film director

0-8021-1556-X GROVE....$22.00

Woody **Allen** & Linda **Sunshine**

The Illustrated Woody Allen Reader

Contains Woody's first recorded monologue (March 1964), his early, hilarious routine, *If the Impressionists Had Been Dentists*, as well as interviews, one-liners, screenplays, and outtakes, many of them unpublished until now

0-679-42072-X KNOPF....$30.00

Woody Allen

Brian **Hamill**

Woody Allen at Work: The Photographs of Brian Hamill

A pictorial overview of Woody Allen's career; images that capture a side of the director that has rarely before been seen. The compilation was selected from over 100,000 images taken by Hamill, Allen's exclusive still photographer on every project since 1977. Complemented by an informative summary of Allen's career by Charles Champlin, it is a portrait of a great director in his element

ESSAY BY CHARLES CHAMPLIN

0-8109-1957-5 ABRAMS....$39.95

Eric **Lax**

Woody Allen: A Biography

A detailed biography of the director and comedian by a long-time associate

0-394-58349-3 KNOPF....$24.00

Pedro **Almadovar**

Almodovar on Almodovar

Almodovar (*Women of the Verge of a Nervous Breakdown, Kika, The Flower of My Secret*) is the best known Spanish director in America, admired by critics for his biting humor and his lavish and indulgent aesthetic

EDITED BY FREDERIC STRAUSS

TRANSLATED BY YVES BAIGNERES

0-571-17544-9 FABER $24.95

Paul Julian **Smith**

Desire Unlimited: The Cinema of Pedro Almodovar

A highly intelligent, and refreshingly free of jargon, reading of the films of one of the most successful Spanish directors of recent years

0-86091-662-6 VERSO PB $17.95

Bill **Landis**

Anger: The Unauthorized Biography of Kenneth Anger

0-06-092214-1 HARPERCOLLINS PB $15.00

Michelangelo **Antonioni**

The Architecture of Vision: Writings and Interviews on Cinema

1-56886-016-1 MARSILIO PB $19.95

William **Arrowsmith**

Antonioni: The Poet of Images

0-19-509270-8 OXFORD $25.00

Sam **Rohdie**

Antonioni

0-85170-273-2 BRITISH FILM INST $49.95

0-85170-274-0 BRITISH FILM INST PB $19.95

Maitland **McDonagh**

Broken Mirrors, Broken Minds: The Dark Dreams of Dario Argento

Pioneering study of the Italian horror director whose films include *Suspiria* and *The Bird with the Crystal Plumage*

0-8065-1514-7 CITADEL PB $18.95

Ingmar **Bergman**

Images: My Life in Film

1-55970-186-2 ARCADE $27.95

1-55970-293-1 ARCADE PB $17.95

The Magic Lantern: An Autobiography

0-14-012850-6 PENGUIN PB $10.95

0-14-010469-0 PENGUIN PB $13.95

Stig **Bjorkman**

Bergman on Bergman: Interviews with Ingmar Bergman

0-306-80520-0 DA CAPO PB $13.95

Martin **Rubin**

Showstoppers: Busby Berkeley and the Tradition of Spectacle

0-231-08054-9 COLUMBIA $34.50

John **Boorman** & others, editors

Projections: Film-Makers on Film-Making

Volume 1

0-571-16729-2 FABER PB $14.95

Volume 2

0-571-16828-0 FABER PB $16.95

Volume 3

0-571-17047-1 FABER PB $14.95

Volume 4 1/2

0-571-17609-7 FABER PB $16.95

Volume 5

0-571-17811-1 FABER PB $16.95

Volume 6

0-571-17853-7 FABER PB $16.95

Stan **Brakhage**

Film at Wit's End: Eight Avant-Garde Filmmakers

Essays on the origins of American independent film making in the '40s, '50s and '60s, featuring Maya Deren, Maria Menken, James Broughton, Christopher MacLaine, Sydney Peterson, Bruce Conner, Jerome Hill, and Ken Jacobs. "A basic book in the canon of experimental cinema" —*Film Quarterly*

0-929701-16-X MCPHERSON PB $12.00

J. Francisco **Aranda**

Luis Bunuel: A Critical Biography

0-306-80028-4 DA CAPO PB $11.95

Luis **Bunuel**

My Last Sigh

An autobiography of the director of *Viridiana* and *The Exterminating Angel*

0-394-72501-8 RANDOM HOUSE PB $15.00

Jose **De La Colina** & Tomas Perez **Turrent**

Objects of Desire: Conversations With Luis Bunuel

0-941419-68-1 MARSILIO $24.00

Tim **Burton**

Burton on Burton

Burton is known for his cinematographic flair and oddly arresting stories of the misunderstood. Included among his many films are *Edward Scissorhands*, *Ed Wood*, and *The Nightmare Before Christmas*

EDITED BY MARK SALISBURY

0-571-17392-6 FABER $22.95

William **Castle**

Step Right Up!: I'm Gonna Scare the Pants Off America

Castle, B-movie mogul extraordinaire, brought us such promotional excesses as a $1,000 insurance policy for anyone scared to death by *Macabre* and electric-buzzer seats for the audiences of *The Tingler*. This is an outrageous, first-hand look into the life and times of a showman who makes Barnum look like an Avon lady

INTRODUCTION BY JOHN WATERS

0-88687-657-5 PHAROS PB $12.95

Chris **Rodley**, editor

Cronenberg on Cronenberg

The director of *Naked Lunch* and *Crash* revealed in interviews focusing on his creative process

0-571-16993-7 FABER PB $10.95

James C. **Robertson**

The Casablanca Man: The Cinema of Michael Curtiz

The Hungarian director of *Casablanca* is finally receiving wider recognition for his brilliant realization of classic Hollywood form in such masterpieces as *Mystery of the Wax Museum* and *The Breaking Point*

0-415-06804-5 ROUTLEDGE $29.95

0-415-11577-9 ROUTLEDGE PB $16.95

David **Bordwell**

The Films of Carl-Theodor Dreyer

An exceptionally rigorous and intelligent formal analysis, elegantly illustrated

0-520-03987-4 CALIFORNIA $50.00

0-520-04450-9 CALIFORNIA PB $17.00

David **Bordwell**

The Cinema of Eisenstein

A scholarly examination of the works of Eisenstein

0-674-13138-X HARVARD PB $32.00

Sergei **Eisenstein**

Beyond the Stars: The Memoirs of Sergei Eisenstein

The Russian master in his own words

See also **RUSSIA AND EASTERN EUROPE** under **NATIONAL CINEMAS**

EDITED BY RICHARD TAYLOR

TRANSLATED BY WILLIAM POWELL

0-85170-460-3 BRITISH FILM INST $75.00

Notes of a Film Director

0-486-22392-2 DOVER PB $8.95

Selected Works: Writings, 1934-47,

See also **RUSSIA AND EASTERN EUROPE** under **NATIONAL CINEMAS**

TRANSLATED BY WILLIAM POWELL

EDITED BY RICHARD TAYLOR

0-85170-530-8 BRITISH FILM INST $55.00

Hollis **Alpert**

Fellini: A Life

1-55778-000-5 MARLOWE PB $9.95

Peter **Bondanella**

The Cinema of Federico Fellini

Bondanella's examination of the Italian master details his work chronologically and discusses the many influences that went into Fellini's movies from neo-realism to metacinema. Includes a wide range of Fellini's drawings and storyboards, as well as interviews

0-691-03196-7 PRINCETON $60.00

0-691-00875-2 PRINCETON PB $19.95

Federico **Fellini**

Fellini on Fellini

The late Fellini describes his method, discusses his personal preferences ("Beautiful asses on bicycle seats." "Mattisse not Magritte.")

TRANSLATED BY ISABEL QUIGLEY

0-306-80673-8 DA CAPO PB $13.95

Charlotte **Chandler**

I, Fellini

High-spirited memoirs gathered during exclusive conversations with Fellini over 14 years provide an unprecedented portrait of the great Italian director. Along the way Fellini discusses Mastroianni, W.C. Fields, the Marx Brothers, and many others

PREFACE BY BILLY WILDER

0-679-44032-1 RANDOM HOUSE $26.50

Paul **Rotha**

Robert J. Flaherty: A Biography

0-8122-7887-9 PENNSYLVANIA $47.95

Ronald L. **Davis**

John Ford: Hollywood's Old Master

A "well-researched study of a great filmmaker and a complex, fascinating man"
—*Richard Widmark*

0-8061-2708-2 OKLAHOMA $29.95

Tag **Gallagher**

John Ford: The Man and His Films

Thoroughgoing review of Ford's films, elaborately researched

0-317-67094-8 CALIFORNIA PB $18.00

Joseph **McBride** & Michael **Wilmington**

John Ford

0-306-80016-0 DA CAPO PB $11.95

Raymond **Bellour**, editor

Jean-Luc Godard: Sound/Image 1974-1992

Much of Godard's work since 1974 has been in video, and is therefore little known to American audiences. This concordant volume to his provocative, experimental work contains essays by film scholars from France, Britain, and the US

0-87070-348-X MOMA $39.95
0-8109-6114-8 MOMA $39.95

Jean **Narboni** & Tom **Milne**, editors

Godard on Godard

A compendium of Godard's inimitably paradoxical pronouncements

See also EARLY CLASSICS under FILM THEORY

0-306-80259-7 DA CAPO PB $12.95

Marshall **Deutelbaum** & Leland **Poague**, editors

A Hitchcock Reader

A collection of essays illustrating the range of intellectual response that Hitchcock's work is currently eliciting

0-8138-0892-8 IOWA PB $21.95

Alfred **Hitchcock**

Hitchcock on Hitchcock: Selected Writings and Interviews

A revealing look at the "master of suspense"

EDITED BY SIDNEY GOTTLIEB

0-520-08528-0 CALIFORNIA $29.95

Janet **Leigh** & Christopher **Nickens**

Psycho: Behind the Scenes of the Classic Thriller

0-517-70112-X HARMONY $22.00

Robert E. **Kapsis**

Hitchcock: The Making of a Reputation

Studying the work of a man who had a life-long need to be regarded as an artist, not just a "thriller" craftsman, Kapsis explores the ever-shifting critical response to the director's work and his eventual triumph in his medium

0-226-42489-8 CHICAGO PB $18.95

Alfred Hitchcock

Tania **Modleski**

The Women Who Knew Too Much: Hitchcock and Feminist Theory

0-416-01711-8 ROUTLEDGE PB $14.95

Stephen **Rebello**

Alfred Hitchcock and the Making of Psycho

0-06-097366-8 HARPERCOLLINS PB $12.00

Tom **Ryall**

Alfred Hitchcock and the British Cinema

During the ten years that the Cinematograph Films Act of 1927 was in force, British directors, actors, and technicians enjoyed continuous employment, and Hitchcock created some of his early masterpieces, among them *The 39 Steps, Sabotage,* and *Young and Innocent*

0-252-01374-3 ILLINOIS $24.95

Donald **Spoto**

The Art of Alfred Hitchcock

The best general study of Hitchcock's work

0-385-15569-7 DOUBLEDAY PB $18.00

The Dark Side of Genius: The Life of Alfred Hitchcock

In case anyone wonders, Hitchcock was not the happiest of men. Spoto spells out the grimmer side of his career and in the process casts new light on many details of his film

0-316-80815-6 LITTLE, BROWN PB $16.95
0-345-31462-X BALLANTINE PB $6.99

François **Truffaut**

Hitchcock

A pioneering book of interviews that can also serve as an introduction to film technique

TRANSLATED BY HELEN G. SCOTT

0-671-60429-5 SIMON & SCHUSTER PB $20.00

Robin **Wood**

Hitchcock's Films Revisited

Wood was one of the first English-language critics to study Hitchcock in detail; now he offers a revised view

0-231-06550-7 COLUMBIA $55.00

Leonard J. **Luff**

Hitchcock and Selznick

An absorbing account of the often troubled collaboration that produced *Rebecca, Notorious,* and other films

1-55584-272-0 GROVE PB $11.95

John **Huston**

An Open Book

0-394-40465-3 KNOPF $1.00

Derek **Jarman**

Chroma

0-87951-574-0 OVERLOOK $19.95

Kevin **Jackson**, editor

The Humphrey Jennings Film Reader

Jennings, a poet and historian, created a series of extraordinary documentaries about World War II and its aftermath, including *Listen to Britain, A Diary for Timothy,* and the magnificent *Fires Were Started*

1-55783-208-0 APPLAUSE THEATRE $39.95

Tom **Dardis**

Keaton: The Man Who Wouldn't Lie Down

0-684-16150-8 SCRIBNERS $4.98

Krzysztof **Kieslowski**

Kieslowski on Kieslowski

The late Kieslowski—best known in America for his *Red, White,* and *Blue* trilogy—was a leading figure in Eastern European cinema of the '70s and '80s

EDITED BY DANUSIA STOK

0-571-17328-4 FABER PB $13.95

Buster **Keaton** & Charles **Samuels**

Buster Keaton: My Wonderful World of Slapstick

INTRODUCTION BY DWIGHT MACDONALD

0-306-80178-7 DA CAPO PB $12.95

Marion **Meade**

Buster Keaton

Through over 200 interviews of Keaton's friends and co-workers, including Billy Wilder, Leni Riefenstahl, Gene Kelly, and Bill Cosby, Meade has drawn an unparalleled portrait of Keaton: his work, his marriages, his alcoholism, and his virtual illiteracy

0-06-017337-8 HARPERCOLLINS $30.00

Gabriella **Oldham**

Keaton's Silent Shorts: Beyond the Laughter

0-8093-1952-7 SOUTHERN ILLINOIS PB $24.95

Buster Keaton

Vincent **Lobrutto**

Stanley Kubrick: A Biography

A look at the enigmatic director of *Lolita, A Clockwork Orange*, and *2001: A Space Odyssey*

1-55611-492-3 FINE $29.95

Akira **Kurosawa**

Something Like an Autobiography

Reminiscences by the director of *Seven Samurai and Ran*

TRANSLATED BY AUDIE E. BOCK

0-394-71439-3 RANDOM HOUSE PB $15.00

Donald **Richie**

The Films of Akira Kurosawa, 3rd Edition

A portrait of Japan's most well recognized and highly regarded director (*Rashomon, The Seven Samurai, Ran*)

0-520-20026-8 CALIFORNIA PB $19.95

Lotte H. **Eisner**

Fritz Lang

Eisner, a friend of Lang, covers all his films, with much attention to technical aspects

0-306-80271-6 DA CAPO PB $14.95

Stephen M. **Silverman**

David Lean

An elaborately produced tribute to the director of *Lawrence of Arabia, Brief Encounter,* and *Great Expectations.* The author has drawn on extensive interviews with Lean to produce the most detailed account of his career to date. Includes 155 illustrations, 50 in color

INTRODUCTION BY KATHERINE HEPBURN

0-8109-3550-3 ABRAMS PB $39.95

Barry **Levinson**

Levinson on Levinson

A distinctly American director best known for his wonderful portrait of wayward Baltimore twenty-somethings, *Diner*

EDITED BY DAVID THOMPSON

0-571-16731-4 FABER PB $11.95

William **Paul**

Ernst Lubitsch's American Comedy

0-231-05681-8 COLUMBIA PB $18.00

Sidney **Lumet**

Making Movies

With 50 Oscar nominations for his 40 films (including the classic *Twelve Angry Men* and *The Verdict*), Lumet is uniquely placed to illuminate the processes of making movies

0-679-43709-6 KNOPF $23.00

0679437969 KNOPF $23.00

0-679-75660-4 VINTAGE PB $12.00

Auguste **Lumiere** & Louis **Lumiere**

Letters: Inventing the Cinema

TRANSLATED BY PIERRE HODGSON

0-571-17545-7 FABER $29.95

Louis **Malle**

Malle on Malle

The late Malle was one of the best directors of his genearation. His films include *Atlantic City* and the Oscar-winning *Au Revoir les Enfants*. This collection of articles and interviews is a wonderful introduction to the man and his work

0-571-16237-1 FABER $19.95

0-571-17880-4 FABER PB $13.95

David **Mamet**

On Directing Film

Pulitzer Prize-winning playwright, screenwriter, and director, Mamet's insights into the making of a film from script to cutting room are now available in paperback. Mamet regales his students with anecdotes from the Yiddish theater, the principles of Aristotle as they apply to movies, and why he believes that *Dumbo* is the perfect film

0-14-012722-4 PENGUIN PB $11.95

It's like climbing the stairs. We don't want to climb a stair we've already climbed… Get on with it. Everybody always says the way to make any movie better is burn the first reel, and it's true.
ON DIRECTING FILM

David Mamet

Chris **Marker**

La Jetée

A frame-by-frame visual reconstruction of Marker's haunting and apocalyptic film, on which Terry Gillian's *Twelve Monkeys* is based

0-942299-67-1 ZONE PB $26.50

Joseph **McBride**

Dreammaker: A Biography of Steven Spielberg

0-684-81167-7 SIMON & SCHUSTER $25.00

Robert E. **Long**

The Films of Merchant Ivory

Ismail Merchant and James Ivory have produced and directed some of the most visually moving films in recent history: *Shakespeare Wallah, Bombay Talkie,* and *A Room With A View* among them. Long's history of their work is lavishly illustrated, in-depth, and altogether a remarkable document

0-8109-3618-6 ABRAMS $49.50

0-8065-1470-1 CITADEL PB $19.95

Donald **Richie**

Ozu: His Life and Films

0-520-03277-2 CALIFORNIA PB $14.95

Pier Paolo Pasolini

David Schwartz **Barth**

Pasolini Requiem

Filmmaker, poet, polemicist, Pasolini was the emblematic figure of the Italian cultural renaissance of the postwar period. This biography incorporates information about Pasolini's murder in 1975 (allegedly at the hands of a young male prostitute) that has only recently come to light

0-679-73349-3 VINTAGE PB $18.00

Sam **Rohdie**

The Passion of Pier Paolo Pasolini

0-253-21010-0 BRITISH FILM INST PB $15.95

David **Weddle**

"If They Move...Kill 'Em!": The Life and Times of Sam Peckinpah

The first major biography of the major filmmaker *(The Getaway, The Wild Bunch)* who was, depending on your tastes, a distressingly sick nihilist or an inspirational, era-defining original. His supercharged, hard-working life provides plenty of grist for Weddle, a film critic for the *LA Times Magazine*

0-8021-1546-2 GROVE $27.50

Yvonne **Rainer**

The Films of Yvonne Rainer

0-253-20542-5 INDIANA PB $5.25

Bernard **Eisenschitz**

Nicholas Ray: An American Journey

Eisenschitz, a critic for *Cashiers du Cinema,* has written a large-scale account of the tumultuous and ultimately tragic life of the director of *Rebel Without a Cause* and *Johnny Guitar*

0-571-14086-6 FABER $24.95
0-571-17830-8 FABER PB $17.95

Nicholas **Ray**

I Was Interrupted: Nicholas Ray on Making Movies

0-520-08233-8 CALIFORNIA $30.00
0-520-20169-8 CALIFORNIA PB $14.00

Ronald **Bergan**

Jean Renoir: Projections of Paradise

0-87951-537-6 OVERLOOK $23.95

Celia **Bertin**

Jean Renoir: A Life in Pictures

0-8018-4184-4 JOHNS HOPKINS $39.95

Jean **Renoir**

Letters

EDITED BY DAVID THOMPSON AND LORRAINE LOBIANCO

0-571-17298-9 FABER $40.00

Alexander **Sesonske**

Jean Renoir: The French Years, 1924-1939

A painstaking account of what many would consider the major phase of Renoir's career. The director wrote of this book: "With Sesonske's book I have my arch of triumph"

0-674-47355-8 HARVARD $30.50
0-674-47360-4 HARVARD PB $16.95

James **Riordan**

Stone: The Controversies, Excesses and Exploits of a Radical Filmmaker

INTRODUCTION BY MICHAEL DOUGLAS

0-7868-6026-X HYPERION $24.95
0-7868-8201-8 HYPERION PB $15.95

Robert **Rodriguez**

Rebel Without a Crew: Or How a 23-Year-Old Filmmaker With $7,000 Became a Hollywood Player

The fabled story of Rodriguez's making of the sub-underground indie fave *El Mariachi*

See also DO IT YOURSELF

0-525-93794-3 DUTTON $22.95
0-452-27187-8 PLUME PB $11.95

Peter **Brunette**

Roberto Rossellini

A detailed study that does justice to the full variety of Rossellini's career, from the early Neorealist classics to the late history films

0-19-504989-6 OLYMPIC PB $14.95

Roberto **Rossellini**

My Method: Writings and Interviews

TRANSLATED BY ANNAPAOLA CANCOGNI

0-941419-65-7 MARSILIO PB $12.95

Mary Pat **Kelly**

Martin Scorsese: A Journey

0-938410-79-2 THUNDER'S MOUTH PB $24.95

Martin **Scorsese**

Scorsese on Scorsese

In a series of detailed interviews, the director takes a film-by-film took at his career, ranging from *Boxcar Bertha* and *Mean Streets* to *After Hours* and *The Last Temptation of Christ*

EDITED BY DAVID THOMPSON & IAN CHRISTIE

0-571-15243-0 FABER PB $13.95
0-571-14103-X FABER PB $17.95

As a child I wanted to be a painter, so I started trying to draw. But I was also fascinated by films, and, having asthma, I would often be taken to movie theatres because they didn't know what else to do with me. Most of all I was amazed by the size of the images on the screen, and I would come back and draw what I saw. And of course I loved biblical epics—only mine weren't just in 70 mm, they were in 75 mm! I planned a gigantic Roman epic, but it only got as far as a gladiatorial fight at the beginning to mark the Emperor's homecoming after a war, painted in watercolors. I still have these strips and when they're framed they look very like the traditional Sicilian puppet shows of knights fighting.

SCORSESE ON SCORSESE

Scorsese on Scorsese: The Update

0-571-17827-8 FABER PB $14.95

Robert S. **Sennett**

Setting the Scene: The Great Hollywood Art Directors

They're written, they're acted, they're directed, and they're produced, but beyond the obvious a wide world of talent creates the look of films, and that talent resides in the art director. From *The Birth of a Nation* to *Batman,* this fascinating volume shows the art and artifice of the people—literally—behind the scenes of cinema

0-8109-3846-4 ABRAMS $39.95

Eric **Sherman**

Directing the Film: Film Directors on Their Art

The filmmaking process from start to finish, in the words of 75 directors

0-918226-15-5 ACROBAT PB $16.95

Don **Siegel**

A Siegel Film: An Autobiography

Siegel is known mostly for his heavily symbolic meditation on Cold War hysteria, the 1956 science-fiction masterpeice, *Invasion of the Body Snatchers*. At the high point of his career, he was recognized by the young crtics at *Cahiers du Cinema*—including Truffault and Godard—as a brilliant *auteur* who brought a consistent style and vision to his films

0-571-17831-6 FABER PB $17.95

James **Curtis**

Between Flops: A Biography of Preston Sturges

The alternately troubled and hilarious life of one of the great American originals, director of *The Lady Eve* and *The Miracle of Morgan's Creek*

0-87910-027-3 PROSCENIUM PB $16.95

Andrei **Tarkovsky**

Sculpting in Time: Reflections on the Cinema

TRANSLATED BY KITTY HUNTER-BLAIR

0-292-77624-1 TEXAS PB $19.95

Rob **Van Scheers**

Paul Verhoeven

TRANSLATED BY ALETTA STEVENS

0-571-17479-5 FABER $24.95

Stephen **Shore** & Lynn **Tillman**

The Velvet Years: Warhol's Factory, 1965-67

1-56025-098-4 THUNDER'S MOUTH PB $24.95

John **Waters**

Shock Value: A Tasteful Book about Bad Taste

1-56025-092-5 THUNDER'S MOUTH PB $12.95

Crackpot

By the director of such camp classics as *Crybaby, Hairspray, Polyester,* and *Pink Flamingos.* Whether he's interviewing Pia Zadora, extolling *The National Enquirer,* describing his class on film studies for jail inmates, or just ranting, the self-proclaimed High Priest of Bad Taste is always funny. "John Waters is the Pope of Trash and his taste in tacky is unexcelled…ladies and gentleman, a very funny man"—William Burroughs

See also DIRECTORS

0-394-75534-0 VINTAGE PB $11.00

Simon **Callow**

Orson Welles: The Road to Xanadu

The first installment of a two-volume biography of Welles by the British actor, taking him up to his first and greatest film triumph, *Citizen Kane*

0-670-86722-5 VIKING $32.95

Robert L. **Carringer**

The Magnificent Ambersons: A Reconstruction

Carringer enables us to get an idea of what Welles's truncated masterpiece might have been

0-520-07857-8 CALIFORNIA $35.00

The Making of Citizen Kane

Carringer focuses less on the singular genius of Orson Welles and more on the interplay between the director and his creative partners. Full of fascinating technical details

0-520-05876-3 CALIFORNIA PB $16.00

Barbara **Leaming**

Orson Welles: A Biography

A long and absorbing account of Welles' very eventful life

0-670-52895-1 VIKING $19.95
0-14-009620-5 PENGUIN PB $4.95
9996145077 TUSQUETS EDITOR PB $27.50

David **Thomson**

Rosebud: The Story of Orson Welles

Showbiz biographer Thomson (*Suspect, Showman: The Life of David O. Selznick, A Biographical Dictionary of Film*) has written the authoritative biography of Welles. A career that found Welles at 23 the phenomenon of theatre and of radio but that seemed to have self-destructed a few years after the release of *Citizen Kane*. The story of how this happened is a superb, thoroughly entertaining American tragedy

0-679-41834-2 KNOPF $30.00

Orson **Welles** & Peter **Bogdanovich**

This Is Orson Welles

Revealing conversations between the legendary filmmaker and his long-time friend Peter Bogdanovich over a period of 15 years. The master's estimation of his own work, and of his colleagues', and his thoughts on subjects such as *Citizen Kane*, the Oscars, and modern directors are entirely absorbing. A collaboration to "set the record straight"—Orson Welles

0-06-016616-9 HARPERPERENNIAL PB $15.00

Maurice **Zolotow**

Billy Wilder in Hollywood

0-87910-070-2 LIMELIGHT PB $18.95

Kevin **Lally**

Wilder Times: The Life of Billy Wilder

Wilder is a biographer's dream. A tireless recounter of anecdotes and witticisms, he is his own best commentator

0-8050-3119-7 HOLT $30.00

0-8050-3120-0 HOLT PB $14.95

Rudolph **Grey**

Nightmare of Ecstasy: The Life and Art of Edward D. Wood, Jr.

Voices from the depths: an oral biography of the director of *Plan 9 from Outer Space* and *The Sinister Urge,* conveying a far more dark and anxious impression than Tim Burton's lighthearted biopic

0-922915-24-5 FERAL HOUSE PB $14.95

Movie Stars

Truman **Capote**

Marlon Brando: Portraits and Film Stills, 1946-1995

In the November 9, 1957, *New Yorker* profile, Truman Capote gained unprecedented access to Brando, digging into the enigmatic persona and reclusive psyche in a way never to be repeated. Here, Capote's interview is illustrated with 87 photographs spanning Brando's entire career, revealing the actor both in portraits by the likes of Cecil Beaton and in marvelous roles in films from *The Wild Ones* to *Last Tango in Paris* and *Don Juan de Marco*

1-55670-463-1 STEWART, TABORI $40.00

Marlon Brando

Peter **Manso**

Brando: The Biography

From his harsh childhood, his dizzying rise to stardom, to his comebacks in *The Godfather* and *Last Tango in Paris* and his agony when his son was convicted of murder, this is the tell-all on Brando

0-7868-6063-4 HYPERION $29.95

Lauren **Bacall**

Lauren Bacall by Myself

0-345-33321-7 BALLANTINE PB $6.99

Lauren Bacall
(credit: ©The Collection of John Kobal)

Paul **Alexander**

Boulevard of Broken Dreams: The Life, Times, and Legend of James Dean

The author of *Rough Magic* plows beyond the Hollywood cliches to put forth the thesis that Dean's anxious public compliance with rigid sexual mores provided the fuel for his explosive, furious acting. The first serious biography of this complicated icon will be of interest to film buffs and pop culture aficionados alike

0-670-84951-0 VIKING $22.95

David **Dalton** & Ron **Cayen**

James Dean: American Icon

INTRODUCTION BY MARTIN SHEEN

0-312-43962-8 ST. MARTIN'S PB $19.95

Val **Holley**

James Dean: The Biography

0-312-13249-2 ST. MARTIN'S $23.95

The secret to Deans "fine, intense perception of the Jim Stark role," wrote Nicholas Ray, was that both he and the character were "jealously seeking an answer to an escape from the surrounding world. In the end, both the character and the actor found that escape, but Dean, in so doing, breached the point of no return." What he had really hoped for, asserted Ray, was the escape achieved by Jim Stark—"a full, complete realization of himself."

JAMES DEAN: THE BIOGRAPHY

Donald **Spoto**

Rebel: The Life and Legend of James Dean

0-06-017656-3 HARPERCOLLINS $25.00

Dennis **Stock**

James Dean Revisited

1-55013-055-2 KEY PORTER PB $19.95

Paul **Chutkow**

Depardieu

The first biography of the one–man industry of French-film acting by a film critic for *NY Times*. From Depardieu's childhood of illiteracy, pennilessness, and severe stuttering to his current status as an international star

0-679-40943-2 KNOPF $24.00

Maria **Riva**

Marlene Dietrich

A painful and almost too-revealing remembrance of Dietrich by her daughter. Riva draws on mountains of material—including her mother's many diaries and her life-long collection of letters—to draw a picture of a compulsively romantic woman; a celebrity intent on controlling her image in every detail; a bigot; and an enormously oppressive mother. An "ultimate act of demystification...completing, rather than competing with, the portrait begun by recent Dietrich biographies...I not only believe every word in Ms. Riva's account; I also came away convinced of her right to tell it as she has"—Molly Haskell, *NY Times Book Review*

0-394-58692-1 KNOPF $27.50

Kirk **Douglas**

The Ragman's Son: An Autobiography

0-671-73789-9 POCKET PB $5.99

Faye **Dunaway** & Betsy **Sharkey**

Looking For Gatsby

The star of *Chinatown*, *Bonnie and Clyde*, *Network*, and numerous other films presents an uncompromising and unapologetic autobiography. Long remaining aloof, Dunaway writes candidly of the poverty of her childhood, her rise to stardom, the co-stars, lovers, husbands, and the continuing difficulty faced by leading ladies in Hollywood

0-684-80841-2 SIMON & SCHUSTER $25.00

Richard **Schickel**

Clint Eastwood: A Biography

0-679-42974-3 KNOPF......$26.00

Paul **Smith**

Clint Eastwood: A Cultural Production

0-8166-1958-1 MINNESOTA......$44.95
0-8166-1960-3 MINNESOTA PB......$17.95

Barry **Paris**

Garbo: A Biography

Drawing on hitherto unavailable letters and taped conversations, as well as interviews with friends and family, Paris recounts Garbo's troubled childhood in Stockholm, her reign as *the* international megastar, and the creeping paranoia that poisoned the last 50 years of her life. More than a celebrity "dish" book, or another appreciation of the "Garbo enigma," this is a groundbreaking study of a complex woman

0-394-58020-6 KNOPF......$35.00

David **Shipman**

Judy Garland: The Secret Life of an American Legend

The sad and astonishing story of the sexual misidentity, the addictions, and the heartaches of this unearthly talent who even at the age of 12 sang like a woman whose heart had been broken. "If you can take it, it's a great story" —*Kirkus Reviews*

0-7868-8026-0 HYPERION PB......$14.95

There was no limit to her talent. Her brain was amazing. She would hear a song, or a page of dialogue, and immediately memorize it. She was the quickest, brightest person I ever worked with.—*Gene Kelly*

JUDY GARLAND: THE SECRET LIFE OF AN AMERICAN LEGEND

Eve **Golden**

Platinum Girl: The Life and Legends of Jean Harlow

1-55859-214-8 ABBEVILLE......$35.00
1-55859-430-2 ABBEVILLE PB......$17.95

Jean Harlow

James **Prideaux**

Knowing Hepburn and Other Curious Experiences

A look at Katharine Hepburn

0-571-19892-9 FABER......$24.95

Katharine **Hepburn**

Me

A charming, conversational book by the legendary star of *The Philadelphia Story* and *The African Queen*

0-679-40051-6 KNOPF......$25.00
0-345-37770-2 BALLANTINE PB......$5.99

Barbara **Leaming**

Katharine Hepburn

The stories that Hepburn herself refused to tell in her best-selling memoir

0-517-59284-3 CROWN......$27.50
0-380-72717-X AVON PB......$7.50

Charlton **Heston**

In The Arena: An Autobiography

0-684-80394-1 SIMON & SCHUSTER......$27.50

Klaus **Kinski**

Kinski Uncut: The Autobiography of Klaus Kinski

The notorious, obsessive memoirs of the actor who worked for Herzog, Leone, and many others

TRANSLATED BY JOACHIM NEUGROSCHEL

0-670-86744-6 VIKING......$26.95

Alexander **Walker**

Vivien: The Life of Vivien Leigh

1-55584-296-8 GROVE PB......$9.95

Shawn **Levy**

King of Comedy: The Life and Art of Jerry Lewis

A respectful biography of a performer and director more often honored in Europe than at home

0-312-13248-4 ST. MARTIN'S......$24.95

Maxine **Marx**

Growing Up with Chico

0-13-367821-0 SIMON & SCHUSTER......$2.98

Harpo **Marx** & Rowland **Barber**

Harpo Speaks!

0-87910-036-2 PROSCENIUM PB......$18.95

Donald **Dewey**

Marcello Mastroianni: His Life and Art

An ultimate look at the great Italian actor who shuns Hollywood and publicity tours in favor of his lovers and most-adored restaurants in Rome. Maybe this explains why his work gets better as he ages

1-55972-158-8 BIRCH LANE......$21.95

George **Barris**

Marilyn—Her Life In Her Own Words: Marilyn Monroe's Revealing Last Words and Photographs

1-55972-306-8 BIRCH LANE......$24.95

Brambilla **Giovanbattista**, editor

Marilyn Monroe: The Life and the Myth

More than 30 years after her death, Marilyn Monroe continues to exert a mythic control over our attention. Here, 400 photographs—150 never before published—and 15 writers present a fresh and contemporary view of her life and her myth. Starting with biographical information, this lush book moves on to examine her image in advertising and art, her influence on fashion, and then ends with a treasure of memorabilia

0-8478-1960-4 RIZZOLI......$60.00

James **Haspiel**

Marilyn: The Ultimate Look at the Legend

"Intimate, touching, and intensely personal…the photographs are dazzling. A tribute in the finest sense"—Liz Smith

0-8050-2965-6 OWLET PB......$19.95

Norman **Mailer**

Marilyn: A Biography

0-88365-731-7 GALAHAD......$19.98

Berniece Baker **Miracle** & Mona Rae **Miracle**

My Sister Marilyn: A Memoir of Marilyn Monroe

Marilyn as sister, daughter, aunt—a real person rather than an iconic sex goddess. Marilyn's half-sister—they shared the same mother—provides an unprecedented, intimate, and empathic view of the person behind the myth

1-56512-070-1 ALGONQUIN......$19.95

Donald **Spoto**

Marilyn Monroe: The Biography

0-06-109166-9 HARPERCOLLINS PB......$6.99

Anthony **Summers**

Goddess: The Secret Lives of Marilyn Monroe

0-451-40014-3 ONYX PB......$4.95

Marianne **Gray**

La Moreau: A Biography of Jeanne Moreau

1-55611-487-7 PENGUIN......$23.95

John **Griggs**

The Films of Gregory Peck

0-8065-1025-0 LYLE STUART PB......$12.95

Vanessa **Redgrave**

Vanessa Redgrave: An Autobiography

The gifted and controversial actress has captivated audiences for over three decades, from Antonioni's *Blow Up* to the recent *Howard's End.* Less celebrated, perhaps, is her political involvement on behalf of the Palestinians. Here, for the first time, the intensely private actress opens up about her acting, her childhood, her romances, and her often misunderstood political life in a performance of depth and honesty

0-679-40216-0 RANDOM HOUSE......$25.00

Ray **Robinson**

American Original: A Life Of Will Rogers

0-19-508693-7 OXFORD......$30.00

Catherine **David**

Simone Signoret

An actress of unusual intellect and political courage whose popularity was based not on sex appeal but on her extraordinary ability to communicate passion. Signoret's 36-year marriage to Yves Montand, who betrayed her for Marilyn Monroe, and her defiant, subsequent decline into premature old age are examined

0-87951-491-4 OVERLOOK $22.95
0-06-087951-581-3 PENGUIN PB $12.95

Roy **Pickard**

Jimmy Stewart: A Life in Film

This biography of the man who, over the past 50 years, has become one of the foremost American icons, focuses on the actor's charmed career during Hollywood's golden era of the '30s and '40s, and shows how his artistic versatility enabled him to rescue that career later when, after the war, he moved into Westerns

0-312-08828-0 ST. MARTIN'S $18.95

Everything about Grace was appealing. I was married but I wasn't dead. She had those big warm eyes and well, if you had ever played a love scene with her, you'd know she wasn't cold. She had an inner confidence. People who have that are not cold. Grace had that twinkle and a touch of larceny in her eyes.—*Jimmy Stewart*

JIMMY STEWART: A LIFE IN FILM

Donald **Spoto**

A Passion For Life: A Biography of Elizabeth Taylor

0-06-109401-3 HARPERCOLLINS PB $6.99

Other Creative Contributors

Michael **Cader**, editor

Saturday Night Live: The Classic Years Special Collector's Edition of Two Videocassettes

0-395-75284-1 DORLING KINDERSLEY PB $16.95

Michael **Caine**

Acting in Film: An Actor's Take on Movie Making

Now in paperback, Caine's straightforward primer is helpful both to actors who want to polish their craft, and to viewers of stage and screen drama who want to unlock some of the secrets of acting for themselves. "No one is more qualified to discuss the craft and business of film acting…[this] is of as much interest to members of the audience as to actors"
—Allen Barra, *NY Times Book Review*

0-936839-86-4 APPLAUSE THEATRE $14.95
1-55783-124-6 APPLAUSE THEATRE PB $8.95

Irving **Lazar**

Swifty: My Life and Good Times

The original "superagent." By the time of his death, Lazar had at one time or another represented nearly every major star of the screen or stage as well as authors and figures like Henry Kissinger and Richard Nixon

0-684-80418-2 SIMON & SCHUSTER $24.50

Kevin **MacDonald**

Emeric Pressburger: The Life and Death of a Screenwriter

0-571-16853-1 FABER $24.95

Kris **Malkiewicz**

Film Lighting

Interviews with leading cinematographers and gaffers

ILLUSTRATED BY LEONARD KONOPELSKI

0-671-76634-1 SIMON & SCHUSTER PB $20.00

Leonard **Maltin**

The Art of the Cinematographer: A Survey and Interviews with Five Masters

0-486-23686-2 DOVER PB $12.95

Leonard Maltin (photo by Andrew Semel)

Pat **McGilligan,** editor

Backstory 2: Interviews With Screenwriters of the '40s and '50s

A follow-up featuring frank interviews with fourteen writers including Richard Brooks, Garson Kanin, Ben Maddow, and Daniel Taradash

0-520-07169-7 CALIFORNIA $34.95

Patrick **McGilligan**

Backstory: Interviews with Screenwriters of Hollywood's Golden Age

The screenwriters interviewed provide a frequently acerbic account of what went on behind the camera

0-520-05689-2 CALIFORNIA PB $16.00

Gabriella **Oldham**

First Cut: Conversations with Film Editors

0-520-07586-2 CALIFORNIA $37.50

Dennis **Potter**

Potter on Potter

Screenwriter Potter was best known for his 1981 *Pennies from Heaven*

0-571-17046-3 FABER PB $11.95

David **Thomson**

Showman: The Life of David O. Selznick

0-394-56833-8 KNOPF $35.00

Ralph **Rosenblum** & Robert **Karen**

When the Shooting Stops...the Cutting Begins: A Film Editor's Story

Enormously entertaining anecdotes about the most underrated of film arts, including revealing stories about working with William Friedkin and Woody Allen

0-306-80272-4 DA CAPO PB $12.95

Dennis **Schaefer** & Larry **Salvato**

Masters of Light: Conversations with Contemporary Cinematographers

0-520-05336-2 CALIFORNIA PB $15.95

Paul **Schrader**

Schrader on Schrader & Other Writings

Schrader first made his name writing criticism in Los Angeles. He eventually became one of Martin Scorsese's favorite screenwriters after he wrote *Taxi Driver* in just eight days

EDITED BY KEVIN JACKSON

0-571-16370-X FABER PB $12.95

Tom **Stempel**

Framework: A History of Screenwriting in the American Film

FOREWORD BY PHILIP DUNNE

0-8264-0411-1 CONTINUUM $22.95

Animation

Joe **Adamson**

Bugs Bunny: Fifty Years and Only One Gray Hare

A sumptuous celebration of half a century of the voracious Bugs, with 200 illustrations, over 150 in color

0-8050-1190-0 HOLT $35.00

Jerry **Beck** & Will **Friedwald**

Looney Tunes and Merrie Melodies: A Complete Illustrated Guide to the Warner Bros. Cartoons

0-8050-0894-2 HOLT PB $15.95

Giannalberto **Bendazzi**

Cartoons: One Hundred Years of Cinema Animation

0-253-20937-4 INDIANA PB $39.95

Leslie **Cabarga**

The Fleischer Story

0-306-80313-5 DA CAPO PB $16.95

Christopher **Finch**

The Art of the Lion King

A lush, sumptuous companion to the animated extravaganza from Disney, in which Simba, a royal lion cub forced into exile by his usurping uncle, must return home to claim his rightful place as King of the Beasts. A wonderful

keepsake produced with the same pride and attention to detail that went into the film. Directed by Don Hahn *(Beauty and the Beast)*, with original artwork that takes its inspiration from African themes and landscapes
FOREWORD BY JAMES EARL JONES
0-7868-6028-6 HYPERION $50.00

The Art of Walt Disney: From Mickey Mouse to the Magic Kingdoms
0-8109-1962-1 ABRAMS $60.00

Chuck **Jones**
Chuck Amok: The Life and Times of an Animated Cartoonist
0-374-12348-9 FS&G $29.00

Norman M. **Klein**
Seven Minutes: The Life and Death of the American Animated Cartoon
The late, lamented cartoon short, which had ceased to exist by the '60s, was an art form as tightly controlled as a minuet—and one fraught with complex pressures. Cartoons reflected changing styles of design, fashion, and economics while evoking the harried nature of daily life. "No one has a view of animation as broad and yet as detailed as Norman Klein's. From the nuances of the art clear out to its richest social implications, he's consistently lucid and stimulating"—Hugh Kenner
See also **THE IMPACT OF THE MEDIA** under **TOPICS IN AMERICAN STUDIES** in **HISTORY OF THE AMERICAS**
0-86091-396-1 VERSO $29.95
1-85984-150-3 VERSO PB $19.95

Leonard **Maltin**
Of Mice and Magic: A History of American Animated Cartoons
0-452-25993-2 NEW AMERICAN LIBRARY PB .. $24.95

Design and Glamour

Margaret J. **Bailey**
Those Glorious Glamorous Years: Classic Hollywood Costume Design of the 1930s
0-8065-0784-5 CITADEL $25.00

Gary **Bernstein**
Portrait Hollywood: Gary Bernstein's Classic Celebrity Photographs
PHOTOGRAPHS BY GARY BERNSTEIN
0-942627-02-4 WODFP $34.95

David **Fahey** & Linda **Rich**
Masters of Starlight: Photographers in Hollywood
Decades of the best portraits and candid shots
0-517-05092-7 OUTLET $12.99

Joel W. **Finler**
Hollywood Movie Stills
1-56833-039-1 MADISON $25.01

Jean **Howard** & James **Watters**
Jean Howard's Hollywood: A Photo Memoir
This engaging book provides an intimate look at the lives of the movie stars, directors, agents and other Hollywood figures in the 1930s, '40s, and '50s. As a a contract player at MGM and the wife of superagent Charles Feldman, Jean Howard entertained and was entertained by such stars as Tyrone Power, Clark Gable, Jennifer Jones, and Darryl Zanuck—and captured them with her camera. They are seen at play and at work, at home and abroad—a view of a lifestyle which no longer exists
0-8109-1190-6 ABRAMS $45.00

John **Margolies** & Emily **Gwathmey**
Ticket to Paradise: American Movie Theaters and How We Had Fun
0-8212-1829-8 BULFINCH $29.95

Michael **Webb**, editor
Hollywood: Legend and Reality
Hollywood wasn't just movies; it was a mode of perceiving the universe. Webb's book offers up some of the artifacts that sprang from that inimitably gaudy mode of perception
0-8212-1588-4 NEW YORK GRAPHIC SOCIETY . $9.98
9-990-79765-X BOOK SALES PB $7.98

Screenplays

Collections

Woody **Allen**
Four Films of Woody Allen
Includes *Annie Hall, Interiors, Manhattan, and Stardust Memories*
0-394-71229-3 RANDOM HOUSE PB $18.00

Jean **Cocteau**
Blood of a Poet & the Testament of Orpheus
0-7145-0580-3 MARION BOYARS PB $12.95

Joel **Coen** & Ethan **Coen**
Barton Fink/Miller's Crossing
Barton Fink is the fanatstic, slightly hallucinatory story of a Hollywood screenwriter with a monumental case of writer's block. *Miller's Crossing* is the Coen's "gangster" picture about the twisted loyalties within the Irish mafia
0-571-12925-0 FABER PB $13.95

William **Goldman**
Four Screenplays With Essays
1-55783-266-8 APPLAUSE THEATRE $25.95
1-55783-265-X APPLAUSE THEATRE PB $18.95

Akira **Kurosawa**
Seven Samurai: And Other Screenplays
0-571-16224-X FABER PB $14.95

Mike **Leigh**
Naked and Other Screenplays
Leigh's scripts are blistering examinations of the darker side of human emotions
0-571-17386-1 FABER PB $18.95

Whit **Stillman**
Barcelona and Metropolitan: Tales of Two Cities
Stillman skewers upper-class American mores with graceful wit and perfect pitch dialogue
0-571-17365-9 FABER PB $13.95

Preston **Sturges**
Five Screenplays by Preston Sturges
EDITED BY DAVID HENDERSON
0-520-05442-3 CALIFORNIA $55.00
0-520-05564-0 CALIFORNIA PB $28.00

THE BUTLER: You see, sir, rich people and theorists, who are usually rich people, think of poverty in the negative...as the lack of riches...as disease might be called the lack of health...but it isn't, sir. Poverty is not the lack of anything, but a positive plague, virulent in itself, contagious as cholera, with filth, criminality, vice and despair as only a few of its symptoms. It is to be stayed away from, even for purposes of study... It is to be shunned.
FIVE SCREENPLAYS BY PRESTON STURGES

Quentin **Tarantino**
Reservoir Dogs & True Romance: Screenplays
Tarantino sold *True Romance*—the road-movie homage to Bruce Lee, comic books, convertibles, Vietnam movies, and Elvis—to director Tony Scott and used the money to help finance *Reservoir Dogs*, the quintessential Tarrantino script, replete with sharp dialogue splattered with pop references, highly stylized violence, and an underlying sense of hipness and humor
0-8021-3355-X GROVE PB $13.00

Sam **Thomas**, editor
Best American Screenplays
Includes *All Quiet on the Western Front, Meet John Doe, Casablanca, Miracle on 34th Street, Rebel Without a Cause, Bonnie and Clyde, The Graduate, Butch Cassidy and the Sundance Kid, Sounder, On Golden Pond, Arthur,* and *The Candidate*
0-517-55542-5 CROWN $35.00

Best American Screenplays 3
0-517-59104-9 CROWN $50.00

Michael **Tolkin**
The Player, The Rapture & The New Age: Three Screenplays
Tolkin's *The Player* is one of the funniest and most knowing satires of the Hollywood system
See also **SINCE 1945** under **20TH-CENTURY AMERICAN FICTION** in **LITERATURE OF THE AMERICAS**
0-8021-3392-4 GROVE PB $13.00

Robert **Towne**
Chinatown, The Last Detail, Shampoo: Screenplays
0-87113-213-3 ATLANTIC MONTHLY PB $12.95

Individual Films

For related reading, see ARTS AND LETTERS under WOMEN'S STUDIES in SOCIAL STUDIES

Scott **Alexander** & Larry **Karaszewski**
Ed Wood
The script of the excellent Tim Burton film that paid homage to the "worst director of all time." Wood is the zany genius behind such classic works as *Plan Nine from Outerspace* and the meditation of gender themes, *Glen or Glenda*. Bela Lugosi, who figured prominently in Wood's pictures, is sensitively depicted as a has-been morphine addict—Martin Landau received an Oscar for this role
0-571-17568-6 FABER PB $12.95

Woody **Allen**
Hannah and Her Sisters
0-394-74749-6 VINTAGE PB $12.00

Paul **Auster**
Smoke and Blue in the Face: Two Films
Novelist Auster's warm homage to his home, Brooklyn. *Smoke* tells the story of Augie, a cigar shop owner, who comes into contact with the varieties of people who live in his neighborhood. *Blue in the Face* is a lighter, more improvised examination of the same characters and themes
See also **SINCE 1945** under **20TH-CENTURY AMERICAN FICTION** in **LITERATURE OF THE AMERICAS**
0-7868-8098-8 HYPERION PB $12.95

John **Berger** & Alain **Tanner**
Jonah Who Will Be Twenty-Five in the Year 2000
TRANSLATED BY MICHAEL PALMER
0-913028-98-3 NORTH ATLANTIC PB $9.95

Les **Blank**
Burden of Dreams
EDITED BY JAMES BOGAN
0-938190-17-2 NORTH ATLANTIC PB $12.95

Robert **Buckner** & Edmund **Joseph**
Yankee Doodle Dandy
EDITED BY PATRICK MCGILLIGAN
0-299-08474-4 WISCONSIN PB $6.95

Luis **Bunuel** & Jean-Claude **Carriere**
Belle De Jour
0-8044-6071-X UNGAR PB $9.95

Luis **Bunuel** & Salvador **Dali**
Un Chien Andalou
One of the masterworks of the surrealist movement as written by two of its leading practitioners
0-571-17372-1 FABER PB $9.95

Ethan **Coen** & Joel **Coen**
Fargo
The Coen brothers, masters of humorous American gothic-noir, send up midwestern values and accents in this story of an ordinary man who, through his own greed, gets himself involved in a plot involving hit men, parking lots, used cars, and a wood-chipper
0-571-17963-0 FABER PB $12.95

David **Cronenberg**
Crash
0-88910-497-2 COACH HOUSE PB $16.95

Julie **Dash**
Daughters of the Dust: The Making of an African-American Woman's Film
Dash's struggle to complete her lush, ambitious first film, *Daughters of the Dust*, is more than just a tale of logistics. It is a revealing study of how an African–American woman artist—the first to make a nationally distributed feature film—fought to create an honest picture of life in the Georgia Sea Islands. Included is Dash's original screenplay, an interview of the filmmaker by critic bell hooks, Dash's production notes, and color stills from the movie
1-56584-030-5 NEW PRESS PB $17.95

Marguerite **Duras**
Hiroshima, Mon Amour
TRANSLATED BY RICHARD SEAVER
0-8021-3104-2 GROVE PB $8.95

Marguerite Duras

Sergei **Eisenstein**
The Battleship Potemkin
TRANSLATED BY GILLON R. AITKEN
0-571-12559-X FABER PB $9.95

Francis **Faragoh** & Robert E. **Lee**
Little Caesar
EDITED BY GERALD PEARY
0-299-08454-X WISCONSIN PB $8.95

Mike **Figgis** & John **O'Brien**
Leaving Las Vegas
Figgis based this haunting story on the late O'Brien's novel. Working with seemingly clichéd characters (an alcoholic with a death wish, a hooker with a heart of gold), they create an unrepentant, harrowing glimpse into the world of the hopeless alcoholic as well as the most enduring love story to come out of Hollywood in years
0-571-17969-X FABER PB $12.95

Erwin **Gelsey**
Gold Diggers of 1933
EDITED BY ARTHUR HOVE
0-299-08084-6 WISCONSIN PB $8.95

Graham **Greene**
The Third Man
0-571-12634-0 FABER PB $12.95

Graham Greene

Sheridan **Gibney**
I Am a Fugitive from a Chain Gang
EDITED BY JOHN O'CONNOR
0-299-08754-9 WISCONSIN PB $6.95

Jean-Luc **Godard**
Breathless
See also **RUTGERS FILM IN PRINT SERIES**
EDITED BY DUDLEY ANDREW
0-8135-1252-2 RUTGERS $30.00
0-8135-1253-0 RUTGERS PB $15.00

Ivan **Goff** & Ben **Roberts**
White Heat
EDITED BY PATRICK MCGILLIGAN
0-299-09674-2 WISCONSIN PB $6.95

Christopher **Hampton**
Carrington
Playwright Hampton's look at the relationship between painter Dora Carrington and writer Lytton Strachey, both prominent figures in the Bloomsbury group
0-571-15336-4 FABER PB $12.95

Total Eclipse
The story of poet Arthur Rimbaud, the young genius of the late 19th century French poetry world, and his reckless relationship with the older, married Paul Verlaine. A tragic tale of insanity and artistic creation
0-571-17873-1 FABER PB $10.95

Hal **Hartley**
Amateur
Another entry in the outrageous Hartley oeuvre. This one concerns itself with an ex-nun who is attempting to write pornography for a living who meets up with an amnesiac criminal
0-571-17213-X FABER PB $12.95

Flirt
0-571-17954-1 FABER PB $12.95

John **Huston**
Juarez
EDITED BY PAUL VANDERWOOD
0-299-08744-1 WISCONSIN PB $8.95

Sergei **Eisenstein**
Ivan the Terrible: Parts 1, 2, 3
0-571-12586-7 FABER PB $14.95

Howard **Koch**
Mission to Moscow
EDITED BY DAVID CULBERT
0-299-08384-5 WISCONSIN PB $6.95

Hanif **Kureishi**
My Beautiful Laundrette
0-571-13981-7 FABER PB $12.95

Claude **Lanzmann**
Shoah: An Oral History of the Holocaust
Complete text of the landmark film
See also **ART AND LITERATURE** under **THE HOLOCAUST** in **WORLD HISTORY AND CURRENT AFFAIRS**
FOREWORD BY SIMONE DE BEAUVOIR
0-306-80665-7 DA CAPO PB $12.95

Ranald **MacDougall**
Mildred Pierce
EDITED BY ALBERT LAVALLEY
0-299-08374-8 WISCONSIN PB $6.95

Louis **Malle**
Au Revoir Les Enfants
TRANSLATED BY ANSELM HOLLO
0-8021-3114-X GROVE PB $6.95

Cormac **McCarthy**
The Gardener's Son: A Screenplay
0-88001-481-4 ECCO $22.00

Seton I. **Miller** & Howard **Koch**
The Sea Hawk
EDITED BY RUDY BEHLMER
0-299-09014-0 WISCONSIN PB $6.95

Sally **Potter**
Orlando
Potter's adaptation of the Virginia Woolf novel
0-571-17295-4 FABER PB $12.95

Casey **Robinson**
Dark Victory
EDITED BY BERNARD F. DICK
0-299-08764-6 WISCONSIN PB $6.95

Now, Voyager
EDITED BY JEANNE ALLEN
0-299-09794-3 WISCONSIN PB $6.95

Martin **Scorsese** & Jay **Cocks**
The Age of Innocence: A Portrait of the Film Based on the Novel by Edith Wharton
1-55704-143-1 NEWMARKET $49.50
1-55704-254-3 NEWMARKET PB $14.95

James **Seymour** & Rian **James**
42nd Street
EDITED BY ROCCO FUMENTO
0-299-08104-4 WISCONSIN PB $6.95

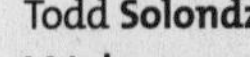

Todd **Solondz**
Welcome to the Dollhouse
The darling of Sundance in 1996 concerns itself with the pre-adolescent angst of its "nerdy" girl protagonist
0-571-19050-2 FABER PB $12.95

John **Steinbeck**
Zapata
This is the original version of Steinbeck's narrative of the life of Emiliano Zapata, "the Little Tiger," a leader of the Mexican revolution, upon which he based his Academy Award-winning script for the Elia Kazin film *Viva Zapata!*. Only recently discovered
See also **FROM THE TURN OF THE CENTURY TO WORLD WAR II** under **20TH-CENTURY AMERICAN FICTION** in **LITERATURE OF THE AMERICAS**
0-14-017322-6 PENGUIN PB $12.95

John Steinbeck

Quentin **Tarantino**
Pulp Fiction
Ex-video store clerk turned master of urban American slang and violent black humor, Tarrantino won an Oscar for this sharply plotted meditation on all things violent, American, and cool
0-7868-8104-6 HYPERION PB $9.95

Harvey **Thew**
The Public Enemy
EDITED BY HENRY COHEN
0-299-08460-4 WISCONSIN $18.95

Emma **Thompson**
The Sense and Sensibility Screenplay & Diaries: Bringing Jane Austen's Novel to Film
Actress Thompson won an Oscar for her adaptation of Jane Austen's novel. Included here is Thompson's account of the creative process behind her enormously risky and successful first stab at screenwriting
1-55704-292-6 NEWMARKET PB $15.95

François **Truffaut** & Claude **de Givray**
La Petite Voleuse
0-571-14175-7 FABER PB $9.95

François Truffaut

Erich **von Stroheim**
Greed
0-571-12581-6 FABER PB $12.95

Film Theory

Film theory once centered on the silent era. The writings of Eisenstein, Pudovkin, Arnheim, and Balazs retained their dominance for decades, and new technical developments like color and wide screen were viewed mostly as commercial aberrations rather than new formal opportunities. Then came André Bazin and the young Turks of *Cahiers du Cinéma* to stir things up, and in their wake a host of structuralists, semioticians, and (especially influential in recent years) feminists. As a result, every analytical truism has been called into question. Nearly everything written about film in recent years bears the imprint of French post-structuralist thought, if only at second or third hand. This is not always a blessing, since it requires continual immersion in terms like "syntagmatic parallelism" and "maximization of the diegetic effect," but there is no question that the semiotic approach has illuminated film in unexpected ways through its reading of narrative codes and generic structures. In the process, attention has shifted from high-minded prescriptions of what cinema ought to do, to focus instead on precise notation of what it actually does.

Early Classics

Richard **Abel**, editor
French Film Theory and Criticism: A History/Anthology
Volume I
1907-1929
0-691-05517-3 PRINCETON $65.00
0-691-00062-X PRINCETON PB $24.95

Volume II
1929-1939
0-691-05518-1 PRINCETON $49.50
0-691-00063-8 PRINCETON PB $21.95

Rudolf **Arnheim**

Film as Art

0-520-00035-8 CALIFORNIA PB $12.00

Nick **Browne**, editor

Cahiers Du Cinema, 1969-1972: The Politics of Representation

0-674-09063-2 HARVARD $38.00

Sergei **Eisenstein**

Film Form

0-15-630920-3 HARCOURT BRACE PB $16.00

The Film Sense

0-15-630935-1 HARCOURT BRACE PB $15.00

Jim **Hillier**, editor

Cahiers Du Cinema: 1950s Neo-Realism, Hollywood, New Wave

The prime years of the most influential of all film magazines; staff writers included Godard, Truffaut, Rohmer, Rivette, and Chabrol

0-674-09062-4 HARVARD $36.00
0-674-09061-6 HARVARD PB $15.50

Jean **Narboni** & Tom **Milne**, editors

Godard on Godard

A compendium of Godard's inimitably paradoxical pronouncements

See also **DIRECTORS**

0-306-80259-7 DA CAPO PB $12.95

Andrew **Sarris**

The American Cinema: Directors and Directions, 1929-1968

Sarris's influential rating of American directors, from the "pantheon" on down, with filmographies up to 1968; a classic statement of the auteurist position

See also **FILM IN AMERICA**

0-306-80728-9 DA CAPO PB $14.95

Dziga **Vertov**

Kino-Eye: The Writings of Dziga Vertov

EDITED BY ANNETTE MICHELSON

0-520-05630-2 CALIFORNIA PB $16.95

Contemporary Theory

David **Bordwell**

Narration in the Fiction Film

0-299-10174-6 WISCONSIN PB $16.95

Leo **Braudy**

The World in a Frame: What We See in Films

0-226-07155-3 CHICAGO PB $11.95

Noel **Burch**

Life to Those Shadows

0-520-07143-3 CALIFORNIA $48.00
0-520-07144-1 CALIFORNIA PB $22.50

Theory of Film Practice

0-691-00329-7 PRINCETON PB $13.95

Stanley **Cavell**

Contesting Tears: The Hollywood Melodrama of the Unknown Woman

See also **GENRES AND THEMES**

0-226-09814-1 CHICAGO $36.00
0-226-09816-8 CHICAGO PB $14.95

The World Viewed: Reflections on the Ontology of Film

0-674-96196-X HARVARD PB $12.95

Michel **Chion**

Audio Vision: Sound on Screen

0-231-07898-6 COLUMBIA $55.00
0-231-07899-4 COLUMBIA PB $17.50

Gilles **Deleuze**

Cinema One: Movement—Image

TRANSLATED BY HUGH TOMLINSON & BARBARA HABBERJAM

0-8166-1400-8 MINNESOTA PB $16.95

Lorraine **Gamman** &
Margaret **Marshment**, editors

The Female Gaze: Women as Viewers of Popular Culture

0-941104-41-9 REAL COMET PB $12.95

T. Jefferson **Kline**

Screening the Text: Intertextuality in New Wave French Cinema

See also **FRANCE** under **NATIONAL CINEMAS**

0-8018-4267-0 JOHNS HOPKINS $37.50

Gerald **Mast** & Marshall **Cohen**, editors

Film Theory and Criticism: Introductory Readings

A definitive collection spanning the history of film from Lumiere and Melies to the French New Wave

0-19-506398-8 OXFORD PB $24.95

Christian **Metz**

Film Language: A Semiotics of the Cinema

TRANSLATED BY MICHAEL TAYLOR

0-19-501762-5 OXFORD $35.00

The Imaginary Signifier: Psychoanalysis and the Cinema

TRANSLATED BY CELIA BRITTON

0-253-20380-5 INDIANA PB $14.95

Philip **Rosen**

Narrative, Apparatus, Ideology: A Film Theory Reader

0-231-05881-0 COLUMBIA PB $21.50

Film Reviewers

Before there were film critics, there were movie reviewers. They had the advantage of working not from a theoretical matrix but out of the daily experience of seeing. If that experience induced little beyond sleepy cynicism in most, a handful turned a journalistic necessity into a minor art form.

Frank D. **Gilroy**

I Wake Up Screening

0-8093-1856-3 SOUTHERN ILLINOIS $39.95
0-8093-1918-7 SOUTHERN ILLINOIS PB $19.95

J. **Hoberman**

Vulgar Modernism

"One of the most intelligent and thought-provoking critics in the United States, though he doesn't always like my films"— Martin Scorsese

0-87722-864-7 TEMPLE $54.95
0-87722-866-3 TEMPLE PB $16.95

Pauline **Kael**

For Keeps: Thirty Years At the Movies

The ultimate collection of the best work of possibly the most accomplished movie reviewer of all time. In her 25 years covering cinema for *New Yorker,* Kael established herself as the strongest voice in the genre. This discriminating collection of her finest reviews captures the essential Kael. "Think of it as the Riverside Shakespeare of...Kael's writing"—*Kirkus Reviews*

0-525-93896-6 DUTTON $34.95

Pauline Kael

Stanley **Kauffmann**

Before My Eyes: Film Criticism and Comment

Essays by the longtime reviewer for *The New Republic*

0-306-80179-5 DA CAPO PB $9.95

Jonathan **Rosenbaum**

Placing Movies: The Practice of Film Criticism

0-520-08632-5 CALIFORNIA $45.00
0-520-08633-3 CALIFORNIA PB $16.00

The Moviegoing Experience

Ian **Breakwell** & Paul **Hammond**, editors

Seeing in the Dark: A Compendium of Cinemagoing

1-85242-166-5 SERPENT'S TAIL PB $15.95

Geoffrey **O'Brien**

The Phantom Empire

O'Brien poses a fundamental question of film criticism: what do we finally internalize from the thousands of moving images that have been projected before our eyes? Captures the unexpected ways in which movies have transformed how we think and how we feel

0 393035492 NORTON $20.00
0-393-31296-8 NORTON PB.............................$12.00

Jonathan **Rosenbaum**

Moving Places: A Life at the Movies

Rosenbaum's family were film exhibitors, and here he offers an unprecedented autobiographical account of how movies seeped into his consciousness on all levels

0-520-08907-3 CALIFORNIA PB.........................$16.00

Do It Yourself

Here are some useful titles for the novice filmmaker.

Daniel **Arijon**

Grammar of the Film Language

1-87950-507-X SAMUEL FRENCH PB $24.95

Edward **Dmytryk**

On Film Editing

0-240-51738-5 FOCAL PB.....................................$22.95

On Screen Directing

0-240-51716-4 FOCAL PB.....................................$22.95

On Screen Writing

0-240-51753-9 FOCAL PB.....................................$22.95

Richard **Levinson**

The Screenwriter's Workbook

A practical, step-by-step guide

0-440-58225-3 DELL PB..$11.95

Art **Linson**

A Pound of Flesh: Perilous Tales of How to Produce Movies in Hollywood

Part practical textbook, part warning to wannabes, part gossip, and entirely entertaining, this no-nonsense book names names while offering anecdotal lessons for Tinsel Town hopefuls. The author is a long-time producer whose hits have included *The Untouchables, Fast Times at Ridgemont High,* and *This Boy's Life*

0-8021-1543-8 GROVE $18.00

Alec **Nisbett**

The Technique of the Sound Studio

0-240-51100-X FOCAL PB.....................................$39.95

Joe **Queenan**

The Unkindest Cut: How a Hatchet-Man Critic Made his Own $7,000 Movie and Put It All on his Credit Card

0-7868-6090-1 HYPERION $22.95
0-7868-8198-4 HYPERION PB $11.95

Karel **Reisz** & Gavin **Millar**

Technique of Film Editing

0-240-50846-7 FOCAL PB $27.50

Robert **Rodriguez**

Rebel Without a Crew: Or How a 23-Year-Old Filmmaker with $7,000 Became a Hollywood Player

The fabled story of Rodriguez's making of the sub-underground indie fave *El Mariachi*

See also **DIRECTORS**

0-525-93794-3 DUTTON $22.95
0-452-27187-8 PLUME PB $11.95

Eric **Sherman**

Frame by Frame: A Handbook For Creative Filmmaking

0-918226-12-0 ACROBAT PB................................$19.95

Reference

Finally there are the lists. Movies and list-making naturally go together, from the ritual of ten-best choices to the current spate of encyclopedic reference works geared to the VCR owner. The following are some of the standouts in a crowded field.

Leslie **Halliwell**

Halliwell's Film and Video Guide: Sixth Edition

Alphabetical film-by-film entries notable for their detailed credits listings

0-684-19051-6 SCRIBNERS PB.............................$19.95

Halliwell's Film Guide 1996

"A knockout compilation of almost everything you could possibly want to know about thousands of movies"—*Chicago Tribune*

0-06-273372-9 HARPERCOLLINS PB $21.00

Halliwell's Filmgoer's and Video Viewer's Companion: Tenth Edition

The most popular, authoritative, and complete reference book for movie and video fans. Updated and revised

0-06-273239-0 HARPER REFERENCE PB $25.00

Leslie L. **Halliwell**

Halliwell's Filmgoer's Companion

Halliwell's thick and well-researched volumes are extremely useful for their data, although the author's opinions are, to say the least, questionable

0-684-18410-9 SCRIBNERS PB.............................$16.95

John **Hulme** & Michael **Wexler**

Baked Potatoes: A Pot Smoker's Guide to Film and Video

A hilariously off-beat guide to videos. Includes a section that features films in which Harry Dean Stanton makes an appearance. Also includes an elaborate rating system and witty annotations

0-385-47837-2 MAIN STREET PB.........................$10.00

Pauline **Kael**

5001 Nights at the Movies: Expanded For the '90s with 800 New Reviews

Makes no attempt to be comprehensive, but Kael's thumbnail critiques are irresistibly readable even when they annoy

0-8050-1367-9 HOLT PB $24.95

Ephraim **Katz**

Film Encyclopedia

Remarkably comprehensive: now revised it is still the best one-volume data source

0-06-273089-4 HARPERCOLLINS PB...................$27.50

Tim **Lucas**

The Video Watchdog Book

A cornucopia of hard-to-find information on fantasy, horror, and garden-variety exploitation from the editor of *Video Watchdog*, an unsung and indispensable guide to cinema's outer and lower reaches

0-9633756-0-1 VIDEO WATCHDOG PB $19.95

Leonard **Maltin**

Leonard Maltin's Movie and Video Guide 1997

An enormously useful guide to over 14,000 movies available on VHS or Laserdisc. With brief reviews from the popular critic

0-452-27681-0 PLUME PB $19.95

Leonard Maltin's Movie Encyclopedia

More than 2,000 entries of vital statistics, awards, and bios on stars, directors, writers, and producers

0-452-27058-8 PLUME PB $19.95

James **Monaco**

The Encyclopedia of Film

Useful biographical guide to directors, stars, producers, and others

0-399-51606-9 PERIGEE PB $18.95

Robert **Moses** & Beth **Rowen**, editors

1997 Information Please Entertainment Almanac

This updated edition of the classic almanac contains full listings of Oscar, Grammy, and Emmy winners; a comprehensive yearbook of the major film, television, and music releases of 1997; essays by leading feature writers and columnists; time lines; film and music festival calendars; photography, and more

See also **ALMANACS AND BOOKS OF FACTS** under **GENERAL INFORMATION** under **REFERENCE** in **BUSINESS AND REFERENCE**

0-395-82855-4 HOUGHTON MIFFLIN PB............$13.95

Raymond **Murray**

Images in the Dark: An Encyclopedia of Gay and Lesbian Film and Video

Over 3,000 reviews and 200 biographies, some well known, some deeply buried. Hundreds of photos and detailed indices

See also **THEATER AND FILM** under **ARTS AND LETTERS** under **GAY, LESBIAN, AND BISEXUAL STUDIES** in **SOCIAL STUDIES**

0-452-27627-6 PLUME PB $19.95

Andrea **Shaw**

Seen That, Now What?: The Ultimate Guide to Finding the Video You Really Want to Watch

A breezy guide to the wide and endless proliferating world of video-to-go, with sidelines on such genres as Female Crime Capers, LA Sick Soul of Modern Life, Techno Horror, and Post-Watergate paranoia

0-684-80011-X FIRESIDE PB..............................$15.95

Michael **Weldon**

The Psychotronic Encyclopedia of Film

Much, much more—over six hundred pages—of Weldon's patented (and now trademark-protected) brand of the bizarre and the sleazy. Even the hardiest explorer may blanch a little at the prospect of *Cycle psycho, Hallucinations in a Deranged Mind, Night of the Bloody Transplant,* and other delights

0-345-34345-X BALLANTJNE PB.......................$20.00

Journalism

The first newspaper in America, *Publick Occurrences*, was founded in 1690: it lasted one issue before Massachusetts authorities shut it down for impertinence. Two thirds of the history of American journalism had been recorded before the storied William Randolph Hearst commandeered his first daily a century ago.

Still, it is this recent century that engages most of our attention, for in its new prominence, what was once referred to only as "the newspaper business" has become a giant industry, a profession, and a socio-political institution.

For related reading, see 20TH-CENTURY AMERICAN ESSAYS AND JOURNALISM in LITERATURE OF THE AMERICAS

For related reading, see 20TH-CENTURY AMERICAN ESSAYS AND JOURNALISM in LITERATURE OF THE AMERICAS

History

Michael **Emery** & Edwin **Emery**

The Press and America: An Interpretive History of the Mass Media

A standard textbook, thick and informative

0-13-739277-X PRENTICE HALL.............................$71.82

Michael **Schudson**

Discovering the News: A Social History of America's Newspapers

Stimulating essays focusing on the concept of objectivity

0-465-01666-9 BASIC BOOKS PB.......................$15.00

The Age of the Printer: 1690-1800

The first century of American journalism was an era of tiny, perishable newspapers trying to make their way in a culture that was not sure it needed the press.

Leonard W. **Levy**

The Emergence of a Free Press

The major study on the origins of the major force in American journalism: freedom of the press

0-19-504240-9 OXFORD PB...............................$12.95

Arthur M. **Schlesinger**, Jr.

Prelude to Independence: The Newspaper War on Britain 1764-1776

The pivotal role of the press in the American Revolution

FOREWORD BY CHARLES AKERS

0-930350-13-8 NORTHEASTERN PB..................$18.95

The Age of the Editor: 1800-1880

The 19th century brought a transition from newspapers for the few—the political and commercial elite—to newspapers for the many. The vehicle for expansion was news: it was either entertaining or useful or, occasionally, both.

News for amusement came on the scene with the penny press of the 1830s. The multifeatured newspaper that we know today arrived with Horace Greeley's *New York Tribune* in the 1840s. And the Civil War marked a major turning point in the history of the American press, creating a monstrous appetite that newspapers and other news media are still trying to sate.

Douglas **Fermer**

James Gordon Bennett and the New York Herald

Biography of the man who invented—and corrupted—news as we know it

0-312-43955-5 ST. MARTIN'S $35.00

Louis M. **Starr**

Bohemian Brigade

How the Civil War, and the reporters who covered it, created a 19th-century news revolution

FOREWORD BY JAMES BOYLAN

0-299-11344-2 WISCONSIN PB..........................$13.50

The Age of the Reporter: Since 1880

Although such innovators as Joseph Pulitzer, William Randolph Hearst, and E.W. Scripps were more famous names, reporters became the key figures in the new urban journalism of the 1880s. They remained the workhorses of the press for the next century. As police reporters, war correspondents, and tenacious investigators, they created the legends of American journalism.

Timothy **Crouse**

The Boys on the Bus: Riding with the Campaign Press Corps

A wry account of the dangers, and joys, of pack journalism

0-345-34015-9 BALLANTINE PB.........................$5.99

Sally Foreman **Griffith**

Hometown News: William Allen White and the Emporia Gazette

A biography of the famous small-town journalist and a social history of small-town life

0-19-505589-6 OXFORD...................................$30.00

Samuel **Hynes**

Reporting World War II: American Journalism, 1938-1946

Volume I

See also **THE UNITED STATES AND WORLD WAR II** under **THE SECOND WORLD WAR** in **WORLD HISTORY AND CURRENT AFFAIRS**

See also **LIBRARY OF AMERICA** in **LITERATURE OF THE AMERICAS**

1-88301-104-3 LIBRARY OF AMERICA.............$35.00

Volume II

See also **THE UNITED STATES AND WORLD WAR II** under **THE SECOND WORLD WAR** in **WORLD HISTORY AND CURRENT AFFAIRS**

See also **LIBRARY OF AMERICA** in **LITERATURE OF THE AMERICAS**

1-88301-105-1 LIBRARY OF AMERICA.............$35.00

Phillip **Knightley**

The First Casualty: From the Crimea to Vietnam—The War Correspondent as Hero, Propagandist, and Myth Maker

On war correspondents of all nationalities, told with more gusto than accuracy

0-15-631130-5 HARCOURT BRACE PB..............$16.95

Stephen R. **MacKinnon** & Oris **Friesen**

China Reporting: An Oral History of American Journalism in the 1930s and 1940s

A fascinating glimpse into one of the American press's first experiences with world revolution

0-520-06967-6 CALIFORNIA PB.........................$14.00

Jack **Stenbuck**

Typewriter Battalion: Dramatic Frontline Dispatches from World War II

See also **THE MEN IN THE FIELD** under **MEMOIRS AND BIOGRAPHIES** under **THE SECOND WORLD WAR** in **WORLD HISTORY AND CURRENT AFFAIRS**

0-688-14190-0 MORROW................................$23.00

Biographies and Memoirs

Brooke **Kroeger**

Nellie Bly: Daredevil, Reporter, Feminist

"Bly's was the thrilling account of a trailblazer—emphasis blaze, as in glory…"
—LA Times

0-8129-2525-4 TIME BOOKS PB.......................$16.00

Brenda **Wineapple**

Genet: The Life of Janet Flanner

0-89919-442-7 TICKNOR & FIELDS $24.95

Ronald **Steel**

Walter Lippman and the American Century

A wonderful portrait of one of journalism's giants, a man who strove to put things in a larger context. But, also, a man who sometimes grew too close to the powerful

0-394-74731-3 VINTAGE PB $22.00

Stan **Cloud** & Lynn **Olson**

The Murrow Boys: Pioneers on the Frontlines of American Journalism

Edward R. Murrow and his team of reporters—Howard K. Smith, William L. Shirer, Charles Collingwood, and others—were the cutting edge of broadcast journalism, first on the radio and then on television

See also **BIOGRAPHIES AND MEMOIRS** under **RADIO**

0-395-68084-0 HOUGHTON MIFFLIN.............$27.95

Thomas **Kunkel**

Genius in Disguise: Harold Ross of The New Yorker

0-679-41837-7 RANDOM HOUSE $25.00

0-7867-0323-7 CARROLL & GRAF PB $14.95

First-Person Accounts

Russell **Baker**

The Good Times

The second installment of Baker's memoirs, covering his early years as a reporter

See also **MEMOIRS AND JOURNALS** under **20TH-CENTURY AMERICAN ESSAYS AND JOURNALISM** in **LITERATURE OF THE AMERICAS**

0-451-17230-2 SIGNET PB $5.99

Ben **Bradlee**

A Good Life

The former executive editor of *Washington Post* offers an account of his old-boy-network waltz from Harvard to the Pacific war, from postwar Paris to Watergate. A portrait of a charmed life, an historical account of our century since the war, and a look inside the world of newspapers and reporting

0-684-80894-3 SIMON & SCHUSTER................$27.50

0-684-82523-6 TOUCHSTONE PB.......................$14.00

Pete **Hamill**

The Drinking Life: A Memoir

0-316-34108-8 LITTLE, BROWN.........................$21.95

Ben **Hecht**

A Child of the Century

The tumultuous life of the journalist, playwright, and screenwriter

INTRODUCTION BY SIDNEY ZION

0-917657-41-1 FINE PB $11.95

Eric **Sevareid**

Not So Wild a Dream

0-8262-1014-7 MISSOURI PB $24.95

H.L. **Mencken**

A Choice of Days

Selections from the Sage of Baltimore's autobiographical volumes, including *Newspaper Days*

See also **HISTORY, POLITICS, AND SOCIETY** under **20TH-CENTURY AMERICAN ESSAYS AND JOURNALISM** in **LITERATURE OF THE AMERICAS**

EDITED BY EDWARD L. GALLIGAN

0-394-74760-7 RANDOM HOUSE PB $7.95

H.L. Mencken

Harrison E. **Salisbury**

Heroes of My Time

Winner of the Pulitzer Prize for his reporting from Moscow in the '50s and the founding editor of *NY Times* Op-Ed page, Salisbury recollects 25 people who have inspired his admiration over the years. They include RFK, Malcolm X, Khruschev, and Zhou En-lai. "Reading these essays is like opening a family album and finding it full of life. Salisbury remains as sharp in recollection as his reporter's eye was in observation"—Bill Moyers

0-8027-1217-7 WALKER $19.95

Journey For Our Times: A Memoir

0-88184-037-8 CARROLL & GRAF PB $10.95

Donald **Woods**

Asking For Trouble

First-person account from the South African reporter who exposed the death of Stephen Biko

0-8446-6324-7 SMITH $25.05

Bob **Woodward** & Carl **Bernstein**

All the President's Men

How two green *Washington Post* reporters toppled a presidency

See also **THE NIXON YEARS** under **US HISTORY, 1945 TO THE PRESENT** in **HISTORY OF THE AMERICAS**

0-671-89441-2 TOUCHSTONE PB......................$12.00

Newspaper Barons

Joseph C. **Goulden**

Fit to Print: A.M. Rosenthal and His Times

0-8184-0474-4 LYLE STUART.............................$21.95

Deborah **Davis**

Katharine the Great: Katharine Graham and the Washington Post

0-915765-43-8 SHERIDAN SQUARE......................$17.95

Michael **Leapman**

Arrogant Aussie: The Rupert Murdoch Story

A look at the man behind the British tabloids and the incessant controversy surrounding him

0-8184-0370-5 LYLE STUART $14.95

William **Shawcross**

Murdoch

An unauthorized portrait of the media mogul whose orgy of acquisitions rewarded him with Fox Film and TV, *The Times* [London], HarperCollins, *TV Guide, New York Magazine.* The frightening story of a lapsed socialist's egomaniacal assault upon the world

0-671-67327-0 TOUCHSTONE PB $27.50

Chalmers M. **Roberts**

In the Shadow of Power: The Story of the Washington Post

0-932020-71-2 SEVEN LOCKS PB........................$16.95

Richard F. **Shepard**

The Paper's Papers: A Reporter's Journey Through the Archives of the New York Times

From his debut as a copy boy in 1946 to his retirement from the cultural news desk in 1991, Shepard has known *The NY Times* as few others ever have been able. This charming book draws on the paper's archives—internal memos, sketches, cartoons, letters—to paint a singular portrait of the institution that guides American news

0-8129-2453-3 TIME BOOKS...............................$30.00

Ambrose Bierce

The Television Age

Linda **Ellerbee**

And So It Goes: Adventures in Television

One of TV newsdom's most irreverent fixtures lets loose on the TV news industry

0-425-10237-8 BERKLEY PB..............................$4.99

Marc **Gunther**

The House That Roone Built: The Inside Story of ABC News

Roone Arledge is the former head of ABC sports who took over the network's news division in 1976. "...Sheds considerable light on the way the Global Village now gets and views its news"—*Kirkus Reviews*

0-316-33151-1 LITTLE, BROWN........................$23.95

Ted **Koppel** & Kyle **Gibson**

Nightline: History in the Making and the Making of Television

0-8129-2478-9 TIME BOOKS..............................$25.00

Gil **Noble**

Black Is the Color of My TV Tube

The autobiographical odyssey of a star black reporter, one of the first in the industry, during the 1960s

0-8184-0297-0 LYLE STUART..............................$12.00

Magazine Journalism

For nearly a century, magazines have been a major force in American journalism, expanding its role far beyond the expectations of the earliest newspaper editors. After the rise of the popular ten-cent magazine in the 1890s, magazine journalism soon struck a rich vein in what was first called the "literature of exposure," and then dubbed "muckraking" by Theodore Roosevelt.

In due course, the news magazine became the dominant form. *Time* was created by Henry Luce—who placed himself in the public eye as the proponent of "the American Century"—and his forgotten partner, Briton Hadden.

The Muckrakers

Ida **Tarbell**

The History of the Standard Oil Company

An abridged edition of a famous expose

0-393-00496-1 NORTON PB..............................$8.95

Life

Philip B. **Kunhardt**, Jr.

Life Laughs Last

0-671-68797-2 FIRESIDE PB..............................$14.00

The New Yorker and Literary Journalism

Scott **Elledge**

E.B. White: A Biography

0-393-30305-5 NORTON PB..............................$13.00

A. J. **Liebling**

Liebling at the New Yorker: Uncollected Essays

0-8263-1535-6 NEW MEXICO..............................$29.95

Norman **Sims**, editor

The Literary Journalists: The New Art of Personal

Interviews and excerpts from literary journalism's leading stylists, including Joan Didion, John McPhee, Sara Davidson, and Tracy Kidder

0-345-31081-0 BALLANTINE PB..............................$11.00

Raymond **Sokolov**

Wayward Reporter: The Life of A.J. Liebling

0-06-014061-5 HARPERCOLLINS..............................$17.95

David **Seideman**

The New Republic: A Voice of Modern Liberalism

Covers the first 25 years of the magazine and its responses to major historical events from labor strikes to Stalinism

FOREWORD BY MARTIN PERETZ

0-275-92015-1 PRAEGER..............................$55.00

E.B. **White**

Writings from the New Yorker: 1927-1976

Short pieces and essays concerning everything from Khrushchev to cicadas, Thoreau to lipstick, and hyphens to sparrows. "There are enough sparkling gems here to show that White was one of the country's greatest literary treasures" —*NY Times*

See also **REPORTING** under **20TH-CENTURY AMERICAN ESSAYS AND JOURNALISM** in **LITERATURE OF THE AMERICAS**

0-06-092123-4 HARPERPERENNIAL PB..............................$13.00

E. B. White (photo by Jim Kalett)

Journalism Today

General Studies

The Associated Press

The Associated Press Stylebook and Libel Manual: The Journalist's Bible

0-201-10433-4 ADDISON WESLEY PB..............................$10.95

Lou **Cannon**

Reporting: An Inside View

Notes from the seasoned *Washington Post* political reporter

0-930302-13-3 CALIFORNIA JOURNAL PB..............................$4.95

Kay **Mills**

A Place in the News: From the Women's Pages to the Front Pages

The recent rise of women in newspapers

0-396-08932-1 COLUMBIA..............................$19.95

Mark **Pedelty**

War Stories: The Culture of Foreign Correspondents

0-415-91123-0 ROUTLEDGE..............................$59.95

0-415-91124-9 ROUTLEDGE PB..............................$16.95

Clint C. **Wilson** & Felix **Gutierrez**

Minorities and Media: Diversity and the End of Mass Communication

Charts the slow progress in the hiring and promotion of minorities in the newsroom

0-8039-2455-0 SAGE PB..............................$18.95

The National Press Corps

Although most national news organizations retain a New York base, the heaviest permanent mass of journalists is the national press corps in Washington. The press has assumed increasing importance with the centralization of American politics in the White House.

Stephen **Hess**

The Washington Reporters

0-8157-3593-6 BROOKINGS PB..............................$9.95

Brigitte Lebens **Nacos**

The Press, Presidents, and Crises

0-231-07064-0 COLUMBIA..............................$35.00

Critical Studies

Ben H. **Bagdikian**

The Media Monopoly

0-8070-6171-9 BEACON PB..............................$10.95

Daniel J. **Boorstin**

Image: A Guide to Pseudo-Events in America

0-689-70280-9 VINTAGE PB $7.95

Herbert **Gans**

Deciding What's News: A Study of CBS Evening News, NBC Nightly News, Newsweek and Time

Serves as a reminder that journalists should try to talk to not just "the knowns" in our phone books, but "the unknowns" as well

0-394-74354-7 RANDOM HOUSE PB $15.00

Todd **Gitlin**

The Whole World Is Watching: Mass Media in the Making and Unmaking of the New Left

Inside look at the new shape of the opposition in a media-saturated society

0-520-04024-4 CALIFORNIA PB $14.95

Edward S. **Herman** & Noam **Chomsky**

Manufacturing Consent: The Political Economy of the Mass Media

The authors argue that an underlying elite consensus largely structures all facets of the news

0-679-72034-0 PANTHEON PB $17.00

Janet **Malcolm**

The Journalist and the Murderer

The complex relation of author Joe McGinniss to Jeffrey MacDonald, the subject of his bestselling book *Fatal Vision,* accused and convicted of murdering his wife and children. Malcolm's analysis puts into question the ethics and motivations of journalists

0-394-58312-4 VINTAGE PB $18.95

Jimmy Breslin

Robert K. Ore **Manoff** & Ore **Michael Schudson**

Reading The News

0-394-74649-X PANTHEON PB $14.00

Michael **Parenti**

Inventing Reality: The Politics of News Media

The press meets the Reagan era

0-312-02013-9 ST. MARTIN'S PB $19.99

Gaye **Tuchman**

Making News: A Study in the Construction of Reality

Sociological study of mass media and American culture

0-02-932960-4 FREE PRESS PB $13.95

The Press and Government

Robert **Scheer**

Thinking Tuna Fish, Talking Death: Essays on the Pornography of Power

See also **HISTORY, POLITICS, AND SOCIETY** under **20TH-CENTURY AMERICAN ESSAYS AND JOURNALISM** in **LITERATURE OF THE AMERICAS**

0-8090-9316-2 HILL & WANG $19.95

0-374-52214-6 NOONDAY PB $11.95

Kathleen J. **Turner**

Lyndon Johnson's Dual War: Vietnam and the Press

Johnson's ultimately unsuccessful struggle to gain the support of the press for the war in Vietnam

See also **THE POLITICS** under **THE VIETNAM WAR** in **HISTORY OF THE AMERICAS**

0-226-81731-8 CHICAGO $25.00

0-226-81732-6 CHICAGO PB $14.95

Censorship and Freedom

For related reading, see LAW in SOCIAL STUDIES

Fred **Friendly**

Minnesota Rag

Near vs. Minnesota, an epoch-making case about a scandal sheet

0-394-71241-2 RANDOM HOUSE PB $8.87

Carl **Jensen** & **Project Censored**

Censored: The News that Didn't Make the News and Why, 1995

The annual compilation of the top 25 stories in America that went unremarked by the mainstream news

1-56858-030-4 FOUR WALLS PB $14.95

Carl **Jensen** & **Project Censored**

Censored: The News that Didn't Make the News and Why, 1996

Jensen, professor of Communication Studies at Sonoma State University, has been keeping an eagle eye out for under-reported stories since 1976—and each year delivers them with a missionary zeal. The top 25 1996 findings by Project Censored—Jensen's stable of watchdogs—include the history of GM's rigged crash tests, NASA's exemption from EPA regulations, and an expose of the POW/MIA myth, and others

INTRODUCTION BY JESSICA MITFORD

CARTOONS BY TOM TOMORROW

1-88836-301-0 FOUR WALLS PB $14.95

Rodney **Smolla**

Suing the Press: Libel, the Media, and Power

From Carol Burnett vs. The National Enquirer to Westermoreland vs. CBS, a study of trends in recent libel cases

0-19-505192-0 OXFORD PB $10.95

The Practitioners: A Sampler

The list below includes collections of various types of journalism—news articles, columns, magazine pieces—from a wide range of American and foreign journalists.

Edna **Buchanan**

Never Let Them See You Cry: More Tales of Murder and Mayhem in Miami

Ace crime-reporter Buchanan is legendary for being first on the scene, and her dispatches set the standard for true-crime writing. Miami's lurid events make fertile material: a flamboyant millionaire gunned down in broad daylight, a corpse that walks, a three-year-old witness, and even a stray duck come to life (or death) in the pages of Buchanan's latest work

See also **MODERN CRIMINAL CASES** under **TRUE CRIME** in **POPULAR READING**

0-425-13824-0 BERKLEY PB $5.99

Bill **Buford**, editor

The Best of Granta Reportage

The preeminent British magazine offers a decade of incisive reportage by writers such as John le Carre (visiting the spy of the century in Switzerland), Martha Gellhorn (in Panama City following the US invasion), Richard Raynor (on the LA riots), and James Fenton (in Saigon). A unique combination of the adventurous and the literary

0-14-014071-9 PENGUIN PB..............................$11.95

Alexander **Cockburn**

Corruptions of Empire

A collection of columns and articles on the Reagan era, from a master of alternative journalism

0-86091-940-4 VERSO PB..................................$17.95

Barbara **Ehrenreich**

The Snarling Citizen

The essayist for *Time* magazine holds the heart of the '90s up to her perceptive and hilarious satire

0-374-26648-4 FS&G..$20.00

Martha **Gelllhorn**

The Face of War

0-87113-211-7 ATLANTIC MONTHLY PB $9.95

Ellen **Goodman**

Value Judgments

The Pulitzer Prize-winning columnist from *The Boston Globe* collects her sharpest, most original pieces on life in America over the past four years. The abortion wars, the 1992 election, and the William Kennedy Smith trial are among her wide-ranging themes

0-374-16571-8 FS&G..$22.00

Oriana **Fallaci**

Interview with History

A collection of fascinating interviews with world leaders by a top journalist

0-395-25223-7 HOUGHTON MIFFLIN PB..........$14.95

Oriana Fallaci (photo by Francesco Scavullo)

Pete **Hamill**

Piecework: Writings on Men and Women, Fools and Heroes, Lost Cities, Vanished Friends, Small Pleasures, Large Calamities, and How the Weather Was

Esquire, *Village Voice*, *Vanity Fair*, *New York*, *The New York Post*—these are just some of the venues where Hamill's tough-minded reporting and penetrating insight have appeared. Collected here—and introduced by Jimmy Breslin—is the author's best work on subjects as varied as the movie business, the mob, foreign affairs, and that den of thieves, the art world

0-316-34104-5 LITTLE, BROWN..........$24.95

Christopher **Hitchens**

For the Sake of Argument: Essays and Minority Reports

Unsparing observations on the political squalor of Washington, the embattled barrios of Central America, Grahame Greene, the "lugubrious" Dr. Kissinger, the "reactionary" Mother Theresa, and the "predictable" P. J. O'Rourke. No-holds-barred politics from the author of *Blood, Class, and Nostalgia*

0-86091-435-6 VERSO..........$27.95
0-86091-628-6 VERSO PB..........$16.95

Molly **Ivins**

Molly Ivins Can't Say That, Can She?

Ivins at her incisive best, covering everything from the S&L debacle to governmental incompetence, Texas, and human folly. Hilarious

0-679-74183-6 VINTAGE PB..........$11.00

Nothin' But Good Times Ahead

The same biting wit and hilarious observations that made *Molly Ivins Can't Say That, Can She?* a bestseller inform this collection. Here she takes on her fellow Texan Ross Perot, President Clinton, and the madness of America's political culture

0-679-42234-X RANDOM HOUSE..........$12.00
0-679-75488-1 VINTAGE PB..........$12.00

Anna **Quindlen**

Living Out Loud

A collection from the Popular syndicated *NY Times* "Life in the '30s" column

0-8041-0527-8 IVY PB..........$5.99

Thinking Out Loud: On the Personal, Political, the Public, and the Private

Sharp and compassionate observations on the contemporary scene from the Pulitzer Prize-winning columnist and author (*Object lessons, Living Out Loud*). "Anna Quindlen's beat is life, and she's one hell of a terrific reporter" —Susan Isaacs

See also **HISTORY, POLITICS, AND SOCIETY** under **20TH-CENTURY AMERICAN ESSAYS AND JOURNALISM** in **LITERATURE OF THE AMERICAS**

0-449-90905-0 FAWCETT PB..........$12.00

Murray **Kempton**

Rebellions, Perversities, and Main Events

As a complex stylist with an unerring eye for the absurd details of life, Kempton has no equal in the newspaper trade

See also **REPORTING** under **20TH-CENTURY AMERICAN ESSAYS AND JOURNALISM** in **LITERATURE OF THE AMERICAS**

0-8129-2294-8 TIME BOOKS..........$27.50
0-8129-2528-9 TIME BOOKS PB..........$16.00

Murray Kempton

Robert B. **Silvers**, Barbara **Epstein** & Rea S. **Hederman**, editors

The First Anthology: Thirty Years of the New York Review of Books

The preeminent American journal of politics and culture celebrates its 30th anniversary with a compendium of some of its finest pieces. Included are such landmark essays as Elizabeth Hardwick's report on the Watts Riots of LA in 1966, Gore Vidal's memorable portrait of Amelia Earhart, Hannah Arendt's "Reflections on Violence" as well as Joseph Brodsky, Robert Hughes, Dwight Macdonald, Susan Sontag, Isaiah Berlin, and more. A touchstone for the ideas that have shaped the past three decades, and an indispensable tutorial on the contemporary world

See also **ANTHOLOGIES** under **20TH-CENTURY AMERICAN ESSAYS AND JOURNALISM** in **LITERATURE OF THE AMERICAS**

0-940322-01-3 NEW YORK REVIEW..........$27.50
0-940322-02-1 CONSORTIUM PB..........$12.95

The Foreign Press

Madeleine K. **Albright**

Poland: The Role of the Press in Political Change

0-275-91559-X PRAEGER PB..........$9.95

Ellen **Mickiewicz**

Split Signals: Television and Politics in the Soviet Union

The first in-depth look at Soviet television and its place in Gorbachev's glasnost campaign focuses on the popularity of broadcast

See also **HISTORY OF TELEVISION** under **TELEVISION**

0-19-506319-8 OXFORD PB..........$9.95
0-19-505463-6 OXFORD PB..........$22.95

Radio

Histories and Reference Works

EriK **Barnouw**

A History of Broadcasting in the United States

Volume 1
A Tower in Babel To 1933

0-19-500474-4 OXFORD..........$50.00

Volume 2
The Golden Web 1933 to 1953

0-19-500475-2 OXFORD..........$50.00

Volume 3
The Image Empire From 1950

0-19-501259-3 OXFORD..........$50.00

Susan J. **Douglas**

Inventing American Broadcasting, 1899-1922

0-8018-3832-0 JOHNS HOPKINS PB..........$15.95

Fairness and Accuracy in Media, editor

The Way Things Aren't: Rush Limbaugh's Reign of Error

Introduced by Molly Ivins, this collection is devoted to documenting the widening gyre between reality and Limbaugh's on-the-record view thereof

1-56584-260-X NEW PRESS PB..........$6.95

Tom **Lewis**

Empire of the Air: The Men Who Made Radio

The amazing story of the inventors and entrepreneurs—Lee De Forest, Edwin Howard Armstrong, David Sarnoff—who created a media empire, published in conjunction with a public television documentary by Ken Burns. The uneasy collaboration between technological genius and commercial exploitation led to sometimes tragic results

0-06-018215-6 HARPERPERENNIAL PB..........$25.00

J. Fred **MacDonald**

Don't Touch That Dial

0-88229-673-6 NELSON-HALL PB $25.95

Lorenzo Wilson **Milam**

Sex and Broadcasting: A Handbook on Building a Radio Station For the Community

The fourth edition of a popular book on independent broadcasting. "[Milam] wrote his book…to give practical advice to anyone who shares his passion for broadcasting, anyone mad enough to build a radio station for love, not money. The book is firmly grounded in practicalities…but it is also wiser and funnier than almost any other book in the field"—*TLS*

0-917320-01-8 MHO & MHO PB $12.95

Robert **Siegel**

The NPR Interviews, 1994

A collection of the incisive, the quirky, the hilarious, the disturbing—the accomplished and groundbreaking interviews conducted by the journalists of National Public Radio. Includes Elizabeth Marshall Thomas, George Gallup, Amos Oz, Desmond Tutu, Donna Shalala, John le Carre, Katha Pollitt, and many more. Fascinating discussions with fascinating people

0-395-70741-2 HOUGHTON MIFFLIN $24.95
0-395-71373-0 HOUGHTON MIFFLIN PB $11.95

Linda **Wertheimer**, editor

Listening to America: Twenty-Five Years in the Life of a Nation, as Heard on National Public Radio

A collection of NPR's interviews and commentaries on the major news stories of our time

0-395-70697-1 HOUGHTON MIFFLIN $24.95
0-395-79153-7 HOUGHTON MIFFLIN PB $14.95

Biographies and Memoirs

Garrison **Keillor**

WLT: A Radio Romance

If ever a book was meant to be read aloud, this is it. Keillor narrates his own work, a history of a fictional Minneapolis radio station. Four cassettes

See also **HUMOR WRITERS** under **HUMOR** in **POPULAR READING**

0-14-010380-5 PENGUIN PB $11.00

Garrison Keillor

LeRoy R. **Bannerman**

Norman Corwin and Radio: The Golden Years

0-8173-0274-3 ALABAMA $32.50

Stan **Cloud** & Lynn **Olson**

The Murrow Boys: Pioneers on the Frontlines of American Journalism

See also **BIOGRAPHIES AND MEMOIRS** under **JOURNALISM**

0-395-68084-0 HOUGHTON MIFFLIN $27.95

Anthony **Slide**

Great Radio Personalities in Historic Photographs

0-911572-72-4 VESTAL PB $12.95

Susan **Stamberg**

Talk: NPR's Susan Stamberg Considers All Things

From the award-winning journalist come 75 highlights from her memorable interviews of the last 20 years. Here presented with clarity, spontaneity, and charm are such luminaries as Rosa Parks, James Baldwin, Robert Altman, Annie Leibovitz, and Helen Hayes. Insightful introductions, sidebars, and asides from the author complete this fascinating retrospective of our recent history

0-399-51873-8 PERIGEE PB $15.00

Television

History of Television

Erik **Barnouw**

Tube of Plenty: The Evolution of American Television

See also **CULTURAL AND SOCIAL HISTORY** under **TOPICS IN AMERICAN STUDIES** in **HISTORY OF THE AMERICAS**

0-19-506484-4 OXFORD PB $16.95

Donald **Bogle**

Blacks in American Films and Television

See also **FILM IN AMERICA** under **FILM**

0-8240-8715-1 GARLAND $85.00

George **Brandt**, editor

British Television Drama in the 1980's

0-521-42723-1 CAMBRIDGE PB $18.95

James **Day**

The Vanishing Vision: The Inside Story of Public Television

0-520-08659-7 CALIFORNIA $29.95

Jane **Feuer** & Paul **Kerr**

MTM: Quality Television

A detailed appraisal of the rise and subsequent decline of the Mary Tyler Moore Studios, which, under the leadership of Grant Tinker created such programs as *The Mary Tyler Moore Show, Lou Grant, The White Shadow, Hill Street Blues,* and *St. Elsewhere*

0-85170-162-0 BRITISH FILM INST $39.95
0-85170-163-9 BRITISH FILM INST PB $19.95

David **Fisher** & Marshall Jon **Fisher**

Tube: The Invention of Television

1-88717-817-1 COUNTERPOINT $30.00

William **Hawes**

American Television Drama: The Experimental Years

0-8173-0276-X ALABAMA $31.50

J. Fred **MacDonald**

Who Shot the Sheriff?: The Rise and Fall of the Television Western

0-275-92326-6 PRAEGER $42.95

Ellen **Mickiewicz**

Split Signals: Television and Politics in the Soviet Union

The first in-depth look at Soviet television and its place in Gorbachev's glasnost campaign focuses on the popularity of broadcast

See also **THE FOREIGN PRESS** under **JOURNALISM**

0-19-506319-8 OXFORD PB $9.95
0-19-505463-6 OXFORD PB $22.95

Joseph H. **Udelson**

The Great Television Race: A History of the American Industry 1925-1941

0-8173-0082-1 ALABAMA PB $17.50

The Shows

Michael **Cader**, editor

The First Twenty Years: Saturday Night Live

The wild and crazy men and women that brought Saturday night to life on the tube, from Gilda Radner and Eddie Murphy to Dana Carvey, captured behind the scenes and on the stage in interview. Included are summaries of skits, photographic records of familiar and reminiscent scenes, all the musical acts that have appeared in 20 years, and a timeline of world events as seen on "Weekend Update"

PHOTOGRAPHS BY EDIE BASKIN

0-395-70895-8 HOUGHTON MIFFLIN $25.00

Mark **Dawidziak**

The Columbo Phile: A Casebook

0-89296-984-9 MYSTERIOUS PB $14.95

Greg **Gattuso**

The "Seinfeld" Universe: An Unauthorized Fan's-Eye View of the Entire Domain

Gattuso is the founder, publisher, and editor of *Nothing*, the only Seinfeld newsletter published in the US. Included in this celebration of the hit NBC sitcom is a history of the show, biographies of the real-life people who inspired the characters, and a tour of Jerry, Elaine, George, and Kramer's New York haunts

0-8065-1744-1 CITADEL PB $9.95

Matt **Groening**

"Matt Groening is the rambunctious, unpredictable, taboo-defying alternative cartoonist who makes Gary Trudeau's Doonesbury seem, by comparison, reminiscent of Mary Worth."—LA Times

Bart Simpson's Guide to Life

Nothing escapes his keen bug-eyed gaze as he probes the mysteries of childhood and beyond

0-06-096975-X HARPERPERENNIAL $12.95

Jon **Hestland**

The Man from U.N.C.L.E. Book

TV's answer to James Bond

INTRODUCTION BY ROBERT VAUGHN

0-312-00052-9 ST. MARTIN'S PB $13.95

John **Javna**

Cult TV: A Viewer's Guide to the Shows America Can't Live Without

0-312-17848-4 ST. MARTIN'S PB $14.95

The TV Theme Song Singalong Songbook Volume 1

0-312-78215-2 ST. MARTIN'S PB $6.95

Suzy **Kalter**

The Complete Book of M*A*S*H

0-8109-1319-4 ABRAMS $35.00

0-8109-8083-5 ABRADALE $19.98

Jeff **Lenburg**

The Three Stooges Scrapbook

0-8065-0946-5 CITADEL PB $16.95

David **Letterman** & **The Late Show with David Letterman Writers**

The First Book of Top Ten Lists from the Late Show with David Letterman

The first of what will no doubt be many, many, many collections of Letterman's Top Ten Lists. Luckily, they're very, very, very funny

0-553-10222-2 BDD $16.00

Tamar **Liebes** & Elihu **Katz**

The Export of Meaning: Cross Cultural Readings of Dallas

0-7456-1295-4 POLITY PB $20.95

Donna **McCrohan**

Archie and Edith, Mike and Gloria: The Tumultuous History of All in the Family

0-89480-527-4 WORKMAN PB $7.95

The Honeymooners' Companion

0-89480-022-1 WORKMAN PB $7.95

Donna **McCrohan** & Peter **Crescenti**

The Honeymooners' Lost Episodes

0-89480-157-0 WORKMAN PB $8.95

Ric **Meyers**

Murder on the Air: Television's Great Mystery Series

0-89296-977-6 MYSTERIOUS PB $12.95

Richard **Meyers**

The TV Detectives

0-498-02236-6 SMITH PB $4.98

Monty Python

Monty Python's Flying Circus: The Complete Television Scripts Volume 1

Even without the visuals, these scripts—the complete text of the 4 Monty Python series first broadcast on BBC between 1969 and 1974—make for compulsive and hilarious reading. Some excerpts from the index give a hint of the contents: Apology for violence and nudity; Appeal on behalf of extremely rich people; the 'Attila the Hun Show;' Beethoven's mynah bird, 'Buying an ant,' Conquistador coffee campaign…and hundreds more

0-679-72647-0 PANTHEON PB $15.00

Outside a shop. A sign roads 'Tudor Job Agency—Jobs a Specialty.' A man enters the shop. Inside it is decorated in Tudor style. The assistant is in Tudor dress.

Assistant (Terry J): Morning, sir, can I help you?

Customer (Graham): Yes, yes… I wondered if you have any part-time vacancies on your books.

Assistant: Part-time, I'll have a look, sir. (He gets out a book and looks through it.) Let me look now. We've got, ah yes, Sir Walter Raleigh is equipping another expedition to Virginia. He needs traders and sailors. Vittlers needed at the Court of Philip of Spain. Oh, yes, and they want master joiners and craftsmen for the building of the Globe Theater.

Customer: I see. Have you anything a bit more modern, you know, like a job on the buses, or digging the underground?

Assistant: Oh no, we only have Tudor jobs.

MONTY PYTHON'S FLYING CIRCUS

Jeff **Rovin**

TV Babylon

Titillating and scandalous stories about the real-lives of TV stars

0-451-16633-7 NEW AMERICAN LIBRARY PB ... $4.99

Jennifer **Saunders**

Absolutely Fabulous

By the creator, writer, and star of the popular British satire of the fabulous world of haute couture, champagne, and plastic surgery

0-671-52714-2 POCKET PB $12.00

Ted **Sennett**

Your Show of Shows

The golden age of TV comedy, with Sid Caesar, Imogene Coca, and others

0-306-80235-X DA CAPO PB $10.95

Stephen **Whitfield** & Gene **Roddenberry**

The Making of Star Trek

0-345-34019-1 BALLANTINE PB $5.99

Celebrity Biographies and Autobiographies

Roseanne **Arnold**

My Lives

The second blockbuster by the formidable Arnold—this one even more ferocious than the first. An "inside Hollywood" tale about the vicissitudes of showbiz, stardom, family, her checkered past, and of course her ever deepening romance with Tom Arnold, all told in irresistible Roseanne style

0-345-37815-6 BALLANTINE $23.00

Coyne Steven **Sanders** & Tom **Gilbert**

Desilu: The Lives of Lucille Ball and Desi Arnaz

Lucy and Desi created *I Love Lucy* to save their marriage; the program succeeded, the marriage didn't. Nonetheless, the two entertainers created the most successful production company of their time. And their show, still popular now, brought Afro-Cuban rhythms and thinly disguised interracial love to American homes. 60 black-and-white photos. "The best dual bio yet of Lucille Ball and Desi Arnaz, backed by hard research and access to private Ball-Arnaz materials and Desilu Studios corporate records"—*Kirkus Reviews*

0-688-11217-X QUILL PB $23.00

Bob **Woodward**

Wired: The Short Life and Fast Times of John Belushi

The excesses of the *Saturday Night Live* star, the struggle for control over his career by agents, managers, and family, and his sudden death from an overdose of cocaine and heroin, by the *Washington Post* editor and coauthor of *All The President's Men*

0-671-64077-1 POCKET PB $5.99

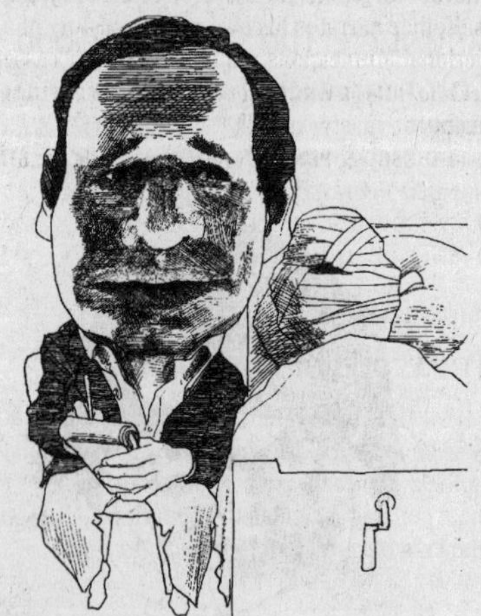

Bob Woodward

Fran **Drescher**

Enter Whining

Star of *The Nanny*

0-06-039155-3 HARPERCOLLINS $22.00

Carol **Burnett**

One More Time

The comedienne's chaotic upbringing and her early career

0-380-70449-8 AVON PB $4.95

Carol Burnett

Jonathan **Margolis**

Cleese Encounters

This comprehensive biography follows John Cleese from his childhood through his days at Cambridge (where the Monty Python troupe was incubated), to his present-day success, including his brilliant *Fawlty Towers* TV series, his self-produced business shorts, and *A Fish Called Wanda,* England's most successful film comedy

0-312-08162-6 ST. MARTIN'S $19.95

Patty **Duke** & Kenneth **Turan**

Call Me Anna: The Autobiography of Patty Duke

The child star's lonely childhood

0-553-27205-5 BDD PB $6.50

Larry **King** & Bill **Gilbert**

How to Talk to Anyone, Anytime, Anywhere: The Secrets of Good Communication

From the master of talk

See also **SELF-MOTIVATION** under **QUALITY OF LIFE** under **SELF-HELP** in **LIFESTYLES AND PRACTICAL ADVICE**

0-517-59905-8 CROWN $20.00

0-517-88453-4 CROWN PB $12.00

Bill **Adler** & Bruce **Cassiday**

The World of Jay Leno: His Humor and His Life

How Leno found his comic voice and developed his schtick, eventually triumphing as one of America's most popular comedians. An informed biography and jokeography of *The Tonight Show* host

1-55972-145-6 BIRCH LANE $15.95

Audrey **Meadows** & Joe **Daley**

Love, Alice: My Life as a Honeymooner

With all the smarts and sensitivity of her performances, Meadows brings America's favorite TV show to life—and what a life, with Gleason and Art Carney constantly on the scene. "A very entertaining book, gracefully written, with a wealth of funny anecdotes....Meadows brings her own wit and charm to backstage stories that will be a treat for her many fans" —*Kirkus Reviews*

0-517-59881-7 CROWN $22.00

Leonard **Nimoy**

I Am Spock

0-7868-6182-7 HYPERION $24.95

Yvonne **Fern**

Gene Roddenberry: The Last Conversation—A Dialogue with the Creator of Star Trek

0-520-08842-5 CALIFORNIA $20.00

Jerry **Seinfeld**

Seinlanguage

The hip creator of the popular show that bears his name extends to us his hilarious observations on the existential angst of the mundane

0-553-09606-0 BANTAM DOUBLEDAY DELL $19.95

I have no plants in my house. They won't live for me. Some of them don't even wait to die, they commit suicide. I once came home and found one hanging from a macrame noose, the pot kicked out from underneath. The note said, "I hate you and your albums."

SEINLANGUAGE

Jerry Seinfeld
(credit: ©1993 Annie Leibovitz)

Television and Society

Geoffrey **Barlow** & Alison **Hill**, editors

Video Violence and Children

The effects of televised mayhem on children

0-312-84571-5 ST. MARTIN'S $24.95

John Thornton **Caldwell**

Televisuality: Style, Crisis, and Authority in American Television

0-8135-2163-7 RUTGERS $55.00

0-8135-2164-5 RUTGERS PB $20.00

Razelle **Frankl**

Televangelism: The Marketing of Popular Religion

The rise of TV ministries and an explanation of their methods, power, and popularity

0-8093-1299-9 SOUTHERN ILLINOIS $29.95

Todd **Gitlin**

Inside Prime-Time

Critical essays on such shows as *Lou Grant* and *Hill Street Blues* by one of the country's finest writers about television

0-394-73787-3 PANTHEON PB $15.10

Hal **Himmelstein**

Television, Myth and the American Mind

0-275-91788-6 PRAEGER PB $18.95

John **Leonard**

Smoke and Mirrors: Violence, Television and the Other America

Television critic Leonard investigates the dialogue of violence between TV and American society

1-56584-226-X NEW PRESS $22.00

Jerry **Mander**

Four Arguments For the Elimination of Television

0-688-08274-2 MORROW PB $8.95

David **Marc**

Bonfire of the Humanities: Essays on Television, Subliteracy, and Long-Term Memory Loss

0-8156-0321-5 SYRACUSE $24.95

Horace **Newcomb**, editor

Television: The Critical View

"Essays on music television, sitcoms, and the ideological structures of television from a variety of approaches including semiotics, communication theory, and institutional analysis"—*Film Quarterly*

0-19-508528-0 OXFORD PB $19.95

Ella **Taylor**

Prime-Time Families: Television Culture in Post-War America

0-520-05867-4 CALIFORNIA $35.00

Martin **Williams**

TV: The Casual Art

Essays by a well-known jazz critic

0-19-502992-5 OXFORD $19.95

Raymond **Williams**

Raymond Williams on Television: The Culture of Television

A collection of Williams' essays for *The Listener*

See also **RECENT MARXIST CRITICISM** under **CULTURAL CRITICISM** under **LITERARY THEORY** in **LITERATURE OF EUROPE, AFRICA, AND ASIA**

EDITED BY ALAN O'CONNOR

0-415-02627-X ROUTLEDGE PB $20.50

Marie **Winn**

The Plug-In Drug: Television, Children and the Family

See also TECHNOLOGY AND EDUCATION under EDUCATION in SOCIAL STUDIES

0-14-007698-0 VIKING PB $10.95

The Business of Television

Ken **Auletta**

Three Blind Mice: How the TV Networks Lost Their Way

Auletta's book is based on a five-year investigation of the television industry and of the networks increasingly embattled by the rise of competitive forces, from cable to videocassettes. The result is an unprecedented inside look at the corporate struggles and programming quandaries of television's giants caught by changing times

0-394-56358-1 VINTAGE PB $23.00

Robert **Goldberg** & Gerald Jay **Goldberg**

Citizen Turner: The Wild Rise of an American Tycoon

The story of Ted Turner

0-15-118008-3 HARCOURT BRACE $27.00

Linda **Seger**

Making a Good Script Great: A Guide to Writing and Re-Writing

The most useful and instructive book on screenwriting

0-396-08935-6 SAMUEL FRENCH $15.95

0-396-08953-4 DODD, MEAD PB $10.95

Advertising

Erik **Barnouw**

The Sponsor: Notes on a Modern Potentate

Advertising and sponsorship and their influence

0-19-502614-4 OXFORD PB $10.95

Edwin **Diamond** & Stephen **Bates**

The Spot: The Rise of Political Advertising on Television

Illustrated

0-262-54065-7 MIT PB $17.50

Reference

Alex **McNeil**

Total Television: A Comprehensive Guide to Programming from 1948 Through 1979

0-14-015736-0 PENGUIN PB $21.95

Videos

To 1929

Kino Video

Movies Begin: A Treasury of Early Cinema

A collection of five cassettes tracing the origins of cinema

6303080995 .... $200.00

Charlie **Chaplin**

Chaplin began his career as a stage dancer and his early experiences informed and influenced both his screen acting and directing. Often noted more for his reputation as the "Little Tramp," Chaplin was a director of tremendous insight and innovation. He is known primarily for his comedies but many of his later films—most notably Limelight*—reflect a politically disillusioned vision.*

Charlie Chaplin at Mutual Studios 1

6302686504 .... $19.99

Charlie Chaplin at Mutual Studios 2

6302686512 .... $19.99

Charlie Chaplin at Mutual Studios 3

6302686520 .... $19.99

The Adventurer/One A.M./A Fair Exhange

6303945740 .... $9.99

The Bank/Shanghaied/Night in the Show

6302630142 .... $19.99

Caught in a Caberet/The Masquerader

6303945716 .... $9.99

The Champion/The Face on the Barroom Floor

6303945724 .... $9.99

Chaplin Collection

Ten cassettes collect a wide range of Chaplin's films

6302767911 .... $49.99

The Gold Rush

(1925) Charlie Chaplin, Mack Swain, Georgia Hale, Tom Murray, Henry Bergman, Betty Morrissey. In what is considered one of his greatest comedies, Chaplin sets out for the blizzards of the Klondike gold rush of 1898. A hilariously sweet view of the chivalrous entrepreneur who wins the woman and the gold

6302420253 .... $19.98

The Gold Rush/Rink/Making a Living

6302959608 .... $9.99

Charlie Chaplin

The Kid/The Idle Class

(1921) Charlie Chaplin, Jackie Coogan. Coogan has his debut role as "The Kid" adopted by Chaplin years ago and now wanted back by his real mother. Also included is another early film, *The Idle Class,* a satirical look at the life of the very rich and the very bored

6302561957 .... $19.98

Pawnshop/His Prehistoric Past

6303945759 .... $9.99

Tillie's Punctured Romance

6302479002 .... $19.99

Vagabond/Immigrant/20 Minutes of Love

6303945732 .... $9.99

Carl Theodor **Dreyer**

The Passion of Joan of Arc

(1928) Maria Falconetti, Eugene Silvain, Antonin Artaud. One of the best films ever made—silent or talkie. Dreyer broke cinematic ground with his daring use of revealing close-ups; Falconetti is simply amazing in the title role. French

6300267210 .... $29.95

Sergei **Eisenstein**

Noted both as a director and a revolutionary film theorist, Eisenstein is widely regarded as Russia's greatest director. His seamless use of montage gives his films a look entirely unlike those of any other director of his era. His most recognized work is the much referenced and imitated Battleship Potemkin*, an epic of the revolution of 1905. The Oddessa Steps sequence of that film is perhaps the most famous scene in film history*

Battleship Potemkin

(1925) Alexander Antonov, Grigori Alexandrov. Eisenstein's masterpiece—the Soviet film that shook the world

6302054273 .... $19.98

October (Ten Days that Shook the World)

(1928) V. Nikandrov, N. Popov. Dazzling reconstruction of the 1917 Russian Revolution featuring brilliant montage work and imagery

6301815831 .... $29.95

Jacques **Feyder**

The Kiss

(1929) Greta Garbo, Conrad Nagel. Passion, infidelity, murder, with highly stylized courtroom scenes

6302048990 ....$29.98

Sidney **Franklin**

Wild Orchids

(1929) Greta Garbo, John Gilbert, Lewis Stone. Illicit love in a tropical setting with, Garbo mesmerizing as ever

6302049024 ....$29.98

Abel **Gance**

Napoleon

(1927) A film of great daring and questionable politics, combining intimacy with dementia, montage with proto-fascism

6300183548 ....$29.95

D.W. **Griffith**

Birth of a Nation

(1915) Lillian Gish, Mae Marsh, Henry Walthall. An important milestone in narrative film, this epic of the American Civil War has become as famous for its frightening glorification of prejudice as it is for its many technical innovations

6302075726 ....$19.98

Griffith: Short Films, Volume 1

6301253175 ....$19.99

Intolerance

(1916) Lillian Gish, Mae Marsh, Robert Harron. Intertwining stories from antiquity to his own era, Griffith offers a powerful meditation on prejudices

6302180007 ....$59.99

Judith of Bethulia/Home Sweet Home

(1913)

6302730791 ....$24.99

Way Down East

(1920) Lillian Gish's outstanding performance outlines a woman's growth from naif to embittered cynic, right up to the famous scene on the ice floe

6301448944 ....$69.95

Alfred **Hitchcock**

Blackmail

(1929) Anny Ondra, Sara Allgood, John Longden, Charles Paton, Donald Calthrop, Cyril Ritchard. Facing both the legal system and a blackmailer, a woman goes on trial for murdering her attacker in self-defense. Noted for Hitchcock's innovative use of sound in this, Britain's first "talkie"

6300158942 ....$9.95

Easy Virtue

(1927) Isabel Jeans, Franklyn Dyall, Eric Bransby Williams, Ian Hunter, Robin Irvine, Violet Farebrother. This melodrama, based on Noel Coward's play, chronicles the noble sufferings of a woman who is the wife of an alcoholic and lover of a man who commits suicide. Hitchcock uses imaginative camera work and astonishing silent narration techniques

6301208498 ....$29.95

The Lodger

(1926) Ivor Novello, Malcolm Keen, Marie Ault. Charged with the cinematic stylings which would distinguish his later works, the master of suspense presents a story of a mysterious stranger, a boarding house, and a series of unexplained murders. Hitchcock's first film

6301164679 ....$49.95

Rupert **Julian**

The Phantom of the Opera

(1925)

6303626424 ....$24.99

Buster **Keaton**

Nicknamed "Buster" by Harry Houdini, Keaton began his show business career early in life, traveling with his family's act, "The Three Keatons." When he was 21 the act broke up, due in large part to his father's excessive drinking and abusiveness. Keaton, by then an established visual comedian, took small roles in several films directed by Fatty Arbuckle before moving on to write screenplays and eventually to direct. The best of his screen comedies combine hilarious sight gags with hallucinatory meditations on themes of isolation, loneliness, and unrealized aspiration.

The General

(1926) Buster Keaton, Marian Mack, Glen Cavender, Jim Farley, Frederick Vroom, Joe Keaton. The best of Buster Keaton's celebrated screen comedies, and one of the funniest films ever made.

6301931742 ....$39.99

Buster Keaton

The Navigator

(1924)

630336652X $29.99

Sherlock Jr./Our Hospitality

6303366511 ....$29.99

Our Hospitality

(1923) Buster Keaton, Natalie Talmadge, Ralph Bushman, Michael Keaton, Buster Keaton, Jr. An innocent young man journeys to his home in the South to claim a family inheritance, only to fall in love with the daughter of a longtime rival family. Keaton is at his pratfall best in this Hatfield-and-McCoy drama

6301931734 ....$39.98

Fritz **Lang**

Siegfried

(1924) Paul Richter, Margarete Schon. Part one of *Die Nibelungen:* a visually dazzling medieval fantasia and Lang's first masterpiece

6302054478 ....$19.98

Kriemhilde's Revenge

(1924) Margarete Schon, Rudolph Klein-Rogge. The second half of Lang's *Die Nibelungen* is harsher and more violent in tone

6302054427 ....$19.95

The Spiders

(1919) A diabolical gang of criminals plan to take over the world, funding it all with the lost treasure of the Incas. Fiends, villains, swooning heroines, and humorous sensibility

6301581083 ....$19.95

F.W. **Murnau**

Nosferatu

(1922) Max Schreck, Greta Schroeder. Murnau's version of Dracula, with its plagues and nocturnal visitations, has the haunting clarity of a recurrent nightmare

6302054443 ....$19.98

Faust

(1926)

6303968198 ....$29.99

Fred **Niblo**

Ben-Hur

(1926) Ramon Novarro, Francis X. Bushman. Hollywood goes to Rome: a magnificently excessive epic, superbly restored (including color sequences)

6301965787 ....$29.95

Blood and Sand

(1922) Rudolph Valentino, Nita Naldi, Lila Lee, George Field, Walter Long. Based on the tragic novel by Vicente Blasco Ibañez, this is the earlier of two versions made by Hollywood. Melodramatic and exotic, the role of Juan, a poor Spanish boy who rises to fame in the bullring, was one of Valentino's most popular vehicles

6302054281 ....$19.98

The Mark of Zorro

(1920) Fairbanks is the masked hero in this, the first of his many swashbuckling roles

6302054435 ....$19.99

G.W. **Pabst**

Pandora's Box

(1928) The ethereal Louise Brooks attracts every crank and would-be lover in Berlin with her beauty, yet somehow finds herself in a London garret with Jack the Ripper

6300149463 ....$19.95

Albert **Parker**

The Black Pirate

(1926) Douglas Fairbanks plays a gentleman who takes to pirating

6304083262 ....$24.99

Giovanni **Pastrone**

Cabiria

(1914) Italia Almirante Manzini, Lidia Quaranta. Tells the story of a Sicilian slave during the second Punic War. An impressive early silent

6301826566 ....$39.99

Vsevolod **Pudovkin**

End of St. Petersburg

(1927) One of the handful of Pudovkin films to be released in the West, this fictional examination of the fall of a city ensured his place among the finest Soviet directors

6302062403 .... $29.95

Joseph **Santley** & Robert **Florey**

The Cocoanuts

(1929) Set in a Florida hotel overrun with jewel thieves, dancing bellhops, and stately dowagers. The Marx brothers' first feature, based on their hit 1925 play

6301337999 .... $19.95

Edward **Sedgwick**

The Cameraman

(1929) Buster Keaton, Marceline Day. Keaton's final silent role is a wonderfully inventive and oddly elegiac

6302004470 .... $29.98

Esther **Shub**

The Fall of the Romanov Dynasty

(1927) Shub created this dramatic montage from forgotten newsreel footage housed in the Moscow archives, covering the years 1913-1917. She deftly juxtaposes the rise of the proletariat with the fall of the Czar

630206242X $29.95

Erich **von Stroheim**

Greed

(1923) Gibson Gowland, ZaSu Pitts, Jean Hersholt. Von Stroheim's masterpiece was hacked from 10 hours to just over two by studio head Irving Thalberg. It is the relentlessly cynical view of a lottery win, based on the Frank Norris novel

6301969146 .... $29.98

Foolish Wives

(1920) Von Stroheim's third feature is a sophisticated tale of blackmail and murder in Monte Carlo

6301581148 .... $29.99

King **Vidor**

The Crowd

(1928) James Murray, Eleanor Boardman, Bert Roach. One of Vidor's finest films portrays the gritty disintegration of the American Dream when a child is killed by a hit-and-run driver. Stunning location work in New York City, including Coney Island in its heyday

6301965744 .... $29.98

Raoul **Walsh**

Thief of Bagdad

(1924) Douglas Fairbanks, Julanne Johnston, Anna May Wong. An adventurous Arabian Nights extravaganza. The sets were six and a half acres of pomp deco chinoiserie

630193170X $39.99

Robert **Wiene**

The Cabinet of Dr. Caligari

(1920) Werner Krauss, Conrad Veidt. The primal German Expressionist psychodrama still unnerves and delights

6301581156 .... $29.95

The '30s

Richard **Boleslawski**

Les Miserables

(1935) Fredric March and Charles Laughton. The best screen version of Victor Hugo's classic

6301798570 .... $59.98

Frank **Borzage**

A Farewell to Arms

(1932) Helen Hayes, Gary Cooper, Adolphe Menjou, Mary Philips, Jack LaRue. An American ambulance-man serving in Italy during World War I falls in love with an English nurse. A tragic tale of love and war based on the Hemingway novel

6300158381 .... $9.99

Clarence **Brown**

Anna Karenina

(1935) Greta Garbo, Fredric March, Basil Rathbone, Freddie Bartholomew, Maureen O'Sullivan, Reginald Denny, May Robson, Reginald Owen. Greta is divine as the passionate Anna who sacrifices her son and her reputation for love in Tolstoy's story set in Russia's imperial era

6301964144 .... $19.98

Tod **Browning**

Dracula

(1931) The original screen version of this horror classic, with a wonderful and frightening performance by Lugosi—the best of his career

6300181278 .... $14.99

Frank **Capra**

Bitter Tea of General Yen

(1933)

6302864496 .... $19.99

It Happened One Night

(1934) Clark Gable, Claudette Colbert, Ward Bond. A hit during the Depression, this romantic comedy showcases Gable as a cynical reporter on the trail of a snobby but sassy fugitive heiress with whom he eventually falls in love

6300137554 .... $19.95

Lost Horizon

(1937) Ronald Colman, Jane Wyatt, Sam Jaffe, Margo. Mass-market Art Deco mysticism amid the snows of Shangri-La

6300140962 .... $19.95

Mr. Smith Goes to Washington

(1936) James Stewart, Jean Arthur, Claude Rains, Edward Arnold. Idealism versus corruption, resolved in characteristic Capra fashion

6300134741 .... $19.95

Charlie **Chaplin**

City Lights

(1931)

6302561833 .... $19.99

Modern Times

(1936) Charlie Chaplin, Paulette Goddard. Chaplin does battle with the dehumanizing industrial world in this satire of life filled with technology, but devoid of all else. A disturbing prediction of our current predicament, lightened by Chaplin's hilarious sight gags

6302561841 .... $19.98

René **Clair**

A Nous la Liberté

(1931) Satire of the cult of technology centering on an escaped prisoner. French

6303184049 .... $14.99

John **Cromwell**

Of Human Bondage

(1934) Bette Davis, Leslie Howard, Alan Hale, Sr., Frances Dee. A sassy Cockney waitress captures a young doctor's interest and almost causes his demise. From the W. Somerset Maugham novel

6300158470 .... $9.99

George **Cukor**

Camille

(1936) Greta Garbo, Robert Taylor, Lionel Barrymore, Elizabeth Allan. In her most popular film, Garbo oozes glamour as a highly sophisticated courtesan dying of consumption. Dumas's 19th-century tear-jerker is the perfect vehicle for Garbo

6301967739 .... $19.98

David Copperfield

(1935) Freddie Bartholomew, Frank Lawton, Lionel Barrymore, W.C. Fields, Edna May Oliver, Basil Rathbone. Featuring an all-star cast, this production of Dickens's classic recounts the exploits of a young man in 19th-century England. Cukor brilliantly condenses the novel for this sharp and colorful rendition

6301967801 .... $19.98

Dinner at Eight

(1933) Jean Harlow, John Barrymore, Lionel Barrymore, Marie Dressler, Wallace Beery. An engaging blend of soap opera and high comedy

6301976347 .... $19.98

Holiday

(1938) Cary Grant, Katharine Hepburn. A social dropout shakes up a wealthy family. Barbed dialogue, high polish, and great depth of feeling

630014108X $19.95

Little Women

(1933) Katharine Hepburn, Spring Byington, Joan Bennett, Frances Dee, Jean Parker. This American favorite based on the novel by Louisa May Alcott follows the adventures of four young women coming of age at the time of the Civil War. Features Katharine Hepburn as the tomboy Jo

6301971590 .... $19.98

The Women

(1939) Joan Crawford, Norma Shearer, Rosalind Russell, Joan Fontaine. Based on the Clare Booth play, this is a smart, funny, wicked look at manners, morals, and men

6301976339 .... $24.98

Michael **Curtiz**

Captain Blood

(1935) Errol Flynn, Olivia de Havilland, Lionel Atwill, Basil Rathbone. Swords and sailing ships, with a memorable Korngold score

6302120527 .... $19.98

Michael **Curtiz** & W.M. **Keighly**

The Adventures of Robinhood

(1939) Errol Flynn, Olivia de Havilland, Basil Rathbone, Claude Rains. Peerless heroism and villainy, in Technicolor

6301963997 ....$19.98

William **Dieterle**

The Hunchback of Notre Dame

(1939) Charles Laughton, Maureen O'Hara, Cedric Hardwicke, Thomas Mitchell, Edmond O'Brien. Filmed on the eve of war, Hugo's novel became something of an anti-Nazi allegory in this splendidly designed version

6301327772 ....$19.98

Alexander **Dovzhenko**

Earth

(1930) This classic story about collective farming in the Soviet Union is also an homage the natural world

630206239X $29.99

Carl-Theodor **Dreyer**

Vampyr

(1932)

6302194288 ....$29.99

Allan **Dwan**

The Iron Mask

(1929) Douglas Fairbanks plays a man who becomes the guardian of Louis XIV

6304083327 ....$24.99

Sergei **Eisenstein**

Alexander Nevksy

(1938) A nationalist epic approved by Stalin—interpreted as anti-German during World War II—resuscitates a 13th-century hero as the savior of Russia from the Teutonic hordes

6301816218 ....$29.95

Que Viva Mexico

(1932) The only film Eisenstein ever directed outside the Soviet Union. This unfinished work was to have been a semi-documentary on the history of Mexico—funds were supplied, and ultimately withdrawn, by Upton Sinclair

6301884450 ....$59.95

Strike

(1924)

6302062454 ....$29.99

George **Fitzmaurice**

Mata Hari

(1932) Greta Garbo, Raymon Novarro, Lionel Barrymore. Garbo as the legendary dancer and spy

6301972252 ....$19.98

Victor **Fleming**

Bombshell

(1933) Jean Harlow, Lee Tracy, Pat O'Brien, Franchot Tone, Una Merkel. Jean Harlow plays herself in this relentlessly fast-paced behind-the-cameras comedy

6301967615 ....$19.98

Gone with the Wind

(1939) Clark Gable, Vivien Leigh, Leslie Howard, Olivia de Havilland, Hatti McDaniel. Never before and never since has a film had such a far-reaching effect on the American imagination. Margaret Mitchell's epic Civil War romance translates into a monumental film achievement

6301970047 ....$89.98

Red Dust

(1932) Jean Harlow, Clark Gable, Mary Astor, Donald Crisp. Romance on a rubber plantation: snappy pre-code comedy

6301978390 ....$19.98

Treasure Island

(1934) Wallace Beery, Jackie Cooper, Lewis Stone, Lionel Barrymore, Otto Kruger, Nigel Bruce. An all-star presentation of Robert Louis Stevenson's 18th-century pirate classic, complete with hoards of buried treasure. Disney's 1950 remake (directed by Byron Haskin) is not quite as amusing, but should be watched for Robert Newton's definitive performance of the roguish Long John Silver

630197638X FLEMING (1934) $19.95

6302271940 HASKIN (1950) $19.95

John **Ford**

"I make Westerns." Accepting Ford's own assessment of his work is to believe the commonly held myth that Ford was an unsubtle director who made films about a world inhabited by two types of people: good guys and bad guys. His 50 years of directing—which are marked by such films as Stagecoach *and* The Searchers*—changed American and world cinema for ages after. Orson Welles, when asked to name the directors who most influenced his own style, remarked, "The old masters…by which I mean John Ford, John Ford, and John Ford."*

Stagecoach

(1939)

630101698X $14.99

Young Mr. Lincoln

(1939)

6301798783 ....$19.99

Edmund **Goulding**

Grand Hotel

(1932) Greta Garbo, John Barrymore, Joan Crawford, Wallace Beery. The definitive "crossroads of destiny" vehicle, source of the Broadway musical—and of several hundred other movies

6301969324 ....$19.99

Victor **Halperin**

White Zombie

(1932) Well-directed low-budget horror fare set on a Haitian sugar plantation

6303307892 ....$12.99

Howard **Hawks**

Bringing Up Baby

(1938) Cary Grant, Katharine Hepburn, Charles Ruggles, May Robson. Grant is an awkward and nervous paleontologist bent on retrieving a dinosaur bone stolen by the dog of a zany socialite, played by Hepburn. However, it is her other pet, a leopard named Baby, that complicates things, wreaking havoc wherever it goes

6301293193 ....$19.98

Scarface

(1932) Paul Muni, Ann Dvorak, Karen Morley, Boris Karloff, George Raft. A truly flawless film that seems to echo with every malevolent nuance of world history—crossing the Capones with the Borgias

6300181316 ....$19.95

Victor **Herman**

Animal Crackers

(1930) The Marx Brothers' second feature, in which they assault the rich at a society party and become involved with a stolen painting

6300181243 ....$19.95

Alfred **Hitchcock**

The 39 Steps

(1935) An appropriately sophisticated mystery surprising for its light comedic touch and witty dialogue

6303346367 ....$24.99

Gregory **Ratoff**

Intermezzo

(1939) Leslie Howard, Ingrid Bergman, Edna Best, Cecil Kellaway, John Halliday. Bergman had won much critical acclaim for her performance in a 1936 Swedish version of this story; Selznick re-created this role for her debut in Hollywood. A story of two musicians, one married, who fall in love while on a tour of the Continent

6301942620 ....$19.98

Erle C. **Kenton**

Island of Lost Souls

(1933) A powerful and genuinely frightening adaptation of H.G. Wells's tale of a mad scientist stranded on an island who turns wild animals into half-human beings

6302843200 ....$14.99

Zoltan **Korda**

The Four Feathers

(1939) The story of a British gentleman's bravery during an uprising in the Sudan

6302453003 ....$19.99

Gregory **La Cava**

Stage Door

(1937) Katharine Hepburn, Ginger Rogers, Adolphe Menjou, Lucille Ball, Eve Arden, Ann Miller. A brilliantly cast ensemble piece about a group of young actresses thrown together in the Big City

6301278410 ....$19.98

Fritz **Lang**

Fury

(1936) Lang's first American film is a harrowing look at small-town lynch mobs. Spencer Tracy stars as a good man corrupted by this claustrophobic scenario

630024721X $9.99

The Testament of Dr. Mabuse

(1932) The story of a criminal, confined to an insane asylum, who continues to exercise control over the underworld he once ruled

6303120733 ....$24.99

Mervyn **Leroy**

The Gold Diggers of 1933

(1933)

630196926X $19.99

Little Caesar
(1930) Edward G. Robinson, Douglas Fairbanks, Jr., Glenda Farrell, Stanley Fields. The first of the talking gangster films. Robinson instantly became a star as a result of his performance as bad-guy Rico Bandello, creating the prototype of the movie mobster
6302120497 ....$19.98

Frank **Lloyd**
Cavalcade
(1933) Diane Wynward, Clive Brook, Una O'Connor. Wonderfully realized performances grace this poignant story of the hardships of two families as they struggle to survive the harrowing aftershocks of World War I and settle into the desperate times of the Depression. From Noel Coward's popular play
6302640520 ....$19.98

Mutiny on the Bounty
(1935) Charles Laughton, Clark Gable, Franchot Tone. Laughton gives an unforgettable performance as the ruthless Captain Bligh in this captivating tale of adventure and treason on the South Seas
630197347X $19.98

Ernst **Lubitsch**
Ninotchka
(1939) Greta Garbo, Melvyn Douglas, Bela Lugosi. The classic sendup of Soviet revolutionary ideology. Garbo stars as a commissar who has come to investigate the decadent activities of trade representatives in Paris
6301973445 ....$19.98

Ruben **Mamoulian**
Queen Christina
(1933) Greta Garbo is a 17th-century Swedish queen who steps down from her throne for the sake of love. Garbo's finest performance
6301978374 ....$19.99

George **Marshall**
Destry Rides Again
(1939) Marlene Dietrich, James Stewart, Charles Winninger, Brian Donlevy, Una Merkel, Mischa Auer, Irene Hervey, Billy Gilbert, Jack Carson. Stewart's character finds it just as difficult to cope with the advances of Dietrich's Frenchie, a spicy saloon gal, as with the roguish villain. This film established the cowboy genre by artfully combining humor, romance, suspense, and action
6300185117 ....$14.95

Leo **McCarey**
The Awful Truth
(1937) Cary Grant, Irene Dunne, Ralph Bellamy, Alexander D'Arcy, Cecil Cunningham. Dunne and Grant demonstrate impeccable comic timing in this classic screwball comedy about a divorced couple who eventually decide to get back together. McCarey won an Academy Award for his outstanding and outlandish direction
6300139727 ....$59.95

Duck Soup
(1933) The Marx Brothers, Margaret Dumont, Edgar Buchanan. Fredonia and Sylvania square off in the Brothers' most inventive film
6300181367 ....$19.95

Norman **McLeod**
Horse Feathers
(1932) Groucho as Professor Wagstaff, and Thelma Todd as the campus widow with whom all are in love
6301221494 ....$19.95

Monkey Business
(1931) The Marx Brothers, Thelma Todd, Ruth Hall, Harry Woods. The Brothers stow away and try to get through immigration by pretending to be Maurice Chevalier, one at a time. Thelma Todd is a magnificent foil to Groucho
6300184072 ....$19.95

Look at me: I worked my way up from nothing to a state of extreme poverty
MONKEY BUSINESS

Kenzi **Mizoguchi**
Osaka Elegy
(1936)
630326171X $29.99

F.W. **Murnau**
Tabu
(1930)
6302420504 ....$39.99

Jean **Renoir**
La Marseillaise
(1938)
6303184235 ....$14.99

The Rules of the Game
(1939) A comedy of manners that contrasts the amorous behavior of aristocrats with that of their servants. French
6302969301 ....$29.99

Leni **Riefenstahl**
Olympiad
(1936)Riefenstahl's two-part documentary, which also served as a powerful piece of Nazi propaganda, records in stunning cinematography the 1936 Berlin Olympics. A masterpiece of technical style

Part 1: Festival of the People
6303695795 ....$14.99

Part 2: Festival of Beauty
6303695809 ....$14.99

Wesley **Ruggles**
Cimarron
(1931) Inspiring Western epic about the impact of Manifest Destiny as seen through one hard-working family who settle on the untamed land of the Oklahoma prairie. Based on Edna Ferber's novel
6301967720 ....$19.98

Mark **Sandrich**
The Gay Divorcee
(1934) Ginger Rogers, Fred Astaire, Edward Everett Horton, Alice Brady, Betty Grable. A musical extravaganza. This remake of the famous Cole Porter show features the popular standard "Night and Day" in its score
6301589378 ....$19.98

William A. **Seiter**
Sons of the Desert
(1933) Laurel and Hardy, in one of their finest and funniest pairings, go behind their wives' backs to a fraternal convention
6302172888 ....$9.99

George **Stevens**
Swing Time
(1936) Fred Astaire and Ginger Rogers as dance partners who spark up a romance while on tour
6304119127 ....$19.99

W.S. **Van Dyke**
The Thin Man
(1934) William Powell, Myrna Loy, Maureen O'Sullivan, Cesar Romero. First and best film incarnation of Nick and Nora Charles. Funny, fast, and brilliantly adapted from the Dashiell Hammett novel
6301978420 ....$19.98

Dziga **Vertov**
Three Songs of Lenin
(1934) Russian
6302062462 ....$29.99

King **Vidor**
Hallelujah
(1929)
6302717760 ....$19.99

Jean **Vigo**
L'Atalante
(1934) A romantic story of a young couple on a barge on the Seine. The film's deceptively simple plot hides a truly innovative style that proved to be far ahead of its time
6302590388 ....$69.99

Josef **von Sternberg**
The Blue Angel
(1930) Emil Jannings, Marlene Dietrich, Kurt Gerron. In her first major role, Dietrich plays the steamy femme fatale who seduces and ultimately destroys a straitlaced schoolteacher
6300267261 ....$29.95

The Docks of New York
(1928) A man falls for the woman he saved from a suicide attempt—set against the backdrop of a dark and hazy waterfront
6300215474 ....$29.99

Morocco
(1930)
6302888190 ....$14.99

Shanghai Express
(1932)
6302888204 ....$14.99

Michel **Waszynski**
The Dybbuk
(1938) A supernatural tale of a young bride's possession by the soul of her true love, set in the Polish shtetl. An all-too-brief glimpse of the Eastern European Jewish culture utterly destroyed in the Second World War
6301585925 ....$59.95

William **Wellman**

Nothing Sacred

(1937) Comedy centering on a cynical reporter who uses a naive girl's "imminent death" to further his journalistic aspirations

6301253191 ....$24.99

James **Whale**

Frankenstein

(1931) Boris Karloff, Colin Clive, Mae Clark. Beautifully designed and richly atmospheric. A frightening performance by Karloff

6300181286 ....$14.95

Bride of Frankenstein

(1935) An impressive sequel

6300183629 ....$14.99

William **Wyler**

Dead End

(1937) An adaptation of the Broadway play depicting the lives of inhabitants of a New York City slum

6302413672 ....$19.99

Wuthering Heights

(1939) Merle Oberon, Laurence Olivier, Flora Robson, David Niven. Brontë's eerie gothic romance takes on a tempestuous tone with Olivier's interpretation of the mysterious Heathcliff. Oberon gives a stunning performance as Cathy in this tale of forbidden love

6302278929 ....$19.98

The '40s

Ludwig **Berger** & others

The Thief of Bagdad

(1940) Amazing Technicolor photography highlights this Arabian Nights tale that has Sabu outsmarting an evil magician

630390047X $39.99

Frank **Capra**

Arsenic and Old Lace

(1944) Cary Grant, Priscilla Lane, Raymond Massey, Peter Lorre, Josephine Hull, Jean Adair. What is so terrible about two darling, little, old spinsters slipping large amounts of arsenic into their guests' wine? Or burying the corpses in the cellar?

6301964012 ....$19.98

It's a Wonderful Life

(1946) James Stewart, Donna Reed, Lionel Barrymore, Gloria Grahame, Henry Travers. Capra's favorite of all his films. Stewart is rescued from taking his own life by a guardian angel who shows him how his death would affect loved ones

630289915X $14.98

Marcel **Carné**

Les Enfants du Paradis

(1945)

6302969603 ....$39.99

Charlie **Chaplin**

The Great Dictator

(1940) Chaplin combines all forms of cinematic comedy in this odd and effective mix of humor and anti-fascist political commentary

630256185X $19.99

Jean **Cocteau**

Beauty and the Beast

(1946) The eclectic Cocteau's stunning, surreal take on the classic myth. French

6302794064 ....$24.99

Les Parents Terribles

(1948)

6303367585 ....$29.99

Orpheus

(1949) Jean Marais, Francois Perier, Maria Casares, Maria Dea, Juliette Greco, Roger Blin. One of many Cocteau masterpieces , this allegorical update of the myth ponders life, love, art, and death. Darkly comic and deeply bizarre, it features an earth-to-heaven Rolls Royce limousine and an entourage of leather-clad motorcyclists. French

630320208X $29.99

George **Cukor**

Gaslight

(1944) Ingrid Bergman, Charles Boyer, Joseph Cotten, Angela Lansbury. A masterpiece of inexorably mounting horror, with impeccable performances by Bergman as the wife slowly driven insane, Boyer as the psychotic husband, and Lansbury as the insolent parlor maid

6301969316 ....$19.98

The Philadelphia Story

(1940) Katharine Hepburn, Cary Grant, James Stewart, Ruth Hussey, Roland Young, John Howard. Definitive performances in Philip Barry's high comedy earn it a place in film history. Brought together again, Grant and Hepburn electrify and enthrall with their chemistry

6301971515 ....$19.98

Michael **Curtiz**

Casablanca

(1942) Humphrey Bogart, Ingrid Bergman, Claude Rains, Peter Lorre. The never-tiresome romance between the lone nightclub owner and his irresistible, yet not-fit-for-the-nightclub-life lover. This movie is quoted more often than Shakespeare and the Bible combined

6302482585 ....$19.98

Vittorio **De Sica**

The Bicycle Thief

(1949) The embodiment of the neorealist aesthetic. An honest everyman is forced to steal a bicycle to ride to work. A striking examination of the conditions of the working class in post-war Italy

6302286875 ....$69.99

Carl Theodor **Dreyer**

Day of Wrath

(1943) A dark story of an elderly woman who is accused by a local pastor of being a witch

6303861709 ....$29.99

Sergei **Eisenstein**

Ivan the Terrible

(1944-46) An operatic treatment of paranoia at the top. Eisenstein's last film, and arguably his finest, intended as a trilogy but never completed

Part 1

6301815785 ....$29.95

Part 2

6304073674 ....$24.99

Ray **Enright**

The Spoilers

(1942) John Wayne, Marlene Dietrich, Randolph Scott, Harry Carey, Russell Simpson, George Cleveland. Dietrich plays the wealthy financial backer of a pair of gold miners (Wayne and Carey) who have struck it rich. The trio must defend their claim against an underhanded gold commissioner

6300183033 ....$14.95

John **Farrow**

The Big Clock

(1948) The editor of a magazine commits a murder which is investigated by his top reporter. A dizzying script turns all the evidence against the reporter in this excellent example of artful pulp

6304153155 ....$14.99

John **Ford**

The Grapes of Wrath

(1940) Henry Fonda, John Carradine, Jane Darwell, Russell Simpson, Charley Grapewin, John Qualen. Fonda stars in this poignant story of migrant farm workers fleeing the Oklahoma dust bowl and encountering prejudice and hostility in the promised land of California. An excellent screen adaptation of the classic Steinbeck novel

6301797906 ....$19.98

How Green Was My Valley

(1941) Walter Pidgeon, Maureen O'Hara, Roddy McDowall, Donald Crisp. This heart-rending film chronicles the bleak lives of Welsh coal miners while telling the story of a large, close-knit family torn apart by mining labor disputes. Handsomely filmed and directed, this film swept the Academy and won six Oscars, including ones for Best Cinematography and Best Director

6302640504 ....$19.98

My Darling Clementine

(1946) Ford's subtle telling of the legend of the O.K Corral

6301798759 ....$14.99

They Were Expendable

6301977246 ....$19.99

Howard **Hawks**

His Girl Friday

(1940) An impeccably played romantic comedy involving various employees of a newspaper

6304078757 ....$24.99

Red River

(1948) Montgomery Clift, in his first role, stars opposite John Wayne in this story of an ill-fated cattle drive

630197705X $14.99

To Have and Have Not

(1944) William Faulkner worked on the screenplay for this adaptation of the Hemingway novel that is highlighted by the chemistry of Humphrey Bogart and Lauren Bacall in their first pairing

6301978110 ....$19.99

The Big Sleep

(1946) Humphrey Bogart, Lauren Bacall, Martha Vickers. Based on Raymond Chandler's "hard-boiled" novel, the astonishingly complex plot required three screenwriters including William Faulkner. Stellar performances, flawless direction, and gritty dialogue have made this a classic of the genre. Bogart's definitive Philip Marlowe

6301967240 .... $19.98

Humphrey Bogart

Alfred **Hitchcock**

Notorious

(1946) Cary Grant, Ingrid Bergman, Claude Rains. The sexy, alcoholic daughter of an infamous Nazi is enlisted by a suave American agent in this dark and complex romantic spy thriller

6301798503 .... $19.98

Rebecca

(1940) Laurence Olivier, Joan Fontaine, Judith Anderson, Nigel Bruce. Hitchcock's first Hollywood film and his only to win an Academy Award for Best Picture. Based on the bestselling gothic romance by Daphne Du Maurier, but Hitchcock's adroit visual storytelling takes the tale far beyond the limits of the original narrative

6301670140 .... $19.98

Spellbound

(1945) Ingrid Bergman, Gregory Peck, Leo G. Carroll, John Emery, Michael Chekhov, Wallace Ford. Bergman, a repressed psychoanalyst, must restore the memory of her amnesiac lover/boss through hypnosis in order to solve the mystery of his identity and clear him from murder charges. Positively Freudian in its campy symbolism, it is the first movie ever to feature psychoanalysis as a major theme. Unforgettable dream sequences designed by Salvador Dali

6301670159 .... $19.98

Alfred Hitchcock

John **Huston**

Across the Pacific

(1942) Humphrey Bogart, Mary Astor, Sydney Greenstreet. Bogie foils a Japanese plot against the Panama Canal; pure escapist fun

6302120446 .... $19.98

Key Largo

(1948) Humphrey Bogart, Edward G. Robinson, Lauren Bacall, Lionel Barrymore. Bogart, a WWII hero disillusioned by wartime killing, reluctantly goes to battle to protect a dame from the mob. Robinson plays the relentless head racketeer who, while soaking in a bathtub and chomping on a cigar, has "the look of a crustacean with its shell off"

6301971965 .... $19.98

The Maltese Falcon

(1941) Humphrey Bogart, Mary Astor, Peter Lorre, Sydney Greenstreet, Elisha Cook. Arguably the best detective film of all time, Bogart's rendering of Dashiell Hammett's romantically cynical antihero Sam Spade is sheer genius. Huston's seamlessly fast-paced directorial debut never loses its charm

6301972023 .... $19.98

Gene **Kelly** & Stanley **Donen**

On the Town

(1949) The story of three sailors who have one day's leave in New York City. Adapted from the Jerome Robbins ballet

6302363306 .... $19.99

Fritz **Lang**

The Woman in the Window

(1944)

6304056931 .... $19.99

David **Lean**

Great Expectations

(1946) John Mills, Valery Hobson, Finlay Currie, Alec Guinness, Bernard Miles, Francis L. Sullivan, Jean Simmons, Martita Hunt. The classic tale of Pip, an orphaned boy, who makes friends with an escaped convict by chance, and is changed forever by the experience

6300988805 .... $19.95

Oliver Twist

(1948) Alec Guinness, John Howard Davies. Guinness plays the dastardly Fagin with a touch of humor and wickedness. A scathing attack on cruelty, child abuse, and the criminal underworld, the film brilliantly captures Dickens

630098883X $19.95

Robert Z. **Leonard**

Pride and Prejudice

(1940) Greer Garson, Laurence Olivier, Edmund Gwenn, Mary Boland, Edna Mae Oliver, Maureen O'Sullivan. Loyal to Jane Austen's 19th-century novel, the mannerly plight of five sisters looking for suitable husbands

6301977688 .... $19.98

Joseph **Lewis**

Gun Crazy

(1949) John Dall, Peggy Cummins. An arid, stylish tale of crime and the American highway. Cummins and Dall give uncompromising performances charged with vivid realism

6301967933 .... $19.98

Joseph L. **Mankiewiecz**

The Ghost and Mrs. Muir

(1947) The fantasy of a woman who falls in love with a ghost

6301586042 .... $19.99

Leo **McCarey**

Going My Way

(1944) Bing Crosby, Barry Fitzgerald, Gene Lockhart, Rise Stevens, William Frawley, Carl "Alfalfa" Switzer. Crosby, a singing priest, brings happiness to a run-down part of town, winning the hearts of a cantankerous old bishop and a gang of tough, streetsmart boys. This light-hearted and charming film will surely win everyone's hearts, especially as Crosby sings the award-winning "Swinging on a Star"

6300181545 .... $19.95

Sir Laurence Olivier

Laurence **Olivier**

Hamlet

(1948) Laurence Olivier, Jean Simmons, Eileen Herlie. A Freudian reading of the play, bathed in late '40s lighting effects; magnificent performances by all

6301026381 .... $19.95

Henry V

(1945) Olivier's brilliantly realized adaptation of Shakespeare's play

6303605494 .... $19.99

Irving **Pichel**

They Won't Believe Me

(1947) Robert Young, Susan Hayward, Jane Greer. A craftily constructed murder plot with a sting in its tail

6301648609 ....$19.98

Michael **Powell**

Black Narcissus

(1946) Visually lush tale of nuns who establish a mission in the Himalayas

6304054211 ....$14.99

Michael **Powell** & Emeric **Pressburger**

The Red Shoes

(1948) The film that inspired almost every character in *A Chorus Line* to enter the world of dance. The 14-minute ballet included in the action is based on Hans Christian Andersen's tale of the same name, and the dramatic relationship of the dance impresario and the young dancer, played by Norma Shearer, echoes Andersen as well

6300217728 ....$14.98

Irving **Rapper**

Now Voyager

(1942) Bette Davis, Claude Rains, Paul Henreid, Gladys Cooper. Psychoanalysis, Henreid's cigarette trick, and Max Steiner's score grace this classic Davis vehicle

630197333X $19.98

Carol **Reed**

The Third Man

(1949) Joseph Cotten, Orson Welles, Alida Valli. British-noir based on the Graham Greene novel and set in postwar Vienna. Masterful camera work, baroque characterization, brilliant dark score

6300158934 ....$9.95

In Italy for thirty years under the Borgias they had warfare, terror, murder, bloodshed—they produced Michelangelo, Leonardo da Vinci and the Renaissance. In Switzerland they had brotherly love, five hundred years of democracy and peace, and what did they produce? The cuckoo clock!—Orson Welles

THE THIRD MAN

Mark **Robson**

The Seventh Victim

(1943) Kim Hunter, Tom Conway, Evelyn Brent. Satanists, bohemians, and psychiatrists in the cultural melting pot of Greenwich Village: a trend-setting chiller

6301327942 ....$19.98

Robert **Rossen**

All the King's Men

(1949) Broderick Crawford, Joanne Dru, John Ireland, Mercedes McCambridge, John Derek. Rossen's adaptation of Robert Penn Warren's Pulitzer Prize-winning novel places Crawford in the role of the Southern demagogue whose uncontrollable greed is the means to his end

6300139409 ....$19.95

Body and Soul

(1947) One of the greatest boxing films ever made. John Garfield stars as a fighter on a Machiavellian mission to reach the top of his sport

6303890342 ....$14.99

George **Seaton**

Miracle on 34th Street

(1947) Edmund Gwenn. One of Hollywood's most endearing films, with Gwenn as the man who may, or may not, be the real Santa Claus. Both Seaton and Gwenn won Academy Awards for their work here

6301442962 ....$14.98

Ben **Sharpsteen** & Hamilton **Luske**

Pinocchio

(1940) Another Disney classic. The story of a lonely old man's wooden puppet who eventually becomes a real little boy. Enchanting

See also **CHILDREN'S VIDEOS**

6302642248 ....$24.95

George **Sidney**

Bathing Beauty

(1944) Red Skelton, Esther Williams, Basil Rathbone, Ethel Smith. Williams shines in the spectacular aquatic finale of her debut film appearance

6302077818 ....$19.98

Robert **Stevenson**

Jane Eyre

(1943) Orson Welles, Joan Fontaine, Margaret O'Brien, Peggy Ann Garner, John Sutton, Sara Allgood, Henry Daniell, Agnes Moorehead, Elizabeth Taylor. Dramatically tailored to Charlotte Brontë's classic. Orson Welles is haunting as the enigmatic and fiery-tempered Rochester

6302878535 ....$19.98

Preston **Sturges**

The Great McGinty

(1940) Brian Donlevy, Muriel Angelus, Akim Tamiroff, Allyn Joslyn, William Demarest, Louis Jean Heydt. Sturges's first film as both writer and director. A bum who becomes state governor is undone by his one temptation to honesty. A sly, satirical look at politics

6300987493 ....$29.95

Hail the Conquering Hero

(1945) Eddie Bracken, William Demarest, Ella Raines, Raymond Walburn. Small-town jingoism goes awry in the funniest comedy to emerge from World War II. Non sequitur and grotesquerie combine when a man turned down for the Marines for hay fever is given a hero's welcome home

6301805046 ....$29.95

The Lady Eve

(1941) Barbara Stanwyck, Henry Fonda, Charles Coburn, Eugene Pallette, William Demarest, Eric Blore, Melville Cooper. Fonda is a somewhat prissy academic who meets up with cardsharp Stanwyck on an ocean liner, jilts her, and gets his comeuppance when she returns disguised as a British society girl

6300185125 ....$29.95

The Miracle of Morgan's Creek

(1943) Betty Hutton, Eddie Bracken, William Demarest, Diana Lynn, Porter Hall. A small-town girl marries and is with child by one of six soldiers, but which one she isn't sure. Religion, mothers, politicians, and everything respectable is called into question in this hectic satire

6300215490 ....$29.95

The Palm Beach Story

(1942) Claudette Colbert, Joel McCrea, Rudy Vallee, Mary Astor, Sig Arno, Robert Warwick, William Demarest, Franklin Panghorn. Colbert runs from her penniless husband only to fall into the arms of an absurd billionaire played by Vallee

6300185206 ....$29.95

Sullivan's Travels

(1941) Joel McCrea, Veronica Lake, Robert Warwick, William Demarest, Franklin Panghorn. A comedy director disguised as a hobo sets out to research poverty for his first "arty" film, only to discover that chain gangs prefer Disney. Wild characterizations and superlative dialogue

6301232291 ....$29.95

Unfaithfully Yours

(1948) Rex Harrison stars as a conductor who suspects his wife is cheating on him in Sturges's very funny comedy

6300247686 ....$59.99

Jacques **Tourneur**

I Walked with a Zombie

(1943) A chilling story about a nurse who goes to the Caribbean to look after a Zombie-like woman. While there she uncovers dark family secrets and encounters local voodoo rituals and legends

6302069122 ....$19.99

Out of the Past

(1947) Robert Mitchum, Kirk Douglas, Jane Greer, Rhonda Fleming. Late '40s mood to spare in this complex tale of pursuit, revenge, and illicit passion

6301491920 ....$19.98

Edgar G. **Ulmer**

Detour

(1945) Total immersion in the film noir aesthetic. The story of a hitchhiker who encounters a dangerous woman

6303038743 ....$12.99

Raoul **Walsh**

They Drive by Night

(1940) George Raft, Ida Lupino, Ann Sheridan, Humphrey Bogart. Part realistic trucker story, part out-of-control murder melodrama

6302120470 ....$19.98

Orson **Welles**

Citizen Kane

(1941) Welles used every trick in the book to come up with this sprawling, wildly imaginative examination of a newspaper magnate resembling (very closely) William Randolph Hearst. Ponders the emptiness of wealth and power, the illusion of the American Dream

6301327748 ....$19.98

The Lady from Shanghai

(1948) Orson Welles, Rita Hayworth, Everett Sloane. A hallucinatory melodrama filled with dreamlike images: the fiesta, the fish tank, the hall of mirrors

6300138135 ....$19.95

Macbeth

(1948) Orson Welles, Jeanette Nolan, Dan O'Herlihy. A low-budget, sometimes off-the-wall adaptation suffused with visual splendor

6300208680 ....$19.98

The Magnificent Ambersons
(1942) Joseph Cotten, Dolores Costello, Anne Baxter, Agnes Moorehead. Somber and exquisite evocation of turn-of-the-century family life. Effective despite the fact that Welles never signed off on the studio's final edit
6301327888 ....$19.98

Raoul **Walsh**

White Heat
(1949) James Cagney, Virginia Mayo, Edmond O'Brien. A gangster flick near-mythological in its exploration of a criminal mother-son bond, in which Cagney makes it to "the top of the world, Ma," before the explosive climax
6301976940 ....$19.98

Billy **Wilder**

Double Indemnity
(1944) A hard-edged tale of adultery and an insurance scam gone wrong. Based on James M. Cain's pulp novel
6300184099 ....$14.98

The Lost Weekend
(1945) Ray Milland, Jane Wyman. The disintegration of an alcoholic writer over a weekend in a peculiarly menacing and surreal New York City. Milland won Best Actor and Wilder took home the Best Director
6301005740 ....$19.95

Wiliam **Wyler**

The Letter
(1940) Adaptation of a W. Somerset Maugham story with Bette Davis as a murderous woman who attempts to beat the rap by employing self-defense as her motive
6300176746 ....$19.98

The Best Years of Our Lives
(1946) Fredric March, Myrna Loy, Teresa Wright, Dana Andrews, Virginia Mayo, Harold Russell, Hoagy Carmichael, Gladys George, Roman Bohnen, Steve Cochran. A classic wartime film which chronicles the return of three veterans and their readjustment to civilian life. Won seven Oscars
6302226899 ....$19.98

Mrs. Miniver
(1942) Greer Garson, Walter Pidgeon, Richard Ney, Dame May Whitty, Teresa Wright. Set in bomb-scarred England, a middle-class family copes with the hardships and dangers of World War II
630197316X $19.98

The '50s

Robert **Aldrich**

Kiss Me Deadly
(1955) Ralph Meeker, Cloris Leachman, Paul Stewart, Albert Dekker. A taut, stylish thriller, hard-edged and apocalyptic
6302109051 ....$19.98

Michael **Anderson**

Around the World in 80 Days
(1956) David Niven, Cantinflas, Shirley MacLaine, Robert Newton. More than 40 cameo appearances by such screen luminaries as Marlene Dietrich and Buster Keaton add to the high-class entertainment and splendor of this delightful adaptation of Jules Verne's tale
6300270130 ....$29.97

Ingmar **Bergman**

The Seventh Seal
(1956) Bergman's metaphysical, symbolic wrestling with themes of God and death is masterful
6303107338 ....$29.99

Smiles of a Summer Night
(1955)
6302919584 ....$29.99

Wild Strawberries
(1957) An aging professor remembers the disappointments of his life. A deeply spiritual film notable for its use of flashback
6302783356 ....$29.99

Richard **Brooks**

Cat on a Hot Tin Roof
(1958) Elizabeth Taylor, Paul Newman, Burl Ives, Judith Anderson, Jack Carson, Madeleine Sherwood. Taylor is uncanny as Tennessee Williams's Cat. A film rife with frustration, obnoxious children, mendacity, and a peculiarly Southern-literature brand of mental squalor
6301966031 ....$19.98

Marcel **Camus**

Black Orpheus
(1959) Breno Mello, Marpessa Dawn. The myth retold against the backdrop of Rio's carnival
6301313607 ....$29.95

René **Clément**

Forbidden Games
(1952) Two children, one an orphan, bury a dead puppy and make a game of building a cemetery. Their innocence causes a feud among the inhabitants of their town. French
6303413161 ....$29.99

Henri Georges **Clouzot**

Diabolique
(1955) The wife and mistress of an abusive headmaster plot his death. French
630296962X $29.99

Wages of Fear
(1953) The manager of a large Central American oilfield tries to deal with a well fire by paying drivers large sums of money to drive across the jungle carrying nitroglycerine. French
6303184189 ....$14.99

Charles **Crichton**

The Lavender Hill Mob
(1951) A bank clerk pulls off a daring heist
6303209963 ....$9.99

George **Cukor**

A Star Is Born
(1954) Judy Garland, James Mason. The restored version of the all-time great tear-jerker. Garland and Mason give two of the finest performances of their careers
6300270211 ....$19.98

Delmer **Daves**

3:10 to Yuma
(1957) A suspenseful Western based on an early Elmore Leonard novel
6303257348 ....$9.99

A Summer Place
(1959) Richard Egan, Dorothy McGuire, Sandra Dee, Arthur Kennedy, Troy Donahue. This story of adultery and teenage infatuation at a Maine coastal resort was a box-office hit, instantly skyrocketing the careers of Sandra Dee and Troy Donahue. Award-winning score and lush photography
6301706587 ....$19.98

Cecil B. **DeMille**

The Ten Commandments
(1956) Well-cast epic of Moses (Charlton Heston) leading the Israelites into the promised land
6300215830 ....$29.99

The Greatest Show on Earth
(1952) James Stewart, Betty Hutton, Charlton Heston, Dorothy Lamour. A true epic within the confines of the Big Top Circus, this picture won DeMille his first Academy Award
6300215938 ....$29.95

Vittorio **De Sica**

Umberto D
(1952) A retired man who, though so destitute he is unable to pay the rent on his apartment, refuses to part with his dog
6303449050 ....$29.99

Stanley **Donen**

Funny Face
(1957) Fred Astaire, Audrey Hepburn, Kay Thompson. Astaire as an Avedon-like fashion photographer who romances Hepburn in Hollywood's version of Paris; great Gershwin songs
6300215598 ....$14.98

Federico **Fellini**

La Strada
(1954) A peasant girl is sold to a brutish street performer and they travel. One of Fellini's more touching films examines the odd and fragile bonds of relationships
6303012094 ....$29.99

Nights of Cabiria
(1957) Giulietta Masina, Francois Perier, Amedeo Nazzari, Franca Marzi, Dorian Gray. An Oscar winner for Best Foreign Film, this inverted fairytale follows the beleaguered life of a waifish Roman call girl who fantasizes about love and legitimacy. Italian
6301526368 ....$19.95

John **Ford**

The Searchers
(1956) John Wayne stars as a man driven to find a relative who was kidnapped by Indians. Elegiac in tone with beautiful sets and a famous final scene shot (Ford claimed out of necessity) through the frame of a door
6300267938 ....$19.99

Wagonmaster
(1950)
6300207390 ....$19.95

Georges **Franju**

Eyes Without a Face

(1959) A man whose daughter was killed in a car accident kills young girls in an effort to reconstruct her face. A cult classic

6301304993 .... $59.99

Samuel **Fuller**

Pickup on South Street

(1953) Richard Widmark, Jean Peters, Thelma Ritter. A pickpocket takes on the Reds in this vigorous and always surprising action classic

630196697X $19.98

Jean-Luc **Godard**

Breathless (A Bout de Souffle)

(1959) Jean Seberg, Jean-Paul Belmondo. The Marshall Plan per Godard. A Parisian hood (Belmondo) falls in love with an American woman living in Paris (Seberg) and is slowly brought down by her jejune, touristic idiocy. Belmondo and Seberg in mythical roles, Godard perfecting his esthetic. A visual love affair with Paris

6301358384 .... $59.95

Howard **Hawks**

Rio Bravo

(1959) A sheriff and a local drunk hold off a group of bandits trying to seize the town. With John Wayne, Dean Martin, and Angie Dickinson rounding out the cast

6300268470 .... $19.99

Alfred **Hitchcock**

North by Northwest

(1959) Cary Grant, Eva Marie Saint, James Mason, Leo G. Carroll, Jessie Royce Landis, Martin Landau. Comedy, adventure, thriller, romance: this engaging story of a dangerous case of mistaken identity refuses to be labeled. Like all great Hitchcock films it opens itself to many levels of interpretation

6301971612 .... $19.98

Rear Window

(1954) James Stewart, Grace Kelly, Thelma Ritter, Raymond Burr. A voyeur is a witness to murder

6300183513 .... $19.95

Strangers on a Train

(1951) Farley Granger, Robert Walker, Ruth Roman, Leo G. Carroll. A psycho "swaps murders" with a tennis pro

6300268586 .... $19.98

Vertigo

(1958) James Stewart, Kim Novak, Barbara Bel Geddes. Hitchcock's ultimate drama of obsession and confusion of identity

6300183521 .... $19.95

John **Huston**

The African Queen

(1951) Humphrey Bogart, Katharine Hepburn, Robert Morley. A romantic adventure whose troubled on-location shooting has become as much a legend as the movie itself

630150528X $19.98

The Asphalt Jungle

(1950) Sterling Hayden, Sam Jaffe, Marilyn Monroe. Character-driven thriller revolving around a group of crooks planning a jewel heist. Brilliantly executed by Huston—often copied, it has never been equalled

6301966430 .... $19.99

Elia **Kazan**

East of Eden

(1955) James Dean, Raymond Massey, Julie Harris, Richard Davalos, Jo Van Fleet, Burl Ives, Albert Dekker. Dean, as the misunderstood teen, jockeys with his brother for his stern father's love. Steinbeck's interpretation of Cain and Abel is explosively emotional on film

6300267865 .... $19.98

On the Waterfront

(1954) Marlon Brando, Eva Marie Saint, Karl Malden, Lee J. Cobb, Rod Steiger. Brando's tough-guy performance makes this one of the most powerful movies of its time and made it the leading contender at the Academy Awards

6300137325 .... $19.95

Panic in the Streets

(1950) Richard Widmark, Paul Douglas, Barbara Bel Geddes, Jack Palance. Action-packed, stylishly executed thriller. Set in steamy New Orleans, the victim of a mob hit is found to be carrying the plague and a frantic hunt begins to find anyone who has been in contact with him, mobsters included

6301863208 .... $39.98

A Streetcar Named Desire

(1951) Vivien Leigh, Marlon Brando, Kim Hunter, Karl Malden, Randy Bond. Kazan and Tennessee Williams; Leigh and Brando. The last word

630027294X $19.98

Gene **Kelly** & Stanley **Donen**

Singin' in the Rain

(1952)

630233683X $19.99

Stanley **Kramer**

On the Beach

(1959) Gregory Peck, Ava Gardner, Fred Astaire, Anthony Perkins, Donna Anderson. Australians await the effects of nuclear fallout from a war that destroyed the rest of the world. Memorable performances mark this poignant telling of Nevil Shute's novel

6302120489 .... $19.98

Stanley **Kubrick**

The Killing

(1956) Sterling Hayden, Coleen Gray, Vince Edwards, Jay C. Flippen, Ted de Corsia, Marie Windsor, Elisha Cook. This early Kubrick classic details an elaborately conceived racetrack robbery. Perfectly paced with a complex and unusual narrative

6301972120 .... $19.98

Akira **Kurosawa**

Kurosawa's 1951 film Rashomon*—an alternating first-person recounting of a murder—won the Grand Prize at the Venice Film Festival, thus introducing Western audiences not only to the genius of Kurosawa, but to the Japanese cinematic tradition as a whole. His films mix the modern with the ancient, incorporate and interpret traditional myths and legends, and push the stylistic envelope of cinematic expression.*

Ikiru

(1952)

6302919649 .... $39.99

Rashomon

(1951) Toshiro Mifune, Machiko Kyo, Masayuki Mori, Takashi Shimura. Questioning the nature of truth, this film takes one particular incident and shows it from the varying perspectives of the people involved. The incident is the rape and murder of a newlywed couple as seen through the eyes of the wife, the husband, the culprit, and a witness

6300149765 .... $19.98

The Seven Samurai

(1954) Takashi Shimura, Toshiro Mifune, Yoshio Inaba. An epic period piece of three and one half hours (in its complete state), it tells the story of seven Samurai hired to defend a farming village from 40 bandits. In 1960, an American version of the story, a Western called *The Magnificent Seven*, was released

6300149315 .... $29.28

Fritz **Lang**

The Big Heat

(1953) Glenn Ford, Gloria Grahame, Lee Marvin. Lang deftly applies his expressionist style to this classic Hollywood story of a determined cop and a femme fatale. Stark cinematography filled with shadow epitomizes the noir aesthetic

0-630-27967-5 .... $59.95

Charles **Laughton**

The Night of the Hunter

(1955) Better known as an actor, this brilliant film was Laughton's only directorial effort

6301973232 .... $19.99

David **Lean**

The Bridge on the River Kwai

(1957) William Holden, Alec Guinness, Jack Hawkins. High drama, psychological tension, and lots of action make this story of British POWs building a bridge for their Japanese captors a real blockbuster

6300135578 .... $19.95

Albert **Lewin**

Pandora and the Flying Dutchman

(1951) An American woman falls in love with the ghost of a Spanish sea captain

6303918476 .... $19.99

Alexander **Mackendrick**

Sweet Smell of Success

(1957) Burt Lancaster, Tony Curtis, Sam Levene, Barbara Nichols. Masterful, brilliantly acted tour of the hellish world of gossip columnists, with some of the best screen dialogue ever written

6301976126 .... $29.98

Joseph L. **Mankiewicz**

All About Eve

(1950) Bette Davis, Anne Baxter, George Sanders, Celeste Holm, Thelma Ritter, Marilyn Monroe. Life in and around the theater, and the constant vying for the spotlight, is the theme of what is considered to be one of the most enjoyable movies ever made. Davis is divine as an aging actress exploited by an aspiring and conniving young actress who longs to be a star

6301797957 .... $19.98

Julius Caesar
(1953) James Mason, Marlon Brando, John Gielgud, Louis Calhern. An odd mix of acting styles works, thanks to Mankiewicz's intelligent direction
6301971140 ....$19.98

Suddenly Last Summer
(1959) Elizabeth Taylor, Katharine Hepburn, Montgomery Clift, Mercedes McCambridge, Albert Dekker, Gary Raymond. Hepburn wants Taylor lobotomized, Taylor saw someone get eaten, Clift wants money for the clinic... Unforgettable Tennessee Williams by a great director
6302655897 ....$19.95

Anthony **Mann**

The Naked Spur
(1953) James Stewart as a bounty hunter who is continually frustrated by the elusiveness of his quarry and the greed of his "partners"
6302032237 ....$19.99

Delbert **Mann**

Marty
(1955) Ernest Borgnine, Betsy Blair, Joe De Santis, Esther Minciotti. A shy, fat, unattractive and insecure Bronx butcher meets a plain-Jane schoolteacher at a dance and a charming love ensues
6301973259 ....$19.98

Rudolph **Mate**

D.O.A.
(1950) Edmond O'Brien, Pamela Britton, Luther Adler, Beverly Campbell, Lynn Baggett. Thrilling, fast-paced, nightmarish film noir. A small-town businessman gets mixed up with big-city corruption and, through clever plot surprises, must solve his own murder
6301042433 ....$19.99

Vincente **Minnelli**

Gigi
(1958) Leslie Caron, Maurice Chevalier, Louis Jourdan, Hermione Gingold, Jacques Bergerac, Eva Gabor. This turn-of-the-century musical is derived from Colette's short novel about a young French girl who is groomed to become a courtesan. Lerner and Loewe create a memorable score with such favorites as "Thank Heaven for Little Girls"
630969804 ....$19.98

An American in Paris
(1951) Gene Kelly, Leslie Caron, Oscar Levant, Nina Foch. Frustrated American artist sojourning in the city of lights falls in love with a French girl amidst delightful Gershwin tunes
6301964284 ....$19.98

The Band Wagon
(1953) Fred Astaire, Cyd Charisse, Jack Buchanan, Oscar Levant, Nanette Fabray. The musical contemplates itself, in this mélange of Faust, Mickey Spillane, and a raft of Dietz-Schwartz tunes
630196635X $19.98

Father of the Bride
(1950) Elizabeth Taylor, Spencer Tracy, Joan Bennett, Don Taylor. In a world where the neighbors always seem to have a bigger house, a fancier car, and a better job, Tracy, an archetypal middle-class banker, is trying to put on a wedding for his darling daughter. Despite the never-ending expenses, his misgivings about his son-in-law, and the smallness of his house, the wedding comes off
6301967852 ....$19.98

Some Came Running
(1958) Frank Sinatra plays a writer who returns to the claustrophobic stillness of small-town America, where he befriends a prostitute brilliantly played by Shirley MacLaine
6302682630 ....$19.99

Kenji **Mizoguchi**

Sansho the Bailiff
(1954) Kinuyo Tanaka, Kyoko Kagawa. Poetic, deeply moving epic of medieval Japan
6301179404 ....$59.95

Ugetsu
Supernatural love and brutal war are among the elements of this masterpiece
6302969425 ....$24.99

Max **Ophuls**

The Earrings of Madame de...
(1953) An upperclass woman sells her earrings and lies to her husband about what she has done
630359316X $19.99

Nicholas **Ray**

In a Lonely Place
6302801133 ....$69.99

Johnny Guitar
(1954)
6303391931 ....$14.99

On Dangerous Ground
(1952) Ida Lupino, Robert Ryan. A blind girl softens a tough cop in this dark and moody film. Ray's exercise in noir contains stunning cinematography and a marvelous Bernard Herrmann score
6301648048 ....$19.98

Rebel Without a Cause
(1955) James Dean's most famous role is that of a misunderstood youth who moves to a new town, has trouble with his parents and the law, befriends a loner in his class, falls for the wrong girl, and eventually winds up in a deadly game of chicken. A heavily psychological examination of familial tensions provides an interesting subtext to the seemingly all-American storyline
6304039514 ....$19.99

Satyajit **Ray**

Pather Panchali
(1955) A stark examination of a poor family living in Bengal
6304104286 ....$19.99

Aparajito
(1956) The son of a poor Indian family goes off to college in Calcutta in this, the second installment of Ray's Apu trilogy
6304104278 ....$19.99

The World of Apu
(1959) The third of Ray's Apu trilogy. A writer suffering under the weight of severe poverty enters into an arranged marriage. When his wife dies, he has a difficult time accepting their only son
6304104294 ....$19.99

Martin **Ritt**

The Long Hot Summer
(1958) Paul Newman, Joanne Woodward, Anthony Franciosa, Orson Welles, Lee Remick, Angela Lansbury. Newman is a drifting handyman who sets the women aflame, but only has eyes for Woodward, the daughter of the rich, tyrannical Big Daddy Varner (played by a stout Welles). This brooding drama, based on a compilation of stories by William Faulkner, was Newman and Woodward's first film together
6301599225 ....$14.98

Roberto **Rossellini**

Voyage in Italy
(1953)
6303593518 ....$19.99

Don **Siegel**

Invasion of the Body Snatchers
(1956) Siegel's science fiction masterpiece is also a symbolic meditation on Cold War hysteria
6300208508 ....$19.99

Douglas **Sirk**

The Tarnished Angels
(1958)
6304021690 ....$14.99

George **Stevens**

A Place in the Sun
(1951) Elizabeth Taylor, Montgomery Clift, Shelley Winters, Raymond Burr. Based on Dreiser's *An American Tragedy*, this is the quintessential seamy-underside-of-the-American-Dream film, with brilliant performances by all—especially Winters as the shrill factory girl whose death precipitates the hero's fall
6300215644 ....$19.95

Robert **Stevenson**

Old Yeller
(1957) Dorothy McGuire, Fess Parker, Tommy Kirk, Kevin Corcoran, Jeff York, Beverly Washburn, Chuck Connors. Set in dusty 1859 Texas, this is the best film ever made about a boy and his loyal dog
6302272947 ....$19.99

François **Truffaut**

Truffaut was a leading figure in the French New Wave. His stint with Godard at the famed Cahiers du Cinema *cemented his reputation as a brilliant theorist and one of cinema's great trendsetters.*

The 400 Blows (Les Quatre Cent Coups)
(1959) Jean-Pierre Leaud, Patrick Auffay, Claire Maurier, Jeanne Moreau. Boy turns to a life of petty crime in response to his totalitarian parents in this poignant and moving film. Leaud's first role in Truffaut's autobiographical series establishes him forever in our psyches
6302784123 ....$39.95

King **Vidor**

War and Peace

(1956) Audrey Hepburn, Henry Fonda, Mel Ferrer, Vittorio Gassman, John Mills, Herbert Lom, Anita Ekberg, Barry Jones, Oscar Homolka, Jeremy Brett, Helmut Dantine. Tolstoy's great novel impressively brought to the screen in historical detail. Magnificent battle scenes
6300215601 ....$29.95

Orson **Welles**

Mr. Arkadin

(1955) Also known as *The Confidential Report*, Welles brought his innovative cinematography and overlapping dialogue to Hitchcock territory with this story of a wealthy banker who hires a man to look into several of his past connections, all of whom seem to be dead
6302633125 ....$39.99

Touch of Evil

(1958) Charlton Heston, Janet Leigh, Orson Welles. The epitaph of noir, this story of law and order in a border town was Welles's first American film in a decade. The exaggerated use of shadow, dramatic angles, along with surreal performances by the all-star cast gives it the quality of an irresistibly entertaining nightmare
6300181855 ....$29.95

Fred McLeod **Wilcox**

Forbidden Planet

(1956) A surprisingly effective science fiction version of Shakespeare's *The Tempest*
6302181569 ....$14.99

Billy **Wilder**

Sabrina

(1954) Audrey Hepburn, William Holden, Humphrey Bogart. Hepburn wins hearts as the chauffeur's daughter who charms the wealthy employer's son and ends up happy and in love
630103144X $14.95

The Seven Year Itch

(1955) Marilyn Monroe, Tom Ewell, Evelyn Keyes. Includes one of the most beloved moments in film history: Marilyn's inability to keep her dress down while standing over a subway grating
6300247007 ....$19.98

Some Like It Hot

(1959) Tony Curtis, Jack Lemmon, Marilyn Monroe, Joe E. Brown. Hiding from the mob, Lemmon and Curtis dress in drag and join Monroe's all-women band
6301978277 ....$19.98

Stalag 17

(1953) William Holden, Don Taylor, Robert Strauss, Harvey Lembeck, Neville Brand, Richard Erdman, Otto Preminger. Holden won an Academy Award for his role as the testosterone-dominated, abrasive, and cynical American POW in a German WWII camp. Based on a successful Broadway play, written by Donald Bevan and Edmund Trzcinski
6300215652 ....$49.95

Sunset Boulevard

(1950) Gloria Swanson, William Holden, Erich von Stroheim, Buster Keaton, Cecil B. DeMille, Anna Q. Nilsson. Holden gets caught in the destructive web of a late-great silent film star (Swanson), when, for the promise of payment, he becomes her lover, her screenwriter, and our window into the fabulously macabre world of Hollywood has-beens
6300215512 ....$14.95

Robert **Wise**

The Day the Earth Stood Still

(1951) A flying saucer carrying a prophetic alien lands in Washington
6302168465 ....$14.99

Edward D. **Wood, Jr.**

Plan 9 from Outer Space

(1959) Wood's obsessively bizarre science fiction film features production values of the lowest denominator
6303170498 ....$9.99

Glen or Glenda

(1953) Stories of transvestites and sex-change operations as told by a director who is either a slightly off-the-wall cult hero or the worst director of all time (depending on who one asks)
6303861229 ....$14.99

William **Wyler**

Ben-Hur

(1959) Charlton Heston, Jack Hawkins, Haya Harareet, Stephen Boyd. The Roman Empire provides ample room for this filmmaker's grandiose scenes, especially apparent in the galley-slave sequence, and the climactic chariot race
6301966821 ....$29.98

Roman Holiday

(1953) Audrey Hepburn, Gregory Peck, Eddie Albert. Shot mostly on location in Rome, this amorous city proves the perfect complement for a charming fairy tale of romance that made Hepburn a star
6300215717 ....$14.95

Fred **Zinnemann**

High Noon

(1952) Gary Cooper stars as a marshal forced to defend his territory
6302484472 ....$19.99

From Here to Eternity

(1953) Burt Lancaster, Deborah Kerr, Frank Sinatra, Montgomery Clift, Donna Reed, Ernest Borgnine. Based on James Jones's novel of army life in Hawaii just before Pearl Harbor. Unparalleled romantic beach scene
630159007 ....$19.95

The '60s

Lindsay **Anderson**

If...

(1968)
6300216128 ....$49.99

Michelangelo **Antonioni**

Blowup

(1966) Much-imitated, stylized tale of a pop-culture photographer's hollow existence
6301966015 ....$19.99

L'Avventura

(1960) Monica Vitti, Gabriele Ferzetti. A woman vanishes, exposing the emptiness of the world she leaves behind
6301326083 ....$29.95

Red Desert

(1964)
6303593232 ....$29.99

Ingmar **Bergman**

Persona

(1966) While himself recovering in the hospital Bergman wrote this story of an actress who refuses to speak and the nurse who cares for her. A sometimes obscure meditation on the value of art and the possibility of living one's life truthfully
6302641888 ....$19.99

Bernardo **Bertolucci**

Before the Revolution

(1964)
630155163X $29.99

John **Boorman**

Point Blank

(1967)
6301971876 ....$19.99

Peter **Brook**

Lord of the Flies

(1963) James Aubrey, Hugh Edwards, Tom Chapin. The late William Golding wrote this allegorical novel of social Darwinism in 1954. A gang of schoolboys is stranded on a desert island and all forms of civilization rapidly break down, reducing them to savages. The screen adaptation by Brook perfectly captures Golding's dark vision of humanity and society
6302891256 ....$29.98

Richard **Brooks**

Elmer Gantry

(1960) Burt Lancaster is remarkable in the role of a small-town evangelist
6301965833 ....$19.99

Luis **Buñuel**

Nazarin

(1961)
6303593186 ....$69.99

Viridiana

(1961)
6302562252 ....$24.99

John **Cassavetes**

Faces

(1968) This uncharacteristically personal and accesible film from Cassavetes examines the nuances of infidelity
6304192312 ....$19.99

George **Cukor**

My Fair Lady

(1964) Audrey Hepburn, Rex Harrison, Stanley Holloway, Wilfrid Hyde-White, Gladys Cooper, Jeremy Brett, Mona Washbourne. This delightful musical version of Shaw's *Pygmalion* has taught the world how to properly pronounce "the rain in Spain falls mainly on the plain" ten times fast
6302135818 ....$29.98

Blake **Edwards**

Breakfast at Tiffany's

(1961) Audrey Hepburn, George Peppard, Patricia Neal, Buddy Ebsen, Mickey Rooney, John McGiver, Martin Balsam. A New York comedy with the ultra-chic Hepburn as Truman Capote's creation, Holly Golightly, the epitome of the uptown party girl

6300215814 ....$14.95

The Pink Panther

(1964) Peter Sellers is the endearingly clumsy, dim-witted, paranoid, and extremely funny Inspector Clouseau

6301972287 ....$14.99

Federico **Fellini**

8 1/2

(1963) Marcello Mastroianni, Claudia Cardinale, Anouk Aimee. Celebrated for its creative and technical ingenuity, Fellini's autobiographical escapade features the director's on-screen alter-ego Mastroianni. A director working on a film entitled *8 1/2* experiences an extreme case of writer's block while recovering in a countryside spa. The title, seemingly cryptic, stems from the fact that this was to be Fellini's ninth film, but he never considered it entirely complete

6301025083 ....$59.95

Fellini Satyricon

(1969) Martin Potter, Hiram Keller, Salvo Randone, Max Born, Fanfulla, Capucine, Alain Cuny, Lucia Bose. A homage to Pasolini's interpretation of myths, this psychological film follows the sexual adventures of a Roman student. Visually stunning

6301965752 ....$19.98

Federico Fellini

Juliet of the Spirits

(1965)

6301224698 ....$29.99

La Dolce Vita

(1960) Marcello Mastroianni, Anita Ekberg, Anouk Aimee. A singularly entertaining movie which places Mastroianni on the masthead of a tabloid magazine. Finding himself jettisoned into Rome's fashionable but shallow society, he must reevaluate his calling

6300208591 ....$24.98

John **Ford**

Donovan's Reef

(1963) John Wayne, Lee Marvin, Jack Warden, Cesar Romero. Comic adventure ensues as Wayne, an ex-Navy man, and his freewheeling friends frolic in the Pacific. Underlying the very effective humor is a bleak social commentary on tradition and racism

6300215733 ....$14.95

The Man Who Shot Liberty Valance

(1962) A classic American Western featuring John Wayne and James Stewart

6300215709 ....$14.99

John **Frankenheimer**

The Manchurian Candidate

(1962) A Cold War-era tale of mind control and political assassination

6301972902 ....$19.98

Seven Days in May

(1964)

6302756502 ....$19.99

Jean-Luc **Godard**

Alphaville

(1965) New Wave director Godard's foray into science fiction

6303994083 ....$29.99

Contempt (Le Mépris)

(1963) Brigitte Bardot, Jack Palance, Michel Piccoli, Fritz Lang. Piccoli is a writer working on the script for a Hollywood adaptation of *The Odyssey*

6300148009 ....$19.95

Masculine/Feminine (Masculin/Feminin)

(1966) Jean-Pierre Leaud, Chantal Goya, Catherine Isabelle Duport. In 15 vignettes, Godard explores the relationship between a young radical and a flirtatious young woman

6302149495 ....$69.95

Pierrot le Fou

(1965)

6301910273 ....$59.99

Anthony **Harvey**

The Lion in Winter

(1968) Katharine Hepburn, Peter O'Toole, Anthony Hopkins, Timothy Dalton. Clashing wits and power struggles between King Henry II (O'Toole) and his wife Eleanor of Aquitaine (Hepburn, in an Academy Award-winning performance) form the backbone of this 12th-century English tale. Adapted by James Goldman from his own 1966 Broadway play with intelligent directing and seamless performances

6300147452 ....$14.95

James **Hill**

Born Free

(1966) Virginia McKenna, Bill Travers. Time-tested family film that tells Joy Adamson's story of Elsa, a lion cub raised in captivity by two game wardens, who must fend for herself in the wilds of Kenya. Won two Oscars

6302540437 ....$14.95

Alfred **Hitchcock**

The Birds

(1963) Hitchcock's effects in this film are legendary

6300181340 ....$14.99

Psycho

(1960) Hitchcock's most famous, and lasting, film. A multilayered, psychologically probing play on Freudian themes, multiple personality, and the peculiar American morality of the day

6300181251 ....$14.99

James **Ivory**

Shakespeare Wallah

(1965) A roving Shakespearean troupe struggles gamely on in India after the Raj. The story is loosely based on the Kendals' experiences, and they perform pieces from their bardic repertoire

6300151433 ....$19.95

Norman **Jewison**

In the Heat of the Night

(1967) Sidney Poitier, Rod Steiger. Melodrama of racial tension as a bigoted Mississippi sheriff agrees to collaborate with a black homicide expert from Philadelphia to solve a murder

6301968751 ....$19.98

Elia **Kazan**

Splendor in the Grass

(1961) Natalie Wood, Warren Beatty, Sandy Dennis, Audrey Christie, Phillis Diller. Wood and Beatty (in his debut appearance) as star-crossed lovers whose parents believe they are too young to marry

6300269345 ....$19.98

Masaki **Kobayashi**

Harakiri

(1962) This Samurai period piece won the International Jury Prize at Cannes, and in so doing exposed this powerful director to the Western world

6303261736 ....$39.99

Stanley **Kramer**

Judgment at Nuremberg

(1961) Spencer Tracy, Burt Lancaster, Judy Garland, Montgomery Clift, Maximilian Schell, Marlene Dietrich. Set during the later stages of the Nazi war-crime trials, this thoughtful social drama depicts the moral dilemma of an American judge (Tracy) who must negotiate the shocking moral, legal, and political maze of the Nuremburg trials

6301973372 ....$29.98

Ship of Fools

(1965) Simone Signoret, Vivian Leigh, Jose Ferrer, Werner Klemperer, George Segal, Elizabeth Ashley. An ocean liner headed from Veracruz to Bremerhaven in 1933 is a microcosm of the coming war

6300138984 ....$59.95

Stanley **Kubrick**

2001: A Space Odyssey

(1968) A "letterboxed" (simulated wide-screen) edition does justice to Kubrick's spacious galactic vistas. With only forty minutes of dialogue, and most of it with a computer, the score is necessarily amazing

6302089638 ....$19.98

Dr. Strangelove

(1964) Peter Sellers, George C. Scott, Sterling Hayden. How we learned to stop worrying and love the bomb

6300135691 ....$19.95

Stanley Kubrick

Lolita
(1962) James Mason, Sue Lyon, Peter Sellers, Shelley Winters. A wonderful movie bearing almost no resemblance to Nabokov's novel, with Mason at his best
6301971574 ......$19.95

Spartacus
(1960) A sprawling epic telling of a foiled slave revolt in ancient Rome
6302200342 ......$19.99

Akira **Kurosawa**

Yojimbo
(1961)
6303202055 ......$29.99

David **Lean**

Doctor Zhivago
(1965) Omar Sharif, Julie Christie, Geraldine Chaplin, Rod Steiger, Alec Guinness. A pure-hearted doctor struggles to comprehend events that transpire during the Russian Revolution. This absorbing account, based on the prize-winning novel by Boris Pasternak, is masterfully composed by director David Lean
6301966813 ......$29.98

Lawrence of Arabia
(1962) Peter O'Toole, Alec Guinness, Anthony Quinn, Omar Sharif, Claude Rains. A true spectacle about the powers of the desert as experienced by one enigmatic adventurer. This anniversary edition restores many cuts made over the years
3301436504 ......$29.95

Sergio **Leone**

The Good, the Bad and the Ugly
(1967)
6303050239 ......$29.99

Once Upon a Time in the West
(1968) Henry Fonda, Charles Bronson, Claudia Cardinale, Jason Robards. The movie that put the "opera" back in "horse opera"
6300216098 ......$29.95

Richard **Lester**

Help!
(1965) The Beatles. A wild tale about a group of religious zealots trying to recover a sacred ring from Ringo
6303823351 ......$19.99

Henry **Levin**

Where the Boys Are
(1960) Dolores Hart, George Hamilton, Yvette Mimieux, Jim Hutton, Barbara Nichols, Connie Francis. Spring break in Ft. Lauderdale, '60s style. Francis's first starring role also sees her singing the title tune
6301977963 ......$59.99

Jerry **Lewis**

The Nutty Professor
(1963)
6300215989 ......$14.99

Joseph **Losey**

The Servant
(1963)
6302089875 ......$9.99

Sidney **Lumet**

The Group
(1966) Story of eight graduates of a small, all-women New England college, based on Mary McCarthy's novel
630408434X $19.99

Robert **Mulligan**

To Kill a Mockingbird
(1962) Gregory Peck, Mary Badham, Philip Alford, Brock Peters. Peck won an Academy Award for his performance as a widowed lawyer responsible for two young children in an Alabama town. Harper Lee's Pulitzer Prize-winning story grapples with issues that remain all too relevant today
6300181499 ......$19.95

Mike **Nichols**

The Graduate
(1967) Anne Bancroft, Dustin Hoffman, Katharine Ross, William Daniels, Murray Hamilton, Elizabeth Wilson, Norman Fell, Buck Henry. Thirty years ago this film made an impact that reverberates even today. A recent college grad, directionless and unsure about his future, is seduced by an older woman. Starring a very young and serious Dustin Hoffman
6302540445 ......$19.95

Who's Afraid of Virginia Woolf?
(1966) Elizabeth Taylor, Richard Burton, Sandy, Dennis, George Segal. A potent mix of domestic warfare, booze, verbal fireworks, and vulgar excess, based on the play by Edward Albee
6300268527 ......$19.98

Kihachi **Okamoto**

Sword of Doom
(1966) Tatsuya Nakadai, Toshiro Mifune. "An evil sword is an evil mind": a nightmarish, stylized movie characterized by dreamlike violence
630015002X $19.95

Sergei **Paradjanov**

Shadows of Forgotten Ancestors
(1964) Set in the 19th century, this is a moody tale of love and betrayal
6302969360 ......$29.99

Sam **Peckinpah**

The Wild Bunch
(1969) William Holden, Robert Ryan, Ernest Borgnine, Warren Oates, Ben Johnson. Choreographic violence punctuates Peckinpah's most enduring film
6300267954 ......$19.98

Arthur **Penn**

Bonnie and Clyde
(1967) Warren Beatty and Faye Dunaway star as the legendary American criminals cum folk heroes
6304039522 ......$19.99

Frank **Perry**

Last Summer
(1969) Richard Thomas, Barbara Hershey. A powerful exploration of the sexual awakenings, desires, and frustrations of a group of teenagers playing on the beach at a summer resort
6301802438 ......$59.98

Roman **Polanski**

Knife in the Water
(1962) Polanski's first feature, shot in Poland, lays much of the groundwork for his continuing explorations of sexuality, humiliation, and cruel head games. All of this with three actors and a boat
6300267202 ......$29.95

Repulsion
(1965) Catherine Deneuve. One of the most exquisitely terrifying films ever made. Polanski depicts, in brutal yet delicate detail, Deneuve's mental disintegration as she retreats further and further into her fear of sexual contact
6301686888 ......$29.95

Rosemary's Baby
(1968) Mia Farrow, John Cassavetes, Ruth Gordon, Maurice Evans. The supreme Satanist drama, set in New York City's eerie Dakota building. While there is almost no gore or violence, Polanski's deft direction makes even the tiniest action chilling
6300216101 ......$14.95

Michael **Powell**

Peeping Tom
(1960) A studio cameraman who kills women so he can film the fear on their faces
6302969255 ......$29.99

Otto **Preminger**

Advise and Consent
(1962)
6303118275 ......$19.99

Exodus
(1960) An epic adaptation of the Leon Uris novel focusing on the early days of Israel
6303961630 ......$24.99

Carol **Reed**

Oliver
(1968) Oliver Reed, Harry Secombe. Entertaining musical adaptation of Dickens's classic. Wonderful atmosphere and rousing score make this good family fun
6300138852 ......$19.95

Michael **Reeves**

The Conqueror Worm
(1968)
6303522688 ......$14.99

Tony **Richardson**

Tom Jones

(1963) Albert Finney, Susannah York, Hugh Griffith. An award-winning rendition of the 18th-century classic about a cavorting charmer. An abridged but lively rendition of Fielding's novel

6302292042 .... $19.99

Eric **Rohmer**

My Night at Maud's

(1969)

6304006829 .... $19.99

John **Schlesinger**

Midnight Cowboy

(1969) Jon Voight, Dustin Hoffman, Sylvia Miles, Brenda Vaccaro. Two misguided dreamers (Voight and Hoffman) find friendship as they conjure a plan to get rich by "servicing" wealthy New York women. A dark and moving story

6301971817 .... $19.98

Andrei **Tarkovsky**

Andrei Rublev

(1966)

6302426499 .... $19.99

J. Lee **Thompson**

Cape Fear

(1962) Gregory Peck, Robert Mitchum, Telly Savalas. Mitchum is disturbingly credible as a menacing ex-con who blames his lawyer (Peck) for his incarceration and seeks revenge by tormenting his family. John D. MacDonald's novel *The Executioners* is the basis for the story, and the remarkable score is the work of Bernard Herrmann

63001858OX $19.95

François **Truffaut**

The Bride Wore Black

(1968)

6302180163 .... $19.99

Jules & Jim

(1961)

6302969743 .... $29.99

Shoot the Piano Player

(1962) Charles Aznavour, Marie Dubois, Nicole Berger. A bittersweet tribute to American crime films

6301313593 .... $29.95

François Truffaut

The Wild Child

(1969)

6302180252 .... $19.99

Roger **Vadim**

Barbarella

(1967) Terry Southern's script and Claude Renoir's camerawork provide flashes of brilliance in this high-camp ode to sex in space, starring a pre-Hanoi Jane Fonda

6300216047 .... $14.95

Billy **Wilder**

The Apartment

(1960) Jack Lemmon, Shirley MacLaine, Fred MacMurray. Life outside the nine-to-five; a splendid satire on office politics with Lemmon as the sycophantic insurance clerk who, in search of a promotion, lends his apartment to his superiors for their sleazy affairs

6301963970 .... $19.98

Robert **Wise**

The Sound of Music

(1965) Julie Andrews, Christopher Plummer, Eleanor Parker, Richard Hayden. One of the all-time family favorites; based on the singing von Trapp family. The memorable Rodgers and Hammerstein musical numbers and the simple story are irresistible

6302140897 .... $29.98

Robert **Wise** & Jerome **Robbins**

West Side Story

(1961) Natalie Wood, Rita Moreno. Gang wars between the natives and the Puerto Rican immigrants of a New York City neighborhood provide a dramatic background to this musical love story. Choreography by Robbins, lyrics by Sondheim, music by Bernstein, and plot by Shakespeare

6301978854 .... $19.98

Terence **Young**

Wait Until Dark

(1967) Audrey Hepburn, Alan Arkin, Richard Crenna, Efrem Zimbalist, Jr., Jack Weston, Samantha Jones. Edge-of-your-seat suspense results when the blind Hepburn, alone in her house, is threatened by a psychotic villain. Amazing use of the film medium for capturing interior spaces

6300268683 .... $19.98

Dr. No

(1962)

6303651453 .... $14.99

Fred **Zinnemann**

A Man for All Seasons

(1966) Paul Scofield, Wendy Hiller, Leo McKern, Robert Shaw, Orson Welles, Susannah York, Vanessa Redgrave. Excellent film based on Robert Bolt's play about Thomas More. Literate and thoughtful

6300134571 .... $19.95

The '70s

Woody **Allen**

Annie Hall

(1977) Woody Allen, Diane Keaton, Paul Simon. Melancholy romantic comedy among city folk, exploring Freud, Marshall McLuhan, *The Sorrow and the Pity,* real estate, and the complications of love between neurotics

6301963911 .... $19.98

Woody Allen

Manhattan

(1979) Woody Allen, Diane Keaton, Michael Murphy, Mariel Hemingway, Meryl Streep. A television comedy writer contemplates a change to serious literature in this classic New York picture. "A masterpiece that has become a film for the ages by not seeking to be a film of the moment"—Andrew Sarris

6301971922 .... $19.89

Robert **Altman**

M*A*S*H

(1970) Elliott Gould, Donald Sutherland, Sally Kellerman, Robert Duvall. The original film—about an American mobile medical unit based in Korea during the war—upon which the popular TV series was based. Screenwriter Ring Lardner, Jr. won an Academy Award for the film that became an American phenomenon

6301777387 .... $14.98

McCabe and Mrs. Miller

(1971) A harshly realistic depiction of small town life at the turn of the century

6302816386 .... $14.99

Nashville

(1975) Keith Carradine, Lily Tomlin, Ned Beatty, Henry Gibson, Karen Black. This Altman masterpiece explores the American Dream through slice-of-life depictions of the country music capital

6301936930 .... $29.95

Hal **Ashby**

Harold & Maude

(1972) Quirky cult film that details the love relationship between a death-obsessed 20-year-old and a 79-year-old dynamo. Cat Stevens's music aptly accompanies this comedic original

6300216268 .... $14.95

The Last Detail
(1973) Jack Nicholson, Otis Young, Randy Quaid. A man's movie about men being men. Two sailors are assigned to escort a young soldier from Virginia to a naval prison in New Hampshire. He appeals to their humanity, and they decide to show him a good time before locking him away

630013444X $14.95

John G. **Avildsen**

Rocky
(1976) Sylvester Stallone, Talia Shire, Burt Young, Carl Weathers, Burgess Meredith. Stallone's performance as a tough, uneducated Philadelphia boxer skyrocketed him into stardom in this modern rags-to-riches success story. Stallone also wrote the screenplay

630197767X $19.98

Robert **Benton**

Kramer vs. Kramer
(1979) Dustin Hoffman, Meryl Streep. Exemplary performances by the entire cast bring to life this profoundly moving story of a professional man left alone to care for his young son after his wife leaves them to search for herself

6300134407 .... $19.95

Igmar **Bergman**

Cries and Whispers
(1972)

6302919509 .... $39.99

Bernardo **Bertolucci**

1900
(1977) Gerard Depardieu, Robert De Niro, Dominique Sanda, Burt Lancaster. Encapsulates half a century of Italian history

6301015320 .... $29.95

Last Tango in Paris
(1972) Marlon Brando, Maria Schneider. Bertolucci's masterpiece of narcissism, set in and around an empty apartment in Paris

6301973399 .... $19.98

The Spider's Stratagem
(1970)

6301773640 .... $29.99

Mel **Brooks**

Blazing Saddles
(1974) Brooks's funniest film plays with the conventions of the Hollywood Western

630281622X $14.99

Luis **Buñuel**

One of the most powerfully anti-establishment directors in the history of film, Buñuel is recognized as a major innovator in surrealist cinema. His exchange of dreams and fantasies with Salvador Dali led to the surrealistic short Un Chien Andalou, *which consists of a series of shocking and unrelated images. His* L'Age d'Or *and* Belle de Jour *are particularly barbed and funny assaults on bourgeois morality.*

The Discreet Charm of the Bourgeoisie
(1972)

630240584X $24.99

Tristana
(1970)

6304116594 .... $29.99

Michael **Cimino**

The Deer Hunter
(1978) Robert De Niro, John Cazale, John Savage, Christopher Walken, Meryl Streep. Sober tale of three Pennsylvania steelworkers who volunteer for service in Vietnam and return home to no heroes' welcome in a country heavily disapproving of the war they fought. One of the best films of the '70s

630018627X $29.95

Francis Ford **Coppola**

Apocalypse Now
(1979) May be the best Vietnam film ever made. Coppola based his tale loosely on Conrad's *The Heart of Darkness*. Lush scenery and perfect-pitch dialogue, as well as some of the greatest casting ever

6302413931 .... $29.99

The Godfather
(1972) Marlon Brando, Al Pacino, James Caan, Richard Castellano, John Cazale, Diane Keaton, Talia Shire. Unforgettable film epic that offers an intimate view of a Mafia dynasty, unequaled by any others in the mobster genre. With potent performances by Brando as Don Corleone and Pacino as his calculating son, Michael

6300216292 .... $29.95

Marlon Brando

The Godfather, Part II
(1974) Al Pacino, Robert Duvall, Diane Keaton, Robert De Niro, John Cazale, Talia Shire, Lee Strasberg. Even larger, more complex, and more beautiful than the first

630021639X $29.95

The Godfather Trilogy
(1996 re-release) Remastered and restored

6302610710 .... $199.99

Peter **Davis**

Hearts and Minds
(1974) Highlighting the psychological rather than the political repercussions of the Vietnam conflict, Davis interviews the people whose lives were altered by their war experiences. Contrasts empty rhetoric with personal anguish

6302039525 .... $19.98

Brian **De Palma**

Carrie
(1976) Based on Stephen King's story of a high school girl who, after years of school and abuse, takes her supernatural revenge

630196800X $14.99

Clint **Eastwood**

The Outlaw Josey Wales
(1975)

6300269043 .... $19.99

Rainer Werner **Fassbinder**

Fassbinder was the darling of New German Cinema of the 1970s. His prolific career—he made a total of 41 features—was shortened by his premature death at the age of 36.

The Bitter Tears of Petra von Kant
630204121X $79.99

Fox and His Friends
(1975)

6301551656 .... $79.99

The Marriage of Maria Braun
(1978) Fassbinder's most accessible film

6302348730 .... $79.99

Federico **Fellini**

Amarcord
(1973) Fellini recalls his youth in this semi-autobiographical story of life in provincial Italy

6303522440 .... $39.99

Milos **Forman**

One Flew Over the Cuckoo's Nest
(1975) Jack Nicholson, Will Sampson, Scatman Crothers, Danny De Vito. A powerful look at life in a state insane asylum where catatonia is the preferred state and nonconformity is considered dangerous. Nicholson delivers a stunning performance as the rebellious inmate who attempts to instigate mutiny

6301931033 .... $19.99

Bob **Fosse**

Cabaret
(1972) Directed by legendary dance choreographer Fosse

6302281415 .... $19.99

William **Friedkin**

The French Connection
(1971) Gene Hackman as maverick New York City cop Popeye Doyle who is determined to stop an international narcotics ring. Thrilling chase scenes through the streets of New York

6302238331 .... $14.98

Terry **Gilliam** & Terry **Jones**

Monty Python and the Holy Grail
(1974)

6302293553 .... $19.99

Werner **Herzog**

Aguirre, the Wrath of God
(1972) Lush Amazon location shooting marks this story of a conquistador's search for the seven cities of gold

630195517X $29.99

George Roy **Hill**

The Sting

(1973) Paul Newman, Robert Redford, Robert Shaw, Charles Durning. Newman and Redford play '30s con-men trying to put "the sting" on a New York City mobster who ordered the murder of a friend

6300l8224X $19.95

John **Huston**

Man Who Would Be King

(1975) Michael Caine, Sean Connery, Christopher Plummer. A spirited rendering of Kipling's famous tale

6300251160 .... $19.98

James **Ivory**

Bombay Talkie

(1970) An English woman becomes involved with a star of the Indian cinema and destroys his life. Outstanding bits include a guru showing a slideshow of his triumph in L.A., and a musical rehearsal with zaftig Indian girls dancing on typewriter keys

630015145X $19.95

The Europeans

(1979) An extravagant, freewheeling European countess and her brother visit their wealthy, puritanical American cousins in Henry James's classic of culture clash

6303593569 .... $59.95

Elia **Kazan**

The Last Tycoon

(1976) Robert De Niro, Tony Curtis, Robert Mitchum, Jeanne Moreau, Jack Nicholson. A Hollywood adaptation of Fitzgerald's story about the moral vacancy of Hollywood

6300216675 .... $19.95

Stanley **Kubrick**

Barry Lyndon

(1975) Ryan O'Neal, Marisa Berenson, Patrick Magee. A meticulous, glacially detached meditation on the 18th century: perhaps Kubrick's most original film

6300269426 .... $29.98

A Clockwork Orange

(1971) Highly stylized violence, brilliant use of color, and a slangy pidgin derived from Anthony Burgess's novel mark this futuristic tale of violence, depravity, and Pavlovian behavior modification

6300268101 .... $19.99

George **Lucas**

Star Wars Trilogy

(1977) The complete set of the classic science fiction trilogy with its incredible effects, epic plotting, and Oedipal subtext

6303617700 .... $59.99

Sidney **Lumet**

Murder on the Orient Express

(1974) Albert Finney, Lauren Bacall, Martin Balsam, Ingrid Bergman, Jacqueline Bisset, Jean-Pierre Cassel, Sean Connery, John Gielgud, Anthony Perkins, Vanessa Redgrave, Rachel Roberts, Richard Widmark, Michael York. An Agatha Christie murder mystery with an all-star cast of possible suspects on board a train

6300216721 .... $29.95

Terrence **Malick**

Days of Heaven

(1978) A richly photographed vision of a love triangle set in the Midwest at the turn of the century

6300216969 .... $14.99

Mike **Nichols**

Catch-22

(1970) Alan Arkin, Martin Balsam, Richard Benjamin, Anthony Perkins, Orson Welles, Jon Voight, Art Garfunkel, Jack Gilford, Buck Henry, Bob Newhart, Paula Prentiss, Martin Sheen. Based on the darkly humorous, influential Joseph Heller novel

6301015304 .... $19.95

Nagisa **Oshima**

In the Realm of the Senses

(1976)

6303402097 .... $19.99

Pier Paolo **Pasolini**

Arabian Nights

(1974)

6301149599 .... $79.99

Roman **Polanski**

Chinatown

(1974) Jack Nicholson, Faye Dunaway, John Huston, Diane Ladd, Roman Polanski. Retro noir set in '30s Los Angeles, based on Robert Towne's impeccable screenplay. One of the five best films of the 70's, this has it all: bizarre violence, money, beauty, and depravity

6300216500 .... $19.95

Tess

(1979) Nastassia Kinski, Peter Firth. A young woman is slowly and hauntingly destroyed in this adaptation of Hardy's epic novel. Unrelentingly beautiful cinematography

6300136221 .... $29.95

Sydney **Pollack**

3 Days of the Condor

(1976) Robert Redford plays a reader for the CIA whose entire office is wiped out in a violent attack. He then goes underground and uncovers a sinister plot involving his own government. Excellent '70s spin on bureaucratic paranoia

6300216748 .... $14.99

The Way We Were

(1973) Barbra Streisand, Robert Redford. Twenty years in the lives of a blond buttoned-up writer (Redford) who has fallen hard for his opposite, a frizzy-haired leftist played by the vivacious Streisand. Despite their differences, the chemistry on screen is tangible. Marvin Hamlisch won an Academy Award for his score

6302824419 .... $14.95

Bob **Rafelson**

Five Easy Pieces

(1970) Jack Nicholson stars in this perceptive character study of a talented musician who gives up music for the life of a blue-collar laborer

6302757096 .... $14.99

Eric **Rohmer**

Claire's Knee

(1971) A vacation house in the north of France is the setting for Rohmer's chatty and perceptive exploration of love and desire

6303911366 .... $19.99

Franklin J. **Schaffner**

Patton

(1970) George C. Scott, Karl Malden, Michael Bates. Impressive film biography of the ill-tempered, controlling World War II General. Scott gives a truly amazing performance

6300246817 .... $29.98

Martin **Scorsese**

Mean Streets

(1973)

6300268691 .... $19.99

Taxi Driver

(1976) Paul Schrader's taut and claustrophobic script, which he wrote in just eight days, and Scorsese's perfect pacing make this story of a paranoid cab driver on a misguided quest for greatness and purity one of the best films of the decade

6303686796 .... $9.99

Ridley **Scott**

Alien

(1979) The special effects in this science fiction classic are extremely advanced. Sigourney Weaver crafts her character Ripley into one of the most compelling screen heroines of the genre

6300247171 .... $14.99

Andrei **Tarkovsky**

Solaris

(1972)

630212042X $19.99

François **Truffaut**

Story of Adele H

(1975) French

6302180236 .... $19.99

The '80s

Chantal **Akerman**

Toute une Nuit

(1982)

6301828712 .... $29.99

Woody **Allen**

Another Woman

(1988) Gena Rowlands, Mia Farrow, Ian Holm, Blythe Danner, Gene Hackman, Betty Buckley, Martha Plimpton, John Houseman, Sandy Dennis. A middle-aged professor on sabbatical rents a tiny apartment in New York, where she thinks she's found academic manna. Then a neighbor's confessions to her psychologist—replete with philosophical ponderings on the meaning of life, and the meaning of marriage—begin to permeate the thin walls and shed some light on her own banal existence. Marvelous performances

6301264169 .... $14.98

Broadway Danny Rose
(1984)
6303636381 ....$14.99

The Purple Rose of Cairo
(1985)
6303636403 ....$14.99

Pedro **Almodóvar**

Women on the Verge of a Nervous Breakdown
(1988) Carmen Maura, Antonio Banderas, Julieta Serrano, Maria Barranco, Bossy De Palma. Irreverent and stylish, Almodóvar is the comic genius of Spanish cinema. His first American success is based on Cocteau's *The Human Voice* and tells the story of an actress who has recently been left by her lover. Subplots of Shiite terrorists and spiked gazpacho round out this outrageous comedy
6301536037 ....$19.98

Richard **Attenborough**

Gandhi
(1982) Ben Kingsley, Candice Bergen, Edward Fox, John Gielgud, Trevor Howard, John Mills, Martin Sheen. Kingsley gives an outstanding performance in this beautifully filmed account of the pacifist Indian leader
6301863151 ....$29.95

Hector **Babenco**

Kiss of the Spider Woman
(1985) Based on Manuel Puig's controversial play about two prisoners—one a committed revolutionary, the other a dreaming homosexual window-dresser. Phenomenal performances by William Hurt, Raul Julia, and Sonia Braga
630383258X $14.99

Jean-Jacques **Beineix**

Diva
(1982) A mailman finds himself in an interesting situation when his bootlegged recording of his favorite superstar diva gets mixed up with another tape incriminating gangsters
6304006837 ....$29.99

Bruce **Beresford**

Driving Miss Daisy
(1989) Jessica Tandy, Morgan Freeman, Dan Aykroyd, Patti LuPone, Esther Rolle. A touching account of the relationship between a cantankerously independent Southern gentlewoman and her kind, resilient black chauffeur
6301734734 ....$19.98

Claude **Berri**

Jean de Florette
(1986) Yves Montand, Gerard Depardieu. Marcel Pagnol's Provence brought richly to life
6301094476 ....$19.98

Manon of the Spring
(1986) French. Yves Montand, Emmanuelle Beart. A daughter seeks revenge in the follow-up to *Jean de Florette*
6301094468 ....$19.98

Bernardo **Bertolucci**

The Last Emperor
(1987) John Lone, Joan Chen, Peter O'Toole. Stunning epic drama of the life of Pu Yi, who was Emperor of the Forbidden City at the age of three, chronicling his life from "little god" to puppet emperor under Japan, to quiet gardener in Communist China
6301055845 ....$19.95

Kenneth **Branagh**

Henry V
(1989) Kenneth Branagh, Derek Jacobi, Emma Thompson. A lively, intelligent, earthy presentation of the warrior king
6301863240 ....$89.98

Albert **Brooks**

Lost in America
(1985) Two yuppies give up the good life to travel across America
6300270653 ....$14.99

James L. **Brooks**

Terms of Endearment
(1983) Debra Winger, Shirley Maclaine, Jack Nicholson, Jeff Daniels, John Lithgow, Danny De Vito. A funny tear-jerker—MacLaine and Winger are astounding as a mother and daughter who support, love, and battle each other through the best and worst of times. Based on Larry McMurtry's novel
6300214117 ....$14.95

James **Cameron**

The Terminator
(1984) An apocalyptic film that melds the past and present in its examination of the one man who can save the world and the one woman who can save him
6303566677 ....$19.99

Chen Kaige

Yellow Earth
(1984)
6302917050 ....$19.99

Joel **Coen**

Blood Simple
(1984) The Cohen brothers' slow and darkly comic neo-noir tale skewers many of the genre's conventions
6300184110 ....$14.99

David **Cronenberg**

Dead Ringers
(1988) Twin gynecologists who date the same drug-addicted actress gradually lose touch with reality and become addicted to heroin
6301269780 ....$9.99

Scanners
(1981)
6302353874 ....$9.99

Cameron **Crowe**

Say Anything...
(1989) John Cusack, Ione Skye, Lili Taylor, Joan Cusack, Eric Stoltz, Bebe Neuwirth. Cusack, a regular guy, goes after Skye, class brain and beauty. Surprisingly—or maybe not—she falls for him. Crowe's directorial debut offers a fresh look at post-high school teenage life and love
6301412761 ....$19.98

Brian **De Palma**

Blow Out
(1981) A political candidate in Philadelphia dies in a suspicious car wreck accidentally recorded by a sound specialist played by John Travolta
6303471587 ....$12.99

Robert **Epstein**

The Life and Times of Harvey Milk
(1984) A film that greatly deserved the Academy Award it received. Originally intended to focus on anti-gay legislation, the work was enlarged as a tribute to America's first openly gay politician, following his assassination alongside San Francisco's Mayor Moscone
6300219380 ....$19.95

Federico **Fellini**

And the Ship Sails On
(1983) A ship full of opera stars sets off to bury a compatriot at sea. Wonderful, ludicrous details like a symphony played on wine glasses and divas singing to the stokers enrich this nostalgic piece, set on the eve of World War I
6300136965 ....$59.95

City of Women
(1980) A man dozes on a train, finding himself in a dreamland of militant feminists. Fellini swears that every word uttered at the Women's Lib Conference was lifted from feminist literature
6301599934 ....$79.95

Intervista
(1987) *The* film for Fellini aficionados. A revealing mock-documentary about the making of a film about Fellini in which he produces Kafka's *Amerika*. An illuminating and personal glimpse behind the camera
6302732921 ....$89.95

Milos **Forman**

Amadeus
(1984) Stunning costumes, great music, magnificent acting, and a splendid screenplay made this account of the life of Mozart a sure win for Best Picture
6301932919 ....$19.98

Stephen **Frears**

Dangerous Liaisons
(1988) Glenn Close, John Malkovich, Michelle Pfeiffer, Uma Thurman. An elegant minuet of aristocratic evil
6301334523 ....$19.98

Patrick **Garland**

A Doll's House
(1989) Claire Bloom, Anthony Hopkins. Ibsen's dramatic masterpiece about women's rights and the nuances of marriage remains disturbingly relevant today
6302270553 ....$14.95

Terry **Gilliam**

Brazil
(1985) Director Gilliam was the cartoonist for Monty Python. His unique vision and technical acumen is evidenced here
6300184064 ....$14.99

Serif **Goren**

Yol

(1982) A convict returns home while on "leave" from prison

6302824435 ....$19.99

Lasse **Hallstrom**

My Life as a Dog

(1985) Anton Glanzelius, Manfred Serner, Anki Liden, Tomas von Brimssen. An amazingly mature performance from the child star, Anton Glanzelius, who captures the mischievous and earnest nature of childhood as his character struggles to come to terms with disappointments and events beyond his comprehension

6301228596 ....$19.95

Agnieszka **Holland**

Angry Harvest

(1986) A Jewish woman dodges her fate by escaping the train bound for a Nazi death camp only to be imprisoned by a farmer who becomes obsessed with her. A captivating and paradoxical story wonderfully executed on screen

6300984486 ....$69.95

Hugh **Hudson**

Chariots of Fire

(1981) Ben Cross, Ian Holm, John Gielgud. A wealthy Jew and a devout Scottish divinity scholar, both Oxford students, run for Britain in the 1924 Olympics

6300271498 ....$19.98

John **Huston**

Prizzi's Honor

(1985) Jack Nicholson, Kathleen Turner, Robert Loggia, Anjelica Huston. A satiric look at the workings of a mob family. Huston's brilliant direction highlights the varied strengths of his talented cast

6300262782 ....$29.98

Juzo **Itami**

Tampopo

(1986) The search for the perfect noodle

6301038983 ....$19.98

James **Ivory**

The Bostonians

(1984) Christopher Reeve, Vanessa Redgrave, Madeleine Potter, Jessica Tandy. A tale of subverted passion, and a superb evocation of Henry James's novel. Reeve and Redgrave compete for the attentions of a young suffragette

6302034027 ....$79.98

Maurice

(1987) This beautifully crafted Merchant-Ivory adaptation of the E.M. Forster novel tells the story of a young man attempting to comprehend his homosexuality with unflinching honesty and grace

6301651529 ....$19.98

A Room with a View

(1985) Maggie Smith, Helena Bonham-Carter, Denholm Elliot, Julian Sands, Daniel Day Lewis. The locations—Florence, Tuscany, the Home Counties—are so beautifully shot that this film would be a moving experience with no actors at all. But the superb performances from the entire cast have a sublime effect on nature itself. A fitting tribute to Forster's novel

6300250512 ....$19.98

Terry **Jones**

The Meaning of Life

(1983) Nearly as insightful as Bergman, with some uncanny similarities to *The Seventh Seal*. The Busby Berkeley-esque "Every Sperm is Sacred" song and dance extravanganza is outstanding

6300182797 ....$59.95

Lawrence **Kasdan**

The Big Chill

(1983) Tom Berenger, Glenn Close, Jeff Goldblum, William Hurt, Kevin Kline, Mary Kay Place, Meg Tilly, JoBeth Williams. A group of college friends reunite for the funeral of a friend, and spend the weekend under one roof

6302752337 ....$14.95

Philip **Kaufman**

The Unbearable Lightness of Being

(1987) Daniel Day Lewis, Juliette Binoche, Lena Olin. Loosely based on Milan Kundera's novel, this phenomenal film explores one man's sexual insatiability. Day-Lewis plays a hedonistic neurosurgeon unable to reconcile two polar attributes—weight and lightness—in one woman

6301179501 ....$19.98

Irvin **Kershner**

The Empire Strikes Back

(1980) The best of the trilogy

6301792769 ....$19.99

Stanley **Kubrick**

Full Metal Jacket

(1987) Kubrick's brutal look at the Vietnam conflict

6301021118 ....$19.99

The Shining

(1980) Jack Nicholson, Shelley Duvall, Danny Lloyd, Scatman Crothers. Evil ghosts in a haunted hotel possess the winter innkeeper, turning him violently against his family. Written by Stephen King, this film is high in psychological tension; Nicholson's facial expressions provide a barometer of his madness

6300268675 ....$19.98

Akira **Kurosawa**

Kagemusha

(1980)

6301661737 ....$19.99

Ran

(1985) Kurosawa's variation on Shakespeare's *King Lear* is set in 16-century Japan and contains some of the most gruesome battle scenes in film history. *Ran*, "chaos" in Japanese, prevails as a kingdom is divided

6300248518 ....$29.98

David **Lean**

A Passage to India

(1984) Peggy Ashcroft, Judy Davis, Victor Banerjee, Alec Guinness. From E.M. Forster's novel, this exquisitely acted film details the life of a sexually repressed young woman, who in an attempt to acquaint herself socially with Indian natives ends up accusing an Indian doctor of rape. A powerful allegory of imperialism

6302814138 ....$19.98

Spike **Lee**

Do the Right Thing

(1989) Lee's best film. Examines racial tensions in New York City, using a pizza shop as a microcosm

6301562291 ....$19.99

Barry **Levinson**

Rain Man

(1988) Dustin Hoffman, Tom Cruise. Hoffman won an Oscar for his unbeatable performance as Raymond, an autistic savant with an uncanny talent for remembering seemingly random numbers and trivial facts

6301976681 ....$19.98

Sidney **Lumet**

Prince of the City

(1981) A New York City police officer is victimized after he exposes corruption in his own department

630027182X $24.99

David **Lynch**

The Elephant Man

(1980) Anthony Hopkins, John Hurt, Ann Bancroft. A humanistic look at the suffering of a man born seriously deformed and ostracized by Victorian society. Lynch has vividly re-created post-Industrial Revolution London

6300214044 ....$14.95

Louis **Malle**

Atlantic City

(1980) An aging would-be player (Burt Lancaster) falls in love with a beautiful black-jack dealer and gets mixed up in a messy world of cocaine and fast money

6300214206 ....$14.99

Au Revoir Les Enfants

(1987) An unforgettable and heartbreaking story based on Malle's childhood memory of two young Jewish boys who had to pass for Christians at a boarding school situated in Nazi-occupied France

63121613X $19.98

David **Mamet**

House of Games

(1987) David Mamet's directing debut showcases his trademark urban patter in the story of a psychiatrist who becomes involved with a con man

6304108877 ....$12.99

George **Miller**

The Road Warrior

(1981) Mad Max in a post-apocalyptic Australian wasteland

6302877849 ....$14.99

Errol **Morris**

The Thin Blue Line

(1988) An extraordinary piece of investigative journalism, stylishly edited, argues the case for Randall Adams's innocence of murder charges. Everyone connected to this case appears guilty. The crime, the trial, and the conviction are examined from every possible angle, making it impossible to feel confidence in the jury's decision that Adams killed a police officer in 1976

6301928229 ....$89.99

Sydney **Pollack**

Out of Africa

(1985) Meryl Streep, Robert Redford, Klaus Maria Brandauer. This romantic drama features an unconventionally strong woman (modeled on author Isak Dinesen) who, in her husband's absence, falls in love with a British rogue played by Redford. Although the film has been criticized for romanticizing colonialism in Africa, its rich cinematography and carefully constructed narrative should not be missed

6300185095 .... $19.95

Robert **Redford**

Ordinary People

(1980) Donald Sutherland, Mary Tyler Moore, Judd Hirsch, Timothy Hutton, Elizabeth McGovern. Robert Redford's directorial debut, based on the popular novel by Judith Guest, explores the deterioration of a seemingly normal family coming to terms with tragedy

6306216977 .... $14.95

Carl **Reiner**

All of Me

(1984) Steve Martin, in one of his most hilarious performances, is inhabited by the spirit of a dead woman

6302559545 .... $19.99

Eric **Rohmer**

Pauline at the Beach

(1983) An entertaining comedy of morals about a teenage girl who spends the summer with her older cousin. French

6302405858 .... $24.99

Summer

(1986) A depressed young woman seeks solace on vacation: one of Rohmer's best. French

6300219712 .... $29.95

Paul **Schrader**

Mishima: A Life in Four Chapters

(1985) A thorough—at times astonishing—dramatization of Japan's most controversial post-WWII author, activist, and playwright. Mishima's life is mirrored in the complexity of the narrative. Score by Philip Glass

6300270939 .... $79.99

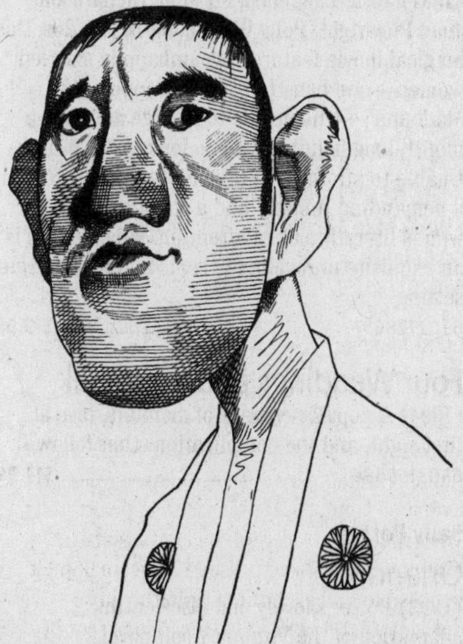

Yukio Mishima

Barbet **Schroeder**

Barfly

(1987) Mickey Rourke, Faye Dunaway. A young, honest, and angst-ridden budding writer prefers heavy drinking and scrapping in L.A. dives to his publisher's lavish estate. The recently deceased Charles Bukowski wrote the semi-autobiographical script with an unheard-of caveat: the director was not allowed to change a word without Bukowski's permission

6301008901 .... $19.98

Martin **Scorsese**

King of Comedy

(1983)

6303982662 .... $19.99

Raging Bull

(1980) Robert De Niro, Cathy Moriarty, Joe Pesci. A black and white rendering of the life of near-great heavywieght fighter Jake La Motta, with superbly choreographed, stop-action fight sequences and a dark subtext of the perils of freindship and desire

6301978900 .... $19.98

Ridley **Scott**

Blade Runner/Directors Cut

(1982) The story of a bounty hunter who hunts androids in a rainy, futuristic, meticulously imagined Los Angeles. This directors cut removes much of the intrusive voice over

6302732778 .... $19.99

Jim **Sheridan**

My Left Foot

(1989) An anguishing account of the Irish writer and painter Cristy Brown who overcomes the obstacles of cerebral palsy. Daniel Day Lewis and Brenda Fricker won Oscars for their roles

6301930584 .... $19.98

Steven **Spielberg**

Raiders of the Lost Ark

(1981) Harrison Ford, Karen Allen, Wolf Kahler, Paul Freeman. A genuinely thrilling film that takes you to the far reaches of the earth with an array of Oscar-winning visual and aural effects. Ford as Indiana Jones, an archaeologist in a race with the Nazis to recover the priceless and powerful Ark of the Covenant

6300214060 .... $14.95

Oliver **Stone**

Platoon

(1986) Tom Berenger, Willem Dafoe, Charlie Sheen, Forest Whitaker, Francesco Quinn. Sheen, an innocent American youth, goes to Vietnam and discovers hell on earth

6301115430 .... $14.98

Giuseppe **Tornatore**

Cinema Paradiso

(1989) Philippe Noiret, Jacques Perrin, Salvatore Cascio, Agnese Nano. Best Foreign Language Film Oscar winner. A small boy's coming of age under the influence of an old projectionist

6302000823 .... $19.98

Daniel **Vigne**

The Return of Martin Guerre

(1982) A peasant returns home to his family after seven years' absence only to find that no one recognizes him or believes he is who he says he is, if indeed he is telling the truth. The basis for the more recent American film *Somersby.* French

6304192266 .... $29.99

Peter **Weir**

Dead Poets Society

(1989) Robin Williams, Robert Sean Leonard, Ethan Hawke. Williams is a vivacious English teacher who brings new meaning to *veni, vedi, vici* as he inspires his students with his passion for poetry at a less-than-passionate New England boarding school. Won a a well-deserved Oscar for Best Screenplay

6301627768 .... $19.99

John **Woo**

The Killer

(1989) Woo, Hong Kong's best-known cinematic export, displays his impressive editing in the seamless action sequences. Occasionally weighed down by the less-than-subtle religious overtones. Cantonese

6302989817 .... $19.95

The '90s

Woody **Allen**

The quintessential New York director who combines self-deprecating humor with incisive comedy on the mores of the urban upper middle class. Allen has distinguished himself as a stand-up comedian, a playwright, a screenwriter, a director, and even as a jazz clarinetist—he has a regular gig on Manhattan's Upper West Side.

Bullets over Broadway

(1994)

6303430546 .... $19.99

Husbands and Wives

(1992)

6302697042 .... $19.99

Manhattan Murder Mystery

(1993)

6303011411 .... $19.99

Robert **Altman**

The Player

(1992) Tim Robbins, Greta Scacchi, Fred Ward, Whoopi Goldberg, Peter Gallagher, Dean Stockwell, Sydney Pollack, Lyle Lovett. A movie about the making of movies, but also an intriguing murder mystery. Its creator Altman is the ultimate insider, with a wicked sense of humor

6302689171 .... $94.95

Bruce **Beresford**

Black Robe

(1991)

6302336562 .... $14.99

Ken **Burns**

Baseball

(1991) A nine-inning boxed set from noted documentary filmmaker Ken Burns. Features Paul Newman, Jason Robards, Bob Costas, plus every baseball legend from Shoeless Joe to Joe DiMaggio. Spans the history of this timeless American sport

6303218725 .... $179.95

The Civil War

(1994) Nine-volume set. The riveting, acclaimed PBS documentary that spawned a national obsession with the War Between the States

6301996135 .... $179.95

Tim **Burton**

Ed Wood

(1994) Burton's homage to the angora-clad director of dreadfully bad (so much so as to be considered classics of sorts) science fiction films

6303407188 .... $9.99

Jane **Campion**

An Angel at My Table

(1990) A psychologically captivating yet humorous depiction of a young woman who's unjustly diagnosed as a schizophrenic and sent to a mental hospital for eight years, this is an engrossing portrait of New Zealand writer Janet Frame

6302290619 .... $19.95

The Piano

(1993) A woman married to a cold-hearted settler in New Zealand has an emotional and spiritual epiphany when she becomes involved with his rival while learning how to play the piano

630307362X $14.99

Chen Kaige

Farewell My Concubine

(1993)

6303187196 .... $19.99

Joel **Coen**

Barton Fink

The hallucinatory story of a Hollywood screenwriter's monumental case of writer's block

6302291879 .... $19.99

Kevin **Costner**

Dances with Wolves

(1990) First-time director Costner netted an Oscar

6302415853 .... $14.98

David **Cronenberg**

Naked Lunch

(1991) Peter Weller, Judy Davis, Ian Holm, Julian Sands, Roy Scheider. An original and surprising Burroughs adaptation to film. Pure Cronenberg—that is, crazily creative. Soundtrack by Ornette Coleman

6302390486 .... $94.98

Terence **Davies**

The Long Day Closes

(1992)

6303023053 .... $19.99

Jan **De Bont**

Speed

(1994) Breakneck pacing and tight plotting make this Keanu Reeves action vehicle an incredible ride

6303257844 .... $14.99

Jonathan **Demme**

The Silence of the Lambs

(1991) Jodie Foster, Anthony Hopkins, Scott Glenn. Sweeping the 1991 Academy Awards, this chilling psycho-thriller brought Hannibal "The Cannibal" Lecter into the nightmares of millions. Hopkins is extraordinary in the role of the imprisoned serial killer, while Foster is impeccable as the young FBI cadet who seeks the jailed doctor's psychiatric expertise to help her catch a serial killer

6302171725 .... $19.98

Clint **Eastwood**

The Unforgiven

(1992) Eastwood won an Oscar for Best Director in this updating of the classic themes of Hollywood Westerns

6302769051 .... $19.99

James **Foley**

Glengarry Glen Ross

(1992) David Mamet's sharp and authentic dialogue shines in this examination of the soullessness of salesmanship

6302732875 .... $14.99

Stephen **Frears**

The Grifters

(1990) A heavy Freudian subtext distinguishes this alternately dramatic and darkly comedic story of small-time con artists. With Annette Bening, John Cusack, and Anjelica Huston

630201770X $9.99

Agnieszka **Holland**

Europa, Europa

(1990) A heart-pounding account of a young Jewish man who comes of age while concealing his identity first from the Russians, then from the Germans

6302405939 .... $79.98

James **Ivory**

Howards End

(1992) Vanessa Redgrave, Helena Bonham-Carter, Emma Thompson, Anthony Hopkins, Jemma Redgrave. A costume drama based on E.M. Forster's famous novel

6302744121 .... $95.95

Emma Thompson

Neil **Jordan**

The Crying Game

(1992) Gender-bending story of an IRA soldier who travels to London to find the girlfriend of a British prisoner he inadvertently killed

6302779421 .... $14.99

Philip **Kaufman**

Henry & June

(1990) Based on the often explicit memoirs of diarist Anaïs Nin, this film delves into the illicit love affair that took place between expatriate American writer Henry Miller and Nin. Stunningly directed, Ward captures the hardboiled honesty and blunt boorishness that made Miller such an unforgettable literary figure

630194531X $19.99

Ang **Lee**

The Wedding Banquet

(1993)

6303201261 .... $96.99

Spike **Lee**

Malcolm X

(1992) Denzel Washington gives a powerful performance

6302787556 .... $24.99

Mike **Leigh**

Life Is Sweet

(1990) A funny portrayal of a working-class couple and their twin daughters by the director of *Naked* and *Secrets and Lies*

6302451930 .... $14.99

Baz **Luhrmann**

Strictly Ballroom

(1992)

6302994063 .... $14.99

Louis **Malle**

Vanya on 42nd Street

(1994)

630349918X $19.99

Mike **Newell**

Enchanted April

(1991) Josie Lawrence, Miranda Richardson, Joan Plowright, Polly Walker. Set in the '20s, this magical movie features two unhappily married women—one hausfrau, one "disappointed Madonna"—who decide to splurge and take a month-long holiday at a gracious castle in Italy. Unable to afford it, they invite two other women, a demanding spinster and a glamorous flapper who is literally sick of attention. What results is an exquisite unraveling of souls in a picturesque setting

6302728657 .... $19.95

Four Weddings and a Funeral

(1994) A popular comedy of manners, love at first sight, and the complications that follow

6303165680 .... $14.99

Sally **Potter**

Orlando

(1992) Potter's lovely and disorienting adaptation of the Virginia Woolf novel

630305904X $19.99

Robert **Redford**

Quiz Show

(1994) A look at the '50s quiz-show scandal that undercut the American public's trust in the media

6303407161 ....$19.99

Martin **Scorsese**

The Age of Innocence

(1993) Lavish costumes and sets dominate this adapatation of Edith Wharton's novel of forbidden love among upper-class New Yorkers

6303026206 ....$14.99

Goodfellas

(1990) Scorsese's reevaluation of the gangster genre traces the fall and decline of the mob brought on by new blood and drugs. He punctuates his point by closing the soundtrack with a Sid Vicious cover of Frank Sinatra's "I Did It My Way"

6302054982 ....$19.99

Tony **Scott**

True Romance

(1994) Christian Slater, Patricia Arquette, Dennis Hopper, Christopher Walken, Gary Oldman. This Quentin Tarantino-scripted road movie receives big-budget treatment by director Scott and the result is mesmerizing: Lush cinematography complements dynamite dialogue as the plot spins out of control toward a '90s version of the Mexican stand-off

6302968119 ....$19.98

Steven **Spielberg**

Schindler's List

(1993) Spielberg's most emotional and committed film tells the true story of Oskar Schindler, a German responsible for saving the lives of hundreds of Jews during the Holocaust

6303168507 ....$29.99

Quentin **Tarantino**

Pulp Fiction

(1994) Tarantino's dialogue is at its gritty, postmodern best and his fractured plotting is dazzling. Took the Grand Jury Prize at Cannes

630395345X $19.99

Quentin Tarantino

Reservoir Dogs

(1992) Harvey Keitel, Tim Roth, Michael Madsen, Chris Penn, Steve Buscemi, Lawrence Tierney, Randy Brooks, Kirk Baltz, Eddie Bunker, Quentin Tarantino, voice of Steven Wright. Tarantino's debut showcases all of his trademarks: horrific but darkly comic violence, wickedly poetic dialogue, and disorientingly brilliant narrative form. His encyclopedic movie-making sensibility allows him to break every rule he knows. Splattered with witty references to classic noir thrillers including *The Killing* and *The Asphalt Jungle,* it examines a botched robbery through flashback. With an excellent ensemble cast

630268644X $19.98

Michael **Tolkin**

The Rapture

(1991) A surreal examination of a beautiful woman's escape from hedonistic boredom into extreme religious zealotry

6303915027 ....$14.99

Giuseppe **Tornatore**

Everybody's Fine

(1991) Marcello Mastroianni, Michele Morgan. From a perceptive and masterful director comes this tale of disillusion. Mastroianni adapts brilliantly to his role as the retired widower and civil servant who voyages throughout Italy to see his five grown children, only to discover that they're all in various states of disrepair. Italian

6302423449 ....$89.95

Rose **Troche**

Go Fish

(1994) Guinivere Turner, V.S. Brodie, T. Wendy McMillan, Migdalia Menendez, Anastasia Sharp. Vividly alive characters and true-to-life depictions of young lesbian love abound in this romantic comedy. Max, young and beautiful, seeks love in the person of Ely, older and less than beautiful, as the comedy of relationships unfolds

6302728541 ....$14.95

John **Woo**

Hard-Boiled

(1992) Woo delivers the best action sequences around

6303158552 ....$19.99

Zhang Yimou

Ju Dou

(1989) Originally banned in China, *Ju Dou* tells the story of a young woman living in the '20s who is forced to marry an elderly, ill-tempered man

6302194253 ....$19.99

Raise the Red Lantern

(1991) Chinese

6302645891 ....$19.99

Children's Videos

Big Bird in China

Big Bird's quest for the legendary Chinese phoenix

0-394-89755-2 ....$14.95

Big Bird in Japan

0-679-82093-0 ....$14.95

Big Bird's Story Time

0-394-88934-7 ....$9.95

Charlie and the Chocolate Factory

Roald Dahl's popular tale made into an entertaining and cautionary movie. Gene Wilder is a diabolical Willie Wonka, and the comeuppance of little Charlie's greedy rivals is just vicious enough to appeal greatly to the 5-11 age group

6300269531 ....$19.98

Charlotte's Web

Voices of Debbie Reynolds, Henry Gibson, Paul Lynde, Agnes Moorehead. E.B. White's story of Wilbur, a runt pig, whose barnyard friends protect him from the frying pan

6300216357 ....$14.95

The Elephant's Child

Jack Nicholson narrates this Kipling adaptation about an elephant encountering the trials of life. Soundtrack by Bobby McFerrin

6302275822 ....$9.95

Fantasia

Hippos, mushrooms, and other suggestively unusual creatures dance to Beethoven, Mozart, and the like

6302158095 ....$24.99

Homeward Bound: The Incredible Journey

Three households pets set out across America to find their owners

6302794390 ....$22.99

How the Grinch Stole Christmas

Boris Karloff narrates this animated 26-minute Dr. Seuss classic

6301969707 ....$12.95

The Lion King

(1994) The endearing tale of Simba, the future King, whose path to the throne is hindered by the travails of youth, a wild gang of hyenas, and a conniving uncle

6303314015 ....$26.99

The Phantom Tollbooth

Part live action, part animation, adapted from the Norton Juster novel of a world where words are hoarded and numbers are eaten

6301971523 ....$19.98

Rudolf the Red Nosed Reindeer

This vintage account of the red nosed reindeer's life was animated by Max Fleischer

6301392884 ....$12.98

Rudyard Kipling: The Elephant's Child

Jack Nicholson narrates this story of a baby elephant as it learns life's hard lessons

0-394-87861-2 ....$9.95

Santa Bear's First Christmas
Santa Bear meets Santa Claus. Score by Michael Hedges
6301404807 ....$9.98

Pinocchio
Another Disney classic. The story of a lonely old man's wooden puppet who eventually becomes a real little boy
See also THE '40S
6302642248 ....$24.95

Shipwrecked
A young boy goes to sea seeking fortune and finds himself battling a pirate for a buried treasure
6302088143 ....$19.95

Snow White and the Seven Dwarfs
The crisp animation in Walt Disney's landmark first feature continues to amaze even in this era of hi-tech cartoons
6303123317 ....$26.99

The Swiss Family Robinson
A Swiss family in search of a new life gets shipwrecked on a tropical island
6302428106 ....$19.99

Thumbelina
Rags-to-riches tale of a tiny girl
6303144837 ....$19.98

Twenty Thousand Leagues Under the Sea
Based on Jules Verne's novel. The lushly Victorian interior of the *Nautilus* is wonderfully rendered and the acting is excellent all around
6301862724 ....$12.95

Watership Down
An animated version of the Richard Adams book, focusing on the secret world of rabbits. With Zero Mostel, John Hurt, and Ralph Richardson providing some of the voices
6300272850 ....$19.98

Part 13

Lifestyles & Practical Advice

Carl Djerassi, inventor of "the pill"

A Warm Prison

The baby is closely confined in a warm dark prison of exquisite, neutral comfort; everything around him is of the same texture and at the same temperature as himself. There is no friction, no sensation, no change. His eyes are ready but there is nothing for him to see. He has no need to breathe or to digest food, so he feels no sensations from within himself. He can sense sound and movement, but muffled by his insulated liquid environment.

—Penelope Leach
Your Baby and Child
1396

Suck Reflex

I mention to women who plan to breast-feed that it may hurt when they begin. The baby's suck reflex can be amazingly strong. Also, breast milk ducts can go into spasms at first and hurt until the milk starts flowing. I reassure mothers-to-be that after a few initial feedings the spasms will stop, and the resultant feeling will be pleasure.

—T. Berry Brazelton, M.D.
Touchpoints
1395

Big Boy

Accept any offers from the older child but don't make too much of the "You're my big boy" line. He may not be feeling at all big. Indeed he is probably feeling that his bigness is his whole trouble; if he were tiny he would be getting all the attention like that beastly baby. To have to help in order to get your approval may be the last straw.

—Penelope Leach
Your Baby and Child
1396

The Rest of Our Lives

Ideally our children will wean us from our habit of making decisions for them, but we're more aware that we made our own parents go cold turkey—by not soliciting, for example, so much as their opinion when it came to decisions like where (or whether) we'd go to college, whom we'd marry, and what we intended to do with the rest of our lives.

—Melinda M. Marshall
Good Enough Mothers
1397

Communication

Michelle: How many people are coming for dinner?
Gary: Don't worry. There'll be enough food.

Ned: Are you leaving now?
Valerie: You can take a nap if you want.

Ned: Are you just about finished?
Valerie: Do you want to have supper now?

—Deborah Tannen, M.D.
You Just Don't Understand
1385

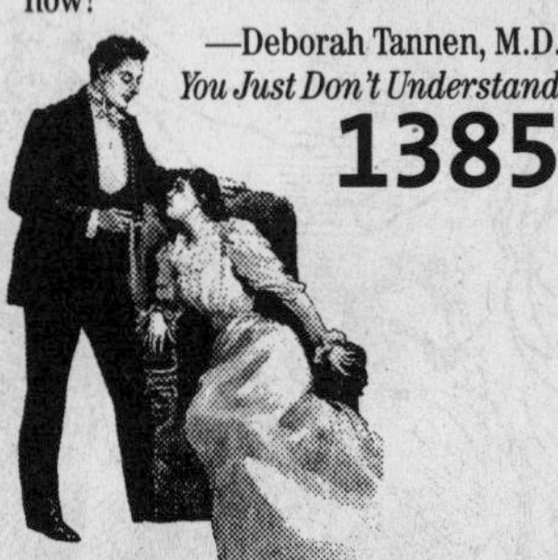

Wild in Bed

Place erotic Japanese prints, elegant, sexy photos, and sensuous statuettes in strategic locations around your bedroom, then draw his attention to them at crucial moments. Maybe that position would be fun.

—Olivia St. Claire
203 Ways to Drive a Man Wild in Bed
1387

Difficult Kisses

Long Kisses: Don't panic. Some people get anxious during long kisses because they feel they're suffocating. Just remember to breathe through your nose and your panic will subside. *Upside-down Kisses:* Don't become confused just because your lover is upside down. Don't worry about the fact that you have somewhat less eye contact with your partner in this position. Do tell your partner how good he/she looks from this angle.

—William Cane
The Art of Kissing
1382

Personal Authenticity

The real you is the arrangement, the organizing power, the knowledge, the intelligence, the impulse of consciousness that designs material stuff to give the appearance of you. Through its own infinite expression it gives the appearance of changing, evolving, declining, decaying, dying. But essentially it stands back from the appearance of change, because intelligence controls change.

—Deepak Chopra
Creating Health
1425

Enough

Is a wide and stable plateau. It is a place of alertness, creativity, and freedom.

—Joe Dominguez and Vicki Robin
Your Money or Your Life
378

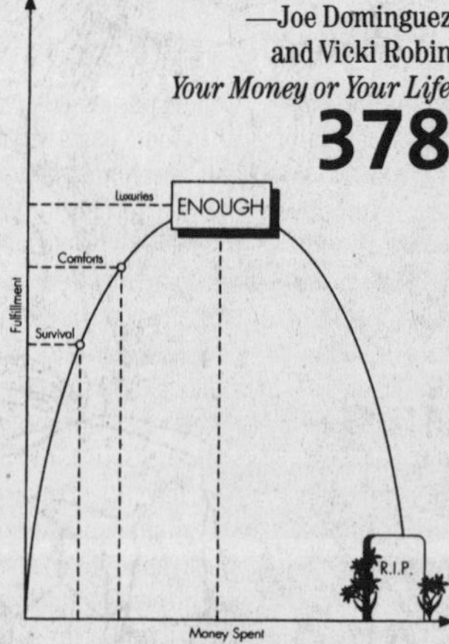

FIGURE 1-3
The Fulfillment Curve: *Enough*

A Losing Battle

Though pestilential offensives may be slowed or halted for a while by one or another of the newer pharmaceutical agents, they will always in time resume, if not in one form, then in another. A skirmish may be won here and there, or a battle prevented by timely use of prophylactic drugs, and some months of stability thereby achieved—but the eventual outcome of the struggle is preordained. The determined microbial aggression will accept nothing less than the unconditional surrender that comes only with the death of their involuntary host.

—Sherwin Nuland
How We Die: Reflections on Life's Final Chapter
1449

Local Afflictions

1 Nasal Reflex

Neurosis was diagnosed by an appearance of swelling in the nose believed to be caused by masturbation. "Mr. F suffers from left-sided neuralgiform headaches, is intolerant of alcohol, has pain in the sternum, dizziness, cannot breathe through the nose when reclining, has a dried-out mouth upon awaking, restless sleep and a suspicious shape to his nose."

—*Complete Letters of Sigmund Freud to Wilhelm Fliess*

464

2 Tamazai

"Among the Yuaneg people in Northern Nigeria, tamazai is described as an illness of the heart and soul curable by music, jokes, and noise. Tamazai victims sit alone in their tents and do not look at others or speak to them. Sometimes they run wildly through the desert." (Susan Rassmussen)

1414

3 Chronic Back Pain

Severe lower-back pain is a prominent complaint in doctors' offices in the United States, though it is rarely encountered in other parts of the world. By definition this syndrome often begins with an accident or injury, but the pain persists long after wounds are healed. Chronic back pain, like other pain disorders, appears closely related to the availability of workman's compensation and disability.

1410

4 Koro

East Asian: "Usually the malady begins with a feeling on the part of the victim that his sex organ is shrinking. Believing that the condition is critical, the victim does whatever he can to stop retractions. A man may be seen holding his penis, anchoring it with some clamping device, or tying it with a string. He is pale, parched, shivering, hyperventilating, palpitating, sweating, fainting. Injury to the sex organ, including bruises, bleeding, and infection often results from the rescue efforts. These reactions are generally the only sequelae of the disorder." (Sheung-tak Cheng)

1420

5 Pa Leng or Frigophobia

Based on a belief in the imbalance of yin and yang, patients develop a morbid fear that their bodies are excessively cold owing to depletion of "hot" yang. These patients bundle up in warm weather, fear "catching cold," avoid going out, and eat only hot foods and tonics.

1425

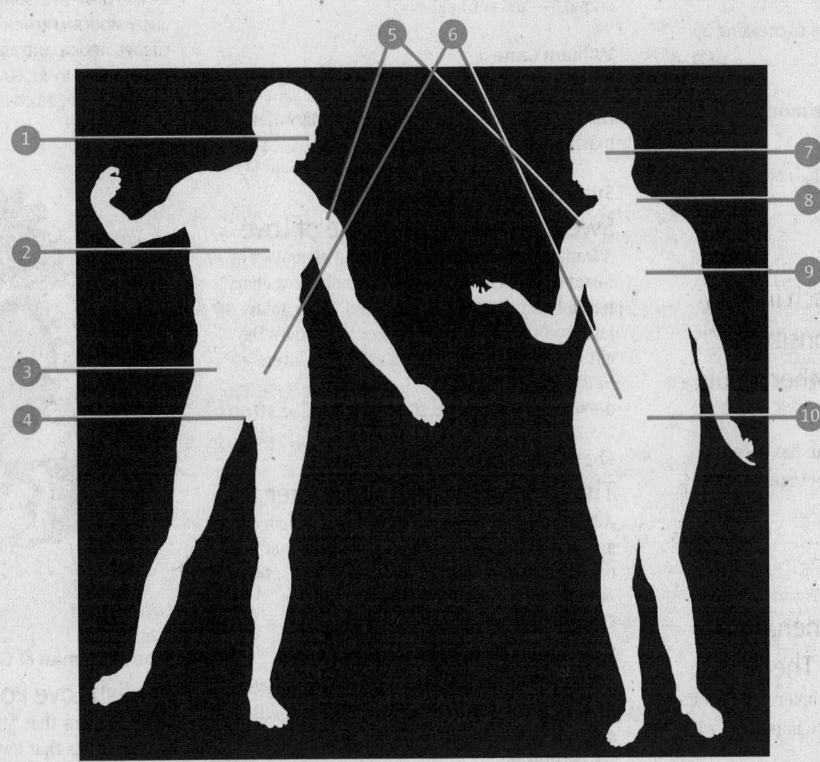

6 Intestinal Melancholy

A disease category popular in the mid-19c, based on the idea that intestinal irritation produces irritation in the brain. On the basis of this diagnosis, psychotic patients were commonly given enemas on admission to mental asylums, often with excellent short-term effect.

1412

7 Shame

In Salman Rushdie's novel *Midnight's Children,* the Muslim narrator's great-grandmother, who has spent her life in *purdah,* sacrifices her modesty in order to run a gem business. The moment she removes her veil because "nobody is going to buy a piece of turquoise from somebody they can't see," she is stricken with a strange disorder, a blush of pathogenic shame that spreads across her face, heating her blood and bringing forth a rash of boils, pimples, and eczema.

839

8 Spondylitis

The hypothesized inflammation of a vertebra was a popular diagnosis in early-19c Europe. Treatment involved leeching, cauterization, and the prescription of bed rest. Large numbers of Victorian women spent years in bed in the effort to rid themselves of the disorder. Though vanished entirely from the West, spondylitis is still common in South Asia, where it afflicts modern housewives. It is treated with Valium.

1410

9 Possession

Women possessed by Zar spirits in some parts of Ethiopia and West Sudan become depressed, lethargic, weak, and infertile. To be cured they must participate in a healing ceremony in which the spirits cause the patients to dance, shout, sing, menace male members of the audience with sticks and swords, and demand gifts of luxury items. One woman, possessed by a spirit, announced she would not be healed until she was given a yellow dress and a can of tuna fish.

1417

10 PMS

A common disorder afflicting middle-class American and European women, but which is unknown in non-Western cultures. Sufferers of the syndrome report headaches, water retention, tearfulness, and shortness of temper during the premenstrual phase of their cycle. Repeated studies have failed to turn up consistent scientific evidence of the disorder.

1418

Courtship, Love, Sex, and Marriage

Finding a Partner

"Love looks not with the eyes, but with the mind, And therefore is winged Cupid painted blind." —William Shakespeare, *A Midsummer Night's Dream*

Amy **Alkon** & others
Free Advice: The Advice Ladies on Love, Dating, Sex, and Relationships
From meeting a potential date to breaking up
0-440-50751-0 DELL PB $13.95

Patricia **Allen** & Sandra **Harmon**
Getting to "I Do"
How to achieve a long-term relationship
0-380-71815-4 AVON PB $12.00

Robin **Gorman Newman**
How to Meet a Mensch in New York: A Decent, Responsible Person Even Your Mother Would Love
For the last ten years, Newman has been immersed in the New York meet/meat market, and she's ready to tell all
1-88549-204-9 CITY & CO. PB $9.95

Dory **Hollander**
101 Lies Men Tell Women, and Why Women Believe Them
Psychologist interviewed 60 women and 35 men to learn why men lie and, more important, why women want to believe them
0-06-017125-1 HARPERCOLLINS $20.00

Margaret **Kent**
How to Marry the Man of Your Choice
How to find a man and transform him into a husband
0-446-34788-4 WARNER PB $5.50

Mindi **Rudan**
Men: The Handbook: How to Meet a Man, How to Marry a Man, How to Mature with a Man
The dos and don'ts of dating and keeping a relationship healthy
1-56790-113-1 COOL HAND PB $12.95

Judith **Sills**
How to Stop Looking For Someone Perfect and Find Someone to Love
Quit looking for the partner your mother would choose and find someone to please you
0-345-32597-4 BALLANTINE PB $5.99

Nita **Tucker** & Randi **Moret**
How Not to Stay Single: 10 Steps to a Great Relationship
The author of *Beyond Cinderella* provides tips for successful matching
0-517-88637-5 CROWN PB $12.00

Courtship and Dating

"Women deprived of the company of men pine, men deprived of the company of women become stupid."—Anton Chekhov

William **Cane**
The Art of Kissing
Instructional, with tips on kissing underwater
0-312-05378-9 ST. MARTIN'S PB $6.95

Susan **Ferraro**
Sweet Talk: The Language of Love
A frank and saucy discussion of the etymology of romantic as well as dirty words. Includes a chapter on how to leave your lover and "Dear John" letters of the famous. "A perfect Valentine's Day gift for language aficionados as well as lovers"—*Publishers Weekly*
0-671-79234-2 SIMON & SCHUSTER $17.00

Sherri **Foxman**
The J-Factor: Male Jerk Counter
A humorous guide for rating the man in your life and how to discern whether he's a keeper or not
04466700944 WARNER PB $4.99

Cynthia **Heimel**
Sex Tips For Girls
A New York City humor columnist gives advice on "The Great Boyfriend Crunch," "Lingerie Dos and Don'ts," and "How to Cure a Broken Heart"
See also **HUMOR**
0-671-47725-0 SIMON & SCHUSTER PB $9.00

Thomas **McKnight** & Robert **Phillips**
Love Tactics: How to Win the One You Want
0-89529-367-6 AVERY PB $7.95

More Love Tactics: How to Win that Special Someone
0-89529-531-8 AVERY PB $8.95

Jenny **Newman**
The Faber Book of Seductions
The most famous seduction scenes in English literature, including passages from Andrew Marvell, Graham Greene, Jane Austen, and Oscar Wilde
0-571-15110-8 FABER PB $19.95

Michael **Newman**
The Complete Guide to Everything Romantic: Unique and Creative Ideas
How to express yourself romantically
0-8065-1547-3 CITADEL $15.95

Love and Romance

"If intelligence were taken out of my life, it would only be more or less reduced. If I had no one to love, it would be ruined." —Henri de Montherlant

Roland **Barthes**
A Lover's Discourse: Fragments
"Barthes surprises us by making love, in its most absurd and sentimental forms, an object of interest"—Jonathan Culler
See also **ESSAYS: PERSONAL, LITERARY, PHILOSOPHICAL** under **MODERN FRENCH LITERATURE** in **LITERATURE OF EUROPE, AFRICA, AND ASIA**
TRANSLATED BY RICHARD HOWARD
0-374-52161-1 FS&G PB $10.95

Lord Byron

John **Betjeman** & Geoffrey **Taylor**, editors
English Love Poems
Classic poems that "crystallize…those thoughts and emotions that love provokes"
0-571-07065-5 FABER PB $12.95

Anne **De Courcy**
The English in Love: Passion Among the Elite
0-88162-267-2 HARPERCOLLINS PB $1.98

Riane **Eisler**
Sacred Pleasure: Sex, Myth, and the Politics of the Body—New Paths to Power and Love
Eisler studies sex and spirituality to point the way to the possibility of a revolutionary, fulfilling equality
See also **SEXUALITY** under **THE FEMALE EXPERIENCE** under **WOMEN'S STUDIES** in **SOCIAL STUDIES**
0-06-250293-X HARPERCOLLINS $25.00
0-06-250283-2 HARPERCOLLINS PB $15.00

Valerie **Frankel** & Ellen **Tien**

The Heartbreak Handbook: How to Survive the Worst Twenty-Four Hours of Your Life and Move On

Quizzes, anecdotes, humor, revenge tactics, and antidotes to love's pain to get you out and on to a new beginning

0-449-90757-0 FAWCETT PB $8.00

Antonia **Fraser**

Love Letters: An Illustrated Anthology

0-517-14266-X CRESCENT $16.99

Erich **Fromm**

The Art of Loving: An Enquiry Into the Nature of Love

Advice on developing the ability to love without fear

0-8095-9110-3 BORGO $29.00

Willard **Gaylin** & Ethel **Person**

Passionate Attachments: Thinking About Love

0-02-911430-6 FREE PRESS $27.95

Geoffrey **Grigson**, editor

The Faber Book of Love Poems

Shakespeare, Dickinson, Lawrence, and others on love, from early expectations to final renunciation

0-571-13118-2 FABER PB $12.95

Shere **Hite**

Women and Love: A Cultural Revolution in Progress

Hite's much-contested work is an analysis of the stages of falling in love, having a relationship, and getting married

See also **SEXUALITY**

0-312-91378-8 ST. MARTIN'S PB $5.95

Marla Hamburg **Kennedy**

Kissing: Photographs and Essays on the Wonderful Act of Kissing

0-9630570-4-9 D.A.P. $16.95

Courtney **Long**

Love Awaits: African American Women Talk About Sex, Love, and Life

From all kinds of backgrounds, 26 women expound on black men and men in general. "Long's own respect and sensitivity toward his Sisters is apparent in his pungent report from the trenches"—*Publishers Weekly*

0-553-09702-4 BDD $21.95

Karen **Lystra**

Searching the Heart: Women, Men, and Romantic Love in Nineteenth-Century America

0-19-505817-8 OXFORD $30.00

Jon **Stallworthy**, editor

A Book of Love Poetry

From Chaucer to e.e. cummings, arranged thematically

0-19-519774-7 OXFORD $30.00

Ethel **Person**

Dreams of Love and Fateful Encounters: The Power of Romantic Passion

"Charts a new topography in which romantic love is seen as a healthy, creative process, an imaginative journey, a powerful agent for change"—Jean Strouse

0-14-012055-6 PENGUIN PB $12.95

Judith **Sills**

Biting the Apple: Women Getting Wise About Love

Bestselling author and clinical psychologist points out how women's self-worth is all-important

0-670-85846-3 VIKING $22.95

Robert **Solomon**

About Love: Reinventing Romance for Our Times

A study of romantic love, and its possibilities in modern times

0-8226-3027-3 LITTLEFIELD ADAMS PB $16.95

Paul **Woods** & Felix **Liddell**, editors

I Hear A Symphony: African Americans Celebrate Love

A collection of essays, poems, letters, speeches, and fiction on the subject of love

0-385-47503-9 ANCHOR PB $19.95

Maintaining a Relationship

"Surely, once the name of jealousy has been applied to an unjust, perverse and unfounded suspicion, that other jealousy which is a just and natural feeling, founded on reason and experience, deserves another name."
—La Bruyère

Aaron T. **Beck**

Love Is Never Enough

Cognitive therapist outlines how couples can resolve conflict

0-06-091604-4 HARPERCOLLINS PB $13.50

Michael **Broder**

The Art of Staying Together: A Couple's Guide to Intimacy and Respect

Common sense for marital conundrums

15628208835 HYPERION $19.95

Stephen **Dowrick**

Intimacy and Solitude

The co-founder of the Women's Press in London contemplates the age-old paradox of intimacy: that to achieve it we must first have mastered the pleasures and pitfalls of solitude. "Offers penetrating insights into some of the most basic paradoxes of human relationships"
—*The London Guardian*

0-393-03627-8 NORTON $21.00

0-393-31361-1 NORTON PB $12.50

Steven **Carter** & Julia **Sokol**

He's Scared; She's Scared: Understanding the Hidden Fears that Sabotage Your Relationships

"Straightforward advice on how to detect commitment phobia and move toward true intimacy"
—*Publishers Weekly*

0-440-50625-5 DELL PB $10.95

Men Who Can't Love: When a Man's Fear Makes Him Run from Commitment (and What a Smart Woman Can Do About It)

Written for a popular audience with useful advice for women

0-87131-517-3 EVANS $15.95

Connell **Cowan**

Women Men Love, Women Men Leave: Why Men Are Drawn to Women—What Makes Them Want to Stay

Difficulties men have forming lasting relationships

0-451-16641-8 NEW AMERICAN LIBRARY PB $5.99

Connell **Cowan** & Melvyn **Kinder**

Smart Women, Foolish Choices

The complex negative issues surrounding women's choices of a love partner, and the unsatisfying unions that result

0-451-15885-7 NEW AMERICAN LIBRARY PB $5.99

Barry **Dym** & Michael L. **Glenn**

Couples: Exploring and Understanding the Cycles of Intimate Relationships

Helps readers understand the evolutionary nature of relationships, and the roles that family, gender, and cultural expectations play in their success. Many non-traditional relationships are examined, including gay and lesbian partnerships

0-06-016713-0 HARPERPERENNIAL PB $20.00

Roger **Fisher** & Scott **Brown**

Getting Together: Building a Relationship as We Negotiate

How to deal with the emotional challenges in relationships

0-14-012638-4 PENGUIN PB $11.95

Susan **Forward** & Joan **Torres**

Men Who Hate Women and the Women Who Love Them

Men's fear of women, and the propensity of certain women to involve themselves in destructive relationships

0-553-28037-6 BDD PB $6.99

Herb **Goldberg**

The New Male-Female Relationship

The new male-female relationship, based on an unselfconscious, playful, and accepting sexuality

0-451-14840-1 NEW AMERICAN LIBRARY PB $5.99

Sheila **Gillooly**

Venus in Spurs: The Secret Female Fear of Commitment, or Why You Head for the Hills When Love Comes to Town

Men are not the only ones who fear tying the knot. The author offers practical suggestions "that entertain as well as instruct"—*Publishers Weekly*

0-8050-3552-4 HOLT..$20.00

John **Gray**

Mars and Venus in Love: Inspiring and Heartfelt Stories of Relationships that Work

Gray's life- and love-enhancing works (*Men Are From Mars, Women Are From Venus*; *What Your Mother Couldn't Tell You and Your Father Didn't Know*; and *Mars and Venus in the Bedroom*), his national seminars, and his infomercials have reached a staggering number of people and transformed him into a phenomenon. Here, a collection of first-person stories show how Gray's spiritual message works for people who have put his principles to the test in their own lives

0-06-017471-4 HARPERCOLLINS......................$18.00

What Your Mother Couldn't Tell You and Your Father Didn't Know

Addresses how couples in the modern world (where both men and women have higher marital expectations than their parents and grandparents) can create peaceful and lasting relationships. Drawing from his extensive work with couples, Gray offers practical ways to change expectations by understanding the differences between the genders

0-06-017162-6 HARPERCOLLINS......................$23.00

Lynn **Harris**

He Loves Me, He Loves Me Not: A Guide to Fudge, Fury, Free Time, and Life Beyond the Breakup

Humor and cartoons for surviving the end of a relationship

CARTOONS BY CHRIS KALB

0-380-78443-2 AVON PB..................................$10.00

John H. **Harvey**

Odyssey of the Heart: The Search for Closeness, Intimacy and Love

Analysis of a close relationship in all its stages from the euphoric beginning to the painful drama of its demise

0-7167-2589-4 FREEMAN PB............................$16.95

Jody **Hayes** & Maureen **Redl**

Smart Love: Changing Painful Patterns, Choosing Satisfying Relationships

0-87477-472-1 TARCHER PB..............................$10.95

Jane Wescheider **Hyman** & Esther R. **Rome**

Sacrificing Ourselves for Love

From the collective that brought forth *Our Bodies, Ourselves*, this discusses how to stop compromising self-esteem and health in order to please others

0-89594-743-9 CROSSING PB...........................$18.95

Harville **Hendrix**

Getting the Love You Want: A Guide for Couples

An enormously successful book designed to help couples communicate better without resorting to an outside counselor. "I know of no better guide for couples who genuinely desire a maturing relationship"—M. Scott Peck

0-06-097292-0 HARPERPERENNIAL PB...........$13.00

Daphne Rose **Kingma**

Coming Apart: Why Relationships End and How to Live Through the Ending of Yours

In her usual pithy prose, Kingma takes the guilt out of breaking up with commonsense advice and healing rituals

0-449-21661-6 CREST PB...................................$5.99

A Garland of Love: Daily Reflections on the Meaning and Magic of Love

Inspirations on love from January 1 through December 31

0-943233-27-5 CONARI PB.................................$9.95

Heart & Soul: Living the Joy, Truth & Beauty of Your Intimate Relationship

Concise wisdom from the queen of hearts

1-57324-001-X CONARI PB.................................$9.95

The Men We Never Knew: How to Deepen Your Relationship with the Man You Love

Mending the gender crisis by explaining the spiritual and intimacy needs of men, of which women are often unaware. "An effective attempt at delving into men's hearts and minds"—*Mademoiselle*

FOREWORD BY JOHN GRAY

0-943233-66-6 CONARI PB...............................$10.95

Thomas Chatterton

Neal H. **Olshan**

Golden Handcuffs: How Women Can Break Free of Financial Dependence in Their Intimate Relationships

Olshan shows how to break the pattern of behavior and crippling state of mind that financial dependence often engenders. He provides a blueprint for equality in dependent relationships, including setting goals, honestly communicating needs, overcoming depression, and becoming more assertive

See also **CAREERS AND MONEY**

1-55972-202-9 BIRCH LANE...............................$17.95

True Love: How to Make Your Relationship Sweeter, Deeper, and More Passionate

More than 60 inspirational messages and suggestions for enhancing love

0-943233-58-5 CONARI......................................$12.95

0-943233-13-5 CONARI PB.................................$9.95

Sherod **Miller** & Daniel **Wachman**

Straight Talk: A New Way to Get Closer to Others by Saying What You Really Mean

Techniques to improve communications skills in every arena, from marriage to parenthood to the office

0-451-16680-9 NEW AMERICAN LIBRARY PB....$5.99

Robin **Norwood**

Women Who Love Too Much: When You Keep Wishing and Hoping He'll Change

Involvement in a destructive relationship may be a manifestation of unconscious psychological needs

0-671-73341-9 POCKET PB.................................$6.99

Bill **O'Hanlon** & Pat **Hudson**

Love Is a Verb: How to Stop Analyzing Your Relationship and Start Making It Great

Husband-wife psychotherapy team emphasizes how couples can move forward by changing patterns and not dwelling on the past. "...examples from the authors' practice and own marriage lend credibility to this helpful self-help book" —*Publishers Weekly*

0-393-03734-7 NORTON....................................$19.95

Stanton **Peele** & Archie **Brodsky**

Love and Addiction

An analysis of the obsession with being in love, often with the wrong person

0-8008-5041-6 TAPLINGER...............................$16.95

Hugh **Prather** & Gayle **Prather**

I Will Never Leave You: How Couples Can Achieve the Power of Lasting Love

Human-potential workshop leaders and married couples present the eight stages of relationships

0-533-09533-1 BDD PB......................................$19.95

Lillian B. **Rubin**

Intimate Strangers: Men and Women Together

A compassionate look at people's fear of being close and its effect on work, parenting, and life in general

0-06-091134-4 HARPERCOLLINS PB................$13.00

Robert **Schwebel**

Who's On Top, Who's On Bottom: How Couples Can Learn to Share Power

The power struggle in couples analyzed with real examples and real solutions

1-55704-197-0 NEWMARKET...........................$19.95

Karen **Shanor**

How to Stay Together When You Have to Be Apart

How to cope with long-distance relationships, working in different cities, separations

0-446-38418-6 WARNER PB $9.95

Marion F. **Solomon**

Lean on Me: The Power of Positive Dependency in Intimate Relationships

Challenging prevailing views, Solomon tells us "loving too much is not a disease." Rather, it is a healthy and necessary component of a complete life

0-671-87010-6 SIMON & SCHUSTER....................$22.00

Janis Abrahms **Spring** & Michael **Spring**

After the Affair: Healing the Pain and Rebuilding Trust When a Partner Has Been Unfaithful

Clinical psychologists draw on over 20 years' experience to help couples reconnect and recommit after trust has been betrayed. "This wise book fills a gap on the self-help shelf"—*Publishers Weekly*

0-06-017236-3 HARPERCOLLINS....................$23.00

Joyce L. **Vedral**

Get Rid of Him

Basic and to the point. Finding the courage to shed the wrong man and start looking for Mr. Right

0-446-39544-7 WARNER PB....................$9.99

Daniel **Wile**

After the Honeymoon: Turning Conflict into Understanding

Learn how to argue and not flee from discord

0-471-85347-X WILEY PB....................$22.95

Steven **Carter** & Julia **Sokol**

Men Like Women Who Like Themselves, (And Other Secrets that the Smartest Women Know)

Relationship experts talk about the importance of self-esteem

See also **SELF-ESTEEM** under **QUALITY OF LIFE** under **SELF-HELP**

0-385-31513-9 DELACORTE....................$21.95

Understanding the Opposite Sex

"Men always want to be a woman's first love, women like to be a man's last romance."
—Oscar Wilde

Douglas **Gillette**

Primal Love: Reclaiming Our Instincts for Lasting Passion

Based on the premise that men and women are different because of their different survival skills before civilization, Gillette explains why there exists such strife between the sexes

0-312-11776-0 ST. MARTIN'S....................$21.95

Warren **Farrell**

Why Men Are the Way They Are

Unravels assumptions for both sexes

0-425-11094-X BERKLEY PB....................$5.99

Françoise **Giroud** & Bernard-Henri **Levy**

Women and Men: A Philosophical Conversation

Bestselling French authors discourse on sex, love, jealousy, infidelity, and seduction with Gallic wit and insight

0-316-31474-9 LITTLE, BROWN....................$22.95

Nancy **Good**

How to Love a Difficult Man

How compromise and sensitivity can help women overcome the problem of loving difficult men

0-312-90963-2 ST. MARTIN'S PB....................$4.50

Gwendolyn Goldsby **Grant**

The Best Kind of Loving: A Black Woman's Guide to Finding Intimacy

Essence columnist and psychologist discusses the cultural differences between black women and men. "Practical, insightful and loaded with case histories"—*Publishers Weekly*

0-06-017088-3 HARPERCOLLINS....................$22.00

0-06-092475-6 HARPERPERENNIAL PB....................$13.00

John **Gray**

Men Are from Mars, Women Are from Venus

In this bestselling work Gray dissects relationships, offering much insight along the way. "It is rare to find a non-fiction book that is a page turner, but John Gray has written one"—Susan Page

0-06-016848-X HARPERCOLLINS....................$25.00

0-06-092416-0 HARPERPERENNIAL PB....................$13.00

Victoria **Houston**

Loving a Younger Man: How Women Are Finding and Enjoying a Better Relationship

0-671-66882-X POCKET PB....................$5.50

Dan **Kiley**

The Peter Pan Syndrome: Men Who Have Never Grown Up

A Peter Pan type avoids responsibility and emotional demands. Suggestions for helping him to grow up

0-380-68890-5 AVON PB....................$5.99

Anne **Moir** & David **Jessel**

Brain Sex: The Real Difference Between Men and Women

The latest in sex difference research applied from the prenatal brain to adult attitudes on love, sex, and marriage. "Literate and entertaining, Moir and Jessel write with clarity and style, documenting their data every step of the way"
—*Kirkus Reviews*

0-8184-0543-0 LYLE STUART....................$17.95

0-385-31183-4 DELL PB....................$12.95

Laurie **Schloff** & Marcia **Yudkin**

He & She Talk: How to Communicate with the Opposite Sex

0-452-27066-9 PLUME PB....................$10.00

Deborah **Tannen**

Gender and Discourse

Five academic essays on language and gender

0-19-508975-8 OXFORD....................$25.00

0-19-510124-3 OXFORD PB....................$10.95

You Just Don't Understand

Discusses how the way men and women talk differ so greatly that often dissension occurs unnessesarily. "Utterly fascinating…it's destined to become a classic in the field of interpersonal relations"—*San Francisco Chronicle*

0-345-37205-0 BALLANTINE PB....................$12.50

Sex

Susan Crain **Bakos**

Kink: The Hidden Sex Lives of Americans

The former *Penthouse* magazine's "Dear Superlady of Sex" discusses America's sexual practices

0-312-11845-7 ST. MARTIN'S....................$19.95

0-312-95684-3 ST. MARTIN'S PB....................$6.99

Lonnie **Barbach**

For Each Other: Sharing Sexual Intimacy

A recommended work on female sexuality and desires

0-451-15271-9 NEW AMERICAN LIBRARY PB....$5.99

For Yourself: Fulfillment of Female Sexuality

From anatomy to erotic pleasure and sexual response

0-451-16681-7 NEW AMERICAN LIBRARY PB....$5.99

Sydney Biddle **Barrows** & Judith **Newman**

Just Between Us Girls: Secrets About Men from the Madam Who Knows

From the Mayflower Madam, based on her women-only seminars, funny and explicit sexual advice

0-312-13993-4 ST. MARTIN'S....................$21.95

Whit **Barry**

Making Love: A Man's Guide

The author's view of what women really want

0-451-16314-1 NEW AMERICAN LIBRARY PB ...$4.99

Pat **Califia**

Public Sex: The Culture of Radical Sex

Controversial writer presents 19 of her essays on sex and politics from 1980 to the present. "Always intelligent but never academic, Califia takes bold, unpopular stances on censorship and sexual freedom"—*Publishers Weekly*

0-939416-89-1 CLEIS PB....................$12.95

Gloria G. **Brame** & others

Different Loving: A Complete Exploration of the World of Sexual Dominance and Submission

0-679-76956-0 VILLARD PB $18.00

David M. **Buss**

The Evolution of Desire: Strategies of Human Mating

0-465-02143-3 BASIC PB $13.00

Rufus C. **Camphausen**

The Encyclopedia of Erotic Wisdom: A Reference Guide to the Symbolism, Techniques, Rituals, Sacred Texts, Anatomy, and History of Sexuality

A comprehensive resource providing access to ancient mysteries of eros and sexuality, from Tantrism and Taoism to the alchemical and Kabbalistic traditions. Extensively cross-referenced with over 100 illustrations

0-89281-321-0 INNER TRADITIONS PB $19.95

Mantak **Chia** & Douglas Abrams **Arava**

The Multi-Orgasmic Man: Sexual Secrets Every Man Should Know

0-06-251335-4 HARPERCOLLINS $20.00

Alex **Comfort**

The Joy of Sex: A Gourmet Guide to Lovemaking

A relaxed guide to sexual pleasure, both erotic and instructive

0-517-58583-9 CROWN $32.00
0-671-77859-5 POCKET PB $20.00

More Joy of Sex: A Lovemaking Companion to the Joy of Sex

Instruction in developing deeper relations through an understanding of the body

0-671-74076-8 POCKET PB $18.00

Theresa L. **Crenshaw**

The Alchemy of Lust: Discovering Our Sex Hormones and How They Determine Who We Love, When We Love, and How Often We Love

Sex therapist explains why our lust waxes and wanes throughout our lifetime

0-399-14041-7 PUTNAM $24.95

Elizabeth **Davis**

Women, Sex & Desire: Exploring Your Sexuality at Every Stage of Life

A midwife discusses aspects of a woman's sexual health, including sexual dysfunction, abuse, and abstinence. "…a rare combination of breadth, practicality, strong—though not rigid—opinion"—*Publishers Weekly*

0-89793-143-2 HUNTER $22.95
0-89793-127-0 HUNTER PB $14.95

Judith **Davis**

Making Love: A Woman's Guide

0-451-16822-4 NEW AMERICAN LIBRARY PB ...$4.99

Barbara **De Angelis**

Real Moments for Lovers

De Angelis's pioneering work offers a wealth of insight into the mystical and transformational capacity of physical love

0-385-31429-9 DELACORTE $14.95

John **D'Emilio** & Estelle B. **Freedman**

Intimate Matters: A History of Sexuality in America

A serious and provocative scholarly study

0-06-091550-1 HARPERCOLLINS PB $14.00

The Diagram Group

Sex: A User's Manual

A book intended to end fears and dispel myths about sex, written by a group of editors, researchers, and artists with the help of physicians

0-425-08972-X BERKLEY PB $6.99

Ronnie **Edell**

The Sexually Satisfied Woman: Five Step Program for Getting Everything You Want in Bed

Sexual sublimity, in five steps, illuminated by exercises, case histories, and a proven approach. Unique in its reliance on the power of the woman

0-452-27468-0 PLUME PB $10.95

Ronn **Elmore**

How to Love a Black Man

Black psychotherapist and LA Radio's "relationship doctor" provides pertinent information on understanding black men

0-446-51878-6 MYSTERIOUS $17.95
0-446-67259-9 WARNER PB $11.99

Thomas C. **Fox**

Sexuality and Catholicism

An excellent survey of Catholic teachings and practice concerning women, birth control, abortion, celibacy, and homosexuality, with discussions of such institutional problems as clerical abuse of children

See also **CONTEMPORARY ISSUES** under **THEOLOGY AND DOCTRINE** under **CHRISTIANITY** in **RELIGION, SPIRITUALITY, AND PHILOSOPHY**

0-8076-1396-7 BRAZILLER $27.50

Nancy **Friday**

Forbidden Flowers

Female sexual fantasies

0-671-74102-0 POCKET PB $6.50

Men in Love, Male Sexual Fantasies: The Triumph of Love over Rage

Men from the ages of 14 to 60 discuss their sexual fantasies. The author's intent is to encourage awareness and acceptance of erotic pleasures

0-440-15903-2 DELL PB $6.99

My Secret Garden

Female sexual fantasies

0-671-74252-3 POCKET PB $6.50

Cary **Friedman**

Marital Intimacy: A Traditional Jewish Approach

Judaism, in contrast to some tenets of Christianity, views sexual intimacy as a pleasure sanctioned by God, and therefore holy. "Friedman's is a fascinating presentation of a sensitive subject and one that is highly recommended"—*Publishers Weekly*

1-56821-461-8 ARONSON $22.50

John **Gray**

Mars and Venus in the Bedroom

An advanced lesson in relationship skills with an emphasis on communicating sexual needs effectively and romantically

0-06-017212-6 HARPERCOLLINS $24.00

Shere **Hite**

The Hite Report

An exploration of female sexuality, from fantasy to practical experience

0-440-13690-3 DELL PB $6.95

Ann **Hooper**

The Ultimate Sex Book

Sex therapist and marriage counselor discusses individual case histories with 300 large-format, lavish color photos that detail sexual exercises and positions

1-56458-063-6 DORLING KINDERSLEY $29.95

Ruth S. **Jacobowitz**

150 Most-Asked Questions About Midlife Sex, Love & Intimacy that Women and Their Partners Really Want to Know

Shares information based on interviews with 15,000 women on subjects pertinent to the maturing woman's sexual happiness

0-688-12890-4 HEARST $15.00
0-688-14767-4 MORROW PB $10.00

Staci **Keith**

Drive Your Woman Wild in Bed: A Lover's Guide to Sex and Romance

Hints for spicing up your love life. Includes 101 best places for a quickie and advice on how to buy lingerie

0-446-67047-2 WARNER PB $11.99

Jennifer **Knopf** & Michael **Seiler**

Uninhibited Sexual Desire

A practical step-by-step guide for sexual enhancement or the rekindling of desire if lost

0-446-39235-9 WARNER PB $12.99

James Vaughn **Kohl** & Robert T. **Francoeur**

The Scent of Eros: Mysteries of Odor in Human Sexuality

0-8264-0677-7 CONTINUUM $24.95

Nitya **Lacroix** & Sakina **Bowhay**

The Art of Sensual Aromatherapy: A Lover's Guide to Using Aromatic Oils and Essences

0-8050-4153-2 HOLT PB $18.95

Thomas **Laqueur**

Making Sex: Body and Gender from the Greeks to Freud

How concepts of human sexuality and the sex organs have drastically changed over the centuries. "Bold, important, and original....The book is very well written, with sly humor and witty metaphor"—Natalie Zemon Davis

0-674-54349-1 HARVARD $34.95

Sherry **Lehman** & Micki **Brook**

It Was Better in the Back Seat: How to Recharge Your Sex Life

Sexy suggestions from couples who have experienced marital renaissance

1-55850-359-5 ADAMS PB $8.95

Howard **Levy** & Akira **Ishihara**

The Tao of Sex: The Essence of Medical Prescriptions (Ishimpo)

An illustrated edition of the 10th-century work. Describes proper positions for sexual intercourse, use of aphrodisiacs, and medical prescriptions for treating sex-related debilities

0-941255-44-1 INTEGRAL PB $15.95

Joan Elizabeth **Lloyd**

Come Play With Me: Games and Toys for Creative Lovers

Scenarios, scripts, and toys for consenting adults

0-446-39538-2 WARNER PB $12.99

Sari **Locker**

Mindblowing Sex in the Real World: Hot Tips for Doing It in the Age of Anxiety

A NYC radio talk-show host offers a concise and chatty sex discussion for those under 30. "[S]he offers a smart, responsible blend of basic technical details, decision-making advice and tips for broadening one's sexual horizons"
—*Publishers Weekly*

0-06-095099-4 HARPERPERENNIAL $10.00

William **Masters** & Virginia **Johnson**

Masters and Johnson on Sex and Human Loving

A survey of current findings on the biological, psychological, and social issues of sexuality. This updated study includes chapters on sexual abuse, contraception, and AIDS

0-316-50160-3 LITTLE, BROWN PB $19.95

Heterosexuality

"An enlightened, remarkable, thorough guide to heterosexual loving and sex...An invaluable sourcebook for couples and singles seeking self-understanding and fulfillment"
—*Publishers Weekly*

0-06-092600-7 HARPERPERENNIAL PB $16.00

Barry **McCarthy** & Emily **McCarthy**

Sexual Awareness: Enhancing Sexual Pleasure

The classic guide to intimacy and pleasure is newly revised and updated to include the latest in clinical research as well as two new chapters on enchancing desire and maintaining arousal in long-term relationships

0-7867-0015-7 CARROLL & GRAF PB $11.95

Graham **Masterson**

More Ways to Drive Your Man Wild in Bed

Tips and insights for you-know-what

0-451-16174-2 NEW AMERICAN LIBRARY PB $5.99

Barry **McCarthy**

Male Sexual Awareness: Increasing Sexual Pleasure

Advice for men on such matters as contraception, pregnancy, and homosexuality

0-88184-348-2 CARROLL & GRAF PB $9.95

Jack **Morin**

The Erotic Mind: Peak Sex, Troublesome Turn-ons, and the Paradoxes of Passion

0-06-016975-3 HARPERCOLLINS $25.00

Charles **Muir** & others

Tantra: The Art of Conscious Loving

The yoga of sex, tantra is an ancient Hindu spiritual system in which sexual love is a sacrament. How gender differences can be a positive force for couples. Finding the "g" spot is a particularly illuminating chapter

0-916515-86-9 MERCURY HOUSE PB $12.95

Brigitte **Nioche**

What Turns Men On: Erotic Techniques to Seduce Him So He Stays Seduced

A study of 5,000 American men reveals what turns them on and off

0-451-16054-1 NEW AMERICAN LIBRARY PB $4.99

Joseph **Nowinski**

A Lifelong Love Affair: Keeping Sexual Desire Alive in Your Relationship

Sex can and should improve with time and result in greater intimacy

0-393-30621-6 NORTON PB $7.95

Susan **Rako**

The Hormone of Desire: The Truth About Sexuality, Menopause and Testosterone

The discussion of the importance of testosterone for a woman's libido

0-517-70342-4 HARMONY $21.00

Domeena **Renshaw**

Seven Weeks to Better Sex

Founder and director of Loyola University's Sex Therapy Clinic "provides excellent guidance to help couples achieve greater closeness, communication and sexual satisfaction"—*Publishers Weekly*

0-679-43546-8 RANDOM HOUSE $22.00
0-440-50752-9 DELL PB $12.95

Saul H. **Rosenthal**

Sex over 40

Addresses both the problems and advantages for middle-age and older men

0-87477-495-0 TARCHER PB $9.95

Olivia **St. Claire**

203 Ways to Drive a Man Wild in Bed

A frankly erotic and intelligently written guide, guaranteed to raise the temperature of any relationship

0-517-59533-8 HARMONY $16.00

Harriet **Schechter** & Vicki **Gibbs**

More Time for Sex: The Organizing Guide for Busy Couples

Checklists, worksheets, quizzes, anecdotes enthusiastically cajole couples to reduce marital minutiae and find time to enjoy each other

0-525-93842-7 DUTTON $17.95

Andrew **Stanway**

The Art of Sensual Loving: A New Approach to Sexual Relationships

Illustrated guide covering attraction and courtship to lovemaking positions. Emphasizes non-intercourse sexuality and the art of arousal

0-88184-507-8 CARROLL & GRAF PB $15.95

A Woman's Guide to Men and Sex

Everything from the psychology of the male ego to foreplay, with over 60 illustrations

0-88184-706-2 CARROLL & GRAF PB $11.95

Stuart **Sovatsky**

Passions of Innocence: Tantric Celibacy and the Mysteries of Eros

Explains how periods of celibacy enhance eroticism. Exercises based on yoga, kundalini, and chakra meditation are included

0-89281-405-5 INNER TRADITIONS PB $14.95

Vinod **Verma**

The Kamasutra for Women: The Modern Woman's Way to Sensual Fulfillment and Health

Written by a neurobiologist and combining both Western medical research and the Indian healing arts of yoga and ayurveda, this update of the *Kamasutra* specifically addresses the full range of female heterosexual experience: menstruation, pregnancy, childbirth, menopause, relationships, sexual techniques, and more. Ancient and modern wisdom, sexual and spiritual

See also **SEXUALITY**

1-56836-141-6 KODANSHA $20.00

Ruth **Westheimer**

Dr. Ruth's Guide to Good Sex

Sexual straight talk from the television personality, which dispels myths and clarifies facts and techniques

0-446-34529-6 WARNER PB $6.50

Glenn **Wilson**

Creative Loving: An Inspiring Guide to the Art of Making Love

0-7867-0320-2 CARROLL & GRAF PB $17.95

Maurice **Yaffe** & Elizabeth **Fenwick**

Sexual Happiness: A Practical Approach

A self-help guide for sex therapy

0-8050-0691-5 HOLT $24.95

Morton **Walker**

Sexual Nutrition: How to Nutritionally Improve, Enhance and Stimulate Your Sexual Appetite

Increasing your libido with healthy "nutridisiacs"

0-89529-565-2 AVERY PB $9.95

Sex & Culture

Michael Vincent **Miller**

Intimate Terrorism: The Deterioration of Erotic Life

Intimate terrorism refers to the conjugal power struggle brought on by America's cultural myths of romance—a disappointment that creates a "culture of abuse"

0-393-03759-2 NORTON $23.00

0-393-31532-0 NORTON PB $13.00

Lawrence **Osborne**

The Poisoned Embrace: A Brief History of Sexual Pessimism

A fascinating and accessible scholarly discussion of the relationship between death and sex in Western culture

0-679-75414-8 VINTAGE PB $12.00

Medieval tales, however, are full of the titillating proximity of sex and the dead. Time and again, we meet people creeping into nunneries at night who unexpectedly meet processions of the dead, like those rumored to roam around the countryside on All Souls' Day, the Day of the Dead. The price of such an encounter was always death by dawn.

THE POISONED EMBRACE: A BRIEF HISTORY OF SEXUAL PESSIMISM

Richard A. **Posner**

Sex and Reason

An incisive examination of the history of sexuality and its social control, from ancient Greece to contemporary Sweden. "Extraordinary....An ambitious and complex undertaking....Posner combines a passion for exposing humbug and pseudoprofundity with an odd but genuine sort of social compassion, a delight in shocking the self-righteous with a love of human diversity and freedom"
—Martha Nussbaum, *The New Republic*

0-674-80279-9 HARVARD $29.95

Donna C. **Stanton**, editor

Discourses of Sexuality: From Aristotle to AIDS

Fourteen scholars, artists, and critics examine the history and meaning of sex in the Western world

0-472-06513-0 MICHIGAN PB $14.95

Timothy **Taylor**

The Prehistory of Sex: Four Million Years of Human Sexual Culture

British archaeologist presents what *Publishers Weekly* calls a "groundbreaking, riveting survey that strongly suggests that sex and love among prehistoric peoples was less bestial than is commonly assumed"

0-553-09694-X BDDL $23.95

1-85702-352-8 MCCLELLAND & STEWART $34.99

Erotica

Lonnie **Barbach**, editor

Pleasures: Women Write Erotica

What do women want? Just what men do, as revealed in these short steamy stories of truth and fantasy

0-06-097002-2 HARPERCOLLINS PB $13.00

Georges **Bataille**

Story of the Eye

"One of the most original and unsettling of those thinkers who, in the wake of Sade and Nietzsche, have confronted the possibility of thought in a world that has lost its myth of transcendence."
—Peter Brooks, *NY Times Book Review*

See also **FICTION** under **MODERN FRENCH LITERATURE** in **LITERATURE OF EUROPE, AFRICA, AND ASIA**

0-87286-209-7 CITY LIGHTS PB $7.95

Susie **Bright**, editor

The Best American Erotica 1995

"Bright...brings us a brand-new, skin-tingling potpourri of stories you won't hear told at the dinner table"—*Publishers Weekly*

0-684-80163-9 TOUCHSTONE PB $12.00

Herotica 1: A Collection of Women's Erotic Fiction

A real "sexual banquet"

0-940208-11-3 DOWN THERE PRESS PB ... $8.50

Susie **Bright** & others, editors

Herotica 2

An intriguing collection of short pieces of women's erotica. A companion volume to the 1988 *Herotica 1*, now an underground classic

0-452-26787-0 PLUMSTOCK PB $11.95

Miriam DeCosta Willis, editor

Erotique Noire/Black Erotica

Gay and straight, funny and raunchy

0-385-42309-8 ANCHOR PB $14.95

Nik **Douglas** & Penny **Slinger**

Sexual Secrets: The Alchemy of Ecstasy

0-89281-266-4 INNER TRADITIONS PB $19.95

Iris **Finz** & Steven **Finz**

Whispered Secrets: The Couple's Guide to Erotic Fantasy

Couples share their imaginative and intimate fantasies

0-451-16401-6 NEW AMERICAN LIBRARY PB $5.99

Charlotte **Hill** & William **Wallace**

Erotica III: The Ultimate Collection of Sexual Art and Literature from Around the World

0-7867-0297-4 CARROLL & GRAF PB $17.95

Maxim **Jakubowski**, editor

Mammoth Book of Erotica

Steamy short stories, in bulk

0-7867-0158-7 CARROLL & GRAF PB $10.95

Marcy **Sheiner**, editor

Herotica 4: A New Collection of Erotic Writing by Women

A collection of 29 stories that covers (or uncovers) just about every sexual experience, including "infidelity, talking dirty, pornography, lesbianism, heterosexuality, group sex, dominance, submission, visions of pleasure on another planet and even a gender-changing vampire"—*Publishers Weekly*

0-452-27181-9 PLUME PB $12.95

Richard Glyn **Jones** & Susan A. **Williams**, editors

The Penguin Book of Erotic Stories by Women

The 31 tales cover 103 years and six continents, arranged chronologically. "In a compilation that includes such diverse authors as Edith Wharton and Kathy Acker, it's a safe bet that each reader will find some of these tales titillating, others curious and still others repulsive"
—*Publishers Weekly*

0-670-86620-2 VIKING $24.95

Richard **Burton**, translator

The Kama Sutra of Vatsyayana

The classic translation as it appeared in 1883

EDITED AND WITH PREFACE BY W.G. ARCHER

0-425-09593-2 BERKLEY PB $5.99

Sir Richard Burton

Alain **Danielou**, translator

The Complete Kama Sutra

"Dildo was translated as 'medicine.' Lesbian was just 'corrupt woman'. No wonder we couldn't follow any of the instructions in the *Kama Sutra.* But now, there's a new translation of the oldest sex manual, the first since the Victorians brought it home and hid it under the mattress"
—*The Guardian Weekend*

0-89281-492-6 INNER TRADITIONS $29.95

0-89281-525-6 INNER TRADITIONS PB $19.95

Phyllis **Kronhausen** & Eberhard **Kronhausen**, editors

Erotic Fantasies: A Study of the Sexual Imagination

Back in print, these mental aphrodisiacs from erotic classics range from early folklore through the Victorians to the present

0-8021-3006-2 GROVE PB $15.95

Lizabeth **Paravisini-Gebert**, editor

Pleasure in the Word: Erotic Writing by Latin American Women

Isabelle Allende and others contribute to a previously taboo subject

0-452-27104-5 PLUME PB $10.95

Donald **McCormick**

Erotic Literature: A Connoisseur's Guide

0-8264-0594-0 CONTINUUM PB $14.95

Shaykh **Nefzawi**

The Illustrated Perfumed Garden: A 90's Adaptation of the Ancient Treatise on Lovemaking

0-7322-5634-8 HARPERCOLLINS PB $26.00

Richard **Burton**, translator

The Perfumed Garden

The classic 16th-century text by Shaykh Nefzawi on seduction and lovemaking

0-89281-443-8 INNER TRADITIONS PB.............$16.95

Anaïs **Nin**

Delta of Venus: Erotica

Seventeen erotic stories written by Nin in the 1940s

0-671-74249-3 POCKET PB..................................$6.99

Little Birds: Erotica

More erotic stories

See also **FICTION SINCE 1945** under **20TH-CENTURY AMERICAN FICTION** in **LITERATURE OF THE AMERICAS**

0-671-68011-0 POCKET PB $5.99

Fiona **Pitt-Kethley**

The Literary Companion to Sex

Sex in the arts, or the art of sex: a rollicking tour through some of the most distinguished erotica ever written. The Bible, Rabelais, Defoe; Joe Orton, John Updike, and Anaïs Nin—organized by historical era, this unique book guides us through literary sex from the ancient world to the 20th century

0-679-42323-0 RANDOM HOUSE $25.00
0-679-76952-8 RANDOM HOUSE PB................$17.00

Lily **Pond** & Richard **Russo**, editors

The Book of Eros: Arts and Letters from *Yellow Silk*

The second volume in the erotic series. "A lagniappe of tasteful but intriguing ecstasies" —*Publishers Weekly*

0-517-79962-6 HARMONY $22.00

John **Preston** & Michael **Lowenthal**, editors

Flesh and the Word 3: An Anthology of Gay Erotic Writing

"The imagery here is often visceral, the language sophisticated and the humor on an even keel with eros"—*Publishers Weekly*

See also **SEX AND SEXUALITY** under **GAY, LESBIAN, AND BISEXUAL STUDIES** in **SOCIAL STUDIES**

0-452-27252-1 PENGUIN PB $13.95

Michele **Slung**, editor

Fever: Sensual Stories by Women Writers

Selections from the *Slow Hand*

0-06-092650-3 HARPERCOLLINS PB $12.00

Slow Hand: Women Writing Erotica

0-06-016592-7 HARPER COLLINS $20.00
0-06-092236-2 HARPER PERENNIAL PB............$17.00

Pauline **Reage**

The Story of O

The author of this classic erotic tale remained anonymous for many years and was only recently reveled to be Reage

0-345-30111-0 BALLANTINE PB $5.99

David **Steinberg**, editor

The Erotic Impulse: Honoring the Sensual Self

A thoughtful collection of poetry, essays, and short fiction celebrating the healing power of sex

0-87477-697-X TARCHER PB..............................$13.95

Weddings

"If it were not for the presents, an elopement would be preferable."—George Ade

Yetta Fisher **Gruen**

Wediquette: The Answers to All Your Wedding Etiquette Questions

0-14-024139-6 PENGUIN PB.............................$10.95

Judith **Martin**

Miss Manners on (Painfully Proper) Weddings

Sprinkled with illustrations and humor, the popular syndicated columnist "upholds the perennial etiquette that contributes to our general civility...."—*Publishers Weekly*

0-517-70187-1 CROWN $14.00

Eleanor **Munro**, editor

Wedding Readings: Centuries of Writing and Rituals on Love and Marriage

0-14-008879-2 PENGUIN PB $12.95

Elizabeth **Post**

Emily Post's Wedding Planner

An update from *the* source, by her daughter

0-06-273018-5 HARPERCOLLINS PB..................$8.00

Carol **Reed-Jones**

Green Weddings that Don't Cost the Earth

Planning a wedding with the environment as focus. Includes recipes, index, bibliography, and illustrations

0-9650833-0-6 PAPER CRANE PRESS PB $10.95

Nicole **Rubel**

Getting Married: A Guide for the Bride-To-Be

A cartoon spoof on planning weddings

0-312-01766-9 ST. MARTIN'S PB.........................$5.95

Martha **Stewart**

Weddings

Lavish photographs and detailed instructions for more than 40 weddings, including such elements as music, flower arrangement, table decorations, and menus

See also **ENTERTAINING**

0-517-55675-8 CLARKSON POTTER.................$70.00

Marriage

"A married couple are well suited when both partners usually feel the need for a quarrel at the same time."—Jean Rostand

Rosalind **Barnett** & Caryl **Rivers**

He Works/She Works: How the New American Family Is Making It Work

A study sponsored by the National Institutes of Health investigated two-income households. Although the study is of white and heterosexual couples, there is valuable insight into the dynamic of all contemporary working couples

0-06-251080-0 HARPERCOLLINS.....................$24.00

Regina **Barreca**

Perfect Husbands and Other Fairy Tales: Demystifying Marriage, Men, and Romance

A witty and engaging account of the evolving roles of husbands and wives in a radically changed world. As provocative as Colette Dowling's *The Cinderella Complex* and Deborah Tannen's *You Just Don't Understand*

See also **THE FEMALE EXPERIENCE** under **WOMEN'S STUDIES** in **SOCIAL STUDIES**

0-517-59538-9 HARMONY...............................$20.00

Dave **Barry**

Dave Barry's Guide to Marriage And/Or Sex

Humor on topics like "How to find somebody to go on dates with and eventually marry someone who is not a total jerk" and "How to argue like a veteran couple"

0-87857-725-4 RODALE PB...............................$8.95

Joyce **Brothers**

What Every Woman Ought to Know About Love and Marriage

Advice from the popular columnist, surprisingly sensible and useful

0-345-32113-8 BALLANTINE PB........................$6.99

Betty **Carter** & Joan K. **Peters**

Love, Honor and Negotiate: Making Your Marriage Work

From a family therapist; this "enlightening handbook will compel couples to reexamine their power games, hidden agendas and sexual and emotional needs"—*Publishers Weekly*

0-671-89624-5 POCKET..................................$23.00

Joel **Crohn**

Mixed Matches: How to Create Successful Interracial, Interethnic, and Interfaith Marriages

A psychotherapist discusses his 14 years of research on how mixed couples cope with each other, children, parents, and society

0-449-90961-1 FAWCETT PB.............................$12.00

William **Lederer** & Don D. **Jackson**

The Miracles of Marriage

FOREWORD BY KARL MENNINGER

0-393-30632-1 NORTON PB $11.00

Ronnie **Edell**

How to Save Your Marriage from an Affair: Seven Steps to Rebuilding a Broken Trust

How to restore marital harmony and bring back love and commitment

0-8217-4886-6 ZEBRA PB $12.00

John **Gottman**

Why Marriages Succeed or Fail

The fruits of decades of research reveal how married couples relate to each other will determine within 94 percent accuracy if the marriage will succeed or not

0-671-86748-2 SIMON & SCHUSTER $21.00
0-684-80241-4 FIRESIDE PB $12.00

Lis **Harris**

Rules of Engagement: Four Couples and American Marriage Today

A staff writer at *The New Yorker* spent several years with four couples of different backgrounds to present an entertaining and illuminating picture of marriage today

0-684-80826-0 SIMON & SCHUSTER $23.00
0-684-82527-9 TOUCHSTONE PB $11.00

Rosanna **Hertz**

More Equal than Others: Women and Men in Dual-Career Marriages

0-520-05804-6 CALIFORNIA $35.00

Bonnie **Maslin**

The Angry Marriage: Overcoming the Rage, Reclaiming the Love

Discover why you fell in love in the first place

1-56282-806-1 HYPERION $19.95
0-7868-8069-4 WARNER PB $12.95

Barry **McCarthy** & Emily **McCarthy**

Intimate Marriage: Developing a Life Partnership

Explains the relationship of self-esteem and success in marriage. Case studies, exercises, and practical information

0-88184-824-7 CARROLL & GRAF PB $10.95

Valerie **Monroe**

In the Weather of the Heart: A Memoir of a Shattered Marriage and a Reckoning with Recovery

"A sensitive memoir and a good antidote for those who believe marriages require little work to be successful"—*Publishers Weekly*

See also **ADDICTION AND RECOVERY** under **SELF-HELP**

0-385-47103-3 DOUBLEDAY $22.50

Charlotte **Myerson**

Goin' to the Chapel: Dreams of Love, Realities of Marriage

From interviewing 100 women about their ideas on marriage and its realities, others can learn how not to be frustrated with sex, careers, kids, and chores

0-465-04180-0 BASIC $20.00

Augustus **Napier**

The Fragile Bond: In Search of an Equal, Intimate and Enduring Marriage

The common crises of modern marriages, based on the author's experience and other case histories

0-06-091598-6 HARPERCOLLINS PB $14.00

Dagmar **O'Connor**

How to Make Love to the Same Person for the Rest of Your Life

The possibility of enjoying emotional commitment and good sex with one person

0-553-26099-5 BDD PB $5.99

Frank **Pittman**

Private Lies: Infidelity and the Betrayal of Intimacy

A frank and nonjudgmental analysis of affairs through anecdote and case histories by a seasoned family therapist

0-393-30707-7 NORTON PB $11.95

Cathleen **Rountree**

The Country of Marriage: Discovering the Secrets of Enduring Love

Interviews of couples who have created long-lasting unions, from the author of *Coming into Our Fullness*

0-06-250842-3 HARPERCOLLINS $22.95

Eileen **Simpson**

Late Love: A Celebration of Marriage After Fifty

Psychotherapist interviewed 50 couples, some as old as 90, who married after 55

0-395-67587-1 HOUGHTON MIFFLIN $21.95
0-395-75533-6 DORLING KINDERSLEY PB $10.95

Richard **Taylor**

Having Love Affairs

Analyzes the nature of affairs through the discussion of fidelity, ethics, ego (male), and etiquette for those involved in or affected by an affair

0-87975-186-X PROMETHEUS PB $19.95

Judith S. **Wallerstein** & Sandra **Blakeslee**

The Good Marriage: How and Why Love Lasts

An exploration of what makes up a successful and lasting marriage

0-446-67248-3 WARNER PB $12.99

Ruth **Westheimer**

Dr. Ruth's Guide for Married Lovers

Adding vitality to romance and sex to keep the love affair in marriage

0-446-34562-8 WARNER PB $4.99

Living Single

Michael **Broder**

The Art of Living Single

The complete guide to enjoying life on your own

0-380-70933-3 AVON PB $5.99

Barbara Levy **Simpson**

Never Married Women

Fifty never-married women born before 1919 talk about day-to-day life, adaptations, and stigmas

0-87722-671-7 TEMPLE PB $12.95

Parenting

Today's parents face old dilemmas and new decisions, and an increasing number of works offer them help; these books reflect recent changes in American family life. New technologies combat infertility, gentler methods of childbirth have evolved, and the traditional "family unit" has changed irrevocably with the prevalence of single working mothers and fathers who are more than mere breadwinners.

Adoption

Elizabeth **Bartholet**

Family Bonds: Adoption and the Politics of Parenting

Bartholet examines the emotional and legal aspects of adoption, and looks at the domestic and international laws that often leave would-be parents childless and deny homes to parentless children. The mother of two adopted children, Bartholet draws on her own triumphs and disappointments as well as the most recent legal rulings. "A seminal volume."—*Kirkus Reviews*

0-395-70064-7 HOUGHTON MIFFLIN PB $10.95

J. Douglas **Bates**

Gift Children: A Story of Race, Family, and Adoption in a Divided America

A white newpaper reporter's memoir of rearing two black girls. "…confronts with exemplary wisdom and integrity the complex issues that face the families of transracial adopted children as they grow up"—Daniel Goldstine, *NY Times*

0-395-63314-1 TICKNOR & FIELDS $21.95

Eric **Blau**

Stories of Adoption: Loss and Reunion

Personal stories of reunions by adoptees, birth-mothers and fathers, and adoptive parents. Photos

0-939165-17-1 NEWSAGE PB $16.95

Edmund **Bolles**

The Penguin Adoption Handbook: A Guide to Creating Your New Family

0-14-046548-0 PENGUIN PB $12.00

Lois **Gilman**

The Adoption Resource Book: All the Things You Need to Know and Ought to Know About Creating an Adoptive Family

Finding support and resources

0-06-273043-6 HARPERCOLLINS PB $14.00

Merry Bloch **Jones**

Birth Mothers: Women Who Have Relinquished Babies for Adoption Tell Their Stories

1-55652-192-8 CHICAGO REVIEW....................$21.95

Phoebe **Koehler**

The Day We Met You

0-02-750901-X SIMON & SCHUSTER $14.00

Jeanne Warren **Lindsay**

Pregnant? Adoption is an Option

Adoption from the birthparents' side

1-88535-608-0 MORNING GLORY PB $11.95

Lois **Melina**

Raising Adopted Children: A Manual for Adoptive Parents

0-06-096039-6 HARPERCOLLINS PB................$12.50

Carol **Schaefer**

The Other Mother: A True Story

0-939149-75-3 SOPHIA PB $12.95

Judith **Schaffer** & Christina **Lindstrom**

How to Raise an Adopted Child

0-452-26560-6 DUTTON PB..............................$12.95

Robin O. **Sweet** & Patty **Bryan**

Adopt International: Everything You Need to Know to Adopt a Child from Abroad

0-374-52468-8 NOONDAY PB $16.00

Susan **Wadia-Ells**, editor

The Adoption Reader: Birth Mothers, Adoptive Mothers and Adopted Daughters Tell Their Stories

A helpful and vital book about growth and self-understanding

1-87806-765-6 SEAL PB $15.95

Susan Wadia-Ells (photo by Greg Bolosky)

Jan L. **Waldron**

Giving Away Simone: A Memoir of Daughters, Mothers, Adoption, and Reunion

A poignant recounting of a writer's reunion with her 11-year-old daughter, whom she gave up at birth

0-8129-2400-2 TIME BOOKS............................$22.00

Conception

Birth Control

Sherman **Silber**

How Not to Get Pregnant: Your Guide to Simple, Reliable Contraception

0-446-39088-7 WARNER PB $9.95

Beverly **Winikoff** & Suzanne **Wymelenberg**

The Whole Truth About Contraceptives: A Decision-Making Guide for Teenagers to Middle-Agers

0-309-05494-X NATIONAL ACADEMY PB........$14.95

Merryl **Winstein**

Your Fertility Signals: Using Them to Achieve or Avoid Pregnancy, Naturally

Clearly explains ovulation and the natural methods of temperature and other signals to reduce or even eliminate the need for contraceptives

0-9619401-0-7 SMOOTH STONE PB $12.95

Getting Pregnant

Alan **Guttmacher**

Pregnancy, Birth, and Family Planning

Includes a useful chapter on birth-control methods

0-451-16632-9 NEW AMERICAN LIBRARY PB....$5.99

Niels H. **Lauersen** & Colette **Bouchez**

Getting Pregnant: What Couples Need to Know Right Now

This book explains for the layperson the past three years' advancement in fertility research and its breakthroughs

0-449-90667-1 FAWCETT PB $12.95

Elizabeth **Noble**

Having Your Baby by Donor Insemination: A Complete Resource Guide

0-395-45395-X HOUGHTON MIFFLIN PB..........$15.95

How To Get Pregnant

A small book with basic information on fertility

0-446-38642-1 WARNER PB..............................$13.99

Shelly **Lavigne**

How to Make a Boy or Girl Baby!: Over 60 Tried and True Ways

For those who care about the gender of their child

0-440-50657-3 DIAL BOOKS PB $7.95

Miriam **Stoppard**

Conception, Pregnancy, and Birth

Easily accessible text and more than 500 photos and illustrations provide a complete guide to what every parent should know: birthing choices, medical tests, labor, nutrition, exercise, and the partner's role in the birthing practice

1-56458-182-9 DORLING KINDERSLEY $29.95

Toni **Weschler**

Taking Charge of Your Fertility: The Definitive Guide to Natural Birth Control and Pregnancy

Written by a women's health educator, it presents the Fertility Awareness Method of birth control as an alternative to chemical, barrier, and surgical methods

0-06-095053-6 HARPERPERENNIAL PB...........$22.00

Miscarriage

Sherokee **Ilse**

Empty Arms: Coping After Miscarriage, Stillbirth, & Infant Death

0-9609456-4-4 WINTERGREEN PB $5.50

Sherokee **Ilse** & Linda Hammer **Burns**

Miscarriage: A Shattered Dream

0-9609456-3-6 WINTERGREEN PB.......................$7.50

Claudia **Panuthos** & Catherine **Romero**

Ended Beginnings: Healing Childbearing Losses

A guide to emotional healing

0-89789-054-X BERGIN & GARVEY PB..............$14.95

Infertility

Paulette Bates **Alden**

Crossing the Moon: A Journey Through Infertility

How a writer's infertility affected her life

1-88691-308-0 HUNGRY MIND........................$20.00

Gary S. **Berger** & others

The Couple's Guide to Fertility: How New Medical Advances Can Help You Have a Baby

Covers it all, from hormone therapy to surgery. Includes directory of leading fertility specialists and centers

0-385-26390-2 DOUBLEDAY PB.........................$16.95

Lynda **Stephenson**

Give Us a Child: Coping with the Personal Crisis of Infertility

0-310-57931-7 ZONDERVAN PB $9.99

Surrogate Parenting

Liz **Carpenter**

Unplanned Parenthood: The Confessions of a Seventy–something Surrogate Mother

"I wish Liz Carpenter would adopt me. This book tells why"—Bill Moyers

FOREWORD BY ERMA BOMBECK

0-449-90995-6 FAWCETT PB $11.00

Pregnancy

The American College of Obstetrics and Gynecology

Planning for Pregnancy, Birth and Beyond

A thoughtful guide for those considering parenthood; ranges from pre-conception care to postpartem adjustment

0-525-94140-1 DUTTON $23.95

Bill M. **Atalla**

The Thirteen Months of Pregnancy: A Guide for the Pregnant Father

Gives the father-to-be the basics on pregnancy, childbirth, and beyond in a lighthearted format with color cartoon illustrations

0-9631754-5-9 ODDLY ENOUGH PUBLICATIONS$19.95

Maureen **Bard**

Getting Organized for Your New Baby: A Checklist and Planning Guide for Busy Parents to Be

0-671-53477-7 MEADOWBROOK PB $9.00
0-88166-081-7 SIMON & SCHUSTER PB $5.00

Michael **Benson**

Pregnancy Myths: What Not to Expect When You're Expecting

Commonly held beliefs about pregnancy and childbirth are debunked

1-56924-822-2 MARLOWE PB $9.95

Ronald M. **Caplan** & Betty **Rothbart**

Your Pregnancy: Reassuring Answers to the Questions of Mothers to Be

0-688-10826-1 QUILL PB $5.95

Laura **Chester**, editor

Cradle and All: Women Writers on Pregnancy and Birth

An anthology of prose and poetry from 50 contemporary writers, including Joyce Carol Oates, Adrienne Rich, and Erica Jong, capturing the pleasure and pain of motherhood

See also **POETRY ANTHOLOGIES** under **ANTHOLOGIES OF WOMEN'S WRITING** under **WOMEN'S STUDIES** in **SOCIAL STUDIES**

0-571-12989-7 FABER PB $12.95

Joyce Carol Oates

Glade **Curtis**

Your Pregnancy Week-By-Week: Revised and Expanded Edition

The format provides the parents-to-be a close-up look at the developmental changes of the fetus, as well as topics pertinent to each successive week

1-55561-068-4 FISHER PB $12.95

Lindsay **Curtis** & others

Pregnant & Lovin' It

A question-and-answer format gleaned from 2,000 couples who attended the authors' childbirth classes, covering topics from pregnancy testing to contraception after giving birth

0-399-51744-8 PERIGEE PB $8.95

Arlene **Eisenberg**, Heidi Eisenberg **Murkhoff**, Sandee Eisenberg **Hathaway**

What to Eat When You're Expecting

Includes recipes, diet guidelines, and information about how diet reduces the side effects of pregnancy, such as morning sickness and mood swings

0-89480-015-9 WORKMAN PB $8.95

What to Expect When You're Expecting

Attractively designed month-by-month guide

0-89480-769-2 WORKMAN PB $10.95

Richard I. **Feinbloom**

Pregnancy, Birth & the Early Months: A Complete Guide

"Encyclopedic…clear, well-written, and succinct"—*The New England Journal of Medicine*

0-201-58149-3 ADDISON-WESLEY PB $15.00

Tikva **Frymer-Kensky**

Motherprayer: The Pregnant Woman's Spiritual Companion

A collection culled over 16 years of study uses prayers and biblical interpretations from the past to inspire modern thinking on the spiritual dimensions of pregancy, birth, and the female body

1-57322-011-6 PUTNAM $22.00
1-57322-553-3 RIVERHEAD PB $12.00

Geraldine Lux **Flanagan**

The First Nine Months of Life

Black-and-white photographs chronicle the baby in utero

0-671-45975-9 SIMON & SCHUSTER PB $11.00

Clark **Gillespie**

Your Pregnancy Month by Month

A valuable monthly guide, from conception to delivery

0-06-055271-9 HARPERCOLLINS $22.00
0-06-096533-9 HARPERPERENNIAL PB $13.00

Janis **Graham**

Your Pregnancy Companion

In addition to common medical concerns, this well-organized book discusses pregnancy's effect on emotions, lifestyle, and work

0-671-68557-0 POCKET PB $12.00

Tracy **Hotchner**

Pregnancy and Childbirth: Complete Guide for a New Life

A thorough guide (over 700 pages) to all aspects of pregnancy and childbirth

0-380-75946-2 AVON PB $11.00

Pregnancy Pure & Simple: Everything Expectant Parents Need to Know

Practical information presented in a no-nonsense and concise format

0-380-77434-8 AVON PB $10.00

Vicki **Iovine**

The Girlfriends' Guide to Pregnancy: Or, Everything Your Doctor Won't Tell You

"Iovine anticipates every conceivable question, and her responses are warm, wise and witty" —*Publishers Weekly*

0-671-52431-3 POCKET PB $10.00

Robert V. **Johnson**

Mayo Clinic Complete Book of Pregnancy & Baby's First Year

Summoning experts from the clinic's staff in obstetrics, pediatrics, family medicine, and parent education, "The tone throughout is refreshingly sober and unhyped, an antidote to the pushy coziness of some child care tomes…"—*Publishers Weekly*

0-688-11761-9 MORROW $30.00

Elyse Zorn **Karlin** & others

The Complete Baby Checklist: A Total Organizing System for Parents

0-380-76347-8 AVON PB $12.00

Sheila **Kitzinger**

Complete Book of Pregnancy and Childbirth

From a well-known expert and author

0-394-58011-7 KNOPF $22.50

Peter **Mayle**

How To be a Pregnant Father

0-8184-0399-3 LYLE STUART PB $9.95

Sheila **Kitzinger** & Vicky **Bailey**

Pregnancy Day by Day: The Expectant Mother's Diary, Record Book, and Guide

An efficient way to get organized

0-394-58751-0 KNOPF....................................$20.00

Marshall H. **Klaus** & others

Bonding: Building the Foundations of Secure Attachment and Independence

The process of bonding from pregnancy through breastfeeding; includes a discussion of pre-term babies and adoption

0-201-62673-X ADDISON-WESLEY..................$22.00
0-201-44198-5 ADDISON-WESLEY PB..............$12.00

Neils **Lauerson** & Judy **Hendra**

It's Your Pregnancy: An Obstetrician Answers Your Most Intimate Questions about Pregnancy and Childbirth

The authors cover "subjects not addressed in other books, such as the safety of airport scanners, as well as pre-pregnancy considerations, such as fertility and pregnancy over 35"
—*Library Journal*

0-671-50211-5 FIRESIDE PB..............................$12.95

Jennifer **Louden**

The Pregnant Woman's Comfort Book: A Self-Nurturing Guide to Your Emotional Well-Being During Pregnancy and Early Motherhood

Emphasizes the mother-to-be's well-being during pregnancy to lay the foundation for a healthy and happy motherhood

0-06-251165-3 HARPERCOLLINS PB................$14.00

Jacqueline Vincent **Priya**

Birth Traditions & Modern Pregnancy Care

A fascinating exploration of women's knowledge and beliefs about pregnancy, labor, and birth in cultures worldwide

1-85230-321-2 ELEMENT PB..............................$10.95

Margie **Profet**

Protecting Your Baby-to-Be: Preventing Birth Defects Within the First Three Months of Pregnancy

A MacArthur Award-winning evolutionary biologist Profet, has written a revolutionary book that examines how pregnancy sickness, rather than being an unfortunate side effect of the first trimester, actually helps prevent birth defects by shielding the embryo from plant toxins found in many vegetables, herb teas, and other foods. Most important, she comes to the valuable conclusion that we can learn from morning sickness a way to eat that minimizes risks to the embryo. Required reading for all parents-to-be

0-201-40768-X ADDISON-WESLEY...................$20.00

Miriam **Stoppard**

Dr. Miriam Stoppard's Pregnancy and Birth Book

A popular resource

0-345-31908-7 BALLANTINE PB........................$10.00

Baby Names

Alfred **Kolatch**

The Dictionary of First Names

0-399-50570-9 PUTNAM PB..............................$9.95

Linda **Rosenkrantz** &
Pamela Redmond **Satran**

Beyond Jennifer & Jason

Over 200,000 copies of this savvy guide to naming your child have already been sold, but it is now available in a larger, higher quality format. Beware of imitations; this is the original that *The Wall Street Journal* called "The arbiter of hip baby names"

0-312-10426-X ST. MARTIN'S PB........................$11.95

Diet and Exercise During Pregnancy

Mary Abbott **Hess** & Anne Elise **Hunt**

Eating for Two: The Complete Guide to Nutrition During Pregnancy

0-02-065441-3 MACMILLAN PB........................$13.00

Elizabeth **Somer**

Nutrition for a Healthy Pregnancy: The Complete Guide to Eating Before, During, and After Your Pregnancy

This hefty volume offers information on how food can improve fertility and prevent birth defects as well as dietary suggestions to help avoid post-partum depression

0-8050-3775-6 HOLT PB....................................$14.95

Childbirth

Michael D. **Benson**

Birth Day! the Last 24 Hours of Pregnancy

This informative text tells mothers-to-be exactly what to expect in the delivery room, including cesarean sections, induced labor, pain medications, and common medical interventions

1-55778-587-2 MARLOWE PB..........................$10.95

In a society of growing complexity, there is commonly a gap between scientific advancements and a person's ability to cope as a patient... Being familiar with the many aspects of labor and delivery will help you to have a good birth experience. Childbirth in a modern hospital is not a frightening experience, especially if you know what to expect during the twelve to twenty-four hours before you give birth.

BIRTH DAY! THE LAST 24 HOURS OF PREGNANCY

Patricia **Bernstein**

Having a Baby: Mothers Tell Their Stories

0-671-72614-5 POCKET PB..............................$10.00

Diana **Bert**

Having a Baby

The personal accounts of seven friends

0-440-53491-7 DELL PB....................................$9.95

Elisabeth **Bing**

Six Practical Lessons for an Easier Childbirth

0-553-25984-9 BANTAM PB..............................$4.50

Judith Walzer **Leavitt**

Brought to Bed: Childbearing in America, 1750-1950

0-19-505690-6 OXFORD PB..............................$11.95

Richard W. **Wertz** & Dorothy C. **Wertz**

Lying-In: A History of Childbirth in America

See also SPECIAL STUDIES

0-300-04088-1 YALE...$35.00
0-300-04087-3 YALE PB...................................$18.00

Home, Lamaze, and Other Birth Methods

Janet **Balaskas**

Active Birth: The New Approach to Giving Birth Naturally

Only in the modern Western countries have women been made to lie on their backs for childbirth—a position that defies both nature and gravity. This book is designed to help mothers participate actively in pregnancy and childbirth, and to aid childbirth teachers, midwives, and birth partners. It includes stretching exercises and an up-to-date resource section

1-55832-037-7 HARVARD COMMON...............$19.95
1-55832-038-5 HARVARD COMMON PB..........$12.95

Robert A. **Bradley**

Husband-Coached Childbirth

This is the third edition of this popular book; illustrated

0-06-014850-0 HARPERCOLLINS.....................$22.00
0-55337556-3 BDD...$11.95

Ginny **Brinkley** & others

Your Child's First Journey: A Guide to Prepared Birth from Pregnancy to Parenthood

0-89529-372-2 AVERY PB...............................$10.95

Grantly **Dick-Read**

Childbirth Without Fear: The Original Approach to Natural Childbirth, 5th Edition

This classic bestseller revolutionized obstetrics from the '50s' notion of "delivery" to "birth"

0-06-015221-4 HARPERCOLLINS......................$17.95
0-06-080870-5 HARPERCOLLINS PB.................$6.50

Bruce **Flamm**

Birth after Caesarean: The Medical Facts

0-671-79218-0 FIRESIDE PB $11.00

Frederick **Leboyer**

Birth Without Violence

"One of the twenty books that changed the world"—*Utne Reader*

0-89281-545-0 INNER TRADITIONS PB $14.95

Beverly **Savage** & Diana **Simkin**

Preparation for Birth: The Complete Guide to the Lamaze Method

0-345-31230-9 BALLANTINE PB $12.00

Later-Life Pregnancy

Glade B. **Curtis**

Your Pregnancy After 30

1-55561088-9 FISHER PB....................$12.95

Patricia **Mellon-Elibol**

Having a Baby in Your Forties

9-99274851-6 LIFETIME PB $6.95

Postnatal Care

Frank P. **Manginello** & Theresa **Digeronimo**

Your Premature Baby: Everything You Need to Know About the Childbirth Treatment and Parenting of Premature Infants

0-471-53587-7 WILEY PB $15.95

Paula M. **Siegel**

The Next Nine Months: A Guide to Your Body After Giving Birth

For every expectant and new mother, the only guide devoted specifically to the mother's body postpartum—now in a revised and updated edition

0-14-024023-3 PENGUIN PB....................$10.95

Linda **Todd**

You and Your Newborn Baby: A Guide to the First Months After Birth

"A gentle, helpful book that will enable parents to respond to their new baby's needs"
—Sheila Kitzinger

1-55832-055-5 HARVARD COMMON $11.95
1-55832-054-7 HARVARD COMMON PB $5.95

Postpartum

Ann **Dunnewold** & Diane G. **Sanford**

Post Partum Survival Guide

1-87923-780-6 NEW HARBINGER PB $13.95

Elisabeth **Bing** & Libby **Colman**

Losing Weight After Pregnancy

Bing, the childbirth expert who introduced the Lamaze method to America, now outlines specific dietary and exercise guidelines for the different phases of the postpartum year and includes nutritional advice and information for lactating women

1-56282-811-8 HYPERION PB....................$9.95

Katharina **Dalton**

Depression After Childbirth: How to Recognize and Treat Postnatal Illness

0-19-286008-9 OXFORD PB $8.95

Karen R. **Kleiman** & Valerie D. **Raskin**

This Isn't What I Expected: Recognizing and Recovering from Depression and Anxiety After Childbirth

0-553-37075-8 BANTAM PB $12.95

Breastfeeding

Marvin **Eiger** & Sally **Olds**

The Complete Book of Breastfeeding

A clear, practical guide

0-553-26232-7 BDD PB $5.99

Sheila **Kitzinger**

Breastfeeding Your Baby

0-679-72433-8 KNOPF PB $20.00

La Leche League International

The Womanly Art of Breastfeeding: 35th Anniversary Edition

The book that set the standard for new mothers

0-452-26623-8 PLUME $12.95

Child Care

Day Care

Alison **Clarke-Steward**

Daycare

In this revised edition of her 1982 study, Clarke-Steward surveys the political and economic landscape of childcare. Her analysis will help parents make informed choices about daycare and better understand how their choices will affect their lives and their children's

0-674-19405-5 HARVARD....................$24.00
0-674-19406-3 HARVARD PB....................$9.95

Julia **Wrigley**

Other People's Children

Wrigley examines the dilemma that millions of working parents face: the cultural clash between foreign-born babysitters and American parents

0-465-05382-3 BASIC PB $13.00

Pediatric Guides

Barbara **Dixon** & Josleen **Wilson**

Good Health for African-American Kids

Acknowledges the health gap between white and black Americans; nutritionist Dixon advises a family health tree to chart heart disease. Nutrition, home remedies, how to find supportive health care providers, and more

0-517-88269-8 CROWN PB $18.00

Martin **Green**

A Sigh of Relief: First-Aid Handbook for Childhood Emergencies

Simple, clear instructions for common childhood injuries and illnesses

0-553-35180-X BANTAM PB $16.95

Kathi **Kemper**

The Holistic Pediatrician: A Parent's Comprehensive Guide to Safe and Effective Therapies for the 25 Most Common Childhood Ailments

The only book on holistic medicine written by a pediatrician, this scientific guide combines the best traditional and alternative therapies for common childhood problems

0-06-095177-X HARPERCOLLINS PB $18.00

Laura Walther **Nathanson**

The Portable Pediatrician

An authoritative and lively book on how healthfully to navigate the perilous early years. Very parent-friendly, with a glossary of medical terms, in-depth essays on important pediatric concepts, and month-by-month chapters on the well child, from birth to age five

0-06-271562-3 HARPERCOLLINS....................$40.00
0-06-273176-9 HARPERCOLLINS PB....................$20.00

Barton **Schmitt**

Instructions for Pediatric Patients

0-7216-3160-6 W.B. SAUNDERS PB $41.95

Your Child's Health: The Parents' Guide to Symptoms, Emergencies, Common Illness, Behavior and School Problems

"This terrific reference sets a new standard for child care books"—Dr. Daniel Broughton

0-553-35339-X BANTAM PB $17.95

Martha **Sears** & William **Sears**

25 Things Every New Mother Should Know

Simple and clear-headed advice about the problems and questions that often confuse a new parent

See also **FATHERS** under **BEING A PARENT**

1-55832-068-7 HARVARD COMMON....................$14.95

Edward L. **Shor**, editor

Caring for Your School-Age Child: Ages 5 to 12

Encyclopedic, with a wide range of topics that include not only physical ailments but issues such as homework and ADD

0-553-09981-7 BDD $29.95

Lendon H. **Smith**

How to Raise a Healthy Child

Over 30 years of medical practice and consultation distilled in this easy-to-use encyclopedia of pediatric medicine and nutrition. Controversial topics explored, such as immunization, circumcision, cause of SIDS, vitamin therapy, and antibiotics use

0-87131-798-2 EVANS $24.95

Benjamin **Spock** & Michael **Rothenberg**

Dr. Spock's Baby and Child Care

The classic, still indispensable book

0-525-93400-6 DUTTON $25.00
0-671-76060-2 POCKET PB $7.99

Benjamin Spock

Special Children

Jill **Bloom**

Help Me to Help My Child: A Sourcebook for Parents of Learning Disabled Children

Provides a solid overview of the massive array of information available, from legal rights and strategies to the research avenues, and peer and professional help needed by parents in order to become their children's advocates

0-316-09982-1 LITTLE, BROWN PB $11.95

Helen **Featherstone**

A Difference in the Family: Living with a Disabled Child

Help for the family with a handicapped child

0-14-005941-5 VIKING PB $12.95

Laura Shapiro **Kramer**

Uncommon Voyage: Parenting a Special Needs Child in the World of Alternative Medicine

Unconventional medical options are offered

See also **GENERAL** under **PEOPLE WITH DISABILITIES**

0-571-19887-2 FABER $24.95

Miriam **Kaufman**

Easy for You to Say

Adolescents with disabilities or chronic illness discuss sex, family, social activities, and death

See also **GENERAL** under **PEOPLE WITH DISABILITIES**

1-55013-619-4 KEY PORTER PB $15.95

Harold S. **Koplewicz**

It's Nobody's Fault: New Hope and Help for Difficult Children and Their Parents

0-8129-2473-8 TIME BOOKS $25.00

Tom **Sullivan**

Special Parent, Special Child: Parents of Children with Disabilities Share Their Trials, Triumphs, and Hard-Won Wisdom

Parents' stories of their struggle to bring dignity and joy to their children with disabilities

0-87477-782-8 TARCHER $21.95
0-87477-830-1 PUTNAM PB $13.95

Stages of Development

See also JEAN PIAGET under CHILD PSYCHOLOGY in PSYCHOLOGY under SOCIAL STUDIES

General

Clifford **Anderson**

The Stages of Life: A Groundbreaking Look at How We Mature

As a result of a groundbreaking psychoanalytic technique, Anderson identifies the stages of maturation from birth to adulthood, analyzes the behaviors and emotions that aid the process, and gives an essential understanding of its dynamics and pitfalls

0-87113-481-0 GROVE $23.00

T. Berry **Brazelton**

Touchpoints: Your Child's Emotional and Behavioral Development, the Essential Reference

"Move over Dr. Spock"—*NY Times*

0-201-09380-4 ADDISON-WESLEY $24.95
0-201-62690-X ADDISON-WESLEY PB $16.00

Richard **Ferber**

Solve Your Child's Sleep Problems

0-671-62099-1 SIMON & SCHUSTER PB $12.00

Selma **Fraiberg**

The Magic Years: Understanding and Handling the Problems of Early Childhood

An early psychoanalytic classic

0-684-71768-9 MACMILLAN PB $11.00

Jane **Healy**

Your Child's Growing Mind

The standard classic work on the developing mind of a child. Updated to include the most recent research into the brain. Healy charts the mind's development from infancy. What behaviors enhance its growth? How are anomalies, or for that matter disorders, distinguished?

0-385-46930-6 MAIN STREET PB $12.95

Barbara D. **Ingersoll** & Sam **Goldstein**

Lonely, Sad and Angry: A Parent's Guide to Depression in Children and Adolescents

Two psychiatrists bring their experience to a straightforward definition of childhood and adolescent depression

0-385-47641-8 DOUBLEDAY $21.95
0-385-47642-6 MAIN STREET PB $11.95

Sheldon **Lewis** & Sheila Kay **Lewis**

Stress-Proofing Your Child: Mind-Body Exercises to Enhance Your Child's Health

How to get your kid to relax, using guided imagery and affirmations for the psychological pain of life

0-553-35319-5 BANTAM PB $10.95

Ro **Logrippo**

In My World: Designing Living and Learning Environments for the Young

How to create useful and attractive space for kids

0-471-11162-7 WILEY $24.95

Angela **Phillips**

The Trouble with Boys

Phillips warns that the standards by which we raise boys reflect a bygone world where women were dependents rather than equal partners. The result: violence against women, rising crime, broken families

FOREWORD BY ROBERT COLES

0-465-08735-3 BASIC PB $14.00

Infancy

Louise Bates **Ames**

Your One-Year-Old: The Fun-Loving, Fussy 12- to 24-Month-Old

9-993-03962-4 DOUBLEDAY PB $9.95

Your Two Year Old: Terrible or Tender

0-440-50638-7 DELACORTE PB $10.95

T. Berry **Brazelton**

Infants and Mothers: Differences in Development

0-385-29209-0 DELACORTE PB $16.00

Toddlers and Parents: A Declaration of Independence

0-385-29790-4 DELACORTE PB $16.00

Frank **Caplan**, editor

The Second Twelve Months of Life

Month-by-month courses in baby development

0-553-26438-9 BDD PB $6.50

Stanley **Greenspan** & Nancy **Greenspan**

First Feelings: Milestones in the Emotional Development of Your Baby and Child from Birth to Age Four

Overview of early emotional development by child psychiatrists

0-14-011988-4 PENGUIN PB $12.95

Claire B. **Kopp**

Baby Steps: A Parents' Guide to Understanding Behavior During the First Two Years

The result of nearly 30 years of research, this fascinating volume leads parents and caregivers through the changes and milestones in their children's behavior, motor skills, perception, and mental and emotional states during these formative years

0-7167-2390-5 FREEMAN $23.95
0-7167-2499-5 FREEMAN PB $14.95

Penelope **Leach**

Babyhood

How a baby thinks, feels, learns, and expresses needs

0-394-71436-9 KNOPF PB $17.00

Your Baby and Child: From Birth to Age Five

"Well researched, well written and sensitive to both parents' and children's needs in the task of growing up together"—T. Berry Brazelton

0-394-57951-8 KNOPF $29.95
0-679-72425-7 KNOPF PB $19.95

William **Sears**

The Fussy Baby

Care for the difficult, demanding baby

0-451-16327-3 SIGNET PB $4.99

SIDS: A Parent's Guide to Understanding and Preventing Sudden Infant Death Syndrome

"The reassuring guide acknowledges the fierce grip of parental anxiety and counters it with practical steps parents can take to reduce the risk of SIDS"—*Publishers Weekly*

0-316-77953-9 LITTLE, BROWN PB $12.95

Marilyn **Segal** & Don **Adcock**

Your Child At Play: 2 to 3 Years

An informal, anecdotal book on sleeping, eating, and playing

0-937858-54-4 NEWMARKET $21.95
0-937858-53-6 NEWMARKET PB $14.95

Burton L. **White**

The *New* First Three Years of Life

Jam-packed with information. "His blessedly specific list of toys appropriate for each phase may alone be worth the price of the book"—*Publishers Weekly*

0-684-80419-0 FIRESIDE PB $14.00

Linda **Todd**

You and Your Newborn Baby: A Guide to the First Months After Birth

"A gentle, helpful book that will enable parents to respond to their new baby's needs"—Sheila Kitzinger

See also **POSTNATAL CARE** under **CHILDBIRTH**

1-55832-055-5 HARVARD COMMON $11.95
1-55832-054-7 HARVARD COMMON PB $5.95

D.W. **Winnicott**

Babies and Their Mothers

"Winnicott is a major influence on all who have tried to bring emotional and behavioral issues into pediatrics"—T. Berry Brazelton

INTRODUCTION BY DR. BENJAMIN SPOCK

0-201-07677-2 ADDISON-WESLEY PB $10.95

Childhood

Louise Bates **Ames**

Your Four Year Old: Wild and Wonderful

0-385-29143-4 DELACORTE PB $9.95

Your Five Year Old: Sunny and Serene

0-385-29145-0 DELACORTE PB $9.95

Your Six Year Old: Friend or Enemy

0-385-29146-9 DELACORTE PB $9.95

Your Seven Year Old: Life in a Minor Key

0-440-50650-6 DELTA PB $10.95

Robert **Coles**

Their Eyes Meeting the World: The Drawings and Paintings of Children

Harvard professor Coles has been investigating the moral and spiritual development of children for 30 years. Here he examines 55 children's drawings that reveal the subtle yet dramatic influences on race, class, religion, and history. A penetrating portrait on the inner life of children

0-395-61129-6 HOUGHTON MIFFLIN $30.00

It is not hard, looking at children's drawings or paintings, to see the important influences of personal experience, or the influences of race and class and region and historical moment on a boy's, a girl's, sense of what matters in life—the shaping forces upon the particular world a child calls his or her own. Children in urban ghettos have given representation rather sardonically or mournfully to the impoverished tenement-house reality of their neighborhood existence—a broken-down, desperate version of some of Edward Hopper's scenes of city loneliness, or of John Sloan's "Under the El" presentations of a livelier, more hopeful metropolitan scene.

THEIR EYES MEETING THE WORLD: THE DRAWINGS AND PAINTINGS OF CHILDREN

Ronald **Kleinman** & Michael **Jellinek**

Let Them Eat Cake!: The Case Against Controlling What Your Children Eat

Kids love junk food and, since they burn twice the calories of adults, require some lenience. The authors contend that deprivation heightens desire, sugar and chocolate do not cause pediatric hyperactivity and insomnia, lifelong eating habits are not formed in childhood, and provide much more to dispel parental nutrition guilt

0-679-41259-X VILLARD $19.95

Herbert **Kohl**

Should We Burn Babar?: Essays on Children's Literature and the Power of Stories

Kohl illustrates how prevalent sexism and chauvinism are in children's literature, and then suggests useful strategies for detecting bias and protecting children from it

1-56584-258-8 NEW PRESS $18.95

Lawrence **Kutner**

Toddlers and Preschoolers

From the *New York Times* columnist, the second volume in his Parent & Child Series

0-688-10216-6 MORROW $20.00

Alicia F. **Lieberman**

The Emotional Life of the Toddler

Discusses the challenges of raising a toddler and of being one; includes advice on day care, divorce, and shy and active kids

0-02-919021-5 FREE PRESS $24.95

Gareth B. **Matthews**

The Philosophy of Childhood

Imagination, speculation, and endless questions are the tools with which a child inquires into her universe. And yet, by about nine years old, the child's philosophical curiosity tends to fade. Why? Matthews identifies parents' expectations and social demands as the limiting factors of a child's natural inquisitiveness, and suggests ways we can encourage rather than curtail the continued growth of our children's rich philosophical lives

0-674-66480-9 HARVARD $18.95

Grace **Mitchell**

A Very Practical Guide to Discipline with Young Children

A friendly book written by an educator, which takes into consideration the child's point of view and limitations

0-910287-00-7 GRYPHON HOUSE PB $12.95

Gary Paul **Nabhan** & Stephen **Trimble**

The Geography of Childhood: Why Children Need Wild Places

0-8070-8524-3 BEACON $22.00

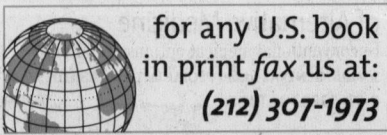

Adolescence

Lawrence **Bauman** & Robert **Ricke**

The Nine Most Troublesome Teenage Problems and How to Solve Them

Direct, practical, and positive advice

0-345-34290-9 BALLANTINE PB $5.99

Robert T. **Bayard** & Jean **Bayard**

How to Deal with Your Acting-Up Teenager: Practical Help for Desperate Parents

"An outstandingly courageous, honest and original approach to teenage acting-out. This book might save your family's sanity and could put your difficult teenager back on the right track"—Louise Bates Ames

0-87131-479-7 EVANS PB $11.95

Mindy **Bingham** & Sandy **Styker**

Things Will Be Different for My Daughter: A Practical Guide to Building Her Self-Esteem

Discusses how girls and women are portrayed by the media and viewed by society. Advice proffered on how to communicate with adolescent daughters, prevent negative female images, build skills, and how girls can build healthy relationships with boys

0-14-024125-6 PENGUIN PB $14.95

Gregory **Bodenhamer**

Parent In Control

Former parole officer outlines a three-point procedure for regaining control of kids. Offers "sound, practical advice on dealing with provocative and manipulative verbal challenges raised by teenagers and early adolescents...." —*Publishers Weekly*

0-684-80777-7 FIRESIDE PB $10.00

Foster W. **Cline** & Jim **Fay**

Parenting Teens with Love & Logic: Parenting Adolescents for Responsible Adulthood

0-89109-695-7 NAVPRESS $18.00

Mihaly **Csikszentmihalyi** & others

Talented Teenagers: The Roots of Success and Failure

The result of an extensive five-year study, this pioneering book examines a group of gifted teenagers in an effort to understand the loss of motivation and diminution of talent that takes place during this troublesome period

0-521-41578-0 CAMBRIDGE $24.95

We cannot increase the inborn gifts of our children, and as individuals we can do little to alter the cultural and societal parameters that affect the unfolding of talent. But if we understood better those elements of the equation over which we have some measure of control, we might be able to protect and nurture the unique human potentials that young people in our families, schools, and communities possess.

TALENTED TEENAGERS: THE ROOTS OF SUCCESS AND FAILURE

David **Elkind**

All Grown Up and No Place to Go: Teenagers in Crisis

"A worthwhile sequel to his *The Hurried Child*—the teenager is quite accurately portrayed as someone who has simultaneously been pushed and left to cope"—Ellen Goodman, *NY Times Book Review*

0-201-48385-8 ADDISON-WESLEY PB $14.00

Grimm Brothers

Adele **Faber** & others

How to Talk So Kids Can Learn: At Home and In School

Sound advice on how to enable children to enjoy learning. The authors operate under the premise that if we want kids to learn we must respect and acknowledge their emotions

See also BEING A PARENT

0-684-81333-5 SCRIBNERS $22.00

0-684-82472-8 FIRESIDE PB $11.00

Don **Fleming** & others

How to Stop the Battle with Your Child: A Practical Guide to Solving Everyday Problems

0-671-76349-0 SIMON & SCHUSTER PB $11.00

Don H. **Fontanelle**

Keys to Parenting Your Teenager

Tips on understanding and appropriately responding to teen behavior and how to establish and maintain positive parenting throughout these rocky years

0-8120-4876-8 BARRONS PB $6.95

Carol **Gilligan** & others

Making Connections: The Relational Worlds of Adolescent Girls at Emma Willard School

A collection of essays that portrays the psychological problems commonly occurring in girls between the ages of 11 and 16

0-674-54041-7 HARVARD PB $12.95

Haim G. **Ginott**

Between Parent & Teenager

0-380-00820-3 AVON PB $5.99

Peggy **Orenstein**

Schoolgirls, Young Women, Self-Esteem, and the Confidence Gap

0-38542576-7 ANCHOR PB $12.95

Robin **Goldstein** & Janet **Gallant**

"Stop Treating Me Like a Kid!": Everyday Parenting: The 10-to 13-Year-Old

0-14-017945-3 PENGUIN PB $9.95

Ben **Kamin**

Raising a Thoughtful Teenager: A Book of Answers and Values for Parents

The Cleveland rabbi, parent, and counselor discusses topics from drugs to sex that most parents are likely to confront

0-525-93984-9 DUTTON $20.95

Tracy **Kidder**

Among Schoolchildren

0-380-71089-7 AVON PB $11.00

Reed **Larson** & Maryse H. **Richards**

Divergent Realities: The Emotional Lives of Mothers, Fathers, and Adolescents

After studying 55 families, the authors present how adults and adolescents view reality differently from each other and why this poses problems

0-465-01663-4 BASIC PB $16.00

Sydney **Lewis**

"A Totally Alien Life-Form"—Teenagers

Interviews with 47 teenagers nationwide blows apart the concept of an indolent Generation X. "A riveting slice-of-life generational portrait" —*Publishers Weekly*

1-56584-282-0 NEW PRESS $25.00

G. Wayne **Miller**

Coming of Age: The True Adventures of Two American Teens

Two teens living in a small town in Rhode Island are shadowed by a journalist during their senior year. "Miller describes the universal experiences of adolescents growing up in a world quite different from that of their parents' youth" —*Publishers Weekly*

0-679-42326-5 RANDOM HOUSE $22.00

Joseph R. **Novello**

What to Do Until the Grownup Arrives: The Art and Science of Raising Teenagers

0-88937-040-0 HOGREFE & HUBER $24.50

Anthony **Wolf**

Get Out of My Life, But First Could You Drive Me and Cheryl to the Mall?: A Parent's Guide to the New Teenager

A clinical psychologist delivers the scoop on teens humorously and wisely

0-374-52322-3 NOONDAY PB $10.00

Teenage Health

Ruth **Bell**

Changing Bodies, Changing Lives

Written in collaboration with members of the Teen Book Project on teenage health problems and concerns. Now in paperback

0-394-75541-3 VINTAGE PB $20.00

Hans Christian Andersen

Consumer Reports

AIDS: Trading Fears for Facts

A guide for teenagers

See also **MEDICAL AND RESEARCH ASPECTS** under **AIDS** under **MEDICINE** in **SCIENCE**

See also **AIDS** under **SPECIFIC HEALTH PROBLEMS** under **HEALTH**

0-89043-269-4 CONSUMER REPORTS PB $4.95

Edsel **Erickson** & Alan **McEvoy**

Teenagers at Risk

A look at why some teenagers are sexually abused

See also **SEXUAL ABUSE** under **SELF-HELP**

1-55691-042-8 LEARNING PUBLICATIONS PB .. $12.95

Marry **Harris** & Wilma **Nachsin**

"My Kid's Allergic to Everything" Dessert Cookbook: Sweets & Treats the Whole Family Will Enjoy

See also **ALLERGIES** under **SPECIFIC HEALTH PROBLEMS** under **HEALTH**

1-55652-303-3 CHICAGO REVIEW PB $11.95

Rosmarie **Hausherr**

Children and the AIDS Virus

0-395-51167-4 CLARION PB $6.95

Polly **Joan**

Preventing Teenage Suicide: The Living Alternative Handbook

A how-to book for parents and guidance counselors

See also **SUICIDE** under **DEATH AND MOURNING** under **SELF-HELP**

0-89885-247-1 HUMAN SCIENCES $30.95

0-89885-349-4 HUMAN SCIENCES PB $18.95

Jeffrey **Nevid**

201 Things You Should Know About AIDS and Other Sexually Transmitted Diseases

In addition to a complete discussion of AIDS and STDs, provides a listing of hotlines for both

See also **AIDS** under **SPECIFIC HEALTH PROBLEMS** under **HEALTH**

0-205-14873-5 ALLYN & BACON PB $15.00

Teenage Pregnancy

Robert W. **Buckingham** & Mary P. **Derby**

"I'm Pregnant, Now What Do I Do?"

A resource for teenagers and their families that presents an even-handed look at all options for teen pregnancy. Includes legal advice, discussion on the father's role, as well as case studies

1-57392-117-3 PROMETHEUS PB $12.95

Leon **Dash**

When Children Want Children: The Urban Crisis of Teenage Childbearing

The problem of teenage pregnancy in a poor neighborhood of Washington

0-14-011789-X PENGUIN PB $11.95

Joelle **Sander**

Before Their Time: Four Generations of Teenage Mothers

"Accessible, instructive, poignant…we finish reading this book moved in heart and soul"—Robert Coles

0-15-111638-5 HARCOURT BRACE $19.95

0-15-611673-1 HARCOURT BRACE PB $9.95

Rickie **Solinger**

Wake Up Little Susie

Shocking documentation of the American double standard in the treatment and perception of pregnant teenagers. Solinger shows how white teenagers are allowed a second chance at respectability owing to the high demand for white adopted children, whereas young black women, with unmarketable children, continue to be villified. "[A] revelatory work with repercussions for today"—*Kirkus Reviews*

0-415-90448-X ROUTLEDGE $35.00

0-415-90894-9 ROUTLEDGE PB $16.95

Beverly **Winikoff** & Suzanne **Wymelenberg**

The Whole Truth About Contraceptives: A Decision-Making Guide for Teenagers to Middle-Agers

See also **BIRTH CONTROL** under **CONCEPTION**

0-309-05494-X NATIONAL ACADEMY PB $14.95

Being a Parent

Lawrence **Balter**

"Not in Front of the Children…": How to Talk to Your Child About Tough Family Matters

"An invaluable resource for parents"—Matilda R. Cuomo, Chair, New York State Citizens Task Force on Child Abuse and Neglect

0-14-015833-2 PENGUIN PB $9.95

T. Berry **Brazelton**

Working and Caring

Interviews, with commentary, on three working families with children

0-201-63271-3 ADDISON-WESLEY PB $13.00

Jay **Belsky** & John **Kelly**

The Transition to Parenthood: How a First Child Changes a Marriage; Why Some Couples Grow Closer and Others Apart

0-440-50698-0 DELL PB $12.95

Polly Bernen **Berends**

Whole Child/Whole Parent

The psychology of parenthood, with practical tips. "The best book I know on the psychology of child raising…because it reveals the essence of what human beings are all about"—From the Foreword by M. Scott Peck.

0-06-091427-0 HARPERCOLLINS PB $16.00

James **Campbell**

Raising Your Child to Be Gifted

How to have a smart kid

1-57129-000-1 BROOKLINE PB $19.95

Marian Wright **Edelman**

The Measure of Our Success: A Letter to My Children and Yours

Edelman, founder and president of the Children's Defense Fund, describes her hopes for the improvement of American children's well-being. "A touching, compelling personal affirmation from one of the nation's most important moral leaders"—Robert Coles

"Profound and moving"—*Library Journal*

0-8070-3106-2 BEACON $15.00

0-06-097546-6 HARPERCOLLINS PB $10.00

Adele **Faber** & others

How to Talk So Kids Can Learn: At Home and In School

Sound advice on how to enable children to enjoy learning. The authors operate under the premise that if we want kids to learn we must respect and acknowledge their emotions

See also **ADOLESCENCE**

0-684-81333-5 SCRIBNERS $22.00

0-684-82472-8 FIRESIDE PB $11.00

Nancy **Fuchs**

Our Share of Night, Our Share of Morning: Parenting as a Spiritual Journey

"Provides a crash course in love, forgiveness and mystery"—*Publishers Weekly*

0-06-251288-9 HARPERCOLLINS $18.00

Ellen **Galinsky**

The Six Stages of Parenthood

How parents grow: interviews and theories

0-201-10529-2 ADDISON-WESLEY PB $17.00

Susan **Ginsberg**, editor

Family Wisdom: The 2,000 Most Important Things Ever Said About Parenting, Children, and Family Life

Quotations ancient and modern on all aspects and from all walks of life on the family

See also **QUOTATIONS**

0-231-10376-X COLUMBIA $19.95

Colleen Davis **Gardephe** & Steve **Ettlinger**

Don't Pick Up the Baby Or You'll Spoil the Child & Other Old Wives' Tales About Pregnancy and Parenting

As prevalent as dirty diapers are old wives' tales, and this intriguing and often amusing book sheds light on 100 of the most common, while offering a sound scientific basis for those that happen to be grounded in fact

0-8118-0242-6 CHRONICLE $9.95

For every child, you will lose a tooth…If you don't get morning sickness, you're having a boy.
DON'T PICK UP THE BABY OR YOU'LL SPOIL THE CHILD & OTHER OLD WIVES' TALES ABOUT PREGNANCY AND PARENTING

Christina **Hardyment**

Perfect Parents: Baby-Care Advice Past and Present

Advice in a historical context and support for the contemporary parent to be selective about advice

0-19-286172-7 OXFORD PB $12.95

Peggy J. **Jenkins**

Nurturing Spirituality in Children: Simple Hands-On Activities

By using common household objects as visual aids Jenkins presents parents with five-minute lessons to help kids with their spiritual and mental growth

1-88522-323-4 BEYOND WORDS PB $10.95

Sheila **Kitzinger** & Celia **Kitzinger**

Tough Questions: Talking Straight with Your Kids About the Real World

A well-known authority on pregnancy and childbirth collaborates with her daughter in discussing how to talk to children about the moral and social problems of the contemporary world

1-55832-032-6 HARVARD COMMON PB $12.95

Penelope **Leach**

Children First

Leach shows us that mouthing platitudes about "family values" isn't enough: we have to create new structures in our economic and social systems which will make children a priority—and those efforts must begin at home

0-679-42133-5 KNOPF $22.00
0-679-75466-0 RANDOM HOUSE PB $12.00

Jean **Liedloff**

The Continuum Concept

Spiritual and philosophical approaches to the daily task of being parents

0-201-05071-4 ADDISON-WESLEY PB $12.00

Barbara **Mathias** & Mary Ann **French**

50 Ways to Raise a Nonracist Child

This groundbreaking, one-of-a-kind guide provides parents with the practical tools they need to deal with one of today's most explosive issues

0-06-273322-2 HARPERCOLLINS PB $10.00

Kathleen **McCue**

How to Help Children Through a Parent's Serious Illness

McCue draws on her long experience in children's counseling to map a coping strategy for this, possibly a parent's most difficult task

0-312-11350-1 ST. MARTIN'S $18.95
0-312-14619-1 ST. MARTIN'S PB $11.95

Mickey **Michaels**

Survival Guide for Parents: How to Avoid Screwing Up Your Kids or Losing Your Own Sanity

Psychologist and single mom offers pointers

0-9644761-1-8 POSSIBILITY PB $9.95

Vanessa **Ochs**

Safe and Sound: Protecting Your Child in an Unpredictable World

How to draw the line between commonsense caution and overprotection. The chapters are arranged in stages of a child's life from prenatal to teenager and provide sensible advice on when to let go

0-14-017880-5 PENGUIN PB $10.95

Alex J. **Packer**

Parenting One Day at a Time: Using the Tools of Recovery to Become Better Parents and Raise Better Children

How to amend the hurts from addiction

0-440-50520-8 DELL PB $9.95

Linda **Pollock**

A Lasting Relationship: Parents and Children over Three Centuries

An absorbing collection of first-hand accounts of child care in England and America, from 1600 to 1906. The voices of many ordinary people mingle with those of Queen Victoria, Elizabeth Gaskell, Fanny Burney, Thomas Jefferson, and many others.

0-87451-507-6 NEW ENGLAND PB $17.95

James Boswell talks to his daughter about religion, 1779:

At night, after we were in bed, Veronica spoke out from her little bed and said, "I do not believe there is a god."

"Preserve me," said I, "my dear, what do you mean?"

She answered, "I have *thinket* it many a time, but did not like to speak of it."

I was confounded and uneasy, and tried with the simple arguments that without God there would not be all the things we see. It is He who makes the sun shine.

Said she, "It shines only on good days."

Said I: "God made you."

Said she: "My Mother bore me." It was a strange and alarming thing to her Mother and me to hear our little angel talk thus. But I thought it better just to let the subject drop insensibly tonight. I asked her if she had said her prayers tonight. She said yes, and asked me to put her in mind to say them in the morning. I prayed to God to prevent such thoughts from entering into her mind.

A LASTING RELATIONSHIP: PARENTS AND CHILDREN OVER THREE CENTURIES

Julie A. **Ross**

Practical Parenting for the 21st Century: The Manual You Wish Had Come With Your Child

0-9627226-6-9 EXCALIBUR PB $10.95

Elin **Schoen**

Growing With Your Child: Reflections on Parent Development

Anecdotes on how rearing children can transform a parent's life

0-385-47987-5 MAIN STREET PB $12.95

Martin E.P. **Seligman** & others

The Optimistic Child: How Learned Optimism Protects Children from Depression

Thirty percent of American kids suffer from depression and Seligman outlines a plan of action to raise self-esteem and therefore a contented child

0-395-69380-2 HOUGHTON MIFFLIN $24.95

Ron **Taffel** & Roberta **Israeloff**

Why Parents Disagree and What You Can Do About It: How to Raise Great Kids While You Strengthen Your Marriage

How parents who have differing ideas of parenting can come to agreement

0-380-72046-9 AVON PB $10.00

Jan **Wagner**

Raising Safe Kids in an Unsafe World: 30 Simple Ways to Prevent Your Child from Becoming Abducted or Abused

How to prevent the unthinkable

0-380-78695-8 AVON PB $11.00

D.W. **Winnicott**

Talking to Parents

This collection from the influential British pediatrician is drawn mostly from Winnicott's unpublished talks with parents and concerns questions all parents have about discipline, jealousy, and over-teaching. "Winnicott helped to bridge the gap for me between pediatrics and the dynamics of child development"—Dr. Benjamin Spock

INTRODUCTION BY DR. T. BERRY BRAZELTON

0-201-60893-6 ADDISON-WESLEY $17.95

Thinking About Children

0-201-40700-0 ADDISON-WESLEY $25.00

Anthony E. **Wolf**

It's Not Fair, Jeremy Spencer's Parents Let Him Stay Up All Night!: A Guide to the Tougher Parts of Parenting

0-374-52473-4 NOONDAY PB $10.00

Playtime

Linda Williams **Aber**

101 Activities for Siblings Who Squabble: Projects and Games to Entertain and Keep the Peace

Activity ideas that build relationships among siblings

0-312-13101-1 ST. MARTIN'S PB........................$10.95

Rita **Anderson** & Linda **Neumann**

Partners in Play: Creative Homemade Toys for Toddlers

An age-appropriate how-to on making toys

0-8050-3673-3 HOLT PB....................................$12.95

Steve **Bennet** & Ruth **Bennet**

Cabin Fever: 202 Activities for Turning Your Child's Rainy Days, Snow Days, and Sick Days Into Great Days

Pocket-size and filled with fun and educational activities for all ages

0-14-023909-X PENGUIN PB $6.95

Heidi **Britz-Crecelius**

Children at Play: Using Waldorf Principles to Foster Childhood Development

Recommendations for toys, games, and art supplies that aid in a child's development

0-89281-629-5 INNER TRADITIONS PB $9.95

Alice **Honig**

Playtime Learning Games for Young Children

A guide to playing with children

0-8156-0178-6 SYRACUSE PB...............................$9.95

Mary **Leonhardt**

Keeping Kids Reading: How to Raise Avid Readers in the Video Age

How to help your kids develop an enthusiasm for reading throughout their lives

0-517-70114-6 CROWN....................................$23.00

Allyssa **McCabe**

Language Games to Play with Your Child

Enjoyable and instructive games for children of all ages

0-306-44320-1 INSIGHT....................................$24.95

Vivian Gussin **Paley**

You Can't Say You Can't Play

This MacArthur Prize-winning kindergarten teacher attacks the roots of exclusion, rejection, and loneliness in the life of children and obtains a surprising glimpse into a child's view of the world

See also **TEACHING** under **EDUCATION** in **SOCIAL STUDIES**

0-674-96590-6 HARVARD PB...............................$10.00

The Riverside Mothers' Playgroup

Entertain Me! Creative Ideas for Fun and Games with Your Baby in the First Year

A virtual toy chest of stimulating and healthy games for children under one year. From at-home games and bath-time activities that use common household items to having fun at the check-out line, this field-tested, innovative guide includes tips on baby exercising and lists of fun toys

0-671-74536-0 POCKET PB $10.00

Angela **Wilkes**

Child Magazine's Book of Children's Parties

How to throw an old-fashioned party at home for your kids

1-56458-853-X DORLING KINDERSLEY.............$18.95

Gloria **DeGaetano** & Kathleen **Bander**

Screen Smarts: A Family Guide to Media Literacy

0-395-71550-4 HOUGHTON MIFFLIN PB..........$12.95

Sex Education

Mary **Calderone** & James **Ramey**

Talking with Your Child About Sex: Questions and Answers for Children from Birth to Puberty

0-345-31379-8 BALLANTINE PB..........................$4.99

Inner and Outer Discipline

Jan **Arnow**

Teaching Peace: How to Raise Children to Live in Harmony Without Prejudice, Fear, or Violence

This important book provides a hands-on, down-to-earth approach to teaching children to resist the violence they increasingly encounter in the media and on the streets. Arnow shows how to combat prejudice and prevent conflict while teaching children the values that will help them live peacefully and productively in today's changing world

0-399-52155-0 PERIGEE PB................................$12.00

Barbara **Chernofsky** & Diane **Gage**

Change Your Child's Behavior by Changing Yours: 13 New Tricks to Teach Yourself to Get Kids to Cooperate

"This practical, affectionate technique sure beats a trip to the woodshed"—*Booklist*

0-517-88463-1 CROWN PB $14.00

Foster **Cline** & Jim **Fay**

Parenting with Love and Logic: Teaching Children Responsibility

Lessons kids will need for navigating to and through adulthood

0-89109-311-7 NAVPRESS $18.00

Barbara **Coloroso**

Kids Are Worth It!: Giving Your Child the Gift of Inner Discipline

An approach to parenting based on the simple premise that children have dignity and worth and can take responsibility for their actions

0-380-71954-1 AVON PB.....................................$10.00

Morgan Simone **Daleo**

Curriculum of Love: Cultivating the Spiritual Nature of Children

Based on Christian values but flavored with Eastern philosophy, each of the 10 chapters provides art, storytelling, and music activities to illustrate history, compassion, beauty, balance, joy, harmony, mindfulness, service, self-reliance, and community

0-9648799-4-8 GRACE PB....................................$17.95

Wayne **Dosick**

Golden Rules: Ten Ethical Values Parents Need to Teach Their Children

"America's future depends upon the moral education of our young, and Wayne Dosick has made a serious contribution to the endeavor. Anyone who cares about our children and our country will enjoy *Golden Rules*. It is filled with warmth and wisdom"—Dan Quayle

0-06-251204-8 HARPERCOLLINS $16.00
0-06-251249-8 HARPERCOLLINS PB $12.00

Beatrix Potter

Elizabeth M. **Ellis**

Raising a Responsible Child: How Parents Can Avoid Overindulgent Behavior and Nurture Healthy Children

Based on 18 years of family counseling, Dr. Ellis presents an insightful analysis of what she terms overindulgent parents and underdeveloped children and formulates a plan whereby parents, in controlling *themselves*, can teach their children independence and self-control

1-55972-301-7 BIRCH LANE $18.95
0-8065-1824-3 CITADEL PB $14.95

Mitch **Golant** & Donna G. **Corwin**

The Challenging Child: A Guide for Parents of Exceptionally Strong-Willed Children

Clinical psychologist Golant offers wise, practical advice on how to deal with the nonconforming child in ways that maintain discipline and encourage maturity, yet don't stifle the child's unique personality strengths. Included are discussions of school and social issues, high IQ, Attention Deficit Disorder, allergies, and other factors

0-425-14953-6 BERKELEY PB $10.95

Robert Louis Stevenson

Marilyn E. **Gootman**

The Loving Parents' Guide to Discipline

0-425-14571-9 BERKLEY PB $4.99

Fred G. **Gosman**

Spoiled Rotten: Today's Children and How to Change Them

Citing the most common displays of misbehavior and parenting missteps, this commonsense, real-world guide is a survival manual for the modern parent or caregiver. "It's good healthy commonsense and will reinforce parents to do the obvious thing—I liked it immensely. Bravo!"—T. Berry Brazelton

0-446-39509-9 WARNER PB $12.99

Stanley I. **Greenspan** & Jacqueline **Salmon**

The Challenging Child: How to Understand, Raise, and Enjoy Your "Difficult" Child

Discusses the five child personality types and offers pragmatic advice for parenting each

See also **SPECIAL CHILDREN** under **CHILD CARE**

0-201-62647-0 ADDISON-WESLEY $23.00
0-201-44193-4 ADDISON-WESLEY PB $12.00

Mary Sheedy **Kurchina**

Raising Your Spirited Child: A Guide for Parents Whose Child Is *More* Intense, Sensitive, Perceptive, Persistant, Energetic

Positive support and proven strategies for rearing children who have been traditionally defined as difficult

0-06-016361-5 HARPERPERENNIAL PB $11.00

Grace **Mitchell**

A Very Practical Guide to Discipline with Young Children

A friendly book written by an educator, which takes into consideration the child's point of view and limitations

See also **CHILDHOOD** under **STAGES OF DEVELOPMENT**

0-910287-00-7 GRYPHON HOUSE PB $12.95

Henry A. **Paul**

When Kids Are Mad, Not Bad

Psychiatrist in family and child practice believes that anger is natural and normal and a problem when these feelings are not handled constructively. Analyzes when anger can be a problem and offers suggestions for lessening its effects

0-425-14648-0 BERKLEY PB $5.99

Hugh **Prather** & Gale **Prather**

Spiritual Parenting: A Guide to Understanding and Nuturing the Heart of Your Child

Instilling virtues in your children

0-517-70385-8 HARMONY $23.00

Myrna B. **Shure**

Raising a Thinking Child

Conflict resolution, problem solving, and the satisfactions of independence are the themes of this unique approach to raising children: *ICPS,* or the *I Can Problem Solve* program. Teaches parents the dialogues, games, and techniques to raise healthy, self-confident, and well-adjusted children

0-8050-2758-0 HOLT $22.50
0-671-53463-7 POCKET PB $12.00

Deborah **Spaide**

Teaching Your Kids to Care: How to Discover and Develop the Spirit of Charity in Your Child

From the founder of Kids Care Clubs, this book suggests 100 projects to nurture a kid's wish to help others

0-8065-1637-2 CITADEL PB $9.95

Barbara C. **Unell** & Jerry L. **Wyckoff**

20 Teachable Virtues

Surprisingly unsanctimonious, each chapter addresses fundamental moral lessons for children from Empathy through Loyalty to Cooperating. "This compelling, down-to-earth and useful guide deserves a place on any parenting how-to shelf"—*Publishers Weekly*

0-399-51959-9 PERIGEE PB $12.00

Bettie B. **Youngs**

How to Develop Self-Esteem in Your Child: 6 Vital Ingredients

0-449-90687-6 COLUMBINE PB $10.00

Steven W. **Vannoy**

The 10 Greatest Gifts I Give My Children: Parenting from the Heart

0-671-50227-1 FIRESIDE PB $11.00

Denise Chapman **Weston** & Mark **Weston**

Playful Parenting: Turning the Dilemma of Discipline into Fun and Games

Recipes for solving family problems, with workbook chapter. "Not only is their approach positive rather than punitive, it also has a definite sense of humor"—*Booklist*

0-87477-734-8 TARCHER PB $14.95

Burton L. **White**

Raising a Happy, Unspoiled Child

A fabulously helpful book that stresses the importance of not spoiling your child, mainly because they will be happier

0-684-80134-5 FIRESIDE PB $11.00

Financial Responsibility

Neale **Godfrey** & Carolina **Edwards**

Money Doesn't Grow on Trees: A Parent's Guide to Raising Financially Responsible Children

Godfrey, the chairwoman of the Children's Financial Network and founder of a bank for kids, offers fun tips to help kids save rather than spend

0-671-79805-7 FIRESIDE PB $11.00

Neale **Godfrey** & Tad **Richards**

A Penny Saved: Teaching Your Children the Values and Life-Skills They Will Need to Live in the Real World

"What children don't know about money *can* hurt them" is the main message here. Money games, making change, work, and saving accounts are all addressed in a breezy and accessible format

0-684-80397-6 SIMON & SCHUSTER $18.95
0-684-82480-9 FIRESIDE PB $12.00

Sibling and Family Dynamics

Louise Bates **Ames**

He Hit Me First: When Brothers and Sisters Fight

0-446-39048-8 WARNER PB $11.99

Cynthia **MacGregor**

"Why Do We Need Another Baby?": Helping Your Child Welcome a New Arrival

How to pacify baby-to-be's older siblings

0-8184-0578-3 LYLE STUART $13.95

Adele **Faber** & Elaine **Mazlish**
Siblings Without Rivalry: How to Help Your Children Live Together So You Can Live Too
How to prevent jealousy and conflicts. "A very human book about one of the toughest problems parents have to handle"—Dr. Benjamin Spock
9-992-43513-5 AVON PB $10.00

Kevin **Leman**
The Birth Order Book
How birth order affects children's behavior
0-440-50471-6 DELL PB $10.95

Nancy **Samalin** & Catherine **Whitney**
Loving Each One Best: A Caring and Practical Approach to Raising Siblings
Parenting expert offers helpful tips gleaned from her workshops, seminars, and questionnaires. "This is a good book to have when you're having more than one"—*Publishers Weekly*
0-553-09641-9 BDD $22.95

Mothers

Joan **Anderson**
The Single Mother's Book: A Practical Guide to Managing Your Children, Career, Home Finances, and Everything Else
See also **SINGLE PARENTING**
0-934601-84-4 PEACHTREE PB $13.95

Evelyn **Bassoff**
Between Mothers and Sons: The Making of Vital and Loving Men
Psychologist and *Parents* columnist explores the vital link between mother and son, the imprinting experiences of a man's future effective life. Wise and compassionate, Bassoff looks beyond the silence which surrounds that relationship to introduce a means for its management and enrichment
0-525-93833-8 DUTTON $20.95
0-452-27462-1 PLUME PB $11.95

Mother and Daughters
From the mother's perspective; by a psychiatrist
See also **MOTHERHOOD** under **THE FEMALE EXPERIENCE** under **WOMEN'S STUDIES** in **SOCIAL STUDIES**
0-452-26319-0 PLUME PB $12.95

Mary Frances **Berry**
The Politics of Parenthood: Child Care, Women's Rights, and the Myth of the Good Mother
Berry argues that the lessons of the past, including the experiences of African-Americans and Native Americans, teach that what matters is not who cares for children, but how they are cared for. "An important and comprehensive reference for those involved in both gender battles and the fight for comprehensive child-care" —*Kirkus Reviews*
0-14-023360-1 PENGUIN PB $11.95

Mary Kay **Blakely**
American Mom
A lively account of raising children in these changing times, garnered from 20 years of motherhood. "By her gifts as a writer and her experience as a woman, Mary Kay Blakely is better able to give voice to a whole generation than anyone now publishing"—Gloria Steinem
1-56512-052-3 ALGONQUIN $19.95

Marty **Burns-Wolf** & others
Wear Your Bra on Your Head and Push Up Your Brains: Unconventional Wisdom for Mothers Raising Daughters
0-7867-0328-8 CARROLL & GRAF PB $11.95

Louise **Erdrich**
The Blue Jay's Dance
"Astute, poetic reflections on the powerful mother-daughter relationship from conception through the baby's first year"—*Kirkus Reviews*
See also **SINCE 1945** under **20TH-CENTURY AMERICAN FICTION** in **LITERATURE OF THE AMERICAS**
0-06-017132-4 HARPERCOLLINS $21.00

Katherine **Goldman**
My Mother Worked and I Turned Out Okay
Fully 60 percent of America's mothers work outside the home. Goldman, the daughter of a famous working mother (Lois Wyse), interviewed many adult children of working women, children who have not only survived but succeeded. Her book—and her subjects' entertaining and important observations—is a real guide to working mothers
AFTERWORD BY LOIS WYSE
0-679-41544-0 VILLARD $16.00

> The bad news is your mother's not there when you get home from school. The good news is your mother's not there when you get home from school.
> MY MOTHER WORKED AND I TURNED OUT OKAY

Roseann **Hirsch**
Super Working Mom's Handbook
Helpful lists and tips
0-446-38073-3 WARNER PB $8.95

Anndee **Hochman**
Everyday Acts & Small Subversions: Women Reinventing Family, Community and Home
"A compelling book about the options both straight and lesbian women have—and the complications and freedoms those options offer"—*The Oregonian*
See also **GAY AND LESBIAN PARENTS** under **LOVERS, FAMILIES, AND FRIENDS** under **GAY, LESBIAN, AND BISEXUAL STUDIES** in **SOCIAL STUDIES**
0-933377-25-8 EIGHTH MOUNTAIN PB $12.95

Melinda M. **Marshall**
Good Enough Mothers: Changing Expectations for Ourselves
With incisive commentary from experts, inspiring examples of women who have figured out how to cope
1-56079-253-1 PETERSON'S $18.95
1-56079-433-X PETERSON'S PB $10.95

Jane **Matters**
Single Mothers by Choice: A Guidebook for Single Women Who Are Considering or Have Chosen Motherhood
The founding director of Single Mothers by Choice has fashioned an accessible handbook for this brave and besieged group, whose numbers have increased by 60 percent over the past ten years
0-8129-2246-8 TIME BOOKS PB $15.00

B. Kaye **Olson**
Energy Secrets for Tired Mothers on the Run
From a nurse and stress consultant on how to promote family teamwork for chores, stop unnecessary worrying, eat right, and more
1-55874-250-6 HEALTH COMMUNICATIONS PB $11.95

Shelley **Phillips**
Beyond the Myths: Mother-Daughter Relationships in Psychology, History, Literature and Everyday Life
Challenges the prejudices and myths that paralyze; and gives new understanding to the complicated roles of mothers
0-14-025186-3 PENGUIN PB $14.95

Martha **Sears** & William **Sears**
25 Things Every New Mother Should Know
Simple and clear-headed advice about the problems and questions that often confuse a new parent
1-55832-068-7 HARVARD COMMON $14.95

Claudette **Wassil-Grimm**
Where's Daddy?: How Divorced, Single and Widowed Mothers Can Provide What's Missing When Dad's Missing
"The author covers single parenting issues in a constructive, yet realistic spirit" —*Publishers Weekly*
0-87951-627-5 PENGUIN PB $11.95

Fathers

David **Blankenhorn**
Fatherless America: Confronting Our Most Urgent Social Problem
Predicts that unless the trend of fatherlessness is reversed there will be a "decline of child well-being and the spread of male violence"
0-465-01483-6 BASIC $23.00

Bill **Cosby**
Fatherhood
The popular comedian's wise, warm book about the joys and tribulations of being Dad
0-425-09772-2 BERKELEY PB $11.00

Armin A. **Brott** & Jennifer **Ash**

The Expectant Father: Facts, Tips and Advice for Dads-to-Be

In chronological order, details prenatal through postpartum events with cartoons, lists, resources

1-55859-690-9 ABBEVILLE PB..............................$9.95

Arthur **Coleman** & Libby **Coleman**

The Father: Mythology and Changing Roles

Examines the relatively neglected role of the father, in terms of the modern family and in terms of a man's evolving self-image

0-933029-35-7 CHIRON PB..............................$14.95

Will **Glennon**

Fathering: Strengthening Connection with Your Children No Matter Where You Are

The difficulties of being a long-distance father, emotionally or physically

1-57324-002-8 CONARI PB..............................$10.95

Gerald G. **Jampolsky** & Lee L. **Jampolsky**

Listen to Me: A Book for Men and Women About Fathers and Sons

A collection of letters between a father and son. "Their letters, almost painfully candid, have helped them to a better relationship and may help not only other fathers and sons, but also the women they love and who love them to a new understanding"—*Publishers Weekly*

0-89087-810-2 CELESTIAL ARTS..............................$21.95

Bill **McCoy**

Father's Day: Notes from a New Dad in the Real World

Parents magazine editor thrilled to be a father. "...heartily recommended to all fathers" —*Publishers Weekly*

0-8129-2405-3 TIME BOOKS..............................$22.00

George **Newman**

One Hundred and One Ways to Be a Long-Distance Super-Dad

0-88247-800-1 R & E PB..............................$7.95

Thomas **Oakland** & Edwin **Terry**

Divorced Fathers: Reconstructing a Quality Life

The personal adjustment of the father: his relationship with his children, the legal and financial aspects of divorce

0-89885-101-7 HUMAN SCIENCES..............................$32.95

John R. **Snarey**

How Fathers Care for the Next Generation: A Four-Decade Study

This four-decade, four-generation study spotlights the father's vital effect on the social-emotional, intellectual-academic, and physical-athletic development of children

0-674-40940-X HARVARD..............................$37.50

S. Adams **Sullivan**

The Fathers' Almanac

An informal guide to the care of children

0-385-42625-9 DOUBLEDAY PB..............................$17.95

Charles **Sullivan**, editor

Fathers and Sons: in Literature and Art

This handsomely illustrated volume offers an insightful, provocative collection of literature and art portraying fathers and fatherhood through the ages. Over 100 poems, quotations, and prose passages are paired with paintings, photographs, and sculptures to provide a visually rich, poignant, yet unsentimental occasion for reflection on the relationship between fathers and children

0-8109-3329-2 ABRAMS..............................$29.95

Bruno Bettelheim

Single Parenting

The growing number of single parents has created a need for role models and the wisdom found in the following list of books.

Joan **Anderson**

The Single Mother's Book: A Practical Guide to Managing Your Children, Career, Home Finances, and Everything Else

0-934601-84-4 PEACHTREE PB..............................$13.95

Elissa P. **Benedek** & Catherine F. **Brown**

How to Help Your Child Overcome Your Divorce

Ameliorates the psychological dilemmas sure to plague every family after a marriage breaks up

0-88048-565-5 AMERICAN PSYCHIATRIC..........$22.95

Cherie **Burns**

Stepmotherhood: How to Survive Without Feeling Frustrated, Left Out, or Wicked

For stepmothers and single parents

0-06-097064-2 HARPERCOLLINS PB..............................$11.00

D. Merilee **Clunis** & G. Dorsey **Green**

The Lesbian Parenting Book: A Guide to Creating Families and Raising Children

"Extremely readable, informative and nonjudgemental guide for lesbians interested in relationships and for therapists working with them...A significant contribution"—*Library Journal*

1-87806-768-0 SEAL PB..............................$16.95

Richard **Gardner**

The Parents' Book About Divorce

See also **DIVORCE** under **SELF-HELP**

0-933812-27-2 CREATIVE THERAPEUTICS........$29.95

0-553-28632-3 BDD PB..............................$6.50

Claudia **Jewett**

Helping Children Cope with Separation and Loss

A mix of theory, examples, and advice

1-55832-051-2 HARVARD COMMON PB..........$12.95

Gayle **Kimballe**

Fifty-Fifty Parenting: Sharing Family Rewards and Responsibilities

Includes chapters on stepfamilies and working parents

0-669-14867-9 EQUALITY PRESS PB..............................$9.95

Jane **Matters**

Single Mothers by Choice: A Guidebook for Single Women Who Are Considering or Have Chosen Motherhood

See also **MOTHERS**

0-8129-2246-8 TIME BOOKS PB..............................$15.00

Sara **McLanahan** & Gary **Sandefur**

Growing Up with A Single Parent: What Hurts, What Helps

0-674-36408-2 HARVARD PB..............................$14.00

Julia A. **Ross** & Judy **Corcoran**

Joint Custody with a Jerk: Raising a Child with an Uncooperative Ex

How to deal with prickly situations that an unfriendly divorce can produce

0-312-14113-0 ST. MARTIN'S PB..............................$13.95

Debbie **Taylor**

My Children, My Gold: A Journey to the World of Seven Single Mothers

The author traveled to seven countries to interview seven single mothers. "Taylor has the novelist's flair for picking out the little details that give each profile its heartrending force..." —*Publishers Weekly*

0-520-20145-0 CALIFORNIA PB..............................$15.00

John **Thorndike**

Another Way Home: A Single Father's Story

Single fatherhood, written like a novel

0-517-70542-7 CROWN..............................$24.00

Grandparents

Vicki **Lansky**

101 Ways to Spoil Your Grandchild

From a well-known writer on pediatric topics

0-8092-3231-6 CONTEMPORARY PB..............................$6.95

Lillian **Carson**

The Essential Grandparent: A Guide for Making a Difference

To enhance the rewarding role that is performed by one in six Americans

1-55874-397-9 HEALTH COMMUNICATIONS PB $10.95

Sylvie **de Toledo** & Deborah Edler **Brown**

Grandparents as Parents: A Survival Guide for Raising a Second Family

How to cope with unexpected parenthood, from the court system to finding support groups

1-57230-020-5 GUILFORD PB $16.95

Sue **Johnson** & Julie **Carlson**

Grandloving: Making Memories with Your Grandchildren

Over 200 inexpensive activities to engage all generations; illustrated

1-57749-010-X FAIRVIEW PRESS PB $14.95

Sheila **Kitzinger**

Becoming a Grandmother: A Life Transition

Social anthropologist best known for her childbirth books (*The Complete Book of Pregnancy and Childbirth*) writes professionally and personally about grandmotherhood. She explores the history of grandmothering and gleans pertinent information from interviews of mothers and grandmothers

0-684-19619-0 SCRIBNERS $22.00

Arthur **Kornhaber**

Grandparent Power!

From the "Dr. Spock of Grandparenting," advice on how to connect with grandchildren, along with problem-solving techniques and practical information for traditional and nontraditional families alike

0-517-59805-1 CROWN $20.00

Education & Literature

Sheila **Egoff**, editor

Only Connect: Readings in Children's Literature

Collection of essays by distinguished authors such as P.L. Travers and C.S. Lewis

0-19-540309-6 OXFORD PB $17.95

Estelle S. **Gellman**

School Testing: What Parents and Educators Need to Know

How to understand what testing means and how to interpret scores

0-275-94800-5 PRAEGER $45.00

E. D. **Hirsch** & John **Holdren**

What Your Kindergartener Needs to Know: Preparing Your Child for a Lifetime of Learning

0-385-48117-9 BDD $24.95

Peggy **Kaye**

Games for Writing: Playful Ways to Help Your Child Learn to Write

This volume teaches more than 50 ways to help a child along the often anxious road to writing

0-374-16024-4 FS&G $27.50

0-374-52427-0 NOONDAY PB $13.00

Herbert **Kohl**

"I Won't Learn from You": And Other Inquiries into the Control and Liberation of Learning

In the vanguard of educational theory, Kohl has forged new paths to the heart of the urban school crisis. Now available in book form, his acclaimed essay links the refusal to learn to students' sense that their dignity and self-worth are compromised by their teachers, schools, and society. Also included are three new essays: "The Tattooed Man: Against Stigma," "Beyond Not Learning: An Essay on Creative Maladjustment" and "Provocations: On Powerful Learning Experiences"

0-915943-64-6 MILKWEED PB $5.95

> Not-learning tends to take place when someone has to deal with unavoidable challenges to her or his personal and family loyalties, integrity, and identity…To agree to learn from a stranger who does not respect your integrity causes a major loss of self. The only alternative is to not-learn and reject the stranger's world.
>
> "I WON'T LEARN FROM YOU": AND OTHER INQUIRIES INTO THE CONTROL AND LIBERATION OF LEARNING

Sidney **Ledson**

Raising Brighter Children

0-8027-7299-4 WALKER PB $9.95

Eden Ross **Lipson**

The New York Times Parent's Guide to the Best Books For Children

Cites over 1000 books distinguished by quality rather than popularity. Organized according to reading level

0-8129-1889-4 TIME BOOKS PB $15.00

Perry **Nodelman**

The Pleasures of Children's Literature

0-8013-0219-6 LONGMAN PB $24.75

William F. **Russell**

Classics to Read Aloud to Your Children

Selections from Shakespeare, Twain, Dickens, O. Henry, Cervantes, Hawthorne, and many more, that will enthrall children ages 5 to 12. Each segment is categorized by age group

0-517-58715-7 CROWN PB $10.00

Jim **Trelease**

The New Read-Aloud Handbook

A little classic which encourages parents by positive guidance and interesting insights. Booklists included

0-8446-6172-4 SMITH $22.25

Gifted Children

James **Delisle**

Gifted Children Speak Out

Accounts from gifted children, with discussion guides for parents

0-8027-0752-1 WALKER $14.95

James **Delisle** & Judy **Galbraith**

The Gifted Kids Survival Guide II

For parents and teachers of gifted children, aged 11 to 18; educational and social issues

0-915793-09-1 FREE SPIRIT PB $9.95

Alice **Miller**

The Drama of the Gifted Child

The classic work on exceptional children

0-46501693-6 BASIC PB $12.00

Carol **Takacs**

Enjoy Your Gifted Child

A readable book by an educational psychologist

0-8156-2357-7 SYRACUSE PB $14.95

Ellen **Winner**

Gifted Children: Myths and Realities

0-465-01760-6 BASIC $28.00

Children with Learning Disabilities

Thomas **Armstrong**

The Myth of the A.D.D. Child: 50 Ways to Improve Your Child's Behavior and Attention Span Without Drugs, Labels, or Coercion

Psychologist argues that "these children are *not* disordered" and asserts that the cause of ADD-type behavior is multifaceted and offers parents strategies for coping and helping the child

0-525-93841-9 DUTTON $23.95

Lisa J. **Bain**

A Parents' Guide to Attention Deficit Disorders

Published in conjunction with the Children's Hospital of Philadelphia, this book offers an authoritative guide to one of the most widely diagnosed childhood disorders, characterized by moodiness, inattention, and hyperactivity. Surveys the recommended treatments and examines the social, educational, and family problems that can result from ADD

0-385-30031-X DOUBLEDAY PB $10.00

Bryant J. **Cratty** & Richard L. **Goldman**

Learning Disabilities: Contemporary Viewpoints

Examines the social issues and education of learning disabled children and the effect the disability has on their families

3-7186-0623-2 GORDON AND BREACH $27.95

Stephen W. **Garber** & others

Beyond Ritalin: Facts About Medication and Other Strategies for Helping Children, Adolescents, and Adults with Attention Deficit Disorders

How to alleviate the symptoms of ADD without resorting to drugs. Resource list also included

0-679-45018-1 VILLARD $23.00

Edward M. **Hallowell** & John J. **Ratey**

Driven to Distraction: Recognizing and Coping With Attention Deficit Disorder from Childhood through Adolecence

"A very readable, highly informative and helpful book"—*NY Times Book Review*

0-679-42177-7 PANTHEON $23.00

0-684-80128-0 SIMON & SCHUSTER PB $12.00

Barbara **Ingersoll**

Your Hyperactive Child

A parents' guide to coping with attention-deficit disorders

0-385-24070-8 DOUBLEDAY PB $9.95

Harold **Levinson**

Total Concentration: How to Understand Attention Deficit Disorders

"This is the best book I have seen so far which describes Dyslexia, Learning Disabilities and Attention Deficit Disorders"—*ADD Resources*

0-87131-708-7 EVANS PB $11.95

Harold **Levinson** & Addie **Sanders**

The Upside-Down Kids

The first in a series on dyslexic kids and their parents, written in story form

0-87131-625-0 EVANS $17.95

Turning Around the Upside-Down Kids

The second in the series

0-87131-700-1 EVANS $17.95

Priscilla **Vail**

Smart Kids with School Problems

"Conundrum kids": brilliant in one subject but slow in another

0-452-26242-9 NEW AMERICAN LIBRARY PB ...$11.95

Health

The books listed in this section include general reference books useful in an emergency; drug guides, which detail the side effects of prescribed medicine; and books on medical insurance, hospitals, and home care for the chronically ill.

Medical Consumer Reference

Robert **Berkow**, editor

The Merck Manual

Volume 1
General Medicine

Physicians have been relying on this text—which is now in its 15th edition—since 1899. It is an excellent all-around guide to illnesses and their treatments, with each entry summarizing the signs and symptoms of the disease, diagnostic procedures, alternative prognoses, and appropriate treatment

See also SPECIFIC HEALTH PROBLEMS

0-911910-17-4 MERCK PB $13.50

Volume 2
Obstetrics, Gynecology, Pediatrics, Genetics

See also SPECIFIC HEALTH PROBLEMS

0-911910-15-8 MERCK PB $12.00

Michael E. **Cafferty**

Managed Care and You: The Consumer Guide to Managing Your Health Care

Includes questions to ask before enrolling in a plan; how to choose hospitals, doctors; patients' rights discussed

0-07-600759-6 MCGRAW HILL PB $14.95

Charles **Inlander** & others, editors

The Consumer's Medical Desk Reference: Information Your Doctor Can't or Won't Tell You—Everything You Need to Know for the Best in Health Care

Health insurance coverage, hospitals, medications, and much more about which today's health-care industry consumer should be aware. "Charles Inlander…the Ralph Nader of health care, has been showing patients how to stand up to the medical establishment for decades"
—*US News & World Report*

0-7868-6056-1 HYPERION $24.95

Robert **Keet** & Mary **Nelson**

The Shopper's Guide to the Medical Marketplace

How to get the best care while cutting costs

0-915166-52-6 IMPACT PB $11.95

Ruth **Macklin**

Enemies of Patients

A leading medical ethicist explores the world of modern medicine and the forces that work against patients and doctors alike: hospital administrators, insurance companies, lawyers, the government. "Fascinating and…instructive. An outstanding achievement that should interest general readers as well as health care professionals and bioethicists"
—*New England Journal of Medicine*

0-19-507200-6 OXFORD $30.00

Timothy B. **McCall**

Examining Your Doctor: A Patient's Guide to Avoiding Harmful Medical Care

A physician emphasizes patient education on health as well as how to ensure quality care

1-55972-282-7 BIRCH LANE $22.50

0-8065-1826-X CITADEL PB $16.95

Mark **Miller**, editor

Health Care Choices for Today's Consumer

Defines *all* health care options

FOREWORD BY HILLARY RODHAM CLINTON

1-87932-623-X LIVING PLANET PB $14.95

Mosby

Mosby's Medical Dictionary

Includes a 44-page color atlas of the human body

0-8016-3489-X MOSBY $22.95

Mosby's Medical Encyclopedia

20,000 entries

0-452-26672-6 PLUME PB $18.95

Cathy **Pickney** & Edward **Pickney**

The Patient's Guide to Medical Tests

Covers hospital and outpatient procedures

0-8160-1292-X FACTS ON FILE $27.95

Nancy **Roper**, editor

New American Pocket Medical Dictionary

The 14th edition of a popular portable medical reference, with more than 1,000 new entries

0-684-19031-1 MACMILLAN PB $17.00

Marti Ann **Schwartz**

"Listen to Me, Doctor": Taking Charge of Your Own Health Care

Hodgkin's disease sufferer writes a consumer guide for patients

1-87844-867-6 MACMURRAY & BECK PB $12.95

US News & World Report

America's Best Hospitals

Ranks hospitals nationally in 16 specialty areas from AIDS to urology

0-471-12614-4 WILEY PB $19.95

Donald **Vickery** & James **Fries**

Take Care of Yourself: The Consumer's Guide to Medicine

A best-seller, now in its third edition

0-201-63292-6 ADDISON-WESLEY PB $17.95

John **Walton**

The Oxford Medical Companion

An intelligent, complete, and readable catalog of the medical world, revised and expanded. "Should be enjoyed not only as a useful reference but also as a mine of information about the present, the past, and by extrapolation, the future"—*New England Journal of Medicine*

0-19-262355-9 OXFORD $65.00

Home Health, First-Aid, and Medical Reference

American Medical Association

The American Medical Association Family Medical Guide

Divided into four parts: the healthy body, symptoms and self-diagnosis, explanation of the most common physical and mental illnesses, and caring for the sick at home

0-394-55582-1 RANDOM HOUSE $35.00

The American Medical Association Home Medical Encyclopedia

Hundreds of clear and colorful illustrations accompany the text of this thorough self-help guide to symptoms, diseases, and medical emergencies

0-394-56344-1 RANDOM HOUSE $25.00

William **Bennett**

Your Good Health: How to Stay Well, and What to Do When You're Not

Advice from Harvard Medical School doctors

0-674-96631-7 HARVARD $36.00

A.W.H. **Black**

Black's Medical Dictionary

Detailed entries

0-389-20989-9BARNES & NOBLE....................$95.00

Charles **Clayman**

The American Medical Association Encyclopedia of Medicine

An alphabetical listing of medical terms, with over 5,000 entries and 2,000 illustrations; includes symptoms, diseases, drugs, and treatments

0-394-56528-2 RANDOM HOUSE....................$45.00

Consumers Guide

The Home Remedies Handbook

Safe, practical remedies for more than 100 common ailments from acne to yeast infections are addressed

1-56173-747-X PUBLICATIONS INTERNATIONAL$29.95

Richard **Dawood**

Traveler's Health: How to Stay Healthy all over the World

0-679-74608-0 RANDOM HOUSE PB $18.00

Thomas **Dickey**

The New Wellness Encyclopedia: The Best-Selling Guide to Preventing Disease and Maintaining Your Health and Well-Being

Packed with useful and recent information on the variety of health topics; includes advice for protection against cancer and heart disease; vitamin and mineral charts

0-395-73345-6 DORLING KINDERSLEY PB $19.95

Good Housekeeping

The New Good Housekeeping Family Health and Medical Guide

Written for the layperson, with 16 pages of full-color anatomical charts and over 200 helpful illustrations

0-688-06164-8 HEARST....................................$24.95

H. Winter **Griffith**

Complete Guide to Symptoms, Illnesses & Surgery

This third edition includes 2,082 symptoms, 520 illnesses, and 171 surgeries (with illustrations)

0-399-51942-4 PERIGEE PB $16.95

Johns Hopkins

The Johns Hopkins Medical Handbook and Directory: The Hundred Major Medical Disorders of People over the Age of 50

The latest research on cancer, Alzheimer's, heart disease, glaucoma, and others—detailed coverage with drawings of the 100 disorders most affecting older people. How and where to find state-of-the-art care, with the best courses of treatment

0-929661-04-4 RANDOM HOUSE....................$39.95

Carol **Krausse**

How Healthy Is *Your* Family Tree?: A Complete Guide to Tracing Your Family's Medical and Behavioral History

Using extrapolations from studies on twins, this is an accessible and succinct format to chart both medical and behavioral genetic predispositions

0-02-044165-7 COLLIER PB $12.00

James **Kusick**

A Treasury of Natural First Aid: Remedies from A to Z

Easy-to-find drug-free remedies from a naturopathic health consultant

0-13-063181-7 PRENTICE HALL PB....................$11.95

Merriam-Webster

Webster's Medical Desk Dictionary

A popular reference for the home or medical office

0-87779-025-6 MERRIAM WEBSTER..................$24.95

Lyle J. **Micheli** & Mark **Jenkins**

The Sports Medicine Bible

The director of sports medicine at Boston Children's Hospital, orthopedist for the Boston Ballet, and Harvard Medical School professor shows how to detect and treat sports injuries, and above all how to prevent them

0-06-273143-2 HARPERCOLLINS PB................$20.00

National Safety Council

The First Aid Handbook

Full-color illustrations of the dos and don'ts in medical emergencies from *the* pros

0-86720-846-5 JONES & BARTLETT PB............$10.95

Danette **Nelson-Anderson** & Cynthia **Waters**

Genetic Connection: A Guide to Documenting Your Individual and Family Health History

Knowing your family's medical history and genetic heritage is an essential element in taking charge of your health

0-9639154-3-6 SONTERS PB $34.95

Physician's Desk Reference

The PDR Family Guide to Nutrition and Health

"Throughout, fact is distinguished from myth. . . ."—*Publishers Weekly*

1-56363-135-0 MEDICAL ECONOMICS PB $25.95

Betty A. **Prasher**, editor

The Columbia University College of Physicians and Surgeons Complete Home Medical Guide

Revised and updated

0-517-59610-5 CROWN..................................$50.00

Isadore **Rosenfeld**

Modern Prevention: The New Medicine

Current ideas on how to prevent common illnesses

0-553-27301-9 BDD PB $6.50

Phyllis **Stoffman**

The Family Guide to Preventing & Treating 100 Infectious Illnesses: All You Need to Know to Keep Your Family Healthy

Written by a community health and infection-control nurse; offers parents facts to help in preventing infectious diseases or caring for those afflicted

0-471-00014-0 WILEY PB.................................$18.95

Carol **Turkington**

The Home Health Guide to Poisons and Antidotes

An A to Z guide for more than 600 toxins listing their symptoms and treatments

0-8160-3316-1 FACTS ON FILE PB $12.95

Drug Guides

American Association of Retired Persons

The AARP Pharmacy Service Prescription Drug Handbook

Organized by diseases

0-06-271553-4 HARPERPERENNIAL PB $35.00

Joe **Graedon** & Teresa **Graedon**

The People's Guide to Deadly Drug Interactions

Foods as well as drugs analyzed that may be dangerous when combined

0-312-13243-3 ST. MARTIN'S $25.95

Ellen Hodgson **Brown** & Lynne Paige **Walker**

The Informed Consumer's Pharmacy: The Essential Guide to Prescription and Over-the-Counter Drugs

Compiled by a hospital pharmacist, the book's purpose is to inform the consumer about all the consequences as well as to weigh the benefits and risks of certain drugs

0-88184-586-8 CARROLL & GRAF PB $12.95

Andrew **Chetley**

Problem Drugs

Lists unsafe and ineffective drugs, with special focus on kids, women, and the elderly

1-85649-320-2 ZED PB $22.50

Consumer Reports

The Complete Drug Reference 1996 Edition

Americans spend $20 billion annually on drugs, yet take 50 percent of these drugs incorrectly. "What a good drug reference should be: highly readable, with complete and clear sections describing potential side effects and precautions to take while using a medicine"
—*US News & World Report*

See also **OTHER** under **REFERENCE** in **BUSINESS AND REFERENCE**

0-89043-849-8CONSUMER REPORTS $39.95

John **Fried** & Sharon **Pestka**

The American Druggist's Complete Family Guide to Prescriptions, Pills, and Drugs: Everything You Need to Know to Stock Your Medicine Cabinet and to Use Drugs Safely

Up-to-date reference on pharmaceuticals and drugstore products, tables of generic and brand names, side effects, and other useful information

0-688-12385-6 HEARST PB $19.95

Jeffrey **Jonas** & Ron **Schaumburg**

Everything You Need to Know About Prozac: The Authoritative Guide to America's Most Prescribed Antidepressant

Crucial for an informed decision

0-553-29192-0 BDD PB $4.99

Peter D. **Kramer**

Listening to Prozac: A Psychiatrist Explores Mood-Altering Drugs and the New Meaning of the Self

An expert in the field of drug therapy explores the implications of the drug that is currently prescribed to over 4,000,000 people. "[Kramer is] a warm-spirited, open-minded physician who has a thoughtful, wide-ranging mind…and a voice of earnest, unashamed speculation and reflection—subtle, suggestive, clarifying"—Robert Coles, author of *The Spiritual Life of Children*

See also **DEPRESSION** under **DISORDERS AND TREATMENT** under **PSYCHOLOGY** in **SOCIAL STUDIES**

0-14-015940-1 PENGUIN PB $12.95

James W. **Long** & James J. **Rybacki**

The Essential Guide to Prescription Drugs, 1997

Includes expected minor side effects and more serious effects which require immediate medical attention

0-06-273429-6 HARPERCOLLINS PB.................$20.00

Gesina **Longenecker**

How Drugs Work: Drug Abuse and the Human Body

Full-color diagrams clearly show the effects of drug use/abuse; ideal for teens, parents, educators

1-56276-241-9 ZIFF DAVIS PB $19.95

Physician's Desk Reference

The PDR Family Guide to Prescription Drugs with CD Rom

"Brief, lucid entries on drugs and their side effects"—*Wall Street Journal*

1-56363-134-2 MEDICAL ECONOMICS PB $25.95

Physician's Desk Reference

The 42nd edition of the drug guide on every doctor's desk

1-56363-074-5 MEDICAL ECONOMICS $56.95

Lynn **Sonberg**

The Pill Guide

Alphabetical listing from acetaminophen to warfarin; includes side effects, food and drug interactions, pregnancy, and drugs

0-425-13336-2 BERKLEY PB...................................$5.50

David **Thueson**

Thueson's Guide to Over-the-Counter Drugs: A Symptom-by-Symptom Handbook of the Best Nonprescription Drugs

Pharmacologist simplifies the dizzying array of drugs and manufacturer's claims

1-57224-005-9 NEW HARBINGER PB $13.95

United States Pharmacopeia

The Complete Drug Reference: 1997 Edition

U.S. News and World Report ranks this number one as a drug reference guide. Vital information on more than 5,500 prescription and over-the-counter medications is provided. A full-color, 24-page chart indentifies 1,400 frequently used tablets and capsules. "More comprehensive than *The Physician's Desk Reference*, more consistent and logically organized, and the layout is far easier to read"— *Library Journal*

0-89043-850-1 CONSUMER REPORTS $39.95

Ruth **Winter**

A Consumer's Dictionary of Medicine: Prescription, Over-the-Counter & Herbal Remedies

Covers why particular medications are used, their reported benefits and side effects, interaction with other drugs and foods, overuse, misuse, and abuse

0-517-88046-6 CROWN PB...............................$20.00

Sidney **Wolfe**

Worst Pills, Best Pills: The Older Adult's Guide to Avoiding Drug Induced Death or Illness

Information on nearly 300 of the most commonly prescribed medications

0-937188-52-2 PANTHEON PB...........................$15.00

Hospital and Medical Care

David John **Doukas** & William **Reichel**

Planning for Uncertainty: A Guide to Living Wills and Other Advance Directives for Health Care

This book will help prepare us all for the possibility that someday we may be unable to communicate our health care decisions. As family doctors who have seen the devastating effects of prolonged and useless suffering, the authors are able to give us a clear and reliable guide on how to direct the final details of our lives, and what to take into account—medical choices, legal issues, and family concerns— when we do so

See also **REFERENCE AND PRACTICAL GUIDES** under **LAW** in **SOCIAL STUDIES**

0-8018-4671-4 JOHNS HOPKINS PB..................$13.95

Melvin **Konner**

Medicine at the Crossroads: The Crisis in Health Care

In a passionate call to arms, this anthropologist provides an indictment of American medicine. Why does it cost $6,000 to have a baby? Why do other countries handle AIDS and care for the elderly better than we do? "Konner's arguments…are forceful, and his recommendations for change are specific"—*Kirkus Reviews*

0-679-41545-9 PANTHEON.................................$23.00
0-679-74216-6 VINTAGE PB..............................$13.00

Ira **Schneider** & Ezra **Huber**

Financial Planning for Long Term Care: A Guide for Lawyers, Caregivers, and Consumers

An explanation of Medicare and Medicaid

0-89885-417-2 HUMAN SCIENCES...................$28.95

Robert M. **Youngson**

The Surgery Book: An Illustrated Guide to 73 of the Most Common Operations

Discusses why a specific surgery is necessary; diagrams, procedures, and lists of post-surgery effects

0-312-09398-5 ST. MARTIN'S $27.95

Specific Health Problems

Robert **Berkow**, editor

The Merck Manual Volume 1 General Medicine

0-911910-17-4 MERCK PB $13.50

Volume 2
Obstetrics, Gynecology, Pediatrics, Genetics
0-911910-15-8 MERCK PB $12.00

AIDS

John G. **Bartlett** & Ann K. **Finkbeiner**
The Guide to Living with HIV Infection: Developed at the Johns Hopkins AIDS Clinic, Third Edition
How to negotiate the formidable challenges—medical, legal, psychological, and financial—presented by HIV. It includes updated information on new drugs, transmission of HIV, HIV and women, and much more. "An excellent resource for people with HIV infection, as well as those who live with or love them"—Jane E. Brody, *NY Times*
See also **AIDS AND HEALTH** under **GAY, LESBIAN, AND BISEXUAL STUDIES** in **SOCIAL STUDIES**
0-8018-5358-3 JOHNS HOPKINS $40.00
0-8018-5359-1 JOHNS HOPKINS PB $15.95

Leon **Chaitow** & James **Strohecker**
You Don't Have to Die: Unraveling the AIDS Myth
"...[provides] an interesting alternative to the conventional beliefs about HIV and AIDS"—*Publishers Weekly*
0-9636334-4-9 FUTURE MEDICINE PB $14.95

Consumer Reports
AIDS: Trading Fears for Facts
A guide for teenagers
See also **MEDICAL AND RESEARCH ASPECTS** under **AIDS** under **MEDICINE** in **SCIENCE**
0-89043-269-4 CONSUMER REPORTS PB $4.95

Gena **Corea**
The Invisible Epidemic: The Story of Women and AIDS
The author, who has taken on the medical establishment before in her book *The Mother Machine,* interweaves factual research with personal narratives about AIDS sufferers, their relatives, professional experts, and activists to disclose many alarming truths about the effects of the disease on women. "A powerful report on the AIDS crisis...a long overdue exposé...and a heartfelt call to action"—*Kirkus Reviews*
See also **MEDICAL AND RESEARCH ASPECTS** under **AIDS** under **MEDICINE** in **SCIENCE**
0-06-016648-7 HARPER PERENNIAL PB $23.00

Martin **Delaney** & Peter **Goldblum**
Strategies for Survival: A Gay Men's Health Manual for the Age of AIDS
A comprehensive guide covering gay health
0-312-00558-X ST. MARTIN'S PB $10.95

The Voices of AIDS
An excellent introduction to the disease, with "AIDS Fast Facts"
0-688-05322-X MORROW $15.00
9-995-50251-8 BEECH TREE PB $4.95

Elizabeth **Fee** & Daniel **Fox**
AIDS: The Making of a Chronic Disease
This collection of essays covers the AIDS virus and epidemiology, law, ethics and public policy, those afflicted, and international perspectives
0-520-07569-2 CALIFORNIA $50.00
0-520-07778-4 CALIFORNIA PB $15.95

Michael Thomas **Ford**
100 Questions & Answers About Aids
This candid, well-organized volume asks and answers pointed questions about the plague. "One of the best books explaining HIV disease—to people of any age—that I have ever read"—William B. Rubenstein, ACLU National AIDS Project
0-688-12697-9 MORROW PB $4.95

Rosmarie **Hausherr**
Children and the AIDS Virus
See also **TEENAGE HEALTH** under **STAGES OF DEVELOPMENT** under **PARENTING**
0-395-51167-4 CLARION PB $6.95

Stephen **Joseph**
The Dragon Within the Gates: The Once and Future AIDS Epidemic
As former NYC Health Commissioner, Joseph contends that AIDS is the first major public health issue of our time for which social and political values rather than health requirements have set the agenda. "Steve Joseph was a sane and courageous public official in a time of madness and cowardice. He has written a sane and courageous book"—*Newsweek*
0-7867-0033-5 CARROLL & GRAF PB $9.95

Elisabeth **Kübler-Ross** & Mal **Warshaw**
AIDS: The Ultimate Challenge
An expert on working with the terminally ill offers compassionate advice to those confronting AIDS
See also **MEDICAL AND RESEARCH ASPECTS** under **AIDS** under **MEDICINE** in **SCIENCE**
0-02-089143-1 COLLIER PB $10.00

John **Langone**
AIDS: The Facts
Scientific consensus used to trace the progress of the epidemic and to examine its enigmas
0-316-51414-4 LITTLE, BROWN PB $10.95

Bonnie **Lester**
Women and AIDS: A Practical Guide for Those Who Help Others
0-8245-1348-7 CONTINUUM $15.95

Bettyclare **Moffatt**
When Someone You Love Has AIDS: A Book of Hope for Family and Friends
See also **MEDICAL AND RESEARCH ASPECTS** under **AIDS** under **MEDICINE** in **SCIENCE**
0-8095-6551-X BORGO $27.00

Project Inform
The HIV Drug Book
Up-to-date listing of the drugs, alternative therapies, and experimental treatments used to treat AIDS
0-671-53518-8 POCKET PB $18.00

National Academy of Sciences
Mobilizing Against AIDS: The Unfinished Story of a Virus
See also **MEDICAL AND RESEARCH ASPECTS** under **AIDS** under **MEDICINE** in **SCIENCE**
0-674-57762-0 HARVARD PB $12.95

Jeffrey **Nevid**
201 Things You Should Know About AIDS and Other Sexually Transmitted Diseases
In addition to a complete discussion of AIDS and STDs, provides a listing of hotlines for both
0-205-14873-5 ALLYN & BACON PB $15.00

Walt **Odets**
In the Shadow of the Epidemic: Being HIV-Negative in the Age of AIDS
0-8223-1638-2 DUKE PB $14.95

Laura **Pinsky** & Paul Harding **Douglas**
The Essential HIV Treatment Fact Book
"An amazingly complete medical guide to all aspects of HIV and infection...a thorough tool kit for individual patients..."
—Martin Delaney, *Project Inform*
0-671-72528-9 POCKET PB $14.00

Mary **Romeyn**
Nutrition and HIV: A New Model for Treatment
"Although its focus is on nutrition, this is a truly comprehensive guide to combatting the ravages of HIV infection"—*Publishers Weekly*
0-7879-0107-5 JOSSEY-BASS PB $18.95

William **Rubenstein** & others
The Rights of People Who Are HIV Positive
The authoritative ACLU guide to the rights of people living with HIV disease and AIDS
0-8093-1991-8 SOUTHERN ILLINOIS $34.95
0-8093-1992-6 SOUTHERN ILLINOIS PB $13.95

Susan **Sontag**
Illness as Metaphor and AIDS and Its Metaphors
0-385-26705-3 ANCHOR PB $9.95

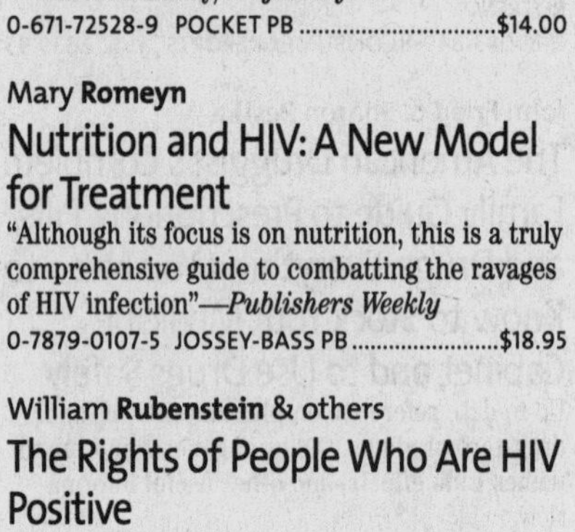

Susan Sontag

Nick **Siano**

No Time to Wait: A Complete Guide to Treating, Managing and Living with HIV Infection

Current information and strategies to deal with the virus, covering psychological, physical, and spiritual needs

0-553-37176-2 BANTAM PB $13.95

Allergies

Marry **Harris** & Wilma **Nachsin**

"My Kid's Allergic to Everything" Dessert Cookbook: Sweets & Treats the Whole Family Will Enjoy

1-55652-303-3 CHICAGO REVIEW PB $11.95

Marjorie **Jones**

The Allergy Self-Help Cookbook

Over 325 natural foods recipes, free from wheat, milk eggs, corn, yeast, sugar, and other common food-allergy substances

See also **DIETS FOR SPECIAL HEALTH PROBLEMS** under **SPECIAL DIETS** under **DIET AND NUTRITION**

0-87596-109-6 RODALE PB $15.95

Nelson Lee **Novick**

You Can Do Something About Your Allergies

A medical doctor's approach that includes the latest on prescription drugs for treatment

0-553-57267-9 BDD PB $5.99

Gheron G. **Randolph** & Ralph W. **Moss**

An Alternative Approach to Allergies: The New Field of Clinical Ecology Unravels the Environmental Causes of Mental and Physical Ills

Hidden as well as overt addictions are discussed, as is the modern environment as possible causes of illness

0-06-091693-1 HARPERCOLLINS PB $13.50

William **Walsh**

The Food Allergy Book: The Foods that Cause You Pain & Discomfort & How to Take Them Out of Your Diet

Identifies common allergens in foods and beverages, with practical tips on grocery shopping and dining out as well as recipes

0-9631544-7-8 CHRONIMED PB $12.95

Alzheimer's Disease

Donna **Cohen** & Carl **Eisdorfer**

The Loss of Self: A Family Resource for the Care of Alzheimer's Disease and Related Disorders

0-393-02263-3 NORTON $19.95

0-452-25946-0 NEW AMERICAN LIBRARY PB....$12.95

Harriet **Hodgson**

Alzheimer's: Finding the Words

A helpful communication guide to detect symptoms, cope with personality changes, and effectively communicate with the patient

1-56561-071-7 CHRONIMED PB $10.95

Marilynn **Larkin**

When Someone You Love Has Alzheimer's: What You Must Know, What You Can Do, What You Should Expect

Strategies for dealing with memory loss and behavior problems; planning meals, exercise, and long-term care, as well as how to maintain the sanity of the caregiver

0-440-21660-5 DELL PB $4.99

Nancy **Mace** & Peter **Rabins**

The 36-Hour Day: A Family Guide to Caring for Persons with Alzheimer's Disease, Related Dementing Illnesses, and Memory Loss in Later Life

Longtime bestseller

0-8018-4033-3 JOHNS HOPKINS $38.95

0-8018-4034-1 JOHNS HOPKINS PB $11.95

Rose **Oliver** & Frances **Bock**

Coping with Alzheimer's: A Caregiver's Emotional Survival Guide

Written by two psychiatrists, sound, practical advice on providing maximum care for the person with Alzheimer's while inflicting minimum emotional strain on oneself

0-87980-424-6 WILSHIRE PB $10.00

Lenore S. **Powell** & Katie **Courtice**

Alzheimer's Disease

Caring for someone with Alzheimer's disease is draining emotionally and physically. This book, which resulted from a therapist's work with caregivers, helps such people overcome their frustration, fears, and other burdens. And it provides up-to-date advice on nursing homes, health plans, and patient-choice laws. *New York Times* has called it both "excellent" and "indispensable"

0-201-63201-2 ADDISON-WESLEY PB $15.00

Judah **Ronch**

Alzheimer's Disease: A Practical Guide for Those Who Help Others

A resource for family members, friends, nurses, physicians, counselors, and other caregivers

0-8245-1283-9 CONTINUUM $17.95

0-8245-1284-7 CONTINUUM PB $12.95

Margaret **Shawver**

What's Wrong with Grandma?: A Family's Experience with Alzheimer's

A child's first-person narrative that reflects the frustration, sadness, and anger of watching a loved one gradually succumb to this baffling disease

1-57392-107-6 PROMETHEUS $14.95

Jitka **Zgola**

Doing Things: A Guide to Programming Activities for Persons with Alzheimer's Disease and Related Disorders

Intended for professional caregivers but also a useful guide for the patient's families

0-8018-3467-8 JOHNS HOPKINS PB $12.95

Arthritic Diseases

Lauri **Aesoph**

How to Eat Away Arthritis

Foods for a cure

0-13-242900-4 PRENTICE HALL $24.95

0-13-242892-X PRENTICE HALL PB $14.95

Dale **Alexander**

Arthritis & Common Sense

In print since 1954, now in large-print format, this classic provides meals and supplements specifically designed for the arthritic

0-671-42791-1 SIMON & SCHUSTER PB $11.00

Arthritis Foundation

Understanding Arthritis: What It Is, How It's Treated, How to Cope with It

The traditional viewpoint, including a critical look at nonmedical treatments

0-684-18736-1 MACMILLAN PB $12.00

Derrick **Brewerton**

All About Arthritis: Past, Present, Future

History of arthritis research by a contributor to the field

0-674-01615-7 HARVARD $29.95

Darlene **Cohen**

Arthritis—Stop Suffering, Start Moving

A certified movement therapist shows how to overcome pain and get flexible with at-home exercises

0-8027-7466-0 WALKER PB $14.95

Collin **Doug** & Jane **Banks**

New Hope for the Arthritic

Emphasizes the connection between diet and arthritis; includes recipes and menus

0-345-32728-4 BALLANTINE PB $4.95

Gwen **Ellert**

The Arthritis Exercise Book: Gentle Joint-by-Joint Exercises to Keep You Flexible and Independent

Fifty easy, relaxing, stretching, and strengthening exercises designed by a nurse and rheumatoid arthritis sufferer to alleviate joint pain

0-8092-4094-7 CONTEMPORARY PB $14.95

J.T. **Scott**

Arthritis and Rheumatism: The Facts

0-19-261168-2 OXFORD $21.95

Michael Reed **Gach**

Arthritis Relief at Your Fingertips: Your Guide to Easing Aches and Pains *Without* Drugs

Fully illustrated with black-and-white photos and diagrams for every joint, discusses diet and exercise. "...helps the reader relearn what to do when conventional drugs aren't the answer"
—*Utne Reader*

0-446-39156-5 WARNER PB $15.99

Kate **Loring** & James **Fries**

The Arthritis Help Book: A Tested Self-Management Program for Coping with Your Arthritis

Recommended by the Arthritis Foundation for use in its classes

0-201-52402-3 ADDISON-WESLEY PB $10.95

Tammi L. **Shlotzhauer** & James L. **McGuire**

Living with Rheumatoid Arthritis

Explanation of the disease, coping strategies, nutrition and exercise, and lifestyle changes for both patient and family

0-8018-5185-8 JOHNS HOPKINS PB $15.95

Dava **Sobel** & Arthur **Klein**

Arthritis: What Works

Jam-packed with both orthodox and nutritional treatments

0-312-92719-3 ST. MARTIN'S PB $6.99

Asthma

Vincent **Friedewald**

Ask the Doctor: Asthma

Explains what asthma is and isn't in a well-organized format

0-8362-7023-1 ANDREWS & MCMEEL PB $8.95

Eric **Gershwin** & E.L. **Klingelhofer**

Asthma: Stop Suffering, Start Living

New strategies for controlling asthma that include diet, medication, and exercise

0-201-60847-2 ADDISON-WESLEY PB $13.00

Nancy **Sander**

A Parent's Guide to Asthma: How You Can Help Your Child Control Asthma at Home, School, and Play

Founder of the National Asthma and Allergy Network presents all aspects of care and management

0-452-27216-5 PLUME PB $10.95

Myra B. **Shayevitz** & Berton R. **Shayevitz**

Living Well with Chronic Asthma, Bronchitis, and Emphysema: A Complete Guide to Coping with Chronic Lung Disease

How to manage symptoms and live a fulfilled life

0-89043-416-6 CONSUMER REPORTS $18.95

Allan **Weinstein**

Asthma: The Complete Guide for Patients and Their Families

0-449-21562-8 FAWCETT PB $5.99

Back Problems

American Medical Association

Pocket Guide to Back Pain

Causes, prevention, and treatment in this handy edition

0-679-75560-8 RANDOM HOUSE PB $4.99

Stephen **Hochschuler**

Back in Shape: A Back Owner's Manual

Numerous black-and-white illustrations provide exercise program developed by the Texas Back Institute to reduce pain and prevent future injury

0-395-56273-2 HOUGHTON MIFFLIN PB $13.95

Stephanie **Levin-Gervasi**

The Back Pain Sourcebook

Explains spine physiology, conditions, prevention, and standard and alternative treatments

1-56565-205-3 LOWELL $25.00
1-56565-472-2 LOWELL PB $16.00

Leon **Root**

No More Aching Back!: Dr. Root's 15-Minutes-A-Day Program for a Healthy Back

Renowned orthopedic surgeon and best-selling co-author of *Oh, My Aching Back,* Dr. Leon Root presents a simple program designed to reduce or eliminate most back pain

0-451-17091-1 NEW AMERICAN LIBRARY PB $5.99

Glenn **Rothfield** & Suzanne **LeVert**

Natural Medicine for Back Pain: The Best Alternative Methods for Banishing Backache

A medical doctor discusses acupressure, chiropractics, nutrition, and yoga

0-87596-288-2 RODALE PB $11.95

Cancer

Ronald E. **Aigotti**

The People's Cancer Guide Book

A physician communicates in nonmedical language information relative to all cancers, from causes to treatments

0-9648656-0-2 BELLETRIST PB $29.95

Oliver **Alabaster**

The Power of Prevention: A Personal Plan to Reduce Your Risk of Cancer Up to 70%

0-929693-01-9 SAVILLE PB $15.00

Roberta **Altman**

Waking Up, Fighting Back: The Politics of Breast Cancer

0-316-03532-7 LITTLE, BROWN $24.95

Lisa J. **Bain**

A Parent's Guide to Childhood Cancer

Besides the medical aspects addressed, the family's emotional considerations are considered. "Bain's guide is an excellent starting point and sourcebook for parents anywhere"
—*Publishers Weekly*

FOREWORD BY C. EVERETT KOOP

0-440-50692-1 BANTAM PB $13.95

Harold **Benjamin**

The Wellness Community Guide to Fighting for Recovery from Cancer

Publishers Weekly calls it an "empowering, emphatic guide" that emphasizes the mind/body relation for recovery

0-87477-794-1 TARCHER PB $12.95

Jeanne Munn **Bracken**

Children with Cancer: A Comprehensive Reference Guide for Parents

From practical tips to sophisticated medical facts, written by a librarian whose son survived cancer. "A remarkable job....The technical information is clearly stated, up-to-date and accurate....But, most of all, this is a human book"
—*LA Times*

0-19-503482-1 OXFORD $35.00

Gerald **Dermer**

The Immortal Cell: Why Cancer Research Fails

Why science is losing the war on cancer

0-89529-582-2 AVERY PB $11.95

Malin **Dollinger** & others

Everyone's Guide to Cancer Therapy: How Cancer Is Diagnosed, Treated, and Managed Day to Day

"This may be a landmark book: it provides, in one place, so much of what the cancer patient must know to make informed decisions"
—*Publishers Weekly*

0-8362-2427-2 ANDREWS & MCMEEL PB $19.95

Ron **Falcone**

The Complete Guide to Alternative Cancer Therapies: What You Need to Know to Make an Informed Choice

Presents pros and cons for standard cancer treatments as well as 17 different holistic therapies

0-8065-1553-8 CITADEL PB $12.95

Richard A. **Evans**

Making the Right Choice: Treatment Options in Cancer Surgery

A cancer surgeon discusses ten types of cancers and treatment with conservative surgeries

0-89529-644-6 AVERY PB $14.95

Mae **Eydie** & Chris **Loeffler**

How I Conquered Cancer Naturally

Breast cancer survivor writes about her lifestyle and dietary regimen

0-89529-518-0 AVERY PB $7.95

Errol **Friedberg**

Cancer Answers: Encouraging Answers to 25 Questions You Were Always Afraid to Ask

Clearly written, concise answers to commonly asked questions

0-7167-7023-7 FREEMAN PB $10.95

Lucy **Grealy**

Autobiography of a Face

Of her disfigurement from cancer treatment, Grealy writes: "I've spent fifteen years being treated for nothing other than looking different from everyone else. It was the pain from that, from feeling ugly, that I'd always viewed as the great tragedy in my life. The fact that I had cancer seemed minor in comparison"

See also **MEMOIRS AND JOURNALS** under **20TH-CENTURY AMERICAN ESSAYS AND JOURNALISM** in **LITERATURE OF THE AMERICAS**

0-395-65780-6 HOUGHTON MIFFLIN $19.95

0-06-097673-X HARPERPERENNIAL PB $12.00

Lucy Grealy (photo by Lorin Klaris)

Glenna **Halvorson-Boyd** & Lisa K. **Hunter**

Dancing in Limbo: Making Sense of Life After Cancer

"If someone you love has been treated for cancer, this insightful journal of life after cancer will be invaluable"—George N. Peters, past president, American Cancer Society

0-7879-0103-2 JOSSEY-BASS $21.00

Jill **Ireland**

Life Wish

How the glamorous movie actress (and wife of Charles Bronson) coped with breast cancer

0-515-09609-1 JOVE PB $4.95

Wendy Schlessel **Harpham**

After Cancer: A Guide to Your New Life

Question-and-answer format by an MD as well as cancer survivor who discusses life's practicalities with the disease

0-06-097678-0 HARPERPERENNIAL PB $13.00

Diagnosis: Cancer—Your Guide Through the First Few Months

Answers to common questions for the new cancer patient as well as resources and other practical information

0-393-30892-8 NORTON PB $10.95

Don **Hawkins** & others

When Cancer Comes: Mobilizing Physical, Emotional, and Spiritual Resources to Combat One of Life's Most Dreaded Diseases

A Christian approach to surviving

0-8024-09498 MOODY $18.99

Edward **Larschan** & Richard **Larschan**

The Diagnosis Is Cancer: A Psychological and Legal Resource Handbook for Cancer Patients, Their Families, and Helping Professionals

0-915950-77-4 BULL PB $9.95

John **Laszlo**

The Cure of Childhood Leukemia: Into the Age of Miracles

Stories of those who contributed to the cure as well as the parents and their children who survived. "Their stories are harbingers of hope" —*Publishers Weekly*

0-8135-2186-6 RUTGERS $29.95

0-8135-2385-0 RUTGERS PB $16.95

Michael **Lerner**

Choices in Healing: Integrating the Best of Conventional and Complementary Approaches to Cancer

For both cancer patient and health professional. On the entire cycle of cancer as well as all manner of healing modalities available

0-262-12180-8 MIT $27.50

0-262-62104-5 MIT PB $17.50

Lawrence **LeShan**

You Can Fight for Your Life: Emotional Factors in the Treatment of Cancer

How emotions affect recovery

0-87131-494-0 EVANS PB $12.95

Christina **Middlebrook**

Seeing the Crab: A Memoir of Dying Before I Do

A bestseller about living with cancer and its treatment

0-465-07493-6 BASIC $22.00

Joyce Slayton **Mitchell**

Winning the Cancer Battle

Information on chemotherapy drugs and their side effects, as well as tips on nutrition and coping skills, written by a survivor

0-393-30713-1 NORTON PB $11.00

Linus **Pauling** & Ewan **Cameron**

Cancer and Vitamin C

Updated and expanded resource on the efficacy of the vitamin as a preventative and adjunct therapy

0-940159-21-X CAMINO PB $13.95

Ross **Pelton** & Lee **Overholser**

Alternatives in Cancer Therapy: The Complete Guide to Non-Traditional Treatments

Information on research, side effects, availability, and efficacy of non-traditional therapies. "The definitive guide...."—Earl Mindell

0-671-79623-2 FIRESIDE PB $12.00

M. Steven **Piver** & Gene **Wilder**

Gilda's Disease: Sharing Personal Experiences and a Medical Perspective on Ovarian Cancer

Thoughts from the husband of one of TV's best loved comediennes and from a medical doctor. With photos

1-57392-089-4 PROMETHEUS $22.95

Kedar N. **Prasad**

Vitamins in Cancer Prevention & Treatment: A Practical Guide

"...a useful and well-organized antidote to the mass of irresponsible information about vitamins"—Frank L. Meyskeus, Jr., MD, Director, Cancer Prevention and Control

0-89281-483-7 INNER TRADITIONS PB $9.95

Reynolds **Price**

A Whole New Life: An Illness and a Healing

Well-known writer documents his battle with a tumor in his spinal cord

0-452-27473-7 PENGUIN PB $10.95

Gary L. **Schine** & Ellen **Berlinsky**

Cancer Cure: The Complete Guide to Finding and Getting the Best Care There Is

"A fine guide and reference source from someone who has lived the experience and learned how to teach others"—Bernie Siegel

1-57566-024-5 KENSINGTON PB $13.00

Wendy Schlessel **Harpham**

After Cancer: A Guide to Your New Life

Written for lay readers by a doctor who is also a cancer survivor, this easy-to-use book guides us from the discovery and treatment of cancer to the medical, practical, and psychological issues of recovery. "This is 'must' reading for anyone coping with the aftermath of cancer treatments, as well as for their families and friends" —*Publishers Weekly*

0-393-03664-2 NORTON $23.00

Alice **Trillin**
Dear Bruno
Deals with the issue of cancer in children
ILLUSTRATIONS BY EDWARD KOREN
1-56584-057-7 NEW PRESS $12.00

Sidney J. **Winawer** & others
Cancer Free: The Comprehensive Cancer Prevention Program
Prevention includes learning about one's genetic background, diet, environmental pollutants, and scheduling periodic tests and screenings
0-671-79967-3 SIMON & SCHUSTER $25.00
0-684-81512-5 FIRESIDE PB........................$14.00

Chronic Fatigue Syndrome

Katrina **Berne**
Running on Empty: Living with Chronic Fatigue Immune Dysfunction Syndrome
An award-winning self-help book for both patients and health-care professionals
0-89793-100-9 HUNTER PB $13.95

Deepak **Chopra**
Boundless Energy: The Complete Mind/Body Program for Overcoming Chronic Fatigue
From the mind/body guru
0-517-79974-X HARMONY........................$15.00
0-517-88491-7 HARMONY PB........................$11.00

Karyn **Feiden**
Hope and Help for Chronic Fatigue Syndrome
Written in conjunction with the Chronic Fatigue Syndrome/Chronic Fatigue Immune Dysfunction Syndrome network to provide the latest information on research
0-671-75944-2 FIRESIDE PB $11.00

Richard **Podell**
Doctor, Why Am I So Tired?
Discusses organic as well as environmental health issues that may cause chronic fatigue
0-449-14578-6 FAWCETT PB $4.99

Edward **Shorter**
From Paralysis to Fatigue: A History of Psychosomatic Illness in the Modern Era
A study of the manner in which symptoms of disease have changed to meet the expectations of doctors—from 19th-century "spinal irritation" to present-day "chronic fatigue syndrome."
"Building on his vast and learned research in three languages, [Shorter] has created a compelling and sometimes poignant picture of our unending sruggle against illness in a medicocentric world"—*NY Times Book Review*
See also **HISTORIES AND INTRODUCTIONS** under **PSYCHOLOGY** in **SOCIAL STUDIES**
0-02-928667-0 FREE PRESS PB $14.95

Colds

Charles **Inlander** & Cynthia K. **Moran**
77 Ways to Beat Colds and Flu
For those who have no clue as to what to do
0-553-57420-5 BDD PB $4.99

Lloyd R. **Stark**
The Ultimate Cause and Preventive Cure for the Common Cold
0-9639123-0-5 MOJAVE PB $12.95

Cosmetic Surgery

John A. **Byrne**
Informed Consent
"Byrne brings to vivid life the human costs of the breast-implant calamity....A first-rate take on corporate responsibility—at once disturbing and engrossing"—*Kirkus Reviews*
0-07-009625-2 MCGRAW HILL........................$22.00
0-07-011784-5 MCGRAW HILL PB $12.95

Joyce **Nash**
What Your Doctor Can't Tell You About Cosmetic Surgery
A help in making an informed decision
1-57224-032-6 NEW HARBINGER PB $13.95

Jan **Willis**
Beautiful Again: Restoring Your Image & Enhancing Body Changes
Addresses the effects of chemotherapy, burns, and long-term illnesses
0-929173-13-9 HEALTH PRESS PB $20.00

Dental Care

Thomas **McGuire**
Tooth Fitness: Your Guide to Healing Teeth
Preventive dental care; discusses fluoride and mercury as well as cosmetic dentistry
0-9638321-2-3 ST MICHAELS PB $16.95

Jerry **Taintor** & Mary **Taintor**
The Oral Report: The Consumer's Common Sense Guide to Better Dental Care
0-8160-1392-6 FACTS ON FILE $18.95

Diabetes

Jerry **Edelwich** & Archie **Brodsky**
Diabetes: Caring for Your Emotions as Well as Your Health
0-201-10608-6 ADDISON-WESLEY PB $15.00

Benjamin **Beaser**
The Joslin Guide to Diabetes: A Program for Managing Your Treatment
"The book belongs in the hands of all diabetics and those who share in their care and well-being"—*Publishers Weekly*
0-684-80208-2 FIRESIDE PB $15.00

Dorothy **Borni**
Diabetes in the Family
A guide to a healthy lifestyle, with meal plans
0-13-208463-5 PRENTICE HALL PB $9.95

Lester **Henry** & Kirk **Johnson**
The Black Health Library Guide to Diabetes
For the one in 10 African Americans who suffer from diabetes
0-8050-2285-6 HOLT $22.50

International Diabetes Center
Learning to Live Well with Diabetes
Comprehensive guide to diabetes management, written by 25 professionals
0-937721-79-4 DIABETES CENTER PB $24.95

Janet **Meirelles**
Diabetes Is Not a Piece of Cake
Focuses on family, friends, and co-workers to give the dos and don'ts in social and emergency situations for those with diabetes
1-88492-975-3 INDUSTRY BOOKS PB................$15.95

Katherine **Middleton** & Mary **Hess**
The Art of Cooking for the Diabetic
See also **DIETS FOR SPECIAL HEALTH PROBLEMS** under **SPECIAL DIETS** under **DIET AND NUTRITION**
0-8092-4653-8 CONTEMPORARY PB................$14.95
0-451-17574-3 SIGNET PB........................$6.99

Charles **Peterson** & Lois **Jovanovic**
The Diabetes Self-Care Method
0-929923-29-4 LOWELL PB $12.95

Julian **Whitaker**
Reversing Diabetes
From a Pritikin Longevity Center doctor, a lifestyle plan which promises to reduce or even eliminate dependence on insulin or oral drugs
0-446-38563-8 WARNER PB........................$14.99

Digestive Disorders

James **Scala**
Eating Right for a Bad Gut: The Complete Nutritional Guide to Ileitis, Colitis, Crohn's Disease and Inflammatory Bowel Disease
How to develop a personal food-testing program, reduce stress, get fit, and learn about vitamin supplements
0-452-26766-8 PLUME PB........................$13.95

Deepak **Chopra**

Perfect Digestion: The Key to Balanced Living

An Ayurvedic approach to the gut

0-517-79975-8 HARMONY $15.00

Henry D. **Janowitz**

Indigestion: Living Better with Upper Intestinal Problems from Heartburn to Ulcers and Gallstones

The whole array of the causes, symptoms, and treatments of gastrointestinal ailments, explained in an accessible, interesting, even humorous manner. Helpful examples and everything an indigestion sufferer needs to know make this a "a must have"—*Library Journal*

0-19-508554-X OXFORD PB $9.95

David **Potterton**

All About Irritable Bowel Syndrome: And Its Treatment Without Drugs

From a naturopath

0-572-02165-8 ATRIUM PB $7.95

Elaine Fantle **Shimberg**

Relief from IBS (Irritable Bowel Syndrome)

Former sufferer of IBS covers all aspects, including kids with IBS

0-345-36712-X BALLANTINE PB $5.99

Stanley **Weinberger**

Healing Within: The Complete Guide to Colon Health

Discusses the holistic process for cleansing, eliminating parasites and candida

0-9616184-2-6 C.H.C. PUB PB $12.95

Eating Disorders: Anorexia and Bulimia

Hilda **Bruch**

Conversations with Anorexics

Written by a psychiatry professor, a leading authority on the emotional aspects of anorexia

1-56821-261-5 ARONSON PB $30.00

Eating Disorders: Obesity, Anorexia Nervosa, and the Person Within

0-465-01782-7 BASIC BOOKS PB $20.00

Joan Jacobs **Brumberg**

Fasting Girls: The Emergence of Anorexia Nervosa as a Modern Disease

An excellent history, by a Cornell professor

0-674-29501-3 HARVARD $35.50

0-452-26327-1 PLUME PB $14.95

Kim **Chernin**

The Obsession: Reflections on the Tyranny of Slenderness

"Eloquently written, passionate in its rhetoric and consistently absorbing"—*NY Times*

0-06-090967-6 HARPERPERENNIAL PB $12.00

Lindsey **Hull** & Leigh **Cohn**

Bulimia: A Guide to Recovery

Understanding and overcoming the binge/purge syndrome

0-936077-17-4 GURZE PB $12.95

Ira **Sacker** & Marc **Zimmer**

Dying to Be Thin

0-446-38417-8 WARNER PB $14.99

Michele **Siegel**

Surviving an Eating Disorder: Strategies for Family and Friends

"A lucid and comprehensive book that I am certain will be helpful to those whose lives have been affected"—Craig Johnson

0-06-091553-6 HARPERCOLLINS PB $12.50

Brett **Silverstein** & Deborah **Perlick**

The Cost of Competence: Gender Ambivalence, Eating Disorders and Depression in Women

Two psychologists study the connection among talent, depression, and eating disorders in women. Their conclusion: cultural prejudices and our ways of raising children lead women to equate thinness with success and femininity with failure

See also **THE FEMALE EXPERIENCE** under **WOMEN'S STUDIES** in **SOCIAL STUDIES**

0-19-506986-2 OXFORD $25.00

William **White** & Marlene **Boskind**

Bulimarexia: The Binge/Purge Cycle

Explains the dynamics of the disorder and includes how to recognize symptoms, pros and cons of drug therapy, and nutritional advice

0-393-30117-6 NORTON PB $12.95

Epilepsy

Anthony **Hopkins**

Epilepsy: The Facts

0-19-262548-9 OXFORD PB $16.95

Adrienne **Richard** & Joel **Reiter**

Epilepsy: A New Approach

A unique self-help program for sufferers. "I am firmly convinced that if everyone who suffers from epilepsy reads and follows this book we could restore healthy life to hundreds of thousands of people"
—Robert Ornstein, *The Healing Brain*

0-8027-7465-2 WALKER PB $11.95

Eye Care

William **Bates**

The Bates Method for Better Eyesight Without Glasses

Daily eye exercises as an alternative to eyeglasses

0-8050-0241-3 HOLT PB $8.95

Earlyne **Chaney**

The EYES Have It: A Self-help Manual for Better Vision

Incorporates Bates's system, yoga, acupressure, homeopathy, and light techniques

0-87728-621-3 WEISER PB $9.95

James **Collins**

Your Eyes: An Owner's Manual

Information on contact lenses, surgery, and 100 common eye disorders and their treatments

0-13-182379-5 PRENTICE HALL PB $10.95

Robert-Michael **Kaplan**

The Power Behind Your Eyes: Improving Your Eyesight with Integrated Vision Therapy

"…an important book that can help you create a new vision for your life"—Deepak Chopra

0-89281-536-1 INNER TRADITIONS PB $16.95

Seeing Without Glasses: Improving Your Vision Naturally

Exciting alternative treatments

1-88522-302-1 BEYOND WORDS $19.95

0-941831-97-3 BEYOND WORDS PB $12.95

Jacob **Liberman**

Take Off Your Glasses and See: A Mind/Body Approach to Expanding Your Eyesight and Your Insight

Promotes the connection of inner and outer vision

0-517-88604-9 CROWN PB $14.00

Walter **Zinn**

Complete Guide to Eyecare, Eyeglasses & Contact Lenses

From prevention of childhood eye injury to aging vision by eyecare specialists

0-8119-0786-4 LIFETIME PB $14.95

Feet and Knees

Devaki **Berkson**

The Foot Book: Healing the Body Through Foot Reflexology

A holistic guide to foot care using a number of alternative therapies

0-06-092296-6 HARPERPERENNIAL PB $11.50

Glenn **Copeland** & Stan **Solomon**
The Foot Book: Relief for Overused, Abused, & Ailing Feet
Sports podiatrist discusses specific concerns, footwear, and solutions to common foot problems
0-471-55840-0 WILEY PB $12.95

James **Fox** & Rick **McGuire**
Save Your Knees
0-440-50011-7 DELL PB $11.95

Howard **Kiernan**
The Knee Book: Everything You Need to Know About Knee Disorders, Treatment Options, and Maintenance Programs
Illustrated guide to the joint most affected by America's craze for high-impact exercise
0-517-59889-2 CROWN $16.00

Gary **Null** & Howard **Robbins**
How to Keep Your Feet and Legs Healthy for a Lifetime
A special section for walkers, runners, and joggers
1-88836-330-4 SEVEN STORIES PB $14.95

Headaches and Migraines

Seymour **Diamond** & others
The Hormone Headache: New Ways to Prevent, Manage, and Treat Migraines and Other Headaches
Guide to controling hormone-linked headache pain
0-02-008315-7 MACMILLAN PB $11.95

Charles B. **Inlander** & Porter **Schimer**
Headaches: 47 Ways to Stop the Pain
A People's Medical Society Book lists prescriptions and medications as well as alternative relief
0-8027-1314-9 WALKER $16.95
0-8027-7473-3 WALKER PB $8.95

Lawrence **Robbins** & Susan S. **Lang**
Headache Help: A Complete Guide to Understanding Headaches and the Medicines that Relieve Them
Emphasis on self-help, with special chapters on headaches suffered by women and children
0-395-70751-X DORLING KINDERSLEY PB $10.95

Oliver **Sacks**
Migraine
"His commentary is so erudite, so gracefully written, that even those people fortunate enough never to have had a migraine in their lives should find it compelling"—*NY Times*
See also **THE NEUROSCIENCES AND THE BRAIN** under **BIOLOGY** under **LIFE SCIENCES** in **SCIENCE**
0-520-08101-3 CALIFORNIA $35.00
0-520-08223-0 CALIFORNIA PB $15.95

Oliver Sacks

Joel **Saper** & Kenneth **Magge**
Freedom from Headaches
0-671-25404-9 SIMON & SCHUSTER PB $11.00

Heart Disease

American Heart Association
Your Heart: An Owner's Manual
Illustrated guidelines for diet, exercise, lifestyle; includes self-tests, charts, diagrams
0-13-359324-X PRENTICE HALL $27.95

Doc Lew **Childre**, composer
Heart Zones
The first album of self-help music ever to make *Billboard's* charts and designed to reduce stress, fatigue, and anxiety. A compilation of specific chords and rhythms chosen and arranged for their effects on the brain. According to its creator, "The music is to create an energetic ebullience and clarity. Like a psychological cup of coffee without the side effects"
6-30331434-1 REAL MUSIC CD $16.98
6-30331448-1 REAL MUSIC CST $10.98

Self-Empowerment: The Heart Approach to Stress Management
The man behind the "Heart Zones" music offers new techniques for effectively dealing with everyday stress
1-87905-234-2 PLANETARY PUBLICATIONS PB $13.95

Norman **Cousins**
The Healing Heart: Antidotes to Panic and Helplessness
The importance of a patient's role in recovering from a massive heart attack
0-393-01816-4 NORTON $13.95

Vincent **Friedewald**
Ask Your Doctor: Hypertension
Compact and basic source for information as well as worksheets on home monitoring
0-8362-7022-3 ANDREWS & MCMEEL PB $8.95

Jack **Gillis**
The Heart Attack Prevention & Recovery Handbook
How to assess your chances for a heart attack or prevent another
0-88179-118-0 HARTLEY & MARKS PB $10.95

Robert E. **Kowalski**
8 Steps to a Healthy Heart
Emphasizes the mental aspects of cardiovascular well-being
0-446-39458-0 WARNER PB $13.99

Siegfried J. **Kra**
What Every Woman Must Know About Heart Disease: A No-Nonsense Approach to Diagnosing, Treating, and Preventing the #1 Killer of Women
"...warning call about women's vulnerabilty and an introduction to the subject"
—*Publishers Weekly*
0-446-51986-3 MYSTERIOUS $22.95
0-446-39532-3 WARNER PB $14.99

John A. **McDougall** & Mary **McDougall**
The McDougall Program for a Healthy Heart: A Life-Saving Approach to Preventing and Treating Heart Disease
With meal plans and recipes, this program will appeal to those who are motivated and who are experiencing heart problems
0-525-93868-0 DUTTON $24.95

Marvin **Moser** & Brenda **Becker**
Week by Week to a Strong Heart: A Realistic Action Plan to Help Save Your Life
Easy-to-follow program designed to ease heart attack sufferers into a healthy lifestyle
0-380-72089-2 AVON PB $5.50

Ralph **Myerson**
How Your Heart Works
A part of the How It Works series. Full-color illustrations illuminate the cause of heart problems and disease
1-56276-238-9 ZIFF DAVIS PB $19.95

Fredric J. **Pashkow** & Charlotte **Libov**
50 Essential Things to Do When the Doctor Says It's Heart Disease
Emphasizes women and heart disease while employing a cheery tone
0-452-27101-0 PENGUIN PB $10.95

Glenn **Rothfeld** & Suzanne **LeVert**
Natural Medicine for Heart Disease: The Best Alternative Methods for Prevention and Treatment
Practical instruction from a medical doctor
0-87596-289-0 RODALE PB $11.95

Marc A. **Silver**

Success with Heart Failure: Help and Hope for Those with Congestive Heart Failure

"...an excellent resource for patients and doctors dealing with heart failure...presented in a sensitive manner"—Bernie Siegel

0-306-44767-3 INSIGHT $23.95

Harvey **Simon**

Conquering Heart Disease: New Ways to Live Well Without Drugs or Surgery

A drug-free and nonsurgical cardiovascular health plan

0-316-79172-5 LITTLE, BROWN PB $13.95

Texas Heart Institute

Heart Owner's Handbook

Answers every question anybody could possibly have about the heart

0-471-05982-X WILEY $29.95
0-471-04420-2 WILEY PB $16.95

Art **Ulene**

Count Out Cholesterol: Level 30 Percent in Only 30 Days

0-915233-97-5 ULYSSES PB $14.95

Julian **Whitaker**

Reversing Heart Disease

The prevention and treatment of cardiac problems without surgery

0-446-38548-4 WARNER PB $13.99

Lupus

Henrietta **Aladjem**

Understanding Lupus: What It Is, How to Treat It, How to Cope With It

0-684-18349-8 MACMILLAN PB $11.95

Sheldon Paul **Blau** & Dodi **Schultz**

Living with Lupus: All the Knowledge You Need to Help Yourself

Latest research covered that includes treatments in addition to standard drug approaches, special section on lupus and kids and teens; resource list

0-201-60809-X ADDISON-WESLEY PB $11.00

Laura **Chester**

Lupus Novice: Toward Self-Healing

A poet stricken with lupus writes of her journey to healing

0-88268-037-4 STATION HILL $16.95

Joanna Baumer **Permut**

Embracing the Wolf: A Lupus Victim and Her Family

An honest and personal view from one who is chronically ill

0-87797-166-8 LARLIN $14.95

Daniel J. **Wallace**

The Lupus Book

An LA-based specialist "blends clinical information with practical advice"—*Publishers Weekly*

0-19-508443-8 OXFORD $25.00

Robert **Yocum**

My Adventures with Lupus: Living with a Chronic Illness

Inspiring words from a sufferer and a survivor

1-88218-045-3 GRIFFIN PB $12.95

Lyme Disease

Denise **Lang** & Derrick **DeSilva**

Coping with Lyme Disease: A Practical Guide to Dealing with Diagnosis and Treatment

Recognizing, treatment, getting support, and a chapter on children and pregnant women

0-8050-2650-9 HOLT PB $12.95

Multiple Sclerosis

Judy **Graham**

Multiple Sclerosis: A Self-Help Guide to Its Management

Rewritten and updated to include current data on diet supplements, yoga, exercise, and hyperbaric oxygen treatment by an MS patient

0-89281-242-7 INNER TRADITIONS PB $12.95

Louis **Rosner**

Multiple Sclerosis: New Hope and Practical Advice for People with MS and Their Families

"The best patient-oriented book on multiple sclerosis"—*The New England Journal of Medicine*

0-671-77809-9 FIRESIDE PB $11.00

Pain

Gayle **Backstrom** & Bernard R. **Rubin**

When Muscle Pain Just Won't Go Away: The Relief Handbook for Fibromyalgia and Chronic Muscle Pain

Identifying symptoms, latest research, treatment, coping, and numerous resource lists

0-87833-891-8 TAYLOR PB $12.95

Ben **Benjamin** & Gail **Border**

Listen to Your Pain: The Active Person's Guide to Understanding, Identifying, and Treating Pain and Injury

Organized by symptoms

0-14-006687-X VIKING PB $17.95

Barry **Bittman**

Reprogramming Pain: Transform Pain and Suffering into Health and Success

Encourages chronic pain sufferers to decide to live without pain as the first step, as well as 10 steps to help achieve that goal

1-56750-208-3 ABLEX PB $18.95

The Natural Medicine Collective with Therese Digeronimo

The Natural Way of Healing Chronic Pain

Drug-free therapies and prevention of migraine to arthritis

0-440-21658-3 DELL PB $4.99

Prevention Magazine

The Prevention Pain-Relief System: A Total Program for Relieving Any Pain in Your Body

Healing every pain from ankle sprains to toothaches using medical science and alternative medicine. A well-organized resource with charts, diagrams, and comprehensive index

0-553-56491-9 BDD PB $6.99

Richard A. **Sternbach**

Mastering Pain: A Twelve-Step Program for Coping with Chronic Pain

From the premise of mind over matter, these 12 steps aid in the control of pain. "Advice that might be more important than your medicine cabinet when it comes to living with pain" —*USA Weekend*

0-345-35428-1 BALLANTINE PB $5.99

Parkinson's Disease

Glenna Wotton **Atwood**

Living Well With Parkinson's: An Inspirational, Informative Guide for Parkinsonians and Their Loved Ones

One woman's story of coping with the disease as well as useful resource lists

0-471-52539-1 WILEY PB $14.95

Sandi **Gordon**

Parkinson's: A Personal Story of Acceptance

Stricken in her youth, a mother of four writes about her struggle with this debilitating disease

0-8283-1949-9 BRANDEN PB $12.95

J. Thomas **Hutton** & Raye Lynee **Dippel**

Caring for the Parkinson Patient: A Practical Guide

From the publisher's Golden Age series, a collection of 14 essays by nurses, neurologists, psychologists and other specialists who shed light on this mysterious disease

0-87975-562-8 PROMETHEUS PB $16.95

Abraham **Lieberman** & Frank **Williams**

Parkinson's Disease: The Complete Guide for Patients and Caregivers

From the chairman and executive director of the American Parkinson's Disease Association and other health care professionals features a guide to symptoms and side effects and a state-by-state resource list

0-671-76819-0 FIRESIDE PB $11.00

Dwight **McGoon**

The Parkinson's Handbook

A practical guide from a Mayo Clinic surgeon with Parkinson's

0-393-31143-0 NORTON PB $10.95

J.M.S. **Pearce**

Parkinson's Disease and Its Management

Concise review of current knowledge for those advanced in this subject

0-19-262177-7 OXFORD $37.50

Skin Care and Disorders

Joseph P. **Bark**

Your Skin: An Owner's Guide

A general guide to a wide range of skin problems

0-13-199663-0 PRENTICE HALL PB $10.95

Barney **Kenet** & Patricia **Lawler**

Saving Your Skin: Prevention, Early Detection, and Treatment of Melanoma and Other Skin Cancers

An illustrated guide to the deadliest skin cancer

1-56858-009-6 FOUR WALLS PB $14.95

Marc **Lappe**

The Body's Edge: Our Cultural Obsession with Skin

See also **BIOLOGY AND HUMAN BEHAVIOR** under **BIOLOGY** under **LIFE SCIENCES** in **SCIENCE**

0-8050-4208-3 HOLT $22.50

Norman **Levine**

Skin Healthy: Everyone's Guide to Great Skin

A comprehensive guide for women and men of all ages

0-87833-900-0 TAYLOR PB $12.95

Mervyn **Mitton**

Herbal Remedies: Skin Problems

Safe home treatments for a variety of problems

0-572-01710-3 FOULSHAM PB $9.95

Sleep Disorders

Consumer Reports

Sleep: Problems and Solutions

0-89043-055-1 CONSUMER REPORTS $15.95

Alexander **Borbely**

Secrets of Sleep

The latest word on sleep, dreams, and sleep disorders by one of the world's leading sleep researchers

0-465-07593-2 BASIC BOOKS PB $16.00

Deepak **Chopra**

Restful Sleep: The Complete Mind-Body Program for Overcoming Insomnia

How to fall asleep easily, feel rested, eliminate insomnia, and achieve a healthy balance between rest and activity

0-517-59923-6 HARMONY $15.00

0-517-88457-7 CROWN PB $11.00

William **Dement**

Some Must Watch While Some Must Sleep: Exploring the World of Sleep

What sleep research has taught us about our sleeping habits

0-393-09001-9 NORTON PB $5.95

Roger **Fritz**

Sleep Disorders: America's Hidden Nightmare

How our country's sleep deprivation is a detriment to health and safety

FOREWORD BY WILLIAM DEMENT

0-9635137-0-2 NATIONAL SLEEP ALERT PB $12.95

Sandy **Jones**

Crying Baby, Sleepless Nights: Why Your Baby Is Crying and What You Can Do About It

This comprehensive, sympathetic guide answers questions about what your baby's crying means and reveals how to recognize infant allergies and colic and how overwrought parents can get some rest!

1-55832-045-8 HARVARD COMMON PB $9.95

Charles **McPhee**

Stop Sleeping Through Your Dreams: A Guide to Awakening Consciousness During Dream Sleep

How lucid dreaming may improve mental health

0-8050-2500-6 HOLT $22.50

Ray **Sahelian**

Melatonin: Nature's Sleeping Pill

A family physician's experiences prescribing the hormone for his patients' sleep disorders and other ailments

0-9639755-7-9 BE HAPPIER PRESS PB $13.95

Stress

Rosalind **Barnett**

Gender and Stress

An investigation of the cause of stress, and how men and women experience it differently

0-02-901380-1 FREE PRESS $50.00

Herbert **Benson** & William **Proctor**

Beyond the Relaxation Response

Meditation as a means of alleviating stress and easing physical ills

0-425-08183-4 BERKLEY PB $4.99

Herbert **Benson** & Eileen M. **Stuart**

The Wellness Book: The Comprehensive Guide to Treating Stress-Related Illness

Associate professor of medicine at Harvard details methods of stress management, nutrition, and exercise that can be used to combat high blood pressure, cardiovascular disease, the symptoms of cancer and AIDS, infertility, and chronic pain

1-55972-092-1 BIRCH LANE $24.95

0-671-79750-6 FIRESIDE PB $14.00

Joan **Borysenko**

Minding the Body, Mending the Mind

A Harvard Medical School instructor presents the scientific rationale behind her acclaimed stress-reduction program and shares the experiences of her patients

0-553-34556-7 BANTAM PB $13.95

Edward **Charlesworth** & Ronald **Nathan**

Stress Management: A Comprehensive Guide to Wellness

0-345-32734-9 BALLANTINE PB $5.99

Doc Lew **Childre**

Freeze-Frame: Fast Action Stress Relief

Identifies the impact of stress on our health, physical and emotional, and illustrates the key steps of transforming stress into positive action and peace of mind. "A powerful tool that can be used by anyone to manage internal stress and dramatically improve the body's physiology" —Joseph Z. Davids, MD, American College of Cardiology

1-87905-239-3 PLANETARY PUBLICATIONS PB .$9.95

Alix **Krista**

Book of Stress Survival: Identifying and Reducing the Stress in Your Life

A colorful illustrated guide

0-671-63026-1 FIRESIDE PB $14.00

Valerie **O'Hara**

Wellness at Work: Building Resilience to Job Stress

Create a personal "stress profile," learn to relax through breathing, improve communication skills, and other tips to cope in the workplace

1-57224-030-X NEW HARBINGER PB $14.95

Robert M. **Sapolsky**

Why Zebras Don't Get Ulcers: A Guide to Stress, Stress-Related Diseases and Coping

Clues to why people get sick when they worry and how to prevent it. "First-rate science for the nonscientist … certain to reduce stress…." —*Kirkus Reviews*

0-7167-2391-3 FREEMAN....$21.95
0-7167-2718-8 FREEMAN PB....$14.95

Hans **Selye**

The Stress of Life

A classic work by the founder of the International Institute of Stress; includes new research

0-07-056212-1 MCGRAW HILL PB....$9.95

Stress Without Distress

How to use stress as a positive force

0-538-21251-9 SOUTH-WESTERN PB....$22.95

Robert E. **Thayer**

The Origin of Everyday Moods: Managing Energy, Tension, and Stress

A pioneering researcher in biopsychology, Thayer here looks at the sources of tiredness and tension and our unexamined self-medication for dealing with them. What we eat—and drink—how we sleep and exercise, the rhythms of our day: all these things, Thayer shows, govern our moods, and yet the techniques to use them to enhance rather than depress are simple and easy to learn. This in-depth exploration brings readers to a new understanding of the biology of mood and offers powerful techniques to break self-destructive habits and enrich productivity and enjoyment

0-19-508791-7 OXFORD....$24.00

David **Zemach-Bersin** & others

Relaxercise: The Easy New Way to Health & Fitness

Feldenkrais teacher-trainers illustrate simple ways to relax and relieve stress

See also **AEROBICS AND GENERAL FITNESS** under **FITNESS**

0-06-250992-6 HARPERCOLLINS PB....$22.00

Stroke

William H. **Bergquist** & others

Stroke Survivors

Seventy intimate stories by those who survived as well as from family, caregivers, and professionals

1-55542-669-7 JOSSEY-BASS....$25.00

Jennifer **Hay**

Stroke: Questions You Have—Answers You Need

The number one cause of disability in the US is discussed along with prevention, rehabilitation, and resources

1-88260-622-1 PEOPLES MEDICAL SOCIETY PB$10.95

Marilyn **Larkin**

When Someone You Love Has a Stroke: What You Must Know, What You Can Do, What You Should Expect

Strategies for dealing with speech and language problems, mood swings, medication, nutrition, as well as advice on how caregivers can maintain their own emotional equilibrium

0-440-21666-4 DELL PB....$4.99

Behavioral Disorders

Lucinda **Bassett**

From Panic to Power

0-06-017320-3 HARPERCOLLINS....$23.00

R. Reid **Wilson**

Don't Panic: Taking Control of Anxiety Attacks

A highly successful and remarkably effective resource for readers suffering from panic attacks—one of the leading emotional disorders in America

0-06-095160-5 HARPERCOLLINS PB....$14.00

Harold **Levinson**

Total Concentration: How to Understand Attention Deficit Disorders

"This is the best book I have seen so far which describes Dyslexia, Learning Disabilities and Attention Deficit Disorders"—*ADD Resources*

See also **CHILDREN WITH LEARNING DISABILITIES** under **EDUCATION** under **PARENTING**

0-87131-708-7 EVANS PB....$11.95

Environmental Medicine

Herbert **Needleman** & Philip **Landrigan**

Raising Children Toxic Free: How to Keep Your Child Safe from Lead, Asbestos, Pesticides, and Other Environmental Hazards

Two leading experts on environmental disease offer a guide to the pollutants most necessary, and most difficult, to avoid

FOREWORD BY T. BERRY BRAZELTON

0-374-24643-2 FS&G....$20.00
0-374-52392-4 FS&G PB....$12.00

Doris J. **Rapp**

Is This Your Child's World?: How You Can Fix the Schools and Homes that Are Making Your Children Sick

0-553-10513-2 BDD....$24.95

Richard H. **Stapleton**

Lead Is a Silent Hazard

How to identify sources and avoid contamination

FOREWORD BY SENATOR BILL BRADLEY

0-8027-1303-3 WALKER....$22.95
0-8027-7449-0 WALKER PB....$11.95

Arthur C. **Upton** & Eden **Graber**, editors

The New York University Medical Center Family Guide to Environmental Health

From sick building syndrome to second-hand smoke, everyone faces a daily maze of environmental hazards. Find out what the dangers are and what you can do to minimize your risks by recognizing and understanding the symptoms and warning signs. Includes appendices listing environmental laws, addresses and phone numbers

0-671-76815-8 SIMON & SCHUSTER....$32.50

Women's Health

Mary **Ballweg** & Susan **Deutsch**

Overcoming Endometriosis: New Help from the Endometriosis Association

0-86553-190-0 CONGDON & WEED PB....$14.95

Gail **Burton**

Candida Control Cookbook: 1996 Revised Updated Information

How to control candida through food, now in its third edition

0-944031-67-6 ATRIUM PB....$13.95

Karen J. **Carlson** & others

The Harvard Guide to Women's Health

0-674-36768-5 HARVARD....$39.95
0-674-36769-3 HARVARD PB....$24.95

William **Crook**

The Yeast Connection and the Woman

New information, with emphasis on mind/body connection, lifestyle, and exercise

0-933478-22-4 PROFESSIONAL BOOKS PB....$17.95

Edward B. **Diethrich** & Carol **Cohan**

Women and Heart Disease: What You Can Do to Fight the Number One Killer of American Women

Women have been largely ignored in cardiac research and 250,000 women die needlessly every year. This important book presents specific preventive guidelines as well as a self-diagnostic test

0-345-38620-5 BALLANTINE PB....$10.00

Alice D. **Domar** & Henry **Dreher**

Healing Mind, Healthy Woman: Take Control of Your Well-Being Using the Mind-Body Control

From Harvard Medical School's Division of Behavioral Medicine, a repertoire of therapeutic methods for women. Includes programs addressing infertility, high-risk pregnancy, menopause, eating disorders, breast cancer, and more. With case histories showing the benefits of the mind-body connection for taking control of health and well-being

0-8050-4134-6 HOLT....$25.00

Paula **Doress-Worters** & Diana Laskin **Siegal**

The New Ourselves, Growing Older: Women Aging with Knowledge and Power

From the Boston Women's Health Book Collective, a comprehensive volume on health and medical issues for women over 40

0-671-87297-4 TOUCHSTONE PB $18.00

Sylvia **Gearing**

Female Executive Stress Syndrome: The Working Woman's Guide to a Balanced *and* Successful Life

The first national study of women in corporations shares top female execs' secrets for success

1-56530-144-7 SUMMIT $24.95

Larrian **Gillespie**

You Don't Have to Live with Cystitis: A Woman Urologist Tells How to Avoid It—And What to Do About It

Alternatives to the standard medical treatments for cystitis

0-380-70486-2 AVON PB $10.00

Ann Louise **Gittleman** & J. Lynne **Dodson**

Super Nutrition for Women: A Food-Wise Guide for Health, Beauty, Energy, and Immunity

A readable, common-sense, information-packed guide that debunks earlier health approaches created with men in mind. "A comprehensive up-to-date compendium of useful advice on the health requirements for women"—Gary Null

0-553-35328-4 BANTAM PB $13.95

Bernadine **Healy**

A New Prescription for Women's Health: Staying Strong and Healthy from Nine to Ninety-Nine

Former director of National Institutes of Health presents an information-packed and controversial wakeup call for women to take charge of their health and well-being, both personally and politically

0-670-85550-2 VIKING $24.95

Ada **Kahn** & Linda Hughey **Holt**

Midlife Health: A Woman's Guide to Feeling Good

0-380-70719-5 AVON PB $5.99

Susan M. **Lark**

Heavy Menstrual Flow & Anemia: Self-Help Book

Self-evaluation workbook and customized self-help programs for alleviating symptoms naturally as well as information on drug and medical therapies

0-89087-774-2 CELESTIAL ARTS PB $16.95

Nancy **Lonsdorff** & others

A Woman's Best Medicine: Health, Happiness, and Long Life Through Maharishi Ayur-Veda

The application of ancient wisdom to women's health concerns

0-87477-785-2 TARCHER PB $14.95

Joseph **Martorano** & others

Unmasking PMS: The Complete PMS Medical Treatment Plan

Thorough

0-87131-692-7 EVANS $21.95

0-425-14401-1 BERKLEY PB $5.99

Kerry **McGinn**

The Informed Woman's Guide to Breast Health: Breast Changes that Are Not Cancer

0-923521-24-0 BULL PB $12.95

Jane **Porcino**

Growing Older, Getting Better: A Handbook for Women in the Second Half of Life

0-8245-1312-6 CROSSROAD PB $16.95

Judith **Reichman**

I'm Too Young to Get Old: Health Care for Women After Forty

0-8129-2417-7 TIME BOOKS $25.00

Carolyn D. **Runowicz** & Donna **Haupt**

To Be Alive: A Woman's Guide to a Full Life After Cancer

"Stories about her patients enliven the text and reinforce her urgings that the cancer survivor take care of herself and get on with her life" —*Publishers Weekly*

0-8050-2958-3 HOLT $22.50

Nancy **Sander**

Women's Bodies, Women's Wisdom: Creating Physical & Emotional Health & Healing

Founder of the holistic health center Women to Women uses mind/body medicine to heal by recognizing the body's own logic and wisdom

0-553-08120-9 BDD $29.95

Tracy Chutorian **Semler**

The Women's Healthcare Companion

Drawing on personal stories and statistics, this volume deals with all the major themes affecting a woman's health

0-06-273248-X HARPERPERENNIAL PB $16.00

Diane **Stein**

The Natural Remedy Book for Women

Using all forms of natural healing, from acupressure to vitamins; resources and index

0-89594-525-8 CROSSING PB $16.95

Nancy **Snyderman** & Margaret **Blackstone**

Nancy Snyderman's Guide to Good Health: What Every Forty-Plus Woman Should Know about Her Changing Body

Good Morning America's medical correspondent proffers professional expertise and personal anecdotes on such subjects as heart disease, cancer, pregnancy, menopause, depression

0-688-12979-X MORROW $25.00

Miriam **Stoppard**

Every Woman's Medical Handbook

Easy-to-use directory of conditions, diseases, procedures, and symptoms

0-345-37356-1 BALLANTINE PB $15.00

Elizabeth **Vliet**

Screaming to Be Heard: Hormonal Connections Women Suspect...and Doctors Ignore

Many physical ailments are often dismissed as neurotic. Vliet outlines the symptoms that may be hormonal

0-87131-784-2 EVANS $24.95

Kate **Weinstein**

Living with Endometriosis: How to Cope with the Physical and Emotional Challenges

0-201-19810-X ADDISON-WESLEY PB $16.00

Stanley **West** & Paula **Dranov**

The Hysterectomy Hoax

Of the more than 600,000 hysterectomies that are performed in the US each year, only 10 percent are necessary. Dr. West explains why hysterectomies are so often the surgeon's *first* resort, and what women must know to ask in order to make the right choice. "A gynecologist's emphatic appeal to women to refuse to have hysterectomies unless their lives are at stake..." —*Kirkus Reviews*

0-385-46820-2 DOUBLEDAY PB $12.95

Lynda **Wharton**

Natural Women's Health: A Guide to Healthy Living for Women of Any Age

How a woman's body works through pregnancy and menopause explained by a naturopath and acupuncturist

1-57224-007-5 NEW HARBINGER PB $13.95

Josleen **Wilson**

Woman: Your Body, Your Health: The Essential Guide for Well-Being

Four-color illustrations of every aspect of women's physical development and change from puberty through old age

0-15-698150-5 HBJ PB $19.95

Georgia **Witkin**

The Female Stress Syndrome: How to Become Stress-Wise in the '90s

Why women experience stress differently from men and how they can learn to cope

1-55704-098-2 NEWMARKET PB $12.95

African-American Women's Health

Sylvia **Dunnavant**

Celebrating Life: African–American Women Speak Out About Breast Cancer

Inspirational words from an often-ignored group

0-9643211-4-9 U.S.F.I. PB $19.95

Linda **Villarosa**, editor

Body & Soul: The Black Women's Guide to Physical Health & Emotional Well-Being

A unique resource that emphasizes the mind/body connection for spiritual and physical well-being and addresses specific health issues of black American females. Illustrated with resource lists

FOREWORD BY ANGELA Y. DAVIS & JUNE JORDAN

0-06-095085-4 HARPERPERENNIAL PB $20.00

Evelyn C. **White**, editor

The Black Women's Health Book: Speaking for Ourselves

Forty-one writings that address the unique health issues, both physical and emotional, of black women in America. Contributions range from the highly personal experience to the specifically medical; informative on menopause, breast feeding, fibroids, HIV, and skin-color issues. "Lord I love this book. Ms. White and all the contributors were speaking for and to me. I might not live any longer after reading this, but I will live better"—Maya Angelou

1-87806-740-0 SEAL PB $16.95

Breast Cancer

Robert **Kradjian**

Save Yourself from Breast Cancer

Breast surgeon stresses abandoning high-fat diets to avoid cancer

0-425-14390-2 BERKELEY PB $12.00

Joyce **Wadler**

My Breast: One Woman's Cancer Story

Based on widely acclaimed *New York Magazine* pieces, Wadler describes her horrified suspicion of breast cancer: its confirmation, her agonized decision about treatment, and her final recovery. This book contains insights of tremendous value to all women and is also a highly readable, vivid, and inspiring true story

0-671-87970-7 POCKET PB $5.50

Susan M. **Love** & Karen **Lindsey**

Dr. Susan Love's Breast Book

Fully revised and updated, this is a "highly readable book that educates, supports and encourages women to become their own advocates of breast health"—*Publishers Weekly*

0-201-40835-X ADDISON-WESLEY PB $17.00

Rosalind **MacPhee**

Picasso's Woman: A Breast Cancer Story

Poet MacPhee chronicles an extraordinary tale of friendship, love, motherhood, and facing death following a breast cancer diagnosis

AFTERWORD BY KATHY LATOUR

1-56836-138-6 KODANSHA $20.00

Lucille M. **Pederson** & Janet M. **Trigg**

Breast Cancer: A Family Survival Guide

A study of nine women and their families from detection through treatment and how they coped; reading lists and appendices

0-89789-438-3 BERGIN & GARVEY PB $19.95

Carol Ann **Rinzler**

Estrogen and Breast Cancer: A Warning to Women

The author shows a direct link between the rise in cancer and the use of estrogen in ERT and birth-control pills

0-02-603491-3 MACMILLAN $22.00

Betty **Rollin**

First You Cry

Inspiring personal account of breast cancer and its consequences

0-06-104235-8 HARPERCOLLINS PB $5.50

Charles **Simone**

Breast Health: What You Need to Know

In its 400 pages covers all the bases and even includes a chapter on male breast cancer

0-89529-660-8 AVERY PB $15.95

Diana **Stumm**

Recovering from Breast Surgery: Excercises to Strengthen Your Body and Relieve Pain

Physical therapist discusses the often-overlooked emotional and physical problems following surgery; includes exercises, stretches, and massage

0-89793-180-7 HUNTER PB $11.95

Menopause

Sandra **Cabot**

Smart Medicine for Menopause: Hormone Replacement Therapy and Its Natural Alternatives

Australian MD clearly makes a case for naturally occurring hormones and discusses male menopause

0-89529-628-4 AVERY PB $9.95

Winnifred B. **Cutler** & Celso-Ramon **Garcia**

Menopause: A Guide for Women and the Men Who Love Them

"In language accessible to lay people, the authors present the physiological facts about the menopausal process and discuss symptoms from hot flashes to insomnia to more serious possible side effects such as osteoporosis and cancer" —*Publishers Weekly*

0-393-30995-9 NORTON PB $13.95

Germaine **Greer**

The Change: Women, Aging and the Menopause

Greer takes on the ambiguities and half-truths surrounding menopause and aging, challenging women to question the status quo "truths," and proposing a new "art of aging" based on acknowledgment of women's new needs and desires. Greer's *The Female Eunuch* changed how we think about women and sex; her new book will prove every bit as important

0-449-90853-4 FAWCETT PB $12.50

Dee **Ito**

Without Estrogen: Natural Remedies for Menopause and Beyond

Ito explores safe, natural options for the millions of women who prefer not to take estrogen, with its side effects and health risks, for menopause. An alternative, in-depth blueprint for greater health and energy in the post-reproductive years

0-517-58825-0 RANDOM HOUSE $20.00

0-517-88406-2 CROWN PB $12.00

Susan M. **Lark**

The Estrogen Decision: Self-Help Book—Revised & Updated

In-depth discussion of menopause with particular focus on the pros and cons of estrogen and progesterone replacement therapy

0-89087-776-9 CELESTIAL ARTS PB $17.95

Mary Jane **Minkin** & Carol V. **Wright**

What Every Woman Needs to Know About Menopause

The authoritative guide to physical and emotional well-being during the premenopausal, menopausal, and postmenopausal years, based on a leading gynecologist's 20 years of experience. "This book is essential for every woman and her physician to read. Delving into every aspect of menopause, it is intelligent and candid and also warm and compassionate" —Karen L. Giblen

FOREWORD BY FREDERICK NAFTOLIN

0-300-06573-6 YALE $25.00

Isaac **Schiff** & Ann **Parson**

The Massachusetts General Hospital Guide to Menopause

What steps should be taken to reduce the symptoms of menopause? How can the postmenopausal years be made healthier? When is hormone replacement therapy right, and what alternatives are available? This comprehensive, up-to-date compendium of information is designed to help understand, cope, and, if necessary, choose treatment throughout menopause

0-8129-2318-9 KIPLINGER PB $15.00

Susan **Perry** & Katherine A. **O'Hanlan**

Natural Menopause: The Complete Guide

"*Natural Menopause* offers the most authoritative and wide-ranging explanation of the basics of menopause yet published"
—*San Francisco Chronicle*

0-201-47987-7 ADDISON-WESLEY PB $14.00

Rosetta **Reitz**

Menopause: A Positive Approach

A classic, written to alleviate fears and smash stereotypes about this misunderstood phase of maturation

0-14-005120-1 VIKING PB $11.95

Edna Copeland **Ryneveld**

Secrets of a Natural Menopause: A Positive Drug-Free Approach

A resource combining diet, vitamins, minerals, homeopathy, yoga, and meditation for alleviating or preventing menopausal symptoms

1-56718-596-7 LLEWELLYN PB $12.95

Judith **Sachs**

What Women Should Know About Menopause

Basic facts, with glossary and resource list

0-440-20643-X DELL PB $4.99

Gail **Sheehy**

The Silent Passage

Like Germaine Greer, Sheehy describes menopause as the "gateway to a second adulthood." A highly welcome book with case histories and concrete medical and psychological advice to women

0-679-41388-X RANDOM HOUSE $16.00
0-671-79931-2 POCKET PB $6.50

Gail Sheehy
(photo credit: ©Sara Barrett)

Lynne **Taetzsch**, editor

Hot Flashes: Women Writers on the Change of Life

Twenty personal essays and five poems illuminate the experience of menopause in this insightful book. Germaine Greer, Marge Piercy, Gloria Steinem, Ellen Gilchrist provide insight into the physical, emotional, and societal aspects of the change of life

0-571-19871-6 FABER $22.95

Nancy Lee **Teaff** & Kim Wright **Wiley**

Perimenopause: Preparing for the Change

Not an event but a process, menopause symptoms can start a good 15 years before onset. How to make the transition gentle and worry-free

1-55958-579-X PRIMA $22.95

Susan **Weed**

Menopausal Years—The Wise Woman Way

Herbal remedies for relieving symptoms

0-9614620-4-3 ASH TREE PB $9.95

Men's Health

American Diabetes Association

The American Dietetic Association Family Cookbook: The American Tradition

0-671-76695-3 SIMON & SCHUSTER $23.00

Robert **Arnot**

Dr. Bob Arnot's Guide to Turning Back the Clock

Staying fit in middle age. "[Arnot] has found a way to make health and fitness good fun as well as good for you"—Dean Ornish

0-316-05189-6 LITTLE, BROWN $22.95

Sarah **Brewer**

The Complete Book of Men's Health

Illustrated guide to the male body from backache to prostate cancer

0-7225-3219-9 HARPERCOLLINS PB $16.00

Dudley Seth **Danoff**

Superpotency: How to Get It, Use It, and Maintain It for a Lifetime

A Beverly Hills urologist discusses impotency and how to overcome it as well as specific techniques for prolonging sexual performance

0-446-39512-9 WARNER PB $10.99

Doug **Dollemore** & Mark **Guiliucci**

Age Erasers for Men: Hundreds of Fast and Easy Ways to Beat the Years

How to stay young from middle age on

0-[illegible]96-213-0 ST. MARTIN'S $27.95

James H. **Gilbaugh**, Jr.

Men's Private Parts: An Owner's Manual

Told in a straightforward, no-nonsense style, this invaluable guide offers information on AIDS, no-scalpel vasectomy, diagnosis and treatment of prostate cancer, urinary problems, penile injuries, hormones, sperm production, and more. "This book could save your life"—Harvey Mackay, author of *Swim with the Sharks*

0-517-88064-4 CROWN PB $12.00

Ann Louise **Gittleman**

Super Nutrition for Men: Why Male Nutrition is Often Mal-Nutrition

Addresses the stresses unique to men in today's world

0-87131-793-1 EVANS $19.95

Nancy **Mayer**

The Male Mid-Life Crisis: Fresh Starts After 40

Insightful case histories of every possible scenario American men at 40 and older face and how to rise to the challenges of responsible maturation

0-451-16634-5 SIGNET PB $5.95

Men's Health Magazine

How a Man Stays Young

Addresses all issues for those approaching middle age

0-87596-156-8 RODALE PB $14.95

Michael **Murray**

Male Sexual Vitality: How You Can Benefit from Diet, Vitamins, Minerals, Herbs, Exercise and Other Natural Methods

Impotence, infertility, prostate and urinary tract health are primarily dealt with; both medical and natural treatments discussed

1-55958-428-9 PRIMA PB $8.95

Kenneth **Purvis**

The Male Sexual Machine: An Owner's Manual

Straightforward, thorough, and accurate information on male sexual anatomy, functions, and health. Purvis provides enlightenment on the subject of andrology—gynecology's male-oriented counterpart—that is sure to be helpful to men, and to women, everywhere

0-312-07031-4 ST. MARTIN'S $18.95

George **Ryan**

Reclaiming Male Sexuality: A Guide to Potency, Vitality, and Prowess

For a flagging libido

0-87131-809-1 EVANS PB $14.95

Neil **Wertheimer**, editor

Total Health for Men: How to Prevent and Treat the Health Problems that Trouble Men the Most

From the managing editor of Men's Health Books. "Wertheimer delivers a well-researched, accessibly written reference...."
—*Publishers Weekly*

0-87596-309-9 RODALE $31.95

Georgia **Witkin**

The Male Stress Syndrome: How to Survive Stress in the '90s

A do-it-yourself guide from a stress expert

1-55704-205-5 NEWMARKET PB $12.95

Prostate Cancer

Martin **Gelbard** & William **Bentley**

Prostate Problems: Every Man's Concern

A general discussion of prostate health

0-671-88465-4 FIRESIDE PB $12.00

Don **Kaltenbach** & Tim **Richards**

Prostate Cancer: A Survivor's Guide

American Cancer Society Award winner written by a former patient with expert medical advice from leading professionals

0-9640088-1-5 PROSTATE CANCER GUIDE PB .$16.95

Michael **Korda**

Man-to-Man: Surviving Prostate Cancer

The celebrated author and editor-in-chief of Simon & Schuster offers a harrowing, intensely intimate, and ultimately hopeful account of his experience with prostate cancer. Frank, informative, and moving, Korda tells his story with unparalleled honesty and intensity

0-679-44844-6 RANDOM HOUSE......................$20.00

Sheldon **Marks**

Prostate & Cancer: A Family Guide to Diagnosis, Treatment, and Survival

Urologist outlines detection, treatment, and prevention

1-55561-078-1 FISHER PB $14.95

William **Martin**

My Prostate and Me: Dealing with Prostate Cancer

"...emotional, humorous, factual, and straight to the point. It should be required reading for all men over 40 and for the people who love them"—Bob Dole

1-56977-888-4 NATIONAL BOOK NETWORK....$17.95

W. Scott **McDougal** with P.J. **Skerrett**

Prostate Disease: The Massachusetts General Hospital Guide

Norman Schwarzkopf, Jerry Lewis, Timothy Leary, and Bob Dole have in common a diagnosis of the most common cancer and the leading cancer killer of men: prostate cancer. This guide from the Massachusetts General Hospital answers all the questions about this curable disease: diagnosis, treatment options, surgery, radiation therapy, hormone therapy, and, most important, coping

0-8129-2319-7 TIME BOOKS PB $14.00

Stephen **Rous**

The Prostate Book: Sound Advice on Symptoms and Treatment

An expert discusses in nontechnical language the causes, symptoms, and surgical and nonsurgical treatment of the most common prostate problems

0-393-02592-6 NORTON $22.95

Anthony **Sattilaro** & Tom **Monte**

Recalled by Life: The Story of My Recovery from Cancer

The story of a physician who successfully overcame cancer of the prostate with a macrobiotic diet

0-380-65573-X AVON PB....................................$5.99

Aging

Mark H. **Beers** & Stephen **Urice**

Aging in Good Health: A Complete Essential Medical Guide for Older Men and Women and Their Families

Covers the basics of aging, common problems, and the warning signs of diseases

0-671-72822-9 POCKET PB $10.00

Wayne **Booth**, editor

The Art of Growing Older: Writers on Living and Aging

02260654909 CHICAGO PB.............................$14.95

Deepak **Chopra**

Ageless Body, Timeless Mind: The Quantum Alternative to Growing Old

Combining ancient wisdom with the latest scientific data, he shows how many of the effects of the aging process are avoidable and suggests ways to prevent physical vitality, creativity, memory, and self-esteem from waning with the passing years

0-517-59257-6 HARMONY...............................$23.00

0-517-59818-3 RANDOM HOUSE PB $12.50

Thomas R. **Cole** & Mary G. **Winkler**

The Oxford Book of Aging: Reflections on the Journey of Life

Two hundred and fifty pieces discuss the later stages of life. Illuminating and profound, from Schopenhauer's observation that "disillusion is the chief characteristic of old age" to Florida Scott-Maxwell's comment that age "is an intense and varied experience, almost beyond our capacity at times, but something to be carried high"

0-19-507369-X OXFORD $25.00

Betty **Friedan**

The Fountain of Age

"A book that explodes the myths of aging—just as, 30 years ago, Friedan exploded the myth of the contented housewife"—*Kirkus Review*

See also AGING under THE FEMALE EXPERIENCE under WOMEN'S STUDIES in SOCIAL STUDIES

0-671-40027-4 SIMON & SCHUSTER $25.00

0-671-89853-1 TOUCHSTONE PB $15.00

Sharon R. **Kaufman**

The Ageless Self: Sources of Meaning in Late Life

A study of 60 elderly women and men proving that spirit often compensates for a weak body. "A book that no novelist or indeed any caring person with a fondness for human interiors could resist"—Paul West

0-299-10864-3 WISCONSIN PB $11.95

Florence **Lieberman** & Morris **Collen**, editors

Aging in Good Health: A Quality Lifestyle for the Later Years

An anthology of essays from geriatric healthcare professionals concerning all aspects of aging

0-306-44502-6 INSIGHT $26.95

Vernon **Mark** & Jeffrey **Mark**

Brain Power: A Neurosurgeon's Complete Program to Maintain and Enhance Brain Fitness Throughout Your Life

The prevention of brain power loss as well as diet, nutrition, and exercise programs for boosting gray matter

0-395-55001-7 HOUGHTON MIFFLIN PB..........$12.95

Sandra Halderman **Martz**, editor

Grow Old Along with Me: The Best Is Yet to Be

From the author of *When I Am an Old Woman I Shall Wear Purple*, this is a beautiful collection of short fiction, poems, and photographs by women and men over 50

0-918949-86-6 PAPIER-MACHE PB...................$12.00

Howell **Raines**

Fly Fishing Through the Midlife Crisis

From a Pulitzer Prize-winning journalist and *New York Times* editorial page director, thoughtful musing on lost youth and new found pleasures

0-688-10346-4 MORROW................................$22.00

Reader's Digest

Live Longer, Live Better: Adding Years to Your Life and Life to Your Years

Advice for preventing disease and fulfulling lifelong dreams

0-89577-578-6 READER'S DIGEST....................$35.00

Magda **Rosenberg**

Sixty-Plus and Fit Again: Exercises for Older Men and Women

Not only for older people, but for those who care for the elderly

0-87131-224-7 EVANS.....................................$12.95

Fritz E. **Schmere** & Sally Patterson **Tubach**

The Challenge of Age: A Guide to Growing Older in Health and Happiness

Sprinkled with wise quotes, this readable survey of the issues of aging combines medical advice with practical information; resource lists also included

0-8245-1296-0 CROSSROAD PB........................$14.95

Gail **Sheehy**

New Passages: Mapping Your Life Across Time

This sequel to *The Silent Passage* traces the radical changes that we undergo in our 20s, 30s, and 40s and maps out the second adulthood of middle life

0-394-58913-0 RANDOM HOUSE........................$25.00

Roy **Walford** & Lisa **Walford**

The Anti-Aging Plan: Strategies and Recipes for Extending Your Healthy Years

By the physician for Biosphere 2, a book culled from the experience of that experiment's diet, which, in six months, decreased the average weight in men by 26 pounds and in women by 19, cholesterol levels by 68 points, and blood pressure from 110/75 to 90/58—dramatic changes that no other sustainable diet has ever been shown to produce. Includes hundreds of recipes while teaching the principles of nutrient-rich caloric limitation

1-56858-049-5 FOUR WALLS PB $12.95

Mark E. **Williams**

The American Geriatric Society's Complete Guide to Aging & Health

Comprehensive resource for those who wish for a healthy old age; also for caregivers of the elderly

0-517-59539-7 HARMONY $40.00

Melatonin

Steven **Bock** & Michael **Boyette**

Stay Young the Melatonin Way: The Natural Plan for Better Sex, Better Sleep, Better Health & Longer Life

A readable and helpful introduction to the wonder hormone

0-525-94115-0 PENGUIN $18.95
0-452-27525-3 PLUME PB $10.95

Suzanne **Levert**

Melatonin: The Anti-Aging Hormone

The question-and-answer format covers all the bases

0-380-78304-5 AVON PB $5.99

Walter **Pierpaoli** & others

The Melatonin Miracle: Nature's Age-Reversing, Disease Fighting, Sex Enhancing Hormone

Well-written explanation of the hormone's powers by the world's leading researcher; includes age-appropriate dosages

0-7838-1603-0 GK HALL $23.95
0-671-53435-1 POCKET PB $6.99

Russel J. **Reiter** & Jo **Robinson**

Your Body's Natural Wonder Drug: Melatonin

An easy read by a neuroendocrinologist

0-553-10017-3 BDD $22.95

Ray **Sahelian**

Melatonin: Nature's Sleeping Pill

A family physician's experiences prescribing the hormone for his patients' sleep disorders and other ailments

See also **SLEEP DISORDERS** under **SPECIFIC HEALTH PROBLEMS**

0-9639755-7-9 BE HAPPIER PRESS PB $13.95

Mental Fitness and Memory

Connirhe **Andreas** & Steve **Andreas**

Heart of the Mind: Engaging Your Inner Power to Change with Neuro-Linguistic Programming

From overcoming stage fright to allergies, phobias, traumas; just about every human trial can be helped with this technique

0-911226-31-1 REAL PEOPLE PB $10.50

Gillian **Butler** & Tony **Hope**

Managing Your Mind: The Mental Fitness Guide

Tackles specific areas such as memory enhancement, sleeping problems, smoking, and alcohol abuse

0-19-510379-3 OXFORD $19.95
0-19-511125-7 OXFORD PB $10.95

Tony **Buzan**

Make the Most of Your Mind

How to untap the unused bulk of your brain

0-671-49519-4 SIMON & SCHUSTER PB $10.00

Use Both Sides of Your Brain

The third edition of the classic work for reading and studying faster and more effectively, and how to increase overall memory

0-452-26603-3 DUTTON PB $11.95

Use Your Perfect Memory

Improve memory for names, numbers, dates, speeches, poetry, entire books, languages, and dreams

0-452-26606-8 DUTTON PB $11.95

Bobbi **De Porter** & Mike **Hernacki**

Quantum Learning: Unleashing the Genius in You

Motivation, note-taking techniques, learning style, memory tricks, and other tips for the student and nonstudent

0-440-50427-9 DELL PB $11.95

Edward **deBono**

deBono's Thinking Course

Cognitive thinker and inventor of "lateral thinking" explains how to improve thinking and therefore problem solving

0-8160-3178-9 FACTS ON FILE PB $12.95

Priscilla **Donovan** & Jacquelyn **Wonder**

The Forever Mind: Eight Ways to Unleash the Powers of Your Mature Mind

In the belief that mental powers sharpen, not deteriorate with age, this program ensures that the older brain gets more vital

0-688-14623-6 QUILL PB $12.00

Marilyn vos **Savant** & Leonore **Fleischer**

Brain Building in Just 12 Weeks

The person with the highest IQ in the world explains how to build vocabulary, learn creative problem solving, and improve concentration, logic, and insight

0-553-35348-9 BANTAM PB $11.95

Hans **Eysenck**

Test Your IQ

Explains the significance of the test, how it works, and how to take it

0-14-024962-1 PENGUIN PB $9.95

Peter **Russell**

The Brain Book

An introduction to how the brain functions as well as how to use it

0-452-26723-4 DUTTON PB $13.95

Marsha **Sinetar**

Developing a 21st Century Mind

A how-to for creative thinking and evolving beyond mere coping skills

0-345-37648-X BALLANTINE PB $5.99

Dennis **Swiercinsky**

50 Ways You Can Improve Your Memory: Improve and Gain Confidence in Everyday Memory

Neuropsychologist presents simple techniques for memory, thinking, and problem solving

0-9641311-0-2 WORLD WISDOM PB $9.95

Kevin **Trudeau**

Mega Memory

Based on the TV program

0-688-13582-X MORROW $23.00

Carol **Turkington**

12 Steps to a Better Memory

Besides the basic memory-building techniques, it also offers how to prevent memory loss

0-02-860579-9 ARCO PB $9.95

Anna **Wise**

The High-Performance Mind: Mastering Brainwaves for Insight, Healing, and Creativity

"…a superb introduction to the tools and techniques of brainwave training—learning to alter our brainwaves into high-performance patterns and move into peak states on demand"
—Michael Hutchinson, *Megabrain*

0-87477-806-9 TARCHER $24.95
0-87477-850-6 TARCHER PB $14.95

Health Care for the Aging

Claire **Berman**

Caring for Yourself While Caring for Your Aging Parents: How to Help, How to Survive

Many resources inform this much-needed guide. "Berman delivers sensible advice and practical help"—*Publishers Weekly*

0-8050-3734-9 HOLT $22.50

Robert **Butler** & Myrna **Lewis**

Aging and Mental Health

Butler is the former director of the National Institute on Aging and Lewis is a psychologist and gerontologist; together they present the specific problems of the elderly and their mental afflictions

0-675-20920-X MERRILL PB $41.00

Molly **Mettler**

Healthwise for Life: Medical Self-Care for Healthy Aging

Large print and many illustrations present common-sense advice for independent living

1-87793-002-4 HEALTHWISE PB.....................$18.95

Donald J. **Murphy**

Honest Medicine: Shattering the Myths About Aging and Health Care

An overview of geriatric healthcare and health advice. "His appraisal of the medical system is reasoned and well-considered; the book will make deciding what to do a little clearer"
—*Publishers Weekly*

0-87113-587-6 GROVE.....................$23.00
0-87113-658-9 ATLANTIC MONTHLY PB.....................$12.00

Carolyn **Rob** & Janet **Reynolds**

The Caregiver's Guide: Helping Elderly Relatives Cope with Health and Safety Problems

A sensible, basic, and reassuring collection of information that takes a "Dr. Spock" approach to care of the elderly. Provides essential recommendations for maintaining the comfort and independence of an aging friend or relative, handling medical emergencies, locating social services, and recognizing how aging affects medical symptoms

0-395-58780-8 HOUGHTON MIFFLIN PB.....................$13.95

Harriet Sarnoff **Schiff**

How Did I Become My Parent's Parent?

0-670-85543-X VIKING.....................$22.95

Care of the Disabled and Chronically Ill

Greg **Anderson**

Healing Wisdom: Insight, Wit, and Inspiration for Anyone Facing Illness

0-452-27164-9 PLUME PB.....................$8.95

Cappy **Caposella** & Sheila **Warnock**

Share the Care: How to Organize a Support Group to Care for Someone Who Is Seriously Ill

Explains how to arrange a surrogate family of all ages to care for the dying

0-684-81136-7 FIRESIDE PB.....................$13.00

Lucille **Carlton**

In Sickness and Health: Sex, Love, and Chronic Illness

Suggestions for the ailing or aging on reclaiming sexual intimacy. She also covers impotence and depression. A helpful resource directory included

0-385-31525-2 DELACORTE.....................$18.95

Rosalynn **Carter**

Helping Yourself Help Others: A Book for Caregivers

Carter began the Rosalynn Carter Institute for Human Development primarily to combat what she sees as a national crisis in caregiving. Carter outlines problems of those administering home care for people with chronic health problems: isolation, burnout, anger, and helplessness

0-8129-2591-2 TIME BOOKS PB.....................$14.00

Martha **Cleveland**

Living Well: A Twelve-Step Response to Chronic Illness and Disability

A retired psychologist uses the 12 steps from AA to find emotional and spiritual healing for those suffering from chronic illness

0-345-38519-5 BALLANTINE PB.....................$4.99

Suzanne **LeVert**

When Your Child Has a Chronic Illness: What You Must Know, Do, Expect

Communication, food, education, care, self-esteem are all covered in this sensitive and well-thought-out guide

0-440-21667-2 DELL PB.....................$4.99

Rodger **McFarlane** & Philip **Bashe**

Everyday Angels: A No-Nonsense Guide to Caring for the Seriously Ill and the Dying

0-684-80143-4 SIMON & SCHUSTER.....................$25.00

Sefra **Pitzele**

We Are Not Alone: Learning to Live with Chronic Illness

Useful, supportive information for the everyday problems of the chronically ill

0-89480-139-2 WORKMAN PB.....................$10.95

Irene **Pollin** & Susan K. **Golant**

Taking Charge: How to Master the Eight Most Common Fears of Long-Term Illness

How to master both the illness and the medical care system for both patient and family

0-8129-2258-1 TIME BOOKS.....................$23.00
0-8129-2700-1 TIME BOOKS PB.....................$14.00

Tieneke **Van Bentheim** & Saskia **Bos**

Caring for the Sick at Home

Nonclinical aspects of caring for the sick and the elderly, including psychological insight

0-88010-254-3 ANTHROPOSOPHIC PB.....................$12.95

David **Spiegel**

Living Beyond Limits: A Scientific Mind/Body Approach to Facing Life-Threatening Illness

The interaction of mind and body in the healing process and the importance and consequent beneficial results of accepting the facts of chronic illness are brilliantly examined in this major contribution to one of today's most pressing health issues. "David Spiegel is a pioneer on the new frontier of healing"—Bill Moyers

See also **MIND-BODY HEALING** under **HOLISTIC MEDICINE**

0-449-90940-9 FAWCETT PB.....................$12.50

Holistic Medicine

Since ancient times, societies worldwide have placed a strong emphasis on the healing powers of spiritual leaders, sacred locations, and particular herbs and potions. The current era is witnessing a return to reliance on alternative methods of healing among many people, along with a parallel emphasis on the power of individuals to heal themselves.

General

Richard **Carlson** & Benjamin **Shield**, editor

Healers on Healing

Norman Cousins, Ram Dass, Bernie Siegel, and 34 other health luminaries explore the mysterious nature of healing

0-87477-494-2 TARCHER PB.....................$14.95

Norman **Cousins**

Anatomy of an Illness: As Perceived by the Patient

Natural healing and the importance of the patient's attitude, based on the author's own recovery from a crippling disease

0-553-34365-3 BANTAM PB.....................$11.95

Larry **Dossey**

Healing Words: The Power of Prayer and the Practice of Medicine

0-06-250252-2 HARPERCOLLINS PB.....................$12.00

Prayer Is Good Medicine: How to Reap the Healing Benefits of Prayer

"Dossey shows us how we can create a lasting partnership between faith and medicine"
—Deepak Chopra.

See also **INSPIRATIONAL** under **SPIRITUALITY** in **RELIGION, SPIRITUALITY, AND PHILOSOPHY**

0-06-251423-7 HARPERCOLLINS.....................$20.00

Space, Time, and Medicine

Holistic medicine, by a noted Dallas doctor

0-394-71091-6 SHAMBHALA PB.....................$18.00

East West Journal

The Shopper's Guide to Natural Foods

0-89529-233-5 AVERY PB.....................$12.95

Joy **Gardner**

The New Healing Yourself: Natural Remedies for Adults and Children

From aches and pains to warts, tried and true simple remedies for relief. Includes healthful recipes and a resource list

0-89594-354-9 CROSSING PB.....................$12.95

Robert M. **Giller** & Kathy **Mathews**

Natural Prescriptions

A practitioner of preventive medicine dispenses instructions for treatment of almost every common ailment from acne to preventing wrinkles with vitamins, herbs, diet, and lifestyle advice. An excellent resource for drug-free healing

0-517-58689-4 RANDOM HOUSE $25.00

Ralph **Golan**

Optimal Wellness: Where Mainstream and Alternative Medicine Meet

A teacher of naturopathic medicine examines the causes of chronic illness and discusses alternative as well as conventional therapies

0-345-35874-0 FAWCETT PB $20.00

Elson **Haas**

Staying Healthy with the Seasons

Culling from ancient cultures and modern science to teach individuals the process of disease and healing for prevention and wellness

0-89087-306-2 CELESTIAL ARTS PB $14.95

James **Lynch** & Anita Weil **Bell**

Dr. Lynch's Holistic Self-Health Program: Three Months to Total Well-Being

A three-month program designed to realize the individual's power to heal

0-452-27150-9 PLUME PB $11.95

Mark **Mayell** & **Natural Health Magazine**

52 Simple Steps to Natural Health: A Week-by-Week Guide to More Healthful Living

Authors suggest that one can change one's life one week at a time. The 52 chapters cover almost all aspects of mental, spiritual, and physical health. "...convenient and inspiring"
—*Publishers Weekly*

0-671-88061-6 POCKET PB $14.00

Paul **Pitchford**

Healing with Whole Foods: Oriental Traditions and Modern Nutrition

Over 300 vegan recipes, oriental medicines, guidelines on nutrients, weight loss, and other topics

0-938190-64-4 NORTH ATLANTIC PB $29.95

Meir **Schneider** & others

The Handbook of Self-Healing: Your Personal Program for Better Health and Increased Vitality

The author, who cured himself of congenital blindness, now presents special regimens and exercises for all parts of the body for either disease prevention or cure

0-14-019331-6 ARKANA PB...............................$19.95

Julian **Whitaker**

Dr. Whitaker's Guide to Health and Healing

Prevention, natural remedies, and discussion of American health-care problems

1-55958-495-5 PRIMA.......................................$24.95

Dana **Ullman**

The One Minute or So Healer: 500 Quick and Simple Ways to Heal Yourself Naturally

"Written for the average health consumer, it is both instructive and funny... one of the best health bargains in town"
—*Townsend Letter for Doctors*

0-87477-667-8 TARCHER PB...............................$9.95

Andrew **Weil**

Health and Healing: Understanding Conventional and Alternative Medicine

From one of the leaders in the field

0-395-73100-3 DORLING KINDERSLEY PB $11.95

Alternative Therapies

Dylana **Accolla** & Peter **Yates**

Back to Balance: A Holistic Self-Help Guide to Eastern Remedies

This handbook shows how to treat common ailments through natural and safe remedies from the East. Therapies include shiatsu massage, diet, herbs, meditation, and more. Alphabetically arranged for easy reference, this is a splendid introduction to the techniques of Eastern medicine for promoting health and inner harmony

4-7700-1923-8 KODANSHA PB $22.00

Lendon H. **Smith**

Happiness Is a Healthy Life

A wise and witty collection of comments and observations on health by the popular author, a medical doctor who was pilloried for researching and promoting alternative health therapies

0-87983-547-8 KEATS PB $10.95

General

Mark **Bricklin**

The Practical Encyclopedia of Natural Healing

0-14-013864-1 PENGUIN PB..............................$14.95

Burton Goldberg Group

Alternative Medicine: The Definitive Guide

"This book is long overdue...if you are interested in alternative medicine of any kind and want the security of authenticity in this field"—Deepak Chopra

0-9636334-3-0 FUTURE MEDICINE $59.95

William **Collinge**

The American Holistic Health Association Complete Guide to Alternative Medicine

"A balanced view and comprehensive scope distinguish this guide"—*Publishers Weekly*

0-446-51817-4 MYSTERIOUS.............................$24.95

Fred M. **Frohock**

Healing Powers: Alternative Medicine, Spiritual Communities, and the State

Do people's religious beliefs give them access to healing powers that the medical establishment cannot or will not accept? Through the fictional voice of "Luke," a child with cancer, the author probes the philosophical chasm that separates scientific medicine and alternative care

0-226-26584-6 CHICAGO $29.95
0-226-26585-4 CHICAGO PB.............................$14.95

Norman **Gevitz**, editor

Other Healers

Over 60 million Americans have, at some point, relied on osteopathy, homeopathy, acupuncture, and other non-allopathic medical treatments. Nine authors evaluate some of these alternative practices

0-8018-3710-3 JOHNS HOPKINS PB.................$15.95

James S. **Gordon**

Manifesto for a New Medicine: Your Guide to Healing Partnerships and the Wise Use of Alternative Therapies

The first book to integrate the full range of alternative healing practices into the medical mainstream. Supported by unassailable credentials, Dr. Gordon guides readers through homeopathy, guided imagery, chiropraxy, herbalism, acupuncture, massage therapy, and more, showing how to integrate these practices with traditional medical therapy for a true healing partnership

0-201-48383-1 ADDISON-WESLEY.....................$25.00

Bill **Gottlieb**

New Choices in Natural Healing: Over 1,800 of the Best Self-Help Remedies from the World of Alternative Medicine

"...this volume offers a clear, concise introduction to a wide range of complementary healing practices from around the world"
—*Publishers Weekly*

0-87596-257-2 RODALE...................................$27.95

Laura Shapiro **Kramer**

Uncommon Voyage: Parenting a Special Needs Child in the World of Alternative Medicine

Unconventional medical options are offered

See also **SPECIAL CHILDREN** under **CHILD CARE** under **PARENTING**

0-571-19887-2 FABER.......................................$24.95

Pat **Lazarus**

Healing the Mind the Natural Way: Nutritional Solutions to Psychological Problems

A practitioner who uses the fascinating nutritional approach to healing called orthomolecular psychiatry, wherein the body is used to treat the mind. "Lazarus offers a unique, informative addition to consumer medical literature"—*Publishers Weekly*

0-87477-752-6 PUTNAM PB $15.95

Kenneth **Meadows**

Earth Medicine: Revealing Hidden Teachings of the Native American Medicine Wheel

1-85230-668-8 ELEMENT PB $16.95

Michael **Murray** & Joseph **Pizzorno**

Encyclopedia of Natural Medicine

Learn how to use herbs, vitamins, minerals, diet, and other naturopathic remedies safely and effectively for hundreds of ailments

1-55958-091-7 PRIMA PB $19.95

Katrina **Raphaell**

Crystal Healing: The Therapeutic Application of Crystals and Stones

0-943358-30-2 AURORA PB $14.95

Acupuncture/Acupressure

Yoshio **Manaka** & Ian **Urquhart**

The Layman's Guide to Acupuncture

INTRODUCTION BY JAMES RESTON

0-8348-0107-8 WEATHERHILL PB $10.95

David J. **Nickel**

Acupressure for Athletes: Newly Revised Edition

"Health professionals, trainers, coaches, athletes, and fitness enthusiasts have come to appreciate acupressure, for it is a natural, drug-free, noninvasive healing system without side effects"—*Sports Fitness*

0-8050-0128-X HOLT PB $10.95

Aromatherapy

Jane **Dye**

Aromatherapy for Women & Children: Pregnancy and Childbirth

Chatty, well-written resource emphasizes use and special properties of essential oils beneficial to women; bibliography

0-85207-226-0 DANIEL PB $23.95

Danielle **Ryman**

Aromatherapy: The Complete Guide to Plant & Flower Essences for Health & Beauty

An A to Z listing of 80 of the most effective oils and plants for massage, bath, inhalants, facial saunas, lotions, poultices, and cooking, as well as aromatherapy treatment for 100 common ailments

0-553-37166-5 BANTAM PB $11.95

Carol **Schiller** & David **Schiller**

500 Formulas for Aromatherapy: Mixing Oils for Every Use

A handy manual, from breath freshners to lice removers

0-8069-0584-0 STERLING PB $12.95

Marcel **Lavabre**

Aromatherapy Workbook

Helpful in determining which oils are best for you

0-89281-346-6 INNER TRADITIONS PB $12.95

Susanne **Fischer-Rizzi**

Complete Aromatherapy Handbook: Essential Oils for Radiant Health

Clear and easy to read; details essential oils from Angelica to Ylang-Ylang with history and usage for both mental and physical needs. Illustrated

0-8069-8222-5 STERLING PB $16.95

Robert B. **Tisserand**

The Art of Aromatherapy: The Healing & Beautifying Properties of the Essential Oils of Flowers & Herbs

A classic. From history and use in ancient Egypt to present day, 29 essences described in detail—tastes, glossary, indexes of therapeutic uses and properties

0-89281-001-7 INNER TRADITIONS PB $12.95

Ayurvedic

Deepak **Chopra**

Creating Health: How to Wake Up the Body's Intelligence

This revised edition of Chopra's classic work introduces the reader to the basics of Ayurveda, the 6,000-year-old tradition of health care from India, which Dr. Chopra, then the chief of staff for the New England Memorial Hospital, brought to national attention. "Chopra communicates excitement on the cutting edge of today's mind/body medicine with the sophistication of a medical insider"—*Harvard Magazine*

0-395-75515-8 HOUGHTON MIFFLIN PB $11.95

Scott **Gerson**

Ayurveda: The Ancient Indian Healing Art

Introduction to the system of holistic healing used in India for over 6,000 years

1-85230-335-2 ELEMENT PB $9.95

Maya **Tiwari**

Ayurveda Secrets of Healing

"...an authoritative compendium on the ancient wisdom and knowledge of healing that will be of immense value to health professionals as well as those interested in healing themselves" —Deepak Chopra

0-914955-15-2 LOTUS LIGHT PB $22.95

Chinese Medicine

Ted **Kaptchuk**

The Web that Has No Weaver: Understanding Chinese Medicine

0-8092-2933-1 CONGDON & WEED PB $18.95

Wee Yeow **Chin** & Hsuan **Keng**

An Illustrated Dictionary of Chinese Medicinal Herbs

A handsome, exhaustive reference with over 270 photographs. Indexed both by Western and Chinese names, each entry describes the history and use of the herb in a variety of cultures. A comprehensive guide for herbalists, gardeners, botanists, and students and practitioners of the healing arts

0-916360-53-9 C.R.C.S. $32.95

Jake **Fratkin**

Chinese Herbal Patent Formulas: A Practical Guide

Over 200 formulas organized in traditional categories with Chinese characters and pronunciation, by symptom and pathology; indispensable when buying from Chinese herbalists

0-9626078-2-7 SHYA PB $17.95

Claude **Larre**

Rooted in Spirit: The Heart of Chinese Medicine

A translation of Chapter 8 from *The Yellow Emperor's Classic of Internal Medicine*, wherein the spiritual and metaphysical aspects of Chinese medicine are illuminated

0-88268-120-6 TALMAN PB $19.95

Henry C. **Lu**

Chinese Systems of Natural Cures

Ancient Chinese remedies of herbs and foods to cure what ails you

0-8069-0616-2 STERLING PB $10.95

Legendary Chinese Healing Herbs

More than 100 Chinese medicinal herbs are described, including essential information on their distinct flavors and healing properties. Each plant, finely illustrated, is accompanied by the classic Chinese tale that details its mythological origins

0-8069-8230-6STERLING PB $9.95

Daniel **Reid**

Chinese Herbal Medicine

A colorful, well-organized, and well-respected presentation of the vast and confusing art of Chinese herbal healing

0-87773-398-8 SHAMBHALA PB $25.00

Charles **Windridge**

The Fountain of Health: An A-Z of Traditional Chinese Medicine

An encyclopedia of healing from the Chinese perspective

1-85158-635-0 MAINSTREAM PB $19.95

Nancy **Zi**

The Art of Breathing: A Course of Six Simple Lessons to Improve Performance and Well-Being

Taps the power of the chi yi method of controlled breathing

1-88487-262-X VIVI PB $9.95

Flower Remedies

Edward **Bach** & F.J. **Wheeler**
The Bach Flower Remedies
An explanation of the 38 remedies designed to treat "spiritual and psychological disharmonies" with the essences of flowers and plants
0-87983-193-6 KEATS PB $10.95

Donn **Cunningham**
Flower Remedies Handbook: Emotional Healing & Growth with Bach & Other Flower Essences
Well-researched book contains folklore, Latin names, uses, astrological correlations, as well as index, sources, bibliography
0-8069-8204-7 STERLING PB $12.95

Nora **Weeks**
The Medical Discoveries of Edward Bach, Physician
The fascinating story written by the doctor's assistant of the discovery and development of his 38 flower remedies
0-87983-642-3 KEATS PB $9.95

Healing Hands

Robert O. **Becker** & Gary **Selden**
The Body Electric: Electromagnetism and the Foundation of Life
0-688-06971-1 MORROW PB $11.00

Barbara Ann **Brennan**
Hands of Light: A Guide to Healing Through the Human Energy Field
"This book is a must for all aspiring healers and health-care givers"—Elisabeth Kübler-Ross
0-553-34539-7 BANTAM PB $23.95

Dan **Menkin**
Transformation Through Bodywork: Using Touch Therapies for Inner Peace
An exploration of several types of bodywork as tools for healing, self-discovery, finding and creating a sense of ease
See also **PERSONAL AND PSYCHIC DEVELOPMENT** under **SPIRITUALITY** under **SPIRITUALITY** in **RELIGION, SPIRITUALITY, AND PHILOSOPHY**
1-87918-134-7 BEAR PB $16.00

Ric A. **Weinman**
Your Hands Can Heal: Learn to Channel Healing Energy
Workbook based on the author's classes presents exercises for learning how to use the body's energy to help treat illness; the section on color is particularly fascinating
0-14-019361-8 ARKANA PB $10.95

Richard Rainbow **Pavek**
Handbook of SHEN
Introduces the SHEN (Specific Human Energy Nexus) method of treatment for both physical and mental well-being. Written by the originator
0-9618646-0-5 SHEN THERAPY PB $14.95

Dolores **Krieger**
The Therapeutic Touch: How to Use Your Hands to Help or to Heal
0-671-76537-X SIMON & SCHUSTER PB $11.00

Herbal Remedies

Stephen Harrod **Buhner**
Sacred Plant Medicine: Explorations in the Practice of Indigenous Herbalism
The historical use of plants and how the sacredness of plants is experienced by indigenous cultures. Color plates of 19 plant species, recipes, and prayers to invoke before harvesting
1-57098-091-8 ROBERTS RINEHART PB $18.95

Michael **Castleman**
The Healing Herbs: The Ultimate Guide to the Curative Power of Nature's Medicines
History, description, illustrations, storage, buying of 100 herbs; prevention and treatment guide; references and index
0-553-56988-0 BDD PB $6.99

Nicholas **Culpeper**
Culpeper's Color Herbal
The renowned 17th-century astrologer-physician's 300-year-old botanical text has been updated with practical, modern information by respected herbalist David Potterton. Filled with full-color illustrations
0-8069-8568-2 STERLING PB $19.95

Stephen **Fulder**
The Book of Ginseng: And Other Herbs for Vitality
For 7,000 years this herb has been regarded as both restorative and prophylactic. Well known for its ability to preserve male sexual potency and to assist women through menopause and for general weakness of all kinds
0-89281-491-8 INNER TRADITIONS PB $14.95

Rosemary **Gladstar**
Herbal Healing for Women: Simple Home Remedies for Women of All Ages
For adolescents, remedies for irregular menstrual cycles and acne; for women of childbearing age, safe treatments for PMS and morning sickness; for older women, the easing of osteoporosis and reduced estrogen. Practical step-by-step instructions from an expert herbalist. Recipes for oils, salves, teas, and more included. "The most complete women's herbal guide I have ever read"—Dr. Earl Mindell, author of *Earl Mindell's Herbal Bible*
0-671-76767-4 FIRESIDE PB $12.00

Terry **Lemerond**
The Healing Power of Herbs: The Enlightened Person's Guide to the Wonders of Medicinal Herbs
Revised and expanded second edition of botanical medicine, chemical composition, pharmacology, clinical applications, dosage, and toxicity. Detailed references of sources
1-55958-700-8 PRIMA PB $15.95

Frank J. **Lipp**
Herbalism
0-316-52750-5 LITTLE, BROWN PB $14.95

Mark **Mayell**
Off-The-Shelf Natural Health: How to Use Herbs and Nutrients to Stay Well
The former editor of *Natural Health* magazine stresses how general health can be enhanced with commonly available supplements, vitamins, herbs, and homeopathy. "An extensive resource section caps off this densely packed yet eminently readable reference"–*Publishers Weekly*
0-553-37457-5 BANTAM PB $14.95

Michael **Moore**
Los Remedios
A practical guide to the herbal remedies used by generations of Southwesterners of varying backgrounds and cultures. Beautifully illustrated
1-87861-006-6 RED CRANE PB $9.95

Robert A. **Nelson**
Hemp: The Complete Guide to the Commercial, Medicinal, Psychotropic Uses of the World's Most Extraordinary Plant
0-89281-541-8 INNER TRADITIONS PB $19.95

Jack **Ritchason**
The Little Herb Encyclopedia: The Handbook of Nature's Remedies for a Healthier Life
Besides herbs from A to Z, includes glossary, herb combinations, Chinese herbs, and herbs for children and babies
0-913923-89-3 WOODLAND PB $14.95

Jeanne **Rose**
Jeanne Rose's Modern Herbal
0-399-51394-9 PERIGEE PB $11.00

Michael **Tierra**
The Way of Herbs
Descriptions, use, dosage for over 140 Western herbs, 31 Chinese herbs; how to buy, grow, store, and use for treatment
0-671-72403-7 POCKET PB $6.99

Homeopathy

Peter **Chappell**

Emotional Healing with Homeopathy: A Self-Help Manual

A unique source for those already familiar with homeopathy. Discusses trauma from emotional upsets in which homeopathic remedies can alleviate the symptoms

1-85230-487-1 ELEMENT PB $13.95

Richard **Grossinger**

Planet Medicine: From Stone Age Shamanism to Post-Industrial Healing

Grossinger's penetrating, discursive analysis of homeopathy includes chapters on "Healing, Language and Sexuality," "The Political and Spiritual Basis of Medicine," and "How to Choose a Healer." "His lucid, informative and sympathetic account demonstrates how homeopathic theory is itself a critique of standard medical practice"—*Publishers Weekly*

1-55643-093-0 NORTH ATLANTIC PB $16.95

Colin **Lessell**

The World Traveller's Manual of Homeopathy

Over 100 maladies and disorders discussed that a world traveler may encounter, from sunburn to malaria to snakebite

0-85207-242-2 DANIEL PB $33.95

Lyle W. **Morgan**

Homeopathic Medicine: First-Aid and Emergency Care

This is the book to take along on vacation, covering treatments for everything from motion sickness to shock. A practical, quick-reference handbook rather than an in-depth study, structured to provide immediate first-aid remedies

0-89281-249-4 INNER TRADITIONS PB $10.95

Barry **Rose**

The Family Health Guide to Homeopathy

Diagnoses over 200 common ailments, with over 100 remedies, in an easy-to-use format, with diagrams and colorful illustrations

FOREWORD BY YEHUDI MENUHIN

0-89087-695-9 CELESTIAL ARTS PB $32.95

George **Vithoulkas**

The Science of Homeopathy

The principles of homeopathy in practical application

0-8021-5120-5 GROVE PB $14.95

Light Therapy

Jacob **Liberman**

Light: Medicine of the Future

Fascinating study on the modern problem of mal-illumination

FOREWORD BY JOHN OTT

1-87918-101-0 BEAR PB $16.95

John N. **Ott**

Health and Light: The Effects of Natural and Artificial Light on Man and Other Living Things

How light affects health and emotions, from the main proponent of the field

0-89804-098-1 ARIEL PB $10.95

S.G. **Ouseley**

Colour Meditations

0-85243-062-0 ARIEL PB $6.95

Mind-Body Healing

Jeanne **Achterberg**

Imagery in Healing: Shamanism and Modern Medicine

A history and discussion of shamanism as the medicine of the imagination—the healing power of the mind on the body

0-394-73031-3 RANDOM HOUSE PB $16.00

Greg **Anderson**

The 22 Non-Negotiable Laws of Wellness

Discusses how attitude, job, and emotions in addition to diet and lifestyle contribute to good health and mental happiness

0-06-251235-8 HARPERCOLLINS $17.00
0-06-251238-2 HARPERCOLLINS PB $12.00

Marc Ian **Barash**

The Healing Path: A Soul Approach to Illness

Thryoid cancer sufferer finds the healing power of spirituality

0-14-019486-X PENGUIN PB $11.95

Deepak **Chopra**

Perfect Health: The Complete Mind/Body Guide

A paperback edition of a book that sold out its first hardcover printing in less than three weeks. Chopra's approach is based on the idea of preventing health problems by combining Western medicine with ancient Eastern techniques. "Dr. Chopra takes the old mind/body controversy to new levels of complexity and fascination"
—*San Francisco Chronicle*

0-517-58421-2 HARIMANDER PB $14.00

Kenneth **Cooper**

It's Better to Believe

Faith as the impetus for a healthy lifestyle

0-7852-8314-5 NELSON $22.99

Jason **Elias** & Katherine **Ketcham**

In the House of the Moon: Reclaiming the Feminine Spirit of Healing

Psychotherapist uses Eastern medical traditions to help remedy all manner of female ailments

0-446-51816-6 WARNER $22.95

Louise **Hay**

You Can Heal Your Life

10th edition of successful mental healing techniques for mind and body

1-561-70094-0 HAY HOUSE $16.95

Steven **Locke** & Douglas **Colligan**

The Healer Within: The Medicine of Mind and Body

The mind and immunity

9-993-90896-7 MENTOR PB $5.99

Robert **Masters**

Neurospeak: Transforming Your Body While You Read

An explanation of, and guide to, psychophysical reeducation, or using words to create physical changes in the body. "In an era of intellectualizing, specializing, and loss of touch with our bodies, *Neurospeak* offers us a lighted path—a path that can lead to an integration and coordination of brain and body"—Bernie Siegel

0-8356-0707-0 QUEST PB $12.00

Bill **Moyers**

Healing and the Mind

PBS commentator Moyers travels around the globe exploring medical treatments that rely on the power of the mind rather than on modern medicine's high-tech miracles

0-385-46870-9 DOUBLEDAY $25.00

Andrea **Olsen** & Caryn **McHose**

Bodystories: A Guide to Experiential Anatomy

Anatomical, anecdotal, massage information for dancers, teachers, athletes, or anyone interested in the body and how it works. Unique art by prominent contemporary artists provocatively illustrates this uncategorizable book

See also DANCE PRINTS, PHOTOGRAPHS, AND FILMS under DANCE in PERFORMING ARTS AND MEDIA

0-88268-106-0 STATION HILL PB $24.95

Emerikus **Padus**

The Complete Guide to Your Emotions and Your Health: Hundreds of Proven Techniques to Harmonize Mind and Body for Happy, Healthy Living

The executive editor of *Prevention* magazine quotes experts in the mind/body field (Bernie Siegel among others); exercises from journals to reading poetry to learn the gentle art of self-healing. Psychological first aid. Almost 600 pages—just about everything the '90s have devised

0-87596-144-4 RODALE $26.95

Ernest Lawrence **Rossi**

The Psychobiology of Mind-Body Healing: New Concepts of Therapeutic Hypnosis

"Supplies the missing link between the theory that the mind can make a significant difference in dealing with disease and the clinical observations of physicians that the theory works in enough cases to be taken seriously"
—Norman Cousins

0-393-30554-6 NORTON PB $10.95

Martin **Rush**

Decoding the Secret Language of Your Body: The Many Ways Our Bodies Send Us Messages

Psychiatrist believes that every illness can be linked to an emotional event

0-671-87238-9 FIRESIDE PB $11.00

Bernie **Siegel**

Love, Medicine, and Miracles

A surgeon stresses the importance of the patient's mind and emotions and offers a non-medical means of overcoming illness; a runaway best-seller

0-06-092467-5 HARPERPERENNIAL PB $13.00

David **Spiegel**

Living Beyond Limits: A Scientific Mind/Body Approach to Facing Life-Threatening Illness

The interaction of mind and body in the healing process and the importance and consequent beneficial results of accepting the facts of chronic illness are brilliantly examined in this major contribution to one of today's most pressing health issues, "David Spiegel is a pioneer on the new frontier of healing"—Bill Moyers

0-449-90940-9 FAWCETT PB $12.50

Andrew **Weil**

Spontaneous Healing: How to Enlist and Enhance the Body's Own Gifts for Maintaining and Healing Itself

Considers the nature of the healing process that exists in us all

0-679-43607-3 KNOPF $23.00

Immune System

Stuart **Berger**

Dr. Berger's Immune Power Diet

A diet aimed at improving the immune system

See also **DIET PLANS** under **WEIGHT-LOSS DIETS** under **DIET AND NUTRITION**

0-451-14111-3 NEW AMERICAN LIBRARY PB....$5.99

Henry **Dreher**

The Immune Power Personality: 7 Traits You Can Develop to Stay Healthy

Provides the means to cope with stress to develop the powers of resilience and to enhance the immune system

0-525-93838-9 DUTTON $23.95

0-452-27546-6 PLUME PB $13.95

Donna **Gates** & Linda **Schatz**

The Body Ecology Diet: Recovering Your Health and Rebuilding Your Immunity

For sufferers of allergies, candidiasis, and various immune disorders, this book "brings us into the era of whole-body therapy. I don't think the authors left anything out"—Lendon H. Smith

0-9638458-8-8 B.E.D. PB $19.95

William **Clark**

At War Within: The Double-Edged Sword of Immunity

Describes the immune system as a high-wire act that if unbalanced can possibly kill us

0-19-509286-4 OXFORD $25.00

Carlye **Hirshberg** & Marc Ian **Barasch**

Remarkable Recovery: What Extraordinary Healings Tell Us About Getting Well and Staying Well

Fascinating stories and history of medicine's study of the body's immune system. Why people recover from terminal illness against the odds

1-57322-000-0 PUTNAM.................................$23.95

Elinor **Levy** & Tom **Monte**

The Ten Best Tools to Boost Your Immune System

0-395-69460-4 HOUGHTON MIFFLIN PB..........$12.95

Michael **Schmidt** & others

Beyond Antibiotics: 50 (or so) Ways to Boost Immunity and Avoid Antibiotics

Discusses the overuse of antibiotics and how to avoid them

1-55643-180-5 NORTH ATLANTIC PB...............$18.95

Carlson **Wade**

Immune Power Boosters: Your Key to Feeling Younger, Living Longer

Immunity as the missing link in health and longevity considerations

0-13-451592-7 PRENTICE HALL PB...................$11.95

Diet and Nutrition

Americans have been increasingly concerned with diet and nutrition as key factors in the prevention of disease. New eating styles recognize this link and, together with exercise, are seen as vital prescriptions for the health and well-being of the human animal. These books address a range of nutritional issues, such as vitamins and health foods and the special needs of heart patients, hypertensives, and diabetics.

Lendon H. **Smith**

Feed Your Body Right: Understanding Your Individual Body Chemistry for Proper Nutrition Without Guesswork

The author of the best-selling *Feed Your Kids Right* and *Feed Yourself Right* puts the art of healing in your own hands. The premise is simple and compelling: because each of us has a unique body chemistry, generic health regimens often fail. Dr. Smith presents a program that is safe and sensible, and which teaches you to learn and listen to your body's nutritional needs for optimum health and longevity

0-87131-741-9 EVANS $19.95

Special Diets

Jane **Brody**

Jane Brody's Good Food Book: Living the High-Carbohydrate Way

A guide to changing and maintaining eating habits for health and slimness that includes a low-fat, high-carbohydrate plan with 350 easy-to-prepare recipes

0-393-02210-2 NORTON....................................$25.00

0-553-34618-0 BANTAM PB $16.95

Sonja **Connor** & William **Connor**

The New American Diet: The Lifetime Family Eating Plan for Good Health

Diet and health plan (high-carbohydrate, low-fat) aimed at health and disease prevention; includes almost 350 recipes

0-671-75503-X FIRESIDE PB.............................$14.00

Michael **Eades** & Mary Dan **Eades**

Protein Power

Family medicine and weight-loss medical doctors make a case for high-protein and low-carbo eating plan to prevent overproduction of insulin, which in turn controls fat storage. Recipes and other helpful information

0-553-10183-8 BDD $21.95

Barbara **Gibbons**

The International Slim Gourmet Cookbook

International cuisine for weight loss and maintenance without dieting

0-88365-867-4 BUDGET BOOK..........................$8.98

Ann Louise **Gittleman**

Super Nutrition for Men: Why Male Nutrition is Often Mal-Nutrition

Addresses the stresses unique to men in today's world

See also **MEN'S HEALTH** under **HEALTH**

0-87131-793-1 EVANS $19.95

Carolyn **Nostrand**

Junk Food to Real Food: A Blueprint for Healthier Eating

To ease the transition to healthy eating, menus, recipes, eating-out tips, and fast-cooking techniques are offered

0-87983-627-X KEATS PB $16.95

David **Reuben**

Quick Weight-Gain Program: Safe, Easy Weight Gain for Every Age and Situation

Recipes and nutritional advice for those who are too thin

0-517-70205-3 CROWN $23.00

Joel **Robertson** & Tom **Monte**

Peak Performance Living: Easy, Drug-Free Ways to Alter Your Own Brain Chemistry and Achieve Optimal Health

By correcting our neurochemical imbalances with corresponding changes in diet, exercise, and lifestyles we can boost energy, intellectual abilities, and even self-esteem

0-06-251233-1 HARPERCOLLINS $23.00

Low Cholesterol

American Heart Association

The American Heart Association Cookbook

Popular and useful, with fat-cholesterol charts

0-8129-2282-4 TIME BOOKS PB $16.00

Ron **Goor** & Nancy **Goor**

Eater's Choice: A Food Lover's Guide to Lower Cholesterol

Includes recipes

0-395-70813-3 HOUGHTON MIFFLIN PB $14.95

Robert **Kowalski**

The Eight-Week Cholesterol Cure: How to Lower Your Blood Cholesterol by Up to 40 Percent Without Drugs or Deprivation

Lowering blood cholesterol with the wonders of oat bran

0-06-091471-8 HARPERCOLLINS PB $13.00

The Revolutionary Cholesterol Breakthrough: How to Eat Everything You Want and Have Your Heart Thank You for It

How to block unwanted fats by using certain products, antioxidants, soluble fiber, and niacin

0-8362-1044-1 ANDREWS & MCMEEL $24.95

Joseph **Piscatella**

Choices for a Healthy Heart

Prescriptive measures and recipes

0-89480-138-4 WORKMAN PB $16.95

Eli **Roth** & Sandra **Streicher-Lankin**

Good Cholesterol, Bad Cholesterol

Written by cardiovascular specialists to explain the confusion about cholesterol and show how to adapt to a good and low cholesterol diet

0-7615-0010-3 PRIMA PB $10.95

Richard **Trubo** & **Prevention Magazine**

Cholesterol Cures: From Almonds and Antioxidants to Garlic, Golf, Wine and Yogurt—325 Quick and Easy Ways to Lower Cholesterol and Live Longer

"...hundreds of nuggets of practical advice from nutritionists and physicians and findings from researchers are gathered in 60 main entries" —*Publishers Weekly*

0-87596-284-X NOT OUR PUBLICATIONS $27.95

0-87596-399-4 RODALE PB $15.95

Diets for Special Health Problems

Michael E. **DeBakey** & others

The Living Heart Diet

Cookbook and heart disease data have been completely revised since the 1984 edition. Compiled by Baylor College of Medicine heart specialists; presents more than 300 recipes and menus

0-684-81188-X FIRESIDE PB $16.00

Joel **Fuhrman**

Fasting and Eating for Health: A Medical Doctor's Program for Conquering Disease

Fasting procedure outlined as well as specific fasts for specific ailments

0-312-13071-6 ST. MARTIN'S $23.95

Richard F. **Heller** & Rachael F. **Heller**

Healthy for Life: The Scientific Breakthrough Program for Looking, Feeling and Staying Healthy Without Deprivation

Diet plan to control too much insulin

0-525-93733-1 DUTTON $24.95

Marjorie **Jones**

The Allergy Self-Help Cookbook

Over 325 natural foods recipes, free from wheat, milk eggs, corn, yeast, sugar, and other common food-allergy substances

0-87596-109-6 RODALE PB $15.95

Katherine **Middleton** & Mary **Hess**

The Art of Cooking for the Diabetic

0-8092-4653-8 CONTEMPORARY PB $14.95

0-451-17574-3 SIGNET PB $6.99

Earl **Mindell**

Earl Mindell's Food as Medicine

What foods to eat to help prevent a variety of maladies from colds to cancer

0-671-79755-7 FIRESIDE PB $13.00

Earl Mindell's Soy Miracle

Besides discussion of soy's efficacy for many types of ailments, he lists types of soy products, where to find them, and how to incorporate them into your diet

0-671-89820-5 FIRESIDE PB $12.00

Arlene **Monk** & Marion **Franz**

Convenience Food Facts: Help for the Healthy Meal Planner

Dietary help for the diabetic

0-937721-77-8 CHRONIMED PB $10.95

Gary **Null**

Nutrition and the Mind

Preventive health writer and radio personality explores alcoholism through thyroid disorders and other ailments commonly misdiagnosed as mental disease. Based on interviews with 25 MDs on their nutrition-based approaches

1-88836-324-X SEVEN STORIES PB $14.95

Helen Cassidy **Page** & others

The Stanford Life Plan for a Healthy Heart

A four-part guide to the ticker: heart disease primer, nutritional guide, shopping and meal planning guide, and cookbook

0-8118-1045-3 CHRONICLE $29.95

Diane **Reader**

Pass the Pepper Please!: Healthy Meal Planning for People on Sodium-Restricted Diets

0-937721-17-4 CHRONIMED PB $3.95

Isadore **Rosenfeld**

Doctor, What Should I Eat?: Nutrition Prescriptions for Ailments in Which Diet Can Really Make a Difference

Discusses what diet can and cannot do for cancer, Parkinson's disease, multiple sclerosis, heart disease, chronic fatigue syndrome

0-679-42818-6 RANDOM HOUSE $25.00

Carlson **Wade**

Eat Away Illness: How to Age-Proof Your Body with Antioxidant Foods

All kinds of ailments can be treated by a proper diet

0-13-224817-4 PRENTICE HALL PB $11.95

Jonathan V. **Wright**

Dr. Wright's Guide to Healing with Nutrition

Presents 75 case histories to illustrate the role of nutrition in helping a variety of problems

0-87983-530-3 KEATS PB $18.95

Children and Adolescents

Boston Children's Hospital & others

Parents' Guide to Nutrition

This comprehensive guide covers breastfeeding to teenage eating disorders. "Full of common sense advice and reassurance"—*NY Times*

0-201-05739-5 ADDISON-WESLEY PB $12.95

Michael **Jacobson** & Bruce **Maxwell**

What Are We Feeding Our Kids?

A wakeup call to start healthful eating strategies for children

1-56305-101-X WORKMAN PB $8.95

Michael D. **LeBow**

Overweight Teenagers: Don't Bear the Burden Alone

A psychologist from the Manitoba Obesity Clinic emphasizes gradual behavioral changes and goal setting to make weight loss plausible

0-306-45047-X INSIGHT $23.95

Bonnie L. **Lukes**

How to Be a Reasonably Thin Teenage Girl Without Starving, Losing Your Friends or Running Away from Home

A good bet to avoid teenage diet disorders; written specifically for teens

0-679-31269-5 ATHENEUM $12.95

Laura Walther **Nathanson**

Kid Shapes: A Guide to Helping Your Kids Control Their Weight

Pediatrician dispenses advice on this culturally loaded and highly emotional problem

0-06-270135-5 HARPERCOLLINS $17.50

Robin O. **Sweet** & Thomas **Bloom**

The Well-Fed Baby: Easy Healthful Recipes for the First 12 Months

How to make your own fresh and healthful foods

0-02-045370-1 MACMILLAN PB $12.00

Middle and Later Years

Neal **Barnard**

Eat Right, Live Longer: Using the Natural Power of Foods to Age-Proof Your Body

Vegetarian and walking regime designed to lose weight, strengthen the immune system, maintain strong bones, and to protect veins and arteries

0-517-79950-2 HARMONY $24.00

0-517-88778-9 CROWN PB $13.00

Michael **Colgan**

The New Nutrition: Medicine for the Millennium

How to compensate for environmental degradation by ingesting certain nutrients

0-9695272-4-1 APPLE PB $14.95

Linus **Pauling**

How to Live Longer and Feel Better

Vitamins and health, by the famous pioneer in the field

0-380-70289-4 AVON PB $6.50

Diets for Women

Susie **Orbach**

Fat Is a Feminist Issue: The Anti-Diet Guide to Permanent Weight Loss

Fatness as a response: how to change this response into thinness

0-425-14145-4 BERKELEY PB $9.00

Sandra **Cabot**

The Body-Shaping Diet: A Leading Woman's Health Specialist Reveals the Hormonal Secrets that Can Change Your Shape Forever

Determine if you are a lymphatic, android, gynecoid, or thyroid type; learn how each determines body shape and how to lose weight with this knowledge

0-446-51872-7 WARNER $19.95

0-446-60290-6 WARNER PB $6.50

Monica **Dixon**

Love the Body You Were Born With: A Ten-Step Workbook for Women

Worksheets help women set goals and rethink their attitude to their body

0-399-51975-0 BERKELEY PB $13.00

Dolores **Riccio**

Superfoods for Women

Categorized by foods for illnesses that are specific to females, with an introductory chapter that lists healthful foods and their virtues

0-446-51795-X MYSTERIOUS $21.95

Elizabeth **Somer**

Nutrition for Women: The Complete Guide

Athletes, pregnant and breastfeeding women, seniors, those with anemia, AIDS—every type, age, or scenario is represented. "An excellent source. Highly recommended"
—*Library Journal*

0-8050-3563-X HOLT PB $15.95

Jean Perry **Spodnik** & Barbara **Gibbons**

The 35 Plus Diet For Women: Kaiser Permanente Clinic's Breakthrough Metabolism Diet

For the changing metabolism of the over-35 woman: high protein, low carbohydrate, low fat, no sugar

0-671-73213-7 POCKET PB $5.99

Debra **Waterhouse**

Outsmarting the Female Fat Cell: The First Weight-Control Program Designed *Specifically* for Women

Explains why women's weight problems are different from men's and what they can do about it

0-446-60129-2 WARNER PB $5.99

Why Women Need Chocolate

Takes the guilt out of cravings and puts them in perspective

0-7868-6051-0 HYPERION $19.95

0-7868-8134-8 HYPERION PB $10.95

Sports Nutrition

Liz **Applegate**

Power Foods: High Performance Nutrition for High Performance People

Nutrition columnist for *Runner's World* magazine believes that an athlete's diet can benefit everyone who has an active life

0-87596-219-X RODALE PB $13.95

Anita **Bean**

The Complete Guide to Sports Nutrition

Diet for all performance levels. Discusses fuel and fluid intake, and includes recipes for optimum energy

0-7136-3605-X A & C BLACK PB $15.95

L. **Burke**

The Complete Guide to Food for Sports Performance

Unique in that it categorizes nutrition needs by individual sport

1-86373-073-7 ALLEN & UNWIN PB $16.95

Nancy **Clark**

Nancy Clark's Sports Nutrition Guidebook: Eating to Fuel Your Lifestyle

Registered dietician dispenses nutrition advice for weekend athletes as well as professionals. Tables, charts, 103 recipes, as well as information on carbo loading

0-88011-326-X LEISURE PB $14.95

Michael **Colgon**

Optimum Sports Nutrition: Your Competitive Edge

Well-known sports nutritionist puts up-to-date information in one easy-to-read source

0-9624840-5-9 ADVANCED RESEARCH PRESS PB $24.95

Ellington **Darden**

The Nautilus Diet: Ten Weeks to a Brand-New Body

Uses strength training and a descending calorie regimen; includes recipes, menus, and photos that illustrate weight-losing exercises

0-316-17284-7 LITTLE, BROWN PB $16.95

Robert **Haas**

Eat to Succeed: The Haas Maximum Performance Program

High-carbohydrate performance plans

0-451-40088-7 ONYX PB $5.99

Eat to Win: The Sports Nutrition Bible

From a sports nutritionist: high-carbohydrate, low-cholesterol eating for a moderate-to-active sports life

See also **AEROBICS AND GENERAL FITNESS** under **FITNESS**

0-451-15509-2 SIGNET PB $5.99

Frederick C. **Hatfield**

Ultimate Sports Nutrition: A Scientific Approach to Peak Athletic Performance

How to lose *and* gain weight, as well as which nutrients to take

0-8092-4887-5 CONTEMPORARY PB $14.95

Health for Life

The Human Fuel Handbook: Nutrition for Peak Athletic Performance

From an explanation of how the body converts food to fuel to eating for a bodybuilding contest, this is a complete and comprehensible guide for all athletes

0-944831-17-6 HEALTH FOR LIFE PB $24.95

Susan M. **Kleiner** & Maggie **Greenwood**

High-Performance Nutrition: The Total Eating Plan to Maximize Your Workout

Espouses complex carbos and low fats in general. Discusses nutrition for vegetarian athletes, pregnant women, and senior athletes

0-471-11520-7 WILEY PB $16.95

Weight-loss Diets

The following books offer alternative weight loss diets—some focus on one central idea, such as the use of dietary fiber; others propose a high-protein, low-carbohydrate plan.

Diane **Epstein** & Kathleen **Thompson**

Feeding on Dreams: Why America's Diet Industry Doesn't Work and What Will Work for You

From condemnation of the diet industry to a self-designed diet plan, this book lets you control and enjoy food again

0-02-536191-0 MACMILLAN $20.00
0-380-72521-5 AVON PB $5.99

Terry Nicholetti **Garrison** & David **Levitsky**

Fed-Up: Liberating Ourselves from the Diet/Weight Prison

Beginning with a detailed explanation of the diet industry, our culture's preoccupation with food and rigid standards of beauty, and progressing through the latest research on health and weight, *Fed-Up* shows how to replace dieting with healthy lifestyles

0-88184-964-2 CARROLL & GRAF PB $9.95

Ann Louise **Gittleman** & others

Your Body Knows Best: The Revolutionary Eating Plan that Helps You Achieve Your Optimal Weight and Energy Level for Life

Because we all burn fat differently, not any one diet will work for everybody. Gittleman (*Beyond Pritikin*) introduces the concept of genetic background, blood type, and metabolism to help determine an appropriate and workable diet regime

0-671-87592-2 POCKET $23.00

Stephen **George** & Jeff **Bredenberg**

Fight Fat: A Total Lifestyle Program for Men to Stay Slim and Healthy

The authors and the editors of *Men's Health* books present a healthful weight program specifically designed for men

0-87596-278-5 RODALE PB $14.95

Rosemary **Green**

Diary of a Fat Housewife: A True Story of Humor, Heartbreak, and Hope

A personal look at weight loss

0-446-51789-5 WARNER $21.95
0-446-60281-7 WARNER PB $5.99

Psychological Approaches

Denise **Austin**

JumpStart: The 21-Day Plan to Lose Weight, Get Fit, and Increase Your Energy and Enthusiasm for Life

An ESPN regular maintains that attitude is the only way to achieve positive results. This she guarantees in 21 days for those who follow her program

0-684-80220-1 SIMON & SCHUSTER $23.00

Thomas **Cash**

What Do You See When You Look In the Mirror?: Helping Yourself to a Positive Body Image

Cognitive-therapy approach to help readers understand the psychology of physical appearance and how it affects their lives

0-553-37450-8 BANTAM PB $11.95

Robert K. **Cooper** & Leslie L. **Cooper**

Low-Fat Living: Turn Off the Fat Makers, Turn On the Fat Burners for Longevity, Energy, Weight Loss, Freedom from Disease

Emphasizes skill in controlling food intake rather than will power. *Publishers Weekly* calls this "a cheerful, action-oriented program for lifestyle change"

0-87596-295-5 RODALE $27.95

Molly **Groger**

Eating Awareness Training: The Natural Way to Permanent Weight Loss

Not a diet book per se; the author maintains that by listening to the body one can control caloric intake. "Safe, sound, effective…and what's more, it could last a lifetime"—*McCall's*

0-671-55486-7 SUMMIT PB $9.00

Gabe **Mirkin**

Getting Thin: All About Fat—How You Lose It, How You Keep It Off for Good

0-316-57439-2 LITTLE, BROWN PB $12.95

Stephen **Gullo**

Thin Tastes Better: Control Your Food Triggers and Lose Weight Without Feeling Deprived

How to view weight control as positive rather than a grind

0-517-70006-9 RANDOM HOUSE $22.00
0-694-51639-2 HARPER AUDIO $18.00

Rachel **Heller** & Richard **Heller**

The Carbohydrate Addict's Program for Success

Workbook to help addicts overcome their insatiable desire for certain foods

0-452-26933-4 PLUME PB $12.00

Shad **Helmstetter** & Bob **Schwartz**

Self-Talk for Weight Loss: Lose Weight, Keep It Off, and Never Diet Again

Using self-talk technique for weight control instead of dieting

0-942540-10-7 BREAKTHRU $22.95

Jane **Hirschmann** & Carol **Munter**

Overcoming Overeating: Living Free in a World of Food

A program for ending the compulsive eater's addictive relationship to food

0-449-90407-5 FAWCETT PB $11.00

Steven **Lamm** & Gerald Secor **Couzens**

Thinner at Last: The New Medicine that Releases Your Brain's Power to Bring About Permanent Weight Loss

The ultimate psychological diet

0-684-81368-8 SIMON & SCHUSTER $23.00
0-684-83035-3 FIRESIDE PB $13.00

Richard **Podell** & William **Proctor**

The G-Index Diet

A diet designed to make you feel satisfied so as to avoid binging

0-446-36576-9 WARNER PB $5.99

Susan **Powter**

Food

The last word in motivational and informational books on food

0-671-89225-8 SIMON & SCHUSTER $24.00
0-671-56756-X POCKET PB $5.99

Stop the Insanity!

The national TV star tells how she emerged from her depression, or "fat coma", as she calls it, weighing 260 pounds, and how she devised a method to put her life—and body—in order. A step-by-step anecdotal guide for physical strength and mental fitness

0-671-52292-2 POCKET PB $6.99

Doreen **Virtue**

Constant Craving: What Your Food Cravings Mean and How to Overcome Them

An intriguing look at food cravings and personality

1-56170-124-6 HAY HOUSE PB $12.95

Judith **Rodin**

Body Traps: Breaking the Binds that Keep You from Feeling Good About Your Body

A straightforward and honest investigation of the traps and psychic distortions that befall people in pursuit of the beauty ideal, from Yale's Eating Disorders Clinic. "Dr. Rodin is one of the leading pioneers, researchers, and educators in understanding life-enhancing and self-destructive behaviors…Her writing resonates with both passion and an uncompromising investigative spirit"—Dean Ornish

0-688-12836-X QUILL PB $12.00

Geneen **Roth**

Appetites: On the Search for True Nourishment

"The gift of this book is its soul-baring honesty in touching our longing. Geneen grapples with the demons of appetite, and wins us over with her humanity, her laughter, and a wise, knowing heart"—Jack Kornfield

See also **PERSONAL AND PSYCHIC DEVELOPMENT** under **SPIRITUALITY** under **SPIRITUALITY** in **RELIGION, SPIRITUALITY, AND PHILOSOPHY**

0-525-94076-6 PENGUIN $20.95

Richard **Simmons**

Richard Simmons' Never Give Up: Inspirations, Reflections, Stories of Hope

Forty true stories of people who overcame obesity from the energetic and compassionate Simmons, told to inspire and encourage others who are intent on losing weight

0-446-60085-7 WARNER PB $5.99

Evelyn **Tribole** & Elyse **Resch**

Intuitive Eating: A Recovery Book for the Chronic Dieter

How to make peace with food and still maintain a healthy lifestyle

0-312-13097-X ST. MARTIN'S $21.95
0-312-95721-1 ST. MARTIN'S PB $6.99

Diet Plans

Louis J. **Aronne** & Fred **Graver**

Weigh Less, Live Longer

The head of the Weight Control Center at New York Hospital dispenses what he's learned as well as menus and recipes for weight maintenance

0-471-58112-7 WILEY $22.95

Covert **Bailey**

Smart Eating: Choosing Wisely, Living Lean

From the author of *Fit or Fat*, a program designed to create a "smart eating food target" to incorporate the theories he expounds: low fat and sugar, high fiber, and variety; includes recipes

0-395-75283-3 DORLING KINDERSLEY $19.95

Thomas J. **Bassler** & Robert **Burger**

The Whole Life Diet

Program for a lifestyle of nutrition and exercise

0-87131-305-7 EVANS $9.95

Robert **Atkins**

Dr. Atkins' Diet Revolution

A high-protein diet

0-553-27157-1 BDD PB $6.50

Dr. Atkins' *New* Diet Revolution

The bestselling diet plan updated 20 years later

0-87131-763-X EVANS PB $12.95

Robert **Atkins** & Fran **Gare**

Dr. Atkins' *New* Diet Cookbook

Besides 200 recipes, a carbo counter, menu plans, and guide to nutritional supplementation, includes a medical update on the Atkins diet

0-87131-794-X EVANS PB $12.95

Stuart **Berger**

Dr. Berger's Immune Power Diet

A diet aimed at improving the immune system

0-451-14111-3 NEW AMERICAN LIBRARY PB $5.99

Janet M. **Chiavetta**

Eat, Drink and Be Healthy: A Guide to Healthful Eating and Weight Control

"Healthy indulgences is what this book gives you. Perfect!"—Lynn Fischer, host *Low Cholesterol Gourmet*

1-55591-199-4 FULCRUM PB $18.95

Craig **Claiborne** & Pierre **Franey**

Craig Claiborne's Gourmet Diet

Delicious, innovative, low-sodium, modified-fat, modified-cholesterol recipes from the *New York Times* chef

0-345-33635-6 BALLANTINE PB $5.99

Jenny **Craig** & Brenda **Wolfe**

Jenny Craig's What Have You Got to Lose?

Recipes and inspiration from the popular weight-loss queen

1-55958-301-0 PRIMA PB $14.00

Harvey **Diamond** & Marilyn **Diamond**

Fit for Life

A highly controversial natural body cycle, permanent weight-loss plan whose cardinal rule is only fruit before noon

0-446-30015-2 WARNER PB $6.99

Anne M. **Fletcher**

Thin for Life: 10 Keys to Success from People Who Have Lost Weight and Kept It Off

"*Thin for Life* can lead you down the path of sensible weight control"—Jane Brody

1-88152-730-1 CHAPTERS $24.95

Martin **Katahn**

The Rotation Diet: Lose a Pound a Day and Never Gain It Back

More than 100 recipes designed for this 21-day diet plan

0-553-27667-0 BDD PB $6.50

Karen **Kreps** & Richard **Smith**

The 60-Day Diet Diary

A cheerful diet account

0-440-57946-5 DELL PB $5.95

Lawrence **Le Shan**

Meditating to Attain a Healthy Body Weight

Mind/body work for weight control

0-553-37372-2 DOUBLEDAY PB $9.95

John A. **McDougall** & Mary **McDougall**

The McDougall Program for Maximum Weight Loss

Features more than 100 recipes as well as sound advice for all manner of weight problems. "Lifesaving information"—Dean Ornish

0-452-27380-3 PLUME PB $11.95

Peter **Miller**

The Hilton Head Metabolism Diet

In a nutshell: "Fat people do not eat more than slim people. Fat people just do not burn fat as well as slim people"—Dr. Peter Miller

0-446-34528-8 WARNER PB $5.99

Joyce **Nash**

Maximize Your Body Potential: 16 Weeks to a Lifetime of Effective Weight Management

0-915950-69-3 BULL PB $18.95

Jean **Nidetch**

Weight Watchers Fast and Fabulous Cookbook

0-452-26473-1 NEW AMERICAN LIBRARY PB ..$12.00

Nathan **Pritikin** & Patrick **McGrady**

The Pritikin Program for Diet and Exercise

The best selling weightlessness and longevity plan

0-553-27192-X BDD PB $5.95

Barry **Sears** & Bill **Lawren**

The Zone

A biochemist recommends a diet based on individual metabolism to reduce cholesterol and to aid in weight control

0-06-039150-2 HARPERCOLLINS $24.00
0-06-101000-6 HARPERCOLLINS PB $5.99

Art **Ulene**

Take It Off! Keep It Off!

Based on the premise that obesity is a chronic disease and not simply a person's lack of willpower, this 28-day plan is a start for a permanent weight-control program

1-56975-025-4 ULYSSES PB $9.95

Roy **Walford**

The 120-Year Diet: How to Double Your Vital Years

Longevity through high-nutrient, low-caloric eating

0-671-74474-7 POCKET PB $5.95

Eric **Witt** & Carol **Wirth**

Bodystat: How to Reset Your Fat Thermostat Permanently

Dispels weight-loss myths, encourages low-fat diets, and explains the importance of setting a goal for body weight

0-670-85955-9 VIKING $22.95

Vegetarianism and Natural Foods

Gabriel **Cousens**
Conscious Eating
Explains how what we eat affects our physical, as well as our mental, emotional, and spiritual health
0-9644584-0-3 ATRIUM PB $19.95

Ellen **Klavan**
The Vegetarian Fact Finder: Ages 6 to 16
More and more parents are hearing from their children a desire to be a vegetarian. This comprehensive reference discusses the who, what, why, and how of vegetarianism
ILLUSTRATED BY ADRIENNE HARTMAN
0-9641262-1-4 LITTLE BOOK ROOM $19.95

Paulette **Mitchell**
The New American Vegetarian Menu Cookbook: From Everyday Dining to Elegant Entertaining
Imaginative ideas
0-87857-501-4 RODALE....................$17.95

Gary **Null**
The Vegetarian Handbook: Eating Right for Total Health
A convincing and gentle argument to eat no meat
0-312-03948-4 ST. MARTIN'S PB....................$10.95

Laurel **Robertson**
The New Laurel's Kitchen
A new age classic: cookbook and guide
See also **VEGETARIAN** under **SPECIAL DIETS** under **FOOD** in **FOOD, TRAVEL, AND LEISURE**
0-89815-166-X TEN SPEED PB $29.95

Anthony **Sattilaro** & Tom **Monte**
Living Well Naturally
Grains and vegetable diet from a doctor who recovered from cancer
0-395-39389-2 HOUGHTON MIFFLIN PB $10.95

Lisa **Tracy**
The Gradual Vegetarian
0-440-53124-1 DELL PB....................$12.95

Vitamins and Dietary Supplements

Ruth **Adams**
The Big Family Guide to All the Vitamins
In its 18th printing
0-87983-583-4 KEATS PB....................$17.95

Johanna **Budwig**
Flax Oil as a True Aid
This formerly hard-to-find book is now readily available
0-9695272-1-7 APPLE PB....................$5.95

James **Balach** & Phyllis A. **Balach**
Prescription for Nutritional Healing
A practical reference to drug-free remedies using herbs, vitamins, minerals, and food supplements. A comprehensive self-help guide for just about every ailment and disease
0-89529-429-X AVERY PB....................$16.95

Emanuel **Cheraskin**
The Vitamin C Controversy: Questions and Answers
More than 50 questions are answered by one of the leaders in vitamin C research
0-942333-01-2 BIO COMMUNICATIONS PB.....$12.95

Kenneth **Cooper**
Dr. Kenneth H. Cooper's Antioxidant & Revolution
Discusses free radicals and their destructive nature; daily doses of antioxidant vitamins and food; low-intensity exercise; and generally how living an antioxidant way can delay the signs of aging and reduce risk of cancer and heart disease
0-7852-8313-7 NELSON....................$22.99

Mary Dan **Eades**
The Doctor's Complete Guide to Vitamins and Minerals
Lists and discusses vitamins as well as what's appropriate for various ailments
0-440-21502-1 DELL PB....................$5.99

H. Winter **Griffith**
Complete Guide to Vitamins, Minerals, and Supplements
1-55561-006-4 FISHER PB $14.95

Patricia **Hausman**
The Right Dose: How to Take Vitamins and Minerals Safely
0-345-35877-5 BALLANTINE PB....................$5.95

Joseph **Levy**
Vitamins: Their Use and Abuse
0-87140-616-0 NORTON....................$8.95

Shari **Lieberman** & Nancy **Bruning**
The Real Vitamin and Mineral Book
A complete and up-to-date source that provides the ODA (Optimum Daily Allowance) well above the government's minimal RDA
0-89529-449-4 AVERY PB....................$9.95

Earl **Mindell**
Earl Mindell's Vitamin Bible
Revised and expanded edition by the vitamin guru
0-446-36184-4 WARNER PB....................$6.50

Shaping Up with Vitamins
Supplements for athletes as well as vitamins to alleviate a multitude of common (and not so common) ailments
0-446-30952-4 WARNER PB....................$5.99

Patrick **Quillin**
Healing Nutrients
0-679-72187-8 VINTAGE PB....................$13.00

Jack **Ritchason**
The Vitamin and Health Encyclopedia: The Handbook of Vitamins for Your Healthy Life
From every angle, this discussion by a naturopathic physician is an excellent source for prevention and relieving symptoms
0-913923-92-3 WOODLAND PB....................$7.95

Ronald F. **Schmid**
Native Nutrition
Eating according to ancestral wisdom
0-89281-482-9 HEARD PB....................$14.95

Harold **Silverman** & others
The Vitamin Book: A No-Nonsense Consumer Guide
Includes daily requirements, dosages, toxicity, and uses for over 35 vitamins
0-553-27435-X BDD PB....................$5.99

Elizabeth **Somer** & **Health Media of America**
The Essential Guide to Vitamins and Minerals
The compact edition includes a unique section on how alcohol, cigarettes, and medications affect vitamin status
0-06-273045-2 HARPERPERENNIAL PB $15.00

Carlson **Wade**
Bee Pollen and Your Health
Besides treating allergies and digestion, pollen may also be used in beauty aids
0-87983-184-7 KEATS PB....................$4.50

Hasnain **Walji**
Vitamin Guide: Essential Nutrients for Healthy Living
An overall look at our need for vitamins for health and well-being
1-85230-375-1 ELEMENT PB....................$9.95

Reference Books and Nutrient Counters

Jean **Anderson** & Barbara **Deskins**
The Nutrition Bible
Publishers Weekly calls this a "comprehensive work [which] has something to offer both the serious researcher and the casual browser." Food writer and nutritionist present just about everything to do with food
0-688-11619-1 MORROW $30.00

Robert **Crayhon**
Robert Crayhon's Nutrition Made Simple: A Comprehensive Guide to the Latest Findings in Optimal Nutrition
A one-volume, readable, information-packed resource from the radio personality and nutritionist
0-87131-767-2 EVANS $19.95

Jean **Carper**

The All-in-One Calorie Counter

Calorie counts for 8,800 food items including junk, health, and restaurant food

0-553-26326-9 BDD PB $4.95

Jean Carper's Total Nutrition Guide: The Complete Official Report on Healthful Eating

0-553-34350-5 BANTAM PB $14.95

Ronald **Deutsch** & Judi **Morrill**

Realities of Nutrition: Completely Revised

The basics of the science of nutrition explained lucidly and with illustrations. "...belongs next to Dr. Spock and the dictionary on your bookshelf"—*The Detroit Free Press*

0-923521-25-9 BULL PB..$24.95

Susan **Finn** & Linda Stern **Kass**

The Real Life Nutrition Book: Making the Right Food Choices Without Changing Your Life-Style

A nutritionist addresses today's busy lifestyle with tips on how to plan and prepare healthful meals

0-14-013174-4 PENGUIN PB..$15.00

Elson **Haas**

Staying Healthy with Nutrition: The Complete Guide to Diet & Nutritional Medicine

The mother of all nutrition encyclopedias

0-89087-481-6 CELESTIAL ARTS PB..$34.95

John **Kirschmann** & Lavon **Dunne**

Nutrition Almanac

Guide to how nutrients work, sources of calories, food composition, diet, and health

0-07-034912-6 MCGRAW HILL PB..$15.95

Barbara **Kraus**

Calories and Carbohydrates

A dictionary listing of over 8,000 brand names and basic foods with their caloric and carbohydrate counts

0-452-26936-9 PENGUIN PB..$12.95

0-451-17532-8 SIGNET PB..$5.99

Annette **Natow** & Jo-Ann **Heslin**

The Cholesterol Counter, Third Edition

This handy guide keeps track of the cholesterol in 10,000 entries including name brands, chain restaurants, and "take-out"

0-671-75173-5 POCKET PB..$5.99

Corinne T. **Netzer**

The Corinne Netzer Encyclopedia of Food Values

Calories, protein, carbohydrates, total fat, saturated fat, cholesterol, sodium, and fiber are broken down in 40,000 listings in this unique and complete resource; vitamins and minerals are also included

0-440-50367-1 DELL..$26.95

Paul **Saltman**

The University of California San Diego Nutrition Book

0-316-76981-9 LITTLE, BROWN PB..$13.95

Elizabeth **Somer**

Food & Mood: The Complete Guide to Eating Well & Feeling Your Best

Glossary, tables, quizzes, and menus complete this information-packed book on nutrition, eating disorders, diet, and supplements to lessen fatigue and elevate mood

0-8050-3125-1 HOLT..$25.00

Louise **Tenney**

Louise Tenney's Nutritional Guide with Food Combining

Explains proper food combining for maximum nutrition and to avoid digestive difficulties

0-913923-90-7 WOODLAND PB..$14.95

Art **Ulene**

The Nutribase Guide to Carbohydrates, Calories & Fat in Your Food

Fat and carbohydrates in over 30,000 foods given in grams as well as a total calorie count

0-89529-632-2 AVERY PB..$5.95

The Nutribase Nutrition Facts Desk Reference

Over 40,000 food product listings categorized by calories, fats, salt, etc., as well as a breakdown of fast food and restaurant meals

0-89529-623-3 AVERY PB..$17.95

Leah **Wallach**

Food Values: Cholesterol and Fats

These books contain values for more than 8,000 foods, including brand-name products, fast foods, prepared foods, fresh foods, health foods, and beverages

0-06-273125-4 HARPERCOLLINS PB..$6.50

Fitness

Aerobics and General Fitness

Judy **Alter**

Stretch & Strengthen

Illustrates 100 exercises that provide a unique balance of stretching and strengthening every part of the body for the sedentary beginner to professional athlete

0-395-36263-6 HOUGHTON MIFFLIN..$17.95

American College of Sports Medicine

ACSM Fitness Book

Full-color photos and diagrams to inspire a lifetime commitment to fitness

0-88011-460-6 LEISURE PB..$13.95

Karen **Andes**

A Woman's Book of Strength: An Empowering Guide to Total Mind/Body Fitness

A spiritual guide to fitness

0-399-51899-1 PERIGEE PB..$12.00

Bob **Anderson**

Stretching for Everybody

If you can't exercise, at least stretch

0-394-73874-8 SHELTER PB..$13.00

Covert **Bailey**

Smart Exercise: Burning Fat, Getting Fit

PBS TV star dispels myths, dispenses advice and useful information on how our bodies function, and gives tips on exercise and weight training

0-395-47043-9 HOUGHTON MIFFLIN..$19.95

0-395-66114-5 DORLING KINDERSLEY PB..$9.95

Bicycling Magazine

Training for Fitness and Endurance

Concise and compact guide to stretching, nutrition, and workouts

0-87857-899-4 RODALE PB..$8.95

Kurt **Brungardt**

The Complete Book of Abs

Over 100 exercises for the belly as well as diet and workout regimes

0-679-74435-5 VILLARD PB..$20.00

The Complete Book of Butt and Legs

Over 100 butt, thigh, and leg exercises with machines and in water; anatomy and nutrition discussed

0-679-75481-4 VILLARD PB..$20.00

Brian **Chichester** & others

Powerfully Fit: Dozens of Ways to Boost Strength, Increase Endurance, and Chisel Your Body

Hundreds of illustrated exercises that also share the secrets of top athletes

0-87596-279-3 RODALE PB..$14.95

Kenneth **Cooper**

The Aerobics Program for Total Well-Being

The man who started America running now brings you the ultimate fitness program

0-553-34677-6 BANTAM PB..$16.95

Bob **Delmonteque**

Lifelong Fitness: How to Look Great at Any Age

Information on dramatically delaying the effects of aging. Covers topics such as endurance, maintaining strength, nutrition for longevity, and coping with injuries

0-446-39488-2 WARNER PB..$14.99

Corinna **Everson**

Cory Everson's Work Out

Six-time Ms. Olympia shows how it's done

0-399-51684-0 PERIGEE PB $15.95

Corinna **Everson** & Carole **Jacobs**

Cory Everson's Fat-Free & Fit: A Complete Program for Fitness, Exercise, and Healthy Living

Weight lifting, aerobics, low-fat meal plans

0-399-51858-4 PERIGEE PB $15.00

Robert **Haas**

Eat to Win: The Sports Nutrition Bible

From a sports nutritionist: high-carbohydrate, low-cholesterol eating for a moderate-to-active sports life

See also **SPORTS NUTRITION**

0-451-15509-2 SIGNET PB $5.99

Philip **Maffetone** & Matthew **Mantel**

The High Performance Heart: An Updated Edition

How to incorporate the heart monitor in your workout for either general fitness or competition

0-933201-64-8 BICYCLE MAGAZINE PB $10.95

Dan **Millman**

The Inner Athlete: Mind, Body, and Spirit

"An innovative approach to fitness that applies Eastern philosophies to the Western concepts of physical well-being"—*Publishers Weekly*

0-913299-97-9 STILLPOINT PB $12.95

Sport Stretch

With illustrations, 26 specific sports listed including the 12 best stretches for each

0-88011-381-2 LEISURE PB $15.95

Milton **Trager** & Cathy **Hammond**

Movement as a Way to Agelessness: A Guide to Trager Mentastics

Mentastics or "mental gymnastics", by the man who created the benign use of body and movement

0-88268-167-2 STATION HILL PB $15.95

John **Yacenda**

Fitness Cross Training

Full-color photos and tips on training for running, cycling, swimming, walking, aerobics, and weight training

0-87322-770-0 HUMAN KINETICS PB $14.95

David **Zemach-Bersin** & others

Relaxercise: The Easy New Way to Health & Fitness

Feldenkrais teacher-trainers illustrate simple ways to relax and relieve stress

See also **STRESS**

0-06-250992-6 HARPERCOLLINS PB $22.00

Bicycling

Bicycling Magazine

Cycling for Women

From nutrition to bike maintenance

0-87857-811-0 RODALE PB $8.95

Nutrition for Cyclists

Discussion of carbos and liquid energy food from those who know

0-87857-935-4 RODALE PB $6.95

Chris **Carmichael** & Edmund **Burke**

Fitness Cycling

Full-color pictures and easy-to-difficult workouts

0-87322-460-4 HUMAN KINETICS PB $14.95

Greg **LeMond** & Kent **Gordis**

Greg Lemond's Complete Book of Bicycling

One of the best cycling books by the American winner of the 1986 Tour de France

See also **CYCLING** under **RECREATIONAL AND OTHER SPORTS** under **SPORTS** in **FOOD, TRAVEL, AND LEISURE**

0-399-51594-1 PERIGEE PB $14.00

Peter **Nye**

Heart of Lions: The History of American Bicycle Racing

Stories of the good old days when American cyclists were equals to Jack Dempsey and Ty Cobb

See also **CYCLING** under **RECREATIONAL AND OTHER SPORTS** under **SPORTS** in **FOOD, TRAVEL, AND LEISURE**

FOREWORD BY ERIC HEIDEN

0-393-30576-7 NORTON PB $14.00

David Brunn **Perry**

Bike Cult: The Ultimate Guide to Human-Powered Vehicles

From the editor of Transportation Alternative's *City Cyclist* and US Cycling Team racer, this is the most comprehensive book available on HPVs, from bicycles to rollerblades, Leonardo to Schwinn

1-56858-027-4 FOUR WALLS PB $23.95

John **Schubert**

Richard's Cycling for Fitness

From road etiquette to race training; also includes how to buy a bike

0-345-34117-1 BALLANTINE PB $11.00

Oprah **Winfrey** & Bob **Green**

Make the Connection: Ten Steps to a Better Body—and a Better Life

Oprah's own exercise and fitness program includes tips on looking and feeling better, from making the commitment to nutrition to how to work out. Generously illustrated with color photographs

0-7868-6256-4 HYPERION PB $18.95

Bodybuilding and Weight Training

Ellington **Darden**

The Nautilus Book

0-8092-4074-2 CONTEMPORARY PB $12.95

Corinna **Everson** & Jeff **Everson**

Superflex: Ms. Olympia's Guide to Building a Strong and Sexy Body

Simple exercises for the beginner, using weights to sculpt the butt, breasts, back, thighs, and legs

0-8092-4865-4 CONTEMPORARY PB $13.95

Peter **Grymkowski** & others

The Gold's Gym Training Encyclopedia

More than 300 exercises using either free weights or machines. Clearly described and illustrated, body part by body part

0-8092-5446-8 CONTEMPORARY PB $14.95

Frederick **Hatfield**

Hardcore Bodybuilding: A Scientific Approach

For bodybuilding pros or those who seriously strength train for other sports

0-8092-3728-8 CONTEMPORARY PB $18.95

Toni **Kiana**

Kiana's Body Sculpting

Cheesecake pictures illustrate chapters divided into problem body areas: Flabby Triceps, Jiggly Thighs. Lots of recipes

0-312-11570-9 ST. MARTIN'S PB $13.95

William J. **Kraemer** & Steven **Fleck**

Strength Training for Young Adults

Over 100 strength-training exercises especially for kids 7 to 18

0-87322-396-9 HUMAN KINETICS PB $17.95

Tom **Kubistant**

Mind Pump: The Psychology of Bodybuilding

A systematic mental training approach for bodybuilders

0-88011-296-4 LEISURE PB $15.95

Charles T. **Kuntzleman**

Home Gym Fitness: Free Weight Workouts

Basic and clearly written for those who prefer to work out in the privacy of the home

0-8092-5273-2 CONTEMPORARY PB $9.95

Anja **Langer** & Bill **Reynolds**

Body Flex—Body Magic

A bodybuilding champ shares her secrets; there's a special section on training during pregancy

0-8092-3930-2 CONTEMPORARY PB $15.95

Christopher **Norris**

Weight Training: Principles & Practice

Explains proper use of weights and machines; an ideal companion for the gym

0-7136-3771-4 A&C BLACK PB $20.95

Gladys **Portugues** & Joyce **Vedral**

Hard Bodies

Women's weight training workout fully illustrated to exhibit correct positions with free weights and machines

0-440-53424-0 DELL PB $15.95

Hard Bodies Express Workout

For those in a hurry and interested in body sculpting through weights

0-440-53426-7 DELL PB $14.95

Bill **Reynolds**

Weight Training for Beginners

Principles of weight-training explained with lots of pictures of correct lifting, by the former editor of *Flex* magazine

0-8092-5728-9 CONTEMPORARY PB $8.95

Beth **Rothenberg** & Oscar **Rothenberg**

Touch Training for Strength

Describes Systematic T.O.U.C.H. Training, a unique program to stay focused on the correct development of muscles

0-87322-437-X HUMAN KINETICS PB $13.95

Arnold **Schwarzenegger** & Bill **Dobbins**

Arnold Schwarzenegger's Encyclopedia of Modern Bodybuilding

Complete information on training principles, competition strategy, and nutrition

0-671-63381-3 FIRESIDE PB $22.00

Joyce L. **Vedral**

Bottoms Up!

An easy and perky exercise program from a prolific fitness writer who concentrates on the female body's strengths and problems

0-446-39421-1 WARNER PB $12.99

Definition: Shape Without Bulk in 15 Minutes a Day!

The latest in strength training for women from Vedral; fully illustrated

0-446-67069-3 WARNER PB $14.99

Nick **Whitehead**

Learn Weight Training in a Weekend

Four-color illustrations of muscle groups clearly explain what's happening during each exercise. An excellent beginner's guide

0-679-40953-X KNOPF $16.00

Martial Arts

The martial arts are ancient systems of self-defense devised in China by monks and peasants as a means of protection against bandits and soldiers. Handed down from generation to generation, these slowly evolving disciplines are taught throughout the world and help the practitioner develop confidence, discipline, and strength. Though it's difficult (if not impossible) to become proficient from reading a book, we've included some of the best how-to guides to show the reader the particulars of the most common martial arts (karate, judo, t'ai chi, aikido), as well as to help students refine techniques with which they may already be familiar. Also, you'll find some inspirational biographies of the great masters and interesting accounts by Westerners who traveled east to learn the ways of the warrior.

Black Belt Magazine

The Legendary Bruce Lee

Explores Lee's spartan training regime, the principles of *jeet kune do,* as well as the reality behind the man

0-89750-106-3 OHARA PB $10.95

David **Chow** & Richard **Spangler**

Kung Fu: History, Philosophy and Technique

Black-and-white photos illustrate 23 lessons as well as the masters of Kung Fu and philosophers briefly explained

0-86568-011-6 UNIQUE PB $14.95

Taisen **Deshimaru**

The Zen Way to the Martial Arts

A Japanese master reveals the secrets of the samurai that provide wisdom to students of the martial arts or to any reader interested in Zen

0-14-019344-8 DUTTON PB $11.95

Donn **Draeger** & Robert **Smith**

Comprehensive Asian Fighting Arts

An illustrated encyclopedia of martial arts, covering most of the major schools, their historical and mythical backgrounds, and commonly used terms. It is the most useful and complete reference of its kind

0-87011-436-0 KODANSHA PB $22.00

Judith **Fein**

How to Fight Back and Win: The Joy of Self-Defense

The 20 lessons are presented as if the reader is in class. Offers fighting-skill technique, assault prevention, and personal safety

0-929523-28-8 TORRANCE PB $16.95

0-929523-30-X TORRANCE PUBLISHING PB $6.95

Gichin **Funakoshi**

Karate-Do: My Way of Life

In this brief, simple autobiography, Funakoshi, known in Japan as "the father of modern karate" tells of his lifetime of studying, practicing, and teaching. He describes the austere beauty romanticizing the skills he developed

0-87011-463-8 KODANSHA PB $8.00

E.J. **Harrison**

The Fighting Spirit of Japan

An in-depth study of judo, karate, aikido, and jujitsu, written by an English journalist who spent 20 years in Japan

0-87951-154-0 OVERLOOK PB $10.95

Eugen **Herrigel**

Zen in the Art of Archery

This remarkable book discusses how the practice of archery helps toward an understanding of Zen. Eugen Herrigel spent a five-year apprenticeship in Japanese archery that resulted in his deep understanding of Zen and this wonderful book, written long before martial arts became a fad. Although not specially about martial arts, it captures the philosophy of training that distinguishes Asian martial arts from Western fencing or boxing

0-679-72297-1 VINTAGE PB $10.00

0-394-71663-9 VINTAGE PB $4.95

Joe **Hyams**

Zen in the Martial Arts

The author recounts his more than 25 years of experience in the martial arts under such masters as Ed Parker and Bruce Lee, and reveals how the application of Zen principles develops physical expertise and mental discipline

0-553-27559-3 BDD PB $5.50

Isao **Inokuma** & Nobuyuki **Sato**

Best Judo

Joint effort by two of Japan's foremost judo instructors

0-87011-786-6 KODANSHA PB $26.00

Herman **Kauz**

Tai Chi Handbook: Exercise, Meditation and Self-Defense

0-385-09370-5 DOUBLEDAY PB $14.95

Bruce **Klickstein**

Living Aikido

0-938190-85-7 NORTH ATLANTIC PB $16.95

T. T. **Liang**

T'ai Chi Ch'uan for Health and Self-Defense: Philosophy and Practice

For those who have already mastered the basic postures

0-394-72461-5 RANDOM HOUSE PB $9.00

Yagyu **Munenori**

The Sword and the Mind

A translation of the classic treatise on swordsmanship

TRANSLATED BY HIROAKI SATO

0-87951-256-3 OVERLOOK PB $11.95

Miyamoto **Musashi**

A Book of Five Rings

Attributed to a legendary swordsman

0-553-27096-6 BDD PB $5.99

0-87773-998-6 SHAMBHALA PB $6.00

Mark **Salzman**

Iron and Silk

The Chinese adventures of a young martial arts master "produce the gulp of feeling you might get from an unusually fine short story"
—*NY Times*

See also CHINA

0-394-75511-1 VINTAGE PB $11.00

Mitsugi **Saotome**

The Principles of Aikido

Over 1,000 black-and-white photos illustrate basic techniques. Includes lectures by the founder, Morihei Saotome

0-87773-409-7 SHAMBHALA PB $25.00

Robert C. **Sohn**

Tao and T'ai Chi Kung

How the practice and philosophy of T'ai Chi are integrated for achieving meditative calm and how it helps certain ailments

0-89281-217-6 INNER TRADITIONS PB $14.95

Bill **Sosa** & Bryan **Robbins**

The Essence of Aikido

Guide to one of the youngest of the martial arts

0-86568-097-3 UNIQUE PB $10.95

John **Stevens**

Abundant Peace: The Biography of Morihei Ueshiba, Founder of Aikido

Considered by many to be the greatest martial artist of the 20th century

0-87773-350-3 SHAMBHALA PB $20.00

John **Stone** & Ron **Meyer**

Aikido in America

These 14 interviews with American martial artists describe Aikido's evolution to its American version, yet essentially keeping its Japanese essence

1-88331-927-7 NORTH ATLANTIC PB $16.95

Carol **Wiley**

Women in the Martial Arts

Twenty-three essays by women whose lives have been changed through the discipline of martial arts

1-55643-136-8 NORTH ATLANTIC PB $12.95

Running

The books on this list explain how many miles to run and how fast, which shoes to wear, and what to eat—in short, everything the runner needs to reach his or her potential. Also included are books on how to prepare for races, from a 10K to a marathon. Others deal with the psychological and philosophical side of the sport, while the rest are yarns to motivate the mind when the body says no.

Richard **Benyo**

Making the Marathon Your Event

A serious approach to the ultimate running challenge

0-679-73930-0 RANDOM HOUSE PB $13.00

Tom **Derderian**

Boston Marathon: The History of the World's Premier Running Event

Marathon race freaks relive the drama from 1897 to present

FOREWORDS BY JOAN BENOIT SAMUELSON AND BILL RODGERS

0-87322-491-4 HUMAN KINETICS PB $21.95

Richard L. **Brown** & Joe **Henderson**

Fitness Running

For those who need a running program spelled out

0-87322-451-5 HUMAN KINETICS PB $14.95

Jean **Couch**

The Runner's Yoga Book: A Balanced Approach to Fitness

Over 400 photographs and illustations of yoga stretches to help prevent sports injuries and to improve athletic agility. Easy to do

0-9627138-1-3 RODMELL PR PB $18.95

Bill **Dellinger** & Bill **Freeman**

The Competitive Runner's Training Book: Techniques and Strategies to Prepare Any Runner for Any Race

Legendary running coach shares the secrets of his "Oregon System" for competing

0-02-028340-7 MACMILLAN PB $7.95

George **Dintiman** & Robert **Ward**

Sport Speed: The #1 Speed Improvement Program For Athletes

0-88011-325-1 LEISURE PB $15.95

Joe **Ellis** & Joe **Henderson**

Running Injury Free: How to Prevent, Treat and Recover from Dozens of Painful Problems

If you run more than 15 miles per week and wish to increase mileage or speed

0-87596-221-1 RODALE PB $14.95

James **Fixx**

The Complete Book of Running

A virtual encyclopedia that covers every aspect of the sport

0-394-41159-5 RANDOM HOUSE $24.00

Jeff **Galloway**

Galloway's Book on Running

"If there were a literary Olympics, Galloway's book would take gold in the distance events"
—Sports Fitness

0-394-72709-6 SHELTER PB $13.00

Bob **Glover** & Pete **Schuder**

The New Competitive Runners Handbook

A complete program, with strategies for the 10K and marathon

0-14-046837-4 PENGUIN PB $15.95

Bob **Glover** & Jack **Shepherd**

The Runner's Handbook: The Classic Fitness Guide for Beginning and Intermediate Runners

For those planning to take up running. From proper stretching to shoes, it covers every facet

0-14-046713-0 PENGUIN PB $12.95

Hal **Higdon**

Boston: A Century of Running

With over 200 photos "Higdon [*Run Fast*] has put together an absorbing history"
—Publishers Weekly

0-87596-283-1 RODALE $40.00

Allan **Lawrence** & Mark **Scheid**

Running and Racing After 35

For the mature runner, provides schedules to bring a runner up to competition level; chapters on the psychology of running; Q & A

0-316-51675-9 LITTLE, BROWN PB $13.95

Fred **Lebow** & Gloria **Auerbuch**

The NY Road Runner's Club Complete Book of Running: Updated Edition

"It's the last word on running"
—Detroit Free Press

0-679-74861-X RANDOM HOUSE PB $16.00

Barry **Lewis**

Running the TransAmerica Footrace

The event and behind-the-scenes doings

FOREWORD BY TED CORBITT

0-8117-2582-0 STACKPOLE PB $14.95

Eric **Newsholme** & others

Keep on Running: The Science of Training and Performance

Complete compendium for the serious runner emphasizing biochemistry, nutrition, physiology, and psychology

0-471-94314-2 WILEY PB $17.95

Tim **Noakes**

Lore of Running: Discover the Science and Spirit of Running

Physician and research scientist in exercise physiology presents personal experience and professional expertise

0-88011-438-X HUMAN KINETICS PB $22.95

Mark **Will-Weber**

The Quotable Runner: Great Moments of Wisdom, Inspiration, Wrongheadedness, and Humor

A comprehensive collection of quotes on running from such commentators as Chairman Mao, Winston Churchill, Bill Clinton, and hundreds of others. Sections of the book include Pain, Records, Women and Running, Coaches, Eating, Training, Winning, Losing, and Hills—among other subjects

See also **RUNNING** under **SPORTS** in **FOOD, TRAVEL, AND LEISURE**

1-55821-420-8 LYONS & BURFORD $20.00

Gary **Null** & Howard **Robbins**

How to Keep Your Feet and Legs Healthy for a Lifetime

A special section for walkers, runners, and joggers

See also **FEET AND KNEES** under **SPECIFIC HEALTH PROBLEMS** under **HEALTH**

1-88836-330-4 SEVEN STORIES PB $14.95

Walking

Included here are several fine books on sportwalking that tell you how fast, how far, and how long you need to go to get the most out of your mile.

American Heart Association
The Healthy Heart Walking Book: A Complete Program for a Lifetime of Fitness
Assesses fitness level, designs programs, and supplies a personal diary
0-02-860447-4 MACMILLAN PB........................$14.95

Mark **Fenton** & Seth **Bauer**
The 90-Day Fitness Walking Program
From the editors of *Walking Magazine*, perfect for the first-time exerciser
0-399-51898-3 PERIGEE PB...............................$10.00

Therese **Iknoian**
Fitness Walking
Four-color photos and workout plans to motive any couch potato
0-87322-553-8 HUMAN KINETICS PB.................$14.95

Anne **Kashiwa** & James **Rippe**
Fitness Walking for Women
Advice from a walking-clinic instructor
0-399-51407-4 PERIGEE PB...............................$11.00

Suzanne **Levine**
Walk It Off!
Formerly overweight podiatrist shares her secrets for permanent weight loss
0-452-26535-5 PLUME PB $10.95

Casey **Myers**
Walking: A Complete Guide to the Complete Exercise
Discusses the four paces of walking: stroll, brisk walk, aerobic walk, and race walking
0-679-73777-4 RANDOM HOUSE PB................$12.00

Ruth **Rudner**
Walking
"Solid, thorough, and accurate—a compendium of essential information about America's most popular, most accessible, and most rewarding fitness activity"—Seth Bauer, editor, *Walking Magazine*
0-87322-668-2 HUMAN KINETICS PB $13.95

Les **Snowdon** & Maggie **Humphries**
The Walking Diet: Walk Back to Fitness in 30 Days
For all fitness levels and ages; combines a walking program with a low-fat, high-fiber diet plan
0-87951-596-1 OVERLOOK PB $11.95

Gary **Yanker**
Walkshaping: Indoors or Outdoors, Six Weeks to a Better Body
Walk-clinic specialist developed this benign form of body shaping
0-688-13813-6 HEARST $20.00

Gary **Yanker** & Kathy **Burton**
Walking Medicine: The Lifetime Guide to Preventive & Therapeutic Exercisewalking Programs
The complete "bible of walking" from the foremost authority
0-07-072265-X MCGRAW HILL PB $16.95

Mark **Bricklin** & Maggie **Spilner**
Prevention's Practical Encyclopedia of Walking for Health: From Age Reversal to Weight Loss, the Most Complete Guide Ever Written
Discusses all manner of ailments and topics from aging to zoo walking
0-87596-165-7 RODALE PB.................................$13.95

Swimming

Marianne **Brems**
The Fit Swimmer: 120 Workout and Training Tips
Stop counting laps and learn how to create your own fitness program
0-8092-5454-9 CONTEMPORARY PB.................$11.95

Cecil M. **Colwin**
Swimming: Into the 21st Century
"The book is a must for coaches but will also be of interest to swimmers who want to be inspired while being instructed at the same time"
—*Swim Canada*
See also **SWIMMING** under **WATER SPORTS** under **SPORTS** in **FOOD, TRAVEL, AND LEISURE**
0-87322-456-6 HUMAN KINETICS PB.................$19.95

MaryBeth Pappas **Gaines**
Fantastic Water Workouts: Low Impact Water Exercises for Health and Fitness
Drawings illustrate 90 fun and effective workout exercises
0-87322-458-2 HUMAN KINETICS PB..............$14.95

Dick **Hannula**
Coaching Swimming Successfully
"Organized and succinct, this book will benefit all coaches who read and study it"—Peter Daland, President, American Swim Coaches Association
0-87322-492-2 HUMAN KINETICS PB..............$18.95

John **Jerome**
Staying with It: On Becoming an Athlete
A personal account of Jerome's quest, starting with laps in a pool and culminating in competitive success
0-670-66876-1 VIKING $14.95

Jane **Katz**
The New W.E.T. Workout: Water Exercise Techniques for Strengthening, Toning, and Lifetime Fitness
0-8160-3268-8 FACTS ON FILE $21.95
0-8160-3342-0 FACTS ON FILE PB $14.95

Jane **Katz** & Nancy **Bruning**
Swimming for Total Fitness: A Progressive Aerobic Program
Contains over 80 workouts gradually increasing from 100 yards to two miles
See also **SWIMMING** under **WATER SPORTS** under **SPORTS** in **FOOD, TRAVEL, AND LEISURE**
0-385-46821-0 DOUBLEDAY PB.........................$17.95

Jean G. **Larrabee**
Coaching Swimming Effectively
Part of the American Coaching Effectiveness Program (ACEP) Level I series, with technique diagrams and planning guides
0-87322-080-3 HUMAN KINETICS PB $18.00

John **Leonard**
Rookie Coaches Swimming Guide
Covers all the basics for coaching kids: philosophy, injuries, and motivation
0-87322-645-3 HUMAN KINETICS PB $9.95

Edward J. **Shea**
Swimming for Seniors
Discusses health benefits for the older swimmer; clear diagrams for proper stroke as well as for in and out-of-water exercises
0-88011-271-9 LEISURE PB.................................$13.95

Davis G. **Thomas**
Advanced Swimming: Steps to Success
Second-level swimming book brings strokes up to competitive level
0-88011-389-8 LEISURE PB.................................$15.95

Katherine **Vaz** & Chip **Zempel**
Swim, Swim: A Complete Handbook for Fitness Swimmers
Advice for the novice to master competitor from the editors of *Swim* magazine
5-75358-001-7 CONTEMPORARY PB $7.95

Triathlons

Mark **Allen** & Bob **Babbitt**
Mark Allen's Total Triathlete
Photos and personal training schedule from a champion
0-8092-4589-2 CONTEMPORARY PB....................$12.95

Steven **Jonas**
Triathloning for Ordinary Mortals
Written by a former nonathlete who began endurance sports at middle age
0-393-30279-2 NORTON PB $12.95

Dave **Scott**
Dave Scott's Triathlon Training
From the five-time Ironman winner
0-671-60473-2 SIMON & SCHUSTER PB $12.95

Tony **Svensson**
Total Triathlon Almanac—3: The Essential Training Tool and Information Source for the Triathlete and Duathlete
0-9634568-7-3 ATRIUM PB $16.95

Scott **Tinley**

Finding the Wheel's Hub: Tales and Thoughts on the Endurance Athletic Lifestyle

Legendary triathlete's ruminations on the grueling sport

0-9634568-5-7 TRIMARKET PB..........$9.95

Scott **Tinley** & Mike **Plant**

Scott Tinley's Winning Triathlon

Action photos, stories, tips, and inspiration from a world-class triathlete

0-8092-5117-5 CONTEMPORARY PB..........$13.95

Glenn **Town** & Todd **Kearney**

Swim, Bike, Run

For both beginners and veterans, men and women

See also **EXERCISE AND FITNESS** under **RECREATIONAL AND OTHER SPORTS** under **SPORTS** in **FOOD, TRAVEL, AND LEISURE**

FOREWORD BY SCOTT TINLEY

0-87322-513-9 HUMAN KINETICS PB..........$15.95

Yoga

Beryl Bender **Birch**

Power Yoga: The Total Strength and Flexibility Workout

Astanga yoga for athletes to prevent or heal injury. "Birch's credibility supports her passionate advocacy"—*Publishers Weekly*

0-02-058351-6 FIRESIDE PB..........$15.00

Birram **Choudong** & Bonnie **Reynolds**

Birram's Beginning Yoga Class

0-87477-082-3 TARCHER PB..........$13.95

Alice **Christensen**

20-Minute Yoga Workouts

Workouts for busy people as well as for when you are not feeling well. "Her well-designed approach, explained in lucid, focused prose, allows readers to refer easily to what they need"—*Publishers Weekly*

0-345-38845-3 FAWCETT PB..........$12.95

The American Yoga Association Beginner's Manual

Three easy 10-week programs of exercise, breathing, and meditation

0-671-61935-7 FIRESIDE PB..........$15.00

The American Yoga Association Wellness Book

The founder of the American Yoga Association presents a yoga program

1-57566-025-3 KENSINGTON PB..........$18.95

T.K.V. **Desikachar**

The Heart of Yoga: Developing a Personal Practice

Viniyoga is highlighted here; includes translation of Patanjali's ancient work *Yoga Sutra*

0-89281-533-7 INNER TRADITIONS PB..........$19.95

James **Hewitt**

The Complete Yoga Book: Yoga of Breathing, Yoga of Posture and Yoga of Meditation

0-8052-0969-7 SCHOCKEN PB..........$16.00

Richard **Hittleman**

Richard Hittleman's Introduction to Yoga: Beginning and Intermediate Exercises for Peace and Physical Fulfillment

Begins with basic positions and advances at individual's own pace

0-553-27428-7 BDD PB..........$5.99

Richard Hittleman's Yoga: 28–Day Exercise Plan

Over 500 step-by-step black-and-white photos for each of the 28 days

0-553-27748-0 BDD PB..........$6.99

Aladar **Kogler**

Yoga for Every Athlete: Secrets of an Olympic Coach

Yoga exercises for peak performance in any of 30 different sports

1-56718-387-5 LLEWELLYN PB..........$16.95

Lucy **Lidell**

The Sivananda Companion to Yoga

A comprehensive guide to the postures, breathing exercises, diet, relaxation, and meditation techniques

0-671-47088-4 SIMON & SCHUSTER PB..........$14.00

Ramamurti **Mishra**

Fundamentals of Yoga: A Handbook of Theory, Practice and Application

0-517-56422-X JULIAN PB..........$13.95

A.G. **Mohan**

Yoga For Body, Breath and Mind: A Guide to Personal Reintegration

A breath-oriented approach to yoga presents over 300 illustrations and photos to develop your own yoga routine

0-915801-51-5 RUDRA PB..........$16.95

Robin **Monro**

Yoga for Common Ailments

From asthma to PMS, yoga as developed by the Vivekananda Yoga Therapy and Research Foundation

0-671-70528-8 FIRESIDE PB..........$12.95

Paddy **O'Brien**

Yoga for Women: Complete Mind and Body Fitness

From adolescence through pregnancy to old age

1-85538-426-4 HARPERCOLLINS PB..........$15.00

Wallace **Slater**

Simplified Course of Hatha Yoga

This slim volume contains selected exercises for busy people. Perfect size for a purse or briefcase

0-8356-0138-2 THEOSOPHICAL PB..........$5.95

Mary **Stewart**

Yoga Over 50: The Way to Vitality, Health, and Energy in the Prime of Life

Yoga is a low-impact and non-competitive means of keeping the mind and body supple and relaxed

0-671-88510-3 FIRESIDE PB..........$15.00

Louise **Taylor**

A Woman's Book of Yoga: A Journal for Health and Self-Discovery

"Taylor, a yoga practitioner, provides an extremely clear, progressive introduction to hatha yoga...This is a good self-help manual for teaching oneself yoga"—*Library Journal*

0-8048-1829-0 TUTTLE PB..........$16.95

Swami **Vishnu-Devananda**

The Complete Illustrated Book of Yoga

Over 140 black-and-white photos of fundamental yoga postures

0-517-88431-3 CROWN PB..........$16.00

Kareen **Zebroff**

Yoga for Everyone

Four-color photos clearly illustrate basic postures. Perfect for the beginner

0-572-02127-5 FOULSHAM PB..........$15.95

Massage

Mark E. **Beck**

Milady's Theory and Practice, Second Edition

A comprehensive resource that covers the art and business of massage with over 700 drawings, anatomy tables, bibliography, and history, as well as chapters on equipment and sports massage

1-56253-120-4 MILADY..........$46.95

Mario-Paul **Cassar**

Massage Made Easy

Besides four-color step-by-step techniques, discusses reflexology and acupressure

1-88260-617-5 PEOPLES MEDICAL SOCIETY PB $14.95

Thomas **Claire**

Bodywork: What Type of Massage to Get—and How to Make the Most of It

A complete guide to the many massage therapies available today, with background, resources, glossary, bibliography, notes, and index

0-688-12581-6 MORROW..........$25.00

Nicola **Hall**
Reflexology for Women: Restore Harmony and Balance Through Precise Massaging Techniques
Foot massage to alleviate specific female concerns and problems: menstruation, pregnancy side effects, menopause, water retention, and more
0-7225-2868-X HARPERCOLLINS PB $15.00

Linda **Hartley**
Wisdom of the Body Moving
Mind/body centering by the pioneer in the field
1-55643-174-0 NORTH ATLANTIC PB $18.95

Joan **Johnson**
The Healing Art of Sports Massage
Step-by-step guide for speedy recovery from all types of sports and athletic injuries
0-87596-186-X RODALE PB $16.95

Deane **Juhan**
Job's Body: A Handbook for Bodywork
Strategies for releasing tension and thereby enhancing health
0-88268-134-6 STATION HILL PB $25.95

Nitya **Lacroix**
Learn Massage in a Weekend
Four-color photos illustrate technique; a perfect start for the beginner
0-679-41675-7 KNOPF $16.00

Lucinda **Lidell** & others
The Book of Massage: The Complete Step-By-Step Guide to Eastern and Western Techniques
Four-color photos discuss the healing aspects of massage as well as the techniques of Shiatsu and reflexology
0-671-54139-0 SIMON & SCHUSTER PB $14.00

Jeffrey **Maitland**
Spacious Body: Explorations in Somatic Ontology
Master Rolfer's views on the nature of being—not for the novice
1-55643-188-0 NORTH ATLANTIC PB $12.95

Clare **Maxwell-Hudson**
The Complete Book of Massage
Massage for all ages (even for babies); how to use essential oils and how to self-massage
0-394-75975-3 RANDOM HOUSE PB $17.00

Jack **Meagher** & Pat **Boughton**
Sports Massage
A program to increase performance and endurance in 15 sports; includes on-the-spot emergency techniques
0-88268-096-X STATION HILL PB $16.95

Elaine **Stillerman**
Encyclopedia of Bodywork A-Z
From a licensed massage therapist of the Swedish Institute
0-8160-3187-8 FACTS ON FILE $35.00

Susan **Mumford**
The Complete Guide to Massage: A Step-by-Step Approach to Total Body Relaxation
The four-color photos clearly illustrate technique for head-to-toe massage
0-452-27518-0 PLUME PB $16.95

Stephanie **Rick**
The Reflexology Workout: Hand & Foot Massage for Super Health and Rejuvenation
How to stimulate pressure points for eight specific areas such as weight control, stress, and cardiovascular; includes discussion of specific ailments as well
0-517-88485-2 CROWN PB $14.00

Ida **Rolf**
Rolfing: Reestablishing the Natural Alignment and Structural Integration of the Human Body for Vitality and Well-Being
The 600 musculature and skeletal drawings help explain the process to loosen and reorganize connective tissue. For the untrained layperson as well as the pro
0-89281-335-0 INNER TRADITIONS PB $22.95

Yochanan **Rywerant**
The Feldenkrais Method: Teaching by Handling
The authorized edition of the training manual of basic techniques and the theories behind them
0-87983-554-0 KEATS PB $11.95

Peijian **Shen**
Massage for Pain Relief: A Step-by-Step Guide
0-679-76954-4 RANDOM HOUSE PB $14.00

Rosie **Spiegel**
Bodies & Health Consciousness
Integrates the practices of Rolfing and yoga
0-9637824-0-1 S.R.G. PB $24.95

Pauline **Wells**
The Reflexology & Color Therapy Workbook
A unique book that combines the study of color and hand and foot pressure for healing
1-85230-347-6 ELEMENT PB $14.95

Ouida **West**
The Magic of Massage: A New and Holistic Approach
Massage for couples, children, and even pets
0-8038-9278-0 HASTINGS PB $15.95

Christine **Wildwood**
The Aromatherapy and Massage Book
Color photos describe step-by-step techiques and the use of 30 essential oils
0-7225-2975-9 HARPERCOLLINS PB $19.00

Beauty and Grooming

Kevyn **Aucoin**
The Art of Makeup
Makeup artist reveals celebrity beauty secrets, lavishly illustrated by top fashion photographers
0-06-017186-3 HARPERCOLLINS $60.00

Sallie **Batson**
Great Hair! Your Complete Hair Care and Styling Guide
How to pick a salon, find the right style, and tips on quick dos
0-425-15022-4 BERKLEY PB $4.99

Paula **Begoun**
Don't Go Shopping for Hair Care Products Without Me
Learn how to avoid wasting money on expensive hair care products
1-87798-815-4 BEGINNING PRESS PB $14.95

Don't Go to the Cosmetics Counter Without Me: An Eye-Opening Guide to Brand Name Cosmetics, Second Edition
"Paula has made it her business to demystify ingredients and explain which cosmetics live up to their claims and their price tags"—*LA Times*
1-87798-809-X BEGINNING PRESS PB $13.95

Wilma **Bergfeld** & Shelagh Ryan **Masline**
A Woman Doctor's Guide to Skin Care
A dermatologist discusses the skin's anatomy, function, makeup, and problems for every generation
0-7868-8100-3 HYPERION PB $9.95

Hilary **Boddie**
The Herbal Beauty and Health Book: Safe and Natural Ways to Enhance Your Beauty
How to prepare herbs for healthy remedies and beauty treatments
1-55958-693-1 PRIMA PB $12.95

Lonnice Brittenum **Bonner**
Good Hair: For Colored Girls Who've Considered Weaves When the Chemicals Became Too Ruff
A humorous and helpful look at the beauty and diversity of African American women's hair
0-51788-151 CROWN PB $10.00

Deb **Carpenter**
Nature's Beauty Kit: Cosmetic Recipes You Can Make at Home
Herbs, flowers, essential oils for cleansers, lotions, masks, splashes, lip gloss, and even hair-coloring tints
1-55591-221-4 FULCRUM PB $9.95

Kaz **Cooke**

Real Gorgeous: The Truth About Body and Beauty

A reference from Australian columnist and film-maker on beauty products "shoots [as] straight from the hip as Dr. Ruth when discussing body image"—*Publishers Weekly*

0-393-31355-7 NORTON PB $13.00

Janice **Cox**

Natural Beauty at Home

More than 200 easy-to-make and use recipes for skin and hair

0-8050-3313-0 HOLT PB $17.95

Jessica **Harris**

The World Beauty Book: How We Can All Look and Feel Wonderful Using the Natural Beauty Secrets of Women of Color

Presents old ways of beauty enhancement from the "worldwide sisterhood of non-Western women of color." "Although specifically aimed at women of color, Harris's exploration of this strand of folk wisdom is likely to intrigue any woman"—*Publishers Weekly*

0-06-251092-4 HARPERCOLLINS PB $14.00

Thomas **Hayden** & James **Williams**

Milady's Black Cosmetology

Skin and hair care for African-American women

0-87350-377-5 MILADY PB $28.95

Carolynn **Hillman**

Love Your Looks: How to Stop Criticizing and Start Appreciating Your Appearance

The book is a result of the author's self-esteem workshops stressing how women should examine the source of their negative self-assessment in order to restore confidence

0-684-81138-3 FIRESIDE PB..............................$12.00

Rex **Hilverdink**

Making Up

A thorough guide to make-up styles and techniques

0-517-56955-8 CLARKSON POTTER PB $20.00

Elsa **Klensch** & Beryl **Meyer**

Style

The CNN fashion correspondent discusses all the arcane tidbits every woman should probably know

0-399-52152-6 BERKELEY PB $14.00

Darlene **Mathis**

Women of Color: The Multicultural Guide to Fashion and Beauty

Unique and comprehensive

0-345-38929-8 BALLANTINE $23.00

Mary **Quant**

Ultimate Makeup & Beauty

The definitive guide from one of the 20th century's most famous fashion creators

0-7894-1056-7 DK $24.95

Sidra **Shaukat**

Skin and Body Care: The Natural, Cruelty-free Way to Beauty

How to make your own moisturizers and beauty preparations from beeswax, honey, herbs, yogurt, and other natural ingredients

1-85230-350-6 ELEMENT PB..............................$9.95

People with Disabilities

General

Edward D. **Berkowitz**

Disabled Policy: America's Programs for the Handicapped

0-521-38930-5 CAMBRIDGE PB..............................$19.95

Susan E. **Browne** & Nanci **Stern**, editors

With the Power of Each Breath: A Disabled Women's Anthology

0-939416-06-9 CLEIS PB $10.95

Foundation for Children with Learning Disabilities

The FCLD Learning Disabilities Resource Guide: A State-by-State Directory of Programs and Services

0-8147-2579-1 NYU $50.00

Alan **Gartner** & Tom **Joe**

Images of the Disabled—Disabling Images

0-275-92178-6 PRAEGER $55.00

David **Goode**

A World Without Words: The Social Construction of Children Born Deaf and Blind

1-56639-215-2 TEMPLE..............................$59.95

1-56639-216-0 TEMPLE PB..............................$19.95

John **Hockenberry**

Moving Violations: A Memoir: War Zones, Wheelchairs, and Declaration of Independence

Paraplegic news correspondent tells his harrowing and humorous story

0-7868-6078-2 HYPERION $24.95

Miriam **Kaufman**

Easy for You to Say

Adolescents with disabilities or chronic illness discuss sex, family, social activities, and death

See also SPECIAL CHILDREN

1-55013-619-4 KEY PORTER PB $15.95

Lauri **Klobas**

Disability Drama in Television and Film

Over 400 chronological entries with critiques of television programs and film noting stereotypical or positive depictions of disabilities

0-89950-309-8 MCFARLAND..............................$65.00

Harlan **Lane**

The Wild Boy of Aveyron

0-674-95300-2 HARVARD PB..............................$15.95

Robert M. **Levy** & Leonard **Rubenstein**

The Rights of People with Mental Disabilities

The authoritative ACLU guide to the rights of people with mental illness and mental retardation

0-8093-1989-6 SOUTHERN ILLINOIS..............$34.95

0-8093-1990-X SOUTHERN ILLINOIS PB $13.95

Chalda **Maloff** & Susan M. **Wood**

Business and Social Etiquette with Disabled People: A Guide to Getting Along with Persons Who Have Impairments of Mobility, Vision, Hearing or Speech

FOREWORD BY MEL TILLIS

0-398-05463-0 THOMAS $39.95

Thomas H. **Powell** & Peggy A. **Ogle**

Brothers and Sisters: A Special Part of Exceptional Families

Provides successful strategies for helping siblings of the disabled cope with and benefit from their unique role in the exceptional family

0-933716-45-1 BROOKES PB $18.00

Donna **Williams**

Like Color to the Blind: Soul Searching and Soul Finding

Williams (*Nobody Nowhere*, *Somebody Somewhere*) has previously chronicled her autistic childhood and her growth out of the sheltered bubble of autism into the real world. Here she tells the powerful sequel to the story, the emotional transformation of love and marriage that followed her emergence. "Donna Williams isn't just teaching us what it is like to be autistic. She is teaching us what it is like to be human"—*NY Times Book Review*

0-8129-2640-4 TIME BOOKS..............................$24.00

Mary **Willmuth** & Lillian **Holcomb**, editors

Women with Disabilities: Formal Voices

An anthology of essays by leaders in occupational and physical therapy, particularly useful for clinicians

1-56023-046-0 HAWORTH PB..............................$19.95

Blindness and Visual Impairment

John H. **Dobree** & Eric **Boulter**
Blindness and Visual Handicap: The Facts
0-19-261328-6 OXFORD $13.95

Robert V. **Hine**
Second Sight
0-520-08195-1 CALIFORNIA $22.50

Helen **Keller**
The Story of My Life
An inspiring personal account
0-451-52447-0 NEW AMERICAN LIBRARY PB ...$4.99

Deborah **Kendrick**
Jobs To Be Proud of: Profiles of Workers Who Are Blind or Visually Impaired
0-89128-258-0 AMERICAN FOUNDATION FOR THE BLIND PB $21.95

Berthold **Lowenfeld**
Berthold Lowenfeld on Blindness and Blind People
0-89128-101-0 AMERICAN FOUNDATION FOR THE BLIND PB $21.95

Rami **Rabby** & Diane **Croft**
Take Charge: A Strategic Guide for Blind Job Seekers
0-939173-16-6 NATIONAL BRAILLE PRESS PB ..$19.95

Dean W. **Tuttle** & Naomi R. **Tuttle**
Self-Esteem and Adjusting with Blindness: The Process of Responding to Life's Demands
0-398-04887-8 THOMAS $46.95
0-398-06598-5 THOMAS PB $37.95

Deafness

"Deaf people can do anything—except hear."
King Jordan, President, Gallaudet University

Evelyn **Cherow**
Hearing Impaired Children and Youth with Developmental Disabilities: An Interdisciplinary Foundation for Service
0-913580-97-X GALLAUDET $29.95

Debbie L. **Cole**
Sign Language and the Health Care Professional
0-89464-417-3 KRIEGER PB $13.00

John C. **Denmark**
Deafness and Mental Health
1-85302-212-8 KINGSLEY PB $24.95

Lennard J. **Davis**
Enforcing Normalcy: Disability, Deafness and the Body
Discussion of the concept of "normal" and cultural assumptions governing our conception of people with disabilities
1-85984-007-8 VERSO PB $17.00

Jack R. **Gannon**
The Week the World Heard Gallaudet
0-930323-54-8 GALLAUDET $29.95
0-930323-50-5 GALLAUDET PB $19.95

Leonard G. **Lane**
The Gallaudet Survival Guide to Signing
A pocket-size dictionary of more than 500 words in American Sign Language
0-930323-34-3 GALLAUDET PB $3.50

Oliver **Sacks**
Seeing Voices: A Journey into the World of the Deaf
0-520-06083-0 CALIFORNIA $22.00

Oliver Sacks

Jerome D. **Schein**
At Home Among Strangers
Views the unique culture of deaf people, their families, and organizations
0-930323-51-3 GALLAUDET $24.95

David A. **Stewart**
Deaf Sport: The Impact of Sports Within the Deaf Community
0-930323-74-2 GALLAUDET $24.95

Bonnie Poitras **Tucker**
The Feel of Silence
1-56639-352-3 TEMPLE PB $19.95

John **Van Cleve** & Barry **Crouch**
A Place of Their Own: Creating a Deaf Community in America
0-930323-49-1 GALLAUDET PB $14.95

Barbara **Willigan** & Susan **King**
Mental Health Services for the Deaf
9-994-52041-5 GALLAUDET PB $15.95

Environments

Bettyann B. **Raschko**
Housing Interiors For the Disabled and Elderly
0-442-22001-4 VAN NOSTRAND REINHOLD PB $47.95

Employment

Jeffrey G. **Allen**
Successful Job Search Strategies for the Disabled
0-471-59234-X WILEY $49.95

Bertram J. **Black**
Work and Mental Illness: Transitions to Employment
0-8018-3565-8 JOHNS HOPKINS $40.00

Carl F. **Calkins** & Hill M. **Walker**
Social Competence for Workers with Developmental Disabilities: A Guide to Enhancing Employment
1-55766-034-4 BROOKES PB $35.00

Walter P. **Christian**, editor
Programming Effective Human Services: Strategies for Institutional Change and Client Transition
0-306-41526-7 PLENUM $59.50

John **Fish**
Disabled Youth and Employment
92-64-14152-9 ORGANIZATION FOR ECONOMIC COOPERATION AND DEVELOPMENT PB $13.00

Malcolm **Harper** & Willi **Momm**
Self-Employment for Disabled People: Experiences from Africa and Asia
92-2-106457-3 INTERNATIONAL LABOR PB $12.00

Mary **Hopkins-Best** & others
Reaching the Hidden Majority: A Leader's Guide to Career Preparation for Disabled Women and Girls
0-910328-42-0 CARROLL $26.95

Caven S. **McLoughlin**
Getting Employed, Staying Employed: Development and Training for Persons with Severe Handicaps
An exhaustive manual for both the job seeker and the professional vocational counselor
0-933716-70-2 BROOKES PB $24.00

Health, Exercise, and Therapy

Donna B. **Bernhardt**, editor

Recreation for the Disabled Child

For both the professional and parents

0-86656-263-X HAWORTH....................................$39.95

David D. **Burns**

Feeling Good: The New Mood Therapy

See especially the chapters "Depression and Inventory Scale" and "Dysfunctional Attitudes Scale"

See also COGNITIVE THERAPY

0-688-03633-3 MORROW....................................$25.00

Conway Greene

Sports, Everyone!: Recreation and Sports for the Physically Handicapped

Resource for clubs, camps, college, and travel; information for over 100 sports and activities

1-88466-910-7 CONWAY GREENE PB....................$16.95

Lauren J. **Lieberman** & Jim F. **Cowart**

Games for People with Sensory Impairments: Strategies for Including Individuals of All Ages

0-87322-890-1 HUMAN KINETICS PB..................$17.00

Kevin F. **Lockette**

Conditioning with Physical Disabilities

In conjunction with the Rehabilitation Institute of Chicago; exercises for all levels and classifications of physical disabilities; over 250 illustrations

0-87322-614-3 HUMAN KINETICS PB..................$22.95

Gerald G. **May**

Care of Mind, Care of Spirit: A Psychiatrist Explores Spiritual Dimension

0-06-065533-X HARPERCOLLINS PB....................$15.50

Mary Alice **Ross**

Fitness for the Aging Adult with Visual Impairment

0-89128-125-8 AMERICAN FOUNDATION FOR THE BLIND PB..$19.95

Jules C. **Weiss**, editor

Expressive Therapy with Elders and the Disabled: Touching the Heart of Life

This therapy works through the difficulties of finding a new and positive lifestyle

0-86656-266-4 HAWORTH....................................$39.95

0-86656-372-5 HAWORTH PB..............................$19.95

Sex

Ann **Craft**, editor

Practical Issues in Sexuality and Learning Disabilities

0-415-05735-3 ROUTLEDGE PB..........................$18.95

Lydia **Fegan** & Anne **Rauch**

Sexuality and People with Intellectual Disabilities

1-55766-140-5 BROOKES PB..............................$32.00

Ken **Kroll** & Erica Levy **Klein**

Enabling Romance: A Guide to Love, Sex, and Relationships for the Disabled (and the People Who Love Them)

0-933149-78-6 WOODBINE PB............................$15.95

Karin Melberg **Schwier**

Couples with Intellectual Disabilities Talk About Living & Loving

Collection of profiles of people with disabilities who speak intimately about their lovers and partners

0-933149-65-4 WOODBINE PB............................$15.95

Thomas O. **Mooney**

Sexual Options for Paraplegics and Quadriplegics

0-316-57937-8 LITTLE, BROWN PB....................$29.95

Self-Help

Life Crisis: General

Public demand for information and advice on coping with such serious problems as addiction, rape, and suicide has increased dramatically in recent years. Along with the rise in these crises are books on healing, especially the daily affirmations filled with wise words to mull over.

Maria **Arapakis**

SoftPower!: How to Speak Up, Set Limits, and Say No Without Losing Your Lover, Your Job, or Your Friends

Help in finding the balance between being powerful and overpowering, knowing when to defend your position and when to let go, and how to accomplish these goals without alienating those around you

0446301034 WARNER PB $11.99

Max **De Pree**

Dear Zoe

0-06-251375-3 HARPERCOLLINS.......................$18.00

0-06-251390-7 HARPERCOLLINS PB.................$10.00

Melody **Beattie**

Codependent No More: How to Stop Controlling Others and Start Caring for Yourself

A popular, helpful guide

0-06-255446-8 HAZELDEN PB...........................$12.00

Harold H. **Bloomfield** & Robert K. **Cooper**

The Power of 5

Authors are convinced that everyone can reinvent his or her life with consistent attitude adjustments that take only 5 minutes or even 5 seconds. Topics include diet, exercise, energy management, and everyday spirituality

0-87596-201-7 RODALE....................................$24.95

0-87596-363-3 RODALE PB................................$12.95

Harold H. **Bloomfield** & Leonard **Felder**

Making Peace with Your Parents: The Key to Enriching Your Life & All Your Relationships

From resentment to forgiveness, this explores the most fundamental of all relationships. "Dr. Bloomfield's book is worth thousands of dollars of therapy"—Elisabeth Kübler-Ross

0-345-30904-9 BALLANTINE PB........................$5.95

Deepak **Chopra**

The Way of the Wizard: 20 Lessons for Living a Magical Life

Deepak Chopra's *The Seven Spiritual Laws of Success* and *Ageless Body, Timeless Mind* were both *New York Times* bestsellers and, more important, vastly enhanced the quality of life for millions. Here, Chopra elucidates 20 principles of spiritual alchemy for discovering and mastering the full—indeed, the boundless—possibilities of the world around us

0-517-70434-X HARMONY................................$15.95

Dianne **Hales** & Robert E. **Hales**

Caring for the Mind: The Comprehensive Guide to Mental Health

Specific disorders discussed with case histories, symptoms, and treatment. This "...thorough guide [is] particularly helpful for readers seeking information for themselves or for those whom they love"—*Publishers Weekly*

0-553-09146-8 BDD..$39.95

Harry **Harrison** & Melissa **Harrison**

Both Sides of Recovery

Considers the couple's role and problems as more important than the addict or co–dependent

0-8091-3633-3 PAULIST PB..............................$12.95

Ann **Kliman**

Crisis: Psychological First Aid for Recovery and Growth

The first general guide to deal with such crises as death, divorce, rape, and illness from a psychological and emotional perspective. The author, a clinical psychologist, includes case histories

1-56821-208-9 ARONSON PB............................$27.50

Harold S. **Kushner**

When Bad Things Happen to Good People

A best-selling guide to crisis management, from a noted rabbi

See also **SELF-HELP**

0-380-67033-X AVON PB $10.00

Angelyn **Miller**

The Enabler: When Helping Harms the One You Love

Enabling and codependency do not necessarily have to exist in families with chemical dependencies. Helping too much can be disastrous. Provides useful case studies and worksheets

0-345-36848-7 BALLANTINE PB $4.95

Stanton **Peele**

Diseasing of America: How We Allowed Recovery Zealots and the Treatment Industry to Convince Us We Are Out of Control

Refutes the notion that drug and alcohol addiction is a disease as promoted by AA, NA, and drug-treatment centers

0-02-874014-9 LEXINGTON PB $14.95

Elayne **Rapping**

The Culture of Recovery: Making Sense of the Self-Help Movement in Women's Lives

Examines the self-help phenomenon and finds that feminism is at the core of the recovery movement

0-8070-2716-2 BEACON $24.00

Rachel Naomi **Remen**

Kitchen Table Wisdom: Stories that Heal

A compilation of instructive stories from real life

1-57322-042-6 RIVERHEAD $22.95

Lillian B. **Rubin**

The Transcendent Child: Tales of Triumph Over the Past

In a refreshing antidote to the cult of the victim, Rubin collects tales of triumph over harsh and painful pasts. Doing so, she asks and answers the difficult question of how some people manage to transcend the tragedy and hardship of their lives and find an adult identity based on success rather than victimization. "No one listens and makes the rest of the world hear like Lillian Rubin"—Michael Rogin

0-465-08669-1 BASIC $23.00

Karen Kissel **Wegela**

How to Be a Help Instead of a Nuisance: Practical Approaches to Giving Support, Service and Encouragement to Others

From the director of contemplative psychology at the Naropa Institute, a step-by-step and concisely written handbook to offer real help to distressed clients, friends, or relatives

1-57062-150-0 SHAMBHALA PB $13.00

Lewis B. **Smedes**

Forgive and Forget: Healing the Hurts We Don't Deserve

"First rate....Smedes does a masterful job of conveying the emotional dimensions involved....The author's honest self-disclosure adds enormously. Highly recommended" —*Library Journal*

0-06-067431-8 HARPERCOLLINS PB $11.00

Heidi H. **Spencer**

"Did I Do Something Wrong?": A Supportive Guide for Parents and Loved Ones of People in Therapy

Psychotherapist discusses the guilt often felt when an intimate undergoes counseling and advises how friends and family can help during this sometimes painful process

0-88282-128-8 NEW HORIZON PB $13.95

Addiction and Recovery

Stephen **Braun**

Buzz: The Science and Lore of Alcohol and Caffeine

"If it weren't for coffee," said David Letterman, "I'd have no identifiable personality whatsoever." Award-winning science writer Braun takes us on a fascinating and informative tour through the science and mythology of the world's most popularly used substances. Along the way he shows up the myth that alcohol kills brain cells, traces its mimicry of drugs ranging from cocaine to Valium, and visits with coffee drinkers Bach, Kant, Rousseau, and Voltaire

0-19-509289-9 OXFORD $25.00

Patrick **Carnes**

A Gentle Path Through the Twelve Steps: The Classic Guide for All People in the Process of Recovery—Revised Edition

Workbook format includes basic information about addiction and recovery as well as specific exercises to aid in the process of recovery

1-56838-058-5 COMPCARE PB $14.95

Gerald **Gillespie**

The 12-Step Kabbalah Method to End Your Addiction: A New, Proven Approach to Cure Dependence on Alcohol, Drugs, Nicotine, & Compulsive Disorders

1-56171-960-9 ATRIUM $23.95

Wilfrid **Sheed**

In Love With Daylight: A Memoir of Recovery

Critic, essayist, and novelist documents his recovery from polio, depression, and drug and alcohol abuse. Eschewing outside help, he relied on himself to find the path to health. "...a two-year ordeal he describes with wit and gallantry"—*Publishers Weekly*

0-671-79215-6 SIMON & SCHUSTER $23.00

Robert **Hemfelt** & Richard **Fowler**

Serenity: A Companion for Twelve-Step Recovery

Includes 84 meditations, seven for each of the 12 steps, and comes with New Testament psalms and proverbs

0-8407-1542-0 NELSON PB $9.99

Patrick **Fanning** & John **O'Neill**

The Addiction Workbook

For quitting drinking and drugs and how to avoid a relapse

1-87923-736-9 NEW HARBINGER PB.................$11.95

Valerie **Monroe**

In the Weather of the Heart: A Memoir of a Shattered Marriage and a Reckoning with Recovery

"A sensitive memoir and a good antidote for those who believe marriages require little work to be successful"—*Publishers Weekly*

0-385-47103-3 DOUBLEDAY $22.50

Alex J. **Packer**

Parenting One Day at a Time: Using the Tools of Recovery to Become Better Parents and Raise Better Children

How to amend the hurts of addiction

See also **BEING A PARENT** under **PARENTING**

0-440-50520-8 DELL PB $9.95

Bryan E. **Robinson**

Work Addiction: Hidden Legacies of Adult Children

How to determine the difference between healthy work and compulsive overworking with self-tests; provides recovery options

1-55874-023-6 HEALTH COMMUNICATIONS PB$8.95

Jack **Trimpey**

The Small Book: A Revolutionary Alternative for Overcoming Alcohol and Drug Dependence

The agnostic or atheist's answer to A.A.'s *The Big Book*. Trimpey is the founder of a secular alternative to 12-step programs, Rational Recovery, emphasizing the strength and rationality of the individual rather than relying on a "higher power." This is a new approach to recovery, and the basis for a movement that's gone national since its founding in 1986

0-440-50725-1 DELL PB $12.95

Alcohol Abuse

Clark **Vaughan**

Addictive Drinking: The Road to Recovery for Problem Drinkers and Those Who Love Them

The medical and emotional effects of alcoholism, primarily directed to the abuser

0-670-10479-5 VIKING $14.95

Al-Anon
Al-Anon Faces Alcoholism
An explanation of the organization that helps families of alcoholics
0-910034-55-9 AL-ANON $7.50

Alcoholics Anonymous
Alcoholics Anonymous
The text for the AA program. At 575 pages, it is known as "the Big Book"
0-916856-18-6 ALCOHOLICS ANONYMOUS PB $4.60

Frank **Dwyer**
The Annotated AA Handbook: A Companion to the AA Bible
The Big Book clarified
1-56980-075-8 BARRICADE PB $20.00

Herbert **Fingarette**
Heavy Drinking: The Myth of Alcoholism as a Disease
A UCLA professor's critical look at the efficacy of various alcoholic treatment programs
0-520-06290-6 CALIFORNIA..............................$29.95

Guy **Kettelhack**
Sober and Free: Making Your Recovery Work for You
A recovering alcoholic contends that there are many paths to sobriety other than AA
0-684-81120-0 FIRESIDE PB $11.00

Jean **Kinney** & Gwen **Leaton**
Understanding Alcohol
A guide to alcohol problems and their treatment
0-8016-2627-7 MOSBY PB..................................$19.95

Audrey **Kishline**
Moderate Drinking: The Moderation Management Guide for People Who Want to Reduce Their Drinking
Controversial self-help program that suggests moderation rather than abstinence. This is the official handbook for Moderation Management (MM), a support network to help people reduce their drinking
0-517-88656-1 CROWN PB $14.00

Arnold **Ludwig**
Understanding the Alcoholic's Mind: The Nature of Craving and How to Control It
0-19-504878-4 OXFORD $25.00

George **Valliant**
The Natural History of Alcoholism
An excellent, somewhat technical, book
0-674-60376-1 HARVARD PB $14.95

Bill **W.**
A Simple Program: A Contemporary Translation of the Original Big Book of Alcoholics Anonymous
An update of AA's core text
0-7868-8136-4 HYPERION PB..............................$9.95

Families of Alcoholics

Timmen **Cermak**
A Time to Heal: The Road to Recovery for Adult Children of Alcoholics
0-87477-745-3 TARCHER PB..............................$14.95

Herbert **Gravitz** & Julie **Bowden**
Recovery: A Guide for Adult Children of Alcoholics
Questions and answers on topics ranging from the definition of alcoholism to successful intervention
0-671-64528-5 FIRESIDE PB...............................$10.00

William J. **Sonnenstuhl**
Working Sober: The Transformation of an Occupational Drinking Culture
The interrelationship between some occupations and alcoholism
0-8014-3267-7 I.L.R. $35.00
0-8014-8348-4 I.L.R. PB $14.95

Sharon **Wegsheider**
Another Chance: Hope and Health for Alcoholic Families
Explores the patterns of families of alcoholics, offering suggestions for intervention and recovery
0-8314-0072-2 SCIENCE & BEHAVIOR PB..........$17.95

Barbara **Wood**
Children of Alcoholism: The Struggle for Self and Intimacy in Adult Life
Strategies for intervention and step-by-step principles for therapists on how best to create an environment to help patients
0-8147-9222-7 NYU PB $18.50

Drug Abuse

Riving A. **Cohen**
Addiction: The High-Low Trap
The physiological aspects of a variety of drugs discussed as well as recovery from them
0-929173-10-4 HEALTH PRESS PB.....................$13.95

Robert **DuPont**, Jr.
Getting Tough on Gateway Drugs: A Guide for the Family
Includes case histories, research, and practical advice for dealing with drug abuse
0-88048-046-7 AMERICAN PSYCHIATRIC PB.....$12.95

Dan **Ellis**
Growing Up Stoned
A serious exploration of the family's role in drug addiction, treatments, and therapies
0-932194-35-4 HEALTH COMMUNICATIONS PB $8.95

Roger **Weiss** & Steven **Mirin**
Cocaine
Includes sections on intervention by family and coworkers, treatment programs, and a list of treatment facilities
0-88048-549-3 AMERICAN PSYCHIATRIC $21.50

Sexual Addiction

Ann Wilson **Schaef**
Escape from Intimacy: Untangling the "Love" Addictions of Sex, Romance, Relationships
Defines intimate addictions and incorporates the 12-step program for recovery
0-06-254873-5 HARPERCOLLINS PB $14.00

Smoking

Patricia **Allison** & Jack **Yost**
Hooked, But Not Helpless: Ending Your Love/Hate Relationship with Nicotine
Tips and techniques for quitting and a discussion of why most stop-smoking programs fail
0-9623683-2-6 BRIDGECITY PB $14.95

Tom **Ferguson**
The No-Nag, No-Guilt, Do-It-Your-Own-Way Guide to Quitting Smoking
A how-to, step by step
0-345-35578-4 BALLANTINE PB $5.99

Peggy **Holmes** & Peter **Holmes**
Out of the Ashes: Help for People Who Have Stopped Smoking
Meditations for ex-smokers and those who desire to quit
0-925190-57-8 FAIRVIEW PB.............................$10.95

Martin **Katahn**
How to Quit Smoking Without Gaining Weight
Author of *The T-Factor Diet* advises those who are worried about weight gain when quitting smoking with tricks and tips to avoid this problem
0-393-03714-2 NORTON...................................$12.95

Brad **Roder**
For Smokers Only: How Smokeless Tobacco Can Save Your Life
Based on the premise that it's the smoke and not the nicotine that causes disease, this book presents a smokeless program for quitting
0-945819-77-3 SULZBURGER & GRAHAM PB...$11.99

Terry **Rustin**
Quit and Stay Quit: A Personal Program to Stop Smoking
A medical doctor offers a nicotine recovery plan
1-56838-109-3 HAZELDEN PB $12.95

Meditations

John Beverley **Butcher**
The Tao of Jesus: A Book of Days for the Natural Year
0-06-061188-X HARPERCOLLINS PB $14.00

Paula Peisner **Coxe**
Finding Love: Let Your Heart Be Your Guide
Discusses all types of love, from self–love to the love of nature
1-57071-031-7 SOURCEBOOKS PB $7.95

Jan Johnson **Drantell**
Healing Hearts: Meditations for Women Living with Divorce
A daily companion for coping with a broken marriage
0-553-35172-9 BANTAM PB $8.95

Alan **Epstein**
How to Have More Love in Your Life: Everyday Actions for Nourishing Heart and Soul
"…offers suggestions to enrich our lives and imaginations, which will, in turn, he assures, make us more loving—and lovable"
—*Publishers Weekly*
0-670-85445-X VIKING $17.95

Mary **Hayes-Grieco**
The Kitchen Mystic: Spiritual Lessons Hidden in Everyday Life
A collection of short essays that synthesizes 12-step, holistic, Judeo-Christian, and earth religions
0-89486-814-4 HAZELDEN PB $7.00

Hazelden
Today's Gift: Daily Meditations for Families
The purpose is to give families a few minutes together and encourage discussion
0-89486-302-9 HAZELDEN PB $11.00

A Woman's Spirit
Picks up where *Each Day a New Beginning* left off for those women continuing the sober life
0-06-255282-1 HARPERCOLLINS PB $14.00

Sally **Hill** & Valerie **Deilgat**
New Clothes from Old Threads: Daily Reflections for Recovering Adults
Using childhood fables for new lessons with 12-step messages
0-941405-10-9 RECOVERY PB $9.95

Jon **Kabat-Zinn**
Wherever You Go There You Are: Mindfulness Meditation in Everyday Life
Draws on the Buddhist concept of "mindfulness"—of living fully in the moment
0-7868-8070-8 HYPERION PB $12.95

Dalai Lama

Sally **Coleman** & Nancy **Hull-Mast**
Our Best days
Daily meditations for everyone
0-942421-28-0 PARKSIDE PB $7.95

Earnie **Larsen** & Carol **Hegarty**
Believing in Myself: Daily Meditations for Healing and Building Self-Esteem
Based on the premise that raising self-esteem is essential to recovery
0-671-76616-3 SIMON & SCHUSTER PB $9.00

Days of Healing, Days of Joy: Daily Meditations for Adult Children
From the Hazelden Meditation Series based on the 12 steps
0-06-255449-2 HAZELDEN PB $13.00

Jonathon **Lazear**
Meditations for Men Who Do Too Much
"An excellent tool for men who are ready to go deeper than pay checks and meetings. A joy to read…and pass on"
—Melody Beattie, *Codependent No More*
0-671-75908-6 FIRESIDE PB $9.00

Rokelle **Lerner**
Affirmations for the Inner Child
How to "reparent" your inner child to experience life anew
1-55874-054-6 HEALTH COMMUNICATIONS PB$6.95

Daily Affirmations for Adult Children of Alcoholics
Positive affirmations from a psychotherapist…
0-932194-27-3 HEALTH COMMUNICATIONS PB$7.95

Stephen **Levine** & Ondrea **Levine**
Embracing the Beloved: Relationship as a Path of Awakening
Free-form poetry and practical meditation techniques on the healing potential of love and the family
0-385-42526-0 DOUBLEDAY..............................$21.95

Frank **Minirth** & others
Walk Through the Next 365 Days with the Serenity Prayer
Daily devotional prayers for change
0-8407-3236-8 NELSON PB $8.99

Norman Vincent **Peale**
Positive Thinking Every Day: An Inspiration for Each Day of the Year
From the man who began it all, wise words culled from his nine bestselling books
0-671-86891-8 FIRESIDE PB $9.00

M. Scott **Peck**
Meditations from the Road: Daily Reflections from *The Road Less Traveled* and *The Different Drum*
Quotes from the author's bestselling books as a daily companion
0-671-79799-9 FIRESIDE PB $9.00

Paula **Peisner**
Finding Time: Breathing Space for Women Who Do Too Much
Tips in the form of wise quotes and examples
0-942061-33-0 SOURCEBOOKS PB $7.95

Elizabeth **Roberts** & Elias **Amidon**, editors
Life Prayers: From Around the World
Poetry, political wisdom, and commemorations from Hildegard of Bingen, Gary Snyder, Nelson Mandela, and sources including Native American chants and classical Chinese verse
See also **INSPIRATIONAL** under **SPIRITUALITY** under **SPIRITUALITY** in **RELIGION, SPIRITUALITY, AND PHILOSOPHY**
0-06-251377-X HARPERCOLLINS PB $15.00

Anne Wilson **Schaef**
Meditations for People Who (May) Worry Too Much
The sequel to *Meditations for Women Who Do Too Much*
0-345-39406-2 BALLANTINE PB..........................$12.00

Native Wisdom for White Minds: Daily Reflections Inspired by the Native Peoples of the World
Quotes collected from Native elders worldwide
0-345-39405-4 BALLANTINE PB $10.00

Gary **Smalley** & John **Trent**
Giving the Blessing: Daily Thoughts on the Joy of Giving
How to give a blessing each day
0-8407-4557-5 NELSON PB $7.99

Starting Over: Meditations for Divorced Women
A year's companion to help heal a broken heart and to welcome the change and challenge of a new start
0-440-50595-X BANTAM PB $8.95

Perry **Tilleraas**
The Color of Light: Daily Meditations for All of Us Living with AIDS
Inspiration for living one day at a time
0-89486-511-0 HAZELDEN PB $11.00

Sue Patton **Thoele**

The Woman's Book of Confidence: Meditations for Trusting & Accepting Ourselves

Trusting intuitive wisdom for support spiritually, psychologically, and emotionally

0-943233-37-2 CONARI PB $9.95

The Woman's Book of Courage: Meditations for Empowerment & Peace of Mind

Words of wisdom for women who wish to enhance their personal power

0-943233-17-8 CONARI PB $9.95

Ellen Sue **Stern**

I Do: Meditations for Brides

For the ups and downs of marriage

0-440-50494-5 DELL PB........................$8.99

In My Prime: Meditations for Women in Midlife

For those facing menopause, meditations for every day of the year

0-440-50596-8 BANTAM PB........................$8.95

David **Viscott**

Finding Your Strength in Difficult Times: A Book of Meditations

A collection of readings from a psychiatrist

0-8092-3723-7 CONTEMPORARY PB..................$8.00

Susan **Ward**

Daily Affirmations for Compulsive Eaters: Beyond Feast or Famine

Towards developing a positive relationship to food

1-55874-076-7 HEALTH COMMUNICATIONS PB$7.95

Battered Women

Lee **Bowker**

Ending the Violence: A Guidebook Based on the Experiences of One Thousand Battered Women

This book of interviews examines the resources available to the victims: police, courts, doctors, agencies, and counselors

0-918452-86-4 LEARNING PUBLICATIONS PB..$12.95

Suzette Haden **Elgin**

You Can't Say That To Me!: Stopping the Pain of Verbal Abuse—An 8-Step Program

"Elgin offers an accessible, extremely pragmatic approach to verbal abuse"—*Publishers Weekly*

0-471-00395-6 WILEY........................$34.95

Patricia **Evans**

The Verbally Abusive Relationship: How to Recognize It and How to Respond

Based on the theory that all domestic violence begins with verbal abuse, it examines cultural notions of power and how women can respond and prevent further abuse

1-55850-133-9 ADAMS PB........................$7.95

Edward **Gondolf**

Men Who Batter: An Integrated Approach for Stopping Wife Abuse

Advice for the abusive male

0-918452-79-1 LEARNING PUBLICATIONS PB .$19.95

Lynn **Hawker** & Terry **Bicehouse**

End The Pain: Solutions for Stopping Domestic Violence

Dispels the myths of domestic violence to uncover true psychological and psychosocial reasons; answers questions as to why it is tolerated

0-935016-11-2 BARCLAY PB........................$12.95

Del **Martin**

Battered Wives

History of the subject and specific advice for victims. Includes a guide to shelters

0-912078-70-7 VOLCANO PB........................$12.95

Ginny **McCarthy**

Getting Free: A Handbook for Women in Abusive Relationships

A comprehensive look at how to get emergency help from the police, the law, and doctors

0-931188-37-7 SEAL PB........................$12.95

Alan **McEvoy** & Jeff **Brookings**

Helping Battered Women: A Volunteer's Handbook for Assisting Victims of Marital Violence

Practical guide for volunteers and professionals: shelters, telephone counseling, and helping the children of battered women

1-55691-067-3 LEARNING PUBLICATIONS PB ..$11.95

Mary Susan **Miller**

No Visible Wounds: Identifying Nonphysical Abuse of Women by Their Men

Exposes the subtler forms of wife abuse and concludes with options for getting out

0-8092-3546-3 CONTEMPORARY........................$19.95

0-449-91079-2 FAWCETT PB........................$12.00

Brian K. **Ogawa**

Walking on Eggshells: Practical Counsel for Women In or Leaving a Violent Relationship

Presents various violent scenarios and how to respond

1-88424-411-4 VOLCANO PB........................$8.95

Stephanie **Rodriguez**

Time to Stop Pretending: A Mother's Story of Domestic Violence, Homelessness, Poverty and Escape

A moving account of one woman's stuggle to escape her abusive home

0-8397-8060-5 ERIKSSON........................$19.95

Linda **Rouse**

You Are Not Alone: A Guide for Battered Women

Patterns of abusive relationships, the causes of battering, and information on shelter, medical, and legal services

0-918452-73-2 LEARNING PUBLICATIONS PB..$12.95

Lenore E. **Walker**

The Battered Woman

"In addition to carefully written but inevitably disturbing case studies, Professor Walker's book includes sections on preventative remedies, including safehouses, and a careful discussion of psychotherapy"—*NY Times*

See also **RAPE, INCEST, AND BATTERED WOMEN**

0-06-090742-8 HARPERCOLLINS PB..................$12.50

The Battered Woman Syndrome

0-8261-4320-2 SPRINGER........................$36.95

Child Abuse

Vincent **Fontana**

Somewhere a Child Is Crying: Maltreatment—Causes and Prevention

A book filled with shocking case histories and a directory of child-abuse programs

0-451-62699-0 NEW AMERICAN LIBRARY PB ...$4.99

Eliana **Gil**

Outgrowing the Pain

A self-help book that uses cartoons effectively

0-440-50006-0 DELL PB........................$8.95

Ruth **Kempe** & Henry **Kempe**

Child Abuse

A discussion of abuse and treatment, the results of the authors' work with abused children and their parents

0-674-11426-4 HARVARD PB........................$8.95

Suzanne **Stutman**

Broken Feather: A Journey of Healing

How one woman dealt with childhood abuse

0-9648261-0-0 MANOR HOUSE $42.00

0-9648261-1-9 MANOR HOUSE PB..................$42.00

Sexual Abuse

Kenneth M. **Adams**

Silently Seduced: When Parents Make Their Children Partners—Understanding Covert Incest

For those who have experienced "psychological marriage" to a parent

1-55874-131-3 HEALTH COMMUNICATIONS PB$7.95

Ellen **Bass** & Louise **Thornton**, editors

I Never Told Anyone: Writing by Women Survivors of Child Sexual Abuse

A collection of personal accounts

0-06-096573-8 HARPERCOLLINS PB $12.00

Edsel **Erickson** & Alan **McEvoy**

Teenagers at Risk

A look at why some teenagers are sexually abused

See also **TEENAGE HEALTH**

1-55691-042-8 LEARNING PUBLICATIONS PB..$12.95

Susan **Forward** & Craig **Buck**

Betrayal of Innocence: Incest and Its Devastation

Includes case histories and chapters devoted to each type of incest

0-14-011002-X PENGUIN PB $10.95

Sylvia **Fraser**

My Father's House: A Memoir of Incest and Healing

Beautifully written account by a woman who had been sexually abused by her father

0-06-097218-1 HARPERCOLLINS PB $12.00

Anne Stirling **Hastings**

From Generation to Generation: Understanding Sexual Attraction to Children

Understanding those who are attracted to children will end the generation-to-generation curse of sexual abuse

0-9637891-4-7 PRINTED VOICE PB $9.95

Judith **Herman**

Father-Daughter Incest

An academic study of women as victims within families

See also **RAPE, INCEST, AND BATTERED WOMEN** under **THE FEMALE EXPERIENCE** under **WOMEN'S STUDIES** in **SOCIAL STUDIES**

0-674-29506-4 HARVARD PB..............................$12.95

William E. **Prendergast**

Sexual Abuse of Children and Adolescents: A Preventative Guide for Parents, Teachers, and Counselors

In-depth and comprehensive

0-8264-0892-3 CONTINUUM $29.95

Wendy Ann **Wood**

Triumph Over Darkness: Understanding and Healing the Trauma of Childhood Sexual Abuse

Help for moving beyond the trauma of sexual abuse

0-941831-86-8 BEYOND WORDS PB $12.95

Death and Mourning

Philippe **Ariés**

Western Attitudes Toward Death from the Middle Ages to the Present

Four essays illuminate Western culture's evolution of death from the familiar to the frightening

0-8018-1762-5 JOHNS HOPKINS PB $10.95

Barbara Lazear **Ascher**

Landscape Without Gravity: A Memoir of Grief

The intelligent, unflinching chronicle of the author's coming to terms with her wild, sometimes estranged brother's death from AIDS. "A warm, witty, very human voice"—Annie Dillard

0-671-79676-3 DELPHINEUM..........................$20.00

0-14-023495-0 PENGUIN PB $9.95

Jan Selliken **Bernard** & Miriam **Schneider**

The True Work of Dying: A Practical and Compassionate Guide to Easing the Dying Process

From two nurses

0-380-97329-4 AVON...$22.00

Sandi **Caplan** & Gordon **Lang**

Grief's Courageous Journey: A Workbook

Step-by-step journal exercises for personal use or ideal as a facilitator's guide for a grief support group

1-57224-017-2 NEW HARBINGER PB $12.95

Lisa **Carlson**

Caring for Your Own Dead

A unique how-to book

0-942679-01-6 UPPER ACCESS PB $12.95

David **Carroll**

Living with Dying: A Loving Guide for Family and Close Friends

Question-and-answer format deals with the practical aspects of death with special sections on a dying child and a person with AIDS. "A helpful and honest book"—Elisabeth Kübler-Ross

1-55778-356-X MARLOWE PB $12.95

Tom **Crider**

Give Sorrow Words: A Father's Passage Through Grief

1-56512-116-3 ALGONQUIN $16.95

Richard Lewis **Detrich** & Nicola J. **Steele**

How to Recover from Grief

How to deal with the confusion and fear that accompany grief

0-8170-1237-0 JUDSON PB...............................$15.00

Polly Young **Eisendrath**

The Gifts of Suffering: A Guide to Resilience and Renewal

How loss and adversity can help make you strong

0-201-47964-8 ADDISON-WESLEY.................$20.00

D.J. **Enright**

The Oxford Book of Death

A wide-ranging anthology of literary and philosophical commentary on death

0-19-282013-3 OXFORD PB...............................$12.95

Victoria **Frigo** & others

You Can Help Someone Who's Grieving: A How-To Healing Handbook

0-14-025907-4 PENGUIN PB $9.95

E.J. **Gold**

The American Book of the Dead

From a Human Potential advocate who leads a journey toward death based on the *Tibetan Book of the Dead*

0-06-251310-9 HARPERCOLLINS PB $13.00

Earl A. **Grollman**

Bereaved Children and Teens: A Support Guide for Parents and Professionals

Rabbi and author of *Talking About Death*, Grollman has culled advice from various experts who share the view that kids are often forgotten mourners and excluded from the grieving process

0-8070-2306-X BEACON $27.50

Concerning Death: A Practical Guide for the Living

0-8070-2765-0 BEACON PB $16.00

Evan **Imber-Black** & Janine **Roberts**

Rituals for Our Times and Our Relationships

Sympathetic and accessible

0-06-092210-9 HARPERPERENNIAL PB $13.00

Elisabeth **Kübler-Ross**

Living with Death and Dying

An essential book for patients and their families

0-02-567140-5 MACMILLAN $10.95

On Life After Death

Four inspirational essays: "Living and Dying," "There Is No Death," "Life, Death, and Life After Death," and "Death of a Parent"

0-89087-653-3 CELESTIAL ARTS PB..............$7.95

Questions and Answers on Death and Dying

From the respected doctor who has specialized in the terminally ill

0-02-089142-3 COLLIER PB...........................$9.00

Working It Through

Describes the author's experience running innovative workshops on dying

0-02-022000-6MACMILLAN PB $7.00

Clarence **Miller**

The Funeral Book: An Insider Reveals How to Save Money and Reduce Stress While Planning a Funeral

1-88500-302-1 REED PB...$7.95

Ernest **Morgan**

Dealing Creatively with Death: A Manual of Death Education and Simple Burial

Discusses funerals, grief, and bereavement in a frank, straightforward way

PREFACE BY JESSICA MITFORD

0-935016-79-1 BARCLAY PB..............................$11.95

Sherwin B. **Nuland**

How We Die: Reflections on Life's Final Chapter

A rare book that demythologizes death not with tired homilies but with an unflinching look at its reality. Rooted in both medical science and personal experience, Dr. Nuland's account, for instance, "of the decline and death of his grandmother—with whom he shared a bedroom until he was in his late teens and she was in her nineties—is unforgettable"—*Kirkus Reviews*

0-679-41461-4 KNOPF........................$24.00
0-679-74244-1 VINTAGE PB........................$13.00

Morrie **Schwartz**

Letting Go: Morrie's Reflections on Living While Dying

The story of a confrontation with terminal illness and death which came out of interviews with Schwartz—a retired university professor facing Lou Gehrig's Disease—on ABC's "Nightline" and NPR's "Talk of the Nation"

See also **GENERAL BOOKS** under **SPIRITUALITY** under **SPIRITUALITY** in **RELIGION, SPIRITUALITY, AND PHILOSOPHY**

0-8027-1315-7 WALKER........................$18.00

Carol **Staudacher**

Beyond Grief: A Guide for Recovering from the Death of a Loved One

0-934986-43-6 NEW HARBINGER PB........................$13.95

Ganga **Stone**

Start the Conversation: The Only Book You'll Ever Need About Death

Lessons for the terminally ill

0-446-51959-6 WARNER........................$22.95

Judy **Tatelbaum**

The Courage to Grieve: Creative Living, Recovery, and Growth Through Grief

0-06-091185-9 HARPERCOLLINS PB........................$12.00

Roberta **Temes**

Living with an Empty Chair: A Guide Through Grief

Includes useful bibliographies at the end of each chapter

0-88282-110-5 NEW HORIZON........................$15.95
0-8290-1773-9 IRVINGTON PB........................$9.95

Patricia **Weenolsen**

The Art of Dying

Dying with grace and dignity

FOREWORD BY BERNIE SIEGEL

0-312-14278-1 ST. MARTIN'S........................$22.95

Savine **Weizman** & Phyllis **Kamm**

About Mourning: Support and Guidance for the Bereaved

A thorough exploration of the mourning process

0-89885-136-X HUMAN SCIENCES........................$36.95
0-89885-309-5 HUMAN SCIENCES PB........................$20.95

Death of a Spouse

Lynn **Caine** & Eleanor **Friede**

Being a Widow

A candid guide to the problems of widowhood, from the initial shock of death to the first steps toward a new life

0-14-013025-X PENGUIN PB........................$11.95

Scott **Campbell** & Phyllis **Silverman**

Widower

Case histories

0-89503-140-X BAYWOOD........................$34.95

Earl **Goethals**

What Helped Me When My Loved One Died

0-8070-3229-8 BEACON PB........................$12.95

C.S. **Lewis**

Grief Observed

Lewis's effort to console himself after the death of his wife—and to defend against his loss of belief in God. "The author has done something I believed impossible—assuaged his own grief by conveying it"—Anne Freemantle

0-06-065284-5 HARPERCOLLINS PB........................$10.00

Morton A. **Lieberman**

Doors Close, Doors Open: Widows, Grieving and Growing

Interviews with more than 700 widows to learn how they coped with their loss; includes a chapter on widowers as well

0-399-14141-3 PUTNAM........................$23.95

Ted **Menten**

Going Solo: Widows Tell Their Stories of Love, Loss, and Rediscovery

Elegant and inspiring essays from women who have lost their husbands

1-56138-611-1 RUNNING PRESS........................$12.95

Ellen Sue **Stern**

Living With Loss: Meditations for Grieving Widows

Daily meditations as a companion during mourning

0-440-50598-4 BANTAM PB........................$8.95

Death of a Parent

Marc **Angel**

The Orphaned Adult: Confronting the Death of a Parent

Religious and philosophical insights from a rabbi

0-89885-334-6 HUMAN SCIENCES........................$26.95

Eda **Le Shan**

Learning to Say Good-Bye

A well-written book for adults who have lost parents

0-380-40105-3 AVON PB........................$8.00

Katherine **Donnelly**

Recovering from the Loss of a Parent: Adult Sons and Daughters Reveal How They Overcame Their Grief

Fascinating accounts of dealing with grief

0-425-13916-6 BERKLEY PB........................$5.99

Maxine **Harris**

The Loss that Is Forever: The Lifelong Impact of the Early Death of a Mother or Father

0-452-27268-8 PLUME PB........................$12.95

Fiona **Marshall**

Losing a Parent: A Personal Guide to Coping With that Special Grief that Comes With Losing a Parent

A resource guide to cope emotionally and practically

1-55561-056-0 FISHER PB........................$12.95

Edward **Myers**

When a Parent Dies: A Guide for Adults

A practical guide, with resources for the bereaved

0-14-009211-0 PENGUIN PB........................$11.95

Death of a Child

Mark **Cosman**

In the Wake of Death: Surviving the Loss of a Child

How a father dealt with the murder of his daughter

0-688-14336-9 MORROW........................$22.00

Deborah L. **Davis**

Empty Cradle, Broken Heart: Surviving the Death of Your Baby

Covers every aspect, from emotional to physical changes as well as deciding to have another child

1-55591-063-7 FULCRUM PB........................$12.95

Douglas **Hobbie**

Being Brett: Chronicle of a Daughter's Death

"…it is a book that will help readers edge close to the heart of the matter: what it means to live, to lose (or lose someone), to leave this world all too soon, or be left behind by someone dearly loved"—Robert Coles

0-8050-2520-0 HOLT........................$22.50

Elisabeth **Kübler-Ross**

On Children and Death

Advice for parents on confronting the illness and death of a child

0-02-089144-X COLLIER PB........................$10.00

Irving **Leon**

When a Baby Dies: Psychotherapy for Pregnancy and Newborn Loss

0-300-05230-8 YALE PB $15.00

Janet Deveson **Lord**

When a Baby Suddenly Dies: Cot Death—The Impact and Effects

An Australian mother who lost her baby to SIDS covers all aspects of the mysterious killer

0-85572-162-6 SEVEN HILLS PB $13.95

Harriet **Schiff**

The Bereaved Parent

Includes a section on the effect of the loss on siblings and the parents' marriage

0-14-005043-4 VIKING PB $11.95

Suicide

Sol **Gordon**

When Living Hurts

Practical advice for helping those who are severely depressed and contemplating suicide

0-8074-0310-5 U.A.H.C. PB $10.00

Earl **Grollman**

Suicide: Prevention, Intervention, Postvention

Offers prevention strategies and help for the victim's family

0-8070-2707-3 BEACON PB $14.00

Richard A. **Heckler**

Waking Up, Alive: The Descent, the Suicide Attempt and the Return to Life

Heckler looks at the descent into isolation and pain that culminates in a rational attempt at suicide, and the new strength of hope that can emerge in the wake of such an attempt: "wake up alive." "This remarkable and exciting book is a pleasure to read and a treasure to contemplate. It is about recovery and the fructifying role of realistic hope. I enthusiastically recommend it"—Edwin S. Schneidman

0-399-13945-1 PUTNAM $23.95

Polly **Joan**

Preventing Teenage Suicide: The Living Alternative Handbook

A how-to book for parents and guidance counselors

0-89885-247-1 HUMAN SCIENCES $30.95
0-89885-349-4 HUMAN SCIENCES PB $18.95

Paul **Quinnett**

Suicide—The Forever Decision: A Book for Those Thinking About Suicide, and for Those Who Know, Love, or Counsel Them

A clearly written, straightforward book to deter people from suicide; includes case studies

0-8245-1352-5 CONTINUUM PB $9.95

Herbert **Hendin**

Suicide in America

Discusses the ethics of euthanasia

See also **ASSISTED SUICIDE**

0-393-03688-X NORTON $23.00

Assisted Suicide

Herbert **Hendin**

Suicide in America

Discusses the ethics of euthanasia

0-393-03688-X NORTON $23.00

T. Patrick **Hill** & David **Shirley**

A Good Death: Taking More Control at the End of Your Life

From the Director of Education at Choice in Dying, a complete resource for all aspects of dying with dignity

0-201-06223-2 ADDISON-WESLEY PB $11.95

Stephen **Jamison**

Final Acts of Love: Families, Friends, and Assisted Dying

"Here is the inside story on assisted dying: its pathos and tenderness, plus the tribulations. A unique and impressive tool"
—Derek Humphry, *Final Exit*

0-87477-816-6 PUTNAM $23.95
0-87477-849-2 TARCHER PB $13.95

Gerald **Larue**

Playing God: Deciding Your Life and Death

1-55921-145-8 MOYER BELL $24.95

Lonny **Shavelson**

A Chosen Death: The Dying Confront Assisted Suicide

Emergency room physician and photojournalist recalls friends and patients who opted for physician-assisted suicide

0-684-80100-0 SIMON & SCHUSTER $23.00

Depression

Harold H. **Bloomfield** & Peter **McWilliams**

How to Heal Depression

By defining what depression is, the cure is relatively manageable. Going one step further than other books on the topic, it deals with the importance of nutrition and exercise

0-931580-39-0 PRELUDE $14.95
0-931580-61-7 PRELUDE PB $5.95

Richard **Brodie**

Getting Past OK: A Straightforward Guide to Having a Fantastic Life

Advice, encouragement, and good cheer for getting out of life's ruts. "Incredibly useful!"
—Bill Gates, CEO, Microsoft

0-9636001-0-9 INTEGRAL PB $9.95
0-446-67188-6 WARNER PB $10.99

Robert **Benson**

Between the Dreaming and the Coming True

Elegant bundles of wisdom illuminate one man's struggle with depression. "Benson has given us that rare gift, a thought-provoking record of his own spiritual quest for God through the dark night of depression"—*Publishers Weekly*

See also **PERSONAL AND PSYCHIC DEVELOPMENT** under **SPIRITUALITY** under **SPIRITUALITY** in **RELIGION, SPIRITUALITY, AND PHILOSOPHY**

0-06-060973-7 HARPERCOLLINS $18.00
0-06-060900-1 HARPERCOLLINS PB $10.00

Mark **Gold** & Lois **Morris**

The Good News About Depression

0-553-34511-7 BANTAM PB $14.95

John **Greist** & James **Jefferson**

Depression and Its Treatment

0-446-32718-2 WARNER PB $3.95

Cheri **Huber**

Being Present in the Darkness: Using Depression as a Tool for Self Discovery

How to heal yourself using the lessons of depression

0-399-52223-9 PERIGEE PB $10.00

Kay Redfield **Jamison**

An Unquiet Mind

Professor of psychiatry at Johns Hopkins and foremost authority on manic-depressive illness, Jamison offers a remarkable personal testimony about her own lifelong struggle with manic-depression. Vivid, direct, and witty, Dr. Jamison's memoir traces the growth and effect of her illness—an illness that finally led to a suicide attempt—and the slow and courageous process of mastering that illness through knowledge, medication, and self-discipline. An exhilarating and readable memoir

See also **DEPRESSION** under **DISORDERS AND TREATMENT** under **PSYCHOLOGY** in **SOCIAL STUDIES**

0-679-44374-6 KNOPF $22.00
0-679-76330-9 RANDOM HOUSE PB $12.00

Earnie **Larsen** & Cara A. **Macken**

Overcoming Depressive Living Syndrome: How to Enjoy Life, Not Just Endure It

Interactive exercises, self-evaluation tools, and diagrams by the leading authority on this malady

0-89243-868-1 TRIUMPH PB $12.95

Donald **McKnew**, Jr

Why Isn't Johnny Crying?: Coping with Depression in Children

0-393-30240-7 NORTON PB $5.95

Caroline Adams **Miller**

Bright Words for Dark Days: Meditations for Women Who Get the Blues

From witty to profound, these daily meditations are aimed at understanding the cause and effect of depression

0-553-37181-9 BANTAM PB $9.95

Michael T. **Murray**

Natural Alternatives to Prozac

A concise and reasoning approach to the simple things one can do to alleviate anxiety and depression, without pharmaceuticals

0-688-14684-8 MORROW $20.00

John **Nelson** & Andrea **Nelson**, editors

Sacred Sorrows: Embracing and Transforming Depression

A collection of inspiring essays by authors who have struggled with depression includes William Styron, Eric Fromm, and many others

0-87477-822-0 TARCHER PB..............................$14.95

William Styron

Michael J. **Norden**

Beyond Prozac: Antidotes for Modern Times

Beyond Prozac, says Norden, lie many innovative natural remedies that combat depression in much the same way as the controversial drug. Light therapies, melatonin, specialized diets, acupuncture, and sleep deprivation are just some of the therapies that Norden discusses along with other alternative drugs and the successes and failures of Prozac itself

0-06-039151-0 HARPERCOLLINS.....................$23.00

Demitri **Papolos** & Janice **Papolos**

Overcoming Depression

0-06-096594-0 HARPERPERENNIAL PB $15.00

Maggie **Scarf**

Unfinished Business

An interesting analysis of the causes of depression in women

0-345-34248-8 BALLANTINE PB..........................$6.99

Tracy **Thompson**

The Beast: A Reckoning with Depression

Washington Post reporter chronicles her descent into depression and her heroic and honest resiliency to mental health. "It is a journey that is powerful, wrenching, and rare in its unflinching honest and steely-eyed self-examination"—Susan Faludi

0-399-14077-8 PUTNAM....................................$23.95

Elizabeth **Wurtzel**

Prozac Nation: Young and Depressed in America

This is a harrowing, if at times hilarious, account of what is becoming an all-too-common occurrence among today's young people

0-395-68093-X HOUGHTON MIFFLIN...............$19.95

1-57322-512-6 RIVERHEAD PB.........................$12.00

Divorce

Constance **Ahrons**

The Good Divorce: Keeping Your Family Together When Your Marriage Comes Apart

Based on a recent study that focused on normal divorced families: develops the concept that the binucleate family is a viable cultural alternative

0-06-092634-1 BASIC PB $13.00

Dawn Bradley **Berry**

The Divorce Sourcebook

Covers the logistical, legal, economic, and emotional aspects of divorce; includes a state-by-state appendix

1-56565-335-1 LOWELL.....................................$25.00

1-56565-474-9 LOWELL PB $16.00

George **Feifer**

Divorce: An Oral Portrait

A comforting collection of true stories on a wide range of circumstances and reactions to the end of a marriage

1-56584-272-3 NEW PRESS $25.00

Richard **Gardner**

The Parents' Book About Divorce

See also **SINGLE PARENTING**

0-933812-27-2 CREATIVE THERAPEUTICS $29.95

0-553-28632-3 BDD PB $6.50

Penny **Kaganoff** & Susan **Spano**, editors

Women on Divorce: A Bedside Companion

Fourteen provocative essays by notable writers offer a woman's perspective on divorce. Ellen Gilchrist considers the psychology of mate selection, Perri Klass discusses divorce as gossip, and Ann Patchett reflects on the end of her strict Catholic marriage. Plus essays by Anne Roiphe, Mary Morris, Francine Prose, and others

0-15-100114-6 HARCOURT BRACE $22.00

Gloria **Lintermans**

The Newly Divorced Book of Protocol: How to Be Civil When You Hate Their Guts

An encyclopedia for the newly divorced; covers a wide range of topics with a humorous edge

1-56980-037-5 BARRICADE $17.95

Catherine **Napolitane** & Victoria **Pelligrino**

Living and Loving After Divorce

The importance of relearning independence and the ability to trust

0-451-14988-2 NEW AMERICAN LIBRARY PB ...$4.99

Harvey **Rosenstock**

Journey Through Divorce: Five Stages Toward Recovery

Based on clinical studies and personal experience; the predictable stages of divorce

0-89885-403-2 HUMAN SCIENCES...................$24.95

Elliot **Samuelson**

The Divorce Law Handbook: A Comprehensive Guide to Matrimonial Law

Clear information from a matrimonial attorney

0-89885-411-3 HUMAN SCIENCES PB $20.95

Daniel **Sitarz**

Divorce Yourself: The National No-Fault Divorce Kit

This bestselling, critically acclaimed legal reference on divorce offers detailed instructions, checklists, worksheets, and explanations for every step of a divorce in all 50 states and Washington, DC

0-935755-13-6 NOVA PB.................................$24.95

Diane **Vaughan**

Uncoupling

The patterns that move couples apart, with one person initiating the separation

0-679-73002-8 VINTAGE PB.............................$13.00

Judith **Wallerstein** & Sandra **Blakeslee**

Second Chances: Men, Women and Children a Decade After Divorce

0-89919-949-6 HOUGHTON MIFFLIN PB $10.95

Judith **Wallerstein** & Joan **Kelly**

Surviving the Breakup: How Children and Parents Cope with Divorce

0-465-08344-7 BASIC PB $14.50

Robert **Weiss**

Marital Separation: Managing After a Marriage Ends

How to contend with the end of a marriage and the difficult transition to single life

0-465-09723-5 BASIC BOOKS PB.....................$18.00

Ellie **Wymand**

Men on Divorce: Conversations with Ex-Husbands

Based on extensive interviews with 45 divorced men; discusses the pain and difficulties men experience as a result of divorce, including issues such as part-time parenting, sexual politics, sharing family friends, and grief

1-56170-096-7 HAY HOUSE PB.........................$12.00

Elissa P. **Benedek** & Catherine F. **Brown**

How to Help Your Child Overcome Your Divorce

To ameliorate the psychological dilemmas sure to plague every family after a marriage fails

See also **SINGLE PARENTING** under **BEING A PARENT** under **PARENTING**

0-88048-565-5 AMERICAN PSYCHIATRIC.........$22.95

Rape

Pauline **Bart** & Patricia **O'Brien**
Stopping Rape: Successful Survival Strategies
0-8077-6212-1 ELSEVIER PB..............................$17.95

Dianna **Booher**
Rape: What Would You Do If...?
0-671-49485-6 MESSNER PB..............................$4.95

Cynthia **Carosella**, editor
Who's Afraid of the Dark?: A Forum of Truth, Support, and Assurance for Those Affected by Rape
A rape survivor offers advice on rape and its aftermath through a collection of writings from women and men who have been raped
See also **RAPE, INCEST, AND BATTERED WOMEN**
0-06-095072-2 HARPERPERENNIAL PB $12.00

David **Finkelhor** & Kersti **Yllo**
License to Rape: Sexual Abuse of Wives
An examination of the history and theory of rape in marriage, with testimony from victims
0-02-910401-7 FREE PRESS PB..............................$16.95

Linda **Ledray**
Recovering from Rape
0-8050-2928-1 OWLET PB..............................$12.95

Alan **McEvoy** & Jeff **Brookings**
If She Is Raped: A Book for Husbands, Fathers, and Male Friends
Includes case studies and community outreach services
1-55691-062-2 LEARNING PUBLICATIONS PB..$12.95

Diana **Russell**
Rape in Marriage
INTRODUCTION BY SUSAN BROWNMILLER
0-253-35055-7 INDIANA..............................$39.95
0-253-20563-8 INDIANA PB..............................$16.95

Rosalind **Wiseman**
Defending Ourselves: A Guide to Prevention, Self-Defense, and Recovery from Rape
The founder and director of Woman's Way, a self-defense program, discusses in full all aspects of rape, how to protect yourself, and what to do if assaulted
See also **RAPE, INCEST, AND BATTERED WOMEN** under **THE FEMALE EXPERIENCE** under **WOMEN'S STUDIES** in **SOCIAL STUDIES**
0-374-52415-7 NOONDAY PB..............................$10.00

Quality of Life

Stephen R. **Covey** & others
First Things First: A Principle-Centered Approach to Time and Life Management
An insightful study that tells us how to break free of entrenched, time-squandering habits, how to relocate the sources of personal passion and drive, and how successfully to delegate power. A must for business people and anyone who seeks to expand the parameters of his or her personal achievement
0-671-86441-6 SIMON & SCHUSTER..............................$23.00

Harriet **Lerner**
Life Preservers: Staying Afloat in Love and Life
New Woman magazine advice columnist answers life's big and little questions
0-06-017420-X HARPERCOLLINS..............................$23.50

Nancy **Mayer**
The Male Mid-Life Crisis: Fresh Starts After 40
Insightful case histories of every possible scenario American men at 40 and older face and how to rise to the challenges of responsible maturation
See also **MEN'S HEALTH** under **HEALTH**
0-451-16634-5 SIGNET PB..............................$5.95

Simon **Speyer**
You Can Be Driven Sane: Know Yourself & Heal Yourself—A Journal of Self-Discovery
1-56171-337-6 ATRIUM PB..............................$5.50

Joyce L. **Vedral**
Look In, Look Up, Look Out: Be the Person You Were Meant to Be
Prolific author and exercise expert reveals her personal psychic system for nurturing the soul, based on the premise of trusting yourself more
0-446-51863-8 WARNER..............................$22.95

Values

Pema **Chodron**
Start Where You Are: A Guide to Compassionate Living
This how-to uses a framework of 59 Tibetan Buddhist maxims that help the individual to let go of fear and, starting with the self, to live with compassion as a driving value
0-87773-880-7 SHAMBHALA PB..............................$12.00

Laurent **Daloz** & others
Common Fire: Lives of Commitment in a Complex World
The motivations of over 100 people who work for societal betterment are revealed by four educational researchers
0-8070-2004-4 BEACON..............................$25.00

Eileen R. **Hannegan**
When Money Is Not Enough: Fulfillment in Work
How to find meaning in work
1-88522-314-5 BEYOND WORDS PB..............................$10.95

Kerry M. **Olitzky** & Rachel T. **Sabath**
Striving Toward Virtue: A Contemporary Guide for Jewish Ethical Behavior
Authors drawe from Judaism's ethical roots to discuss topics such as "Gossip: the Ecology of Words" and "Senseless Hatred: Committing to Love"
0-881-25534-5 KTAV..............................$23.00

Sidney B. **Simon**
In Search of Values: 31 Strategies for Finding Out What Really Matters Most to You
The best-selling author of *Values Clarification* serves up an intriguing group of exercises (such as writing your own obituary) designed to reveal to us what we actually believe. If this sounds frightening, it's not. Dr. Simon's methods are adventurous and playful, and the dividends they yield can be challenging, even profound
0-446-39437-8 WARNER PB..............................$8.99

Self-Motivation

Dale **Carnegie**
How to Win Friends and Influence People
0-671-72365-0 POCKET PB..............................$6.99

Jimmy **Carter** & Rosalynn **Carter**
Everything to Gain: Making the Most of the Rest of Your Life
1-55728-388-5 ARKANSAS PB..............................$20.00

Jimmy Carter

Carole **Hyatt** & Linda **Gottlieb**
When Smart People Fail: Rebuilding Yourself for Success
0-14-010727-4 PENGUIN PB..............................$12.00

Barry Neil **Kaufman**

Out-Smarting Your Karma and Other Pre-Ordained Conditions

An illustrated book of poignant thoughts on topics ranging from pride and sorrow to meditation and perspective

1-88725-404-8 EPIC CENTURY PB $9.95

Larry **King** & Bill **Gilbert**

How to Talk to Anyone, Anytime, Anywhere: The Secrets of Good Communication

From the master of talk

See also **CELEBRITY BIOGRAPHIES AND AUTOBIOGRAPHIES** under **TELEVISION** in **PERFORMING ARTS AND MEDIA**

0-517-59905-8 CROWN $20.00
0-517-88453-4 CROWN PB $12.00

Norman Vincent **Peale**

The Power of Positive Thinking

0-13-686445-7 SIMON & SCHUSTER $20.00
0-449-21493-1 FAWCETT PB $5.99

Why Some Positive Thinkers Get Powerful Results

0-449-21359-5 CREST PB $5.99

You Can Get It If You Want

0-671-66072-1 SIMON & SCHUSTER $12.00

Anthony **Robbins**

Unlimited Power: The New Science of Personal Achievement

0-684-82436-1 SIMON & SCHUSTER $23.00

David **Schwartz**

The Magic of Getting What You Want

0-425-10391-9 BERKELEY PB $12.00

David **Seabury**

The Art of Selfishness: Fill Your Life with Confidence and Success

99914-73-04-1 POCKET PB $4.95

Self-Esteem

Nathaniel **Branden**

Honoring the Self: Self-Esteem and Personal Transformation

How to nurture self-esteem in children and more on the ethics of rational self-interest

0-553-26814-7 BDD PB $6.99

The Six Pillars of Self-Esteem

Outlines six facets that define the author's guide to living better through self-reliance and personal responsibility

0-553-37439-7 BDD PB $12.95

Albert **Ellis** & Robert A. **Harper**

A New Guide to Rational Living

Rational-emotive therapy processes for self-therapy

0-87980-042-9 WILSHIRE PB $10.00

Jack **Canfield** & Jacqueline **Miller**

Heart at Work: Stories and Strategies for Building Self-Esteem and Reawakening the Soul at Work

Inspiring personal testimonies from Nelson Mandela, Mother Theresa, and others

0-07-011643-1 MCGRAW HILL PB $14.95

Steven **Carter** & Julia **Sokol**

Men Like Women Who Like Themselves (And Other Secrets that the Smartest Women Know)

Relationship experts talk about the importance of self-esteem

0-385-31513-9 DELACORTE $21.95

Joyce Brothers

How to Get Whatever You Want Out of Life

0-345-34747-1 BALLANTINE PB $5.99

Janet **Landman**

Regret: The Persistence of the Possible

This book takes both a scholarly and humane look at that most gnawing and melancholic emotions. Lack of education, Landman discovers, is what people regret most, followed by type of employment and marriage. Exploring virtually every discipline of thought, especially great literary works, she sees the varying ways regret is regarded. The imaginative strength of regret, she concludes, is how we "accomplish the task of becoming fully human"

0-19-507178-6 OXFORD $30.00

Ferenc **Mate**

A Reasonable Life: Toward a Simpler, Secure, More Humane Existence

In this rousing plea for a fundamental change in American values and behavior, Mate examines modern society's deteriorating quality of life and the resulting alienation of the individual. He offers inspiring solutions to make personal changes and take back control of our lives

0-920256-25-2 NORTON $17.95

Mildred **Newman** & Bernard **Berkowitz**

How to Be Your Own Best Friend

0-345-34239-9 BALLANTINE PB $4.95

Gail **Sheehy**

Passages

0-553-27106-7 BDD PB $7.50

Pathfinders

0-553-27084-2 BDD PB $6.99

Sidney **Simon**

Getting Unstuck: Breaking Through the Barriers to Change

0-446-39024-0 WARNER PB $11.99

Gloria **Steinem**

Revolution from Within

In this national bestseller Steinem—writer, activist, and founder of *Ms.* magazine—turns her revolutionary ardor to the issue of self-esteem. *Revolution from Within* is a moving personal journey and an authoritative public statement

0-316-81247-1 LITTLE, BROWN PB $11.95

My hope is that each time you come upon a story of mine, you will turn inward and listen to a story told by your own inner voice. These last three years have taught me that, like the spider spinning her web, we create much of the outer world from within ourselves. "The universe as we know it," as Teilhard de Chardin said and as the new physics confirms, "is a joint product of the observer and the observed." We make progress by a constant spiraling back and forth between the inner world and the outer one, the personal and the political, the self and the circumstance. Nature doesn't move in a straight line, and as part of nature, neither do we.

REVOLUTION FROM WITHIN

Letting Go of Guilt, Fear, or Anger

Robert **Alberti** & Michael **Emmons**

Your Perfect Right: A Guide to Assertive Living

Now in its seventh edition, this book is "…filled with a wealth of examples on how to cope with everyday situations…counters feelings of futility"—*LA Times*

0-915166-12-7 IMPACT PB $12.95

Robert **Anthony**

The Ultimate Secrets of Total Self-Confidence

A step-by-step to be more creative and abandon fear, worry, and guilt

0-425-10170-3 BERKELEY PB $5.50

Sharon Anthony **Bower** & Gordon H. **Bower**

Asserting Yourself: A Practical Guide for Positive Change

This updated edition contains exercises, scripts, and more tips

0-201-57088-2 ADDISON WESLEY PB $12.95

Gary **Hankins** & Carol **Hankins**

Prescription for Anger: Coping With Angry Feelings and Angry People

Insights from a national authority in the field on such topics as why letting all your anger out is *not* the healthiest way to express it, and other tips on anger management whether it comes from within or without

0-446-36392-8 WARNER PB $6.50

Gerald **Jampolsky**

Goodbye to Guilt: Releasing Fear Through Forgiveness

0-553-34574-5 BANTAM PB $11.95

Susan **Jeffers**

Feel the Fear...And Do It Anyway

0-449-90292-7 FAWCETT PB $12.00

Harold **Kushner**

How Good Do We Have to Be?: A New Understanding of Guilt and Forgiveness

The prolific rabbi offers a new way of interpreting Adam and Eve's eating from the Tree of Knowledge as a brave step toward self-knowledge rather than an act of disobedience

0-316-50741-5 LITTLE, BROWN $21.45

Craig B. **Mardus**

How to Make Worry Work for You

Techniques and exercises to help convert the energy used for worrying into fuel for creative, productive activity

0-446-51967-7 WARNER PB $14.95

Reneau Z. **Peurifoy**

Anxiety, Phobias, & Panic

Techniques in mastering fears—everything from mild anxieties to severe phobias—from an internationally recognized specialist

0-446-67053-7 WARNER PB $10.99

Manuel **Smith**

When I Say No, I Feel Guilty

0-553-26390-0 BDD PB $6.99

Part 14

Business & Reference

T. Boone Pickens

A

Abominable Snowman or Yeti:
Manlike creature associated with the Himalayas. Known through tracks ascribed to it and alleged encounters, it is supposedly 6 to 7 feet tall and covered with long hair. While many scholars dismiss it as a myth, others claim it may be a kind of ape.
—*The Concise Columbia Encyclopedia*
1473

Buckeye
An American name for the different species of horse chestnut, *desculus,* native to the U.S.
—*The National Gardening Association Dictionary of Horticulture*
1574

Charleyhorse
This popular term is harmless as sex-linked terms go. The problem is not with the term per se, but with the fact that it is one of hundreds of male-oriented terms that give the language an overwhelming male "voice." There is nothing wrong with using male expressions, as long as they are balanced with female expressions.
—*The Dictionary of Bias-Free Usage*
441

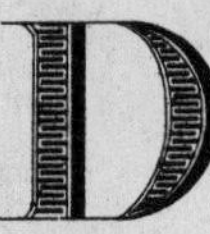

Discomfort
Agony. The supposedly comforting language of dentistry. If your dentist, drill at the ready, informs you that you may feel a little discomfort, it is time to grip the arms of the chair and think pure thoughts. —*A Dictionary of Euphemisms*
1478

Embolalia
Meaningless babbling, var. embololalia.
—*Penguin Dictionary of Psychology*
480

Klop, Klap
Rhymes with "slop." German: "blow," "hit." 1. A blow; to hit. "Give him a klop; you're closer." 2. More colorfully, to klop is to yammer, to yak, to blab on at great length and without mercy. "He klopped me in kop" means either "He knocked me in the head," or, better, "He talked my ears off." "All day long he klops about his troubles." "Klop der kop in der vant" means "Beat your head against the wall." —Leo Rosten *The Joys of Yiddish*
995

Limbo
(Lt. *limbus;* lit. "body, hem of a garment") In Roman Catholic theology the state and place of the dead who, though excluded from the beatific vision, were not guilty of personal sin. Theologians distinguished between (1) the *limbus patrus,* in which Old Testament saints remained until the resurrection of Christ, and (2) the *limbus infantum,* in which persons dying in original sin, but innocent of personal guilt, enjoy full natural happiness.
360

Mesopotamia
In ancient Mesopotamia, the most widely consumed alcoholic drink at all periods was probably beer. However, grape wine is already mentioned in cuneiform texts preserved on clay tablets from Ur dating to approximately 2750 B.C. A drinking song in ancient Sumer (c. 200 B.C.) lists all the implements required for making beer and wine.
—*The Oxford Companion to Wine*
1508

Ninel (f.)
Russian: modern coinage adopted by patriotic Russian citizens, representing Lenin spelled backwards. Pet form: Nelya. —*Oxford Dictionary of First Names*
1478

"Only time will tell"
A cliché especially of broadcast news journalism and used by reporters to round off a story when they can't think of anything else to say. The proverbial expression has existed since 1539. *Time Magazine* quoted Edwin Newman, a former NBC-TV correspondent, on a continuing weakness of TV news: "There are too many correspondents standing outside buildings and saying 'Time will tell'."
—*The Dictionary of Cliches*
1480

Upper Sandusky
Village, of Wyandot Co., NW Cen. Ohio, 18 m. NNW of Marion; pop. (1980) 5967
—*Geographical Dictionary*
1476

Violence
"Great men have reaching hands; oft have I struck
Those that I never saw, and struck them dead."
—Lord Say
2 Henry VI
790

Warts
See adulterer cures warts; corpse's hand cures; cross cures; counting wart cure; elder protects against and cures disease; gooseberry thorn; iron cures; knots used in cures; moon, pointing at; moonlight "washes" warts away; pins cure warts; tree disease transferred to; warts.
—*A Dictionary of Superstitions*
324

Xmas \'kris-məs *also* 'eks-məs\ *n* [*X* (symbol for *Christ,* fr. the Gk letter chi (X), initial of *Christos* Christ) + *-mas* (in *Christmas*)] (1551): CHRISTMAS.
—*Webster's Tenth Collegiate English Dictionary*
1477

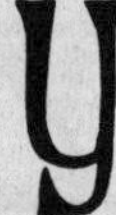

Yggdrasil
In Norse Myth, the giant ash tree which is the foundation of the Universe. Its deepest reaches are in NIFLHEIM, and the serpent NIDHOGG continually gnaws at its roots.
—*Putnam's Concise Mythological Dictionary*
325

F

Foia
V.t.; foiable. In the slang of administrative lawyers, foiable documents are subject to disclosure under the freedom of information act and citizens may foia (= seek to obtain them) under that Act. Common in oral use, there is little written evidence of these terms.
—*Dictionary of Modern Legal Usage*
1478

Grumness (grumnes)
[f. GRUM + -ness] The quality of being "grum." 1675 WYCHERLEY *Country Wife I:* "Well, Jack, by thy long absence from the Towne, the grumness of thy countenance, and the slovenliness of thy habit; I shou'd give thee joy, shou'd I not, of Marriage?"
—*Oxford English Dictionary*
1478

Haunch of Venison, The
A poetical epistle to Lord Clare by Oliver Goldsmith, written about 1770, published 1776.
—*The Oxford Companion to English Literature*
873

Illin
v. (1980s–1990s) Suffering from severe stress.
—*Juba to Jive: A Dictionary of African-American Slang*
257

Jealous
Put the right fingertip at the corner of the mouth and give it a twist.
Memory aid: The little finger suggests J, which causes the mouth to open and drool with jealousy.
—*The Pocket Book of Signing*
1442

Placebo
(Lat., I shall please, or be acceptable). The first antiphon at Vespers of the Office of the Dead began with the words *Placebo Domino in regione vivorum,* "I will walk before the Lord in the land of the living." Those who hoped to get something out of the relatives of the deceased used to make a point of attending this service and singing the Placebo, so the term came to refer to sycophants.
—*Brewer's Dictionary of Phrase and Fable*
1478

Quarrels
Contemplative and bookish men must of necessitie be more quarrelsome than others, because they contend not about matter of fact, nor can determine their controversies by any certain witnesses, nor judges. But as long as they goe towards peace that is Truth, it is no matter which way.
—John Donne, *The Columbia Dictionary of Quotation*
1481

R

Rags and Tatters
They are symbolic of wounds and gashes in the soul. More precise meanings are derived from the actual garment which is in tatters.
—*A Dictionary of Symbols*
1133

-estial
Agrestial, bestial, celestial, supercelestial.
—*New Rhyming Dictionary and Poets Handbook*
1480

Thief
Or rascal GANEF—thieves' vocabulary or similar half-secret language CANT, ARGOT.
—*Illustrated Reverse Dictionary*
1478

Z

Zhu Da [joo dah]
(c. 1625–1705) Born in Nanchang. A descendent of the Ming royal house, he entered a Buddhist monastery on the collapse of the Ming dynasty, and may have feigned madness to survive the purges of the Manchu conquerors. The individualism of his ink paintings of flowers, birds, fish, and landscapes appealed to the Japanese, and his style has become synonymous with Zen painting in Japan.
—*The Cambridge Biographical Encyclopedia*
1474

Business, Industry, and Finance

For related reading, see ECONOMIC HISTORY under TOPICS IN AMERICAN STUDIES in HISTORY OF THE AMERICAS

Seth **Goldin**, editor

The 1997 Information Please Business Almanac

Whatever you need to know to make you more efficient and your business more profitable is probably among the 754 topics described in this ingenious annual. Information, travel, packaging, international currency exchange rates, phone numbers of government officials around the world, shipping, and drug testing—it's all here

0-395-82851-1 HOUGHTON MIFFLIN PB $22.95

Management: Theory and Practice

Roger E. **Allen**

Winnie-The-Pooh on Management

Back to basics with management consultant Allen. An amusing and valuable guide that uses the characters of A.A. Milne to illustrate such principles as good communication, setting clear objectives, strong leadership, and the need for accurate information—the enduring basics of prudent management

0-525-93898-2 DUTTON $17.95

Kenneth **Blanchard** & Spencer **Johnson**

The One Minute Manager

Business advice by parable

0-688-02632-X MORROW $15.00
0-425-09847-8 BERKELEY PB..............................$10.95

David **Bollier**

Aiming Higher: 25 Stories of How Companies Prosper by Combining Sound Management and Social Vision

This collection emphasizes the philosophy that "those businesses which actively serve their many constituencies in creative, morally thoughtful ways also...serve their shareholders best. Companies...do well by doing good" —from the foreword by Norman Lear

0-8144-0319-0 AMACOM $24.95

Dawn-Marie **Driscoll** & others

The Ethical Edge

An instructional volume which maps out the high road for businesses and other organizations wishing to establish an atmosphere of social responsibility

1-57101-051-3 MASTER MEDIA $24.95

Gary **Hamel** & C.K. **Prahalad**

Competing for the Future

"The year's best management book" —*Business Week*

0-87584-716-1 MCGRAW HILL PB $12.95

Barbara J. **Braham**

Managing Stress: Keeping Calm Under Fire

This well-known lecturer and consultant provides a step-by step program to help managers and employees keep their professional and private lives calm and productive

1-55623-855-X IRWIN...$17.00

Creating a Learning Organization

1-56052-351-4 CRISP PB $9.95

Tom **Chappell**

The Soul of a Business

The president of Tom's of Maine and a graduate of Harvard Divinity School provides a blueprint, by way of personal experience, of how a business can survive and thrive while incorporating concern for its workers and environmental awareness with its quest for profits. An inspiring business model for the '90s

0-553-37415-X BANTAM PB................................$11.95

Anne **Donnellon**

Team Talk: The Power of Language in Team Dynamics—Listening Between the Lines to Improve Team Performance

An analysis of team conversations to aid in understanding the challenges of cross-functional teamwork

0-87584-619-X HARVARD BUSINESS................$24.95

Wayne **Dosick**

The Business Bible: The Ten Commandments for Creating an Ethical Workplace

According to the author, "ethical business" is not an oxymoron but rather a pragmatic strategy for long-term profit and growth. In ten anecdotal chapters, Rabbi Dosick combines ancient wisdom and modern business theory to the benefit of everyone

0-688-12237-X MORROW..................................$18.00

Peter F. **Drucker**

The Concept of the Corporation

Drucker's classic study of the management structure of General Motors, and the relevance of GM's organization for other large companies

1-56000-625-0 TRANSACTION PB $21.95

Management: Tasks, Responsibilities, Practices

A long book full of concise, engaging essays that address the question, "What does the manager have to know, or at least have to understand, to be equal to his task?"

0-88730-615-2 HARPERCOLLINS PB $18.00

Masaaki **Imai**

Gemba Kaizen: Going Back to the Basics of Management

0-07-031446-2 HARVARD BUSINESS................$24.95

Michael **Hammer**

Beyond Reengineering: How the Process-Centered Organization Is Reshaping Our Work and Our Lives

A manual with fresh insights on how to detect busywork, how to tap worker imagination, and in general how to transform the workplace from a competitive mechanistic atmosphere to a place that fosters entrepreneurial team players. The authors use case histories from such companies as Showtime Networks, GTE Corp., Aetna Life, American Standard, and General Electric

0-88730-729-9 HARPERCOLLINS $25.00

Gay **Hendricks** & Kate **Ludeman**

The Corporate Mystic: A Guide for Visionaries with Their Feet on the Ground

Corporate consultants for 25 years, the authors of this book assert that corporate leaders of the 21st century will necessarily be problem-solvers who inspire commitment, speak plainly, listen well, manage projects, and create wealth. Concludes with four exercises for attaining the abundance-producing mysticism

0-553-09953-1 BDD..$22.95

Jennifer **James**

Thinking in the Future Tense: Leadership Skills for a New Age

0-684-81098-0 SIMON & SCHUSTER...............$23.00

Laurie Beth **Jones**

Jesus CEO: Using Ancient Wisdom for Visionary Leadership

Guidance tips on inspiring and managing others from a management consultant

0-7868-8126-7 HYPERION PB $10.95

John P. **Kotter**

Leading Change

An accessible guide for making the transition from the overmanagement of the '80s to an emphasis on leadership in the '90s, (management being associated with maintenance of the status quo, and leadership with generating change). Written by a Harvard Business School professor and author of *A Force for Change*

0-87584-747-1 HARVARD BUSINESS PB $24.95

Tom **Peters**

Thriving on Chaos: Handbook for a Management Revolution

The co-author of *In Search of Excellence* reconsiders and declares, "There are no excellent companies." Still, the classic Peters formula—valuable insights and advice packaged in easy-to-digest lists

0-394-56784-6 KNOPF.......................................$30.00
0-06-097184-3 HARPERCOLLINS PB..................$17.00

Tom **Peters** & Nancy **Austin**

A Passion for Excellence: The Leadership Difference

More lessons for corporate success, this time with a focus on individual management champions

0-394-54484-6 RANDOM HOUSE.....................$30.00
0-446-38639-1 WARNER PB..............................$14.99

Bob **Losyk**

Managing a Changing Workforce: Achieving Outstanding Service with Today's Employees

"If business wants to provide outstanding service," writes Bob Losyk of Innovative Training Solutions, "then new ways must be found to motivate a workforce with new beliefs, values, attitudes, and behaviors. This book was written as a blueprint to achieve these objectives." Drawing on experience with clients such as Taco Bell, American Express, IBM, Marriott, and Hyatt, Losyk gives invaluable insight into motivating and rewarding today's workforce

0-9647393-4-8 WORKPLACE TRENDS $24.95

Richard **Luecke**

Scuttle Your Ships Before Advancing: And Other Lessons from History on Leadership and Change for Today's Managers

The success and failures of military strategists, politicians, and explorers are offered as insightful management techniques in this practical guide—from Cortès and Martin Luther to American Presidents Truman and Kennedy. "This work is fun to read, educational and gripping, rare traits in a 'business' work" —*Publishers Weekly*

0-19-508408-X OXFORD $25.00

James F. **Moore**

The Death of Competition: Leadership and Strategy in the Age of Business Ecosystems

The president of GeoPartners Research, Inc., and regular contributor to *The Wall Street Journal* and *The New York Times* looks beyond the age of business competition to explain the alliance-based relationships of the modern business world. Using the metaphor of ecology, he explains the cooperation-competition relationships of Apple, Intel, Microsoft, and IBM, and looks at how co-existence and co-evolution work within "business ecosystems." The result of such a model, he shows, is new values for customers and new competitive positions for companies

9-99610-319-6 HARPERCOLLINS......................$42.00
0-88730-809-0 HARPERCOLLINS PB.................$25.00

Jan **Morrison**

The Second Curve: Managing the Velocity of Change

For CEOs and management who take strategic planning seriously. A detailed study of how corporations can avoid falling behind by identifying and embracing changes in technology, demographics, and newly emerging markets and respond accordingly

0-345-40541-2 BALLANTINE $25.00

National Research Council

Enhancing Organizational Performance

0-309-05397-8 NATIONAL ACADEMY $29.95

Wess **Roberts**

Leadership Secrets of Attila the Hun

0-446-39106-9 WARNER PB...............................$10.99

Tom **Peters** & Robert **Waterman**

In Search of Excellence: Lessons from America's Best-Run Companies

The book that triggered the boom in management advice. It remains without peer for its seriousness of purpose, extensive research, and common-sense wisdom

0-446-38507-7 WARNER PB................................$15.99

J. David **Pincus** & J. Nicholas **DeBonis**

Top Dog: A Different Kind of Book About Becoming an Excellent Leader

0-07-050188-2 HARVARD BUSINESS PB...........$14.95

Michael E. **Porter**

Competitive Advantage: Creating and Sustaining Superior Performance

The celebrated Harvard Business School professor follows up his book on industry analysis with a study of the "value chain" and how companies build competitive strength

0-02-925090-0 FREE PRESS...............................$37.50

Competitive Strategy: Techniques for Analyzing Industries and Competitors

The bible of corporate strategy. Porter explains how to use his "five-forces" model to understand competition within industries

0-02-925360-8 FREE PRESS $37.50

John E. **Rehfield**

Alchemy of a Leader: Combining Western and Japanese Management Skills to Transform Your Company

The most effective new work ethic, like so much else in the world, is a multicultural one. Rehfield, one of the few Westerners to hold senior executive positions in Japanese companies, explains a new system of management skills for managers who need a fresh approach, blending the best in Western and Japanese business strengths. "John Rehfield is a trailblazer among American executives of companies 'fathered' in Japan"—*The Wall Street Journal*

0-471-00836-2 WILEY...$22.95

Frederick F. **Reichheld** & Thomas **Teal**

The Loyalty Effect: The Hidden Force Behind Growth, Profits and Lasting Value

The director of Bain & Co., a strategy consulting firm in Boston, demonstrates how the practice of loyalty contributes to long-term profit growth

0-87584-448-0 HARVARD BUSINESS.................$24.95

Al **Ries**

Focus: The Future of Your Company Depends on It

A how-to for managers in the position of having to divest, and some important considerations for those who are contemplating diversification

0-88730-764-7 HARPERCOLLINS......................$25.00

Wess **Roberts** & Bill **Ross**

Make It So: Leadership Lessons from Star Trek—The Next Generation

Advice on successful business management using the hit show as a springboard, and the character Jean-Luc Picard as the role model for leadership

0-671-52098-9 POCKET PB $12.00

Joseph **Romm**

Lean and Clean Management: How to Boost Profits and Productivity by Reducing Pollution

Reducing inefficiency and waste doesn't just save money and salve consciences, it also allows companies to boost profits and raise productivity. This visionary new book uses case histories from Dow Chemical, Baxter Healthcare, Boeing Aircraft, and others to show how waste-free lean management is the future of American business

1-56836-037-1 KODANSHA...............................$23.00

Robert H. **Rosen** & Paul B. **Brown**

Leading People: Transforming Business from the Inside Out

36 professionals who possess the outlined principles of wisdom, trust, participation, learning, diversity, creativity, integrity, and community are analyzed to demonstrate how these qualities make them good leaders. This treatise for corporate leadership recommends caring, empowerment, and social responsibility over traditional hierarchical styles

See also **CORPORATE LEADERSHIP AND CEO BIOGRAPHIES**

0-670-85874-9 VIKING.......................................$24.95

Peter B. **Scott-Morgan** & Arun **Maira**

Learning to Change and Changing to Learn: Managing for the 21st Century

0-07-057720-X HARVARD BUSINESS.................$24.95

Richard F. **Vancil**

Passing the Baton: Managing the Process of CEO Succession

CEOs, former CEOs, heirs apparent, and outside directors describe how chief executive officers transfer power to their successors

0-07-103273-8 HARVARD BUSINESS.................$24.95

Larraine D. **Segil**

Intelligent Business Alliances: How to Profit Using Today's Most Important Strategic Tools

An invaluable resource for managers involved in or contemplating an alliance to help prevent them from becoming a part of the 55 percent statistic of failed business alliances

0-8129-2466-5 TIME BOOKS $25.00

Randall P. **White** & others

The Future of Leadership: Riding the Corporate Rapids into the 21st Century

The authors develop an approach to leadership that emphasizes an acceptance of uncertainty and a case-by-case approach to decision-making

0-273-62206-4 PITMAN $25.00

Wellford W. **Wilms**

Restoring Prosperity: How Workers and Managers Are Forging a New Culture of Cooperation

0-8129-2030-9 TIME BOOKS $25.00

Shoshana **Zuboff**

In the Age of the Smart Machine: The Future of Work and Power

A dense but pioneering analysis of how information technology changes the structure of companies and the relationship between management and labor

0-465-03211-7 BASIC PB $18.50

Corporate Leadership and CEO Biographies

Henry **Ford**

Today and Tomorrow

Henry Ford's vision of manufacturing, politics, and society. First published in 1926, the book still holds lessons for managers struggling to understand Japanese production efficiency

0-915299-36-4 PRODUCTIVITY.........................$30.00

Henry Ford

Elkan **Blout**, editor

The Power of Boldness: Ten Master Builders of American Industry Tell Their Success Stories

0-309-05446-X NATIONAL ACADEMY $29.95

0-309-05445-1 NATIONAL ACADEMY PB.........$18.95

Elizabeth **Brayer**

George Eastman: A Biography

A thorough biography of the man who made photography accessible to everyone

0-8018-5263-3 JOHNS HOPKINS.......................$39.95

Mark **Fisher**

The Millionaire's Secrets: Life Lessons in Wisdom and Wealth

A parable about a 32-year-old ad man who meets a mysterious millionaire and is given formulas for financial success

0-684-80281-3 SIMON & SCHUSTER.................$18.95

Edward Jay **Epstein**

The Three Lives of Armand Hammer

See also **BIOGRAPHIES** under **US HISTORY, 1945 TO THE PRESENT** in **HISTORY OF THE AMERICAS**

0-679-44802-0 RANDOM HOUSE.....................$30.00

Lee **Iacocca** & others

Iacocca: An Autobiography

The CEO saga that started it all. Candid, sassy, funny, insightful—qualities lacking in so many of the executive biographies it inspired

0-553-25147-3 BDD PB...$6.99

Talking Straight

Pointed reflections on Washington, trade with Japan, Wall Street, and other issues on the Chrysler chairman's mind

0-553-27805-3 BDD PB...$5.99

Robert **Jackall**

Moral Mazes: The World of Corporate Managers

0-19-506080-6 OXFORD PB...............................$10.95

Geoffrey **James**

Business Wisdom of the Electronic Elite: 34 Strategies that CEOs at Microsoft, COMPAQ, Sun, Hewlett-Packard, and Other Top Companies Are Using to Create a New American Corporate Culture

The transformation of the corporate workplace by upstarts such as Bill Gates and Mitch Kapor from battlefield to ecosystem

0-679-44855-1 RANDOM HOUSE.....................$25.00

Joseph **Jaworski**

Synchronicity: The Inner Path of Leadership

Following a midlife crisis, a top Shell Oil executive blazes a path of psychospiritual discovery and shares his resultant insights on leadership

1-88105-294-X BERRETT-KOEHLER..................$24.95

Art **Kleiner**

The Age of Heretics: Heroes, Outlaws, and the Forerunners of Corporate Change

The corporate mavericks of the 1950s, '60s, and '70s, and their managerial innovations which set them apart are showcased

0-385-41576-1 DOUBLEDAY.............................$29.95

Akio **Morita** & others

Made in Japan: Akio Morita and the Sony Corporation

One of Japan's most creative business leaders tells his company's story and reflects on technology, world trade, and differences between his country and the US

See also **ECONOMICS AND BUSINESS** under **JAPAN** in **WORLD HISTORY AND CURRENT AFFAIRS**

0-451-15171-2 NEW AMERICAN LIBRARY PB ...$6.99

Donald **Trump** & others

Trump: The Art of the Deal

"I like thinking big. I always have. To me, it's very simple; if you're going to be thinking anyway, you might as well think big"

0-446-35325-6 WARNER PB...............................$5.95

Donald Trump

Roger Lowenstein Buffett: The Making of an American Capitalist

0-385-48491-7 DOUBLEDAY PB.......................$14.95

Alfred P. **Sloan**

My Years with General Motors

Management insights from one of the true giants of American business

0-385-04235-3 DOUBLEDAY PB.......................$18.95

Thomas **Teal**, editor

First Person: Tales of Management, Courage and Tenacity

With an introduction by Thomas Teal

0-87584-674-2 HARVARD BUSINESS..............$19.95

James **Wallace** & Jim **Erickson**

Hard Drive: Bill Gates and the Making of the Microsoft Empire

The fascinating history of the nation's largest software company and the rise of Bill Gates to become one of the richest men in the world. A behind-the-scenes account of the world of computers, and a delightful story of how this tycoon made it. "A biting biography and computer industry exposé"—*Publishers Weekly*

0-471-56886-4 WILEY.......................................$22.95

Jeffrey **Sonnenfeld**

Hero's Farewell: What Happens When CEOs Retire

An analysis of one of the least understood aspects of executive life. Sonnenfeld draws on dozens of case histories to identify four "styles" of how CEOs give up (often reluctantly) the power and privilege to which they are accustomed

See also **RETIREMENT** under **BUSINESS ADVICE** under **INVESTING, TAXES, AND BUSINESS ADVICE**

0-19-505091-6 OXFORD $30.00

Companies and Industries

Stephen **Fenichell**

Plastic: The Making of a Synthetic Century

A celebration of its role in modern society, covering everything from its inception to current applications

0-88730-732-9 HARPERCOLLINS $25.00

John P. **Hoerr**

And the Wolf Finally Came: The Decline of the American Steel Industry

A sensitive and sophisticated analysis of labor-management relations, with a focus on US Steel's operations in the Monongahela Valley outside Pittsburgh

0-8229-3572-4 PITTSBURGH $49.95
0-8229-5398-6 PITTSBURGH PB $22.50

Charles **Kenney**

Riding the Runaway Horse: The Rise and Decline of Wang Laboratories

Kenney, a reporter for the *Boston Globe*, details the rise and fall of an extraordinary computer company. Tracing the history of Wang from its inception as a one-room business in 1951 to its excesses of power during the '80s, when the company flag flew high over Boston's Route 128

0-316-48919-0 LITTLE, BROWN $22.95

Tracy **Kidder**

The Soul of a New Machine

A book that defined a new genre of business writing. Kidder sketches a tale of heartache and exhilaration as a group of Data General engineers design a computer whose success may determine the fate of their company

See also **THE COMPUTER REVOLUTION** under **THE COMPUTER REVOLUTION AND ARTIFICIAL INTELLIGENCE** in **SCIENCE**

0-380-71115-X AVON PB $12.00

Edwin **Green**

Banking: An Illustrated History

0-7148-2570-0 PHAIDON $25.00

D. Quinn **Mills** & G. Bruce **Friesen**

Promises: An Unconventional View of What Went Wrong at IBM

Harvard business professor and a "knowledge manager" trace the ups and downs of the company that was once an icon in the high-tech world

0-87584-654-8 HARVARD BUSINESS $22.95

Brock **Yates**

The Critical Path: Inventing an Automobile and Reinventing the Corporation

The story of Chrysler's venture with its latest generation of minivans and how it shifted the company from a traditional vertical management system to project teams

0-316-96708-4 LITTLE, BROWN $24.95

Steven **Levy**

Insanely Great: The Life and Times of Macintosh, the Computer that Changed Everything

A techno-biography of the machine that put a mouse in millions of homes and offices. From R&D to analysis of the Mac's impact on computing, this is an informative and colorful history

0-14-023237-0 PENGUIN PB $9.95

Fred **Moody**

I Sing the Body Electronic: A Year with Microsoft on the Multimedia Frontier

"A first-rate work...rendering the look and feel of life inside Microsoft"—*NY Times Book Review*

0-670-84875-1 VIKING $23.95
0-14-017655-1 PENGUIN PB $12.95

Only two emotions seem to surface among Microsoft employees when Gates's name is mentioned. One is awe, the other is fear. He is revered as an unrivaled genius both at technology and at business strategy. Employees called before him know they will be grilled mercilessly not only on the technical details of their project, but on its market potential and profitability as well. No one ever hopes to slip an unresolved issue past him.

I SING THE BODY ELECTRONIC: A YEAR WITH MICROSOFT ON THE MULTIMEDIA FRONTIER

Thomas **Petzinger**

Hard Landing: How the Epic Contest for Power and Profits Plunged the Airlines into Chaos

What *Den of Thieves* did for Wall Street, Petzinger does here for the busy and byzantine men's club that runs the world's airline industry. From the sale of People Express to the battles between British Airways and Virgin Air, this is a story both riveting and informative. A primer in modern business and a fascinating history of the world's largest industry

0-8129-2186-0 TIME BOOKS $30.00
0-8129-2835-0 TIME BOOKS PB $16.00

John **Naisbitt**

Megatrends: 10 New Directions Transforming Our Lives

A futuristic account of the forces moving America from an industrial economy rooted in the Northeast to a decentralized, high-tech, information society

0-446-35681-6 WARNER PB $6.50

The Japanese Challenge and America's Economic Future

For related reading, see JAPAN in WORLD HISTORY AND CURRENT AFFAIRS

James **Abegglen** & George **Stalk**, Jr.

Kaisha, the Japanese Corporation: How Marketing, Money and Manpower Strategy, Not Management Style, Make the Japanese World Pacesetters

Abegglen, a longtime resident of Tokyo, is a leading authority on Japanese business

See also **ECONOMICS AND BUSINESS** under **JAPAN** in **WORLD HISTORY AND CURRENT AFFAIRS**

0-465-03712-7 BASIC PB $17.00

David **Halberstam**

The Reckoning

Halberstam compares the humbling of Ford Motor Company with the rise of Japan's Nissan

See also **ECONOMICS AND BUSINESS** under **JAPAN** in **WORLD HISTORY AND CURRENT AFFAIRS**

0-380-70447-1 AVON PB $6.50

Robert H. **Hayes** & others

Dynamic Manufacturing: Creating the Learning Organization

Three of this country's most respected experts on manufacturing, all of them professors at the Harvard Business School, offer detailed prescriptions for the rebirth of US competitiveness

0-02-914211-3 FREE PRESS $37.50

John **Hillkirk** & Gary **Jacobson**

Xerox, American Samurai: The Behind-the-Scenes Story of How a Corporate Giant Beat the Japanese at Their Own Game

A well-reported account of how Xerox almost lost its position as world leader in the industry it invented, and how it launched a successful comeback

0-02-033830-9 MACMILLAN PB $13.95

Johnny **Johansson** & Ikujiro **Nonaka**

Relentless: The Japanese Way of Marketing

Important insights for Western marketers into Japanese marketing success, which the authors assert is due to their concentration on the consumer's needs and desires

0-88730-805-8 HARPERCOLLINS $22.00

Chalmers **Johnson**

Miti and the Japanese Miracle: The Group of Industrial Policy, 1925-1975

The classic study of Japanese economic planning; dense but worth the effort

See also **ECONOMICS AND BUSINESS** under **JAPAN** in **WORLD HISTORY AND CURRENT AFFAIRS**

0-8047-1206-9 STANFORD PB $16.95

R. Taggart **Murphy**

The Weight of the Yen

Drawing on his 15 years as an American investment banker in Japan, the author provides an analysis of how Japan became the world's largest creditor while the U.S. became the world's biggest debtor

0-393-03832-7 NORTON $25.00

William **Ouchi**

Theory Z: How American Business Can Meet the Japanese Challenge

One of the earliest, and still one of the best, explanations of quality circles, worker participation, and the other human dimensions of the Japanese management style

0-380-71944-4 AVON PB $11.50

Japan and U.S.

Michael J. **Piore** & Charles F. **Sabel**

The Second Industrial Divide: Possibilities for Prosperity

Two MIT economists explain the decline of American manufacturing and offer prescriptions for renewal

0-465-07561-4 BASIC BOOKS PB $19.50

Clyde V. **Prestowitz**, Jr.

Trading Places: How We Allowed Japan to Take the Lead

A former high-ranking Commerce Department official makes a convincing case for get-tough trade policies with Japan

See also **ECONOMICS AND BUSINESS** under **JAPAN** in **WORLD HISTORY AND CURRENT AFFAIRS**

0-465-08679-9 BASIC PB $18.00

Lester **Thurow**

Head to Head

One of America's most distinguished economists gives a vivid account of the battle between the US and Japan and a newly integrated Europe for economic dominance. He provides suggestions on how America can change its economic ways and once again regain its position in the world. "Mr. Thurow's urgency compels attention....I suspect Americans will have to find a uniquely American way to meet the challenge" —*NY Times Book Review*

0-446-39497-1 WARNER PB $13.99

Ezra **Vogel**

Japan as Number One: Lesson For America

How Japan's political, social, and economic institutions contribute to its global economic dominance

0-674-47215-2 HARVARD $25.00
0-06-132055-2 HARPERCOLLINS PB $18.90

Wall Street and Corporate Finance

Marshall E. **Blume** & others

Revolution on Wall Street

This intriguing look at the bastion of American finance shows the New York Stock Exchange in chaos and ill-equipped to face the future. With unprecedented access to the NYSE's archives, the authors provide an in-depth analysis of how Wall Street may have gambled its future by trading short-term profits for long-term rewards. "A perceptive, unsparing analysis of a colossus in crisis"—*Kirkus Reviews*

0-393-03526-3 NORTON $27.50

Connie **Bruck**

The Predators' Ball: The Junk Bond Raiders and the Man Who Staked Them

A glimpse inside Michael Milken's securities empire and the giant deals he engineered. Intelligent analysis game and entertaining stories, including feared raider Carl Icahn's Monopoly game with real money

See also **THE BUSINESS BARONS** under **ECONOMIC HISTORY** under **TOPICS IN AMERICAN STUDIES** in **HISTORY OF THE AMERICAS**

0-14-012090-4 PENGUIN PB $12.95

Bryan **Burrough** & John **Helyar**

Barbarians at the Gate: The Fall of RJR Nabisco

The largest corporate takeover in American history covered in detail by two business reporters; the gripping story of buyout kings, Wall Street institutions, and gigantic corporations caught in a struggle for power

See also **THE BUSINESS BARONS** under **ECONOMIC HISTORY** under **TOPICS IN AMERICAN STUDIES** in **HISTORY OF THE AMERICAS**

0-06-016172-8 HARPERCOLLINS PB $22.50

Dwight **Crane** & Robert **Eccles**

Doing Deals: Investment Banks at Work

Wall Street anthropology: a unique analysis of investment bankers' customs, values, and work habits

0-07-103232-0 HARVARD BUSINESS $35.00

Benjamin **Graham**

Benjamin Graham: The Memoirs of the Dean of Wall Street

0-07-024269-0 HARVARD BUSINESS $27.95

Moira **Johnson**

Takeover: The New Wall Street Warriors—The Men, the Money, the Impact

Blow-by-blow accounts of major takeovers engineered by the likes of Sir James Goldsmith, Carl Icahn, and T. Boone Pickens

0-87795-784-3 MORROW $3.98

Gene **Marcial**

Secrets of the Street

0-07-040256-6 HARVARD BUSINESS PB $10.95

Nick **Leeson**

Rogue Trader: How I Brought Down Barings Bank and Shook the Financial World

The financial scandal that caused the collapse of one of England's oldest financial institutions

0-316-51856-5 LITTLE, BROWN $24.95

Michael **Lewis**

Liar's Poker: Rising Through the Wreckage of Salomon Brothers

A very funny account of a money-minded young man's rise up the greasy pole of Salomon Brothers—from $48,000-a-year trainee (in 1984) to institutional bond salesman in Salomon's London office earning $225,000 (in 1987). Richard L. Stern, a senior editor at *Forbes*, writes: "He's obviously as good a writer as he was a bond salesman"

0-393-02750-3 NORTON $18.95
0-14-014345-9 PENGUIN PB $11.95

The Money Culture

The author of the outstanding *Liar's Poker*, Lewis relates more tales from his days as a trainee at Salomon Brothers, investment banker, and financial journalist in London and later Japan. "A wry, wicked account...falls somewhere between *Wealth of Nations* and *Animal House*"—*Newsweek*

See also **WALL STREET CULTURE OF THE '80S AND '90S** under **ECONOMIC HISTORY** under **TOPICS IN AMERICAN STUDIES** in **HISTORY OF THE AMERICAS**

0-393-03037-7 PENGUIN PB $19.95

Louis **Lowenstein**

What's Wrong with Wall Street: Short-Term Gain and the Absentee Shareholder

Criticisms of the misguided practices and priorities of the investment world and their debilitating effects on the corporate heartland

0-201-17169-4 ADDISON-WESLEY $17.95
0-201-51796-5 ADDISON-WESLEY PB $10.95

Business and Society

Tad **Crawford**

The Secret Life of Money: The Hidden Meaning of Giving, Receiving, Hoarding, Spending, Borrowing, Lending, Earning and Inheriting

Money talks, and often in very subtle ways. Crawford listens to the many voices of money from ancient Greece and the Bible to Native American tales. What he hears is a tale of power and of spirituality, of the fatalism of gambling and the obsession of hoarding

See also **SELF-ESTEEM** under **QUALITY OF LIFE** under **SELF-HELP** in **LIFESTYLES AND PRACTICAL ADVICE**

0-87477-786-0 TARCHER $24.95
1-88055-951-X ALLWORTH PB $14.95

David **Dorsey**

The Force

An inside look at the business world of middle America

0-345-37625-0 FAWCETT PB $12.50

James **Grant**

Money of the Mind: How the 1980s Got that Way

Keen observations on how credit collided with fiscal irresponsibility to produce the roller-coaster that was the '80s. This is a witty, incisive, and often irreverent look at economic history from the turn of the century to the present

0-374-16979-9 FS&G..$30.00

Paul **Hawken**

The Ecology of Commerce

When best-selling author Hawken first proposed his radical theory in the pages of *INC. Magazine*, the response was an avalanche of mail. Simply stated, he argues that the business community is the last and only entity powerful enough to reverse global environmental and social degradation. By manufacturing products in innovative ways, reeducating the consumer, and restoring the relationship between government and business, there is hope for a better future

0-88730-704-3 HARPERPERENNIAL PB...........$14.00

Paul Hawken (photo by Jim Sano)

Charles **Handy**

The Age of Paradox

Sequel to the best-selling *The Age of Unreason*, this book argues that society in general and business in particular needs a new ethic—one based on a renewed humanism and a redefined capitalism. But the new business practices—the minimalist organization, portfolio careers, and wealth based on information—bring about their own paradoxes. "The most forward-looking book of 1990's best books....An eloquent handbook for contemplating, coping with, and capitalizing on enveloping change"—*Business Week*

0-87584-425-1 HARVARD BUSINESS...............$24.95
0-87584-643-2 MCGRAW HILL PB....................$12.95

Paul **Weaver**

The Suicidal Corporation: How Big Business Has Failed America

Bitter confessions of a neoconservative magazine writer who joined Ford Motor Company to fight for capitalism, only to discover that Ford was less interested in capitalism than in profits—and in getting along with the political powers-that-be

0-671-52378-3 SIMON & SCHUSTER.................$18.95

Lawrence J. **White**

The S&L Debacle: Public Policy Lessons for Bank and Thrift Regulation

"An indispensable resource for anyone seriously concerned with learning from the S&L debacle"—Paul Volcker

0-19-506733-9 OXFORD $24.95

Hung Jury

Richard **Kluger**

Ashes to Ashes: America's Hundred Year Cigarette War, the Public Health, and the Unabashed Triumph of Philip Morris

A timely and important history of the corporate superpower Philip Morris, purveyor of society's most widespread instrument of self-destruction—and most profitable consumer product

0-394-57076-6 KNOPF.......................................$35.00

The International Marketplace

David L. **James**

The Executive Guide to Asia-Pacific Communications

Executive interviews, extensive personal experience, and a unique survey of 400 experts on Asia-Pacific business practices make this an indispensable guide for those eager to exploit business opportunities across the Pacific. The author, a corporate lawyer, multinational executive, diplomat, and government consultant, has worked in the region for over 20 years

1-56836-040-1 KODANSHA PB..........................$16.00

Andrew **Krieger** & Edward **Claflin**

The Money Bazaar: Inside the Trillion Dollar World of Currency Trading

The comparative worth of the dollar can influence everything from how difficult it is to find a job to the cost of goods and services. Here is an insider's view of the volatile, unregulated, and immensely profitable arena where a global elite dictates the relative values of the world's currencies. Krieger and Claflin detail how going off the gold standard spawned an economic roller-coaster, and what we can do to regain control of our financial destiny

0-8129-1861-4 TIME BOOKS..............................$22.00

Paul R. **Krugman**

Pop Internationalism

From the author of *The Age of Diminished Expectations*, this compilation of his essays argues against the popular assertion that government and business need to forge a partnership in order to effectively compete in a global economy, pointing instead to the domestic problems which are the true cause of the slowed growth in Americans' real income

See also **ECONOMIC DEVELOPMENT AND INTERNATIONAL TRADE** under **ECONOMICS** in **SOCIAL STUDIES**

0-262-11210-8 MIT..$22.50

Paul **Volcker** & Toyoo **Gyohten**

Changing Fortunes: The World's Money and the Threat to American Leadership

Volcker, former chairman of the Federal Reserve, and Gyohten, Vice Minister of Japan's International Finance Ministry, are unusually well-placed to survey the evolution of international monetary systems. Their clear and insightful analysis is particularly timely, useful, and readable. "If you have any interest at all in international finance, this is the book to read. No one is better qualified to tell this story, and none has told it better"—Robert Z. Lawrence, Professor of International Economics, Harvard

0-8129-2018-X TIME BOOKS PB........................$25.00

Larry **Kahaner**

Competitive Intelligence: From Black Ops to Boardrooms—How Businesses Gather, Analyze, and Use Information to Succeed in the Global Marketplace

The how-to for setting up a CI division to ethically and legally spy on the competition

0-684-81074-3 SIMON & SCHUSTER $24.00

Homeless Uncle Sam

William C. **Taylor** & Alan M. **Webber**

Going Global: Four Entrepreneurs Map the New World Marketplace

Two former editors of the *Harvard Business Review* join forces to profile four pioneers in the new global economy. Ranging from Whirlpool to Nestlè and Kleiner, Perkins, Caufield and Byers (the venture capital firm), the authors present a vision for business in the new global world of instant communications, borderless corporations, and fluid capital

See also **ENTREPRENEURSHIP** under **BUSINESS ADVICE** under **INVESTING, TAXES, AND BUSINESS ADVICE**

0-670-86308-4 VIKING......................................$22.95

Investing, Taxes, and Business Advice

For related reading, see BUSINESS, INDUSTRY, AND FINANCE

Personal Finance

Janet **Bamford**
Complete Guide to Managing Your Money
Advice on investments, banking, taxes, insurance, budgeting, and other aspects of finance
0-89043-465-4 CONSUMER REPORTS $29.95

Norman F. **Dacey**
How to Avoid Probate
0-02-008181-2 HARPERPERENNIAL PB $24.95

Debt Free: The National Bankruptcy Kit
From the Legal Self-Help series
0-935755-18-7 NOVA PB $17.95

Peter H. **Engel**
Budgeting and Finance
0-07-001567-8 MCGRAW HILL PB $12.00

John **Hannah**
Using Dollars and Sense
0-88022-164-X QUE PB.......................................$19.95

Linda **Kelley**
Two Incomes and Still Broke?: It's Not How Much You Make, But How Much You Keep
The grim fact so many Americans have learned is that a second income does not necessarily mean more money. Kelley explains the counter-intuitive economics of this, showing how taxes, social security, transportation, childcare, and many other expenses serve to diminish a second income, how to calculate these costs, and how to make clear decisions on financial arrangements for working couples
0-8129-2569-6 TIME BOOKS.............................$20.00

Beth **Kobliner**
Get a Financial Life: Personal Finance in Your Twenties and Thirties
Advice on banking, investing, insurance, retirement, buying versus renting a home, and taxes from a *Money* magazine contributor
0-684-81213-4 FIRESIDE PB $11.00

Jack Lenor **Larsen**
Jack Lenor Larsen's Guide to Material Wealth
1-55859-007-2 ABBEVILLE $40.00

Kenneth M. **Morris** & Alan S. **Siegel**
The Wall Street Journal Guide to Understanding Personal Finance
This jargon-free, no-nonsense primer takes the mystery out of your financial options. The authors, acknowledged masters of communication in the financial world, lay out the pros and cons of credit, mortgages, investing, and college planning
0-671-87964-2 FIRESIDE PB $14.95

Michael **Moynihan**
The Coming American Renaissance: How to Benefit from America's Economic Resurgence
Extrapolating from recent upward economic trends, the author predicts an optimistic financial future for Americans and offers personal, practical advice on how to most benefit from it
0-684-81207-X SIMON & SCHUSTER................$23.00

Jerrold **Mundis**
Earn What You Deserve: How to Stop Underearning and Start Thriving
Concrete steps for treating underearning from the author of *How to Get Out of Debt, Stay Out of Debt, and Live Prosperously*
0-553-57222-9 BDD PB $5.99

Joel G. **Siegel**
Dictionary of Personal Finance
Written specifically for the layperson, this guide offers much-needed illumination on mortgages, annuities, and other financial instruments. Also included are sections on consumer tips, information on government and consumer agencies, as well as annuity tables
0-02-897394-1 MACMILLAN PB $20.00

John **Ventura**
Beating the Paycheck to Paycheck Blues
Help in getting out of the hand-to-mouth cycle
0-7931-2325-9 DEARBORN PB $17.95

Investment Advice

Nancy **Dunnan**
Dun and Bradstreet's Guide to Your Investment Dollar
0-06-273288-9 HARPERCOLLINS PB $19.00

Karen **Ferguson** & Kate **Blackwell**
Pensions in Crisis: Why the System Is Failing America and How You Can Protect Your Future
1-55970-331-8 ARCADE PB................................$12.95

Harold **Gourges**
Total Financial Planning: A Guide for Financial Advisors and Serious Investors
0-13-925272-X PRENTICE HALL $64.95

Sandra **Hildreth**
The A to Z of Wall Street: 2500 Terms for the Street-Smart Investor
Dictionary of Wall Street terms, from boiler room to Q-tip trust. For example: a "Goldbug" is an analyst who recommends gold as a haven for investors concerned about possible disaster in the world economy
0-88462-711-X LONGMAN PB $16.95

Gary L. **Klott**
The New York Times Complete Financial Guide to the 1990s
Discusses the environmental, social, and political changes of the decade and how to profit from them
0-8129-1814-2 TIME BOOKS $22.50

Lion of Credit

Janet **Lowe**
Value Investing Made Easy: Benjamin Graham's Classic Investment Strategy Explained for Everyone
0-07-038859-8 MCGRAW HILL...........................$22.95

Lawrence **Lynn**, editor
How to Invest Today: A Beginner's Guide to the World of Investments
Making money is one thing, keeping it is another. This sensible guide to investment, estate planning, stocks, bonds, insurance, mutual funds, retirement planning, and more is everything the beginning investor needs. Written by a team of professionals and financial writers, *How to Invest Today* is an up-to-date, practical, and highly readable account of financial markets and instruments and how to use them
0-8050-3733-0 HOLT $23.00

Burton G. **Malkiel**
A Random Walk Down Wall Street
The classic, surefooted, irreverent, and vastly informative guide to investing offers sensible advice to maximize gains and minimize losses in a variety of markets: bonds, money market funds, real estate, gold, and collectibles. Among the smartest books on Wall Street available—you no longer need the pros
0-393-31529-0 NORTON PB.................................$15.95

G. Michael **Moebs** & Eva **Moebs**
Pricing Financial Services
An explanation of value, competition, and cost-plus analysis for pricing financial services
0-87094-594-7 IRWIN $50.00

Joseph **Tique** & Joseph **Lisanti**
The Dividend Rich Investor
0-07-064639-2 HARVARD BUSINESS................$22.95

John **Tracy**

How to Read a Financial Report: Wringing Cash Flow and Other Vital Signs Out of the Numbers

This clear and concise book explains the basics of cash flow analysis and how to use financial ratios to evaluate a company's performance

0-471-59391-5 WILEY PB $16.95

John **Train**

The Money Masters: Nine Great Investors—Their Winning Strategies and How You Can Apply Them

0-06-091405-X HARPERCOLLINS PB $12.00

Preserving Capital and Making It Grow

0-517-54766-X CROWN $17.95

John F. **Wasik**

The Investment Club Book

Thousands of Americans are forming investment clubs these days, pooling their money to place in the stock market, and many are beating Wall Street wizards at their own game. This complete guide offers everything needed to found an investment club and get it running, including invaluable guidelines for evaluating a Wall Street offering and timing a buy or a sell

0-446-67147-9 WARNER PB $11.99

Henry **Weingarten**

Investing by the Stars: Using Astrology in the Financial Markets

0-07-068999-7 HARVARD BUSINESS $24.95

Commodities and Futures Trading

George **Angell**

Winning in the Futures Market

The Chicago floor trader writes about the futures market in simple, step-by-step terms

1-55738-146-1 PROBUS PB $21.95

David **Gardner** & Thomas **Gardner**

The Motley Fool Investment Guide: How the Fools Beat Wall Street's Wise Men and How You Can Too

0-684-82703-4 FIRESIDE PB $12.00

Kirk **Kazanjian**

Wall Street's Picks for 1997

With expert recommendations from William Berger, Elizabeth Bramwell, Philip Carret, William Donoghue, Gail Dudack, and many more

0-7931-2348-8 DEARBORN PB $19.95

James P. **O'Shaugnessy**

What Works on Wall Street

0-07-047985-2 HARVARD $29.95

Gold

Timothy **Green**

The Prospect for Gold

A short but comprehensive look at the history of the precious metal: its discovery, its use, its role in the global economy, and its value as an investment in the current market

0-8027-1002-6 WALKER $29.95

0-471-84367-9 WILEY $45.00

Mutual Funds and Money Market Funds

Richard **Dorf**

The New Mutual Fund Investment Advisor: Everything You Need to Know About Investing in No-Loads

1-55738-157-7 PROBUS $24.95

Hrach **Alexanian**, editor

Morningstar Mutual Fund 500: An In-Depth Look at 500 Select Mutual Funds from the Leading Authority in Mutual Fund Analysis, 1994

A thorough and unbiased overview of the 500 best-performing mutual funds in 1994. Readers can reference performance ratings, manager profiles, portfolio holdings and statistics, and operations information. With data laid out simply and efficiently, this is an accessible guide to a mazelike topic

0-7863-0136-8 IRWIN PB $35.00

Bucks on the Line

Bernard **Seligman**

Money Market Funds

0-275-91728-2 GREENWOOD $47.95

Bonds

Edward **Altman** & Scott **Nammacher**

Investment in Junk Bonds: Inside the High-Yield Debt Market

An explanation in simple terms

0-471-84886-7 WILEY $24.95

David **Darst**

The Complete Bond Book: A Guide to All Types of Fixed-Income Securities

The technical aspects of bonds, from government and corporate to tax-exempt

0-07-017390-7 MCGRAW HILL $49.95

Standard & Poor's

Standard & Poor's Stock and Bond Guide: 1996 Edition

A time-honored tool of the best brokers, this unique volume includes: 1995 year-end prices; S&P's earnings estimates for stock; S&P's rankings and ratings of stocks; S&P's closely watched debt ratings for more than 6,000 bonds; as well as detailed data on 700 mutual funds and information on virtually any stock traded

0-07-047985-2 HARVARD BUSINESS $29.95

0-07-052238-3 MCGRAW HILL PB $22.95

Foreign Markets

A. K. **Chrystal** & Robert **Sedgwick**, editors

Exchange Rates and the Open Economy

0-312-01583-6 ST. MARTIN'S $45.00

Paul **Smith**

Comparative Financial Systems

0-275-90905-0 PRAEGER $49.95

Dale **Strand**

The Business Traveler's World Guide: Key Information on 150 Cities Around the World

0-07-061997-2 HARVARD BUSINESS PB $19.95

Aron **Viner**

Inside Japanese Financial Markets

1-55623-020-6 IRWIN $50.00

L. Fargo **Wells**

Selling to the World: Your Fast and Easy Guide to Exporting and Importing

0-07-069302-1 MCGRAW HILL PB $16.95

Tax Preparation

Warren **Esanu**

Consumer Reports Guide to Income Tax Preparation 1997

0-89043-855-2 CONSUMER REPORTS PB $14.99

H&R Block Staff

H&R Block Income Tax Guide and Workbook, 1997

0-684-82594-5 FIRESIDE PB $14.00

J.K. **Lasser**

J.K. Lasser's Your Income Tax, 1997

0-0286-1381-3 MACMILLAN $14.95

Price Waterhouse Staff
The Price Waterhouse Personal Tax Advisor 1995-1996
0-7863-0500-2 IRWIN PB....................$14.95

Jeff **Schnepper**
How to Pay Zero Taxes: Your Guide to Deductions, Shelters, Investments, and Other Strategies
0-07-055557-5 MCGRAW HILL PB....................$14.95

Business Advice

Geoff **Burch**
The Art and Science of Business Persuasion: Mastering the Power of Getting What You Want
1-55972-354-8 BIRCH LANE....................$19.95

Laurence A. **Canter** & Martha S. **Siegel**
How to Make a Fortune on the Information Superhighway
The basics for using the Internet to sell your products, from structuring ads and opening "stores" to coping with various forms of abuse and vandalism by netters resistant to the practice of cyberselling
0-0627-2065-1 HARPERCOLLINS PB....................$13.00

Ann **Cavoukian** & Don **Tapscott**
Who Knows: Safeguarding Your Privacy in a Networked World
0-07-063320-7 HARVARD BUSINESS....................$24.95

James **Champy** & Nitin **Nohria**
Fast Forward: The Best Ideas on Managing Business Change
16 essays, by such business notables as Peter Drucker, on the ideas most likely to affect the shape of businesses in the future. Featuring two original essays by the authors
0-87584-673-4 MCGRAW HILL....................$24.95

Mary J. **Cronin**
The Internet Strategy Handbook: Lessons from the New Frontier of Business
A compilation of advice on the Internet from corporate pioneers
0-87584-631-9 HARVARD BUSINESS....................$39.95
0-87584-720-X HARVARD BUSINESS PB....................$29.95

Kevin **Davis**
Getting into Your Customer's Head: Secrets of Selling Your Competitors Don't Know
A step-by-step strategy to help win the sale which explores the different roles the salesperson takes on with the customer in each phase of it
0-8129-2628-5 TIME BOOKS....................$25.00

Richard F. **Gerson**
Great Customer Service for Your Small Business
1-56052-364-6 CRISP PB....................$15.95

Avinash K. **Dixit** & Barry J. **Nalebuff**
Thinking Strategically: The Competitive Edge in Business, Politics, and Everyday Life
This 1991 *Financial Times* "Top Ten" favorite is without a doubt the best "strategic game" book on the market. It is included in the curriculum of the nation's top business schools and is currently Tokyo's best-selling business book. Written in clear, lay terms, it is remarkably readable. "A gem of a book"—Burton G. Malkiel, author of *A Random Walk Down Wall Street*
0-393-96101-X NORTON PB....................$10.95

The conductor of an orchestra in the Soviet Union (during the Stalin era) was traveling by train to his next engagement and was looking over the score of the music he was to conduct that night. Two KGB officers saw what he was reading and, thinking that the musical notation was some secret code, arrested him as a spy. He protested that it was only Tchaikovsky's Violin Concerto, but to no avail. On the second day of his imprisonment, the interrogator walked in smugly and said, "You had better tell us all. We have caught your friend Tchaikovsky, and he is already talking." So begins one telling of the prisoner's dilemma, perhaps the best-known strategic game. Let us develop the story to its logical conclusion. Suppose the KGB has actually arrested someone whose only offense is that he is called Tchaikovsky, and are separately subjecting him to the same kind of interrogation. If the two innocents withstand this treatment, each will be sentenced to three years imprisonment....

THINKING STRATEGICALLY: THE COMPETITIVE EDGE IN BUSINESS, POLITICS, AND EVERYDAY LIFE

Roger J. **Dow** & Susan P. **Cook**
Turned On: Eight Proven Principles for Energizing Your Customers, People and Profits
A pragmatic guide filled with concrete examples that help elucidate its eight business insights, such as "Build a Strong Foundation" and "Make Every Customer Feel Special"
0-88730-766-3 HARPERPERENNIAL....................$25.00

First Books for Business
Negotiating
0-07-001566-X MCGRAW HILL PB....................$12.00

Sales and Marketing
0-07-001568-1 MCGRAW HILL PB....................$12.00

Supervising and Managing People
0-07-001569-4 HARVARD BUSINESS PB....................$12.00

J.K. Lasser Institute
How to Run a Small Business: Seventh Edition
Retail, wholesale, manufacturing, or franchise, this volume contains information to start a new business or improve an existing one. From finance and inventory control to mailing lists and temp services, this guide has been fully revised for the '90s
0-07-036576-8 MCGRAW HILL....................$27.95

Guy **Kawasaki**
How to Drive Your Competition Crazy: Creating Disruption for Fun and Profit
MacWorld columnist and Apple Computer Fellow offers advice on marketing
0-7868-8163-1 HYPERION PB....................$12.95

Jay Conrad **Levinson** & Seth **Godin**
The Guerrilla Marketing Handbook
0-395-50013-2 HOUGHTON MIFFLIN PB....................$16.95

Jay Conrad **Levinson** & Charles **Rubin**
Guerrilla Marketing Online Weapons: 100 Low-Cost, High-Impact Weapons for Online Profits and Prosperity
Ideas for advertising, promotions, special events, planning and service
0-395-77019-X HOUGHTON MIFFLIN PB....................$12.95

U.S. Dollar

Harvey **Mackay**
Swim with Sharks Without Being Eaten Alive: Outsell, Outmanage, Outmotivate and Outnegotiate Your Competition
0-688-07473-1 MORROW....................$20.00

Jeff **Monassebian**
A Survival Guide to Computer Contracts
A comprehensive map to buying computer technology, with tips on how to steer clear of potential legal and business pitfalls
0-9650971-7-X APPLICATION PB....................$24.95

Charles C. **Poirier** & Steven E. **Reiter**
Supply Chain Optimization
In order for companies to keep themselves from going out of business, the authors explain the need for companies to eliminate every inefficiency within their delivery systems, and redefine and reengineer supply chains to establish mutually beneficial networks extending from the original supply to final consumption
1-88105-293-1 BERRETT-KOEHLER....................$32.95

Daniel **Sitarz**

Incorporate Your Business: The National Corporation Kit

From the Small Business Library

0-935755-26-8 NOVA $29.95

0-935755-09-8 NOVA PB $18.95

Sam **Stovall**

Sector Investing 1996 Edition

See also **CAREERS FOR WOMEN** under **CAREERS**

0-07-065521-9 MCGRAW HILL $14.95

Entrepreneurship

Bob **Adams**

Adams Streetwise Small Business Start-Up

406 pages of clearly written information organized in such a way it can be read in entirety at the outset of a business venture or as specific needs and questions arise

1-55850-581-4 ADDAMM PB $16.95

Peter **Bieler** & Suzanne **Costas**

This Business Has Legs: How I Used Infomercial Marketing to Create the $1,000,000,000 Thighmaster Exerciser Craze: An Entrepreneurial Adventure Story

A firsthand account of how one person used the TV infomercial to build a highly successful product, with a relatively small initial outlay of cash

0-471-14749-4 WILEY $24.95

Hattie **Bryant**

Small Business Today Guide to Beating the Odds

More an inspirational than a how-to, this guide provides interviews with successful entrepreneurs and short vignettes of their companies. Also features a solid chapter on developing a business plan

0-7615-0344-7 PRIMA PB $16.95

Ben **Cohen** & Jerry **Greenfield**

Starting and Running a Socially Responsible Business

Business advice from the creators of Ben & Jerry's ice cream

0-684-83499-5 SIMON & SCHUSTER $24.00

The Complete Book of Small Business Legal Forms

From the Legal Self-Help series

0-935755-03-9 NOVA PB $17.95

John **Kao**

Jamming: The Art and Discipline of Business Creativity

Creative entrepreneurship through several techniques described here by a Harvard Business School professor. Includes how to audit and manage creativity, and how to clear the mind, thereby rendering it receptive to the improvisational process

0-88730-746-9 HARPERCOLLINS $23.00

Peter F. **Drucker**

Innovation and Entrepreneurship: Practice and Principles

The world's leading student of big business turns his attention to the new entrepreneurial forces fueling economic growth

0-88730-618-7 HARPERCOLLINS PB $13.50

Alice **Bredin**

The Virtual Office: What Telecommuters and Entrepreneurs Need to Succeed in Today's Nontraditional Workplace

The author of the syndicated newspaper column "Working at Home" has created a step-by-step guide for creating a home, or "virtual," office

0-471-12059-6 WILEY PB $16.95

Paul **Edwards** & Sarah **Edwards**

Working from Home

On the subject of home-based business, this gets as close as possible to everything you need to know, from office layout to maintaining personal relationships. A must for anyone considering working out of the home

0-87477-764-X PUTNAM PB $15.95

Jo **Frohbieter-Mueller**

Stay Home and Mind Your Own Business: How to Manage Your Time, Space, Personal Obligations, Money, Business, and Yourself While Working at Home

0-932620-83-3 BETTERWAY PB $12.95

Working Solo Sourcebook: Essential Resources for Independent Entrepreneurs

Twelve hundred essential resources for the "Lone Eagle"—the fastest-growing segment of the business world—culled largely from the 15-year entrepreneurial experience of this successful woman. Includes effective training programs, government agencies for small businesses, professional associations and conferences, technological resources, and much more—all in user-friendly organization

1-88328-250-0 PORTICO $24.95

1-88328-260-8 PORTICO PB $14.95

Terri **Lonier**

Working Solo

Named the best business book for independent entrepreneurs by *INC. Magazine* (April 1994)

1-88328-240-3 PORTICO PB $14.95

Rebecca **Maddox**

Inc. Your Dreams

A practical and inspiring approach for women who want to create a business—and a more fulfilling life—by a leading female entrepreneur

See also **CAREERS FOR WOMEN** under **CAREERS**

0-14-023537-X PENGUIN PB $11.95

Judith **McQuown**

Incorporate Yourself: How to Profit by Setting Up Your Own Corporation

0-88730-611-X HARPERCOLLINS PB $13.00

Ronald E. **Merrill** & Henry D. **Sedgwick**

The New Venture Handbook

The authors offer their own experiences to illustrate points in this highly readable resource on starting and running a business

0-8144-5087-3 AMACOM $26.95

0-8144-7892-1 AMACOM PB $18.95

Jim **Schell**

The Entrepreneur Magazine Small Business Advisor

A self-scoring test designed to measure entrepreneurial aptitude starts out this book, and yields, if not accurate results, a good list of skills needed for success in small business ventures. Strong detail on a variety of subjects in a nuts-and-bolts approach

0-471-14841-5 WILEY $34.95

0-471-14842-3 WILEY PB $19.95

Martin **Shenkman** & Ivan **Taback**

Starting a Limited Liability Company

Only for those individuals who are most serious about starting this newest form of business organization

0-471-13357-4 WILEY $55.00

0-471-13365-5 WILEY PB $19.95

Simplified Small Business Accounting

From the Small Business Library

0-935755-15-2 NOVA PB $19.95

William C. **Taylor** & Alan M. **Webber**

Going Global: Four Entrepreneurs Map the New World Marketplace

See also **THE INTERNATIONAL MARKETPLACE** under **BUSINESS, INDUSTRY, AND FINANCE**

0-670-86308-4 VIKING $22.95

Venture Capital

David **Gladstone**

Venture Capital Investing: The Complete Handbook for Investing in Small Private Businesses for Outstanding Profits

0-13-941428-2 PRENTICE HALL $39.95

Retirement

Forest **Bowman**

The Complete Retirement Handbook

0-8131-1710-0 KENTUCKY $25.00

David **Cleary** & Virginia **Cleary**

Retire Smart

Based on the experiences of retirees, this volume provides a roadmap to avoiding the pitfalls and hazards of the golden years, from money management and housing to avoiding scams and maintaining good health

1-88055-909-9 ALLWORTH PB $12.95

Jeffrey **Sonnenfeld**

Hero's Farewell: What Happens When CEOs Retire

See also **CORPORATE LEADERSHIP AND CEO BIOGRAPHIES** under **BUSINESS, INDUSTRY, AND FINANCE**

0-19-505091-6 OXFORD $30.00

Real Estate

For related reading, see THE HOME in ARCHITECTURE, DESIGN, AND HOMES

Daniel **De Benedictis**

The Complete Real Estate Advisor

Written by a real estate lawyer, this excellent step-by-step guide contains savvy warnings to both buyer and seller

0-671-62908-5 POCKET PB $9.95

Joseph **Howell**

Real Estate Development Syndication

0-275-91010-5 PRAEGER $49.95
0-275-91774-6 PRAEGER PB $14.95

Hollis **Norton**

The New Real Estate Game: Building Wealth Under the New Tax Laws

0-8092-4577-9 CONTEMPORARY PB $14.95

Buying a Home

Julie **Garton-Good**

The Home–Buying Game: A Quick and Easy Way to Get the Best Home for Your Money

0-7931-1646-5 DEARBORN PB $14.95

Ilyce R. **Glink**

10 Steps to Home Ownership: A Workbook for First-Time Buyers

Following the hugely successful *100 Questions Every First-Time Home Buyer Should Ask*, this essential workbook takes virgin buyers through the essential choices that precede buying a house. Deciding on renting versus owning, figuring the affordable range of purchase prices, planning for down payment and closing costs, fixing credit problems, choosing mortgages, and much more make this the complete guide to buying a first home

0-8129-2531-9 TIMES BOOKS PB $15.00

100 Questions Every Home-Seller Should Ask

0-812-92406-1 TIME BOOKS PB $14.00

100 Questions Every Home-Buyer Should Ask With Answers from Top Brokers Around the World

0-812-92283-2 TIME BOOKS PB $14.00

Robert **Irwin**

Making Mortgages Work for You

A guide to all types of mortgage financing, with useful payment tables

See also **BUYING A HOUSE** under **THE HOME** in **ARCHITECTURE, DESIGN, AND HOMES**

0-07-032129-9 MCGRAW HILL $24.95
0-07-032128-0 MCGRAW HILL PB $14.95

Careers

Career Opportunities

Peterson's

The Hidden Job Market 1997: 2000 Fast Growing High Technology Companies that are Hiring Now

From environmental consulting to genetic engineering, this will help nearly anyone locate a job. Each listing includes contacts within the organization, projected openings, fax and phone numbers, all that is useful for job seekers

1-56079-644-8 PETERSON'S PB $18.95

Richard **Lathrop**

Who's Hiring Who

Extensive practical advice on resumes, interviews, and job searches

0-89815-298-4 TEN SPEED PB $11.95

Martha **Leape** & Susan **Vacca**

The Harvard Guide to Careers

Introductions to various careers, trade associations, and sources for the job-hunter or the new graduate

0-674-37563-7 HARVARD PB $8.95

William **Lewis** & Nancy **Schuman**

Fast-Track Careers: A Guide to the Highest Paying Jobs

Concentrates on careers in finance, advertising, media, real estate, and other high-powered areas

0-471-83801-2 WILEY PB $14.95

National Academy Press

Careers in Science & Engineering: A Student Planning Guide to Graduate School and Beyond

0-309-05393-5 NATIONAL ACADEMY PB $11.95

John **Wright**

The American Almanac of Jobs and Salaries

A fact-filled almanac that includes standard jobs, as well as those in government, the arts, the sciences, and health care

0-380-77219-1 AVON PB $18.00

James McGrath **Morris** & Laura **Adler**

Grant Seeker's Guide, 4th Edition

1-55921-139-3 MOYER BELL PB $39.95

Jill R. **Shellow** & Nancy C. **Stella**, editors

The Grant Seeker's Guide

From the National Network for Grantmakers, this is the most complete reference available for researching grants of all kinds. Includes listings of corporations and foundations that fund social change projects, the how-tos of fundraising, and many other helpful hints

0-918825-84-9 MOYER BELL $24.95

Job Success

In addition to more standard tips on how to enjoy success in a current job, there are several new books that advocate creating one's own job security in a time when there is little provided by employers. Some focus on making oneself an indispensable employee, while others demonstrate how to glean the kind of skills that are transferable from one job to another in the event of downsizing or reorganization.

Tony **Alessandra** & Michael J. **O'Connor**

The Platinum Rule: Discover the Four Basic Business Personalities—and How They Can Lead You to Success

A how-to on reading people for success in business and industry

0-446-51970-7 WARNER $22.95

Nancy **Anderson**

Work with Passion: How to Do What You Love for a Living

Advice on attaining career goals, with examples

0-88184-212-5 CARROLL & GRAF PB $9.95

Laurie Beth **Jones**

The Path: Creating Your Mission Statement for Work and for Life

The follow-up to *Jesus, CEO*

0-7868-6227-0 HYPERION $16.95

Jack **Canfield** & Jacqueline **Miller**

Heart at Work: Stories and Strategies for Building Self-Esteem and Reawakening the Soul at Work

Inspiring personal testimonies from Nelson Mandela, Mother Theresa, and others

See also **WESTERN** under **20TH-CENTURY SPIRITUAL LEADERS** under **SPIRITUALITY** under **SPIRITUALITY** in **RELIGION, SPIRITUALITY, AND PHILOSOPHY**

See also **SELF-ESTEEM** under **QUALITY OF LIFE** under **SELF-HELP** in **LIFESTYLES AND PRACTICAL ADVICE**

0-07-011643-1 MCGRAW HILL PB $14.95

Sonya **Hamlin**

How to Talk So People Listen: The Real Key to Job Success

0-06-091573-0 HARPERCOLLINS PB $12.00

Judith **Briles**

Gender Traps: Confronting Confrontophobia, Toxic Bosses, & Other Landmines at Work

A guide for working women focuses on 10 gender traps, workplace problems that range from prejudice to sabotage

See also **ECONOMICS** under **FEMINIST THEORY** under **WOMEN'S STUDIES** in **SOCIAL STUDIES**

0-07-007895-5 MCGRAW HILL $19.95

Barbara **Hemphill**

Taming the Paper Tiger: Organizing the Paper in Your Life

"A must read for anyone who spends more than five minutes a day shuffling paper"—Kenneth Blanchard

0-938721-19-4 KIPLINGER PB $11.95

Adrienne **Mendell**

How Men Think: Making It in a Man's World

A psychologist's guide for female professionals trying to understand male behavior patterns in the workplace

0-449-90978-6 FAWCETT PB $11.00

Shane **Murphy**

The Achievement Zone: Eight Skills for Winning All the Time from the Playing Field to the Boardroom

A private corporate consultant details the skills needed to enter the "achievement zone," which the author likens to the sports notion of being "in the zone," where everything goes right for an athlete

0-399-14096-4 PUTNAM $24.95

Deborah **Tannen**

Talking from 9 to 5: How Women's and Men's Conversational Styles Affect Who Gets Heard, Who Gets Credit, and What Gets Done at Work

A fascinating look at the subtleties of speech and how it may affect your job as well as your relationships

See also **GENDER STUDIES** in **SOCIAL STUDIES**

0-380-71783-2 AVON PB $12.50

Rick **Jarow**

Creating the Work You Love: Courage, Commitment, and Career

0-89281-542-6 INNER TRADITIONS PB $14.95

Denis **Waitley**

The New Dynamics of Goal Setting: Flextactics for a Fast-Changing Future

With the advent of the downsizing trend in the 1980s came the loss of job security. The author encourages workers to accept this as an ongoing condition and use it to their advantage, and provides specific strategies for doing so

0-688-12668-5 MORROW $25.00

Kate **White**

Why Good Girls Don't Get Ahead but Gutsy Girls Do: 9 Secrets Every Career Woman Should Know

The *Redbook* editor-in-chief shares her knowledge and strategies for success

0-446-67215-7 WARNER PB $12.99

Neal **Whitten**

Becoming an Indispensable Employee in a Disposable World

Guidance and encouragement of real value to employees and employers alike. Whitten shows how to counter negative employee beliefs and to develop the skills—self-belief and responsibility, meeting customer expectations, balancing professional and personal lives—to render each and every employee indispensable to the workplace

0-13-603812-3 PRENTICE HALL $19.95

0-446-51775-5 WARNER $19.95

Diane **Tracy**

Take this Job and Love It: A Personal Guide to Career Empowerment

An eminently practical four-step program that shows how to reclaim a positive, more satisfying relationship with your job. In examining and addressing the career dilemmas of eight emblematic employees, Tracy, acclaimed seminar leader and author of *The Power Pyramid*, is able to isolate—and exorcise—the demons that make us loathe our work

0-07-065254-6 MCGRAW HILL $19.95

Terrie **Williams**

The Personal Touch: What You Really Need to Succeed in Today's Fast-Paced Business World

"She's handled some of the top and some of the most visible talent...and she's pulled it off with great expertise and apparent ease. Listen to her—she has a lot to say!" So says Sidney Ganis of Columbia Pictures about Terrie Williams's success in public relations. The book is endorsed equally by Bill Cosby, David Dinkins, and many others. A straightforward and easy-to-use guide to doing well in business while doing good

0-446-51775-5 WARNER $19.95

Getting a Job

Laurence G. **Boldt**

How to Find the Work You Love

The author of the bestselling *Zen and the Art of Making a Living* shows here that technical and marketplace changes have made the chances for finding a truly satisfying career better than ever. But how to find that career? Bolt provides a remarkable guide addressing not only how to get the work you love, but managing personal resources in the quest to discover what that work is

See also **CAREER CHANGE**

0-14-019524-6 ARKANA PB $9.95

Linda **Linn**

Landing Your First Real Job

0-07-038061-9 HARVARD BUSINESS PB $12.95

Everett **Harkins** & others

After College Guide to Life

Finding a job, budgeting, cooking, shopping, stress management, and friendship maintenance are among the many topics covered. A thoughtful gift for graduates launching into the real world

0-9634987-0-3 ALCOVE PB $12.95

Andrea **Kay**

Interview Strategies that Will Get You the Job You Want

1-55870-411-6 BETTERWAY PB $12.99

Michael **Novak**

Business as a Calling: Work and the Examined Life

An analysis and exploration of the spiritual aspects of business for those who "have enough to live by, but not enough to live for"

0-684-82748-4 FREE PRESS $22.50

Kathryn **Petras** & Ross **Petras**

The Only Job-Hunting Guide You'll Ever Need

A step-by-step approach for job hunters and career switchers

0-671-63648-0 SIMON & SCHUSTER PB $14.00

Resumes

Juvenal **Angel**

The Complete Resume Book and Job Search Guide

Four hundred sample resumes for a variety of jobs

0-671-72564-5 POCKET PB $5.99

Marian **Faux**

The Complete Resume Guide

Two hundred job categories with sample resumes; includes sections for those over 40 and for the handicapped

0-02-860028-2 ARCO PB $8.95

Interviews

Jeffrey **Allen**

How to Turn an Interview into a Job

0-671-62134-3 SIMON & SCHUSTER PB $9.00

Richard **Beatty**

The Five-Minute Interview

Based on the theory that the first five minutes of an interview are the most crucial; sample questions and practice exercises

0-471-84034-3 WILEY PB $14.95

John **Marcus**

The Complete Job Interview Handbook

Ways to obtain an interview, commonly asked questions and replies, suggestions for negotiating salaries

0-06-273266-8 HARPERPERENNIAL PB $10.00

Jack **Biegeleisen**

Make Your Job Interview a Success: A Guide for the Career-Minded Job Seeker

Includes cardinal rules for interviews (such as punctuality), ways to muff an interview, good advice for writing resumes, and sample questions

0-13-552852-6 MACMILLAN PB........................$11.00

Anthony **Medley**

Sweaty Palms: The Neglected Art of Being Interviewed

A well-organized guide with cartoons

0-89815-403-0 TEN SPEED PB............................$8.95

Career Change

Laurence G. **Boldt**

How to Find the Work You Love

See also GETTING A JOB

0-14-019524-6 ARKANA PB................................$9.95

Richard **Bolles**

What Color Is Your Parachute?

The classic work on job hunting and career change. Witty, with unusual graphics and amusing exercises for evaluating one's life and goals

0-89815-568-1 TEN SPEED PB...........................$14.95

William **Bridges**

Jobshift

The American workplace has changed, and many of the jobs that are gone simply aren't coming back. Bridges, named one of the ten most popular executive development consultants by *The Wall Street Journal,* outlines the technological and economic forces that have produced these changes. He goes on to describe the companies of the future, and, most important, teaches employees how to manage and market themselves for a successful career in our new society

0-201-62667-5 ADDISON-WESLEY..................$22.00

0-201-48933-3 ADDISON-WESLEY PB.............$13.00

John **Crystal** & Richard **Bolles**

Where Do I Go from Here with My Life?

An intelligent book in an unusual design to help in making career decisions

0-89815-084-1 TEN SPEED PB...........................$17.95

Faith **Popcorn** & Lys **Marigold**

Clicking: 16 Trends to Future Fit Your Life, Your Work, and Your Business

An upbeat manual that helps individuals identify, adapt to and utilize current trends

0-88730-694-2 HARPERCOLLINS.....................$26.00

Downsizing

Nina **Schuyler**

The Unemployment Survival Handbook

From practical advice for cutting through the red tape in obtaining unemployment benefits to dealing with the emotional and financial stress of job loss. This complete guide is a must read for everyone who has been "downsized," "laid off," "excessed," or "de-hired"

1-88055-908-0 ALLWORTH PB...........................$9.95

Careers for Women

Mindy **Bingham** & Sandy **Stryker**

More Choices: A Strategic Planning Guide for Mixing Career and Family

Questionnaires to help women decide whether or how to mix a career with raising a family

0-911655-28-X ADVOCACY PB.........................$16.95

Constance **Glaser** & Barbara Steinberg **Smalley**

Swim with the Dolphins: How Women Can Succeed in Corporate America on their Own Terms

An exploration of how traditional "feminine" characteristics can be assets in the business world

0-446-51802-6 WARNER..................................$19.95

0-446-671844 WARNER PB..............................$12.99

Betty **Harragan**

Games Mother Never Taught You: Corporate Gamesmanship for Women

A commonsense advice book for women just starting out in the corporate world

0-446-35703-0 WARNER PB................................$6.50

Mona **Harrington**

Women Lawyers: Rewriting the Rules

A graduate of Harvard Law School probes the perpetually frustrating status of women in the quintessential "boy's club" profession, also giving voice to those women who have fallen off the traditional lawyering track. "The author's great contribution here is quoting women at length as they describe in intimate detail what brought them to–and often what drove them away from–the practice of law. An important and incisive study"—*Kirkus Reviews*

0-394-58025-7 KNOPF...................................$24.00

Rebecca **Maddox**

Inc. Your Dreams

See also ENTREPRENEURSHIP under BUSINESS ADVICE under INVESTING, TAXES, AND BUSINESS ADVICE

0-14-023537-X PENGUIN PB.............................$11.95

Sam **Stovall**

Sector Investing 1996 Edition

See also INVESTING, TAXES, AND BUSINESS ADVICE

0-07-065521-9 MCGRAW HILL...........................$14.95

Joyce **Ward**

Finding Your Financial Freedom: Every Woman's Guide to Success

0-7931-2346-1 DEARBORN PB...........................$16.95

0-380-77219-1 AVON PB..................................$18.00

Business Careers

John A. **Thompson** & Catharine A. **Henningsen**

The Portable Executive: Building Your Own Job Security—From Corporate Dependency to Self-Direction

Pragmatic self-marketing strategies for the downsized executive

0-671-86904-3 SIMON & SCHUSTER...............$23.00

0-684-81891-4 SIMON & SCHUSTER PB..........$12.00

Ron **Tepper**

Become a Top Consultant: How the Experts Do It

How to determine the market, build a business, and set fees. Includes case histories

0-471-81706-6 WILEY.......................................$21.95

Terrie **Williams** & Joe **Cooney**

The Personal Touch: What You Really Need to Succeed in Today's Fast-paced Business World

With forewords by Bill Cosby and Jonathan Tisch, this paperback edition of Williams's best-selling volume offers timely and simple strategies for business success. The president of a renowned public relations agency, Williams offers the benefit of her vast experience in a clear and intelligent manner that allows application to one's own business challenges. "A required primer in how to turn unique talents into the building blocks of success"
—*Michael Fuchs*

0-446-67158-4 WARNER PB.............................$11.99

Secretarial Jobs

Diana **Booher**

The New Secretary: How to Handle People as Well as You Handle Paper

0-8160-1160-5 FACTS ON FILE.........................$22.95

Lillian **Doris** & Bessemoy **Miller**

Complete Secretary's Handbook

0-13-159674-8 PRENTICE HALL........................$24.95

Sarah **Taintor** & Kate **Monro**

The Secretary's Handbook

0-02-610211-0 MACMILLAN..............................$19.95

INTRODUCTION BY JOHN NAISBITT

0-930807-21-9 FUND RAISING INSTITUTE......$30.00

Advertising and Marketing

Toron **Douglas**

The Complete Guide to Advertising

A good reference work

0-89009-784-4BOOK SALES............................$16.98

Theodore **Levitt**
The Marketing Imagination
A collection of influential essays by the most highly acclaimed marketing scholar of the last 30 years
0-02-919090-8 FREE PRESS PB....................$16.95

Sales

Joe **Girard** & Stanley **Brown**
How to Sell Anything to Anybody
Personal tips: brash, but interesting
0-446-38532-8 WARNER PB....................$11.99

Tom **Hopkins**
How to Master the Art of Selling
Best-seller by a millionaire salesman on everything from phone techniques to "power closes"
0-446-38636-7 WARNER PB....................$14.99

Chuck **Lewis**
You're Gonna Love It: Witty, Fast-Paced Observations on a Career in Sales
0-89815-138-4 TEN SPEED PB....................$7.95

Bradley J. **Morgan**, editor
Marketing and Sales Career Directory
0-8103-5609-0 GALE....................$39.00
0-8103-9430-8 VISIBLE INK PB....................$17.95

Mark H. **McCormack**
On Selling
The author of the bestselling *What They Don't Teach You at Harvard Business School* conducts a training course that includes the standard wisdom of selling along with some less orthodox practices, such as "unselling," and letting the customer who needs to have a sense of control say no
9-7871-0904-5 DOVE HOUSE....................$19.95

Linda **Richardson**
Sales Coaching
0-07-052382-7 HARVARD BUSINESS....................$19.95

Writing as a Career

Elizabeth **Benedict**
The Joy of Writing Sex: A Guide for Fiction Writers
"Elizabeth Benedict's magical mystery tour of sex between the pages manages at once to be instructive, entertaining and literary. She gives the term 'word play' new meaning"—Michael Dorris
1-88491-021-1 STORY PRESS....................$16.99

Robert W. **Bly**
Secrets of a Freelance Writer
0-8050-1192-7 HOLT PB....................$10.95

Kirsten **Holm**, editor
1997 Writer's Market: Where and How to Sell What You Write
An extremely useful reference
0-89879-742-X WRITER'S DIGEST....................$27.99

Richard **Curtis**
How to Be Your Own Literary Agent: The Business of Getting Your Book Published
Advice from a successful agent on negotiation and other business aspects of the literary world
0-395-36142-7 HOUGHTON MIFFLIN PB.........$10.95

Edisol W. **Dotson**
Putting Out: The Essential Publishing Resource Guide for Gay & Lesbian Writers
A timely resource that lists 500 book and magazine publishers, newspapers, agents. Includes editors' phone numbers, advice on agenting a manuscript, information on the submission and publishing processes, on reading contracts, and marketing your work
0-939416-86-7 CLEIS....................$29.95
0-939416-87-5 CLEIS PB....................$12.95

Diane **Gage** & Marcia **Coppess**
Get Published: Top Magazine Editors Tell You How
0-8050-2689-4 HOLT PB....................$16.95

Jean **Kent** & Candace **Shelton**
The Romance Writer's Phrase Book
Handy phrases organized by emotions, sex, parts of the body, physical characteristics, and more
0-399-51002-8 PERIGEE PB....................$9.00

Suzanne **Lipsett**
Surviving a Writer's Life
"Sure to be snapped up by the countless…writers looking for insights into the wonderful world of writing and it will serve them well"
—*The Bloomsbury Review*
0-06-250658-7 HARPERCOLLINS PB....................$10.00

Donald **Maass**
The Career Novelist: A Literary Agent Offers Strategies for Success
Help with choosing agents, marketing, the various genre options, and publishing
0-435-08693-6 HEINEMANN PB....................$15.95

Mickey **Pearlman**
Listen to Their Voices: Twenty Interviews with Women Who Write
"Makes us feel as if we've kicked off our shoes and sat down across the table with some of the best writers in America"—Rosellen Brown
0-395-68197-9 HOUGHTON MIFFLIN PB.........$10.95

Publishing

Marvin **Arth** & Helen **Ashmore**
The Newsletter Editor's Desk Book
A well-organized manual, with concrete advice
0-9630222-2-9 NATIONAL BOOK NETWORK PB $17.95

Dian Dincin **Buchman** & Seli **Groves**
Writer's Digest Guide to Manuscript Formats
A simple and clear guide for all types of manuscript presentation
See also **WRITING GUIDES** under **REFERENCE**
0-89879-293-2 WRITER'S DIGEST....................$19.99

Gerald **Gross**
Editors on Editing
Advice on editing, from the practical to the theoretical
0-8021-3263-4 GROVE PB....................$16.95

Dan **Poytner**
The Self-Publishing Manual
0-915516-90-X PARA PUBLICATION PB....................$19.95

University of Chicago
The Chicago Manual of Style: 14th Edition
The standard. For over 80 years, this reference has been used by American authors, editors, and proofreaders for its chapters on preparing and editing copy for publication
See also **USAGE AND STYLE MANUALS** under **WRITING GUIDES** under **REFERENCE**
0-226-10389-7 CHICAGO....................$40.00
0-941159-96-5 PROFESSIONAL BUSINESS PB..$11.95

Miscellaneous Jobs

Ragnar **Benson**
Action Careers: Employment in the High-Risk Job Market
Describes unusual careers: from bodyguard to explosives handler, missionary, rodeo cowboy, and private eye
0-8065-1079-X CITADEL PB....................$9.95

Shelly **Field**
Career Opportunities in the Music Industry
Short descriptions of 80 careers in music, from business management to conducting; includes lists of music publishers, agencies, and record companies
0-8160-2401-4 FACTS ON FILE....................$27.50

Deborah **Hoover**
Supporting Yourself as an Artist: A Practical Guide
Sources of support, as well as information for media artists, visual artists, craft artists, poets, playwrights, composers, and choreographers
0-19-505972-7 OXFORD PB....................$10.95

Public Speaking

Ron **Hoff**
Say It in Six: How to Say Exactly What You Mean in Six Minutes or Less
The author of *I Can See You Naked* explains how to achieve brevity, an important and necessary skill for doing business in the '90s
0-8362-1041-7 ANDREWS & MCMEEL PB........$10.95

First Books for Business

Business Presentations and Public Speaking

0-07-001565-1 HARVARD BUSINESS PB..........$12.00

William **Hendricks** & others

Secrets of Power Presentations

Filled with checklists, questionnaires and information on everything from booking rooms for presentations to organizing and delivering talks

1-56414-242-6 CAREER PB..........$16.99

Terri **Mandel**

Power Schmoozing: The New Etiquette for Social and Business Success

Advice from the owner of the marketing and publicity firm the Mulholland Group

0-07-039887-9 HARVARD BUSINESS PB..........$12.95

Jo **Sprague** & Douglas **Stuart**

The Speaker's Handbook

0-15-583173-9 HARCOURT BRACE..........$33.92

Marian **Woodall**

Thinking on Your Feet—How to Communicate Under Pressure

Tips from a consultant and speech coach on how to prepare for the post-presentation queries

0-941-15996-5 PROBA..........$11.95

Education: Practical Advice

Guides for Parents

Alice **Drum** & Richard **Kneedler**

Funding a College Education: Finding the Right School for Your Child and the Right Fit for Your Budget

Featuring numerous worksheets on what financial aid is available and how to apply for it

0-87584-628-9 MCGRAW HILL PB..........$14.95

Erlene B. **Wilson**

Money for College: A Guide to Financial Aid for African-American Students

Foundation, corporate, private, and university scholarship listings

0-452-27276-9 PLUME PB..........$15.95

Public and Private Schools

Charles **Harrison**

Public Schools USA: A Comparative Guide to School Districts

1-56079-081-4 PETERSON'S..........$44.95

Peterson's Guides

Peterson's Guide to Private Secondary Schools, 1996-1997

The most complete guide to both boarding and day schools

1-560-79586-7 PETERSON'S PB..........$29.95

College Guides

Barry **Beckham**

The Black Student's Guide to Colleges

0-931761-07-7 BECKHAM PB..........$16.95

Laurie **Blum**

Free Money for College: A Guide to More than 1,000 Grants and Scholarships for Undergraduate Schools

0-8160-3101-0 FACTS ON FILE..........$24.95
0-8160-3498-2 FACTS ON FILE PB..........$14.95

Daniel J. **Cassidy** & Michael J. **Alves**

The Scholarship Book

A comprehensive listing of sources for undergraduate financial aid

0-13-799545-8 PRENTICE HALL PB..........$21.95

The College Board

The College Handbook 1997: The Official College Board Guide to 3,300 Two- and Four-year Colleges

"The College Handbook…is the most comprehensive"—*Rolling Stone*

0-87447-542-2 CLGX..........$21.95

Edward **Fiske**

The Fiske Guide to Colleges, 1997

A newly renamed and revised edition of a first-rate guide by the *New York Times* education writer

0-8129-2757-5 TIME BOOKS PB..........$19.00

Peterson's Guides

Paying Less for College 1997: The Complete Guide to More than $36 Billion in Financial Aid

This book guides would-be students to an understanding of the financial-aid process, showing them how to select both colleges and financial-aid plans to suit their needs. It includes information on 3,000 state and federal financial aid programs

1-56079-650-2 PETERSON'S PB..........$26.95

Charles J. **Shields**

The College Guide for Parents

0-87447-316-0 COLLEGE BOARD PB..........$12.95

Janet **Spencer** & Sandra **Maleson**

The Complete Guide to College Visits

Covering over 250 colleges and universities, this book provides easily accessible tour and class schedules, information on faculty interviews, driving instructions, places to stay, and local attractions. "In one place here's all the available, but often hard-to-get, nuts and bolts of visiting colleges. It fills a real need"—Jonathan Reider

0-8065-1320-9 VILLARD PB..........$19.95

Graduate and Professional Schools

Laurie **Blum**

Free Money for Graduate School

0-8160-3562-8 FACTS ON FILE..........$24.95
0-8160-3463-6 FACTS ON FILE PB..........$14.95

Sally F. **Goldfarb**

Inside the Law Schools: A Guide by Students for Students

0-452-27014-6 PLUME PB..........$12.00

Eugene **Miller**

Barron's Guide to Graduate Business Schools

0-8120-4863-6 BARRONS PB..........$14.95

T.C. **Moore**, editor

Peterson's Guide to Graduate and Professional Programs, 1997

1-56079-651-0 PETERSON'S PB..........$27.95

The National Research Council

Student Guide to the Research-doctorate Programs in the United States

0-309-05444-3 NATIONAL ACADEMY PB..........$19.95

Saul **Wischnitzer**, editor

Barron's Guide to Medical and Dental Schools

0-8120-1631-9 BARRONS PB..........$14.95

Testing

The College Board

8 *Real* SATs

Included in this handbook are test-taking tips from the test makers, PSATs, and real SATs

0-87447-550-3 CLGX PB..........$16.95

Thomas H. **Martinson**

ACT Supercourse

Guide to the American College Testing exam

0-671-86604-4 ARCO PB..........$17.00

SAT Supercourse

0-671-86402-5 ARCO PB..........$17.00

LSAT Supercourse
How to prepare for the Law School Admissions Test
0-671-84849-6 MACMILLAN PB $18.00

Fred **O'Brechtetal**
How to Prepare For the ACT
A standard guide for the American College Testing exam
0-8120-4692-7 BARRONS PB $11.95

David **Owen**
None of the Above: Behind the Myth of Scholastic Aptitude
Not a guide as much as an expose of what's wrong with the much-vaunted test
0-395-35540-0 HOUGHTON MIFFLIN..............$16.95

Adam **Robinson**
Cracking the System: The GRE
The Princeton Review meets the Graduate Record Exam
0-394-74342-3 RANDOM HOUSE PB..................$9.95

Adam **Robinson** & John **Katzman**
Princeton Review: Cracking the SAT and PSAT
Based on a systematized coaching program for improving test scores through intelligent guessing and other test-taking methods
0-679-73907-6 VILLARD PB...............................$15.00

Murray **Rockowitz**
How to Prepare for the GED
Preparation for the high school diploma equivalency test
0-8120-4397-9 BARRONS PB.............................$12.95

College Admissions

Christopher **Georges** & Gigi **Georges**
100 Successful College Application Essays
Using essays from applicants who were admitted to various colleges, this book offers advice and guidance on how to write an essay that can help win admission
0-451-62835-7 NEW AMERICAN LIBRARY PB ...$4.99

Reference

One-Volume Encyclopedias

Benet
Benet's Reader's Encyclopedia: Third Edition
Biographies of writers, artists, musicians, and philosophers; plot summaries, character sketches, myths, legends, folklore; literary awards; important movements and schools of literature
0-06-181088-6 HARPERCOLLINS.....................$45.50

Alan **Axlerod** & Charles **Phillips**
What Every American Should Know About American History: 200 Events that Shaped the Nation
The crash course, palm-sized. "Cogently written, concisely thorough and admirably informative"—*Library Journal*
See also **GENERAL HISTORIES** under **SURVEYS OF US HISTORY** in **HISTORY OF THE AMERICAS**
1-55850-309-9 ADAMS PB..................................$10.95

Barron's
Barron's Student's Concise Encyclopedia
Full-color maps and illustrations plus unique sections on life skills for teens and young adults
0-8120-6329-5 BARRONS $29.95

Cyril Leslie **Beeching**
A Dictionary of Dates
Interesting facts and historical tidbits for each day of the year, from the London *Observer's* weekly dates column writer
0-19-285274-4 OXFORD PB...............................$10.95

Chas S. **Clifton**, editor
Encyclopedia of Heresies and Heretics
The tradition of heretics in Christianity is a long one that includes not only madmen and witches, but also Augustine, Joan of Arc, and early followers of St. Francis of Assisi—the history of heresy is ultimately and fascinatingly intertwined with the history of the Church of Rome
See also **REFERENCE** under **CHRISTIANITY** in **RELIGION, SPIRITUALITY, AND PHILOSOPHY**
0-87436-600-3 ABC CLIO $50.00

David **Crystal**, editor
The Cambridge Encyclopedia
The most up-to-date general reference book, with over 30,000 entries and over 750 line drawings, illustrations, and maps, printed in two colors throughout
0-521-44429-2 CAMBRIDGE $49.95

The Cambridge Encyclopedia of the English Language
Beginning with the Anglo-Saxon origins of English and following its evolution throughout the world, Crystal takes particular care to allow the language to "speak for itself" by using quotations, newspaper clippings, poems, advertisements, cartoons, and other types of illustrative material
0-521-40179-8 CAMBRIDGE $49.95

Bonnie L. **Hendricks**, editor
International Encyclopedia of Horse Breeds
See also **HORSE BREEDS** under **HORSES** under **PETS** in **FOOD, TRAVEL, AND LEISURE**
See also **ANIMALS** under **NATURE STUDY** in **SCIENCE**
FOREWORD BY ANTHONY A. DENT
0-8061-2753-8 OKLAHOMA..............................$65.00

Robert **Ingpen** & Philip **Wilkinson**
Encyclopedia of Mysterious Places
0-670-82794-0 VIKING $29.95

E. D. **Hirsch**, Jr. & others, editors
The Dictionary of Cultural Literacy
Revised and updated, this new edition provides a wealth of essential facts in fields that include politics, technology, medicine, history, and literature. Also includes new subjects based on readers' suggestions from the first edition, such as multiculturalism and African-American history. The only reference book to appear on the bestseller list
See also **READING AND LITERACY** under **EDUCATION** in **SOCIAL STUDIES**
0-395-65597-8 HOUGHTON MIFFLIN $24.95

Barbara **Chernow** & George **Vallasi**, editors
The Columbia Encyclopedia: Fifth Edition
The largest, most comprehensive single-volume encyclopedia available. Contains 50,000 articles and 65,000 cross-references in 3,000 pages. This stunning edition contains 60 percent new or revised material. "An incomparable one-volume omnifactotum"—John Updike. "The standard of excellence as a guide to essential facts"
—*NY Times Book Review*
0-395-62438-X COLUMBIA.....................$125.00

Columbia Encyclopedia
The Concise Columbia Encyclopedia
Perfect for home or office
0-395-62439-8 COLUMBIA.......................$49.95

Paul **Lagasse**, editor
The Concise Columbia Encyclopedia: Third Edition
The paperback edition of the widely praised *Concise Encyclopedia* is designed to provide the most current information in all fields of knowledge. "Among desk encyclopedias it is the standout choice...the cream of the crop"—Kenneth F. Kister
0-395-75184-5 DORLING KINDERSLEY PB $19.95

Thomas H. **Johnson**, editor
The Oxford Companion to American History
One-volume reference, sister volume to *The Oxford Companion to American Literature*
0-19-500597-X OXFORD.....................................$55.00

Don **Lessem** & Donald F. **Glut**, editors
The Dinosaur Society Dinosaur Encyclopedia
They may have died in an ice age, but it's no news that dinosaurs are hotter than ever. Ideal for dinosaur fanciers of all ages, this lavishly illustrated guide includes depictions of more than 600 species as well as detailed information regarding restoration, research, and behavior
See also **YOUNG ADULT NONFICTION** in **BOOKS FOR YOUNG READERS**
0-679-41770-2 RANDOM HOUSE $25.00

Hilary **McGlynn**, editor
Random House Concise Encyclopedia
A best-selling reference
0-679-76454-2 RANDOM HOUSE PB................$18.00

Merriam-Webster
Merriam-Webster's Encyclopedia of Literature
In conjunction with the editors of the *Encyclopaedia Brittanica*, with 10,000 entries and 250 illustrations
0-87779-042-6 MERRIAM WEBSTER................$39.95

Bruce M. **Metzger** &
Michael D. **Coogan**, editors
The Oxford Companion to the Bible
Far more comprehensive than "standard Bible dictionaries," this guide features not only traditional definitions, references, and maps, but more than 700 articles by 250 scholars relating to everything from homosexuality in the Bible and the Bible's influence on literature to women's issues and extended entries on concepts such as immortality, sin, and the Holy Spirit
See also **THE BIBLE** under **REFERENCE** under **CHRISTIANITY** in **RELIGION, SPIRITUALITY, AND PHILOSOPHY**
0-19-504645-5 OXFORD....................................$55.00

Richard **Milner**
The Encyclopedia of Evolution: Humanity's Search for Its Origins
Did you know that early New England farmers believed that the fossilized "bird tracks" of the Connecticut Valley were made by Noah's ravens? Or that the sentimental movie classic *It's a Wonderful Life* reflects crucial evolutionary ideas? Trivia mixes with history mixes with theory and scholarship in this entertaining volume
See also **BIOLOGY** under **LIFE SCIENCES** in **SCIENCE**
0-8050-2717-3 OWLET PB.................................$25.00

The New York Public Library
The New York Public Library Desk Reference: Second Edition
This invaluable, extensively indexed reference guide features answers to the most frequently asked questions from students, researchers, teachers, business executives, and scholars. Divided into 26 categories, this fully revised volume of the national bestseller includes lists, tables, sidebars, charts, and statistics
0-671-85014-8 MACMILLAN..............................$40.00

The New York Public Library Student's Desk Reference
This edition is edited especially for students on the junior high and middle school level. It features 27 categories, from math to etiquette and law to chemistry
0-671-85013-X MACMILLAN..............................$20.00

Oxford University
The New Encyclopedia of Science Volume I Matter and Energy
Seasoned science journalists render this exhaustive collection readable; academic overseers ensure its accuracy
See also **REFERENCE** under **SCIENTIFIC THOUGHT AND DISCOVERY** under **SCIENCE AND TECHNOLOGY** in **SCIENCE**
0-19-521085-9 OXFORD $35.00

Volume II Animal Life
See also **REFERENCE** under **SCIENTIFIC THOUGHT AND DISCOVERY** under **SCIENCE AND TECHNOLOGY** in **SCIENCE**
0-19-521084-0 OXFORD $35.00

George **Perkins** & others, editors
Benet's Reader's Encyclopedia of American Literature
Comprehensive volume on the literature of North America and Latin America
0-06-270027-8 HARPERCOLLINS......................$47.50

Doris **Weatherford**
American Women's History: An A-to-Z of People, Organizations, Issues and Events
An inspirational volume that emphasizes the human by profiling such exemplary American women as Grace Abbott, the first advocate of prenatal care; Susan B. Anthony, who was arrested when she cast a presidential vote in 1872; and such pioneer artists in their fields as singer Marian Anderson and novelist Willa Cather
See also **REFERENCE** under **WOMEN'S STUDIES** in **SOCIAL STUDIES**
0-671-85028-8 MACMILLAN PB.......................$18.00

Bruce **Wetterau**, editor
World History: A Dictionary of Important People, Places, and Events from Ancient Times to the Present
A quick, versatile guide to historical events, places, and figures in world politics, science, business, art, et al. Will fill a much-needed gap on the reference shelves of high school students and scholars alike. More than 10,000 entries
0-8050-2350-X HOLT $60.00

Prentice Hall
Webster's New World Encyclopedia, College Edition
Five hundred maps, charts, graphs, and illustrations complement 20,000 entries
0-671-85016-4 MACMILLAN $35.00

Roy **Willis**, editor
World Mythology
The myths of birth, loss, death, famine, abundance, longing, greed, love, and power comprise a portrait of the emotional and imaginative landscape of humankind. Common mythological themes from diverse corners of the world are linked and explored, both as aspects of a single unified psyche and as rich regional expressions of their own. 500 photographs, charts, and maps
See also **GENERAL INTRODUCTIONS** under **MYTHOLOGY AND FOLKLORE** in **RELIGION, SPIRITUALITY, AND PHILOSOPHY**
0-8050-2701-7 HOLT $45.00

General Information

Biographical Dictionaries

Mark Mayo **Boatner**
Biographical Dictionary of World War II
See also **THE MEN IN THE FIELD** under **MEMOIRS AND BIOGRAPHIES** under **THE SECOND WORLD WAR** in **WORLD HISTORY AND CURRENT AFFAIRS**
0-89141-548-3 PRESIDIO PB $50.00

Matthew **Bruccoli**, editor
The Concise Dictionary of American Biography
0-8103-1818-0 GALE......................................$380.00

David **Crystal**
The Cambridge Biographical Dictionary
0-521-56780-7 CAMBRIDGE PB........................$16.95

The Cambridge Biographical Encyclopedia
Heavily cross-referenced and illustrated; lists 16,000 bios as well as 50 essays that illuminate prominent people and events
0-521-43421-1 CAMBRIDGE $49.95

Deborah G. **Felder**
The 100 Most Influential Women of All Time: A Ranking Past and Present
From social reformers to scientists, educators, labor leaders, artists, performers, and sports figures, Felder has ranked the 100 most influential women of history in a detailed and insightful biographical compendium. Lucille Ball clocks in at 100, Sandra Day O'Connor at 86, Coco Chanel at 50, Simone de Beauvoir at 15, and Eleanor Roosevelt outdistances a field that also includes the Virgin Mary (10) and Marie Curie (2)
See also **REFERENCE** under **WOMEN'S STUDIES** in **SOCIAL STUDIES**
0-8065-1726-3 CITADEL..................................$24.95

John S. **Bowman**, editor
Cambridge Dictionary of American Biography
Nearly 9,000 entries cover American figures from Colonial times to the present. Over 90 consultants' contributions and a useful index by occupation make this comprehensive and easy to use
0-521-40258-1 CAMBRIDGE $44.95

Pierre **Grimal**
A Concise Dictionary of Classical Mythology
TRANSLATED BY A.R. MAXWELL-HYSLOP
0-631-16696-3 BLACKWELL.............................$36.95

Merriam-Webster
Webster's New Biographical Dictionary
Perfect for every home or office reference shelf
0-87779-543-6 MERRIAM WEBSTER $27.95

Magnus **Magnusson**, editor

Chambers Biographical Dictionary

0-550-10640-5 LAROUSSE $50.00

Peter **Parker** & Frank **Kermode**, editors

A Reader's Guide to Twentieth-Century Writers

The distinguished critics Parker and Kermode offer over 1,000 biographical entries of all the major literary figures of the century the world over. Each entry offers biography, critical assessment, a full bibliography, and other essential information, such as literary brawls, libel actions, honors, and difficulties with drink, drugs, lovers, and publishers. A splendid, lively, and readable guide to the literature and writers of our century

See also **GENERAL STUDIES** under **WORLD LITERATURE: WORLD LITERATURE SURVEYS AND ANTHOLOGIES** in **LITERATURE OF EUROPE, AFRICA, AND ASIA**

0-19-521215-0 OXFORD $35.00

Don Michael **Randel**, editor

The Harvard Biographical Dictionary of Music

0-674-37299-9 HARVARD $39.95

The Reader's Digest

Who's Who in the Bible

An illustrated A-to-Z format provides concise and in-depth portraits of over 500 biblical characters, from prophets to beggars. With color maps, genealogies, and ample documentation

See also **THE BIBLE** under **REFERENCE** under **CHRISTIANITY** in **RELIGION, SPIRITUALITY, AND PHILOSOPHY**

0-89577-618-9 READER'S DIGEST $32.00

Harriet L. **Tiger**, editor

Who's Who in America 1997, 51st Edition

The book everyone wants to be in

0-8379-0175-8 MARQUIS $489.95

Marquis Who's Who

Who's Who in the World 1997, 14th Edition

0-8379-1117-6 MARQUIS $359.95

Almanacs and Books of Facts

Michael **Barone** & Grand **Ujifusa**

The Almanac of American Politics, 1996

Maps, statistics, names, profiles, and data that includes detailed information on every elected official from governor to president and the regions they represent. "The Bible of American politics..."—George F. Will

0-89234-067-3 TIME BOOKS $64.95

Peter **Bernstein** & Christopher **Ma**

The Practical Guide to Practically Everything: Information You Can Really Use

Over 450 experts on a wide range of subjects with resources and statistics in an easy-to-find format

0-679-75491-1 RANDOM HOUSE PB $13.95

Russell **Ash**

The Top Ten of Everything 1996

0-7894-0338-2 DORLING KINDERSLEY PB $16.95

David **Brownstone** & Irene **Franck**

Timelines of War: A Chronology of Warfare from 100,000 B.C. to the Present

An easy-to-use, unique overview of the entire history of war, revolutions, coups, and rebellions. Extensive, detailed, and visually friendly chronologies provide both far-reaching comprehension and quick reference

0-316-11403-0 LITTLE, BROWN $29.95

Cambridge University Press

The Cambridge Factfinder

Over 180,000 facts and figures, 300 maps and diagrams, fully indexed

0-521-46991-0 CAMBRIDGE PB $14.95

Central Intelligence Agency

The World Factbook 1996-1997

Every nation in the world is included along with a map, climate, government, recent disputes, population, environment, literacy rate, religion, legal system, and much more. Also contains appendices on the United Nations, international organizations, weights and measures, and geographic names

1-57488-014-4 BRASSEY'S DEFENSE $32.95

Joel **Drieger**, editor

The Oxford Companion to Politics of the World

Economics, women's issues, underdevelopment and deindustrialization, human rights, ethnic and civil conflict, and more—discussed here by experts from 40 different countries

0-19-505934-4 OXFORD $55.00

Macmillan

The Macmillan Dictionary of Measurement

From coins and currencies to music and sports, proves anything can and is measured

0-02-525750-1 MACMILLAN $27.50

Guinness Books

The Guinness Book of Records 1996

The record of records, this illustrated compendium of those who have gone the distance–juggled longer, ran faster, made the highest house of cards–remains the standard by which young and old measure their dreams against life's fantastic possibilities

0-8160-2861-3 FACTS ON FILE $24.95

Otto **Johnson**, editor

1997 Information Please Almanac

More than a thousand pages of facts, essays, maps, and photos that touch upon almost every field of inquiry, with particular emphasis on the transforming events and discoveries of the past year. A browser's delight

0-395-82859-7 HOUGHTON MIFFLIN $24.95
0-395-82858-9 HOUGHTON MIFFLIN PB $10.95

Howard **Rheingold**

The Millennium Whole Earth Catalog: Access to Tools and Ideas for the Twenty-First Century

The most up-to-date information for this century and beyond, by the cultural prophets of *The Whole Earth Catalog*. "A table of contents to the Zeitgeist—or the coolest Yellow Pages around"—*Kirkus Reviews*. "Implicit on every page is the...assumption that we're all intelligent, curious, and capable of educating ourselves, given access to the right tools" —*Outside Magazine*

See also **PRACTICAL ADVICE** under **NATURAL RESOURCES AT RISK** under **THE ENVIRONMENT** in **SCIENCE**

FOREWORD BY STEWART BRAND

0-06-251141-6 HARPERCOLLINS $50.00

Les **Krantz**

America by the Numbers: Facts and Figures from the Weighty to the Way-Out

Krantz (*The Best and Worst of Everything*) has masterminded this quirky compendium of statistics, data, and surveys on the way Americans live and what really, alas, concerns us. What are the ten rarest mammals in America? Next to sleep and sex what are the most popular activities in the bedroom?

0-395-65970-1 HOUGHTON MIFFLIN PB $10.95

Robert **Moses** & Beth **Rowen**, editors

1997 Information Please Entertainment Almanac

This updated edition of the classic almanac contains full listings of Oscar, Grammy, and Emmy winners; a comprehensive yearbook of the major film, television, and music releases of 1995; essays by leading feature writers and columnists; time lines; film and music festival calendars; photography, and more

See also **REFERENCE** under **FILM** in **PERFORMING ARTS AND MEDIA**

0-395-82855-4 HOUGHTON MIFFLIN PB $13.95

Alice **Siegel** & Margo McLoone **Basta**, editors

The Information Please Kids' Almanac

...and for kids...

See also **OTHER OR MISCELLANEOUS** in **BOOKS FOR YOUNG READERS**

0-395-58801-4 HOUGHTON MIFFLIN PB $9.95

Rand McNally

World Facts & Maps, Concise International Review: 1997 Edition

Facts and locator maps for every country. Includes hot spots of 41 centers of conflict and other pertinent demographic information

See also **ATLASES** under **GEOGRAPHICAL INFORMATION**

0-528-83881-4 RAND MCNALLY PB $10.95

Bruce **Wetterau**

The New York Public Library Book of Chronologies

The timeline format from the Big Bang to the present with the library's usual thoroughness

0-671-89265-7 MACMILLAN PB $16.00

James **Trager**

The People's Chronology: A Year By Year Record of Human Events from Prehistory to the Present

"...a wonderful compendium of the striking events and anecdotes that have customarily been left out of serious history"—*NY Times*

0-8050-3134-0 OWLET PB $25.00

Amy **Wallace** & David **Wallechinsky**

The Book of Lists: The '90s Edition

0-316-92029-0 L.B. PB $6.99

World Almanac

The World Almanac and Book of Facts 1996

"*The World Almanac* is the most useful reference book known to modern man"—*LA Times*

See also **HISTORICAL AND POLITICAL ATLASES** under **GEOGRAPHICAL INFORMATION**

0-88687-781-4 ST. MARTIN'S $24.95
0-88687-780-6 ST. MARTIN'S PB $9.95

John **Wright**, editor

The Universal Almanac: 1996

Odd entries in addition to useful facts. "An almanac for the '90s"—*Chicago Tribune*

0-8362-0549-9 ANDREWS & MCMEEL PB $9.95

Ted **Yanak** & Pam **Cornelison**

The Great American History Fact Finder

"This crisp and readable volume provides first-rate ready reference for anyone wanting the essential facts on salient persons, dates, and incidents in American history"—Arthur M. Schlesinger, Jr.

0-395-61715-4 HOUGHTON MIFFLIN PB $14.95

Yankee Press

Old Farmer's Almanac

1-57198-027-X YANKEE PRESS $17.95

Geographical Information

Geographical Dictionaries

Archie **Hobson**

The Cambridge Gazetteer of the United States and Canada: A Dictionary of Places

Alphabetically arranged dictionary of places with populations over 16,000; 20 color maps

0-521-41579-9 CAMBRIDGE $49.95

Merriam-Webster

Webster's New Geographical Dictionary

Useful for making those prickly distinctions of location and spelling

0-87779-446-4 MERRIAM WEBSTER $24.95

Mauro **Talocci**, editor

Guide to the Flags of the World

Besides being a useful reference tool

0-688-13561-7 QUILL PB $16.00

John **Small** & Michael **Witherick**

A Modern Dictionary of Geography

0-340-49317-8 ROUTLEDGE $45.00
0-340-49318-6 ROUTLEDGE PB $16.95

Atlases

Reader's Digest

Reader's Digest Atlas of the World

0-528-83539-4 RAND MCNALLY $39.95

John **Bartholomew**, editor

The Times Atlas

The ninth edition of the definitive world atlas, whose oversize pages provide a close-up view of every region of the globe. The uniquely informative index contains over 210,000 annotated entries

0-8129-1874-6 TIME BOOKS $159.95

Hammond

Hammond Atlas of the World

0-8437-1175-2 HAMMOND $69.95

Hammond New Century World Atlas

0-8437-1197-3 HAMMOND PB $19.95

National Geographic

National Geographic Atlas of the World: Book and Magnified Sheet

Fact-filled, beautifully photographed, *National Geographic* atlases explore our country and our world with physical maps, political maps, time zones, demographic, geographic, and economic information, and more

0-87044-835-8 NATIONAL GEOGRAPHIC $100.00

National Geographic Picture Atlas of Our World

0-87044-960-5 NATIONAL GEOGRAPHIC $25.00

New York Times

New York Times Atlas of the World: New Family Edition

Full-color relief maps of the countries, world regions, and a 30,000-entry index of place names

0-8129-2075-9 TIME BOOKS $37.50

Oxford University Press

Oxford Encyclopedic World Atlas: Country-By-Country Coverage

Full-color maps and profiles for every country in the world

0-19-521170-7 OXFORD $39.95

Rand McNally

The New International Atlas

0-528-83214-X RAND MCNALLY $150.00

Quick Reference Atlas with CD

128 pages of highly detailed world maps

0-528-52018-0 RAND MCNALLY $39.95

Rand McNally: The United States in Old Maps and Prints

Oversize book with fascinating series of maps chronicling the discovery and gradual exploration of America

See also **HISTORICAL AND POLITICAL ATLASES**

0-528-83619-6 RAND MCNALLY $50.00

Rand McNally Road Atlas, 1996: United States, Canada, Mexico

0-528-81468-0 RAND MCNALLY PB $9.95

Rand McNally World Atlas of Nations

0-528-83698-6 RAND MCNALLY $22.95

World Facts & Maps, Concise International Review: 1997 Edition

See also **ALMANACS AND BOOKS OF FACTS** under **GENERAL INFORMATION**

0-528-83881-4 RAND MCNALLY PB $10.95

Peter **Smith**, editor

The Times Atlas of the World: Comprehensive Edition

Over 245 pages of maps, 210,000 entries, fully revised to include the 15 Soviet republics and changes in Yugoslavia and Eastern Europe

0-8129-2077-5 TIME BOOKS $175.00

The Times Atlas of the World: Expanded, Designed and Produced Using the Exclusive Bartholomew System

Maps, city plans, and enormous amounts of new information in the celebrated Bartholomew System atlas, digitally produced for instant updating at the moment of printing. Includes nine pages of star charts, planetary maps, and geographical comparison charts

0-8129-2604-8 TIME BOOKS $100.00

The New York Times

The New York Times Atlas of the World: 4th Revised Concise Edition

One hundred forty-six pages of maps with up-to-date world changes. "Visually superior" —*Washington Post*

0-8129-2420-7 TIME BOOKS $75.00
0-8129-2266-2 TIME BOOKS PB $22.50

Times/Bartholomew

The New York Times Traveler's Pocket Atlas

The source again, in pocket-size format. Perfect for traveling; affordable and convenient

0-8129-2421-5 TIME BOOKS PB $10.00

Denis **Wood**

The Power of Maps

See also **EARTH SCIENCES** in **SCIENCE**

0-89862-492-4 GUILFORD $39.95
0-89862-493-2 GUILFORD PB $17.95

Historical and Political Atlases

Hammond

Atlas of United States History
0-8437-1142-6 HAMMOND $12.95

Atlas of World History
0-8437-1143-4 HAMMOND $12.95

The Times Atlas of World History: Fourth Edition
0-7230-0534-6 HAMMOND $95.00

Geoffrey **Barraclough**, editor

The Times Atlas of World History
With over 600 maps and illustrations, this magnificent volume provides a total immersion crash-course in the major doings of *Homo sapiens*. *The Toronto Star* calls it "a smashingly extravagant and wonderful family gift"
0-7230-0304-1 HAMMOND $85.00

The Economist

The Economist Desk Companion
Perhaps the most illustrious international publication in the world measures, converts, and calculates just about everything. Answers thousands of questions with "practically every statistic you ever wanted to know"—*Rocky Mountain News*
0-8050-2380-1 HOLT $40.00

Eric **Homberger** & Alice **Hudson**, editors

The Historical Atlas of New York City
Even if you are not a New Yorker, this will intrigue you
See also **NEW YORK** under **AMERICAN CITIES (ALPHABETICAL BY SUBJECT)** under **AMERICAN PEOPLE AND PLACES** in **HISTORY OF THE AMERICAS**
0-8050-2649-5 HOLT $45.00

Michael **Kidron** & Ronald **Segal**, editors

The State of the World Atlas: A Unique Visual Survey of Global Political, Economic and Social Trends
"Unique and uniquely beautiful…tells us more about the world today than a dozen statistical abstracts or scholarly tomes"—*LA Times*
0-14-025204-5 PENGUIN PB $16.95

Colin **McEvedy**, editor

The Penguin Atlas of Medieval History
See also **REFERENCE** under **THE VARIETIES OF CIVILIZATION** in **WORLD HISTORY AND CURRENT AFFAIRS**
0-14-051249-7 PENGUIN PB $12.95

The Penguin Atlas of Modern History: To 1815
See also **REFERENCE** under **THE VARIETIES OF CIVILIZATION** in **WORLD HISTORY AND CURRENT AFFAIRS**
0-14-051153-9 VIKING PB $10.95

The Penguin Atlas of North American History: To 1870
See also **REFERENCE** under **THE VARIETIES OF CIVILIZATION** in **WORLD HISTORY AND CURRENT AFFAIRS**
0-14-051128-8 PENGUIN PB $11.95

The Penguin Atlas of Recent History
See also **REFERENCE** under **THE VARIETIES OF CIVILIZATION** in **WORLD HISTORY AND CURRENT AFFAIRS**
0-14-051154-7 PENGUIN PB $11.95

James **McPherson**, editor

The Atlas of the Civil War
Every battle plotted on full-color maps by Pulitzer Prize-winning historian also includes hundreds of photos and personal accounts. Recommended by *Library Journal*
0-02-579050-1 MACMILLAN $40.00

R.I. **Moore**, editor

Atlas of World History
Well-written text accompanies 102 pages of color maps designed especially for this atlas
0-528-83498-3 RAND MCNALLY PB $24.95

Rand McNally

Rand McNally: The United States in Old Maps and Prints
Oversize book with fascinating series of maps chronicling the discovery and gradual exploration of America
See also **ATLASES**
0-528-83619-6 RAND MCNALLY $50.00

Chris **Scarre**, editor

Smithsonian Timelines of the Ancient World
Unique time charts explain, for example, what was happening in the Americas when the pyramids were being built in Egypt. Or the state of Chinese technology when the wheel first appeared in Mesopotamia. From prehistory to the Renaissance
1-56458-305-8 DORLING KINDERSLEY $49.95

Gordon G. **Summers**

History Atlas of the Vietnam War
INTRODUCTION AND CONCLUSION BY STANLEY KARNOW
0-395-72223-3 HOUGHTON MIFFLIN $39.95

Michael J. **Weiss**

Latitudes & Attitudes: An Atlas of American Tastes, Trends, Politics, and Passions
Unique atlas of America's cultural landscape, with 88 color maps and 211 consumer market profiles
0-316-92908-5 LITTLE, BROWN PB $14.95

World Almanac

The World Almanac and Book of Facts 1996
"The *World Almanac* is the most useful reference book known to modern man"—*LA Times*
See also **ALMANACS AND BOOKS OF FACTS** under **GENERAL INFORMATION**
0-88687-781-4 ST. MARTIN'S $24.95
0-88687-780-6 ST. MARTIN'S PB $9.95

English-Language Dictionaries

Webster's

All of these editions are direct descendants of Noah Webster's venerable–but eccentric–19th-century dictionary of the American language

Webster's New World College Dictionary: Revised and Updated
0-02-860333-8 MACMILLAN $22.95

Webster's New World Compact School and Office Dictionary: Updated Edition
Based on Webster's *New World Dictionary: Third College Edition*
0-02-860311-7 MACMILLAN PB $7.95

Webster's New World Dictionary, Third College Edition
AP and UPI dictionary of choice
0-671-89448-X POCKET PB $11.00

Webster's New World Dictionary and Thesaurus
Thesaurus printed on lower half of each page for the dictionary words above
0-02-860574-8 MACMILLAN $19.95

Merriam-Webster

The Merriam-Webster Dictionary: Home and Office Edition
Includes a style guide for punctuation, bibliography, and grammar
0-87779-606-8 MERRIAM WEBSTER PB.....$9.95

Merriam-Webster's Collegiate Dictionary: Tenth Edition
The standard dictionary used by editors and proofreaders
0-87779-710-2 MERRIAM WEBSTER $25.95

Webster's Compact Dictionary
0-87779-488-X MERRIAM WEBSTER..........$6.50

Webster's Tenth New Collegiate Dictionary
Webster's Tenth has become the standard for writers and editors, a clear and comprehensive arbiter of spelling and usage
0-87779-509-6 MERRIAM WEBSTER $18.95

Webster's Third New International Dictionary
0-87779-206-2 MERRIAM WEBSTER......$109.95

The Merriam-Webster Dictionary: New Edition
The paperback dictionary based on *Webster's Third New International Dictionary, Unabridged*
0-87779-911-3 MERRIAM WEBSTER PB $5.99

Oxford University Press

The Compact Edition of the Oxford English Dictionary: Supplement to the Oxford English Dictionary, Volume 3

Words that have come into common usage in the English-speaking world since 1884

0-19-861211-7 OXFORD $125.00

The Concise Oxford Dictionary: Ninth Edition

0-19-861320-2 OXFORD $29.95

The Concise Oxford Dictionary of Current English

0-19-861319-9 OXFORD $27.50

The Little Oxford Writer's Shelf

Boxed set includes *The Little Oxford Dictionary* and *The Little Oxford Thesaurus*

0-19-521076-X OXFORD PB $23.90

The New Shorter Oxford English Dictionary

With 500,000 definitions, 83,000 illustrative quotations, and countless etymological explanations, this two-volume, fullsize type OED is the most authoritative dictionary you can fit on your desk. "*The New Shorter Oxford English Dictionary*, in its immense reach and profound wealth, has no rival for utility and potential enlightenment" —*Harold Bloom*

0-19-861271-0 OXFORD $125.00

The Oxford Dictionary of Current English: New Edition

0-19-283127-5 OXFORD PB $7.95

The Oxford Encyclopedic English Dictionary: Second Edition

0-19-521158-8 OXFORD $35.00

The Oxford English Dictionary: The Compact Edition

An essential reference book in two volumes, boxed with a magnifying glass, and containing the complete text of the first edition multi-volume *Oxford English Dictionary* in smaller print

0-19-861186-2 OXFORD $350.00

The Oxford Modern English Dictionary

A handy one-volume reference with over 90,000 entries drawn from the database of the *Oxford English Dictionary*. Thorough definitions, with contemporary usage notes, word origins, and illustrative phrases and sentences

0-19-861267-2 OXFORD $19.95

Oxford Pocket English Dictionary

0-19-861256-7 OXFORD $15.95

American Heritage

American Heritage College Dictionary

A panel of 173 members, including writer Ann Tyler, makes this one of the more lively dictionaries available

0-395-66918-9 HOUGHTON MIFFLIN $24.95

The American Heritage Desk Dictionary

0-395-31256-6 HOUGHTON MIFFLIN $15.95

The American Heritage Dictionary: Second College Edition

0-395-32944-2 HOUGHTON MIFFLIN $17.95

American Heritage Dictionary of the English Language: Third Edition

Sixteen thousand new words and meanings bring this edition of the popular reference book up to date. Easy to use and finely illustrated, this vast volume also contains word etymologies and helpful notes on proper word usage

0-395-44895-6 HOUGHTON MIFFLIN..............$45.00

0-440-21861-6 LAUREL AVE. PB........................$5.99

The American Heritage Dictionary of the English Language, Third Edition: Print and CD-Rom Edition

The classical and elegant book and lively reference, illustrated and definitive, now available in a print and CD-ROM edition. The CD-ROM runs either on a CD-ROM player or downloads to disk, and can be configured to both the PC and Macintosh platforms

0-395-71146-0 HOUGHTON MIFFLIN $75.00

The American Heritage Dictionary of the English Language: User's Guide

0-395-20515-8 HOUGHTON MIFFLIN PB $3.32

Random **House**

The Random House Unabridged Dictionary: Second Edition

One of the most comprehensive dictionaries

0-679-42917-4 RANDOM HOUSE..................$100.00

Barbara Ann **Kipfer**, editor

Webster's 21st Century Large-Print Dictionary

0-385-31643-7 DELTA $19.95

Random House

Random House Unabridged Dictionary: Second Edition

One of the most comprehensive dictionaries currently available

0-679-45026-2 RANDOM HOUSE....................$50.00

0-679-44046-1 RANDOM HOUSE....................$79.00

Random House Webster's College Dictionary

Thumb-indexed

0-679-43886-6 RANDOM HOUSE $23.95

Random House Webster's School & Office Dictionary: Newly Revised and Updated

Based on the 1995 edition of Random House's *Webster's College Dictionary*

0-679-76158-6 RANDOM HOUSE PB $10.95

Specialized Dictionaries

Josefa Heifetz **Byrne**

Mrs. Byrne's Dictionary of Unusual, Obscure, and Preposterous Words

Thousands of the weirder words in English, from "ablewhackers" to "zoanthropy"

1-55972-233-9 CAROL.......................................$18.95

0-8065-0498-6 LYLE STUART PB......................$10.95

Bob **Cotton** & Richard **Oliver**

The Cyberspace Lexicon: An Illustrated Dictionary of Terms from Multimedia to Virtual Reality

New technologies emerge with pulsant quickness, and the infinitude of cyberspace becomes more chaotic daily. More than a dictionary, it is a meticulous, illustrated explanation of everything from interactive media to arcade games to virtual reality. "In addition to the 800 concise dictionary entries are illustrated features that range from computer animation, electronic books, and Nintendo to virtual sex. An essential guide"—*Library Journal*

See also **THE CYBERNETIC SOCIETY** under **THE COMPUTER REVOLUTION AND ARTIFICIAL INTELLIGENCE** in **SCIENCE**

See also **REFERENCE** under **THE COMPUTER REVOLUTION AND ARTIFICIAL INTELLIGENCE** in **SCIENCE**

0-714-83267-0 PHAIDON PB $29.99

Michael **Curl**

The Anagram Dictionary

0-7090-5864-0 ATRIUM PB................................$13.95

R. Terry **Ellmore**

NTC's Mass Media Dictionary

More than 20,000 authoritative definitions regarding the media from, "abaxial" to the "Zworykin Prize"

0-8442-3186-X N.T.C. PB..................................$24.95

Stephen **Glazier**

Random House's Word Menu

How to find the right word when you only know its meaning

0-679-40030-3 RANDOM HOUSE.......................$22.00

James Orchard **Halliwell**

Dictionary of Archaic and Provincial Words

Facsimile edition from 1850 contains references to more than 51,000 words

0-404-03055-6 AMS..$90.00

R.W. **Holder**

A Dictionary of Euphemisms: How Not to Say What You Mean

A guide to the art of understatement and evasion. "A very funny collection"—*Financial Times*

0-19-869275-7 OXFORD $25.00

0-19-280051-5 OXFORD PB..............................$10.00

Don M. **Randel**, editor

The New Harvard Dictionary of Music

"Drawing on the latest musical research and buttressed by a large group of advisers and readers, Professor Randel has provided concise, accurate, and literate entries pertaining to the entire field of music"— Philip Gossett, University of Chicago

See also **REFERENCE** under **WESTERN CLASSICAL MUSIC** in **PERFORMING ARTS AND MEDIA**

0-674-61525-5 BELKNAP $39.95

Adrian **Room**

NTC's Dictionary of Changes in Meanings: A Comprehensive Reference to the Major Changes in Meanings in English Words

Over 1,300 words explored in their historical nuances

0-8442-5135-6 N.T.C. PB $14.95

Richard **Weiner**, editor

Webster's New World Dictionary of Media and Communication

Definitions from all fields of the media compiled by a PR executive

0-13-969759-4 MACMILLAN $29.95

Computer Dictionaries

American Heritage

The American Heritage Dictionary of Computer Words: An A to Z Guide to Today's Computer

See also **REFERENCE** under **THE COMPUTER REVOLUTION AND ARTIFICIAL INTELLIGENCE** in **SCIENCE**

0-395-72834-7 HOUGHTON MIFFLIN PB $11.95

Douglas **Downing** & Michael A. **Covington**

Dictionary of Computer and Internet Terms: 5th Edition

The most up-to-date dictionary on this fast-changing world

0-8120-9811-0 BARRONS PB $9.95

Microsoft

Microsoft Press Computer Dictionary: Second Edition

More that 5,000 clearly written entries compiled by a team of computer and business professionals as well as academics

See also **REFERENCE** under **THE COMPUTER REVOLUTION AND ARTIFICIAL INTELLIGENCE** in **SCIENCE**

1-55615-597-2 MICROSOFT PB $19.95

Oxford University

Dictionary of Computing: Third Edition

For both the neophyte and the seasoned professional, this is the ultimate, user-friendly reference work on the burgeoning vocabulary of the computerati. Profusely illustrated

0-19-286131-X OXFORD PB $11.95

Eric S. **Raymond**, editor

The New Hacker's Dictionary: Third Edition

"...not only a useful guidebook to very much unofficial technical terms and street tech slang, but also a de facto ethnography of the early years of the hacker culture"—*Mondo 2000*

0-262-68092-0 MIT PB $16.50

Merriam-Webster's New Book of Word Histories

Over 1,500 words of curious origin

0-87779-603-3 MERRIAM WEBSTER PB $9.95

Etymological Dictionaries

John **Algeo**, editor

Fifty Years Among the New Words: A Dictionary of Neologisms

"Algeo's lucid introduction systematically explains the processes by which new words are formed...The entries proper [are] models of the lexicographer's art"—*Wilson Library Bulletin*

0-521-41377-X CAMBRIDGE $64.95

0521449711 CAMBRIDGE PB $24.95

E. Cobham **Brewer**

Brewer's Dictionary of Phrase and Fable

The classic reference for the origin and meaning of words and expressions

0-06-272022-8 HARPERCOLLINS $20.00

Robert K. **Barnhart**, editor

The Barnhart Concise Dictionary of Etymology: The Origins of American English Words

"A combination of readability with scholarship...exceptional quality"
—*American Library Association*

0-06-270084-7 HARPERCOLLINS $50.00

Ivor H. **Evans**, editor

Brewer's Dictionary of Phrase and Fable

Terms and phrases from mythology, literature, history, folk tales, customs, philosophy, science, and magic. "It retains the serendipitous charm which has kept the book going for a century..."—*TLS* [London]

0-06-270133-9 HARPERCOLLINS $45.00

T.F. **Hoad**, editor

The Concise Oxford Dictionary of English Etymology

Seventeen thousand entries; a concise guide to word origins

0-19-283098-8 OXFORD PB $15.95

William **Morris** & Mary **Morris**

Morris Dictionary of Word and Phrase Origins

FOREWORD BY ISAAC ASIMOV

0-06-015862-X HARPERCOLLINS $35.00

John **Kennedy**, editor

Word Stems: A Dictionary

This classic dictionary provides the sources for thousands of English words from Latin, Greek, and ten other languages. An invaluable resource for students, writers, puzzlers, and anyone else interested in deepening their understanding of the English language

1-56947-051-0 SOHO PB $12.00

Jeremy **Marshall** &
Mrs. Fred **McDonald**, editors

Questions of English

What does the "corned" mean in corned beef? How many words are there in English? A fascinating and useful guide to the finer points of English. Illustrated in cartoon format makes a potentially dull subject lively

See also **USAGE AND STYLE MANUALS** under **WRITING GUIDES**

0-19-869292-7 OXFORD PB $7.95

Oxford University

Oxford Dictionary of English Etymology

0-19-861112-9 OXFORD $65.00

Idiomatic Phrases and Expressions

Harry **Collis**

101 American English Idioms: Understanding and Speaking English Like an American

Cleverly illustrated, this whimsical collection of American idiomatic speech is useful to all levels of English knowledge

0-8442-5446-0 NATIONAL TEXTBOOK CO PB $6.95

Eugene **Ehrlich**, editor

The Harper Dictionary of Foreign Terms: Third Edition

More than 15,000 words and phrases from over 50 languages and culled from many disciplines

0-06-273162-9 HARPERCOLLINS PB $15.00

Daphne M. **Gulland** & David G. **Hinds-Howell**

The Penguin Dictionary of English Idioms

Explains meanings and origins and gives examples of our more colorful idioms; particularly useful for the foreign student

0-14-051135-0 VIKING PB $12.50

E.M. **Kirkpatrick** & C.M. **Schwartz**, editors

The Wordsworth Dictionary of Idioms

Compact guide to British English idiomatic phrases

1-85326-309-5 JOHNSON PB $17.00

Adam **Makkai** & others, editors

Handbook of Commonly Used American Idioms

Plastic-covered, pocket-size listing of 2,500 idioms. Invaluable for ESL students

0-8120-9239-2 BARRONS PB $7.95

James **Rogers**
The Dictionary of Cliches
"Not to beat around the bush, or hedge the bet, this is a must-read for every Tom, Dick, and Harry under the sun!"—*People*
See also SLANG DICTIONARIES
0-517-06020-5 OUTLET $8.99
0-345-33814-6 BALLANTINE PB $5.99

Jesse **Sheidlower**, editor
The F-Word
"Want the F-word? Try [a book full] of it"—*Entertainment Weekly*. The history and current usage of the most censored word in English
See also SLANG DICTIONARIES
0-679-76427-5 RANDOM HOUSE PB..................$12.95

Richard A. **Spears**, editor
Essential American Idioms
More than 1,500 expressions specially selected for the non–native speaker
0-8442-5153-4 NATIONAL TEXTBOOK CO PB....$9.95

Richard A. **Spears** & others
NTC's Dictionary of Everyday American English Expressions
Divided between "Topic and Situation" and "Word and Concept," this practical guide to more than 7,000 expressions is indispensable to native and nonnative English speakers
0-8442-5779-6 NATIONAL TEXTBOOK PB.........$12.95

Pictorial Dictionaries

Dorling **Kindersley**, editor
Ultimate Visual Dictionary
Over 30,000 terms, 5,000 color photos, 1,000 illustrations with detailed explanations. "The book is a feast for the eyes"—*Library Journal*
1-56458-648-0 DORLING KINDERSLEY $39.95

G.F. **Lamb**, editor
Shakespeare Quotations
Over 2,100 quotes in 197 topic categories, as well as quotes and a bio about the Bard and a dictionary of his characters
0-7523-5004-8 LAROUSSE PB $10.95

Macmillan
The Macmillan Visual Desk Reference
A unique reference, facts in a single volume presented through diagrams, charts, illustrations, maps, timelines, and other graphics
0-02-531310-X MACMILLAN $29.95

The Macmillan Visual Dictionary
Divided into 28 chapters from the human body to the house
0-02-578115-4 MACMILLAN $60.00
0-02-860810-0 MACMILLAN PB $24.95

Oxford University
Oxford American Dictionary
0-380-51052-9 AVON PB...................................$12.50

Oxford American Dictionary: Heald Colleges Edition
0-380-60772-7 AVON PB $4.99

The Oxford Color Dictionary
Based on *The Little Oxford Dictionary*, with easy-to-read color highlights
0-19-860020-8 OXFORD PB $7.95

The Oxford-Duden Pictorial English Dictionary: New Edition
0-19-861311-3 OXFORD PB...............................$18.95

Rhyming Dictionaries and Poetic Handbooks

Babette **Deutsch**
The Poetry Handbook: A Dictionary of Terms
0-06-463548-1 BARNES & NOBLE PB $12.00

Rosalind **Fergusson**, editor
The Penguin Rhyming Dictionary
Organized by spelling and on phonic principles
0-14-051136-9 VIKING PB $13.95

Burges **Johnson**
New Rhyming Dictionary Poet's Handbook
0-06-272014-7 HARPERPERENNIAL PB............$15.00

Lewis **Turco**
The New Book of Forms: A Handbook of Poetics
0-87451-381-2 NEW ENGLAND PB $17.95

Clement **Wood**, editor
The Complete Rhyming Dictionary: Revised Edition
In addition to 10,000 new entries, this classic incorporates *The Poet's Craft Book*, a guide to the technique and forms of poetry
0-385-41350-5 DOUBLEDAY...............................$25.00
0-440-21205-7 DELL PB $6.99

Spelling Dictionaries

Merriam-Webster
Webster's Instant Word Guide
A dictionary without definitions
0-87779-273-9 MERRIAM WEBSTER...................$6.50

New World Dictionary
Misspeller's Dictionary
0-671-46864-2 MACMILLAN PB $5.00

Harry **Shaw**
Spell It Right
0-06-097048-0 HARPERCOLLINS PB..................$5.95

Slang Dictionaries

Robert **Chapman**
New Dictionary of American Slang
0-06-181157-2 HARPERCOLLINS $35.00

John **Ayto** & John **Simpron**
Oxford Dictionary of Modern Slang
From the co-editor of *The Oxford English Dictionary*, a collection of 5,000 terms with historical reference and definition, from "buzz off," which appeared in 1914, to "wilding"
0-19-280007-8 OXFORD PB $9.95

Robert **Chapman**, editor
Thesaurus of American Slang
Over 17,000 alphabetically arranged slang words with usage examples and synonyms
0-06-272010-4 HARPERCOLLINS PB $14.00

Jonathon **Green**, editor
The Slang Thesaurus
Rhyming, paraphrases for American and Australian slang
0-14-051205-5 PENGUIN PB $13.95

J.E. **Lighter**, editor
Random House Historical Dictionary of American Slang Vol I
"Will do for nonstandard English what the *Oxford English Dictionary* did for the whole language"—William Safire
0-394-54427-7 RANDOM HOUSE $55.00
9-995-40468-0RANDOM HOUSE PB..................$25.00

Esther **Lewin** & Albert E. **Lewin**, editors
The Thesaurus of Slang
0-8160-1742-5 FACTS ON FILE $50.00

Oxford University
The Oxford Dictionary of Current Idiomatic English
0-19-431150-3 OXFORD $21.95

Eric **Partridge**, editor
A Dictionary of Slang and Unconventional English
0-02-594980-2 MACMILLAN $75.00

James **Rogers**
The Dictionary of Cliches
See also IDIOMATIC PHRASES AND EXPRESSIONS
0-517-06020-5 OUTLET $8.99
0-345-33814-6 BALLANTINE PB $5.99

Jesse **Sheidlower**, editor
The F-Word
See also IDIOMATIC PHRASES AND EXPRESSIONS
0-679-76427-5 RANDOM HOUSE PB.................$12.95

Richard A. **Spears**, editor
Forbidden American English: A Serious Compilation of Taboo American English
This unique dictionary of 1,400 words and phrases of offensive and inflammatory vocabulary, with usage examples
0-8442-5152-6 PASSPORT PB $9.95

Karen **Watts**, editor
21st Century Dictionary of Slang
Five thousand contemporary slang terms covering 40 subject areas
0-440-21551-X DELL PB $5.99

NTC's American Idioms Dictionary: Second Edition
Here are 12,000 examples of usage for over 8,500 idiomatic phrases
0-8442-0826-4 NATIONAL TEXTBOOK CO PB...$12.95

NTC's Dictionary of American Slang and Colloquial Expressions
More than 10,000 definitions of terms and expressions likely to be heard in movies, TV, on the street, and on college campuses
0-8442-0828-0 PASSPORT PB $12.95

Tony **Thorne**, editor
The Dictionary of Contemporary Slang
A potpourri of over 5,000 of the raciest and most raffish expressions from around the English-speaking world: the puns, metaphors, obscenities, and euphemisms that have enriched our vocabulary in the past half-century
0-679-73706-5 PANTHEON PB $16.00

Thesauruses

American Heritage
Roget's II: The New Thesaurus: Third Edition
The new edition of the classic thesaurus, based on the lexicographical foundation of the *American Heritage Dictionary*
0-395-68722-5 HOUGHTON MIFFLIN..............$16.95

Roget's International Thesaurus
A new edition of the indispensable reference book for writers and word fanciers. Contains slang and informal speech, foreign words and phrases, scientific terms, and labels indicating levels of usage and fields of use
0-06-270014-6 HARPERCOLLINS....................$19.95
0-06-272037-6 HARPERCOLLINS PB.................$13.50

S.I. **Hayakawa**, editor
Choose the Right Word: A Modern Guide to Synonyms
0-06-272028-7 HARPERCOLLINS PB $16.00

Charles **Laird**, editor
Webster's New World Thesaurus: New Revised Edition
0-13-948126-5 MACMILLAN PB......................$12.95

William D. **Lutz**, editor
The Cambridge Thesaurus of American English
Lutz *(Doublespeak)* has compiled an up-to-date collection of over 200,000 synonyms and antonyms, with special attention given to idiomatic expressions and slang
0-521-41427-X CAMBRIDGE..............................$17.95

Random House
The Random House Thesaurus: College Edition
0-679-41780-X RANDOM HOUSE.......................$17.00

J.I. **Rodale**, editor
The Synonym Finder
Updated and revised, containing over 1,000,000 synonyms
0-446-37029-0 WARNER PB..............................$13.99

Webster
Webster's New World Thesaurus
0-671-60437-6 MACMILLAN..............................$17.95

Quotations and Proverbs

Quotations

Rosie **Gonzalez**
The Fire in Our Souls: Quotations of Wisdom and Inspiration by Latino-Americans
FOREWORD BY EDWARD JAMES OLMOS
0-452-27684-5 PLUME PB $10.95

Robert **Andrews**, editor
The Columbia Dictionary of Quotations
From the profound to the provocative, and then to the humorous, this essential reference guide contains more than 18,000 quotations—1,000 never before included in such a book—and 1,500 subjects. Among those mentioned are Shakespeare, Twain, Malcolm X, Tallulah Bankhead, Henry Kissinger, Andrea Dworkin, Desmond Tutu
See also PROVERBS
0-231-07194-9 COLUMBIA $34.95

Famous Lines: A Columbia Dictionary of Familiar Quotations
The most up-to-date collection
0-231-10218-6 COLUMBIA $29.95

Bartlett
Bartlett's Familiar Quotations
Now in its 16th edition
0-316-08277-5 LITTLE, BROWN..........................$45.00

M.J. **Cohen** & J.M. **Cohen**, editors
The New Penguin Dictionary of Quotations
Newly revised to include more 20th-century contributions
0-14-051244-6 PENGUIN PB $14.95

Elza **Dinwiddie-Boyd**, editor
In Our Own Words: A Treasury of Quotations from the African-American Community
Inspirational and humorous offerings from black history and culture
0-380-77910-2 AVON PB $12.00

H.L. **Mencken**, editor
New Dictionary of Quotations on Historical Principles from Ancient and Modern Sources
0-394-40079-8 RANDOM HOUSE.......................$75.00

Susan **Ginsberg**, editor
Family Wisdom: The 2,000 Most Important Things Ever Said About Parenting, Children, and Family Life
Quotations on all aspects and from all walks of life, ancient and modern, on the family
See also BEING A PARENT under PARENTING in LIFESTYLES AND PRACTICAL ADVICE
0-231-10376-X COLUMBIA................................$19.95

Brian **MacArthur**, editor
The Penguin Book of Twentieth-Century Speeches
0-14-023234-6 PENGUIN PB $13.95

This is pre-eminently the time to speak the truth, the whole truth, frankly and boldly. Nor need we shrink from honestly facing conditions in our country today. This great nation will endure as it has endured, will revive and will prosper. So first of all let me assert my firm belief that the only thing we have to fear is fear itself—nameless, unreasoning, unjustified terror which paralyzes needed efforts to convert retreat into advance—Franklin D. Roosevelt, first inaugural
THE PENGUIN BOOK OF TWENTIETH-CENTURY SPEECHES

Oxford University
The Concise Oxford Dictionary of Quotations
The best from the large collection (see below)
0-19-281324-2 OXFORD PB $9.95

The Oxford Dictionary of Quotations
Twenty thousand quotations from more than 3,000 well-known sources—Aristotle to Monty Python. "What makes this book unusual is its tilt toward British and foreign literature, as well as its insightful feminist quotations"—*NY Times*
0-19-866185-1 OXFORD $39.95

Elaine **Partnow**, editor
The New Quotable Woman: The Definitive Treasury of Notable Words by Women from Eve to the Present
Over 15,000 quotes from more than 2,500 women on every subject imaginable
See also REFERENCE under WOMEN'S STUDIES in SOCIAL STUDIES
0-452-01099-3 PLUME PB $15.00

Philanthropic Service for Institutions
Words of Wisdom for Writers, Speakers, & Leaders
Two thousand seven hundred sayings on a virtuous life of service, love, and generosity
0-9643585-0-6 PHILANTHROPIC SERVICE FOR INSTITUTIONS $14.95

Dorothy Winbush **Riley**, editor
My Soul Looks Back, 'Less I Forget
"A groundbreaking collection, inspiring, powerful, and important"—*The Chicago Defender*
0-06-272057-0 HARPERCOLLINS PB $14.00

Elyse **Sommer** & Dorrie **Weiss**, editors

Metaphors Dictionary

Collection of 6,500 colorful comparative phrases from the ancients to present day in 500 themes. "The most comprehensive work of its kind" —*Booklist*

0-7876-0619-7 VISIBLE INK PB....................$29.95

Jon **Winokur**, editor

A Curmudgeon's Garden of Love

0-452-26551-7 PLUME PB....................$8.00

The Portable Curmudgeon

A small book of irreverent quotations, anecdotes, and interviews from an illustrious list of grouches

0-453-00565-9 NEW AMERICAN LIBRARY........$17.00

The Return of the Portable Curmudgeon

0-452-27030-8 PLUME PB....................$10.95

Proverbs

Robert **Andrews**, editor

The Columbia Dictionary of Quotations

See also **QUOTATIONS**

0-231-07194-9 COLUMBIA....................$34.95

The Concise Columbia Dictionary of Quotations

"Browsable...readable...provocative...sassier and more up-to-date than most"—*Washington Post*

0-231-06990-1 COLUMBIA....................$19.95

Anne **Bertram**, editor

NTC's Dictionary of Proverbs and Clichés

Nine hundred old and new proverbs with each expression defined and usage examples given

0-8442-5159-3 N.T.C....................$16.95

0-8442-5158-5 N.T.C. PB....................$12.95

Rosalind **Fergusson**, editor

The Penguin Dictionary of Proverbs

0-14-051118-0 PENGUIN PB....................$13.95

Linda **Flavell** & Roger **Flavell**

Dictionary of Proverbs and Their Origins

Origins and histories for over 400 proverbs, some dating over 2,000 years

1-85626-141-7 TRAFALGAR SQUARE PB...........$12.95

Leonard Roy **Frank**, editor

Influencing Minds: A Reader in Quotations

A unique collection of quotes from writers and philosophers on the subject of the mind

0-922915-25-3 FERAL HOUSE PB....................$12.95

Carole **McKenzie**, editor

Quotable Sex

"Women should be obscene and not heard"—John Lennon. A must-have for all collections

0-312-95405-0 ST. MARTIN'S PB....................$4.99

Colin **Jarman**, editor

The Guinness Book of Poisonous Quotes

"The fastest way to a man's heart is through his chest"—Roseanne. One of many notable acid wits included here

0-8092-3681-8 CONTEMPORARY....................$12.95

Oxford University

The Concise Oxford Dictionary of Proverbs

0-19-866177-0 OXFORD....................$35.00

0-19-281880-5 OXFORD PB....................$8.95

The Oxford Dictionary of English Proverbs

0-19-869118-1 OXFORD....................$55.00

Ned **Sherrin**, editor

The Oxford Dictionary of Humorous Quotations

Thematically organized from Actors and Acting to Sex

0-19-214244-5 OXFORD....................$39.95

Aphorisms, Toasts and Jokes

Aphorisms

Oxford University

The Oxford Book of Aphorisms

"...fascinating...[the reader] will experience the delight of having his worst fears for the human race confirmed with brevity and style"—Quentin Crisp

0-19-214111-2 OXFORD....................$29.95

0-19-282015-X OXFORD PB....................$12.95

Toasts and Jokes

Paul **Dickson**, editor

Toasts: Over 1,500 of the Best Toasts, Sentiments, Blessings, and Graces

Never be at a loss for words

0-517-58412-3 CROWN....................$19.00

Writing Guides

Edward **Bailey**

Plain English at Work: A Guide to Business Writing and Speaking

There is nothing in business as important as communication, and nothing in communication as important as writing skills. This well-arranged guide presents the essentials of style, organization, and layout for business presentations, memos, and speeches, all centered around the use of clear and concise English

0-19-510449-8 OXFORD....................$19.95

Dian Dincin **Buchman** & Seli **Groves**

Writer's Digest Guide to Manuscript Formats

A simple and clear guide for all types of manuscript presentation

See also **PUBLISHING** under **CAREERS**

0-89879-293-2 WRITER'S DIGEST....................$19.99

Robin A. **Cormier**

Error-Free Writing: A Lifetime Guide to Flawless Business Writing

A step-by-step approach for writing and producing reports, brochures, newsletters, and proposals

0-13-303587-5 PRENTICE HALL....................$29.95

0-13-303595-6 PRENTICE HALL PB....................$14.95

Elizabeth **Preston**

Preparing Your Manuscript

Punctuation, grammar, proofreading, and other important details

0-87116-144-3 WRITER PB....................$10.00

William **Zinsser**

On Writing Well: An Informal Guide to Writing Nonfiction

0-06-272027-9 HARPERCOLLINS PB....................$12.00

Usage and Style Manuals

Walter **Achtert** & Joseph **Gibaldi**

MLA Style Manual

The official style book of the Modern Language Association

0-87352-136-6 MLA....................$22.00

John **Bremner**

Words on Words: A Dictionary for Writers and Others Who Care About Words

0-231-04493-3 COLUMBIA PB....................$18.00

Frederick **Crews**

The Random House Handbook

0-07-013636-X MCGRAW HILL....................$36.80

H.W. **Fowler**

A Dictionary of Modern English Usage: Second Edition

0-19-281389-7 OXFORD PB....................$11.95

Constance **Hale**

Wired Style: Principles of English Usage in the Digital Age

1-88886-901-1 HRDWR $17.95

Joseph **Gibaldi**

MLA Handbook for Writers of Research Papers: Fourth Edition

The only guide for most college students

0-87352-565-5 MLA PB $13.50

Karen Elizabeth **Gordon**

The Deluxe Transitive Vampire: The Ultimate Handbook of Grammar for the Innocent, the Eager, and the Doomed

An *illustrated* grammar book remarkable for its conciseness and humor. "A book to sink your fangs into"—*William Safire*

0-679-41860-1 PANTHEON $22.00

Jeremy **Marshall** & Mrs. Fred **McDonald**, editors

Questions of English

See also **ETYMOLOGICAL DICTIONARIES** under **SPECIALIZED DICTIONARIES**

0-19-869292-7 OXFORD PB $7.95

David **Olsen**

The Words You Should Know: 1,200 Essential Words Every Educated Person Should Be Able to Use and Define

Concise definitions and sentence examples of confusing but common words such as "affect" and "effect"

1-55850-018-9 ADAMS PB $6.95

Oxford University Press

The Oxford Dictionary of English Usage

0-19-280024-8 OXFORD PB $8.95

The Oxford Dictionary of English Grammar

0-190-86131-148 OXFORD PB $11.95

Harry **Shaw**

Errors in English and Ways to Correct Them: The Practical Approach to Correct Word Usage, Sentence Structure, Spelling, Punctuation, and Grammar

Specifically designed to improve skills by using exercises, methods of study, and clear examples. Points out the most common errors "everyone makes" and encourages readers to pinpoint their own consistent errors

0-06-461044-6 HARPERCOLLINS PB $11.00

Peggy **Smith**

Letter Perfect: A Guide to Practical Proofreading

An easy-to-learn system that uses 12 basic marks and also covers the fundamentals of grammar, punctuation, typography, and editorial style

0-935012-17-6 EDITORIAL EXPERTS PB $24.95

Mary **Stoughton**

Substance & Style: Instruction & Practice in Copyediting

A self-teaching tool for copyeditors offers a practical course in grammar, punctuation, and clear writing

0-935012-11-7 EDITORIAL EXPERTS PB $35.00

Andrea **Sutcliffe**, editor

The New York Public Library Writer's Guide to Style and Usage

One-volume resource covers split infinitives to book production. "A sensible and sensitive authority from real-world editors!" —Arthur Plotnick, *The Elements of Editing*

0-06-270064-2 HARPERCOLLINS $37.50

William **Strunk**, Jr. & E. B. **White**

The Elements of Style

The classic manual of style

0-02-418200-1 PRENTICE HALL PB $7.95

University of Chicago

The Chicago Manual of Style: 14th Edition

The standard. For over 80 years, this reference has been used by American authors, editors, and proofreaders for its chapters on preparing and editing copy for publication

See also **PUBLISHING** under **CAREERS**

0-226-10389-7 CHICAGO $40.00

Kenneth G. **Wilson**

The Columbia Guide to Standard American English

Solves the knottiest grammatical problems clearly. No one should be without it. "An extraordinarily valuable tool"—Judy Woodruff

0-231-06988-X COLUMBIA $29.95
0-231-06989-8 COLUMBIA PB $16.95

William **Zinsser**

Writing to Learn: How to Write and Think Clearly About Any Subject At All

0-06-272040-6 HARPERCOLLINS PB $11.00

Grammar and Punctuation Guides

Karen **Gordon**

The Well-Tempered Sentence: A Punctuation Handbook for the Innocent, the Eager, and Doomed

0-395-62883-0 TICKNOR & FIELDS $14.95

Philip **Gucker**

Essential English Grammar

0-486-21649-7 DOVER PB $4.95

Margaret **Schertzer**

The Elements of Grammar

0-02-015440-2 COLLIER PB $7.00

Harry **Shaw**

Punctuate It Right!

0-06-461045-4 HARPERCOLLINS PB $11.00

Research Guides

Jacques **Barzun** & Henry **Graff**

The Modern Researcher

How to research essays, articles, and books. Covers everything from fact finding and unbiased writing to the art of quoting and the rules of footnotes

0-395-64494-1 HOUGHTON MIFFLIN $24.95

Maureen **Croteau** & Wayne **Worcester**

The Essential Researcher: A Complete, Up-to-Date, One-Volume Sourcebook for Journalists, Writers, Students and Everyone Who Needs Facts Fast

Government, history, sports, disasters, religion, popular culture, census figures, and other topics presented clearly

0-06-273040-1 HARPERPERENNIAL PB $20.00

Joseph **Gibaldi** & Walter **Achtert**

The MLA Handbook for Writers of Research Papers

From the mandarins of English

0-87352-379-2 MLA PB $10.25

Student Writing Guides

John C. **Hodges**, Winfred **Bryan**, & Suzanne **Strobeck**

Harbrace College Handbook

With its easy reference, clear statement of grammatical rules and examples of sentence structure, Harbrace College Handbook remains an excellent writing resource

0-155-00119-1 HARCC $30.26

Sharon **Sorenson**

Webster's New World Student Writing Handbook

0-13-951955-6 MACMILLAN PB $16.00

University of Chicago

Students' Guide for Writing College Papers

0-226-81623-0 CHICAGO PB $8.95

About Language

Mortimer **Adler**

Some Questions About Language

The humanist philosopher connects language to the way we live

0-8126-9178-4 OPEN COURT PB $14.95

R.E. **Asher** & J.M. **Simpson**, editors

Encyclopedia of Language and Linguistics

A compilation of over 2,000 articles from 1,000 contributors in more than 50 countries makes this 10-volume set the most exhaustive source ever compiled. "Detailed coverage of virtually every language group over the past 3,000

years...topics as diverse as bird song, computer languages...[t]his work is one of the best...in reference publishing"—*Library Journal*
0-08-035943-4 ELSEVIER $2,975.00

Charles **Funk**
Horsefeathers and Others Curious Words
0-06-091352-5 HARPERCOLLINS PB $8.00

Charles **Barber**
The English Language
From Indo-European roots to the present day, Barber covers the history of the English language as well as major theoretical and technical concepts of historical linguistics. Chapters on the nature of language and its evolution are followed by a chronological survey, while short passages from different periods are given as examples
0-521-41620-5 CAMBRIDGE $49.95
0-521-42622-7 CAMBRIDGE PB $17.95

Frederick **Bodmer**
The Loom of Language
0-393-30034-X NORTON PB $16.95

Roger **Brown**
Words and Things
See also **LANGUAGE THEORY** under **LINGUISTICS** in **SOCIAL STUDIES**
0-02-904810-9 FREE PRESS PB $13.95

Stuart **Chase**
The Tyranny of Words
How professions and disciplines impose their will through specialized vocabularies
0-15-692394-7 HARCOURT BRACE PB $7.95

Bernard **Comrie** & others
Atlas of Languages: The Origin and Development of Languages
0-8160-3388-9 FACTS ON FILE $35.00

David **Feldman**
Who Put the Butter in Butterfly? Other Fearless Investigations into Our Illogical Language
0-06-091661-3 HARPERCOLLINS PB $11.00

Charles **Funk**
Hog on Ice & Other Curious Expressions
0-06-091259-6 HARPERCOLLINS PB $10.00

Thereby Hangs a Tale: Stories of Curious Word Origins
0-06-272049-X HARPERCOLLINS PB $10.00

Geoffrey **Hughes**
Words in Time: A Social History of the English Vocabulary
The fascinating origin of words: "blurb" comes from "Miss Linda Blurb," who appeared on an American book cover around 1900; and more
See also **CULTURAL AND SOCIAL LIFE** under **TOPICS IN BRITISH HISTORY** under **GREAT BRITAIN AND IRELAND** in **WORLD HISTORY AND CURRENT AFFAIRS**
0-631-17321-8 BLACKWELL PB $20.95

Winfred P. **Lehmann**
Language: An Introduction
See also **LANGUAGE THEORY** under **LINGUISTICS** in **SOCIAL STUDIES**
0-07-554251-X RANDOM HOUSE PB $34.15

James **Lipton**
An Exaltation of Larks
Definitions and origins of collective nouns, some familiar (a pride of lions) and some less so (a murder of crows)
0-14-017096-0 PENGUIN PB $12.50

Robert **McCrum**
The Story of English
A companion volume to the public television series. "The study of the language will never be the same again after the publication of this book. It travels at the speed of a bullet train to every corner of the globe where English is spoken. It also authentically describes the mysterious power of older dazzling forms of the language"—Robert Burchfield, Editor in Chief, *The Oxford Dictionaries*
See also **LANGUAGE AND SOCIETY** under **LINGUISTICS** in **SOCIAL STUDIES**
0-14-015405-1 PENGUIN PB $22.95

Lawrence **McNamee** & Kent **Biffle**
A Few Words: A Cornucopia of Questions and Answers Concerning Language
0-87833-615-X TAYLOR PB $8.95

Leonard **Michaels** & Christopher **Ricks**
The State of the Language
A collection of essays, with contributions from M.F.K. Fisher, Anthony Burgess, Angela Carter, and Ishmael Reed, among others
See also **LITERARY ESSAYISTS** under **LITERARY CRITICISM** in **LITERATURE OF EUROPE, AFRICA, AND ASIA**
0-520-05906-9 CALIFORNIA $40.00

Fred **West**
The Way of Language: An Introduction
0-15-595130-0 HARCOURT BRACE PB $18.62

Foreign-Language Dictionaries

International Book Centre
Arabic-English Modern Dictionary
0-86685-287-5 INTERNATIONAL BOOK CENTRE$45.00

Oxford University
Oxford English-Arabic Dictionary of Current Usage
0-19-864312-8 OXFORD $85.00

A.H. **Yacobian**
English-Armenian, Armenian-English Dictionary
0-87559-004-7 P SHALOM $37.50

Beijing Foreign Language Institute
Pinyin Chinese-English Dictionary
0-471-86796-9 WILEY PB $59.95

Shi-Chiu **Liang**, editor
New Practical Chinese-English Dictionary
0-917056-53-1 CHANG & TSUI $42.50
0-917056-54-X CHANG & TSUI PB $21.95

Nina **Trnka**
Czech-English, English-Czech Concise Dictionary
0-87052-981-1 HIPPOCRENE PB $11.95

Collins-Robert
Collins-Robert French Dictionary
The $50.00 version is unabridged
0-06-275521-8 HARPERCOLLINS $22.00
0-06-275519-6 HARPERCOLLINS $50.00

Cassell
Cassell's French Dictionary: French-English, English-French
0-02-522620-7 MACMILLAN $24.95
0-02-522670-3 MACMILLAN PB $12.95

J.E. **Mansion**, editor
Harrap's Standard French-English Dictionary Volume 1
0-13-383068-3 MACMILLAN $55.00

Cassell
Cassell's German Dictionary: German-English, English-German
0-02-522930-3 MACMILLAN $27.00
0-02-522650-9 MACMILLAN PB $13.95

Langenscheidt
Langenscheidt German Standard Dictionary
0-88729-043-4 LANGENSCHEIDT $17.95

Reuven **Sivan** & others, editors
The New Bantam-Megiddo Hebrew Dictionary
0-553-26387-0 BDD PB $6.99

Avraham **Zilkha**
Modern Hebrew-English Dictionary
0-300-04647-2 YALE $40.00
0-300-04648-0 YALE PB $18.00

Asia Society
A Practical Hindi-English Dictionary
0-88386-380-4 SOUTH ASIA $16.00

Cambridge University
Chambers English-Hindi Dictionary
0-8364-1474-8 SOUTH ASIA $18.50

The Concise Cambridge Italian Dictionary
0-14-051064-8 VIKING PB $14.95

Cassell
Cassell's Italian Dictionary: Italian-English, English-Italian
0-02-522540-5 MACMILLAN $24.95

Sansoni-Harrap
Sansoni-Harrap Standard Italian and English Dictionary
Volume 1: Italian-English, A-L
0-13-382540-X MACMILLAN $59.95
Volume 2: Italian-English, M-Z
0-13-382557-4 MACMILLAN $59.95
Volume 3: English-Italian, A-L
0-13-382565-5 MACMILLAN $59.95
Volume 4: English-Italian, M-Z
0-13-382573-6 MACMILLAN PB $59.95

Kodansha
Kodansha English-Japanese Dictionary
0-87011-672-X KODANSHA PB $45.95

Kodansha Japanese-English Dictionary
0-87011-671-1 KODANSHA PB $45.95

Andrew **Nelson**
Modern Reader's Japanese-English Character Dictionary
0-8048-0408-7 TUTTLE $69.95

Charles **Tuttle**
Concise English-Korean Dictionary Romanized
0-8048-0118-5 TUTTLE PB $8.95

Oxford University
Oxford Latin Dictionary
0-19-864224-5 OXFORD $225.00

E.D. **Gabrielsen**
Norwegian-English, English-Norwegian Pocket Dictionary
0-7818-0199-0 HIPPOCRENE PB $14.95

Abbas **Aryanpur-Kashani** & others
The Combined New Persian-English and English-Persian Dictionary
0-939214-28-8 MAZDA $49.95

Routledge, Chapman & Hall
A Comprehensive Persian-English Dictionary: Including the Arabic Words and Phrases to Be Met with in Persian Literature
0-7100-2152-6 ROUTLEDGE $151.50

Iwo C. **Pogonowski**
Polish-English, English-Polish Dictionary
0-7818-0183-4 HIPPOCRENE PB $16.95

Collins
Collins Pocket Portuguese-English Dictionary
0-87052-980-3 HIPPOCRENE PB $19.95

Stanford University
Portuguese-English Dictionary
0-8047-0480-5 STANFORD $49.50

M.A. **O'Brien**, editor
New Russian-English and English-Russian Dictionary
0-486-20208-9 DOVER PB $9.95

Oxford University
The Oxford English-Russian Dictionary
0-19-864117-6 OXFORD PB $89.00

The Oxford Russian-English Dictionary
0-19-864193-1 OXFORD PB $29.95

Practical Sanskrit Dictionary: With Transliteration, Accentuation, and Etymological Analysis Throughout
0-19-864303-9 OXFORD $85.00

South Asia
Sanskrit-English Dictionary
81-208-0069-9 SOUTH ASIA $58.00

Branislav **Grujic**
Serbo-Croatian/English, English/Serbo-Croatian Dictionary
0-87557-074-7 SAPHROGRAPH $42.50

American Heritage
The American Heritage Spanish Dictionary
0-395-32429-7 HOUGHTON MIFFLIN $22.95

Cassell
Cassell's Spanish Dictionary: Spanish-English, English-Spanish
0-02-522910-9 MACMILLAN $22.95
0-02-522660-6 MACMILLAN PB $13.00

Simon & Schuster
Simon & Schuster International Dictionary: English-Spanish, Spanish-English
0-671-21267-2 MACMILLAN $55.00

University of Chicago
The University of Chicago Spanish Dictionary
0-226-10400-1 CHICAGO $23.95
0-226-10402-8 CHICAGO PB $8.95

Oxford University
Standard Swahili-English Dictionary
0-19-864403-5 OXFORD $59.00

Prisma
Prisma's Modern Swedish-English and English-Swedish Dictionary
0-8166-1734-1 MINNESOTA $69.95

Prisma's English-Swedish Dictionary
0-8166-1733-3 MINNESOTA PB $19.95

Prisma's Swedish-English Dictionary
0-8166-1732-5 MINNESOTA PB $19.95

Uriel **Weinreich**, editor
Modern English-Yiddish, Yiddish-English Dictionary
0-8052-0575-6 SCHOCKEN PB $30.00

Other

Robert **Christgau**
Christgau's Record Guide: Rock Albums of the '80s
Christgau's compressed, highly informed style is fully in evidence in these 2,800 capsule reviews
See also **REFERENCE** under **ROCK** in **PERFORMING ARTS AND MEDIA**
0-306-80582-0 DA CAPO PB $17.95

Rock Albums of the '70s: A Critical Guide
"[Christgau] can say in 50 words what others may need 500 to 5,000 words to say... You'll not find a reviewer who so passionately suffers to comprehend the essence of even the most superfluous recordings"—*Newsday*
See also **REFERENCE** under **ROCK** in **PERFORMING ARTS AND MEDIA**
0-306-80409-3 DA CAPO PB $15.95

Consumer Reports
The Complete Drug Reference 1996 Edition
Americans spend $20 billion annually on drugs, yet take 50 percent of these drugs incorrectly. "What a good drug reference should be: highly readable, with complete and clear sections describing potential side effects and precautions to take while using a medicine"
—*US News & World Report*
See also **DRUG GUIDES** under **HEALTH** in **LIFESTYLES AND PRACTICAL ADVICE**
0-89043-849-8 CONSUMER REPORTS $39.95

Janice **Jorgensen**, editor
Encyclopedia of Consumer Brands
This unique three-volume set highlights 600 of America's most popular and influential brands that have been around since 1950. Each entry gives a history, sales and market share, competition, ownership, and more
1-55862-335-3 ST. JAMES $200.00

Amy **Dacyczyn**

The Tightwad Gazette: Promoting Thrift as a Viable Alternative Lifestyle

How to recycle everything from coat hangers to dryer lint, and many more money-saving tips that make sound economic and ecological sense, from the founder of the hugely popular newsletter *Tightwad Gazette*

0-679-74388-X RANDOM HOUSE PB..................$11.99

Fortune & Hoover's Handbooks

Fortune Guide to the 100 Fastest-Growing Companies in America

From hardware superstores to software designers, this guide from the editors of *Fortune* magazine identifies and explains the success of America's 100 fastest-growing companies. Includes company profiles, financial and employment data, products, addresses and telephone numbers of company officers, and much more

1-87875-395-9 WARNER $14.95

Jack **Gillis**

The Car Book 1996

Gillis is the Director of Public Affairs for the Consumer Federation of America. *The Car Book* gives you the upper hand in dealing with showroom sharks and helps with tire selection, insurance, safety features, unnecessary options, and, most important, deciding on the best model for your needs

0-06-273282-X HARPERCOLLINS PB..................$12.95

Paul **Katzka** & Bill **Yankus**

Autointelligence New Car, Decision Maker Volume II: Large, Luxury, & High Performance Cars, Sports Utility Vehicles, Station Wagons and Compact Vans

See also **CARS** under **BOATS, CARS, PLANES, AND TRAINS** in **FOOD, TRAVEL, AND LEISURE**

0-679-74410-X RANDOM HOUSE PB...............$12.00

Bob Scher

The Little Know-How Book: Everything You Need to Know to Get By in Life from Changing a Tire to Figuring a Tip to Tying Your Shoes

Learn to build a fire, make friends with any dog, jumpstart a car, and solve that dilemma that's plagued generations: tying a shoe so it stays tied

0-517-88031-8 CROWN PB..................................$9.00

Part 15

Food, Travel, & Leisure

Captain Kidd

Games Sacred and Profane

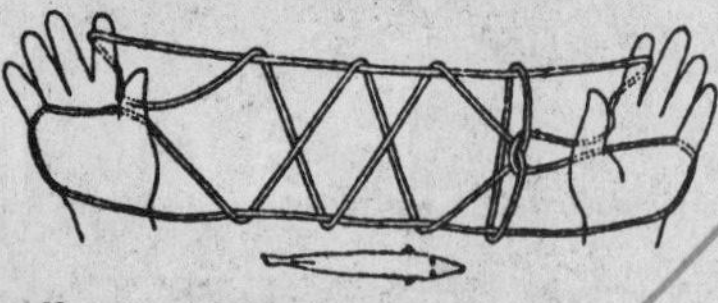

Cat's Cradle
The origin of string figures is impossible to date, but children's games and rhymes are surprisingly ancient, and the near-universality of string figures in world culture suggests that ever since fingers first met string, they've woven shapes to tell stories, play tricks, or just show off.

1594

2050 BC: Tomb at Beni Hasan, Egypt
"Never did I miss a moment of bliss," boasts a tombstone. For Egyptians, these moments include games, dances, and sports of all kinds. The walls of this tomb are covered with step-by-step paintings of wrestling matches (depicting 122 couples in all, and as detailed as a textbook), which demonstrate the full range of techniques known today.

1552

1500 BC: The Sweet Science
Boxing, as practiced by boys on the isle of Thera (now Santorini) in the Aegean.

1553

776 BC: The First Olympiad
A local celebration of Olympian Zeus that begins with sacrifices and ends with footraces soon becomes the focus not just of secular sportsmanship and national rivalry, but also of a cult of athletic stardom familiar to us today.

21

600 BC: The Spartan Women
In the rest of Greece women are veiled, secluded, and excluded from participating in almost all sporting events; married women are forbidden to even watch the Olympic games. But Spartan custom requires women to dance, wrestle, run, and throw the discus and javelin—all in the nude. "These public processions of the maidens, and their appearing naked in exercises and dances, were incitements to marriage, operating upon the young with the rigor and certainty, as Plato says, of love if not of mathematics." (Plutarch)

20

490 BC: Pheidippides
Runs 26 miles to Athens bearing news of victory at Marathon. Not until the first modern Olympics in 1891 will his feat be honored by running the "marathon."

1557

100: Lunch Hour at the Colosseum
Morning is for combat with wild beasts and afternoon is for gladiators, but during the noon lunch recess entertainment is provided by the condemned. Urged on by whips, hot irons, and the stamping, screaming, crowd —"Whip him to meet his wounds!"—an armed prisoner must kill an unarmed one, then be himself disarmed to take his turn, until hundreds lie dead. "In the morning they throw men to the lions and bears; at noon, they throw them to the spectators." (Seneca)

23

1200: Whose National Pastime?
Shrovetide stoolball, ancestor of cricket and baseball, is a chance for peasants—particularly women—to celebrate springtime at the Easter fair. "Although modern baseball is primarily American, urban, and male, its roots are medieval, English, rural, and female." (William Baker)

1549

1300: The Daughters of Artemis
Stickball and football are out of the question for European gentlewomen, but they ride, hunt stags with a bow, and hunt with falcons.

1548

1427: Paris
Tennis is all the rage. Margot of Hainault comes to town, outplays all the men, and causes a sensation.

1558

1876: Women (The Shape of Things to Come)
"They are not one jot less than I am,
They are tann'd in the face by shining suns and blowing winds,
Their flesh has the old divine suppleness and strength,
They know how to swim, row, ride, wrestle, shoot, run, strike,
retreat, advance, resist, defend themselves…"

—Walt Whitman
"A Woman Waits For Me"

619

1900: Modern Sports
These are marked by secularization, bureaucratization, and above all a mania for quantification. Largely a British invention, they encourage the discipline and zeal that can unite the classes and nations of a diverse state. Soccer serves this purpose for much of the world. A variant of soccer developed at Rugby gave rise to American football, which plays a similar role in the U.S.

1554

1996: The New Spartans
In politics we may follow Athens, but in our new ideal of an athletic, muscular beauty for women as well as men we now resemble Sparta.

1434

1000BC · 1500BC · 500BC · AD1 · AD500 · AD1500 · AD1900 · AD1996

1 The Gastronome
A complete lack of caution is perhaps one of the true signs of a real gourmet: he has no need for it, being filled as he is with a God-given and intelligently self-cultivated sense of gastronomical freedom.

—M.F.K. Fisher
The Art of Eating
1490

2 Fried Squirrel: Tennessee
Make sure all the hair is cleaned off the squirrel. Cut it up. If it's old and tough, put it in the pressure cooker for 15–20 minutes. Salt and pepper it. Cover w/flour and fry in a cast-iron skillet on a medium fire until brown and tender. This is a real sweet meat. You can smother a squirrel just like a chicken.

—Ernest Matthew Mickler
White Trash Cooking
1492

3 Wig: The Carolinas
2 pounds of wheat flour, 1/2 lb. of butter, 1/2 lb. of sugar, one pint of milk; mix these ingredients well together, and add three tablespoonfuls of good yeast, a little cinnamon and rosewater; cover the mixture, and set it in a warm place to rise; when light , bake in rings, and split and butter them while hot.

—Sarah Rutledge
The Carolina Housewife 1847, Biscuits, Spoonbread, and Sweet Potato Pie
1493

4 Coffee James Joyce: Dublin
2 jiggers Irish Whiskey in a balloon wine glass
1 teaspoon sugar
Pour in black coffee, stir; as contents revolve, add jigger cream slowly in circular motion. Allow cream to float on top of coffee. Do not stir again. Excellent for after-dinner conversation.

—Gertrude Stein
Alice B. Toklas Cookbook
1490

5 Soup: Canterbury
To make blaunche porre. Tak whyte lekys & perboyle hem & hewe hem smale with oynouns. Cast it in good broth & sethe it up with smale bryddys. Coloure it with safferoun; powdur yt with pouder douce.

—Maggie Black
The Medieval Cookbook
1490

6 Spiced Stuffed Sheep Stomach: Scotland
But mark the Rustic, haggis-fed
The trembling earth resounds hes tread,
Clap in his walie nieve a blade,
He'll mak it whissle;
An' legs, an'arms, an' heads will sned,
Like taps o' thrissle
Ye pow'rs wha mak mankind your care,
And dish them out their bill o' fare
Auld Scotland wants nae skinking ware
That jaups in luggies;
But, if ye wish her grateful' pray'r,
Gie her a haggis!

—Robert Burns
(in Joan and John Digby
Food for Thought)
1490

7 The Truffle: France
The truffle-hunting pig is usually a sow. At other seasons she produces her annual litter of a dozen piglets. Sows are better at the job than hogs or castrated pigs; they are gentler and less capricious. A truffle-hunting sow will have been trained from the age of a few weeks by being occasionally fed poor quality truffles, which she loves. However, she may sometimes develop a perverse taste for their poor quality, and then she ignores the best truffles and heads straight for rotting tubers.

—Maguelonne Toussaint-Samat
The History of Food
1491

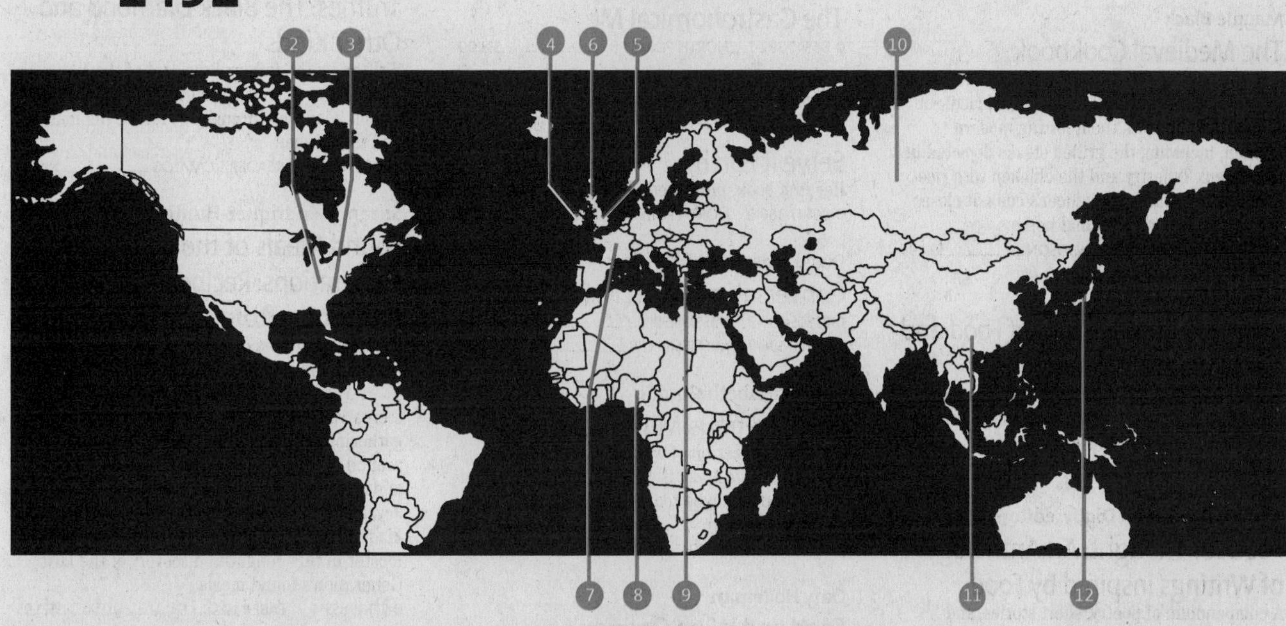

8 Palm-Wine: Nigeria
When it was early in the morning of the next day, I had no palm-wine to drink at all, and throughout that day I felt not so happy as before; I was seriously sat down in my parlor, but when it was the third day that I had no palm-wine at all, all my friends did not come to my house at all, all my friends did not come to my house again, they left me there alone, because there was no palm-wine for them to drink.

—Amos Tutuola
The Palm-Wine Drinkard
999

9 Fish Sauce: Greece
"Here is lordly Garum, a costly gift, made from the blood of a still-gasping mackerel." The Greek and Roman fish sauce has a rather unattractive sound. The smell given off during its production was so bad that making garum in urban areas was sometimes outlawed.

—Andrew Dalby and Sally Granger
The Classical Cookbook
1490

10 Pork Preserves: Russia
First cut off the head (*Sperva otrezyvaetsya golova*). Set aside a fine, whole head with attractive ears for Easter. Salt and smoke the head; halve less attractive ones. Salt and smoke the lower jaws which are extraordinarily tasty for garnishing sauces (#529). Or use them to prepare Jowls #2686. Remove the brains from the upper part of the head and use them while they are stilll fresh. Use the head itself for jellied meat (*studen*).

—Evgenia Molokhodets
A Gift to a Young Housewife
1498

11 Health Food: Southern China
In the fourth month, too, they gather to share a ritual meal, in this case the flavored liquid in which the Buddha's image has been washed outside the temple gate, and then eat sweet rice cakes cooked with a hundred herbs. Some say this will cure delirium. At the summer solstice, they cook and eat dog meat, to keep away malaria, and at the coming of the winter share a broth of meat, peaches and mustard greens, to keep any other sicknesses away.

—Jonathan Spence
God's Chinese Son
141

12 Elegance: Japan
A white coat worn over a violet waistcoat.
Duck eggs.
Shaved ice mixed with liana syrup and put in a new silver bowl.

—*The Pillow Book of Sei Shonagon*
1020

Food

"Of all the books produced since the remote ages by human talents and industry those only that treat of cooking are, from a moral point of view, above suspicion. The intention of every other piece of prose may be discussed and even mistrusted, but the purpose of a cookery book is one and unmistakable. Its object can conceivably be no other than to increase the happiness of mankind."—Joseph Conrad

Books on Food

Brigid **Allen**, editor

Food: An Oxford Anthology

This anthology will delight any cook or gourmet with its wealth of literary comment and opinion on food—from biblical selections to George Orwell

0-19-212327-0 OXFORD $30.00

Maggie **Black**

The Medieval Cookbook

An illustrated survey of the Middle Ages and its food, this book draws 80 recipes from medieval sources and updates them for the modern kitchen, including the grilled steaks depicted in the Bayeux Tapestry and the chicken with rice and almonds made by Chaucer's cook. It closes with a chapter on medicinal herbs

0-500-01548-1 THAMES & HUDSON $24.95

Andrew **Dalby**

Siren Feasts: A History of Food and Gastronomy in Greece

Serious food history buffs will enjoy this study of Greek foodstuffs and culinary attitudes from prehistory to the present day

0-415-11620-1 ROUTLEDGE $39.95

John **Digby** & Joan **Digby**, editors

Food for Thought: An Anthology of Writings Inspired by Food

A compendium of poetry, short stories, and excerpts that you can snack on for years to come

0-88001-469-5 ECCO PB $15.00

M.F.K. **Fisher**

The Art of Eating

To some this is the best collection of essays about food written thus far in the 20th-century. The book is serious but not pedantic, much of it relating to her early years of living in Provence

See also **AMERICAN FOOD WRITERS** under **AMERICAN COOKERY**

0-02-032220-8 MACMILLAN PB $19.95

The Boss Dog

This collection of six previously unpublished tales chronicles the adventures of a single mother and her two young daughters in Aix-en-Provence. Witty and delightful, Fisher conveys the soul of the town: its moods, festivals, foods, and foibles

0-86547-465-6 NORTH POINT $16.95
0-679-73860-6 PANTHEON PB $10.00

M.F.K. Fisher

Consider the Oyster

0-86547-335-8 NORTH POINT PB $9.00

Dubious Honors

0-86547-414-1 NORTH POINT PB $9.95

The Gastronomical Me

0-86547-392-7 NORTH POINT PB $13.00

Here Let Us Feast

0-86547-206-8 NORTH POINT PB $15.00

Serve It Forth

Her first book, published in 1937

0-86547-369-2 NORTH POINT PB $12.00

David **Lazar** & M.F.K. **Fisher**

Conversations with M.F.K. Fisher

0-87805-595-9 MISSISSIPPI $39.50
0-87805-596-7 MISSISSIPPI PB $15.95

Karen Elizabeth **Gordon**

The Ravenous Muse

A macabe selection of writings involving food. "*The Ravenous Muse* is good for everyone's night table, though maybe too rich for bedtime" —Diane Johnson

0-679-41861-X PANTHEON $20.50

Gary **Holleman**

Food and Wine Online

From accessing the Web to ratings of the services and bulletin boards offered

0-442-02007-4 VAN NOSTRAND REINHOLD PB $29.95

Michel **Jordan**

The Good Cook's Book of Days: A Food Lover's Journal

Not a cookbook, but a beautifully illustrated journal to keep track of your culinary triumphs and inspirations

0-201-40659-4 ADDISON-WESLEY $25.00

Douglas **Messerli**, editor

The Sun and Moon Guide to Eating Through Literature

The original and innovative West Coast press takes us on an avant-garde literary tour of the tongue. Ron Padgett cooks spaghetti, Vaclav Havel sits down to beefsteak with sweet-sour gravy, and Harry Mathews writes on country cooking. Paul Auster, Thomas Pynchon, Iris Murdoch, Vladimir Nabokov, and a whole literary soiree of hungry writers focus their skills on food. Bountifully illustrated with reproductions from Warhol, Ruscha, Oldenburg, and more

1-55713-178-3 SUN & MOON $29.95

Sidney Wilfred **Mintz**

Tasting Food, Tasting Freedom: On Eating, Power and the Past

"This savvy anthropologist smuggles his nourishing essays both ways across a little-known frontier. It is the border between what people choose to eat and macroeconomics, even war and peace"—Phillip Morrison

0-8070-4628-0 BEACON $22.00

Simon **Rae**, editor

The Faber Book of Drink, Drinkers, and Drinking

"On reading Mr. Rae's anthology...I felt by turns queasy, horrified, and slightly foxed" —Christopher Howse, *Spectator*

0-571-16821-3 FABER PB $15.95

Jean-Marie **Rocchia**

Truffles: The Black Diamond and Other Kinds

Written by the former President of the National Association of Trufficulteurs, this book will take you on a journey through the forest, the market, and the kitchen

2-87923-050-0 READER'S CATALOG $39.95

Suzanne **Rodriquez-Hunter**

Found Meals of the Lost Generations: Recipes and Anecdotes from 1920's Paris

Hemingway writes of hungrily eyeing a street pigeon while strolling through Paris in his poorest days, but beyond the starving artist stereotype, Paris of the '20s was notable for gatherings of that epoch's greatest talents around the table. Accompany Gertrude Stein and Alice B. Toklas with a jugged hare; James Joyce and Sylvia Beach and a ham braising in Madiera; and Josephine Baker serving grilled lobster in this delightful discovery of the Lost Generation's found meals

0-571-19855-4 FABER $21.95

James Joyce

Waverly **Root**

Food: An Authoritative Visual History and Dictionary of the Foods of the World

0-7651-9791-X SMITHMARK $24.98

Colin **Spencer** & Claire **Clifton**, editors

The Faber Book of Food

0-571-16467-6 FABER $24.95
0-571-17887-1 FABER PB $15.95

Maguelonne **Toussaint-Samat**

A History of Food

The classic history of eating, now available in paperback. "Indispensable, endless and endlessly fascinating. Not a book to digest at one or several sittings. Savor it...one small slice at a time, accompanied by a very fine wine"—*NY Times Book Review.* "This book is not only impressive for the knowledge it provides, it is unique in its integration of historical anecdotes and factual data. It is a marvelous reference to a great many topics"—Raymond Blanc

TRANSLATED BY ANTHEA BELL

0-631-17741-8 BLACKWELL $59.95
0-631-19497-5 BLACKWELL PB $25.95

James **Trager**

The Food Chronology: A Food Lover's Compendium of Events and Anecdotes, from Prehistory to the Present

A book to flip through at leisure; a fun compendium of food-related events, product introductions, restaurant demises, and much more, from prehistory to the present

See also ENTERTAINING

0-8050-3389-0 HOLT $40.00

Bob **Young** & Al **Stankus**

Jazz Cooks: Portraits and Recipes of the Greats

More than 90 top international jazz musicians are featured in this mouth-watering, toe tapping volume celebrating jazz music, jazz musicians and, of course, jazz's favorite foods. Highlighting each musician's favorite recipe, the authors engross us with biographical anecdotes and a taste of musical history. Deborah Feingold's striking photographic portraits of these jazz greats are unforgettable. "So gather those ingredients, adjust that chef's hat, and turn on the stereo. I think you'll enjoy these culinary riffs"—Bob Young

1-55670-192-6 STEWART, TABORI PB $24.95

Al Stankus and Bob Young

The Basics

Jean **Anderson**, editor

1,001 Secrets of Great Cooks

Short cuts and quick tips on cooking, baking, shopping, kitchen equipment, and menus

0-399-52153-4 BERKELEY PB $12.00

Janet **Bailey**

Keeping Food Fresh

Can it be frozen? How long will it keep? This convenient guide will answer all of your concerns

0-06-272503-3 HARPERCOLLINS PB $15.00

Francis **Bissell**

The Book of Food: A Cook's Guide to Over 1,000 Exotic and Everyday Ingredients

The photos in this award-winning reference make this a real stand-out

0-8050-3006-9 HOLT $40.00

Julia **Child**

From Julia Child's Kitchen

Julia Child introduced classical French cuisine to the American kitchen and changed our lives forever. Her books are amusing, intelligent, and energetic

0-394-48071-6 RANDOM HOUSE $39.95

In Julia's Kitchen with Master Chefs

Twenty-six great cooks from across America join Julia Child in her own kitchen and share, with her and for us, their secrets. The result is 150 superb recipes, tendered for us in Julia's clear writing and familiar voice. From Zarela Martinez's *poblanos rellenos* to Madhur Jaffrey's shrimp in spicy cocunut sauce and Leah Chase's southern fried chicken, this is a masterful book that every cook will want at arm's reach

0-679-43896-3 KNOPF $35.00

The Way to Cook

The definitive word from the American master, combining classic techniques with free-style American cooking. The emphasis is on light, fresh, and simple preparations. More than 600 color photographs accompany the 800 recipes for everything from fish and fresh vegetables to hamburger buns and exotic chocolate cakes

0-679-74765-6 KNOPF PB $35.00

Ann **Creber**

The World's Finest Food

Over 180 recipes from 12 countries-from Mexico to China, France to Morocco, Italy to Russia, Spain and Thailand—have been selected for this culinary grand tour. Beautifully designed and illustrated, this is *the* introduction to easy multiculturalism of the palate

PHOTOGRAPHY BY PHIL WYMANT

1-55670-374-0 STEWART, TABORI $45.00

Marion **Cunningham**

Fannie Farmer Cookbook, 13th Ed.

A special 100th-Anniversary edition with new foward and commemorative jacket

0-679-45081-5 KNOPF $30.00

Sharon Tyler **Herbst**

The New Food Lover's Companion: Comprehensive Definitions of over 3000 Food, Wine, and Culinary Terms

A convenient reference

0-8120-1520-7 BARRONS PB $12.95

Barbara **Kafka**

Microwave Gourmet

Nearly 600 recipes

0-380-71251-2 AVON PB $5.95

Roasting: A Simple Art

Exceptionally well-covered and delicious study of an often overlooked cooking method

0-688-13135-2 MORROW $25.00

Christopher **Kimball**

The Cook's Bible

The founder and editor of *Cook's Magazine* brings his tradition of rigorously-tested recipes and clear, in-depth discussions to this volume of American favorites

0-316-49371-6 LITTLE, BROWN $29.95

Harold **MaGee**

On Food and Cooking

The whys of cooking explained in a captivating combination of history and science

0-02-034621-2 COLLIER PB $21.00

Jacques **Manière**

Cuisine a la Vapeur: Art of Cooking with Steam

"With Stephanie Lyness's attentive translation/interpretation, the age-old art of steaming takes on a revitalized life of its own. Few cooking methods are as delicate or gentle, rewarding cooks with pure, intense flavors, exceptional moistness, food that's succulant, tender, and memorable"—Patricia Wells

TRANSLATED AND INTERPRETED BY STEPHANIE LYNESS

0-688-10507-6 MORROW $25.00

Marilyn M. **Moore**

Meat and Potatoes: and Other Comfort Foods from the Wooden Spoon Kitchen

0-87113-606-6 GROVE $20.00

Jacques **Pepin**

La Methode: An Illustrated Guide to the Fundamental Methods of Cooking

Instructions and detailed photos for the dedicated amateur as well as the professional

0-671-70711-6 POCKET PB $25.00

Irma **Rombauer** & Marion **Becker**

The Joy of Cooking

From meat loaf to a definition of the mangosteen, this all-purpose volume, originally published in 1931 and since revised and enlarged many times, becomes a member of the family in most kitchens. "An invaluable reference work where techniques, cooking procedures, solid information about measurements, temperatures and even proper table settings are concerned"—Craig Clairborne

0-02-604570-2 MACMILLAN $25.00
0-452-26332-8 PLUME PB $13.95

David **Rosengarten** & others

The Dean & Deluca Cookbook

An enormous compendium of the recipes that have made the store famous, plus extremely informative sidebars on the basic and exotic ingredients that are its backbone

0-679-77003-8 RANDOM HOUSE PB $23.00

Julee **Rosso**

The Silver Palate Good Times Cookbook

Winning menus for special occasions. Note the swordfish marinated with lime and coriander and blueberry pie with cinnamon lattice crust

See also **ENTERTAINING**

0-89480-832-X WORKMAN $22.95
0-89480-831-1 WORKMAN PB $14.95

Michele **Urvater**

Monday to Friday Cookbook

Urvater blows away the notion of beginner recipes being necessarily boring; the book is jam-packed with exciting flavors as well as tips to help you manuveur with ease through the kitchen

1-56305-748-4 WORKMAN PB $14.95

American Cookery

James **Beard**

Probably the most inspiring American food writer and chef of the 20th century. Teaching, writing, and sharing his unwavering enthusiasm for food into his '80s, Beard left an indelible mark on American cuisine.

Delights and Prejudices

0-689-00007-3 SIMON & SCHUSTER $59.40

James Beard's American Cookery

0-316-08566-9 LITTLE, BROWN PB $21.95

James Beard's Theory and Practice of Good Cooking

0-517-11860-2 RANDOM HOUSE $9.99

Julia **Child**

Julia Child: Cooking with the Master Chefs

This companion book to the PBS series brings 50 recipes of America's master chefs home. Recipes have been edited for home cooking. 80 photographs

0-679-74829-6 KNOPF PB $17.95

Merle **Ellis**

The Great American Meat Cookbook

536 recipes from our forefathers as well as contemporaries chronicling American culinary history

0-394-58835-5 KNOPF $30.00

Fannie Merritt **Farmer**

The Original Boston Cooking School Cook Book, 1896

Reprinted in honor of the book's 100th anniversary

0-88363-196-2 LEVIN $18.96

Jim **Heimann**

Car Hops and Curb Service: A History of American Drive-In Restaurants 1920-1960

Photographs and text work together to preserve the memory of the nearly-extinct, drive-in restaurant

0-8118-1115-8 CHRONICLE PB $17.95

Hal **Kendig**, editor

James Beard's Simple Foods

"This is James Beard…at his entertaining, conversational, and educational best"—Julia Child. In this never-before-published collection of recipes, the late Beard presents a back-to-basics primer for newcomers and experienced gourmets alike. Written in the unpretentious, easy-to-execute style that made Beard's writing as legendary as his culinary artistry, this unique collection is sure to delight

FOREWORD BY JULIA CHILD

0-02-508070-9 MACMILLAN $22.00

Chef Waldy **Malouf** & Molly **Finn**

The Hudson River Valley Cookbook: A Leading American Chef Savors the Region's Bounty

Chef Malouf's intensely flavored cuisine demonstrates that it is possible to create gourmet food without importing hard-to-find ingredients. These recipes will be marvelous no matter where you live

0-201-62253-X ADDISON-WESLEY $27.50

Ernest Matthew **Mickler**

Sinkin Spells, Hot Flashes, Fits and Cravin's

"Like the cherished White Trash Cookbook, these dishes are likely to either set the teeth on edge or send a Proustian reverie wafting out of the kitchen"—*Booklist*

0-89815-268-2 TEN SPEED PB $14.95

White Trash Cooking

"I have never seen a sociological document of such beauty"—Harper Lee

0-89815-189-9 TEN SPEED PB $17.95

William **Rice**

Steak Lover's Cookbook

Bill Rice has left no cut overlooked; a passionate steak-lover, he has come up with the "Best-Ever" recipes for each cut as well as inspired variations, and thrown in a few side dishes to complement your meal

0-7611-0080-6 WORKMAN PB $13.95

Waverly **Root** & Richard **De Rochemont**

Eating in America: A History

"Not only a browser's paradise but a pungently controversial history"—*Bon Appetit*

0-88001-399-0 ECCO PB $18.00

Martha Adams **Rubin**

Countryside, Garden & Table

A true celebration of nature's bounty and centered around the changing seasons, this is much more than just a gardening cookbook. Divided into chapters representing each month, Rubin discusses the land, the garden, and the kitchen, providing practical tips and philosophical meditations on living close to the earth. Stocked full with her favorite recipes, all of which feature the foods of the harvest, she provides numerous menus for seasonal party planning

See also **VEGETABLES AND FRUIT** under **THE OUTDOORS**

1-55591-137-4 FULCRUM $19.95

Amelia **Simmons**

The First American Cookbook

A facsimile of *American Cookery* (1796)

0-486-24710-4 DOVER PB $3.95

Raymond **Sokolov**

Fading Feast: A Compendium of Disappearing American Regional Foods

1-56792-037-3 NATL BOOK NETWORK PB $15.95

American Food Writers

Craig **Claiborne**

Craig Claiborne's New New York Times Cookbook

A basic but imaginative collection of recipes by the former food writer for the *The New York Times.* The pasta with ginger and garlic sauce is memorable

0-517-12235-9 RANDOM HOUSE $15.99

Robert **Clark**

The Solace of Food: A Life of James Beard

Previously published in hardcover as *James Beard: A Biography*

FOREWORD BY JULIA CHILD

1-88364-204-3 STEERFORTH PB $16.00

Laurie **Colwin**

Home Cooking

"A home cook, like you and me, whose charm and lack of pretension make her wonderfully human and a welcome companion as she chatters on about the small culinary accomplishments and discoveries that occur in her kitchen"—*Chicago Tribune*

0-06-097522-9 HARPERPERENNIAL PB $11.00

More Home Cooking: A Writer Returns to the Kitchen

0-06-092578-7 HARPERPERENNIAL PB $12.00

M.F.K. **Fisher**

The Art of Eating

To some this is the best collection of essays about food written thus far in the 20th-century. The book is serious but not pedantic, much of it relating to her early years of living in Provence

0-02-032220-8 MACMILLAN PB $19.95

The Boss Dog

This collection of six previously unpublished tales chronicles the adventures of a single mother and her two young daughters in Aix-en-Provence. Witty and delightful, Fisher conveys the soul of the town: its moods, festivals, foods, and foibles

0-86547-465-6 NORTH POINT $16.95

0-679-73860-6 PANTHEON PB $10.00

Serve It Forth

Her first book, published in 1937

0-86547-369-2 NORTH POINT PB $12.00

To Begin Again: Stories and Memoirs, 1908-1929

0-679-75082-7 PANTHEON PB $12.00

David **Lazar** & M.F.K. **Fisher**

Conversations with M.F.K. Fisher

0-87805-595-9 MISSISSIPPI $39.50

0-87805-596-7 MISSISSIPPI PB $15.95

A.J. **Liebling**

Between Meals: An Appetite for Paris

The great journalist on his favorite subjects: wine, food and Paris

See also **HISTORY, POLITICS, AND SOCIETY** under **20TH-CENTURY AMERICAN ESSAYS AND JOURNALISM** in **LITERATURE OF THE AMERICAS**

0-679-60142-2 MODERN LIBRARY $12.50

0-86547-236-X NORTH POINT PB $11.00

Anne **Mendelson**

Stand Facing the Stove: The Story of the Women Who Gave America the Joy of Cooking

A biography of the mother and daughter who created the bestselling trade cookbook ever, intertwining culinary history, publishing intrique, and social history within their portraits

0-8050-2904-4 HOLT $29.95

Molly **O'Neill**

A Well-Seasoned Appetite: Recipes from an American Kitchen

The food columnist for *The New York Times Magazine* and author of *The New York Cookbook* offers a set of essays on the pleasures of seasonal cooking. Incorporating recipes and techniques adapted to the offerings of each season, O'Neill makes a convincing argument against the year-round sameness of global agribusiness and for the rhythmic variation of tastes and cuisines by season

0-670-85574-X VIKING $25.95

John **Thorne** & Matt Lewis **Thorne**

Outlaw Cook

The author insists that eating well consistently means learning to cook for oneself. Eschewing culinary jargon, he describes the evolution of his own tastes and culinary skills, and urges readers into the kitchen. "So far from the usual run of gushing food-writers as to make M.F.K. Fisher look a little precious"—*Kirkus Reviews*

0-86547-479-6 NORTH POINT PB $10.00

Serious Pig: In Search of Some American Culinary Roots

Another refreshing collection of food essays from the eclectic pair

0-86547-502-4 NORTH POINT $25.00

New England and the Atlantic Seaboard

Sarah Leah **Chase**

The Open-House Cookbook

The owner of a Nantucket gourmet shop offers up many wonderful recipes. The tone is breezy and the recipes appetizing—as in steak, mushroom, and hearts of palm salad with Bearnaise mayonnaise, deep-dish broccoli pizza, and white chocolate brownies

See also **ENTERTAINING**

0-89480-465-0 WORKMAN PB $12.95

Mystic Seaport Museum

Saltwater Foodways: New Englanders and Their Food, at Sea and Ashore, in the 19th Century

0-913372-72-2 MYSTIC SEAPORT MUSEUM $39.95

Amy Bess **Miller** &
Persis Wellington **Fuller**, editors

The Best of Shaker Cooking

Shaker cookery at its simplest and most authentic

0-02-035045-7 MACMILLAN PB $14.00

Jasper **White**

Jasper White's Cooking from New England

White was one of the first and most visionary of chefs to recognize the importance of the New England culinary tradition and to re-create it using his ingenuity

0-06-092399-7 HARPERPERENNIAL PB $16.00

The South

Ella **Brennan** & Dick **Brennan**

The Commander's Palace New Orleans Cookbook

The recipes that made this New Orleans landmark famous

0-517-55049-0 CROWN $20.00

Linda **Crawford**

The Catfish Book

The last word on the subject: everything you'll ever need to know about this southern staple, for anglers, cooks, diners, and the merely curious

0-87805-502-9 MISSISSIPPI PB $10.95

John **Egerton**

Southern Food: At Home, on the Road, in History

A lively, handsomely illustrated celebration; a history, restaurant guide, and recipe book all in one

0-8078-4417-9 NORTH CAROLINA PB $18.95

Sheila **Ferguson**

Soul Food: Classic Cuisine from the Deep South

1-55584-420-0 GROVE PB $18.95

Mrs. **Fisher**

What Mrs. Fisher Knows About Old Southern Cooking

Delicious Southern recipes in the first published cookbook written by an African American

1-55709-403-9 APPLEWOOD PB $8.95

Damon Lee **Fowler**

Classical Southern Cooking: A Celebration of the Cuisine of the South

In the South, American urban sprawl has hidden classical regional cuisines under a transcontinental barrage of, in Damon Lee Fowler's words, "fast-food diners, instant coffee, instant pudding...and, God help us, nondairy topping." This passionate book rediscovers the glorious melange of European, African, and Native American cuisine that once filled the tables of the Old South: venison stew, okra and tomatoes, sauteed ham with red-eye gravy, and apple meringue pie are some of the recipes that, accompanied with warm recollections and forgotten lore, inform this collection

0-517-59353-X CROWN $30.00

Camille **Glenn**

The Heritage of Southern Cooking

A recipe tour of Southern cuisine from one of the South's foremost cooking teachers. Try the Kentucky-style ham in cream or Baltimore barbecue chicken

0-89480-117-1 WORKMAN PB $16.95

Karen **Hess**

The Carolina Rice Kitchen

An important study of the rice plantation in America and its social, economic and cultural reverberations

0-87249-666-X SOUTH CAROLINA $24.95

Wilbert **Jones**

The New Soul Food Cookbook: Healthier Recipes for Traditional Favorites

1-55972-317-3 BIRCH LANE $14.95

Edna **Lewis**

The Taste of Country Cooking

The recipe and reminiscences of a brilliant cook from Virginia. The chicken with dumplings is unforgettable, as is her fresh peach cobbler with nutmeg sauce

0-394-73215-4 RANDOM HOUSE PB $19.50

Sally **Morrison**

Cross Creek Kitchens: Seasonal Recipes and Reflections

0-937404-50-0 TRIAD $24.95

Bill **Neal**

Biscuits, Spoonbread, and Sweet Potato Pie

Classic Southern baked goods like Carolina Rice Bread, Pecan Pie, and Robert E. Lee Cake from a knowledgeable Southerner

0-679-76580-8 RANDOM HOUSE PB $18.00

Alex **Patout**

Patout's Cajun Home Cooking

0-394-54725-X RANDOM HOUSE $27.50

Paul **Prudhomme**

Chef Paul Prudhomme's Louisiana Kitchen

The owner and chef of K-Paul's restaurant in New Orleans shares the recipes he has made famous, among them blackened redfish, deep-fried crayfish (also called Cajun popcorn), and coffee cookies

0-688-02847-0 MORROW $23.00

The Prudhomme Family Cookbook: Old-Time Louisiana Recipes

0-688-07549-5 MORROW $19.95

Kathy **Starr**

The Soul of Southern Cooking

0-87805-421-9 MISSISSIPPI $35.00

The Midwest

Beth **Dooley** & Lucia **Watson**

Savoring the Seasons of the Northern Heartland

"The lore alone, not to mention good food, makes (this book) worth having"
—Lynn Rosetto Kasper

06784411755 KNOPF $25.00

The Southwest

Leland **Atkinson**

Cocina!: A Hands-On Guide to the Techniques of Southwestern Cooking

Provides instructions on steaming tamales, preparing moles, smoking, drying, roasting and more

0-89815-841-9 TEN SPEED $19.95

Barrie **Kavasch**

Enduring Harvests

Native American foods and celebrations

1-56440-737-3 GLOBE PEQUOT PB $14.95

Emeril **Lagasse**

Louisiana Real and Rustic

This zany chef puts aside his urge to innovate to give you a more genuine representation of this region's fare

0-688-12721-5 MORROW $25.00

Emeril **Lagasse** & Jessie **Tirsch**

Emeril's New New Orleans Cooking

Lagasse's passion and energy is reflected brilliantly in his interpretations of his native food

See also **AMERICAN CHEFS**

0-688-11284-6 MORROW $23.00

The West

John **Ash** & Sid **Goldstein**

From the Earth to the Table: John Ash's Wine Country Cuisine

Chef of the kitchens at Fetzer, Ash favors cuisine that is naturally complemented by wine, and his suggestions are most helpful

0-525-94000-6 DUTTON $29.95

Michael **Bauer** & Fran **Irwin**, editors

New California Classics: Great Recipes from The San Francisco Chronicle

A collection of recipes pulled from the best newspaper food section in the country

0-8118-1445-9 CHRONICLE PB $18.95

Beverly **Cox** & Martin **Jacobs**

Spirit of the West: Cooking from Ranch House and Range

Hearty, homey food that is enriched by the influence of Native Americans, Mexicans, and wide backgrounds of settlers

1-88518-321-6 ARTISAN $35.00

Rachel **Laudan**

The Food of Paradise: Exploring Hawaii's Culinary Heritage

Laudan explores the American, Chinese, Japanese, Korean, Polynesian and Portuguese influences on Hawaiian cuisine by visiting markets, fairs, family restaurants and lunch-wagons in this lavishly photographed volume

0-8248-1708-7 HAWAII $38.95
0-8248-1778-8 HAWAII PB $24.95

Cathy **Luchetti**

Home on the Range: A Culinary History of the American West

A decade ago, Luchetti published the best-selling *Women of the West;* here she writes of the frontier roots of American cooking. Some of America's most characteristic foods were cooked by early settlers, and this book covers the cuisine of cowboys, the gold rush, the trading-post, the plantation, and seaman's fare

0-679-74484-3 RANDOM HOUSE PB $25.00

Diane Rossen **Worthington**

The California Cook

Fresh, relaxed cuisine that captures the best of the ingredients and attitude of the Pacific coast

0-553-09179-4 BANTAM DOUBLEDAY DELL $27.95

Quick and Easy

Pierre **Franey**

The 60-Minute Gourmet

The former chef of Le Pavillon in New York City collects his columns from the *NY Times* for cooking by the clock. The recipes are superb, from cheese souffle to pork chops with orange, and they can actually be prepared in an hour

0-449-90194-7 FAWCETT PB $12.00

Pierre **Franey** & Bryan **Miller**

Cuisine Rapide

The companion volume to Franey's PBS television series

0-8129-1746-4 TIME BOOKS $22.50

Marie **Simmons** & Richard **Sax**

Lighter, Quicker, Better

0-688-13871-3 MORROW $25.00

Nigel **Slater**

Real Fast Food: 350 Recipes Ready-To-Eat in 30 Minutes

Fast and filled with simple fresh ideas

0-87951-642-9 OVERLOOK $23.95

Anne **Willan**

In and Out of the Kitchen: Fresh, Fast, and Easy Meals in 15 Minutes

No matter how much one loves to cook, there are times when nothing is more needed than a quick, easy, and delicious dinner. Willan, the proprietor of the famous La Varenne Cooking School, provides 100 recipes that can be prepared in 15 minutes or less. Red wine gazpacho with mint, deviled crab souffle, baked ham with apple and cream, and chocolate mousse with orange are just some of the specialties included

0-8478-1913-2 RIZZOLI $25.00

American Chefs

Paul **Bertolli** & Alice **Waters**

Chez Panisse Cooking

The first book of Chez Panisse main course recipes since the original *Chez Panisse Menu Cookbook*

See also **BUSINESS AND REFERENCE**

0-679-75535-7 RANDOM HOUSE PB $18.00

Daniel **Boulud**

Cooking with Daniel Boulud

Four-star chef Boulud has cooked at the finest restaurants in Europe and America, including serving as Executive Chef at Le Cirque. In this

lavishly illustrated volume, he adapts 250 of his favorite recipes for the home kitchen, allowing them to be prepared without arduous techniques or expensive equipment
0-679-40409-0 RANDOM HOUSE $40.00

Ellen **Brown**
Southwest Tastes: From the PBS Television Series "Great Chefs of the West"
Forty-four chefs contribute recipes from five western states, including *enchiladas verdes*, barbecued pork with tequilla casserole, and caramel custard flavored with orange
0-929714-04-0 H.P. $29.95
0-929714-24-5 GREAT CHEFS PB $24.95

David **Burke**
Cooking with David Burke
Chef of the Park Avenue Cafe in New York City, Burke blends his French training with American regional specialties to come up with his own innovative, dazzling cuisine
0-394-58343-4 KNOPF $30.00

Mary **Cleaver** & others
The Tribeca Cookbook
New York's Les Halles of 100 years ago, the "Triangle Below Canal Street" now boasts some of the great city's greatest restaurants: Montrachet, Chanterelle, and other names well known to the denizens of restaurant waiting lists. This charming collection brings 12 restaurants together to create six menus for each of the four seasons. An original and altogether delightful book
0-89815-634-3 TEN SPEED $25.95

Bobby **Flay**
Bobby Flay's Bold American Food
Signature food from New York's Mesa Grill
0-446-51724-0 WARNER $34.95

Larry **Forgione**
An American Place
0-688-08716-7 MORROW $30.00

Hubert **Keller**
Hubert Keller's Cuisine
The chef of Fleur-de-Lys in San Fransisco brings his widely-acclaimed Franco-California cooking to your kitchen
0-89815-807-9 TEN SPEED $35.00

Emeril **Lagasse** & Jessie **Tirsch**
Emeril's New New Orleans Cooking
Lagasse's passion and energy is reflected brilliantly in his interpretations of his native food
0-688-11284-6 MORROW $23.00

Michael **Lomonaco** & Donna **Forsman**
The '21' Cookbook
0-385-47570-5 DOUBLEDAY $35.00

Mark **Miller**
Coyote Cafe
0-89815-245-3 TEN SPEED $27.95

Coyote's Pantry
0-89815-494-4 TEN SPEED $25.95

Danny **Meyer** & Michael **Romano**
The Union Square Cafe Cookbook
0-06-017013-1 HARPERCOLLINS $30.00

Daniel Meyer and Michael Romano

Mark Miller's Indian Market Cookbook
0-89815-620-3 TEN SPEED $35.00

Mark **Miller** & Andrew **MacLauchlan**
Flavored Breads from the Famous Coyote Cafe
0-89815-862-1 TEN SPEED PB $19.95

Mary Sue **Milliken** & Susan **Feniger**
City Cuisine
0-688-13177-8 HEARST PB $14.95

Mesa Mexicana
0-688-10649-8 MORROW $17.95

Patrick **O'Connell**
The Inn at Little Washington: A Consuming Passion
Chef O'Connell's elegant French-inspired cuisine has drawn much attention to his inn in the Shenandoah Valley; this volume reveals thorough recipes and photos what makes this spot so outstanding
0-679-44736-9 RANDOM HOUSE $50.00

Charlie **Palmer** & Judith **Choate**
Great American Food
Charlie Palmer of Aureole fame shares with you his signature cuisine based on seasonal American foods presented beautifully. Judith Choate assists in adapting the recipes to your home kitchen
0-679-43794-0 RANDOM HOUSE $50.00

Cindy **Pawlcyn**
Fog City Diner Cookbook
American diner food reinterpreted from this San Francisco restaurant
0-89815-493-6 TEN SPEED $27.95

Wolfgang **Puck**
Adventures in the Kitchen
Puck, founder of L.A.'s famed Spago and purveyor of designer pizza to the stars, presents recipes from his four landmark California restaurants. Included are such outrageously decadent offerings as soft-shell crab tempura with cilantro vinaigrette, grilled quail with wild rice risotto, spicy scallop pizza, and whiskey, fudge cake
0-394-55895-2 RANDOM HOUSE $30.00

The Wolfgang Puck Cookbook
Recipes from Los Angeles' Spago and Chinois restaurants by their inspired creator. Don't miss the watercress salad with barbecued chicken breast or the lobster with sweet ginger and fried baby spinach leaves or Puck's famous grilled chicken with garlic and parsley. Not for the beginner but essential for any serious cook
0-394-53366-6 RANDOM HOUSE $23.00

Douglas **Rodriquez**
Nuevo Latino
Rodriguez started the upscale Latino craze in New York with his exotic and startling dishes. Warning: these are delicious, but labor-intensive plated dishes
0-89815-752-8 TEN SPEED $27.95

Anne **Rosenzweig**
The Arcadia Seasonal Mural and Cookbook
Recipes by the founder of New York's Arcadia restaurant
0-8109-1843-9 ABRAMS $14.95

Debbie **Shore** & others
Home Food: 44 Great American Chefs Cook 160 Recipes on Their Night Off
Menus and interviews give the reader a personal look at the chef outside the spotlight. These chefs don't slack off on their days off
0-517-59778-0 CLARKSON POTTER $25.00

Andre **Soltner** & Seymour **Britchky**
The Lutece Cookbook
The long-awaited cookbook from the chef-proprietor of New York's most famous French restaurant, Lutece. Soltner delivers a singular testament to classic French cuisine: chilled sorrel soup; terrine of guinea hen with wild mushrooms; beef tenderloin in a brioche crust; and praline *Bombe*, all taught in Soltner's entertaining, experienced voice
See also **CLASSIC FRENCH CUISINE** under **FRENCH COOKERY**
0-679-42273-0 KNOPF $35.00

Joachim **Splichal**
Patina Cookbook
Recipes and photos take the reader through a day in the life of a chef
0-00-255474-7 COLLINS SAN FRANCISCO $27.00

Charlie **Trotter**
Charlie Trotter's Vegetables
Not for the hesitant; this is complicated, involved food that will pay you back in gustatory and visual delight
0-89815-628-9 TEN SPEED $50.00

Jean-George **Vongerichten**
Simple Cuisine
Vongerichten pioneered the use of essences and infusions; here he will share his secrets and some inspirations too
0-02-860991-3 MACMILLAN PB $16.00

Alice **Waters**
The Chez Panisse Menu Cookbook
One of the most influential American cookbooks, this classic has profoundly changed the way

Americans cook and eat. The superb recipes, mingling the flavors and techniques of Provence and California, have inspired countless cooks, both professional and amateur. Not for beginners but essential for amateurs and professionals

0-394-51787-3 RANDOM HOUSE $26.00
0-679-75818-6 RANDOM HOUSE PB $16.00

Roy **Yamaguchi** & John **Harrisson**

Roy's Feasts from Hawaii

Yamaguchi adds innovation to Hawaii's already vibrant and brilliantly flavored cuisine

0-89815-637-8 TEN SPEED $27.95

French Cookery

Henri **De Toulouse-Lautrec** & Maurice **Joyant**

The Art of Cuisine: The Inventive Cooking of Toulouse-Lautrec

0-8050-4110-9 HOLT $35.00

Pierre **Franey** & others

A Chef's Tale: A Memoir of Food, France and America

Franey writes of growing up in Burgundy and of his classical education in cooking—eventually becoming the top chef at Le Pavillon and La Cote Basque—two of the most famous French restaurants in America. Includes 100 classic and modern French recipes

0-394-58600-X KNOPF $25.00

Robert **Freson**

The Taste of France

A picture book with recipes, capturing the quintessence of France and its cuisine. Exceptional photos

1-55670-369-4 STEWART, TABORI PB $24.95

Ermine **Herscher**

Picasso Bon Vivant

140 drawings and photographs surround the regional recipes the artist enjoyed

0-8478-1969-8 RIZZOLI $35.00

Shirley **King**

Pampille's Table: Recipes and Writings from the French Countryside

A mouthwatering and highly entertaining translation and adaption of Marthe Daudet's 1919 classic *Les Bons Plats de France.* Do try the savoy cake

0-571-19889-9 FABER $24.95

Waverley **Root**

The Food of France

Not a cookbook but an essential background to French gastronomy

0-679-73897-5 VINTAGE PB $14.00

Jeanne **Strang**

Goose Fat and Garlic

A mouth-watering selection of recipes from Southwest France

1-85626-120-4 TRAFALGAR SQUARE PB $16.95

Patricia **Wells**

Bistro Cooking

A selection of mouth-watering home-style French dishes assembled by a former *New York Times* food writer. Included are hearty recipes for rabbit, potatoes au gratin, varied terrines, and fruit tarts—which make one eager to go to France. This is the everyday fare found in the local restaurants, not the more elaborate creations of the master chefs of the grand establishments

0-89480-622-X WORKMAN $22.95
0-89480-623-8 WORKMAN PB $12.95

Patricia Wells at Home in Provence: Recipes Inspired by Her Farmhouse in France

A delicious invitation that's much more affordable than her courses

0-684-81569-9 SCRIBNERS $40.00

Patricia **Wells** & Joel **Robuchon**

Simply French

0-688-14356-3 HEARST PB $20.00

Classic French Cuisine

Auguste **Escoffier**

Escoffier: A Complete Guide to Modern Cooking

A translation of *Le Guide Culinaire*, this is the classic guide to French haute cuisine

0-517-50662-9 CROWN $16.00

Andre **Soltner** & Seymour **Britchky**

The Lutece Cookbook

See also **AMERICAN CHEFS** under **AMERICAN COOKERY**

0-679-42273-0 KNOPF $35.00

Famous French Chefs

Joel **Robuchon** & Nicholas **Rabaudy**

Joel Robuchon Cooking Through the Seasons

0-8478-1899-3 RIZZOLI $40.00

Alain **Senderens** & Eventhia **Senderens**

The Three-Star Recipes of Alain Senderens

Fine fish and shellfish recipes, among many others, from the master chef of the renowned Parisian restaurants L'Archestrate and Lucas Carton. Try the roast lobster with vanilla butter sauce and the mixed fried dinner with garlic mayonnaise. Not for the beginner

0-688-06668-2 MORROW PB $3.98

Roger **Verge** & Martine **Anglade**

Roger Verge's Vegetables

Gorgeously photographed and presented in an oversized format, these recipes could turn even an avowed vegetable hater into a fan

1-88518-304-6 ARTISAN $35.00

French Cooking Lessons

Julia **Child**

Mastering the Art of French Cooking

Volume 1

The classic preparations, including clear instructions, drawings, and superb recipes. The French basics adapted to the American kitchen

0-394-53399-2 RANDOM HOUSE $50.00
0-394-72178-0 RANDOM HOUSE PB $30.00

Volume 2

An extraordinary book, particularly the chapters on pastry. Recommended for the accomplished cook

0-394-72177-2 RANDOM HOUSE PB $25.00

Madeleine **Kamman**

In Madeleine's Kitchen

Recipes from a gifted and opinionated professional with unwavering standards

INTRODUCTION BY JAMES BEARD

0-02-009745-X MACMILLAN PB $19.95

Madeleine Cooks

From her television series; very French, with straightforward, basic recipes

0-688-06203-2 MORROW $22.95

When French Women Cook: A Gastronomic Memoir

A tour of eight regions of France

0-689-70620-0 MACMILLAN PB $16.00

Italian Cookery

Pellegrino **Artusi**

The Art of Eating Well

A brand-new translation of the classic that first appeared in Italy in 1891. While the translation retains Artusi's voice, the translator's annotations make the recipes accessible to today's cook

See also ITALY under **WINE AND BEVERAGES**

0-679-43056-3 RANDOM HOUSE $25.00

Anne **Bianchi**

From the Tables of Tuscan Women

An inviting selection of recipes from Lucca accompanied by portraits of Zacchesians

0-88001-425-3 ECCO $26.00

Zuppa! Soups from the Italian Countryside

0-88001-513-6 ECCO $25.00

Giuliano **Bugialli**

The Fine Art of Italian Cooking

A classic reference

0-8129-1838-X TIME BOOKS $27.00

Giuliano Bugialli's Classic Techniques of Italian Cooking

A well researched and fascinating collection of recipes

0-671-69069-8 FIRESIDE PB $22.00

Giuliano Bugialli's Foods of Italy
The splendor of Italian cooking, with striking color photographs. Expensive but worth it for the many original and well presented recipes
0-941434-52-4 STEWART, TABORI $50.00
1-55670-370-8 STEWART, TABORI PB $24.95

Giuliano Bugialli's Foods of Tuscany
1-55670-200-0 STEWART, TABORI $50.00

Guiliano **Bugialli**
The Foods of Sicily and Sardinia and the Smaller Islands
Lamb with saffron and artichokes, tuna in vinegar sauce, and jasmine gelato are just a tiny fraction of the tempting dishes from this region
0-8478-1924-8 RIZZOLI $50.00

Arrigo **Cipriani**
The Harry's Bar Cookbook
Cipriani, son of the restaurant's founder, shares his favorite reminiscenses about and recipes originated by the expatriate's care that counted the Windsors and Hemingway among its patrons. From the famed fresh peach and champagne Bellini cocktail to delicate, paper-thin beef carpaccio and elegant risotto Primavera, all Harry's Bar innovations, the more than 200 recipes in this book reveal the secrets that kept the customers satisfied
0-553-07030-4 BDD $40.00

Elizabeth **David**
Italian Food
This handsome volume, with remarkable color plates, celebrates Italy and Italian cooking. Reading the text is almost like going on the journey itself
0-7651-9651-4 SMITHMARK $19.98

Julia **della Croce**
Antipasti: The Little Dishes of Italy
The widely read author of *Pasta Classica* turns her attention to the classic, unparalleled appetizers of northern Italy, recipes that are increasingly served as side dishes or meals in themselves. Porcini mushrooms, roasted peppers, black olives, Tuscan style shrimp, and prosciutto: these are simple foods whose delectability relies on the traditional quality of their ingredients
0-8118-0218-3 CHRONICLE PB $18.95

Iliria Gozzini **Giacosa**
A Taste of Ancient Rome
The dishes Romans ate—and sometimes still do—from a Rustic Barley Soup with Ham to Truffles in Herbed Vinaigrette. Includes a guide to preserving fruits and vegetables, and a history of Roman eating, drinking, and entertaining. "More than just a cookbook [this book] is a fascinating portrait of everyday life in ancient Rome"—*Il tempo*
0-226-29030-1 CHICAGO PB $29.95

Marcella **Hazan**
Essentials of Italian Cooking
A compilation of Hazan's *The Classic Italian Cookbook* and *More Classic Italian Cooking,* widely considered the finest of Italian cookbooks, in a single volume. Now Hazan has rewritten each recipe, greatly reducing reliance on cooking fats and emphasizing the simple, natural tastes of ingredients. "Marcella Hazan is synonymous with Italian cusine"—James Beard
0-394-58404-X KNOPF $30.00

Marcella's Italian Kitchen
"Of all Marcella Hazan's marvelous books, this may be the best—personal, elegant, inventive, flavorful"—Barbara Kafka
0-679-76437-2 KNOPF PB $19.95

Vianna **LaPlace** & Evan **Kleiman**
Cucina Fresca
225 simple delicious recipes to serve cold or at room temperature
0-06-096211-9 HARPERCOLLINS PB $16.00

Cucina Rustica
0-688-07764-1 MORROW $23.00

Pasta Fresca
0-688-07763-3 MORROW $19.95

Pino **Luongo** & others
A Tuscan in the Kitchen: Recipes and Tales from My Home
With stories of the Tuscan countryside intermixed with recipes of the simple and robust foods characteristic of the region. The recipes leave out measurements, oven temperatures, and most directions—he believes that cooking is a creative process and encourages experimentation. The photographs of Tuscany add to an already superb experience
0-517-56916-7 CLARKSON POTTER $24.95

Fred **Plotkin**
Italy for the Gourmet Traveller
So filled with information it needs its own carry-on bag
0-316-71070-9 LITTLE, BROWN PB $19.95

Ruth **Rogers** & Rose **Gray**
The Rogers and Gray Italian Country Cookbook
Nineteen weeks on the *Times(London)* bestseller list, this is "the culinary bible for a new generation of cooks." The Independent credited it with "raising Italian home cooking to an art form," while The Guardian described it as "a forerunner in introducing the most authentic and best Italian food in London." Delightful and simple recipes using only a few straightforward ingredients and resulting in original and authentic dishes
0-679-45001-7 RANDOM HOUSE $40.00

Waverley **Root**
The Food of Italy
A cultural history of Italian cooking that remains unequaled
0-679-73896-7 VINTAGE PB $16.00

Catherine **Scorsese** & Georgia **Downard**
Italianamerican: The Scorcese Family Cookbook
0-679-44282-0 RANDOM HOUSE $20.00

Richard Camillo **Sidoli**
The Cooking of Parma
Rustic mixes with refined in this survey of the cuisines of the city of Parma and the surrounding mountains
0-8478-1926-4 RIZZOLI $30.00

The Strawpaper Press
Authentic Italian Kitchen: Pasta
A whimsical-looking book fashioned after the out-of-print Im Bocca series and filled with unusual, mouth-watering recipes
0-9642027-1-9 INDT PUBLISHERS GROUP $15.95
0-9642027-0-0 INDT PUBLISHERS GROUP $17.95

Ann **Taruschio** & Franco **Taruschio**
Bruschetta
1-85793-474-1 ABBEVILLE $24.95
0-7892-0096-1 ABBEVILLE $17.95

Faith **Willinger**
Red, White and Greens: The Italian Way with Vegetables
0-06-018366-7 HARPERCOLLINS $25.00

British and Irish Cookery

Alison **Armstrong**
The Joyce of Cooking
"This is a joyous book celebrating the best of Irish cooking. Food's an essential part of [James] Joyce's writing, which has enabled Armstrong to write a strong new cookbook, with heat and intelligence, using quotes from his work"—Shirley King
0-930794-85-0 STATION HILL $18.95

Paul **Rankin** & Jeanne **Rankin**
Gourmet Ireland
This Michelin-starred team demonstrates that there is much more to Irish cuisine than tea and soda bread
1-56426-073-9 COLE PB $17.95

C. Anne **Wilson**
Food & Drink in Britain: From the Stone Age to the 19th-century
A history of British cuisine written by one of England's foremost culinary historians
0-89733-364-0 ACADEMY CHICAGO $25.00

Mediterranean and Middle Eastern Cookery

Ayla **Algar**
Classical Turkish Cooking: Traditional Turkish Food for the American Kitchen
These savory, piquant and delicately sweet recipes from the cuisine of Turkey retain all the flavor and variety of the region's ancient culinary tradition, but have been adapted for preparation with ingredients readily available in North America. The dishes described include a magnificent green olive, walnut, and pomegranate salad; elegant quince dolmas with cinnamon sauce; trout stuffed with pine nuts, currants, herbs and sweet spices; and rose petal, violet, and almond sherbets
0-06-016317-8 HARPERCOLLINS $32.00

Batmanglij
New Food of Life
Ancient Persian and modern Iranian cooking and ceremonies
0-934211-34-5 MAGE $44.95

Persian Cooking for a Healthy Kitchen
0-934211-40-X MAGE $32.50

Anissa **Helou**
Lebanese Cuisine
A comprehensive collection of authentic Lebanese recipes—stews, kebabs, yoghurt dishes—the first available in English
0-312-13111-9 ST. MARTIN'S $22.95

Aglaia **Kremezi**
Foods of Greece
This over-sized volume is filled with glossy photographs and recipes that wil transport you to the Mediterranean
1-55670-204-3 STEWART, TABORI $50.00

Gulseren **Ramazanoglu**
Turkish Cooking
975-7489-05-0 BOSPHORUS PB $14.95

Claudia **Roden**
A Book of Middle Eastern Food
0-394-71948-4 VINTAGE PB $16.00

Sonia **Uvezian**
Cuisine of Armenia
Back in print after many years, this is still the definitive guide
0-7818-0417-5 HIPPOCRENE PB $14.95

Paula **Wolfert**
The Cooking of the Eastern Mediterranean: 215 Healthy, Vibrant, and Inspired Recipes
"Wolfert...is blessed with a passion for food, an unerring eye and palate and an enviable ability to transport her reader to the ends of the earth"—Jean Anderson, *Food & Wine Magazine*
0-06-016651-7 HARPERCOLLINS $30.00

Couscous and Other Good Food from Morocco
Don't miss the lamb tagine with raisins, almonds, and honey
0-06-091396-7 HARPERCOLLINS PB $17.00

Mostly Mediterranean
Previously published as *Paula Wolfert's World of Food*
0-14-025769-1 PENGUIN PB $16.95

Other European Cookery

Jean **Anderson**
The Food of Portugal
The author has spent a lifetime learning about Portugal; this is the definitive work
0-688-04363-1 MORROW $24.95
0-688-13415-7 MORROW PB $15.00

Penelope **Casas**
Delicioso!: The Regional Cooking of Spain
Covering seven culinary regions of Spain, Casas offers over 400 carefully planned recipes. Pepper and eggplant pie from Navarra. Cocido from the central plains. Squid-ink paella from the southeastern coast. Mojos from the Canary Islands. The perfect book for newcomers and aficionados of Spanish cooking alike
0-679-43055-5 KNOPF $30.00

Foods and Wines of Spain
A fascinating cookbook by an expert cook and scholar. Note the white gazpacho recipe and chicken in a sauce of chorizo and red wine
0-394-51348-7 RANDOM HOUSE $30.00

Mari **Kaneva-Johnson**
The Melting Pot: Balkan Food and Cookery
0-907325-57-2 READER'S CATALOG $35.00

Alicia **Rios** & Lourdes **March**
The Heritage of Spanish Cooking
Like Heritage of Italian Cooking and *The Heritage of French Cooking,* this book is both a collection of authentic recipes and a culinary history. It draws on historical menus and sources to portray Spanish cooking's evolution, and includes Moorish and Jewish recipes and many regional specialties. Period illustrations and photographs of each dish
0-517-16544-9 RANDOM HOUSE $19.99
0-679-41628-5 RANDOM HOUSE $45.00

Carol **Robertson**
Turkish Cooking: A Journey Through Turkey
Culled from her extensive travels throughout Turkey, Robertson offers 85 recipes from one of the most aesthetically complex, practically simple, and gustatorily satisfying cuisines of the world. From the mainstay of the Turkish meal, hors d'oeuvres such as fried mussels and stuffed grape leaves, to entrees, like raki shrimp with feta cheese, and traditional desserts, such as baklava, this is a splendid addition to any kitchen
PHOTOGRAPHS BY DAVID ROBERTSON
1-88331-938-2 NORTH ATLANTIC $24.95

Mimi **Sheraton**
German Cookbook
The basic book for German cuisine
0-394-40138-7 RANDOM HOUSE $29.95

Joyce **Toomre**
Classic Russian Cooking: Elena Molokhovet's A Gift to Young Housewives
0-253-36026-9 INDIANA $39.95

Anne **Volokh** & Mavis **Manus**
The Art of Russian Cuisine
From pirogi to baking powder and buckwheat blini. The standard work, comprehensive and exciting
0-02-038102-6 MACMILLAN PB $16.95

Ruth Van **Waerebeck**
Everybody Eats Well in Belgium
0-7611-0106-3 WORKMAN $24.95
1-56305-411-6 WORKMAN PB $14.95

Kosher

Cara **DeSilva**, editor
The Women of Terezin
An amazing compilation of recipes written from memories in the concentration camps of Terezin, this is "a cookbook from hell. But it is also a book of hope, for it shows in its wan way how human beings can morally bear the worst treatment ever imagined"
1-56821-902-4 ARONSON $24.00

Anne **London** & Bertha Kahn **Bishor**
The Complete American Jewish Cookbook
Over 3500 tested kosher recipes, with chapters on holiday and modern Jewish cooking
0-06-091590-0 HARPERCOLLINS PB $18.00

Gil **Marks**
The World of Jewish Cooking: More Than 500 Traditional Recipes from Alsace to Yemen
The former editor of Kosher Gourmet Magazine has compiled kosher festive and everyday recipes from 24 communities around the world
0-684-82491-4 SIMON & SCHUSTER $30.00

Helen **Nash**
Helen Nash's Kosher Kitchen
An up-to-date approach, with lighter variations on traditional dishes
0-394-57026-X RANDOM HOUSE $25.00

Joan **Nathan**
The Jewish Holiday Kitchen
Almost 200 recipes from the US, Israel, and elsewhere for the Sabbath, holidays, weddings, and other special occasions
0-8052-0900-X SCHOCKEN PB $20.00

Claudia **Roden**
A Book of Jewish Food: An Odyssey from Samarkland to New York
Describes the development of both Ashkenazic and Sephardic Jewish communities through recipes from around the world. Meticulously researched by a highly-respected scholar, this will become a classic
0-394-53258-9 KNOPF $35.00

Evelyn **Rose**
The New Complete International Jewish Cookbook
An encyclopedic celebration of Jewish home cooking. Includes a section on how to prepare for Passover and the Seder meals, and informative chapters on Jewish festivals and their food
0-679-74460-6 CROWN PB $19.00

Raymond **Sokolov**
The Jewish-American Kitchen
RECIPES BY SUSAN R. FRIEDLAND
0-517-08913-0 OUTLET $19.99
1-55670-096-2 STEWART, TABORI $30.00

Robert **Sternberg**

The Sephardic Kitchen: The Healthy Food and Rich Culture of the Mediterranean Jews

Filled with fresh, flavorful, vegetable-full recipes and interlaced with a fascinating collection of anecdotes and history, this both will appeal to historians as well as cooks who are looking to expand their repetoire with lighter dishes

0-06-017691-1 HARPERCOLLINS $30.00

African Cookery

Hildegonda J. **Duckitt**

Traditional South African Cookery

Traditional recipes, both British and Dutch-inspired, from colonial Africa

0-7818-0490-6 HIPPOCRENE $10.95

Jessica B. **Harris**

The Welcome Table: African-American Heritage Cooking

0-671-79360-8 SIMON & SCHUSTER $24.00

Daniel **Mesfin**

Exotic Ethiopian Cooking

0-9616345-2-9 ETHIOPIAN COOKBOOK PB $15.99

Asian Cookery

Jennifer **Brennan**

The Cuisines of Asia

A very useful introduction to the cuisines of China, India, Indonesia, Japan, Korea, Malaysia and Singapore, the Philippines, Thailand, and Vietnam

0-312-03977-8 ST. MARTIN'S PB $15.95

Copeland **Marks** & Aung **Thein**

The Burmese Kitchen

0-87131-768-0 EVANS PB $12.95

Jacki **Passamore**

Lett's Companion to Asian Food and Cooking

Not a cookbook but an extraordinary detailed and illustrated guide to Asian ingredients and techniques

1-85238-151-5 READER'S CATALOG $27.50

The Noodle Shop Cookbook

150 fun recipes that incorporate a wide variety of Asian noodles and flavorings

0-02-594705-2 MACMILLAN $25.00

Rosa Lo San **Ross**

Beyond Bok Choy

Well-illustrated and expertly described, this book will guide you through your nearest Asian market

1-88518-323-2 ARTISAN $25.00

China

Eileen Yin-Fei **Lo**

The Dim Sum Dumpling Book

Chinese dumplings, buns, rolls and dipping sauces

0-02-090295-6 MACMILLAN PB $15.00

From the Earth: Chinese Vegetarian Cooking

"This passionate guide will turn even an Argentine gaucho into a kitchen-Buddhist" —George Lang

0-02-632985-9 MACMILLAN $25.00

Nina **Simonds**

China Express

Simonds *(Chinese Seasons, China's Food)* is on a crusade to create a lexicon of recipes for the Westerner who can't afford the shopping and preparing time required for traditional Chinese dishes. She has succeeded brilliantly, instructing us in the making of pan-fried noodles, sweet and sour shrimp, braised game hens, and steamed lemon cake without having to venture beyond our local markets. "Simonds just might put Chinese takeout out of business" *—Publishers Weekly*

0-688-11478-4 MORROW $25.00

Classic Chinese Cuisine

Splendid recipes, not for the beginner, from a young but accomplished American student of Chinese cooking

1-88152-731-X CHAPTERS $29.95

1-88152-732-8 CHAPTERS PB $19.95

Barbara **Tropp**

The Modern Art of Chinese Cooking

The first-rate recipes and information on substitutes, storing, and even wines make this essential

0-688-14611-2 HEARST PB $17.95

Japan

Kinjiro **Omae** & Yuzuru **Tachibana**

The Book of Sushi

FOREWORD BY JEAN-PIERRE RAMPAL

4-7700-1954-8 KODANSHA PB $9.95

Shizuo **Tsuji**

Japanese Cooking: A Simple Art

The intricacies of Japanese cooking with detailed illustrations

INTRODUCTION BY M.F.K. FISHER

0-87011-399-2 KODANSHA $40.00

Practical Japanese Cooking Easy & Elegant

0-87011-762-9 KODANSHA $35.00

Eri **Yamaguchi**

The Well-Flavored Vegetable: New and Traditional Japanese Methods of Preparing Vegetables

Ways to prepare vegetables without cooking: pickling, marinating and so forth

0-87011-861-7 KODANSHA $17.95

India

Yamuna **Devi**

Lord Krishna's Cuisine: The Art of Indian Vegetarian Cooking

0-525-24564-2 DUTTON $35.00

Yamuna's Table: Healthful Vegetarian Cuisine Inspired by the Flavors of India

Devi's *Lord Krishna's Cuisine* is the number-one guide to authentic Indian foods. Her new book adapts Indian flavors and techniques to such low-fat and easy recipes as chilled avocado bisque with tangerine cream, and roast potato salad with cilantro, mustard seed, lemon juice, and pistachios. "Many cross-cultural cuisines seem arbitrary; Devi's is both well-grounded and inspired"*—Kirkus Reviews*

0-525-93487-1 DUTTON $23.00

Madhur **Jaffrey**

Indian Cookery

First published to accompany Jaffrey's BBC series, these recipes, with color photographs, are authentic and easy to prepare

0-8120-2700-0 BARRONS PB $14.95

An Invitation to Indian Cooking

One of the best guides to Indian cooking

0-394-71191-2 VINTAGE PB $12.00

Madhur Jaffrey's Spice Kitchen: Fifty Recipes Introducing Indian Spices and Aromatic Seeds

Jaffrey has introduced thousands of Americans to the easy, delicious, inexpensive and low-fat Indian cuisine. Her new book takes the mystery out of distinctive Indian seasonings, teaching the use of cardamom pods, fenugreek, coriander, cumin seeds, and other essential spices. A pleasure to read and to cook with

0-517-59698-9 RANDOM HOUSE $15.00

Chandra **Padmanabhan**

Dakshin: Vegetarian Cuisine form South India: An Earthly Delight Cookbook

0-207-18477-1 HARPERCOLLINS $26.00

Camellia **Panjabi**

The Great Curries of India

This exotic collection of recipes covers all the regions of India centering on the mainstay of the Indian meal, the curry. Fifty authentic regional recipes guide you from the basics of curry making to the finished, elegant product in easy-to-follow steps. "I shall be very surprised if your copy of this astonishing book is not very soon covered in gravy stains from repeated use—happy souvenirs of glorious meals cooked from it and eaten with abandon and relish" —Paul Levy

0-684-80383-6 SIMON & SCHUSTER $30.00

Julie **Sahni**

Classic Indian Cooking

A sensitive approach with particularly clear text

0-688-03721-6 MORROW $25.00

Classic Indian Vegetarian and Grain Cooking
Intelligent and expert. Try the stuffed cauliflower with tart tomato-coriander sauce, carrot salad with peanuts and mustard seeds, and tandoor bread
0-688-04995-8 MORROW $25.00

Southeast Asia

Reynaldo **Alejandro**
The Philippine Cookbook
A useful book on this lesser-known cuisine. Don't miss the ginger tea recipe
0-399-51144-X PERIGEE PB $13.95

Jennifer **Brennan**
The Original Thai Cookbook
In addition to fabulous recipes, Brennan spices the text up with culture, customs, anecdotes and history and provides a pronunciation guide and ingredient glossary
0-399-51033-8 PERIGEE PB $13.00

Binh **Duong** & Marcia **Kisel**
Simple Art of Vietnamese Cooking
Vietnamese food has been called a hybrid of the best of Chinese and French cuisine: delicate in its textures, provocative in its flavors, yet composed of surprisingly simple ingredients. This long-overdue introduction to the pleasures of Vietnamese cooking features more than 150 recipes including coral lobster, sweet potato nests with shrimp, and the ever-popular beef-based Hanoi soup
0-13-812124-9 SIMON & SCHUSTER $30.00

Marc **Millon**
Flavours of Korea: Stories and Recipes from a Korean Grandmother's Kitchen
A tour with recipes
0-233-98635-9 ANDRE DEUTSCH PB $17.95

Sri **Owen**
Indonesian Regional Cooking
0-312-11832-5 ST. MARTIN'S $18.95

Carol Slevah **Rajah**
Makan-Lah!: The Fine Art of Malay Cuisine
Nonya, Chinese, Indian, and Colonial influences have been incorporated into traditional Malaysian cooking to create a fascinating, mouth-watering world of tastes. This book will open that world to you
0-207-18717-7 HARPERCOLLINS $27.00

Nicole **Routhier**
The Foods of Vietnam
PHOTOGRAPHS BY MARTIN JACOBS
1-55670-095-4 STEWART, TABORI $40.00

Puangkram **Schmitz** & Michael **Worman**
Practical Thai Cooking
0-87011-727-0 KODANSHA $25.00

Latin American and Caribbean Cookery

Christopher **Idone**
Brazil: A Cook's Tour
Not only a cookbook but a photographic journey and hand travel guide, with listings of markets, restaurants, shops and lodging
0-517-59555-9 CLARKSON POTTER $30.00

Maria Josefa Lluria De **O'Higgins**
A Taste of Old Cuba: More Than 150 Recipes for Delicious, Authentic, and Traditional Dishes
Pre-Castro memories and traditional cuisine
0-06-016964-8 HARPERCOLLINS $25.00

Elisabeth Lambert **Ortiz**
The Complete Book of Caribbean Cooking
Some simple recipes, some exotic—all easy to prepare
0-345-33256-3 BALLANTINE PB $5.95

Felipe **Rojas-Lombardi**
The Art of South American Cooking
A comprehensive guide to the best of Latin cuisine, by a chef of international renown. Includes recipes for honey-fried rabbit, butterflied leg of lamb with cilantro, hazelnut and lemon "manna" cookies, and a garlic, ginger, and malagueta pepper-spiced Brazilian chicken soup. "Chef Felipe is without question one of the most creative chefs in this country. He is a genius with inspiration"—Craig Claiborne
0-06-016425-5 HARPERCOLLINS $32.50

Caroline **Sullivan**
Classic Jamaican Cooking: Traditional Recipes and Herbal Remedies
1-89795-915-X INBOOK PB $14.95

Mexico

Rick **Bayless**
Rick Bayless's Mexican Kitchen
Bayless is not only an award-winning chef, but a widely-respected authority on Mexican food and foodways. In this second book, he will walk you through ingredients and techniques as he teaches you over 200 dishes
0-684-80006-3 SCRIBNERS $35.00

Rick **Bayless** & Deanne **Bayless**
Authentic Mexican: Regional Cooking from the Heart of Mexico
A splendid compendium of information and recipes, such as cold chicken and avocado with chile chipotle, minced pork with almonds, raisins and sweet spices, and Mexican tomato-colored rice with vegetables
0-688-04394-1 MORROW $27.50

Reed **Hearon**
Bocaditos: The Little Dishes of Mexico
"Little mouthfuls" of explosive flavor and tantalizing textures can enliven a party or just perk up snack time
0-8118-1009-7 CHRONICLE PB $14.95

Diana **Kennedy**
The Art of Mexican Cooking
An adventurous new book from the authority on Mexican cuisine, which explains the right ingredients and techniques for the most popular foods, from simple to sophisticated. Included are more than 200 recipes, with 100 how-to photographs, for such items as black soup, coffee-flavored flan, and an array of sauces
PHOTOGRAPHS BY MICHAEL CALDERWOOD
0-553-05706-5 BDD $24.95

The Cuisines of Mexico
The definitive work
FOREWORD BY CRAIG CLAIBORNE
0-06-091561-7 HARPERCOLLINS PB $20.00

Mexican Regional Cooking
An unsurpassable collection
0-06-092069-6 HARPERCOLLINS PB $20.00

The Tortilla Book, Revised Edition
0-06-092124-2 HARPERPERENNIAL PB $15.00

Guadalupe **Rivera** & Marie-Pierre **Kolle**
Frida's Fiestas: Recipes and Recollections of Life with Frida Kahlo
The rich and full life of the celebrated Mexican artist Kahlo is illustrated by her stepdaughter in a memoir organized around the 12 culinary celebrations of the artist's year. From the anniversary of her marriage to Diego Rivera to the Day of the Dead, this wonderful book takes us from chiles stuffed with picadillo to chicken in pipian sauce, introducing a world of festive Mexican cuisine through the life of the artist
0-517-59235-5 CLARKSON POTTER $35.00

Baking

Elizabeth **Alston**
Biscuits and Scones: 72 Recipes-From Breakfast Biscuits to Homey Desserts
Homey, delicious items, including ham or smoked-turkey biscuits and zesty gingerbread scones
See also BREAKFAST AND TEA FOOD
0-517-56345-2 CLARKSON POTTER $11.00

Muffins: 60 Sweet and Savory Recipes from Old Favorites to New
A pretty, pocket-size collection of such treats as nutmeg and sticky pecan muffins and a wonderful blueberry muffin recipe
See also BREAKFAST AND TEA FOOD
0-517-55587-5 CROWN $11.00

Marion **Cunningham**
The Fannie Farmer Baking Book
American baking at its best. Her kind voice will walk you through every step to insure success every time
0-517-14829-3 RANDOM HOUSE $12.99

Linda **Dannenberg**
Paris Boulangerie-Patisserie: Recipes from Thirteen Outstanding French Bakeries
Like the cafe, the French bakery/pastry shop defines both the diet and aesthetic of that food-loving country. Here, a gastronomic tour of the finest exemplars of Gallic baking provides a cornucopia of treats. Dozens of practical recipes, 150 full-color photographs, and sugar-high recipes for such delicacies as *mousse au caramel et aux poires* and *croissants aux amandes*
PHOTOGRAPHS BY GUY BOUCHET
0-517-59221-5 CLARKSON POTTER $35.00

Jim **Fobel**
The Old-Fashioned Baking Book
Finally back in print; this collection of traditional American recipes is gladly welcomed back
0-9627403-6-5 LAKE ISLE PB $14.95

Dorie **Greenspan**
Baking With Julia Child
Based on the PBS Series Hosted by Julia Child
0-688-14657-0 MORROW $40.00

Nick **Malgieri**
How to Bake
An highly-respected pastry teacher, Malgieri has a gift for giving clear and concise instructions, guaranteeing your success in the kitchen
0-06-016819-6 HARPERCOLLINS $35.00

Breads

Jeffrey **Alford** & Naomi **Duguid**
Flatbreads and Flavors
"A stunning book that takes us on an enthralling journey to extraordinary places. On the way we find a mass of precious information to collectors of truly delectable recipes"—Clandra Rodez
0-688-11411-3 MORROW $30.00

Jerome **Assire**
The Book of Bread
Extravagantly photographed tour of breads of the world
FOREWORD BY RAYMOND CALVEL
2-08-013625-9 ABBEVILLE $45.00
2-08-013533-3 ABBEVILLE $55.00

James **Beard**
Beard on Bread
One of the first books on the pleasures of baking bread, and still one of the best. Accessible, detailed recipes, with magnificent line drawings. The monkey bread recipe alone is worth the price
0-345-29550-1 BALLANTINE PB $5.99

James Beard

Edward Espe **Brown**
The Tassajara Bread Book
Revised and updated and still very good
0-394-74196-X SHAMBHALA PB $10.00

Bernard **Clayton**, Jr.
The New Complete Book of Breads
An exhaustive compendium of yeasted bread recipes from around the world
0-671-60222-5 SIMON & SCHUSTER $30.00

Elizabeth **David** & Wendy **Jones**
English Bread and Yeast Cookery
Revered food writer Elizabeth David embarks on a scholarly study of the history of bread and gives over 200 recipes
0-9643600-0-4 NATL BOOK NETWORK $25.00

Carol **Field**
Focaccia
An in-depth look at this wildly popular flatbread
0-8118-0854-8 CHRONICLE $22.95
0-8118-0604-9 CHRONICLE PB $14.95

Beth **Hensperger** & Joyce Oudkerk **Pool** (Pht)
The Art of Quick Breads: Simple Everyday Baking
Sweet or savory, from perfect buttermilk biscuits to a marbled chestnut sour cream coffeecake, Hensperger has a recipe for every occassion. Excellent directions and source list
0-8118-0353-8 CHRONICLE PB $18.95

Daniel **Leader** & Judith **Blahnik**
Bread Alone
Two purists of the hearth—one a renowned baker of Woodstock, New York—serve up 88 rich, ancient recipes for the flavorful loaves of life. Their sourdough is guaranteed to succeed, and people have been known to drive 50 miles for their health loaf which you can now bake yourself
0-688-09261-6 MORROW $25.00

Marilyn **Moore**
The Wooden Spoon Bread Book: The Secrets of Successful Baking
A friendly collection of simpler loaves, muffins, and doughnuts. Note the lovely and unusual sourdough doughnuts
0-87113-505-1 ATLANTIC MONTHLY PB $15.00
0-87113-150-1 ATLANTIC MONTHLY PB $19.95

Joe **Ortiz**
The Village Baker
Regional European and American breads adapted for the home baker by the bread baker of Gayle's Bakery in Capitola, CA
0-89815-489-8 TEN SPEED $27.95

Laurel **Robertson**
The Laurel's Kitchen Bread Book: A Guide to Whole-Grain Breadmaking
Only whole grains. Try the buttermilk whole wheat and herb cottage loaf
0-394-72434-8 RANDOM HOUSE PB $21.00

Amy **Scherber** & Toy Kim **Dupree**
Amy's Bread
Artisanal breads modified for the home baker
0-688-12401-1 MORROW $23.00

Nancy **Silverton**
Breads from the La Brea Bakery
Breads for the serious home baker or artisinal bread professional
0-679-40907-6 VILLARD $30.00

Ed **Wood**
World Sourdoughs from Antiquity
A history of sourdough from around the world from a forensic pathologist who's been studying them for over 50 years. Includes over 85 recipes
0-89815-843-5 TEN SPEED PB $16.95

Grains

Brigit Legere **Binns**
Polenta
Cornmeal mush taken to gustatory heights
0-8118-1185-9 CHRONICLE PB $14.95

Kevin **Graham**
Grains, Rice, and Beans
1-88518-308-9 ARTISAN $30.00

Bert **Greene**
The Grains Cookbook
Greene's usual outstanding collection of recipes filled with his amusing and reassuring commentary
0-89480-612-2 WORKMAN PB $15.95

Sri **Owen**
The Rice Book
An in-depth look at the history and uses of rice around the world, with particular emphasis on Southeast Asia and plenty of adventurous recipes
0-312-10532-0 ST. MARTIN'S $24.95
0-312-14132-7 ST. MARTIN'S PB $15.95

Barbecue

Jane **Butel**

Finger Lickin', Rib Stickin' Great Tastin' Hot and Spicy Barbecue

What more can we say?

0-89480-208-9 WORKMAN PB........$6.95

Chris **Schlesinger** & John **Willoughby**

The Thrill of the Grill: Techniques, Recipes, & Down-Home Barbecue

The definitive work on grilling, with enough recipes and ideas to last several summers

0-688-08832-5 MORROW........$25.00

Philip **Schulz**

Cooking with Fire and Smoke

0-671-73309-5 FIRESIDE PB........$12.00
0-671-55234-1 FIRESIDE PB........$17.95

Jeanne **Voltz**

Barbecued Ribs and Other Great Feeds

The last word on barbecue: ribs, steaks, chicken, and many other combinations; interesting and fun

0-394-73487-4 KNOPF........$11.95

Breakfast and Tea Food

Elizabeth **Alston**

Biscuits and Scones: 72 Recipes-From Breakfast Biscuits to Homey Desserts

Homey, delicious items, including ham or smoked-turkey biscuits and zesty gingerbread scones

See also **BAKING**

0-517-56345-2 CLARKSON POTTER........$11.00

Muffins: 60 Sweet and Savory Recipes from Old Favorites to New

A pretty, pocket-size collection of such treats as nutmeg and sticky pecan muffins and a wonderful blueberry muffin recipe

See also **BAKING**

0-517-55587-5 CROWN........$11.00

Carole **Manchester**

French Tea: The Pleasures of the Table

Whoever said that tea was a peculiarly English institution obviously never set foot in Paris. A former fashion consultant for *Vogue* and *Elle* describes the finest teas, gives recipes for the madeleines and macaroons that best accompany them, and throws in a guide to the best *salons de the* in France. Beautiful, elegant, and a bargain

See also **ALES AND BEERS** under **WINE AND BEVERAGES**
See also **TEA AND COFFEE** under **WINE AND BEVERAGES**

0-688-11355-9 HEARST........$17.00

Sara **Perry**

The Tea Book

The author of *The Complete Coffee Book* now presents perhaps the most complete guide to tea available. This handsome volume features 60 recipes for preparing hot and iced tea, as well as recipes for baked goods and desserts. Also includes sections on the history of tea, tea lore, preparation, and ceremonies throughout the world

See also **TEA AND COFFEE** under **WINE AND BEVERAGES**

0-8118-0336-8 CHRONICLE PB........$12.95

Lucy **Wing**

Country Mornings Cookbook

Flapjacks, red flannel hash, and a plethora of muffins and cakes for the ultimate American breakfast experience. Part of the *Country Living* series

0-688-06639-9 HEARST........$23.95

Cheese

Pierre **Androuet**

Guide to Cheeses

0-85628-240-5 ELLIS PB........$19.95

Ricki **Carroll** & Robert **Carroll**

Cheese Making Made Easy

Methods and sources to get you started

0-88266-267-8 STOREY PB........$12.95

Steven **Jenkins**

Cheese Primer

Copiously photographed and intimately described, you will know cheese better than ever before

0-89480-762-5 WORKMAN PB........$15.95

Bernard **Nantet**, editor

Cheeses of the World: An Illustrated Guide for Gourmets

This glossy oversized volume is filled with as much information as beauty

0-8478-1599-4 RIZZOLI........$45.00

Desserts

Lee **Bailey**

Lee Bailey's Country Desserts: Cakes, Cookies, Ice Creams, Pies, Puddings and More

Filled with beautiful photographs and appealing recipes. Don't miss the fresh peach cake, tangerine mousse, and pear-raspberry cobbler; and fruit combinations are only part of the selection. The cookie chapter is good, too

0-517-88444-5 CROWN PB........$16.00

The Eating Well Dessert Cookbook: 150 Recipes to Bring Dessert Back into Your Life

Fresh-tasting desserts that rely on natural ingredients rather than artificial fats and sweetners

1-88494-310-1 ARTISAN PB........$15.95

Maida **Heatter**

Heatter has gained renown among foodies as one of the greats when it comes to dessert cooking (she's Wolfgang Puck's favorite dessert chef). And while her recipes are elegant to a point just short of decadence, the clarity and thoroughness of her writing is such that even beginners can produce these culinary masterpieces with confidence. No cook's shelf should be without at least one of these volumes.

Maida Heatter's Best Dessert Book Ever

From sponge cakes and cobblers to tartlets and mousse, another cornucopia of dessert delights from the number one specialist in after-dinner treats

0-394-57832-5 RANDOM HOUSE........$24.95

Maida Heatter's Book of Great Chocolate Desserts

Temptations from this best-selling expert on desserts. The Palm Beach brownies are notoriously well-liked

0-679-76533-6 RANDOM HOUSE PB........$15.00

Maida Heatter's Book of Great Desserts

Invaluable for dessert lovers

0-679-40509-7 RANDOM HOUSE........$25.00
0-394-49111-4 RANDOM HOUSE........$25.00

Maida Heatter's Brand New Book of Great Cookies

Everything under the sun in the cookie line is covered here, from biscotti to drop cookies, meringues, fruit bars, and brownies. A staple for any sweet-toothed cook

0-679-43874-2 RANDOM HOUSE........$25.00

Emily **Luchetti**

Four-Star Desserts

The former pastry chef of Stars brings us a second volume of her casually elegant American desserts

0-06-017315-7 HARPERCOLLINS........$32.50

Stars Desserts

A cornmeal poundcake studded with jucy blackberries and a bittersweet chocolate "pudding" that is really a molten, self-saucing cake are just hints of Luchetti's genius in the kitchen

0-06-092218-4 HARPERPERENNIAL PB........$22.50

Judy **Rosenberg** & Barbara **Maslen**

Rosie's Bakery: All-Butter, Fresh Cream, Sugar-Packed Baking Book

0-89480-723-4 WORKMAN PB........$13.95

Michel **Roux**

Michel Roux's Finest Desserts

A renown chef brings us restaurant quality desserts

0-8478-1857-8 RIZZOLI........$40.00

Richard **Sax**

Classic Home Desserts

1-88152-752-2 CHAPTERS........$35.00

Lindsey Remolif **Shere**

Chez Panisse Desserts

0-394-53860-9 RANDOM HOUSE........$27.00

Lisa **Yockelson**

Cobblers, Crisps, and Deep-Dish Pies (American Baking Classics)

0-06-016749-1 HARPERCOLLINS........$15.00

Lisa **Yockelson**

Layer Cakes and Sheet Cakes (American Baking Classics)

From hurry-up sheet cakes to towering 3-layer masterpieces, Yockelson has captured the best of American cake baking in her easy to follow recipes

0-06-017195-2 HARPERCOLLINS $15.00

Lisa **Yockelson** & Wendy **Wheeler** (Ilt)

A Country Baking Treasury: Pies, Cakes, Cookies

Combines her previous books, *Country Cakes, Country Pies,* and *Country Cookies* into one volume

0-06-017296-7 HARPERCOLLINS $25.00

Cookies

Rose Levy **Beranbaum**

Rose's Christmas Cookies

Meticulous testing, recipe writing, and illustration give Berenbaum's books a reputation for being the best in their fields. These 60 recipes will take you well beyond just Christmas

0-688-10136-4 MORROW $25.00

Sharon Tyler **Herbst**

The Joy of Cookies

FOREWORD BY BERT GREENE

0-8120-4518-1 BARRONS PB $14.95

Judy **Rosenberg**

Rosie's Bakery: Chocolate-Packed, Jam-Filled, Butter-Rich, No-Holds-Barred Cookie Book

Never one for restraint, Judy has included 150 new recipes for her famous desserts

1-56305-506-6 WORKMAN PB $12.95

Chocolate

Carole **Bloom**

Truffles, Candies, and Confections: Elegant Candymaking in the Home

Thankfully this invaluable guide is back in print again, and in paperback

0-89594-833-8 CROSSING PB $14.95

Jeanne **Bourin**

Book of Chocolate

2-08-013588-0 ABBEVILLE $50.00

Chantal **Coady**

The Chocolate Companion: A Connoisseur's Guide to the World's Finest Chocolates

The world's greatest chocolates are at your fingertips with this marvelous guide; phone and fax numbers are provided so they can be sped your way

0-684-80374-7 SIMON & SCHUSTER $20.00

Sophie D. **Coe** & Michael D. **Coe**

The True History of Chocolate

From Mayan hieroglyphs to the letters of Madame de Sevigne, from the empire of Montezuma to the kingdom of Hershey bars. Includes recipes and 100 illustrations

See also **FOOD AND PHARMACEUTICALS** under **PERSPECTIVES IN HISTORY** under **THE VARIETIES OF CIVILIZATION** in **WORLD HISTORY AND CURRENT AFFAIRS**

0-500-01693-3 THAMES & HUDSON $27.50

Alice **Medrick**

Chocolate and the Art of Low-Fat Desserts

This California pastry chef manages to cut down the fat without sacrificing an iota of taste

0-446-51666-X WARNER $35.00

Cocolat: Extraordinary Chocolate Desserts

One hundred percent decadent

0-446-51419-5 WARNER $35.00

Ice Cream

Gail **Damerow**

Ice Cream: The Whole Scoop

The most comprehensive guide to making frozen desserts of all sorts

0-944435-29-7 GLENBRIDGE PB $16.95

Caroline **Liddell** & Robin **Weir**

Frozen Desserts: The Definitive Guide to Making Ice Creams, Ices, Sorbets, Gelati, and Other Frozen Desserts

0-312-14343-5 ST. MARTIN'S PB $13.95

Pies, Tarts, and Cakes

Rose Levy **Beranbaum**

The Cake Bible

"One of the very few books that…would serve as textbook and inspiration for a generation of dessert makers"—*NY Times*

0-688-04402-6 MORROW $27.95

Lisa **Cherkasky**, Photographer & Renee **Comet**, Photographer

The Artful Pie: Unforgettable Recipes For Creative Cooks

A playful, beautifully designed book, as enticing on the coffee table as it is useful in the kitchen. Among Lisa Cherkasky's favorites: cool lime pie with a bracing splash of tequila, brandy spiked cranberry pear streudel, and apple butter pie with a surprising dash of chili

1-57630-022-6 CHAPTERS PB $17.95

Ceri **Hadda**

Cupcakes

Seventy recipes, homey or sophisticated, low-fat or high-fat, plus over 30 fillings and frostings for endless variations

0-671-86436-X SIMON & SCHUSTER $18.95

Colette **Peters**

Colette's Cakes

If you want detailed instructions on how to make a cake in the shape of a Gothic cathedral—to scale, no less—this is the book to buy. Peters, who has been known to use exacto blades, power drills, and edible paint to construct her confections, provides step-by-step instructions for a variety of whimsical, eye-catching, and downright bizzare baked goods

0-316-70205-6 LITTLE, BROWN $24.95

Maury **Rubin**

Book of Tarts

Sophisticated flavors and eccentric presentations on the best tart crust you've ever made from the owner of City Bakery in New York

0-688-12254-X MORROW $25.00

Martha **Stewart**

Martha Stewart's Pies and Tarts

Appealing photos and recipes, such as chocolate pecan lattice tart, almost too pretty to eat

0-517-55751-7 CLARKSON POTTER $22.95

0-517-58953-2 CLARKSON POTTER PB $18.00

Game

John **Ash** & Sid **Goldstein**

American Game Cookbook: A Contemporary Guide to Preparing Farm-Raised Game Birds and Meats

Game farms have made exotic fowl and meats widely available to the non-hunter, and this is an excellent resource for those who want to cook on the wild side. From boar-based borscht to roast lacquered duck with muscat-tamarind sauce, the recipes contained herein are delicious

0-201-57005-X ARIS $25.00

Angus **Cameron** & Judith **Jones**

The L.L. Bean Game & Fish Cookbook

The classic, with over 800 recipes, ranging from trout and moose to grouse and pheasant. A compendium of information about all aspects of game and fish with hundreds of provocative and useful recipes

0-394-51191-3 RANDOM HOUSE $25.00

Pasta and Pizza

Lorenza **de'Medici**

Lorenza's Pasta

Detailed sections on making fresh pasta as well as preparing dried pasta from a celebrated Italian author and cooking teacher

0-517-70440-4 CLARKSON POTTER $40.00

Giuliano **Hazan**

The Classic Pasta Cookbook

Hazan learned the skills of his trade from one of the great Italian chefs of our time: his mother Marcella. In this extremely practical cookbook he explains the difference between dried and fresh pasta (including the sauces that best accompany each) and provides a full range of simple, authentic recipes

1-56458-292-2 DORLING KINDERSLEY $24.95

Silvio **Rizzi** & others

The Pasta Bible

Over 1,000 illustrations of pasta types and production techniques from all over the world

0-670-86996-1 PENGUIN $29.95

Evelyne **Slomon**

The Pizza Book: Everything There Is to Know About the World's Greatest Pie

This young chef makes pizza-making easy and fun. Calzone recipes include hearty eggplant and sausage, shrimp and pesto; and savory goat cheese and onion

0-8129-1113-X TIME BOOKS $22.00

Alice **Waters** & Patricia **Curtan**

Chez Panisse Pasta, Pizza and Calzone

Innovative recipes from one of America's great restaurants: fettuccine with wild mushrooms and prosciutto, and pizza with caramelized onions, gorgonzola and rosemary. For the sophisticated cook, but worth the effort

0-679-75536-5 RANDOM HOUSE PB $14.00

Seafood

James **Beard**

James Beard's New Fish Cookery

A revised and updated version of the 1954 classic

0-316-08500-6 LITTLE, BROWN PB $15.95

Mark **Bittman**

Fish: The Complete Guide to Buying and Cooking

An A-Z reference of essential information and innovative recipes specifically matched to showcase the particular fish

0-02-510775-5 MACMILLAN $27.50

Jane **Brody**

Jane Brody's Good Seafood Book

An expert on great food that is also good food, the celebrated Brody guides us through the world of edible marine life with sure and practical advice. How to select, store, clean, and cook the delicious low-fat alternative to meat; how to avoid the problems fish pose; plus 250 recipes for appetizers, soups, salads, and entrees

0-393-03687-1 NORTON $27.50

Alan **Davidson**

Seafood: A Connoisseur's Guide and Cookbook

0-671-67011-5 FIRESIDE PB $29.95

Joan **Foley** & Joe **Foley**

The Chesapeake Bay Fish and Fowl Cookbook

A superb regional cookbook; the chapter on crabs is especially good

0-02-539560-2 MACMILLAN $17.95

Shirley **King**

Fish: The Basics

A clear, concise guide arranged by type of fish

1-88152-796-4 CHAPTERS PB $19.95

A.J. **McClane**

McClane's North American Fish Cookery

Plain-speaking information about fish. Note the tilefish fillets with orange sauce, clam fritters, and the "hangtown" fry

0-8050-1065-3 HOLT $27.95

Howard **Mitcham**

Clams, Mussels, Oysters, Scallops, and Snails: A Cookbook and a Memoir

"Cape Cod's Master Seafood Chef" is overflowing with ideas and opinions on how to enjoy shellfish

0-940160-47-1 PARNASSUS PB $12.50

Anton **Mosimann** & Holger **Hofmann**

Shellfish

Beautifully illustrated, with intriguing, recipes from the chef of London's Dorchester Hotel

0-688-06630-5 HEARST $30.00

Mary Ethelyn **Orso**

The Crab Lover's Book: Recipes & More

Includes recipes, folklore and lots of practical information pertaining to blue, stone, Alaskan King and Dungeness crabs

0-87805-796-X MISSISSIPPI PB $16.95

James **Peterson**

Fish and Shellfish

Peterson's exceptional coverage makes this THE reference for both the home cook and the professional

0-688-12737-1 MORROW $40.00

Jean **Reardon** & Ruth **Ebling**

Oysters: A Culinary Celebration

All you need to know

0-940160-26-9 PARNASSUS $25.00

Sauces and Seasonings

Leslie **Brenner** & Katherine **Kinsolving**

Essential Flavors

Vibrantly-flavored oils, vinegars, and reductions to add verve to everything

0-670-85523-5 VIKING $24.95

Dave **DeWitt**

The Hot Sauce Bible

Definitely the most comprehensive source, listing over 2,000 international bottled sauces, over 175 recipes for making your own, plus history, web sites, and sources

0-89594-760-9 CROSSING PB $20.00

Maggie **Klein**

The Feast of the Olive: Cooking with Olives and Olive Oil

Over 75 recipes; note the recipe for chicken with leeks and olives

0-8118-0523-9 CHRONICLE PB $10.95

Michel **Roux**

Michel Roux: Sauces

0-8478-1970-1 RIZZOLI $35.00

Mark **Miller**

The Great Salsa Book

Far-ranging in bases and Scoville units, these 100 recipes provide something for every ocassion

0-89815-517-7 TEN SPEED PB $14.95

Lambert Elisabeth **Ortiz**

The Encyclopedia of Herbs, Spices, and Flavorings

750 photos of over 200 flavorings

1-56458-065-2 DORLING KINDERSLEY $34.95

Julie **Sahni**

Savoring Spices and Herbs

The pleasure of Julie Sahni's book is more than the authoritative information and brilliant insights into combining flavors. It is the brilliance of her cooking and the ease with which she helps us achieve the same results

0-688-06976-2 MORROW $25.00

Chris **Slesinger** & John **Willoughby**

Salsas, Sambals, Chutneys, and Chowchows: Intensely Flavored "Little Dishes" From Around the World

Put a little kick into your next meal with one of these easily prepared accoutrements

0-688-14270-2 HEARST PB $15.00

Soups

Lindsey **Baeham**

A Celebration of Soup

The chapter on garnishes alone is enough reason to buy the book

0-14-046970-2 PENGUIN PB $26.95

James **Peterson**

Splendid Soups

Peterson's previous *Sauces* won the James Beard Award for Best Cookbook of 1991. 400 entries introduce several basic soup genres on which the user can experiment and not be constrained by strict recipes. This is, after all, how all fine soups are made

0-553-07505-5 BDD $29.95

Margaret **Romagnoli** & G. Franco **Romagnoli**

Zuppa: A Seventeen-Region Tour of the Soups of Italy

Soups provide a delicious excuse to take us on a tour of the landscape, history, foods and people of each region. Includes 144 recipes

0-8050-3834-5 HOLT $25.00

0-8050-3833-7 HOLT $25.00

Susan **Wyler**

Simply Stews: More Than 100 Savory One-Pot Meals

Over 100 recipes to keep you thoroughly warm and satisfied

0-06-095144-3 HARPERPERENNIAL PB $14.00

Vegetables and Salads

Lindsey **Bareham**

In Praise of the Potato: Recipes from Around the World

With dishes such as The Four Season's Transylvanian potato soup with a white ruffled petticoat, Bareham develops a potato potential we never knew existed

0-87951-497-3 OVERLOOK PB........$13.95

Georgeanne **Brennan**

Down to Earth: Great Recipes for Root Vegetables

These often-overlooked vegetables are brought to new heights

0-8118-0670-7 CHRONICLE PB........$16.95

Bert **Greene**

Greene on Greens

Vegetables arranged A to Z, with appealing recipes. Fun and informative

0-89480-659-9 WORKMAN PB........$16.95

Mort **Rosenblum**

Olives: Life and Lore of the Noble Fruit

A correspondent-turned-olive-farmer shares his obsession with olives, writing abouit their history, production, and political importance as well as the respect and passion they inspire in their growers

0-86547-503-2 NORTH POINT........$42.00

Colin **Spencer**

The Vegetable Book: A Detailed Guide to Identifying, Using and Cooking Over 100 Vegetables

0-8478-1971-X RIZZOLI........$40.00

Sylvia **Thompson**

The Kitchen Garden Book

A wealth of recipes for every edible part of the plant, from broccoli's delicious leaves to carrot tops

0-553-09956-6 BDD........$27.95

Alice **Waters**

Chez Panisse Vegetables

Alice Waters—acclaimed restaurateur, bestselling author, and consultant to the White House—offers 300 of the best vegetable recipes from the world-famous Chez Panisse. Concentrating on seasonal, organic, local vegetables, organized alphabetically and with chapters on growing and buying seasonal produce, this is as pleasurable a book to read as it is to cook from

0-06-017147-2 HARPERCOLLINS........$35.00

Fruits

Elizabeth **Riely**

A Feast of Fruits

Riley provides more than 340 healthy recipes for fruit, covering everything from low-fat appetizers to delicious low-calorie desserts. More than 40 different varieties of fruit insures easy, year-round menu planning. Each section features information on the fruit's history, cultivation, nutritional content, methods of storage, and selection

0-02-601961-2 MACMILLAN........$25.00
0-02-861019-9 MACMILLAN PB........$15.00

Nicole **Routhier**

Nicole Routhier's Fruit Cookbook

An enormous compendium of information and recipes sweet and savory

1-56305-565-1 WORKMAN PB........$15.95
0-7611-0504-2 WORKMAN PB........$8.95

Elizabeth **Schneider**

Uncommon Fruits and Vegetables

The culinary sleuth of the plant kingdom answers all your questions and provides a few recipes for each plant explored

0-06-091669-9 HARPERCOLLINS PB........$20.00

Norman **Van Aken** & John **Harrison**

The Great Exotic Fruit Book

Large, full-color photos of both whole fruit and cross-section plus delicious recipes

0-89815-688-2 TEN SPEED PB........$15.95

Entertaining

For related reading, see THE HOME in ARCHITECTURE, DESIGN, AND HOMES

Lee **Bailey**

Lee Bailey's Country Weekends

Great taste and style, excellent menus

0-517-88447-X CROWN PB........$16.00

The Way I Cook

Bailey's beautiful books have been gathered into a single volume, plus 100 recipes never before published

0-517-59751-9 CLARKSON POTTER........$30.00

Jean Anthelme **Brillat-Savarin**

The Physiology of Taste

A reproduction of the beautiful Arion Press limited edition with illustrations by Wayne Thiebauld and the only inprint M.F.K. Fisher translation available

TRANSLATED BY M.F.K. FISHER
ILLUSTRATIONS BY WAYNE THIEBAUD

1-88717-809-0 COUNTERPOINT........$55.00
0-14-044614-1 PENGUIN PB........$12.95

Lora **Brody**

The Entertaining Survival Guide: A Handbook for the Hesitant Host

Ms. Brody will help you get a party of any size off without a hitch

0-688-12295-7 MORROW........$20.00

Margaret **Caselton**

The Gracious Table

Everything you need to know about setting the table/creating a mood

0-8478-1949-3 RIZZOLI........$30.00

Sarah Leah **Chase**

The Open-House Cookbook

The owner of a Nantucket gourmet shop offers up many wonderful recipes. The tone is breezy and the recipes appetizing—as in steak, mushroom, and hearts of palm salad with Bearnaise mayonnaise, deep-dish broccoli pizza, and white chocolate brownies

See also **NEW ENGLAND AND THE ATLANTIC SEABOARD** under **AMERICAN COOKERY**

0-89480-465-0 WORKMAN PB........$12.95

Anton **Edelmann**

Canapés and Frivolities

Innovative flavors and presentations make this the book to reach for when you really want to impress

1-85145-824-7 TRAFALGAR SQUARE PB........$24.95

The Editors of ***Gourmet***

Gourmet's Holidays and Celebrations

Easy, crowd-pleasing recipes for big occasions, developed with an emphasis on health, including Southern turkey with pecan and rice stuffing, a poached egg and salmon Easter brunch, and a light Christmas supper. Complete with wine suggestions, dessert and preserve recipes, this splendid collection also features suggestions for gifts of food

0-679-41767-2 RANDOM HOUSE........$25.00

Barbara **Kafka**

Party Food

Entertaining without knife and fork

0-688-11184-X MORROW........$25.00

Julee **Rosso**

The Silver Palate Good Times Cookbook

Winning menus for special occasions. Note the swordfish marinated with lime and coriander and blueberry pie with cinnamon lattice crust

See also **THE BASICS**

0-89480-832-X WORKMAN........$22.95
0-89480-831-1 WORKMAN PB........$14.95

Nicole **Routhier**

Cooking Under Wraps: The Art of Wrapping Hors d'Oeuvres, Main Courses, & Desserts

0-688-14610-4 HEARST PB........$18.00

Martha **Stewart**

Martha Stewart's Hors D'oeuvres: The Creation and Presentation of Fabulous Finger Food

Party hors d'oeuvres by theme. Note the outdoor barbecue, for one: cocktail ribs, with a sauce spiced with pepper flakes, barbecued chicken wings, a grilled sausages, with pina coladas and daiquiris to wash it all down. Attractive and helpful photos

0-517-58950-8 CLARKSON POTTER PB........$18.00

Martha Stewart's Menus For Entertaining

Rediscover the pleasures of hospitality with Martha. Step-by-step photographs show how to cook, decorate, and serve the delightful offerings of the renowned Connecticut and East Hampton denizen

0-517-59099-9 CLARKSON POTTER........$30.00

James **Trager**

The Food Chronology: A Food Lover's Compendium of Events and Anecdotes, From Prehistory to the Present

A book to flip through at leisure; a fun compendium of food-related events, product introductions, restaurant demises, and much more, from prehistory to the present

See also **BOOKS ON FOOD**

0-8050-3389-0 HOLT $40.00

Roger **Verge**

Roger Verge's Entertaining in the French Style

A beautiful book, with advice for presenting a French meal

See also **ENTERTAINING** under **HOME ENTERTAINING** under **THE HOME** in **ARCHITECTURE, DESIGN, AND HOMES**

0-941434-90-7 STEWART, TABORI $60.00

Peri **Wolfman** & Charles **Gold**

Great Settings

Exceptionally beautiful place settings, imaginative ideas, and sources around the country

0-517-70106-5 CLARKSON POTTER $30.00

The Perfect Setting Cookbook

0-8109-3737-9 ABRAMS $14.95

Preserving and Canning

Janet **Greene**

Putting Food By

The classic guide to pickling, preserving canning, freezing, and storing; with recipes

0-8289-0645-9 GREENE PB $8.95
0-452-26899-0 PENGUIN PB $13.95

Carol **Hupping**

Stocking Up: America's Classic Preserving Guide, Completely Revised and Updated

Canning, freezing, drying, pickling, cheese and butter making and anything else you need to know to make your pantry complete

0-671-69395-6 FIRESIDE PB $17.95

Special Diets

For related reading, see DIET AND NUTRITION in LIFESTYLES AND PRACTICAL ADVICE

Beth **Kidder**

The Milk-Free Kitchen: Living Well Without Dairy Products

Living dairy-free with children in the house can be difficult, but Kidder handles it with ease and creativity

0-8050-1836-0 HOLT PB $17.95

Jax Peters **Lowell**

Against the Grain

Wheat-free cooking

0-8050-3625-3 HOLT PB $14.95

Aaron **Maree**

Sweet Health

Desserts for diets that restrict sugar, cholesterol, gluten, salt, lactose, and fat but don't employ artificial ingredients from a prominent Australian dessert chef

0-207-18428-3 HARPERCOLLINS $19.00

Vegetarian

Dara **Goldstein**

The Vegetarian Hearth: Recipes and Reflections for the Cold Season

Cold-weather recipes, many inspired by Eastern European and Scandinavian countries

0-06-018760-3 HARPERCOLLINS $25.00

Barbara **Grunes** & Virginia **Van Vynkt**

All-American Vegetarian: A Regional Harvest of Low-Fat Recipes

More than 200 splendid vegetarian recipes combine traditional cuisines from the length and breadth of North America with cutting-edge, low-fat cooking techniques. Fresh tomato soup swirled with spinach cream, rye-caraway crepes with glazed onions, saffron noodle squares, and layered canyon cornbread are just a few of the enticing recipes collected in this informative book

0-8050-3509-5 HOLT $25.00

Jean **Hewitt**

The New York Times New Natural Foods Cookbook

Not strictly vegetarian, but a solid source on a variety of natural foods

0-380-62687-X AVON PB $10.00

Mollie **Katzen**

The Enchanted Broccoli Forest & Other Timeless Delicacies

More recipes from the Moosewood cook

0-89815-079-5 TEN SPEED $19.95
0-89815-078-7 TEN SPEED PB $16.95

The Moosewood Cookbook, Revised Edition

Charming, with hand-lettered recipes from the Moosewood Restaurant in Ithaca, New York

0-89815-503-7 TEN SPEED $21.95
0-89815-490-1 TEN SPEED PB $16.95

New Recipes from Moosewood Restaurant

Two hundred recipes, this time with some potions for fish

0-89815-208-9 TEN SPEED PB $15.95

Pam **Krauss**, editor

Moosewood Restaurant's Low-Fat Favorites

A brand new update on their already famous cuisine

0-517-70210-X CLARKSON POTTER $32.50
0-517-88494-1 CLARKSON POTTER PB $22.00

Frances **Lappe**

Diet For a Small Planet: 20th Anniversary Edition

Classic vegetarian text, including information on combining grains, legumes, and dairy for complete protein; with recipes

0-345-37366-9 BALLANTINE PB $15.00
0-345-32120-0 BALLANTINE PB $6.99

Deborah **Madison** & Edward Espe **Brown**

The Greens Cookbook: Vegetarian Cuisine from the Celebrated Restaurant

Cooking from the renowned vegetarian restaurant in San Francisco. Note the mushroom lasagna, goat cheese and sundried tomato toasts, and the cherry apricot crumble

0-553-05195-4 BDD $28.50

Moosewood Collective

Moosewood Restaurant Cooks At Home: Fast and Easy Recipes For Any Day

The Moosewood Collective from Ithaca, NY, has long been at the vanguard of meatless, whole-food cookbooks. This new volume concentrates on time- and energy-saving recipes—whole meals that can be prepared in a half hour. Includes an invaluable guide to recommended convenience foods, from canned beans to pre-baked pizza crusts

0-671-67992-9 FIRESIDE PB $16.00

Sundays at Moosewood Restaurant

Ethnic menus

0-671-67990-2 FIRESIDE PB $21.50

Vasantha **Prasad**

Indian Vegetarian Cooking for the American Kitchen

0-679-76438-0 RANDOM HOUSE PB $18.00

Steven **Raichlen**

High-Flavor, Low-Fat Vegetarian Cooking

The author of the award winning *High-Flavor, Low-Fat Cooking* uses his sophisticated techniques for intensely flavored, innovative meat-free cuisine

0-670-85782-3 VIKING $24.95

Laurel **Robertson**

The New Laurel's Kitchen

A new age classic: cookbook and guide

See also **VEGETARIANISM AND NATURAL FOODS** under **DIET AND NUTRITION** in **LIFESTYLES AND PRACTICAL ADVICE**

0-89815-166-X TEN SPEED PB $29.95

Lorna **Sass**

Lorna Sass' Complete Vegetarian Kitchen

Originally published under the title *Recipes From an Ecological Kitchen*, this superb low-fat vegan book is now available in paperback

0-688-14185-4 HEARST PB $16.00

William **Shurtleff**

The Book of Tofu

Recipes for making your own soyfoods as well as incorporating them into dishes

0-89815-095-7 TEN SPEED PB $19.95

William **Shurtleff** & Akiko **Aoyagi**

The Book of Miso: Savory, High-Protein Seasoning

0-89815-097-3 TEN SPEED PB $16.95

Annie **Somerville**

Fields of Green: New Vegetarian Recipes from the Celebrated Greens Restaurant

Healthy, simple, and delicious are the key words for this collection of over 300 vegetarian delights. Written by the executive chef at San Francisco's famed Green Restaurant, these recipes are destined to become culinary classics. Also included are special sections on finding the best seasonal produce, low-fat cooking, organic gardening, and a produce glossary

0-553-09139-5 BDD $28.50

Anna **Thomas**

The New Vegetarian Epicure, Plain and Fancy

Thomas has updated her *Vegetarian Epicure, Vols 1 and 2,* to a stunning array of recipes tasteful enough for entertaining but simple enough for a hot summer day

0-679-42714-7 KNOPF $30.00

0-679-76588-3 KNOPF PB $19.00

Vegetarian Epicure, Book Two

A vegetarian classic for both beginning and experienced cooks

0-394-41363-6 RANDOM HOUSE PB $12.50

Vegetarian Times Editors

The Complete Vegetarian Times Cookbook

0-02-621745-7 MACMILLAN $29.95

Vegetarian Times Vegetarian Entertaining

0-02-861324-4 MACMILLAN $27.50

Low-Fat

Nancy **Baggett** & Ruth **Glick**

100% Pleasure: From Appetizers to Desserts, the Low-Fat Cookbook For People who Love to Eat

Dangerous-looking dishes done up wholesomely. Cheesecake, steak, dumplings, gravy, and chili need be off-limits no more, explain the authors—if you stick to a logical system of diet tips so effective that you won't miss what you once considered the "real thing"

0-87596-368-4 RODALE PB $15.95

Eating Well Secrets of Low-Fat Cooking: 100 Techniques & 200 Recipes for Great Healthy Food

Rigorously tested methods and recipes are trademarks of this magazine; bringing all of this knowledge together under one cover is a boon to those who want to lighten their mealtimes

1-88494-311-X ARTISAN $24.95

Jill **O'Connor**

Sweet Nothings: Over 50 Luscious, Low Fat, Low Calorie Desserts

Sacrifice nothing—except calories and fat. From world class chocolate chip cookies to perfectly deliciously parfaits, the former pastry chef at the legendary Golden Door Spa and frequent contributor to *Bon Appetit* and *Food and Wine* reveals the secrets of healthy decadence. Using innovative fat substitutes and unique preparation techniques, these original dessert recipes are well under 30 percent fat and 200 calories each

0-8118-0289-2 CHRONICLE PB $12.95

Steven **Raichlen**

High-Flavor, Low-Fat Cooking

"[Raichlen] has definitely traded fat for flavor in this superb new cookbook for anyone interested in good taste"-John Mariani, author of *America Eats Out*

0-14-024123-X PENGUIN PB $18.95

Martha **Stewart**

Martha Stewart's Healthy Cooking

Martha may irk some people, but it can't be denied that she excels at providing inspiration and ideas, something many of us desperately need in this area. This sensible volume contains over 150 illustrated recipes plus plenty of lifestyle tips

0-517-57702-X CLARKSON POTTER $32.50

Cooking for Children

Lisa **Chaney**

Investigating Food in History

A wonderfully illustrated and entertaining book on the history of food for children

0-7078-0149-4 TRAFALGAR SQUARE PB $6.95

Rena **Coyle**

My First Baking Book

Even very young children can enjoy making these well-chosen and illustrated recipes

0-89480-579-7 WORKMAN PB $9.95

My First Cookbook

Written by a mother, with her three-year old by her side. Fun and reliable

0-89480-846-X WORKMAN PB $10.95

Marion **Cunningham**

Cooking With Children

An ambitious book for seriously interested children

0-679-42297-8 KNOPF $18.00

Denice **Skrepcinski** & others

Cody Coyote Cooks: A Southwest Cookbook for Kids

1-88367-237-6 TRICYCLE $14.95

Jean **Pare**

Kids Cooking

Heavy-duty pages and colorful plastic measuring spoons make this an exciting and indestructible first cookbook

1-89545-544-8 COMPANYS COMING PB $10.95

Alice **Waters**

Fanny at Chez Panisse

Whimsically illustrated, this is based on Fanny's life growing up in her mom's restaurant. Recipes require adult help

0-06-016896-X HARPERCOLLINS $25.00

Angela **Wilkes**

The Children's Step-By-Step Cook Book

The large and informative photographs help to make the recipes in this volume especially accessible to budding chefs

1-56458-474-7 DORLING KINDERSLEY $18.95

Wine and Beverages

General Books on Wine

Leon **Adams**

The Commonsense Book of Wine

A revised and updated edition of the standard work that helped to demystify the world of wine

0-932664-76-8 WINE GUILD PB $8.95

Leslie **Brenner**

Fear of Wine: An Introductory Guide to the Grape

Observations, outrageous dreams, and strange, but at least somewhat true, stories: the brilliant and hilarious star of the runaway television hit contributes to the new genre of books by comedians

ILLUSTRATED BY LETTIE TEAGUE

0-553-37464-8 BANTAM PB $11.95

Gordon **Brown**

Classic Spirits of the World

In chapters that range from a history of distillation to a country-by-country survey of brands, this is the most comprehensive independent guide to whiskeys, brandies, vodka, gin, rum, tequila, aquavit, schnapps, bitters, and liqueurs from all over the globe. Tasting notes, photographs, history

See also **WHISKEY AND OTHER SPIRITS**

0-7892-0165-8 ABBEVILLE $29.95

Oz **Clarke**

Oz Clarke's Wine Atlas: Wines and Wine Regions of the World

The acclaimed wine correspondent for London's *Daily Telegraph*, Clarke has become world renowned for his authoritative, sometimes opinionated, always witty pronouncements on the world of wine. Here, 70 large-scale color

maps detail the major wine-producing regions of the world, from France and California to Australia and Chile, each map accompanied by Clarke's erudite commentary
0-316-14697-8 LITTLE, BROWN $60.00

Michael **Edwards**
The Champagne Companion
Over 100 champagnes are listed, with background information, tasting notes, and vintage ratings
See also **CHAMPAGNE AND ALSACE** under **FRANCE**
1-56138-440-2 RUNNING PRESS $24.95

Barbara **Ensrud**
Best Wine Buys for $12 and Under: A Guide for the Frugal Connoisseur
Discerning, discriminating, and *exclusively* interested in good wines that cost under $12, Ensrud's new book is the indispensable guide to everyday wines. Organized by region, grape variety, and type, it covers the world of wine from bargaining with merchants to reading labels. She shows how to negotiate the world of wine without going broke, and how to complement a more expensive palate with exceptional *vins ordinaires*
0-679-75662-0 VILLARD PB $9.95

Frank **Henriques**
The Signet Encyclopedia of Wine
A complete guide to brand names, vineyards, vintages, and varieties, covering some 20,000 wines
0-452-25669-0 OLYMPIC PB $2.98

Ron **Herbst** & Sharon Tyler **Herbst**
Wine Lover's Companion
Handy purse-sized reference book for wine terms and types
0-8120-1479-0 BARRONS PB $11.95

Hugh **Johnson**
Hugh Johnson's Modern Encyclopedia of Wine
"One of the most useful and attractive wine books ever published" —*NY Times*
0-671-73638-8 SIMON & SCHUSTER $35.00

Hugh Johnson's Pocket Encyclopedia of Wine, 1989
A quick reference guide that discusses modem wines, winemakers, and wine enjoyment
0-671-88635-5 FIRESIDE $12.00

Hugh Johnson's Pocket Encyclopedia of Wine 1996
0-671-68701-8 SIMON & SCHUSTER PB $9.95

Vintage: The Story of Wine
0-671-79182-6 FIRESIDE PB $25.00

The World Atlas of Wine
A country-by-country, region-by-region format offer's the first complete mapping of the world's great wine areas
0-671-88674-6 SIMON & SCHUSTER $50.00

Hugh **Johnson**, editor
Touring in Wine Country: Alsace
Series Editor Hugh Johnson has overseen the production of these excellent guides. Light and slim though packed with wine, food, restaurant and lodging information, you will not want to leave these guides at home
1-85732-581-8 ANTIQUE COLLECTORS $21.95

Steven **Kolpan** & others
Exploring Wine: The Culinary Institute of America's Tour of Wines of the World
The perfect gift for the wine lover, from the prestigious Culinary Institute of America. "There is no finer book on the market with regard to the subject of wine and food"
—Sharon McCarthy, Wine Consultant.
"The wines of the world as well as the world of wine unfolded before my very eyes"
—Robin Insley, Oldways Foundation
0-442-01831-2 VAN NOSTRAND REINHOLD $59.95

Tom **Maresca**
Mastering Wine
An updated edition of Maresca's 1985 Cliquot Prize-winning book, this offers affordable ways to learn about wines—through programmed tastings of red, white, rose, and sparkling vintages, or by region or class—allowing the reader's own tastes to dictate steps. A delightful gift for the holidays
0-8021-3298-7 GROVE PB $12.95

The Right Wine
Maresca's unusual book teaches readers to decide for themselves why wines do or do not work with different foods. Straightforward advice on how wines mature, what wines to keep, and other practical issues, *The Right Wine* is written with an eye toward the drinker's taste and pleasure. "Maresca writes entertainingly…A fine job"—Robert M. Parker. "Charming, chatty, and useful"—Anthony Dias Blue
0-8021-3297-9 GROVE PB $12.95

Joni C. **McNutt**, editor
In Praise of Wine: An Offering of Hearty Toasts, Quotations, Witticisms, Poetry & Proverbs Throughout History
"The rule is, don't give in until the wine gives out"—Euripides: a suitable epigraph for this delightful collection of quotations from such enthusiastic wine drinkers as Homer and Madame Pompadour, Isak Dinesen and W. C. Fields. The perfect gift for the oenophile
0-88496-372-1 CAPRA PB $12.95

Jancis **Robinson**
Jancis Robinson's Guide to Wine Grapes
Endless grape varieties are indentified in this handy pocket-sized reference
0-19-866232-7 OXFORD $13.95

Jancis Robinson's Wine Course
Clear instruction from one of the world's most respected wine experts
0-7892-0256-5 ABBEVILLE $29.95
0-563-37098-X BBC $50.00

Jancis **Robinson**, editor
The Oxford Companion to Wine
For novice and connoisseur, the "undisputed mistress of the kingdom of wines" *(Madame Figaro)* and columnist for the *Wine Spectator* and *Financial Times* defines every wine-related term imaginable
0-19-866159-2 OXFORD $60.00

Frank **Schoonmaker**
The New Frank Schoonmaker Encyclopedia of Wine
A classic reference work, revised in 1988—concise, easy-to-use, and up-to-date. "The finest quick reference work in the literature of wine"—*NY Times*
COMPLETELY REVISED BY ALEXIS BESPALOFF
0-688-05749-7 MORROW $22.95

Commentaries

Gerald **Asher**
Vintage Tales: Reflections on Wine
Asher has been the wine editor of *Gourmet* for the past 24 years. In his trademark relaxed, informal style, Asher evaluates wines from around the world and gives advice on serving, tasting, and enjoying wines
0-8118-1267-7 CHRONICLE $22.95

Christine **Atkinson**
Secret Vineyards of France
0-87052-585-9 HIPPOCRENE $24.95

Leonard **Bernstein**
The Official Guide to Wine Snobbery
A seriocomic reference book
0-688-01605-7 MORROW PB $10.00

Thomas **Jefferson**
Thomas Jefferson's European Travel Diaries
The record of a delightful backroads odyssey in 1787 and 1788 through the major wine regions of France, northern Italy, and Germany
0-9615964-3-0 SEVEN LOCKS PB $7.95

At Pommard and Volnay I observed [laborers] eating good wheat bread; at Mersault, rye. I asked the reason of this difference. They told me that the white wines fail in quality much more often than the red and remain on hand. The farmer therefore cannot afford to feed his laborer so well. At Meursault only white wines are made because there is too much stone for he red. On such slight circumstances depends the condition of man!
THOMAS JEFFERSON'S EUROPEAN TRAVEL DIARIES

Thomas Jefferson

Daniel **Johnnes** & Michael **Stephenson**

Daniel Johnnes's Top 200 Wines: An Expert's Guide to Maximum Enjoyment for Your Dollar

The sommelier of Manhattan's celebrated Montrachet shares his knowledge and taste with an eye on the pocketbook

See also **WINE TASTING** under **TECHNICAL BOOKS**

0-14-051316-7 PENGUIN PB $14.95

Kermit **Lynch**

Adventures on the Wine Route: A Wine Buyer's Tour of France

"Colorful portraits of some idiosyncratic vintners and commentaries on their wines make for some of the finest reading since Joseph Wechsberg ate and drank his way through France"
—Robert M. Parker

0-374-52266-9 NOONDAY PB $14.00

Reminton **Norman**

Rhone Renaissance: The Finest Rhone and Rhone Style Wines from France and the New World

0-932664-95-4 WINE APPRECIATION GUILD $50.00

Robert M. **Parker**

Parker's Wine Buyer's Guide, 4th Edition

Ratings, prices vintage information of over 7,500 wines

0-684-80283-X FIRESIDE PB $25.00

Ralph **Steadman**

The Grapes of Ralph: Wine According to Ralph Steadman

Steadman is a genius in the art of caricature; what more worthy subject than wine could he choose to turn his pen on?

0-15-100245-2 HARCOURT BRACE $35.00

Bernard **Watney** & Homer **Babbidge**

Corkscrews For Collectors

Whimsical and sophisticated designs for corkscrews

See also **OTHER** under **COLLECTIBLES** in **ARCHITECTURE, DESIGN, AND HOMES**

0-85667-113-4 SOTHEBY PARKE BERNET $39.95

France

More books have been written about French wine than any other. It is worth remembering that the entire French wine industry came close to extinction in the late 19th-century thanks to an indefatigable sap-eating aphid, the grape phylloxera, which was accidentally introduced to France from North America. Europe's vineyards were saved by the wide-scale grafting of vulnerable vines onto resistant North American root stocks. To this day, in many areas of France, each new vine planted is still grafted in this way.

Asa **Briggs**

Haut-Brion: An Illustrious Lineage

A history of some of France's greatest wines by a well-respected wine historian and critic

0-571-17118-4 FABER PB $14.95

Jacqueline **Friedrich**

A Wine and Food Guide to the Loire

A lively, opinionated description of over 600 wineries and their winemakers, plus details of the surrounding countryside and regional food specialties

0-8050-4390-X HOLT $27.50

Rosemary **George**

French Country Wines

Covers wines of the South-West, Midi, Provence, Corsica, Savoy, Yura and Paris

0-571-13894-2 FABER $24.95
0-571-15311-9 FABER PB $14.95

Alexis **Lichine**

Alexis Lichine's Guide to the Wines and Vineyards of France

An invaluable companion for anyone embarking on this journey, be it in armchair or automobile. This discursive guide provides information and anecdotes about the wines as well as descriptions of hotels and restaurants

0-394-74440-3 KNOPF PB $14.95

Thomas **Matthews** & Sarah **Matthews**

A Village in the Vineyards

A fascinating account of a year spent in Ruch, a tiny village in the heart of Bordeaux, which exists for and because of wine. New Yorkers Thomas and Sarah Matthews take us into the lives of the villagers, hearing the gossip and learning how wine is made in this community caught between modernity and age-old traditions

0-374-28381-8 FS&G $23.00

Paul **Strang**

Wines of South-West France

"...a grand tour of vineyards upstream from bordeaux, mixing sound history, shrewd analysis, and delightful anecdotes. The pen-portraits of the wine-makers along the way are beautifully painted...the list of growers and their phone numbers is alone worth the price of the book"
—Michael Edwards

1-85626-222-7 TRAFALGAR SQUARE PB $17.95

Roger **Voss** & Julian **Jeffs**, editor

Wines of the Loire

0-571-16485-4 FABER $29.95
0-571-16486-2 FABER PB $14.95

Bordeaux

John **Baxevanis**

The Wines of Bordeaux and Western France

Explicit and helpful diagrams and photographs guide the reader through not only Bordeaux, but also the Loire, Bergerac, Cahors, Gaillac, and Bearn

0-8476-7490-8 ROWMAN & LITTLEFIELD $50.50

Jeffrey **Benson** & Alastair **Mackenzie**

Sauternes: A Study of the Great Sweet Wines of Bordeaux

A specialized look at the history, gastronomy, and vintages, with tasting notes and a glossary

0-85667-360-9 SOTHEBY PARKE BERNET $39.95

Stephen **Brook**

Sauternes and Other Sweet Wines of Bordeaux

Detailed profiles of all classified growths of Sauternes and Barsac and information on how these wines are made

0-571-17317-9 FABER PB $15.95

Clive **Coates**

Grands Vins: The Finest Chateaux of Bordeaux and Their Wines

Details the history, varieties, vintages, and idiosyncrasies of just about every fine Bordeaux wine made in the past 30 years

0-520-20220-1 CALIFORNIA $55.00

Nicholas **Faith**

Chateau Margaux

A visit to the Haut-Medoc chateau, with production details, menus, and recipes

0-86565-106-X VENDOME $50.00

David **Peppercorn**

Bordeaux

A rare combination of a professional's experience, a true wineman's passion, and a historian's eye

0-571-13699-0 FABER $39.95
0-571-13654-0 FABER PB $24.95

Burgundy and Beaujolais

Michael **Buller**

In Beaujolais

Award winning-author of *The Winemakers Year: Four Seasons in Bordeaux,* Buller now transports readers to the source of the delightful wine, Beaujolais. Text and photos bring back the vineyard, the growers, the villages and cafes of this wine-lover's paradise

PHOTOGRAPHS BY PIERRE COTTIN

0-500-01584-8 THAMES & HUDSON $35.00

Anthony **Hanson**

Burgundy

The most up-to-date and complete book on Burgundy available today

0-571-15389-5 FABER $40.00

Guy **Jacquemont** & Paul **Mereaud**

Beaujolais: The Complete Guide

An inviting look at the history, cellars, and chateaux of the insufficiently known Beaujolais region

INTRODUCTION BY PAUL BOCUSE

0-316-45598-9 LITTLE, BROWN $19.98

Richard **Olney**

Romanee-Conti

0-8478-1927-2 RIZZOLI $35.00

Champagne and Alsace

Michael **Edwards**

The Champagne Companion

Over 100 champagnes are listed, with background information, tasting notes, and vintage ratings

See also **GENERAL BOOKS ON WINE**

1-56138-440-2 RUNNING PRESS $24.95

Germany

Ian **Jamieson**

German Wines

This historical tour of Germany's wine-producing regions will make the often confusing world of German wine much clearer

0-571-14154-4 FABER $29.95

Italy

Philip **Dallas**

Italian Wines

A bright look at the civilization that has imbibed wine for 4000 years and made it for 2500, with assessments of today's major producers

0-571-15390-9 FABER $24.95
0-571-15179-5 FABER PB $13.95

Hugh **Johnson**, editor

Touring in Wine Country: Tuscany

1-85732-582-6 ANTIQUE COLLECTORS PB $21.95

Spain and Portugal

Though Spain is the world's third largest wine producer, it has been a rare subject of books, except for sherries. In recent years, the spreading popularity of the good Rioja wines of northern Spain have managed to enhance the country's standing in the wine league. Portugal's wine renown is founded primarily on the port wines, but the country also produces tasty white *vinho verde* and sturdy new red wines.

Jan **Read**

The Pocket Guide to Spanish Wines

An essential reference book with advice on quality, variety, value, and reliability

0-671-47194-5 SIMON & SCHUSTER $6.95

The Wines of Portugal

"Mr. Read is completely at home on this territory and the information is not available elsewhere"—*Guardian*

0-571-15003-9 FABER PB $11.95

Wines of Spain

"None can rival the author's detailed knowledge of the country's wines"—*Financial Times*

0-571-14621-X FABER PB $13.95

Sherry, Port, Madeira, Sweet, and Dessert Wines

Noel **Cossart**

Madeira: The Island Vineyard

A teamed and comprehensive introduction to the island's famous product

0-903432-33-1 CHRISTIE'S WINE $24.00

Julian **Jeffs**

Sherry

An examination by a true aficionado with plenty of colorful early history, ranging from Chaucer's tipple to modem export statistics

0-571-16445-5 FABER $29.95
0-571-16447-1 FABER PB $14.95

North America

A number of books on American wines consist of tasting notes on current releases and are therefore soon out of date; others are local touring guides. Most of the wine production of the United States originates in California, ranging from mass-produced gallons to high-quality cabernets and chardonnays.

Corbet **Clark**

American Wines of the Northwest: A Guide to the Wines of Washington, Oregon, and Idaho

0-688-11276-5 QUILL PB $14.00

Linda **Collison** & Bob **Russell**

Rocky Mountain Wineries: A Travel Guide to the Wayside Vineyards

If you never thought of tasting wine while in New Mexico, Colorado, Idaho, Arizona, Utah, or Montana, you will after you read this book. The combination of serious craft winemakers and the favorable climate at more than 4,000 feet leads to some very good wines

0-87108-848-7 PRUETT PB $16.95

Anthony **Dias Blue**

American Wine

"A voluminous, courageous undertaking. A most informative and interesting reference work for everyone's vinous bookshelf"—Alexis Lichine

0-06-015914-6 HARPERCOLLINS $15.98

Buyer's Guide to American Wines

Quality ratings for more than 5000 currently available wines

0-06-273158-0 HARPERCOLLINS PB $15.00

John **Doerper**

Wine Country: California's Napa & Sonoma Valleys

This pocket-sized guide is packed with the most up-to-date information available on individual wineries. In addition, it lists restaurant and lodging options

1-87886-784-9 COMPASS GUIDES PB $18.95

Sarah Jane **English**

The Wines of Texas: A Guide and a History

Ms. English takes us on a well-researched and lively tour of Texas vineyards, historical and present-day. She also provides excellent touring information, and even offers some wine-inspired recipes to complement her wine and food matching advice

1-57168-054-3 EAKINS $16.95

Paul **Gregutt** & Jeff **Prather**

Northwest Wines: A Pocket Guide to the Wines of Washington, Oregon, and Idaho

"The most authoritative and consumer-oriented guide to the wines of Washington, Oregon, and Idaho. Wine enthusiasts will find this a must purchase" —Robert M. Parker, Jr., *The Wine Advocate*

0-912365-97-8 SASQUATCH PB $9.95

James **Halliday**

The Wine Atlas of California

A splendid, authoritative guide to the nine wine regions of California where, undisputedly, some of the world's finest vintages are made. With amazing, computer-generated topographical maps and wise commentary by Halliday, Australia's most respected writer on wines

0-670-84950-2 VIKING $50.00

James **Laube**

Wine Spectator's California Wine

Ratings of over 7,000 wines plus discussions on winemakers and vintages

1-88165-925-9 RUNNING PRESS $39.95

Jon **Palmer**

Wineries of the Mid-Atlantic

"Should be useful to East Coast wine fans who can't make it to the Napa Valley or the Finger Lakes"—Frank Prial

0-8135-1346-4 RUTGERS $30.00
0-8135-1351-0 RUTGERS PB $12.95

Cyril **Ray**

Robert Mondavi of the Napa Valley

A warm portrait of a master Californian vintner—and character

0-446-38322-8 WARNER PB $12.95

Norman S. **Roby** & Charles E. **Olken**

The New Connoisseur's Handbook of California Wines: Second Edition

The most comprehensive listing available, this volume features every one of the 680 labels currently available, as well as thousands of tasting notes and ratings. "An invaluable reference book"—Frank J. Prial, *NY Times*

0-679-44486-6 KNOPF $27.50

Dennis **Schaefer**

Vintage Talk: Conversations with California's New Winemakers

Wine connoisseurs know that this is the beginning of a "golden age" for California wines. This book explores the world of Californian wines by talking to many among the energetic and knowledgeable generation of young winemakers. In their own words, reflections on a life committed to the vineyard, and to the philosophy of producing new classics

0-88496-360-8 CAPRA PB $15.95

Marguerite **Thomas**

Wineries of the Eastern States

Over 130 wineries from the Finger Lakes to the Shenandoah Valley are discussed. Maps and directories make touring easy

0-936399-77-5 BERKSHIRE PB $17.95

Southern Hemisphere

John **Beeston**

A Concise History of Australian Wine

An extremely readable account of the development and ascendancy of the wine industry in Australia

1-86373-621-2 ALLEN & UNWIN PB $17.95

Oliver **Mayo**

Wines of Australia

An agronomist and vineyard owner's history of the development of the country's wine trade, with a survey of all current wine regions

0-571-16395-5 FABER $24.95

Technical Books

James **Page-Roberts**

Vines and Wines in a Small Garden: From Planting to Bottling

A unique and easy-to-follow guide to growing vines that not only add color and foliage to gardens but also yield fruit for delicious, healthy, additive-free wine. From planting and pruning, to making and bottling the wine, Page-Roberts stresses the ease of the process and the satisfaction of the product. A splendid new adventure for gardeners and oenophiles

0-7892-0076-7 ABBEVILLE $24.95

Emile **Peynaud**

Knowing and Making Wine

A complete and informative guide to oenology for professionals and curious amateurs alike by the noted researcher and teacher

0-471-88149-X WILEY $64.95

Philip **Wagner**

Grapes Into Wine: The Art of Winemaking in America

A popular handbook for winemakers

0-394-73172-7 RANDOM HOUSE PB $18.00

Wine Tasting

Daniel **Johnnes** & Michael **Stephenson**

Daniel Johnnes's Top 200 Wines: An Expert's Guide to Maximum Enjoyment for Your Dollar

The sommelier of Manhattan's celebrated Montrachet shares his knowledge and taste with an eye on the pocketbook

See also **COMMENTARIES**

0-14-051316-7 PENGUIN PB $14.95

Andrew **Sharp**

Winetaster's Secrets

A step-by-step guide to the art of wine tasting. For the serious wine enthusiast, a very thorough and approachable manual to help you through the complexities of tasting, describing, and accurately appraising all types of wine

1-89562-936-5 WARWICK PB $14.95

Brian **St. Pierre** & Deborah **Jones**

A Perfect Glass of Wine: Choosing, Serving, and Enjoying Great Wines

Wine should not be intimidating! The object of this book is to give you enough solid knowledge so that you will be able to choose and serve wines intelligently with a minimum of worry

0-8118-1295-2 CHRONICLE $24.95

Whiskey and Other Spirits

John **Booth**

A Toast to Ireland: A Celebration of Traditional Irish Drinks

A history of Irish whiskey, poitin and Guiness in a photo and memorabilia filled volume

1-57098-062-4 ROBERTS RINEHART PB $18.95

Gordon **Brown**

Classic Spirits of the World

In chapters that range from a history of distillation to a country-by-country survey of brands, this is the most comprehensive independent guide to whiskeys, brandies, vodka, gin, rum, tequila, aquavit, schnapps, bitters, and liqueurs from all over the globe. Tasting notes, photographs, history

See also **GENERAL BOOKS ON WINE**

0-7892-0165-8 ABBEVILLE $29.95

The Whisky Trails: A Geographical Guide to Scotch Whisky

Photos and descriptions that include telephone numbers, directions, and business hours make this guide as useable as it is enjoyable

1-56138-490-9 RUNNING PRESS $24.95

Michael **Jackson**

Michael Jackson's Complete Guide to Single-Malt Scotchs

Alphabetical listing of over 300 different malts from 120 distilleries. With tasting notes and labels

1-56138-519-0 RUNNING PRESS $24.95

William **Pokhlebkin** & Renfrey **Clarke**, translator

A History of Vodka

In his search for the origin of his country's national drink, Pokhlebkin investigates everything from biology and technology to politics and cuisine

0-86091-359-7 VERSO $29.95

Gary **Regan** & Mardee Haidin **Regan**

The Book of Bourbon: And Other Fine American Whiskeys

Tasting notes on over 100 Whiskeys rounded out with history and anecdotes

1-88152-789-1 CHAPTERS $29.95

Cocktails

Sally Ann **Berk**

The California Health-Bar Drink Guide/Nearly 750 Nutritious and Delicious Non-Alcoholic Drinks

Non-alcoholic will never mean boring now; this book provides over 700 recipes for alchohol-free drinks with names like "Honey Don't" and "Kid Galahad"

1-88482-227-4 BLACK DOG $9.98

Barnaby **Conrad**

The Martini: An Illustrated History of an American Classic

0-8118-0717-7 CHRONICLE $24.95

Mr. **Boston**

The Mr. Boston Official Bartender's Guide: 50th Anniversary Edition

0-446-67042-1 WARNER $9.99

Michael **Jackson**

Michael Jackson's Bar and Cocktail Companion: The Connoisseur's Handbook

A slim, classy volume of drink recipes and directions for setting up a bar

1-56138-603-0 RUNNING PRESS $17.95

Fred **Powell**, editor

Bartender's Standard Manual

0-517-29305-6 OUTLET $5.99

Ales and Beers

Christopher **Finch**

Beer: Connoisseur's Guide to the World's Best

A lavishly illustrated history of beer, and a guide to the different brews

0-89659-913-2 ABBEVILLE $29.95

Michael **Jackson**

Michael Jackson's Beer Companion: The World's Great Beer Styles, Gastronomy, and Traditions

Beer, beer, and more beer. Styles, traditions, recipes, and menus featuring beer. From the author of *The New World Guide to Beer, The Complete Guide to Single Malt Scotch,* and *The World Guide to Whiskey*

1-56138-288-4 RUNNING PRESS $35.00

The New World Guide to Beer

A beer drinker's world tour

0-89471-884-3 RUNNING PRESS $22.98

The Simon & Schuster Pocket Guide to Beer: The Connoisseur's Companion to over 1500 Beers of the World

Lists over 1500 beers worldwide in a convenient pocket-size book

0-684-83062-0 FIRESIDE PB $13.00

Denis **Kelly**

Real Beer and Good Eats

A history of American beer and pub fare. From pickled oysters and quail with sweet stout gravy, a colonial favorite, to the present-day saloon fare of fish fries, onion soup, and soft pretzels, *Real Beer and Good Eats* provides recipes for the foods that traditionally accompany frothy ales. With appendixes on How Beer is Made, World Beer Styles, and Brewing Beer at Home, this is a necessary read for a country recently rediscovering the pleasures of micro-breweries and home-brewed ale

0-394-58267-5 KNOPF $27.50

Gregory J. **Noonan**

New Brewing Lager Beer: The Most Comprehensive Book for Home- And Microbrewers

A careful guide to the trickier process of brewing good lager beer, approachable enough for serious amatuers and comprehensive enough for small-scale professionals

0-937381-46-2 BREWERS PB $14.95

Charlie **Papazian**

The Home Brewer's Companion

THE authoritative guide to every step of the brewing process. Includes recipes from around the world

0-380-77287-6 AVON PB $11.00

Christine P. **Rhodes**, editor

The Encyclopedia of Beer

Ales, stouts, bocks, lambics, lagers, pale ales; with over 150 microbreweries producing dozens of distinctive varieties of brews, the world of beer in America has become as complex, and as fascinating, as that of wine. This encyclopedia covers the entire world of today's beer boom including breweries worldwide, various beer styles, ingredients and flavorings, brands from Abbey Beer to Zip City, and much more

0-8050-3799-3 HOLT $35.00

Home Brewing

William **Mares**

Making Beer

0-679-75502-0 KNOPF PB $17.00

0-394-72328-7 KNOPF PB $15.00

Dave **Miller**

The Complete Handbook of Home Brewing

0-88266-517-0 GARDEN WAY PB $11.95

Tea and Coffee

Dawn L. **Campbell**

The Tea Book

From the familiar Earl Grey to Moroccan Mint, Thai Iced Cha, Polish Esencja, Myanmar Pickled, and many, many more

1-56554-074-3 PELICAN $16.95

Kit **Chow** & Ione **Kramer**

All the Tea in China

An in-depth look at tea in China, from regional preferences to the art of ceramics, with detailed descriptions of 50 famous Chinese teas

0-8351-2194-1 CHINA BOOKS PB $14.95

Kenneth **Davids** & Ken **Davids**

Home Coffee Roasting: Romance & Revival

You can enjoy the exquisite aroma of fresh-roasted coffee and the satisfaction of roasting it to your exact specifications in your own home

0-312-14111-4 ST. MARTIN'S PB $14.95

Corby **Kummer**

The Joy of Coffee

Everything you need for the perfect cup of coffee

1-88152-753-0 CHAPTERS $22.00

Carole **Manchester**

French Tea: The Pleasures of the Table

Whoever said that tea was a peculiarly English institution obviously never set foot in Paris. A former fashion consultant for *Vogue* and *Elle* describes the finest teas, gives recipes for the madeleines and macaroons that best accompany them, and throws in a guide to the best *salons de the* in France. Beautiful, elegant, and a bargain

See also **BREAKFAST AND TEA FOOD**

0-688-11355-9 HEARST $17.00

Tea in the East

Instructions for brewing and recipes for appropriate snacks, as well as a list of places to take tea when you are in Udaipur, New Delhi, or just Connecticut

0-688-13243-X MORROW $23.00

Bo **Niles** & Veronica **McNiff**

The New York Book of Tea: Where to Take Tea and Buy Tea & Teaware

Whether you want the *a la francaise*, or a "haiku" tea, this book will direct you to the perfect spot

See also **NEW YORK CITY** under **NEW ENGLAND & THE MID-ATLANTIC STATES** under **GUIDES TO MEXICO, THE UNITED STATES, AND CANADA** under **TRAVEL GUIDES**

1-88549-206-5 CITY & CO. $15.00

Sara **Perry**

The Tea Book

The author of *The Complete Coffee Book* now presents perhaps the most complete guide to tea available. This handsome Volume features 60 recipes for preparing hot and iced tea, as well as recipes for baked goods and desserts. Also includes sections on the history of tea, tea lore, preparation, and ceremonies throughout the world

See also **BREAKFAST AND TEA FOOD** under **FOOD**

0-8118-0336-8 CHRONICLE PB $12.95

Michael **Smith**

The Afternoon Tea Book

History and traditional recipes

0-02-010351-4 MACMILLAN PB $10.95

Travel Literature

Anthologies

Patricia **Craig**, editor

The Oxford Book of Travel Stories

Charles Dickens, Edith Wharton, Evelyn Waugh and many other authors of renown fill the pages of this delightful collection

0-19-214253-4 OXFORD $27.50

Kevin **Crossley-Holland**, editor

The Oxford Book of Travel Verse

Surprises with the new and comforts with the familiar

0-19-214156-2 OXFORD PB $21.95

Larry **Dark**, editor

The Literary Traveler: Great Contemporary Stories of Travel and Self-Discovery

Traveling is not only a calculated movement through space, but also an inward activity, as proven in Dark's stunning new compilation, that includes contributions from Paul Theroux, Sue Miller, Mavis Gallant, Paul Bowles, William Trevor, Harold Brodkey, Alice Munro, and James Lasdun

0-670-84578-7 VIKING $22.95

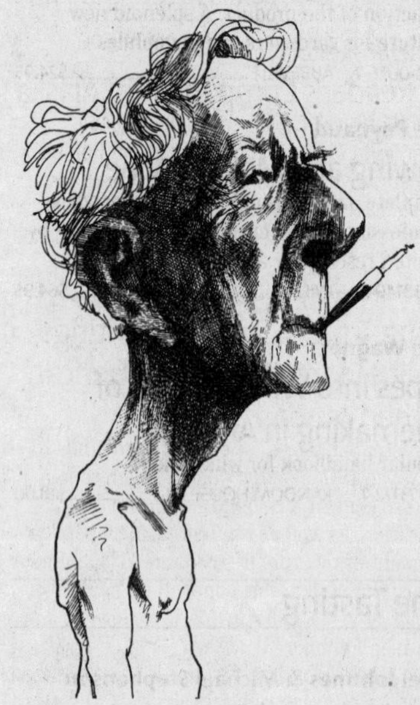

Paul Bowles

Paul **Fussell**

Abroad: British Literary Traveling Between the Wars

An excellent survey of the flowering of travel books between the wars

0-19-502767-1 OXFORD $25.00

Katherine **Govier**, editor

Without a Guide: Contemporary Women's Travel Adventures

A collection of travel essays from Alice Walker, E. Annie Proulx, and others

See also **ANTHOLOGIES OF WOMEN'S WRITING** under **WOMEN'S STUDIES** in **SOCIAL STUDIES**

1-88691-304-8 CONSORTIUM PB $16.00

Robin **Hanbury-Tenison**, editor

The Oxford Book of Exploration

Hailed by the London *Sunday Times* as "the greatest explorer of the last twenty years," Hanbury-Tenison now explores the impact, motivations, and even failures of the history's greatest explorers, front Marco polo to Teddy Roosevelt

0-19-214208-9 OXFORD $35.00

Natania **Jansz** & Miranda **Davies**, editors

More Women Travel: Adventures and Advice from More than 60 Countries

This collection can serve both as guide and literature for the traveler, with its presentation of travel information and alternating essays, which beautifully deliver a sense of place. Usual and unusual travel locations are featured, as well as information about what safety precautions women should take in each place

1-85828-098-2 ROUGH GUIDES PB $14.95

Stuart **Miller**

The Other Islands of New York: A Historical Companion

A collection of stories from New York's 40 islands other than Manhattan

See also **NORTH AMERICA**

0-88150-336-3 BACKCOUNTRY PB $17.00

Alan **Ryan**, editor

The Reader's Companion to Alaska

A compilation of travel writing by dogsled runner John Muir, humor writer Erma Bombeck, and many others on the largest, and perhaps wildest, state in America

0-15-600368-6 HARCOURT BRACE PB $15.00

Mary Suzanne **Schriber**

Telling Travels: Selected Writings by Nineteenth Century American Women Abroad

When "steam palaces" opened foreign lands to safe travel, 19th-century women began to join the great century's colonial expansion and exploration, as well as the increasingly popular enjoyment of tourism. Henry James's Isabelle Archer inhabited a world opened up by Harriet Beecher Stowe, Catharine Maria Sedgwick, and Constance Fenimore Woolson

0-87580-195-1 NORTHERN ILLINOIS $35.00

0-87580-561-2 NORTHERN ILLINOIS PB $18.50

Travel Essays

Tim **Cahill**

Jaguars Ripped My Flesh

The offbeat encounters of the nervy travel writer in his latest collection of essays

0-679-77079-8 VINTAGE PB $13.00

John **Caldwell**

Desperate Voyage

0-924486-20-1 SHERIDAN PB $14.95

Bruce **Chatwin**

Anatomy of Restlessness: Selected Writings 1969-1989

See also **20TH-CENTURY BRITISH ESSAYS AND OTHER PROSE** in **LITERATURE OF THE BRITISH ISLES**

0-670-86859-0 VIKING $23.95

Antoine **de Saint-Exupery**

Airman's Odyssey

TRANSLATED BY STUART GILBERT & LEWIS GALANTIERE

0-15-603733-5 HARCOURT BRACE PB $12.00

Michael **Flanagan**

Stations: An Imagined Journey

Flanagan innovatively combines photographs, newspaper clips, diaries, and reminiscences to recreate the lost world of a mythical railroad line, intertwining his fable with a poignant love story

0-679-43547-6 PANTHEON $21.00

Keath **Fraser**

Bad Trips

0-679-72908-9 VINTAGE PB $13.00

Pico **Iyer**

Falling Off the Map: Some Lonely Places of the World

The author of *Video Night in Kathmandu* now shares his journeys through "the places that don't fit in," such as North Korea's 105-story hotel in a land virtually devoid of tourists or the strange, and often darkly comedic, results of geographic or psychic isolation

0-679-74612-9 VINTAGE PB $11.00

Henry **James**

"There is, I think, no more nutritive or suggestive truth...than that of the perfect dependence of the 'moral' sense of a work of art on the amount of felt life concerned in producing it. The question comes back thus, obviously, to the kind and degree of the artist's prime sensibility, which is the soil out of which his subject springs. The quality and capacity of that soil, its ability to 'grow' with due freshness and straightness any vision of life, represents, strongly or weakly, the projected morality. That element is but another name for the more or less close connexion of the subject with some mark made on the intelligence, with some sincere experience."—From the preface to the New York Edition of The Portrait of a Lady

Travel Writings: The Continent

There are books in the hundreds ready to tell you where to eat, shop, sleep and be seen; I defy you to name any which will provide better company than James"—*LA Times*

See also **LIBRARY OF AMERICA** in **LITERATURE OF THE AMERICAS**

EDITED BY RICHARD HOWARD

0-940450-77-1 LIBRARY OF AMERICA $35.00

Henry James

Travel Writings: Great Britain and America

Includes *English Hours, The American Scene* and *Other Travels*

EDITED BY RICHARD HOWARD

0-940450-76-3 LIBRARY OF AMERICA $35.00

Kathlyn Maurean **Liscomb**

Learning from Mt. Hua: A Chinese Physician's Illustrated Travel Record and Painting Theory

0-521-41112-2 CAMBRIDGE $85.00

Beryl **Markham**

West with the Night

Written by the aviator who became the first person to fly alone east to west across the Atlantic. "With the skill of someone who has filled long nights with stories, Markham recounts her adventure—discoveries, rescues, and narrow escapes, the glint of an airplane abandoned in the desert, the look of a lion about to pounce"—*Nation*

0-86547-118-5 NORTH POINT PB $13.00

Jan **Morris**

Destinations

More essays on travel, reprinted from *Rolling Stone*

0-19-503069-9 OXFORD PB $9.95

Journeys

"A mystery tour" whose stops range from Santa Fe, New Mexico, to Cetinje, Yugoslavia

0-19-503452-X OXFORD $25.00

Michael **Palin**

Around the World in 80 Days

The Monty Python star retraces the route of Phileas Fogg, traveling by ship, barge, and camel. The companion volume to a BBC television series

0-563-20826-0 PARKWEST $24.95

Freya **Stark**

The Journey's Echo

Extracts from the great traveler's many books, ranging from the *Letters from Syria* (1927-28) to *Riding to the Tigris* (1958)

0-88001-218-8 ECCO PB $8.95

Edith **Wharton** & Sarah **Bird**, editor

The first woman to win the Pulitzer Prize, Edith Wharton was an immensely popular writer in her day. She depicts the life of the American upper class—a class into which she was born—with irony and satire, exposing its lack of compassion and its stifling of human happinness.

Edith Wharton Abroad: Selected Travel Writings, 1888-20

0-312-12417-1 ST. MARTIN'S $22.95

0-312-16120-4 ST. MARTIN'S PB $14.95

Edith Wharton

Great Britain and Ireland

Though the selection is disappointingly small, the available accounts present widely diverging views of one small country; compare, for instance, J.B. Priestley's travels in the '30s with those of Beryl Bainbridge 50 years later along the same route.

Anthony **Bailey**

A Walk Through Wales

"As a portrait of Wales today, this book is unmatched"—*New Yorker*

0-06-118008-4 HARPERPERENNIAL PB $12.00

Paul **Bailey**, editor

The Oxford Book of London

The life and growth of the city from the Middle Ages to present day, chronicled through the works of such renowned authors as Charles Dickens, Ben Johnson, William Wordsworth, George Bernard Shaw, Daniel Defoe, John Evelyn, and Samuel Pepys

See also **LONDON** under **TOPICS IN BRITISH HISTORY** under **GREAT BRITAIN AND IRELAND** in **WORLD HISTORY AND CURRENT AFFAIRS**

0-19-214192-9 OXFORD $25.00

0-19-283244-1 OXFORD PB $13.95

Bill **Bryson**

Notes from a Small Island: An Affectionate Portrait of Britain

After his 20-year residence in England, American journalist Bryson takes a farewell tour via public transportation and foot, recording his witty, detailed observations about the towns and villages along the way

0-688-14725-9 MORROW $25.00

John **Hillaby**

Journey Through Britain

A much-loved author who travels the world on foot takes on his own country

1-85089-683-6 DUAL DOLPHIN $69.95

Carl Philip **Moritz**

Journeys of a German in England

A walking tour taken in 1782

0-907871-50-X HIPPOCRENE PB $11.95

Jan **Morris**

Oxford

Written in the early '60s, this book (with *The World of Venice)* established Jan Morris as a distinguished travel writer

0-19-282065-6 OXFORD PB $13.95

J.B. **Priestley**

English Journey

London to the Tyne and back again in 1933, in search of "little England" and "that inner growing tradition of the English spirit"

0-226-68212-9 CHICAGO $29.95

Israel **Shenker**

In the Footsteps of Johnson and Boswell: A Modern Day Journey Through Scotland

The writings of Johnson and Boswell serve as points of departure for each chapter of this chronicle

0-395-3185-6 HOUGHTON MIFFLIN $14.95

A.N. **Wilson**, editor

The Norton Book of London

The various eyes of Dickens, Dostoyevsky, Joe Orton, and Martin Amis give us a unique view of London through the centuries

0-393-03631-6 NORTON $30.00

Ireland

Dervla **Murphy**

A Place Apart

An Irishwoman visits Northern Ireland in an attempt to understand the passions that separate the two countries

0-7195-3476-3 DEVIN-ADAIR $15.00

Niall **Williams** & Christine **Breen**

O Come Ye Back to Ireland: Our First Year in County Clare

0-939149-22-2 SOPHIA PB $9.95

Arthur **Young**

A Tour in Ireland: With General Observations on the Present State of That Kingdom Made in the Years 1776, 1777 and 1778

A shrewd account of 18th-century Ireland

0-85640-303-2 BLACKSTAFF $14.95

Europe

Travelers have long been drawn to Italy as a repository of classical civilization, and youthful British aristocrats commonly rounded out their education by gaining first-hand knowledge of France and Greece as well. In the 19th-century, the advent of the railroad and a growing appreciation of the beauties of the Natural Sublime enabled voyagers to wander farther afield.

American visitors joined the British and European contingents when steamships began plying the New York-Liverpool route in 1819. Thus, two closely linked worlds began to record and examine myths and realities.

John **Ash**

A Byzantine Journey

0-679-40934-3 RANDOM HOUSE $25.00

Hilaire **Belloc**

The Path to Rome

An account of Belloc's journey from France to Rome on foot. In later years he wrote, "I hate writing. I wouldn't have written a word if I could have helped it. I only wrote for money. *The Path to Rome* is the only book I ever wrote for love"

See also **19TH-CENTURY PROSE** under **THE 19TH-CENTURY** in **LITERATURE OF THE BRITISH ISLES**

0-89526-784-5 LAB FOR EDUCATION PB $8.95

Hilaire Belloc

Ina **Caro**

The Road From the Past

Traveling through history in France

0-15-600363-5 HARCOURT BRACE PB $15.00

Charles **Dickens**

"Chesterton asserted that time would show that Dickens was not merely one of the Victorians, but incomparably the greatest English writer of his time; and Shaw coupled his name with that of Shakespeare. It is the conviction of the present writer that both these judgments were justified. Dickens—though he cannot of course pretend to the rank where Shakespeare has few companions—was nevertheless the greatest dramatic writer that the English had had since Shakespeare, and he created the largest and most varied world."—Edmund Wilson in The Wound and the Bow

Pictures from Italy

Dickens didn't leave his social conscience behind when he traveled abroad; in Italy he found the effects of years of political turmoil at odds with "the beauties, natural and artificial, of which it is full to overflowing"

0-88001-164-5 ECCO PB $7.50

George **Gissing**

After a long period of neglect, George Gissing's powerfully realistic, relentlessly pessimistic novels have been rediscovered.

By the Ionian Sea: Notes of a Ramble in Southern Italy

0-8101-6010-2 MARLBORO PB $13.95

Johann Wolfgang von **Goethe**

Italian Journey: 1786-1788

"*Italian Journey* is not only a description of places, persons and things, but also a psychological document of the first importance dealing with a life crisis which, in various degrees of intensity, we all experience somewhere between the ages of thirty-five and forty-five"—W.H. Auden

See also **ENLIGHTENMENT, STURM UND DRANG, AND CLASSICISM** under **GERMAN LITERATURE** in **LITERATURE OF EUROPE, AFRICA, AND ASIA**

TRANSLATED BY W.H. AUDEN & ELIZABETH MAYER

0-14-044233-2 PENGUIN PB $11.95

Johann Wolfgang von Goethe

Barbara Grizzuti **Harrison**

Italian Days

A mixture of history, politics, folkore, food, and the arts—with local anecdotes and personal reflection

0-395-55131-5 TICKNOR & FIELDS PB $15.95

Henry **James**

A Little Tour in France

See also **THE 19TH-CENTURY: AFTER THE CIVIL WAR** under **AMERICAN LITERATURE TO 1900** in **LITERATURE OF THE AMERICAS**

0-374-18956-0 FS&G $18.95

1-55584-129-5 GROVE $24.95

D.H. **Lawrence**

The intemperate, tubercular, coal miner's son looked like a satyr, at times filled his writing with crazed messianism, was accused by Bertrand Russell and others of espousing fascism, and—by loosening the sexual clamp on the English novel of the 1910s, '20s, and '30s—excited the imaginations of several generations of readers. Among the editions listed below, the Cambridge series presents new texts incorporating recent research.

D.H. Lawrence and Italy

A collection of three of his most evocative books on Italy: *Twilight in Italy, Sea and Sardinia*, and the posthumously published *Etruscan Places*

See also **20TH-CENTURY BRITISH ESSAYS AND OTHER PROSE** in **LITERATURE OF THE BRITISH ISLES**

0-14-009520-9 VIKING PB $13.99

The dancers on the right wall move with a strange, powerful alertness onwards. They are men dressed only in a loose coloured scarf, or in the gay handsome chlamys draped as a mantle. The subulo plays the double flute the Etruscans loved so much, touching the stops with big, exaggerated hands, the man behind him touches the seven-stringed lyre, the man in front turns round and signals with his left hand, holding a big wine-bowl in his right. And so they move on, on their long, sandalled feet, past the little berried olive-trees, swiftly going with their limbs full of life, full of life to the tips.

D.H. LAWRENCE AND ITALY

J.B.S. **Morritt**

A Grand Tour: Letters and Journals, 1794-1796

An enthusiastic and typical young Grand Tourist travels through Europe as far as Constantinople

0-7126-0993-8 DAVID & CHARLES PB $11.95

Richard **Stoneman**, editor

A Literary Companion to Travel in Greece

0-89236-298-7 GETTY MUSEUM PB $17.95

Colm **Toibin**

The Sign of the Cross: Travels in Catholic Europe

0-679-44203-0 PANTHEON $24.00

Mark **Twain**

The Innocents Abroad

Shrewd observation and typical Twain humor in this familiar book about the New World encountering the Old on a trip to Europe and the Holy Land

See also **THE 19TH-CENTURY: AFTER THE CIVIL WAR** under **AMERICAN LITERATURE TO 1900** in **LITERATURE OF THE AMERICAS**

0-451-52502-7 NEW AMERICAN LIBRARY PB $5.95

Henry **Miller**

The Colossus of Maroussi

Miller's idiosyncratic account of his first visit to Greece in the late '30s captures the essence of people and place like almost no other writer

0-8112-0109-0 NEW DIRECTIONS PB $9.95

Henry Miller

Edith **Wharton**

The first woman to win the Pulitzer Prize, Edith Wharton was an immensely popular writer in her day. She depicts the life of the American upper class—a class into which she was born—with irony and satire, exposing its lack of compassion ans its stifling of human happinness.

A Motor-Flight Through France

First published in 1908 and long unavailable, this book began as a series of articles for *The Atlantic Monthly.* Wharton's reflections on her travels through the French countryside in a 1904 Panhard-Levassor car recreated a long-lost way of life, little changed from that of medieval times

0-87580-163-3 NORTHERN ILLINOIS $28.00

0-87580-553-1 NORTHERN ILLINOIS PB $15.00

The motor-car has restored the romance of travel from all the compulsions and contacts of the railway, the bondage to fixed hours and the beaten track, the approach to each town through the area of ugliness and desolation created by the railway itself.

A MOTOR-FLIGHT THROUGH FRANCE

Europe Since 1945

Ann **Barry**

At Home in France: Tales of an American and Her House Abroad

The story of a former *New Yorker* editor who purchases a home in the fairy-tale village of Carennac, and her time there over two years. She takes her readers on excursions into Brittany and Provence, to back road inns and markets, to Gothic churches and a majestic chateaux

0-345-39201-9 BALLANTINE $20.00

James **Bentley**

The Most Beautiful Villages of Dordogne

38 towns and villages along this 293-mile river in France are highlighted in 258 color photos by Hugh Palmer

0-500-54201-5 THAMES & HUDSON $40.00

Lawrence **Durrell**

Prospero's Cell: A Guide to the Landscape and Manners of the Island Corfu

See also **20TH-CENTURY BRITISH ESSAYS AND OTHER PROSE** in **LITERATURE OF THE BRITISH ISLES**

1-56924-766-8 MARLOWE PB $10.95

Reflections on a Marine Venus: A Companion to the Landscape of Rhodes

1-56924-791-9 MARLOWE PB $10.95

Patrick Leigh **Fermor**

Between the Woods and the Water: From the Middle Danube to the Iron Gates

Conclusion of the trip begun in *A Time of Gifts*

0-14-009430-X PENGUIN PB $11.00

Mani: Travel in the Southern Peloponnese
A seldom-visited region of Greece explored in a quest to seek out the relationship between the Greeks, their history, and the land
0-14-011511-0 VIKING PB $9.00

Roumeli: Travels in Northern Greece
Wanderings in the "contracting wilderness" of central Greece, with its remote monasteries and local legends of Lord Byron
1-85089-212-1 ABC CLIO $19.95

A Time of Gifts: On Foot to Constantinople from the Hook of Holland
A young traveler tries his luck on the open road
0-14-004947-9 PENGUIN PB $11.95

M.F.K. **Fisher**

Long Ago in France: The Years in Dijon
No one writes about France with the richness and verve of M.F.K. Fisher, as she proves once again in this memoir. "M.F.K. Fisher represents a type of American artist still cherished in the national imagination, one who has knocked around the world, and so understands lives lived under many different conditions"
—Patricia Storace, *NY Review of Books*
See also **MEMOIRS AND JOURNALS** under **20TH-CENTURY AMERICAN ESSAYS AND JOURNALISM** in **LITERATURE OF THE AMERICAS**
0-671-75514-5 TOUCHSTONE PB $10.00

Two Towns in Provence
Includes *Map of Another Town* and *A Considerable Town*
0-394-71631-0 VINTAGE PB $16.00

Ford Madox **Ford**

Provence: From Minstrels to the Machine
"The expansiveness and exuberance of spirit, the embracing knowledge of the place, that show forth in Ford's love affair with Provence will always give this book a joyous life of its own"—Eudora Welty
See also **20TH-CENTURY BRITISH ESSAYS AND OTHER PROSE** in **LITERATURE OF THE BRITISH ISLES**
0-88001-413-X ECCO PB $13.00

Ford Madox Ford

Christina **Hardyment**

Heidi's Alp
An English family seeks out the locales of their favorite fairy stories across the Continent, often with humorous and instructive results
0-87113-178-1 ATLANTIC MONTHLY PB $7.95

Barbara Grizzuti **Harrison**

The Islands of Italy: Sicily, Sardinia, and the Aeolian Isles
Harrison extends the vision of *Italian Days* to the island worlds of Sicily, Sardinia, and the Aeolian Islands, from Taormina to the Sopramente hills
PHOTOGRAPHS BY SHEILA NARDULLI
0-395-59302-6 TICKNOR & FIELDS $40.00

John **Hillaby**

Journey Through Europe
An ambitious, recent walking tour
0-586-08141-0 ACADEMY CHICAGO PB $7.00

Robert **Hughes**

Barcelona
Extensive historical research, intimate personal experience, and a dazzling prose style combine to make it, "like [E.M.] Forster's *Alexandria* and Mary McCarthy's *Venice Observed* a classic of the genre of urban history"
—*NY Times Book Review*
0-394-58027-3 KNOPF $27.50

Dzevad **Karahasan**

Sarajevo, Exodus of a City
The tragedy of the great city, in a personal account. "A must read for every contemporary person"—*Die Makische Allgemeine*
1-56836-057-6 KODANSHA PB $10.00

David **Leavitt** & Mark **Mitchell**

Italian Pleasures
The authors' collected essays sing the praises of their adopted country
0-8118-1227-8 CHRONICLE $16.95

J.G. **Links**

Venice For Pleasure
An unusual walking guide to Venice, favoring ordinary pleasures over historical obligations. "Not only the best guide-book to that city ever written, but the best guide-book to *any* city ever written"—*The Times* [London]
1-55921-048-6 MOYER BELL PB $12.95

Peter **Mayle**

Toujours Provence
Mayle's charming and evocative sequel to *A Year in Provence* now in paperback. "Picking up [*Toujours Provence*] is like returning to a country inn where you know the owner, where they save your favorite room for you, and the bartender remembers your name"
—*NY Times Book Review*
0-679-40253-5 KNOPF $23.00
0-679-73604-2 VINTAGE PB $11.00

A Year in Provence
The popular first book in Mayle's delightful series on life in rural France
0-679-73114-8 VINTAGE PB $11.00

Peter Mayle

A Year in Provence, Toujours Provence: Boxed Set
These bestsellers are now available in a beautiful slipcase. Photos and text bring the landscapes, peoples, and places of the South of France back home to the armchair travelers. "Peter Mayle [is] something of a wonder…chronicling the scene around him in irresistible prose"—*Time*
0-679-74943-8 VINTAGE PB $23.00

Mary **McCarthy**

The Stones of Florence
A perceptive look into the spirit of one of Italy's greatest cities
See also **RENAISSANCE CITIES** under **RENAISSANCE ITALY AND THE COMING OF HUMANISM** under **MEDIEVAL AND RENAISSANCE EUROPE** in **WORLD HISTORY AND CURRENT AFFAIRS**
0-15-185079-8 HARCOURT BRACE $49.95
0-15-685081-8 HARCOURT BRACE PB $19.95

Venice Observed
A companion to her book *The Stones of Florence*, both published in the '50s
0-15-693521-X HARCOURT BRACE PB $8.00

Lucy **McCauley**

Traveler's Tales Spain
A sampler from a variety of travelers—teachers, musicians, writers—which ultimately guides the would-be traveler to what to seek out, what to avoid, when in Spain
1-88521-107-4 TRAVELER'S TALES PB $17.95

Sara **Midda**

The South of France: A Book of Days
1-56305-367-5 WORKMAN $13.95

John **Miller** & Kirsten **Miller**

Venice: Tales of the City
Thomas Mann, Edith Wharton, Orson Welles, Casanova, Jeanette Winterson, and Jean Paul Sartre are among the prestigious list of authors represented in this volume
0-8118-0471-2 CHRONICLE $13.95

Farley **Mowat**
Aftermath: Travels in a Postwar World
The author's wartime steps are retraced
1-57098-103-5 ROBERTS RINEHART $22.95

Dervla **Murphy**
Transylvania and Beyond: A Travel Memoir
Murphy travels through Romania just after the fall of Communism when the country's still reeling from its sudden liberation. "This book is more than just a record of a journey, but also an insight into the soul of the country" —*Travel Books Worldwide*
0-87951-603-8 OVERLOOK PB $13.95

Cees **Nooteboom**
The Roads to Santiago: Essays
Twenty-five essays by the winner of the 1993 European Literary Prize recount explorations of Spain over three decades. Nooteboom describes the shrine of the Black Madonna of Guadalupe, reflects on the life and work of Velazquez from the Prado, and admires the under-appreciated Zurbaran
See also **DUTCH LITERATURE** in **LITERATURE OF EUROPE, AFRICA, AND ASIA**
TRANSLATED BY INA RILKE
0-15-100197-9 HARCOURT BRACE $24.00

James **O'Reilly**, editor
Travelers' Tales France
1-88521-102-3 O'REILLY PB $17.95

Tim **Parks**
An Italian Education: The Further Adventures of an Expatriate in Verona
A compelling look into the byzantine complexity of Italian society and the foibles, rituals, and moral contradictions of family life. The sequel to *Italian Neighbors*
0-8021-1508-X GROVE $22.00
0-380-72760-9 AVON PB $12.50

John **Pemble**
Venice Rediscovered
An exploration of how American and European outsiders developed an obsession with preserving this dying city at all costs
0-19-820501-5 CLARENDON $25.00

Kate **Ratliffe**
A Culinary Journey in Gascony: Recipes and Stories from My French Canal Boat
A fine layering of travel writing and fabulous recipes from the author's tour, by way of an old Dutch barge, down her favorite canal in southwestern France
0-89815-753-6 TEN SPEED PB $16.95

Elizabeth **Romer**
The Tuscan Year: Life and Food in an Italian Valley
The daily routines, including food preparation, form the framework of this portrait of a family situated between Umbria and Tuscany
0-86547-478-8 NORTH POINT $20.00

Mort **Rosenblum**
The Secret Life of the Seine
"I greatly enjoyed *The Secret Life of the Seine*, not only for its erudition and its sense of fun, but for its bold exploration down France's central artery and into its heart"—Paul Theroux
0-201-62461-3 ADDISON-WESLEY $21.00
0-201-48941-4 ADDISON-WESLEY PB $12.00

Edmund **White** & Hubert **Sorin**, illustrator
Our Paris: Sketches From Memory
White, in collaboration with the French artist Sorin, offers a light-hearted and irreverent tour of their neighborhood, the Chatelet, from the ultra-chic couturiers to the prostitutes of the Rue St. Denis. Underlying the delightful and affectionate narrative is the theme of Sorin's AIDS, rendering this book a tribute to the courage with which the couple celebrated their life in the city of light
0-679-44166-2 KNOPF $22.00

Freda **White**
Three Rivers of France: Dordogne, Lot, Tarn
This classic guide, published in 1952, remains a great piece of travel writing
1-85145-754-2 TRAFALGAR SQUARE PB $22.95

Paul **Wilson**, editor
Prague: A Traveler's Literary Companion
Twenty-four stories are arranged by the areas of the city they illuminate, exposing the richness and irony inevitable in a city that blends Czech, German, and Jewish cultures
See also **HUNGARIAN LITERATURE** under **EASTERN EUROPEAN LITERATURE** in **LITERATURE OF EUROPE, AFRICA, AND ASIA**
1-88351-301-4 CONSORTIUM PB $12.95

The Commonwealth of Independent States

There have been few published accounts of travel in Russia, and as a result it remains in the minds of many Westerners a land of myth and rumor. The writers who have penetrated the layers of mystery and red tape are worth a read by anyone planning to essay the journey.

Yuz **Aleshkovsky**
A Ring in a Case
0-8101-1138-1 NORTHWESTERN $24.95

Lloyd **Jones**
Biografi: A Traveler's Tale
"*Biografi* is travel writing as it should be: with an intellectual and emotional investment in the country which is subject [Albania]"—*TLS*
See also **EASTERN EUROPE** under **EUROPE SINCE 1945** in **WORLD HISTORY AND CURRENT AFFAIRS**
0-374-11318-1 FS&G $19.00
0-15-600128-4 HARVEST PB $10.95

Henry **Seebohm**
The Birds of Siberia: The Yenesei
More natural adventures in old Russia
0-86299-260-5 HIPPOCRENE PB $5.95

Laurens **Van Der Post**
A widely traveled writer who states that he has walked over more of Africa than anyone else alive, Van der Post spent many years among the bushmen and writes feelingly of their myths and legends.
Journey Into Russia
0-933280-25-4 ISLAND PB $16.95

Asia

Ian **Buruma**
God's Dust: A Modern Asian Journey
Deep familiarity with customs of both east and west makes Buruma one of the most qualified observers of the thriving Pacific Rim. *God's Dust* is a tour of Burma, Thailand, the Philippines, Malaysia, Singapore, Taiwan, South Korea, and Japan
0-374-52235-9 NOONDAY PB $11.00

Ian Buruma

Eric **Hansen**
The Traveler: An American Odyssey in the Himalayas
Acclaimed travel-writer Hansen gives a loving testimonial to the passion and purity that inspired Hugh Swift's writings, while 56 of Swift's magnificent full-color photographs are an eloquent record of an extraordinary traveler
0-87156-350-9 SIERRA CLUB PB $18.00

Eleanor Holgate **Lattimore**
Turkestan Reunion
Eleanor Lattimore takes a separate, highly challenging route through China before joining her husband for an epic journey through the homelands of the Mongols and over the Himalayas to India
1-56836-053-3 KODANSHA PB $14.00

Owen **Lattimore** & Orville **Schell**
High Tartary
Completes a splendid husband-and-wife travel and adventure trilogy, and remains one of the best books on Chinese Turkestan, with its rich, exotic history, its lush valleys, great trade caravans, the beckoning "Mountains of Heaven"

and the snow bound high passes of the massive barrier of the Karakorum range

1-56836-054-1 KODANSHA PB $15.00

James **O'Reilly** & Larry **Habegger**, editors

Travelers' Tales Thailand

"*Travelers' Tales Thailand* is the first title in a new revolutionary style of travel guidebooks…It is an enriching and absorbing collection, and a perfect travelling companion for anyone going to this exotic land"—*Times News Service*

1-88521-105-8 O'REILLY PB $17.95

Jeremy **Seal**

A Fez of the Heart: Travels Around Turkey in Search of a Hat

This engaging and funny travelogue creates an inroad to a country defined by the tension between modernity and tradition, and its antithetical European and Islamic influences

0-15-600393-7 HARVEST PB $14.00

Andrew **Wilson**

Abode of Snow

In 1873 Scottish explorer Wilson traversed the Himalayan crest zone, a virtually unheard of trip at the time. His descriptions of the "flaming stars" over the snowy peaks, of encounters with an uncomprehending native population that had never seen the likes of this traveler, and of altitude sickness, snow blindness, and hunger make for a unique account of a purer time

1-55921-100-8 MOYER BELL PB $12.95

The Near and Middle East

When Wilfred Thesiger set off, in the '50s, to cross the Empty Quarter of Arabia because he "craved for adventure in savage lands," he was conscious of being the latest in a long line of British explorers who had found the savagery and beauty of the desert irresistible. The books of these British Arabists present a powerful and seductive picture of desert life before the discovery and exploitation of oil rendered it ever more precarious.

The Arabian desert may have been magnetic, but the British had been turning their attention eastward even before Napoleon's 1798 expedition to Egypt. The most notable early traveler, Alexander Kinglake, made a typical, relatively unadventurous journey to the eastern Mediterranean and the Near East in 1835. *Eothen*, his impressionistic account of the voyage, is written in a self-deprecating, ironic style that echoes in his literary heirs today.

Richard **Burton**

Personal Narrative of a Pilgrimage to Al-Madinah and Meccah

Volume 1

The preeminent Victorian orientalist, fluent in Arabic, disguised himself in 1853 to become the first Englishman to visit the sacred cities of Mecca and Medina

0-486-21217-3 DOVER PB $10.95

Volume 2

0-486-21218-1 DOVER PB $10.95

Robert **Byron**

The Road to Oxiana

Persia and Afghanistan in the early '30s, described in a rich mixture of scholarship and adventure narrative

See also **20TH-CENTURY BRITISH ESSAYS AND OTHER PROSE** in **LITERATURE OF THE BRITISH ISLES**

0-19-503067-2 OXFORD PB $13.95

Sir John **Chardin**

Travels in Persia, 1673-1677

0-486-25636-7 DOVER PB $9.95

Christopher **Dickey**

Expats: Travels in Arabia, from Tripoli to Teheran

A timely exploration from the Western perspective of the tensions, hardships, and pleasures of life in the Middle East

0-87113-463-2 ATLANTIC MONTHLY PB $10.95

Tony **Horwitz**

Baghdad Without a Map: And Other Misadventures in Arabia

A *Wall Street Journal* reporter with an eye for humorous detail travels through Israel and 13 Muslim countries

0-525-24960-5 PLUME PB $18.95

The traditional Islamic ban on representation of the human form had been overcome in Baghdad, in a very big way. Saddam's face perched on the dashboards of taxis, on the walls of every shop and every office, on clock faces, on ashtrays, on calendars, on billboards at every major intersection—sometimes four pictures to an intersection. Some of the portraits covered entire building fronts. And to ensure that your eye didn't ignore the pictures from sheer repetition, Saddam appeared in innumerable guises: in military fatigues festooned with medals, in Bedouin garb atop a charging steed, in pilgrim's robes praying at Mecca, in a double-breasted suit and aviator sunglasses, looking cool and sophisticated.

BAGHDAD WITHOUT A MAP: AND OTHER MISADVENTURES IN ARABIA

Mary S. **Lovell**

Rebel Heart: The Scandalous Life of Jane Digby

The life of Digby, a British aristocrat who, married at 18, was scandalously divorced at 21. With every door in London closed to her, she lived a maverick lifestyle, eventually settling in Arabia where she married a sheik

0-393-03895-5 NORTON $25.00

V.S. **Naipaul**

Among the Believers: An Islamic Journey

A foremost novelist, essayist, and frequently controversial socio-political critic, born of Indian parents in Trinidad, but a British resident since the '50s, provides commentary conducted through Iran, Pakistan, Malaysia, and Indonesia to the "Islamic Winter" of the final chapter

See also **FUNDAMENTALISM** under **CONTEMPORARY POLITICS AND SOCIETY** under **THE CONTEMPORARY MIDDLE EAST** in **WORLD HISTORY AND CURRENT AFFAIRS**

0-394-71195-5 RANDOM HOUSE PB $15.00

V.S. Naipaul

Christopher **Pick**, editor

Embassy to Constantinople: The Travels of Lady Mary Wortley Montagu

Letters full of keen observations from a prominent British traveler in 18th-century Turkey

0-941533-41-7 NEW AMSTERDAM $30.00

0-460-87235-4 EVERYMAN'S PB $10.95

Nitza **Rosovsky**, editor

City of the Great King: Jerusalem from David to the Present

A single magnificent volume brings to life the majestic story of the world's holiest city. From its natural scenic splendor to its architectural fascination, Rosovsky's portrait also tells the city's history and the history of its centrality to the three monotheisms. A splendid book for travelers and armchair travelers alike

See also **GENERAL HISTORIES** under **JEWISH HISTORY** in **WORLD HISTORY AND CURRENT AFFAIRS**

0-674-13190-8 HARVARD $39.95

Mary Lee **Settle** & Jan **Norris**

Turkish Reflections: A Biography of a Place

The author of *The Beulah Quintet* and *Blood Ties* embarks on a tour of a country where she lived for three years in the early '70s, and gives a sympathetic account of the country and its people. "A diverting mixture of travelogue, history, polemic and contemporary portrait" —Roderick Conway Morris, *NY Times Book Review*

0-671-77997-4 TOUCHSTONE PB $11.00

Freya **Stark**

Baghdad Sketches

0-910395-81-0 MARLBORO PB $11.95

John Lloyd **Stephens**

Incidents of Travel in Egypt, Arabia Petraea, and the Holy Land

Stephens—who went on to become one of the great pioneers of Central American exploration—published this account of his Middle Eastern travels in 1837, leading an enthusiastic Edgar Allan Poe to declare: "He is a traveler with whom we shall like to take other journeys"

0-486-29155-3 DOVER PB $14.95

Peter **Theroux**

Sandstorms: Days and Nights in Arabia

An inside account of a journalist's years in Saudi Arabia, recounted in a tone of ironic detachment. Theroux evokes more contradictions than he can resolve, but his book is full of unexpected insights into one of the world's most sealed-off societies

0-393-02841-0 NORTON $18.95

Wilfred **Thesiger**

Arabian Sands

Travels made from 1945 to 1950 among the Bedu of the Empty Quarter—a way of life "doomed" in Thesiger's eyes by encroaching technology

0-14-009514-4 VIKING PB $12.95

Central Asia

Marco Polo's tale of his 20-year travels in the service of Kublai Khan in the late 13th century revealed an exotic world of which the West had little inkling. Some of his destinations—parts of Burma, for instance—were not visited again by Europeans for another 600 years.

Travelers still encounter strenuous difficulties in that remote area known as the Roof of the World, where the very act of traveling is often more important than the arrival at a destination.

Fred **Burnaby**

On Horseback Through Asia Minor

Northern Turkey in the winter of 1876-77, and the Russian threat again. Back home, the book solidified Burnaby's status as a popular hero

0-87052-211-6 HIPPOCRENE PB $5.95

A Ride to Khiva: Travels and Adventures in Central Asia

A captain in the Royal Horse Guards investigates a perceived Russian threat to the British Empire's Indian borders in Turkestan

0-405-03010-X ARNO $23.95

Alexandra **David-Neel**

Magic and Mystery in Tibet

Spiritual life and practices among the lamas in the early 20th-century, as described by a Frenchwoman who became fluent in Tibetan and lived as a Buddhist for many years

0-486-22682-4 DOVER PB $8.95

My Journey to Lhasa

A gripping account of the successful attempt to become the first white woman (and one of the first whites) to enter Lhasa (in disguise) in 1923

0-8070-5903-X BEACON PB $15.00

Carroll **Dunham** & Ian **Baker**

Tibet: Reflections from the Wheel of Life

This remarkable volume documents people in different life stages to give an intimate perspective on the Tibetan cycle of birth, death, and rebirth. Set in Tibet's stunning mountain vistas, and against the ongoing Tibetan struggle to win independence from China, this book portrays the many faces of a fascinating culture

PHOTOGRAPHY BY THOMAS L. KELLY

FOREWORD BY THE DALAI LAMA

1-55859-218-0 ABBEVILLE $55.00

Lee **Feigon**

Demystifying Tibet: Unlocking the Secrets of the Land of the Snows

A scholarly, unromantic look at this vast land and its people, featuring the author's well researched argument against China's historical claim to sovereignity over Tibet. Also noteworthy is his stunning description of contemporary Lhasa

See also **TIBET** under **CHINA** in **WORLD HISTORY AND CURRENT AFFAIRS**

1-56663-089-4 DEE $27.50

Peter **Fleming**

Bayonets to Lhasa

By one of the great British 20th-century adventurers

0-19-583862-9 OXFORD PB $11.95

Philip **Glazebrook**

Journey to Khiva: A Writer's Search for Central Asia

The keenly observant author of *Journey to Kars* travels across the crumbling Soviet empire in search of the elusive essence of Central Asia. On the way to the near-mythic cities of Tashkent, Bokhara, and Khiva, we glimpse the ghosts of Victorian adventurers and Czarist armies. "This book is pure pleasure" —Anne McElvoy, *The Times* [London]

1-56836-011-8 KODANSHA $23.00

1-56836-074-6 KODANSHA PB $14.00

Heinrich **Harrer**

Return to Tibet

Harrer returns to Tibet in 1980

0-7089-1488-8 ULVERSCROFT $21.95

Brian **Harris**

Tibetan Voices: A Traditional Memoir

A chronicle of the near-extinct Himalayan Buddhist culture

0-7649-0020-X POMEGRANATE $45.00

0-7649-0004-8 POMEGRANATE PB $31.95

Sven **Hedin**

My Life as an Explorer: The Great Adventurer's Classic Memoir

From the author of *The Silk Road* and *The Wandering Lake*, this is the epic memoir that helped make him a worldwide celebrity and best-selling author in his own time. "An account of an astonishing number of adventures…and of perils, a tenth of which would satisfy most men"—*New York Tribune*

1-56836-142-4 KODANSHA PB $15.00

Peregrine **Hodson**

Under a Sickle Moon: A Journey Through Afghanistan

0-7089-1773-9 ULVERSCROFT $15.95

Peter **Hopkirk**

Foreign Devils on the Silk Road: The Search for the Lost Cities and Treasures of Chinese Central Asia

See also **ASIA** under **THE ARCHAEOLOGY OF CIVILIZATIONS** under **ARCHAEOLOGY** in **WORLD HISTORY AND CURRENT AFFAIRS**

0-87023-435-8 MASSACHUSETTS PB $17.95

Evariste-Regis **Huc** & Joseph **Gabet**

Travels in Tartary, Tibet and China, 1844-1846

A French missionary's travels, marked by good narrative style and an eye for anthropological detail

0-486-25438-0 DOVER PB $16.95

Pico **Iyer**

Video Night in Kathmandu and Other Reports from the Not-So-Far East

A *Time* correspondent attempts to unravel what happens when East meets West in Asia in a witty and perceptive look at "tourist culture" and beyond

0-679-72216-5 VINTAGE PB $13.00

Owen **Lattimore**

The Desert Road to Turkestan

Lattimore's account of traveling in a camel caravan through inner Mongolia, published in 1929, reveals the lives and customs of "camel pullers" and Chinese traders

See also **MEMOIRS** under **CHINA** in **WORLD HISTORY AND CURRENT AFFAIRS**

1-56836-070-3 KODANSHA PB $16.00

Theodore **Levin**

The Hundred Thousand Fools of God: Musical Travels in Central Asia (and Queens, NY)

The author's encounters with musicians from Uzbekistan and Tajikistan, and with emigres who have ended up in Queens

0-253-33206-0 INDIANA $35.00

Robin **Magowan**

Fabled Cities of Central Asia: Samarkand, Bukhara, Khiva

PHOTOGRAPHS BY VADIM GIPPENREITER

0-89659-964-7 ABBEVILLE $65.00

Peter **Matthiessen**

The Snow Leopard

Matthiessen in the Himalayas in search of an endangered cat; winner of the National Book Award

See also **MAMMALS** under **ANIMALS** under **NATURE STUDY** in **SCIENCE**

0-14-010266-3 PENGUIN PB $12.95

Geoffrey **Moorhouse**

To the Frontier

A modern traveler's extreme experiences in this 1983 journey in Pakistan, across the Punjab to the northwest frontier

0-03-000454-3 HOLT $2.98

Dervla **Murphy**

Full Tilt: Ireland to India with a Bicycle

In fulfillment of a childhood dream, Murphy pedaled through some of the world's wildest terrain

0-87951-236-9 VIKING $17.95

0-89924-064-X LYNX HOUSE PB $11.95

The Waiting Land
In her characteristic, understated way, Murphy describes her journey by air, bicycle and foot, warmly rendering the people and land of Nepal in a diary format
0-87951-305-5 OVERLOOK PB $13.95

Where the Indus Is Young
In 1974, Murphy took her six-year old daughter with her to "Little Tibet"—Baltistan in Kashmir—through the Indus Gorge in winter
1-85089-207-5 ABC CLIO $19.95

Sheila **Paine**
The Afghan Amulet: Travels from the Hindu Kush to Razgrad
0-312-11236-X ST. MARTIN'S $21.95

Frances **Parsons**
I Didn't Hear the Dragon Roar
The adventures of a deaf art history lecturer traveling through China and Tibet
See also **CHINA**
0-930323-41-6 GALLAUDET $17.95

Nicholas **Shoumatoff** & Nina **Shoumatoff**
Around the Roof of the World
Excerpts of travel writing on central Asia spanning nearly a century, with the editors' translations of selections by four Russian writers. Illustrated
0-472-10741-0 MICHIGAN $29.95

Stuart **Stevens**
Night Train to Turkestan
A 1986 trip with friends along China's ancient Silk Road, following Peter Fleming's itinerary of 50 years before
0-87113-190-0 ATLANTIC MONTHLY PB $12.00

India

Jonah **Blank**
Arrow of the Blue-Skinned God: Retracing the Ramayana Through India
American journalist Blank physically retraces the steps of the Rama who, 3,000 years ago, crossed the subcontinent to turn himself into a god. "What Hollywood attempted on the big screen with casts of thousands in *Gandhi* and *A Passage to India* Jonah Blank has achieved in 350 stylistically rich pages"
—*LA Times Book Review*
0-385-47203-X BANTAM PB $12.00

Christopher **Ondaatje**
Sindh Revisited: A Journey in the Footsteps of Captain Sir Richard Francis Burton
An account of the author's years spent in India attempting to ferret out the secrets of the famous explorer's seven years in India. It additionally provides a fascinating contrast between contemporary India and that of the time of Burton's writings
See also **THE BRITISH PERIOD** *under* **THE INDIAN SUBCONTINENT** *in* **WORLD HISTORY AND CURRENT AFFAIRS**
0-00-255436-4 HARPERCOLLINS $30.00

Robyn **Davidson**
Desert Places
The author travels through the Indian desert with Rabari nomads, experiencing both the pleasures and abject poverty of their way of life
067008400777 VIKING $23.95

E.M. **Forster**
The Hill of Devi
Life in India as private secretary to the Maharajah of Dewas
See also **20TH-CENTURY BRITISH ESSAYS AND OTHER PROSE** *in* **LITERATURE OF THE BRITISH ISLES**
0-8419-5828-9 HOLMES & MEIER $55.00
0-15-640265-3 HARCOURT BRACE PB $4.95

Alexander **Frater**
Chasing the Monsoon: A Modern Pilgrimage Through India
Chief travel correspondent for *The Observer*, Frater follows the path of the monsoon and its yearly impact on people from its "burst" on the beaches of Trivandrum, through Delhi, Calcutta, and on to the finale in Cherrapunji, called the "wettest place on earth" by *The Guinness Book of World Records*. "One of the most remarkable travel books in recent memory"—*Newsweek*. "A brilliantly amusing book"
—*NY Times Book Review*
0-8050-2052-7 HOLT PB $14.95

Andrew **Harvey**
A Journey in Ladakh
A young English poet's pilgrimage to Ladakh in northern India in 1981, to see "one of the last places on earth … where a Tibetan Buddhist society can be experienced"
0-395-36670-4 HOUGHTON MIFFLIN PB $12.95

Dervla **Murphy**
On a Shoestring to Coorg: An Experience of South India
The latest in Murphy's series of acclaimed travel writings is her account of a trip to India taken with her five-year old daughter. She lives among the villagers and partakes in their life, in a landscape of dense forests, mountains, paddy fields and coffee plantations
0-87951-372-1 OVERLOOK $19.95

V.S. **Naipaul**
An Area of Darkness
Harsh observation of the subcontinent that met with little Indian popularity in the late '60s
0-14-002895-1 PENGUIN PB $11.95

James **O'Reilly**, editor
Travelers' Tales India
1-88521-101-5 O'REILLY PB $17.95

Tal **Streeter**
A Kite Journey Through India
A look at India through the nation's kite-flying passion
0-8348-0301-1 WEATHERHILL PB $39.95

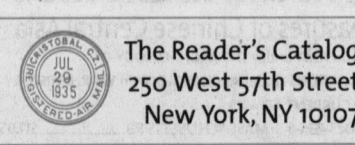

China

Wade **Brackenbury**
Yak Butter and Black Tea: A Journey Into Forbidden China
An account of travel through China's restricted Drung valley
1-56512-148-1 ALGONQUIN $19.95

John **DeFrancis**
In the Footsteps of Genghis Khan
A story of traveling through China in the '30s when it seemed like the Wild West. The author—now a professor of Chinese—traveled 1,000 miles across the Gobi by camel, was imprisoned by a Muslim warlord, and experienced many other near-misses
0-8248-1493-2 HAWAII $29.95

Robert **Easton**
China Caravans: An American Adventure in Old China
Easton vividly recreates the travels of Fred Meyer Schroder in China, Mongolia, and Tibet between 1912 and 1920
0-8095-4034-7 BORGO $22.95

Peter **Jenkins**
Across China
His adventurous trip across Tibet, China, and Mongolia
0-449-21456-7 FAWCETT PB $5.95

Jan **Morris**
Hong Kong
A great travel writer's montage of imperial history and modern capitalism shows the precipitous contrasts between primitive poverty and outrageous wealth
See also **HONG KONG** *under* **SOUTHEAST ASIA AND THE PHILIPPINES** *in* **WORLD HISTORY AND CURRENT AFFAIRS**
0-679-72486-9 VINTAGE PB $15.00

James **O'Reilly**, editor
Travelers' Tales Hong Kong
1-88521-103-1 O'REILLY PB $17.95

Martin **Palmer**
Travels Through Sacred China
Palmer has written a guide not only to the places but also to the spiritual dimensions of China: from the mountains and cities to the household shrines. He introduces the reader to the spirit of Tao, and brings to life the culture and traditions of China
1-85538-494-9 HARPERCOLLINS PB $16.00

Frances **Parsons**
I Didn't Hear the Dragon Roar
The adventures of a deaf art history lecturer traveling through China and Tibet
See also **CENTRAL ASIA**
0-930323-41-6 GALLAUDET $17.95

Mark **Salzman**
Iron and Silk
The Chinese adventures of a young martial arts master "produce the gulp of feeling you might get from an unusually fine short story" —*NY Times*
See also **MARTIAL ARTS** *under* **FITNESS** *in* **LIFESTYLES AND PRACTICAL ADVICE**
0-394-75511-1 VINTAGE PB $11.00

Bill **Porter**

Road to Heaven: Encounters with Chinese Hermits

Combining travel, religion, philosophy, culture, and history, the author presents a fascinating view of the men and women who have abandoned society in search of a higher meaning

INCLUDES PHOTOGRAPHS BY STEVE JOHNSTON AND BILL PORTER

1-56279-041-2 MERCURY HOUSE PB $14.00

Vikram **Stevens**

From Heaven Lake: Travels Through Sinkiang and Tibet

Hitchhiking home from Nanjing to Delhi via Tibet and Nepal

0-7089-1290-7 ULVERSCROFT $16.95
0-394-75218-X VINTAGE PB $11.00

Paul **Theroux**

Riding the Iron Rooster: By Train Through China

The book that put Theroux on the travel writer's map

See also **TRAINS** under **BOATS, CARS, PLANES, AND TRAINS**

0-8041-0454-9 IVY PB $6.99

Simon **Winchester**

The River at the Center of the World: A Journey Up the Yangtze and Back in Chinese Time

The author probes Chinese essence in his journey up the Yangtze

0-8050-3888-4 HOLT $27.50

Japan

Alan **Booth**

Looking for the Lost: Journeys Through a Vanishing Japan

1-56836-065-7 KODANSHA $25.00
1-56836-148-3 KODANSHA PB $15.00

The Roads to Sata

Booth walked the miles from the northernmost point of Japan (Cape Soya) to the southernmost (Cape Sata)

0-670-80776-1 VIKING $20.95

J.D. **Brown**

The Sudden Disappearance of Japan: Journeys Through a Hidden Land

Following the classic 19th-century itinerary of Percival Lowell, Brown (*Digging to China*) searches for the fugitive, disappearing soul of Japan—that of Shinto temples, tea ceremonies, and bonsai gardens

FOREWORD BY PICO IYER

0-88496-381-0 CAPRA PB $12.95

Cathy N. **Davidson**

36 Views of Mount Fuji: On Finding Myself in Japan

"As enjoyable a read as *A Year In Provence*" —Louise DeSalvo, *Virginia Woolf*

0-452-27240-8 PLUME PB $11.95

Charles **Danziger**

The American Who Couldn't Say Noh: Everything You Need to Know About Japan But Had No One to Ask

When Danziger was plopped into a minuscule dormitory room in Japan he had no idea what he was in for. The proverbially ignorant American, however, had his eyes and ears open, and his entertaining observations on the vicissitudes of life in the Land of the Rising Sun make for provocative reading

4-7700-1681-6 KODANSHA $20.00

Lafcadio **Hearn**

Glimpses of Unfamiliar Japan

Hearn was an acute observer and vivid describer of late 19th-century Japan

0-8048-1145-8 TUTTLE PB $16.95

Donald **Richie**

The Inland Sea

A film historian long resident in Japan writes sensitively and knowledgeably about its great interior waterways

4-7700-1751-0 KODANSHA PB $9.00

Korea and Southeast Asia

Isabella **Bird**

Korea and Her Neighbors

Bird made four visits to Korea in the last decade of the 19th-century, and her account touches on contemporary politics (especially the Sino-Japanese War) as well as on customs and daily life

0-7103-0135-9 KEGAN & PAUL PB $29.95

Michael **Buckley**

Vietnam, Cambodia and Laos Handbook

Buckley's experience of Asian travel—he researched the four Lonely Planet guides—is reflected in this handbook to traveling in Southeast Asia. From an overview of history, culture, and geography to health considerations and transportation, this guide covers the nightclubs of Saigon as thoroughly as the war zone of Cambodia

See also **MOON HANDBOOKS** under **GENERAL GUIDES** under **TRAVEL GUIDES**

1-56691-029-3 MOON PB $18.95

Peter **Matthiessen**

Under the Mountain Wall

Two seasons with tribesmen of New Guinea

See also **ESSAYS, MEDITATIONS, AND CLASSICS** under **NATURE STUDY** in **SCIENCE**

See also **RESEARCH AND METHODOLOGY** under **GENERAL ANTHROPOLOGICAL STUDIES** under **ANTHROPOLOGY** in **SOCIAL STUDIES**

0-14-025270-3 PENGUIN PB $12.95

Redmond **O'Hanlon**

Into the Heart of Borneo

"A learned and sensitive book as well as a knockout force"—*NY Review of Books*

0-394-75540-5 VINTAGE PB $12.00

Hickman **Powell**

The Last Paradise

Even 70 years ago, Westerners thought that Bali was the last Eden, soon to be despoiled by tourism and civilization

0-19-582537-3 OXFORD PB $9.95

Tobias **Schneebaum**

Where the Spirits Dwell: An Odyssey in the Jungle of New Guinea

Schneebaum's singular travels to some of the most primitive corners of the world constitute not only an awe-inspiring travelogue, but also an extraordinarily honest and literate account of his journey, spiritual and sexual, toward self-realization and acceptance

0-8021-0019-8 GROVE $17.95
0-8021-3166-2 GROVE PB $10.95

Zoe **Schramm-Evans**

A Phoenix Rising: Impressions of Vietnam

From rice paddies in the countryside to the opium dens of Ho Chi Minh City, from the Mekong Delta to the streets of Hanoi, Schramm-Evans discovers a country with a rich, ancient culture just opening to the explosive force of Western capitalism: a beautiful country in flux. Urban, rural, and intimate portaits of Vietnam

0-04-440976-1 HARPERCOLLINS $20.00

Rudolph **Wurlitzer**

Hard Travel to Sacred Places

An odyssey through the Buddhist sacred places in Cambodia, Thailand, and Burma in the wake of the author's son's tragic death. "An extraordinary illumination of dark corners and dangerous roads, an inspiring record of two amazing journeys one into the real world, the other into the soul. It has the attributes of a classic"— Michael Herr

1-57062-024-5 SHAMBHALA $15.00
1-57062-117-9 SHAMBHALA PB $10.00

Africa

Bartle **Bull**

Safari: A Chronicle of Adventure

0-14-016885-0 PENGUIN PB $29.95

Peter **Matthiessen**

African Silences

The author of the classic *The Snow Leopard* writes of his two journeys through the ravaged equatorial African wilderness

0-679-40021-4 VINTAGE PB $20.00

North Africa

Ffyona **Campbell**

On Foot Through Africa

In her latest trek, the author of *Feet of Clay* walks over 30 miles a day for over two years through both the jungle and desert of Africa

1-85797-813-7 ORION PB $13.95

Amitav **Ghosh**

In an Antique Land

A vivid account of ancient and modern Egypt, in which the author-historian uncovers the life of a slave who lived 800 years ago. Combining history with cultural investigation, travel writing with storytelling, Ghosh explains the strange and intense relationship that developed across centuries between his subject and himself

See also EGYPT under THE CONTEMPORARY MIDDLE EAST in WORLD HISTORY AND CURRENT AFFAIRS

See also 20TH-CENTURY LITERATURE OF THE INDIAN SUBCONTINENT under LITERATURES OF INDIA in LITERATURE OF EUROPE, AFRICA, AND ASIA

0-679-72783-3 VINTAGE PB $13.00

By the time the trading nations of the Indian Ocean began to realize that their old understandings had been rendered defunct by the Europeans it was already too late. In 1509 AD the fate of that ancient trading culture was sealed in a naval engagement that was sadly, perhaps pathetically, evocative of its ethos: a transcontinental fleet, hastily put together by the Muslim potentate of Gujarat, the Hindu ruler of Calicut, and the Sultan of Egypt was attached and defeated by a Portuguese force off the shores of Diu, in Gujarat. As always, the determination of a small, united band of soldiers triumphed easily over the rich confusions that accompany a culture of accommodation and compromise.

IN AN ANTIQUE LAND

William **Golding**

An Egyptian Journal

The Nobel prize-winning novelist takes a trip down the Nile

See also 20TH-CENTURY BRITISH ESSAYS AND OTHER PROSE in LITERATURE OF THE BRITISH ISLES

0-571-12547-6 FABER PB $12.95

Walter **Harris**

Morocco That Was

0-907871-40-2 HIPPOCRENE PB $14.95

Wyndham **Lewis**

Publisher, novelist, painter, and ferocious critic, Lewis was described by Ezra Pound as "the only English writer who can be compared to Dostoevsky." His work, much of it long out of print, has been republished in recent years.

Journey Into Barbary

Morocco in 1931: the writer and painter's escape from "dying European society" into a search for "the mirages of the great electric desert"

See also 20TH-CENTURY BRITISH ESSAYS AND OTHER PROSE in LITERATURE OF THE BRITISH ISLES

See also THE EARLY 20TH-CENTURY under 20TH-CENTURY BRITISH AND IRISH FICTION in LITERATURE OF THE BRITISH ISLES

EDITED BY C.J. FOX

0-87685-519-2 BLACK SPARROW $25.00
0-87685-518-4 BLACK SPARROW PB $14.00

John **Miller** & Kirsten **Miller**

Cairo: Tales of the City

0-8118-0492-5 CHRONICLE $12.95

Dervla **Murphy**

In Ethiopia With a Mule

This journey on a mule named Jock is plagued by illness, three robberies, and rough terrain, but is ultimately rewarded with the seasoned travel writer's great affection for the Ethiopian people

0-00-654798-2 FLAMINGO PB $15.95

Sub-Saharan Africa

Richard F. **Burton**

Wanderings in West Africa

An account, first published in 1863, of the famous adventurer's travels along the West African coast, with the detailed ethnographic descriptions that shocked his contemporaries and that are now prized for their first-hand observation

0-486-26890-X DOVER PB $13.95

Edward **Hoagland**

African Calliope: A Journey to the Sudan

1-55821-370-8 LYONS & BURFORD PB $14.95

Mary **Kingsley**

Travels in West Africa

A Victorian lady proves that one didn't have to be a "heroic male" to explore successfully

0-460-87394-6 EVERYMAN'S PB $6.95

Doris **Lessing**

African Laughter: Four Visits to Zimbabwe

In 1982, Doris Lessing returned to Zimbabwe, from which she'd once been exiled for opposition to a white minority government. This book describes what she found: a struggling economy, AIDS, environmental degradation, some thriving communal enterprises, and blacks and whites—as well as blacks and blacks—still struggling to overcome divisions created by racism and civil war

0-06-016854-4 HARPERPERENNIAL PB $25.00

Dervla **Murphy**

The Urimwi Road: From Kenya to Zimbabwe

A recounting of her 3,000 mile bike trek creates a picture of a country plagued by AIDS (*urimwi* is the Swahili word for AIDS) and Ebola epidemics, drought and economic hardship, and equally the exceptional beauty of its land and the abiding hope of its people

0-87951-671-2 OVERLOOK PB $13.95

Laurens **van der Post**

A widely traveled writer who states that he has walked over more of Africa than anyone else alive, Van der Post spent many years among the bushmen and writes feelingly of their myths and legends.

The Lost World of the Kalahari

"A journey in a great wasteland and a search for some pure remnant of the unique and almost vanished First People of my native land, the Bushmen of Africa," writes Van der Post

See also SOUTHERN AFRICA under REGIONAL HISTORIES under AFRICA in WORLD HISTORY AND CURRENT AFFAIRS

0-15-653706-0 HARCOURT BRACE PB $11.00

North America

Stephen **Brock**

Maple Leaf Rag

Humorous, good-natured account of a cross-Canada trek

0-7089-2100-0 ULVERSCROFT $17.95

Bill **Bryson**

The Lost Continent: Travels in Small-Town America

"...the kind of book Steinbeck might have written if he'd traveled with David Letterman instead of Charlie the Poodle"
—*New York Magazine*

0-06-092008-4 HARPERPERENNIAL PB $13.00

Carl Lamson **Carmer**, editor

Tavern Lamps Are Burning: Literary Journeys Through Six Regions and Four Centuries of New York

With over 100 different authors represented, this anthology includes the writings of Edith Wharton and Washington Irving

0-8232-1697-7 FORDHAM $35.00
0-8232-1698-5 FORDHAM PB $19.95

Thurston **Clarke**

California Fault: Searching for the Spirit of a State

The chronicle of a journey that follows the length of the San Andreas fault

0-345-38566-7 BALLANTINE $24.00

Andrei **Codrescu**

Road Scholar: Coast to Coast Late in the Century

NPR's Codrescu goes on the road in this funny, captivating, and off-beat view of America. From a drive-through wedding in Las Vegas to the black-garbed scene in New York's East Village, Codrescu drives his 1968 Cadillac convertible into the heart and heartlands of the American experience

PHOTOGRAPHS BY DAVID GRAHAM

1-56282-878-9 HYPERION $19.95
0-7868-8081-3 HYPERION PB $12.95

David **Darlington**

The Mojave: A Portrait of the Definitive American Desert

A sparkling narrative about the land that houses the Joshua tree and the desert tortoise, and the sweep of attitudes regarding it from its use in the past as dumping ground, to its present status as refuge and recreational area

0-8050-1631-7 HOLT $25.00

Josie **Dew**

Travels In a Strange State: Cycling Across the U.S.A.

Insights and observations from the POV of a bicycle seat, by the author of *The Wind In My Wheels*

0-316-18222-2 LITTLE, BROWN PB $7.95

Murray **Dubin**

South Philadelphia: Mummers, Memories, and the Melrose Diner

The story of the city's first neighborhood as told by the *Philadelphia Inquirer* reporter

1-56639-429-5 TEMPLE $29.95

Dayton **Duncan**

Out West

On the trail of the Lewis and Clark Expedition

0-14-008362-6 PENGUIN PB $10.95

Peter **Genovese**

Jersey Diners

A travelogue of Jersey's all night hot-spots

0-8135-2350-8 RUTGERS $29.95

Eric **Hiscock**

Sou'west in Wanderer IV

0-19-217528-9 OXFORD $22.50

Diamond **Jenness**

Arctic Odyssey: The Diary of Diamond Jenness, 1913-1916

The journal of a young New Zealand ethnologist who accompanied the Stefansson expedition along the Arctic coast of Alaska and Canada. Jenness's early encounters with the Inuit people prompted keen observations that are among the few primary documents recording their traditional way of life. Includes 74 photographs, 103 line drawings, and 32 maps

0-660-12906-X CANADIAN MUSEUM $65.00

David **Lamb**

Over the Hills: A Midlife Escape Across America by Bicycle

The author of *Stolen Season* takes to the road

0-8129-2579-3 TIME BOOKS $23.00

Andrew H. **Malcolm** & Roger **Straus**

Mississippi Currents: Journeys Through Time and a Valley

An exploration of how America's largest river has shaped the land around it. With photos and text

0-688-11940-9 MORROW $30.00

W.S. **Merwin**

Travels

Merwin is one of our most honored and read poets, and *Travels* is among "the most beautiful and moving collections of his career. [He] displays his narrative gifts to provide us with a book of deep historical resonance and luminous poetic grace"—*LA Times Book Review*

See also **POETRY SINCE 1945** under **20TH-CENTURY AMERICAN POETRY** in **LITERATURE OF THE AMERICAS**

0-679-41890-3 KNOPF $20.00

0-679-75277-3 KNOPF PB $14.00

Stuart **Miller**

The Other Islands of New York: A Historical Companion

A collection of stories from New York's 40 islands other than Manhattan

See also **ANTHOLOGIES**

0-88150-336-3 BACKCOUNTRY PB $17.00

V.S. **Naipaul**

A Turn in the South

A recent work relating Naipaul's impressions of the American South

0-394-56477-4 KNOPF $18.95

Joseph **O'Connor**

Sweet Liberty: Travels in Irish America

Portraits of Ireland's American counterparts

1-57098-105-1 ROBERTS RINEHART $24.95

Tim **Palmer**

The Sierra Nevada: A Mountain Journey

A journey through the Lake Tahoe casinos and Yosemite campgrounds and into the mountains

0-933280-54-8 ISLAND $35.00

0-933280-53-X ISLAND PB $16.95

Jonathan **Raban**

Bad Land: An American Romance

See also **20TH-CENTURY BRITISH ESSAYS AND OTHER PROSE** in **LITERATURE OF THE BRITISH ISLES**

0-679-44254-5 PANTHEON $25.00

Lucy **Rees**

The Maze: A Desert Journey

A Welsh couple seeking peace after a personal tragedy travels to Arizona in search of a stone carving on the Hopi reservation reputed to be identical to a stone in Cornwall called the Cretan Maze

0-88150-369-X COUNTRYMAN $21.00

Alan **Ryan**, editor

The Reader's Companion to Alaska

A compilation of travel writing by dogsled runner John Muir, humor writer Erma Bombeck, and many others on the largest, and perhaps wildest, state in America

See also **ANTHOLOGIES**

0-15-600368-6 HARCOURT BRACE PB $15.00

Peter **Stark**

Driving to Greenland: Arctic Travel, Nordic Sport, and Other Ventures in the Heart of Winter

Ski jumping, luging, the Arctic: a world of snow and ice from *New Yorker* writer who thrives on cold. Stark joins the ranks of hands-on journalists who willingly, shamelessly, risk life and limb at extreme sports.... [He] brings you to places you never dreamed of going, takes all the lumps, and gets you home safe and sound" —*Kirkus Reviews*

1-55821-320-1 LYONS & BURFORD $22.95

John **Steinbeck**

Travels with Charley in Search of America

A poodle, a novelist, and a van named Rocinante in search of America in 1961

0-453-00897-6 HIGHBRIDGE AUDIO $30.00

0-14-005320-4 VIKING PB $6.95

Philip **Stevick**

Imagining Philadelphia: Travelers' Views of the City from 1800 to Present

A sampling of outsiders' observations on the city of brotherly love

0-8122-3377-8 PENNSYLVANIA $22.95

Bradford **Washburn** & David **Roberts**

Mount Mckinley: The Conquest of Denali

A vivid history of the adventurers who pitted themselves against the highest peak in North America, told dramatically by two men who successfully scaled it. 120 illustrations and 8 maps

PREFACE BY ANSEL ADAMS

0-8109-3611-9 ABRAMS $60.00

19th-Century Travelers

Isabella **Bird**

The Englishwoman in America

A young Victorian's honest though sometimes prejudiced impression of Canada and America in the 1850s

0-299-03520-4 WISCONSIN $20.00

A Lady's Life in the Rocky Mountains

Bird returned 20 years after her first visit to journey by horseback through the Rockies, producing an excellent portrait of outdoor life in the American West

0-89174-025-2 COMSTOCK PB $5.95

W.C. **Corsan**

Two Months in the Confederate States: An Englishman's Travels Through the South

An account of an English hardware salesman's travels in the deep South in the autumn of 1862, augmented by the notes of Benjamin H. Trask, the Mariners' Museum's librarian in Newport News, VA

0-8071-2037-5 LSU $26.95

Frances **Trollope**

Domestic Manners of the Americans

The novelist's mother ventured to America in 1827 and produced such a scathing report that her book allegedly set back US-British relations a generation

0-8446-3090-X SMITH $28.80

The Caribbean and Central America

David Rains **Wallace**

Adventuring in Central America: Guatemala, Belize, Honduras, El Salvador, Nicaragua, Costa Rica, Panama

See also **HIGH ADVENTURE TRAVEL** under **SPECIALIZED GUIDES** under **TRAVEL GUIDES**

See also **AUSTRALIA AND NEW ZEALAND** under **SIERRA CLUB GUIDES** under **GENERAL GUIDES** under **TRAVEL GUIDES**

0-87156-473-4 SIERRA CLUB PB $16.00

Jason **Wilson**

Traveler's Literary Companions: South & Central America Including Mexico

Over 250 extracts from novels, poems, and short stories from writers such as Moritz Thomsen on Peru, Rudyard Kipling on Brazil, Graham Greene on Argentina, and many, many others. With a foreword by Margaret Drabble

See also **SOUTH AMERICA**

0-8442-8973-6 PASSPORT PB $17.95

The Caribbean

Michael **Anthony**
All That Glitters: The Caribbean
See also **CARIBBEAN LITERATURE** in **LITERATURE OF THE AMERICAS**
0-435-98034-3 HEINEMANN PB $7.95

Mary **Bond**
Far Afield in the Caribbean
A naturalist's wife does some exploring on her own
0-915180-13-8 HARROWOOD $6.95

V.S. **Naipaul**
Middle Passage
A satirical version of Caribbean life
See also **THE MIDDLE GENERATION** under **20TH-CENTURY BRITISH AND IRISH FICTION** in **LITERATURE OF THE BRITISH ISLES**
0-14-002920-6 PENGUIN PB $10.00

Alan **Ryan**, editor
The Reader's Companion to Cuba
A collection of some of the best travel writing on the land of the mambo, cigars and fine rum
0-15-600468-2 HARCOURT BRACE PB $15.00

Pico **Iyer**
Cuba and the Night
0-679-44052-6 KNOPF $22.00
0-679-76075-X VINTAGE PB $12.00

Mexico

Frances **Calderon de la Barca**
Life in Mexico During a Residence of Two Years
Letters from the Scottish wife of the first Spanish envoy to the independent country, 1838-40
0-404-14517-5 AMS $27.50

James **O'Reilly**, editor
Travelers' Tales Mexico
1-88521-100-7 O'REILLY PB $17.95

Donald G. **Schueler**
The Temple of the Jaguar: Travels in the Yucatan
Shattered by the AIDS-related death of his lover, noted reporter and travel author Schueler journeys to the Yucatan Peninsula in search of the elusive jaguar. More than incisive travelogue, this is a message of hope and renewed faith
0-87156-651-6 SIERRA CLUB $25.00

John Lloyd **Stephens**
Incidents of Travel in Yucatan
Originally published in 1843, Stephens reveals Yucatan villages of 150 years ago, when cacao beans were used for money
See also **MEXICO AND CENTRAL AMERICA: GENERAL WORKS** under **NATIVE AMERICAN CULTURES: CENTRAL AND SOUTH AMERICA** in **HISTORY OF THE AMERICAS**
NEW EDITION BY KARL ACKERMAN
1-56098-652-2 SMITHSONIAN $36.50
1-56098-651-4 SMITHSONIAN PB $13.95

Ronald **Wright**
Time Among the Maya: Travels in Belize, Guatemala, and Mexico
"Wright is an acute and indefatigable observer, bound to be compared to Peter Matthiessen and Paul Theroux"—*LA Times*
0-8050-1470-5 HOLT PB $15.95

Central America

Peter **Canby**
The Heart of the Sky: Travels Among the Maya
More than seven million Mayans live in Mexico and Central America a thousand years after the disappearance of their urban centers, with a culture that has survived intact. "Canby makes us feel we have just begun to comprehend a rich, profoundly different and endangered culture"—*Times Book Review*
1-56836-026-6 KODANSHA PB $13.00

Salman **Rushdie**
The Jaguar Smile: A Nicaraguan Journey
Vivid literary journalism and "the view from underneath" based on a three-week trip in 1986 by the renowned and exiled Anglo-Indian author
See also **20TH-CENTURY LITERATURE OF THE INDIAN SUBCONTINENT** under **LITERATURES OF INDIA** in **LITERATURE OF EUROPE, AFRICA, AND ASIA**
0-670-81757-0 VIKING $12.95

South America

Roberta **Allen**
Amazon Dream
"...I have tried to preserve a little piece of the Peruvian Amazon, to preserve what this place was to me. The Peruvian Amazon as I saw it in the fall of 1987 no longer exists"—From the Author's Note
0-87286-270-4 CITY LIGHTS PB $9.95

Bruce **Chatwin**
In Patagonia
A modern masterpiece of travel writing
0-671-40045-2 SUMMIT $9.95
0-14-011291-X PENGUIN PB $11.95

Alma **Guillermoprieto**
Samba
An intimate look at the heart of Brazilian life. The author spent a year training in a village samba school in preparation for Rio's Carnival parade. "Eloquent and persuasive in bringing it all to life"—*New Yorker*
See also **MUSIC OF THE AMERICAS** under **WORLD MUSIC: OTHER TRADITIONS** in **PERFORMING ARTS AND MEDIA**
See also **SOCIAL AND FOLK DANCING** under **SPECIAL TOPICS** under **DANCE** in **PERFORMING ARTS AND MEDIA**
0-679-73256-X VINTAGE PB $12.00

Joe **Kane**
Running the Amazon
The story of the first people to float the entire Amazon, encountering everything from deadly rapids to Maoist guerrillas
0-394-55331-4 KNOPF $19.95
0-679-72902-X VINTAGE PB $12.00

Peter **Matthiessen**
The Cloud Forest: A Chronicle of the South American Wilderness
A journey through wild terrain from the Amazon rain forest to Tierra del Fuego
See also **ESSAYS, MEDITATIONS, AND CLASSICS** under **NATURE STUDY** in **SCIENCE**
0-8446-6605-X SMITH $19.80
0-14-009549-7 PENGUIN PB $11.95

Peter Matthiessen

Dervla **Murphy**
Eight Feet in the Andes
Murphy retraces Pizarro's path by mule through Peru's mountains with her nine-year-old daughter
0-87951-262-8 OVERLOOK PB $13.95

Redmond **O'Hanlon**
In Trouble Again: A Journey Between the Orinoco and the Amazon
The story of "O'Hanlon hacking his way up an unmapped tributory of the Amazon, fearful of ending his days in someone's cooking pot" —Jonathan Raban
See also **SOUTH AMERICA** under **NATIVE AMERICAN CULTURES: CENTRAL AND SOUTH AMERICA** in **HISTORY OF THE AMERICAS**
0-679-72714-0 VINTAGE PB $12.00

Paul **Rambali**
In the Cities & Jungles of Brazil
From the author of *French Blues*, a vivid, impressionistic portrait of the teeming giant of South America that strips away the cliches. From street urchins to corrupt politicians, endangered tribes to voodoo cults, this account is as intelligent and as complex as its multifarious subject. "Reveals a fine sensuality, a compelling lust for Brazil's odorous, overripe surface"—Alma Guillermoprieto, *TLS*
0-8050-3078-6 HOLT PB $12.95

Paul **Theroux**
The Old Patagonian Express
By train from Boston to Patagonia, as described by an expert on rail travel
See also **TRAINS** under **BOATS, CARS, PLANES, AND TRAINS**
0-395-52105-X HOUGHTON MIFFLIN PB $12.95

Jason **Wilson**, editor

Traveler's Literary Companions: South & Central America Including Mexico

Over 250 extracts from novels, poems, and short stories from writers such as Moritz Thomsen on Peru, Rudyard Kipling on Brazil, Graham Greene on Argentina, and many, many others. With a foreword by Margaret Drabble

See also THE CARIBBEAN AND CENTRAL AMERICA

0-8442-8973-6 PASSPORT PB $17.95

Australia, New Zealand, and the South Pacific

Barbara Marie **Brewster**

Down Under All Over: A Love Affair with Australia

From its sheep farms to its opal mines, Australia is enthusiastically rendered in a way that evokes the magic of the land and its peoples

0-9628608-0-8 4 WINDS PB $14.95

Ffyona **Campbell**

Feet of Clay

A chronicle of her epic walk across Australia

0-7493-0807-9 MANDARIN PB $13.95

Bruce **Chatwin**

The Songlines

This fascinating picture of the interaction between the Aborigine and Anglo cultures in Australia is also a philosophical meditation on the human potential of "nomadism"

See also THE MIDDLE GENERATION under 20TH-CENTURY BRITISH AND IRISH FICTION in LITERATURE OF THE BRITISH ISLES

0-14-009429-6 PENGUIN PB $12.95

Enoch Carter **Cloud**

Enoch's Voyage: Life on a Whaleship, 1851-1854

A decent young man is in over his head on a whaling voyage from New England via Portugal's Cape of Good Hope, New Zealand and the South Pacific. Fresh and unusual; rich insights into pressured, small group living which is set off by the great danger and huge rewards of the hunt

EDITED BY ELIZABETH MCLEAN

1-55921-079-6 MOYER BELL $24.95

Captain James **Cook**

Explorations of Captain James Cook in the Pacific, as Told by Selections of His Own Journals, 1768-1779

See also CAPTAIN COOK under POLYNESIA under AUSTRALIA, NEW ZEALAND, AND POLYNESIA in WORLD HISTORY AND CURRENT AFFAIRS

0-486-22766-9 DOVER PB $9.95

Robyn **Davidson**

Tracks

The extraordinary journey of a young woman and four camels across 1700 miles of Australian outback

0-394-72167-5 RANDOM HOUSE PB $12.00
0-679-76287-6 VINTAGE PB $12.00

Robert Louis **Stevenson**

In the South Seas

Firsthand impressions of the Marquesas and the Paumotus and Gilbert Islands

See also POLYNESIA under AUSTRALIA, NEW ZEALAND, AND POLYNESIA in WORLD HISTORY AND CURRENT AFFAIRS
See also 19TH-CENTURY PROSE under THE 19TH-CENTURY in LITERATURE OF THE BRITISH ISLES

0-7103-0140-5 ROUTLEDGE PB $25.50

Paul **Theroux**

The Happy Isles of Oceania: Paddling the Pacific

Beginning his travels on the islands of New Zealand, the author of *The Mosquito Coast* hikes and kayaks through New Guinea, Melanesian Fiji, and Somoa, ending his long journey in Hawaii

0-449-90858-5 FAWCETT PB $12.95

Sea Travels

Maria **Coffey**

A Boat In Our Baggage: Around the World With a Kayak

The chronicle of a husband and wife who travel to various locations all over the world in their kayak, which folds up to fit in a canvas bag

0-349-10631-2 ABACUS PB $15.95

John O. **Coote**, editor

The Norton Book of the Sea

INTRODUCTION BY HAMMOND INNES

0-393-02778-3 NORTON $22.50

David **Cordingly**

Under the Black Flag: The Romance of Life Among the Pirates

"This is the most authoritative and highly literate account of these pernicious people that I've ever read"—Patrick O'Brian

0-679-42560-8 RANDOM HOUSE $25.00

Thor **Heyerdahl**

Kon-Tiki: Across the Pacific by Raft

0-671-72652-8 WASHINGTON PB $5.99

Robin **Knox-Johnston**

A World of My Own

Against incredible odds and mounting hardships, 29-year-old Knox-Johnston sailed his tiny ketch, *Suhaili,* around the world in ten-and-a-half months. Culled from the ship's log and diaries, this tale of single-handed seamanship is more than a noteworthy sea adventure: this is the tale of one man's single-minded determination

0-393-02900-X NORTON $29.95

J. **Marriott**

Disaster At Sea

0-87052-450-X HIPPOCRENE $25.00
0-87052-764-9 HIPPOCRENE PB $9.95

Tim **Severin**

The Jason Voyage: The Quest of the Golden Fleece

The voyage of a 20-oared galley, a replica of the *Argo* of Greek mythology, from Greece to Soviet Georgia

0-7089-8359-6 ULVERSCROFT $23.95

Joshua **Slocum**

Sailing Alone Around the World

The account of the first man to sail solo around; he left Boston in 1895 and returned to Newport in 1898

0-486-20326-3 DOVER PB $5.95

Travel Photography

For related reading, see PHOTOGRAPHY in ART

Susan **McCartney**

Travel Photography: A Complete Guide to How to Shoot and Sell

A guide to travel photography and its potential profits. How to photograph people and locations as well as what equipment, lighting, techniques, and film to use. It discusses editing, creating a portfolio, and self-promotion, and includes ten assignments for developing skills. "Destined-to-be-dog-eared"—*Booklist*

1-88055-900-5 ALLWORTH PB $22.95

Jeremy **Stafford-Deitsch**

Reef: A Safari Through the Coral World

Veteran marine explorer and photographer Stafford-Deitsch takes readers on a remarkable journey to some of the world's most beautiful, mysterious, and environmentally fragile "undersea landscapes." More than 100 photographs, maps, and drawings as well as chapters on the formation of reefs, marine life, and environmental concerns. Awarded Best Science Book for General Readers by *Library Journal*

See also OCEANOGRAPHY under EARTH SCIENCES in SCIENCE

0-87156-541-2 SIERRA CLUB PB $20.00

Africa

Creina **Bond**

Okavango: Sea and Land, Land of Water

One of Earth's last wildernesses is captured in 200 color photographs

PHOTOGRAPHS BY PETER JOHNSON AND ANTHONY BANNISTER

0-312-14384-2 ST. MARTIN'S $35.00

Angela **Fischer**

Africa Adorned

0-8109-1823-4 ABRAMS $65.00

Tepilitole **Saitoiti**

Maasai

PHOTOGRAPHS BY CAROL BECKWITH

0-8109-8099-1 ABRADALE $34.98

Marian **Van Ofelen**

Nomads of Niger

PHOTOGRAPHS BY CAROL BECKWITH

0-8109-8125-4 ABRADALE $29.98
0-8109-0734-8 ABRADALE $49.50

Alberto **Siliotti**
Egypt: Splendors of an Ancient Civilization
A photo journey up the Nile highlights national monuments and treasures
See also **EGYPT** under **THE ANCIENT NEAR EAST** under **ARCHAEOLOGY** in **WORLD HISTORY AND CURRENT AFFAIRS**
0-500-01647-X THAMES & HUDSON $50.00

Asia and the Pacific

China

Cecil **Beaton**
Chinese Diary and Album
A wartime chronicle of Britain and its allies in the Far East, as depicted by the great portrait and fashion photographer. 100 halftones
0-19-585428-4 OXFORD $24.95

Emily **Hahn**
China to Me
0-306-70695-4 DA CAPO $56.50

Weng **Wan-go** & Yang **Boda**
Palace Museum, Peking: Treasures of the Forbidden City
0-8109-1477-8 ABRAMS $75.00

Japan

Melissa **Banta** & Susan **Taylor**, editors
A Timely Encounter: 19th-Century Photographs of Japan
A selection of 61 hand-colored albumen photographs recording 19th-century Japanese life at a moment of abrupt transition from traditional to modern. The accompanying text fills in the historical background of the images
0-87365-810-8 NORTHEASTERN PB $16.95

Donald **Richie**
Introducing Japan
4-7700-1791-X KODANSHA PB $15.00

India and Nepal

Cecil **Beaton**
Indian Diary and Album
A companion volume to *Chinese Diary and Album*, abounding in observed detail. 100 halftones
0-19-212299-1 OXFORD $24.95

Keith **Dowman**
Power Places of Kathmandu: Hindu and Buddhist Holy Sites in the Sacred Valley of Nepal
Power places—the focal points of divine energy—in the mystical Kathmandu Valley are pictured in 108 magnificent color plates, evoking the mystery and grandeur of Nepal's "Abode of the Gods." An extraordinary guide for adventurers and armchair travelers alike
PHOTOGRAPHS BY KEVIN BUBRISKI
0-89281-540-X INNER TRADITIONS $39.95

Kyuya **Fukada**
Himalayas
PHOTOGRAPHS BY YOSHIKAZU SHIRAKAURA
0-8109-8065-7 ABRADALE $49.98

Raghubir **Singh**
Bombay: Gateway of India
A great photographer, in conversation with V.S. Naipaul, tours the gateway to India, and captures the essence of its energy
0-89381-583-7 APERTURE $40.00

Other Asian Countries

Leonard **Lueras**
Bali: The Ultimate Island
PHOTOGRAPHS BY R. IAN LOYD
0-312-14547-0 ST. MARTIN'S $45.00

Roland **Michaud** & Sabrina **Michaud**
Afghanistan: Paradise Lost
0-500-27393-6 THAMES & HUDSON PB $17.95

Europe

Bill **Bryson**
Neither Here Nor There: Travels in Europe
The author of *The Lost Continent* and *The Mother Tongue* retraces his steps from the journey he took as a young man in the early '70s. "Splendidly provocative…so hilarious and simultaneously honest that he's got to be, if not forgiven, at least excused for stepping on toes" —Brad Hooper, *Booklist*
0-380-71380-2 AVON PB $12.00

Britain and Ireland

Michael **Buselle**
England: The Four Color Seasons
England's seasonal landscapes are captured in these full-color photographs
1-55859-649-6 CRCSI $29.95
1-85793-815-1 TRAFALGAR SQUARE PB $22.95

Robert **Cameron** & Alistair **Cooke**
Above London
0-918684-10-2 CAMERON $29.50

Jacqueline **O'Brien** & Desmond **Guinness**
Dublin: A Grand Tour
Beauty is general in this magnificent city, toured here with the authors of *Great Irish Houses and Castles* and presented in a lavishly photographed, beautifully presented portrait. The text traces the development of the city's architectural and decorative styles—a lovely vision of one of the world's remarkable cosmopolises by two of its most appreciative denizens
0-8109-3216-4 ABRAMS $65.00

France

Robert **Cameron** & Pierre **Salinger**
Above Paris
0-918684-19-6 CAMERON $29.50

Marie-Ange **Guillaume**
Provence
Featuring exquisite images—a field of glowing sunflowers juxtaposed against a magenta sky and haunting stonework from the time of the Romans—this collection represents the two decades photographers Bullaty and Lomeo have dedicated to portraying the stunning light, textures, and colors of Provence
1-55859-557-0 ABBEVILLE $45.00

June **Hargrove**
Statues of Paris
0-86565-121-3 VENDOME $150.00

Louisa **Jones**
Provence: A Country Almanac
In the manner of an old-fashioned farmer's guide, this beautifully photographed and designed book tells you what life in the south of France is all about with information on local festivals, gardens, markets, history, customs, and cold remedies
1-55670-278-7 STEWART, TABORI $24.95

Jean-Pierre **Le Dantec** & Denise **Le Dantec**
Paris in Bloom
A lavish photographic treatment of the French capital's parks and gardens in all seasons, from the formal elegance of Saint-Cloud to the mysterious ruins of the Parc Monceau. Includes a comprehensive treatment of history, botany, and legends, as well as up-to-date maps and touring information
2-08-013518-X ABBEVILLE $24.98

Frederic **Raphael**
France: The Four Color Seasons
Full-color photographs by Michael Buselle render the French landscape by seasonal turns
1-85793-820-8 TRAFALGAR SQUARE PB $22.95

John **Russell**
Paris
FOREWORD BY ROSAMOND BERNIER
0-8109-8090-8 ABRADALE $24.98

Sam **Walden** & Solvi **Dos Santos**
Provence: The Art of Living
FOREWORD BY SIR TARENCE CONRAD
1-55670-449-6 STEWART, TABORI $50.00

Paul **Walshe**
French Farmhouses and Cottages (Country Series)
France's regional charms through the photographs of John Miller
0-8478-1507-2 RIZZOLI $27.50
0-297-83562-9 WEIDENFELD & NICOLSON PB $17.95

Italy

Attilio **Boccazzi-Varotto**
Venice 360 Degrees
0-679-44284-7 RANDOM HOUSE $70.00

Dominique **Fernandez**
Rome: Mirror of the Centuries
PHOTOGRAPHS BY PAOLO MARTON
0-86565-049-7 VENDOME $50.00

Hugh **Palmer**
The Most Beautiful Villages of Tuscany
TEXT BY JAMES BENTLEY
0-500-01664-X THAMES & HUDSON $40.00

Spain

Nicholas **Luard**
Landscape in Spain
0-8212-1706-2 LITTLE, BROWN $9.98

The Middle East

Sarah **Kochav**
Israel: Splendors of the Holy Land
0-500-01668-2 THAMES & HUDSON $50.00

The Americas

Richard **Brown**
Richard Brown's New England
Full color photographs throughout
1-55209-070-1 FIREFLY $40.00

Bruce **Chatwin** & Paul **Theroux**
Nowhere is a Place: Travels in Patagonia
One of America's best landscape photographers, Jeff Grass, teams up over 50 of his color photos with text by the well-known travel writers
0-87156-359-2 SIERRA CLUB PB $18.00

David **Dunbar**
Yosemite National Park
PHOTOGRAPHED BY JERRY PAVIA
0-7892-0131-3 ABBEVILLE PB $11.95

John **Margolies**
Home Away From Home: Motels in America
A wonderfully illustrated record of an icon in the American landscape, the motel. With more than 200 photographs and an authoritative text, Margolies brings to new life the singularly American innovation of housing that competes, sometimes bizarrely, for the trade of passing motorists. From "Kozy Kottages" and teepee-shaped bungalows, to today's chains, this lovely gift book documents an American roadscape
0-8212-2162-0 BULFINCH $29.95

Walter F. **Morris**, Jr.
Living Maya
PHOTOGRAPHS BY JEFFREY JAY FOX
0-8109-1298-8 ABRAMS $49.50

Stan **Patey**
The Coast of New England
Aerial color photographs lend a bird's eye view of New England's landscape from Connecticut to Maine
0-07-048770-7 MCGRAW HILL $49.95

Olive **Pierce**
Up River: The Story of a Maine Fishing Community
WITH WORD PICTURES BY CAROLYN CHUTE
0-87451-756-7 NEW ENGLAND PB $19.95

Lawrence Clark **Powell**
Photographs of the Southwest
PHOTOGRAPHS BY ANSEL ADAMS
0-8212-0699-0 BULFINCH $50.00

Galen **Rowell**
Poles Apart: Parallel Visions of the Arctic and Antarctic
0-520-20174-4 CALIFORNIA $39.95

T.H. **Watkins**
American Landscape
PHOTOGRAPHS BY DAVID MUENCH
0-932575-30-7 GRAPHIC ARTS $42.50

American Cities

Bill **Kurtis**
Chicago
PHOTOGRAPHS BY SANTI VISALLI
0-8478-0842-4 RIZZOLI $55.00

Charles **Dufour**, editor
New Orleans
PHOTOGRAPHS BY BERNARD HERMANN
0-8071-0799-9 LSU $24.95

Robert **Cameron**
Above New York
0-918684-42-0 CAMERON $29.50

Lloyd **Ultan**
The Bronx in the Innocent Years: 1890-1925
0-941980-32-4 BRONX CITY HISTORICAL SOC. $25.00

Harvey **Wang**
Harvey Wang's New York
The supervisor of a kosher bakery, a woodwind repairman, a boxing trainer, a sign painter, a blacksmith, a bowling alley mechanic, a mannequin maker: these are some of the trades and crafts whose practitioners Harvey Wang has lovingly photographed in this poignant book about a vanishing New York
0-393-30692-5 NORTON PB $9.95

"I avoid iron because it's too heavy," Max's only concession to age is that he needs one of the grandkids to drive him and his booty to Irving's Scrap Metal on Ditmars Avenue in Brooklyn, where it is sorted, weighed, and exchanged for cash. "I retired ten years ago. After I gave up working, I needed something to do. I would pick up old television sets, not because I needed it, but just to keep busy. I can't sit still on a chair reading comics or walk around the streets doing nothing..."
HARVEY WANG'S NEW YORK

William **Younger**
Old Brooklyn in Early Photographs, 1865-1929
0-486-23587-4 DOVER PB $13.95

Robert **Bernhardi**
Great Buildings of San Francisco
0-8446-5736-0 SMITH $11.00

Herb **Caen**
San Francisco
PHOTOGRAPHS BY MORTON BEEBE
0-8109-1608-8 ABRAMS $49.50

Robert **Cameron**
Above San Francisco
TEXT BY HERB CAEN
0-918684-28-5 CAMERON $29.50

Above Washingtion
INTRODUCTION BY ALISTAIR COOKE
0-918684-08-0 CAMERON $29.50

Bill **Harris**
Washington, D.C.
PHOTOGRAPHS BY J.C. SUARES
0-517-01748-2 CRESCENT $8.99

Charles **Kelly**
Washington, D.C., Then and Now: 69 Sites Photographed in the Past Present
0-486-24586-1 DOVER PB $11.95

Travel Guides

General Guides

Baedeker Guides

This series for independent travelers includes A to Z listings of sights as well as museum floor plans and pullout maps. City and region guides are pocket-size.

Asia

Baedeker
Bangkok
0-13-057985-8 BAEDEKER GUIDES PB $10.95

Japan
0-13-056382-X BAEDEKER GUIDES $15.95

Europe

Baedeker

Netherlands, Belgium, and Luxembourg
0-13-611419-9 SIMON & SCHUSTER PB $9.95

Rail Guide to Europe
See also **RAIL TRAVEL** under **SPECIALIZED GUIDES**
0-13-055971-7 BAEDEKER GUIDES PB $18.00

Belgium Guide
0-02-861351-1 BAEDEKER GUIDES PB $23.95

Guide to Crete
0-02-861364-3 BAEDEKER GUIDES PB $15.95

Germany Guide
0-02-861362-7 BAEDEKER GUIDES PB $24.95

Berlin
0-13-367996-9 PRENTICE HALL PB $10.95

Germany
0-13-055830-3 BAEDEKER GUIDES PB $15.95

Lisbon Guide
0-02-861352-X BAEDEKER GUIDES PB $15.95

Scandinavia Guide
0-02-861356-2 BAEDEKER GUIDES PB $24.95

Madrid
0-13-058033-3 PRENTICE HALL PB $10.95

Eastern Europe

Baedecker

St. Petersberg Guide
0-02-861357-0 BAEDEKER GUIDES PB $15.95

Blue Guides

With their in-depth, well-researched information on the arts and history, these guidebooks are for the intellectual. They include maps, floor plans, and detailed itineraries.

Europe

England
0-393-31340-9 NORTON PB $24.00

Florence
0-393-31274-7 NORTON PB $17.95

Greece: Maps and Plans (6th Ed.)
0-393-31273-9 NORTON PB $25.00

Ireland (7th Ed)
0-393-31343-3 NORTON PB $19.95

Rome and Environs
0-393-31259-3 NORTON PB $21.95

Oxford and Cambridge (4th Ed)
0-393-31344-1 NORTON PB $16.95

Portugal
0-393-31416-2 NORTON PB $19.95

Austria
0-393-30364-0 NORTON $18.95
0-393-30365-9 NORTON PB $17.95

Scotland (11th Ed)
0-393-31417-0 NORTON PB $24.95

Southern Italy
0-393-31418-9 NORTON PB $24.95

Sweden
0-393-31271-2 NORTON PB $24.00

Tuscany
0-393-31401-4 NORTON PB $24.95

Umbria
0-393-31402-2 NORTON PB $19.95

Western Germany
0-393-31196-1 NORTON PB $21.95

Eastern Europe

Albania
0-393-31421-9 NORTON PB $19.95

Budapest
0-393-31422-7 NORTON PB $19.95

Bob **Dent**

Hungary
This new edition covers Budapest, the Danube Bend, Lake Balaton, and many less well-known areas of what is becoming one of Europe's most enticing destinations
0-393-30687-9 NORTON PB $22.50

Paul **Blanchard**

Yugoslavia
0-393-30485-X NORTON PB $18.95

Africa

Tunisia
0-393-31419-7 NORTON PB $19.95

The Middle East

Jordan
0-393-31420-0 NORTON PB $21.95

Fodor's Guides

This series covers more countries and areas than any other. Each guidebook includes listings in a variety of price ranges for hotels, restaurants, shops, and sights, as well as background information on history and culture.

Fodor's

Caribbean '97: The Complete Guide to Choosing and Enjoying the Perfect Island Vacation
0-679-03193-6 FODOR'S PB $18.50

Central and South America

Fodor's

Belize & Guatemala
The complete guide with beaches, Maya ruins and dive sites
0-679-03309-2 FODOR'S PB $12.50

Costa Rica: The Complete Guide
Includes excursions to Panama
0-679-03197-9 FODOR'S PB $13.00

Brazil
0-679-01605-8 RANDOM HOUSE PB $8.95

Central America
0-679-01613-9 RANDOM HOUSE PB $15.95

Australia and New Zealand

Fodor's

Australia '97
0-679-03172-3 FODOR'S PB $19.50

Australia and New Zealand 1996
0-679-02972-9 FODOR'S PB $19.00

Australia, New Zealand and the South Pacific
0-679-01598-1 RANDOM HOUSE PB $15.95

Europe

Fodor's

Great Britain '97
0-679-03226-6 FODOR'S PB $18.50

Ireland
0-679-03238-X FODOR'S PB $18.00

London: The Complete Guide
0-679-03245-2 FODOR'S PB $13.50

Scotland: The Complete Guide
From historic cities to the wild highlands
0-679-03282-7 FODOR'S PB $18.50

Europe '97: The Complete Guide
0-679-03200-2 FODOR'S PB $21.00

Touring Europe: Flexible Day-By-Day Itineraries for Independent Travelers
0-679-02767-X FODOR'S PB $15.00

Vienna and The Danube Valley
0-679-02592-8 FODOR'S PB $11.00

Switzerland
0-679-01704-6 RANDOM HOUSE PB $13.95

Exploring France
0-679-03206-1 FODOR'S PB $21.00

Exploring Paris
0-679-03211-8 FODOR'S PB $21.00

France
Includes phrasebook, dictionary and audio cassette
0-679-02234-1 FODOR'S $27.50

France '97
Includes walking tours of Paris, chateaux excursions and the best of every province
0-679-03221-5 FODOR'S PB $18.50

Paris: With Excursions to Chartres, Fontainbleau, and Versailles
EDITED BY WILLIAM ZINSSER
0-679-02074-8 FODOR'S PB $11.00

Paris: The Complete Guide
Includes walking tours
0-679-03266-5 FODOR'S PB $13.50

Provence and the Riveria: The Complete Guide
0-679-03304-1 FODOR'S PB $10.00

Exploring Germany
0-679-03207-X FODOR'S PB $21.00

Germany '97
0-679-03223-1 FODOR'S PB $20.00

Munich
0-679-03318-1 FODOR'S PB $9.00

Italy '97
0-679-03239-8 FODOR'S PB $19.00

Exploring Rome
0-679-03213-4 FODOR'S PB $21.00

Exploring Spain
0-679-03216-9 FODOR'S PB $21.00

Spain '97
Includes coverage of Mallorca, the Canary Islands and Morrocco
0-679-03287-8 FODOR'S PB $18.50

Madrid & Barcelona
0-679-03247-9 FODOR'S PB $13.00

Switzerland '97
This complete guide includes mountain drives, alpine hikes and city walking tours
0-679-03289-4 FODOR'S PB $19.50

Eastern Europe

Fodor's

Eastern Europe
Covers Hungary, Poland, Romania, Slovakia, the Czech Republic and Bulgaria
0-679-03199-5 FODOR'S PB $19.50

Scandinavia

Fodor's

Scandinavian Cities
0-679-01959-6 FODOR'S PB $9.00

Former Soviet States

Fodor's

Moscow, St. Petersburg, Kiev
0-679-03050-6 FODOR'S PB $19.00

Exploring Moscow & St. Petersburg
0-679-01870-0 FODOR'S PB $16.00

Southeast Asia

Fodor's

Southeast Asia
0-679-02762-9 FODOR'S PB $18.50

Asia

Fodor's

Korea
0-679-02310-9 FODOR'S PB $15.50

Japan
0-679-02523-5 FODOR'S PB $20.00

Tokyo
0-679-02349-6 FODOR'S PB $13.00

Japan '94: With the Best of Tokyo, Kyoto and Old Japan
0-679-02523-5 FODOR'S PB $20.00

The Middle East

Fodor's

Egypt
0-679-03007-7 FODOR'S PB $21.00

Exploring Israel
0-679-03009-3 FODOR'S PB $21.00

Jordan and the Holy Land
0-679-01665-1 FODOR'S PB $12.95

India and the Subcontinent

Fodor's

India, Nepal and Sri Lanka
0-679-01917-0 FODOR'S PB $19.00

North Africa

Fodor's

Kenya & Tanzania
0-679-02309-7 FODOR'S PB $16.00

Insight Guides

Illustrated with color photographs, these guides emphasize each country's history, people, and sites.

Insight

Bavaria
0-395-78832-3 APA PB $12.95

Milan
0-395-78419-0 APA PB $12.95

Ireland
0-395-73437-1 APA PB $7.95

Wild West (1996)
0-395-73386-3 APA PB $23.95

Central and South America

Insight

Buenos Aires
0-395-80969-X APA PB $21.95

Europe

Insight

Mallorca
0-395-73440-1 APA PB $7.95

Burgundy
0-395-78834-X APA PB $7.95

Dublin
0-13-468091-X APA PB $14.95

Provence
0-395-78835-8 APA PB $7.95

Tenerife
0-395-73447-9 APA PB $7.95

Madrid
0-395-78418-2 APA PB $12.95

Switzerland
0-395-78836-6 APA PB $7.95

Madeira (Insight Compact Guides)
0-395-73439-8 APA PB $7.95

Sicily
0-395-82689-6 APA PB $22.95

Bath & Surroundings
0-395-78839-0 APA PB $7.95

Former Soviet States

Insight

Moscow
0-395-66436-5 APA PB $21.95

Southeast Asia

Insight

Bali
0-395-73450-9 APA PB $7.95

Burma Myanmar (9th Ed, 1996)
0-395-75503-4 APA PB $22.95

Asia

Insight

Beijing
0-395-78837-4 APA PB $7.95

Bhutan
0-395-73400-2 APA PB $12.95

East Asia
0-395-66251-6 APA PB $23.95

Indonesia
0-13-457391-9 APA PB $16.95

The Middle East

Insight

Israel
0-13-506296-9 ARA PB $19.95

Turkish Coast (Insight Compact Guides)
0-395-78046-2 APA PB $7.95

Turkey
0-395-73448-7 APA PB $7.95

Istanbul
0-395-78417-4 APA PB $12.95

Knopf Guides

Practical, portable, and handsomely designed, the Knopf Guides are distinguished by their wealth of illustrations, maps, visual guides, and information.

Knopf

Egypt
From the Temple of Luxor to the life of the Nile and Cairo nightlife
0-679-75566-7 KNOPF PB $25.00

Provence
Arles to restaurant menus, a celebration of Europe's sweetest corner
See also **EUROPE** under **OTHER TRAVEL GUIDES**
0-679-75066-5 KNOPF PB $25.00

Restaurants of Paris
Illustrated, informative, and discriminating from the inexpensive to luxurious; opens up the labyrinthine mysteries of the Parisian table
See also **RESTAURANTS** under **SPECIALIZED GUIDES**
0-679-75578-0 KNOPF PB $25.00

Knopf Guide to Paris
Four new Knopf Guides provide in-depth information on four new destinations, each containing more than 1000 drawings, paintings, photographs, maps, and an astonishing wealth of detail. Welcome additions to a super travel series
0-679-76453-4 KNOPF PB $25.00

The Louvre
See also **MUSEUMS AND ART** under **SPECIALIZED GUIDES**
0-679-76452-6 KNOPF PB $25.00

Ireland
0-679-76203-5 KNOPF PB $25.00

Bali
Over 1,000 drawings, paintings, photographs, and maps—as well as a wealth of historical, cultural, and practical information—introduce the traveler to Bali. 140 pages of itineraries allow structured planning, and tours for four or ten-day stays encompass the entire country
0-679-75565-9 KNOPF PB $25.00

The Traveler's Guide to Art: Great Britain and Ireland
See also **RESTAURANTS** under **SPECIALIZED GUIDES**
0-394-72426-7 OUTLET $14.95

Amsterdam
0-679-74914-4 KNOPF PB $25.00

Athens
0-679-75064-9 KNOPF PB $25.00

Florence
0-679-74915-2 KNOPF $25.00

Istanbul and Northwest Turkey
0-679-74916-0 KNOPF PB $25.00

The Loire Valley
0-679-76449-6 KNOPF PB $25.00

Naples and Pompeii
0-679-76451-8 KNOPF PB $25.00

Rajasthan
0-679-76591-3 KNOPF PB $25.00

St. Petersburg
0-679-76202-7 KNOPF PB $25.00

London
0-679-74917-9 KNOPF PB $25.00

Morocco
0-679-75313-3 KNOPF PB $25.00

New York
0-679-75065-7 KNOPF PB $25.00

Prague
0-679-75437-7 KNOPF PB $25.00

Rome
0-679-75067-3 KNOPF PB $25.00

San Francisco
0-679-74913-6 KNOPF PB $25.00

Thailand
0-679-75063-0 KNOPF PB $25.00

Venice
0-679-74918-7 KNOPF PB $25.00

Vienna
0-679-75068-1 KNOPF PB $25.00

The Route of the Mayas
0-679-75569-1 KNOPF PB $25.00

Let's Go Guides

Created by the Harvard Student Agencies, these guides are popular with students and low-budget travelers. They include information on places to stay, restaurants, sightseeing, and where to get student discounts.

The Americas

Let's Go

The Budget Guide to Central America
0-312-14648-5 ST. MARTIN'S PB $16.99

The Budget Guide to Ecuador & the Galapagos Islands
0-312-14650-7 ST. MARTIN'S PB $16.99

The Budget Guide to New York City
0-312-14661-2 ST. MARTIN'S PB $13.99

Europe

Let's Go

The Budget Guide to Britain & Ireland
Includes Alpine hikes, mountain drives and city walking tours
0-312-14645-0 ST. MARTIN'S PB $17.99

The Budget Guide to France 1997
0-312-14652-3 ST. MARTIN'S PB $17.99

The Budget Guide to Germany
0-312-14653-1 ST. MARTIN'S PB $17.99

The Budget Guide to Greece & Turkey
Includes coverage of Cyprus
0-312-14654-X ST. MARTIN'S PB $17.99

The Budget Guide to Ireland
0-312-14656-6 ST. MARTIN'S PB $16.99

The Budget Guide to Italy
0-312-14658-2 ST. MARTIN'S PB $17.99

The Budget Guide to Europe
0-312-14651-5 ST. MARTIN'S PB $18.99

The Budget Guide to London
0-312-14659-0 ST. MARTIN'S PB $13.99

London: Map Guide
0-312-13766-4 ST. MARTIN'S PB $7.95

The Budget Guide to Paris
0-312-14662-0 ST. MARTIN'S PB $13.99

Paris: Map Guide
0-312-13767-2 ST. MARTIN'S PB $7.95

The Budget Guide to Rome
0-312-14663-9 ST. MARTIN'S PB $13.99

The Budget Guide to Spain & Portugal
Includes coverage of Morocco
0-312-14666-3 ST. MARTIN'S PB $17.99

The Budget Guide to Switzerland & Austria
0-312-14667-1 ST. MARTIN'S PB $17.99

Eastern Europe

Let's Go
The Budget Guide to Eastern Europe
0-312-14649-3 ST. MARTIN'S PB $18.99

Southeast Asia

Let's Go
The Budget Guide to Southeast Asia
0-312-14664-7 ST. MARTIN'S PB $18.99

The Middle East

Let's Go
The Budget Guide to Israel & Egypt
Includes coverage of Jordan, Syria and the West Bank
0-312-14657-4 ST. MARTIN'S PB $17.99

India and the Subcontinent

Let's Go
The Budget Guide to India & Nepal
0-312-14655-8 ST. MARTIN'S PB $18.99

Lonely Planet Guides

This series includes the "Travel Survival Kit" and "On a Shoestring" titles. The Asian and South Pacific series are the most popular of these guides. Used primarily by independent budget-minded travelers who want more than a list of places to stay, the guides include sightseeing information as well as practical information.

Lonely Planet
Antarctica
0-86442-415-9 LONELY PLANET $15.95

Central and South America

Lonely Planet
Bolivia
0-86442-396-9 LONELY PLANET $19.95

Central America
0-86442-122-2 LONELY PLANET PB $16.95

Costa Rica
0-86442-106-0 LONELY PLANET PB $11.95

Cuba
0-86442-403-5 LONELY PLANET $15.95

Andrew **Draffen** & others
Brazil
0-86442-317-9 LONELY PLANET PB $17.95

Lonely Planet
Ecuador & the Galapagos
0-86442-348-9 LONELY PLANET $17.95

Chile and Easter Island: A Travel Survival Kit
0-908086-99-7 LONELY PLANET PB $8.95

Colombia: A Travel Survival Kit
0-86442-002-1 LONELY PLANET PB $11.95

Ecuador and the Galapagos Islands: A Travel Survival Kit
0-908086-79-2 LONELY PLANET PB $7.95

South America on a Shoestring
0-908086-75-X LONELY PLANET PB $14.95

Peru
0-86442-332-2 LONELY PLANET PB $17.95

South America on a Shoestring
0-86442-401-9 LONELY PLANET $29.95

Australia and New Zealand

Lonely Planet
Australia
"This probably ought to be the first guidebook anybody going Down Under picks up"
—LA Times
0-86442-233-4 LONELY PLANET PB $23.95

Australia: A Travel Survival Kit
Over 800 pages of information for the adventurous, with full details on traveling in the most remote regions of Australia
0-86442-040-4 LONELY PLANET PB $19.95

New Zealand
0-86442-204-0 LONELY PLANET PB $17.95

New Zealand: A Travel Survival Kit
0-86442-020-X LONELY PLANET PB $8.95

Tasmania
0-86442-384-5 LONELY PLANET $14.95

Europe

Lonely Planet
Central Europe on a Shoestring
0-86442-420-5 LONELY PLANET $21.95

France
0-86442-331-4 LONELY PLANET $19.95

Paris City Guide
0-86442-431-0 LONELY PLANET $12.95

Mediterranean Europe on a Shoestring
0-86442-428-0 LONELY PLANET $24.95

Scandinavian & Baltic Europe on a Shoestring
0-86442-434-5 LONELY PLANET $17.95

Western Europe on a Shoestring
0-86442-438-8 LONELY PLANET $24.95

Eastern Europe

Lonely Planet
Eastern Europe
0-86442-116-8 LONELY PLANET PB $21.95

Eastern Europe on a Shoestring
0-86442-423-X LONELY PLANET $24.95

Prague: City Guide
0-86442-212-1 LONELY PLANET PB $9.95

Romania and Moldova
0-86442-329-2 LONELY PLANET PB $17.95

Scandinavia

Lonely Planet
Denmark
0-86442-330-6 LONELY PLANET PB $17.95

Southeast Asia

Lonely Planet
Bali & Lombok
0-86442-446-9 LONELY PLANET $15.95

Cambodia
0-86442-447-7 LONELY PLANET $12.95

Indonesia: A Travel Survival Kit
0-908086-81-4 LONELY PLANET PB $14.95

Laos
0-86442-381-0 LONELY PLANET PB $15.95

Laos Travel Atlas
0-86442-375-6 LONELY PLANET $12.95

The Philippines: A Travel Survival Kit
0-908086-92-X LONELY PLANET PB $8.95

Southeast Asia on a Shoestring
0-86442-056-0 LONELY PLANET PB $14.95

Malaysia, Singapore and Brunei: A Travel Survival Kit
0-86442-022-6 LONELY PLANET PB $9.95

Seoul City Guide
0-86442-385-3 LONELY PLANET $11.95

Sri Lanka
0-86442-476-0 LONELY PLANET $11.95

Jakarta: City Guide
0-86442-290-3 LONELY PLANET PB $9.95

Java
0-86442-314-4 LONELY PLANET PB $14.95

Southeast Asia
"Probably the most popular traveler's manual ever"—*Village Voice*
0-86442-226-1 LONELY PLANET PB $21.95

Asia

Lonely Planet

China
0-86442-363-2 LONELY PLANET PB $27.95

Old Kyoto: A Guide to Traditional Shops, Restaurants, and Inns
See also **SHOPPING** under **SPECIALIZED GUIDES**
See also **RESTAURANTS** under **SPECIALIZED GUIDES**
0-87011-757-2 KODANSHA PB $15.00

Thailand
"Cummings knows his way around this country like a Buddhist monk knows his way around a temple"—*Toronto Star*
0-86442-252-0 LONELY PLANET PB $18.95

Hong Kong
0-86442-426-4 LONELY PLANET PB $12.95

Japan
0-86442-271-7 LONELY PLANET PB $8.95

Lonely Planet: Lost Japan
0-86442-370-5 LONELY PLANET PB $10.95

China: a Travel Survival Kit
0-86442-003-X LONELY PLANET PB $17.95

Hong Kong, Macau and Canton: A Travel Survival Kit
0-908086-74-1 LONELY PLANET PB $7.95

Japan: A Travel Survival Kit
0-908086-70-9 LONELY PLANET PB $12.95

Korea: A Travel Survival Kit
0-86442-021-8 LONELY PLANET PB $8.95

Mongolia: A Travel Survival Kit
0-86442-180-X LONELY PLANET PB $13.95

North-East Asia on a Shoestring
0-908086-35-0 LONELY PLANET PB $7.95

Taiwan: A Travel Survival Kit
Oriented to the independent, low-budget traveler
0-86442-014-5 LONELY PLANET PB $8.95

Thailand
0-86442-170-2 LONELY PLANET PB $17.95

Tibet: A Travel Survival Kit
0-908086-88-1 LONELY PLANET PB $7.95

Malaysia, Singapore & Brunei
0-86442-393-4 LONELY PLANET $17.95

Burma: A Travel Survival Kit
0-86442-017-X LONELY PLANET PB $8.95

Thailand: A Travel Survival Kit
0-908086-95-4 LONELY PLANET PB $8.95

Singapore City Guide
0-86442-400-0 LONELY PLANET $11.95

The Middle East

Lonely Planet

Arab Gulf States
0-86442-390-X LONELY PLANET $17.95

Egypt
0-86442-395-0 LONELY PLANET $17.95

Egypt and the Sudan: A Travel Survival Kit
0-86442-001-3 LONELY PLANET PB $9.95

Iran
0-86442-136-2 LONELY PLANET PB $14.95

Israel and Palestinian Territories
0-86442-399-3 LONELY PLANET $17.95

Jerusalem City Guide
0-86442-298-9 LONELY PLANET $11.95

Jordan & Syria
0-86442-427-2 LONELY PLANET $15.95

Jordan and Syria: A Travel Survival Kit
0-86442-172-9 LONELY PLANET PB $14.95

Gates of Damascus
TRANSLATED BY SAM GARRETT
0-86442-368-3 LONELY PLANET PB $10.95

Lebanon
0-86442-350-0 LONELY PLANET PB $13.95

Istanbul City Guide
0-86442-388-8 LONELY PLANET $11.95

Trekking in Turkey: A Travel Survival Kit
0-86442-037-4 LONELY PLANET PB $9.95

Turkey
0-86442-364-0 LONELY PLANET $19.95

Middle East on a Shoestring
0-86442-407-8 LONELY PLANET $19.95

Yemen: A Travel Survival Kit
0-86442-006-4 LONELY PLANET PB $8.95

India and the Subcontinent

Lonely Planet

New Delhi: City Guide
0-86442-349-7 LONELY PLANET PB $9.95

Indian Himalayas
0-86442-413-2 LONELY PLANET $17.95

Rajasthan
0-86442-470-1 LONELY PLANET $15.95

Trekking in Karakoram and Hindukush
0-86442-360-8 LONELY PLANET PB $14.95

Bangladesh: A Travel Survival Kit
0-908086-60-1 LONELY PLANET PB $7.95

India: A Travel Survival Kit
0-908086-93-8 LONELY PLANET PB $17.95

Kathmandu and the Kingdom of Nepal: A Travel Survival Kit
0-86442-024-2 LONELY PLANET PB $8.95

Pakistan: A Travel Survival Kit
0-86442-167-2 LONELY PLANET PB $15.95

Sri Lanka: A Travel Survival Kit
0-86442-000-5 LONELY PLANET PB $8.95

Trekking in the Indian Himalaya
0-86442-093-5 LONELY PLANET PB $10.95

Trekking in the Nepal Himalaya
0-908086-66-0 LONELY PLANET PB $7.95

Nepal
0-86442-397-7 LONELY PLANET $15.95

Sri Lanka
0-86442-169-9 LONELY PLANET PB $13.95

Maldives and Islands of the East Indian Ocean: A Travel Survival Kit
A brief but information-packed guide to the 2,000 islands south of India. The author writes: "There are no wonderful cities or towns, no great edifices, events or rail journeys… So you'd better like the sea because you'll be seeing a lot of it, whether you choose to simply lie beside it or get right into it and join the marine life"
0-86442-084-6 LONELY PLANET PB $9.95

Africa

Lonely Planet

Africa on a Shoestring
0-908086-89-X LONELY PLANET PB $14.95

East Africa: A Travel Survival Kit
0-86442-005-6 LONELY PLANET PB $9.95

North Africa: A Travel Survival Kit
0-86442-258-X LONELY PLANET PB $19.95

West Africa: A Travel Survival Kit
0-86442-028-5 LONELY PLANET PB $12.95

Ethiopia, Eritrea, and Djibouti
0-86442-292-X LONELY PLANET PB $14.95

Pacific Islands

Lonely Planet

Vanuatu
0-86442-293-8 LONELY PLANET PB $13.95

Fiji: A Travel Survival Kit
0-908086-87-3 LONELY PLANET PB $7.95

Islands in the Clouds: Travels in the Highlands of New Guinea
0-86442-369-1 LONELY PLANET PB $10.95

Micronesia: A Travel Survival Kit
0-86442-019-6 LONELY PLANET PB $8.95

Papua New Guinea: A Travel Survival Kit
0-86442-048-X LONELY PLANET PB $11.95

Tahiti & French Polynesia
0-86442-287-3 LONELY PLANET $14.95

Tahiti and French Polynesia: A Travel Survival Kit
0-86442-049-8 LONELY PLANET PB $9.95

Tonga
"Amid the wealth of pertinent information are pearls of wisdom"—*Yachting*
0-86442-242-3 LONELY PLANET PB $11.95

Michelin Guides

These classic French guidebooks come in two series: the Red Guides list selected hotels and restaurants with an international rating system; the Green Guides provide historical, cultural, and sightseeing information with a star rating system. Each guide includes several good maps. The Michelin list is too extensive for us to list all titles conveniently here, we are, of course, happy to take orders for any book not listed

Michelin

Auvergne
2-06-030403-2 MICHELIN PB $20.00

Brussels
2-06-151301-8 MICHELIN PB $18.00

Europe
2-06-159101-9 MICHELIN PB $20.00

Flandres, Artois and Picardie
2-06-033804-2 MICHELIN PB $20.00

Chateaux of the Loire Valley
2-06-132204-2 MICHELIN PB $20.00

England—The West Country
2-06-701541-9 MICHELIN PB $20.00

Normandy
2-06-134802-5 MICHELIN PB $20.00

Provence
2-06-137503-0 MICHELIN PB $20.00

The Pyrenees
2-06-136601-5 MICHELIN PB $20.00

Scandinavia
Includes coverage of Finland
2-06-156701-0 MICHELIN PB $20.00

Scotland
2-06-157503-X MICHELIN PB $20.00

Venice
2-06-158701-1 MICHELIN PB $18.00

Wales
2-06-151001-9 MICHELIN PB $20.00

Moon Handbooks

Central & South America

Moon Handbooks

Baja Handbook: The Mexican Peninsula
1-56691-052-8 MOON PB $15.95

Belize Handbook
1-56691-030-7 MOON PB $15.95

Cabo Handbook: La Paz to Cabo San Lucas
1-56691-028-5 MOON PB $14.95

Cancun Handbook: Mexico's Caribbean Coast
1-56691-050-1 MOON PB $13.95

Central Mexico Handbook: Mexico City, Guadalajara, and Other Colonial Cities
1-56691-023-4 MOON PB $15.95

Costa Rica Handbook
1-56691-035-8 MOON PB $19.95

Northern Mexico Handbook: The Sea of Cortez to the Gulf of Mexico
1-56691-022-6 MOON PB $16.95

Mexico Handbook
1-56691-031-5 MOON PB $21.95

Pacific Mexico Handbook: Acapulco, Puerto Vallarta, Oaxaca, Guadalajara, Mazatlan
1-56691-032-3 MOON PB $16.95

Pacific Mexico Handbook/from the Coast to the Mountains
1-56691-005-6 MOON PB $15.95

Puerto Vallarta Handbook
1-56691-025-0 MOON PB $14.95

Yucatan Peninsula Handbook: The Gulf of Mexico to the Caribbean Sea
1-56691-024-2 MOON PB $15.95

The United States & Canada

Moon Handbooks

Alaska-Yukon Handbook
1-56691-016-1 MOON PB $14.95

Atlantic Canada Handbook: New Brunswick, Nova Scotia, Prince Edward Island, and Newfoundland
1-56691-007-2 MOON PB $17.95

Alberta and the Northwest Territories Handbook: Including Banff, Jasper, and the Canadian Rockies
1-56691-067-6 MOON PB $17.95

Arizona Traveler's Handbook
1-56691-071-4 MOON PB $17.95

British Columbia Handbook: Canada's West Coast
1-56691-014-5 MOON PB $15.95

California Downhill: A Skier's Handbook
0-918373-10-7 MOON PB $7.95

Catalina Island Handbook: A Guide to California's Channel Islands
0-918373-75-1 MOON PB $10.95

Colorado Handbook: Denver, Aspen, Durango, Mesa Verde, and Rocky Mountain National Parks
1-56691-044-7 MOON PB $18.95

Georgia Handbook
Includes Atlanta, Savannah, and the Blue Ridge Mountains
1-56691-039-0 MOON PB $17.95

Hawaii Handbook: The All-Island Guide
1-56691-000-5 MOON PB $19.95

Big Island of Hawaii Handbook: Including Hawaii Volcanoes National Park, the Kona Coast, and Waipio
1-56691-006-4 MOON PB $13.95

Honolulu and Waikiki Handbook: The Island of Oahu
1-56691-058-7 MOON PB $14.95

Idaho Handbook
1-56691-061-7 MOON PB $14.95

Kauai Handbook: Including the Island of Niihau
1-56691-001-3 MOON PB $13.95

Maui Handbook: Including Molokai and Lanai
1-56691-057-9 MOON PB $14.95

Maui Handbook Including Molokai and Lanai
0-918373-60-3 MOON PB $11.95

New Mexico Handbook
1-56691-015-3 MOON PB $14.95

Montana Handbook
Includes Glacier National Park
1-56691-049-8 MOON PB $17.95

Nevada Handbook
1-56691-064-1 MOON PB $16.95

Northern California Handbook
Includes San Francisco, Wine Country, Big Sur, Yosemite, Redwood
0-918373-84-0 MOON PB $19.95

Oregon Handbook
1-56691-010-2 MOON PB $16.95

Texas Handbook
1-56691-063-3 MOON PB $17.95

Road Trip USA: Cross-Country Adventures on America's Two-Lane Highways
1-56691-036-6 MOON PB $22.50

Utah Handbook
1-56691-068-4 MOON PB $16.95

Washington Handbook
Includes Seattle, Mt. Rainier, and Olympic National Park
1-56691-045-5 MOON PB $18.95

Wyoming Handbook
Includes Yellowstone and Grand Teton National Parks
0-918373-98-0 MOON PB $14.95

Washington Handbook
1-56691-055-2 MOON PB $15.95

The Caribbean

Moon Handbooks

Caribbean Handbook: The Virgin, Leeward, and Windward Islands
1-56691-027-7 MOON PB $16.95

Jamaica Handbook
1-56691-070-6 MOON PB $15.95

Guide to Puerto Rico and the Virgin Islands
Including the Dominican Republic
0-918373-08-5 PUBLISHERS GROUP WEST PB $8.95

General Guides

Moon Handbooks

Backpacking: A Hedonist's Guide
0-918373-00-X MOON PB $7.95

Blueprint for Paradise
0-918373-38-7 MOON PB $14.95

Moon Handbook: A 21st-Century Travel Guide
1-56691-066-8 MOON PB $10.00

Moonbooks Travel Catalog: The Portable Store for Independent Travelers
0-918373-07-7 MOON PB $2.95

The Practical Nomad: Planning for the Trip of a Lifetime
1-56691-076-5 MOON PB $13.95

Staying Healthy in Asia, Africa, and Latin America
1-56691-026-9 MOON PB $11.95

The South Pacific

Moon Handbooks

Australia Handbook
1-56691-072-2 MOON PB $21.95

Bali Handbook
1-56691-073-0 MOON PB $19.95

Fiji Islands Handbook
1-56691-038-2 MOON PB $13.95

Fiji Islands Handbook
0-918373-92-1 MOON PB $11.95

Finding Fiji
0-918373-03-4 MOON PB $6.95

Indonesia Handbook
1-56691-062-5 MOON PB $25.00

Micronesia Handbook
0-918373-06-9 MOON PB $8.95

Micronesia Handbook: Guide to the Caroline, Gilbert, Mariana, and Marshall Islands
0-918373-80-8 MOON PB $11.95

Micronesia Handbook
1-56691-077-3 MOON PB $14.95

New Zealand Handbook
1-56691-033-1 MOON PB $19.95

Outback Australia Handbook
1-56691-047-1 MOON PB $18.95

Philippines Handbook
1-56691-004-8 MOON PB $17.95

South Pacific Handbook
Another outstanding Moon guide for independent-minded traveler. Stanley's sure grasp of Pacific history provides a rich sense of context for the far-flung cultures of Fiji, Tonga, Tahiti, New Caledonia, and many others
1-56691-040-4 MOON PB $22.95

South Pacific Handbook
0-918373-99-9 MOON PB $19.95

Tahiti-Polynesia Handbook
1-56691-037-4 MOON PB $13.95

Tahiti-Polynesia Handbook
0-918373-87-5 MOON PB $11.95

Southeast Asia

Moon Handbooks

Bangkok Handbook
1-56691-059-5 MOON PB $13.95

Hong Kong Handbook: Including MacAu and Guangzhou
1-56691-056-0 MOON PB $15.95

Nepal Handbook
1-56691-041-2 MOON PB $18.95

Southeast Asia Handbook
1-56691-002-1 MOON PB $21.95

Thailand Handbook
For both shoestring travelers and the well-to-do, Parkes provides in-depth information on the best of Thailand's cuisines and the adventures of river travel and hill tribe trekking. 120 maps, a suggested reading list, and a Thai primer
1-56691-042-0 MOON PB $19.95

Vietnam, Cambodia and Laos Handbook
Buckley's experience of Asian travel—he researched the four Lonely Planet guides—is reflected in this handbook to traveling in Southeast Asia. From an overview of history, culture, and geography to health considerations and transportation, this guide covers the nightclubs of Saigon as thoroughly as the war zone of Cambodia
See also **KOREA AND SOUTHEAST ASIA** under **ASIA** under **TRAVEL LITERATURE**
1-56691-029-3 MOON PB $18.95

Other

Moon Handbooks

Japan Handbook
0-918373-70-0 MOON PB $22.50

Nepali Aama: Portrait of a Nepalese Hill Woman
0-918373-74-3 MOON PB $13.95

Pakistan Handbook
1-56691-069-2 MOON PB $22.50

Moscow-St. Petersburg Handbook
Including the Golden Ring
0-918373-91-3 MOON PB $13.95

South Korea Handbook
0-918373-20-4 MOON PB $14.95

Rick Steves' Guides

Geared to the young and independent who generally rely on public transportation and moderate budgets, these guides include a very thorough historical and cultural background for each region.

Rick Steves

Europe Through the Back Door
Includes 40 of Europe's most fascinating, least-visited places, along with all basic travel information
1-56261-260-3 JOHN MUIR PB $18.95

Europe, 1996
1-56261-261-1 JOHN MUIR PB $17.95

Baltics & Russia, 1996
1-56261-276-X JOHN MUIR PB $9.95

France, Belgium & The Netherlands, 1996
1-56261-262-X JOHN MUIR PB $13.95

Germany, Austria & Switzerland, 1996
1-56261-263-8 JOHN MUIR PB $13.95

Great Britain, 1996
1-56261-264-6 JOHN MUIR PB $13.95

Italy
1-56261-265-4 JOHN MUIR PB $13.95

Scandinavia
1-56261-266-2 JOHN MUIR PB $13.95

Spain & Portugal
1-56261-267-0 JOHN MUIR PB $13.95

Rough Guides

The intent of these guidebooks is to steer the traveler away from an insular, tourist-oriented experience of other countries and toward one that is more authentic, one in which the traveler temporarily becomes a part of each place. Individual books in this series are categorized as "Read-before-you-leave" or "Take-along" and all are concise and compact.

Central and South America

Rough Guides

Guatemala and Belize
1-85828-189-X ROUGH GUIDES PB $16.95

Peru
1858281423. ROUGG PB $17.95

Guatemala and Belize
EDITED BY BRIAN KEENAN
0-13-764150-8 ROUGH GUIDES PB $14.00

Europe

Rough Guides

Britain
A guide to England, Scotland and Wales
1-85828-208-X ROUGH GUIDES PB $19.95

Cyprus
1-85828-182-2 ROUGH GUIDES PB $16.95

Ireland
1-85828-179-2 ROUGH GUIDES PB $17.95

Italy
1-85828-167-9 ROUGH GUIDES PB $19.95

Rhodes and the Eastern Aegean
1-85828-120-2 ROUGH GUIDES PB $14.95

Portugal
0-7102-0967-3 SIMON & SCHUSTER PB $11.95

Eastern Europe

Rough Guides

Bulgaria
1-85828-183-0 ROUGH GUIDES PB $16.95

Poland
1-85828-168-7 ROUGH GUIDES PB $17.95

Southeast Asia

Rough Guides

Hong Kong and Macao
1-85828-187-3 ROUGH GUIDES PB $14.95

Vietnam
1-85828-191-1 ROUGH GUIDES PB $15.95

The Middle East

Rough Guides

Egypt
1-85828-188-1 ROUGH GUIDES PB $17.95

India and the Subcontinent

Rough Guides

Nepal
1-85828-190-3 ROUGH GUIDES PB $17.95

Africa

Rough Guides

Kenya
1-85828-192-X ROUGH GUIDES PB $18.95

Morocco
1-85828-169-5 ROUGH GUIDES PB $17.95

The Rough Guide to Kenya
0-7102-0616-X ROUTLEDGE PB $12.95

West Africa
1-85828-014-1 PENGUIN PB $24.95

Time Out Guides

This British series features practical and cultural information, as well as money—and time-saving tips. Though oriented toward the low-budget traveler, it also offers useful information to those on larger budgets.

Time Out

Budapest Guide
0-14-025416-1 PENGUIN PB $14.95

New York Guide
0-14-024872-2 PENGUIN PB $14.95

Rome Guide
0-14-024875-7 PENGUIN PB $14.95

San Francisco Guide
0-14-025417-X PENGUIN PB $14.95

Sierra Club Guides

Illustrated with hundreds of enticing color photographs, each book also includes maps, addresses, phone numbers, appendices for indigenous plant and animal identification, and trail information, making it the leading guide through many natural worlds around the planet.

Central and South America

Sierra Club

Adventuring in Belize
A guide to the islands, waters and inland parks
See also **HIGH ADVENTURE TRAVEL** under **SPECIALIZED GUIDES**
0-87156-592-7 SIERRA CLUB PB $15.00

Australia and New Zealand

Sierra Club

Adventuring in New Zealand

See also **HIGH ADVENTURE TRAVEL** under **SPECIALIZED GUIDES**

0-87156-571-4 SIERRA CLUB PB $15.00

Tahiti: A Complete Travel Guide to All of the Islands

For Tahiti, Bora Bora, Moorea, and other islands

0-87052-363-5 HIPPOCRENE PB $9.95

Adventuring in Central America: Guatemala, Belize, Honduras, El Salvador, Nicaragua, Costa Rica, Panama

Includes coverage of Guatemala, Belize, Honduras, El Salvador, Nicaragua, Costa Rica and Panama

See also **HIGH ADVENTURE TRAVEL** under **SPECIALIZED GUIDES**

See also **THE CARIBBEAN AND CENTRAL AMERICA**

0-87156-473-4 SIERRA CLUB PB $16.00

Europe

Sierra Club

Wild Britain

0-87156-475-0 SIERRA CLUB PB $16.00

Wild Ireland

0-87156-427-0 SIERRA CLUB PB $16.00

Smithsonian Guides

From the autumn foliage in the Berkshires to the untouched forests of Northern Wisconsin, the Smithsonian Guides offer a good introduction to parks, wilderness preserves, nature sanctuaries, and scenic wonders in America. Maps, phone numbers and addresses make arranging the trip easy, and activities from hiking to birdwatching make it worth the work of getting there.

Steve **Barth** & Kim **Heacox**

The Smithsonian Guides to Natural America: The Pacific: Hawaii and Alaska

0-679-76155-1 SMITHSONIAN PB $19.95

Daniel Jack **Chasan**

The Smithsonian Guides to Natural America: The Pacific Northwest Washington and Oregon

0-679-76313-9 SMITHSONIAN PB $19.95

Dwight **Holing**

The Smithsonian Guides to Natural America: The Far West-California and Nevada

0-679-76473-9 SMITHSONIAN PB $19.95

Bruce **Hopkins**

The Smithsonian Guides to Natural America: Central Appalachians

PHOTOGRAPHY BY WILLARD AND KATHY CLAY

0-679-76474-7 SMITHSONIAN PB $19.95

Susan **Lamb** & Tom **Bean**

The Smithsonian Guides to Natural America: The Southern Rockies-Colorado and Utah

0-679-76472-0 SMITHSONIAN PB $19.95

William Bryant **Logan** & others

The Smithsonian Guide to Historic America: The Pacific States

1-556-70006-3 STEWART, TABORI PB $18.95

Jake **Page**

The Smithsonian Guides to Natural America: The Southwest: New Mexico and Arizona

0-679-76154-3 SMITHSONIAN PB $19.95

John **Ross**

The Smithsonian Guides to Natural America: The Atlantic Coast & Blue Ridge: Delaware, Maryland, the District of Columbia, Virginia, and North Carolina

0-679-76314-7 RANDOM HOUSE PB $19.95

Thomas **Schmidt** & others

The Smithsonian Guides to Natural America: The Northern Rockies: Idaho, Montana, Wyoming

0-679-76312-0 SMITHSONIAN PB $19.95

Lansing **Shepard**

The Smithsonian Guides to Natural America: Northern Plains: Minnesota, North Dakota, South Dakota

0-679-76477-1 SMITHSONIAN PB $19.95

Michele **Strutin**

The Smithsonian Guides to Natural America: The Great Lakes

PHOTOGRAPHY BY GARY IRVING

0-679-76476-3 RANDOM HOUSE PB $19.95

Michele **Strutin** & Tony **Arruza**

The Smithsonian Guides to Natural America: Southeast

0679764800 SMITHSONIAN PB $10.00

Eugene **Walter** & Jonathan **Wallen**, editors

The Smithsonian Guides to Natural America: Mid Atlantic States: Pennsylvania, New York, New Jersey

0-679-76478-X SMITHSONIAN PB $19.95

W.D. **Wetherell** & Len **Jenshel**

The Smithsonian Guides to Natural America: Northern New England: Vermont, New Hampshire, and Maine

0-679-76153-5 SMITHSONIAN PB $19.95

Mel **White** & Jim **Bones**

The Smithsonian Guides to Natural America: South Central States: Texas, Oklahoma, Arkansas, Louisana, Mississippi

0-679-76479-8 SMITHSONIAN PB $19.95

Suzanne **Winckler** & Michael **Forsberg**

The Smithsonian Guides to Natural America: Heartland

0-679-76481-X SMITHSONIAN PB $19.95

Other Travel Guides

Central and South America

John **Brooks**, editor

The South American Handbook: Including Caribbean, Mexico, and Central America

0-13-823717-4 RAND MCNALLY $28.95

Paul **Glassman**

Costa Rica Guide

0-930016-18-1 TRAVEL LINE LIBRARY EDITION $13.95

0-930016-09-2 PASSPORT PB $12.95

Guatemala Guide

0-930016-08-4 PASSPORT PB $16.95

Larry **Rice**

Baja to Patagonia: Latin American Adventures

Part adventurer, part naturalist, ecotourist Rice takes us to the outer reaches of Latin America. Offers off-the-beaten-track adventure: kayaking in the fjords of southern Chile, hiking in Venezuela's rain forest, and skiing in Argentina

See also **HIGH ADVENTURE TRAVEL** under **SPECIALIZED GUIDES**

1-55591-113-7 FULCRUM PB $15.95

John **Whitman**

The Best Mexican and Central American Travel Tips

See also **MEXICO** under **GUIDES TO MEXICO, THE UNITED STATES, AND CANADA**

0-06-273268-4 HARPERPERENNIAL PB $15.00

Australia and New Zealand

Penguin

The Penguin Guide to Australia

0-14-019905-5 PENGUIN PB $11.95

Europe

Birnbaum

Europe '95

0-06-278125-1 HARPERPERENNIAL PB $20.00

Europe For Business Travelers '94

0-06-278126-X HARPERCOLLINS PB $14.00

Eric **Bredesen**

Moto Europa: The Complete Guide to European Motoring

"Moto Europa is a remarkable piece of research that explains virtually everything imaginable about driving in Europe... Bredesen boggles the mind"—*Times*

0-9641488-3-8 SEREN PB $15.95

Ken **Anderson** & others, editors

The Watering Holes of Scotland

With over 250 recommended hotels, a resume of restaurants, a glossary of golf courses, heritage, price guides, color maps of each area, and a selection of fine art

1-87134-956-7 TEMERON PB $32.95

Karen **Brown**

Karen Brown's Irish Country Inns

0-446-38808-4 WARNER PB $12.95

Karen Brown's Spanish Country Inns and Paradors

0-446-38813-0 WARNER PB $12.95

Chronicle

Cheap Eats in London

See also **RESTAURANTS** under **SPECIALIZED GUIDES**

0-87701-762-X CHRONICLE PB $9.95

Penguin

The Penguin Guide to England and Wales

0-14-019901-2 PENGUIN PB $12.95

Hillary **Pubenstien**, editor

Europe's Wonderful Little Hotels and Inns, 1996: Great Britain and Ireland

Interesting places to stay in Europe's biggest cities and most out-of-the-way places. Guides include detailed information about rates, services, restrictions, and locations. "There's no substiute for these invaluable handbooks—civilized of attitude, fun to read"—Jan Morris

0-312-13489-4 ST. MARTIN'S PB $18.99

Tim **Stilwell**

Stilwell's Scotland Bed and Breakfast

With over 1,400 bed and breakfasts, maps, and a currency conversion table

See also **RESTAURANTS** under **SPECIALIZED GUIDES**

0-9521909-6-6 STILLWELL PB $11.95

Richard Saul **Wurman**

London Access: Third Edition

0-06-277051-9 ACCESS PB $18.00

Karen **Brown**

Karen Brown's English, Welsh and Scottish Country Inns

0-446-38817-3 WARNER PB $12.95

Chronicle

Cheap Sleeps in London

0-87701-775-1 CHRONICLE PB $9.95

Judi **Culbertson** & Tom **Randall**

Permanent Londoners: An Illustrated Biographical Guide to the Cemeteries of London

0-8027-7471-7 WALKER PB $16.95

Europe

0-13-761644-9 ROUGH GUIDES PB $18.00

Josephine **Fletcher-Watson**, editor

The National Trust Handbook 1993

Dedicated to the preservation of historic places and properties in England, Wales, and Northern Ireland, The National Trust is the largest private landowner in Britain. From castles to gardens to lighthouses, each entry includes a brief description and travel directions. Includes line drawings

See also **HISTORICAL SITES AND NATIONAL PARKS** under **SPECIALIZED GUIDES**

0-7078-0160-5 TRAFALGAR SQUARE PB $8.95

Access

Paris Access

0-671-62577-2 ACCESS PB $14.95

Geoffrey **Barlow**

Travels in the Loire Valley

1-85391-039-2 DAVID & CHARLES PB $13.95

Douglas **Botting**

Wild France

0-87156-476-9 SIERRA CLUB PB $16.00

Karen **Brown**

Karen Brown's French Country Inns and Chateaux

0-930328-18-3 GLOBE PEQUOT PB $19.95

Chronicle

Cheap Eats in Paris

See also **RESTAURANTS** under **SPECIALIZED GUIDES**

0-8118-0057-1 CHRONICLE PB $9.95

Cheap Sleeps in Paris

0-8118-0058-X CHRONICLE PB $9.95

Judi **Culbertson** & Tom **Randall**

Permanent Parisians: An Illustrated Biographical Guide to the Cemeteries of Paris

See also **HISTORICAL SITES AND NATIONAL PARKS** under **SPECIALIZED GUIDES**

0-8027-7470-9 WALKER PB $16.95

Larry **Dark**, editor

Provence

Arles to restaurant menus, a celebration of Europe's sweetest corner

See also **KNOPF GUIDES**

0-679-75066-5 KNOPF PB $25.00

Henri **Gault** & Christian **Millau**

The Best of France

1-88106-609-6 GAULT MILLAU PB $20.00

Robert **Hamburger** & Barbara **Hamburger**

Paris Bistros and Wine Bars: A Select Guide

An exhaustive roundup of the most authentic way to eat in Paris, including reviews, ratings, dinner and wine suggestions, geographical listing by arrondissement, phrase and menu glossaries, an additional listing of wine bars, and more

See also **RESTAURANTS** under **SPECIALIZED GUIDES**

0-88001-417-2 ECCO PB $18.00

Penguin

The Penguin Guide to France

0-14-019902-0 PENGUIN PB $14.95

Karen **Brown**

Karen Brown's German Country Inns and Castles

0-446-38815-7 WARNER PB $12.95

Access

Rome Access

0-671-62578-0 ACCESS PB $14.95

Birnbaum

Italy

0-06-278131-6 HARPERCOLLINS PB $18.00

Chronicle

Cheap Eats in Italy

See also **RESTAURANTS** under **SPECIALIZED GUIDES**

0-8118-0207-8 CHRONICLE PB $9.95

Judi **Culbertson** & Tom **Randall**

Permanent Italians: An Illustrated Biographical Guide to the Cemeteries of Italy

These original and insightful guides introduce the traveler to their destinations by way of birthplaces, cemeteries, places of residence, and other biographical details of the country's great historical figures

See also **HISTORICAL SITES AND NATIONAL PARKS** under **SPECIALIZED GUIDES**

0-8027-7431-8 WALKER PB $16.95

Henri **Gault** & Christian **Millau**

The Best of Italy

0-13-074030-6 GAULT MILLAU PB $16.95

Paul **Hofmann**

Roma: The Smart Traveler's Guide to the Eternal City

0-8050-3002-6 HOLT PB $12.95

Penguin

The Penguin Guide to Italy

0-14-019903-9 PENGUIN PB $14.95

Stuart **Miller**

Understanding Europeans, Second Edition

1-56261-294-8 JOHN MUIR PB $14.95

Ian **Robertson**

Austria

0-393-30836-7 NORTON PB $22.95

Frederich V. **Grunfeld**

Wild Spain

0-87156-477-7 SIERRA CLUB PB $16.00

Ira **Spring** & Harvey **Edwards**

100 Hikes in the Alps

0-916890-72-4 MOUNTAINEERS PB $10.95

Ben **Weinreb** & Christopher **Hibbert**, editors

The London Encyclopaedia

0-312-05213-8 ST. MARTIN'S $49.95

Former Soviet States

Robert **Greenall**

An Explorer's Guide to Moscow

"A book which in many ways sets the standard for guides to post-Soviet Russia… Well-written, topical, even-handed, accurate"
—*The Sunday Times*

0-939010-51-8 ZEPHYR PB $14.95

Firth **Maier**

Trekking in Russia & Central Asia: A Traveler's Guide

With an emphasis on including locations not found in other Russian and East Asian guides, Maier provides 50 treks at all skill levels, cultural background information, 61 maps, travel conditions, accommodations, food, Russian phrases and terms

0-89886-355-4 MOUNTAINEERS PB $16.95

Paul E. **Richardson**, editor

Where in Moscow: The Ultimate Directory, Including Maps, Telephone Listings, and Essential Goods and Services, Fifth Edition

1-88010-028-2 RUSSIAN INFO SERVICES PB $13.50

Asia

Chris **Bates** & Ling-Li **Bates**

Culture Shock! Taiwan: A Guide to Customs and Etiquette

A look at the geographical diversity and cultural depth of this often-stereotyped country

1-55868-175-2 GRAPHIC ARTS PB $12.95

Victor **Chan**

Tibet Handbook

Using exhaustively researched itineraries and meticulous maps, Chan chronicles Tibetan literature and religious history, going so far as to include an introductory course and phrasebook in Tibetan.

0-918373-90-5 MOON PB $30.00

David Hatcher **Childress**

Lost Cities of China, Central Asia and India

0-932813-07-0 ADVENTURES UNLIMITED PB $14.95

Frederick **Fisher**

China

0-671-87896-4 MACMILLAN PB $18.00

Fodor

Fodor's '96 Hong Kong and Macau

0-679-03030-1 RANDOM HOUSE PB $14.00

Roger **Grigsby**

China by Bike: Taiwan, Hong Kong, China's East Coast

0-89886-410-0 MOUNTAINEERS PB $14.95

Paul **Hunt**

Hiking in Japan: An Adventurer's Guide to the Mountain Trails

0-87011-893-5 KODANSHA PB $17.00

Fredric **Kaplan**

The China Guidebook: 1989 Edition

0-395-48679-3 HOUGHTON MIFFLIN PB $16.95

Richard **Kennedy**

Good Tokyo Restaurants

See also **RESTAURANTS** under **SPECIALIZED GUIDES**

4-7700-1710-3 KODANSHA PB $9.00

0-87011-702-5 KODANSHA PB $7.95

Kimiko **Nagasawa** & Camy **Condon**

Eating Cheap in Japan: The Gaijin Gourmet's Guide to Ordering in Non-Tourist Restaurants

See also **RESTAURANTS** under **SPECIALIZED GUIDES**

4-07-971548-X TUTTLE PB $9.95

Robert Young **Pelton** & Wink **Dulles**

Fielding's Guide to the Far East 1996: China, Hong Kong, Japan, Macau, North Korea, South Korea, and Taiwan

1-56952-032-1 FIELDING PB $18.95

Sally **Rodwell**

Historic Hong Kong

Features ten expeditions to historic places in Hong Kong as well as easy-to-read historical backgrounds

962-217-212-1 CHINA BOOKS PB $17.95

Robert **Strauss** & Tamsin **Turnbull**

The Trans-Siberian Rail Guide, Fourth Edition

0-9520900-1-5 HUNTER PB $17.95

Taylor & Francis

All-Asia Guide

962-7010-25-1 TAYLOR & FRANCIS PB $20.00

The Middle East

Samuel **Heilman**

A Walker in Jerusalem

Award-winning guide with detailed itinerary for various tours in Jerusalem area

0-8276-0556-0 JEWISH PUB PB $14.95

Bazak

Bazak Guide to Israel, 1989-90

0-06-096317-4 HARPER & ROW PB $14.95

Bernard **McDonagh** & John (Ilt) **Flower**

Turkey: Atlas, Maps and Plans

0-393-31195-3 NORTON PB $27.50

Bernard **McDonagh**

Blue Guide: Turkey—the Aegean and Mediterranean Coasts

From Bursa in the northwest to Antakya in the far southeast, this massive (nearly 600 pages) new entry in the Blue Guide series offers, as always, a comprehensive guide to history, art, and architecture, and a detailed itinerary to be followed by car or public transportation

0-393-30489-2 NORTON PB $19.95

Africa

Nina **Casimati**

Guide to East Africa: Kenya, Tanzania, the Seychelles

0-87052-246-9 HIPPOCRENE PB $11.95

Michael **Haag**

Guide to West Africa

0-87052-244-2 HIPPOCRENE PB $11.95

Hunter Publishing

Traveller's Guide to Central and Southern Africa

0-905268-48-2 HUNTER PB $12.95

Peter **Morris**

Rough Guide to Tunisia

0-7102-0148-6 ROUTLEDGE PB $7.95

Kim **Naylor**

Africa: The Nile Route

0-903-90922-2 LASCELLES PB $12.95

Specialized Guides

High Adventure Travel

Sierra Club Guides

Adventuring in Alaska

0-87156-472-6 SIERRA CLUB PB $15.00

Adventuring in Belize

A guide to the islands, waters and inland parks

0-87156-592-7 SIERRA CLUB PB $15.00

John **Annerino**

Hiking the Grand Canyon

Information on 100 of the best trails, required equipment, hiking techniques, safety, weather, clothing, as well as tips on rafting and pack-animal excursions. Also included here are special sections on Native American history, natural history, and geology

0-87156-589-7 SIERRA CLUB PB $15.00

Sierra Club

Adventure Travel California Guide

0-679-77142-5 SIERRA CLUB PB........................$9.95

Sierra Club Guides

Adventuring in the San Francisco Bay Area

0-87156-353-3 SIERRA CLUB PB........................$15.00

Sierra Club

Adventuring in New Zealand

0-87156-571-4 SIERRA CLUB PB........................$15.00

Larry **Rice**

Baja to Patagonia: Latin American Adventures

Part adventurer, part naturalist, ecotourist Rice takes us to the outer reaches of Latin America. Offers off-the-beaten-track adventure: kayaking in the fjords of southern Chile, hiking in Venezuela's rain forest, and skiing in Argentina

1-55591-113-7 FULCRUM PB........................$15.95

Sierra Club Guides

Adventuring in Florida

Includes coverage of the Georgia Sea Islands and the Okefenokee Swamp

0-87156-373-8 SIERRA CLUB PB........................$15.00

David Rains **Wallace**

Adventuring in Central America: Guatemala, Belize, Honduras, El Salvador, Nicaragua, Costa Rica, Panama

Includes coverage of Guatemala, Belize, Honduras, El Salvador, Nicaragua, Costa Rica and Panama

See also **AUSTRALIA AND NEW ZEALAND** under **SIERRA CLUB GUIDES** under **GENERAL GUIDES**

See also **THE CARIBBEAN AND CENTRAL AMERICA**

0-87156-473-4 SIERRA CLUB PB........................$16.00

Guides for Women Travelers

Marybeth **Bond**

Travelers' Tales: A Woman's World

"We think anyone who reads this collection—woman or man—will never feel quite the same about travel again, or about what it means to be a woman in this world"—*Travelers' Tales Catalog*

1-88521-106-6 O'REILLY PB........................$17.95

Cristalyn **Brannen** & Tracey **Wilen**

Doing Business With Japanese Men

A must-read for any woman in the position of conducting business in Japan

1-88065-604-3 STONE BRIDGE PB........................$9.95

Feminist Press at CUN

China For Women: Travel and Culture

Personal essays by a variety of Chinese women as well as valuable information on how to travel and act

1-55861-112-6 FEMINIST PRESS PB........................$17.95

Susan **Hawthorne** & Renate **Klein**

Australia For Women: Travel and Culture

1-55861-095-2 FEMINIST PRESS PB........................$17.95

Jurate **Kazickas** & Lynn **Sherr**

Susan B. Anthony Slept Here: A Guide to American Women's Monuments

See also **UNITED STATES** under **GUIDES TO MEXICO, THE UNITED STATES, AND CANADA**

0-8129-2223-9 TIME BOOKS PB........................$20.00

Linda **White**

The Independent Woman's Guide to Europe

The major and minor aspects of culture shock, from tipping and transportation to shopping and specialty vacations, for the woman traveling alone

1-55591-087-4 FULCRUM PB........................$13.95

Thalia **Zepatos**

Adventures in Good Company: The Complete Guide to Women's Tours and Outdoor Trips

"This is THE best women's travel resource we've seen, ever….It's authoritative; it's supportive; it's amusing; it really does have it all"
—Pamela Robin Brandt, *Daily News*

0-933377-28-2 EIGHTH MOUNTAIN........................$24.95
0-933377-27-4 EIGHTH MOUNTAIN PB........................$16.95

A Journey of One's Own

An insightful book for women traveling alone. Contains practical advice (how to deal with sexual harassment, staying healthy, etc.), as well as ruminative essays on the need for solitary adventures, and cross-cultural encounters

0-933377-21-5 EIGHTH MOUNTAIN........................$24.95
0-933377-20-7 EIGHTH MOUNTAIN PB........................$14.95

Family

Bubbles **Fisher**

The Candy Apple: New York For Kids

See also **NEW YORK CITY** under **NEW ENGLAND & THE MID-ATLANTIC STATES** under **GUIDES TO MEXICO, THE UNITED STATES, AND CANADA**

0-13-114224-0 SIMON & SCHUSTER PB........................$11.95

Fodor

Fodor's Fun in New York City

See also **UNITED STATES** under **GUIDES TO MEXICO, THE UNITED STATES, AND CANADA**

0-679-01633-3 RANDOM HOUSE PB........................$6.95

Ann **Banks**

Children's Travel Journal

Part activity center, part diary, the *Journal* provides a structured workbook in which children can record their experiences and impressions of traveling. Composed of 24 sheets of heavyweight paper and spiral bound with a durable plastic cover, this journal will last through the rigors of any trip

0-9641126-2-0 LITTLEBOOK........................$14.95

Alfred **Gingold** & Helen **Rogan**

Cool Parent's Guide to All of New York

From the Whitney Museum to the annual Tibetan festival—this guidebook will delight parents as much as it does kids

See also **NEW YORK CITY** under **NEW ENGLAND & THE MID-ATLANTIC STATES** under **GUIDES TO MEXICO, THE UNITED STATES, AND CANADA**

1-88549-235-9 CITY & CO. PB........................$12.95

Evelyn **Kaye**

Family Travel

Exciting, unusual, and affordable vacation ideas for children, teenagers, and parents

0-9626231-3-X BLUE PENGUIN PB........................$19.95

Vicki **Lansky**

Trouble-Free Travel With Children: Helpful Hints for Parents on the Go

Tips on everything from planning through traveling abroad, plus important resource information

9167-73140 BOOK PEDDLERS PB........................$6.95

Carole Terwilliger **Meyers**

The Family Travel Guide

Family travel hot spots, adventure vacations, and how-to details as well as anecdotes to help families avoid some of the pitfalls of traveling with children

0-917120-14-0 CAROUSEL PB........................$16.95

Sanford **Portnoy** & Joan **Portnoy**

How to Take Great Trips with Your Kids

0-916782-51-4 HARVARD COMMON PB........................$8.95

Maureen **Wheeler**

Travel With Children

0-86442-299-7 LONELY PLANET PB........................$11.95

Museums and Art

Alliance for the Arts

New York City Culture Catalog

0-8109-2578-8 ABRAMS PB........................$12.95

Botond **Bognar**

The Japan Guide

See also **ASIA** under **20TH-CENTURY ARCHITECTURE** in **ARCHITECTURE, DESIGN, AND HOMES**

1-87827-133-4 PRINCETON ARCHITECTURAL PB..$24.95

Gerardo **Brown-Manrique**

The Ticino Guide

0-910413-46-0 PRINCETON ARCHITECTURAL PB...$17.95

Knopf Guides

The Louvre

See also **KNOPF GUIDES** under **GENERAL GUIDES**

0-679-76452-6 KNOPF PB....$25.00

Susan **Rappaport**

1997 Traveler's Guide to Art Museum Exhibitions

Offers art museum exhibition schedules for the year ahead in one volume, listing more than 125 museums in the US, Canada, and Europe

0-8109-6329-9 ABRAMS PB....$12.95

1995 Traveler's Guide to Art Museum Exhibitions

0-8109-2586-9 ABRAMS PB....$12.95

Arlene **Sanderson**, editor

Wright Sites: A Guide to Frank Lloyd Wright Public Places

See also **FRANK LLOYD WRIGHT** under **20TH-CENTURY INDIVIDUAL ARCHITECTS** under **20TH-CENTURY ARCHITECTURE** in **ARCHITECTURE, DESIGN, AND HOMES**

1-56898-041-8 PRINCETON ARCHITECTURAL PB...$12.95

Restaurants

Craig **Allen**

Eating Out in Barcelona and Catalunya

Finally, a culinary guide to this region with sophisticated tastes

1-56656-151-5 INTERLINK PB....$13.95

Chronicle

Cheap Eats in London

See also **EUROPE** under **OTHER TRAVEL GUIDES** under **GENERAL GUIDES**

0-87701-762-X CHRONICLE PB....$9.95

Tim **Stilwell**

Stilwell's Scotland Bed & Breakfast

With over 1,400 bed and breakfasts, maps, and a currency conversion table

0-9521909-6-6 STILLWELL PB....$11.95

Eugene **Zagat** & Nina **Zagat**

Zagat Los Angeles Restaurant Survey

0-943421-07-1 ZAGAT SURVEY PB....$9.95

A. **Laban**

Cheap Chow Chicago

A guide to spending little while eating well in the windy city

1-55652-267-3 CHICAGO REVIEW PB....$9.95

Judith **Connor** & Mayumi **Yoshida**

Old Kyoto: A Guide to Traditional Shops, Restaurants, and Inns

See also **ASIA** under **LONELY PLANET GUIDES** under **GENERAL GUIDES**

0-87011-757-2 KODANSHA PB....$15.00

Joyce **Lafray**

The Guide to Florida's Best Restaurants

0-89815-727-7 TEN SPEED PB....$11.95

Chronicle

Cheap Eats in Paris

See also **EUROPE** under **OTHER TRAVEL GUIDES** under **GENERAL GUIDES**

0-8118-0057-1 CHRONICLE PB....$9.95

Larry **Dark**, editor

Restaurants of Paris

Illustrated, informative, and discriminating, inexpensive to luxurious, opens up the labyrinthine mysteries of the Parisian table

0-679-75578-0 KNOPF PB....$25.00

Robert **Hamburger** & Barbara **Hamburger**

Paris Bistros and Wine Bars: A Select Guide

An exhaustive roundup of the most authentic way to eat in Paris, including reviews, ratings, dinner and wine suggestions, geographical listing by arrondissement, phrase and menu glossaries, an additional listing of wine bars, and more

See also **EUROPE** under **OTHER TRAVEL GUIDES** under **GENERAL GUIDES**

0-88001-417-2 ECCO PB....$18.00

Patricia **Wells**

The Food Lover's Guide to France

A resident's perspective

0-89480-306-9 WORKMAN PB....$15.95

Chronicle

Cheap Eats in Italy

0-8118-0207-8 CHRONICLE PB....$9.95

Sandra A. **Gustafson**

Cheap Eats in Italy: The Savy Traveler's Guide to the Best Meals at the Best Prices

A guide to more than 150 inexpensive restaurants

0-8118-1070-4 CHRONICLE PB....$10.95

Japan Travel Bureau

Eating in Japan

An illustrated guide

4-533-00456-3 BOOKS NIPPAN PB....$17.95

Richard **Kennedy**

Good Tokyo Restaurants

See also **ASIA** under **OTHER TRAVEL GUIDES** under **GENERAL GUIDES**

4-7700-1710-3 KODANSHA PB....$9.00

0-87011-702-5 KODANSHA PB....$7.95

Knopf

The Traveler's Guide to Art: Great Britain and Ireland

0-394-72426-7 OUTLET....$14.95

Pamela **Lanier**

The Complete Guide to Bed and Breakfasts, Inns and Guesthouses in the U.S. and Canada

See also **CANADA** under **GUIDES TO MEXICO, THE UNITED STATES, AND CANADA**

0-912528-82-6 JOHN MUIR PB....$13.95

Sandra A. **Gustafson**

Cheap Eats in London: The Savvy Traveler's Guide to the Best Meals at the Best Prices

0-8118-4283-5 CHRONICLE PB....$10.95

Nancy **Zaslavsky**

A Cook's Tour of Mexico: Authentic Recipes from the Country's Best Open-Air Markets, City Fondas and Home Kitchens

A cookbook with invaluable and up-to-date information on markets and restaurants

0-312-13454-1 ST. MARTIN'S....$27.50

Bryan **Miller**

The New York Times Guide to Restaurants in New York City

0-8129-1735-9 TIME BOOKS PB....$12.95

Kimiko **Nagasawa** & Camy **Condon**

Eating Cheap in Japan: The Gaijin Gourmet's Guide to Ordering in Non-Tourist Restaurants

4-07-971548-X TUTTLE PB....$9.95

Eugene **Zagat** & **Nina Zagat,**

Zagat New Orleans Restaurant Survey

See also **THE SOUTH** under **GUIDES TO MEXICO, THE UNITED STATES, AND CANADA**

0-943421-04-7 ZAGAT SURVEY PB....$8.95

Eric **Asimov**

$25 and Under, 1997: A Guide to the Best Inexpensive Restaurants in New York

A New York City columnist has compiled a list of his favorites

0-06-273401-6 HARPERCOLLINS PB....$10.95

Sylvia **Carter** & Peter M. **Gianotti**

Eats NYC: A Guide to the Best, Cheapest, Most Interesting Restaurants in New York

A particular emphasis on affordability takes us into the boroughs often: A great guide for the adventurous

0-8362-0809-9 ANDREWS & MCMEEL PB....$8.95

Molly **O'Neill**

New York Cookbook

Still an invaluable refernce for sources of ethnic specialties and ingredients throughout Manhattan and the boroughs

1-56305-337-3 WORKMAN....$27.95

0-89480-698-X WORKMAN PB....$17.95

Bo **Niles** & Veronica **McNiff**

The New York Book of Tea: Where to Take Tea and Buy Tea & Teaware

Whether you want the *a la francaise*, or a "haiku" tea, this book will direct you to the perfect spot

1-88549-206-5 CITY & CO. $15.00

Patricia **Wells** & Peter **Turnley**

The Food Lover's Guide to Paris

A detailed guide from a resident expert

1-56305-326-8 WORKMAN PB $15.95

Betty **Rundback**

Bed and Breakfast U.S.A.: 1996

With over 1,200 listings, this may be the best book on how to choose a good B&B anywhere in America. For low budgets (hundreds of listings under $50 for two) to more expensive ones, the rates in this edition are guaranteed for a year

See also **UNITED STATES** under **GUIDES TO MEXICO, THE UNITED STATES, AND CANADA**

0-452-26926-1 PLUME PB $14.00

Penelope **Casas**

Discovering Spain: An Uncommon Guide

Spain's culinary maven takes us on an extensive tour

0-679-76569-7 KNOPF PB $25.00

Jane **Stern** & Michael **Stern**

Road Food and Good Food

0-394-74396-2 HARPERPERENNIAL PB $12.95

Jennifer Trainer **Thompson**

Trail of Flame: The Off-The-Wall Guide to Spicy Restaurants Across America

For true chili-pepper addicts

0-89815-750-1 TEN SPEED PB $11.95

Eugene **Zagat** & Nina **Zagat**

Zagat Boston Restaurant Survey

See also **BOSTON** under **NEW ENGLAND & THE MID-ATLANTIC STATES** under **GUIDES TO MEXICO, THE UNITED STATES, AND CANADA**

0-943421-03-9 ZAGAT SURVEY PB $8.95

Zagat New York City Restaurant Survey

0-943421-09-8 ZAGAT SURVEY PB $9.95

Zagat Washington, D.C. Restaurant Survey

See also **WASHINGTON, D.C.** under **NEW ENGLAND & THE MID-ATLANTIC STATES** under **GUIDES TO MEXICO, THE UNITED STATES, AND CANADA**

0-943421-01-2 ZAGAT SURVEY PB $8.95

Shopping

Judith **Connor** & Mayumi **Yoshida**

Old Kyoto: A Guide to Traditional Shops, Restaurants, and Inns

See also **ASIA** under **LONELY PLANET GUIDES** under **GENERAL GUIDES**

0-87011-757-2 KODANSHA PB $15.00

Historical Sites and National Parks

Devereux **Butcher**

Exploring Our National Parks and Monuments

0-87645-122-9 ROBERTS RINEHART PB $14.95

Josephine **Fletcher-Watson**, editor

The National Trust Handbook 1993

Dedicated to the preservation of historic places and properties in England, Wales, and Northern Ireland, The National Trust is the largest private landowner in Britain. From castles to gardens to lighthouses, each entry includes a brief description and travel directions. Includes line drawings

See also **EUROPE** under **OTHER TRAVEL GUIDES** under **GENERAL GUIDES**

0-7078-0160-5 TRAFALGAR SQUARE PB $8.95

Fodor

Fodor's National Parks of the West: A Complete Guide to the Thirty Best-Loved National Parks and Monuments in the Western United States and Canada

EDITED BY WILLIAM ZINSSER

0-679-02192-2 RANDOM HOUSE PB $17.00

Judi **Culbertson** & Tom **Randall**

Permanent Parisians: An Illustrated Biographical Guide to the Cemeteries of Paris

0-8027-7470-9 WALKER PB $16.95

Michael **Frome**

National Park Guide 1994

0-671-88418-2 MACMILLAN PB $16.00

Judi **Culbertson** & Tom **Randall**

Permanent Italians: An Illustrated Biographical Guide to the Cemeteries of Italy

These original and insightful guides introduce the traveler to their destinations by way of birthplaces, cemeteries, places of residence, and other biographical details of the country's great historical figures

0-8027-7431-8 WALKER PB $16.95

Marcia **Kelly** & Jack **Kelly**

Sanctuaries: The West Coast and Southwest—a Guide to Lodgings in Monasteries, Abbeys, and Retreats of the United States

Ninety profiles of religious and nonsectarian sanctuaries in California, Arizona, Colorado, New Mexico, Oregon, and Washington. The entries give complete information on each place: its history, size, ritual aims, fees and accommodations

0-517-88007-5 RANDOM HOUSE PB $15.00

Charles E. **Little**

Discover America: The Smithsonian Book of National Parks

A splendid photographic homage and an authoritative guide, this volume covers the 368 national parks, monuments, battlefields, and wilderness preserves in America. Descriptions of the parks start with geological forces that shaped the land, then explore their uses as the land was settled, and the political forces that made the national park system what it is today

0-89599-050-4 SMITHSONIAN $34.95

Rand **McNally**

Rand McNally Great National Park Vacations

0-13-750712-7 RAND MCNALLY $12.95

Arthur P. **Miller** & Marjorie **Miller**

Trails Across America: Traveler's Guide to Our National Scenic and Historic Trails

From the Iditarod to the Appalachian Trail, this is a complete guide to the nationwide system of scenic and historic trails. Colorful description, ready reference, and informative maps

1-55591-235-4 FULCRUM PB $19.95

Eric **Nash**

New York's 50 Best Secret Architectural Treasures

See also **NEW YORK CITY** under **NEW ENGLAND & THE MID-ATLANTIC STATES** under **GUIDES TO MEXICO, THE UNITED STATES, AND CANADA**

1-88549-231-6 CITY & CO. PB $9.95

Henry **Reuss**

The Unknown South of France: A History Buff's Guide

An entertaining guide to the archaeology and history of the ancient lands of Aquitania, Languedoc, and Provence, arranged chronologically. Also lists inns and restaurants. "The most interesting and unusual guidebook I have seen for a long time"
—Arthur M. Schlesinger, Jr.

1-55832-030-X HARVARD COMMON PB $12.95

John F. **Sears**

Sacred Places: American Tourist Attractions in the Nineteenth Century

Sears has discovered unexpected fascinations in the relations between 19th-century Americans and their native scenery. A new national identity took shape against the background of "sacred places" like Niagara Falls, the Hudson Valley, the White Mountains, Yosemite, and Yellowstone—while a profitable tourist industry also

flourished. The book is enriched by profuse illustrations and unusual source materials
0-19-505350-8 OXFORD $27.95

Frank E. **Vandiver**
Civil War Battlefields and Landmarks
With over 150 illustrations and a fluently written text, campaign maps, then-and-now photographs, statistical tables, eyewitness accounts, sidebars, biographical sketches, and the official National Parks Service maps, this is an essential guide to the theater of the American Civil War
0-679-44898-5 RANDOM HOUSE $25.00

Rail Travel

Baedeker
Rail Guide to Europe
0-13-055971-7 BAEDEKER GUIDES PB $18.00

Charles **Jacobs** & Babette **Jacobs**
Great Railtrips of the World
0-912640-35-9 TRAVEL DIGESTS PB $11.95

Guides to Mexico, the United States, and Canada

Canada

Baedecker
Canada Guide
0-02-861350-3 BAEDEKER GUIDES PB $24.95

Birnbaum
Birnbaum's Canada
0-395-48168-6 HOUGHTON MIFFLIN PB $12.95

Fodor's
Canada '97
Complete guide to the mountains, coasts, prairies, cities and wilderness
0-679-03190-1 FODOR'S PB $19.00

Fodor's Canada
0-679-01608-2 RANDOM HOUSE PB $14.95

Pamela **Lanier**
The Complete Guide to Bed and Breakfasts, Inns and Guesthouses in the U.S. and Canada
See also **RESTAURANTS** under **SPECIALIZED GUIDES**
0-912528-82-6 JOHN MUIR PB $13.95

Lonely Planet
Canada
0-86442-409-4 LONELY PLANET $21.95

Canada: A Travel Survival Kit
0-86442-042-0 LONELY PLANET PB $10.95

Felicity **Munn**
Travel-Smart Trip Planner: Eastern Canada
1-56261-254-9 JOHN MUIR PB $14.95

Penguin
The Penguin Guide to Canada
0-14-019906-3 PENGUIN PB $12.95

Sandra W. **Soule**
USA and Canada
See also **UNITED STATES**
0-312-08133-2 ST. MARTIN'S PB $19.95

Lonely Planet
Victoria
0-86442-361-6 LONELY PLANET PB $15.95

Mexico

Baedecker Guides
Mexico Guide
0-02-861359-7 BAEDEKER GUIDES PB $23.95
0-02-861366-X BAEDEKER GUIDES PB $24.95

Berkeley Guides
Mexico
0-679-03182-0 FODOR'S PB $17.95

Birnbaum
Birnbaum's Mexico
0-395-48162-7 HOUGHTON MIFFLIN PB $12.95

Rebecca **Burns**
Hidden Mexico: An Adventure's Guide to the Beaches and Coasts
0-915233-05-3 ULYSSES PB $12.95

Bob **Burleson** & David **Riskind**
Backcountry Mexico: A Traveler's Guide and Phrasebook
0-292-70755-X TEXAS PB $14.95

Fodor's
Cancun, Cozumel, Yucatan Peninsula: The Complete Guide
0-679-03191-X FODOR'S PB $13.00

Fodor's
Fodor's Mexico
0-679-01673-2 RANDOM HOUSE PB $13.95

Fodor's
Mexico: The Complete Guide
0-679-03249-5 FODOR'S PB $18.50

E.J. **Guarino**
The Other Mexico: A Guide to Ancient Wonders and Modern Pleasures in Mexico
0-914846-36-1 GOLDEN WEST PB $9.00

Let's Go
The Budget Guide to Mexico
0-312-14660-4 ST. MARTIN'S PB $13.99

Lonely Planet
Mexico: A Travel Survival Kit
0-86442-047-1 LONELY PLANET PB $17.95

John **Noble**
Mexico
0-86442-166-4 LONELY PLANET $19.95

John **Whitman**
The Best Mexican and Central American Travel Tips
See also **CENTRAL AND SOUTH AMERICA** under **OTHER TRAVEL GUIDES** under **GENERAL GUIDES**
0-06-273268-4 HARPERPERENNIAL PB $15.00

United States

Birnbaum
Birnbaum's United States
0-395-48169-4 HOUGHTON MIFFLIN PB $12.95

Devereux **Butcher**
Exploring Our National Parks and Monuments
See also **HISTORICAL SITES AND NATIONAL PARKS** under **SPECIALIZED GUIDES**
0-87645-122-9 ROBERTS RINEHART PB $14.95

Fodor's
Fodor's Budget Travel in America
0-679-01097-1 RANDOM HOUSE PB $11.95

Fodor's Fun in New York City
See also **FAMILY** under **SPECIALIZED GUIDES**
0-679-01633-3 RANDOM HOUSE PB $6.95

Fodor's Great American Vacations: 50 Affordable, Health-Conscious Trips to the Country's Best-Loved Travel Destinations
EDITED BY WILLIAM ZINSSER
0-679-02174-4 FODOR'S PB $14.00

Fodor's
USA '97
Guide to the best of everything in all fifty states
0-679-03295-9 FODOR'S PB $21.00

Jurate **Kazickas** & Lynn **Sherr**
Susan B. Anthony Slept Here: A Guide to American Women's Monuments
See also **GUIDES FOR WOMEN TRAVELERS** under **SPECIALIZED GUIDES**
0-8129-2223-9 TIME BOOKS PB $20.00

Brian **Keenan**
U.S.A.
0-13-766726-4 ROUGH GUIDES PB $18.00

Let's Go
The Budget Guide to the USA
0-312-14668-X ST. MARTIN'S PB $19.99

The Reader's Catalog
250 West 57th Street
New York, NY 10107

Charles E. **Little**

Discover America: The Smithsonian Book of National Parks

A splendid photographic homage and an authoritative guide, this volume covers the 368 national parks, monuments, battlefields, and wilderness preserves in America. Descriptions of the parks start with geological forces that shaped the land, then explore their uses as the land was settled, and the political forces that made the national park system what it is today

PHOTOGRAPHS BY DAVID MUENCH

0-89599-050-4 SMITHSONIAN............$34.95

Trails Across America: Traveler's Guide to Our National Scenic and Historic Trails

From the Iditarod to the Appalachian Trail, this is a complete guide to the nationwide system of scenic and historic trails. Colorful description, ready reference, and informative maps

See also **HISTORICAL SITES AND NATIONAL PARKS** under **SPECIALIZED GUIDES**

1-55591-235-4 FULCRUM PB............$19.95

Betty **Rundback**

Bed and Breakfast U.S.A.: 1996

With over 1,200 listings, this may be the best book on how to choose a good B&B anywhere in America. For low budgets (hundreds of listings under $50 for two) to more expensive ones, the rates in this edition are guaranteed for a year

0-452-26926-1 PLUME PB............$14.00

John F. **Sears**

Sacred Places: American Tourist Attractions in the Nineteenth Century

Sears has discovered unexpected fascinations in the relations between 19th-century Americans and their native scenery. A new national identity took shape against the background of "sacred places" like Niagara Falls, the Hudson Valley, the White Mountains, Yosemite, and Yellowstone—while a profitable tourist industry also flourished. The book is enriched by profuse illustrations and unusual source materials

0-19-505350-8 OXFORD............$27.95

Sandra W. **Soule**

USA and Canada

0-312-08133-2 ST. MARTIN'S PB............$19.95

New England & the Mid-Atlantic States

Michael **Durham**

The Smithsonian Guide to Historic America: The Mid-Atlantic States

1-55670-060-1 STEWART, TABORI............$24.95
1-55670-050-4 STEWART, TABORI PB............$18.95

Robert **Finch**

The Smithsonian Guides to Natural America: Southern New England

State-of-the-art maps, directions, phone numbers, and addresses make arranging the trip easy, and activities from hiking to birdwatching make it worth the work of getting there

PHOTOGRAPHY BY JONATHAN WALLEN

0-679-76475-5 RANDOM HOUSE PB............$19.95

Fodor's

Fodor's New England

0-679-01676-7 RANDOM HOUSE PB............$13.95

Angus Kress **Gillespie** & Michael Aaron **Rockland**

Looking For America on the New Jersey Turnpike

0-8135-1466-5 RUTGERS............$18.95
0-8135-1955-1 RUTGERS PB............$11.95

Marcia **Kelly**

Sanctuaries: The Northeast

This series arrives in time to aid that growing number of people who are choosing tanquility and spiritual renewal for vacations and weekends

0-517-57727-5 RANDOM HOUSE PB............$15.00

Tim **Mulligan**

The Hudson River Valley: From Saratoga Springs to New York City—a History and Guide, 1992-93 Edition

The most thorough guide available to a region rich in the pleasures of history and landscape. "Eloquent, amusing, and sensible" —*Washington Post*

0-679-73737-5 RANDOM HOUSE PB............$12.00

Vance **Muse**

The Smithsonian Guide to Historic America: Northern New England

1-55670-049-0 STEWART, TABORI............$24.95
1-55670-066-0 STEWART, TABORI PB............$18.95

Fodor's

New England: A Four-Season Guide

0-679-03261-4 FODOR'S PB............$18.00

Lonely Planet

New England

0864422652. LONELY PLANET PB............$15.95

Sandra W. **Soule**

The Middle Atlantic

0-312-06281-8 ST. MARTIN'S PB............$14.95

New England

0-312-08130-8 ST. MARTIN'S PB............$16.95

Elizabeth **Squier**

Guide to the Recommended Country Inns of New England

0-87106-819-2 GLOBE PEQUOT PB............$10.95

Fodor's

Virginia

1-87886-795-4 FODOR'S............$42.00

Henry **Wiencek**

The Smithsonian Guide to Historic America: Virginia and the Capital Region

1-55670-058-X STEWART, TABORI............$24.95

Anne E. **Wright**

Travel-Smart Trip Planner: New England

1-56261-256-5 JOHN MUIR PB............$14.95

Boston

Fodor's

Fodor's Boston

0-679-01604-X RANDOM HOUSE PB............$7.95

Fodor's

Exploring Boston

0-679-03201-0 FODOR'S PB............$21.00

Let's Go

Boston: Map Guide

0-312-13765-6 ST. MARTIN'S PB............$7.95

Eugene **Zagat** & Nina **Zagat**

Zagat Boston Restaurant Survey

See also **RESTAURANTS** under **SPECIALIZED GUIDES**

0-943421-03-9 ZAGAT SURVEY PB............$8.95

New York City

Applause

New York's Guide to the Performing Arts

1-55783-096-7 APPLAUSE THEATRE PB............$15.95

Berkeley Editors

On the Loose, On the Cheap, Off the Beaten Path in New York City '97

0-679-03135-9 FODOR'S PB............$15.00

Bubbles **Fisher**

The Candy Apple: New York for Kids

See also **FAMILY** under **SPECIALIZED GUIDES**

0-13-114224-0 SIMON & SCHUSTER PB............$11.95

Fodor's

Fodor's New York City

0-679-01679-1 RANDOM HOUSE PB............$9.95

Sunday in New York

2,076 relaxing, uplifting, caloric, historic, hip and romantic, weekend things to do

0-679-02100-0 FODOR'S PB............$11.00

Alfred **Gingold** & Helen **Rogan**
Cool Parent's Guide to All of New York
From the Whitney Museum to the annual Tibetan festival—this guidebook will delight parents as much as it does kids
See also **FAMILY** under **SPECIALIZED GUIDES**
1-88549-235-9 CITY & CO. PB $12.95

Let's Go
New York City: Map Guide
0-312-13764-8 ST. MARTIN'S PB $7.95

Bryan **Miller**
The New York Times Guide to Restaurants in New York City
See also **RESTAURANTS** under **SPECIALIZED GUIDES**
0-8129-1735-9 TIME BOOKS PB $12.95

Eric **Nash**
New York's 50 Best Secret Architectural Treasures
See also **HISTORICAL SITES AND NATIONAL PARKS** under **SPECIALIZED GUIDES**
1-88549-231-6 CITY & CO. PB $9.95

Bo **Niles** & Veronica **McNiff**
The New York Book of Tea: Where to Take Tea and Buy Tea & Teaware
Whether you want the *á la francaise*, or a "haiku" tea, this book will direct you to the perfect spot
See also **ALES AND BEERS** under **WINE AND BEVERAGES**
1-88549-206-5 CITY & CO. $15.00

Rough Guides
New York
1-85828-073-7 ROUGH GUIDES PB $13.95

Access
New York City Access: Fifth Edition
0-06-277052-7 ACCESS PB $18.00

Eugene **Zagat** & Nina **Zagat**
Zagat New York City Restaurant Survey
0-943421-09-8 ZAGAT SURVEY PB $9.95

Washington, D.C.

Fodor's
Fodor's Washington, D.c.
0-679-01714-3 RANDOM HOUSE PB $7.95

Washington DC '97
Complete guide includes monuments, museums, Arlington, Annapolis and the city's best restaurants
0-679-03322-X FODOR'S PB $14.00

Let's Go
The Budget Guide to Washington, D.C
0-312-14669-8 ST. MARTIN'S PB $13.99

Henry **Wiencek**
The Smithsonian Guide to Historic America: Virginia and the Capital Region
1-55670-059-8 STEWART, TABORI $24.95

Eugene **Zagat** & Nina **Zagat**
Zagat Washington, D.C. Restaurant Survey
0-943421-01-2 ZAGAT SURVEY PB $8.95

The South

John **Bowen**
Adventuring Along the Southeast Coast: The Sierra Club Travel Guide to the Low Country, Beaches and Barrier Islands of North Carolina, South Carolina, and Georgia
Organized to ease travel plans, this volume includes sightseeing opportunities, historical attractions, wildlife refuges, as well as a comprehensive bibliography and appendices with helpful phone numbers
0-87156-553-6 SIERRA CLUB PB $15.00

Fodor's
The Carolinas and the Georgia Coast
0-679-03194-4 FODOR'S PB $10.00

Florida
0-13-761651-1 ROUGH GUIDES PB $14.00

Fodor's Florida
0-679-01623-6 RANDOM HOUSE PB $10.95

Lonely Planet
Florida
0-86442-374-8 LONELY PLANET $19.95

Miami City Guide
0-86442-373-X LONELY PLANET $11.95

Rough Guides
Florida
1-85828-184-9 ROUGH GUIDES PB $16.95

Fodor's
Fodor's The American South
0-679-01696-1 RANDOM HOUSE PB $12.95

Fodor's The Carolinas and The Georgia Coast
0-679-01493-4 RANDOM HOUSE PB $8.95

William **Logan** & Vance **Muse**
The Smithsonian Guide to Historic America: The Deep South
1-55670-069-5 STEWART, TABORI $24.95
1-55670-068-7 STEWART, TABORI PB $18.95

Fodor's
Fodor's New Orleans
0-679-01678-3 RANDOM HOUSE PB $8.95

Miami & the Keys '97
Includes coverage of Ft. Lauderdale, Palm Beach and the Everglades
0-679-03250-9 FODOR'S PB $13.00

New Orleans: The Complete Guide
0-679-03262-2 FODOR'S PB $13.50

Lonely Planet
New Orleans City Guide
0-86442-430-2 LONELY PLANET $11.95

Michelin Green Guides
Guide to Florida
2-06-152801-5 MICHELIN PB $20.00

Sierra Club
Adventuring in Florida
Includes coverage of the Georgia Sea Islands and the Okefenokee Swamp
See also **HIGH ADVENTURE TRAVEL** under **SPECIALIZED GUIDES**
0-87156-373-8 SIERRA CLUB PB $15.00

Sandra W. **Soule**
The South
0-312-08131-6 ST. MARTIN'S PB $14.95

Karl **Teuschl**
Florida
0-395-78241-4 APA PB $7.95

Joy **Williams**
The Florida Keys: A History and Guide 1993-1994 Edition
"A magnificent, tragi-comic guide…one of the best guidebooks ever written"
—Condé-Nast Traveler
0-679-75773-2 RANDOM HOUSE PB $13.00
0-679-75088-6 RANDOM HOUSE PB $12.00

Eugene **Zagat** & Nina **Zagat**,
Zagat New Orleans Restaurant Survey
0-943421-04-7 ZAGAT SURVEY PB $8.95

The West

Access
Las Vegas Access
0-671-60335-3 PRENTICE HALL PB $9.95

John **Annerino**
Hiking the Grand Canyon
Information on 100 of the best trails, required equipment, hiking techniques, safety, weather, clothing, as well as tips on rafting and pack-animal excursions. Also included here are special sections on Native American history, natural history, and geology
See also **HIGH ADVENTURE TRAVEL** under **SPECIALIZED GUIDES**
0-87156-589-7 SIERRA CLUB PB $15.00

Fodor's
Fodor's: Arizona '97
Complete guide to the Grand Canyon, major cities, the Red Rocks and Native communities
0-679-03171-5 FODOR'S PB $15.50

Applause

The Los Angeles Guide to the Performing Arts
1-55783-153-X APPLAUSE THEATRE PB $15.95

Wayne **Bernhardson** & Scott **Wayne**

Baja: California
"It's hard to see how one small volume could possibly hold more useful information"
—*The San Diego Tribune*
0-86442-214-8 LONELY PLANET PB $14.95

Fodor's

Exploring California
0-679-03202-9 FODOR'S PB $21.00

Fodor's California
0-679-01607-4 RANDOM HOUSE PB $12.95

Fodor's Los Angeles, Orange Country, Palm Springs
0-679-01671-6 RANDOM HOUSE PB $8.95

California '97
Complete guide with coastal drives, national parks, major cities and the Napa Valley
0-679-03188-X FODOR'S PB $18.00

Los Angeles: The Complete Guide
0-679-03246-0 FODOR'S PB $14.50

San Diego: The Complete Guide
0-679-03278-9 FODOR'S PB $13.50

San Francisco '97
Includes coverage of the wine country
0-679-03279-7 FODOR'S PB $14.00

Henri **Gault**

The Best of San Francisco
0-13-076084-6 PRENTICE HALL PB $14.95

Henri **Gault** & Christian **Millau**

The Best of Los Angeles
0-13-076068-4 PRENTICE HALL PB $14.95

Let's Go

The Budget Guide to California
Includes coverage of Hawaii
See also **HAWAII**
0-312-14647-7 ST. MARTIN'S PB $17.99

Michelin Green Guides

San Fransisco
2-06-159501-4 MICHELIN PB $18.00

Rough Guides

California
1-85828-181-4 ROUGH GUIDES PB $16.95

San Francisco
1-85828-185-7 ROUGH GUIDES PB $14.95

Sierra Club

Adventure Travel California Guide
0-679-77142-5 SIERRA CLUB PB $9.95

Adventuring in the San Francisco Bay Area
0-87156-353-3 SIERRA CLUB PB $15.00

Kim **Weir**

Northern California Handbook
A complete 746-page guide, includes 54 maps, accommodation and dining suggestions, suggested walking tours, and plenty of historical and cultural background
0-918373-43-3 MOON PB $16.95

Eugene **Zagat** & Nina **Zagat**

Zagat Los Angeles Restaurant Survey
See also **RESTAURANTS** under **SPECIALIZED GUIDES**
0-943421-07-1 ZAGAT SURVEY PB $9.95

California and the West Coast: Second Edition
0-671-84754-6 ROUGH GUIDES PB $17.00

Sierra Club

The Sierra Club Guide to the Natural Areas of New Mexico, Arizona and Nevada
0-87156-753-9 RANDOM HOUSE PB $12.00

Fodor's

Fodor's Arizona
0-679-01596-5 RANDOM HOUSE PB $8.95

Fodor's Colorado
0-679-01616-3 RANDOM HOUSE PB $8.95

Fodor's Las Vegas
0-679-01628-7 RANDOM HOUSE PB $6.95

Fodor's National Parks of the West: A Complete Guide to the Thirty Best-Loved National Parks and Monuments in the Western United States and Canada
See also **HISTORICAL SITES AND NATIONAL PARKS** under **SPECIALIZED GUIDES**
EDITED BY WILLIAM ZINSSER
0-679-02192-2 RANDOM HOUSE PB $17.00

Fodor's New Mexico
0-679-01542-6 RANDOM HOUSE PB $7.95

Fodor's the Rockies: U.S. and Canada
0-679-01553-1 RANDOM HOUSE PB $8.95

Richard **Harris**

Travel-Smart Trip Planner: The American Southwest
1-56261-251-4 JOHN MUIR PB $14.95

Marcia **Kelly** & Jack **Kelly**

Sanctuaries: The West Coast and Southwest—a Guide to Lodgings in Monasteries, Abbeys, and Retreats of the United States
Ninety profiles of religious and nonsectarian sanctuaries in California, Arizona, Colorado, New Mexico, Oregon, and Washington. The entries give complete information on each place: its history, size, ritual aims, fees and accommodations
0-517-88007-5 RANDOM HOUSE PB $15.00

John **Perry** & Jane Greverus **Perry**

The Sierra Club Guide to the Natural Areas of Idaho, Montana, and Wyoming
0-87156-781-4 SIERRA CLUB PB $14.00

Rough Guides

The Rockies
1-85828-201-2 ROUGH GUIDES PB $26.95

Sandra W. **Soule**

The Rocky Mountains and the Southwest
0-312-06563-9 ST. MARTIN'S PB $13.95

The West Coast
0-312-08132-4 ST. MARTIN'S PB $15.95

Bill **Weir**

Utah Handbook
0-918373-05-0 MOON PB $10.95

The Pacific Northwest & Alaska

Sierra Club

Adventuring in Alaska
See also **HIGH ADVENTURE TRAVEL** under **SPECIALIZED GUIDES**
0-87156-472-6 SIERRA CLUB PB $15.00

Jim **DuFresne**

Alaska: A Travel Survival Kit
The third edition of an excellent guidebook featuring 70 maps and detailed information on wilderness and wildlife
0-86442-101-X LONELY PLANET PB $12.95

Let's Go

The Budget Guide to Alaska & The Pacific Northwest
0-312-14644-2 ST. MARTIN'S PB $17.99

Lonely Planet

Alaska: A Travel Survival Kit
0-908086-77-6 LONELY PLANET PB $8.95

The Midwest

Fodor's

Fodor's '97 Chicago
0-679-03195-2 FODOR'S PB $13.50

Henri **Gault** & Christian **Millau**

The Best of Chicago
0-13-072836-5 GAULT MILLAU PB $15.95

Anthony **Hitchcock** & Jean **Lindgren**, editors

Country Inns, Lodges and Historic Hotels: The Midwest and the Rocky Mountain States
0-89102-376-3 FRANKLIN PB $8.95

David **Lowe**

Lost Chicago
0-517-46888-3 CRESCENT $16.99

Michelin Green Guides
Chicago
2-06-159401-8 MICHELIN PB $18.00

Sandra W. **Soule**
The Midwest
0-312-06282-6 ST. MARTIN'S PB $12.95

Suzanne **Winckler**
The Smithsonian Guide to Historic America: The Great Lake States
1-55670-072-5 STEWART, TABORI $24.95
1-55670-071-7 STEWART, TABORI PB $18.95

Hawaii

Access
Hawaii Access
0-13-001157-6 PRENTICE HALL PB $12.95

J.D. **Bisignani**
Hawaii Handbook
Over 700 pages of remarkably detailed information about all the islands of Hawaii. A book for those who want to go beyond the glitzy and pre-packaged
0-918373-39-5 PUBLISHERS GROUP WEST PB $14.95

Let's Go
The Budget Guide to California
Includes coverage of Hawaii
See also THE WEST
0-312-14647-7 ST. MARTIN'S PB $17.99

Fodor's
Fodor's Hawaii
0-679-01656-2 RANDOM HOUSE PB $11.95

Fodor's
Hawaii: The Complete Guide
0-679-03228-2 FODOR'S PB $17.00

Maui: The Complete Guide
Includes scenic drives, beaches, shops and resorts
0-679-03248-7 FODOR'S PB $10.00

Rough Guides
Hawaii
1-85828-206-3 ROUGH GUIDES PB $16.95

Arnold **Schuchter**
Travel-Smart Trip Planner: Hawaii
1-56261-255-7 JOHN MUIR PB $14.95

Caribbean and Latin America

APA Productions
Insight Guide: Bahamas
0-13-056276-9 PRENTICE HALL PB $16.95

Fodor's
The Bahamas: The Complete Guide
0-679-03174-X FODOR'S PB $12.50

Glenda **Bendure** & Ned **Friary**
Eastern Caribbean
0-86442-235-0 LONELY PLANET PB $16.95

Birnbaum
Birnbaum's Caribbean: Bermuda and the Bahamas
0-395-48163-5 HOUGHTON MIFFLIN PB $12.95
0-395-51141-0 HOUGHTON MIFFLIN PB $13.95

Fodor's
Caribbean Ports of Call 1997
Dining, shopping and entertainment highlights of every Caribbean island
0-679-03317-3 FODOR'S PB $9.95

Condé Nast Traveler
Condé Nast Traveler Caribbean Resort and Cruise Ship Finder
0-679-02850-1 FODOR'S PB $14.00

Fodor's
Fodor's Bahamas
0-679-01600-7 RANDOM HOUSE PB $8.95

Fodor's Bermuda
0-679-01603-1 RANDOM HOUSE PB $8.95

Fodor's Caribbean
0-679-01612-0 RANDOM HOUSE PB $13.95

Fodor's Saint Martin
0-679-01636-8 RANDOM HOUSE PB $6.95

Fodor's Virgin Islands
0-679-01712-7 RANDOM HOUSE PB $8.95

Lonely Planet
Jamaica
0-86442-372-1 LONELY PLANET PB $17.95

Monika **Latzel** & Jurgen **Reiter**
Dominican Republic (Insight Compact Guides)
0-395-78838-2 APA PB $7.95

Penguin
The Penguin Guide to the Caribbean
0-14-019900-4 PENGUIN PB $9.95

Fodor's
Pocket Puerto Rico Guide
0-679-03273-8 FODOR'S PB $8.50

Jonathan **Runge**
Rum and Reggae: What's Hot and What's Not in the Caribbean
The unofficial bible for American travelers to the Caribbean, now revised and expanded to include every island in the magic sea. Runge descends into a volcano on St. Vincent, parties nonstop at the carnival in Tobago, windsurfs off Barbados, and more
See also MUSIC OF THE AMERICAS under WORLD MUSIC: OTHER TRADITIONS in PERFORMING ARTS AND MEDIA
0-679-74716-8 RANDOM HOUSE PB $17.00
0-312-01509-7 RANDOM HOUSE PB $9.95

David **Schwab**, editor
Caribbean (The Lesser Antilles, 1996)
0-395-75499-2 APA PB $22.95

Fodor's
U.S. and British Virgin Islands: The Complete Guide
0-679-03294-0 FODOR'S PB $13.50

Phrasebooks

Berlitz Phrasebooks

Berlitz
Berlitz Arabic Phrasebook
2-8315-0901-7 BERLITZ PB $6.95

Dutch Phrasebook
2-8315-0885-1 BERLITZ PB $6.95

Finnish Phrasebook
2-8315-0896-7 BERLITZ PB $6.95

French Phrasebook
2-8315-0880-0 BERLITZ PB $6.95

German Phrasebook
2-8315-0883-5 BERLITZ PB $6.95

Greek Phrasebook
2-8315-0903-3 BERLITZ PB $6.95

Hebrew Phrasebook
2-8315-0872-X BERLITZ PB $6.95

Hungarian Phrasebook
2-8315-0919-X BERLITZ PB $6.95

Japanese Phrasebook
2-8315-0898-3 BERLITZ PB $6.95

Norwegian Phrasebook
2-8315-0897-5 BERLITZ PB $6.95

Polish Phrasebook
2-8315-0876-2 BERLITZ PB $6.95

Portuguese Phrasebook
2-8315-0899-1 BERLITZ PB $6.95

Russian Phrasebook
2-8315-0910-6 BERLITZ PB $6.95

Spanish Phrasebook
2-8315-0888-6 BERLITZ PB $6.95

Swedish Phrasebook
2-8315-0886-X BERLITZ PB $6.95

Turkish Phrasebook
2-8315-0844-4 BERLITZ PB $5.95

Lonely Planet Phrasebooks

Lonely Planet
Burmese Phrasebook
0-86442-026-9 LONELY PLANET PB $2.95

China Phrasebook
0-86442-086-2 LONELY PLANET PB $4.95

Korean Phrasebook
0-86442-060-9 LONELY PLANET PB $2.95

Nepal Phrasebook
0-86442-145-1 LONELY PLANET PB $4.95

Papua New Guinea Phrasebook
0-908086-90-3 LONELY PLANET PB $2.95

Philipino Phrasebook
0-86442-064-1 LONELY PLANET PB $2.95

Sri Lanka Phrasebook
0-908086-94-6 LONELY PLANET PB $2.95

Tibet Phrasebook
0-86442-346-2 LONELY PLANET PB $5.95

Boats, Cars, Planes, and Trains

For related reading, see MILITARY AFFAIRS in WORLD HISTORY AND CURRENT AFFAIRS

Boats

Jan **Adkins**
The Craft of Sail: A Primer of Sailing
0-8027-7214-5 WALKER PB $10.95

Clifford W. **Ashley**
The Ashley Book of Knots
0-385-04025-3 DOUBLEDAY $60.00

Jill **Bobrow**
Classic Yacht Interiors
0-393-03274-4 NORTON $50.00

Bill **Brogdon**
Boat Navigation for the Rest of Us: Finding Your Way by Eye and Electronics
0-07-008164-6 INTERNATIONAL MARINE PB $18.95

Norman **Brouwer**
International Register of Historic Ships
0-930248-04-X NATL MARITIME HIST SOCIETY $57.75
0-930248-05-8 NATL MARITIME HIST SOCIETY PB $37.75

Howard **Chapelle**
American Small Sailing Craft
0-393-03143-8 NORTON $40.00

Wyn Craig **Wade**
The Titanic
Called by some critics the definitive story
0-14-016691-2 PENGUIN PB $12.95

Charles **Davis**
American Sailing Ships: Their Plans and History
0-8446-6136-8 SMITH $17.80
0-486-24658-2 DOVER PB $7.95

George **Dow**
Whale Ships and Whaling: A Pictorial History
0-486-24808-9 DOVER PB $10.95

Francis **Holland**
America's Lighthouses: An Illustrated History
0-486-25576-X DOVER PB $11.95

Octavius **Howe** & Frederick **Matthews**
American Clipper Ships, 1833-1858
Volume 1
0-486-25115-2 DOVER PB $10.95
Volume 2
0-486-25116-0 DOVER PB $12.95

Cynthia **Kaul**
Harbors of Enchantment: A Yachtmen's Anthology
0-393-02761-9 NORTON $50.00

Gary **Kinder**
Ship of Gold in the Deep Blue Sea: The History and Discovery of the World's Richest Shipwreck
In 1857, the *SS Central America* went down 200 miles off the Carolina coast, and with it sunk hundreds of millions of dollars worth of California gold. This engrossing account draws on eyewitness accounts and diaries to piece together the history of the ship, the disaster, and the captivating story of the wreck's rediscovery and salvage
0-87113-464-0 GROVE $24.00

F. Alexander **Magoun**
The Frigate Constitution and Other Historic Ships
0-486-25524-7 DOVER PB $12.95

Ferenc **Mate**
The World's Best Sailboats
0-920256-11-2 NORTON $50.00

Benjamin **Mendlowitz**
The Book of Wooden Boats
A collection of 100 of the best images from Mendlowitz's previous *Calendar of Wooden Boats*, this book adds more than 100 additional new views of beautiful, traditional canoes, rowboats, sailboats, working boats, and yachts. A text by marine historian and restorer Maynard Bray accompanies each photo
0-393-03417-8 NORTON $55.00

William **Miller**
The First Great Ocean Liners in Photographs: 180 Views, 1897-1927
0-486-24574-8 DOVER PB $12.95

Peter **Neill**, editor
America: Art and Artifacts from America's Great Nautical Collection
0-8109-1527-8 ABRAMS $45.00

Joel **White**
Wood, Water and Light: Classic Wooden Boats
PHOTOGRAPHS BY BENJAMIN MENDLOWITZ
0-393-03327-9 NORTON $50.00

Cars

Automobile Quarterly Staff
Corvette: A Piece of the Action
0-915038-44-7 MOTORBOOKS INTL $39.95

Chilton's Automotives
Chilton's Easy Car Care
0-8019-8042-9 CHILTON PB $17.95

Essential Car Care
0-8118-0600-6 CHRONICLE PB $9.95

James J. **Flink**
The Automobile Age
A sweeping social history of the car and its impact on American society
See also **INDUSTRIAL REVOLUTIONS** under **HISTORY OF SCIENCE AND TECHNOLOGY** under **TOPICS IN AMERICAN STUDIES** in **HISTORY OF THE AMERICAS**
0-262-56055-0 MIT PB $19.00
0263560500 MIT PB $16.95

Jay **Hirsch**
Great American Dream Machines: Classic Cars of the '50s and '60s
0-679-72160-6 RANDOM HOUSE PB $25.00

Paul **Katzka** & Bill **Yankus**
Autointelligence New Car, Decision Maker: Large, Luxury, & High Performance Cars, Sports Utility Vehicles, Station Wagons and Compact Vans
See also **OTHER** under **REFERENCE** in **BUSINESS AND REFERENCE**
0-679-74410-X RANDOM HOUSE PB $12.00

David **Lewis** & Laurence **Goldstein**, editors
The Automobile and American Culture
0-472-08044-X MICHIGAN PB $21.95

Ralph **Nader** & Clarence **Ditlow**
The Lemon Book: Auto Rights
An extensive, clearly written consumer's manual offering step-by-step instructions on how to avoid purchasing a car that turns out to be a lemon, and how to cope with the less than satisfactory automobile you may already own
1-55921-020-6 MOYER BELL PB $12.95

National Auto Museum of France
The Schlumpf Automobile Collection
0-88740-192-9 SCHIFFER PB $19.95

Antoine Prunet
The Ferrari Legend: The Road Cars
0-393-01475-4 NORTON $45.00

Lucille Treganowan & Gina Catanzarite
Lucille's Car Care: Everything You Need to Know from Under the Hood—by America's Most Trusted Mechanic
0-7868-6201-7 HYPERION $19.95

Motorcycles

Keith Code
The Soft Science of Road Racing Motorcycles
0-918226-11-2 ACROBAT PB $19.95

A Twist of the Wrist: The Motorcycle Road Racers Handbook
0-918226-08-2 MOTORBOOKS INTL PB $19.95

Jerry Hatfield
American Racing Motorcycles
0-87938-355-0 MOTORBOOKS INTL PB $19.96

Bruce Johns & David Edmundson
Motorcycles: Fundamentals, Service, Repair
0-87006-654-4 GOODHEART-WILCOX $36.60

David Wright
The Harley-Davidson Motor Company: An Official Eighty-Year History
0-87938-764-5 MOTORBOOKS INTL $24.95

Patricia Zonker
Murdercycles
0-88229-553-5 NELSON-HALL $24.95

Airplanes

Richard Allen
Revolution in the Sky: The Lockheeds of Aviation's Golden Age
0-88740-584-3 SCHIFFER $37.50

Walter Boyne
Smithsonian Book of Flight
0-89599-020-2 SMITHSONIAN $35.00
0-517-11850-5 WINGS $24.99

C.D. Bryan
The National Air and Space Museum
0-8109-1380-1 ABRAMS $65.00

Amelia Earhart
The Fun of It
1-55888-980-9 OMNIGRAPHICS $42.00

Last Flight
0-609-80032-9 CROWN PB $12.00

Rene Francillon
Lockheed Aircraft Since 1913
0-87021-897-2 NAVAL INSTITUTE $37.95

Donald H. Walter
Building Your Own Airplane
This book covers the entire range of questions and issues related to building an airplane
0-8138-1308-5 IOWA STATE PB $19.95

Balloons

Tom Crouch
The Eagle Aloft: Two Centuries of the Balloon in America
0-87474-346-X SMITHSONIAN $62.00

A. Hildebrant
Balloons and Airships
0-85409-879-8 CHARLES RIVER $25.00

Wolfgang Langewiesche
Stick and Rudder: An Explanation of the Art of Flying
0-07-036240-8 TAB $22.95

Trains

Abrams Editors
Steam, Steel and Stars: America's Last Steam Railroad
0-8109-1645-2 ABRAMS PB $45.00

Don Ball
America's Railroads: The Second Generation
0-393-01416-9 NORTON $55.00

Robert Hedin
The Great Machines: Poems and Songs of the American Railroad
0-87745-550-3 IOWA PB $17.50

Geoffrey Moorhouse & Brian Hollingsworth
Rail Across India: A Photographic Journey
0-89659-652-4 ABBEVILLE $85.00

John Stilgoe
Metropolitan Corridor: Railroads and the American Scene
0-300-03481-4 YALE PB $20.00

Paul Theroux
The Old Patagonian Express
By train from Boston to Patagonia
See also SOUTH AMERICA under TRAVEL LITERATURE
0-395-52105-X HOUGHTON MIFFLIN PB $12.95

Riding the Iron Rooster: By Train Through China
The book that put Theroux on the travel writer's map
See also CHINA under ASIA under TRAVEL LITERATURE
0-8041-0454-9 IVY PB $6.99

Sports

Scott Brown & Will Collier
The Uncivil War: Alabama vs. Auburn, 1981-1994
The rivalry that split an entire state
1-55853-354-0 RUTLEDGE HILL PB $12.95

Walter Byers & Charles Hammer
Unsportsmanlike Conduct: Exploiting College Athletes
0-472-10666-X MICHIGAN $27.50

Sports Illustrated
Sports Illustrated 1996 Sports Almanac
The best-selling sports almanac's fifth annual volume, fully revised and filled with more stats, pictures, stories than ever before. Includes complete coverage of all major sports, articles and profiles, records and awards, photographs, and much more
0-316-80883-0 LITTLE, BROWN PB $11.95

Allen Guttmann
Women's Sports: A History
The history of women's sports from antiquity to the present. Guttman examines the roles of such outstanding female athletes as "Babe" Didrikson, Gertrude Ederle, Wilma Rudolph, and Mary Decker Slaney. "[Allen Guttman is] our most distinguished contemporary thinker on the nature and role of sport in society"—A. Bartlett Giamatti
0-231-06957-X COLUMBIA PB $16.50

Allen Guttmann
A Whole New Ball Game: An Interpretation of American Sports
A history and analysis of the place of sports in American culture
0-8078-4220-6 NORTH CAROLINA PB $15.95

Women's Sports: A History
A comprehensive look at women in sports, from medieval football to the cultural impact of the Gibson Girl
0-231-06956-1 COLUMBIA PB $29.95

Anne Janette Johnson
Great Women in Sports
An encyclopedia of the greatest female athletes in modern history. Covers sports across the board
0-7876-0873-4 VISIBLE INK PB $17.95

Mariah Burton **Nelson**

The Stronger Women Get, the More Men Love Football: Sexism and the American Culture of Sports

A former player on the Women's Pro Basketball League argues that male hegemony in sports make men fear strong women, which in turn causes prejudice and violence against them

See also FEMINIST THEORY under **WOMEN'S STUDIES** in **SOCIAL STUDIES**

0-15-181393-0 HARCOURT BRACE $22.95
0-380-72527-4 AVON PB $11.00

Randy **Roberts** & James **Olson**

Winning Is the Only Thing: Sports in America Since 1945

0-8018-3830-4 JOHNS HOPKINS $38.95

John **Slaughter** & Richard **Lapchick**

The Rules of the Game: Ethics in College Sports

0-02-897401-8 ORYX $19.95

Jess R. **White**, editor

Sports Rules Encyclopedia

Everything. If you don't know anything about the rules of sports, but would like to be able to converse with other human beings, you need this. If you think you know everything about sports guidelines (you don't), you still need this book

0-87322-457-4 HUMAN KINETICS PB $19.95

Sportswriters and Sportscasters

Frank **Deford**, editor

The Best American Sports Writing, 1996

Culled from over 400 periodicals, this irresistible collection includes not only a full range of sports coverage, but everything from features to exposés and from the controversial to the tragic. "This collection proves that some of the best current American journalism is on the sports pages"—*Publishers Weekly*

SERIES EDITED BY GLENN STOUT

0-395-70072-8 HOUGHTON MIFFLIN PB $24.95

Dan **Jenkins**, editor

The Best American Sports Writing, 1995

From profiles of O.J. Simpson and Jennifer Capriati to studies of NFL End Zone celebrations, anorexia among female gymnasts, and the art of cleaning fish (not to mention the joys of motherhood, spousal abuse, delinquent child support, and other pressing social issues), the premier sports anthology returns with another uniformly fascinating collection. "Glenn Stout's annual American sportswriting series is a venerable institution"—*Boston Globe*

SERIES EDITED BY GLENN STOUT

0-395-70069-8 HOUGHTON MIFFLIN PB $12.95

Tom **Boswell**, editor

The Best American Sports Writing, 1994

Offers a lively, varied, and immensely readable selection of sports writing. From the US Open to a girl's high school basketball team in Massachusetts and the tragic plane crash in which the entire Zambian soccer team died, this volume covers the world of sports in the best prose in which it is reported. "Glenn Stout's annual American sportswriting series is a venerable institution"—*Boston Globe*

0-395-63325-7 HOUGHTON MIFFLIN PB $11.95

Howard **Cosell** & Peter **Bonventure**

I Never Played the Game

Cosell proclaims his place at the center of American sports and manages to offend his usual quota of former colleagues in this autobiography

0-380-70159-6 AVON PB $5.99

Charles **Fountain**

Sportswriter: The Life and Times of Grantland Rice

0-19-506176-4 OXFORD $27.50

Jim **Murray**

Jim Murray: The Autobiography of the Pulitzer Prize-Winning Sports Columnist

For more than 40 years Murray has been America's most beloved and celebrated sports writer. Now, in this opinionated, witty biography he shares the story of his life and experiences with such sports greats as Muhammad Ali, Magic Johnson, and Al Davis, among others

0-02-860430-X MACMILLAN PB $12.95

Blackie **Sherrod**

The Blackie Sherrod Collection

INTRODUCTION BY DAN JENKINS

0-87833-606-0 TAYLOR $14.95

Red **Smith**

The Red Smith Reader

FOREWORD BY TERENCE SMITH

0-393-31002-7 NORTON PB $8.95

Bob **Verdi**

The Bob Verdi Collection

INTRODUCTION BY MIKE ROYKO

0-87833-608-7 TAYLOR $14.95

Rich **Westcott**

Philadelphia's Old Ballparks

The old drawings, narratives, and grainy photographs evoke a time when ball players stuck with one ballclub throughout their careers and simply knocked the ball out of the ballpark

1-56639-454-6 TEMPLE $29.95

Baseball

Baseball is a consuming passion and, a commitment of six months or more, from the first February workout to the last pitch of the World Series in October. In its greatest books, baseball emerges as not just a daily obsession, but as a metaphor for life—our yearning for our lost youth, our pastoral beginnings.

Hank **Aaron** & Lonnie **Wheeler**

I Had a Hammer: The Hank Aaron Story

The autobiography of the greatest home run hitter in baseball history

See also **ATHLETES AND ENTERTAINERS** under **BLACK VOICES, BLACK LIVES** under **AFRICAN-AMERICAN STUDIES** in **HISTORY OF THE AMERICAS**

0-06-016321-6 HARPERCOLLINS PB $21.95

Peter C. **Bjarkman**, editor

Encyclopedia of Major League Baseball: National League

Like its companion, the National League edition contains extensive histories of all its teams. The opening essay shows why the NL has proved to be baseball's truest source of innovation. "Edited and introduced by a knowledgeable historian…well done"—*ALA Booklist*

0-88184-974-X CARROLL & GRAF PB $14.95

Thomas **Boswell**

The Heart of the Order

The most recent collection from the *Washington Post's* great beat reporter

0-14-012987-1 PENGUIN PB $11.95

John **Feinstein**

Play Ball: The Life and Troubled Times of Major League Baseball

The author of *Hard Courts* and *A Season on the Brink* spent 1992 examining major league baseball first hand. He takes a hard look at who really controls the game, and explains the pressures behind many of the sport's big decisions. He also offers a detailed accounting of the Fay Vincent affair and intimate views of some of the game's most interesting personalities

0-517-15304-1 RANDOM HOUSE PB $3.99

Dan **Gutman**

The Way Baseball Works

Graphically illustrated and well written, this stunning volume dissects and explains every aspect of baseball. From the physics of a pitch to the design of a ball park; from how TV directors orchestrate a game and the business of baseball to the art of the stolen base and the best way to get autographs, this is every fan's ideal guide to the national pastime

INTRODUCTION BY TIM MCCARVER, PRODUCED IN COOPERATION WITH THE NATIONAL BASEBALL HALL OF FAME

0-684-81606-7 SIMON & SCHUSTER $30.00

Christopher **Lehmann-Haupt**

Me and DiMaggio

A *NY Times* editor pursues a dream by following the Yankees for a season

0-671-50504-1 SIMON & SCHUSTER $2.98

Ron **McCulloch**

How Baseball Began

Starting in the 16th century and continuing through the first modern World Series game in 1903, this is the definitive history of the American pastime

1-89562-944-6 WARWICK PB $18.95

Larry **Moffi**

This Side of Cooperstown: An Oral History of Major League Baseball in the '50s

0-87745-521-X IOWA $24.95

Larry **Moffi** & Jonathan **Kronstadt**

Crossing The Line: Black Major Leaguers, 1947-1959

0-87745-529-5 IOWA PB $11.95

Daniel **Okrent**

The Ultimate Baseball Book

0-395-36145-1 HOUGHTON MIFFLIN PB $19.95

Daniel **Okrent** & Steve **Wulf**

Baseball Anecdotes

A history of baseball, featuring stories of the great players, the great plays, and Yogi's wit

0-19-504396-0 OXFORD $25.00
0-19-504396-0 OXFORD $21.95
0-06-273206-4 HARPERPERENNIAL PB $13.00

Dan **Riley**

The Dodgers Reader

From the "bums" of Ebbetts Field to the star-studded Los Angeles team, this is the best writing on some of baseball's finest, all in one volume. Writers such as Roger Kahn, Red Smith, Jim Murray, Scott Ostler, and Tom Boswell describe a dazzling cast of players and supporting characters, from Jackie Robinson and Red Barber to Steve Garvey and Tommy LaSorda

0-395-58778-6 HOUGHTON MIFFLIN PB $9.95

The whole country was stirred by their high deeds and thwarted longings… The team was awesomely good and yet defeated. Their skills lifted every man's spirit and their defeat joined them with every man's existence.—*Roger Khan on the 1956 Dodgers*

THE DODGERS READER

Tom **Seaver** & Lee **Lowenfish**

The Art of Pitching

Preparation, mechanics, trick pitches, and maintenance from one of baseball's greatest pitchers

0-688-13226-X MORROW PB $12.95

Joseph **Wallace**

The Baseball Anthology

Babe Ruth to Barry Bonds; the 1869 Red Stockings to the 1993 Blue Jays. Over 200 high-quality photos, drawings, and cartoons come to life in the interviews and essays of writers who have followed baseball with the attention and earnestness of ardent fans. In the dugout with Joe DiMaggio, on the diamond with Red Smith; *New Yorker's* Roger Angell on the 1981 strike, Sparky Anderson on the soul of the game…this varied celebration of baseball contains something for everyone

0-8109-3135-4 ABRAMS $45.00

Joel **Zoss** & John **Bowman**

Diamonds in the Rough: The Untold Story of Baseball

0-8092-3234-0 CONTEMPORARY PB $16.95

Baseball Statistics

Until recently, the notion that baseball fans had a limited appetite for statistics was widespread among book publishers. The market is now flooded with offering statistics in raw form and books that analyze the reams of information now available.

Mcmillan **Editors**

The Baseball Encyclopedia: The Complete and Definitive Record of Major League Baseball, Ninth Edition

Macmillan's "Baseball Bible" remains unchallenged worldwide as the authoritative, complete source for baseball statistics. Featuring all up-to date listing of players in the All American Girls Professional Baseball League

0-02-579041-2 MACMILLAN $55.00

Joseph **Reichler**, editor

The Baseball Encyclopedia

The final word on baseball statistics; updated every three years

0-02-601930-2 MACMILLAN $39.95

Sporting News

Official Baseball Register, 1989

Like having the back of every active player's baseball card in one book: career batting, pitching, fielding, and personal statistics in both the minors and the majors

0-89204-486-1 SPORTING NEWS PB $12.95

John **Thorn** & Pete **Palmer**

Total Baseball

This is the one you'll find by the cash register of the best bars—there to settle the most heated and arcane disputes among ardent fans. More than 2,300 pages of statistics and history for every player and team in the major leagues from the beginning of organized baseball. "The best book on stats and history"—Phil Rizzuto

0-670-86099-9 VIKING $59.95

Baseball Instruction

Statistics are largely irrelevant to these instructional books, for the game's great thinkers and great athletes inhabit two separate worlds. As a great hitter and sage of the diamond once said, "Who can hit and think at the same time?"

Rod **Delmonico**

Offensive Baseball Drills

Includes 68 hitting, baserunning, and team drills

0-87322-865-0 HUMAN KINETICS PB $14.95

Al **Goldis** & Rich **Wolff**

Breaking Into the Big Leagues

For athletes who believe they have major league baseball ability

0-88011-298-0 LEISURE PB $12.95

Pat **Jordan**

Sports Illustrated Pitching: The Keys to Excellence

A very good book for young players

0-452-26101-5 NEW AMERICAN LIBRARY PB $9.95
1-56800-073-1 SPORTS ILLUSTRATED PB $10.95

Pete **Rose** & Bob **Hertzel**

Pete Rose's Winning Baseball

Pete Rose doesn't know more about baseball than the average fan; he just applies the common wisdom with greater spirit and determination

0-8092-8102-3 CONTEMPORARY PB $2.98

Ted **Williams** & John **Underwood**

The Science of Hitting

Unquestionably the most authoritative book on hitting, written by the master; a must-read

0-671-62103-3 SIMON & SCHUSTER PB $10.95

Baseball Biographies

Baseball biographies are a mixed bag: some cover a retired star's entire life and attempt to put his achievements in meaningful perspective; others merely reflect on one season (usually a winning one), offering a brilliant chapter from an entire career. The biographies listed here focus on the greats of the past.

Roy **Campanella**

It's Good to be Alive

0-8032-6363-5 NEBRASKA PB $10.95

Charles **Alexander**

Ty Cobb

0-19-503598-4 OXFORD PB $12.95

Ty Cobb

Jack **Moore**

Joe DiMaggio: Yankee Clipper

0-275-92712-1 PRAEGER PB $11.95

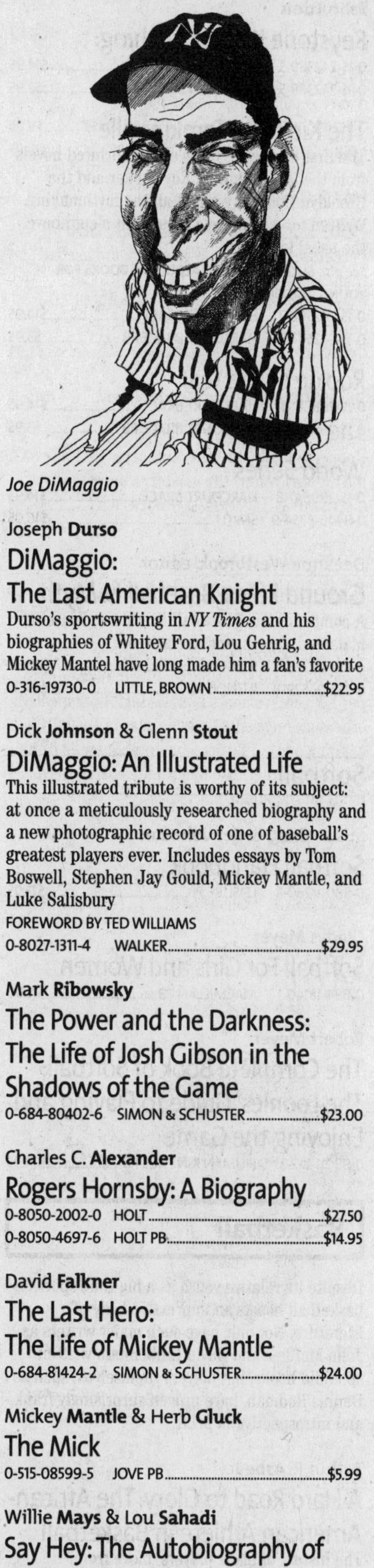
Joe DiMaggio

Joseph **Durso**
DiMaggio: The Last American Knight
Durso's sportswriting in *NY Times* and his biographies of Whitey Ford, Lou Gehrig, and Mickey Mantel have long made him a fan's favorite
0-316-19730-0 LITTLE, BROWN $22.95

Dick **Johnson** & Glenn **Stout**
DiMaggio: An Illustrated Life
This illustrated tribute is worthy of its subject: at once a meticulously researched biography and a new photographic record of one of baseball's greatest players ever. Includes essays by Tom Boswell, Stephen Jay Gould, Mickey Mantle, and Luke Salisbury
FOREWORD BY TED WILLIAMS
0-8027-1311-4 WALKER $29.95

Mark **Ribowsky**
The Power and the Darkness: The Life of Josh Gibson in the Shadows of the Game
0-684-80402-6 SIMON & SCHUSTER $23.00

Charles C. **Alexander**
Rogers Hornsby: A Biography
0-8050-2002-0 HOLT $27.50
0-8050-4697-6 HOLT PB $14.95

David **Falkner**
The Last Hero: The Life of Mickey Mantle
0-684-81424-2 SIMON & SCHUSTER $24.00

Mickey **Mantle** & Herb **Gluck**
The Mick
0-515-08599-5 JOVE PB $5.99

Willie **Mays** & Lou **Sahadi**
Say Hey: The Autobiography of Willie Mays
0-671-67836-1 POCKET PB $4.50

Buck **O'Neil** & others
I Was Right on Time
FOREWORD BY KEN BURNS
0-684-80305-4 SIMON & SCHUSTER $23.00

Jackie **Robinson**
I Never Had It Made: An Autobiography
0-88001-419-9 ECCO $24.00

Jackie **Robinson** & Jules **Tygiel**
The Jackie Robinson Readers: Writings By and About Jackie Robinson
See also **ATHLETES AND ENTERTAINERS** under **BLACK VOICES, BLACK LIVES** under **AFRICAN-AMERICAN STUDIES** in **HISTORY OF THE AMERICAS**
0-525-94096-0 DUTTON $25.00

Rachel **Robinson** & Lee **Daniels**
Jackie Robinson: An Intimate Portrait
Published in the fall of 1997
0-8109-3792-1 ABRAMS $29.95

Sharon **Robinson**
Stealing Home: An Intimate Family Portrait by the Daughter of Jackie Robinson
0-06-017191-X HARPERCOLLINS $24.00

Robert **Creamer**
Babe: The Legend Comes to Life
A thoughtful, well-researched, well-written biography of baseball's greatest player
0-671-76070-X FIRESIDE PB $12.00

Lawrence **Ritter** & Mark **Rucker**
The Babe: A Life in Pictures
9-991-65872-6 TICKNOR & FIELDS $40.00

Duke **Snider** & Bill **Gilbert**
The Duke of Flatbush
His days in center field
0-8217-2469-X ZEBRA $17.95
0-8217-3615-9 ZEBRA PB $4.95

Ted **Williams** & John **Underwood**
My Turn At Bat: The Story of My Life
0-671-63423-2 FIRESIDE PB $11.00

Group Biographies

Arthur R. **Ashe** Jr.
A Hard Road to Glory: The African-American Athlete in Baseball
1-56743-035-X AMISTAD PB $9.95

Harvey **Frommer**
New York City Baseball: The Last Golden Age, 1947-1957
Until the next golden age, that is
0-15-665500-4 HARCOURT BRACE PB $9.95

Barbara **Gregorich**
Women At Play: The Story of Women in Baseball
Drawing on pioneering original research with many of the women who made baseball history, *Women at Play* is the extraordinary untold story that the hit film *A League of their Own* only touched upon
0-15-698297-8 HARCOURT BRACE PB $14.95

David **Halberstam**
October 1964
Following his #1 best selling *Summer of '49*, Halberstam returns to the world of baseball with a portrait of the last season of the great Yankee dynasty, and the drama of an electrifying championship season. Great writing and great journalism combine in this unforgettable image of one of the sport's highest and most ennobling moments
0-679-41560-2 VILLARD $24.00

The Summer of 'Forty-Nine
0-380-72146-5 AVON PB $10.00

Roger **Kahn**
The Boys of Summer
The story of the '50s Brooklyn Dodgers, carried to the present
0-06-091416-5 HARPERCOLLINS PB $14.00

The Era: 1947-1957, When the Yankees, the New York Giants, and the Brooklyn Dodgers Ruled the World
The author of *The Boys of Summer* chronicles the evolution of the national pastime through its most glorious and tumultuous decade when the New York teams won 9 out of 11 World Series. Beginning with the first game of Jackie Robinson's glorious career, and on to the signing of Campanella and Newcombe, the retirement of the Yankee Clipper, the stardom of Berra, Mantle, Snider, and Mays, *The Era* concludes with the momentous uprooting of both the Giants and the Brooklyn Dodgers. "Kahn knows where the bodies are buried and allows his audience a joyous read as he digs them up"
—*Publishers Weekly*
0-395-56155-8 TICKNOR & FIELDS $23.95

Frederick **Turner**
When the Boys Came Back: Baseball and 1946
0-8050-2645-2 HOLT $27.50

Picture Books

Constance **McCabe** & Neal **McCabe**
Baseball's Golden Age: The Photographs of Charles M. Conlon
Here are more than 200 classic baseball photos—from 1904 to 1942—by the legendary photographer Charles M. Conlon. Selected from archives of *Sporting News*, the photos include rare action shots of Ty Cobb, Shoeless Joe Jackson, Honus Wagner, and Joe DiMaggio, as well as those umpires, coaches, and fans. Accompanying the photos are trivia-packed stories that further enliven these greats
0-8109-3130-3 ABRAMS $35.00

Lawrence **Ritter** & Donald **Honig**
The Image of Their Greatness
0-517-55422-4 CROWN PB $24.95

Geoffrey C. **Ward** & Ken **Burns**

Baseball: An Illustrated History

The companion volume to the recent PBS documentary covers the entire history of baseball, not only in stunning images but in insightful analysis

0-679-40459-7 KNOPF $60.00

Insider Accounts

Beginning in the early '60s, several players who had hardly left their stamp on the game—at least, not on the playing field—made a splash with memoirs recalling often sordid (but always fascinating) details of life in the big leagues.

Jim **Brosnan**

The Long Season

Brosnan was a well-traveled relief pitcher with a wry sense of humor and a taste for martinis. This excellent book was the first to treat baseball players as adults who carry adult baggage

0-941372-01-4 HOLTZMAN $24.95

Bill **Lee** & Dick **Lally**

The Wrong Stuff

Baseball's biggest flake and only presidential candidate

0-670-76724-7 VIKING $15.95

Baseball Fiction

Baseball has attracted the wild mythmakers more than the gritty realists.

Robert **Coover**

The Universal Baseball Association, Inc.

In this tale of fate and imagination, a bachelor accountant brings a baseball league of his own creation to life every night on his kitchen table

See also **SINCE 1945** under **20TH-CENTURY AMERICAN FICTION** in **LITERATURE OF THE AMERICAS**

0-452-26030-2 NEW AMERICAN LIBRARY PB $10.95

Mark **Harris**

Bang the Drum Slowly

A dying baseball player

0-8032-7221-9 NEBRASKA PB $8.95

The Southpaw

"By far the best "serious" baseball novel published"—*San Francisco Chronicle*

0-8032-7220-0 NEBRASKA PB $12.95

A Ticket For a Seamstitch

Completes the baseball tetralogy begun by *The Southpaw, Bang the Drum Slowly*, and *It Looked Like For Ever*

0-8032-7224-3 NEBRASKA PB $7.95

W.P. **Kinsella**

The Iowa Baseball Confederacy

The 1908 Chicago Cubs make a road trip to Iowa and play a game of over 2000 innings that has been forgotten by the record books

0-345-34230-5 BALLANTINE PB $5.99

Shoeless Joe

Based on the career of the player who was thrown out of the major leagues for his involvement in the 1919 Black Sox scandal; source of the movie *Field of Dreams*

0-345-34256-9 BALLANTINE PB $5.99

Ring **Lardner**

Haircut & Other Stories

Only one baseball story in this collection, but it's the classic "Alibi Ike"

INTRODUCTION BY WILFRID SNEED

0-02-022344-7 COLLIER PB $9.95

You Know Me Al: A Busher's Letters

The classic baseball novel. "With the surest touch, the sharpest insight, he lets Jack Keefe the baseball player cut his own outline, fill in his own depths, until the figure of the foolish, boastful, innocent athlete lives before us" —Virginia Woolf

See also **FROM THE TURN OF THE CENTURY TO WORLD WAR II** under **20TH-CENTURY AMERICAN FICTION** in **LITERATURE OF THE AMERICAS**

INTRODUCTION BY WILFRID SHEED

0-02-022342-0 COLLIER PB $9.95

Bernard **Malamud**

The Natural

"An allegory about the rise and fall of a baseball player who can't quite overcome his own pride or the chicanery of modern life"—*Booklist*

0-380-72084-1 AVON PB $12.00

0-380-50609-2 AVON PB $5.99

Bernard Malamud

Philip **Roth**

The Great American Novel

A ride through the mythical Patriot League, featuring unbeatable rookie hurler Gil Gamesh and iron-willed umpire Mike the Mouth Masterson

0-679-74906-3 VINTAGE PB $13.00

Ernest **Thayer**

Casey At the Bat: A Centennial Edition

Possibly the best-known American poem

0-689-31945-2 ATHENEUM $15.00

0-8114-8357-6 RAINTREE/STECK-VAUGHN PB $4.95

John **Tunis**

Keystone Kids

0-15-242389-3 HARCOURT BRACE $14.95

0-15-242388-5 HARCOURT BRACE PB $3.95

The Kid from Tomkinsville

The first in a series of recently reprinted novels from the '40s, following Roy Tucker and the Brooklyn Dodgers without all the mythmaking. Written for a young age group, but a cut above the usual kid's fare

See also **SUGGESTED READ ALOUDS** in **BOOKS FOR YOUNG READERS**

0-15-242568-3 HARCOURT BRACE $14.95

0-15-242567-5 HARCOURT BRACE PB $3.95

Rookie of the Year

0-15-268881-1 HARCOURT BRACE $14.95

0-15-268880-3 HARCOURT BRACE PB $3.95

World Series

0-15-299647-8 HARCOURT BRACE $14.95

0-8446-6354-9 SMITH $16.05

Deeanne **Westbrook**, editor

Ground Rules: Baseball & Myth

A compendium of baseball literature. Kinsella, Malamud, essays, and narratives

0-252-02226-2 ILLINOIS $49.95

0-252-06529-8 ILLINOIS PB $19.95

Softball

Susan **Craig** & Ken **Johnson**

Softball Handbook

0-88011-260-3 LEISURE PB $15.95

Gladys **Meyer**

Softball For Girls and Women

0-684-18140-1 MACMILLAN PB $11.00

Robert **Meyer**

The Complete Book of Softball: The Loonies' Guide to Playing and Enjoying the Game

0-88011-212-3 HUMAN KINETICS PB $14.95

Basketball

Despite its relative youth as a big-time sport, basketball boasts an impressive body of literature. Not only have such major writers as John McPhee and David Halberstam written splendid books, but players themselves, such as Dennis Rodman, have proven surprisingly frank and introspective in print.

Arthur R. **Ashe** Jr.

A Hard Road to Glory: The African-American Athlete in Basketball

The history of black players' move from "omission to domination." Includes a huge reference section

1-56743-037-6 AMISTAD PB $9.95

Faye Young **Miller** & Wayne **Coffey**

Winning Basketball for Girls

0-8160-2776-5 FACTS ON FILE PB $11.95

Sidney **Goldstein**

The Basketball Player's Bible: A Comprehensive and Systematic Guide to Playing

1-88435-713-X GOLAU PB $19.95

Professional Basketball

David **Halberstam**

The Breaks of the Game

A splendid account of a year in the life of the Portland Trailblazers and of the varied personalities who make up a professional basketball team

0-345-29625-7 BALLANTINE PB $5.99

Michael **Jordan**

I Can't Accept Not Trying: Michael Jordan on the Pursuit of Excellence

0-06-251190-4 HARPERCOLLINS PB $12.00

Elbert S. **Maloney**

The Official NBA Basketball Encyclopedia: The Complete History and Statistics of Professional Basketball

FOREWORD BY JULIUS ERVING

0-394-58039-7 VILLARD $29.95

Reggie **Miller** & Gene **Wojciechowski**

I Love Being the Enemy: A Season on the Court with the NBA's Best Shooter and Sharpest Tongue

0-684-81389-0 SIMON & SCHUSTER $23.00

James **Naismith**

Basketball: Its Origin and Development

0-8032-8370-9 NEBRASKA PB $10.00

David S. **Neft** & Richard M. **Cohen**

The Sports Encyclopedia: Pro Basketball

Less expensive and less exhaustive than *The Baseball Encyclopedia;* full player and team statistics since 1901 are organized by season

0-312-10551-7 ST. MARTIN'S PB $19.99

Scott **Ostler** & Steve **Springer**

Winnin' Times: The Magical Journey of the Los Angeles Lakers

A snapshot of a dynasty. An entertaining, inside-the-locker-room look at the Laker's 1986-1987 championship season

0-02-594080-5 MACMILLAN $17.95

Spud **Webb** & Reid **Slaughter**

Spud Webb: Flying High

The little man in the land of the giants

0-8314-0317-9 HARPERCOLLINS $3.98

College Basketball

Peter C. **Bjarkman**

Hoopla: A Century of College Basketball

1-57028-039-8 MASTERS $22.95

John **McPhee**

A Sense of Where You Are: A Profile of Bill Bradley At Princeton

A look at the New York Knicks star and New Jersey senator in his days as a collegiate perfectionist, written by one of *New Yorker's* master stylists

0-374-51485-2 FS&G PB $10.00

Bert **Nelli**

The Winning Tradition: A History of Kentucky Wildcat Basketball

0-8131-1519-1 KENTUCKY $20.00

Billy **Packer** & Roland **Lazenby**

Hoops!: Confessions of a College Basketball Analyst

0-8092-5305-4 CONTEMPORARY $13.95

Basketball Instruction

Larry **Bird** & John **Bischoff**

Bird on Basketball: How-To Strategies from the Great Celtics Champion

0-201-14209-0 ADDISON-WESLEY PB $13.00

Howard **Garfinkel**

Five Star Basketball Drills

The paces through which Garf and his well-known counselors put the nation's best high school players at his famed summer camp

0-940279-58-4 MASTERS PB $14.95

0-940279-22-3 MASTERS PB $14.95

Roland **Lazenby**

Championship Basketball: Top Coaches Present Their Winning Strategies and Techniques For Players and Coaches

0-8092-4874-3 CONTEMPORARY PB $11.95

John **Wooden**

Practical Modern Basketball

By the coaching genius who guided UCLA to ten national titles and molded Bill Walton and Kareem Abdul-Jabbar

0-02-429470-5 MACMILLAN $64.00

Boxing and Wrestling

Arthur R. **Ashe** Jr.

A Hard Road to Glory: The African-American Athlete in Boxing

1-56743-036-8 AMISTAD PB $9.95

Phil **Berger**

Blood Season: Mike Tyson and the World of Boxing

This successful journalist centers on Tyson, but goes into the history of the sport, its great fighters, and the promoters behind them, through to the present status of boxing as a sport, now at its nadir

1-56858-069-X FOUR WALLS PB $13.95

E.A. **Carmean**, Jr.

Bellows: The Boxing Pictures

Bellows as a leading American painter in the first quarter of this century, and his work captured boxing's brutal beauty

0-295-96320-4 WASHINGTON PB $9.95

Nat **Fleisher**

A Pictorial History of Boxing from the Bare-Knuckle Days to the Present

The resident geniuses of the original Ring magazine take a step up in class with this copious photographic salute

0-8065-1048-X CITADEL $19.95

0-8065-1427-2 CITADEL PB $19.95

Joe **Frazier** & Phil **Berger**

Smokin' Joe: The Autobiography

0-02-860847-X MACMILLAN $23.95

Thomas **Hauser** & Muhammad **Ali**

Muhammad Ali: In Perspective

See also **ATHLETES AND ENTERTAINERS** under **BLACK VOICES, BLACK LIVES** under **AFRICAN-AMERICAN STUDIES** in **HISTORY OF THE AMERICAS**

0-00-649124-3 COLLINS SAN FRANCISCO PB $25.00

Peter **Heller**

"In This Corner...!": Forty-Two World Champions Tell Their Stories

0-306-80603-7 DA CAPO PB $15.95

Tom **Jarman** & Reid **Hanley**

Wrestling for Beginners

0-8092-5656-8 CONTEMPORARY PB $12.95

A.J. **Liebling**

The Sweet Science

One of the best books ever written about boxing, this is a collection of fighters' portraits that Liebling composed for *New Yorker.* Includes his famous pieces on young Marciano and the venerable Mongoose, Archie Moore

0-941372-06-5 HOLTZMAN $24.95

Mark **Mysnyk** & others

Winning Wrestling Moves

Instruction with photos

0-87322-482-5 HUMAN KINETICS PB $19.95

Joyce Carol **Oates**

On Boxing

. The well-known novelist and essayist takes on this, our "self-destructive" and "most dramatically 'masculine' sport"

0-88001-385-0 ECCO PB $13.00

United States **Wrestling**
Rookie Coaches Wrestling Guide: American Coaching Effectiveness Program
Endorsed by the U.S. Wrestling Federation
0-88011-421-5 LEISURE PB $9.95

Football

Football books have been streaming out of American publishing houses ever since *McMahon!*, *Snake* and John Madden's *Hey Wait a Minute! (I Wrote a Book!)* took control of the *New York Times* best-seller list. College fans will also find virtually every Top Ten powerhouse celebrated between hard covers.

John **Madden**
One Knee Equals Two Feet (and Everything Else You Need to Know About Football)
More reminiscences and ramblings
0-515-09193-6 JOVE PB $5.99

Bud **Wilkinson**
Sports Illustrated Football: Defense
1-56800-003-0 SPORTS ILLUSTRATED PB $10.95

Sports Illustrated Football Winning Offense
From Oklahoma's coach in the glory years of the '50s
1-56800-002-2 SPORTS ILLUSTRATED PB $11.95

Biographies

Mike **Ditka** & Don **Pierson**
Ditka: An Autobiography
Once the Bears' bone-cracking tight end, now their bone-cracking coach
FOREWORD BY TOM LANDRY
0-933893-07-8 BONUS $16.95
0-933893-38-8 BONUS PB $7.95

Mickey **Herskowitz**
The Legend of Bear Bryant
The great Alabama coach, mentor to Joe Namath and Ken Stabler
0-89015-910-6 EAKINS PB $15.95

David **Kopay** & Perry Deane **Young**
The David Kopay Story
The autobiography of the football running back, the first professional athlete publicly to reveal his homosexuality. "A dazzling and wonderful book"—Merle Miller
See also **BIOGRAPHIES** under **GAY, LESBIAN, AND BISEXUAL STUDIES** in **SOCIAL STUDIES**
FOREWORD BY DICK SCHAAP
1-55611-080-4 FINE PB $9.95

John **Madden**
Hey, Wait a Minute! (I Wrote a Book!)
The reminiscences and ramblings of the colorful ex-Raiders coach and CBS commentator. The best-seller that started it all
0-345-32507-9 BALLANTINE PB $4.95

Dan **Marino** & Steve **Delsohn**
Marino!
0-00-225108-6 HARPERCOLLINS $50.00

The Business of Football

Ed **Linn** & Mel **Durslag**
The One Hundred Million Dollar Game
How pro football, aided and abetted by television and commercial sponsors, became the most lucrative of all big-time sports
0-671-47054-X SIMON & SCHUSTER $16.95

Michael **Oriard**
Reading Football
0-8078-2083-0 NORTH CAROLINA $32.50

College Football

Bob **Waldstein** & others
Saturday Afternoon Madness
Two guys quit their jobs and spend the Fall driving a used funeral limousine to tailgate parties around the country. The great spirit of the hoopla of college football pervades
0-9648571-0-3 FOUR HORSEMEN PB $13.95

Encyclopedias and Reference Books

Bruce **Nash** & Allan **Zullo**
The Football Hall of Shame
0-671-72922-5 POCKET PB $2.95

David S. **Neft**
The Sports Encyclopedia: Pro Football, the Modern Era 1960-1989
0-312-03433-4 ST. MARTIN'S PB $16.95

David S. **Neft**, editor
The Football Encyclopedia: Second Edition
Seventeen years of research resulting in a cornucopia of football facts: scores of *every* game from 1920 to 1993; complete seasonal statistics of players, complete team rosters; lifetime statistical leaders for every category of players. *The* book for the pigskin fan. "One can hardly imagine any competitor usurping this book's preeminance"—*The Sporting News.* "A monumental work"—*San Francisco Chronicle*
0-312-11435-4 ST. MARTIN'S $49.95

Mark **Sabljak** & Martin **Greenberg**
Who's Who in the Super Bowl: The Performance of Every Player in Super Bowls I to XX
9-991-78292-3 BOOK SALES PB $1.98

Golf

Dick **Beach** & Bob **Ford**
Golf: The Body, The Mind, The Game
0-679-43958-7 VILLARD $19.00

Thomas **Boswell**
Strokes of Genius
A great writer on the greatest shots ever made
0-14-011368-1 PENGUIN PB $11.00

Mike **Bryan**
Dogleg Madness
A notable new novel; takes on the history and sociology of golf
0-87113-330-X ATLANTIC MONTHLY PB $8.95

Bobby **Jones**
Bobby Jones on Golf
A broad look at the game of golf
0-385-42419-1 DOUBLEDAY PB $15.00

Bobby **Jones** & O.B. **Keeler**
Down the Fairway
Possibly the best golf book ever written
0-940889-00-5 CLASSICS OF GOLF $25.00

R.R. **Knudson**
Babe Didrikson: Athlete of the Century
0-14-032095-4 VIKING PB $4.99

Tony **Lema** & G.S. **Brown**
Golfer's Gold
An amusing look at the pro tour
0-940889-17-X CLASSICS OF GOLF $25.00

Charles **MacDonald**
Scotland's Gift—Golf
0-940889-07-2 CLASSICS OF GOLF $25.00

Michael **Murphy**
Golf in the Kingdom
Murphy has been called the Carlos Casteneda of golf writers; a fictional account of a golfer who finds enlightenment
0-670-34529-6 ARKANA $22.95
0-14-019450-9 ARKANA PB $12.95

Captain Bruce Warren **Ollstein**
Combat Golf: The Competitor's Field Manual for Winning Against Any Opponent
0-670-86802-7 VIKING $15.95

Harvey **Penick**
The Game For a Lifetime: More Lessons and Teachings
The great Penick, called by *Sports Illustrated* "the Socrates of the Golf World," in a posthumous volume with his longtime friend Bud Shrake. Here he ranges from encouraging youngsters to learn and enjoy the game to offering senior golfers specific advice. And throughout, he provides trademark wisdom and gentle spirit in a fitting final work
WITH BUD SHRAKE
0-684-80059-4 SIMON & SCHUSTER $21.00

George **Peper**, editor

Golf in America: The First 100 Years of Golf Heroes, Major Championships, and Players of the Decade

0-8109-8123-8 ABRADALE $24.98
0-8109-1032-2 ABRADALE $45.00

George **Plimpton**

The Bogey Man

A new paperback edition of a sports classic—the world of the golf tour as lived and told by a master stylist. Plimpton recounts golf legends, adventures, sporting tips and theories he heard from pros, caddies and fans, with humor and insight and a great love for the game. "Plimpton will interest the man who can't tell a pitching wedge from a putter...This is really a book about a kind of madness with rules, and anyone can appreciate the appeal of that"—*Newsweek*

1-55821-241-8 LYONS & BURFORD PB $15.95

George Plimpton

Gene **Sarazen** & Herbert Warren **Wind**

30 Years of Championship Golf

0-940889-13-7 CLASSICS OF GOLF $25.00

Laurence **Sheehan**

A Passion For Golf: Treasures and Traditions of the Game

A season-by-season celebration of the passionate world of golf. The great clubhouses from Scotland to the States; the beautiful vistas of the world's most famous courses; the legendary heroes from Ben Hogan to Arnold Palmer—this is a stunning panorama of the emerald fairway

FOREWORD BY ARNOLD PALMER

0-517-59363-7 CLARKSON POTTER $30.00

Lee **Trevino** & Sam **Blair**

The Snake in Sandtrap (and Other Misadventures on the Golf Tour)

A quick read by a prolific tipster

0-8050-0368-1 HOLT PB $9.95

John **Updike**

Golf Dreams: Writings on Golf

0-679-45058-0 KNOPF $23.00

John Updike

US Golf Association

Golf Rules in Pictures

An illustrated rule book

0-399-51799-5 PERIGEE PB $10.00

Carl A. **Vigeland**

Stalking the Shark

0-393-03795-9 NORTON $25.00

Golf Instruction

Jonathan **Abrahams**

First Tee: A Beginner's Guide to Golf

ILLUSTRATIONS BY BARRY ROSS

1-55821-445-3 LYONS & BURFORD PB $15.95

Tommy **Armour**

How to Play Your Best Golf All the Time

Tips from the Silver Scot

0-940889-02-1 CLASSICS OF GOLF $25.00
0-671-21150-1 SIMON & SCHUSTER PB $7.95

Percy **Boomer**

On Learning Golf

The underground classic; noted for its famous description of the swing through "feel"

0-940889-22-6 CLASSICS OF GOLF $25.00
0-394-41008-4 RANDOM HOUSE $20.00

Julius **Boros**

Swing Easy, Hit Hard

1-55821-416-X LYONS & BURFORD PB $14.95

Richard **Coop** & **Bill Fields**

Mind Over Golf: Play Your Best by Thinking Smart

Dr. Coop's newest book provides the keys that all golfers, amateur and professional alike, need in order to improve their attitude and their overall game

0-02-527830-4 MACMILLAN $20.00

Ernie **Els**

How to Build a Classic Golf Swing

The number-two ranked golfer in the world joins forces with the instruction editor of *Golf World* magazine to teach the fundamentals of the classic swing. Concise tips and swing-sequence illustrations teach grip, aim, stance, posture, and go on to reveal Els' seven secrets to hitting the ball farther off the tee. Readable, instructive, and always entertaining

0-06-270088-X HARPERCOLLINS $27.50

Nick **Faldo**

Faldo: A Swing For Life

An entertaining and invaluable guide from the golf great, a three-time winner of the British Open and two-time Masters-winner. Faldo offers a comprehensive discussion of every aspect of the game from swing to putting to the essentials of psychology on and *off* the course. A must for any private collection or golf club library

0-670-85605-3 VIKING $27.95
0-297-83278-6 WEIDENFELD & NICOLSON $34.95

Claude "Butch" **Harmon** & John **Andrisani**

The Four Cornerstones of Winning Golf

FORWARD BY GREG NORMAN

0-684-80792-0 SIMON & SCHUSTER $25.00

Ben **Hogan**

Ben Hogan's Power Golf

An expert practitioner of the perfect swing

0-671-72905-5 POCKET PB $5.99

Modern Fundamentals of Golf

Hogan's landmark book from 1957

0-940889-18-8 CLASSICS OF GOLF $25.00
0-671-61297-2 SIMON & SCHUSTER PB $10.00

John **Jacobs** & Ken **Bowden**

Practical Golf

Easy to read and well-illustrated

0-689-70634-0 MACMILLAN PB $15.95

Ernest **Jones**

Swing the Clubhead

Jones uses simplified imagery to expound his particular theories of the swing

0-914178-91-1 GOLF DIGEST $13.95

David **Leadbetter**

David Leadbetter's Faults and Fixes

One of the world's most respected golf coaches and bestselling author of *The Golf Swing,* addresses the 50 most common errors players make. Hooks, slices, inaccuracy in putting, and common psychological errors are among the "faults" he "fixes." Fully illustrated

0-06-272005-8 HARPERPERENNIAL PB $19.95

Nancy **Lopez** & Don **Wade**

Nancy Lopez's Complete Golfer

One of the few books written by and for women golfers

0-8092-4711-9 CONTEMPORARY PB $15.95

Jack **Nicklaus**

Golf My Way

An overall examination of his techniques

0-671-22278-3 SIMON & SCHUSTER PB $12.00

My 55 Ways to Lower Your Golf Score
A series of tips rather than a detailed study
0-671-55395-X SIMON & SCHUSTER PB $10.00

Tom **Watson**
Getting Up and Down
Techniques and tricks of the short game
0-394-75300-3 VINTAGE PB $14.00

Golf Courses

F.W. **Hawtree**
The Golf Course: Planning, Design, Construction and Management
A primer on creating resort, club, and public courses
0-419-12250-8 CHAPMAN & HALL $66.95

Brian **McCallen**
Golf Resorts of the World: The Best Places to Stay and Play
For players of all abilities, here is a superbly photographed guide to the best golf vacations. This review presents 96 outstanding resorts chosen by the editorial board of *Golf Magazine*. Organized geographically, including information for the non-golfer too, this guide covers 64 resorts in the US and 34 in the Caribbean, Canada, Europe, Australia, and Asia
0-8109-3372-1 ABRAMS $49.50

Robert **McCord**
The 499 Best Public Golf Courses in the United States, Canada, Mexico, and the Caribbean
The ultimate guide to the public golf courses of all 50 states plus Canada, Mexico, and the Caribbean. Each entry gives all the necessary information to contact each course, plus a description of the course, its facilities, policies, fees, travel directions, motels, local attractions, and much more
0-679-76903-X RANDOM HOUSE PB $20.00

George **Peper**
Golf Courses of the PGA Tour
A beautifully illustrated book from *Golf* magazine
0-8109-3380-2 ABRAMS $49.50

Golf Humor

John **Feinstein**
A Good Walk Spoiled: Days and Nights on the PGA Tour
0-316-27737-1 LITTLE, BROWN PB $13.95

Dan **Jenkins**
The Dogged Victims of Inexorable Fate
A collection of clever pieces written for *Sports Illustrated*
0-940889-03-X CLASSICS OF GOLF $25.00

Rex **Lardner**
Downhill Lies and Other Falsehoods: Or How to Play Dirty Golf
One of the funniest books of the genre
0-8015-2198-X DUTTON PB $5.95

Leslie **Nielsen**
Bad Golf My Way
The comic personality brings his focus to the game of golf. Once again under the guise of good intention, Nielsen shows the reader how best to be the worst golfer on the course
0-385-48351-1 BDD $19.95

P.G. **Wodehouse**
Fore!: The Best of P.G. Wodehouse on Golf
0-89919-358-7 HOUGHTON MIFFLIN PB $11.95

P.G. Wodehouse

Ice Hockey

Howard **Berger**
On the Road: An Inside View of Life With an NHL Team
The Toronto sports broadcaster goes on tour with the Maple Leafs, leaving behind a trail of brutal training, injuries, the fear of being "sent down," and the glory of the games
1-89562-951-9 WARWICK PB $14.95

Bruce **Cooper** & Gene **Hart**
The Hockey Trivia Book
0-88011-233-6 HUMAN KINETICS PB $12.95

Jack **Falla**
Sports Illustrated Hockey: Learn to Play the Modern Way
Probably the best of the instructional books
1-56800-004-9 SPORTS ILLUSTRATED PB $12.95

Zander **Hollander** & Hal **Bock**, editors
The Complete Encyclopedia of Hockey
FOREWORD BY JOHN ZIEGLER
0-8103-8869-3 GALE $55.00
0-8103-9419-7 VISIBLE INK PB $22.95

George **Plimpton**
Open Net
Plimpton's brief and bruising sojourn with the Boston Bruins, under the tutelage of Jerry Cheevers
1-55821-242-6 LYONS & BURFORD PB $12.95

Gerald A. **Walford**
Youth Hockey: For Parents and Players
0-940279-89-4 MASTERS PB $12.95

David **Whitaker**
Coaching Hockey
Begins with the fundamentals of skating and puck-handling moves up to game strategies and coaching. Diagrams and statistics
1-85223-556-X CROWOOD PB $29.95

Horse Racing and Equestrian Sports

Horse Racing

Edward L. **Bowen**
The Jockey Club's Illustrated History of Thoroughbred Racing in America
A beautiful collection of paintings and photographs of the history, horses, and people involved in horseracing
0-8212-2059-4 BULFINCH $60.00

William **Nack**
Secretariat: The Making of a Champion
The horse whose records at Churchill Downs, Pimlico and Belmont still stand. "This book is supposed to be about a horse and racing. It misses the mark entirely and ends up, I think, as major reading"—Jimmy Breslin
0-306-80317-8 DA CAPO PB $13.95

Guy St. John **Williams** & Francis **Hyland**
The Irish Derby: 1866-1979
Another beautifully illustrated volume. The top winners may not have much to say, but they do make for a pretty picture
0-85131-358-2 SPORTING BOOK CENTER $40.00

Handicapping

Tom **Ainslie**
Ainslie's Encyclopedia of Thoroughbred Handicapping
0-688-00466-0 MORROW PB $14.95

Tom Ainslie's Complete Guide to Thoroughbred Racing
The most important book on the subject. Clearly explains everything one needs to handicap a race, without burdening the reader with "foolproof" methods
0-671-65655-4 FIRESIDE PB $13.00

Andrew **Beyer**
Picking Winners: A Horseplayer's Guide to Handicapping
A good how-to for gamblers who would rather have been statisticians, by the guru of speed handicappers
0-395-70132-5 HOUGHTON MIFFLIN PB $12.95

The Winning Horseplayer: A Revolutionary Approach to Thoroughbred Handicapping and Betting
A pleasant and amusing introduction to thoroughbred racing and to the handicapping methods of this Harvard dropout and *Washington Post* racing writer
0-395-70131-7 HOUGHTON MIFFLIN PB $12.95

James **Quinn**
The Best of Thoroughbred Handicapping: Advice on Handicapping from the Experts
0-688-07012-4 MORROW $22.00

Equestrian Sports

Riding

Anthony **Crossley**
Dressage: The Seat, Aids and Exercises
See also **DRESSAGE AND SHOW JUMPING** under **HORSES** under **PETS**
1-85310-329-2 VOYAGEUR PB $17.95

Judy **Richter**
Pony Talk: A Complete Learning Guide For Young Riders
One of the country's top teachers covers the fundamentals of proper horsemanship, including grooming, horse shows, and lessons. Photographs complement and illustrate the text
0-87605-849-7 HOWELL $22.00

Running

Garth **Battista**, editor
The Runner's Literary Companion
All the best short stories, poetry, and excerpts from novels about running—from Homer to W. H. Auden to Joyce Carol Oates, also includes cult novelists John L. Parker *(Once a Runner)* and Brian Glanville *(The Olympian)* and a number of obscure but excellent finds. And, of course, the bitter monologue of Colin Smith, protagonist of *The Loneliness of the Long-Distance Runner.* "Indispensable for hard-core road warriors, of significant interest to sports fiction fans in general, and may well contain enough surprises to appeal to readers in the mainstream" —*Publishers Weekly*
1-55821-335-X LYONS & BURFORD $23.00
0-14-025353-X PENGUIN PB $12.95

Tom **Derderian**
Boston Marathon: The First Century of the World's Premier Running Event
0-88011-479-7 HUMAN KINETICS PB $21.95

Richard **Harris**
Marathon: A Story of Endurance and Friendship
0-393-02765-1 NORTON $18.95

David **Martin** & Peter **Coe**
Training Distance Runners
0-87322-727-1 HUMAN KINETICS PB $19.95

Lyle J. **Micheli** & Mark **Jenkins**
Healthy Runner's Handbook
Includes an excellent section on recognizing and repairing injuries
0-88011-524-6 HUMAN KINETICS PB $16.95

Michael **Sandrock**
Running With the Legends: With the Training and Racing Insights from 21 Great Runners
Biographies of the best, past and present, along with their tips, perspectives, stories of competition, and coaching theories
0-87322-493-0 HUMAN KINETICS PB $19.95

Mark **Will-Weber**
The Quotable Runner: Great Moments of Wisdom, Inspiration, Wrongheadedness, and Humor
A comprehensive collection of quotes on running from such commentators as Chairman Mao, Winston Churchill, Bill Clinton, and hundreds of others. Sections of the book include Pain, Records, Women and Running, Coaches, Eating, Training, Winning, Losing, and Hills—among other subjects
See also **RUNNING** under **FITNESS** in **LIFESTYLES AND PRACTICAL ADVICE**
1-55821-420-8 LYONS & BURFORD $20.00

Sailing

Henry **Beard** & Roy **McKie**
Sailing
0-89480-144-9 WORKMAN PB $5.95

Bob **Bond**
The Handbook of Sailing
0-679-74063-5 KNOPF PB $26.00

Halsey **Herreshoff**, editor
The Sailor's Handbook
0-316-35948-3 LITTLE, BROWN $19.95

Elbert S. **Maloney**
Chapman Piloting, Seamanship and Small Boat Handling
0-688-11684-1 MORROW $50.00
0-688-09127-X MORROW PB $29.95

Larry **Pardey** & Lin **Pardey**
The Self-Sufficient Sailor
0-393-03269-8 PARADISE CAY $30.00

Sailboat Racing

Dennis **Conner** & Bruce **Stannard**
Comeback: My Race For the America's Cup
FOREWORD BY WALTER CRONKITE
0-312-01749-9 ST. MARTIN'S PB $7.95

Buddy **Melges** & Charles **Mason**
Sailing Smart: Winning Techniques, Tactics, and Strategies
0-8050-0351-7 HOLT PB $10.95

Jeff **Toghill**
Yacht Racing For Beginners
0-393-30297-0 NORTON PB $6.95

Stuart **Walker**
Advanced Racing Tactics
0-393-30333-0 NORTON PB $19.95

Tactics of Small Boat Racing
0-393-30801-4 NORTON PB $17.00

Skiing

Steve **Barnett**
The Best Ski Touring in America
Describes 31 classic ski tours of the best wilderness skiing in the United States, Canada, and Mexico
0-8446-6306-9 SMITH $18.75

Jeff **Bennett** & Scott **Downey**
The Complete Snowboarder
0-07-005142-9 MCGRAW HILL PB $14.95

John **Caldwell**
The New Cross-Country Ski Book
"The Bible of the sport"—*Boston Globe*
0-8446-6310-7 SMITH $20.80

Karl **Gamma**
The Handbook of Skiing
0-679-74316-2 KNOPF PB $21.00

Laurie **Gullion**
The Cross-Country Primer
1-55821-083-0 LYONS & BURFORD PB $15.95

Martin **Heckelman**
The New Guide to Skiing
0-393-30609-7 NORTON PB $15.95

Paul **Parker**

Free Heel-Skiing: The Secrets of Telemark and Parallel Techniques

For beginners and intermediate skiers

0-930031-18-0 CHELSEA GREEN PB........$19.95

Lito **Tejada-Flores**

Breakthrough on Skis: How to Get Out of the Intermediate Rut

"A rarity: a book by a ski instructor who can really write"—*Skiing Magazine*

0-679-75081-9 VINTAGE PB........$13.00

Soccer

Kurt **Ascherman** & Jim **San Marco**

Coaching Kids to Play Soccer

A complete guide to youth coaching, for both the experienced coach and the clueless parent who has just been drafted to take charge of a team

0-671-63936-6 FIRESIDE PB........$7.95

Andres **Cantor**

Goooal!: A Celebration of Soccer

From a master commentator

0-684-81440-4 SIMON & SCHUSTER........$23.00

Brian **Glanville**

The Story of the World Cup

From 1930 on, the championship rounds of international football (soccer) have drawn more fans than any other sporting event. Statistics, teams, individual players' histories, commentary. Bobby Moore, British mid-fielder in 1962, '66, and '70, calls this "the definitive history"

0-571-16979-1 FABER PB........$15.95

Tennis

E. Digby **Baltzell**

Sporting Gentlemen: Men's Tennis from the Age of Honor to the Cult of the Superstar

A history of tennis and its changes as a reflection of society

0-02-901315-1 FREE PRESS........$30.00

Peter **Bodo**

The Courts of Babylon: Tales of Greed and Glory in a Harsh New World of Professional Tennis

0-684-81296-7 SCRIBNERS........$25.00

Bud **Collins**

Bud Collins' Modern Encyclopedia of Tennis

The eminent broadcaster shares his view of the "Gentleman's Sport"

0-8103-8988-6 GALE........$39.95

0-8103-9443-X VISIBLE INK PB........$14.95

Fred **Stolle** & Kenneth **Wydro**

Tennis Down Under

Tennis in Australia

FOREWORD BY JOHN NEWCOMBE

0-915765-18-7 NATIONAL PRESS........$12.95

Jay **Jennings**, editor

Tennis and the Meaning of Life: A Literary Anthology of the Game

An anthology of writings on tennis, with contributions by Ring Lardner, W. Somerset Maugham, Paul Theroux, William Trevor, and over 20 others

1-55821-378-3 LYONS & BURFORD........$24.00

John **McPhee**

Levels of the Game

A narrative of a US Open semifinal between Arthur Ashe and Clark Graebner, with an eye for the contrasting styles and backgrounds of the players. A masterful account

0-374-18568-9 FS&G........$18.95

0-374-51526-3 FS&G PB........$9.00

Ilie **Nastase**

Break Point

One of tennis's premier bad boys tries his hand at fiction in this story of murder and intrigue on the international circuit

0-312-09514-7 ST. MARTIN'S........$15.95

Tennis Biographies

Arthur **Ashe**

Days of Grace: A Memoir

0-679-42396-6 RANDOM HOUSE........$24.00

0-345-38681-7 BALLANTINE PB........$6.99

Adrianne **Blue**

Martina: The Lives and Times of Martina Navratilova

The most recent biography of the greatest female tennis star to play the game

1-55972-300-9 BIRCH LANE........$19.95

Martina **Navratilova** & George **Vecsey**

Martina

Even with eight Wimbledon titles under her belt, she remains one of the most misunderstood figures in sports. Here she writes candidly of her youth in Czechoslovakia, her emigration to the West, her bisexuality, and her well-known entourage of friends

See also **BIOGRAPHIES** under **GAY, LESBIAN, AND BISEXUAL STUDIES** in **SOCIAL STUDIES**

0-449-20982-2 FAWCETT PB........$5.99

Martina Navratilova

Monica **Seles** & Ann **Richardson**

Monica: From Fear to Victory

Sixteen pages of pictures. Begins with her stabbing in 1993 and chronicles her recovery and return to the proffessional circuit

0-06-018645-3 HARPERCOLLINS........$23.00

Tennis Instruction

Arthur **Ashe** & Alexander **McNab**

Arthur Ashe on Tennis

Invaluable pointers on strokes, strategy, psychology, and wisdom from the late Davis Cup captain, reaching pro, writer, and champion of the game alike

0-679-43797-5 KNOPF........$20.00

0-380-72715-3 AVON PB........$10.00

Vic **Braden** & Bill **Bruns**

Vic Braden's Quick Fixes: Expert Cures For Common Tennis Problems

The latest book by the most visible teaching pro in America

0-316-10515-5 LITTLE, BROWN PB........$14.95

Lewis **Brewer**, editor

Professional Tennis Drills

Seventy-five drills from US Tennis Association professionals, covering strokes and footwork, conditioning, and game strategy

0-684-18298-X MACMILLAN PB........$13.00

Other Team Sports

Cricket

Keith **Andrew**

The Skills of Cricket

1-85223-237-4 CROWOOD PB........$16.95

Michael **Rundell**

The Dictionary of Cricket

0-19-866198-3 OXFORD........$19.95

Field Hockey

Jenny **John**

Field Hockey Handbook

0-88839-043-2 HANCOCK HOUSE PB........$8.95

Lacrosse

Lacrosse is a truly American sport, slowly breaking out of its Northeast prep school stronghold.

Jim **Hinkson**

Lacrosse Team Strategies

1-89562-955-1 FIREFLY PB........$16.95

Bob **Scott**

Lacrosse: Technique and Tradition

Instructional overview of the sport by the former coach of the Hopkins powerhouse, with an emphasis on strategy

0-8018-2060-X JOHNS HOPKINS PB $16.95

David **Urick**

Lacrosse: Fundamentals for Winning

A Sports Illustrated volume containing helpful pictures and diagrams for play, good organization, and most importantly: when and how it is legal to "chop check," "slap check," or "wrap check"

1-56800-071-5 SPORTS ILLUSTRATED PB $12.95

Rugby

Jim **Greenwood**

Think Rugby: A Guide to Purposeful Team Play

0-7136-3781-1 A&C BLACK PB $24.95

Total Rugby: Fifteen-Man Rugby for Coach and Player

0-7136-3443-X A&C BLACK PB $24.95

Bruce **Walsh**

Strength Training for Rugby

0-86417-293-1 SEVEN HILLS PB $13.95

Volleyball

Bob **Bertucci**, editor

The AVCA Volleyball Manual Handbook: The Official Handbook of the American Volleyball Coaches' Association

0-940279-11-8 MASTERS PB $17.95

Stuart **Biddle** & others

Volleyball Training

1-85223-880-1 CROWOOD PB $19.95

Karch **Kiraly**

Karch Kiraly's Championship Volleyball

0-684-81466-8 FIRESIDE PB $13.00

Jeff **Lucas**

Pass, Set, Crush: Volleyball Illustrated

A shot-by-shot guide with detailed illustrations

0-9615088-6-8 EUCLID NORTHWEST PB $24.95

Arie **Selenger**

Arie Selenger's Power Volleyball

A big book of technique and strategy from the coach of the 1984 US Women's Olympic team

0-312-04915-3 ST. MARTIN'S PB $18.95

Racket Sports

Tony **Grice**

Badminton: Steps to Success

Detailed instruction

0-87322-613-5 HUMAN KINETICS PB $14.95

Larry **Hodges**

Table Tennis: Steps to Success

0-87322-403-5 HUMAN KINETICS PB $14.95

Jahangir **Khan**

Learn Squash and Racquetball in a Weekend

0-679-42753-8 KNOPF $16.00

Gordon **Steggal** & Peter **Hirst**

Table Tennis: The Skills of the Game

1-85223-159-9 CROWOOD PB $17.95

Winter Sports

Peter **Stark** & Steven M. **Krauzer**

Winter Adventure: A Complete Guide to Winter Sports

Begat of the National Public Television show, "Trailside"

0-393-31400-6 NORTON PB $17.95

Figure Skating

Ricky **Harris**

Choreography and Style For Ice Skaters

0-312-05401-7 ST. MARTIN'S PB $10.95

Thomas **Lynch**

Skating with Heather Grace

0-394-74756-9 KNOPF PB $13.00

John **Petkevich**

Sports Illustrated Figure Skating: Championship Techniques

1-56800-070-7 SPORTS ILLUSTRATED PB $12.95

Joan **Ryan**

Little Girls in Pretty Boxes: The Making and Breaking of Elite Gymnasts and Figure Skaters

A private look at the pressure to succeed and potential for heartbreak of these young athletes. Many specific examples of our most vaunted professional youngsters. For anyone who wants to know what Bela Karolyi is like when not beaming in front of a camera. A stunning insider account.

See also **GYMNASTICS** under **OLYMPIC SPORTS**

0-446-67250-5 WARNER PB $12.99

Water Sports

Rowing, Canoeing, and Kayaking

Lloyd **Armstead**

Whitewater Rafting in North America

A guide to 200 outstanding adventures from Canada to Costa Rica. Each river write-up includes information on the trip's length, difficulty, cost, location, and reliable local outfitters

1-56440-362-9 GLOBE PEQUOT PB $16.95

James **Davidson** & John **Rugge**

The Complete Wilderness Paddler

0-394-71153-X VINTAGE PB $13.00

Jay **Evans**

The Kayaking Book

0-452-26941-5 PLUME PB $13.95

David **Halberstam**

The Amateurs

Here, the distinguished author of *October 1964*, provides a narrative of four men on the amateur rowing circuit. He focuses on the single scull trials in 1984 to compete for the Olympic Games. Excellent sportswriting by an author who brings out the drama in sports

0-449-91003-2 FAWCETT PB $10.00

Stephen **Kiesling**

The Shell Game: Reflections on Rowing

0-9638461-9-1 NORDIC KNIGHT PB $11.95

John **McPhee**

The Survival of the Bark Canoe

McPhee takes a traditional bark canoe through the backcountry of Maine

0-374-27207-7 FS&G $18.95
0-374-51693-6 FS&G PB $9.00

Joel W. **Rogers**

The Hidden Coast: Kayak Explorations from Alaska to Mexico

From the Prince William Sound to Mexico's La Manzanilla, this is the ultimate guide for the Pacific coast sea kayaker. Extensively illustrated with color photos

See also **CANOEING, RAFTING, AND KAYAKING** under **CAMPING AND MOUNTAINEERING** under **THE OUTDOORS**

0-88240-403-2 ALASKA NORTHWEST PB $19.95

Diving

Richard A. **Clinchy** III

Dive/First Responder

0-8016-7525-1 MOSBY PB $32.95

Greg **Louganis** & Eric **Marcus**
Breaking the Surface
The autobiography of the Olympic Gold Medalist who courageously revealed to the world that he is HIV positive
0-679-43703-7 RANDOM HOUSE $23.00
0-452-27590-3 PLUME PB $12.95

Ron **O'Brien**
Ron O'Brien's Diving for Gold
Head coach of the U.S. Olympic team since 1972, he is the pre-eminent genius of diving
FOREWORD BY GREG LOUGANIS
0-88011-448-7 LEISURE PB $19.95

Skin and Scuba Diving

Richard **Clinchy** & Glen **Egstrom**
Jeppesen's Open Water Sport Diver Manual
0-8016-9035-8 MOSBY PB $17.95

John L. **Culliney** & Edward S. **Crockett**
Exploring Underwater: The Sierra Club Guide to Scuba and Snorkling
Equipment, techniques, and dangers for beginners
0-87156-270-7 SIERRA CLUB PB $15.00

Dennis **Graver**
Scuba Diving
0-87322-431-0 HUMAN KINETICS PB $19.95

Surfing

Nick **Carroll**, editor
The Next Wave: The World of Surfing
A full-color exploration of the coasts of the world, in search of the gnarly wave. Carroll surveys the history of surfing from the '60s onward
1-55859-162-1 ABBEVILLE $29.98

Trevor **Cralle**
Surfin'Ary: A Dictionary of Surfing Terms and Surfspeak
A lexical companion to the world's most slang-oriented sport. "Hang ten" and don't be a "Barney"
0-89815-422-7 TEN SPEED PB $19.95

Daniel **Duane**
Caught Inside: A Surfer's Year on the California Coast
Remarkably prescient account of a year-long trek to explore the Pacific Coast and all its beauty. Ostensibly a surf journal, it also captures the seasonal beat of the land and its effect on the narrator
0-86547-494-X NORTH POINT $21.00

Doug **Werner**
Longboarder's Start-Up: A Guide to Longboard Surfing
1-88465-406-1 TRCKS PB $9.95

Swimming

Laurel **Blossom**
Splash: Great Writing About Swimming
With a preface by George Plimpton and writings by authors such as John Cheever, Laurie Colwin, Doris Lessing, John Updike, Calvin Trillin. Don't miss Anne Sexton's entry: "The Nude Swim." Definitely not a dry read
0-88001-449-0 ECCO $26.00

Cecil M. **Colwin**
Swimming: Into the 21st Century
"The book is a must for coaches but will also be of interest to swimmers who want to be inspired while being instructed at the same time"
—*Swim Canada*
See also SWIMMING under FITNESS in LIFESTYLES AND PRACTICAL ADVICE
0-87322-456-6 HUMAN KINETICS PB $19.95

Jane **Katz** & Nancy **Bruning**
Swimming for Total Fitness: A Progressive Aerobic Program
Contains over 80 workouts gradually increasing from 100 yards to two miles
0-385-46821-0 DOUBLEDAY PB $17.95

Steve **Tarpinian**
The Essential Swimmer
A comprehensive program for success with swimming
1-55821-386-4 LYONS & BURFORD PB $12.95

Waterskiing and Windsurfing

Jeremy **Evans**
Complete Guide to Windsurfing
0-8160-1527-9 FACTS ON FILE $21.95

Bruce **Kistler**
Hit It!: Your Guide to Waterskiing Fun
FOREWORD BY BRUCE JENNER
0-88011-313-8 LEISURE PB $11.95

Rob **Reichenfeld**
Windsurfing: Step by Step to Success
1-85223-746-5 CROWOOD PB $22.95

Olympic Sports

Douglas **Collins** & James A. **Michener**
Olympic Dreams: 100 Years of Excellence: An Official Publication of the United States Olympic Committee
0-7893-0030-3 RIZZOLI PB $25.00

Larry **Siddons**
The Olympics at 100: A Celebration in Pictures
0-02-860346-X MACMILLAN PB $19.95

Jane **Leder**
Grace & Glory: A Century of Women in the Olympics
Athletes' biographies and pictures. Explains the historical significance of women's inclusion in the competition
EDITED BY SIOBAHN DRUMMOND & ELIZABETH RATHBURN
1-57243-116-4 TRIUMPH $19.95

David **Wallechinsky**
Sports Illustrated Presents the Complete Book of Summer Olympics 1996
0-316-92094-0 LITTLE, BROWN PB $15.95

Michael T. **Wise** & others, editors
Chronicle of the Olympics, 1896-1996
Huge and comprehensive, with a multitude of pictures
0-7894-0608-X DORLING KINDERSLEY $29.95

Gymnastics

Rik **Feeney**
Gymnastics: A Guide for Parents and Athletes
Good beginner's manual for kids who enjoy tumbling and their parents who think they might have a career in it
0-940279-43-6 MASTERS PB $14.95

Bela **Karolyi** & Nancy Ann **Richardson**
Feel No Fear: The Power, Passion, and Politics of a Life in Gymnastics
The gymastics world from the viewpoint of its greatest coach
0-7868-8020-1 HYPERION PB $13.95

Trevor **Low**
Gymnastics: Floor, Vault, Beam and Bar
1-85223-752-X CROWOOD PB $17.95

Dominque **Moceanu**
Dominique Moceanu: An American Champion: An Autobiography
An autobiography by one of America's darlings of the 1996 Olympic Games in Atlanta
0-553-09773-3 BANTAM $14.95

Joan **Ryan**
Little Girls in Pretty Boxes: The Making and Breaking of Elite Gymnasts and Figure Skaters
A private look at the pressure to succeed and potential for heartbreak of these young athletes. Many specific examples of our most vaunted professional youngsters. For anyone who wants to know what Bela Karolyi is like when not beaming in front of a camera. A stunning insider account.
See also FIGURE SKATING under WINTER SPORTS
0-446-67250-5 WARNER PB $12.99

Track and Field

Arthur R. **Ashe**, Jr.

A Hard Road to Glory: The African-American Athlete in Track & Field

1-56743-039-2 AMISTAD PB $9.95

Roger **Bannister**

The Four-Minute Mile

1-55821-027-X LYONS & BURFORD PB $12.95

William J. **Bowerman** & William H. **Freeman**

High-Performance Training for Track and Field

0-88011-390-1 LEISURE PB $24.00

Gerry A. **Carr**

Fundamentals of Track and Field

0-88011-388-X LEISURE PB $24.00

John **Randolph**, editor

Championship Track and Field by the Experts: Field Events

0-918438-15-2 HUMAN KINETICS PB $14.00

Jim **Santos** & Ken **Shannon**

Sports Illustrated Track: The Field Events

Another in the reliable Sports Illustrated series

1-56800-031-6 SPORTS ILLUSTRATED PB $10.95

Recreational and Other Sports

Archery

Wayne C. **McKinney** & Mike W. **McKinney**

Archery

0-697-10413-3 BROWN PB $11.15

Auto Racing

Bob **Bondurant** & John **Blakemore**

Bob Bondurant on High Performance Driving

0-87938-751-3 MOTORBOOKS INTL PB $15.95

Robin **MacGowan** & Graham **Watson**

Kings of the Road: A Portrait of Racers and Racing

0-88011-297-2 LEISURE $25.95

Bowling

Carmen **Salvino** & Frederick **Klein**

Fast Lanes

After turning pro at age 17, Salvino was a part of bowling's rise to television success and became a member of its Hall of Fame

0-933893-46-9 BONUS PB $9.95

Cycling

Ed **Burke**

Serious Cycling

Complex manual for training

0-87322-759-X HUMAN KINETICS PB $18.95

Tom **Cuthbertson**

Anybody's Bike Book

0-8446-6305-0 SMITH $20.05

Greg **LeMond** & Kent **Gordis**

Greg LeMond's Complete Book of Bicycling

One of the best cycling books by the American winner of the 1986 Tour de France

See also **BICYCLING** under **FITNESS** in **LIFESTYLES AND PRACTICAL ADVICE**

0-399-51594-1 PERIGEE PB $14.00

Peter **Nye**

Heart of Lions: The History of American Bicycle Racing

Stories of the good old days when American cyclists were equals to Jack Dempsey and Ty Cobb

FOREWORD BY ERIC HEIDEN

0-393-30576-7 NORTON PB $14.00

Bob **Woodward**

Mountain Biking: The Complete Guide

Another in the reliable Sports Illustrated series

1-56800-072-3 SPORTS ILLUSTRATED PB $12.95

Exercise and Fitness

Bob **Anderson** & others

Getting in Shape: Workout Programs for Men and Women

0-679-75609-4 SHELTER PB $19.95

Bob **Jackson-Paris** & Bob **Paris**

Natural Fitness

A "bodybuilding superstar" gives his keys to a healthy and totally balanced lifestyle based around exercise

0-446-67029-4 WARNER PB $13.99

George **McGlynn**

Dynamics of Fitness: A Practical Approach

0-697-24651-5 BROWN & BENCHMARK PB $11.15

Keli **Roberts**

Fitness Hollywood: The Trainer to the Stars Shares Her Body-Shaping Secrets

What the celebrities do and how you can mimic them with successful fitness exercies. Who wouldn't want to have Cher's body…

1-56530-147-1 SUMMIT $19.95

Silvanada Yoga Vedanta Center

Learn Yoga in a Weekend

0-679-42751-1 KNOPF $16.00

Suzanne **Schlosberg**

The Ultimate Workout Log: An Exercise Diary and Fitness Guide

Anyone who has struggled to maintain a consistent exercise routine will welcome this helpftul, motivating book. *The Ultimate Workout Log* keeps you in shape with specially designed pages to note goals and evaluate performance. Also includes injury prevention guidelines, calorie-burning charts, cardiovascular tips, diagrams of muscle groups, and other essential fitness information

0-395-66599-X HOUGHTON MIFFLIN PB $11.95

David R. **Stutz**, editor & **Consumer Reports**,

40+ Guide to Fitness: A Physician's Exercise and Sports Program

Team physician for the Chicago White Sox and Baltimore Orioles, a 40+ athlete himself, Dr. Stutz knows whence he speaks. With its emphasis on minimizing injury and its special instructions for people with lower-back pain, heart condition, neurological disorders, and respiratory problems, *40+ Guide to Fitness* proves of immense value to enthusiasts who intend to stay competitive, as well as for those who are sedentary and want to get in shape

0-89043-578-2 CONSUMER REPORTS PB $16.95

Glenn **Town** & Todd **Kearney**

Swim, Bike, Run

For both beginners and veterans, men and women

See also **TRIATHLONS** under **FITNESS** in **LIFESTYLES AND PRACTICAL ADVICE**

FOREWORD BY SCOTT TINLEY

0-87322-513-9 HUMAN KINETICS PB $15.95

Fencing

Aldo **Nadi** & others

The Living Sword: A Fencer's Autobiography

Apparently the James Bond of swordsmanship, Nadi vanquished his adversaries with chilling technical skill and a wit as sharp as his epee, then celebrated victory with fine wine and women

1-88452-820-1 LAUREATE PB $17.95

A.T. **Simmonds** & E.D. **Morton**

Fencing to Win

Different theories, styles, and weapons presented by two fencing coaches

0-948253-69-X SPORTSMANS $17.95

Pool and Billiards

Robert **Byrne**

Byrne's Standard Book of Pool and Billiards

This is a sourcebook for beginners to advanced players which covers what you need to know in order to play nearly every existing cue game. "A tremendous work."—Al Gilbert, seven-time U.S. Billiards Champion

0-15-614972-9 HARCOURT BRACE PB $18.00

Byrne's Treasury of Trick Shots in Pool and Billiards
0-15-115224-1 HARCOURT BRACE $19.95
0-15-614973-7 HARCOURT BRACE PB $19.00

Robert **Byrne** & others, editors
Byrne's Book of Great Pool Stories
Leo Tolstoy, Wallace Stegner, James Kelman, Andrew Vachss, and others contribute thrilling, tragic and comedic tales of battles fought on the felt. A must for anyone who would like to remind themselves of the beauty of the game
0-15-600223-X HARVEST PB $18.00

Ray **Martin** & Rosser **Reeves**
The 99 Critical Shots in Pool
0-8129-2241-7 TIME BOOKS PB $14.00

David **McCumber**
Playing Off the Rail: A Pool Hustler's Journey
Going on the road with a professional shark, McCumber turns from journalist to "stakehorse"—the guy who supplies the money for the games. Suspenseful and very funny
0-679-42374-5 RANDOM HOUSE $25.00

Steve **Mizerak**
Steve Mizerak's Pocket Billiards: Tips and Trick Shots
A man whose grin says it all. Includes a section on hustling
0-517-12332-0 WINGS $6.99

Michael Ian **Shamos**
Pool: History, Strategies, and Legends
Shamos, curator of Pittsburgh's Billiard Archive, reveals techniques for better play, including choosing a cue, using chalk, and testing a table
1-56799-061-4 FRIEDMAN/FAIRFAX PB $12.95

John **Spencer**
Snooker
Part of the "Teach Yourself" series
EDITED BY CLIVE EVERTON
0-8442-3940-2 N.T.C. PB $9.95

Rodeo

Kristine **Fredriksson**
American Rodeo: From Buffalo Bill to Big Business
0-89096-565-X TEXAS A & M PB $15.95

Ron **Tyler**
The Rodeo of John A. Stryker
0-88426-050-X ENCINO $20.00

Shooting

Art **Blatt**
Gun Digest Book of Trap and Skeet Shooting
0-87349-030-4 D.B.I. PB $16.95

The Outdoors

Recent literature on the outdoors ranges from philosophical and meditative treatises, memoirs of adventure, and studies in ecology, to field guides, camping tips, hunting and fishing manuals, and cookbooks.

For related reading, see NATURE STUDY in SCIENCE

Essays

Edward **Abbey**

"What entertains many and exasperates others is Abbey's unique prose voice. Alternately misanthropic and sentimental, enraged and hilarious, it is the voice of a full-blooded man airing his passions."—Peter Carlson
Desert Solitaire
See also **HISTORY, POLITICS, AND SOCIETY** under **20TH-CENTURY AMERICAN ESSAYS AND JOURNALISM** in **LITERATURE OF THE AMERICAS**
See also **THE SOUTHWEST AND THE DESERT** under **REGIONAL GUIDES AND STUDIES** under **NATURE STUDY** in **SCIENCE**
0-8165-1057-1 ARIZONA $36.00
0-345-32649-0 BALLANTINE PB $5.95
0-671-69588-6 TOUCHSTONE PB $11.00

Rick **Bass**
The Lost Grizzlies: A Search for Survivors in the Wilderness of Colorado
Bass, an acclaimed nature writer whose fiction has appeared in *The Paris Review* and *Esquire*, tells the story of his search for evidence of Colorado's grizzly bears, long thought to be extinct. Bass describes the dangers of the trail, the mystery and beauty of the animal, and the courage and hope of the search. "In [Bass's] chest beats the heat of both the poet and the hunter"—*Chicago Sun-Times*
0-395-71759-0 HOUGHTON MIFFLIN $22.95

Stephen **Bodio**
A Rage For Falcons
By a columnist and editor of *Gray's Sporting Journal*
See also **BIRDS** under **ANIMALS** under **NATURE STUDY** in **SCIENCE**
0-87108-826-6 PRUETT PB $12.95

Jay **Cassell**, editor
The Best of Sports Afield: The Greatest Outdoor Writing of the 20th-century
A tribute to a century of outdoor life, this anthology spans over a century of writing, from the Alaska gold rush to Teddy Roosevelt's early concern with game animals to the modern views of hunters and fishers. Includes pieces by Gordon MacQurrie, P.J. O'Rourke, Jim Harrison, Earle Stanley Gardner, and Thomas McGuane
0-87113-644-9 ATLANTIC MONTHLY $25.00

Alston **Chase**
Playing God in Yellowstone: The Destruction of America's First National Park
The most iconoclastic book on conservation policy in decades, with implications that go beyond Yellowstone
0-15-672036-1 HARCOURT BRACE PB $14.00

David **Duncan**
The River Why
A comic novel, whimsical yet serious, on man and nature as seen through the eyes of a fly-fishing fanatic
See also **SINCE 1945** under **20TH-CENTURY AMERICAN FICTION** in **LITERATURE OF THE AMERICAS**
0-87156-321-5 SIERRA CLUB $22.00
0-553-34486-2 BANTAM PB $11.95

Bill **Gilbert**
Our Nature
0-8032-7023-2 NEBRASKA PB $7.50

Ted **Kerasote**
Navigations: One Man Explores the Americas and Discovers Himself
A reflective, highly personal book on travel and wilderness
0-8117-1013-0 STACKPOLE $16.95

Gretchen **Legler**
All the Powerful Invisible Things: A Sportswoman's Notebook
Pushcart Prize-winning Legler offers a moving chronicle of outdoor life. From the politics of hunting to family, sexuality, and ecology, this intimate mediation on the natural world is also a moving description of a woman's journey of self discovery
1-87806-769-9 SEAL PB $12.95

Gretchen Legler

Aldo **Leopold**
A Sand County Almanac: And Sketches Here and There
Essays on changes in the Wisconsin countryside and other observations by this pioneering conservationist. Awarded the John Burroughs Medal of the American Museum of Natural History (1978)
0-19-505305-2 OXFORD $25.00

Norman **Maclean**

A River Runs Through It & Other Stories

0-226-50055-1 CHICAGO $17.95
0-226-50057-8 CHICAGO PB $9.95

Norman Maclean

Thomas **McGuane**

"It's time we recognized Thomas McGuane as a national resource."—The Boston Globe

An Outside Chance: Essays on Sport

Broad-based essays by a master prose stylist

0-395-50084-2 HOUGHTON MIFFLIN $19.95
0-374-10472-7 HOUGHTON MIFFLIN PB $10.95

Roderick **Nash**

Wilderness and the American Mind

See also **ENVIRONMENTAL HISTORY** under **THE ENVIRONMENT** in **SCIENCE**
See also **INTELLECTUAL HISTORY** under **TOPICS IN AMERICAN STUDIES** in **HISTORY OF THE AMERICAS**

0-300-02910-1 YALE PB $16.00

Daniel G. **Payne**

Voices in the Wilderness: American Nature Writing and Environmental Politics

0-87451-752-4 NEW ENGLAND PB $15.95

James **Vickery**

Wilderness Visionaries

Biographies of Muir, Olson, Thoreau, and others

1-55971-435-2 NORTHWORD PB $9.95

Guides

Reader's Digest

Encyclopedia of Animals

An international team of experts enhance 600 color photographs with detailed coverage of all varieties of mammals, birds, reptiles, and amphibians, on the ground and in the air. A precious sourcebook and an endlessly fascinating browse from cover to cover

1-87513-749-1 READER'S DIGEST $50.00

Sierra Club Guides

The Sierra Club Naturalist's Guides are skillfully written, well-printed, and beautifully illustrated. They also include species identification.

Michael **Berrill** & Deborah **Berrill**

A Sierra Club Naturalist's Guide to the North Atlantic Coast: Cape Cod to Newfoundland

0-87156-243-X RANDOM HOUSE PB $16.00

Glena **Daniel** & Jerry **Sullivan**

A Sierra Club Naturalist's Guide to the North Woods of Michigan, Wisconsin, Minnesota and Southern Ontario

0-87156-277-4 RANDOM HOUSE PB $16.00

Michael **Godfrey**

A Sierra Club Naturalist's Guide to the Piedmont of Eastern North America

0-87156-744-X SIERRA CLUB PB $14.00

Neil **Jorgensen**

A Sierra Club Naturalist's Guide to Southern New England

0-87156-183-2 RANDOM HOUSE PB $18.00

Dean **Krakel II**

Downriver: A Yellowstone Journey

0-87156-708-3 SIERRA CLUB $16.95

Peggy **Larson** & Lane **Larson**

A Sierra Club Naturalist's Guide to the Deserts of the Southwest

0-87156-186-7 SIERRA CLUB PB $12.00

Bill **Perry**

A Sierra Club Naturalist's Guide to the Middle Atlantic Coast: Cape Hatteras to Cape Cod

0-87156-816-0 RANDOM HOUSE PB $14.00

John **Perry** & Jane **Perry**

The Sierra Club Guide to the Natural Areas of Colorado and Utah

0-87156-832-2 SIERRA CLUB PB $10.00

Stephen **Whitney**

A Sierra Club Naturalist's Guide to the Sierra Nevada

0-87156-216-2 RANDOM HOUSE PB $18.00

Mammals

James **Halfpenny**

Field Guide to Mammal Tracking in North America

This handy sourcebook details how to follow the trail of various mammals, even through snow and mud. "May be the most useful new work on the subject in 30 years"—*Outside* magazine

0-933472-98-6 JOHNSON PB $14.95

John A. **Murray**

Grizzly Bears: An Illustrated Field Guide

Murray has spent 18 years researching grizzlies in North America. Here he explains how to identify the bear and its signs, discusses habitat, diet, and ursine society, and offers ideas for protecting these bears into the next century

1-57098-029-2 ROBERTS RINEHART PB $14.95

Birds

ABA Staff

Birdfinding in Forty National Forests and Grasslands

This guide, produced in cooperation between the U.S. Department of Agriculture Forest Service and the American Birding Association, tells you what you need to know to bird in our national forests and preserves. Printed on recycled paper

1-87878-829-9 AMBIR PB $12.95

John **Bull** & John **Farrand**

The Audubon Society Guides to North American Birds: Eastern Region

0-394-41405-5 KNOPF PB $18.00

John James Audubon

Jon **Curson** & others

Warblers of the Americas: An Identification Guide

116 species of warbler, native to North, Central, and South America. Described in this definitive guide. Color plates

0-395-70998-9 HOUGHTON MIFFLIN $40.00

Pete **Dunne**

The Wind Masters: The Lives of North American Birds of Prey

An inside look at the lives of all 34 species of day-flying raptors in North America. An intriguing natural history narrative

0-395-65235-9 HOUGHTON MIFFLIN $22.95

Peter **Dunne** & others

Hawks in Flight: The Flight Identification of North American Migrant Raptors

How to identify the 23 most common raptor species in North America, using a new system of classification by general appearance while the bird is on the wing. "A landmark"
—Roger Tory Peterson

0-395-51022-8 HOUGHTON MIFFLIN PB $11.95

Joan **Dunning**

Secrets of the Nest: The Family Life of North American Birds

Charmingly illustrated with line drawings and watercolors, this is an intimate look at the society of birds

0-395-62035-X HOUGHTON MIFFLIN $27.50
0-395-71820-1 DORLING KINDERSLEY PB $15.95

Paul **Ehrlich** & others

The Birder's Handbook: A Field Guide to the Natural History of North American Birds

This is the ideal volume to accompany your identification field guide. "Field guides will help you recognize birds. This book will help you to understand them"
—David S. Wilcove, *The Wilderness Society*

0-671-65989-8 FIRESIDE PB $17.00

Joseph **Forshaw** & Terence **Lindsey**

Birding: A Nature Company Guide

Here is a volume filled with colorful photos, illustrations, and information of and about America's birds and birders. Suitable for the amateur or expert

0-7835-4752-8 TIME BOOKS $29.95

Steven **Magde**

Waterfowl: An Identification Guide to the Ducks, Geese and Swans of the World

More than 700 birds are illustrated in full-color paintings in this volume. Includes 150 distribution maps

See also **BIRDS** under **ANIMALS** under **NATURE STUDY** in **SCIENCE**

INTRODUCTION BY ROGER TORY PETERSON
0-395-46726-8 HOUGHTON MIFFLIN PB $29.95

Laura C. **Martin**

The Folklore of Birds

Fascinating information about many types of birds, including natural history, fable, and spiritual beliefs concerning our feathered friends

1-56440-872-8 GLOBE PEQUOT PB $15.95

Roger Troy **Peterson**

Atlantic Coastal Birds

The fastest and easiest tool yet for identifying birds. Organized by type or place, and using the Peterson identification system to pinpoint the key features that distinguish one bird from another, Flash Guides are slim, durable, and unfold in a flash. Includes 50 to 100 species per guide, with brief surveys of each bird's distinctive habits and habitats

0-395-79286-X HOUGHTON MIFFLIN PB $7.95

Backyard Birds

0-395-79290-8 HOUGHTON MIFFLIN PB $7.95

Eastern Mountain Birds

0-395-79288-6 HOUGHTON MIFFLIN PB $7.95

Hawks

0-395-79291-6 HOUGHTON MIFFLIN PB $7.95

Pacific Coastal Birds

0-395-79287-8 HOUGHTON MIFFLIN PB $7.95

Western Mountain Birds

0-395-79289-4 HOUGHTON MIFFLIN PB $7.95

Donald **Stokes** & Lilliane **Stokes**

Stokes Field Guide to Birds: Eastern Region

0-316-81810-0 LITTLE, BROWN PB $16.95
0-316-81809-7 LITTLE, BROWN PB $16.95

Clay **Sutton** & Patricia Taylor **Sutton**

How to Spot Hawks & Eagles

The Suttons discuss types of raptor, how they differ, birding equipment, and where to find these magnificent birds in the United States and Canada. Includes color photos, species-by-species descriptions, range maps, and guides to major migration routes

1-57630-001-3 CHAPTERS $24.95
1-57630-000-5 CHAPTERS PB $15.95

Don **True**

Hummingbirds of North America: Attracting, Feeding, and Photographing

From feeder formulas to nesting habits, this is a thorough guide to all types of hummingbirds. "Here in one book is all you could hope to know about our hummingbirds North of the border"
—Roger Tory Peterson

0-8263-1572-0 NEW MEXICO PB $24.95

Sea Creatures

Herbert **Boschung**, editor

The Audubon Society Field Guide to North American Fishes, Whales, and Dolphins

0-394-53405-0 KNOPF PB $19.00

Harold **Feinberg**

The Simon & Schuster Guide to Shells

0-671-25320-4 SIMON & SCHUSTER PB $15.00

Eugene **Kaplan**

A Field Guide to Coral Reefs of the Caribbean and Florida

0-395-46811-6 HOUGHTON MIFFLIN PB $16.95

Stephen **Leatherwood** & Randall **Reeves**

The Sierra Club Handbook of Whales and Dolphins

0-87156-340-1 RANDOM HOUSE PB $18.00

Norman **Meinkoth**

The Audubon Society Field Guide to North American Seashore Creatures

0-394-51993-0 KNOPF $19.00

Percy **Morris**

A Field Guide to Pacific Coast Shells

0-395-08029-0 HOUGHTON MIFFLIN $21.95
0-395-18322-7 HOUGHTON MIFFLIN PB $15.95

Harrold **Rehder**

The Audubon Society Field Guide to North American Seashells

0-394-51913-2 KNOPF PB $19.00

Reptiles and Amphibians

John **Coborn**

Atlas of Snakes

The ultimate snake book, superbly illustrated in color

0-86622-749-0 T.F.H. $129.95

The Mini-Atlas of Snakes of the World

This volume, an abridged version of Coborn's classic "Atlas," illustrates over 500 species of snake, and includes more than 950 color photos. Contains an easy-to-use system of symbols that indicates each snake's feeding habits, method of reproduction, potential harmfulness, and average adult length

0-86622-601-X T.F.H. $59.95

Roger **Conant**

A Field Guide to Reptiles and Amphibians of Eastern and Central North America

0-395-37022-1 HOUGHTON MIFFLIN $24.95
0-395-19979-4 HOUGHTON MIFFLIN PB $17.95

Insects

R. **Arnett** & R. **Jacques**, Jr.

The Simon & Schuster Guide to Insects

0-671-25014-0 SIMON & SCHUSTER PB $15.00

David **Carter**

Butterflies and Moths

From the Adonis Blue to the Madagascan Sunset Moth, here is a straightforward guide for the butterfly enthusiast. Contains more than 600 color photos

1-56458-062-8 DORLING KINDERSLEY PB $17.95

Robert Michael **Pyle**

Handbook for Butterfly Watchers

For the amateur to the expert lepidopterist, this is a beautifully illustrated and well-written field guide. "Pyle is America's butterfly guru"
—*Whole Earth Review*

0-395-61629-8 HOUGHTON MIFFLIN PB $12.95

Erik D. **Stoops** & Jeffrey L. **Martin**

Scorpions and Venomous Insects of the Southwest

What you need to know about dangerous scorpions, spiders, ticks, centipedes, millipedes, fire ants, "killer" bees, wasps, beetles, mosquitoes, fleas, lice, and moths

0-914846-87-6 GOLDEN WEST PB..........$9.95

Trees, Plants, and Fungi

Alan **Bessette**, editor

Mushrooms of North America in Color: A Field Guide Companion to Seldom-Illustrated Fungi

0-8156-2666-5 SYRACUSE..........$39.95

Tom **Brown**

Tom Brown's Guide to Wild Edible and Medicinal Plants

0-425-10063-4 BERKELEY PB..........$12.00

Timothy **Coffey**

The History and Folklore of North American Wildflowers

A reference work which provides ethnobotanical information on the popular lore, social hsitory, and practical uses of almost 700 native wildflowers

0-395-51593-9 HOUGHTON MIFFLIN PB..........$14.95

The History and Folklore of North American Wildflowers

0-8160-2624-6 FACTS ON FILE..........$40.00

Thomas S. **Elias** & Peter A. **Dykeman**

Edible Wild Plants: A North American Field Guide

A season-by-season guide that offers instruction in identifying, gathering, and preparing edible wild plants. Here's how to make wild grape jelly, gather pine nuts, and create real "marsh mallow" candy

0-8069-7488-5 STERLING PB..........$16.95

Douglas B. **Elliott**

Wild Roots: A Forager's Guide to the Edible and Medicinal Roots, Tubers, Corms, and Rhizomes of North America

Elliot has combined plant lore and knowledge into a beautifully illustrated book. Here is information on edible and medicinal plants, as well as those that can be used to make teas, toothpaste, shampoos, and dyes

0-89281-538-8 HEALING ARTS PB..........$14.95

David W. **Fischer** & Alan E. **Bessette**

Edible Wild Mushrooms of North America: A Field-To-Kitchen Guide

Information on how to eat over 100 species of wild mushrooms safely, using color photos and detailed, non-technical descriptions. Includes 70 recipes, from Salmon with Black Trumpets and Horseradish Sauce to Puffballs Parmesan

0-292-72079-3 TEXAS..........$35.00
0-292-72080-7 TEXAS PB..........$22.95

Steven **Foster**

A Field Guide to Medicinal Plants: Eastern and Central North America

0-395-46722-5 HOUGHTON MIFFLIN PB..........$16.95

Edward **Knobel**

Field Guide to the Grasses, Sedges and Rushes of the United States

Accurate line drawing depictions, clear text, and a useful categorization system make this a handy volume. Each illustration shows the whole plant and a spikelet

0-486-23505-X DOVER PB..........$3.95

Carol **Levine**

A Guide to Wildflowers in Winter: Herbaceous Plants of Northeastern North America

A beautifully illustrated field guide that will allow amateur botanists to continue their pursuits into the Fall and Winter months. Features extensive illustrated entires on 391 species of plant

0-300-06207-9 YALE..........$40.00
0-300-06560-4 YALE PB..........$20.00

Michael **Moore**

Los Remedios

This comprehensive guide details the primary and secondary medicinal uses of 172 medicinal plants. Includes usefulness rating, precise dosage instructions, preparation methods, and sources for purchase

See also **HERBAL REMEDIES** under **ALTERNATIVE THERAPIES** under **HOLISTIC MEDICINE** under **HEALTH** in **LIFESTYLES AND PRACTICAL ADVICE**

1-87861-006-6 RED CRANE PB..........$9.95

Lee **Peterson**

A Field Guide to Eastern Edible Wild Plants

See also **TREES, PLANTS, AND FUNGI** under **NATURE STUDY** in **SCIENCE**

0-395-20445-3 HOUGHTON MIFFLIN..........$24.95
0-395-31870-X HOUGHTON MIFFLIN PB..........$15.95

Antony Armstrong-Jones **Snowdon**

Wild Flowers

Portrait-style photographs of 39 wildflowers, with a descriptive page of text on each

0-517-70565-6 CLARKSON POTTER..........$14.50

Camping and Mountaineering

Nessmuk

Woodcraft and Camping

0-486-21145-2 DOVER PB..........$4.95

Ernest Thompson **Seton**

Two Little Savages

0-486-20985-7 DOVER PB..........$7.95

Hiking and Backpacking

Michael **Abel**

Backpacking Made Easy

Everything the beginner needs to consider before setting out on an extended hike, from optimum sleeping bag construction to the several types of bears to be found in North America

0-87961-040-9 NATUREGRAPH PB..........$6.95

Colin **Fletcher**

The Complete Walker III: The Joys and Techniques of Hiking and Backpacking

An updated and enlarged edition of the book *Field and Stream* called "the hiker's bible." Covers everything from new types of hiker's clothing to why it most often makes sense to eschew a tent

0-394-72264-7 RANDOM HOUSE PB..........$19.00

David **Ganci**

Desert Hiking

0-89997-168-7 WILDERNESS PB..........$13.95

Bruce **Hampton** & David **Cole**

Soft Paths: How to Enjoy the Wilderness Without Harming It

A revised and updated edition of the National Outdoor Leadership School's classic on low-impact hiking and camping. "The authors have done a great service to the protection of our great outdoors"—George T. Frampton, Jr., Assistant Secretary for Fish, Wildlife, and Parks

0-8117-3092-1 STACKPOLE PB..........$14.95

David **Harmon** & Amy S. **Rubin**

Llamas on the Trail: A Packer's Guide

Ideas for both the neophyte and experienced pack tripper on selection, training, and conditioning of llamas, as well as packing equipment, planning trips, and getting into the backcountry

0-87842-251-X MOUNTAIN PB..........$15.00

John **Hart**

Walking Softly in the Wilderness: The Sierra Club Guide to Backpacking

A revised and updated edition that covers everything from boot and foot care to camping in snow and ice

0-87156-813-6 SIERRA CLUB PB..........$15.00

Michael **Hodgson**

Camping for Mere Mortals

A light-hearted look at camping, from the hazards of wilderness cookery to the utter uselessness of camouflage toilet paper

0-934802-35-1 I.C.S. PB..........$6.99

Thomas E. **Huggler**

The Camper's and Backpacker's Bible

An up-to-date guide to campcraft, trip planning, and equipment such as tents, cookware, and other gear now available for outdoor exploration

0-385-47194-7 BANTAM PB..........$12.95

Frank **Logue**
Knots for Hikers and Backpackers
Every kind of knot for the outdoors, with tips on using rope to ford streams, pitch an A-frame tarp shelter, and keep food away from bears
0-89732-146-4 MENRP PB........$4.95

Eric **Seaborg** & Ellen **Dudley**
Hiking and Backpacking
This is a collection of hiking tips from the PBS series *Trailside*. The handy volume contains information on everything from dealing with hypothermia to entertaining young hikers
0-87322-506-6 HUMAN KINETICS PB........$12.95

David Raines **Wallace**, editor
The Walker's Companion
A handbook that encourages the amateur naturalist to make the most of even a modest walk. This is a lavishly illustrated volume which contains information on everything from whale-watching to volcanoes
0-7835-4754-4 TIME BOOKS........$29.95

Canoeing, Rafting, and Kayaking

Michael P. **Ghiglieri**
Canyon
Professional river guide Ghiglieri describes a rafting trip covering 228 miles of the Grand Canyon, from Lee's Ferry to Diamond Creek. A great ride
0-8165-1286-8 ARIZONA PB........$15.95

Kim **Grumbo**
A River Runner's Guide to the History of the Grand Canyon
Grumbo has logged over 30,000 miles on the Colorado River, the water responsible for the creation of the Grand Canyon. Includes photos of the early river men, their boats, and their monuments
0-933472-61-7 JOHNSON........$9.95

Laurie **Guillion**
Canoeing
A complete sourcebook authored by an experienced canoe tour guide. Covers safety guidelines, equipment options, flexibility and strengthening exercises for the canoer, and much more
0-87322-443-4 HUMAN KINETICS PB........$12.95

Cecil **Kuhne**
Whitewater Rafting: An Introductory Guide
1-55821-317-1 LYONS & BURFORD PB........$16.95

Joel W. **Rogers**
The Hidden Coast: Kayak Explorations from Alaska to Mexico
From the Prince William Sound to Mexico's La Manzanilla, this is the ultimate guide for the Pacific coast sea kayaker. Extensively illustrated with color photos
See also **ROWING, CANOEING, AND KAYAKING** under **WATER SPORTS** under **SPORTS**
0-88240-403-2 ALASKA NORTHWEST PB........$19.95

To Read Around the Campfire

E.M. **Freeman**, editor
Campfire Chillers
Nine classic ghost stories to read aloud in the night-time woods, from *The Black Cat* to *The Monkey's Paw*
1-56440-475-7 GLOBE PEQUOT PB........$9.95

Michael **Hodgson**, editor
No Shit! There I Was: A Collection of Wild Stories from Wild People
A great volume to throw in your backpack when you're heading out to the trailhead. Chock-full of outrageous tales from the backcountry
0-934802-97-1 I.C.S. PB........$11.99

The Wilderness in Winter

Alan M. **Cvancara**
Exploring Nature in Winter: A Guide to Activities, Adventures, and Projects for the Winter Naturalist
Weather prediction, winter astronomy, snowshoeing, birding, botany, and survival are all subjects considered in this volume. Includes a chapter on the wonders of snow
0-8027-7385-0 WALKER PB........$17.95

Sally **Edwards** & Melissa **McKenzie**
Snowshoeing
The authors, avid snowshoers who founded a sport snowshoe manufacturing company, discuss fundamental techniques, safety guidelines, and a training plan to get fit for the sport. Also covered are 45 of the world's best snowshoeing destinations
0-87322-767-0 HUMAN KINETICS PB........$13.95

David **McClung** & Peter **Schaerer**
The Avalanche Book
A revised and thoroughly updated edition of the classic, first published by the U.S. Forest Service in 1976. Includes chapters on avalanche formation, prediction, terrain, motion, and effects, as well as the most up-to-date information available on safety and rescue
See also **SURVIVAL**
0-89886-364-3 MOUNTAINEERS PB........$19.95

Ernest **Wilkinson**
Snow Caves for Fun and Survival
Detailed instructions for building quick, comfortable, and safe snowcaves from an experienced Colorado guide. Also includes information on constructing igloos and lean-tos, and winter camp foods, clothing, tools, and safety
1-55566-095-9 JOHNSON PB........$9.95

Wilderness Cookery

Sierra **Adare**
Backcountry Cooking: Feasts for Hikers, Hoofers, and Floaters
Hearty recipes for the outdoor appetite, from breakfast biscuits and gravy to blue corn bread and chile rellenos. Complete grocery lists for several types of trip are included from rafting to trekking, with tips for pre-trip preparation and in-the-field cooking techniques
1-88660-902-0 UNKNOWN PB........$16.95

Claudia **Axcell** & others
Simple Foods for the Pack: The Sierra Club Guide to Delicious Natural Foods for the Trail
The revised edition of an outstanding food book for the hiker. Includes 180 trail-tested recipes, from Moroccan Couscous to Salmon in Tomato-Orange Sauce, plus tips on packing foods and suggestions on utensils and staple ingredients
0-87156-757-1 RANDOM HOUSE PB........$9.00

Valerie **Brunell** & Ralph **Swain**
Wilderness Ranger Cookbook: A Collection of Backcountry Recipes by U.S. Forest Service Wilderness Rangers
Dandelion Salad, Backcountry Scones, and even a Crab and Cheese Curry grace the pages of this handy book. Also included: the full text of the 1964 Wilderness Act, a map of the National Wilderness Preservation System, and more
1-56044-038-4 FALCON PB........$7.95

Don **Jacobson** & Don **Mauer**
The One-Pan Gourmet Cooks Light: A Low-Fat Guide to Outdoor Cooking
If s'mores and creamed chipped beef aren't on your training table, this is the book to consult before your next backpacking trip. 150 recipes include a light Chicken Moussaka, Goulash, and a combination of Pork, Pesto, Peppers, and Pasta
1-57034-033-1 I.C.S. PB........$11.95

Dorcas S. **Miller**
Good Food for Camp and Trail: All-Natural Recipes for Delicious Meals Outdoors
Tips on home dehydrating, cooking at altitude, and more, plus recipes for Mulligatawny Soup, Tortellini Stew, and homemade Biscuit Mix and more
0-87108-811-8 PRUETT PB........$14.95

Prater & Mendenhall
Gorp, Glop and Glue Stew
A wide variety of recipes for outdoor foods, from Papaya-Licorice Gorp to Mouse Soup, contributed by rock climbers, mountaineers, nature photographers, and other backcountry habitués. Includes information on the cooks as well as the comestibles.
0-89886-017-2 MOUNTAINEERS PB........$12.95

Sukey **Richard** & others, editors
Nols Cookery
Information on nutrition, menu planning, stoves and equipment, cooking over open fires, altitude, bears, and minimum impact camping from the National Outdoor Leadership School. Recipes include Apple Pie Cake, Potato Cheese Soup, Spicy Peanut Gado-Gado Sauce, and Empanadas
0-8117-3083-2 STACKPOLE PB........$8.95

Wilderness First Aid

Tod **Schimelpfenig** & Linda **Lindsey**

Nols Wilderness First Aid

0-8117-3084-0 NATOU PB $14.95

Buck **Tilton**

Backcountry First Aid and Extended Care: With a New Section of Advice to International Travelers

0-934802-99-8 I.C.S. PB $3.95

Buck **Tilton** & Frank **Hubbell**

Medicine for the Backcountry

An in-depth compendium on recognizing, treating, and most importantly preventing common wilderness accidents and injuries. Covers everything from respiratory problems to altitude sickness

1-57034-002-1 I.C.S. PB $12.99

Mountaineering

John **Bachar** & Steve **Boga**

Free Climbing With John Bachar

Free climbing is rock climbing in which technical equipment is used only as a backup measure for safety, not as an aid in the climb itself. Bachar, a renowned free-climber, here discusses the history, technique, practice, and ethics of the sport

0-8117-2517-0 STACKPOLE PB $10.95

John **Barry** & Nigel **Shepherd**

Rock Climbing

Covers basic techniques to expert skills, and includes 30 step-by-step diagrams and 70 color photos

0-8117-2231-7 STACKPOLE PB $18.95

Chris **Bonington**

The Climbers: A History of Mountaineering

From the Victorian pioneers Whymper and Mummery to Reinhold Messner, first man to climb all 14 of the world's 8000 meter peaks (soloing on one of them), Bonington examines the rich history of mountain climbing as sport. The companion book to the BBC series

0-563-20918-6 BBC $29.95

Greg **Child**

Mixed Emotions: Mountaineering Writings

An extremely personal examination of climbing's inherent exhiliration, as well as the tragedy it can engender, by a world-renowned mountaineer. "Child illuminates the shadowy heart of the mad pursuit that is climbing" —David Roberts

0-89886-363-5 MOUNTAINEERS PB $14.95

Stefan **Glowacs** & Uli **Wiesmeier**

Rocks Around the World

A chronicle of the world's ultimate free-climbing challenges, from Yosemite's Salath Wall to Australia's Mount Arapiles. Stunning color photos that could induce acrophobia in a Wallenda

0-87156-885-3 SIERRA CLUB PB $25.00

Andrew J. **Kaufman** & William L. **Putnam**

K2: The 1939 Tragedy

A thoroughly researched narrative examining the mysterious assault on K2 that became a legendary tragedy. "A 'must-read' for all Himalayophiles"—Dee Molanar, member 1953 K2 Expedition

0-89886-373-2 MOUNTAINEERS PB $18.95

Jon **Krakauer**

Eiger Dreams: Ventures Among Men and Mountains

Tales of journeys up Denali, Devil's Thumb, K2, and Everest. "Krakauer conveys well the formidable, even terrifying aspects of the sport....Likely to please not only the mountain maniacs but adventure-buffs in general" —*Kirkus Reviews*

1-55821-411-9 OAKNO PB $14.95

Michael **Laughman**

Learning to Rock Climb

A clearly written and illustrated guide to the sport, covering equipment, techniques, teminology, and ethics. "A new level of insight, comprehensiveness, and simplicity....brilliantly illustrated"—*American Alpine Journal*

0-87156-281-2 RANDOM HOUSE PB $14.00

John **Long**

Rock Jocks, Wall Rats, and Hang Dogs: Rock Climbing on the Edge of Reality

The legends of rock-climbing, as related by the sport's answer to Hunter S. Thompson. "Long is the genuine article"—*Outside* Magazine

0-671-88466-2 FIRESIDE PB $11.00

Jeff **Lowe**

Ice World: Techniques and Experiences of Modern Ice Climbing

Covered here are novice and advanced climbing techniques, an overview of the world's best climbs, expert advice on clothing and gear, a history of the sport, and much more. 250 chilling photos

0-89886-471-2 MOUNTAINEERS $39.95
0-89886-446-1 MOUNTAINEERS PB $29.95

Richard G. **Mitchell**, Jr.

Mountain Experience: The Psychology and Sociology of Adventure

0-226-53224-0 CHICAGO $18.00

Ed **Peters**, editor

Mountaineering: The Freedom of the Hills

This book, now in its fifth edition, has been the bible of the climbing set for three decades. Includes expanded chapters on recent developments in equipment and technique, a new chapter on winter and expedition climbing, and 350 new illustrations

0-89886-201-9 MOUNTAINEERS $32.00
0-89886-309-0 MOUNTAINEERS PB $22.95

Phil **Powers**

Nols Wilderness Mountaineering

Powers, a National Outdoor Leadership School guide, gives cogent advice here on avalanches, climbing movement, glacier travel, crevasse rescue, and more. "A superb, portable handbook of mountaineering basics"—*Climbing*

0-8117-3086-7 STACKPOLE PB $14.95

Steve **Roper** & Allen **Steck**

Fifty Classic Climbs of North America

From Lotus Flower Tower to Shiprock, these are North America's premiere climbs, chosen on the basis of striking presentation from afar, significant climbing history, and excellence of the climb itself. Includes maps, specifications, logistical information, and 180 photos

0-87156-884-5 SIERRA CLUB PB $25.00

John **Roskelley**

Stories Off the Wall

Roskelley, who has been called the leading American mountaineer of his generation, here chronicles his youth climbing in Spokane, Washington, his two decades in the Himalayas; and climbs in Yosemite, Russia, and more

0-89886-349-X MOUNTAINEERS $22.95

Neville **Shulman**

Zen in the Art of Climbing Mountains

Shulman, who had never before climbed, relied on the simple Zen philosophy outlined in this book during his ascent of Mont Blanc, Western Europe's highest and deadliest peak

0-8048-1775-8 TUTTLE PB $12.95

Joe **Simpson**

Touching the Void

At the top of a 21,000-foot Andean peak, a climber breaks his leg falling from an ice ledge, only to have his rope cut hours later by his partner as a last-ditch effort to prevent both their deaths. This is the tale of the grueling three days that followed, and how both men survived

0-06-091654-0 HARPERCOLLINS PB $12.00

Kevin **Walker**

Learn Rock Climbing in a Weekend

Forty eight hours is all it takes, according to this rigorously structured volume, to acquaint oneself thoroughly with the fundamentals of rock climbing. Includes sections on basic eduipment, safety, appropriate clothing, obstacles, rapelling, and the all-important "mountain code"

0-679-40951-3 KNOPF $16.00

Orienteering

June **Fleming**

Staying Found: The Complete Map & Compass Handbook

A simple, thorough guide to orienting oneself in the wilderness by the author of *The Well-Fed Backpacker*

0-89886-397-X MOUNTAINEERS PB $12.95

Don **Geary**

Using a Map and Compass

How to use a topographical map and a compass to bushwack into the real, trailless wilderness, without despoiling it

0-8117-2591-X STACKPOLE PB $14.95

Cliff **Jacobson**

The Basic Essentials of Map and Compass

0-934802-42-4 I.C.S. PB $5.99

Bob **Newman**

Land Navigation for Outdoor Enthusiasts

0-89732-178-2 MENRP PB $4.95

Survival

Bart **Blankenship** & Robin **Blankenship**

Earth Knack: Stone Age Skills for the 21st Century

0-87905-733-5 GIBBS SMITH PB $14.95

Gary **Brown**

The Great Bear Almanac

1-55821-210-8 LYONS & BURFORD $30.00
1-55821-474-7 LYONS & BURFORD PB $22.95

Safe Travel in Bear Country

1-55821-349-X LYONS & BURFORD PB $10.95

Tom **Brown**

Tom Brown's Field Guide to City and Suburban Survival

0-425-09172-4 BERKLEY PB $12.00

Tom **Brown** & others

Tom Brown's Field Guide to Nature and Survival for Children

0-425-11106-7 BERKLEY PB $12.00

Allan F. **MacFarlan**

Exploring the Outdoors With Indian Secrets

0-8117-2183-3 STACKPOLE PB $14.95

David **McClung** & Peter **Schaerer**

The Avalanche Book

A revised and thoroughly updated edition of the classic, first published by the U.S. Forest Service in 1976. Includes chapters on avalanche formation, prediction, terrain, motion, and effects, as well as the most up-to-date information available on safety and rescue

See also **THE WILDERNESS IN WINTER**

0-89886-364-3 MOUNTAINEERS PB $19.95

Len **McDougall**

Made for the Outdoors: Over 40 Do-It-Yourself Projects for the Great Outdoors

1-55821-329-5 LYONS & BURFORD PB $12.95

Hugh **McManners**

The Complete Wilderness Training Book

1-56458-488-7 DORLING KINDERSLEY $29.95

Raymond **Mears**

The Outdoor Survival Handbook

0-312-09359-4 ST. MARTIN'S PB $13.95

James **Wilkerson**, editor

Medicine For Mountaineering

0-89886-331-7 MOUNTAINEERS PB $18.95

John **Wiseman**

The SAS of Survival Handbook

Wiseman, who served for 26 years with the Special Air Service, an elite unit of the British Army, here outlines their complete survival course. Gives outstanding, often fascinating advice on everything from sizing up your survival chances in a variety of terrains to finding edible plants, surviving at sea, and even making a compass out of a razor blade and a piece of string

0-00-217185-6 HARPERCOLLINS PB $20.00

Bird Watching

Bird watching has become one of the largest outdoor sports in America, with an estimated eight million enthusiasts.

Jack **Connor**

Season at the Point: The Birds and Birders of Cape May

The birds and birders of Cape May evoked in a book filled with the mystery and excitement of the millions of migrating birds converging on their wintering grounds

0-87113-475-6 ATLANTIC MONTHLY PB $11.95

John **Farrand, Jr.**

Eastern Birds

Farrand's books are indispensable sources.

0-07-019976-0 MCGRAW HILL PB $17.95

How to Identify Birds

0-07-019975-2 MCGRAW HILL PB $17.95

Western Birds

0-07-019977-9 MCGRAW HILL $17.95

George **Harrison**

Backyard Bird Watcher

0-671-66374-7 SIMON & SCHUSTER PB $12.00

Konrad **Lorenz**

King Solomon's Ring

A seminal work by the founder of modern ethology

See also **ANIMAL BEHAVIOR** under **ANIMALS** under **NATURE STUDY** in **SCIENCE**

FOREWORD BY JULIAN HUXLEY

0-451-62831-4 NEW AMERICAN LIBRARY PB $3.99

Hunting

Hunting Essays

Sydney **Lea**

Hunting the Whole Way Home

Lea's tales and essays reveal the natural world in an intoxicating manner. Here is narrative on grouse and trout, fathers and sons, marriage and friendship

0-87451-689-7 NEW ENGLAND $24.95
0-87451-737-0 NEW ENGLAND PB $12.95

Michael **McIntosh**

Shotguns and Shooting: A Celebration of the Gun

The definitive volume on shotgun history, development, and the manner in which the finest guns are fabricated

0-924357-48-7 COUNTRYSPORT $30.00

James A. **Swan**

In Defense of Hunting

Environmental psychologist Swan explores the human impulse to hunt. "Whether or not you're a hunter, you won't have to read very far before you realize this is an important contribution to this highly controversial subject"
—Dick Murdoch, *Marin Independent Journal*

0-06-251237-4 HARPERCOLLINS PB $13.00

Guns

Chuck **O'Connor**

Big Game Rifle

1-57157-000-4 SAFAP $37.50

Birds

Bruce **Bowlen**

The Orvis Wing Shooting Handbook

0-941130-05-3 LYONS & BURFORD PB $10.95

Guy **de la Valdene**

For Handful of Feathers

"Beautifully conceived and written, valuable for its insights into quail behavior and its thoughtful address of hunting ethics, a new classic for the sportsman's canon"—*Kirkus Reviews*

0-87113-618-X ATLANTIC MONTHLY $18.00

Guy **De la Valdene**

Making Game: An Essay on Woodcock

A literate book about woodcock

0-944439-14-4 CLARK CITY $24.95

Chris **Dorsey**

The Grouse Hunter's Almanac

0-89658-135-7 VOYAGEUR $24.95
0-89658-261-2 VOYAGEUR PB $18.95

Charles **Fergus**

The Upland Equation: A Modern Bird Hunter's Code

This book-length essay offers a fresh, thoughtfully reasoned philosophy for the contemporary hunter. "Deserves space in every thoughtful sportsman's library"—Robert F. Jones, *Shooting Sportsman Magazine*

1-55821-363-5 LYONS & BURFORD $20.00

George Bird **Grinnell**

American Duck Shooting

0-8117-2427-1 STACKPOLE PB $19.95

Steve **Grooms**

Pheasant Hunter's Harvest

1-55821-089-X LYONS & BURFORD $22.95

Tom **Huggler**

Grouse of North America: A Cross-Continental Hunting Guide

1-55971-074-8 WILLOW CREEK $19.95

Burton **Spiller**

Drummer in the Woods

0-8117-2320-8 STACKPOLE PB $16.95

Dennis **Walrod**

Hunter's Guide: Solid Facts, Observations, and Insights on How to Hunt the Ruffed Grouse

0-8117-0772-5 STACKPOLE $18.95

Charles **Waterman**

Gun Dogs and Bird Guns: A Charley Waterman Reader

Thoughtful essays, not "how-to"

0-924357-52-5 COUNTRYSPORT $30.00

Frank **Woolner**

Timberdoodle: A Guide to Woodcock

0-941130-52-5 LYONS & BURFORD $18.95

Deer and Big Game

Bob **Brister**

Shotgunning: The Art and the Science

The best on the subject

0-8329-1840-7 NEW WIN $18.95

Peter **Capstick**

Safari–The Last Adventure: How You Can Share in It

0-312-69657-4 ST. MARTIN'S $19.95

George **Laycock**

The Deer Hunter's Bible

0-385-19985-6 DOUBLEDAY PB $12.00

Wesley **Murphey**

Blacktail Deer Hunting Adventures

0-9641320-4-4 LSTCR PB $12.95

Jack **Thomas** & Dale **Toweill**, editors

Elk of North America: Ecology and Management

0-8117-0571-4 STACKPOLE $49.95

Robert **Wegner**

Deer and Deer Hunting: The Serious Hunter's Guide Volume 1

0-8117-2585-5 STACKPOLE PB $18.95

Hunting Dogs and Falconry

Diana **Durman-Walters**

The Modern Falconer

The essential volume for those interested in falconry. Provides comprehensive information on raptor breeding, falconry schools, the pairing of birds with gundogs, and choosing the appropriate environment and quarry for your bird

1-85310-368-3 COUNTRYSPORT $35.00

Kenneth **Roebuck**

Gun-Dog Training: Pointing Dogs

0-8117-0778-4 STACKPOLE $16.95
0-8117-0714-8 STACKPOLE $16.95

Richard **Wolters**

Game Dog: The Hunter's Retriever

A columnist for *Gun Dog* magazine, Wolters is a leader in applying cutting edge animal behavior theory to dog training. "Wolters has produced a solid book that will be of great help to anyone training his retriever to work. He is an acknowledged master in the field and an excellent instructor"—*Dog Fancy*

0-525-93299-2 DUTTON $20.00

Gun Dog: Revolutionary Rapid Training Method

"One of the most valuable, probably THE most valuable, training tools the average amateur could have"—*Sports Afield*

0-525-24549-9 DUTTON $24.95

Water Dog

"Anyone who wants to try turning his dog into a well-mannered retriever will do well with *Water Dog*"—*NY Times*

0-525-24734-3 DUTTON $24.95
0-525-24430-1 DUTTON $20.00

Richard A. **Wolters**

Game Dog: The Hunter's Retriever for Upland Birds and Waterfowl: A Concise New Training Method

0-525-93942-3 DUTTON $24.95

Dressing Game

Teresa **Marrone**

Dressing and Cooking Wild Game

0-86573-020-2 DE COSSE $19.95

Fishing

Harold **Blaisdell**

The Philosophical Fisherman

0-941130-13-4 LYONS & BURFORD PB $12.95

Muriel **Foster**

Muriel Foster's Fishing Diary

This charming facsimile of an extraordinary fisherwoman's diary brings a sought-after collector's book to a general audience. From her first 1913 entry at Little Loch Broom in Scotland and through her 35-year log of fishing, lures, birds, dogs, and descriptions, this beautifully illustrated diary is a must for any angler

0-670-86868-X STUDIO $34.95

John **Gierach**

Another Lousy Day in Paradise

0-684-82424-8 SIMON & SCHUSTER $22.00

Trout Bum

"A brilliant collection of narrative essays about flies, fly rods, float tubes, and just plain fishing"—*Rod & Reel*

0-671-64413-0 FIRESIDE PB $11.00

John Inglis **Hall**

Fishing a Highland Stream

This is the finest kind of memoir: the enchanting portrait of a place of remote beauty—"a bard little burn" of a river, and the lonely, crafted pleasure of fishing it. Born in 1910, Half has been a fisherman since the age of four, and he's been casting a fly into the Truim for almost as long

1-55821-287-6 LYONS & BURFORD $19.95

Nick **Lyons**, editor

The Little Book of Fishing

INTRODUCTION BY NICK LYONS

0-87113-568-X GROVE $16.00

Odell **Shepard**

Thy Rod and Thy Reel

0-8329-0364-7 WINCHESTER PB $12.95

Izaak **Walton**

The Compleat Angler

Walton's treatise on fishing is one of the most treasured books in English

See also **PROSE** under **THE EARLY 17TH CENTURY** in **LITERATURE OF THE BRITISH ISLES**

0-88001-406-7 ECCO $23.00

Trout, Fly-fishing, and Fly-tying

Sheridan **Anderson**

Curtis Creek Manifesto

A charmingly illustrated comic book with useful information on everything from the life cycle of the mayfly to tips on splinting broken rods

0-936608-06-4 VIRGINIA PB $7.95

Rick **Bass**

Platte River

Haunting novellas set in remote Montana by "the best young writer to come along in many years"—Annie Dillard. "Three fascinating long stories from the greatly gifted avatar of the

outdoors....Beautifully written and filled with radiant imagery and a powerful sense of the mysteries of nature—human and otherwise"—*Kirkus Reviews.* "Finely detailed, complex characters, simple men and women crafted with sympathy and understanding"
—*Publishers Weekly*

See also **SINCE 1945** under **20TH-CENTURY AMERICAN FICTION** in **LITERATURE OF THE AMERICAS**

0-395-68080-8 HOUGHTON MIFFLIN $19.95

Cathy **Beck**

Cathy Beck's Fly-Fishing Handbook

Beck brings her popular fishing wisdom to a clearly written, practical, and utterly engaging volume that covers all the basic elements of the sport: tackle, clothing, accessories, techniques, spirit, and ethics. With a particular emphasis on the fastest-growing segment of the fly-fishing world—women—this is a key guide to the popular sport

ILLUSTRATED BY ROD WALINCHUS

1-55821-471-2 LYONS & BURFORD PB $20.00
1-55821-340-6 LYONS & BURFORD PB $24.95

Terry **Brykczynski** & David **Reuther**

The Armchair Angler

Roy Blount Jr., Nick Lyons, Ernest Hemingway, Zane Grey, Thomas McGuane—these are just a few of the writers who address, in this single volume, that compelling subject, the elusive trout. "An anthology that all who love angling in print will cherish, and a perfect gift for the angler in your life"—*Philadelphia Inquirer*

0-02-017801-8 BUDGET BOOK PB $15.00

Silvio **Calabi**

The Illustrated Encyclopedia of Fly-Fishing: A Complete A-Z of Terminology, Tackle and Techniques

An A-Z compendium of fly-fishing tackle, vocabulary, and technique. "The most richly informative book on fly-fishing ever published"—*The Bookwatch*

0-8050-3809-4 HOLT PB $19.95

David M. **Carroll**

Trout Reflections: A Natural History of the Trout and Its World

A lyrical and expert account of the parallel seasons of the trout and its fishermen, enlivened with watercolors and line drawings. Naturalist and angler Carroll eloquently sings the praises of the sport and its quarry, with plenty of serious attention to the natural rhythms and beauties of the angler's surroundings. A must for the serious fisherman

0-312-09464-7 ST. MARTIN'S $18.95
0-312-14142-4 ST. MARTIN'S PB $11.95

Michael **Checchio**

A Clean, Well-Lighted Stream

A collection of essays previously published in *Gray's Sporting Journal*, *San Francisco Focus*, and *California Fly Fisher*, among other journals. This volume chronicles Checchio's fishing adventures from Zane Grey's creek to Mendocino

1-56947-045-6 SOHO $23.00

F-Stop **Fitzgerald**

Fly-Fishing Logbook

This beautiful and useful logbook has entry places for location, water, weather conditions, flies, equipment, fish, and more. Accompanied by Fitzgerald's celebrated photographs

0-8212-2163-9 BULFINCH $14.95

Paul N. **Fling** & Donald L. **Puterbaugh**

Fly-Fisherman's Primer

A valuable guide for the beginning fly-fisher, answering such questions as whether or not to snap your wrist when casting and whether chest or hip waders will prove the better choice on your first fishing trip

0-8069-7890-2 STERLING PB $12.95

John **Gierach**

Dances With Trout

Vintage Gierach essays on fishing and hunting adventures around the world. "These well-crafted gems sparkle"—*Kirkus Reviews*

0-671-77920-6 FIRESIDE PB $11.00

Sex, Death, and Fly-Fishing

An engaging look at the sweet mystery of life. "If Mark Twain were alive and a modern-day fisherman, he still would be hard put to top John Gierach"—*Sports Illustrated*

0-671-68437-X FIRESIDE PB $11.00

Where the Trout Are All As Long As Your Leg

New York Times columnist Gierach, "the bohemian equivalent of a country gentleman," takes readers on a tour of secret Montana pools and rattlesnake-riddled brooks in the search for trout and the meaning of life

0-671-75455-6 FIRESIDE PB $9.00

The View from Rat Lake

"Gierach writes with more knowledge and more humour about all the joys, vicissitudes, horrors, and hallelujahs of pursuing fish than almost anyone else laboring the craft today"
—John Nichols

0-671-67581-8 FIRESIDE PB $11.00

Terry **Heffernan**, editor

Fly Fishing Tales: Literary Bait by Angling Authors

Connoisseurs of trout literature will thrill to these eight classic stories of big-game fly fishing. Among the famous anglers who contribute: Thomas McGuane, Ernest Hemingway, Zane Grey, and "master word handler" Robert Traver, author of *Anatomy of a Murder.* With paintings by Winslow Homer and 18 still-life photographs of the gear of such famous fly-casters as Herbert Hoover and Bing Crosby, this handsome volume makes an excellent Father's Day gift

INTRODUCTION BY JOHN RANDOLPH

0-670-85343-7 STUDIO $14.95

John **Holt**

Chasing Fish Tales: A Freewheeling Year in the Life of an Angler

Holt's wonderful year of fishing from Montana to Morocco is enough to make any angler weak with envy. A passionate account

0-924357-36-3 COUNTRYSPORT $35.00

Dave **Hughes**

Wet Flies: Tying and Fishing Soft-Hackles, Winged and Wingless Wets, and Fuzzy Nymphs

Essential information on tying and fishing

0-8117-1868-9 STACKPOLE $32.95

David **Hughes**

Fly Fishing Basics

An illustrated volume that provides a thorough grounding in technique for the neophyte

0-8117-2439-5 STACKPOLE PB $12.95

Charles **Jardine**

The Classic Guide to Fly-Fishing for Trout/The Fly-Fishers Book of Quarry, Tackle, and Techniques

A comprehensive volume offering valuable information on trout, tackle, and techniques. Photos of more than 600 flies and step-by-step instructions for tying each of them

0-394-58719-7 RANDOM HOUSE $40.00

Ted **Leeson**

The Habit of Rivers: Reflections on Trout Streams and Fly Fishing

A moving account of Leeson's years fishing for trout and steelhead in the Northwest. "Leeson's work belongs on the shelf next to that of Annie Dillard, Barry Lopez, and others of their stripe (and speckle)"—*Publishers Weekly*

1-55821-300-7 LYONS & BURFORD $22.95
0-14-024260-0 PENGUIN PB $10.95

Nick **Lyons**

A Flyfisher's World

0-87113-628-7 ATLANTIC MONTHLY $23.00

Spring Creek

This richly humorous and perceptive account of the angler's passion explores the secrets and challenges of one of the continent's best trout rivers. "Spring Creek shows what fishing writing can be. Nick Lyons has written a genuinely literate and deeply felt book"
—Thomas McGuane

See also **ESSAYS, MEDITATIONS, AND CLASSICS** under **NATURE STUDY** in **SCIENCE**

0-87113-612-0 GROVE PB $11.00

Nick Lyons

Grant **McClintock** & Mike **Crockett**

Flywater

Knockout photos of fish, fishing men and fishing women, and some of the most incredible stretches of water in America

1-55821-339-2 LYONS & BURFORD $39.95

Tom **McNally**

The Complete Book of Fly Fishing

Tips on fishing for everything from trout to sailfish with flies. "To say that any single book about a subject so diverse as fly fishing is 'complete' is tall talk, but this one delivers" —*Flyfisher*

0-87742-345-8 TAB $29.95

John **Merwin**

The New American Trout Fishing

A new bible for America's ten million trout fishermen and women, with advice on where to find good fishing and how to develop sound fishing instincts and technique. Includes plenty of patterns for fly-tying, useful knots, and information on the latest in both technology and equipment. From the former editor of *Fly Fisherman*

0-02-584382-6 MACMILLAN $30.00

John **Merwin**, editor

Well-Cast Lines: The Fisherman's Quotation Book

Quoting everyone from Cervantes to Annie Dillard, Merwin has proved once again that "some of the best fishing is not done in water but in print"

0-684-81151-0 FIRESIDE PB $10.00

Steven **Meyers**

San Juan River Chronicle: Personal Remembrances of One of America's Best-Known Trout Streams

A loving and lovely chronicle of fishing one of America's premier trout streams. In quiet prose Meyers, a celebrated fly-fishing guide, captures the willow-lined channels, rising trout, the setting of sandstone canyons and sage, and the colorful and varied people who gather to pay homage to the fine and delicate art of angling. Sure to stand out among classics of fly fishing

1-55821-277-9 LYONS & BURFORD $19.95

Harry **Middleton**

The Earth Is Enough: Growing Up in a World of Fly Fishing, Trout, & Old Men

In 1965, a tragic loss leads 12-year-old Harry to the Ozarks. "This is a grand true story and its wonderful old men are classic American characters"—Annie Dillard

0-87108-874-6 PRUETT PB $18.00

Shaun **Morey**

Incredible Fishing Stories

Much more than the one that got away—from the rattlesnake who jumped aboard to the fisherman whose thumb turned up in a Mackinaw trout's belly

1-56305-637-2 WORKMAN PB $8.95

Holly **Morris**, editor

A Different Angle: Fly Fishing Stories by Women

This anthology includes fresh prose by E. Annie Proulx, Pam Houston, Lorian Hemingway, Joan Wulff, Margot Page, and others; spans fishing from New York's Battenkill to Outer Mongolia

See also **ANTHOLOGIES OF WOMEN'S WRITING** under **WOMEN'S STUDIES** in **SOCIAL STUDIES**

1-87806-763-X SEAL $22.95
0-425-15134-4 BERKELEY PB $12.00

Holly Morris

Uncommon Waters: Women Write About Fishing

Over 18 million women fish in the United States. In this anthology, 34 women anglers share their meditative moments and bracing adventures in essays, stories and poems. "A book of beauty, vision and depth"—*Fly Fisherman*

1-87806-710-9 SEAL PB $14.95

I often think of fishing when I'm writing. You put out a little bait and wait. Sometimes you get a nibble, sometimes nothing. You stare at the still blank piece of paper, like the smooth unruffled surface of water, waiting for some sign of life, some inspiration....If you're patient and lucky, words may start to surface. Sometimes they're keepers; often they're not.—*Joan Ackermann*
UNCOMMON WATERS: WOMEN WRITE ABOUT FISHING

Jennifer **Olsson**

Cast Again: Tales of a Fly-Fishing Guide

Drawing on her long experience as a licensed Montana and Yellowstone Park fishing guide, Olsson offers a collection of hilarious and colorful tales. Together they make up the story of a woman's life built around the ethics, beauty, and rhythm of fly fishing, and a deeply insightful reflection on the sport

1-55821-442-9 LYONS & BURFORD $19.95

Margot **Page**

Little Rivers: Tales of a Woman Angler

Twelve essays tell the tale of a woman's coming into her own as an angler and more. Handsomely illustrated

1-55821-367-8 LYONS & BURFORD $16.95
0-380-72650-5 AVON PB $9.00

James **Prosek**

Trout: An Illustrated History

This prodigious celebration of the mysterious and beautiful trout captures, in over 70 original watercolors, varieties from the Apache to the rainbow, redband, golden, cutthroat, and other species and subspecies, of which some are already extinct. Passionate and accurate, this must-have for the serious angler is by a 20-year-old undergraduate at Yale who is already considered "a fair bid to become the Audubon of the fishing world"—*NY Times*

See also **AQUATIC LIFE** under **ANIMALS** under **NATURE STUDY** in **SCIENCE**

0-679-44453-X KNOPF $27.50

Howell **Raines**

Fly Fishing Through the Midlife Crisis

0-385-47519-5 ANCHOR PB $12.95

Steve **Raymond**

The Year of the Trout

The sequel to Raymond's acclaimed *Year of the Angler*. "The blend of personal experience, philosophy, advice, and history make this a book that will be cherished by those who seek the elusive trout"—*American Field*

1-57061-022-3 SASQUATCH PB $12.95

Ken **Reinard**

The Colonial Angler's Manual of Flyfishing & Flytying

The story of how a mild-mannered fisherman became Historic Williamsburgh's "Colonial Angler." Packed with information the author has gathered on how people fished in 18th-Century America

1-56523-039-6 FOX CHAPEL PB $19.95

John **Roberts**

Collins Illustrated Dictionary of Trout Flies

From the Loop-wing Dun to the Treacle Parkin, this guide covers over 1000 dressings and their variations. 32 color plates

0-00-218491-5 HARPERCOLLINS $29.00

Anthony J. **Route**

Flyfishing Alaska

Route, Alaska's premiere fly-fishing writer, has worked as a fisheries technician, guide, sport-fishing consultant, and commercial fly-tier. He also teaches fly-fishing at the University of Alaska

1-55566-150-5 JOHNSON PB $17.95

Paul **Schullery**

American Fly-Fishing

0-941130-32-0 LYONS & BURFORD $40.00

Richard **Talleur**

Mastering the Art of Fly-Tying

0-8117-0907-8 STACKPOLE $34.95

Zack **Taylor**, editor

Fly Fishing With MacQuarrie

MacQuarrie, known as "the Bard of the Brule," is a little known marvel in angling literature. His timeless stories of trout fishing in Ireland are gathered together here for the first time

1-57223-025-8 WILLOW CREEK $19.50

Rod **Walinchus**

Fly Fishing the North Platte River: An Angler's Guide

Covers the 150 miles of river from its entrance to Wyoming to the town of Casper. Includes special fishing techniques and tackle requirements, as well as some North Platte fly patterns

0-87108-834-7 PRUETT PB $18.50

Rod **Walinchus** & Tom **Travis**

Fly Fishing the Yellowstone River: An Angler's Guide

An indispensable volume by two of Montana's top fishing guides. Includes hatch charts, recommended fly patterns, access information, and many maps, photos, and drawings

0-87108-861-4 PRUETT PB $25.00

Philip **White**

Trout: Fly Fishing, Fly Tying

0-8478-1868-3 RIZZOLI $35.00

Joan **Wulff**

Joan Wulff's Fly-Casting Techniques

0-941130-38-X LYONS & BURFORD PB $29.95

Joan Salvato **Wulff**

Joan Wulff's Fly Fishing: Expert Advice from a Woman's Perspective

Valuable information for anglers of all ability levels from the doyenne of the sport. "Joan Wulff is the Margot Fonteyn of fly fishing" —Judy Muller, ABC News

0-8117-1654-6 STACKPOLE $19.95

Bait, Bottom, and Saltwater Fishing

Dan **Aadland**

Treading Lightly With Pack Animals: A Guide to Low-Impact Travel in the Backcountry

Here's how to enlist the help of a pack animal, be it a llama, dog, horse, or goat, without creating environmental havoc in the fragile wilderness

0-87842-297-8 MOUNTAIN PB $15.00

Erwin **Bauer**

The Bass Fisherman's Bible

0-385-24690-0 DOUBLEDAY PB $12.00

Saltwater Fisherman's Bible

0-385-26444-5 DOUBLEDAY PB $12.95

Steven A. **Griffin**

The Fishing Sourcebook: Your One-Stop Resource for Everything to Feed Your Fishing Habit

A one-stop compendium for the angler, with information on everything from fishing videos to fishing clubs, as well as the correct way to relate a fishing story

1-56440-752-7 GLOBE PEQUOT PB $18.95

John **Hersey**

Blues

"*Blues* is, of course, about much more than the pleasures and techniques of fishing; it is…about interconnections—the ties between mankind and the natural world, among others" *New Yorker*

0-394-55960-6 KNOPF $16.95

0-394-75702-5 RANDOM HOUSE PB $12.00

Henry **Lyman**

Bluefishing

0-941130-58-4 LYONS & BURFORD PB $10.95

Steven D. **Price**

The Ultimate Fishing Guide

Indispensable information for the angler on a multitude of subjects, from catch limits to clothing. For fresh and saltwater, bait and fly-fishing enthusiasts

0-06-273290-0 HARPERPERENNIAL PB $20.00

Herbert A. **Schaffner**

Freshwater Game Fish of North America

A catalog of America's most sought-after fish, from bass to whitefish. Includes information on eating habits, and hiding spots, as well as the most effective tackle, bait, and lures for each type

1-56799-153-X FRIEDMAN/FAIRFAX PB $14.95

Tim **Smith** & Mark **Herrick**

Buck Wilder's Small Fry Fishing Guide: A Complete Introduction to the World of Fishing for Small Fry

A full-color comic-book-style guide for all ages that provides tips on catching everything from the muskellunge to the smelt

0-9643793-0-9 ALEXANDER & SMITH PB $12.95

Gardening

It is possible to be a very good gardener without opening a single book, but most lovers of plants and trees always want to know more. Appreciation of classic works on cultivation, design, and the history of gardens is increasing, and many titles can be enjoyed apart from their value as practical guides.

Starting Out

Some novice gardeners do not know quite where to begin. Confronted with an old, overgrown yard or a bald, rough-graded site around a new house, they often tend to do either too much or too little. The following titles provide practical help in a cheerful, competent way.

John **Brookes**

The Garden Book

A complete guide to creating gardens by a leading English garden designer

0-517-58948-6 CROWN PB $24.00

Hugh **Johnson**

Principles of Gardening

0-684-83524-X SIMON & SCHUSTER $40.00

Rita **Buchanan** & Roger **Holmes**

Taylor's Master Guide to Gardening

"A masterwork…infused with a love of gardening…A book as comprehensive, as easy to use, and as beautiful as this doesn't come along often"—*Fine Gardening*

0-395-64995-1 HOUGHTON MIFFLIN $60.00

Cheryl **Merser**

A Starter Garden: The Guide For the Horticulturally Hapless

Helpful, literate, and enjoyable, this empathetic guide takes the first time gardener from square one to a finished, beautiful garden—without breaking the bank. From tools and basic skills to the best starter plants, this is the first garden book for the horticulturally inexperienced—or hopeful

0-06-096933-4 HARPERPERENNIAL PB $14.00

Marina **Schinz** & Gabrielle **van Zuylen**

Start a Garden

0-8118-0561-1 CHRONICLE PB $9.95

Martha **Stewart**

Martha Stewart's Gardening: Month by Month

A practical and comprehensive yearly planning guide for amateur gardeners at every level of expertise. Illustrated with color photos of Stewart at work in her own Connecticut garden, the book outlines how and when to order and buy supplies, prepare and care for tools, germinate seeds, and countless other steps towards perfecting nature

PHOTOGRAPHS BY ELIZABETH ZESCHIN

0-517-57413-6 CLARKSON POTTER $50.00

Roy **Strong**

Successful Small Gardens

Innovative ideas and pithy advice characterize this handbook for small and manageable areas, from backyards to vegetable and water gardens

0-8478-1839-X RIZZOLI $29.95

Practical Matters for Gardeners

Ann **Bonar**

Fragrance

How to arrange scented plants in order to create maximum aromatic impact throughout the year

1-55859-553-8 ABBEVILLE $9.95

Lauren **Brown**

Grasses: An Identification Guide

0-395-62881-4 HOUGHTON MIFFLIN PB $11.95

Nancy **Bubel**

The New Seed-Starters Handbook

An encyclopedia of more than 200 plants to grow from seeds with details on planting and care

0-87857-752-1 RODALE PB $15.95

Lewis **Hill**

Cold-Climate Gardening: How to Extend Your Growing Season by At Least 30 Days

0-88266-441-7 GARDEN WAY PB $14.95

Lewis **Hill**

Pruning Simplified

0-88266-417-4 GARDEN WAY PB $14.95

Secrets of Plant Propagation: Starting Your Own Flowers, Vegetables, Fruits, Berries, Shrubs, Trees, and Houseplants

See also VEGETABLES AND FRUIT

0-88266-370-4 GARDEN WAY PB $14.95

Ann **Lovejoy**

The Year in Bloom: Gardening For All Seasons in the Pacific Northwest

An enthusiastic and practical approach to gardening

0-912365-11-0 SASQUATCH PB $11.95

Mimi **Luebbermann**

Climbing Vines: Simple Secrets For Glorious Gardens—Indoors and Out

This simple guide covers all variety of wall or fence-covering vines

0-8118-0723-1 CHRONICLE PB $12.95

Harriet **Morse**

Gardening in the Shade

The revision of a standard work, with gardens in all degrees of shade: light, half, and full

0-917304-16-0 INTL SPECIALIZED PB $13.95

Reader's Digest

Reader's Digest Guide to Creative Gardening

0-276-35223-8 READER'S DIGEST $32.00

The Royal Horticultural Society

The Royal Horticultural Society Plant and Record Book

In a convenient month-by-month format, this notebook is the perfect way for gardeners to keep track of their spade work. Divided into seven different plant categories with room to record suppliers' addresses, this useful text discusses different types of gardens and suggests helpful color schemes

0-517-59402-1 RANDOM HOUSE $18.00

Diana **Saville**

Color

Suggestions for planting with color in mind in the garden, both in and out of season. Ideas adaptable to a variety of needs and tastes

1-55859-551-1 ABBEVILLE $9.95

George **Schenk**

The Complete Shade Gardener

A fine nurseryman shows how to make the most of limited sunlight

0-395-35397-1 HOUGHTON MIFFLIN $24.95
0-395-57426-9 HOUGHTON MIFFLIN PB $19.95

Solomon M. **Skolnick**

The Home Gardener's Source

The source for any home gardener—an indispensable, information-packed volume listing how and where to order *everything*

0-679-75477-6 RANDOM HOUSE PB $17.00

Patricia **Thorpe**

Growing Pains: Remaking Your Older Garden

Learn how to deal with overplanting, discover the drawbacks of perennials, and consider the ecological questions that even experienced gardeners must face. This is the book for the already-established garden and gardener, the one that will aid you in reassessment and help you finally to achieve the garden you have been working toward all along

0-15-176652-5 HARCOURT BRACE $22.95

Growing Pains: Time and Change in the Garden

"All gardens," says Thorpe, "need serious reassessment and replanting every seven to ten years." Midlife advice for the garden, from the expert

0-15-600201-9 HARVEST PB $14.00

Reference

John I. **Alber** & Delores M. **Alber**

Baby-Safe Houseplants & Cut Flowers

This acclaimed, scrupulously researched guide "may be one of the best gifts you can give to new parents"—*The Oakland Press*. Includes information on how to find safe and attractive plants, plants to avoid, and steps to take if a child eats a poisonous plant

0-88266-869-2 GARDEN WAY PB $12.95

Liberty **Bailey**

Hortus Third: A Concise Dictionary of Plants Cultivated in the United States and Canada

A comprehensive 4000-page compendium of American gardening with thousands of entries and the last word in nomenclature and spelling

0-02-505470-8 MACMILLAN $150.00

Christopher **Brickell**, editor

American Horticultural Society Encyclopedia of Garden Plants

0-02-557920-7 MACMILLAN $59.95

Christopher **Brickell** & others

The American Horticultural Society Encyclopedia of Gardening

Containing more than 3,000 specially commissioned full-color photographs and illustrations and accompanied by 500 step-by-step photographic series of basic and advanced gardening techniques, this definitive guide contains all the practical advice every amateur or professional needs to make a garden flourish. Includes tips on growing fruits and vegetables as well as tending a lawn

1-56458-291-4 DORLING KINDERSLEY $59.95

John **Brookes**

The Book of Garden Design

A reference bible for gardeners, this massive volume outlines the mechanics of garden design "from the ground up." More than 500 photographs and illustrations demonstrate each step, from site evaluation to employment of color, texture, and specific plants. Includes hundreds of case studies from Europe and the Americas

See also LANDSCAPE AND GARDEN DESIGN

0-02-516695-6 MACMILLAN $45.00

Basil **Caplan**

The Complete Manual of Organic Gardening

This encyclopedic guide covers all aspects of natural gardening methods: cultivation without artificial fertilizers or pesticides, how to improve soil content and make compost, combating plant diseases and destructive insects. Now you can have hearty fruits, vegetables, and herbs without chemicals

See also ORGANIC GARDENING AND COMPOSTING

1-55859-644-5 ABBEVILLE $49.95

Ruth Rogers **Clausen** & Nicolas H. **Ekstrom**

Perennials For American Gardens

More than 3000 species are included in this comprehensive, stunningly illustrated reference

0-394-55740-9 RANDOM HOUSE $50.00

Alan **Coombes**

Dictionary of Plant Names

A useful and surprisingly entertaining garden reference book from a noted botanist

0-88192-023-1 TIMBER PB $10.95

Gordon **Courtright**

Trees and Shrubs For Temperate Climates

The standard reference for landscape plants in temperate zones. Includes hundreds of plants readily available in retail nurseries, with information on their requirements and growth; 800 color photographs

See also TREES AND SHRUBS under SPECIFIC PLANTS

0-88192-097-5 TIMBER $49.95

Tanya **Denckla**

The Organic Gardener's Home Reference: A Plant-By-Plant Guide to Growing Fresh, Healthy Food

0-88266-840-4 STOREY $29.95
0-88266-839-0 STOREY PB $19.95

Ken **Druse**

New York City Gardener

It *is* possible to be an urban gardener. And this guide provides all the information—from how to handle peat moss, to where to buy bulbs

1-88549-227-8 RC PB $15.00

Patrick **Goode** & Michael **Lancaster**, editors

The Oxford Companion to Gardens

A highly accurate and entertaining reference book covering the history and design of gardens all over the world

0-19-866123-1 OXFORD $55.00

Alfred Byrd **Graf**

Hortica: A Color Cyclopedia of Garden Flora in All Climates and Indoor Plants

This is the third in Dr. Graf's series of pictorial encyclopedias; it contains 8,000 photos and describes over 10,000 plants and trees, including their native habitats and climactic preferences. The most comprehensive work of its kind

See also **ART BOOKS**

0-02-544995-8 ROEHRS $250.00

The National Gardening Association

Dictionary of Horticulture

By the same publisher as *National Gardening* magazine, this is the first dictionary to explain every gardening term. With 18,000 entries and 5,000 cross-references, arranged alphabetically, and compiled by experts on everything from dirt and cover tools to insects and chemicals, this is an unendingly useful 796-page tool

0-670-84992-8 VIKING $29.95

Roger **Phillips** & Martin **Rix**

The Random House Book of Perennials

Volume One

Early Perennials

An exhaustive guide to the ultimate flowers for the busy gardener. These two magnificent volumes, organized by seasonal flowering periods, feature information on selection, planting, and cultivation of some 5,000 flowering plants from around the world. The two books include over 3,000 full-color photographs

0-679-73797-9 RANDOM HOUSE PB $27.50

Volume Two

Late Perennials

An exhaustive guide to the ultimate flowers for the busy gardener. These two magnificent volumes, organized by seasonal flowering periods, feature information on selection, planting, and cultivation of some 5,000 flowering plants from around the world. The two books include over 3,000 full-color photographs

0-679-73798-7 RANDOM HOUSE PB $27.50

Alec **Pridgeon**, editor

The Illustrated Encyclopedia of Orchids

See also **FLOWERING PLANTS** under **SPECIFIC PLANTS**

0-88192-267-6 TIMBER $39.95

Mary Helen **Ray** & Robert P. **Nicholls**, editors

The Traveler's Guide to American Gardens

More than 1000 varied public gardens, organized by location

0-8078-1787-2 NORTH CAROLINA $22.50

Reader's Digest

Reader's Digest Illustrated Guide to Gardening

0-89577-829-7 READER'S DIGEST $30.00

William T **Stearn**

Botanical Latin: History, Grammar, Syntax, Terminology and Vocabulary

0-88192-321-4 TIMBER $39.95

Donald **Wyman**, editor

Taylor's Guide to Houseplants

0-395-43091-7 HOUGHTON MIFFLIN PB $19.95

Patrick **Synge**, editor

Dictionary of Gardening

This four-volume work plus supplement is easy to use as all cultivars are listed alphabetically. Excellent drawings throughout

0-19-869116-5 OXFORD $74.00

Donald **Wyman**

Wyman's Gardening Encyclopedia

A new edition of the classic reference book. An excellent, well-organized one-volume work

0-02-632070-3 MACMILLAN $65.00

Landscape and Garden Design

For related reading, see LANDSCAPE ARCHITECTURE AND GARDEN DESIGN in ARCHITECTURE, DESIGN, AND HOMES

Elisabeth **Arter**

Cottage Garden

How to use the many possibilities of the old-fashioned "cottage" garden in contemporary settings

1-55859-547-3 ABBEVILLE $9.95

Adrian **Bloom**

Winter Garden Glory: How to Get the Best from Your Garden from Autumn Through to Spring

0-00-412892-3 HARPERCOLLINS $25.00

Jean **Breskind**

Backyard Design: Making the Most of the Space Around Your House

A fresh, comprehensive look at how to design the perfect American backyard, with instructions for hundreds of projects

0-8212-1776-3 BULFINCH $29.95

John **Brookes**

The Book of Garden Design

A reference bible for gardeners, this massive volume outlines the mechanics of garden design "from the ground up." More than 500 photographs and illustrations demonstrate each step, from site evaluation to employment of color, texture, and specific plants. Includes hundreds of case studies from Europe and the Americas

See also **REFERENCE**

0-02-516695-6 MACMILLAN $45.00

The Country Gardenbook

The most recent and beautifully illustrated British book on elegant but low-maintenance landscaping

0-517-56704-0 CROWN $40.00

Emily **Brown**

Landscaping with Perennials

0-88192-063-0 TIMBER $39.95

Guy **Cooper** & Gordon **Taylor**

English Herb Gardens

See also **ENGLISH GARDENS** under **GARDEN HISTORY**

See also **HERBS** under **VEGETABLES AND FRUIT**

0-8478-0689-8 RIZZOLI $27.50

Cassandra **Danz**

Mrs. Greenthumbs: How I Turned a Boring Yard Into a Glorious Garden and How You Can Too

From the host of her own gardening radio program comes a book on how to bring beauty to a garden even with limited time and resources. Proceeding on a month-by-month basis, she covers everything front pruning to fall clean-up and replanting, with time-saving tips, occasional philosophy, even some insight into botany's erotic aspects

See also **CONTEMPORARY AMERICAN WRITERS** under **ESSAYS, MEMOIRS, AND REFLECTIONS**

0-517-88010-5 CROWN PB $12.00

Chet **Davis**

Cutting Gardens

0-671-85043-1 MACMILLAN PB $9.00

Michael **Dirr**

Manual of Woody Landscape Plants

0-87563-347-1 STIPES $45.80

0-87563-344-7 STIPES PB $35.80

Photographic Manual For Woody Landscape Plants

See also **ART BOOKS**

0-87563-156-8 STIPES PB $26.00

Robert **Ditchfield**

Arches and Pergolas

Since most gardens bloom at knee-level, Ditchfield shows how to add a "higher dimension" to a garden with climbing plants, arches, and pergolas

1-55859-550-3 ABBEVILLE $9.95

William **Douglas**

Garden Design: History, Principles, Elements, Practice

Beautifully photographed tours of the best work of contemporary designers, along with a thorough treatment of garden design basics

0-8317-5157-6 SMITHMARK $19.98

Ken **Druse**

The Collector's Garden: Designing with Extraordinary Plants

Three-time Quill and Trowel Award winner Ken Druse's natural gardening secrets have garnered a faithful readership worldwide. Here, a lushly illustrated volume introduces us to 21 people and their gardens, all revolving around the design possibilities of extraordinary plants. Includes a source guide for locating hard-to-find items

0-517-79983-9 CLARKSON POTTER $45.00

Brent **Elliot**

The Country House Garden: From the Archives of Country Life: 1897-1939

1-85732-697-0 ANTIQUE COLLECTORS $60.00

Barbara **Gallup** & Deborah **Reich**

The Complete Book of Topiary

From modest windowsill projects to tree tunnels; a lively book by the American topiary specialist

0-89480-318-2 WORKMAN PB $12.95

Melanie **Fleischmann**

American Border Gardens

Border gardens are the most common American garden, but until now no one book focused on them. Here are 18 border gardens that go well beyond the old standard mix of lawn-edging perennials. Showing numerous ways to group perennials, bulbs, annuals, and grasses, this distinguished volume includes tips on soil testing and preparation, planting, transplanting, and color combining. 125 color photos

See also **ART BOOKS**

0-517-57646-5 CLARKSON POTTER $30.00

Ann **Halpin** & Betty **MacKey**

Cutting Gardens

0-671-74441-0 SIMON & SCHUSTER $27.50

Peter **Holland**

Traditional Garden Woodwork

0-7063-7451-7 WARD LOCK PB $16.95

Geoffrey **Jellicoe** & Susan **Jellicoe**

The Landscape of Man: Shaping the Environment from Prehistory to the Present Day

A brilliant and entertaining classic that ranges over philosophy, art, and literature as they pertain to landscape history

See also **ENVIRONMENTAL HISTORY** under **THE ENVIRONMENT** in **SCIENCE**

0-500-27431-2 THAMES & HUDSON PB $24.95

H. Peter **Loewer**

Thoreau's Garden: Native Plants for the American Landscape

0-8117-1728-3 STACKPOLE $22.95

Mildred **Mathias**, editor

Flowering Plants in the Landscape

See also **FLOWERING PLANTS** under **SPECIFIC PLANTS**

0-520-05414-8 CALIFORNIA PB $21.95

Charles **Moore**

The Poetics of Gardens

A knowledgeable, instructive, and entertaining book on garden history and design; gardens from different cultures and parts of the world with over 500 illustrations

See also **GARDEN HISTORY**

0-262-13231-1 MIT $47.50

0-262-63153-9 MIT PB $19.95

John **Simonds**

Landscape Architecture: A Manual of Site Planning and Design

0-07-057448-0 MCGRAW HILL $73.00

Elizabeth **Stell** & C. Colston **Burrell**

Landscaping With Perennials

0-87596-663-2 RODALE $24.95

David **Stevens**

The Outdoor Room: Garden Design for Living

0-679-43467-4 RANDOM HOUSE $40.00

Kenneth **Turner**

Kenneth Turner's Flower Style: The Art of Floral Design and Decoration

0-8021-1479-2 GROVE $35.00

Rosemary **Verey**

Secret Gardens: Revealed by Their Owners

0-8212-2074-8 BULFINCH $45.00

Sara Jane **von Trapp**

Landscape Doctor: Plans & Do-It-Yourself Remedies For Home Planting Problems

Easy remedies and inspiring ideas to turn any outdoor area—entrances, gardens, fences—into a pleasure to behold. Clearly illustrated by a leading horticultural illustrator, this readable, practical, sensible guide is an elementary education in landscaping

1-88152-738-7 CHAPTERS $29.95

1-88152-739-5 CHAPTERS PB $19.95

Donald **Wyman**

Taylor's Guide to Garden Design

0-395-46784-5 HOUGHTON MIFFLIN PB $19.95

Taylor's Guide to Ground Covers, Vines, and Grasses

0-395-43094-1 HOUGHTON MIFFLIN PB $19.95

Specific Plants

Gordon **Courtright**

Tropicals

A visual dictionary of tropical trees, shrubs, and vines for those with gardens in California and the south; also of use to greenhouse owners

See also **FLOWERING PLANTS**

0-88192-332-X TIMBER PB $24.95

Jack **Kramer**

300 Extraordinary Plants For Home and Garden

Illustrated with 150 color photographs, this is a stunning collection of exotic plants including cacti, succulents, gesneriads, South African bulbs, and orchids. The author describes each plant and gives detailed directions on indoor and outdoor care and includes a list of reputable places from which to buy these amazing plants

PHOTOGRAPHY BY CHARLES FITCH & JERRY PAVIA

1-55859-382-9 ABBEVILLE $45.00

Trees and Shrubs

Gordon **Courtright**

Trees and Shrubs For Temperate Climates

The standard reference for landscape plants in temperate zones. Includes hundreds of plants readily available in retail nurseries, with information on their requirements and growth; 800 color photographs

See also **ART BOOKS** and **REFERENCE**

0-88192-097-5 TIMBER $49.95

The Garden Club of America

Plants That Merit Attention: Shrubs

0-88192-347-8 TIMBER $59.95

The Garden Club of America

Plants That Merit Attention: Trees

0-917304-75-6 TIMBER $49.95

D. M. Van **Gelderen**

Conifers: The Illustrated Encyclopedia

0-88192-354-0 TIMBER $125.00

Grow Great Annuals

0-8118-0574-3 CHRONICLE PB $9.95

Lewis **Hill** & Nancy **Hill**

Successful Perennial Gardening: A Practical Guide

A comprehensive handbook on care and cultivation; includes a descriptive catalog of the best garden perennials

0-88266-472-7 GARDEN WAY PB $16.95

Alan **Mitchell**

The Trees of North America

0-8160-1806-5 FACTS ON FILE $35.00

Stella **Otto**

The Backyard Orchardist: A Complete Guide to Growing Fruit Trees in the Home Garden

See also **VEGETABLES AND FRUIT**

0-9634520-3-7 OTTOG PB $14.95

Roger **Phillips**

Trees of North America and Europe: A Photographic Guide to More Than 500 Trees

0-394-73541-2 RANDOM HOUSE PB $27.50

Wayne **Sinclair**

Diseases of Trees and Shrubs

0-8014-1517-9 CORNELL $59.50

J.D. **Vertrees**

Japanese Maples

0-88192-048-7 TIMBER $40.00

Donald **Wyman**

Trees For American Gardens

0-02-632201-3 MACMILLAN $50.00

Flowering Plants

Paul **Aden**, editor

The Hosta Book

A definitive sourcebook on one of the most versatile of perennials

0-88192-260-9 TIMBER PB $19.95

Peter **Arnold**

Orchids

0-8478-1810-1 RIZZOLI $40.00

David **Bassett**
Delphiniums
0-304-32022-6 CASSELL PB $5.95

Elizabeth **Blackadder** & Deborah **Kellaway**
Irises and Other Flowers
0-8109-3328-4 ABRAMS $19.95

Jim **Fisk**
Clematis: The Queen of Climbers
0-304-34327-7 CASSELL PB $19.95

Fred **Galle**
Azaleas
An up-to-date and complete guide to the species
0-88192-012-6
INTL SPECIALIZED BOOK SERVICE $69.95
0-88192-091-6 TIMBER $75.00

Harold **Greer** & Homer **Salley**
The Rhododendron Hybrids
The parentage of nearly 5000 hybrids; an authoritative reference
0-88192-184-X TIMBER $59.95

Michael **Jefferson-Brown** & Harris **Howland**
The Gardener's Guide to Growing Lilies
0-88192-315-X TIMBER $29.95

Noel **Kingsbury**
The New Perennial Garden
This environmentally friendly approach to temperate-zone gardening teaches the techniques of designing, planning, and planting perennial groupings that will virtually look after themselves. Comprehensive descriptions of habitats and suggestions for appropriate plant communities lead the reader through all the essential techniques of a revolutionary new approach to ecologically sound gardens requiring minimal upkeep
0-8050-4673-9 HOLT $40.00

Brian **Mathew**
Lilies: A Romantic History With a Guide to Cultivation
1-56138-304-X RUNNING PRESS $12.95

Mildred **Mathias**, editor
Flowering Plants in the Landscape
See also **LANDSCAPE AND GARDEN DESIGN**
0-520-05414-8 CALIFORNIA PB $21.95

Alec **Pridgeon**, editor
The Illustrated Encyclopedia of Orchids
See also **REFERENCE**
0-88192-267-6 TIMBER $39.95

J.N. **Rentoul**
Growing Orchids: The Specialist Orchid Grower
See also **INDOOR GARDENING**
0-88192-085-1 TIMBER $34.95
9-99411-513-8 AM. ORCHID SOCIETY PB $24.95

Growing Orchids: The Cattleyas and Other Epiphytes
0-917304-20-9 INTL SPECIALIZED BOOK SERVICE $34.95

Growing Orchids: The Australasian Families
0-88192-020-7 TIMBER $34.95
0-88192-021-5 TIMBER PB $22.95

Homer **Salley** & Harold **Greer**
Rhododendron Hybrids: A Guide to Their Origins
0-88192-061-4 TIMBER $55.00

Graham Stuart **Thomas**
Perennial Garden Plants: Or the Modern Florilegium: A Concise Account of Herbaceous Plants
One of Britain's great gardeners discusses plants and the best way to grow them
0-88192-167-X TIMBER $39.95
0-460-04575-X TIMBER $39.95

Roses

Peter **Beales**
Visions of Roses: Using Roses in over 30 Beautiful Gardens
0-8212-2318-6 BULFINCH $40.00

Laura **Cerwinske**
The Book of the Rose
For its beauty, fragrance, and above all, symbolism, the rose is universally revered. This book celebrates the flower, following its history from Persian and Indian cultivation to the gardens of Empress Josephine. It includes over 120 fine reproductions of roses in art—from illuminated manuscripts to William Morris's wallpapers. The perfect holiday gift for gardner and reader alike
0-500-01535-X THAMES & HUDSON $35.00

Rayford **Clayton**
The Rose Bible
Early to modern, hybrid teas to grandifloras, bushes to climbers: this is the bible of rose growers and a delight for any gardener. Engaging, opinionated, lavishly illustrated, how to grow, maintain, or dream—that is, create hybrids—of roses
FOREWORD BY MARTHA STEWART
PHOTOGRAPHS BY ROBERT GALYEAN
0-517-58821-8 HARMONY $50.00

Taylor Guides
Taylor's Guide to Roses
The best book on this subject: a fine all-around guide to rose culture for the average gardener
0-395-69459-0 HOUGHTON MIFFLIN PB $19.95

Stirling **Macoboy**
The Ultimate Rose Book
Featured here are more than 1,500 roses from around the world. Divided into three categories—old garden, modern garden, and miniature—each is accompanied by photos and text that provide classification, international code, and common name, as well as details of appearance, fragrance, parentage, and time of flowering. A huge and beautiful rose-lover's reference
0-8109-3920-7 ABRAMS $49.50

Sean **McCann**
Miniature Roses
0-304-34799-X CASSELL PB $19.95

Roger **Phillips** & Martyn **Rix**
Roses: Over 1400 Roses in Full-Colour Photographs
Fourteen hundred varieties from around the world; includes a detailed description of origin and parentage, appearance, and growing conditions
0-394-75867-6 RANDOM HOUSE PB $27.50

Ferns, Cacti, and Carnivorous Plants

F. Gordon **Foster**
Ferns to Know and Grow
0-88192-234-X TIMBER PB $22.95

David **Jones**
Encyclopedia of Ferns
0-88192-054-1 TIMBER $69.95

James **Pietropaolo** & Patricia **Pietropaolo**
Carnivorous Plants of the World
0-88192-356-7 TIMBER PB $22.95

Indoor Gardening

John **Brookes**
The Indoor Garden Book
1-56458-527-1 DORLING KINDERSLEY PB $14.95

David **Du Puy** & Phillip **Cribb**
The Genus Cymbidium
A comprehensive study of one of the most popular orchids grown
0-88192-119-X TIMBER $59.95

J.N. **Rentoul**
Growing Orchids: The Specialist Orchid Grower
See also **FLOWERING PLANTS** under **SPECIFIC PLANTS** under **GARDENING**
0-88192-085-1 TIMBER $34.95
9994115138 AMERICAN ORCHID SOCIETY PB $24.95

Growing Orchids II: The Cattleyas and Other Epiphytes
0-917304-20-9
INTL SPECIALIZED BOOK SERVICE $34.95

Growing Orchids IV: The Australasian Families
0-88192-020-7 TIMBER $34.95
0-88192-021-5 TIMBER PB $22.95

David M. **Tucker**
Kitchen Gardening in America
The first history of a 10,000-year-old tradition practiced by 29 million Americans today. This highly readable exploration uses historical changes like Darwinism and the Enlightenment to explain how the culture and philosophy of the craft were formed, and examines the evolution of the plants, tools, and fertilizers of the kitchen gardener
0-8138-1888-5 IOWA STATE $24.95

Indoor Gardens

Rob **Proctor**
The Indoor Potted Bulb
0-671-77951-6 SIMON & SCHUSTER $20.00

Donald **Wyman**
Taylor's Guide to House-Plants
0-317-53568-4 HOUGHTON MIFFLIN PB $18.95

Bonsai

Herb L. **Gustafson**
Keep Your Bonsai Alive & Well
0-8069-1310-X STERLING PB $9.95

Miniature Living Bonsai Landscapes: The Art of Saikei
0-8069-0734-7 STERLING $29.95

Amy **Liang**
The Living Art of Bonsai: Principles & Techniques of Cultivation & Propagation
0-8069-8781-2 STERLING PB $24.95

Nippon Bonsai Association
Classic Bonsai of Japan
0-87011-933-8 KODANSHA $100.00

Butterfly and Bird Gardens

Alcinda **Lewis**, editor
Butterfly Gardens: Luring Nature's Loveliest Pollinators to Your Yard
0-945352-88-3 HARPERCOLLINS PB $7.95

Marcus **Schneck**
Creating a Butterfly Garden: A Guide to Attracting and Identifying Bufferfly Visitors
0-671-89246-0 FIRESIDE PB $8.95

Tony **Soper**
The Bird Table Book: How to Attract Wild Birds to Your Garden
0-7153-0053-9 DAVID & CHARLES $19.95

Contained Gardens

Kenneth **Beckett** & others
The Contained Garden, Revised Edition
More than 400 of the best plants for growing in containers, from traditional herbs and shrubs to new species, with planting advice and ideas for display. Full-color illustrations and photos
0-14-046940-0 PENGUIN PB $19.95

Chuck **Crandall** & Barbara **Crandall**
Movable Harvests: Fruits, Vegetables, Berries: The Simplicity & Bounty of Container Gardens
1-88152-769-7 CHAPTERS $29.95
1-88152-770-0 CHAPTERS PB $19.95

David **Joyce**
The Complete Container Garden
0-89577-848-3 READER'S DIGEST $30.00

Window Box Gardening
Over 100 step-by-step photographs, shot on location and showing a range of sills from the Mediterranean to Alpine troughs. Joyce gives a wealth of original ideas for both the novice and the experienced gardener. The options for small-scale planting are carefully examined in a focused plant guide, with advice on color scheme, form, texture, and fragrance
1-56440-292-4 GLOBE PEQUOT $22.95

Rob **Proctor**
The Outdoor Potted Bulb
0-671-87034-3 SIMON & SCHUSTER $20.00

Jim **Wilson**
Landscaping with Container Plants
"A thorough, utterly practical guide to container gardening. With its beautiful photographs and Wilson's essential practicality and colorful humor, this book is both a joy to read and a pleasure to use"—*Christian Science Monitor*
0-395-70133-3 HOUGHTON MIFFLIN PB $28.00

Rock Gardens

Katharine **Ferguson**, editor
Rock Gardens
1-89556-594-4 FIREFLY PB $10.95

H. Lincoln **Foster**
Rock Gardening: A Guide to Growing Alpines and Other Wildflowers in the American Garden
0-917304-29-2 TIMBER PB $24.95

John **Kelly**
Rock Gardens
0-7063-7489-4 WARD LOCK $12.95

Water Gardens

Jacqueline **Heriteau** & Charles **Thomas**
Water Gardens: How to Design, Install, Plant and Maintain a Home Water Garden
0-395-70935-0 DORLING KINDERSLEY PB $18.95

Archie **Skinner** & David **Arscott**
The Stream Garden: Create and Plant Your Own Natural-Looking Water Feature
0-7063-7477-0 WARD LOCK PB $14.95

Perry D. **Slocum** & others
Water Gardening: Water Lilies and Lotuses
0-88192-335-4 TIMBER $59.95

Xeriscape Gardens

Connie Lockhart **Ellefson** & others
Xeriscape Gardening: Water Conservation for the American Landscape
0-02-614125-6 MACMILLAN $30.00

Jim **Knopf**
The Xeriscape Flower Gardener: A Waterwise Guide for the Rocky Mountain Region
1-55566-077-0 JOHNSON PB $16.95

Organic Gardening and Composting

Basil **Caplan**
The Complete Manual of Organic Gardening
This encyclopedic guide covers all aspects of natural gardening methods: cultivation without artificial fertilizers or pesticides, how to improve soil content and make compost, combating plant diseases and destructive insects. Now you can have hearty fruits, vegetables, and herbs without chemicals
See also **REFERENCE** under **GARDENING**
1-55859-644-5 ABBEVILLE $49.95

Tom **Christopher** & Marty **Asher**
Compost This Book!: The Art of Composting for Your Yard, Your Community, and the Planet
0-87156-596-X SIERRA CLUB PB $12.00

Mark **Cullen** & Lorraine **Johnson**
The Urban/Suburban Composter: The Complete Guide to Backyard, Balcony, and Apartment Composting
0-312-10530-4 ST. MARTIN'S PB $13.95

Tanya **Denckla**
The Organic Gardener's Home Reference: A Plant-By-Plant Guide to Growing Fresh, Healthy Food
See also **REFERENCE** under **GARDENING**
0-88266-840-4 STOREY $29.95
0-88266-839-0 STOREY PB $19.95

Lady **Muck**
Magic Muck: The Complete Guide to Compost
1-85793-261-7 TRAFALGAR SQUARE $17.95

Sara **Stein**
Noah's Garden: Restoring the Ecology of Our Own Backyards
With a fresh eye and thoughtful insights, Stein looks at the ecology of gardens and shares her quest to create outside spaces that are not only ecologically sound, but welcoming to humans as well as to animals
0-395-65373-8 HOUGHTON MIFFLIN $21.95
0-395-70940-7 HOUGHTON MIFFLIN PB $10.95

Vegetables and Fruit

Suzanne **Ashworth**
Seed to Seed: Seed Saving Techniques for the Vegetable Gardener
0-9613977-7-2 SEED SAVER PB $20.00

Sam **Bittman**
The Salad Lover's Garden
The easiest and most successful techniques to growing gorgeous greens
0-385-41415-3 MAIN STREET PB $15.00

Fern Marshall **Bradley**, editor
Rodale's Garden Answers: Vegetables, Fruits, and Herbs: At-A-Glance Solutions for Every Gardening Problem
0-87596-639-X RODALE $27.95

Nora **Carey**
Perfect Preserves: Provisions from the Kitchen Garden
Voted one of the "Most Beautiful Food and Wine Books of the Year" by *Food Arts*, this is a wonderfully photographed compendium of preserving methods. Fruits, vegetables, and flowers, bottled, salted, oil-cured, pickled, frozen, dried, and more. "All you need to know about [preserving] good things from the garden"—*People Weekly*
PHOTOGRAPHS BY MICK HALES
1-55670-401-1 STEWART, TABORI PB $24.95

David **Chambers** & Lucinda **Mays**
Vegetable Gardening
0-679-41434-7 PANTHEON PB $25.00

Lewis **Hill**
Fruits and Berries For the Home Garden
0-88266-763-7 HARPERCOLLINS PB $16.95

Secrets of Plant Propagation: Starting Your Own Flowers, Vegetables, Fruits, Berries, Shrubs, Trees, and Houseplants
See also **PRACTICAL MATTERS FOR GARDENERS** under **GARDENING**
0-88266-370-4 GARDEN WAY PB $14.95

Shepherd **Ogden**
Step by Step Organic Vegetable Gardening
0-06-092225-7 HARPERPERENNIAL PB $16.00

Stella **Otto**
The Backyard Berry Book: A Hands-On Guide to Growing Berries, Brambles, and Vine Fruit in the Home Garden
0-9634520-6-1 OTTO GRAPHICS PB $15.95

The Backyard Orchardist: A Complete Guide to Growing Fruit Trees in the Home Garden
See also **TREES AND SHRUBS** under **SPECIFIC PLANTS** under **GARDENING**
0-9634520-3-7 OTTO GRAPHICS PB $14.95

Roger **Phillips** & Martyn **Rix**
The Random House Book of Vegetables
This is the preeminent guide to the history, characteristics, and cultivation of more than 650 vegetables from around the world. Starting a compost heap, preventing potato blight, deciding on which lettuces to plant and when to plant them—it's all here, as well as the organic vs. non-organic controversy and tips on fertilization and cultivation
0-679-75024-X RANDOLPH PB $25.00

Martha Adams **Rubin**
Countryside, Garden & Table
A true celebration of nature's bounty and centered around the changing seasons, this is much more than a just a gardening cookbook. Divided into chapters representing each month, Rubin discusses the land, the garden, and the kitchen, providing practical tips and philosophical meditations on living close to the earth. Stocked full with her favorite recipes, all of which feature the foods of the harvest, she provides numerous menus for seasonal party planning
See also **AMERICAN COOKERY** under **FOOD**
1-55591-137-4 FULCRUM $19.95

Miranda **Smith**
Backyard Fruits and Berries: Everything You Need to Know About Planting and Growing Fruits and Berries in Your Own Backyard
0-87596-638-1 RODALE $25.95

Allan A. **Swenson**
Fruit Trees for the Home Gardener
1-55821-308-2 LYONS & BURFORD PB $14.95

Sylvia **Thompson**
The Kitchen Garden
Using the organic French Intensive Method, Thompson steers the reader through the process of building a kitchen garden from seed catalog to harvest
0-553-08138-1 BANTAM DOUBLEDAY DELL $27.95

Donald **Wyman**
Taylor's Guide to Vegetables and Herbs
See also **HERBS**
0-395-43092-5 HOUGHTON MIFFLIN PB $19.95

Herbs

James **Adams**
Landscaping with Herbs
Covers a range of garden designs, formal and informal, traditional and modern, fragrant and wild
0-88192-073-8 TIMBER $32.95

Henry **Beston**
Herbs and the Earth
The newest edition of Beston's classic treatise on herbs, filled with indispensable information, history, folklore, and wisdom. With woodcuts by John Howard Benson, and a new introduction by John Swain, this is an affectionate exploration through the world of herbs
0-87923-827-5 NATIONAL BOOK NETWORK $17.95

Ann **Bonar** & Daphne **MacCarthy**
How to Grow & Use Herbs
9-995-28020-5 WARD LOCK PB $10.95

Rita **Buchanan**, editor
Taylor's Guide to Herbs
0-395-68081-6 HOUGHTON MIFFLIN PB $19.95

Guy **Cooper** & Gordon **Taylor**
English Herb Gardens
See also **ENGLISH GARDENS** under **GARDEN HISTORY**
See also **LANDSCAPE AND GARDEN DESIGN** under **GARDENING**
0-8478-0689-8 RIZZOLI $27.50

Thomas **Debaggio**
Growing Herbs from Seed, Cutting & Root: An Adventure in Small Miracles
0-934026-96-3 INTERWEAVE PB $9.95

Claire **Kowalchik** & William **Hyeton**, editors
Rodale's Illustrated Encyclopedia of Herbs
Comprehensive information and illustrations on more than 140 herbs. A matchless source
0-87857-699-1 RODALE $26.95

Lise **Manniche**
An Ancient Egyptian Herbal
0-292-70415-1 TEXAS PB $19.95

John **Mason**
Growing Herbs
0-916638-50-2 MEYBK PB $15.95

Barbara **Seagall**
The Herb Garden Month-By-Month
0-7153-0060-1 DAVID & CHARLES $24.95

Emelie **Tolley** & Chris **Mead**
Gardening with Herbs
This book shows not only the beautiful gardening effects that can be created with herbs, but how to do so while maintaining a useful and delicious collection of pot-herbs
0-517-58332-1 CLARKSON POTTER $45.00

Emelie **Tolley** & Chris **Mead**

Herbs: Gardens, Decorations, and Recipes

An elegant book on how to set up a simple but sophisticated herb garden, with ideas for gardeners in all climates

0-517-55244-2 CLARKSON POTTER..............$35.00

Jim **Wilson**

Landscaping With Herbs

0-395-62237-9 HOUGHTON MIFFLIN..............$35.00
0-395-70941-5 DORLING KINDERSLEY PB..............$19.95

Donald **Wyman**

Taylor's Guide to Vegetables and Herbs

0-395-43092-5 HOUGHTON MIFFLIN PB..............$19.95

Wild Gardening

Henry **Art**

A Garden of Wildflowers: 101 Native Species and How to Grow Them

Excellent for beginners

0-88266-405-0 GARDEN WAY PB..............$18.95

Richard **Austin**

Wild Gardening

A general overview for the novice gardener with handy lists of sources

0-671-62022-3 SIMON & SCHUSTER..............$12.98

Roger **Holmes**, editor

Taylor's Guide to Natural Gardening

Offering ecologically minded gardeners a selection of wildflowers and native plants to employ in their yards, this guide describes the six natural botanical regions of the US and urges a regional approach to plant selection. Styles derived from meadows, woodlands, and prairies are highlighted. It also offers a detailed plant encyclopedia, and information on how to attract wildlife to your garden

0-395-60729-9 HOUGHTON MIFFLIN PB..............$19.95

Harry **Phillips**

Growing and Propagating Wild Flowers

0-8078-4131-5 NORTH CAROLINA PB..............$17.95

Yvonne **Rees**

Practical Wildflower Gardening

1-85223-778-3 CROWOOD PB..............$8.95

William **Robinson**

The Wild Garden

A British classic written in 1870 by an early advocate of this style of planting

0-88192-284-6 TIMBER..............$24.95

Violet **Stevenson**

The Wild Garden

How to grow the best of these plants in settings that enhance their natural beauty

0-14-046710-6 PENGUIN PB..............$17.95

James **Young** & Cheryl **Young**

Collecting, Processing and Germinating Seeds of Wildland Plants

Technical information on this delightful activity

0-88192-057-6 TIMBER..............$24.95

Garden Pests and Pest Control

Anna **Carr**

Rodale's Color HandBook of Garden Insects

A clear guide for the average gardener

0-87857-460-3 RODALE PB..............$16.95

Warren **Johnson** & H.H. **Lyon**

Insects That Feed on Trees and Shrubs: An Illustrated Practical Guide

0-8014-2602-2 COMSTOCK..............$56.50

Pascal **Pirone**

Diseases and Pests of Ornamental Plants

0-471-07249-4 WILEY..............$79.95

Garden History

Charles **Moore**

The Poetics of Gardens

A knowledgeable, instructive, and entertaining book on garden history and design; gardens from different cultures and parts of the world with over 500 illustrations

See also **LANDSCAPE AND GARDEN DESIGN** under **GARDENING**

0-262-13231-1 MIT..............$47.50
0-262-63153-9 MIT PB..............$19.95

Christopher **Thacker**

The History of Gardens

A fast-moving and clearly written scholarly text

0-520-03736-7 CALIFORNIA..............$55.00
0-520-05629-9 CALIFORNIA PB..............$24.95

American Gardens

Diana **Balmori**

Beatrix Farrand's American Landscapes: Her Gardens and Campuses

The designer of Dumbarton Oaks and many other important private gardens and public sites

See also **AMERICAN** under **LANDSCAPE ARCHITECTURE AND GARDEN DESIGN** in **ARCHITECTURE, DESIGN, AND HOMES**

0-89831-003-2 TIMBER PB..............$24.95

Michael J. **Caduto** & Joseph **Bruchac**

Native American Gardening: Stories, Projects and Recipes for Families

The authors of the best-selling Keepers of the Earth series present a gardening activity book for families. Centering around the Native American approach to gardening, this lovely book combines stories, activities, and recipes to teach the techniques of native farmers—seed preservation, natural pest control—and introduces the relationship between people and gardens

FOREWORD BY GARY PAUL NABHAN

1-55591-148-X FULCRUM PB..............$15.95

Lester **Collins**

Innisfree: An American Garden

0-8109-3464-7 ABRAMS..............$35.00

Mac **Griswold** & Eleanor **Weller**

The Golden Age of American Gardens: Proud Owners, Private Estates, 1890-1940

A tribute to the age of the grand estate gardens and their illustrious owners. More than 500 gardens are featured, from Marjorie Merriweather Post's Floridian Mar-a-Lago to the du Pont's Pennsylvania Longwood and Huntington's California San Merino Ranch. Illustrated with over 100 reproductions of glass lantern slides created for the Garden Club of America

0-8109-3358-6 ABRAMS..............$75.00

Adrian **Higgins**

The Secret Gardens of Georgetown: Behind the Walls of Washington's Most Historic Neighborhood

0-316-36084-8 LITTLE, BROWN..............$40.00

In the Garden: Colonial Williamsburg Foundation

Each of these handy pocket planners measures 5 1/8 x 4 1/8 inches, features 12 full-color illustrations, saddle-stitched for a year-long life span, and includes daily write-on boxes. Beautiful photos feature the highlights of the gardens of Colonial Williamsburg

See also **ART BOOKS**

1-55550-393-4 UNIVERSE..............$4.95

Ann **Leighton**

American Gardens in the 18th Century: For Use Or For Delight

0-87023-531-1 MASSACHUSETTS PB..............$20.95

American Gardens of the 19th-Century: For Comfort and Affluence

0-87023-532-X MASSACHUSETTS..............$40.00
0-87023-533-8 MASSACHUSETTS PB..............$18.95

Early American Gardens: For Meate or Medicine

A vivid and carefully researched history of American gardens written by a practical and witty gardener

0-87023-530-3 MASSACHUSETTS PB..............$18.95

Denise **Magnani**

The Winterthur Garden: Henry Francis Du Pont's Romance With the Land

0-8109-3779-4 ABRAMS..............$39.95

Laura C. **Martin**
Southern Gardens: A Gracious History and Travelers Guide
A tour of 33 gardens throughout the South, arranged chronologically to illustrate different periods of southern history. Beginning with the Elizabethan Gardens at Roanoke and working toward Atlanta's famed and recent Gardens for peace, this magnificent volume includes garden histories, notes on cultivation, historical prints, and 200 large-format color photos of the gardens
1-55859-323-3 ARTABRAS $19.98

Tovah **Martin**
Tasha Tudor's Garden
PHOTOGRAPHS BY
0-395-43609-5 HOUGHTON MIFFLIN $35.00

Patricia **O'Gorman** & Bob **Schalkwijk**
Patios and Gardens of Mexico
0-8038-0210-2 ARCHITECTURAL $40.00

Nancy Goslee **Power**
The Gardens of California: Four Centuries of Design from Mission to Modern
0-517-58381-X CLARKSON POTTER $50.00

Ogden **Tanner**
Gardens of the Hudson River Valley: An Illustrated Guide
PHOTOGRAPHS BY TED SPIEGEL
0-8109-2643-1 ABRAMS PB $19.95

Celia **Thaxter**
An Island Garden
A facsimile edition; the creation of Celia Thaxton's beautiful garden on Appledore Island, off the coast of New Hampshire. With paintings by Childe Hassam
0-395-48591-6 HOUGHTON MIFFLIN $21.95
0-395-74547-0 HOUGHTON MIFFLIN PB $12.95

British, Scottish, and Irish Gardens

Richard **Bisgrove**
The Gardens of Gertrude Jekyll
Gertrude Jekyll was an important innovator in the English gardening tradition and influenced planting worldwide. Many of her gardens have disappeared, but over 1,000 of her detailed plans survive. The author has selected the best of these to show how Jekyll's ideas remain relevant. They are depicted in watercolors and 150 photographs that, in themselves, are works of art
0-316-09657-1 LITTLE, BROWN $45.00

Jane **Brown**
Sissinghurst: Portrait of a Garden
0-297-83350-2 WEIDENFELD & NICOLSON PB $19.95

Tim **Buxbaum**
Scottish Garden Buildings: From Food to Folly
1-85158-113-8 TRAFALGAR SQUARE $34.95

David R. **Coffin**
The English Garden: Meditation and Memorial
0-691-03432-X PRINCETON $35.00

Guy **Cooper** & Gordon **Taylor**
English Herb Gardens
See also **HERBS** under **VEGETABLES AND FRUIT**
0-8478-0689-8 RIZZOLI $27.50

Findhorn Community
The Findhorn Garden
0-06-090520-4 HARPERCOLLINS PB $16.00

Mireille **Galinou**, editor
London's Pride: The Glorious History of the Capital's Gardens
1-85470-032-4 TRAFALGAR SQUARE $29.95

John **Harris**
The Palladian Revival: Lord Burlington, His Villa and Garden at Chiswick
0-300-05983-3 YALE $55.00

James **Howley**
The Follies and Garden Buildings of Ireland
0-300-05577-3 YALE $65.00

Gertrude **Jekyll**
Colour Schemes For the Flower Garden: The Illustrated Gertrude Jekyll
A new, illustrated edition of a classic by one of the greatest English gardeners, containing new color photographs, hitherto unpublished designs, and new illustrations. Miss Jekyll's planting plans have also been redrawn and interpreted in color
0-907462-17-0 ANTIQUE COLLECTORS $29.50
0-88162-066-1 OLYMPIC PB $4.98

The Gardener's Essential Gertrude Jekyll
0-87923-599-3 GODINE PB $13.95

Gertrude **Jekyll** & George S. **Elgood**
Classic English Gardens
0-8317-1310-0 SMITHMARK $24.98

Alvilde **Lees-Milne**, editor
The New Englishwoman's Garden
0-7011-3492-5 CHATTO & WINDOWS PB $22.95

William **Robinson**
The English Flower Garden
A reprint of the English 19th-century classic, updated for contemporary gardeners by Graham Stuart Thomas
0-89831-000-8 TIMBER $35.00

A.A. **Tait**
The Landscape Garden in Scotland, 1735-1835
0-85224-581-5 EDINBURGH PB $20.00

French Gardens

Francesca **Crespi**, editor
A Walk in Monet's Garden: A Pop-Up Book
Provides a unique tour of Giverny, relating its significance to Monet's life and art
0-8212-2195-7 BULFINCH $19.95

Bernd H. **Dams** & Andrew **Zega**
Pleasure Pavillions and Follies in the Gardens of the Ancien Régime
A major contribution to our knowledge of the imaginative garden follies built for the pleasure of the pre-Revolutionary Bourbon kings. The authors' watercolor renderings reconstruct these magnificent structures, and their text brings the vanished world that created them vividly to life
See also **EUROPEAN** under **LANDSCAPE ARCHITECTURE AND GARDEN DESIGN** in **ARCHITECTURE, DESIGN, AND HOMES**
2-08-013561-9 ABBEVILLE $50.00

Marguerite **Duval**
The King's Garden
An imaginative account of the French kings' botanical gardens and their search for exotic plants
0-8139-0916-3 VIRGINIA $20.00

Derek **Fell**
The Impressionist Garden: Ideas and Inspiration from the Gardens and Paintings of the Impressionists
0-517-59851-5 RANDOM HOUSE $35.00

Richard **Goodman**
French Dirt: The Story of a Garden in the South of France
0-06-097505-9 HARPERCOLLINS PB $12.00

Dorothee **Imbert**
Modernist Garden in France
0-300-04716-9 YALE $60.00

Diana **Ketcham**
Le Desert De Retz: A Late Eighteenth-Century French Folly Garden, the Artful Landscape of Monsieur De Monville
0-262-11186-1 MIT $42.50

Pierre André **Lablaude**
The Gardens of Versailles
A history of the evolution of taste, art, and philosophy, as seen through the development of the grounds around the famous palace, from the hunting park of Louis XIII to the grand schemes of Le Nôtre for Louis XIV
50-302-00659-1 SOTHEBY'S $40.00
1-85759-043-0 SOTHEBY'S $39.95

Louis XIV

Vivian **Russell**
Gardens of the Riviera
0-8478-1778-4 RIZZOLI $45.00

Marie-Francoise **Valery**
French Garden Style
0-517-14242-2 CRESCENT $24.99

Gardens in Normandy
From Monet's garden at Giverny to the Bois de Moutiers at Varengeville, a breathtaking tour from the gardens in the fertile Seine valley to the cliffs over the English Channel
PHOTOGRAPHY BY VINCENT MOTTE & CHRISTIAN SARRAMON
2-08-013579-1 ABBEVILLE $50.00

Allen **Weiss**
Mirrors of Infinity: The French Formal Garden and 17th-Century Metaphysics
Unanimously acclaimed for its remarkable ability to combine philosophical insights and social history with analyses of 17th-century French gardens such as Vaux-le-Vicomte, Chantilly, and Versailles
See also **EUROPEAN** under **LANDSCAPE ARCHITECTURE AND GARDEN DESIGN** in **ARCHITECTURE, DESIGN, AND HOMES**
1-56898-050-7 PRINCETON ARCHIT PB $14.95

Pierre **Wittmer**
Caillebotte and His Garden at Yerres
0-8109-3167-2 ABRAMS $95.00

Kenneth **Woodbridge**
Princely Gardens: The Origins and Development of the French Formal Style
0-8478-0684-7 RIZZOLI $45.00

Italian Gardens

Gianni Berengo **Gardin** & others
Secret Gardens in Venice
9-995-47848-X ANTIQUE COLLECTORS $50.00

Claudia **Lazzaro**
Italian Renaissance Gardening: From the Conventions of Planting, Design, and Ornament to the Grand Gardens
0-300-04765-7 YALE $60.00

Elisabeth Blair **MacDougall**
Fountains, Statues, and Flowers: Studies in Italian Gardens of the 16th and 17th Centuries
0-88402-216-1 DUMBARTON OAKS $50.00

Elisabth **MacDougall** & Nicolas **Sapieha**
Gardens of Naples
0-935748-95-4 SOTHEBY'S $60.00

Islamic Gardens

John **Brookes**
Gardens of Paradise: The History and Design of the Great Islamic Gardens
One of England's foremost landscape designers traces the spread of the Islamic image of a garden paradise through India, Persia, Turkey, Egypt, Sicily, North Africa, and Muslim Spain
See also **ASIAN** under **LANDSCAPE ARCHITECTURE AND GARDEN DESIGN** in **ARCHITECTURE, DESIGN, AND HOMES**
See also **ISLAMIC ART AND ARCHITECTURE** in **ART**
0-941533-07-7 NEW AMSTERDAM $36.00

James L. **Wescoat** & Joachim **Wolschke-Bulmahn**, editors
Mughal Gardens: Sources, Places, Representations, and Prospects
0-88402-235-8 DUMBARTON OAKS $47.00

Chinese Gardens

David **Engel**
Creating a Chinese Garden
FOREWORD BY SIR HAROLD ACTON
0-88192-025-8 TIMBER $38.95

R. Stewart **Johnston**
Scholar Gardens of China: A Study and Analysis of the Spatial Design of the Chinese Private Garden
0-521-39477-5 CAMBRIDGE $159.95

Pierre **Rambach** & Susanne **Rambach**
Gardens of Longevity in China and Japan
0-8478-0837-8 RIZZOLI $85.00

Maggie **Keswick**
The Chinese Garden
A persuasive and interesting book, with a section on garden architecture
See also **GARDENS** under **CHINA** under **EAST ASIAN ART** in **ART**
0-312-13382-0 ST. MARTIN'S $50.00

Japanese Gardens

Judy **Glattstein**
Enhance Your Garden with Japanese Plants: A Practical Sourcebook
ILLUSTRATED BY HIDEO SHIMIZU
1-56836-137-8 KODANSHA PB $25.00

Sadao **Hibi**
A Celebration of Japanese Gardens
4-7661-0744-6 GRAPHIC SHA $44.95

Preston L. **Houser** & Mizuno **Katsuhiko**
The Tea Garden: Kyoto's Culture Enclosed
4-8381-0116-3 BOOKS NIPPAN PB $19.95

Teiji **Itoh**
The Gardens of Japan
0-87011-648-7 KODANSHA $175.00

Paul **Lesniewicz**
Bonsai: The Complete Guide to Art and Technique
Covers all the essentials; with color photographs, drawings, and a convenient chart of Japanese terms
0-7137-1362-3 BLANDFORD $27.95

Kiyoshi **Seike**
A Japanese Touch For Your Garden
4-7700-1661-1 KODANSHA PB $22.00

Harry **Tomlinson**
The Complete Book of Bonsai: A Practical Guide to Its Art and Cultivation
A comprehensive guide to this ancient indoor gardening technique
1-55859-118-4 ABBEVILLE $35.00

Essays, Memoirs, and Reflections

Jennifer **Ackerman**
Notes from the Shore
"Ackerman, blessed with a naturalist's eye for detail and a poet's soul, beautifully captures the ebb and flow of life at this edge of marsh, sand, and sea"—*People*
0-14-017788-4 PENGUIN PB $11.95

Joe **Eck** & Wayne **Winterrowd**
A Year at North Hill: Four Seasons in a Vermont Garden
0-316-20916-3 LITTLE, BROWN $35.00
0-8050-4614-3 HOLT PB $19.95

John **Jerome**

Stone Work: Reflections on Serious Play and Other Aspects of Country Life

0-87451-762-1 NEW ENGLAND PB $11.95

Allen **Lacy**, editor

The American Gardener

An instructive sampler of American writing on gardening, from Jefferson's notes on growing oak trees to the best of the modern essayists

0-374-10404-2 FS&G $18.95

William **Lishman**

Father Goose: One Man, a Gaggle of Geese, and Their Real-Life Incredible Journey South

Made famous by an enormously popular *20/20* segment that earned, in Barbara Walters's words "the largest, warmest [audience response] I've seen in 15 years," this is the story of a sculptor who adopted a gaggle of geese, flew with them in an ultralight, and taught them to migrate. Illustrated with more than 60 color photographs, this unique book cannot fail to delight anyone who ever admired a soaring flock of migratory birds

PHOTOGRAPHS BY JOSEPH DUFF

0-517-70182-0 CROWN $25.00

Beth **Powning**

Home: Chronicle of a North Country Life

1-55670-460-7 STEWART, TABORI $22.50

Veronica **Ray**

Zen Gardening: A Down-to-Earth Philosophy

In the relationship with a garden Veronica Ray finds a mirror of our relationship with all the world. Drawing on the words of great writers, artists, and Zen thinkers, Ray explores this relationship as a reconnection of the timeless and spiritual bond to the earth

0-425-15299-5 BERKELEY PB $10.00

Sara **Stein**

My Weeds: A Gardener's Botany

A thoughtful and informative book, combining experience and technical knowledge

0-395-70817-6 HOUGHTON MIFFLIN PB $11.95

Delta **Willis**

The Sand Dollar and the Slide Rule: Drawing Blueprints from Nature

"Charming and adroit. Dusty facts sparkle in their new juxtaposition"—*The Washington Times*

0-201-48831-0 ADDISON-WESLEY PB $12.00

Contemporary American Writers

Florence **Bellis**

Gardening and Beyond

A down-to-earth book that discusses with charm and clarity such difficult topics as soil structure, and many other scientific subjects

0-88192-015-0 INTL SPECIALIZED BOOK $14.95

Cassandra **Danz**

Mrs. Greenthumbs: How I Turned a Boring Yard Into a Glorious Garden and How You Can Too

From the host of her own gardening radio program comes a book on how to bring beauty to a garden even with limited time and resources. Proceeding on a month-by-month basis, she covers everything front pruning to fall clean-up and replanting, with time-saving tips, occasional philosophy, even some insight into botany's erotic aspects

See also **LANDSCAPE AND GARDEN DESIGN** under **GARDENING**

0-517-88010-5 CROWN PB $12.00

Marcy **Houle**

The Prairie Keepers: Secrets of the Grasslands

"This lively record of the delicate ways humans alter seemingly untouched ground is a particularly effective portrait of an ecosystem"—*NY Times Book Review*

0-201-40821-X ADDISON-WESLEY PB $11.00

Allen **Lacy**

Farther Afield: Gardener's Excursions

0-374-15355-8 FS&G $17.95
0-374-52063-1 FS&G PB $8.95

Home Ground: A Gardener's Miscellany

0-395-60730-2 HOUGHTON MIFFLIN PB $12.95

Bonnie **Marranca**

American Garden Writing

Letters, journals, and essays by such diverse figures as George Washington, Henry David Thoreau, and Edith Wharton offer a unique view of American garden history

1-55554-029-5 PAJ PUBLICATIONS $23.95

Henry **Mitchell**

The Essential Earthman

The *Washington Post* garden columnist's best work

0-395-68632-6 HOUGHTON MIFFLIN PB $11.95

Eleanor **Perenyi**

Green Thoughts: A Writer in the Garden

Clear, pithy, and practical. A classic

0-394-71714-7 RANDOM HOUSE PB $13.00

Anne **Raver**

Deep in the Green: An Exploration of Country Pleasures

"The subjects are universal, tangible and genuine. Ms. Raver's insights are flawless" —*NY Times*

0-679-43483-6 KNOPF $25.00
0-679-76798-3 VINTAGE PB $13.00

Contemporary British Writers

Russell **Page**

The Education of a Gardener

A worldly and brilliant landscape designer writes about gardening for beginner and expert alike

0-00-271374-8 HARPERCOLLINS PB $15.00

Christopher **Brickell** & Fay **Sharman**

The Vanishing Garden: A Conservation Guide to Garden Plants

0-88192-030-4 TIMBER $24.95

Charles **Elliot**

The Transplanted Gardener

"There is an old story," writes Elliot, "about an American tourist who asked the gardener at a grand English house how he made the lawn look so nice. He was told that it was simple, you only had to mow it and roll it for three hundred years." This lovely and singular collection of essays not only celebrates the beauty of English gardens, it also captures the utter madness and single-minded eccentricity with which British gardeners approach their national obsession

1-55821-417-8 LYONS & BURFORD $22.95

Rosemary **Verey**

Rosemary Verey's Making of a Garden

From the heart of the Cotswolds Verey, celebrated garden author and proprietor of one of England's most famous gardens, offers the distillation of her 30 years' experience as a gardener and designer. From herbs and vegetables, to statues and fountains, this book contains a wealth of gardening wisdom, illustrated with watercolor designs and explicated in the best of British prose

0-8050-3956-2 HOLT $45.00

Art Books

Gordon **Courtright**

Trees and Shrubs For Temperate Climates

The standard reference for landscape plants in temperate zones. Includes hundreds of plants readily available in retail nurseries, with information on their requirements and growth. 800 color photographs

See also **TREES AND SHRUBS** under **SPECIFIC PLANTS** under **GARDENING**
See also **REFERENCE** under **GARDENING**

0-88192-097-5 TIMBER $49.95

Michael **Dirr**

Photographic Manual For Woody Landscape Plants

See also **LANDSCAPE AND GARDEN DESIGN** under **GARDENING**

0-87563-156-8 STIPES PB $26.00
0-87563-153-3 STIPES PB $19.80

Melanie **Fleischmann**

American Border Gardens

Border gardens are the most common American garden, but until now no one book focused on them. Here are 18 border gardens that go well beyond the old standard mix of lawn-edging perennials. Showing numerous ways to group perennials, bulbs, annuals, and grasses, this distinguished volume includes tips on soil testing and preparation, planting, transplanting, and color combining. 125 color photos

0-517-57646-5 CLARKSON POTTER $30.00

Melanie **Fleischmann**

Focus on Flowers

1-55859-540-6 ABBEVILLE $10.95

Alfred Byrd **Graf**

Hortica: A Color Cyclopedia of Garden Flora in All Climates and Indoor Plants

This is the third in Dr. Graf's series of pictorial encyclopedias; it contains 8,000 photos and describes over 10,000 plants and trees, including their native habitats and climactic preferences. The most comprehensive work of its kind

See also **REFERENCE** under **GARDENING**

0-02-544995-8 ROEHRS $250.00

Debra **Heimerdinger**

Re-Arrangements: A Book of Flowers

Fitting celebration of the luxurious-and literary-quality of flowers, this collection gives a new twist to the photography of flowers. Images of flowers in non-traditional settings are perfectly matched with text from Colette's sensuous *Flowers and Fruit*

0-8118-0267-1 CHRONICLE $22.95

In the Garden: Colonial Williamsburg Foundation

Each of these handy pocket planners measures 5 1/8 x 4 1/8 inches, features 12 full-color illustrations, saddle-stitched for a year-long life span, and includes daily write-on boxes. Beautiful photos feature the highlights of the gardens of Colonial Williamsburg

See also **AMERICAN GARDENS** under **GARDEN HISTORY**

1-55550-393-4 UNIVERSE $4.95

Frances **Mallary** & Peter **Mallary**

A Redouté Treasury: 468 Watercolors from Les Liliacees

Considered to be among the most exact and beautiful botanical prints ever made

0-86565-067-5 BOOK SALES $22.98

Rosemary **Verey**

The Garden in Winter

A superbly illustrated book of gardens in England, Europe, and the United States

0-88192-337-0 TIMBER PB $24.95

William **Warren**

Balinese Gardens

A beautifully illustrated tour through the lush gardens of the Indonesian archipelago, in which lofty volcanic mountains tower over orchards and gardens nestled in the grounds of temples, palaces, hotels, and private houses. 270 full-color photographs and lively text reveal a little-known world of floral landscape and design

PHOTOGRAPHS BY TETTONI, LUCA INVERNIZZI

0-500-01680-1 THAMES & HUDSON $50.00

Pets

The overwhelming majority of pet books focuses on particular species and favorite breeds. There is, however, a small but interesting body of literature that takes a more general view of pets and their role in human society.

Bruce **Fogle**

Pets and Their People

A lucid introduction, both practical and philosophical, to the bonds between humans and animals

0-670-55052-3 VIKING $14.95

James **Herriot**

All Creatures Great and Small

Best-selling memoirs of a Yorkshire country veterinarian with a genuine love of life and a natural storyteller's gift

0-312-08498-6 ST. MARTIN'S $18.95

0-553-26812-0 BDD PB $6.99

Amy **Marder**

Your Healthy Pet: A Practical Guide For Choosing and Raising Happier, Healthier Dogs and Cats

Prevention magazine's pet care columnist gives expert advice on flea-fighting, allergy control, slimming down diets, and other matters related to the vigor and longevity of your cat or dog. Includes a valuable and informative discussion of which health problems to watch out for in different breeds. An excellent and highly readable handbook

0-87596-185-1 RODALE PB $14.95

Jeffrey Moussaieff **Masson** & Susan **McCarthy**

When Elephants Sleep: The Emotional Lives of Animals

"A masterpiece, the most comprehensive and compelling argument for animal sensibility that I've yet seen "—Elizabeth Marshall Thomas, *The Hidden Life of Dogs*

See also **ZOOLOGY** under **NATURAL HISTORY** under **LIFE SCIENCES** in **SCIENCE**

0-385-31425-6 DOUBLEDAY $23.95

Harriet **Ritvo**

The Animal Estate: The English and Other Creatures in the Victorian Age —Seven Case Studies Showing How Animals Have Been Made to Embody Human Values and Institutions

0-674-03707-3 HARVARD PB $12.95

Janet **Ruckert**

The Four-Footed Therapist: How Your Pet Can Help You Solve Your Problems

The therapeutic value of companion animals

0-89815-185-6 TEN SPEED PB $7.95

Pet Care and Pet Loss

Howard **Bronson**

Dog Gone: Coping With the Loss of a Pet

Help for those in mourning for a beloved pet. "Grieving pet lovers and just pet lovers in general are realizing enormous benefits in this book"—Louise Morgan, D.M.V., Brewster Veterinary Hospital

0-9616807-8-4 BESTL PB $9.95

Warren **Eckstein** & Fay **Eckstein**

Understanding Your Pet: The Eckstein Method of Pet Therapy and Behavior Training

How to deal with pet behavior problems by looking at the family's life

0-517-14906-0 RANDOM HOUSE $7.99

Michael **Fox**

The New Animal Doctor's Answer Book

A valuable reference, which answers more than 1000 questions about the care and behavior of cats, dogs, fish, birds, rabbits, hamsters, and other pets. Written by the author of the popular newspaper column "The Animal Doctor"

1-55704-035-4 NEWMARKET PB $14.95

Peter **Roach**

The Complete Book of Pet Care

A practical, up-to-date household reference book by an Australian veterinarian; with sections on birds, cats, dogs, fish, guinea pigs, horses, mice, rabbits, and reptiles

0-87605-484-X MACMILLAN PB $17.95

Dogs

The dog, a domesticated wolf, is generally thought to have been mankind's first pet. Originally a hunting ally, by 7000 BC he was a domesticated friend as well. The superior quality and quantity of dog books attests to the abiding hold of canines on mankind's affection and imagination. Today it is estimated that 40 percent of all American households own a dog. Howell Book House is the outstanding publisher of dog literature, offering the most serious, comprehensive and up-to-date books. Denlingers, though smaller, also publishes quality dog books.

American Kennel Club Staff

The Complete Dog Book

The indispensable dog book: America's official guide to the purebred dog, a superb compendium dedicated to "acquainting the public with the appearance and qualification of each breed, and guiding owners in keeping their dogs healthy, happy and well-balanced"

0-87605-464-5 HOWELL $27.50

Konrad Z. **Lorenz**

Man Meets Dog

"A warm humanity, a kindly humor, and a deep thoughtfulness shine through almost every word Konrad Lorenz writes"—*New Yorker*

1-56836-051-7 KODANSHA PB $12.00

Elizabeth M. **Schuler**, editor
Simon and Schuster's Guide to Dogs
Identifying pictures and characteristics of over 300 breeds, including all those not recognized by the American Kennel Club
0-671-25527-4 SIMON & SCHUSTER PB $14.00

Carrie **Shook**
What to Name Your Dog
An entertaining book, with thousands of imaginative names
0-87605-807-1 HOWELL PB $10.95

Dog Behavior and Psychology

Matthew **Margolis** & Mordecai **Siegal**
Woof! My Twenty-Five Years of Training Dogs
The best-selling authors of *Good Dog, Bad Dog* and *When Good Dogs Do Bad Things* reminisce about 25 years in dog training. We meet dogs of the rich and famous—Whoopie Goldberg, Cher, and James Stewart—help housebreak Poofie the Park Avenue Pekingese and observe Margolis's howling success on the *Tonight* show with Johnny Carson
0-517-59148-0 CROWN $20.00

Myrna M. **Milani**
The Body Language and Emotion of Dogs
The former president of the New Hampshire Veterinary Association offers the fruits of her considerable experience to help dog owners understand the complex lives of their pets. Based on case histories, Milani gives advice on canine behavioral problems while showing owners how properly and sensitively to respond to the physical and emotional needs of their pets, Sure to strengthen the pet-owner relationship
0-688-06239-3 MORROW $17.95
0-688-12841-6 QUILL PB $12.00

Desmond **Morris**
Dogwatching
Random observations and little-known facts by a celebrated author and zoologist
0-517-56519-6 DILITHIUM $13.00
0-517-88055-5 CROWN PB $8.00

Kate **Petty**
Dogs: First Pets
0-8120-1484-7 BARRONS PB $4.95

Clarence **Pfaffenberger**
New Knowledge of Dog Behavior
A clear exposition of the four critical stages of development in a puppy's life
0-87605-704-0 HOWELL $21.95

James **Serpell**, editor
The Domestic Dog: Its Evolution, Behaviour, and Interactions with People
ILLUSTRATED BY PRISCILLA BARRETT
0-521-41529-2 CAMBRIDGE $69.95
0-521-42537-9 CAMBRIDGE PB $19.95

Bill **Tarrant**
The Magic of Dogs
Combining his love of dogs with the exactitude of his vast scientific knowledge, the author of the most popular dog column in America (*Field and Stream*) offers this complete and detailed appreciation of the canine, from a biological study of the dog's physical and mental capabilities to the processes of training, caring, and loving
1-55821-365-1 LYONS & BURFORD $22.95

David **Taylor**
You and Your Dog
0-394-72983-8 RANDOM HOUSE PB $16.00

Elizabeth Marshall **Thomas**
The Hidden Life of Dogs
Thomas, renowned anthropologist, novelist, and ethologist, solves the dog mystery: what do they want? Do they dream or fantasize? By observing her "pack" of 11 over 30 years she watched them parent, navigate cities and country, work out hierarchy, and negotiate territory. In short, she discovered what dogs are. "A model of steady, intellectually courageous, and imaginatively fastidious thought about animals. [Her] observations are as quick and decisive and meaningful as, those of a confident husky. An exquisite book"—Vicki Hearne, author of *Bandit: Dossier of A Dangerous Dog*
0-395-66958-8 HOUGHTON MIFFLIN $18.95

This is a book about dog consciousness. To some people, the subject might seem anthropomorphic simply by definition, since in the past even scientists have been led to believe that only human beings have thoughts or emotions. Of course, nothing could be further from the truth.
THE HIDDEN LIFE OF DOGS

Dog Training

Ted **Baer**
Communicating With Your Dog: Twenty Magic Words
Baer uses a 20-word command vocabulary and simple hand signals that utilize your dog's basic willingness to please as a foundation for obedience training. Winner of the Dog Writer's Association of America Award
0-8120-4203-4 BARRONS PB $10.95

Carol **Benjamin**
Dog Problems
How to control and correct undesirable behavior patterns
0-87605-514-5 HOWELL PB $14.00

Mother Knows Best: The Natural Way to Train Your Dog
Benjamin uses a dog's "pack animal" behavior pattern as the basis for her renowned training techniques. Covers everything from basic puppy training to structured obedience exercises
0-87605-666-4 HOWELL $22.95

Carol Lea **Benjamin**
Surviving Your Dog's Adolescence: A Positive Training Program
This humane guide offers a hands-on approach to overcoming those wild years—five months to three years—when dogs may start exhibiting aggressive, destructive, or other anti-social behavior. Covers everything from training programs to commands and selection of equipment
See also **DOG BEHAVIOR AND PSYCHOLOGY**
0-87605-742-3 HOWELL $20.00

Kate Delano **Condax**
101 Training Tips For Your Dog
Two innovative new books draw on the cutting edge of animal behavior research. The authors show that both dogs' and cats' inborn behaviors and abilities—pack mentality, establishment of dominance—can be used in behavior modification, and that even an old dog or cat can learn the new tricks of proper and peaceful habits
0-440-50568-2 DELL PB $8.95

Shirlee **Kalstone**
How to Housebreak Your Dog in 7 Days
Includes easy-to-follow instructions for apartment and house dwellers, with hour-by-hour schedules. Advice on choosing between the paper-training and housebreaking methods for your dog
0-553-34615-6 BANTAM PB $5.99

Brian **Kilcommons** & Sarah **Wilson**
Childproofing Your Dog: A Complete Guide to Preparing Your Dog for the Children in Your Life
A step-by-step, photo-illustrated guide to everything from how to train an older dog to accept an infant to teaching kids safety rules and dog care. Special section offers tips for helping dog-phobic kids
0-446-67016-2 WARNER PB $9.99

William **Koehler**
Koehler Method of Dog Training
A standard text by the former Disney animal trainer
0-87605-785-7 HOWELL $25.95
0-7838-1871-8 GK HALL PB $23.95

Monks of the Brotherhood of St. Francis.
How to Be Your Dog's Best Friend: A Training Manual for Dog Owners
The Monks of New Skete, an Upstate New York monastery, support themselves by raising German Shepherds and training a variety of breeds. "The Monks of New Skete have turned out a book on virtually every phase of dog care, understanding, and training"—*The Washington Post*
0-316-60491-7 LITTLE, BROWN $22.95

The Art of Raising a Puppy
Advice on everything from choosing the right breed to solving common puppy problems
0-316-57839-8 LITTLE, BROWN $22.95

Margaret **Pearsall**
The Pearsall Guide to Successful Dog Training
Obedience from the dog's point of view
0-87605-759-8 HOWELL $25.95

Mordecai **Siegal** & Matthew **Margolis**

Good Dog, Bad Dog

Self-help reference for dog training. "It will be read and revered for many years to come" —Roger Caras

0-8050-1094-7 HOLT $22.50

When Good Dogs Do Bad Things

Even the best dogs have their moments when they're not carrying in slippers or bringing brandy to lost mountaineers. Here is an assortment of proven behavior modification techniques for correcting more than 30 problems ranging from excessive barking to destructive chewing

0-316-79012-5 LITTLE, BROWN PB $12.95

Barbara **Woodhouse**

Dog Training My Way

Woodhouse presents her six-and-a-half hour dog (and owner) training course. "Woodhouse knows how to win the hearts and minds of dogs" —*Washington Star*

0-425-08108-7 BERKLEY PB $5.50

No Bad Dogs: Training Dogs the Woodhouse Way

Simple and effective techniques from the host of the TV series "Training Dogs the Woodhouse Way", which has a devoted international following. Woodhouse has successfully trained over 17,000 dogs using this method

0-671-54185-4 SUMMIT PB $11.00

Health and Care

Carol Lea **Benjamin**

Second-Hand Dog: How to Turn Yours Into a First-Rate Pet

The special needs of dogs adopted from shelters or rescued from the streets

0-87605-735-0 HOWELL PB $6.95

Marty L. **Brennan** & Norma **Eckroate**

Pet Guides

These fascinating pet guides emphasize a holistic approach to pet care. Combining alternative remedies to traditional veterinarian practices uch as herbal treatments, homeopathy, and acupuncture, with the latest scientific information on everything from training and traveling to diet and grooming, these guides are sure to answer your every question

0-452-27019-7 PLUME PB $15.95

Jane **Buckle**

How to Massage Your Dog

Describes techniques for massaging everything from a dog's face and head to its paws and tail. Includes information on the use of oils, types of stroke, and adapting massage to the special needs of the elderly, hyperactive, or newly adopted canine

0-87605-645-1 HOWELL $9.95

Delbert **Carlson** & James **Giffin**

Dog Owner's Home Veterinary Handbook

The leader in the field of professional dog doctoring. Covers every health need your dog will face in its lifetime

0-87605-537-4 HOWELL $25.00

Tim **Hawcroft**

First Aid For Dogs

The knowledgeable author of the *Howell Books for Dog and Cat Care* teaches you when to call the vet and when to treat your pet at home. Deals with poisoning, accidents, fight injuries, and coaches you in assembling a priority first-aid kit for common—and not so common—mishaps. A great resource for pet owners, urban or rural

0-87605-546-3 HOWELL PB $10.00

William **Kay** & Elizabeth **Randolph**

The Complete Book of Dog Health: The Animal Medical Center

0-87605-455-6 HOWELL PB $15.00

Chris C. **Pinney**

Caring for Your Older Dog

The complete sourcebook for those who want to ensure longevity and quality of life for an aging canine. Detailed advice and reassurance on everything from hearing loss to euthanasia

0-8120-9149-3 BARRONS PB $8.95

Sheldon **Rubin**

Practical Guide to Dog Care

Rubin joins with the editors of *Consumer Guide* in this concise sourcebook that covers everything from choosing a suitable breed to coping with canine medical emergencies

0-451-18575-7 SIGNET PB $4.99

Leon **Whitney** & George **Whitney**

Complete Book of Dog Care

A thorough, classic guide

0-385-15547-6 DOUBLEDAY PB $13.95

Grooming

Charlotte **Gold**

Grooming Dogs For Profit

A professional groomer covers all aspects of the grooming business

0-87605-618-4 HOWELL $22.95

Ben **Stone** & Pearl **Stone**

The Stone Guide to Dog Grooming For All Breeds

A comprehensive guide with fall grooming instructions and techniques for all AKC breeds

0-87605-403-3 HOWELL $32.95

Breeding and Showing

George G. **Alston** & Connie **Vanacore**

The Winning Edge: Show Ring Secrets

How to make your dog stand out from the crowd at any show. The bedtime reading of champions, copiously illustrated

0-87605-834-9 HOWELL $25.95

Robert **Forsyth** & Jane **Forsyth**

The Forsyth Guide to Successful Dog Showing

A concise guide by two renowned handlers

0-87605-523-4 HOWELL $19.95

Nancy **Baer** & Steven **Duno**

Choosing a Dog: A Guide to Picking the Perfect Breed

A thorough and helpful guide to to the behavioral profiles and needs of all breeds recognized by the American Kennel Club. Illustrated

0-425-14958-7 BERKELEY PB $12.00

Alvin **Grossman**

The Standard Book of Dog Breeding

0-944875-18-1 DORAL $26.50

Mary **Smith**

The Joy of Breeding Your Own Show Dog

A serious introduction to a complex art

0-87605-413-0 HOWELL $22.95

Popular Breeds

Clara **Tice**

ABC Dogs

Whether you know the alphabet already or are just learning it, this is an enchanting tour of dog breeds from Afghan to Ulmer. Tice's classic illustrations, formally published in the original *Vanity Fair* magazine between 1914 and 1926, are classics of the genre: whimsical lithographs that are complemented by perceptive discussions of the origins and foibles of each breed

0-8109-1958-3 ABRAMS $12.95

Tetsu **Yamazaki**

Legacy of the Dog: The Ultimate Illustrated Guide to Over 200 Breeds

An extensively illustrated (900 color photos) guide to 200 dog breeds, some rarely seen outside their homelands. Includes information on characteristics, care and exercise, and puppies and training

0-8118-1123-9 CHRONICLE $45.00

0-8118-1069-0 CHRONICLE PB $24.95

Constance **Miller** & Edward **Gilbert**, Jr.

The New Complete Afghan Hound

0-87605-001-1 HOWELL $25.95

Robert **Berndt**

Your Beagle

0-87714-034-0 DENLINGERS $13.95

Billie **McFadden**

The New Boxer

0-87605-062-3 HOWELL $25.95

E. Ruth **Terry**

The New Chihuahua

0-87605-125-5 HOWELL $25.95

L.J. Kip **Kopatch**

The Complete Chow Chow

0-87605-102-6 HOWELL $25.95

Collie Club of America
New Collie
0-87605-130-1 HOWELL $25.95

George **Roos**
Collie Concept
0-931866-36-7 ALPINE $26.95

Lois **Meistrell**
The New Dachsund
0-87605-107-7 HOWELL $25.95

Alfred **Treen** & Esmeralda **Treen**
The Dalmatian: Coach Dog—Firehouse Dog
0-87605-109-3 HOWELL $24.00

Joanna **Walker**
The New Doberman Pinscher
0-87605-113-1 HOWELL $25.95

Jane **Bennett**
The New Complete German Shepherd Dog
0-87605-151-4 HOWELL $25.95

Gertrude **Fischer**
The New Complete Golden Retriever
0-87605-185-9 HOWELL $25.95

Evelyn **Schneider**
The Golden Retriever
0-87714-122-3 DENLINGERS $29.95

Helen **Warwick**
The New Complete Labrador Retriever
0-87605-230-8 HOWELL $25.95

Anna **Nicholas** & Joan **Brearley**
The Book of the Pekingese
0-87666-348-X T.F.H. $39.95

Frank **Sabella**
Your Poodle: Standard, Miniature and Toy
0-87714-023-5 DENLINGERS $13.95

Shirley **Thomas**
The New Pug
0-87605-264-2 HOWELL $25.95

Esther **Wolf**
Your Pug
0-87714-001-4 DENLINGERS $13.95

Paul **Strang** & Eve **Olsen**
The Chinese Shar-Pei
9-99273-452-3 DENLINGERS PB $19.95
0-87714-072-3 DENLINGERS PB $29.95

Joan **Gordon** & Janet **Bennett**
The Complete Yorkshire
0-87605-361-4 HOWELL $25.95

D. Brian **Plummer**
The Complete Jack Russell Terrier
0-85115-121-3 HOWELL $22.95

John **Remer**, Jr., editor
The New Bull Terrier
0-87605-096-8 HOWELL $25.95

John **Marvin**
The Complete West Highland Terrier
0-87605-355-X HOWELL $25.95

The New Complete Scottish Terrier
0-87605-306-1 HOWELL $25.95

Dog Stories and Humor

Sharon **Beals**
What Dogs Do
A charming collection of black-and-white photos depicting everything from a guard-dog Chihuahua to a Dalmatian wannabe
0-8118-1023-2 CHRONICLE $7.95

Roger **Caras**
Roger Caras' Treasury of Great Dog Stories
Stories about dogs, from Jack London and Mark Twain to R.K. Narayan and Francoise Sagan. Essential for any dog lover
0-88365-764-3 GALAHAD $10.98

John **Donegan**
Dog Almighty!
Satirical, good-natured cartoons
0-87605-466-1 HOWELL $7.95

Vicki **Hearne**
Adam's Task: Calling Animals by Name
An examination of the moral implications of animal training. "A fascinating and often surprising discussion of human-animal encounters"—*Atlantic Monthly*
See also **ANIMALS** under **NATURE STUDY** in **SCIENCE**
0-06-097634-9 HARPERPERENNIAL PB $13.00

Animal Happiness
Hearne, perhaps America's most articulate and outspoken animal trainer, has assembled cameos of a variety of our fellow creatures here. "Smart, passionate, and challenging"—*Kirkus Reviews*
See also **ANIMALS** under **NATURE STUDY** in **SCIENCE**
0-06-092606-6 HARPERPERENNIAL PB $12.00

Amy **Hempel** & Jim **Shepard**
Unleashed: Poems by Writer's Dogs
A who's who of literary dogdom, including poetic selections from the canine companions of Edward Albee, John Irving, Linda Barry, and more
0-517-70140-5 CROWN $19.00

James **Herriot**
James Herriot's Dog Stories
A collection of all the dog stories from the best-selling author
0-312-43968-7 ST. MARTIN'S $19.95
0-312-92558-1 ST. MARTIN'S PB $6.99

Donald **McCaig**
Eminent Dogs Dangerous Men
From the author of *Nop's Trials*, this is a wonderfully readable journey into the heart of human-canine history. "McCaig has given us, at last, a serious dog book for grownups" —Vicki Hearne
0-06-098114-8 CURLEY PB $12.00

John **McCormack**
Fields and Pastures New: My First Year As a Country Vet
In November of 1963, McCormack moved to Choctaw County, Alabama, to become the region's first trained vet. "A heartwarming read for the animal lover"—James Herriot
0-449-22536-4 CREST PB $5.99

Willie **Morris**
My Dog Skip
The moving story of a boy, his dog, and small-town America. "True artistry and exquisite writing"—*Winston Groom*
See also **MEMOIRS AND JOURNALS** under **20TH-CENTURY AMERICAN ESSAYS AND JOURNALISM** in **LITERATURE OF THE AMERICAS**
0-679-44144-1 RANDOM HOUSE $15.00
0-679-76722-3 VINTAGE PB $9.00

The New Yorker
The New Yorker Book of Dog Cartoons
Dogs in an endless variety of incarnations—drawn from 65 years of *New Yorker*—by Charles Addams, George Booth, Roz Chast, Edward Koren, Edward Sorel, Saul Steinberg, and James Thurber
See also **NEW YORKER ANTHOLOGIES** under **COMICS OF THE '50S AND '60S** under **COMICS** in **POPULAR READING**
0-679-41680-3 KNOPF $20.00
0-679-76542-5 KNOPF PB $9.00

Louise **Shattuck**
From Riches to Bitches (and a Cadillac For Your Vet): Being a Mirthful Recounting of the Carry-On Kennel Chronicles
0-87605-548-X HOWELL $19.95

Illustrated Dog Books

Life Magazine, editor
A Dog's Life: A Book of Classic Photographs
Classic photographs from the pages of *Life* capture the essence of dogs in all seasons. With an introduction by the ultimate canine photographer, William Wegman, this is a delightful addition to any photography—or dog-lover's collection
INTRODUCTION BY WILLIAM WEGMAN
0-316-52691-6 LITTLE, BROWN $14.95

Ruth **Silverman**, editor
The Dog Observed: Photographs, 1844-1983
A wonderful book of photographs by some of the world's greatest photographers, such as Diane Arbus and Richard Avedon
0-87701-499-X CHRONICLE PB $16.95

Cats

Domesticated since prehistoric times, cats were once used as retrievers in hunting. The modern domestic and the Egyptian cat are both thought to derive from a type of North African wildcat. The personality of the cat, with its air of mystery and independence, has always been fascinating, and the literature on cats reflects this mystique.

Dr. **Zodicat**

Zodicat Speaks: Discover Your Cat's Astrological Signature

0-670-86858-2 VIKING..........$12.95

Cat Breeds

David **Alderton**

Cats

1-56458-073-3 DORLING KINDERSLEY..........$29.95
1-56458-070-9 DORLING KINDERSLEY PB..........$17.95

Joan **Brearley**

All About Himalayan Cats

0-86622-080-1 T.F.H...........$17.95

Kate **Faler**

This Is the Abyssinian Cat

0-87666-866-X T.F.H...........$35.95

Richard H. **Gebhardt**

The Complete Cat Book

International all-breed judge Gebhardt covers every aspect of purchasing and caring for a cat. Includes standards for over 40 breeds, with color photos of each type

0-87605-919-1 HOWELL PB..........$19.95

Harper Collins

Harper's Illustrated Book of Cats: A Guide to Every Breed Recognized in America

A comprehensive and essential book on cats, as there is no single governing body (such as the American Kennel Club for dogs) that regulates breeds and standards for cats

0-06-273165-3 HARPERCOLLINS PB..........$16.00

Health and Care

Marty L. **Brennan** & Norma **Eckroate**

The New Natural Cat: A Complete Guide For Finicky Owners

A revised and expanded edition of the classic handbook, this volume covers everything from holistic cat care to changing scratching and biting behavior. Includes a new encyclopedia of 40 common health problems

0-452-26517-7 DUTTON PB..........$15.95

Cat Fanciers' Association

Cat Encyclopedia

Covers care, health, food, travel, first aid, all clearly organized with appendices and glossaries, illustrated

0-684-80186-8 SIMON & SCHUSTER..........$30.00

Delbert G. **Carlson** & James M. **Giffin**

Cat Owner's Home Veterinary Handbook

This revised edition includes a signs and symptoms index, plus hundreds of helpful photos and illustrations. An encyclopedic book for every cat owner's library

0-87605-796-2 HOWELL..........$24.95

Carol Himsel **Daly**

Caring for Your Sick Cat

Covers everything from prenatal care and kitten delivery to broken bones. Special hints on caring for cats just released from the hospital

0-8120-1726-9 BARRONS PB..........$9.95

Andrew **Edney** & David **Taylor**

Cat Care: 101 Essential Tips

This pocket-sized volume covers everything from how to deal with feline houseplant eating to treating a cat who has been poisoned. Color photos

1-56458-986-2 DORLING KINDERSLEY PB..........$6.95

Teri **Goodman**

Purr-Fect Dishes: Whisker-Licking and Nutritious Recipes for Your Favorite Feline

A collection of recipes for your favorite cat, from Salmon Quenelles with Shrimp Sauce to Roast Duck Breast with Lo Mein Noodles. Yummy

0-688-12813-0 HEARST..........$14.95

Tim **Hawcroft**

First Aid For Cats

0-87605-907-8 HOWELL PB..........$10.00

Jim **Humphries**

Dr. Jim's Animal Clinic for Cats: What People What to Know

The author's experience as host of a syndicated radio call-in show and cable TV "Pet Care Magazine", as well as his 15 years in private practice, have given this question-and-answer format book both readability and authority

0-87605-790-3 HOWELL PB..........$15.00

Brian **Kilcommons** & Sarah **Wilson**

Good Owners, Great Cats

From the best-selling animal trainer—the only American protege of the celebrated British trainer Barbara Wodehouse—the definitive guide to keeping your feline healthy, happy, and well-behaved. From kitten-proofing the home to grooming, health care, and playing, this is the only guide to owning a cat you will ever need

See also **PSYCHOLOGY, BEHAVIOR, AND TRAINING**

0-446-51807-7 WARNER..........$19.95

Kate **Petty**

Cats: First Pets

0-8120-1485-5 BARRONS PB..........$4.95

Mordecai **Siegal**

The Cornell Book of Cats: A Comprehensive Medical Reference For Every Cat and Kitten

0-394-56787-0 VILLARD..........$30.00

David **Taylor**

You and Your Cat

0-394-72984-6 RANDOM HOUSE PB..........$16.00

Psychology, Behavior, and Training

Bill **Fleming** & Judy **Petersen-Fleming**

The Tiger on Your Couch: What the Big Cats Can Teach You About Living in Harmony With Your House Cat

The authors, wild animal behaviorists, offer tips, photos, facts and stories about cats large and small. "If one has just one cat book allowed, this would be my top choice" —Betty White

0-688-13508-0 QUILL PB..........$12.00

Brian **Kilcommons** & Sarah **Wilson**

Good Owners, Great Cats

From the best-selling animal trainer—the only American protege of the celebrated British trainer Barbara Wodehouse—the definitive guide to keeping your feline healthy, happy, and well-behaved. From kitten-proofing the home to grooming, health care, and playing, this is the only guide to owning a cat you will ever need

See also **HEALTH AND CARE**

0-446-51807-7 WARNER..........$19.95

Jo **Loeb** & Paul **Loeb**

You Can Train Your Cat

0-671-73906-9 POCKET PB..........$5.50

Myrna **Milani**

The Body Language and Emotion of Cats

A behavioral approach to improving one's relations with cats

0-688-12840-8 QUILL PB..........$12.00

Desmond **Morris**

Catwatching

Observations and thoughts on the double life of cats, from a seasoned observer

0-517-12065-8 CRESCENT..........$17.99
0-517-88053-9 CROWN PB..........$8.00

Debra **Pirotin** & Sherry **Cohen**

No Naughty Cats: The First Guide to Intelligent Cat Training

0-449-21005-7 HARPERCOLLINS PB..........$4.99

Alice **Rhea**

Good Cats, Bad Habits: The Complete A-To-Z Guide for When Your Cat Misbehaves

An A-Z guide for the owner of the imperfectly behaved kitty. Instructions on alleviating hairballs, introducing your cat safely to a baby, stopping flowerbed digging, and more

0-684-81113-8 FIRESIDE PB..........$12.00

Carin **Smith**

101 Training Tips For Your Cat

0-440-50567-4 DELL PB..........$8.95

Roz **Riddle**

The City Cat: How to Live Healthily and Happily with Your Indoor Pet

0-449-21022-7 FAWCETT PB $4.99

Elizabeth Marshall **Thomas**

The Tribe of Tiger: Cats and Their Culture

From the author of *The Hidden Life of Dogs*, this insightful study of feline life is a must even for the non-cat lover. "Formidable woman. Wonderful book" —Christopher Lehmann-Haupt

0-671-79965-7 SIMON & SCHUSTER $20.00
0-684-80454-9 TOUCHSTONE PB $12.00

Legends, Stories, and Entertainments

Cleveland **Amory**

The Best Cat Ever

The author of *The Cat and the Curmudgeon* and *The Cat Who Came for Christmas* concludes his delightful trilogy with reminiscences about his charmed life as a friend of Kate Hepburn and the Duke of Windsor, as both he and his wise, unsentimental cat, Polar Bear, enter their autumnal years

0-316-03744-3 LITTLE, BROWN $19.95
0-316-03762-1 LITTLE, BROWN PB $10.95

The Cat Who Came for Christmas

A humorous best-selling memoir of a strange feline friend

0-14-099706-7 PENGUIN PB $8.95
0-14-011342-8 VIKING PB $7.95

Cleveland Amory's Compleat Cat

Includes *The Cat Who Came for Christmas, The Cat and the Curmudgeon,* and *The Best Cat Ever*, the three beloved books concerning Amory's adventures with Polar Bear the cat

1-88482-228-2 BLACK DOG $12.98

Brandt **Aymar**, editor

The Personality of the Cat

An anthology of cat commentary from T.S. Eliot, Colette, Kipling, and many more. Includes artwork by Picasso, Manet, Gustave Doré, and other cat fanciers

0-517-00016-4 CRESCENT $9.99

Felicity **Bast**, editor &
Robert **Anderson**, illustrator

The Poetical Cat

W.H. Auden, Elizabeth Bishop, William Carlos Williams, and William Butler Yeats are some of the poets whose work, inspired by cats, is collected in this witty, spirited volume. A perfect gift for the cat lover

0-374-23533-3 FS&G $20.00

Henry **Beard**

French For Cats

0-679-40676-X VILLARD $10.00

Poetry For Cats: The Definitive Anthology of Distinguished Feline Verse

Beard has brought your cat through beginning and advanced French, and you'd think that would be enough. But no. Now he introduces the feline composition of great—and neglected—pet poets: Whitman's "Leaves of Catnip," Thomas's "Do Not Go Gentle to that Damned Vet," and, of course, the celebrated "Love Song of J. Alfred Housecat" by T. S. Eliot. Inventive, parodic poetry by the best-selling author of those strange and lovely little books, *French for Cats* and *Advanced French for Cats*

0-679-43582-4 VILLARD $12.95

T.S. Eliot

Tom **Bianchi**

Living with Dickens

"The camera, to Dickens, is another cat toy, a signal that he will now get my undivided attention. This fortunate circumstance has allowed me to make this record of our lives together." So writes Bianchi in explaining these delightful photographs of the imperious, curious, infinitely playful cat of his household

0-312-10491-X ST. MARTIN'S PB $13.95

John R. F. **Breen**, editor

Who's Who of Cats

This Is Not A Listing Of The Feline Rich And Famous, But Rather 496 Mini-Biographies Of "The Cats Next Door" By Their Owners And Friends. A Volume For The Truly Cat-Mad

1-56305-629-1 WORKMAN PB $7.95

Michael **Cader**

Meditations For Cats Who Do Too Much: Learning to Take Things One Life At a Time

Compulsive behavior, eating disorders, and chronic fatigue are only a few of the maladies facing felines today. From chasing your own tail to coping with the compulsion to sit on each piece of furniture, everyday, this handy self-help guide is the essential manual for all nine lives

0-14-017799-X PENGUIN PB $5.95

Louis **Camuti**

My Patients Are Under the Bed

The popular memoirs and anecdotes of a cat doctor

0-671-55450-6 SIMON & SCHUSTER PB $10.00

Roger A. **Caras**

The Cats of Thistle Hiss: A Mostly Peaceable Kingdom

The story of the ten-plus cats who make their homes on Caras's Maryland farm. "This is one big enjoyable read" —*Kirkus Reviews*

0-671-75462-9 SIMON & SCHUSTER $22.00
0-684-80061-6 FIRESIDE PB $11.00

Jacqueline **Damian**

Sasha's Tail

Damian is the Boswell to cat Sasha's Johnson in this charming memoir. "Reading *Sasha's Tail* is almost as wonderful as having a real cat purring in your lap"—Susan Fromberg Schaeffer

0-393-03731-2 NORTON $19.95

Robert **De Laroche** & Jean-Michel **Labat**

The Secret Life of Cats

Color photos of diverse cats and a plethora of cat-related artwork from throughout the ages decorate this thought-provoking look at the influence of the feline on human history. Translated from the French

0-8120-6513-1 BARRONS $18.95

Paul **Gallico** & Suzanne **Szasz**

The Silent Miaow: A Manuel For Kittens, Strays, and Homeless Cats

Fictional "guide" for cats on how to win their way into a household and take over the family

0-517-55683-9 CROWN PB $12.00

Peter **Gethers**

A Cat Abroad: The Further Adventures of Norton, the Cat Who Went to Paris, and His Human

The funny and often touching sequel to *The Cat Who Went to Paris* finds the delightful Norton, a Scottish Fold, again on the continent in a charming adventure

0-517-59110-3 CROWN $16.00

James **Herriot**

James Herriot's Cat Stories

A felinophile's delight, this collection of stories from the author of *All Creatures Great and Small* is illustrated with charming watercolors

ILLUSTRATIONS BY LESLEY HOLMES

0-312-11342-0 ST. MARTIN'S $16.95

Joyce Carol **Oates** & Daniel **Halpern**, editors

The Sophisticated Cat: An Anthology

An irresistible and amazingly diverse collection of stories and poems about cats by such varied writers as Balzac, Keats, Chekhov, Colette, Twain, Hemingway, Wallace Stevens, and Angela Carter

0-525-93522-3 PLUME PB $23.00

Richard **Stephens** & Kim **Smith**, editors

Mysterious Cat Stories

A delightful compilation of fiction, legends, and reminiscenses—dating from the 13th century to now—about the most supernatural of beasts. Among the stories are Bram Stoker's *The Jewel of the Seven Stars,* Washington Irving's *Sir Walter Scott's Cat,* as well as contributions from Edgar Allen Poe, Cervantes, and Saki

0-88184-948-0 CARROLL & GRAF $19.95

Patrick R. **Tobin** & Christine R. **Doley**

Petted by the Light: The Most Profound and Complete Feline Near-Death Experiences Ever

At last! A "Mew Age" handbook to the feline near-death experience! This unprecedented collection allows cats to share their tales of the afterlife, tales that, if taken seriously, could solve some of the most tenacious problems of the world: cat and mouse hatred, high rate of unwanted litters, overcrowded animal shelters. A delicious parody of the national bestseller

1-55972-314-9 BIRCH LANE $9.95

Illustrated Cat Books

Heather **Busch** & Burton **Silver**

Why Cats Paint: A Theory of Feline Aesthetics

From angst-ridden cat portraitists to moody felines who sculpt in wool and sofa stuffing, here is the deeper side of cat creativity exposed. "Sets cat art in a coherent framework, yet permits the cats to speak for themselves" —*L.A. Art Times*

0-89815-623-8 TEN SPEED $18.95
0-89815-612-2 TEN SPEED PB $16.95

Juliet **Clutton-Brock**

Cats: Ancient and Modern

This is the ultimate cat-fancier gift, depicting 7,000 years of feline domesticity in lore, history, pictures, and literature from around the world. "A beautiful, intelligent, well written, and fascinating book"—Harriet Ritvo, MIT

0-674-10407-2 HARVARD $16.95

Susan **Herbert**

Medieval Cats

Herbert meticulously inserts felines into scenes based on authentic works from the 13th to 16th centuries

0-8212-2215-5 THAMES & HUDSON $14.95

Oliver **Herford**

The Rubaiyat of a Persian Kitten

First published in 1904, this long-lost treasure chronicles the adventures of a tiny cat whose empty bowl leads him on a search for milk. Original illustrations

0-8478-1707-5 RIZZOLI $14.95

Ronald **Searle**

Searle's Cats

0-89815-263-1 TEN SPEED PB $9.95

Hans **Silvester**

Cats in the Sun

Silvester spent three years chronicling the lives of cats in the Greek Islands in these handsome photographs. "The finest pictures ever taken of cats"—*The Atlantic Monthly*

0-8118-1384-3 CHRONICLE $10.95
0-8118-1093-3 CHRONICLE PB $18.95

Richard **Surman**

College Cats of Oxford and Cambridge

From Polly Flinders of Oriel to Trinity's Burbage, the feline Oxbridge inhabitants give their human counterparts a run for their money in the charm and eccentricity departments. From the author of *Cathedral Cats*

0-00-627869-8 HARPERCOLLINS $16.00

Horses

Recent years have seen an increase in the popularity of equestrian sports in the United States, and many new books cover the field.

Eadward **Muybridge**

Animals in Motion

This classic, ground-breaking collection of animal stop-motion photos forever settled the ancient question of whether or not horses ever simultaneously have all four feet off the ground during the course of a natural stride in any gait. Includes 4000 high speed shots of 34 different animals and birds, most against ruled backgrounds

See also **PHOTOGRAPHERS** under **PHOTOGRAPHY** in **ART**

EDITED BY LEWIS S. BROWN

0-486-20203-8 DOVER $29.95

Steven **Price**, editor

The Whole Horse Catalog

A complete up-to-date sensible handbook

0-671-86681-8 FIRESIDE PB $18.00
0-671-54196-X SIMON & SCHUSTER PB $16.00

M.A. **Stoneridge**

A Horse of Your Own

A complete guide for horse owners and riders

0-385-26385-6 DOUBLEDAY $29.95

George **Stubbs**

Anatomy of the Horse: A Sourcebook for Artists & Designers

0-8317-8043-6 SMITHMARK $14.98

Horse Breeds

There are over 150 registered breeds of horses. Unlike a thoroughbred dog, a thoroughbred horse is a specific breed that traces its ancestry to England in the 1660s. The thoroughbred line has produced the most valuable horses in the world, dominating flat and steeplechase racing as well as hunter/jumper horse shows and dressage competition. The graceful, fine-featured Arabian is one of the oldest breeds. The Quarter Horse, the classic "western" horse, is so named because of its ability to run one-quarter of a mile faster than any other breed.

Anthony **Amaral**

Mustang: The Life and Legends of Nevada's Wild Horses

0-87417-046-X NEVADA $12.95

Glynn **Haynes**

The American Paint Horse

0-8061-2144-0 OKLAHOMA PB $19.95

Bonnie L. **Hendricks**, editor

International Encyclopedia of Horse Breeds

See also **ONE-VOLUME ENCYCLOPEDIAS** under **REFERENCE** in **BUSINESS AND REFERENCE**
See also **ANIMALS** under **NATURE STUDY** in **SCIENCE**

FOREWORD BY ANTHONY A. DENT

0-8061-2753-8 OKLAHOMA $65.00

Robbee **Huseth**

Equine Expressions from the Kentucky Horse Park

This small book features lovely color photos of America's favorite 26 breeds, with a history of each. Includes quotations from, among others, Shakespeare and Xenophon on the subject of horses

0-87905-653-3 GIBBS SMITH $14.95

Bill **Richardson** & Dana **Richardson**

The Appaloosa

0-87980-182-4 WILSHIRE PB $7.00

Reginald **Summerhays**

The Arabian Horse

0-87980-183-2 WILSHIRE PB $7.00

Equine Management, Health, and Care

Gaydell **Collier**

Basic Horse Care

0-385-26199-3 DOUBLEDAY PB $15.95

Tim **Hawcroft**

The Complete Book of Horse Care

Reliable information on many aspects of horse care, with color photos

0-947116-77-X HOWELL $27.95

Horace **Hayes**

Veterinary Notes For Horse Owners

The most thorough and professional book on the subject

0-671-76561-2 ARCO $35.00

Bruce **Mills** & Barbara **Carne**

A Basic Guide to Horse Care and Management

0-87605-871-3 HOWELL $18.95

Meriel **Buxton**

The Pony Club: Dream and Reality

A history of one of the world's premiere equestrian associations

0-948253-70-3 SPORTSMANS PB $34.95

Pony Club Staff

Choosing and Buying a Pony

0-900226-38-2 HALFH $18.95

Gymkhanas and Rally Games

0-900226-42-0 HALFH PB $18.95

Hunting

0-900226-34-X HALFH $17.95

The Manual of Horsemanship
The Pony Club approach to horsemanship is hands-on and thorough. These manuals, respectively from the British and United States Pony Clubs and the British Horse Society, will not only teach one to ride independently and well, but how to care for a horse from the ground up
0-900226-39-0 HALFH $27.95

The Pony Club Manual of Horsemanship: Basics for Beginners-D Level
See also **HORSEMANSHIP**
0-87605-952-3 HOWELL $17.00

The Pony Club Quiz Book
0-900226-29-3 HALFH PB $12.95

The United States Pony Club Manual of Horsemanship: Intermediate Horsemanship C Level
0-87605-977-9 HOWELL $17.00

David W. **Ramey**
Horsefeathers: Facts Versus Myths About Your Horse's Health
Dispels such misinformation as the need to wrap a leg in the "right" direction, the need to walk a horse with colic, and whether or not cribbing qualifies as a "vice," plus the overdiagnosis of navicular disease
0-87605-986-8 HOWELL $25.00

Breeding

M. Phyllis **Lose**
Blessed Are the Brood Mares
An essential book on breeding and foaling
0-87605-848-9 HOWELL $27.50

Training

Gaydell **Collier**
Basic Training For Horses: English and Western
Specific instructions for safe, step-by-step training methods
0-385-26238-8 DOUBLEDAY PB $19.95

Carolyn **Henderson** & Lynn **Russell**
Breaking and Schooling: Training Your Horse from the Ground Up
Advice on everything from buying a young horse to re-training an ex-racehorse. 50 photos illustrate techniques discussed
1-55821-419-4 LYONS & BURFORD PB $18.95

John **Lyons**
Lyons on Horses: John Lyons' Proven Conditioned-Response Training Program
Lyons' philosophy of gentle persuasion to elicit conditioned responses from horses is highly effective in overcoming such equine habits as biting, spooking, and head-tossing. Discusses round pen training, trailer loading, halter breaking, and more
0-385-41398-X DOUBLEDAY $27.95

Alois **Podhajsky**
Complete Training of Horse and Rider in the Principles of Classical Horsemanship
A classic from the former director of the Spanish Riding School
0-87980-235-9 WILSHIRE PB $10.00

Grooming and Showing

Susan **Harris**
Grooming to Win: How to Groom, Trim, Braid, and Prepare Your Horse For Show
From the author of the U.S. Pony Club manuals, here is everything you need to know to make your horse look its best when preparing for competition
0-87605-892-6 HOWELL $29.95

Jane **Holderness-Roddam**
Preparing for a Show
Covers what needs to get done before those all-important moments in the ring, so that both horse and rider can concentrate on competition
0-901366-09-9 HALFH PB $12.00

Kathleen **Obenland**
Show Ring Success: A Rider's Guide to Winning Strategies
How to catch the judge's eye for your, and your horse's, positive qualities
0-87605-965-5 HOWELL $24.00

Charlene **Strickland**
Show Grooming
What you need to know so that your horse will look polished and crisp for showing
0-914327-57-7 BRKTP PB $29.95

Horsemanship

The British Horse Society
Riding Class
An excellent manual on riding for young equestrians
0-87605-860-8 HOWELL $16.95

George **Morris**
Hunter Seat Equitation
From the successful instructor who gave us the "Morris method"
0-385-15253-1 DOUBLEDAY $17.95

Pony Club Staff
The Pony Club Manual of Horsemanship: Basics for Beginners-D Level
See also **EQUINE MANAGEMENT, HEALTH, AND CARE**
0-87605-952-3 HOWELL $17.00

The United States Pony Club Manual of Horsemanship: Intermediate Horsemanship C Level
See also **EQUINE MANAGEMENT, HEALTH, AND CARE**
0-87605-977-9 HOWELL $17.00

Sally **Swift**
Centered Riding
The classic volume from one of the most creative trainers in America. "Wonderfully imaginative in finding just the right psychological images to go beyond the mere mechanics of riding…indispensable"—*Lliam Steinkraus*
0-312-12734-0 ST. MARTIN'S $18.95

Dressage and Show Jumping

Gary J. **Benson** & Phil **Maggitti**
In the Irons: Show Jumping, Dressage and Eventing in North America
0-87605-967-1 HOWELL $50.00

R.L. French **Blake**
Dressage For Beginners
0-395-24399-8 HOUGHTON MIFFLIN PB $10.95

Jonathan **Burton** & Darlene **Sordillo**
How to Ride a Winning Dressage Test: The Judge's Guide to Step-By-Step Improvement
Takes you through every official test used in dressage and combined competition
0-395-38217-3 HOUGHTON MIFFLIN PB $13.95

Meriel **Buxton**
The World of Hunting
0-948253-53-3 SPOPR $34.95

Judy **Cammaerts**
Dressage Test Technique
1-87208-251-3 HALFH PB $12.00

Kathy **Connelly** & Marietta **Whittlesey**
Dressage Insights: Excerpts from Experts
0-939481-38-3 HALFH $28.95

Sarah **Cotton**
Cross-Country Jumping: Preparation and Training for Both Horse and Rider
0-7134-7120-4 BATSFORD $24.95

Anthony **Crossley**
Dressage: The Seat, Aids and Exercises
See also **RIDING** under **EQUESTRIAN SPORTS** under **HORSE RACING AND EQUESTRIAN SPORTS** under **SPORTS**
1-85310-329-2 VOYAGEUR PB $17.95

Ferdi **Eilberg**
Dressage for the Event Horse
1-87208-241-6 HALFH $32.95

Anne **Kursinski** & Miranda **Lorraine**

Anne Kursinski's Riding and Jumping Clinic: A Step-By-Step Course for Winning in the Hunter and Jumper Rings

0-385-47405-9 DOUBLEDAY $30.00

Pat **Parelli**

Natural Horse-Man-Ship

Parelli has taught 15,000 students the basics of western riding on three continents. This is his six-part guide to becoming a more natural equestrian

0-911647-27-9 WESHO PB $14.95

James C. **Wofford**

Training the Three-Day-Event Horse and Rider

The three-day-event is one of the most rigorous tests of the skills, grace, and stamina of both horse and rider in the equestrian world today, comprising as it does segments of grueling cross-country obstacles, exacting dressage work, and the split-second precision of stadium jumping. This is a thorough volume that outlines what it takes to compete successfully in this demanding competition at all levels

0-385-42520-1 DOUBLEDAY $27.95

Western Riding

J.P. **Forget**

The Complete Guide to Western Horsemanship

Covers the discipline of western horsemanship, with information for riders of all ability levels on the psychology of riding, barrel racing technique, and much more

0-87605-982-5 HOWELL $30.00

Charlene **Strickland**

Western Riding: Showing Rodeo Events Reining Roping Trail Riding

A comprehensive introduction to all aspects of western riding, with hints on everything from roping to trail riding, what to wear for showing, and buying your first horse

0-88266-890-0 STOREY $24.95

Birds

Today approximately 60 million Americans practice the hobby of aviculture, ranging from the canary owner to the breeder of exotic swans and pheasants.

Ernest **Choate**

The Dictionary of American Bird Names

0-87645-121-0 HARVARD COMMON $17.95

W.B. **Lockwood**

The Oxford Book of British Bird Names

0-19-214155-4 OXFORD $18.95

Matthew **Vriends**

Simon and Schuster's Guide to Pet Birds

Includes information on 206 species of cage and aviary birds, illustrated in color

0-671-50696-X SIMON & SCHUSTER PB $15.00

Bird Species

The most popular pet birds today in the United States are canaries, budgerigars, finches, and parrots. Cockatiels, cockatoos, lovebirds, macaws, and parakeets are all members of the parrot family.

Karl **Diefenbach**

The World of Cockatoos

0-86622-034-8 T.F.H. $35.95

Rosemary **Low**

Parrots: Their Care and Breeding

0-7137-1437-9 BLANDFORD $90.00

Arthur **Freud**

The Complete Parrot

An entertaining and educational volume packed with parrot lore and color photos. Includes a discussion of conservation measures being taken in light of the widespread destruction of natural parrot habitat

0-87605-905-1 HOWELL $34.95

Mattie Sue **Athan**

Guide to a Well-Behaved Parrot

Practical advice on dealing with the behaviorally-challenged bird. Covers parrot body language, aggression, screaming, biting, and more

0-8120-4996-9 BARRONS PB $9.95

Feyerabend

Parakeets

An intriguing book that covers everything from styles of antique birdcages to teaching your budgie tricks, including playing dead and fortune telling with cards

0-86622-148-4 T.F.H. PB $5.95

Matthew M. **Vriends**

Lovebirds: Everything About Housing, Care, Nutrition, Breeding, and Diseases

0-8120-9014-4 BARRONS PB $6.95

Breeding, Health, and Care

Gary **Gallerstein**

The Bird Owner's Home Health and Care Handbook

Well organized and informative

0-87605-820-9 HOWELL $17.95

Sheldon **Gerstenfeld**

The Bird Book

0-201-03909-5 ADDISON-WESLEY PB $9.95

Sheldon L. **Gerstenfeld**

The Bird Care Book: All You Need to Know to Keep Your Bird Healthy and Happy

Gerstenfeld, the head of Philadelphia's Chestnut Hill Veterinary Hospital and Bird Clinic, offers up-to-date advice on the anatomy, nutrition, taming, and exercise of birds. A general manual, this is a volume that should certainly be consulted in case of bird emergencies but it should also be considered a must-read by anyone who is thinking about buying a bird as a pet

0-201-09559-9 ADDISON-WESLEY PB $15.00

Annette **Wolter** & Monika **Wegler**

The Complete Book of Parakeet Care: Expert Advice on Proper Management

This handy volume discusses the origins of parakeets in the Australian Outback, and gives advice on their breeding, care, and health maintenance. 160 color photos show many types of parakeets, both in capitivity and in the wild

0-8120-1688-2 BARRONS PB $14.95

Garden Birds

John **Dennis**

A Complete Guide to Bird Feeding

0-394-47937-8 KNOPF PB $18.95

Walter **Schutz**

How to Attract, House, and Feed Birds: 48 Plans For Bird Feeders and Houses You Can Make

With step-by-step drawings, photographs, and directions

0-02-011910-0 MACMILLAN PB $9.95

John **Terres**

Songbirds in Your Garden

0-06-091377-0 ALGONQUIN PB $10.95

Fish

In the United States today there are over five million hobbyists who maintain aquariums. Tetra Press publishes well-organized, informative books on fish. Tropical Fish Hobbyists also publishes some useful literature; the subjects include tropical, cold-water, and marine species suitable for the home aquarium.

Herbert **Axelrod**

Exotic Tropical Fishes

How to care for these fish at home; tips on aquariums

0-7938-0027-7 T.F.H. $39.95

Brian **Curtis**

Life Story of the Fish

0-486-20929-6 DOVER PB $6.95

Bethen **Penzes** & Istvan **Tolg**

Goldfish and Ornamental Carp

0-8120-9286-4 BARRONS PB $14.95

Simon & Schuster
Simon & Schuster's Guide to Freshwater and Marine Aquarium Fish
0-671-22809-9 SIMON & SCHUSTER PB $14.00

The Aquarium

Herbert **Axelrod**
Breeding Aquarium Fishes: A Complete Introduction
0-86622-294-4 T.F.H. PB $8.95

Gordon **Kay**
The Tropical Marine Fish Survival Manual
A detailed guide to setting up and maintaining the successful seawater aquarium. Includes a directory of 33 fish families, containing 109 species
0-8120-9372-0 BARRONS PB $16.95

Dick **Mills**
You and Your Aquarium
0-394-72985-4 RANDOM HOUSE PB $17.00

Gina **Sandford**
An Illustrated Encyclopedia of Aquarium Fish
Discusses 700 species of freshwater and marine fish, with tips on feeding, breeding, and designing and stocking environmentally suitable aquariums
See also **FISH SPECIES**
0-87605-947-7 HOWELL $29.95

Ulrich **Schliewen**
Aquarium Fish
Over 300 color photographs illustrate virtually every type of freshwater fish available today, from the upside-down catfish to the wrestling halfbeak. Includes tips on vegetation, food, water pH and temperature, and tank size appropriate to each type
See also **FISH SPECIES**
0-8120-1350-6 BARRONS PB $13.95

Peter W. **Scott**
The Complete Aquarium
0-7894-0013-8 HOUGHTON MIFFLIN PB $16.95

Gunther **Sterba**, editor
The Aquarium Encyclopedia
From a major pioneer in fish research
0-262-19207-1 MIT $45.00

Reptiles and Lizards

R.D. **Bartlett** & Patricia P. **Bartlett**
Geckos: Everything About Selection, Care, Nutrition, Diseases, Breeding, and Behavior
Everything the gecko-phile needs to know about selection, care, and behavior. Color photos
0-8120-9082-9 BARRONS PB $6.95

Richard D. **Bartlett** & Patricia P. **Bartlett**
Chameleons: Everything About Selection, Care, Nutrition, Diseases, Breeding, and Behavior
Answers to questions on chameleon physiology, health, feeding, and more. Illustrated with color photos
0-8120-9157-4 BARRONS PB $6.95

John **Coborn**
Caring for Green Iguanas: Breeding, Feeding & Selection
A useful sourcebook for owners of one of the world's most popular reptile pets. Includes color photos of iguanas in action, both in captivity and in the wild
0-7938-0255-5 T.F.H. PB $7.95

Ray **Hunziker**
Leopard Geckos
A guide to "eyelid" geckos, this informative book gives cogent advice on proper feeding, handling, housing and more
0-7938-0258-X T.F.H. PB $9.95

Harald **Jes**
Lizards in the Terrarium
0-8120-3925-4 BARRONS PB $6.95

Ronald G. **Markel**
Kingsnakes: Care and Breeding in Captivity
A very popular serpentine pet, the kingsnake comes in a variety of colors and patterns. This volume offers information on housing, feeding, and breeding these handsome reptiles
0-7938-0273-3 T.F.H. PB $9.95

Ronald G. **Markel** & Richard D. **Bartlett**
Kingsnakes and Milksnakes
0-8120-4240-9 BARRONS PB $6.95

Rabbits, Hamsters, Gerbils, and Guinea Pigs

Kate **Petty**
Gerbils: First Pets
0-8120-9081-0 BARRONS PB $3.95

Wanda L. **Curran**
Your Guinea Pig: A Kid's Guide to Raising and Showing
How to do everything from grooming to soothing the sniffles
0-88266-889-7 STOREY PB $12.95

Kate **Petty**
Guinea Pigs: First Pets
Books in this series have short, easy-to-read text and lots of informative illustrations for young pet owners and animal lovers
0-8120-9080-2 BARRONS PB $3.95

Hamsters: First Pets
0-8120-1472-3 BARRONS PB $3.95

Marinell **Harriman**
House Rabbit Handbook: How to Live With an Urban Rabbit
Excellent advice on housetraining, bunny-proofing, and even hand-feeding orphaned litters
0-940920-12-3 DROLL PB $8.95

Kate **Petty**
Rabbits: First Pets
0-8120-1473-1 BARRONS PB $3.95

Exotic Pets

James **McKay**
Complete Guide to Ferrets
Contains advice on housing and equipment, showing, hunting with the ferret, ferret racing and more. A listing of useful organizations in the UK, US, and Europe included
1-85310-433-7 VOYAGEUR PB $21.95

E. Lynn **Morton** & Chuck **Morton**
Ferrets: Everything About Purchase, Care, Nutrition, Diseases, Behavior, and Breeding
Expert answers to a variety of ferret-related questions, clearly written for the younger pet owner. Color photos
0-8120-9021-7 BARRONS PB $6.95

Matthew M. **Vriends**
Hedgehogs: How to Take Care of Them and Understand Them
Advice on the care and maintenance of the African Pygmy Hedgehog, a pet gaining popularity in Europe and America. Thoroughly illustrated
0-8120-1141-4 BARRONS PB $6.95

Farm Animals

Richard E. **Bonney**
Beekeeping: A Practical Guide
Bonney offers useful information for both the novice and experienced beekeeper on everything from acquiring bees to preventing tracheal mites. Includes important recommendations for dealing with Africanized bees
0-88266-861-7 GARDEN WAY PB $16.95

Roger A. **Morse**
The New Complete Guide to Beekeeping
Morse, a professor of agriculture at Cornell University, gives sound advice on all aspects of beekeeping, including how to select a good apiary site, sell honey, and rear queen honey bees
0-88150-315-0 COUNTRYMAN PB $15.00

Gail **Damerow**
Your Chickens: A Kid's Guide to Raising and Showing
0-88266-823-4 GARDEN WAY PB $12.95

Ulrich **Jaudas** & Matthew M. **Vriends**

The New Goat Handbook: Housing, Care, Feeding, Sickness, and Breeding

A concise, clearly written volume for the prospective goat owner. Offers advice on purchasing, caring for, feeding, and even understanding goats

0-8120-4090-2 BARRONS PB $9.95

Games and Puzzles

Martin **Daniels**

Cunning Stunts: The Best 50 Pub Tricks and Brain Teasers

How to drink another glass of bubbly from an empty champagne bottle, slice a banana without damaging the peel, and even pour seven liqueurs into a glass without their mixing together

0-572-02051-1 FOULSHAM PB $7.95

Chess

Andras **Adojan** & Jeno **Dory**

Winning with the Grunfeld

An analysis of the Grunfeld Defense, an aggressive defense ideal for the tournament player, written by two Hungarian champions

0-02-016080-1 COLLIER PB $10.95

Alexander **Alekhine**

My Best Games of Chess, 1908-1937

The triumphs of Alexander Alekhine, the world champion from 1927-1935 and again from 1937-1946

0-486-24941-7 DOVER PB $12.95

Mikhail **Botvinnik**

Half a Century of Chess

1-85744-122-2 SIMON & SCHUSTER PB $24.95

Mikhail **Botvinnik** & Yakov **Estrin**

The Grunfeld Defense

An essential book on this strategy

0-931462-84-3 CHESS PB $6.50

José **Capablanca**

My Chess Career

One of the best chess biographies

0-486-21548-2 DOVER PB $7.95

Primer of Chess

A classic introduction by one of the game's great players

1-85744-165-6 CADOGON PB $15.95
0-15-673900-3 HARCOURT BRACE PB $10.00

Irving **Chernev**

Capablanca's Best Chess Endings: 60 Complete Games

0-486-24249-8 DOVER PB $7.95

Combinations: The Heart of Chess

0-486-21744-2 DOVER PB $6.95

Reuben **Fine**, editor

Basic Chess Endings

"The definitive work on the end game which all serious students of the game have been waiting for"—*NY Times*

0-679-14002-6 MCKAY PB $20.00

The World's Greatest Chess Games

The greatest games ever played, compiled and annotated by the renowned chess author and grand master

0-486-24512-8 DOVER PB $9.95

Bobby **Fischer**

Bobby Fischer Teaches Chess

An introduction to the game by the youngest international grand master in chess history

0-553-26315-3 BDD PB $6.99

David **Hooper** & Ken **Whyld**

The Oxford Companion to Chess

A comprehensive chess encyclopedia, with a history of the game and an analysis of strategies and moves

0-19-280049-3 OXFORD $19.95

Israel **Horowitz** & Alexandra **Mark**

Chess For Beginners

An introduction to the game by the chess editor of the *NY Times* and former US Open champion

0-671-21184-6 SIMON & SCHUSTER PB $9.00

Kenneth **Howard**

Classic Chess Problems

An essential book for all chess players

0-486-22522-4 DOVER PB $5.95

Raymond **Keene**

Chess for Absolute Beginners

0-8050-2945-1 HOLT PB $15.00

Walter **Korn** & Nick **De Firmian**, editors

Modern Chess Openings

The chess player's bible, this is the only chess book regularly kept up to date since it was first published more than 50 years ago

0-8129-1785-5 MCKAY PB $23.00

Alexander **Kotov**

Think Like a Grandmaster: Algebraic Edition

0-7134-3160-1 BATSFORD PB $24.95

Edward **Lasker**

Chess For Fun and Chess For Blood

0-486-20146-5 DOVER PB $6.95

Common Sense in Chess

0-679-14006-9 MCKAY PB $5.95

Lasker's Manual of Chess

One of the most thorough studies of chess by the great modern chess player

0-486-20640-8 DOVER PB $8.95

Johann **Lowenthal**

Morphy's Games of Chess

0-486-20386-7 DOVER PB $8.95

James **Mason**

Art of Chess

A recent revision of the famous general study of the game

0-486-20463-4 DOVER PB $8.95

Ludek **Pachman**

Decisive Games in Chess History

Sixty-five games from important matches and tournaments played in the last 100 years

0-486-25323-6 DOVER PB $8.95

Modern Chess Strategy

A classic study of chess strategy by the Czech grand master

0-486-20290-9 DOVER PB $7.95

Fred **Reinfeld**

The Complete Book of Chess Stratagems

0-486-20690-4 DOVER PB $5.95

Samuel **Reshevsky**

The Art of Positional Play

0-679-14101-4 MCKAY PB $15.00

Richard **Reti**

Masters of the Chessboard

The last and most important work of the well-known chess writer, this book contains 70 games by 23 chess masters

0-486-23384-7 DOVER PB $8.95

Modern Ideas in Chess

A classic of chess literature, which includes a history of the evolution of the game

0-486-20638-6 DOVER PB $8.95

Siegbert **Tarrasch**

The Game of Chess

A classic instruction book by a legendary grand master

0-486-25447-X DOVER PB $10.95

A. **Tartakower**

U.S. Chess Federation's Official Rules of Chess

An essential volume for every serious player

0-8129-2217-4 MCKAY PB $16.00

A. **Tartakower** & J. **Du Mont**

Five Hundred Master Games of Chess

One of the great collections of chess games in English

0-486-23208-5 DOVER PB $14.95

Fred **Waitzkin**

Searching For Bobby Fischer: The Father of a Prodigy Observes the World of Chess

Here is the biography that inspired the film version of Josh Waitzkin's rise to chess stardom, from his first game at age six to his historic match in Russia

0-14-023038-6 PENGUIN PB $11.95

Ken **Whyld**

Chess: The Records

The results of all the great matches, with cross tables for 120 tournaments

0-85112-455-0 OLYMPIC PB $7.98

Other Board Games

Backgammon

Millard **Hopper**

Win At Backgammon

The basics of the game, illustrated with many diagrams and containing a description of gambling conventions

0-486-22894-0 DOVER PB $3.95

Checkers

Millard **Hopper**

Win At Checkers

Advice from the Unrestricted Checker Champion of the World

0-486-20363-8 DOVER PB $3.95

Fred **Reinfeld**

How to Win At Checkers

More tips on improving your game

0-87980-068-2 WILSHIRE PB $7.00

Go

Kaoru **Iwamoto**

Go For Beginners

An introduction to the ancient Japanese game of territory

0-394-73331-2 RANDOM HOUSE PB $12.00

Shigemi **Kishikawa**

Steppingstones to Go

The basics of go, written for the Westerner

0-8048-0547-4 TUTTLE PB $11.95

O. **Korschelt**

The Theory and Practice of Go

The classic treatise on go, first published in 1880 in a German magazine

0-8048-0572-5 TUTTLE $16.95
0-8048-1660-3 TUTTLE PB $11.95

Mah-Jongg

Shozo **Kanai** & Margaret **Farrell**

Mah-Jongg For Beginners

A guide to the game, based on the rules and regulations of the Mah-Jongg Association of Japan

0-8048-0391-9 TUTTLE $10.95

Kitty **Strauser** & Lucille **Evans**

Mah-Jongg Anyone?: A Manual of Modern Play

0-8048-0390-0 TUTTLE $12.95

Eleanor **Whitney**

Mah-Jongg Handbook: How to Play, Score and Win the Modern Game

0-8048-0392-7 TUTTLE $16.95

Other

R.C. **Bell**

Board and Table Games from Many Civilizations

A revised edition of this classic work, originally published in the '60s, in which the rules and strategies for 182 games are explained

0-486-23855-5 DOVER PB $9.95

C.F. **Jayne**

String Figures and How to Make Them

0-8446-2318-0 SMITH PB $17.00

Crossword Puzzles

"It may seem that crossword-solving is a very trivial pursuit, yet it has been claimed that crosswords extend one's vocabulary, stimulate the mind, and even encourage a healthy skepticism towards accepting things at their face value. They are predominantly a solitary pastime, although lone solvers are likely to find that bystanders want to help, even if no help is wanted."—Tony Augarde, *The Oxford Guide to Word Games*.

Eugene T. **Maleska**, editor

The New York Times Daily Crossword Puzzles: Volume 38

...the latest volume

0-8129-2450-9 TIME BOOKS PB $8.50

Will **Weng**, editor

The Will Weng Crossword Puzzle Omnibus Volume 1

These are collections of the daily *NY Times* puzzles (also published annually in spiral-bound editions), which are among the most popular and challenging crosswords in the county. They are shorter and less difficult than the Sunday *NY Times* puzzles

0-8129-0733-7 RANDOM HOUSE PB $11.00

The New York Times Sunday Crossword Puzzle Omnibus Volume 2

0-8129-1791-X TIME BOOKS PB $11.00

Reference Books

John **Griffiths**, editor

Cassell's Crossword Finisher

Twenty-one thousand words and names of three to seven letters have been fed into a computer in order to provide the word combinations presented in this book

0-304-34030-8 CASSELL PB $16.95

Merriam-Webster

Webster's Official Crossword Puzzle Dictionary

Comprehensive and authoritative crossword puzzle dictionary, containing specialized lists to aid in the "answer word" search

0-87779-021-3 MERRIAM WEBSTER $17.95

Tom **Pulliam** & Clare **Grundman**, editors

The New York Crossword Puzzle Dictionary

Contains over 600,000 words as well as thousands of names of famous people and fictional characters. Especially useful when doing *NY Times* puzzles

0-8129-1131-8 TIME BOOKS $21.00
0-446-38265-5 WARNER PB $15.99

Andrew **Swanfeldt**

Crossword Puzzle Dictionary

More than 365,000 words covered in the sixth edition of this popular dictionary

0-06-270090-1 HARPERCOLLINS $23.00
0-06-272053-8 HARPERCOLLINS PB $15.00
0-06-091313-4 HARPERCOLLINS PB $5.99

Word Games

A. Ross **Eckler**

Word Recreations: Games and Diversions from Word Ways

0-486-23854-7 DOVER PB $5.95

Thomas **Middleton**

New York Times Acrostics Volume 7

0-8129-2704-4 TIME BOOKS PB $9.00

The Official Scrabble Players Dictionary

The third edition

0-87779-220-8 MERRIAM WEBSTER $17.95
0-87779-915-6 MERRIAM WEBSTER PB $5.99

Robert **Schachner**

The Official Scrabble Word-Finder

This book contains thousands of words arranged for easy access

0-02-029802-1 MACMILLAN PB $7.00

Juliet **Snape** & Charles **Snape**

The Great Double Maze Book

0-8109-2623-7 ABRAMS PB $12.95

Quiz Books and Brainteasers

For related reading, see MATHEMATICS in SCIENCE

Alastair **Brotchie**

A Book of Surrealist Games

From Automatic Writing to Fumage, these are the "games" invented and played by Magritte, Max Ernst, André Breton, and others of the Surrealist school

1-57062-084-9 SHAMBHALA PB $10.00

Dell Puzzle Magazines

Dell Book of Logic Problems Volume 6

Each volume contains 75 brainteasers. Call for other volumes

0-440-50738-3 DELL PB $10.99

Marvin **Grosswirth**

The Mensa Genius Quiz Book Volume 1

Quizzes and puzzles that challenge readers to test their intelligence

0-201-05959-2 ADDISON-WESLEY PB $9.00

Volume 2

0-201-05958-4 ADDISON-WESLEY PB $9.00

Richard **Lederer** & Michael **Gilleland**

Literary Trivia: Fun and Games For Book Lovers

0-679-75380-X VINTAGE PB $11.00

Rosalind **Moore**, editor

The Dell Book of Logic Problems Volume 1

Each volume contains 75 brainteasers

0-440-51891-1 DELL PB $10.99

Louis **Phillips**

The Most Challenging Quiz Book Ever

Who recorded the first record to sell a million copies? What network TV show was the first to air an interracial kiss? This is trivia for the master

0-679-77090-9 RANDOM HOUSE PB $12.00

Abbie **Salny**

The Mensa Book of Words, Word Games, Puzzles and Oddities

Lexicographical brainteasers, from the MENSA group

0-06-096208-9 HARPERCOLLINS PB $8.00

Abbie **Salny** & Lewis Burke **Frumkes**

Mensa Think-Smart Book

Quizzes and exercises designed to strengthen the mind

0-06-091255-3 HARPERCOLLINS PB $9.00

Card Games

Tom **Ainslie**

Ainslie's Complete Hoyle: Rules, Strategics, Scoring, Bidding, Betting

Includes 1800 entries and all popular card games, with variations and strategies

0-671-24779-4 SIMON & SCHUSTER PB $16.00

Peter **Arnold**

Book of Card Games

One hundred fifty games are explained in this compendium, including Bridge, Pinochle, Piquet, and 17 types of Solitaire or Patience. Two-color illustrations

0-87052-730-4 HIPPOCRENE PB $16.95

Walter **Gibson**

Hoyle's Modern Encyclopedia of Card Games

A thorough guide to card games, with the bask rules and popular variations of each game

0-385-07680-0 DOUBLEDAY PB $12.95

Richard L. **Frey**

According to Hoyle: Official Rules of More Than 200 Popular Games of Skill and Chance With Expert Advice

From Backgammon to word games, this volume covers it all

0-449-21112-6 FAWCETT PB $5.99

Joseph **Leeming**

Games and Fun with Playing Cards

0-486-23977-2 DOVER PB $3.95

Albert **Morehead**, editor

The Complete Book of Solitaire and Patience Games

0-553-26240-8 BDD PB $5.99

Official Rules of Card Games

Up-to-date rules of over 300 card games, including the New International Laws of Contract Bridge

0-449-21381-1 FAWCETT PB $5.99

Albert **Morehead** & Geoffrey **Mott-Smith**, editors

Hoyle's Rules of Games

0-451-16309-5 NEW AMERICAN LIBRARY PB $5.99

David **Parlett**

A History of Card Games

The history of such well-known games as Bridge and Poker, as well as lesser known entertainments such as Yellow Dwarf and Slippery Sam. "A compelling piece of cultural history"—Michael Dummett

0-19-282905-X OXFORD PB $10.95

John **Scarne**

Scarne's Encyclopedia of Card Games

The histories and variations of the world's greatest card games

0-06-273155-6 HARPERCOLLINS PB $16.00

Bridge

George **Coffin**

Bridge Play from A to Z

A thorough and useful book for all players

0-486-23891-1 DOVER PB $6.95

Jonathan **Davis**

Learn Bridge in a Weekend

0-679-42752-X KNOPF $16.00

Tony **Forrester**

Improve Your Bridge at Home

Forrester, Bridge columnist for *The Daily Telegraph*, here writes for the intermediate player. Includes self-testing quizzes

0-7134-7779-2 TRAFALGAR SQUARE PB $16.95

Richard **Frey**

How to Win At Contract Bridge in 10 Easy Lessons

The author of *According to Hoyle* clearly explains winning contract bridge techniques

0-449-20995-4 FAWCETT PB $5.99

Charles **Goren**

Contract Bridge For Beginners

A beginner's book that introduces the novice player to the "point count" method of bidding

0-671-21052-1 SIMON & SCHUSTER PB $9.00

Goren's New Bridge Complete

The revised edition of the classic bridge book

0-385-23324-8 DOUBLEDAY $29.95

Alan **Hiron** & Maureen **Hiron**

Easy Guide to Bridge

The perfect starter book for the absolute beginner

1-85744-509-0 CADOGON PB $11.95

Mark **Horton**

Step by Step: Signalling

How to use the most popular forms of encouraging and discouraging signals in Bridge play

0-7134-7640-0 BATSFORD PB $16.95

James **Jacoby**

Jacoby on Bridge

A guide for all levels of bridge players, written by the first player to ever amass 1000 points in one year

0-671-66884-6 POCKET PB $5.99

Patrick **Jourdain**

Play the Game: Bridge

A clear, concise, and easy-to-use handbook. Includes numerous sample hands and game situations

0-7137-2408-0 BLANDFORD PB $8.95

Edgar **Kaplan**

Winning Contract Bridge

A world-renowned expert explains techniques that helped him win many championships

0-486-24559-4 DOVER PB $9.95

Fred **Karpin**

Bridge Strategy At Trick One

An indispensable guide to playing winning bridge, concentrating on strategy at trick one, when many hands are decided

0-486-23296-4 DOVER PB $6.95

Zia **Mahmood**

Declarer Play

FORWARD BY OMAR SHARIF

0-00-218471-0 HARPERCOLLINS PB $8.00

Defence

FORWARD BY OMAR SHARIF

0-00-218469-9 HARPERCOLLINS PB $8.00

Freddie **North**

Conventional Bidding Explained

North makes clear nearly 30 bidding conventions and five key defense systems, rating each

0-7134-7643-5 BATSFORD PB $16.95

Terence **Reese** & David **Bird**

Make a Start at Bridge

A clear, easy introduction to Bridge for those who don't know a trump from a trick

0-571-17112-5 FABER PB $10.95

William **Root**

Commonsense Bidding

A renowned expert's guide to basic bidding

0-517-88430-5 CROWN PB $15.00

How to Defend a Bridge Hand

The world's leading bridge teacher covers opening leads, third-hand play, attitude signals, discarding and deception, and every other essential defensive angle of the game. Not for experts or beginners, but for the 90 percent of players in between. With an introduction by Alan Truscott, Bridge Editor of *NY Times*

0-517-59160-X CROWN $25.00

0-517-88393-7 CROWN PB $16.00

Alfred **Sheinwold**

Five Weeks to Winning Bridge

From valuing your hand to hold-up play, this book explains it all. "The best Bridge book ever written"—Albert H. Morehead, Former Bridge editor, *NY Times*

0-671-68770-0 POCKET PB $6.50

Alan **Truscott**

Contract Bridge for Beginners and Intermediate Players

A beginner's book that introduces the novice player to the "point count" method of bidding

0-8119-0755-4 LIFETIME PB $8.95

Louis **Watson**

The Play of the Hand At Bridge

The classic guide to all aspects of playing strategy, written by one of the world's foremost authorities on contract bridge

0-06-463209-1 BARNES & NOBLE PB $14.00

Gin Rummy

F. George **Fraed**

Gin Rummy at Its Best from Beginner to Expert

Advice for players of all abilities from a Gin Rummy International Champion

0-9630463-1-4 SMIDA PB $10.95

Sam **Fry**

Gin Rummy: How to Play and Win

Advice for all levels of player on Gin Rummy and its variations, including Oklahoma Gin and Hollywood Gin

0-486-23630-7 DOVER PB $2.95

Poker

John **Archer**

An Expert's Guide to Winning At Poker

0-87980-362-2 WILSHIRE PB $10.00

Mike **Caro**

The Body Language of Poker

0-89746-100-2 CAROL PB $18.95

Maverick's Guide to Poker

First published in conjunction with the '60s TV series, this entertaining volume has been re-released as a companion to the feature film

0-8048-3032-0 TUTTLE PB $5.95

Andy **Nelson**

Poker One Hundred and One Ways to Win

How to master high-powered Poker techniques, from reading opponents to coping with check raises. Special section on tournament play

0-945983-22-0 POKER PB $17.95

Terence **Reese** & Anthony **Watkins**

How to Win At Poker

0-87980-070-4 WILSHIRE PB $7.00

Jeff **Rubens**

Win At Poker

A complete guide to poker, starting with the fundamentals and moving step-by-step to more complex areas of the game

0-486-24626-4 DOVER PB $5.95

John **Scarne**

Scarne's Guide to Modern Poker

The rules of all 117 forms of poker, presented by today's greatest gambling expert

0-671-53076-3 SIMON & SCHUSTER PB $11.00

Peter O. **Steiner**

Thursday-Night Poker: How to Understand, Enjoy, and Win

If you're a weekly or monthly player, this book may save you hundreds of dollars in a year. "Forget the casinos, it's all here"—Frank Conroy

0-679-76020-2 RANDOM HOUSE PB $16.00

Blackjack

J. Edward **Allen**

The Basics of Winning Blackjack

Covers everything from odds to non-counting strategies in simple language

0-940685-24-8 CARDZ PB $3.95

Richard **Canfield**

Blackjack: Your Way to Riches

How to be a winning player

0-8184-0498-1 LYLE STUART PB $12.95

Lance **Humble** & Carl **Cooper**

The World's Greatest Blackjack Book

A comprehensive guide, updated to include the rules of play in Atlantic City

0-385-15382-1 DOUBLEDAY PB $10.95

Jerry **Patterson**

Blackjack: A Winner's Handbook

"This vitamin-packed work might also be labeled 'Current Guide to 50 Blackjack Systems.' It could also be your very best guideline to selecting the system you wish to play—complex or simplified"—*Gambler's Book Club*

0-399-51598-4 PERIGEE PB $10.00

Lawrence **Revere**

Playing Blackjack as a Business

Accurate and up-to-date guide to blackjack, with strategies devised by Julian Braun of the IBM Corporation

0-8184-0064-1 LYLE STUART PB $15.95

Frank **Scoblete**

Best Blackjack

Tells you what you need to know to take advantage of sloppy dealers, count cards, and conserve your bankroll

1-56625-057-9 BONUS PB $14.95

Ken **Uston**

Million Dollar Blackjack

Blackjack advice from the man who once made $27,000 in 45 minutes at Las Vegas' Fremont Casino

0-89746-068-5 CAROL PB $16.95

Magic Tricks

Harry **Blackstone**

The Blackstone Book of Magic and Illusion

1-55704-182-2 NEWMARKET $35.00

1-55704-177-6 NEWMARKET PB $19.95

Blackstone's Tricks Anyone Can Do

One of the great magicians of the 20th-century reveals the secrets of 200 magic tricks

0-8065-0862-0 LYLE STUART PB $8.95

J.C. **Cannell**

The Secrets of Houdini

A rational explanation of Houdini's tricks, written by a personal friend of the magician's and published shortly after Houdini's death

0-486-22913-0 DOVER PB $7.95

Nelson **Downs**

The Art of Magic

A compilation of renowned magic tricks, along with transcriptions of appropriate patter to use while performing these tricks

0-486-24005-3 DOVER PB $7.95

Walter **Gibson**

The New Magician's Manual

Thirty-six tricks explained

0-486-23113-5 DOVER PB $8.95

Harry **Houdini**

Houdini on Magic

Houdini's own account of some of his most famous feats, with instructions for performing 44 stage tricks

0-486-20384-0 DOVER PB $6.95

Jean **Hugard**, editor

Encyclopedia of Card Tricks

An explanation of over 600 professional card tricks

0-486-21252-1 DOVER PB $8.95

Jean **Hugard** & Frederick **Brave**

Expert Card Techniques: Close-Up Table Magic

A definitive work on card tricks, with step-by-step instructions

0-486-21755-8 DOVER PB $9.95

Bob **Longe**

World's Greatest Card Tricks

Card control, false cuts, forces and glides are all covered, as are the classic sleights-of-hand that employ them

0-8069-5991-6 STERLING PB $4.95

Part 16

Books for Young Readers

Beatrix Potter

If You Were Young In...

1600 · 1650 · 1700 · 1750 · 1800 · 1850 · 1900 · 1950 · 1990

1400: The Boy Serving at Table
Against the post let not thy back abide,
Neither make thy mirror of the wall.
Pickt not thy nose, and, most especial,
Be well ware, and set hereon thy thought,
Before thy sovereign scratch nor rub
thee nought. —John Lydgate
The Oxford Book of Children's Verse

1617

1744: The Pretty Songs of Tommy Thumb
Piss a Bed,
Piss a Bed,
Barley Butt,
Your Bum is so heavy
You can't get up.
—Mother Goose

1605

1771: Hymn for Saturday
A Lark's nest, then your playmate begs
You'd spare herself and speckled eggs;
Soon she shall ascend and sing
Your praises to the eternal King.
—Christopher Smart
The Oxford Book of Children's Verse

1617

1865: You Are Old, Father William
"You are old," said the youth, "as I mentioned before,
And have grown most uncommonly fat;
Yet you turned a back-somersault in at the door—
Pray, what is the reason of that?"
—Lewis Carroll

1647

1939: The Naming of Cats
When you notice a cat in profound meditation,
The reason, I tell you, is always the same:
His mind is engaged in a rapt contemplation
Of the thought, of the thought, of the thought
of his name:
His ineffable effable
Effanineffable
Deep and inscrutable singular Name.
—T.S. Eliot

1624

1984: Remember?
Remember me?
I am the girl
with the dark skin
whose shoes are thin
I am the girl
with rotted teeth
I am the dark
rotten-toothed girl
with the wounded eye
and the melted ear.
—Alice Walker

1643

1600: Mother Goose
Golden slumbers kiss your eyes,
Smiles awake you when you rise,
Sleep, pretty wanton; do not cry,
And I will sing you a lullaby:
Rock them, rock them, lullaby.
—Thomas Dekker

1608

1715: Against Idleness and Mischief
How doth the little busy bee
Improve each shining hour,
And gather honey all the day
From every opening flower! —Isaac Watts
The Oxford Book of Children's Verse

1617

1760: Sonnets for the Cradle
Three wise men of Gotham
They went to Sea in a Bowl,
And if the Bowl had been stronger
My Song had been longer.
—Mother Goose

1606

1846: The Jumblies
They sailed to the Western Sea, they did,
To a land all covered with trees,
And they bought an Owl, and a useful
Cart,
And a pound of Rice, and a Cranberry
Tart,
And a hive of silvery Bees.
And they bought a Pig, and some green
Jackdaws,
And forty bottles of Ring-Bo-Ree,
And no end of Stilton Cheese.
—Edward Lear

1615

1924: When We Were Very Young
Once upon a time there were three
little foxes
Who didn't wear stockings, and they
didn't wear sockses,
But they all had handkerchiefs to
blow their noses,
And they kept their handkerchiefs in
cardboard boxes. —A.A. Milne

1617

1955: The Lord of the Rings
One Ring to rule them all,
One Ring to find them,
One Ring to bring them all
and in the darkness bind them
In the Land of Mordor where the Shadows lie. —J.R.R. Tolkien

1652

1989: Sometimes Even Parents Win
There was a young lady from Gloucester
Who complained that her parents both
bossed her;
So she ran off to Maine.
Did her parents complain?
Not at all–they were glad to have lost her.
—John Ciardi

1624

One day little Sal went with her mother to blueberry hill to pick blueberries.
—Robert McCloskey
Blueberries for Sal
1616

The Queen and her Ladies-in-waiting
Sat at the window and sewed.
She cried, "Look! who's that handsome man?"
They answered, "Mr. Toad."
—Kenneth Grahame
The Wind in The Willows
1635

"You have put on a lot of weight since the last time you were here, Lowly," says Nurse Nora.
—Richard Scarry
Best First Book Ever
1607

"I can eat you, don't you see?"
"I don't care!"
"And you will be inside of me."
"I don't care!"
"Then you'll never have to bother."
"I don't care"
"With a mother and a father."
"I don't care." —Maurice Sendak
Pierre
1607

His real name was Alastair Roderic Craigellachie Dalhousie Gowan Donnybristle MacMac, but that took too long to say, so everybody just called him Wee Gillis.
—Munroe Leaf
Wee Gillis
1617

Wilbur admired the way Charlotte managed. He was particularly glad that she always put her victim to sleep before eating it. "It's real thoughtful of you to do that, Charlotte," he said. "Yes," she replied in her sweet, musical voice, "I always give them an anaesthetic so they won't feel pain. It's a little service I throw in."
—E.B. White
Charlotte's Web
1626

The door flew open, in he ran,
The great, long, red-legg'd scissar-man.
Oh! children, see! the tailor's come
And caught our little Suck-a-Thumb.
—Heinrich Hoffmann-Donner
Slovenly Peter, or Cheerful Stories and Funny Pictures for Good Little Folks
1653

"I meant what I said
And I said what I meant…
An elephant's faithful
One hundred percent!"
—Dr. Seuss
Horton Hatches the Egg
1620

Long John Silver: "It was a master surgeon, him that ampytated me—out of college and all—Latin by the bucket, and what not, but he was hanged like a dog, and sun-dried like the rest, at Corso castle."
—Robert Louis Stevenson
Treasure Island
1625

Then—they saw the Groke. Everybody saw her. She sat motionless on the sandy path at the bottom of the steps and stared at them with round, expressionless eyes.
—Tove Jansson
Finn Family Moomintroll
1636

He didn't want to get lost in the woods. So he made a very small forest, with just one tree in it.
—Crockett Johnson
Harold and the Purple Crayon
1606

Mother Goose for the Mirthless

"The average collection of 200 traditional nursery rhymes contains approximately 100 rhymes which personify all that is glorious and ideal for the child. Unfortunately, the remaining 100 rhymes harbor unsavory elements. The incidents below occur in the average collection and may be accepted as a reasonably conservative estimate based on the general survey of this type of literature.

Death by choking, 2 cases
Death by devouring, 1 case
Death by squeezing, 1 case
Death by shriveling, 1 case
Death by starvation, 1 case
Death by boiling, 1 case
Death by hanging, 1 case
Death by drowning, 1 case
Death (unclassified), 21 cases
Threats of death, 5 cases
Murder (unclassified), 8 allusions
Physical violence (unclassified), 23 cases
Cutting a human being in half, 1 case
Breaking of limbs, 4 cases
Severing of limbs, 7 cases
Desire to have a limb severed, 1 case
Maimed people and animals, 12 cases
Self-inflicted injury, 2 cases
Bleeding heart, 1 allusion
Devouring human flesh, 1 case
Kidnapping, 1 case

Cruelty to human beings and animals, 12 cases
Killing domestic animals, 4 cases
Whipping and lashing, 8 cases
Blood, 3 allusions
Stealing and general dishonesty, 14 cases
Undertakers, 1 allusion
Graves, 2 allusions
Body snatching, 1 case
Lunacy, 1 case
Misery and sorrow, 16 allusions
Poverty and want, 9 allusions
Drunkenness, 1 case
Cursing, 4 cases
Scorning the blind, 1 case
Scorning prayer, 1 case
Children lost or abandoned, 9 cases
House burning, 2 cases
Quarreling, 5 allusions
Unlawful imprisonment, 2 cases
Racial discrimination, 2 cases
Marriage as a form of death, 1 allusion

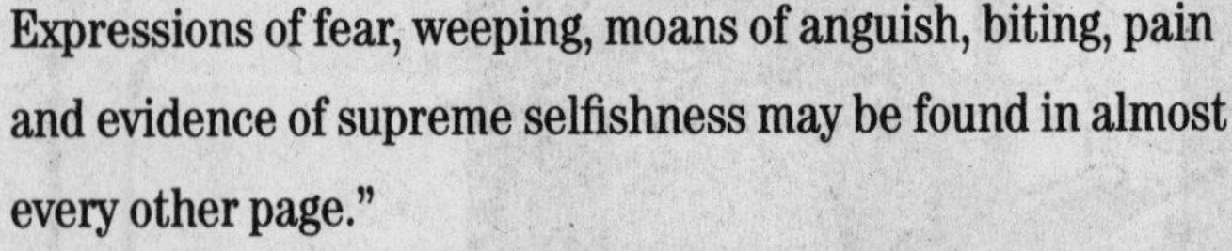

Expressions of fear, weeping, moans of anguish, biting, pain and evidence of supreme selfishness may be found in almost every other page."

—Geoffrey Handley-Taylor (1952)

Quoted (with dissent) by William and Ciel Baring-Gould in *The Annotated Mother Goose*

1608

Books for Children Under Five

A book to a baby is a thing to chew on, throw out of the crib, or pull about; and a sturdily made cloth book is an excellent toy. Once children become old enough to make out the pictures, books are satisfying for other reasons. For the toddler, looking at books is a pleasurable activity. "Reading" allows the child to climb into Mommy's or Daddy's lap with the book, cuddle up, and help turn the pages. Small children know that the adult is paying special attention to them; it's a good feeling. With luck the pictures are interesting, too.

The best books are those with uncluttered, self-explanatory pictures and very brief text. Very small children like to hear you "read," but they can't grasp more than one short line at a time. Successful baby books are distinguished by simplicity; bad ones try to do too much or introduce material that young children shouldn't need to understand—and won't anyway.

After outgrowing baby books, a child is ready for Margaret Wise Brown's magical bedtime books, written during the '40s. You can then begin to collect picture books by authors such as Nancy Tafuri and Frank Asch, whose best books have the same effortless and loving quality.

Children just out of the toddling stage like to participate when they are read to by touching the pictures, lifting flaps, or finding hidden pictures.

A child of three gets pleasure out of seeing and describing things. The illustrations of trains, buses, and cars in Donald Crews's and Byron Barton's books provide a visually stimulating way to keep a child entertained.

Though parents may be eager to introduce their four-year-olds to the picture-book classics of their own childhoods, Madeline and Babar require a bit of sitting still. As they do when crawling, walking, or talking, children take their own sweet time before they are ready to listen to the beginning, middle, and end of a story. However, children this age love the repetition common to the simpler folktales from Europe, Africa, and elsewhere. Young children also find poetry, as Jack Prelutsky has said, "as delightful and surprising as being tickled or catching a snowflake on a mitten."

Aliki

Dinosaurs Are Different

ILLUSTRATED BY ALIKI
0-690-04456-9 CROWELL $15.00
0-06-445056-2 TROPHY PB $4.95

Joan Walsh **Anglund**

Baby's First Book

0-394-87470-6 RANDOM HOUSE $4.99

Kerry **Argent** & Rod **Trinca**

One Wooly Wombat

An Australian counting and ABC book, full of wacky paintings of koalas, echidnas, and other denizens of the outback
ILLUSTRATED BY KERRY ARGENT
0-916291-00-6 KANE/MILLER $12.95
0-916291-10-3 KANE/MILLER PB $6.95

Jim **Arnosky**

Every Autumn Comes the Bear

0-399-22508-0 PUTNAM $15.95

Frank **Asch**

Bear's Bargain

Frank Asch has such an appealingly simple style of illustration that his books will suit the youngest threes, even though his stories have involving plots. In this one Little Bird will show Bear how to fly, if Bear will show him how to grow bigger
0-671-67838-8 ALADDIN PB $4.95

Goodbye House

Aided by a wise daddy, a little bear says goodbye to his first family home
0-671-67054-9 PRENTICE HALL $12.95
0-671-67927-9 ALADDIN PB $4.95

Happy Birthday, Moon

0-671-66455-7 ALADDIN PB $4.95

Esther **Averill**

Jenny's Birthday Book

0-06-020251-3 HARPERCREST $14.95

Molly G. **Bang**

Ten, Nine, Eight

A counting book, this countdown to bedtime is sufficiently soothing that the rhymes seem just right for the very young. A Caldecott Honor Book for 1984
0-688-00906-9 GREENWILLOW $16.00
0-688-10480-0 MULBERRY PB $4.95

Judi **Barrett**

Animals Should Definitely Not Wear Clothing

A humorous little essay on why camels, hens, lions, and so on look better without it
See also BOOKS FOR AGES FIVE, SIX, AND SEVEN
ILLUSTRATED BY RON BARRETT
0-689-20592-9 ATHENEUM $13.95
0-689-70807-6 ALADDIN PB $4.95

Judith **Barrett**

Cloudy with a Chance of Meatballs

0-689-30647-4 ATHENEUM $16.00

Byron **Barton**

Airport

0-690-04169-1 HARPERCREST $14.89

Dinosaurs, Dinosaurs

0-694-00269-0 CAROUSEL $10.95

Planes (Chunky Board Book)

0-694-00603-3 HARPERFESTIVAL $2.95

Trains

0-690-04534-4 HARPERCREST $13.89

Trains (Chunky Board Book)

0-694-00601-7 HARPERFESTIVAL $2.95

Trucks

0-690-04530-1 HARPERCREST $13.89

Caroline Feller **Bauer**

My Mom Travels a Lot

Funny things happen when Mom is away (Dad is in charge)—and nice things, too. The best thing is that Mom always comes back
0-14-050545-8 VIKING PB $4.99

Ludwig **Bemelmans**

Mad About Madeline

One of the most beloved children's characters of all time, Madeline has captured the imagination and hearts of the young around the world. Now all six of her adventures are available in this handsomely bound volume. Full-color illustrations throughout.
INTRODUCTION BY ANNA QUINDLEN
0-670-85187-6 VIKING $29.95

Madeline

Bemelmans had a good ear for rhyme and a lovely if wacky illustrative style. Madeline lives in an old house in Paris, and her healthy streak of mischief is a trial to poor Miss Clavell. But she is all indignation when injustice occurs, especially when animals are the victims.
A Caldecott Honor Book for 1940
See also BOOKS FOR AGES FIVE, SIX, AND SEVEN
0-14-050198-3 VIKING PB $4.99

Madeline and the Bad Hat

0-670-44614-9 VIKING $14.99
0-14-050206-8 VIKING PB $4.99

Madeline's House: Madeline, Madeline's Rescue, Madeline and the Bad Hat

Bemelmans's stories of Parisian schoolgirl Madeline and her wonderful adventures, illustrated whimsically by the author
0-14-095028-1 VIKING PB $12.95

Madeline in London

0-670-44648-3 VIKING $15.00
0-14-050199-1 VIKING PB $4.99

Sandra **Boynton**

But Not the Hippopotamus

These quirkily humorous pictures make a pleasant change for adults; the lulling text is just what toddlers want to hear
0-671-44904-4 LITTLE SIMON $3.95

The Going to Bed Book

0-671-44902-8 LITTLE SIMON $3.95

Moo Baa La La La

0-671-44901-X LITTLE SIMON $3.95

Jan **Brett**

Annie and the Wild Animals

0-395-37800-1 HOUGHTON MIFFLIN $14.95

Norman **Bridwell**

Clifford at the Circus

Clifford behaves as dogs do, but because he is as big and as red as a firehouse, he and his owners are perpetually in trouble. With their few words and simple illustrations, Bridwell's picture books are understood even by children under four
0-590-44293-7 SCHOLASTIC PB $2.99

Clifford Gets a Job

0-590-44296-1 SCHOLASTIC PB $2.99

Clifford the Big Red Dog

0-590-40743-0 SCHOLASTIC $10.95
0-590-44297-X SCHOLASTIC PB $2.99

Clifford the Small Red Puppy

0-590-44294-5 SCHOLASTIC PB $2.50

Norman **Bridwell**
Clifford's Good Deeds
0-590-44292-9 SCHOLASTIC PB $2.99

Raymond **Briggs**
Father Christmas
Father Christmas grumbles a lot but still gets up and down chimneys. Detailed little pictures are arranged in stories that are really elongated strip cartoons
0-14-050125-8 VIKING PB $4.50

The Snowman
A wordless book that appeals to older children as well: a boy and a snowman go on a mysterious journey
0-7214-1109-6 LADYBIRD $3.50

Marc **Brown**, editor
Hand Rhymes
Finger rhymes of several vintages encourage counting, rhyming, and singing
0-525-44201-4 DUTTON $14.99

Marc **Brown** & Stephen **Krensky**
Dinosaurs Beware: A Safety Guide
Pictures of frenetic dinosaurs help kids learn the positives along with the negatives and distinguish rational from irrational fears
0-316-11219-4 LITTLE, BROWN PB $7.95

Margaret Wise **Brown**
Big Red Barn
0-06-020748-5 HARPERCOLLINS $14.95

A Child's Good Night Book
A Caldecott Honor Book for 1944
ILLUSTRATED BY JEAN CHARLOT
0-06-021028-1 HARPERCOLLINS $10.95

Goodnight Moon
Goodnight socks and goodnight clocks; the sleepy bunny hero of this classic lullaby book has bid goodnight to children since 1947
ILLUSTRATED BY CLEMENT HURD
0-06-020705-1 HARPERCOLLINS $13.95
0-06-443017-0 HARPERCOLLINS PB $4.95

Goodnight Moon

Margaret Wise Brown Treasury
0-307-16175-7 WESTERN $6.00

The Runaway Bunny
An adventurous little bunny tells his mother he is going to run away; his mother's response makes for an unforgettable fantasy
ILLUSTRATED BY CLEMENT HURD
0-06-443018-9 TROPHY PB $4.95
0-06-020765-5 HARPERCOLLINS $13.95

Wait Till the Moon Is Full
A calming little book about how good it is to go to sleep
ILLUSTRATED BY GARTH WILLIAMS
0-06-020800-7 TROPHY PB $15.00

Ruth **Brown**
The Big Sneeze
An almost wordless picture book about a sneeze that causes a sequence of unexpected events
0-688-04665-7 MORROW $16.00

Virginia Lee **Burton**
Little House
0-395-18156-9 HOUGHTON MIFFLIN $14.95

Mike Mulligan and His Steam Shovel: Story and Pictures
0-395-16961-5 HOUGHTON MIFFLIN $14.95

Rod **Campbell**
Dear Zoo
A humorous lift-the-flap book: the author asks the zoo for a pet, and the zoo sends one inappropriate animal after another
0-02-716440-3 LITTLE SIMON $10.95
0-14-050446-X VIKING PB $49.99

Lion

Eric **Carle**
Papa, Please Get the Moon for Me
The book unfolds as the story progresses. A younger child will request help with the activity, but the book is fascinating
0-88708-177-0 SIMON & SCHUSTER $5.95

The Very Busy Spider
As they listen, children use their fingers to trace the growth of the spider's web until the story reaches its triumphant conclusion
0-399-21166-7 PHILOMEL $19.95

The Very Hungry Caterpillar
Children help the caterpillar turn into a beautiful butterfly by turning half pages or putting small fingers through inviting holes in the stiff pages—a more varied participation than the conventional "lift the flap" books
0-399-21301-5 PUTNAM $5.95
0-399-20853-4 PUTNAM $18.95

The Very Quiet Cricket
Children love this book, which leads up to a surprising—and audible—ending. Preschool
ILLUSTRATED BY ERIC CARLE
0-399-21885-8 PHILOMEL $19.95

Nancy White **Carlstrom**
Jesse Bear, What Will You Wear?
"A rose between my toes," suggests Jesse Bear. A rhyming account of Jesse Bear's day, from dawn to dusk—and a very satisfying one
ILLUSTRATED BY BRUCE DEGEN
0-689-80930-1 SIMON & SCHUSTER $6.99
0-689-80623-X ALADDIN PB $4.95

David **Carter**
How Many Bugs in a Box!
Odd creatures with witty names pop up and ask to be counted
0-671-64965-5 LITTLE SIMON $12.95

Kay **Chorao**
The Baby's Good Morning Book
Short verse selections appear in the companion volume to *The Baby's Story Book*
0-525-44257-X DUTTON $13.95

The Baby's Story Book
0-14-055738-5 PUFFIN PB $5.99

Miriam **Cohen**
Will I Have a Friend?
0-02-722790-1 SIMON & SCHUSTER $14.00

Donald **Crews**
Flying
Real-looking trains, buses, and trucks, with lots of activity and extremely simple text. Although suitable for older children, Crews's lively illustrations hold the attention of threes and fours
0-688-09235-7 MULBERRY PB $4.95

Freight Train
0-688-80165-X MORROW $16.00
0-688-11701-5 MULBERRY PB $3.95

School Bus
0-688-02807-1 MORROW $16.00
0-688-12267-1 MULBERRY PB $4.95

Ten Black Dots/Redesigned
0-688-06067-6 MORROW $16.00

Truck
A Caldecott Honor Book for 1981
0-688-80244-3 MORROW $16.00
0-688-10481-9 MULBERRY PB $3.95

Ermanno **Cristini** & Luigi **Puricelli**
In the Pond
0-907234-43-7 SIMON & SCHUSTER $12.95

In the Woods
Two wordless picture books introduce younger children to different wildlife habitats. An identification key appears at the back of each book
0-907234-31-3 SIMON & SCHUSTER $12.95

Lydia **Dabcovich**
Sleepy Bear
0-14-054785-1 DUTTON PB $4.99

Alexandra **Day**

Carl Goes Shopping

The star of *Good Dog, Carl* accompanies Mom and her baby on a trip to the department store in this action-filled, wordless treat. For children under 5

0-374-31110-2 FS&G $12.95

Good Dog, Carl

0-689-80748-1 SIMON & SCHUSTER PB $5.95

Bruce **Degen**

Jamberry

0-06-021416-3 HARPERCOLLINS $14.95

Demi

Cuddly Chick

0-448-19154-7 GROSSETT & DUNLAP $6.95

Downy Duckling

0-448-19153-9 GROSSETT & DUNLAP $6.95

Fluffy Bunny

0-448-19151-2 GROSSETT & DUNLAP $6.95

Tomie **dePaola**, editor

Tomie dePaola's Favorite Nursery Tales

Children out of the nursery too will enjoy these popular folk stories and fairy tales

0-399-21319-8 PUTNAM $24.95

Tomie dePaola's Mother Goose

A handsome and comprehensive collection of rhymes

0-399-21258-2 PUTNAM $24.95

Christine **Dubov**

Aleksandra, Where Are Your Toes?

PHOTOGRAPHS BY JOSEF SCHNEIDER

0-312-01717-0 ST. MARTIN'S $3.95

Kate **Duke**

The Guinea Pig ABC

Rambunctious guinea pigs star in this lively ABC primer

0-14-054756-8 DUTTON PB $5.99

Phoebe **Dunn**

Baby's Animal Friends

Very young children may learn to identify these uncluttered images with ease

0-394-89583-5 RANDOM HOUSE $3.25

I'm a Baby

0-394-88605-4 RANDOM HOUSE $3.99

Cooper **Edens**, editor

The Glorious Mother Goose

The classic rhymes are accompanied by reproductions of illustrations from the 17th-century to the present

0-689-31434-5 ATHENEUM $18.00

Lois **Ehlert**

Growing Vegetable Soup

0-15-232581-6 HARCOURT BRACE PB $20.00

Planting a Rainbow

0-15-262609-3 HARCOURT BRACE $15.00

Red Leaf, Yellow Leaf

0-15-266197-2 HARCOURT BRACE $15.00

Marie Hall **Ets**

Gilberto and the Wind

0-670-34025-1 VIKING $14.99

In the Forest: Story and Pictures

0-14-050180-0 PUFFIN PB $4.99

Play with Me

0-670-55977-6 VIKING $13.95

Muriel **Feelings**

Moja Means One: Swahili Counting Book

ILLUSTRATED BY TOM FEELINGS

0-14-055296-0 PUFFIN PB $18.99

Douglas **Florian**

City Street

0-688-09543-7 GREENWILLOW $15.00

Margot **Fonteyn**

Swan Lake

The great dancer offers a splendid retelling of the ballet. The illustrations do full justice to the story's melancholy romanticism. For ages 8, 9, and up

See also **FICTION** under **BOOKS FOR EIGHTS, NINES, AND UP**

ILLUSTRATED BY TRINA SCHART HYMAN

0-15-200600-1 HARCOURT BRACE $14.95

Don **Freeman**

Corduroy

Corduroy is Lisa's toy teddy bear and she takes him everywhere. Of course she loses him too, but he is indestructible

0-670-24133-4 VIKING $13.99

0-14-050173-8 VIKING PB $4.99

A Pocket for Corduroy

0 140503528 VIKING $3.99

Wanda **Gag**

The ABC Bunny

0-698-20465-4 PUTNAM PB $6.95

Millions of Cats

Published in 1928, Wanda Gag's classic storybook describes a little old couple who must cope with an explosive feline population when they try to adopt just one cat

0-698-20091-8 MCCANN $11.95

0-698-20637-1 PUTNAM PB $4.95

Paul **Galdone**

Cat Goes Fiddle-I-Fee

A retelling of an old English rhyme in which children are introduced to the characteristic sounds of farm animals

0-89919-336-6 CLARION $14.95

The Gingerbread Boy

Galdone's illustrated versions of traditional tales are characteristically jaunty and good-humored. The big animated figures and vivid colors will please the very young

0-395-28799-5 CLARION $14.95

0-89919-163-0 CLARION PB $5.95

Three Little Kittens

Two rhyming stories accompanied by vigorous illustrations

0-89919-426-5 HOUGHTON MIFFLIN $14.95

Walter **Gerrold**

Mother Goose's Nursery Rhymes

0-679-42815-1 RANDOM HOUSE $13.95

Gail **Gibbons**

Boat Book

0-8234-0478-1 HOLIDAY HOUSE $15.95

Fire! Fire!

0-690-04416-X HARPERCREST $14.89

Trains

0-8234-0640-7 HOLIDAY HOUSE $15.95

Mirra **Ginsburg**

Good Morning, Chick

ILLUSTRATED BY BYRON BARTON

0-688-84284-4

GREENWILLOW LIBRARY EDITION $13.95

Mushroom in the Rain

A storybook about animals who take refuge under an amazing mushroom, with bold and satisfying illustrations by José Aruego and Ariane Dewey

0-689-71441-6 ALADDIN PB $3.95

Norman **Gorbaty**

Baby Animals Say Hello

0-394-88241-5 RANDOM HOUSE PB $4.99

Eric **Hill**

Spot Goes to the Beach

Spot is a rotund puppy, and young listeners participate in his adventures by lifting a flap at the appropriate moment

0-399-21247-7 PUTNAM $12.95

Spot Goes to the Farm

0-399-21434-8 PUTNAM $12.95

Spot's Baby Sister

0-399-21640-5 PUTNAM $12.95

Spot's Big Book of Words

0-399-21563-8 PUTNAM $10.95

Spot's First Walk

0-399-20838-0 PUTNAM $11.95

Spot's Walk in the Woods: A Lift the Flap Rebus Book

0-399-22528-5 PUTNAM $12.95

Where's Spot?

"There's a magic about Spot all children respond to"—*Parents*

0-399-20758-9 PUTNAM $12.95

Tana **Hoban**

26 Letters and 99 Cents

Bright, colorful photographs provide a simultaneous introduction to the alphabet and to counting money

0-688-06362-4

GREENWILLOW LIBRARY EDITION $15.95

A Children's Zoo

A petting zoo photographed as though the animals are seen through the eyes of the young visitors

0-688-05202-9 GREENWILLOW $16.00

Tana **Hoban**

I Read Signs

Hoban photographs scenes or objects in close-up, and children find a shape, color, or object that fits a prechosen concept. Pre-kindergarten children enter wholeheartedly into the game, and Hoban's sense of the unexpected makes the pictures fun to look at many times over.

0-688-02317-7 MORROW $16.00
0-688-07331-X MORROW PB $4.95

Is It Red? Is It Yellow? Is It Blue?

0-688-80171-4 GREENWILLOW $16.00
0-688-07034-5 MORROW PB $4.95

Is It Rough? Is It Smooth? Is It Shiny?

0-688-03823-9 GREENWILLOW $18.00

Look Again!

0-02-744050-8 SIMON & SCHUSTER $15.00

Of Colors and Things

0-688-07534-7 GREENWILLOW $16.00
0-688-04585-5 MULBERRY PB $4.95

Shirley **Hughes**

Colors

Illustrated in a lovely, soft style. Threes to fives will find plenty to look at

0-688-04206-6 LOTHROP, LEE, & SHEPHERD $4.95

Crockett **Johnson**

Harold and the Purple Crayon

Harold sets off with his mighty purple crayon to draw himself an adventure. This masterful little book moves with terrific speed as Harold uses a few brief crayon strokes to put himself in and out of situations

0-06-022935-7 HARPERCOLLINS $12.95
0-06-443022-7 TROPHY PB $4.95

Harold's Circus

0-06-443024-3 TROPHY PB $4.95

Harold's Trip to the Sky

0-06-443025-1 TROPHY PB $3.95

Satoshi **Kitamura**

When Sheep Cannot Sleep

Woolly the sheep is wide awake, and his night-time adventures give young readers all sorts of things to count

0-374-38311-1 FS&G $14.00

Ruth **Krauss**

The Carrot Seed

See also **NONFICTION** under **BOOKS FOR EIGHTS, NINES, AND UP**

ILLUSTRATED BY CROCKETT JOHNSON

0-06-023350-8 HARPERCOLLINS $13.95
0-06-443210-6 TROPHY PB $4.95

Dorothy **Kunhardt**

Pat the Bunny

First and best of its kind; fashioned after the ever-popular toy. The baby-sized activities are easy, varied, and fun

0-307-12000-7 GOLDEN PB $8.00

Edward **Lear**

The Owl and the Pussy-Cat: And Other Nonsense Poems

ILLUSTRATED BY MICHAEL HAGUE

1-55858-467-6 NORTH SOUTH $18.95

Barbro **Lindgren**

Sam's Ball

Sam is a funny-looking fellow, but you will learn to like him. Unlike some other fictional two-year-olds, he possesses annoying qualities as well as charm; there is a wealth of stubborn energy behind his everyday exploits

ILLUSTRATED BY EVA ERIKSSON

0-688-02359-2 MORROW $6.95

Sam's Bath

ILLUSTRATED BY EVA ERIKSSON

0-688-02362-2 MORROW $6.95

Sam's Potty

ILLUSTRATED BY EVA ERIKSSON

0-688-06603-8 MORROW $6.95

Sam's Teddy Bear

ILLUSTRATED BY EVA ERIKSSON

0-688-01270-1 MORROW $6.95

Margaret **Mahy** & Patricia **MacCarthy**

17 Kings and 42 Elephants

0-8037-0458-5 DUTTON $15.99

Bill **Martin**

Brown Bear, Brown Bear, What Do You See?

ILLUSTRATED BY ERIC CARLE

0-8050-1744-5 HOLT $15.95

Bill **Martin**, Jr. & John **Archambault**

Chicka Chicka Boom Boom

In rollicking rhyme, the letters of the alphabet race each other to the top of the coconut tree. An ideal introduction to the ABCs. For children under 5

ILLUSTRATED BY LOIS EHLERT

0-671-67949-X SIMON & SCHUSTER $14.00

Mercer **Mayer**

A Boy, a Dog and a Frog

Three small-format, wordless books with precise and humorous observations

0-14-054611-1 DIAL BOOKS PB $3.99

Faith **McNulty**

The Lady and the Spider

An unusual early reading book

ILLUSTRATED BY BOB MARSTALL

0-06-024192-6 HARPERCREST LIBRARY EDITION $14.89
0-06-443152-5 TROPHY PB $4.95

Iona **Opie**

Oxford Dictionary of Nursery Rhymes

EDITED BY PETER OPIE

0-19-869111-4 OXFORD $47.50

Iona **Opie** & Peter **Opie**

Tail Feathers from Mother Goose

Previously unpublished Mother Goose rhymes, lavishly illustrated by British and American artists

99912-4-964-8
LITTLE, BROWN LIBRARY EDITION $16.99

Hiawyn **Oram**

In the Attic

A little child goes up into an attic that isn't there and sees various fanstastic sights

ILLUSTRATED BY SATOSHI KITAMURA

0-8050-0779-2 HOLT $13.95
0-8050-0780-6 HOLT PB $5.95

Helen **Oxenbury**

All Fall Down

These are commendably uncomplicated board books, dealing with everyday situations the very young will recognize

0-02-769040-7 LITTLE SIMON $6.95

The Car Trip

0-14-050377-3 PUFFIN PB $3.99

Clap Hands

0-02-769030-X LITTLE SIMON $6.95

The Dancing Class

0-14-054934-X PUFFIN PB $3.99

Dressing

0-671-42113-1 LITTLE SIMON $3.95

Eating Out

0-14-054948-X PUFFIN PB $3.99

Playing

0-671-42109-3 LITTLE SIMON $4.95

Shopping Trip

0-8037-7939-9 DIAL BOOKS $3.95

Tickle Tickle

0-02-769020-2 LITTLE SIMON $6.95

Jerry **Pallotta**

Icky Bug Counting Book

ILLUSTRATED BY RALPH MASIELLO

0-88106-497-1 CHARLESBRIDGE $14.95

Dorothy Hinshaw **Patent**

Baby Horses

PHOTOGRAPHY BY WILLIAM MUNOZ

0-87614-690-6 CAROL $17.50

Jack **Prelutsky**

Ride a Purple Pelican

ILLUSTRATED BY GARTH WILLIAMS

0-688-04031-4 MORROW $17.95

Jack **Prelutsky**, editor

Read-Aloud Rhymes for the Very Young

One of a handful of contemporary poets who write for children, Prelutsky is a distinguished anthologist and the editor of *The Random House Book of Poetry for Children,* the best available collection for elementary school children

ILLUSTRATED BY MARC BROWN

0-394-87218-5 KNOPF $19.00

H.A. **Rey**

Curious George Gets a Medal

0-395-16973-9 HOUGHTON MIFFLIN $14.95

Curious George Takes a Job

0-395-15086-8 HOUGHTON MIFFLIN $14.95

The Adventures of Curious George/ Boxed Set of Miniature Books
0-395-73518-1 HOUGHTON MIFFLIN PB $10.00

Anybody at Home?
0-395-07045-7 HOUGHTON MIFFLIN PB $2.95

Curious George
0-395-69803-0 HOUGHTON MIFFLIN PB $19.95

Curious George/Carry Along Book and Cassette
0-395-66490-X HOUGHTON MIFFLIN PB $7.95

Feed the Animals
0-395-07063-5 HOUGHTON MIFFLIN PB $2.95

See the Circus
0-395-07068-6 HOUGHTON MIFFLIN PB $2.95

Eve **Rice**

Benny Bakes a Cake
0-688-11579-9 GREENWILLOW $14.00

Sam Who Never Forgets
0-688-84088-4 MORROW $13.95
0-688-07335-2 MORROW PB $3.95

Anne **Rockwell**

Happy Birthday to Me
0-02-777680-8 SIMON & SCHUSTER $10.95

Fred **Rogers**

Going to the Potty
A straight-faced and sensible picture book about toilet training that asks and answers questions from the child's point of view
ILLUSTRATED BY JIM JUDKIS
0-399-21297-3 PUTNAM PB $6.95

Michael **Rosen**

We're Going on a Bear Hunt
A family ventures out in search of adventure—only to find it. In this oversized picture book, the traditional chant is retold in glorious watercolors. For children under 5
ILLUSTRATIONS BY HELEN OXENBURY
0-689-50476-4 MCELDERRY $16.00

Cynthia **Rylant**

Henry and Mudge: The First Book of Their Adventures
"Warm, loving and gently philosophical, these stories about an only child and his closest companion deserve a place in every library collection"—*Kirkus Reviews*
ILLUSTRATED BY SUCIE STEVENSON
0-02-778001-5 SIMON & SCHUSTER $13.00
0-689-71399-1 ALADDIN PB $3.95

Henry and Mudge and the Bedtime Thumps: The Ninth Book of Their Adventures (Ready-to-Read)
ILLUSTRATED BY SUCIE STEVENSON
0-02-778006-6 SIMON & SCHUSTER $14.00
0-689-80162-9 ALADDIN PB $3.99

Henry and Mudge and the Best Day of All
ILLUSTRATED BY SUCIE STEVENSON
0-02-778012-0 SIMON & SCHUSTER $14.00

Henry and Mudge and the Careful Cousin (The Henry and Mudge Books, Bk 13)
ILLUSTRATED BY SUCIE STEVENSON
0-02-778021-X SIMON & SCHUSTER $14.00

Henry and Mudge and the Forever Sea (Henry and Mudge Adventures, Bk 6)
"The Ryland and Stevenson combo offers a sixth aventure as brisk and invigorating as the ocean breezes when Henry, Henry's father, and Henry's massive woofer, Mudge, head for the ocean in four more lively stories…Propelled by the perky illustrations, new readers…will tag right along on this jaunt" —*Booklist*
ILLUSTRATED BY SUCIE STEVENSON
0-689-71701-6 ALADDIN PB $3.95

Henry and Mudge and the Happy Cat (The Henry and Mudge Adventures, Bk 8)
ILLUSTRATED BY SUCIE STEVENSON
0-689-71791-1 ALADDIN PB $3.95

Henry and Mudge and the Long Weekend: Ready-To-Read Level 2
ILLUSTRATED BY SUCIE STEVENSON
0-689-80885-2 ALADDIN PB $3.99

Henry and Mudge and the Long Weekend (Henry and Mudge Adventures, Bk 11)
ILLUSTRATED BY SUCIE STEVENSON
0-02-778013-9 SIMON & SCHUSTER $13.00

Henry and Mudge and the Wild Wind (Henry and Mudge Adventures, Bk 12)
ILLUSTRATED BY SUCIE STEVENSON
0-02-778014-7 SIMON & SCHUSTER $13.00

Henry and Mudge Get the Cold Shivers: The Seventh Book of Their Adventures
ILLUSTRATED BY SUCIE STEVENSON
0-689-71849-7 ALADDIN PB $3.95

Henry and Mudge in Puddle Trouble: The Second Book of Their Adventures
Henry and Mudge celebrate spring in this lively and comical book
0-689-71400-9 ALADDIN PB $3.95

Henry and Mudge in the Green Time
0-689-71582-X ALADDIN PB $3.95

Henry and Mudge in the Sparkle Days (The Henry and Mudge Books, Bk 5)
ILLUSTRATED BY SUCIE STEVENSON
0-689-71752-0 ALADDIN PB $3.95

Henry and Mudge/Book and Toy
0-689-71648-6 LITTLE SIMON $19.95

Henry and Mudge Take the Big Test: The Tenth Book of Their Adventures
ILLUSTRATED BY SUCIE STEVENSON
0-02-778009-0 SIMON & SCHUSTER $12.95

Henry and Mudge Under the Yellow Moon
"Three easy-to-read stories that celebrate the fall…The special friendship between this small boy and his enormous dog shines through in both the simple text and in the energetic watercolors. All three are on target in their humor and in the way that they speak directly to the concerns of children. Young readers are sure to enjoy the time they spend with Henry and Mudge" —*School Library Journal*
0-689-71580-3 ALADDIN PB $3.95

Ruth **Sawyer**

Journey Cake, Ho
0-14-050275-0 VIKING PB $4.99

Richard **Scarry**

Best First Book Ever
0-394-84250-2 RANDOM HOUSE $14.00

Maurice **Sendak**

Chicken Soup with Rice
0-06-025535-8 HARPERCREST $13.89

Hector Protector & As I Went over the Water
0-06-443237-8 TROPHY PB $7.95

One Was Johnny: A Counting Book
Johnny was one, then he became 10, then he became one again. As the house of the once solitary Johnny fills to the ceiling, enjoy Sendak's humorous characterizations
0-06-025540-4 HARPERCREST LIBRARY EDITION $13.89
0-06-443251-3 TROPHY PB $4.95

Pierre: A Cautionary Tale in Five Chapters and a Prologue
0-06-443252-1 TROPHY PB $4.95

Dr. **Seuss**

Cat in the Hat
See also **BOOKS FOR AGES FIVE, SIX, AND SEVEN**
0-394-90001-4 RANDOM LIBRARY $11.99

Fox in Socks
0-394-90038-3 RANDOM LIBRARY $11.99

Hop on Pop
0-394-90029-4 RANDOM LIBRARY $11.99

Peter **Sis**

Waving
People wave, and others wave back. Children count the participants in these bright illustrations
0-688-07159-7 GREENWILLOW $12.95
0-688-07160-0 MORROW LIBRARY EDITION $5.00

Esphyr **Slobodkina**

Caps for Sale: A Tale of a Peddler, Some Monkeys, and Their Monkey Business
0-06-025778-4 HARPERCREST $13.89

Esphyr **Slobodkina**

Caps for Sale

A peddler's caps are stolen by a treeful of monkeys in a classic little storybook with few words and funny illustrations

0-201-09147-X HARPERCOLLINS $13.95
0-06-443143-6 TROPHY PB $4.95

John **Stadler**

Hooray for Snail!

0-690-04413-5 CROWELL LIBRARY EDITION $14.89

Nancy **Tafuri**

Have You Seen My Duckling?

See also BOOKS FOR AGES FIVE, SIX, AND SEVEN

0-688-02797-0 GREENWILLOW $15.95
0-688-10994-2 MULBERRY PB $4.95

Who's Counting?

Children count the animals seen by an inquisitive puppy. Another lovely book

0-688-06130-3 GREENWILLOW $16.00

Olive **Wadsworth**

Over in the Meadow

A counting rhyme cheerfully illustrated for the threes and fours

ILLUSTRATED BY EZRA JACK KEATS

0-590-44848-X SCHOLASTIC PB $4.95

Shigeo **Watanabe**

How Do I Put It On?

Rather purposeful about introducing notions of autonomy and self-reliance—questionable goals for children this young. But the illustrations are nicely done, and the little bear hero is appealing

ILLUSTRATED BY YASUO OHTOMO

0-399-20761-9 PHILOMEL $10.99

Rosemary **Wells**

Fritz and the Mess Fairy

0-8037-0981-1 DIAL BOOKS $14.00

Max's Chocolate Chicken

0-8037-0585-9 DIAL BOOKS $9.95

Morris's Disappearing Bag: A Christmas Story

0-14-054664-2 DIAL BOOKS PB $4.99

Noisy Nora

0-8037-6638-6 DIAL BOOKS $11.99

Colin **West**

Ten Little Crocodiles

Crocodiles become larger in numbers, then smaller in numbers in an Australian artist's funny pictures

1-56402-463-6 CANDLEWICK PB $4.99

Nadine Bernard **Westcott**

The Lady with the Alligator Purse

0-316-93135-7 JOY STREET $15.95

Brian **Wildsmith**

Animal Shapes

0-19-272174-7 OXFORD PB $6.95

Brian Wildsmith's Mother Goose

0-19-272180-1 OXFORD PB $11.95

Squirrels

0-19-272105-4 OXFORD PB $11.95

Vera B. **Williams**

"More More More," Said the Baby: 3 Love Stories

0-688-14736-4 MULBERRY PB $4.95

Audrey **Wood**

Oh My Baby Bear!

0-15-257698-3 HARCOURT BRACE $13.95

Audrey **Wood** & Don **Wood**

Little Mouse, the Red Ripe Strawberry, and the Big Hungry Bear

0-85953-182-1 CHILDS PLAY $13.99

Blanche Fisher **Wright**

The Original Mother Goose

Recently reissued in a handsome cloth-bound edition, this is a superior collection of timeless nursery rhymes. Enlivened with Blanche Fisher Wright's beloved and evocative color illustrations from the 1916 edition, this volume is a treasure that is every child's legacy

1-56138-113-6 RUNNING PRESS $14.95

Jane **Yolen**

The Emperor and the Kite

ILLUSTRATED BY ED YOUNG

0-399-22512-9 SANCS PB $5.95

Sky Dogs

ILLUSTRATED BY BARRY MOSER

0-15-200776-8 VOYAGER PB $5.00

Jane **Yolen**, editor

The Lullaby Songbook

Musical arrangements by Adam Stemple

ILLUSTRATED BY CHARLES MIKOLAYDAK

0-15-249903-2 HARCOURT BRACE $13.95

Jane **Yolen** & John **Schoenherr**

Owl Moon

0-399-21457-7 PHILOMEL $15.95

Margot **Zemach**

The Little Red Hen

Stars a determined Little Red Hen doing everything for and by herself

0-374-34621-6 FS&G $14.00
0-374-44511-7 SUNBURST PB $4.95

Books for Ages Five, Six, and Seven

Though children are still lookers and listeners when they enter kindergarten and first grade, they are advanced verbally and soon become readers. Picture books presenting funny situations are strong favorites, but children of six and seven also enjoy classic fairy tales, folktales, and modern fantasy tales. Many stories that children first meet when they are in preschool or kindergarten remain favorites for two or three years thereafter. The picture books selected are those which children in the early elementary grades can read themselves.

Verna **Aardema**

Bimwili and the Zimwi (My Bear Books)

0-8037-0212-4 DUTTON $14.99

Bringing the Rain to Kapiti Plain

An African folktale told in the manner of "The House that Jack Built"

ILLUSTRATED BY BEATRIZ VIDAL

0-8037-0809-2 DIAL BOOKS $15.99
0-14-054616-2 DIAL BOOKS PB $4.99

Why Mosquitoes Buzz in People's Ear's: A West African Tale

All the African animals must suffer after a mishap occurs to one of their children. The animal king settles the case, and the scapegoat mosquito is punished. Caldecott Medal 1976

ILLUSTRATED BY DIANE DILLON

0-8037-6089-2 DIAL BOOKS $15.99
0-8037-6088-4 DIAL BOOKS PB $4.99

Karen **Ackerman**

Song and Dance Man

ILLUSTRATED BY STEPHEN GAMMELL

0-394-99330-6
RANDOM LIBRARY LIBRARY EDITION $15.99

Arnold **Adoff**, editor

My Black Me: A Beginning Book of Black Poetry

0-525-45216-8 DUTTON $14.99

Aesop

Aesop's Fables

Full-color illustrations make this an especially good introduction to Aesop for young children

ILLUSTRATED BY MICHAEL HAGUE

0-89009-350-4 BOOK SALES $6.98
0-8050-0210-3 HOLT $14.95

Janet **Ahlberg** & Allan **Ahlberg**

Each Peach Pear Plum

Set on a summer afternoon in the country, this favorite story reveals a host of nursery rhyme characters

0-670-28705-9 VIKING $12.95

The Jolly Postman

Letters that the reader pulls out of the book are addressed to fairy tale characters. Children familiar with traditional stories will find the idea intriguing

0-316-02036-2 LITTLE, BROWN $17.95

Martha **Alexander**

Blackboard Bear

Blackboard Bear emerges from a chalk drawing and becomes a little boy's companion. Bear is a wonderful, if silent, friend, but he often gets his master into trouble. A nice little fable about the pleasures and dangers of imagination

0-8045-6507-4 SPOEKEN ARTS $14.45

Aliki

Digging Up Dinosaurs

Distinguished by small, delicate illustrations, this is a fascinating account of hunts for extinct monsters and should appeal to a broad age group

0-06-445078-3 TROPHY PB $4.95

Feelings

Sketches, poems, and anecdotes in a picture book that for a child is second-best to a flesh-and-blood confidant. Funny without making fun of children's fears and attachments

0-688-03831-X GREENWILLOW $16.00
0-688-06518-X GREENWILLOW PB $4.95

A Medieval Feast

A scrupulously accurate little picture book about a fictional event (a royal visit) and a factual account of what went on in a medieval household

0-06-446050-9 TROPHY PB $5.95

Harry **Allard**

Miss Nelson Is Missing

Miss Nelson's homeroom is inhabited by a bunch of really naughty kids. The situation isn't resolved until nice Miss Nelson becomes horrid Miss Swamp, and some well-behaved children start longing for her return

ILLUSTRATED BY JAMES MARSHALL

9-992-66164-X WESTON WOOD PB $4.80

Miss Nelson Is Missing

With Cassette

9-996-40174-X WESTON WOOD $14.80

The Stupids Have a Ball

ILLUSTRATED BY JAMES MARSHALL

0-676-30227-0 AMERICAN SCHOOL $18.66

The Stupids Step Out

The Stupids put on their sneakers when it's time for bed and vacuum the carpet with a lawn mower. Goofily good-natured, the Stupids will appeal to kids who don't care how silly the jokes are

ILLUSTRATED BY JAMES MARSHALL

0-39-525377-2 HOUGHTON MIFFLIN PB $5.95

Harry **Allard** & James **Marshall**

Miss Nelson Has a Field Day

The substitute teacher, Coach Swamp, strikes terror in the hearts of the incompetent footballers from homeroom 207

ILLUSTRATED BY JAMES MARSHALL

0-395-52138-6 HOUGHTON MIFFLIN PB $7.95

Hans Christian **Andersen**

The Fir Tree

ILLUSTRATED BY MARCEL IMSAND & RITA MARSHALL

0-87191-949-4 CREATIVE ED LIBRARY EDITION $13.95
0-8249-8389-0 IDEALS CHILDRENS PB $2.95

The Little Mermaid

A mermaid falls in love with a prince and makes thankless sacrifices for him

ILLUSTRATED BY MICHAEL HOGUE

1-88539-417-9 BLUESTAR COMMUNICATION $25.00

Hans Christian Andersen

The Princess and the Pea

Andersen's little comedy about an ungrateful guest who more than gets away with it

ILLUSTRATED BY SUCIE STEVENSON

0-385-41375-0 YEARLING PB $15.00

Thumbelina

Thumbelina is as small as her name suggests, and her first suitors are equally small and very ugly. But after many tribulations, determined little Thumbelina is rewarded with a husband

ILLUSTRATED BY LISBETH ZWERGER

0-8362-4926-7 ANDREWS & MCMEEL $6.95
0-88708-006-5 SIMON & SCHUSTER $16.00

The Tinderbox

Barry Moser's expressive watercolors bring out the dramatic undertones of Andersen's fairy tale, which he has transposed to the post-Civil War era

ADAPTED AND ILLUSTRATED BY BARRY MOSER

0-689-50458-6 MCELDERRY $14.95
0-316-03938-1 LITTLE, BROWN LIBRARY EDITION $14.95

The Ugly Duckling

With cassette

ILLUSTRATED BY DANIEL SAN SOUCI

0-89565-474-1 CHILDS WORLD LIBRARY EDITION $19.93

The Ugly Duckling

Andersen's masterpiece is the story we like to think is autobiographical

ILLUSTRATED BY LORINDA BRYAN CAVLEY

0-15-692528-1 HARCOURT BRACE PB $4.95

The Wild Swans

An oversized picture book with colored pages. A young woman saves her 12 brothers by putting herself in terrible danger

RETOLD BY AMY EHRLICH

ILLUSTRATED BY SUSAN JEFFERS

0-8037-9381-2 DIAL BOOKS $16.95
0-89375-481-1 TROLL PB $1.95

Maya **Angelou**

My Painted House, My Friendly Chicken, and Me

PHOTOGRAPHY BY MARGARET COURTNEY-CLARKE

0-517-59667-9 CROWN $16.00

Maya **Angelou** & Jean-Michel **Basquiat**

Life Doesn't Frighten Me

An unusual mixture of forms, uniquely appropriate for children. The dynamic combination of the strength and courage of Angelou's poems and the daring of Basquiat's full-color artwork, together, in this unique book, compose a testament to courage

See also POETRY SINCE 1945 under 20TH-CENTURY AMERICAN POETRY in LITERATURE OF THE AMERICAS

EDITED BY SARA JANE BOYERS

1-55670-288-4 STEWART, TABORI $15.95

Mitsumasa **Anno**

All in a Day

International illustrators paint a picture of life in eight countries

0-399-61292-0 PHILOMEL LIBRARY EDITION $15.99

Anno's Alphabet: An Adventure in Imagination

The alphabet book to buy for a child who is past the letter-learning stage. The pages contain one charming surprise after another—wooden, three-dimensional letters, and smoothly rendered illustrations with many fanciful touches

0-690-00540-7 HARPERCREST LIBRARY EDITION $16.00

Anno's Counting Book

The landscape fills up as children turn the pages and are asked to count flocks of birds, numbers of houses, and so on

0-690-01287-X CROWELL $16.00
0-06-443123-1 TROPHY PB $5.95

Anno's Mysterious Multiplying Jar

Objects emerge from Anno's handsome jar and start multiplying. Mathematicians call the process factoring. For readers it's a counting game and visual feast combined

0-399-20951-4 PUTNAM $18.95

Richard **Atwater** & Florence **Atwater**

Mr. Popper's Penguins

ILLUSTRATED BY ROBERT LAWSON

0-316-05842-4 LITTLE, BROWN $16.95

Esther **Averill**

The Fire Cat

0-06-444038-9 TROPHY PB $3.75

Natalie **Babbitt**

Bub, Or the Very Best Thing

0-06-205044-3 HARPERCOLLINS $15.95

Barbara **Bader**

Aesop and Company: With Scenes from His Legendary Life

ILLUSTRATED BY ARTHUR GEISERT

0-395-50597-6 HOUGHTON MIFFLIN $16.95

Debra **Barracca** & Sal **Barracca**

The Adventures of Taxi Dog

"My name is Maxi, I ride in a taxi around New York City all day. I sit next to Jim (I belong to him), but it wasn't always this way." Thus begins the tale of a homeless dog who spends his days (and nights) in a cab helping soon-to-be-moms and dads get to the hospital, singing along with performers, and entertaining passengers. With 19 lively full-color illustrations, this is a book certain to be read over and over. Ages 4-8

0-8037-0671-5 DIAL BOOKS $14.99

Judi **Barrett**

Animals Should Definitely Not Wear Clothing

A humorous little essay on why camels, hens, lions, and so on look better without it

See also BOOKS FOR CHILDREN UNDER FIVE

ILLUSTRATED BY RON BARRETT

0-689-20592-9 ATHENEUM $13.95
0-689-70807-6 ALADDIN PB $4.95

Cloudy with a Chance of Meatballs

The little town of Chewandswallow enjoys an edible climate. The weather takes a turn for the worse and the inhabitants of Chewandswallow seek a safe haven

0-689-70749-5 MACMILLAN PB $4.99

Graeme **Base**

The Sign of the Seahorse: A Tale of Greed and High Adventure in Two Acts

The bestselling author and illustrator (*Animalia, The Eleventh Hour*) offers a sweeping story of adventure and intrigue set in the lovely but fragile world of a coral reef. Base portrays "a fully imagined underwater world where…each believably fishy face is also a witty human caricature"—*Kirkus Reviews*

0-8109-3825-1 ABRAMS $19.95

Ludwig **Bemelmans**

Madeline

Bemelmans had a good ear for rhyme and a lovely if wacky illustrative style. Madeline lives in an old house in Paris, and her healthy streak of mischief is a trial to poor Miss Clavell. But she is all indignation when injustice occurs, especially when animals are the victims. A Caldecott Honor Book for 1940

See also BOOKS FOR CHILDREN UNDER FIVE

0-14-050198-3 VIKING PB $4.99

Madeline's Rescue

Caldecott Medal 1954

0-670-44716-1 VIKING $15.99
0-14-050207-6 VIKING PB $4.99

Nathaniel **Benchley**

Oscar Otter

0-06-444025-7 TROPHY PB $3.50

Sam the Minuteman

0-06-444107-5 TROPHY PB $3.75

Small Wolf

ILLUSTRATED BY JOAN SANDIN

0-06-020491-5 HARPERCOLLINS $14.95

Melvin **Berger** & Gilda **Berger**

Telephones, Televisions, and Toilets: How They Work—And What Can Go Wrong

ILLUSTRATED BY DON MADDEN

0-8249-8608-3 IDEAP PB $4.50

Where Does the Mail Go?: A Book About the Postal System

ILLUSTRATED BY GEOFFREY BRITTINGHAM

1-57102-022-5 IDEALS $12.00

Cari **Best**

Red Light, Green Light, Mama and Me

ILLUSTRATED BY NIKI DALY

0-531-09452-9 ORCHARD $14.95

Christina **Bjork**

Linnea in Monet's Garden

Two unusual, inventive approaches to gardening

ILLUSTRATED BY LENA ANDERSON

91-29-58314-4 FS&G $13.00

Linnea's Windowsill Garden

91-29-59064-7 FS&G $13.00

Judy **Blume**

The One in the Middle Is the Green Kangaroo

Squeezed in like peanut butter between the oldest and youngest kids of the family, this "middle" child finds ways to make himself visible

0-02-711055-9 SIMON & SCHUSTER $14.95
0-440-40668-4 YEARLING PB $5.99

Jo Ellen **Bogart**

Daniel's Dog

Since Daniel's baby sister was born, his mother hasn't had much time for him, but now he has Lucy, the "ghost" dog sent by his dead grandmother. In text and in full-color pictures, this is a warm story which will speak especially to those in unsettling situations. For ages 5-8

ILLUSTRATED BY JANET WILSON

0-590-43402-0 SCHOLASTIC PB $11.95

Sandra **Boynton**

Hippos Go Berserk

Boisterous hippos arrive at a party and must somehow be counted

0-689-80854-2 SIMON & SCHUSTER $14.00

Jan **Brett**

Armadillo Rodeo

0-399-22803-9 PUTNAM $15.95

Goldilocks and the Three Bears

The distinctly Russian bears wear their colorful costumes with a half-comic dignity

0-399-22033-X DODD, MEAD $15.95

The Brothers Grimm

Dear Mili: An Old Tale

ILLUSTRATED BY MAURICE SENDAK

0-374-31762-3 FS&G $16.95

The Brothers Grimm

Hansel and Gretel

ILLUSTRATED BY SUSAN JEFFERS

0-14-054636-7 DUTTON PB $5.99

Red Riding Hood

A sturdy heroine and a witty ending to the traditional Grimm story. Caldecott Honor Book 1988

RETOLD AND ILLUSTRATED BY JAMES MARSHALL

0-8037-0344-9 DUTTON $14.99

Marc **Brown** & Laurene K. **Brown**

Dinosaurs Divorce: A Guide For Changing Families

Dinosaurs act out the roles played by parents and young children in real-life separations

0-316-10996-7 LITTLE, BROWN PB $6.95

Marcia **Brown**

Let's Go Swimming with Mr. Sillypants

0-517-59030-1 CROWN PB $5.99

Stone Soup

The pleasant old-fashioned story about the miraculous soup pot

0-87499-053-X LIVE OAK $22.95
0-689-71103-4 ALADDIN PB $5.99

Ashley **Bryan**

Turtle Knows Your Name

0-689-71728-8 ALADDIN PB $4.95

Eve **Bunting**

How Many Days to America?: A Thankgiving Story

ILLUSTRATED BY BETH PECK

0-395-54777-6 CLARION PB $5.95

The Mother's Day Mice

Mice brothers set off to find the perfect gift in an exceptionally pretty book that also has a nicely consoling point

0-89919-895-3 HOUGHTON MIFFLIN PB $8.95

Scary, Scary Halloween

Trick-or-treaters are pursued by a mysterious sheeted creature

ILLUSTRATED BY JAN BRETT

0-89919-799-X CLARION PB $5.95

John **Burningham**

Come Away from the Water, Shirley

Shirley's prosaic parents don't notice that she is having the most extraordinary daydreams. Short on text, but unusually sophisticated for a picture book

0-690-01361-2 HARPERCREST LIBRARY EDITION $14.89

Mr. Gumpy's Outing

An eccentric English gentleman is accompanied by the oddest group of people and animals

0-8050-0708-3 HOLT $15.95
0-8050-1315-6 HOLT PB $5.95

Betsy **Byars**

The Blossoms Meet the Vulture Lady

ILLUSTRATED BY JACQUELINE ROGERS

0-440-40677-3 YEARLING PB $3.50

Jeannette **Caines**

I Need a Lunch Box

ILLUSTRATED BY PAT CUMMINGS

0-06-443341-2 TROPHY PB $4.95

Carol **Carrick**

Patrick's Dinosaurs

When Patrick and his older brother visit the zoo, Patrick's brother is too busy showing off to see prehistoric monsters. But Patrick does; giant dinosaurs loom over the elephant house and swim in the zoo's lake until Patrick finally reaches home safely

ILLUSTRATED BY DONALD CARRICK

0-89919-189-4 HOUGHTON MIFFLIN $14.95

0-395-66496-9 HOUGHTON MIFFLIN PB $8.95

What Happened to Patrick's Dinosaurs?

Patrick comes up with an explanation for the dinosaurs' disappearance

ILLUSTRATED BY DONALD CARRICK

0-89919-406-0 HOUGHTON MIFFLIN $15.95

Lewis **Carroll**

Alice's Adventures in Wonderland

With pictures by the author and creator of *Gorilla*

ILLUSTRATED BY ANTHONY BROWNE

0-312-01821-5 ST. MARTIN'S $14.95

Judith **Caseley**

Dear Annie

0-688-10010-4 GREENWILLOW $15.00

Priscilla Twice

0-688-13305-3 GREENWILLOW $15.00

Bennett **Cerf**

Bennett Cerf's Book of Riddles

ILLUSTRATED BY ROY MCKIE

0-394-80015-X RANDOM HOUSE $7.99

Ann Nolan **Clark**

In My Mother's House

ILLUSTRATED BY VELINO HERRARA

0-670-83917-5 VIKING $15.95

Secret of the Andes

0-14-030926-8 VIKING PB $4.99

Vicki **Cobb**

Lots of Rot

0-397-31939-8 LIPPINCOTT $15.89

Science Experiments You Can Eat

Chemistry demonstrated in kitchen experiments designed for children 10 and up

See also **YOUNG ADULT NONFICTION**

ILLUSTRATED BY DAVID CAIN

0-06-023534-9 HARPERCOLLINS $15.00

Why Doesn't the Earth Fall Up?: And Other Not Such Dumb Questions About Motion

ILLUSTRATED BY TED ENIK

0-525-67253-2 LODESTAR $14.99

Vicki **Cobb** & Marylin **Hafner**

Feeding Yourself

0-397-32325-5 LIPPINCOTT $12.89

Eleanor **Coerr**

The Josefina Story Quilt

0-06-021348-5 HARPERCOLLINS $14.95

Miriam **Cohen**

Liar, Liar, Pants on Fire!

Cohen's ongoing saga of Jim and his classmates offers brief, realistic slices of first-grade life, with much humor and surprisingly rounded characterizations

ILLUSTRATED BY LILLIAN HOBAN

0-440-44755-0 YEARLING PB $3.25

Lost in the Museum

ILLUSTRATED BY LILLIAN HOBAN

0-440-44780-1 DELL PB $2.95

Starring First Grade

ILLUSTRATED BY LILLIAN HOBAN

0-688-04030-6 MORROW LIBRARY EDITION $16.93

When Will I Read?

ILLUSTRATED BY LILLIAN HOBAN

0-688-80073-4 MORROW $16.00

0-688-84073-6 MORROW LIBRARY EDITION $15.93

Babette **Cole**

Princess Smartypants

0-399-21409-7 PUTNAM $15.95

Joanna **Cole**

Bony-Legs

0-590-40516-0 SCHOLASTIC PB $3.99

Doctor Change

Doctor Change is a magician whose name is all too appropriate in the eyes of his runaway apprentice

ILLUSTRATED BY DONALD CARRICK

0-688-06136-2 MORROW LIBRARY EDITION $12.88

How You Were Born

0-688-05801-9 MULBERRY PB $4.95

Hungry, Hungry Sharks

ILLUSTRATED BY ATRICIA WYNNE

0-394-87471-4 RANDOM HOUSE PB $3.99

The Magic School Bus at the Water Works

Ruled by an eccentric teacher, Cole's imaginary pupils reluctantly accompany Miss Frizzle on trips where fantastical adventures introduce solid scientific information. Second and third graders will enjoy these funny, imaginative, and irreverent science books

See also **NONFICTION** under **BOOKS FOR EIGHTS, NINES, AND UP**

ILLUSTRATED BY BRUCE DEGEN

0-590-43739-9 SCHOLASTIC $14.95

0-590-40360-5 SCHOLASTIC PB $4.95

The Magic School Bus Inside the Earth

ILLUSTRATED BY BRUCE DEGEN

0-590-40759-7 SCHOLASTIC $14.95

The New Baby at Your House

ILLUSTRATED BY HELLA HAMMID

0-688-07418-9 MORROW PB $5.95

Chris **Conover**

Froggie Went A-Courting

0-374-42474-8 FS&G PB $4.95

Barbara **Cooney**

Hattie and the Wild Waves

0-670-83056-9 VIKING $14.95

Miss Rumphius

0-670-47958-6 VIKING $14.99

Susan **Cooper** & Warwick **Hutton**

The Selkie Girl

0-689-50390-3 MCELDERRY $14.95

Helen **Craig**

Angelina's Christmas

0-517-57188-9 CROWN $5.99

Helen **Craig** & Katharine **Holabird**

Angelina and the Princess

Angelina is a child mouse and the heroine of a series that begins with her dancing lessons. Despite setbacks along the way, Angelina remains unspoiled when she finally realizes her ambitions

0-517-55273-6 CROWN $16.00

Angelina at the Fair

0-517-55744-4 CROWN $15.00

Angelina Ballerina

0-517-55083-0 CROWN $16.00

Angelina on Stage

0-517-56073-9 CROWN $16.00

Jamie Lee **Curtis**

When I Was Little: A Four Year Old's Memoir of Her Youth

Yes, *that* Jamie Lee Curtis. Actor, director, and mom. Now she can add author to her list of bonafides with this delightful story of a little girl, able to go down the slide by herself, and all the other joys of being four years old

ILLUSTRATED BY LAURA CORNELL

0-06-021079-6 HARPERCREST LIBRARY EDITION $14.89

Paula **Danziger**

Amber Brown Goes Fourth

"This appealing chapter book will please those who have met Amber in her earlier adventures…An enjoyable, accessible, and well-written story" —*The Horn Book Magazine*

0-590-93425-2 LITTLE APPLE PB $2.99

Amber Brown Is not a Crayon

"Danziger reaches out to a younger audience in this funny, touching slice of third-grade life, told in the voice of a fiesty, lovable heroine." —*School Library Journal*

Comes with Amber Brown Key Chain

0-399-22509-9 PUTNAM $13.95

0-590-45899-X SCHOLASTIC PB $2.99

Amber Brown Wants Extra Credit

0-399-22900-0 PUTNAM $13.95

Ingri **D'Aulaire** & Edgar P. **D'Aulaire**

Biographies free of obvious historical cliches. Children up to nine will appreciate the narratives and brightly crayoned illustrations.

Abraham Lincoln

Winner of the Caldecott Medal 1940

0-8045-6619-4 SPOEKEN ARTS PB $15.00

0-440-40690-0 YEARLING PB $10.95

Columbus
9992485418 SPOEKEN ARTS PB $15.00

D'Aulaire's Norse Gods & Giants
0-385-23692-1 DELACORTE PB $17.95

D'Aulaire's Book of Greek Myths
These classic retellings of Greek and Norse myths are wonderful read-aloud stories for young children and are candidates for an older child's permanent collection

ILLUSTRATED BY INGRI AND EDGAR P. D'AULAIRE

0-385-01583-6 DOUBLEDAY $24.95
0-440-40694-3 BANTAM PB $16.95

Jean **de Brunhoff**

Babar and His Children
0-394-80577-1 RANDOM HOUSE $13.00

The Story of Babar
Babar begins life as an ordinary little elephant. Then, in a series of swiftly drawn events, he loses his mother, runs out of the jungle, meets the Old Lady, and learns to dress and think like a human. Thereafter Babar is only short steps away from becoming king and founding Celesteville. Meanwhile, Zephir the monkey and Arthur, Celeste's heedless little brother, are always up to something. A classic for over 50 years.

0-394-80575-5 RANDOM HOUSE $13.00

Laurent **de Brunhoff**

Babar and the Ghost
Laurent de Brunhoff is Jean's son and successor, and his books are pale shadows of the first Babar series. Nevertheless, the characters remain lovable regardless of the plots

0-394-87908-2 RANDOM HOUSE PB $3.99

Walter **De La Mare**

The Turnip
ILLUSTRATED BY KEVIN HAWKES

0-87923-934-4 GODINE $18.95

Tomie **De Paola**

Bill and Pete
Bill is a Nile crocodile, and Pete the plover is his friend and toothbrush. Threatened with becoming a crocodile suitcase, Bill is rescued by Pete. Bill's adventures are pictured in bold, bright illustrations

0-399-22402-5 PUTNAM PB $5.95

Charlie Needs a Cloak
0-671-66467-0 ALADDIN PB $5.95

Oliver Button Is a Sissy
0-15-257852-8 HARCOURT BRACE $11.95

Merry Christmas, Strega Nona
0-15-253183-1 HARCOURT BRACE $14.95

Nana Upstairs and Nana Downstairs
0-399-21417-8 PUTNAM $14.95

Strega Nona
Strega Nona is the local witch. When her foolish assistant Anthony tries to replicate her magic, the results are calamitous—and hilarious. Caldecott Honor Book 1976

0-671-66283-X SIMON & SCHUSTER $15.00
0-671-66606-1 ALADDIN PB $6.95

Tomie **De Paola** & Tony **Johnston**

Badger and the Magic Fan: A Japanese Folktale
0-399-21945-5 PUTNAM $13.95

Beatrice Schenk **De Regniers**

May I Bring a Friend?
ILLUSTRATED BY BENI MONTRESOR

0-689-71353-3 ALADDIN PB $4.95

Arthur **Dorros**

Abuela
ILLUSTRATED BY ELISA KLEVEN

0-525-44750-4 DUTTON $15.99

Ann **Durell**, editor

The Diane Goode Book of American Folk Tales and Songs
ILLUSTRATIONS BY DIANE GOODE

0-525-44458-0 DUTTON $15.95

Philip D. **Eastman**

Are You My Mother?
A nonsense easy reader from a collaborator of Dr. Seuss. Some odd creatures get asked before the problem is resolved

0-394-80018-4 RANDOM HOUSE $7.99

Amy **Ehrlich**

The Story of Hanukkah
ILLUSTRATIONS BY ORI SHERMAN

0-8037-0615-4 DIAL BOOKS $14.95

Eugene **Field**

Wynken, Blynken and Nod
Night sailors Wynken, Blynken, and Nod are pictured as contemporary children in this version of the classic bedtime poem

ILLUSTRATED BY SUSAN JEFFERS

0-14-054794-0 UNICORN PB $4.99

Valerie **Flournoy**

The Patchwork Quilt
0-8037-0097-0 DUTTON $15.99

Mem **Fox**

Koala Lou
ILLUSTRATED BY PAMELA LOFTS

0-15-200502-1 HARCOURT BRACE $13.95

Possum Magic
ILLUSTRATED BY JULIE VIVAS

0-15-200572-2 HARCOURT BRACE $14.00

Tough Boris
ILLUSTRATED BY KATHRYN BROWN

0-15-289612-0 HARCOURT BRACE $15.00

Ina R. **Friedman**

How My Parents Learned to Eat
The young heroine recounts how her mother and father—Japanese and American respectively—met, fell in love, and finally learned to eat with knife and fork as well as chopsticks

ILLUSTRATED BY ALLAN SAY

0-395-66488-8 HOUGHTON MIFFLIN $7.95

Anita **Ganeri**

Creatures that Glow
A splendid book for young readers that takes a dramatic look at creatures that glow in the dark. Stunning illustrations printed on black backgrounds will fascinate children, whether they're marveling at deep-sea luminescent fish or fireflies, funghis, or bacteria. Clear, concise text and annotation accompany the photos to make this an informative, educational, and entertaining introduction to fascinating life forms

0-8109-4027-2 ABRAMS $19.95

Ruth Stiles **Gannett**

The Dragons of Blueland
ILLUSTRATED BY RUTH CHRISMAN GANNETT

0-394-89050-7 KNOPF PB $4.99

My Father's Dragon
A little boy tells a story about an island visited by his father, who discovers a dragon endowed with human traits. Newbery Honor Book 1949

0-394-89048-5 KNOPF PB $4.99

Jack **Gantos**

Rotten Ralph
The stories of a well-behaved little girl and her rotten cat Ralph

0-395-29202-6 HOUGHTON MIFFLIN PB $5.95

Rotten Ralph's Rotten Christmas
0-395-60285-8 HOUGHTON MIFFLIN PB $5.95

Christian **Garrison**

The Dream Eater
ILLUSTRATED BY DIANE GOODE

0-689-71058-5 ALADDIN PB $4.95

Arthur **Geisert**

Pigs from A to Z
A commendably different alphabet book. Pigs build an elaborate tree house, while the reader finds the letters hidden in the curiously drawn black-and-white illustrations

0-395-77874-3 HOUGHTON MIFFLIN PB $7.95

Roy **Gerrard**

Sir Cedric
Since Sir Cedric the Good is a knight, he defeats sinister opponents and rescues ladies—specifically one Fat Matilda, whom he marries. Gerrard tells his tale in a bouncy rhyming narrative and colorful, eccentric pictures

0-374-36959-3 FS&G $14.95
0-374-46659-9 FS&G PB $4.95

Gail **Gibbons**

Flying
A straightforward history from ancient times to the present

0-8234-0599-0 HOLIDAY HOUSE $15.95

Trucks
0-06-443069-3 TROPHY PB $4.95

Paul **Goble**

Brave Eagle's Account of the Fetterman Fight
The story of the battle over the Bozeman Trail, the shortest route to Montana's goldfields, which cut through the heart of lands reserved for the Sioux, Cheyenne, and Arapaho people. Told by 19-year-old Brave Eagle, who fought under Sioux Chief Red Cloud, this moving account is drawn from Red Cloud's speeches, published Indian statements, and the historians' information. Includes 39 color illustrations

0-8032-7032-1 NEBRASKA PB $9.95

The Death of the Iron Horse
Trains as they used to be, by a winner of the Caldecott Medal
0-02-737830-6 SIMON & SCHUSTER $14.95

The Gift of the Sacred Dog
The horse is the sacred dog, according to Indian lore that dates back to the conquistadors
0-02-736560-3 SIMON & SCHUSTER $15.00
0-02-043280-1 MACMILLAN PB $4.95

The Girl Who Loved Wild Horses
Based on Indian legend, the story of a girl who so loves wild horses that she is transformed into a mare. Caldecott Medal 1979
0-02-736570-0 SIMON & SCHUSTER $14.95
0-689-71696-6 ALADDIN PB $4.95

Red Hawk's Account of Custer's Last Battle
Back in print, Goble's first book describes Custer's Last Stand from the viewpoint of a 15-year-old Oglala warrior who fought at the Little Bighorn. Contains 43 color illustrations. "Beautifully illustrated and written with verve and authenticity...the realities conveyed to young readers are the closest to the final layer of truth that one can hope for"—*NY Times*
0-8032-7033-X NEBRASKA PB $9.95

Barbara Diamond **Goldin** & Seymour **Chwast**
Just Enough Is Plenty
0-670-81852-6 VIKING $12.95

Eloise **Greenfield**
Nathaniel Talking
Coretta Scott King Award for illustration
ILLUSTRATED BY JAN SPIVEY GILCHRIST
086312002 CHILDREN'S PRESS $11.95

Night on Neighborhood Street
ILLUSTRATED BY JAN SPIVEY GILCHRIST
0-8037-0778-9 DIAL BOOKS $13.89

Michael **Hague**
A Child's Book of Prayers
Twenty familiar prayers interpreted by Michael Hague's illustrations
0-8050-0211-1 HOLT $14.95

Gail E. **Haley**
A Story, A Story
Spider stories in African folklore describe defenseless men or animals outwitting others or succeeding against great odds. Anansi the spider man is just such a hero as he proves clever enough to purchase a golden box of stories from the sky god. Caldecott Medal Book 1971
0-689-71201-4 ALADDIN PB $4.95

Donald **Hall**
Ox-Cart Man
A New England farmer gathers the family's produce for the journey to the market town. The story describes a bygone era when families produced food and clothes, and the children helped. Caldecott Medal 1980
ILLUSTRATED BY BARBARA COONEY
0-670-53328-9 VIKING $15.99
0-14-050441-9 VIKING PB $4.99

Donald Hall

Martin **Handford**
Where's Waldo?
As wandering Waldo moves from picture to picture, children search the crowded pages to find him. An original idea, and the oversized pictures are great fun
1-56402-576-4 CANDLEWICK PB $4.99

Brett **Harvey**
My Prairie Year: Based on the Diary of Elenore Plaisted
ILLUSTRATED BY DEBORAH RAY KOGAN
0-8234-1028-5 HOLIDAY HOUSE PB $5.95

Clint **Hatchett**
The Glow-in-the-Dark Night Sky Book
Brief exposure to the light makes the color pictures glow, so that children can take the book outdoors when sky gazing
ILLUSTRATED BY STEPHEN MARCHESI
0-394-89113-9 RANDOM HOUSE $14.00

Ruth **Heller**
Chickens Aren't the Only Ones
Bold and attractive illustrations introduce children to the egg-laying creatures, not forgetting such oddities as the duckbilled platypus
0-8045-6651-8 SPOKEN ARTS $20.90

How to Hide a Crocodile
A picture book that describes the way animals are camouflaged in the wild
0-8045-6568-6 SPOKEN ARTS $16.90

Kevin **Henkes**
Sheila Rae, the Brave
0-688-07155-4 GREENWILLOW $15.00

Patricia **Hermes**
Kevin Corbett Eats Flies
A boy's attempt to set straight a family situation leads to a bizarrely humorous "habit"
ILLUSTRATED BY CAROL NEWSOM
9-9928-6748-5
HARCOURT BRACE LIBRARY EDITION $5.00
0-671-69183-X POCKET PB $2.99

Amy **Hest**
The Purple Coat
Grandpa understands a little girl's desire for a different-colored winter coat, in a story set in New York City in the 1940s. The illustrations are fascinating
ILLUSTRATED BY AMY SCHWARTZ
0-02-743640-3 SIMON & SCHUSTER $14.95
0-689-71634-6 ALADDIN PB $4.95

Dubose **Heyward**
Country Bunny and the Little Gold Shoes
A delightful story about love and endurance. A little country bunny delivering Easter eggs for the Easter Bunny sprains her ankle. Despite the pain, she climbs to the top of a huge mountain to deliver an egg to the small child that lives there. As a reward, she is given a pair of golden shoes which transport her back to her own children in time for Easter morning
0-395-15990-3 HOUGHTON MIFFLIN $14.95

Robert L. **Hillerich**, editor
The American Heritage Picture Dictionary
Big pictures introduce 900 words selected from the vocabulary of preschoolers and kindergarten children
ILLUSTRATED BY MAGGIE SWANSON
0-395-69585-6 HOUGHTON MIFFLIN $11.95

Lillian **Hoban**
Arthur's Christmas Cookies
With cassette
0-06-444055-9 TROPHY PB $3.75

Arthur's Honey Bear
If growing up means selling a favorite toy, Arthur would rather not do so. An easy reader
1-55994-219-3 HARPER AUDIO PB $7.95
0-06-444033-8 TROPHY PB $3.75

Russell **Hoban**
A Baby Sister for Frances
ILLUSTRATED BY LILLIAN HOBAN
0-06-022335-9 HARPERCOLLINS $15.00

Best Friends for Frances
Russell Hoban and Lillian Hoban had a long and distinguished collaboration as the authors and illustrators of numerous picture books, of which the Frances series is the most popular. The Hobans have sensitive ears and eyes for stories that make young children laugh but also provoke questions
ILLUSTRATED BY LILLIAN HOBAN
0-06-022327-8 HARPERCOLLINS $15.00
0-06-443008-1 TROPHY PB $4.95

A Birthday for Frances
Extraordinary things happen to Frances, a cuddly badger, but Mama and Papa are always there to help
ILLUSTRATED BY LILLIAN HOBAN
0-06-443007-3 TROPHY PB $4.95

Bread and Jam for Frances
ILLUSTRATED BY LILIAN HOBAN
0-06-022359-6 HARPERCOLLINS $15.00

Riddley Walker
0-330-26645-4 TRANS-ATLANTIC PB $16.95

Bryan **Hodgson**

The World of Baby Animals

Extraordinary full-color photographs from some of the world's finest nature photographers document the care and feeding of the newborn, the rearing of young babies, and their ceaseless play throughout the natural world: young elephants being spoiled, kangaroos in their mother's pouches, a giraffe learning to stand in the moments after its birth, a young brown bear cub being taught how to catch his dinner, and more

0-88363-795-2 LEVIN $25.00

Syd **Hoff**

Danny and the Dinosaur

Cartoonish early reading books from the 1960s. Both are funny

0-06-022465-7 HARPERCOLLINS $14.95
0-06-444002-8 TROPHY PB $3.75

Sammy the Seal

0-06-444028-1 TROPHY PB $3.75

Mary **Hoffman**

Amazing Grace

ILLUSTRATED BY CAROLINE BINCH

0-8037-1040-2 DIAL BOOKS $14.99

Nonny **Hogrogian**

One Fine Day

A variation on the familiar folk stories in which one action must lead to another so the narrative comes to the proper conclusion. The fun for children is remembering the sequence as the fox loses his tail to an irate old lady and gets it back again. Caldecott Medal 1972

0-02-744000-1 SIMON & SCHUSTER $14.95
0-02-043620-3 ALADDIN PB $4.95

Lee Bennett **Hopkins**

Side by Side: Poems to Read Together

0-671-73622-1 ALADDIN PB $9.95

Thacher **Hurd**

The Pea Patch Jig

0-06-443383-8 TROPHY PB $4.95

Pat **Hutchins**

Don't Forget the Bacon

0-688-08743-4 MULBERRY PB $4.95

The Doorbell Rang

0-688-13101-8 MULBERRY PB $18.95

Rosie's Walk

Rosie the hen is in big trouble from a fox who's trailing right behind her, but she never looks up to notice. Meanwhile the fox meets with a series of comical misadventures every time he tries to close in. An amusing wordless story

0-02-043750-1 ALADDIN PB $4.95

Warwick **Hutton**

Adam and Eve

Three retold stories, illustrated with Hutton's luminous watercolor paintings

0-689-50433-0 MCELDERRY $14.95

Moses in the Bulrushes

0-689-50393-8 MCELDERRY $14.95

William **Joyce**

George Shrinks

0-06-023070-3 HARPERCOLLINS $15.00
0-06-443129-0 TROPHY PB $4.95

Mavis **Jukes**

Blackberries in the Dark

A boy visits his widowed grandmother soon after the death of a beloved grandpa. A picture book with an ambitious text

ILLUSTRATED BY THOMAS B. ALLEN

0-679-86570-5 BULLSEYE PB $3.99

Like Jake and Me

ILLUSTRATED BY LLOYD BLOOM

0-394-89263-1 KNOPF PB $7.99

Maira **Kalman**

Chicken Soup, Boots

A book about jobs designed to introduce young children to different occupations

0-670-85201-5 VIKING $15.00

Max in Hollywood, Baby

"The ongoing saga of Max the dog—in words, in pictures, in typography—has vaulted across genres, between audiences and beyond expectations. It's the graphic novel of the '90s, and it's truly for all ages" —*Booklist*

0-670-84479-9 VIKING $15.00

Max Makes a Million

0-670-83545-5 VIKING $17.00

Ooh LA LA (Max in Love)

0-670-84163-3 VIKING $16.99

Swami on Rye: Max in India

0-670-85646-0 VIKING $16.00

Mollie **Katzen** & Ann **Henderson**

Pretend Soup and Other Real Recipes: A Cookbook for Preschoolers & Up

From the ever-imaginative Ten Speed Press, this delightful book by the famed *Moosewood Cookbook* author brings the world of real cooking to real children. Extensively tested, these easy-to-follow recipes provide perfect structured play for children (with an adult helper), and, illustrated with whimsical watercolors, invite children to bring their natural delight to the kitchen, as well as illustrating the real rewards of patience, counting, reading, and science. A lovely idea

1-88367-206-6 TRICYCLE $16.95

Mollie Katzen (photo by Terry McCarthy)

Ezra Jack **Keats**

Apt. 3

0-689-71059-3 ALADDIN PB $4.95

Dreams

Roberto looks out his window one night only to find Archie's cat trapped by a huge dog! What happens next and who saves Archie's cat is incredible

0-689-71599-4 ALADDIN PB $5.99

God Is in the Mountain

0-8050-3168-5 HOLT $15.95

Goggles!

Caldecott Honor Book 1970

0-689-71157-3 MACMILLAN PB $4.95

Jennie's Hat

0-06-443072-3 TROPHY PB $5.95

John Henry: An American Legend

0-394-89052-3 KNOPF PB $5.99

Kitten for a Day

0-689-71737-7 ALADDIN PB $4.95

A Letter to Amy

0-06-443063-4 TROPHY PB $5.95

The Little Drummer Boy

0-689-71158-1 ALADDIN PB $4.95

Louie's Search

0-689-71354-1 ALADDIN PB $4.95

Maggie and the Pirate

0-590-44852-8 SCHOLASTIC PB $5.95

Pet Show

0-689-71159-X ALADDIN PB $4.95

Peter's Chair/Mini Book and Doll

0-694-00685-8 HARPERCOLLINS $14.95

Regards to the Man in the Moon

0-689-71160-3 ALADDIN PB $3.95

Snowy Day

0-590-73323-0 SCHOLASTIC PB $19.95
0-14-050182-7 VIKING PB $4.99

The Trip

"Keats…has surpassed even his award winners here…The effect is tenderness and uncommon beauty" —*Publishers Weekly*

0-688-07328-X MORROW PB $4.95

Whistle for Willie

Willie wants to whistle so badly but he has to wait to learn. A nice description of the affection between a father and his son

0-14-050202-5 VIKING PB $4.99

Steven **Kellogg**

Best Friends

Louise Jenkins is Katie's best friend—and also a traitor. The theme of best friend turned worst enemy is nicely explored in an amusing book

0-8037-0099-7 DUTTON $15.99

Chicken Little

The old story given a modern twist

RETOLD AND ILLUSTRATED BY STEVEN KELLOGG

0-688-07045-0 MORROW PB $4.95

The Island of the Skog

On National Rodent Day a tribe of hard-pressed mice decides to set off in search of an uninhabited island. Kellogg's sweet, woolly-headed heroes take possession of their island after a last, scary adventure

0-8037-3842-0 DIAL BOOKS $15.99
0-14-054649-9 DIAL BOOKS PB $5.99

Much Bigger than Martin

0-14-054666-9 DIAL BOOKS PB $5.99

The Mysterious Tadpole

A boy's pet tadpole keeps on growing, precipitating a series of ever more outrageous situations

ILLUSTRATED BY STEVEN KELLOGG

0-14-054870-X DIAL BOOKS PB $5.99

Pecos Bell: A Tall Tale

0-688-05871-X MORROW $16.00

Pinkerton, Behave!

Pinkerton is an affectionate and awkward Great Dane puppy who will not learn how to behave. The resulting mayhem is the subject of funny illustrations

0-8037-6573-8 DIAL BOOKS $16.99
0-14-054687-1 DIAL BOOKS PB $5.99

Prehistoric Pinkerton

0-8037-0322-8 DUTTON $14.99

A Rose for Pinkerton

Rose the kitten joins the household and wins the pet show after Pinkerton disrupts one of the show's snootier exhibits

0-8037-7502-4 DIAL BOOKS $14.99
0-8037-0060-1 DUTTON PB $4.99

X.J. **Kennedy** & Dorothy **Kennedy**

Talking Like the Rain: A Read-to-Me Book of Poems

ILLUSTRATED BY JANE DYER

0-316-48889-5 LITTLE, BROWN $19.95

Rudyard **Kipling**

The Cat that Walked by Himself

ILLUSTRATED BY WILLIAM STOBBS

0-85953-309-3 CHILDS PLAY PB $6.99

Rudyard Kipling

The Elephant's Child

ILLUSTRATED BY JOHN ROWE

1-558-58369-6 NORTH-SOUTH $14.95

How the Camel Got His Hump

ILLUSTRATED BY QUENTIN BLAKE

0-88708-097-9 PICTURE BOOK STUDIO $19.95

How the Rhinoceros Got His Skin

ILLUSTRATED BY JENNY THORNE

0-88708-083-9 PICTURE BOOK STUDIO $19.95
0-88708-078-2 SIMON & SCHUSTER $14.95

William **Kurelek**

A Prairie Boy's Winter

A picture book version of the life that Laura Ingalls Wilder, author of *Little House on the Prairie,* might have led had she been a boy and been part of a family that had fewer worries about "getting by." The illustrations are charming

ILLUSTRATED BY WILLIAM KURELEK

0-395-17708-1 HOUGHTON MIFFLIN $14.95
0-395-36609-7 HOUGHTON MIFFLIN PB $6.95

Karla **Kuskin**

The Philharmonic Gets Dressed

A charming and ingenious introduction to ordinary people who make music

ILLUSTRATED BY MARC SIMONT

0-06-023622-1 HARPERCOLLINS $14.95
0-06-443124-X TROPHY PB $4.95

Patricia **Lauber**

Great Whales: The Gentle Giants

ILLUSTRATED BY PIETER FOLKENS

0-8050-2894-3 HOLT PB $4.95

Ursula K. **Le Guin**

Catwings

ILLUSTRATED BY S.D. SCHINDLER

0-590-42833-0 SCHOLASTIC PB $2.99

Catwings Return

ILLUSTRATED BY S.D. SCHINDLER

0-590-42832-2 SCHOLASTIC PB $2.99

Munro **Leaf**

The Story of Ferdinand

Ah, Ferdinand the bull, who only wants to sniff the flowers! Children will be happy that Ferdinand sits down during the bullfight and lives out his life in peace

ILLUSTRATED BY ROBERT LAWSON

0-14-050234-3 VIKING PB $4.99

Edward **Lear**

A Book of Nonsense

0-679-41798-2 KNOPF $12.95

The Owl and the Pussy-Cat & Other Nonsense

0-575-04709-7 TRAFALGAR SQUARE $15.95

Theo **LeSieg**

I Wish that I Had Duck Feet

A boy's comic fantasies in a 1950s classic. With cassette

ILLUSTRATED BY ROY MCKIE

0-394-80040-0 RANDOM HOUSE $7.99

Julius **Lester**

How Many Spots Does a Leopard Have?: And Other Tales

ILLUSTRATED BY DAVID SHANNON

0-590-41972-2 SCHOLASTIC PB $5.95

Elizabeth **Levy**

Something Queer at the Haunted School

Elizabeth Levy has written over 50 books for children. Among them are the award-winning *Keep Ms. Sugarman in the Fourth Grade* and the *Something Queer* series

0-440-48461-8 DELL PB $3.50

Something Queer at the Library

0-440-48120-1 DELL PB $3.50

Something Queer at the Scary Movie

ILLUSTRATED BY MORDICAI GERSTEIN

0-7868-1056-4 HYPERION PB $4.95

Something Queer in Outer Space

ILLUSTRATED BY MORDICAI GERSTEIN

1-56282-279-9 DISNEY PB $4.95

Something Queer in the Cafeteria

ILLUSTRATED BY MORDICAI GERSTEIN

0-7868-1000-9 HYPERION PB $4.95

Something Queer Is Going On

0-440-47974-6 YEARLING PB $3.50

Astrid **Lindgren**

The Children of Noisy Village

The Swedish farm children in this fictional village are all fast friends. The creator of Pippi Longstocking writes of their goings-on

0-14-032609-X VIKING PB $5.99

Leo **Lionni**

Alexander and the Wind-Up Mouse

Alexander is a clockwork mouse who wants to be free. His friend is a real mouse who has his own dreams

0-394-82911-5 KNOPF PB $5.99

Swimmy

0-394-81713-3 KNOPF $16.00
0-394-82620-5 KNOPF PB $5.99

Myra Cohen **Livingston**, editor

I Like You, If You Like Me: Poems of Friendship

0-689-50408-X MCELDERRY $14.95

Arnold **Lobel**

The Book of Pigericks

Limericks are easily remembered (and composed) by anyone who is 8 or 9, and Lobel's are amusing

0-06-443163-0 TROPHY PB $5.95

Days with Frog and Toad

With cassette

1-55994-227-4 HARPER AUDIO $7.95
0-06-444058-3 TROPHY PB $3.75

Arnold **Lobel**

Fables

Children will love the bear who dresses up in saucepan headgear and the camel with ballet shoes. Caldecott Medal 1980

0-06-023974-3 HARPERCREST LIBRARY EDITION $14.89
0-06-443046-4 TROPHY PB $5.95

Frog and Toad All Year

With cassette

1-55994-228-2 CAROUSEL $7.95
0-06-444059-1 TROPHY PB $3.75

Frog and Toad Are Friends

The first book in a tender (and funny) series of stories about an abiding friendship. Short chapters can be read as separate stories to help beginning readers along. Caldecott Honor Book 1971

0-590-04529-6 TROPHY PB $3.75

Frog and Toad Together

With cassette

0-06-023959-X HARPERCOLLINS $14.95
0-06-444021-4 TROPHY PB $3.75

Ming Lo Moves the Mountain

0-688-10995-0 MULBERRY PB $4.95

Mouse Soup

0-06-444041-9 TROPHY PB $3.75

On Market Street

This award-winning collaboration introduces the shopkeepers of Market Street, whose elaborate costumes are made up of their wares. Caldecott Honor Book 1982

ILLUSTRATED BY ANITA LOBEL

0-688-80309-1 GREENWILLOW $16.00
0-688-08745-0 MULBERRY PB $4.95

Owl at Home

0-06-444034-6 TROPHY PB $3.75

Small Pig

0-06-444120-2 TROPHY PB $3.75

Uncle Elephant

0-06-444104-0 TROPHY PB $3.75

Whiskers and Rhymes

0-688-08291-2 MORROW PB $4.95

Alice **Low**, editor

The Family Read-Aloud Christmas Treasury

ILLUSTRATIONS BY MARC BROWN

0-316-53284-3 LITTLE, BROWN PB $12.95

Golden **MacDonald**

The Little Island

ILLUSTRATED BY LEONARD WEISGARD

0-440-40830-X YEARLING PB $5.99

Hana **MacHotka**

Breathtaking Noses

0-688-09527-5 MORROW $14.93

Pasta Factory

0-395-60197-5 HOUGHTON MIFFLIN $14.95

Edward **Marshall**

Fox All Week

ILLUSTRATED BY JAMES MARSHALL

0-14-036187-1 DIAL BOOKS PB $4.99

Fox and His Friends

ILLUSTRATED BY JAMES MARSHALL

0-14-037007-2 PUFFIN PB $3.50

James **Marshall**

The Cut-Ups

0-14-050637-3 VIKING PB $4.99

The Cut-Ups Crack Up

0-14-055318-5 PUFFIN PB $4.99

Fox Be Nimble

0-14-036842-6 PUFFIN PB $3.50

Fox on Stage

0-14-038032-9 PUFFIN PB $3.50

Fox on the Job

0-14-037602-X PUFFIN PB $3.50

Fox Outfoxed

0-8037-1036-4 DIAL BOOKS $11.99

George and Martha

George is a bit plodding, Martha is sharp-tongued and decisive. They experience the usual fallings-out and makings-up common to close friends. They are hippopotami. Marshall's brief and witty text is easy for beginning readers.

0-395-16619-5 HOUGHTON MIFFLIN $14.95
0-395-45739-4 HOUGHTON MIFFLIN PB $7.95

George and Martha Back in Town

0-395-47946-0 HOUGHTON MIFFLIN PB $5.95

George and Martha Round and Round

0-395-58410-8 HOUGHTON MIFFLIN PB $5.95

George and Martha Tons of Fun

0-395-42646-4 HOUGHTON MIFFLIN PB $5.95

Goldilocks and the Three Bears

0-8037-0542-5 DIAL BOOKS $14.99

Hansel and Gretel

0-14-050836-8 PUFFIN PB $4.99

Old Mother Hubbard and Her Wonderful Dog

0-374-45611-9 SUNBURST PB $4.95

Pocketful of Nonsense

0-307-17552-9 ARTIW $12.95

Rats on the Range and Other Stories

0-8037-1385-1 DIAL BOOKS $12.89

Rats on the Roof and Other Stories

With charming illustrations by the author, this chapter book is filled with stories of silly sheep and other Marshallian animals designed to entertain both parent and child. Ages 6 to 10

0-8037-0834-3 DIAL BOOKS $13.00
0-8037-0835-1 DIAL BOOKS LIBRARY EDITION $12.89

Speedboat

0-395-68977-5 HOUGHTON MIFFLIN PB $5.95

The Three Little Pigs

0-8037-0591-3 DUTTON $14.99
0-14-055742-3 PUFFIN PB $4.99

Three Up a Tree

0-14-037003-X PUFFIN PB $3.50

Yummers!

The heroine is Emilie the Pig, whose gustatory adventures are unusual

0-395-14757-3 HOUGHTON MIFFLIN $14.95

Yummers Too: The Second Course

0-395-53967-6 HOUGHTON MIFFLIN PB $5.95

Sharon Bell **Mathis**

The Hundred Penny Box

0-14-032169-1 VIKING PB $4.99

Marianna **Mayer**

Turandot

ILLUSTRATED BY WINSLOW PELMS

0-688-09073-7 MORROW $16.00

The Twelve Dancing Princesses

ILLUSTRATED BY K.Y. CRAFT

0-688-14392-X MULBERRY PB $4.95

Mercer **Mayer**

What Do You Do With a Kangaroo?

0-590-44850-1 SCHOLASTIC PB $3.95

Robert **McCloskey**

Blueberries for Sal

A Caldecott Honor Book for 1949

0-14-050169-X VIKING PB $4.99

Make Way for Ducklings

McCloskey comes up with the perfect solution to the problem of bringing up a brood of ducklings in the center of Boston. Caldecott Medal 1942

0-14-050171-1 VIKING PB $4.99

One Morning in Maine

0-14-050174-6 VIKING PB $4.99

Gerald **McDermott**

Anansi the Spider: A Tale from the Ashanti

A West African folktale retold in simple words and pictured in big geometric illustrations

0-8050-0310-X HOLT $15.95
0-8050-0311-8 HOLT PB $5.95

Arrow to the Sun: A Pueblo Indian Tale

0-14-050211-4 VIKING PB $5.99

Raven: A Trickster Tale from the Pacific Northwest

0-15-265661-8 HARCOURT BRACE $14.95

Patricia C. **McKissack**

A Million Fish...More or Less

ILLUSTRATED BY DENA SCHUTZER

0-679-88086-0 DRAGONFLY PB $6.99

Patricia C. **McKissack** & Rachel **Isadora**

Flossie and the Fox

0-8037-0250-7 DUTTON $14.99

Patricia **McKissack** & Jerry **Pinkney**

Mirandy and Brother Wind

0-394-88765-4 KNOPF $17.00

Bruce **McMillan**

Eating Fractions

0-590-43770-4 SCHOLASTIC $15.95

Gian-Carlo **Menotti**

Amahl and the Night Visitors

A retelling of the libretto of Menotti's Christmas opera

ILLUSTRATED BY MICHELE LEMIEUX

0-688-05426-9 MORROW $19.95

Eve **Merriam**

Holloween ABC

ILLUSTRATED BY LANE SMITH

0-02-766870-3 SIMON & SCHUSTER $14.95

Norman **Messenger**

Making Faces

The perfect gift for children of all ages, a mix and match book that can create 65,000 different faces, from the hilarious to the surreal. Great fun

1-56458-111-X DORLING KINDERSLEY $14.95

Mercer **Meyer**

Frog Goes to Dinner

0-14-054633-2 DIAL BOOKS PB $3.99

There's a Nightmare in My Closet

And it's not going to stay there, either. Boy and monster make friends, but the ending suggests that other things may be in store

0-8037-8682-4 DIAL BOOKS $15.99

0-14-054712-6 DUTTON PB $5.99

There's an Alligator Under My Bed

Meyer's sequel features a realistic alligator who just happens to live you know where

0-8037-0374-0 DUTTON $14.99

A.A. **Milne**

Now We Are Six

See also **FICTION** under **BOOKS FOR EIGHTS, NINES, AND UP**

ILLUSTRATED BY ERNEST H. SHEPARD

0-525-44446-7 DUTTON $10.99

0-14-036124-3 PUFFIN PB $3.99

When We Were Very Young

See also **FICTION** under **BOOKS FOR EIGHTS, NINES, AND UP**

ILLUSTRATED BY ERNEST H. SHEPARD

0-525-44445-9 DUTTON $10.99

0-525-44961-2 DUTTON $20.00

0-14-036123-5 PUFFIN PB $3.99

Winnie-the-Pooh

Milne's quintessentially British fantasy either tends to inspire devotion or leave readers wondering what the fuss is all about. Distinguished by puns and other wordplay, the comedy is invariably deft and amusing. But readers (or listeners) who are not wholehearted members of the Pooh fan club may simply grow tired of all those words. Children who like Pooh in moderation will enjoy the more straight-forward sections, such as the first chapter of *The House at Pooh Corner*, in which Tigger makes his appearance

See also **FICTION** under **BOOKS FOR EIGHTS, NINES, AND UP**

ILLUSTRATED BY ERNEST H. SHEPARD

0-525-44443-2 DUTTON $10.99

0-14-036121-9 PUFFIN PB $3.99

Else Holmelund **Minarik**

Father Bear Comes Home

ILLUSTRATED BY MAURICE SENDAK

0-06-024230-2 HARPERCOLLINS $14.95

0-06-444014-1 TROPHY PB $3.75

A Kiss for Little Bear

0-06-444050-8 TROPHY PB

Little Bear

The consoling illustrations and quiet text make this a classic among easy-to-read books and a splendid read-aloud picture book for children up to five. Mother Bear is large, tolerant, and powerful, Baby Bear has big dreams

ILLUSTRATED BY MAURICE SENDAK

0-06-024240-X HARPERCOLLINS $14.95

0-06-444004-4 TROPHY PB $3.75

Little Bear's Friend

0-06-444051-6 TROPHY PB $3.75

Little Bear's Visit

With cassette

ILLUSTRATED BY MAURICE SENDAK

9-992-92973-1 WESTON WOOD $23.00

0-06-444023-0 TROPHY PB $3.75

No Fighting, No Bitting!

Another Minarik title, this time without Little Bear

ILLUSTRATED BY MAURICE SENDAK

0-06-444015-X TROPHY PB $3.75

Clement **Moore**

The Night Before Christmas

The beloved story of Old Saint Nick with busy and colorful illustrations

ILLUSTRATED BY TOMIE DE PAOLA

0-8234-0414-5 HOLIDAY HOUSE $15.95

0-8234-0417-X HOLIDAY HOUSE PB $6.95

The Night Before Christmas

A humorous illustrated edition

ILLUSTRATED BY JAMES MARSHALL

0-590-45977-5 SCHOLASTIC PB $4.95

Ann **Morris**

Bread, Bread, Bread

PHOTOGRAPHY BY KEN HEYMAN

0-688-12275-2 MULBERRY PB $4.95

Hats, Hats, Hats

PHOTOGRAPHY BY KEN HEYMAN

0-688-12274-4 MULBERRY PB $4.95

Loving

PHOTOGRAPHY BY KEN HEYMAN

0-688-13613-3 MULBERRY PB $4.95

Arlene **Mosel**

Tikki Tikki Tembo

0-8050-1166-8 HOLT PB $5.95

Munro **Leaf**

Wee Gillis

Unfortunately, this classic is currently out of print

0-670-75608-3 VIKING $12.95

Roxie **Munro**

The Inside-Outside Book of New York City

Bold and detailed pictures show the exteriors and interiors of celebrated buildings

0-14-050454-0 PUFFIN PB $4.99

The Inside-Outside Book of Washington D.C.

0-525-44298-7 DUTTON $13.95

Robert **Munsch**

Boy in the Drawer

0-920236-36-7 FIREFLY PB $4.95

Moira's Birthday

0-920303-83-8 ANNIC PB $4.95

Purple, Green and Yellow

ILLUSTRATED BY HELENE DESPUTEAUX

1-55037-256-4 ANNIC PB $5.95

Jill **Murphy**

Five Minutes' Peace

Mother Elephant's children won't leave her alone, even when she decides to take a bath. It takes longer than five minutes to get them to understand why Mother needs time off

1-85430-355-4 MAGI $16.95

Margaret W. **Musgrove**

Ashanti to Zulu: African Traditions

An alphabet book with a difference. The 26 distinct African tribal customs beautifully pictured in full color span the entire continent. Winner of the Caldecott Medal 1977

ILLUSTRATED BY DIANE & LEO DILLON

0-8037-0357-0 DIAL BOOKS $17.99

0-14-054604-9 DIAL BOOKS PB $4.99

Rolf **Myller**

How Big Is a Foot?

0-440-40495-9 YOUYE PB $3.50

Trinka Hakes **Noble**

The Day Jimmy's Boa Ate the Wash

Jimmie's class goes off on a bus trip to a farm, and the boa goes too. The adventures become wilder and funnier as the tall tale progresses

ILLUSTRATED BY STEVEN KELLOGG

0-8037-1723-7 DIAL BOOKS $15.99

0-14-054623-5 DUTTON PB $4.99

Laura **Numeroff**

If You Give a Mouse a Cookie

0-06-024587-5 HARPERCREST $13.89

Iona **Opie** & Peter **Opie**

I Saw Esau: The Schoolchild's Pocket Book

ILLUSTRATED BY MAURICE SENDAK

1-56402-046-0 CANDLEWICK $19.95

Iona **Opie** & Peter **Opie**, editors

The Oxford Book of Children's Verse

0-19-282349-3 OXFORD PB $14.95

Mary Pope **Osborne**

American Tall Tales

0-679-80089-1 KNOPF $20.00

Peggy **Parish**

Amelia Bedelia

Amelia Bedelia is the amicable, muddleheaded housekeeper who interprets orders literally by dusting the parlor with talcum and changing the towels by cutting them up. Of course she is saved by her pie-making and general affability. The series will appeal to readers who are past beginner books

ILLUSTRATED BY FRITZ SIEBEL

0-06-020186-X HARPERCOLLINS $14.95

Amelia Bedelia and the Surprise Shower
With cassette
ILLUSTRATED BY FRITZ SIEBEL
1-55994-216-9 HARPER AUDIO $7.95
0-06-444019-2 TROPHY PB $3.75

Amelia Bedelia Goes Camping
0-688-04057-8 MORROW $16.00
0-380-70067-0 AVON PB $3.99

Amelia Bedelia Helps Out
ILLUSTRATED BY LYNN SWEAT
0-688-80231-1 MORROW $15.00
0-380-53405-3 AVON PB $3.99

Nancy Winslow **Parker** &
Joan Richards **Wright**

Bugs
In an original approach, this introduction to insects combines facts with humorous rhymes and bright pictures
ILLUSTRATED BY NANCY WINSLOW PARKER
0-688-06624-0 MORROW LIBRARY EDITION $15.93
0-688-08296-3 MORROW PB $4.95

Francine **Patterson**

Koko's Kitten
Koko the gorilla lives with the animal behaviorist who taught her sign language, and she is able to communicate with humans. A few years ago Koko was given a stray kitten as a pet, and this unusual picture book is a photographed record of her odd but affectionate attachment to it
PHOTOGRAPHS BY RONALD H. COHN
0-590-40952-2 SCHOLASTIC $14.95
0-590-44425-5 SCHOLASTIC PB $4.95

Patricia **Pearse**

See How You Grow
Children open sections of the illustrations to answer questions about where babies come from and how they themselves are developing
ILLUSTRATED BY EDWINA RIDDELL
0-8120-5936-0 BARRONS $14.95

Bill **Peet**

Buford the Little Bighorn
0-395-34067-5 HOUGHTON MIFFLIN PB $5.95

Ella
0-395-27269-6 HOUGHTON MIFFLIN PB $5.95

The Whingdingdilly
0-395-31381-3 HOUGHTON MIFFLIN PB $5.95

The Wump World
0-395-31129-2 HOUGHTON MIFFLIN PB $5.95

Ian **Penney**

Ian Penney's Book of Fairy Tales
From the widely praised author of *Ian Penney's Book of Nursery Rhymes,* which *Publishers Weekly* called "an aesthetic marvel," this is an enchanting collection of fairy tales accompanied by delightful illustrations. "Rapunzel," "Hansel and Gretel," "Sleeping Beauty," and other favorites and, as an added attraction, a hidden acorn in each large picture, for children to look for while they listen
0-8109-3740-9 ABRAMS $14.95

Ian Penney's Book of Nursery Rhymes
0-8109-3733-6 ABRAMS $14.95

Charles **Perrault**

Cinderella
A retelling fashioned from relatively few words. This Cinderella will hold the attention of the fours as well as the fives. Caldecott Medal 1955
RETOLD AND ILLUSTRATED BY MARCIA BROWN
0-684-12676-1 ATHENEUM $14.00
0-689-71261-8 ALADDIN PB $4.95

Cinderella
A subtle retelling in an oversized version
RETOLD BY AMY EHRLICH
ILLUSTRATED BY SUSAN JEFFERS
0-87191-945-1 CREATIVE EDUCATION $13.95
0-8037-0205-1 DUTTON $16.99

Puss in Boots
This newest rendition of Perrault's classic will no doubt capture many awards for its boldness of design, refreshing perspective on visualization, and sheer wit
ILLUSTRATED BY FRED MARCELLINO
0-374-36160-6 FS&G $16.00
0-89919-192-4 HOUGHTON MIFFLIN PB $6.95

Puss in Boots
ILLUSTRATED BY YAN THOMAS
1-85697-624-6 KINGFISHER $9.95

The Sleeping Beauty
EDITED AND ILLUSTRATED BY WARREN CHAPPELL
0-8317-1719-X SMITHMARK $7.98

Andrea Davis **Pinkney**

Alvin Ailey
ILLUSTRATED BY BRIAN PINKNEY
0-7868-1077-7 HYPERION PB $4.95

D. Marcus **Pinkwater**

The Hoboken Chicken Emergency
A farcical romp initiated by the bringing home of a 266-pound, six-foot-two Thanksgiving chicken
0-671-66447-6 ALADDIN PB $4.95

Daniel **Pinkwater**

Aunt Lulu
0-689-71413-0 ALADDIN PB $3.95

I Was a Second Grade Werewolf
0-14-055718-0 UNICORN PB $4.99

Daniel Manus **Pinkwater**

Guys from Space
0-689-71590-0 ALADDIN PB $3.95

Watty **Piper**

The Little Engine that Could
I think I can, I think I can. The youngest members of the picture-book audience will like the simplified pictures and catchy text
ILLUSTRATED BY RICHARD WALZ
0-448-40520-2 GROSSETT & DUNLAP $5.95
0-448-18963-1 PRICE, STERN, & SLOAN $9.95

Patricia **Polacco**

Chicken Sunday
0-399-22133-6 PHILOMEL $15.95

Just Plain Fancy
0-440-40937-3 YEARLING PB $4.99

Mrs. Katz and Tush
0-440-40936-5 YEARLING PB $5.99

Rechenka's Eggs
ILLUSTRATED BY PATRICIA POLACCO
0-698-11385-3 PPRST PB $5.95

Leo **Politi**

Song of the Swallows
0-689-71140-9 ALADDIN PB $4.95

Three Stalks of Corn
0-689-71782-2 ALADDIN PB $4.95

Charlotte **Pomerantz**

The Chalk Doll
ILLUSTRATED BY FRANE LESSAC
0-06-443333-1 TROPHY PB $4.95

The Tamarindo Puppy: And Other Poems
ILLUSTRATED BY BYRON BARTON
0-688-11514-4 MULBERRY PB $4.95

Joyce **Pope**

Do Animals Dream?: Children's Questions About Animals Most Often Asked of the Natural History Museum
A fascinating question-and-answer book containing unusual information
99914-1-407-X VIKING $17.99

Beatrix **Potter**

The Complete Adventures of Peter Rabbit
Beatrix Potter was always at great pains to render accurately the animals she so loved and was a fierce critic of her own work. When describing and illustrating her stories she preferred to use places and people (human and animal) she knew. Hence a convincingly rabbitty Peter is chased through an authentic garden by the angry Mr. MacGregor, and we know he is going to put Peter in a pie if he catches him. Four of Potter's tales in one volume, with her original illustrations
0-7232-2951-1 VIKING $13.00
0-14-050444-3 VIKING PB $6.99

The Complete Tales of Beatrix Potter
Peter Rabbit, Mrs. Tiggywinkle, Benjamin Bunny—the characters of Beatrix Potter have delighted generations of children, and are now available complete in one handsome volume. Illustrated with the author's esteemed watercolor paintings
0-7232-3618-6 WARNER $35.00

The Peter Rabbit Pop-Up Book
0-7232-2950-3 WARNER $12.95

The Tailor of Gloucester
0-7232-3462-0 WARNER $5.95
0-7232-3487-6 WARNER PB $2.25

The Tale of Benjamin Bunny
0-7232-3463-9 WARNER $5.95
0-486-28538-3 DOVER PB $1.00

Beatrix Potter

The Tale of Jemima Puddle-Duck
0-7232-3468-X WARNER $5.95
0-7232-3493-0 WARNER PB $2.25

The Tale of Johnny Townmouse
0-7232-3472-8 VIKING $5.95
0-7232-3497-3 WARNER PB $2.25

The Tale of Little Pig Robinson
0-7232-3478-7 WARNER $5.95
0-7232-3503-1 WARNER PB $2.25

The Tale of Mr. Jeremy Fisher
0-7232-3466-3 WARNER $5.95
0-7232-3491-4 WARNER PB $2.25

The Tale of Mrs. Tiggy-Winkle
0-7232-3465-5 WARNER $5.95
0-7232-3490-6 WARNER PB $2.25

The Tale of Peter Rabbit
0-7232-3460-4 WARNER $5.95
0-590-41101-2 SCHOLASTIC PB $2.50

The Tale of Pigling Bland
0-7232-3474-4 WARNER $5.95
0-7232-3499-X WARNER PB $2.25

The Tale of Squirrel Nutkin
0-7232-3461-2 WARNER $5.95
0-486-29033-6 DOVER PB $1.00

The Tale of Tom Kitten
0-7232-3467-1 WARNER $5.95
0-7232-3492-2 WARNER PB $2.25

The Tale of Two Bad Mice
0-517-07241-6 DERRYDALE $3.99
0-7232-3464-7 WARNER $5.95

The Tale of Ginger and Pickles
0-7232-3477-9 WARNER $5.95

Jack **Prelutsky**

The Dragons Are Singing Tonight
ILLUSTRATED BY PETER SIS
0-688-09645-X GREENWILLOW $16.00

The New Kid on the Block
ILLUSTRATED BY JAMES STEVENSON
0-688-02271-5 GREENWILLOW $17.95

Tyrannosaurus Was a Beast
ILLUSTRATED BY ARNOLD LOBEL
0-688-06442-6 GREENWILLOW $15.00

Jack **Prelutsky** & Arnold **Lobel**

The Terrible Tiger
0-689-71300-2 ALADDIN PB $3.95

Alice **Provensen** & Martin **Provensen**

The Glorious Flight Across the Channel with Louis Bleriot
Winner of the Caldecott Medal 1984
0-670-34259-9 VIKING $16.99
0-14-050729-9 VIKING PB $5.99

Arthur **Ransome**, editor

The Fool of the World and the Flying Ship: A Russian Tale
The Fool of the World sets off to marry the Czar's daughter and gathers up a crew of foolish people who turn out to possess odd and irreplaceable talents. Caldecott Medal Book 1968
ILLUSTRATED BY URI SHULEVITZ
0-374-32442-5 FS&G $16.00
0-374-42438-1 FS&G PB $6.95

Ellen **Raskin**

Spectacles
Before and after the dreaded visit to the eye doctor. A book characterized by inspired nonsense
0-689-71271-5 ALADDIN PB $4.95

Mary **Rayner**

Garth Pig and the Ice Cream Lady
Plump little pig hero Garth Pig doesn't know that the genial ice cream seller is really a hungry wolf
0-689-30598-2 ATHENEUM $14.95

Mr. and Mrs. Pig's Evening Out
0-689-30530-3 ATHENEUM $14.95

Mrs. Pig Gets Cross and Other Stories
0-525-44705-9 DUTTON PB $5.95

Mrs. Pig's Bulk Buy
Mrs. Pig is so fed up with the piglets' eating fads that she devises a whole new menu based on their favorite food
0-689-30831-0 ATHENEUM $14.95

Faith **Ringgold**

Tar Beach
0-517-58030-6 CROWN $18.00

Faith **Ringgold** & Erin **McCormack**, editor

Dinner at Aunt Connie's House
0-7868-1150-1 DISNEY PB $4.95

Fred **Rogers**

Going to the Hospital
PHOTOGRAPHS BY JIM JUDKIS
0-399-21530-1 PUTNAM PB $6.95

The New Baby
PHOTOGRAPHS BY JIM JUDKIS
0-399-21238-8 PUTNAM PB $6.95

Cynthia **Rylant**

Night in the Country
Nighttime sights and sounds by the Caldecott prize-winning author
ILLUSTRATED BY MARY SZILAGYI
0-02-777210-1 SIMON & SCHUSTER $14.95

The Relatives Came
An ebullient crowd of relatives from West Virginia comes for a visit and reawakens a family's affection. Caldecott Honor Book 1986
ILLUSTRATED BY STEPHEN GAMMELL
0-02-777220-9 SIMON & SCHUSTER $14.95

When I Was Young in the Mountains
0-14-054875-0 DUTTON PB $4.99

Florence **Sakade**

Japanese Children's Favorite Stories
0-8048-0284-X TUTTLE $16.95

Robert **San Souci**

The Talking Eggs
0-8037-0619-7 DUTTON $15.99

Flip **Schulke** & Penelope Ortner **McPhee**

King Remembered
The story of Martin Luther King's life; with photos
0-393-02256-0 NORTON $22.95
0-671-62018-5 POCKET PB $12.00

Amy **Schwartz**

Bea and Mr. Jones
Bea dislikes school and Mr. Jones is frustrated by his job as an advertising executive. Parent and child swap places—with very surprising results
0-689-71796-2 ALADDIN PB $3.95

David M. **Schwartz**

How Much Is a Million?
This unconventional counting book takes readers off on adventures asking them to imagine huge numbers rather than enumerate them
ILLUSTRATED BY STEPHEN KELLOGG
0-688-04049-7 MORROW $17.00
0-688-09933-5 MULBERRY PB $4.95

If You Made a Million
ILLUSTRATED BY STEVEN KELLOGG
0-688-13634-6 MULBERRY PB $4.95

Jon **Scieszka**

Stinky Cheese Man
0-14-054896-3 DUTTON PB $10.00

The True Story of the 3 Little Pigs
ILLUSTRATED BY LANE SMITH
0-14-054451-8 PUFFIN PB $4.99

Jon **Scieszka**

The Frog Prince—Continued

In this original spin on the familiar fairy tale, Scieszka has taken the frog prince story past "and they lived happily ever after." The Princess nags the frog prince while he mopes about the castle until he finally decides to find a witch to turn him back into a frog—which turns out not to be so easy. Steve Johnson's witty and detailed illustrations make this book a happy marriage of story and art. Ages 5 and up

0-670-83421-1 VIKING $14.95

Okay, so they weren't so happy.
In fact, they were miserable.
"Stop sticking your tongue out like that," nagged the Princess.
"How come you never want to go down to the pond anymore?" whined the Prince.
The Prince and the Princess were so unhappy.
They didn't know what to do.
THE FROG PRINCE—CONTINUED

Maurice **Sendak**

In the Night Kitchen

Maurice Sendak won the 1970 Hans Christian Andersen award for his substantial and lasting contributions to children's literature. He has said that he has always had more trouble with the text of his children's books than the pictures, describing how his stories come to him "in bits and pieces of memories that don't seem related for a very long time, but something in me determines they will be closely related: they are going to work together come hell and high water." Sendak pushes dream logic to its limit in a hauntingly beautiful book that confronts and transcends some basic anxieties of early childhood

0-06-026668-6 HARPERCOLLINS $15.95
0-06-443436-2 TROPHY PB $5.95

Kenny's Window

0-06-443209-2 TROPHY PB $4.95

Outside Over There

Sendak calls this the last book in the trilogy begun by *Where the Wild Things Are* and *In the Night Kitchen.* But this stunning story with its illustrations of fat children and grumpy little girls may puzzle some young readers

0-06-025523-4 HARPERCOLLINS $20.00

We Are All in the Dumps with Jack and Guy

These two illustrated nursery rhymes tell the story of how Jack and Guy made their way out of the dumps to rescue a little kid and bring him home. Classic Sendak, only new

0-06-205014-1 HARPERCOLLINS $20.00
0-06-205015-X HARPERCREST LIBRARY EDITION $19.89

Where the Wild Things Are

Familiarity has tamed the Wild Things somewhat, but young readers are still likely to be startled by the curiously menacing monsters created out of a hodgepodge of mythical and real beasts

See also **FICTION** under **BOOKS FOR EIGHTS, NINES, AND UP**

0-06-025492-0 HARPERCOLLINS $15.00
0-06-443178-9 TROPHY PB $4.95

Dr. **Seuss**

And to Think that I Saw It on Mulberry Street

Dr. Seuss's first children's book, published in 1937

0-394-84494-7 RANDOM HOUSE $14.00

The 500 Hats of Bartholomew Cubbins

Bartholomew almost loses his head when the King insists he take off his hat to royalty

0-394-94484-4
RANDOM LIBRARY LIBRARY EDITION $15.99

The Cat in the Hat

The master of meaningful nonsense, Dr. Seuss has led millions of American children by the hand and into the world of I Can Read By Myself.
With cassette

0-394-80001-X RANDOM HOUSE $7.99

Dr. Seuss (Theodor Geisel) (credit: ©Czeslaw)

The Cat in the Hat Comes Back

With cassette

0-394-80002-8 RANDOM HOUSE $7.99

Dr. Seuss's Sleep Book

0-394-90091-X RANDOM LIBRARY $15.99

Fox in Socks

With cassette

0-394-88322-5 RANDOM HOUSE PB $8.95

Fox in Socks

0-394-80038-9 RANDOM HOUSE $7.99

Green Eggs and Ham

With cassette

0-394-80016-8 RANDOM HOUSE $7.99
0-394-89220-8 RANDOM HOUSE PB $8.95

Hop on Pop

With cassette

0-394-80029-X RANDOM HOUSE $7.99
0-394-89222-4 RANDOM HOUSE PB $8.95

Horton Hatches the Egg

0-394-80077-X RANDOM HOUSE $14.00

Horton Hears a Who

"A person's a person, no matter how small," and sometimes he or she needs help. Seuss's rhyming story describes a courageous Horton caring for his "person," even though the situation gets him into all kinds of trouble

0-394-80078-8 RANDOM HOUSE $14.00

How the Grinch Stole Christmas

A Christmas classic for over 30 years

0-394-07845-4 AMERICAN SCHOOL $18.66

If I Ran the Circus

0-394-80080-X RANDOM HOUSE $14.00

If I Ran the Zoo

Bored with ordinary lions and tigers, the new zookeeper searches out a Gusset, a Gherkin, a Gasket, and a Gootch along with some other exotic breeds

0-394-80081-8 RANDOM HOUSE $14.00

The Lorax

0-394-82337-0 RANDOM HOUSE $14.00

Oh, the Places You'll Go

0-679-84736-7 RANDOM HOUSE $20.00

Oh, Say Can You Say?

With cassette

0-394-84255-3 RANDOM HOUSE $7.99

Oh, the Thinks You Can Think

With cassette

0-394-83129-2 RANDOM HOUSE $7.99

One Fish Two Fish Red Fish Blue Fish

0-394-80013-3 RANDOM HOUSE $7.99

Scrambled Eggs Super!

Salamagoox eggs mixed with Tittle Topped Goose eggs—not quite fine enough, as we would expect from Seuss's nonsense verse

0-394-80085-0 RANDOM HOUSE $14.00

Six by Seuss

0-679-87921-8 RANDOM HOUSE $8.00

Thidwick the Big-Hearted Moose

0-394-80086-9 RANDOM HOUSE $14.00

Yertle the Turtle & Other Stories

An imperious king insists on climbing on the shoulders of his subjects. The precarious pyramid rests on the back of one small turtle who finally realizes there's no reason to be the fellow at the bottom of the heap

0-394-80087-7 RANDOM HOUSE $14.00

Marcia **Sewall**

The Pilgrims of Plymouth

A young (fictional) Pilgrim's first-person account of the eventful Mayflower voyage and the settlers' first Thanksgiving

0-689-31250-4 ATHENEUM $15.95

Marjorie W. **Sharmat**

Gila Monsters Meet You at the Airport

The real and imaginary adventures of a boy who is moving to another part of the country

ILLUSTRATED BY BYRON WON

0-02-782450-0 SIMON & SCHUSTER $14.95
0-689-71383-5 ALADDIN PB $4.95

Mitchell Is Moving

Mitchell the dinosaur's irresistible desire to move house annoys his resourceful friend Martha, who works out the situation to satisfy them both. First- or second-graders can read this story for themselves

ILLUSTRATED BY JOSE ARUEGO & ARIANE DEWEY

0-02-045260-8 MICROSOFT PB $3.95

Nate the Great and the Sticky Case
ILLUSTRATED BY MARC SIMONT
0-440-46289-4 DELL PB $3.99

Mitchell **Sharmat**
Gregory, the Terrible Eater
Mom and Dad enjoy the usual goat staples such as tin cans; by their standards Gregory has peculiar eating habits
ILLUSTRATED BY JOSE ARUEGO & ARIANE DEWEY
0-02-782250-8 SIMON & SCHUSTER $15.00
0-590-43350-4 SCHOLASTIC PB $4.99

Paul **Showers**
How Many Teeth?
0-06-445098-8 HARPERCOLLINS PB $4.95

What Happens to a Hamburger
0-06-445013-9 TROPHY PB $4.95

Your Skin and Mine
ILLUSTRATED BY KATHLENN KUCHENA
0-06-445102-X HARPERCOLLINS PB $4.95

Uri **Shulevitz**
Rain Rain Rivers
A deceptively simple picture book depicts rain in town, rain in the country, rain everywhere
0-374-46195-3 FS&G PB $3.95

Diane **Siebert**
Heartland
ILLUSTRATIONS BY WENDELL MINOR
0-690-04730-4 CROWELL $16.00

Shel **Silverstein**
Falling Up: Poems and Drawings
See also **FICTION** under **BOOKS FOR EIGHTS, NINES, AND UP**
0-06-024802-5 HARPERCOLLINS $16.95

The Giving Tree
Classic story by one of the best children's storytellers of this century. Shel Silverstein tells the story of lifelong love and the power of friendship in this tale about a boy and a tree
See also **FICTION** under **BOOKS FOR EIGHTS, NINES, AND UP**
0-06-025665-6 HARPERCOLLINS $14.95

A Light in the Attic
See also **FICTION** under **BOOKS FOR EIGHTS, NINES, AND UP**
0-06-025673-7 HARPERCOLLINS $16.95

Where the Sidewalk Ends: Poems and Drawings
Possibly the most popular book of verse published in the last 20 years; the cautionary verse is exceptionally good
See also **FICTION** under **BOOKS FOR EIGHTS, NINES, AND UP**
0-06-025667-2 HARPERCOLLINS $16.95

Seymour **Simon**
Our Solar System
0-688-09992-0 MORROW $20.00

Volcanoes
0-688-14029-7 MULBERRY PB $5.95

David **Small**
Imogene's Antlers
0-517-56242-1 CROWN PB $5.99

Clare **Smallman** & Edwina **Riddell**
Outside In
A companion picture book to the out-of-print *See How You Grow*. This time children lift the flaps to glimpse under the skin and learn the whereabouts of bones, muscles, and organs
0-8120-5760-0 BARRONS $14.95

Donald J. **Sobol**
Encyclopedia Brown and the Case of the Mysterious Handprints
Ten solve-it-yourself mysteries from a long-lived series started in the 1960s
ILLUSTRATED BY GAIL OWEN
0-688-04626-6 MORROW $16.00
0-553-15739-6 BDD PB $3.99

Peter **Spier**
Noah's Ark
A translation of a 17th-century Dutch poem precedes pages of wordless, and glorious, illustrations
0-385-09473-6 DOUBLEDAY $15.95
0-440-40693-5 YEARLING PB $6.99

William **Steig**
Brave Irene
A plucky little girl braves a blizzard to deliver the duchess's ball gown in one of Steig's most successful books for children
0-374-30947-7 FS&G $17.00
0-374-40927-7 FS&G PB $4.95

Caleb and Kate
0-374-41038-0 FS&G PB $4.95

Doctor De Soto
Steig invests his enchanting frogs, mice, and rabbits with a gravity that makes his humor as convincing as his talent for fantasy. One takes great pleasure in the way a Steig picture book looks and sounds
0-374-31803-4 FS&G $16.00
0-374-41810-1 SUNBURST PB $4.95

Gorky Rises
Gorky the frog experiments with a potion that includes a hefty dash of his father's cologne and all of a sudden he's able to fly. As so often happens in Steig's books, one discovers that magic can have logic of its own
0-374-42784-4 SUNBURST PB $4.95

Solomon the Rusty Nail
Solomon finds he can turn himself into a rusty nail, but the real consequences are unforeseen. This rabbit's adventures make for an inspired nonsense-fantasy
0-374-37131-8 FS&G $16.00
0-374-46903-2 FS&G PB $5.95

Spinky Sulks
Convinced that his family doesn't love him, Spinky develops a massive case of the sulks
0-374-38321-9 FS&G $15.00

Sylvester and the Magic Pebble
Sylvester is a young donkey who finds an attractive red pebble and the apparent ability to transform himself at will. Caldecott Medal 1970
0-671-66154-X SIMON & SCHUSTER $14.00
0-671-66269-4 ALADDIN PB $5.95

John **Steptoe**
Mufaro's Beautiful Daughters: An African Tale
Based on a traditional African tale. Caldecott Honor Book 1988
0-688-04045-4 LOTHROP, LEE, & SHEPHERD $16.00

The Story of the Jumping Mouse
An Indian legend retold to create the character of an unselfish mouse who gives his all and is rewarded by eternal life in a far-off land
0-688-01902-1 LOTHROP, LEE, & SHEPHERD $16.00

Janet **Stevens**
The Tortoise and the Hare
A sassy hare and a lovable tortoise are the heroes of Stevens's funny illustrations
0-8234-0510-9 HOLIDAY HOUSE $15.95

James **Stevenson**
Could Be Worse
A nice old grandpa is challenged by his grandchildren and comes up with a whopping tale about the things he had to do when he was young
0-688-07035-3 MORROW PB $3.95

What's Under My Bed
Grandpa is awakened and exorcises all the things that are smelly or shaking like jelly
0-688-02325-8 MORROW $16.00
0-688-09350-7 MULBERRY PB $3.95

Robert Louis **Stevenson**
A Child's Garden of Verses
0-679-41799-0 KNOPF $12.95

Catherine **Stock**
Sophie's Bucket
0-15-277162-X VOYAGEUR PB $4.95

Where Are You Going Manyoni?
0-688-10352-9 MORROW $15.00

Rosemary **Sutcliff**
The Minstrel and the Dragon Pup
ILLUSTRATED BY EMMA CHICHESTER CLARK
1-56402-603-5 CANDLEWICK PB $6.99

Nancy **Tafuri**
All Year Long
Children count the days and watch the months and seasons change along with them. This is one counting book children won't tire of easily
0-688-01416-X MORROW LIBRARY EDITION $13.95

Early Morning in the Barn
A wordless book, aside from the characteristic sounds of the farm animals, with bold and splendid illustrations. Tafuri's books have just the right balance of clarity and tenderness
0-688-02328-2 GREENWILLOW $17.00
0-688-11710-4 MULBERRY PB $3.95

Have You Seen My Duckling?
See also **BOOKS FOR CHILDREN UNDER FIVE**
0-688-02797-0 GREENWILLOW $15.95

Ernest L. **Thayer**
Casey at the Bat
ILLUSTRATED BY BARRY MOSER
0-8446-5613-5 SMITH $18.75

James **Thurber**

Many Moons

A spoiled princess demands the moon and the kingdom is turned upside down as the king's wise men try to get it for her. Then a good-hearted young lad comes along and invents an acceptable solution. Caldecott Medal 1944

See also **FICTION** under **BOOKS FOR EIGHTS, NINES, AND UP**

0-15-251873-8 HARCOURT BRACE $15.00
0-15-656980-9 HARCOURT BRACE PB $6.00

Alvin R. **Tresselt**

Mitten: An Old Ukrainian Folktale

0-688-09238-1 MULBERRY PB $4.95

White Snow, Bright Snow

ILLUSTRATED BY ROGER DUVOISIN

0-688-41161-4 MORROW $16.00

Autumn Harvest

0-688-51155-4 MORROW $16.93

Jack **Tworkov**

Camel Who Took a Walk

0-525-27393-X DUTTON $13.95

Tomi **Ungerer**

The Beast of Monsieur Racine

Monsieur Racine finds a strange animal digging up his tidy garden and loses his heart to a beast that looks like an old mop with a nose

0-374-30640-0 FS&G $15.95
0-374-40570-0 FS&G PB $5.95

Chris **Van Allsburg**

The Garden of Abdul Gasazi

A bad-mannered dog breaks into an enchanter's garden and leads a little boy into an adventure. Caldecott Honor Book 1980
Book & Cassette

0-395-71254-8 HOUGHTON MIFFLIN $24.95

Jumanji

Two children play a jungle board game that they must finish despite the consequences. There are some scary moments before the children are out of danger. Caldecott Medal 1982

0-395-30448-2 HOUGHTON MIFFLIN $17.95
0-590-54551-5 SCHOLASTIC PB $4.95

The Polar Express

This picture book about a Christmas-time train ride to the North Pole is also a fable about children's belief in inexplicable worlds. Caldecott Medal 1986

0-395-38949-6 HOUGHTON MIFFLIN $17.95

Two Bad Ants

0-395-48668-8 HOUGHTON MIFFLIN $17.95

The Widow's Broom

What happens when a witch's broom loses its power of flight? Van Allsburg (*The Polar Express*) has created another spellbinding tale, illustrated in his inimitable style. "One of Van Allsburg's best: an intriguing, well-told tale with elegantly structured art, resonant with significance and lightened with sly humor" —*Kirkus Reviews*

0-395-64051-2 HOUGHTON MIFFLIN $17.95

Nancy **Van Laan**

Possum Come A-Knockin'

A funny and flavorful picture book by the wonderful *New Yorker* cartoonist. "A raucous romp"—*The Horn Book Guide*

ILLUSTRATED BY GEORGE BOOTH

0-394-82206-4
RANDOM LIBRARY LIBRARY EDITION $12.95

Jean **Van Leeuwen**

Amanda Pig and Her Big Brother Oliver

Van Leeuwen's series of easy-to-read books about Amanda Pig and her family

0-14-037008-0 PUFFIN PB $3.50

Amanda Pig on Her Own

When big brother Oliver leaves for school, Amanda tries to play by herself. But the games she always played with Oliver are no fun without him. Amanda thinks she will never have fun again

ILLUSTRATED BY ANN SCHWENINGER

0-8037-0893-9 DIAL BOOKS $9.95
0-14-037144-3 PUFFIN PB $3.50

Amanda Pig, School Girl

ILLUSTRATED BY ANN SCHWENINGER

0-8037-1981-7 DIAL BOOKS $25.00

More Tales of Amanda Pig

Amanda Pig is growing up. She's big enough to care for Sallie Rabbit and her other stuffed animals. She's big enough to help Oliver make a bubble bath. But she's not to big to share a big hug in the big chair with Mother

ILLUSTRATED BY ANN SCHWENINGER

0-14-037603-8 PUFFIN PB $3.50

More Tales of Oliver Pig

ILLUSTRATED BY ARNOLD LOBEL

0-14-036554-0 PUFFIN PB $3.50

Oliver, Amanda, and Grandmother Pig

0-14-036207-X DIAL BOOKS PB $4.99

Oliver Pig at School

ILLUSTRATED BY ANN SCHWENINGER

0-8037-0813-0 DIAL BOOKS $10.95
0-14-037145-1 PUFFIN PB $3.50

Tales of Amanda Pig

ILLUSTRATED BY ANN SCHWENINGER

0-14-036840-X PUFFIN PB $3.50

Tales of Oliver Pig

ILLUSTRATED BY ARNOLD LOBEL

0-14-036549-4 PUFFIN PB $3.50

Gabrielle **Vincent**

Ernest and Celestine

Ernest is a fatherly-looking bear, Celestine is a childlike mouse. They inhabit an old-fashioned house in France in amicable fashion and have numerous adventures

0-688-06525-2 MORROW PB $3.95

Judith **Viorst**

Alexander and the Terrible, Horrible, No Good, Very Bad Day

Alexander has one of those days. Viorst makes us laugh but doesn't spoil the story by pasting on a sunny ending

ILLUSTRATED BY RAY CRUZ

0-689-30072-7 ATHENEUM $14.00
0-689-71173-5 ALADDIN PB $4.99

Alexander, Who Used to Be Rich Last Sunday

Another monologue from Alexander, whose dollar disappears in a series of misadventures

ILLUSTRATED BY RAY CRUZ

0-689-71199-9 ALADDIN PB $3.95

Earrings

ILLUSTRATED BY NOLA LANGNER MALONE

0-689-71669-9 ALADDIN PB $4.95

The Good-Bye Book

A little boy tries everything within his power to stop his parents from leaving. The author knows what bothers children and what doesn't, and is blessed with an observant sense of humor

ILLUSTRATED BY KAY CHORAO

0-689-31308-X ATHENEUM $16.00

The Tenth Good Thing About Barney

Barney is the family cat, and when he dies the children are angry and sad. An unsentimental picture book about necessary losses and grief

ILLUSTRATED BY ERIK BLEGVAD

0-689-20688-7 ATHENEUM $13.95
0-689-71203-0 ALADDIN PB $3.95

Julie **Vivas**

The Nativity

Vivas gives the Nativity story a contemporary setting and a light-hearted interpretation

0-15-200535-8 HARCOURT BRACE $13.95

Bernard **Waber**

The House on East 88th Street

A family moves into a New York City brownstone—and finds Lyle the crocodile in the bathtub. The mysterious Lyle is very fond of caviar and was once the star of a sideshow

0-395-19970-0 HOUGHTON MIFFLIN PB $5.95

Ira Sleeps Over

0-395-20503-4 HOUGHTON MIFFLIN PB $4.95

Lovable Lyle
Lyle has to prove he's lovable when someone in the neighborhood tries to scare him away
0-395-19858-5 HOUGHTON MIFFLIN $15.95

Lyle, Lyle Crocodile
0-395-66502-7 HOUGHTON MIFFLIN PB $8.95

Rosemary **Wells**

Benjamin and Tulip
Tulip is the little girl who does whatever she pleases and gets other people into trouble. Benjamin finally realizes what he is up against and acts accordingly. Delightfully observant and humorous
0-8037-2057-2 DIAL BOOKS $12.00

Hazel's Amazing Mother
Mother is someone to be relied on, and she arrives on the scene at just the right moment
0-8037-0209-4 DIAL BOOKS $14.99

Max's Bath
Max is a sassy baby rabbit whose sister is his bugaboo. The illustrations are amusing, but the relatively advanced vocabulary may put the dialogue beyond the comprehension of many youngsters
0-8037-0162-4 DUTTON $4.50

Max's Birthday
0-8037-0163-2 DUTTON $4.50

Max's Breakfast
0-8037-0161-6 DUTTON $4.50

Timothy Goes to School
One of the very best books about a child's desire to fit in. Sympathetic and humorous
0-14-054715-0 DUTTON PB $4.99

Ruth **Westheimer**

Cat
1-56458-241-8 DORLING KINDERSLEY PB $6.95

Dinosaur
1-56458-247-7 DORLING KINDERSLEY PB $6.95

Dog
1-56458-242-6 DORLING KINDERSLEY PB $6.95

David **Wiesner**

Free Fall
0-688-10990-X MULBERRY PB $4.95

June 29, 1999
0-395-72767-7 CLARION PB $5.95

Laura Ingalls **Wilder**

Christmas in the Big Woods (My First Little House Books)
ILLUSTRATED BY RENEE GRAEF
0-06-024752-5 HARPERCOLLINS $11.95

Dance at Grandpa's (My First Little House Books)
ILLUSTRATED BY RENEE GRAEF
0-06-443372-2 TROPHY PB $4.95

Going to Town (My First Little House Books)
ILLUSTRATED BY RENEE GRAEF
0-06-023012-6 HARPERCOLLINS $11.95
0-06-443452-4 TROPHY PB $4.95

Happy Birthday, Laura! (My First Little House Books)
ILLUSTRATED BY RENEE GRAEF
0-694-00730-7 HARPERCOLLINS $5.95

Summertime in the Big Woods (My First Little House Books)
ILLUSTRATED BY RENEE GRAEF
0-06-025934-5 HARPERCOLLINS $11.95

Winter Days in the Big Woods (My First Little House Books)
ILLUSTRATED BY GARTH WILLIAMS
0-06-443373-0 HARPERCOLLINS PB $4.95

Nancy **Willard**

Pish, Posh, Said Hieronymus Bosch
A playful fantasy about the wildly unusual household of 15th-century Flemish painter Hieronymus Bosch, as imagined by the author of *A Visit to William Blake's Inn* and visualized by the award-winning illustrators of *Aida*
ILLUSTRATED BY THE DILLONS
0-15-262210-1 HARCOURT BRACE $18.95

Sailing to Cythera
The first book of the Anatole Series
ILLUSTRATED BY DAVID MCPHAIL
0-15-269961-9 HARCOURT BRACE PB $5.95

Uncle Terrible: More Adventures of Anatole
"Her images are invigorating, her fantasy convincing, and she can write on numerous levels simultaneously"—*NY Times*
ILLUSTRATED BY DAVID MCPHAIL
0-15-292794-8 HARCOURT BRACE PB $5.95

Barbara **Williams**

Albert's Toothache
ILLUSTRATED BY KAY CHORAO
0-14-054733-9 DUTTON PB $4.99

Karen Lynn **Williams**

Galimoto
ILLUSTRATED BY CATHERINE STOCK
0-688-10991-8 MULBERRY PB $4.95

Vera B. **Williams**

Stringbean's Trip to the Shining Sea
ILLUSTRATED BY JENNIFER WILLIAMS
0-590-44851-X SCHOLASTIC PB $4.95

A Chair for My Mother
After their home is destroyed, a grandmother, mother, and daughter start over with courage and affection. Caldecott Honor Book 1983
0-688-00914-X GREENWILLOW $16.00
0-688-04074-8 GREENWILLOW PB $4.95

Cherries and Cherry Pits
0-688-10478-9 MULBERRY PB $4.95

Music, Music for Everyone
0-688-07811-7 MORROW PB $3.95

Something Special for Me
0-688-06526-0 MORROW PB $4.95

Three Days on a River in a Red Canoe
0-688-04072-1 GREENWILLOW PB $5.95

Diane **Wolkstein**

The Banza: A Haitian Story
0-14-054605-7 DUTTON PB $4.99

The Magic Orange Tree and Other Haitian Folktales
0-8052-1077-6 SCHOCKEN PB $10.00

Diane **Wolkstein** & Robert Andrew **Parker**

The Magic Wings: A Tale from China
0-14-054769-X DUTTON PB $4.99

Audrey **Wood**

Heckedy Peg
ILLUSTRATED BY DON WOOD
0-15-233679-6 HARCOURT BRACE PB $6.00

King Bidgood's in the Bathtub
The court must persuade stubborn King Bidgood to leave his much-too-comfortable and luxurious bathtub. Caldecott Honor Book 1987
ILLUSTRATED BY DON WOOD
0-15-242730-9 HARCOURT BRACE $15.00

The Napping House
ILLUSTRATED BY DON WOOD
0-15-256708-9 HARCOURT BRACE $15.00

Weird Parents
A loopy book about loopy parents who continually embarrass their child: wearing odd clothes, laughing too loudly in the movies, doing a chicken walk in front of a crowd … the kind of things that drive every child nuts. Children ages 4 to 8—and their parents—will relate to the story and to the author's wild and colorful illustrations
0-8037-0648-0 DIAL BOOKS $14.99

Valerie **Worth**

All the Small Poems
0-374-40344-9 SUNBURST PB $4.95

Taro **Yashima**

Crow Boy
0-14-050172-X VIKING PB $4.99

Umbrella
A little Japanese girl growing up in New York City waits for rain to come so she can try out her new umbrella. An appealingly gentle story
0-14-050240-8 PUFFIN PB $4.99

Jane **Yolen**

Commander Toad and the Big Black Hole
0-698-20594-4 PUTNAM PB $6.95

Arthur **Yorinks**

Hey, Al
Al the janitor and his dog are offered a new life in paradise, but the gift is not all that it seems. Caldecott Medal 1987
ILLUSTRATED BY RICHARD EGIELSKI
0-374-33060-3 FS&G $16.00
0-374-42985-5 SUNBURST PB $4.95

Louis the Fish
0-374-34658-5 FS&G $13.95

Ed **Young**

Cat and Rat: The Legend of the Chinese Zodiac

0-8050-2977-X HOLT $15.95

Ed **Young**, translator

Lon Po Po: A Red Riding Hood Story from China

0-399-21619-7 PHILOMEL $15.95

Charlotte **Yue** & David **Yue**

The Igloo

0-395-62986-1 SANDPIPER PB $4.95

Harriet **Ziefert**

A New Coat for Anna

A little girl's mother gets her a new coat. It's an act of courage and determination for a poor family living in Europe after World War II

ILLUSTRATED BY ANITA LOBEL

0-394-89861-3 KNOPF PB $5.99

Gene **Zion**

Harry and the Lady Next Door

Harry the sometimes grubby dog in an easy-to-read adventure

ILLUSTRATED BY MARGARET B. GRAHAM

0-06-444008-7 TROPHY PB $3.75

Harry the Dirty Dog

0-06-443009-X TROPHY PB $4.95

Charlotte **Zolotow**

Mr. Rabbit and the Lovely Present

ILLUSTRATED BY MAURICE SENDAK

0-06-026945-6 HARPERCOLLINS $14.95
0-06-443020-0 TROPHY PB $4.95

My Grandson Lew

0-06-026962-6 HARPERCREST $15.89

The Quarreling Book

0-06-443034-0 TROPHY PB $4.95

The Sleepy Book

A bedtime book by an author of consistently excellent work

ILLUSTRATED BY IISE PLUME

0-06-026968-5 HARPERCREST LIBRARY EDITION $14.89
0-06-443239-4 TROPHY PB $5.95

When I Have a Little Girl

I'm going to let her do all the things you won't let me do, such as...

ILLUSTRATED BY HILARY KNIGHT

0-06-443175-4 TROPHY PB $4.95

William's Doll

William wants a doll; when father objects, grandmother comes to the rescue

ILLUSTRATED BY WILLIAM PENE DU BOIS

0-06-027047-0 HARPERCOLLINS $14.95
0-06-443067-7 TROPHY PB $4.95

Read Alouds

Brian **Alderson**

The Arabian Nights: Or, Tales Told by Sheherezade During a Thousand Nights and One Night

ILLUSTRATED BY MICHAEL FOREMAN

0-688-14219-2 MORROW $20.00

Richard **Atwater** & Florence **Atwater**

Mr. Popper's Penguins

ILLUSTRATED BY ROBERT LAWSON

0-316-05842-4 LITTLE, BROWN $16.95

William J. **Bennett**, editor

The Book of Virtues for Young People: A Treasury of Great Moral Stories

0-382-24923-2 SILVER, BURDETT $16.95

Sheila **Burnford**

The Incredible Journey

Separated from their owners, two dogs and a cat trek through 250 miles of dangerous Canadian wilderness to get back home

0-553-15616-0 BDD PB $4.50

Ann **Cameron**

The Stories Julian Tells

Julian thinks he knows everything, and his smaller sidekick brother, Huey, believes everything Julian says. And Julian says some very odd things

ILLUSTRATED BY ANN STRUGNELL

0-394-82892-5 RANDOM HOUSE PB $3.99

Eleanor **Cameron**

Stowaway to the Mushroom Planet

0-316-12541-5 LITTLE, BROWN PB $6.95

The Wonderful Flight to the Mushroom Planet

ILLUSTRATED BY ROBERT HENNEBERGER

0-316-12537-7 LITTLE, BROWN $15.95

John **Ciardi**

The Hopeful Trout and Other Limericks

ILLUSTRATED BY SUSAN MEDDAUGH

0-395-61616-6 HOUGHTON MIFFLIN PB $5.95

Beverly **Cleary**

Beezus and Ramona

ILLUSTRATED BY LOUIS DARLING

0-380-70918-X CAMELOT PB $3.99

Ellen Tebbits

Ellen has to wait until a new little girl moves into town to acquire her very special friend. A quiet, humorous book set in a '50s small town.

ILLUSTRATED BY LOUIS DARLING

0-688-21264-6 MORROW $16.00
0-380-70913-9 CAMELOT PB $4.50

Ramona and Her Mother

0-380-70952-X AVON PB $4.50

Harold **Courlander** & George **Herzog**

Cow-Tail Switch and Other West African Stories

0-8050-0298-7 HOLT PB $8.95

Ingri **D'Aulaire** & Edgar P. **D'Aulaire**

D'Aulaire's Norse Gods & Giants

0-385-23692-1 DELACORTE PB $17.95

D'Aulaire's Book of Greek Myths

These classic retellings of Greek and Norse myths are wonderful read-aloud stories for young children and are candidates for an older child's permanent collection.

ILLUSTRATED BY INGRI D'AULAIRE EDGAR P. D'AULAIRE

0-385-01583-6 DOUBLEDAY $24.95
0-440-40694-3 BANTAM PB $16.95

William Pene **Du Bois**

The Twenty-One Balloons

A balloonist lands abruptly on an uninhabited Pacific island and is welcomed by a colony of formally dressed people living in an advanced civilization. An unlikely, imaginative, and funny parable about what it is like to live on the edge of disaster. Winner of a Newbery Medal 1947

0-670-73441-1 VIKING $15.99
0-14-032097-0 VIKING PB $3.99

T.S. **Eliot**

Old Possum's Book of Practical Cats

Illustrated

0-15-168656-4 HARCOURT BRACE $13.00
0-15-668568-X HARCOURT BRACE PB $6.00

Ruth Stiles **Gannett**

The Dragons of Blueland

ILLUSTRATED BY RUTH CHRISMAN GANNETT

0-394-89050-7 KNOPF PB $4.99

My Father's Dragon

A little boy tells a story about an island visited by his father, who discovers a dragon endowed with human traits. Newbery Honor Book 1949

0-394-89048-5 KNOPF PB $4.99

Virginia **Hamilton**

In the Beginning: Creation Stories from Around the World

ILLUSTRATED BY BARRY MOSER

0-15-238740-4 HARCOURT BRACE $22.95

The People Could Fly: American Black Folktales

ILLUSTRATED BY DIANE DILLON & LEO DILLON

0-679-84336-1 KNOPF PB $12.00

Rudyard **Kipling**

Just So Stories

Animal fables that retain their magic

See also **19TH-CENTURY FICTION** under **THE 19TH-CENTURY** in **LITERATURE OF THE BRITISH ISLES**

EDITED WITH AN INTRODUCTION BY PETER LEVI

0-88680-333-0 CLARK PB $3.50
0-14-043302-3 PENGUIN PB $2.95

Julius **Lester**

More Tales of Uncle Remus: Further Adventures of Brer Rabbit, His Friends, Enemies, and Others

0-8037-0419-4 DIAL BOOKS $16.99

The Tales of Uncle Remus: The Adventures of Brer Rabbit
0-8037-0271-X DUTTON $18.99

Julius **Lester** & Jerry **Pinkney**, illustrator

Further Tales of Uncle Remus: The Misadventures of Brer Rabbit, Brer Fox, Brer Wolf
0-8037-0610-3 DIAL BOOKS $17.99

Astrid **Lindgren**

Pippi Goes on Board
0-14-030959-4 VIKING PB $3.99

Pippi in the South Seas
0-14-030958-6 VIKING PB $3.99

Pippi Longstocking
Pippi is the little Swedish girl who lives all by herself with a pet monkey and a big horse. She does exactly as she pleases and has a humorous time doing it

ILLUSTRATED BY LOUIS GLANZMAN

0-14-030957-8 VIKING PB $3.99

Betty **MacDonald**

Hello Mrs. Piggle-Wiggle
0-06-440149-9 TROPHY PB $4.50

Mrs. Piggle-Wiggle
0-06-440148-0 TROPHY PB $4.50

A.A. **Milne**

Now We Are Six
See also **FICTION** under **BOOKS FOR EIGHTS, NINES, AND UP**

ILLUSTRATED BY ERNEST H. SHEPARD

0-525-44960-4 DUTTON $20.00

0-14-036124-3 PUFFIN PB $3.99

When We Were Very Young
ILLUSTRATED BY ERNEST H. SHEPARD

0-525-44961-2 DUTTON $20.00

0-14-036123-5 PUFFIN PB $3.99

Winnie-the-Pooh
ILLUSTRATED BY ERNEST H. SHEPARD

0-525-43035-0 DUTTON $9.95

0-525-44443-2 DUTTON $10.99

0-14-036121-9 PUFFIN PB $3.99

A.A. Milne

The World of Christopher Robin
ILLUSTRATED BY ERNEST H. SHEPARD

0-525-44448-3 DUTTON $19.99

E. **Nesbit**

The Enchanted Castle
0-14-036743-8 PUFFIN PB $3.99

Five Children and It
Turn-of-the-century stories concerning a tribe of children and the sand-fairy who grants their wishes. The dialogue is dated but the situations are still deliciously funny

0-14-036735-7 PUFFIN PB $3.99

The Railway Children
When their father goes away for a little while, three children and their mother leave their home in London for a small house in the country. Soon they begin to wonder where their father is and will he ever return. Adapted into a popular children's film

ILLUSTRATED BY C.E. BROCK

0-14-036671-7 PUFFIN PB $3.99

The Story of the Treasure Seekers
ILLUSTRATED BY CECIL LESLIE

0-14-036706-3 PUFFIN PB $3.99

Mary **Norton**

The Borrowers
Pod, Homily, and Arrietty live in a wonderful old house in the country. Rather, they live under the house, in a home of their own furnished with cotton reels, safety pins, and other things filched from the human inhabitants. It's cozy enough but the girl, Arrietty, is lonely and curious. Where are the other Borrowers or are they the last ones? What does Pa do when Borrowing? A compulsive read, the story of the Borrowers comes close to tragedy when Arrietty befriends a human

ILLUSTRATED BY BETH KRUSH & JOE KRUSH

0-15-209987-5 HARCOURT BRACE $13.95

0-15-200086-0 HARCOURT BRACE PB $4.95

The Borrowers Afield
ILLUSTRATED BY BETH KRUSH & JOE KRUSH

0-15-210166-7 HARCOURT BRACE $14.00

0-15-210535-2 HARCOURT BRACE PB $5.00

The Borrowers Afloat
ILLUSTRATED BY BETH KRUSH & JOE KRUSH

0-15-210345-7 HARCOURT BRACE $15.00

0-15-210534-4 HARCOURT BRACE PB $6.00

The Borrowers Aloft
ILLUSTRATED BY BETH KRUSH & JOE KRUSH

0-15-210524-7 HARCOURT BRACE $14.00

0-15-210533-6 HARCOURT BRACE PB $4.95

The Borrowers Avenged
ILLUSTRATED BY BETH KRUSH & JOE KRUSH

0-15-210530-1 HARCOURT BRACE $15.00

0-15-210532-8 HARCOURT BRACE PB $5.00

Howard **Pyle**

The Wonder Clock: Or Four and Twenty Marvelous Tales
0-486-21446-X DOVER PB $8.95

Salman **Rushdie**

Haroun and the Sea of Stories
"Salman Rushdie has in his own veins the flow of the Sea of Stories, fantastical, funny, whooping through drama and comedy, good and evil, personified in creatures delightful or frightening"—Nadine Gordimer

See also **THE MIDDLE GENERATION** under **20TH-CENTURY BRITISH AND IRISH FICTION** in **LITERATURE OF THE BRITISH ISLES**

See also **20TH-CENTURY LITERATURE OF THE INDIAN SUBCONTINENT** under **LITERATURES OF INDIA** in **LITERATURE OF EUROPE, AFRICA, AND ASIA**

0-14-015737-9 PENGUIN PB $11.95

And in the depths of the city, beyond an old zone of ruined buildings that looked like broken hearts, there lived a happy young fellow by the name of Haroun, the only child of the storyteller Rashid Khalifa, whose cheerfulness was famous throughout that unhappy metropolis, and whose never-ending stream of tall, short and winding tales had earned him not one but two nicknames. To his admirers he was Rashid the Ocean of Notions, as stuffed with cheery stories as the sea was full of glumfish; but to his jealous rivals he was the Shah of Blah.

HAROUN AND THE SEA OF STORIES

Robert Louis **Stevenson**

Kidnapped
See also **19TH-CENTURY FICTION** under **THE 19TH-CENTURY** in **LITERATURE OF THE BRITISH ISLES**

0-00-273017-0 HARPERCOLLINS PB $12.00

The Strange Case of Dr. Jekyll and Mr. Hyde
An elegant new edition of the classic statement of the dual-identity theme

See also **EARLY SCIENCE FICTION** under **SCIENCE FICTION AND FANTASY** in **POPULAR READING**

ILLUSTRATED BY BARRY MOSER

INTRODUCTION BY JOYCE CAROL OATES

0-89968-552-8 BUCCANEER $16.95

0-8032-4212-3 NEBRASKA $25.00

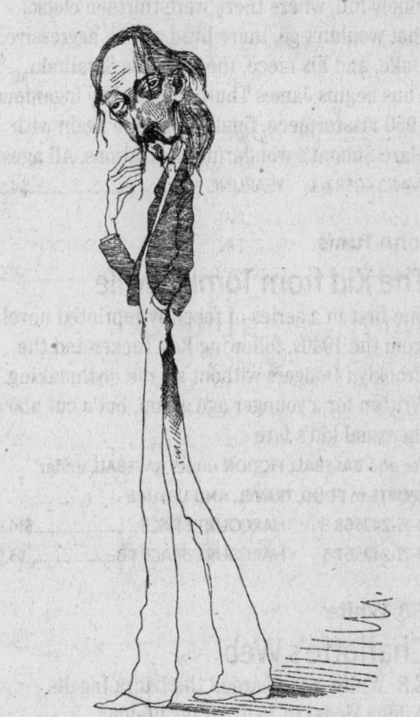

Robert Louis Stevenson

Treasure Island
The novel that revolutionized popular fiction by inventing a more realistic style of adventure story

EDITED BY EMMA LETLEY

0-19-281681-0 OXFORD PB $5.95

George **Selden**

A Cricket in Times Square

A lovely little fantasy about a cricket and a boy whose Italian family runs a Times Square newsstand. Newbery Honor Book

ILLUSTRATED BY GARTH WILLIAMS

0-374-31650-3 FS&G $16.00
0-440-41563-2 DELL PB $4.99

Isaac Bashevis **Singer**

The Power of Light: Eight Stories of Hanukkah

The late Nobel Prize-winning author presents eight autobiographically inspired tales, one for each night of Hanukkah. His simple yet powerful tales of the triumph of love are further enhanced by Irene Lieblich's full-color illustrations, culled from memories of her childhood village near Singer's own in Poland. All ages

See also **SABBATH AND HOLIDAYS** under **HOW-TO: RITUAL AND PRACTICE** under **JUDAISM** in **RELIGION, SPIRITUALITY, AND PHILOSOPHY**

See also **ISAAC BASHEVIS SINGER** under **YIDDISH LANGUAGE AND LITERATURE** in **LITERATURE OF EUROPE, AFRICA, AND ASIA**

ILLUSTRATED BY IRENE LIEBLICH

0-374-36099-5 SUNBURST $15.00
0-374-45984-3 FS&G PB $8.95

Stories for Children

See also **ISAAC BASHEVIS SINGER** under **YIDDISH LANGUAGE AND LITERATURE** in **LITERATURE OF EUROPE, AFRICA, AND ASIA**

0-374-37266-7 FS&G $22.95
0-374-46489-8 SUNBURST PB $13.00

James **Thurber**

The Thirteen Clocks

"Once upon a time, in a gloomy castle on a lonely hill, where there were thirteen clocks that wouldn't go, there lived a cold, aggressive Duke, and his niece, the Princess Saralinda…" Thus begins James Thurber's quirkily ingenious 1950 masterpiece, finally available again with Marc Simont's wonderful illustrations. All ages

0-440-40582-3 YEARLING PB $4.99

John **Tunis**

The Kid from Tomkinsville

The first in a series of recently reprinted novels from the 1940s, following Roy Tucker and the Brooklyn Dodgers without all the mythmaking. Written for a younger age group, but a cut above the usual kid's fare

See also **BASEBALL FICTION** under **BASEBALL** under **SPORTS** in **FOOD, TRAVEL, AND LEISURE**

0-15-242568-3 HARCOURT BRACE $14.95
0-15-242567-5 HARCOURT BRACE PB $3.95

E.B. **White**

Charlotte's Web

E.B. White was awarded the Laura Ingalls Wilder Medal in 1970 for his lifelong contributions to children's literature.
No pig ever had a truer friend, and no one was ever as affectionate, loyal, and skillful as Charlotte A. Cavatica, the spider

ILLUSTRATED BY GARTH WILLIAMS

0-06-026385-7 HARPERCOLLINS $13.95
0-06-440055-7 HARPERCOLLINS PB $4.50

Stuart Little

Humorous episodes in the life of a mouse who goes out into the world dressed as a man

ILLUSTRATED BY GARTH WILLIAMS

0-06-026395-4 HARPERCOLLINS $13.95
0-06-440056-5 TROPHY PB $4.50

The Trumpet of the Swan

ILLUSTRATED BY EDWARD FRASCINO

0-06-026397-0 HARPERCOLLINS $13.95
0-06-440048-4 TROPHY PB $4.50

Laura Ingalls **Wilder**

The Little House Books

Wilder's vivid re-creations of pioneer life are classics of children's literature. From the "Big Woods" to the prairie, she gives detailed accounts of her family's struggles to survive on the changing frontier, providing generations of young readers a personal vision of American life in the nineteenth century. Boxed set

See also **FICTION** under **BOOKS FOR EIGHTS, NINES, AND UP**

0-06-440040-9 TROPHY PB $35.55

Vera B. **Williams**

Scooter

0-688-09376-0 GREENWILLOW $15.00

Diane **Wolkstein**

The Magic Orange Tree and Other Haitian Folktales

0-8052-1077-6 SCHOCKEN PB $10.00

Valerie **Worth**

All the Small Poems

0-374-40344-9 SUNBURST PB $4.95

While not great children's literature, the popular Goosebump series by R.L. Stine does provide early individual reading experiences for children over eight years old. At this age, kids like to be scared—but not too much—and this series fits the bill perfectly. Kids can trade and re-read individual books until they're ready for the next series created for preteen readers.

R.L. **Stine**

Scream of the Evil Genie

0-5908-4773-2 APPLE PB $3.99

Be Careful What You Wish For

0-5909-3955-6 APPLE PB $3.99

Beware, the Snowman

0-5905-6888-4 APPLE PB $3.99

Books for Eights, Nines, and Up

Children at this age are home-centered, and family fiction is popular. Those who have put picture books behind them still half believe in magic and enjoy fantasy and fairy tales. Children usually become better readers by leaps and bounds and are more than capable of enjoying books by themselves. But they still like to be read to—and why not, when they can listen to *The Little House on the Prairie* or *Abel's Island*?

Nonfiction

Arnold **Adoff**

Black Is Brown Is Tan

0-06-020083-9 HARPERCOLLINS $15.00

Sports Pages

The experiences and dreams of young athletes expressed in verse

See also **FICTION**

0-397-32103-1 HARPERCREST LIBRARY EDITION $14.89
0-06-446098-3 TROPHY PB $6.95

Jim **Arnosky**

Crinkleroot's Guide to Walking in Wild Places

See also **FICTION**

0-689-71753-9 ALADDIN PB $5.95

Robert D. **Ballard**

Exploring the Bismarck: The Real-Life Quest to Find Hitler's Greatest Battleship

The short but deadly career of this warship is recounted, by four of its crewmen, from its launching through one of the greatest sea chases and momentous battles of World War II. Ballard then details the search for and dramatic discovery of the ship's remains with the underwater vehicle *Argo*, the same craft that discovered the Titanic. Filled with paintings, archival and new photographs, excellent diagrams and maps, the book also contains a full-color poster

0-394-22054-4 RANDOM HOUSE $14.00

Ann **Banks**

Children's Travel Journal

Part activity center, part diary, the journal provides a structured workbook in which children can record their experiences and impressions of traveling. Composed of 24 sheets of heavyweight paper and spiral-bound with a durable plastic cover, this journal will last through the rigors of any trip

0-964-11262-0 LITTLE BOOK ROOM $14.95

Byrd **Baylor**

If You Are a Hunter of Fossils

ILLUSTRATED BY PETER PARNALL

0-684-16419-1 ATHENEUM $14.95
0-689-70773-8 ALADDIN PB $4.95

Linda **Beech**

Scholastic's the Magic School Bus Meets the Rot Squad: A Book of Decomposition

ILLUSTRATED BY CAROLYN BRACKEN

0-590-40023-1 SCHOLASTIC PB $2.50

Michael J. **Benton**

The Dinosaur Encyclopedia

For knowledgeable children older than nine

ILLUSTRATED BY JIM CHANNELL

0-671-51046-0 POCKET PB $7.95

Claire G. **Berman**

So What Am I Doing in a Step-Family?

The pitfalls and advantages of step-families discussed by a respected authority. For children ten and younger

ILLUSTRATED BY DICK WILSON

0-8184-0325-X LYLE STUART $12.00

N.J. **Berrill** & Jacquelyn **Berrill**

1001 Questions Answered About the Seashore

How crabs breathe, what crabs see, how to find sand eels and grunions, what mollusk shells are made of

0-486-23366-9 DOVER PB $7.95

Franklyn M. **Branley**

Is There Life in Outer Space?

ILLUSTRATED BY DON MADDEM

0-06-445049-X TROPHY PB $4.95

Barbara **Braun**

A Weekend with Diego Rivera

0-8478-1749-0 RIZZOLI $19.95

Polly Schoyer **Brooks**

Queen Eleanor, Independent Spirit of the Medieval World: A Biography of Eleanor of Aquitaine

0-397-31995-9 HARPERCREST $14.89

David **Burnie**

The Concise Encyclopedia of the Human Body

0-7894-0204-1 DORLING KINDERSLEY $19.95

Marilyn **Burns**

The Book of Think: Or, How to Solve a Problem Twice Your Size

0-316-11743-9 LITTLE, BROWN PB $11.95

The I Hate Mathematics! Book

0-316-11740-4 LITTLE, BROWN $17.95
0-316-11741-2 LITTLE, BROWN PB $11.95

Math for Smarty Pants: Or Who Says Mathematicians Have Little Pig Eyes

0-316-11738-2 LITTLE, BROWN $17.95
0-316-11739-0 LITTLE, BROWN PB $11.95

Michele **Byam**

Arms and Armor

One of a series of juvenile reference books illustrated throughout by full-color photographs. The text is reasonably technical but the pictures will interest children under 14

PHOTOGRAPHS BY DAVE KING

0-394-89622-X KNOPF $19.00

Stephanie **Calmenson** & Joanna **Cole**

Miss Mary Mack

0-688-09749-9 MORROW PB $6.95

Beverly **Cleary**

A Girl from Yamhill

0-688-07800-1 MORROW $19.95
0-380-72740-4 CAMELOT PB $4.99

Miriam **Chaikin**

Ask Another Question: The Story and Meaning of Passover

The history of Passover from the Exodus to today, with explanations of the holiday's songs, rituals, and symbols

ILLUSTRATED BY MARVIN FRIEDMAN

0-89919-423-0 HOUGHTON MIFFLIN PB $6.95

Joanna **Cole**

Going Batty: A Book About Bats

ILLUSTRATED BY BRUCE DEGEN

0-590-73872-0 SCHOLASTIC PB $2.99

Magic School Bus: Inside the Earth

0-590-88129-9 SCHOLASTIC PB $3.50

The Magic School Bus: Inside the Human Body

ILLUSTRATED BY BRUCE DEGEN

0-590-41427-5 SCHOLASTIC PB $4.95

The Magic School Bus at the Water Works

Ruled by an eccentric teacher, Cole's imaginary pupils reluctantly accompany Miss Frizzle on trips where fantastical adventures introduce solid scientific information. Second and third graders will enjoy these funny, imaginative, and irreverent science books

See also BOOKS FOR AGES FIVE, SIX, AND SEVEN

ILLUSTRATED BY BRUCE DEGEN

0-590-43739-9 SCHOLASTIC $14.95
0-590-40360-5 SCHOLASTIC PB $4.95

Magic School Bus Briefcase

0-590-22300-3 SCHOLASTIC PB $24.75

The Magic School Bus in the Haunted Museum: A Book About Sound

ILLUSTRATED BY BRCE DEGEN

0-590-48412-5 SCHOLASTIC PB $2.50

The Magic School Bus in the Time of the Dinosaurs

ILLUSTRATED BY BRUCE DEGEN

0-590-44689-4 SCHOLASTIC PB $4.95

The Magic School Bus Inside a Beehive

ILLUSTRATED BY BRUCE DEGEN

0-590-44684-3 SCHOLASTIC $15.95

The Magic School Bus Inside a Hurricane

ILLUSTRATED BY BRUCE DEGEN

0-590-44686-X SCHOLASTIC $14.95
0-590-44687-8 SCHOLASTIC PB $4.95

The Magic School Bus Lost in the Solar System

ILLUSTRATED BY BRUCE DEGEN

0-590-41429-1 SCHOLASTIC PB $4.95

The Magic School Bus on the Ocean Floor

ILLUSTRATED BY BRUCE DEGEN

0-590-41431-3 SCHOLASTIC PB $4.95

The Magic School Bus Plants Seeds: A Book About How Living Things Grow

ILLUSTRATED BY BRUCE DEGEN

0-590-22296-1 SCHOLASTIC PB $2.99

Out of This World: A Book About Bats

ILLUSTRATED BY BRUCE DEGEN

0-590-92156-8 SCHOLASTIC PB $2.99

Scholastic's the Magic School Bus: Hello Out There: A Sticker Book About the Solar System

0-590-88128-0 SCHOLASTIC PB $3.50

Scholastic's the Magic School Bus Blows Its Top: A Book About Volcanoes

ILLUSTRATED BY BRUCE DEGEN

0-590-50835-0 SCHOLASTIC PB $2.99

Scholastic's the Magic School Bus Gets All Dried Up: A Book About Deserts

ILLUSTRATED BY BRUCE DEGEN

0-590-50831-8 SCHOLASTIC PB $2.99

Scholastic's the Magic School Bus Gets Ants in Its Pants: A Book About Ants

ILLUSTRATED BY BRUCE DEGEN

0-590-40024-X SCHOLASTIC PB $2.99

Scholastic's the Magic School Bus Gets Eaten: A Book About Food Chains

ILLUSTRATED BY BRUCE DEGEN

0-590-48414-1 SCHOLASTIC PB $2.99

Joanna **Cole** & Beth **Nadler**

Scholastic's the Magic School Bus: Inside Ralphie, A Book About Germs

0-590-40025-8 SCHOLASTIC PB $2.50

Molly **Cone**

Come Back, Salmon: How a Group of Dedicated Kids Adopted Pigeon Creek and Brought It Back to Life

PHOTOGRAPHY BY SIDNEE WHEELWRIGHT

0-87156-489-0 SIERRA CLUB PB $6.95

Pam **Conrad**

Pedro's Journal: A Voyage With Christopher Columbus, August 3, 1492-February 14, 1493

ILLUSTRATED BY PETER KOEPPEN

0-590-46206-7 SCHOLASTIC PB $2.95

Roald **Dahl**

Boy: Tales of Childhood

The story of Dahl's childhood told with the breakneck humor his fans have learned to expect

0-14-031890-9 PENGUIN PB $4.99

Roald **Dahl**

Going Solo

0-14-032528-X PUFFIN PB $4.99

Margaret **Davidson**

The Story of Jackie Robinson, the Bravest Man in Baseball

0-440-40019-8 DELL PB $3.50

Mary **Elting**

The Macmillan Book of Dinosaurs and Other Prehistoric Creatures

The cleanly written text contains information about the history of discoveries that young enthusiasts might not easily find elsewhere

ILLUSTRATED BY JOHN HAMBERGER

0-02-043000-0 ALADDIN PB $8.95

Bill **Farnsworth**

The Illustrated Children's Bible

0-15-232876-9 HARCOURT BRACE $19.95

The Illustrated Children's Old Testament

0-15-238220-8 HARCOURT BRACE $14.95

David **Fassler** & Kelly **McQueen**

What's a Virus, Anyway?: The Kids Book About AIDS

0-914525-15-8 WATERFRONT PB $8.95

Leonard Everett **Fisher**

The Great Wall of China

The making of an ancient monument described in an illustrated book for children eight and nine

0-02-735220-X ATHENEUM $15.95

Paul **Fleischman**

Joyful Noise: Poems for Two Voices

ILLUSTRATED BY ERIC BEDDOWS

0-06-446093-2 HARPERCOLLINS PB $3.95

Townsend's Warbler

0-06-021875-4 HARPERCREST $12.89

Jean **Fritz**

Shh! We're Writing the Constitution

0-399-21404-6 PUTNAM PB $8.95

Where Do You Think You're Going, Christopher Columbus?

0-399-20734-1 PUTNAM PB $8.95

Jean **Fritz** & others

The World in 1492

0-8050-1674-0 HOLT $19.95

Beverly **Gherman**

Agnes de Mille: Dancing Off the Earth

"With many black-and-white photographs, this biography of the American dancer and choreographer *(Rodeo, Oklahoma!,* and *Carousel)* is written crisply and sympathetically" —*Publishers Weekly* Ages 9 and up

0-02-043240-2 ALLADIN PB $5.95

Patricia Reilly **Giff**

Mother Teresa: Sister to the Poor

ILLUSTRATED BY TED LEWIN

0-14-032225-6 VIKING PB $4.99

John S. **Goodall**

The Story of a Main Street

0-689-50436-5 MCELDERRY $14.95

Aylette **Jenness**

Come Home with Me: A Multicultural Treasure Hunt

The first in the new *Kids Bridge* series, this multicultural adventure story is based on the acclaimed exhibit in the Children's Museum of Boston. Kids eight and older hunt for ethnic objects and learn about other cultures, using the "interactive" method of flipping back and forth in the book searching for clues

1-56584-064-X NEW PRESS $16.95

Jamie **Jobb**

The Night Sky Book: An Everyday Guide to Every Night

Explore such wonders as constellations, meteors, auroras, and zodiacal light

ILLUSTRATED BY LINDA BENNETT

0-316-46552-6 LITTLE, BROWN PB $12.95

James Weldon **Johnson**

Lift Every Voice and Sing

Widely known as the African-American national anthem, *Lift Every Voice and Sing* was written for children to celebrate Abraham Lincoln's birthday, and tells the story of the struggle for equality in America. This handsome new version couples Johnson's beloved lyrics with prints by Elizabeth Catlett, and includes an introduction by James Haskins

0-8027-8250-7 WALKER $14.95

0-8027-7442-3 WALKER PB $6.95

Susan **Kalbfleish**

Jump! the New Jump Rope Book

An illustrated book on the techniques of jumping rope

0-688-06930-4 MORROW PB $6.95

Ruth **Krauss**

The Carrot Seed

See also **BOOKS FOR CHILDREN UNDER FIVE**

ILLUSTRATED BY CROCKETT JOHNSON

0-06-023350-8 HARPERCOLLINS $13.95

0-06-443210-6 TROPHY PB $4.95

Jill **Krementz**

How It Feels When Parents Divorce

Illustrated interviews with children presented in their own words; intended for teenagers but helpful for younger children too

0-394-75855-2 KNOPF PB $15.00

Mary D. **Lankford**

Hopscotch Around the World

ILLUSTRATED BY KAREN MILONE

0-688-14745-3 BEECH TREE PB $5.95

Patricia **Lauber**

Dinosaurs Walked Here & Other Stories Fossils Tell

0-02-754510-5 SIMON & SCHUSTER $16.95

Volcano: The Eruption and Healing of Mt. St. Helena

A stunning full-color photo-essay

0-02-754500-8 SIMON & SCHUSTER $16.95

Eda **LeShan**

When Grownups Drive You Crazy

Sample topics: When parents forget how old you are; brothers and sisters; favoritism

0-02-756340-5 MACMILLAN LIBRARY EDITION $5.00

Judith **Levey**, editor

Macmillan Dictionary for Children

0-02-761561-8 SIMON & SCHUSTER $15.00

Sarah **Lovett**

Extremely Weird Primates

1-56261-018-X JOHN MUIR PB $9.95

Extremely Weird Spiders

1-56261-289-1 JOHN MUIR PB $5.95

David **Macaulay**

Castle

Macaulay describes people building great buildings in places as remote as ancient Egypt and as close at hand as today's New York City. The pictures are glorious; detailed pen-and-ink illustrations offer new perspectives each time a page is turned. Macaulay doesn't write (or illustrate) down, so younger children may need to ask a fascinated adult to share the books with them Caldecott Honor Book 1978

0-395-25784-0 HOUGHTON MIFFLIN $16.95

Unbuilding

0-395-29457-6 HOUGHTON MIFFLIN $16.95

0-395-45425-5 HOUGHTON MIFFLIN PB $7.95

Underground

0-395-34065-9 HOUGHTON MIFFLIN PB $8.95

The Way Things Work

A whimsical demystification of the principles and workings of common devices, with many four-color illustrations

See also **SCIENCE AND TECHNOLOGY** in **SCIENCE**

0-395-42857-2 HOUGHTON MIFFLIN $29.95

Betsy **Maestro**

The Story of the Statue of Liberty

An admirably clear picture-book history

ILLUSTRATED BY GIULIO MAESTRO

0-688-08746-9 MULBERRY PB $5.95

0-688-05774-8 MORROW LIBRARY EDITION $16.93

Peter **Mayle**

What's Happening to Me: The Answer to the World's Most Embarrassing Questions

Amusing and quite informative

ILLUSTRATED BY ARTHUR ROBBINS & PAUL WALTER

0-8184-0312-8 LYLE STUART PB $9.95

Where Did I Come From?

A broadly humorous approach to sex and puberty with comic book illustrations. Includes pages on intercourse

ILLUSTRATED BY ARTHUR ROBBINS & PAUL WALTER

0-8184-0253-9 LYLE STUART PB $9.95

James **Martin**

Chameleons: Dragons in the Trees

0-517-58388-7 CROWN $15.00

Henri **Matisse** & Florian **Rodari**

A Weekend with Matisse

TRANSLATED BY JOAN KNIGHT

0-8478-1792-X RIZZOLI $19.95

Sara **Midda**

Growing Up and Other Vices

A whimsical volume illustrates the pitfalls and watersheds of childhood with beautiful little pictures: Things you are supposed to grow out of, behavior toward various creatures, behavior toward adults (avoid rolling eyes in disgust or boredom). From the bestselling artist of *In and Out of the Garden* and *Sara Midda's South of France*

1-56305-728-X WORKMAN $13.95

Jacqueline **Morley**

An Egyptian Pyramid

From the *Inside Story* series: a pictorial journey through ancient Egyptian life, not just pyramids and mummification but farming, amusements, social structure, and religious ceremonies. A straightforward, informative survey of a fascinating culture

0-87226-346-0 BEDRICK LIBRARY EDITION $18.95

Dokuihtei **Nakano**

Easy Origami

Origami is a good way to learn to follow instructions. The projects include folded paper animals, puppets, and masks

0-670-80382-0 PUFFIN PB $13.00

Ogden **Nash**

The Adventures of Isabel

ILLUSTRATED BY JAMES MARSHALL

0-316-59883-6 LITTLE, BROWN PB $5.95

Natural History Museum Staff

Rocks and Minerals

PHOTOGRAPHS BY COLIN KEATES & ANDREAS EINSIEDEL

0-394-89621-1 KNOPF $19.00

Bruce **Ogilvie** & Douglas **Waitley**

Rand McNally Children's Atlas of the World

0-528-83455-X RAND MCNALLY $14.95

Steve **Parker** & Giuliano **Fornari**

The Body Atlas

One of Europe's leading anatomical illustrators takes young readers on an irresistible, labyrinthine voyage of the human body. The lively text includes facts about how hair grows, why funny bones are so vulnerable, and why tickling yourself doesn't work

1-56458-224-8 DORLING KINDERSLEY $19.95

Dorothy Hinshaw **Patent**

Feathers

PHOTOGRAPHY BY WILLIAM MUNOZ

0-525-65081-4 COBBLE HILL $15.99

What Good Is a Tail?

PHOTOGRAPHY BY WILLIAM MUNOZ

0-525-65148-9 COBBLE HILL $13.99

Bill **Peet**

Bill Peet: An Autobiography

Peet worked for over 30 years as an animator with the Disney Studio and as a creator of many books for children. This autobiography is full of his own illustrations. For young adult readers

See also **YOUNG ADULT NONFICTION**

0-395-50932-7 HOUGHTON MIFFLIN $17.95
0-395-68982-1 HOUGHTON MIFFLIN PB $10.95

Lila **Perl**

Don't Sing Before Breakfast, Don't Sleep in the Moonlight: Everyday Superstitions and How They Began

ILLUSTRATED BY ERIKA WEIHS

0-89919-504-0 HOUGHTON MIFFLIN $14.95

The Great Ancestor Hunt: The Fun of Finding Out Who You Are

0-395-54790-3 CLARION PB $7.95

Mummies, Tombs, and Treasure

The mysteries of ancient Egypt

0-89919-407-9 HOUGHTON MIFFLIN $15.95

Richard **Platt**

Stephen Biesty's Cross-Sections Castle

ILLUSTRATED BY STEPHEN BIESTY

1-56458-467-4 DORLING KINDERSLEY $16.95

Stephen Biesty's Incredible Cross-Sections

ILLUSTRATED BY STEPHEN BIESTY

0-679-81411-6 KNOPF $22.00

Gilles **Plazy**

A Weekend with Rousseau

0-8478-1717-2 RIZZOLI $19.95

Chris **Raschka**

Charlie Parker Played Be-Bop

0-531-05999-5 ORCHARD $14.95

Sally **Ride** & Susan **Okie**

To Space and Back

An account of space flight by a crew member of the Space Shuttle who rode, ate, slept, and worked in space

0-688-06159-1 LOTHROP, LEE, & SHEPHERD $19.00

Colin A. **Ronan**

The Skywatcher's Handbook: Night and Day, What to Look for in the Heavens Above

Colorfully illustrated with material on galaxies, constellations, eclipses, sunspots, mirages, cloud formations, weather maps, equipment, and technology

0-517-57326-1 CROWN PB $15.00

Skira-Venturi **Rosabianca**

Weekend with Degas

0-8478-1439-4 RIZZOLI $19.95

Carl **Sandburg**

Rainbows Are Made

0-15-265481-X HARCOURT BRACE PB $8.95

Alvin **Schwartz**

The Cat's Elbow & Other Secret Languages

To speak Cat's Elbow add extra letters to the words. Then look up King Tut and Medieval Greek

ILLUSTRATED BY MARGOT ZEMACH

0-374-41054-2 FS&G PB $3.95

Lynne Sharon **Schwartz**

The Four Questions

ILLUSTRATIONS BY ORI SHERMAN

0-8037-0601-4 PENGUIN LIBRARY EDITION $5.00

Marcia **Sewall**

People of the Breaking Day

0-689-31407-8 ATHENEUM $15.95

Anna **Sewell**

Black Beauty: The Autobiography of a Horse

ILLUSTRATED BY FRITZ EICHENBERG

0-448-40942-9 GROSSETT & DUNLAP $14.95

Ilana **Shamir** & Shlomo **Shavit**, editors

The Young Readers Encyclopedia of Jewish History

0-670-81738-4 VIKING LIBRARY EDITION $17.95

Alice **Siegel** & Margo **McLoone Basta**

The Information Please Kids' Almanac

This newest addition to the *Information Please* series offers 15 fact-filled chapters on the environment, history, mythology, computers, languages, famous people, sports, nutrition, and more. Lavishly illustrated and packed with useful and curious information, this is a superb resource for today's child

0-395-64737-1 HOUGHTON MIFFLIN PB $16.95

Seymour **Simon**

Jupiter

Big colorful photographs from NASA's archives accompany clear, simple texts. The series will appeal to children up to eleven

0-688-05796-9 MORROW $16.00
0-688-08403-6 MORROW PB $5.95

Mars

0-688-06584-8 MORROW $18.00
0-688-09928-9 MULBERRY PB $5.95

Stars

0-688-09237-3 MULBERRY PB $5.95

The Sun

0-688-05857-4 MORROW $17.00
0-688-09236-5 MULBERRY PB $5.95

Winter Across America

0-7868-0019-4 HYPERION $14.95

Donald J. **Sobol**

The Wright Brothers at Kitty Hawk

ILLUSTRATED BY WAYNE BLICKENSTAFF

0-590-42904-3 SCHOLASTIC PB $2.95

Diane **Stanley** & Peter **Vennema**

Good Queen Bess: The Story of Elizabeth I of England

The life of Queen Elizabeth—her rise to power, her conflict with Mary, Queen of Scots, her defeat of the Spanish Armada—illustrated with gouaches based on the style of English Renaissance painting. Ages 6-9

ILLUSTRATED BY DIANE STANLEY

0-02-786810-9 SIMON & SCHUSTER $16.95

Sara **Stein**

The Evolution Book: The Story of 400 Million Years of Life on Earth

An overstuffed paperback encourages children 10 and up to observe, experiment, and do projects. Each section introduces a phase in the Earth's evolution and then suggests explanatory observations and experiments

0-89480-927-X WORKMAN PB $12.95

The Science Book

A companion to *The Evolution Book* that offers many introductory activities in the earth sciences

0-89480-120-1 WORKMAN PB $9.95

Charles **Sullivan**, editor

Children of Promise: African-American Literature and Art for Young People

An anthology specially designed for young readers, presenting an extraordinary range of writing and art by and about African-Americans. Includes selections by Gwendolyn Brooks, W.E.B. DuBois, Langston Hughes, Frederick Douglass's Countee Cullen, and others, with art by Romare Bearden, August Saint-Gaudens, Charles Searles, and Jacob Lawrence, among many others. 80 illustrations, 40 in full color

0-8109-3170-2 ABRAMS $24.95

Barbara **Taylor**

Shoreline

1-56458-213-2 DORLING KINDERSLEY $9.95

Marvin **Terban**

Eight Ate: A Feast of Homonym Riddles

The illustrations are great fun

ILLUSTRATED BY GIULIO MAESTRO

0-89919-067-7 HOUGHTON MIFFLIN $14.95

0-89919-086-3 HOUGHTON MIFFLIN PB $6.95

Merriam Webster Editors

The Webster's II New Riverside Children's Dictionary

Special features include over 250 word histories. For young readers aged eight to twelve

0-395-37884-2 HOUGHTON MIFFLIN PB $12.95

Angela **Wilkes**, editor

French Picture Dictionary

Designed for children embarking on a second language

0-8442-1405-1 NATIONAL TEXTBOOK COMPANY $9.95

Charlotte **Yue** & David **Yue**

The Pueblo

A well-written book about the ceremonial, spiritual, and cultural life of the Pueblo Indians

0-395-54961-2 HOUGHTON MIFFLIN PB $6.95

Jill **Wright** & David **Wright**

The Simon & Schuster Young Readers' Atlas

EDITED BY WENDY BARISH

ILLUSTRATED BY MIKE SAUNDERS & DAVID WRIGHT

0-671-50657-9 WANDERER PB $7.95

Fiction

Arnold **Adoff**

Sports Pages

The experiences and dreams of young athletes expressed in verse

See also **NONFICTION**

0-397-32103-1 HARPERCREST LIBRARY EDITION $14.89

0-06-446098-3 TROPHY PB $6.95

Aesop

Aesop's Fables

ILLUSTRATED BY HEIDI HOLDER

0-670-10643-7 VIKING $16.00

Fables

STEPHEN GOODEN, ILLUSTRATOR

ROGER L'ESTRANGE, TRANSLATOR

0-679-41790-7 KNOPF $12.95

Joan **Aiken**

The Wolves of Willoughby Chase

American by birth and English by adoption, Aiken writes historical adventures that appeal to the child with a sophisticated vocabulary. At her best she recreates the past with an inventive mixture of fact and fantasy

See also **YOUNG ADULT FICTION**

0-440-49603-9 YEARLING PB $4.50

Brian **Alderson**

The Arabian Nights: Or, Tales Told by Sheherezade During a Thousand Nights and One Night

ILLUSTRATED BY MICHAEL FOREMAN

0-688-14219-2 MORROW $20.00

Lloyd **Alexander**

The Book of Three

Alexander's magnificent saga of a young swineherd who takes on the forces of darkness to save the world is humorous, swashbuckling, and spine-tingling. The set includes the book and four cassettes

0-8072-7348-1 LISTEN LIBRARY PB $33.98

Hans Christian **Andersen**

Michael Hague's Favourite Hans Christian Andersen Fairy Tales

The larger print makes the text extremely accessible to young readers. A perfect first Andersen collection for the eights and nines

ILLUSTRATED BY MICHAEL HAGUE

0-8050-0659-1 HOLT $19.95

Andersen's Fairy Tales

0-448-06005-1 PRICE, STERN, & SLOAN $15.95

The Nightingale

Zwerger's carefully defined illustrations are usually drawn in soft colors, and her retold fairy stories are very lovely to look at

ILLUSTRATED BY LISBETH ZWERGER

0-907234-57-7 SIMON & SCHUSTER $14.95

0-88335-579-5 MILLIKEN PB $4.95

Maya **Angelou**

All God's Children Need Traveling Shoes

Black Americans search for an African home in the 1960s

0-679-73404-X VINTAGE PB $9.00

Now Sheba Sings the Song

Black women of all ages are evoked in this poem

0-452-27143-6 PLUME PB $11.95

Anonymous

The Arabian Nights

ILLUSTRATED BY EARLE GOODENOW

0-448-06006-X GROSSETT & DUNLAP $14.95

Jim **Arnosky**

Crinkleroot's Guide to Walking in Wild Places

See also **NONFICTION**

0-689-71753-9 ALADDIN PB $5.95

Jeannine **Atkins**

Aani and the Tree Huggers

ILLUSTRATED BY PINTO VENANTIUS

1-88000-024-5 LEE & LOW $14.95

Avi

Poppy

ILLUSTRATED BY BRIAN FLOCA

0-531-09483-9 ORCHARD $15.95

The True Confessions of Charlotte Doyle

0-531-05893-X ORCHARD $15.95

Natalie **Babbitt**

The Eyes of the Amaryllis

0-374-42238-9 FS&G PB $3.95

The Search for Delicious

0-374-46536-3 FS&G PB $3.95

Tuck Everlasting

Suppose you could live forever, would you want to? The legend of the Fountain of Youth updated to 19th-century New England

0-374-37848-7 FS&G $15.00

0-374-48009-5 FS&G PB $4.95

Edith **Bagnold**

National Velvet

Wishes are granted in this classic story of a skinny girl and a mixed-breed horse who train, fight, and scheme to become winners

0-380-71235-0 FLARE PB $3.99

Lynne Reid **Banks**

I, Houdini: The Amazing Story of an Escape-Artist Hamster

0-380-70649-0 CAMELOT PB $4.50

The Mystery of the Cupboard
ILLUSTRATED BY TOM NEWSOM
0-688-12138-1 MORROW $15.00

The Return of the Indian
0-385-23497-X DOUBLEDAY $15.95

The Secret of the Indian
0-385-26292-2 DOUBLEDAY $15.95

Lynne Reid **Banks** & Nancy E. **Krulik**

The Indian in the Cupboard: Omri's Scrapbook
0-590-50983-7 SCHOLASTIC PB $2.95

J.M. **Barrie**

Peter Pan
Includes cassette recording by Lynn Redgrave
0-553-21178-1 BDD PB $3.50

Peter Pan
F.D. BEDFORD, ILLUSTRATOR
0-679-41792-3 KNOPF $12.95
9-992-71409-3 VIKING LIBRARY EDITION $5.00

Graeme **Base**

The Eleventh Hour: A Curious Mystery
When Horace the elephant turns 11, he celebrates by inviting his friends to a party where a curious mystery will be revealed. For ages 8, 9, and up
0-8109-0851-4 ABRAMS $18.95

L. Frank **Baum**

Dorothy and the Wizard of Oz
ILLUSTRATED BY JOHN R. NEILL
0-486-24714-7 DOVER PB $6.95

L. Frank Baum

The Emerald City of Oz
0-345-33464-7 BALLANTINE PB $4.99
0-486-25681-2 DOVER PB $6.95

Glinda of Oz
0-345-33394-2 BALLANTINE PB $4.99

The Land of Oz
In a worthy sequel to *The Wizard of Oz,* Baum leaves Dorothy back home in Kansas. New characters include Jack Pumpkinhead, the Saw-Horse, and Mr. H.M. Woggle Bug
ILLUSTRATED BY JOHN R. NEILL
0-345-33568-6 BALLANTINE PB $4.99

The Magic of Oz
0-8488-0787-1 AMEREON $20.95

Ozma of Oz
0-486-24779-1 DOVER PB $6.95

The Patchwork Girl of Oz
0-345-33290-3 DEL RAY PB $4.99
0-486-26514-5 DOVER PB $6.95

Rinkitink in Oz
0-345-33317-9 BALLANTINE PB $4.95

The Road to Oz
0-486-25208-6 DOVER PB $6.95

Scarecrow of Oz
0-8488-0707-3 AMEREON $20.95

Tik Tok of Oz
0-345-33435-3 BALLANTINE PB $4.99

The Tin Woodman of Oz
0-345-33436-1 BALLANTINE PB $4.99

The Wizard of Oz
The first and greatest American fairy story was the *The Wizard of Oz,* and the Oz books make wonderful bedtime story books for children as young as seven or eight and will be read with pleasure by older children as well. *The Land of Oz* and *Ozma of Oz* are in many respects just as inventive as the original title, but a number of the later books pale by comparison.
The original text whimsically re-illustrated in full color. A lovely gift book for the young Oz reader
ILLUSTRATED BY MICHAEL HAGUE
0-03-061661-1 HOLT $19.95
0-590-44089-6 SCHOLASTIC PB $2.95

The Wizard of Oz
0-345-33590-2 BALLANTINE PB $4.99
0-14-035001-2 PUFFIN PB $2.99

The Wonderful Wizard of Oz
W.W. DENSLOW, ILLUSTRATOR
0-679-41794-X KNOPF $12.95
0-8446-1610-9 SMITH $20.05

John **Bellairs**

The House with a Clock in Its Walls
0-8446-6758-7 SMITH $17.75

Betsy **Byars**

The Pinballs
0-06-447150-0 TROPHY PB $3.99

John **Bierhorst**

Doctor Coyote
ILLUSTRATED BY WENDY WATSON
0-689-80739-2 ALADDIN PB $5.99

John **Bierhorst**, editor

The Monkey's Haircut & Other Stories Told by the Maya
Twenty-two traditional stories
ILLUSTRATED BY ROBERT ANDREW PARKER
0-688-04269-4 MORROW $15.00

The Naked Bear: Folktales of the Iroquois
ILLUSTRATED BY DIRK ZIMMER
0-688-06422-1 MORROW $15.00

Joan W. **Blos**

A Gathering of Days
0-689-71419-X ALADDIN PB $3.95

Judy **Blume**

Blubber
Accurately describes the social dynamics of the fifth grade
0-02-711010-9 SIMON & SCHUSTER $15.00
0-440-40707-9 YEARLING PB $3.50

Freckle Juice
When class clown Sharon offers Nicky her secret recipe for freckle juice, Nicky just can't pass up the opportunity
ILLUSTRATED BY SONIA LISKER
0-440-42813-0 YEARLING PB $3.99

Starring Sally J. Freedman as Herself
A Jewish girl from New Jersey spends a year growing up in Florida just after the close of World War II. Her daydreams mix with her increasingly shrewd observations about herself, her friends, and family
0-02-711070-2 SIMON & SCHUSTER $15.95
0-440-48253-4 DELL PB $3.99

Superfudge
Voted the most popular children's book of 1983 by Children's Choices, a nationwide readers' survey
0-525-40522-4 DUTTON $13.99
0-440-48433-2 YEARLING PB $3.99

Tales of a Fourth Grade Nothing
A nine-year-old is "given" a little sister and soon decides that she is expendable. But some things about little sister are lovable too
ILLUSTRATED BY ROY DOTY
0-525-40720-0 DUTTON $13.99
0-440-48474-X DELL PB $3.99

Michael **Bond**

A Bear Called Paddington
The first story in a long series about the celebrated bear from Peru dressed in rain hat, duffel coat, and wellies found in London's Paddington Station
ILLUSTRATED BY PEGGY STATION
0-440-40483-5 YEARLING PB $3.99

Paddington Helps Out
ILLUSTRATED BY PEGGY FORTNUM
0-395-06639-5 HOUGHTON MIFFLIN $13.95

Lucy Maria **Boston**

The Children of Green Knowe
ILLUSTRATED BY PETER BOSTON
0-15-217151-7 HARCOURT BRACE PB $3.95

Carol Ryrie **Brink**

Caddie Woodlawn
ILLUSTRATED BY TRINA SCHART HYMAN
0-689-71370-3 ALADDIN PB $3.95

Bill **Brittain**

Dr. Dredd's Wagon of Wonders
Alarming things happen in the little New England town of Coven Tree when the straight-talking inhabitants fall victim to Dr. Hugh Dredd's sinister manipulations
ILLUSTRATED BY ANDREW GLASS
0-06-440289-4 HARPERCOLLINS PB $3.50

Wings
0-06-440612-1 TROPHY PB $4.50

The Wish Giver: 3 Tales of Coven Tree
Newbery Honor Book 1984
ILLUSTRATED BY ANDREW GLASS
0-06-020686-1 HARPERCREST LIBRARY EDITION $13.89
0-06-440168-5 HARPERCOLLINS PB $4.50

Joseph **Bruchac**

The Boy Who Lived with Bears and Other Iroquois Stories
0-06-021287-X HARPERCOLLINS $15.95

Joseph **Bruchac** & Gayle **Ross**

The Girl Who Married the Moon: Tales from Native North America
0-8167-3480-1 BRIDGEWATER $13.95

Pearl S. **Buck**

The Big Wave
0-06-440171-5 TROPHY PB $3.95

Clyde Robert **Bulla**

Pirate's Promise
ILLUSTRATED BY PETER BURCHARD
0-06-440457-9 TROPHY PB $3.95

Pocahontas and the Strangers
Pocahontas is a little girl, a young woman, and John Smith's bride in this interesting retelling
ILLUSTRATED BY PETER BURCHARD
0-590-43481-0 SCHOLASTIC PB $3.99

Shoeshine Girl
ILLUSTRATED BY LEIGH GRANT
0-06-440228-2 TROPHY PB $3.95

Sword in the Tree
0-690-79909-8 HARPERCREST $14.89

Frances Hodgson **Burnett**

Little Lord Fauntleroy
0-89966-288-9 BUCCANEER $21.95

A Little Princess
1-56138-742-8 COURAGE $5.98
0-440-40386-3 BDD PB $3.99

The Secret Garden
A turn-of-the-century masterpiece about a little orphan girl who comes to live in a big house in the north of England. An unforgettable evocation of the magic that occurs when people learn to love one another
ILLUSTRATED BY TASHA TUDOR
0-397-32165-1 HARPERCOLLINS $15.00
0-06-440188-X TROPHY PB $4.50

Sheila **Burnford**

The Incredible Journey
Separated from their owners, two dogs and a cat trek through 250 miles of dangerous Canadian wilderness to get back home
0-553-15616-0 BDD PB $4.50

Oliver **Butterworth**

The Enormous Egg
ILLUSTRATED BY LOUIS DARLING
0-316-11904-0 LITTLE, BROWN $16.95
0-316-11920-2 LITTLE, BROWN PB $4.95

Betsy **Byars**

The Burning Questions of Bingo Brown
0-14-032479-8 PUFFIN PB $3.99

Cracker Jackson
Eleven-year-old Cracker cares very much about his former babysitter, who's in serious trouble. The story deals with problems encountered by responsible children when confronting an unjust adult world
0-14-031881-X VIKING PB $3.99

The Not-Just-Anybody Family
The maverick Blossom family includes a rodeo rider (Mom) and a boy who flies off the roof when the police come looking for Grandpa—odd heroes dealt with honestly and humorously
0-440-45951-6 YEARLING PB $3.99

The Pinballs
Called pinballs because they are always being shuffled around, two boys and a girl meet in a group foster home. An odd and healing friendship develops
0-06-440198-7 HARPERCOLLINS PB $3.95

Jeannette **Caines**

Just Us Women
0-06-443056-1 TROPHY PB $4.95

Mary **Calhoun**

Katie John
0-06-020951-8 HARPERCREST $13.89

Ann **Cameron**

Julian, Dream Doctor
ILLUSTRATED BY ANN STRUGNELL
0-679-80524-9 RANDOM HOUSE PB $3.99

More Stories Julian Tells
ILLUSTRATED BY ANN STRUGNELL
0-394-82454-7 RANDOM HOUSE PB $3.99

The Stories Huey Tells
ILLUSTRATED BY ROBERTA SMITH
0-679-86732-5 KNOPF $15.00

The Stories Julian Tells
Julian thinks he knows everything, and his smaller sidekick brother, Huey, believes everything Julian says. And Julian says some very odd things
ILLUSTRATED BY ANN STRUGNELL
0-394-82892-5 RANDOM HOUSE PB $3.99

Eleanor **Cameron**

The Court of the Stone Children
0-14-034289-3 PUFFIN PB $4.99

Stowaway to the Mushroom Planet
0-316-12541-5 LITTLE, BROWN PB $6.95

The Wonderful Flight to the Mushroom Planet
ILLUSTRATED BY ROBERT HENNEBERGER
0-316-12537-7 LITTLE, BROWN $15.95

Peter **Carey**

The Big Bazoohley
ILLUSTRATED BY ABIRA ALI
0-8050-3855-8 HOLT $14.95

Natalie Savage **Carlson**

The Family Under the Bridge
ILLUSTRATED BY GARTH WILLIAMS
0-06-440250-9 TROPHY PB $3.95

Sylvia **Cassedy**

Behind the Attic Wall
An unrepentant orphan, kicked out of several foster homes, settles with relatives and thereby enters a house of friendly ghosts who become her family
0-380-69843-9 CAMELOT PB $3.99

Richard **Chase**, editor

The Jack Tales
ILLUSTRATED BY BERKELEY WILLIAMS, JR.
0-395-66951-0 HOUGHTON MIFFLIN PB $5.95

Anton **Chekhov**

Kashtanka
ILLUSTRATED BY GENNADY SPIRIN
0-15-200539-0 GULLIVER $16.00

Grace **Chetwin**

The Riddle and the Rune
0-02-718312-2 MACMILLAN LIBRARY EDITION $5.00

Sook Nyul **Choi**

Year of Impossible Goodbyes
0-440-40759-1 YEARLING PB $3.99

John **Ciardi**

The Hopeful Trout and other Limericks
ILLUSTRATED BY SUSAN MEDDAUGH
0-395-61616-6 HOUGHTON MIFFLIN PB $5.95

Beverly **Cleary**

Beezus and Ramona
ILLUSTRATED BY LOUIS DARLING
0-380-70918-X CAMELOT PB $3.99

Ellen Tebbits
Ellen has to wait until a new little girl moves into town to acquire her very special friend. A quiet, humorous book set in a 1950s small town
ILLUSTRATED BY LOUIS DARLING
0-688-21264-6 MORROW $16.00
0-380-70913-9 CAMELOT PB $4.50

Henry Huggins
Henry and his impossibly dirty mutt Ribsy live in Small Town, USA, in this old-fashioned and funny book
ILLUSTRATED BY LOUIS DARLING
0-688-21385-5 MORROW $16.00
0-380-70912-0 CAMELOT PB $4.50

Muggie Maggie

The author who brought us Ramona Quimby and Henry Huggins now gives us Maggie Schultz, who is about to enter third grade. "Fans who have eagerly awaited a new Cleary novel will find this story wrought with the same understanding and sympathetic humor that have warmed the hearts of two generations of readers"
—*Publishers Weekly*. Ages 7 and up

ILLUSTRATED BY KAY LIFE

0-688-08553-9 MORROW $15.00

Ramona and Her Father

Beverly Cleary has been awarded the Laura Ingalls Wilder Medal for 40 years of distinguished writing for children. Energetic eight-year-old Ramona tries to set things right when Dad loses his job, but helping him is much harder than the television says. Written with tenderness as well as humor. Newbery Honor Book 1978

ILLUSTRATED BY ALAN TIEGREEN

0-688-22114-9 MORROW $16.00

Ramona Forever

0-688-03785-2 MORROW $16.00

Ramona and Her Mother

0-380-70952-X AVON PB $4.50

Ramona Quimby, Age Eight

ILLUSTRATED BY ALAN TIEGREEN

0-688-00477-6 MORROW $16.00

Ramona the Brave

ILLUSTRATED BY ALAN TIEGREEN

0-688-22015-0 MORROW $16.00

Ramona the Pest

0-688-21721-4 MORROW $16.00

0-380-70954-6 CAMELOT PB $3.99

Ribsy

In a sequel to *Henry Huggins*, the search is on for the beloved, lost Ribsy

0-380-70955-4 CAMELOT PB $3.99

Eleanor **Coerr**

Mieko and the Fifth Treasure

0-399-22434-3 PUTNAM $14.95

Sadako and the Thousand Paper Cranes

0-399-20520-9 PUTNAM $14.95

Barbara **Cohen**

The Canterbury Tales

Retellings of selections from Chaucer, beautifully illustrated

ILLUSTRATED BY TRINA HYMAN

0-688-06201-6 LOTHROP, LEE, & SHEPHERD $18.00

Molly's Pilgrim

0-688-02103-4 LOTHROP, LEE, & SHEPHERD $16.00

James Lincoln **Collier**

Jump Ship to Freedom

0-440-44323-7 YEARLING PB $4.50

Carlo **Collodi**

Pinnocchio

0-14-035037-3 PENGUIN PB $3.50

Harold **Courlander**

People of the Short Blue Corn: Tales and Legends of the Hopi Indians

ILLUSTRATED BY ENRICO ARNO

0-8050-3511-7 HOLT PB $9.95

Harold **Courlander** & George **Herzog**

Cow-Tail Switch and Other West African Stories

0-8050-0298-7 HOLT PB $8.95

Marie **Craft**

Cupid and Psyche

ILLUSTRATED BY KINUKO CRAFT

0-688-13163-8 MORROW $16.00

Paul **Creswick**

Robin Hood

Wyeth's magnificent paintings bring the legendary outlaw to vivid life, in this classic edition of the tale. All ages

ILLUSTRATED BY N. C. WYETH

0-684-18162-2 ATHENEUM $24.95

Karen **Cushman**

Catherine, Called Birdy

0-395-68186-3 CLARION $14.95

The Midwife's Apprentice

0-395-69229-6 CLARION $10.95

Roald **Dahl**

The BFG

A most extraordinary cast of characters including the Queen of England, the Head of the Army, the Head of the Air Force, the orphan Sophie, the Fleshlumper, and Bone Cruncher, the Childchewer, and the BFG (Big Friendly Giant)

ILLUSTRATED BY QUENTIN BLAKE

0-679-42813-5 KNOPF $13.95

0-14-034019-X VIKING PB $4.99

Roald Dahl

Charlie and the Chocolate Factory

A magical tour where the selfish and undeserving are nastily punished and the good are sumptuously rewarded

ILLUSTRATED BY JOSEPH SCHINDELMAN

0-394-81011-2 KNOPF $17.00

0-14-032869-6 VIKING PB $4.99

Charlie and the Great Glass Elevator

The uncharacteristically tame sequel contains one haunting nightmare image—the elevator that doesn't stop at the top floor

ILLUSTRATED BY JOSEPH SCHINDELMAN

0-394-92472-X KNOPF LIBRARY EDITION $18.99

0-14-032870-X VIKING PB $4.99

Danny, Champion of the World

0-14-032873-4 VIKING PB $4.99

The Enormous Crocodile

This bad-tempered crocodile is too greedy for his own good. Children either respond enthusiastically to Dahl's boisterous moralizing, or they just don't find him funny at all

ILLUSTRATED BY QUENTIN BLAKE

0-14-036556-7 PUFFIN PB $3.99

James and the Giant Peach

Poor James is tormented by two horrible aunts. But with characteristic vigor Dahl devises their horrid fate, while James goes on to extraordinary adventures

ILLUSTRATED BY NANCY BURHHARDT

0-394-81282-4 RANDOM HOUSE $16.00

0-679-98090-3 KNOPF LIBRARY EDITION $17.99

Matilda

ILLUSTRATED BY QUENTIN BLAKE

0-14-037985-1 PUFFIN PB $4.99

The Twits

ILLUSTRATED BY QUENTIN BLAKE

0-14-034640-6 PUFFIN PB $3.99

The Witches

Real witches are very ordinary people, and that is why they are so hard to catch, says the witch-catching, cigar-smoking grandmother heroine of this fantasy about a witches' convention at an otherwise ordinary seaside hotel

ILLUSTRATED BY QUENTIN BLAKE

0-374-38457-6 FS&G $16.00

0-14-034020-3 VIKING PB $4.99

Alice **Dalgliesh**

The Bears on Hemlock Mountain

ILLUSTRATED BY HELEN SEWELL

0-689-71604-4 ALADDIN PB $4.95

The Courage of Sarah Noble

0-684-18830-9 ATHENEUM $14.00

Mark Daniel **Daniel**, editor

A Child's Treasury of Poems

An anthology of 19th- and early 20th-century poetry, with 100 full-color and black-and-white reproductions of rarely seen paintings and engravings. A stunning collection

0-8037-0330-9 DUTTON $17.99

9-9911-7322-6 DUTTON LIBRARY EDITION $5.00

Beatrice Schenk **de Regniers**, editor

Sing a Song of Popcorn

An anthology of favorite poems, illustrated by nine Caldecott-winning artists

0-590-43974-X SCHOLASTIC $18.95

Antoine **De Saint-Exupery**

The Little Prince: Boxed Deluxe Gift Book

At half a century after its first publication, *The Little Prince* still captivates young and old alike.

This commemorative, gilt-edged edition ($50.00 edition below) includes a satin bookmark, new samples of the author's artwork, and facsimile pages of the original manuscript

0-15-243820-3 HARCOURT BRACE $50.00
0-15-652820-7 HARCOURT BRACE PB $4.95

Madame **de Villeneuve**

Beauty and the Beast: A Tale of Love's Sacrifice

ILLUSTRATED BY ETIENNE DELESSERT
0-87191-946-X CREATIVE ED LIBRARY EDITION $13.95

Charles **Dickens**

A Christmas Carol

A new edition of the yuletide favorite with fine watercolor illustrations. Awarded first place in the New York Book Show in 1991 and two critics' prizes at the Bologna Children's Fair. "One of the year's best children's books"—*NY Times*

See also **19TH-CENTURY FICTION** under **THE 19TH-CENTURY** in **LITERATURE OF THE BRITISH ISLES**

ILLUSTRATED BY ROBERTO INNOCENTI
0-15-100200-2 CREATIVE EDUCATION $19.95

Charles Dickens

A Christmas Carol: Being a Ghost Story of Christmas

An illustrated version that characterizes Scrooge, Tiny Tim, and all the rest as animals

ILLUSTRATED BY MERCER MAYER
0-87104-228-2 NEW YORK PUBLIC LIBRARY $20.00

Michael **Dorris**

Morning Girl

1-56282-284-5 HYPERION $12.95

William Pene **Du Bois**

The Twenty-One Balloons

A balloonist lands abruptly on an uninhabited Pacific island and is welcomed by a colony of formally dressed people living in an advanced civilization. An unlikely, imaginative, and funny parable about what it is like to live on the edge of disaster. Winner of a Newbery Medal 1947

0-670-73441-1 VIKING $15.99
0-14-032097-0 VIKING PB $3.99

Edward **Eager**

Half Magic

Eager's fantasy stories appeal because the magic is kindly even when matters are temporarily out of control

ILLUSTRATED BY N.M. BODECKER
0-15-233078-X HARCOURT BRACE $15.00
0-15-233081-X HARCOURT BRACE PB $6.00

Knight's Castle

ILLUSTRATED BY N.M. BODECKER
0-15-243105-5 HARCOURT BRACE PB $3.95

Magic by the Lake

ILLUSTRATED BY N.M. BODECKER
0-15-250444-3 HARCOURT BRACE PB $6.00

Magic or Not?

0-15-251160-1 HARCOURT BRACE PB $3.95

Seven-Day Magic

ILLUSTRATED BY N.M. BODECKER
0-15-272916-X HARCOURT BRACE PB $5.00

The Time Garden

ILLUSTRATED BY N.M. BODECKER
0-15-288193-X HARCOURT BRACE PB $6.00

The Well-Wishers

ILLUSTRATED BY N.M. BODECKER
0-15-294994-1 HARCOURT BRACE PB $6.00

Elizabeth **Enright**

Gone-Away Lake

Boy and girl cousins rediscover a lost world when they find two old people left behind by time and circumstance. Newbery Medal 1957

ILLUSTRATED BY BETH & JOE KRUSH
0-15-231649-3 HARCOURT BRACE PB $6.00

Saturdays

0-8050-0291-X HOLT $12.95

Thimble Summer

0-440-48681-5 DELL PB $3.99

Elizabeth **Enright** & others

Return to Gone-Away

0-15-266377-0 HARCOURT BRACE PB $4.95

Eleanor **Estes**

The Hundred Dresses

Every day Wanda comes to school in the same washed-out, blue dress, yet she tells the other children she has closets full of clothes. Her Cinderella dreams become real in this story

0-15-642350-2 HARCOURT BRACE PB $5.00

The Hundred Dresses

ILLUSTRATED BY LOUIS SLOBODKIN
0-15-237374-8 HARCOURT BRACE $15.00

Moffats

ILLUSTRATED BY LOUIS SLOBODKIN
0-15-255095-X HARCOURT BRACE $16.00

Bernard **Evslin**

Adventures of Ulysses

0-590-42599-4 SCHOLASTIC PB $4.50

Walter **Farley**

The Black Stallion

The Black Stallion series chronicles the bloodline of a champion.

ILLUSTRATED BY KEITH WARD
0-679-81343-8 RANDOM HOUSE PB $4.99

Black Stallion

0-394-90601-2 RANDOM LIBRARY $13.99

The Black Stallion and the Girl

0-679-82021-3 RANDOM HOUSE PB $4.99

The Black Stallion's Blood Bay Colt

0-679-81347-0 RANDOM HOUSE PB $4.99

Jules **Feiffer**

A Barrel of Laughs

"Wickedly funny" (*Booklist*), "wonderfully wise"(*SLJ*), Feiffer's tells the story of Prince Roger's quest, in preparation for becoming king, in which he must seek to turn himself from carefree and hilarious to sober and serious. Awful and awfully funny, the journey—illustrated with Feiffer's unforgettable cartooning—proceeds through the Forever Forest, the Dastardly Divide, the Valley of Vengeance, and the Sea of Screams. A wise and unforgettably funny fairy-tale epic

0-06-205098-2 HARPERCOLLINS $14.95

The Man in the Ceiling

In his first book for children, Pulitzer Prize-winning cartoonist Feiffer tells the story of Jimmy, a boy with a dream to become a cartoonist. Discouraged by some and ignored by others, he persists, working hard to make his dream come true despite mistakes and setbacks. Illustrations by the author

0-06-205035-4 HARPERCOLLINS $15.00

Rachel **Field**

Hitty: Her First Hundred Years

0-02-734840-7 SIMON & SCHUSTER $15.00

John D. **Fitzgerald**

The Great Brain

An 11-year-old con artist has adventurous schemes

ILLUSTRATED BY MERCER MAYER
0-440-43071-2 YEARLING PB $3.99

The Great Brain at the Academy

0-440-43113-1 DELL PB $3.99

Louise **Fitzhugh**

Harriet the Spy

Though she calls herself a spy, this very independent New York schoolgirl who takes notes on the behavior of her friends, family, and neighbors could also be a future novelist. When it first appeared, the book was criticized by adults for its frankness, but young readers rapidly made it popular. The success of the feature film adaptation has served to cement that popularity

0-06-440660-1 TROPHY PB $4.50

Nobody's Family Is Going to Change

0-374-45523-6 SUNBURST PB $4.95

Paul **Fleischman**

Bull Run

ILLUSTRATED BY DAVID FRAMPTON
0-06-440588-5 TROPHY PB $4.95

Sid **Fleischman**

The Whipping Boy

When the bored prince decides to run away he takes his whipping boy along, but the adventure soon turns into a misadventure when the two are kidnapped. Newbery Medal 1987

ILLUSTRATED BY PETER SIS
0-688-06216-4 MORROW $16.00
0-8167-1038-4 TROLL PB $3.95

Ian **Fleming**

Chitty Chitty Bang Bang

When Jemima and Jeremy, twin children of inventor Caractacus Pott, are kidnapped by a ring of international thugs, the world's most famous car comes to their rescue. A family favorite

0-394-81948-9 BULLSEYE PB $3.99

Commander Pott sat gripping the wheel and chuckling with excitement and delight. "I told you so!" he shouted against the roar of the wind. "She's got ideas of her own. She's a magical car. Don't worry! She'll look after us!"

He carefully turned the wheel to see what would happen. And, sure enough, the nose of the car followed what he did and after curving about a bit to get the feel of the steering, Commander Pott made straight for the tall steeple of Canterbury Cathedral in the distance, soaring over the long line of cars in which the poor people were roasting in the sunshine and sniffing up the disgusting gas fumes of the cars in front.

CHITTY CHITTY BANG BANG

Ian Fleming

Margot **Fonteyn**

Swan Lake

The great dancer offers a splendid retelling of the ballet, for those in search of a more traditional version than the Mark Helprin adaptation listed below. The illustrations do full justice to the story's melancholy romanticism. For ages 8, 9, and up

See also **BOOKS FOR CHILDREN UNDER FIVE**

ILLUSTRATED BY TRINA SCHART HYMAN

0-15-200600-1 HARCOURT BRACE $14.95

Kathryn **Forbes**

Mama's Bank Account

0-15-656377-0 HARCOURT BRACE PB $7.00

Paula **Fox**

The Little Swineherd and Other Tales

ILLUSTRATED BY ROBERT BYRD

0-525-45398-9 DUTTON $16.99

Maurice's Room

Maurice collects things, and not even mean dogs deter him in his own urban treasure hunt

ILLUSTRATED BY INGRID FETZ

0-689-71216-2 ALADDIN PB $3.95

Monkey Island

From the winner of the Newbery Award Medal and Hans Christian Andersen award, *Monkey Island* is the truthful and moving story of a homeless boy in New York City. "*Monkey Island* has the power and simplicity of truth and the universality of a fable"—*LA Times*

0-531-05962-6 ORCHARD $15.95

0-531-08562-7 ORCHARD LIBRARY EDITION $16.99

Paula **Fox** & Floriano **Vecchi**

Amzat and His Brothers: Three Italian Folktales

"Stories are like a great rope that ties the generations together… [They] do not disappear. They last longer than anything else," writes the author in her preface to these three wise and delightful tales. Fox, winner of the Newbery and the Hans Christian Andersen medals, found these stories in the Tuscan village of Pianoro Vecchio. Her unique wit infuses them with new life and meaning

ILLUSTRATED BY EMILY ARNOLD MCCULLY

0-531-05462-4 ORCHARD $16.95

0-531-08612-7 ORCHARD LIBRARY EDITION $17.99

Jean **Fritz**

The Great Little Mansion

0-399-21768-1 PUTNAM $15.95

John R. **Gardiner**

Stone Fox

A boy takes on responsibility for the family farm when his grandmother falls ill and must help save the farm from foreclosure. Hard on a sensitive child. Newbery Medal Winner 1980

ILLUSTRATED BY MARCIA SEWALL

0-690-03983-2 CROWELL $14.95

0-06-440132-4 TROPHY PB $3.95

Leon **Garfield**

Shakespeare Stories

Twelve plays in narrative form, presented without undue simplification and with a strong sense of the dramatic

ILLUSTRATED BY MICHAEL FOREMAN

0-395-56397-6 HOUGHTON MIFFLIN $24.95

Smith

A 12-year-old pickpocket steals the motive for a murder and finds himself hunted down for a piece of paper he can't read

0-7451-0448-7 CHIVERS NORTH AMERICA $16.95

Doris **Gates**

Blue Willow

ILLUSTRATED BY PAUL LANTZ

0-670-17557-9 VIKING $14.99

Jean Craighead **George**

Julie

ILLUSTRATED BY WENDELL MINOR

0-06-440573-7 TROPHY PB $4.50

Julie of the Wolves

0-06-021944-0 HARPERCREST $14.89

Patricia Reilly **Giff**

Rat Teeth

0-440-47457-4 DELL PB $3.25

Frank **Gilbreth**, Jr. & Ernestine Gilbreth **Carey**

Cheaper by the Dozen

0-553-27250-0 BDD PB $4.99

Rumer **Godden**

Doll's House

ILLUSTRATED BY TASHA TUDOR

0-14-030942-X VIKING PB $4.99

Kenneth **Grahame**

The Reluctant Dragon

A short and funny fantasy about a reluctant dragon who is engaged to fight by St. George himself

ILLUSTRATED BY MICHAEL HAGUE

0-03-064031-8 HOLT $15.95

0-8050-0802-0 HOLT PB $6.95

The Wind in the Willows

0-679-41802-4 KNOPF $13.95

0-440-40385-5 BDD PB $3.99

0-14-036685-7 PUFFIN PB $3.99

Jacob **Grimm** & Wilhelm **Grimm**

The Juniper Tree: And Other Tales from Grimm

A superior two-volume edition of Grimm's *Household Stories* beautifully translated and matched by evocative line drawings. A marvelous present for an intelligent child

TRANSLATED BY LORE SEGAL & RANDALL JARRELL

ILLUSTRATED BY MAURICE SENDAK

0-374-51358-9 FS&G PB $9.95

Grimm Brothers

Snow-White and the Seven Dwarfs

A fine edition distinguished by an outstanding translation

TRANSLATED BY RANDALL JARRELL

ILLUSTRATED BY NANCY EKHOLM BURKERT

0-374-37099-0 FS&G $17.00

0-374-46868-0 FS&G PB $5.95

Virginia **Hamilton**

Her Stories: African American Folktales, Fairy Tales and True Tales

A collection for children

See also **AFRICAN-AMERICAN** under **THE WESTERN HEMISPHERE** under **MYTHOLOGY AND FOLKLORE** in **RELIGION, SPIRITUALITY, AND PHILOSOPHY**

0-590-47370-0 SCHOLASTIC $19.95

In the Beginning: Creation Stories from Around the World
ILLUSTRATED BY BARRY MOSER
0-15-238740-4 HARCOURT BRACE $22.95

The People Could Fly: American Black Folktales
ILLUSTRATED BY DIANE & LEO DILLON
0-679-84336-1 KNOPF PB $12.00

Carolyn **Haywood**

B Is for Betsy
ILLUSTRATED BY CAROLYN HAYWOOD & JOE YAKOVETIC
0-15-204975-4 HARCOURT BRACE $14.00
0-15-204977-0 HARCOURT BRACE PB $3.95

Betsy and Billy
ILLUSTRATED BY CAROLYN HAYWOOD & JOE YAKOVETIC
0-15-206765-5 HARCOURT BRACE $12.95
0-15-206768-X HARCOURT BRACE PB $3.95

Florence Parry **Heide** & Judith Heide **Gilliland**

The Day of Ahmed's Secret
The streets of Cairo come to life in this simple but evocative story about an Egyptian boy who journeys through the city delivering butane gas on his donkey cart
ILLUSTRATED BY TED LEWIN
0-688-08894-5 LOTHROP, LEE, & SHEPHERD $16.00
0-688-08895-3 MORROW LIBRARY EDITION $15.93

Mark **Helprin**

Swan Lake
Novelist Mark Helprin (*Winter's Tale, Ellis Island*) has expanded the classic ballet into a poetic adventure novella, and Chris Van Allsburg (*The Polar Express*) has illustrated it with a series of unforgettable paintings, richly shaded and brilliantly composed. For ages 8, 9, and up
ILLUSTRATED BY CHRIS VAN ALLBURG
0-395-49858-9 HOUGHTON MIFFLIN $19.95

Frances Mary **Hendry**

Quest for a Maid
0-374-46155-4 SUNBURST PB $4.95

Marguerite **Henry**

King of the Wind
Newbery Medal 1949
ILLUSTRATED BY WESLEY DENNIS
0-02-743629-2 SIMON & SCHUSTER $14.00
0-689-71486-6 ALADDIN PB $3.95

Stormy: Misty's Foal
ILLUSTRATED BY WESLEY DENNIS
0-689-71487-4 ALADDIN PB $3.95

O. **Henry**

The Gift of the Magi
0-671-64706-7 SIMON & SCHUSTER $14.00

E.T.A. **Hoffman**

The Nutcracker
The beloved 19th-century Christmas fantasy; Sendak's illustrations suggest the story's more disturbing and fantastic elements
TRANSLATED BY RALPH MANHEIM
ILLUSTRATED BY MAURICE SENDAK
1-56138-764-9 COURAGE $9.98

James **Howe**

Bunnicula: A Rabbit Tale of Mystery
0-689-80659-0 ALADDIN PB $3.99

Celery Stalks at Midnight
0-380-69054-3 AVON PB $4.50

Dew Drop Dead
The fourth mystery in the popular Sebastian Barth Mystery series uses rural Connecticut as a background for a tension-filled story of a murdered homeless man. Ages 8-12
0-689-31425-6 ATHENEUM $14.00

Howliday Inn
0-380-64543-2 AVON PB $3.99

Johanna **Hurwitz**

The Adventures of Ali Baba Bernstein
David changes his name to honor his favorite story book, *The Arabian Nights.* Thereafter his adventures fit his new personality
0-688-04161-2 MORROW $15.00
0-688-04345-3 MORROW LIBRARY EDITION $14.93

Aldo Applesauce
ILLUSTRATED BY JOHN WALLNER
0-14-034083-1 VIKING PB $3.99

Class Clown
Lucas is the smartest kid in Mrs. Hockaday's third grade, but he is always in trouble. Lucas eventually shows just how smart he is in a way that makes everyone happy
ILLUSTRATED BY SHEILA HAMANAKA
0-688-06723-9 MORROW $16.00

Joseph **Jacobs**

English Fairytales
0-679-42809-7 KNOPF $13.95

Brian **Jacques**

The Bellmaker: A Novel of Redwall
0-441-00315-X ACE PB $5.99

The Great Redwall Feast
ILLUSTRATED BY CHRISTOPHER DENISE
0-399-22707-5 PHILOMEL $18.95

Mariel of Redwall
ILLUSTRATED BY GARY CHALK
9-995-68730-5 AVON PB $5.50

Martin the Warrior
0-441-00186-6 ACE PB $5.99

Mattimeo
ILLUSTRATED BY GARY CHALK
9-995-61318-2 AVON PB $5.50

Mossflower
ILLUSTRATED BY GARY CHALK
0-380-70828-0 AVON PB $5.50

The Outcast of Redwall: A Tale from Redwall
ILLUSTRATED BY ALLEN CURLESS
0-399-22914-0 PHILOMEL $19.95

The Pearls of Lutra
0-399-22946-9 PHILOMEL $25.00

Redwall
0-380-70827-2 AVON PB $5.50

Salamandastron
ILLUSTRATED BY GARY CHALK
0-441-00031-2 ACE PB $5.99

Seven Strange & Ghostly Tales
0-380-71906-1 CAMELOT PB $3.99

John **Jakes**

Susanna of the Alamo: A True Story
A 19th-century Texas girl is the heroine of this authentic adventure story
ILLUSTRATED BY PAUL BACON
0-15-200592-7 HARCOURT BRACE $13.95
0-15-200595-1 HARCOURT BRACE PB $6.00

Will **James**

Smokey the Cow Horse
0-689-71682-6 ALADDIN PB $3.95

Paul B. **Janeczko**, editor

This Delicious Day
Sixty-five poems by Ogden Nash, John Ciardi, Lillian Moore, and others
0-531-05724-0 FRANKLIN WATTS $14.95

Tove **Jansson**

Finn Family Moomintroll
0-374-42307-5 FS&G PB $4.95

Norton **Juster**

The Phantom Tollbooth
A bored, uninspired schoolboy takes an adventurous drive through a toy tollbooth and begins a magical journey into a world of numbers and letters. Along the way, he learns to appreciate life and the many exciting things it has to offer
ILLUSTRATED BY JULES FEIFFER
0-394-82037-1 RANDOM HOUSE PB $4.99

Carol **Kendall**

Gammage Cup
ILLUSTRATED BY ERIK BLEGVAD
0-15-230575-0 HARCOURT BRACE PB $3.95

X.J. **Kennedy**

Brats
Ingenious and fun
ILLUSTRATED BY JAMES WATTS
0-689-50392-X MCELDERRY $14.00

Ken **Kesey**

The Sea Lion
A tale of a young, crook-backed orphan boy who proves himself in the harsh life of the sea. The pastel images float beneath the text, giving a visual feel of the vast and ghostly mythic Northwest Coast. All ages
ILLUSTRATED BY NEIL WALDMAN
0-14-054950-1 PUFFIN PB $4.99

Eric A. **Kimmel**

The Spotted Pony: A Collection of Hanukkah Stories
ILLUSTRATED BY EVERETT LEONARD
0-8234-0936-8 HOLIDAY HOUSE $15.95

Dick **King-Smith**

Babe: The Gallant Pig

ILLUSTRATED BY MARY RAYNER

0-679-88361-4 BULLSEYE PB.......$3.99

Rudyard **Kipling**

The Jungle Book

A handsome new edition, illustrated in color, introduces another generation to the adventures of Mowgli and his jungle compatriots. An essential addition to the library of any young reader

0-06-106286-3 HARPERCOLLINS PB.......$4.99

Just So Stories

The full text edition, illustrated by Kipling himself

See also **19TH-CENTURY FICTION** under **THE 19TH-CENTURY** in **LITERATURE OF THE BRITISH ISLES**

0-14-035075-6 PENGUIN PB.......$2.99

Jim **Kjelgaard**

Big Red

A brisk 1945 adventure about a country boy and the training of a champion red setter

ILLUSTRATED BY CARL PFEUFFER

0-8234-0007-7 HOLIDAY HOUSE.......$16.95

0-553-15434-6 SKYLARK PB.......$4.50

Outlaw Red

ILLUSTRATED BY CARL PFEUFFER

0-553-15686-1 BDD PB.......$3.99

Kenneth **Koch** & Kate **Farrell**, editors

Talking to the Sun: An Illustrated Anthology of Poems for Young People

A lavishly illustrated collection with artwork from the collection of the Metropolitan Museum of Art

0-8050-0144-1 HOLT.......$24.95

Kenneth Koch

E.L. **Konigsburg**

From the Mixed-Up Files of Mrs. Basil E. Frankweiler

Two precocious suburban children run away to New York and make their home in the Metropolitan Museum of Art. An original story told with a humorous purposefulness, telling children they are far more resourceful than they usually imagine. Newbery Medal 1968

0-689-20586-4 ATHENEUM.......$15.00

0-440-43180-8 DELL PB.......$4.99

Journey to an 800 Number

A speedily told story of a miniature preppy and his animal trainer dad

0-689-30901-5 ATHENEUM.......$15.00

A Proud Taste for Scarlet and Miniver

0-440-47201-6 DELL PB.......$4.50

Selma **Lagerlof**

The Wonderful Adventures of Nils

0-486-28611-8 DOVER PB.......$6.95

Albert **Lamorisse**

The Red Balloon

The adventures of a solitary little boy and his red balloon told in stills made from the sad and charming French film of the same name. In the end the hero escapes a gang of bullies and soars off into the skies of Paris

0-385-14297-8 DOUBLEDAY PB.......$10.95

Andrew **Lang**

The Blue Fairy Book

See also **YOUNG ADULT FICTION**

0-486-21437-0 DOVER PB.......$7.95

The Yellow Fairy Book

0-486-21674-8 DOVER PB.......$7.95

Eleanor F. **Lattimore**

Little Pear: The Story of a Little Chinese Boy

0-15-246685-1 HARCOURT BRACE PB.......$6.00

Robert **Lawson**

Ben and Me: A New and Astonishing Life of Benjamin Franklin as Written by His Good Mouse Amos

0-316-51730-5 LITTLE, BROWN PB.......$5.95

Rabbit Hill

0-14-031010-X VIKING PB.......$3.99

Lois **Lenski**

Strawberry Girl

Story of a "strawberry family" in rural 1940s Florida and a way of life that has long disappeared. Newbery Medal 1946

ILLUSTRATED BY LOIS LENSKI

0-397-30109-X LIPPINCOTT.......$16.00

Julius **Lester**

More Tales of Uncle Remus: Further Adventures of Brer Rabbit, His Friends, Enemies, and Others

0-8037-0419-4 DIAL BOOKS.......$16.99

The Tales of Uncle Remus: The Adventures of Brer Rabbit

0-8037-0271-X DUTTON.......$18.99

Julius **Lester** & Jerry **Pinkney**, illustrator

Further Tales of Uncle Remus: The Misadventures of Brer Rabbit, Brer Fox, Brer Wolf

0-8037-0610-3 DIAL BOOKS.......$17.99

C.S. **Lewis**

The Chronicles of Narnia

Intended to be read aloud, the *Chronicles of Narnia* will fascinate advanced nine-year-olds with strong narrative and engagingly odd characters. Older children can begin to decipher the mix of Christian theology, Arthurian myth, and classical mythology in these allegorical adventure stories, which deal with grander themes than are usual in children's literature

ILLUSTRATED BY PAULINE BAYNES

0-06-447119-5 HARPERCOLLINS PB.......$27.75

The Lion, the Witch, and the Wardrobe

Lewis's enthralling adventure story and well-veiled Christian allegory, in which four British schoolchildren find the door to a magical land through an abandoned wardrobe.

ILLUSTRATED BY PAULINE BAYNES

0-06-023481-4 HARPERCOLLINS.......$15.00

Prince Caspian

ILLUSTRATED BY PAULINE BAYNES

0-02-044430-3 HARPERCOLLINS PB.......$7.95

The Voyage of the Dawn Treader

0-02-044440-0 HARPERCOLLINS PB.......$7.95

The Silver Chair

ILLUSTRATED BY PAULINE BAYNES

0-06-023495-4 HARPERCOLLINS.......$15.00

The Horse and His Boy

ILLUSTRATED BY PAULINE BAYNES

0-06-440501-X HARPERCOLLINS PB.......$5.95

The Magician's Nephew

ILLUSTRATED BY PAULINE BAYNES

0-02-044390-0 HARPERCOLLINS PB.......$5.95

The Last Battle

ILLUSTRATED BY PAULINE BAYNES

0-06-440503-6 HARPERCOLLINS PB.......$5.95

Astrid **Lindgren**

Pippi Longstocking

Pippi is the little Swedish girl who lives all by herself with a pet monkey and a big horse. She does exactly as she pleases and has a terrific time doing it

ILLUSTRATED BY LOUIS GLANZMAN

0-14-030957-8 VIKING PB.......$3.99

Barbro **Lindgren**

The Wild Baby

0-688-00601-9 MORROW LIBRARY EDITION.......$15.93

Janet Taylor **Lisle**

Afternoon of the Elves

0-531-05837-9 ORCHARD.......$14.95

0-531-08437-X ORCHARD LIBRARY EDITION.......$15.99

Hugh **Lofting**

The Story of Doctor Dolittle

Doctor Dolittle understands what animals are saying. He doesn't care about money except for the few pennies needed to feed his many animal house guests. Written in the 1920s, and long out of print, *Dolittle* has been revised and reissued so that children can again enjoy these eloquent fantasies about the need to care for others

0-440-48307-7 YEARLING PB.......$3.99

The Voyages of Doctor Dolittle

Newbery Medal 1923

0-440-40002-3 BDD PB.......$4.99

Bette Bao **Lord**

In the Year of the Boar and Jackie Robinson

A Chinese immigrant in a working-class Brooklyn neighborhood learns English, the piano, and stickball, in that order

ILLUSTRATED BY MARC SIMONT

0-06-440175-8 TROPHY PB $4.50

Lois **Lowry**

Anastasia, Absolutely

0-395-74521-7 HOUGHTON MIFFLIN $13.95

Anastasia Again!

0-440-40009-0 YEARLING PB $3.99

Anastasia, Ask Your Analyst

0-440-40289-1 YEARLING PB $3.99

Anastasia at this Address

0-440-40652-8 YEARLING PB $3.99

Anastasia at Your Service

0-440-40290-5 YEARLING PB $3.99

Anastasia Has the Answers

0-440-40087-2 YEARLING PB $3.99

Anastasia Krupnik

Ten-year-old Anastasia writes down all her trials and confusions in her secret green notebook. The Anastasia books are a delightful series of adventures that look honestly and optimistically at the life of a maturing young girl

84-239-2779-2 LECTORUM PB $9.75

0-440-40852-0 YEARLING PB $3.99

Anastasia on Her Own

The challenges involved when 11- or 12-year-olds take on new responsibilities

0-440-40291-3 YEARLING PB $3.50

Number the Stars

Newbery Medal winner for the most distinguished contribution to American literature for children

0-395-51060-0 HOUGHTON MIFFLIN $14.95

0-440-40327-8 DELL PB $4.99

Switcharound

Boy and girl siblings go off on an unexpected visit to their father and are given responsibilities they don't enjoy

0-440-48415-4 DELL PB $3.50

Alison **Lurie**, editor

The Oxford Book of Modern Fairy Tales

See also **ANTHOLOGIES** under **SUPERNATURAL FANTASY AND HORROR** under **SCIENCE FICTION AND FANTASY** in **POPULAR READING**

0-19-214218-6 OXFORD $30.00

0-19-282385-X OXFORD PB $14.95

Betty **MacDonald**

Hello Mrs. Piggle-Wiggle

0-06-440149-9 TROPHY PB $4.50

Mrs. Piggle-Wiggle

0-06-440148-0 TROPHY PB $4.50

George **MacDonald**

Castle Warlock

1-88108-403-5 JOHANNESEN $16.00

At the Back of the North Wind

A young boy is literally swept off his feet as readers are drawn into a greater belief in the supernatural with each imaginative adventure

1-88108-407-8 JOHANNESEN $16.00

Donal Gran

1-88108-402-7 JOHANNESEN $16.00

The Golden Key

ILLUSTRATED BY MAURICE SENDAK

AFTERWORD BY W.H. AUDEN

0-374-42590-6 SUNBURST PB $4.95

Guild Court: A London Story

A group of mismatched characters, from a street orphan to an uptown lawyer, interact together. They eventually find themselves forced to choose a path of faith…or else

1-88108-410-8 JOHANNESEN $16.00

Home Again/The Elect Lady

1-88108-411-6 JOHANNESEN $16.00

The Light Princess and Other Fairy Tales

A selection of Victorian fairy tales

1-88108-416-7 JOHANNESEN $16.00

Paul Faber, Surgeon

1-88108-408-6 JOHANNESEN $16.00

Princess and Curdie

A sequel to *The Princess and the Goblin*

1-88108-415-9 JOHANNESEN $20.00

The Princess and the Goblin

A Victorian fairy tale where children of the light battle the darkness of the underground world. The first of the *Princess* books

1-88108-414-0 JOHANNESEN $20.00

The Princess and the Goblin

0-688-06604-6 MORROW $22.00

Ranald Bannerman's Boyhood

1-88108-413-2 JOHANNESEN $20.00

A Rough Shaking

A young boy is orphaned when his parents are killed in an earthquake. He learns survival skills through his relationships with small animals

1-88108-404-3 JOHANNESEN $16.00

Sir Gibbie

1-88108-401-9 JOHANNESEN $18.00

There and Back

A young man searching for his parents encounters love and jealousy in Victorian England

1-88108-405-1 JOHANNESEN $16.00

The Vicar's Daughter

1-88108-409-4 JOHANNESEN $16.00

What's Mine's Mine

1-88108-400-0 JOHANNESEN $18.00

The Wise Woman/Gutta Percha Willie

This book is a must-read for all parents, parents-to-be, and children ages 7 and up

1-88108-417-5 JOHANNESEN $16.00

Suse **MacDonald**

Alphabatics

Animated letters invite children to look by moving up, moving down, or even leaving the page. Caldecott Honor Book 1987

0-02-761520-0 SIMON & SCHUSTER $16.95

Patricia **MacLachlan**

Baby

0-440-41145-9 BDD PB $3.99

Journey

0-440-40809-1 YEARLING PB $3.99

Sarah, Plain and Tall

Sarah answers Papa's advertisement for a mail-order bride, but the children are afraid she will not want to stay. Newbery Medal 1986

0-06-024101-2 HARPERCOLLINS $12.95

0-06-447149-7 TROPHY PB $2.25

Jan **Mark**, editor

The Oxford Book of Children's Stories

0-19-214228-3 OXFORD $30.00

Bill **Martin**, Jr. & others

Knots on a Counting Rope

0-8050-0571-4 HOLT $15.95

Marianna **Mayer**

Baba Yaga and Vasilisa the Brave

ILLUSTRATED BY K.Y. CRAFT

0-688-08500-8 MORROW $16.00

Gretchen W. **Mayo**

Star Tales

0-8027-7345-1 WALKER PB $5.95

Robert **McCloskey**

Homer Price

"This is a real boy, thinking out loud and living out these rich and hilarious dilemmas with solemn and devastating humor…The American comic genius in its top form" —James Daugherty

0-670-37729-5 VIKING $15.99

Robin **McKinley**

The Blue Sword

Newbery Honor Book 1983

0-688-00938-7 MORROW $16.00

0-441-06880-4 ACE PB $5.50

The Outlaws of Sherwood

0-688-07178-3 GREENWILLOW $15.00

0-441-64451-1 ACE PB $5.50

Patricia **McKissack**

The Dark-Thirty: Southern Tales of the Supernatural

ILLUSTRATED BY BRIAN PINKNEY

0-679-81863-4 KNOPF $16.00

Jean **Merrill**

Pushcart War

0-440-47147-8 YEARLING PB $4.50

The Toothpaste Millionaire

ILLUSTRATED BY JAN PALMER

0-395-66954-5 HOUGHTON MIFFLIN PB $4.95

A.A. **Milne**

The Collected Edition: The World of Christopher Robin

Pooh was just a teddy bear when he first appeared in print. The hero, Milne's son Christopher Robin, is a small boy doing things small boys did 60 years ago. Contemporary children of the appropriate ages (six and under) won't understand all of it, but the rhymes do keep bouncing along

ILLUSTRATED BY ERNEST H. SHEPARD

0-525-44452-1 DUTTON $39.98

The House at Pooh Corner

Tigger drops in for breakfast, and Christopher Robin goes away to the place nobody knows

ILLUSTRATED BY ERNEST H. SHEPARD

0-525-44444-0 DUTTON $10.99
0-14-036122-7 PUFFIN PB $3.99

Now We Are Six

See also **BOOKS FOR AGES FIVE, SIX, AND SEVEN**

ILLUSTRATED BY ERNEST H. SHEPARD

0-525-44960-4 DUTTON $20.00
0-14-036124-3 PUFFIN PB $3.99

The Pooh Story Book

Pooh in large format with large print and color illustrations. The book contains one chapter from *Winnie-the-Pooh* and two from *The House at Pooh Corner*, two classics written when young children apparently had a longer attention span and a larger vocabulary

ILLUSTRATED BY ERNEST H. SHEPARD

0-525-37546-5 DUTTON $13.99

A.A. Milne

When We Were Very Young

ILLUSTRATED BY ERNEST H. SHEPARD

0-525-44961-2 DUTTON $20.00
0-14-036123-5 PUFFIN PB $3.99

Winnie-the-Pooh

Milne's quintessentially British fantasy either tends to inspire devotion or leave readers wondering what the fuss is all about. Distinguished by puns and other wordplay, the comedy is invariably deft and amusing. But readers (or listeners) who are not wholehearted members of the Pooh fan club may simply grow tired of all those words.
Children who like Pooh in moderation will enjoy the more straightforward sections, such as the first chapter of *The House at Pooh Corner*, in which Tigger makes his appearance.

See also **BOOKS FOR AGES FIVE, SIX, AND SEVEN**

ILLUSTRATED BY ERNEST H. SHEPARD

0-525-44443-2 DUTTON $10.99
0-14-036121-9 PUFFIN PB $3.99

The World of Christopher Robin

ILLUSTRATED BY ERNEST H. SHEPARD

0-525-44448-3 DUTTON $19.99

The World of Winnie-the-Pooh & House at Pooh Corner

A collected edition with special color illustrations

ILLUSTRATED BY ERNEST H. SHEPARD

0-525-44447-5 DUTTON $19.99

L. M. **Montgomery**

Anne of Green Gables

An orphan is sent to a surly farm family and proves her worth. A classic

0-679-44475-0 EVERYMAN'S $13.95
0-14-036741-1 PUFFIN PB $3.99

Anne of Avonlea

The same endearing character that decades of children loved in *Anne of Green Gables* is now a young woman. Still one of the most beloved children's series in print

0-553-21314-8 BDD PB $2.95

Anne of Windy Poplars

0-553-48065-0 BDD PB $3.50

Anne Lindbergh **Morrow**

Hunky-Dory Dairy

ILLUSTRATED BY JULIE BRINCKLOE

0-15-237449-3 HARCOURT BRACE $14.95

Farley **Mowat**

Owls in the Family

0-553-15585-7 BDD PB $3.99

Phyllis R. **Naylor**

Reluctantly Alice

0-440-40685-4 YEARLING PB $3.50

Phyllis Reynolds **Naylor**

The Agony of Alice

0-440-40051-1 YEARLING PB $3.99

Alice in April

Alice worries about the responsiblities of turning 13

0-440-40944-6 YEARLING PB $3.50

Alice in Between

0-440-41064-9 BDD PB $3.99

Alice in Lace

0-689-80358-3 ATHENEUM $15.00

Alice in Rapture, Sort of

0-440-40462-2 YEARLING PB $3.50

Alice the Brave

It's August and the whole gang is having a great time swimming and frolicking at the pool—except Alice, who is afraid of deep water

ILLUSTRATED BY ELIZABETH SAYLES

0-689-80598-5 ALADDIN PB $3.99

All but Alice

0-440-40918-7 YEARLING PB $3.50

Shiloh

"Fueled by the love and trust of Shiloh, Marty displays a wisdom and strength beyond his years. Naylor offers a moving and powerful look at the best and the worst of human nature as well as the shades of gray that color most of life's dilemmas" —*Booklist*, starred review

0-440-40752-4 YEARLING PB $4.99

E. **Nesbit**

The Enchanted Castle

0-14-036743-8 PUFFIN PB $3.99

The Five Children and It

ILLUSTRATED BY H.R. MILLAR

0-89967-036-9 BUCCANEER $21.95

Five Children and It

0-14-036735-7 PUFFIN PB $3.99

The Railway Children

When their father goes away for a little while, three children and their mother leave their home in London for a small house in the country. Soon they begin to wonder where their father is and will he ever return. Adapted into a popular children's film

ILLUSTRATED BY C.E. BROCK

0-14-036671-7 PUFFIN PB $3.99

The Story of the Treasure Seekers

ILLUSTRATED BY CECIL LESLIE

0-14-036706-3 PUFFIN PB $3.99

Joan Lowery **Nixon**

And Maggie Makes Three

0-15-250355-2 HARCOURT BRACE $12.95

Ursula **Nordstrom**

The Secret Language

A little girl goes to boarding school, is miserable, makes friends, and learns self-confidence. The calmly written story has a real ring of truth

0-06-440022-0 TROPHY PB $3.95

Sterling **North**

Rascal

ILLUSTRATED BY JOHN SCHOENHERR

0-14-034445-4 PUFFIN PB $3.99

Mary **Norton**

Bed-Knob and Broomstick: A Combined Edition of the Magic Bed-Knob & Bonfires and Broomsticks

ILLUSTRATED BY ERIK BLEGVAD

0-15-206231-9 HARCOURT BRACE PB $3.95

Mary **Norton**

The Borrowers

Pod, Homily, and Arrietty live in a wonderful old house in the country. Rather, they live under the house, in a home of their own furnished with cotton reels, safety pins, and other things filched from the human inhabitants. It's cozy enough but the girl, Arrietty, is lonely and curious. Where are the other Borrowers, or are they the last ones? What does Pa do when Borrowing? A compulsive read, the story of the Borrowers comes close to tragedy when Arrietty befriends a human

ILLUSTRATED BY BETH & JOE KRUSH

0-15-209987-5 HARCOURT BRACE $13.95
0-15-200086-0 HARCOURT BRACE PB $4.95

The Borrowers Afield

ILLUSTRATED BY BETH & JOE KRUSH

0-15-210166-7 HARCOURT BRACE $14.00
0-15-210535-2 HARCOURT BRACE PB $5.00

The Borrowers Afloat

ILLUSTRATED BY BETH & JOE KRUSH

0-15-210345-7 HARCOURT BRACE $15.00
0-15-210534-4 HARCOURT BRACE PB $6.00

The Borrowers Aloft

ILLUSTRATED BY BETH & JOE KRUSH

0-15-210524-7 HARCOURT BRACE $14.00
0-15-210533-6 HARCOURT BRACE PB $4.95

The Borrowers Avenged

ILLUSTRATED BY BETH & JOE KRUSH

0-15-210530-1 HARCOURT BRACE $15.00
0-15-210532-8 HARCOURT BRACE PB $5.00

Naomi Shihab **Nye**

This Same Sky: A Collection of Poems from Around the World

Nye *(Different Ways to Pray, Hugging the Jukebox)* has selected 129 extraordinary poetic voices from around the world for this anthology. From Chinese poet Gu Cheng to Israeli Yehuda Amichai to Bangladeshi Farhad Mazhar, each work is unique yet connected to the others under "this same sky." An unusual and unusally moving anthology

0-02-768440-7 SIMON & SCHUSTER $17.00

Robert C. **O'Brien**

Mrs. Frisby and the Rats of NIMH

Laboratory rats observe people from their cages, escape, and use their observations to create a society based on human technology. A haunting fantasy about love, loyalty, and sacrifice. Newbery Medal 1972

0-689-20651-8 ATHENEUM $16.00
0-689-71068-2 ALADDIN PB $3.95

The Secret of NIMH

0-590-41708-8 SCHOLASTIC PB $3.99

Scott **O'Dell**

Island of the Blue Dolphins

An American Indian girl is left on her tribe's abandoned Pacific island. Her survival and courage are gripping. Newbery Medal 1961

0-395-53680-4 HOUGHTON MIFFLIN $18.95
0-440-43988-4 DELL PB $4.99

Mary **O'Hara**

My Friend Flicka

0-06-080902-7 HARPERCOLLINS PB $5.50

Doris **Orgel**

Sarah's Room

An old-fashioned, pleasantly simple rhyming book accompanied by early Sendak illustrations

ILLUSTRATIONS BY MAURICE SENDAK

0-06-443238-6 HARPERCOLLINS PB $4.95

Barbara **Park**

Almost Starring Skinnybones

0-394-82591-8 BULLSEYE PB $3.99

Skinnybones

Skinnybones makes up for a diminutive physique with his one-liners. His Little League team hasn't won in years, but Skinnybones scores an unexpected success

0-394-94988-9
RANDOM LIBRARY LIBRARY EDITION $13.99
0-394-82596-9 BULLSEYE PB $3.99

Katherine **Paterson**

The Great Gilly Hopkins

A social worker has just about given up on Gilly when she places her with a new and surprising foster family. Gilly's unhappiness is skillfully depicted without condoning her intolerably bad behavior. Newbery Honor Book 1978

0-690-03837-2 CROWELL LIBRARY EDITION $14.00
0-06-440201-0 TROPHY PB $4.50

The King's Equal

ILLUSTRATED BY VLADIMIR VAGIN

0-06-443396-X TROPHY PB $6.95

Lyddie

0-14-037389-6 PUFFIN PB $3.99

Of Nightingales that Weep

ILLUSTRATED BY HARU WELLS

0-06-440282-7 TROPHY PB $4.50

Gary **Paulsen**

Dogsong

An Eskimo boy's life is grim until he enters a dog-sleigh race. Newbery Honor Book 1986

See also YOUNG ADULT FICTION

0-02-770180-8 SIMON & SCHUSTER $16.00
0-14-032235-3 VIKING PB $4.99

The River

0-440-40753-2 YEARLING PB $4.50

Phillipa **Pearce**

Tom's Midnight Garden

Provoked by an old lady's memories, a boy travels back into time

0-06-440445-5 HARPERCOLLINS PB $4.95

Robert **Peck**

Soup

The first in a series about the audacious schemes of two boys who live in a small Vermont town in the '30s. Fun, good-natured

ILLUSTRATED BY CHARLES ROBINSON

0-440-48186-4 DELL PB $3.99

Eleanor H. **Porter**

Pollyanna

0-14-035023-3 VIKING PB $3.50

Howard **Pyle**

The Story of the Champions of the Round Table

0-684-18171-1 ATHENEUM $19.95
0-486-21883-X DOVER PB $8.95

The Wonder Clock: Or Four and Twenty Marvelous Tales

0-486-21446-X DOVER PB $8.95

Ellen **Raskin**

The Mysterious Disappearance of Leon (I Mean Noel)

0-14-032945-5 VIKING PB $4.99

Wilson **Rawls**

Summer of the Monkeys

0-385-11450-8 DOUBLEDAY $15.95
0-553-29818-6 STARFIVE PB $4.99

Where the Red Fern Grows

A young boy receives a team of coon dogs as pets. The emotional story of the relationship between them makes this a must-read for children of all ages

0-440-41267-6 YEARLING PB $4.99

Mordecai **Richler**

A popular Montreal writer notable for his ability to elicit sympathy for unsympathetic characters.

Jacob Two-Two and the Dinosaur

Jacob Two-Two's exotic pet becomes the interest of politicians and scientists. A funny and sophisticated story, written with a plainly satirical bite

ILLUSTRATED BY NORMAN EYOLFSON

0-679-87042-3 BULLSEYE PB $3.99

Jacob Two-Two Meets the Hooded Fang

A short, sharply conceived, and verbally adept story about a little boy's bizarrely comic adventure

0-679-85403-7 RANDOM HOUSE PB $3.50

Willo Davis **Roberts**

To Grandmother's House We Go

Threatened with separation and placement in foster homes, Rosie, Nathan, and Kevin run away to a grandmother they have never met. They are soon involved in a well-written and satisfying mystery. Ages 8-12

0-689-31594-5 ATHENEUM $16.00
0-689-71838-1 ALADDIN PB $3.95

Barbara **Robinson**

The Best Christmas Pageant Ever

How the terrible Herdman kids come to be the stars of the Christmas pageant and the consequences. Told for laughs, and lots of them. Children don't seem to mind the sentimental ending

ILLUSTRATED BY JUDITH GLYNN BROWN

0-06-025043-7 HARPERCOLLINS $14.95
0-06-447044-X HARPERCOLLINS PB $3.95

Thomas **Rockwell**

How to Eat Fried Worms

A boy intends to do exactly that in a consistently funny story

0-440-44545-0 DELL PB $4.50

Mary **Rodgers**

Freaky Friday

Annabel changes into her mother and finds it's tougher being Mom than she'd imagined

0-06-025048-8 HARPERCOLLINS $15.95
0-06-440046-8 HARPERCOLLINS PB $4.50

Summer Switch

A boy on his way to camp finds himself traveling instead to Hollywood in the body of his scriptwriter father. A captivating fantasy theme explored with characteristic humor

0-06-025058-5 HARPERCOLLINS $14.95

Jane **Rosenberg**

Dance Me a Story: Twelve Tales from the Classic Ballets

The plots of great ballets, unfolded with the dancer's point of view in mind

INTRODUCTION BY MERRILL ASHLEY

0-500-27739-7 HUDSON ANNEX PB $15.95

Salman **Rushdie**

Haroun and the Sea of Stories

"Salman Rushdie has in his own veins the flow of the Sea of Stories, fantastical, funny, whooping through drama and comedy, good and evil, personified in creatures delightful or frightening"—Nadine Gordimer

See also **THE MIDDLE GENERATION** under **20TH-CENTURY BRITISH AND IRISH FICTION** in **LITERATURE OF THE BRITISH ISLES**

See also **20TH-CENTURY LITERATURE OF THE INDIAN SUBCONTINENT** under **LITERATURES OF INDIA** in **LITERATURE OF EUROPE, AFRICA, AND ASIA**

0-14-015737-9 PENGUIN PB $11.95

And in the depths of the city, beyond an old zone of ruined buildings that looked like broken hearts, there lived a happy young fellow by the name of Haroun, the only child of the storyteller Rashid Khalifa, whose cheerfulness was famous throughout that unhappy metropolis, and whose never-ending stream of tall, short and winding tales had earned him not one but two nicknames. To his admirers he was Rashid the Ocean of Notions, as stuffed with cheery stories as the sea was full of glumfish; but to his jealous rivals he was the Shah of Blah.

HAROUN AND THE SEA OF STORIES

Carl **Sandburg** & others

Rootabaga Stories, Part One

0-15-269065-4 HARCOURT BRACE PB $5.00

Rootabaga Stories, Part Two

0-15-269063-8 HARCOURT BRACE PB $5.95

Alvin **Schwartz**

More Scary Stories to Tell in the Dark: Collected and Retold from Folklore

ILLUSTRATED BY STEPHEN GAMMELL

0-397-32081-7 LIPPINCOTT $14.95
0-06-440177-4 TROPHY PB $3.95

Scary Stories to Tell in the Dark

Short folk tales that children will enjoy reading at Halloween

ILLUSTRATED BY STEPHEN GAMMELL

0-397-31926-6 LIPPINCOTT $14.95
0-06-440170-7 HARPERCOLLINS PB $3.95

Scary Stories 3: More Tales to Chill Your Bones

Just when you thought it was safe to turn the lights out, here comes another spooky set of 25 spine-tingling tales about swamp creatures, strange dreams, and other disturbing phenomena. Ages 9 and up

0-06-021794-4 HARPERCOLLINS $14.95
0-06-440418-8 HARPERCOLLINS PB $3.95

Jon **Scieszka**

Knights of the Kitchen Table

ILLUSTRATED BY LANE SMITH

0-14-034603-1 PUFFIN PB $2.99

Math Curse

ILLUSTRATED BY LANE SMITH

0-670-86194-4 VIKING $16.99

The Good, the Bad, and the Goofy

ILLUSTRATED BY LANE SMITH

0-14-036170-7 PUFFIN PB $2.99

Pete **Seeger**

Abiyoyo: South African Lullaby and Folk Story

A little boy and his father make a dreaded giant disappear

ILLUSTRATED BY MICHAEL HAYS

0-02-781490-4 SIMON & SCHUSTER $16.00

Lore **Segal**

Mrs. Lovewright and Purrless Her Cat

The irritable Mrs. Lovewright becomes a different person once she accepts the friendship of a stubborn cat

0-394-86817-X KNOPF $14.00

Tell Me a Mitzi

0-374-37392-2 FS&G $17.00
0-374-47502-4 SUNBURST PB $5.95

Tor **Seidler**

The Wainscott Weasel

ILLUSTRATED BY FRED MARCELLINO

0-06-205911-4 TROPHY PB $9.95

George **Selden**

Chester Cricket's New Home

ILLUSTRATED BY GARTH WILLIAMS

0-440-41246-3 DELL PB $3.99

A Cricket in Times Square

A lovely little fantasy about a cricket and a boy whose Italian family runs a Times Square newsstand. Newbery Honor Book

ILLUSTRATED BY GARTH WILLIAMS

0-374-31650-3 FS&G $16.00
0-440-41563-2 DELL PB $4.99

Harry Kitten and Tucker Mouse

Animal heroes encounter the perilous New York City streets as they search for a new home

ILLUSTRATED BY GARTH WILLIAMS

0-374-32860-9 FS&G $16.00

Maurice **Sendak**

Higglety Pigglety Pop: Or, There Must Be More to Life

0-06-443021-9 TROPHY PB $5.95

Where the Wild Things Are

Familiarity has tamed the Wild Things somewhat, but young readers are still likely to be startled by the curiously menacing monsters created out of a hodgepodge of mythical and real beasts

See also **BOOKS FOR AGES FIVE, SIX, AND SEVEN**

0-06-025492-0 HARPERCOLLINS $15.00
0-06-025493-9 HARPERCREST $14.89
0-06-443178-9 TROPHY PB $4.95

Anna **Sewell**

Black Beauty

Sewell's affecting novel about a horse is adapted by an accomplished children's writer and illustrated by a Caldecott Medal winner.

EDITED BY ROBIN MCKINLEY

ILLUSTRATED BY SUSAN JEFFERS

0-88411-065-6 AMEREON $19.95
0-140-36684-9 PUFFIN PB $3.99

Marjorie Weinman **Sharmat**

Nate the Great and the Fishy Prize

Nate the Great is a popular boy detective whose faithful hound Sludge invariably helps him solve his cases

ILLUSTRATED BY MARC SIMONT

0-440-40039-2 DELL PB $3.99

Nate the Great and the Lost List

ILLUSTRATED BY MARC SIMONT

0-698-20646-0 MCCANN $13.95

Nate the Great and the Missing Key

ILLUSTRATED BY MARC SIMONT

0-440-46191-X DELL PB $3.50

Nate the Great and the Snowy Trail

ILLUSTRATED BY MARC SIMONT

0-440-46276-2 DELL PB $3.50

Margaret **Sidney**

Five Little Peppers & How They Grew

0-14-035127-2 VIKING PB $3.99

Shel **Silverstein**

Falling Up: Poems and Drawings

See also **BOOKS FOR AGES FIVE, SIX, AND SEVEN**

0-06-024802-5 HARPERCOLLINS $16.95

The Giving Tree

Classic story by one of the best children's storytellers of this century. Shel Silverstein tells the story of lifelong love and the power of friendship in this tale about a boy and a tree

See also **BOOKS FOR AGES FIVE, SIX, AND SEVEN**

0-06-025665-6 HARPERCOLLINS $14.95

A Light in the Attic

See also **BOOKS FOR AGES FIVE, SIX, AND SEVEN**

0-06-025673-7 HARPERCOLLINS $16.95

Where the Sidewalk Ends: Poems and Drawings

Possibly the most popular book of verse published in the last 20 years; the cautionary verse is exceptionally good

See also **BOOKS FOR AGES FIVE, SIX, AND SEVEN**

0-06-025667-2 HARPERCOLLINS $16.95

Isaac Bashevis **Singer**

The Power of Light: Eight Stories of Hanukkah

The late Nobel Prize-winning author presents eight autobiographically inspired tales, one for each night of Hanukkah. His simple yet powerful tales of the triumph of love are further enhanced by Irene Lieblich's full-color illustrations, culled from memories of her childhood village near Singer's own in Poland. All ages

See also **SABBATH AND HOLIDAYS** under **HOW-TO: RITUAL AND PRACTICE** under **JUDAISM** in **RELIGION, SPIRITUALITY, AND PHILOSOPHY**

See also **ISAAC BASHEVIS SINGER** under **YIDDISH LANGUAGE AND LITERATURE** in **LITERATURE OF EUROPE, AFRICA, AND ASIA**

ILLUSTRATED BY IRENE LIEBLICH

0-374-36099-5 SUNBURST $15.00
0-374-45984-3 FS&G PB $8.95

Stories For Children

See also **ISAAC BASHEVIS SINGER** under **YIDDISH LANGUAGE AND LITERATURE** in **LITERATURE OF EUROPE, AFRICA, AND ASIA**

0-374-37266-7 FS&G $22.95
0-374-46489-8 SUNBURST PB $13.00

Doris **Smith**

Return to Bitter Creek

0-14-032223-X VIKING PB $4.99

Doris Buchanan **Smith**

A Taste of Blackberries

0-690-80512-8 HARPERCREST $13.89

Zilpha Keatley **Snyder**

Black and Blue Magic

A boy named after Harry Houdini is too clumsy to imitate the stage magic his father once performed but learns about an infinitely more powerful magic from a figure out of the past. A refreshingly unpretentious fantasy

0-689-71848-9 ALADDIN PB $3.95

Zilpha Keatly **Snyder**

The Egypt Game

Newbery Honor Book 1968

0-689-30006-9 ATHENEUM $16.00
0-440-42225-6 DELL PB $4.99

The Famous Stanley Kidnapping Case

A mystery adventure about an unorthodox family

0-440-42485-2 DELL PB $3.99

Zilpha Keatley **Snyder**

The Witches of Worm

Newbery Honor Book 1974

ILLUSTRATED BY ALTON RAIBLE

0-689-30066-2 ATHENEUM $16.00
0-440-49727-2 YEARLING PB $3.99

Virginia **Sorensen**

Miracles on Maple Hill

When a family goes to live on a farm in Pennsylvania they learn to love the land and each other. Newbery Medal 1957

ILLUSTRATED BY BETH AND JOE KRUSH

0-15-254561-1 HARCOURT BRACE PB $6.00

Gary **Soto**

Baseball in April and Other Stories

0-15-205721-8 HARCOURT BRACE PB $6.00

Elizabeth **Speare**

Calico Captive

0-440-41156-4 DELL PB $4.50

Elizabeth George **Speare**

The Sign of the Beaver

Newbery Honor Book 1984

0-395-33890-5 HOUGHTON MIFFLIN $14.95
0-440-47900-2 DELL PB $4.50

The Witch of Blackbird Pond

Set in 17th-century New England, this is a surprisingly unflattering depiction of the unpleasant aspects of the colonists' hard work, thrift, and self-sufficiency. Newbery Medal 1959

0-395-07114-3 HOUGHTON MIFFLIN $14.95
0-440-99577-9 LAUREL LEAF PB $4.99

Jerry **Spinelli**

Maniac Magee: A Novel

0-06-447151-9 TROPHY PB $2.25

Johanna **Spyri**

Heidi

A freshly illustrated version of the tale of the Swiss orphan, her ornery grandpa, and her beloved mountains

ILLUSTRATED BY RUTH SANDERSON

0-88301-389-4 PENDULUM PB $2.95

William **Steig**

Abel's Island

Abel is an unlikely Robinson Crusoe. But there he is, a dandy mouse, marooned on an uninhabited island. Steig's text is as elegant as his illustrations. Newbery Honor Book 1977

0-374-40016-4 FS&G PB $4.95

The Real Thief

0-374-46208-9 FS&G PB $3.95

Robert Louis **Stevenson**

Kidnapped

See also **19TH-CENTURY FICTION** under **THE 19TH-CENTURY** in **LITERATURE OF THE BRITISH ISLES**

0-00-273017-0 HARPERCOLLINS PB $12.00

Robert Louis Stevenson

Treasure Island

The novel that revolutionized popular fiction by inventing a more realistic style of adventure story

See also **19TH-CENTURY FICTION** under **THE 19TH-CENTURY** in **LITERATURE OF THE BRITISH ISLES**

EDITED BY EMMA LETLEY

0-19-281681-0 OXFORD PB $5.95

The Strange Case of Dr. Jekyll and Mr. Hyde

An elegant new edition of the classic statement of the dual-identity theme

See also **EARLY SCIENCE FICTION** under **SCIENCE FICTION AND FANTASY** in **POPULAR READING**

ILLUSTRATED BY BARRY MOSER

INTRODUCTION BY JOYCE CAROL OATES

0-89968-552-8 BUCCANEER $16.95
0-8032-4212-3 NEBRASKA $25.00

Mary **Stolz**

Stealing Home

0-06-440528-1 HARPERCOLLINS PB $4.50

Rosemary **Sutcliff**

Black Ships Before Troy: The Story of the Iliad

ILLUSTRATED BY ALAN LEE

0-385-31069-2 DELACORTE $19.95

Mildred **Taylor**

Let the Circle Be Unbroken

0-14-034892-1 PUFFIN PB $4.50

The Road to Memphis

0-14-036077-8 PUFFIN PB $3.99

Roll of Thunder, Hear My Cry

Cassie Logan is raised by a family determined not to surrender their freedom or humanity because they are black

See also **YOUNG ADULT FICTION**

0-8037-7473-7 DIAL BOOKS $15.99
0-14-034893-X PUFFIN PB $4.99

The Well: David's Story

0-8037-1802-0 DIAL BOOKS $14.99

Sydney **Taylor**

All-of-a-Kind Family Downtown

0-929093-01-1 TAYLP $14.95

All-of-a-Kind Family Uptown

0-929093-03-8 MADISON $14.95

All-of-A-Kind Family

These five little girls are a "stepping stone" family, each one two years apart. Their Lower East Side neighborhood is full of lively people, and the family celebrates the Jewish holidays with much ceremony

ILLUSTRATED BY HELEN JOHN

0-8446-6253-4 SMITH $17.55
0-440-40059-7 YEARLING PB $3.99

More All-of-a-Kind Family

0-929093-02-X ALPHA $15.95

Marvin **Terban**

I Think I Thought & Other Tricky Verbs

Tricky verbs reviewed with the help of amusing illustrations

ILLUSTRATED BY GIULIO MAESTRO

0-89919-290-4 HOUGHTON MIFFLIN PB $6.95

Albert **Terhune**

Lad: A Dog

0-14-036474-9 PUFFIN PB $4.99

Jane Resh **Thomas**

Saying Good-Bye to Grandma

A sensitive portrait of a girl attending her grandmother's funeral

ILLUSTRATED BY MARCIA SEWALL

0-89919-645-4 CLARION $15.95

0-395-54779-2 CLARION PB $6.95

James **Thurber**

Many Moons

A spoiled princess demands the moon and the kingdom is turned upside down as the king's wise men try to get it for her. Then a good-hearted young lad comes along and invents an acceptable solution. Caldecott Medal 1944

See also **BOOKS FOR AGES FIVE, SIX, AND SEVEN**

0-15-251873-8 HARCOURT BRACE $15.00

0-15-656980-9 HARCOURT BRACE PB $6.00

P.L. **Travers**

Mary Poppins

The fearsome British nanny recast as good fairy: enchantment mixed with never-speak-with-your-mouth-full morality

0-440-40406-1 DELL PB $4.50

Wallace **Tripp**

Marguerite, Go Wash Your Feet!

A collection of poetic nonsense, illustrated with cartoonish verve. For children eight and up

ILLUSTRATED BY WALLACE TRIPP

0-395-35392-0 HOUGHTON MIFFLIN $17.95

John **Tunis**

The Kid from Tomkinsville

The first in a series of recently reprinted novels from the 1940s, following Roy Tucker and the Brooklyn Dodgers without all the mythmaking. Written for a younger age group, but a cut above the usual kid's fare

See also **BASEBALL FICTION** under **BASEBALL** under **SPORTS** in **FOOD, TRAVEL, AND LEISURE**

0-15-242568-3 HARCOURT BRACE $14.95

0-15-242567-5 HARCOURT BRACE PB $3.95

Janwillem **Van De Wetering**

Hugh Pine

A short, charming fable about the difficulties involved in making decisions for others; the hero is a porcupine in a red hat

0-688-11799-6 BEECH TREE PB $3.95

Alice **Walker**

Finding the Green Stone

From the celebrated author of *The Color Purple*

ILLUSTRATED BY CATHERINE DECTER

0-15-227538-X HARCOURT BRACE $17.00

Barbara Brooks **Wallace**

Peppermints in the Parlor

A little girl comes to her wealthy aunt's home to discover terrible and sinister changes. A first-rate novel, peopled by two wicked spinsters, their pathetic elderly guests, and a courageous heroine

0-689-71680-X ALADDIN PB $3.95

Jill Paton **Walsh**

The Green Book

Child refugees travel by spaceship to settle on an unexplored planet

ILLUSTRATED BY LLOYD BLOOM

0-374-32778-5 FS&G $13.00

0-374-42802-6 FS&G PB $3.95

Gertrude Chandler **Warner**

The Boxcar Children (Boxcar Children, No 1)

0-8075-0852-7 WHITMAN PB $3.95

Gloria **Whelan** & Leslie W. **Bowman**

Night of the Full Moon (Stepping Stone Books)

0-679-87276-0 RANDOM HOUSE PB $3.99

E.B. **White**

Charlotte's Web

E.B. White was awarded the Laura Ingalls Wilder Medal in 1970 for his lifelong contributions to children's literature. No pig ever had a truer friend, and no one was ever as affectionate, loyal, and skillful as Charlotte A. Cavatica, the spider

ILLUSTRATED BY GARTH WILLIAMS

0-06-026385-7 HARPERCOLLINS $13.95

0-06-440055-7 HARPERCOLLINS PB $4.50

E.B. White Boxed Set: Charlotte's Web, The Trumpet of the Swan, and Stuart Little

White's beloved children's stories concern a gifted piglet saved from the slaughter by a spider, a mute swan who learns to communicate with a trumpet, and a dapper mouse-child who sets out to see the world in a toy automobile

0-06-440061-1 TROPHY PB $13.50

Stuart Little

Humorous episodes in the life of a mouse who goes out into the world dressed as a man

ILLUSTRATED BY GARTH WILLIAMS

0-06-026395-4 HARPERCOLLINS $13.95

0-06-440056-5 TROPHY PB $4.50

The Trumpet of the Swan

ILLUSTRATED BY EDWARD FRASCINO

0-06-026397-0 HARPERCOLLINS $13.95

0-06-440048-4 TROPHY PB $4.50

Kate Douglas **Wiggin**

Rebecca of Sunnybrook Farm

0-89966-354-0 BUCCANEER $22.95

0-14-035046-2 PENGUIN PB $2.95

Laura Ingalls **Wilder**

The Little House Books

Wilder's vivid re-creations of pioneer life are classics of children's literature. From the "Big Woods" to the prairie, she gives detailed accounts of her family's struggles to survive on the changing frontier, providing generations of young readers a personal vision of American life in the 19th-century. Boxed set

0-06-440040-9 TROPHY PB $35.55

Little House in the Big Woods

ILLUSTRATED BY GARTH WILLIAMS

0-06-026430-6 HARPERCOLLINS $15.95

0-06-440001-8 TROPHY PB $4.50

Little House on the Prairie

The *Little House* series chronicles a childhood in Wisconsin and on the family homestead in De Smeet Territory. The family shares the pleasures and dangers of prairie life as well as chores required to make the homestead productive

ILLUSTRATED BY GARTH WILLIAMS

0-06-026445-4 HARPERCOLLINS $15.95

0-06-440002-6 TROPHY PB $4.50

Farmer Boy

Not a *Little House* book but the story of Wilder's husband's childhood on a farm in New York

ILLUSTRATED BY GARTH WILLIAMS

0-06-026425-X HARPERCOLLINS $15.95

0-06-440003-4 TROPHY PB $4.50

On the Banks of Plum Creek

ILLUSTRATED BY GARTH WILLIAMS

0-06-026470-5 HARPERCOLLINS $15.95

0-06-440004-2 TROPHY PB $4.50

By the Shores of Silver Lake

ILLUSTRATED BY GARTH WILLIAMS

0-06-026416-0 HARPERCOLLINS $15.95

0-06-440005-0 TROPHY PB $4.50

The Long Winter

ILLUSTRATED BY GARTH WILLIAMS

0-06-026460-8 HARPERCOLLINS $15.95

0-06-440006-9 TROPHY PB $4.50

Little Town on the Prairie

ILLUSTRATED BY GARTH WILLIAMS

0-06-026450-0 HARPERCOLLINS $15.95

0-06-440007-7 TROPHY PB $4.50

Laura Ingalls Wilder's: The Early Years Collection/The Long Winter/By the Shores of Silver Lake

ILLUSTRATED BY GARTH WILLIAMS

0-06-440476-5 TROPHY PB $22.50

Laura Ingalls Wilder

These Happy Golden Years

0-06-440008-5 TROPHY PB $4.50

On the Way Home

0-06-440080-8 TROPHY PB $3.95

Margery Bianco **Williams**

The Velveteen Rabbit: Or How Toys Become Real

A celebrated fantasy from the 1920s about a toy rabbit who is loved by a boy, cast aside, and changed into a "real" rabbit as a reward for his loyalty and forbearance. Children may cry over it; adults may sense something wrong in the author's failure to castigate the wrongdoers

ILLUSTRATED BY MICHAEL HAGUE

0-8050-0209-X HOLT $13.95

0-590-42805-5 SCHOLASTIC PB $2.99

Oscar **Wilde**

The Selfish Giant

A giant creates a perpetual winter out of his garden because is too selfish to share it with anyone

ILLUSTRATED BY SAELIG GALLAGHER

0-86315-212-0 ANTHROPOSOPHIC $15.95

0-399-22448-3 PUTNAM $15.95

Oscar Wilde

Vera B. **Williams**

Scooter

0-688-09376-0 GREENWILLOW $15.00

Elizabeth **Winthrop**

The Battle for the Castle

0-440-40942-X YEARLING PB $4.50

The Castle in the Attic

A boy learns to deal with a powerful magic associated with the gift of a miniature castle

ILLUSTRATED BY TRINA S. HYMAN

0-440-40941-1 YEARLING PB $4.50

Virginia **Woolf**

Nurse Lugton's Curtain

Originally found in Virginia Woolf's manuscript for *Mrs. Dalloway,* this story was written for her niece in the early '20s. In this edition, Julie Vivas's paintings give an inspired slant to this quirky story of wild animals and tiny towns that come alive in the nurse's curtain material as she sleeps. Ages 6 to 10

0-15-200545-5 HARCOURT BRACE $14.95

Johann **Wyss**

The Swiss Family Robinson

0-448-06022-1 PRICE, STERN, & SLOAN $16.95

0-451-52481-0 SIGNET PB $4.95

Laurence **Yep**

Dragonwings

Moon Shadow comes to San Francisco at the turn of the century to join the father he has never seen. Ordinary Chinese immigrants, they realize an extraordinary dream in a story based on American history. Newbery Honor Book 1975

See also **YOUNG ADULT FICTION**

0-06-440085-9 TROPHY PB $4.95

Jane **Yolen**

The Girl Who Cried Flowers & Other Tales

ILLUSTRATED BY DAVID PALLADINI

9-995-25011-X WESTON WOOD $9.00

Jane **Yolen**, editor

Favorite Folktales from Around the World

Straightforward translations for children who no longer require a picture on every page

0-394-75188-4 PANTHEON PB $18.00

Young Adult Nonfiction

American Heritage

American Heritage Student's Dictionary

For students aged 12 to 15

0-395-55857-3 HOUGHTON MIFFLIN $17.95

Rhoda **Blumberg**

Commodore Perry in the Land of the Shogun

A much praised recounting of Commodore Perry's forced opening of 19th-century Japan to the West; a fascinating account of a medieval country and its American "conquerors"

0-688-03723-2 LOTHROP, LEE, & SHEPHERD $17.00

The Incredible Journey of Lewis and Clark

The story of the explorers who set out to chart the vast wilderness west of the Mississippi

0-688-14421-7 BEECH TREE PB $9.95

Maurice **Burton**

Birds

A critical survey of preservation and conservation

0-8160-1063-3 FACTS ON FILE $15.95

Robert **Burton** & Maurice **Burton**

Beginnings of Life

Explores the genetics and heredity of plants and animals

0-8160-1070-6 FACTS ON FILE $15.95

Jimmy **Carter**

Talking Peace: A Vision for the Next Generation

President Carter's personal strategies for achieving peace and ensuring human rights in more than 30 major conflicts raging in the world today. An excellent book for younger readers with an interest in politics and the world

0-525-44959-0 PENGUIN $16.99

Jimmy Carter

Giovanni **Castelli**

The First Civilizations

A brief social history with descriptions of the ancient world's tools, homes, weapons, and food

0-911745-59-9 BEDRICK LIBRARY EDITION $18.95

Miriam **Chaikin**

A Nightmare in History: The Holocaust, 1933-1945

Chaikin deals with her terrible subject without shrillness. Children 10 and up will understand the narrative and contemporary photographs

0-395-61580-1 CLARION PB $7.95

Vicki **Cobb**

Science Experiments You Can Eat

Chemistry demonstrated in kitchen experiments designed for children 10 and up

See also **BOOKS FOR AGES FIVE, SIX, AND SEVEN**

ILLUSTRATED BY DAVID CAIN

0-06-023534-9 HARPERCOLLINS $15.00

Susan **Cohen**

Teenage Competition: A Survival Guide

Young adults discuss familiar forms of competition and talk about ways to survive the stresses

0-87131-487-8 EVANS $13.95

Bruno **Dagens**

Angkor: Heart of the Asian Empire

0-8109-2801-9 ABRAMS PB $12.95

Red **Foley**

Red Foley's Best Baseball Book Ever: New for '94

Updated annually, this collection of baseball facts and trivia comes with stickers of many baseball stars

0-671-87577-9 SIMON & SCHUSTER PB $8.95

Michael **Folsom** & Marcia **Folsom**

The Macmillan Book of How Things Work

ILLUSTRATED BY BRAD HAMMANN

0-689-71139-5 ALADDIN PB $9.95

Anne **Frank**

The Diary of a Young Girl, the Definitive Edition

This edition of Anne Frank's diary restores 30 percent of material previously excised by her father

See also **FIRST-PERSON ACCOUNTS** under **THE HOLOCAUST** in **WORLD HISTORY AND CURRENT AFFAIRS**

0-385-47378-8 DOUBLEDAY $25.00

Russell **Freedman**

Eleanor Roosevelt: A Life of Discovery

0-89919-862-7 CLARION $17.95

Indian Chiefs

Portraits of six chiefs of Western tribes by a renowned authority on American Indian culture

0-8234-0625-3 HOLIDAY HOUSE $19.95

Jean **Fritz**

Homesick: My Own Story

A skillfully constructed autobiographical account of Fritz's childhood in pre-Revolutionary China, where the author was both one of the privileged and a "foreign devil". A Newberry Honor Book for 1982

0-440-43683-4 DELL PB $4.50

James **Giblin**

When Plague Strikes: The Black Death, Smallpox, AIDS

ILLUSTRATED BY DAVID FRAMPTON

0-06-025854-3 HARPERCOLLINS $14.95

James Cross **Giblin**

The Riddle of the Rosetta Stone: Key to Ancient Egypt

0-06-446137-8 TROPHY PB $5.95

Jane **Goodall**

My Life with the Chimpanzees

The English naturalist tells the story of "her" wild and endangered chimpanzees

0-671-66095-0 POCKET PB $2.99

0-663-56245-7 SILVER, BURDETT, & GINN PB $3.66

William D. **Halsey**

Macmillan Dictionary for Students

A concise dictionary; includes maps, glossary place names, and brief biographies

0-02-761560-X SIMON & SCHUSTER $18.00

Robie H. **Harris**

It's Perfectly Normal: A Book About Changing Bodies, Growing Up, Sex, and Sexual Health

ILLUSTRATED BY MICHAEL EMBERLEY

1-56402-199-8 CANDLEWICK $19.95

Dorothy **Hoobler** & Thomas **Hoobler**

Mandela: The Man, the Struggle, the Triumph

A young reader's biography of a man who lead the struggle against apartheid in South Africa, and was destined to become one of that country's most inspiring leaders

0-531-11141-5 FRANKLIN WATTS $22.70

Quang Nhuong **Huynh**

The Land I Lost: Adventures of a Boy in Vietnam

Not about the war but about encounters with crocodiles and snakes and other adventures

ILLUSTRATED BY MAI VO-DINH

0-06-440183-9 TROPHY PB $3.95

Margaret Oldroyd **Hyde** & Elizabeth H. **Forsyth**

AIDS: What Does It Mean to You?

Includes medical as well as personal information, and a technical glossary

0-8027-8202-7 WALKER $13.95

Ilse **Koehn**

Mischling, Second Degree: My Childhood in Nazi Germany

Through one-quarter Jewish, the author posed as an "Aryan" child while her world dissolved into chaos. A first-hand account of World War II

0-688-84110-4

GREENWILLOW LIBRARY EDITION $14.93

Don **Lessem** & Donald F. **Glut**, editors

The Dinosaur Society Dinosaur Encyclopedia

They may have died in an ice age, but it's no news that dinosaurs are hotter than ever. Ideal for dinosaur fanciers of all ages, this lavishly illustrated guide includes depictions of more than 600 species as well as detailed information regarding restoration, research, and behavior

See also **ONE-VOLUME ENCYCLOPEDIAS** under **REFERENCE** in **BUSINESS AND REFERENCE**

0-679-41770-2 RANDOM HOUSE $25.00

Ellen **Levine**

Freedom's Children: Young Civil Rights Activists Tell Their Own Stories

0-399-21893-9 PUTNAM $16.95

Saul **Levine** & Kathleen **Wilcox**

Dear Doctor

A question-and-answer introduction to medical topics of interest to young adults

0-688-07095-7 MORROW LIBRARY EDITION $12.93

Russell **Freedman**

Lincoln: A Photobiography

An ambitious book with far more information than usual in juvenile biographies. The illustrations are from contemporary sources. For attentive readers 11 and up. Newbery Medal 1988

See also **YOUNG ADULT FICTION**

See also **LINCOLN** under **THE LEADERS** under **THE CIVIL WAR AND RECONSTRUCTION**

0-395-51848-2 CLARION PB $7.95

Jean **Little**

Little by Little: A Writer's Education

0-14-032325-2 PUFFIN PB $6.99

Cornelia **Meigs**

Invincible Louisa

A celebrated short biography of Louisa May Alcott, the author of *Little Women*

0-316-56590-3 LITTLE, BROWN $17.95

0-590-44818-8 SCHOLASTIC PB $2.95

Merriam Webster Staff

Webster's School Dictionary

0-87779-280-1 MERRIAM WEBSTER $15.95

Jim **Murphy**

The Boys' War: Confederate and Union Soldiers Talk About the Civil War

Through first-hand accounts, photographs, portraits, and narrative, we hear young voices tell of their eager enlistment, their fear and bravery in the battlefield, and their final disillusionment. Ages 12 and up

0-89919-893-7 CLARION $15.95

0-395-66412-8 CLARION PB $7.95

As we lay there and the shells were flying over us…I thought what a foolish boy I was to run away and get into such a mess as I was in. I would have been glad to have seen my father coming after me.—Elisha Stockwell, 15-year-old Union soldier

THE BOYS' WAR: CONFEDERATE AND UNION SOLDIERS TALK ABOUT THE CIVIL WAR

Laurie **Nadel**

Corazon Aquino: Journey to Power

0-671-63950-1 MESSNER LIBRARY EDITION $13.98

Rose **Neufeld**

Exploring Non-Traditional Jobs for Women

PHOTOGRAPHS BY WILLIAM NEUFELD

0-8239-0971-9 ROSEN LIBRARY EDITION $14.95

Dorothy Hinshaw **Patent**

How Smart Are Animals?

The author reviews the latest research which challenges the traditional belief that animals live by instinct and reflex alone. Ages 12 and up

0-15-236770-5 HARCOURT BRACE $17.95

Bill **Peet**

Bill Peet: An Autobiography

Peet worked for over 30 years as an animator with the Disney Studio and as a creator of many books for children. This autobiography is full of his own illustrations. For young adult readers

See also **NONFICTION** under **BOOKS FOR EIGHTS, NINES, AND UP**

0-395-50932-7 HOUGHTON MIFFLIN $17.95

0-395-68982-1 HOUGHTON MIFFLIN PB $10.95

Ann **Petry**

Harriet Tubman: Conductor on the Underground Railroad

0-06-446181-5 TROPHY PB $4.50

Richard **Platt**

The Smithsonian Visual Timeline of Inventions

1-56458-675-8 DORLING KINDERSLEY $16.95

Janet R. **Price** & others

The Rights of Students: The Basic ACLU Guide to a Student's Rights

Issues relating to personal appearance, corporal punishment, sex discrimination, school records, and the right to a public education

0-8093-1423-1 SOUTHERN ILLINOIS PB $7.95

Doreen **Rappaport**

Living Dangerously: American Women Who Risked Their Lives for Adventure

0-06-025109-3 HARPERCREST.....$14.89

Doreen **Rappaport**, editor

American Women: Their Lives in Their Words

0-06-446127-0 HARPERCOLLINS PB.....$7.95

Barbara **Rogasky**

Smoke and Ashes: The Story of the Holocaust

0-8234-0878-7 HOLIDAY HOUSE PB.....$12.95

Cynthia R. **Samuels**

It's a Free Country: A Young Person's Guide to Politics and Elections

0-689-31416-7 ATHENEUM LIBRARY EDITION.....$5.00

Jacqueline **Tivers** & Michael **Day**

The Viking Children's World Atlas: An Introductory Atlas for Young People

0-670-85481-6 VIKING.....$11.99
0-14-031874-7 PUFFIN PB.....$5.99

Usborne

The Usborne Book of World Geography

0-86020-193-7 E.D.C......$17.95

The Usborne Book of World History

0-86020-959-8 E.D.C......$24.95

The Usborne Science Encyclopedia

0-7460-0419-2 E.D.C. PB.....$14.95

The Running Press Kits

Jim **Becker** & Andy **Mayer**

Build Your Own Radio

Everything you need to build a working AM radio, with easy instructions and text about the world of radio

1-56138-071-7 RUNNING PRESS.....$19.95

Ted **Daeschler**

The Dinosaur Hunter's Kit

Learn how fossils are located, collected, and studied from this 64-page book and then do it yourself! Complete with replica fossil of an Apatosaurus (formerly called Brontosaurus) buried in a slab of rock, an excavation tool, paints, and a brush

0-89471-804-5 RUNNING PRESS.....$18.95

Matt **Liddle**

Make Your Own Book Kit

All the materials and instructions needed for children to create their own books. Bind the pages, illustrate, write, and design a cover!

1-56138-337-6 RUNNING PRESS.....$18.95

Tim **Lutz**

Gem Hunter's Kit

Geologist Tim Lutz describes the best ways to locate, identify, and collect gems and minerals. The kit contains an excavation tool, gem tray, and sample gems and minerals embedded in rock for a practice dig

0-89471-828-2 RUNNING PRESS.....$18.95

Young Adult Fiction

The current crop of fictional children are more adult than adults. They are a resourceful bunch who cope with preadolescence, divorce, family finances, and the inconsistencies of parents and step-parents.

Douglas **Adams**

Hitchhiker's Guide to the Galaxy

See also **CONTEMPORARY SCIENCE FICTION** under **SCIENCE FICTION AND FANTASY** in **POPULAR READING**

0-345-39180-2 BALLANTINE PB.....$6.99

The Illustrated Hitchhiker's Guide to the Galaxy

The perennially attractive cult classic, now illustrated with state-of-the-art digital graphics that do not alter the original ascii set—that is, the text

See also **CONTEMPORARY SCIENCE FICTION** under **SCIENCE FICTION AND FANTASY** in **POPULAR READING**

0-517-59924-4 HARMONY.....$42.00

Life, the Universe and Everything

See also **CONTEMPORARY SCIENCE FICTION** under **SCIENCE FICTION AND FANTASY** in **POPULAR READING**

0-345-39182-9 BALLANTINE PB.....$6.99

The Restaurant at the End of the Universe

See also **CONTEMPORARY SCIENCE FICTION** under **SCIENCE FICTION AND FANTASY** in **POPULAR READING**

0-345-39181-0 BALLANTINE PB.....$6.99

So Long and Thanks for All the Fish

0-345-39183-7 BALLANTINE PB.....$10.01

Richard **Adams**

Watership Down

The quest of a band of Berkshire rabbits for a new home has allegorical overtones but treats the conditions of wildlife with astonishing fidelity. "His true achievement lies in the altogether enchanting civilization he has created"—Peter S. Prescott

See also **THE '70S** under **THE GREAT FICTION BESTSELLERS 1930-1995** in **POPULAR READING**

See also **THE MIDDLE GENERATION** under **20TH-CENTURY BRITISH AND IRISH FICTION** in **LITERATURE OF THE BRITISH ISLES**

0-02-700030-3 MACMILLAN.....$40.00
0-380-00293-0 AVON PB.....$5.99

Joan **Aiken**

The Wolves of Willoughby Chase

American by birth and English by adoption, Aiken writes historical adventures that appeal to the child with a sophisticated vocabulary. At her best she recreates the past with an inventive mixture of fact and fantasy

See also **FICTION** under **BOOKS FOR EIGHTS, NINES, AND UP**

0-440-49603-9 YEARLING PB.....$4.50

Louisa May **Alcott**

Little Women

In 19th-century New England, Jo, Beth, Meg, and Amy March struggle in the face of genteel poverty, keeping their spirits up and their unusually affectionate household going

0-553-21275-3 BDD PB.....$3.95
0-14-036668-7 PUFFIN PB.....$3.99

William **Armstrong**

Sounder

A sharecropper steals to feed his family and is forcibly arrested—dividing the family and injuring Sounder, the great coon dog. Set in the 19th-century South, the story shifts to the search by the sharecropper's young son for his missing father and faithful Sounder's role in the boy's odyssey. Newbery Medal 1970

0-06-020143-6 HARPERCOLLINS.....$14.95
0-06-440020-4 TROPHY PB.....$4.50

Christine **Arnothy**

I Am Fifteen— And I Don't Want to Die

Christine is caught in the middle of a war-torn city

0-590-44630-4 POINT PB.....$3.50

Avi

Place Called Ugly

Faced with the destruction of his summer home, the hero decides to fight the developers in a story about hard choices and compromises

0-380-72423-5 FLARE PB.....$3.99

Marion Dane **Bauer**

On My Honor

Courage and friendship are central to this excellent junior novel about an apparent drowning and a boy's coming to terms with death. Newbery Honor Book 1987

0-440-46633-4 YEARLING PB.....$3.99

Marion Dane **Bauer**, editor

Am I Blue?: Coming Out from the Silence

0-06-024253-1 HARPERCOLLINS.....$15.00

Nina **Bawden**

Humbug

0-14-036586-9 PUFFIN PB.....$3.99

Patricia **Beatty**

Charley Skedaddle

0-688-06687-9 MORROW.....$16.00

Jayhawker

0-688-09850-9 MORROW.....$16.00

Lupita Manana

0-688-11497-0 BEECH TREE PB.....$4.95

William J. **Bennett**, editor

The Book of Virtues for Young People: A Treasury of Great Moral Stories

0-382-24923-2 SILVER, BURDETT.....$16.95

Francesca L. **Block**

Cherokee Bat and the Goat Guys

0-06-447095-4 TROPHY PB $3.95

Francesca Lia **Block**

Missing Angel Juan

0-06-447120-9 TROPHY PB $3.95

Weetzie Bat

0-06-447068-7 HARPERCOLLINS PB $3.95

Witch Baby

0-06-447065-2 HARPERCOLLINS PB $4.50

Judy **Blume**

Are You There, God? It's Me, Margaret

A long monologue about growing and growing up from the viewpoint of an inexperienced half-Jewish, half-gentile 11-year old

0-440-90419-6 LAUREL LEAF PB $3.99

Forever

One of Blume's most popular young adult novels. The story centers around Katherine, a young woman and her experiences with first love and sex

0-02-711030-3 SIMON & SCHUSTER $16.00
0-671-69530-4 POCKET PB $5.50

Just as Long as We're Together

A seventh-grade girl moves to a Connecticut suburb and acquires two unconventional bosom buddies. When her home life alters she needs her new friends more than ever

0-531-08329-2 ORCHARD LIBRARY EDITION $17.99

Then Again, Maybe I Won't

A boy's growing up is interrupted by his parents' new emphasis on social status and his sister's budding sexuality

0-440-48659-9 DELL PB $4.50

Tiger Eyes

A father's murder is followed by the bereaved family's visit to unfamiliar relatives. A confessional monologue of sadness mixed with caustic observations and the recounting of a first affair

0-02-711080-X SIMON & SCHUSTER $16.00
0-440-98469-6 DELL PB $4.50

Nancy **Bond**

A String on the Harp

When an American boy visiting Wales accidentally discovers the tuning key to the harp of Taliesin, his life is invaded by fragments of the past

0-14-032376-7 VIKING PB $5.99

Bruce **Books**

Midnight Hour Encores

Sib and her father travel around the country so she can meet her hippie mother, who abandoned her when she was born

0-06-447021-0 TROPHY PB $4.50

The Moves Make the Man

The one black student to integrate the biggest white school in a North Carolina town meets up with its hero, the school's showcase athlete

0-06-447022-9 TROPHY PB $4.50

Betsy **Byars**

The Summer of the Swans

Charlie is an autistic 12-year-old, Sara his older, protective sister. When Charlie disappears, Sarah's life changes more than she knows

0-670-68190-3 VIKING $15.99
0-14-031420-2 VIKING PB $3.99

Lewis **Carroll**

Alice in Wonderland & Alice Through the Looking Glass

Charles Dodgson, who took the pen name Lewis Carroll, was a mathematics don at an Oxford college, a composer of amateur nonsense verse, and an excellent but equally unprofessional photographer. However, it was his genius as a humorist and logician that created his legacy to the literature of childhood. Few other children's books have been read for so long, by so many, with so much pleasure. The collected edition is a reminder that American children commonly read the first Alice but not the second. Are they put off by the idea of a plot based on a chess game? Or do they find the verbal nonsense in *Through the Looking Glass* overwhelming?

ILLUSTRATED BY JOHN TENNIEL

0-448-06004-3 GROSSETT & DUNLAP $15.95

Alice's Adventures in Wonderland

See also **19TH-CENTURY FICTION** under **THE 19TH-CENTURY** in **LITERATURE OF THE BRITISH ISLES**

ILLUSTRATED BY JOHN TENNIEL

0-14-035038-1 PUFFIN PB $2.99

Alice's Adventures in Wonderland

With muted pictures that hint at Victorian styles

ILLUSTRATED BY MICHAEL HAGUE

0-03-002037-9 HOLT $19.95

Alice's Adventures in Wonderland & Through the Looking-Glass

0-451-52320-2 NEW AMERICAN LIBRARY PB $3.95

Alice's Adventures in Wonderland & Through the Looking-Glass

See also **19TH-CENTURY FICTION** under **THE 19TH-CENTURY** in **LITERATURE OF THE BRITISH ISLES**

EDITED BY ROGER L. GREEN
ILLUSTRATED BY JOHN TENNIEL

0-19-281620-9 OXFORD PB $4.95

Jabberwocky

ILLUSTRATED BY GRAME BASE

0-8109-1150-7 ABRAMS $16.95

Alice **Childress**

A Hero Ain't Nothin' but a Sandwich

A Harlem adolescent uses heroin regularly. His story is told in a sequence of forceful first-person narratives

0-380-00132-2 AVON PB $4.25

Rainbow Jordan

0-380-58974-5 AVON PB $3.99

John **Christopher**

The City of Gold and Lead

Further adventures involving the Tripods

0-02-042701-8 ALADDIN PB $3.95

The Pool of Fire

Will and his free compatriots must carry out the destruction of the Master's three great cities before Tripods and Masters utterly destroy the earth

0-02-718350-5 SIMON & SCHUSTER $14.95
0-02-042720-4 MICROSOFT PB $3.95

The Tripods Trilogy

A three-volume set including *The White Mountains, The City of Gold and Lead,* and *Pools of Fire*

0-02-042571-6 ALADDIN PB $11.95

The White Mountains

In a 21st-century Europe that has regressed to the Middle Ages, villagers live in the shadow of interplanetary Tripods and undergo a surgical puberty rite

0-02-718360-2 SIMON & SCHUSTER $16.00
0-02-042711-5 ALADDIN PB $3.95

Sandra **Cisneros**

The House on Mango Street

The coming-of-age classic about a Latino girl in Chicago from the celebrated Cisneros. "Marvelous…spare yet luminous…The subtle power of Cisneros's storytelling is evident…She communicates all the rapture and rage of growing up in a modern world"—*San Francisco Chronicle*

See also **NEW WRITERS OF THE '90S** under **20TH-CENTURY AMERICAN FICTION** in **LITERATURE OF THE AMERICAS**

0-679-43335-X KNOPF $21.00
0-679-73477-5 VINTAGE PB $9.00

Beverly **Cleary**

Dear Mr. Henshaw

A 12-year-old boy begins a correspondence with his favorite author—not to show off but because he is lonely. Newbery Medal 1983

0-688-02406-8 MORROW LIBRARY EDITION $15.93

Vera **Cleaver** & Bill **Cleaver**

Where the Lilies Bloom

Eccentric Appalachian children survive the death of their father and subsequent deprivations by bluff and deception

0-06-447005-9 TROPHY PB $4.50

Brock **Cole**

Celine

A 16-year-old girl, Celine, is left with her 22-year-old stepmother. Celine's distinctive voice characterizes this frank, exceptionally well-written novel for young adult readers

0-374-31234-6 FS&G $15.00

Brock **Cole**

The Goats

Two outcasts survive and find inner strength

0-374-32678-9 FS&G $15.00
0-374-42576-0 FS&G PB $3.95

James Lincoln **Collier** & Christopher **Collier**

My Brother Sam Is Dead

In a house divided by the Civil War, Tim mediates between his father and his brother, a 17-year-old who loves war and is destroyed by it

0-02-722980-7 SIMON & SCHUSTER $16.00
0-590-42792-X SCHOLASTIC PB $3.99

Susan **Cooper**

The Dark Is Rising

An evocative fantasy, set in today's Britain, evokes a pre-Christian world in which humankind's guardians battle a malevolent force seeking its destruction

0-689-30317-3 MCELDERRY $16.00
0-689-71087-9 ALADDIN PB $3.95

The Dark Is Rising Sequence/ Silver on the Tree/The Grey King/ Greenwitch/The Dark Is Rising/ Over Sea, Under Stone

0-02-042565-1 ALADDIN PB $19.75

Greenwitch

0-689-30426-9 MCELDERRY $16.00
0-689-71088-7 ALADDIN PB $3.95

The Grey King

0-689-50029-7 MCELDERRY $16.00
0-689-71089-5 MACMILLAN PB $3.95

Silver on the Tree

0-689-50088-2 MCELDERRY $17.00
0-689-71152-2 ALADDIN PB $3.95

Robert **Cormier**

Beyond the Chocolate War

0-440-90580-X DELL PB $4.50

The Chocolate War

A shy freshman is the pawn of a powerful secret society at a Catholic prep school

0-394-82805-4 KNOPF $20.00
0-440-94459-7 LAUREL LEAF PB $4.50

I Am the Cheese

0-440-94060-5 LAUREL LEAF PB $4.50

Stephen **Crane**

The Red Badge of Courage: An Episode of the American Civil War

See also **THE 19TH-CENTURY: AFTER THE CIVIL WAR** under **AMERICAN LITERATURE TO 1900** in **LITERATURE OF THE AMERICAS**

0-679-60044-2 MODERN LIBRARY $13.50
0-679-73223-3 VINTAGE PB $9.50

Margaret **Craven**

I Heard the Owl Call My Name

See also **THE '70S** under **THE GREAT FICTION BESTSELLERS 1930-1995** in **POPULAR READING**

0-440-34369-0 LAUREL LEAF PB $4.99

Sharon **Creech**

Absolutely Normal Chaos

0-06-026989-8 HARPERCOLLINS $14.95

Linda **Crew**

Children of the River

0-440-21022-4 BDD PB $4.50

Paula **Danziger**

Can You Sue Your Parents for Malpractice

0-440-91066-8 DELL PB $3.99

The Pistachio Prescription

0-440-96895-X DELL PB $3.99

The Cat Ate My Gymsuit

Overweight, discontented Marcy Lewis finds her orderly world disrupted by an unconventional young English teacher and pursues a new cause zealously

0-440-41612-4 DELL PB $3.99

The Divorce Express

Phoebe, ninth-grade daughter of divorced parents, shuttles back and forth each week on the bus known as the Divorce Express. When she meets Rosie, another rider on the bus, she finds that she is not alone in her sadness and can even begin to deal with the devastating news that her mother tells her

0-440-92062-0 DELL PB $3.99

Remember Me to Harold Square

0-440-20153-5 DELL PB $3.99

There's a Bat in Bunk Five

Marcy reappears as a counselor in training under the guidance of her beloved teacher

0-440-40098-8 YEARLING PB $3.99

Miguel **de Cervantes**

Don Quixote

A beautiful edition of Cervantes's classic, as adapted for readers of all ages by the distinguished translator Magda Begin. Forty-six full-color illustrations by Spanish artist Manuel Boix

TRANSLATED AND ADAPTED BY MAGDA BEGIN

1-56402-174-2 CANDLEWICK $13.95

His head swam with fantastic images from all the books he had read—bewitchings and spells, hangings and duels, contests and quarrels, romances and dances and every kind of unimaginable occurrence; and these dreamlike things became so real to him that he believed there was no truer story in the world.

In fact, with his wits gone, he soon fell prey to the strangest thought that ever crossed a madman's mind. Namely, that for his personal honor and the greater glory of his country, he should become a wandering knight like those he read about, and ride forth on horseback, fully armed, to seek his fortune, risking body and soul in good deeds that would win him everlasting fame.

DON QUIXOTE

Miguel de Cervantes

Guy **de Maupassant**

Best Short Stories of Guy de Maupassant

0-88411-589-5 AMEREON $19.95

Daniel **DeFoe**

Robinson Crusoe: His Life and Strange Surprizing Adventures

0-679-42819-4 KNOPF $13.95
0-8224-6225-7 LAKE PB $7.12

Ella Carla **Deloria**

Waterlily

0-8032-6579-4 NEBRASKA PB $9.95

Frederick **Douglass**

Escape from Slavery: The Boyhood of Frederick Douglass in His Own Words

See also **THE 19TH-CENTURY: TO THE CIVIL WAR** under **AMERICAN LITERATURE TO 1900** in **LITERATURE OF THE AMERICAS**

ILLUSTRATED BY MICHAEL MCCURDY

0-679-84652-2 KNOPF $15.00
0-679-84651-4 KNOPF PB $6.99

Arthur C. **Doyle**

The Adventures of Sherlock Holmes

ILLUSTRATED BY BARRY MOSER

0-688-10782-6 MORROW $20.00

Gardner **Dozois**, editor

The Year's Best Science Fiction: Fourth Annual Competition

Twenty-seven award-winning short stories

0-312-00710-8 ST. MARTIN'S PB $13.95

Alexandre **Dumas**

Dumas was not only the great yarn-spinner of 19th-century literature, an effortless storyteller with a sure instinct for melodramatic excitement, but a writer able to weave subtler moods into his relentlessly paced stories

Three Musketeers

Countless movie versions later, Dumas' great adventure novel remains fresh and often startling

See also **THE 19TH-CENTURY: ROMANTICISM AND REALISM** under **FRENCH LITERATURE TO 1900** in **LITERATURE OF EUROPE, AFRICA, AND ASIA**

0-448-06024-8 PRICE, STERN, & SLOAN $13.95
0-14-044025-9 PENGUIN PB $8.95

Dan **Fox**

Go in and Out the Window: An Illustrated Songbook for Young People

0-8050-0628-1 HOLT $24.95

Paula **Fox**

One-Eyed Cat

Ned's act of careless cruelty alters his perception of his own life and the sacredness of others'. A subtly written book in which one comes to share his burden. A Newbery Honor Book for 1984

0-02-735540-3 SIMON & SCHUSTER $14.95
0-440-46641-5 DELL PB $3.99

A Place Apart

0-374-45868-5 FS&G PB $3.95

The Slave Dancer

Imprisoned aboard a 19th-century slave ship, a young kidnapped deckhand provides the flute music for the cruel slave "dance," performed as exercise by the shackled captives. A brutal portrait of a small but hellish world

See also **FICTION** under **BOOKS FOR EIGHTS, NINES, AND UP**

0-02-735560-8 SIMON & SCHUSTER $16.00
0-440-96132-7 DELL PB $4.50

Monica **Furlong**

Juniper

0-679-83369-2 RANDOM HOUSE PB $4.99

Wise Child

0-394-82598-5 RANDOM HOUSE PB $4.99

Donald R. **Gallo**, editor

Visions

Nineteen short stories by writers for young adults including Jean Davies Okimoto, Norma Fox Mazer, Ouida Sebestyen, Joan Aiken, and M.E. Kerr

0-440-20208-6 LAUREL LEAF PB $4.99

Nancy **Garden**

Annie on My Mind

0-374-40414-3 FS&G PB $3.95

Jean Craighead **George**

My Side of the Mountain

0-14-034810-7 VIKING PB $4.99

On the Far Side of the Mountain

A worthy sequel to the Newbery Honor Book, *My Side of the Mountain*. Ages 8-12

ILLUSTRATED BY JEAN CRAIGHEAD GEORGE

0-525-44563-3 DUTTON $15.00

Nikki **Giovanni**

"Talent is light, but mature talent is a beacon and Nikki Giovanni has…joined that small band of talented people who try to show us all the way to go home."—LA Times. *Nikki Giovanni is currently a professor of English and creative writing at Virginia Tech*

Ego-Tripping and Other Poems for Young People

ILLUSTRATED BY GEORGE FORD

1-55652-189-8 LAWRENCE HILL PB $9.95

Rumer **Godden**

The Greengage Summer

0-330-32778-X MCCLELLAND & STEWART PB $12.99

Sheila **Gordon**

Middle of Somewhere: A Story of South Africa

Winner of the Jane Addams Peace Award—as was Gordon's previous novel about apartheid, *Waiting for the Rain*—this novel tells the story of a black South African girl whose village is to be forcibly removed to a distant township to make way for a white suburb. "A delicately crafted story…heartbreaking in its intimate portrayal of people clinging to life and dignity amid cruel deprivation"—*The Guardian*

0-531-05908-1 ORCHARD $15.95

Kenneth **Grahame**

The Wind in the Willows

Grahame's lengthy and demanding meditation on freedom is as much about life among river dwellers (animal and human) as it is about the adventures of the incorrigible Mr. Toad. A convincing adventure fantasy

ILLUSTRATED BY ERNEST H. SHEPARD
PREFACE BY MARGARET HODGES

0-684-17957-1 ATHENEUM $19.00
0-689-71310-X SIMON & SCHUSTER PB $4.95

Roger Lancelyn **Green**

King Arthur and His Knights of the Round Table

0-679-42311-7 KNOPF $13.95

Joanne **Greenberg**

I Never Promised You a Rose Garden

0-451-16031-2 NEW AMERICAN LIBRARY PB $4.99

Bette **Greene**

Summer of My German Soldier

A 12-year-old Jewish girl living in a backward Arkansas town forms a destructive friendship with a young German prisoner of war. When rebellious Patty hides the enemy-turned-friend, the town's communal wrath is swift and sure

0-440-21892-6 LAUREL LEAF PB $4.99

Eloise **Greenfield**

Sister

0-690-00497-4 CROWELL $15.00
0-06-440199-5 HARPERCOLLINS PB $3.95

Rosa **Guy**

The Disappearance

Acquitted of murder, a neglected boy is placed with a socially responsible middle-class family, where social tensions are underlined

0-440-92064-7 DELL PB $3.99

The Friends

0-8050-1742-9 HOLT $13.95
0-440-22667-8 BDD PB $3.99

Alex **Haley**

Roots

See also **CLASSIC AUTOBIOGRAPHIES** under **BLACK VOICES, BLACK LIVES** under **AFRICAN-AMERICAN STUDIES** in **HISTORY OF THE AMERICAS**

See also **THE '70S** under **THE GREAT FICTION BESTSELLERS 1930-1995** in **POPULAR READING**

0-385-03787-2 DOUBLEDAY $25.00
0-440-17464-3 DELL PB $6.99

Donald **Hall**, editor

The Oxford Book of Children's Verse in America

For children eleven and up

99912-4-215-5 OXFORD LIBRARY EDITION $5.00

Virginia **Hamilton**

M.C. Higgins the Great

The unexpected visit of two strangers threatens a family living in Ohio coal mining country

0-02-742480-4 SIMON & SCHUSTER $17.00
0-02-043490-1 ALADDIN PB $3.95

Sweet Whispers, Brother Rush

0-399-20894-1 PUTNAM $17.95
0-380-65193-9 AVON PB $3.99

A White Romance

A young woman struggles to leave her girlhood behind and stay free of the prejudices and fears that surround her

0-15-295888-6 HARCOURT BRACE PB $3.95

Karen **Hesse**

Letters from Rifka

0-8050-1964-2 HOLT $14.95

S.E. **Hinton**

The Outsiders

Warfare along class lines begins and ends bloodily in a memorable book

0-440-96769-4 LAUREL LEAF PB $4.50

Rumble Fish

Wildly attached to his older brother Rusty, James apes a precocity he can't live up to. The result is a messy round of fights and escalating troubles

0-440-97534-4 LAUREL LEAF PB $3.99

Tex

Tex's carefree Oklahoma days are numbered as he faces an unexpectedly violent future

0-440-97850-5 LAUREL LEAF PB $4.50

That Was Then, This Is Now

Two inseparable 16-year-old boys, and the experiences and decisions they face

0-440-98652-4 LAUREL LEAF PB $4.99

Minfong **Ho**

Rice Without Rain

Set in rural Thailand in the mid-70s, a 17-year-old girl, Jinda, is the central character of this graphic novel of violent politics. A widely acclaimed book for older children, ages 12 and up

0-688-06355-1 LOTHROP, LEE, & SHEPHERD $14.95

Felice **Holman**

Slake's Limbo

A scrawny, bruised boy takes refuge in the New York City subway and lives 100 days underground

0-684-13926-X ATHENEUM $16.00
0-689-71066-6 ALADDIN PB $3.95

The Wild Children

Finding his family gone, the orphaned Alex starts on a journey that leads him into the midst of *bezprizorni*, the "wild children," as the Soviet authorities called them

0-14-031930-1 PUFFIN PB $4.99

Irene **Hunt**

Across Five Aprils

Rooted in Kentucky, living in southern Illinois, Jethro's family doesn't know where its loyalties lie but is inevitably caught up in the Civil War. A Newbery Honor Book

0-425-10241-6 BERKLEY PB $4.50

M.E. **Kerr**

Dinky Hocker Shoots Smack!

A witty and touching account of two boys, two girls, and their relatives living in New York City in the mercurial early 1970s

0-06-023151-3 HARPERCREST LIBRARY EDITION $15.89
0-06-447006-7 TROPHY PB $4.50

Night Kites

Two people pay a high price for not fitting in

0-06-023254-4 HARPERCREST LIBRARY EDITION $14.89
0-06-447035-0 TROPHY PB $4.50

Rudyard **Kipling**

Just So Stories for Little Children

EDITED BY LISA LEWIS

0-19-282276-4 OXFORD PB $4.95

The Jungle Book

EDITED BY KURT WIESE

0-679-43637-5 KNOPF $13.95

Eric **Knight**

Lassie Come Home

0-440-40760-5 YEARLING PB $3.50

E.L. **Konigsburg**

Throwing Shadows

0-02-044140-1 MACMILLAN PB $3.95

Joseph **Krumgold**

...And Now Miguel

A New Mexican 12-year-old's rite of passage. Newbery Medal 1954

0-06-440143-X TROPHY PB $4.50

Onion John

Newbery Medal 1960

0-06-440144-8 TROPHY PB $4.50

Charles **Lamb** & Mary **Lamb**

Tales from Shakespeare

See also **THE ROMANTIC MOVEMENT** under **THE 19TH-CENTURY** in **LITERATURE OF THE BRITISH ISLES**

0-451-52391-1 NEW AMERICAN LIBRARY PB $5.95

0-14-036677-6 PUFFIN PB $3.99

Charles Lamb

Andrew **Lang**

The Blue Fairy Book

See also **FICTION** under **BOOKS FOR EIGHTS, NINES, AND UP**

0-486-21437-0 DOVER PB $7.95

The Brown Fairy Book

0-486-21438-9 DOVER PB $6.95

The Pink Fairy Book

0-486-21792-2 DOVER PB $7.95

The Rainbow Fairy Book

ILLUSTRATED BY MICHAEL HAGUE

0-688-10878-4 MORROW $20.00

Andrew **Lang** & H. J. **Ford**

The Lilac Fairy Book

0-486-21907-0 DOVER PB $7.95

Ursula **Le Guin**

With 15 novels, 60 short stories, poetry, children's books, criticism, and screenplays to her name—as well as a National Book Award—Le Guin is the preeminent science fiction writer in America, as well as a major literary voice transcending genre classifications

A Wizard of Earthsea

The first volume of her wonderful and haunting fantasy trilogy for children; as good as anything she has written for adults, or perhaps even better

0-689-31720-4 ATHENEUM $16.95

0-553-26250-5 BDD PB $5.99

The Farthest Shore

0-553-26847-3 BDD PB $5.50

The Tombs of Atuan

0-553-27331-0 BDD PB $5.50

Very Far Away from Anywhere Else

A contemporary love story of teenage exiles who share in a private, believable universe

0-689-30525-7 ATHENEUM $15.00

Madeleine **L'Engle**

An Acceptable Time

A new time-travel fantasy from the author of the classic A *Wrinkle in Time*. Polly O'Keefe's quiet autumn is interrupted by mysterious strangers and travel to the past. For young adult readers

0-374-30027-5 FS&G $18.00

0-440-20814-9 LAUREL LEAF PB $4.99

A House Like a Lotus

0-374-33385-8 FS&G $17.00

0-440-93685-3 LAUREL LEAF PB $3.99

Meet the Austins

0-374-34929-0 FS&G $25.01

A Swiftly Tilting Planet

The sequel to *A Wrinkle in Time* tells of the further journeys of the Murrys on behalf of universally beneficent forces

0-440-90158-8 LAUREL LEAF PB $4.99

A Wrinkle in Time

Science-fiction, feminism, and faith; a ground-breaking and unbeatable combination; one of the most original children's books of this century

0-374-38613-7 FS&G $17.00

0-440-99805-0 LAUREL LEAF PB $5.50

The Wrinkle in Time Books

In search of their missing father, three children travel through the realms of time and space encountering phenomenal adventures along the way. Not only are they successful in their quest, but they heroically save the universe from the grasp of evil. Their journeys continue in the following three books. Boxed set of four volumes

0-440-36037-4 BANTAM PB $15.96

A Wind in the Door

The third adventure of the Murry family in the science-fiction series that began with *A Wrinkle in Time*

0-440-48761-7 DELL PB $4.50

Russell **Freedman**

Lincoln: A Photobiography

An ambitious book with far more information than usual in juvenile biographies. The illustrations are from contemporary sources. For attentive readers 11 and up. Newbery Medal 1988

See also **YOUNG ADULT NONFICTION**

See also **LINCOLN** under **THE LEADERS** under **THE CIVIL WAR AND RECONSTRUCTION**

0-395-51848-2 CLARION PB $7.95

Robert **Lipsyte**

The Contender

Seventeen-year-old dropout Alfred Brook finds that getting to the top is less important than how you get there

0-06-447039-3 CAROUSEL PB $4.50

One Fat Summer

A comic "Crisco Kid" finds out how terrifying and exhilarating a summer can be

0-06-023896-8

HARPERCREST LIBRARY EDITION $14.89

Jack **London**

The Call of the Wild

ILLUSTRATED BY PHILIPPE MUNCH

0-670-86796-9 PENGUIN PB $13.99

White Fang

0-14-036667-9 PUFFIN PB $3.99

Lois **Lowry**

Find a Stranger, Say Good Bye

An adopted child blessed with intelligence, good looks, and an affectionate adopted family sets out to find her natural parents, aided by only a few scanty clues

0-395-26459-6 HOUGHTON MIFFLIN $16.95

The Giver

0-440-21907-8 LAUREL LEAF PB $4.99

Rabble Starkey

0-395-43607-9 HOUGHTON MIFFLIN $14.95

0-440-40056-2 YEARLING PB $3.99

A Summer to Die

An account of two girls, one growing up and exploring life, the other dying of leukemia

0-440-21917-5 BDD PB $3.99

Michelle **Magorian**

Good Night, Mr. Tom

0-06-024079-2 HARPERCREST $15.89

Margaret **Mahy**

The Catalogue of the Universe

0-689-50391-1 MCELDERRY $15.95

0-14-036600-8 PUFFIN PB $3.99

The Changeover

A New Zealand girl acquires supernatural abilities through her intimacy with a family of witches, but must fight off demonic possession

0-689-50303-2 MCELDERRY $16.00

0-14-036599-0 PUFFIN PB $3.99

The Tricksters

The story of a warm New Zealand Christmas, a large, intellectual family, and an apparition that can't be explained

0-689-50400-4 MCELDERRY $16.00

99912-5-305-X MACMILLAN LIBRARY EDITION $5.00

Malcolm X & Alex **Haley**

The Autobiography of Malcolm X

A compelling view as a man of color in America, from a childhood of poverty to the jitterbug days of Boston and Harlem. Malcolm X educated himself in prison, where he joined the Nation of Islam. His ultimate rejection of the movement's separatist ideology, after seeing people of all races worship together at Mecca, resulted in his assassination

See also CLASSIC AUTOBIOGRAPHIES under BLACK VOICES, BLACK LIVES under AFRICAN-AMERICAN STUDIES in HISTORY OF THE AMERICAS

0-345-35068-5 BALLANTINE PB $5.99

Sharon Bell **Mathis**

Teacup Full of Roses

A black teenager tries to keep his family together

0-14-032328-7 VIKING PB $4.99

Norma Fox **Mazer**

A, My Name Is Ami

0-590-40054-1 SCHOLASTIC PB $2.25

After the Rain

Newbery Honor Book 1988

0-688-06867-7 MORROW $16.00
0-380-75025-2 AVON PB $4.50

Robin **McKinley**

Beauty: The Retelling of the Story of Beauty and the Beast

A 20th-century version of the evocative folk story of a beautiful woman held captive by a beast

0-06-024149-7 HARPERCOLLINS $16.00

Patricia **McKissack** & Frederick **McKissack**

A Long Hard Journey: The Story of the Pullman Porters

Coretta Scott King Award for text

0-8027-6884-9 WALKER $17.95

Walter Dean **Myers**

Fallen Angels

Richard Perry can't afford college, and street life is harsh. The fictional account of a teenaged black conscript's tour of duty in Vietnam

0-590-40942-5 SCHOLASTIC $14.95

Hoops

Seventeen-year-old Lonnie Jackson has the talent to become a great basketball player but struggles to make his way in a brutal world

0-440-93884-8 DELL PB $3.99

Motown and Didi

0-440-95762-1 DELL PB $3.99

Won't Know Till I Get There

When some good kids stumble into trouble, the judge sentences them to a summer of unpaid service in an old folk's home, in a bouncy story about teenage entrepreneurship

0-14-032612-X VIKING PB $3.99

Beverley **Naidoo**

Chain of Fire

ILLUSTRATED BY ERIC VELASQUEZ

0-06-440468-4 TROPHY PB $4.50

Donna Jo **Napoli**

The Magic Circle

0-14-037439-6 PUFFIN PB $3.99

John **Neufeld**

Lisa, Bright and Dark

0-87599-153-X PHILLIPS $22.95
0-451-16684-1 NEW AMERICAN LIBRARY PB $4.99

Scott **O'Dell**

The Black Pearl

In a pearling seaport off the coast of 19th-century Spanish California, the young Ramon finds that the real and the mythical frequently cross paths

0-395-06961-0 HOUGHTON MIFFLIN $14.95
0-440-41146-7 YEARLING PB $4.50

Carlota

A violent incident throws the heroine's life into confusion and liberates her from her autocratic inheritance

0-395-25487-6 HOUGHTON MIFFLIN $15.95
0-440-90928-7 DELL PB $3.99

Sing Down the Moon

0-440-97975-7 DELL PB $3.99

Zibby **O'Neal**

The Language of Goldfish

People in Northport do not have crazy children, but Carrie is swept up by a force stronger than her mother's social pretensions

0-14-034540-X PUFFIN PB $4.99

Katherine **Paterson**

Bridge to Terabithia

Terabithia is a secret kingdom invented by two unusual children to ease the ordinary hurts of life. The kingdom later becomes a reason for surviving an unexpected tragedy. Newbery Medal 1978

ILLUSTRATED BY DONNA DIAMOND

0-06-440184-7 TROPHY PB $4.50

Jacob Have I Loved

A beautifully written novel about love and envy between sisters, set in a fascinating and difficult community of crabbers on an island in the Chesapeake Bay

0-690-04078-4 CROWELL $14.95
0-06-440368-8 TROPHY PB $4.50

Rebels of the Heavenly Kingdom

0-14-037610-0 PUFFIN PB $3.99

The Sign of the Chrysanthemum

0-06-440232-0 TROPHY PB $4.50

Gary **Paulsen**

Dogsong

An Eskimo boy's life is grim until he enters a dog-sleigh race. Newbery Honor Book 1986

See also FICTION under BOOKS FOR EIGHTS, NINES, AND UP

0-02-770180-8 SIMON & SCHUSTER $16.00
0-689-80409-1 ALADDIN PB $3.95
0-14-032235-3 VIKING PB $4.99

Hatchet

A small plane goes down in the Canadian wilderness, taking with it a 13-year-old boy who must learn how to stay alive. Newbery Honor Book 1987

0-02-770130-1 SIMON & SCHUSTER $16.00
0-689-80882-8 ALADDIN $4.50

Nightjohn

0-440-21936-1 LAUREL LEAF PB $3.99

Woodsong

0-14-034905-7 PUFFIN PB $4.99

Ann **Petry**

Tituba of Salem Village

0-06-440403-X HARPERCOLLINS PB $4.50

Gene S. **Porter**

A Girl of the Limberlost

0-440-43090-9 YEARLING PB $3.95

Chaim **Potok**

The Chosen

Potok's most widely read novel, a story of two Jewish boys in Brooklyn—one modern orthodox and the other Hasidic—who form a friendship in the wake of Israel's war of independence

See also SINCE 1945 under 20TH-CENTURY AMERICAN FICTION in LITERATURE OF THE AMERICAS

0-449-21344-7 FAWCETT PB $6.99

Howard **Pyle**

The Story of King Arthur and His Knights

0-451-52488-8 NEW AMERICAN LIBRARY PB $5.95

Ellen **Raskin**

Westing Game

0-14-034991-X PUFFIN PB $4.99

Carolyn **Reeder**

Shades of Gray

0-380-71232-6 CAMELOT PB $4.50

Johanna **Reiss**

The Upstairs Room

0-06-440370-X TROPHY PB $4.50

Margaret J. **Rostkowski**

After the Dancing Days

An inexperienced 13-year-old becomes nurse and confidante at a veterans' hospital for wounded soldiers and discovers how her uncle died in the First World War

0-06-440248-7 TROPHY PB $4.50

Cynthia **Rylant**

A Blue-Eyed Daisy

Set in the West Virginia mountains, this imaginative story traces four consecutive seasons in a young girl's life after a mining accident changes her relationship with her father

0-02-777960-2 SIMON & SCHUSTER $15.00

A Fine White Dust

0-689-80462-8 ALADDIN PB $3.95

Missing May

0-440-40865-2 YEARLING PB $3.99

Waiting to Waltz: A Childhood

0-02-778000-7 SIMON & SCHUSTER $14.00

J.D. **Salinger**

The Catcher in the Rye

Probably the most famous novel of adolescence

See also SINCE 1945 under 20TH-CENTURY AMERICAN FICTION in LITERATURE OF THE AMERICAS

0-316-76953-3 LITTLE, BROWN $22.95
0-316-76948-7 LITTLE, BROWN PB $5.99

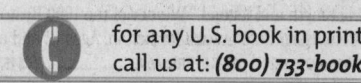

J.D. **Salinger**

Franny and Zooey

Two long stories about the eccentric Glass family

See also **SINCE 1945** under **20TH-CENTURY AMERICAN FICTION** in **LITERATURE OF THE AMERICAS**

0-316-76954-1 LITTLE, BROWN $23.95
0-316-76949-5 LITTLE, BROWN PB $4.99

Nine Stories

See also **SINCE 1945** under **20TH-CENTURY AMERICAN FICTION** in **LITERATURE OF THE AMERICAS**

0-316-76956-8 LITTLE, BROWN $22.95
0-316-76950-4 LITTLE, BROWN PB $4.99

Mari **Sandoz**

Cheyenne Autumn

0-8032-9212-0 NEBRASKA PB $9.95

Budd **Schulberg**

What Makes Sammy Run?

"Brilliantly effective. Sammy is a conquistador of the gutter.....His portrait is vitriolic, never dull, and the comic aspects are given full appreciation"—*NY Times Book Review*

See also **SINCE 1945** under **20TH-CENTURY AMERICAN FICTION** in **LITERATURE OF THE AMERICAS**

0394476187 RANDOM HOUSE $19.95
0-679-73422-8 VINTAGE PB $13.00

Ouida **Sebestyen**

Words by Heart

At the turn of the century a black girl wins local recognition and a Bible-quoting contest, but her success puts her in risky circumstances

0-553-27179-2 BDD PB $3.99

Kate **Seredy**

The Good Master

0-14-030133-X VIKING PB $4.99

The White Stag

0-14-031258-7 VIKING PB $4.99

Zheng **Shensun** & Alice **Low**

A Young Painter: The Life and Paintings of Wang Yani—China's Extraordinary Young Artist

Now 16, Wang Yani has completed in her 14-year career 10,000 paintings of landscapes, animals, and rural Chinese life. 50 full-color reproductions, photographs of the artist at work, and two foldouts give a wonderful sense of her style—a visual festival of monkeys, peacocks, and the world at play

0-590-44906-0 SCHOLASTIC $17.95

Virginia Driving Hawk **Sneve**, editor

Dancing Teepees: Poems of American Indian Youth

ILLUSTRATIONS BY STEPHEN GAMMELL

0-8234-0724-1 HOLIDAY HOUSE $16.95

Jerry **Spinelli**

Maniac Magee

The author says that this book, based on his childhood in Norristown, Pennsylvania, "is about, among other things, the kid as legendary hero..I thought about the world that children inhabit…It's a world that, in many ways, I find indistinguishable from myth and legend." Winner of the 1990 Boston Globe-Horn Book Award for fiction. Ages 12 and up

0-316-80722-2 LITTLE, BROWN $15.95

Suzanne Fisher **Staples**

Haveli

0-679-86569-1 BULLSEYE PB $4.99

Shabanu: Daughter of the Wind

0-679-81030-7 RANDOM HOUSE PB $4.99

John **Steinbeck**

The Grapes of Wrath

The epic story of the Joads, a family of Oklahoma farmers who flee from their farm to California during the dustbowl years of the 1930s. *"The Grapes of Wrath is* the greatest American novel I have ever read"—Dorothy Parker

See also **FROM THE TURN OF THE CENTURY TO WORLD WAR II** under **20TH-CENTURY AMERICAN FICTION** in **LITERATURE OF THE AMERICAS**

0-670-82638-3 VIKING $25.00
0-14-018640-9 PENGUIN PB $11.95

The Red Pony

0-14-017736-1 PENGUIN PB $5.95

Robert Louis **Stevenson**

Treasure Island

0-679-41800-8 KNOPF $12.95

Robert Louis **Stevenson** & others

The Ebb-Tide: A Trio and Quartet of Robert Lewis Stevenson.

Centenary Edition

0-7486-0476-6 EDINBURGH $35.00

Rosemary **Sutcliff**

Dragon Slayer

A retelling of *Beowulf* weaves together mythical events in a fine recreation of Anglo-Saxon England

0-14-030254-9 VIKING PB $4.99

Tristan and Iseult

0-374-47982-8 SUNBURST PB $3.95

Rosemary **Sutcliff** & Alan **Lee**

The Wanderings of Odysseus: The Story of the Odyssey

0-385-32205-4 DELACORTE $22.50

Mildred D. **Taylor**

Roll of Thunder, Hear My Cry

Cassie Logan is raised by a family determined not to surrender their freedom or humanity because they are black

See also **FICTION** under **BOOKS FOR EIGHTS, NINES, AND UP**

0-8037-7473-7 DIAL BOOKS $15.99
0-14-034893-X PUFFIN PB $4.99

J. R. R. **Tolkien**

The Lord of the Rings

A splendid centenary edition for the anniversary of Tolkien's birth, illustrated with 50 specially commissioned paintings from a noted English artist

ILLUSTRATED BY ALAN LEE

0-395-59511-8 HOUGHTON MIFFLIN $70.00

The Lord of the Rings

Part 1: Fellowship of the Rings

0-345-33920-3 BALLANTINE PB $5.99

Part 2: The Two Towers

0-345-33971-1 BALLANTINE PB $5.99

Part 3: The Return of the King

0-345-33973-8 BALLANTINE PB $5.99

James **Thurber**

Lost Princess of Oz

0-345-33367-5 BALLANTINE PB $4.99

James Thurber

Sue **Townsend**

Secret Diary of Adrian Mole, Aged 13 3/4

0-380-86876-8 AVON PB $4.99

Yoshiko **Uchida**

The Invisible Thread: An Autobiography

0-688-13703-2 BEECH TREE PB $4.95

Jar of Dreams

0-689-71672-9 ALADDIN PB $3.95

Jules **Verne**

Verne was a varied and profound writer whose obsession with scientific, geographical, and political information combined with a capacity for broad and potent—and often unconscious—symbolism

Around the World in Eighty Days

0-590-43053-X SCHOLASTIC PB $4.50

A Journey to the Center of the Earth

Verne's first great, popular success describes a geological descent that takes on dreamlike fascination

See also **EARLY SCIENCE FICTION** under **SCIENCE FICTION AND FANTASY** in **POPULAR READING**

See also **THE LATER 19TH-CENTURY: SYMBOLISM, NATURALISM, AND ROOTS OF MODERNISM** under **FRENCH LITERATURE TO 1900** in **LITERATURE OF EUROPE, AFRICA, AND ASIA**

0-8049-0060-4 AIRMONT PB $3.50
0-19-585460-8 OXFORD PB $4.95

The Mysterious Island

TRANSLATED BY LOWELL BAIR

0-553-21434-9 BDD PB $3.95

Twenty Thousand Leagues Under the Sea

EDITED BY PETER COSTELLO

0-460-87354-7 EVERYMAN'S PB $2.95

Cynthia **Voigt**

Building Blocks

A fantasy about a boy and his unappreciated father

0-590-47732-3 POINT PB $3.95

Come a Stranger
0-689-31289-X ATHENEUM $15.95

Dicey's Song
Prematurely responsible for her siblings, Dicey pushes to get herself and the children out of hard times. Newbery Medal 1983
0-689-30944-9 ATHENEUM $17.00
0-449-70276-6 FAWCETT PB $4.50

Homecoming
Five children, abandoned after their mother's death, make their way, mostly on foot, from New England to the eastern shore of Maryland in search of a grandmother they have never seen. The author is a keen observer of both landscape and people, and has written several good sequels
0-689-30833-7 ATHENEUM $17.00
0-449-70254-5 FAWCETT PB $4.99

Izzy, Willy-Nilly
At 15, Isabel Lingaid is popular, pretty, and a cheerleader. A date's drunk-driving accident changes all of that
0-689-31202-4 MACMILLAN $17.00
0-449-70214-6 JUNIPER PB $3.99

Seventeen Against the Dealer
0-689-31497-3 ATHENEUM $15.95
0-449-70375-4 JUNIPER PB $4.50

A Solitary Blue
0-590-47157-0 SCHOLASTIC PB $3.99

Yoko Kawashima **Watkins**
So Far from the Bamboo Grove
0-688-13115-8 BEECH TREE PB $4.95

Lyall **Watson**
The Dreams of Dragons: An Exploration and Celebration of the Mysteries of Nature
The real and the mythical: essays on dragons and on extraordinary natural phenomena
0-89281-372-5 INNER TRADITIONS PB $9.95

Jeane **Webster**
Daddy-Longlegs
0-14-035111-6 PUFFIN PB $3.99

H.G. **Wells**
The Time Machine
0-8125-0504-2 TOR PB $2.99

Seven Science Fiction Novels of H.G. Wells
A comprehensive edition of Wells's greatest speculative works. Includes *The First Men in the Moon, The Island of Dr. Moreau, The War of the Worlds, The Invisible Man, The Time Machine, The Food of the Gods,* and *In the Days of the Comet*
See also **EARLY SCIENCE FICTION** under **SCIENCE FICTION AND FANTASY** in **POPULAR READING**
0-486-20264-X DOVER $29.95

Robert **Westall**
The Kingdom by the Sea
0-374-44060-3 FS&G PB $3.95

T.H. **White**
The Once and Future King
This retelling of King Arthur was the basis for *Camelot,* and contains fascinating information about living in the Dark Ages
See also **FANTASY** under **SCIENCE FICTION AND FANTASY** in **POPULAR READING**
See also **BRITISH AND CELTIC** under **EUROPEAN MYTHOLOGY** under **MYTHOLOGY AND FOLKLORE** in **RELIGION, SPIRITUALITY, AND PHILOSOPHY**
See also **THE EARLY 20TH-CENTURY** under **20TH-CENTURY BRITISH AND IRISH FICTION** in **LITERATURE OF THE BRITISH ISLES**
0-441-62740-4 ACE PB $6.99

Nancy **Willard**
Gutenberg's Gift
ILLUSTRATED BY BRYAN LEISTER
0-15-200783-0 HARCOURT BRACE $20.00

Nancy **Willard** & Jane **Yolen**
Among Angels
ILLUSTRATED BY S. SAELIG GALLAGHER
0-15-100195-2 HARCOURT BRACE $20.00

Rita **Williams-Garcia**
Blue Tights
An American girl joins an African dance company and discovers her heritage
0-525-67234-6 LODESTAR $12.95

G. Clifton **Wisler**
Mr. Lincoln's Drummer
0-525-67463-2 LODESTAR $14.99

The Red Cap
0-14-036936-8 PUFFIN PB $3.99

Virginia Euwer **Wolff**
Make Lemonade
0-590-48141-X POINT PB $3.95

Paul **Yee**
Tales from Gold Mountain: Stories of the Chinese in the New World
Collection of eight original stories based on the frontier history of Chinese immigrants. The gold rush, building the transcontinental railroad, and settling the West are grippingly evoked through pen and brush. Stunning full-color illustrations. All ages
ILLUSTRATED BY SIMON NG
0-02-793621-X SIMON & SCHUSTER $15.95

Laurence **Yep**
Child of the Owl
An assimilated Chinese-American girl joins her thoroughly Chinese grandmother in a tiny San Francisco apartment
0-06-440336-X TROPHY PB $4.50

Dragonwings
Moon Shadow comes to San Francisco at the turn of the century to join the father he has never seen. Ordinary Chinese immigrants, they realize an extraordinary dream in a story based on American history. Newbery Honor Book 1975
See also **FICTION** under **BOOKS FOR EIGHTS, NINES, AND UP**
0-06-440085-9 TROPHY PB $4.95

Paul **Zindel**
Confessions of a Teenage Baboon
Overstuffed with odd characters, this account of a boy's violent coming of age was written by the Pulitzer Prize-winning playwright
0-553-27190-3 BDD PB $4.50

The Effect of Gamma Rays on Man-in-the-Moon Marigolds
See also **THE '70S, '80S, AND '90S** under **20TH-CENTURY AMERICAN DRAMA** in **LITERATURE OF THE AMERICAS**
0-553-28028-7 BDD PB $5.50

My Darling, My Hamburger
0-553-27324-8 BDD PB $3.99

The Pigman
0-553-26321-8 STARFIVE PB $4.99

The Pigman & Me
0-553-56456-0 BDD PB $4.50

The Undertaker's Gone Bananas
0-06-026846-8 HARPERCREST LIBRARY EDITION $16.89
0-553-27189-X BDD PB $3.99

Miscellaneous

L. **Ashman**
Make This Model Castle
0-86020-578-9 E.D.C. PB $9.95

Make This Model Town
0-7460-0181-9 E.D.C. PB $9.95

Helen C. **Challand**
Science Projects and Activities
Includes starting an ant colony and building a camera and telegraph set
0-516-00569-3 CHILDRENS PRESS $19.10

The Free Stuff Editors
Free Stuff for Kids, 1996 Edition
"Will appeal to kids of all ages"
—*New York Daily News*
0-671-53478-5 MEADOWBROOK PB $5.00

Colin **Greer** & Herbert **Kohl**, editors
A Call to Character: A Family Treasury
0-06-017339-4 HARPERCOLLINS $25.00

Heinrich **Hoffman**
Struwwelpeter: Slovenly Peter, Or Pretty Stories and Funny Pictures for Little Children
0-486-28469-7 DOVER PB $5.95

Judith **Morgan** & Neil **Morgan**
Dr. Seuss and Mr. Geisel: A Biography
This authorized biography of the children's writer tells the story of Ted Geisel's life and Dr. Seuss's success
0-679-41686-2 RANDOM HOUSE $25.00

The National Gallery

The National Gallery Christmas Decorations

Culled from the National Gallery's Renaissance art collection, this assortment of over 40 full-color reproductions of angels, cherubs, doves, stars, and landscapes provides lovely holiday ornaments and gift tags. Ideal as an activity book for children, who can "press out," assemble, and hang the decorations with thread

0-316-59890-9 LITTLE, BROWN PB $12.95

Catherine **Roehring**

Fun with Hieroglyphs

A handsomely designed kit for kids who want to send secret messages in an ancient and mysterious language. Included are a book explaining the history and use of Egyptian hieroglyphs, 24 rubber hieroglyph stamps, an ink pad, a hieroglyph alphabet chart, puzzles, and word games. Published with the Metropolitan Museum of Art

0-670-83576-5 PENGUIN $19.95

Alice **Siegel** &
Margo McLoone **Basta**, editors

The Information Please Kids' Almanac

See also **ALMANACS AND BOOKS OF FACTS** under **GENERAL INFORMATION** under **REFERENCE** in **BUSINESS AND REFERENCE**

0-395-58801-4 HOUGHTON MIFFLIN PB $9.95

William **Zinsser**, editor

Worlds of Childhood: The Art and Craft of Writing for Children

0-395-51425-8 HOUGHTON MIFFLIN PB $10.95

Children are extremely tough—they know exactly what's going to frighten their parents, and they don't ask questions that will upset mommy and daddy. They see the signs on their parents' faces: "Uh-oh, distress time coming." I remember from my own childhood that I would never tell my parents anything that disturbed me because it would have upset them. And since you love and honor your parents, you don't want to give them ulcers with questions they can't deal with. So you find out in the back yard, or from the landlady's daughter. But you do find out. Even before television, you found out. Isn't it kinder to give children the bitter pill in a work of art?—*Maurice Sendak*

WORLDS OF CHILDHOOD: THE ART AND CRAFT OF WRITING FOR CHILDREN

Index

The Plan of the Book

History of the Americas 171

Popular Reading 1055

Art 1125

Books for Young Readers 1599

Index

Titles

A

B

C

D

E

F

G

H

I

K

L

M

N

O

P

Q

R

S

T

U

V

W

Z

Index

AUTHORS

A

B

C

E

F

G

H

I

J

K

L

M

N

O

P

S

T

U

W

Z